# REFERENCE ONLY

# PETERSON'S®
# GRADUATE PROGRAMS
# IN THE BIOLOGICAL/BIOMEDICAL
# SCIENCES & HEALTH-RELATED
# MEDICAL PROFESSIONS

# 2021

# CONTENTS

# CONTENTS

# A Note from the Peterson's Editors

The six volumes of Peterson's *Graduate and Professional Programs*, the only annually updated reference work of its kind, provide wide-ranging information on the graduate and professional programs offered by accredited colleges and universities in the United States, U.S. territories, and Canada and by those institutions outside the United States that are accredited by U.S. accrediting bodies. More than 44,000 individual academic and professional programs at nearly 2,300 institutions are listed. Peterson's *Graduate and Professional Programs* have been used for more than fifty years by prospective graduate and professional students, placement counselors, faculty advisers, and all others interested in postbaccalaureate education.

*Graduate & Professional Programs: An Overview* contains information on institutions as a whole, while the other books in the series are devoted to specific academic and professional fields:

- *Graduate Programs in the Biological/Biomedical Sciences & Health-Related Medical Professions*

- *Graduate Programs in Business, Education, Information Studies, Law & Social Work*

- *Graduate Programs in Engineering & Applied Sciences*

- *Graduate Programs in the Humanities, Arts & Social Sciences*

- *Graduate Programs in the Physical Sciences, Mathematics, Agricultural Sciences, the Environment & Natural Resources*

The books may be used individually or as a set. For example, if you have chosen a field of study but do not know what institution you want to attend or if you have a college or university in mind but have not chosen an academic field of study, it is best to begin with the Overview guide.

*Graduate & Professional Programs: An Overview* presents several directories to help you identify programs of study that might interest you; you can then research those programs further in the other books in the series by using the Directory of Graduate and Professional Programs by Field, which lists 500 fields and gives the names of those institutions that offer graduate degree programs in each.

For geographical or financial reasons, you may be interested in attending a particular institution and will want to know what it has to offer. You should turn to the Directory of Institutions and Their Offerings, which lists the degree programs available at each institution. As in the Directory of Graduate and Professional Programs by Field, the level of degrees offered is also indicated.

All books in the series include advice on graduate education, including topics such as admissions tests, financial aid, and accreditation. **The Graduate Adviser** includes two essays and information about accreditation. The first essay, "The Admissions Process," discusses general admission requirements, admission tests, factors to consider when selecting a graduate school or program, when and how to apply, and how admission decisions are made. Special information for international students and tips for minority students are also included. The second essay, "Financial Support," is an overview of the broad range of support available at the graduate level. Fellowships, scholarships, and grants; assistantships and internships; federal and private loan programs, as well as Federal Work-Study; and the GI bill are detailed. This essay concludes with advice on applying for need-based financial aid. "Accreditation and Accrediting Agencies" gives information on accreditation and its purpose and lists institutional accrediting agencies first and then specialized accrediting agencies relevant to each volume's specific fields of study.

With information on more than 40,000 graduate programs in more than 500 disciplines, Peterson's *Graduate and Professional Programs* give you all the information you need about the programs that are of interest to you in three formats: **Profiles** (capsule summaries of basic information), **Displays** (information that an institution or program wants to emphasize), and **Close-Ups** (written by administrators, with more expansive information than the **Profiles**, emphasizing different aspects of the programs). By using these various formats of program information, coupled with **Appendixes** and **Indexes** covering directories and subject areas for all six books, you will find that these guides provide the most comprehensive, accurate, and up-to-date graduate study information available.

Peterson's publishes a full line of resources with information you need to guide you through the graduate admissions process. Peterson's publications can be found at college libraries and career centers and your local bookstore or library—or visit us on the Web at www.petersons.com.

Colleges and universities will be pleased to know that Peterson's helped you in your selection. Admissions staff members are more than happy to answer questions, address specific problems, and help in any way they can. The editors at Peterson's wish you great success in your graduate program search!

# THE GRADUATE ADVISER

# The Admissions Process

Generalizations about graduate admissions practices are not always helpful because each institution has its own set of guidelines and procedures. Nevertheless, some broad statements can be made about the admissions process that may help you plan your strategy.

## Factors Involved in Selecting a Graduate School or Program

Selecting a graduate school and a specific program of study is a complex matter. Quality of the faculty; program and course offerings; the nature, size, and location of the institution; admission requirements; cost; and the availability of financial assistance are among the many factors that affect one's choice of institution. Other considerations are job placement and achievements of the program's graduates and the institution's resources, such as libraries, laboratories, and computer facilities. If you are to make the best possible choice, you need to learn as much as you can about the schools and programs you are considering before you apply.

The following steps may help you narrow your choices.

- Talk to alumni of the programs or institutions you are considering to get their impressions of how well they were prepared for work in their fields of study.
- Remember that graduate school requirements change, so be sure to get the most up-to-date information possible.
- Talk to department faculty members and the graduate adviser at your undergraduate institution. They often have information about programs of study at other institutions.
- Visit the websites of the graduate schools in which you are interested to request a graduate catalog. Contact the department chair in your chosen field of study for additional information about the department and the field.
- Visit as many campuses as possible. Call ahead for an appointment with the graduate adviser in your field of interest and be sure to check out the facilities and talk to students.

## General Requirements

Graduate schools and departments have requirements that applicants for admission must meet. Typically, these requirements include undergraduate transcripts (which provide information about undergraduate grade point average and course work applied toward a major), admission test scores, and letters of recommendation. Most graduate programs also ask for an essay or personal statement that describes your personal reasons for seeking graduate study. In some fields, such as art and music, portfolios or auditions may be required in addition to other evidence of talent. Some institutions require that the applicant have an undergraduate degree in the same subject as the intended graduate major.

Most institutions evaluate each applicant on the basis of the applicant's total record, and the weight accorded any given factor varies widely from institution to institution and from program to program.

## The Application Process

You should begin the application process at least one year before you expect to begin your graduate study. Find out the application deadline for each institution (many are provided in the **Profile** section of this guide). Go to the institution's website and find out if you can apply online. If not, request a paper application form. Fill out this form thoroughly and neatly. Assume that the school needs all the information it is requesting and that the admissions officer will be sensitive to the neatness and overall quality of what you submit. Do not supply more information than the school requires.

The institution may ask at least one question that will require a three- or four-paragraph answer. Compose your response on the assumption that the admissions officer is interested in both what you think and how you express yourself. Keep your statement brief and to the point, but, at the same time, include all pertinent information about your past experiences and your educational goals. Individual statements vary greatly in style and content, which helps admissions officers differentiate among applicants. Many graduate departments give considerable weight to the statement in making their admissions decisions, so be sure to take the time to prepare a thoughtful and concise statement.

If recommendations are a part of the admissions requirements, carefully choose the individuals you ask to write them. It is generally best to ask current or former professors to write the recommendations, provided they are able to attest to your intellectual ability and motivation for doing the work required of a graduate student. It is advisable to provide stamped, preaddressed envelopes to people being asked to submit recommendations on your behalf.

Completed applications, including references, transcripts, and admission test scores, should be received at the institution by the specified date.

Be advised that institutions do not usually make admissions decisions until all materials have been received. Enclose a self-addressed postcard with your application, requesting confirmation of receipt. Allow at least ten days for the return of the postcard before making further inquiries.

If you plan to apply for financial support, it is imperative that you file your application early.

## ADMISSION TESTS

The major testing program used in graduate admissions is the Graduate Record Examinations (GRE®) testing program, sponsored by the GRE Board and administered by Educational Testing Service, Princeton, New Jersey.

The Graduate Record Examinations testing program consists of a General Test and six Subject Tests. The General Test measures critical thinking, verbal reasoning, quantitative reasoning, and analytical writing skills. It is offered as an Internet-based test (iBT) in the United States, Canada, and many other countries.

The GRE® revised General Test's questions were designed to reflect the kind of thinking that students need to do in graduate or business school and demonstrate that students are indeed ready for graduate-level work.

- **Verbal Reasoning**—Measures ability to analyze and evaluate written material and synthesize information obtained from it, analyze relationships among component parts of sentences, and recognize relationships among words and concepts.
- **Quantitative Reasoning**—Measures problem-solving ability, focusing on basic concepts of arithmetic, algebra, geometry, and data analysis.
- **Analytical Writing**—Measures critical thinking and analytical writing skills, specifically the ability to articulate and support complex ideas clearly and effectively.

The computer-delivered GRE® revised General Test is offered year-round at Prometric™ test centers and on specific dates at testing locations outside of the Prometric test center network. Appointments are scheduled on a first-come, first-served basis. The GRE® revised General Test is also offered as a paper-based test three times a year in areas where computer-based testing is not available.

You can take the computer-delivered GRE® revised General Test once every twenty-one days, up to five times within any continuous rolling twelve-month period (365 days)—even if you canceled your

scores on a previously taken test. You may take the paper-based GRE® revised General Test as often as it is offered.

Three scores are reported on the revised General Test:

1. A **Verbal Reasoning score** is reported on a 130–170 score scale, in 1-point increments.

2. A **Quantitative Reasoning score** is reported on a 130–170 score scale, in 1-point increments.

3. An **Analytical Writing score** is reported on a 0–6 score level, in half-point increments.

The GRE® Subject Tests measure achievement and assume undergraduate majors or extensive background in the following six disciplines:

- Biology
- Chemistry
- Literature in English
- Mathematics
- Physics
- Psychology

The Subject Tests are available three times per year as paper-based administrations around the world. Testing time is approximately 2 hours and 50 minutes. You can obtain more information about the GRE® by visiting the ETS website at **www.ets.org** or consulting the *GRE® Information Bulletin*. The *Bulletin* can be obtained at many undergraduate colleges. You can also download it from the ETS website or obtain it by contacting Graduate Record Examinations, Educational Testing Service, P.O. Box 6000, Princeton, NJ 08541-6000; phone: 609-771-7670 or 866-473-4373.

If you expect to apply for admission to a program that requires any of the GRE® tests, you should select a test date well in advance of the application deadline. Scores on the computer-based General Test are reported within ten to fifteen days; scores on the paper-based Subject Tests are reported within six weeks.

Another testing program, the Miller Analogies Test® (MAT®), is administered at more than 500 Controlled Testing Centers in the United States, Canada, and other countries. The MAT® computer-based test is now available. Testing time is 60 minutes. The test consists of 120 partial analogies. You can obtain the *Candidate Information Booklet,* which contains a list of test centers and instructions for taking the test, from **www.milleranalogies.com** or by calling 800-328-5999 (toll-free).

Check the specific requirements of the programs to which you are applying.

# How Admission Decisions Are Made

The program you apply to is directly involved in the admissions process. Although the final decision is usually made by the graduate dean (or an associate) or the faculty admissions committee, recommendations from faculty members in your intended field are important. At some institutions, an interview is incorporated into the decision process.

# A Special Note for International Students

In addition to the steps already described, there are some special considerations for international students who intend to apply for graduate study in the United States. All graduate schools require an indication of competence in English. The purpose of the Test of English as a Foreign Language (TOEFL®) is to evaluate the English proficiency of people who are nonnative speakers of English and want to study at colleges and universities where English is the language of instruction. The TOEFL® is administered by Educational Testing Service (ETS) under the general direction of a policy board established by the College Board and the Graduate Record Examinations Board.

The TOEFL iBT® assesses four basic language skills: listening, reading, writing, and speaking. The Internet-based test is administered at secure, official test centers. The testing time is approximately 4 hours.

The TOEFL® is also offered in a paper-based format in areas of the world where internet-based testing is not available. In 2017, ETS launched a revised TOEFL® paper-based Test, that more closely aligned to the TOEFL iBT® test. This revised paper-based test consists of three sections—listening, reading, and writing. The testing time is approximately 3 hours.

You can obtain more information for both versions of the TOEFL® by visiting the ETS website at **www.ets.org/toefl**. Information can also be obtained by contacting TOEFL® Services, Educational Testing Service, P.O. Box 6151, Princeton, NJ 08541-6151. Phone: 609-771-7100 or 877-863-3546 (toll free).

International students should apply especially early because of the number of steps required to complete the admissions process. Furthermore, many United States graduate schools have a limited number of spaces for international students, and many more students apply than the schools can accommodate.

International students may find financial assistance from institutions very limited. The U.S. government requires international applicants to submit a certification of support, which is a statement attesting to the applicant's financial resources. In addition, international students *must* have health insurance coverage.

# Tips for Minority Students

Indicators of a university's values in terms of diversity are found both in its recruitment programs and its resources directed to student success. Important questions: Does the institution vigorously recruit minorities for its graduate programs? Is there funding available to help with the costs associated with visiting the school? Are minorities represented in the institution's brochures or website or on their faculty rolls? What campus-based resources or services (including assistance in locating housing or career counseling and placement) are available? Is funding available to members of underrepresented groups?

At the program level, it is particularly important for minority students to investigate the "climate" of a program under consideration. How many minority students are enrolled and how many have graduated? What opportunities are there to work with diverse faculty and mentors whose research interests match yours? How are conflicts resolved or concerns addressed? How interested are faculty in building strong and supportive relations with students? "Climate" concerns should be addressed by posing questions to various individuals, including faculty members, current students, and alumni.

Information is also available through various organizations, such as the Hispanic Association of Colleges & Universities (HACU), and publications such as *Diverse Issues in Higher Education* and *Hispanic Outlook* magazine. There are also books devoted to this topic, such as *The Multicultural Student's Guide to Colleges* by Robert Mitchell.

# Financial Support

The range of financial support at the graduate level is very broad. The following descriptions will give you a general idea of what you might expect and what will be expected of you as a financial support recipient.

## Fellowships, Scholarships, and Grants

These are usually outright awards of a few hundred to many thousands of dollars with no service to the institution required in return. Fellowships and scholarships are usually awarded on the basis of merit and are highly competitive. Grants are made on the basis of financial need or special talent in a field of study. Many fellowships, scholarships, and grants not only cover tuition, fees, and supplies but also include stipends for living expenses with allowances for dependents. However, the terms of each should be examined because some do not permit recipients to supplement their income with outside work. Fellowships, scholarships, and grants may vary in the number of years for which they are awarded.

In addition to the availability of these funds at the university or program level, many excellent fellowship programs are available at the national level and may be applied for before and during enrollment in a graduate program. A listing of many of these programs can be found at the Council of Graduate Schools' website, **https://cgsnet.org/**. There is a wealth of information in the "Programs" and "Awards" sections.

## Assistantships and Internships

Many graduate students receive financial support through assistantships, particularly involving teaching or research duties. It is important to recognize that such appointments should not be viewed simply as employment relationships but rather should constitute an integral and important part of a student's graduate education. As such, the appointments should be accompanied by strong faculty mentoring and increasingly responsible apprenticeship experiences. The specific nature of these appointments in a given program should be considered in selecting that graduate program.

### TEACHING ASSISTANTSHIPS

These usually provide a salary and full or partial tuition remission and may also provide health benefits. Unlike fellowships, scholarships, and grants, which require no service to the institution, teaching assistantships require recipients to provide the institution with a specific amount of undergraduate teaching, ideally related to the student's field of study. Some teaching assistants are limited to grading papers, compiling bibliographies, taking notes, or monitoring laboratories. At some graduate schools, teaching assistants must carry lighter course loads than regular full-time students.

### RESEARCH ASSISTANTSHIPS

These are very similar to teaching assistantships in the manner in which financial assistance is provided. The difference is that recipients are given basic research assignments in their disciplines rather than teaching responsibilities. The work required is normally related to the student's field of study; in most instances, the assistantship supports the student's thesis or dissertation research.

### ADMINISTRATIVE INTERNSHIPS

These are similar to assistantships in application of financial assistance funds, but the student is given an assignment on a part-time basis, usually as a special assistant with one of the university's administrative offices. The assignment may not necessarily be directly related to the recipient's discipline.

## RESIDENCE HALL AND COUNSELING ASSISTANTSHIPS

These assistantships are frequently assigned to graduate students in psychology, counseling, and social work, but they may be offered to students in other disciplines, especially if the student has worked in this capacity during his or her undergraduate years. Duties can vary from being available in a dean's office for a specific number of hours for consultation with undergraduates to living in campus residences and being responsible for both counseling and administrative tasks or advising student activity groups. Residence hall assistantships often include a room and board allowance and, in some cases, tuition assistance and stipends. Contact the Housing and Student Life Office for more information.

## Health Insurance

The availability and affordability of health insurance is an important issue and one that should be considered in an applicant's choice of institution and program. While often included with assistantships and fellowships, this is not always the case and, even if provided, the benefits may be limited. It is important to note that the U.S. government requires international students to have health insurance.

## The GI Bill

This provides financial assistance for students who are veterans of the United States armed forces. If you are a veteran, contact your local Veterans Administration office to determine your eligibility and to get full details about benefits. There are a number of programs that offer educational benefits to current military enlistees. Some states have tuition assistance programs for members of the National Guard. Contact the VA office at the college for more information.

## Federal Work-Study Program (FWS)

Employment is another way some students finance their graduate studies. The federally funded Federal Work-Study Program provides eligible students with employment opportunities, usually in public and private nonprofit organizations. Federal funds pay up to 75 percent of the wages, with the remainder paid by the employing agency. FWS is available to graduate students who demonstrate financial need. Not all schools have these funds, and some only award them to undergraduates. Each school sets its application deadline and workstudy earnings limits. Wages vary and are related to the type of work done. You must file the Free Application for Federal Student Aid (FAFSA) to be eligible for this program.

## Loans

Many graduate students borrow to finance their graduate programs when other sources of assistance (which do not have to be repaid) prove insufficient. You should always read and understand the terms of any loan program before submitting your application.

### FEDERAL DIRECT LOANS

**Federal Direct Loans.** The Federal Direct Loan Program offers a variable-fixed interest rate loan to graduate students with the Department of Education acting as the lender. Students receive a new rate with each new loan, but that rate is fixed for the life of the loan. Beginning with loans made on or after July 1, 2013, the interest rate for loans made each July 1st to June 30th period are determined based on the last 10-year Treasury note auction prior to June 1st of that year, plus an added percentage. The interest rate can be no higher than 9.5%.

Beginning July 1, 2012, the Federal Direct Loan for graduate students is an unsubsidized loan. Under the *unsubsidized* program, the grad borrower pays the interest on the loan from the day proceeds are issued and is responsible for paying interest during all periods. If the borrower chooses not to pay the interest while in school, or during the grace periods, deferment, or forbearance, the interest accrues and will be capitalized.

Graduate students may borrow up to $20,500 per year through the Direct Loan Program, up to a cumulative maximum of $138,500, including undergraduate borrowing. No more than $65,500 of the $138,500 can be from subsidized loans, including loans the grad borrower may have received for periods of enrollment that began before July 1, 2012, or for prior undergraduate borrowing. You may borrow up to the cost of attendance at the school in which you are enrolled or will attend, minus estimated financial assistance from other federal, state, and private sources, up to a maximum of $20,500. Grad borrowers who reach the aggregate loan limit over the course of their education cannot receive additional loans; however, if they repay some of their loans to bring the outstanding balance below the aggregate limit, they could be eligible to borrow again, up to that limit.

Under the *subsidized* Federal Direct Loan Program, repayment begins six months after your last date of enrollment on at least a half-time basis. Under the *unsubsidized* program, repayment of interest begins within thirty days from disbursement of the loan proceeds, and repayment of the principal begins six months after your last enrollment on at least a half-time basis. Some borrowers may choose to defer interest payments while they are in school. The accrued interest is added to the loan balance when the borrower begins repayment. There are several repayment options.

**Federal Perkins Loans.** The Federal Perkins Loan is available to students demonstrating financial need and is administered directly by the school. Not all schools have these funds, and some may award them to undergraduates only. Eligibility is determined from the information you provide on the FAFSA. The school will notify you of your eligibility.

Eligible graduate students may borrow up to $8,000 per year, up to a maximum of $60,000, including undergraduate borrowing (even if your previous Perkins Loans have been repaid). The interest rate for Federal Perkins Loans is 5 percent, and no interest accrues while you remain in school at least half-time. Students who are attending less than half-time need to check with their school to determine the length of their grace period. There are no guarantee, loan, or disbursement fees. Repayment begins nine months after your last date of enrollment on at least a half-time basis and may extend over a maximum of ten years with no prepayment penalty.

**Federal Direct Graduate PLUS Loans.** Effective July 1, 2006, graduate and professional students are eligible for Graduate PLUS loans. This program allows students to borrow up to the cost of attendance, less any other aid received. These loans have a fixed interest rate (5.30% for loans first disbursed on or after July 1, 2020, and before July 1, 2021) and interest begins to accrue at the time of disbursement. Beginning with loans made on or after July 1, 2013, the interest rate for loans made each July 1st to June 30th period are determined based on the last 10-year Treasury note auction prior to June 1st of that year. The interest rate can be no higher than 10.5%. The PLUS loans do involve a credit check; a PLUS borrower may obtain a loan with a cosigner if his or her credit is not good enough. Grad PLUS loans may be deferred while a student is in school and for the six months following a drop below half-time enrollment. For more information, you should contact a representative in your college's financial aid office.

**Deferring Your Federal Loan Repayments.** If you borrowed under the Federal Direct Loan Program, Federal Direct PLUS Loan Program, or the Federal Perkins Loan Program for previous undergraduate or graduate study, your payments may be deferred when you return to graduate school, depending on when you borrowed and under which program.

There are other deferment options available if you are temporarily unable to repay your loan. Information about these deferments is provided at your entrance and exit interviews. If you believe you are eligible for a deferment of your loan payments, you must contact your lender or loan servicer to request a deferment. The deferment must be filed prior to the time your payment is due, and it must be re-filed when it expires if you remain eligible for deferment at that time.

## SUPPLEMENTAL (PRIVATE) LOANS

Many lending institutions offer supplemental loan programs and other financing plans, such as the ones described here, to students seeking additional assistance in meeting their education expenses. Some loan programs target all types of graduate students; others are designed specifically for business, law, or medical students. In addition, you can use private loans not specifically designed for education to help finance your graduate degree.

If you are considering borrowing through a supplemental or private loan program, you should carefully consider the terms and be sure to read the fine print. Check with the program sponsor for the most current terms that will be applicable to the amounts you intend to borrow for graduate study. Most supplemental loan programs for graduate study offer unsubsidized, credit-based loans. In general, a credit-ready borrower is one who has a satisfactory credit history or no credit history at all. A creditworthy borrower generally must pass a credit test to be eligible to borrow or act as a cosigner for the loan funds.

Many supplemental loan programs have minimum and maximum annual loan limits. Some offer amounts equal to the cost of attendance minus any other aid you will receive for graduate study. If you are planning to borrow for several years of graduate study, consider whether there is a cumulative or aggregate limit on the amount you may borrow. Often this cumulative or aggregate limit will include any amounts you borrowed and have not repaid for undergraduate or previous graduate study.

The combination of the annual interest rate, loan fees, and the repayment terms you choose will determine how much you will repay over time. Compare these features in combination before you decide which loan program to use. Some loans offer interest rates that are adjusted monthly, quarterly, or annually. Some offer interest rates that are lower during the in-school, grace, and deferment periods and then increase when you begin repayment. Some programs include a loan origination fee, which is usually deducted from the principal amount you receive when the loan is disbursed and must be repaid along with the interest and other principal when you graduate, withdraw from school, or drop below half-time study. Sometimes the loan fees are reduced if you borrow with a qualified cosigner. Some programs allow you to defer interest and/or principal payments while you are enrolled in graduate school. Many programs allow you to capitalize your interest payments; the interest due on your loan is added to the outstanding balance of your loan, so you don't have to repay immediately, but this increases the amount you owe. Other programs allow you to pay the interest as you go, which reduces the amount you later have to repay. The private loan market is very competitive, and your financial aid office can help you evaluate these programs.

# Applying for Need-Based Financial Aid

Schools that award federal and institutional financial assistance based on need will require you to complete the FAFSA and, in some cases, an institutional financial aid application.

If you are applying for federal student assistance, you **must** complete the FAFSA. A service of the U.S. Department of Education, the FAFSA is free to all applicants. Most applicants apply online at **www.fafsa.ed.gov**. Paper applications are available at the financial aid office of your local college.

After your FAFSA information has been processed, you will receive a Student Aid Report (SAR). If you provided an e-mail address on the FAFSA, this will be sent to you electronically; otherwise, it will be mailed to your home address.

Follow the instructions on the SAR if you need to correct information reported on your original application. If your situation changes after you file your FAFSA, contact your financial aid officer to discuss amending

your information. You can also appeal your financial aid award if you have extenuating circumstances.

If you would like more information on federal student financial aid, visit the FAFSA website or download the most recent version of *Do You Need Money for College* at www.studentaid.gov/sites/default/files/do-you-need-money.pdf. This guide is also available in Spanish.

The U.S. Department of Education also has a toll-free number for questions concerning federal student aid programs. The number is 1-800-4-FED AID (1-800-433-3243). If you are hearing impaired, call toll-free, 1-800-730-8913.

# Summary

Remember that these are generalized statements about financial assistance at the graduate level. Because each institution allots its aid differently, you should communicate directly with the school and the specific department of interest to you. It is not unusual, for example, to find that an endowment vested within a specific department supports one or more fellowships. You may fit its requirements and specifications precisely.

# Accreditation and Accrediting Agencies

Colleges and universities in the United States, and their individual academic and professional programs, are accredited by nongovernmental agencies concerned with monitoring the quality of education in this country. Agencies with both regional and national jurisdictions grant accreditation to institutions as a whole, while specialized bodies acting on a nationwide basis—often national professional associations—grant accreditation to departments and programs in specific fields.

Institutional and specialized accrediting agencies share the same basic concerns: the purpose an academic unit—whether university or program—has set for itself and how well it fulfills that purpose, the adequacy of its financial and other resources, the quality of its academic offerings, and the level of services it provides. Agencies that grant institutional accreditation take a broader view, of course, and examine university-wide or college-wide services with which a specialized agency may not concern itself.

Both types of agencies follow the same general procedures when considering an application for accreditation. The academic unit prepares a self-evaluation, focusing on the concerns mentioned above and usually including an assessment of both its strengths and weaknesses; a team of representatives of the accrediting body reviews this evaluation, visits the campus, and makes its own report; and finally, the accrediting body makes a decision on the application. Often, even when accreditation is granted, the agency makes a recommendation regarding how the institution or program can improve. All institutions and programs are also reviewed every few years to determine whether they continue to meet established standards; if they do not, they may lose their accreditation.

Accrediting agencies themselves are reviewed and evaluated periodically by the U.S. Department of Education and the Council for Higher Education Accreditation (CHEA). Recognized agencies adhere to certain standards and practices, and their authority in matters of accreditation is widely accepted in the educational community.

This does not mean, however, that accreditation is a simple matter, either for schools wishing to become accredited or for students deciding where to apply. Indeed, in certain fields the very meaning and methods of accreditation are the subject of a good deal of debate. For their part, those applying to graduate school should be aware of the safeguards provided by regional accreditation, especially in terms of degree acceptance and institutional longevity. Beyond this, applicants should understand the role that specialized accreditation plays in their field, as this varies considerably from one discipline to another. In certain professional fields, it is necessary to have graduated from a program that is accredited in order to be eligible for a license to practice, and in some fields the federal government also makes this a hiring requirement. In other disciplines, however, accreditation is not as essential, and there can be excellent programs that are not accredited. In fact, some programs choose not to seek accreditation, although most do.

Institutions and programs that present themselves for accreditation are sometimes granted the status of candidate for accreditation, or what is known as "preaccreditation." This may happen, for example, when an academic unit is too new to have met all the requirements for accreditation. Such status signifies initial recognition and indicates that the school or program in question is working to fulfill all requirements; it does not, however, guarantee that accreditation will be granted.

## Institutional Accrediting Agencies—Regional

### MIDDLE STATES COMMISSION ON HIGHER EDUCATION

Accredits institutions in Delaware, District of Columbia, Maryland, New Jersey, New York, Pennsylvania, Puerto Rico, and the Virgin Islands.

Dr. Elizabeth Sibolski, President
Middle States Commission on Higher Education
3624 Market Street, Second Floor West
Philadelphia, Pennsylvania 19104
Phone: 267-284-5000
Fax: 215-662-5501
E-mail: info@msche.org
Website: www.msche.org

### NEW ENGLAND ASSOCIATION OF SCHOOLS AND COLLEGES

Accredits institutions in Connecticut, Maine, Massachusetts, New Hampshire, Rhode Island, and Vermont.

Dr. Barbara E. Brittingham, President/Director
Commission on Institutions of Higher Education
3 Burlington Woods Drive, Suite 100
Burlington, Massachusetts 01803-4531
Phone: 855-886-3272 or 781-425-7714
Fax: 781-425-1001
E-mail: cihe@neasc.org
Website: https://cihe.neasc.org

### THE HIGHER LEARNING COMMISSION

Accredits institutions in Arizona, Arkansas, Colorado, Illinois, Indiana, Iowa, Kansas, Michigan, Minnesota, Missouri, Nebraska, New Mexico, North Dakota, Ohio, Oklahoma, South Dakota, West Virginia, Wisconsin, and Wyoming.

Dr. Barbara Gellman-Danley, President
The Higher Learning Commission
230 South LaSalle Street, Suite 7-500
Chicago, Illinois 60604-1413
Phone: 800-621-7440 or 312-263-0456
Fax: 312-263-7462
E-mail: info@hlcommission.org
Website: www.hlcommission.org

### NORTHWEST COMMISSION ON COLLEGES AND UNIVERSITIES

Accredits institutions in Alaska, Idaho, Montana, Nevada, Oregon, Utah, and Washington.

Dr. Sandra E. Elman, President
8060 165th Avenue, NE, Suite 100
Redmond, Washington 98052
Phone: 425-558-4224
Fax: 425-376-0596
E-mail: selman@nwccu.org
Website: www.nwccu.org

### SOUTHERN ASSOCIATION OF COLLEGES AND SCHOOLS

Accredits institutions in Alabama, Florida, Georgia, Kentucky, Louisiana, Mississippi, North Carolina, South Carolina, Tennessee, Texas, and Virginia.

Dr. Belle S. Wheelan, President
Commission on Colleges
1866 Southern Lane
Decatur, Georgia 30033-4097
Phone: 404-679-4500 Ext. 4504
Fax: 404-679-4558
E-mail: questions@sacscoc.org
Website: www.sacscoc.org

### WESTERN ASSOCIATION OF SCHOOLS AND COLLEGES

Accredits institutions in California, Guam, and Hawaii.

Jamienne S. Studley, President
WASC Senior College and University Commission
985 Atlantic Avenue, Suite 100
Alameda, California 94501
Phone: 510-748-9001
Fax: 510-748-9797
E-mail: wasc@wscuc.org
Website: https://www.wscuc.org/

## Institutional Accrediting Agencies—Other

*ACCREDITING COUNCIL FOR INDEPENDENT*
*COLLEGES AND SCHOOLS*
Michelle Edwards, President
750 First Street NE, Suite 980
Washington, DC 20002-4223
Phone: 202-336-6780
Fax: 202-842-2593
E-mail: info@acics.org
Website: www.acics.org

*DISTANCE EDUCATION ACCREDITING COMMISSION (DEAC)*
Leah Matthews, Executive Director
1101 17th Street NW, Suite 808
Washington, DC 20036-4704
Phone: 202-234-5100
Fax: 202-332-1386
E-mail: info@deac.org
Website: www.deac.org

## Specialized Accrediting Agencies

*ACUPUNCTURE AND ORIENTAL MEDICINE*
Mark S. McKenzie, LAc MsOM DiplOM, Executive Director
Accreditation Commission for Acupuncture and Oriental Medicine
8941 Aztec Drive, Suite 2
Eden Prairie, Minnesota 55347
Phone: 952-212-2434
Fax: 301-313-0912
E-mail: info@acaom.org
Website: www.acaom.org

*ALLIED HEALTH*
Kathleen Megivern, Executive Director
Commission on Accreditation of Allied Health Education Programs
(CAAHEP)
25400 US Hwy 19 North, Suite 158
Clearwater, Florida 33763
Phone: 727-210-2350
Fax: 727-210-2354
E-mail: mail@caahep.org
Website: www.caahep.org

*ART AND DESIGN*
Karen P. Moynahan, Executive Director
National Association of Schools of Art and Design (NASAD)
Commission on Accreditation
11250 Roger Bacon Drive, Suite 21
Reston, Virginia 20190-5248
Phone: 703-437-0700
Fax: 703-437-6312
E-mail: info@arts-accredit.org
Website: http://nasad.arts-accredit.org

*ATHLETIC TRAINING EDUCATION*
Pamela Hansen, CAATE Director of Accreditation
Commission on Accreditation of Athletic Training Education (CAATE)
6850 Austin Center Blvd., Suite 100
Austin, Texas 78731-3184
Phone: 512-733-9700
E-mail: pamela@caate.net
Website: www.caate.net

*AUDIOLOGY EDUCATION*
Meggan Olek, Director
Accreditation Commission for Audiology Education (ACAE)
11480 Commerce Park Drive, Suite 220
Reston, Virginia 20191
Phone: 202-986-9500
Fax: 202-986-9550
E-mail: info@acaeaccred.org
Website: https://acaeaccred.org/

*AVIATION*
Dr. Gary J. Northam, President
Aviation Accreditation Board International (AABI)
3410 Skyway Drive
Auburn, Alabama 36830
Phone: 334-844-2431
Fax: 334-844-2432
E-mail: gary.northam@auburn.edu
Website: www.aabi.aero

*BUSINESS*
Stephanie Bryant, Executive Vice President and Chief Accreditation
  Officer
AACSB International—The Association to Advance Collegiate Schools
  of Business
777 South Harbour Island Boulevard, Suite 750
Tampa, Florida 33602
Phone: 813-769-6500
Fax: 813-769-6559
E-mail: stephanie.bryant@aacsb.edu
Website: www.aacsb.edu

*BUSINESS EDUCATION*
Dr. Phyllis Okrepkie, President
International Assembly for Collegiate Business Education (IACBE)
11374 Strang Line Road
Lenexa, Kansas 66215
Phone: 913-631-3009
Fax: 913-631-9154
E-mail: iacbe@iacbe.org
Website: www.iacbe.org

*CHIROPRACTIC*
Dr. Craig S. Little, President
Council on Chiropractic Education (CCE)
Commission on Accreditation
8049 North 85th Way
Scottsdale, Arizona 85258-4321
Phone: 480-443-8877 or 888-443-3506
Fax: 480-483-7333
E-mail: cce@cce-usa.org
Website: www.cce-usa.org

*CLINICAL LABORATORY SCIENCES*
Dianne M. Cearlock, Ph.D., Chief Executive Officer
National Accrediting Agency for Clinical Laboratory Sciences
5600 North River Road, Suite 720
Rosemont, Illinois 60018-5119
Phone: 773-714-8880 or 847-939-3597
Fax: 773-714-8886
E-mail: info@naacls.org
Website: www.naacls.org

*CLINICAL PASTORAL EDUCATION*
Trace Haythorn, Ph.D., Executive Director/CEO
Association for Clinical Pastoral Education, Inc.
One West Court Square, Suite 325
Decatur, Georgia 30030-2576
Phone: 678-363-6226
Fax: 404-320-0849
E-mail: acpe@acpe.edu
Website: www.acpe.edu

*DANCE*
Karen P. Moynahan, Executive Director
National Association of Schools of Dance (NASD)
Commission on Accreditation
11250 Roger Bacon Drive, Suite 21
Reston, Virginia 20190-5248
Phone: 703-437-0700
Fax: 703-437-6312
E-mail: info@arts-accredit.org
Website: http://nasd.arts-accredit.org

## DENTISTRY
Dr. Kathleen T. O'Loughlin, Executive Director
Commission on Dental Accreditation
American Dental Association
211 East Chicago Avenue
Chicago, Illinois 60611
Phone: 312-440-2500
E-mail: accreditation@ada.org
Website: www.ada.org

## DIETETICS AND NUTRITION
Mary B. Gregoire, Ph.D., Executive Director; RD, FADA, FAND
Academy of Nutrition and Dietetics
Accreditation Council for Education in Nutrition and Dietetics (ACEND)
120 South Riverside Plaza
Chicago, Illinois 60606-6995
Phone: 800-877-1600 or 312-899-0040
E-mail: acend@eatright.org
Website: www.eatright.org/cade

## EDUCATION PREPARATION
Christopher Koch, President
Council for the Accreditation of Educator Preparation (CAEP)
1140 19th Street NW, Suite 400
Washington, DC 20036
Phone: 202-223-0077
Fax: 202-296-6620
E-mail: caep@caepnet.org
Website: www.caepnet.org

## ENGINEERING
Michael Milligan, Ph.D., PE, Executive Director
Accreditation Board for Engineering and Technology, Inc. (ABET)
415 North Charles Street
Baltimore, Maryland 21201
Phone: 410-347-7700
E-mail: accreditation@abet.org
Website: www.abet.org

## FORENSIC SCIENCES
Nancy J. Jackson, Director of Development and Accreditation
American Academy of Forensic Sciences (AAFS)
Forensic Science Education Program Accreditation Commission (FEPAC)
410 North 21st Street
Colorado Springs, Colorado 80904
Phone: 719-636-1100
Fax: 719-636-1993
E-mail: njackson@aafs.org
Website: www.fepac-edu.org

## FORESTRY
Carol L. Redelsheimer
Director of Science and Education
Society of American Foresters
10100 Laureate Way
Bethesda, Maryland 20814-2198
Phone: 301-897-8720 or 866-897-8720
Fax: 301-897-3690
E-mail: membership@safnet.org
Website: www.eforester.com

## HEALTHCARE MANAGEMENT
Commission on Accreditation of Healthcare Management Education (CAHME)
Anthony Stanowski, President and CEO
6110 Executive Boulevard, Suite 614
Rockville, Maryland 20852
Phone: 301-298-1820
E-mail: info@cahme.org
Website: www.cahme.org

## HEALTH INFORMATICS AND HEALTH MANAGEMENT
Angela Kennedy, EdD, MBA, RHIA, Chief Executive Officer
Commission on Accreditation for Health Informatics and Information Management Education (CAHIIM)
233 North Michigan Avenue, 21st Floor
Chicago, Illinois 60601-5800
Phone: 312-233-1134
Fax: 312-233-1948
E-mail: info@cahiim.org
Website: www.cahiim.org

## HUMAN SERVICE EDUCATION
Dr. Elaine Green, President
Council for Standards in Human Service Education (CSHSE)
3337 Duke Street
Alexandria, Virginia 22314
Phone: 571-257-3959
E-mail: info@cshse.org
Website: www.cshse.org

## INTERIOR DESIGN
Holly Mattson, Executive Director
Council for Interior Design Accreditation
206 Grandview Avenue, Suite 350
Grand Rapids, Michigan 49503-4014
Phone: 616-458-0400
Fax: 616-458-0460
E-mail: info@accredit-id.org
Website: www.accredit-id.org

## JOURNALISM AND MASS COMMUNICATIONS
Patricia Thompson, Executive Director
Accrediting Council on Education in Journalism and Mass Communications (ACEJMC)
201 Bishop Hall
P.O. Box 1848
University, MS 38677-1848
Phone: 662-915-5504
E-mail: pthomps1@olemiss.edu
Website: www.acejmc.org

## LANDSCAPE ARCHITECTURE
Nancy Somerville, Executive Vice President, CEO
American Society of Landscape Architects (ASLA)
636 Eye Street, NW
Washington, DC 20001-3736
Phone: 202-898-2444
Fax: 202-898-1185
E-mail: info@asla.org
Website: www.asla.org

## LAW
Barry Currier, Managing Director of Accreditation & Legal Education
American Bar Association
321 North Clark Street, 21st Floor
Chicago, Illinois 60654
Phone: 312-988-6738
Fax: 312-988-5681
E-mail: legaled@americanbar.org
Website: https://www.americanbar.org/groups/legal_education/accreditation.html

## LIBRARY
Karen O'Brien, Director
Office for Accreditation
American Library Association
50 East Huron Street
Chicago, Illinois 60611-2795
Phone: 800-545-2433, ext. 2432 or 312-280-2432
Fax: 312-280-2433
E-mail: accred@ala.org
Website: http://www.ala.org/aboutala/offices/accreditation/

MARRIAGE AND FAMILY THERAPY
Tanya A. Tamarkin, Director of Educational Affairs
Commission on Accreditation for Marriage and Family Therapy
    Education (COAMFTE)
American Association for Marriage and Family Therapy
112 South Alfred Street
Alexandria, Virginia 22314-3061
Phone: 703-838-9808
Fax: 703-838-9805
E-mail: coa@aamft.org
Website: www.aamft.org

MEDICAL ILLUSTRATION
Kathleen Megivern, Executive Director
Commission on Accreditation of Allied Health Education Programs
    (CAAHEP)
25400 US Highway 19 North, Suite 158
Clearwater, Florida 33756
Phone: 727-210-2350
Fax: 727-210-2354
E-mail: mail@caahep.org
Website: www.caahep.org

MEDICINE
Liaison Committee on Medical Education (LCME)
Robert B. Hash, M.D., LCME Secretary
American Medical Association
Council on Medical Education
330 North Wabash Avenue, Suite 39300
Chicago, Illinois 60611-5885
Phone: 312-464-4933
E-mail: lcme@aamc.org
Website: www.ama-assn.org

Liaison Committee on Medical Education (LCME)
Heather Lent, M.A., Director
Accreditation Services
Association of American Medical Colleges
655 K Street, NW
Washington, DC 20001-2399
Phone: 202-828-0596
E-mail: lcme@aamc.org
Website: www.lcme.org

MUSIC
Karen P. Moynahan, Executive Director
National Association of Schools of Music (NASM)
Commission on Accreditation
11250 Roger Bacon Drive, Suite 21
Reston, Virginia 20190-5248
Phone: 703-437-0700
Fax: 703-437-6312
E-mail: info@arts-accredit.org
Website: http://nasm.arts-accredit.org/

NATUROPATHIC MEDICINE
Daniel Seitz, J.D., Ed.D., Executive Director
Council on Naturopathic Medical Education
P.O. Box 178
Great Barrington, Massachusetts 01230
Phone: 413-528-8877
E-mail: https://cnme.org/contact-us/
Website: www.cnme.org

NURSE ANESTHESIA
Francis R.Gerbasi, Ph.D., CRNA, COA Executive Director
Council on Accreditation of Nurse Anesthesia Educational Programs
    (CoA-NAEP)
American Association of Nurse Anesthetists
222 South Prospect Avenue
Park Ridge, Illinois 60068-4001
Phone: 847-655-1160
Fax: 847-692-7137
E-mail: accreditation@coa.us.com
Website: http://www.coacrna.org

NURSE EDUCATION
Jennifer L. Butlin, Executive Director
Commission on Collegiate Nursing Education (CCNE)
One Dupont Circle, NW, Suite 530
Washington, DC 20036-1120
Phone: 202-887-6791
Fax: 202-887-8476
E-mail: jbutlin@aacn.nche.edu
Website: www.aacn.nche.edu/accreditation

Marsal P. Stoll, Chief Executive Officer
Accreditation Commission for Education in Nursing (ACEN)
3343 Peachtree Road, NE, Suite 850
Atlanta, Georgia 30326
Phone: 404-975-5000
Fax: 404-975-5020
E-mail: mstoll@acenursing.org
Website: www.acenursing.org

NURSE MIDWIFERY
Heather L. Maurer, M.A., Executive Director
Accreditation Commission for Midwifery Education (ACME)
American College of Nurse-Midwives
8403 Colesville Road, Suite 1550
Silver Spring, Maryland 20910
Phone: 240-485-1800
Fax: 240-485-1818
E-mail: info@acnm.org
Website: www.midwife.org/Program-Accreditation

NURSE PRACTITIONER
Gay Johnson, CEO
National Association of Nurse Practitioners in Women's Health
Council on Accreditation
505 C Street, NE
Washington, DC 20002
Phone: 202-543-9693 Ext. 1
Fax: 202-543-9858
E-mail: info@npwh.org
Website: www.npwh.org

NURSING
Marsal P. Stoll, Chief Executive Director
Accreditation Commission for Education in Nursing (ACEN)
3343 Peachtree Road, NE, Suite 850
Atlanta, Georgia 30326
Phone: 404-975-5000
Fax: 404-975-5020
E-mail: info@acenursing.org
Website: www.acenursing.org

OCCUPATIONAL THERAPY
Heather Stagliano, DHSc, OTR/L, Executive Director
The American Occupational Therapy Association, Inc.
4720 Montgomery Lane, Suite 200
Bethesda, Maryland 20814-3449
Phone: 301-652-6611 Ext. 2682
TDD: 800-377-8555
Fax: 240-762-5150
E-mail: accred@aota.org
Website: www.aoteonline.org

*OPTOMETRY*
Joyce L. Urbeck, Administrative Director
Accreditation Council on Optometric Education (ACOE)
American Optometric Association
243 North Lindbergh Boulevard
St. Louis, Missouri 63141-7881
Phone: 314-991-4100, Ext. 4246
Fax: 314-991-4101
E-mail: accredit@aoa.org
Website: www.theacoe.org

*OSTEOPATHIC MEDICINE*
Director, Department of Accreditation
Commission on Osteopathic College Accreditation (COCA)
American Osteopathic Association
142 East Ontario Street
Chicago, Illinois 60611
Phone: 312-202-8048
Fax: 312-202-8202
E-mail: predoc@osteopathic.org
Website: www.aoacoca.org

*PHARMACY*
Peter H. Vlasses, PharmD, Executive Director
Accreditation Council for Pharmacy Education
135 South LaSalle Street, Suite 4100
Chicago, Illinois 60603-4810
Phone: 312-664-3575
Fax: 312-664-4652
E-mail: csinfo@acpe-accredit.org
Website: www.acpe-accredit.org

*PHYSICAL THERAPY*
Sandra Wise, Senior Director
Commission on Accreditation in Physical Therapy Education (CAPTE)
American Physical Therapy Association (APTA)
1111 North Fairfax Street
Alexandria, Virginia 22314-1488
Phone: 703-706-3245
Fax: 703-706-3387
E-mail: accreditation@apta.org
Website: www.capteonline.org

*PHYSICIAN ASSISTANT STUDIES*
Sharon L. Luke, Executive Director
Accredittion Review Commission on Education for the Physician
    Assistant, Inc. (ARC-PA)
12000 Findley Road, Suite 275
Johns Creek, Georgia 30097
Phone: 770-476-1224
Fax: 770-476-1738
E-mail: arc-pa@arc-pa.org
Website: www.arc-pa.org

*PLANNING*
Jesmarie Soto Johnson, Executive Director
American Institute of Certified Planners/Association of Collegiate
    Schools of Planning/American Planning Association
Planning Accreditation Board (PAB)
2334 West Lawrence Avenue, Suite 209
Chicago, Illinois 60625
Phone: 773-334-7200
E-mail: smerits@planningaccreditationboard.org
Website: www.planningaccreditationboard.org

*PODIATRIC MEDICINE*
Heather Stagliano, OTR/L, DHSc, Executive Director
Council on Podiatric Medical Education (CPME)
American Podiatric Medical Association (APMA)
9312 Old Georgetown Road
Bethesda, Maryland 20814-1621
Phone: 301-581-9200
Fax: 301-571-4903
Website: www.cpme.org

*PSYCHOLOGY AND COUNSELING*
Jacqueline Remondet, Associate Executive Director, CEO of the
Accrediting Unit,
Office of Program Consultation and Accreditation
American Psychological Association
750 First Street, NE
Washington, DC 20002-4202
Phone: 202-336-5979 or 800-374-2721
TDD/TTY: 202-336-6123
Fax: 202-336-5978
E-mail: apaaccred@apa.org
Website: www.apa.org/ed/accreditation

Kelly Coker, Executive Director
Council for Accreditation of Counseling and Related Educational
    Programs (CACREP)
1001 North Fairfax Street, Suite 510
Alexandria, Virginia 22314
Phone: 703-535-5990
Fax: 703-739-6209
E-mail: cacrep@cacrep.org
Website: www.cacrep.org

Richard M. McFall, Executive Director
Psychological Clinical Science Accreditation System (PCSAS)
1101 East Tenth Street
IU Psychology Building
Bloomington, Indiana 47405-7007
Phone: 812-856-2570
Fax: 812-322-5545
E-mail: rmmcfall@pcsas.org
Website: www.pcsas.org

*PUBLIC HEALTH*
Laura Rasar King, M.P.H., MCHES, Executive Director
Council on Education for Public Health
1010 Wayne Avenue, Suite 220
Silver Spring, Maryland 20910
Phone: 202-789-1050
Fax: 202-789-1895
E-mail: Lking@ceph.org
Website: www.ceph.org

*PUBLIC POLICY, AFFAIRS AND ADMINISTRATION*
Crystal Calarusse, Chief Accreditation Officer
Commission on Peer Review and Accreditation
Network of Schools of Public Policy, Affairs, and Administration
(NASPAA-COPRA)
1029 Vermont Avenue, NW, Suite 1100
Washington, DC 20005
Phone: 202-628-8965
Fax: 202-626-4978
E-mail: copra@naspaa.org
Website: accreditation.naspaa.org

*RADIOLOGIC TECHNOLOGY*
Leslie Winter, Chief Executive Officer Joint Review Committee on
Education in Radiologic Technology (JRCERT)
20 North Wacker Drive, Suite 2850
Chicago, Illinois 60606-3182
Phone: 312-704-5300
Fax: 312-704-5304
E-mail: mail@jrcert.org
Website: www.jrcert.org

*REHABILITATION EDUCATION*
Frank Lane, Ph.D., Executive Director
Council for Accreditation of Counseling and Related Educational
    Programs (CACREP)
1001 North Fairfax Street, Suite 510
Alexandria, Virginia 22314
Phone: 703-535-5990
Fax: 703-739-6209
E-mail: cacrep@cacrep.org
Website: www.cacrep.org

## RESPIRATORY CARE

Thomas Smalling, Executive Director
Commission on Accreditation for Respiratory Care (CoARC)
1248 Harwood Road
Bedford, Texas 76021-4244
Phone: 817-283-2835
Fax: 817-354-8519
E-mail: tom@coarc.com
Website: www.coarc.com

## SOCIAL WORK

Dr. Stacey Borasky, Director of Accreditation
Office of Social Work Accreditation
Council on Social Work Education
1701 Duke Street, Suite 200
Alexandria, Virginia 22314
Phone: 703-683-8080
Fax: 703-519-2078
E-mail: info@cswe.org
Website: www.cswe.org

## SPEECH-LANGUAGE PATHOLOGY AND AUDIOLOGY

Kimberlee Moore, Accreditation Executive Director
American Speech-Language-Hearing Association
Council on Academic Accreditation in Audiology and
    Speech-Language Pathology
2200 Research Boulevard #310
Rockville, Maryland 20850-3289
Phone: 301-296-5700
Fax: 301-296-8750
E-mail: accreditation@asha.org
Website: http://caa.asha.org

## TEACHER EDUCATION

Christopher A. Koch, President
National Council for Accreditation of Teacher Education (NCATE)
Teacher Education Accreditation Council (TEAC)
1140 19th Street, Suite 400
Washington, DC 20036
Phone: 202-223-0077
Fax: 202-296-6620
E-mail: caep@caepnet.org
Website: www.ncate.org

## TECHNOLOGY

Michale S. McComis, Ed.D., Executive Director
Accrediting Commission of Career Schools and Colleges
2101 Wilson Boulevard, Suite 302
Arlington, Virginia 22201
Phone: 703-247-4212
Fax: 703-247-4533
E-mail: mccomis@accsc.org
Website: www.accsc.org

## TECHNOLOGY, MANAGEMENT, AND APPLIED ENGINEERING

Kelly Schild, Director of Accreditation
The Association of Technology, Management, and
Applied Engineering (ATMAE)
275 N. York Street, Suite 401
Elmhurst, Illinois 60126
Phone: 630-433-4514
Fax: 630-563-9181
E-mail: Kelly@atmae.org
Website: www.atmae.org

## THEATER

Karen P. Moynahan, Executive Director
National Association of Schools of Theatre Commission
    on Accreditation
11250 Roger Bacon Drive, Suite 21
Reston, Virginia 20190
Phone: 703-437-0700
Fax: 703-437-6312
E-mail: info@arts-accredit.org
Website: http://nast.arts-accredit.org/

## THEOLOGY

Dr. Bernard Fryshman, Executive VP
Emeritus and Interim Executive Director
Association of Advanced Rabbinical and Talmudic Schools (AARTS)
Accreditation Commission
11 Broadway, Suite 405
New York, New York 10004
Phone: 212-363-1991
Fax: 212-533-5335
E-mail: k.sharfman.aarts@gmail.com

Frank Yamada, Executive Director
Association of Theological Schools in the United States
    and Canada (ATS)
Commission on Accrediting
10 Summit Park Drive
Pittsburgh, Pennsylvania 15275
Phone: 412-788-6505
Fax: 412-788-6510
E-mail: ats@ats.edu
Website: www.ats.edu

Dr. Timothy Eaton, President
Transnational Association of Christian Colleges and Schools (TRACS)
Accreditation Commission
15935 Forest Road
Forest, Virginia 24551
Phone: 434-525-9539
Fax: 434-525-9538
E-mail: info@tracs.org
Website: www.tracs.org

## VETERINARY MEDICINE

Dr. Karen Brandt, Director of Education and Research
American Veterinary Medical Association (AVMA)
Council on Education
1931 North Meacham Road, Suite 100
Schaumburg, Illinois 60173-4360
Phone: 847-925-8070 Ext. 6674
Fax: 847-285-5732
E-mail: info@avma.org
Website: www.avma.org

# How to Use These Guides

As you identify the particular programs and institutions that interest you, you can use both the *Graduate & Professional Programs: An Overview* volume and the specialized volumes in the series to obtain detailed information.

- *Graduate Programs in the Biological/Biomedical Sciences & Health-Related Professions*
- *Graduate Programs in Business, Education, Information Studies, Law & Social Work*
- *Graduate Programs in Engineering & Applied Sciences*
- *Graduate Programs the Humanities, Arts & Social Sciences*
- *Graduate Programs in the Physical Sciences, Mathematics, Agricultural Sciences, the Environment & Natural Resources*

Each of the specialized volumes in the series is divided into sections that contain one or more directories devoted to programs in a particular field. If you do not find a directory devoted to your field of interest in a specific volume, consult "Directories and Subject Areas" (located at the end of each volume). After you have identified the correct volume, consult the "Directories and Subject Areas in This Book" index, which shows (as does the more general directory) what directories cover subjects not specifically named in a directory or section title.

Each of the specialized volumes in the series has a number of general directories. These directories have entries for the largest unit at an institution granting graduate degrees in that field. For example, the general Engineering and Applied Sciences directory in the *Graduate Programs in Engineering & Applied Sciences* volume consists of **Profiles** for colleges, schools, and departments of engineering and applied sciences.

General directories are followed by other directories, or sections, that give more detailed information about programs in particular areas of the general field that has been covered. The general Engineering and Applied Sciences directory, in the previous example, is followed by nineteen sections with directories in specific areas of engineering, such as Chemical Engineering, Industrial/Management Engineering, and Mechanical Engineering.

Because of the broad nature of many fields, any system of organization is bound to involve a certain amount of overlap. Environmental studies, for example, is a field whose various aspects are studied in several types of departments and schools. Readers interested in such studies will find information on relevant programs in the *Graduate Programs in the Biological/Biomedical Sciences & Health-Related Professions* volume under Ecology and Environmental Biology and Environmental and Occupational Health; in the *Graduate Programs in the Physical Sciences, Mathematics, Agricultural Sciences, the Environment & Natural Resources* volume under Environmental Management and Policy and Natural Resources; and in the *Graduate Programs in Engineering & Applied Sciences* volume under Energy Management and Policy and Environmental Engineering. To help you find all of the programs of interest to you, the introduction to each section within the specialized volumes includes, if applicable, a paragraph suggesting other sections and directories with information on related areas of study.

## Directory of Institutions with Programs in the Physical Sciences, Mathematics, Agricultural Sciences, the Environment & Natural Resources

This directory lists institutions in alphabetical order and includes beneath each name the academic fields in which each institution offers graduate programs. The degree level in each field is also indicated, provided that the institution has supplied that information in response to Peterson's Annual Survey of Graduate and Professional Institutions.

An M indicates that a master's degree program is offered; a D indicates that a doctoral degree program is offered; an O signifies that other advanced degrees (e.g., certificates or specialist degrees) are offered; and an * (asterisk) indicates that a **Close-Up** and/or **Display** is located in this volume. See the index, "Close-Ups and Displays," for the specific page number.

## Profiles of Academic and Professional Programs in the Specialized Volumes

Each section of **Profiles** has a table of contents that lists the Program Directories, **Displays**, and **Close-Ups**. Program Directories consist of the **Profiles** of programs in the relevant fields, with **Displays** following if programs have chosen to include them. **Close-Ups**, which are more individualized statements, are also listed for those graduate schools or programs that have chosen to submit them.

The **Profiles** found in the 500 directories in the specialized volumes provide basic data about the graduate units in capsule form for quick reference. To make these directories as useful as possible, **Profiles** are generally listed for an institution's smallest academic unit within a subject area. In other words, if an institution has a College of Liberal Arts that administers many related programs, the **Profile** for the individual program (e.g., Program in History), not the entire College, appears in the directory.

Some institutions maintain a "Premium Profile" at Peterson's where prospective students can find more in-depth school program descriptions and information. You can learn more about those schools by visiting **www.petersons.com**

There are some programs that do not fit into any current directory and are not given individual **Profiles**. The directory structure is reviewed annually in order to keep this number to a minimum and to accommodate major trends in graduate education.

The following outline describes the **Profile** information found in the guides and explains how best to use that information. Any item that does not apply to or was not provided by a graduate unit is omitted from its listing. The format of the **Profiles** is constant, making it easy to compare one institution with another and one program with another.

**Identifying Information.** The institution's name, in boldface type, is followed by a complete listing of the administrative structure for that field of study. (For example, University of Akron, Buchtel College of Arts and Sciences, Department of Theoretical and Applied Mathematics, Program in Mathematics.) The last unit listed is the one to which all information in the **Profile** pertains. The institution's city, state, and ZIP code follow.

**Offerings.** Each field of study offered by the unit is listed with all postbaccalaureate degrees awarded. Degrees that are not preceded by a specific concentration are awarded in the general field listed in the unit name. Frequently, fields of study are broken down into subspecializations, and those appear following the degrees awarded; for example, "Offerings in secondary education (M.Ed.), including English education, mathematics education, science education." Students enrolled in the M.Ed. program would be able to specialize in any of the three fields mentioned.

**Professional Accreditation.** Some **Profiles** indicate whether a program is professionally accredited. Because it is possible for a program to receive or lose professional accreditation at any time, students entering fields in which accreditation is important to a career should verify the status of programs by contacting either the chairperson or the appropriate accrediting association.

**Jointly Offered Degrees.** Explanatory statements concerning programs that are offered in cooperation with other institutions are included in the list of degrees offered. This occurs most commonly on a regional basis (for example, two state universities offering a cooperative Ph.D. in special education) or where the specialized nature of the

institutions encourages joint efforts (a J.D./M.B.A. offered by a law school at an institution with no formal business programs and an institution with a business school but lacking a law school). Only programs that are truly cooperative are listed; those involving only limited course work at another institution are not. Interested students should contact the heads of such units for further information.

**Program Availability**. This may include the following: part-time, evening/weekend, online only, blended/hybrid learning, and/or minimal on-campus study. When information regarding the availability of part-time or evening/weekend study appears in the **Profile**, it means that students are able to earn a degree exclusively through such study. Blended/hybrid learning describes those courses in which some traditional in-class time has been replaced by online learning activities. Hybrid courses take advantage of the best features of both face-to-face and online learning.

**Faculty**. Figures on the number of faculty members actively involved with graduate students through teaching or research are separated into full- and part-time as well as men and women whenever the information has been supplied.

**Students**. Figures for the number of students enrolled in graduate and professional programs pertain to the semester of highest enrollment from the 2019-20 academic year. These figures are broken down into full- and part-time and men and women whenever the data have been supplied. Information on the number of matriculated students enrolled in the unit who are members of a minority group or are international students appears here. The average age of the matriculated students is followed by the number of applicants, the percentage accepted, and the number enrolled for fall 2019.

**Degrees Awarded**. The number of degrees awarded in the calendar year is listed. Many doctoral programs offer a terminal master's degree if students leave the program after completing only part of the requirements for a doctoral degree; that is indicated here. All degrees are classified into one of four types: master's, doctoral, first professional, and other advanced degrees. A unit may award one or several degrees at a given level; however, the data are only collected by type and may therefore represent several different degree programs.

**Degree Requirements**. The information in this section is also broken down by type of degree, and all information for a degree level pertains to all degrees of that type unless otherwise specified. Degree requirements are collected in a simplified form to provide some very basic information on the nature of the program and on foreign language, thesis or dissertation, comprehensive exam, and registration requirements. Many units also provide a short list of additional requirements, such as fieldwork or an internship. For complete information on graduation requirements, contact the graduate school or program directly.

**Entrance Requirements**. Entrance requirements are broken down into the four degree levels of master's, doctoral, first professional, and other advanced degrees. Within each level, information may be provided in two basic categories: entrance exams and other requirements. The entrance exams are identified by the standard acronyms used by the testing agencies, unless they are not well known. Other entrance requirements are quite varied, but they often contain an undergraduate or graduate grade point average (GPA). Unless otherwise stated, the GPA is calculated on a 4.0 scale and is listed as a minimum required for admission. Additional exam requirements/recommendations for international students may be listed here. Application deadlines for domestic and international students, the application fee, and whether electronic applications are accepted may be listed here. Note that the deadline should be used for reference only; these dates are subject to change, and students interested in applying should always contact the graduate unit directly about application procedures and deadlines.

**Expenses.** The typical cost of study for the 2019-20 academic year (2018-19 if 2019-20 figures were not available) is given in two basic categories: tuition and fees. Cost of study may be quite complex at a graduate institution. There are often sliding scales for part-time study, a different cost for first-year students, and other variables that make it impossible to completely cover the cost of study for each graduate program. To provide the most usable information, figures are given for full-time study for a full year where available and for part-time study in terms of a per-unit rate (per credit, per semester hour, etc.). Occasionally, variances may be noted in tuition and fees for reasons such as the type of program, whether courses are taken during the day or evening, whether courses are at the master's or doctoral level, or other institution-specific reasons. Respondents were also given the opportunity to provide more specific and detailed tuition and fees information at the unit level. When provided, this information will appear in place of any typical costs entered elsewhere on the university-level survey. Expenses are usually subject to change; for exact costs at any given time, contact your chosen schools and programs directly. Keep in mind that the tuition of Canadian institutions is usually given in Canadian dollars.

**Financial Support**. This section contains data on the number of awards administered by the institution and given to graduate students during the 2019-20 academic year. The first figure given represents the total number of students receiving financial support enrolled in that unit. If the unit has provided information on graduate appointments, these are broken down into three major categories: fellowships give money to graduate students to cover the cost of study and living expenses and are not based on a work obligation or research commitment, research assistantships provide stipends to graduate students for assistance in a formal research project with a faculty member, and teaching assistantships provide stipends to graduate students for teaching or for assisting faculty members in teaching undergraduate classes. Within each category, figures are given for the total number of awards, the average yearly amount per award, and whether full or partial tuition reimbursements are awarded. In addition to graduate appointments, the availability of several other financial aid sources is covered in this section. Tuition waivers are routinely part of a graduate appointment, but units sometimes waive part or all of a student's tuition even if a graduate appointment is not available. Federal Work Study is made available to students who demonstrate need and meet the federal guidelines; this form of aid normally includes 10 or more hours of work per week in an office of the institution. Institutionally sponsored loans are low-interest loans available to graduate students to cover both educational and living expenses. Career-related internships or fieldwork offer money to students who are participating in a formal off-campus research project or practicum. Grants, scholarships, traineeships, unspecified assistantships, and other awards may also be noted. The availability of financial support to part-time students is also indicated here.

Some programs list the financial aid application deadline and the forms that need to be completed for students to be eligible for financial awards. There are two forms: FAFSA, the Free Application for Federal Student Aid, which is required for federal aid, and the CSS PROFILE®.

**Faculty Research**. Each unit has the opportunity to list several keyword phrases describing the current research involving faculty members and graduate students. Space limitations prevent the unit from listing complete information on all research programs. The total expenditure for funded research from the previous academic year may also be included.

**Unit Head and Application Contact**. The head of the graduate program for each unit may be listed with academic title, phone and fax numbers, and e-mail address. In addition to the unit head's contact information, many graduate programs also list a separate contact for application and admission information, followed by the graduate school, program, or department's website. If no unit head or application contact is given, you should contact the overall institution for information on graduate admissions.

# Displays and Close-Ups

Any **Displays** and **Close-Ups** are supplementary insertions submitted by deans, chairs, and other administrators who wish to offer an additional, more individualized statement to readers. A number of graduate school and program administrators have attached a **Display** ad near the **Profile** listing. Here you will find information that an institution or program wants to emphasize. The **Close-Ups** are by their very nature more expansive and flexible than the **Profiles**, and the administrators who have written them may emphasize different aspects of their programs. All of the **Close-Ups** are organized in the same way (with the exception of a few that describe research and training opportunities instead of degree programs), and in each one you will find information on the same basic topics, such as programs of study, research facilities, tuition and fees, financial aid, and application procedures. If an institution or program has submitted a **Close-Up**, a

boldface cross-reference appears below its **Profile**. As with the **Displays**, all of the **Close-Ups** in the guides have been submitted by choice; the absence of a **Display** or **Close-Up** does not reflect any type of editorial judgment on the part of Peterson's, and their presence in the guides should not be taken as an indication of status, quality, or approval. Statements regarding a university's objectives and accomplishments are a reflection of its own beliefs and are not the opinions of the Peterson's editors.

## Appendixes

This section contains two appendixes. The first, "Institutional Changes Since the 2020 Edition," lists institutions that have closed, merged, or changed their name or status since the last edition of the guides. The second, "Abbreviations Used in the Guides," gives abbreviations of degree names, along with what those abbreviations stand for. These appendixes are identical in all six volumes of *Peterson's Graduate and Professional Programs*.

## Indexes

There are three indexes presented here. The first index, "Close-Ups and Displays," gives page references for all programs that have chosen to place **Close-Ups** and **Displays** in this volume. It is arranged alphabetically by institution; within institutions, the arrangement is alphabetical by subject area. It is not an index to all programs in the book's directories of **Profiles**; readers must refer to the directories themselves for **Profile** information on programs that have not submitted the additional, more individualized statements. The second index, "Directories and Subject Areas in Other Books in This Series", gives book references for the directories in the specialized volumes and also includes cross-references for subject area names not used in the directory structure, for example, "Computing Technology (see Computer Science)." The third index, "Directories and Subject Areas in This Book," gives page references for the directories in this volume and cross-references for subject area names not used in this volume's directory structure.

## Data Collection Procedures

The information published in the directories and Profiles of all the books is collected through Peterson's Annual Survey of Graduate and Professional Institutions. The survey is sent each spring to nearly 2,300 institutions offering postbaccalaureate degree programs, including accredited institutions in the United States, U.S. territories, and Canada and those institutions outside the United States that are accredited by U.S. accrediting bodies. Deans and other administrators complete these surveys, providing information on programs in the 500 academic and professional fields covered in the guides as well as overall institutional information. While every effort has been made to ensure the accuracy and completeness of the data, information is sometimes unavailable or changes occur after publication deadlines. All usable information received in time for publication has been included. The omission of any particular item from a directory or Profile signifies either that the item is not applicable to the institution or program or that information was not available. Profiles of programs scheduled to begin during the 2019-20 academic year cannot, obviously, include statistics on enrollment or, in many cases, the number of faculty members. If no usable data were submitted by an institution, its name, address, and program name appear in order to indicate the availability of graduate work.

## Criteria for Inclusion in This Guide

To be included in this guide, an institution must have full accreditation or be a candidate for accreditation (preaccreditation) status by an institutional or specialized accrediting body recognized by the U.S. Department of Education or the Council for Higher Education Accreditation (CHEA). Institutional accrediting bodies, which review each institution as a whole, include the six regional associations of schools and colleges (Middle States, New England, North Central, Northwest, Southern, and Western), each of which is responsible for a specified portion of the United States and its territories. Other institutional accrediting bodies are national in scope and accredit specific kinds of institutions (e.g., Bible colleges, independent colleges, and rabbinical and Talmudic schools). Program registration by the New York State Board of Regents is considered to be the equivalent of institutional accreditation, since the board requires that all programs offered by an institution meet its standards before recognition is granted. A Canadian institution must be chartered and authorized to grant degrees by the provincial government, affiliated with a chartered institution, or accredited by a recognized U.S. accrediting body. This guide also includes institutions outside the United States that are accredited by these U.S. accrediting bodies. There are recognized specialized or professional accrediting bodies in more than fifty different fields, each of which is authorized to accredit institutions or specific programs in its particular field. For specialized institutions that offer programs in one field only, we designate this to be the equivalent of institutional accreditation. A full explanation of the accrediting process and complete information on recognized institutional (regional and national) and specialized accrediting bodies can be found online at **www.chea.org** or at **www.ed.gov/admins/finaid/accred/index.html**.

# DIRECTORY OF INSTITUTIONS WITH PROGRAMS IN THE BIOLOGICAL/BIOMEDICAL SCIENCES & HEALTH-RELATED MEDICAL PROFESSIONS

**ABILENE CHRISTIAN UNIVERSITY**
Communication Disorders — M
Health Services Management and Hospital Administration — M
Nursing and Healthcare Administration — D
Nursing Education — D
Nursing—General — D
Nutrition — M,O
Occupational Therapy — M

**ACADEMY FOR FIVE ELEMENT ACUPUNCTURE**
Acupuncture and Oriental Medicine

**ACADEMY OF CHINESE CULTURE AND HEALTH SCIENCES**
Acupuncture and Oriental Medicine — M

**ACADIA UNIVERSITY**
Biological and Biomedical Sciences—General — M

**ACUPUNCTURE & INTEGRATIVE MEDICINE COLLEGE, BERKELEY**
Acupuncture and Oriental Medicine — M

**ACUPUNCTURE AND MASSAGE COLLEGE**
Acupuncture and Oriental Medicine — M

**ADELPHI UNIVERSITY**
Adult Nursing — M
Biological and Biomedical Sciences—General — M
Health Services Management and Hospital Administration — M
Nursing and Healthcare Administration — M,O
Nursing Education — M,O
Nursing—General — D
Nutrition — M,D,O
Public Health—General — M

**ADLER UNIVERSITY**
Community Health — M

**ADVENTHEALTH UNIVERSITY**
Health Services Management and Hospital Administration — M
Nurse Anesthesia — M
Occupational Therapy — M
Physical Therapy — D
Physician Assistant Studies — M

**ALABAMA AGRICULTURAL AND MECHANICAL UNIVERSITY**
Biological and Biomedical Sciences—General — M,D
Communication Disorders — M
Nutrition — M

**ALABAMA COLLEGE OF OSTEOPATHIC MEDICINE**
Osteopathic Medicine — D

**ALABAMA STATE UNIVERSITY**
Allied Health—General — M,D
Biological and Biomedical Sciences—General — M,D
Microbiology — M,D
Occupational Therapy — M
Physical Therapy — D
Rehabilitation Sciences — M

**ALASKA PACIFIC UNIVERSITY**
Health Services Management and Hospital Administration — M

**ALBANY COLLEGE OF PHARMACY AND HEALTH SCIENCES**
Cell Biology — M
Clinical Laboratory Sciences/Medical Technology — M
Health Services Research — M,D
Molecular Biology — M
Pharmaceutical Sciences — M,D
Pharmacology — M,D
Pharmacy — M,D

**ALBANY MEDICAL COLLEGE**
Allopathic Medicine — D
Bioethics — M,D,O
Cardiovascular Sciences — M,D
Cell Biology — M,D
Immunology — M,D
Microbiology — M,D
Molecular Biology — M,D
Neuroscience — M,D
Nurse Anesthesia — M
Pharmacology — M,D
Physician Assistant Studies — M

**ALBANY STATE UNIVERSITY**
Family Nurse Practitioner Studies — M
Health Services Management and Hospital Administration — M
Nursing Education — M
Nursing—General — M

**ALBERT EINSTEIN COLLEGE OF MEDICINE**
Allopathic Medicine — D
Anatomy — D
Biochemistry — D
Biological and Biomedical Sciences—General — D
Biophysics — D
Cell Biology — D
Clinical Research — D
Computational Biology — D
Developmental Biology — D
Genetics — D
Genomic Sciences — D
Immunology — D
Microbiology — D
Molecular Biology — D
Molecular Genetics — D
Molecular Pharmacology — D
Neuroscience — D
Pathology — D
Physiology — D
Structural Biology — D
Systems Biology — D

**ALBERTUS MAGNUS COLLEGE**
Health Services Management and Hospital Administration — M

**ALBIZU UNIVERSITY - MIAMI**
Communication Disorders — M,D

**ALBIZU UNIVERSITY - SAN JUAN**
Communication Disorders — M,D

**ALCORN STATE UNIVERSITY**
Biological and Biomedical Sciences—General — M
Nursing—General — M

**ALDERSON BROADDUS UNIVERSITY**
Physician Assistant Studies — M

**ALLEN COLLEGE**
Adult Nursing — M,D
Community Health Nursing — M,D
Family Nurse Practitioner Studies — M,D
Gerontological Nursing — M,D
Nursing and Healthcare Administration — M,D
Nursing Education — M,D
Nursing Informatics — M,D
Nursing—General — M,D
Occupational Therapy — M,D
Psychiatric Nursing — M,D
Public Health—General — M,D

**ALLIANT INTERNATIONAL UNIVERSITY - SAN DIEGO**
Neuroscience — M,D,O

**ALLIANT INTERNATIONAL UNIVERSITY– SAN FRANCISCO**
Pharmacology — M

**ALVERNIA UNIVERSITY**
Family Nurse Practitioner Studies — M,D,O
Gerontological Nursing — M,D,O
Nursing and Healthcare Administration — M,D,O
Nursing Education — M,D,O
Nursing—General — M,D,O
Occupational Therapy — M

**ALVERNO COLLEGE**
Family Nurse Practitioner Studies — M,D
Nursing—General — M,D
Psychiatric Nursing — M,D

**AMERICAN ACADEMY OF ACUPUNCTURE AND ORIENTAL MEDICINE**
Acupuncture and Oriental Medicine — M

**AMERICAN COLLEGE OF ACUPUNCTURE AND ORIENTAL MEDICINE**
Acupuncture and Oriental Medicine — M

**AMERICAN COLLEGE OF HEALTHCARE SCIENCES**
Allied Health—General — M,O
Health Promotion — M,O
Nutrition — M,O
Physiology — M,O

**AMERICAN INSTITUTE OF ALTERNATIVE MEDICINE**
Acupuncture and Oriental Medicine — M

**AMERICAN INTERCONTINENTAL UNIVERSITY ONLINE**
Health Services Management and Hospital Administration — M

**AMERICAN INTERNATIONAL COLLEGE**
Family Nurse Practitioner Studies — M,D,O
Nursing and Healthcare Administration — M,D,O
Nursing Education — M,D,O
Occupational Therapy — M,D,O
Physical Therapy — M,D,O

**AMERICAN MUSEUM OF NATURAL HISTORY–RICHARD GILDER GRADUATE SCHOOL**
Biological and Biomedical Sciences—General — D

**AMERICAN PUBLIC UNIVERSITY SYSTEM**
Nursing—General — M,D

**AMERICAN SENTINEL UNIVERSITY**
Health Services Management and Hospital Administration — M
Nursing—General — M

**AMERICAN UNIVERSITY**
Biological and Biomedical Sciences—General — M
Biopsychology — M,D,O
Health Promotion — M,O
Health Services Management and Hospital Administration — M,O
Neuroscience — M,D,O
Nutrition — M,O

**AMERICAN UNIVERSITY OF ARMENIA**
Public Health—General — M

**AMERICAN UNIVERSITY OF HEALTH SCIENCES**
Clinical Research — M

**ANDERSON UNIVERSITY (SC)**
Family Nurse Practitioner Studies — M,D
Health Services Management and Hospital Administration — M

**ANDERSON UNIVERSITY (SC)** *(continued)*
Nursing and Healthcare Administration — M,D
Nursing Education — M,D
Nursing—General — M,D
Psychiatric Nursing — M,D

**ANDREWS UNIVERSITY**
Allied Health—General — M
Biological and Biomedical Sciences—General — M
Communication Disorders — M
Nursing—General — M,D
Nutrition — M,O
Physical Therapy — D
Public Health—General — M,O

**ANGELO STATE UNIVERSITY**
Biological and Biomedical Sciences—General — M
Family Nurse Practitioner Studies — M
Nursing Education — M
Nursing—General — M
Physical Therapy — D

**ANTIOCH UNIVERSITY MIDWEST**
Health Services Management and Hospital Administration — M

**ANTIOCH UNIVERSITY NEW ENGLAND**
Conservation Biology — M,D

**AOMA GRADUATE SCHOOL OF INTEGRATIVE MEDICINE**
Acupuncture and Oriental Medicine — M,D

**APPALACHIAN COLLEGE OF PHARMACY**
Pharmacy — D

**APPALACHIAN STATE UNIVERSITY**
Biological and Biomedical Sciences—General — M
Cell Biology — M
Communication Disorders — M
Molecular Biology — M
Nutrition — M

**AQUINAS INSTITUTE OF THEOLOGY**
Health Services Management and Hospital Administration — M,D,O

**ARCADIA UNIVERSITY**
Physical Therapy — D
Physician Assistant Studies — M
Public Health—General — M

**ARGOSY UNIVERSITY, ATLANTA**
Biopsychology — M,D,O
Health Services Management and Hospital Administration — M,D
Public Health—General — M

**ARGOSY UNIVERSITY, CHICAGO**
Health Services Management and Hospital Administration — M,D
Neuroscience — D
Public Health—General — M

**ARGOSY UNIVERSITY, HAWAII**
Health Services Management and Hospital Administration — M,D,O
Pharmacology — M,O
Public Health—General — M

**ARGOSY UNIVERSITY, LOS ANGELES**
Health Services Management and Hospital Administration — M,D
Public Health—General — M

**ARGOSY UNIVERSITY, NORTHERN VIRGINIA**
Health Services Management and Hospital Administration — M,D,O
Public Health—General — M

**ARGOSY UNIVERSITY, ORANGE COUNTY**
Health Services Management and Hospital Administration — M,D,O
Public Health—General — M

**ARGOSY UNIVERSITY, PHOENIX**
Health Services Management and Hospital Administration — M,D
Neuroscience — D
Public Health—General — M

**ARGOSY UNIVERSITY, SEATTLE**
Health Services Management and Hospital Administration — M,D
Public Health—General — M

**ARGOSY UNIVERSITY, TAMPA**
Health Services Management and Hospital Administration — M,D
Neuroscience — M,D
Public Health—General — M

**ARGOSY UNIVERSITY, TWIN CITIES**
Biopsychology — M,D,O
Health Services Management and Hospital Administration — M,D
Public Health—General — M

**ARIZONA SCHOOL OF ACUPUNCTURE AND ORIENTAL MEDICINE**
Acupuncture and Oriental Medicine — M

**ARIZONA STATE UNIVERSITY AT TEMPE**
Animal Behavior — M,D
Biochemistry — M,D
Biological and Biomedical Sciences—General — M,D
Cell Biology — M,D
Communication Disorders — M,D
Community Health — M,D,O
Conservation Biology — M,D
Evolutionary Biology — M,D
Family Nurse Practitioner Studies — M,D,O
Gerontological Nursing — M,D,O
Health Promotion — M,D
Health Services Management and Hospital Administration — M,D,O
International Health — M,D,O
Microbiology — M,D
Molecular Biology — M,D
Neuroscience — M,D
Nursing and Healthcare Administration — M,D,O
Nursing Education — M,D,O
Nursing—General — M,D,O
Nutrition — M,D
Plant Biology — M,D
Psychiatric Nursing — M,D,O
Public Health—General — M,D,O

**ARKANSAS COLLEGES OF HEALTH EDUCATION**
Biological and Biomedical Sciences—General — M
Osteopathic Medicine — D

**ARKANSAS STATE UNIVERSITY**
Biological and Biomedical Sciences—General — M,O
Communication Disorders — M,O
Health Services Management and Hospital Administration — M,D,O
Molecular Biology — M,D
Nurse Anesthesia — M,D,O
Nursing—General — M,D,O
Occupational Therapy — D
Physical Therapy — D

**ARKANSAS TECH UNIVERSITY**
Nursing—General — M

**ASHLAND UNIVERSITY**
Family Nurse Practitioner Studies — D
Health Services Management and Hospital Administration — M
Nursing—General — D

**ASHWORTH COLLEGE**
Health Services Management and Hospital Administration — M

**ASPEN UNIVERSITY**
Forensic Nursing — M
Nursing and Healthcare Administration — M
Nursing Education — M
Nursing Informatics — M
Nursing—General — M

**ASSUMPTION UNIVERSITY**
Health Services Management and Hospital Administration — M,O

**ATHABASCA UNIVERSITY**
Allied Health—General — M,O
Nursing and Healthcare Administration — M,O
Nursing—General — M,O

**ATLANTIC INSTITUTE OF ORIENTAL MEDICINE**
Acupuncture and Oriental Medicine — M,D

**ATLANTIS UNIVERSITY**
Health Services Management and Hospital Administration — M

**A.T. STILL UNIVERSITY**
Allied Health—General — M,D,O
Biological and Biomedical Sciences—General — M,D
Communication Disorders — M,D,O
Dentistry — M,D,O
Health Services Management and Hospital Administration — M,D,O
International Health — M,D,O
Occupational Therapy — M,D,O
Oral and Dental Sciences — M,D,O
Osteopathic Medicine — M,D
Physical Therapy — M,D,O
Physician Assistant Studies — M,D,O
Public Health—General — M,D,O

**AUBURN UNIVERSITY**
Biochemistry — M,D
Biological and Biomedical Sciences—General — M,D
Botany — M,D
Cell Biology — M,D
Communication Disorders — M,D
Entomology — M,D
Molecular Biology — M,D
Nursing Education — M
Nursing—General — M
Nutrition — M,D,O
Pharmaceutical Sciences — M,D
Pharmacy — D
Plant Pathology — M,D
Veterinary Medicine — D
Zoology — M,D

**AUBURN UNIVERSITY AT MONTGOMERY**
Family Nurse Practitioner Studies — M
Nursing Education — M
Nursing—General — M

**AUGSBURG UNIVERSITY**
Family Nurse Practitioner Studies — M,D
Nursing—General — M,D
Physician Assistant Studies — M
Transcultural Nursing — M,D

**AUGUSTA UNIVERSITY**
Acute Care/Critical Care Nursing — D
Allied Health—General — D
Allopathic Medicine — D
Anatomy — D
Biochemistry — D
Cancer Biology/Oncology — D
Cardiovascular Sciences — D
Cell Biology — D
Clinical Research — M

| | |
|---|---|
| Dentistry | D |
| Environmental and Occupational Health | M |
| Family Nurse Practitioner Studies | D |
| Genomic Sciences | D |
| Gerontological Nursing | D |
| Molecular Medicine | D |
| Neuroscience | D |
| Nurse Anesthesia | D |
| Nursing and Healthcare Administration | M,D |
| Nursing—General | D |
| Occupational Therapy | M |
| Oral and Dental Sciences | M,D |
| Pediatric Nursing | D |
| Pharmacology | D |
| Physical Therapy | D |
| Physician Assistant Studies | M |
| Physiology | D |
| Psychiatric Nursing | D |
| Public Health—General | M |
| Rehabilitation Sciences | D |

**AUSTIN PEAY STATE UNIVERSITY**

| | |
|---|---|
| Biological and Biomedical Sciences—General | M |
| Clinical Laboratory Sciences/Medical Technology | M |
| Family Nurse Practitioner Studies | M |
| Nursing and Healthcare Administration | M |
| Nursing Education | M |
| Nursing Informatics | M |
| Nursing—General | M |
| Public Health—General | M |

**AZUSA PACIFIC UNIVERSITY**

| | |
|---|---|
| Adult Nursing | M,D |
| Family Nurse Practitioner Studies | M,D |
| Gerontological Nursing | M,D |
| Nursing and Healthcare Administration | M,D |
| Nursing Education | M,D |
| Nursing—General | M,D |
| Pediatric Nursing | M,D |
| Physical Therapy | D |
| Psychiatric Nursing | M,D |
| Public Health—General | M |

**BAKER COLLEGE CENTER FOR GRADUATE STUDIES–ONLINE**

| | |
|---|---|
| Health Services Management and Hospital Administration | M,D |
| Occupational Therapy | M,D |

**BALDWIN WALLACE UNIVERSITY**

| | |
|---|---|
| Communication Disorders | M |
| Health Services Management and Hospital Administration | M |
| Physician Assistant Studies | M |
| Public Health—General | M |

**BALL STATE UNIVERSITY**

| | |
|---|---|
| Biological and Biomedical Sciences—General | M,D |
| Communication Disorders | M,D |
| Family Nurse Practitioner Studies | M,D,O |
| Gerontological Nursing | M,D,O |
| Health Promotion | M |
| Neuroscience | M,D,O |
| Nursing Education | M,D,O |
| Nursing—General | M,D,O |
| Nutrition | M |
| Physiology | M |

**BANK STREET COLLEGE OF EDUCATION**

| | |
|---|---|
| Maternal and Child Health | M |

**BARRY UNIVERSITY**

| | |
|---|---|
| Acute Care/Critical Care Nursing | M,O |
| Anatomy | M |
| Biological and Biomedical Sciences—General | M |
| Communication Disorders | M |
| Family Nurse Practitioner Studies | M,O |
| Health Services Management and Hospital Administration | M,O |
| Nurse Anesthesia | M |
| Nursing and Healthcare Administration | M,D,O |
| Nursing Education | M,O |
| Nursing—General | M,D,O |
| Occupational Therapy | M |
| Physician Assistant Studies | M |
| Podiatric Medicine | D |
| Public Health—General | M |

**BARUCH COLLEGE OF THE CITY UNIVERSITY OF NEW YORK**

| | |
|---|---|
| Health Services Management and Hospital Administration | M |

**BASTYR UNIVERSITY**

| | |
|---|---|
| Acupuncture and Oriental Medicine | M,D |
| Maternal and Child Health | M,O |
| Naturopathic Medicine | D,O |
| Nurse Midwifery | M,O |
| Nutrition | M,O |

**BAYLOR COLLEGE OF MEDICINE**

| | |
|---|---|
| Allopathic Medicine | D |
| Biochemistry | D |
| Biological and Biomedical Sciences—General | M,D |
| Biophysics | D |
| Cancer Biology/Oncology | D |
| Cardiovascular Sciences | D |
| Cell Biology | D |
| Clinical Laboratory Sciences/Medical Technology | M,D |
| Computational Biology | D |
| Developmental Biology | D |
| Genetics | D |
| Human Genetics | D |
| Immunology | D |
| Microbiology | D |
| Molecular Biology | D |
| Molecular Biophysics | D |
| Molecular Medicine | D |
| Molecular Physiology | D |
| Neuroscience | D |
| Nurse Anesthesia | D |
| Pharmacology | D |
| Physician Assistant Studies | M |
| Structural Biology | D |
| Translational Biology | D |
| Virology | D |

**BAYLOR UNIVERSITY**

| | |
|---|---|
| Biochemistry | M,D |
| Biological and Biomedical Sciences—General | M,D |
| Communication Disorders | M |
| Community Health | M |
| Ecology | D |
| Health Services Management and Hospital Administration | M |
| Nursing—General | M,D |
| Nutrition | M,D |
| Physiology | M,D |
| Public Health—General | M |

**BAY PATH UNIVERSITY**

| | |
|---|---|
| Health Services Management and Hospital Administration | M |
| Occupational Therapy | M,D |
| Physician Assistant Studies | M |

**BELHAVEN UNIVERSITY (MS)**

| | |
|---|---|
| Health Services Management and Hospital Administration | M |

**BELLARMINE UNIVERSITY**

| | |
|---|---|
| Family Nurse Practitioner Studies | M,D |
| Nursing and Healthcare Administration | M,D |
| Nursing Education | M,D |
| Nursing—General | M,D |
| Physical Therapy | M,D |

**BELLEVUE UNIVERSITY**

| | |
|---|---|
| Health Services Management and Hospital Administration | M |

**BELLIN COLLEGE**

| | |
|---|---|
| Family Nurse Practitioner Studies | M |
| Nursing Education | M |
| Nursing—General | M |

**BELMONT UNIVERSITY**

| | |
|---|---|
| Allied Health—General | M,D |
| Health Services Management and Hospital Administration | M |
| Nursing—General | M,D |
| Occupational Therapy | M,D |
| Pharmaceutical Administration | D |
| Pharmacy | D |
| Physical Therapy | M,D |
| Public Health—General | D |

**BEMIDJI STATE UNIVERSITY**

| | |
|---|---|
| Biological and Biomedical Sciences—General | M |

**BENEDICTINE UNIVERSITY**

| | |
|---|---|
| Health Services Management and Hospital Administration | M |
| Nursing—General | M |
| Nutrition | M |
| Public Health—General | M |

**BENNINGTON COLLEGE**

| | |
|---|---|
| Allied Health—General | O |

**BETHEL UNIVERSITY (IN)**

| | |
|---|---|
| Nursing—General | M |

**BETHEL UNIVERSITY (MN)**

| | |
|---|---|
| Nurse Midwifery | M,D,O |
| Nursing Education | M,D,O |
| Physician Assistant Studies | M,D,O |

**BETHEL UNIVERSITY (TN)**

| | |
|---|---|
| Physician Assistant Studies | M |

**BINGHAMTON UNIVERSITY, STATE UNIVERSITY OF NEW YORK**

| | |
|---|---|
| Biological and Biomedical Sciences—General | M,D |
| Biopsychology | D |
| Community Health Nursing | M,D,O |
| Family Nurse Practitioner Studies | M,D,O |
| Gerontological Nursing | M,D,O |
| Health Services Management and Hospital Administration | M,D |
| Nursing—General | M,D,O |
| Pharmacy | D |
| Psychiatric Nursing | M,D,O |

**BLACK HILLS STATE UNIVERSITY**

| | |
|---|---|
| Genomic Sciences | M |

**BLESSING-RIEMAN COLLEGE OF NURSING & HEALTH SCIENCES**

| | |
|---|---|
| Nursing and Healthcare Administration | M |
| Nursing Education | M |
| Nursing—General | M |

**BLOOMSBURG UNIVERSITY OF PENNSYLVANIA**

| | |
|---|---|
| Adult Nursing | M,D |
| Biological and Biomedical Sciences—General | M |
| Communication Disorders | M,D |
| Community Health | M,D |
| Family Nurse Practitioner Studies | M,D |
| Nurse Anesthesia | M,D |
| Nursing and Healthcare Administration | M,D |
| Nursing—General | M,D |

**BLUFFTON UNIVERSITY**

| | |
|---|---|
| Health Services Management and Hospital Administration | M |

**BOISE STATE UNIVERSITY**

| | |
|---|---|
| Biological and Biomedical Sciences—General | M,D |
| Environmental and Occupational Health | M,O |
| Gerontological Nursing | M,D,O |
| Health Promotion | M,O |
| Molecular Biology | M,D |
| Nursing—General | M,D,O |
| Public Health—General | M,D,O |

**BOSTON COLLEGE**

| | |
|---|---|
| Adult Nursing | M,D |
| Biochemistry | M,D |
| Biological and Biomedical Sciences—General | D |
| Gerontological Nursing | M,D |
| Maternal and Child/Neonatal Nursing | M,D |
| Nurse Anesthesia | M,D |
| Nursing—General | M,D |
| Pediatric Nursing | M,D |
| Psychiatric Nursing | M,D |
| Women's Health Nursing | M,D |

**BOSTON UNIVERSITY**

| | |
|---|---|
| Allied Health—General | M,D |
| Allopathic Medicine | D |
| Anatomy | M,D |
| Biochemistry | M,D |
| Biological and Biomedical Sciences—General | M,D |
| Biophysics | M,D |
| Biopsychology | M |
| Cell Biology | M,D |
| Clinical Research | M |
| Communication Disorders | M,D |
| Genetics | D |
| Genomic Sciences | D |
| Health Services Management and Hospital Administration | M |
| Immunology | D |
| Medical Imaging | M |
| Microbiology | D |
| Molecular Biology | M,D |
| Molecular Medicine | D |
| Neurobiology | M,D |
| Neuroscience | D |
| Nutrition | M,D |
| Occupational Therapy | D |
| Oral and Dental Sciences | M,D |
| Pathology | M,D |
| Pharmaceutical Sciences | D |
| Pharmacology | M,D |
| Physical Therapy | M,D |
| Physician Assistant Studies | M |
| Physiology | M,D |
| Public Health—General | M,D |
| Rehabilitation Sciences | M,D |
| Translational Biology | D |

**BOWIE STATE UNIVERSITY**

| | |
|---|---|
| Family Nurse Practitioner Studies | M |
| Nursing and Healthcare Administration | M |
| Nursing Education | M |
| Nursing—General | M |

**BOWLING GREEN STATE UNIVERSITY**

| | |
|---|---|
| Biological and Biomedical Sciences—General | M,D |
| Communication Disorders | M,D |
| Public Health—General | M |

**BRADLEY UNIVERSITY**

| | |
|---|---|
| Biochemistry | M |
| Biological and Biomedical Sciences—General | M |
| Family Nurse Practitioner Studies | M,D,O |
| Health Services Management and Hospital Administration | M,D,O |
| Nursing and Healthcare Administration | M,D,O |
| Nursing Education | M,D,O |
| Nursing—General | M,D,O |
| Nutrition | M |
| Physical Therapy | D |

**BRANDEIS UNIVERSITY**

| | |
|---|---|
| Biochemistry | M,D |
| Biological and Biomedical Sciences—General | M,D |
| Biophysics | M,D |
| Cell Biology | M,D |
| Genetics | M,D |
| Health Services Management and Hospital Administration | M |
| International Health | M,D |
| Microbiology | M,D |
| Molecular Biology | M,D |
| Neurobiology | M,D |
| Neuroscience | M,D |

**BRANDMAN UNIVERSITY**

| | |
|---|---|
| Health Services Management and Hospital Administration | M |
| Nursing—General | D |

**BRENAU UNIVERSITY**

| | |
|---|---|
| Family Nurse Practitioner Studies | M |
| Health Services Management and Hospital Administration | M |
| Nursing and Healthcare Administration | M |
| Nursing Education | M |
| Occupational Therapy | M |

**BRIAR CLIFF UNIVERSITY**

| | |
|---|---|
| Nursing—General | M,D,O |

**BRIDGEWATER STATE UNIVERSITY**

| | |
|---|---|
| Communication Disorders | M |
| Health Promotion | M |

**BRIGHAM YOUNG UNIVERSITY**

| | |
|---|---|
| Biochemistry | M,D |
| Biological and Biomedical Sciences—General | M,D |
| Communication Disorders | M |
| Developmental Biology | M,D |
| Family Nurse Practitioner Studies | M |
| Health Promotion | M,D |
| Health Services Management and Hospital Administration | M |
| Microbiology | M,D |
| Molecular Biology | M,D |
| Neuroscience | M,D |
| Nursing—General | M |
| Nutrition | M |
| Physiology | M,D |
| Public Health—General | M |

**BROADVIEW UNIVERSITY–WEST JORDAN**

| | |
|---|---|
| Health Services Management and Hospital Administration | M |

**BROCK UNIVERSITY**

| | |
|---|---|
| Allied Health—General | M,D |
| Biological and Biomedical Sciences—General | M,D |
| Neuroscience | M,D |

**BROOKLINE COLLEGE - PHOENIX CAMPUS**

| | |
|---|---|
| Nursing and Healthcare Administration | M |
| Nursing—General | M |

**BROOKLYN COLLEGE OF THE CITY UNIVERSITY OF NEW YORK**

| | |
|---|---|
| Biological and Biomedical Sciences—General | M |
| Communication Disorders | M,D |
| Community Health | M |
| Health Services Management and Hospital Administration | M |
| Nutrition | M |
| Public Health—General | M |

**BROWN UNIVERSITY**

| | |
|---|---|
| Allopathic Medicine | D |
| Biochemistry | M,D |
| Biological and Biomedical Sciences—General | M,D |
| Cell Biology | M,D |
| Community Health | M,D |
| Ecology | D |
| Epidemiology | M,D |
| Evolutionary Biology | D |
| Health Services Research | D |
| Molecular Biology | M,D |
| Molecular Pharmacology | M,D |
| Neuroscience | D |
| Pathobiology | M,D |
| Physiology | M,D |
| Public Health—General | M |

**BRYAN COLLEGE**

| | |
|---|---|
| Health Services Management and Hospital Administration | M |

**BRYAN COLLEGE OF HEALTH SCIENCES**

| | |
|---|---|
| Nurse Anesthesia | M |

**BRYANT UNIVERSITY**

| | |
|---|---|
| Physician Assistant Studies | M |

**BUCKNELL UNIVERSITY**

| | |
|---|---|
| Animal Behavior | M |
| Biological and Biomedical Sciences—General | M |

**BUFFALO STATE COLLEGE, STATE UNIVERSITY OF NEW YORK**

| | |
|---|---|
| Biological and Biomedical Sciences—General | M |
| Communication Disorders | M |
| Nutrition | M |

**BURRELL COLLEGE OF OSTEOPATHIC MEDICINE**

| | |
|---|---|
| Osteopathic Medicine | D |

**BUTLER UNIVERSITY**

| | |
|---|---|
| Pharmaceutical Sciences | M,D |
| Pharmacy | M,D |
| Physician Assistant Studies | M,D |

**CABARRUS COLLEGE OF HEALTH SCIENCES**

| | |
|---|---|
| Occupational Therapy | M |

**CABRINI UNIVERSITY**

| | |
|---|---|
| Biological and Biomedical Sciences—General | M,D |

**CALIFORNIA BAPTIST UNIVERSITY**

| | |
|---|---|
| Adult Nursing | M |
| Communication Disorders | M |
| Family Nurse Practitioner Studies | M |
| Health Promotion | M |
| Health Services Management and Hospital Administration | M |
| Nursing and Healthcare Administration | M |
| Nursing Education | M |
| Nursing—General | M,D |
| Physician Assistant Studies | M |
| Public Health—General | M |

**CALIFORNIA COAST UNIVERSITY**

| | |
|---|---|
| Health Services Management and Hospital Administration | M |

*M—masters degree; D—doctorate; O—other advanced degree; *—Close-Up and/or Display*

**CALIFORNIA HEALTH SCIENCES UNIVERSITY**
Pharmacy — D

**CALIFORNIA INSTITUTE OF TECHNOLOGY**
Biochemistry — M,D
Biological and Biomedical Sciences—General — D
Biophysics — D
Cell Biology — D
Developmental Biology — D
Genetics — D
Immunology — D
Molecular Biology — D
Molecular Biophysics — M,D
Neurobiology — D
Neuroscience — M,D

**CALIFORNIA INTERCONTINENTAL UNIVERSITY**
Health Services Management and Hospital Administration — M,D

**CALIFORNIA NORTHSTATE UNIVERSITY**
Allopathic Medicine — M
Pharmacy — D

**CALIFORNIA POLYTECHNIC STATE UNIVERSITY, SAN LUIS OBISPO**
Biochemistry — M
Biological and Biomedical Sciences—General — M
Nutrition — M

**CALIFORNIA STATE POLYTECHNIC UNIVERSITY, POMONA**
Biological and Biomedical Sciences—General — M

**CALIFORNIA STATE UNIVERSITY, CHICO**
Biological and Biomedical Sciences—General — M
Communication Disorders — M
Health Services Management and Hospital Administration — M
Nursing—General — M
Nutrition — M

**CALIFORNIA STATE UNIVERSITY, DOMINGUEZ HILLS**
Biological and Biomedical Sciences—General — M
Nursing—General — M
Occupational Therapy — M

**CALIFORNIA STATE UNIVERSITY, EAST BAY**
Biochemistry — M
Biological and Biomedical Sciences—General — M
Communication Disorders — M
Health Services Management and Hospital Administration — M

**CALIFORNIA STATE UNIVERSITY, FRESNO**
Biological and Biomedical Sciences—General — M
Communication Disorders — M
Health Promotion — M
Health Services Management and Hospital Administration — M
Nursing—General — M,D
Physical Therapy — D
Public Health—General — M

**CALIFORNIA STATE UNIVERSITY, FULLERTON**
Biological and Biomedical Sciences—General — M
Communication Disorders — M
Environmental and Occupational Health — M
Health Promotion — M
Nurse Anesthesia — M,D
Nursing and Healthcare Administration — M,D
Nursing Education — M,D
Nursing—General — M,D
Public Health—General — M
School Nursing — M,D
Women's Health Nursing — M,D

**CALIFORNIA STATE UNIVERSITY, LONG BEACH**
Biochemistry — M
Biological and Biomedical Sciences—General — M
Communication Disorders — M
Health Services Management and Hospital Administration — M
Microbiology — M
Nursing—General — M,D,O
Nutrition — M
Physical Therapy — D
Public Health—General — M

**CALIFORNIA STATE UNIVERSITY, LOS ANGELES**
Biochemistry — M
Biological and Biomedical Sciences—General — M
Communication Disorders — M
Health Services Management and Hospital Administration — M,O
Nursing—General — M,O
Nutrition — M,O

**CALIFORNIA STATE UNIVERSITY, NORTHRIDGE**
Biochemistry — M
Biological and Biomedical Sciences—General — M
Communication Disorders — M

**CALIFORNIA STATE UNIVERSITY, SACRAMENTO** *(column 2 continues)*

Environmental and Occupational Health — M
Epidemiology — M
Health Services Management and Hospital Administration — M
Industrial Hygiene — M
Physical Therapy — M
Public Health—General — M

**CALIFORNIA STATE UNIVERSITY, SACRAMENTO**
Biochemistry — M
Biological and Biomedical Sciences—General — M
Cell Biology — M
Communication Disorders — M
Conservation Biology — M
Developmental Biology — M
Molecular Biology — M
Nursing—General — M
Physical Therapy — D

**CALIFORNIA STATE UNIVERSITY, SAN BERNARDINO**
Biological and Biomedical Sciences—General — M
Health Services Management and Hospital Administration — M
Nursing—General — M
Public Health—General — M

**CALIFORNIA STATE UNIVERSITY, SAN MARCOS**
Biological and Biomedical Sciences—General — M
Communication Disorders — M
Family Nurse Practitioner Studies — M
Nursing and Healthcare Administration — M
Nursing Education — M
Nursing—General — M
Psychiatric Nursing — M
Public Health—General — M

**CALIFORNIA STATE UNIVERSITY, STANISLAUS**
Conservation Biology — M
Ecology — M
Gerontological Nursing — M
Nursing Education — M
Nursing—General — M

**CALIFORNIA UNIVERSITY OF PENNSYLVANIA**
Communication Disorders — M
Health Services Management and Hospital Administration — M
Nursing and Healthcare Administration — M
Nursing Education — M
Nursing—General — M
Nutrition — M

**CALVIN COLLEGE**
Communication Disorders — M

**CAMBRIDGE COLLEGE**
Health Services Management and Hospital Administration — M
School Nursing — M,D,O

**CAMPBELL UNIVERSITY**
Osteopathic Medicine — D
Pharmaceutical Sciences — M,D
Pharmacy — M,D
Physical Therapy — M,D
Physician Assistant Studies — M,D
Public Health—General — M,D

**CANADIAN COLLEGE OF NATUROPATHIC MEDICINE**
Naturopathic Medicine — D

**CANADIAN MEMORIAL CHIROPRACTIC COLLEGE**
Acupuncture and Oriental Medicine — O
Chiropractic — D,O

**CANISIUS COLLEGE**
Allied Health—General — M,O
Communication Disorders — M,O
Community Health — M,O
Nutrition — M,O

**CAPELLA UNIVERSITY**
Environmental and Occupational Health — M
Epidemiology — D
Gerontological Nursing — M
Health Services Management and Hospital Administration — M,D
Nursing and Healthcare Administration — M
Nursing Education — M,D
Nursing—General — M,D

**CAPITAL UNIVERSITY**
Nursing and Healthcare Administration — M
Nursing—General — M

**CARDINAL STRITCH UNIVERSITY**
Health Services Management and Hospital Administration — M
Nursing—General — M

**CARIBBEAN UNIVERSITY**
Gerontological Nursing — M,D
Pediatric Nursing — M,D

**CARLETON UNIVERSITY**
Biological and Biomedical Sciences—General — M,D
Neuroscience — M,D

**CARLOW UNIVERSITY**
Family Nurse Practitioner Studies — M,O
Health Services Management and Hospital Administration — M

Nursing and Healthcare Administration — M
Nursing Education — M
Nursing—General — D
Women's Health Nursing — M,O

**CARNEGIE MELLON UNIVERSITY**
Biochemistry — M,D
Biological and Biomedical Sciences—General — M,D
Biophysics — M,D
Biopsychology — D
Cell Biology — M,D
Computational Biology — M,D
Developmental Biology — M,D
Genetics — M,D
Health Services Management and Hospital Administration — M
Molecular Biology — M,D
Molecular Biophysics — D
Neurobiology — M,D
Neuroscience — M,D
Structural Biology — M,D

**CARROLL UNIVERSITY**
Occupational Therapy — M
Physical Therapy — D
Physician Assistant Studies — M

**CASE WESTERN RESERVE UNIVERSITY**
Acute Care/Critical Care Nursing — M
Allopathic Medicine — D
Anatomy — M
Anesthesiologist Assistant Studies — M
Biochemistry — M,D
Bioethics — M
Biological and Biomedical Sciences—General — M,D
Biophysics — M,D
Cancer Biology/Oncology — D
Cell Biology — D
Clinical Research — M,D
Communication Disorders — M,D
Dentistry — D
Epidemiology — D
Family Nurse Practitioner Studies — M
Genomic Sciences — D
Gerontological Nursing — M
Health Services Management and Hospital Administration — M
Human Genetics — M,D
Maternal and Child/Neonatal Nursing — M
Medical/Surgical Nursing — M
Microbiology — D
Molecular Biology — D
Molecular Medicine — D
Neuroscience — D
Nurse Anesthesia — M
Nurse Midwifery — M
Nursing Education — M
Nursing—General — M,D
Nutrition — M,D
Oral and Dental Sciences — M,O
Pathology — M,D
Pediatric Nursing — M
Pharmacology — D
Physician Assistant Studies — M
Physiology — M,D
Psychiatric Nursing — M
Public Health—General — M
Virology — D
Women's Health Nursing — M

**THE CATHOLIC UNIVERSITY OF AMERICA**
Biological and Biomedical Sciences—General — M,D
Cell Biology — M,D
Clinical Laboratory Sciences/Medical Technology — M,D
Health Services Management and Hospital Administration — M
Microbiology — M,D
Nursing—General — M,D,O

**CEDAR CREST COLLEGE**
Nursing and Healthcare Administration — M
Nursing Education — M
Nursing—General — M
Nutrition — O

**CEDARS-SINAI MEDICAL CENTER**
Biological and Biomedical Sciences—General — M,D
Medical Imaging — M,D
Translational Biology — M,D

**CEDARVILLE UNIVERSITY**
Family Nurse Practitioner Studies — M,D
Health Services Management and Hospital Administration — M,D
International Health — M,D
Nursing Education — M,D
Pharmacy — M,D

**CENTRAL CONNECTICUT STATE UNIVERSITY**
Biological and Biomedical Sciences—General — M,D
Hospice Nursing — M
Molecular Biology — M,O
Nursing—General — M

**CENTRAL METHODIST UNIVERSITY**
Nursing and Healthcare Administration — M
Nursing Education — M
Nursing—General — M

**CENTRAL MICHIGAN UNIVERSITY**
Allopathic Medicine — D
Biological and Biomedical Sciences—General — M
Communication Disorders — M,D
Conservation Biology — M

**Health Services Management and Hospital Administration** — M,D,O
International Health — M,D,O
Neuroscience — M,D
Nutrition — M,D,O
Physical Therapy — M,D
Physician Assistant Studies — M,D
Rehabilitation Sciences — M,D

**CENTRAL WASHINGTON UNIVERSITY**
Biological and Biomedical Sciences—General — M
Botany — M
Ecology — M
Microbiology — M
Nutrition — M
Physiology — M

**CHAMPLAIN COLLEGE**
Health Services Management and Hospital Administration — M

**CHAPMAN UNIVERSITY**
Communication Disorders — M
Nutrition — M
Pharmaceutical Sciences — M,D
Pharmacy — M,D
Physical Therapy — D
Physician Assistant Studies — M

**CHARLES R. DREW UNIVERSITY OF MEDICINE AND SCIENCE**
Allopathic Medicine — D
Public Health—General — M

**CHATHAM UNIVERSITY**
Biological and Biomedical Sciences—General — M
Environmental Biology — M
Nursing and Healthcare Administration — M,D
Nursing Education — M,D
Nursing—General — M,D
Occupational Therapy — M,D
Physical Therapy — D
Physician Assistant Studies — M

**THE CHICAGO SCHOOL OF PROFESSIONAL PSYCHOLOGY: ONLINE**
Health Services Management and Hospital Administration — M
Pharmacology — M

**CHICAGO STATE UNIVERSITY**
Biological and Biomedical Sciences—General — M
Nursing—General — M
Occupational Therapy — M
Pharmacy — D
Public Health—General — M

**CHRISTIAN BROTHERS UNIVERSITY**
Physician Assistant Studies — M

**THE CITADEL, THE MILITARY COLLEGE OF SOUTH CAROLINA**
Biological and Biomedical Sciences—General — M,O
Medical Microbiology — M,O

**CITY COLLEGE OF THE CITY UNIVERSITY OF NEW YORK**
Biochemistry — M,D
Biological and Biomedical Sciences—General — M,D

**CLAREMONT GRADUATE UNIVERSITY**
Botany — M,D
Computational Biology — M,D
Health Promotion — M,D
Public Health—General — M,D

**CLARION UNIVERSITY OF PENNSYLVANIA**
Communication Disorders — M
Family Nurse Practitioner Studies — M
Health Services Management and Hospital Administration — M
Nursing—General — M

**CLARK ATLANTA UNIVERSITY**
Biological and Biomedical Sciences—General — M,D

**CLARKE UNIVERSITY**
Family Nurse Practitioner Studies — D
Nursing and Healthcare Administration — D
Nursing—General — D
Physical Therapy — D
Psychiatric Nursing — D

**CLARKSON COLLEGE**
Adult Nursing — M,O
Family Nurse Practitioner Studies — M,O
Nursing and Healthcare Administration — M,O
Nursing Education — M,O
Nursing—General — M,O

**CLARKSON UNIVERSITY**
Bioethics — M,O
Biological and Biomedical Sciences—General — M
Health Services Management and Hospital Administration — M,O
Health Services Research — M
Nursing and Healthcare Administration — M,O
Occupational Therapy — M
Physical Therapy — D
Physician Assistant Studies — M

**CLARK UNIVERSITY**
Biochemistry — D
Biological and Biomedical Sciences—General — M,D
Community Health — M
International Health — M

**CLAYTON STATE UNIVERSITY**
Biological and Biomedical
    Sciences—General    M
Family Nurse Practitioner Studies    M
Nursing—General    M

**CLEARY UNIVERSITY**
Health Services Management and
    Hospital Administration    M,O

**CLEMSON UNIVERSITY**
Biological and Biomedical
    Sciences—General    M,D
Clinical Research    M,D,O
Entomology    M,D
Environmental and Occupational
    Health    M,D
Family Nurse Practitioner Studies    M,D,O
Genetics    M,D
Gerontological Nursing    M,D,O
International Health    M,D,O
Microbiology    M
Molecular Biology    D
Nursing—General    M,D,O
Nutrition    M
Plant Biology    M,D
Public Health—General    M,D,O
Toxicology    M,D
Veterinary Sciences    M,D

**CLEVELAND STATE UNIVERSITY**
Allied Health—General    M
Bioethics    M,O
Biological and Biomedical
    Sciences—General    M,D
Communication Disorders    M
Health Services Management and
    Hospital Administration    M
Molecular Medicine    M,D
Nursing Education    D
Nursing—General    M,D
Occupational Therapy    M
Physical Therapy    D
Physician Assistant Studies    M
Public Health—General    M

**CLEVELAND UNIVERSITY–KANSAS CITY**
Chiropractic    D
Health Promotion    M

**COLD SPRING HARBOR LABORATORY**
Biological and Biomedical
    Sciences—General    D

**COLLEGE OF CHARLESTON**
Marine Biology    M

**COLLEGE OF MOUNT SAINT VINCENT**
Family Nurse Practitioner Studies    M,O
Nursing and Healthcare
    Administration    M,O
Nursing Education    M,O
Nursing—General    M,O

**THE COLLEGE OF NEW JERSEY**
International Health    M
Nursing—General    M,O
Public Health—General    M

**THE COLLEGE OF NEW ROCHELLE**
Acute Care/Critical Care Nursing    M,O
Family Nurse Practitioner Studies    M,O
Nursing and Healthcare
    Administration    M,O
Nursing Education    M,O
Nursing—General    M,O

**COLLEGE OF SAINT ELIZABETH**
Health Services Management and
    Hospital Administration    M
Nursing—General    M
Nutrition    M,O
Public Health—General    M

**COLLEGE OF SAINT MARY**
Nursing—General    M
Occupational Therapy    M

**THE COLLEGE OF SAINT ROSE**
Communication Disorders    M

**THE COLLEGE OF ST. SCHOLASTICA**
Nursing—General    M,O
Occupational Therapy    M
Physical Therapy    D

**COLLEGE OF STATEN ISLAND OF THE CITY UNIVERSITY OF NEW YORK**
Adult Nursing    M,O
Biological and Biomedical
    Sciences—General    M
Gerontological Nursing    M,O
Health Services Management and
    Hospital Administration    M
Neuroscience    M
Physical Therapy    D

**COLORADO MESA UNIVERSITY**
Family Nurse Practitioner Studies    M,D,O
Nursing Education    M,D,O
Nursing—General    M,D,O

**COLORADO SCHOOL OF TRADITIONAL CHINESE MEDICINE**
Acupuncture and Oriental Medicine    M

**COLORADO STATE UNIVERSITY**
Biochemistry    M,D
Biological and Biomedical
    Sciences—General    M,D
Botany    M,D
Conservation Biology    M,D
Entomology    M,D
Environmental and Occupational
    Health    M,D

Epidemiology    M,D
Immunology    M,D
Microbiology    M,D
Nutrition    M,D
Occupational Therapy    M,D
Pathology    M,D
Plant Pathology    M,D
Veterinary Medicine    D
Veterinary Sciences    M,D
Zoology    M,D

**COLORADO STATE UNIVERSITY–GLOBAL CAMPUS**
Health Services Management and
    Hospital Administration    M

**COLORADO STATE UNIVERSITY–PUEBLO**
Biochemistry    M
Biological and Biomedical
    Sciences—General    M
Nursing—General    M

**COLUMBIA COLLEGE OF NURSING**
Nursing—General    M

**COLUMBIA SOUTHERN UNIVERSITY**
Environmental and Occupational
    Health    M
Health Services Management and
    Hospital Administration    M

**COLUMBIA UNIVERSITY**
Acute Care/Critical Care Nursing    M,O
Adult Nursing    M,O
Allopathic Medicine    M,D
Anatomy    M,D
Biochemistry    M,D
Bioethics    M
Biological and Biomedical
    Sciences—General    M,D,O
Biophysics    M,D
Cell Biology    M,D
Community Health    M,D
Conservation Biology    M,D
Dentistry    D
Developmental Biology    M,D
Ecology    M,D
Environmental and Occupational
    Health    M,D
Epidemiology    M,D
Evolutionary Biology    M,D
Family Nurse Practitioner Studies    M,O
Genetics    M,D
Gerontological Nursing    M,O
Health Services Management and
    Hospital Administration    M,D
Maternal and Child Health    M,D
Medical Physics    M,D
Microbiology    M,D
Molecular Biology    D
Neurobiology    D
Nurse Anesthesia    M,O
Nurse Midwifery    M,O
Nursing—General    M,D,O
Nutrition    M,D
Occupational Therapy    M,D
Oral and Dental Sciences    M,D,O
Pathobiology    M,D
Pathology    M,D
Pediatric Nursing    M,O
Pharmaceutical Administration    M
Pharmacology    M,D
Physical Therapy    D
Physiology    M,D
Psychiatric Nursing    M,O
Public Health—General    M,D
Structural Biology    D
Toxicology    M,D

**COLUMBUS STATE UNIVERSITY**
Biological and Biomedical
    Sciences—General    M
Family Nurse Practitioner Studies    M
Health Services Management and
    Hospital Administration    M
Nursing and Healthcare
    Administration    M
Nursing Education    M
Nursing Informatics    M
Nursing—General    M

**CONCORDIA UNIVERSITY (CANADA)**
Biological and Biomedical
    Sciences—General    M,D,O
Genomic Sciences    M,D,O

**CONCORDIA UNIVERSITY IRVINE**
Health Services Management and
    Hospital Administration    M
Nursing—General    M

**CONCORDIA UNIVERSITY, ST. PAUL**
Allied Health—General    M,D
Health Services Management and
    Hospital Administration    M
Physical Therapy    M,D

**CONCORDIA UNIVERSITY WISCONSIN**
Family Nurse Practitioner Studies    M,D
Health Services Management and
    Hospital Administration    M
Nursing—General    M,D
Occupational Therapy    M
Pharmacy    M,D
Physical Therapy    D
Rehabilitation Sciences    M

**CONCORD UNIVERSITY**
Health Promotion    M

**COPENHAGEN BUSINESS SCHOOL**
Health Services Management and
    Hospital Administration    M,D

**COPPIN STATE UNIVERSITY**
Family Nurse Practitioner Studies    M,O
Nursing—General    M,O

**CORNELL UNIVERSITY**
Animal Behavior    D
Biochemistry    M,D
Biological and Biomedical
    Sciences—General    D
Biophysics    D
Biopsychology    D
Cell Biology    D
Computational Biology    D
Conservation Biology    D
Developmental Biology    D
Ecology    M,D
Entomology    M,D
Evolutionary Biology    D
Genetics    D
Genomic Sciences    D
Health Services Management and
    Hospital Administration    M,D
Microbiology    D
Molecular Biology    D
Neurobiology    D
Nutrition    M,D
Physiology    M,D
Plant Biology    M,D
Plant Molecular Biology    M,D
Plant Pathology    M,D
Plant Physiology    M,D
Toxicology    M,D
Veterinary Medicine    D

**COX COLLEGE**
Family Nurse Practitioner Studies    M
Nursing and Healthcare
    Administration    M
Nursing Education    M
Nursing—General    M
Occupational Therapy    M

**CREIGHTON UNIVERSITY**
Adult Nursing    M,D,O
Allied Health—General    M,D
Allopathic Medicine    D
Anatomy    M
Bioethics    M
Biological and Biomedical
    Sciences—General    M,D
Dentistry    D
Emergency Medical Services    M
Family Nurse Practitioner Studies    M,D,O
Gerontological Nursing    M,D,O
Health Promotion    M
Health Services Management and
    Hospital Administration    M,D
Immunology    M,D
Maternal and Child/Neonatal
    Nursing    M,D,O
Medical Microbiology    M,D
Nursing and Healthcare
    Administration    M,D,O
Nursing—General    M,D,O
Occupational Therapy    D
Pediatric Nursing    M,D,O
Pharmaceutical Sciences    M,D
Pharmacology    M,D
Pharmacy    D
Physical Therapy    D
Psychiatric Nursing    M,D,O
Public Health—General    M

**CURRY COLLEGE**
Nursing—General    M

**DAEMEN COLLEGE**
Adult Nursing    M,D,O
Community Health    M
Epidemiology    M
Health Services Management and
    Hospital Administration    M
Medical/Surgical Nursing    M,D,O
Nursing and Healthcare
    Administration    M,D,O
Nursing Education    M,D,O
Nursing—General    M,D,O
Physical Therapy    D,O
Physician Assistant Studies    M
Public Health—General    M

**DALHOUSIE UNIVERSITY**
Allopathic Medicine    M,D
Anatomy    M,D
Biochemistry    M,D
Biological and Biomedical
    Sciences—General    M,D
Biophysics    M,D
Botany    M,D
Communication Disorders    M,D
Community Health    M
Developmental Biology    M,D
Ecology    M,D
Environmental Biology    M
Epidemiology    M
Health Services Management and
    Hospital Administration    M,D
Immunology    M,D
Microbiology    M,D
Neuroscience    M,D
Nursing—General    M
Occupational Therapy    M
Oral and Dental Sciences    M
Pathology    M,D
Pharmacology    M,D
Physical Therapy    M,D
Physiology    M,D
Plant Biology    M
Plant Physiology    M

**DALLAS BAPTIST UNIVERSITY**
Health Services Management and
    Hospital Administration    M

**DAOIST TRADITIONS COLLEGE OF CHINESE MEDICAL ARTS**
Acupuncture and Oriental Medicine    M,D

**DARTMOUTH COLLEGE**
Allopathic Medicine    D
Biochemistry    M,D
Biological and Biomedical
    Sciences—General    D
Cell Biology    D
Ecology    D
Environmental Biology    D
Epidemiology    M,D
Evolutionary Biology    D
Health Services Management and
    Hospital Administration    M,D
Health Services Research    M,D
Microbiology    D
Molecular Biology    D
Molecular Medicine    D
Molecular Pathogenesis    D
Neuroscience    D
Public Health—General    M

**DAVENPORT UNIVERSITY**
Health Services Management and
    Hospital Administration    M
Occupational Therapy    M
Public Health—General    M

**DELAWARE STATE UNIVERSITY**
Biological and Biomedical
    Sciences—General    M
Neuroscience    M,D
Nursing—General    M

**DELTA STATE UNIVERSITY**
Biological and Biomedical
    Sciences—General    M
Family Nurse Practitioner Studies    M,D
Health Services Management and
    Hospital Administration    M,D
Nursing Education    M,D
Nursing—General    M,D

**DEPAUL UNIVERSITY**
Biological and Biomedical
    Sciences—General    M,D
Family Nurse Practitioner Studies    M,D
Nursing—General    M,D
Public Health—General    M

**DESALES UNIVERSITY**
Family Nurse Practitioner Studies    M,D,O
Health Services Management and
    Hospital Administration    M
Nurse Anesthesia    M,D,O
Nurse Midwifery    M,D,O
Nursing and Healthcare
    Administration    M,D,O
Nursing Education    M,D,O
Nursing—General    M,D,O

**DES MOINES UNIVERSITY**
Anatomy    M
Biological and Biomedical
    Sciences—General    M
Health Services Management and
    Hospital Administration    M
Osteopathic Medicine    D
Physical Therapy    D
Physician Assistant Studies    M
Podiatric Medicine    D
Public Health—General    M

**DOMINICAN COLLEGE**
Allied Health—General    M,D
Family Nurse Practitioner Studies    M,D
Health Services Management and
    Hospital Administration    M
Occupational Therapy    M
Physical Therapy    M,D

**DOMINICAN UNIVERSITY OF CALIFORNIA**
Biological and Biomedical
    Sciences—General    M
Clinical Laboratory
    Sciences/Medical Technology    M
Occupational Therapy    M

**DONGGUK UNIVERSITY LOS ANGELES**
Acupuncture and Oriental Medicine    M

**DRAGON RISES COLLEGE OF ORIENTAL MEDICINE**
Acupuncture and Oriental Medicine    M

**DRAKE UNIVERSITY**
Pharmacy    M,D

**DREW UNIVERSITY**
Biological and Biomedical
    Sciences—General    M,D,O
Health Services Management and
    Hospital Administration    M,D,O

**DREXEL UNIVERSITY**
Acute Care/Critical Care Nursing    M
Allied Health—General    M,D,O
Allopathic Medicine    D
Biochemistry    M,D
Biological and Biomedical
    Sciences—General    M,D,O
Biopsychology    M,D
Cell Biology    M,D
Emergency Medical Services    M
Epidemiology    M,D,O
Family Nurse Practitioner Studies    M
Genetics    M,D
Immunology    M,D
Microbiology    M,D
Molecular Biology    M,D
Molecular Medicine    M
Neuroscience    M,D

- Nurse Anesthesia M
- Nursing and Healthcare Administration M
- Nursing Education M
- Nursing—General M,D
- Pathobiology M,D
- Pediatric Nursing M
- Pharmaceutical Sciences M
- Pharmacology M,D
- Physical Therapy M,D,O
- Physician Assistant Studies M
- Psychiatric Nursing M
- Public Health—General M,D,O
- Veterinary Sciences M
- Women's Health Nursing M

### DUKE UNIVERSITY
- Acute Care/Critical Care Nursing M,D,O
- Adult Nursing M,D,O
- Allopathic Medicine D
- Anatomy D
- Biochemistry D
- Bioethics M
- Biological and Biomedical Sciences—General D
- Biopsychology D
- Cancer Biology/Oncology D
- Cell Biology D,O
- Clinical Research M
- Computational Biology D,O
- Developmental Biology O
- Ecology D,O
- Environmental and Occupational Health O
- Family Nurse Practitioner Studies M,D,O
- Genetics D
- Genomic Sciences D
- Gerontological Nursing M,D,O
- Immunology D
- International Health M
- Maternal and Child/Neonatal Nursing M,D,O
- Medical Physics M,D
- Microbiology D
- Molecular Biology D,O
- Molecular Biophysics O
- Molecular Genetics D
- Neurobiology D
- Neuroscience D,O
- Nurse Anesthesia M,D,O
- Nursing and Healthcare Administration M,D,O
- Nursing Education M,D,O
- Nursing Informatics M,D,O
- Nursing—General D
- Pathology M,D
- Pediatric Nursing M,D,O
- Pharmacology D
- Physical Therapy D
- Physician Assistant Studies M
- Structural Biology O
- Toxicology O
- Women's Health Nursing M,D,O

### DUQUESNE UNIVERSITY
- Allied Health—General M,D,O
- Bioethics M,D,O
- Biological and Biomedical Sciences—General D
- Communication Disorders M,D
- Family Nurse Practitioner Studies M,D,O
- Forensic Nursing M,O
- Health Services Management and Hospital Administration M,D
- Medicinal and Pharmaceutical Chemistry M,D
- Nursing Education M,D,O
- Nursing—General M,D,O
- Occupational Therapy M,D
- Pharmaceutical Administration M
- Pharmaceutical Sciences M,D
- Pharmacology M,D
- Pharmacy D
- Physical Therapy M,D
- Physician Assistant Studies M,D
- Rehabilitation Sciences M,D

### D'YOUVILLE COLLEGE
- Anatomy M
- Chiropractic D
- Family Nurse Practitioner Studies M,D,O
- Health Services Management and Hospital Administration M,D,O
- Nursing—General M,D,O
- Nutrition M
- Occupational Therapy M
- Pharmacy D
- Physical Therapy D,O
- Physician Assistant Studies M

### EAST CAROLINA UNIVERSITY
- Allied Health—General M,D,O
- Allopathic Medicine D
- Anatomy M,D
- Biochemistry M,D
- Biological and Biomedical Sciences—General M,D
- Biophysics M,D
- Cell Biology M,D
- Communication Disorders M,D
- Dentistry D
- Environmental and Occupational Health M,D,O
- Health Physics/Radiological Health M,D
- Health Promotion M
- Health Services Management and Hospital Administration M,O
- Immunology M,D
- Maternal and Child Health M,D,O
- Medical Physics M,D
- Microbiology M,D
- Molecular Biology M,D
- Nursing—General M,D
- Nutrition M
- Occupational Therapy M,D,O
- Pharmacology M,D
- Physical Therapy D
- Physician Assistant Studies M
- Physiology M,D
- Public Health—General M,D,O
- Rehabilitation Sciences M,D,O
- Toxicology M,D

### EASTERN ILLINOIS UNIVERSITY
- Biological and Biomedical Sciences—General M
- Communication Disorders M
- Nutrition M

### EASTERN KENTUCKY UNIVERSITY
- Allied Health—General M
- Biological and Biomedical Sciences—General M
- Communication Disorders M
- Community Health M
- Ecology M
- Environmental and Occupational Health M
- Family Nurse Practitioner Studies M
- Health Promotion M
- Health Services Management and Hospital Administration M
- Industrial Hygiene M
- Nursing—General M
- Nutrition M
- Occupational Therapy M

### EASTERN MENNONITE UNIVERSITY
- Biological and Biomedical Sciences—General M
- Health Services Management and Hospital Administration M
- Nursing and Healthcare Administration M,D
- Nursing—General M,D
- School Nursing M,D

### EASTERN MICHIGAN UNIVERSITY
- Adult Nursing M,O
- Biological and Biomedical Sciences—General M
- Clinical Research M,O
- Communication Disorders M
- Health Promotion M,O
- Health Services Management and Hospital Administration M,O
- Nursing and Healthcare Administration M,O
- Nursing Education M,O
- Nutrition M
- Occupational Therapy M
- Physician Assistant Studies M
- Physiology M

### EASTERN NEW MEXICO UNIVERSITY
- Biochemistry M
- Biological and Biomedical Sciences—General M
- Communication Disorders M
- Nursing—General M

### EASTERN SCHOOL OF ACUPUNCTURE AND TRADITIONAL MEDICINE
- Acupuncture and Oriental Medicine M

### EASTERN UNIVERSITY
- Health Services Management and Hospital Administration M

### EASTERN VIRGINIA MEDICAL SCHOOL
- Allopathic Medicine D
- Biological and Biomedical Sciences—General M,D
- Medical/Surgical Nursing M
- Physician Assistant Studies M
- Public Health—General M
- Reproductive Biology M
- Vision Sciences O

### EASTERN WASHINGTON UNIVERSITY
- Biological and Biomedical Sciences—General M
- Communication Disorders M
- Dental Hygiene M
- Occupational Therapy M
- Physical Therapy D
- Public Health—General M

### EAST STROUDSBURG UNIVERSITY OF PENNSYLVANIA
- Biological and Biomedical Sciences—General M
- Communication Disorders M
- Public Health—General M
- Rehabilitation Sciences M

### EAST TENNESSEE STATE UNIVERSITY
- Allied Health—General M
- Allopathic Medicine D
- Anatomy D
- Biochemistry D
- Biological and Biomedical Sciences—General M,D
- Communication Disorders M,D
- Community Health M,D,O
- Environmental and Occupational Health M,D,O
- Epidemiology M,D,O
- Family Nurse Practitioner Studies M,D,O
- Gerontological Nursing M,D,O
- Health Services Management and Hospital Administration M,D,O
- International Health M,D,O
- Microbiology M,D
- Nursing and Healthcare Administration M,D,O
- Nursing Education M,D,O
- Nursing—General M,D,O
- Nutrition M
- Pediatric Nursing M,D,O
- Pharmaceutical Sciences D
- Pharmacology D
- Pharmacy D
- Physical Therapy D
- Physiology D
- Psychiatric Nursing M,D,O
- Public Health—General M,D,O
- Women's Health Nursing M,D,O

### EAST WEST COLLEGE OF NATURAL MEDICINE
- Acupuncture and Oriental Medicine M

### EDGEWOOD COLLEGE
- Nursing—General M,D

### EDINBORO UNIVERSITY OF PENNSYLVANIA
- Communication Disorders M
- Family Nurse Practitioner Studies M,D
- Nursing Education M,D
- Nursing—General M,D

### EDP UNIVERSITY OF PUERTO RICO–SAN SEBASTIAN
- Nursing—General M

### EDWARD VIA COLLEGE OF OSTEOPATHIC MEDICINE–CAROLINAS CAMPUS
- Osteopathic Medicine D

### EDWARD VIA COLLEGE OF OSTEOPATHIC MEDICINE–VIRGINIA CAMPUS
- Osteopathic Medicine D

### ELIZABETH CITY STATE UNIVERSITY
- Biological and Biomedical Sciences—General M

### ELIZABETHTOWN COLLEGE
- Occupational Therapy M

### ELMEZZI GRADUATE SCHOOL OF MOLECULAR MEDICINE
- Molecular Medicine D

### ELMHURST UNIVERSITY
- Communication Disorders M
- Health Services Management and Hospital Administration M
- Nursing—General M
- Occupational Therapy M
- Public Health—General M

### ELMS COLLEGE
- Acute Care/Critical Care Nursing M,D
- Biological and Biomedical Sciences—General M
- Family Nurse Practitioner Studies M,D
- Gerontological Nursing M,D
- Health Services Management and Hospital Administration M,O
- Nursing and Healthcare Administration M,D
- Nursing Education M,D
- Nursing—General M,D

### ELON UNIVERSITY
- Physical Therapy D
- Physician Assistant Studies M

### EMBRY-RIDDLE AERONAUTICAL UNIVERSITY–WORLDWIDE
- Environmental and Occupational Health M

### EMMANUEL COLLEGE (UNITED STATES)
- Nursing and Healthcare Administration M,O
- Nursing Education M,O
- Nursing—General M,O

### EMORY & HENRY COLLEGE
- Occupational Therapy M,D
- Physical Therapy M,D
- Physician Assistant Studies M,D

### EMORY UNIVERSITY
- Adult Nursing M
- Allied Health—General M,D
- Allopathic Medicine D
- Anesthesiologist Assistant Studies M
- Animal Behavior D
- Biochemistry D
- Bioethics M
- Biological and Biomedical Sciences—General D
- Cancer Biology/Oncology D
- Cell Biology D
- Clinical Research M
- Developmental Biology D
- Ecology D
- Environmental and Occupational Health M,D
- Epidemiology M,D
- Evolutionary Biology D
- Family Nurse Practitioner Studies M
- Genetics D
- Health Promotion M
- Health Services Management and Hospital Administration M,D
- Health Services Research M,D
- Human Genetics M
- Immunology D
- International Health M
- Microbiology D
- Molecular Biology D
- Molecular Genetics D
- Molecular Pathogenesis D
- Neuroscience D
- Nurse Midwifery M
- Nursing and Healthcare Administration M
- Nursing—General M,D
- Nutrition M,D
- Pediatric Nursing M
- Pharmacology D
- Physical Therapy D
- Physician Assistant Studies M
- Public Health—General M,D
- Women's Health Nursing M

### EMPEROR'S COLLEGE OF TRADITIONAL ORIENTAL MEDICINE
- Acupuncture and Oriental Medicine M,D

### EMPORIA STATE UNIVERSITY
- Biological and Biomedical Sciences—General M
- Botany M
- Cell Biology M
- Environmental Biology M
- Microbiology M
- Zoology M

### ENDICOTT COLLEGE
- Family Nurse Practitioner Studies M,O
- International Health M,O
- Nursing and Healthcare Administration M,O
- Nursing Education M,O
- Nursing—General M,O

### EVERGLADES UNIVERSITY
- Public Health—General M

### FAIRFIELD UNIVERSITY
- Family Nurse Practitioner Studies M,D
- Nurse Anesthesia M,D
- Nursing and Healthcare Administration M,D
- Nursing—General M,D
- Psychiatric Nursing M,D

### FAIRLEIGH DICKINSON UNIVERSITY, FLORHAM CAMPUS
- Biological and Biomedical Sciences—General M
- Gerontological Nursing M
- Health Services Management and Hospital Administration M
- Nursing—General M
- Pharmacology M,O
- Pharmacy D
- Psychiatric Nursing M

### FAIRLEIGH DICKINSON UNIVERSITY, METROPOLITAN CAMPUS
- Biological and Biomedical Sciences—General M
- Clinical Laboratory Sciences/Medical Technology M
- Health Services Management and Hospital Administration M
- Nursing—General M,D,O
- Pharmaceutical Administration M,O

### FAIRMONT STATE UNIVERSITY
- Health Promotion M

### FELICIAN UNIVERSITY
- Adult Nursing M,O
- Family Nurse Practitioner Studies M,O
- Gerontological Nursing M,O
- Health Services Management and Hospital Administration M
- Nursing and Healthcare Administration M,D,O
- Nursing Education M,O
- Nursing—General M,D,O

### FERRIS STATE UNIVERSITY
- Allied Health—General M
- Health Services Management and Hospital Administration M
- Nursing and Healthcare Administration M
- Nursing Education M
- Nursing Informatics M
- Nursing—General M
- Optometry D
- Pharmacy D
- Public Health—General M

### FIELDING GRADUATE UNIVERSITY
- Neuroscience O

### FISK UNIVERSITY
- Biological and Biomedical Sciences—General M

### FITCHBURG STATE UNIVERSITY
- Biological and Biomedical Sciences—General M
- Forensic Nursing M,O

### FIVE BRANCHES UNIVERSITY
- Acupuncture and Oriental Medicine M,D

### FLORIDA AGRICULTURAL AND MECHANICAL UNIVERSITY
- Allied Health—General M,D
- Health Services Research M,D
- Medicinal and Pharmaceutical Chemistry M,D
- Nursing and Healthcare Administration M,D
- Nursing—General M,D
- Occupational Therapy M
- Pharmaceutical Administration M,D
- Pharmaceutical Sciences M,D
- Pharmacology M,D
- Pharmacy D
- Physical Therapy D
- Public Health—General M,D
- Toxicology M,D

### FLORIDA ATLANTIC UNIVERSITY
- Allopathic Medicine M,D
- Biological and Biomedical Sciences—General M,D
- Communication Disorders M
- Health Promotion M
- Health Services Management and Hospital Administration M
- Neuroscience D
- Nursing and Healthcare Administration M,D,O

Nursing—General | M,D,O

**FLORIDA COLLEGE OF INTEGRATIVE MEDICINE**
Acupuncture and Oriental Medicine | M

**FLORIDA GULF COAST UNIVERSITY**
Allied Health—General | M,D
Nurse Anesthesia | M
Nursing Education | M
Occupational Therapy | M
Physical Therapy | D
Physician Assistant Studies | M

**FLORIDA INSTITUTE OF TECHNOLOGY**
Biochemistry | M
Biological and Biomedical
  Sciences—General | M,D
Cell Biology | M
Conservation Biology | M
Ecology | M,D
Health Services Management and
  Hospital Administration | M
Marine Biology | M,D
Molecular Biology | M

**FLORIDA INTERNATIONAL UNIVERSITY**
Adult Nursing | M,D
Allopathic Medicine | M,D
Biological and Biomedical
  Sciences—General | M,D
Communication Disorders | M
Environmental and Occupational
  Health | M,D
Epidemiology | M,D
Health Promotion | M,D
Health Services Management and
  Hospital Administration | M,D
Neuroscience | M,D
Nurse Anesthesia | M,D
Nursing—General | M,D
Nutrition | M,D
Occupational Therapy | M
Pediatric Nursing | M,D
Physical Therapy | D
Physician Assistant Studies | M,D
Psychiatric Nursing | M,D
Public Health—General | M,D

**FLORIDA NATIONAL UNIVERSITY**
Family Nurse Practitioner Studies | M
Health Services Management and
  Hospital Administration | M
Nursing and Healthcare
  Administration | M
Nursing Education | M
Nursing—General | M

**FLORIDA SOUTHERN COLLEGE**
Adult Nursing | M
Family Nurse Practitioner Studies | M
Gerontological Nursing | M
Nursing and Healthcare
  Administration | M
Nursing Education | M
Nursing—General | M

**FLORIDA STATE UNIVERSITY**
Allopathic Medicine | D
Biochemistry | M,D
Biological and Biomedical
  Sciences—General | M,D
Biopsychology | M,D
Cell Biology | M,D
Communication Disorders | M,D
Ecology | M,D
Evolutionary Biology | M,D
Family Nurse Practitioner Studies | D,O
Molecular Biology | M,D
Molecular Biophysics | D
Neuroscience | M,D
Nursing—General | D,O
Nutrition | M,D
Psychiatric Nursing | D,O
Public Health—General | M
Structural Biology | D

**FONTBONNE UNIVERSITY**
Communication Disorders | M

**FORDHAM UNIVERSITY**
Biological and Biomedical
  Sciences—General | M,D,O
Clinical Research | M
Conservation Biology | M,D,O
Health Services Management and
  Hospital Administration | M,D

**FORT HAYS STATE UNIVERSITY**
Biological and Biomedical
  Sciences—General | M
Communication Disorders | M
Nursing—General | M

**FORT VALLEY STATE UNIVERSITY**
Environmental and Occupational
  Health | M
Public Health—General | M

**FRAMINGHAM STATE UNIVERSITY**
Health Services Management and
  Hospital Administration | M
Nursing and Healthcare
  Administration | M
Nursing Education | M
Nursing—General | M
Nutrition | M

**FRANCISCAN MISSIONARIES OF OUR LADY UNIVERSITY**
Family Nurse Practitioner Studies | M
Health Services Management and
  Hospital Administration | M,D
Nurse Anesthesia | D
Nursing—General | M,D

Nutrition | M,D
Physical Therapy | M,D
Physician Assistant Studies | M,D

**FRANCISCAN UNIVERSITY OF STEUBENVILLE**
Nursing—General | M

**FRANCIS MARION UNIVERSITY**
Communication Disorders | M
Family Nurse Practitioner Studies | M
Health Services Management and
  Hospital Administration | M
Nursing Education | M
Nursing—General | M
Physician Assistant Studies | M

**FRANKLIN PIERCE UNIVERSITY**
Health Services Management and
  Hospital Administration | M,D,O
Nursing and Healthcare
  Administration | M,D,O
Nursing Education | M,D,O
Physical Therapy | M,D,O
Physician Assistant Studies | M,D,O

**FRESNO PACIFIC UNIVERSITY**
Family Nurse Practitioner Studies | M
Nursing—General | M

**FRIENDS UNIVERSITY**
Health Services Management and
  Hospital Administration | M

**FROSTBURG STATE UNIVERSITY**
Biological and Biomedical
  Sciences—General | M
Conservation Biology | M
Ecology | M
Nursing and Healthcare
  Administration | M
Nursing Education | M
Nursing—General | M

**GALLAUDET UNIVERSITY**
Communication Disorders | M,D,O
Neuroscience | M,D,O

**GANNON UNIVERSITY**
Environmental and Occupational
  Health | M
Family Nurse Practitioner Studies | M,O
Nurse Anesthesia | M,O
Nursing and Healthcare
  Administration | M
Nursing—General | D
Occupational Therapy | M,D
Physical Therapy | D
Physician Assistant Studies | M

**GARDNER-WEBB UNIVERSITY**
Family Nurse Practitioner Studies | M,D
Nursing—General | M,D
Physician Assistant Studies | M

**GEISINGER COMMONWEALTH SCHOOL OF MEDICINE**
Allopathic Medicine | D
Biological and Biomedical
  Sciences—General | M

**GEORGE FOX UNIVERSITY**
Physical Therapy | D

**GEORGE MASON UNIVERSITY**
Adult Nursing | M,D,O
Biochemistry | M,D
Biological and Biomedical
  Sciences—General | M,D,O
Community Health | M,O
Computational Biology | M,D,O
Epidemiology | M,O
Family Nurse Practitioner Studies | M,D,O
Gerontological Nursing | M,O
Health Promotion | M,O
Health Services Management and
  Hospital Administration | M,D,O
Health Services Research | M,O
International Health | M,O
Neuroscience | M,D,O
Nursing and Healthcare
  Administration | M,D,O
Nursing Education | M,D,O
Nursing—General | M,D,O
Nutrition | M,O
Psychiatric Nursing | M,D,O
Public Health—General | M,O
Rehabilitation Sciences | D,O
Systems Biology | M,D,O

**GEORGETOWN UNIVERSITY**
Acute Care/Critical Care Nursing | M,D
Allopathic Medicine | D
Biochemistry | M,D
Biological and Biomedical
  Sciences—General | D
Epidemiology | M,O
Family Nurse Practitioner Studies | M,D
Health Physics/Radiological Health | M,D
Health Promotion | M,D
Health Services Management and
  Hospital Administration | M,D
Immunology | M,D
Infectious Diseases | M,D
International Health | M,D
Microbiology | M,D
Molecular Biology | M,D
Neuroscience | D
Nurse Anesthesia | M,D
Nurse Midwifery | M,D
Nursing Education | M,D
Nursing—General | M,D
Pharmacology | M,D
Physiology | M,D
Public Health—General | M,D

Radiation Biology | M

**THE GEORGE WASHINGTON UNIVERSITY**
Adult Nursing | M,D,O
Allopathic Medicine | D
Biochemistry | D
Biological and Biomedical
  Sciences—General | M,D
Communication Disorders | M
Community Health | M,D
Environmental and Occupational
  Health | D
Epidemiology | M
Family Nurse Practitioner Studies | M,D,O
Health Services Management and
  Hospital Administration | M,D,O
Health Services Research | M,D,O
Immunology | D
Infectious Diseases | M,D,O
International Health | M,D
Microbiology | M
Molecular Medicine | D
Nursing and Healthcare
  Administration | M,D,O
Nursing—General | M,D,O
Physical Therapy | D
Physician Assistant Studies | M
Public Health—General | M
Systems Biology | D
Toxicology | M,D

**GEORGIA CAMPUS–PHILADELPHIA COLLEGE OF OSTEOPATHIC MEDICINE**
Osteopathic Medicine | D
Pharmacy | D
Physical Therapy | D

**GEORGIA COLLEGE & STATE UNIVERSITY**
Biological and Biomedical
  Sciences—General | M
Health Promotion | M
Nursing—General | M,D,O

**GEORGIA INSTITUTE OF TECHNOLOGY**
Biological and Biomedical
  Sciences—General | M,D
Health Physics/Radiological Health | M,D
Health Services Management and
  Hospital Administration | M,D
Physiology | M,D

**GEORGIA SOUTHERN UNIVERSITY**
Allied Health—General | M,D,O
Biological and Biomedical
  Sciences—General | M
Communication Disorders | M
Community Health | M,D
Environmental and Occupational
  Health | M,D,O
Epidemiology | M,D
Family Nurse Practitioner Studies | M
Health Services Management and
  Hospital Administration | M,D
Nursing Education | O
Nursing—General | O
Nutrition | O
Physical Therapy | D
Psychiatric Nursing | M
Public Health—General | M,D

**GEORGIA SOUTHWESTERN STATE UNIVERSITY**
Family Nurse Practitioner Studies | M,O
Nursing and Healthcare
  Administration | M,O
Nursing Education | M,O
Nursing Informatics | M,O
Nursing—General | M,O

**GEORGIA STATE UNIVERSITY**
Adult Nursing | M,D,O
Allied Health—General | M
Biochemistry | M,D
Biological and Biomedical
  Sciences—General | M,D
Cell Biology | M,D
Communication Disorders | M,D
Environmental Biology | M,D
Family Nurse Practitioner Studies | M,D,O
Health Services Management and
  Hospital Administration | M,D,O
Microbiology | M,D
Molecular Biology | M,D
Molecular Genetics | M,D
Neurobiology | M,D
Neuroscience | D
Nursing and Healthcare
  Administration | M,D,O
Nursing Informatics | M,D,O
Nursing—General | M,D,O
Nutrition | M
Occupational Therapy | M
Pediatric Nursing | M,D,O
Physical Therapy | D
Physiology | M,D
Psychiatric Nursing | M,D,O
Public Health—General | M,D,O
Women's Health Nursing | M,D,O

**GERSTNER SLOAN KETTERING GRADUATE SCHOOL OF BIOMEDICAL SCIENCES**
Biological and Biomedical
  Sciences—General | D
Cancer Biology/Oncology | D

**GODDARD COLLEGE**
Health Promotion | M

**GOLDEY-BEACOM COLLEGE**
Health Services Management and
  Hospital Administration | M

**GOLDFARB SCHOOL OF NURSING AT BARNES-JEWISH COLLEGE**
Acute Care/Critical Care Nursing | M
Gerontological Nursing | M
Nurse Anesthesia | M
Nursing and Healthcare
  Administration | M
Nursing—General | M

**GONZAGA UNIVERSITY**
Nursing—General | M,D
Physiology | M,D

**GOSHEN COLLEGE**
Family Nurse Practitioner Studies | M
Nursing—General | M

**GOUCHER COLLEGE**
Biological and Biomedical
  Sciences—General | O

**GOVERNORS STATE UNIVERSITY**
Communication Disorders | M
Environmental Biology | M
Health Services Management and
  Hospital Administration | M
Nursing—General | M
Occupational Therapy | M
Physical Therapy | D

**GRACELAND UNIVERSITY (IA)**
Family Nurse Practitioner Studies | M,D,O
Gerontological Nursing | M,D,O
Nursing Education | M,D,O
Nursing—General | M,D,O

**THE GRADUATE CENTER, CITY UNIVERSITY OF NEW YORK**
Biochemistry | D
Biological and Biomedical
  Sciences—General | D
Biopsychology | D
Communication Disorders | D
Neuroscience | M,D
Nursing—General | D

**GRAMBLING STATE UNIVERSITY**
Family Nurse Practitioner Studies | M,O
Health Services Management and
  Hospital Administration | M
Nursing—General | M,O

**GRAND CANYON UNIVERSITY**
Acute Care/Critical Care Nursing | M,D,O
Family Nurse Practitioner Studies | M,D,O
Health Services Management and
  Hospital Administration | M,D,O
Nursing Education | M,D,O
Nursing—General | M,D,O
Public Health—General | M,D,O

**GRAND VALLEY STATE UNIVERSITY**
Allied Health—General | M,D
Biological and Biomedical
  Sciences—General | M
Cancer Biology/Oncology | M
Cell Biology | M
Communication Disorders | M
Health Services Management and
  Hospital Administration | M
Molecular Biology | M
Nursing and Healthcare
  Administration | M,D
Nursing—General | M,D
Nutrition | M
Occupational Therapy | M
Physical Therapy | D
Physician Assistant Studies | M
Public Health—General | M

**GRAND VIEW UNIVERSITY**
Nursing and Healthcare
  Administration | M,O
Nursing Education | M,O

**GRANTHAM UNIVERSITY**
Health Services Management and
  Hospital Administration | M
Nursing and Healthcare
  Administration | M
Nursing Education | M
Nursing Informatics | M
Nursing—General | M

**GWYNEDD MERCY UNIVERSITY**
Adult Nursing | M,D
Family Nurse Practitioner Studies | M,D
Gerontological Nursing | M,D
Nursing Education | M,D
Nursing—General | M,D
Oncology Nursing | M,D
Pediatric Nursing | M,D

**HAMPTON UNIVERSITY**
Allied Health—General | M
Biological and Biomedical
  Sciences—General | M
Communication Disorders | M
Community Health Nursing | M,D
Environmental Biology | M
Family Nurse Practitioner Studies | M,D
Medical Physics | M,D
Nursing and Healthcare
  Administration | M,D
Nursing Education | M,D
Nursing—General | M,D
Physical Therapy | D

**HARDING UNIVERSITY**
Allied Health—General | M,D
Communication Disorders | M
Pharmacy | D
Physical Therapy | D
Physician Assistant Studies | M

*M—masters degree; D—doctorate; O—other advanced degree; *—Close-Up and/or Display*

**HARDIN-SIMMONS UNIVERSITY**
- Family Nurse Practitioner Studies M
- Maternal and Child/Neonatal Nursing M
- Nursing Education M
- Nursing—General M
- Physical Therapy D
- Physician Assistant Studies M,D

**HARVARD UNIVERSITY**
- Allopathic Medicine D
- Biochemistry D
- Biological and Biomedical Sciences—General M,D,O
- Biophysics D
- Biopsychology D
- Cell Biology D
- Computational Biology M
- Dentistry M,D,O
- Environmental and Occupational Health M,D
- Epidemiology M,D
- Evolutionary Biology D
- Genetics M,D
- Health Promotion M,D
- Health Services Management and Hospital Administration M,D
- International Health M,D
- Medical Physics D
- Microbiology D
- Molecular Biology D
- Molecular Genetics D
- Molecular Pharmacology D
- Neurobiology D
- Neuroscience D
- Nutrition D
- Oral and Dental Sciences M,D,O
- Pathology D
- Public Health—General M,D*
- Systems Biology D

**HAWAII PACIFIC UNIVERSITY**
- Nursing—General M,D
- Public Health—General M

**HEC MONTREAL**
- Medical Microbiology D

**HERZING UNIVERSITY ONLINE**
- Health Services Management and Hospital Administration M
- Nursing and Healthcare Administration M
- Nursing Education M
- Nursing—General M

**HIGH POINT UNIVERSITY**
- Pharmacy M,D
- Physical Therapy M,D
- Physician Assistant Studies M,D

**HILBERT COLLEGE**
- Health Services Management and Hospital Administration M

**HODGES UNIVERSITY**
- Health Services Management and Hospital Administration M

**HOFSTRA UNIVERSITY**
- Allopathic Medicine D
- Bioethics M,D,O
- Biological and Biomedical Sciences—General M
- Communication Disorders M,D,O
- Family Nurse Practitioner Studies M
- Gerontological Nursing M
- Health Services Management and Hospital Administration M,O
- Medical Physics M
- Molecular Medicine D
- Nursing and Healthcare Administration M,D,O
- Nursing—General M
- Occupational Therapy M,O
- Physician Assistant Studies M
- Psychiatric Nursing M
- Public Health—General M,O

**HOLY FAMILY UNIVERSITY**
- Health Services Management and Hospital Administration M
- Nursing and Healthcare Administration M
- Nursing Education M
- Nursing—General M

**HOLY NAMES UNIVERSITY**
- Family Nurse Practitioner Studies M,O
- Nursing and Healthcare Administration M,O
- Nursing Informatics M,O
- Nursing—General M,O

**HOOD COLLEGE**
- Biological and Biomedical Sciences—General M
- Environmental Biology M,O

**HOUSTON BAPTIST UNIVERSITY**
- Family Nurse Practitioner Studies M
- Nursing—General M
- Pediatric Nursing M

**HOWARD UNIVERSITY**
- Allied Health—General M,D
- Allopathic Medicine D
- Anatomy M,D
- Biochemistry M,D
- Biological and Biomedical Sciences—General M,D
- Biophysics D
- Biopsychology M,D
- Communication Disorders M,D
- Dentistry D,O
- Family Nurse Practitioner Studies M
- Microbiology D
- Molecular Biology M,D
- Nursing Education M
- Nursing—General M
- Nutrition M,D
- Occupational Therapy M,D
- Oral and Dental Sciences D,O
- Pharmacology M,D
- Pharmacy D
- Physical Therapy M,D
- Physician Assistant Studies M,D
- Physiology D
- Public Health—General M

**HUMBOLDT STATE UNIVERSITY**
- Biological and Biomedical Sciences—General M

**HUNTER COLLEGE OF THE CITY UNIVERSITY OF NEW YORK**
- Adult Nursing M
- Animal Behavior M,O
- Biochemistry M,D
- Biological and Biomedical Sciences—General M,D
- Communication Disorders M
- Community Health Nursing M
- Family Nurse Practitioner Studies D
- Gerontological Nursing M,D
- Nursing—General M,D,O
- Nutrition M
- Physical Therapy D
- Psychiatric Nursing M,D,O
- Public Health—General M

**HUNTINGTON UNIVERSITY**
- Occupational Therapy M,D

**HUNTINGTON UNIVERSITY OF HEALTH SCIENCES**
- Nutrition M,D

**HUSSON UNIVERSITY**
- Community Health Nursing M,O
- Family Nurse Practitioner Studies M,O
- Health Services Management and Hospital Administration M
- Nursing—General M,O
- Pharmacology M,D
- Pharmacy M,D
- Physical Therapy D
- Psychiatric Nursing M,O

**ICAHN SCHOOL OF MEDICINE AT MOUNT SINAI**
- Allopathic Medicine D
- Bioethics M
- Biological and Biomedical Sciences—General M,D
- Clinical Research M,D
- Community Health M,D
- Neuroscience M,D
- Public Health—General M,D

**IDAHO STATE UNIVERSITY**
- Allied Health—General M,D,O
- Biological and Biomedical Sciences—General M,D
- Communication Disorders M,D
- Community Health O
- Dental Hygiene M
- Dentistry O
- Health Physics/Radiological Health M,D
- Medical Microbiology M,D
- Medicinal and Pharmaceutical Chemistry M,D
- Microbiology M,D
- Nursing—General M,D
- Occupational Therapy M
- Oral and Dental Sciences O
- Pharmaceutical Administration M,D
- Pharmaceutical Sciences M,D
- Pharmacology M,D
- Pharmacy M,D
- Physical Therapy D
- Physician Assistant Studies M
- Public Health—General M

**IGLOBAL UNIVERSITY**
- Health Services Management and Hospital Administration M

**ILLINOIS COLLEGE OF OPTOMETRY**
- Optometry D

**ILLINOIS INSTITUTE OF TECHNOLOGY**
- Biochemistry M,D
- Biological and Biomedical Sciences—General M,D
- Cell Biology M,D
- Health Physics/Radiological Health M,D
- Medical Imaging M,D
- Microbiology M,D
- Molecular Biology M,D
- Molecular Biophysics M,D

**ILLINOIS STATE UNIVERSITY**
- Animal Behavior M,D
- Bacteriology M,D
- Biochemistry M,D
- Biological and Biomedical Sciences—General M,D
- Biophysics M,D
- Botany M,D
- Cell Biology M,D
- Communication Disorders M
- Conservation Biology M,D
- Developmental Biology M,D
- Ecology M,D
- Entomology M,D
- Evolutionary Biology M,D
- Family Nurse Practitioner Studies M,D,O
- Genetics M,D
- Immunology M,D
- Microbiology M,D
- Molecular Biology M,D
- Molecular Genetics M,D
- Neurobiology M,D
- Neuroscience M,D
- Nursing—General M,D,O
- Parasitology M,D
- Physiology M,D
- Plant Biology M,D
- Plant Molecular Biology M,D
- Structural Biology M,D
- Zoology M,D

**IMMACULATA UNIVERSITY**
- Health Promotion M
- Neuroscience M,D,O
- Nursing and Healthcare Administration M
- Nursing Education M
- Nursing—General M
- Nutrition M

**INDEPENDENCE UNIVERSITY**
- Community Health Nursing M
- Community Health M
- Gerontological Nursing M
- Health Promotion M
- Health Services Management and Hospital Administration M
- Nursing and Healthcare Administration M
- Nursing—General M
- Public Health—General M

**INDIANA STATE UNIVERSITY**
- Biological and Biomedical Sciences—General M,D
- Cell Biology M,D
- Communication Disorders M,D,O
- Ecology M,D
- Environmental and Occupational Health M
- Evolutionary Biology M,D
- Family Nurse Practitioner Studies M,D
- Molecular Biology M,D
- Nursing and Healthcare Administration M,D
- Nursing Education M,D
- Nursing—General M,D
- Occupational Therapy M,D
- Physical Therapy M,D
- Physician Assistant Studies M,D
- Physiology M,D

**INDIANA TECH**
- Health Services Management and Hospital Administration M

**INDIANA UNIVERSITY BLOOMINGTON**
- Biochemistry M,D
- Biological and Biomedical Sciences—General M,D
- Cell Biology M,D
- Communication Disorders M,D
- Community Health M,D
- Ecology M,D,O
- Environmental and Occupational Health M,D
- Epidemiology M,D
- Evolutionary Biology M,D
- Genetics M,D
- Health Promotion M,D
- Health Services Management and Hospital Administration M,D
- Medical Physics M,D
- Microbiology M,D
- Molecular Biology M,D
- Neuroscience D
- Nutrition M,D
- Optometry M,D
- Plant Biology M,D
- Public Health—General M,D
- Toxicology M,D,O
- Zoology M,D

**INDIANA UNIVERSITY EAST**
- Nursing—General M

**INDIANA UNIVERSITY KOKOMO**
- Family Nurse Practitioner Studies M
- Health Services Management and Hospital Administration M,O
- Nursing and Healthcare Administration M
- Nursing Education M
- Nursing—General M

**INDIANA UNIVERSITY NORTHWEST**
- Health Services Management and Hospital Administration M,O

**INDIANA UNIVERSITY OF PENNSYLVANIA**
- Biological and Biomedical Sciences—General M
- Communication Disorders M
- Environmental and Occupational Health M,D
- Health Services Management and Hospital Administration M
- Nursing and Healthcare Administration M
- Nursing Education M
- Nursing—General D
- Nutrition M

**INDIANA UNIVERSITY-PURDUE UNIVERSITY INDIANAPOLIS**
- Acute Care/Critical Care Nursing M
- Allopathic Medicine M,D
- Anatomy M,D
- Biochemistry M,D
- Bioethics M,D,O
- Biological and Biomedical Sciences—General M,D
- Cell Biology M,D
- Community Health M,D,O
- Dentistry M,D,O
- Environmental and Occupational Health M,D,O
- Epidemiology M,D,O
- Family Nurse Practitioner Studies M
- Gerontological Nursing M
- Health Services Management and Hospital Administration M,D,O
- Immunology M,D
- International Health M,D,O
- Microbiology M,D
- Molecular Biology M,D
- Molecular Genetics M,D
- Neurobiology D
- Nursing and Healthcare Administration M,D
- Nursing Education M
- Nursing—General M,D
- Nutrition M,D
- Occupational Therapy M,D
- Pathology M,D
- Pediatric Nursing M
- Pharmacology M,D
- Physical Therapy M,D
- Public Health—General M,D,O
- Rehabilitation Sciences M,D
- Toxicology M,D

**INDIANA UNIVERSITY SOUTH BEND**
- Family Nurse Practitioner Studies M
- Health Services Management and Hospital Administration M,O
- Nursing—General M

**INDIANA WESLEYAN UNIVERSITY**
- Health Services Management and Hospital Administration M,O
- Nursing and Healthcare Administration M
- Nursing Education M
- Nursing—General M
- Occupational Therapy M,D
- Public Health—General M,D

**INSTITUTE OF CLINICAL ACUPUNCTURE AND ORIENTAL MEDICINE**
- Acupuncture and Oriental Medicine M

**INSTITUTE OF PUBLIC ADMINISTRATION**
- Health Services Management and Hospital Administration M,O

**INSTITUTE OF TAOIST EDUCATION AND ACUPUNCTURE**
- Acupuncture and Oriental Medicine M

**INSTITUT FRANCO-EUROPÉEN DE CHIROPRAXIE**
- Chiropractic D

**INSTITUTO TECNOLOGICO DE SANTO DOMINGO**
- Allopathic Medicine M,D
- Bioethics M,O
- Health Promotion M,O
- Maternal and Child Health M,O
- Nutrition M,O

**INTER AMERICAN UNIVERSITY OF PUERTO RICO, ARECIBO CAMPUS**
- Acute Care/Critical Care Nursing M
- Medical/Surgical Nursing M
- Nurse Anesthesia M
- Nursing—General M

**INTER AMERICAN UNIVERSITY OF PUERTO RICO, BARRANQUITAS CAMPUS**
- Acute Care/Critical Care Nursing M
- Biological and Biomedical Sciences—General M
- Medical/Surgical Nursing M
- Nursing—General M

**INTER AMERICAN UNIVERSITY OF PUERTO RICO, BAYAMÓN CAMPUS**
- Ecology M

**INTER AMERICAN UNIVERSITY OF PUERTO RICO, METROPOLITAN CAMPUS**
- Clinical Laboratory Sciences/Medical Technology M
- Microbiology M
- Molecular Biology M

**INTER AMERICAN UNIVERSITY OF PUERTO RICO SCHOOL OF OPTOMETRY**
- Optometry D

**IONA COLLEGE**
- Communication Disorders M
- Health Services Management and Hospital Administration M,O

**IOWA STATE UNIVERSITY OF SCIENCE AND TECHNOLOGY**
- Biological and Biomedical Sciences—General M,D
- Biophysics M,D
- Cell Biology M,D
- Computational Biology M,D
- Developmental Biology M,D
- Ecology M,D
- Entomology M,D
- Evolutionary Biology M,D
- Genetics M,D
- Immunology M,D
- Microbiology M,D
- Molecular Biology M,D
- Molecular Genetics M,D
- Neuroscience M,D
- Nutrition M,D
- Pathology M,D
- Plant Biology M,D
- Plant Pathology M,D
- Structural Biology M,D
- Toxicology M,D
- Veterinary Medicine M
- Veterinary Sciences M,D

### IRELL & MANELLA GRADUATE SCHOOL OF BIOLOGICAL SCIENCES
- Biochemistry D
- Biological and Biomedical Sciences—General D
- Cancer Biology/Oncology D
- Cell Biology D
- Developmental Biology D
- Genetics D
- Immunology D
- Molecular Biology D
- Neuroscience D
- Pharmaceutical Sciences D

### ITHACA COLLEGE
- Allied Health—General M,D
- Communication Disorders M
- Occupational Therapy M
- Physical Therapy D

### JACKSON STATE UNIVERSITY
- Biological and Biomedical Sciences—General M
- Communication Disorders M
- Public Health—General M,D
- Rehabilitation Sciences M

### JACKSONVILLE STATE UNIVERSITY
- Biological and Biomedical Sciences—General M
- Nursing—General M

### JACKSONVILLE UNIVERSITY
- Adult Nursing M,D,O
- Allied Health—General M,D
- Communication Disorders M
- Dentistry M,O
- Family Nurse Practitioner Studies M
- Gerontological Nursing M,D,O
- Nursing and Healthcare Administration M
- Nursing Education M
- Nursing Informatics M
- Nursing—General M,D
- Occupational Therapy D
- Oral and Dental Sciences M,O
- Psychiatric Nursing M

### JAMES MADISON UNIVERSITY
- Biological and Biomedical Sciences—General M
- Communication Disorders M,D
- Family Nurse Practitioner Studies M,D
- Gerontological Nursing M,D
- Nurse Midwifery M,D
- Nursing and Healthcare Administration M,D
- Nursing—General M,D
- Nutrition M
- Occupational Therapy M
- Physician Assistant Studies M
- Physiology M
- Psychiatric Nursing M,D

### JEFFERSON COLLEGE OF HEALTH SCIENCES
- Nursing and Healthcare Administration M
- Nursing Education M
- Nursing—General M
- Occupational Therapy M
- Physician Assistant Studies M

### JOHN CARROLL UNIVERSITY
- Biological and Biomedical Sciences—General M

### JOHN F. KENNEDY UNIVERSITY
- Health Services Management and Hospital Administration M

### JOHN PATRICK UNIVERSITY OF HEALTH AND APPLIED SCIENCES
- Health Physics/Radiological Health M
- Medical Physics M

### JOHNS HOPKINS UNIVERSITY
- Allopathic Medicine D
- Anatomy D
- Biochemistry M,D
- Bioethics M,D
- Biological and Biomedical Sciences—General M,D
- Biophysics D
- Cardiovascular Sciences M,D
- Cell Biology D
- Clinical Research M,D
- Community Health Nursing
- Community Health M,D
- Developmental Biology D
- Environmental and Occupational Health M,D
- Epidemiology M,D
- Evolutionary Biology D
- Family Nurse Practitioner Studies D
- Genetics M,D
- Gerontological Nursing D
- Health Services Management and Hospital Administration M,D
- Immunology M,D
- Infectious Diseases M,D
- International Health M,D
- Microbiology M,D
- Molecular Biology M,D
- Molecular Biophysics M,D
- Molecular Medicine D
- Neuroscience D
- Nursing and Healthcare Administration M,D
- Nursing Education O
- Nursing—General M,D,O
- Nutrition M,D
- Pathobiology D
- Pathology D
- Pediatric Nursing D,O
- Pharmaceutical Sciences M
- Pharmacology D
- Physiology D
- Psychiatric Nursing O
- Public Health—General M,D

### JOHNSON & WALES UNIVERSITY
- Occupational Therapy D
- Physician Assistant Studies M

### KANSAS CITY UNIVERSITY OF MEDICINE AND BIOSCIENCES
- Bioethics M
- Biological and Biomedical Sciences—General M
- Osteopathic Medicine D

### KANSAS STATE UNIVERSITY
- Biochemistry M,D
- Biological and Biomedical Sciences—General M,D
- Communication Disorders M,D,O
- Entomology M,D
- Genetics M,D
- Nutrition M,D
- Pathobiology M,D
- Physiology M,D
- Plant Pathology M,D
- Public Health—General M,D,O
- Veterinary Medicine D
- Veterinary Sciences M,O

### KEAN UNIVERSITY
- Communication Disorders M,D
- Community Health Nursing M
- Health Services Management and Hospital Administration M
- Nursing and Healthcare Administration M
- Nursing—General M
- Occupational Therapy M
- Physical Therapy D

### KEISER UNIVERSITY
- Family Nurse Practitioner Studies M
- Health Services Management and Hospital Administration M
- Nurse Anesthesia M,D
- Nursing—General M
- Occupational Therapy M
- Physician Assistant Studies M

### KENNESAW STATE UNIVERSITY
- Biochemistry M
- Biological and Biomedical Sciences—General M
- Health Services Management and Hospital Administration M
- Nursing and Healthcare Administration M
- Nursing Education M
- Nursing—General M

### KENT STATE UNIVERSITY
- Adult Nursing M,D
- Biological and Biomedical Sciences—General M,D
- Botany M,D
- Cell Biology M,D
- Communication Disorders M,D,O
- Ecology M,D
- Environmental and Occupational Health M,D
- Epidemiology M,D
- Family Nurse Practitioner Studies M,D
- Genetics M,D
- Gerontological Nursing M,D
- Health Promotion M,D
- Health Services Management and Hospital Administration M,D
- Molecular Biology M,D
- Neuroscience M,D
- Nursing and Healthcare Administration M,D
- Nursing Education M,D
- Nursing—General M,D
- Nutrition M
- Pediatric Nursing M,D
- Pharmacology M,D
- Physiology M,D
- Podiatric Medicine D
- Psychiatric Nursing M,D
- Public Health—General M,D

### KETTERING COLLEGE
- Occupational Therapy D
- Physician Assistant Studies M

### KEUKA COLLEGE
- Gerontological Nursing M
- Nursing Education M
- Nursing—General M
- Occupational Therapy M

### KING'S COLLEGE
- Health Services Management and Hospital Administration M
- Physician Assistant Studies M

### KING UNIVERSITY
- Family Nurse Practitioner Studies M,D,O
- Health Services Management and Hospital Administration M
- Nursing and Healthcare Administration M,D,O
- Nursing Education M,D,O
- Nursing—General M,D,O
- Pediatric Nursing M,D,O

### KUTZTOWN UNIVERSITY OF PENNSYLVANIA
- Biological and Biomedical Sciences—General M,D

### LAKE ERIE COLLEGE
- Health Services Management and Hospital Administration M

### LAKE ERIE COLLEGE OF OSTEOPATHIC MEDICINE
- Biological and Biomedical Sciences—General M,D,O
- Osteopathic Medicine M,D,O
- Pharmacy M,D,O

### LAKE FOREST GRADUATE SCHOOL OF MANAGEMENT
- Health Services Management and Hospital Administration M

### LAKEHEAD UNIVERSITY
- Biological and Biomedical Sciences—General M
- Health Services Research M

### LAMAR UNIVERSITY
- Biological and Biomedical Sciences—General M
- Communication Disorders M,D
- Nursing and Healthcare Administration M
- Nursing Education M
- Nursing—General M

### LANDER UNIVERSITY
- Nursing—General M

### LANGSTON UNIVERSITY
- Physical Therapy D

### LA ROCHE UNIVERSITY
- Nurse Anesthesia M,D
- Nursing and Healthcare Administration M
- Nursing Education M
- Nursing—General M

### LA SALLE UNIVERSITY
- Adult Nursing M,D,O
- Communication Disorders M
- Community Health Nursing M,D,O
- Family Nurse Practitioner Studies M,D,O
- Gerontological Nursing M,D,O
- Nurse Anesthesia M,D,O
- Nursing and Healthcare Administration M,D,O
- Nursing Education M,D,O
- Nursing—General M,D,O
- Public Health—General M
- School Nursing M,D,O

### LASELL COLLEGE
- Health Services Management and Hospital Administration M,O
- Rehabilitation Sciences M

### LAURENTIAN UNIVERSITY
- Biochemistry M
- Biological and Biomedical Sciences—General M,D
- Ecology M,D
- Nursing—General M
- Public Health—General D

### LAWRENCE TECHNOLOGICAL UNIVERSITY
- Health Services Management and Hospital Administration M,D,O

### LEBANESE AMERICAN UNIVERSITY
- Pharmacy D

### LEBANON VALLEY COLLEGE
- Communication Disorders M
- Health Services Management and Hospital Administration M
- Physical Therapy D

### LEE UNIVERSITY
- Biological and Biomedical Sciences—General M,O

### LEHIGH UNIVERSITY
- Biochemistry M,D
- Biological and Biomedical Sciences—General M,D
- Cell Biology M,D
- Environmental and Occupational Health M,O
- Health Services Management and Hospital Administration M,O
- Molecular Biology M,D

### LEHMAN COLLEGE OF THE CITY UNIVERSITY OF NEW YORK
- Adult Nursing M
- Biological and Biomedical Sciences—General M
- Communication Disorders M
- Gerontological Nursing M
- Health Promotion M
- Maternal and Child/Neonatal Nursing M
- Nursing—General M
- Nutrition M
- Pediatric Nursing M

### LE MOYNE COLLEGE
- Family Nurse Practitioner Studies M,O
- Nursing and Healthcare Administration M,O
- Nursing Education M,O
- Nursing Informatics M,O
- Nursing—General M,O
- Occupational Therapy M
- Physician Assistant Studies M

### LENOIR-RHYNE UNIVERSITY
- Health Services Management and Hospital Administration M
- Nursing and Healthcare Administration M
- Nursing Education M
- Nursing—General M
- Occupational Therapy M
- Physician Assistant Studies M
- Public Health—General M

### LESLEY UNIVERSITY
- Ecology M,D,O

### LETOURNEAU UNIVERSITY
- Health Services Management and Hospital Administration M

### LEWIS & CLARK COLLEGE
- Communication Disorders M

### LEWIS UNIVERSITY
- Adult Nursing M,D
- Computational Biology M
- Environmental and Occupational Health M
- Family Nurse Practitioner Studies M,D
- Health Services Management and Hospital Administration M
- Nursing and Healthcare Administration M,D
- Nursing Education M,D
- Nursing—General M,D
- School Nursing M,D

### LIBERTY UNIVERSITY
- Anatomy M,D
- Biological and Biomedical Sciences—General M,D
- Biopsychology M,D
- Cell Biology M,D
- Epidemiology M,D
- Family Nurse Practitioner Studies M,D
- Health Promotion M,D,O
- International Health M,D
- Molecular Medicine M,D
- Nursing and Healthcare Administration M,D
- Nursing Education M,D
- Nursing Informatics M,D
- Nursing—General M,D
- Nutrition M,D
- Osteopathic Medicine D
- Public Health—General M,D

### LIFE CHIROPRACTIC COLLEGE WEST
- Chiropractic D

### LIFE UNIVERSITY
- Chiropractic D
- Nutrition M

### LINCOLN MEMORIAL UNIVERSITY
- Family Nurse Practitioner Studies M
- Nurse Anesthesia M
- Nursing—General M
- Osteopathic Medicine D
- Psychiatric Nursing M
- Veterinary Medicine D

### LINDENWOOD UNIVERSITY
- Communication Disorders M,D,O
- Health Promotion M
- Health Services Management and Hospital Administration M,O
- Nursing—General M

### LINDENWOOD UNIVERSITY–BELLEVILLE
- Health Services Management and Hospital Administration M

### LIPSCOMB UNIVERSITY
- Clinical Laboratory Sciences/Medical Technology M
- Health Services Management and Hospital Administration M,O
- Molecular Biology M
- Nutrition M
- Pharmacy M,D

### LOCK HAVEN UNIVERSITY OF PENNSYLVANIA
- Health Promotion M
- Health Services Management and Hospital Administration M
- Physician Assistant Studies M

### LOGAN UNIVERSITY
- Chiropractic D
- Nutrition M,D
- Rehabilitation Sciences M,D

### LOMA LINDA UNIVERSITY
- Adult Nursing M
- Allied Health—General M,D
- Allopathic Medicine M,D
- Anatomy D
- Biochemistry M,D
- Bioethics M,O
- Communication Disorders M,D
- Dentistry M,D,O
- Environmental and Occupational Health M
- Epidemiology M,D
- Gerontological Nursing M
- Health Services Management and Hospital Administration M
- International Health M
- Microbiology M,D
- Nursing and Healthcare Administration M
- Nursing Education M
- Nursing—General D
- Nutrition M,D
- Occupational Therapy M,D
- Oral and Dental Sciences M,O
- Pathology D
- Pediatric Nursing M

*M—masters degree; D—doctorate; O—other advanced degree; *—Close-Up and/or Display*

- Pharmacology D
- Pharmacy D
- Physical Therapy M,D
- Physician Assistant Studies M
- Physiology D
- Public Health—General M,D
- Rehabilitation Sciences M,D

**LONDON METROPOLITAN UNIVERSITY**
- Biological and Biomedical Sciences—General M,D
- Health Services Management and Hospital Administration M,D
- Immunology M,D
- Nutrition M,D
- Pharmacology M,D
- Public Health—General M,D

**LONG ISLAND UNIVERSITY - BRENTWOOD CAMPUS**
- Family Nurse Practitioner Studies M,O
- Health Services Management and Hospital Administration M,O

**LONG ISLAND UNIVERSITY - BROOKLYN**
- Adult Nursing M,O
- Biological and Biomedical Sciences—General M,D,O
- Communication Disorders M,D,O
- Community Health M,D,O
- Family Nurse Practitioner Studies M,O
- Health Services Management and Hospital Administration M,O
- Nursing Education M,O
- Nursing—General M,O
- Occupational Therapy M,D,O
- Pharmaceutical Sciences M,D
- Pharmacology M,D
- Pharmacy M,D
- Physical Therapy M,D,O
- Physician Assistant Studies M,D,O
- Public Health—General M,D,O
- Toxicology M,D

**LONG ISLAND UNIVERSITY - HUDSON**
- Health Services Management and Hospital Administration M,O
- Pharmaceutical Sciences M,O
- Pharmacy M,O

**LONG ISLAND UNIVERSITY - POST**
- Allied Health—General M,O
- Biological and Biomedical Sciences—General M,O
- Communication Disorders M,D,O
- Family Nurse Practitioner Studies M,O
- Health Services Management and Hospital Administration M,O
- Nursing Education M,O
- Nutrition M,O
- Perfusion M,O

**LONGWOOD UNIVERSITY**
- Communication Disorders M

**LOUISIANA COLLEGE**
- Nursing and Healthcare Administration M
- Nursing—General M

**LOUISIANA STATE UNIVERSITY AND AGRICULTURAL & MECHANICAL COLLEGE**
- Biochemistry M,D
- Biological and Biomedical Sciences—General M,D
- Biopsychology M,D
- Communication Disorders M,D
- Entomology M,D
- Medical Physics M,D
- Nutrition M,D
- Plant Pathology M,D
- Toxicology M,D
- Veterinary Medicine D
- Veterinary Sciences M,D

**LOUISIANA STATE UNIVERSITY HEALTH SCIENCES CENTER**
- Allopathic Medicine M,D
- Anatomy D
- Biological and Biomedical Sciences—General D
- Cell Biology D
- Communication Disorders M,D
- Community Health Nursing M,D,O
- Community Health M,D
- Dentistry D
- Developmental Biology D
- Environmental and Occupational Health M,D
- Epidemiology M,D
- Family Nurse Practitioner Studies M,D,O
- Gerontological Nursing M,D,O
- Health Services Management and Hospital Administration M,D
- Human Genetics D
- Immunology D
- Maternal and Child/Neonatal Nursing M,D,O
- Microbiology D
- Neurobiology D
- Neuroscience D
- Nurse Anesthesia M,D,O
- Nursing and Healthcare Administration M,D,O
- Nursing Education M,D,O
- Nursing—General M,D,O
- Occupational Therapy M
- Parasitology D
- Pharmacology D
- Physical Therapy D
- Physician Assistant Studies M
- Physiology D
- Public Health—General M,D

**LOUISIANA STATE UNIVERSITY HEALTH SCIENCES CENTER AT SHREVEPORT**
- Allopathic Medicine D
- Anatomy M,D
- Biochemistry M,D
- Biological and Biomedical Sciences—General M
- Cell Biology M,D
- Immunology M,D
- Microbiology M,D
- Molecular Biology M,D
- Pharmacology M,D
- Physiology M,D

**LOUISIANA STATE UNIVERSITY IN SHREVEPORT**
- Biological and Biomedical Sciences—General M
- Health Services Management and Hospital Administration M
- Public Health—General M

**LOUISIANA TECH UNIVERSITY**
- Biological and Biomedical Sciences—General M,D,O
- Communication Disorders M,D,O
- Molecular Biology M,D,O
- Nutrition M,D,O

**LOURDES UNIVERSITY**
- Nurse Anesthesia M
- Nursing and Healthcare Administration M
- Nursing Education M

**LOYOLA MARYMOUNT UNIVERSITY**
- Bioethics M

**LOYOLA UNIVERSITY CHICAGO**
- Adult Nursing M,D,O
- Biochemistry M,D
- Bioethics M,D,O
- Biological and Biomedical Sciences—General M,D
- Cell Biology M,D
- Clinical Research M
- Family Nurse Practitioner Studies M,D,O
- Health Services Management and Hospital Administration M
- Immunology M,D
- Infectious Diseases M,D,O
- Microbiology M,D
- Molecular Biology M,D
- Molecular Pharmacology M,D
- Molecular Physiology M,D
- Neuroscience M,D
- Nursing and Healthcare Administration M,D,O
- Nursing—General M,D,O
- Nutrition M,D,O
- Physiology M,D
- Public Health—General M,O
- Women's Health Nursing M,D,O

**LOYOLA UNIVERSITY MARYLAND**
- Communication Disorders M

**LOYOLA UNIVERSITY NEW ORLEANS**
- Family Nurse Practitioner Studies M,D
- Nursing—General M,D

**MADONNA UNIVERSITY**
- Adult Nursing M
- Health Services Management and Hospital Administration M
- Hospice Nursing M
- Nursing and Healthcare Administration M
- Nursing—General M

**MAHARISHI INTERNATIONAL UNIVERSITY**
- Physiology D

**MALONE UNIVERSITY**
- Family Nurse Practitioner Studies M
- Nursing—General M

**MANCHESTER UNIVERSITY**
- Genomic Sciences M
- Pharmacy D

**MANHATTANVILLE COLLEGE**
- Biological and Biomedical Sciences—General M,O
- Health Promotion M,O

**MANSFIELD UNIVERSITY OF PENNSYLVANIA**
- Nursing—General M

**MARIAN UNIVERSITY (IN)**
- Family Nurse Practitioner Studies M,D
- Nurse Anesthesia M,D
- Nursing Education M,D
- Nursing—General M,D
- Osteopathic Medicine M,D

**MARIAN UNIVERSITY (WI)**
- Adult Nursing M
- Nursing Education M
- Nursing—General M

**MARIETTA COLLEGE**
- Physician Assistant Studies M

**MARIST COLLEGE**
- Physical Therapy D

**MARQUETTE UNIVERSITY**
- Acute Care/Critical Care Nursing M,D,O
- Adult Nursing M,D,O
- Biological and Biomedical Sciences—General M,D
- Cardiovascular Sciences M,D
- Cell Biology M,D
- Communication Disorders M,O
- Dentistry D
- Developmental Biology M,D
- Ecology M,D
- Family Nurse Practitioner Studies M,D,O
- Genetics M,D
- Gerontological Nursing M,D,O
- Microbiology M,D
- Molecular Biology M,D
- Neuroscience M,D
- Nurse Midwifery M,D,O
- Nursing and Healthcare Administration M,D,O
- Nursing—General M,D,O
- Oral and Dental Sciences M,O
- Pediatric Nursing M,D,O
- Physical Therapy D
- Physician Assistant Studies M
- Physiology M,D
- Rehabilitation Sciences M,D

**MARSHALL B. KETCHUM UNIVERSITY**
- Optometry M,D
- Pharmacy M,D
- Vision Sciences M,D

**MARSHALL UNIVERSITY**
- Allopathic Medicine D
- Biological and Biomedical Sciences—General M,D
- Communication Disorders M
- Health Services Management and Hospital Administration M
- Nurse Anesthesia D
- Nursing—General M,O
- Nutrition M,O
- Pharmacy D
- Physical Therapy D
- Public Health—General M

**MARY BALDWIN UNIVERSITY**
- Nursing—General M
- Occupational Therapy D
- Physical Therapy D
- Physician Assistant Studies M

**MARYLAND UNIVERSITY OF INTEGRATIVE HEALTH**
- Acupuncture and Oriental Medicine M,D,O
- Health Promotion M,O
- Naturopathic Medicine D
- Nutrition M,D,O

**MARYMOUNT UNIVERSITY**
- Allied Health—General M,D,O
- Family Nurse Practitioner Studies M,D,O
- Health Promotion M
- Health Services Management and Hospital Administration M
- Nursing—General M,D,O
- Physical Therapy D

**MARYVILLE UNIVERSITY OF SAINT LOUIS**
- Acute Care/Critical Care Nursing M,D
- Adult Nursing M,D
- Allied Health—General M,D,O
- Communication Disorders M
- Family Nurse Practitioner Studies M,D
- Gerontological Nursing M,D
- Health Services Management and Hospital Administration M,O
- Nursing—General M,D
- Occupational Therapy M
- Pediatric Nursing M,D
- Physical Therapy D

**MARYWOOD UNIVERSITY**
- Communication Disorders M
- Health Services Management and Hospital Administration M
- Nutrition M,O
- Physician Assistant Studies M

**MASSACHUSETTS INSTITUTE OF TECHNOLOGY**
- Biochemistry D
- Biological and Biomedical Sciences—General M,D
- Cell Biology D
- Communication Disorders M,D
- Computational Biology D
- Developmental Biology D
- Environmental Biology M,D,O
- Genetics D
- Genomic Sciences M,D
- Immunology D
- Medical Physics M,D
- Microbiology D
- Molecular Biology M,D,O
- Molecular Toxicology D
- Neurobiology D
- Neuroscience D
- Structural Biology D
- Systems Biology D
- Toxicology M,D

**MAYO CLINIC ALIX SCHOOL OF MEDICINE**
- Allopathic Medicine D

**MAYO CLINIC GRADUATE SCHOOL OF BIOMEDICAL SCIENCES**
- Biochemistry M,D
- Clinical Laboratory Sciences/Medical Technology M,D
- Genetics D
- Immunology D
- Molecular Biology M,D
- Molecular Pharmacology M,D
- Neuroscience M,D
- Physiology M,D
- Virology D

**MAYO CLINIC SCHOOL OF HEALTH SCIENCES**
- Nurse Anesthesia D
- Physical Therapy D

**MCGILL UNIVERSITY**
- Allopathic Medicine M,D
- Anatomy M,D
- Biochemistry M,D
- Bioethics M,D,O
- Biological and Biomedical Sciences—General M,D
- Cell Biology M,D
- Communication Disorders M,D
- Dentistry M,D,O
- Entomology M,D
- Environmental and Occupational Health M,D
- Epidemiology M,D,O
- Family Nurse Practitioner Studies M,D,O
- Human Genetics M,D
- Immunology M,D
- Medical Physics M,D
- Microbiology M,D
- Neuroscience M,D
- Nursing—General M,D,O
- Nutrition M,D,O
- Oral and Dental Sciences M,D,O
- Parasitology M,D,O
- Pathology M,D
- Pharmacology M,D
- Physiology M,D
- Public Health—General M,D
- Rehabilitation Sciences M,D,O

**MCKENDREE UNIVERSITY**
- Nursing and Healthcare Administration M
- Nursing Education M
- Nursing—General M

**MCMASTER UNIVERSITY**
- Biochemistry M,D
- Biological and Biomedical Sciences—General M,D
- Cancer Biology/Oncology M,D
- Cardiovascular Sciences M,D
- Cell Biology M,D
- Genetics M,D
- Health Physics/Radiological Health M,D
- Health Services Research M,D
- Immunology M,D
- Medical Physics M,D
- Molecular Biology M,D
- Neuroscience M,D
- Nursing—General M,D
- Nutrition M,D
- Occupational Therapy M
- Pharmacology M,D
- Physical Therapy M
- Physiology M,D
- Rehabilitation Sciences M,D
- Virology M,D

**MCMURRY UNIVERSITY**
- Family Nurse Practitioner Studies M
- Nursing Education M
- Nursing—General M

**MCNEESE STATE UNIVERSITY**
- Family Nurse Practitioner Studies M
- Health Promotion M
- Nursing Education M
- Nursing—General M,O
- Nutrition M
- Psychiatric Nursing M,O

**MCPHS UNIVERSITY**
- Acupuncture and Oriental Medicine M
- Health Services Management and Hospital Administration M
- Nursing—General M
- Optometry D
- Pharmaceutical Sciences M,D
- Pharmacology M,D
- Pharmacy D
- Physical Therapy D
- Physician Assistant Studies M
- Public Health—General M

**MEDICAL COLLEGE OF WISCONSIN**
- Allopathic Medicine D
- Anesthesiologist Assistant Studies M
- Biochemistry D
- Bioethics M,O
- Biological and Biomedical Sciences—General M,D,O
- Clinical Laboratory Sciences/Medical Technology M
- Clinical Research
- Community Health D
- Neuroscience D
- Pharmacology D
- Pharmacy D
- Physiology D
- Public Health—General M,D,O
- Toxicology D

**MEDICAL UNIVERSITY OF SOUTH CAROLINA**
- Adult Nursing M,D
- Allied Health—General M,D
- Allopathic Medicine D
- Biochemistry M,D
- Biological and Biomedical Sciences—General M,D
- Cancer Biology/Oncology D
- Cardiovascular Sciences D
- Cell Biology D
- Clinical Research M
- Dentistry D
- Developmental Biology D
- Epidemiology M,D
- Family Nurse Practitioner Studies M,D
- Genetics D
- Gerontological Nursing M,D
- Health Services Management and Hospital Administration M,D
- Immunology M,D
- International Health M
- Maternal and Child/Neonatal Nursing M,D
- Medical Imaging D

| | |
|---|---|
| Medicinal and Pharmaceutical Chemistry | D |
| Microbiology | M,D |
| Molecular Biology | M,D |
| Molecular Pharmacology | M,D |
| Neuroscience | M,D |
| Nurse Anesthesia | M |
| Nursing and Healthcare Administration | M |
| Nursing Education | M |
| Nursing—General | D |
| Occupational Therapy | M |
| Pathobiology | D |
| Pathology | M,D |
| Pharmacy | D |
| Physical Therapy | D |
| Physician Assistant Studies | M |
| Rehabilitation Sciences | D |
| Toxicology | D |

**MEHARRY MEDICAL COLLEGE**

| | |
|---|---|
| Allopathic Medicine | D |
| Biochemistry | D |
| Biological and Biomedical Sciences—General | D |
| Cancer Biology/Oncology | D |
| Dentistry | D |
| Environmental and Occupational Health | M |
| Health Services Management and Hospital Administration | M |
| Immunology | D |
| Microbiology | D |
| Neuroscience | D |
| Pharmacology | D |
| Public Health—General | M |

**MEMORIAL UNIVERSITY OF NEWFOUNDLAND**

| | |
|---|---|
| Biochemistry | M,D |
| Biological and Biomedical Sciences—General | M,D,O |
| Biopsychology | M,D |
| Cancer Biology/Oncology | M,D |
| Cardiovascular Sciences | M,D |
| Clinical Research | M |
| Community Health | M,D,O |
| Epidemiology | M,D,O |
| Human Genetics | M,D |
| Immunology | M,D |
| Neuroscience | M,D |
| Nursing—General | M,D |
| Pharmaceutical Sciences | M,D |

**MERCER UNIVERSITY**

| | |
|---|---|
| Allopathic Medicine | M,D |
| Environmental and Occupational Health | M,D |
| Family Nurse Practitioner Studies | M,D,O |
| Gerontological Nursing | M,D,O |
| Nursing and Healthcare Administration | M,D |
| Nursing—General | M,D,O |
| Pharmaceutical Sciences | D |
| Pharmacy | D |
| Physical Therapy | M,D |
| Physician Assistant Studies | M,D |
| Public Health—General | M,D |

**MERCY COLLEGE**

| | |
|---|---|
| Allied Health—General | M,D |
| Communication Disorders | M |
| Health Services Management and Hospital Administration | M |
| Nursing and Healthcare Administration | M |
| Nursing Education | M |
| Nursing—General | M |
| Occupational Therapy | M |
| Physical Therapy | D |
| Physician Assistant Studies | M |

**MERCY COLLEGE OF OHIO**

| | |
|---|---|
| Health Services Management and Hospital Administration | M |
| Nursing—General | M,O |

**MERCYHURST UNIVERSITY**

| | |
|---|---|
| Physician Assistant Studies | M |

**MEREDITH COLLEGE**

| | |
|---|---|
| Nutrition | M,O |

**MERRIMACK COLLEGE**

| | |
|---|---|
| Health Promotion | M |

**MESSIAH UNIVERSITY**

| | |
|---|---|
| Nursing Education | M |

**METHODIST UNIVERSITY**

| | |
|---|---|
| Physician Assistant Studies | M |

**METROPOLITAN STATE UNIVERSITY**

| | |
|---|---|
| Nursing and Healthcare Administration | M,D |
| Nursing Education | M,D |
| Nursing—General | M,D |
| Oral and Dental Sciences | M,D |

**MGH INSTITUTE OF HEALTH PROFESSIONS**

| | |
|---|---|
| Communication Disorders | M,O |
| Gerontological Nursing | M,D,O |
| Nursing Education | M,D,O |
| Nursing—General | M,D,O |
| Occupational Therapy | D |
| Pediatric Nursing | M,D,O |
| Physical Therapy | M,D,O |
| Physician Assistant Studies | M |
| Psychiatric Nursing | M,D,O |
| Women's Health Nursing | M,D,O |

**MIAMI REGIONAL UNIVERSITY**

| | |
|---|---|
| Nursing and Healthcare Administration | M |
| Nursing Education | M |
| Nursing—General | M |

**MIAMI UNIVERSITY**

| | |
|---|---|
| Biochemistry | M,D |
| Biological and Biomedical Sciences—General | M,D |
| Communication Disorders | M |
| Microbiology | M,D |

**MICHIGAN STATE UNIVERSITY**

| | |
|---|---|
| Allopathic Medicine | D |
| Biochemistry | M,D |
| Biological and Biomedical Sciences—General | M,D |
| Cell Biology | M,D |
| Clinical Laboratory Sciences/Medical Technology | M |
| Communication Disorders | M,D |
| Ecology | D |
| Entomology | M,D |
| Epidemiology | M,D |
| Evolutionary Biology | D |
| Genetics | M,D |
| Microbiology | M,D |
| Molecular Biology | M,D |
| Molecular Genetics | M,D |
| Neuroscience | M,D |
| Nursing—General | M,D |
| Nutrition | M,D |
| Osteopathic Medicine | D |
| Pathobiology | M,D |
| Pathology | M,D |
| Pharmacology | M,D |
| Physiology | M,D |
| Plant Biology | M,D |
| Plant Pathology | M,D |
| Public Health—General | M |
| Structural Biology | D |
| Systems Biology | D |
| Toxicology | M,D |
| Veterinary Medicine | D |
| Veterinary Sciences | M,D |
| Zoology | M,D |

**MICHIGAN TECHNOLOGICAL UNIVERSITY**

| | |
|---|---|
| Biochemistry | M,D,O |
| Biological and Biomedical Sciences—General | M,D |
| Molecular Biology | M,D,O |

**MIDAMERICA NAZARENE UNIVERSITY**

| | |
|---|---|
| Nursing and Healthcare Administration | M |
| Nursing Education | M |
| Nursing—General | M |
| Public Health—General | M |

**MIDDLE GEORGIA STATE UNIVERSITY**

| | |
|---|---|
| Gerontological Nursing | M |

**MIDDLE TENNESSEE STATE UNIVERSITY**

| | |
|---|---|
| Biological and Biomedical Sciences—General | M |
| Family Nurse Practitioner Studies | M,O |
| Molecular Biology | D |
| Nursing and Healthcare Administration | M |
| Nursing Education | M |
| Nursing—General | M,O |

**MIDWEST COLLEGE OF ORIENTAL MEDICINE**

| | |
|---|---|
| Acupuncture and Oriental Medicine | M,O |

**MIDWESTERN STATE UNIVERSITY**

| | |
|---|---|
| Biological and Biomedical Sciences—General | M |
| Community Health | M,O |
| Family Nurse Practitioner Studies | M |
| Health Physics/Radiological Health | M |
| Health Services Management and Hospital Administration | M,O |
| Nursing Education | M |
| Nursing—General | M |
| Psychiatric Nursing | M |

**MIDWESTERN UNIVERSITY, DOWNERS GROVE CAMPUS**

| | |
|---|---|
| Biological and Biomedical Sciences—General | M |
| Communication Disorders | M |
| Dentistry | D |
| Occupational Therapy | M |
| Optometry | D |
| Osteopathic Medicine | D |
| Pharmacy | D |
| Physical Therapy | D |
| Physician Assistant Studies | M |

**MIDWESTERN UNIVERSITY, GLENDALE CAMPUS**

| | |
|---|---|
| Allied Health—General | M,D |
| Biological and Biomedical Sciences—General | M |
| Cardiovascular Sciences | M |
| Communication Disorders | M |
| Dentistry | D |
| Nurse Anesthesia | M |
| Occupational Therapy | M |
| Optometry | D |
| Osteopathic Medicine | D |
| Pharmacy | D |
| Physical Therapy | D |
| Physician Assistant Studies | M |
| Podiatric Medicine | D |
| Veterinary Medicine | D |

**MIDWIVES COLLEGE OF UTAH**

| | |
|---|---|
| Nurse Midwifery | M |

**MILLERSVILLE UNIVERSITY OF PENNSYLVANIA**

| | |
|---|---|
| Family Nurse Practitioner Studies | M,D,O |
| Nursing Education | M,D,O |
| Nursing—General | M,D,O |

**MILLIGAN UNIVERSITY**

| | |
|---|---|
| Health Services Management and Hospital Administration | M,O |
| Occupational Therapy | M |
| Physician Assistant Studies | M |

**MILLIKIN UNIVERSITY**

| | |
|---|---|
| Nursing—General | M,D |

**MILLS COLLEGE**

| | |
|---|---|
| Biological and Biomedical Sciences—General | O |

**MILWAUKEE SCHOOL OF ENGINEERING**

| | |
|---|---|
| Cardiovascular Sciences | M |
| Clinical Laboratory Sciences/Medical Technology | M |
| Health Services Management and Hospital Administration | M |
| Nursing and Healthcare Administration | M |
| Perfusion | M |

**MINNESOTA STATE UNIVERSITY MANKATO**

| | |
|---|---|
| Allied Health—General | M,D,O |
| Biological and Biomedical Sciences—General | M |
| Communication Disorders | M |
| Community Health | M,O |
| Family Nurse Practitioner Studies | M,D |
| Nursing Education | M,D |
| Nursing—General | M,D |

**MINNESOTA STATE UNIVERSITY MOORHEAD**

| | |
|---|---|
| Health Services Management and Hospital Administration | M,O |
| Nursing—General | M,O |

**MINOT STATE UNIVERSITY**

| | |
|---|---|
| Communication Disorders | M |

**MISERICORDIA UNIVERSITY**

| | |
|---|---|
| Allied Health—General | M,D |
| Communication Disorders | M |
| Health Services Management and Hospital Administration | M |
| Nursing—General | M,D |
| Occupational Therapy | M,D |
| Physical Therapy | D |

**MISSISSIPPI COLLEGE**

| | |
|---|---|
| Biochemistry | M |
| Biological and Biomedical Sciences—General | M |
| Health Services Management and Hospital Administration | M |

**MISSISSIPPI STATE UNIVERSITY**

| | |
|---|---|
| Biochemistry | M,D |
| Biological and Biomedical Sciences—General | M,D |
| Genetics | M,D |
| Molecular Biology | M,D |
| Nutrition | M,D |
| Veterinary Medicine | D |
| Veterinary Sciences | M,D |

**MISSISSIPPI UNIVERSITY FOR WOMEN**

| | |
|---|---|
| Communication Disorders | M,D,O |
| Nursing—General | M,D,O |
| Public Health—General | M,D,O |

**MISSISSIPPI VALLEY STATE UNIVERSITY**

| | |
|---|---|
| Environmental and Occupational Health | M |

**MISSOURI SOUTHERN STATE UNIVERSITY**

| | |
|---|---|
| Dental Hygiene | M |
| Nursing—General | M |

**MISSOURI STATE UNIVERSITY**

| | |
|---|---|
| Biological and Biomedical Sciences—General | M |
| Cell Biology | M |
| Communication Disorders | M,D |
| Family Nurse Practitioner Studies | M,D |
| Molecular Biology | M |
| Nurse Anesthesia | D |
| Nursing Education | M,D |
| Nursing—General | M,D |
| Nutrition | M,D,O |
| Occupational Therapy | M |
| Physical Therapy | D |
| Physician Assistant Studies | M |
| Public Health—General | M |

**MISSOURI UNIVERSITY OF SCIENCE AND TECHNOLOGY**

| | |
|---|---|
| Biological and Biomedical Sciences—General | M |
| Environmental Biology | M |

**MISSOURI WESTERN STATE UNIVERSITY**

| | |
|---|---|
| Biological and Biomedical Sciences—General | M |
| Nursing and Healthcare Administration | M,O |
| Nursing Education | M,O |
| Nursing—General | M,O |

**MOLLOY COLLEGE**

| | |
|---|---|
| Communication Disorders | M |
| Family Nurse Practitioner Studies | M,D,O |
| Gerontological Nursing | M,D,O |
| Health Services Management and Hospital Administration | M,D,O |
| Nursing Education | M,D,O |
| Nursing—General | M,D,O |
| Pediatric Nursing | M,D,O |
| Psychiatric Nursing | M,D,O |

**MONMOUTH UNIVERSITY**

| | |
|---|---|
| Adult Nursing | M,D,O |
| Communication Disorders | M,D,O |
| Forensic Nursing | M,D,O |
| Gerontological Nursing | M,D,O |
| Nursing—General | M,D,O |

**MONROE COLLEGE**

| | |
|---|---|
| Community Health | M |
| Epidemiology | M |
| Health Services Management and Hospital Administration | M |
| Public Health—General | M |

**MONTANA STATE UNIVERSITY**

| | |
|---|---|
| Biochemistry | M,D |
| Biological and Biomedical Sciences—General | M,D |
| Ecology | M,D |
| Family Nurse Practitioner Studies | M,D,O |
| Immunology | M,D |
| Infectious Diseases | M,D |
| Microbiology | M,D |
| Neuroscience | M,D |
| Nursing and Healthcare Administration | M,D,O |
| Nursing Education | M,D,O |
| Nursing—General | M,D,O |
| Plant Pathology | M,D |
| Psychiatric Nursing | M,D,O |

**MONTANA STATE UNIVERSITY BILLINGS**

| | |
|---|---|
| Health Services Management and Hospital Administration | M |

**MONTANA TECHNOLOGICAL UNIVERSITY**

| | |
|---|---|
| Industrial Hygiene | M |

**MONTCLAIR STATE UNIVERSITY**

| | |
|---|---|
| Biochemistry | M |
| Biological and Biomedical Sciences—General | M |
| Communication Disorders | M,D |
| Ecology | M |
| Evolutionary Biology | M |
| Marine Biology | M |
| Molecular Biology | M,O |
| Nutrition | M,O |
| Pharmacology | M |
| Physiology | M |
| Public Health—General | M |

**MORAVIAN COLLEGE**

| | |
|---|---|
| Acute Care/Critical Care Nursing | M |
| Communication Disorders | M,D |
| Health Services Management and Hospital Administration | M |
| Nursing and Healthcare Administration | M |
| Nursing Education | M |
| Nursing—General | M |

**MOREHEAD STATE UNIVERSITY**

| | |
|---|---|
| Biological and Biomedical Sciences—General | M |
| Health Promotion | M |

**MOREHOUSE SCHOOL OF MEDICINE**

| | |
|---|---|
| Allopathic Medicine | D |
| Biological and Biomedical Sciences—General | M,D |
| Clinical Research | M |
| Public Health—General | M |

**MORGAN STATE UNIVERSITY**

| | |
|---|---|
| Biological and Biomedical Sciences—General | M,D |
| Environmental Biology | D |
| Nursing—General | M,D |
| Public Health—General | M,D |

**MORNINGSIDE COLLEGE**

| | |
|---|---|
| Family Nurse Practitioner Studies | M |
| Gerontological Nursing | M |
| Nursing—General | M |

**MOUNT ALLISON UNIVERSITY**

| | |
|---|---|
| Biochemistry | M |
| Biological and Biomedical Sciences—General | M |

**MOUNT ALOYSIUS COLLEGE**

| | |
|---|---|
| Health Services Management and Hospital Administration | M |

**MOUNT CARMEL COLLEGE OF NURSING**

| | |
|---|---|
| Acute Care/Critical Care Nursing | M,D |
| Adult Nursing | M,D |
| Family Nurse Practitioner Studies | M,D |
| Gerontological Nursing | M,D |
| Nursing and Healthcare Administration | M,D |
| Nursing Education | M,D |
| Nursing—General | M,D |

**MOUNT MARTY UNIVERSITY**

| | |
|---|---|
| Nurse Anesthesia | M |
| Nursing—General | M |

**MOUNT MARY UNIVERSITY**

| | |
|---|---|
| Nursing and Healthcare Administration | M |
| Nutrition | M |
| Occupational Therapy | M,D |

*M—masters degree; D—doctorate; O—other advanced degree; *—Close-Up and/or Display*

**MOUNT MERCY UNIVERSITY**
Nursing and Healthcare Administration M
Nursing Education M
Nursing—General M

**MOUNT ST. JOSEPH UNIVERSITY**
Health Promotion M,O
Health Services Management and Hospital Administration D
Nursing and Healthcare Administration M
Nursing Education M
Nursing—General M,D
Physical Therapy D

**MOUNT SAINT MARY COLLEGE**
Adult Nursing M,O
Nursing and Healthcare Administration M,O
Nursing Education M,O
Nursing—General M,O

**MOUNT SAINT MARY'S UNIVERSITY (CA)**
Health Services Management and Hospital Administration M,D,O
Nursing—General M,D,O
Physical Therapy M,D,O

**MOUNT ST. MARY'S UNIVERSITY (MD)**
Health Services Management and Hospital Administration M

**MOUNT SAINT VINCENT UNIVERSITY**
Nutrition M

**MURRAY STATE UNIVERSITY**
Biological and Biomedical Sciences—General M
Communication Disorders M,O
Environmental and Occupational Health M
Family Nurse Practitioner Studies D
Nurse Anesthesia D
Nursing—General D
Nutrition M,O

**NAROPA UNIVERSITY**
Ecology M

**NATIONAL AMERICAN UNIVERSITY (TX)**
Health Services Management and Hospital Administration M,D
Nursing and Healthcare Administration M,D
Nursing Education M,D
Nursing Informatics M,D

**NATIONAL COLLEGE OF MIDWIFERY**
Nurse Midwifery M,D

**NATIONAL UNIVERSITY**
Biological and Biomedical Sciences—General M,O
Family Nurse Practitioner Studies M,O
Health Promotion M,O
Health Services Management and Hospital Administration M,O
Nurse Anesthesia M,O
Nursing and Healthcare Administration M,O
Nursing Informatics M,O
Psychiatric Nursing M,O
Public Health—General M,O

**NATIONAL UNIVERSITY OF HEALTH SCIENCES**
Acupuncture and Oriental Medicine M,D
Chiropractic M,D
Medical Imaging M,D
Naturopathic Medicine M,D

**NATIONAL UNIVERSITY OF NATURAL MEDICINE**
Acupuncture and Oriental Medicine M,D
Clinical Research M
International Health M
Naturopathic Medicine M,D
Nutrition M

**NAZARETH COLLEGE OF ROCHESTER**
Communication Disorders M
Physical Therapy D

**NEBRASKA METHODIST COLLEGE**
Health Promotion M
Health Services Management and Hospital Administration M
Nursing and Healthcare Administration M
Nursing Education M
Nursing—General M
Occupational Therapy M

**NEBRASKA WESLEYAN UNIVERSITY**
Nursing—General M

**NEUMANN UNIVERSITY**
Adult Nursing M,O
Gerontological Nursing M,O
Nursing—General M,O
Physical Therapy D

**NEW CHARTER UNIVERSITY**
Health Services Management and Hospital Administration M

**NEW ENGLAND COLLEGE**
Health Services Management and Hospital Administration M

**NEW ENGLAND COLLEGE OF OPTOMETRY**
Optometry M,D
Vision Sciences M,D

**NEW ENGLAND INSTITUTE OF TECHNOLOGY**
Occupational Therapy M,D
Public Health—General M

**NEW JERSEY CITY UNIVERSITY**
Allied Health—General M
Community Health M
Health Services Management and Hospital Administration M

**NEW JERSEY INSTITUTE OF TECHNOLOGY**
Biological and Biomedical Sciences—General M,D,O
Health Services Management and Hospital Administration M,D
Medicinal and Pharmaceutical Chemistry M,D,O
Pharmaceutical Administration M,D
Pharmacology M,D

**NEWMAN UNIVERSITY**
Nurse Anesthesia M

**NEW MEXICO INSTITUTE OF MINING AND TECHNOLOGY**
Biological and Biomedical Sciences—General M,D

**NEW MEXICO STATE UNIVERSITY**
Biological and Biomedical Sciences—General M,D
Communication Disorders M,D,O
Entomology M
Family Nurse Practitioner Studies M,D,O
Molecular Biology M,D
Nursing and Healthcare Administration M,D,O
Nursing—General M,D,O
Plant Pathology M
Psychiatric Nursing M,D,O
Public Health—General M,O

**NEW YORK ACADEMY OF ART**
Anatomy M

**NEW YORK CHIROPRACTIC COLLEGE**
Acupuncture and Oriental Medicine M
Anatomy M
Chiropractic D
Nutrition M

**NEW YORK COLLEGE OF HEALTH PROFESSIONS**
Acupuncture and Oriental Medicine M

**NEW YORK COLLEGE OF PODIATRIC MEDICINE**
Podiatric Medicine D

**NEW YORK COLLEGE OF TRADITIONAL CHINESE MEDICINE**
Acupuncture and Oriental Medicine M

**NEW YORK INSTITUTE OF TECHNOLOGY**
International Health O
Nutrition M
Occupational Therapy M
Osteopathic Medicine O
Physical Therapy D
Physician Assistant Studies M

**NEW YORK MEDICAL COLLEGE**
Allopathic Medicine D
Biochemistry M,D
Biological and Biomedical Sciences—General M,D
Cell Biology M,D
Communication Disorders M,D,O
Environmental and Occupational Health M,D,O
Epidemiology M,D,O
Health Services Management and Hospital Administration M,D,O
Immunology M,D
Industrial Hygiene M,D,O
International Health M,D,O
Microbiology M,D
Molecular Biology M,D
Pathology M,D
Pharmacology M,D
Physical Therapy M,D,O
Physiology M,D
Public Health—General M,D,O

**NEW YORK UNIVERSITY**
Acute Care/Critical Care Nursing M,D,O
Adult Nursing M,D,O
Allopathic Medicine M,D
Biological and Biomedical Sciences—General M,D
Cancer Biology/Oncology M,D
Clinical Research M
Communication Disorders M,D
Community Health M,D
Computational Biology D
Dentistry D
Developmental Biology M,D
Family Nurse Practitioner Studies M,D,O
Genetics M,D
Gerontological Nursing M,D,O
Health Promotion M,D,O
Health Services Management and Hospital Administration M,D,O
Immunology M,D
International Health M,D
Microbiology M,D
Molecular Biology M,D
Molecular Genetics M,D
Neurobiology M,D
Neuroscience D
Nurse Midwifery M,D,O
Nursing and Healthcare Administration M,O
Nursing Education M,O
Nursing Informatics M,O
Nursing—General M,D,O
Nutrition M,D
Occupational Therapy M,D
Oral and Dental Sciences M,D,O
Pediatric Nursing M,D,O
Physical Therapy M,D,O
Plant Biology M,D
Psychiatric Nursing M,D,O
Public Health—General M,D
Rehabilitation Sciences M,D

**NIAGARA UNIVERSITY**
Health Services Management and Hospital Administration M

**NICHOLLS STATE UNIVERSITY**
Environmental Biology M
Family Nurse Practitioner Studies M
Marine Biology M
Nursing and Healthcare Administration M
Nursing Education M
Nursing—General M
Psychiatric Nursing M

**NORTH CAROLINA AGRICULTURAL AND TECHNICAL STATE UNIVERSITY**
Biological and Biomedical Sciences—General M
Nutrition M

**NORTH CAROLINA CENTRAL UNIVERSITY**
Biological and Biomedical Sciences—General M
Communication Disorders M

**NORTH CAROLINA STATE UNIVERSITY**
Biochemistry D
Biological and Biomedical Sciences—General M,D,O
Cell Biology M,D
Entomology M,D
Epidemiology M,D
Genomic Sciences M,D
Infectious Diseases M,D
Microbiology M,D
Nutrition M,D
Pathology M,D
Pharmacology M,D
Plant Biology M,D
Veterinary Sciences M,D

**NORTH DAKOTA STATE UNIVERSITY**
Biochemistry M,D
Biological and Biomedical Sciences—General M,D
Botany M,D
Cell Biology D
Community Health M
Conservation Biology M,D
Entomology M,D
Genomic Sciences M,D
Infectious Diseases M
Microbiology M,D
Molecular Biology D
Molecular Pathogenesis M,D
Nursing—General D
Nutrition M,D
Pathology M,D
Pharmacy M,D
Plant Pathology M,D
Public Health—General M
Zoology M,D

**NORTHEASTERN ILLINOIS UNIVERSITY**
Biological and Biomedical Sciences—General M
Cell Biology M
Ecology M
Molecular Biology M

**NORTHEASTERN STATE UNIVERSITY**
Communication Disorders M
Nursing and Healthcare Administration M
Nursing Education M
Occupational Therapy M
Optometry D

**NORTHEASTERN UNIVERSITY**
Acute Care/Critical Care Nursing M,D,O
Allied Health—General M,D,O
Biological and Biomedical Sciences—General M,D
Communication Disorders M,D,O
Family Nurse Practitioner Studies M,D,O
Gerontological Nursing M,D,O
Marine Biology M,D
Maternal and Child/Neonatal Nursing M,D,O
Nurse Anesthesia M,D,O
Nursing and Healthcare Administration M,D,O
Nursing—General M,D,O
Nutrition M
Pediatric Nursing M,D,O
Pharmaceutical Sciences M,D,O
Pharmacology M,D,O
Pharmacy M,D,O
Psychiatric Nursing M,D,O
Public Health—General M,D,O

**NORTHEAST OHIO MEDICAL UNIVERSITY**
Allopathic Medicine D
Bioethics M,D,O
Health Services Management and Hospital Administration M,D,O
Pharmaceutical Administration M,D,O
Pharmaceutical Sciences M,D,O
Pharmacy D
Public Health—General M,D,O

**NORTHERN ARIZONA UNIVERSITY**
Allied Health—General M,D,O
Biological and Biomedical Sciences—General M,D
Communication Disorders M
Family Nurse Practitioner Studies M,D,O
Health Services Management and Hospital Administration D
Nursing—General M,D,O
Occupational Therapy D
Physical Therapy D
Physician Assistant Studies M

**NORTHERN ILLINOIS UNIVERSITY**
Biochemistry M,D
Biological and Biomedical Sciences—General M,D
Communication Disorders M,D
Nursing—General M,D
Nutrition M
Physical Therapy M,D
Public Health—General M

**NORTHERN KENTUCKY UNIVERSITY**
Allied Health—General M
Nursing—General M,D,O

**NORTHERN MICHIGAN UNIVERSITY**
Biological and Biomedical Sciences—General M
Clinical Laboratory Sciences/Medical Technology M
Molecular Genetics M
Nursing—General D

**NORTH PARK UNIVERSITY**
Adult Nursing M
Nursing and Healthcare Administration M
Nursing—General M

**NORTHWESTERN HEALTH SCIENCES UNIVERSITY**
Acupuncture and Oriental Medicine M
Chiropractic D
Nutrition M

**NORTHWESTERN STATE UNIVERSITY OF LOUISIANA**
Health Physics/Radiological Health M
Nursing—General M

**NORTHWESTERN UNIVERSITY**
Allopathic Medicine
Biochemistry D
Biological and Biomedical Sciences—General D
Biophysics D
Biopsychology D
Cell Biology D
Clinical Laboratory Sciences/Medical Technology M
Clinical Research M,O
Communication Disorders M,D
Developmental Biology D
Epidemiology D
Health Services Management and Hospital Administration M,D
Health Services Research D
International Health M
Molecular Biology D
Neurobiology M,D
Neuroscience D
Physical Therapy D
Physiology M
Plant Biology M,D
Public Health—General M
Rehabilitation Sciences D
Structural Biology D
Systems Biology D

**NORTHWEST MISSOURI STATE UNIVERSITY**
Biological and Biomedical Sciences—General M,O

**NORTHWEST NAZARENE UNIVERSITY**
Nursing and Healthcare Administration M

**NORWICH UNIVERSITY**
Nursing and Healthcare Administration M
Nursing Education M
Nursing—General M

**NOTRE DAME OF MARYLAND UNIVERSITY**
Pharmacy D

**NOVA SOUTHEASTERN UNIVERSITY**
Adult Nursing M,D
Allied Health—General M,D
Allopathic Medicine D
Anesthesiologist Assistant Studies M,D
Biological and Biomedical Sciences—General M,D
Communication Disorders M,D
Dentistry M,D
Family Nurse Practitioner Studies M,D
Gerontological Nursing M,D
Marine Biology M,D
Nursing Education M,D
Nursing Informatics M,D
Nursing—General M,D
Nutrition M,D,O
Occupational Therapy M,D
Optometry M,D
Osteopathic Medicine M,D,O
Pharmacy M,D
Physical Therapy M,D
Physician Assistant Studies M,D
Psychiatric Nursing M,D
Public Health—General M,D,O

**OAKLAND UNIVERSITY**
Allied Health—General M,D,O
Biological and Biomedical Sciences—General M,D,O
Environmental and Occupational Health M
Family Nurse Practitioner Studies M,O
Gerontological Nursing M,O
Medical Physics M,D
Nurse Anesthesia M,O
Nursing—General M,D,O
Public Health—General M

## OCCIDENTAL COLLEGE
Biological and Biomedical
  Sciences—General — M

## OHIO CHRISTIAN UNIVERSITY
Health Services Management and
  Hospital Administration — M

## OHIO DOMINICAN UNIVERSITY
Health Services Management and
  Hospital Administration — M
Physician Assistant Studies — M

## OHIO NORTHERN UNIVERSITY
Pharmacy — D

## THE OHIO STATE UNIVERSITY
Allied Health—General — M
Allopathic Medicine — D
Anatomy — M,D
Biochemistry — M,D
Biological and Biomedical
  Sciences—General — M,D
Biophysics — M,D
Cell Biology — M,D
Communication Disorders — M,D
Dental Hygiene — M,D
Dentistry — M,D
Developmental Biology — M,D
Ecology — M,D
Entomology — M,D
Evolutionary Biology — M,D
Genetics — M,D
Health Services Management and
  Hospital Administration — M,D
Microbiology — M,D
Molecular Biology — M,D
Molecular Genetics — M,D
Neuroscience — D
Nursing—General — M,D
Nutrition — M,D
Occupational Therapy — M
Optometry — M,D
Oral and Dental Sciences — M,D
Pharmaceutical Administration — M,D
Pharmacology — M,D
Pharmacy — M,D
Physical Therapy — D
Plant Pathology — M,D
Public Health—General — M,D
Rehabilitation Sciences — D
Veterinary Sciences — M,D

## OHIO UNIVERSITY
Biochemistry — M,D
Biological and Biomedical
  Sciences—General — M,D
Cell Biology — M,D
Communication Disorders — M,D
Ecology — M,D
Environmental Biology — M,D
Evolutionary Biology — M,D
Family Nurse Practitioner Studies — M,D
Health Services Management and
  Hospital Administration — M
Microbiology — M,D
Molecular Biology — D
Neuroscience — M,D
Nursing and Healthcare
  Administration — M,D
Nursing Education — M,D
Nursing—General — M,D
Nutrition — M
Osteopathic Medicine — D
Physical Therapy — D
Physiology — M,D
Plant Biology — M,D
Public Health—General — M

## OKLAHOMA BAPTIST UNIVERSITY
Nursing Education — M
Nursing—General — M

## OKLAHOMA CHRISTIAN UNIVERSITY
Health Services Management and
  Hospital Administration — M

## OKLAHOMA CITY UNIVERSITY
Nursing Education — M,D
Nursing—General — M,D

## OKLAHOMA STATE UNIVERSITY
Biochemistry — M,D
Biological and Biomedical
  Sciences—General — M,D
Botany — M,D
Communication Disorders — M
Ecology — M,D
Entomology — M,D
Evolutionary Biology — M,D
Microbiology — M,D
Molecular Biology — M,D
Molecular Genetics — M,D
Nutrition — M,D
Plant Biology — M,D
Plant Pathology — M,D
Veterinary Medicine — D
Veterinary Sciences — M,D

## OKLAHOMA STATE UNIVERSITY CENTER FOR HEALTH SCIENCES
Biological and Biomedical
  Sciences—General — M,D
Health Services Management and
  Hospital Administration — M
Osteopathic Medicine — D
Toxicology — M

## OKLAHOMA WESLEYAN UNIVERSITY
Nursing and Healthcare
  Administration — M
Nursing Education — M

## OLD DOMINION UNIVERSITY
Adult Nursing — M,D
Allied Health—General — M,D
Biochemistry — M,D
Biological and Biomedical
  Sciences—General — M,D
Communication Disorders — M
Community Health — M
Dental Hygiene — M
Ecology — D
Environmental and Occupational
  Health — M
Family Nurse Practitioner Studies — M
Gerontological Nursing — M,D
Health Promotion — M
Health Services Research — M
Immunology — M
Industrial Hygiene — M
Maternal and Child/Neonatal
  Nursing — M
Microbiology — M
Nurse Anesthesia — D
Nursing and Healthcare
  Administration — M,D
Nursing Education — M,D
Nursing—General — D
Pediatric Nursing — M,D
Physical Therapy — D
Public Health—General — M
Rehabilitation Sciences — D

## OLIVET NAZARENE UNIVERSITY
Family Nurse Practitioner Studies — M
Nursing—General — M

## OREGON COLLEGE OF ORIENTAL MEDICINE
Acupuncture and Oriental Medicine — M,D

## OREGON HEALTH & SCIENCE UNIVERSITY
Allopathic Medicine — D
Biochemistry — M,D
Biological and Biomedical
  Sciences—General — M,D,O
Biopsychology — D
Cancer Biology/Oncology — D
Cell Biology — D
Clinical Research — M,O
Community Health Nursing — M,O
Computational Biology — M,D,O
Dentistry — D,O
Developmental Biology — D
Family Nurse Practitioner Studies — M
Genetics — D
Gerontological Nursing — M
Health Services Management and
  Hospital Administration — M,O
Immunology — D
Microbiology — D
Molecular Biology — M,D
Molecular Medicine — M,D
Neuroscience — D
Nurse Anesthesia — M
Nurse Midwifery — M
Nursing and Healthcare
  Administration — M
Nursing Education — M,O
Nursing—General — M,D,O
Nutrition — M,O
Oral and Dental Sciences — M,D,O
Pediatric Nursing — M
Pharmacology — D
Physician Assistant Studies — M
Physiology — D
Psychiatric Nursing — M

## OREGON STATE UNIVERSITY
Allied Health—General — M,D
Biochemistry — M,D
Biological and Biomedical
  Sciences—General — M,D
Biophysics — M,D
Botany — M,D
Cell Biology — M,D
Computational Biology — M,D
Conservation Biology — M,D
Ecology — M,D
Environmental and Occupational
  Health — M,D
Environmental Biology — M,D
Epidemiology — M,D
Genetics — M,D
Genomic Sciences — M,D
Health Physics/Radiological Health — M,D
Health Promotion — M,D
Health Services Management and
  Hospital Administration — M,D
Immunology — M,D
International Health — M,D
Medical Imaging — M,D
Medical Physics — M,D
Microbiology — M,D
Molecular Biology — M,D
Molecular Toxicology — M,D
Nutrition — M,D
Parasitology — M,D
Pharmaceutical Sciences — M,D
Pharmacy — D
Physiology — M,D
Plant Molecular Biology — D
Plant Pathology — M,D
Plant Physiology — M,D
Public Health—General — M,D
Systems Biology — M,D
Toxicology — M,D
Veterinary Medicine — D
Virology — M,D

## OTTERBEIN UNIVERSITY
Family Nurse Practitioner Studies — M,D,O
Nurse Anesthesia — M,D,O

Nursing and Healthcare
  Administration — M,D,O
Nursing Education — M,D,O
Nursing—General — M,D,O

## OUR LADY OF THE LAKE UNIVERSITY
Communication Disorders — M
Health Services Management and
  Hospital Administration — M

## PACE UNIVERSITY
Biochemistry — M
Biological and Biomedical
  Sciences—General — M,O
Communication Disorders — M
Family Nurse Practitioner Studies — M,D,O
Health Services Management and
  Hospital Administration — M
Molecular Biology — M
Nursing and Healthcare
  Administration — M,D,O
Nursing—General — M,D,O
Physician Assistant Studies — M

## PACIFIC COLLEGE OF ORIENTAL MEDICINE
Acupuncture and Oriental Medicine — M,D

## PACIFIC COLLEGE OF ORIENTAL MEDICINE–CHICAGO
Acupuncture and Oriental Medicine — M

## PACIFIC COLLEGE OF ORIENTAL MEDICINE-NEW YORK
Acupuncture and Oriental Medicine — M

## PACIFIC LUTHERAN UNIVERSITY
Family Nurse Practitioner Studies — D
Nursing—General — M,D

## PACIFIC NORTHWEST UNIVERSITY OF HEALTH SCIENCES
Osteopathic Medicine — D

## PACIFIC UNIVERSITY
Communication Disorders — M,D
Health Services Management and
  Hospital Administration — M
Occupational Therapy — D
Optometry — M,D
Pharmacy — D
Physical Therapy — M,D
Physician Assistant Studies — M
Vision Sciences — M,D

## PALM BEACH ATLANTIC UNIVERSITY
Family Nurse Practitioner Studies — M,D
Nursing and Healthcare
  Administration — M,D
Nursing—General — M,D
Pharmacy — D

## PALMER COLLEGE OF CHIROPRACTIC
Anatomy — M
Chiropractic — M
Clinical Research — M

## PALO ALTO UNIVERSITY
Biopsychology — D

## PARKER UNIVERSITY
Chiropractic — D

## PARK UNIVERSITY
Health Services Management and
  Hospital Administration — M,O
International Health — M,O

## PENN STATE GREAT VALLEY
Health Services Management and
  Hospital Administration — M,O

## PENN STATE HARRISBURG
Health Services Management and
  Hospital Administration — M,D,O

## PENN STATE HERSHEY MEDICAL CENTER
Allopathic Medicine — M,D
Anatomy — M,D
Biochemistry — M,D
Biological and Biomedical
  Sciences—General — M,D
Cell Biology — D
Developmental Biology — D
Genomic Sciences — M,D
Health Services Research — M
Immunology — M,D
Molecular Genetics — M,D
Molecular Medicine — D
Molecular Toxicology — D
Neurobiology — D
Neuroscience — M,D
Public Health—General — M,D
Veterinary Sciences — M
Virology — M,D

## PENN STATE UNIVERSITY PARK
Biochemistry — M,D
Biological and Biomedical
  Sciences—General — M,D
Biopsychology — M,D
Cell Biology — M,D
Communication Disorders — M,D,O
Ecology — M,D
Entomology — M,D
Health Services Management and
  Hospital Administration — M,D
Molecular Biology — M,D
Nursing—General — M,D
Nutrition — M,D
Pathobiology — M,D
Physiology — M,D
Plant Biology — M,D
Plant Pathology — M,D

## PENNSYLVANIA COLLEGE OF HEALTH SCIENCES
Health Services Management and
  Hospital Administration — M
Nursing and Healthcare
  Administration — M
Nursing Education — M

## PENSACOLA CHRISTIAN COLLEGE
Nursing—General — M,D,O

## PFEIFFER UNIVERSITY
Health Services Management and
  Hospital Administration — M

## PHILADELPHIA COLLEGE OF OSTEOPATHIC MEDICINE
Biological and Biomedical
  Sciences—General — M
Biopsychology — M,D,O
Health Services Management and
  Hospital Administration — M,D,O
Osteopathic Medicine — D
Physician Assistant Studies — M
Public Health—General — M,D,O

## PHOENIX INSTITUTE OF HERBAL MEDICINE & ACUPUNCTURE
Acupuncture and Oriental Medicine — M

## PITTSBURG STATE UNIVERSITY
Biological and Biomedical
  Sciences—General — M,D
Nursing Education — M,D
Nursing—General — M,D

## PLYMOUTH STATE UNIVERSITY
Health Promotion — M,O

## POINT LOMA NAZARENE UNIVERSITY
Acute Care/Critical Care Nursing — M
Biological and Biomedical
  Sciences—General — M
Family Nurse Practitioner Studies — M
Gerontological Nursing — M
Health Services Management and
  Hospital Administration — M
Nursing—General — M,D,O
Pediatric Nursing — M

## POINT PARK UNIVERSITY
Health Services Management and
  Hospital Administration — M

## PONCE HEALTH SCIENCES UNIVERSITY
Biological and Biomedical
  Sciences—General — D
Epidemiology — M,D
Public Health—General — M,D

## PONTIFICAL CATHOLIC UNIVERSITY OF PUERTO RICO
Biological and Biomedical
  Sciences—General — M
Clinical Laboratory
  Sciences/Medical Technology — O
Medical/Surgical Nursing — M
Nursing—General — M
Psychiatric Nursing — M

## PONTIFICIA UNIVERSIDAD CATOLICA MADRE Y MAESTRA
Allopathic Medicine — D

## PORTLAND STATE UNIVERSITY
Biological and Biomedical
  Sciences—General — M,D
Communication Disorders — M
Health Promotion — M,D
Health Services Management and
  Hospital Administration — M,D,O
Public Health—General — M,D

## POST UNIVERSITY
Health Services Management and
  Hospital Administration — M

## PRAIRIE VIEW A&M UNIVERSITY
Nursing—General — M,D

## PRESBYTERIAN COLLEGE
Pharmacy — D

## PRINCETON UNIVERSITY
Computational Biology — D
Ecology — D
Evolutionary Biology — D
Marine Biology — D
Molecular Biology — D
Neuroscience — D

## PURDUE UNIVERSITY
Allied Health—General — M,D
Anatomy — M,D
Biochemistry — M,D
Biological and Biomedical
  Sciences—General — M,D
Biophysics — D
Botany — M,D
Cancer Biology/Oncology — D
Cell Biology — M,D
Communication Disorders — M,D
Developmental Biology — M,D
Ecology — M,D
Entomology — M,D
Environmental and Occupational
  Health — M,D
Epidemiology — M,D
Evolutionary Biology — D
Family Nurse Practitioner Studies — M,D,O
Genetics — M,D
Genomic Sciences — D
Gerontological Nursing — M,D,O
Health Physics/Radiological Health — M,D
Immunology — M,D
Medical Physics — M,D

- Medicinal and Pharmaceutical Chemistry D
- Microbiology M,D
- Molecular Biology D
- Molecular Pharmacology D
- Neurobiology M,D
- Neuroscience D
- Nursing—General M,D,O
- Nutrition M,D
- Pathobiology M,D
- Pathology M,D
- Pediatric Nursing M,D,O
- Pharmaceutical Administration M,D,O
- Pharmaceutical Sciences M,D,O
- Pharmacology M,D
- Pharmacy D
- Physiology M,D
- Plant Pathology M,D
- Public Health—General M,D
- Systems Biology D
- Toxicology M,D
- Veterinary Medicine D
- Veterinary Sciences M,D
- Virology M,D

**PURDUE UNIVERSITY FORT WAYNE**
- Adult Nursing M,O
- Biological and Biomedical Sciences—General M
- Family Nurse Practitioner Studies M,O
- Gerontological Nursing M,O
- Nursing and Healthcare Administration M,O
- Nursing Education M,O
- Nursing—General M,O

**PURDUE UNIVERSITY GLOBAL**
- Health Services Management and Hospital Administration M,O
- Nursing and Healthcare Administration M
- Nursing Education M
- Nursing—General M

**PURDUE UNIVERSITY NORTHWEST**
- Acute Care/Critical Care Nursing M
- Adult Nursing M
- Biological and Biomedical Sciences—General M
- Family Nurse Practitioner Studies M
- Nursing and Healthcare Administration M
- Nursing—General M

**QUEENS COLLEGE OF THE CITY UNIVERSITY OF NEW YORK**
- Biological and Biomedical Sciences—General M,O
- Communication Disorders M,O
- Neuroscience M
- Nutrition M,O

**QUEEN'S UNIVERSITY AT KINGSTON**
- Allopathic Medicine D
- Biological and Biomedical Sciences—General M,D
- Epidemiology M,D
- Family Nurse Practitioner Studies M,D,O
- Health Promotion M,D
- Molecular Medicine M,D
- Nursing—General M,D,O
- Occupational Therapy M,D
- Pathology M,D
- Pediatric Nursing M,D,O
- Physical Therapy M,D
- Public Health—General M,D
- Rehabilitation Sciences M,D
- Women's Health Nursing M,D,O

**QUEENS UNIVERSITY OF CHARLOTTE**
- Nursing and Healthcare Administration M
- Nursing Education M
- Nursing—General M

**QUINNIPIAC UNIVERSITY**
- Adult Nursing D
- Allied Health—General M
- Allopathic Medicine D
- Anesthesiologist Assistant Studies M
- Biological and Biomedical Sciences—General M
- Cardiovascular Sciences M
- Cell Biology M
- Community Health D
- Family Nurse Practitioner Studies D
- Health Physics/Radiological Health M
- Health Services Management and Hospital Administration M
- Molecular Biology M
- Nurse Anesthesia D
- Nursing and Healthcare Administration D
- Nursing—General D
- Pathology M
- Perfusion M
- Physician Assistant Studies M

**RADFORD UNIVERSITY**
- Communication Disorders M
- Nursing—General D
- Occupational Therapy M
- Physical Therapy D

**RAMAPO COLLEGE OF NEW JERSEY**
- Family Nurse Practitioner Studies M
- Nursing and Healthcare Administration M
- Nursing Education M
- Nursing—General M

**REGENT UNIVERSITY**
- Health Services Management and Hospital Administration M,D,O

**REGIS COLLEGE (MA)**
- Family Nurse Practitioner Studies M,D,O
- Health Services Management and Hospital Administration M,D,O
- Nursing Education M,D,O
- Nursing—General M,D,O
- Occupational Therapy M,D,O

**REGIS UNIVERSITY**
- Allied Health—General M,D,O
- Biological and Biomedical Sciences—General M
- Environmental Biology M
- Health Services Management and Hospital Administration M,D,O
- Maternal and Child/Neonatal Nursing M,D,O
- Nursing and Healthcare Administration M,D,O
- Nursing Education M,D,O
- Occupational Therapy M,D,O
- Pharmacy M,D,O
- Physical Therapy M,D,O

**RENSSELAER POLYTECHNIC INSTITUTE**
- Biochemistry M,D
- Biological and Biomedical Sciences—General M,D
- Biophysics M,D

**RESURRECTION UNIVERSITY**
- Nursing—General M

**RHODE ISLAND COLLEGE**
- Biological and Biomedical Sciences—General M,O
- Health Services Management and Hospital Administration M
- Nursing—General M,D

**RICE UNIVERSITY**
- Biochemistry M,D
- Cell Biology M,D
- Ecology M,D
- Evolutionary Biology M,D
- Health Services Management and Hospital Administration M

**RIVIER UNIVERSITY**
- Family Nurse Practitioner Studies M,D
- Nursing and Healthcare Administration M,D
- Nursing Education M,D
- Nursing—General M,D
- Psychiatric Nursing M,D
- Public Health—General M,D

**ROBERT MORRIS UNIVERSITY**
- Nursing—General M,D

**ROBERT MORRIS UNIVERSITY ILLINOIS**
- Health Services Management and Hospital Administration M

**ROBERTS WESLEYAN COLLEGE**
- Health Services Management and Hospital Administration M
- Nursing and Healthcare Administration M
- Nursing Education M
- Nursing Informatics M
- Nursing—General M

**ROCHESTER INSTITUTE OF TECHNOLOGY**
- Biological and Biomedical Sciences—General M
- Environmental and Occupational Health M
- Health Services Management and Hospital Administration M,O

**THE ROCKEFELLER UNIVERSITY**
- Biological and Biomedical Sciences—General M,D*

**ROCKHURST UNIVERSITY**
- Communication Disorders M
- Health Services Management and Hospital Administration M,O
- Occupational Therapy M
- Physical Therapy D

**ROCKY MOUNTAIN COLLEGE**
- Occupational Therapy D
- Physician Assistant Studies M

**ROCKY MOUNTAIN UNIVERSITY OF HEALTH PROFESSIONS**
- Communication Disorders D
- Family Nurse Practitioner Studies D
- Occupational Therapy D
- Physical Therapy D
- Physician Assistant Studies M
- Physiology D

**ROCKY VISTA UNIVERSITY**
- Biological and Biomedical Sciences—General M
- Osteopathic Medicine D
- Physician Assistant Studies M

**ROGER WILLIAMS UNIVERSITY**
- Health Services Management and Hospital Administration M

**ROLLINS COLLEGE**
- Public Health—General M

**ROOSEVELT UNIVERSITY**
- Pharmacy D

**ROSALIND FRANKLIN UNIVERSITY OF MEDICINE AND SCIENCE**
- Allied Health—General M,D,O
- Allopathic Medicine D
- Anatomy D
- Biochemistry D
- Biological and Biomedical Sciences—General M,D
- Biophysics M,D
- Cell Biology D
- Health Promotion M
- Health Services Management and Hospital Administration M,O
- Immunology D
- Microbiology D
- Molecular Biology D
- Molecular Pharmacology M,D
- Neuroscience D
- Nurse Anesthesia D
- Nutrition M
- Pathology M
- Pharmacy D
- Physical Therapy M,D
- Physician Assistant Studies M
- Physiology M,D
- Podiatric Medicine D

**ROSEMAN UNIVERSITY OF HEALTH SCIENCES**
- Dentistry M,D,O
- Pharmacy D

**ROWAN UNIVERSITY**
- Allopathic Medicine D
- Biological and Biomedical Sciences—General M
- Health Promotion M
- Nursing—General M
- Osteopathic Medicine D
- Pharmaceutical Sciences M
- School Nursing M,D,O

**RUSH UNIVERSITY**
- Allopathic Medicine D
- Anatomy M,D
- Biochemistry M,D
- Cell Biology M,D
- Clinical Laboratory Sciences/Medical Technology M
- Communication Disorders M,D
- Health Services Management and Hospital Administration M,D
- Immunology M,D
- Medical Physics M,D
- Microbiology M,D
- Neuroscience M,D
- Nutrition M
- Occupational Therapy D
- Perfusion M
- Pharmaceutical Sciences M,D
- Pharmacology M,D
- Physical Therapy M
- Physician Assistant Studies M
- Physiology D
- Virology M,D

**RUTGERS UNIVERSITY - CAMDEN**
- Biological and Biomedical Sciences—General M
- Computational Biology M,D
- Family Nurse Practitioner Studies D
- Gerontological Nursing D
- Health Services Management and Hospital Administration M,O
- Nursing—General D
- Physical Therapy D
- Public Health—General M,O

**RUTGERS UNIVERSITY - NEWARK**
- Adult Nursing M,D,O
- Allied Health—General M,D,O
- Allopathic Medicine D
- Biochemistry M,D
- Biological and Biomedical Sciences—General M,D,O
- Biopsychology D
- Cell Biology D
- Clinical Laboratory Sciences/Medical Technology M
- Computational Biology M
- Dentistry M,D,O
- Epidemiology M,O
- Family Nurse Practitioner Studies M,D,O
- Health Physics/Radiological Health M
- Health Services Management and Hospital Administration M,D,O
- Immunology D
- Medical Imaging M
- Microbiology D
- Molecular Biology M,D
- Molecular Genetics D
- Molecular Medicine D
- Molecular Pathology D
- Neuroscience D
- Nurse Anesthesia M,D,O
- Nursing Informatics M
- Nursing—General M,D,O
- Nutrition M,D,O
- Occupational Health Nursing M,D,O
- Oral and Dental Sciences M,D,O
- Pathology D
- Pharmaceutical Administration M
- Pharmacology D
- Physical Therapy D
- Physician Assistant Studies M
- Physiology D
- Public Health—General M,O
- Transcultural Nursing M,D,O
- Women's Health Nursing M,D,O

**RUTGERS UNIVERSITY - NEW BRUNSWICK**
- Allopathic Medicine D
- Biochemistry M,D
- Biological and Biomedical Sciences—General M,D
- Biopsychology D
- Cancer Biology/Oncology M,D
- Cell Biology M,D
- Clinical Laboratory Sciences/Medical Technology M
- Computational Biology D
- Developmental Biology M,D
- Ecology M,D
- Entomology M,D
- Environmental and Occupational Health M,D,O
- Environmental Biology M,D
- Epidemiology M,D,O
- Evolutionary Biology M,D
- Genetics M,D
- Health Services Management and Hospital Administration M,D,O
- Immunology M,D
- Marine Biology M,D
- Medical Microbiology M,D
- Medicinal and Pharmaceutical Chemistry M,D
- Microbiology M,D
- Molecular Biology M,D
- Molecular Biophysics D
- Molecular Genetics M,D
- Molecular Pharmacology M,D
- Molecular Physiology M,D
- Neuroscience M,D
- Nutrition M,D
- Pharmaceutical Sciences M,D
- Pharmacy M,D
- Physiology M,D
- Plant Biology M,D
- Plant Molecular Biology M,D
- Plant Pathology M,D
- Public Health—General M,D
- Reproductive Biology M,D
- Systems Biology D
- Toxicology M,D
- Translational Biology M
- Virology M,D

**SACRED HEART UNIVERSITY**
- Communication Disorders M
- Family Nurse Practitioner Studies M,D,O
- Molecular Biology M
- Nursing and Healthcare Administration M,D,O
- Nursing Education M,D,O
- Nursing—General M,D,O
- Nutrition M
- Occupational Therapy M
- Physical Therapy D
- Physician Assistant Studies M
- Public Health—General M

**SAGE GRADUATE SCHOOL**
- Family Nurse Practitioner Studies M
- Gerontological Nursing M,O
- Health Services Management and Hospital Administration M
- Nursing Education D
- Nursing—General M,D,O
- Nutrition M,O
- Occupational Therapy M
- Physical Therapy D
- Psychiatric Nursing M,O

**SAGINAW VALLEY STATE UNIVERSITY**
- Family Nurse Practitioner Studies M,D
- Health Services Management and Hospital Administration M
- Nursing—General M
- Occupational Therapy M

**ST. AMBROSE UNIVERSITY**
- Communication Disorders M
- Health Services Management and Hospital Administration M,D
- Occupational Therapy D
- Physical Therapy D
- Physician Assistant Studies M
- Public Health—General M

**SAINT ANTHONY COLLEGE OF NURSING**
- Nursing—General M

**ST. CATHERINE UNIVERSITY**
- Adult Nursing M,D
- Gerontological Nursing M,D
- Health Services Management and Hospital Administration M
- International Health M
- Nursing Education M,D
- Nursing—General M,D
- Occupational Therapy M,D
- Pediatric Nursing M,D
- Physical Therapy D
- Physician Assistant Studies M
- Public Health—General M

**ST. CLOUD STATE UNIVERSITY**
- Biological and Biomedical Sciences—General M
- Communication Disorders M

**SAINT FRANCIS MEDICAL CENTER COLLEGE OF NURSING**
- Family Nurse Practitioner Studies M,D,O
- Gerontological Nursing M,D,O
- Maternal and Child/Neonatal Nursing M,D,O
- Medical/Surgical Nursing M,D,O
- Nursing and Healthcare Administration M,D,O
- Nursing Education M,D,O
- Nursing—General M,D,O
- Psychiatric Nursing M,D,O

**SAINT FRANCIS UNIVERSITY**
- Biological and Biomedical Sciences—General M
- Cancer Biology/Oncology M
- Nursing and Healthcare Administration M
- Nursing Education M
- Nursing—General M
- Occupational Therapy M
- Physical Therapy D
- Physician Assistant Studies M

**ST. FRANCIS XAVIER UNIVERSITY**
- Biological and Biomedical Sciences—General M

**ST. JOHN FISHER COLLEGE**
Biological and Biomedical
    Sciences—General    M
Nursing—General    M,D,O
Pharmacy    D

**ST. JOHN'S UNIVERSITY (NY)**
Biological and Biomedical
    Sciences—General    M,D
Communication Disorders    M,D
Pharmaceutical Administration    M
Pharmaceutical Sciences    M,D
Pharmacy    M,D
Public Health—General    M
Toxicology    M

**ST. JOSEPH'S COLLEGE, LONG ISLAND CAMPUS**
Adult Nursing    M
Gerontological Nursing    M
Health Services Management and
    Hospital Administration    M
Nursing Education    M
Nursing—General    M

**ST. JOSEPH'S COLLEGE, NEW YORK**
Adult Nursing    M
Gerontological Nursing    M
Health Services Management and
    Hospital Administration    M
Nursing Education    M
Nursing—General    M

**SAINT JOSEPH'S COLLEGE OF MAINE**
Family Nurse Practitioner Studies    M,O
Health Services Management and
    Hospital Administration    M
Nursing and Healthcare
    Administration    M,O
Nursing Education    M,O
Nursing—General    M,O

**SAINT JOSEPH'S UNIVERSITY**
Biological and Biomedical
    Sciences—General    M
Communication Disorders    M,D,O
Health Services Management and
    Hospital Administration    M,O

**SAINT LEO UNIVERSITY**
Health Services Management and
    Hospital Administration    M,D

**ST. LOUIS COLLEGE OF PHARMACY**
Pharmacy    D

**SAINT LOUIS UNIVERSITY**
Allied Health—General    M,D,O
Allopathic Medicine    D
Anatomy    M,D
Biochemistry    D
Bioethics    D,O
Biological and Biomedical
    Sciences—General    M,D
Communication Disorders    M
Community Health    M
Computational Biology    M
Dentistry    M
Health Services Management and
    Hospital Administration    M,D
Immunology    D
Microbiology    D
Molecular Biology    D
Nursing—General    M,D,O
Nutrition    M
Occupational Therapy    M
Oral and Dental Sciences    M
Pathology    D
Pharmacology    D
Physical Therapy    M,D
Physician Assistant Studies    M
Physiology    D
Public Health—General    M,D

**SAINT MARY-OF-THE-WOODS COLLEGE**
Health Services Management and
    Hospital Administration    M
Nursing—General    M

**SAINT MARY'S COLLEGE**
Adult Nursing    D
Communication Disorders    M
Family Nurse Practitioner Studies    D
Gerontological Nursing    D
Nursing—General    D

**SAINT MARY'S UNIVERSITY OF MINNESOTA**
Health Services Management and
    Hospital Administration    M
Nurse Anesthesia    M

**ST. NORBERT COLLEGE**
Health Services Management and
    Hospital Administration    M

**SAINT PETER'S UNIVERSITY**
Adult Nursing    M,D,O
Health Services Management and
    Hospital Administration    M
Nursing and Healthcare
    Administration    M,D,O
Nursing—General    M,D,O

**ST. THOMAS UNIVERSITY - FLORIDA**
Health Services Management and
    Hospital Administration    M,O

**SAINT VINCENT COLLEGE**
Nurse Anesthesia    M,D

**SAINT XAVIER UNIVERSITY**
Communication Disorders    M
Health Services Management and
    Hospital Administration    M,O

---

Nursing—General    M,O

**SALEM STATE UNIVERSITY**
Gerontological Nursing    M
Nursing and Healthcare
    Administration    M
Nursing Education    M
Nursing—General    M
Occupational Therapy    M

**SALISBURY UNIVERSITY**
Biological and Biomedical
    Sciences—General    M
Family Nurse Practitioner Studies    D
Nursing and Healthcare
    Administration    M,D
Nursing Education    M
Nursing—General    M,D
Physiology    M

**SALUS UNIVERSITY**
Communication Disorders    M,D,O
Occupational Therapy    M,O
Optometry    D
Physician Assistant Studies    M
Public Health—General    M
Rehabilitation Sciences    M,O
Vision Sciences    M

**SALVE REGINA UNIVERSITY**
Health Services Management and
    Hospital Administration    M,O
Nursing—General    D

**SAMFORD UNIVERSITY**
Communication Disorders    M,D
Family Nurse Practitioner Studies    M,D
Health Services Management and
    Hospital Administration    M
Nurse Anesthesia    M,D
Nursing and Healthcare
    Administration    M,D
Nursing Informatics    M,D
Nursing—General    M
Nutrition    M
Pharmacy    D
Physical Therapy    M,D
Public Health—General    M

**SAM HOUSTON STATE UNIVERSITY**
Allied Health—General    M
Biological and Biomedical
    Sciences—General    M
Nutrition    M

**SAMUEL MERRITT UNIVERSITY**
Family Nurse Practitioner Studies    M,D,O
Nurse Anesthesia    M,D,O
Nursing and Healthcare
    Administration    M,D,O
Nursing—General    M,D,O
Occupational Therapy    D
Physical Therapy    D
Physician Assistant Studies    M
Podiatric Medicine    D

**SAN DIEGO STATE UNIVERSITY**
Biochemistry    M,D
Biological and Biomedical
    Sciences—General    M,D
Cell Biology    M,D
Communication Disorders    M,D
Ecology    M,D
Emergency Medical Services    M,D
Environmental and Occupational
    Health    M,D
Epidemiology    M,D
Health Physics/Radiological Health    M
Health Promotion    M,D
Health Services Management and
    Hospital Administration    M,D
International Health    M,D
Microbiology    M
Molecular Biology    M
Nursing—General    M
Nutrition    M
Pharmaceutical Administration    M
Physical Therapy    D
Public Health—General    M,D
Toxicology    M,D

**SANFORD BURNHAM PREBYS MEDICAL DISCOVERY INSTITUTE**
Biological and Biomedical
    Sciences—General    D

**SAN FRANCISCO STATE UNIVERSITY**
Acute Care/Critical Care Nursing    M,O
Biochemistry    M
Biological and Biomedical
    Sciences—General    M
Cell Biology    M
Communication Disorders    M
Community Health Nursing    M,O
Community Health    M
Developmental Biology    M
Ecology    M
Family Nurse Practitioner Studies    M,O
Health Services Management and
    Hospital Administration    M
Marine Biology    M
Microbiology    M
Molecular Biology    M
Nursing and Healthcare
    Administration    M,O
Nursing—General    M,O
Pediatric Nursing    M,O
Physical Therapy    D
Physiology    M
Public Health—General    M
Women's Health Nursing    M,O

**SAN JOSE STATE UNIVERSITY**
Biological and Biomedical
    Sciences—General    M

---

Communication Disorders    M
Ecology    M
Gerontological Nursing    M,O
Microbiology    M
Molecular Biology    M
Nursing and Healthcare
    Administration    M,O
Nursing Education    M,O
Nursing—General    M,O
Nutrition    M
Occupational Therapy    M
Physiology    M

**SAN JUAN BAUTISTA SCHOOL OF MEDICINE**
Allopathic Medicine    M,D
Public Health—General    M,D

**SARAH LAWRENCE COLLEGE**
Human Genetics    M
Public Health—General    M

**SAYBROOK UNIVERSITY**
Nutrition    M,D,O

**THE SCRIPPS RESEARCH INSTITUTE**
Biological and Biomedical
    Sciences—General    D

**SEATTLE INSTITUTE OF EAST ASIAN MEDICINE**
Acupuncture and Oriental Medicine    M

**SEATTLE PACIFIC UNIVERSITY**
Adult Nursing    M,O
Family Nurse Practitioner Studies    M,O
Gerontological Nursing    M,O
Nursing and Healthcare
    Administration    M,O
Nursing Education    M,O
Nursing Informatics    M,O
Nursing—General    M,O

**SEATTLE UNIVERSITY**
Nursing—General    D

**SETON HALL UNIVERSITY**
Adult Nursing    M,D
Allied Health—General    D
Allopathic Medicine    D
Biochemistry    M,D
Biological and Biomedical
    Sciences—General    M,D
Communication Disorders    M
Gerontological Nursing    M,D
Health Services Management and
    Hospital Administration    M,D
International Health    M,O
Microbiology    M,D
Molecular Biology    M,D
Neuroscience    M,D
Nursing and Healthcare
    Administration    M,D
Nursing Education    M,D
Nursing—General    M,D
Occupational Therapy    M
Pediatric Nursing    M,D
Physical Therapy    D
Physician Assistant Studies    M
School Nursing    M,D

**SETON HILL UNIVERSITY**
Health Services Management and
    Hospital Administration    M
Oral and Dental Sciences    M,O
Physician Assistant Studies    M

**SHAWNEE STATE UNIVERSITY**
Occupational Therapy    M

**SHENANDOAH UNIVERSITY**
Adult Nursing    M,D,O
Allied Health—General    M,D,O
Family Nurse Practitioner Studies    M,D,O
Gerontological Nursing    M,D,O
Health Services Management and
    Hospital Administration    M,D,O
Nurse Midwifery    M,D,O
Nursing and Healthcare
    Administration    M,D,O
Nursing Education    M,D,O
Nursing—General    M,D,O
Occupational Therapy    M
Pharmacy    D
Physical Therapy    D
Physician Assistant Studies    M,D,O
Psychiatric Nursing    M,D,O
Public Health—General    M,D,O

**SHERMAN COLLEGE OF CHIROPRACTIC**
Chiropractic    D

**SHIPPENSBURG UNIVERSITY OF PENNSYLVANIA**
Biological and Biomedical
    Sciences—General    M
Health Services Management and
    Hospital Administration    M,D,O

**SIENA HEIGHTS UNIVERSITY**
Health Services Management and
    Hospital Administration    M,O

**SIMMONS UNIVERSITY**
Family Nurse Practitioner Studies    M,D
Health Promotion    M,D,O
Health Services Management and
    Hospital Administration    M
Nursing—General    M,D,O
Nutrition    M
Physical Therapy    M,D,O
Public Health—General    M,D,O

**SIMON FRASER UNIVERSITY**
Biochemistry    M,D,O

---

Biological and Biomedical
    Sciences—General    M,D,O
Entomology    M,D,O
International Health    M,D,O
Molecular Biology    M,D,O
Public Health—General    M,D,O
Toxicology    M,D,O

**SLIPPERY ROCK UNIVERSITY OF PENNSYLVANIA**
Physical Therapy    D
Physician Assistant Studies    M
Public Health—General    M

**SMITH COLLEGE**
Biological and Biomedical
    Sciences—General    M

**SONOMA STATE UNIVERSITY**
Biochemistry    M
Biological and Biomedical
    Sciences—General    M
Family Nurse Practitioner Studies    M
Health Promotion    M
Nursing—General    M
Occupational Therapy    M
Physical Therapy    M

**SOUTH BAYLO UNIVERSITY**
Acupuncture and Oriental Medicine    M

**SOUTH CAROLINA STATE UNIVERSITY**
Allied Health—General    M
Biological and Biomedical
    Sciences—General    M
Communication Disorders    M
Health Services Management and
    Hospital Administration    M
Nutrition    M

**SOUTH COLLEGE**
Pharmacy    D
Physician Assistant Studies    M

**SOUTH DAKOTA STATE UNIVERSITY**
Biochemistry    M,D
Biological and Biomedical
    Sciences—General    M,D
Microbiology    M,D
Nursing—General    M,D
Nutrition    M,D
Pharmaceutical Sciences    M,D
Pharmacy    D
Veterinary Sciences    M,D

**SOUTHEASTERN LOUISIANA UNIVERSITY**
Biological and Biomedical
    Sciences—General    M
Communication Disorders    M
Nursing—General    M,D

**SOUTHEASTERN OKLAHOMA STATE UNIVERSITY**
Environmental and Occupational
    Health    M

**SOUTHEASTERN UNIVERSITY (FL)**
Health Services Management and
    Hospital Administration    M,D

**SOUTHEAST MISSOURI STATE UNIVERSITY**
Biological and Biomedical
    Sciences—General    M
Communication Disorders    M
Nursing—General    M

**SOUTHERN ADVENTIST UNIVERSITY**
Acute Care/Critical Care Nursing    M,D
Adult Nursing    M,D
Family Nurse Practitioner Studies    M,D
Gerontological Nursing    M,D
Health Services Management and
    Hospital Administration    M
Nursing Education    M,D
Nursing—General    M,D
Psychiatric Nursing    M,D

**SOUTHERN ARKANSAS UNIVERSITY– MAGNOLIA**
Psychiatric Nursing    M

**SOUTHERN CALIFORNIA UNIVERSITY OF HEALTH SCIENCES**
Acupuncture and Oriental Medicine    M,D
Chiropractic    D

**SOUTHERN COLLEGE OF OPTOMETRY**
Optometry    D

**SOUTHERN CONNECTICUT STATE UNIVERSITY**
Biological and Biomedical
    Sciences—General    M
Communication Disorders    M
Family Nurse Practitioner Studies    M,D
Nursing Education    M,D
Nursing—General    M,D
Public Health—General    M

**SOUTHERN ILLINOIS UNIVERSITY CARBONDALE**
Biochemistry    M,D
Biological and Biomedical
    Sciences—General    M,D
Communication Disorders    M
Community Health    M
Health Services Management and
    Hospital Administration    M
Medical Physics    M
Microbiology    M,D
Molecular Biology    M,D
Nutrition    M
Pharmacology    M,D
Physician Assistant Studies    M

---

Physiology M,D
Plant Biology M,D
Zoology M,D

**SOUTHERN ILLINOIS UNIVERSITY EDWARDSVILLE**
Biological and Biomedical Sciences—General M
Communication Disorders M
Dentistry D
Family Nurse Practitioner Studies M,D,O
Nurse Anesthesia D
Nursing and Healthcare Administration M,O
Nursing Education M,O
Nursing—General M,D,O
Pharmacy D

**SOUTHERN METHODIST UNIVERSITY**
Biological and Biomedical Sciences—General M,D
Cell Biology M,D
Health Promotion M,D
Molecular Biology M,D
Physiology M,D

**SOUTHERN NAZARENE UNIVERSITY**
Health Services Management and Hospital Administration M
Nursing and Healthcare Administration M
Nursing Education M
Nursing—General M

**SOUTHERN NEW HAMPSHIRE UNIVERSITY**
Health Services Management and Hospital Administration M,D,O
Nursing and Healthcare Administration M,O
Nursing Education M,O
Nursing—General M,O

**SOUTHERN UNIVERSITY AND AGRICULTURAL AND MECHANICAL COLLEGE**
Biochemistry M
Biological and Biomedical Sciences—General M
Communication Disorders M
Family Nurse Practitioner Studies M,D,O
Gerontological Nursing M,D,O
Nursing and Healthcare Administration M,D,O
Nursing Education M,D,O
Nursing—General M,D,O

**SOUTH UNIVERSITY - COLUMBIA**
Health Services Management and Hospital Administration M
Nursing—General M
Pharmacy D

**SOUTH UNIVERSITY - MONTGOMERY**
Health Services Management and Hospital Administration M
Nursing—General M

**SOUTH UNIVERSITY - RICHMOND**
Nursing—General M

**SOUTH UNIVERSITY - SAVANNAH**
Anesthesiologist Assistant Studies M
Health Services Management and Hospital Administration M
Nursing Education M
Nursing—General M
Pharmacy D
Physician Assistant Studies M

**SOUTH UNIVERSITY - TAMPA**
Adult Nursing M
Family Nurse Practitioner Studies M
Health Services Management and Hospital Administration M
Nursing Education M
Nursing—General M
Physician Assistant Studies M

**SOUTH UNIVERSITY - VIRGINIA BEACH**
Family Nurse Practitioner Studies M
Nursing—General M

**SOUTH UNIVERSITY - WEST PALM BEACH**
Family Nurse Practitioner Studies M
Health Services Management and Hospital Administration M
Nursing—General M
Occupational Therapy D

**SOUTHWEST ACUPUNCTURE COLLEGE**
Acupuncture and Oriental Medicine M

**SOUTHWEST BAPTIST UNIVERSITY**
Health Services Management and Hospital Administration M
Physical Therapy D

**SOUTHWEST COLLEGE OF NATUROPATHIC MEDICINE AND HEALTH SCIENCES**
Naturopathic Medicine D

**SOUTHWESTERN OKLAHOMA STATE UNIVERSITY**
Microbiology M
Pharmaceutical Administration D
Pharmacy D

**SPALDING UNIVERSITY**
Adult Nursing M,D,O
Family Nurse Practitioner Studies M,D,O
Nursing and Healthcare Administration M,D,O
Nursing Education M,D,O
Nursing—General M,D,O
Occupational Therapy M
Pediatric Nursing M,D,O

**SPRING ARBOR UNIVERSITY**
Nursing—General M

**SPRINGFIELD COLLEGE**
Health Promotion M,D,O
Occupational Therapy M
Physical Therapy D
Physician Assistant Studies M

**SPRING HILL COLLEGE**
Nursing and Healthcare Administration M,O
Nursing—General M,O

**STANBRIDGE UNIVERSITY**
Nursing—General M
Occupational Therapy M

**STANFORD UNIVERSITY**
Allopathic Medicine D
Biochemistry D
Biological and Biomedical Sciences—General M,D
Biophysics D
Clinical Research M,D
Developmental Biology M,D
Ecology M,D
Epidemiology M,D
Genetics D
Health Services Research M,D
Immunology D
Microbiology D
Physiology D
Structural Biology D
Systems Biology D

**STATE UNIVERSITY OF NEW YORK AT FREDONIA**
Biological and Biomedical Sciences—General M,O
Communication Disorders M,O

**STATE UNIVERSITY OF NEW YORK AT NEW PALTZ**
Communication Disorders M

**STATE UNIVERSITY OF NEW YORK AT PLATTSBURGH**
Communication Disorders M

**STATE UNIVERSITY OF NEW YORK COLLEGE AT CORTLAND**
Communication Disorders M
Community Health M

**STATE UNIVERSITY OF NEW YORK COLLEGE AT ONEONTA**
Biological and Biomedical Sciences—General M
Nutrition M

**STATE UNIVERSITY OF NEW YORK COLLEGE AT POTSDAM**
Community Health M

**STATE UNIVERSITY OF NEW YORK COLLEGE OF ENVIRONMENTAL SCIENCE AND FORESTRY**
Biochemistry M,D
Conservation Biology M,D
Ecology M,D
Entomology M,D
Environmental Biology M,D
Plant Pathology M,D

**STATE UNIVERSITY OF NEW YORK COLLEGE OF OPTOMETRY**
Optometry D
Vision Sciences D

**STATE UNIVERSITY OF NEW YORK COLLEGE OF TECHNOLOGY AT DELHI**
Nursing and Healthcare Administration M
Nursing Education M
Nursing—General M

**STATE UNIVERSITY OF NEW YORK DOWNSTATE MEDICAL CENTER**
Allopathic Medicine M,D
Biological and Biomedical Sciences—General M,D
Cell Biology D
Community Health M
Family Nurse Practitioner Studies M,O
Medical/Surgical Nursing M,O
Molecular Biology D
Neuroscience D
Nurse Anesthesia M
Nurse Midwifery M,O
Nursing—General M,O
Occupational Therapy M
Public Health—General M

**STATE UNIVERSITY OF NEW YORK EMPIRE STATE COLLEGE**
Nursing Education M

**STATE UNIVERSITY OF NEW YORK POLYTECHNIC INSTITUTE**
Family Nurse Practitioner Studies M,O
Nursing Education M,O

**STATE UNIVERSITY OF NEW YORK UPSTATE MEDICAL UNIVERSITY**
Allopathic Medicine D
Anatomy M,D
Biochemistry M,D
Biological and Biomedical Sciences—General M,D
Cell Biology M,D
Clinical Laboratory Sciences/Medical Technology M
Family Nurse Practitioner Studies M,O
Immunology M,D
Microbiology M,D
Molecular Biology M,D
Neuroscience D
Nursing—General M,O

Pharmacology D
Physical Therapy D
Physiology M,D
Public Health—General M

**STEPHEN F. AUSTIN STATE UNIVERSITY**
Biological and Biomedical Sciences—General M
Communication Disorders M
Family Nurse Practitioner Studies M
Nursing—General M

**STEPHENS COLLEGE**
Physician Assistant Studies M,O

**STEVENS INSTITUTE OF TECHNOLOGY**
Biochemistry M,D,O
Pharmaceutical Sciences M,O

**STEVENSON UNIVERSITY**
Biological and Biomedical Sciences—General M
Health Services Management and Hospital Administration M
Nursing and Healthcare Administration M
Nursing Education M
Nursing—General M

**STOCKTON UNIVERSITY**
Communication Disorders M
Nursing—General M
Occupational Therapy M
Physical Therapy D

**STONY BROOK UNIVERSITY, STATE UNIVERSITY OF NEW YORK**
Adult Nursing M,D,O
Allopathic Medicine D
Anatomy D
Biochemistry M,D
Bioethics
Biological and Biomedical Sciences—General M,D,O
Biophysics D
Cell Biology D
Community Health M,D,O
Dentistry D,O
Developmental Biology M,D
Ecology M,D
Evolutionary Biology M,D
Family Nurse Practitioner Studies M,D,O
Genetics D
Gerontological Nursing M,D,O
Health Promotion M,O
Health Services Management and Hospital Administration M,D,O
Immunology M,D
Maternal and Child/Neonatal Nursing M,D,O
Medical Physics M,D
Microbiology D
Molecular Biology M,D
Molecular Genetics D
Molecular Physiology D
Neuroscience M,D
Nurse Midwifery M,D,O
Nursing and Healthcare Administration M,D,O
Nursing Education M,O
Nursing—General M,D,O
Nutrition M,O
Occupational Therapy M,D,O
Oral and Dental Sciences M,D,O
Pathology M,D
Pediatric Nursing M,D,O
Pharmacology M,D
Physical Therapy M,D,O
Physician Assistant Studies M,D,O
Physiology D
Psychiatric Nursing M,D,O
Public Health—General M,O
Rehabilitation Sciences M,D,O
Structural Biology D
Women's Health Nursing M,D,O

**STRATFORD UNIVERSITY (VA)**
Health Services Management and Hospital Administration M,D

**STRAYER UNIVERSITY**
Health Services Management and Hospital Administration M

**SUFFOLK UNIVERSITY**
Community Health M
Health Services Management and Hospital Administration M

**SULLIVAN UNIVERSITY**
Pharmacy D

**SUL ROSS STATE UNIVERSITY**
Biological and Biomedical Sciences—General M

**SUNY BROCKPORT**
Biological and Biomedical Sciences—General M,O
Community Health M
Health Services Management and Hospital Administration M,O
Public Health—General M

**SWEDISH INSTITUTE, COLLEGE OF HEALTH SCIENCES**
Acupuncture and Oriental Medicine M

**SYRACUSE UNIVERSITY**
Biological and Biomedical Sciences—General M,D
Communication Disorders M,D
Environmental and Occupational Health O
Health Services Management and Hospital Administration O
International Health M
Neuroscience M,D

Nutrition M,D

**TARLETON STATE UNIVERSITY**
Biological and Biomedical Sciences—General M
Clinical Laboratory Sciences/Medical Technology M
Nursing and Healthcare Administration M
Nursing Education M
Nursing—General M
Public Health—General M

**TEACHERS COLLEGE, COLUMBIA UNIVERSITY**
Biological and Biomedical Sciences—General M,D
Communication Disorders M,D,O
Community Health M,D,O
Neuroscience M,D
Nursing and Healthcare Administration M,D
Nursing Education M,D,O
Nutrition M,D,O
Physiology M,D

**TEMPLE UNIVERSITY**
Adult Nursing D
Allied Health—General M,D
Allopathic Medicine D
Biological and Biomedical Sciences—General M,D
Communication Disorders M,D
Dentistry D
Environmental and Occupational Health M,D
Epidemiology M,D
Family Nurse Practitioner Studies D
Health Services Management and Hospital Administration M
Medicinal and Pharmaceutical Chemistry M,D
Nursing—General M,D
Occupational Therapy M,D
Oral and Dental Sciences M,O
Pharmaceutical Administration M
Pharmaceutical Sciences M,D
Pharmacy M,D
Podiatric Medicine D
Public Health—General M,D
Rehabilitation Sciences M,D

**TENNESSEE STATE UNIVERSITY**
Allied Health—General M,D,O
Biological and Biomedical Sciences—General M,D
Communication Disorders M
Family Nurse Practitioner Studies M,O
Nursing—General M,O
Occupational Therapy M
Physical Therapy D
Public Health—General M

**TENNESSEE TECHNOLOGICAL UNIVERSITY**
Acute Care/Critical Care Nursing D
Biological and Biomedical Sciences—General M,D
Family Nurse Practitioner Studies M,D
Gerontological Nursing D
Health Promotion M
Nursing and Healthcare Administration M,D
Nursing Education M
Nursing—General M,D
Psychiatric Nursing D
Women's Health Nursing D

**TEXAS A&M INTERNATIONAL UNIVERSITY**
Biological and Biomedical Sciences—General M
Family Nurse Practitioner Studies M
Nursing—General M

**TEXAS A&M UNIVERSITY**
Allopathic Medicine M,D
Biochemistry M,D
Biological and Biomedical Sciences—General M,D
Dentistry M,D,O
Entomology M,D
Environmental and Occupational Health M,D
Epidemiology M,D
Family Nurse Practitioner Studies M
Forensic Nursing M
Health Services Management and Hospital Administration M,D
Health Services Research M,D
Marine Biology M,D
Microbiology M,D
Nursing Education M
Nursing—General M
Nutrition M,D
Oral and Dental Sciences M,D,O
Pharmacy D
Plant Pathology M,D
Public Health—General M,D
Veterinary Medicine M,D
Veterinary Sciences M,D

**TEXAS A&M UNIVERSITY–COMMERCE**
Biological and Biomedical Sciences—General M,O

**TEXAS A&M UNIVERSITY–CORPUS CHRISTI**
Biological and Biomedical Sciences—General M,D
Family Nurse Practitioner Studies M
Health Services Management and Hospital Administration M,D
Marine Biology M,D
Nursing and Healthcare Administration M,D
Nursing Education M,D

Nursing—General M,D

**TEXAS A&M UNIVERSITY–KINGSVILLE**
Biological and Biomedical
   Sciences—General M
Communication Disorders M

**TEXAS CHIROPRACTIC COLLEGE**
Chiropractic D

**TEXAS CHRISTIAN UNIVERSITY**
Adult Nursing M,O
Allied Health—General M,D,O
Biochemistry M,D
Biological and Biomedical
   Sciences—General M,D
Biophysics M,D
Communication Disorders M
Family Nurse Practitioner Studies D
Gerontological Nursing M,O
Neuroscience M
Nurse Anesthesia D
Nursing and Healthcare
   Administration M,D,O
Nursing Education M,O
Nursing—General M,D,O
Pediatric Nursing M,D,O

**TEXAS HEALTH AND SCIENCE UNIVERSITY**
Acupuncture and Oriental Medicine M,D
Health Services Management and
   Hospital Administration M,D

**TEXAS SOUTHERN UNIVERSITY**
Biological and Biomedical
   Sciences—General M
Health Services Management and
   Hospital Administration M
Pharmaceutical Sciences M,D
Pharmacy D
Toxicology M,D

**TEXAS STATE UNIVERSITY**
Allied Health—General M,D
Biochemistry M
Biological and Biomedical
   Sciences—General M
Communication Disorders M
Conservation Biology M
Family Nurse Practitioner Studies M
Health Services Management and
   Hospital Administration M
Marine Biology M,D
Nutrition M
Physical Therapy D

**TEXAS TECH UNIVERSITY**
Biological and Biomedical
   Sciences—General M,D
Health Services Management and
   Hospital Administration M,D
Microbiology M,D
Nutrition M,D
Toxicology M,D
Zoology M,D

**TEXAS TECH UNIVERSITY HEALTH SCIENCES CENTER**
Acute Care/Critical Care Nursing M,D,O
Allopathic Medicine D
Biological and Biomedical
   Sciences—General M,D
Cell Biology M,D
Communication Disorders M,D
Family Nurse Practitioner Studies M,D,O
Gerontological Nursing M,D,O
Health Services Management and
   Hospital Administration M
Molecular Pathology M
Nursing and Healthcare
   Administration M,D,O
Nursing Education M,D,O
Nursing—General M,D,O
Occupational Therapy M
Pediatric Nursing M,D,O
Pharmaceutical Sciences M
Pharmacy D
Physical Therapy D
Physician Assistant Studies M
Rehabilitation Sciences D

**TEXAS TECH UNIVERSITY HEALTH SCIENCES CENTER EL PASO**
Allopathic Medicine D
Biological and Biomedical
   Sciences—General M
Nursing—General M

**TEXAS WESLEYAN UNIVERSITY**
Nurse Anesthesia M,D

**TEXAS WOMAN'S UNIVERSITY**
Acute Care/Critical Care Nursing M,D
Adult Nursing M,D
Allied Health—General M,D
Biological and Biomedical
   Sciences—General M,D
Communication Disorders M
Dental Hygiene M,D
Family Nurse Practitioner Studies M,D
Gerontological Nursing M,D
Health Services Management and
   Hospital Administration M
Molecular Biology M,D
Nursing and Healthcare
   Administration M,D
Nursing Education M,D
Nursing—General M,D
Nutrition M,D
Occupational Therapy M,D
Pediatric Nursing M,D
Physical Therapy D
Women's Health Nursing M,D

**THOMAS EDISON STATE UNIVERSITY**
Nursing and Healthcare
   Administration M
Nursing Education M
Nursing Informatics M
Nursing—General M,D
Public Health—General M

**THOMAS JEFFERSON UNIVERSITY**
Allopathic Medicine D
Biochemistry D
Biological and Biomedical
   Sciences—General M,D,O
Cancer Biology/Oncology D
Cell Biology M,D
Clinical Laboratory
   Sciences/Medical Technology M
Clinical Research M,O
Developmental Biology M
Genetics D
Genomic Sciences D
Health Physics/Radiological Health M
Health Services Management and
   Hospital Administration M,D,O
Health Services Research M,D,O
Human Genetics M
Immunology D
Infectious Diseases O
Medical Imaging M
Medical Physics M
Microbiology M,D
Molecular Pharmacology D
Neuroscience D
Nurse Midwifery M
Nursing—General M,D
Occupational Therapy M
Pharmacology M
Pharmacy D
Physical Therapy D
Physician Assistant Studies M
Public Health—General M,O
Toxicology M

**THOMAS UNIVERSITY**
Nursing—General M

**TIFFIN UNIVERSITY**
Health Services Management and
   Hospital Administration M

**TOURO UNIVERSITY CALIFORNIA**
Osteopathic Medicine M,D
Pharmacy M,D
Public Health—General M,D

**TOWSON UNIVERSITY**
Allied Health—General M
Biological and Biomedical
   Sciences—General M
Communication Disorders M,D
Environmental and Occupational
   Health D
Health Services Management and
   Hospital Administration M,O
Occupational Therapy M
Physician Assistant Studies M

**TRENT UNIVERSITY**
Biological and Biomedical
   Sciences—General M,D

**TREVECCA NAZARENE UNIVERSITY**
Health Services Management and
   Hospital Administration M
Physician Assistant Studies M

**TRIDENT UNIVERSITY INTERNATIONAL**
Clinical Research M,D,O
Environmental and Occupational
   Health M,D,O
Health Services Management and
   Hospital Administration M,D,O
International Health M,D,O

**TRINE UNIVERSITY**
Physical Therapy D
Physician Assistant Studies M

**TRINITY INTERNATIONAL UNIVERSITY**
Bioethics M,D

**TRINITY UNIVERSITY**
Health Services Management and
   Hospital Administration M

**TRINITY WASHINGTON UNIVERSITY**
Nursing—General M
Occupational Therapy M
Public Health—General M

**TRINITY WESTERN UNIVERSITY**
Health Services Management and
   Hospital Administration M,O
Nursing—General M

**TROPICAL AGRICULTURE RESEARCH AND HIGHER EDUCATION CENTER**
Conservation Biology M,D

**TROY UNIVERSITY**
Adult Nursing M,D
Biological and Biomedical
   Sciences—General M,O
Family Nurse Practitioner Studies M,D
Health Services Management and
   Hospital Administration M
Maternal and Child Health M,D
Nursing Informatics M,D
Nursing—General M,D

**TRUETT MCCONNELL UNIVERSITY**
Biological and Biomedical
   Sciences—General M

**TRUMAN STATE UNIVERSITY**
Communication Disorders M

**TUFTS UNIVERSITY**
Allopathic Medicine D
Biochemistry D
Biological and Biomedical
   Sciences—General M,D,O
Cancer Biology/Oncology D
Cell Biology D
Clinical Laboratory
   Sciences/Medical Technology M,D,O
Dentistry D
Developmental Biology D
Environmental and Occupational
   Health M,D
Epidemiology M,D
Genetics D
Health Services Management and
   Hospital Administration M,D,O
Immunology D
Infectious Diseases M,D
Microbiology D
Molecular Biology D
Molecular Medicine D
Neuroscience D
Nutrition M,D,O
Occupational Therapy M,D,O
Oral and Dental Sciences M,D
Pathology M,D
Physician Assistant Studies M,D,O
Public Health—General M,D,O
Reproductive Biology M,D
Structural Biology D
Veterinary Medicine M,D

**TULANE UNIVERSITY**
Allopathic Medicine D
Biochemistry M
Biological and Biomedical
   Sciences—General M,D
Cell Biology M,D
Community Health M,D
Ecology M,D
Environmental and Occupational
   Health M,D
Epidemiology M,D
Evolutionary Biology M,D
Health Promotion M
Health Services Management and
   Hospital Administration M,D
Human Genetics M
Immunology M
International Health M,D
Microbiology M
Molecular Biology M,D
Neuroscience M
Parasitology M,D,O
Pharmacology M
Physiology M,D
Public Health—General M,D
Structural Biology M,D

**TUSCULUM UNIVERSITY**
Family Nurse Practitioner Studies M
Nursing—General M

**TUSKEGEE UNIVERSITY**
Biological and Biomedical
   Sciences—General M,D
Nutrition M
Occupational Therapy M
Veterinary Medicine M,D
Veterinary Sciences M,D

**UNB FREDERICTON**
Biological and Biomedical
   Sciences—General M,D
Health Services Research M
Nursing Education M
Nursing—General M

**UNIFORMED SERVICES UNIVERSITY OF THE HEALTH SCIENCES**
Allopathic Medicine M,D
Biological and Biomedical
   Sciences—General M,D
Cell Biology M,D
Environmental and Occupational
   Health M,D
Family Nurse Practitioner Studies M,D
Gerontological Nursing M,D
Health Services Management and
   Hospital Administration M,D
Immunology D
Infectious Diseases D
International Health M,D
Molecular Biology M,D
Neuroscience D
Nurse Anesthesia M,D
Nursing—General M,D
Psychiatric Nursing M,D
Public Health—General M,D
Women's Health Nursing M,D
Zoology M,D

**UNION COLLEGE (NE)**
Physician Assistant Studies M

**UNION INSTITUTE & UNIVERSITY**
Health Promotion M
Health Services Management and
   Hospital Administration M

**UNION UNIVERSITY**
Family Nurse Practitioner Studies M,D,O
Nurse Anesthesia M,D,O
Nursing and Healthcare
   Administration M,D,O
Nursing Education M,D,O
Nursing—General M,D,O
Pharmacy D

**UNITED STATES UNIVERSITY**
Family Nurse Practitioner Studies M

**UNIVERSIDAD ADVENTISTA DE LAS ANTILLAS**
Medical/Surgical Nursing M

**UNIVERSIDAD AUTONOMA DE GUADALAJARA**
Allopathic Medicine D
Environmental and Occupational
   Health M,D

**UNIVERSIDAD CENTRAL DEL CARIBE**
Allopathic Medicine M,D
Anatomy M,D
Biochemistry M,D
Biological and Biomedical
   Sciences—General M,D
Cell Biology M,D
Immunology M,D
Microbiology M,D
Molecular Biology M,D
Pharmacology M,D
Physiology M,D

**UNIVERSIDAD CENTRAL DEL ESTE**
Allopathic Medicine D
Dentistry D

**UNIVERSIDAD DE CIENCIAS MEDICAS**
Allopathic Medicine M,D,O
Anatomy M,D,O
Biological and Biomedical
   Sciences—General M,D,O
Community Health M,D,O
Environmental and Occupational
   Health M,D,O
Health Services Management and
   Hospital Administration M,D,O
Pharmacy M,D,O

**UNIVERSIDAD DE IBEROAMERICA**
Acute Care/Critical Care Nursing M,D
Allopathic Medicine M,D
Health Services Management and
   Hospital Administration M,D
Neuroscience M,D

**UNIVERSIDAD DE LAS AMÉRICAS PUEBLA**
Clinical Laboratory
   Sciences/Medical Technology M

**UNIVERSIDAD DEL TURABO**
Adult Nursing M,O
Communication Disorders M
Environmental Biology M,D
Family Nurse Practitioner Studies M,O
Health Promotion M
Naturopathic Medicine D

**UNIVERSIDAD IBEROAMERICANA**
Allopathic Medicine D
Dentistry M,D

**UNIVERSIDAD METROPOLITANA**
Nursing and Healthcare
   Administration M,O
Nursing—General M,O
Oncology Nursing M,O

**UNIVERSIDAD NACIONAL PEDRO HENRIQUEZ URENA**
Allopathic Medicine D
Dentistry D
Ecology M

**UNIVERSITÉ DE MONCTON**
Biochemistry M
Biological and Biomedical
   Sciences—General M
Nutrition M

**UNIVERSITÉ DE MONTRÉAL**
Allopathic Medicine D
Biochemistry M,D,O
Bioethics M,D,O
Biological and Biomedical
   Sciences—General M,D
Cell Biology M,D
Communication Disorders M,O
Community Health M,D,O
Dental Hygiene O
Environmental and Occupational
   Health M
Genetics O
Health Services Management and
   Hospital Administration M,O
Immunology M,D
Microbiology M,D
Molecular Biology M,D
Neuroscience M,D
Nursing—General M,D,O
Nutrition M,D,O
Occupational Therapy O
Optometry D
Oral and Dental Sciences M,O
Pathology M,D
Pharmaceutical Sciences M,D,O
Pharmacology M,D
Physiology M,D
Public Health—General M,D,O
Rehabilitation Sciences O
Toxicology O
Veterinary Medicine M,D
Veterinary Sciences M,D
Virology D
Vision Sciences M,O

**UNIVERSITÉ DE SHERBROOKE**
Allopathic Medicine D
Biochemistry M,D
Biological and Biomedical
   Sciences—General M,D,O
Biophysics M,D
Cell Biology M,D

---

*M—masters degree; D—doctorate; O—other advanced degree; *—Close-Up and/or Display*

Clinical Laboratory
  Sciences/Medical Technology — M,D
Immunology — M,D
Microbiology — M,D
Pharmacology — M,D
Physiology — M,D
Radiation Biology — M,D

## UNIVERSITÉ DU QUÉBEC À CHICOUTIMI
Genetics — M

## UNIVERSITÉ DU QUÉBEC À MONTRÉAL
Biological and Biomedical
  Sciences—General — M,D
Environmental and Occupational
  Health — O

## UNIVERSITÉ DU QUÉBEC À RIMOUSKI
Nursing—General — M,O

## UNIVERSITÉ DU QUÉBEC À TROIS-RIVIÈRES
Biophysics — M,D
Chiropractic — D
Nursing—General — M,O

## UNIVERSITÉ DU QUÉBEC EN ABITIBI-TÉMISCAMINGUE
Biological and Biomedical
  Sciences—General — M,D

## UNIVERSITÉ DU QUÉBEC EN OUTAOUAIS
Nursing—General — M,O

## UNIVERSITÉ DU QUÉBEC, INSTITUT NATIONAL DE LA RECHERCHE SCIENTIFIQUE
Biological and Biomedical
  Sciences—General — M,D
Immunology — M,D
Medical Microbiology — M,D
Microbiology — M,D
Virology — M,D

## UNIVERSITY AT ALBANY, STATE UNIVERSITY OF NEW YORK
Biological and Biomedical
  Sciences—General — M,D
Environmental and Occupational
  Health — M,D
Epidemiology — M,D
Health Services Management and
  Hospital Administration — M,D,O
Neuroscience — M,D
Public Health—General — M,D
Toxicology — M,D

## UNIVERSITY AT BUFFALO, THE STATE UNIVERSITY OF NEW YORK
Adult Nursing — M,D,O
Allied Health—General — M,D,O
Allopathic Medicine — D
Anatomy — M,D
Biochemistry — M,D
Biological and Biomedical
  Sciences—General — M,D
Biophysics — M,D
Cancer Biology/Oncology — M
Cell Biology — M,D
Clinical Laboratory
  Sciences/Medical Technology — M
Communication Disorders — M,D
Community Health — M,D,O
Dentistry — D
Ecology — M,D,O
Epidemiology — M,D
Evolutionary Biology — M,D,O
Family Nurse Practitioner Studies — M,D,O
Genetics — M,D
Genomic Sciences — M,D
Gerontological Nursing — M,D,O
Health Services Management and
  Hospital Administration — M,D
Immunology — M,D
Medical Physics — M,D
Medicinal and Pharmaceutical
  Chemistry — M,D
Microbiology — M,D
Molecular Biology — M,D
Molecular Biophysics — M,D
Molecular Pharmacology — M,D
Neuroscience — M,D
Nurse Anesthesia — M,D,O
Nursing and Healthcare
  Administration — M,D,O
Nursing—General — M,D,O
Nutrition — M,D,O
Occupational Therapy — M
Oral and Dental Sciences — M,D,O
Pathology — M,D
Pharmaceutical Sciences — M,D
Pharmacology — M,D
Pharmacy — D
Physical Therapy — D
Physiology — M,D
Psychiatric Nursing — M,D,O
Public Health—General — M,D
Rehabilitation Sciences — O
Structural Biology — M,D
Toxicology — M,D

## THE UNIVERSITY OF AKRON
Biological and Biomedical
  Sciences—General — M,D
Communication Disorders — M,D
Nursing—General — M,D

## THE UNIVERSITY OF ALABAMA
Biological and Biomedical
  Sciences—General — M,D
Communication Disorders — M
Community Health — M
Health Promotion — M,D
Nursing—General — M,D
Nutrition — M

## THE UNIVERSITY OF ALABAMA AT BIRMINGHAM
Adult Nursing — M,D
Allied Health—General — M,D,O
Allopathic Medicine — D
Biochemistry — D
Biological and Biomedical
  Sciences—General — M,D
Cancer Biology/Oncology — D
Cell Biology — D
Clinical Laboratory
  Sciences/Medical Technology — M,D
Community Health — M
Dentistry — D
Developmental Biology — D
Environmental and Occupational
  Health — M,D
Epidemiology — M,D
Family Nurse Practitioner Studies — M,D
Genetics — D
Genomic Sciences — D
Gerontological Nursing — D
Health Promotion — D
Health Services Management and
  Hospital Administration — M,D
Health Services Research — M,D
Immunology — D
Industrial Hygiene — M,D
Maternal and Child Health — M,D
Microbiology — D
Molecular Biology — D
Molecular Medicine — D
Neuroscience — M,D
Nurse Anesthesia — M,D
Nursing and Healthcare
  Administration — M,D
Nursing Informatics — M,D
Nursing—General — M,D
Nutrition — M,D
Occupational Therapy — M,O
Optometry — M
Oral and Dental Sciences — M
Pathobiology — D
Pediatric Nursing — M,D
Pharmacology — M,D
Physical Therapy — D
Physician Assistant Studies — M
Psychiatric Nursing — M,D
Public Health—General — M,D
Rehabilitation Sciences — M,D
Structural Biology — D
Toxicology — M,D
Vision Sciences — M,D
Women's Health Nursing — M,D

## THE UNIVERSITY OF ALABAMA IN HUNTSVILLE
Acute Care/Critical Care Nursing — M,D,O
Biological and Biomedical
  Sciences—General — M
Family Nurse Practitioner Studies — M,D,O
Gerontological Nursing — M,D,O
Health Services Management and
  Hospital Administration — M,D,O
Nursing Education — M,D,O
Nursing—General — M,D,O

## UNIVERSITY OF ALASKA ANCHORAGE
Biological and Biomedical
  Sciences—General — M
Nursing—General — M,D,O
Physician Assistant Studies — M
Public Health—General — M

## UNIVERSITY OF ALASKA FAIRBANKS
Biochemistry — M,D
Biological and Biomedical
  Sciences—General — M,D,O
Marine Biology — M,D
Neuroscience — M,D

## UNIVERSITY OF ALBERTA
Allopathic Medicine — D
Biochemistry — M,D
Biological and Biomedical
  Sciences—General — M,D
Cancer Biology/Oncology — M,D
Cell Biology — M,D
Clinical Laboratory
  Sciences/Medical Technology — M,D
Communication Disorders — M
Community Health — M,D
Conservation Biology — M,D
Dental Hygiene — O
Dentistry — D
Ecology — M,D
Environmental and Occupational
  Health — M,D
Environmental Biology — M,D
Epidemiology — M,D
Evolutionary Biology — M,D
Genetics — M,D
Health Physics/Radiological Health — M,D
Health Promotion — M,O
Health Services Management and
  Hospital Administration — M,D
Health Services Research — M,D
Immunology — M,D
International Health — M,D
Maternal and Child/Neonatal
  Nursing — D
Medical Microbiology — M,D
Medical Physics — M,D
Microbiology — M,D
Molecular Biology — M,D
Neuroscience — M,D
Nursing—General — M,D
Occupational Therapy — M,D
Oral and Dental Sciences — M,D
Pathology — M,D
Pharmaceutical Sciences — M,D
Pharmacology — M,D
Pharmacy — M,D
Physical Therapy — M,D
Physiology — M,D

Plant Biology — M,D
Public Health—General — M,D
Rehabilitation Sciences — M,D
Vision Sciences — M,D

## THE UNIVERSITY OF ARIZONA
Allopathic Medicine — M,D
Biochemistry — M,D
Biological and Biomedical
  Sciences—General — M,D
Cancer Biology/Oncology — D
Cell Biology — D
Communication Disorders — M,D,O
Ecology — M,D
Entomology — M,D
Epidemiology — M,D
Evolutionary Biology — M,D
Family Nurse Practitioner Studies — M,D,O
Genetics — M,D
Immunology — D
Medical Physics — M
Microbiology — D
Molecular Biology — D
Molecular Medicine — M,D
Neuroscience — D
Nursing—General — M,D,O
Nutrition — M,D
Perfusion — M,D
Pharmaceutical Sciences — M,D
Pharmacology — M,D
Pharmacy — D
Physiology — M,D
Plant Pathology — M,D
Public Health—General — M,D

## UNIVERSITY OF ARKANSAS
Biological and Biomedical
  Sciences—General — M,D
Cell Biology — M,D
Communication Disorders — M
Community Health — M,D
Entomology — M,D
Health Promotion — M,D
Molecular Biology — M,D
Nursing—General — M
Plant Pathology — M

## UNIVERSITY OF ARKANSAS AT LITTLE ROCK
Biological and Biomedical
  Sciences—General — M

## UNIVERSITY OF ARKANSAS FOR MEDICAL SCIENCES
Allopathic Medicine — D
Biochemistry — M,D,O
Biological and Biomedical
  Sciences—General — M,D,O
Communication Disorders — M,D
Environmental and Occupational
  Health — M,D,O
Epidemiology — M,D,O
Health Physics/Radiological Health — M,D
Health Promotion — M,D,O
Health Services Management and
  Hospital Administration — M,D,O
Health Services Research — M,D,O
Immunology — M,D,O
Microbiology — M,D,O
Molecular Biology — M,D,O
Molecular Biophysics — M,D,O
Neurobiology — M,D,O
Nursing—General — D
Nutrition — M,D,O
Pharmacology — M,D,O
Pharmacy — M,D
Physician Assistant Studies — M,D
Physiology — M,D,O
Public Health—General — M,D,O
Toxicology — M,D,O

## UNIVERSITY OF ARKANSAS-FORT SMITH
Health Services Management and
  Hospital Administration — M

## UNIVERSITY OF BALTIMORE
Health Services Management and
  Hospital Administration — M

## UNIVERSITY OF BRIDGEPORT
Acupuncture and Oriental Medicine — M
Chiropractic — D
Dental Hygiene — M
Naturopathic Medicine — D
Nutrition — M
Physician Assistant Studies — M

## THE UNIVERSITY OF BRITISH COLUMBIA
Allopathic Medicine — M,D
Biochemistry — M,D
Biopsychology — M,D
Botany — M,D
Cell Biology — M,D
Communication Disorders — M,D
Dentistry — D
Developmental Biology — M,D
Genetics — M,D
Health Services Management and
  Hospital Administration — M,D
Immunology — M,D
Infectious Diseases — M,D
Microbiology — M,D
Molecular Biology — M,D
Neuroscience — M,D
Nursing—General — M,D
Nutrition — M,D
Occupational Therapy — M
Oral and Dental Sciences — M,D
Pathology — M,D
Pharmaceutical Sciences — M,D
Pharmacology — M,D
Pharmacy — M,D
Physical Therapy — M
Public Health—General — M,D

Plant Biology — M,D
Public Health—General — M,D
Rehabilitation Sciences — M,D
Vision Sciences — M,D

## THE UNIVERSITY OF ARIZONA
Allopathic Medicine — M,D
Biochemistry — M,D

Rehabilitation Sciences — M,D
Reproductive Biology — M,D
Zoology — M,D

## UNIVERSITY OF CALGARY
Allopathic Medicine — D
Biochemistry — M,D
Biological and Biomedical
  Sciences—General — M,D
Cancer Biology/Oncology — M,D
Cardiovascular Sciences — M,D
Community Health — M,D
Genetics — M,D
Immunology — M,D
Infectious Diseases — M,D
Microbiology — M,D
Molecular Biology — M,D
Molecular Genetics — M,D
Neuroscience — M,D
Nursing—General — M,D,O
Pathology — M,D
Physiology — M,D

## UNIVERSITY OF CALIFORNIA, BERKELEY
Allopathic Medicine —
Biochemistry — D
Biological and Biomedical
  Sciences—General — D
Biophysics — D
Cell Biology — D
Clinical Research — O
Environmental and Occupational
  Health — M,D
Epidemiology — M,D
Health Services Management and
  Hospital Administration — D
Immunology — M,D
Infectious Diseases — M,D
Microbiology — D
Molecular Biology — D
Molecular Toxicology — D
Neuroscience — D
Nutrition — M,D
Optometry — D,O
Physiology — M,D
Plant Biology — D
Public Health—General — M,D
Vision Sciences — M,D

## UNIVERSITY OF CALIFORNIA, DAVIS
Allopathic Medicine — D
Animal Behavior — D
Biochemistry — M,D
Biophysics — M,D
Cell Biology — M,D
Clinical Research — M
Developmental Biology — M,D
Ecology — M,D
Entomology — M,D
Epidemiology — M,D
Evolutionary Biology — D
Genetics — M,D
Immunology — M,D
Maternal and Child Health — M
Microbiology — M,D
Molecular Biology — M,D
Neuroscience — D
Nutrition — M,D
Pathology — M,D
Pharmacology — M,D
Physiology — M,D
Plant Biology — M,D
Plant Pathology — M,D
Toxicology — M,D
Veterinary Medicine — D
Veterinary Sciences — M,O
Zoology — M,D

## UNIVERSITY OF CALIFORNIA, IRVINE
Allopathic Medicine — D
Anatomy — M,D
Biochemistry — M,D
Biological and Biomedical
  Sciences—General — M,D
Biophysics — D
Cell Biology — M,D
Computational Biology — M,D
Developmental Biology — M,D
Ecology — M,D
Environmental and Occupational
  Health — M,D
Epidemiology — M,D
Evolutionary Biology — M,D
Genetics — D
Health Services Management and
  Hospital Administration — M
Medicinal and Pharmaceutical
  Chemistry — D
Microbiology — M,D
Molecular Biology — M,D
Molecular Genetics — M,D
Neurobiology — M,D
Neuroscience — D
Nursing—General — M
Pathology — D
Pharmaceutical Sciences — D
Physiology — D
Public Health—General — M,D
Systems Biology — D
Toxicology — M,D
Translational Biology — M

## UNIVERSITY OF CALIFORNIA, LOS ANGELES
Allopathic Medicine — D
Anatomy — M,D
Biochemistry — M,D
Biological and Biomedical
  Sciences—General — M,D
Cell Biology — M,D
Clinical Research — M
Community Health — M,D
Dentistry — D,O
Developmental Biology — M,D
Ecology — M,D

Environmental and Occupational
    Health — M,D
Epidemiology — M,D
Evolutionary Biology — M,D
Health Services Management and
    Hospital Administration — M,D
Human Genetics — M,D
Immunology — M,D
Medical Physics — M,D
Microbiology — M,D
Molecular Biology — M,D
Molecular Genetics — M,D
Molecular Pathology — D
Molecular Physiology — D
Molecular Toxicology — D
Neurobiology — M,D
Neuroscience — D
Nursing—General — M,D
Oral and Dental Sciences — M,D
Pathology — M,D
Pharmacology — M,D
Physiology — M,D
Public Health—General — M,D

### UNIVERSITY OF CALIFORNIA, MERCED
Biochemistry — M,D
Biological and Biomedical
    Sciences—General — M,D
Systems Biology — M,D

### UNIVERSITY OF CALIFORNIA, RIVERSIDE
Allopathic Medicine — D
Biochemistry — M,D
Biological and Biomedical
    Sciences—General — M,D
Botany — M,D
Cell Biology — M,D
Developmental Biology — M,D
Entomology — M,D
Evolutionary Biology — M,D
Genetics — D
Genomic Sciences — D
International Health — M,D
Microbiology — M,D
Molecular Biology — M,D
Neuroscience — D
Plant Biology — M,D
Plant Molecular Biology — M,D
Plant Pathology — M,D
Toxicology — M,D

### UNIVERSITY OF CALIFORNIA, SAN DIEGO
Allopathic Medicine — D
Biochemistry — M,D
Biological and Biomedical
    Sciences—General — M,D
Biophysics — M,D
Clinical Laboratory
    Sciences/Medical Technology — M,D
Clinical Research — M
Communication Disorders — D
Epidemiology — D
Health Services Management and
    Hospital Administration — M
International Health — D
Neuroscience — M,D
Pharmacy — D
Public Health—General — D
Systems Biology — D

### UNIVERSITY OF CALIFORNIA, SAN FRANCISCO
Allopathic Medicine — D
Biochemistry — D
Biological and Biomedical
    Sciences—General — D
Biophysics — D
Cell Biology — D
Dentistry — D
Developmental Biology — D
Genetics — D
Genomic Sciences — D
Medical Imaging — M
Medicinal and Pharmaceutical
    Chemistry — D
Molecular Biology — D
Neuroscience — D
Nursing—General — M,D
Oral and Dental Sciences — M,D
Pharmaceutical Sciences — D
Pharmacology — D
Pharmacy — D
Physical Therapy — D

### UNIVERSITY OF CALIFORNIA, SANTA BARBARA
Biochemistry — D
Biophysics — D
Cell Biology — M,D
Developmental Biology — M,D
Ecology — M,D
Evolutionary Biology — M,D
Marine Biology — M,D
Molecular Biology — M,D
Neuroscience — D

### UNIVERSITY OF CALIFORNIA, SANTA CRUZ
Biochemistry — M,D
Cell Biology — M,D
Developmental Biology — M,D
Ecology — M,D
Environmental Biology — M,D
Evolutionary Biology — M,D
Microbiology — M,D
Molecular Biology — M,D
Toxicology — M,D

### UNIVERSITY OF CENTRAL ARKANSAS
Adult Nursing — M,O

Biological and Biomedical
    Sciences—General — M
Communication Disorders — M,D
Family Nurse Practitioner Studies — M,O
Nursing and Healthcare
    Administration — M,O
Nursing Education — M,O
Nursing—General — M,O
Nutrition — M
Occupational Therapy — M
Physical Therapy — D

### UNIVERSITY OF CENTRAL FLORIDA
Allopathic Medicine — M,D
Biological and Biomedical
    Sciences—General — M,D,O
Communication Disorders — M,O
Conservation Biology — M,D,O
Health Services Management and
    Hospital Administration — M,O
Nursing—General — M,D,O
Physical Therapy — D
Physiology — M,O

### UNIVERSITY OF CENTRAL MISSOURI
Biological and Biomedical
    Sciences—General — M,D,O
Communication Disorders — M,D,O
Environmental and Occupational
    Health — M,D,O
Industrial Hygiene — M,D,O
Nursing—General — M,D,O

### UNIVERSITY OF CENTRAL OKLAHOMA
Biological and Biomedical
    Sciences—General — M
Communication Disorders — M
Health Promotion — M
Nursing—General — M
Nutrition — M

### UNIVERSITY OF CHARLESTON
Pharmacy — D
Physician Assistant Studies — M

### UNIVERSITY OF CHICAGO
Allopathic Medicine — D
Anatomy — D
Biological and Biomedical
    Sciences—General — D
Biophysics — D
Cancer Biology/Oncology — D
Cell Biology — D
Developmental Biology — D
Ecology — D
Evolutionary Biology — D
Genetics — D
Genomic Sciences — D
Health Promotion — M,D
Health Services Management and
    Hospital Administration — M,O
Human Genetics — D
Immunology — D
Medical Physics — D
Microbiology — D
Molecular Biology — D
Molecular Biophysics — D
Neurobiology — D
Neuroscience — D
Nutrition — D
Systems Biology — D

### UNIVERSITY OF CINCINNATI
Acute Care/Critical Care Nursing — M,D
Adult Nursing — M,D
Allopathic Medicine — D
Biochemistry — M,D
Biological and Biomedical
    Sciences—General — M,D,O
Biophysics — D
Cancer Biology/Oncology — D
Cell Biology — D
Communication Disorders — M,D
Developmental Biology — D
Environmental and Occupational
    Health — M,D
Epidemiology — M,D
Genomic Sciences — M,D
Gerontological Nursing — M,D
Health Physics/Radiological Health — M
Health Promotion — M
Health Services Research — M
Immunology — M,D
Industrial Hygiene — M,D
Maternal and Child/Neonatal
    Nursing — M,D
Medical Imaging — M,D
Medical Physics — M
Microbiology — M,D
Molecular Biology — M,D
Molecular Genetics — M,D
Molecular Medicine — D
Molecular Toxicology — M,D
Neuroscience — D
Nurse Anesthesia — M,D
Nurse Midwifery — M,D
Nursing and Healthcare
    Administration — M,D
Nursing—General — M,D
Nutrition — M,D
Occupational Health Nursing — M,D
Pathobiology — D
Pathology — D
Pediatric Nursing — M,D
Pharmaceutical Sciences — M,D
Pharmacology — D
Pharmacy — D
Physical Therapy — D
Public Health—General — M,D
Systems Biology — D
Women's Health Nursing — M,D

### UNIVERSITY OF COLORADO BOULDER
Biochemistry — M,D
Cell Biology — M,D
Communication Disorders — M,D
Developmental Biology — M,D
Ecology — M,D
Evolutionary Biology — M,D
Molecular Biology — M,D
Physiology — M,D

### UNIVERSITY OF COLORADO COLORADO SPRINGS
Adult Nursing — M,D
Gerontological Nursing — M,D
Nursing—General — M,D

### UNIVERSITY OF COLORADO DENVER
Adult Nursing — M,D
Allopathic Medicine — D
Anatomy — M,D
Anesthesiologist Assistant Studies — M
Biochemistry — D
Biological and Biomedical
    Sciences—General — M,D
Biophysics — M
Cancer Biology/Oncology — M,D
Cell Biology — M,D
Clinical Laboratory
    Sciences/Medical Technology — M,D
Clinical Research — M,D
Community Health — M,D,O
Computational Biology — M,D
Dentistry — D,O
Developmental Biology — M,D
Ecology — M
Environmental and Occupational
    Health — M,D
Epidemiology — M,D
Family Nurse Practitioner Studies — M,D
Genetics — D
Genomic Sciences — D
Health Services Management and
    Hospital Administration — M
Health Services Research — M,D
Immunology — D
International Health — M
Microbiology — D
Molecular Biology — D
Molecular Genetics — D
Neuroscience — D
Nurse Midwifery — M,D
Nursing and Healthcare
    Administration — M,D
Nursing—General — M,D
Oral and Dental Sciences — D,O
Pediatric Nursing — M,D
Pharmaceutical Sciences — D
Pharmacology — D
Pharmacy — D
Physical Therapy — D
Physician Assistant Studies — M
Psychiatric Nursing — M,D
Public Health—General — M,D
Rehabilitation Sciences — D
Systems Biology — M,D
Toxicology — D
Women's Health Nursing — M,D

### UNIVERSITY OF CONNECTICUT
Biophysics — M,D
Biopsychology — M,D
Botany — M,D
Cell Biology — M,D
Communication Disorders — M,D
Developmental Biology — M,D
Ecology — M,D
Environmental and Occupational
    Health — O
Family Nurse Practitioner Studies — M
Genetics — M,D
Genomic Sciences — M,D
Gerontological Nursing — M,O
Health Services Management and
    Hospital Administration — M,D
Maternal and Child/Neonatal
    Nursing — M,O
Medicinal and Pharmaceutical
    Chemistry — M,D
Microbiology — M,D
Molecular Biology — M,D
Neurobiology — M,D
Neuroscience — M,D
Nursing—General — M,D,O
Nutrition — M,D
Pathobiology — M,D
Pharmaceutical Sciences — M,D
Pharmacology — M,D
Pharmacy — D
Physical Therapy — D
Physiology — M,D
Structural Biology — M,D
Toxicology — M,D

### UNIVERSITY OF CONNECTICUT HEALTH CENTER
Allopathic Medicine — D
Anatomy — D
Biochemistry — D
Biological and Biomedical
    Sciences—General — D
Cell Biology — D
Clinical Research — M
Dentistry — D,O
Developmental Biology — D
Genetics — D
Immunology — D
Molecular Biology — D
Neuroscience — D
Oral and Dental Sciences — D
Public Health—General — M

### UNIVERSITY OF COLORADO BOULDER
### UNIVERSITY OF DALLAS
Health Services Management and
    Hospital Administration — M,D

### UNIVERSITY OF DAYTON
Biochemistry — M
Biological and Biomedical
    Sciences—General — M,D
Physical Therapy — D
Physician Assistant Studies — M

### UNIVERSITY OF DELAWARE
Adult Nursing — M,O
Biochemistry — M,D
Biological and Biomedical
    Sciences—General — M,D
Cancer Biology/Oncology — M,D
Cell Biology — M,D
Communication Disorders — M
Developmental Biology — M,D
Ecology — M,D
Entomology — M,D
Evolutionary Biology — M,D
Family Nurse Practitioner Studies — M,D
Genetics — M,D
Gerontological Nursing — M,D
Health Promotion — M
HIV/AIDS Nursing — M,O
Maternal and Child/Neonatal
    Nursing — M,O
Microbiology — M,D
Molecular Biology — M,D
Neuroscience — D
Nursing and Healthcare
    Administration — M,O
Nursing—General — M,O
Nutrition — M
Oncology Nursing — M,O
Pediatric Nursing — M,O
Physical Therapy — D
Physiology — M,D
Psychiatric Nursing — M,O
Women's Health Nursing — M,O

### UNIVERSITY OF DENVER
Biological and Biomedical
    Sciences—General — M,D
Cell Biology — M,D
Ecology — M,D
Evolutionary Biology — M,D
Health Services Management and
    Hospital Administration — M,O
International Health — M,D,O
Molecular Biology — M,D

### UNIVERSITY OF DETROIT MERCY
Allied Health—General — M,D,O
Dentistry — M,D,O
Family Nurse Practitioner Studies — M,D,O
Health Services Management and
    Hospital Administration — M,D,O
Nurse Anesthesia — M,D,O
Nursing Education — M,D,O
Nursing—General — M,D,O
Oral and Dental Sciences — M,D,O
Physician Assistant Studies — M,D,O

### UNIVERSITY OF EAST-WEST MEDICINE
Acupuncture and Oriental Medicine — M,D

### UNIVERSITY OF EVANSVILLE
Health Services Management and
    Hospital Administration — M
Physical Therapy — D

### THE UNIVERSITY OF FINDLAY
Health Services Management and
    Hospital Administration — M,D
Occupational Therapy — M,D
Pharmacy — M,D
Physical Therapy — M,D
Physician Assistant Studies — M,D

### UNIVERSITY OF FLORIDA
Allied Health—General — M,D,O
Allopathic Medicine — D
Biochemistry — D
Biological and Biomedical
    Sciences—General — M,D
Botany — M,D
Cell Biology — M,D
Clinical Laboratory
    Sciences/Medical Technology — M,D
Clinical Research — M,D,O
Communication Disorders — M,D
Dentistry — D,O
Ecology — M,D,O
Environmental and Occupational
    Health — M,D
Epidemiology — M,D,O
Genetics — D
Health Services Management and
    Hospital Administration — M,D
Health Services Research — M,D
Immunology — D
International Health — M,D
Medical Physics — M,D,O
Medicinal and Pharmaceutical
    Chemistry — M,D
Microbiology — M,D
Molecular Biology — M,D
Molecular Genetics — M
Neuroscience — D
Nursing—General — M,D
Nutrition — M,D
Occupational Therapy — M,D
Oral and Dental Sciences — M,D,O
Pharmaceutical Administration — M,D
Pharmaceutical Sciences — M,D
Pharmacology — M,D
Pharmacy — M,D
Physical Therapy — D
Physician Assistant Studies — M

---

*M—masters degree; D—doctorate; O—other advanced degree; *—Close-Up and/or Display*

Physiology M,D
Plant Biology M,D
Plant Molecular Biology M,D
Plant Pathology M,D
Public Health—General M,D,O
Rehabilitation Sciences D
Toxicology M,D,O
Veterinary Medicine D
Veterinary Sciences M,D,O
Zoology M,D

### UNIVERSITY OF GEORGIA
Biochemistry M,D
Biological and Biomedical Sciences—General D
Cell Biology M,D
Communication Disorders M,D,O
Ecology M,D
Entomology M,D
Environmental and Occupational Health M,D
Genetics M,D
Genomic Sciences M,D
Health Promotion M,D
Infectious Diseases D
Microbiology M,D
Molecular Biology M,D
Neuroscience D
Nutrition M,D
Pathology M,D
Pharmaceutical Administration D
Pharmaceutical Sciences M,D
Pharmacology M,D
Pharmacy M,D,O
Physiology M,D
Plant Biology M,D
Plant Pathology M,D
Public Health—General D
Veterinary Medicine M,D

### UNIVERSITY OF GUAM
Biological and Biomedical Sciences—General M
Marine Biology M

### UNIVERSITY OF GUELPH
Acute Care/Critical Care Nursing M,D,O
Anatomy M,D
Anesthesiologist Assistant Studies M,D,O
Biochemistry M,D
Biological and Biomedical Sciences—General M,D
Biophysics M,D
Botany M,D
Cardiovascular Sciences M,D,O
Cell Biology M,D
Ecology M,D
Emergency Medical Services M,D,O
Entomology M,D
Environmental Biology M,D
Epidemiology M,D
Evolutionary Biology M,D
Immunology M,D,O
Infectious Diseases M,D,O
Medical Imaging M,D,O
Microbiology M,D
Molecular Biology M,D
Molecular Genetics M,D
Neuroscience M,D,O
Nutrition M,D
Pathology M,D,O
Pharmacology M,D
Physiology M,D
Plant Pathology M,D
Toxicology M,D
Veterinary Medicine M,D,O
Veterinary Sciences M,D,O
Vision Sciences M,D,O
Zoology M,D

### UNIVERSITY OF HARTFORD
Community Health Nursing M
Neuroscience M
Nursing Education M
Nursing—General M
Physical Therapy M,D

### UNIVERSITY OF HAWAII AT HILO
Conservation Biology M
Marine Biology M
Nursing—General D
Pharmaceutical Sciences D
Pharmacology M
Pharmacy D

### UNIVERSITY OF HAWAII AT MANOA
Adult Nursing M,D,O
Allopathic Medicine D
Biological and Biomedical Sciences—General M,D
Botany M,D
Communication Disorders M
Community Health Nursing M,D,O
Developmental Biology M,D
Entomology M,D
Epidemiology D
Family Nurse Practitioner Studies M,D,O
Genetics M,D
Marine Biology M,D
Medical Microbiology M,D
Microbiology M,D
Molecular Biology M,D
Nursing and Healthcare Administration M,D,O
Nursing—General M,D,O
Nutrition M,D
Physiology M,D
Plant Pathology M,D
Public Health—General M,D,O
Reproductive Biology M,D
Zoology M,D

### UNIVERSITY OF HOLY CROSS
Biological and Biomedical Sciences—General M,D
Health Services Management and Hospital Administration M,D

### UNIVERSITY OF HOUSTON
Biochemistry M,D
Biological and Biomedical Sciences—General M,D
Communication Disorders M
Family Nurse Practitioner Studies M
Nursing and Healthcare Administration M
Nursing Education M
Nursing—General M
Nutrition M,D
Optometry D
Pharmaceutical Administration M,D
Pharmaceutical Sciences M,D
Pharmacology M,D
Pharmacy M,D
Vision Sciences M,D

### UNIVERSITY OF HOUSTON–CLEAR LAKE
Biological and Biomedical Sciences—General M
Health Services Management and Hospital Administration M

### UNIVERSITY OF HOUSTON–VICTORIA
Biological and Biomedical Sciences—General M

### UNIVERSITY OF IDAHO
Biochemistry M,D
Biological and Biomedical Sciences—General M,D
Computational Biology M,D
Entomology M,D
Microbiology M,D
Plant Pathology M,D
Veterinary Sciences M,D

### UNIVERSITY OF ILLINOIS AT CHICAGO
Acute Care/Critical Care Nursing M,O
Adult Nursing M,O
Allied Health—General M,D,O
Allopathic Medicine D
Anatomy M
Biochemistry D
Biological and Biomedical Sciences—General M,D
Biophysics M,D
Cell Biology M,D
Community Health Nursing M,O
Community Health M,D
Dentistry D
Environmental and Occupational Health M,D
Epidemiology M,D
Family Nurse Practitioner Studies M,O
Genetics D
Gerontological Nursing M,O
Health Services Management and Hospital Administration M,D
Health Services Research M,D
Immunology D
Maternal and Child/Neonatal Nursing M,O
Medicinal and Pharmaceutical Chemistry M,D
Microbiology D
Molecular Biology D
Molecular Genetics D
Neuroscience M,D
Nurse Midwifery M,O
Nursing and Healthcare Administration M,O
Nursing—General M,D,O
Nutrition M,D
Occupational Health Nursing M,O
Occupational Therapy M,D
Oral and Dental Sciences M,D
Pediatric Nursing M,O
Pharmaceutical Administration M,D
Pharmaceutical Sciences M,D
Pharmacology D
Pharmacy D
Physical Therapy M,D
Physiology M,D
Public Health—General M,D
School Nursing M,O
Toxicology M,D
Women's Health Nursing M,O

### UNIVERSITY OF ILLINOIS AT SPRINGFIELD
Biological and Biomedical Sciences—General M
Community Health M,O
Environmental and Occupational Health M,O
Epidemiology M,O
Public Health—General M,O

### UNIVERSITY OF ILLINOIS AT URBANA-CHAMPAIGN
Biochemistry M,D
Biological and Biomedical Sciences—General M,D
Biophysics M,D
Cell Biology D
Communication Disorders M,D
Community Health M,D
Computational Biology M,D
Conservation Biology M,D
Developmental Biology D
Ecology M,D
Entomology M,D
Evolutionary Biology M,D
Health Services Management and Hospital Administration M,D
Microbiology M,D
Molecular Physiology M,D
Neuroscience D
Nutrition M,D
Pathobiology M,D
Physiology M,D
Plant Biology M,D
Public Health—General M,D
Rehabilitation Sciences M,D
Veterinary Medicine D
Veterinary Sciences M,D
Zoology M,D

### UNIVERSITY OF INDIANAPOLIS
Biological and Biomedical Sciences—General M
Family Nurse Practitioner Studies M,D
Maternal and Child/Neonatal Nursing M,D
Nurse Midwifery M,D
Nursing and Healthcare Administration M,D
Nursing Education M,D
Nursing—General M,D
Occupational Therapy M,D
Physical Therapy M,D
Public Health—General M
Women's Health Nursing M,D

### THE UNIVERSITY OF IOWA
Allopathic Medicine D
Anatomy D
Bacteriology M,D
Biochemistry M,D
Biological and Biomedical Sciences—General M,D
Biophysics M,D
Cell Biology M,D
Clinical Research M,D
Communication Disorders M,D
Community Health M,D
Computational Biology M,D,O
Dentistry M,D,O
Environmental and Occupational Health M,D,O
Epidemiology M,D
Evolutionary Biology M,D
Genetics M,D
Health Services Management and Hospital Administration M,D
Immunology M,D
Industrial Hygiene M,D,O
Medicinal and Pharmaceutical Chemistry M,D
Microbiology M,D
Molecular Biology D
Neurobiology M,D
Neuroscience D
Nursing—General M,D
Oral and Dental Sciences M,D,O
Pathology M
Pharmaceutical Sciences M,D
Pharmacology M,D
Pharmacy M,D
Physical Therapy M,D
Physician Assistant Studies M
Physiology M,D
Public Health—General M,D,O
Radiation Biology M
Rehabilitation Sciences M,D
Toxicology M,D
Translational Biology M,D
Virology M,D

### UNIVERSITY OF JAMESTOWN
Physical Therapy D

### THE UNIVERSITY OF KANSAS
Adult Nursing M,D,O
Allied Health—General M,D,O
Allopathic Medicine D
Anatomy M,D
Biochemistry D
Biological and Biomedical Sciences—General D
Biophysics D
Cancer Biology/Oncology M,D
Cell Biology M,D
Clinical Research M
Communication Disorders M,D
Community Health Nursing M,D,O
Community Health M,D,O
Computational Biology D
Developmental Biology D
Ecology M,D
Epidemiology M
Evolutionary Biology M,D
Gerontological Nursing M,D,O
Health Promotion M,D,O
Medicinal and Pharmaceutical Chemistry M,D
Microbiology M,D
Molecular Biology D
Neuroscience M,D
Nurse Anesthesia D
Nurse Midwifery M,D,O
Nursing—General M,D,O
Nutrition M,D,O
Occupational Therapy M,D
Pathology M,D
Pharmacology M,D
Pharmacy M,D
Physical Therapy D
Physiology D
Psychiatric Nursing M,D,O
Public Health—General M
Rehabilitation Sciences M,D
Toxicology M,D

### UNIVERSITY OF KENTUCKY
Allied Health—General M,D
Allopathic Medicine D
Anatomy D
Biochemistry D
Biological and Biomedical Sciences—General M,D
Clinical Research M
Communication Disorders M
Dentistry D
Entomology M,D
Epidemiology D
Health Physics/Radiological Health M
Health Promotion M,D
Health Services Management and Hospital Administration M
Immunology D
Medical Physics M
Microbiology D
Neurobiology D
Nursing—General D
Nutrition M,D
Oral and Dental Sciences M
Pharmaceutical Sciences M,D
Pharmacology D
Pharmacy D
Physical Therapy D
Physician Assistant Studies M
Physiology D
Plant Pathology M,D
Public Health—General M,D
Rehabilitation Sciences D
Toxicology M,D
Veterinary Sciences M,D

### UNIVERSITY OF LA VERNE
Health Services Management and Hospital Administration M,D,O
Health Services Research M
Public Health—General M

### UNIVERSITY OF LETHBRIDGE
Biochemistry M,D
Biological and Biomedical Sciences—General M,D
Molecular Biology M,D
Neuroscience M,D
Nursing—General M,D

### UNIVERSITY OF LOUISIANA AT LAFAYETTE
Biological and Biomedical Sciences—General M,D
Communication Disorders M,D
Environmental Biology M,D
Evolutionary Biology M,D
Family Nurse Practitioner Studies M,D
Nursing and Healthcare Administration M
Nursing Education M,D
Nursing—General M,D

### UNIVERSITY OF LOUISIANA AT MONROE
Biological and Biomedical Sciences—General M
Communication Disorders M
Occupational Therapy M
Pharmacy D
Toxicology D

### UNIVERSITY OF LOUISVILLE
Allopathic Medicine D
Anatomy M,D
Biochemistry M,D
Bioethics M,D
Biological and Biomedical Sciences—General M,D
Communication Disorders M,D
Community Health M
Dentistry M,D
Environmental and Occupational Health M,D
Environmental Biology M,D
Epidemiology M,D
Family Nurse Practitioner Studies M,D
Gerontological Nursing M,D
Health Promotion D
Health Services Management and Hospital Administration M
Immunology M,D
Maternal and Child/Neonatal Nursing M,D
Microbiology M,D
Molecular Genetics M,D
Neurobiology M,D
Nursing and Healthcare Administration M,D
Nursing Education M,D
Nursing—General M,D
Oral and Dental Sciences M,D
Pharmacology M,D
Physiology M,D
Psychiatric Nursing M,D
Public Health—General M,D
Toxicology M,D
Women's Health Nursing M,D

### UNIVERSITY OF LYNCHBURG
Allopathic Medicine D
Health Promotion M
Physical Therapy D
Physician Assistant Studies M
Public Health—General M

### UNIVERSITY OF MAINE
Biological and Biomedical Sciences—General M,D
Botany M,D
Communication Disorders M
Entomology M,D
Family Nurse Practitioner Studies M,O
Microbiology M,D
Molecular Biology M,D
Nursing Education M,O
Nursing—General M,O
Plant Pathology M,D
Zoology M,D

### UNIVERSITY OF MANAGEMENT AND TECHNOLOGY
Health Services Management and Hospital Administration M

### THE UNIVERSITY OF MANCHESTER
Biochemistry M,D
Biological and Biomedical Sciences—General M,D
Biophysics M,D

Cancer Biology/Oncology — M,D
Cell Biology — M,D
Communication Disorders — M,D
Dentistry — M,D
Developmental Biology — M,D
Ecology — M,D
Environmental Biology — M,D
Evolutionary Biology — M,D
Genetics — M,D
Immunology — M,D
Microbiology — M,D
Molecular Biology — M,D
Molecular Genetics — M,D
Neurobiology — M,D
Neuroscience — M,D
Nurse Midwifery — M,D
Nursing—General — M,D
Optometry — M,D
Oral and Dental Sciences — M,D
Pharmaceutical Sciences — M,D
Pharmacology — M,D
Pharmacy — M,D
Physiology — M,D
Public Health—General — M,D
Structural Biology — M,D
Toxicology — M,D
Vision Sciences — M,D

## UNIVERSITY OF MANITOBA
Allopathic Medicine — M
Anatomy — M,D
Biochemistry — M,D
Biological and Biomedical Sciences—General — M,D,O
Botany — M,D
Cancer Biology/Oncology — M
Community Health — M,D,O
Dentistry — D
Ecology — M,D
Entomology — M,D
Human Genetics — M,D
Immunology — M,D
Infectious Diseases — M,D
Maternal and Child Health — M
Medical Microbiology — M,D
Microbiology — M,D
Nursing—General — M
Nutrition — M,D
Occupational Therapy — M,D
Oral and Dental Sciences — M,D
Pathology — M
Pharmaceutical Sciences — M,D
Pharmacology — M,D
Physical Therapy — M,D
Physiology — M,D
Plant Physiology — M,D
Rehabilitation Sciences — M,D
Zoology — M,D

## UNIVERSITY OF MARY
Bioethics — M
Cardiovascular Sciences — M
Communication Disorders — M
Family Nurse Practitioner Studies — M,D
Health Services Management and Hospital Administration — M
Nursing and Healthcare Administration — M,D
Nursing Education — M,D
Nursing—General — M,D
Occupational Therapy — M
Physical Therapy — D

## UNIVERSITY OF MARY HARDIN-BAYLOR
Family Nurse Practitioner Studies — M,D,O
Nursing Education — M,D,O
Nursing—General — M,D,O
Physical Therapy — D

## UNIVERSITY OF MARYLAND, BALTIMORE
Allied Health—General — M
Allopathic Medicine — D
Biochemistry — M,D
Biological and Biomedical Sciences—General — M,D,O
Cancer Biology/Oncology — D
Cell Biology — M,D
Clinical Laboratory Sciences/Medical Technology — M
Clinical Research — M,D,O
Community Health Nursing — M
Dentistry — D,O
Epidemiology — M,D,O
Family Nurse Practitioner Studies — M,D,O
Genomic Sciences — M,D
Gerontological Nursing — M,D,O
Health Services Research — M,D
Human Genetics — M,D
Immunology — D
International Health — M,D,O
Maternal and Child/Neonatal Nursing — M,D,O
Microbiology — D
Molecular Biology — M,D
Molecular Medicine — D
Molecular Pharmacology — D
Molecular Toxicology — D
Neurobiology — D
Neuroscience — D
Nurse Anesthesia — M,D,O
Nursing and Healthcare Administration — M,D,O
Nursing Education — M,D,O
Nursing Informatics — M,D,O
Nursing—General — M,D,O
Oral and Dental Sciences — M,D,O
Pathology — M
Pediatric Nursing — M,D
Pharmaceutical Administration — M,D
Pharmaceutical Sciences — D

Pharmacology — M
Pharmacy — M,D
Physical Therapy — D
Psychiatric Nursing — M,D,O
Rehabilitation Sciences — D
Toxicology — M,D

## UNIVERSITY OF MARYLAND, BALTIMORE COUNTY
Biological and Biomedical Sciences—General — M,D
Cell Biology — D
Epidemiology — M,D,O
Health Services Management and Hospital Administration — M,D,O
Molecular Biology — M,D
Neuroscience — D

## UNIVERSITY OF MARYLAND, COLLEGE PARK
Biochemistry — M,D
Biological and Biomedical Sciences—General — M,D
Biophysics — D
Cell Biology — M,D
Communication Disorders — M,D
Computational Biology — D
Conservation Biology — M
Ecology — M,D
Entomology — M,D
Environmental and Occupational Health — M
Epidemiology — M,D
Evolutionary Biology — M,D
Genomic Sciences — D
Health Services Management and Hospital Administration — M,D
Maternal and Child Health — M,D
Molecular Biology — D
Molecular Genetics — M,D
Neuroscience — M,D
Nutrition — M,D
Plant Biology — M,D
Public Health—General — M,D
Veterinary Medicine — D
Veterinary Sciences — M,D

## UNIVERSITY OF MARYLAND EASTERN SHORE
Pharmaceutical Sciences — M,D
Pharmacy — M,D
Physical Therapy — D
Rehabilitation Sciences — M
Toxicology — M,D

## UNIVERSITY OF MARYLAND GLOBAL CAMPUS
Health Services Management and Hospital Administration — M

## UNIVERSITY OF MASSACHUSETTS AMHERST
Adult Nursing — M,D
Animal Behavior — M,D
Biochemistry — M,D
Biological and Biomedical Sciences—General — M,D
Cell Biology — M,D
Communication Disorders — M,D
Community Health Nursing — M,D
Community Health — M,D
Developmental Biology — D
Environmental and Occupational Health — M,D
Environmental Biology — M,D
Epidemiology — M,D
Evolutionary Biology — M,D
Family Nurse Practitioner Studies — M,D
Genetics — M,D
Gerontological Nursing — M,D
Health Services Management and Hospital Administration — M,D
Microbiology — M,D
Molecular Biophysics — D
Neuroscience — M,D
Nursing and Healthcare Administration — M,D
Nursing—General — M,D
Nutrition — M,D
Physiology — M,D
Plant Biology — M,D
Plant Molecular Biology — M,D
Plant Physiology — M,D
Public Health—General — M,D

## UNIVERSITY OF MASSACHUSETTS BOSTON
Biological and Biomedical Sciences—General — M,D
Nursing—General — M,D
Vision Sciences — M

## UNIVERSITY OF MASSACHUSETTS DARTMOUTH
Biochemistry — M,D
Biological and Biomedical Sciences—General — M,D
Community Health Nursing — M,D
Health Services Management and Hospital Administration — M
Marine Biology — M,D
Nursing—General — M,D

## UNIVERSITY OF MASSACHUSETTS LOWELL
Allied Health—General — M,D
Biochemistry — M,D
Biological and Biomedical Sciences—General — M,D
Clinical Laboratory Sciences/Medical Technology — M
Family Nurse Practitioner Studies — M
Gerontological Nursing — M

## UNIVERSITY OF MASSACHUSETTS MEDICAL SCHOOL
Adult Nursing — M,D,O
Allopathic Medicine — D
Biochemistry — M,D
Biological and Biomedical Sciences—General — M,D
Cancer Biology/Oncology — M,D
Clinical Research — M,D
Computational Biology — M,D
Family Nurse Practitioner Studies — M,D,O
Gerontological Nursing — M,D,O
Health Services Research — M,D
Immunology — M,D
Microbiology — M,D
Molecular Pharmacology — M,D
Neuroscience — M,D
Nursing and Healthcare Administration — M,D,O
Nursing Education — M,D,O
Nursing—General — M,D,O
Translational Biology — M,D

## UNIVERSITY OF MEMPHIS
Allied Health—General — M,D
Biological and Biomedical Sciences—General — M,D
Communication Disorders — M,D
Environmental and Occupational Health — M,D
Epidemiology — M,O
Family Nurse Practitioner Studies — M,D
Health Promotion — M,O
Health Services Management and Hospital Administration — M,D
Nursing and Healthcare Administration — M,O
Nursing Education — M,O
Nursing—General — M,O
Nutrition — M,O
Public Health—General — M,D

## UNIVERSITY OF MIAMI
Acute Care/Critical Care Nursing — M,D
Adult Nursing — M,D
Allopathic Medicine — D
Biochemistry — D
Biological and Biomedical Sciences—General — M,D
Biophysics — D
Cancer Biology/Oncology — D
Cell Biology — D
Community Health — M,D
Developmental Biology — D
Environmental and Occupational Health — M
Epidemiology — M,D
Evolutionary Biology — M,D
Family Nurse Practitioner Studies — M,D
Genetics — M,D
Health Services Management and Hospital Administration — M,D
Immunology — D
Marine Biology — M,D
Microbiology — D
Molecular Biology — D
Neuroscience — M,D
Nurse Anesthesia — M,D
Nurse Midwifery — M,D
Nursing—General — M,D
Nutrition — M
Pharmacology — D
Physical Therapy — D
Physiology — D
Public Health—General — M,D

## UNIVERSITY OF MICHIGAN
Allopathic Medicine — D
Biochemistry — M,D
Biological and Biomedical Sciences—General — M,D
Biophysics — D
Biopsychology — D
Cancer Biology/Oncology — M,D
Cell Biology — M,D
Clinical Research — M
Dental Hygiene — M
Dentistry — D
Developmental Biology — M,D
Ecology — M,D
Environmental and Occupational Health — M,D
Epidemiology — M,D
Evolutionary Biology — M,D
Health Physics/Radiological Health — M,D,O
Health Promotion — M,D
Health Services Management and Hospital Administration — M,D
Human Genetics — M,D
Immunology — M,D
Industrial Hygiene — M,D
International Health — M,D
Medicinal and Pharmaceutical Chemistry — D
Microbiology — M,D
Molecular Biology — M,D
Molecular Pathology — M,D
Neuroscience — D
Nursing—General — M,D,O
Nutrition — M,D
Oral and Dental Sciences — M,D
Pathology — D
Pediatric Nursing — M,D
Pharmaceutical Administration — D
Pharmaceutical Sciences — D
Pharmacology — M,D
Pharmacy — D

Health Physics/Radiological Health — M
Health Promotion — D
Nursing—General — M,D
Physical Therapy — D

## UNIVERSITY OF MICHIGAN–FLINT
Biological and Biomedical Sciences—General — M,D,O
Family Nurse Practitioner Studies — M,D,O
Health Services Management and Hospital Administration — M,O
Neuroscience — D,O
Nurse Anesthesia — M,D,O
Nursing—General — M,D,O
Physical Therapy — D,O
Psychiatric Nursing — M,D,O
Public Health—General — M

## UNIVERSITY OF MINNESOTA, DULUTH
Allopathic Medicine — D
Biochemistry — M,D
Biological and Biomedical Sciences—General — M,D
Biophysics — M,D
Communication Disorders — M
Immunology — M,D
Medical Microbiology — M,D
Molecular Biology — M,D
Pharmacology — M,D
Pharmacy — M,D
Physiology — M,D
Toxicology — M,D

## UNIVERSITY OF MINNESOTA ROCHESTER
Computational Biology — M,D
Occupational Therapy — M,D

## UNIVERSITY OF MINNESOTA, TWIN CITIES CAMPUS
Allopathic Medicine — M,D
Animal Behavior — M,D
Biochemistry — D
Biological and Biomedical Sciences—General — M
Biophysics — M,D
Biopsychology — D
Cancer Biology/Oncology — D
Cell Biology — M,D
Clinical Laboratory Sciences/Medical Technology — M
Clinical Research — M
Communication Disorders — M,D
Community Health — M
Conservation Biology — M,D
Dentistry — D
Developmental Biology — M,D
Ecology — M,D
Entomology — M,D
Environmental and Occupational Health — M,D,O
Epidemiology — M,D
Evolutionary Biology — M,D
Family Nurse Practitioner Studies — M,D
Genetics — M,D
Gerontological Nursing — M,D
Health Services Management and Hospital Administration — M,D
Health Services Research — M,D
Immunology — D
Industrial Hygiene — M,D
Infectious Diseases — M,D
International Health — M
Maternal and Child Health — M
Medical Physics — M,D
Medicinal and Pharmaceutical Chemistry — M,D
Microbiology — D
Molecular Biology — M,D
Neurobiology — M,D
Neuroscience — M,D
Nurse Anesthesia — M,D
Nurse Midwifery — M,D
Nursing and Healthcare Administration — M,D
Nursing Informatics — M,D
Nursing—General — M,D
Nutrition — M,D
Occupational Health Nursing — M,D
Occupational Therapy — M
Oral and Dental Sciences — M,D,O
Pediatric Nursing — M,D
Pharmaceutical Administration — M,D
Pharmaceutical Sciences — M,D
Pharmacology — M,D
Pharmacy — M,D
Physical Therapy — M,D
Physiology — D
Plant Biology — M,D
Plant Pathology — M,D
Psychiatric Nursing — M,D
Public Health—General — M,D,O
Structural Biology — D
Toxicology — M,D
Veterinary Medicine — D
Veterinary Sciences — M,D
Virology — D
Women's Health Nursing — M,D

Physiology — M,D
Public Health—General — M,D
Toxicology — M,D

## UNIVERSITY OF MISSISSIPPI
Biological and Biomedical Sciences—General — M,D
Communication Disorders — M,D
Health Promotion — M,D
Medicinal and Pharmaceutical Chemistry — M,D
Nutrition — M,D
Pharmaceutical Administration — M,D
Pharmaceutical Sciences — M,D
Pharmacology — M,D
Pharmacy — M,D
Toxicology — M,D

---

M—masters degree; D—doctorate; O—other advanced degree; *—Close-Up and/or Display

**UNIVERSITY OF MISSISSIPPI MEDICAL CENTER**

| | |
|---|---|
| Allied Health—General | M |
| Allopathic Medicine | D |
| Anatomy | M,D |
| Biochemistry | D |
| Biological and Biomedical Sciences—General | M,D |
| Biophysics | D |
| Dentistry | M,D |
| Microbiology | D |
| Neuroscience | D |
| Nursing—General | M,D |
| Occupational Therapy | M |
| Oral and Dental Sciences | M,D |
| Pathology | D |
| Pharmacology | D |
| Physical Therapy | M |
| Physiology | D |
| Toxicology | D |

**UNIVERSITY OF MISSOURI**

| | |
|---|---|
| Adult Nursing | M,D,O |
| Allopathic Medicine | D |
| Anatomy | M,D |
| Biochemistry | M,D |
| Biological and Biomedical Sciences—General | M,D,O |
| Communication Disorders | M,D |
| Conservation Biology | M,D,O |
| Ecology | M,D |
| Entomology | M,D |
| Evolutionary Biology | M,D |
| Family Nurse Practitioner Studies | M,D,O |
| Gerontological Nursing | M,D,O |
| Health Physics/Radiological Health | M |
| Health Promotion | M,O |
| Health Services Management and Hospital Administration | M,O |
| Immunology | D |
| International Health | M,O |
| Microbiology | D |
| Neuroscience | M,D,O |
| Nursing and Healthcare Administration | M,D,O |
| Nursing—General | M,D,O |
| Nutrition | M,D |
| Pathobiology | M,D |
| Pathology | M,D |
| Pediatric Nursing | M,D,O |
| Pharmacology | M,D |
| Physiology | M,D |
| Plant Biology | M,D |
| Psychiatric Nursing | M,D,O |
| Public Health—General | M,O |
| Veterinary Medicine | M,D |
| Veterinary Sciences | M |

**UNIVERSITY OF MISSOURI–KANSAS CITY**

| | |
|---|---|
| Adult Nursing | M,D |
| Allopathic Medicine | M,D |
| Biochemistry | D |
| Biological and Biomedical Sciences—General | M,D |
| Biophysics | D |
| Cell Biology | D |
| Dental Hygiene | M,D,O |
| Dentistry | M,D,O |
| Family Nurse Practitioner Studies | M,D |
| Gerontological Nursing | M,D |
| Maternal and Child/Neonatal Nursing | M,D |
| Molecular Biology | D |
| Nursing and Healthcare Administration | M,D |
| Nursing Education | M,D |
| Nursing—General | M,D |
| Oral and Dental Sciences | M,D,O |
| Pediatric Nursing | M,D |
| Pharmacy | D |
| Women's Health Nursing | M,D |

**UNIVERSITY OF MISSOURI–ST. LOUIS**

| | |
|---|---|
| Adult Nursing | D,O |
| Biochemistry | M,D |
| Biological and Biomedical Sciences—General | M,D,O |
| Family Nurse Practitioner Studies | D,O |
| Gerontological Nursing | D,O |
| Neuroscience | M,D,O |
| Nursing—General | D,O |
| Pediatric Nursing | D,O |
| Psychiatric Nursing | D,O |
| Women's Health Nursing | D,O |

**UNIVERSITY OF MOBILE**

| | |
|---|---|
| Nursing and Healthcare Administration | M,D |
| Nursing Education | M,D |
| Nursing—General | M,D |

**UNIVERSITY OF MONTANA**

| | |
|---|---|
| Animal Behavior | M,D,O |
| Biochemistry | D |
| Biological and Biomedical Sciences—General | M,D |
| Cell Biology | D |
| Communication Disorders | M,O |
| Community Health | M |
| Developmental Biology | D |
| Ecology | M,D |
| Immunology | D |
| Medicinal and Pharmaceutical Chemistry | M,D |
| Microbiology | D |
| Molecular Biology | D |
| Neuroscience | M,D |
| Pharmaceutical Sciences | M,D |
| Pharmacy | M,D |
| Physical Therapy | D |
| Public Health—General | M,O |
| Toxicology | M,D |
| Zoology | M,D |

**UNIVERSITY OF MONTEVALLO**

| | |
|---|---|
| Communication Disorders | M |

**UNIVERSITY OF MOUNT OLIVE**

| | |
|---|---|
| Nursing—General | M |

**UNIVERSITY OF MOUNT UNION**

| | |
|---|---|
| Physical Therapy | D |
| Physician Assistant Studies | M |

**UNIVERSITY OF NEBRASKA AT KEARNEY**

| | |
|---|---|
| Biological and Biomedical Sciences—General | M |
| Communication Disorders | M |

**UNIVERSITY OF NEBRASKA AT OMAHA**

| | |
|---|---|
| Biological and Biomedical Sciences—General | M,O |
| Communication Disorders | M |

**UNIVERSITY OF NEBRASKA–LINCOLN**

| | |
|---|---|
| Biochemistry | M,D |
| Biological and Biomedical Sciences—General | M,D |
| Biopsychology | M,D |
| Communication Disorders | M,D |
| Entomology | M,D |
| Health Promotion | M,D |
| Nutrition | M,D |
| Toxicology | M,D |
| Veterinary Sciences | M,D |

**UNIVERSITY OF NEBRASKA MEDICAL CENTER**

| | |
|---|---|
| Allied Health—General | M,D,O |
| Allopathic Medicine | D,O |
| Anatomy | M,D |
| Biochemistry | M |
| Biological and Biomedical Sciences—General | M,D |
| Cancer Biology/Oncology | D |
| Cell Biology | M,D |
| Clinical Laboratory Sciences/Medical Technology | M,O |
| Dentistry | M,D,O |
| Environmental and Occupational Health | D |
| Epidemiology | D |
| Genetics | M,D |
| Health Promotion | D |
| Health Services Management and Hospital Administration | M,D |
| Health Services Research | M,D |
| Immunology | M,D |
| Infectious Diseases | M,D |
| Molecular Biology | M |
| Molecular Genetics | M,D |
| Molecular Medicine | D |
| Neuroscience | D |
| Nursing—General | D |
| Nutrition | O |
| Oral and Dental Sciences | M,D |
| Pathology | M,D |
| Perfusion | M |
| Pharmaceutical Sciences | M,D |
| Pharmacology | D |
| Pharmacy | D |
| Physical Therapy | D |
| Physician Assistant Studies | M |
| Physiology | D |
| Public Health—General | M |
| Toxicology | D |

**UNIVERSITY OF NEVADA, LAS VEGAS**

| | |
|---|---|
| Allied Health—General | M,D,O |
| Biochemistry | M,D |
| Biological and Biomedical Sciences—General | M,D |
| Community Health | M,D,O |
| Dentistry | M,D,O |
| Family Nurse Practitioner Studies | M,D,O |
| Health Physics/Radiological Health | M,D,O |
| Health Services Management and Hospital Administration | M |
| Nursing Education | M,D,O |
| Nursing—General | M,D,O |
| Nutrition | M,D |
| Oral and Dental Sciences | M,D,O |
| Physical Therapy | D |
| Public Health—General | M,D,O |

**UNIVERSITY OF NEVADA, RENO**

| | |
|---|---|
| Allopathic Medicine | D |
| Biochemistry | M,D |
| Biological and Biomedical Sciences—General | M |
| Cell Biology | M,D |
| Communication Disorders | M,D |
| Conservation Biology | D |
| Ecology | D |
| Environmental and Occupational Health | M,D |
| Evolutionary Biology | D |
| Molecular Biology | M,D |
| Molecular Pharmacology | D |
| Nursing—General | M,D |
| Nutrition | M |
| Physiology | D |
| Public Health—General | M,D |

**UNIVERSITY OF NEW BRUNSWICK SAINT JOHN**

| | |
|---|---|
| Biological and Biomedical Sciences—General | M,D |

**UNIVERSITY OF NEW ENGLAND**

| | |
|---|---|
| Biological and Biomedical Sciences—General | M |
| Dentistry | D |
| Health Services Management and Hospital Administration | M,D,O |
| Nurse Anesthesia | M,D |
| Nutrition | M,D,O |
| Occupational Therapy | M,D |
| Osteopathic Medicine | D |
| Pharmacy | D |
| Physical Therapy | M,D |
| Physician Assistant Studies | M,D |
| Public Health—General | M,D,O |

**UNIVERSITY OF NEW HAMPSHIRE**

| | |
|---|---|
| Biochemistry | M,D |
| Biological and Biomedical Sciences—General | M,D |
| Communication Disorders | M |
| Conservation Biology | M |
| Evolutionary Biology | D |
| Family Nurse Practitioner Studies | M,D,O |
| Genetics | M,D |
| Marine Biology | M,D |
| Microbiology | M,D |
| Nursing—General | M,D,O |
| Nutrition | M,D |
| Occupational Therapy | M,O |
| Psychiatric Nursing | M,D,O |
| Public Health—General | M,O |

**UNIVERSITY OF NEW HAVEN**

| | |
|---|---|
| Cell Biology | M |
| Ecology | M |
| Environmental and Occupational Health | M |
| Molecular Biology | M |

**UNIVERSITY OF NEW MEXICO**

| | |
|---|---|
| Allied Health—General | M,D,O |
| Allopathic Medicine | D |
| Biochemistry | M,D |
| Biological and Biomedical Sciences—General | M,D |
| Cell Biology | M,D |
| Clinical Laboratory Sciences/Medical Technology | M,O |
| Communication Disorders | M |
| Community Health | M |
| Dental Hygiene | M |
| Epidemiology | M |
| Genetics | M,D |
| Health Services Management and Hospital Administration | M |
| Microbiology | M,D |
| Molecular Biology | M,D |
| Neuroscience | M,D |
| Nursing—General | M,D |
| Nutrition | M |
| Occupational Therapy | M |
| Pathology | M,D |
| Pharmaceutical Sciences | M,D |
| Pharmacy | D |
| Physical Therapy | D |
| Physician Assistant Studies | M |
| Physiology | M,D |
| Public Health—General | M |
| Toxicology | M,D |

**UNIVERSITY OF NEW ORLEANS**

| | |
|---|---|
| Biological and Biomedical Sciences—General | M |
| Health Services Management and Hospital Administration | M |

**UNIVERSITY OF NORTH ALABAMA**

| | |
|---|---|
| Health Promotion | M |
| Health Services Management and Hospital Administration | M |
| Nursing—General | M |

**THE UNIVERSITY OF NORTH CAROLINA AT CHAPEL HILL**

| | |
|---|---|
| Adult Nursing | M,D,O |
| Allopathic Medicine | D |
| Biochemistry | M,D |
| Biological and Biomedical Sciences—General | M,D |
| Biophysics | M,D |
| Biopsychology | D |
| Botany | M,D |
| Cell Biology | M,D |
| Clinical Research | M,D |
| Computational Biology | D |
| Dental Hygiene | M,D |
| Dentistry | D |
| Developmental Biology | M,D |
| Ecology | M,D |
| Environmental and Occupational Health | M,D |
| Epidemiology | M,D |
| Evolutionary Biology | M,D |
| Family Nurse Practitioner Studies | M,D,O |
| Genetics | M,D |
| Gerontological Nursing | M,D,O |
| Health Promotion | M |
| Health Services Management and Hospital Administration | M,D |
| Immunology | M,D |
| Maternal and Child Health | M,D |
| Microbiology | M,D |
| Molecular Biology | M,D |
| Molecular Physiology | D |
| Neurobiology | D |
| Neuroscience | D |
| Nursing and Healthcare Administration | M,D,O |
| Nursing Education | M,D,O |
| Nursing Informatics | M,D,O |
| Nursing—General | M,D,O |
| Nutrition | M,D |
| Occupational Health Nursing | M |
| Oral and Dental Sciences | M,D |
| Pathology | D |
| Pediatric Nursing | M,D,O |
| Pharmaceutical Administration | M,D |
| Pharmaceutical Sciences | M,D |
| Pharmacology | D |
| Pharmacy | M,D |
| Psychiatric Nursing | M,D,O |
| Public Health—General | M,D |
| Toxicology | M,D |

**THE UNIVERSITY OF NORTH CAROLINA AT CHARLOTTE**

| | |
|---|---|
| Acute Care/Critical Care Nursing | M,D,O |
| Biological and Biomedical Sciences—General | M,D |
| Community Health | M,D,O |
| Family Nurse Practitioner Studies | M,D,O |
| Gerontological Nursing | M,D,O |
| Health Services Management and Hospital Administration | M,D,O |
| Health Services Research | D |
| Nurse Anesthesia | M,D,O |
| Nursing and Healthcare Administration | M,D,O |
| Nursing Education | M,D,O |
| Nursing—General | M,D,O |
| Public Health—General | M,D,O |

**THE UNIVERSITY OF NORTH CAROLINA AT GREENSBORO**

| | |
|---|---|
| Adult Nursing | M,D,O |
| Biochemistry | M |
| Biological and Biomedical Sciences—General | M |
| Communication Disorders | M,D |
| Community Health | M,D |
| Gerontological Nursing | M,D,O |
| Nurse Anesthesia | M,D,O |
| Nursing and Healthcare Administration | M,D,O |
| Nursing Education | M,D,O |
| Nursing—General | M,D,O |
| Nutrition | M,D |

**THE UNIVERSITY OF NORTH CAROLINA AT PEMBROKE**

| | |
|---|---|
| Health Services Management and Hospital Administration | M |
| Nursing and Healthcare Administration | M |
| Nursing Education | M |
| Nursing—General | M |

**THE UNIVERSITY OF NORTH CAROLINA WILMINGTON**

| | |
|---|---|
| Biological and Biomedical Sciences—General | M,D |
| Clinical Research | M,D,O |
| Family Nurse Practitioner Studies | M,D,O |
| Marine Biology | M,D |
| Nursing Education | M,D,O |
| Nursing—General | M,D,O |

**UNIVERSITY OF NORTH DAKOTA**

| | |
|---|---|
| Biological and Biomedical Sciences—General | M,D |
| Clinical Laboratory Sciences/Medical Technology | M,D |
| Communication Disorders | M |
| Community Health Nursing | M,D,O |
| Family Nurse Practitioner Studies | M,D,O |
| Genetics | M,D |
| Gerontological Nursing | M,D,O |
| Nurse Anesthesia | M,D,O |
| Nursing Education | M,D,O |
| Nursing—General | M,D,O |
| Occupational Therapy | M |
| Physical Therapy | D |
| Physician Assistant Studies | M |
| Psychiatric Nursing | M,D,O |
| Public Health—General | M |
| Zoology | M,D |

**UNIVERSITY OF NORTHERN BRITISH COLUMBIA**

| | |
|---|---|
| Community Health | M,D,O |

**UNIVERSITY OF NORTHERN COLORADO**

| | |
|---|---|
| Acute Care/Critical Care Nursing | M,D |
| Biological and Biomedical Sciences—General | M |
| Communication Disorders | M,D |
| Community Health | M |
| Family Nurse Practitioner Studies | M,D |
| Health Services Management and Hospital Administration | M |
| International Health | M |
| Nursing Education | M,D |
| Nursing—General | M,D |
| Public Health—General | M |
| Rehabilitation Sciences | M,D |

**UNIVERSITY OF NORTHERN IOWA**

| | |
|---|---|
| Allied Health—General | M,D |
| Biological and Biomedical Sciences—General | M |
| Communication Disorders | M |
| Community Health | M |
| Health Promotion | M |

**UNIVERSITY OF NORTH FLORIDA**

| | |
|---|---|
| Allied Health—General | M,D,O |
| Biological and Biomedical Sciences—General | M |
| Communication Disorders | M |
| Community Health | M,O |
| Family Nurse Practitioner Studies | M,D,O |
| Health Services Management and Hospital Administration | M |
| Nurse Anesthesia | M,D,O |
| Nursing—General | M,D,O |
| Nutrition | M |
| Physical Therapy | M,D |
| Public Health—General | M,O |

**UNIVERSITY OF NORTH GEORGIA**

| | |
|---|---|
| Family Nurse Practitioner Studies | M,O |
| Nursing Education | M |
| Physical Therapy | D |

**UNIVERSITY OF NORTH TEXAS**

| | |
|---|---|
| Biochemistry | M,D,O |
| Biological and Biomedical Sciences—General | M,D,O |
| Communication Disorders | M,D,O |
| Health Services Management and Hospital Administration | M,D,O |
| Molecular Biology | M,D,O |

**UNIVERSITY OF NORTH TEXAS HEALTH SCIENCE CENTER AT FORT WORTH**

| | |
|---|---|
| Anatomy | M,D |
| Biochemistry | M,D |
| Biological and Biomedical Sciences—General | M,D |
| Cancer Biology/Oncology | M,D |
| Epidemiology | M,D,O |
| Genetics | M,D |
| Health Services Management and Hospital Administration | M,D,O |
| Health Services Research | M,D,O |
| Immunology | M,D |
| International Health | M,D,O |
| Microbiology | M,D |
| Neuroscience | M,D |
| Osteopathic Medicine | D |
| Pharmaceutical Sciences | M,D |
| Pharmacology | M,D |
| Physical Therapy | M,D |
| Physician Assistant Studies | M,D |
| Physiology | M,D |
| Public Health—General | M,D,O |
| Rehabilitation Sciences | M,D |

**UNIVERSITY OF NOTRE DAME**

| | |
|---|---|
| Biochemistry | M,D |
| Biological and Biomedical Sciences—General | M,D |
| Cell Biology | M,D |
| Ecology | M,D |
| Evolutionary Biology | M,D |
| Genetics | M,D |
| Molecular Biology | M,D |
| Parasitology | M,D |
| Physiology | M,D |

**UNIVERSITY OF OKLAHOMA**

| | |
|---|---|
| Biochemistry | M,D |
| Ecology | M,D |
| Evolutionary Biology | M,D |
| Health Promotion | M,D |
| Health Services Management and Hospital Administration | M,O |
| Microbiology | M,D |
| Neurobiology | M,D |
| Plant Biology | M,D |
| Structural Biology | M,D |

**UNIVERSITY OF OKLAHOMA HEALTH SCIENCES CENTER**

| | |
|---|---|
| Allied Health—General | M,D,O |
| Allopathic Medicine | D |
| Biochemistry | M,D |
| Biological and Biomedical Sciences—General | M,D |
| Biopsychology | M,D |
| Cell Biology | M,D |
| Communication Disorders | M,D,O |
| Dentistry | D,O |
| Environmental and Occupational Health | M,D |
| Epidemiology | M,D |
| Health Physics/Radiological Health | M,D |
| Health Promotion | M,D |
| Health Services Management and Hospital Administration | M,D |
| Immunology | M,D |
| Medical Physics | M,D |
| Microbiology | M,D |
| Molecular Biology | M,D |
| Neuroscience | M,D |
| Nursing—General | M |
| Nutrition | M |
| Occupational Therapy | M |
| Oral and Dental Sciences | M |
| Pathology | D |
| Pharmaceutical Sciences | M,D |
| Pharmacy | D |
| Physical Therapy | M |
| Physician Assistant Studies | M |
| Physiology | M,D |
| Public Health—General | M,D |
| Radiation Biology | M,D |
| Rehabilitation Sciences | M |

**UNIVERSITY OF OREGON**

| | |
|---|---|
| Biochemistry | M,D |
| Biological and Biomedical Sciences—General | M,D |
| Biopsychology | M,D |
| Communication Disorders | M,D |
| Ecology | M,D |
| Evolutionary Biology | M,D |
| Genetics | M,D |
| Marine Biology | M,D |
| Molecular Biology | M,D |
| Neuroscience | M,D |
| Physiology | M,D |

**UNIVERSITY OF OTTAWA**

| | |
|---|---|
| Allopathic Medicine | M,D |
| Biochemistry | M,D |
| Biological and Biomedical Sciences—General | M,D |
| Cell Biology | M,D |
| Communication Disorders | M |
| Community Health | D,O |
| Epidemiology | M |
| Health Services Management and Hospital Administration | M |
| Health Services Research | D,O |
| Immunology | M,D |
| Microbiology | M,D |
| Molecular Biology | M,D |
| Nursing—General | M,D,O |
| Public Health—General | D |
| Rehabilitation Sciences | M |

**UNIVERSITY OF PENNSYLVANIA**

| | |
|---|---|
| Acute Care/Critical Care Nursing | M |
| Adult Nursing | M |
| Allopathic Medicine | D |
| Biochemistry | D |
| Bioethics | M |
| Biological and Biomedical Sciences—General | M,D |
| Cancer Biology/Oncology | D |
| Cell Biology | D |
| Clinical Laboratory Sciences/Medical Technology | M |
| Computational Biology | D |
| Dentistry | D |
| Developmental Biology | D |
| Environmental and Occupational Health | M |
| Epidemiology | M |
| Family Nurse Practitioner Studies | M,O |
| Genetics | D |
| Genomic Sciences | D |
| Gerontological Nursing | M |
| Health Services Management and Hospital Administration | M,D |
| Health Services Research | M |
| Human Genetics | M |
| Immunology | D |
| International Health | M |
| Maternal and Child/Neonatal Nursing | M |
| Medical Physics | M,D |
| Microbiology | D |
| Molecular Biology | D |
| Molecular Biophysics | D |
| Neuroscience | D |
| Nurse Anesthesia | M |
| Nurse Midwifery | M |
| Nursing and Healthcare Administration | M,D |
| Nursing—General | M,D,O |
| Pediatric Nursing | M |
| Pharmacology | D |
| Physiology | D |
| Psychiatric Nursing | M |
| Public Health—General | M |
| Veterinary Medicine | D |
| Virology | D |
| Women's Health Nursing | M |

**UNIVERSITY OF PHOENIX - BAY AREA CAMPUS**

| | |
|---|---|
| Gerontological Nursing | M,D |
| Health Services Management and Hospital Administration | M,D |
| Nursing and Healthcare Administration | M,D |
| Nursing Education | M,D |
| Nursing Informatics | M,D |
| Nursing—General | M,D |

**UNIVERSITY OF PHOENIX - CENTRAL VALLEY CAMPUS**

| | |
|---|---|
| Community Health | M |
| Health Services Management and Hospital Administration | M |
| Nursing—General | M |

**UNIVERSITY OF PHOENIX - HAWAII CAMPUS**

| | |
|---|---|
| Community Health | M |
| Family Nurse Practitioner Studies | M |
| Health Services Management and Hospital Administration | M |
| Nursing Education | M |
| Nursing—General | M |

**UNIVERSITY OF PHOENIX - HOUSTON CAMPUS**

| | |
|---|---|
| Health Services Management and Hospital Administration | M |
| Nursing—General | M |

**UNIVERSITY OF PHOENIX - LAS VEGAS CAMPUS**

| | |
|---|---|
| Allied Health—General | M |

**UNIVERSITY OF PHOENIX–ONLINE CAMPUS**

| | |
|---|---|
| Family Nurse Practitioner Studies | M,O |
| Health Services Management and Hospital Administration | M,D,O |
| Nursing Education | M,O |
| Nursing—General | M,D,O |

**UNIVERSITY OF PHOENIX - PHOENIX CAMPUS**

| | |
|---|---|
| Family Nurse Practitioner Studies | M,O |
| Gerontological Nursing | M,O |
| Health Services Management and Hospital Administration | M,O |
| Nursing Education | M,O |
| Nursing Informatics | M,O |
| Nursing—General | M,O |

**UNIVERSITY OF PHOENIX - SACRAMENTO VALLEY CAMPUS**

| | |
|---|---|
| Family Nurse Practitioner Studies | M |
| Health Services Management and Hospital Administration | M |
| Nursing Education | M |
| Nursing—General | M |

**UNIVERSITY OF PHOENIX - SAN ANTONIO CAMPUS**

| | |
|---|---|
| Health Services Management and Hospital Administration | M |
| Nursing—General | M |

**UNIVERSITY OF PHOENIX - SAN DIEGO CAMPUS**

| | |
|---|---|
| Nursing Education | M |
| Nursing—General | M |

**UNIVERSITY OF PIKEVILLE**

| | |
|---|---|
| Health Services Management and Hospital Administration | M |
| Optometry | D |
| Osteopathic Medicine | D |

**UNIVERSITY OF PITTSBURGH**

| | |
|---|---|
| Allopathic Medicine | D |
| Bioethics | M |
| Biological and Biomedical Sciences—General | M,D |
| Cell Biology | D |
| Clinical Laboratory Sciences/Medical Technology | D |
| Clinical Research | M,O |
| Communication Disorders | M,D |
| Community Health | M,D,O |
| Dentistry | M,D,O |
| Developmental Biology | D |
| Ecology | D |
| Environmental and Occupational Health | M,D |
| Epidemiology | M,D |
| Evolutionary Biology | D |
| Family Nurse Practitioner Studies | M,D |
| Gerontological Nursing | D |
| Health Services Management and Hospital Administration | M,D,O |
| Health Services Research | M |
| Human Genetics | M,D,O |
| Immunology | D |
| Infectious Diseases | M,D |
| International Health | M,D,O |
| Microbiology | M,D |
| Molecular Biology | D |
| Molecular Biophysics | D |
| Neuroscience | D |
| Nurse Anesthesia | D |
| Nurse Midwifery | D |
| Nursing and Healthcare Administration | M,D |
| Nursing—General | D |
| Nutrition | M |
| Occupational Therapy | M,D |
| Oral and Dental Sciences | M,D,O |
| Pharmaceutical Administration | M |
| Pharmaceutical Sciences | M,D |
| Pharmacy | D |
| Physical Therapy | M,D |
| Physician Assistant Studies | M,D |
| Public Health—General | M,D,O |
| Rehabilitation Sciences | M,D |
| Structural Biology | D |
| Systems Biology | D |

**UNIVERSITY OF PORTLAND**

| | |
|---|---|
| Family Nurse Practitioner Studies | M,D |
| Health Services Management and Hospital Administration | M |
| Nursing Education | M,D |
| Nursing—General | M,D |

**UNIVERSITY OF PRINCE EDWARD ISLAND**

| | |
|---|---|
| Anatomy | M,D |
| Bacteriology | M,D |
| Biological and Biomedical Sciences—General | M,D |
| Epidemiology | M,D |
| Immunology | M,D |
| Parasitology | M,D |
| Pathology | M,D |
| Pharmacology | M,D |
| Physiology | M,D |
| Toxicology | M,D |
| Veterinary Medicine | D |
| Veterinary Sciences | M,D |
| Virology | M,D |

**UNIVERSITY OF PUERTO RICO AT MAYAGÜEZ**

| | |
|---|---|
| Biological and Biomedical Sciences—General | M |

**UNIVERSITY OF PUERTO RICO AT RIO PIEDRAS**

| | |
|---|---|
| Biological and Biomedical Sciences—General | M,D |
| Cell Biology | M,D |
| Ecology | M,D |
| Evolutionary Biology | M,D |
| Genetics | M,D |
| Molecular Biology | M,D |
| Neuroscience | M,D |
| Nutrition | M |

**UNIVERSITY OF PUERTO RICO - MEDICAL SCIENCES CAMPUS**

| | |
|---|---|
| Acute Care/Critical Care Nursing | M |
| Adult Nursing | M |
| Allied Health—General | M,D,O |
| Allopathic Medicine | D |
| Anatomy | M,D |
| Biochemistry | M,D |
| Biological and Biomedical Sciences—General | M,D |
| Clinical Laboratory Sciences/Medical Technology | M,O |
| Clinical Research | M,O |
| Communication Disorders | M,D |
| Community Health Nursing | M |
| Dentistry | D |
| Environmental and Occupational Health | M,D |
| Epidemiology | M |
| Family Nurse Practitioner Studies | M |
| Gerontological Nursing | M |
| Health Promotion | O |
| Health Services Management and Hospital Administration | M |
| Health Services Research | M |
| Industrial Hygiene | M |
| Maternal and Child Health | M |
| Maternal and Child/Neonatal Nursing | M |
| Microbiology | M,D |
| Nurse Midwifery | M,O |
| Nursing—General | M |
| Nutrition | M,D,O |
| Occupational Therapy | M |
| Oral and Dental Sciences | O |
| Pediatric Nursing | M |
| Pharmaceutical Sciences | M,D |
| Pharmacology | M,D |
| Pharmacy | M,D |
| Physical Therapy | M |
| Physiology | M,D |
| Psychiatric Nursing | M |
| Toxicology | M,D |

**UNIVERSITY OF PUGET SOUND**

| | |
|---|---|
| Occupational Therapy | M,D |
| Physical Therapy | D |

**UNIVERSITY OF REDLANDS**

| | |
|---|---|
| Communication Disorders | M |

**UNIVERSITY OF REGINA**

| | |
|---|---|
| Biochemistry | M,D |
| Biological and Biomedical Sciences—General | M,D |
| Biophysics | M,D |
| Cancer Biology/Oncology | M,D |
| Health Services Management and Hospital Administration | M,D,O |
| Nursing—General | M,D |

**UNIVERSITY OF RHODE ISLAND**

| | |
|---|---|
| Acute Care/Critical Care Nursing | M,D,O |
| Adult Nursing | M,D,O |
| Biochemistry | M,D |
| Biological and Biomedical Sciences—General | M,D |
| Cell Biology | M,D |
| Clinical Laboratory Sciences/Medical Technology | M,D |
| Communication Disorders | M |
| Ecology | M,D |
| Evolutionary Biology | M,D |
| Family Nurse Practitioner Studies | M,D,O |
| Gerontological Nursing | M,D,O |
| Health Services Management and Hospital Administration | M,D,O |
| Marine Biology | M,D |
| Medical Physics | M,D |
| Medicinal and Pharmaceutical Chemistry | M,D |
| Microbiology | M,D |
| Molecular Biology | M,D |
| Molecular Genetics | M,D |
| Nursing Education | M,D,O |
| Nursing—General | M,D,O |
| Nutrition | M |
| Pharmaceutical Sciences | M,D |
| Pharmacology | M,D |
| Pharmacy | D |
| Physical Therapy | D |
| Toxicology | M,D |

**UNIVERSITY OF ROCHESTER**

| | |
|---|---|
| Acute Care/Critical Care Nursing | M,D |
| Adult Nursing | M,D |
| Allopathic Medicine | D |
| Anatomy | D |
| Biochemistry | D |
| Biological and Biomedical Sciences—General | M,D |
| Biophysics | D |
| Clinical Research | M |
| Computational Biology | M,D |
| Ecology | M,D |
| Epidemiology | D |
| Family Nurse Practitioner Studies | M,D |
| Genetics | M,D |
| Genomic Sciences | D |
| Gerontological Nursing | M,D |
| Health Services Management and Hospital Administration | M,D |
| Health Services Research | D |
| Immunology | M,D |
| Maternal and Child/Neonatal Nursing | M,D |
| Microbiology | M,D |
| Molecular Biology | M,D |
| Neurobiology | D |
| Neuroscience | D |
| Nursing and Healthcare Administration | M,D |
| Nursing Education | M,D |
| Nursing—General | M,D |
| Oral and Dental Sciences | M |
| Pathology | D |
| Pediatric Nursing | M,D |
| Pharmacology | M,D |
| Physiology | M,D |
| Psychiatric Nursing | M,D |
| Public Health—General | M |
| Structural Biology | D |
| Toxicology | D |

**UNIVERSITY OF ST. AUGUSTINE FOR HEALTH SCIENCES**

| | |
|---|---|
| Health Services Management and Hospital Administration | M |
| Nursing and Healthcare Administration | M |
| Nursing Education | M |
| Nursing Informatics | M |
| Nursing—General | M,D |
| Occupational Therapy | M,D |
| Physical Therapy | D |

**UNIVERSITY OF ST. FRANCIS (IL)**

| | |
|---|---|
| Family Nurse Practitioner Studies | M,D,O |
| Health Services Management and Hospital Administration | M,O |
| Nursing and Healthcare Administration | M,D,O |
| Nursing Education | M,D,O |
| Nursing—General | M,D,O |
| Physician Assistant Studies | M,O |

*M—masters degree; D—doctorate; O—other advanced degree; *—Close-Up and/or Display*

Psychiatric Nursing — M,D,O

### UNIVERSITY OF SAINT FRANCIS (IN)
Environmental and Occupational
  Health — M
Family Nurse Practitioner Studies — M,D,O
Health Services Management and
  Hospital Administration — M
Nurse Anesthesia — M,D,O
Nursing—General — M,D,O
Physician Assistant Studies — M

### UNIVERSITY OF SAINT JOSEPH
Biochemistry — M
Biological and Biomedical
  Sciences—General — M
Family Nurse Practitioner Studies — M
Nursing Education — M,D
Nursing—General — M,D
Nutrition — M
Pharmacy — D
Psychiatric Nursing — M,D
Public Health—General — M

### UNIVERSITY OF SAINT MARY
Health Services Management and
  Hospital Administration — M
Nursing and Healthcare
  Administration — M
Nursing Education — M
Nursing—General — M
Physical Therapy — D

### UNIVERSITY OF ST. THOMAS (MN)
Health Services Management and
  Hospital Administration — M

### UNIVERSITY OF SAN DIEGO
Adult Nursing — M,D
Family Nurse Practitioner Studies — M,D
Gerontological Nursing — M,D
Nursing and Healthcare
  Administration — M,D
Nursing—General — M,D
Pediatric Nursing — M,D
Psychiatric Nursing — M,D

### UNIVERSITY OF SAN FRANCISCO
Biological and Biomedical
  Sciences—General — M
Health Services Management and
  Hospital Administration — M
Nursing—General — D
Public Health—General — M

### UNIVERSITY OF SASKATCHEWAN
Allopathic Medicine — D
Anatomy — M,D
Biochemistry — M,D
Biological and Biomedical
  Sciences—General — M,D
Cell Biology — M,D
Community Health — M,D
Dentistry — D
Epidemiology — M,D
Immunology — M,D
Microbiology — M,D
Nursing—General — M,D
Nutrition — M,D
Pathology — M,D
Pharmacology — M,D
Pharmacy — M,D
Physiology — M,D
Reproductive Biology — M,D
Toxicology — M,D,O
Veterinary Medicine — M,D
Veterinary Sciences — M,D

### THE UNIVERSITY OF SCRANTON
Biochemistry — M
Family Nurse Practitioner Studies — M,D,O
Health Services Management and
  Hospital Administration — M
Nurse Anesthesia — M,D,O
Nursing and Healthcare
  Administration — M,D,O
Nursing—General — M,D,O
Occupational Therapy — M
Physical Therapy — D

### UNIVERSITY OF SIOUX FALLS
Health Services Management and
  Hospital Administration — M

### UNIVERSITY OF SOUTH AFRICA
Acute Care/Critical Care Nursing — M,D
Health Services Management and
  Hospital Administration — M,D
Maternal and Child/Neonatal
  Nursing — M,D
Medical/Surgical Nursing — M,D
Nurse Midwifery — M,D
Public Health—General — M,D

### UNIVERSITY OF SOUTH ALABAMA
Allied Health—General — M,D
Allopathic Medicine — D
Biological and Biomedical
  Sciences—General — M,D
Communication Disorders — M,D
Environmental and Occupational
  Health — M
Nursing and Healthcare
  Administration — M,D,O
Nursing Education — M,D,O
Nursing—General — M,D,O
Occupational Therapy — M
Physical Therapy — D
Physician Assistant Studies — M
Toxicology — M

### UNIVERSITY OF SOUTH CAROLINA
Acute Care/Critical Care Nursing — M,O
Adult Nursing — M
Allopathic Medicine — D
Biochemistry — M,D
Biological and Biomedical
  Sciences—General — M,D,O

Cell Biology — M,D
Communication Disorders — M,D
Community Health Nursing — M
Developmental Biology — M
Ecology — M,D
Environmental and Occupational
  Health — M,D
Epidemiology — M,D
Evolutionary Biology — M,D
Family Nurse Practitioner Studies — M
Health Promotion — M,D,O
Health Services Management and
  Hospital Administration — M,D
Industrial Hygiene — M,D
Medical/Surgical Nursing — M,D
Molecular Biology — M
Nurse Anesthesia — M
Nursing and Healthcare
  Administration — M,O
Nursing—General — M,O
Pediatric Nursing — M
Pharmaceutical Sciences — M,D
Pharmacy — D
Psychiatric Nursing — M,O
Public Health—General — M,D
Rehabilitation Sciences — M
Women's Health Nursing — M

### UNIVERSITY OF SOUTH DAKOTA
Allied Health—General — M,D,O
Allopathic Medicine — D,O
Bioethics — D,O
Biological and Biomedical
  Sciences—General — M,D
Cardiovascular Sciences — M,D
Cell Biology — M,D
Communication Disorders — M,D
Health Services Management and
  Hospital Administration — M,O
Immunology — M,D
Microbiology — M,D
Molecular Biology — M,D
Neuroscience — M,D
Occupational Therapy — M,D
Pharmacology — M,D
Physical Therapy — D
Physician Assistant Studies — M
Physiology — M,D
Public Health—General — M

### UNIVERSITY OF SOUTHERN CALIFORNIA
Allopathic Medicine — D
Biochemistry — M
Biological and Biomedical
  Sciences—General — M,D,O
Biophysics — M,D
Cancer Biology/Oncology — D
Cell Biology — M,D
Clinical Research — M,D,O
Computational Biology — D
Dentistry — D
Developmental Biology — D
Environmental and Occupational
  Health — M
Environmental Biology — M,D
Epidemiology — M,D
Evolutionary Biology — D
Genomic Sciences — D
Health Promotion — M
Health Services Management and
  Hospital Administration — M,D
Health Services Research — D
Immunology — M
International Health — M,O
Marine Biology — M,D
Medical Imaging — M,D
Medical Microbiology — D
Microbiology — M
Molecular Biology — D
Molecular Medicine — M,D
Molecular Pharmacology — M,D
Neurobiology — M,D
Neuroscience — M,D
Nurse Anesthesia — D
Occupational Therapy — M,D
Oral and Dental Sciences — M,D,O
Pathology — M
Pharmaceutical Administration — M
Pharmaceutical Sciences — M,D,O
Pharmacy — D
Physical Therapy — M
Physician Assistant Studies — M
Physiology — M
Public Health—General — M
Toxicology — M

### UNIVERSITY OF SOUTHERN INDIANA
Family Nurse Practitioner Studies — M,D,O
Health Services Management and
  Hospital Administration — M
Nursing and Healthcare
  Administration — M,D,O
Nursing Education — M,D,O
Nursing—General — M,D,O
Occupational Therapy — M
Psychiatric Nursing — M,D,O

### UNIVERSITY OF SOUTHERN MAINE
Adult Nursing — M,D,O
Biological and Biomedical
  Sciences—General — M
Family Nurse Practitioner Studies — M,D,O
Gerontological Nursing — M,D,O
Health Services Management and
  Hospital Administration — M
Nursing and Healthcare
  Administration — M,D,O
Nursing Education — M,D,O
Nursing—General — M,D,O
Occupational Therapy — M
Psychiatric Nursing — M,D,O
Public Health—General — M,O

### UNIVERSITY OF SOUTHERN MISSISSIPPI
Communication Disorders — M,D
Epidemiology — M
Health Services Management and
  Hospital Administration — M
Nursing—General — M,D,O
Public Health—General — M

### UNIVERSITY OF SOUTH FLORIDA
Acute Care/Critical Care Nursing — M,D
Adult Nursing — M,D,O
Allopathic Medicine — M,D
Bioethics — O
Biological and Biomedical
  Sciences—General — M,D
Cancer Biology/Oncology — M,D
Cardiovascular Sciences — O
Cell Biology — M,D
Clinical Research — M
Communication Disorders — M,D,O
Community Health — O
Computational Biology — M,D
Ecology — M,D
Environmental and Occupational
  Health — O
Environmental Biology — M,D
Epidemiology — O
Evolutionary Biology — M,D
Family Nurse Practitioner Studies — M,D,O
Gerontological Nursing — M,D,O
Health Services Management and
  Hospital Administration — O
International Health — O
Maternal and Child Health — O
Microbiology — M,D
Molecular Biology — M,D
Neuroscience — D,O
Nurse Anesthesia — M,D,O
Nursing Education — M,D,O
Nursing—General — M,D,O
Nutrition — O
Occupational Health Nursing — M,D,O
Oncology Nursing — M,D,O
Pediatric Nursing — M,D,O
Pharmaceutical Sciences — M,D
Pharmacy — M,D,O
Physical Therapy — D
Physiology — M,D
Public Health—General — M,D,O
Rehabilitation Sciences — D
Toxicology — O

### THE UNIVERSITY OF TAMPA
Adult Nursing — M
Family Nurse Practitioner Studies — M
Nursing—General — M
Nutrition — M

### THE UNIVERSITY OF TENNESSEE
Anatomy — M,D
Animal Behavior — M,D
Biochemistry — M,D
Bioethics — M,D
Biological and Biomedical
  Sciences—General — M,D
Communication Disorders — M,D,O
Community Health — M,D
Ecology — M,D
Entomology — M,D
Evolutionary Biology — M,D
Genetics — M,D
Genomic Sciences — M,D
Health Promotion — M
Health Services Management and
  Hospital Administration — M
Microbiology — M,D
Nursing—General — M,D
Nutrition — M
Physiology — M,D
Plant Pathology — M,D
Plant Physiology — M,D
Public Health—General — M
Veterinary Medicine — D

### THE UNIVERSITY OF TENNESSEE AT CHATTANOOGA
Family Nurse Practitioner Studies — M,D,O
Gerontological Nursing — M,D,O
Nurse Anesthesia — M,D,O
Nursing Education — M,D,O
Nursing—General — M,D,O
Occupational Therapy — D
Physical Therapy — D

### THE UNIVERSITY OF TENNESSEE AT MARTIN
Nutrition — M

### THE UNIVERSITY OF TENNESSEE HEALTH SCIENCE CENTER
Allied Health—General — M,D
Allopathic Medicine — D
Biological and Biomedical
  Sciences—General — M,D
Clinical Laboratory
  Sciences/Medical Technology — M,D
Communication Disorders — M,D
Dentistry — D
Epidemiology — M,D
Family Nurse Practitioner Studies — D,O
Gerontological Nursing — D,O
Health Services Research — M,D
Nursing—General — M,D,O
Occupational Therapy — M,D
Oral and Dental Sciences — M,D
Pathology — M,D
Pediatric Nursing — D,O
Pharmaceutical Sciences — M,D
Pharmacology — M,D
Pharmacy — M,D
Physical Therapy — M,D
Physician Assistant Studies — M,D
Psychiatric Nursing — D,O

### THE UNIVERSITY OF TENNESSEE–OAK RIDGE NATIONAL LABORATORY
Biological and Biomedical
  Sciences—General — M,D
Genomic Sciences — M,D

### THE UNIVERSITY OF TEXAS AT ARLINGTON
Biological and Biomedical
  Sciences—General — M,D
Family Nurse Practitioner Studies — M,D
Health Services Management and
  Hospital Administration — M
Nursing and Healthcare
  Administration — M,D
Nursing Education — M,D
Nursing—General — M,D

### THE UNIVERSITY OF TEXAS AT AUSTIN
Adult Nursing — M,D
Allopathic Medicine — D
Animal Behavior — D
Biochemistry — D
Biological and Biomedical
  Sciences—General — M,D
Biopsychology — D
Cell Biology — D
Clinical Laboratory
  Sciences/Medical Technology — M,D
Communication Disorders — M,D
Community Health Nursing — M,D
Ecology — D
Evolutionary Biology — D
Family Nurse Practitioner Studies — M,D
Gerontological Nursing — M,D
Maternal and Child/Neonatal
  Nursing — M,D
Medicinal and Pharmaceutical
  Chemistry — M,D
Microbiology — D
Molecular Biology — D
Neurobiology — D
Neuroscience — D
Nursing and Healthcare
  Administration — M,D
Nursing Education — M,D
Nursing—General — M,D
Nutrition — M,D
Pediatric Nursing — M,D
Pharmaceutical Sciences — M,D
Pharmacology — M,D
Pharmacy — D
Plant Biology — M,D
Psychiatric Nursing — M,D
Toxicology — M,D

### THE UNIVERSITY OF TEXAS AT DALLAS
Biochemistry — M,D
Biological and Biomedical
  Sciences—General — M,D
Cell Biology — M,D
Communication Disorders — M,D
Health Services Management and
  Hospital Administration — M,D
Molecular Biology — M,D
Neuroscience — M,D

### THE UNIVERSITY OF TEXAS AT EL PASO
Allied Health—General — D
Biochemistry — M,D
Biological and Biomedical
  Sciences—General — M,D
Communication Disorders — M
Family Nurse Practitioner Studies — M,D,O
Health Services Management and
  Hospital Administration — M,D,O
Nursing and Healthcare
  Administration — M,D,O
Nursing Education — M,D,O
Nursing—General — M,D,O
Occupational Therapy — M
Physical Therapy — D
Public Health—General — M,O

### THE UNIVERSITY OF TEXAS AT SAN ANTONIO
Biological and Biomedical
  Sciences—General — M,D
Cell Biology — M,D
Ecology — M
Molecular Biology — M,D
Neurobiology — M,D
Translational Biology — M,D

### THE UNIVERSITY OF TEXAS AT TYLER
Biological and Biomedical
  Sciences—General — M
Environmental and Occupational
  Health — M
Family Nurse Practitioner Studies — M,D
Health Services Management and
  Hospital Administration — M
Nursing and Healthcare
  Administration — M,D
Nursing Education — M,D
Nursing—General — M,D
Pharmacy — D

### THE UNIVERSITY OF TEXAS HEALTH SCIENCE CENTER AT HOUSTON
Allopathic Medicine — D
Biochemistry — M,D
Biological and Biomedical
  Sciences—General — M,D
Cancer Biology/Oncology — M,D
Cell Biology — M,D
Community Health — M,D,O
Dentistry — M,D
Environmental and Occupational
  Health — M,D,O
Epidemiology — M,D,O
Genetics — M,D
Genomic Sciences — M,D
Health Promotion — M,D,O

| | |
|---|---|
| Health Services Management and Hospital Administration | M,D,O |
| Immunology | M,D |
| Infectious Diseases | M,D |
| Maternal and Child Health | M,D,O |
| Medical Physics | M,D |
| Microbiology | M,D |
| Neuroscience | M,D |
| Nursing—General | M,D |
| Pharmacology | M,D |
| Public Health—General | M,D,O |

### THE UNIVERSITY OF TEXAS HEALTH SCIENCE CENTER AT SAN ANTONIO

| | |
|---|---|
| Acute Care/Critical Care Nursing | M,D,O |
| Allopathic Medicine | M,D |
| Biochemistry | M,D |
| Biological and Biomedical Sciences—General | D |
| Cell Biology | M,D |
| Clinical Laboratory Sciences/Medical Technology | D |
| Clinical Research | M |
| Communication Disorders | M,D |
| Community Health Nursing | M,D,O |
| Dentistry | M,D,O |
| Family Nurse Practitioner Studies | M,D,O |
| Gerontological Nursing | M,D,O |
| Immunology | M,D |
| Medical Physics | D |
| Microbiology | M,D |
| Molecular Medicine | M,D |
| Neuroscience | D |
| Nursing and Healthcare Administration | M,D,O |
| Nursing Education | M,D,O |
| Nursing—General | M,D,O |
| Occupational Therapy | M,D |
| Pediatric Nursing | M,D,O |
| Pharmacology | D |
| Physical Therapy | M,D |
| Physician Assistant Studies | M,D |
| Psychiatric Nursing | M,D,O |
| Structural Biology | M,D |
| Toxicology | M |

### THE UNIVERSITY OF TEXAS HEALTH SCIENCE CENTER AT TYLER

| | |
|---|---|
| Health Services Management and Hospital Administration | M |
| Public Health—General | M |

### THE UNIVERSITY OF TEXAS MD ANDERSON CANCER CENTER

| | |
|---|---|
| Genetics | M |

### THE UNIVERSITY OF TEXAS MEDICAL BRANCH

| | |
|---|---|
| Allied Health—General | M,D |
| Allopathic Medicine | D |
| Biochemistry | D |
| Biological and Biomedical Sciences—General | M,D |
| Biophysics | D |
| Cell Biology | M,D |
| Clinical Laboratory Sciences/Medical Technology | M,D |
| Computational Biology | D |
| Immunology | M,D |
| Microbiology | M,D |
| Molecular Biophysics | D |
| Neuroscience | D |
| Nursing—General | M,D |
| Occupational Therapy | M |
| Pathology | D |
| Pharmacology | M,D |
| Physical Therapy | M,D |
| Physician Assistant Studies | M |
| Physiology | M,D |
| Public Health—General | M |
| Rehabilitation Sciences | D |
| Structural Biology | D |
| Toxicology | M,D |
| Translational Biology | M,D |

### THE UNIVERSITY OF TEXAS OF THE PERMIAN BASIN

| | |
|---|---|
| Biological and Biomedical Sciences—General | M |

### THE UNIVERSITY OF TEXAS RIO GRANDE VALLEY

| | |
|---|---|
| Allopathic Medicine | D |
| Biological and Biomedical Sciences—General | M |
| Clinical Laboratory Sciences/Medical Technology | M |
| Communication Disorders | M |
| Health Services Management and Hospital Administration | M |
| Nutrition | M |
| Occupational Therapy | M |
| Physician Assistant Studies | M |

### THE UNIVERSITY OF TEXAS SOUTHWESTERN MEDICAL CENTER

| | |
|---|---|
| Allopathic Medicine | D |
| Biochemistry | D |
| Biological and Biomedical Sciences—General | M,D |
| Cancer Biology/Oncology | D |
| Cell Biology | D |
| Developmental Biology | D |
| Genetics | D |
| Immunology | D |
| Microbiology | D |
| Molecular Biophysics | D |
| Neuroscience | D |
| Nutrition | M |
| Physical Therapy | D |
| Physician Assistant Studies | M |

### UNIVERSITY OF THE CUMBERLANDS

| | |
|---|---|
| Physician Assistant Studies | M |

### UNIVERSITY OF THE DISTRICT OF COLUMBIA

| | |
|---|---|
| Cancer Biology/Oncology | M |
| Communication Disorders | M |
| Nutrition | M |

### UNIVERSITY OF THE INCARNATE WORD

| | |
|---|---|
| Biological and Biomedical Sciences—General | M |
| Health Services Management and Hospital Administration | M,D |
| Nursing—General | M,D |
| Nutrition | M |
| Optometry | D |
| Osteopathic Medicine | M,D |
| Pharmacy | D |
| Physical Therapy | D |

### UNIVERSITY OF THE PACIFIC

| | |
|---|---|
| Biological and Biomedical Sciences—General | M |
| Communication Disorders | M,D |
| Dentistry | M,D,O |
| Pharmaceutical Sciences | M,D |
| Pharmacy | D |
| Physical Therapy | M,D |

### UNIVERSITY OF THE SACRED HEART

| | |
|---|---|
| Environmental and Occupational Health | M |
| Occupational Health Nursing | M |

### UNIVERSITY OF THE SCIENCES

| | |
|---|---|
| Biochemistry | M,D |
| Cell Biology | M |
| Health Services Management and Hospital Administration | M,D |
| Medicinal and Pharmaceutical Chemistry | M,D |
| Occupational Therapy | M,D |
| Pharmaceutical Administration | M |
| Pharmaceutical Sciences | M,D |
| Pharmacology | M,D |
| Pharmacy | D |
| Physical Therapy | D |
| Public Health—General | M |
| Toxicology | M,D |

### THE UNIVERSITY OF TOLEDO

| | |
|---|---|
| Allopathic Medicine | M,D,O |
| Biochemistry | M,D |
| Biological and Biomedical Sciences—General | M,D,O |
| Cancer Biology/Oncology | M,D |
| Cardiovascular Sciences | M,D |
| Communication Disorders | M,D,O |
| Community Health Nursing | M,O |
| Ecology | M,D |
| Environmental and Occupational Health | M,D,O |
| Epidemiology | M,O |
| Family Nurse Practitioner Studies | M,O |
| Genomic Sciences | M,O |
| Health Promotion | M,D,O |
| Health Services Management and Hospital Administration | M,O |
| Immunology | M,D |
| Industrial Hygiene | M,D,O |
| International Health | M,O |
| Medical Physics | M,D |
| Medicinal and Pharmaceutical Chemistry | M,D |
| Neuroscience | M,D |
| Nursing and Healthcare Administration | M,O |
| Nursing Education | M,O |
| Nursing—General | M,D,O |
| Nutrition | M,O |
| Occupational Therapy | M,D |
| Oral and Dental Sciences | M |
| Pathology | M,O |
| Pediatric Nursing | M,O |
| Pharmaceutical Administration | M |
| Pharmaceutical Sciences | M |
| Pharmacology | M,D |
| Pharmacy | M,D |
| Physical Therapy | M,D |
| Physician Assistant Studies | M |
| Public Health—General | M,D,O |

### UNIVERSITY OF TORONTO

| | |
|---|---|
| Allopathic Medicine | M,D |
| Biochemistry | M,D |
| Bioethics | M,D |
| Biophysics | M,D |
| Cell Biology | M,D |
| Communication Disorders | M,D |
| Community Health | M,D |
| Dentistry | D |
| Ecology | M,D |
| Environmental and Occupational Health | M,D |
| Epidemiology | M,D |
| Evolutionary Biology | M,D |
| Health Physics/Radiological Health | M,D |
| Health Promotion | M,D |
| Health Services Management and Hospital Administration | M |
| Immunology | M,D |
| Molecular Genetics | M,D |
| Nursing—General | M,D |
| Nutrition | M,D |
| Occupational Therapy | M |
| Oral and Dental Sciences | M,D |
| Pathobiology | M,D |
| Pharmaceutical Sciences | M,D |
| Pharmacology | M,D |
| Physical Therapy | M |
| Physiology | M,D |
| Public Health—General | M,D |
| Rehabilitation Sciences | M,D |
| Systems Biology | M,D |

### THE UNIVERSITY OF TULSA

| | |
|---|---|
| Biological and Biomedical Sciences—General | M,D |
| Communication Disorders | M |
| Family Nurse Practitioner Studies | D |
| Gerontological Nursing | D |
| Nursing—General | D |
| Rehabilitation Sciences | M |

### UNIVERSITY OF UTAH

| | |
|---|---|
| Allopathic Medicine | D |
| Anatomy | D |
| Biochemistry | M,D |
| Biological and Biomedical Sciences—General | M,D,O |
| Cancer Biology/Oncology | M,D |
| Clinical Laboratory Sciences/Medical Technology | M |
| Communication Disorders | M,D |
| Dentistry | D |
| Gerontological Nursing | M,O |
| Health Services Management and Hospital Administration | M,D |
| Health Services Research | M,D |
| Human Genetics | M,D |
| Medical Physics | M,D |
| Medicinal and Pharmaceutical Chemistry | M,D |
| Molecular Biology | D |
| Neurobiology | D |
| Neuroscience | D |
| Nursing—General | M,D |
| Nutrition | M,D |
| Occupational Therapy | M,D |
| Pathology | M,D |
| Pharmaceutical Administration | M,D |
| Pharmaceutical Sciences | M,D |
| Pharmacology | D |
| Pharmacy | M,D |
| Physical Therapy | D |
| Physician Assistant Studies | M |
| Physiology | M,D |
| Public Health—General | M,D |
| Rehabilitation Sciences | D |
| Toxicology | D |

### UNIVERSITY OF VERMONT

| | |
|---|---|
| Allied Health—General | M,D,O |
| Allopathic Medicine | M,D,O |
| Biochemistry | M,D |
| Biological and Biomedical Sciences—General | M,D |
| Cell Biology | D |
| Clinical Laboratory Sciences/Medical Technology | M,D,O |
| Communication Disorders | M |
| Community Health | M |
| Entomology | M,D,O |
| Environmental and Occupational Health | M,O |
| Epidemiology | M,O |
| Health Promotion | M |
| Health Services Management and Hospital Administration | M,O |
| International Health | M,O |
| Molecular Biology | D |
| Neuroscience | D |
| Nursing—General | M,D,O |
| Nutrition | M |
| Pathology | M |
| Pharmacology | M,D |
| Physical Therapy | D |
| Plant Biology | M,D |
| Plant Pathology | M,D,O |
| Public Health—General | M,O |
| Rehabilitation Sciences | D |
| Veterinary Sciences | M,D |

### UNIVERSITY OF VICTORIA

| | |
|---|---|
| Biochemistry | M,D |
| Biological and Biomedical Sciences—General | M,D |
| Family Nurse Practitioner Studies | M,D |
| Medical Physics | M,D |
| Microbiology | M,D |
| Nursing and Healthcare Administration | M,D |
| Nursing Education | M,D |
| Nursing—General | M,D |

### UNIVERSITY OF VIRGINIA

| | |
|---|---|
| Acute Care/Critical Care Nursing | M,D |
| Allopathic Medicine | M,D |
| Biochemistry | D |
| Biological and Biomedical Sciences—General | M,D |
| Biophysics | M,D |
| Cell Biology | D |
| Clinical Research | M |
| Communication Disorders | M,D |
| Community Health | M,D |
| Health Services Management and Hospital Administration | M |
| Health Services Research | M |
| Microbiology | D |
| Molecular Genetics | D |
| Molecular Physiology | M,D |
| Neuroscience | D |
| Nursing and Healthcare Administration | M,D |
| Nursing—General | M,D |
| Pathology | D |
| Pharmacology | D |
| Physiology | D |
| Psychiatric Nursing | M,D |
| Public Health—General | M,D |

### UNIVERSITY OF WASHINGTON

| | |
|---|---|
| Allopathic Medicine | D |
| Animal Behavior | M,D |
| Biochemistry | D |
| Bioethics | M |
| Biological and Biomedical Sciences—General | M,D |
| Biophysics | D |
| Cell Biology | D |
| Clinical Laboratory Sciences/Medical Technology | M |
| Clinical Research | M,D |
| Communication Disorders | M,D |
| Community Health | M,D |
| Dentistry | M,D,O |
| Ecology | M,D |
| Environmental and Occupational Health | M,D |
| Epidemiology | M,D |
| Genetics | M,D,O |
| Genomic Sciences | D |
| Health Services Management and Hospital Administration | M |
| Health Services Research | M,D |
| Immunology | D |
| Infectious Diseases | D |
| International Health | M,D |
| Maternal and Child Health | M,D |
| Medicinal and Pharmaceutical Chemistry | D |
| Microbiology | D |
| Molecular Biology | D |
| Molecular Medicine | D |
| Neurobiology | D |
| Neuroscience | M,D |
| Nursing—General | M,D,O |
| Nutrition | M,D |
| Occupational Therapy | M,D |
| Oral and Dental Sciences | M,D,O |
| Pathobiology | D |
| Pathology | D |
| Pharmaceutical Sciences | M,D |
| Pharmacology | D |
| Pharmacy | M,D |
| Physical Therapy | M,D |
| Physiology | D |
| Public Health—General | M |
| Rehabilitation Sciences | M,D |
| Structural Biology | D |
| Toxicology | M,D |
| Veterinary Sciences | M |

### UNIVERSITY OF WASHINGTON, BOTHELL

| | |
|---|---|
| Nursing—General | M |

### UNIVERSITY OF WASHINGTON, TACOMA

| | |
|---|---|
| Community Health Nursing | M |
| Nursing and Healthcare Administration | M |
| Nursing Education | M |
| Nursing—General | M |

### UNIVERSITY OF WATERLOO

| | |
|---|---|
| Biochemistry | M,D |
| Biological and Biomedical Sciences—General | M,D |
| Optometry | M,D |
| Public Health—General | M,D |
| Vision Sciences | M,D |

### THE UNIVERSITY OF WEST ALABAMA

| | |
|---|---|
| Conservation Biology | M |

### THE UNIVERSITY OF WESTERN ONTARIO

| | |
|---|---|
| Allopathic Medicine | M,D |
| Anatomy | M,D |
| Biochemistry | M,D |
| Biological and Biomedical Sciences—General | M,D |
| Biophysics | M,D |
| Cell Biology | M,D |
| Communication Disorders | M |
| Dentistry | D |
| Epidemiology | M,D |
| Health Services Management and Hospital Administration | M,D |
| Immunology | M,D |
| Microbiology | M,D |
| Neuroscience | M,D |
| Nursing—General | M,D |
| Occupational Therapy | M |
| Oral and Dental Sciences | M |
| Pathology | M,D |
| Physical Therapy | M,O |
| Physiology | M,D |

### UNIVERSITY OF WESTERN STATES

| | |
|---|---|
| Chiropractic | D |

### UNIVERSITY OF WEST FLORIDA

| | |
|---|---|
| Biological and Biomedical Sciences—General | M |
| Health Promotion | M |
| Health Services Management and Hospital Administration | M |
| Nursing—General | M |
| Public Health—General | M |

### UNIVERSITY OF WINDSOR

| | |
|---|---|
| Biochemistry | M,D |
| Biological and Biomedical Sciences—General | M,D |
| Biopsychology | M,D |
| Nursing—General | M |

### UNIVERSITY OF WISCONSIN–EAU CLAIRE

| | |
|---|---|
| Adult Nursing | M,D |
| Communication Disorders | M |
| Family Nurse Practitioner Studies | M,D |
| Gerontological Nursing | M,D |
| Nursing and Healthcare Administration | M,D |
| Nursing Education | M,D |

*M—masters degree; D—doctorate; O—other advanced degree; *—Close-Up and/or Display*

Nursing—General M,D

## UNIVERSITY OF WISCONSIN–GREEN BAY
Nursing and Healthcare Administration M

## UNIVERSITY OF WISCONSIN–LA CROSSE
Biological and Biomedical Sciences—General M
Cancer Biology/Oncology M
Cell Biology M
Community Health M
Medical Microbiology M
Microbiology M
Molecular Biology M
Nurse Anesthesia M
Occupational Therapy M
Physical Therapy D
Physician Assistant Studies M
Physiology M
Public Health—General M
Rehabilitation Sciences M

## UNIVERSITY OF WISCONSIN–MADISON
Adult Nursing D
Allopathic Medicine D
Bacteriology M
Biochemistry M,D
Biological and Biomedical Sciences—General
Biophysics D
Biopsychology D
Botany M,D
Cancer Biology/Oncology D
Cell Biology D
Clinical Research M,D
Communication Disorders M,D
Conservation Biology M
Ecology M
Entomology M,D
Environmental Biology M,D
Epidemiology M,D
Genetics M,D
Gerontological Nursing D
Medical Microbiology D
Medical Physics M,D
Microbiology D
Molecular Biology D
Molecular Pathology D
Neuroscience D
Nursing—General M,D
Nutrition M,D
Occupational Therapy M
Pathology D
Pediatric Nursing D
Pharmaceutical Administration M,D
Pharmaceutical Sciences M,D
Pharmacology D
Pharmacy D
Physical Therapy D
Physician Assistant Studies M
Physiology M,D
Plant Pathology M,D
Psychiatric Nursing D
Public Health—General M
Toxicology M,D
Veterinary Medicine M,D
Veterinary Sciences M,D
Zoology M,D

## UNIVERSITY OF WISCONSIN–MILWAUKEE
Allied Health—General M,D,O
Biochemistry M,D
Biological and Biomedical Sciences—General M,D
Cell Biology M,D
Communication Disorders M
Community Health D
Environmental and Occupational Health M,D,O
Epidemiology M,D,O
Family Nurse Practitioner Studies M,D,O
Health Promotion M,D,O
Health Services Management and Hospital Administration M,D
Medical Imaging D
Microbiology M,D
Molecular Biology M,D
Nursing—General M,D,O*
Nutrition M,D
Occupational Therapy M
Physical Therapy M,D
Public Health—General M,D,O
Rehabilitation Sciences D

## UNIVERSITY OF WISCONSIN–OSHKOSH
Adult Nursing M
Biological and Biomedical Sciences—General M
Botany M
Family Nurse Practitioner Studies M
Health Services Management and Hospital Administration M
Microbiology M
Nursing—General M
Zoology M

## UNIVERSITY OF WISCONSIN–PARKSIDE
Health Promotion M
Molecular Biology M

## UNIVERSITY OF WISCONSIN–RIVER FALLS
Communication Disorders M

## UNIVERSITY OF WISCONSIN–STEVENS POINT
Communication Disorders M,D
Health Promotion M
Nutrition M

## UNIVERSITY OF WISCONSIN–STOUT
Conservation Biology M
Industrial Hygiene M

Nutrition M

## UNIVERSITY OF WISCONSIN–WHITEWATER
Communication Disorders M
Environmental and Occupational Health M

## UNIVERSITY OF WYOMING
Botany M,D
Cell Biology D
Communication Disorders M,D
Community Health M,D
Computational Biology D
Ecology M,D
Entomology M,D
Genetics D
Health Promotion M
Health Services Management and Hospital Administration
Microbiology D
Molecular Biology M
Nursing—General M
Nutrition M
Pathobiology M
Pharmacy M,D
Physiology M,D
Reproductive Biology M
Zoology M,D

## UNIVERSITÉ LAVAL
Allopathic Medicine D,O
Anatomy O
Anesthesiologist Assistant Studies O
Biochemistry M,D,O
Biological and Biomedical Sciences—General M,D,O
Cancer Biology/Oncology O
Cardiovascular Sciences O
Cell Biology M,D
Communication Disorders M,D
Community Health M,D,O
Dentistry M
Emergency Medical Services O
Environmental and Occupational Health O
Epidemiology M,D
Health Physics/Radiological Health O
Immunology M,D
Infectious Diseases O
Microbiology M,D
Molecular Biology M,D
Neurobiology M,D
Nursing—General M,D,O
Nutrition M,D
Oral and Dental Sciences M,O
Pathology O
Pharmaceutical Sciences M,D,O
Physiology M,D
Plant Biology M,D

## URBANA UNIVERSITY–A BRANCH CAMPUS OF FRANKLIN UNIVERSITY
Nursing—General M

## URSULINE COLLEGE
Adult Nursing M,D
Family Nurse Practitioner Studies M,D
Gerontological Nursing M,D
Medical/Surgical Nursing M,D
Nursing Education M,D
Nursing—General M,D

## UTAH STATE UNIVERSITY
Biochemistry M,D
Biological and Biomedical Sciences—General M,D
Communication Disorders M,D,O
Ecology M,D
Health Promotion M,D
Nutrition M,D
Public Health—General M,D
Toxicology M,D
Veterinary Sciences M,D

## UTAH VALLEY UNIVERSITY
Nursing—General M

## UTICA COLLEGE
Health Services Management and Hospital Administration M
Occupational Therapy M
Physical Therapy D

## VALDOSTA STATE UNIVERSITY
Communication Disorders M,D,O
Family Nurse Practitioner Studies M
Gerontological Nursing M
Health Services Management and Hospital Administration M
Nursing—General M
Psychiatric Nursing M

## VALPARAISO UNIVERSITY
Health Services Management and Hospital Administration M
Nursing Education M,D,O
Nursing—General M,D,O
Physician Assistant Studies M,D,O
Public Health—General M,D,O

## VAN ANDEL INSTITUTE GRADUATE SCHOOL
Genetics D
Molecular Genetics D

## VANDERBILT UNIVERSITY
Allopathic Medicine M,D
Biochemistry M,D
Biological and Biomedical Sciences—General M,D
Biophysics M,D
Cell Biology M,D
Communication Disorders M,D
Developmental Biology M,D
Health Services Management and Hospital Administration M
Human Genetics D

Immunology M,D
Microbiology M,D
Molecular Biology M,D
Molecular Physiology M,D
Nursing—General M,D,O
Pathology D
Pharmacology M,D
Public Health—General M

## VANGUARD UNIVERSITY OF SOUTHERN CALIFORNIA
Nursing—General M

## VILLANOVA UNIVERSITY
Adult Nursing M,D,O
Biological and Biomedical Sciences—General M
Family Nurse Practitioner Studies M,D,O
Gerontological Nursing M,D,O
Health Services Management and Hospital Administration M,D,O
Nurse Anesthesia M,D,O
Nursing Education M,D,O
Nursing—General M,D,O
Pediatric Nursing M,D,O

## VIRGINIA COMMONWEALTH UNIVERSITY
Adult Nursing M,D,O
Allied Health—General D
Allopathic Medicine D
Anatomy M
Biochemistry M,D
Biological and Biomedical Sciences—General M,D,O
Clinical Laboratory Sciences/Medical Technology M,D
Community Health M,D
Dentistry M,D
Epidemiology M,D
Family Nurse Practitioner Studies M,D,O
Health Physics/Radiological Health D
Health Services Management and Hospital Administration M,D
Health Services Research D
Human Genetics M,D
Immunology M,D
Medical Physics M,D
Medicinal and Pharmaceutical Chemistry M,D
Microbiology M,D
Molecular Biology M,D
Molecular Genetics M,D
Neurobiology M
Neuroscience M,D,O
Nurse Anesthesia M,D
Nursing and Healthcare Administration M,D,O
Nursing Education M,D,O
Nursing—General M,D,O
Occupational Therapy M,D
Pediatric Nursing M,D,O
Pharmaceutical Administration M,D
Pharmaceutical Sciences M,D
Pharmacology M,D,O
Pharmacy D
Physical Therapy M,D
Physiology M,D
Psychiatric Nursing M,D,O
Public Health—General M
Rehabilitation Sciences D
Systems Biology D
Toxicology M,D,O
Women's Health Nursing M,D,O

## VIRGINIA INTERNATIONAL UNIVERSITY
Health Services Management and Hospital Administration M,O

## VIRGINIA POLYTECHNIC INSTITUTE AND STATE UNIVERSITY
Allopathic Medicine D
Biochemistry M,D
Biological and Biomedical Sciences—General M,D
Entomology M,D
Genetics M,D
Nutrition M,D
Plant Pathology M,D
Plant Physiology M,D
Public Health—General M,D
Translational Biology M,D
Veterinary Medicine M,D
Veterinary Sciences M,D

## VIRGINIA STATE UNIVERSITY
Biological and Biomedical Sciences—General M
Community Health M,D

## VIRGINIA UNIVERSITY OF INTEGRATIVE MEDICINE
Acupuncture and Oriental Medicine M,D,O
Nutrition M,D,O

## VITERBO UNIVERSITY
Health Services Management and Hospital Administration M
Nursing—General D

## WAGNER COLLEGE
Family Nurse Practitioner Studies M,D,O
Microbiology M
Nursing Education M,D,O
Nursing—General M,D,O

## WAKE FOREST UNIVERSITY
Allopathic Medicine D
Anatomy D
Biochemistry D
Biological and Biomedical Sciences—General M,D
Cancer Biology/Oncology D
Clinical Laboratory Sciences/Medical Technology M
Genomic Sciences D
Immunology D

Microbiology D
Molecular Genetics D
Molecular Medicine M,D
Neurobiology D
Neuroscience D
Nurse Anesthesia M
Pharmacology D
Physiology D
Translational Biology M,D

## WALDEN UNIVERSITY
Adult Nursing M,D,O
Clinical Research M,D,O
Community Health M,D,O
Epidemiology M,D,O
Family Nurse Practitioner Studies M,D,O
Gerontological Nursing M,D,O
Health Promotion M,D,O
Health Services Management and Hospital Administration M,D,O
International Health M,D,O
Nursing and Healthcare Administration M,D,O
Nursing Education M,D,O
Nursing Informatics M,D,O
Nursing—General M,D,O
Public Health—General M,D,O

## WALLA WALLA UNIVERSITY
Biological and Biomedical Sciences—General M

## WALSH UNIVERSITY
Adult Nursing M
Health Services Management and Hospital Administration M
Nursing and Healthcare Administration M,D
Nursing Education M,D
Nursing—General M,D
Physical Therapy D

## WASHBURN UNIVERSITY
Nursing and Healthcare Administration M,D,O
Nursing—General M,D,O

## WASHINGTON ADVENTIST UNIVERSITY
Health Services Management and Hospital Administration M
Nursing and Healthcare Administration M
Nursing Education M
Nursing—General M

## WASHINGTON STATE UNIVERSITY
Allopathic Medicine M,D
Biochemistry M,D
Bioethics M,D,O
Biological and Biomedical Sciences—General M,D
Biophysics M,D
Communication Disorders M
Community Health M,D,O
Entomology M,D
Family Nurse Practitioner Studies M,D,O
Genetics M,D
Health Services Management and Hospital Administration M
Immunology M,D
Infectious Diseases M,D
Neuroscience M,D
Nursing—General M,D,O
Nutrition M
Pharmacy D
Plant Pathology M,D
Psychiatric Nursing M,D,O
Veterinary Medicine D
Veterinary Sciences M,D

## WASHINGTON UNIVERSITY IN ST. LOUIS
Allopathic Medicine D
Biochemistry D
Bioethics M
Biological and Biomedical Sciences—General D
Cell Biology D
Clinical Research M
Communication Disorders M,D
Computational Biology D
Developmental Biology D
Ecology D
Environmental Biology D
Epidemiology M,D
Evolutionary Biology D
Genetics M,D
Genomic Sciences D
Health Services Research M,O
Human Genetics D
Immunology D
International Health M,D
Microbiology D
Molecular Biology D
Molecular Biophysics D
Molecular Genetics D
Molecular Pathogenesis D
Neuroscience D
Occupational Therapy M,D
Physical Therapy D
Plant Biology D
Public Health—General M,D
Rehabilitation Sciences D
Systems Biology D

## WAYLAND BAPTIST UNIVERSITY
Health Services Management and Hospital Administration M,D

## WAYNESBURG UNIVERSITY
Health Services Management and Hospital Administration M,D
Nursing and Healthcare Administration M,D
Nursing Education M,D
Nursing Informatics M,D
Nursing—General M,D

**WAYNE STATE UNIVERSITY**
Acute Care/Critical Care Nursing M,D
Adult Nursing M,D
Biological and Biomedical Sciences—General M,D
Communication Disorders M,D
Community Health Nursing M,D
Computational Biology M,D
Gerontological Nursing M,D
Health Services Management and Hospital Administration M,D
Health Services Research M,D
Maternal and Child/Neonatal Nursing M,D
Medical Imaging M,D,O
Medicinal and Pharmaceutical Chemistry M,D
Neuroscience M,D
Nurse Anesthesia M,D,O
Nurse Midwifery M,D
Nursing—General M,D
Nutrition M,D,O
Occupational Therapy M,D,O
Pediatric Nursing M,D,O
Pharmaceutical Sciences M,D
Pharmacology M,D
Pharmacy D
Physical Therapy M,D,O
Physician Assistant Studies M,D,O
Psychiatric Nursing M,D
Toxicology M,D
Women's Health Nursing M,D

**WEBER STATE UNIVERSITY**
Health Physics/Radiological Health M
Health Services Management and Hospital Administration M
Nursing and Healthcare Administration M
Nursing Education M
Nursing—General M

**WEBSTER UNIVERSITY**
Communication Disorders M
Health Services Management and Hospital Administration M,D,O
Nurse Anesthesia D
Nursing Education M
Nursing—General M

**WEILL CORNELL MEDICINE**
Biochemistry M,D
Biological and Biomedical Sciences—General M,D
Biophysics M,D
Cell Biology M,D
Computational Biology D
Epidemiology M
Health Services Management and Hospital Administration M
Health Services Research M
Immunology M,D
Molecular Biology M,D
Neuroscience M,D
Pharmacology M,D
Physician Assistant Studies M
Physiology M,D
Structural Biology M,D
Systems Biology M,D

**WESLEYAN UNIVERSITY**
Biochemistry D
Biological and Biomedical Sciences—General D
Cell Biology D
Developmental Biology D
Ecology D
Evolutionary Biology D
Genetics D
Genomic Sciences D
Molecular Biology D
Molecular Biophysics D
Neurobiology D

**WESLEY COLLEGE**
Nursing—General M
Occupational Therapy M

**WEST COAST UNIVERSITY**
Family Nurse Practitioner Studies M,D
Health Services Management and Hospital Administration M,D
Nursing—General M,D
Occupational Therapy M,D
Pharmacy M,D
Physical Therapy M,D

**WESTERN CAROLINA UNIVERSITY**
Biological and Biomedical Sciences—General M
Communication Disorders M
Health Services Management and Hospital Administration M
Nursing—General M,D,O
Physical Therapy D

**WESTERN CONNECTICUT STATE UNIVERSITY**
Adult Nursing M,D
Gerontological Nursing M,D
Health Services Management and Hospital Administration M
Nursing Education D
Nursing—General M,D

**WESTERN GOVERNORS UNIVERSITY**
Health Services Management and Hospital Administration M
Nursing and Healthcare Administration M
Nursing Education M
Nursing Informatics M

**WESTERN ILLINOIS UNIVERSITY**
Biological and Biomedical Sciences—General M,O
Communication Disorders M
Ecology D
Marine Biology M,O
Public Health—General M
Zoology M,O

**WESTERN KENTUCKY UNIVERSITY**
Biological and Biomedical Sciences—General M
Communication Disorders M
Health Services Management and Hospital Administration M
Nursing—General M
Physical Therapy D
Public Health—General M

**WESTERN MICHIGAN UNIVERSITY**
Biological and Biomedical Sciences—General M,D,O
Communication Disorders M,D
Health Services Management and Hospital Administration M,D,O
Nursing—General M
Occupational Therapy M
Physician Assistant Studies M
Physiology M
Rehabilitation Sciences M
Vision Sciences M

**WESTERN MICHIGAN UNIVERSITY HOMER STRYKER MD SCHOOL OF MEDICINE**
Allopathic Medicine D

**WESTERN NEW ENGLAND UNIVERSITY**
Occupational Therapy D
Pharmacy D

**WESTERN NEW MEXICO UNIVERSITY**
Occupational Therapy M

**WESTERN UNIVERSITY OF HEALTH SCIENCES**
Allied Health—General M,D
Biological and Biomedical Sciences—General M
Dentistry D
Nursing and Healthcare Administration M
Nursing—General M,D
Optometry D
Osteopathic Medicine D
Pharmaceutical Sciences M
Pharmacy D
Physical Therapy D
Physician Assistant Studies M
Podiatric Medicine D
Veterinary Medicine D

**WESTERN WASHINGTON UNIVERSITY**
Biological and Biomedical Sciences—General M
Communication Disorders M

**WESTFIELD STATE UNIVERSITY**
Physician Assistant Studies M

**WEST LIBERTY UNIVERSITY**
Biological and Biomedical Sciences—General M
Physician Assistant Studies M
Zoology M

**WESTMINSTER COLLEGE (UT)**
Family Nurse Practitioner Studies M
Nurse Anesthesia M
Nursing—General M
Public Health—General M

**WEST TEXAS A&M UNIVERSITY**
Biological and Biomedical Sciences—General M
Communication Disorders M
Family Nurse Practitioner Studies M
Nursing—General M

**WEST VIRGINIA SCHOOL OF OSTEOPATHIC MEDICINE**
Osteopathic Medicine D

**WEST VIRGINIA UNIVERSITY**
Allopathic Medicine M,D
Biochemistry M,D
Biological and Biomedical Sciences—General M,D
Cancer Biology/Oncology M,D
Communication Disorders M,D
Dental Hygiene M,D
Dentistry M,D
Developmental Biology M,D
Entomology M,D
Environmental and Occupational Health M,D
Epidemiology M,D
Genetics M,D
Immunology M,D
Industrial Hygiene M,D
Molecular Biology M,D
Nursing—General M,D,O
Nutrition M,D
Occupational Therapy M,D
Oral and Dental Sciences M,D
Pathology M,D
Pharmaceutical Sciences D
Pharmacy D
Physical Therapy M,D
Plant Pathology M,D
Public Health—General M,D

**WEST VIRGINIA WESLEYAN COLLEGE**
Family Nurse Practitioner Studies M,D,O
Nurse Midwifery M,D,O
Nursing and Healthcare Administration M,D,O
Nursing—General M,D,O
Psychiatric Nursing M,D,O

**WHEELING JESUIT UNIVERSITY**
Nursing—General M
Physical Therapy D

**WICHITA STATE UNIVERSITY**
Allied Health—General M,D
Biological and Biomedical Sciences—General M
Communication Disorders M,D
Nursing—General M,D
Physical Therapy D
Physician Assistant Studies M

**WIDENER UNIVERSITY**
Health Services Management and Hospital Administration M
Nursing—General M,D,O
Physical Therapy M,D

**WILFRID LAURIER UNIVERSITY**
Biological and Biomedical Sciences—General M
Health Promotion M
Neuroscience M,D

**WILLIAM CAREY UNIVERSITY**
Nursing—General M
Osteopathic Medicine D
Pharmacy D

**WILLIAM JAMES COLLEGE**
Community Health M,D,O
International Health M,D,O

**WILLIAM WOODS UNIVERSITY**
Health Services Management and Hospital Administration M,D,O

**WILMINGTON UNIVERSITY**
Adult Nursing M,D
Family Nurse Practitioner Studies M,D
Gerontological Nursing M,D
Health Services Management and Hospital Administration M,D
Nursing and Healthcare Administration M,D
Nursing—General M,D

**WILSON COLLEGE**
Health Services Management and Hospital Administration M
Nursing and Healthcare Administration M
Nursing Education M
Nursing—General M

**WINGATE UNIVERSITY**
Health Services Management and Hospital Administration M
Pharmacy D
Physical Therapy D
Physician Assistant Studies M

**WINONA STATE UNIVERSITY**
Acute Care/Critical Care Nursing M,D,O
Adult Nursing M,D,O
Family Nurse Practitioner Studies M,D,O
Gerontological Nursing M,D,O
Nursing and Healthcare Administration M,D,O
Nursing Education M,D,O
Nursing—General M,D,O

**WINSTON-SALEM STATE UNIVERSITY**
Family Nurse Practitioner Studies M,D
Health Services Management and Hospital Administration M
Nursing Education M,D
Nursing—General M,D
Occupational Therapy M
Physical Therapy D

**WINTHROP UNIVERSITY**
Biological and Biomedical Sciences—General M
Nutrition M,O

**WONGU UNIVERSITY OF ORIENTAL MEDICINE**
Acupuncture and Oriental Medicine M

**WON INSTITUTE OF GRADUATE STUDIES**
Acupuncture and Oriental Medicine M,O

**WOODS HOLE OCEANOGRAPHIC INSTITUTION**
Marine Biology D

**WORCESTER POLYTECHNIC INSTITUTE**
Biochemistry M,D
Biological and Biomedical Sciences—General M,D
Computational Biology M,D

**WORCESTER STATE UNIVERSITY**
Communication Disorders M
Community Health Nursing M
Health Services Management and Hospital Administration M
Nursing Education M
Occupational Therapy M

**WRIGHT STATE UNIVERSITY**
Acute Care/Critical Care Nursing M
Adult Nursing M
Allopathic Medicine D
Anatomy M
Biochemistry M
Biological and Biomedical Sciences—General M,D
Family Nurse Practitioner Studies M
Gerontological Nursing M
Health Promotion M
Immunology M
Maternal and Child/Neonatal Nursing M
Microbiology M
Molecular Biology M
Neuroscience M
Nursing and Healthcare Administration M
Nursing—General M
Pediatric Nursing M
Pharmacology M
Physiology M
Psychiatric Nursing M
Public Health—General M
School Nursing M
Toxicology M

**XAVIER UNIVERSITY**
Health Services Management and Hospital Administration M*
Nursing—General M,D,O
Occupational Therapy M

**XAVIER UNIVERSITY OF LOUISIANA**
Pharmacy D

**YALE UNIVERSITY**
Allopathic Medicine D
Biochemistry D
Biological and Biomedical Sciences—General D
Biophysics D
Cell Biology D
Computational Biology D
Developmental Biology D
Ecology D
Environmental and Occupational Health M,D
Epidemiology M,D
Evolutionary Biology D
Genetics D
Genomic Sciences D
Health Services Management and Hospital Administration M,D
Immunology D
Infectious Diseases D
International Health M,D
Microbiology D
Molecular Biology D
Molecular Biophysics D
Molecular Medicine D
Molecular Physiology D
Neurobiology D
Neuroscience D
Nursing—General M,D,O
Pathology M,D
Pharmacology D
Physician Assistant Studies M
Physiology D
Plant Biology D
Public Health—General M,D
Virology D

**YESHIVA UNIVERSITY**
Communication Disorders M

**YORK COLLEGE OF PENNSYLVANIA**
Gerontological Nursing M
Health Services Management and Hospital Administration M
Nurse Anesthesia M
Nursing—General M

**YORK COLLEGE OF THE CITY UNIVERSITY OF NEW YORK**
Pharmaceutical Sciences M
Physician Assistant Studies M

**YORK UNIVERSITY**
Biological and Biomedical Sciences—General M,D
Nursing—General M

**YO SAN UNIVERSITY OF TRADITIONAL CHINESE MEDICINE**
Acupuncture and Oriental Medicine M

**YOUNGSTOWN STATE UNIVERSITY**
Anatomy M
Biochemistry M
Biological and Biomedical Sciences—General M
Environmental Biology M
Health Services Management and Hospital Administration M
Microbiology M
Molecular Biology M
Nursing—General M
Physical Therapy D
Physiology M
Public Health—General M

*M—masters degree; D—doctorate; O—other advanced degree; *—Close-Up and/or Display*

# ACADEMIC AND PROFESSIONAL PROGRAMS IN THE BIOLOGICAL AND BIOMEDICAL SCIENCES

# Section 1
# Biological and Biomedical Sciences

This section contains a directory of institutions offering graduate work in biological and biomedical sciences, followed by in-depth entries submitted by institutions that chose to prepare detailed program descriptions. Additional information about programs listed in the directory but not augmented by an in-depth entry may be obtained by writing directly to the dean of a graduate school or chair of a department at the address given in the directory.

Programs in fields related to the biological and biomedical sciences may be found throughout this book. In the other guides in this series:

**Graduate Programs in the Humanities, Arts & Social Sciences**
See *Psychology and Counseling* and *Sociology, Anthropology, and Archaeology*

**Graduate Programs in the Physical Sciences, Mathematics, Agricultural Sciences, the Environment & Natural Resources**
See *Chemistry, Marine Sciences and Oceanography,* and *Mathematical Sciences*

**Graduate Programs in Engineering & Applied Sciences**
See *Agricultural Engineering and Bioengineering, Biomedical Engineering and Biotechnology, Civil and Environmental Engineering, Management of Engineering and Technology,* and *Ocean Engineering*

## CONTENTS

# Biological and Biomedical Sciences—General

**Acadia University,** Faculty of Pure and Applied Science, Department of Biology, Wolfville, NS B4P 2R6, Canada. Offers M Sc. *Degree requirements:* For master's, comprehensive exam, thesis. *Entrance requirements:* For master's, minimum B-average in last 2 years of major. Additional exam requirements/recommendations for international students: required—TOEFL (minimum score 580 paper-based; 93 iBT), IELTS (minimum score 6.5).

**Adelphi University,** College of Arts and Sciences, Department of Biology, Garden City, NY 11530-0701. Offers biology (MS); biotechnology (MS). *Program availability:* Part-time, evening/weekend. *Degree requirements:* For master's, thesis or alternative. *Entrance requirements:* For master's, bachelor's degree in biology or allied sciences, essay, 3 letters of recommendation, official transcripts. Additional exam requirements/recommendations for international students: required—TOEFL (minimum score 550 paper-based; 80 iBT), IELTS (minimum score 6.5). Electronic applications accepted. *Expenses:* Contact institution.

**Alabama Agricultural and Mechanical University,** School of Graduate Studies, College of Agricultural, Life and Natural Sciences, Department of Biological and Environmental Sciences, Huntsville, AL 35811. Offers biology (MS); plant and soil science (MS, PhD). *Program availability:* Evening/weekend. Terminal master's awarded for partial completion of doctoral program. *Degree requirements:* For master's, thesis optional; for doctorate, one foreign language, thesis/dissertation optional. *Entrance requirements:* For master's, GRE General Test, BS in agriculture; for doctorate, GRE General Test, master's degree. Additional exam requirements/recommendations for international students: required—TOEFL (minimum score 500 paper-based; 61 iBT). Electronic applications accepted.

**Alabama State University,** College of Science, Mathematics and Technology, Department of Biological Sciences, Montgomery, AL 36101-0271. Offers biology (MS); microbiology (PhD). *Faculty:* 13 full-time (4 women), 7 part-time/adjunct (4 women). *Students:* 8 full-time (3 women), 11 part-time (7 women); includes 13 minority (12 Black or African American, non-Hispanic/Latino; 1 Asian, non-Hispanic/Latino), 4 international. Average age 29. 17 applicants, 41% accepted, 4 enrolled. In 2019, 3 master's, 1 doctorate awarded. *Degree requirements:* For master's, one foreign language, comprehensive exam, thesis; for doctorate, 3 foreign languages, thesis/dissertation. *Entrance requirements:* For master's, GRE General Test, GRE Subject Test, writing competency test. Additional exam requirements/recommendations for international students: required—TOEFL (minimum score 500 paper-based). *Application deadline:* For fall admission, 4/15 for domestic and international students; for spring admission, 11/15 for domestic and international students; for summer admission, 3/15 for domestic and international students. Applications are processed on a rolling basis. Application fee: $25. Electronic applications accepted. Application fee is waived when completed online. *Financial support:* Fellowships, research assistantships, scholarships/grants, tuition waivers (partial), and unspecified assistantships available. Financial award application deadline: 6/30; financial award applicants required to submit FAFSA. *Unit head:* Dr. Boakai K. Robertson, Chair, 334-229-4467, Fax: 334-229-1007, E-mail: bkrobertson@alasu.edu. *Application contact:* Dr. Ed Brown, Dean of Graduate Studies, 334-229-4274, Fax: 334-229-4928, E-mail: wperson@alasu.edu.
Website: http://www.alasu.edu/academics/colleges—departments/science-mathematics-technology/biological-sciences-department/index.aspx

**Albert Einstein College of Medicine,** Graduate Programs in the Biomedical Sciences, Bronx, NY 10461. Offers PhD, MD/PhD. *Degree requirements:* For doctorate, thesis/dissertation. *Entrance requirements:* For doctorate, GRE General Test. Additional exam requirements/recommendations for international students: required—TOEFL. Electronic applications accepted.

**Albert Einstein College of Medicine,** Medical Scientist Training Program, Bronx, NY 10461. Offers MD/PhD.

**Alcorn State University,** School of Graduate Studies, School of Arts and Sciences, Department of Biological Sciences, Lorman, MS 39096-7500. Offers MS.

**American Museum of Natural History–Richard Gilder Graduate School,** Program in Comparative Biology, New York, NY 10024. Offers PhD. *Degree requirements:* For doctorate, thesis/dissertation, qualifying examination. *Entrance requirements:* For doctorate, GRE General Test (taken within the past five years); GRE Subject Test (recommended), BA, BS, or equivalent degree from accredited institution; official transcripts; essay. Additional exam requirements/recommendations for international students: required—TOEFL (minimum score 600 paper-based; 100 iBT), IELTS (minimum score 7).

**American University,** College of Arts and Sciences, Department of Biology, Washington, DC 20016-8007. Offers biology (MS); biotechnology (MA). *Program availability:* Part-time. *Degree requirements:* For master's, comprehensive exam, thesis (for some programs). *Entrance requirements:* For master's, GRE General Test, GRE Subject Test, statement of purpose, transcripts, 2 letters of recommendation, resume. Additional exam requirements/recommendations for international students: required—TOEFL. Electronic applications accepted. *Expenses:* Contact institution.

**Andrews University,** School of Graduate Studies, College of Arts and Sciences, Department of Biology, Berrien Springs, MI 49104. Offers MAT, MS. *Faculty:* 7 full-time (3 women). *Students:* 7 full-time (4 women), 1 part-time (0 women); includes 2 minority (1 Black or African American, non-Hispanic/Latino; 1 Hispanic/Latino), 2 international. Average age 26. *Degree requirements:* For master's, comprehensive exam, thesis. *Entrance requirements:* For master's, GRE Subject Test. Additional exam requirements/recommendations for international students: required—TOEFL (minimum score 550 paper-based). *Application deadline:* Applications are processed on a rolling basis. Application fee: $60. Electronic applications accepted. *Financial support:* Fellowships, research assistantships, teaching assistantships, career-related internships or fieldwork, Federal Work-Study, and institutionally sponsored loans available. Financial award application deadline: 3/15. *Unit head:* Dr. Robert Zdor, Chairman, 269-471-3243. *Application contact:* Jillian Panagot, Director, University Admissions, 800-253-2874, Fax: 269-471-6321, E-mail: graduate@andrews.edu.

**Angelo State University,** College of Graduate Studies and Research, College of Science and Engineering, Department of Biology, San Angelo, TX 76909. Offers MS. *Program availability:* Part-time, evening/weekend. *Degree requirements:* For master's, comprehensive exam, thesis optional. *Entrance requirements:* For master's, GRE General Test, essay. Electronic applications accepted.

**Appalachian State University,** Cratis D. Williams School of Graduate Studies, Department of Biology, Boone, NC 28608. Offers cell and molecular biology (MS). *Program availability:* Part-time. *Degree requirements:* For master's, comprehensive exam, thesis. *Entrance requirements:* For master's, GRE General Test, 3 letters of recommendation. Additional exam requirements/recommendations for international students: required—TOEFL (minimum score 570 paper-based; 79 iBT), IELTS (minimum score 6.5). Electronic applications accepted.

**Arizona State University at Tempe,** College of Liberal Arts and Sciences, School of Life Sciences, Tempe, AZ 85287-4601. Offers animal behavior (PhD); applied ethics (biomedical and health ethics) (MA); biology (MS, PhD), including biology, biology and society, complex adaptive systems science (PhD), plant biology and conservation (MS); environmental life sciences (PhD); evolutionary biology (PhD); history and philosophy of science (PhD); human and social dimensions of science and technology (PhD); microbiology (PhD); molecular and cellular biology (PhD); neuroscience (PhD). Terminal master's awarded for partial completion of doctoral program. *Degree requirements:* For master's, thesis (for some programs), interactive Program of Study (iPOS) submitted before completing 50 percent of required credit hours; for doctorate, variable foreign language requirement, comprehensive exam, thesis/dissertation, interactive Program of Study (iPOS) submitted before completing 50 percent of required credit hours. *Entrance requirements:* For master's and doctorate, GRE, minimum GPA of 3.0 or equivalent in last 2 years of work leading to bachelor's degree. Additional exam requirements/recommendations for international students: required—TOEFL (minimum score 600 paper-based; 100 iBT). Electronic applications accepted.

**Arkansas Colleges of Health Education,** Program in Biomedicine, Fort Smith, AR 72916. Offers MS.

**Arkansas State University,** Graduate School, College of Sciences and Mathematics, Department of Biological Sciences, State University, AR 72467. Offers biological sciences (MA); biology (MS); biology education (MSE, SCCT); biotechnology (PSM). *Program availability:* Part-time. *Degree requirements:* For master's, comprehensive exam, thesis (for some programs); for SCCT, comprehensive exam. *Entrance requirements:* For master's, GRE General Test, appropriate bachelor's degree, letters of reference, interview, official transcripts, immunization records, statement of educational objectives and career goals, teaching certificate (for MSE); for SCCT, GRE General Test or MAT, interview, master's degree, letters of reference, official transcript, personal statement, immunization records. Additional exam requirements/recommendations for international students: required—TOEFL (minimum score 550 paper-based; 79 iBT), IELTS (minimum score 6), PTE (minimum score 56). Electronic applications accepted.

**A.T. Still University,** Kirksville College of Osteopathic Medicine, Kirksville, MO 63501. Offers biomedical sciences (MS); osteopathic medicine (DO). *Accreditation:* AOsA. *Faculty:* 147 full-time (95 women), 61 part-time/adjunct (23 women). *Students:* 710 full-time (311 women), 10 part-time (3 women); includes 143 minority (17 Black or African American, non-Hispanic/Latino; 46 Asian, non-Hispanic/Latino; 41 Hispanic/Latino; 1 Native Hawaiian or other Pacific Islander, non-Hispanic/Latino; 38 Two or more races, non-Hispanic/Latino). Average age 27. 4,388 applicants, 9% accepted, 180 enrolled. In 2019, 7 master's, 173 doctorates awarded. *Degree requirements:* For master's, thesis; for doctorate, Level 1 and 2 COMLEX-PE and CE exams. *Entrance requirements:* For master's, GRE, MCAT, or DAT, minimum undergraduate GPA of 2.65 (cumulative and science); for doctorate, MCAT, bachelor's degree with minimum GPA of 2.8 (cumulative and science) or 90 semester hours with minimum GPA of 3.5 (cumulative and science) and MCAT (minimum score 500). *Application deadline:* For fall admission, 2/1 for domestic students; for summer admission, 2/1 for domestic students. Applications are processed on a rolling basis. Application fee: $70. Electronic applications accepted. *Financial support:* In 2019–20, 194 students received support, including 10 fellowships with full tuition reimbursements available (averaging $58,290 per year); Federal Work-Study and scholarships/grants also available. Financial award application deadline: 6/1; financial award applicants required to submit FAFSA. *Unit head:* Dr. Margaret Wilson, Dean, 660-626-2354, Fax: 660-626-2080, E-mail: mwilson@atsu.edu. *Application contact:* Donna Sparks, Director, Admissions Processing, 660-626-2117, Fax: 660-626-2969, E-mail: admissions@atsu.edu.
Website: http://www.atsu.edu/kcom/

**Auburn University,** Graduate School, College of Sciences and Mathematics, Department of Biological Sciences, Auburn, AL 36849. Offers botany (MS); zoology (MS). *Program availability:* Part-time. *Faculty:* 44 full-time (22 women), 2 part-time/adjunct (1 woman). *Students:* 56 full-time (35 women), 70 part-time (39 women); includes 27 minority (10 Black or African American, non-Hispanic/Latino; 4 Asian, non-Hispanic/Latino; 5 Hispanic/Latino; 8 Two or more races, non-Hispanic/Latino), 23 international. Average age 28. 102 applicants, 48% accepted, 44 enrolled. In 2019, 26 master's, 6 doctorates awarded. *Degree requirements:* For master's, thesis (for some programs); for doctorate, thesis/dissertation. *Entrance requirements:* For master's and doctorate, GRE General Test. Additional exam requirements/recommendations for international students: required—iTEP; recommended—TOEFL (minimum score 550 paper-based; 79 iBT), IELTS (minimum score 6.5). *Application deadline:* Applications are processed on a rolling basis. Application fee: $60 ($70 for international students). Electronic applications accepted. *Expenses: Tuition, area resident:* Full-time $9828; part-time $546 per credit hour. Tuition, state resident: full-time $9828; part-time $546 per credit hour. Tuition, nonresident: full-time $29,484; part-time $1638 per credit hour. *International tuition:* $29,744 full-time. Tuition and fees vary according to course load, program and reciprocity agreements. *Financial support:* In 2019–20, 61 fellowships with tuition reimbursements, 28 research assistantships with tuition reimbursements (averaging $22,237 per year), 81 teaching assistantships with tuition reimbursements (averaging $27,166 per year) were awarded. Financial award application deadline: 3/15; financial award applicants required to submit FAFSA. *Unit head:* Dr. Scott R. Santos, Chair, 334-844-7410, Fax: 334-844-1645, E-mail: santos@auburn.edu. *Application contact:* Dr. George Flowers, Dean of the Graduate School, 334-844-2125.
Website: http://www.auburn.edu/cosam/departments/biology/

**Austin Peay State University,** College of Graduate Studies, College of Science, Technology, Engineering and Mathematics, Department of Biology, Clarksville, TN 37044. Offers clinical laboratory science (MS). *Program availability:* Part-time. *Faculty:* 12 full-time (5 women). *Students:* 10 full-time (4 women), 22 part-time (13 women); includes 7 minority (2 Black or African American, non-Hispanic/Latino; 2 Hispanic/Latino; 3 Two or more races, non-Hispanic/Latino), 3 international. Average age 27. 21 applicants, 100% accepted, 6 enrolled. In 2019, 4 master's awarded. *Degree requirements:* For master's, comprehensive exam, thesis optional. *Entrance requirements:* For master's, GRE General Test, 3 letters of recommendation, minimum undergraduate GPA of 2.75. Additional exam requirements/recommendations for international students: required—TOEFL (minimum score 500 paper-based). *Application deadline:* For fall admission, 8/5 priority date for domestic students. Applications are processed on a rolling basis. Application fee: $45 ($55 for international students). Electronic applications accepted. *Financial support:* Research assistantships with full tuition reimbursements, career-related internships or fieldwork, Federal Work-Study, institutionally sponsored loans, scholarships/grants, and unspecified assistantships

available. Support available to part-time students. Financial award application deadline: 7/1; financial award applicants required to submit FAFSA. *Unit head:* Dr. Don Dailey, Chair, 931-221-7781, Fax: 931-221-6323, E-mail: daileyd@apsu.edu. *Application contact:* Megan Mitchell, Coordinator of Graduate Admissions, 800-859-4723, Fax: 931-221-7641, E-mail: gradadmissions@apsu.edu.
Website: http://www.apsu.edu/biology/

**Ball State University,** Graduate School, College of Sciences and Humanities, Department of Biology, Program in Biology, Muncie, IN 47306. Offers MA, MS. *Program availability:* Part-time. *Entrance requirements:* For master's, minimum baccalaureate GPA of 2.75 or 3.0 in latter half of baccalaureate, transcripts of all prior coursework, three letters of recommendation. Additional exam requirements/recommendations for international students: required—TOEFL (minimum score 550 paper-based; 79 iBT), IELTS (minimum score 6.5). Electronic applications accepted. *Expenses: Tuition, area resident:* Full-time $7506; part-time $417 per credit hour. Tuition, nonresident: full-time $20,610; part-time $1145 per credit hour. *Required fees:* $2126. Tuition and fees vary according to course load, campus/location and program.

**Ball State University,** Graduate School, College of Sciences and Humanities, Interdepartmental Program in Environmental Sciences, Muncie, IN 47306. Offers environmental science (PhD), including biology, chemistry, geological sciences. *Program availability:* Part-time. *Degree requirements:* For doctorate, thesis/dissertation. *Entrance requirements:* For doctorate, GRE General Test, minimum cumulative GPA of 3.0 (chemistry), 3.2 (biology and geological sciences); acknowledged arrangement for doctoral environmental sciences research with faculty mentor; three letters of recommendation. Additional exam requirements/recommendations for international students: required—TOEFL (minimum score 550 paper-based; 79 iBT), IELTS (minimum score 6.5). Electronic applications accepted. *Expenses: Tuition, area resident:* Full-time $7506; part-time $417 per credit hour. Tuition, nonresident: full-time $20,610; part-time $1145 per credit hour. *Required fees:* $2126. Tuition and fees vary according to course load, campus/location and program.

**Barry University,** College of Health Sciences, Programs in Biology and Biomedical Sciences, Miami Shores, FL 33161-6695. Offers biology (MS); biomedical sciences (MS). *Program availability:* Part-time, evening/weekend. *Degree requirements:* For master's, comprehensive exam, thesis (for some programs). *Entrance requirements:* For master's, GRE General Test or Florida Teacher's Certification Exam (biology); GRE General Test, MCAT, or DAT (biomedical sciences). Electronic applications accepted.

**Baylor College of Medicine,** Graduate School of Biomedical Sciences, Houston, TX 77030-3498. Offers MS, PhD, MD/PhD. Terminal master's awarded for partial completion of doctoral program. *Degree requirements:* For master's, thesis; for doctorate, thesis/dissertation, public defense. *Entrance requirements:* For doctorate, GRE General Test, GRE Subject Test (strongly recommended), minimum GPA of 3.0. Additional exam requirements/recommendations for international students: required—TOEFL. Electronic applications accepted.

**Baylor University,** Graduate School, College of Arts and Sciences, Department of Biology, Waco, TX 76798. Offers MA, MS, PhD. *Program availability:* Part-time. *Entrance requirements:* For master's and doctorate, GRE General Test. Additional exam requirements/recommendations for international students: required—TOEFL.

**Bemidji State University,** School of Graduate Studies, Bemidji, MN 56601. Offers biology (MS); education (MS); English (MA, MS); environmental studies (MS); mathematics (MS); mathematics (elementary and middle level education) (MS); special education (M Sp Ed). *Program availability:* Part-time, online learning. *Degree requirements:* For master's, comprehensive exam, thesis (for some programs). *Entrance requirements:* For master's, GRE; GMAT, letters of recommendation, letters of interest. Additional exam requirements/recommendations for international students: required—TOEFL (minimum score 550 paper-based; 80 iBT). Electronic applications accepted. *Expenses:* Contact institution.

**Binghamton University, State University of New York,** Graduate School, Harpur College of Arts and Sciences, Department of Biological Sciences, Binghamton, NY 13902-6000. Offers MA, MS, PhD. *Program availability:* Part-time. Terminal master's awarded for partial completion of doctoral program. *Degree requirements:* For master's, thesis; for doctorate, comprehensive exam, thesis/dissertation. *Entrance requirements:* For master's and doctorate, GRE General Test. Additional exam requirements/recommendations for international students: required—TOEFL (minimum score 550 paper-based; 100 iBT). Electronic applications accepted.

**Bloomsburg University of Pennsylvania,** School of Graduate Studies, College of Science and Technology, Department of Biological and Allied Health Sciences, Program in Biology, Bloomsburg, PA 17815-1301. Offers MS. *Degree requirements:* For master's, thesis optional. *Entrance requirements:* For master's, minimum QPA of 3.0, 2 letters of recommendation, personal statement, undergraduate degree in biology. Additional exam requirements/recommendations for international students: required—TOEFL (minimum score 550 paper-based), IELTS. Electronic applications accepted.

**Boise State University,** College of Arts and Sciences, Department of Biological Sciences, Boise, ID 83725-1515. Offers biology (MA, MS); biomolecular sciences (PhD); raptor biology (MS). *Program availability:* Part-time. *Students:* 50 full-time (36 women), 10 part-time (5 women); includes 6 minority (4 Hispanic/Latino; 1 Native Hawaiian or other Pacific Islander, non-Hispanic/Latino; 1 Two or more races, non-Hispanic/Latino), 4 international. *Degree requirements:* For master's, thesis. *Entrance requirements:* For master's, GRE General Test, minimum GPA of 3.0. Additional exam requirements/recommendations for international students: required—TOEFL, IELTS. Electronic applications accepted. *Expenses: Tuition, area resident:* Full-time $7110; part-time $470 per credit hour. Tuition, state resident: full-time $7110; part-time $470 per credit hour. Tuition, nonresident: full-time $24,030; part-time $827 per credit hour. *International tuition:* $24,030 full-time. *Required fees:* $2536. Tuition and fees vary according to course load and program. *Financial support:* Research assistantships, teaching assistantships, institutionally sponsored loans, and unspecified assistantships available. Financial award application deadline: 1/15; financial award applicants required to submit FAFSA. *Unit head:* Dr. Kevin Feris, Chair, 208-426-4267, E-mail: kevinferis@boisestate.edu. *Application contact:* Dr. Ian Roberts, Graduate Coordinator, 208-426-3208, E-mail: iroberts@boisestate.edu.
Website: https://www.boisestate.edu/biology/

**Boston College,** Morrissey Graduate School of Arts and Sciences, Department of Biology, Chestnut Hill, MA 02467-3800. Offers PhD, MBA/MS. *Degree requirements:* For doctorate, thesis/dissertation. *Entrance requirements:* For doctorate, GRE General Test, GRE Subject Test. Additional exam requirements/recommendations for international students: required—TOEFL (minimum score 600 paper-based; 100 iBT), IELTS (minimum score 8). Electronic applications accepted.

**Boston University,** Graduate School of Arts and Sciences, Department of Biology, Boston, MA 02215. Offers MA, PhD. *Students:* 68 full-time (44 women), 12 part-time (9 women); includes 16 minority (1 Black or African American, non-Hispanic/Latino; 6 Asian, non-Hispanic/Latino; 5 Hispanic/Latino; 4 Two or more races, non-Hispanic/Latino), 17 international. Average age 26. 210 applicants, 12% accepted, 8 enrolled. In 2019, 11 master's, 5 doctorates awarded. Terminal master's awarded for partial completion of doctoral program. *Degree requirements:* For master's, thesis (for some programs); for doctorate, comprehensive exam, thesis/dissertation. *Entrance requirements:* For master's and doctorate, 3 letters of recommendation, transcripts, personal statement, curriculum vitae. Additional exam requirements/recommendations for international students: required—TOEFL (minimum score 550 paper-based; 84 iBT). *Application deadline:* For fall admission, 12/2 for domestic and international students. Application fee: $95. Electronic applications accepted. *Financial support:* In 2019–20, 64 students received support, including 8 fellowships with full tuition reimbursements available (averaging $23,340 per year), 17 research assistantships with full tuition reimbursements available (averaging $23,340 per year), 28 teaching assistantships with full tuition reimbursements available (averaging $23,340 per year); Federal Work-Study, scholarships/grants, traineeships, and health care benefits also available. Financial award application deadline: 12/2. *Unit head:* Kim McCall, Chair, 617-353-5444, Fax: 617-358-0442, E-mail: kmccall@bu.edu. *Application contact:* Christina Honeycutt, Academic Administrator, 617-353-2432, Fax: 617-353-6340, E-mail: cjhoney@bu.edu.
Website: http://www.bu.edu/biology/

**Boston University,** School of Medicine, Graduate Medical Sciences, Program in Biomedical Sciences, Boston, MA 02215. Offers PhD. *Entrance requirements:* For doctorate, GRE. *Financial support:* Fellowships, research assistantships, and teaching assistantships available. *Unit head:* Dr. Deborah Stearns-Kurosawa, Associate Provost, 617-358-9518, Fax: 617-358-2913, E-mail: gmsbusm@bu.edu. *Application contact:* GMS Office of Admissions, 617-358-9518, Fax: 617-358-2913, E-mail: gmsbusm@bu.edu.
Website: http://www.bumc.bu.edu/gms/pibs/

**Bowling Green State University,** Graduate College, College of Arts and Sciences, Department of Biological Sciences, Bowling Green, OH 43403. Offers MS, PhD. *Program availability:* Part-time. *Degree requirements:* For master's, thesis or alternative; for doctorate, comprehensive exam, thesis/dissertation. *Entrance requirements:* For master's and doctorate, GRE General Test. Additional exam requirements/recommendations for international students: required—TOEFL. Electronic applications accepted.

**Bradley University,** The Graduate School, College of Liberal Arts and Sciences, Department of Biology, Peoria, IL 61625-0002. Offers MS. *Program availability:* Part-time. *Faculty:* 14 full-time (9 women). *Students:* 5 applicants, 40% accepted. In 2019, 3 master's awarded. *Degree requirements:* For master's, comprehensive exam, thesis. *Entrance requirements:* For master's, GRE. Additional exam requirements/recommendations for international students: required—TOEFL (minimum score 550 paper-based; 79 iBT), IELTS (minimum score 6.5), PTE (minimum score 58). *Application deadline:* For fall admission, 5/15 priority date for domestic and international students; for spring admission, 10/15 priority date for domestic and international students. Applications are processed on a rolling basis. Application fee: $40 ($50 for international students). Electronic applications accepted. *Expenses: Tuition:* Part-time $930 per credit hour. *Financial support:* Research assistantships, scholarships/grants, tuition waivers (partial), and unspecified assistantships available. Support available to part-time students. Financial award application deadline: 4/1. *Unit head:* Sherri Morris, Chair, 309-677-3016, E-mail: sjmorris@bradley.edu. *Application contact:* Rachel Webb, Director of On-Campus Graduate Admissions and International Student and Scholar Services, 309-677-2375, E-mail: rkwebb@bradley.edu.
Website: http://www.bradley.edu/academic/departments/biology/

**Brandeis University,** Graduate School of Arts and Sciences, Department of Biochemistry, Waltham, MA 02454. Offers biochemistry and biophysics (MS, PhD); biochemistry and biophysics and quantitative biology (PhD). *Program availability:* Part-time. *Faculty:* 11 full-time (6 women). *Students:* 39 full-time (19 women); includes 12 minority (5 Asian, non-Hispanic/Latino; 4 Hispanic/Latino; 3 Two or more races, non-Hispanic/Latino), 9 international. Average age 26. 72 applicants, 31% accepted, 8 enrolled. In 2019, 6 doctorates awarded. Terminal master's awarded for partial completion of doctoral program. *Degree requirements:* For master's, thesis; for doctorate, comprehensive exam, thesis/dissertation. *Entrance requirements:* For master's, transcripts, letters of recommendation, resume, statement of purpose; for doctorate, transcripts, letters of recommendation, resume, statement of purpose, program questions. Additional exam requirements/recommendations for international students: required—TOEFL, IELTS, PTE. *Application deadline:* For fall admission, 12/1 priority date for domestic students. Applications are processed on a rolling basis. Application fee: $75. Electronic applications accepted. *Financial support:* In 2019–20, 10 teaching assistantships (averaging $3,550 per year) were awarded; fellowships, research assistantships, scholarships/grants, and health care benefits also available. *Unit head:* Dr. Dagmar Ringe, Director of Graduate Studies, 781-736-4902, E-mail: ringe@brandeis.edu. *Application contact:* Maryanna Aldrich, Administrator, 781-736-2352, E-mail: scigradoffice@brandeis.edu.
Website: http://www.brandeis.edu/gsas/programs/bio.html

**Brandeis University,** Graduate School of Arts and Sciences, Department of Biology, Waltham, MA 02454-9110. Offers genetics (PhD); microbiology (PhD); molecular and cell biology (MS, PhD); molecular biology (PhD); neurobiology (PhD); quantitative biology (PhD). *Program availability:* Part-time. *Faculty:* 28 full-time (14 women), 1 part-time/adjunct (0 women). *Students:* 44 full-time (26 women), 1 (woman) part-time; includes 15 minority (1 American Indian or Alaska Native, non-Hispanic/Latino; 7 Asian, non-Hispanic/Latino; 7 Hispanic/Latino), 10 international. Average age 27. 202 applicants, 22% accepted, 12 enrolled. In 2019, 9 master's, 6 doctorates awarded. Terminal master's awarded for partial completion of doctoral program. *Degree requirements:* For master's, thesis optional; for doctorate, comprehensive exam, thesis/dissertation. *Entrance requirements:* For master's, transcripts, letters of recommendation, resume, statement of purpose; for doctorate, transcripts, letters of recommendation, resume, program questions, statement of purpose. Additional exam requirements/recommendations for international students: required—TOEFL, IELTS, PTE. *Application deadline:* For fall admission, 12/1 priority date for domestic and international students; for spring admission, 10/15 for domestic students, 11/15 for international students. Applications are processed on a rolling basis. Application fee: $75. Electronic applications accepted. *Financial support:* In 2019–20, 50 fellowships with full tuition reimbursements (averaging $35,000 per year), 21 teaching assistantships (averaging $3,550 per year) were awarded; research assistantships, scholarships/grants, health care benefits, and tuition waivers also available. Support available to part-time students. *Unit head:* Dr. Michael Marr, Director of Graduate Studies, 781-736-2481, E-mail: mmarr@brandeis.edu. *Application contact:* Maryanna Aldrich, Administrator, 781-736-2352, E-mail: scigradoffice@brandeis.edu.
Website: http://www.brandeis.edu/gsas/programs/mcbio.html

**Brandeis University,** Graduate School of Arts and Sciences, Department of Neuroscience, Waltham, MA 02454-9110. Offers neuroscience (MS, PhD); quantitative biology (PhD). *Program availability:* Part-time. *Faculty:* 26 full-time (12 women). *Students:* 60 full-time (29 women), 2 part-time (0 women); includes 18 minority (2 Black or African American, non-Hispanic/Latino; 1 American Indian or Alaska Native, non-Hispanic/Latino; 3 Asian, non-Hispanic/Latino; 9 Hispanic/Latino; 3 Two or more races, non-Hispanic/Latino), 13 international. Average age 27. 169 applicants, 27% accepted, 13 enrolled. In 2019, 13 master's, 7 doctorates awarded. Terminal master's awarded for

partial completion of doctoral program. *Degree requirements:* For master's, thesis optional; for doctorate, comprehensive exam, thesis/dissertation. *Entrance requirements:* For master's, transcripts, letters of recommendation, resume, statement of purpose; for doctorate, transcripts, letters of recommendation, resume, program questions, statement of purpose. Additional exam requirements/recommendations for international students: required—TOEFL, IELTS, PTE. *Application deadline:* For fall admission, 12/1 priority date for domestic and international students. Applications are processed on a rolling basis. Application fee: $75. Electronic applications accepted. *Financial support:* In 2019–20, 64 fellowships with full tuition reimbursements (averaging $35,000 per year), 10 teaching assistantships (averaging $3,550 per year) were awarded; scholarships/grants, health care benefits, and tuition waivers also available. Support available to part-time students. *Unit head:* Dr. Susan Birren, Director of Graduate Studies, 781-736-2680, E-mail: birren@brandeis.edu. *Application contact:* Maryanna Aldrich, Administrator, 781-736-2352, E-mail: scigradoffice@brandeis.edu.
Website: http://www.brandeis.edu/gsas/programs/neuroscience.html

**Brandeis University,** Graduate School of Arts and Sciences, Department of Physics, Waltham, MA 02454-9110. Offers physics (MS, PhD); quantitative biology (PhD). *Program availability:* Part-time. *Faculty:* 17 full-time (4 women), 1 part-time/adjunct (0 women). *Students:* 54 full-time (21 women); includes 6 minority (2 Asian, non-Hispanic/Latino; 3 Hispanic/Latino; 1 Two or more races, non-Hispanic/Latino), 28 international. Average age 26. 184 applicants, 11% accepted, 13 enrolled. In 2019, 2 master's, 6 doctorates awarded. *Degree requirements:* For master's, thesis optional; for doctorate, comprehensive exam, thesis/dissertation. *Entrance requirements:* For master's and doctorate, General GRE (Subject GRE is recommended), transcripts, letters of recommendation, resume, statement of purpose. Additional exam requirements/recommendations for international students: required—TOEFL, IELTS, PTE. *Application deadline:* For fall admission, 1/15 priority date for domestic and international students. Applications are processed on a rolling basis. Application fee: $75. Electronic applications accepted. *Financial support:* In 2019–20, 75 fellowships with full tuition reimbursements (averaging $31,000 per year), 33 teaching assistantships (averaging $3,550 per year) were awarded; research assistantships, scholarships/grants, and health care benefits also available. *Unit head:* Dr. Craig Blocker, Director of Graduate Studies, 781-736-2879, E-mail: blocker@brandeis.edu. *Application contact:* Maryanna Aldrich, Administrator, 781-736-2352, E-mail: scigradoffice@brandeis.edu.
Website: http://www.brandeis.edu/gsas/programs/physics.html

**Brigham Young University,** Graduate Studies, College of Life Sciences, Department of Biology, Provo, UT 84602. Offers biological science education (MS); biology (MS, PhD). *Faculty:* 25 full-time (3 women). *Students:* 36 full-time (17 women); includes 5 minority (3 Hispanic/Latino; 2 Native Hawaiian or other Pacific Islander, non-Hispanic/Latino), 5 international. Average age 29. 23 applicants, 70% accepted, 9 enrolled. In 2019, 2 master's, 5 doctorates awarded. *Degree requirements:* For master's, comprehensive exam, thesis, prospectus, defense of research, defense of thesis; for doctorate, comprehensive exam, thesis/dissertation, prospectus, defense of research, defense of dissertation. *Entrance requirements:* For master's and doctorate, minimum cumulative GPA of 3.0 for undergraduate degree. Additional exam requirements/recommendations for international students: required—TOEFL (minimum score 580 paper-based; 85 iBT), IELTS (minimum score 7), E3PT, CAE. *Application deadline:* For fall admission, 1/15 for domestic and international students. Application fee: $50. Electronic applications accepted. *Financial support:* In 2019–20, 28 students received support, including 2 fellowships with full tuition reimbursements available (averaging $30,000 per year), 38 research assistantships with full and partial tuition reimbursements available (averaging $5,517 per year), 36 teaching assistantships with full and partial tuition reimbursements available (averaging $6,668 per year); institutionally sponsored loans, scholarships/grants, tuition waivers (full and partial), and unspecified assistantships also available. Financial award application deadline: 3/1; financial award applicants required to submit FAFSA. *Unit head:* Dr. Richard Gill, Chair, 801-422-3856, E-mail: rgill@byu.edu. *Application contact:* Gentri Glaittli, Graduate Program Manager, 801-422-7137, E-mail: biogradmanager@byu.edu.
Website: http://biology.byu.edu/

**Brock University,** Faculty of Graduate Studies, Faculty of Mathematics and Science, Program in Biological Sciences, St. Catharines, ON L2S 3A1, Canada. Offers M Sc, PhD. *Program availability:* Part-time. *Degree requirements:* For master's, thesis; for doctorate, thesis/dissertation. *Entrance requirements:* For master's, honors B Sc in biology, minimum undergraduate GPA of 3.0; for doctorate, M Sc. Additional exam requirements/recommendations for international students: required—TOEFL (minimum score 550 paper-based; 80 iBT), IELTS (minimum score 6.5), TWE (minimum score 4). Electronic applications accepted.

**Brooklyn College of the City University of New York,** School of Education, Program in Middle Childhood Science Education, Brooklyn, NY 11210-2889. Offers biology (MA); chemistry (MA); earth science (MA); general science (MA); physics (MA). *Program availability:* Part-time, evening/weekend. *Entrance requirements:* For master's, LAST, interview, previous course work in education and mathematics, resume, 2 letters of recommendation, essay. Additional exam requirements/recommendations for international students: required—TOEFL (minimum score 500 paper-based; 61 iBT). Electronic applications accepted.

**Brooklyn College of the City University of New York,** School of Natural and Behavioral Sciences, Department of Biology, Brooklyn, NY 11210-2889. Offers MA. *Degree requirements:* For master's, one foreign language, comprehensive exam, thesis. *Entrance requirements:* For master's, minimum GPA of 3.0, 2 letters of recommendation. Additional exam requirements/recommendations for international students: required—TOEFL (minimum score 500 paper-based; 61 iBT). Electronic applications accepted.

**Brown University,** Graduate School, Division of Biology and Medicine, Providence, RI 02912. Offers AM, M Sc, MA, MPH, Sc M, MD, PhD, MD/PhD. *Program availability:* Part-time. Terminal master's awarded for partial completion of doctoral program. *Degree requirements:* For doctorate, thesis/dissertation. *Entrance requirements:* For master's and doctorate, GRE General Test. Additional exam requirements/recommendations for international students: required—TOEFL. Electronic applications accepted.

**Bucknell University,** Graduate Studies, College of Arts and Sciences, Department of Biology, Lewisburg, PA 17837. Offers MS. *Degree requirements:* For master's, thesis. *Entrance requirements:* For master's, GRE General Test, GRE Subject Test, minimum GPA of 3.0. Additional exam requirements/recommendations for international students: required—TOEFL (minimum score 600 paper-based).

**Buffalo State College, State University of New York,** The Graduate School, School of Natural and Social Sciences, Department of Biology, Buffalo, NY 14222-1095. Offers biology (MA); secondary education (MS Ed), including biology. *Program availability:* Evening/weekend. *Degree requirements:* For master's, thesis (for some programs), project. *Entrance requirements:* For master's, minimum GPA of 2.75. Additional exam requirements/recommendations for international students: required—TOEFL (minimum score 550 paper-based).

**Cabrini University,** Academic Affairs, Radnor, PA 19087. Offers accounting (M Acc); autism spectrum disorder (M Ed); biological sciences (MS), including civic leadership; criminology and criminal justice (MA); curriculum, instruction, and assessment (M Ed); educational leadership (M Ed, Ed D), including curriculum and instructional leadership (Ed D), preK-12 leadership (Ed D); English as a second language (M Ed); organizational leadership (DBA, PhD); preK to 4 (M Ed); reading specialist (M Ed); secondary education (M Ed), including biology, chemistry, English, English/communication, mathematics, social studies; special education grades 7-12 (M Ed); special education preK-8 (M Ed); teaching and learning (M Ed). *Program availability:* Part-time, evening/weekend. *Degree requirements:* For master's, comprehensive exam (for some programs), thesis (for some programs); for doctorate, comprehensive exam (for some programs), thesis/dissertation. *Entrance requirements:* For master's, professional resume, personal statement, two recommendations, official transcripts; for doctorate, official transcripts, minimum master's GPA of 3.0, two recommendations, interview with admissions committee. Additional exam requirements/recommendations for international students: required—TOEFL (minimum score 80 iBT). Electronic applications accepted. Application fee is waived when completed online. *Expenses:* Contact institution.

**California Institute of Technology,** Division of Biology and Biological Engineering, Pasadena, CA 91125-0001. Offers biochemistry and molecular biophysics (PhD); cell biology and biophysics (PhD); developmental biology (PhD); genetics (PhD); immunology (PhD); molecular biology (PhD); neurobiology (PhD). *Degree requirements:* For doctorate, thesis/dissertation, qualifying exam. *Entrance requirements:* For doctorate, GRE General Test. Additional exam requirements/recommendations for international students: required—TOEFL. Electronic applications accepted.

**California Polytechnic State University, San Luis Obispo,** College of Science and Mathematics, Department of Biological Sciences, San Luis Obispo, CA 93407. Offers MS. *Program availability:* Part-time. *Faculty:* 9 full-time (3 women). *Students:* 25 full-time (18 women), 10 part-time (5 women); includes 6 minority (2 Hispanic/Latino; 4 Two or more races, non-Hispanic/Latino), 1 international. Average age 26. 70 applicants, 37% accepted, 18 enrolled. In 2019, 20 master's awarded. *Entrance requirements:* For master's, GRE. Additional exam requirements/recommendations for international students: required—TOEFL (minimum score 80 iBT). *Application deadline:* For fall admission, 2/1 for domestic and international students. Applications are processed on a rolling basis. Application fee: $55. Electronic applications accepted. *Expenses:* Tuition, state resident: full-time $7176; part-time $4164 per year. Tuition, nonresident: full-time $18,690; part-time $8916 per year. *Required fees:* $4206; $3185 per unit. $1061 per term. *Financial support:* Fellowships, research assistantships, teaching assistantships, career-related internships or fieldwork, Federal Work-Study, and unspecified assistantships available. Support available to part-time students. Financial award application deadline: 3/2; financial award applicants required to submit FAFSA. *Unit head:* Dr. Emily Taylor, Graduate Coordinator, 805-756-2616, Fax: 805-756-1419, E-mail: etaylor@calpoly.edu. *Application contact:* Dr. Emily Taylor, Graduate Coordinator, 805-756-2616, Fax: 805-756-1419, E-mail: etaylor@calpoly.edu.
Website: http://bio.calpoly.edu/

**California State Polytechnic University, Pomona,** Program in Biological Sciences, Pomona, CA 91768-2557. Offers biological science (MS). *Program availability:* Part-time, evening/weekend. *Entrance requirements:* Additional exam requirements/recommendations for international students: required—TOEFL (minimum score 550 paper-based). Electronic applications accepted. *Expenses:* Contact institution.

**California State University, Chico,** Office of Graduate Studies, College of Natural Sciences, Department of Biological Sciences, Chico, CA 95929-0722. Offers MS. *Degree requirements:* For master's, thesis, independent research project resulting in a thesis. *Entrance requirements:* For master's, GRE, identification of faculty mentor, 2 letters of recommendation, statement of purpose, curriculum vitae, department letter of recommendation access waiver form. Additional exam requirements/recommendations for international students: required—TOEFL (minimum score 550 paper-based; 80 iBT), IELTS (minimum score 6.5), PTE (minimum score 59). Electronic applications accepted.

**California State University, Dominguez Hills,** College of Natural and Behavioral Sciences, Department of Biology, Carson, CA 90747-0001. Offers MS. *Program availability:* Part-time, evening/weekend. *Degree requirements:* For master's, thesis. *Entrance requirements:* For master's, minimum GPA of 2.75. Additional exam requirements/recommendations for international students: required—TOEFL (minimum score 550 paper-based). Electronic applications accepted.

**California State University, East Bay,** Office of Graduate Studies, College of Science, Department of Biological Sciences, Hayward, CA 94542-3000. Offers marine science (MA, MS), including biological science, marine science (MS). *Program availability:* Part-time. *Degree requirements:* For master's, thesis. *Entrance requirements:* For master's, GRE General and Subject Tests, minimum GPA of 3.0 in field, 2.75 overall; 3 letters of reference; statement of purpose. Additional exam requirements/recommendations for international students: required—TOEFL (minimum score 550 paper-based). Electronic applications accepted.

**California State University, Fresno,** Division of Research and Graduate Studies, College of Science and Mathematics, Department of Biology, Fresno, CA 93740-8027. Offers biology (MS); biotechnology (MBT). *Program availability:* Part-time, evening/weekend. *Degree requirements:* For master's, thesis. *Entrance requirements:* For master's, GRE General Test, GRE Subject Test, minimum GPA of 2.5 in last 60 units. Additional exam requirements/recommendations for international students: required—TOEFL. Electronic applications accepted. *Expenses:* Tuition, state resident: full-time $4012; part-time $2506 per semester.

**California State University, Fullerton,** Graduate Studies, College of Natural Science and Mathematics, Department of Biological Science, Fullerton, CA 92831-3599. Offers biology (MS); biotechnology (MBT). *Program availability:* Part-time. *Entrance requirements:* For master's, GRE General and Subject Tests, MCAT, or DAT, minimum GPA of 3.0 in biology.

**California State University, Fullerton,** Graduate Studies, College of Natural Science and Mathematics, Department of Chemistry and Biochemistry, Fullerton, CA 92831-3599. Offers biology (MS); chemistry (MA, MS). *Program availability:* Part-time. *Degree requirements:* For master's, thesis, departmental qualifying exam. *Entrance requirements:* For master's, minimum GPA of 2.5 in last 60 units of course work, major in chemistry or related field.

**California State University, Long Beach,** Graduate Studies, College of Natural Sciences and Mathematics, Department of Biological Sciences, Long Beach, CA 90840. Offers biology (MS); microbiology (MS). *Program availability:* Part-time. *Entrance requirements:* For master's, GRE Subject Test, minimum GPA of 3.0. Electronic applications accepted.

**California State University, Los Angeles,** Graduate Studies, College of Natural and Social Sciences, Department of Biological Sciences, Los Angeles, CA 90032-8530. Offers biology (MS). *Program availability:* Part-time, evening/weekend. *Degree requirements:* For master's, comprehensive exam or thesis. *Entrance requirements:* Additional exam requirements/recommendations for international students: required—TOEFL (minimum score 500 paper-based). *Expenses: Tuition, area resident:* Full-time $7176; part-time $4164 per year. Tuition, state resident: full-time $7176; part-time

$4164 per year. Tuition, nonresident: full-time $14,304; part-time $8916 per year. *International tuition:* $14,304 full-time. *Required fees:* $1037.76; $1037.76 per unit. Tuition and fees vary according to degree level and program.

**California State University, Northridge,** Graduate Studies, College of Science and Mathematics, Department of Biology, Northridge, CA 91330. Offers MS. *Degree requirements:* For master's, thesis, seminar. *Entrance requirements:* For master's, GRE Subject Test, GRE General Test. Additional exam requirements/recommendations for international students: required—TOEFL.

**California State University, Sacramento,** College of Natural Sciences and Mathematics, Department of Biological Sciences, Sacramento, CA 95819. Offers biological conservation (MS); molecular and cellular biology (MS); stem cell (MA). *Program availability:* Part-time. *Students:* 38 full-time (12 women), 24 part-time (8 women); includes 19 minority (14 Asian, non-Hispanic/Latino; 4 Hispanic/Latino; 1 Native Hawaiian or other Pacific Islander, non-Hispanic/Latino), 1 international. Average age 29. 68 applicants, 44% accepted, 23 enrolled. In 2019, 13 master's awarded. *Degree requirements:* For master's, comprehensive exam (for some programs), thesis (for some programs), thesis or project; writing proficiency exam. *Entrance requirements:* For master's, GRE, bachelor's degree in biology or equivalent; minimum GPA of 2.75 in all biology courses, 3.0 in all upper-division biology courses. Additional exam requirements/recommendations for international students: required—TOEFL (minimum score 550 paper-based; 80 iBT); recommended—IELTS (minimum score 7). *Application deadline:* For fall admission, 2/1 for domestic students, 1/1 for international students. Applications are processed on a rolling basis. Application fee: $70. Electronic applications accepted. *Expenses:* Contact institution. *Financial support:* Teaching assistantships, career-related internships or fieldwork, Federal Work-Study, and scholarships/grants available. Support available to part-time students. Financial award application deadline: 3/1; financial award applicants required to submit FAFSA. *Unit head:* Dr. Shannon Datwyler, Chair, 916-278-6535, Fax: 916-278-6993, E-mail: datwyler@csus.edu. *Application contact:* Jose Martinez, Graduate Admissions Supervisor, 916-278-7871, E-mail: martinj@skymail.csus.edu. Website: http://www.csus.edu/bios

**California State University, San Bernardino,** Graduate Studies, College of Natural Sciences, Program in Biology, San Bernardino, CA 92407. Offers MS. *Program availability:* Part-time. *Faculty:* 11 full-time (3 women). *Students:* 7 full-time (5 women), 19 part-time (9 women); includes 16 minority (1 Asian, non-Hispanic/Latino; 15 Hispanic/Latino). Average age 27. 23 applicants, 35% accepted, 8 enrolled. In 2019, 7 master's awarded. *Application deadline:* For fall admission, 5/1 for domestic students; for winter admission, 10/16 for domestic students; for spring admission, 1/22 for domestic students. Application fee: $55. *Unit head:* Dr. Michael Chao, Chair, 909-537-5388, E-mail: mchao@csusb.edu. *Application contact:* Dr. Dorota Huizinga, Dean of Graduate Studies, 909-537-3064, E-mail: dorota.huizinga@csusb.edu.

**California State University, San Marcos,** College of Science and Mathematics, Program in Biology, San Marcos, CA 92096-0001. Offers MS. *Program availability:* Part-time. *Entrance requirements:* For master's, GRE General Test, minimum GPA of 2.75 in mathematics and science or 3.0 in last 35 units of mathematics and science, bachelor's degree in the biological or related sciences. Additional exam requirements/recommendations for international students: required—TOEFL, TWE. *Expenses: Tuition, area resident:* Full-time $7176. Tuition, state resident: full-time $7176. Tuition, nonresident: full-time $18,640. *International tuition:* $18,640 full-time. *Required fees:* $1960.

**Carleton University,** Faculty of Graduate Studies, Faculty of Science, Department of Biology, Ottawa, ON K1S 5B6, Canada. Offers M Sc, PhD. *Degree requirements:* For master's, thesis, seminar; for doctorate, comprehensive exam, thesis/dissertation, seminar. *Entrance requirements:* For master's, honors degree in science; for doctorate, M Sc. Additional exam requirements/recommendations for international students: required—TOEFL.

**Carnegie Mellon University,** Mellon College of Science, Department of Biological Sciences, Pittsburgh, PA 15213-3891. Offers biochemistry (PhD); biophysics (PhD); cell and developmental biology (PhD); computational biology (MS, PhD); genetics (PhD); molecular biology (PhD); neuroscience (PhD); structural biology (PhD). *Degree requirements:* For doctorate, comprehensive exam, thesis/dissertation. *Entrance requirements:* For doctorate, GRE General Test, GRE Subject Test, interview. Electronic applications accepted.

**Case Western Reserve University,** School of Graduate Studies, Department of Biology, Cleveland, OH 44106. Offers MS, PhD. *Program availability:* Part-time. *Faculty:* 26 full-time (15 women), 3 part-time/adjunct (2 women). *Students:* 64 full-time (27 women), 5 part-time (4 women); includes 9 minority (4 Asian, non-Hispanic/Latino; 4 Hispanic/Latino; 1 Two or more races, non-Hispanic/Latino), 25 international. Average age 27. 72 applicants, 74% accepted, 19 enrolled. In 2019, 16 master's, 8 doctorates awarded. Terminal master's awarded for partial completion of doctoral program. *Degree requirements:* For master's, thesis or alternative; for doctorate, thesis/dissertation. *Entrance requirements:* For master's and doctorate, GRE General Test, GRE Subject Test, statement of objectives; three letters of recommendation. Additional exam requirements/recommendations for international students: required—TOEFL (minimum score 577 paper-based; 90 iBT); recommended—IELTS (minimum score 7). *Application deadline:* For fall admission, 12/15 priority date for domestic students. Applications are processed on a rolling basis. Application fee: $50. Electronic applications accepted. *Financial support:* Fellowships, research assistantships, teaching assistantships, career-related internships or fieldwork, Federal Work-Study, scholarships/grants, health care benefits, tuition waivers, unspecified assistantships, and stipends available. Financial award application deadline: 12/15; financial award applicants required to submit CSS PROFILE or FAFSA. *Unit head:* Mark Willis, Professor and Chair, Department of Biology, 216-368-4358, Fax: 216-368-4762, E-mail: mark.willis@case.edu. *Application contact:* Tyler Cajka, Student Service Specialist, E-mail: txc492@case.edu. Website: http://biology.case.edu/

**Case Western Reserve University,** School of Medicine and School of Graduate Studies, Graduate Programs in Medicine, Medical Scientist Training Program, Cleveland, OH 44106. Offers MD/PhD. *Entrance requirements:* Additional exam requirements/recommendations for international students: required—TOEFL. Electronic applications accepted.

**The Catholic University of America,** School of Arts and Sciences, Department of Biology, Washington, DC 20064. Offers biotechnology (MS); cell and microbial biology (MS, PhD), including cell biology; clinical laboratory science (MS, PhD); MSLS/MS. *Program availability:* Part-time. *Faculty:* 10 full-time (4 women), 3 part-time/adjunct (1 woman). *Students:* 16 full-time (13 women), 36 part-time (19 women); includes 11 minority (4 Black or African American, non-Hispanic/Latino; 3 Asian, non-Hispanic/Latino; 4 Two or more races, non-Hispanic/Latino), 33 international. Average age 31. 46 applicants, 65% accepted, 12 enrolled. In 2019, 15 master's, 8 doctorates awarded. Terminal master's awarded for partial completion of doctoral program. *Degree requirements:* For master's and doctorate, comprehensive exam. *Entrance requirements:* For master's and doctorate, GRE General Test, GRE Subject Test,

statement of purpose, official copies of academic transcripts, three letters of recommendation. Additional exam requirements/recommendations for international students: required—TOEFL (minimum score 550 paper-based; 80 iBT). *Application deadline:* For fall admission, 7/15 priority date for domestic students, 7/1 for international students; for spring admission, 11/15 priority date for domestic students, 11/1 for international students. Applications are processed on a rolling basis. Application fee: $55. Electronic applications accepted. *Expenses:* Contact institution. *Financial support:* Fellowships, research assistantships, teaching assistantships, Federal Work-Study, scholarships/grants, tuition waivers (full and partial), and unspecified assistantships available. Financial award application deadline: 2/1; financial award applicants required to submit FAFSA. *Unit head:* Dr. Venigalla Rao, Chair, 202-319-5271, Fax: 202-319-5721, E-mail: rao@cua.edu. *Application contact:* Dr. Steven Brown, Director of Graduate Admissions, 202-319-5057, Fax: 202-319-6533, E-mail: cua-admissions@cua.edu.
Website: http://biology.cua.edu/

**Cedars-Sinai Medical Center,** Graduate Programs, Los Angeles, CA 90048. Offers biomedical and translational sciences (PhD); magnetic resonance in medicine (MS). *Degree requirements:* For doctorate, comprehensive exam, thesis/dissertation. *Entrance requirements:* For doctorate, GRE, 3 letters of recommendation. Additional exam requirements/recommendations for international students: required—TOEFL (minimum score 550 paper-based; 80 iBT), IELTS (minimum score 6.5). Electronic applications accepted.

**Central Connecticut State University,** School of Graduate Studies, School of Engineering, Science and Technology, Department of Biology, New Britain, CT 06050-4010. Offers MA, DNP-A. *Program availability:* Part-time, evening/weekend. *Degree requirements:* For master's, comprehensive exam, thesis or alternative. *Entrance requirements:* For master's, minimum undergraduate GPA of 2.7, essay, letters of recommendation. Additional exam requirements/recommendations for international students: required—TOEFL (minimum score 550 paper-based; 79 iBT); recommended—IELTS (minimum score 6.5). Electronic applications accepted.

**Central Michigan University,** College of Graduate Studies, College of Science and Engineering, Department of Biology, Mount Pleasant, MI 48859. Offers biology (MS); conservation biology (MS). *Faculty:* 42 full-time (17 women). *Students:* 8 full-time (6 women), 40 part-time (19 women); includes 5 minority (2 Hispanic/Latino; 3 Two or more races, non-Hispanic/Latino), 7 international. Average age 26. 53 applicants, 62% accepted, 20 enrolled. In 2019, 24 master's awarded. *Degree requirements:* For master's, thesis optional, Plan A requires 30 credits and a thesis. *Entrance requirements:* Additional exam requirements/recommendations for international students: required—This section should be directed towards Admissions Processing as these are their requirements. *Application deadline:* For fall admission, 2/1 for domestic and international students; for spring admission, 10/1 for domestic and international students. Applications are processed on a rolling basis. Application fee: $50. *Expenses: Tuition, area resident:* Full-time $12,267; part-time $8178 per year. Tuition, state resident: full-time $12,267; part-time $8178 per year. Tuition, nonresident: full-time $12,267; part-time $8178 per year. *International tuition:* $16,110 full-time. *Required fees:* $225 per semester. Tuition and fees vary according to degree level and program. *Financial support:* In 2019–20, 32 students received support, including 18 research assistantships with full tuition reimbursements available (averaging $13,900 per year), 21 teaching assistantships with full tuition reimbursements available (averaging $13,900 per year). Financial award application deadline: 2/1. *Unit head:* Dr. Tracy Galarowicz, 989-774-3227, Fax: 989-774-3462, E-mail: galar1tl@cmich.edu. *Application contact:* Dr. Tom Gehring, 989-774-3227, Fax: 989-774-3462, E-mail: gehri1tm@cmich.edu. Website: www.cmich.edu

**Central Washington University,** School of Graduate Studies and Research, College of the Sciences, Department of Biological Sciences, Ellensburg, WA 98926. Offers botany (MS); microbiology and parasitology (MS); stream ecology and fisheries (MS); terrestrial ecology (MS). *Program availability:* Part-time. *Entrance requirements:* For master's, GRE General Test, minimum GPA of 3.0. Additional exam requirements/recommendations for international students: required—TOEFL (minimum score 550 paper-based; 79 iBT). Electronic applications accepted.

**Chatham University,** Program in Biology, Pittsburgh, PA 15232-2826. Offers environmental biology (MS); human biology (MS). *Program availability:* Part-time. *Degree requirements:* For master's, thesis optional. *Entrance requirements:* For master's, 3 letters of recommendation. Additional exam requirements/recommendations for international students: required—TOEFL (minimum score 600 paper-based; 100 iBT), IELTS (minimum score 7), TWE. Electronic applications accepted. Application fee is waived when completed online. *Expenses: Tuition:* Part-time $1017 per credit. *Required fees:* $30 per credit. Tuition and fees vary according to program.

**Chicago State University,** School of Graduate and Professional Studies, College of Arts and Sciences, Department of Biological Sciences, Chicago, IL 60628. Offers MS. *Program availability:* Part-time, evening/weekend. *Entrance requirements:* For master's, minimum GPA of 3.0, 15 credit hours in biological sciences.

**The Citadel, The Military College of South Carolina,** Citadel Graduate College, School of Science and Mathematics, Department of Biology, Charleston, SC 29409. Offers biology (MA); environmental studies (Graduate Certificate). *Accreditation:* NCATE (one or more programs are accredited). *Program availability:* Part-time, evening/weekend. *Faculty:* 11 full-time (4 women), 10 part-time/adjunct (6 women). *Students:* 10 part-time (7 women); includes 2 minority (1 Black or African American, non-Hispanic/Latino; 1 American Indian or Alaska Native, non-Hispanic/Latino). In 2019, 6 master's awarded. *Entrance requirements:* For master's, GRE or MAT, Submission of an official transcript reflecting the highest degree earned from a regionally accredited college or university; for Graduate Certificate, Submission of an official transcript reflecting the highest degree earned from a regionally accredited college or university. Additional transcripts may be required depending on undergraduate course requirements by program. Additional exam requirements/recommendations for international students: required—TOEFL (minimum score 550 paper-based; 79 iBT). *Application deadline:* Applications are processed on a rolling basis. Application fee: $40. Electronic applications accepted. *Financial support:* Federal Work-Study, scholarships/grants, tuition waivers (partial), and Athletics available. Financial award applicants required to submit FAFSA. *Unit head:* John Weinstein, Biology Department Head, 843-953-7796, Fax: 843-953-7264, E-mail: john.weinstein@citadel.edu. *Application contact:* Caroline Schlatt, Assistant Director of Enrollment Management, 843-953-0523, Fax: 843-953-7630, E-mail: cschlatt@citadel.edu.
Website: http://www.citadel.edu/root/biology

**The Citadel, The Military College of South Carolina,** Citadel Graduate College, Zucker Family School of Education, Charleston, SC 29409. Offers elementary/secondary school administration and supervision (M Ed); elementary/secondary school counseling (M Ed); interdisciplinary STEM education (M Ed); literacy education (M Ed, Graduate Certificate); middle grades (MAT), including English, mathematics, science, social studies; physical education (grades K-12) (MAT); school superintendency (Ed S); secondary education (MAT), including biology, English, mathematics, social studies; student affairs (Graduate Certificate); student affairs and college counseling (M Ed).

## Biological and Biomedical Sciences—General

*Accreditation:* NCATE. *Program availability:* Part-time, evening/weekend, 100% online, blended/hybrid learning. *Faculty:* 16 full-time (10 women), 10 part-time/adjunct (7 women). *Students:* 37 full-time (27 women), 166 part-time (128 women); includes 55 minority (42 Black or African American, non-Hispanic/Latino; 1 Asian, non-Hispanic/Latino; 8 Hispanic/Latino; 4 Two or more races, non-Hispanic/Latino). In 2019, 120 master's, 27 other advanced degrees awarded. *Entrance requirements:* For master's, Submission of an official transcript of the baccalaureate degree and all other undergraduate or graduate work directly from each regionally accredited college and university, 3.0 cum GPA; for other advanced degree, Official transcript reflecting the highest degree earned from a regionally accredited college or university, 2.5 cum GPA. Additional exam requirements/recommendations for international students: required—TOEFL (minimum score 550 paper-based; 79 iBT). *Application deadline:* Applications are processed on a rolling basis. Application fee: $40. Electronic applications accepted. *Expenses:* MEd Higher Education Leadership, MEd Interdisciplinary STEM Education, MS Instructional Systems Design and Performance Improvement, Certificate Higher Education Leadership: $695 per credit hour. $165 per semester in fees ($75 Technology Fee + $75 Infrastructure Fee + $15 Registration Fee). *Financial support:* In 2019–20, 21,283 students received support. Federal Work-Study, scholarships/grants, tuition waivers (partial), and Athletics available. Financial award applicants required to submit FAFSA. *Unit head:* Evan Ortlieb, Zucker Family School of Education Dean, 843-953-5097, Fax: 843-953-7258, E-mail: eortlieb@citadel.edu. *Application contact:* Carl Hill, Assistant Director of Enrollment Management, 843-953-6808, Fax: 843-953-7630, E-mail: chill9@citadel.edu.
Website: http://www.citadel.edu/root/education-graduate-programs

**City College of the City University of New York,** Graduate School, Division of Science, Department of Biology, New York, NY 10031-9198. Offers MS, PhD. *Program availability:* Part-time. Terminal master's awarded for partial completion of doctoral program. *Degree requirements:* For master's, thesis or alternative; for doctorate, one foreign language, thesis/dissertation, teaching experience. *Entrance requirements:* For doctorate, GRE General Test. Additional exam requirements/recommendations for international students: required—TOEFL (minimum score 500 paper-based; 61 iBT). Electronic applications accepted.

**Clark Atlanta University,** School of Arts and Sciences, Department of Biology, Atlanta, GA 30314. Offers MS, PhD. *Program availability:* Part-time. Terminal master's awarded for partial completion of doctoral program. *Degree requirements:* For master's, one foreign language, thesis; for doctorate, 2 foreign languages, thesis/dissertation. *Entrance requirements:* For master's, GRE General Test, minimum GPA of 2.5; for doctorate, GRE General Test, minimum graduate GPA of 3.0. Additional exam requirements/recommendations for international students: required—TOEFL (minimum score 500 paper-based; 61 iBT). Electronic applications accepted.

**Clarkson University,** School of Arts and Sciences, Program in Basic Science, Potsdam, NY 13699. Offers basic science (MS), including biology. *Students:* 2 full-time (0 women), 1 (woman) part-time; includes 2 minority (1 Black or African American, non-Hispanic/Latino; 1 Asian, non-Hispanic/Latino). 3 applicants, 100% accepted, 2 enrolled. In 2019, 5 master's awarded. *Entrance requirements:* For master's, GRE. Additional exam requirements/recommendations for international students: required—TOEFL (minimum score 550 paper-based, 80 iBT) or IELTS (6.5). *Application deadline:* Applications are processed on a rolling basis. Application fee: $50. Electronic applications accepted. *Expenses: Tuition:* Full-time $24,984; part-time $1388 per credit hour. *Required fees:* $225. Tuition and fees vary according to campus/location and program. *Financial support:* Scholarships/grants and unspecified assistantships available. *Unit head:* Dr. Charles Thorpe, Dean of the School of Arts and Sciences, 315-268-6544, E-mail: cthorpe@clarkson.edu. *Application contact:* Daniel Capogna, Director of Graduate Admissions & Recruitment, 518-631-9910, E-mail: graduate@clarkson.edu.
Website: https://www.clarkson.edu/academics/graduate

**Clark University,** Graduate School, Department of Biology, Worcester, MA 01610-1477. Offers MA, PhD. Terminal master's awarded for partial completion of doctoral program. *Degree requirements:* For doctorate, thesis/dissertation. *Entrance requirements:* For doctorate, GRE General Test. Additional exam requirements/recommendations for international students: required—TOEFL (minimum score 575 paper-based; 90 iBT), IELTS (minimum score 6.5). Electronic applications accepted. *Expenses: Tuition:* Full-time $47,650; part-time $4765 per course. *Required fees:* $1850.

**Clayton State University,** School of Graduate Studies, College of Arts and Sciences, Program in Education, Morrow, GA 30260-0285. Offers biology (MAT); English (MAT); history (MAT); mathematics (MAT). *Accreditation:* NCATE. *Entrance requirements:* For master's, GRE, GACE, 2 official copies of transcripts, 3 recommendation letters, statement of purpose. Additional exam requirements/recommendations for international students: required—TOEFL (minimum score 550 paper-based). Electronic applications accepted.

**Clemson University,** Graduate School, College of Science, Department of Biological Sciences, Clemson, SC 29634. Offers biological sciences (MS, PhD); biological sciences for science educators (MBS); environmental toxicology (MS, PhD); microbiology (MS, PhD). *Program availability:* Part-time, 100% online. *Faculty:* 48 full-time (22 women), 5 part-time/adjunct (0 women). *Students:* 72 full-time (40 women), 221 part-time (148 women); includes 39 minority (7 Black or African American, non-Hispanic/Latino; 2 American Indian or Alaska Native, non-Hispanic/Latino; 4 Asian, non-Hispanic/Latino; 14 Hispanic/Latino; 1 Native Hawaiian or other Pacific Islander, non-Hispanic/Latino; 11 Two or more races, non-Hispanic/Latino), 11 international. Average age 34. 206 applicants, 76% accepted, 122 enrolled. In 2019, 111 master's, 8 doctorates awarded. *Degree requirements:* For master's, comprehensive exam (for some programs), thesis (for some programs); for doctorate, comprehensive exam, thesis/dissertation. *Entrance requirements:* For master's and doctorate, GRE General Test, unofficial transcripts, letters of recommendation. Additional exam requirements/recommendations for international students: required—TOEFL (minimum score 102 paper-based; 102 iBT); recommended—IELTS (minimum score 7.5), TSE (minimum score 72). *Application deadline:* For fall admission, 12/10 priority date for domestic and international students. Applications are processed on a rolling basis. Application fee: $80 ($90 for international students). Electronic applications accepted. *Expenses:* Full-Time Student per Semester: Tuition: $4600 (in-state), $9525 (out-of-state), Fees: $598; Graduate Assistant Per Semester: $1144; Part-Time Student Per Credit Hour: $556 (in-state), $1106 (out-of-state), Fees: $617; other fees apply depending on program, credit hours, campus & residency. Doctoral Base Fee per Semester: $4938 (in-state), $10405 (out-of-state). *Financial support:* In 2019–20, 59 students received support, including 5 fellowships with full and partial tuition reimbursements available (averaging $3,622 per year), 11 research assistantships with full and partial tuition reimbursements available (averaging $23,227 per year), 43 teaching assistantships with full and partial tuition reimbursements available (averaging $22,326 per year); unspecified assistantships also available. Financial award application deadline: 12/10. *Unit head:* Dr. Saara Dewalt, Department Chair, 864-656-1112, E-mail: saarad@clemson.edu. *Application contact:* Jay Lyn Martin, Graduate Student Services Coordinator, 864-656-3587, E-mail: jaylyn@clemson.edu.
Website: http://www.clemson.edu/science/departments/biosci/

**Cleveland State University,** College of Graduate Studies, College of Sciences and Health Professions, Department of Biological, Geological, and Environmental Sciences, Cleveland, OH 44115. Offers MS, PhD. *Program availability:* Part-time. *Faculty:* 18 full-time (5 women), 54 part-time/adjunct (22 women). *Students:* 59 full-time (39 women), 11 part-time (7 women); includes 10 minority (6 Black or African American, non-Hispanic/Latino; 1 American Indian or Alaska Native, non-Hispanic/Latino; 2 Hispanic/Latino; 1 Two or more races, non-Hispanic/Latino), 23 international. Average age 28. 56 applicants, 54% accepted, 16 enrolled. In 2019, 8 master's, 8 doctorates awarded. Terminal master's awarded for partial completion of doctoral program. *Entrance requirements:* For master's, GRE General Test, 3 letters of recommendation; for doctorate, GRE General Test, 3 letters of recommendation; 1-2 page essay; statement of career goals and research interests. Additional exam requirements/recommendations for international students: required—TOEFL (minimum score 550 paper-based; 78 iBT), IELTS. *Application deadline:* Applications are processed on a rolling basis. Application fee: $40. Electronic applications accepted. *Expenses:* Tuition, state resident: full-time $10,215; part-time $6810 per credit hour. Tuition, nonresident: full-time $17,496; part-time $11,664 per credit hour. *International tuition:* $19,316 full-time. Tuition and fees vary according to degree level and program. *Financial support:* In 2019–20, 33 students received support, including 1 fellowship with full tuition reimbursement available (averaging $21,000 per year), 10 research assistantships with full tuition reimbursements available (averaging $11,800 per year), 14 teaching assistantships with full tuition reimbursements available (averaging $9,500 per year); tuition waivers (full and partial) and unspecified assistantships also available. Financial award applicants required to submit FAFSA. *Unit head:* Dr. Crystal M. Weyman, Chairperson/Professor, 216-687-6971, Fax: 216-687-6972, E-mail: c.weyman@csuohio.edu. *Application contact:* Dr. Girish C. Shukla, Associate Professor and Graduate Program Director, 216-687-2395, Fax: 216-687-6972, E-mail: g.shukla@csuohio.edu.
Website: http://www.csuohio.edu/sciences/bges

**Cold Spring Harbor Laboratory,** School of Biological Sciences, Cold Spring Harbor, NY 11724. Offers PhD. *Faculty:* 55 full-time (11 women). *Students:* 44 full-time (22 women); includes 7 minority (1 Black or African American, non-Hispanic/Latino; 2 Asian, non-Hispanic/Latino; 3 Hispanic/Latino; 1 Two or more races, non-Hispanic/Latino), 22 international. Average age 27. 202 applicants, 13% accepted, 8 enrolled. In 2019, 9 doctorates awarded. *Degree requirements:* For doctorate, comprehensive exam, thesis/dissertation, lab rotations, teaching experience, qualifying exam, postdoctoral proposals. *Entrance requirements:* For doctorate, GRE (recommended). *Application deadline:* For fall admission, 12/1 for domestic and international students. Application fee: $60. Electronic applications accepted. *Financial support:* In 2019–20, 44 students received support, including 44 fellowships with full tuition reimbursements available (averaging $34,000 per year); scholarships/grants, traineeships, health care benefits, and tuition waivers (full) also available. Financial award application deadline: 12/1. *Unit head:* Dr. Alexander Gann, Dean, 516-367-6890. *Application contact:* Dr. Alexander Gann, Dean, 516-367-6890.
Website: https://www.cshl.edu/education/phd-program/

**College of Staten Island of the City University of New York,** Graduate Programs, Division of Science and Technology, Program in Biology, Staten Island, NY 10314-6600. Offers biology (MS), including biotechnology, general biology. *Program availability:* Part-time, evening/weekend. *Faculty:* 10. *Students:* 37. 48 applicants, 46% accepted, 13 enrolled. In 2019, 17 master's awarded. *Degree requirements:* For master's, 30 credits (for general biology and biotechnology tracks). *Entrance requirements:* For master's, GRE (recommended), BS in Biology degree from an accredited college, overall GPA of 2.75 (B-), GPA of 3.0 (B) in undergraduate science and mathematics courses, 2 letters of recommendation. Additional exam requirements/recommendations for international students: required—TOEFL (minimum score 550 paper-based; 79 iBT), IELTS (minimum score 6.5). *Application deadline:* For fall admission, 7/1 for domestic students, 4/25 for international students; for spring admission, 11/25 for domestic and international students. Applications are processed on a rolling basis. Application fee: $75. Electronic applications accepted. *Expenses: Tuition, area resident:* Full-time $11,090; part-time $470 per credit. Tuition, state resident: full-time $11,090; part-time $470 per credit. Tuition, nonresident: full-time $20,520; part-time $855 per credit. *International tuition:* $20,520 full-time. *Required fees:* $559; $181 per semester. Tuition and fees vary according to program. *Unit head:* Dr. Jianying Gu, Biotechnology Coordinator, 718-982-4123, E-mail: jianying.gu@csi.cuny.edu. *Application contact:* Sasha Spence, Associate Director for Graduate Admissions, 718-982-2019, Fax: 718-982-2500, E-mail: sasha.spence@csi.cuny.edu.
Website: http://csicuny.smartcatalogiq.com/en/current/Graduate-Catalog/Graduate-Programs-Disciplines-and-Offerings-in-Selected-Disciplines/Biology-MS

**College of Staten Island of the City University of New York,** Graduate Programs, School of Education, Program in Adolescence Education, Staten Island, NY 10314-6600. Offers adolescence education (MS Ed), including biology, English, mathematics, social studies. *Program availability:* Part-time, evening/weekend. *Faculty:* 24. *Students:* 82. 36 applicants, 83% accepted, 25 enrolled. In 2019, 30 master's awarded. *Degree requirements:* For master's, thesis, educational research project supervised by faculty; Sequence 1 consists of a minimum of 33-38 graduate credits among 11 courses. Sequence 2 consists of a minimum of 46-53 graduate credits. *Entrance requirements:* For master's, Sequence 1: NYS initial teaching; Sequence 2: 32 approved academic credits in appropriate subject area. Relevant bachelor's degree, overall GPA at or above 3.0, two letters of recommendation, one-or-two-page personal statement. Additional exam requirements/recommendations for international students: required—TOEFL (minimum score 550 paper-based; 79 iBT), IELTS (minimum score 6.5). *Application deadline:* For fall admission, 4/25 for domestic and international students; for spring admission, 11/25 for domestic and international students. Applications are processed on a rolling basis. Application fee: $75. Electronic applications accepted. *Expenses: Tuition, area resident:* Full-time $11,090; part-time $470 per credit. Tuition, state resident: full-time $11,090; part-time $470 per credit. Tuition, nonresident: full-time $20,520; part-time $855 per credit. *International tuition:* $20,520 full-time. *Required fees:* $559; $181 per semester. Tuition and fees vary according to program. *Unit head:* Diane Brescia, 718-982-3877, E-mail: diane.brescia@csi.cuny.edu. *Application contact:* Sasha Spence, Associate Director for Graduate Admissions, 718-982-2019, Fax: 718-982-2500, E-mail: sasha.spence@csi.cuny.edu.
Website: http://csicuny.smartcatalogiq.com/en/current/Graduate-Catalog/Graduate-Programs-Disciplines-and-Offerings-in-Selected-Disciplines/Adolescence-Educatio

**Colorado State University,** College of Natural Sciences, Department of Biology, Fort Collins, CO 80523-1878. Offers botany (MS, PhD). *Faculty:* 31 full-time (12 women), 2 part-time/adjunct (both women). *Students:* 12 full-time (6 women), 26 part-time (12 women); includes 6 minority (1 Asian, non-Hispanic/Latino; 4 Hispanic/Latino; 1 Two or more races, non-Hispanic/Latino), 3 international. Average age 30. 31 applicants, 32% accepted, 8 enrolled. In 2019, 5 master's, 5 doctorates awarded. Terminal master's awarded for partial completion of doctoral program. *Degree requirements:* For master's, thesis, defense; for doctorate, comprehensive exam, thesis/dissertation. *Entrance requirements:* For master's and doctorate, transcripts, minimum GPA of 3.0; recommendation letters. Additional exam requirements/recommendations for international students: required—TOEFL (minimum score 550 paper-based; 80 iBT), IELTS (minimum score 6.5). *Application deadline:* For fall admission, 1/1 for domestic

and international students; for spring admission, 10/1 for domestic and international students. Application fee: $60 ($70 for international students). Electronic applications accepted. *Expenses:* Tuition, state resident: full-time $10,520; part-time $5844 per credit hour. Tuition, nonresident: full-time $25,791; part-time $14,328 per credit hour. International tuition: $25,791 full-time. *Required fees:* $2512.80. Part-time tuition and fees vary according to course level, course load, degree level, program and student level. *Financial support:* In 2019–20, 80 students received support, including 8 research assistantships with full and partial tuition reimbursements available (averaging $20,858 per year), 78 teaching assistantships with full and partial tuition reimbursements available (averaging $20,340 per year); fellowships with full and partial tuition reimbursements available, career-related internships or fieldwork, health care benefits, and unspecified assistantships also available. Financial award applicants required to submit FAFSA. *Unit head:* Dr. Deborah Garrity, Department Chair and Professor, 970-491-2513, Fax: 970-491-0649, E-mail: deborah.garrity@colostate.edu. *Application contact:* Dorothy Ramirez, Graduate Coordinator, 970-491-1923, Fax: 970-491-0649, E-mail: dramirez@colostate.edu.
Website: http://www.biology.colostate.edu/

**Colorado State University,** College of Veterinary Medicine and Biomedical Sciences, Department of Biomedical Sciences, Fort Collins, CO 80523-1680. Offers biomedical sciences (PhD); reproductive technology (MS). *Faculty:* 35 full-time (12 women), 2 part-time/adjunct (1 woman). *Students:* 95 full-time (61 women), 37 part-time (21 women); includes 29 minority (1 Black or African American, non-Hispanic/Latino; 1 American Indian or Alaska Native, non-Hispanic/Latino; 4 Asian, non-Hispanic/Latino; 20 Hispanic/Latino; 3 Two or more races, non-Hispanic/Latino), 11 international. Average age 26. 200 applicants, 60% accepted, 80 enrolled. In 2019, 75 master's, 5 doctorates awarded. Terminal master's awarded for partial completion of doctoral program. *Degree requirements:* For master's, comprehensive exam (for some programs), thesis (for some programs); for doctorate, comprehensive exam (for some programs), thesis/dissertation. *Entrance requirements:* For master's and doctorate, GRE, minimum GPA of 3.0; bachelor's degree; resume/curriculum vitae; statement of purpose; recommendations. Additional exam requirements/recommendations for international students: required—TOEFL (minimum score 550 paper-based; 80 iBT), IELTS (minimum score 6.5). *Application deadline:* For fall admission, 4/1 for domestic and international students; for spring admission, 9/1 for domestic and international students; for summer admission, 1/1 for domestic and international students. Applications are processed on a rolling basis. Application fee: $60 ($70 for international students). Electronic applications accepted. *Expenses:* Contact institution. *Financial support:* In 2019–20, 21 research assistantships (averaging $24,617 per year), 7 teaching assistantships (averaging $24,816 per year) were awarded; fellowships, scholarships/grants, traineeships, health care benefits, and unspecified assistantships also available. *Unit head:* Dr. Colin Clay, Department Head, 970-491-3259, E-mail: colin.clay@colostate.edu. *Application contact:* Erin Bisenius, Graduate Education Coordinator, 970-491-6188, E-mail: erin.bisenius@colostate.edu.
Website: https://vetmedbiosci.colostate.edu/bms/

**Colorado State University-Pueblo,** College of Science and Mathematics, Pueblo, CO 81001-4901. Offers applied natural science (MS), including biochemistry, biology, chemistry. *Program availability:* Part-time, evening/weekend. *Degree requirements:* For master's, comprehensive exam (for some programs), thesis (for some programs), internship report (if non-thesis). *Entrance requirements:* For master's, GRE General Test (minimum score 1000), 2 letters of reference, minimum GPA of 3.0. Additional exam requirements/recommendations for international students: required—TOEFL (minimum score 500 paper-based), IELTS (minimum score 5).

**Columbia University,** College of Physicians and Surgeons, New York, NY 10032. Offers M Phil, MA, MS, DN Sc, DPT, Ed D, MD, OTD, PhD, Adv C, MBA/MS, MD/DDS, MD/MPH, MD/MS, MD/PhD, MPH/MS. *Program availability:* Part-time. *Entrance requirements:* For master's, GRE General Test. Additional exam requirements/recommendations for international students: required—TOEFL. *Expenses:* Contact institution.

**Columbia University,** Graduate School of Arts and Sciences, Department of Biological Sciences, New York, NY 10027. Offers PhD. *Degree requirements:* For doctorate, comprehensive exam, thesis/dissertation, teaching experience. *Entrance requirements:* For doctorate, GRE General Test, GRE Subject Test (recommended), letters of recommendation. Additional exam requirements/recommendations for international students: required—TOEFL (minimum score 600 paper-based; 100 iBT). *Expenses:* Tuition: Full-time $47,600; part-time $1880 per credit. One-time fee: $105.

**Columbus State University,** Graduate Studies, College of Letters and Sciences, Department of Earth and Space Sciences, Columbus, GA 31907-5645. Offers natural sciences (MS), including biology, chemistry, environmental science, geosciences. *Program availability:* Part-time, evening/weekend. *Degree requirements:* For master's, thesis. *Entrance requirements:* For master's, GRE General Test, minimum GPA of 3.0. Additional exam requirements/recommendations for international students: required—TOEFL (minimum score 550 paper-based; 79 iBT). Electronic applications accepted. *Expenses: Tuition, area resident:* Full-time $210; part-time $210 per credit hour. Tuition, state resident: full-time $210; part-time $210 per credit hour. Tuition, nonresident: full-time $817; part-time $817 per credit hour. *International tuition:* $817 full-time. *Required fees:* $802.50. Tuition and fees vary according to course load, degree level and program.

**Concordia University,** School of Graduate Studies, Faculty of Arts and Science, Department of Biology, Montréal, QC H3G 1M8, Canada. Offers biology (M Sc, PhD); biotechnology and genomics (Diploma). *Degree requirements:* For master's, thesis; for doctorate, thesis/dissertation, pedagogical training. *Entrance requirements:* For master's, honors degree in biology; for doctorate, M Sc in life science.

**Cornell University,** Graduate School, Biomedical and Biological Sciences PhD Program, Ithaca, NY 14853. Offers PhD. *Degree requirements:* For doctorate, comprehensive exam, thesis/dissertation. *Entrance requirements:* For doctorate, GRE General Test. Additional exam requirements/recommendations for international students: required—TOEFL (minimum score 550 paper-based; 77 iBT). Electronic applications accepted. *Expenses:* Contact institution.

**Creighton University,** School of Medicine and Graduate School, Graduate Programs in Medicine, Department of Biomedical Sciences, Omaha, NE 68178-0001. Offers MS, PhD, MD/PhD. Terminal master's awarded for partial completion of doctoral program. *Degree requirements:* For master's, thesis; for doctorate, thesis/dissertation. *Entrance requirements:* For master's, GRE General Test (minimum 50th percentile), three recommendations; for doctorate, GRE General Test (minimum score: 50th percentile), three recommendations. Additional exam requirements/recommendations for international students: required—TOEFL. Electronic applications accepted.

**Dalhousie University,** Faculty of Graduate Studies and Faculty of Medicine, Graduate Programs in Medicine, Halifax, NS B3H 4R2, Canada. Offers M Sc, PhD. *Degree requirements:* For master's, thesis; for doctorate, thesis/dissertation. *Entrance requirements:* Additional exam requirements/recommendations for international students: required—1 of 5 approved tests: TOEFL, IELTS, CANTEST, CAEL, Michigan English Language Assessment Battery. Electronic applications accepted. *Expenses:* Contact institution.

**Dalhousie University,** Faculty of Science, Department of Biology, Halifax, NS B3H 4R2, Canada. Offers M Sc, PhD. Terminal master's awarded for partial completion of doctoral program. *Degree requirements:* For master's, thesis; for doctorate, thesis/dissertation. *Entrance requirements:* Additional exam requirements/recommendations for international students: required—TOEFL, IELTS, CANTEST, CAEL, or Michigan English Language Assessment Battery. Electronic applications accepted.

**Dartmouth College,** Guarini School of Graduate and Advanced Studies, Graduate Programs in Biological Sciences, Graduate Program in Molecular and Cellular Biology, Department of Biological Sciences, Hanover, NH 03755. Offers PhD, MBA/PhD, MD/PhD. *Entrance requirements:* For doctorate, GRE General Test, letters of recommendation. Electronic applications accepted.

**Delaware State University,** Graduate Programs, Department of Biological Sciences, Program in Biological Sciences, Dover, DE 19901-2277. Offers MS. *Entrance requirements:* For master's, GRE, prerequisite undergraduate courses. Additional exam requirements/recommendations for international students: required—TOEFL.

**Delta State University,** Graduate Programs, College of Arts and Sciences, Division of Biological and Physical Sciences, Cleveland, MS 38733-0001. Offers natural sciences (MSNS). *Program availability:* Part-time. *Degree requirements:* For master's, research project or thesis. *Entrance requirements:* For master's, GRE General Test. *Expenses: Tuition, area resident:* Full-time $7501; part-time $417 per credit hour. Tuition, state resident: full-time $7501; part-time $417 per credit hour. Tuition, nonresident: full-time $7501; part-time $417 per credit hour. *International tuition:* $7501 full-time. *Required fees:* $170; $9.45 per credit hour. $9.45 per semester.

**DePaul University,** College of Science and Health, Chicago, IL 60604-2287. Offers applied mathematics (MS); applied statistics (MS); biological sciences (MA, MS); chemistry (MS); environmental science (MS); mathematics education (MA); mathematics for teaching (MS); nursing (MS); nursing practice (DNP); physics (MS); polymer and coatings science (MS); psychology (MS); pure mathematics (MS); science education (MS); MA/PhD. *Accreditation:* AACN. Electronic applications accepted.

**Des Moines University,** College of Osteopathic Medicine, Program in Biomedical Sciences, Des Moines, IA 50312-4104. Offers MS.

**Dominican University of California,** School of Health and Natural Sciences, Program in Biological Sciences, San Rafael, CA 94901-2298. Offers MS. *Degree requirements:* For master's, thesis. *Entrance requirements:* For master's, GRE, BS in biology, biological sciences or biomedical sciences; minimum GPA of 3.0 in last 60 units. Additional exam requirements/recommendations for international students: required—TOEFL (minimum score 550 paper-based; 80 iBT), IELTS (minimum score 6.5). Electronic applications accepted. *Expenses:* Contact institution.

**Drew University,** Caspersen School of Graduate Studies, Madison, NJ 07940-1493. Offers conflict resolution and leadership (Certificate), including community leadership, moderation, peace building; education (M Ed); finance (MA); history and culture (MA, PhD), including American history, book history, British history, European history, intellectual history, Irish history, print culture, public history; K-12 education (MAT), including art, biology, chemistry, elementary education, English, French, Italian, math, secondary education, special education, teacher of students with disabilities; liberal studies (M Litt, D Litt), including history, Irish/Irish-American studies, literature (M Litt, MMH, D Litt, DMH, CMH); religion, spirituality, teaching in the two-year college, writing; medical humanities (MMH, DMH, CMH), including arts, health, healthcare, literature (M Litt, MMH, D Litt, DMH, CMH), scientific research; poetry (MFA). *Program availability:* Part-time, evening/weekend. Terminal master's awarded for partial completion of doctoral program. *Degree requirements:* For master's and other advanced degree, thesis (for some programs); for doctorate, one foreign language, comprehensive exam (for some programs), thesis/dissertation. *Entrance requirements:* For master's, PRAXIS Core and Subject Area tests (for MAT), GRE/GMAT (for MFin MS in Data Analytics), resume, transcripts, writing sample, personal statement, letters of recommendation; for doctorate, GRE (PhD in history and culture), resume, transcripts, writing sample, personal statement, letters of recommendation; for other advanced degree, resume, transcripts, personal statement. Additional exam requirements/recommendations for international students: required—TOEFL (minimum score 587 paper-based; 80 iBT), IELTS (minimum score 6), TWE (minimum score 4). Electronic applications accepted.

**Drexel University,** College of Arts and Sciences, Department of Biology, Philadelphia, PA 19104-2875. Offers biological sciences (MS, PhD). *Program availability:* Part-time. *Degree requirements:* For doctorate, thesis/dissertation. *Entrance requirements:* For master's and doctorate, GRE General Test. Additional exam requirements/recommendations for international students: required—TOEFL. Electronic applications accepted.

**Drexel University,** College of Medicine, Biomedical Graduate Programs, Philadelphia, PA 19129. Offers MLAS, MMS, MS, PhD, Certificate, MD/PhD. *Program availability:* Part-time. Terminal master's awarded for partial completion of doctoral program. *Degree requirements:* For master's, comprehensive exam; for doctorate, thesis/dissertation, qualifying exam. *Entrance requirements:* For master's and doctorate, GRE General Test. Additional exam requirements/recommendations for international students: required—TOEFL. Electronic applications accepted. *Expenses:* Contact institution.

**Drexel University,** College of Medicine, MD/PhD Program, Philadelphia, PA 19104-2875. Offers MD/PhD. Electronic applications accepted.

**Drexel University,** School of Biomedical Engineering, Science and Health Systems, Program in Biomedical Science, Philadelphia, PA 19104-2875. Offers MS, PhD. *Degree requirements:* For master's, thesis (for some programs); for doctorate, thesis/dissertation. Electronic applications accepted.

**Duke University,** Graduate School, Department of Biology, Durham, NC 27708. Offers PhD. *Degree requirements:* For doctorate, one foreign language, thesis/dissertation. *Entrance requirements:* For doctorate, GRE General Test, GRE Subject Test (recommended). Additional exam requirements/recommendations for international students: required—TOEFL (minimum score 577 paper-based; 90 iBT) or IELTS (minimum score 7). Electronic applications accepted.

**Duquesne University,** Bayer School of Natural and Environmental Sciences, Department of Biological Sciences, Pittsburgh, PA 15282-0001. Offers PhD. *Degree requirements:* For doctorate, thesis/dissertation. *Entrance requirements:* For doctorate, GRE General Test; GRE Subject Test in biology, biochemistry, or cell and molecular biology (recommended), BS or MS in biological sciences or related field, 3 letters of recommendation, statement of purpose, official transcripts. Additional exam requirements/recommendations for international students: required—TOEFL (minimum score 95 iBT), TOEFL (minimum score 95 iBT) or IELTS. Electronic applications accepted. *Expenses:* Contact institution.

**East Carolina University,** Brody School of Medicine, Office of Research and Graduate Studies, Greenville, NC 27858-4353. Offers anatomy and cell biology (PhD); biochemistry and molecular biology (PhD); biomedical science (MS); microbiology and immunology (PhD); pharmacology and toxicology (PhD); physiology (PhD). *Students:*

102 full-time (44 women), 1 part-time (0 women); includes 16 minority (4 Black or African American, non-Hispanic/Latino; 7 Asian, non-Hispanic/Latino; 4 Hispanic/Latino; 1 Two or more races, non-Hispanic/Latino), 13 international. Average age 28. 83 applicants, 40% accepted, 20 enrolled. In 2019, 3 master's, 10 doctorates awarded. *Degree requirements:* For doctorate, comprehensive exam, thesis/dissertation. *Entrance requirements:* For doctorate, GRE General Test. Additional exam requirements/recommendations for international students: required—some international applicants may be required to demonstrate English proficiency via the TOEFL, IELTS, or PTE exam.; recommended—TOEFL (minimum score 78 iBT), IELTS (minimum score 6.5), TSE (minimum score 65). *Application deadline:* For fall admission, 8/15 for domestic students; for spring admission, 12/20 for domestic students. Applications are processed on a rolling basis. Application fee: $75. Electronic applications accepted. *Expenses: Tuition, area resident:* Full-time $4749; part-time $185 per credit hour. Tuition, state resident: full-time $4749; part-time $185 per credit hour. Tuition, nonresident: full-time $17,898; part-time $864 per credit hour. *International tuition:* $17,898 full-time. *Required fees:* $2787. *Financial support:* Fellowships available. Financial award application deadline: 6/1. *Unit head:* Dr. Russ Price, Associate Dean, 252-744-9346, E-mail: pricest17@ecu.edu. *Application contact:* Dr. Russ Price, Associate Dean, 252-744-9346, E-mail: pricest17@ecu.edu.
Website: http://www.ecu.edu/cs-dhs/bsomresearchgradstudies/index.cfm

**East Carolina University,** Graduate School, Thomas Harriot College of Arts and Sciences, Department of Biology, Greenville, NC 27858-4353. Offers biology (MS); molecular biology and biotechnology (MS). *Program availability:* Part-time. *Application deadline:* For fall admission, 6/1 priority date for domestic students, 3/1 priority date for international students; for spring admission, 10/15 priority date for domestic students. *Expenses: Tuition, area resident:* Full-time $4749; part-time $185 per credit hour. Tuition, state resident: full-time $4749; part-time $185 per credit hour. Tuition, nonresident: full-time $17,898; part-time $864 per credit hour. *International tuition:* $17,898 full-time. *Required fees:* $2787. *Financial support:* Application deadline: 3/1. *Unit head:* Dr. David Chalcraft, Chair, 252-328-2797, E-mail: chalcraftd@ecu.edu. *Application contact:* graduate School Admissions, 252-328-6012, Fax: 252-328-6071, E-mail: gradschool@ecu.edu.
Website: https://biology.ecu.edu/

**Eastern Illinois University,** Graduate School, College of Liberal Arts and Sciences, Department of Biological Sciences, Charleston, IL 61920. Offers MS. *Program availability:* Part-time, evening/weekend. *Degree requirements:* For master's, comprehensive exam (for some programs), thesis (for some programs). *Entrance requirements:* For master's, GMAT or GRE. Additional exam requirements/recommendations for international students: required—TOEFL (minimum score 500 paper-based; 61 iBT), IELTS (minimum score 6). Electronic applications accepted.

**Eastern Kentucky University,** The Graduate School, College of Arts and Sciences, Department of Biological Sciences, Richmond, KY 40475-3102. Offers biological sciences (MS); ecology (MS). *Program availability:* Part-time. *Degree requirements:* For master's, thesis. *Entrance requirements:* For master's, GRE General Test, minimum GPA of 2.5.

**Eastern Mennonite University,** Program in Biomedicine, Harrisonburg, VA 22802-2462. Offers MA. Electronic applications accepted.

**Eastern Michigan University,** Graduate School, College of Arts and Sciences, Department of Biology, Ypsilanti, MI 48197. Offers community college biology teaching (MS); general biology (MS). *Program availability:* Part-time, evening/weekend, online learning. *Faculty:* 21 full-time (6 women). *Students:* 13 full-time (7 women), 26 part-time (18 women); includes 7 minority (1 Black or African American, non-Hispanic/Latino; 4 Hispanic/Latino; 2 Two or more races, non-Hispanic/Latino), 2 international. Average age 27. 41 applicants, 78% accepted, 16 enrolled. In 2019, 11 master's awarded. *Entrance requirements:* For master's, GRE General Test, GRE Subject Test. Additional exam requirements/recommendations for international students: required—TOEFL. *Application deadline:* Applications are processed on a rolling basis. Application fee: $45. *Financial support:* Fellowships, research assistantships with full tuition reimbursements, teaching assistantships with full tuition reimbursements, career-related internships or fieldwork, Federal Work-Study, institutionally sponsored loans, scholarships/grants, tuition waivers (partial), and unspecified assistantships available. Support available to part-time students. Financial award applicants required to submit FAFSA. *Unit head:* Dr. Marianne Laporte, Department Head, 734-487-4242, Fax: 734-487-9235, E-mail: mlaporte@emich.edu. *Application contact:* Dr. Cara Shillilngton, Graduate Coordinator, 734-487-4433, Fax: 734-487-9235, E-mail: cshilling@emich.edu.
Website: http://www.emich.edu/biology

**Eastern New Mexico University,** Graduate School, College of Liberal Arts and Sciences, Department of Biology, Portales, NM 88130. Offers MS. *Program availability:* Part-time. *Degree requirements:* For master's, comprehensive exam, thesis optional. *Entrance requirements:* For master's, GRE, minimum GPA of 3.0, 2 letters of recommendation, statement of research interest, bachelor's degree related to field of study or proof of common knowledge. Additional exam requirements/recommendations for international students: required—TOEFL (minimum score 550 paper-based; 79 iBT), IELTS (minimum score 6). Electronic applications accepted. *Expenses: Tuition, area resident:* Full-time $5283; part-time $389.25 per credit hour. Tuition, state resident: full-time $5283; part-time $389.25 per credit hour. Tuition, nonresident: full-time $7007; part-time $389.25 per credit hour. *International tuition:* $7007 full-time. *Required fees:* $36; $35 per semester. One-time fee: $25.

**Eastern Virginia Medical School,** Doctoral Program in Biomedical Sciences, Norfolk, VA 23501-1980. Offers PhD. *Degree requirements:* For doctorate, thesis/dissertation. *Entrance requirements:* For doctorate, GRE General Test. Additional exam requirements/recommendations for international students: required—TOEFL. Electronic applications accepted. *Expenses:* Contact institution.

**Eastern Virginia Medical School,** Master's Program in Biomedical Sciences Research, Norfolk, VA 23501-1980. Offers MS. *Degree requirements:* For master's, comprehensive exam (for some programs), thesis optional. *Entrance requirements:* For master's, GRE. Additional exam requirements/recommendations for international students: required—TOEFL. Electronic applications accepted. *Expenses:* Contact institution.

**Eastern Virginia Medical School,** Master's Program in Clinical Embryology and Andrology, Norfolk, VA 23501-1980. Offers MS. *Program availability:* Online learning. *Entrance requirements:* Additional exam requirements/recommendations for international students: required—TOEFL (minimum score 550 paper-based; 80 iBT). Electronic applications accepted. *Expenses:* Contact institution.

**Eastern Virginia Medical School,** Medical Master's Program in Biomedical Sciences, Norfolk, VA 23501-1980. Offers MS. *Entrance requirements:* For master's, MCAT. Electronic applications accepted. *Expenses:* Contact institution.

**Eastern Washington University,** Graduate Studies, College of Science, Technology, Engineering and Mathematics, Department of Biology, Cheney, WA 99004-2431. Offers MS. *Faculty:* 15 full-time (7 women). *Students:* 22 full-time (13 women); includes 1 minority (American Indian or Alaska Native, non-Hispanic/Latino). Average age 29. 20 applicants, 70% accepted, 9 enrolled. In 2019, 9 master's awarded. *Degree requirements:* For master's, comprehensive exam, thesis. *Entrance requirements:* For master's, GRE General Test, minimum GPA of 3.0. Additional exam requirements/recommendations for international students: required—TOEFL (minimum score 580 paper-based; 92 iBT), IELTS (minimum score 7), PTE (minimum score 63). *Application deadline:* For fall admission, 4/1 priority date for domestic students; for spring admission, 1/15 for domestic students. Applications are processed on a rolling basis. Application fee: $75. Electronic applications accepted. *Financial support:* In 2019–20, 14 students received support. Teaching assistantships with partial tuition reimbursements available, career-related internships or fieldwork, Federal Work-Study, institutionally sponsored loans, scholarships/grants, health care benefits, tuition waivers (partial), and unspecified assistantships available. Support available to part-time students. Financial award application deadline: 2/1; financial award applicants required to submit FAFSA. *Unit head:* Dr. Robin O'Quinn, Associate Professor, 509-359-2339, E-mail: biologymasters@ewu.edu. *Application contact:* Dr. Robin O'Quinn, Associate Professor, 509-359-2339, E-mail: biologymasters@ewu.edu.
Website: http://www.ewu.edu/cshe/programs/biology.xml

**East Stroudsburg University of Pennsylvania,** Graduate and Extended Studies, College of Arts and Sciences, Department of Biological Sciences, East Stroudsburg, PA 18301-2999. Offers biology (MS). *Program availability:* Part-time, evening/weekend. *Degree requirements:* For master's, comprehensive exam, thesis or alternative. *Entrance requirements:* For master's, GRE, resume, undergraduate major in life science (or equivalent), completion of organic chemistry (minimum two semesters), 3 letters of recommendation, letter of intent. Additional exam requirements/recommendations for international students: recommended—TOEFL (minimum score 560 paper-based; 83 iBT), IELTS. Electronic applications accepted.

**East Tennessee State University,** College of Graduate and Continuing Studies, College of Arts and Sciences, Department of Biological Sciences, Johnson City, TN 37614. Offers biology (MS); biomedical sciences (MS); microbiology (MS). *Degree requirements:* For master's, comprehensive exam, thesis. *Entrance requirements:* For master's, GRE General Test or GRE Subject Test, minimum GPA of 3.0, undergraduate degree in life or physical sciences, two letters of recommendation; course in calculus and/or course in probability and statistics (recommended). Additional exam requirements/recommendations for international students: required—TOEFL (minimum score 550 paper-based; 79 iBT). Electronic applications accepted.

**East Tennessee State University,** Quillen College of Medicine, Department of Biomedical Sciences, Johnson City, TN 37614. Offers anatomy (PhD); biochemistry (PhD); microbiology (PhD); pharmaceutical sciences (PhD); pharmacology (PhD); physiology (PhD); quantitative biosciences (PhD). *Degree requirements:* For doctorate, comprehensive exam, thesis/dissertation, comprehensive qualifying exam; one-year residency. *Entrance requirements:* For doctorate, GRE General Test, GRE Subject Test, 3 letters of recommendation, minimum of 60 credit hours beyond the baccalaureate degree. Additional exam requirements/recommendations for international students: required—TOEFL (minimum score 550 paper-based; 79 iBT). Electronic applications accepted. *Expenses:* Contact institution.

**Elizabeth City State University,** Master of Science in Biology Program, Elizabeth City, NC 27909-7806. Offers biological sciences (MS); biology education (MS). *Program availability:* Part-time, evening/weekend. *Degree requirements:* For master's, thesis. *Entrance requirements:* For master's, GRE, minimum GPA of 3.0, 3 letters of recommendation, 2 official transcripts from all undergraduate/graduate schools attended, typewritten one-page expository description of student educational preparation, research interests and career aspirations. Additional exam requirements/recommendations for international students: required—TOEFL (minimum score 550 paper-based, 80 iBT) or IELTS ( minimum score 6.5). Electronic applications accepted.

**Elms College,** Division of Natural Sciences, Mathematics and Technology, Chicopee, MA 01013-2839. Offers biomedical sciences (MS). *Faculty:* 6 full-time (3 women), 4 part-time/adjunct (1 woman). *Students:* 21 full-time (14 women), 1 (woman) part-time; includes 3 minority (2 Black or African American, non-Hispanic/Latino; 1 Asian, non-Hispanic/Latino). Average age 27. 38 applicants, 79% accepted, 12 enrolled. In 2019, 24 master's awarded. *Entrance requirements:* Additional exam requirements/recommendations for international students: required—TOEFL (minimum score 80 iBT). *Application deadline:* Applications are processed on a rolling basis. Electronic applications accepted. *Financial support:* Applicants required to submit FAFSA. *Unit head:* Dr. Beryl Hoffman, Co-Chair, Division of Natural Sciences and Mathematics, 413-265-2216, E-mail: hoffmanb@elms.edu. *Application contact:* Nancy Davis, Director, Office of Graduate and Continuing Education Admissions, 413-265-2456, E-mail: grad@elms.edu.

**Emory University,** Laney Graduate School, Division of Biological and Biomedical Sciences, Atlanta, GA 30322-1100. Offers PhD. *Degree requirements:* For doctorate, comprehensive exam, thesis/dissertation. *Entrance requirements:* For doctorate, GRE General Test, minimum GPA of 3.0 in science course work (recommended). Additional exam requirements/recommendations for international students: required—TOEFL. Electronic applications accepted. *Expenses:* Contact institution.

**Emporia State University,** Department of Biological Sciences, Emporia, KS 66801-5415. Offers botany (MS); environmental biology (MS); forensic science (MS); general biology (MS); microbial and cellular biology (MS); zoology (MS). *Program availability:* Part-time. *Degree requirements:* For master's, comprehensive exam or thesis. *Entrance requirements:* For master's, GRE, appropriate undergraduate degree, interview, letters of reference. Additional exam requirements/recommendations for international students: required—TOEFL (minimum score 520 paper-based; 68 iBT). Electronic applications accepted. *Expenses: Tuition, area resident:* Full-time $6394; part-time $266.41 per credit hour. Tuition, state resident: full-time $6394; part-time $266.41 per credit hour. Tuition, nonresident: full-time $20,128; part-time $828.66 per credit hour. *International tuition:* $20,128 full-time. *Required fees:* $2183; $90.95 per credit hour. Tuition and fees vary according to campus/location and program.

**Fairleigh Dickinson University, Florham Campus,** Maxwell Becton College of Arts and Sciences, Department of Biological and Allied Health Sciences, Program in Biology, Madison, NJ 07940-1099. Offers MS.

**Fairleigh Dickinson University, Metropolitan Campus,** University College: Arts, Sciences, and Professional Studies, School of Natural Sciences, Program in Biology, Teaneck, NJ 07666-1914. Offers MS.

**Fisk University,** Division of Graduate Studies, Department of Biology, Nashville, TN 37208-3051. Offers MA. *Program availability:* Part-time. *Degree requirements:* For master's, comprehensive exam, thesis. *Entrance requirements:* For master's, GRE. Electronic applications accepted.

**Fitchburg State University,** Division of Graduate and Continuing Education, Programs in Biology and Teaching Biology (Secondary Level), Fitchburg, MA 01420-2697. Offers biology (MA). *Accreditation:* NCATE. *Program availability:* Part-time, evening/weekend. *Entrance requirements:* Additional exam requirements/recommendations for international students: required—TOEFL (minimum score 550 paper-based; 79 iBT). Electronic applications accepted. *Expenses:* Contact institution.

**Florida Atlantic University,** Charles E. Schmidt College of Medicine, Boca Raton, FL 33431-0991. Offers biomedical science (MS); medicine (MD). *Program availability:* Part-time. *Faculty:* 35 full-time (13 women), 1 part-time/adjunct (0 women). *Students:* 286 full-time (146 women), 31 part-time (18 women); includes 139 minority (27 Black or African American, non-Hispanic/Latino; 1 American Indian or Alaska Native, non-Hispanic/Latino; 53 Asian, non-Hispanic/Latino; 52 Hispanic/Latino; 6 Two or more races, non-Hispanic/Latino), 2 international. Average age 25. 3,233 applicants, 4% accepted, 87 enrolled. In 2019, 30 master's, 55 doctorates awarded. *Degree requirements:* For master's, thesis (for some programs); for doctorate, comprehensive exam. *Entrance requirements:* For master's, GRE, minimum GPA of 3.0; for doctorate, MCAT, AMCAS application, letters of recommendation, interview. *Application deadline:* For fall admission, 5/1 for domestic students, 3/15 for international students; for spring admission, 10/1 for domestic and international students. Application fee: $30. Electronic applications accepted. *Expenses:* Contact institution. *Financial support:* Fellowships and research assistantships available. Financial award applicants required to submit FAFSA. *Unit head:* Marc Kantorow, Assistant Dean, Graduate Programs, 561-297-2142, E-mail: mkantoro@health.fau.edu. *Application contact:* Marc Kantorow, Assistant Dean, Graduate Programs, 561-297-2142, E-mail: mkantoro@health.fau.edu. Website: http://med.fau.edu/

**Florida Atlantic University,** Charles E. Schmidt College of Science, Department of Biological Sciences, Boca Raton, FL 33431-0991. Offers biology (MS, MST). *Program availability:* Part-time. *Faculty:* 43 full-time (18 women), 1 (woman) part-time/adjunct. *Students:* 103 full-time (65 women), 61 part-time (29 women); includes 41 minority (7 Black or African American, non-Hispanic/Latino; 4 Asian, non-Hispanic/Latino; 23 Hispanic/Latino; 7 Two or more races, non-Hispanic/Latino), 12 international. Average age 28. 117 applicants, 39% accepted, 46 enrolled. In 2019, 36 master's awarded. *Entrance requirements:* For master's, GRE General Test, minimum GPA of 3.0. Additional exam requirements/recommendations for international students: required—TOEFL (minimum score 500 paper-based; 61 iBT), IELTS (minimum score 6). *Application deadline:* For fall admission, 3/15 for domestic and international students; for spring admission, 10/1 for domestic and international students. Application fee: $30. *Expenses: Tuition:* Full-time $20,536; part-time $371.82 per credit hour. Tuition and fees vary according to program. *Financial support:* Fellowships, research assistantships, teaching assistantships, career-related internships or fieldwork, and Federal Work-Study available. *Unit head:* Sarah Milton, Interim Chair, 561-297-3327, E-mail: smilton@fau.edu. *Application contact:* Sarah Milton, Interim Chair, 561-297-3327, E-mail: smilton@fau.edu. Website: http://www.science.fau.edu/biology/

**Florida Institute of Technology,** College of Engineering and Science, Program in Biological Sciences, Melbourne, FL 32901-6975. Offers biological sciences (PhD); biotechnology (MS); ecology (MS). *Program availability:* Part-time. *Degree requirements:* For doctorate, comprehensive exam, thesis/dissertation, dissertations seminar, publications. *Entrance requirements:* For doctorate, GRE General Test, resume, 3 letters of recommendation, minimum GPA of 3.2, statement of objectives. Additional exam requirements/recommendations for international students: required—TOEFL (minimum score 550 paper-based; 79 iBT). Electronic applications accepted.

**Florida International University,** College of Arts, Sciences, and Education, Department of Biological Sciences, Miami, FL 33199. Offers MS, PhD. *Program availability:* Part-time. *Faculty:* 56 full-time (21 women), 55 part-time/adjunct (27 women). *Students:* 109 full-time (53 women), 5 part-time (3 women); includes 41 minority (4 Black or African American, non-Hispanic/Latino; 1 American Indian or Alaska Native, non-Hispanic/Latino; 2 Asian, non-Hispanic/Latino; 28 Hispanic/Latino; 6 Two or more races, non-Hispanic/Latino), 22 international. Average age 29. 94 applicants, 26% accepted, 22 enrolled. In 2019, 4 master's, 14 doctorates awarded. *Degree requirements:* For master's, thesis; for doctorate, comprehensive exam, thesis/dissertation. *Entrance requirements:* For master's, GRE General Test, 2 letters of recommendation, minimum GPA of 3.0, faculty sponsor; for doctorate, GRE General Test, 3 letters of recommendation, faculty sponsor with dissertation advisor status, minimum GPA of 3.0. Additional exam requirements/recommendations for international students: required—TOEFL (minimum score 550 paper-based; 80 iBT). *Application deadline:* For fall admission, 2/1 priority date for domestic and international students; for spring admission, 8/1 priority date for domestic and international students. Applications are processed on a rolling basis. Application fee: $30. Electronic applications accepted. *Expenses: Tuition, area resident:* Full-time $8912; part-time $446 per credit hour. Tuition, state resident: full-time $8912; part-time $446 per credit hour. Tuition, nonresident: full-time $21,393; part-time $992 per credit hour. *Required fees:* $2194. *Financial support:* Institutionally sponsored loans and scholarships/grants available. Financial award application deadline: 3/1; financial award applicants required to submit FAFSA. *Unit head:* Dr. Steven Oberbauer, Chair, 305-348-2580, Fax: 305-348-1986, E-mail: steven.oberbauer@fiu.edu. *Application contact:* Nanett Rojas, Manager, Admissions Operations, 305-348-7464, Fax: 305-348-7441, E-mail: gradadm@fiu.edu. Website: http://casgroup.fiu.edu/biology/

**Florida International University,** Herbert Wertheim College of Medicine, Miami, FL 33199. Offers biomedical sciences (PhD); medicine (MD); physician assistant studies (MPAS). *Accreditation:* LCME/AMA. *Faculty:* 75 full-time (36 women), 76 part-time/adjunct (23 women). *Students:* 632 full-time (366 women), 1 (woman) part-time; includes 416 minority (41 Black or African American, non-Hispanic/Latino; 112 Asian, non-Hispanic/Latino; 235 Hispanic/Latino; 28 Two or more races, non-Hispanic/Latino), 7 international. Average age 26. 5,124 applicants, 4% accepted, 171 enrolled. In 2019, 44 master's, 124 doctorates awarded. *Entrance requirements:* For doctorate, MCAT (minimum score of 25), minimum overall GPA of 3.0; 3 letters of recommendation, 2 from basic science faculty (biology, chemistry, physics, math) and 1 from any other faculty member. *Application deadline:* For fall admission, 12/15 for domestic students. Application fee: $160. Electronic applications accepted. *Expenses:* Contact institution. *Financial support:* Institutionally sponsored loans and scholarships/grants available. Financial award application deadline: 3/1; financial award applicants required to submit FAFSA. *Unit head:* Dr. Robert Sackstein, Dean, E-mail: med.admissions@fiu.edu. *Application contact:* Cristina M. Arabatzis, Assistant Director of Admissions, 305-348-0639, Fax: 305-348-0650, E-mail: carabatz@fiu.edu. Website: http://medicine.fiu.edu/

**Florida State University,** The Graduate School, College of Arts and Sciences, Department of Biological Science, Tallahassee, FL 32306-4295. Offers cell and molecular biology (MS, PhD); ecology and evolutionary biology (MS, PhD); science teaching (MST). *Faculty:* 48 full-time (13 women). *Students:* 137 full-time (73 women); includes 23 minority (4 Black or African American, non-Hispanic/Latino; 1 American Indian or Alaska Native, non-Hispanic/Latino; 2 Asian, non-Hispanic/Latino; 1 Hispanic/Latino; 15 Two or more races, non-Hispanic/Latino), 30 international. Average age 30. 168 applicants, 38% accepted, 60 enrolled. In 2019, 3 master's, 11 doctorates awarded. Terminal master's awarded for partial completion of doctoral program. *Degree requirements:* For master's, comprehensive exam (for some programs), thesis (for some programs), teaching experience, seminar presentations; for doctorate, comprehensive exam, thesis/dissertation, teaching experience, seminar presentations. *Entrance requirements:* For master's and doctorate, GRE General Test, minimum upper-division

GPA of 3.0. Additional exam requirements/recommendations for international students: required—TOEFL (minimum score 600 paper-based; 92 iBT). *Application deadline:* For fall admission, 12/1 priority date for domestic students, 12/1 for international students. Application fee: $30. Electronic applications accepted. *Financial support:* In 2019–20, 111 students received support, including 10 fellowships with full tuition reimbursements available (averaging $30,000 per year), 82 teaching assistantships with full tuition reimbursements available (averaging $23,000 per year); scholarships/grants, traineeships, and unspecified assistantships also available. Financial award application deadline: 12/1; financial award applicants required to submit FAFSA. *Unit head:* Dr. Thomas A. Houpt, Professor and Associate Chair, 850-644-4906, Fax: 850-644-4783, E-mail: houpt@bio.fsu.edu. *Application contact:* Crystal Goodwin, Graduate Coordinator, 850-644-3023, Fax: 850-644-9829, E-mail: cgoodwin@bio.fsu.edu. Website: http://www.bio.fsu.edu/

**Florida State University,** The Graduate School, College of Arts and Sciences, Department of Scientific Computing, Tallahassee, FL 32306-4120. Offers computational science (MS, PhD), including atmospheric science (PhD), biochemistry (PhD), biological science (PhD), computational science (PhD), geological science (PhD), materials science (PhD), physics (PhD). *Program availability:* Part-time. *Faculty:* 9 full-time (1 woman), 2 part-time/adjunct (1 woman). *Students:* 34 full-time (6 women); includes 5 minority (2 Asian, non-Hispanic/Latino; 2 Hispanic/Latino; 1 Two or more races, non-Hispanic/Latino), 12 international. Average age 25. 65 applicants, 46% accepted, 8 enrolled. In 2019, 4 master's, 8 doctorates awarded. Terminal master's awarded for partial completion of doctoral program. *Degree requirements:* For master's, comprehensive exam (for some programs), thesis (for some programs); for doctorate, comprehensive exam, thesis/dissertation. *Entrance requirements:* For master's and doctorate, GRE General Test, knowledge of at least one object-oriented computing language, 3 letters of recommendation, resume, statement of purpose. Additional exam requirements/recommendations for international students: required—TOEFL (minimum score 550 paper-based; 80 iBT). *Application deadline:* For fall admission, 4/15 for domestic and international students. Applications are processed on a rolling basis. Application fee: $30. Electronic applications accepted. *Financial support:* In 2019–20, 30 students received support, including 6 research assistantships with full tuition reimbursements available (averaging $26,670 per year), 12 teaching assistantships with full tuition reimbursements available (averaging $23,000 per year); scholarships/grants, health care benefits, tuition waivers (full), and unspecified assistantships also available. Financial award application deadline: 1/15. *Unit head:* Dr. Gordon Erlebacher, Chair, 850-644-7024, E-mail: gerlebacher@fsu.edu. *Application contact:* Karey Fowler, Academic Program Specialist, 850-644-0143, Fax: 850-644-0098, E-mail: kgfowler@fsu.edu. Website: http://www.sc.fsu.edu

**Fordham University,** Graduate School of Arts and Sciences, Department of Biological Sciences, New York, NY 10458. Offers biological sciences (MS, PhD); conservation biology (Graduate Certificate). *Program availability:* Part-time, evening/weekend. *Students:* 40 full-time (27 women), 6 part-time (4 women); includes 5 minority (4 Asian, non-Hispanic/Latino; 1 Hispanic/Latino), 6 international. Average age 29. 88 applicants, 26% accepted, 15 enrolled. In 2019, 5 master's, 10 doctorates, 1 other advanced degree awarded. Terminal master's awarded for partial completion of doctoral program. *Degree requirements:* For master's, one foreign language, comprehensive exam, thesis optional; for doctorate, one foreign language, comprehensive exam, thesis/dissertation. *Entrance requirements:* For master's and doctorate, GRE General Test, GRE Subject Test (recommended). Additional exam requirements/recommendations for international students: required—TOEFL (minimum score 550 paper-based). *Application deadline:* For fall admission, 1/4 priority date for domestic students; for spring admission, 11/1 for domestic students. Application fee: $70. Electronic applications accepted. *Financial support:* In 2019–20, 15 students received support, including 4 fellowships with tuition reimbursements available (averaging $31,000 per year), 42 teaching assistantships with tuition reimbursements available (averaging $29,270 per year); research assistantships, Federal Work-Study, scholarships/grants, tuition waivers (full and partial), and unspecified assistantships also available. Financial award application deadline: 1/4; financial award applicants required to submit FAFSA. *Unit head:* Dr. Silvia Finnemann, Ph.D., Associate Chair of Graduate Studies, 718-817-3630, E-mail: finnemann@fordham.edu. *Application contact:* Garrett Marino, Director of Graduate Admissions, 718-817-4419, Fax: 718-817-3566, E-mail: gmarino10@fordham.edu.

**Fort Hays State University,** Graduate School, Peter Werth College of Science, Technology and Mathematics, Department of Biological Sciences, Program in Biology, Hays, KS 67601-4099. Offers MS. *Program availability:* Part-time. *Degree requirements:* For master's, comprehensive exam, thesis optional. *Entrance requirements:* Additional exam requirements/recommendations for international students: required—TOEFL (minimum score 550 paper-based). Electronic applications accepted.

**Frostburg State University,** College of Liberal Arts and Sciences, Department of Biology, Frostburg, MD 21532-1099. Offers applied ecology and conservation biology (MS); fisheries and wildlife management (MS). *Program availability:* Part-time, evening/weekend. *Degree requirements:* For master's, thesis. *Entrance requirements:* For master's, GRE General Test, resume. Additional exam requirements/recommendations for international students: required—TOEFL. Electronic applications accepted.

**Geisinger Commonwealth School of Medicine,** Graduate Programs in Medicine, Scranton, PA 18509. Offers biomedical sciences (MBS). *Program availability:* Part-time, evening/weekend. *Entrance requirements:* For master's, MCAT, DAT, GRE, bachelor's degree; coursework in biology with lab, organic chemistry with lab, inorganic chemistry with lab, physics with lab, and English; official transcripts; three letters of recommendation. Electronic applications accepted.

**George Mason University,** College of Science, School of Systems Biology, Manassas, VA 22030. Offers bioinformatics and computational biology (MS, PhD, Certificate); bioinformatics management (MS); biology (MS); biosciences (PhD). *Degree requirements:* For master's, comprehensive exam (for some programs), research project or thesis; for doctorate, comprehensive exam, thesis/dissertation. *Entrance requirements:* For master's, GRE, resume; 3 letters of recommendation; expanded goals statement; 2 copies of official transcripts; bachelor's degree in related field with minimum GPA of 3.0 in last 60 hours; for doctorate, GRE, self-assessment form; resume; 3 letters of recommendation; expanded goals statement; 2 copies of official transcripts; bachelor's degree in related field with minimum GPA of 3.0 in last 60 hours; for Certificate, resume; 2 copies of official transcripts. Additional exam requirements/recommendations for international students: required—TOEFL (minimum score 575 paper-based; 88 iBT), IELTS (minimum score 6.5), PTE (minimum score 59). Electronic applications accepted.

**George Mason University,** Schar School of Policy and Government, Program in Biodefense, Arlington, VA 22030. Offers MS, PhD, Certificate. *Program availability:* Evening/weekend, 100% online. *Degree requirements:* For master's, thesis, project; for doctorate, comprehensive exam, thesis/dissertation. *Entrance requirements:* For master's, GRE (taken in the past five years), transcripts from all previous institutions attended in the U.S.; goals statement; two letters of recommendation; current resume; writing sample; for doctorate, GRE (taken in the past five years), official transcript from all colleges and universities attended; current resume; two letters of recommendation;

statement of goals (not to exceed 500 words); writing sample (approximately 10-25 pages in length). Additional exam requirements/recommendations for international students: required—TOEFL (minimum score 575 paper-based; 88 iBT), IELTS (minimum score 6.5), PTE (minimum score 59). Electronic applications accepted. *Expenses:* Contact institution.

**Georgetown University,** Graduate School of Arts and Sciences, Department of Biology, Washington, DC 20057. Offers PhD. Terminal master's awarded for partial completion of doctoral program. *Degree requirements:* For doctorate, comprehensive exam, thesis/dissertation. *Entrance requirements:* For doctorate, GRE General Test, GRE Subject Test (biology). Additional exam requirements/recommendations for international students: required—TOEFL (minimum score 550 paper-based). Electronic applications accepted.

**The George Washington University,** Columbian College of Arts and Sciences, Department of Biological Sciences, Washington, DC 20052. Offers MS, PhD. *Program availability:* Part-time, evening/weekend. Terminal master's awarded for partial completion of doctoral program. *Degree requirements:* For master's, comprehensive exam; for doctorate, thesis/dissertation, general exam. *Entrance requirements:* For master's and doctorate, GRE General Test, minimum GPA of 3.0. Additional exam requirements/recommendations for international students: required—TOEFL (minimum score 550 paper-based; 80 iBT). Electronic applications accepted.

**The George Washington University,** Columbian College of Arts and Sciences, Institute for Biomedical Sciences, Washington, DC 20037. Offers biochemistry and systems biology (PhD); microbiology and immunology (PhD); molecular medicine (PhD), including molecular and cellular oncology, neurosciences, pharmacology and physiology. *Program availability:* Part-time, evening/weekend. *Entrance requirements:* For doctorate, GRE General Test, minimum GPA of 3.0. Additional exam requirements/recommendations for international students: required—TOEFL (minimum score 600 paper-based; 80 iBT). Electronic applications accepted.

**Georgia College & State University,** The Graduate School, College of Arts and Sciences, Department of Biology, Milledgeville, GA 31061. Offers MS. *Program availability:* Part-time. *Faculty:* 26 full-time (12 women). *Students:* 16 full-time (9 women), 7 part-time (6 women); includes 8 minority (4 Black or African American, non-Hispanic/Latino; 1 Asian, non-Hispanic/Latino; 2 Hispanic/Latino; 1 Two or more races, non-Hispanic/Latino). Average age 24. 13 applicants, 100% accepted, 9 enrolled. In 2019, 7 master's awarded. *Degree requirements:* For master's, thesis or alternative, minimum GPA of 3.0, 7 years to complete degree. *Entrance requirements:* For master's, for regular status: GRE (minimum score of 800 under the old system and 286 under the new scoring system), bach degree from accredited institution with 30 hours of undergraduate course work in biological science, transcripts. *Application deadline:* For fall admission, 7/1 priority date for domestic students, 4/1 for international students; for spring admission, 11/1 priority date for domestic students, 9/1 for international students; for summer admission, 4/1 priority date for domestic students. Applications are processed on a rolling basis. Application fee: $40. Electronic applications accepted. *Expenses:* Contact institution. *Financial support:* In 2019–20, 17 students received support. Traineeships and unspecified assistantships available. Support available to part-time students. Financial award application deadline: 7/1; financial award applicants required to submit FAFSA. *Unit head:* Dr. Indiren Pillay, Chair, 478-445-0809, E-mail: indiren.pillayll@gcsu.edu. *Application contact:* Dr. Alfred Mead, Graduate Coordinator, 478-445-1091, E-mail: al.mead@gcsu.edu.

**Georgia Institute of Technology,** Graduate Studies, College of Sciences, School of Biological Sciences, Atlanta, GA 30332. Offers applied physiology (PhD); biology (MS, PhD); prosthetics and orthotics (MS). *Program availability:* Part-time. *Faculty:* 47 full-time (10 women), 1 part-time/adjunct (0 women). *Students:* 206 full-time (117 women), 15 part-time (3 women); includes 39 minority (7 Black or African American, non-Hispanic/Latino; 1 American Indian or Alaska Native, non-Hispanic/Latino; 20 Asian, non-Hispanic/Latino; 7 Hispanic/Latino; 4 Two or more races, non-Hispanic/Latino), 111 international. Average age 27. 287 applicants, 41% accepted, 59 enrolled. In 2019, 62 master's, 19 doctorates awarded. Terminal master's awarded for partial completion of doctoral program. *Degree requirements:* For master's, thesis; for doctorate, thesis/dissertation, qualifying exam. *Entrance requirements:* For master's and doctorate, GRE General Test. Additional exam requirements/recommendations for international students: required—TOEFL (minimum score 600 paper-based; 100 iBT), IELTS (minimum score 7.5). *Application deadline:* For fall admission, 12/1 priority date for domestic and international students. Applications are processed on a rolling basis. Application fee: $75 ($85 for international students). Electronic applications accepted. *Expenses: Tuition, area resident:* Full-time $14,064; part-time $586 per credit hour. Tuition, state resident: full-time $14,064; part-time $586 per credit hour. Tuition, nonresident: full-time $29,140; part-time $1215 per credit hour. *International tuition:* $29,140 full-time. *Required fees:* $2024; $840 per semester. $2096. Tuition and fees vary according to course load. *Financial support:* In 2019–20, 7 fellowships, 94 research assistantships, 42 teaching assistantships were awarded; career-related internships or fieldwork, Federal Work-Study, institutionally sponsored loans, tuition waivers (full and partial), and unspecified assistantships also available. Support available to part-time students. Financial award application deadline: 7/1; financial award applicants required to submit FAFSA. *Unit head:* Todd Streelman, School Chair, 404-894-3700, Fax: 404-894-0519, E-mail: todd.streelman@biology.gatech.edu. *Application contact:* Marla Bruner, Director of Graduate Studies, 404-894-1610, Fax: 404-894-1609, E-mail: gradinfo@mail.gatech.edu.
Website: https://biosciences.gatech.edu

**Georgia Southern University,** Jack N. Averitt College of Graduate Studies, College of Science and Mathematics, Program in Biology, Statesboro, GA 30460. Offers MS. *Program availability:* Part-time. *Faculty:* 56 full-time (22 women). *Students:* 34 full-time (20 women), 13 part-time (7 women); includes 5 minority (2 Black or African American, non-Hispanic/Latino; 2 Hispanic/Latino; 1 Two or more races, non-Hispanic/Latino), 3 international. Average age 26. 25 applicants, 80% accepted, 19 enrolled. In 2019, 13 master's awarded. *Degree requirements:* For master's, comprehensive exam (for some programs), thesis (for some programs), public exit seminar; terminal exam; non-thesis option (course-based). *Entrance requirements:* For master's, GRE General Test, minimum GPA of 2.8, BS in Biology or closely related field, 2 letters of reference. Additional exam requirements/recommendations for international students: recommended—TOEFL (minimum score 550 paper-based; 80 iBT), IELTS (minimum score 6). *Application deadline:* For fall admission, 4/1 priority date for domestic and international students; for spring admission, 11/15 priority date for domestic and international students. Applications are processed on a rolling basis. Application fee: $50. Electronic applications accepted. *Expenses: Tuition, area resident:* Full-time $4986; part-time $277 per credit hour. Tuition, nonresident: full-time $19,890; part-time $1105 per credit hour. *International tuition:* $19,890 full-time. *Required fees:* $2114; $1057 per semester. $1057 per semester. Tuition and fees vary according to course load, campus/location and program. *Financial support:* In 2019–20, 39 students received support, including 13 research assistantships with full tuition reimbursements available (averaging $10,500 per year), 31 teaching assistantships with full tuition reimbursements available (averaging $10,500 per year); career-related internships or fieldwork, Federal Work-Study, scholarships/grants, tuition waivers (full), and unspecified assistantships also available. Support available to part-time students. Financial award application deadline: 4/1; financial award applicants required to submit FAFSA. *Unit head:* Dr. Checo Colon-Gaud, Program Director, 912-478-0053, Fax: 912-478-0845, E-mail: jccolongaud@georgiasouthern.edu.
Website: http://www.bio.georgiasouthern.edu

**Georgia State University,** College of Arts and Sciences, Department of Biology, Atlanta, GA 30302-3083. Offers applied and environmental microbiology (MS, PhD), including applied and environmental microbiology, bioinformatics (MS); cellular and molecular biology and physiology (MS, PhD), including bioinformatics (MS), cellular and molecular biology and physiology; molecular genetics and biochemistry (MS, PhD), including bioinformatics (MS), molecular genetics and biochemistry; neurobiology and behavior (MS, PhD), including bioinformatics (MS), neurobiology and behavior. *Program availability:* Part-time. *Faculty:* 41 full-time (19 women), 1 (woman) part-time/adjunct. *Students:* 199 full-time (123 women), 30 part-time (18 women); includes 111 minority (59 Black or African American, non-Hispanic/Latino; 29 Asian, non-Hispanic/Latino; 15 Hispanic/Latino; 8 Two or more races, non-Hispanic/Latino), 62 international. Average age 28. 155 applicants, 60% accepted, 62 enrolled. In 2019, 80 master's, 14 doctorates awarded. Terminal master's awarded for partial completion of doctoral program. *Degree requirements:* For master's, comprehensive exam (for some programs), thesis optional; for doctorate, comprehensive exam, thesis/dissertation. *Entrance requirements:* For master's, GRE. *Application deadline:* For fall admission, 6/1 priority date for domestic and international students; for spring admission, 10/1 priority date for domestic and international students. Applications are processed on a rolling basis. Application fee: $50. Electronic applications accepted. *Expenses: Tuition, area resident:* Full-time $7164; part-time $398 per credit hour. Tuition, state resident: full-time $7164; part-time $398 per credit hour. Tuition, nonresident: full-time $22,662; part-time $1259 per credit hour. *International tuition:* $22,662 full-time. *Required fees:* $2128; $312 per credit hour. Tuition and fees vary according to course load and program. *Financial support:* In 2019–20, fellowships with full tuition reimbursements (averaging $2,200 per year), research assistantships with full tuition reimbursements (averaging $20,000 per year), teaching assistantships with full tuition reimbursements (averaging $5,400 per year) were awarded; unspecified assistantships also available. Financial award application deadline: 3/1; financial award applicants required to submit FAFSA. *Unit head:* Dr. Geert de Vries, Director of Biology, Associate Vice President for Research and Economic Development, 404-413-5658, Fax: 404-4133518, E-mail: devries@gsu.edu. *Application contact:* Dr. Geert de Vries, Director of Biology, Associate Vice President for Research and Economic Development, 404-413-5658, Fax: 404-4133518, E-mail: devries@gsu.edu.
Website: http://biology.gsu.edu/

**Georgia State University,** College of Education and Human Development, Department of Middle and Secondary Education, Atlanta, GA 30302-3083. Offers curriculum and instruction (Ed D); English education (MAT); mathematics education (M Ed, MAT); middle level education (MAT); reading, language and literacy education (M Ed, MAT), including reading instruction (M Ed); science education (M Ed, MAT), including biology (MAT), broad field science (MAT), chemistry (MAT), earth science (MAT), physics (MAT); social studies education (M Ed, MAT), including economics (MAT), geography (MAT), history (MAT), political science (MAT); teaching and learning (PhD), including language and literacy, mathematics education, music education, science education, social studies education, teaching and teacher education. *Accreditation:* NCATE. *Program availability:* Part-time, evening/weekend, online learning. *Faculty:* 20 full-time (16 women), 8 part-time/adjunct (all women). *Students:* 184 full-time (117 women), 195 part-time (144 women); includes 218 minority (157 Black or African American, non-Hispanic/Latino; 22 Asian, non-Hispanic/Latino; 27 Hispanic/Latino; 12 Two or more races, non-Hispanic/Latino), 3 international. Average age 34. 123 applicants, 61% accepted, 46 enrolled. In 2019, 122 master's, 18 doctorates awarded. *Entrance requirements:* For master's, GRE; GACE I (for initial teacher preparation programs), baccalaureate degree or equivalent, resume, goals statement, two letters of recommendation, minimum undergraduate GPA of 2.5; proof of initial teacher certification in the content area (for M Ed); for doctorate, GRE, resume, goals statement, writing sample, two letters of recommendation, minimum graduate GPA of 3.3, interview. *Application deadline:* For fall admission, 1/15 priority date for domestic and international students; for spring admission, 10/1 for domestic and international students. Application fee: $50. Electronic applications accepted. *Expenses: Tuition, area resident:* Full-time $7164; part-time $398 per credit hour. Tuition, state resident: full-time $7164; part-time $398 per credit hour. Tuition, nonresident: full-time $22,662; part-time $1259 per credit hour. *International tuition:* $22,662 full-time. *Required fees:* $2128; $312 per credit hour. Tuition and fees vary according to course load and program. *Financial support:* In 2019–20, fellowships with full tuition reimbursements (averaging $19,667 per year), research assistantships with full tuition reimbursements (averaging $5,436 per year), teaching assistantships with full tuition reimbursements (averaging $2,779 per year) were awarded; career-related internships or fieldwork, Federal Work-Study, scholarships/grants, health care benefits, tuition waivers (full and partial), and unspecified assistantships also available. Financial award application deadline: 3/15. *Unit head:* Dr. Gertrude Marilyn Tinker Sachs, Chair, 404-413-8384, Fax: 404-413-8063, E-mail: gtinkersachs@gsu.edu. *Application contact:* Shaleen Tibbs, Administrative Specialist, 404-413-8385, Fax: 404-413-8063, E-mail: stibbs@gsu.edu.
Website: http://mse.education.gsu.edu/

**Gerstner Sloan Kettering Graduate School of Biomedical Sciences,** Program in Cancer Biology, New York, NY 10021. Offers PhD. *Degree requirements:* For doctorate, comprehensive exam, thesis/dissertation. *Entrance requirements:* For doctorate, transcripts, 3 letters of recommendation, GRE optional. Additional exam requirements/recommendations for international students: required—TOEFL. Electronic applications accepted.

**Goucher College,** Post-Baccalaureate Premedical Program, Baltimore, MD 21204-2794. Offers Certificate. *Entrance requirements:* For degree, GRE, SAT or ACT. Electronic applications accepted. *Expenses:* Contact institution.

**The Graduate Center, City University of New York,** Graduate Studies, Program in Biology, New York, NY 10016-4039. Offers PhD. *Degree requirements:* For doctorate, thesis/dissertation, teaching experience. *Entrance requirements:* For doctorate, GRE General Test. Additional exam requirements/recommendations for international students: required—TOEFL. Electronic applications accepted.

**Grand Valley State University,** College of Liberal Arts and Sciences, Biology Department, Allendale, MI 49401-9403. Offers MS. *Program availability:* Part-time. *Faculty:* 22 full-time (9 women). *Students:* 22 full-time (14 women), 19 part-time (9 women); includes 1 minority (American Indian or Alaska Native, non-Hispanic/Latino). Average age 27. 13 applicants, 100% accepted, 12 enrolled. In 2019, 11 master's awarded. *Degree requirements:* For master's, comprehensive exam, thesis or alternative. *Entrance requirements:* For master's, GRE General Test, 3 letters of reference, 500-word essay, minimum GPA of 3.0. Additional exam requirements/recommendations for international students: required—TOEFL (minimum iBT score of 80), IELTS (6.5), or Michigan English Language Assessment Battery (77). *Application deadline:* For winter admission, 1/15 priority date for domestic students. Applications are processed on a rolling basis. Application fee: $30. Electronic applications accepted.

*Expenses:* $702 per credit hour, 33 credit hours. *Financial support:* In 2019–20, 27 students received support, including 4 fellowships, 16 research assistantships with full and partial tuition reimbursements available (averaging $8,000 per year); career-related internships or fieldwork, scholarships/grants, and unspecified assistantships also available. Financial award application deadline: 1/15. *Unit head:* Dr. Janet Vigna, Director, 616-331-2592, Fax: 616-331-3446, E-mail: vignaj@gvsu.edu. *Application contact:* Dr. Eric Snyder, Graduate Program Director, 616-331-2417, Fax: 616-331-3446, E-mail: snydeeri@gvsu.edu.

**Grand Valley State University,** College of Liberal Arts and Sciences, Department of Biomedical Sciences, Allendale, MI 49401-9403. Offers MHS. *Program availability:* Part-time. *Faculty:* 20 full-time (5 women), 1 (woman) part-time/adjunct. *Students:* 9 full-time (6 women), 14 part-time (7 women); includes 4 minority (1 Black or African American, non-Hispanic/Latino; 1 Asian, non-Hispanic/Latino; 2 Hispanic/Latino), 4 international. Average age 25. 29 applicants, 69% accepted, 12 enrolled. In 2019, 7 master's awarded. *Degree requirements:* For master's, comprehensive exam, project or thesis. *Entrance requirements:* For master's, GRE General Test, MCAT, or DAT, minimum GPA of 3.0; 3 letters of reference; completion of undergraduate courses in anatomy, physiology, microbiology, and statistics; coursework in chemistry (recommended); personal statement. Additional exam requirements/recommendations for international students: required—TOEFL (minimum iBT score of 80), IELTS (6.5), or Michigan English Language Assessment Battery (77). *Application deadline:* For fall admission, 2/1 priority date for domestic and international students. Applications are processed on a rolling basis. Application fee: $30. Electronic applications accepted. *Expenses:* $702 per credit hour, 33 credit hours. *Financial support:* In 2019–20, 1 student received support, including 1 research assistantship with full and partial tuition reimbursement available (averaging $8,000 per year); fellowships, scholarships/grants, and unspecified assistantships also available. Financial award application deadline: 2/1. *Unit head:* Dr. Daniel Bergman, Chair, 616-331-8837, Fax: 616-331-2090, E-mail: bergmand@gvsu.edu. *Application contact:* Dr. Christopher Pearl, Graduate Program Director/Recruiting Contact, 616-331-3221, Fax: 616-331-2090, E-mail: pearlch@gvsu.edu.

**Hampton University,** School of Science, Department of Biological Sciences, Hampton, VA 23668. Offers biology (MS); environmental science (MS). *Program availability:* Part-time. *Students:* 7 full-time (6 women); includes 5 minority (all Black or African American, non-Hispanic/Latino), 1 international. Average age 24. 15 applicants, 40% accepted, 5 enrolled. In 2019, 1 master's awarded. *Degree requirements:* For master's, comprehensive exam (for some programs), thesis optional. *Entrance requirements:* For master's, GRE General Test. *Application deadline:* For fall admission, 6/1 priority date for domestic students, 6/1 for international students; for spring admission, 11/1 priority date for domestic students, 11/1 for international students; for summer admission, 4/1 priority date for domestic students, 2/1 priority date for international students. Applications are processed on a rolling basis. Application fee: $35. Electronic applications accepted. *Financial support:* Fellowships, research assistantships, teaching assistantships, career-related internships or fieldwork, Federal Work-Study, institutionally sponsored loans, scholarships/grants, and stipends available. Support available to part-time students. Financial award application deadline: 6/30; financial award applicants required to submit FAFSA. *Unit head:* Dr. Jermel Watkins, Chair, 757-727-5267, E-mail: jermel.watkins@hamptonu.edu. *Application contact:* Dr. Jermel Watkins, Chair, 757-727-5267, E-mail: jermel.watkins@hamptonu.edu.

**Harvard University,** Extension School, Cambridge, MA 02138-3722. Offers applied sciences (CAS); biotechnology (ALM); educational technologies (ALM); educational technology (CET); English for graduate and professional studies (DGP); environmental management (ALM, CEM); information technology (ALM); journalism (ALM); liberal arts (ALM); management (ALM, CM); mathematics for teaching (ALM); museum studies (ALM); premedical studies (Diploma); publication and communication (CPC). *Program availability:* Part-time, evening/weekend. *Degree requirements:* For master's, thesis. *Entrance requirements:* For master's, 3 completed graduate courses with grade of B or higher. Additional exam requirements/recommendations for international students: required—TOEFL (minimum score 600 paper-based), TWE (minimum score 5). *Expenses:* Contact institution.

**Harvard University,** Graduate School of Arts and Sciences, Department of Organismic and Evolutionary Biology, Cambridge, MA 02138. Offers biology (PhD). *Degree requirements:* For doctorate, 2 foreign languages, public presentation of thesis research, exam. *Entrance requirements:* For doctorate, GRE General Test, GRE Subject Test (recommended), 7 courses in biology, chemistry, physics, mathematics, computer science, or geology. Additional exam requirements/recommendations for international students: required—TOEFL.

**Harvard University,** Graduate School of Arts and Sciences, Division of Medical Sciences, Boston, MA 02115. Offers biological chemistry and molecular pharmacology (PhD); cell biology (PhD); genetics (PhD); microbiology and molecular genetics (PhD); pathology (PhD), including experimental pathology. *Degree requirements:* For doctorate, thesis/dissertation. *Entrance requirements:* For doctorate, GRE General Test, GRE Subject Test. Additional exam requirements/recommendations for international students: required—TOEFL.

**Harvard University,** Harvard T.H. Chan School of Public Health, PhD Program in Biological Sciences in Public Health, Boston, MA 02115. Offers PhD. *Students:* 49 full-time (0 women). Average age 29. In 2019, 9 doctorates awarded. *Degree requirements:* For doctorate, qualifying examination, dissertation/defense. *Entrance requirements:* For doctorate, GRE General Test. Additional exam requirements/recommendations for international students: recommended—TOEFL (minimum score 600 paper-based; 100 iBT), IELTS (minimum score 7). Electronic applications accepted. *Financial support:* Fellowships, research assistantships, teaching assistantships, institutionally sponsored loans, health care benefits, and tuition waivers (full) available. Financial award application deadline: 1/1. *Unit head:* Tatevik Holmgren, Assistant Director, 617-432-4397, E-mail: bph@hsph.harvard.edu. *Application contact:* Tatevik Holmgren, Assistant Director, 617-432-4397, E-mail: bph@hsph.harvard.edu.
Website: http://www.hsph.harvard.edu/admissions/degree-programs/doctor-of-philosophy/phd-in-biological-sciences-and-public-health/

**See Display on page 602 and Close-Up on page 655.**

**Hofstra University,** College of Liberal Arts and Sciences, Programs in Biology, Hempstead, NY 11549. Offers biology (MA, MS); urban ecology (MA, MS). *Program availability:* Part-time, evening/weekend. *Students:* 5 full-time (3 women), 4 part-time (all women); includes 4 minority (1 Asian, non-Hispanic/Latino; 2 Hispanic/Latino; 1 Two or more races, non-Hispanic/Latino). Average age 25. 21 applicants, 71% accepted, 5 enrolled. In 2019, 9 master's awarded. *Degree requirements:* For master's, thesis, minimum GPA of 3.0. *Entrance requirements:* For master's, GRE, bachelor's degree in biology or equivalent, 2 letters of recommendation, essay. Additional exam requirements/recommendations for international students: required—TOEFL (minimum score 550 paper-based; 80 iBT); recommended—IELTS (minimum score 6.5). *Application deadline:* Applications are processed on a rolling basis. Application fee: $75. Electronic applications accepted. *Expenses: Tuition:* Full-time $25,164; part-time $1398 per credit. *Required fees:* $580; $165 per semester. Tuition and fees vary according to course load, degree level and program. *Financial support:* In 2019–20, 11 students received support, including 8 fellowships with full and partial tuition reimbursements available (averaging $7,443 per year); research assistantships with full and partial tuition reimbursements available, career-related internships or fieldwork, Federal Work-Study, institutionally sponsored loans, scholarships/grants, tuition waivers (full and partial), unspecified assistantships, and scholarships and endowed scholarships also available. Support available to part-time students. Financial award applicants required to submit FAFSA. *Unit head:* Dr. Peter Daniel, Chairperson, 516-463-6718, Fax: 516-463-5112, E-mail: peter.c.daniel@hofstra.edu. *Application contact:* Sunil Samuel, Assistant Vice President of Admissions, 516-463-4723, Fax: 516-463-4664, E-mail: graduateadmission@hofstra.edu.
Website: http://www.hofstra.edu/hclas

**Hood College,** Graduate School, Program in Biomedical Science, Frederick, MD 21701-8575. Offers biotechnology/molecular biology (MS). *Program availability:* Part-time, evening/weekend. *Degree requirements:* For master's, thesis or alternative, mock grant proposal (A). *Entrance requirements:* For master's, bachelor's degree in biology, biochemistry or chemistry; minimum GPA of 2.75; undergraduate coursework required includes completion of the following with a grade B or better: microbiology, organic chemistry, pre-Calculus, upper level genetics, cell biology; essay. Additional exam requirements/recommendations for international students: required—TOEFL (minimum score 575 paper-based; 89 iBT), IELTS (minimum score 6). Electronic applications accepted. *Expenses:* Contact institution.

**Howard University,** Graduate School, Department of Biology, Washington, DC 20059-0002. Offers MS, PhD. *Program availability:* Part-time. *Degree requirements:* For master's, thesis, qualifying exams; for doctorate, thesis/dissertation, qualifying exams. *Entrance requirements:* For master's and doctorate, GRE General Test, minimum GPA of 3.0. Additional exam requirements/recommendations for international students: required—TOEFL. Electronic applications accepted.

**Humboldt State University,** Academic Programs, College of Natural Resources and Sciences, Department of Biological Sciences, Arcata, CA 95521-8299. Offers MS. *Program availability:* Part-time. *Faculty:* 21 full-time (6 women), 15 part-time/adjunct (12 women). *Students:* 18 full-time (14 women), 37 part-time (20 women); includes 7 minority (3 Asian, non-Hispanic/Latino; 4 Hispanic/Latino). Average age 28. 48 applicants, 46% accepted, 18 enrolled. In 2019, 9 master's awarded. *Degree requirements:* For master's, project or thesis. *Entrance requirements:* For master's, GRE General Test, appropriate bachelor's degree, minimum GPA of 2.5, 3 letters of recommendation. Additional exam requirements/recommendations for international students: required—TOEFL (minimum score 500 paper-based). *Application deadline:* For fall admission, 2/15 for domestic and international students. Applications are processed on a rolling basis. Application fee: $55. *Expenses:* Tuition, state resident: full-time $7176; part-time $4164 per term. *Required fees:* $2120; $1672 per term. *Financial support:* Application deadline: 3/1; applicants required to submit FAFSA. *Unit head:* Dr. Amy Sprowles, Department Chair, 707-826-3245, Fax: 707-826-3201, E-mail: amy.sprowles@humboldt.edu. *Application contact:* Dr. Erik S Jules, Biological Sciences Graduate Coordinator, 707-826-3346, Fax: 707-826-3201, E-mail: erik.jules@humboldt.edu.
Website: http://www.humboldt.edu/biosci/programs/grad.html

**Hunter College of the City University of New York,** Graduate School, School of Arts and Sciences, Department of Biological Sciences, New York, NY 10065-5085. Offers MA, PhD. *Program availability:* Part-time. Terminal master's awarded for partial completion of doctoral program. *Degree requirements:* For master's, one foreign language, comprehensive exam or thesis. *Entrance requirements:* For master's, GRE, 1 year of course work in organic chemistry (including laboratory), college physics, and calculus; undergraduate major in biology, botany, physiology, zoology, chemistry or physics. Additional exam requirements/recommendations for international students: required—TOEFL.

**Icahn School of Medicine at Mount Sinai,** Graduate School of Biomedical Sciences, New York, NY 10029-6504. Offers biomedical sciences (MS, PhD); clinical research education (MS, PhD); community medicine (MPH); genetic counseling (MS); neurosciences (PhD); MD/PhD. Terminal master's awarded for partial completion of doctoral program. *Degree requirements:* For master's, thesis; for doctorate, comprehensive exam, thesis/dissertation. *Entrance requirements:* For master's, GRE General Test; for doctorate, GRE General Test, GRE Subject Test, 3 years of college pre-med course work. Additional exam requirements/recommendations for international students: required—TOEFL. Electronic applications accepted.

**Idaho State University,** Graduate School, College of Science and Engineering, Department of Biological Sciences, Pocatello, ID 83209-8007. Offers biology (MNS, MS, DA, PhD); clinical laboratory science (MS); microbiology (MS). *Accreditation:* NAACLS. *Program availability:* Part-time. *Degree requirements:* For master's, comprehensive exam, thesis; for doctorate, comprehensive exam, thesis/dissertation, 9 credits of internship (for DA). *Entrance requirements:* For master's, GRE General Test, minimum GPA of 3.0 in all upper division classes; for doctorate, GRE General Test, GRE Subject Test (biology), diagnostic exam (DA), minimum GPA of 3.0 in all upper division classes. Additional exam requirements/recommendations for international students: required—TOEFL (minimum score 550 paper-based; 80 iBT). Electronic applications accepted.

**Illinois Institute of Technology,** Graduate College, College of Science, Department of Biology, Chicago, IL 60616. Offers applied life sciences (MS); biochemistry (MS); biology (MS, PhD); cell and molecular biology (MS); microbiology (MS); molecular biochemistry and biophysics (MS, PhD). *Program availability:* Part-time, evening/weekend, online learning. Terminal master's awarded for partial completion of doctoral program. *Degree requirements:* For master's, comprehensive exam, thesis (for some programs); for doctorate, comprehensive exam, thesis/dissertation. *Entrance requirements:* For master's, GRE General Test (minimum score 300 Quantitative and Verbal, 2.5 Analytical Writing), minimum undergraduate GPA of 3.0; for doctorate, GRE General Test (minimum score 310 Quantitative and Verbal, 3.0 Analytical Writing); GRE Subject Test (strongly recommended), minimum undergraduate GPA of 3.0. Additional exam requirements/recommendations for international students: required—TOEFL (minimum score 550 paper-based; 80 iBT). Electronic applications accepted.

**Illinois State University,** Graduate School, College of Arts and Sciences, School of Biological Sciences, Normal, IL 61790. Offers animal behavior (MS); bacteriology (MS); biochemistry (MS); biological sciences (MS); biology (PhD); biophysics (MS); biotechnology (MS); botany (MS, PhD); cell biology (MS); conservation biology (MS); developmental biology (MS); ecology (MS, PhD); entomology (MS); evolutionary biology (MS); genetics (MS, PhD); immunology (MS); microbiology (MS, PhD); molecular biology (MS); molecular genetics (MS); neurobiology (MS); neuroscience (MS); parasitology (MS); physiology (MS, PhD); plant biology (MS); plant molecular biology (MS); plant sciences (MS); structural biology (MS); zoology (MS, PhD). *Program availability:* Part-time. *Faculty:* 26 full-time (6 women), 7 part-time/adjunct (2 women). *Students:* 51 full-time (33 women), 15 part-time (8 women). Average age 27. 71 applicants, 28% accepted, 9 enrolled. In 2019, 14 master's, 3 doctorates awarded. *Degree requirements:* For master's, thesis or alternative; for doctorate, variable foreign language requirement, thesis/dissertation, 2 terms of residency. *Entrance requirements:* For master's, GRE General Test, minimum GPA of 2.6 in last 60 hours of course work;

for doctorate, GRE General Test. *Application deadline:* Applications are processed on a rolling basis. Application fee: $50. *Expenses: Tuition, area resident:* Full-time $7956; part-time $9767 per year. Tuition, nonresident: full-time $9233; part-time $17,592 per year. *Required fees:* $1797. *Financial support:* In 2019–20, 20 research assistantships, 41 teaching assistantships were awarded; Federal Work-Study, tuition waivers (full), and unspecified assistantships also available. Financial award application deadline: 4/1. *Unit head:* Dr. Craig Gatto, School Director, 309-438-3087, E-mail: cgatto@IllinoisState.edu. *Application contact:* Dr. Ben Sadd, Assistant Chair for Graduate Studies, 309-438-2651, E-mail: bmsadd@IllinoisState.edu.
Website: http://www.bio.ilstu.edu/

**Indiana State University,** College of Graduate and Professional Studies, College of Arts and Sciences, Department of Biology, Terre Haute, IN 47809. Offers cellular and molecular biology (PhD); ecology, systematics and evolution (PhD); life sciences (MS); physiology (PhD); science education (MS). *Degree requirements:* For master's, thesis optional; for doctorate, comprehensive exam, thesis/dissertation. *Entrance requirements:* For master's and doctorate, GRE General Test. Electronic applications accepted.

**Indiana University Bloomington,** University Graduate School, College of Arts and Sciences, Department of Biology, Bloomington, IN 47405. Offers biology teaching (MAT); biotechnology (MA); evolution, ecology, and behavior (MA, PhD); genetics (PhD); microbiology (MA, PhD); molecular, cellular, and developmental biology (PhD); plant sciences (MA, PhD); zoology (MA, PhD). Terminal master's awarded for partial completion of doctoral program. *Degree requirements:* For master's, thesis, oral defense; for doctorate, thesis/dissertation, oral defense. *Entrance requirements:* For master's and doctorate, GRE General Test. Additional exam requirements/recommendations for international students: required—TOEFL (minimum score 100 iBT). Electronic applications accepted.

**Indiana University of Pennsylvania,** School of Graduate Studies and Research, College of Natural Sciences and Mathematics, Department of Biology, Program in Biology, Indiana, PA 15705. Offers MS. *Program availability:* Part-time. *Faculty:* 9 full-time (2 women). *Students:* 11 full-time (8 women), 13 part-time (8 women); includes 1 minority (Two or more races, non-Hispanic/Latino), 6 international. Average age 25. 29 applicants, 79% accepted, 8 enrolled. In 2019, 23 master's awarded. *Degree requirements:* For master's, comprehensive exam, thesis optional. *Entrance requirements:* For master's, 2 letters of recommendation, official transcripts, goal statement. Additional exam requirements/recommendations for international students: required—TOEFL (minimum score 550 paper-based; 80 iBT), IELTS (minimum score 6.5), TOEFL or IELTS. *Application deadline:* Applications are processed on a rolling basis. Application fee: $50. Electronic applications accepted. *Expenses: Tuition, area resident:* Full-time $9288; part-time $516 per credit. Tuition, nonresident: full-time $13,932; part-time $774 per credit. *Required fees:* $4454. One-time fee: $115 full-time. Tuition and fees vary according to course load and program. *Financial support:* In 2019–20, 3 fellowships (averaging $333 per year), 6 research assistantships with tuition reimbursements (averaging $9,214 per year) were awarded; career-related internships or fieldwork, Federal Work-Study, scholarships/grants, and unspecified assistantships also available. Financial award application deadline: 4/15; financial award applicants required to submit FAFSA. *Unit head:* Dr. Cuong Diep, Graduate Coordinator, 724-357-2357, E-mail: Cuong.Diep@iup.edu. *Application contact:* Dr. Cuong Diep, Graduate Coordinator, 724-357-2357, E-mail: Cuong.Diep@iup.edu.
Website: http://www.iup.edu/grad/biology/default.aspx

**Indiana University-Purdue University Indianapolis,** School of Science, Department of Biology, Indianapolis, IN 46202. Offers MS, PhD. *Program availability:* Part-time, evening/weekend. Terminal master's awarded for partial completion of doctoral program. *Degree requirements:* For master's, thesis (for some programs); for doctorate, thesis/dissertation. *Entrance requirements:* For master's and doctorate, GRE General Test.

**Inter American University of Puerto Rico, Barranquitas Campus,** Program in Education, Barranquitas, PR 00794. Offers curriculum and teaching (M Ed), including biology, English as a second language, history, Spanish; educational leadership and management (MA); elementary education (M Ed); information and library service technology (M Ed); special education (MA). *Accreditation:* TEAC. *Program availability:* Part-time, evening/weekend. *Degree requirements:* For master's, 2 foreign languages, comprehensive exam, thesis (for some programs). *Entrance requirements:* For master's, GRE or EXADEP, bachelor's degree or its equivalent from accredited institution, official academic transcript from institution that conferred bachelor's degree, minimum GPA of 2.5, two recommendation letters, interview (for some programs), essay (for some programs). Electronic applications accepted. *Expenses:* Contact institution.

**Iowa State University of Science and Technology,** Department of Biomedical Sciences, Ames, IA 50011. Offers MS, PhD. *Entrance requirements:* For master's and doctorate, GRE General Test. Additional exam requirements/recommendations for international students: required—TOEFL (minimum score 590 paper-based; 79 iBT), IELTS (minimum score 6.5). Electronic applications accepted.

**Irell & Manella Graduate School of Biological Sciences,** Graduate Program, Duarte, CA 91010. Offers brain metastatic cancer (PhD); cancer and stem cell metabolism (PhD); cancer biology (PhD); cancer biology and developmental therapeutics (PhD); cell biology (PhD); chemical biology (PhD); chromosomal break repair (PhD); diabetes and pancreatic progenitor cell biology (PhD); DNA repair and cancer biology (PhD); germline epigenetic remodeling and endocrine disruptors (PhD); hematology and hematopoietic cell transplantation (PhD); hematology and immunology (PhD); inflammation and cancer (PhD); micrornas and gene regulation in cardiovascular disease (PhD); mixed chimerism for reversal of autoimmunity (PhD); molecular and cellular biology (PhD); molecular biology and genetics (PhD); nanoparticle mediated twist1 silencing in metastatic cancer (PhD); neuro-oncology and stem cell biology (PhD); neuroscience (PhD); RNA directed therapies for HIV-1 (PhD); small RNA-induced transcriptional gene activation (PhD); stem cell regulation by the microenvironment (PhD); translational oncology and pharmaceutical sciences (PhD); tumor biology (PhD). *Degree requirements:* For doctorate, comprehensive exam, thesis/dissertation, qualifying exams, two advanced courses. *Entrance requirements:* For doctorate, GRE General Test; GRE Subject Test (recommended), 2 years of course work in chemistry (general and organic); 1 year of course work each in biochemistry, general biology, and general physics; 2 semesters of course work in mathematics; significant research laboratory experience. Additional exam requirements/recommendations for international students: required—TOEFL. Electronic applications accepted.

**Jackson State University,** Graduate School, College of Science, Engineering and Technology, Department of Biology, Jackson, MS 39217. Offers biology (MS); environmental science (MS). *Program availability:* Part-time, evening/weekend. *Degree requirements:* For master's, comprehensive exam, thesis. *Entrance requirements:* For master's, GRE General Test. Additional exam requirements/recommendations for international students: required—TOEFL (minimum score 520 paper-based; 67 iBT).

**Jacksonville State University,** Graduate Studies, School of Science, Department of Biology, Jacksonville, AL 36265-1602. Offers MS. *Program availability:* Part-time, evening/weekend. *Degree requirements:* For master's, comprehensive exam, thesis (for some programs). *Entrance requirements:* For master's, GRE General Test or MAT. Additional exam requirements/recommendations for international students: required—TOEFL (minimum score 500 paper-based; 61 iBT). Electronic applications accepted.

**James Madison University,** The Graduate School, College of Science and Mathematics, Program in Biology, Harrisonburg, VA 22807. Offers MS. *Program availability:* Part-time. *Students:* 16 full-time (10 women), 3 part-time (1 woman); includes 5 minority (1 Black or African American, non-Hispanic/Latino; 1 Asian, non-Hispanic/Latino; 3 Two or more races, non-Hispanic/Latino). Average age 30. In 2019, 11 master's awarded. Application fee: $60. Electronic applications accepted. *Financial support:* In 2019–20, 16 students received support. Fellowships, Federal Work-Study, and assistantships (averaging $7911) available. Financial award application deadline: 3/1; financial award applicants required to submit FAFSA. *Unit head:* Dr. Joanna B. Mott, Department Head, 540-568-6225, E-mail: mottjb@jmu.edu. *Application contact:* Lynette D. Michael, Director of Graduate Admissions and Student Records, 540-568-6131 Ext. 6395, E-mail: michaeld@jmu.edu.
Website: http://www.jmu.edu/biology/index.shtml

**John Carroll University,** Graduate School, Department of Biology, University Heights, OH 44118. Offers MA, MS. *Degree requirements:* For master's, thesis, seminar. *Entrance requirements:* Additional exam requirements/recommendations for international students: required—TOEFL. *Application deadline:* For fall admission, 2/15 for domestic and international students. Electronic applications accepted. *Financial support:* Scholarships/grants and unspecified assistantships available. Financial award applicants required to submit FAFSA. *Unit head:* Dr. Christopher A. Sheil, Chair, 216-397-3088, Fax: 216-397-4482, E-mail: csheil@jcu.edu. *Application contact:* Dr. Ralph A. Saporito, Graduate Program Director, 216-397-4492, Fax: 216-397-4482, E-mail: rsaporito@jcu.edu.
Website: https://jcu.edu/academics/biology/graduate

**Johns Hopkins University,** National Institutes of Health Sponsored Programs, Baltimore, MD 21218. Offers biology (PhD), including biochemistry, biophysics, cell biology, developmental biology, genetic biology, molecular biology; cell, molecular, and developmental biology and biophysics (PhD). *Degree requirements:* For doctorate, comprehensive exam, thesis/dissertation. *Entrance requirements:* Additional exam requirements/recommendations for international students: required—TOEFL (minimum score 600 paper-based). Electronic applications accepted.

**Johns Hopkins University,** School of Medicine, Graduate Programs in Medicine, Baltimore, MD 21218. Offers MA, PhD. *Degree requirements:* For doctorate, thesis/dissertation. *Entrance requirements:* Additional exam requirements/recommendations for international students: required—TOEFL. Electronic applications accepted. *Expenses:* Contact institution.

**Johns Hopkins University,** Zanvyl Krieger School of Arts and Sciences, Chemistry-Biology Interface Program, Baltimore, MD 21218. Offers chemical biology (MS, PhD). Terminal master's awarded for partial completion of doctoral program. *Degree requirements:* For master's, comprehensive exam, 8 one-semester courses, oral exam; for doctorate, comprehensive exam, thesis/dissertation, 8 one-semester courses, research proposal, oral exam. *Entrance requirements:* For doctorate, GRE General Test; GRE Subject Test in biochemistry, cell and molecular biology, biology or chemistry (strongly recommended), 3 letters of recommendation, transcripts, statement of purpose, resume/curriculum vitae, interview. Additional exam requirements/recommendations for international students: required—TOEFL (minimum score 600 paper-based). Electronic applications accepted. *Expenses:* Contact institution.

**Johns Hopkins University,** Zanvyl Krieger School of Arts and Sciences, Program in Cell, Molecular, Developmental Biology, and Biophysics, Baltimore, MD 21218. Offers PhD. Terminal master's awarded for partial completion of doctoral program. *Degree requirements:* For doctorate, comprehensive exam, thesis/dissertation. *Entrance requirements:* For doctorate, GRE General Test. Additional exam requirements/recommendations for international students: required—TOEFL (minimum score 600 paper-based), IELTS, TWE. Electronic applications accepted.

**Kansas City University of Medicine and Biosciences,** College of Biosciences, Kansas City, MO 64106-1453. Offers bioethics (MA); biomedical sciences (MS). *Program availability:* Part-time. *Degree requirements:* For master's, comprehensive exam, thesis (for some programs). *Entrance requirements:* For master's, MCAT, GRE.

**Kansas State University,** Graduate School, College of Arts and Sciences, Division of Biology, Manhattan, KS 66506. Offers biology (MS). Terminal master's awarded for partial completion of doctoral program. *Degree requirements:* For master's, thesis; for doctorate, thesis/dissertation. *Entrance requirements:* For master's, GRE General Test, minimum undergraduate GPA of 3.0; for doctorate, GRE General Test, minimum GPA of 3.0. Additional exam requirements/recommendations for international students: required—TOEFL (minimum score 550 paper-based). Electronic applications accepted.

**Kansas State University,** Graduate School, College of Veterinary Medicine, Department of Diagnostic Medicine/Pathobiology, Manhattan, KS 66506. Offers biomedical science (MS); diagnostic medicine/pathobiology (PhD). Terminal master's awarded for partial completion of doctoral program. *Degree requirements:* For doctorate, thesis/dissertation. *Entrance requirements:* For master's and doctorate, interviews. Additional exam requirements/recommendations for international students: required—TOEFL (minimum score 550 paper-based). Electronic applications accepted.

**Kennesaw State University,** College of Science and Mathematics, Program in Integrative Biology, Kennesaw, GA 30144. Offers MS. *Students:* 27 full-time (15 women), 3 part-time (2 women); includes 12 minority (9 Black or African American, non-Hispanic/Latino; 1 Asian, non-Hispanic/Latino; 2 Hispanic/Latino). Average age 25. 34 applicants, 62% accepted, 18 enrolled. In 2019, 12 master's awarded. *Degree requirements:* For master's, thesis. *Entrance requirements:* For master's, GRE, two letters of recommendation, official transcript, statement of interest. Additional exam requirements/recommendations for international students: required—TOEFL (minimum score 80 iBT), IELTS (minimum score 6.5). *Application deadline:* For fall admission, 2/1 for domestic and international students. Application fee: $60. Electronic applications accepted. *Expenses: Tuition, area resident:* Full-time $7104; part-time $296 per credit hour. Tuition, state resident: full-time $7104; part-time $296 per credit hour. Tuition, nonresident: full-time $25,584; part-time $1066 per credit hour. *International tuition:* $25,584 full-time. *Required fees:* $2006; $1706 per unit. $853 per semester. *Financial support:* Applicants required to submit FAFSA. *Application contact:* Admissions Counselor, 470-578-4377, Fax: 470-578-9172, E-mail: ksugrad@kennesaw.edu.
Website: http://csm.kennesaw.edu/msib/

**Kent State University,** College of Arts and Sciences, Department of Biological Sciences, Kent, OH 44242. Offers biological sciences (MA, MS, PhD), including botany (MS, PhD), cell biology (MS, PhD), ecology (MS, PhD), physiology (MS, PhD). *Program availability:* Part-time. *Faculty:* 19 full-time (5 women), 2 part-time/adjunct (1 woman). *Students:* 51 full-time (35 women), 9 part-time (4 women); includes 1 minority (Two or more races, non-Hispanic/Latino), 10 international. Average age 29. 53 applicants, 38% accepted, 14 enrolled. In 2019, 8 master's, 9 doctorates awarded. Terminal master's awarded for partial completion of doctoral program. *Degree requirements:* For master's, thesis (for some programs), departmental seminar presentation about research (for MS);

for doctorate, thesis/dissertation, departmental seminar presentation about research, admitted to doctoral candidacy following written and oral candidacy. *Entrance requirements:* For master's, GRE, minimum GPA of 3.0, official transcripts, goal statement, three letters of recommendation, list of up to five potential faculty advisors, undergraduate coursework roughly equivalent to a biology minor, acceptance of student by a faculty advisor; for doctorate, GRE; After completing the required coursework, students complete the doctoral program by being admitted to candidacy, by proposing a research project to the faculty, and by completing and defending that research with a written dissertation before a faculty committee, official transcripts, goal statement, three letters of recommendation, list of up to five potential faculty advisors, baccalaureate degree with strong background in biology and related subjects such as chemistry and mathematics, acceptance of the student by a faculty advisor. Additional exam requirements/recommendations for international students: required—TOEFL (minimum score 94 iBT), IELTS (minimum score 7), PTE (minimum score 65), Michigan English Language Assessment Battery (minimum score 82). *Application deadline:* For fall admission, 12/15 for domestic students, 12/5 for international students. Applications are processed on a rolling basis. Application fee: $45 ($70 for international students). Electronic applications accepted. *Financial support:* Research assistantships with full tuition reimbursements, teaching assistantships with full tuition reimbursements, Federal Work-Study, scholarships/grants, health care benefits, and unspecified assistantships available. Financial award application deadline: 12/15. *Unit head:* Dr. James L. Blank, Dean, 330-672-2650, E-mail: jblank@kent.edu. *Application contact:* Dr. Heather K. Caldwell, Associate Professor and Graduate Coordinator, 330-672-3636, E-mail: hcaldwel@kent.edu.
Website: http://www.kent.edu/biology

**Kent State University,** College of Arts and Sciences, School of Biomedical Sciences, Kent, OH 44242-0001. Offers biological anthropology (PhD); biomedical mathematics (MS, PhD); cellular and molecular biology (MS, PhD), including cellular biology and structures, molecular biology and genetics; neurosciences (MS, PhD); pharmacology (MS, PhD); physiology (MS, PhD). *Faculty:* 17 full-time (8 women). *Students:* 73 full-time (48 women), 2 part-time (1 woman); includes 9 minority (2 Black or African American, non-Hispanic/Latino; 1 Asian, non-Hispanic/Latino; 3 Hispanic/Latino; 3 Two or more races, non-Hispanic/Latino), 53 international. Average age 29. 78 applicants, 17% accepted, 9 enrolled. In 2019, 2 master's, 5 doctorates awarded. *Degree requirements:* For master's, thesis; for doctorate, comprehensive exam, thesis/dissertation. *Entrance requirements:* For master's, GRE, bachelor's degree, transcripts, minimum GPA of 3.0 undergraduate GPA, goal statement, three letters of recommendation, academic preparation adequate to perform graduate work in the desired field (typically two years of chemistry, one year of mathematics, one year of physics and courses in anthropology, biology and psychology); for doctorate, GRE, master's degree, minimum GPA of 3.0, transcripts, goal statement, three letters of recommendation. Additional exam requirements/recommendations for international students: required—TOEFL (minimum score 100 iBT), IELTS (minimum score 7), PTE (minimum score 68), Michigan English Language Assessment Battery (minimum score 85). *Application deadline:* For fall admission, 1/1 for domestic students, 12/15 for international students. Applications are processed on a rolling basis. Application fee: $45 ($70 for international students). Electronic applications accepted. *Financial support:* Research assistantships with full tuition reimbursements, teaching assistantships, health care benefits, and unspecified assistantships available. Financial award application deadline: 1/1. *Unit head:* Dr. Ernest J. Freeman, Director, School of Biomedical Sciences, 330-672-2363, E-mail: efreema2@kent.edu. *Application contact:* School of Biomedical Sciences, 330-6722263, Fax: 330-6729391.
Website: http://www.kent.edu/biomedical/

**Kutztown University of Pennsylvania,** College of Education, Program in Secondary Education, Kutztown, PA 19530-0730. Offers biology (M Ed); curriculum and instruction (M Ed); English (M Ed); mathematics (M Ed); middle level (M Ed); social studies (M Ed); teaching (M Ed); transformational teaching and learning (Ed D). *Accreditation:* NCATE. *Program availability:* Part-time, evening/weekend, 100% online, blended/hybrid learning. *Faculty:* 6 full-time (4 women), 2 part-time/adjunct (0 women). *Students:* 29 full-time (17 women), 80 part-time (56 women); includes 11 minority (2 Black or African American, non-Hispanic/Latino; 7 Hispanic/Latino; 2 Two or more races, non-Hispanic/Latino), 1 international. Average age 34. 91 applicants, 86% accepted, 40 enrolled. In 2019, 31 master's awarded. *Degree requirements:* For master's, comprehensive exam, thesis optional; for doctorate, thesis/dissertation. *Entrance requirements:* For master's, GRE General Test, minimum undergraduate major GPA of 3.0, 3 letters of recommendation, copy of PRAXIS II or valid instructional I or II teaching certificate; for doctorate, master's or specialist degree in education or related field from regionally-accredited institution of higher learning with minimum graduate GPA of 3.25, significant educational experience, employment in an education setting (preferred). Additional exam requirements/recommendations for international students: required—TOEFL (minimum score 550 paper-based, 79 iBT), IELTS (minimum score 6.5), or PTE (minimum score 53). *Application deadline:* For fall admission, 8/1 for domestic and international students; for spring admission, 12/1 for domestic and international students. Application fee: $35. Electronic applications accepted. *Expenses: Tuition, area resident:* Full-time $9288; part-time $515 per credit. Tuition, state resident: full-time $9288. Tuition, nonresident: full-time $13,932; part-time $774 per credit. *Required fees:* $1688; $94 per credit. *Financial support:* Career-related internships or fieldwork, Federal Work-Study, scholarships/grants, and unspecified assistantships available. Financial award application deadline: 3/1; financial award applicants required to submit FAFSA. *Unit head:* Dr. Georgeos Sirrakos, Department Chair, 610-683-4279, Fax: 610-683-1338, E-mail: sirrakos@kutztown.edu. *Application contact:* Dr. Patricia Walsh Coates, Graduate Coordinator, 610-638-4289, Fax: 610-683-1338, E-mail: coates@kutztown.edu.
Website: https://www.kutztown.edu/academcs/graduate-programs/secondary-education.htm

**Lake Erie College of Osteopathic Medicine,** Professional Programs, Erie, PA 16509-1025. Offers biomedical sciences (Postbaccalaureate Certificate); medical education (MS); osteopathic medicine (DO); pharmacy (Pharm D). *Accreditation:* ACPE; AOsA. *Degree requirements:* For doctorate, comprehensive exam, National Osteopathic Medical Licensing Exam, Levels 1 and 2; for Postbaccalaureate Certificate, comprehensive exam, North American Pharmacist Licensure Examination (NAPLEX). *Entrance requirements:* For doctorate, MCAT, minimum GPA of 3.2, letters of recommendation; for Postbaccalaureate Certificate, PCAT, letters of recommendation, minimum GPA of 3.5. Electronic applications accepted.

**Lakehead University,** Graduate Studies, Department of Biology, Thunder Bay, ON P7B 5E1, Canada. Offers M Sc. *Program availability:* Part-time, evening/weekend. *Degree requirements:* For master's, thesis, department seminary, oral examination. *Entrance requirements:* For master's, minimum B average. Additional exam requirements/recommendations for international students: required—TOEFL.

**Lamar University,** College of Graduate Studies, College of Arts and Sciences, Department of Biology, Beaumont, TX 77710. Offers MS. *Program availability:* Part-time, evening/weekend. *Faculty:* 15 full-time (6 women), 4 part-time/adjunct (all women). *Students:* 9 full-time (6 women), 2 part-time (both women); includes 1 minority (Asian, non-Hispanic/Latino), 1 international. Average age 24. 11 applicants, 73% accepted, 7 enrolled. In 2019, 2 master's awarded. *Degree requirements:* For master's, thesis. *Entrance requirements:* For master's, GRE General Test, minimum GPA of 2.5 in last 60 hours of undergraduate course work. Additional exam requirements/recommendations for international students: required—TOEFL (minimum score 550 paper-based; 79 iBT), IELTS (minimum score 6.5). *Application deadline:* Applications are processed on a rolling basis. Application fee: $25 ($50 for international students). Electronic applications accepted. *Expenses: Tuition, area resident:* Full-time $6324; part-time $351 per credit. Tuition, state resident: full-time $6324; part-time $351 per credit. Tuition, nonresident: full-time $13,920; part-time $773 per credit. *International tuition:* $13,920 full-time. *Required fees:* $2462; $327 per credit. Tuition and fees vary according to course load, campus/location and reciprocity agreements. *Financial support:* In 2019–20, 10 students received support, including 3 teaching assistantships (averaging $6,200 per year). *Unit head:* Dr. Randall Terry, Department Chair, 409-880-8262, Fax: 409-880-7147. *Application contact:* Celeste Contreas, Director, Admissions and Academic Services, 409-880-8888, Fax: 409-880-7419, E-mail: gradmissions@lamar.edu.
Website: http://artssciences.lamar.edu/biology

**Laurentian University,** School of Graduate Studies and Research, Programme in Biology, Sudbury, ON P3E 2C6, Canada. Offers biology (M Sc); boreal ecology (PhD). *Program availability:* Part-time. *Degree requirements:* For master's, thesis. *Entrance requirements:* For master's, honors degree with second class or better.

**Lee University,** Program in Education, Cleveland, TN 37320-3450. Offers art (MAT); curriculum and instruction (M Ed, Ed S); early childhood (MAT); educational leadership (M Ed, Ed S); elementary education (MAT); English and math (MAT); English and science (MAT); English and social studies (MAT); higher education administration (MS); history (MAT); history and economics (MAT); math and science (MAT); math and social studies (MAT); middle grades (MAT); science and social studies (MASW); secondary education (MAT); Spanish (MAT); special education (M Ed, MAT); TESOL (MAT). *Accreditation:* NCATE. *Program availability:* Part-time. *Faculty:* 13 full-time (5 women), 9 part-time/adjunct (6 women). *Students:* 24 full-time (15 women), 72 part-time (46 women); includes 14 minority (8 Black or African American, non-Hispanic/Latino; 1 Hispanic/Latino; 5 Two or more races, non-Hispanic/Latino), 1 international. Average age 29. 44 applicants, 86% accepted, 33 enrolled. In 2019, 60 master's, 3 other advanced degrees awarded. *Degree requirements:* For master's, variable foreign language requirement, thesis optional, internship. *Entrance requirements:* For master's, MAT or GRE General Test, minimum undergraduate GPA of 2.75, 3 letters of recommendation, interview, writing sample, official transcripts, background check; for Ed S, minimum undergraduate and master's GPA of 2.75, official transcripts for undergraduate and master's degrees. Additional exam requirements/recommendations for international students: required—TOEFL (minimum score 61 iBT). *Application deadline:* For fall admission, 6/1 priority date for domestic and international students; for spring admission, 11/1 priority date for domestic and international students; for summer admission, 4/1 priority date for domestic and international students. Applications are processed on a rolling basis. Application fee: $25. Electronic applications accepted. *Expenses: Tuition:* Full-time $13,590; part-time $755 per credit hour. *Required fees:* $25. Tuition and fees vary according to program. *Financial support:* In 2019–20, 40 students received support. Career-related internships or fieldwork, Federal Work-Study, institutionally sponsored loans, scholarships/grants, and unspecified assistantships available. Financial award application deadline: 3/1; financial award applicants required to submit FAFSA. *Unit head:* Dr. William Kamm, Director, 423-614-8544, E-mail: wkamm@leeuniversity.edu. *Application contact:* Jeffery McGirt, Director of Graduate Enrollment, 423-614-8691, Fax: 423-614-8317, E-mail: jmcgirt@leeuniversity.edu.
Website: http://www.leeuniversity.edu/academics/graduate/education

**Lehigh University,** College of Arts and Sciences, Department of Biological Sciences, Bethlehem, PA 18015. Offers biochemistry (PhD); cell and molecular biology (PhD); integrative biology (PhD); molecular biology (MS). *Program availability:* 100% online, MS MBio Program Only. *Faculty:* 24 full-time (11 women), 1 (woman) part-time/adjunct. *Students:* 36 full-time (18 women), 23 part-time (16 women); includes 12 minority (1 Black or African American, non-Hispanic/Latino; 1 American Indian or Alaska Native, non-Hispanic/Latino; 2 Asian, non-Hispanic/Latino; 7 Hispanic/Latino; 1 Two or more races, non-Hispanic/Latino), 9 international. Average age 28. 53 applicants, 57% accepted, 22 enrolled. In 2019, 9 master's, 7 doctorates awarded. Terminal master's awarded for partial completion of doctoral program. *Degree requirements:* For master's, thesis optional; for doctorate, comprehensive exam, thesis/dissertation. *Entrance requirements:* For master's, bachelor's degree in a life science or chemistry with a GPA of 3.0 or higher, 2 letters of recommendation, official transcripts of previous educational experience; for doctorate, GRE General Test, Three letters of recommendation, curriculum vitae, official transcripts, minimum Bachelor's degree or equivalent, personal statement. Additional exam requirements/recommendations for international students: required—TOEFL (minimum score 85 iBT). *Application deadline:* For fall admission, 7/15 for domestic and international students; for spring admission, 12/1 for domestic and international students; for summer admission, 4/30 for domestic and international students. Application fee: $75. Electronic applications accepted. *Financial support:* In 2019–20, 39 students received support, including 2 fellowships with full tuition reimbursements available (averaging $29,000 per year), 14 research assistantships with full tuition reimbursements available (averaging $29,000 per year), 18 teaching assistantships with full tuition reimbursements available (averaging $29,000 per year); tuition waivers (full and partial) and partially reimbursed health care benefits also available. Financial award application deadline: 1/1. *Unit head:* Dr. Linda Lowe-Krentz, Chairperson, 610-758-5084, Fax: 610-758-4004, E-mail: lij0@lehigh.edu. *Application contact:* Dr. Amber Rice, Graduate Coordinator, 610-758-5509, Fax: 610-758-4004, E-mail: amr511@lehigh.edu.
Website: http://www.lehigh.edu/~inbios/

**Lehman College of the City University of New York,** School of Natural and Social Sciences, Department of Biological Sciences, Bronx, NY 10468-1589. Offers biology (MA). *Program availability:* Part-time, evening/weekend. Terminal master's awarded for partial completion of doctoral program. *Expenses: Tuition, area resident:* Full-time $5545; part-time $470 per credit. Tuition, nonresident: part-time $855 per credit. *Required fees:* $240.

**Liberty University,** School of Health Sciences, Lynchburg, VA 24515. Offers anatomy and cell biology (PhD); biomedical sciences (MS); epidemiology (MPH); exercise science (MS), including clinical, community physical activity, human performance, nutrition; global health (MPH); health promotion (MPH); medical sciences (MA), including biopsychology, business management, health informatics, molecular medicine, public health; nutrition (MPH). *Program availability:* Part-time, online learning. *Students:* 820 full-time (588 women), 889 part-time (612 women); includes 611 minority (402 Black or African American, non-Hispanic/Latino; 10 American Indian or Alaska Native, non-Hispanic/Latino; 43 Asian, non-Hispanic/Latino; 85 Hispanic/Latino; 1 Native Hawaiian or other Pacific Islander, non-Hispanic/Latino; 70 Two or more races, non-Hispanic/Latino), 67 international. Average age 32. 2,610 applicants, 33% accepted, 406 enrolled. In 2019, 445 master's awarded. *Degree requirements:* For master's, thesis (for some programs); for doctorate, thesis/dissertation. *Entrance requirements:* For doctorate, MAT or GRE, minimum GPA of 3.25 in master's program, 2-3 recommendations, writing

samples (for some programs), letter of intent, professional vitae. Additional exam requirements/recommendations for international students: required—TOEFL (minimum score 600 paper-based; 100 iBT). Application fee: $50. *Expenses: Tuition:* Full-time $545; part-time $410 per credit hour. One-time fee: $50. *Financial support:* In 2019–20, 918 students received support. Federal Work-Study available. Financial award applicants required to submit FAFSA. *Unit head:* Dr. Ralph Linstra, Dean. *Application contact:* Jay Bridge, Director of Admissions, 800-424-9595, Fax: 800-628-7977, E-mail: gradadmissions@liberty.edu.
Website: https://www.liberty.edu/health-sciences/

**London Metropolitan University,** Graduate Programs, London, United Kingdom. Offers applied psychology (M Sc); architecture (MA); biomedical science (M Sc); blood science (M Sc); cancer pharmacology (M Sc); computer networking and cyber security (M Sc); computing and information systems (M Sc); conference interpreting (MA); counter-terrorism studies (M Sc); creative, digital and professional writing (MA); crime, violence and prevention (M Sc); criminology (M Sc); curating contemporary art (MA); data analytics (M Sc); digital media (MA); early childhood studies (MA); education (MA, Ed D); financial services law, regulation and compliance (LL M); food science (M Sc); forensic psychology (M Sc); health and social care management and policy (M Sc); human nutrition (M Sc); human resource management (MA); human rights and international conflict (MA); information technology (M Sc); intelligence and security studies (M Sc); international oil, gas and energy law (LL M); international relations (MA); interpreting (MA); learning and teaching in higher education (MA); legal practice (LL M); media and entertainment law (LL M); organizational and consumer psychology (M Sc); psychological therapy (M Sc); psychology of mental health (M Sc); public health (M Sc); public policy and management (MPA); security studies (M Sc); social work (M Sc); spatial planning and urban design (MA); sports therapy (M Sc); supporting older children and young people with dyslexia (MA); teaching languages (MA), including Arabic, English; translation (MA); woman and child abuse (MA).

**Long Island University - Brooklyn,** Richard L. Conolly College of Liberal Arts and Sciences, Brooklyn, NY 11201-8423. Offers biology (MS); chemistry (MS); clinical psychology (PhD); creative writing (MFA); English (MA); media arts (MA, MFA); political science (MA); psychology (MA); social science (MS); United Nations (Advanced Certificate); urban studies (MA); writing and production for television (MFA). *Program availability:* Part-time. Terminal master's awarded for partial completion of doctoral program. *Degree requirements:* For master's, comprehensive exam (for some programs), thesis (for some programs); for doctorate, thesis/dissertation. *Entrance requirements:* For doctorate, GRE. Additional exam requirements/recommendations for international students: required—TOEFL (minimum score 550 paper-based, 79 iBT) or IELTS. Electronic applications accepted.

**Long Island University - Post,** College of Liberal Arts and Sciences, Brookville, NY 11548-1300. Offers applied mathematics (MS); behavior analysis (MA); biology (MS); criminal justice (MS); earth science (MS); English (MA); environmental sustainability (MS); genetic counseling (MS); history (MA); interdisciplinary studies (MA, MS); political science (MA); psychology (MA). *Program availability:* Part-time, evening/weekend, blended/hybrid learning. Terminal master's awarded for partial completion of doctoral program. *Degree requirements:* For master's, comprehensive exam (for some programs), thesis (for some programs). *Entrance requirements:* Additional exam requirements/recommendations for international students: required—TOEFL, IELTS, or PTE. Electronic applications accepted.

**Long Island University - Post,** School of Health Professions and Nursing, Brookville, NY 11548-1300. Offers biomedical science (MS); cardiovascular perfusion (MS); clinical lab sciences (MS); clinical laboratory management (MS); dietetic internship (Advanced Certificate); family nurse practitioner (MS, Advanced Certificate); forensic social work (Advanced Certificate); gerontology (Advanced Certificate); health administration (MPA); non-profit management (Advanced Certificate); nursing education (MS); nutrition (MS); public administration (MPA); social work (MSW). *Program availability:* Part-time, blended/hybrid learning. *Degree requirements:* For master's, comprehensive exam (for some programs), thesis (for some programs). *Entrance requirements:* Additional exam requirements/recommendations for international students: required—TOEFL (minimum score 85 iBT) or IELTS (7.5). Electronic applications accepted.

**Louisiana State University and Agricultural & Mechanical College,** Graduate School, College of Science, Department of Biological Sciences, Baton Rouge, LA 70803. Offers biochemistry (MS, PhD); biological science (MS, PhD); science (MNS).

**Louisiana State University Health Sciences Center,** School of Graduate Studies in New Orleans, New Orleans, LA 70112-2223. Offers PhD, MD/PhD. *Faculty:* 159 full-time (45 women). *Students:* 76 full-time (44 women); includes 17 minority (5 Black or African American, non-Hispanic/Latino; 6 Asian, non-Hispanic/Latino; 4 Hispanic/Latino; 2 Two or more races, non-Hispanic/Latino), 8 international. Average age 26. 85 applicants, 19% accepted, 12 enrolled. In 2019, 13 doctorates awarded. Terminal master's awarded for partial completion of doctoral program. *Degree requirements:* For doctorate, comprehensive exam, thesis/dissertation. *Entrance requirements:* For doctorate, GRE General Test. Additional exam requirements/recommendations for international students: recommended—TOEFL, IELTS. *Application deadline:* For fall admission, 4/1 for domestic and international students. Applications are processed on a rolling basis. Application fee: $30. Electronic applications accepted. *Expenses:* Contact institution. *Financial support:* In 2019–20, 70 students received support. Tuition waivers (full) and unspecified assistantships available. Financial award application deadline: 4/1. *Unit head:* Dr. Joseph M. Moerschbaecher, III, Dean, 504-568-2211, Fax: 504-568-2361. *Application contact:* Leigh Smith-Vaniz, Coordinator of Student Affairs, 504-568-2211, Fax: 504-568-5588, E-mail: lsmi30@lsuhsc.edu.
Website: http://graduatestudies.lsuhsc.edu

**Louisiana State University Health Sciences Center at Shreveport,** Master of Science in Biomedical Sciences Program, Shreveport, LA 71130-3932. Offers MS. Terminal master's awarded for partial completion of doctoral program. *Degree requirements:* For master's, thesis, seminar and journal club presentations, research component. *Entrance requirements:* For master's, GRE. Additional exam requirements/recommendations for international students: required—TOEFL, IELTS.

**Louisiana State University in Shreveport,** College of Arts and Sciences, Program in Biological Sciences, Shreveport, LA 71115-2399. Offers MS. *Program availability:* Part-time, evening/weekend. *Degree requirements:* For master's, comprehensive exam (for some programs), thesis optional. *Entrance requirements:* For master's, GRE. Additional exam requirements/recommendations for international students: required—TOEFL (minimum score 550 paper-based; 61 iBT). Electronic applications accepted.

**Louisiana Tech University,** Graduate School, College of Applied and Natural Sciences, Ruston, LA 71272. Offers biology (MS); dietetics (Graduate Certificate); health informatics (MHI); molecular science and nanotechnology (MS, PhD). *Program availability:* Part-time. *Degree requirements:* For master's, comprehensive exam (for some programs), thesis (for some programs); for doctorate, comprehensive exam, thesis/dissertation. *Entrance requirements:* For master's and doctorate, GRE General Test, transcript with bachelor's degree awarded; for Graduate Certificate, transcript with bachelor's degree awarded. Additional exam requirements/recommendations for international students: required—TOEFL (minimum score 550 paper-based; 80 iBT), IELTS (minimum score 6.5). Electronic applications accepted. *Expenses: Tuition, area resident:* Full-time $6592; part-time $400 per credit. Tuition, state resident: full-time $6592; part-time $400 per credit. Tuition, nonresident: full-time $13,333; part-time $681 per credit. *International tuition:* $13,333 full-time. *Required fees:* $3011; $3011 per unit.

**Louisiana Tech University,** Graduate School, College of Education, Ruston, LA 71272. Offers counseling and guidance (MA), including clinical mental health counseling, human services, orientation and mobility; counseling psychology (PhD); curriculum and instruction (M Ed); cyber education (Graduate Certificate); dynamics of domestic and family violence (Graduate Certificate); early childhood education - PreK-3 (MAT); educational leadership (M Ed, Ed D); elementary education and special education mild/moderate grades 1-5 (MAT); higher education administration (Graduate Certificate); industrial/organizational psychology (MA, PhD); kinesiology (MS); middle school education (MAT), including mathematics; orientation and mobility (Graduate Certificate); rehabilitation teaching for the blind (Graduate Certificate); secondary education (MAT), including agriculture, biology, business, chemistry, English; special education: visually impaired (MAT); teacher leader education (Graduate Certificate); visual impairments - blind education (Graduate Certificate). *Accreditation:* NCATE. *Program availability:* Part-time. *Degree requirements:* For master's, thesis; for doctorate, thesis/dissertation. *Entrance requirements:* For master's and doctorate, GRE General Test. Additional exam requirements/recommendations for international students: required—TOEFL (minimum score 550 paper-based; 80 iBT), IELTS (minimum score 6.5). Electronic applications accepted. *Expenses: Tuition, area resident:* Full-time $6592; part-time $400 per credit. Tuition, state resident: full-time $6592; part-time $400 per credit. Tuition, nonresident: full-time $13,333; part-time $681 per credit. *International tuition:* $13,333 full-time. *Required fees:* $3011; $3011 per unit.

**Loyola University Chicago,** Graduate School, Department of Biology, Chicago, IL 60660. Offers biology (MA); cellular & molecular oncology (MS). *Faculty:* 21 full-time (8 women). *Students:* 85 full-time (47 women), 2 part-time (both women); includes 40 minority (12 Black or African American, non-Hispanic/Latino; 18 Asian, non-Hispanic/Latino; 7 Hispanic/Latino; 3 Two or more races, non-Hispanic/Latino), 2 international. Average age 25. 331 applicants, 37% accepted, 62 enrolled. In 2019, 58 master's awarded. *Entrance requirements:* For master's, GRE General Test, GRE Subject Test, 3 letters of recommendation, BS in biology. Additional exam requirements/recommendations for international students: required—TOEFL. *Application deadline:* For fall admission, 6/1 for domestic and international students. Applications are processed on a rolling basis. Electronic applications accepted. *Expenses: Tuition:* Full-time $18,540; part-time $1033 per credit hour. *Required fees:* $904; $230 per credit hour. *Financial support:* In 2019–20, 7 students received support, including 7 fellowships with full tuition reimbursements available (averaging $16,000 per year); Federal Work-Study and institutionally sponsored loans also available. Financial award application deadline: 2/1; financial award applicants required to submit FAFSA. *Unit head:* Dr. Terry Grande, Graduate Program Director, 773-583-5649, Fax: 773-508-3646, E-mail: tgrande@luc.edu. *Application contact:* Jill Schur, Director of Graduate Enrollment Management, 312-915-8902, E-mail: gradinfo@luc.edu.
Website: http://www.luc.edu/biology/

**Loyola University Chicago,** Graduate School, Integrated Program in Biomedical Sciences, Maywood, IL 60660. Offers biochemistry and molecular biology (MS, PhD); cell and molecular physiology (MS, PhD); infectious disease and immunology (MS); integrative cell biology (MS, PhD); microbiology and immunology (MS, PhD); molecular pharmacology and therapeutics (MS, PhD); neuroscience (MS, PhD). *Students:* Average age 25. 773 applicants, 34% accepted, 122 enrolled. In 2019, 46 master's, 12 doctorates awarded. *Degree requirements:* For master's, thesis; for doctorate, comprehensive exam, thesis/dissertation. *Entrance requirements:* For doctorate, GRE. Additional exam requirements/recommendations for international students: required—TOEFL (minimum score 94 iBT), IELTS (minimum score 7.5). *Application deadline:* For fall admission, 2/7 for domestic students. Applications are processed on a rolling basis. Electronic applications accepted. *Expenses:* Contact institution. *Financial support:* In 2019–20, 20 students received support. Schmitt Fellowships and yearly tuition scholarships (averaging $25,032) available. Financial award application deadline: 6/15; financial award applicants required to submit FAFSA. *Unit head:* Dr. Leanne L. Cribbs, Associate Dean, Graduate Education, 708-327-2817, Fax: 708-216-8216, E-mail: lcribbs@luc.edu. *Application contact:* Margarita Quesada, Graduate Program Secretary, 708-216-3532, Fax: 708-216-8216, E-mail: mquesad@luc.edu.
Website: http://ssom.luc.edu/graduate_school/degree-programs/ipbsphd/

**Manhattanville College,** School of Education, Program in Middle Childhood/Adolescence Education (Grades 5-12), Purchase, NY 10577-2132. Offers biology and special education (MPS); chemistry and special education (MPS); education for sustainability (Advanced Certificate); English and special education (MPS); literacy and special education (MPS); literacy specialist (MPS); math and special education (MPS); mathematics (Advanced Certificate); middle childhood/adolescence ed science (biology or chemistry grades 5-12) or (physics grades 7-12) (MAT); middle childhood/adolescence education (grades 5-12) English (MAT, Advanced Certificate); middle childhood/adolescence education (grades 5-12) mathematics (MAT, Advanced Certificate); middle childhood/adolescence education (grades 5-12) science (biology chemistry, physics, earth science) (Advanced Certificate); middle childhood/adolescence education (grades 5-12) social studies (MAT, Advanced Certificate); physics (MAT, Advanced Certificate); social studies (MAT); social studies and special education (MPS); special education generalist (MPS). *Program availability:* Part-time, evening/weekend. *Faculty:* 3 full-time (2 women), 17 part-time/adjunct (11 women). *Students:* 21 full-time (13 women), 25 part-time (16 women); includes 9 minority (4 Black or African American, non-Hispanic/Latino; 1 Asian, non-Hispanic/Latino; 4 Hispanic/Latino). Average age 29. 10 applicants, 80% accepted, 5 enrolled. In 2019, 15 master's, 4 other advanced degrees awarded. *Degree requirements:* For master's, comprehensive exam (for some programs), thesis (for some programs), student teaching, research seminars, portfolios, internships, writing assessment; for Advanced Certificate, comprehensive exam (for some programs). *Entrance requirements:* For master's, for programs leading to certification, candidates must submit scores from GRE or MAT(Miller Analogies Test), minimum undergraduate GPA of 3.0, all transcripts from all colleges and universities attended, 2 letters of recommendation, interview, essay (2-3 page personal statement that describes reasons for choosing education as profession and personal philosophy of education), proof of immunization (for those born after 1957). Additional exam requirements/recommendations for international students: required—TOEFL or IELTS are required. Manhattanville College now accepts the Duolingo English Test with a required score of 105; recommended—TOEFL (minimum score 600 paper-based; 110 iBT), IELTS (minimum score 8). *Application deadline:* Applications are processed on a rolling basis. Application fee: $75. Electronic applications accepted. *Expenses:* $935 per credit, $45 technology fee, and $60 registration fee. *Financial support:* In 2019–20, 18 students received support. Teaching assistantships, scholarships/grants, tuition waivers, and unspecified assistantships available. Support available to part-time students. Financial award application deadline: 3/15; financial award applicants required to submit FAFSA. *Unit head:* Dr. Shelley Wepner, Dean, 914-323-3153, Fax: 914-323-5493, E-mail: Shelley.Wepner@mville.edu. *Application contact:* Alissa Wilson, Director, Graduate Admissions, 914-323-

3150, Fax: 914-694-1732, E-mail: Alissa.Wilson@mville.edu. Website: http://www.mville.edu/programs#/search/19

**Marquette University,** Graduate School, College of Arts and Sciences, Department of Biological Sciences, Milwaukee, WI 53201-1881. Offers cell biology (MS, PhD); developmental biology (MS, PhD); ecology (MS, PhD); epithelial physiology (MS, PhD); genetics (MS, PhD); microbiology (MS, PhD); molecular biology (MS, PhD); muscle and exercise physiology (MS, PhD); neuroscience (PhD). Terminal master's awarded for partial completion of doctoral program. *Degree requirements:* For master's, comprehensive exam, thesis, 1 year of teaching experience or equivalent; for doctorate, thesis/dissertation, 1 year of teaching experience or equivalent, qualifying exam. *Entrance requirements:* For master's and doctorate, GRE General Test, GRE Subject Test, official transcripts from all current and previous colleges/universities except Marquette, statement of professional goals and aspirations, three letters of recommendation. Additional exam requirements/recommendations for international students: required—TOEFL (minimum score 530 paper-based). Electronic applications accepted.

**Marshall University,** Academic Affairs Division, College of Science, Department of Biological Science, Huntington, WV 25755. Offers MA, MS. *Degree requirements:* For master's, thesis (for some programs). *Entrance requirements:* For master's, GRE General Test.

**Marshall University,** Joan C. Edwards School of Medicine and Academic Affairs Division, Program in Biomedical Sciences, Huntington, WV 25755. Offers MS, PhD. Terminal master's awarded for partial completion of doctoral program. *Degree requirements:* For master's, comprehensive exam, thesis optional; for doctorate, thesis/dissertation, written and oral qualifying exams. *Entrance requirements:* For master's, GRE General Test or MCAT (medical science), 1 year of course work in biology, physics, chemistry, and organic chemistry and associated labs; for doctorate, GRE General Test, 1 year of course work in biology, physics, chemistry, and organic chemistry and associated labs. Additional exam requirements/recommendations for international students: required—TOEFL (minimum score 525 paper-based). *Expenses:* Contact institution.

**Massachusetts Institute of Technology,** School of Engineering, Harvard-MIT Health Sciences and Technology Program, Cambridge, MA 02139. Offers health sciences and technology (SM, PhD, Sc D), including bioastronautics (PhD, Sc D), bioinformatics and integrative genomics (PhD, Sc D), medical engineering and medical physics (PhD, Sc D), speech and hearing bioscience and technology (PhD, Sc D). Terminal master's awarded for partial completion of doctoral program. *Degree requirements:* For doctorate, comprehensive exam, thesis/dissertation. *Entrance requirements:* For doctorate, GRE General Test. Additional exam requirements/recommendations for international students: required—TOEFL, IELTS. Electronic applications accepted.

**Massachusetts Institute of Technology,** School of Science, Department of Biology, Cambridge, MA 02139. Offers biochemistry (PhD); biological oceanography (PhD); biology (PhD); biophysical chemistry and molecular structure (PhD); cell biology (PhD); computational and systems biology (PhD); developmental biology (PhD); genetics (PhD); immunology (PhD); microbiology (PhD); molecular biology (PhD); neurobiology (PhD). *Degree requirements:* For doctorate, comprehensive exam, thesis/dissertation, teaching assistantship during two semesters. *Entrance requirements:* For doctorate, GRE General Test. Additional exam requirements/recommendations for international students: required—TOEFL, IELTS. Electronic applications accepted.

**McGill University,** Faculty of Graduate and Postdoctoral Studies, Faculty of Medicine, Department of Medicine, Montréal, QC H3A 2T5, Canada. Offers experimental medicine (M Sc, PhD), including bioethics (M Sc), experimental medicine.

**McGill University,** Faculty of Graduate and Postdoctoral Studies, Faculty of Science, Department of Biology, Montréal, QC H3A 2T5, Canada. Offers bioinformatics (M Sc, PhD); environment (M Sc, PhD); neo-tropical environment (M Sc, PhD).

**McMaster University,** Faculty of Health Sciences, Department of Biochemistry and Biomedical Sciences, Hamilton, ON L8S 4M2, Canada. Offers M Sc, PhD. Terminal master's awarded for partial completion of doctoral program. *Degree requirements:* For master's, thesis; for doctorate, comprehensive exam, thesis/dissertation. *Entrance requirements:* For master's and doctorate, minimum B+ average. Additional exam requirements/recommendations for international students: required—TOEFL (minimum score 550 paper-based).

**McMaster University,** Faculty of Health Sciences and School of Graduate Studies, Program in Medical Sciences, Hamilton, ON L8S 4M2, Canada. Offers blood and vascular (M Sc, PhD); genetics and cancer (M Sc, PhD); immunity and infection (M Sc, PhD); metabolism and nutrition (M Sc, PhD); neurosciences and behavioral sciences (M Sc, PhD); physiology/pharmacology (M Sc, PhD); MD/PhD. *Degree requirements:* For master's, thesis; for doctorate, comprehensive exam, thesis/dissertation. *Entrance requirements:* For master's, honors B Sc, B+ average in related field; for doctorate, M Sc, minimum B+ average. Additional exam requirements/recommendations for international students: required—TOEFL (minimum score 580 paper-based; 92 iBT).

**McMaster University,** School of Graduate Studies, Faculty of Science, Department of Biology, Hamilton, ON L8S 4M2, Canada. Offers M Sc, PhD. *Program availability:* Part-time. *Degree requirements:* For master's, thesis; for doctorate, comprehensive exam, thesis/dissertation. *Entrance requirements:* Additional exam requirements/recommendations for international students: required—TOEFL (minimum score 550 paper-based).

**Medical College of Wisconsin,** Graduate School, Milwaukee, WI 56226. Offers MA, MPH, MS, PhD, Graduate Certificate, MD/PhD. *Program availability:* Part-time, evening/weekend, 100% online. *Students:* 241 full-time (136 women), 68 part-time (46 women); includes 47 minority (15 Black or African American, non-Hispanic/Latino; 1 American Indian or Alaska Native, non-Hispanic/Latino; 13 Asian, non-Hispanic/Latino; 14 Hispanic/Latino; 4 Two or more races, non-Hispanic/Latino), 75 international. Average age 29. 353 applicants, 49% accepted, 82 enrolled. In 2019, 44 master's, 35 doctorates, 4 other advanced degrees awarded. *Degree requirements:* For master's, comprehensive exam (for some programs), thesis (for some programs); for doctorate, comprehensive exam, thesis/dissertation. *Entrance requirements:* For master's and doctorate, GRE General Test. Additional exam requirements/recommendations for international students: required—TOEFL. *Application deadline:* For fall admission, 1/15 priority date for domestic students, 1/15 for international students; for spring admission, 12/1 priority date for domestic students, 12/1 for international students. Applications are processed on a rolling basis. Application fee: $50. Electronic applications accepted. *Expenses:* $1,250 per credit for PhD students; $1,056 per credit for masters, certificate and non-degree seeking students; $950 per credit for Masters of Public Health students; $42,000 per year flat fee for Master of Medical Physiology students; $155 per year fees for full-time students. *Financial support:* In 2019–20, 226 students received support, including 177 research assistantships with full tuition reimbursements available (averaging $30,480 per year); career-related internships or fieldwork, Federal Work-Study, institutionally sponsored loans, scholarships/grants, traineeships, health care benefits, unspecified assistantships, and full tuition scholarship plus cost of living stipend (for all full-time PhD seekers) also available. Financial award application deadline: 2/15;

financial award applicants required to submit FAFSA. *Unit head:* Dr. Ravindra P. Misra, Dean, 414-955-8218, Fax: 414-955-6555, E-mail: gradschool@mcw.edu. *Application contact:* Anthony Perez, Associate Director - Graduate School, 414-9554407, E-mail: anperez@mcw.edu.
Website: http://www.mcw.edu/graduateschool.htm

**Medical College of Wisconsin,** Interdisciplinary Program in Biomedical Sciences, Milwaukee, WI 53226. Offers PhD. *Students:* 40 full-time (26 women); includes 2 minority (1 Black or African American, non-Hispanic/Latino; 1 Hispanic/Latino), 15 international. Average age 25. 99 applicants, 42% accepted, 20 enrolled. *Application deadline:* For fall admission, 12/15 priority date for domestic students. Applications are processed on a rolling basis. Application fee: $50. Electronic applications accepted. *Expenses:* $1250 per credit PhD students; $1056 per credit Masters students; $155 per year full time students fees. *Financial support:* In 2019–20, 40 students received support, including fellowships with full tuition reimbursements available (averaging $30,000 per year), research assistantships with full tuition reimbursements available (averaging $30,000 per year); tuition waivers (full) and unspecified assistantships also available. Financial award application deadline: 2/1; financial award applicants required to submit FAFSA. *Unit head:* Dr. Joseph C. Besharse, Director, 414-955-8063, Fax: 414-955-6517, E-mail: biomed@mcw.edu. *Application contact:* Dr. Joseph C. Besharse, Director, 414-955-8063, Fax: 414-955-6517, E-mail: biomed@mcw.edu.
Website: http://www.mcw.edu/BiomedicalGraduateProgram.htm

**Medical University of South Carolina,** College of Graduate Studies, Charleston, SC 29425. Offers MS, PhD, DMD/PhD, MD/PhD, Pharm D/PhD. Terminal master's awarded for partial completion of doctoral program. *Degree requirements:* For master's, thesis; for doctorate, thesis/dissertation, oral and written exams. *Entrance requirements:* For doctorate, GRE General Test, interview. Additional exam requirements/recommendations for international students: required—TOEFL (minimum score 600 paper-based; 100 iBT). Electronic applications accepted. *Expenses:* Contact institution.

**Meharry Medical College,** School of Graduate Studies, Program in Biomedical Sciences, Nashville, TN 37208-9989. Offers biochemistry and cancer biology (PhD); microbiology and immunology (PhD); neuroscience (PhD); pharmacology (PhD); MD/PhD. *Degree requirements:* For doctorate, comprehensive exam, thesis/dissertation. *Entrance requirements:* For doctorate, GRE General Test, GRE Subject Test. Additional exam requirements/recommendations for international students: required—TOEFL. *Application deadline:* For fall admission, 6/1 for domestic students. Applications are processed on a rolling basis. Application fee: $65. *Financial support:* Fellowships and research assistantships available. Financial award application deadline: 4/15; financial award applicants required to submit FAFSA.

**Memorial University of Newfoundland,** Faculty of Medicine and School of Graduate Studies, Graduate Programs in Medicine, St. John's, NL A1C 5S7, Canada. Offers M Sc, PhD, Diploma, MD/PhD. *Program availability:* Part-time. *Degree requirements:* For master's, thesis; for doctorate, comprehensive exam, thesis/dissertation, oral defense of thesis. *Entrance requirements:* For master's, MD or B Sc; for doctorate, MD or M Sc; for Diploma, bachelor's degree in health-related field. Additional exam requirements/recommendations for international students: required—TOEFL (minimum score 550 paper-based). Electronic applications accepted.

**Memorial University of Newfoundland,** School of Graduate Studies, Department of Biology, St. John's, NL A1C 5S7, Canada. Offers M Sc, PhD. *Program availability:* Part-time. *Degree requirements:* For master's, thesis; for doctorate, comprehensive exam, thesis/dissertation, oral defense of thesis. *Entrance requirements:* For master's, honors degree (minimum 2nd class standing) in related field; for doctorate, M Sc. Electronic applications accepted.

**Miami University,** College of Arts and Science, Department of Biology, Oxford, OH 45056. Offers MA, MAT, MS, PhD. *Program availability:* Online learning. Electronic applications accepted.

**Michigan State University,** College of Human Medicine and The Graduate School, Graduate Programs in Human Medicine, East Lansing, MI 48824. Offers biochemistry and molecular biology (MS, PhD); epidemiology (MS, PhD); microbiology (MS); microbiology and molecular genetics (PhD); pharmacology and toxicology (MS, PhD); physiology (MS, PhD); public health (MPH). *Entrance requirements:* Additional exam requirements/recommendations for international students: required—TOEFL.

**Michigan State University,** College of Osteopathic Medicine and The Graduate School, Graduate Studies in Osteopathic Medicine, East Lansing, MI 48824. Offers biochemistry and molecular biology (MS, PhD); microbiology (MS); microbiology and molecular genetics (PhD); pharmacology and toxicology (MS, PhD), including integrative pharmacology (MS), pharmacology and toxicology, pharmacology and toxicology–environmental toxicology (PhD); physiology (MS, PhD).

**Michigan State University,** College of Veterinary Medicine and The Graduate School, Graduate Programs in Veterinary Medicine, Program in Comparative Medicine and Integrative Biology, East Lansing, MI 48824. Offers comparative medicine and integrative biology (MS, PhD); comparative medicine and integrative biology–environmental toxicology (PhD). *Entrance requirements:* Additional exam requirements/recommendations for international students: required—TOEFL. Electronic applications accepted.

**Michigan Technological University,** Graduate School, College of Sciences and Arts, Department of Biological Sciences, Houghton, MI 49931. Offers MS, PhD. *Program availability:* Part-time. *Faculty:* 32 full-time (13 women), 4 part-time/adjunct. *Students:* 32 full-time (20 women), 5 part-time; includes 3 minority (1 Black or African American, non-Hispanic/Latino; 2 Two or more races, non-Hispanic/Latino), 11 international. Average age 29. 135 applicants, 32% accepted, 12 enrolled. In 2019, 12 master's, 2 doctorates awarded. Terminal master's awarded for partial completion of doctoral program. *Degree requirements:* For master's, comprehensive exam (for some programs), thesis (for some programs); for doctorate, comprehensive exam, thesis/dissertation. *Entrance requirements:* For master's and doctorate, statement of purpose, personal statement, official transcripts, 2 letters of recommendation, resume/curriculum vitae. Additional exam requirements/recommendations for international students: required—TOEFL (minimum score 85 iBT) or IELTS (recommended minimum score of 6.5); recommended—TOEFL (minimum score 85 iBT), IELTS (minimum score 6.5). *Application deadline:* For fall admission, 1/15 priority date for domestic and international students; for spring admission, 9/15 priority date for domestic and international students. Applications are processed on a rolling basis. Electronic applications accepted. *Expenses:* Tuition, area resident: Full-time $19,206; part-time $1067 per credit. Tuition, state resident: full-time $19,206; part-time $1067 per credit. Tuition, nonresident: full-time $19,206; part-time $1067 per credit. International tuition: $19,206 full-time. *Required fees:* $248; $248 per unit. $124 per semester. Tuition and fees vary according to course load and program. *Financial support:* In 2019–20, 24 students received support, including 3 fellowships with tuition reimbursements available (averaging $16,590 per year), 7 research assistantships with tuition reimbursements available (averaging $16,590 per year), 8 teaching assistantships with tuition reimbursements available (averaging $16,590 per year); career-related internships or fieldwork, Federal Work-Study, scholarships/grants, health care benefits, unspecified assistantships, and cooperative program also available. Financial award applicants required to submit

## Biological and Biomedical Sciences—General

FAFSA. *Unit head:* Dr. Chandrashekhar P. Joshi, Department Chair, 906-487-2738, Fax: 906-487-3167, E-mail: cpjoshi@mtu.edu. *Application contact:* Tori Connors, Departmental Coordinator, 906-487-1628, Fax: 906-487-3167, E-mail: tconnors@mtu.edu.
Website: http://www.mtu.edu/biological/

**Middle Tennessee State University,** College of Graduate Studies, College of Basic and Applied Sciences, Department of Biology, Murfreesboro, TN 37132. Offers MS. *Program availability:* Part-time, evening/weekend, online learning. *Degree requirements:* For master's, comprehensive exam, thesis. *Entrance requirements:* For master's, GRE. Additional exam requirements/recommendations for international students: required—TOEFL (minimum score 525 paper-based; 71 iBT) or IELTS (minimum score 6). Electronic applications accepted.

**Midwestern State University,** Billie Doris McAda Graduate School, College of Science and Mathematics, Department of Biology, Wichita Falls, TX 76308. Offers MS. *Program availability:* Part-time, evening/weekend. *Degree requirements:* For master's, comprehensive exam, thesis. *Entrance requirements:* For master's, GRE General Test, MAT or GMAT. Additional exam requirements/recommendations for international students: required—TOEFL (minimum score 550 paper-based). Electronic applications accepted.

**Midwestern University, Downers Grove Campus,** College of Graduate Studies, Master of Arts Program in Biomedical Sciences, Downers Grove, IL 60515-1235. Offers MA. *Entrance requirements:* For master's, GRE General Test, MCAT, PCAT, DAT, OAT or other professional exam, bachelor's degree, minimum cumulative GPA of 2.75.

**Midwestern University, Downers Grove Campus,** College of Graduate Studies, Program in Biomedical Sciences, Downers Grove, IL 60515-1235. Offers MBS. *Program availability:* Part-time. *Entrance requirements:* For master's, GRE General Test, MCAT or PCAT, 2 letters of recommendation.

**Midwestern University, Glendale Campus,** College of Health Sciences, Arizona Campus, MA Program in Biomedical Sciences, Glendale, AZ 85308. Offers MA. *Entrance requirements:* For master's, GRE General Test, MCAT, or other professional exam, bachelor's degree, minimum cumulative GPA of 2.75.

**Midwestern University, Glendale Campus,** College of Health Sciences, Arizona Campus, MBS Program in Biomedical Sciences, Glendale, AZ 85308. Offers MBS. *Expenses:* Contact institution.

**Mills College,** Graduate Studies, Pre-Medical Studies Program, Oakland, CA 94613-1000. Offers Certificate. *Program availability:* Part-time. *Entrance requirements:* For degree, SAT/ACT or GRE General Test, bachelor's degree in a non-science area. Additional exam requirements/recommendations for international students: required—TOEFL (minimum score 550 paper-based; 80 iBT) or IELTS (minimum score 6). Electronic applications accepted. *Expenses:* Contact institution.

**Minnesota State University Mankato,** College of Graduate Studies and Research, College of Science, Engineering and Technology, Department of Biological Sciences, Mankato, MN 56001. Offers biology (MS); biology education (MS); environmental sciences (MS). *Program availability:* Part-time. *Degree requirements:* For master's, one foreign language, comprehensive exam, thesis or alternative. *Entrance requirements:* For master's, minimum GPA of 3.0 during previous 2 years of course work. Additional exam requirements/recommendations for international students: required—TOEFL. Electronic applications accepted.

**Mississippi College,** Graduate School, College of Arts and Sciences, School of Science and Mathematics, Department of Biological Sciences, Clinton, MS 39058. Offers biological science (M Ed); biology (MCS); biology-biological sciences (MS); biology-medical sciences (MS). *Program availability:* Part-time. *Degree requirements:* For master's, comprehensive exam, thesis optional. *Entrance requirements:* For master's, GRE General Test, minimum GPA of 2.5. Additional exam requirements/recommendations for international students: recommended—TOEFL, IELTS. Electronic applications accepted.

**Mississippi State University,** College of Arts and Sciences, Department of Biological Sciences, Mississippi State, MS 39762. Offers biological sciences (MS, PhD); general biology (MS). *Program availability:* Blended/hybrid learning. *Faculty:* 24 full-time (8 women), 1 part-time/adjunct (0 women). *Students:* 48 full-time (23 women), 31 part-time (26 women); includes 6 minority (2 Black or African American, non-Hispanic/Latino; 1 Asian, non-Hispanic/Latino; 1 Hispanic/Latino; 2 Two or more races, non-Hispanic/Latino), 24 international. Average age 30. 52 applicants, 50% accepted, 21 enrolled. In 2019, 18 master's, 4 doctorates awarded. Terminal master's awarded for partial completion of doctoral program. *Degree requirements:* For master's, one foreign language, thesis, comprehensive oral or written exam; for doctorate, one foreign language, thesis/dissertation, comprehensive oral or written exam. *Entrance requirements:* For master's, GRE General Test, minimum GPA of 2.75 on last 60 hours of undergraduate courses; for doctorate, GRE General Test. Additional exam requirements/recommendations for international students: required—TOEFL (minimum score 550 paper-based; 79 iBT); recommended—IELTS (minimum score 6.5). *Application deadline:* For fall admission, 7/1 for domestic students, 5/1 for international students; for spring admission, 11/1 for domestic students, 9/1 for international students. Applications are processed on a rolling basis. Application fee: $60 ($80 for international students). Electronic applications accepted. *Expenses:* Tuition, area resident: Full-time $8880; part-time $456 per credit hour. Tuition, state resident: full-time $8880. Tuition, nonresident: full-time $23,840; part-time $1236 per credit hour. *Required fees:* $110; $11.12 per credit hour. Tuition and fees vary according to course load. *Financial support:* In 2019–20, 8 research assistantships with partial tuition reimbursements (averaging $17,375 per year), 51 teaching assistantships with partial tuition reimbursements (averaging $16,482 per year) were awarded; Federal Work-Study, institutionally sponsored loans, scholarships/grants, and unspecified assistantships also available. Financial award application deadline: 4/1; financial award applicants required to submit FAFSA. *Unit head:* Dr. Angus Dawe, Professor and Head, 662-325-3120, Fax: 662-325-7939, E-mail: dawe@biology.msstate.edu. *Application contact:* Angie Campbell, Admissions and Enrollment Assistant, 662-325-9514, E-mail: acampbell@grad.msstate.edu.
Website: http://www.biology.msstate.edu

**Missouri State University,** Graduate College, College of Natural and Applied Sciences, Department of Biology, Springfield, MO 65897. Offers biology (MS); natural and applied science (MNAS), including biology (MNAS, MS Ed); secondary education (MS Ed), including biology (MNAS, MS Ed). *Degree requirements:* For master's, comprehensive exam, thesis or alternative. *Entrance requirements:* For master's, GRE (MS, MNAS), 24 hours of course work in biology (MS); minimum GPA of 3.0 (MS, MNAS); 9-12 teacher certification (MS Ed). Additional exam requirements/recommendations for international students: required—TOEFL (minimum score 550 paper-based; 79 iBT), IELTS (minimum score 6). Electronic applications accepted. *Expenses: Tuition, area resident:* Full-time $2600; part-time $1735 per credit hour. Tuition, nonresident: full-time $5240; part-time $3495 per credit hour. *International tuition:* $5240 full-time. *Required fees:* $530; $438 per credit hour. Tuition and fees vary according to class time, course level, course load, degree level, campus/location and program.

**Missouri University of Science and Technology,** Department of Biological Sciences, Rolla, MO 65409. Offers applied and environmental biology (MS). *Faculty:* 10 full-time (3 women). *Students:* 10 full-time (6 women), 6 part-time (5 women); includes 1 minority (Hispanic/Latino), 6 international. Average age 28. 19 applicants, 68% accepted, 7 enrolled. In 2019, 8 master's awarded. *Entrance requirements:* For master's, GRE (minimum score 600 quantitative, 4 writing). Additional exam requirements/recommendations for international students: required—TOEFL (minimum score 570 paper-based). Application fee: $50. *Expenses:* Tuition, state resident: full-time $7839; part-time $435.50 per credit hour. Tuition, nonresident: full-time $22,169; part-time $1231.60 per credit hour. *International tuition:* $22,169 full-time. *Required fees:* $649.76. One-time fee: $119. Tuition and fees vary according to course load and program. *Financial support:* In 2019–20, 6 research assistantships (averaging $1,810 per year), 1 teaching assistantship (averaging $1,814 per year) were awarded; institutionally sponsored loans and unspecified assistantships also available. *Unit head:* Dr. David Duvernell, Chair, 573-341-6988, Fax: 573-341-4821, E-mail: duvernelld@mst.edu. *Application contact:* Debbie Schwertz, Admissions Coordinator, 573-341-6013, Fax: 573-341-6271, E-mail: schwertz@mst.edu.
Website: http://biosci.mst.edu/

**Missouri Western State University,** Program in Applied Science, St. Joseph, MO 64507-2294. Offers chemistry (MAS); engineering technology management (MAS); industrial life science (MAS); sport and fitness management (MAS). *Accreditation:* AACSB. *Program availability:* Part-time. *Students:* 24 full-time (10 women), 21 part-time (5 women); includes 11 minority (3 Black or African American, non-Hispanic/Latino; 1 American Indian or Alaska Native, non-Hispanic/Latino; 1 Hispanic/Latino; 6 Two or more races, non-Hispanic/Latino), 8 international. Average age 26. 19 applicants, 89% accepted, 15 enrolled. In 2019, 18 master's awarded. *Entrance requirements:* Additional exam requirements/recommendations for international students: recommended—TOEFL (minimum score 79 iBT), IELTS (minimum score 6). *Application deadline:* For fall admission, 7/15 for domestic and international students; for spring admission, 11/1 for domestic and international students; for summer admission, 4/29 for domestic and international students. Applications are processed on a rolling basis. Application fee: $45 ($50 for international students). Electronic applications accepted. *Expenses:* Tuition, state resident: full-time $6469.02; part-time $359.39 per credit hour. Tuition, nonresident: full-time $11,581; part-time $643.39 per credit hour. *Required fees:* $345.20; $99.10 per credit hour. Tuition and fees vary according to course load, campus/location and program. *Financial support:* Scholarships/grants and unspecified assistantships available. Support available to part-time students. *Unit head:* Dr. Susan Bashinski, Dean of the Graduate School, 816-271-4394, Fax: 816-271-4525, E-mail: graduate@missouriwestern.edu. *Application contact:* Dr. Susan Bashinski, Dean of the Graduate School, 816-271-4394, Fax: 816-271-4525, E-mail: graduate@missouriwestern.edu.

**Montana State University,** The Graduate School, College of Letters and Science, Department of Cell Biology and Neuroscience, Bozeman, MT 59717. Offers biological sciences (PhD); neuroscience (MS, PhD). *Program availability:* Part-time. *Degree requirements:* For master's, comprehensive exam; for doctorate, comprehensive exam, thesis/dissertation. *Entrance requirements:* For master's and doctorate, GRE General Test. Additional exam requirements/recommendations for international students: required—TOEFL (minimum score 550 paper-based). Electronic applications accepted.

**Montclair State University,** The Graduate School, College of Science and Mathematics, Program in Biology, Montclair, NJ 07043-1624. Offers biological science/education (MS); biology (MS); ecology and evolution (MS); physiology (MS).

**Morehead State University,** Graduate School, College of Science, Department of Biology and Chemistry, Morehead, KY 40351. Offers biology (MS), including regional analysis & public policy; biology regional analysis (MS). *Program availability:* Part-time. *Faculty:* 14 full-time (2 women), 2 part-time/adjunct (0 women). *Students:* 2 full-time (1 woman), 2 part-time (0 women). 3 applicants, 67% accepted, 2 enrolled. In 2019, 1 master's awarded. *Degree requirements:* For master's, comprehensive exam, thesis optional. *Entrance requirements:* For master's, GRE, minimum 2.5 cumulative GPA, 3.0 upper division biology courses. Additional exam requirements/recommendations for international students: required—TOEFL (minimum score 525 paper-based; 173 iBT). *Application deadline:* Applications are processed on a rolling basis. Application fee: $30. Electronic applications accepted. *Expenses:* Tuition, area resident: Part-time $570 per credit hour. Tuition, state resident: part-time $570 per credit hour. Tuition, nonresident: part-time $570 per credit hour. *Required fees:* $14 per credit hour. *Financial support:* Teaching assistantships, career-related internships or fieldwork, and unspecified assistantships available. Financial award applicants required to submit FAFSA. *Unit head:* Dr. Charles Lydeard, Department Chair Biology & Chemistry, 606-783-2945, E-mail: c.lydeard@moreheadstate.edu. *Application contact:* Dr. Charles Lydeard, Department Chair Biology & Chemistry, 606-783-2945, E-mail: c.lydeard@moreheadstate.edu.
Website: https://www.moreheadstate.edu/biochem

**Morehouse School of Medicine,** Graduate Programs in Biomedical Sciences, Atlanta, GA 30310-1495. Offers biomedical research (MS); biomedical sciences (PhD); biomedical technology (MS); medical sciences (MS). *Degree requirements:* For master's, thesis (for some programs); for doctorate, thesis/dissertation. *Entrance requirements:* For doctorate, GRE General Test. Additional exam requirements/recommendations for international students: required—TOEFL (minimum score 550 paper-based). Electronic applications accepted. *Expenses:* Contact institution.

**Morgan State University,** School of Graduate Studies, School of Computer, Mathematical, and Natural Sciences, Department of Biology, Baltimore, MD 21251. Offers bioenvironmental science (PhD); biology (MS). *Faculty:* 26 full-time (11 women), 2 part-time/adjunct (1 woman). *Degree requirements:* For master's, comprehensive exam, thesis. *Entrance requirements:* For master's, minimum GPA of 3.0. *Application deadline:* For fall admission, 2/1 priority date for domestic students; for spring admission, 10/1 priority date for domestic students. *Expenses:* Tuition, state resident: full-time $455; part-time $455 per credit hour. Tuition, nonresident: full-time $894; part-time $894 per credit hour. *Required fees:* $82; $82 per credit hour. *Financial support:* In 2019–20, 13 students received support. Fellowships with full and partial tuition reimbursements available, teaching assistantships with full and partial tuition reimbursements available, Federal Work-Study, scholarships/grants, tuition waivers (full and partial), and unspecified assistantships available. Financial award application deadline: 2/1. *Unit head:* Dr. Cleo Hughes-Darden, Department Chief, 443-885-3632, E-mail: cleo.hughesdarden@morgan.edu. *Application contact:* Dr. Jahmaine Smith, Director of Admissions, 443-885-3185, Fax: 443-885-8226, E-mail: gradapply@morgan.edu.
Website: https://www.morgan.edu/biology

**Mount Allison University,** Department of Biology, Sackville, NB E4L 1E4, Canada. Offers M Sc. *Degree requirements:* For master's, thesis. *Entrance requirements:* For master's, honors degree.

**Murray State University,** Jesse D. Jones College of Science, Engineering and Technology, Department of Biology, Murray, KY 42071. Offers MS. *Program availability:* Part-time. *Entrance requirements:* For master's, GRE or GMAT, minimum university

GPA of 2.75. Additional exam requirements/recommendations for international students: required—TOEFL (minimum score 527 paper-based; 71 iBT). Electronic applications accepted.

**National University,** College of Letters and Sciences, La Jolla, CA 92037-1011. Offers biology (MS); counseling psychology (MA), including licensed professional clinical counseling, marriage and family therapy; creative writing (MFA); English (MA); film studies (MA); forensic and crime scene investigations (Certificate); forensic sciences (MFS); human behavior (MA); mathematics for educators (MS); performance psychology (MA); strategic communications (MA). *Program availability:* Part-time, evening/weekend, 100% online, blended/hybrid learning. *Degree requirements:* For master's, thesis (for some programs). *Entrance requirements:* For master's, interview, minimum GPA of 2.5. Additional exam requirements/recommendations for international students: required—TOEFL (minimum score 550 paper-based; 79 iBT), IELTS (minimum score 6). Electronic applications accepted. *Expenses: Tuition:* Full-time $442; part-time $442 per unit.

**New Jersey Institute of Technology,** College of Science and Liberal Arts, Newark, NJ 07102. Offers applied mathematics (MS); applied physics (MS, PhD); applied statistics (MS, Certificate); biology (MS, PhD); biostatistics (MS); chemistry (MS, PhD); environmental and sustainability policy (MS); environmental science (MS, PhD); history (MA, MAT); materials science and engineering (MS, PhD); mathematical and computational finance (MS); mathematical sciences (PhD); pharmaceutical chemistry (MS); professional and technical communications (MS); technical communication essentials (Certificate). *Program availability:* Part-time, evening/weekend. *Faculty:* 159 full-time (42 women), 156 part-time/adjunct (61 women). *Students:* 197 full-time (80 women), 58 part-time (14 women); includes 58 minority (18 Black or African American, non-Hispanic/Latino; 22 Asian, non-Hispanic/Latino; 16 Hispanic/Latino; 2 Two or more races, non-Hispanic/Latino), 130 international. Average age 29. 401 applicants, 63% accepted, 73 enrolled. In 2019, 54 master's, 10 doctorates, 1 other advanced degree awarded. Terminal master's awarded for partial completion of doctoral program. *Degree requirements:* For master's, thesis (for some programs); for doctorate, thesis/dissertation. *Entrance requirements:* For master's and doctorate, GRE General Test, Minimum GPA of 3.0, personal statement, 3 letters of recommendation, and transcripts. Additional exam requirements/recommendations for international students: required—TOEFL (minimum score 550 paper-based; 79 iBT), IELTS (minimum score 6.5). *Application deadline:* For fall admission, 6/1 priority date for domestic students, 5/1 priority date for international students; for spring admission, 11/15 priority date for domestic and international students. Applications are processed on a rolling basis. Application fee: $75. Electronic applications accepted. *Expenses:* $23,828 per year (in-state), $33,744 per year (out-of-state). *Financial support:* In 2019–20, 147 students received support, including 13 fellowships with full tuition reimbursements available (averaging $24,000 per year), 41 research assistantships with full tuition reimbursements available (averaging $24,000 per year), 87 teaching assistantships with full tuition reimbursements available (averaging $24,000 per year); scholarships/grants, traineeships, health care benefits, and unspecified assistantships also available. Financial award application deadline: 1/15. *Unit head:* Dr. Kevin Belfield, Dean, 973-596-3676, Fax: 973-565-0586, E-mail: kevin.d.belfield@njit.edu. *Application contact:* Stephen Eck, Director of Admissions, 973-596-3300, Fax: 973-596-3461, E-mail: admissions@njit.edu.
Website: http://csla.njit.edu/

**New Mexico Institute of Mining and Technology,** Center for Graduate Studies, Department of Biology, Socorro, NM 87801. Offers biology (MS); geobiology (PhD). *Program availability:* Part-time. *Degree requirements:* For master's, thesis. *Entrance requirements:* For master's, GRE General Test. Additional exam requirements/recommendations for international students: required—TOEFL (minimum score 540 paper-based). Electronic applications accepted.

**New Mexico State University,** College of Arts and Sciences, Department of Biology, Las Cruces, NM 88003-8001. Offers behavioral, ecological & evolutionary biology (PhD); biology (MS); biotechnology (MS). *Program availability:* Part-time. *Faculty:* 19 full-time (9 women). *Students:* 48 full-time (27 women), 5 part-time (3 women); includes 19 minority (1 American Indian or Alaska Native, non-Hispanic/Latino; 5 Asian, non-Hispanic/Latino; 11 Hispanic/Latino; 2 Two or more races, non-Hispanic/Latino), 15 international. Average age 30. 28 applicants, 50% accepted, 8 enrolled. In 2019, 10 master's, 4 doctorates awarded. *Degree requirements:* For master's, thesis (for some programs), defense or oral exam; for doctorate, comprehensive exam, thesis/dissertation, qualifying exam. *Entrance requirements:* For master's and doctorate, GRE. Additional exam requirements/recommendations for international students: required—TOEFL (minimum score 550 paper-based; 79 iBT), IELTS (minimum score 6.5). *Application deadline:* For fall admission, 1/15 priority date for domestic and international students; for spring admission, 9/30 priority date for domestic and international students. Applications are processed on a rolling basis. Application fee: $40 ($50 for international students). Electronic applications accepted. *Financial support:* In 2019–20, 47 students received support, including 6 fellowships (averaging $4,844 per year), 17 research assistantships (averaging $20,182 per year), 31 teaching assistantships (averaging $18,983 per year); career-related internships or fieldwork, Federal Work-Study, scholarships/grants, traineeships, health care benefits, and unspecified assistantships also available. Support available to part-time students. Financial award application deadline: 3/1. *Unit head:* Dr. Michele K. Nishiguchi, Department Head, 575-646-3611, Fax: 575-646-5665, E-mail: nish@nmsu.edu. *Application contact:* Dr. Jennifer Curtiss, Associate Professor, 575-646-3611, Fax: 575-646-5665, E-mail: curtij01@nmsu.edu. Website: http://bio.nmsu.edu

**New York Medical College,** Graduate School of Basic Medical Sciences, Valhalla, NY 10595. Offers biochemistry and molecular biology (MS, PhD); cell biology (MS, PhD); microbiology and immunology (MS, PhD); pathology (MS, PhD); pharmacology (MS, PhD); physiology (MS, PhD); MD/PhD. *Program availability:* Part-time, evening/weekend. *Faculty:* 98 full-time (24 women). *Students:* 141 full-time (90 women), 17 part-time (3 women); includes 68 minority (16 Black or African American, non-Hispanic/Latino; 32 Asian, non-Hispanic/Latino; 15 Hispanic/Latino; 1 Native Hawaiian or other Pacific Islander, non-Hispanic/Latino; 4 Two or more races, non-Hispanic/Latino), 19 international. Average age 26. 351 applicants, 62% accepted, 86 enrolled. In 2019, 28 master's, 5 doctorates awarded. Terminal master's awarded for partial completion of doctoral program. *Degree requirements:* For master's, thesis; for doctorate, comprehensive exam, thesis/dissertation. *Entrance requirements:* For master's, GRE General Test, MCAT, or DAT, OAT. Additional exam requirements/recommendations for international students: required—TOEFL (minimum score 90 iBT), TOEFL or IELTS; one of the two exams are required. *Application deadline:* For fall admission, 6/1 priority date for domestic students, 5/1 priority date for international students. Applications are processed on a rolling basis. Application fee: $75 ($100 for international students). Electronic applications accepted. *Expenses:* $1200 credit and $620 fees. *Financial support:* In 2019–20, 400 students received support. Federal Work-Study, scholarships/grants, unspecified assistantships, and Student Federal Loans available. Financial award application deadline: 4/30; financial award applicants required to submit FAFSA. *Unit head:* Dr. Marina K Holz, Dean, 914-594-4110, Fax: 914-594-4944, E-mail: mholz@nymc.edu. *Application contact:* Valerie Romeo-Messana, Director of Admissions, 914-594-4110, Fax: 914-594-4944, E-mail: v_romeomessana@nymc.edu.
Website: https://www.nymc.edu/graduate-school-of-basic-medical-sciences-gsbms/gsbms-academics/

**New York University,** Graduate School of Arts and Science, Department of Biology, New York, NY 10012-1019. Offers biology (PhD); biomedical journalism (MS); cancer and molecular biology (PhD); computational biology (PhD); computers in biological research (MS); developmental genetics (PhD); general biology (MS); immunology and microbiology (PhD); molecular genetics (PhD); neurobiology (PhD); oral biology (MS); plant biology (PhD); recombinant DNA technology (MS); MS/MBA. *Program availability:* Part-time. Terminal master's awarded for partial completion of doctoral program. *Degree requirements:* For master's, thesis or alternative, qualifying paper; for doctorate, comprehensive exam, thesis/dissertation. *Entrance requirements:* For master's and doctorate, GRE General Test. Additional exam requirements/recommendations for international students: required—TOEFL, IELTS.

**New York University,** Graduate School of Arts and Science, Department of Environmental Medicine, New York, NY 10012-1019. Offers MS, PhD. *Program availability:* Part-time. Terminal master's awarded for partial completion of doctoral program. *Degree requirements:* For master's, thesis or alternative; for doctorate, one foreign language, thesis/dissertation, oral and written exams. *Entrance requirements:* For master's and doctorate, GRE General Test, minimum GPA of 3.0; bachelor's degree in biological, physical, or engineering science. Additional exam requirements/recommendations for international students: required—TOEFL, IELTS.

**New York University,** School of Medicine and Graduate School of Arts and Science, Medical Scientist Training Program, New York, NY 10012-1019. Offers MD/PhD. Electronic applications accepted. *Expenses:* Contact institution.

**North Carolina Agricultural and Technical State University,** The Graduate College, College of Science and Technology, Department of Biology, Greensboro, NC 27411. Offers biology (MS); biology education (MAT). *Program availability:* Part-time, evening/weekend. *Degree requirements:* For master's, comprehensive exam, thesis (for some programs), qualifying exam. *Entrance requirements:* For master's, GRE General Test, personal statement.

**North Carolina Central University,** College of Arts and Sciences, Department of Biological and Biomedical Sciences, Durham, NC 27707-3129. Offers MS. *Degree requirements:* For master's, one foreign language, comprehensive exam, thesis. *Entrance requirements:* For master's, GRE, minimum GPA of 3.0 in major, 2.5 overall. Additional exam requirements/recommendations for international students: required—TOEFL.

**North Carolina State University,** College of Veterinary Medicine, Program in Comparative Biomedical Sciences, Raleigh, NC 27695. Offers cell biology (MS, PhD); infectious disease (MS, PhD); pathology (MS, PhD); pharmacology (MS, PhD); population medicine (MS, PhD). *Program availability:* Part-time. *Degree requirements:* For master's, thesis; for doctorate, thesis/dissertation. *Entrance requirements:* For master's and doctorate, GRE General Test. Additional exam requirements/recommendations for international students: required—TOEFL (minimum score 550 paper-based). Electronic applications accepted. *Expenses:* Contact institution.

**North Carolina State University,** Graduate School, College of Agriculture and Life Sciences, Raleigh, NC 27695. Offers MBAE, MFG, MFM, MFS, MMB, MN, MP, MS, PhD, Certificate. *Program availability:* Part-time. Electronic applications accepted.

**North Dakota State University,** College of Graduate and Interdisciplinary Studies, College of Science and Mathematics, Department of Biological Sciences, Fargo, ND 58102. Offers biology (MS); botany (MS, PhD); zoology (MS, PhD). *Entrance requirements:* For master's and doctorate, GRE General Test. Additional exam requirements/recommendations for international students: required—TOEFL. Electronic applications accepted. Tuition and fees vary according to program and reciprocity agreements.

**Northeastern Illinois University,** College of Graduate Studies and Research, College of Arts and Sciences, Program in Biology, Chicago, IL 60625. Offers biology (MS), including cell biology, ecology, molecular biology, organismal biology. *Program availability:* Part-time, evening/weekend. *Degree requirements:* For master's, comprehensive exam, thesis optional. *Entrance requirements:* For master's, minimum GPA of 2.75. Additional exam requirements/recommendations for international students: required—TOEFL (minimum score 550 paper-based; 79 iBT). Electronic applications accepted.

**Northeastern University,** College of Science, Boston, MA 02115-5096. Offers applied mathematics (MS); bioinformatics (MS); biology (PhD); biotechnology (MS); chemistry and chemical biology (MS, PhD); environmental science and policy (MS); marine and environmental sciences (PhD); marine biology (MS); mathematics (MS, PhD); operations research (MSOR); physics (MS, PhD); psychology (PhD). *Program availability:* Part-time. Terminal master's awarded for partial completion of doctoral program. *Degree requirements:* For master's, comprehensive exam (for some programs), thesis; for doctorate, comprehensive exam (for some programs), thesis/dissertation. *Entrance requirements:* For master's, GRE General Test. Electronic applications accepted. *Expenses:* Contact institution.

**Northern Arizona University,** College of Environment, Forestry, and Natural Sciences, Department of Biological Sciences, Flagstaff, AZ 86011. Offers biology (MS, PhD). *Degree requirements:* For master's, variable foreign language requirement, comprehensive exam (for some programs), thesis, oral defense, individualized research; for doctorate, variable foreign language requirement, comprehensive exam, thesis/dissertation, oral defense, individualized research. *Entrance requirements:* For master's and doctorate, GRE General Test. Additional exam requirements/recommendations for international students: required—TOEFL (minimum score 80 iBT), IELTS (minimum score 6.5). Electronic applications accepted.

**Northern Illinois University,** Graduate School, College of Liberal Arts and Sciences, Department of Biological Sciences, De Kalb, IL 60115-2854. Offers MS, PhD. *Program availability:* Part-time. *Faculty:* 30 full-time (6 women), 7 part-time/adjunct (1 woman). *Students:* 22 full-time (12 women), 22 part-time (14 women); includes 4 minority (1 Asian, non-Hispanic/Latino; 3 Hispanic/Latino), 11 international. Average age 30. 63 applicants, 35% accepted, 8 enrolled. In 2019, 15 master's, 6 doctorates awarded. Terminal master's awarded for partial completion of doctoral program. *Degree requirements:* For master's, comprehensive exam, thesis optional; for doctorate, thesis/dissertation, candidacy exam, dissertation defense. *Entrance requirements:* For master's, GRE General Test, bachelor's degree in related field, minimum GPA of 2.75; for doctorate, GRE General Test, bachelor's or master's degree in related field; minimum undergraduate GPA of 2.75, graduate 3.2. Additional exam requirements/recommendations for international students: required—TOEFL (minimum score 550 paper-based). *Application deadline:* For fall admission, 6/1 for domestic students, 5/1 for international students; for spring admission, 11/1 for domestic students, 10/1 for international students. Applications are processed on a rolling basis. Application fee: $40. Electronic applications accepted. *Financial support:* In 2019–20, 8 research assistantships with full tuition reimbursements, 32 teaching assistantships with full tuition reimbursements were awarded; fellowships with full tuition reimbursements,

career-related internships or fieldwork, Federal Work-Study, scholarships/grants, tuition waivers (full), and unspecified assistantships also available. Support available to part-time students. Financial award applicants required to submit FAFSA. *Unit head:* Dr. Barrie P. Bode, Chair, 815-753-1753, Fax: 815-753-0461, E-mail: bodebp@niu.edu. *Application contact:* Dr. Thomas Sims, Director of Graduate Studies, 815-753-7873.
Website: http://www.bios.niu.edu/

**Northern Michigan University,** Office of Graduate Education and Research, College of Arts and Sciences, Department of Biology, Marquette, MI 49855-5301. Offers biology (MS); integrated biosciences (MS). *Program availability:* Part-time. *Degree requirements:* For master's, thesis. *Entrance requirements:* For master's, GRE, minimum GPA of 3.0; references; coursework in biology and other sciences; faculty member as mentor. Additional exam requirements/recommendations for international students: required—TOEFL (minimum score 500 paper-based; 61 iBT), IELTS (minimum score 6). *Application deadline:* For fall admission, 5/1 for domestic students; for winter admission, 12/1 for domestic students; for spring admission, 3/17 for domestic students. Applications are processed on a rolling basis. Application fee: $50. Electronic applications accepted. *Financial support:* Application deadline: 3/1; applicants required to submit FAFSA. *Unit head:* Dr. John Rebers, Department Head, 906-227-1585, E-mail: jrebers@nmu.edu. *Application contact:* Dr. Kate Teeter, Biology Graduate Director, 906-227-2177, E-mail: kteeter@nmu.edu.
Website: http://www.nmu.edu/biology/

**Northwestern University,** Feinberg School of Medicine, Combined MD/PhD Medical Scientist Training Program, Evanston, IL 60208. Offers MD/PhD. *Accreditation:* LCME/AMA. Electronic applications accepted.

**Northwestern University,** Feinberg School of Medicine, Driskill Graduate Program in Life Sciences, Chicago, IL 60611. Offers biostatistics (PhD); epidemiology (PhD); health and biomedical informatics (PhD); health services and outcomes research (PhD); healthcare quality and patient safety (PhD); translational outcomes in science (PhD). *Degree requirements:* For doctorate, comprehensive exam, thesis/dissertation, written and oral qualifying exams. *Entrance requirements:* For doctorate, GRE General Test. Additional exam requirements/recommendations for international students: required—TOEFL (minimum score 600 paper-based). Electronic applications accepted.

**Northwestern University,** The Graduate School, Interdisciplinary Biological Sciences Program (IBiS), Evanston, IL 60208. Offers biochemistry (PhD); bioengineering and biotechnology (PhD); biotechnology (PhD); cell and molecular biology (PhD); developmental and systems biology (PhD); nanotechnology (PhD); neurobiology (PhD); structural biology and biophysics (PhD). *Degree requirements:* For doctorate, thesis/dissertation, qualifying exam. *Entrance requirements:* For doctorate, GRE General Test. Additional exam requirements/recommendations for international students: required—TOEFL (minimum score 600 paper-based). Electronic applications accepted.

**Northwest Missouri State University,** Graduate School, College of Arts and Sciences, Maryville, MO 64468-6001. Offers biology (MS); elementary mathematics specialist (MS Ed); English (MA); English education (MS Ed); English pedagogy (MA); geographic information science (MS, Certificate); history (MS Ed); mathematics (MS); mathematics education (MS Ed); teaching: science (MS Ed). *Program availability:* Part-time. *Faculty:* 18 full-time (8 women). *Students:* 10 full-time (5 women), 47 part-time (23 women); includes 6 minority (2 American Indian or Alaska Native, non-Hispanic/Latino; 1 Asian, non-Hispanic/Latino; 1 Hispanic/Latino; 1 Native Hawaiian or other Pacific Islander, non-Hispanic/Latino; 1 Two or more races, non-Hispanic/Latino), 1 international. Average age 31. 17 applicants, 65% accepted, 9 enrolled. In 2019, 25 master's, 6 other advanced degrees awarded. *Degree requirements:* For master's, comprehensive exam. *Entrance requirements:* For master's, GRE General Test, writing sample. Additional exam requirements/recommendations for international students: required—TOEFL (minimum score 550 paper-based; 79 iBT). *Application deadline:* For fall admission, 7/1 for domestic and international students; for spring admission, 11/15 for domestic and international students. Applications are processed on a rolling basis. Application fee: $0 ($75 for international students). Electronic applications accepted. *Expenses:* Contact institution. *Financial support:* Research assistantships with full tuition reimbursements, teaching assistantships with full tuition reimbursements, and administrative assistantships, tutorial assistantships available. Financial award application deadline: 4/1; financial award applicants required to submit FAFSA. *Unit head:* Dr. Michael Steiner, Associate Provost-UG Studies & Dean, 660-562-1197. *Application contact:* Dr. Michael Steiner, Associate Provost-UG Studies & Dean, 660-562-1197.
Website: https://www.nwmissouri.edu/academics/departments.htm

**Nova Southeastern University,** College of Medical Sciences, Fort Lauderdale, FL 33314-7796. Offers biomedical sciences (MBS). *Program availability:* Part-time. *Faculty:* 36 full-time (18 women), 1 part-time/adjunct (0 women). *Students:* 51 full-time (31 women); includes 33 minority (3 Black or African American, non-Hispanic/Latino; 11 Asian, non-Hispanic/Latino; 17 Hispanic/Latino; 2 Two or more races, non-Hispanic/Latino), 3 international. Average age 25. 350 applicants, 11% accepted, 40 enrolled. In 2019, 7 master's awarded. *Entrance requirements:* For master's, Complete a minimum of four semester hours with a minimum of a C in both Biology and Chemistry. Successful completion of Organic Chemistry I and II is recommended. Complete a minimum of three semester hours with a minimum of a C in English or Composition. A minimum cumulative GPA of 2.5 on a 4.0 scale. Letters of recommendation. *Application deadline:* Applications are processed on a rolling basis. Application fee: $50. *Expenses:* 43709. *Financial support:* Application deadline: 4/15; applicants required to submit FAFSA. *Unit head:* Dr. Harold E. Laubach, Dean, 954-262-1303, Fax: 954-262-1802, E-mail: harold@nova.edu. *Application contact:* Dr. Lori B. Dribin, Assistant Dean for Student Affairs, 954-262-1341, Fax: 954-262-1802, E-mail: lorib@nova.edu.

**Nova Southeastern University,** Halmos College of Natural Sciences and Oceanography, Fort Lauderdale, FL 33314-7796. Offers biological sciences (MS), including health studies; marine biology and oceanography (PhD), including marine biology, oceanography. *Program availability:* Part-time, evening/weekend, blended/hybrid learning. *Faculty:* 63 full-time (16 women), 60 part-time/adjunct (27 women). *Students:* 39 full-time (25 women), 118 part-time (88 women); includes 33 minority (11 Black or African American, non-Hispanic/Latino; 6 Asian, non-Hispanic/Latino; 12 Hispanic/Latino; 4 Two or more races, non-Hispanic/Latino), 10 international. Average age 27. 86 applicants, 49% accepted, 26 enrolled. In 2019, 48 master's, 2 doctorates awarded. *Degree requirements:* For master's, thesis; for doctorate, comprehensive exam, thesis/dissertation, departmental qualifying exam. *Entrance requirements:* For master's, GRE General Test, 3 letters of recommendation; BS/BA in natural science (for marine biology program); BS/BA in biology (for biological sciences program); minor in the natural sciences or equivalent (for coastal zone management and marine environmental sciences); for doctorate, GRE General Test, master's degree. Additional exam requirements/recommendations for international students: required—TOEFL (minimum score 550 paper-based); recommended—IELTS. *Application deadline:* Applications are processed on a rolling basis. Application fee: $50. Electronic applications accepted. *Expenses:* Contact institution. *Financial support:* In 2019–20, 101 students received support, including 6 fellowships with full and partial tuition reimbursements available (averaging $25,000 per year), 40 research assistantships with full and partial tuition reimbursements available (averaging $20,000 per year), 8 teaching assistantships with tuition reimbursements available (averaging $15,000 per year); career-related internships or fieldwork, Federal Work-Study, scholarships/grants, health care benefits, tuition waivers (full and partial), and unspecified assistantships also available. Support available to part-time students. Financial award application deadline: 4/15; financial award applicants required to submit FAFSA. *Unit head:* Dr. Richard Dodge, Dean, 954-262-3600, Fax: 954-262-4020, E-mail: dodge@nsu.nova.edu. *Application contact:* Dr. Bernhard Riegl, Chair, Department of Marine and Environmental Sciences, 954-262-3600, Fax: 954-262-4020, E-mail: rieglb@nova.edu.
Website: http://cnso.nova.edu

**Oakland University,** Graduate Study and Lifelong Learning, College of Arts and Sciences, Department of Biological Sciences, Rochester, MI 48309-4401. Offers biological and biomedical sciences (PhD); biology (MA, MS); biomedical sciences (Graduate Certificate). *Program availability:* Part-time. *Degree requirements:* For master's, thesis. *Entrance requirements:* For master's, GRE Subject Test, GRE General Test, minimum GPA of 3.0. Additional exam requirements/recommendations for international students: required—TOEFL (minimum score 550 paper-based). Electronic applications accepted. *Expenses:* Contact institution.

**Occidental College,** Department of Biology, Los Angeles, CA 90041-3314. Offers MA. *Program availability:* Part-time. *Degree requirements:* For master's, thesis, final exam. *Entrance requirements:* For master's, GRE General Test, GRE Subject Test, minimum GPA of 3.0. Additional exam requirements/recommendations for international students: required—TOEFL (minimum score 625 paper-based). *Expenses:* Contact institution.

**The Ohio State University,** College of Medicine, Biomedical Sciences Graduate Program, Columbus, OH 43210. Offers PhD. *Degree requirements:* For doctorate, thesis/dissertation. *Entrance requirements:* For doctorate, GRE General Test. Additional exam requirements/recommendations for international students: required—TOEFL (minimum score 600 paper-based; 100 iBT), Michigan English Language Assessment Battery (minimum score 86); recommended—IELTS (minimum score 8). Electronic applications accepted.

**The Ohio State University,** Graduate School, College of Arts and Sciences, Division of Natural and Mathematical Sciences, Department of Mathematics, Columbus, OH 43210. Offers actuarial and quantitative risk management (MAQRM); computational sciences (MMS); mathematical biosciences (MMS); mathematics (PhD); mathematics for educators (MMS). *Degree requirements:* For master's, thesis optional; for doctorate, one foreign language, thesis/dissertation. *Entrance requirements:* For master's, GRE General Test; for doctorate, GRE General Test (recommended), GRE Subject Test (mathematics). Additional exam requirements/recommendations for international students: required—TOEFL (minimum score 550 paper-based; 79 iBT), Michigan English Language Assessment Battery (minimum score 82); recommended—IELTS (minimum score 7). Electronic applications accepted.

**Ohio University,** Graduate College, College of Arts and Sciences, Department of Biological Sciences, Athens, OH 45701-2979. Offers biological sciences (MS, PhD); cell biology and physiology (MS, PhD); ecology and evolutionary biology (MS, PhD); exercise physiology and muscle biology (MS, PhD); microbiology (MS, PhD); neuroscience (MS, PhD). Terminal master's awarded for partial completion of doctoral program. *Degree requirements:* For master's, comprehensive exam, thesis, 1 quarter of teaching experience; for doctorate, comprehensive exam, thesis/dissertation, 2 quarters of teaching experience. *Entrance requirements:* For master's, GRE General Test, names of three faculty members whose research interests most closely match the applicant's interest; for doctorate, GRE General Test, essay concerning prior training, research interest and career goals, plus names of three faculty members whose research interests most closely match the applicant's interest. Additional exam requirements/recommendations for international students: required—TOEFL (minimum score 620 paper-based; 105 iBT) or IELTS (minimum score 7.5). Electronic applications accepted.

**Oklahoma State University,** College of Arts and Sciences, Department of Integrative Biology, Stillwater, OK 74078. Offers MS, PhD. *Faculty:* 18 full-time (3 women). *Students:* 6 full-time (5 women), 48 part-time (22 women); includes 7 minority (6 Hispanic/Latino; 1 Two or more races, non-Hispanic/Latino), 3 international. Average age 27. 24 applicants, 67% accepted, 10 enrolled. In 2019, 9 master's, 7 doctorates awarded. *Entrance requirements:* For master's and doctorate, GRE General Test. Additional exam requirements/recommendations for international students: required—TOEFL (minimum score 550 paper-based; 79 iBT). *Application deadline:* For fall admission, 3/1 priority date for international students; for spring admission, 8/1 priority date for international students. Applications are processed on a rolling basis. Application fee: $50 ($75 for international students). Electronic applications accepted. *Expenses: Tuition, area resident:* Full-time $4148.10; part-time $2765.40 per credit hour. Tuition, state resident: full-time $4148.10; part-time $2765.40 per credit hour. Tuition, nonresident: full-time $15,775; part-time $10,516.80 per credit hour. *International tuition:* $15,775.20 full-time. *Required fees:* $2196.90; $122.05 per credit hour. Tuition and fees vary according to course load, campus/location and program. *Financial support:* In 2019–20, 17 research assistantships (averaging $2,034 per year), 43 teaching assistantships (averaging $2,446 per year) were awarded; career-related internships or fieldwork, Federal Work-Study, scholarships/grants, health care benefits, tuition waivers (partial), and unspecified assistantships also available. Support available to part-time students. Financial award application deadline: 3/1; financial award applicants required to submit FAFSA. *Unit head:* Dr. Jason Belden, Interim Department Head, 405-744-1718, Fax: 405-744-7824, E-mail: jbelden@okstate.edu. *Application contact:* Dr. Sheryl Tucker, Dean, 405-744-6368, Fax: 405-744-0355, E-mail: gradi@okstate.edu.
Website: http://integrativebiology.okstate.edu/

**Oklahoma State University Center for Health Sciences,** Program in Biomedical Sciences, Tulsa, OK 74107-1898. Offers MS, PhD, DO/PhD. *Degree requirements:* For master's, thesis; for doctorate, thesis/dissertation, comprehensive, oral and written exam. *Entrance requirements:* For master's, GRE General Test, minimum GPA of 3.0; for doctorate, GRE General Test, MCAT, minimum GPA of 3.0. Additional exam requirements/recommendations for international students: required—TOEFL (minimum score 79 iBT). Electronic applications accepted. *Expenses:* Contact institution.

**Old Dominion University,** College of Sciences, Master of Science in Biology Program, Norfolk, VA 23529. Offers biology (MS); microbiology and immunology (MS). *Program availability:* Part-time. *Degree requirements:* For master's, comprehensive exam, thesis optional, 31 credits. *Entrance requirements:* For master's, GRE General Test, MCAT, minimum GPA of 3.0. Additional exam requirements/recommendations for international students: required—TOEFL (minimum score 550 paper-based; 79 iBT). Electronic applications accepted.

**Old Dominion University,** College of Sciences, Program in Biomedical Sciences, Norfolk, VA 23529. Offers PhD. *Degree requirements:* For doctorate, comprehensive exam, thesis/dissertation. *Entrance requirements:* For doctorate, GRE General Test, minimum GPA of 3.0. Additional exam requirements/recommendations for international students: required—TOEFL (minimum score 84 iBT). Electronic applications accepted.

**Oregon Health & Science University,** School of Medicine, Graduate Programs in Medicine, Portland, OR 97239-3098. Offers MBA, MBI, MCR, MPAS, MS, MSCNU, PhD, Certificate. *Program availability:* Part-time. Terminal master's awarded for partial completion of doctoral program. *Entrance requirements:* Additional exam requirements/

recommendations for international students: required—TOEFL, IELTS. Electronic applications accepted.

**Oregon State University,** College of Science, Program in Integrative Biology, Corvallis, OR 97331. Offers behavioral ecology (MS, PhD). Terminal master's awarded for partial completion of doctoral program. *Entrance requirements:* For master's and doctorate, GRE. Additional exam requirements/recommendations for international students: required—TOEFL (minimum score 80 iBT), IELTS (minimum score 6.5). Electronic applications accepted.

**Oregon State University,** Interdisciplinary/Institutional Programs, Program in Comparative Health Sciences, Corvallis, OR 97331. Offers biomedical sciences (MS, PhD). *Entrance requirements:* For master's and doctorate, GRE. Additional exam requirements/recommendations for international students: required—TOEFL (minimum score 80 iBT), IELTS (minimum score 6.5).

**Pace University,** School of Education, New York, NY 10038. Offers adolescent education (MST), including biology, chemistry, earth science, English, foreign languages, mathematics, physics, social studies; childhood education (MST); early childhood development, learning and intervention (MST); educational technology studies (MS); inclusive adolescent education (MST), including biology, chemistry, earth science, English, foreign languages, mathematics, physics, social studies; integrated instruction for educational technology (Certificate); integrated instruction for literacy and technology (Certificate); literacy (MS Ed); special education (MS Ed). *Accreditation:* NCATE. *Program availability:* Part-time, evening/weekend, 100% online, blended/hybrid learning. *Degree requirements:* For master's and Certificate, certification exams. *Entrance requirements:* For master's, GRE (for initial certification programs only), teaching certificate (for MS Ed in literacy and special education programs only). Additional exam requirements/recommendations for international students: required—TOEFL (minimum score 88 iBT), IELTS or PTE. Electronic applications accepted. *Expenses:* Contact institution.

**Penn State Hershey Medical Center,** College of Medicine, Graduate School Programs in the Biomedical Sciences, Hershey, PA 17033. Offers MPH, MS, Dr PH, PhD, MD/PhD, PhD/MBA. Terminal master's awarded for partial completion of doctoral program. *Degree requirements:* For master's, thesis or alternative; for doctorate, comprehensive exam, thesis/dissertation, oral exam. *Entrance requirements:* For master's, GRE; for doctorate, GRE, minimum GPA of 3.0. Additional exam requirements/recommendations for international students: required—TOEFL (minimum score 550 paper-based; 81 iBT). Electronic applications accepted. *Expenses:* Contact institution.

**Penn State University Park,** Graduate School, Eberly College of Science, Department of Biology, University Park, PA 16802. Offers MS, PhD.

**Penn State University Park,** Graduate School, Intercollege Graduate Programs, Program in Molecular, Cellular, and Integrative Biosciences, University Park, PA 16802. Offers MS, PhD.

**Philadelphia College of Osteopathic Medicine,** Graduate and Professional Programs, Graduate Programs in Biomedical Sciences, Philadelphia, PA 19131. Offers MS. *Program availability:* Evening/weekend. *Faculty:* 25 full-time (14 women). *Students:* 119 full-time (67 women); includes 36 minority (9 Black or African American, non-Hispanic/Latino; 7 Asian, non-Hispanic/Latino; 20 Two or more races, non-Hispanic/Latino). Average age 24. 424 applicants, 44% accepted, 82 enrolled. In 2019, 17 master's awarded. *Degree requirements:* For master's, thesis optional. *Entrance requirements:* For master's, GRE, MCAT, DAT, OAT, PCAT, pre-medical prerequisite coursework; biochemistry (recommended). Additional exam requirements/recommendations for international students: required—TOEFL (minimum score 79 iBT). *Application deadline:* Applications are processed on a rolling basis. Application fee: $75. Electronic applications accepted. *Expenses:* Contact institution. *Financial support:* In 2019–20, 59 students received support. Federal Work-Study, institutionally sponsored loans, and scholarships/grants available. Financial award application deadline: 3/15; financial award applicants required to submit FAFSA. *Unit head:* Dr. Marcus Bell, Chair, 215-871-6834, Fax: 215-871-6865, E-mail: marcusbe@pcom.edu. *Application contact:* Kevin A. Zajac, Assistant Director of Admissions, 215-871-6700, Fax: 215-871-6719, E-mail: kevinzaj@pcom.edu.
Website: http://www.pcom.edu

**Pittsburg State University,** Graduate School, College of Arts and Sciences, Department of Biology, Pittsburg, KS 66762. Offers MS. *Degree requirements:* For master's, thesis or alternative. *Entrance requirements:* For master's, letter of intent. Additional exam requirements/recommendations for international students: required—TOEFL (minimum score 520 paper-based; 68 iBT), IELTS (minimum score 6), PTE (minimum score 47). Electronic applications accepted. *Expenses:* Contact institution.

**Point Loma Nazarene University,** Department of Biology, San Diego, CA 92106. Offers MS. *Program availability:* Part-time. *Faculty:* 5 full-time (4 women), 1 part-time/adjunct (0 women). *Students:* 2 full-time (1 woman), 26 part-time (20 women); includes 9 minority (2 Asian, non-Hispanic/Latino; 5 Hispanic/Latino; 1 Native Hawaiian or other Pacific Islander, non-Hispanic/Latino; 1 Two or more races, non-Hispanic/Latino), 3 international. Average age 34. 6 applicants, 100% accepted, 4 enrolled. In 2019, 8 master's awarded. *Degree requirements:* For master's, comprehensive exam (for some programs), thesis (for some programs). *Entrance requirements:* For master's, major field test in biology or GRE Subject Test (biology), BA/BS in science field, letters of recommendation, essay, interview. Additional exam requirements/recommendations for international students: required—TOEFL. *Application deadline:* For fall admission, 7/26 priority date for domestic students; for spring admission, 11/29 priority date for domestic students; for summer admission, 5/23 priority date for domestic students. Application fee: $50. Electronic applications accepted. *Expenses:* $765 per unit. *Financial support:* In 2019–20, 2 students received support. Available to part-time students. Applicants required to submit FAFSA. *Unit head:* Dr. Dianne Anderson, Director of Master's Program in Biology, 619-849-2705, E-mail: DianneAnderson@pointloma.edu. *Application contact:* Maira Lopes, Enrollment Advisor, 619-948-2885, E-mail: mairalopes@pointloma.edu.
Website: https://www.pointloma.edu/graduate-studies/programs/general-biology-ms

**Ponce Health Sciences University,** PhD Program in Biomedical Sciences, Ponce, PR 00732-7004. Offers PhD. *Degree requirements:* For doctorate, one foreign language, comprehensive exam, thesis/dissertation. *Entrance requirements:* For doctorate, GRE General Test, proficiency in Spanish and English, minimum overall GPA of 3.0, 3 letters of recommendation, minimum of 35 credits in science.

**Pontifical Catholic University of Puerto Rico,** College of Sciences, Department of Biology, Ponce, PR 00717-0777. Offers environmental sciences (MS). *Degree requirements:* For master's, thesis. *Entrance requirements:* For master's, GRE, 2 letters of recommendation, interview, minimum GPA of 2.75.

**Portland State University,** Graduate Studies, College of Liberal Arts and Sciences, Department of Biology, Portland, OR 97207-0751. Offers MA, MS, PhD. *Faculty:* 25 full-time (12 women), 7 part-time/adjunct (4 women). *Students:* 49 full-time (31 women), 8 part-time (5 women); includes 12 minority (3 Asian, non-Hispanic/Latino; 2 Hispanic/Latino; 7 Two or more races, non-Hispanic/Latino), 2 international. Average age 32. 36 applicants, 39% accepted, 12 enrolled. In 2019, 8 master's, 3 doctorates awarded. *Degree requirements:* For master's, one foreign language, thesis; for doctorate, thesis/dissertation. *Entrance requirements:* For master's, GRE General Test, GRE Subject Test, minimum GPA of 3.0 in upper-division course work or 2.75 overall, 2 letters of reference; for doctorate, GRE General Test, GRE Subject Test, minimum GPA of 3.5 in science. Additional exam requirements/recommendations for international students: required—TOEFL (minimum score 550 paper-based; 80 iBT). *Application deadline:* For fall admission, 2/15 for domestic and international students; for winter admission, 9/1 for domestic students, 7/1 for international students; for spring admission, 11/1 for domestic and international students. Application fee: $65. *Expenses: Tuition, area resident:* Full-time $13,020; part-time $6510 per year. Tuition, state resident: full-time $13,020; part-time $6510 per year. Tuition, nonresident: full-time $19,830; part-time $9915 per year. *International tuition:* $19,830 full-time. *Required fees:* $1226. One-time fee: $350. Tuition and fees vary according to course load, program and reciprocity agreements. *Financial support:* In 2019–20, 13 research assistantships with full and partial tuition reimbursements (averaging $18,876 per year), 30 teaching assistantships with full and partial tuition reimbursements (averaging $21,764 per year) were awarded; Federal Work-Study, scholarships/grants, tuition waivers (full and partial), and unspecified assistantships also available. Support available to part-time students. Financial award application deadline: 3/1; financial award applicants required to submit FAFSA. *Unit head:* Dr. Michael Bartlett, Chair, 503-725-3858, E-mail: micb@pdx.edu. *Application contact:* Dr. Jeff Singer, Chair, Graduate Affairs Committee, E-mail: jsinger@pdx.edu.
Website: https://www.pdx.edu/biology/

**Purdue University,** Graduate School, Biomedical Sciences Interdisciplinary Graduate Program, West Lafayette, IN 47907. Offers PhD. *Students:* 11 full-time (7 women); includes 2 minority (both Asian, non-Hispanic/Latino), 6 international. Average age 27. 20 applicants, 35% accepted, 6 enrolled. *Degree requirements:* For doctorate, thesis/dissertation, seminars, teaching experience. *Entrance requirements:* For doctorate, GRE General Test (minimum scores: verbal 550, quantitative 700), minimum undergraduate GPA of 3.0. Additional exam requirements/recommendations for international students: required—TOEFL (minimum score 550 paper-based; 77 iBT); recommended—TWE. *Application deadline:* For fall admission, 12/15 priority date for domestic and international students. Applications are processed on a rolling basis. Application fee: $60 ($75 for international students). Electronic applications accepted. *Financial support:* Fellowships, research assistantships, and teaching assistantships available. Support available to part-time students. *Unit head:* Harm HogenEsch, Head of the Graduate Program, 765-496-3485, Fax: 765-496-1261, E-mail: hogenesch@purdue.edu. *Application contact:* Sandra M. May, Graduate Contact for Admissions, 765-494-7054, E-mail: smmay@purdue.edu.
Website: http://www.gradschool.purdue.edu/BSDT/

**Purdue University,** Graduate School, College of Science, Department of Biological Sciences, West Lafayette, IN 47907. Offers cell and developmental biology (PhD); genetics (MS); microbiology (MS, PhD); neurobiology (MS, PhD). *Faculty:* 43 full-time (14 women), 6 part-time/adjunct (1 woman). *Students:* 117 full-time (58 women), 10 part-time (6 women); includes 24 minority (5 Black or African American, non-Hispanic/Latino; 12 Asian, non-Hispanic/Latino; 4 Hispanic/Latino; 3 Two or more races, non-Hispanic/Latino), 56 international. Average age 27. 146 applicants, 32% accepted, 27 enrolled. In 2019, 7 master's, 18 doctorates awarded. Terminal master's awarded for partial completion of doctoral program. *Degree requirements:* For master's, thesis (for some programs); for doctorate, thesis/dissertation, seminars, teaching experience. *Entrance requirements:* For master's, GRE General Test (minimum analytical writing score of 3.5), minimum undergraduate GPA of 3.0; for doctorate, GRE General Test (minimum analytical writing score of 3.5), minimum undergraduate GPA of 3.5. Additional exam requirements/recommendations for international students: required—TOEFL minimum score 600 paper-based; 107 iBT (for MS), 80 iBT (for PhD). *Application deadline:* For fall admission, 12/7 for domestic and international students. Applications are processed on a rolling basis. Application fee: $60 ($75 for international students). Electronic applications accepted. *Financial support:* Fellowships, research assistantships, and teaching assistantships available. Support available to part-time students. Financial award application deadline: 2/15; financial award applicants required to submit FAFSA. *Unit head:* Janice P. Evans, Head, 765-494-4407, E-mail: janiceevans@purdue.edu. *Application contact:* Georgina E. Rupp, Graduate Coordinator, 765-494-8142, E-mail: ruppg@purdue.edu.
Website: http://www.bio.purdue.edu/

**Purdue University,** Graduate School, PULSe - Purdue University Life Sciences Program, West Lafayette, IN 47907. Offers biomolecular structure and biophysics (PhD); biotechnology (PhD); chemical biology (PhD); chromatin and regulation of gene expression (PhD); integrative neuroscience (PhD); integrative plant sciences (PhD); membrane biology (PhD); microbiology (PhD); molecular evolutionary and cancer biology (PhD); molecular evolutionary genetics (PhD); molecular virology (PhD). *Students:* 37 full-time (23 women); includes 7 minority (1 Black or African American, non-Hispanic/Latino; 2 Asian, non-Hispanic/Latino; 4 Hispanic/Latino), 22 international. Average age 25. 162 applicants, 36% accepted, 19 enrolled. *Entrance requirements:* For doctorate, GRE, minimum undergraduate GPA of 3.0. Additional exam requirements/recommendations for international students: required—TOEFL (minimum score 550 paper-based; 77 iBT). *Application deadline:* For fall admission, 1/15 priority date for domestic and international students. Applications are processed on a rolling basis. Application fee: $60 ($75 for international students). Electronic applications accepted. *Financial support:* In 2019–20, research assistantships with tuition reimbursements (averaging $22,500 per year), teaching assistantships with tuition reimbursements (averaging $22,500 per year) were awarded. *Application contact:* Lindsey Springer, Graduate Contact for Admissions, 765-496-9667, E-mail: lbcampbe@purdue.edu.
Website: http://www.gradschool.purdue.edu/pulse

**Purdue University Fort Wayne,** College of Arts and Sciences, Department of Biology, Fort Wayne, IN 46805-1499. Offers MS. *Program availability:* Part-time, evening/weekend. *Degree requirements:* For master's, thesis optional. *Entrance requirements:* For master's, GRE General Test, minimum GPA of 3.0, major or minor in biology, three letters of recommendation. Additional exam requirements/recommendations for international students: required—TOEFL (minimum score 550 paper-based; 79 iBT), TWE. Electronic applications accepted.

**Purdue University Northwest,** Graduate Studies Office, School of Engineering, Mathematics, and Science, Department of Biological Sciences, Hammond, IN 46323-2094. Offers biology (MS); biology teaching (MS); biotechnology (MS). *Entrance requirements:* For master's, GRE. Additional exam requirements/recommendations for international students: required—TOEFL. Electronic applications accepted.

**Queens College of the City University of New York,** Division of Education, Department of Secondary Education and Youth Services, Queens, NY 11367-1597. Offers adolescent biology (MAT); art (MS Ed); biology (MS Ed, AC); chemistry (MS Ed, AC); earth sciences (MS Ed, AC); English (MS Ed, AC); French (MS Ed); Italian (MS Ed, AC); literacy education (MS Ed); mathematics (MS Ed, AC); music (MS Ed, AC); physics (MS Ed, AC); social studies (MS Ed, AC); Spanish (MS Ed, AC). *Program availability:* Part-time, evening/weekend. *Degree requirements:* For master's, research project. *Entrance requirements:* For master's, GRE, minimum GPA of 3.0. Additional exam

requirements/recommendations for international students: required—TOEFL, IELTS. Electronic applications accepted.

**Queens College of the City University of New York,** Mathematics and Natural Sciences Division, Department of Biology, Queens, NY 11367-1597. Offers MA. *Program availability:* Part-time. *Degree requirements:* For master's, thesis, qualifying exam. *Entrance requirements:* For master's, minimum GPA of 3.0. Additional exam requirements/recommendations for international students: required—TOEFL (minimum score 100 iBT), IELTS (minimum score 7). Electronic applications accepted.

**Queen's University at Kingston,** School of Graduate Studies, Faculty of Arts and Science, Department of Biology, Kingston, ON K7L 3N6, Canada. Offers M Sc, PhD. *Program availability:* Part-time. *Degree requirements:* For master's, thesis; for doctorate, comprehensive exam, thesis/dissertation. *Entrance requirements:* Additional exam requirements/recommendations for international students: required—TOEFL.

**Quinnipiac University,** School of Health Sciences, Program in Biomedical Sciences, Hamden, CT 06518-1940. Offers MHS. *Program availability:* Part-time, evening/weekend. *Degree requirements:* For master's, comprehensive exam, thesis optional. *Entrance requirements:* For master's, minimum GPA of 2.75; bachelor's degree in biological, medical, or health sciences. Additional exam requirements/recommendations for international students: required—TOEFL (minimum score 575 paper-based; 90 iBT), IELTS (minimum score 6.5). Electronic applications accepted. *Expenses: Tuition:* Part-time $1055 per credit. *Required fees:* $945 per semester. Tuition and fees vary according to course load and program.

**Regis University,** Regis College, Denver, CO 80221-1099. Offers biomedical sciences (MS); developmental practice (MDP); education (MA); environmental biology (MS). *Accreditation:* TEAC. *Program availability:* Part-time. *Degree requirements:* For master's, thesis (for some programs), capstone presentation. *Entrance requirements:* For master's, official transcript reflecting baccalaureate degree awarded from U.S.-based regionally-accredited college or university. Additional exam requirements/recommendations for international students: required—TOEFL (minimum score 550 paper-based; 82 iBT). Electronic applications accepted. *Expenses:* Contact institution.

**Rensselaer Polytechnic Institute,** Graduate School, School of Science, Program in Biology, Troy, NY 12180-3590. Offers MS, PhD. *Faculty:* 21 full-time (6 women), 2 part-time/adjunct (1 woman). *Students:* 26 full-time (14 women); includes 4 minority (1 Black or African American, non-Hispanic/Latino; 1 American Indian or Alaska Native, non-Hispanic/Latino; 1 Hispanic/Latino; 1 Two or more races, non-Hispanic/Latino), 3 international. Average age 27. 66 applicants, 23% accepted, 8 enrolled. In 2019, 2 master's, 5 doctorates awarded. Terminal master's awarded for partial completion of doctoral program. *Degree requirements:* For master's, comprehensive exam, thesis optional; for doctorate, comprehensive exam, thesis/dissertation. *Entrance requirements:* For master's and doctorate, GRE. Additional exam requirements/recommendations for international students: required—TOEFL (minimum score 570 paper-based; 88 iBT), IELTS (minimum score 6.5), PTE (minimum score 60). *Application deadline:* For fall admission, 1/1 priority date for domestic and international students. Applications are processed on a rolling basis. Application fee: $75. Electronic applications accepted. *Financial support:* In 2019–20, research assistantships (averaging $23,000 per year), teaching assistantships (averaging $23,000 per year) were awarded; fellowships also available. Financial award application deadline: 1/1. *Unit head:* Dr. George Makhatadze, Graduate Program Director, 518-276-4417, E-mail: makhag@rpi.edu. *Application contact:* Jarron Decker, Director of Graduate Admissions, 518-276-6216, Fax: 518-276-4072, E-mail: gradadmissions@rpi.edu. Website: https://science.rpi.edu/biology/graduate

**Rhode Island College,** School of Graduate Studies, Faculty of Arts and Sciences, Department of Biology, Providence, RI 02908-1991. Offers biology (MA); modern biological sciences (CGS). *Program availability:* Part-time. *Faculty:* 6 full-time (3 women). *Students:* 4 part-time (1 woman). Average age 27. In 2019, 1 master's, 1 other advanced degree awarded. *Degree requirements:* For master's, thesis. *Entrance requirements:* For master's, GRE General and Subject Tests. Additional exam requirements/recommendations for international students: required—TOEFL (minimum score 550 paper-based; 80 iBT). *Application deadline:* For fall admission, 3/1 for domestic students. Applications are processed on a rolling basis. Application fee: $50. *Expenses: Tuition, area resident:* Part-time $462 per credit hour. Tuition, state resident: part-time $462 per credit hour. *Required fees:* $720. One-time fee: $140. *Financial support:* Teaching assistantships, career-related internships or fieldwork, Federal Work-Study, scholarships/grants, health care benefits, and unspecified assistantships available. Support available to part-time students. Financial award application deadline: 5/15; financial award applicants required to submit FAFSA. *Unit head:* Dr. Daniel Hewins, Chair, 401-456-8010, E-mail: biology@ric.edu. *Application contact:* Dr. Daniel Hewins, Chair, 401-456-8010, E-mail: biology@ric.edu. Website: http://www.ric.edu/biology/Pages/default.aspx

**Rochester Institute of Technology,** Graduate Enrollment Services, College of Science, School of Life Sciences, Rochester, NY 14623-5603. Offers MS. *Program availability:* Part-time. *Entrance requirements:* For master's, GRE (for some programs), minimum GPA of 3.0 (recommended). Electronic applications accepted. *Expenses:* Contact institution.

**The Rockefeller University,** The David Rockefeller Graduate Program in Bioscience, New York, NY 10021-6399. Offers MS, PhD. *Faculty:* 74 full-time (13 women). *Students:* 248 full-time (108 women); includes 60 minority (9 Black or African American, non-Hispanic/Latino; 2 American Indian or Alaska Native, non-Hispanic/Latino; 29 Asian, non-Hispanic/Latino; 19 Hispanic/Latino; 1 Native Hawaiian or other Pacific Islander, non-Hispanic/Latino; 78 international. Average age 28. 1,098 applicants, 7% accepted, 27 enrolled. In 2019, 9 master's, 30 doctorates awarded. Terminal master's awarded for partial completion of doctoral program. *Degree requirements:* For master's, thesis; for doctorate, thesis/dissertation. *Entrance requirements:* For doctorate, three letters of recommendation, official college or university transcripts, personal essay. *Application deadline:* For fall and winter admission, 12/1 for domestic and international students. Application fee: $50. Electronic applications accepted. Application fee is waived when completed online. *Financial support:* In 2019–20, 248 students received support, including 248 fellowships with full tuition reimbursements available; institutionally sponsored loans, scholarships/grants, traineeships, and health care benefits also available. *Unit head:* Dr. Sidney Strickland, Dean of Graduate and Postgraduate Studies/Vice President, 212-327-8086, Fax: 212-327-8505, E-mail: phd@rockefeller.edu. *Application contact:* Kristen Cullen, Graduate Admissions Administrator/Registrar, 212-327-8086, Fax: 212-327-8505, E-mail: phd@rockefeller.edu. Website: http://www.rockefeller.edu/graduate/

See Display below and Close-Up on page 91.

**Rocky Vista University,** Program in Biomedical Sciences, Parker, CO 80134. Offers MS. *Entrance requirements:* For master's, GRE, MCAT, PCAT, or DAT, U.S. citizenship or permanent residency, bachelor's degree, minimum science and overall GPA of 2.75, resume, two letters of recommendation.

**Rosalind Franklin University of Medicine and Science,** College of Health Professions, Department of Interprofessional Healthcare Studies, Biomedical Sciences Program, North Chicago, IL 60064-3095. Offers MS. *Entrance requirements:* For master's, MCAT, DAT, OAT, PCAT or GRE, BS in chemistry, physics, biology. Additional exam requirements/recommendations for international students: required—TOEFL.

## The David Rockefeller Graduate Program
*Ph.D. Program in the Biological Sciences*

The Rockefeller University is the world's leading biomedical research university. Our unique Ph.D. program provides advanced training in the life sciences to exceptional graduate students from around the world. Our program offers:

- a flexible, hands-on academic experience with freedom to explore different areas of science
- 70 independent laboratories led by world-class faculty
- close in-lab mentorship and individualized support and guidance from the dean's office
- a collegial culture that encourages interdisciplinary collaboration
- modern facilities and state-of-the-art research support

Graduate students pay no tuition. They receive a yearly stipend, free health and dental insurance, subsidized housing on or adjacent to the university's verdant 16-acre New York City campus, and an annual research allowance for travel and lab support.

The nation's first institute devoted to medical research, The Rockefeller University is dedicated to conducting innovative, high-quality research to improve the understanding of life for the benefit of humanity. The university's faculty have produced pioneering achievements in biology and medicine for 119 years, and have been recognized with 25 Nobel Prizes and 22 Lasker Awards.

**Rosalind Franklin University of Medicine and Science,** School of Graduate and Postdoctoral Studies - Interdisciplinary Graduate Program in Biomedical Sciences, North Chicago, IL 60064-3095. Offers MS, PhD, DPM/PhD, MD/PhD. Terminal master's awarded for partial completion of doctoral program. *Degree requirements:* For master's, comprehensive exam, thesis, publication; for doctorate, comprehensive exam, thesis/dissertation. *Entrance requirements:* For master's and doctorate, GRE General Test. Additional exam requirements/recommendations for international students: required—TOEFL, TWE. Electronic applications accepted. *Expenses:* Contact institution.

**Rowan University,** Graduate School, College of Science and Mathematics, Department of Biological Science, Glassboro, NJ 08028-1701. Offers MS. Electronic applications accepted. *Expenses: Tuition, area resident:* Part-time $715.50 per semester hour. Tuition, state resident: part-time $715.50 per semester hour. Tuition, nonresident: part-time $715.50 per semester hour. *Required fees:* $161.55 per semester hour.

**Rutgers University - Camden,** Graduate School of Arts and Sciences, Program in Biology, Camden, NJ 08102. Offers MS. *Program availability:* Part-time, evening/weekend. *Degree requirements:* For master's, comprehensive exam, thesis (for some programs), 30 credits. *Entrance requirements:* For master's, GRE General Test, GRE Subject Test (recommended), 3 letters of recommendation; statement of personal, professional and academic goals; biology or related undergraduate degree (preferred). Additional exam requirements/recommendations for international students: required—TOEFL, IELTS. Electronic applications accepted.

**Rutgers University - Newark,** Graduate School of Biomedical Sciences, Newark, NJ 07107. Offers PhD, Certificate, DMD/PhD, MD/PhD. *Program availability:* Part-time, evening/weekend. Terminal master's awarded for partial completion of doctoral program. *Degree requirements:* For doctorate, thesis/dissertation, qualifying exam. *Entrance requirements:* For doctorate, GRE General Test. Additional exam requirements/recommendations for international students: required—TOEFL. Electronic applications accepted.

**Rutgers University - Newark,** Graduate School, Program in Biology, Newark, NJ 07102. Offers MS, PhD. *Program availability:* Part-time, evening/weekend. Terminal master's awarded for partial completion of doctoral program. *Degree requirements:* For master's, comprehensive exam, thesis optional; for doctorate, thesis/dissertation, qualifying exam. *Entrance requirements:* For master's, GRE General Test, minimum undergraduate B average; for doctorate, GRE General Test, GRE Subject Test, minimum B average. Electronic applications accepted.

**Rutgers University - Newark,** Graduate School, Program in Computational Biology, Newark, NJ 07102. Offers MS. *Entrance requirements:* For master's, GRE, minimum undergraduate B average. Additional exam requirements/recommendations for international students: required—TOEFL.

**Rutgers University - New Brunswick,** Graduate School-New Brunswick, BioMaPS Institute for Quantitative Biology, Piscataway, NJ 08854-8097. Offers computational biology and molecular biophysics (PhD). *Degree requirements:* For doctorate, comprehensive exam, thesis/dissertation. *Entrance requirements:* For doctorate, GRE. Additional exam requirements/recommendations for international students: required—TOEFL. Electronic applications accepted.

**Rutgers University - New Brunswick,** Graduate School of Biomedical Sciences, Piscataway, NJ 08854-5635. Offers biochemistry and molecular biology (MS, PhD); biomedical engineering (MS, PhD); biomedical science (MS); cellular and molecular pharmacology (MS, PhD); clinical and translational science (MS); environmental sciences/exposure assessment (PhD); molecular genetics, microbiology and immunology (MS, PhD); neuroscience (MS, PhD); physiology and integrative biology (MS, PhD); toxicology (PhD); MD/PhD. Terminal master's awarded for partial completion of doctoral program. *Degree requirements:* For master's, thesis (for some programs), ethics training; for doctorate, comprehensive exam, thesis/dissertation, ethics training. *Entrance requirements:* For master's, GRE General Test, MCAT, DAT; for doctorate, GRE General Test. Additional exam requirements/recommendations for international students: required—TOEFL. Electronic applications accepted.

**St. Cloud State University,** School of Graduate Studies, College of Science and Engineering, Department of Biology, St. Cloud, MN 56301-4498. Offers MA, MS. *Degree requirements:* For master's, comprehensive exam (for some programs), thesis or alternative. *Entrance requirements:* For master's, GRE General Test, minimum GPA of 2.75. Additional exam requirements/recommendations for international students: recommended—TOEFL (minimum score 550 paper-based), IELTS (minimum score 6.5). Electronic applications accepted.

**Saint Francis University,** Medical Science Program, Loretto, PA 15940-0600. Offers MMS. *Program availability:* Part-time, evening/weekend, 100% online. *Faculty:* 2 full-time (both women). *Students:* 34 full-time (22 women), 41 part-time (29 women); includes 44 minority (4 Black or African American, non-Hispanic/Latino; 4 Asian, non-Hispanic/Latino; 35 Hispanic/Latino; 1 Native Hawaiian or other Pacific Islander, non-Hispanic/Latino). Average age 31. 59 applicants, 100% accepted, 57 enrolled. In 2019, 66 master's awarded. *Degree requirements:* For master's, thesis or alternative, successful completion of affiliate PA program, minimum GPA of 2.8 in program. *Entrance requirements:* For master's, enrollment in affiliate PA program, bachelor's degree with minimum GPA of 2.5, resume, transcript. Additional exam requirements/recommendations for international students: recommended—TOEFL (minimum score 80 iBT). *Application deadline:* For fall admission, 6/15 for domestic students; for spring admission, 11/15 for domestic students; for summer admission, 3/15 for domestic students. Applications are processed on a rolling basis. Electronic applications accepted. *Expenses:* 850 per credit, 33 credits. *Financial support:* Available to part-time students. Applicants required to submit FAFSA. *Unit head:* Dr. Theresa Horner, Assistant Professor/Chair - Public Health/MMS, 814-471-1314, E-mail: thorner@francis.edu. *Application contact:* Dr. Theresa Horner, Assistant Professor/Chair - Public Health/MMS, 814-471-1314, E-mail: thorner@francis.edu.
Website: http://francis.edu/master-of-medical-science/

**St. Francis Xavier University,** Graduate Studies, Department of Biology, Antigonish, NS B2G 2W5, Canada. Offers M Sc. *Degree requirements:* For master's, thesis. *Entrance requirements:* For master's, 2 letters of recommendation. Additional exam requirements/recommendations for international students: required—TOEFL (minimum score 580 paper-based). *Expenses: Tuition, area resident:* Part-time $1731 Canadian dollars per course. Tuition, state resident: part-time $1731 Canadian dollars per course. Tuition, nonresident: part-time $1988 Canadian dollars per course. *International tuition:* $3976 Canadian dollars full-time. *Required fees:* $185 Canadian dollars per course. Tuition and fees vary according to course level, course load, degree level and program.

**St. John Fisher College,** Ralph C. Wilson Jr. School of Education, Program in Adolescence Education and Special Education, Rochester, NY 14618-3597. Offers adolescence education: biology with special education (MS Ed); adolescence education: chemistry with special education (MS Ed); adolescence education: English with special education (MS Ed); adolescence education: French with special education (MS Ed); adolescence education: math with special education (MS Ed); adolescence education: physics with special education (MS Ed); adolescence education: social studies with special education (MS Ed); adolescence education: Spanish with special education (MS Ed). *Program availability:* Part-time, evening/weekend. *Faculty:* 7 full-time (6 women), 3 part-time/adjunct (all women). *Students:* 10 full-time (6 women), 1 part-time (0 women); includes 10 minority (all Black or African American, non-Hispanic/Latino). Average age 25. 17 applicants, 76% accepted, 7 enrolled. In 2019, 18 master's awarded. *Degree requirements:* For master's, field experiences, student teaching. *Entrance requirements:* For master's, LAST, 2 letters of recommendation, personal statement, current resume. Additional exam requirements/recommendations for international students: required—TOEFL (minimum score 575 paper-based; 80 iBT). *Application deadline:* Applications are processed on a rolling basis. Application fee: $30. Electronic applications accepted. *Expenses:* Contact institution. *Financial support:* Scholarships/grants available. Financial award applicants required to submit FAFSA. *Unit head:* Whitney Rapp, Program Director, 585-899-3813, E-mail: wrapp@sjfc.edu. *Application contact:* Michelle Gosier, Director of Transfer and Graduate Admissions, 585-385-8064, E-mail: mgosier@sjfc.edu.

**St. John's University,** St. John's College of Liberal Arts and Sciences, Department of Biological Sciences, Queens, NY 11439. Offers MS, PhD. *Program availability:* Part-time, evening/weekend. *Degree requirements:* For master's, variable foreign language requirement, comprehensive exam, thesis optional; for doctorate, variable foreign language requirement, comprehensive exam, thesis/dissertation. *Entrance requirements:* For master's, GRE, letters of recommendation, transcripts, resume, personal statement; for doctorate, GRE General Test, letters of recommendation, transcripts, resume, personal statement. Additional exam requirements/recommendations for international students: required—TOEFL (minimum score 80 iBT), IELTS (minimum score 6.5). Electronic applications accepted.

**Saint Joseph's University,** College of Arts and Sciences, Department of Biology, Philadelphia, PA 19131-1395. Offers MA, MS. *Program availability:* Part-time. *Faculty:* 9 full-time (4 women), 1 (woman) part-time/adjunct. *Students:* 4 full-time (3 women), 17 part-time (10 women); includes 7 minority (6 Black or African American, non-Hispanic/Latino; 1 Asian, non-Hispanic/Latino), 2 international. Average age 24. 21 applicants, 81% accepted, 11 enrolled. In 2019, 6 master's awarded. *Degree requirements:* For master's, comprehensive exam (for some programs), thesis (for some programs), minimum GPA of 3.0, completion of degree within 5 years. *Entrance requirements:* For master's, GRE, 2 letters of recommendation, transcript, personal statement, resume. Additional exam requirements/recommendations for international students: required—TOEFL (minimum score 550 paper-based; 80 iBT), IELTS (minimum score 6.5). *Application deadline:* For fall admission, 3/15 priority date for domestic and international students; for spring admission, 11/1 for international students. Applications are processed on a rolling basis. Application fee: $35. Electronic applications accepted. *Expenses:* Total cost to complete the program is based on 30 credits. *Financial support:* In 2019–20, 11 students received support. Scholarships/grants and unspecified assistantships available. Financial award application deadline: 5/1; financial award applicants required to submit FAFSA. *Unit head:* Dr. Edwin Li, Graduate Director, 610-660-1888, E-mail: eli@sju.edu. *Application contact:* Graduate Admissions, College of Arts and Sciences, 610-660-1101, E-mail: graduate@sju.edu.
Website: https://www.sju.edu/degree-programs/biology-mams

**Saint Louis University,** Graduate Programs, College of Arts and Sciences and Graduate Programs, Department of Biology, St. Louis, MO 63103. Offers MS, MS-R, PhD. *Degree requirements:* For master's, comprehensive exam, thesis (for some programs); for doctorate, thesis/dissertation, preliminary exams. *Entrance requirements:* For master's, GRE General Test, letters of recommendation, resume; for doctorate, GRE General Test, letters of recommendation, resumé, statement, transcripts. Additional exam requirements/recommendations for international students: required—TOEFL (minimum score 550 paper-based). Electronic applications accepted.

**Saint Louis University,** Graduate Programs, School of Medicine, Graduate Programs in Biomedical Sciences, St. Louis, MO 63103. Offers MS-R, PhD. *Degree requirements:* For doctorate, comprehensive exam, thesis/dissertation. *Entrance requirements:* For doctorate, GRE. Additional exam requirements/recommendations for international students: required—TOEFL. Electronic applications accepted. *Expenses:* Contact institution.

**Salisbury University,** Program in Applied Biology, Salisbury, MD 21801-6837. Offers applied biology (MS). *Program availability:* Part-time. *Faculty:* 11 full-time (7 women). *Students:* 5 full-time (3 women), 4 part-time (2 women); includes 2 minority (1 Asian, non-Hispanic/Latino; 1 Native Hawaiian or other Pacific Islander, non-Hispanic/Latino). Average age 24. 2 applicants, 100% accepted, 1 enrolled. In 2019, 2 master's awarded. *Degree requirements:* For master's, comprehensive exam, thesis optional. *Entrance requirements:* For master's, GRE required for students that did not earn their undergraduate degree at SU, transcripts; resume or CV; personal statement; minimum GPA of 3.0; three letters of recommendation; undergraduate degree in biology or related field with appropriate prerequisites. Additional exam requirements/recommendations for international students: required—TOEFL (minimum score 550 paper-based; 79 iBT). *Application deadline:* For fall admission, 3/1 for domestic and international students; for spring admission, 10/1 for domestic and international students. Application fee: $65. Electronic applications accepted. *Expenses:* Contact institution. *Financial support:* In 2019–20, 1 student received support, including 11 teaching assistantships with full tuition reimbursements available (averaging $13,000 per year); career-related internships or fieldwork and scholarships/grants also available. Support available to part-time students. Financial award application deadline: 3/1; financial award applicants required to submit FAFSA. *Unit head:* Dr. Dana Price, Graduate Program Director, 410-543-6498, E-mail: dlprice@salisbury.edu. *Application contact:* Dr. Dana Price, Graduate Program Director, 410-543-6498, E-mail: dlprice@salisbury.edu.
Website: https://www.salisbury.edu/explore-academics/programs/graduate-degree-programs/applied-biology-masters/

**Sam Houston State University,** College of Sciences, Department of Biological Sciences, Huntsville, TX 77341. Offers MA, MS. *Program availability:* Part-time. *Degree requirements:* For master's, comprehensive exam, thesis (for some programs). *Entrance requirements:* For master's, GRE General Test, letters of recommendation, statement of purpose. Additional exam requirements/recommendations for international students: required—TOEFL (minimum score 550 paper-based; 78 iBT), IELTS (minimum score 6.5). Electronic applications accepted.

**San Diego State University,** Graduate and Research Affairs, College of Sciences, Department of Biology, San Diego, CA 92182. Offers biology (MA, MS), including ecology (MS), molecular biology (MS), physiology (MS), systematics/evolution (MS); cell and molecular biology (PhD); ecology (MS, PhD); microbiology (MS). Terminal master's awarded for partial completion of doctoral program. *Degree requirements:* For master's, thesis; for doctorate, thesis/dissertation. *Entrance requirements:* For master's, GRE General Test, GRE Subject Test, resume or curriculum vitae, 2 letters of recommendation. Additional exam requirements/recommendations for international students: required—TOEFL. Electronic applications accepted.

**Sanford Burnham Prebys Medical Discovery Institute,** Graduate School of Biomedical Sciences, La Jolla, CA 92037. Offers PhD. *Degree requirements:* For doctorate, thesis/dissertation. *Entrance requirements:* For doctorate, GRE General Test.

Additional exam requirements/recommendations for international students: recommended—TOEFL, IELTS.

**San Francisco State University,** Division of Graduate Studies, College of Science and Engineering, Department of Biology, San Francisco, CA 94132-1722. Offers cell and molecular biology (MS); ecology, evolution, and conservation biology (MS); interdisciplinary marine and estuarine science (MS); marine biology (MS); microbiology (MS); physiology and behavioral biology (MS); science (PSM), including biotechnology, stem cell science. *Application deadline:* Applications are processed on a rolling basis. *Expenses: Tuition, area resident:* Full-time $7176; part-time $4164 per year. Tuition, state resident: full-time $7176; part-time $4164 per year. Tuition, nonresident: full-time $16,680; part-time $396 per unit. *International tuition:* $16,680 full-time. *Required fees:* $1524; $1524 per unit. $762 per semester. Tuition and fees vary according to degree level and program. *Unit head:* Dr. Laura Burrus, Chair, 415-338-7680, Fax: 415-338-6136, E-mail: lburrus@sfsu.edu. *Application contact:* Giovanna Tuccori, Graduate Program Assistant, 415-405-3591, Fax: 415-338-6136.
Website: http://biology.sfsu.edu/

**San Jose State University,** Program in Biological Sciences, San Jose, CA 95192-0001. Offers biological sciences (MA, MS); molecular biology and microbiology (MS); organismal biology, conservation and ecology (MS); physiology (MS). *Program availability:* Part-time. *Entrance requirements:* For master's, GRE. Electronic applications accepted. *Expenses: Tuition, area resident:* Full-time $7176; part-time $4164 per credit hour. Tuition, state resident: full-time $7176; part-time $4164 per credit hour. Tuition, nonresident: full-time $7176; part-time $4165 per credit hour. *International tuition:* $7176 full-time. *Required fees:* $2110; $2110.

**The Scripps Research Institute,** Kellogg School of Science and Technology, La Jolla, CA 92037. Offers chemical and biological sciences (PhD). *Degree requirements:* For doctorate, thesis/dissertation. *Entrance requirements:* For doctorate, GRE General Test, GRE Subject Test, 3 letters of recommendation, official transcripts. Additional exam requirements/recommendations for international students: required—TOEFL. Electronic applications accepted.

**Seton Hall University,** College of Arts and Sciences, Department of Biological Sciences, South Orange, NJ 07079-2697. Offers biology (MS); biology/business administration (MS); microbiology (MS); molecular bioscience (PhD); molecular bioscience/neuroscience (PhD). *Program availability:* Part-time, evening/weekend. *Degree requirements:* For master's, thesis optional; for doctorate, comprehensive exam, thesis/dissertation. *Entrance requirements:* For master's, GRE or undergraduate degree (BS in biological sciences) with minimum GPA of 3.0 from accredited U.S. institution; for doctorate, GRE. Additional exam requirements/recommendations for international students: required—TOEFL. Electronic applications accepted.

**Shippensburg University of Pennsylvania,** School of Graduate Studies, College of Arts and Sciences, Department of Biology, Shippensburg, PA 17257-2299. Offers MS. *Program availability:* Part-time, evening/weekend. *Faculty:* 9 full-time (5 women). *Students:* 14 full-time (7 women), 10 part-time (7 women); includes 1 minority (Black or African American, non-Hispanic/Latino), 1 international. Average age 27. 30 applicants, 87% accepted, 14 enrolled. In 2019, 7 master's awarded. *Degree requirements:* For master's, thesis optional, oral thesis defense, seminar, minimum QPA of 3.0. *Entrance requirements:* For master's, minimum IELTS score of 6.5 or a TOEFL score of 80 (for international students), minimum GPA of 2.75; essay; 500-word statement of purpose; 33 credits of course work in biology; minimum of 3 courses with labs including both inorganic and organic chemistry or biochemistry; completion of math through calculus (including a statistics course) and/or a year of physics optional. Additional exam requirements/recommendations for international students: required—TOEFL (minimum score 80 iBT), IELTS (minimum score 6.5), TOEFL (minimum iBT score 80) or IELTS (minimum score 6.5). *Application deadline:* For fall admission, 4/30 for international students; for spring admission, 9/30 for international students. Applications are processed on a rolling basis. Application fee: $45. Electronic applications accepted. *Expenses:* Tuition, state resident: part-time $516 per credit. Tuition, nonresident: part-time $774 per credit. *Required fees:* $149 per credit. *Financial support:* In 2019–20, 12 students received support. Career-related internships or fieldwork, scholarships/grants, unspecified assistantships, and resident hall director and student payroll positions available. Support available to part-time students. Financial award application deadline: 3/1; financial award applicants required to submit FAFSA. *Unit head:* Dr. Tim J. Maret, Professor and Program Coordinator, 717-477-1401, Fax: 717-477-4064, E-mail: tjmare@ship.edu. *Application contact:* Maya T. Mapp, Director of Admissions, 717-477-1231, Fax: 717-477-4016, E-mail: mtmapp@ship.edu.
Website: http://www.ship.edu/biology/

**Simon Fraser University,** Office of Graduate Studies and Postdoctoral Fellows, Faculty of Science, Department of Biological Sciences, Burnaby, BC V5A 1S6, Canada. Offers bioinformatics (Graduate Diploma); biological sciences (M Sc, PhD); environmental toxicology (MET); pest management (MPM). *Degree requirements:* For master's, thesis; for doctorate, thesis/dissertation, candidacy exam; for Graduate Diploma, practicum. *Entrance requirements:* For master's, minimum GPA of 3.0 (on scale of 4.33) or 3.33 based on last 60 credits of undergraduate courses; for doctorate, minimum GPA of 3.5 (on scale of 4.33); for Graduate Diploma, minimum GPA of 2.5 (on scale of 4.33) or 2.67 based on last 60 credits of undergraduate courses. Additional exam requirements/recommendations for international students: recommended—TOEFL (minimum score 580 paper-based; 93 iBT), IELTS (minimum score 7), TWE (minimum score 5). Electronic applications accepted.

**Smith College,** Graduate and Special Programs, Department of Biological Sciences, Northampton, MA 01063. Offers MAT, MS. *Program availability:* Part-time. *Students:* 7 part-time (5 women); includes 1 minority (Black or African American, non-Hispanic/Latino), 1 international. Average age 29. 15 applicants, 40% accepted, 5 enrolled. In 2019, 2 master's awarded. *Degree requirements:* For master's, thesis (for some programs). *Entrance requirements:* Additional exam requirements/recommendations for international students: required—TOEFL (minimum score 595 paper-based; 97 iBT), IELTS (minimum score 7.5). *Application deadline:* For fall admission, 1/15 for domestic and international students. Application fee: $60. *Expenses: Tuition:* Full-time $36,940; part-time $1690 per credit. *Required fees:* $90. Full-time tuition and fees vary according to course load, degree level and program. *Financial support:* In 2019–20, 7 students received support, including 5 research assistantships with full tuition reimbursements available (averaging $13,850 per year); fellowships, scholarships/grants, and human resources employee benefit also available. Support available to part-time students. Financial award application deadline: 1/15; financial award applicants required to submit CSS PROFILE or FAFSA. *Unit head:* Jesse Bellemare, Graduate Student Advisor, 413-585-3812, E-mail: jbellema@smith.edu. *Application contact:* Ruth Morgan, Program Coordinator, 413-585-3050, Fax: 413-585-3054, E-mail: rmorgan@smith.edu.
Website: http://www.smith.edu/biology/

**Sonoma State University,** School of Science and Technology, Department of Biology, Rohnert Park, CA 94928. Offers biochemistry (MA). *Program availability:* Part-time. *Degree requirements:* For master's, thesis or alternative, oral exam. *Entrance requirements:* For master's, GRE General Test, GRE Subject Test, minimum GPA of 3.0. Additional exam requirements/recommendations for international students: required—TOEFL (minimum score 500 paper-based).

**South Carolina State University,** College of Graduate and Professional Studies, Department of Education, Orangeburg, SC 29117-0001. Offers early childhood education (MAT); education (M Ed); elementary education (M Ed, MAT); English (MAT); general science/biology (MAT); mathematics (MAT); secondary education (M Ed), including biology education, business education, counselor education, English education, home economics education, industrial education, mathematics education, science education, social studies education; special education (M Ed), including emotionally handicapped, learning disabilities, mentally handicapped. *Accreditation:* NCATE. *Program availability:* Part-time, evening/weekend. *Degree requirements:* For master's, thesis optional, departmental qualifying exam. *Entrance requirements:* For master's, GRE General Test, NTE, interview, teaching certificate. Electronic applications accepted.

**South Dakota State University,** Graduate School, College of Agriculture, Food and Environmental Sciences, Department of Animal Science, Brookings, SD 57007. Offers animal science (MS, PhD); biological sciences (PhD). *Program availability:* Part-time. *Degree requirements:* For master's, thesis, oral exam; for doctorate, comprehensive exam, thesis/dissertation, preliminary oral and written exams. *Entrance requirements:* Additional exam requirements/recommendations for international students: required—TOEFL (minimum score 550 paper-based; 79 iBT).

**South Dakota State University,** Graduate School, College of Agriculture, Food and Environmental Sciences, Department of Veterinary and Biomedical Sciences, Brookings, SD 57007. Offers biological sciences (MS, PhD). *Program availability:* Part-time, evening/weekend. *Degree requirements:* For master's, thesis (for some programs), oral exam; for doctorate, comprehensive exam, thesis/dissertation, preliminary oral and written exams. *Entrance requirements:* Additional exam requirements/recommendations for international students: required—TOEFL (minimum score 525 paper-based; 71 iBT).

**South Dakota State University,** Graduate School, College of Natural Sciences, Department of Biology and Microbiology, Brookings, SD 57007. Offers biological sciences (MS, PhD). *Program availability:* Part-time. *Degree requirements:* For master's, thesis (for some programs), oral exam; for doctorate, comprehensive exam, thesis/dissertation, oral exam. *Entrance requirements:* For master's and doctorate, GRE General Test. Additional exam requirements/recommendations for international students: required—TOEFL (minimum score 600 paper-based; 100 iBT).

**South Dakota State University,** Graduate School, College of Pharmacy and Allied Health Professions, Department of Pharmaceutical Sciences, Brookings, SD 57007. Offers biological science (MS); pharmaceutical sciences (PhD). *Degree requirements:* For master's, thesis, oral exam; for doctorate, comprehensive exam, thesis/dissertation, oral exam. *Entrance requirements:* For master's and doctorate, GRE General Test. Additional exam requirements/recommendations for international students: required—TOEFL (minimum score 550 paper-based).

**South Dakota State University,** Graduate School, Jerome J. Lohr College of Engineering, Department of Agricultural and Biosystems Engineering, Brookings, SD 57007. Offers biological sciences (MS, PhD); engineering (MS). *Program availability:* Part-time. *Degree requirements:* For master's, thesis (for some programs), oral exam; for doctorate, thesis/dissertation, preliminary oral and written exams. *Entrance requirements:* For master's and doctorate, engineering degree. Additional exam requirements/recommendations for international students: required—TOEFL (minimum score 550 paper-based; 79 iBT).

**Southeastern Louisiana University,** College of Science and Technology, Department of Biological Sciences, Hammond, LA 70402. Offers biological sciences (MS). *Faculty:* 13 full-time (6 women). *Students:* 23 full-time (16 women), 3 part-time (1 woman); includes 2 minority (1 Asian, non-Hispanic/Latino; 1 Hispanic/Latino), 1 international. Average age 25. 16 applicants, 100% accepted, 12 enrolled. In 2019, 11 master's awarded. *Degree requirements:* For master's, comprehensive exam, thesis optional. *Entrance requirements:* For master's, minimum GRE score of 297 on the GRE general exam (verbal and quantitative), minimum GPA of 3.0 (4.0 scale) for all undergrad work, minimum of 30 semester hours of undergrad biology courses, 2 letters of recommendation, CV, letter of intent. Additional exam requirements/recommendations for international students: required—TOEFL (minimum score 500 paper-based; 61 iBT). *Application deadline:* For fall admission, 2/1 priority date for domestic and international students; for spring admission, 12/1 priority date for domestic students, 10/1 priority date for international students. Applications are processed on a rolling basis. Application fee: $20 ($30 for international students). Electronic applications accepted. *Expenses: Tuition, area resident:* Full-time $6684; part-time $489 per credit hour. Tuition, state resident: full-time $6684; part-time $489 per credit hour. Tuition, nonresident: full-time $19,162; part-time $1183 per credit hour. *International tuition:* $19,162 full-time. *Required fees:* $2124. *Financial support:* In 2019–20, 26 students received support, including 1 fellowship with tuition reimbursement available (averaging $2,500 per year), 6 research assistantships with tuition reimbursements available (averaging $9,917 per year), 14 teaching assistantships with tuition reimbursements available (averaging $10,721 per year); career-related internships or fieldwork, institutionally sponsored loans, traineeships, and unspecified assistantships also available. Financial award application deadline: 5/1; financial award applicants required to submit FAFSA. *Unit head:* Dr. Christopher Beachy, Department Head, 985-549-3740, Fax: 985-549-3851, E-mail: biology@southeastern.edu. *Application contact:* Office of Admissions, 985-549-5637, Fax: 985-549-5632, E-mail: admissions@southeastern.edu.
Website: http://www.southeastern.edu/acad_research/depts/biol

**Southeast Missouri State University,** School of Graduate Studies, Department of Biology, Cape Girardeau, MO 63701-4799. Offers MNS. *Program availability:* Part-time. *Degree requirements:* For master's, comprehensive exam (for some programs), thesis (for some programs), thesis and oral defense, or research paper and comprehensive exam. *Entrance requirements:* For master's, minimum undergraduate GPA of 2.5, 2.75 in last 30 hours of undergraduate course work in science and mathematics; 2 letters of recommendation; faculty sponsor agreement. Additional exam requirements/recommendations for international students: required—TOEFL (minimum score 550 paper-based; 79 iBT), IELTS (minimum score 6), PTE (minimum score 53). Electronic applications accepted. *Expenses:* Tuition, state resident: full-time $6989; part-time $291.20 per credit hour. Tuition, nonresident: full-time $13,061; part-time $544.20 per credit hour. *International tuition:* $13,061 full-time. *Required fees:* $955; $39.80 per credit hour. Tuition and fees vary according to degree level.

**Southern Connecticut State University,** School of Graduate Studies, School of Arts and Sciences, Department of Biology, New Haven, CT 06515-1355. Offers MS. *Program availability:* Part-time, evening/weekend. *Degree requirements:* For master's, thesis optional. *Entrance requirements:* For master's, previous course work in biology, chemistry, and mathematics; interview. Electronic applications accepted.

**Southern Illinois University Carbondale,** Graduate School, College of Science, Biological Sciences Program, Carbondale, IL 62901-4701. Offers MS. *Degree requirements:* For master's, thesis or alternative. *Entrance requirements:* For master's,

GRE General Test, minimum GPA of 2.7. Additional exam requirements/recommendations for international students: required—TOEFL.

**Southern Illinois University Carbondale,** Graduate School, Graduate Programs in Medicine, Carbondale, IL 62901-4701. Offers molecular, cellular and systemic physiology (MS); molecular, cellular, and systemic physiology (PhD); pharmacology (MS, PhD); physician assistant studies (MSPA). Terminal master's awarded for partial completion of doctoral program. *Degree requirements:* For master's, thesis; for doctorate, thesis/dissertation. *Entrance requirements:* For master's, GRE, minimum GPA of 3.0; for doctorate, GRE, minimum GPA of 3.25. Additional exam requirements/recommendations for international students: required—TOEFL.

**Southern Illinois University Edwardsville,** Graduate School, College of Arts and Sciences, Department of Biological Sciences, Program in Biology, Edwardsville, IL 62026. Offers MA, MS. *Program availability:* Part-time, evening/weekend. *Degree requirements:* For master's, thesis (for some programs). *Entrance requirements:* For master's, GRE. Additional exam requirements/recommendations for international students: required—TOEFL (minimum score 550 paper-based; 79 iBT), IELTS (minimum score 6.5). Electronic applications accepted.

**Southern Methodist University,** Dedman College of Humanities and Sciences, Department of Biological Sciences, Dallas, TX 75275. Offers molecular and cellular biology (MA, MS, PhD). Terminal master's awarded for partial completion of doctoral program. *Degree requirements:* For master's, thesis (for MS), oral exam; for doctorate, thesis/dissertation, qualifying exam. *Entrance requirements:* For master's and doctorate, GRE General Test (minimum score 1200), minimum GPA of 3.0. Additional exam requirements/recommendations for international students: required—TOEFL (minimum score 550 paper-based). Electronic applications accepted.

**Southern University and Agricultural and Mechanical College,** Graduate School, College of Sciences and Engineering, Program in Biology, Baton Rouge, LA 70813. Offers MS. *Degree requirements:* For master's, comprehensive exam, thesis. *Entrance requirements:* For master's, GRE General Test. Additional exam requirements/recommendations for international students: required—TOEFL (minimum score 525 paper-based).

**Stanford University,** School of Humanities and Sciences, Department of Biology, Stanford, CA 94305-2004. Offers MS, PhD. *Expenses: Tuition:* Full-time $52,479; part-time $34,110 per unit. *Required fees:* $672; $224 per quarter. Tuition and fees vary according to program and student level. Website: http://www.stanford.edu/dept/biology/

**Stanford University,** School of Medicine, Graduate Programs in Medicine, Stanford, CA 94305-2004. Offers MS, PhD. *Expenses: Tuition:* Full-time $52,479; part-time $34,110 per unit. *Required fees:* $672; $224 per quarter. Tuition and fees vary according to program and student level.

**State University of New York at Fredonia,** College of Liberal Arts and Sciences, Fredonia, NY 14063-1136. Offers biology (MS); English (MA); English education 7-12 (MA); interdisciplinary studies (MA, MS); math education (MS Ed); professional writing (CAS); speech pathology (MS); MA/MS. *Program availability:* Part-time, evening/weekend. *Degree requirements:* For master's, comprehensive exam (for some programs), thesis (for some programs). *Entrance requirements:* For master's, GRE. Additional exam requirements/recommendations for international students: required—TOEFL (minimum score 79 iBT), IELTS (minimum score 6.5). Electronic applications accepted.

**State University of New York College at Oneonta,** Graduate Programs, Department of Biology, Oneonta, NY 13820-4015. Offers biology (MS); lake management (MS). *Program availability:* Part-time, evening/weekend. *Degree requirements:* For master's, comprehensive exam. *Entrance requirements:* For master's, GRE General Test, GRE Subject Test.

**State University of New York Downstate Medical Center,** School of Graduate Studies, Brooklyn, NY 11203-2098. Offers MS, PhD, MD/PhD. *Degree requirements:* For doctorate, thesis/dissertation. *Entrance requirements:* For doctorate, GRE. Additional exam requirements/recommendations for international students: required—TOEFL.

**State University of New York Upstate Medical University,** College of Graduate Studies, Syracuse, NY 13210. Offers MPH, MS, PhD, MD/PhD. Terminal master's awarded for partial completion of doctoral program. *Degree requirements:* For master's, thesis; for doctorate, comprehensive exam, thesis/dissertation. *Entrance requirements:* For master's, GRE General Test, interview; for doctorate, GRE General Test, telephone interview. Additional exam requirements/recommendations for international students: required—TOEFL. Electronic applications accepted.

**Stephen F. Austin State University,** Graduate School, College of Sciences and Mathematics, Department of Biology, Nacogdoches, TX 75962. Offers MS. *Degree requirements:* For master's, comprehensive exam, thesis optional. *Entrance requirements:* For master's, GRE General Test, minimum GPA of 2.8 in last 60 hours, 2.5 overall. Additional exam requirements/recommendations for international students: required—TOEFL.

**Stevenson University,** Master of Forensic Science, Stevenson, MD 21153. Offers biology (MS); chemistry (MS); crime scene investigation (MS). *Program availability:* Part-time. *Faculty:* 1 full-time (0 women), 12 part-time/adjunct (5 women). *Students:* 23 full-time (22 women), 61 part-time (52 women); includes 47 minority (31 Black or African American, non-Hispanic/Latino; 4 Asian, non-Hispanic/Latino; 8 Hispanic/Latino; 4 Two or more races, non-Hispanic/Latino). Average age 28. 53 applicants, 66% accepted, 24 enrolled. In 2019, 15 master's awarded. *Degree requirements:* For master's, thesis or alternative, thesis or a formal scientific paper. *Entrance requirements:* For master's, personal statement (3-5 paragraphs), official college transcript from degree-granting institution, bachelor's degree in a natural science from a regionally accredited institution, minimum cumulative GPA of 3.0 on a 4.0 scale in past academic work. *Application deadline:* For fall admission, 8/9 priority date for domestic students; for spring admission, 1/11 priority date for domestic students; for summer admission, 5/1 priority date for domestic students. Applications are processed on a rolling basis. Electronic applications accepted. *Expenses:* $695 per credit. *Financial support:* Unspecified assistantships available. Financial award applicants required to submit FAFSA. *Unit head:* Carolyn Johnson, Department Chair & Professor, 443-352-4074, E-mail: CHJOHNSON@stevenson.edu. *Application contact:* Amanda Millar, Director, Admissions, 443-333-3334, Fax: 443-394-0538, E-mail: amillar@stevenson.edu. Website: https://www.stevenson.edu/online/academics/online-graduate-programs/forensic-science/

**Stony Brook University, State University of New York,** Stony Brook Medicine, Renaissance School of Medicine and Graduate School, Graduate Programs in Medicine, Stony Brook, NY 11794. Offers MS, PhD, Advanced Certificate. *Students:* 122 full-time (69 women), 11 part-time (10 women); includes 57 minority (13 Black or African American, non-Hispanic/Latino; 21 Asian, non-Hispanic/Latino; 19 Hispanic/Latino; 4 Two or more races, non-Hispanic/Latino), 15 international. 162 applicants, 49% accepted, 53 enrolled. In 2019, 53 master's, 11 doctorates awarded. *Degree requirements:* For doctorate, thesis/dissertation, exam. *Entrance requirements:* For

doctorate, GRE General Test. Additional exam requirements/recommendations for international students: required—TOEFL. *Application deadline:* For fall admission, 1/15 for domestic students; for spring admission, 10/1 for domestic students. Application fee: $100. Electronic applications accepted. *Expenses:* Contact institution. *Financial support:* In 2019–20, 28 fellowships, 33 research assistantships were awarded; teaching assistantships, career-related internships or fieldwork, and Federal Work-Study also available. Financial award application deadline: 3/15. *Unit head:* Dr. Kenneth Kaushansky, Dean and Senior Vice President of Health Sciences, 631-444-2121, Fax: 631-632-6621. *Application contact:* Melissa Jordan, Assistant Dean, 631-632-9712, Fax: 631-632-7243, E-mail: melissa.jordan@stonybrook.edu.

**Stony Brook University, State University of New York,** Stony Brook Medicine, Renaissance School of Medicine, Medical Scientist Training Program, Stony Brook, NY 11794-8651. Offers MD/PhD. *Entrance requirements:* Additional exam requirements/recommendations for international students: required—TOEFL. *Application deadline:* For fall admission, 12/1 for domestic students. *Expenses: Tuition, area resident:* Full-time $11,310; part-time $471 per credit. Tuition, state resident: full-time $11,310; part-time $471 per credit. Tuition, nonresident: full-time $23,100; part-time $963 per credit. *International tuition:* $23,100 full-time. *Required fees:* $2247.50. *Financial support:* Tuition waivers (full) available. *Unit head:* Dr. Michael A. Frohman, Director, 631-444-3050, Fax: 631-444-9749, E-mail: michael.frohman@stonybrook.edu. *Application contact:* Alison Gibbons, Program Administrator, 631-444-3051, Fax: 631-444-3492, E-mail: alison.gibbons@stonybrook.edu. Website: https://renaissance.stonybrookmedicine.edu/mstp/program

**Sul Ross State University,** College of Arts and Sciences, Department of Biology, Alpine, TX 79832. Offers MS. *Program availability:* Part-time. *Degree requirements:* For master's, thesis optional. *Entrance requirements:* For master's, GRE General Test, minimum GPA of 2.5 in last 60 hours of undergraduate work.

**SUNY Brockport,** School of Arts and Sciences, Department of Biology, Brockport, NY 14420-2997. Offers MS, PSM. *Program availability:* Part-time. *Faculty:* 5 full-time (1 woman). *Students:* 7 full-time (3 women), 12 part-time (6 women); includes 4 minority (1 Black or African American, non-Hispanic/Latino; 3 Asian, non-Hispanic/Latino). 12 applicants, 67% accepted, 7 enrolled. In 2019, 5 master's awarded. *Degree requirements:* For master's, comprehensive exam, thesis or alternative. *Entrance requirements:* For master's, letters of recommendation, minimum GPA of 3.0, scientific writing sample, statement of objectives. Additional exam requirements/recommendations for international students: required—TOEFL (minimum score 550 paper-based; 79 iBT), IELTS (minimum score 6.5). *Application deadline:* For fall admission, 7/15 priority date for domestic and international students; for spring admission, 11/15 priority date for domestic and international students; for summer admission, 6/15 priority date for domestic and international students. Application fee: $50. Electronic applications accepted. *Expenses: Tuition, area resident:* Part-time $471 per credit hour. Tuition, nonresident: part-time $963 per credit hour. *Financial support:* In 2019–20, 8 teaching assistantships with full tuition reimbursements (averaging $6,000 per year) were awarded; Federal Work-Study, scholarships/grants, and unspecified assistantships also available. Support available to part-time students. Financial award application deadline: 3/15; financial award applicants required to submit FAFSA. *Unit head:* Dr. Rey Sia, Chairperson, 585-395-2783, Fax: 585-395-2741, E-mail: rsia@brockport.edu. *Application contact:* Dr. Adam Rich, Graduate Program Director, 585-395-5740, Fax: 585-395-2741, E-mail: arich@brockport.edu. Website: http://www.brockport.edu/biology/graduate/

**SUNY Brockport,** School of Education, Health, and Human Services, Department of Education and Human Development, Brockport, NY 14420-2997. Offers adolescence education (MS Ed), including adolescence biology education, adolescence chemistry education, adolescence English, adolescence mathematics, adolescence physics, adolescence physics education, adolescence social studies education; bilingual education (MS Ed, AGC); childhood curriculum specialist (MS Ed); inclusive generalist education (MS Ed, AGC, Advanced Certificate), including biology (MS Ed, AGC), chemistry (MS Ed), English (MS Ed, Advanced Certificate), mathematics (MS Ed, Advanced Certificate), science (MS Ed, Advanced Certificate), social studies (MS Ed, Advanced Certificate); literacy education B-12 (MS Ed). *Accreditation:* NCATE. *Faculty:* 15 full-time (11 women), 7 part-time/adjunct (4 women). *Students:* 68 full-time (38 women), 262 part-time (196 women); includes 9 minority (2 Black or African American, non-Hispanic/Latino; 1 American Indian or Alaska Native, non-Hispanic/Latino; 2 Asian, non-Hispanic/Latino; 4 Hispanic/Latino). 130 applicants, 77% accepted, 82 enrolled. In 2019, 107 master's, 13 AGCs awarded. *Entrance requirements:* For master's, minimum GPA of 3.0, letters of recommendation, interview (for some programs); statement of objectives, current resume. Additional exam requirements/recommendations for international students: required—TOEFL (minimum score 550 paper-based; 79 iBT), IELTS (minimum score 6.5). *Application deadline:* For fall admission, 3/15 priority date for domestic and international students; for spring admission, 10/15 priority date for domestic and international students; for summer admission, 3/15 priority date for domestic and international students. Application fee: $80. Electronic applications accepted. *Expenses: Tuition, area resident:* Part-time $471 per credit hour. Tuition, nonresident: part-time $963 per credit hour. *Financial support:* In 2019–20, 1 fellowship with full tuition reimbursement (averaging $7,500 per year), 1 teaching assistantship with full tuition reimbursement (averaging $6,000 per year) were awarded; Federal Work-Study, scholarships/grants, and unspecified assistantships also available. Support available to part-time students. Financial award application deadline: 3/15; financial award applicants required to submit FAFSA. *Unit head:* Dr. Janka Szilagyi, Chairperson, 585-395-5945, Fax: 585-395-2172, E-mail: jszilagy@brockport.edu. *Application contact:* Buffie Edick, Graduate Program Director, 585-395-2326, Fax: 585-395-2172, E-mail: bedick@brockport.edu. Website: https://www.brockport.edu/academics/education_human_development/department.html

**Syracuse University,** College of Arts and Sciences, Department of Biology, Syracuse, NY 13244. Offers biology (MS, PhD); neuroscience (PhD). Terminal master's awarded for partial completion of doctoral program. *Entrance requirements:* For master's and doctorate, GRE General Test, GRE Subject Test (recommended), BS or BA, at least a minimal background in both physical and biological sciences, three letters of recommendation, personal statement, transcripts. Additional exam requirements/recommendations for international students: required—TOEFL (minimum score 100 iBT). Electronic applications accepted.

**Syracuse University,** School of Education, Programs in Science Education, Syracuse, NY 13244. Offers biology (MS); chemistry (MS, PhD). *Program availability:* Part-time. *Degree requirements:* For doctorate, comprehensive exam, thesis/dissertation. *Entrance requirements:* For master's, GRE General Test or MAT, official transcripts from previous academic institutions, 3 letters of recommendation (preferably from faculty), personal statement that makes a clear and compelling argument for why applicant wants to teach secondary science; for doctorate, GRE General Test or MAT, master's degree, interview. Additional exam requirements/recommendations for international students: required—TOEFL (minimum score 100 iBT). Electronic applications accepted.

**Tarleton State University,** College of Graduate Studies, College of Science and Technology, Department of Biological Sciences, Stephenville, TX 76402. Offers biology

(MS). *Program availability:* Part-time. *Faculty:* 9 full-time (3 women). *Students:* 9 full-time (6 women), 20 part-time (14 women); includes 9 minority (3 Black or African American, non-Hispanic/Latino; 4 Hispanic/Latino; 2 Two or more races, non-Hispanic/Latino), 1 international. Average age 26. 11 applicants, 64% accepted, 5 enrolled. In 2019, 4 master's awarded. *Degree requirements:* For master's, comprehensive exam, thesis (for some programs). *Entrance requirements:* For master's, GRE General Test, minimum GPA of 2.5. Additional exam requirements/recommendations for international students: required—TOEFL (minimum score 520 paper-based; 69 iBT); recommended—IELTS (minimum score 6), TSE (minimum score 50). *Application deadline:* For fall admission, 8/15 priority date for domestic students; for spring admission, 1/7 for domestic students. Applications are processed on a rolling basis. Application fee: $50 ($130 for international students). Electronic applications accepted. *Expenses:* Tuition, state resident: part-time $221.73 per credit hour. Tuition, nonresident: part-time $636.73 per credit hour. *Required fees:* $198 per credit hour. $100 per semester. Tuition and fees vary according to degree level. *Financial support:* Research assistantships, teaching assistantships, career-related internships or fieldwork, and Federal Work-Study available. Support available to part-time students. Financial award application deadline: 5/1; financial award applicants required to submit FAFSA. *Unit head:* Dr. Max Sanderford, Department Head, 254-968-9162, E-mail: sanderford@tarleton.edu. *Application contact:* Wendy Weiss, Graduate Admissions Coordinator, 254-968-9104, Fax: 254-968-9670, E-mail: weiss@tarleton.edu.
Website: https://www.tarleton.edu/biology/index.html

**Teachers College, Columbia University,** Department of Mathematics, Science and Technology, New York, NY 10027-6696. Offers biology 7-12 (MA); chemistry 7-12 (MA); communication and education (MA, Ed D); computing in education (MA); earth science 7-12 (MA); instructional technology and media (Ed M, MA, Ed D); mathematics education (Ed M, MA, Ed D, Ed DCT, PhD); physics 7-12 (MA); science and dental education (MA); science education (Ed M, MS, Ed DCT, PhD); supervisor/teacher of science education (MA); technology specialist (MA). *Faculty:* 13 full-time (8 women). *Students:* 166 full-time (124 women), 188 part-time (113 women); includes 122 minority (40 Black or African American, non-Hispanic/Latino; 1 American Indian or Alaska Native, non-Hispanic/Latino; 50 Asian, non-Hispanic/Latino; 23 Hispanic/Latino; 8 Two or more races, non-Hispanic/Latino), 120 international. 476 applicants, 51% accepted, 125 enrolled. *Unit head:* Dr. Erica Walker, Chair, 212-678-8246, E-mail: ewalker@tc.edu. *Application contact:* Kelly Sutton Skinner, Director of Admission and New Student Enrollment, 212-678-3710, E-mail: kms2237@tc.columbia.edu.
Website: http://www.tc.columbia.edu/mathematics-science-and-technology/

**Temple University,** College of Science and Technology, Department of Biology, Philadelphia, PA 19122-6096. Offers biology (MS, PSM, PhD); biotechnology (MS). *Program availability:* Part-time. *Faculty:* 45 full-time (16 women), 1 part-time/adjunct (0 women). *Students:* 95 full-time (47 women), 13 part-time (4 women); includes 30 minority (3 Black or African American, non-Hispanic/Latino; 17 Asian, non-Hispanic/Latino; 8 Hispanic/Latino; 2 Two or more races, non-Hispanic/Latino), 22 international. 99 applicants, 62% accepted, 34 enrolled. In 2019, 29 master's, 3 doctorates awarded. *Degree requirements:* For master's, thesis (for some programs); for doctorate, thesis/dissertation. *Entrance requirements:* For master's, GRE (optional for P.S.M. in Biotechnology), baccalaureate degree in a related discipline, statement of goals, letters of recommendation; for doctorate, GRE, statement of goals, baccalaureate degree in a related discipline, 3 letters of recommendation. Additional exam requirements/recommendations for international students: required—TOEFL (minimum score 90 iBT), IELTS (minimum score 6.5), PTE (minimum score 61), one of three is required. Application fee: $60. *Expenses:* Contact institution. *Financial support:* Fellowships, research assistantships, teaching assistantships, Federal Work-Study, and health care benefits available. Financial award applicants required to submit FAFSA. *Unit head:* Robert W Sanders, Chairperson/Professor, 215-204-2056, E-mail: robert.sanders@temple.edu. *Application contact:* Richard Waring, Graduate Chair, 215-204-7119, E-mail: richard.waring@temple.edu.
Website: https://bio.cst.temple.edu/

**Temple University,** Lewis Katz School of Medicine, Philadelphia, PA 19122-6096. Offers biomedical sciences (MS); MD/MA; MD/MBA; MD/MPH; MD/PhD. *Faculty:* 22 full-time (9 women). *Students:* 994 full-time (542 women), 24 part-time (19 women); includes 438 minority (108 Black or African American, non-Hispanic/Latino; 186 Asian, non-Hispanic/Latino; 117 Hispanic/Latino; 1 Native Hawaiian or other Pacific Islander, non-Hispanic/Latino; 26 Two or more races, non-Hispanic/Latino), 23 international. 8,346 applicants, 6% accepted, 248 enrolled. In 2019, 44 master's, 214 doctorates awarded. Terminal master's awarded for partial completion of doctoral program. *Entrance requirements:* For doctorate, MCAT (for MD). Additional exam requirements/recommendations for international students: required—TOEFL, IELTS, PTE, one of three is required. Application fee: $60. Electronic applications accepted. *Expenses:* Contact institution. *Financial support:* Fellowships, research assistantships, Federal Work-Study, institutionally sponsored loans, scholarships/grants, and health care benefits available. Financial award applicants required to submit FAFSA. *Unit head:* Larry R. Kaiser, Dean, 215-707-8773, E-mail: sks@temple.edu. *Application contact:* Jacob Ufberg, Associate Dean of Admissions, 215-707-5308, E-mail: medadmissions@temple.edu.
Website: http://www.temple.edu/medicine/

**Tennessee State University,** The School of Graduate Studies and Research, College of Agriculture, Human and Natural Sciences, Department of Biological Sciences, Nashville, TN 37209-1561. Offers PhD. *Degree requirements:* For doctorate, thesis/dissertation. *Entrance requirements:* For doctorate, GRE General Test, GRE Subject Test.

**Tennessee Technological University,** College of Graduate Studies, College of Arts and Sciences, Department of Biology, Cookeville, TN 38505. Offers fish, game, and wildlife management (MS). *Program availability:* Part-time. *Faculty:* 22 full-time (2 women). *Students:* 4 full-time (0 women), 20 part-time (8 women), 1 international. 14 applicants, 57% accepted, 6 enrolled. In 2019, 8 master's awarded. *Degree requirements:* For master's, thesis. *Entrance requirements:* For master's, GRE. Additional exam requirements/recommendations for international students: required—TOEFL (minimum score 527 paper-based; 71 iBT), IELTS (minimum score 5.5), PTE (minimum score 48), or TOEIC (Test of English as an International Communication). *Application deadline:* For fall admission, 8/1 for domestic students, 5/1 for international students; for spring admission, 12/1 for domestic students, 10/1 for international students; for summer admission, 5/1 for domestic students, 2/1 for international students. Applications are processed on a rolling basis. Application fee: $35 ($40 for international students). Electronic applications accepted. *Expenses: Tuition, area resident:* Part-time $597 per credit hour. Tuition, state resident: part-time $597 per credit hour. Tuition, nonresident: part-time $1323 per credit hour. *Financial support:* In 2019–20, 7 research assistantships, 14 teaching assistantships (averaging $7,500 per year) were awarded. Financial award application deadline: 4/1. *Unit head:* Dr. Chris Brown, Interim Chairperson, 931-372-3134, Fax: 931-372-6257, E-mail: cabrown@tntech.edu. *Application contact:* Shelia K. Kendrick, Coordinator of Graduate Studies, 931-372-3808, Fax: 931-372-3497, E-mail: skendrick@tntech.edu.

**Tennessee Technological University,** College of Graduate Studies, College of Interdisciplinary Studies, School of Environmental Studies, Department of Environmental Sciences, Cookeville, TN 38505. Offers agriculture (PhD); biology (PhD); chemistry (PhD); geosciences (PhD); integrated research (PhD). *Program availability:* Part-time. *Students:* 4 full-time (3 women), 20 part-time (11 women); includes 3 minority (1 Asian, non-Hispanic/Latino; 2 Two or more races, non-Hispanic/Latino), 4 international. 22 applicants, 73% accepted, 10 enrolled. In 2019, 5 doctorates awarded. *Degree requirements:* For doctorate, comprehensive exam, thesis/dissertation. *Entrance requirements:* For doctorate, GRE. Additional exam requirements/recommendations for international students: required—TOEFL (minimum score 527 paper-based; 71 iBT), IELTS (minimum score 5.5), PTE (minimum score 48), or TOEIC (Test of English as an International Communication). *Application deadline:* For fall admission, 7/1 for domestic students, 5/1 for international students; for spring admission, 12/1 for domestic students, 10/2 for international students; for summer admission, 5/1 for domestic students, 2/1 for international students. Applications are processed on a rolling basis. Application fee: $35 ($40 for international students). Electronic applications accepted. *Expenses: Tuition, area resident:* Part-time $597 per credit hour. Tuition, state resident: part-time $597 per credit hour. Tuition, nonresident: part-time $1323 per credit hour. *Financial support:* Fellowships, research assistantships, and teaching assistantships available. Financial award application deadline: 4/1. *Unit head:* Dr. Hayden Mattingly, Interim Director, 931-372-6246, E-mail: hmattingly@tntech.edu. *Application contact:* Shelia K. Kendrick, Coordinator of Graduate Studies, 931-372-3808, Fax: 931-372-3497, E-mail: skendrick@tntech.edu.

**Texas A&M International University,** Office of Graduate Studies and Research, College of Arts and Sciences, Department of Biology and Chemistry, Laredo, TX 78041. Offers biology (MS). *Degree requirements:* For master's, comprehensive exam, thesis (for some programs). *Entrance requirements:* Additional exam requirements/recommendations for international students: required—TOEFL (minimum score 79 iBT).

**Texas A&M University,** College of Science, Department of Biology, College Station, TX 77843. Offers biology (PhD); microbiology (MS, PhD). *Faculty:* 36. *Students:* 124 full-time (64 women), 7 part-time (3 women); includes 20 minority (3 Black or African American, non-Hispanic/Latino; 1 American Indian or Alaska Native, non-Hispanic/Latino; 5 Asian, non-Hispanic/Latino; 10 Hispanic/Latino; 1 Two or more races, non-Hispanic/Latino), 44 international. Average age 28. 91 applicants, 57% accepted, 40 enrolled. In 2019, 4 master's, 9 doctorates awarded. *Degree requirements:* For master's, comprehensive exam (for some programs), thesis optional; for doctorate, comprehensive exam, thesis/dissertation. *Entrance requirements:* For master's and doctorate, statement of purpose, letters of recommendation, curriculum vitae. Additional exam requirements/recommendations for international students: required—TOEFL. *Application deadline:* For fall admission, 12/1 for domestic students. Application fee: $65 ($90 for international students). Electronic applications accepted. *Expenses:* Contact institution. *Financial support:* In 2019–20, 126 students received support, including 12 fellowships with tuition reimbursements available (averaging $25,944 per year), 60 research assistantships with tuition reimbursements available (averaging $14,952 per year), 80 teaching assistantships with tuition reimbursements available (averaging $6,789 per year); career-related internships or fieldwork, institutionally sponsored loans, scholarships/grants, traineeships, health care benefits, tuition waivers (full and partial), and unspecified assistantships also available. Support available to part-time students. Financial award application deadline: 4/1; financial award applicants required to submit FAFSA. *Unit head:* Dr. Tom McKnight, Department Head, 979-845-3896, Fax: 979-845-2891, E-mail: mcknight@bio.tamu.edu. *Application contact:* Dr. Rene Garcia, Professor & Graduate Advisor, 979-845-2989, E-mail: gradadvising@bio.tamu.edu.
Website: http://www.bio.tamu.edu/

**Texas A&M University–Commerce,** College of Science and Engineering, Commerce, TX 75429. Offers biological sciences (MS); broadfield science biology (MS); broadfield science chemistry (MS); broadfield science physics (MS); chemistry (MS); computational linguistics (Graduate Certificate); computational science (MS); computer science (MS); environmental science (Graduate Certificate); mathematics (MS); physics (MS); technology management (MS). *Program availability:* Part-time. *Faculty:* 38 full-time (7 women), 6 part-time/adjunct (0 women). *Students:* 118 full-time (53 women), 197 part-time (86 women); includes 71 minority (18 Black or African American, non-Hispanic/Latino; 1 American Indian or Alaska Native, non-Hispanic/Latino; 12 Asian, non-Hispanic/Latino; 32 Hispanic/Latino; 8 Two or more races, non-Hispanic/Latino), 118 international. Average age 31. 303 applicants, 70% accepted, 99 enrolled. In 2019, 226 master's awarded. *Degree requirements:* For master's, comprehensive exam, thesis optional. *Entrance requirements:* For master's, GRE, official transcripts, letters of recommendation, resume, statement of goals. Additional exam requirements/recommendations for international students: required—TOEFL (minimum score 550 paper-based; 79 iBT), IELTS (minimum score 6), PTE (minimum score 53). *Application deadline:* For fall admission, 6/1 priority date for international students; for spring admission, 10/15 priority date for international students; for summer admission, 3/15 priority date for international students. Applications are processed on a rolling basis. Application fee: $50 ($75 for international students). Electronic applications accepted. *Expenses:* Contact institution. *Financial support:* In 2019–20, 56 students received support, including 47 research assistantships with partial tuition reimbursements available (averaging $3,080 per year), 130 teaching assistantships with partial tuition reimbursements available (averaging $3,359 per year); scholarships/grants, health care benefits, and unspecified assistantships also available. Financial award application deadline: 5/1; financial award applicants required to submit FAFSA. *Unit head:* Dr. Brent L. Donham, Dean, 903-886-5321, Fax: 903-886-5199, E-mail: brent.donham@tamuc.edu. *Application contact:* Dayla Burgin, Graduate Student Services Coordinator, 903-886-5134, E-mail: dayla.burgin@tamuc.edu.
Website: https://new.tamuc.edu/science-engineering/

**Texas A&M University–Corpus Christi,** College of Graduate Studies, College of Science and Engineering, Program in Biology, Corpus Christi, TX 78412. Offers MS, PhD. *Program availability:* Part-time, evening/weekend. *Degree requirements:* For master's, comprehensive exam, thesis. *Entrance requirements:* For master's, GRE (taken within 5 years), essay (up to 1,000 words), 3 letters of recommendation. Additional exam requirements/recommendations for international students: required—TOEFL (minimum score 550 paper-based; 79 iBT), IELTS (minimum score 6.5). Electronic applications accepted.

**Texas A&M University–Kingsville,** College of Graduate Studies, College of Arts and Sciences, Department of Biological and Health Sciences, Kingsville, TX 78363. Offers biology (MS). *Entrance requirements:* Additional exam requirements/recommendations for international students: required—TOEFL (minimum score 550 paper-based; 79 iBT); recommended—IELTS (minimum score 6). Electronic applications accepted.

**Texas Christian University,** College of Science and Engineering, Department of Biology, Fort Worth, TX 76129-0002. Offers MA, MS, PhD. *Program availability:* Part-time. *Faculty:* 14 full-time (4 women). *Students:* 21 full-time (11 women); includes 2 minority (1 Asian, non-Hispanic/Latino; 1 Hispanic/Latino), 2 international. Average age 27. 18 applicants, 61% accepted, 11 enrolled. In 2019, 10 master's awarded. *Degree requirements:* For master's, thesis (for some programs); for doctorate, thesis/dissertation. *Entrance requirements:* For master's, GRE General Test. Additional exam

requirements/recommendations for international students: required—TOEFL (minimum score 560 paper-based). *Application deadline:* For fall admission, 1/1 priority date for domestic students, 1/15 for international students; for spring admission, 9/15 priority date for domestic students, 8/15 for international students. Applications are processed on a rolling basis. Application fee: $60. Electronic applications accepted. Full-time tuition and fees vary according to program. *Financial support:* In 2019–20, 20 students received support, including 19 teaching assistantships with full tuition reimbursements available (averaging $16,500 per year); scholarships/grants also available. Financial award application deadline: 1/1. *Unit head:* Dr. Giri Akkaraju, Chairperson, 817-257-8777, E-mail: g.akkaraju@tcu.edu. *Application contact:* Dr. Amanda Hale, Professor, 817-257-6182, E-mail: a.hale@tcu.edu.
Website: http://www.bio.tcu.edu/

**Texas Southern University,** School of Science and Technology, Department of Biology, Houston, TX 77004-4584. Offers MS. *Program availability:* Part-time, evening/weekend. *Degree requirements:* For master's, one foreign language, comprehensive exam, thesis. *Entrance requirements:* For master's, GRE General Test, minimum GPA of 2.5. Additional exam requirements/recommendations for international students: required—TOEFL. Electronic applications accepted.

**Texas State University,** The Graduate College, College of Science and Engineering, Program in Biology, San Marcos, TX 78666. Offers MA, MS. *Program availability:* Part-time. *Degree requirements:* For master's, comprehensive exam, thesis (for some programs). *Entrance requirements:* For master's, official GRE (general test only) required with competitive scores in the verbal reasoning and quantitative reasoning sections, baccalaureate degree in biology or related discipline from regionally-accredited university with minimum GPA of 3.0 on last 60 undergraduate semester hours, current curriculum vitae, statement of purpose with aspirations and academic goals, 3 letters of recommendation, thesis only students letter of intent to mentor from Biology Faculty member. Additional exam requirements/recommendations for international students: required—TOEFL (minimum score 550 paper-based; 78 iBT), IELTS (minimum score 6.5). Electronic applications accepted.

**Texas Tech University,** Graduate School, College of Arts and Sciences, Department of Biological Sciences, Lubbock, TX 79409-3131. Offers biology (MS, PhD); environmental sustainability and natural resource management (PSM); microbiology (MS); zoology (MS, PhD). *Program availability:* Part-time, blended/hybrid learning. *Faculty:* 45 full-time (16 women). *Students:* 131 full-time (71 women), 21 part-time (12 women); includes 22 minority (4 Black or African American, non-Hispanic/Latino; 1 Asian, non-Hispanic/Latino; 11 Hispanic/Latino; 6 Two or more races, non-Hispanic/Latino), 66 international. Average age 29. 80 applicants, 48% accepted, 34 enrolled. In 2019, 13 master's, 6 doctorates awarded. *Degree requirements:* For master's, comprehensive exam, thesis or alternative; for doctorate, comprehensive exam, thesis/dissertation. *Entrance requirements:* For master's and doctorate, GRE General Test. Additional exam requirements/recommendations for international students: required—TOEFL (minimum score 550 paper-based; 79 iBT). *Application deadline:* For fall admission, 6/1 priority date for domestic students, 1/15 priority date for international students; for spring admission, 9/1 priority date for domestic students, 6/15 priority date for international students. Applications are processed on a rolling basis. Application fee: $65. Electronic applications accepted. *Expenses:* Contact institution. *Financial support:* In 2019–20, 140 students received support, including 114 fellowships (averaging $1,560 per year), 22 research assistantships (averaging $19,738 per year), 114 teaching assistantships (averaging $17,489 per year); Federal Work-Study and health care benefits also available. Financial award application deadline: 2/15; financial award applicants required to submit FAFSA. *Unit head:* Dr. John Zak, Professor, Chair and Associate Dean, 806-834-2682, Fax: 806-742-2963, E-mail: john.zak@ttu.edu. *Application contact:* Dr. Lou Densmore, Graduate Adviser, 806-834-6479, Fax: 806-742-2963, E-mail: lou.densmore@ttu.edu.
Website: www.depts.ttu.edu/biology/

**Texas Tech University Health Sciences Center,** Graduate School of Biomedical Sciences, Lubbock, TX 79430-0002. Offers MS, PhD, MD/PhD, MS/PhD. Terminal master's awarded for partial completion of doctoral program. *Degree requirements:* For master's, thesis; for doctorate, thesis/dissertation. *Entrance requirements:* For master's and doctorate, GRE General Test, minimum GPA of 3.0. Additional exam requirements/recommendations for international students: required—TOEFL (minimum score 550 paper-based). Electronic applications accepted.

**Texas Tech University Health Sciences Center El Paso,** Graduate School of Biomedical Sciences, El Paso, TX 79905. Offers MS.

**Texas Woman's University,** Graduate School, College of Arts and Sciences, Department of Biology, Denton, TX 76204. Offers biology (MS); molecular biology (PhD). *Program availability:* Part-time. *Faculty:* 14 full-time (10 women). *Students:* 2 full-time (both women), 29 part-time (21 women); includes 3 minority (1 Asian, non-Hispanic/Latino; 2 Hispanic/Latino), 20 international. Average age 34. 18 applicants, 11% accepted, 1 enrolled. In 2019, 16 master's, 3 doctorates awarded. Terminal master's awarded for partial completion of doctoral program. *Degree requirements:* For master's, thesis or alternative, professional paper or thesis; oral defense of thesis or professional paper; for doctorate, comprehensive exam, thesis/dissertation, 1-year residency; dissertation defense and oral exam by the dissertation committee. *Entrance requirements:* For master's, 3 letters of reference; letter of interest; for doctorate, 3 letters of reference, letter of interest, bachelor's degree in Biology. Additional exam requirements/recommendations for international students: required—TOEFL (minimum score 79 iBT); recommended—IELTS (minimum score 7.5), TSE (minimum score 53). *Application deadline:* For fall admission, 4/1 for domestic and international students; for spring admission, 11/1 for domestic and international students. Application fee: $50 ($75 for international students). Electronic applications accepted. *Expenses:* All are estimates. Tuition for 10 hours = $2,763; Fees for 10 hours = $1,342. Biology courses require an additional $25/SCH not included in the estimates above. *Financial support:* In 2019–20, 21 students received support, including 7 research assistantships (averaging $15,715 per year), 12 teaching assistantships (averaging $12,657 per year); career-related internships or fieldwork, health care benefits, and unspecified assistantships also available. Support available to part-time students. Financial award application deadline: 3/1; financial award applicants required to submit FAFSA. *Unit head:* Dr. Juliet Spencer, Chair, 940-898-2351, Fax: 940-898-2382, E-mail: biology@twu.edu. *Application contact:* Korie Hawkins, Associate Director of Admissions, Graduate Recruitment, 940-898-3188, Fax: 940-898-3081, E-mail: admissions@twu.edu.
Website: http://www.twu.edu/biology

**Thomas Jefferson University,** Jefferson College of Life Sciences, Philadelphia, PA 19107. Offers MS, PhD, Certificate, MD/PhD. *Program availability:* Part-time, evening/weekend. Terminal master's awarded for partial completion of doctoral program. *Degree requirements:* For master's, thesis; for doctorate, comprehensive exam, thesis/dissertation. *Entrance requirements:* For master's, GRE or MCAT; for doctorate, GRE or MCAT, minimum GPA of 3.2. Additional exam requirements/recommendations for international students: required—TOEFL (minimum score 100 iBT), IELTS (minimum score 7). Electronic applications accepted.

**Towson University,** Jess and Mildred Fisher College of Science and Mathematics, Program in Biology, Towson, MD 21252-0001. Offers MS. *Program availability:* Part-time, evening/weekend. *Students:* 17 full-time (10 women), 26 part-time (9 women); includes 21 minority (9 Black or African American, non-Hispanic/Latino; 4 Asian, non-Hispanic/Latino; 7 Hispanic/Latino; 1 Two or more races, non-Hispanic/Latino), 4 international. *Entrance requirements:* For master's, GRE General Test (for thesis students), minimum GPA of 3.0; 24 credits in related course work; 3 letters of recommendation; minimum 24 units in biology; coursework in chemistry, organic chemistry, and physics; personal statement; official transcripts. *Application deadline:* For fall admission, 1/17 for domestic students, 5/15 for international students; for spring admission, 10/15 for domestic students, 12/1 for international students. Applications are processed on a rolling basis. Application fee: $45. Electronic applications accepted. *Expenses: Tuition, area resident:* Full-time $7920; part-time $439 per credit. Tuition, nonresident: full-time $16,344; part-time $908 per credit. *International tuition:* $16,344 full-time. *Required fees:* $2628; $146 per credit. $876 per term. *Financial support:* Application deadline: 4/1. *Unit head:* Dr. Peko Tsuji, Program Director, 410-704-4117, E-mail: ptsuji@towson.edu. *Application contact:* Coverley Beidleman, Assistant Director of Graduate Admissions, 410-704-5630, Fax: 410-704-3030, E-mail: grads@towson.edu.
Website: https://www.towson.edu/fcsm/departments/biology/gradbiology/

**Trent University,** Graduate Studies, Program in Applications of Modeling in the Natural and Social Sciences, Peterborough, ON K9J 7B8, Canada. Offers applications of modeling in the natural and social sciences (MA); biology (M Sc, PhD); chemistry (M Sc); computer studies (M Sc); geography (M Sc, PhD); physics (M Sc). *Program availability:* Part-time. *Degree requirements:* For master's, thesis. *Entrance requirements:* For master's, honours degree.

**Trent University,** Graduate Studies, Program in Environmental and Life Sciences, Department of Biology, Peterborough, ON K9J 7B8, Canada. Offers M Sc, PhD. *Program availability:* Part-time. *Degree requirements:* For master's, thesis; for doctorate, thesis/dissertation. *Entrance requirements:* For master's, honours degree; for doctorate, master's degree.

**Troy University,** Graduate School, College of Arts and Sciences, Program in Biomedical Sciences, Troy, AL 36082. Offers MS, Certificate. *Program availability:* Part-time, evening/weekend. *Faculty:* 2 full-time (1 woman). *Students:* 4 full-time (2 women), 14 part-time (8 women); includes 6 minority (5 Black or African American, non-Hispanic/Latino; 1 Asian, non-Hispanic/Latino), 3 international. Average age 27. 8 applicants, 50% accepted, 4 enrolled. In 2019, 8 master's awarded. *Degree requirements:* For master's, comprehensive exam. *Entrance requirements:* For master's, GRE 290 (recommended:150 verbal, 140 quantitative) and GRE writing score. If student has taken the MCAT (recommended: 487), DAT (recommended: 16) or equivalent professional exam, then this may be substituted for the GRE, Official transcripts; Bachelor's degree from a regionally accredited college of university and achieved a minimum of 2.5 GPA in all undergraduate courses; Two letters of recommendations and 500-word personal statement that addresses applicant's professional goals. Additional exam requirements/recommendations for international students: required—TOEFL (minimum score 523 paper-based; 70 iBT), IELTS (minimum score 6). *Application deadline:* For fall admission, 6/1 for international students; for spring admission, 10/15 for international students. Applications are processed on a rolling basis. Application fee: $50. Electronic applications accepted. *Expenses: Tuition, area resident:* Full-time $7650; part-time $2550 per semester hour. Tuition, state resident: full-time $7650; part-time $2550 per semester hour. Tuition, nonresident: full-time $15,300; part-time $5100 per semester hour. *International tuition:* $15,300 full-time. *Required fees:* $856; $352 per semester hour. $176 per semester. *Financial support:* In 2019–20, 6 students received support. Fellowships, research assistantships, teaching assistantships, career-related internships or fieldwork, Federal Work-Study, scholarships/grants, traineeships, tuition waivers, and unspecified assistantships available. Support available to part-time students. Financial award application deadline: 3/1; financial award applicants required to submit FAFSA. *Unit head:* Dr. Sig Harden, Division Chair, 334-670-3660, Fax: 334-670-3626, E-mail: sbharden@troy.edu. *Application contact:* Haley McKinnon, Director of Graduate Admissions, 334-670-3178, Fax: 334-670-3912, E-mail: hmckinnon@troy.edu.
Website: https://www.troy.edu/academics/academic-programs/biology-biomedical-sciences.html

**Truett McConnell University,** Pilgram Marpeck School of Science, Technology, Engineering and Mathematics, Cleveland, GA 30528. Offers biology (MS). *Program availability:* Part-time. *Students:* 3 full-time (1 woman); includes 1 minority (Hispanic/Latino). Average age 26. 2 applicants. *Degree requirements:* For master's, thesis. *Entrance requirements:* For master's, GRE, minimum STEM GPA of 3.0, personal statement, letters of recommendation, GRE test in the 55th percentile, min of 24 hours in biology. *Application deadline:* For fall admission, 8/1 for domestic students; for spring admission, 12/1 for domestic students; for summer admission, 5/1 for domestic students. Applications are processed on a rolling basis. Electronic applications accepted. *Expenses: Tuition:* Full-time $6300; part-time $350 per credit hour. *Required fees:* $1010; $1010. Tuition and fees vary according to course load. *Financial support:* Applicants required to submit FAFSA. *Unit head:* Dr. Robert Bowen, Dean, 706-865-2134 Ext. 6400, E-mail: rbowen@truett.edu. *Application contact:* Timothy Agee, Graduate Admissions Coordinator, 706-865-2134 Ext. 4305, E-mail: tagee@truett.edu.
Website: https://truett.edu/degrees/master-science-biology/

**Tufts University,** Cummings School of Veterinary Medicine, North Grafton, MA 01536. Offers animals and public policy (MS); biomedical sciences (PhD), including digestive diseases, infectious diseases, neuroscience and reproductive biology, pathology; conservation medicine (MS); veterinary medicine (DVM); DVM/MPH; DVM/MS. *Accreditation:* AVMA (one or more programs are accredited). *Degree requirements:* For master's, thesis (for some programs); for doctorate, comprehensive exam, thesis/dissertation (for some programs). *Entrance requirements:* For master's and doctorate, GRE General Test. Additional exam requirements/recommendations for international students: required—TOEFL or IELTS. Electronic applications accepted. *Expenses:* Contact institution.

**Tufts University,** Graduate School of Arts and Sciences, Department of Biology, Medford, MA 02155. Offers biology (MS, PhD); soft materials robotics (PhD). *Program availability:* Part-time. Terminal master's awarded for partial completion of doctoral program. *Degree requirements:* For master's, thesis (for some programs); for doctorate, comprehensive exam, thesis/dissertation. *Entrance requirements:* For master's and doctorate, GRE General Test. Additional exam requirements/recommendations for international students: required—TOEFL (minimum score 550 paper-based; 80 iBT), IELTS (minimum score 6.5). Electronic applications accepted. *Expenses:* Contact institution.

**Tufts University,** Graduate School of Biomedical Sciences, Boston, MA 02111. Offers MS, PhD, Certificate, DVM/PhD, MD/PhD. *Faculty:* 197 full-time (72 women), 17 part-time/adjunct (4 women). *Students:* 208 full-time (125 women), 1 part-time; includes 50 minority (7 Black or African American, non-Hispanic/Latino; 23 Asian, non-Hispanic/Latino; 12 Hispanic/Latino; 8 Two or more races, non-Hispanic/Latino), 48 international. Average age 32. 788 applicants, 50 enrolled. In 2019, 24 master's, 34 doctorates

awarded. Terminal master's awarded for partial completion of doctoral program. *Degree requirements:* For master's, comprehensive exam (for some programs), thesis; for doctorate, thesis/dissertation. *Entrance requirements:* For master's, GRE General Test, letters of reference, resume, personal statement; for doctorate and Certificate, letters of reference, resume, personal statement. Additional exam requirements/recommendations for international students: required—TOEFL or IELTS to demonstrate English proficiency. *Application deadline:* For fall admission, 12/1 priority date for domestic and international students. Application fee: $90. Electronic applications accepted. *Expenses:* Contact institution. *Financial support:* In 2019–20, 170 research assistantships with full tuition reimbursements (averaging $35,000 per year) were awarded. Financial award application deadline: 12/1. *Unit head:* Dr. Dan Jay, Dean, 617-636-6767, Fax: 617-636-0375, E-mail: daniel.jay@tufts.edu. *Application contact:* Jeff Miller, Admissions Coordinator, 617-636-6767, Fax: 617-636-0375, E-mail: gsbs-admissions@tufts.edu.
Website: http://gsbs.tufts.edu/

**Tulane University,** School of Medicine, Graduate Programs in Biomedical Sciences, New Orleans, LA 70118-5669. Offers MS, PhD, MD/PhD. *Degree requirements:* For doctorate, thesis/dissertation. *Entrance requirements:* For master's, GRE General Test, minimum B average in undergraduate course work; for doctorate, GRE General Test. Additional exam requirements/recommendations for international students: required—TOEFL. *Expenses:* Contact institution.

**Tuskegee University,** Graduate Programs, College of Arts and Sciences, Department of Biology, Tuskegee, AL 36088. Offers MS. *Degree requirements:* For master's, thesis. *Entrance requirements:* For master's, GRE General Test, GRE Subject Test. Additional exam requirements/recommendations for international students: required—TOEFL (minimum score 500 paper-based).

**Tuskegee University,** Graduate Programs, Program in Integrative Biosciences, Tuskegee, AL 36088. Offers PhD. *Degree requirements:* For doctorate, thesis/dissertation. *Entrance requirements:* For doctorate, GRE General Test, GRE Subject Test, minimum cumulative GPA of 3.0, 3.4 in upper-division courses; 3 letters of recommendation; resume or curriculum vitae. Additional exam requirements/recommendations for international students: required—TOEFL (minimum score 500 paper-based). Electronic applications accepted.

**UNB Fredericton,** School of Graduate Studies, Faculty of Science, Applied Science, and Engineering, Biology, Fredericton, NB E3B 5A3, Canada. Offers M Sc, PhD. *Program availability:* Part-time. *Faculty:* 29 full-time (10 women). *Students:* 42 full-time (25 women), 13 part-time (9 women), 14 international. Average age 29. In 2019, 7 master's, 4 doctorates awarded. *Degree requirements:* For master's, thesis; for doctorate, thesis/dissertation. *Entrance requirements:* For master's, minimum GPA of 3.0; undergraduate degree (B Sc or equivalent preferred); for doctorate, minimum GPA of 3.0; undergraduate and/or master's degree in related discipline. Additional exam requirements/recommendations for international students: required—TWE (minimum score 4), TOEFL (minimum score 600 paper-based) or IELTS (minimum score 7). *Application deadline:* For fall admission, 3/1 for domestic students. Applications are processed on a rolling basis. Application fee: $50 Canadian dollars. Electronic applications accepted. *Expenses: Tuition, area resident:* Full-time $6975 Canadian dollars; part-time $3423 Canadian dollars per year. Tuition, state resident: full-time $6975 Canadian dollars; part-time $3423 Canadian dollars per year. Tuition, Canadian resident: full-time $6975 Canadian dollars; part-time $3423 Canadian dollars per year. *International tuition:* $12,435 Canadian dollars full-time. *Required fees:* $92.25 Canadian dollars per term. Full-time tuition and fees vary according to degree level, campus/location, program, reciprocity agreements and student level. *Financial support:* Fellowships, research assistantships with tuition reimbursements, and teaching assistantships available. Financial award application deadline: 1/15. *Unit head:* Dr. Les C. Cwynar, Director of Graduate Studies, 506-452-6197, Fax: 506-453-3583, E-mail: biodogs@unb.ca. *Application contact:* Dr. Les C. Cwynar, Director of Graduate Studies, 506-452-6197, Fax: 506-453-3583, E-mail: biodogs@unb.ca.
Website: http://go.unb.ca/gradprograms

**Uniformed Services University of the Health Sciences,** F. Edward Hebert School of Medicine, Graduate Programs in the Biomedical Sciences and Public Health, Bethesda, MD 20814. Offers emerging infectious diseases (PhD); medical and clinical psychology (PhD), including clinical psychology, medical psychology; medicine (MS, PhD), including health professions education; molecular and cell biology (MS, PhD); neuroscience (PhD); preventive medicine and biometrics (MPH, MS, MSPH, MTMH, PhD), including environmental health sciences (PhD), healthcare administration and policy (MS), medical zoology (PhD), public health (MPH, MSPH), tropical medicine and hygiene (MTMH). Terminal master's awarded for partial completion of doctoral program. *Degree requirements:* For master's, comprehensive exam, thesis or alternative; for doctorate, comprehensive exam, thesis/dissertation, qualifying exam. *Entrance requirements:* For master's, GRE General Test; for doctorate, GRE General Test, minimum GPA of 3.0. Electronic applications accepted. *Expenses:* Contact institution.

**Universidad Central del Caribe,** School of Medicine, Program in Biomedical Sciences, Bayamón, PR 00960-6032. Offers anatomy and cell biology (MA, MS); biochemistry (MS); biomedical sciences (MA); cellular and molecular biology (PhD); microbiology and immunology (MA, MS); pharmacology (MS); physiology (MS).

**Universidad de Ciencias Medicas,** Graduate Programs, San Jose, Costa Rica. Offers dermatology (SP); family health (MS); health service center administration (MHA); human anatomy (MS); medical and surgery (MD); occupational medicine (MS); pharmacy (Pharm D). *Program availability:* Part-time. *Degree requirements:* For master's, thesis; for doctorate and SP, comprehensive exam. *Entrance requirements:* For master's, MD or bachelor's degree; for doctorate, admissions test; for SP, admissions test, MD.

**Université de Moncton,** Faculty of Sciences, Department of Biology, Moncton, NB E1A 3E9, Canada. Offers M Sc. *Degree requirements:* For master's, one foreign language, thesis. *Entrance requirements:* For master's, minimum GPA of 3.0. Electronic applications accepted.

**Université de Montréal,** Faculty of Arts and Sciences, Department of Biological Sciences, Montréal, QC H3C 3J7, Canada. Offers M Sc, PhD. *Program availability:* Part-time. *Degree requirements:* For master's, thesis; for doctorate, thesis/dissertation, general exam. *Entrance requirements:* For doctorate, MS in biology or related field. Electronic applications accepted.

**Université de Montréal,** Faculty of Medicine, Programs in Biomedical Sciences, Montréal, QC H3C 3J7, Canada. Offers M Sc, PhD. *Degree requirements:* For master's, thesis; for doctorate, thesis/dissertation, general exam. *Entrance requirements:* For master's and doctorate, proficiency in French, knowledge of English. Electronic applications accepted.

**Université de Sherbrooke,** Faculty of Medicine and Health Sciences, Graduate Programs in Medicine, Sherbrooke, QC J1H 5N4, Canada. Offers M Sc, PhD. *Program availability:* Part-time. Terminal master's awarded for partial completion of doctoral program. *Degree requirements:* For master's, thesis; for doctorate, thesis/dissertation. Electronic applications accepted. *Expenses:* Contact institution.

**Université de Sherbrooke,** Faculty of Sciences, Department of Biology, Sherbrooke, QC J1K 2R1, Canada. Offers M Sc, PhD, Diploma. *Degree requirements:* For master's, thesis; for doctorate, comprehensive exam, thesis/dissertation. *Entrance requirements:* For doctorate, master's degree. Electronic applications accepted.

**Université du Québec à Montréal,** Graduate Programs, Program in Biology, Montréal, QC H3C 3P8, Canada. Offers M Sc, PhD. *Program availability:* Part-time. *Degree requirements:* For master's, thesis; for doctorate, thesis/dissertation. *Entrance requirements:* For master's, appropriate bachelor's degree or equivalent, proficiency in French; for doctorate, appropriate master's degree or equivalent, proficiency in French.

**Université du Québec en Abitibi-Témiscamingue,** Graduate Programs, Program in Environmental Sciences, Rouyn-Noranda, QC J9X 5E4, Canada. Offers biology (MS); environmental sciences (PhD); sustainable forest ecosystem management (MS).

**Université du Québec, Institut National de la Recherche Scientifique,** Graduate Programs, Armand-Frappier Santé Biotechnologie, Laval, QC H7V 1B7, Canada. Offers applied microbiology (M Sc); biology (PhD); experimental health sciences (M Sc); virology and immunology (M Sc, PhD). *Program availability:* Part-time. *Faculty:* 46 full-time. *Students:* 157 full-time (94 women), 9 part-time (4 women), 100 international. Average age 30. 23 applicants, 96% accepted, 21 enrolled. In 2019, 19 master's, 20 doctorates awarded. *Degree requirements:* For master's, thesis; for doctorate, thesis/dissertation. *Entrance requirements:* For master's, appropriate bachelor's degree, proficiency in French; for doctorate, appropriate master's degree, proficiency in French. *Application deadline:* For fall admission, 3/30 for domestic and international students; for winter admission, 11/1 for domestic and international students; for spring admission, 3/1 for domestic and international students. Application fee: $45 Canadian dollars. Electronic applications accepted. *Financial support:* In 2019–20, fellowships (averaging $16,500 per year) were awarded; research assistantships also available. *Unit head:* Claude Guertin, Director, 450-687-5010, Fax: 450-686-5501, E-mail: claude.guertin@iaf.inrs.ca. *Application contact:* Sean Otto, Registrar, 418-654-2518, Fax: 418-654-3858, E-mail: sean.otto@inrs.ca.
Website: http://www.iaf.inrs.ca

**University at Albany, State University of New York,** College of Arts and Sciences, Department of Biological Sciences, Albany, NY 12222-0001. Offers forensic biology (MS). *Program availability:* Part-time, blended/hybrid learning. *Faculty:* 28 full-time (11 women), 10 part-time/adjunct (7 women). *Students:* 38 full-time (23 women), 35 part-time (23 women); includes 14 minority (3 Black or African American, non-Hispanic/Latino; 3 Asian, non-Hispanic/Latino; 6 Hispanic/Latino; 2 Two or more races, non-Hispanic/Latino), 14 international. 37 applicants, 59% accepted, 15 enrolled. In 2019, 12 master's awarded. *Degree requirements:* For master's, one foreign language. *Entrance requirements:* For master's, transcripts of all schools attended; statement of background and goals; departmental questionnaire; resume; names and contact information for 3 recommenders. Additional exam requirements/recommendations for international students: required—TOEFL (minimum score 550 paper-based). *Application deadline:* For fall admission, 1/15 priority date for domestic students, 5/1 for international students; for spring admission, 11/15 for domestic and international students. Applications are processed on a rolling basis. Application fee: $75. Electronic applications accepted. *Expenses: Tuition, area resident:* Full-time $11,530; part-time $480 per credit hour. Tuition, nonresident: full-time $23,530; part-time $980 per credit hour. *International tuition:* $23,530 full-time. *Required fees:* $2185; $96 per credit hour. Part-time tuition and fees vary according to course load and program. *Financial support:* Fellowships, research assistantships, teaching assistantships, and minority assistantships available. Financial award application deadline: 5/1. *Unit head:* Richard cunningham, Chair, 518-442-4300, Fax: 518-442-4354, E-mail: rcunningham@albany.edu. *Application contact:* Michael DeRensis, Director, Graduate Admissions, 518-442-3980, Fax: 518-442-3922, E-mail: graduate@albany.edu.
Website: https://www.albany.edu/biology

**University at Albany, State University of New York,** School of Public Health, Department of Biomedical Sciences, Albany, NY 12222-0001. Offers MS, PhD. *Faculty:* 5 full-time (1 woman), 24 part-time/adjunct (8 women). *Students:* 17 full-time (11 women), 19 part-time (10 women); includes 7 minority (1 Asian, non-Hispanic/Latino; 2 Hispanic/Latino; 4 Two or more races, non-Hispanic/Latino), 8 international. 75 applicants, 56% accepted, 18 enrolled. In 2019, 2 master's, 3 doctorates awarded. *Degree requirements:* For master's, thesis; for doctorate, comprehensive exam, thesis/dissertation. *Entrance requirements:* For master's and doctorate, transcripts of all schools attended; statement of background and goals; departmental questionnaire; resume; names and contact information for 3 recommenders. Additional exam requirements/recommendations for international students: required—TOEFL (minimum score 600 paper-based). *Application deadline:* For fall admission, 1/15 for domestic and international students; for winter admission, 4/1 for domestic and international students; for spring admission, 11/15 for domestic and international students. Applications are processed on a rolling basis. Application fee: $75. Electronic applications accepted. *Expenses: Tuition, area resident:* Full-time $11,530; part-time $480 per credit hour. Tuition, nonresident: full-time $23,530; part-time $980 per credit hour. *International tuition:* $23,530 full-time. *Required fees:* $2185; $96 per credit hour. Part-time tuition and fees vary according to course load and program. *Financial support:* Fellowships with full tuition reimbursements, research assistantships with full tuition reimbursements, teaching assistantships with tuition reimbursements, scholarships/grants, traineeships, health care benefits, tuition waivers (partial), and unspecified assistantships available. Financial award application deadline: 1/15. *Unit head:* Dr. Janice Pata, Chair, 518-402-2750, E-mail: ipata@albany.edu. *Application contact:* Dr. Janice Pata, Chair, 518-402-2750, E-mail: ipata@albany.edu.
Website: https://www.albany.edu/sph/programs/ms-biomedical-sciences

**University at Buffalo, the State University of New York,** Graduate School, College of Arts and Sciences, Department of Biological Sciences, Buffalo, NY 14260. Offers MA, MS, PhD. Terminal master's awarded for partial completion of doctoral program. *Degree requirements:* For master's, independent research project, written report, oral presentation; for doctorate, comprehensive exam, thesis/dissertation, thesis research, oral defense. *Entrance requirements:* For master's, GRE (for MS); GRE, MCAT, DAT, or equivalent test (for MA), solid foundation in biology, math through calculus, chemistry through organic, general physics; for doctorate, GRE, solid foundation in biology, math through calculus, chemistry through organic, general physics; previous research experience. Additional exam requirements/recommendations for international students: required—TOEFL (minimum score 95 iBT) or IELTS (minimum score 6.5). Electronic applications accepted. *Expenses: Tuition, area resident:* Full-time $11,310; part-time $471 per credit hour. Tuition, state resident: full-time $11,310; part-time $471 per credit hour. Tuition, nonresident: full-time $23,100; part-time $963 per credit hour. *International tuition:* $23,100 full-time. *Required fees:* $2820.

**University at Buffalo, the State University of New York,** Graduate School, Jacobs School of Medicine and Biomedical Sciences, Graduate Programs in Medicine and Biomedical Sciences, PhD Program in Biomedical Sciences, Buffalo, NY 14203. Offers PhD. *Students:* 11 full-time (6 women); includes 4 minority (1 Black or African American, non-Hispanic/Latino; 1 Asian, non-Hispanic/Latino; 2 Hispanic/Latino), 1 international. 309 applicants, 13% accepted, 11 enrolled. *Degree requirements:* For doctorate, comprehensive exam, thesis/dissertation. *Entrance requirements:* For doctorate, 3

letters of recommendation; CV/Resume; Personal Statement. Additional exam requirements/recommendations for international students: required—TOEFL (minimum score 600 paper-based; 100 iBT), IELTS (minimum score 7.5). *Application deadline:* For fall admission, 12/1 priority date for domestic and international students. Applications are processed on a rolling basis. Application fee: $85. Electronic applications accepted. *Expenses: Tuition, area resident:* Full-time $11,310; part-time $471 per credit hour. Tuition, state resident: full-time $11,310; part-time $471 per credit hour. Tuition, nonresident: full-time $23,100; part-time $963 per credit hour. *International tuition:* $23,100 full-time. *Required fees:* $2820. *Financial support:* In 2019–20, 11 students received support, including 4 fellowships (averaging $5,000 per year), 11 research assistantships with full tuition reimbursements available (averaging $27,000 per year); scholarships/grants and health care benefits also available. Financial award application deadline: 12/1. *Unit head:* Dr. Andrew Gulick, Director, 716-829-3398, Fax: 716-829-2437, E-mail: smbs-gradprog@buffalo.edu. *Application contact:* Elizabeth A. White, Director, Graduate Enrollment, 716-829-3399, Fax: 716-829-2437, E-mail: bethw@buffalo.edu.
Website: http://medicine.buffalo.edu/phdprogram

**The University of Akron,** Graduate School, Buchtel College of Arts and Sciences, Department of Biology, Akron, OH 44325. Offers biology (MS); integrated bioscience (PhD). *Program availability:* Part-time. *Degree requirements:* For master's, thesis optional, oral defense of thesis, oral exam, seminars; for doctorate, thesis/dissertation, oral defense of dissertation, seminars. *Entrance requirements:* For master's, GRE General Test, GRE Subject Test (biology), or MCAT, baccalaureate degree in biology or equivalent training; minimum GPA of 3.0 overall and in biology (minimum 32 semester credit hours or equivalent); competence in chemistry and mathematics; letter of interest indicating proposed area of specialization and possible advisers; for doctorate, GRE General Test, minimum GPA of 3.0; three letters of recommendation; career goals and research interest statement. Additional exam requirements/recommendations for international students: required—TOEFL (minimum score 79 iBT), IELTS (minimum score 6.5). Electronic applications accepted.

**The University of Alabama,** Graduate School, College of Arts and Sciences, Department of Biological Sciences, Tuscaloosa, AL 35487. Offers MS, PhD. *Faculty:* 34 full-time (16 women), 1 (woman) part-time/adjunct. *Students:* 73 full-time (34 women), 1 (woman) part-time; includes 6 minority (2 Black or African American, non-Hispanic/Latino; 4 Two or more races, non-Hispanic/Latino), 19 international. Average age 27. 90 applicants, 26% accepted, 11 enrolled. In 2019, 11 master's, 6 doctorates awarded. Terminal master's awarded for partial completion of doctoral program. *Degree requirements:* For master's, comprehensive exam, thesis optional; for doctorate, comprehensive exam, thesis/dissertation, written and oral candidacy exams. *Entrance requirements:* For master's and doctorate, GRE General Test, minimum GPA of 3.0. Additional exam requirements/recommendations for international students: required—TOEFL (minimum score 550 paper-based; 80 iBT). *Application deadline:* For fall admission, 12/5 priority date for domestic and international students; for spring admission, 12/5 priority date for domestic students, 9/5 priority date for international students. Applications are processed on a rolling basis. Application fee: $50 ($60 for international students). Electronic applications accepted. *Expenses: Tuition, area resident:* Full-time $10,780; part-time $440 per credit hour. Tuition, nonresident: full-time $30,250; part-time $1550 per credit hour. *Financial support:* In 2019–20, 23 fellowships with full tuition reimbursements (averaging $18,000 per year), 21 research assistantships with full tuition reimbursements (averaging $21,000 per year), 52 teaching assistantships with full tuition reimbursements (averaging $17,000 per year) were awarded; scholarships/grants, health care benefits, and unspecified assistantships also available. Financial award application deadline: 7/1; financial award applicants required to submit FAFSA. *Unit head:* Dr. Behzad Mortazavi, Professor and Department Chair, 205-348-9810, E-mail: bmortazavi@ua.edu. *Application contact:* Dr. Christina Staudhammer, Graduate Program Director, 205-348-1538, Fax: 205-348-1786, E-mail: cstaudhammer@ua.edu.
Website: http://bsc.ua.edu

**The University of Alabama at Birmingham,** College of Arts and Sciences, Program in Biology, Birmingham, AL 35294. Offers MS, PhD. *Faculty:* 23 full-time (10 women), 1 part-time/adjunct. *Students:* 42 full-time (21 women), 12 part-time (7 women); includes 4 minority (2 Black or African American, non-Hispanic/Latino; 1 Asian, non-Hispanic/Latino; 1 Two or more races, non-Hispanic/Latino), 16 international. Average age 28. 33 applicants, 45% accepted, 9 enrolled. In 2019, 16 master's, 7 doctorates awarded. Terminal master's awarded for partial completion of doctoral program. *Degree requirements:* For master's, comprehensive exam (for some programs), thesis (for some programs); for doctorate, thesis/dissertation. *Entrance requirements:* For master's and doctorate, GRE General Test, previous course work in biology, calculus, organic chemistry, and physics; letters of recommendation. Additional exam requirements/recommendations for international students: required—TOEFL, TWE. *Application deadline:* For fall admission, 3/1 for domestic students; for spring admission, 10/15 for domestic students. Applications are processed on a rolling basis. Application fee: $45 ($60 for international students). Electronic applications accepted. *Financial support:* Fellowships with full tuition reimbursements, research assistantships with full tuition reimbursements, teaching assistantships with full tuition reimbursements, career-related internships or fieldwork, Federal Work-Study, institutionally sponsored loans, scholarships/grants, traineeships, tuition waivers (full), and unspecified assistantships available. Support available to part-time students. *Unit head:* Dr. Stephen A. Watts, Graduate Program Director, 205-934-8308, Fax: 205-975-6097, E-mail: sawatts@uab.edu. *Application contact:* Susan Noblitt Banks, Director of Graduate School Operations, 205-934-8227, Fax: 205-934-8413, E-mail: gradschool@uab.edu.
Website: http://www.uab.edu/cas/biology/graduate-program

**The University of Alabama at Birmingham,** Joint Health Sciences, Program in Basic Medical Sciences, Birmingham, AL 35294. Offers MSBMS. *Entrance requirements:* For master's, GRE. Electronic applications accepted.

**The University of Alabama in Huntsville,** School of Graduate Studies, College of Science, Department of Biological Sciences, Huntsville, AL 35899. Offers biology (MS); biotechnology science and engineering (PhD); education (MS). *Program availability:* Part-time. *Degree requirements:* For master's, comprehensive exam, thesis or alternative, oral and written exams. *Entrance requirements:* For master's, GRE General Test, previous course work in biochemistry and organic chemistry, minimum GPA of 3.0. Additional exam requirements/recommendations for international students: required—TOEFL (minimum score 550 paper-based; 80 iBT), IELTS (minimum score 6.5). Electronic applications accepted.

**University of Alaska Anchorage,** College of Arts and Sciences, Department of Biological Sciences, Anchorage, AK 99508. Offers MS. *Program availability:* Part-time. *Degree requirements:* For master's, comprehensive exam, thesis. *Entrance requirements:* For master's, GRE General Test, GRE Subject Test, bachelor's degree in biology, chemistry or equivalent science. Additional exam requirements/recommendations for international students: required—TOEFL (minimum score 550 paper-based).

**University of Alaska Fairbanks,** College of Natural Science and Mathematics, Department of Biology and Wildlife, Fairbanks, AK 99775-6100. Offers biological

sciences (MS, PhD); wildlife biology and conservation (MS). *Program availability:* Part-time. *Degree requirements:* For master's, comprehensive exam, thesis, oral defense of thesis; for doctorate, comprehensive exam, thesis/dissertation, oral defense of dissertation. *Entrance requirements:* For master's and doctorate, GRE General Test, GRE Subject Test (biology), bachelor's degree from accredited institution with minimum cumulative undergraduate and major GPA of 3.0. Additional exam requirements/recommendations for international students: required—TOEFL (minimum score 550 paper-based; 79 iBT), TWE. Electronic applications accepted.

**University of Alberta,** Faculty of Graduate Studies and Research, Department of Biological Sciences, Edmonton, AB T6G 2E1, Canada. Offers environmental biology and ecology (M Sc, PhD); microbiology and biotechnology (M Sc, PhD); molecular biology and genetics (M Sc, PhD); physiology and cell biology (M Sc, PhD); plant biology (M Sc, PhD); systematics and evolution (M Sc, PhD). Terminal master's awarded for partial completion of doctoral program. *Degree requirements:* For master's, thesis; for doctorate, thesis/dissertation. *Entrance requirements:* Additional exam requirements/recommendations for international students: required—TOEFL.

**University of Alberta,** Faculty of Medicine and Dentistry and Faculty of Graduate Studies and Research, Graduate Programs in Medicine, Edmonton, AB T6G 2E1, Canada. Offers M Sc, MD, PhD. *Program availability:* Part-time. *Degree requirements:* For doctorate, thesis/dissertation (for some programs).

**The University of Arizona,** College of Agriculture and Life Sciences, School of Animal and Comparative Biomedical Sciences, Tucson, AZ 85721. Offers MS, PhD. *Degree requirements:* For master's, thesis; for doctorate, comprehensive exam, thesis/dissertation. *Entrance requirements:* For master's and doctorate, GRE, minimum GPA of 3.0, 3 letters of recommendation, letter of intent. Additional exam requirements/recommendations for international students: required—TOEFL (minimum score 550 paper-based; 79 iBT). Electronic applications accepted.

**The University of Arizona,** College of Science, Program in Applied Biosciences, Tucson, AZ 85721. Offers PSM. *Program availability:* Part-time. *Degree requirements:* For master's, thesis or alternative, internship, colloquium, business courses. *Entrance requirements:* For master's, 3 letters of recommendation. Additional exam requirements/recommendations for international students: required—TOEFL (minimum score 600 paper-based; 90 iBT). Electronic applications accepted.

**University of Arkansas,** Graduate School, J. William Fulbright College of Arts and Sciences, Department of Biological Sciences, Fayetteville, AR 72701. Offers MA, MS, PhD. *Students:* 52 full-time (24 women), 10 part-time (6 women); includes 8 minority (1 American Indian or Alaska Native, non-Hispanic/Latino; 5 Hispanic/Latino; 2 Two or more races, non-Hispanic/Latino), 8 international. 11 applicants, 100% accepted. In 2019, 8 master's, 6 doctorates awarded. *Degree requirements:* For doctorate, one foreign language, thesis/dissertation. *Entrance requirements:* For master's and doctorate, GRE Subject Test. *Application deadline:* For fall admission, 8/1 for domestic students, 4/1 for international students; for spring admission, 12/1 for domestic students, 10/1 for international students; for summer admission, 4/15 for domestic students, 3/1 for international students. Applications are processed on a rolling basis. Application fee: $60. Electronic applications accepted. *Financial support:* In 2019–20, 27 research assistantships, 8 teaching assistantships were awarded; fellowships with tuition reimbursements, career-related internships or fieldwork, and Federal Work-Study also available. Support available to part-time students. Financial award application deadline: 4/1; financial award applicants required to submit FAFSA. *Unit head:* Dr. David S. McNabb, Department Chair, 479-575-3787, E-mail: dmcnabb@uark.edu. *Application contact:* Michele Evans White, 479-575-4706, E-mail: mevanswh@uark.edu.
Website: https://fulbright.uark.edu/departments/biology/

**University of Arkansas at Little Rock,** Graduate School, College of Arts, Letters, and Sciences, Department of Biology, Little Rock, AR 72204-1099. Offers MS.

**University of Arkansas for Medical Sciences,** Graduate School, Little Rock, AR 72205. Offers biochemistry and molecular biology (MS, PhD); bioinformatics (MS, PhD); cellular physiology and molecular biophysics (MS, PhD); clinical nutrition (MS); interdisciplinary biomedical sciences (MS, PhD, Certificate); interdisciplinary toxicology (MS); microbiology and immunology (PhD); neurobiology and developmental sciences (PhD); pharmacology (PhD); MD/PhD. *Program availability:* Part-time. Terminal master's awarded for partial completion of doctoral program. *Degree requirements:* For master's, comprehensive exam (for some programs), thesis (for some programs); for doctorate, thesis/dissertation. *Entrance requirements:* For master's and doctorate, GRE. Additional exam requirements/recommendations for international students: required—TOEFL. Electronic applications accepted. *Expenses:* Contact institution.

**University of Calgary,** Cumming School of Medicine and Faculty of Graduate Studies, Program in Medical Science, Calgary, AB T2N 1N4, Canada. Offers cancer biology (M Sc, PhD); critical care medicine (M Sc, PhD); joint injury and arthritis (M Sc, PhD); molecular and medical genetics (M Sc, PhD); mountain medicine and high altitude physiology (M Sc, PhD); pathologists' assistant (M Sc, PhD). *Degree requirements:* For master's, thesis; for doctorate, thesis/dissertation, candidacy exam. *Entrance requirements:* For master's, minimum undergraduate GPA of 3.2; for doctorate, minimum graduate GPA of 3.2. Additional exam requirements/recommendations for international students: required—TOEFL (minimum score 600 paper-based). Electronic applications accepted.

**University of Calgary,** Faculty of Graduate Studies, Faculty of Science, Program in Biological Science, Calgary, AB T2N 1N4, Canada. Offers M Sc, PhD. *Program availability:* Part-time. *Degree requirements:* For master's, thesis; for doctorate, thesis/dissertation, candidacy exam. *Entrance requirements:* Additional exam requirements/recommendations for international students: required—TOEFL. Electronic applications accepted.

**University of California, Berkeley,** Graduate Division, College of Letters and Science, Department of Integrative Biology, Berkeley, CA 94720. Offers PhD. *Degree requirements:* For doctorate, thesis/dissertation, oral qualifying exam. *Entrance requirements:* For doctorate, GRE General Test, GRE Subject Test, 3 letters of recommendation. Additional exam requirements/recommendations for international students: required—TOEFL. Electronic applications accepted.

**University of California, Irvine,** School of Biological Sciences, Irvine, CA 92697. Offers MS, PhD, MD/PhD. *Students:* 365 full-time (210 women), 2 part-time (1 woman); includes 141 minority (9 Black or African American, non-Hispanic/Latino; 1 American Indian or Alaska Native, non-Hispanic/Latino; 65 Asian, non-Hispanic/Latino; 63 Hispanic/Latino; 3 Two or more races, non-Hispanic/Latino), 72 international. Average age 27. 1,056 applicants, 26% accepted, 120 enrolled. In 2019, 71 master's, 36 doctorates awarded. *Entrance requirements:* For master's and doctorate, GRE General Test, GRE Subject Test, minimum GPA of 3.0. Additional exam requirements/recommendations for international students: required—TOEFL (minimum score 550 paper-based). *Application deadline:* For fall admission, 12/15 for domestic and international students. Applications are processed on a rolling basis. Application fee: $120 ($140 for international students). Electronic applications accepted. *Financial support:* Fellowships with full tuition reimbursements, research assistantships with full tuition reimbursements, teaching assistantships with full tuition reimbursements, career-

related internships or fieldwork, institutionally sponsored loans, scholarships/grants, traineeships, health care benefits, and unspecified assistantships available. Financial award application deadline: 3/1; financial award applicants required to submit FAFSA. *Unit head:* Prof. Frank Laferla, Dean, 949-824-5315, Fax: 949-824-3035, E-mail: laferla@uci.edu. *Application contact:* Prof. R. Michael Mulligan, Associate Dean, 949-824-8433, Fax: 949-824-4709, E-mail: rmmullig@uci.edu.
Website: http://www.bio.uci.edu/

**University of California, Los Angeles,** David Geffen School of Medicine and Graduate Division, Graduate Programs in Medicine, Los Angeles, CA 90095. Offers MS, PhD, MD/PhD. Terminal master's awarded for partial completion of doctoral program. *Degree requirements:* For doctorate, thesis/dissertation, written and oral qualifying exams. Electronic applications accepted. *Expenses:* Contact institution.

**University of California, Los Angeles,** Graduate Division, College of Letters and Science, Department of Ecology and Evolutionary Biology, Los Angeles, CA 90095. Offers MA, PhD. Terminal master's awarded for partial completion of doctoral program. *Degree requirements:* For master's, comprehensive exam or thesis; for doctorate, thesis/dissertation, oral and written qualifying exams; 3 quarters of teaching experience. *Entrance requirements:* For master's and doctorate, GRE General Test, GRE Subject Test (biology), bachelor's degree; minimum undergraduate GPA of 3.0 (or its equivalent if letter grade system not used). Additional exam requirements/recommendations for international students: required—TOEFL. Electronic applications accepted.

**University of California, Merced,** Graduate Division, School of Natural Sciences, Merced, CA 95343. Offers applied mathematics (MS, PhD); chemistry and chemical biology (MS, PhD); physics (MS, PhD); quantitative and systems biology (MS, PhD), including molecular and cellular biology (PhD). *Faculty:* 79 full-time (32 women). *Students:* 255 full-time (104 women), 1 (woman) part-time; includes 83 minority (5 Black or African American, non-Hispanic/Latino; 25 Asian, non-Hispanic/Latino; 44 Hispanic/Latino; 9 Two or more races, non-Hispanic/Latino), 77 international. Average age 28. 292 applicants, 43% accepted, 54 enrolled. In 2019, 13 master's, 23 doctorates awarded. Terminal master's awarded for partial completion of doctoral program. *Degree requirements:* For master's, variable foreign language requirement, comprehensive exam, thesis or alternative, oral defense; for doctorate, variable foreign language requirement, comprehensive exam, thesis/dissertation, oral defense. *Entrance requirements:* For master's and doctorate, GRE. Additional exam requirements/recommendations for international students: required—TOEFL (minimum score 550 paper-based; 80 iBT); recommended—IELTS (minimum score 6.5). *Application deadline:* For fall admission, 1/15 for domestic and international students. Application fee: $105 ($125 for international students). Electronic applications accepted. *Expenses: Tuition, area resident:* Full-time $11,442; part-time $5721 per semester. Tuition, state resident: full-time $11,442; part-time $5721 per semester. Tuition, nonresident: full-time $26,544; part-time $13,272 per semester. *International tuition:* $26,544 full-time. *Required fees:* $564 per semester. *Financial support:* In 2019–20, 233 students received support, including 9 fellowships with full tuition reimbursements available (averaging $22,005 per year), 56 research assistantships with full tuition reimbursements available (averaging $21,420 per year), 168 teaching assistantships with full tuition reimbursements available (averaging $21,911 per year); scholarships/grants, traineeships, and health care benefits also available. *Unit head:* Dr. Elizabeth Dumont, Dean, 209-228-4487, Fax: 209-228-4060, E-mail: edumont@ucmerced.edu. *Application contact:* Tsu Ya, Director of Graduate Admissions and Academic Services, 209-228-4521, Fax: 209-228-6906, E-mail: tya@ucmerced.edu.

**University of California, Riverside,** Graduate Division, Department of Evolution, Ecology, and Organismal Biology, Riverside, CA 92521-0102. Offers evolution, ecology and organismal biology (MS, PhD). Terminal master's awarded for partial completion of doctoral program. *Degree requirements:* For master's, thesis, oral defense of thesis; for doctorate, comprehensive exam, thesis/dissertation, 3 quarters of teaching experience, qualifying exams. *Entrance requirements:* For master's and doctorate, GRE General Test, minimum GPA of 3.2. Additional exam requirements/recommendations for international students: required—TOEFL (minimum score 550 paper-based, 80 iBT) or IELTS; recommended—TWE. Electronic applications accepted.

**University of California, Riverside,** Graduate Division, Program in Biomedical Sciences, Riverside, CA 92521-0102. Offers PhD. *Degree requirements:* For doctorate, thesis/dissertation, qualifying exams. *Entrance requirements:* For doctorate, GRE General Test, minimum GPA of 3.2. Additional exam requirements/recommendations for international students: required—TOEFL (minimum score 550 paper-based; 80 iBT). Electronic applications accepted. *Expenses:* Contact institution.

**University of California, San Diego,** Graduate Division, Department of Physics, La Jolla, CA 92093. Offers biophysics (PhD); computational neuroscience (PhD); computational science (PhD); multi-scale biology (PhD); physics (MS, PhD); quantitative biology (PhD). *Students:* 166 full-time (26 women), 2 part-time (1 woman). 566 applicants, 22% accepted, 22 enrolled. In 2019, 9 master's, 23 doctorates awarded. *Degree requirements:* For doctorate, comprehensive exam, thesis/dissertation, 1-quarter teaching assistantship. *Entrance requirements:* For doctorate, GRE General Test, GRE Subject Test, statement of purpose, three letters of reference. Additional exam requirements/recommendations for international students: required—TOEFL (minimum score 550 paper-based; 80 iBT), IELTS (minimum score 7). *Application deadline:* For fall admission, 12/18 for domestic students. Application fee: $105 ($125 for international students). Electronic applications accepted. *Financial support:* Fellowships, research assistantships, teaching assistantships, scholarships/grants, and unspecified assistantships available. Financial award applicants required to submit FAFSA. *Unit head:* Brian Maple, Chair, 858-534-6857, E-mail: chair@physics.ucsd.edu. *Application contact:* Saixious Dominguez-Kilday, Graduate Admissions Coordinator, 858-534-3293, E-mail: skilday@physics.ucsd.edu.
Website: http://physics.ucsd.edu/

**University of California, San Diego,** Graduate Division, Division of Biological Sciences, La Jolla, CA 92093-0348. Offers anthropogeny (PhD); bioinformatics (PhD); biology (PhD); interdisciplinary environmental research (PhD); multi-scale biology (PhD); quantitative biology (PhD). *Students:* 411 full-time (239 women), 7 part-time (3 women); includes 184 minority (8 Black or African American, non-Hispanic/Latino; 2 American Indian or Alaska Native, non-Hispanic/Latino; 109 Asian, non-Hispanic/Latino; 18 Hispanic/Latino; 47 Two or more races, non-Hispanic/Latino), 117 international. 569 applicants, 37% accepted, 146 enrolled. In 2019, 30 doctorates awarded. *Degree requirements:* For doctorate, comprehensive exam, thesis/dissertation, 3 quarters of teaching assistantship. *Entrance requirements:* Additional exam requirements/recommendations for international students: required—TOEFL (minimum score 550 paper-based; 80 iBT), IELTS (minimum score 7). *Application deadline:* For fall admission, 12/3 for domestic students. Application fee: $105 ($125 for international students). Electronic applications accepted. *Financial support:* Fellowships with full tuition reimbursements, research assistantships with full tuition reimbursements, teaching assistantships with full tuition reimbursements, scholarships/grants, traineeships, and unspecified assistantships available. Financial award applicants required to submit FAFSA. *Unit head:* Andrew Chisholm, Chair, 858-534-7783. *Application contact:* Melody Bayzar, Program Coordinator, 858-534-0181, E-mail: biogradprog@ucsd.edu.
Website: http://biology.ucsd.edu/

**University of California, San Diego,** School of Medicine and Graduate Division, Graduate Studies in Biomedical Sciences, La Jolla, CA 92093-0685. Offers anthropogeny (PhD); bioinformatics (PhD); biomedical science (PhD); multi-scale biology (PhD). *Students:* 171 full-time (96 women). 702 applicants, 14% accepted, 34 enrolled. In 2019, 24 doctorates awarded. *Degree requirements:* For doctorate, comprehensive exam, thesis/dissertation, 1-quarter teaching assistantship. *Entrance requirements:* For doctorate, As of 2018, applicants are no longer required to submit scores for either the GRE General or Subject Tests. Applicants can optionally submit scores for the GRE General Test (verbal, quantitative, and analytical sections) and/or an applicable GRE Subject Test (Biology, Biochemistry (discontinued December 2016), or Chemistry). Additional exam requirements/recommendations for international students: required—TOEFL (minimum score 550 paper-based; 80 iBT), IELTS (minimum score 7). *Application deadline:* For fall admission, 11/27 for domestic students. Application fee: $105 ($125 for international students). Electronic applications accepted. *Financial support:* Fellowships, research assistantships, teaching assistantships, scholarships/grants, traineeships, unspecified assistantships, and stipends available. Financial award applicants required to submit FAFSA. *Unit head:* Asa Gustafsson, Chair, 858-822-5569, E-mail: abgustafsson@ucsd.edu. *Application contact:* Leanne Nordeman, Graduate Coordinator, 858-534-3982, E-mail: biomedsci@ucsd.edu.
Website: http://biomedsci.ucsd.edu

**University of California, San Diego,** School of Medicine, Medical Scientist Training Program, La Jolla, CA 92093. Offers MD/PhD. *Financial support:* Fellowships, research assistantships, scholarships/grants, and traineeships available. Financial award applicants required to submit FAFSA. *Unit head:* Paul A. Insel, Director, 858-534-2295. *Application contact:* Mary Alice Kiisel, Assistant, 858-534-0689, E-mail: mstp@ucsd.edu.

**University of California, San Francisco,** Graduate Division, Biomedical Sciences Graduate Program, San Francisco, CA 94143. Offers PhD. *Degree requirements:* For doctorate, thesis/dissertation. *Entrance requirements:* For doctorate, GRE General Test, three letters of recommendation, official transcripts. Additional exam requirements/recommendations for international students: required—TOEFL, IELTS.

**University of California, San Francisco,** School of Medicine, San Francisco, CA 94143-0410. Offers MD, PhD, MD/MPH, MD/MS, MD/PhD. *Accreditation:* LCME/AMA (one or more programs are accredited). *Entrance requirements:* For doctorate, MCAT (for MD), interview (for MD). Electronic applications accepted. *Expenses:* Contact institution.

**University of Central Arkansas,** Graduate School, College of Natural Sciences and Math, Department of Biological Science, Conway, AR 72035-0001. Offers MS. *Program availability:* Part-time. *Degree requirements:* For master's, comprehensive exam, thesis optional. *Entrance requirements:* For master's, GRE General Test, minimum GPA of 2.7. Additional exam requirements/recommendations for international students: required—TOEFL (minimum score 550 paper-based; 80 iBT). Electronic applications accepted.

**University of Central Florida,** College of Sciences, Department of Biology, Orlando, FL 32816. Offers conservation biology (Certificate). *Program availability:* Part-time, evening/weekend. *Students:* 55 full-time (27 women), 6 part-time (2 women); includes 6 minority (1 Black or African American, non-Hispanic/Latino; 2 Asian, non-Hispanic/Latino; 1 Hispanic/Latino; 2 Two or more races, non-Hispanic/Latino), 9 international. Average age 29. 38 applicants, 34% accepted, 12 enrolled. In 2019, 8 master's, 4 doctorates awarded. *Degree requirements:* For master's, comprehensive exam, thesis or alternative, field exam. *Entrance requirements:* For master's, GRE General Test, minimum GPA of 3.0 in last 60 hours, letters of recommendation, resume, personal/professional statement; for doctorate, GRE General Test, letters of recommendation, resume, personal/professional statement. Additional exam requirements/recommendations for international students: required—TOEFL. *Application deadline:* For fall admission, 1/15 priority date for domestic students. Application fee: $30. Electronic applications accepted. *Financial support:* In 2019–20, 54 students received support, including 20 fellowships with partial tuition reimbursements available (averaging $9,210 per year), 7 research assistantships with partial tuition reimbursements available (averaging $6,146 per year), 51 teaching assistantships with partial tuition reimbursements available (averaging $8,061 per year); career-related internships or fieldwork, Federal Work-Study, institutionally sponsored loans, health care benefits, tuition waivers (partial), and unspecified assistantships also available. Financial award application deadline: 3/1; financial award applicants required to submit FAFSA. *Unit head:* Dr. Graham Worthy, Chair, 407-823-2141, Fax: 407-823-5769, E-mail: graham.worthy@ucf.edu. *Application contact:* Associate Director, Graduate Admissions, 407-823-2766, Fax: 407-823-6442, E-mail: gradadmissions@ucf.edu.
Website: https://sciences.ucf.edu/biology/

**University of Central Missouri,** The Graduate School, Warrensburg, MO 64093. Offers accountancy (MA); accounting (MBA); applied mathematics (MS); aviation safety (MA); biology (MS); business administration (MBA); career and technology education (MS); college student personnel administration (MS); communication (MA); computer information systems and information technology (MS); computer science (MS); counseling (MS); criminal justice and criminology (MS); educational leadership (Ed S); educational leadership and policy analysis (Ed D); educational technology (MS, Ed S); elementary and early childhood education (MSE); English (MA); english language learners - teaching english as a second language (MA); environmental studies (MA); finance (MBA); history (MA); industrial hygiene (MS); industrial management (MS); information systems (MBA); kinesiology (MS); library science and information services (MS); literacy education (MSE); marketing (MBA); mathematics (MS); music (MA); occupational safety management (MS); professional leadership - adult, career, and technical education (Ed S); professional leadership - counseling (Ed S); psychology (MS); rural family nursing (MS); school administration (MSE); social gerontology (MS); sociology (MA); special education (MSE); speech language pathology (MS); teaching (MAT); technology (MS); technology management (PhD); theatre (MA). *Accreditation:* ASHA. *Program availability:* Part-time, 100% online, blended/hybrid learning. *Faculty:* 236 full-time (113 women), 97 part-time/adjunct (61 women). *Students:* 787 full-time (448 women), 1,459 part-time (997 women); includes 213 minority (72 Black or African American, non-Hispanic/Latino; 5 American Indian or Alaska Native, non-Hispanic/Latino; 27 Asian, non-Hispanic/Latino; 59 Hispanic/Latino; 50 Two or more races, non-Hispanic/Latino), 574 international. Average age 30. 1,477 applicants, 68% accepted, 664 enrolled. In 2019, 831 master's, 93 other advanced degrees awarded. *Degree requirements:* For master's and Ed S, comprehensive exam (for some programs), thesis (for some programs). *Entrance requirements:* For master's, A GRE or GMAT test score may be required by some of the programs, A minimum GPA, letters of recommendation, a statement of purpose may be required by some of the programs; for Ed S, A master's degree is required for the application of an Education Specialist's degree program. Additional exam requirements/recommendations for international students: required—TOEFL (minimum score 550 paper-based; 79 iBT). *Application deadline:* For fall admission, 6/1 priority date for domestic and international students; for spring admission, 10/15 priority date for domestic and international students; for summer admission, 4/1 priority date for domestic and international students. Applications are

processed on a rolling basis. Application fee: $30 ($75 for international students). Electronic applications accepted. *Expenses: Tuition, area resident:* Full-time $7524; part-time $313.50 per credit hour. Tuition, state resident: full-time $7524; part-time $313.50 per credit hour. Tuition, nonresident: full-time $15,048; part-time $627 per credit hour. *International tuition:* $15,048 full-time. *Required fees:* $915; $30.50 per credit hour. *Financial support:* In 2019–20, 89 students received support. Research assistantships, teaching assistantships, career-related internships or fieldwork, Federal Work-Study, scholarships/grants, unspecified assistantships, and administrative and laboratory assistantships available. Support available to part-time students. Financial award application deadline: 4/1; financial award applicants required to submit FAFSA. *Unit head:* Shellie Hewitt, Director of Graduate and International Student Services, 660-543-4621, Fax: 660-543-4778, E-mail: hewitt@ucmo.edu. *Application contact:* Shellie Hewitt, Director of Graduate and International Student Services, 660-543-4621, Fax: 660-543-4778, E-mail: hewitt@ucmo.edu.
Website: http://www.ucmo.edu/graduate/

**University of Central Oklahoma,** The Jackson College of Graduate Studies, College of Mathematics and Science, Department of Biology, Edmond, OK 73034-5209. Offers MS. *Program availability:* Part-time. *Degree requirements:* For master's, thesis. *Entrance requirements:* For master's, GRE General Test, GRE Subject Test (biology), faculty commitment to mentor. Additional exam requirements/recommendations for international students: required—TOEFL (minimum score 550 paper-based; 79 iBT), IELTS (minimum score 6.5). Electronic applications accepted.

**University of Chicago,** Division of the Biological Sciences, Biochemistry and Molecular Biology Department, Chicago, IL 60637. Offers PhD, MD/PhD. *Degree requirements:* For doctorate, thesis/dissertation, ethics class, 2 teaching assistantships. *Entrance requirements:* For doctorate, GRE General Test, transcripts, statement of purpose, 3 letters of recommendation. Additional exam requirements/recommendations for international students: required—TOEFL (minimum score 600 paper-based; 104 iBT), IELTS (minimum score 7). Electronic applications accepted.

**University of Cincinnati,** Graduate School, College of Medicine, Graduate Programs in Biomedical Sciences, Cincinnati, OH 45221. Offers MS, PhD, Graduate Certificate. Terminal master's awarded for partial completion of doctoral program. *Degree requirements:* For master's, thesis; for doctorate, thesis/dissertation, qualifying exam. *Entrance requirements:* For master's and doctorate, GRE General Test. Additional exam requirements/recommendations for international students: required—TOEFL (minimum score 600 paper-based; 100 iBT). Electronic applications accepted. *Expenses:* Contact institution.

**University of Cincinnati,** Graduate School, College of Medicine, Medical Scientist Training Program, Cincinnati, OH 45221. Offers MD/PhD. Electronic applications accepted.

**University of Cincinnati,** Graduate School, McMicken College of Arts and Sciences, Department of Biological Sciences, Cincinnati, OH 45221-0006. Offers MS, PhD. *Program availability:* Part-time. Terminal master's awarded for partial completion of doctoral program. *Degree requirements:* For master's, thesis; for doctorate, comprehensive exam, thesis/dissertation. *Entrance requirements:* For master's and doctorate, GRE General Test, BS in biology, chemistry, or equivalent. Additional exam requirements/recommendations for international students: required—TOEFL (minimum score 600 paper-based; 100 iBT). Electronic applications accepted.

**University of Colorado Denver,** College of Liberal Arts and Sciences, Department of Integrative Biology, Denver, CO 80217. Offers biology (MS); integrative and systems biology (PhD). *Program availability:* Part-time. *Degree requirements:* For master's, comprehensive exam, thesis, 30-32 credit hours; for doctorate, comprehensive exam, thesis/dissertation. *Entrance requirements:* For master's, GRE General Test (minimum score in 50th percentile in each section), BA/BS from accredited institution awarded within the last 10 years; minimum undergraduate GPA of 3.0; prerequisite courses: 1 year each of general biology and general chemistry; 1 semester each of general genetics, general ecology, and cell biology; and a structure/function course; for doctorate, GRE, minimum undergraduate GPA of 3.2, three letters of recommendation, official transcripts from all universities and colleges attended. Additional exam requirements/recommendations for international students: required—TOEFL (minimum score 537 paper-based; 75 iBT); recommended—IELTS (minimum score 6.5). Electronic applications accepted. Tuition and fees vary according to course load, program and reciprocity agreements.

**University of Colorado Denver,** School of Medicine, Biomedical Sciences Program, Aurora, CO 80045. Offers MS, PhD. Terminal master's awarded for partial completion of doctoral program. *Degree requirements:* For master's and doctorate, comprehensive exam. *Entrance requirements:* For master's, GRE, three letters of recommendation; for doctorate, GRE, minimum undergraduate GPA of 3.0; prerequisite coursework in organic chemistry, biology, biochemistry, physics, and calculus; letters of recommendation; interview. Additional exam requirements/recommendations for international students: required—TOEFL (minimum score 550 paper-based; 80 iBT). Electronic applications accepted. Tuition and fees vary according to course load, program and reciprocity agreements.

**University of Connecticut Health Center,** Graduate School and School of Medicine, Combined Degree Program in Biomedical Sciences, Farmington, CT 06030. Offers MD/PhD. *Entrance requirements:* Additional exam requirements/recommendations for international students: required—TOEFL (minimum score 600 paper-based). *Expenses:* Contact institution.

**University of Connecticut Health Center,** Graduate School, Programs in Biomedical Sciences, Farmington, CT 06030. Offers PhD, DMD/PhD, MD/PhD. *Degree requirements:* For doctorate, comprehensive exam, thesis/dissertation. *Entrance requirements:* For doctorate, GRE General Test. Additional exam requirements/recommendations for international students: required—TOEFL (minimum score 600 paper-based). Electronic applications accepted.

**University of Connecticut Health Center,** Graduate School, Programs in Biomedical Sciences - Integrated, Farmington, CT 06030. Offers PhD, DMD/PhD, MD/PhD. *Degree requirements:* For doctorate, comprehensive exam, thesis/dissertation. *Entrance requirements:* For doctorate, GRE General Test. Additional exam requirements/recommendations for international students: required—TOEFL (minimum score 600 paper-based). Electronic applications accepted.

**University of Dayton,** Department of Biology, Dayton, OH 45469. Offers MS, PhD. Terminal master's awarded for partial completion of doctoral program. *Degree requirements:* For master's, comprehensive exam, thesis; for doctorate, comprehensive exam, thesis/dissertation, candidacy exam, one first-author paper accepted/published. *Entrance requirements:* For master's and doctorate, GRE, minimum undergraduate GPA of 3.0. Additional exam requirements/recommendations for international students: required—TOEFL (minimum score 550 paper-based; 80 iBT); recommended—IELTS. Electronic applications accepted. *Expenses:* Contact institution.

**University of Delaware,** College of Arts and Sciences, Department of Biological Sciences, Newark, DE 19716. Offers biotechnology (MS); cancer biology (MS, PhD); cell and extracellular matrix biology (MS, PhD); cell and systems physiology (MS, PhD);

developmental biology (MS, PhD); ecology and evolution (MS, PhD); microbiology (MS, PhD); molecular biology and genetics (MS, PhD). Terminal master's awarded for partial completion of doctoral program. *Degree requirements:* For master's, thesis, preliminary exam; for doctorate, comprehensive exam, thesis/dissertation, preliminary exam. *Entrance requirements:* For master's and doctorate, GRE General Test. Additional exam requirements/recommendations for international students: required—TOEFL (minimum score 600 paper-based); recommended—TWE. Electronic applications accepted.

**University of Denver,** Division of Natural Sciences and Mathematics, Department of Biological Sciences, Denver, CO 80208. Offers biology, ecology and evolution (MS, PhD); biomedical sciences (PSM); cell and molecular biology (MS, PhD). *Program availability:* Part-time. *Faculty:* 23 full-time (10 women), 2 part-time/adjunct (both women). *Students:* 12 full-time (7 women), 31 part-time (18 women); includes 6 minority (4 Hispanic/Latino; 2 Two or more races, non-Hispanic/Latino), 3 international. Average age 25. 100 applicants, 34% accepted, 18 enrolled. In 2019, 9 master's, 6 doctorates awarded. Terminal master's awarded for partial completion of doctoral program. *Degree requirements:* For master's, thesis; for doctorate, comprehensive exam, thesis/dissertation. *Entrance requirements:* For master's and doctorate, GRE General Test, bachelor's degree in biology or related field, transcripts, personal statement, three letters of recommendation. Additional exam requirements/recommendations for international students: required—TOEFL (minimum score 550 paper-based; 80 iBT). *Application deadline:* For fall admission, 1/2 priority date for domestic and international students. Applications are processed on a rolling basis. Application fee: $65. Electronic applications accepted. *Expenses:* Contact institution. *Financial support:* In 2019–20, 43 students received support, including 9 research assistantships with tuition reimbursements available (averaging $16,589 per year), 26 teaching assistantships with tuition reimbursements available (averaging $18,869 per year); Federal Work-Study, institutionally sponsored loans, scholarships/grants, and unspecified assistantships also available. Support available to part-time students. Financial award application deadline: 2/15; financial award applicants required to submit FAFSA. *Unit head:* Dr. Joe Angleson, Associate Professor and Chair, 303-871-3463, E-mail: jangleso@du.edu. *Application contact:* Randi Flageolle, Assistant to the Chair, 303-871-3457, E-mail: rflageol@du.edu.
Website: http://www.du.edu/nsm/departments/biologicalsciences

**University of Florida,** College of Medicine and Graduate School, Interdisciplinary Program in Biomedical Sciences, Gainesville, FL 32610-0229. Offers MS, PhD, MD/PhD. *Degree requirements:* For doctorate, comprehensive exam, thesis/dissertation. *Entrance requirements:* For doctorate, GRE General Test, minimum GPA of 3.0, biochemistry before enrollment. Additional exam requirements/recommendations for international students: required—TOEFL, IELTS. Electronic applications accepted. *Expenses:* Contact institution.

**University of Georgia,** Biomedical and Health Sciences Institute, Athens, GA 30602. Offers neuroscience (PhD). *Entrance requirements:* For doctorate, GRE, official transcripts, 3 letters of recommendation, statement of interest. Additional exam requirements/recommendations for international students: required—TOEFL.

**University of Guam,** Office of Graduate Studies, College of Natural and Applied Sciences, Program in Biology, Mangilao, GU 96923. Offers tropical marine biology (MS). *Degree requirements:* For master's, comprehensive exam, thesis. *Entrance requirements:* For master's, GRE General Test, GRE Subject Test. Additional exam requirements/recommendations for international students: required—TOEFL.

**University of Guelph,** Office of Graduate and Postdoctoral Studies, College of Biological Science, Guelph, ON N1G 2W1, Canada. Offers M Sc, PhD. *Program availability:* Part-time. *Degree requirements:* For master's, thesis (for some programs); for doctorate, comprehensive exam (for some programs), thesis/dissertation. *Entrance requirements:* Additional exam requirements/recommendations for international students: required—TOEFL (minimum score 550 paper-based). Electronic applications accepted.

**University of Hawaii at Manoa,** John A. Burns School of Medicine and Office of Graduate Education, Graduate Programs in Biomedical Sciences, Honolulu, HI 96822. Offers MS, PhD. *Program availability:* Part-time. Terminal master's awarded for partial completion of doctoral program. *Degree requirements:* For master's, thesis optional; for doctorate, comprehensive exam, thesis/dissertation. *Entrance requirements:* For master's and doctorate, GRE General Test. Additional exam requirements/recommendations for international students: required—TOEFL (minimum score 500 paper-based; 61 iBT), IELTS (minimum score 5). *Expenses:* Contact institution.

**University of Holy Cross,** Graduate Programs, New Orleans, LA 70131-7399. Offers biomedical sciences (MS); Catholic theology (MA); counseling (MA, PhD), including community counseling (MA), marriage and family counseling (MA), school counseling (MA); educational leadership (M Ed); executive leadership (Ed D); management (MS), including healthcare management, operations management; teaching and learning (M Ed). *Accreditation:* ACA; NCATE. *Program availability:* Part-time, evening/weekend, online learning. *Degree requirements:* For master's, thesis. *Entrance requirements:* For master's, GRE General Test, minimum GPA of 2.7.

**University of Houston,** College of Natural Sciences and Mathematics, Department of Biology and Biochemistry, Houston, TX 77204. Offers biochemistry (MA, PhD); biology (MA). Terminal master's awarded for partial completion of doctoral program. *Degree requirements:* For master's, comprehensive exam (for some programs), thesis optional; for doctorate, comprehensive exam (for some programs), thesis/dissertation. *Entrance requirements:* For master's and doctorate, GRE. Additional exam requirements/recommendations for international students: required—TOEFL (minimum score 550 paper-based; 79 iBT), IELTS (minimum score 6.5). Electronic applications accepted.

**University of Houston–Clear Lake,** School of Science and Computer Engineering, Program in Biological Sciences, Houston, TX 77058-1002. Offers MS. *Program availability:* Part-time, evening/weekend. *Entrance requirements:* For master's, GRE General Test. Additional exam requirements/recommendations for international students: required—TOEFL (minimum score 550 paper-based).

**University of Houston–Victoria,** School of Arts and Sciences, Program in Biomedical Sciences, Victoria, TX 77901-4450. Offers biological sciences (MS); biomedical sciences (MS); forensic science (MS).

**University of Idaho,** College of Graduate Studies, College of Science, Department of Biological Sciences, Moscow, ID 83844-2282. Offers biology (MS, PhD); microbiology, molecular biology and biochemistry (PhD). *Faculty:* 18 full-time (7 women). *Students:* 27 full-time (14 women). Average age 27. In 2019, 2 master's, 2 doctorates awarded. *Degree requirements:* For master's, thesis; for doctorate, thesis/dissertation. *Entrance requirements:* For master's and doctorate, GRE, minimum GPA of 3.0. Additional exam requirements/recommendations for international students: required—TOEFL (minimum score 79 iBT). *Application deadline:* For fall admission, 12/1 for domestic students. Applications are processed on a rolling basis. Application fee: $60. Electronic applications accepted. *Expenses:* Tuition, state resident: full-time $7753.80; part-time $502 per credit hour. Tuition, nonresident: full-time $26,990; part-time $1571 per credit hour. *Required fees:* $2122.20; $47 per credit hour. *Financial support:* Research assistantships and teaching assistantships available. Financial award applicants

required to submit FAFSA. *Unit head:* Dr. James J. Nagler, Chair, 208-885-6280, Fax: 208-885-7905, E-mail: biosci@uidaho.edu. *Application contact:* Dr. James J. Nagler, Chair, 208-885-6280, Fax: 208-885-7905, E-mail: biosci@uidaho.edu.
Website: https://www.uidaho.edu/sci/biology

**University of Illinois at Chicago,** College of Liberal Arts and Sciences, Department of Biological Sciences, Chicago, IL 60607-7128. Offers MS, PhD. *Degree requirements:* For master's, thesis; for doctorate, thesis/dissertation, preliminary exam. *Entrance requirements:* For master's and doctorate, GRE General Test, GRE Subject Test, previous course work in physics, calculus, and organic chemistry; minimum GPA of 2.75. Additional exam requirements/recommendations for international students: required—TOEFL. Electronic applications accepted. *Expenses:* Contact institution.

**University of Illinois at Chicago,** College of Medicine, Graduate Programs in Medicine, Chicago, IL 60607-7128. Offers MHPE, MS, PhD, MD/MS, MD/PhD. *Program availability:* Part-time. Terminal master's awarded for partial completion of doctoral program. *Degree requirements:* For master's, thesis; for doctorate, thesis/dissertation. *Entrance requirements:* For master's and doctorate, GRE General Test. *Expenses:* Contact institution.

**University of Illinois at Springfield,** Graduate Programs, College of Liberal Arts and Sciences, Program in Biology, Springfield, IL 62703-5407. Offers MS. *Program availability:* Part-time. *Faculty:* 8 full-time (2 women). In 2019, 1 master's awarded. *Degree requirements:* For master's, oral presentation of the written thesis or comprehensive examination. *Entrance requirements:* Additional exam requirements/recommendations for international students: required—TOEFL (minimum score 500 paper-based; 61 iBT). *Application deadline:* Applications are processed on a rolling basis. Application fee: $60 ($75 for international students). Electronic applications accepted. *Expenses: Tuition, area resident:* Full-time $7896; part-time $329 per credit hour. Tuition, nonresident: full-time $16,200; part-time $675 per credit hour. *Required fees:* $2735.60; $130.65 per credit hour. *Financial support:* In 2019–20, research assistantships with full tuition reimbursements (averaging $10,562 per year), teaching assistantships with full tuition reimbursements (averaging $10,652 per year) were awarded; fellowships, career-related internships or fieldwork, Federal Work-Study, scholarships/grants, health care benefits, and unspecified assistantships also available. Support available to part-time students. Financial award application deadline: 11/15; financial award applicants required to submit FAFSA. *Unit head:* Dr. Michael Lemke, Program Administrator, 217-206-6630, Fax: 217-206-7205, E-mail: lemke.michael@uis.edu. *Application contact:* Dr. Michael Lemke, Program Administrator, 217-206-6630, Fax: 217-206-7205, E-mail: lemke.michael@uis.edu.
Website: http://www.uis.edu/biology

**University of Illinois at Urbana-Champaign,** Graduate College, College of Liberal Arts and Sciences, School of Chemical Sciences, Champaign, IL 61820. Offers MA, MS, PhD, MS/JD, MS/MBA. *Expenses:* Contact institution.

**University of Illinois at Urbana-Champaign,** Graduate College, College of Liberal Arts and Sciences, School of Integrative Biology, Champaign, IL 61820. Offers MS, MST, PSM, PhD. *Program availability:* Part-time, online learning.

**University of Indianapolis,** Graduate Programs, Shaheen College of Arts and Sciences, Department of Biology, Indianapolis, IN 46227-3697. Offers human biology (MS). *Program availability:* Part-time, evening/weekend. *Degree requirements:* For master's, thesis. *Entrance requirements:* For master's, GRE General Test, 3 letters of recommendation; minimum GPA of 3.0; BA/BS in anthropology, biology, human biology or closely-related field; resume. Additional exam requirements/recommendations for international students: required—TOEFL (minimum score 550 paper-based).

**The University of Iowa,** Graduate College, College of Liberal Arts and Sciences, Department of Biology, Iowa City, IA 52242-1324. Offers biology (MS, PhD); cell and developmental biology (MS, PhD); evolution (MS, PhD); genetics (MS, PhD); neurobiology (MS, PhD). Terminal master's awarded for partial completion of doctoral program. *Degree requirements:* For master's, thesis optional, exam; for doctorate, comprehensive exam, thesis/dissertation. *Entrance requirements:* For master's and doctorate, GRE General Test, minimum GPA of 3.0. Additional exam requirements/recommendations for international students: required—TOEFL (minimum score 600 paper-based; 100 iBT). Electronic applications accepted.

**The University of Iowa,** Roy J. and Lucille A. Carver College of Medicine and Graduate College, Graduate Programs in Medicine, Iowa City, IA 52242-1316. Offers MA, MPAS, MS, DPT, PhD, JD/MHA, MBA/MHA, MD/JD, MD/PhD, MHA/MA, MHA/MS, MPH/MHA, MS/MA, MS/MS. *Program availability:* Part-time. *Degree requirements:* For doctorate, thesis/dissertation. Electronic applications accepted. *Expenses:* Contact institution.

**The University of Iowa,** Roy J. and Lucille A. Carver College of Medicine and Graduate College, Medical Scientist Training Program, Iowa City, IA 52242. Offers MD/PhD. *Faculty:* 87 full-time (28 women). *Students:* 73 full-time (31 women); includes 24 minority (3 Black or African American, non-Hispanic/Latino; 1 American Indian or Alaska Native, non-Hispanic/Latino; 10 Asian, non-Hispanic/Latino; 9 Hispanic/Latino; 1 Two or more races, non-Hispanic/Latino). Average age 28. 202 applicants, 9% accepted, 8 enrolled. *Application deadline:* For fall admission, 12/15 priority date for domestic students. Applications are processed on a rolling basis. Application fee: $60. Electronic applications accepted. *Expenses:* Contact institution. *Financial support:* In 2019–20, 73 students received support, including 29 fellowships with full tuition reimbursements available (averaging $30,500 per year), 40 research assistantships with full tuition reimbursements available (averaging $30,500 per year); scholarships/grants, traineeships, health care benefits, unspecified assistantships, and travel awards also available. *Unit head:* Dr. Steven R. Lentz, Director, 319-356-4048, Fax: 319-335-6634, E-mail: steven-lentz@uiowa.edu. *Application contact:* Jessica Jensen, Administrative Coordinator, 319-335-8303, Fax: 319-335-6634, E-mail: mstp@uiowa.edu.
Website: https://medicine.uiowa.edu/mstp/

**The University of Kansas,** University of Kansas Medical Center, School of Medicine, Interdisciplinary Graduate Program in Biomedical Sciences (IGPBS), Kansas City, KS 66160. Offers PhD, MD/PhD. *Students:* 17 full-time (11 women); includes 3 minority (1 Asian, non-Hispanic/Latino; 1 Hispanic/Latino; 1 Two or more races, non-Hispanic/Latino), 6 international. Average age 25. 112 applicants, 33% accepted, 17 enrolled. Terminal master's awarded for partial completion of doctoral program. *Degree requirements:* For doctorate, comprehensive exam, thesis/dissertation. *Entrance requirements:* Additional exam requirements/recommendations for international students: required—TOEFL. *Application deadline:* For fall admission, 12/1 priority date for domestic and international students. Applications are processed on a rolling basis. Application fee: $60. Electronic applications accepted. *Expenses:* Tuition, state resident: full-time $9989. Tuition, nonresident: full-time $23,950. *International tuition:* $23,950 full-time. *Required fees:* $984; $81.99 per credit hour. Tuition and fees vary according to course load, campus/location and program. *Financial support:* Research assistantships with full tuition reimbursements, teaching assistantships with full tuition reimbursements, scholarships/grants, and unspecified assistantships available. Financial award application deadline: 3/1; financial award applicants required to submit FAFSA. *Unit head:* Dr. Michael Werle, Director, E-mail: mwerle@kumc.edu. *Application contact:* Martin J. Graham, Coordinator, 913-588-2719, Fax: 913-588-5242, E-mail: mgraham4@kumc.edu.
Website: http://www.kumc.edu/igpbs.html

**University of Kentucky,** Graduate School, College of Arts and Sciences, Program in Biology, Lexington, KY 40506-0032. Offers MS, PhD. *Degree requirements:* For master's, comprehensive exam, thesis optional; for doctorate, comprehensive exam, thesis/dissertation. *Entrance requirements:* For master's, GRE General Test, minimum undergraduate GPA of 2.75; for doctorate, GRE General Test, minimum graduate GPA of 3.0. Additional exam requirements/recommendations for international students: required—TOEFL (minimum score 550 paper-based). Electronic applications accepted.

**University of Kentucky,** Graduate School, Graduate School Programs from the College of Medicine, Lexington, KY 40506-0032. Offers MS, PhD, MD/PhD. *Degree requirements:* For master's, comprehensive exam, thesis (for some programs); for doctorate, comprehensive exam, thesis/dissertation. *Entrance requirements:* For master's, GRE General Test, minimum undergraduate GPA of 2.75; for doctorate, GRE General Test, minimum undergraduate GPA of 3.0. Additional exam requirements/recommendations for international students: required—TOEFL (minimum score 550 paper-based). Electronic applications accepted.

**University of Lethbridge,** School of Graduate Studies, Lethbridge, AB T1K 3M4, Canada. Offers addictions counseling (M Sc); agricultural biotechnology (M Sc); agricultural studies (M Sc, MA); anthropology (MA); archaeology (M Sc, MA); art (MA, MFA); biochemistry (M Sc); biological sciences (M Sc); biomolecular science (PhD); biosystems and biodiversity (PhD); Canadian studies (MA); chemistry (M Sc); computer science (M Sc); computer science and geographical information science (M Sc); counseling (MC); counseling psychology (M Ed); dramatic arts (MA); earth, space, and physical science (PhD); economics (MA); education (MA, PhD); educational leadership (M Ed); English (MA); environmental science (M Sc); evolution and behavior (PhD); exercise science (M Sc); French (MA); French/German (MA); French/Spanish (MA); general education (M Ed); geography (M Sc, MA); German (MA); health sciences (M Sc); individualized multidisciplinary (M Sc, MA); kinesiology (M Sc, MA); management (M Sc), including accounting, finance, human resource management and labor relations, information systems, international management, marketing, policy and strategy; mathematics (M Sc); music (M Mus, MA); Native American studies (MA); neuroscience (M Sc, PhD); new media (MA, MFA); nursing (M Sc, MN); philosophy (MA); physics (M Sc); political science (MA); psychology (M Sc, MA); religious studies (MA); sociology (MA); theatre and dramatic arts (MFA); theoretical and computational science (PhD); urban and regional studies (MA); women and gender studies (MA). *Program availability:* Part-time, evening/weekend. *Degree requirements:* For master's, thesis (for some programs); for doctorate, comprehensive exam, thesis/dissertation. *Entrance requirements:* For master's, GMAT (for M Sc in management), bachelor's degree in related field, minimum GPA of 3.0 during previous 20 graded semester courses, 2 years' teaching or related experience (M Ed); for doctorate, master's degree, minimum graduate GPA of 3.5. Additional exam requirements/recommendations for international students: required—TOEFL (minimum score 580 paper-based; 93 iBT). Electronic applications accepted.

**University of Louisiana at Lafayette,** College of Sciences, Department of Biology, Lafayette, LA 70504. Offers biology (MS); environmental and evolutionary biology (PhD). Terminal master's awarded for partial completion of doctoral program. *Degree requirements:* For master's, thesis; for doctorate, 2 foreign languages, comprehensive exam, thesis/dissertation. *Entrance requirements:* For master's, GRE General Test, minimum GPA of 2.75; for doctorate, GRE General Test, GRE Subject Test, minimum GPA of 3.0. Additional exam requirements/recommendations for international students: required—TOEFL (minimum score 550 paper-based). Electronic applications accepted. *Expenses: Tuition, area resident:* Full-time $5511; part-time $1630 per credit hour. Tuition, state resident: full-time $5511; part-time $1630 per credit hour. Tuition, nonresident: full-time $19,239; part-time $2409 per credit hour. *Required fees:* $46,637.

**University of Louisiana at Monroe,** Graduate School, College of Arts, Education, and Sciences, Department of Biology, Monroe, LA 71209-0001. Offers MS. *Faculty:* 5 full-time (2 women), 1 (woman) part-time/adjunct. *Students:* 31 full-time (14 women), 4 part-time (3 women); includes 6 minority (4 Black or African American, non-Hispanic/Latino; 1 Asian, non-Hispanic/Latino; 1 Two or more races, non-Hispanic/Latino), 3 international. Average age 25. 18 applicants, 67% accepted, 10 enrolled. In 2019, 10 master's awarded. *Degree requirements:* For master's, thesis optional. *Entrance requirements:* For master's, GRE General Test, minimum GPA of 2.75. Additional exam requirements/recommendations for international students: required—TOEFL (minimum score 500 paper-based; 61 iBT); recommended—IELTS (minimum score 5.5). *Application deadline:* For fall admission, 8/1 for domestic students, 6/1 for international students; for spring admission, 1/1 for domestic students, 11/1 for international students; for summer admission, 6/1 for domestic students, 3/1 for international students. Applications are processed on a rolling basis. Application fee: $40. Electronic applications accepted. *Expenses: Tuition, area resident:* Full-time $6489. Tuition, state resident: full-time $6489. Tuition, nonresident: full-time $18,989. *Required fees:* $2748. Tuition and fees vary according to course load and program. *Financial support:* In 2019–20, 27 students received support. Teaching assistantships with full tuition reimbursements available, career-related internships or fieldwork, Federal Work-Study, scholarships/grants, and unspecified assistantships available. Financial award application deadline: 2/15; financial award applicants required to submit FAFSA. *Unit head:* Dr. Chris Gissendanner, School of Sciences & CAES Graduate Coordinator, 318-342-3314, Fax: 318-342-1790, E-mail: gissendanner@ulm.edu. *Application contact:* Dr. Chris Gissendanner, School of Sciences & CAES Graduate Coordinator, 318-342-3314, Fax: 318-342-1790, E-mail: gissendanner@ulm.edu.
Website: http://www.ulm.edu/biology/

**University of Louisville,** Graduate School, College of Arts and Sciences, Department of Biology, Louisville, KY 40292-0001. Offers biology (MS); environmental biology (PhD). *Program availability:* Part-time. *Faculty:* 22 full-time (8 women), 7 part-time/adjunct (3 women). *Students:* 37 full-time (18 women), 7 part-time (4 women); includes 11 minority (2 Asian, non-Hispanic/Latino; 5 Hispanic/Latino; 4 Two or more races, non-Hispanic/Latino), 8 international. Average age 30. 25 applicants, 36% accepted, 7 enrolled. In 2019, 7 master's, 5 doctorates awarded. Terminal master's awarded for partial completion of doctoral program. *Degree requirements:* For master's, comprehensive exam, thesis (for some programs); for doctorate, comprehensive exam, thesis/dissertation. *Entrance requirements:* For master's, GRE, MCAT, or DAT, Two letters of reference, official transcripts; for doctorate, GRE, Two letters of reference, official transcripts. Additional exam requirements/recommendations for international students: required—TOEFL (minimum score 550 paper-based; 79 iBT), IELTS can be used in place of the TOEFL; recommended—IELTS (minimum score 6.5). *Application deadline:* For fall admission, 1/15 priority date for domestic and international students; for spring admission, 12/1 for domestic and international students; for summer admission, 4/15 for domestic and international students. Applications are processed on a rolling basis. Application fee: $65. Electronic applications accepted. *Expenses: Tuition, area resident:* Full-time $13,000; part-time $723 per credit hour. Tuition, state resident: full-time $13,000; part-time $723 per credit hour. Tuition, nonresident: full-time $27,114; part-time $1507 per credit hour. *International tuition:* $27,114 full-time. *Required fees:* $196. Tuition and fees vary according to program and reciprocity agreements. *Financial*

*support:* In 2019–20, 43 students received support, including 5 fellowships with full tuition reimbursements available (averaging $22,000 per year), 2 research assistantships with full tuition reimbursements available (averaging $22,000 per year), 28 teaching assistantships with full tuition reimbursements available (averaging $22,000 per year); health care benefits and unspecified assistantships also available. Financial award application deadline: 1/15. *Unit head:* Dr. Perri Eason, Professor and Chair, 502-852-6771, Fax: 502-852-0725, E-mail: perri.eason@louisville.edu. *Application contact:* Dr. Sarah Emery, Professor and Director of Graduate Studies, 502-852-5940, E-mail: sarah.emery@louisville.edu.
Website: http://louisville.edu/biology

**University of Maine,** Graduate School, College of Natural Sciences, Forestry, and Agriculture, Department of Molecular and Biomedical Sciences, Orono, ME 04469. Offers microbiology (PhD). *Faculty:* 10 full-time (5 women). *Students:* 24 full-time (14 women), 6 part-time (5 women); includes 3 minority (1 Black or African American, non-Hispanic/Latino; 1 Asian, non-Hispanic/Latino; 1 Two or more races, non-Hispanic/Latino), 7 international. Average age 29. 41 applicants, 46% accepted, 8 enrolled. In 2019, 2 master's, 3 doctorates awarded. *Degree requirements:* For master's, thesis (for some programs); for doctorate, comprehensive exam, thesis/dissertation. *Entrance requirements:* For master's and doctorate, GRE General Test. Additional exam requirements/recommendations for international students: required—TOEFL (minimum score 580 paper-based; 92 iBT), IELTS (minimum score 7). *Application deadline:* For fall admission, 1/15 for domestic and international students; for spring admission, 9/15 for domestic and international students. Applications are processed on a rolling basis. Application fee: $65. Electronic applications accepted. *Expenses: Tuition, area resident:* Full-time $8100; part-time $450 per credit hour. Tuition, state resident: full-time $8100; part-time $450 per credit hour. Tuition, nonresident: full-time $26,388; part-time $1466 per credit hour. *International tuition:* $26,388 full-time. *Required fees:* $1257; $278 per semester. Tuition and fees vary according to course load. *Financial support:* In 2019–20, 60 students received support, including 1 fellowship with full tuition reimbursement available (averaging $34,000 per year), 49 research assistantships with full tuition reimbursements available (averaging $22,000 per year), 10 teaching assistantships with full tuition reimbursements available (averaging $15,850 per year); tuition waivers (full and partial) also available. Financial award application deadline: 3/1; financial award applicants required to submit FAFSA. *Unit head:* Dr. Robert Gundersen, Chair, 207-581-2802, Fax: 207-581-2801. *Application contact:* Scott G. Delcourt, Assistant Vice President for Graduate Studies and Senior Associate Dean, 207-581-3291, Fax: 207-581-3232, E-mail: graduate@maine.edu.
Website: http://umaine.edu/biomed/

**University of Maine,** Graduate School, College of Natural Sciences, Forestry, and Agriculture, School of Biology and Ecology, Orono, ME 04469. Offers biological sciences (PhD); botany and plant pathology (MS); entomology (MS); zoology (MS, PhD). *Program availability:* Part-time. *Faculty:* 30 full-time (16 women), 2 part-time/adjunct (1 woman). *Students:* 84 full-time (54 women), 12 part-time (6 women); includes 9 minority (1 Black or African American, non-Hispanic/Latino; 1 American Indian or Alaska Native, non-Hispanic/Latino; 1 Asian, non-Hispanic/Latino; 5 Hispanic/Latino; 1 Two or more races, non-Hispanic/Latino), 21 international. Average age 30. 62 applicants, 40% accepted, 22 enrolled. In 2019, 12 master's, 12 doctorates awarded. Terminal master's awarded for partial completion of doctoral program. *Degree requirements:* For master's, thesis (for some programs); for doctorate, comprehensive exam, thesis/dissertation. *Entrance requirements:* For master's and doctorate, GRE General Test. Additional exam requirements/recommendations for international students: required—TOEFL (minimum score 80 iBT), IELTS (minimum score 6.5). *Application deadline:* For fall admission, 2/1 priority date for domestic students. Applications are processed on a rolling basis. Application fee: $65. Electronic applications accepted. *Expenses: Tuition, area resident:* Full-time $8100; part-time $450 per credit hour. Tuition, state resident: full-time $8100; part-time $450 per credit hour. Tuition, nonresident: full-time $26,388; part-time $1466 per credit hour. *International tuition:* $26,388 full-time. *Required fees:* $1257; $278 per semester. Tuition and fees vary according to course load. *Financial support:* In 2019–20, 108 students received support, including 1 fellowship with full tuition reimbursement available (averaging $25,000 per year), 79 research assistantships with full tuition reimbursements available (averaging $15,825 per year), 23 teaching assistantships with full tuition reimbursements available (averaging $15,825 per year); career-related internships or fieldwork, Federal Work-Study, institutionally sponsored loans, tuition waivers (full and partial), and unspecified assistantships also available. Financial award application deadline: 3/1; financial award applicants required to submit FAFSA. *Unit head:* Dr. Andrei Aloykhin, Director, 207-581-2977, Fax: 207-581-2537. *Application contact:* Scott G. Delcourt, Assistant Vice President for Graduate Studies and Senior Associate Dean, 207-581-3291, Fax: 207-581-3232, E-mail: graduate@maine.edu.
Website: http://sbe.umaine.edu/

**University of Maine,** Graduate School, Graduate School of Biomedical Science and Engineering, Orono, ME 04469. Offers bioinformatics (PSM); biomedical engineering (PhD); biomedical science (PhD). *Faculty:* 182 full-time (60 women). *Students:* 47 full-time (26 women), 1 part-time (0 women); includes 2 minority (1 Hispanic/Latino; 1 Two or more races, non-Hispanic/Latino), 9 international. Average age 30. 111 applicants, 17% accepted, 15 enrolled. In 2019, 7 doctorates awarded. *Degree requirements:* For doctorate, comprehensive exam, thesis/dissertation. *Entrance requirements:* For doctorate, GRE General Test, master's degree. Additional exam requirements/recommendations for international students: required—TOEFL (minimum score 80 iBT), IELTS (minimum score 6.5), PTE (minimum score 60). *Application deadline:* For fall admission, 1/1 priority date for domestic and international students. Applications are processed on a rolling basis. Application fee: $65. Electronic applications accepted. *Expenses: Tuition, area resident:* Full-time $8100; part-time $450 per credit hour. Tuition, state resident: full-time $8100; part-time $450 per credit hour. Tuition, nonresident: full-time $26,388; part-time $1466 per credit hour. *International tuition:* $26,388 full-time. *Required fees:* $1257; $278 per semester. Tuition and fees vary according to course load. *Financial support:* In 2019–20, 47 students received support, including 1 fellowship with tuition reimbursement available (averaging $34,000 per year), 41 research assistantships with full tuition reimbursements available (averaging $20,000 per year), 5 teaching assistantships with full tuition reimbursements available (averaging $15,825 per year); career-related internships or fieldwork, scholarships/grants, and unspecified assistantships also available. Financial award application deadline: 3/1; financial award applicants required to submit FAFSA. *Unit head:* Scott G Delcourt, Assistant Vice President for Graduate Studies and Senior Associate Dean, 207-581-3291, Fax: 207-581-3232, E-mail: graduate@maine.edu. *Application contact:* Scott G Delcourt, Assistant Vice President for Graduate Studies and Senior Associate Dean, 207-581-3291, Fax: 207-581-3232, E-mail: graduate@maine.edu.
Website: http://gsbse.umaine.edu/

**The University of Manchester,** School of Biological Sciences, Manchester, United Kingdom. Offers adaptive organismal biology (M Phil, PhD); animal biology (M Phil, PhD); biochemistry (M Phil, PhD); bioinformatics (M Phil, PhD); biomolecular sciences (M Phil, PhD); biotechnology (M Phil, PhD); cell biology (M Phil, PhD); cell matrix research (M Phil, PhD); channels and transporters (M Phil, PhD); developmental biology (M Phil, PhD); environmental biology (M Phil, PhD); evolutionary biology (M Phil, PhD); gene expression (M Phil, PhD); genetics (M Phil, PhD); history of science, technology and medicine (M Phil, PhD); immunology (M Phil, PhD); integrative neurobiology and behavior (M Phil, PhD); membrane trafficking (M Phil, PhD); microbiology (M Phil, PhD); molecular and cellular neuroscience (M Phil, PhD); molecular biology (M Phil, PhD); molecular cancer studies (M Phil, PhD); neuroscience (M Phil, PhD); ophthalmology (M Phil, PhD); optometry (M Phil, PhD); organelle function (M Phil, PhD); pharmacology (M Phil, PhD); physiology (M Phil, PhD); plant sciences (M Phil, PhD); stem cell research (M Phil, PhD); structural biology (M Phil, PhD); systems neuroscience (M Phil, PhD); toxicology (M Phil, PhD).

**The University of Manchester,** School of Chemical Engineering and Analytical Science, Manchester, United Kingdom. Offers biocatalysis (M Phil, PhD); chemical engineering (M Phil, PhD); chemical engineering and analytical science (M Phil, D Eng, PhD); colloids, crystals, interfaces and materials (M Phil, PhD); environment and sustainable technology (M Phil, PhD); instrumentation (M Phil, PhD); multi-scale modeling (M Phil, PhD); process integration (M Phil, PhD); systems biology (M Phil, PhD).

**The University of Manchester,** School of Materials, Manchester, United Kingdom. Offers advanced aerospace materials engineering (M Sc); advanced metallic systems (PhD); biomedical materials (M Phil, M Sc, PhD); ceramics and glass (M Phil, M Sc, PhD); composite materials (M Sc, PhD); corrosion and protection (M Phil, M Sc, PhD); materials (M Phil, PhD); metallic materials (M Phil, M Sc, PhD); nanostructural materials (M Phil, M Sc, PhD); paper science (M Phil, M Sc, PhD); polymer science and engineering (M Phil, M Sc, PhD); technical textiles (M Sc); textile design, fashion and management (M Phil, M Sc, PhD); textile science and technology (M Phil, M Sc, PhD); textiles (M Phil, PhD); textiles and fashion (M Ent).

**The University of Manchester,** School of Medicine, Manchester, United Kingdom. Offers M Phil, PhD.

**University of Manitoba,** Faculty of Graduate Studies, Faculty of Science, Department of Biological Sciences, Winnipeg, MB R3T 2N2, Canada. Offers botany (M Sc, PhD); ecology (M Sc, PhD); zoology (M Sc, PhD).

**University of Manitoba,** Max Rady College of Medicine and Faculty of Graduate Studies, Graduate Programs in Medicine, Winnipeg, MB R3T 2N2, Canada. Offers M Sc, MPH, PhD, G Dip, MD/PhD. *Accreditation:* LCME/AMA. *Program availability:* Part-time. *Expenses:* Contact institution.

**University of Maryland, Baltimore,** Graduate School, Graduate Program in Life Sciences, Baltimore, MD 21201. Offers biochemistry and molecular biology (MS, PhD), including biochemistry; cellular and molecular biomedical science (MS); clinical research (Postbaccalaureate Certificate); epidemiology (PhD); gerontology (PhD); molecular medicine (PhD), including applied pharmacology and toxicology, cancer biology, genome biology, molecular and cellular physiology; molecular microbiology and immunology (PhD); neuroscience (PhD); physical rehabilitation science (PhD); toxicology (MS, PhD); MD/MS; MD/PhD. *Degree requirements:* For master's, comprehensive exam (for some programs), thesis (for some programs); for doctorate, comprehensive exam, thesis/dissertation. *Entrance requirements:* For master's and doctorate, GRE. Additional exam requirements/recommendations for international students: required—TOEFL (minimum score 80 iBT); recommended—IELTS (minimum score 7). Electronic applications accepted.

**University of Maryland, Baltimore County,** The Graduate School, College of Natural and Mathematical Sciences, Department of Biological Sciences, Program in Biological Sciences, Baltimore, MD 21250. Offers MS, PhD. *Faculty:* 26 full-time (11 women). *Students:* 45 full-time (26 women), 5 part-time (1 woman); includes 13 minority (2 Black or African American, non-Hispanic/Latino; 5 Asian, non-Hispanic/Latino; 4 Hispanic/Latino; 2 Two or more races, non-Hispanic/Latino), 11 international. Average age 29. 66 applicants, 38% accepted, 14 enrolled. In 2019, 2 master's, 5 doctorates awarded. Terminal master's awarded for partial completion of doctoral program. *Degree requirements:* For master's, thesis; for doctorate, thesis/dissertation. *Entrance requirements:* For master's, GRE General Test, minimum GPA of 3.0; for doctorate, GRE General Test, GRE Subject Test, minimum GPA of 3.0. Additional exam requirements/recommendations for international students: required—TOEFL (minimum score 80 iBT), IELTS (minimum score 6.5). *Application deadline:* For fall admission, 4/15 priority date for domestic and international students. Application fee: $50. Electronic applications accepted. *Expenses: Tuition, area resident:* Full-time $659. Tuition, state resident: full-time $659. Tuition, nonresident: full-time $1132. *International tuition:* $1132 full-time. *Required fees:* $140; $140 per credit hour. *Financial support:* In 2019–20, 42 students received support, including 1 fellowship with full tuition reimbursement available (averaging $24,000 per year), 12 research assistantships with full tuition reimbursements available (averaging $24,000 per year), 29 teaching assistantships with full tuition reimbursements available (averaging $24,000 per year); health care benefits also available. *Unit head:* Dr. Michelle Starz-Gaiano, Director, 410-455-2217, Fax: 410-455-3875, E-mail: biograd@umbc.edu. *Application contact:* Brandy Darcey, Graduate Program Coordinator, 410-455-3669, E-mail: bdarcey@umbc.edu.

**University of Maryland, College Park,** Academic Affairs, College of Computer, Mathematical and Natural Sciences, Department of Biology, PhD Program in Biological Sciences, College Park, MD 20742. Offers behavior, ecology, evolution, and systematics (PhD); computational biology, bioinformatics, and genomics (PhD); molecular and cellular biology (PhD); physiological systems (PhD). *Degree requirements:* For doctorate, comprehensive exam, thesis/dissertation, thesis work presentation in seminar. *Entrance requirements:* For doctorate, GRE General Test; GRE Subject Test in biology (recommended), academic transcripts, statement of purpose/research interests, 3 letters of recommendation. Additional exam requirements/recommendations for international students: required—TOEFL. Electronic applications accepted.

**University of Maryland, College Park,** Academic Affairs, College of Computer, Mathematical and Natural Sciences, Department of Biology, Program in Biology, College Park, MD 20742. Offers MS, PhD. *Program availability:* Part-time, evening/weekend. Terminal master's awarded for partial completion of doctoral program. *Degree requirements:* For master's, comprehensive exam, thesis optional; for doctorate, thesis/dissertation, oral exam.

**University of Maryland, College Park,** Academic Affairs, College of Computer, Mathematical and Natural Sciences, Program in Life Sciences, College Park, MD 20742. Offers MLS. *Degree requirements:* For master's, scholarly paper. *Entrance requirements:* For master's, 1 year of teaching experience, letters of recommendation. Electronic applications accepted.

**University of Massachusetts Amherst,** Graduate School, College of Natural Sciences, Department of Animal Biotechnology and Biomedical Sciences, Amherst, MA 01003. Offers MS, PhD. *Program availability:* Part-time. Terminal master's awarded for partial completion of doctoral program. *Degree requirements:* For master's, thesis or alternative; for doctorate, comprehensive exam, thesis/dissertation. *Entrance requirements:* For doctorate, GRE General Test. Additional exam requirements/recommendations for international students: required—TOEFL (minimum score 550 paper-based; 80 iBT), IELTS (minimum score 6.5). Electronic applications accepted.

## *Biological and Biomedical Sciences—General*

**University of Massachusetts Boston,** College of Science and Mathematics, Program in Biology, Boston, MA 02125-3393. Offers MS, PhD. *Program availability:* Part-time, evening/weekend. *Entrance requirements:* For master's, GRE General Test, GRE Subject Test, minimum GPA of 2.75.

**University of Massachusetts Boston,** College of Science and Mathematics, Program in Biotechnology and Biomedical Sciences, Boston, MA 02125-3393. Offers MS. *Program availability:* Part-time, evening/weekend. *Entrance requirements:* For master's, GRE General Test, GRE Subject Test, minimum GPA of 2.75, 3.0 in science and math.

**University of Massachusetts Boston,** College of Science and Mathematics, Program in Integrative Biosciences, Boston, MA 02125-3393. Offers PhD.

**University of Massachusetts Dartmouth,** Graduate School, College of Arts and Sciences, Department of Biology, North Dartmouth, MA 02747-2300. Offers biology (MS); integrative biology (PhD); marine biology (MS). *Program availability:* Part-time. *Faculty:* 20 full-time (9 women), 2 part-time/adjunct (both women). *Students:* 13 full-time (8 women), 13 part-time (6 women); includes 4 minority (1 Asian, non-Hispanic/Latino; 2 Hispanic/Latino; 1 Two or more races, non-Hispanic/Latino), 1 international. Average age 29. 16 applicants, 50% accepted, 4 enrolled. In 2019, 6 master's awarded. *Degree requirements:* For master's, comprehensive exam, thesis; for doctorate, comprehensive exam, thesis/dissertation. *Entrance requirements:* For master's and doctorate, GRE, statement of purpose (300-600 words), resume, official transcripts, 3 letters of recommendation. Additional exam requirements/recommendations for international students: required—TOEFL (minimum score 80 iBT). *Application deadline:* For fall admission, 8/15 for domestic students, 7/15 for international students. Application fee: $60. Electronic applications accepted. *Expenses: Tuition, area resident:* Full-time $16,390; part-time $682.92 per credit. Tuition, state resident: full-time $16,390; part-time $682.92 per credit. Tuition, nonresident: full-time $29,578; part-time $1232.42 per credit. *Required fees:* $575. *Financial support:* In 2019–20, 8 research assistantships (averaging $8,993 per year), 10 teaching assistantships (averaging $13,875 per year) were awarded; tuition waivers (full) also available. Financial award application deadline: 3/1; financial award applicants required to submit FAFSA. *Unit head:* Whitney Hable, Graduate Program Director, Biology/Marine Biology, 508-999-8206, E-mail: whable@umassd.edu. *Application contact:* Scott Webster, Director of Graduate Studies and Admissions, 508-999-8604, Fax: 508-999-8183, E-mail: graduate@umassd.edu.
Website: http://www.umassd.edu/cas/biology

**University of Massachusetts Lowell,** College of Sciences, Department of Biological Sciences, Lowell, MA 01854. Offers MS. *Program availability:* Part-time. *Degree requirements:* For master's, thesis. *Entrance requirements:* For master's, GRE General Test. Electronic applications accepted.

**University of Massachusetts Medical School,** Graduate School of Biomedical Sciences, Worcester, MA 01655. Offers biomedical sciences (PhD), including biochemistry and molecular pharmacology, bioinformatics and computational biology, cancer biology, immunology and microbiology, interdisciplinary, neuroscience, translational science; biomedical sciences (millennium program) (PhD); clinical and population health research (PhD); clinical investigation (MS). *Faculty:* 1,258 full-time (525 women), 372 part-time/adjunct (238 women). *Students:* 344 full-time (198 women), 1 (woman) part-time; includes 73 minority (12 Black or African American, non-Hispanic/Latino; 1 American Indian or Alaska Native, non-Hispanic/Latino; 45 Asian, non-Hispanic/Latino; 15 Hispanic/Latino), 120 international. Average age 29. 581 applicants, 23% accepted, 56 enrolled. In 2019, 6 master's, 49 doctorates awarded. Terminal master's awarded for partial completion of doctoral program. *Degree requirements:* For master's, comprehensive exam, thesis; for doctorate, comprehensive exam, thesis/dissertation. *Entrance requirements:* For master's, MD, PhD, DVM, or PharmD; for doctorate, bachelor's degree. Additional exam requirements/recommendations for international students: required—TOEFL, IELTS, TOEFL (minimum score 100 IBT) or IELTS (minimum score 7.0). *Application deadline:* For fall admission, 12/1 for domestic and international students. Applications are processed on a rolling basis. Application fee: $80. Electronic applications accepted. Application fee is waived when completed online. *Expenses:* Contact institution. *Financial support:* In 2019–20, 22 fellowships with full tuition reimbursements (averaging $33,061 per year), 322 research assistantships with full tuition reimbursements (averaging $32,850 per year) were awarded; institutionally sponsored loans and scholarships/grants also available. Financial award application deadline: 5/15. *Unit head:* Dr. Mary Ellen Lane, Dean, 508-856-4018, E-mail: maryellen.lane@umassmed.edu. *Application contact:* Dr. Kendall Knight, Assistant Vice Provost for Admissions, 508-856-5628, Fax: 508-856-3659, E-mail: kendall.knight@umassmed.edu.
Website: http://www.umassmed.edu/gsbs/

**University of Memphis,** Graduate School, College of Arts and Sciences, Department of Biology, Memphis, TN 38152. Offers MS, PhD. *Students:* 26 full-time (16 women), 17 part-time (11 women); includes 7 minority (2 Black or African American, non-Hispanic/Latino; 2 Asian, non-Hispanic/Latino; 3 Hispanic/Latino), 8 international. Average age 30. 12 applicants, 83% accepted, 5 enrolled. In 2019, 11 master's, 3 doctorates awarded. Terminal master's awarded for partial completion of doctoral program. *Degree requirements:* For master's, comprehensive exam, thesis (for some programs); for doctorate, one foreign language, comprehensive exam, thesis/dissertation. *Entrance requirements:* For master's, GRE General Test; for doctorate, GRE General Test, Master's degree. Additional exam requirements/recommendations for international students: required—TOEFL (minimum score 550 paper-based; 79 iBT). *Application deadline:* For fall admission, 2/1 for domestic and international students; for spring admission, 9/15 for domestic and international students. Applications are processed on a rolling basis. Application fee: $35 ($60 for international students). Electronic applications accepted. *Expenses: Tuition, area resident:* Full-time $9216; part-time $512 per credit hour. Tuition, state resident: full-time $9216; part-time $512 per credit hour. Tuition, nonresident: full-time $12,672; part-time $704 per credit hour. *International tuition:* $16,128 full-time. *Required fees:* $1530; $85 per credit hour. Tuition and fees vary according to program. *Financial support:* Research assistantships with full tuition reimbursements, teaching assistantships with full tuition reimbursements, Federal Work-Study, scholarships/grants, and unspecified assistantships available. Financial award application deadline: 2/1; financial award applicants required to submit FAFSA. *Unit head:* Dr. David Freeman, Chair, 901-678-2959, Fax: 901-678-4457, E-mail: dfreemn1@memphis.edu. *Application contact:* Dr. Omar Skalli, Graduate Studies Coordinator, 901-678-2581, Fax: 901-678-4457, E-mail: grad_studies_coordinator@memphis.edu.
Website: http://www.memphis.edu/biology/

**University of Miami,** Graduate School, College of Arts and Sciences, Department of Biology, Coral Gables, FL 33124. Offers biology (MS, PhD); genetics and evolution (MS, PhD). Terminal master's awarded for partial completion of doctoral program. *Degree requirements:* For master's, comprehensive exam (for some programs), thesis (for some programs); for doctorate, thesis/dissertation, oral and written qualifying exam. *Entrance requirements:* For master's, GRE General Test, 3 letters of recommendation, research papers; for doctorate, GRE General Test, 3 letters of recommendation, research papers, sponsor letter. Additional exam requirements/recommendations for international students: required—TOEFL (minimum score 550 paper-based; 59 iBT). Electronic applications accepted.

**University of Michigan,** Medical School and Rackham Graduate School, Medical Scientist Training Program, Ann Arbor, MI 48109. Offers MD/PhD. *Accreditation:* LCME/AMA. Electronic applications accepted.

**University of Michigan,** Rackham Graduate School, Program in Biomedical Sciences (PIBS), Ann Arbor, MI 48109-5619. Offers MS, PhD. *Degree requirements:* For doctorate, thesis/dissertation, oral defense of dissertation, preliminary exam. *Entrance requirements:* For doctorate, 3 letters of recommendation, personal statement, academic statement of purpose (aka research statement), transcripts that resulted in a degree. Additional exam requirements/recommendations for international students: required—TOEFL (minimum score 84 iBT). Electronic applications accepted. *Expenses:* Contact institution.

**University of Michigan–Flint,** College of Arts and Sciences, Program in Biology, Flint, MI 48502-1950. Offers MS. *Program availability:* Part-time. *Faculty:* 20 full-time (11 women), 9 part-time/adjunct (6 women). *Students:* 3 full-time (0 women), 8 part-time (5 women); includes 2 minority (both Asian, non-Hispanic/Latino). Average age 31. 16 applicants, 56% accepted, 3 enrolled. In 2019, 7 master's awarded. *Degree requirements:* For master's, thesis optional, Thesis is optional. *Entrance requirements:* For master's, GRE, bachelor's degree in biology or related life science from accredited institution; minimum overall undergraduate and prerequisite GPA of 3.0; completion of following prerequisites at an accredited university: cell biology, ecology, general physics, and genetics. Additional exam requirements/recommendations for international students: required—TOEFL (minimum score 84 iBT), IELTS (minimum score 6.5). *Application deadline:* For fall admission, 8/1 for domestic students, 5/1 for international students; for winter admission, 11/15 for domestic students, 10/1 for international students; for spring admission, 3/15 for domestic students, 1/1 for international students; for summer admission, 5/15 for domestic students. Applications are processed on a rolling basis. Application fee: $55. Electronic applications accepted. *Expenses:* Contact institution. *Financial support:* Federal Work-Study, scholarships/grants, and unspecified assistantships available. Support available to part-time students. Financial award application deadline: 3/1; financial award applicants required to submit FAFSA. *Unit head:* Dr. Randall Duncan, Chair, 810-762-3360, Fax: 810-762-3360, E-mail: duncanra@umich.edu. *Application contact:* Matt Bohlen, Associate Director of Graduate Programs, 810-762-3171, Fax: 810-766-6789, E-mail: mbohlen@umflint.edu.
Website: https://www.umflint.edu/graduateprograms/biology

**University of Minnesota, Duluth,** Graduate School, Swenson College of Science and Engineering, Department of Biology, Integrated Biosciences Program, Duluth, MN 55812-2496. Offers MS, PhD. Terminal master's awarded for partial completion of doctoral program. *Degree requirements:* For master's, thesis, seminar; for doctorate, comprehensive exam, thesis/dissertation, written and oral exam, seminar, written thesis. *Entrance requirements:* For master's, GRE, 1 year of biology, physics, and chemistry; 1 semester of calculus; for doctorate, GRE, 1 year each of chemistry, biology, physics, calculus, and advanced chemistry. Additional exam requirements/recommendations for international students: required—TOEFL (minimum score 550 paper-based; 79 iBT). Electronic applications accepted.

**University of Minnesota, Twin Cities Campus,** Graduate School, College of Biological Sciences, Biological Science Program, Minneapolis, MN 55455-0213. Offers MBS. *Program availability:* Part-time, evening/weekend. *Entrance requirements:* For master's, 2 years of work experience. Electronic applications accepted. *Expenses:* Contact institution.

**University of Mississippi,** Graduate School, College of Liberal Arts, University, MS 38677. Offers anthropology (MA); biology (MS, PhD); chemistry (MS, DA, PhD); creative writing (MFA); documentary expression (MFA); economics (MA, PhD); English (MA, PhD); experimental psychology (PhD); history (MA, PhD); mathematics (MS, PhD); modern languages (MA); music (MM); philosophy (MA); physics (MA, MS, PhD); political science (MA, PhD); Southern studies (MA); studio art (MFA). *Program availability:* Part-time. *Faculty:* 481 full-time (215 women), 71 part-time/adjunct (40 women). *Students:* 509 full-time (258 women), 55 part-time (21 women); includes 89 minority (40 Black or African American, non-Hispanic/Latino; 13 Asian, non-Hispanic/Latino; 25 Hispanic/Latino; 11 Two or more races, non-Hispanic/Latino), 157 international. Average age 29. In 2019, 119 master's, 51 doctorates awarded. *Degree requirements:* For doctorate, thesis/dissertation. *Entrance requirements:* For master's, GRE General Test, minimum GPA of 3.0; for doctorate, GRE General Test. Additional exam requirements/recommendations for international students: required—TOEFL. *Application deadline:* Applications are processed on a rolling basis. Application fee: $50. Electronic applications accepted. *Expenses:* Tuition, state resident: full-time $8718; part-time $484.25 per credit hour. Tuition, nonresident: full-time $24,990; part-time $1388.25 per credit hour. *Required fees:* $100; $4.16 per credit hour. *Financial support:* Fellowships, research assistantships, teaching assistantships, career-related internships or fieldwork, Federal Work-Study, institutionally sponsored loans, scholarships/grants, and unspecified assistantships available. Financial award application deadline: 3/1; financial award applicants required to submit FAFSA. *Unit head:* Dr. Lee Michael Cohen, Dean, 662-915-7177, Fax: 662-915-5792, E-mail: libarts@olemiss.edu. *Application contact:* Tameka Smith, Graduate Activities Specialist for Admissions, 662-915-7474, Fax: 662-915-7577, E-mail: gschool@olemiss.edu.
Website: ventress@olemiss.edu

**University of Mississippi Medical Center,** School of Graduate Studies in Health Sciences, Jackson, MS 39110. Offers MS, PhD, MD/PhD. *Program availability:* Part-time, online only, 100% online. *Faculty:* 211 full-time (85 women). *Students:* 191 full-time (103 women), 20 part-time (14 women); includes 84 minority (41 Black or African American, non-Hispanic/Latino; 25 Asian, non-Hispanic/Latino; 10 Hispanic/Latino; 8 Two or more races, non-Hispanic/Latino), 1 international. 346 applicants, 42% accepted, 125 enrolled. In 2019, 80 master's, 20 doctorates awarded. Terminal master's awarded for partial completion of doctoral program. *Degree requirements:* For master's, thesis (for some programs); for doctorate, comprehensive exam, thesis/dissertation, first authored publication. *Entrance requirements:* For master's and doctorate, GRE. Additional exam requirements/recommendations for international students: required—TOEFL (minimum score 550 paper-based; 79 iBT); recommended—IELTS (minimum score 6.5), TSE (minimum score 53). *Application deadline:* For fall admission, 6/1 for domestic and international students; for spring admission, 10/1 for domestic and international students; for summer admission, 4/1 for domestic and international students. Applications are processed on a rolling basis. Application fee: $25. Electronic applications accepted. *Financial support:* In 2019–20, 60 students received support, including research assistantships with full and partial tuition reimbursements available (averaging $28,000 per year), teaching assistantships (averaging $28,000 per year). Financial award application deadline: 4/15; financial award applicants required to submit FAFSA. *Unit head:* Sydney Murphy, PhD, Associate Dean, 601-984-1206, Fax: 601-815-9440, E-mail: smurphy@umc.edu. *Application contact:* Michael Ryan, Associate Dean, 601-984-1842, Fax: 601-815-9440, E-mail: mjryan@umc.edu.
Website: https://www.umc.edu/graduateschool/GraduateSchool_Home.html

**University of Missouri,** College of Veterinary Medicine and Office of Research and Graduate Studies, Graduate Programs in Veterinary Medicine, Department of Biomedical Sciences, Columbia, MO 65211. Offers biomedical sciences (MS, PhD); comparative medicine (MS); veterinary medicine and surgery (MS); DVM/PhD. *Entrance*

*requirements:* For master's and doctorate, GRE General Test, minimum GPA of 3.0; 10 hours each of biology and chemistry; 3 hours each of physics, biochemistry, and calculus.

**University of Missouri,** Office of Research and Graduate Studies, College of Arts and Science, Division of Biological Sciences, Columbia, MO 65211. Offers evolutionary biology and ecology (MA, PhD). Terminal master's awarded for partial completion of doctoral program. *Entrance requirements:* For master's and doctorate, GRE General Test (minimum score 1200 verbal and quantitative), minimum GPA of 3.0. Additional exam requirements/recommendations for international students: required—TOEFL.

**University of Missouri,** School of Medicine and Office of Research and Graduate Studies, Graduate Programs in Medicine, Columbia, MO 65211. Offers MHA, MS, PhD, Certificate. *Program availability:* Part-time. *Degree requirements:* For doctorate, thesis/ dissertation. *Entrance requirements:* For master's and doctorate, GRE General Test, minimum GPA of 3.0. Additional exam requirements/recommendations for international students: required—TOEFL. *Expenses:* Contact institution.

**University of Missouri–Kansas City,** School of Biological Sciences, Kansas City, MO 64110-2499. Offers biology (MA); cell biology and biophysics (PhD); cellular and molecular biology (MS); molecular biology and biochemistry (PhD). *Program availability:* Part-time, evening/weekend. *Degree requirements:* For doctorate, comprehensive exam, thesis/dissertation. *Entrance requirements:* For master's, GRE, minimum GPA of 3.0; for doctorate, GRE General Test. Additional exam requirements/recommendations for international students: required—TOEFL (minimum score 550 paper-based; 80 iBT).

**University of Missouri–St. Louis,** College of Arts and Sciences, Department of Biology, St. Louis, MO 63121. Offers MS, PhD, Certificate. *Program availability:* Part-time. *Degree requirements:* For master's, thesis or alternative; for doctorate, thesis/ dissertation, 1 semester of teaching experience. *Entrance requirements:* For master's, 3 letters of recommendation; for doctorate, GRE General Test, 3 letters of recommendation. Additional exam requirements/recommendations for international students: required—TOEFL (minimum score 79 iBT), IELTS (minimum score 6.5). Electronic applications accepted. *Expenses: Tuition, area resident:* Full-time $9005.40; part-time $6003.60 per credit hour. *Tuition, state resident:* Full-time $9005.40; part-time $6003.60 per credit hour. Tuition, nonresident: full-time $22,108; part-time $14,738.40 per credit hour. *International tuition:* $22,108 full-time. Tuition and fees vary according to course load.

**University of Montana,** Graduate School, College of Health Professions and Biomedical Sciences, Skaggs School of Pharmacy, Department of Biomedical and Pharmaceutical Sciences, Missoula, MT 59812. Offers biomedical sciences (PhD); medicinal chemistry (MS, PhD); molecular and cellular toxicology (MS, PhD); neuroscience (PhD); pharmaceutical sciences (MS). *Accreditation:* ACPE. *Degree requirements:* For master's, oral defense of thesis; for doctorate, research dissertation defense. *Entrance requirements:* For master's and doctorate, GRE General Test. Additional exam requirements/recommendations for international students: required—TOEFL (minimum score 540 paper-based). Electronic applications accepted.

**University of Montana,** Graduate School, College of Humanities and Sciences, Division of Biological Sciences, Missoula, MT 59812. Offers cellular, molecular and microbial biology (PhD), including cellular and developmental biology, microbial evolution and ecology, microbiology and immunology, molecular biology and biochemistry; organismal biology and ecology (MS, PhD); systems ecology (MS, PhD). Terminal master's awarded for partial completion of doctoral program. *Degree requirements:* For master's, thesis; for doctorate, thesis/dissertation. *Entrance requirements:* For master's and doctorate, GRE General Test. Additional exam requirements/recommendations for international students: required—TOEFL.

**University of Nebraska at Kearney,** College of Natural and Social Sciences, College of Arts and Sciences, Kearney, NE 68849. Offers biology (MS); science/math education (MA Ed). *Program availability:* Part-time, evening/weekend, 100% online, blended/ hybrid learning. *Faculty:* 18 full-time (7 women). *Students:* 35 full-time (25 women), 257 part-time (179 women); includes 44 minority (9 Black or African American, non-Hispanic/ Latino; 1 American Indian or Alaska Native, non-Hispanic/Latino; 9 Asian, non-Hispanic/ Latino; 18 Hispanic/Latino; 7 Two or more races, non-Hispanic/Latino), 1 international. Average age 40. 73 applicants, 92% accepted, 52 enrolled. In 2019, 67 master's awarded. *Degree requirements:* For master's, comprehensive exam, thesis optional. *Entrance requirements:* For master's, GRE (for thesis option and for online program applicants if undergraduate GPA is below 2.75), letter of interest. Additional exam requirements/recommendations for international students: required—TOEFL (minimum score 550 paper-based; 79 iBT), IELTS (minimum score 6.5). *Application deadline:* For fall admission, 7/10 for domestic students, 5/10 for international students; for spring admission, 11/10 for domestic students, 9/10 for international students; for summer admission, 4/15 for domestic students, 1/10 for international students. Applications are processed on a rolling basis. Application fee: $45. Electronic applications accepted. *Expenses:* Contact institution. *Financial support:* In 2019–20, 10 students received support, including 4 research assistantships with full tuition reimbursements available (averaging $10,980 per year), 6 teaching assistantships with full tuition reimbursements available (averaging $10,980 per year); career-related internships or fieldwork, scholarships/grants, health care benefits, and unspecified assistantships also available. Support available to part-time students. Financial award application deadline: 2/28; financial award applicants required to submit FAFSA. *Unit head:* Dr. Paul Twig, Graduate Program Chair, 308-865-8315, E-mail: twiggp@unk.edu. *Application contact:* Brian Peterson, Coordinator, Online MA Program, 308-865-1589, E-mail: msbiology@ unk.edu.
Website: https://www.unk.edu/academics/biology/index.php

**University of Nebraska at Omaha,** Graduate Studies, College of Arts and Sciences, Department of Biology, Omaha, NE 68182. Offers biology (MS); business for bioscientists (Certificate). *Program availability:* Part-time. *Degree requirements:* For master's, comprehensive exam (for some programs), thesis (for some programs). *Entrance requirements:* For master's, GRE General Test, minimum GPA of 3.0, transcripts, 24 undergraduate biology hours, 3 letters of recommendation, statement of purpose. Additional exam requirements/recommendations for international students: required—TOEFL, IELTS, PTE. Electronic applications accepted.

**University of Nebraska–Lincoln,** Graduate College, College of Agricultural Sciences and Natural Resources, School of Veterinary Medicine and Biomedical Sciences, Lincoln, NE 68588. Offers veterinary science (MS). *Program availability:* Online learning. *Degree requirements:* For master's, thesis optional; for doctorate, comprehensive exam, thesis/dissertation. *Entrance requirements:* For master's, GRE General Test; for doctorate, GRE General Test, MCAT, or VCAT. Additional exam requirements/ recommendations for international students: required—TOEFL (minimum score 550 paper-based). Electronic applications accepted.

**University of Nebraska–Lincoln,** Graduate College, College of Arts and Sciences, School of Biological Sciences, Lincoln, NE 68588. Offers MA, MS, PhD. *Degree requirements:* For master's, thesis optional; for doctorate, comprehensive exam, thesis/ dissertation. *Entrance requirements:* For master's and doctorate, GRE General Test. Additional exam requirements/recommendations for international students: required— TOEFL (minimum score 550 paper-based). Electronic applications accepted.

**University of Nebraska Medical Center,** Interdisciplinary Graduate Program in Biomedical Sciences, Omaha, NE 68198-5840. Offers MS, PhD. *Degree requirements:* For doctorate, comprehensive exam, thesis/dissertation. *Entrance requirements:* Additional exam requirements/recommendations for international students: required— TOEFL (minimum score 95 iBT); recommended—IELTS (minimum score 7). Electronic applications accepted. *Expenses:* Contact institution.

**University of Nebraska Medical Center,** Medical Sciences Interdepartmental Area, Omaha, NE 68198. Offers applied behavior analysis (PhD); clinical translational research (MS, PhD); health practice and medical education research (MS); oral biology (MS, PhD). *Program availability:* Part-time. Terminal master's awarded for partial completion of doctoral program. *Degree requirements:* For master's, comprehensive exam, thesis; for doctorate, comprehensive exam, thesis/dissertation. *Entrance requirements:* For master's, GRE General Test; for doctorate, GRE General Test, MCAT, DAT, LSAT. Additional exam requirements/recommendations for international students: required—TOEFL (minimum score 550 paper-based; 80 iBT), IELTS. Electronic applications accepted. *Expenses:* Contact institution.

**University of Nevada, Las Vegas,** Graduate College, College of Sciences, School of Life Sciences, Las Vegas, NV 89154-4004. Offers biological sciences (MS, PhD). *Program availability:* Part-time. *Faculty:* 16 full-time (7 women), 2 part-time/adjunct (0 women). *Students:* 47 full-time (31 women), 7 part-time (5 women); includes 15 minority (7 Asian, non-Hispanic/Latino; 6 Hispanic/Latino; 2 Two or more races, non-Hispanic/ Latino), 6 international. Average age 31. 48 applicants, 38% accepted, 13 enrolled. In 2019, 6 master's, 5 doctorates awarded. *Degree requirements:* For master's, thesis; for doctorate, comprehensive exam, thesis/dissertation. *Entrance requirements:* For master's and doctorate, GRE General Test, bachelor's degree. Additional exam requirements/recommendations for international students: required—TOEFL (minimum score 550 paper-based; 80 iBT), IELTS (minimum score 7). *Application deadline:* For fall admission, 1/15 for domestic and international students. Application fee: $60 ($95 for international students). Electronic applications accepted. *Expenses:* Contact institution. *Financial support:* In 2019–20, 47 students received support, including 1 fellowship with full tuition reimbursement available (averaging $20,000 per year), 13 research assistantships with full tuition reimbursements available (averaging $19,095 per year), 33 teaching assistantships with full tuition reimbursements available (averaging $21,743 per year); institutionally sponsored loans, scholarships/grants, health care benefits, and unspecified assistantships also available. Financial award application deadline: 3/15; financial award applicants required to submit FAFSA. *Unit head:* Dr. Frank Van Breukelen, Director/Professor, 702-895-3944, Fax: 702-895-3956, E-mail: lifesciences.chair@unlv.edu. *Application contact:* Dr. Helen Wing, Graduate Coordinator, 702-895-5382, Fax: 702-895-3956, E-mail: lifesciences.gradcoord@ unlv.edu.
Website: http://sols.unlv.edu/

**University of Nevada, Reno,** Graduate School, College of Science, Department of Biology, Reno, NV 89557. Offers MS. *Degree requirements:* For master's, thesis optional. *Entrance requirements:* For master's, GRE General Test, minimum GPA of 2.75. Additional exam requirements/recommendations for international students: required—TOEFL (minimum score 500 paper-based; 61 iBT), IELTS (minimum score 6). Electronic applications accepted.

**University of New Brunswick Saint John,** Department of Biology, Saint John, NE E2L 4L5, Canada. Offers M Sc, PhD. *Program availability:* Part-time. *Faculty:* 20 full-time (7 women). *Students:* 30 full-time (18 women), 9 part-time (5 women), 8 international. In 2019, 10 master's, 7 doctorates awarded. *Degree requirements:* For master's, thesis; for doctorate, comprehensive exam, thesis/dissertation. *Entrance requirements:* For master's, B Sc, minimum GPA of 3.0; for doctorate, M Sc, minimum GPA of 3.0. Additional exam requirements/recommendations for international students: required— TOEFL (minimum score 600 paper-based), TWE (minimum score 4). *Application deadline:* For fall admission, 2/15 for domestic and international students. Applications are processed on a rolling basis. Application fee: $50 Canadian dollars. Electronic applications accepted. *Expenses: Tuition, area resident:* Full-time $6975 Canadian dollars; part-time $3423 Canadian dollars per year. Tuition, state resident: full-time $6975 Canadian dollars; part-time $3423 Canadian dollars per year. Tuition, Canadian resident: full-time $6975 Canadian dollars; part-time $3423 Canadian dollars per year. *International tuition:* $12,435 Canadian dollars full-time. *Required fees:* $132.75 Canadian dollars; $92.25 Canadian dollars per term. Tuition and fees vary according to campus/location, program and student level. *Financial support:* Fellowships, research assistantships, teaching assistantships, scholarships/grants, and unspecified assistantships available. Financial award application deadline: 1/15. *Unit head:* Dr. Jeff Houlahan, Director of Graduate Studies, 506-648 5967, Fax: 506-648-5811, E-mail: jeffhoul@unb.ca. *Application contact:* Stacey Hines, Secretary, 506-648 5565, Fax: 506-648-5811, E-mail: shines@unb.ca.
Website: http://go.unb.ca/gradprograms

**University of New England,** College of Arts and Sciences, Biddeford, ME 04005-9526. Offers biological sciences (MS); marine sciences (MS). *Program availability:* Part-time. *Faculty:* 31 full-time (18 women), 1 part-time/adjunct (0 women). *Students:* 16 full-time (12 women), 9 part-time (6 women); includes 1 minority (Black or African American, non-Hispanic/Latino). Average age 28. In 2019, 12 master's awarded. *Application deadline:* Applications are processed on a rolling basis. Electronic applications accepted. *Financial support:* Fellowships, research assistantships, teaching assistantships, career-related internships or fieldwork, scholarships/grants, traineeships, and unspecified assistantships available. Financial award application deadline: 5/1; financial award applicants required to submit FAFSA. *Unit head:* Dr. Jonathan H. Millen, Dean, College of Arts and Sciences, 207-602-2371, E-mail: jmillen@une.edu. *Application contact:* Scott Steinberg, Vice President of University Admissions, 207-221-4225, Fax: 207-523-1925, E-mail: ssteinberg@une.edu.
Website: http://www.une.edu/cas/programs/graduate

**University of New Hampshire,** Graduate School, College of Life Sciences and Agriculture, Department of Biological Sciences, Durham, NH 03824. Offers integrative and organismal biology (MS, PhD); marine biology (MS, PhD). *Program availability:* Part-time. *Students:* 14 full-time (7 women), 17 part-time (9 women); includes 4 minority (1 Asian, non-Hispanic/Latino; 1 Hispanic/Latino; 2 Two or more races, non-Hispanic/ Latino), 2 international. Average age 27. 36 applicants, 25% accepted, 7 enrolled. In 2019, 8 master's awarded. *Entrance requirements:* For master's and doctorate, GRE General Test. Additional exam requirements/recommendations for international students: required—TOEFL (minimum score 550 paper-based; 80 iBT), IELTS, PTE. *Application deadline:* For fall admission, 1/15 priority date for domestic students, 8/1 for international students. Application fee: $65. Electronic applications accepted. *Financial support:* In 2019–20, 26 students received support, including 1 fellowship, 2 research assistantships, 23 teaching assistantships. Financial award application deadline: 2/15. *Unit head:* Bonnie Brown, Chair, 603-862-2100. *Application contact:* Diane Lavalliere, Senior Academic and Student Support Assistant, 603-862-2100, E-mail: diane.lavalliere@unh.edu.
Website: http://www.colsa.unh.edu/dbs

**University of New Mexico,** Graduate Studies, College of Arts and Sciences, Program in Biology, Albuquerque, NM 87131-2039. Offers MS, PhD. *Degree requirements:* For

master's, comprehensive exam, thesis optional; for doctorate, comprehensive exam, thesis/dissertation. *Entrance requirements:* For master's and doctorate, GRE General Test, minimum GPA of 3.2, letters of recommendation. Additional exam requirements/recommendations for international students: required—TOEFL (minimum score 550 paper-based; 79 iBT). Electronic applications accepted. *Expenses:* Tuition, state resident: full-time $7633; part-time $972 per year. Tuition, nonresident: full-time $22,586; part-time $3840 per year. *International tuition:* $23,292 full-time. *Required fees:* $8608. Tuition and fees vary according to course level, course load, degree level, program and student level.

**University of New Mexico,** Graduate Studies, Health Sciences Center, Program in Biomedical Sciences, Albuquerque, NM 87131-5196. Offers biochemistry and molecular biology (MS, PhD); cell biology and physiology (MS, PhD); molecular genetics and microbiology (MS, PhD); neuroscience (MS, PhD); pathology (MS, PhD); toxicology (MS, PhD). *Program availability:* Part-time. Terminal master's awarded for partial completion of doctoral program. *Degree requirements:* For master's, thesis; for doctorate, comprehensive exam, thesis/dissertation, qualifying exam at the end of year 1/core curriculum. *Entrance requirements:* For master's and doctorate, GRE General Test, minimum undergraduate GPA of 3.0. Additional exam requirements/recommendations for international students: required—TOEFL. Electronic applications accepted. *Expenses:* Tuition, state resident: full-time $7633; part-time $972 per year. Tuition, nonresident: full-time $22,586; part-time $3840 per year. *International tuition:* $23,292 full-time. *Required fees:* $8608. Tuition and fees vary according to course level, course load, degree level, program and student level.

**University of New Orleans,** Graduate School, College of Sciences, Department of Biological Sciences, New Orleans, LA 70148. Offers MS. *Degree requirements:* For master's, one foreign language, thesis. *Entrance requirements:* For master's, GRE General Test. Additional exam requirements/recommendations for international students: required—TOEFL (minimum score 550 paper-based; 79 iBT), IELTS (minimum score 6.5). Electronic applications accepted.

**The University of North Carolina at Chapel Hill,** Graduate School, College of Arts and Sciences, Department of Biology, Chapel Hill, NC 27599. Offers botany (MA, MS, PhD); cell biology, development, and physiology (MA, MS, PhD); cell motility and cytoskeleton (PhD); ecology and behavior (MA, MS, PhD); genetics and molecular biology (MA, MS, PhD); morphology, systematics, and evolution (MA, MS, PhD). Terminal master's awarded for partial completion of doctoral program. *Degree requirements:* For master's, comprehensive exam, thesis (for some programs); for doctorate, comprehensive exam, thesis/dissertation. *Entrance requirements:* For master's, GRE General Test, GRE Subject Test, 2 semesters of calculus or statistics; 2 semesters of physics, organic chemistry; 3 semesters of biology; for doctorate, GRE General Test, GRE Subject Test, 2 semesters calculus or statistics, 2 semesters physics, organic chemistry, 3 semesters of biology. Additional exam requirements/recommendations for international students: required—TOEFL (minimum score 550 paper-based). Electronic applications accepted.

**The University of North Carolina at Chapel Hill,** School of Medicine and Graduate School, Biological and Biomedical Sciences Program, Chapel Hill, NC 27599. Offers MS, Au D, DPT, PhD, MD/PhD. *Faculty:* 498 full-time (175 women), 119 part-time/adjunct (37 women). *Students:* 458 full-time (273 women); includes 97 minority (29 Black or African American, non-Hispanic/Latino; 4 American Indian or Alaska Native, non-Hispanic/Latino; 40 Asian, non-Hispanic/Latino; 10 Hispanic/Latino; 1 Native Hawaiian or other Pacific Islander, non-Hispanic/Latino; 13 Two or more races, non-Hispanic/Latino), 60 international. Average age 26. In 2019, 7 master's, 87 doctorates awarded. Terminal master's awarded for partial completion of doctoral program. *Degree requirements:* For doctorate, comprehensive exam, thesis/dissertation. *Entrance requirements:* Additional exam requirements/recommendations for international students: required—TOEFL. *Application deadline:* For fall admission, 12/3 priority date for domestic and international students. Applications are processed on a rolling basis. Application fee: $65. Electronic applications accepted. *Financial support:* In 2019–20, 100 fellowships with full and partial tuition reimbursements (averaging $32,000 per year), 100 research assistantships with full tuition reimbursements (averaging $32,000 per year) were awarded; teaching assistantships with full tuition reimbursements, career-related internships or fieldwork, health care benefits, and tuition waivers (full) also available. *Unit head:* Dr. David McDonald, Director, 919-843-3387, E-mail: david.mcdonald@unc.edu. *Application contact:* Jeffrey Steinbach, Assistant Director of Admissions, 919-843-7129, E-mail: jsteinba@email.unc.edu.
Website: https://bbsp.unc.edu/

**The University of North Carolina at Charlotte,** College of Liberal Arts and Sciences, Department of Biological Sciences, Charlotte, NC 28223-0001. Offers biology (MS), including molecular, cellular and developmental (mcd) biology; environmental, ecology and evolutionary (e3b) biology. *Program availability:* Part-time. *Faculty:* 28 full-time (12 women). *Students:* 46 full-time (27 women), 12 part-time (10 women); includes 8 minority (4 Black or African American, non-Hispanic/Latino; 3 Asian, non-Hispanic/Latino; 1 Hispanic/Latino), 13 international. Average age 28. 43 applicants, 42% accepted, 10 enrolled. In 2019, 9 master's, 8 doctorates awarded. Terminal master's awarded for partial completion of doctoral program. *Degree requirements:* For master's, comprehensive exam, thesis (for some programs); for doctorate, thesis/dissertation, qualifying exam (oral and written). *Entrance requirements:* For master's, BS or BA from accredited university; minimum overall GPA of 3.0; personal statement, previous biological sciences coursework, major in with biological sciences or minimum of 24 hours in biological sciences; for doctorate, BS or BA from accredited university; minimum overall GPA of 3.0; personal statement on why pursing doctorate degree and brief highlights of research; previous biological sciences coursework, major in with biological sciences or minimum of 24 hours in biological sciences. Additional exam requirements/recommendations for international students: required—TOEFL (minimum score 557 paper-based; 83 iBT), IELTS (minimum score 6.5), TOEFL (minimum score 557 paper-based, 83 iBT) or IELTS (6.5). *Application deadline:* For fall admission, 1/15 priority date for domestic students; for spring admission, 10/1 priority date for domestic students. Applications are processed on a rolling basis. Application fee: $75. Electronic applications accepted. *Expenses:* Tuition, state resident: full-time $4337. Tuition, nonresident: full-time $17,771. *Required fees:* $3093. Tuition and fees vary according to course load, degree level and program. *Financial support:* In 2019–20, 42 students received support, including 7 fellowships (averaging $49,388 per year), 11 research assistantships (averaging $11,418 per year), 24 teaching assistantships (averaging $15,043 per year); career-related internships or fieldwork, institutionally sponsored loans, scholarships/grants, and unspecified assistantships also available. Support available to part-time students. Financial award application deadline: 1/1; financial award applicants required to submit FAFSA. *Unit head:* Dr. Christine Richardson, Department Chair and Professor, 704-687-8683, E-mail: c.richardson@uncc.edu. *Application contact:* Kathy B. Giddings, Director of Graduate Admissions, 704-687-5503, Fax: 704-687-1668, E-mail: gradadm@uncc.edu.
Website: http://biology.uncc.edu/

**The University of North Carolina at Greensboro,** Graduate School, College of Arts and Sciences, Department of Biology, Greensboro, NC 27412-5001. Offers MS. *Degree requirements:* For master's, thesis. *Entrance requirements:* For master's, GRE General Test, GRE Subject Test. Additional exam requirements/recommendations for international students: required—TOEFL. Electronic applications accepted.

**The University of North Carolina Wilmington,** College of Arts and Sciences, Department of Biology and Marine Biology, Wilmington, NC 28403-3297. Offers biology (MS); marine biology (MS, PhD). *Program availability:* Part-time. *Faculty:* 37 full-time (11 women). *Students:* 16 full-time (15 women), 59 part-time (36 women); includes 7 minority (2 Black or African American, non-Hispanic/Latino; 1 Asian, non-Hispanic/Latino; 3 Hispanic/Latino; 1 Two or more races, non-Hispanic/Latino), 5 international. Average age 28. 70 applicants, 33% accepted, 18 enrolled. In 2019, 8 master's, 2 doctorates awarded. *Degree requirements:* For master's, comprehensive exam, thesis; for doctorate, comprehensive exam, thesis/dissertation. *Entrance requirements:* For master's, GRE General Test, 3 recommendations, research interests form and statement, resume or curriculum vitae, baccalaureate degree from biology-related field; for doctorate, GRE General Test, 3 recommendations, resume or curriculum vitae, summary of MS thesis research, statement of PhD research interests, copies of publications, master's degree or BS and 1 year of completed work in the MS in biology program. Additional exam requirements/recommendations for international students: required—TOEFL (minimum score 79 iBT), IELTS (minimum score 6.5). *Application deadline:* For fall admission, 5/15 for domestic students; for spring admission, 11/15 for domestic students. Applications are processed on a rolling basis. Application fee: $75. Electronic applications accepted. *Expenses: Tuition, area resident:* Full-time $4719; part-time $326 per credit hour. Tuition, state resident: full-time $4719; part-time $326 per credit hour. Tuition, nonresident: full-time $18,548; part-time $1099 per credit hour. *Required fees:* $2738. Tuition and fees vary according to program. *Financial support:* Research assistantships with tuition reimbursements, teaching assistantships with tuition reimbursements, and scholarships/grants available. Support available to part-time students. Financial award application deadline: 1/1; financial award applicants required to submit FAFSA. *Unit head:* Dr. Heather Koopman, Chair, 910-962-7199, E-mail: koopmanh@uncw.edu. *Application contact:* Lisa Noah, Graduate Administrative Assistant, 910-962-3489, E-mail: noahl@uncw.edu.
Website: http://www.uncw.edu/bio/graduate.html

**University of North Dakota,** Graduate School, College of Arts and Sciences, Department of Biology, Grand Forks, ND 58202. Offers biology (MS); fisheries/wildlife (PhD); genetics (PhD); zoology (PhD). Terminal master's awarded for partial completion of doctoral program. *Degree requirements:* For master's, thesis, final exam; for doctorate, comprehensive exam, thesis/dissertation, final exam. *Entrance requirements:* For master's, GRE General Test, GRE Subject Test, minimum GPA of 3.0; for doctorate, GRE General Test, GRE Subject Test, minimum GPA of 3.5. Additional exam requirements/recommendations for international students: required—TOEFL (minimum score 550 paper-based; 79 iBT), IELTS (minimum score 6.5). Electronic applications accepted.

**University of Northern Colorado,** Graduate School, College of Natural and Health Sciences, School of Biology, Program in Biological Sciences, Greeley, CO 80639. Offers MS. *Program availability:* Part-time. *Degree requirements:* For master's, comprehensive exam. *Entrance requirements:* For master's, GRE General Test, 3 letters of recommendation. Electronic applications accepted.

**University of Northern Iowa,** Graduate College, College of Humanities, Arts and Sciences, Department of Biology, Cedar Falls, IA 50614. Offers MS. *Program availability:* Part-time. *Degree requirements:* For master's, comprehensive exam (for some programs), thesis or alternative. *Entrance requirements:* For master's, minimum GPA of 3.0; 3 letters of recommendation. Additional exam requirements/recommendations for international students: required—TOEFL (minimum score 500 paper-based; 61 iBT). Electronic applications accepted.

**University of North Florida,** College of Arts and Sciences, Department of Biology, Jacksonville, FL 32224. Offers MA, MS. *Program availability:* Part-time. *Degree requirements:* For master's, thesis (for some programs). *Entrance requirements:* For master's, GRE General Test, minimum GPA of 3.0 in last 60 hours, letters of recommendation. Additional exam requirements/recommendations for international students: required—TOEFL (minimum score 570 paper-based). Electronic applications accepted.

**University of North Texas,** Toulouse Graduate School, Denton, TX 76203-5459. Offers accounting (MS); applied anthropology (MA, MS); applied behavior analysis (Certificate); applied geography (MA); applied technology and performance improvement (M Ed, MS); art education (MA); art history (MA); arts leadership (Certificate); audiology (Au D); behavior analysis (MS); behavioral science (PhD); biochemistry and molecular biology (MS); biology (MA, MS); biomedical engineering (MS); business analysis (MS); chemistry (MS); clinical health psychology (PhD); communication studies (MA, MS); computer engineering (MS); computer science (MS); counseling (M Ed, MS), including clinical mental health counseling (MS), college and university counseling, elementary school counseling, secondary school counseling; creative writing (MA); criminal justice (MS); curriculum and instruction (M Ed); decision sciences (MBA); design (MA, MFA), including fashion design (MFA), innovation studies, interior design (MFA); early childhood studies (MS); economics (MS); educational leadership (M Ed, Ed D); educational psychology (MS, PhD), including family studies (MS), gifted and talented (MS), human development (MS), learning and cognition (MS), research, measurement and evaluation (MS); electrical engineering (MS); emergency management (MPA); engineering technology (MS); English (MA); English as a second language (MA); environmental science (MS); finance (MBA, MS); financial management (MPA); French (MA); health services management (MBA); higher education (M Ed, Ed D); history (MA, MS); hospitality management (MS); human resources management (MPA); information science (MS); information systems (PhD); information technologies (MBA); interdisciplinary studies (MA, MS); international studies (MA); international sustainable tourism (MS); jazz studies (MM); journalism (MA, MJ, Graduate Certificate), including interactive and virtual digital communication (Graduate Certificate), narrative journalism (Graduate Certificate), public relations (Graduate Certificate); kinesiology (MS); linguistics (MA); local government management (MPA); logistics (PhD); logistics and supply chain management (MBA); long-term care, senior housing, and aging services (MA); management (PhD); marketing (MBA); mathematics (MA, MS); mechanical and energy engineering (MS, PhD); music (MA), including ethnomusicology, music theory, musicology, performance; music composition (PhD); music education (MM Ed, PhD); nonprofit management (MPA); operations and supply chain management (MBA); performance (MM, DMA); philosophy (MA); political science (MA); professional and technical communication (MA); radio, television and film (MA, MFA); rehabilitation counseling (Certificate); sociology (MA); Spanish (MA); special education (M Ed); speech-language pathology (MA); strategic management (MBA); studio art (MFA); teaching (M Ed); MBA/MS. *Program availability:* Part-time, evening/weekend, online learning. Terminal master's awarded for partial completion of doctoral program. *Degree requirements:* For master's, variable foreign language requirement, comprehensive exam (for some programs), thesis (for some programs); for doctorate, variable foreign language requirement, comprehensive exam (for some programs), thesis/dissertation; for other advanced degree, variable foreign language requirement, comprehensive exam (for some programs). *Entrance requirements:* For master's and doctorate, GRE, GMAT. Additional exam requirements/recommendations for

international students: required—TOEFL (minimum score 550 paper-based; 79 iBT). Electronic applications accepted.

**University of North Texas Health Science Center at Fort Worth,** Graduate School of Biomedical Sciences, Fort Worth, TX 76107-2699. Offers biochemistry and cancer biology (MS, PhD); biotechnology (MS); cell biology, immunology and microbiology (MS, PhD); clinical research management (MS); forensic genetics (MS); genetics (MS, PhD); integrative physiology (MS, PhD); medical sciences (MS); pharmaceutical sciences and pharmacotherapy (MS, PhD); pharmacology and neuroscience (MS, PhD); structural anatomy and rehabilitation sciences (MS, PhD); DO/MS; DO/PhD. Terminal master's awarded for partial completion of doctoral program. *Degree requirements:* For master's, thesis; for doctorate, thesis/dissertation. *Entrance requirements:* For master's and doctorate, GRE General Test. Additional exam requirements/recommendations for international students: required—TOEFL. *Expenses:* Contact institution.

**University of Notre Dame,** The Graduate School, College of Science, Department of Biological Sciences, Notre Dame, IN 46556. Offers aquatic ecology, evolution and environmental biology (MS, PhD); cellular and molecular biology (MS, PhD); genetics (MS, PhD); physiology (MS, PhD); vector biology and parasitology (MS, PhD). Terminal master's awarded for partial completion of doctoral program. *Degree requirements:* For master's, comprehensive exam, thesis; for doctorate, comprehensive exam, thesis/dissertation, candidacy exam. *Entrance requirements:* For master's and doctorate, GRE General Test. Additional exam requirements/recommendations for international students: required—TOEFL (minimum score 600 paper-based; 80 iBT). Electronic applications accepted.

**University of Oklahoma Health Sciences Center,** College of Medicine and Graduate College, Graduate Programs in Medicine, Oklahoma City, OK 73190. Offers biochemistry and molecular biology (MS, PhD), including biochemistry, molecular biology; cell biology (MS, PhD); medical sciences (MS); microbiology and immunology (MS, PhD), including immunology, microbiology; neuroscience (MS, PhD); pathology (PhD); physiology (MS, PhD); psychiatry and behavioral sciences (MS, PhD), including biological psychology; radiological sciences (MS, PhD), including medical radiation physics; MD/PhD. *Program availability:* Part-time. Terminal master's awarded for partial completion of doctoral program. *Degree requirements:* For doctorate, thesis/dissertation. *Entrance requirements:* For doctorate, GRE General Test, 3 letters of recommendation. Additional exam requirements/recommendations for international students: required—TOEFL. *Expenses:* Contact institution.

**University of Oregon,** Graduate School, College of Arts and Sciences, Department of Biology, Eugene, OR 97403. Offers ecology and evolution (MA, MS, PhD); marine biology (MA, MS, PhD); molecular, cellular and genetic biology (PhD); neuroscience and development (PhD). Terminal master's awarded for partial completion of doctoral program. *Degree requirements:* For master's, thesis (for some programs); for doctorate, thesis/dissertation. *Entrance requirements:* For master's and doctorate, GRE General Test, minimum GPA of 3.2. Additional exam requirements/recommendations for international students: required—TOEFL.

**University of Ottawa,** Faculty of Graduate and Postdoctoral Studies, Faculty of Science, Ottawa-Carleton Institute of Biology, Ottawa, ON K1N 6N5, Canada. Offers M Sc, PhD. *Program availability:* Part-time. *Degree requirements:* For master's, thesis, seminar; for doctorate, comprehensive exam, thesis/dissertation, seminar. *Entrance requirements:* For master's, honors B Sc degree or equivalent, minimum B average; for doctorate, honors B Sc with minimum B+ average or M Sc with minimum B+ average. Electronic applications accepted.

**University of Pennsylvania,** Perelman School of Medicine, Biomedical Graduate Studies, Philadelphia, PA 19104. Offers MS, PhD, MD/PhD, VMD/PhD. *Faculty:* 1,191 full-time (364 women). *Students:* 922 full-time (539 women), 141 part-time (90 women); includes 389 minority (43 Black or African American, non-Hispanic/Latino; 3 American Indian or Alaska Native, non-Hispanic/Latino; 172 Asian, non-Hispanic/Latino; 137 Hispanic/Latino; 2 Native Hawaiian or other Pacific Islander, non-Hispanic/Latino; 32 Two or more races, non-Hispanic/Latino; 99 international. 2,423 applicants, 14% accepted, 183 enrolled. In 2019, 62 master's, 94 doctorates awarded. *Unit head:* Dr. Kelly Jordan-Sciutto, Director, 215-898-1585. *Application contact:* Aislinn Wallace, Associate Director, 215-746-6349.
Website: http://www.med.upenn.edu/bgs/

**University of Pennsylvania,** School of Arts and Sciences, Graduate Group in Biology, Philadelphia, PA 19104. Offers PhD. *Faculty:* 49 full-time (13 women), 3 part-time/adjunct (1 woman). *Students:* 54 full-time (31 women), 1 part-time (0 women); includes 5 minority (3 Asian, non-Hispanic/Latino; 2 Hispanic/Latino), 29 international. Average age 27. 159 applicants, 18% accepted, 15 enrolled. In 2019, 8 doctorates awarded. Application fee: $90.
Website: http://www.bio.upenn.edu

**University of Pittsburgh,** Kenneth P. Dietrich School of Arts and Sciences, Department of Biological Sciences, Pittsburgh, PA 15260. Offers ecology and evolution (PhD); molecular, cellular, and developmental biology (PhD). *Program availability:* Online learning. *Faculty:* 36 full-time (14 women). *Students:* 69 full-time (43 women); includes 9 minority (4 Black or African American, non-Hispanic/Latino; 3 Hispanic/Latino; 2 Two or more races, non-Hispanic/Latino), 9 international. Average age 23. 316 applicants, 8% accepted, 11 enrolled. In 2019, 6 doctorates awarded. *Degree requirements:* For doctorate, comprehensive exam, thesis/dissertation, Completion of Research Integrity Module. *Entrance requirements:* Additional exam requirements/recommendations for international students: required—TOEFL (minimum score 90 paper-based), IELTS (minimum score 7). *Application deadline:* For fall admission, 12/2 priority date for domestic students, 12/9 priority date for international students. Applications are processed on a rolling basis. Application fee: $0 ($75 for international students). Electronic applications accepted. *Financial support:* In 2019–20, 56 fellowships with full tuition reimbursements (averaging $36,108 per year), 109 research assistantships with full tuition reimbursements (averaging $30,840 per year), 32 teaching assistantships with full tuition reimbursements (averaging $30,375 per year) were awarded; Federal Work-Study, traineeships, and health care benefits also available. *Unit head:* Dr. Jeffrey G. Lawrence, Professor/Chair, 412-624-4350, Fax: 412-624-4759, E-mail: jlawrenc@pitt.edu. *Application contact:* Cathleen M. Barr, Graduate Administrator, 412-624-4268, Fax: 412-624-4349, E-mail: cbarr@pitt.edu.
Website: http://www.biology.pitt.edu

**University of Pittsburgh,** School of Medicine, Graduate Programs in Medicine, Biomedical Sciences Master's Program, Pittsburgh, PA 15260. Offers MS. *Degree requirements:* For master's, comprehensive exam, capstone project. *Entrance requirements:* Additional exam requirements/recommendations for international students: required—TOEFL (minimum score 100 iBT), IELTS (minimum score 7). Electronic applications accepted. *Expenses:* Contact institution.

**University of Pittsburgh,** School of Medicine, Graduate Programs in Medicine, Interdisciplinary Biomedical Graduate Program, Pittsburgh, PA 15260. Offers PhD. *Degree requirements:* For doctorate, comprehensive exam, thesis/dissertation. *Entrance requirements:* For doctorate, GRE General Test, minimum GPA of 3.2, 3 letters of recommendation, official transcripts, baccalaureate degree. Additional exam requirements/recommendations for international students: required—TOEFL (minimum

score 600 paper-based; 100 iBT), IELTS (minimum score 7). Electronic applications accepted. *Expenses:* Contact institution.

**University of Prince Edward Island,** Faculty of Science, Charlottetown, PE C1A 4P3, Canada. Offers environmental sciences (M Sc, PhD); human biology (M Sc); molecular and macromolecular sciences (M Sc, PhD); sustainable design engineering (M Sc). *Degree requirements:* For master's, thesis. *Entrance requirements:* Additional exam requirements/recommendations for international students: required—TOEFL (minimum score 550 paper-based; 80 iBT), Canadian Academic English Language Assessment, Michigan English Language Assessment Battery, Canadian Test of English for Scholars and Trainees.

**University of Puerto Rico at Mayagüez,** Graduate Studies, College of Arts and Sciences, Department of Biology, Mayagüez, PR 00681-9000. Offers MS. *Program availability:* Part-time. *Degree requirements:* For master's, one foreign language, comprehensive exam, thesis. *Entrance requirements:* For master's, BS in biology or its equivalent; minimum GPA of 3.0 in biology courses. Electronic applications accepted.

**University of Puerto Rico at Rio Piedras,** College of Natural Sciences, Department of Biology, San Juan, PR 00931-3300. Offers ecology/systematics (MS, PhD); evolution/genetics (MS, PhD); molecular/cellular biology (MS, PhD); neuroscience (MS, PhD). *Program availability:* Part-time. *Degree requirements:* For master's, one foreign language, comprehensive exam, thesis; for doctorate, one foreign language, comprehensive exam, thesis/dissertation. *Entrance requirements:* For master's, GRE Subject Test, interview, minimum GPA of 3.0, letter of recommendation; for doctorate, GRE Subject Test, interview, master's degree, minimum GPA of 3.0, letter of recommendation.

**University of Puerto Rico - Medical Sciences Campus,** School of Medicine, Biomedical Sciences Graduate Program, San Juan, PR 00936-5067. Offers MS, PhD. Terminal master's awarded for partial completion of doctoral program. *Degree requirements:* For master's, one foreign language, thesis; for doctorate, one foreign language, comprehensive exam, thesis/dissertation. *Entrance requirements:* For master's and doctorate, GRE General Test, GRE Subject Test, interview, 3 letters of recommendation, minimum GPA of 3.0. Electronic applications accepted. *Expenses:* Contact institution.

**University of Regina,** Faculty of Graduate Studies and Research, Faculty of Science, Department of Biology, Regina, SK S4S 0A2, Canada. Offers M Sc, PhD. *Program availability:* Part-time. *Faculty:* 17 full-time (6 women), 15 part-time/adjunct (1 woman). *Students:* 35 full-time (26 women), 4 part-time (3 women). Average age 25. 23 applicants, 39% accepted. In 2019, 8 master's, 6 doctorates awarded. *Degree requirements:* For master's, thesis; for doctorate, comprehensive exam, thesis/dissertation. *Entrance requirements:* For master's, 4 years Bachelor's degree in biology or related program; for doctorate, completion of Master's degree. Additional exam requirements/recommendations for international students: required—TOEFL (minimum score 580 paper-based; 80 iBT), IELTS (minimum score 6.5), PTE (minimum score 59), other options are CAEL, MELAB, Cantest and U of R ESL. *Application deadline:* Applications are processed on a rolling basis. Application fee: $100. Electronic applications accepted. *Expenses: Tuition:* Full-time $6684 Canadian dollars. *Required fees:* $100 Canadian dollars; $3351.45 Canadian dollars per trimester. $1117.15 Canadian dollars per semester. Tuition and fees vary according to course level, course load, degree level and program. *Financial support:* Fellowships, research assistantships, teaching assistantships, career-related internships or fieldwork, Federal Work-Study, scholarships/grants, unspecified assistantships, and travel award and Graduate Scholarship Base Funds available. Support available to part-time students. Financial award application deadline: 9/30. *Unit head:* Dr. Richard Manson, Department Head, 306-337-2417, Fax: 306-337-2410, E-mail: Richard.Manzon@uregina.ca. *Application contact:* Dr. Harold Weger, Graduate coordinator, 306-585-4479, Fax: 306-337-2410, E-mail: Harold.Weger@uregina.ca.
Website: http://www.uregina.ca/science/biology/

**University of Rhode Island,** Graduate School, College of the Environment and Life Sciences, Department of Biological Sciences, Kingston, RI 02881. Offers cell and molecular biology (MS, PhD); earth and environmental sciences (MS, PhD); ecology and ecosystem sciences (MS, PhD); evolutionary and marine biology (MS, PhD); sustainable agriculture and food systems (MS, PhD). *Program availability:* Part-time. *Faculty:* 20 full-time (10 women). *Students:* 108 full-time (68 women), 22 part-time (15 women); includes 12 minority (6 Black or African American, non-Hispanic/Latino; 4 Asian, non-Hispanic/Latino; 1 Hispanic/Latino; 1 Two or more races, non-Hispanic/Latino), 22 international. In 2019, 12 master's, 10 doctorates awarded. *Entrance requirements:* Additional exam requirements/recommendations for international students: required—TOEFL. *Application deadline:* For fall admission, 1/15 for domestic and international students. Application fee: $65. Electronic applications accepted. *Expenses: Tuition,* area resident: Full-time $13,734; part-time $763 per credit. Tuition, state resident: full-time $13,734; part-time $763 per credit. Tuition, nonresident: full-time $26,512; part-time $1473 per credit. International tuition: $26,512 full-time. *Required fees:* $1780; $52 per credit. $35 per term. One-time fee: $165. *Financial support:* In 2019–20, 24 research assistantships with tuition reimbursements (averaging $9,961 per year), 1 teaching assistantship with tuition reimbursement (averaging $7,521 per year) were awarded. Financial award application deadline: 1/15; financial award applicants required to submit FAFSA. *Unit head:* Dr. Alison Roberts, Chair, E-mail: bio_chair@etal.uri.edu. *Application contact:* Bethany Jenkins, Graduate Program Director, 401-874-7551, E-mail: bdjenkins@uri.edu.
Website: http://web.uri.edu/bio/

**University of Rochester,** School of Arts and Sciences, Department of Biology, Rochester, NY 14627. Offers biology (MS); ecology, genetics, and genomics (PhD); molecular, cellular, and developmental biology evolution (PhD). *Program availability:* Part-time. *Faculty:* 24 full-time (8 women). *Students:* 47 full-time (22 women), 1 (woman) part-time; includes 6 minority (1 Black or African American, non-Hispanic/Latino; 2 Asian, non-Hispanic/Latino; 3 Hispanic/Latino), 20 international. Average age 27. 98 applicants, 34% accepted, 12 enrolled. In 2019, 8 master's, 8 doctorates awarded. Terminal master's awarded for partial completion of doctoral program. *Degree requirements:* For master's, comprehensive exam (for some programs), thesis (for some programs); for doctorate, thesis/dissertation, qualifying exam. *Entrance requirements:* For master's and doctorate, personal statement, transcripts, three letters of recommendation. Additional exam requirements/recommendations for international students: required—TOEFL (minimum score 600 paper-based; 100 iBT), IELTS. *Application deadline:* For fall admission, 12/1 for domestic and international students. Application fee: $60. Electronic applications accepted. *Financial support:* In 2019–20, 40 students received support, including 5 fellowships (averaging $30,080 per year), 20 research assistantships (averaging $28,000 per year), 15 teaching assistantships (averaging $28,000 per year); health care benefits and tuition waivers (full) also available. Financial award application deadline: 12/1. *Unit head:* Michael Welte, Professor and Chair, 585-276-3897, E-mail: michael.welte@rochester.edu. *Application contact:* Cynthia Landry, Administrative Assistant, 585-275-7991, E-mail: cynthia.landry@rochester.edu.
Website: https://www.sas.rochester.edu/bio/graduate/index.html

*Biological and Biomedical Sciences—General*

**University of Rochester,** School of Medicine and Dentistry, Graduate Programs in Medicine and Dentistry, Interdepartmental Program in Translational Biomedical Science, Rochester, NY 14627. Offers PhD.

**University of Saint Joseph,** Department of Biology, West Hartford, CT 06117-2700. Offers MS. *Program availability:* Part-time, online learning. *Degree requirements:* For master's, comprehensive exam, thesis or alternative. *Entrance requirements:* For master's, 2 letters of recommendation. Electronic applications accepted. Application fee is waived when completed online.

**University of San Francisco,** College of Arts and Sciences, Program in Biology, San Francisco, CA 94117. Offers MS. *Faculty:* 8 full-time (3 women). *Students:* 11 full-time (8 women), 2 part-time (both women); includes 8 minority (2 Asian, non-Hispanic/Latino; 4 Hispanic/Latino; 2 Two or more races, non-Hispanic/Latino), 1 international. Average age 25. 47 applicants, 15% accepted, 7 enrolled. In 2019, 2 master's awarded. *Degree requirements:* For master's, thesis. *Entrance requirements:* For master's, GRE General Test, GRE Subject Test (recommended), BS in biology or the equivalent. Additional exam requirements/recommendations for international students: required—TOEFL (minimum score 100 iBT), IELTS (minimum score 7), PTE (minimum score 65). *Application deadline:* For fall admission, 3/15 for domestic and international students; for spring admission, 10/15 for domestic and international students. Applications are processed on a rolling basis. Application fee: $55. Electronic applications accepted. Application fee is waived when completed online. *Financial support:* Research assistantships with full tuition reimbursements, teaching assistantships with full tuition reimbursements, career-related internships or fieldwork, and institutionally sponsored loans available. Financial award applicants required to submit FAFSA. *Unit head:* Dr. John Paul, Graduate Director, 415-422-5470, E-mail: jrpaul@usfca.edu. *Application contact:* Information Contact, 415-422-5101, E-mail: asgraduate@usfca.edu.
Website: https://www.usfca.edu/arts-sciences/graduate-programs/biology

**University of Saskatchewan,** College of Graduate and Postdoctoral Studies, College of Arts and Science, Department of Biology, Saskatoon, SK S7N 5A2, Canada. Offers M Sc, PhD. *Degree requirements:* For master's, thesis (for some programs); for doctorate, comprehensive exam (for some programs), thesis/dissertation. *Entrance requirements:* Additional exam requirements/recommendations for international students: required—TOEFL (minimum score 80 iBT); recommended—IELTS (minimum score 6.5). Electronic applications accepted.

**University of Saskatchewan,** Western College of Veterinary Medicine and College of Graduate and Postdoctoral Studies, Graduate Programs in Veterinary Medicine, Department of Veterinary Biomedical Sciences, Saskatoon, SK S7N 5A2, Canada. Offers veterinary anatomy (M Sc); veterinary biomedical sciences (M Vet Sc); veterinary physiological sciences (M Sc, PhD). *Degree requirements:* For master's, thesis; for doctorate, comprehensive exam (for some programs), thesis/dissertation. *Entrance requirements:* Additional exam requirements/recommendations for international students: required—TOEFL (minimum score 80 iBT); recommended—IELTS (minimum score 6.5). Electronic applications accepted.

**University of South Alabama,** College of Arts and Sciences, Department of Biology, Mobile, AL 36688. Offers MS. *Program availability:* Part-time. *Faculty:* 5 full-time (2 women). *Students:* 8 full-time (5 women), 1 (woman) part-time; includes 3 minority (all Black or African American, non-Hispanic/Latino). Average age 27. 3 applicants, 100% accepted, 2 enrolled. In 2019, 4 master's awarded. *Degree requirements:* For master's, comprehensive exam, thesis. *Entrance requirements:* For master's, GRE. Additional exam requirements/recommendations for international students: required—TOEFL (minimum score 600 paper-based; 100 iBT). *Application deadline:* For fall admission, 7/1 priority date for domestic students, 6/1 priority date for international students; for spring admission, 12/1 priority date for domestic students, 11/1 priority date for international students; for summer admission, 5/1 priority date for domestic students, 4/1 priority date for international students. Applications are processed on a rolling basis. Application fee: $35. Electronic applications accepted. *Expenses: Tuition, area resident:* Part-time $442 per credit hour. Tuition, state resident: full-time $10,608; part-time $442 per credit hour. Tuition, nonresident: full-time $21,216; part-time $884 per credit hour. *Financial support:* Fellowships, research assistantships, teaching assistantships, career-related internships or fieldwork, Federal Work-Study, institutionally sponsored loans, scholarships/grants, and unspecified assistantships available. Support available to part-time students. Financial award application deadline: 3/31; financial award applicants required to submit FAFSA. *Unit head:* Dr. Tim Sherman, Chair, Biology, 251-460-6331, E-mail: tsherman@southalabama.edu. *Application contact:* Dr. Tim Sherman, Chair, Biology, 251-460-6331, E-mail: tsherman@southalabama.edu.
Website: http://www.southalabama.edu/colleges/artsandsci/biology/

**University of South Alabama,** College of Medicine and Graduate School, Interdisciplinary Graduate Program in Basic Medical Sciences, Mobile, AL 36688-0002. Offers PhD. *Faculty:* 26 full-time (9 women). *Students:* 45 full-time (31 women); includes 8 minority (5 Black or African American, non-Hispanic/Latino; 1 American Indian or Alaska Native, non-Hispanic/Latino; 1 Asian, non-Hispanic/Latino; 1 Hispanic/Latino), 14 international. Average age 29. 15 applicants, 93% accepted, 14 enrolled. In 2019, 9 doctorates awarded. *Degree requirements:* For doctorate, comprehensive exam, thesis/dissertation. *Entrance requirements:* For doctorate, GRE. Additional exam requirements/recommendations for international students: required—TOEFL (minimum score 600 paper-based; 100 iBT). *Application deadline:* For fall admission, 3/31 for domestic and international students. Application fee: $75. Electronic applications accepted. *Expenses:* Contact institution. *Financial support:* Fellowships, research assistantships, teaching assistantships, career-related internships or fieldwork, institutionally sponsored loans, scholarships/grants, and unspecified assistantships available. Support available to part-time students. Financial award application deadline: 3/31; financial award applicants required to submit FAFSA. *Unit head:* Dr. Mark Taylor, Director of Graduate Studies, 251-460-6153, Fax: 251-460-6071, E-mail: mtaylor@southalabama.edu. *Application contact:* Angie O'Neal, Academic Advisor, 251-460-6153, Fax: 251-461-6071, E-mail: aoneal@southalabama.edu.
Website: https://www.southalabama.edu/colleges/com/doctoral-program/

**University of South Alabama,** Graduate School, Program in Environmental Toxicology, Mobile, AL 36688-0002. Offers basic medical sciences (MS); biology (MS); chemistry (MS); environmental toxicology (MS); exposure route and chemical transport (MS). *Faculty:* 4 full-time (0 women). *Students:* 7 full-time (5 women), 4 part-time (1 woman); includes 1 minority (Black or African American, non-Hispanic/Latino), 1 international. Average age 26. 2 applicants, 50% accepted, 1 enrolled. In 2019, 3 master's awarded. *Degree requirements:* For master's, comprehensive exam, thesis optional, research project or thesis. *Entrance requirements:* For master's, GRE. Additional exam requirements/recommendations for international students: required—TOEFL (minimum score 525 paper-based; 71 iBT). *Application deadline:* For fall admission, 7/1 for domestic students, 3/1 for international students; for spring admission, 12/1 for domestic students, 11/1 for international students. Application fee: $50. Electronic applications accepted. *Expenses: Tuition, area resident:* Part-time $442 per credit hour. Tuition, state resident: full-time $10,608; part-time $442 per credit hour. Tuition, nonresident: full-time $21,216; part-time $884 per credit hour. *Financial support:* Fellowships, research assistantships, teaching assistantships, career-related internships or fieldwork, Federal Work-Study, institutionally sponsored loans, scholarships/grants, and unspecified assistantships available. Support available to part-time students. Financial award application deadline: 3/31; financial award applicants required to submit FAFSA. *Unit head:* Dr. Sean Powers, Chair, Marine Sciences, 251-460-7136, E-mail: spowers@disl.org. *Application contact:* Dr. David Forbes, Graduate Coordinator/Director, Environmental Toxicology, 251-460-6181, E-mail: dforbes@southalabama.edu.
Website: https://www.southalabama.edu/colleges/graduateschool/etox/

**University of South Carolina,** The Graduate School, College of Arts and Sciences, Department of Biological Sciences, Columbia, SC 29208. Offers biology (MS, PhD); biology education (IMA, MAT); ecology, evolution and organismal biology (MS, PhD); molecular, cellular, and developmental biology (MS, PhD). Terminal master's awarded for partial completion of doctoral program. *Degree requirements:* For master's, one foreign language, thesis (for some programs); for doctorate, one foreign language, thesis/dissertation. *Entrance requirements:* For master's and doctorate, GRE General Test, minimum GPA of 3.0 in science. Electronic applications accepted.

**University of South Carolina,** School of Medicine and The Graduate School, Graduate Programs in Medicine, Columbia, SC 29208. Offers biomedical science (MBS, PhD); genetic counseling (MS); nurse anesthesia (MNA); rehabilitation counseling (MRC, Certificate), including psychiatric rehabilitation (Certificate), rehabilitation counseling (MRC). Terminal master's awarded for partial completion of doctoral program. *Degree requirements:* For master's, comprehensive exam, thesis (for some programs), practicum; for doctorate, comprehensive exam, thesis/dissertation. *Entrance requirements:* For master's, doctorate, and Certificate, GRE General Test. Electronic applications accepted. *Expenses:* Contact institution.

**University of South Carolina,** School of Medicine and The Graduate School, Graduate Programs in Medicine, Graduate Program in Biomedical Science, Doctoral Program in Biomedical Science, Columbia, SC 29208. Offers PhD. *Degree requirements:* For doctorate, comprehensive exam, thesis/dissertation. *Entrance requirements:* For doctorate, GRE General Test. Electronic applications accepted.

**University of South Carolina,** School of Medicine and The Graduate School, Graduate Programs in Medicine, Graduate Program in Biomedical Science, Master's Program in Biomedical Science, Columbia, SC 29208. Offers MBS. *Degree requirements:* For master's, comprehensive exam, thesis. *Entrance requirements:* For master's, GRE General Test. Electronic applications accepted.

**University of South Dakota,** Graduate School, College of Arts and Sciences, Department of Biology, Vermillion, SD 57069. Offers MS, PhD. *Degree requirements:* For master's, comprehensive exam (for some programs), thesis (for some programs); for doctorate, comprehensive exam, thesis/dissertation. *Entrance requirements:* For master's, GRE Subject Test, GRE General Test, minimum GPA of 2.7; for doctorate, GRE General Test, GRE Subject Test, minimum GPA of 2.7. Additional exam requirements/recommendations for international students: required—TOEFL (minimum score 550 paper-based; 70 iBT). Electronic applications accepted.

**University of South Dakota,** Graduate School, Sanford School of Medicine and Graduate School, Biomedical Sciences Graduate Program, Vermillion, SD 57069. Offers cardiovascular research (MS, PhD); cellular and molecular biology (MS, PhD); molecular microbiology and immunology (MS, PhD); neuroscience (MS, PhD); physiology and pharmacology (MS, PhD). Terminal master's awarded for partial completion of doctoral program. *Degree requirements:* For master's, thesis; for doctorate, comprehensive exam, thesis/dissertation. *Entrance requirements:* For master's and doctorate, GRE General Test, minimum GPA of 3.0. Additional exam requirements/recommendations for international students: required—TOEFL (minimum score 550 paper-based; 80 iBT), IELTS (minimum score 6). Electronic applications accepted. *Expenses:* Contact institution.

**University of Southern California,** Graduate School, Dana and David Dornsife College of Letters, Arts and Sciences, Department of Biological Sciences, Los Angeles, CA 90089. Offers biology (MS); computational molecular biology (MS); integrative and evolutionary biology (PhD); marine biology and biological oceanography (MS, PhD), including marine and environmental biology (MS), marine biology and biological oceanography (PhD); molecular and computational biology (PhD), including biology, computational biology and bioinformatics, molecular biology; neurobiology (PhD). Terminal master's awarded for partial completion of doctoral program. *Degree requirements:* For master's, comprehensive exam (for some programs), research paper; for doctorate, thesis/dissertation, qualifying examination, dissertation defense. *Entrance requirements:* For master's, GRE, 3 letters of recommendation, personal statement, resume, minimum GPA of 3.0; for doctorate, GRE, 3 letters of recommendation, resume, minimum GPA of 3.0. Additional exam requirements/recommendations for international students: required—TOEFL (minimum score 600 paper-based; 100 iBT). Electronic applications accepted.

**University of Southern California,** Keck School of Medicine and Graduate School, Graduate Programs in Medicine, Los Angeles, CA 90089-9031. Offers MPAP, MPH, MS, PhD, Certificate. *Faculty:* 514 full-time (175 women), 59 part-time/adjunct (31 women). *Students:* 1,070 full-time (754 women), 95 part-time (73 women); includes 631 minority (67 Black or African American, non-Hispanic/Latino; 10 American Indian or Alaska Native, non-Hispanic/Latino; 322 Asian, non-Hispanic/Latino; 160 Hispanic/Latino; 11 Native Hawaiian or other Pacific Islander, non-Hispanic/Latino; 61 Two or more races, non-Hispanic/Latino), 168 international. Average age 26. 2,397 applicants, 38% accepted, 413 enrolled. In 2019, 421 master's, 34 doctorates awarded. Terminal master's awarded for partial completion of doctoral program. *Entrance requirements:* For master's, GRE General Test, minimum GPA of 3.0; for doctorate, GRE General Test (minimum combined Verbal and Quantitative score of 1000), minimum GPA of 3.0. Additional exam requirements/recommendations for international students: required—TOEFL (minimum score 600 paper-based; 100 iBT). *Application deadline:* Applications are processed on a rolling basis. Application fee: $90. Electronic applications accepted. *Expenses:* Contact institution. *Financial support:* Fellowships, research assistantships, teaching assistantships, career-related internships or fieldwork, Federal Work-Study, institutionally sponsored loans, scholarships/grants, traineeships, and health care benefits available. Support available to part-time students. Financial award applicants required to submit CSS PROFILE or FAFSA. *Unit head:* Dr. Ite Offringa, Associate Dean for Graduate Affairs, 323-442-1607, Fax: 323-442-1199, E-mail: ilaird@usc.edu. *Application contact:* Marisela Zuniga, Administrative Coordinator, 323-442-1607, Fax: 323-442-1199, E-mail: mzuniga@usc.edu.
Website: http://keck.usc.edu/

**University of Southern Maine,** College of Science, Technology, and Health, Program in Biology, Portland, ME 04103. Offers MS. *Expenses: Tuition, area resident:* Full-time $864; part-time $432 per credit hour. Tuition, state resident: full-time $864; part-time $432 per credit hour. Tuition, nonresident: full-time $2372; part-time $1186 per credit hour. *Required fees:* $141; $108 per credit hour. Tuition and fees vary according to course load.

**University of South Florida,** College of Arts and Sciences, Department of Cell Biology, Microbiology, and Molecular Biology, Tampa, FL 33620-9951. Offers biology (MS), including cell biology, microbiology and molecular biology; cancer biology (PhD); cancer chemical biology (PhD); cancer immunology and immunotherapy (PhD); cell and

molecular biology (PhD); microbiology (MS). *Faculty:* 21 full-time (8 women). *Students:* 85 full-time (50 women), 4 part-time (all women); includes 10 minority (1 Black or African American, non-Hispanic/Latino; 3 Asian, non-Hispanic/Latino; 4 Hispanic/Latino; 2 Two or more races, non-Hispanic/Latino), 35 international. Average age 27. 178 applicants, 15% accepted, 20 enrolled. In 2019, 12 master's, 12 doctorates awarded. *Degree requirements:* For master's, thesis or alternative; for doctorate, comprehensive exam, thesis/dissertation. *Entrance requirements:* For master's and doctorate, GRE General Test, minimum GPA of 3.0, extensive background in biology or chemistry. Additional exam requirements/recommendations for international students: required—TOEFL (minimum score 570 paper-based; 79 iBT) or IELTS (minimum score 6.5). *Application deadline:* For fall admission, 11/30 priority date for domestic and international students; for spring admission, 7/1 priority date for domestic students, 7/1 for international students. Application fee: $30. *Financial support:* In 2019–20, 9 students received support. Career-related internships or fieldwork, health care benefits, and unspecified assistantships available. Financial award application deadline: 4/1. *Unit head:* Dr. James Garey, Professor/Chair, 813-974-7103, Fax: 813-974-1614, E-mail: garey@usf.edu. *Application contact:* Dr. Kenneth Wright, Associate Professor of Cancer Biology, H. Lee Moffitt Cancer Center and Research Institute, 813-745-3918, Fax: 813-974-1614, E-mail: ken.wright@moffitt.org.
Website: http://biology.usf.edu/cmmb/

**University of South Florida,** College of Arts and Sciences, Department of Integrative Biology, Tampa, FL 33620-9951. Offers biology (MS), including ecology and evolution, environmental and ecological microbiology, physiology and morphology. *Program availability:* Part-time. *Faculty:* 12 full-time (4 women). *Students:* 27 full-time (15 women), 3 part-time (all women); includes 5 minority (1 Black or African American, non-Hispanic/Latino; 2 Asian, non-Hispanic/Latino; 2 Hispanic/Latino), 3 international. Average age 32. 37 applicants, 24% accepted, 6 enrolled. In 2019, 4 master's, 3 doctorates awarded. *Degree requirements:* For master's, comprehensive exam, thesis (for some programs); for doctorate, comprehensive exam, thesis/dissertation. *Entrance requirements:* For master's, GRE: Preferred scores of 155V (69th percentile), 150Q (38th percentile), 4.5AW, minimum GPA of 3.0; Acceptance by faculty member; 3 letters of recommendation (see student recommendation form on department website); statement of research and professional goals; TA application; It is expected that candidates will have completed courses equivalent to those required for the BS in Biology at USF; for doctorate, GRE: 155+ (70%)V, 150+ (70%)Q, 4.5 (70%) AW, Bachelor of Science required. It is expected that candidates for the Ph.D. degree will have completed courses equivalent to those required for the B.S. in Biology at U.S.F. Acceptance by a faculty member in the Department of Integrative Biology is mandatory. Additional exam requirements/recommendations for international students: required—TOEFL. *Application deadline:* For fall admission, 11/30 priority date for domestic and international students; for spring admission, 7/1 priority date for domestic and international students. Application fee: $30. Electronic applications accepted. *Financial support:* In 2019–20, 11 students received support. Research assistantships, teaching assistantships, and unspecified assistantships available. Financial award application deadline: 6/30; financial award applicants required to submit FAFSA. *Unit head:* Dr. Valerie Harwood, Professor and Chair, 813-974-1524, Fax: 813-974-3263, E-mail: vharwood@usf.edu. *Application contact:* Dr. Stephen Deban, Associate Professor and Graduate Program Director, 813-974-2242, E-mail: sdeban@usf.edu.
Website: http://biology.usf.edu/ib/grad/

**University of South Florida,** Morsani College of Medicine and College of Graduate Studies, Graduate Programs in Medical Sciences, Tampa, FL 33620-9951. Offers bioinformatics and computational biology (MSBCB). *Faculty:* 1 (woman) full-time. *Students:* 355 full-time (207 women), 229 part-time (145 women); includes 283 minority (71 Black or African American, non-Hispanic/Latino; 2 American Indian or Alaska Native, non-Hispanic/Latino; 89 Asian, non-Hispanic/Latino; 103 Hispanic/Latino; 2 Native Hawaiian or other Pacific Islander, non-Hispanic/Latino; 16 Two or more races, non-Hispanic/Latino), 48 international. Average age 28. 898 applicants, 57% accepted, 323 enrolled. In 2019, 227 master's, 13 doctorates awarded. Terminal master's awarded for partial completion of doctoral program. *Degree requirements:* For master's, comprehensive exam, thesis; for doctorate, comprehensive exam, thesis/dissertation. *Entrance requirements:* For master's, GRE General Test or GMAT, bachelor's degree or equivalent from regionally-accredited university with minimum GPA of 3.0 in upper-division sciences coursework; prerequisites in general biology, general chemistry, general physics, organic chemistry, quantitative analysis, and integral and differential calculus; for doctorate, GRE General Test, bachelor's degree from regionally-accredited university with minimum GPA of 3.0 in upper-division sciences coursework; 3 letters of recommendation; personal interview; 1-2 page personal statement; prerequisites in biology, chemistry, physics, organic chemistry, quantitative analysis, and integral/differential calculus. Additional exam requirements/recommendations for international students: required—TOEFL (minimum score 550 paper-based; 79 iBT) or IELTS (minimum score 6.5). *Application deadline:* For fall admission, 2/1 priority date for domestic students, 2/1 for international students. Application fee: $30. Electronic applications accepted. *Expenses:* Contact institution. *Financial support:* In 2019–20, 106 students received support. *Unit head:* Dr. Michael Barber, Professor/Associate Dean for Graduate and Postdoctoral Affairs, 813-974-9908, Fax: 813-974-4317, E-mail: mbarber@health.usf.edu. *Application contact:* Dr. Eric Bennett, Graduate Director, PhD Program in Medical Sciences, 813-974-1545, Fax: 813-974-4317, E-mail: esbennet@health.usf.edu.
Website: http://health.usf.edu/nocms/medicine/graduatestudies/

**The University of Tennessee,** Graduate School, College of Arts and Sciences, Program in Life Sciences, Knoxville, TN 37996. Offers genome science and technology (MS, PhD); plant physiology and genetics (MS, PhD). *Degree requirements:* For doctorate, one foreign language, thesis/dissertation. *Entrance requirements:* For master's and doctorate, GRE General Test, minimum GPA of 2.7. Additional exam requirements/recommendations for international students: required—TOEFL. Electronic applications accepted.

**The University of Tennessee,** Graduate School, Intercollegiate Programs, Program in Comparative and Experimental Medicine, Knoxville, TN 37996. Offers MS, PhD. *Degree requirements:* For master's, thesis; for doctorate, thesis/dissertation. *Entrance requirements:* For master's and doctorate, GRE General Test, minimum GPA of 2.7. Additional exam requirements/recommendations for international students: required—TOEFL. Electronic applications accepted.

**The University of Tennessee Health Science Center,** College of Graduate Health Sciences, Memphis, TN 38163. Offers biomedical engineering (MS, PhD); biomedical sciences (PhD); dental sciences (MDS); epidemiology (MS); health outcomes and policy research (PhD); laboratory research and management (MS); nursing science (PhD); pharmaceutical sciences (PhD); pharmacology (MS); speech and hearing science (PhD); DDS/PhD; DNP/PhD; MD/PhD; Pharm D/PhD. Terminal master's awarded for partial completion of doctoral program. *Degree requirements:* For master's, comprehensive exam, thesis; for doctorate, thesis/dissertation, oral and written preliminary and comprehensive exams. *Entrance requirements:* For master's and doctorate, GRE General Test, minimum GPA of 3.0. Additional exam requirements/recommendations for international students: recommended—TOEFL (minimum score 79 iBT), IELTS (minimum score 6.5). Electronic applications accepted. *Expenses:* Contact institution.

**The University of Tennessee–Oak Ridge National Laboratory,** Graduate Program in Genome Science and Technology, Knoxville, TN 37966. Offers life sciences (MS, PhD). *Degree requirements:* For master's, thesis; for doctorate, comprehensive exam, thesis/dissertation. *Entrance requirements:* For master's and doctorate, GRE General Test. Additional exam requirements/recommendations for international students: required—TOEFL. Electronic applications accepted.

**The University of Texas at Arlington,** Graduate School, College of Science, Department of Biology, Arlington, TX 76019. Offers biology (MS); quantitative biology (PhD). *Program availability:* Part-time, evening/weekend. *Degree requirements:* For master's, thesis, oral defense of thesis; for doctorate, comprehensive exam, thesis/dissertation, oral defense of dissertation. *Entrance requirements:* For master's and doctorate, GRE General Test. Additional exam requirements/recommendations for international students: required—TOEFL (minimum score 550 paper-based; 79 iBT). Electronic applications accepted.

**The University of Texas at Austin,** Graduate School, College of Natural Sciences, School of Biological Sciences, Austin, TX 78712-1111. Offers ecology, evolution and behavior (PhD); microbiology (PhD); plant biology (MA, PhD). *Entrance requirements:* For master's and doctorate, GRE General Test. Electronic applications accepted.

**The University of Texas at Dallas,** School of Natural Sciences and Mathematics, Department of Biological Sciences, Richardson, TX 75080. Offers bioinformatics and computational biology (MS); biotechnology (MS); molecular and cell biology (MS, PhD). *Program availability:* Part-time, evening/weekend. *Faculty:* 20 full-time (5 women), 6 part-time/adjunct (4 women). *Students:* 128 full-time (81 women), 12 part-time (7 women); includes 29 minority (1 Black or African American, non-Hispanic/Latino; 19 Asian, non-Hispanic/Latino; 7 Hispanic/Latino; 2 Two or more races, non-Hispanic/Latino), 77 international. Average age 28. 309 applicants, 25% accepted, 38 enrolled. In 2019, 36 master's, 7 doctorates awarded. *Degree requirements:* For master's, thesis optional; for doctorate, thesis/dissertation, publishable paper. *Entrance requirements:* For master's and doctorate, GRE (minimum combined score of 1000 on verbal and quantitative). Additional exam requirements/recommendations for international students: required—TOEFL (minimum score 550 paper-based; 80 iBT). *Application deadline:* For fall admission, 7/15 for domestic students, 5/1 priority date for international students; for spring admission, 11/15 for domestic students, 9/1 priority date for international students. Applications are processed on a rolling basis. Application fee: $50 ($100 for international students). Electronic applications accepted. *Expenses: Tuition, area resident:* Full-time $16,504. Tuition, state resident: full-time $16,504. Tuition, nonresident: full-time $34,266. Tuition and fees vary according to course load. *Financial support:* In 2019–20, 86 students received support, including 1 fellowship with partial tuition reimbursement available (averaging $500 per year), 16 research assistantships with partial tuition reimbursements available (averaging $25,200 per year), 69 teaching assistantships with partial tuition reimbursements available (averaging $18,173 per year); career-related internships or fieldwork, Federal Work-Study, institutionally sponsored loans, scholarships/grants, and unspecified assistantships also available. Support available to part-time students. Financial award application deadline: 4/30; financial award applicants required to submit FAFSA. *Unit head:* Dr. Tae Hoon Kim, Department Head, 972-883-6032, Fax: 972-883-4551, E-mail: biology@utdallas.edu. *Application contact:* Nancy Yu, Graduate Support Assistant, 972-883-4794, Fax: 972-883-4551, E-mail: biology@utdallas.edu.
Website: https://biology.utdallas.edu/

**The University of Texas at El Paso,** Graduate School, College of Science, Department of Biological Sciences, El Paso, TX 79968-0001. Offers bioinformatics (MS); biological sciences (MS, PhD). *Program availability:* Part-time, evening/weekend. *Degree requirements:* For master's, thesis; for doctorate, thesis/dissertation. *Entrance requirements:* For master's, GRE, minimum GPA of 3.0, letters of recommendation; for doctorate, GRE, statement of purpose, letters of recommendation. Additional exam requirements/recommendations for international students: required—TOEFL; recommended—IELTS. Electronic applications accepted.

**The University of Texas at San Antonio,** College of Sciences, Department of Biology, San Antonio, TX 78249-0617. Offers biology (MS); biotechnology (MS); cell and molecular biology (PhD); neurobiology (PhD). Terminal master's awarded for partial completion of doctoral program. *Degree requirements:* For master's, comprehensive exam, thesis or alternative; for doctorate, comprehensive exam, thesis/dissertation. *Entrance requirements:* For master's, GRE General Test, bachelor's degree with 18 credit hours in field of study or in another appropriate field of study; for doctorate, GRE General Test, 3 letters of recommendation, statement of purpose, resume. Additional exam requirements/recommendations for international students: required—TOEFL (minimum score 500 paper-based; 100 iBT), IELTS (minimum score 5). Electronic applications accepted.

**The University of Texas at Tyler,** College of Arts and Sciences, Department of Biology, Tyler, TX 75799-0001. Offers biology (MS); interdisciplinary studies (MSIS). *Faculty:* 7 full-time (1 woman). *Students:* 11 full-time (8 women), 7 part-time (6 women); includes 4 minority (1 Asian, non-Hispanic/Latino; 1 Hispanic/Latino; 2 Two or more races, non-Hispanic/Latino). Average age 28. 15 applicants, 60% accepted, 8 enrolled. In 2019, 6 master's awarded. *Degree requirements:* For master's, comprehensive exam, thesis, oral qualifying exam, thesis defense. *Entrance requirements:* For master's, GRE General Test, GRE Subject Test, bachelor's degree in biology or equivalent. Additional exam requirements/recommendations for international students: required—TOEFL. *Application deadline:* For fall admission, 8/17 priority date for domestic students, 7/1 priority date for international students; for spring admission, 12/21 priority date for domestic students, 11/1 priority date for international students. Applications are processed on a rolling basis. Application fee: $25 ($50 for international students). Electronic applications accepted. *Financial support:* In 2019–20, 2 research assistantships (averaging $10,000 per year), 10 teaching assistantships (averaging $10,000 per year) were awarded; scholarships/grants also available. Financial award application deadline: 7/1; financial award applicants required to submit FAFSA. *Unit head:* Dr. Lance Williams, Chair, 903-565-5878, E-mail: lwilliams@uttyler.edu. *Application contact:* Dr. Lance Williams, Chair, 903-565-5878, E-mail: lwilliams@uttyler.edu.
Website: http://www.uttyler.edu/biology/

**The University of Texas Health Science Center at Houston,** MD Anderson UTHealth Graduate School, Houston, TX 77225-0036. Offers biochemistry and cell biology (PhD); biomedical sciences (MS); cancer biology (PhD); genetic counseling (MS); genetics and epigenetics (PhD); immunology (PhD); medical physics (MS, PhD); microbiology and infectious diseases (PhD); neuroscience (PhD); quantitative sciences (PhD); therapeutics and pharmacology (PhD); MD/PhD. Terminal master's awarded for partial completion of doctoral program. *Degree requirements:* For master's, thesis; for doctorate, thesis/dissertation. *Entrance requirements:* For master's and doctorate, GRE General Test. Additional exam requirements/recommendations for international students: required—TOEFL. Electronic applications accepted.

## Biological and Biomedical Sciences—General

**The University of Texas Health Science Center at San Antonio,** Graduate School of Biomedical Sciences, Integrated Biomedical Sciences Program, San Antonio, TX 78229-3900. Offers PhD. *Degree requirements:* For doctorate, comprehensive exam, thesis/dissertation.

**The University of Texas Medical Branch,** Graduate School of Biomedical Sciences, Galveston, TX 77555. Offers MA, MMS, MPH, MS, PhD, MD/PhD. Terminal master's awarded for partial completion of doctoral program. *Degree requirements:* For master's, comprehensive exam (for some programs), thesis or alternative; for doctorate, comprehensive exam, thesis/dissertation. *Entrance requirements:* For master's and doctorate, GRE General Test, 3 letters of recommendation. Additional exam requirements/recommendations for international students: required—TOEFL (minimum score 550 paper-based; 80 iBT), IELTS (minimum score 6.5). Electronic applications accepted. *Expenses:* Contact institution.

**The University of Texas of the Permian Basin,** Office of Graduate Studies, College of Arts and Sciences, Department of Biology, Odessa, TX 79762-0001. Offers MS. *Program availability:* Part-time, evening/weekend. *Degree requirements:* For master's, comprehensive exam, thesis or alternative. *Entrance requirements:* For master's, GRE General Test. Additional exam requirements/recommendations for international students: required—TOEFL (minimum score 550 paper-based).

**The University of Texas Rio Grande Valley,** College of Sciences, Department of Biology, Edinburg, TX 78539. Offers MS. *Program availability:* Part-time. *Faculty:* 20 full-time (7 women). *Students:* 54 full-time (30 women), 29 part-time (19 women); includes 56 minority (1 Black or African American, non-Hispanic/Latino; 1 Asian, non-Hispanic/Latino; 54 Hispanic/Latino), 10 international. Average age 26. 31 applicants, 77% accepted, 21 enrolled. In 2019, 23 master's awarded. *Degree requirements:* For master's, comprehensive exam (for some programs), thesis (for some programs), Thesis for thesis students; exam for non-thesis students. *Entrance requirements:* For master's, GRE is required not minimum score, 3.0 in last 60 hours. Must have 15 hours in upper division Biological Science courses. Letter of intent and 2 letters o recommendation. Additional exam requirements/recommendations for international students: required—TOEFL (minimum score 550 paper-based; 79 iBT), IELTS (minimum score 6.5), TOEFL or IELTS. *Application deadline:* For spring admission, 11/30 priority date for international students; for summer admission, 4/1 priority date for domestic and international students. Applications are processed on a rolling basis. Application fee: $50 ($100 for international students). Electronic applications accepted. *Expenses: Tuition, area resident:* Full-time $5959; part-time $440 per credit hour. Tuition, state resident: full-time $5959. Tuition, nonresident: full-time $5959. *International tuition:* $13,321 full-time. *Required fees:* $1169; $185 per credit hour. *Financial support:* In 2019–20, 55 students received support, including 17 fellowships (averaging $17,388 per year), 16 teaching assistantships (averaging $15,000 per year); scholarships/grants and unspecified assistantships also available. *Unit head:* Dr. Kristine Lowe, Chair/Professor, 956-665-8749, Fax: 956-665-3537, E-mail: kristine.lowe@utrgv.edu. *Application contact:* Dr. Robert Keith Dearth, Graduate Program Coordinator/Associate Professor, 956-665-8750, Fax: 956-665-3537, E-mail: robert.dearth@utrgv.edu.
Website: https://www.utrgv.edu/biology/

**The University of Texas Southwestern Medical Center,** Southwestern Graduate School of Biomedical Sciences, Clinical Science Program, Dallas, TX 75390. Offers MCS, MSCS. *Program availability:* Part-time. *Degree requirements:* For master's, 1-year clinical research project. *Entrance requirements:* For master's, graduate degree in biomedical science. Electronic applications accepted.

**The University of Texas Southwestern Medical Center,** Southwestern Graduate School of Biomedical Sciences, Division of Basic Science, Dallas, TX 75390. Offers biological chemistry (PhD); biomedical engineering (MS, PhD); cancer biology (PhD); cell regulation (PhD); genetics and development (PhD); immunology (PhD); integrative biology (PhD); molecular biophysics (PhD); molecular microbiology (PhD); neuroscience (PhD); MD/PhD. *Degree requirements:* For doctorate, thesis/dissertation, qualifying exam. *Entrance requirements:* For doctorate, GRE General Test, research experience. Additional exam requirements/recommendations for international students: required—TOEFL. Electronic applications accepted.

**The University of Texas Southwestern Medical Center,** Southwestern Graduate School of Biomedical Sciences, Medical Scientist Training Program, Dallas, TX 75390. Offers PhD, MD/PhD. Electronic applications accepted.

**University of the Incarnate Word,** School of Mathematics, Science, and Engineering, San Antonio, TX 78209-6397. Offers applied statistics (MS); biology (MA, MS); mathematics (MA), including teaching; multidisciplinary sciences (MA); nutrition (MS). *Program availability:* Part-time, evening/weekend. *Faculty:* 2 full-time (1 woman), 1 part-time/adjunct (0 women). *Students:* 19 full-time (17 women), 5 part-time (3 women); includes 14 minority (1 Black or African American, non-Hispanic/Latino; 13 Hispanic/Latino), 3 international. 15 applicants, 87% accepted, 5 enrolled. In 2019, 18 master's awarded. *Degree requirements:* For master's, comprehensive exam (for some programs), thesis optional, capstone. *Entrance requirements:* For master's, GRE, recommendation letter. Additional exam requirements/recommendations for international students: required—TOEFL (minimum score 560 paper-based; 83 iBT). *Application deadline:* Applications are processed on a rolling basis. Application fee: $20. Electronic applications accepted. *Expenses: Tuition:* Full-time $11,520; part-time $960 per credit hour. *Required fees:* $1128; $94 per credit hour. Tuition and fees vary according to degree level, campus/location, program and student level. *Financial support:* Research assistantships, Federal Work-Study, scholarships/grants, tuition waivers (partial), and unspecified assistantships available. Financial award applicants required to submit FAFSA. *Unit head:* Dr. Carlos A. Garcia, Dean, 210-829-2717, Fax: 210-829-3153, E-mail: cagarci9@uiwtx.edu. *Application contact:* Jessica Delarosa, Director of Admissions, 210-8296005, Fax: 210-829-3921, E-mail: admis@uiwtx.edu.
Website: https://www.uiw.edu/smse/index.html

**University of the Pacific,** College of the Pacific, Department of Biological Sciences, Stockton, CA 95211-0197. Offers MS. *Degree requirements:* For master's, thesis. *Entrance requirements:* For master's, GRE General Test, GRE Subject Test. Additional exam requirements/recommendations for international students: required—TOEFL.

**The University of Toledo,** College of Graduate Studies, College of Medicine and Life Sciences, Interdepartmental Programs, Toledo, OH 43606-3390. Offers bioinformatics and proteomics/genomics (MSBS); biomarkers and bioinformatics (Certificate); biomarkers and diagnostics (PSM); human donation sciences (MSBS); medical sciences (MSBS); MD/MSBS. *Degree requirements:* For master's, thesis or alternative. *Entrance requirements:* For master's, GRE, minimum undergraduate GPA of 3.0, three letters of recommendation, statement of purpose, transcripts from all prior institutions attended, resume; for Certificate, minimum undergraduate GPA of 3.0, three letters of recommendation, statement of purpose, transcripts from all prior institutions attended, resume. Additional exam requirements/recommendations for international students: required—TOEFL (minimum score 550 paper-based; 80 iBT). Electronic applications accepted.

**The University of Toledo,** College of Graduate Studies, College of Natural Sciences and Mathematics, Department of Biological Sciences, Toledo, OH 43606-3390. Offers biology (MS, PhD). *Program availability:* Part-time. *Degree requirements:* For master's, thesis or alternative; for doctorate, thesis/dissertation. *Entrance requirements:* For master's and doctorate, GRE General Test, GRE Subject Test, minimum cumulative point-hour ratio of 2.7 for all previous academic work, three letters of recommendation, statement of purpose, transcripts from all prior institutions attended. Additional exam requirements/recommendations for international students: required—TOEFL (minimum score 550 paper-based; 80 iBT). Electronic applications accepted.

**The University of Toledo,** College of Graduate Studies, College of Natural Sciences and Mathematics, Department of Environmental Sciences, Toledo, OH 43606-3390. Offers biology (MS, PhD), including ecology; geology (MS), including earth surface processes. *Program availability:* Part-time. *Degree requirements:* For master's, thesis or alternative. *Entrance requirements:* For master's, GRE General Test, minimum cumulative point-hour ratio of 2.7 for all previous academic work, three letters of recommendation, statement of purpose, transcripts from all prior institutions attended. Additional exam requirements/recommendations for international students: required—TOEFL (minimum score 550 paper-based; 80 iBT). Electronic applications accepted.

**The University of Tulsa,** Graduate School, College of Engineering and Natural Sciences, Department of Biological Science, Tulsa, OK 74104-3189. Offers MS, MTA, PhD, JD/MS. *Program availability:* Part-time. Terminal master's awarded for partial completion of doctoral program. *Degree requirements:* For master's, thesis, oral exams; for doctorate, comprehensive exam, thesis/dissertation. *Entrance requirements:* For master's and doctorate, GRE General Test. Additional exam requirements/recommendations for international students: required—TOEFL (minimum score 550 paper-based; 80 iBT), IELTS (minimum score 6). Electronic applications accepted. *Expenses: Tuition:* Full-time $22,896; part-time $1272 per credit hour. *Required fees:* $6 per credit hour. Tuition and fees vary according to course load and program.

**University of Utah,** Graduate School, College of Science, School of Biological Sciences, Salt Lake City, UT 84112. Offers doctor of philosophy (PhD); masters of science (MS). *Faculty:* 36 full-time (6 women). *Students:* 84 full-time (46 women), 15 part-time (7 women); includes 14 minority (5 Asian, non-Hispanic/Latino; 8 Hispanic/Latino; 1 Two or more races, non-Hispanic/Latino), 22 international. Average age 27. 138 applicants, 16% accepted, 12 enrolled. In 2019, 2 master's, 8 doctorates awarded. *Degree requirements:* For master's, comprehensive exam, thesis, 30 credit hours of coursework; for doctorate, comprehensive exam, thesis/dissertation. *Entrance requirements:* Additional exam requirements/recommendations for international students: required—TOEFL (minimum score 550 paper-based; 80 iBT). *Application deadline:* For fall admission, 12/1 priority date for domestic and international students. Application fee: $55 ($65 for international students). Electronic applications accepted. Application fee is waived when completed online. *Expenses:* Tuition, state resident: full-time $7085; part-time $272.51 per credit hour. Tuition, nonresident: full-time $24,937; part-time $959.12 per credit hour. *Required fees:* $880.52; $880.52 per semester. Tuition and fees vary according to degree level, program and student level. *Financial support:* In 2019–20, 72 students received support, including 12 fellowships with full tuition reimbursements available (averaging $12,750 per year), 36 research assistantships with full tuition reimbursements available (averaging $12,389 per year), 21 teaching assistantships with full tuition reimbursements available (averaging $14,143 per year); scholarships/grants, traineeships, health care benefits, and unspecified assistantships also available. Financial award application deadline: 4/15; financial award applicants required to submit FAFSA. *Unit head:* Dr. M. Denise Dearing, Director, 801-585-0622, Fax: 801-581-4668, E-mail: denise.dearing@utah.edu. *Application contact:* Shannon Nielsen, Administrative Program Coordinator, 801-581-5636, Fax: 801-581-4668, E-mail: shannon.nielsen@bioscience.utah.edu.
Website: http://www.biology.utah.edu

**University of Utah,** School of Medicine and Graduate School, Graduate Programs in Medicine, Salt Lake City, UT 84112-1107. Offers M Phil, M Stat, MPAS, MPH, MS, MSPH, PhD, Certificate. *Program availability:* Part-time. *Degree requirements:* For doctorate, thesis/dissertation. *Entrance requirements:* For doctorate, MCAT. Electronic applications accepted. *Expenses:* Tuition, state resident: full-time $7085; part-time $272.51 per credit hour. Tuition, nonresident: full-time $24,937; part-time $959.12 per credit hour. *Required fees:* $880.52; $880.52 per semester. Tuition and fees vary according to degree level, program and student level.

**University of Vermont,** Graduate College, College of Arts and Sciences, Department of Biology, Burlington, VT 05405. Offers biology (MS, PhD); biology education (MST). *Degree requirements:* For master's, thesis; for doctorate, thesis/dissertation. *Entrance requirements:* For master's and doctorate, GRE General Test. Additional exam requirements/recommendations for international students: required—TOEFL (minimum score 550 paper-based, 90 iBT) or IELTS (6.5). Electronic applications accepted.

**University of Vermont,** Graduate College, Cross-College Interdisciplinary Program, Cellular, Molecular and Biomedical Sciences Program, Burlington, VT 05405. Offers PhD. *Degree requirements:* For doctorate, thesis/dissertation. *Entrance requirements:* For doctorate, GRE General Test. Additional exam requirements/recommendations for international students: required—TOEFL (minimum score 550 paper-based; 100 iBT), IELTS (minimum score 7). Electronic applications accepted.

**University of Vermont,** The Robert Larner, MD College of Medicine and Graduate College, Graduate Programs in Medicine, Program in Medical Science, Burlington, VT 05405. Offers MS. *Entrance requirements:* For master's, MCAT or GRE. Additional exam requirements/recommendations for international students: required—TOEFL (minimum iBT score of 90) or IELTS (6.5). Electronic applications accepted.

**University of Victoria,** Faculty of Graduate Studies, Faculty of Science, Department of Biology, Victoria, BC V8W 2Y2, Canada. Offers M Sc, PhD. *Degree requirements:* For master's, thesis, seminar; for doctorate, thesis/dissertation, seminar, candidacy exam. *Entrance requirements:* For master's and doctorate, GRE General Test, minimum B+ average in previous 2 years of biology course work. Additional exam requirements/recommendations for international students: required—TOEFL (minimum score 575 paper-based), IELTS (minimum score 7). Electronic applications accepted.

**University of Virginia,** College and Graduate School of Arts and Sciences, Department of Biology, Charlottesville, VA 22903. Offers MA, MS, PhD. *Degree requirements:* For master's, thesis; for doctorate, thesis/dissertation. *Entrance requirements:* For master's and doctorate, GRE General Test, GRE Subject Test (recommended), 2 letters of recommendation. Additional exam requirements/recommendations for international students: required—TOEFL (minimum score 600 paper-based; 90 iBT), IELTS (minimum score 7). Electronic applications accepted.

**University of Virginia,** School of Medicine, Department of Molecular Physiology and Biological Physics, Program in Biological and Physical Sciences, Charlottesville, VA 22903. Offers MS. *Entrance requirements:* For master's, GRE General Test. Additional exam requirements/recommendations for international students: required—TOEFL. Electronic applications accepted.

**University of Washington,** Graduate School, College of Arts and Sciences, Department of Biology, Seattle, WA 98195. Offers PhD.

**University of Washington,** Graduate School, School of Medicine, Graduate Programs in Medicine, Seattle, WA 98195. Offers MA, MOT, MPO, MS, DPT, PhD. *Program*

*availability:* Part-time. *Degree requirements:* For doctorate, thesis/dissertation. *Entrance requirements:* For doctorate, GRE. Electronic applications accepted. *Expenses:* Contact institution.

**University of Waterloo,** Graduate Studies and Postdoctoral Affairs, Faculty of Science, Department of Biology, Waterloo, ON N2L 3G1, Canada. Offers M Sc, PhD. *Program availability:* Part-time. *Degree requirements:* For master's, thesis, seminar; for doctorate, comprehensive exam, thesis/dissertation, seminar. *Entrance requirements:* For master's, honor's degree; for doctorate, master's degree. Additional exam requirements/recommendations for international students: required—TOEFL, IELTS, PTE. Electronic applications accepted.

**The University of Western Ontario,** School of Graduate and Postdoctoral Studies, Faculty of Science, Department of Biology, London, ON N6A 3K7, Canada. Offers M Sc, PhD. *Degree requirements:* For master's, thesis; for doctorate, thesis/dissertation. *Entrance requirements:* For doctorate, M Sc or equivalent. Additional exam requirements/recommendations for international students: required—TOEFL.

**University of West Florida,** Hal Marcus College of Science and Engineering, Department of Biology, Pensacola, FL 32514-5750. Offers MS. *Degree requirements:* For master's, thesis. *Entrance requirements:* For master's, GRE (minimum score: verbal 450, quantitative 550), official transcripts; BS in biology or related field; letter of interest; three letters of recommendation from individuals who can evaluate applicant's academic ability. Additional exam requirements/recommendations for international students: required—TOEFL (minimum score 550 paper-based).

**University of Windsor,** Faculty of Graduate Studies, Faculty of Science, Department of Biological Sciences, Windsor, ON N9B 3P4, Canada. Offers M Sc, PhD. *Program availability:* Part-time. *Degree requirements:* For master's, thesis; for doctorate, comprehensive exam, thesis/dissertation. *Entrance requirements:* For master's and doctorate, minimum B average. Additional exam requirements/recommendations for international students: required—TOEFL (minimum score 560 paper-based). Electronic applications accepted.

**University of Wisconsin–La Crosse,** College of Science and Health, Department of Biology, La Crosse, WI 54601. Offers aquatic sciences (MS); biology (MS); cellular and molecular biology (MS); clinical microbiology (MS); microbiology (MS); nurse anesthesia (MS); physiology (MS). *Accreditation:* AANA/CANAEP. *Program availability:* Part-time. *Faculty:* 19 full-time (7 women). *Students:* 12 full-time (6 women), 39 part-time (15 women); includes 2 minority (1 Black or African American, non-Hispanic/Latino; 1 Asian, non-Hispanic/Latino). Average age 28. 37 applicants, 68% accepted, 19 enrolled. In 2019, 19 master's awarded. *Degree requirements:* For master's, comprehensive exam, thesis. *Entrance requirements:* For master's, GRE General Test, minimum GPA of 2.85. Additional exam requirements/recommendations for international students: required—TOEFL (minimum score 550 paper-based; 79 iBT). *Application deadline:* For fall admission, 2/1 priority date for domestic and international students; for spring admission, 1/4 priority date for domestic and international students. Applications are processed on a rolling basis. Electronic applications accepted. *Financial support:* Research assistantships with partial tuition reimbursements, Federal Work-Study, scholarships/grants, health care benefits, and tuition waivers (partial) available. Support available to part-time students. Financial award application deadline: 3/15; financial award applicants required to submit FAFSA. *Unit head:* Dr. Michael Abler, Department Chair, 608-785-6962, E-mail: mabler@uwlax.edu. *Application contact:* Jennifer Weber, Senior Student Services Coordinator Graduate Admissions, 608-785-8939, E-mail: admissions@uwlax.edu.
Website: http://uwlax.edu/biology/

**University of Wisconsin–Madison,** School of Medicine and Public Health, Medical Scientist Training Program, Madison, WI 53705-2221. Offers MD/PhD. *Accreditation:* LCME/AMA.

**University of Wisconsin–Milwaukee,** Graduate School, College of Engineering and Applied Science, Biomedical and Health Informatics Program, Milwaukee, WI 53201-0413. Offers health information systems (PhD); health services management and policy (PhD); knowledge based systems (PhD); medical imaging and instrumentation (PhD); public health informatics (PhD). *Degree requirements:* For doctorate, comprehensive exam, thesis/dissertation. *Entrance requirements:* For doctorate, GRE, GMAT or MCAT. Additional exam requirements/recommendations for international students: required—TOEFL (minimum score 600 paper-based; 79 iBT), IELTS (minimum score 6.5). Electronic applications accepted.

**University of Wisconsin–Milwaukee,** Graduate School, College of Health Sciences, Department of Biomedical Sciences, Milwaukee, WI 53201-0413. Offers MS. *Accreditation:* APTA. *Entrance requirements:* Additional exam requirements/recommendations for international students: required—TOEFL (minimum score 550 paper-based; 79 iBT), IELTS (minimum score 6.5).

**University of Wisconsin–Milwaukee,** Graduate School, College of Health Sciences, Program in Health Sciences, Milwaukee, WI 53201-0413. Offers health sciences (PhD), including diagnostic and biomedical sciences, disability and rehabilitation, health administration and policy, human movement sciences, population health. *Degree requirements:* For doctorate, comprehensive exam, thesis/dissertation. *Entrance requirements:* For doctorate, GRE. Additional exam requirements/recommendations for international students: required—TOEFL (minimum score 600 paper-based), IELTS (minimum score 6.5).

**University of Wisconsin–Milwaukee,** Graduate School, College of Letters and Science, Department of Biological Sciences, Milwaukee, WI 53201-0413. Offers cellular and molecular biology (MS, PhD); microbiology (MS, PhD). *Degree requirements:* For master's, thesis; for doctorate, thesis/dissertation, 1 foreign language or data analysis proficiency. *Entrance requirements:* For master's and doctorate, GRE General Test. Additional exam requirements/recommendations for international students: required—TOEFL (minimum score 550 paper-based; 79 iBT), IELTS (minimum score 6.5). Electronic applications accepted.

**University of Wisconsin–Oshkosh,** Graduate Studies, College of Letters and Science, Department of Biology and Microbiology, Oshkosh, WI 54901. Offers biology (MS), including botany, microbiology, zoology. *Degree requirements:* For master's, comprehensive exam, thesis. *Entrance requirements:* For master's, GRE General Test, minimum GPA of 3.0, BS in biology. Additional exam requirements/recommendations for international students: required—TOEFL (minimum score 550 paper-based; 79 iBT). Electronic applications accepted.

**Université Laval,** Faculty of Medicine, Graduate Programs in Medicine, Québec, QC G1K 7P4, Canada. Offers M Sc, PhD, Diploma. *Degree requirements:* For doctorate, comprehensive exam, thesis/dissertation. *Entrance requirements:* For doctorate, knowledge of French, comprehension of written English; for Diploma, knowledge of French. Electronic applications accepted.

**Université Laval,** Faculty of Sciences and Engineering, Department of Biology, Programs in Biology, Québec, QC G1K 7P4, Canada. Offers M Sc, PhD. Terminal master's awarded for partial completion of doctoral program. *Degree requirements:* For master's, thesis; for doctorate, comprehensive exam, thesis/dissertation. *Entrance*

*requirements:* For master's and doctorate, knowledge of French and English. Electronic applications accepted.

**Utah State University,** School of Graduate Studies, College of Science, Department of Biology, Logan, UT 84322. Offers biology (MS, PhD); ecology (MS, PhD). *Program availability:* Part-time. *Degree requirements:* For master's, thesis; for doctorate, thesis/dissertation. *Entrance requirements:* For master's and doctorate, GRE General Test, minimum GPA of 3.0. Additional exam requirements/recommendations for international students: required—TOEFL (minimum score 575 paper-based).

**Vanderbilt University,** Department of Biological Sciences, Nashville, TN 37240-1001. Offers MS, PhD. *Faculty:* 21 full-time (5 women). *Students:* 56 full-time (28 women); includes 12 minority (3 Black or African American, non-Hispanic/Latino; 2 Asian, non-Hispanic/Latino; 4 Hispanic/Latino; 3 Two or more races, non-Hispanic/Latino), 13 international. Average age 27. 63 applicants, 27% accepted, 6 enrolled. In 2019, 1 master's, 8 doctorates awarded. Terminal master's awarded for partial completion of doctoral program. *Degree requirements:* For master's, thesis; for doctorate, thesis/dissertation, final and qualifying exams. *Entrance requirements:* For master's and doctorate, GRE General Test. Additional exam requirements/recommendations for international students: required—TOEFL (minimum score 570 paper-based; 88 iBT). *Application deadline:* For fall admission, 1/15 for domestic and international students. Electronic applications accepted. *Expenses: Tuition:* Full-time $51,018; part-time $2087 per hour. *Required fees:* $542. Tuition and fees vary according to program. *Financial support:* Fellowships with tuition reimbursements, research assistantships with full tuition reimbursements, teaching assistantships with full tuition reimbursements, Federal Work-Study, institutionally sponsored loans, scholarships/grants, traineeships, and health care benefits available. Financial award application deadline: 1/15; financial award applicants required to submit CSS PROFILE or FAFSA. *Unit head:* Dr. Douglas McMahon, Chair, 615-322-2008, Fax: 615-343-6707, E-mail: douglas.g.mcmahon@vanderbilt.edu. *Application contact:* Julian Hillyer, Director of Graduate Studies, 615-343-2065, E-mail: julian.hillyer@vanderbilt.edu.
Website: http://sitemason.vanderbilt.edu/biosci/grad/

**Villanova University,** Graduate School of Liberal Arts and Sciences, Department of Biology, Villanova, PA 19085-1699. Offers MA, MS. *Program availability:* Part-time, evening/weekend. *Entrance requirements:* For master's, GRE General Test, minimum GPA of 3.0, 3 recommendation letters. Electronic applications accepted.

**Virginia Commonwealth University,** Graduate School, College of Humanities and Sciences, Department of Biology, Richmond, VA 23284-9005. Offers MS. *Program availability:* Part-time. *Degree requirements:* For master's, thesis. *Entrance requirements:* For master's, GRE General Test, BS in biology or related field. Additional exam requirements/recommendations for international students: required—TOEFL (minimum score 600 paper-based; 100 iBT) or IELTS (minimum score 6.5).

**Virginia Commonwealth University,** Graduate School, School of Life Sciences, Richmond, VA 23284-9005. Offers M Env Sc, MS, PhD. *Entrance requirements:* For master's and doctorate, GRE. Additional exam requirements/recommendations for international students: required—TOEFL (minimum score 600 paper-based; 100 iBT). Electronic applications accepted.

**Virginia Commonwealth University,** Medical College of Virginia-Professional Programs, School of Medicine, Graduate Programs in Medicine, Richmond, VA 23284-9005. Offers MPH, MS, PhD, Certificate, MD/MPH, MD/PhD. *Program availability:* Part-time. Terminal master's awarded for partial completion of doctoral program. *Degree requirements:* For doctorate, thesis/dissertation, comprehensive oral and written exams. *Entrance requirements:* For doctorate, GRE General Test, MCAT.

**Virginia Commonwealth University,** Program in Pre-Medical Basic Health Sciences, Richmond, VA 23284-9005. Offers Postbaccalaureate Certificate. *Entrance requirements:* For degree, GRE, MCAT or DAT, course work in organic chemistry, minimum undergraduate GPA of 2.8. Additional exam requirements/recommendations for international students: required—TOEFL (minimum score 600 paper-based). Electronic applications accepted.

**Virginia Polytechnic Institute and State University,** Graduate School, College of Science, Blacksburg, VA 24061. Offers biological sciences (MS, PhD); biomedical technology development and management (MS); chemistry (MS, PhD); data analysis and applied statistics (MA); economics (PhD); geosciences (MS, PhD); mathematics (MS, PhD); physics (MS, PhD); psychology (MS, PhD); statistics (MS, PhD). *Faculty:* 375 full-time (118 women), 2 part-time/adjunct (1 woman). *Students:* 544 full-time (221 women), 37 part-time (15 women); includes 75 minority (14 Black or African American, non-Hispanic/Latino; 1 American Indian or Alaska Native, non-Hispanic/Latino; 20 Asian, non-Hispanic/Latino; 31 Hispanic/Latino; 9 Two or more races, non-Hispanic/Latino), 216 international. Average age 27. 962 applicants, 33% accepted, 138 enrolled. In 2019, 75 master's, 69 doctorates awarded. *Degree requirements:* For master's, comprehensive exam (for some programs), thesis (for some programs); for doctorate, comprehensive exam (for some programs), thesis/dissertation (for some programs). *Entrance requirements:* For master's and doctorate, GRE/GMAT. Additional exam requirements/recommendations for international students: required—TOEFL (minimum score 90 iBT). *Application deadline:* For fall admission, 8/1 for domestic students, 4/1 for international students; for spring admission, 1/1 for domestic students, 9/1 for international students. Applications are processed on a rolling basis. Application fee: $75. Electronic applications accepted. *Expenses:* Tuition, state resident: full-time $13,700; part-time $761.25 per credit hour. Tuition, nonresident: full-time $27,614; part-time $1534 per credit hour. *Required fees:* $886.50 per term. Tuition and fees vary according to campus/location and program. *Financial support:* In 2019–20, 5 fellowships with full tuition reimbursements (averaging $25,988 per year), 281 research assistantships with full tuition reimbursements (averaging $15,597 per year), 370 teaching assistantships with full tuition reimbursements (averaging $18,225 per year) were awarded; unspecified assistantships also available. Financial award application deadline: 3/1; financial award applicants required to submit FAFSA. *Unit head:* Dr. Sally C. Morton, Dean, 540-231-5422, Fax: 540-231-3380, E-mail: scmorton@vt.edu. *Application contact:* Allison Craft, Executive Assistant, 540-231-6394, Fax: 540-231-3380, E-mail: crafta@vt.edu.
Website: http://www.science.vt.edu/

**Virginia State University,** College of Graduate Studies, College of Natural and Health Sciences, Department of Biology, Petersburg, VA 23806-0001. Offers MS. *Degree requirements:* For master's, one foreign language, thesis. *Entrance requirements:* For master's, GRE General Test.

**Wake Forest University,** Graduate School of Arts and Sciences, Department of Biology, Winston-Salem, NC 27109. Offers MS, PhD. *Program availability:* Part-time. *Degree requirements:* For master's, one foreign language, thesis; for doctorate, 2 foreign languages, comprehensive exam, thesis/dissertation. *Entrance requirements:* For master's and doctorate, GRE General Test. Additional exam requirements/recommendations for international students: required—TOEFL (minimum score 79 iBT). Electronic applications accepted.

**Wake Forest University,** School of Medicine and Graduate School of Arts and Sciences, Graduate Programs in Medicine, Winston-Salem, NC 27109. Offers MS, PhD,

MD/PhD. *Degree requirements:* For master's, thesis; for doctorate, thesis/dissertation. *Entrance requirements:* For master's and doctorate, GRE General Test. Additional exam requirements/recommendations for international students: required—TOEFL. Electronic applications accepted. *Expenses:* Contact institution.

**Walla Walla University,** Graduate Studies, Department of Biological Sciences, College Place, WA 99324. Offers biology (MS). *Degree requirements:* For master's, thesis. *Entrance requirements:* For master's, GRE General Test, GRE Subject Test, minimum GPA of 2.75, three letters of recommendation, official transcripts. Additional exam requirements/recommendations for international students: required—TOEFL (minimum score 550 paper-based; 79 iBT). Electronic applications accepted.

**Washington State University,** College of Arts and Sciences, School of Biological Sciences, Pullman, WA 99164-4236. Offers MS, PhD. *Degree requirements:* For master's, comprehensive exam (for some programs), thesis, oral exam; for doctorate, comprehensive exam, thesis/dissertation, oral exam. *Entrance requirements:* For master's and doctorate, GRE General Test, GRE Subject Test (recommended), three letters of recommendation, official transcripts from each university-level school attended, minimum GPA of 3.0. Additional exam requirements/recommendations for international students: required—TOEFL, IELTS.

**Washington University in St. Louis,** The Graduate School, Division of Biology and Biomedical Sciences, St. Louis, MO 63130-4899. Offers biochemistry (PhD); computational and molecular biophysics (PhD); computational and systems biology (PhD); developmental, regenerative, and stem cell biology (PhD); evolution, ecology and population biology (PhD), including ecology, environmental biology, evolutionary biology, genetics; human and statistical genetics (PhD); immunology (PhD); molecular cell biology (PhD); molecular genetics and genomics (PhD); molecular microbiology and microbial pathogenesis (PhD); neurosciences (PhD); plant and microbial biosciences (PhD); MD/PhD. *Degree requirements:* For doctorate, thesis/dissertation. *Entrance requirements:* For doctorate, GRE General Test, GRE Subject Test. Additional exam requirements/recommendations for international students: required—TOEFL. Electronic applications accepted.

**Wayne State University,** College of Liberal Arts and Sciences, Department of Biological Sciences, Detroit, MI 48202. Offers biological sciences (MA, MS, PhD); molecular biotechnology (MS). *Entrance requirements:* For master's, GRE (for MS applicants), minimum GPA of 3.0; adequate preparation in biological sciences and supporting courses in chemistry, physics and mathematics; curriculum vitae; personal statement; three letters of recommendation (two for MA); for doctorate, GRE, curriculum vitae, statement of goals and career objectives, three letters of reference, bachelor's or master's degree in biological or other science. Additional exam requirements/recommendations for international students: required—TOEFL (minimum score 550 paper-based; 79 iBT), TWE (minimum score 5.5), Michigan English Language Assessment Battery (minimum score 85); recommended—IELTS (minimum score 6.5). Electronic applications accepted. *Expenses: Tuition:* Full-time $34,567.

**Weill Cornell Medicine,** Weill Cornell Graduate School of Medical Sciences, New York, NY 10065. Offers MS, PhD. Terminal master's awarded for partial completion of doctoral program. *Degree requirements:* For master's, comprehensive exam, thesis (for some programs); for doctorate, thesis/dissertation, final exam. *Entrance requirements:* For doctorate, GRE General Test. Additional exam requirements/recommendations for international students: required—TOEFL. Electronic applications accepted. *Expenses:* Contact institution.

**Weill Cornell Medicine,** Weill Cornell/Rockefeller/Sloan-Kettering Tri-Institutional MD-PhD Program, New York, NY 10065. Offers MD/PhD. Electronic applications accepted. *Expenses:* Contact institution.

**Wesleyan University,** Graduate Studies, Department of Biology, Middletown, CT 06459. Offers cell and developmental biology (PhD); evolution and ecology (PhD); genetics and genomics (PhD), including bioinformatics; neurobiology and behavior (PhD). Terminal master's awarded for partial completion of doctoral program. *Degree requirements:* For doctorate, comprehensive exam, thesis/dissertation, public seminar. *Entrance requirements:* For doctorate, GRE, official transcripts, three recommendation letters, essay. Additional exam requirements/recommendations for international students: required—TOEFL. Electronic applications accepted.

**Western Carolina University,** Graduate School, College of Arts and Sciences, Department of Biology, Cullowhee, NC 28723. Offers MS. *Program availability:* Part-time. *Degree requirements:* For master's, thesis. *Entrance requirements:* For master's, GRE General Test, appropriate undergraduate degree, 3 letters of recommendation, statement of research interest, including the names of two faculty whose research is of interest. Additional exam requirements/recommendations for international students: required—TOEFL (minimum score 550 paper-based, 79 iBT) or IELTS (6.5). Electronic applications accepted. *Expenses:* Contact institution.

**Western Illinois University,** School of Graduate Studies, College of Arts and Sciences, Department of Biological Sciences, Macomb, IL 61455-1390. Offers biology (MS); environmental GIS (Certificate); zoo and aquarium studies (Certificate). *Program availability:* Part-time. *Entrance requirements:* Additional exam requirements/recommendations for international students: required—TOEFL (minimum score 550 paper-based; 80 iBT); recommended—IELTS. Electronic applications accepted.

**Western Kentucky University,** Graduate School, Ogden College of Science and Engineering, Department of Biology, Bowling Green, KY 42101. Offers MS. *Program availability:* Online learning. *Degree requirements:* For master's, comprehensive exam, thesis optional, research tool. *Entrance requirements:* For master's, GRE General Test, minimum GPA of 2.75. Additional exam requirements/recommendations for international students: required—TOEFL (minimum score 555 paper-based; 79 iBT).

**Western Michigan University,** Graduate College, College of Arts and Sciences, Department of Biological Sciences, Kalamazoo, MI 49008. Offers MS, PhD. *Degree requirements:* For master's, thesis; for doctorate, thesis/dissertation.

**Western Michigan University,** Graduate College, College of Arts and Sciences, Department of Interdisciplinary Arts and Sciences, Kalamazoo, MI 49008. Offers science education (MA, PhD), including biological sciences (PhD), chemistry (PhD), geosciences (PhD), physical geography (PhD), physics (PhD), science education (PhD). *Degree requirements:* For doctorate, thesis/dissertation.

**Western University of Health Sciences,** Graduate College of Biomedical Sciences, Pomona, CA 91766. Offers biomedical sciences (MS); medical sciences (MS). *Faculty:* 8 full-time (1 woman), 7 part-time/adjunct (2 women). *Students:* 74 full-time (45 women), 12 part-time (6 women); includes 69 minority (6 Black or African American, non-Hispanic/Latino; 32 Asian, non-Hispanic/Latino; 21 Hispanic/Latino; 1 Native Hawaiian or other Pacific Islander, non-Hispanic/Latino; 9 Two or more races, non-Hispanic/Latino), 1 international. Average age 26. 346 applicants, 23% accepted, 66 enrolled. In 2019, 38 master's awarded. *Degree requirements:* For master's, comprehensive exam, thesis (for some programs). *Entrance requirements:* For master's, GRE, MCAT, OAT, or DAT, minimum overall GPA of 3.0; letters of recommendation; personal statement; resume; BS in pharmacy, chemistry, biology or related scientific area, transcript. Additional exam requirements/recommendations for international students: required—TOEFL (minimum score 89 iBT). *Application deadline:* Applications are processed on a rolling basis. Application fee: $50. Electronic applications accepted. *Expenses:* Contact institution. *Financial support:* In 2019–20, 31 students received support. Scholarships/grants available. Financial award application deadline: 3/2; financial award applicants required to submit FAFSA. *Unit head:* Dr. Guru Betageri, Acting Dean of Graduate College of Biomedical Sciences, 909-469-5682, E-mail: gbetageri@westernu.edu. *Application contact:* Daniell Mendoza, Office of Admissions, 909-469-5541, Fax: 909-469-5335, E-mail: admissions@westernu.edu.
Website: http://www.westernu.edu/biomedical-sciences/

**Western University of Health Sciences,** Graduate College of Biomedical Sciences, Master of Science in Biomedical Sciences Program, Pomona, CA 91766-1854. Offers biomedical sciences (MS). *Faculty:* 6 full-time (0 women), 3 part-time/adjunct (1 woman). *Students:* 41 full-time (26 women), 12 part-time (6 women); includes 40 minority (1 Black or African American, non-Hispanic/Latino; 22 Asian, non-Hispanic/Latino; 7 Hispanic/Latino; 1 Native Hawaiian or other Pacific Islander, non-Hispanic/Latino; 9 Two or more races, non-Hispanic/Latino), 1 international. Average age 26. 143 applicants, 31% accepted, 33 enrolled. In 2019, 14 master's awarded. *Degree requirements:* For master's, comprehensive exam (for some programs), thesis. *Entrance requirements:* For master's, GRE, MCAT, or DAT, minimum overall GPA of 2.5; 3 letters of recommendation are recommended; personal statement; resume; BS in pharmacy, chemistry, biology or related scientific area, transcripts. Additional exam requirements/recommendations for international students: required—TOEFL (minimum score 92 iBT). *Application deadline:* For fall admission, 6/15 for domestic and international students. Application fee: $50. Electronic applications accepted. *Expenses:* Tuition is $16,600 and student body fee is $40. *Financial support:* In 2019–20, 1 student received support. Scholarships/grants available. Financial award application deadline: 3/2; financial award applicants required to submit FAFSA. *Unit head:* Dr. Ed Wagner, Director, 909-469-5239, E-mail: ewagner@westernu.edu. *Application contact:* Alberto Espejo, Admission Counselor, 909-469-5540, Fax: 909-469-5570, E-mail: aespejo@westernu.edu.
Website: https://www.westernu.edu/biomedical-sciences/biomedical-sciences-academics/biomedical-sciences-msbs/

**Western University of Health Sciences,** Graduate College of Biomedical Sciences, Master of Science in Medical Sciences Program, Pomona, CA 91766-1854. Offers medical sciences (MS). *Faculty:* 2 full-time (1 woman), 4 part-time/adjunct (1 woman). *Students:* 33 full-time (19 women); includes 29 minority (5 Black or African American, non-Hispanic/Latino; 10 Asian, non-Hispanic/Latino; 14 Hispanic/Latino). Average age 27. 203 applicants, 17% accepted, 33 enrolled. In 2019, 24 master's awarded. *Degree requirements:* For master's, comprehensive exam, thesis (for some programs). *Entrance requirements:* For master's, GRE, MCAT, OAT, or DAT, minimum overall GPA of 2.5; letters of recommendation; personal statement; resume; transcripts; bachelor's degree. Additional exam requirements/recommendations for international students: required—TOEFL (minimum score 89 iBT). *Application deadline:* For fall admission, 4/15 for domestic and international students. Applications are processed on a rolling basis. Application fee: $50. Electronic applications accepted. *Expenses:* Contact institution. *Financial support:* In 2019–20, 24 students received support. Scholarships/grants available. Financial award application deadline: 3/2; financial award applicants required to submit FAFSA. *Unit head:* Marcos Villa, Director, Master of Medical Sciences Program, 909-469-8562, Fax: 909-469-5577, E-mail: mvilla@westernu.edu. *Application contact:* Julie Smith, Admission Counselor, 909-469-5442, Fax: 909-469-5570, E-mail: jasmith@westernu.edu.
Website: http://prospective.westernu.edu/medical-sciences/welcome-4/

**Western Washington University,** Graduate School, College of Sciences and Technology, Department of Biology, Bellingham, WA 98225-5996. Offers MS. *Program availability:* Part-time. *Degree requirements:* For master's, thesis. *Entrance requirements:* For master's, GRE General Test, GRE Subject Test (biology), minimum GPA of 3.0 in last 60 semester hours or last 90 quarter hours. Additional exam requirements/recommendations for international students: required—TOEFL (minimum score 567 paper-based). Electronic applications accepted.

**West Liberty University,** College of Sciences, West Liberty, WV 26074. Offers biology (MA, MS); biomedical science (MA); physician assistant studies (MS); zoo science (MA, MS).

**West Texas A&M University,** College of Agriculture and Natural Sciences, Department of Life, Earth and Environmental Sciences, Program in Biology, Canyon, TX 79015. Offers MS. *Program availability:* Part-time. *Degree requirements:* For master's, comprehensive exam, thesis optional. *Entrance requirements:* For master's, GRE General Test. Additional exam requirements/recommendations for international students: required—TOEFL (minimum score 550 paper-based). Electronic applications accepted.

**West Virginia University,** Eberly College of Arts and Sciences, Morgantown, WV 26506. Offers biology (MS, PhD); chemistry (MS, PhD); communication studies (MA, PhD); computational statistics (PhD); creative writing (MFA); English (MA, PhD); forensic and investigative science (MS); forensic science (PhD); geography (MA); geology (MA, PhD); history (MA, PhD); legal studies (MLS); mathematics (MS); physics (MS, PhD); political science (MA, PhD); professional writing and editing (MA); psychology (MA); public administration (MPA); social work (MSW); sociology (MA, PhD); statistics (MS). *Program availability:* Part-time, evening/weekend, online learning. Terminal master's awarded for partial completion of doctoral program. *Degree requirements:* For master's, thesis (for some programs); for doctorate, comprehensive exam, thesis/dissertation. *Entrance requirements:* For master's and doctorate, GRE. Additional exam requirements/recommendations for international students: required—TOEFL (minimum score 600 paper-based); recommended—TWE. Electronic applications accepted.

**West Virginia University,** School of Medicine, Morgantown, WV 26506. Offers biochemistry and molecular biology (PhD); biomedical science (MS); cancer cell biology (PhD); cellular and integrative physiology (PhD); exercise physiology (MS, PhD); health sciences (MS); immunology (PhD); medicine (MD); occupational therapy (MOT); pathologists assistant' (MHS); physical therapy (DPT). *Accreditation:* AOTA; LCME/AMA. *Program availability:* Part-time, evening/weekend. *Entrance requirements:* Additional exam requirements/recommendations for international students: required—TOEFL. Electronic applications accepted. *Expenses:* Contact institution.

**Wichita State University,** Graduate School, Fairmount College of Liberal Arts and Sciences, Department of Biological Sciences, Wichita, KS 67260. Offers MS. *Program availability:* Part-time.

**Wilfrid Laurier University,** Faculty of Graduate and Postdoctoral Studies, Faculty of Science, Department of Biology, Waterloo, ON N2L 3C5, Canada. Offers integrative biology (M Sc). *Degree requirements:* For master's, thesis. *Entrance requirements:* For master's, honours BA in last two years of undergraduate studies with a minimum B average. Additional exam requirements/recommendations for international students: required—TOEFL (minimum score 89 iBT). Electronic applications accepted.

**Winthrop University,** College of Arts and Sciences, Department of Biology, Rock Hill, SC 29733. Offers MS. *Program availability:* Part-time. *Degree requirements:* For master's, thesis optional. *Entrance requirements:* For master's, GRE General Test. Additional exam requirements/recommendations for international students: required—

TOEFL (minimum score 550 paper-based; 79 iBT). Electronic applications accepted. *Expenses: Tuition, area resident:* Full-time $7659; part-time $641 per credit hour. Tuition, state resident: full-time $7659; part-time $641 per credit hour. Tuition, nonresident: full-time $14,753; part-time $1234 per credit hour.

**Worcester Polytechnic Institute,** Graduate Admissions, Department of Biology and Biotechnology, Worcester, MA 01609-2280. Offers MS, PhD. *Program availability:* Part-time, blended/hybrid learning. Terminal master's awarded for partial completion of doctoral program. *Degree requirements:* For master's, thesis (for some programs); for doctorate, comprehensive exam, thesis/dissertation, qualifying exam. *Entrance requirements:* For master's and doctorate, GRE General Test, 3 letters of recommendation, statement of purpose. Additional exam requirements/ recommendations for international students: required—TOEFL (minimum score 563 paper-based; 84 iBT), IELTS (minimum score 7). Electronic applications accepted.

**Wright State University,** Graduate School, College of Science and Mathematics, Department of Biological Sciences, Dayton, OH 45435. Offers biological sciences (MS). *Degree requirements:* For master's, thesis optional. *Entrance requirements:* Additional exam requirements/recommendations for international students: required—TOEFL.

**Wright State University,** Graduate School, College of Science and Mathematics and Boonshoft School of Medicine, Program in Biomedical Sciences, Dayton, OH 45435. Offers PhD. *Degree requirements:* For doctorate, thesis/dissertation. *Entrance requirements:* For doctorate, GRE General Test. Additional exam requirements/ recommendations for international students: required—TOEFL.

**Yale University,** Yale School of Medicine and Graduate School of Arts and Sciences, Combined Program in Biological and Biomedical Sciences (BBS), New Haven, CT 06520. Offers PhD, MD/PhD. *Degree requirements:* For doctorate, thesis/dissertation. *Entrance requirements:* For doctorate, GRE General Test. Additional exam requirements/recommendations for international students: required—TOEFL. Electronic applications accepted. *Expenses:* Contact institution.

**York University,** Faculty of Graduate Studies, Faculty of Science, Program in Biology, Toronto, ON M3J 1P3, Canada. Offers M Sc, PhD. *Program availability:* Part-time, evening/weekend. *Degree requirements:* For master's, thesis or alternative; for doctorate, comprehensive exam, thesis/dissertation, preliminary exam. Electronic applications accepted.

**Youngstown State University,** College of Graduate Studies, College of Science, Technology, Engineering and Mathematics, Department of Biological Sciences, Youngstown, OH 44555-0001. Offers environmental biology (MS); molecular biology, microbiology, and genetics (MS); physiology and anatomy (MS). *Program availability:* Part-time. *Degree requirements:* For master's, comprehensive exam, thesis, oral review. *Entrance requirements:* For master's, GRE General Test, minimum GPA of 2.7. Additional exam requirements/recommendations for international students: required— TOEFL.

# THE ROCKEFELLER UNIVERSITY
*Graduate Programs*

## Programs of Study

Graduate education leading to the Ph.D. is offered to outstanding students regarded as potential leaders in their scientific fields. The University's research covers a wide range of biomedical and related sciences, including biochemistry, biophysics, chemical biology, and structural biology; cancer biology; cell biology; genetics and genomics; immunology, virology and microbiology; mechanisms of human disease; neurosciences and behavior; organismal biology and evolution; physical, mathematical and computational biology; stem cells, development, regeneration and aging, as summarized by the faculty list in this description. Students work closely with a faculty of active scientists and are encouraged to learn through a combination of course work, tutorial guidance, and apprenticeship in research laboratories. Graduate Fellows spend the first two years engaged in a flexible combination of courses geared toward academic qualification while conducting research in laboratories pertaining to their area of scientific interest. They choose a laboratory for thesis research by the end of the first year and devote their remaining time to pursuit of significant experimental or theoretical research, culminating in a dissertation and thesis defense. Students can spend full time in research; there are no teaching or other service obligations.

The faculties of the Rockefeller University, Weill Cornell Medical College, and the Sloan Kettering Institute collaborate in offering a combined M.D./Ph.D. program in the biomedical sciences to about 150 students. This program, conducted on the adjacent campuses of these three institutions in New York City, normally requires six or seven years of study and leads to an M.D. degree conferred by Weill Cornell Medical College and a Ph.D. degree conferred by either the Rockefeller University, the Weill Cornell Graduate School, or the Gerstner Sloan Kettering Graduate School, depending upon the organizational affiliation of the student's adviser.

## Research Facilities

The Rockefeller University supports its 78 laboratories with strong, centralized scientific facilities, providing convenient access to key technologies and services. These include centralized resource centers devoted to bioimaging, cryo-electron microscopy, high-performance computing, genomics, precision fabrication, high-throughput screening, flow cytometry, and more. Rockefeller scientists are also supported by dedicated administration, which includes specialists in information technology, laboratory safety, technology transfer, grants management, and public affairs. The university's physical infrastructure, set on a 16-acre Manhattan campus, includes 565,000 square feet of lab space, along with faculty and administrative offices, event facilities and housing.

## Financial Aid

Each student accepted into the Ph.D. program receives a stipend ($42,950 in 2020-21) that is adequate to meet all living expenses. Students also receive an annual budget of $1,500 that can be used for travel, books and journals, computer purchases, and lab supplies.

## Cost of Study

The University provides full remission of all tuition and fees for all accepted students.

## Living and Housing Costs

On-campus housing is available for all students at subsidized rates. The stipend is designed to cover the cost of food, housing, and other basic living expenses. Students may elect to live off campus, but rents in the vicinity are very high.

## Student Group

There are 230 graduate students, of whom 183 are enrolled in the Ph.D. program and 47 in the Ph.D. phase of the combined M.D./Ph.D. program. It is the policy of the Rockefeller University to support equality of educational opportunity. No individual is denied admission to the University or otherwise discriminated against with respect to any program of the University because of creed, color, national or ethnic origin, race, sex, or disability.

## Student Outcomes

Graduates of the Rockefeller University have excelled in their professions. Two graduates have been awarded the Nobel Prize, and 31 graduates are members of the National Academy of Sciences. Most Ph.D. graduates move to postdoctoral positions at academic and research centers and subsequently have careers in academics, biotechnology, and the pharmaceutical industry. A few graduates have pursued careers in medicine, law, and business. Almost all M.D. and Ph.D. graduates first complete residencies in medical specialties, and most become medical scientists at major academic and medical research centers.

## Location

The University is situated between 63rd and 68th streets in Manhattan, overlooking the East River. Despite its central metropolitan location, the 16-acre campus offers a peaceful respite from New York's busy streets, with landscaped gardens and ample outdoor seating. In addition to administrative and residential buildings, there are 565,000 square feet of laboratory space and a forty-bed research hospital that serves as a clinical research center. Rockefeller students can take advantage of the resources of New York City's many other vibrant institutions, including

nearby New York Presbyterian Hospital, Weill Cornell Medicine, and the Sloan-Kettering Institute for Cancer Research.

## The University

The Rockefeller University is dedicated to benefiting humankind through scientific research and its application. Founded in 1901 by John D. Rockefeller as the Rockefeller Institute for Medical Research, it rapidly became a source of major scientific innovation in treating and preventing human disease. Since 1954, the institute has extended its function by offering graduate work at the doctoral level to a select group of qualified students.

Laboratories, rather than departments, are the fundamental units of the University. The absence of departmental barriers between laboratories encourages interdisciplinary, problem-oriented approaches to research and facilitates intellectual interaction and collaboration. The collegial atmosphere fosters independence and initiative in students. In addition to the 230 doctoral students, there are 261 postdoctoral associates and fellows and a faculty of 78 full, associate, and assistant professors on campus who head laboratories.

## Applying

Applications for the M.D./Ph.D. program must be completed by October 23; those for the Ph.D. program must be completed by December 1. Applicants are required to submit a research statement that describes a meaningful research experience. The student should identify the 'big picture question' of the experiment and explain how the experiments were designed to answer it. The student should also include a brief discussion of what would have been done next if he or she were to continue working on the experiment. Official transcripts must be uploaded to the application. At least three letters of recommendation should be submitted GRE General and Subject Test scores are no longer required. MCAT scores are required for the M.D./Ph.D. program. Further information about each program and details on application procedures may be obtained from the programs' respective websites. This information is also available on the University website, from which application forms and instructions can be downloaded (https://www.rockefeller.edu/education-and-training/graduate-program-in-bioscience/admissions/).

## Correspondence and Information

Kristen E. Cullen, M.A.
Graduate Admissions Administrator and Registrar
The David Rockefeller Graduate Program
The Rockefeller University
1230 York Avenue, Box 177
New York, New York 10065
Phone: 212-327-8086
E-mail: phd@rockefeller.edu
Website:  http://graduate.rockefeller.edu
          https://www.facebook.com/rockefelleruniversity
          https://twitter.com/rockefelleruniv

## LABORATORY HEADS AND THEIR RESEARCH

C. David Allis, Ph.D. (Chromatin Biology and Epigenetics). Studies the role of DNA packaging proteins in gene expression and DNA replication and repair.

Gregory Alushin, Ph.D. (Biophysics). Using cryo-electron microscopy to determine how molecules change their structure in response to pushing or pulling forces.

Cori Bargmann, Ph.D. (Neural Circuits and Behavior). Studies the relationship between genes, neural circuits and behavior in *C. elegans*.

Paul Bieniasz, Ph.D. (Retrovirology) Studies the biology and evolution of retroviruses, including HIV, and genetics of host-virus interactions.

Kivanc Birsoy, Ph.D. (Cancer Cell Metabolism). Investigating cellular metabolism with an emphasis on cancer and metabolic disorders.

Sean Brady, Ph.D. (Genetically Encoded Small Molecules). Discovers and characterizes new small molecules from microbial sources.

Jan L. Breslow, M.D. (Biochemical Genetics and Metabolism). Investigates the genetic basis of atherosclerotic disease.

Ali Brivanlou, Ph.D. (Stem Cell Biology and Molecular Embryology).Researches the molecular events and cellular interactions that establish cell fate in vertebrate embryogenesis.

Junyue Cao, Ph.D. (Single Cell Genomics and Population Dynamics). Develops single cell genomic techniques to study the mechanisms of healthy tissue development and disease.

Jean-Laurent Casanova, M.D., Ph.D. (Human Genetics of Infectious Diseases). Researches the genetic basis of pediatric infectious diseases.

Brian T. Chait, D.Phil. (Mass Spectrometry and Gaseous Ion Chemistry). Uses mass spectrometry as a tool for studying biomolecules and protein interactions.

Jue Chen, Ph.D. (Membrane Biology and Biophysics). Combines structural and function techniques to study ABC membrane transporter proteins in health and disease.

Nam-Hai Chua, Ph.D. (Plant Molecular Biology). Studies molecular signaling pathways involved in plants' response to stress, light and infection.

Joel Cohen, Ph.D., Dr.P.H. (Populations). Studies interactions among groups of living beings in order to develop concepts helpful for understanding populations.

## The Rockefeller University

Paul Cohen, M.D., Ph.D. (Molecular Metabolism). Investigates the molecular basis for metabolic disease related to obesity.

Barry Coller, M.D. (Blood and Vascular Biology). Investigates the role of blood platelets and the mechanisms of blood cell adhesion in vascular disease.

Frederick P. Cross, Ph.D. (Cell Cycle Genetics). Investigates the molecular basis of cell cycle control.

Robert B. Darnell, M.D., Ph.D. (Molecular Neuro-Oncology). Works to understand human autoimmune responses to cancer and neurologic disease.

Seth Darst, Ph.D. (Molecular Biophysics). Investigates the structure, function and regulation of the bacterial transcription machinery.

Titia de Lange, Ph.D. (Cell Biology and Genetics). Studies how telomeres protect chromosome ends from the DNA damage response.

Vincent A. Fischetti, Ph.D. (Bacterial Pathogenesis and Immunology). Investigates bacterial infectious disease and the use of phage enzymes to block infection.

Winrich Freiwald, Ph.D. (Neural Systems). Researches the neural processes of object recognition and attention.

Jeffrey M. Friedman, M.D., Ph.D. (Molecular Genetics). Studies the molecular mechanisms that regulate food intake and body weight.

Elaine Fuchs, Ph.D. (Mammalian Cell Biology and Development). Investigates molecular mechanisms of skin stem cells, how they make and repair tissues, and how cancers develop.

Hironori Funabiki, Ph.D. (Chromosome and Cell Biology). Studies signaling events in chromosome segregation in mitosis.

Charles D. Gilbert, M.D., Ph.D. (Neurobiology). Studies neural mechanisms of visual perception, learning and memory.

Konstantin A. Goulianos, Ph.D. (Experimental High-Energy Physics). Studies interactions among basic constituents of matter in order to explore the evolution and fate of the universe.

Mary E. Hatten, Ph.D. (Developmental Neurobiology). Investigates mechanisms of neuronal differentiation and migration during embryonic development.

Nathaniel Heintz, Ph.D. (Molecular Biology). Investigates histological and functional aspects of the mammalian brain in health and disease.

David D. Ho, M.D. (Dynamics of HIV/SIV Replication). Pursues the development of drugs and vaccines to prevent HIV transmission.

A. James Hudspeth, M.D., Ph.D. (Sensory Neuroscience). Studies neural mechanisms of hearing and pursues treatments for hearing loss.

Erich Jarvis, Ph.D. (Neurobiology). Studies the mechanisms behind vocal learning, with an emphasis on the molecules that guide neuronal connections from motor learning pathways to vocal neurons.

Tarun Kapoor, Ph.D. (Chemistry and Cell Biology). Investigates molecular and physical mechanisms of cell division.

Sebastian Klinge, Ph.D. (Protein and Nucleic Acid Chemistry). Studies the structure and function of macromolecular complexes involved in eukaryotic ribosome assembly.

Bruce W. Knight Jr. (Biophysics). Develops mathematical descriptions of the nerve networks involved in visual perception.

Mary Jeanne Kreek, M.D. (Biology of Addictive Diseases). Investigates the genetic basis of, and novel treatments for, addictive diseases.

Daniel Kronauer, Ph.D. (Insect Social Evolution). Studies evolution in insect societies at the level of the gene, individual, and colony.

James G. Krueger, M.D., Ph.D. (Investigative Dermatology). Uses psoriasis as a model to investigate the pathogenesis of inflammatory disease and autoimmunity.

Stanislas Leibler, Ph.D. (Living Matter). Conducts quantitative analyses of microbial systems on cellular and population levels.

Albert J. Libchaber, Ph.D. (Experimental Condensed-Matter Physics). Applies mathematical models to biological systems at organismal, cellular, and molecular levels.

Shixin Liu, Ph.D. (Nanoscale Biophysics and Biochemistry). Investigates the interactions between biological machines, such as the transcription and translation apparatuses in bacteria.

Roderick MacKinnon, M.D. (Molecular Neurobiology and Biophysics). Studies principles underlying electricity in biology, particularly the passage of ions across cell membranes.

Marcelo Magnasco, Ph.D. (Mathematical Physics). Creates computational and mathematical models to describe neurophysiological systems and living organisms.

Gaby Maimon, Ph.D. (Integrative Brain Function). Studies electrical activity and computation underlying behavior in *Drosophila*.

Luciano Marraffini, Ph.D. (Bacteriology). Investigates the exchange of genetic material among bacteria.

Bruce S. McEwen, Ph.D. (Neuroendocrinology). Studies molecular mechanisms underlying effects of stress and sex hormones on the brain.

Daniel Mucida, Ph.D. (Mucosal Immunology). Investigates mechanisms of immune activity and tolerance in intestinal mucosa.

Fernando Nottebohm, Ph.D. (Animal Behavior). Investigates the biology of vocal learning and neuronal replacement in songbirds.

Michel C. Nussenzweig, M.D., Ph.D. (Molecular Immunology). Studies molecular aspects of adaptive and innate immune responses.

Michael O'Donnell, Ph.D. (DNA Replication). Studies molecular mechanisms of DNA replication, recombination, and repair.

Priya Rajasethupathy, Ph.D. (Neurobiology). Investigates genetic and circuit level mechanisms that underlie disturbances in memory processing.

Jeffrey V. Ravetch, M.D., Ph.D. (Molecular Genetics and Immunology). Investigates mechanisms of the functional diversity of antibodies in host defense and immunotherapy.

Charles Rice, Ph.D. (Virology). Investigates mechanisms of hepatitis C virus infection and replication.

Viviana Risca, Ph.D. (Biophysics). Uses sequencing, microscopy, and computation to study the dynamic three-dimensional organization of eukaryotic genomes.

Jeremy Rock, Ph.D. (Host-Pathogen Biology). Studies the biology of *Mycobacterium tuberculosis* infection.

Robert G. Roeder, Ph.D. (Biochemistry and Molecular Biology). Studies the proteins and enzymes that execute and regulate gene transcription.

Michael P. Rout, Ph.D. (Cellular and Structural Cell Biology). Researches the structure of nuclear pore complexes and their role in oncogenic and developmental defects.

Vanessa Ruta, Ph.D. (Neurophysiology and Behavior). Investigates neural circuits that underlie innate and learned behaviors.

Thomas P. Sakmar, M.D. (Chemical Biology and Signal Transduction). Conducts biological and chemical investigations of G protein coupled receptors.

Shai Shaham, Ph.D. (Developmental Genetics). Investigates the role of glial cells in nervous system development and function.

Amy Shyer, Ph.D. (Multicellular mechanics and Tissue Morphogenesis). Studies the mechanical forces and molecular cues that guide tissue formation in the developing vertebrate embryo.

Eric Siggia, Ph.D. (Theoretical Condensed-Matter Physics). Uses bioinformatics to study regulatory patterns in gene expression.

Sanford M. Simon, Ph.D. (Cellular Biophysics). Uses imaging techniques and other biophysical tools to study single events in biological systems.

Agata Smogorzewska, M.D., Ph.D. (Genome Maintenance). Uses Fanconia anemia as a backdrop to investigate DNA repair mechanisms in aging and cancer.

Hermann Steller, Ph.D. (Apoptosis and Cancer Biology). Investigates signaling pathways underlying apoptosis.

Sidney Strickland, Ph.D. (Neurobiology and Genetics). Investigates neurovascular dysfunction in Alzheimer's disease and hemorrhagic stroke.

Alexander Tarakhovsky, M.D., Ph.D. (Immune Cell Epigenetics and Signaling). Investigates the epigenetic control of immune gene expression.

Sohail Tavazoie, M.D., Ph.D. (Systems Cancer Biology). Uses a variety of laboratory and clinical approaches to study the processes of cancer metastasis.

Thomas Tuschl, Ph.D. (RNA Molecular Biology). Investigates gene regulatory mechanisms triggered by double-stranded RNA and RNA-binding proteins.

Alipasha Vaziri, Ph.D. (Neurotechnology and Biophysics). Develops and applies new optical imaging techniques with the goal of creating functional images of neural circuits.

Gabriel Victora, Ph.D. (Lymphocyte Dynamics). Investigates the molecular mechanisms behind the immune response.

Ekaterina Vinogradova, Ph.D. (Chemical Immunology and Proteomics). Uses chemical proteomic technologies to study immune protein function and find new targets for therapies.

Leslie Vosshall, Ph.D. (Neurogenetics and Behavior). Investigates how odor stimuli are processed and perceived.

Thomas Walz, Ph.D. (Structural Biology). Using cryo-electron microscopy to understand how the protein structure of membranes enables them to perform their functions.

Michael W. Young, Ph.D. (Genetics). Investigates the genetic regulation of biological clocks that underlie many activities of living organisms.

Li Zhao, Ph.D. (Evolutionary Biology). Using CRISPR-Cas 9 genome editing to investigate the biological function of de novo genes; Investigates the role of natural selection in the origin of genes.

# Section 2
# Anatomy

This section contains a directory of institutions offering graduate work in anatomy. Additional information about programs listed in the directory may be obtained by writing directly to the dean of a graduate school or chair of a department at the address given in the directory.

For programs offering related work, see also in this book *Allied Health; Biomedical Sciences; Cell, Molecular, and Structural Biology; Dentistry and Dental Sciences; Genetics, Developmental Biology, and Reproductive Biology; Neuroscience and Neurobiology; Pathology and Pathobiology; Physiology; Veterinary Medicine and Sciences;* and *Zoology.* In another guide in this series:

**Graduate Programs in the Humanities, Arts & Social Sciences**
See *Sociology, Anthropology, and Archaeology*

## CONTENTS

## Program Directory

# Anatomy

**Albert Einstein College of Medicine,** Graduate Programs in the Biomedical Sciences, Department of Anatomy and Structural Biology, Bronx, NY 10461. Offers anatomy (PhD); MD/PhD. *Degree requirements:* For doctorate, thesis/dissertation. *Entrance requirements:* For doctorate, GRE General Test. Additional exam requirements/recommendations for international students: required—TOEFL. Electronic applications accepted.

**Augusta University,** Program in Cellular Biology and Anatomy, Augusta, GA 30912. Offers PhD. *Degree requirements:* For doctorate, comprehensive exam, thesis/dissertation. *Entrance requirements:* For doctorate, GRE General Test. Additional exam requirements/recommendations for international students: required—TOEFL (minimum score 550 paper-based; 79 iBT).

**Barry University,** School of Podiatric Medicine, Program in Anatomy, Miami Shores, FL 33161-6695. Offers MS. *Entrance requirements:* For master's, GRE.

**Boston University,** College of Health and Rehabilitation Sciences: Sargent College, Programs in Human Physiology, Boston, MA 02215. Offers MS, PhD. *Faculty:* 9 full-time (6 women), 7 part-time/adjunct (3 women). *Students:* 7 full-time (5 women), 4 part-time (3 women); includes 1 minority (Asian, non-Hispanic/Latino), 3 international. Average age 23. 40 applicants, 48% accepted, 7 enrolled. In 2019, 11 master's awarded. Terminal master's awarded for partial completion of doctoral program. *Entrance requirements:* Additional exam requirements/recommendations for international students: required—TOEFL. Application fee: $95. Electronic applications accepted. *Financial support:* Research assistantships, career-related internships or fieldwork, Federal Work-Study, institutionally sponsored loans, scholarships/grants, and unspecified assistantships available. Support available to part-time students. Financial award applicants required to submit FAFSA. *Unit head:* Dr. Paula Quatromoni, Chair, 617-353-5797, Fax: 617-353-7567, E-mail: paulaq@bu.edu. *Application contact:* Sharon Sankey, Assistant Dean, Student Services, 617-353-2713, Fax: 617-353-7500, E-mail: ssankey@bu.edu.

**Boston University,** School of Medicine, Graduate Medical Sciences, Department of Anatomy and Neurobiology, Boston, MA 02118. Offers MA, PhD, MD/PhD. *Program availability:* Part-time. Terminal master's awarded for partial completion of doctoral program. *Degree requirements:* For master's, thesis; for doctorate, thesis/dissertation. *Application deadline:* For fall admission, 1/15 for domestic students; for spring admission, 10/15 for domestic students. *Unit head:* Dr. Mark Moss, Chairman, 617-638-4200, Fax: 617-638-4216. *Application contact:* GMS Admissions Office, 617-358-9518, Fax: 617-358-2913, E-mail: gmsbusm@bu.edu.
Website: http://www.bumc.bu.edu/anatneuro/

**Case Western Reserve University,** School of Medicine and School of Graduate Studies, Graduate Programs in Medicine, Department of Anatomy, Cleveland, OH 44106. Offers applied anatomy (MS); MD/MS. *Program availability:* Part-time. *Degree requirements:* For master's, comprehensive exam, thesis (for some programs). *Entrance requirements:* For master's, GRE General Test. Additional exam requirements/recommendations for international students: required—TOEFL.

**Columbia University,** College of Physicians and Surgeons, Department of Anatomy and Cell Biology, New York, NY 10032. Offers anatomy (M Phil, MA, PhD); anatomy and cell biology (PhD); MD/PhD. Terminal master's awarded for partial completion of doctoral program. *Degree requirements:* For doctorate, thesis/dissertation, oral exam. *Entrance requirements:* For master's and doctorate, GRE General Test. Additional exam requirements/recommendations for international students: required—TOEFL. *Expenses: Tuition:* Full-time $47,600; part-time $1880 per credit. One-time fee: $105.

**Creighton University,** School of Medicine and Graduate School, Graduate Programs in Medicine, Program in Clinical Anatomy, Omaha, NE 68178-0001. Offers MS. *Degree requirements:* For master's, comprehensive exam, thesis or alternative. *Entrance requirements:* For master's, GRE, MCAT or DAT. Additional exam requirements/recommendations for international students: required—TOEFL. Electronic applications accepted.

**Dalhousie University,** Faculty of Graduate Studies, Department of Medical Neuroscience, Halifax, NS B3H 4H7, Canada. Offers anatomy and neuroscience (M Sc, PhD). *Degree requirements:* For doctorate, thesis/dissertation. *Entrance requirements:* For master's and doctorate, 4 year honors degree or equivalent, minimum A- average. Additional exam requirements/recommendations for international students: required—1 of 5 approved tests: TOEFL, IELTS, CANTEST, CAEL, Michigan English Language Assessment Battery. Electronic applications accepted.

**Des Moines University,** College of Osteopathic Medicine, Program in Anatomy, Des Moines, IA 50312-4104. Offers MS.

**Duke University,** Graduate School, Department of Evolutionary Anthropology, Durham, NC 27708. Offers cellular and molecular biology (PhD); gross anatomy and physical anthropology (PhD), including comparative morphology of human and non-human primates, primate social behavior, vertebrate paleontology; neuroanatomy (PhD). *Degree requirements:* For doctorate, one foreign language, thesis/dissertation. *Entrance requirements:* For doctorate, GRE General Test. Additional exam requirements/recommendations for international students: required—TOEFL (minimum score 577 paper-based; 90 iBT) or IELTS (minimum score 7). Electronic applications accepted.

**D'Youville College,** Program in Anatomy, Buffalo, NY 14201-1084. Offers MS.

**East Carolina University,** Brody School of Medicine, Office of Research and Graduate Studies, Greenville, NC 27858-4353. Offers anatomy and cell biology (PhD); biochemistry and molecular biology (PhD); biomedical science (MS); microbiology and immunology (PhD); pharmacology and toxicology (PhD); physiology (PhD). *Students:* 102 full-time (44 women), 1 part-time (0 women); includes 16 minority (4 Black or African American, non-Hispanic/Latino; 7 Asian, non-Hispanic/Latino; 4 Hispanic/Latino; 1 Two or more races, non-Hispanic/Latino), 13 international. Average age 28. 83 applicants, 40% accepted, 20 enrolled. In 2019, 3 master's, 10 doctorates awarded. *Degree requirements:* For doctorate, comprehensive exam, thesis/dissertation. *Entrance requirements:* For doctorate, GRE General Test. Additional exam requirements/recommendations for international students: required—some international applicants may be required to demonstrate English proficiency via the TOEFL, IELTS, or PTE exam.; recommended—TOEFL (minimum score 78 iBT), IELTS (minimum score 6.5), TSE (minimum score 65). *Application deadline:* For fall admission, 8/15 for domestic students; for spring admission, 12/20 for domestic students. Applications are processed on a rolling basis. Application fee: $75. Electronic applications accepted. *Expenses: Tuition, area resident:* Full-time $4749; part-time $185 per credit hour. Tuition, state resident: full-time $4749; part-time $185 per credit hour. Tuition, nonresident: full-time $17,898; part-time $864 per credit hour. *International tuition:* $17,898 full-time. *Required fees:* $2787. *Financial support:* Fellowships available. Financial award application deadline: 6/1. *Unit head:* Dr. Russ Price, Associate Dean, 252-744-9346, E-mail: pricest17@ecu.edu. *Application contact:* Dr. Russ Price, Associate Dean, 252-744-9346, E-mail: pricest17@ecu.edu.
Website: http://www.ecu.edu/cs-dhs/bsomresearchgradstudies/index.cfm

**East Tennessee State University,** Quillen College of Medicine, Department of Biomedical Sciences, Johnson City, TN 37614. Offers anatomy (PhD); biochemistry (PhD); microbiology (PhD); pharmaceutical sciences (PhD); pharmacology (PhD); physiology (PhD); quantitative biosciences (PhD). *Degree requirements:* For doctorate, comprehensive exam, thesis/dissertation, comprehensive qualifying exam; one-year residency. *Entrance requirements:* For doctorate, GRE General Test, GRE Subject Test, 3 letters of recommendation, minimum of 60 credit hours beyond the baccalaureate degree. Additional exam requirements/recommendations for international students: required—TOEFL (minimum score 550 paper-based; 79 iBT). Electronic applications accepted. *Expenses:* Contact institution.

**Howard University,** Graduate School, Department of Anatomy, Washington, DC 20059-0002. Offers MS, PhD. *Degree requirements:* For master's, comprehensive exam, thesis, teaching experience; for doctorate, comprehensive exam, thesis/dissertation, teaching experience. *Entrance requirements:* For master's and doctorate, GRE General Test, minimum GPA of 3.0. Additional exam requirements/recommendations for international students: required—TOEFL (minimum score 550 paper-based). Electronic applications accepted.

**Indiana University-Purdue University Indianapolis,** Indiana University School of Medicine, Department of Anatomy and Cell Biology, Indianapolis, IN 46202. Offers MS, PhD, MD/PhD. *Degree requirements:* For master's, thesis or alternative; for doctorate, thesis/dissertation. *Entrance requirements:* For master's and doctorate, GRE General Test. Additional exam requirements/recommendations for international students: required—TOEFL. Electronic applications accepted. *Expenses:* Contact institution.

**Johns Hopkins University,** School of Medicine, Graduate Programs in Medicine, Center for Functional Anatomy and Evolution, Baltimore, MD 21218. Offers PhD. *Degree requirements:* For doctorate, comprehensive exam, thesis/dissertation, oral exams. *Entrance requirements:* For doctorate, GRE. Additional exam requirements/recommendations for international students: required—TOEFL. Electronic applications accepted.

**Liberty University,** School of Health Sciences, Lynchburg, VA 24515. Offers anatomy and cell biology (PhD); biomedical sciences (MS); epidemiology (MPH); exercise science (MS), including clinical, community physical activity, human performance, nutrition; global health (MPH); health promotion (MPH); medical sciences (MA), including biopsychology, business management, health informatics, molecular medicine, public health; nutrition (MPH). *Program availability:* Part-time, online learning. *Students:* 820 full-time (588 women), 889 part-time (612 women); includes 611 minority (402 Black or African American, non-Hispanic/Latino; 10 American Indian or Alaska Native, non-Hispanic/Latino; 43 Asian, non-Hispanic/Latino; 85 Hispanic/Latino; 1 Native Hawaiian or other Pacific Islander, non-Hispanic/Latino; 70 Two or more races, non-Hispanic/Latino), 67 international. Average age 32. 2,610 applicants, 33% accepted, 406 enrolled. In 2019, 445 master's awarded. *Degree requirements:* For master's, thesis (for some programs); for doctorate, thesis/dissertation. *Entrance requirements:* For doctorate, MAT or GRE, minimum GPA of 3.25 in master's program, 2-3 recommendations, writing samples (for some programs), letter of intent, professional vitae. Additional exam requirements/recommendations for international students: required—TOEFL (minimum score 600 paper-based; 100 iBT). Application fee: $50. *Expenses: Tuition:* Full-time $545; part-time $410 per credit hour. One-time fee: $50. *Financial support:* In 2019–20, 918 students received support. Federal Work-Study available. Financial award applicants required to submit FAFSA. *Unit head:* Dr. Ralph Linstra, Dean. *Application contact:* Jay Bridge, Director of Admissions, 800-424-9595, Fax: 800-628-7977, E-mail: gradadmissions@liberty.edu.
Website: https://www.liberty.edu/health-sciences/

**Loma Linda University,** School of Medicine, Programs in Pathology and Human Anatomy, Loma Linda, CA 92350. Offers human anatomy (PhD); pathology (PhD). *Accreditation:* NAACLS. *Program availability:* Part-time. Terminal master's awarded for partial completion of doctoral program. *Degree requirements:* For doctorate, 2 foreign languages, thesis/dissertation. *Entrance requirements:* For doctorate, GRE General Test. Additional exam requirements/recommendations for international students: required—TOEFL (minimum score 550 paper-based).

**Louisiana State University Health Sciences Center,** School of Graduate Studies in New Orleans, Department of Cell Biology and Anatomy, New Orleans, LA 70112-2223. Offers cell biology and anatomy (PhD), including clinical anatomy, development, cell, and neurobiology; MD/PhD. *Degree requirements:* For doctorate, comprehensive exam, thesis/dissertation. *Entrance requirements:* For doctorate, GRE General Test, minimum undergraduate GPA of 3.0. Additional exam requirements/recommendations for international students: recommended—TOEFL, IELTS.

**Louisiana State University Health Sciences Center at Shreveport,** Department of Cellular Biology and Anatomy, Shreveport, LA 71130-3932. Offers MS, PhD, MD/PhD. Terminal master's awarded for partial completion of doctoral program. *Degree requirements:* For master's, thesis; for doctorate, thesis/dissertation. *Entrance requirements:* For master's and doctorate, GRE General Test. Additional exam requirements/recommendations for international students: required—TOEFL.

**McGill University,** Faculty of Graduate and Postdoctoral Studies, Faculty of Medicine, Department of Anatomy and Cell Biology, Montréal, QC H3A 2T5, Canada. Offers M Sc, PhD.

**New York Academy of Art,** Master of Fine Arts Program, New York, NY 10013-2911. Offers anatomy (MFA); drawing (MFA); fine arts (MFA), including anatomy; painting (MFA); printmaking (MFA); sculpture (MFA). *Accreditation:* NASAD. *Degree requirements:* For master's, thesis. *Entrance requirements:* For master's, portfolio, essay, two letters of recommendation, curriculum vitae or resume, official undergraduate transcripts. Additional exam requirements/recommendations for international students: required—TOEFL (minimum score 550 paper-based; 80 iBT), IELTS (minimum score 6.5). Electronic applications accepted. Application fee is waived when completed online. *Expenses:* Contact institution.

**New York Chiropractic College,** Program in Clinical Anatomy, Seneca Falls, NY 13148-0800. Offers MS. *Degree requirements:* For master's, thesis. *Entrance requirements:* For master's, minimum GPA of 3.0, DC, bachelor's degree or equivalent. Electronic applications accepted.

**New York Chiropractic College,** Program in Human Anatomy and Physiology Instruction, Seneca Falls, NY 13148-0800. Offers MS. *Program availability:* Online learning.

**The Ohio State University,** College of Medicine, School of Health and Rehabilitation Sciences, Program in Anatomy, Columbus, OH 43210. Offers MS, PhD. Terminal master's awarded for partial completion of doctoral program. *Degree requirements:* For master's, thesis (for some programs); for doctorate, thesis/dissertation. *Entrance requirements:* For master's and doctorate, GRE General Test (suggested minimum score in 50th percentile). Additional exam requirements/recommendations for international students: required—TOEFL (minimum score 600 paper-based; 100 iBT), Michigan English Language Assessment Battery (minimum score 86); recommended—IELTS (minimum score 8). Electronic applications accepted.

**Palmer College of Chiropractic,** Division of Graduate Studies, Davenport, IA 52803-5287. Offers clinical research (MS). *Program availability:* Part-time. *Degree requirements:* For master's, 2 mentored practicum projects. *Entrance requirements:* For master's, GRE General Test, minimum GPA of 2.5, bachelor's and doctoral-level health professions degrees. Additional exam requirements/recommendations for international students: required—TOEFL. Electronic applications accepted. *Expenses:* Contact institution.

**Penn State Hershey Medical Center,** College of Medicine, Graduate School Programs in the Biomedical Sciences, Program in Anatomy, Hershey, PA 17033. Offers MS, PhD, MD/PhD. Terminal master's awarded for partial completion of doctoral program. *Degree requirements:* For master's, thesis or alternative; for doctorate, comprehensive exam, thesis/dissertation. *Entrance requirements:* For master's and doctorate, GRE General Test or MCAT, minimum GPA of 3.0. Additional exam requirements/recommendations for international students: required—TOEFL (minimum score 81 iBT). Electronic applications accepted.

**Purdue University,** School of Veterinary Medicine and Graduate School, Graduate Programs in Veterinary Medicine, Department of Basic Medical Sciences, West Lafayette, IN 47907. Offers anatomy (MS, PhD); pharmacology (MS, PhD); physiology (MS, PhD). *Program availability:* Part-time. Terminal master's awarded for partial completion of doctoral program. *Degree requirements:* For master's, thesis; for doctorate, thesis/dissertation. *Entrance requirements:* For master's and doctorate, GRE General Test. Additional exam requirements/recommendations for international students: required—TOEFL. Electronic applications accepted.

**Rosalind Franklin University of Medicine and Science,** School of Graduate and Postdoctoral Studies - Interdisciplinary Graduate Program in Biomedical Sciences, Department of Cell Biology and Anatomy, North Chicago, IL 60064-3095. Offers PhD, MD/PhD. Terminal master's awarded for partial completion of doctoral program. *Degree requirements:* For doctorate, comprehensive exam, thesis/dissertation, original research project. *Entrance requirements:* For doctorate, GRE General Test, minimum GPA of 3.0. Additional exam requirements/recommendations for international students: required—TOEFL, TWE.

**Rush University,** Graduate College, Division of Anatomy and Cell Biology, Chicago, IL 60612-3832. Offers MS, PhD, MD/MS, MD/PhD. Terminal master's awarded for partial completion of doctoral program. *Degree requirements:* For master's, thesis; for doctorate, comprehensive exam, thesis/dissertation, preliminary exam, dissertation proposal. *Entrance requirements:* For master's, GRE General Test, minimum GPA of 3.0, bachelor's degree in biology or chemistry (preferred), interview; for doctorate, GRE General Test, minimum GPA of 3.0, interview. Additional exam requirements/recommendations for international students: required—TOEFL. Electronic applications accepted.

**Saint Louis University,** Graduate Programs, School of Medicine, Graduate Programs in Biomedical Sciences and Graduate Programs, Center for Anatomical Science and Education, St. Louis, MO 63103. Offers anatomy (MS-R, PhD). *Degree requirements:* For master's, comprehensive exam, thesis; for doctorate, comprehensive exam, thesis/dissertation, departmental qualifying exams. *Entrance requirements:* For master's, GRE General Test, letters of recommendation, resume; for doctorate, GRE General Test, letters of recommendation, resumé, goal statement, transcripts. Additional exam requirements/recommendations for international students: required—TOEFL (minimum score 525 paper-based).

**State University of New York Upstate Medical University,** College of Graduate Studies, Program in Cell and Developmental Biology, Syracuse, NY 13210. Offers anatomy (MS, PhD); MD/PhD. Terminal master's awarded for partial completion of doctoral program. *Degree requirements:* For master's, thesis; for doctorate, comprehensive exam, thesis/dissertation. *Entrance requirements:* For master's, GRE General Test, interview; for doctorate, GRE General Test, telephone interview. Additional exam requirements/recommendations for international students: required—TOEFL. Electronic applications accepted.

**Stony Brook University, State University of New York,** Stony Brook Medicine, Renaissance School of Medicine and Graduate School, Graduate Programs in Medicine, Department of Anatomical Sciences, Stony Brook, NY 11794-8081. Offers PhD. *Faculty:* 11 full-time (4 women). *Students:* 3 full-time (2 women). Average age 25. 2 applicants, 50% accepted. *Degree requirements:* For doctorate, comprehensive exam, thesis/dissertation. *Entrance requirements:* For doctorate, GRE General Test, GRE Subject Test, BA in life sciences, minimum GPA of 3.0. Additional exam requirements/recommendations for international students: required—TOEFL. *Application deadline:* For fall admission, 1/15 for domestic students; for spring admission, 10/1 for domestic students. Application fee: $100. *Expenses:* Contact institution. *Financial support:* Fellowships, research assistantships, teaching assistantships, and Federal Work-Study available. Financial award application deadline: 3/15. *Unit head:* Dr. Susan Larson, Professor and Chair, 631-444-3115, Fax: 631-444-3947, E-mail: susan.larson@stonybrook.edu. *Application contact:* Dr. Maureen O'Leary, Professor and Graduate Program Director, 631-444-3114, Fax: 631-444-3947, E-mail: maureen.oleary@stonybrook.edu.
Website: https://renaissance.stonybrookmedicine.edu/anatomy

**Universidad Central del Caribe,** School of Medicine, Program in Biomedical Sciences, Bayamón, PR 00960-6032. Offers anatomy and cell biology (MA, MS); biochemistry (MS); biomedical sciences (MA); cellular and molecular biology (PhD); microbiology and immunology (MA, MS); pharmacology (MS); physiology (MS).

**Universidad de Ciencias Medicas,** Graduate Programs, San Jose, Costa Rica. Offers dermatology (SP); family health (MS); health service center administration (MHA); human anatomy (MS); medical and surgery (MD); occupational medicine (MS); pharmacy (Pharm D). *Program availability:* Part-time. *Degree requirements:* For master's, thesis; for doctorate and SP, comprehensive exam. *Entrance requirements:* For master's, MD or bachelor's degree; for doctorate, admissions test; for SP, admissions test, MD.

**University at Buffalo, the State University of New York,** Graduate School, Jacobs School of Medicine and Biomedical Sciences, Graduate Programs in Medicine and Biomedical Sciences, Department of Pathology and Anatomical Sciences, Buffalo, NY 14203. Offers anatomical sciences (MA, PhD); computational cell biology, anatomy, and pathology (PhD); pathology (MA, PhD). *Faculty:* 14 full-time (2 women). *Students:* 16 full-time (6 women); includes 2 minority (1 American Indian or Alaska Native, non-Hispanic/Latino; 1 Asian, non-Hispanic/Latino), 1 international. Average age 29. 26 applicants, 27% accepted, 3 enrolled. In 2019, 2 master's, 2 doctorates awarded. *Degree requirements:* For master's, thesis; for doctorate, thesis/dissertation. *Entrance requirements:* For master's and doctorate, 3 letters of recommendation. Additional exam requirements/recommendations for international students: required—TOEFL (minimum score 600 paper-based; 100 iBT). *Application deadline:* For fall admission, 5/1 priority date for domestic students, 3/1 priority date for international students. Applications are processed on a rolling basis. Application fee: $85. Electronic applications accepted. *Expenses:* Contact institution. *Financial support:* In 2019–20, 7 students received support, including 1 research assistantship with full tuition reimbursement available (averaging $24,900 per year), 1 teaching assistantship with full tuition reimbursement available (averaging $24,900 per year); Federal Work-Study, scholarships/grants, health care benefits, and unspecified assistantships also available. Financial award application deadline: 2/1; financial award applicants required to submit FAFSA. *Unit head:* Dr. John E. Tomaszewski, Department Chair, 716-829-2846, Fax: 716-829-2911, E-mail: johntoma@buffalo.edu. *Application contact:* Lannette M. Garcia, Assistant for Academic Activity, 716-829-5204, E-mail: ubpathad@buffalo.edu.
Website: http://medicine.buffalo.edu/departments/pathology.html

**University of California, Irvine,** School of Medicine and School of Biological Sciences, Department of Anatomy and Neurobiology, Irvine, CA 92697. Offers biological sciences (MS, PhD); MD/PhD. *Students:* 15 full-time (9 women), 3 part-time (2 women); includes 8 minority (5 Asian, non-Hispanic/Latino; 3 Hispanic/Latino), 2 international. Average age 28. *Entrance requirements:* For master's and doctorate, GRE General Test, GRE Subject Test. Additional exam requirements/recommendations for international students: required—TOEFL (minimum score 550 paper-based). *Application deadline:* For fall admission, 1/15 priority date for domestic students, 1/15 for international students. Applications are processed on a rolling basis. Application fee: $120 ($140 for international students). Electronic applications accepted. *Financial support:* Fellowships, research assistantships with full tuition reimbursements, teaching assistantships, institutionally sponsored loans, traineeships, health care benefits, and unspecified assistantships available. Financial award application deadline: 3/1; financial award applicants required to submit FAFSA. *Unit head:* Prof. Christine Gall, Interim Chair, 949-824-8652, Fax: 949-824-1255, E-mail: cmgall@uci.edu. *Application contact:* David Lyon, Director of Graduate Studies, 949-824-0447, E-mail: dclyon@uci.edu.
Website: http://anatomy.uci.edu/

**University of California, Los Angeles,** David Geffen School of Medicine and Graduate Division, Graduate Programs in Medicine, Department of Neurobiology, Los Angeles, CA 90095. Offers MS, PhD. Terminal master's awarded for partial completion of doctoral program. *Degree requirements:* For master's, comprehensive exam; for doctorate, thesis/dissertation, oral and written qualifying exams; 2 quarters of teaching experience. *Entrance requirements:* For doctorate, GRE General Test; GRE Subject Test, bachelor's degree; minimum undergraduate GPA of 3.0 (or its equivalent if letter grade system not used). Additional exam requirements/recommendations for international students: required—TOEFL. Electronic applications accepted.

**University of Chicago,** Division of the Biological Sciences, Department of Organismal Biology and Anatomy, Chicago, IL 60637. Offers integrative biology (PhD). *Degree requirements:* For doctorate, thesis/dissertation, ethics class, 2 teaching assistantships, preliminary examinations. *Entrance requirements:* For doctorate, GRE General Test, transcripts, statement of purpose, 3 letters of recommendation. Additional exam requirements/recommendations for international students: required—TOEFL (minimum score 600 paper-based; 104 iBT), IELTS (minimum score 7). Electronic applications accepted.

**University of Colorado Denver,** School of Medicine, Program in Cell Biology, Stem Cells, and Development, Aurora, CO 80045. Offers cell biology, stem cells, and developmental biology (PhD); modern human anatomy (MS). *Degree requirements:* For doctorate, comprehensive exam, thesis/dissertation, at least 30 credit hours of coursework and 30 credit hours of thesis research; laboratory rotations. *Entrance requirements:* For doctorate, GRE, minimum GPA of 3.0; 3 letters of reference; prerequisite coursework in organic chemistry, biology, biochemistry, physics and calculus; research experience (highly recommended). Additional exam requirements/recommendations for international students: required—TOEFL (minimum score 550 paper-based; 80 iBT). Tuition and fees vary according to course load, program and reciprocity agreements.

**University of Connecticut Health Center,** Graduate School, Programs in Biomedical Sciences, Program in Skeletal Biology and Regeneration, Farmington, CT 06030. Offers PhD, DMD/PhD, MD/PhD. *Degree requirements:* For doctorate, comprehensive exam, thesis/dissertation. *Entrance requirements:* For doctorate, GRE General Test. Additional exam requirements/recommendations for international students: required—TOEFL (minimum score 600 paper-based). Electronic applications accepted.

**University of Guelph,** Ontario Veterinary College and Office of Graduate and Postdoctoral Studies, Graduate Programs in Veterinary Sciences, Department of Biomedical Sciences, Guelph, ON N1G 2W1, Canada. Offers morphology (M Sc, DV Sc, PhD); neuroscience (M Sc, DV Sc, PhD); pharmacology (M Sc, DV Sc, PhD); physiology (M Sc, DV Sc, PhD); toxicology (M Sc, DV Sc, PhD). *Program availability:* Part-time. *Degree requirements:* For master's, thesis; for doctorate, comprehensive exam, thesis/dissertation. *Entrance requirements:* For master's, honors B Sc, minimum 75% average in last 20 courses; for doctorate, M Sc with thesis from accredited institution. Additional exam requirements/recommendations for international students: required—TOEFL (minimum score 550 paper-based; 89 iBT). Electronic applications accepted.

**University of Illinois at Chicago,** College of Medicine, Graduate Programs in Medicine, Department of Anatomy and Cell Biology, Chicago, IL 60607. Offers MS, MD/PhD. *Degree requirements:* For master's, preliminary oral examination, dissertation and oral defense. *Entrance requirements:* For master's, GRE General Test, minimum GPA of 2.75, 3 letters of recommendation. Additional exam requirements/recommendations for international students: required—TOEFL (minimum score 550 paper-based). Electronic applications accepted.

**The University of Iowa,** Roy J. and Lucille A. Carver College of Medicine and Graduate College, Graduate Programs in Medicine, Department of Anatomy and Cell Biology, Iowa City, IA 52242-1316. Offers PhD. *Degree requirements:* For doctorate, comprehensive exam, thesis/dissertation. *Entrance requirements:* For doctorate, GRE General Test, minimum GPA of 3.0. Additional exam requirements/recommendations for international students: required—TOEFL (minimum score 600 paper-based; 100 iBT). Electronic applications accepted.

**The University of Kansas,** University of Kansas Medical Center, School of Medicine, Department of Anatomy and Cell Biology, Kansas City, KS 66160. Offers MS, PhD, MD/PhD. *Faculty:* 29. *Students:* 8 full-time (7 women), 4 international. Average age 28. In 2019, 1 master's, 2 doctorates awarded. Terminal master's awarded for partial completion of doctoral program. *Degree requirements:* For master's, thesis; for doctorate, comprehensive exam, thesis/dissertation. *Entrance requirements:* For

master's and doctorate, GRE. Additional exam requirements/recommendations for international students: required—TOEFL. *Expenses:* Tuition, state resident: full-time $9989. Tuition, nonresident: full-time $23,950. *International tuition:* $23,950 full-time. *Required fees:* $984; $81.99 per credit hour. Tuition and fees vary according to course load, campus/location and program. *Financial support:* Fellowships, research assistantships with full tuition reimbursements, teaching assistantships with full tuition reimbursements, institutionally sponsored loans, scholarships/grants, health care benefits, and unspecified assistantships available. Financial award application deadline: 3/1; financial award applicants required to submit FAFSA. *Unit head:* Dr. Dale R. Abrahamson, Chairman, 913-588-0702, Fax: 913-588-2710, E-mail: dabrahamson@kumc.edu. *Application contact:* Dr. Julie A. Christianson, Assistant Professor, 913-945-6430, Fax: 913-588-5677, E-mail: jchristianson@kumc.edu.
Website: http://www.kumc.edu/school-of-medicine/anatomy-and-cell-biology.html

**University of Kentucky,** Graduate School, Graduate School Programs from the College of Medicine, Program in Anatomy and Neurobiology, Lexington, KY 40506-0032. Offers PhD. *Degree requirements:* For doctorate, comprehensive exam, thesis/dissertation. *Entrance requirements:* For doctorate, GRE General Test, minimum undergraduate GPA of 2.75. Additional exam requirements/recommendations for international students: required—TOEFL (minimum score 550 paper-based). Electronic applications accepted.

**University of Louisville,** School of Medicine, Department of Anatomical Sciences and Neurobiology, Louisville, KY 40292-0001. Offers MS, PhD, MD/PhD. *Faculty:* 16 full-time (5 women), 2 part-time/adjunct (0 women). *Students:* 24 full-time (7 women), 4 part-time (2 women); includes 2 minority (1 Asian, non-Hispanic/Latino; 1 Hispanic/Latino), 3 international. Average age 30. 29 applicants, 52% accepted, 10 enrolled. In 2019, 9 master's, 6 doctorates awarded. Terminal master's awarded for partial completion of doctoral program. *Degree requirements:* For master's, thesis (for some programs); for doctorate, comprehensive exam, thesis/dissertation. *Entrance requirements:* For master's and doctorate, GRE General Test (Verbal + Quantitative score of 300), Minimum GPA 3.0. Additional exam requirements/recommendations for international students: required—TOEFL (minimum score 550 paper-based; 79 iBT). *Application deadline:* For fall admission, 2/15 priority date for domestic and international students. Application fee: $65. Electronic applications accepted. *Expenses: Tuition, area resident:* Full-time $13,000; part-time $723 per credit hour. Tuition, state resident: full-time $13,000; part-time $723 per credit hour. Tuition, nonresident: full-time $27,114; part-time $1507 per credit hour. *International tuition:* $27,114 full-time. *Required fees:* $196. Tuition and fees vary according to program and reciprocity agreements. *Financial support:* In 2019–20, 25 students received support, including 6 fellowships with full tuition reimbursements available (averaging $25,000 per year); health care benefits and unspecified assistantships also available. Financial award application deadline: 2/15. *Unit head:* Dr. William Guido, Professor and Chair, 502-852-5165, Fax: 502-852-6228, E-mail: w0guid01@gwise.louisville.edu. *Application contact:* Dr. Patrick Moore, Admissions Director, 502-852-1311, E-mail: jpmoor03@louisville.edu.
Website: http://louisville.edu/medicine/departments/anatomy

**University of Manitoba,** Max Rady College of Medicine and Faculty of Graduate Studies, Graduate Programs in Medicine, Department of Human Anatomy and Cell Science, Winnipeg, MB R3T 2N2, Canada. Offers M Sc, PhD. *Degree requirements:* For master's, thesis; for doctorate, one foreign language, thesis/dissertation.

**University of Mississippi Medical Center,** School of Graduate Studies in Health Sciences, Department of Anatomy, Jackson, MS 39216-4505. Offers clinical anatomy (MS, PhD); MD/PhD. *Degree requirements:* For doctorate, comprehensive exam, thesis/dissertation, first authored publication. *Entrance requirements:* For doctorate, GRE General Test, minimum GPA of 3.0, personal statement. Additional exam requirements/recommendations for international students: required—TOEFL.

**University of Missouri,** School of Medicine and Office of Research and Graduate Studies, Graduate Programs in Medicine, Department of Pathology and Anatomical Sciences, Columbia, MO 65211. Offers MS, PhD. *Entrance requirements:* For master's, GRE (minimum Verbal and Analytical score of 1250), letters of recommendation, minimum GPA of 3.5. Additional exam requirements/recommendations for international students: required—TOEFL. Electronic applications accepted.

**University of Nebraska Medical Center,** Interdisciplinary Graduate Program in Biomedical Sciences, Department of Genetics, Cell Biology and Anatomy, Omaha, NE 68198. Offers genetics, cell biology and anatomy (PhD); medical anatomy (MS); molecular genetics and cell biology (MS). Terminal master's awarded for partial completion of doctoral program. *Degree requirements:* For master's, comprehensive exam, thesis (for some programs); for doctorate, comprehensive exam, thesis/dissertation. *Entrance requirements:* For master's, GRE General Test (MCAT or DAT acceptable for MS in medical anatomy); for doctorate, GRE General Test. Additional exam requirements/recommendations for international students: required—TOEFL (minimum score 550 paper-based; 80 iBT). Electronic applications accepted. *Expenses:* Contact institution.

**University of North Texas Health Science Center at Fort Worth,** Graduate School of Biomedical Sciences, Fort Worth, TX 76107-2699. Offers biochemistry and cancer biology (MS, PhD); biotechnology (MS); cell biology, immunology and microbiology (MS, PhD); clinical research management (MS); forensic genetics (MS); genetics (MS, PhD); integrative physiology (MS, PhD); medical sciences (MS); pharmaceutical sciences and pharmacotherapy (MS, PhD); pharmacology and neuroscience (MS, PhD); structural anatomy and rehabilitation sciences (MS, PhD); DO/MS; DO/PhD. Terminal master's awarded for partial completion of doctoral program. *Degree requirements:* For master's, thesis; for doctorate, thesis/dissertation. *Entrance requirements:* For master's and doctorate, GRE General Test. Additional exam requirements/recommendations for international students: required—TOEFL. *Expenses:* Contact institution.

**University of Prince Edward Island,** Atlantic Veterinary College, Graduate Program in Veterinary Medicine, Charlottetown, PE C1A 4P3, Canada. Offers anatomy (M Sc, PhD); bacteriology (M Sc, PhD); clinical pharmacology (M Sc, PhD); clinical sciences (M Sc, PhD); epidemiology (M Sc, PhD), including reproduction; fish health (M Sc, PhD); food animal nutrition (M Sc, PhD); immunology (M Sc, PhD); microanatomy (M Sc, PhD); parasitology (M Sc, PhD); pathology (M Sc, PhD); pharmacology (M Sc, PhD); physiology (M Sc, PhD); toxicology (M Sc, PhD); veterinary science (M Vet Sc); virology (M Sc, PhD). *Program availability:* Part-time. *Degree requirements:* For master's, thesis; for doctorate, thesis/dissertation. *Entrance requirements:* For master's, DVM, B Sc honors degree, or equivalent; for doctorate, M Sc. Additional exam requirements/recommendations for international students: required—TOEFL (minimum score 550 paper-based; 80 iBT). *Expenses:* Contact institution.

**University of Puerto Rico - Medical Sciences Campus,** School of Medicine, Biomedical Sciences Graduate Program, Department of Anatomy and Neurobiology, San Juan, PR 00936-5067. Offers anatomy (MS, PhD). *Degree requirements:* For master's, one foreign language, comprehensive exam, thesis; for doctorate, one foreign language, comprehensive exam, thesis/dissertation. *Entrance requirements:* For master's and doctorate, GRE General Test, GRE Subject Test, interview, minimum GPA of 3.0, 3 letters of recommendation. Electronic applications accepted.

**University of Rochester,** School of Medicine and Dentistry, Graduate Programs in Medicine and Dentistry, Department of Neurobiology and Anatomy, Programs in Neurobiology and Anatomy, Rochester, NY 14627. Offers PhD, MD/MS. *Degree requirements:* For doctorate, thesis/dissertation, qualifying exam. *Entrance requirements:* For doctorate, GRE General Test.

**University of Saskatchewan,** College of Medicine, Department of Anatomy, Physiology and Pharmacology, Saskatoon, SK S7N 5A2, Canada. Offers anatomy and cell biology (M Sc, PhD); pharmacology (M Sc, PhD); physiology (M Sc, PhD). *Degree requirements:* For master's, thesis; for doctorate, thesis/dissertation. *Entrance requirements:* Additional exam requirements/recommendations for international students: required—TOEFL.

**University of Saskatchewan,** Western College of Veterinary Medicine and College of Graduate and Postdoctoral Studies, Graduate Programs in Veterinary Medicine, Department of Veterinary Biomedical Sciences, Saskatoon, SK S7N 5A2, Canada. Offers veterinary anatomy (M Sc); veterinary biomedical sciences (M Vet Sc); veterinary physiological sciences (M Sc, PhD). *Degree requirements:* For master's, thesis; for doctorate, comprehensive exam (for some programs), thesis/dissertation. *Entrance requirements:* Additional exam requirements/recommendations for international students: required—TOEFL (minimum score 80 iBT); recommended—IELTS (minimum score 6.5). Electronic applications accepted.

**The University of Tennessee,** Graduate School, College of Agricultural Sciences and Natural Resources, Department of Animal Science, Knoxville, TN 37996. Offers animal anatomy (PhD); breeding (MS, PhD); management (MS, PhD); nutrition (MS, PhD); physiology (MS, PhD). *Program availability:* Part-time. *Degree requirements:* For master's, thesis; for doctorate, thesis/dissertation. *Entrance requirements:* For master's and doctorate, GRE General Test, minimum GPA of 2.7. Additional exam requirements/recommendations for international students: required—TOEFL. Electronic applications accepted.

**University of Utah,** School of Medicine and Graduate School, Graduate Programs in Medicine, Department of Neurobiology and Anatomy, Salt Lake City, UT 84112-1107. Offers PhD. *Program availability:* Part-time. Terminal master's awarded for partial completion of doctoral program. *Degree requirements:* For doctorate, comprehensive exam, thesis/dissertation. *Entrance requirements:* For doctorate, GRE General Test. Additional exam requirements/recommendations for international students: required—TOEFL. *Expenses:* Tuition, state resident: full-time $7085; part-time $272.51 per credit hour. Tuition, nonresident: full-time $24,937; part-time $959.12 per credit hour. *Required fees:* $880.52; $880.52 per semester. Tuition and fees vary according to degree level, program and student level.

**The University of Western Ontario,** Schulich School of Medicine and Dentistry, Department of Anatomy and Cell Biology, London, ON N6A 3K7, Canada. Offers anatomy and cell biology (M Sc, PhD); clinical anatomy (M Sc). *Degree requirements:* For master's, thesis; for doctorate, comprehensive exam, thesis/dissertation. *Entrance requirements:* For master's, honors degree or equivalent in biological sciences; for doctorate, master's degree. Additional exam requirements/recommendations for international students: required—TOEFL.

**Université Laval,** Faculty of Medicine, Post-Professional Programs in Medical Studies, Québec, QC G1K 7P4, Canada. Offers anatomy–pathology (DESS); anesthesiology (DESS); cardiology (DESS); care of older people (Diploma); clinical research (DESS); community health (DESS); dermatology (DESS); diagnostic radiology (DESS); emergency medicine (Diploma); family medicine (DESS); general surgery (DESS); geriatrics (DESS); hematology (DESS); internal medicine (DESS); maternal and fetal medicine (Diploma); medical biochemistry (DESS); medical microbiology and infectious diseases (DESS); medical oncology (DESS); nephrology (DESS); neurology (DESS); neurosurgery (DESS); obstetrics and gynecology (DESS); ophthalmology (DESS); orthopedic surgery (DESS); oto-rhino-laryngology (DESS); palliative medicine (Diploma); pediatrics (DESS); plastic surgery (DESS); psychiatry (DESS); pulmonary medicine (DESS); radiology–oncology (DESS); thoracic surgery (DESS); urology (DESS). *Degree requirements:* For other advanced degree, comprehensive exam. *Entrance requirements:* For degree, knowledge of French. Electronic applications accepted.

**Virginia Commonwealth University,** Medical College of Virginia-Professional Programs, School of Medicine, Graduate Programs in Medicine, Department of Anatomy and Neurobiology, Richmond, VA 23284-9005. Offers MS. *Degree requirements:* For master's, thesis. *Entrance requirements:* For master's, GRE, MCAT or DAT. Electronic applications accepted.

**Wake Forest University,** School of Medicine and Graduate School of Arts and Sciences, Graduate Programs in Medicine, Department of Neurobiology and Anatomy, Winston-Salem, NC 27109. Offers PhD, MD/PhD. *Degree requirements:* For doctorate, thesis/dissertation. *Entrance requirements:* For doctorate, GRE General Test. Additional exam requirements/recommendations for international students: required—TOEFL. Electronic applications accepted.

**Wright State University,** Graduate School, College of Science and Mathematics, Department of Neuroscience, Cell Biology, and Physiology, Dayton, OH 45435. Offers anatomy (MS); physiology and neuroscience (MS). *Degree requirements:* For master's, thesis optional. *Entrance requirements:* Additional exam requirements/recommendations for international students: required—TOEFL.

**Youngstown State University,** College of Graduate Studies, College of Science, Technology, Engineering and Mathematics, Department of Biological Sciences, Youngstown, OH 44555-0001. Offers environmental biology (MS); molecular biology, microbiology, and genetics (MS); physiology and anatomy (MS). *Program availability:* Part-time. *Degree requirements:* For master's, comprehensive exam, thesis, oral review. *Entrance requirements:* For master's, GRE General Test, minimum GPA of 2.7. Additional exam requirements/recommendations for international students: required—TOEFL.

# Section 3
# Biochemistry

This section contains a directory of institutions offering graduate work in biochemistry, followed by an in-depth entry submitted by an institution that chose to prepare a detailed program description. Additional information about programs listed in the directory but not augmented by an in-depth entry may be obtained by writing directly to the dean of a graduate school or chair of a department at the address given in the directory.

For programs offering related work, see also in this book *Allied Health; Biological and Biomedical Sciences; Biophysics; Botany and Plant Biology; Cell, Molecular, and Structural Biology; Genetics, Developmental Biology, and Reproductive Biology; Microbiological Sciences; Neuroscience and Neurobiology; Nutrition; Pathology and Pathobiology; Pharmacology and Toxicology; Pharmacy and Pharmaceutical Sciences;* and *Physiology.* In the other guides in this series:

**Graduate Programs in the Physical Sciences, Mathematics, Agricultural Sciences, the Environment & Natural Resources**

See *Agricultural and Food Sciences, Chemistry,* and *Physics*

**Graduate Programs in Engineering & Applied Sciences**

See *Agricultural Engineering and Bioengineering, Biomedical Engineering and Biotechnology, Chemical Engineering,* and *Materials Sciences and Engineering*

## CONTENTS

**Program Directory**

# Biochemistry

**Albert Einstein College of Medicine,** Graduate Programs in the Biomedical Sciences, Department of Biochemistry, Bronx, NY 10461. Offers PhD, MD/PhD. *Degree requirements:* For doctorate, thesis/dissertation. *Entrance requirements:* For doctorate, GRE General Test. Additional exam requirements/recommendations for international students: required—TOEFL.

**Arizona State University at Tempe,** College of Liberal Arts and Sciences, Department of Chemistry and Biochemistry, Tempe, AZ 85287-1604. Offers biochemistry (MS, PhD); chemistry (MS, PhD); nanoscience (PSM). Terminal master's awarded for partial completion of doctoral program. *Degree requirements:* For master's, thesis, interactive Program of Study (iPOS) submitted before completing 50 percent of required credit hours; for doctorate, comprehensive exam, thesis/dissertation, interactive Program of Study (iPOS) submitted before completing 50 percent of required credit hours. *Entrance requirements:* For master's and doctorate, GRE, minimum GPA of 3.0 or equivalent in last 2 years of work leading to bachelor's degree. Additional exam requirements/ recommendations for international students: required—TOEFL, IELTS, or PTE. Electronic applications accepted.

**Auburn University,** Graduate School, College of Sciences and Mathematics, Department of Chemistry and Biochemistry, Auburn, AL 36849. Offers analytical chemistry (MS, PhD); biochemistry (MS, PhD); inorganic chemistry (MS); organic chemistry (PhD); physical chemistry (MS, PhD). *Program availability:* Part-time. *Faculty:* 31 full-time (7 women), 4 part-time/adjunct (2 women). *Students:* 60 full-time (27 women), 34 part-time (14 women); includes 9 minority (5 Black or African American, non-Hispanic/Latino; 2 Asian, non-Hispanic/Latino; 1 Hispanic/Latino; 1 Two or more races, non-Hispanic/Latino), 58 international. Average age 29. 40 applicants, 48% accepted, 17 enrolled. In 2019, 1 master's, 14 doctorates awarded. *Degree requirements:* For master's, thesis (for some programs); for doctorate, thesis/ dissertation, oral and written exams. *Entrance requirements:* For master's and doctorate, GRE General Test. Additional exam requirements/recommendations for international students: recommended—TOEFL (minimum score 550 paper-based; 79 iBT). *Application deadline:* Applications are processed on a rolling basis. Application fee: $60 ($70 for international students). Electronic applications accepted. *Expenses: Tuition, area resident:* Full-time $9828; part-time $546 per credit hour. Tuition, state resident: full-time $9828; part-time $546 per credit hour. Tuition, nonresident: full-time $29,484; part-time $1638 per credit hour. *International tuition:* $29,744 full-time. Tuition and fees vary according to course load, program and reciprocity agreements. *Financial support:* In 2019–20, 23 fellowships with tuition reimbursements, 32 research assistantships with tuition reimbursements (averaging $26,183 per year), 57 teaching assistantships with tuition reimbursements (averaging $25,854 per year) were awarded. Financial award application deadline: 3/15; financial award applicants required to submit FAFSA. *Unit head:* Dr. Doug Goodwin, Chair, 334-844-69992, Fax: 334-844-6959, E-mail: goodwdc@auburn.edu. *Application contact:* Dr. George Flowers, Dean of the Graduate School, 334-844-2125.
Website: http://www.auburn.edu/cosam/departments/chemistry/

**Augusta University,** Program in Biochemistry and Cancer Biology, Augusta, GA 30912. Offers PhD. *Degree requirements:* For doctorate, comprehensive exam, thesis/ dissertation. *Entrance requirements:* For doctorate, GRE General Test. Additional exam requirements/recommendations for international students: required—TOEFL (minimum score 550 paper-based; 79 iBT). Electronic applications accepted.

**Baylor College of Medicine,** Graduate School of Biomedical Sciences, Department of Biochemistry and Molecular Biology, Houston, TX 77030-3498. Offers PhD, MD/PhD. *Degree requirements:* For doctorate, thesis/dissertation, public defense. *Entrance requirements:* For doctorate, GRE General Test, GRE Subject Test (strongly recommended), minimum GPA of 3.0. Additional exam requirements/recommendations for international students: required—TOEFL. Electronic applications accepted.

**Baylor College of Medicine,** Graduate School of Biomedical Sciences, Interdepartmental Program in Cell and Molecular Biology, Houston, TX 77030-3498. Offers biochemistry (PhD); cell and molecular biology (PhD); genetics (PhD); human genetics (PhD); immunology (PhD); microbiology (PhD); virology (PhD); MD/PhD. *Degree requirements:* For doctorate, thesis/dissertation, public defense. *Entrance requirements:* For doctorate, GRE General Test, GRE Subject Test (strongly recommended), minimum GPA of 3.0. Additional exam requirements/recommendations for international students: required—TOEFL. Electronic applications accepted.

**Baylor University,** Graduate School, College of Arts and Sciences, Department of Chemistry and Biochemistry, Waco, TX 76798. Offers biochemistry (MS, PhD); chemistry (MS, PhD). Terminal master's awarded for partial completion of doctoral program. *Degree requirements:* For master's, thesis or alternative; for doctorate, comprehensive exam, thesis/dissertation. *Entrance requirements:* For doctorate, GRE General Test, transcripts, 3 letters of recommendation, personal statement. Additional exam requirements/recommendations for international students: required—TOEFL (minimum score 90 iBT). Electronic applications accepted. *Expenses:* Contact institution.

**Boston College,** Morrissey Graduate School of Arts and Sciences, Department of Chemistry, Chestnut Hill, MA 02467-3800. Offers biochemistry (PhD); inorganic chemistry (PhD); organic chemistry (PhD); physical chemistry (PhD); science education (MST). *Degree requirements:* For doctorate, thesis/dissertation, qualifying exam. *Entrance requirements:* For doctorate, GRE General Test, GRE Subject Test. Additional exam requirements/recommendations for international students: required—TOEFL (minimum score 600 paper-based; 100 iBT), IELTS (minimum score 8). Electronic applications accepted.

**Boston University,** Graduate School of Arts and Sciences, Molecular Biology, Cell Biology, and Biochemistry Program (MCBB), Boston, MA 02215. Offers MA, PhD. *Students:* 34 full-time (19 women), 2 part-time (both women); includes 7 minority (3 Black or African American, non-Hispanic/Latino; 3 Hispanic/Latino; 1 Two or more races, non-Hispanic/Latino), 9 international. Average age 27. 220 applicants, 9% accepted, 5 enrolled. In 2019, 10 master's, 4 doctorates awarded. Terminal master's awarded for partial completion of doctoral program. *Degree requirements:* For master's, thesis (for some programs); for doctorate, comprehensive exam, thesis/dissertation, teaching requirement. *Entrance requirements:* For master's and doctorate, 3 letters of recommendation, transcripts, personal statement. Additional exam requirements/ recommendations for international students: required—TOEFL (minimum score 550 paper-based; 84 iBT). *Application deadline:* For fall admission, 12/10 for domestic and international students. Application fee: $95. Electronic applications accepted. *Financial support:* In 2019–20, 31 students received support, including 3 fellowships with full tuition reimbursements available (averaging $23,340 per year), 5 research assistantships with full tuition reimbursements available (averaging $23,340 per year), 5 teaching assistantships with full tuition reimbursements available (averaging $23,440

per year); Federal Work-Study, scholarships/grants, traineeships, and health care benefits also available. Financial award application deadline: 12/10; financial award applicants required to submit FAFSA. *Unit head:* Thomas Gilmore, Director, 617-353-2432, Fax: 617-353-6340, E-mail: gilmore@bu.edu. *Application contact:* Christina Honeycutt, Academic Administrator, 617-353-2432, Fax: 617-353-6340, E-mail: cjhoney@bu.edu.
Website: http://www.bu.edu/mcbb/

**Bradley University,** The Graduate School, College of Liberal Arts and Sciences, Mund-Lagowski Department of Chemistry and Biochemistry, Peoria, IL 61625-0002. Offers biochemistry (MS); chemistry (MS). *Program availability:* Part-time, evening/weekend. *Faculty:* 10 full-time (2 women). *Students:* 5 full-time (2 women), 6 part-time (3 women); includes 4 minority (2 Asian, non-Hispanic/Latino; 2 Hispanic/Latino), 2 international. Average age 25. 5 applicants, 60% accepted, 2 enrolled. In 2019, 4 master's awarded. *Degree requirements:* For master's, comprehensive exam, thesis. *Entrance requirements:* Additional exam requirements/recommendations for international students: required—TOEFL (minimum score 550 paper-based; 79 iBT), IELTS (minimum score 6.5), PTE (minimum score 58). *Application deadline:* For fall admission, 5/15 priority date for domestic students; for spring admission, 10/15 priority date for domestic students. Applications are processed on a rolling basis. Application fee: $40 ($50 for international students). Electronic applications accepted. *Expenses:* Tuition: Part-time $930 per credit hour. *Financial support:* In 2019–20, 1 student received support, including 1 research assistantship with partial tuition reimbursement available (averaging $4,185 per year); scholarships/grants, tuition waivers (partial), and unspecified assistantships also available. Support available to part-time students. Financial award application deadline: 4/1. *Unit head:* Michelle Fry, Chairperson, 309-677-3744, E-mail: mfry@bradley.edu. *Application contact:* Rachel Webb, Director of On-Campus Graduate Admissions and International Student and Scholar Services, 309-677-2375, E-mail: rkwebb@bradley.edu.
Website: http://www.bradley.edu/academic/departments/chemistry/

**Brandeis University,** Graduate School of Arts and Sciences, Department of Biochemistry, Waltham, MA 02454. Offers biochemistry and biophysics (MS, PhD); biochemistry and biophysics and quantitative biology (PhD). *Program availability:* Part-time. *Faculty:* 11 full-time (6 women). *Students:* 39 full-time (19 women); includes 12 minority (5 Asian, non-Hispanic/Latino; 4 Hispanic/Latino; 3 Two or more races, non-Hispanic/Latino), 9 international. Average age 26. 72 applicants, 31% accepted, 8 enrolled. In 2019, 6 doctorates awarded. Terminal master's awarded for partial completion of doctoral program. *Degree requirements:* For master's, thesis; for doctorate, comprehensive exam, thesis/dissertation. *Entrance requirements:* For master's, transcripts, letters of recommendation, resume, statement of purpose; for doctorate, transcripts, letters of recommendation, resume, statement of purpose, program questions. Additional exam requirements/recommendations for international students: required—TOEFL, IELTS, PTE. *Application deadline:* For fall admission, 12/1 priority date for domestic students. Applications are processed on a rolling basis. Application fee: $75. Electronic applications accepted. *Financial support:* In 2019–20, 10 teaching assistantships (averaging $3,550 per year) were awarded; fellowships, research assistantships, scholarships/grants, and health care benefits also available. *Unit head:* Dr. Dagmar Ringe, Director of Graduate Studies, 781-736-4902, E-mail: ringe@brandeis.edu. *Application contact:* Maryanna Aldrich, Administrator, 781-736-2352, E-mail: scigradoffice@brandeis.edu.
Website: http://www.brandeis.edu/gsas/programs/bio.html

**Brigham Young University,** Graduate Studies, College of Physical and Mathematical Sciences, Department of Chemistry and Biochemistry, Provo, UT 84602. Offers biochemistry (MS, PhD); chemistry (MS, PhD). *Faculty:* 35 full-time (3 women). *Students:* 115 full-time (40 women); includes 57 minority (5 Black or African American, non-Hispanic/Latino; 37 Asian, non-Hispanic/Latino; 4 Hispanic/Latino; 11 Two or more races, non-Hispanic/Latino), 50 international. Average age 30. 63 applicants, 54% accepted, 22 enrolled. In 2019, 4 master's, 22 doctorates awarded. *Degree requirements:* For master's, thesis, proficiency exams; for doctorate, thesis/dissertation, proficiency exams. *Entrance requirements:* For master's and doctorate, GRE General Test, minimum GPA of 3.0. Additional exam requirements/recommendations for international students: required—TOEFL (minimum score 580 paper-based; 85 iBT), IELTS (minimum score 7), E3PT. *Application deadline:* For fall admission, 1/1 priority date for domestic students, 1/5 priority date for international students. Application fee: $50. *Financial support:* In 2019–20, 107 students received support, including 18 fellowships with full tuition reimbursements available (averaging $25,000 per year), 40 research assistantships with full tuition reimbursements available (averaging $25,000 per year), 49 teaching assistantships with full tuition reimbursements available (averaging $25,000 per year); scholarships/grants and supplementary awards also available. Financial award application deadline: 1/5. *Unit head:* Dr. David V. Dearden, Chair, 801-422-2355, Fax: 801-422-0153, E-mail: david_dearden@byu.edu. *Application contact:* Amy M. Royer, Graduate Program Administrator, 801-422-0249, Fax: 801-422-4855, E-mail: amy@chem.byu.edu.
Website: http://www.chem.byu.edu/

**Brown University,** Graduate School, Division of Biology and Medicine, Department of Molecular Biology, Cell Biology, and Biochemistry, Providence, RI 02912. Offers MA, PhD. *Program availability:* Part-time. Terminal master's awarded for partial completion of doctoral program. *Degree requirements:* For master's, thesis (for some programs); for doctorate, one foreign language, thesis/dissertation, preliminary exam. *Entrance requirements:* For master's and doctorate, GRE General Test, GRE Subject Test. Additional exam requirements/recommendations for international students: required—TOEFL. Electronic applications accepted.

**California Institute of Technology,** Division of Biology and Biological Engineering and Division of Chemistry and Chemical Engineering, Biochemistry and Molecular Biophysics Graduate Option, Pasadena, CA 91125-0001. Offers PhD. *Degree requirements:* For doctorate, thesis/dissertation, qualifying exam. *Entrance requirements:* For doctorate, GRE General Test. Additional exam requirements/recommendations for international students: required—TOEFL. Electronic applications accepted.

**California Institute of Technology,** Division of Chemistry and Chemical Engineering, Pasadena, CA 91125-0001. Offers biochemistry and molecular biophysics (MS, PhD); chemical engineering (MS, PhD); chemistry (MS, PhD). Terminal master's awarded for partial completion of doctoral program. *Degree requirements:* For master's, thesis; for doctorate, thesis/dissertation. *Entrance requirements:* For doctorate, GRE, BS. Additional exam requirements/recommendations for international students: required—TOEFL; recommended—IELTS, TWE. Electronic applications accepted. *Expenses:* Contact institution.

**California Polytechnic State University, San Luis Obispo,** College of Science and Mathematics, Department of Chemistry and Biochemistry, San Luis Obispo, CA 93407. Offers polymers and coating science (MS). *Program availability:* Part-time. *Faculty:* 3 full-time (0 women). *Students:* 5 full-time (3 women), 5 part-time (0 women); includes 7 minority (2 Asian, non-Hispanic/Latino; 2 Hispanic/Latino; 3 Two or more races, non-Hispanic/Latino), 1 international. Average age 23. 10 applicants, 70% accepted, 4 enrolled. In 2019, 5 master's awarded. *Entrance requirements:* For master's, GRE. Additional exam requirements/recommendations for international students: required—TOEFL (minimum score 80 iBT). *Application deadline:* For fall admission, 4/1 for domestic and international students; for spring admission, 2/1 for domestic students. Applications are processed on a rolling basis. Application fee: $55. Electronic applications accepted. *Expenses:* Tuition, state resident: full-time $7176; part-time $4164 per year. Tuition, nonresident: full-time $18,690; part-time $8916 per year. *Required fees:* $4206; $3185 per unit. $1061 per term. *Financial support:* Fellowships, research assistantships, career-related internships or fieldwork, Federal Work-Study, and scholarships/grants available. Support available to part-time students. Financial award application deadline: 3/2; financial award applicants required to submit FAFSA. *Unit head:* Dr. Raymond Fernando, Graduate Coordinator, 805-756-2395, E-mail: rhfernan@calpoly.edu. *Application contact:* Dr. Raymond Fernando, Graduate Coordinator, 805-756-2395, E-mail: rhfernan@calpoly.edu. Website: http://www.chemistry.calpoly.edu/

**California State University, East Bay,** Office of Graduate Studies, College of Science, Department of Chemistry and Biochemistry, Hayward, CA 94542-3000. Offers biochemistry (MS). *Degree requirements:* For master's, comprehensive exam or thesis. *Entrance requirements:* For master's, minimum GPA of 2.6 in field during previous 2 years of course work. Additional exam requirements/recommendations for international students: required—TOEFL (minimum score 550 paper-based). Electronic applications accepted.

**California State University, Long Beach,** Graduate Studies, College of Natural Sciences and Mathematics, Department of Chemistry and Biochemistry, Long Beach, CA 90840. Offers biochemistry (MS); chemistry (MS). *Program availability:* Part-time. *Degree requirements:* For master's, thesis, departmental qualifying exam. Electronic applications accepted.

**California State University, Los Angeles,** Graduate Studies, College of Natural and Social Sciences, Department of Chemistry and Biochemistry, Los Angeles, CA 90032-8530. Offers analytical chemistry (MS). *Program availability:* Part-time, evening/weekend. *Degree requirements:* For master's, one foreign language, comprehensive exam or thesis. *Entrance requirements:* Additional exam requirements/recommendations for international students: required—TOEFL. *Expenses: Tuition,* area resident: Full-time $7176; part-time $4164 per year. Tuition, state resident: full-time $7176; part-time $4164 per year. Tuition, nonresident: full-time $14,304; part-time $8916 per year. *International tuition:* $14,304 full-time. *Required fees:* $1037.76; $1037.76 per unit. Tuition and fees vary according to degree level and program.

**California State University, Northridge,** Graduate Studies, College of Science and Mathematics, Department of Chemistry and Biochemistry, Northridge, CA 91330. Offers biochemistry (MS); chemistry (MS), including chemistry, environmental chemistry. *Degree requirements:* For master's, thesis. *Entrance requirements:* For master's, GRE General Test or minimum GPA of 3.0. Additional exam requirements/recommendations for international students: required—TOEFL. Electronic applications accepted.

**California State University, Sacramento,** College of Natural Sciences and Mathematics, Department of Chemistry, Sacramento, CA 95819. Offers biochemistry (MS); chemistry (MS). *Program availability:* Part-time. *Degree requirements:* For master's, thesis or project; qualifying exam; writing proficiency exam. *Entrance requirements:* For master's, minimum GPA of 2.5 during previous 2 years of course work, BA in chemistry or equivalent. Additional exam requirements/recommendations for international students: required—TOEFL (minimum score 550 paper-based; 80 iBT); recommended—IELTS, TSE. Electronic applications accepted. *Expenses:* Contact institution.

**Carnegie Mellon University,** Mellon College of Science, Department of Biological Sciences, Pittsburgh, PA 15213-3891. Offers biochemistry (PhD); biophysics (PhD); cell and developmental biology (PhD); computational biology (MS, PhD); genetics (PhD); molecular biology (PhD); neuroscience (PhD); structural biology (PhD). *Degree requirements:* For doctorate, comprehensive exam, thesis/dissertation. *Entrance requirements:* For doctorate, GRE General Test, GRE Subject Test, interview. Electronic applications accepted.

**Carnegie Mellon University,** Mellon College of Science, Department of Chemistry, Pittsburgh, PA 15213-3891. Offers atmospheric chemistry (PhD); bioinorganic chemistry (PhD); bioorganic chemistry and chemical biology (PhD); biophysical chemistry (PhD); catalysis (PhD); green and environmental chemistry (PhD); materials and nanoscience (PhD); renewable energy (PhD); sensors, probes, and imaging (PhD); spectroscopy and single molecule analysis (PhD); theoretical and computational chemistry (PhD). *Program availability:* Part-time. Terminal master's awarded for partial completion of doctoral program. *Degree requirements:* For doctorate, thesis/dissertation, departmental qualifying and oral exams, teaching experience. *Entrance requirements:* For doctorate, GRE General Test, GRE Subject Test. Additional exam requirements/recommendations for international students: required—TOEFL. Electronic applications accepted.

**Case Western Reserve University,** School of Medicine and School of Graduate Studies, Graduate Programs in Medicine, Department of Biochemistry, Cleveland, OH 44106. Offers biochemistry (MS, PhD); JD/MS. *Program availability:* Part-time. Terminal master's awarded for partial completion of doctoral program. *Degree requirements:* For master's, thesis (for some programs); for doctorate, thesis/dissertation. *Entrance requirements:* For master's and doctorate, GRE General Test. Additional exam requirements/recommendations for international students: required—TOEFL. Electronic applications accepted.

**City College of the City University of New York,** Graduate School, Division of Science, Department of Chemistry, Program in Biochemistry, New York, NY 10031-9198. Offers MS, PhD. Terminal master's awarded for partial completion of doctoral program. *Degree requirements:* For doctorate, one foreign language, thesis/dissertation. *Entrance requirements:* For doctorate, GRE. Additional exam requirements/recommendations for international students: required—TOEFL (minimum score 550 paper-based; 79 iBT). Electronic applications accepted.

**Clark University,** Graduate School, Gustav H. Carlson School of Chemistry, Worcester, MA 01610-1477. Offers biochemistry (PhD); chemistry (PhD). *Faculty:* 9 full-time (1 woman). *Students:* 11 full-time (4 women); includes 1 minority (Hispanic/Latino), 8 international. Average age 27. 75 applicants, 23% accepted, 10 enrolled. Terminal master's awarded for partial completion of doctoral program. *Degree requirements:* For doctorate, one foreign language, thesis/dissertation. *Entrance requirements:* For doctorate, GRE General Test. Additional exam requirements/recommendations for international students: required—TOEFL (minimum score 575 paper-based; 90 iBT), IELTS (minimum score 6.5). *Application deadline:* For fall admission, 1/15 priority date for domestic students. Application fee: $75. Electronic applications accepted. *Expenses: Tuition:* Full-time $47,650; part-time $4765 per course. *Required fees:* $1850. *Financial*

*support:* Fellowships, research assistantships, teaching assistantships, and tuition waivers (full) available. *Unit head:* Dr. Shuanghong Huo, Chair, 508-793-7533, E-mail: shuo@clarku.edu. *Application contact:* Rene Baril, Managerial Secretary, 508-793-7130, Fax: 528-793-7117, E-mail: mbaril@clarku.edu. Website: http://www.clarku.edu/departments/chemistry/

**Colorado State University,** College of Natural Sciences, Department of Biochemistry and Molecular Biology, Fort Collins, CO 80523-1870. Offers MS, PhD. Terminal master's awarded for partial completion of doctoral program. *Degree requirements:* For master's, comprehensive exam, thesis optional; for doctorate, comprehensive exam, thesis/dissertation, preliminary exam. *Entrance requirements:* For master's, minimum GPA of 3.0, personal statement; for doctorate, GRE, BS/BA with minimum GPA of 3.0, statement of purpose, research interests. Additional exam requirements/recommendations for international students: required—TOEFL (minimum score 550 paper-based; 50 iBT). Electronic applications accepted. *Expenses:* Tuition, state resident: full-time $10,520; part-time $5844 per credit hour. Tuition, nonresident: full-time $25,791; part-time $14,328 per credit hour. *International tuition:* $25,791 full-time. *Required fees:* $2512.80. Part-time tuition and fees vary according to course level, course load, degree level, program and student level.

**Colorado State University-Pueblo,** College of Science and Mathematics, Pueblo, CO 81001-4901. Offers applied natural science (MS), including biochemistry, biology, chemistry. *Program availability:* Part-time, evening/weekend. *Degree requirements:* For master's, comprehensive exam (for some programs), thesis (for some programs), internship report (if non-thesis). *Entrance requirements:* For master's, GRE General Test (minimum score 1000), 2 letters of reference, minimum GPA of 3.0. Additional exam requirements/recommendations for international students: required—TOEFL (minimum score 500 paper-based), IELTS (minimum score 5).

**Columbia University,** College of Physicians and Surgeons, Department of Biochemistry and Molecular Biophysics, New York, NY 10032. Offers biochemistry and molecular biophysics (M Phil) (PhD); biophysics (PhD); MD/PhD. *Degree requirements:* For doctorate, one foreign language, thesis/dissertation. *Entrance requirements:* For master's and doctorate, GRE General Test. Additional exam requirements/recommendations for international students: required—TOEFL. *Expenses: Tuition:* Full-time $47,600; part-time $1880 per credit. One-time fee: $105.

**Cornell University,** Graduate School, Graduate Fields of Agriculture and Life Sciences, Field of Biochemistry, Molecular and Cell Biology, Ithaca, NY 14853. Offers biochemistry (PhD); biophysics (PhD); cell biology (PhD); molecular biology (PhD). *Degree requirements:* For doctorate, comprehensive exam, thesis/dissertation, 2 semesters of teaching experience. *Entrance requirements:* For doctorate, GRE General Test, GRE Subject Test (biology, chemistry, physics, biochemistry, cell and molecular biology), 3 letters of recommendation. Additional exam requirements/recommendations for international students: required—TOEFL (minimum score 600 paper-based; 77 iBT). Electronic applications accepted.

**Cornell University,** Graduate School, Graduate Fields of Agriculture and Life Sciences, Field of Plant Biology, Ithaca, NY 14853. Offers cytology (MS, PhD); paleobotany (MS, PhD); plant biochemistry (MS, PhD); plant cell biology (MS, PhD); plant ecology (MS, PhD); plant molecular biology (MS, PhD); plant morphology, anatomy and biomechanics (MS, PhD); plant physiology (MS, PhD); systematic botany (MS, PhD). *Degree requirements:* For doctorate, comprehensive exam, thesis/dissertation. *Entrance requirements:* For doctorate, GRE General Test, GRE Subject Test in biology (recommended), 3 letters of recommendation. Additional exam requirements/recommendations for international students: required—TOEFL (minimum score 610 paper-based; 77 iBT). Electronic applications accepted.

**Cornell University,** Graduate School, Graduate Fields of Arts and Sciences, Field of Chemistry and Chemical Biology, Ithaca, NY 14853. Offers analytical chemistry (PhD); bio-organic chemistry (PhD); biophysical chemistry (PhD); chemical biology (PhD); chemical physics (PhD); inorganic chemistry (PhD); materials chemistry (PhD); organic chemistry (PhD); organometallic chemistry (PhD); physical chemistry (PhD); polymer chemistry (PhD); theoretical chemistry (PhD). *Degree requirements:* For doctorate, comprehensive exam, thesis/dissertation. *Entrance requirements:* For doctorate, GRE General Test, GRE Subject Test (chemistry), 3 letters of recommendation. Additional exam requirements/recommendations for international students: required—TOEFL (minimum score 600 paper-based; 77 iBT). Electronic applications accepted.

**Dalhousie University,** Faculty of Medicine, Department of Biochemistry and Molecular Biology, Halifax, NS B3H 4R2, Canada. Offers M Sc, PhD. *Degree requirements:* For master's, thesis, demonstrating/teaching experience, oral defense, seminar; for doctorate, comprehensive exam, thesis/dissertation, demonstrating/teaching experience, oral defense, seminar, 2 short grant proposals in year 3. *Entrance requirements:* For master's and doctorate, GRE. Additional exam requirements/recommendations for international students: required—1 of 5 approved tests: TOEFL, IELTS, CANTEST, CAEL, Michigan English Language Assessment Battery. Electronic applications accepted. *Expenses:* Contact institution.

**Dartmouth College,** Guarini School of Graduate and Advanced Studies, Department of Chemistry, Hanover, NH 03755. Offers biophysical chemistry (MS); chemistry (PhD). *Entrance requirements:* For doctorate, GRE General Test, GRE Subject Test. Additional exam requirements/recommendations for international students: required—TOEFL. Electronic applications accepted.

**Dartmouth College,** Guarini School of Graduate and Advanced Studies, Graduate Programs in Biological Sciences, Graduate Program in Molecular and Cellular Biology, Department of Biochemistry, Hanover, NH 03755. Offers PhD, MBA/PhD, MD/PhD. *Entrance requirements:* For doctorate, GRE General Test, letters of recommendation, minimum GPA of 3.0. Electronic applications accepted.

**Drexel University,** College of Medicine, Biomedical Graduate Programs, Program in Biochemistry, Philadelphia, PA 19104-2875. Offers MS, PhD, MD/PhD. *Program availability:* Part-time. Terminal master's awarded for partial completion of doctoral program. *Degree requirements:* For master's, comprehensive exam, thesis; for doctorate, thesis/dissertation, qualifying exam. *Entrance requirements:* For master's, GRE General Test, minimum GPA of 2.75; for doctorate, GRE General Test, minimum GPA of 3.0. Additional exam requirements/recommendations for international students: required—TOEFL. Electronic applications accepted.

**Duke University,** Graduate School, Department of Biochemistry, Durham, NC 27710. Offers crystallography of macromolecules (PhD); enzyme mechanisms (PhD); lipid biochemistry (PhD); membrane structure and function (PhD); molecular genetics (PhD); neurochemistry (PhD); nucleic acid structure and function (PhD); protein structure and function (PhD). *Degree requirements:* For doctorate, thesis/dissertation. *Entrance requirements:* For doctorate, GRE General Test, GRE Subject Test (recommended). Additional exam requirements/recommendations for international students: required—TOEFL (minimum score 577 paper-based; 90 iBT) or IELTS (minimum score 7). Electronic applications accepted.

**East Carolina University,** Brody School of Medicine, Office of Research and Graduate Studies, Greenville, NC 27858-4353. Offers anatomy and cell biology (PhD); biochemistry and molecular biology (PhD); biomedical science (MS); microbiology and

immunology (PhD); pharmacology and toxicology (PhD); physiology (PhD). *Students:* 102 full-time (44 women), 1 part-time (0 women); includes 16 minority (4 Black or African American, non-Hispanic/Latino; 7 Asian, non-Hispanic/Latino; 4 Hispanic/Latino; 1 Two or more races, non-Hispanic/Latino), 13 international. Average age 28. 83 applicants, 40% accepted, 20 enrolled. In 2019, 3 master's, 10 doctorates awarded. *Degree requirements:* For doctorate, comprehensive exam, thesis/dissertation. *Entrance requirements:* For doctorate, GRE General Test. Additional exam requirements/recommendations for international students: required—some international applicants may be required to demonstrate English proficiency via the TOEFL, IELTS, or PTE exam.; recommended—TOEFL (minimum score 78 iBT), IELTS (minimum score 6.5), TSE (minimum score 65). *Application deadline:* For fall admission, 8/15 for domestic students; for spring admission, 12/20 for domestic students. Applications are processed on a rolling basis. Application fee: $75. Electronic applications accepted. *Expenses: Tuition, area resident:* Full-time $4749; part-time $185 per credit hour. Tuition, state resident: full-time $4749; part-time $185 per credit hour. Tuition, nonresident: full-time $17,898; part-time $864 per credit hour. *International tuition:* $17,898 full-time. *Required fees:* $2787. *Financial support:* Fellowships available. Financial award application deadline: 6/1. *Unit head:* Dr. Russ Price, Associate Dean, 252-744-9346, E-mail: pricest17@ecu.edu. *Application contact:* Dr. Russ Price, Associate Dean, 252-744-9346, E-mail: pricest17@ecu.edu.
Website: http://www.ecu.edu/cs-dhs/bsomresearchgradstudies/index.cfm

**Eastern New Mexico University,** Graduate School, College of Liberal Arts and Sciences, Department of Physical Sciences, Portales, NM 88130. Offers chemistry (MS), including analytical chemistry, biochemistry, organic chemistry, physical chemistry. *Program availability:* Part-time. *Degree requirements:* For master's, thesis optional, seminar, oral and written comprehensive exams. *Entrance requirements:* For master's, ACS placement examination, minimum GPA of 3.0; 2 letters of recommendation; personal statement of career goals; bachelor's degree with minimum of one year each of general, organic, and analytical chemistry. Additional exam requirements/recommendations for international students: required—TOEFL (minimum score 550 paper-based; 79 iBT), IELTS (minimum score 6). Electronic applications accepted. *Expenses: Tuition, area resident:* Full-time $5283; part-time $389.25 per credit hour. Tuition, state resident: full-time $5283; part-time $389.25 per credit hour. Tuition, nonresident: full-time $7007; part-time $389.25 per credit hour. *International tuition:* $7007 full-time. *Required fees:* $36; $35 per semester. One-time fee: $25.

**East Tennessee State University,** Quillen College of Medicine, Department of Biomedical Sciences, Johnson City, TN 37614. Offers anatomy (PhD); biochemistry (PhD); microbiology (PhD); pharmaceutical sciences (PhD); pharmacology (PhD); physiology (PhD); quantitative biosciences (PhD). *Degree requirements:* For doctorate, comprehensive exam, thesis/dissertation, comprehensive qualifying exam; one-year residency. *Entrance requirements:* For doctorate, GRE General Test, GRE Subject Test, 3 letters of recommendation, minimum of 60 credit hours beyond the baccalaureate degree. Additional exam requirements/recommendations for international students: required—TOEFL (minimum score 550 paper-based; 79 iBT). Electronic applications accepted. *Expenses:* Contact institution.

**Emory University,** Laney Graduate School, Division of Biological and Biomedical Sciences, Program in Biochemistry, Cell and Developmental Biology, Atlanta, GA 30322. Offers PhD. *Degree requirements:* For doctorate, comprehensive exam, thesis/dissertation. *Entrance requirements:* For doctorate, GRE General Test, minimum GPA of 3.0 in science course work (recommended). Additional exam requirements/recommendations for international students: required—TOEFL. Electronic applications accepted.

**Florida Institute of Technology,** College of Engineering and Science, Program in Biochemistry, Melbourne, FL 32901-6975. Offers MS. *Program availability:* Part-time. *Degree requirements:* For master's, comprehensive exam (for some programs), thesis optional, Thesis or Non-Thesis option; 30 credit hours. *Entrance requirements:* For master's, GRE General Test and Chemistry Subject test are recommended, undergraduate degree in biochemistry, chemistry, or related area. Additional exam requirements/recommendations for international students: required—TOEFL (minimum score 550 paper-based; 79 iBT). Electronic applications accepted.

**Florida State University,** The Graduate School, College of Arts and Sciences, Department of Chemistry and Biochemistry, Tallahassee, FL 32306-4390. Offers analytical chemistry (MS, PhD); biochemistry (MS, PhD); inorganic chemistry (MS, PhD); materials chemistry (PhD); organic chemistry (MS, PhD); physical chemistry (MS, PhD). Terminal master's awarded for partial completion of doctoral program. *Degree requirements:* For master's, thesis (for some programs); for doctorate, thesis/dissertation. *Entrance requirements:* For master's and doctorate, GRE General Test (minimum scores: 150 verbal, 151 quantitative), minimum upper-division GPA of 3.1 in undergraduate course work. Additional exam requirements/recommendations for international students: required—TOEFL (minimum score 80 iBT). Electronic applications accepted.

**Florida State University,** The Graduate School, College of Arts and Sciences, Department of Scientific Computing, Tallahassee, FL 32306-4120. Offers computational science (MS, PhD), including atmospheric science (PhD), biochemistry (PhD), biological science (PhD), computational science (PhD), geological science (PhD), materials science (PhD), physics (PhD). *Program availability:* Part-time. *Faculty:* 9 full-time (1 woman), 2 part-time/adjunct (1 woman). *Students:* 34 full-time (6 women); includes 5 minority (2 Asian, non-Hispanic/Latino; 2 Hispanic/Latino; 1 Two or more races, non-Hispanic/Latino), 12 international. Average age 25. 65 applicants, 46% accepted, 8 enrolled. In 2019, 4 master's, 8 doctorates awarded. Terminal master's awarded for partial completion of doctoral program. *Degree requirements:* For master's, comprehensive exam (for some programs), thesis (for some programs); for doctorate, comprehensive exam, thesis/dissertation. *Entrance requirements:* For master's and doctorate, GRE General Test, knowledge of at least one object-oriented computing language, 3 letters of recommendation, resume, statement of purpose. Additional exam requirements/recommendations for international students: required—TOEFL (minimum score 550 paper-based; 80 iBT). *Application deadline:* For fall admission, 4/15 for domestic and international students. Applications are processed on a rolling basis. Application fee: $30. Electronic applications accepted. *Financial support:* In 2019–20, 30 students received support, including 6 research assistantships with full tuition reimbursements available (averaging $26,670 per year), 12 teaching assistantships with full tuition reimbursements available (averaging $23,000 per year); scholarships/grants, health care benefits, tuition waivers (full), and unspecified assistantships also available. Financial award application deadline: 1/15. *Unit head:* Dr. Gordon Erlebacher, Chair, 850-644-7024, E-mail: gerlebacher@fsu.edu. *Application contact:* Karey Fowler, Academic Program Specialist, 850-644-0143, Fax: 850-644-0098, E-mail: kgfowler@fsu.edu.
Website: http://www.sc.fsu.edu

**George Mason University,** College of Science, Department of Chemistry and Biochemistry, Fairfax, VA 22030. Offers MS, PhD. *Degree requirements:* For master's, comprehensive exam (for some programs), thesis (for some programs); for doctorate, comprehensive exam, thesis/dissertation, exit seminar. *Entrance requirements:* For doctorate, GRE, BS or MS in chemistry or related discipline. Additional exam requirements/recommendations for international students: required—TOEFL (minimum score 575 paper-based; 88 iBT), IELTS (minimum score 6.5), PTE (minimum score 59). Electronic applications accepted.

**Georgetown University,** Graduate School of Arts and Sciences, Department of Biochemistry and Molecular and Cellular Biology, Washington, DC 20057. Offers MS, PhD. *Degree requirements:* For doctorate, comprehensive exam, thesis/dissertation. *Entrance requirements:* For doctorate, GRE General Test. Additional exam requirements/recommendations for international students: required—TOEFL.

**Georgetown University,** Graduate School of Arts and Sciences, Department of Chemistry, Washington, DC 20057. Offers analytical chemistry (PhD); biochemistry (PhD); computational chemistry (PhD); inorganic chemistry (PhD); materials chemistry (PhD); organic chemistry (PhD); theoretical chemistry (PhD). Terminal master's awarded for partial completion of doctoral program. *Degree requirements:* For doctorate, comprehensive exam, thesis/dissertation. *Entrance requirements:* For doctorate, GRE General Test. Additional exam requirements/recommendations for international students: required—TOEFL.

**The George Washington University,** Columbian College of Arts and Sciences, Institute for Biomedical Sciences, Program in Biochemistry and Systems Biology, Washington, DC 20037. Offers PhD. Terminal master's awarded for partial completion of doctoral program. *Degree requirements:* For doctorate, thesis/dissertation, general exam. *Entrance requirements:* For doctorate, GRE General Test, interview, minimum GPA of 3.0. Additional exam requirements/recommendations for international students: required—TOEFL (minimum score 600 paper-based). Electronic applications accepted.

**Georgia State University,** College of Arts and Sciences, Department of Biology, Program in Molecular Genetics and Biochemistry, Atlanta, GA 30302-3083. Offers bioinformatics (MS); molecular genetics and biochemistry (MS, PhD). *Program availability:* Part-time. Terminal master's awarded for partial completion of doctoral program. *Entrance requirements:* For master's and doctorate, GRE. *Application deadline:* Applications are processed on a rolling basis. Application fee: $50. Electronic applications accepted. *Expenses: Tuition, area resident:* Full-time $7164; part-time $398 per credit hour. Tuition, state resident: full-time $7164; part-time $398 per credit hour. Tuition, nonresident: full-time $22,662; part-time $1259 per credit hour. *International tuition:* $22,662 full-time. *Required fees:* $2128; $312 per credit hour. Tuition and fees vary according to course load and program. *Financial support:* Fellowships and research assistantships available. Financial award application deadline: 12/3. *Unit head:* Dr. Geert de Vries, Chair, 404-413-5658, Fax: 404-413-3518, E-mail: devries@gsu.edu. *Application contact:* Dr. Geert de Vries, Chair, 404-413-5658, Fax: 404-413-3518, E-mail: devries@gsu.edu.
Website: http://biology.gsu.edu/

**Georgia State University,** College of Arts and Sciences, Department of Chemistry, Atlanta, GA 30302-3083. Offers analytical chemistry (MS, PhD); biochemistry (MS, PhD); bioinformatics (MS, PhD); biophysical chemistry (PhD); computational chemistry (MS, PhD); geochemistry (PhD); organic/medicinal chemistry (MS, PhD); physical chemistry (MS). *Program availability:* Part-time. *Faculty:* 24 full-time (5 women), 1 part-time/adjunct (0 women). *Students:* 141 full-time (57 women), 6 part-time (1 woman); includes 36 minority (19 Black or African American, non-Hispanic/Latino; 9 Asian, non-Hispanic/Latino; 5 Hispanic/Latino; 3 Two or more races, non-Hispanic/Latino), 76 international. Average age 29. 111 applicants, 38% accepted, 34 enrolled. In 2019, 28 master's, 24 doctorates awarded. Terminal master's awarded for partial completion of doctoral program. *Degree requirements:* For master's, one foreign language, comprehensive exam (for some programs), thesis (for some programs); for doctorate, one foreign language, comprehensive exam, thesis/dissertation. *Entrance requirements:* For master's and doctorate, GRE. *Application deadline:* For fall admission, 7/1 priority date for domestic and international students; for winter admission, 11/15 priority date for domestic and international students; for spring admission, 4/15 priority date for domestic and international students. Applications are processed on a rolling basis. Application fee: $50. Electronic applications accepted. *Expenses: Tuition, area resident:* Full-time $7164; part-time $398 per credit hour. Tuition, state resident: full-time $7164; part-time $398 per credit hour. Tuition, nonresident: full-time $22,662; part-time $1259 per credit hour. *International tuition:* $22,662 full-time. *Required fees:* $2128; $312 per credit hour. Tuition and fees vary according to course load and program. *Financial support:* Fellowships with full tuition reimbursements, research assistantships with full tuition reimbursements, and teaching assistantships with full tuition reimbursements available. Financial award applicants required to submit FAFSA. *Unit head:* Dr. Donald Hamelberg, Professor; Chair, 404-413-5564, Fax: 404-413-5505, E-mail: dhamelberg@gsu.edu. *Application contact:* Dr. Donald Hamelberg, Professor; Chair, 404-413-5564, Fax: 404-413-5505, E-mail: dhamelberg@gsu.edu.
Website: http://chemistry.gsu.edu/

**The Graduate Center, City University of New York,** Graduate Studies, Program in Biochemistry, New York, NY 10016-4039. Offers PhD. *Degree requirements:* For doctorate, thesis/dissertation, field experience. *Entrance requirements:* For doctorate, GRE General Test. Additional exam requirements/recommendations for international students: required—TOEFL. Electronic applications accepted.

**Harvard University,** Graduate School of Arts and Sciences, Department of Chemistry and Chemical Biology, Cambridge, MA 02138. Offers biochemical chemistry (PhD); inorganic chemistry (PhD); organic chemistry (PhD); physical chemistry (PhD). *Degree requirements:* For doctorate, thesis/dissertation, cumulative exams. *Entrance requirements:* For doctorate, GRE General Test, GRE Subject Test. Additional exam requirements/recommendations for international students: required—TOEFL.

**Harvard University,** Graduate School of Arts and Sciences, Division of Medical Sciences, Boston, MA 02115. Offers biological chemistry and molecular pharmacology (PhD); cell biology (PhD); genetics (PhD); microbiology and molecular genetics (PhD); pathology (PhD), including experimental pathology. *Degree requirements:* For doctorate, thesis/dissertation. *Entrance requirements:* For doctorate, GRE General Test, GRE Subject Test. Additional exam requirements/recommendations for international students: required—TOEFL.

**Howard University,** College of Medicine, Department of Biochemistry and Molecular Biology, Washington, DC 20059-0002. Offers biochemistry and molecular biology (PhD); biotechnology (MS); MD/PhD. *Program availability:* Part-time. *Degree requirements:* For master's, externship; for doctorate, comprehensive exam, thesis/dissertation. *Entrance requirements:* For master's and doctorate, GRE General Test, minimum GPA of 3.0.

**Howard University,** Graduate School, Department of Chemistry, Washington, DC 20059-0002. Offers analytical chemistry (MS, PhD); atmospheric (MS, PhD); biochemistry (MS, PhD); environmental (MS, PhD); inorganic chemistry (MS, PhD); organic chemistry (MS, PhD); physical chemistry (MS, PhD). Terminal master's awarded for partial completion of doctoral program. *Degree requirements:* For master's, comprehensive exam, thesis, teaching experience; for doctorate, comprehensive exam, thesis/dissertation, teaching experience. *Entrance requirements:* For master's, GRE General Test, minimum GPA of 2.7; for doctorate, GRE General Test, minimum GPA of 3.0. Additional exam requirements/recommendations for international students: required—TOEFL. Electronic applications accepted.

**Hunter College of the City University of New York,** Graduate School, School of Arts and Sciences, Department of Chemistry, Program in Biochemistry, New York, NY 10065-5085. Offers MA, PhD. *Program availability:* Part-time. *Degree requirements:* For master's, comprehensive exam or thesis. *Entrance requirements:* For master's, GRE General Test, 1 year of course work in chemistry, quantitative analysis, organic chemistry, physical chemistry, biology, biochemistry lecture and laboratory. Additional exam requirements/recommendations for international students: required—TOEFL.

**Illinois Institute of Technology,** Graduate College, College of Science, Department of Biology, Chicago, IL 60616. Offers applied life sciences (MS); biochemistry (MS); biology (MS, PhD); cell and molecular biology (MS); microbiology (MS); molecular biochemistry and biophysics (MS, PhD). *Program availability:* Part-time, evening/weekend, online learning. Terminal master's awarded for partial completion of doctoral program. *Degree requirements:* For master's, comprehensive exam, thesis (for some programs); for doctorate, comprehensive exam, thesis/dissertation. *Entrance requirements:* For master's, GRE General Test (minimum score 300 Quantitative and Verbal, 2.5 Analytical Writing), minimum undergraduate GPA of 3.0; for doctorate, GRE General Test (minimum score 310 Quantitative and Verbal, 3.0 Analytical Writing); GRE Subject Test (strongly recommended), minimum undergraduate GPA of 3.0. Additional exam requirements/recommendations for international students: required—TOEFL (minimum score 550 paper-based; 80 iBT). Electronic applications accepted.

**Illinois State University,** Graduate School, College of Arts and Sciences, School of Biological Sciences, Normal, IL 61790. Offers animal behavior (MS); bacteriology (MS); biochemistry (MS); biological sciences (MS); biology (PhD); biophysics (MS); biotechnology (MS); botany (MS, PhD); cell biology (MS); conservation biology (MS); developmental biology (MS); ecology (MS, PhD); entomology (MS); evolutionary biology (MS); genetics (MS, PhD); immunology (MS); microbiology (MS, PhD); molecular biology (MS); molecular genetics (MS); neurobiology (MS); neuroscience (MS); parasitology (MS); physiology (MS, PhD); plant biology (MS); plant molecular biology (MS); plant sciences (MS); structural biology (MS); zoology (MS, PhD). *Program availability:* Part-time. *Faculty:* 26 full-time (6 women), 7 part-time/adjunct (2 women). *Students:* 51 full-time (33 women), 15 part-time (8 women). Average age 27. 71 applicants, 28% accepted, 9 enrolled. In 2019, 14 master's, 3 doctorates awarded. *Degree requirements:* For master's, thesis or alternative; for doctorate, variable foreign language requirement, thesis/dissertation, 2 terms of residency. *Entrance requirements:* For master's, GRE General Test, minimum GPA of 2.6 in last 60 hours of course work; for doctorate, GRE General Test. *Application deadline:* Applications are processed on a rolling basis. Application fee: $50. *Expenses: Tuition, area resident:* Full-time $7956; part-time $9767 per year. Tuition, nonresident: full-time $9233; part-time $17,592 per year. *Required fees:* $1797. *Financial support:* In 2019–20, 20 research assistantships, 41 teaching assistantships were awarded; Federal Work-Study, tuition waivers (full), and unspecified assistantships also available. Financial award application deadline: 4/1. *Unit head:* Dr. Craig Gatto, School Director, 309-438-3087, E-mail: cgatto@IllinoisState.edu. *Application contact:* Dr. Ben Sadd, Assistant Chair for Graduate Studies, 309-438-2651, E-mail: bmsadd@IllinoisState.edu.
Website: http://www.bio.ilstu.edu/

**Indiana University Bloomington,** University Graduate School, College of Arts and Sciences, Biochemistry Graduate Program, Bloomington, IN 47405. Offers PhD. *Degree requirements:* For doctorate, comprehensive exam, thesis/dissertation. *Entrance requirements:* For doctorate, GRE. Additional exam requirements/recommendations for international students: required—TOEFL (minimum score 550 paper-based; 79 iBT), Test of English Proficiency for International Associate Instructor Candidates (TEPAIC).

**Indiana University Bloomington,** University Graduate School, College of Arts and Sciences, Department of Chemistry, Bloomington, IN 47405. Offers analytical chemistry (PhD); chemical biology (PhD); chemistry (MAT); inorganic chemistry (PhD); materials chemistry (PhD); organic chemistry (PhD); physical chemistry (PhD); MSES/MS. Terminal master's awarded for partial completion of doctoral program. *Degree requirements:* For master's, thesis; for doctorate, thesis/dissertation. *Entrance requirements:* For master's and doctorate, GRE General Test, GRE Subject Test. Additional exam requirements/recommendations for international students: required—TOEFL. Electronic applications accepted.

**Indiana University-Purdue University Indianapolis,** Indiana University School of Medicine, Department of Biochemistry and Molecular Biology, Indianapolis, IN 46202. Offers MS, PhD, MD/MS, MD/PhD. Terminal master's awarded for partial completion of doctoral program. *Degree requirements:* For master's, thesis; for doctorate, thesis/dissertation. *Entrance requirements:* For master's and doctorate, GRE General Test, GRE Subject Test (recommended), previous course work in organic chemistry. Additional exam requirements/recommendations for international students: required—TOEFL. Electronic applications accepted.

**Indiana University-Purdue University Indianapolis,** School of Science, Department of Chemistry and Chemical Biology, Indianapolis, IN 46202. Offers MS, PhD, MD/PhD. *Program availability:* Part-time, evening/weekend. Terminal master's awarded for partial completion of doctoral program. *Degree requirements:* For master's, thesis (for some programs); for doctorate, comprehensive exam, thesis/dissertation. *Entrance requirements:* For master's and doctorate, minimum GPA of 3.0. Additional exam requirements/recommendations for international students: required—TOEFL (minimum score 106 iBT). Electronic applications accepted.

**Irell & Manella Graduate School of Biological Sciences,** Graduate Program, Duarte, CA 91010. Offers brain metastatic cancer (PhD); cancer and stem cell metabolism (PhD); cancer biology (PhD); cancer biology and developmental therapeutics (PhD); cell biology (PhD); chemical biology (PhD); chromosomal break repair (PhD); diabetes and pancreatic progenitor cell biology (PhD); DNA repair and cancer biology (PhD); germline epigenetic remodeling and endocrine disruptors (PhD); hematology and hematopoietic cell transplantation (PhD); hematology and immunology (PhD); inflammation and cancer (PhD); micrornas and gene regulation in cardiovascular disease (PhD); mixed chimerism for reversal of autoimmunity (PhD); molecular and cellular biology (PhD); molecular biology and genetics (PhD); nanoparticle mediated twist1 silencing in metastatic cancer (PhD); neuro-oncology and stem cell biology (PhD); neuroscience (PhD); RNA directed therapies for HIV-1 (PhD); small RNA-induced transcriptional gene activation (PhD); stem cell regulation by the microenvironment (PhD); translational oncology and pharmaceutical sciences (PhD); tumor biology (PhD). *Degree requirements:* For doctorate, comprehensive exam, thesis/dissertation, qualifying exams, two advanced courses. *Entrance requirements:* For doctorate, GRE General Test; GRE Subject Test (recommended), 2 years of course work in chemistry (general and organic); 1 year of course work each in biochemistry, general biology, and general physics; 2 semesters of course work in mathematics; significant research laboratory experience. Additional exam requirements/recommendations for international students: required—TOEFL. Electronic applications accepted.

**Johns Hopkins University,** Bloomberg School of Public Health, Department of Biochemistry and Molecular Biology, Baltimore, MD 21205. Offers MHS, Sc M, PhD. *Program availability:* Part-time. *Degree requirements:* For master's, thesis; for doctorate, comprehensive exam, thesis/dissertation, oral and written exams. *Entrance requirements:* For master's, MCAT or GRE, 3 letters of recommendation, curriculum vitae; for doctorate, GRE General Test, 3 letters of recommendation, curriculum vitae. Electronic applications accepted.

**Johns Hopkins University,** National Institutes of Health Sponsored Programs, Baltimore, MD 21218. Offers biology (PhD), including biochemistry, biophysics, cell biology, developmental biology, genetic biology, molecular biology; cell, molecular, and developmental biology and biophysics (PhD). *Degree requirements:* For doctorate, comprehensive exam, thesis/dissertation. *Entrance requirements:* Additional exam requirements/recommendations for international students: required—TOEFL (minimum score 600 paper-based). Electronic applications accepted.

**Johns Hopkins University,** School of Medicine, Graduate Programs in Medicine, Department of Biological Chemistry, Baltimore, MD 21205. Offers PhD. *Degree requirements:* For doctorate, thesis/dissertation. *Entrance requirements:* For doctorate, GRE General Test. Additional exam requirements/recommendations for international students: required—TOEFL. Electronic applications accepted.

**Johns Hopkins University,** School of Medicine, Graduate Programs in Medicine, Program in Biochemistry, Cellular and Molecular Biology, Baltimore, MD 21205. Offers PhD. *Degree requirements:* For doctorate, comprehensive exam, thesis/dissertation. *Entrance requirements:* Additional exam requirements/recommendations for international students: required—TOEFL. Electronic applications accepted.

**Kansas State University,** Graduate School, College of Arts and Sciences, Department of Biochemistry and Molecular Biophysics, Manhattan, KS 66506. Offers MS, PhD. *Degree requirements:* For master's, thesis; for doctorate, thesis/dissertation, preliminary exam. *Entrance requirements:* For master's, GRE General Test, minimum GPA of 3.0 for junior and senior year; for doctorate, GRE General Test, minimum undergraduate GPA of 3.0 or an excellent postgraduate record. Additional exam requirements/recommendations for international students: required—TOEFL (minimum score 550 paper-based; 79 iBT). Electronic applications accepted.

**Kennesaw State University,** College of Science and Mathematics, Program in Chemical Sciences, Kennesaw, GA 30144. Offers biochemistry (MS); chemistry (MS). *Students:* 17 full-time (8 women), 2 part-time (1 woman); includes 8 minority (3 Black or African American, non-Hispanic/Latino; 1 Asian, non-Hispanic/Latino; 2 Hispanic/Latino; 2 Two or more races, non-Hispanic/Latino), 2 international. Average age 26. 25 applicants, 48% accepted, 12 enrolled. In 2019, 5 master's awarded. *Degree requirements:* For master's, thesis. *Entrance requirements:* For master's, GRE. Additional exam requirements/recommendations for international students: required—TOEFL (minimum score 80 iBT), IELTS (minimum score 6.5). *Application deadline:* For fall admission, 4/1 for domestic and international students. Application fee: $60. Electronic applications accepted. *Expenses: Tuition, area resident:* Full-time $7104; part-time $296 per credit hour. Tuition, state resident: full-time $7104; part-time $296 per credit hour. Tuition, nonresident: full-time $25,584; part-time $1066 per credit hour. *International tuition:* $25,584 full-time. *Required fees:* $2006; $1706 per unit. $853 per semester. *Financial support:* Applicants required to submit FAFSA. *Unit head:* Dr. Chris Dockery, Assistant Department Chair, 470-578-2047, E-mail: mscb@kennesaw.edu. *Application contact:* Admissions Counselor, 470-578-4377, Fax: 470-578-9172, E-mail: ksugrad@kennesaw.edu.
Website: http://csm.kennesaw.edu/chemistry-biochemistry/programs/mscb.php

**Laurentian University,** School of Graduate Studies and Research, Programme in Chemistry and Biochemistry, Sudbury, ON P3E 2C6, Canada. Offers analytical chemistry (M Sc); biochemistry (M Sc); environmental chemistry (M Sc); organic chemistry (M Sc); physical/theoretical chemistry (M Sc). *Program availability:* Part-time. *Degree requirements:* For master's, thesis or alternative. *Entrance requirements:* For master's, honors degree with minimum second class.

**Lehigh University,** College of Arts and Sciences, Department of Biological Sciences, Bethlehem, PA 18015. Offers biochemistry (PhD); cell and molecular biology (PhD); integrative biology (PhD); molecular biology (MS). *Program availability:* 100% online, MS MBio Program Only. *Faculty:* 24 full-time (11 women), 1 (woman) part-time/adjunct. *Students:* 36 full-time (18 women), 23 part-time (16 women); includes 12 minority (1 Black or African American, non-Hispanic/Latino; 1 American Indian or Alaska Native, non-Hispanic/Latino; 2 Asian, non-Hispanic/Latino; 7 Hispanic/Latino; 1 Two or more races, non-Hispanic/Latino), 9 international. Average age 28. 53 applicants, 57% accepted, 22 enrolled. In 2019, 9 master's, 7 doctorates awarded. Terminal master's awarded for partial completion of doctoral program. *Degree requirements:* For master's, thesis optional; for doctorate, comprehensive exam, thesis/dissertation. *Entrance requirements:* For master's, bachelor's degree in a life science or chemistry with a GPA of 3.0 or higher, 2 letters of recommendation, official transcripts of previous educational experience; for doctorate, GRE General Test, Three letters of recommendation, curriculum vitae, official transcripts, minimum Bachelor's degree or equivalent, personal statement. Additional exam requirements/recommendations for international students: required—TOEFL (minimum score 85 iBT). *Application deadline:* For fall admission, 7/15 for domestic and international students; for spring admission, 12/1 for domestic and international students; for summer admission, 4/30 for domestic and international students. Application fee: $75. Electronic applications accepted. *Financial support:* In 2019–20, 39 students received support, including 2 fellowships with full tuition reimbursements available (averaging $29,000 per year), 14 research assistantships with full tuition reimbursements available (averaging $29,000 per year), 18 teaching assistantships with full tuition reimbursements available (averaging $29,000 per year); tuition waivers (full and partial) and partially reimbursed health care benefits also available. Financial award application deadline: 1/1. *Unit head:* Dr. Linda Lowe-Krentz, Chairperson, 610-758-5084, Fax: 610-758-4004, E-mail: lij0@lehigh.edu. *Application contact:* Dr. Amber Rice, Graduate Coordinator, 610-758-5509, Fax: 610-758-4004, E-mail: amr511@lehigh.edu.
Website: http://www.lehigh.edu/~inbios/

**Loma Linda University,** School of Medicine, Programs in Biochemistry and Microbiology, Loma Linda, CA 92350. Offers biochemistry (MS, PhD); microbiology (PhD). *Program availability:* Part-time. *Degree requirements:* For master's, thesis or alternative; for doctorate, thesis/dissertation. *Entrance requirements:* For master's and doctorate, GRE General Test. Additional exam requirements/recommendations for international students: required—TOEFL (minimum score 550 paper-based).

**Louisiana State University and Agricultural & Mechanical College,** Graduate School, College of Science, Department of Biological Sciences, Baton Rouge, LA 70803. Offers biochemistry (MS, PhD); biological science (MS, PhD); science (MNS).

**Louisiana State University Health Sciences Center at Shreveport,** Department of Biochemistry and Molecular Biology, Shreveport, LA 71130-3932. Offers MS, PhD, MD/PhD. *Degree requirements:* For master's, thesis; for doctorate, thesis/dissertation. *Entrance requirements:* For master's and doctorate, GRE General Test. Additional exam requirements/recommendations for international students: required—TOEFL (minimum score 100 iBT), IELTS (minimum score 7). Electronic applications accepted. *Expenses:* Contact institution.

**Loyola University Chicago,** Graduate School, Integrated Program in Biomedical Sciences, Maywood, IL 60660. Offers biochemistry and molecular biology (MS, PhD); cell and molecular physiology (MS, PhD); infectious disease and immunology (MS);

*Biochemistry*

integrative cell biology (MS, PhD); microbiology and immunology (MS, PhD); molecular pharmacology and therapeutics (MS, PhD); neuroscience (MS, PhD). *Students:* Average age 25. 773 applicants, 34% accepted, 122 enrolled. In 2019, 46 master's, 12 doctorates awarded. *Degree requirements:* For master's, thesis; for doctorate, comprehensive exam, thesis/dissertation. *Entrance requirements:* For doctorate, GRE. Additional exam requirements/recommendations for international students: required—TOEFL (minimum score 94 iBT), IELTS (minimum score 7.5). *Application deadline:* For fall admission, 2/7 for domestic students. Applications are processed on a rolling basis. Electronic applications accepted. *Expenses:* Contact institution. *Financial support:* In 2019–20, 20 students received support. Schmitt Fellowships and yearly tuition scholarships (averaging $25,032) available. Financial award application deadline: 6/15; financial award applicants required to submit FAFSA. *Unit head:* Dr. Leanne L. Cribbs, Associate Dean, Graduate Education, 708-327-2817, Fax: 708-216-8216, E-mail: lcribbs@luc.edu. *Application contact:* Margarita Quesada, Graduate Program Secretary, 708-216-3532, Fax: 708-216-8216, E-mail: mquesad@luc.edu. Website: http://ssom.luc.edu/graduate_school/degree-programs/ipbsphd/

**Massachusetts Institute of Technology,** School of Science, Department of Biology, Cambridge, MA 02139. Offers biochemistry (PhD); biological oceanography (PhD); biology (PhD); biophysical chemistry and molecular structure (PhD); cell biology (PhD); computational and systems biology (PhD); developmental biology (PhD); genetics (PhD); immunology (PhD); microbiology (PhD); molecular biology (PhD); neurobiology (PhD). *Degree requirements:* For doctorate, comprehensive exam, thesis/dissertation, teaching assistantship during two semesters. *Entrance requirements:* For doctorate, GRE General Test. Additional exam requirements/recommendations for international students: required—TOEFL, IELTS. Electronic applications accepted.

**Massachusetts Institute of Technology,** School of Science, Department of Chemistry, Cambridge, MA 02139. Offers biological chemistry (PhD); inorganic chemistry (PhD); organic chemistry (PhD); physical chemistry (PhD). *Degree requirements:* For doctorate, comprehensive exam, thesis/dissertation, teaching assistantship during two semesters. *Entrance requirements:* For doctorate, GRE General Test. Additional exam requirements/recommendations for international students: required—TOEFL, IELTS. Electronic applications accepted.

**Mayo Clinic Graduate School of Biomedical Sciences,** Program in Biochemistry and Molecular Biology, Rochester, MN 55905. Offers MS, PhD. Terminal master's awarded for partial completion of doctoral program. *Degree requirements:* For master's, thesis; for doctorate, comprehensive exam, thesis/dissertation, oral defense of dissertation, qualifying oral and written exam. *Entrance requirements:* For doctorate, GRE, 1 year of chemistry, biology, calculus, and physics. Additional exam requirements/recommendations for international students: required—TOEFL. Electronic applications accepted.

**McGill University,** Faculty of Graduate and Postdoctoral Studies, Faculty of Medicine, Department of Biochemistry, Montréal, QC H3A 2T5, Canada. Offers M Sc, PhD.

**McGill University,** Faculty of Graduate and Postdoctoral Studies, Faculty of Science, Department of Chemistry, Montréal, QC H3A 2T5, Canada. Offers chemical biology (M Sc, PhD); chemistry (M Sc, PhD).

**McMaster University,** Faculty of Health Sciences, Department of Biochemistry and Biomedical Sciences, Hamilton, ON L8S 4M2, Canada. Offers M Sc, PhD. Terminal master's awarded for partial completion of doctoral program. *Degree requirements:* For master's, thesis; for doctorate, comprehensive exam, thesis/dissertation. *Entrance requirements:* For master's and doctorate, minimum B+ average. Additional exam requirements/recommendations for international students: required—TOEFL (minimum score 550 paper-based).

**Medical College of Wisconsin,** Graduate School, Department of Biochemistry, Milwaukee, WI 53226. Offers PhD, MD/PhD. *Students:* 16 full-time (10 women); includes 1 minority (Asian, non-Hispanic/Latino), 2 international. Average age 27. 2 applicants, 100% accepted, 2 enrolled. In 2019, 4 doctorates awarded. *Degree requirements:* For doctorate, comprehensive exam, thesis/dissertation. *Entrance requirements:* For doctorate, GRE, official transcripts, three letters of recommendation. Additional exam requirements/recommendations for international students: required—TOEFL. *Application deadline:* For fall admission, 1/15 for domestic and international students. Applications are processed on a rolling basis. Application fee: $50. Electronic applications accepted. *Expenses:* $1250 per credit PhD students; $1056 per credit Masters students; $155 per year full time students fees. *Financial support:* In 2019–20, 15 students received support, including fellowships with full tuition reimbursements available (averaging $30,000 per year), research assistantships with full tuition reimbursements available (averaging $30,000 per year); career-related internships or fieldwork and institutionally sponsored loans also available. Financial award application deadline: 2/15; financial award applicants required to submit CSS PROFILE or FAFSA. *Unit head:* Dr. John Corbett, Chair, 414-955-8768, Fax: 414-955-6555, E-mail: jcorbett@mcw.edu. *Application contact:* Recruitment Office, 414-955-4402, Fax: 414-955-6555, E-mail: gradschoolrecruit@mcw.edu. Website: http://www.mcw.edu/biochemistry.htm

**Medical University of South Carolina,** College of Graduate Studies, Department of Biochemistry and Molecular Biology, Charleston, SC 29425. Offers MS, PhD, MD/PhD. Terminal master's awarded for partial completion of doctoral program. *Degree requirements:* For master's, thesis, oral exam/thesis defense; for doctorate, thesis/dissertation, oral and written exams/dissertation defense. *Entrance requirements:* For master's, GRE General Test; for doctorate, GRE General Test, interview, minimum GPA of 3.0. Additional exam requirements/recommendations for international students: required—TOEFL (minimum score 600 paper-based; 100 iBT). Electronic applications accepted.

**Meharry Medical College,** School of Graduate Studies, Program in Biomedical Sciences, Biochemistry and Cancer Biology Emphasis, Nashville, TN 37208-9989. Offers PhD, MD/PhD. *Degree requirements:* For doctorate, comprehensive exam, thesis/dissertation. *Entrance requirements:* For doctorate, GRE. *Application deadline:* For fall admission, 6/1 for domestic students. Applications are processed on a rolling basis. Application fee: $65. *Financial support:* Fellowships available. Financial award application deadline: 4/15. *Unit head:* Dr. Armandla Ramesh, Associate Professor, 615-327-6486, E-mail: aramesh@mmc.edu. *Application contact:* Dr. Armandla Ramesh, Associate Professor, 615-327-6486, E-mail: aramesh@mmc.edu. Website: https://home.mmc.edu/school-of-graduate-studies-research/biochemistry-cancer-biology/

**Memorial University of Newfoundland,** School of Graduate Studies, Department of Biochemistry, St. John's, NL A1C 5S7, Canada. Offers biochemistry (M Sc, PhD); food science (M Sc, PhD). *Program availability:* Part-time. *Degree requirements:* For master's, thesis; for doctorate, comprehensive exam, thesis/dissertation, oral defense of thesis. *Entrance requirements:* For master's, 2nd class degree in related field; for doctorate, M Sc. Electronic applications accepted.

**Miami University,** College of Arts and Science, Department of Chemistry and Biochemistry, Oxford, OH 45056. Offers MS, PhD.

**Michigan State University,** College of Human Medicine and The Graduate School, Graduate Programs in Human Medicine, East Lansing, MI 48824. Offers biochemistry and molecular biology (MS, PhD); epidemiology (MS, PhD); microbiology (MS); microbiology and molecular genetics (PhD); pharmacology and toxicology (MS, PhD); physiology (MS, PhD); public health (MPH). *Entrance requirements:* Additional exam requirements/recommendations for international students: required—TOEFL.

**Michigan State University,** College of Osteopathic Medicine and The Graduate School, Graduate Studies in Osteopathic Medicine, East Lansing, MI 48824. Offers biochemistry and molecular biology (MS, PhD); microbiology (MS); microbiology and molecular genetics (PhD); pharmacology and toxicology (MS, PhD), including integrative pharmacology (MS), pharmacology and toxicology, pharmacology and toxicology-environmental toxicology (PhD); physiology (MS, PhD).

**Michigan State University,** The Graduate School, College of Natural Science, Department of Biochemistry and Molecular Biology, East Lansing, MI 48824. Offers biochemistry and molecular biology (MS, PhD); biochemistry and molecular biology/environmental toxicology (PhD). *Entrance requirements:* Additional exam requirements/recommendations for international students: required—TOEFL. Electronic applications accepted.

**Michigan State University,** The Graduate School, College of Natural Science, MSU-DOE Plant Research Laboratory, East Lansing, MI 48824. Offers biochemistry and molecular biology (PhD); cellular and molecular biology (PhD); crop and soil sciences (PhD); genetics (PhD); microbiology and molecular genetics (PhD); plant biology (PhD); plant physiology (PhD). *Degree requirements:* For doctorate, comprehensive exam, thesis/dissertation, laboratory rotation, defense of dissertation. *Entrance requirements:* For doctorate, GRE General Test, acceptance into one of the affiliated department programs; 3 letters of recommendation; bachelor's degree or equivalent in life sciences, chemistry, biochemistry, or biophysics; research experience. Electronic applications accepted.

**Michigan Technological University,** Graduate School, Interdisciplinary Programs, Houghton, MI 49931. Offers automotive systems and controls (Graduate Certificate); biochemistry and molecular biology (PhD); computational science and engineering (PhD); data science (Graduate Certificate); sustainability (Graduate Certificate). *Program availability:* Part-time. *Faculty:* 132 full-time, 6 part-time/adjunct. *Students:* 57 full-time (20 women), 19 part-time; includes 7 minority (3 Black or African American, non-Hispanic/Latino; 1 American Indian or Alaska Native, non-Hispanic/Latino; 1 Asian, non-Hispanic/Latino; 2 Two or more races, non-Hispanic/Latino), 42 international. Average age 30. 475 applicants, 29% accepted, 25 enrolled. In 2019, 23 master's, 10 doctorates, 36 other advanced degrees awarded. Terminal master's awarded for partial completion of doctoral program. *Degree requirements:* For master's, comprehensive exam (for some programs), thesis (for some programs); for doctorate, comprehensive exam, thesis/dissertation. *Entrance requirements:* For master's, doctorate, and Graduate Certificate, GRE, statement of purpose, personal statement, official transcripts, 2-3 letters of recommendation. Additional exam requirements/recommendations for international students: required—TOEFL or IELTS. *Application deadline:* Applications are processed on a rolling basis. Electronic applications accepted. *Expenses: Tuition, area resident:* Full-time $19,206; part-time $1067 per credit. *Tuition, state resident:* full-time $19,206; part-time $1067 per credit. *Tuition, nonresident:* full-time $19,206; part-time $1067 per credit. *International tuition:* $19,206 full-time. *Required fees:* $248; $248 per unit. $124 per semester. Tuition and fees vary according to course load and program. *Financial support:* In 2019–20, 54 students received support, including 9 fellowships with tuition reimbursements available (averaging $16,590 per year), 14 research assistantships with tuition reimbursements available (averaging $16,590 per year), 10 teaching assistantships with tuition reimbursements available (averaging $16,590 per year); career-related internships or fieldwork, Federal Work-Study, scholarships/grants, health care benefits, unspecified assistantships, and cooperative program also available. Financial award applicants required to submit FAFSA. *Unit head:* Dr. Will H Cantrell, Dean of the Graduate School, 906-487-3007, Fax: 906-487-2284, E-mail: cantrell@mtu.edu. *Application contact:* Ashli Wells, Assistant Director of Graduate Enrollment Services, 906-487-3513, Fax: 906-487-2284, E-mail: aesniego@mtu.edu.

**Mississippi College,** Graduate School, College of Arts and Sciences, School of Science and Mathematics, Department of Chemistry and Biochemistry, Clinton, MS 39058. Offers MCS, MS. *Program availability:* Part-time. *Degree requirements:* For master's, comprehensive exam, thesis (for some programs). *Entrance requirements:* For master's, GRE. Additional exam requirements/recommendations for international students: recommended—TOEFL, IELTS. Electronic applications accepted.

**Mississippi State University,** College of Agriculture and Life Sciences, Department of Biochemistry, Molecular Biology, Entomology and Plant Pathology, Mississippi State, MS 39762. Offers biochemistry (MS, PhD); entomology (MS, PhD); plant pathology (MS, PhD). *Faculty:* 36 full-time (9 women). *Students:* 39 full-time (19 women), 8 part-time (4 women); includes 4 minority (1 Black or African American, non-Hispanic/Latino; 1 Asian, non-Hispanic/Latino; 2 Hispanic/Latino), 14 international. Average age 31. 24 applicants, 33% accepted, 3 enrolled. In 2019, 3 master's, 4 doctorates awarded. Terminal master's awarded for partial completion of doctoral program. *Degree requirements:* For master's, thesis (for some programs), final oral exam; for doctorate, thesis/dissertation, preliminary oral and written exam. *Entrance requirements:* For master's, GRE General Test, minimum GPA of 2.75; for doctorate, GRE. Additional exam requirements/recommendations for international students: required—TOEFL (minimum score 500 paper-based; 61 iBT); recommended—IELTS (minimum score 5.5). *Application deadline:* For fall admission, 7/1 for domestic students, 5/1 for international students; for spring admission, 11/1 for domestic students, 9/1 for international students. Applications are processed on a rolling basis. Application fee: $60 ($80 for international students). Electronic applications accepted. *Expenses: Tuition, area resident:* Full-time $8880; part-time $456 per credit hour. *Tuition, state resident:* full-time $8880. *Tuition, nonresident:* full-time $23,840; part-time $1236 per credit hour. *Required fees:* $110; $11.12 per credit hour. Tuition and fees vary according to course load. *Financial support:* In 2019–20, 29 research assistantships with full tuition reimbursements (averaging $16,492 per year) were awarded; Federal Work-Study, institutionally sponsored loans, and unspecified assistantships also available. Financial award application deadline: 4/1; financial award applicants required to submit FAFSA. *Unit head:* Dr. Jeffrey Dean, Professor and Head, 662-325-2640, Fax: 662-325-8664, E-mail: jd1891@msstate.edu. *Application contact:* Ryan King, Admissions and Enrollment Assistant, 662-325-8951, E-mail: rjk101@grad.msstate.edu. Website: http://www.biochemistry.msstate.edu

**Montana State University,** The Graduate School, College of Letters and Science, Department of Chemistry and Biochemistry, Bozeman, MT 59717. Offers biochemistry (MS, PhD); chemistry (MS, PhD). *Program availability:* Part-time. *Degree requirements:* For master's, comprehensive exam, thesis (for some programs); for doctorate, comprehensive exam, thesis/dissertation. *Entrance requirements:* For master's and doctorate, GRE General Test, transcripts, letter of recommendation. Additional exam requirements/recommendations for international students: required—TOEFL (minimum score 550 paper-based). Electronic applications accepted.

**Montclair State University,** The Graduate School, College of Science and Mathematics, Program in Pharmaceutical Biochemistry, Montclair, NJ 07043-1624. Offers MS. *Program availability:* Part-time, evening/weekend. *Entrance requirements:* For master's, GRE General Test, 24 undergraduate credits in chemistry, 2 letters of recommendation, essay. Electronic applications accepted.

**Mount Allison University,** Department of Chemistry and Biochemistry, Sackville, NB E4L 1E4, Canada. Offers chemistry (M Sc). *Degree requirements:* For master's, thesis. *Entrance requirements:* For master's, honors degree in chemistry.

**New York Medical College,** Graduate School of Basic Medical Sciences, Valhalla, NY 10595. Offers biochemistry and molecular biology (MS, PhD); cell biology (MS, PhD); microbiology and immunology (MS, PhD); pathology (MS, PhD); pharmacology (MS, PhD); physiology (MS, PhD); MD/PhD. *Program availability:* Part-time, evening/weekend. *Faculty:* 98 full-time (24 women). *Students:* 141 full-time (90 women), 17 part-time (3 women); includes 68 minority (16 Black or African American, non-Hispanic/Latino; 32 Asian, non-Hispanic/Latino; 15 Hispanic/Latino; 1 Native Hawaiian or other Pacific Islander, non-Hispanic/Latino; 4 Two or more races, non-Hispanic/Latino), 19 international. Average age 26. 351 applicants, 62% accepted, 86 enrolled. In 2019, 28 master's, 5 doctorates awarded. Terminal master's awarded for partial completion of doctoral program. *Degree requirements:* For master's, thesis; for doctorate, comprehensive exam, thesis/dissertation. *Entrance requirements:* For master's, GRE General Test, MCAT, or DAT, OAT. Additional exam requirements/recommendations for international students: required—TOEFL (minimum score 90 iBT), TOEFL or IELTS; one of the two exams are required. *Application deadline:* For fall admission, 6/1 priority date for domestic students, 5/1 priority date for international students. Applications are processed on a rolling basis. Application fee: $75 ($100 for international students). Electronic applications accepted. *Expenses:* $1200 credit and $620 fees. *Financial support:* In 2019–20, 400 students received support. Federal Work-Study, scholarships/grants, unspecified assistantships, and Student Federal Loans available. Financial award application deadline: 4/30; financial award applicants required to submit FAFSA. *Unit head:* Dr. Marina K Holz, Dean, 914-594-4110, Fax: 914-594-4944, E-mail: mholz@nymc.edu. *Application contact:* Valerie Romeo-Messana, Director of Admissions, 914-594-4110, Fax: 914-594-4944, E-mail: v_romeomessana@nymc.edu. Website: https://www.nymc.edu/graduate-school-of-basic-medical-sciences-gsbms/gsbms-academics/

**North Carolina State University,** Graduate School, College of Agriculture and Life Sciences, Department of Molecular and Structural Biochemistry, Raleigh, NC 27695. Offers PhD. *Degree requirements:* For doctorate, thesis/dissertation. *Entrance requirements:* For doctorate, GRE General Test. Additional exam requirements/recommendations for international students: required—TOEFL. Electronic applications accepted.

**North Dakota State University,** College of Graduate and Interdisciplinary Studies, College of Science and Mathematics, Department of Chemistry and Biochemistry, Program in Biochemistry, Fargo, ND 58102. Offers MS, PhD. *Program availability:* Part-time. *Entrance requirements:* Additional exam requirements/recommendations for international students: required—TOEFL (minimum score 550 paper-based). Electronic applications accepted. Tuition and fees vary according to program and reciprocity agreements.

**Northern Illinois University,** Graduate School, College of Liberal Arts and Sciences, Department of Chemistry and Biochemistry, De Kalb, IL 60115-2854. Offers MS, PhD. *Faculty:* 16 full-time (1 woman), 3 part-time/adjunct (1 woman). *Students:* 36 full-time (12 women), 9 part-time (3 women); includes 6 minority (1 Black or African American, non-Hispanic/Latino; 2 Asian, non-Hispanic/Latino; 2 Hispanic/Latino; 1 Two or more races, non-Hispanic/Latino), 22 international. Average age 29. 62 applicants, 52% accepted, 11 enrolled. In 2019, 3 master's, 10 doctorates awarded. Terminal master's awarded for partial completion of doctoral program. *Degree requirements:* For master's, comprehensive exam, thesis optional, research seminar; for doctorate, one foreign language, thesis/dissertation, candidacy exam, dissertation defense, research seminar. *Entrance requirements:* For master's, GRE General Test, bachelor's degree in mathematics or science, minimum GPA of 2.75; for doctorate, GRE General Test, bachelor's degree in mathematics or science; minimum undergraduate GPA of 2.75, 3.2 graduate. Additional exam requirements/recommendations for international students: required—TOEFL (minimum score 550 paper-based). *Application deadline:* For fall admission, 6/1 for domestic students, 5/1 for international students; for spring admission, 11/1 for domestic students, 10/1 for international students. Applications are processed on a rolling basis. Application fee: $40. Electronic applications accepted. *Financial support:* In 2019–20, 12 research assistantships with full tuition reimbursements, 32 teaching assistantships with full tuition reimbursements were awarded; fellowships with full tuition reimbursements, career-related internships or fieldwork, Federal Work-Study, scholarships/grants, tuition waivers (full), and unspecified assistantships also available. Support available to part-time students. Financial award applicants required to submit FAFSA. *Unit head:* Dr. Ralph Wheeler, Chair, 815-753-1181, Fax: 815-753-4802, E-mail: rwheeler@niu.edu. *Application contact:* Graduate School Office, 815-753-0395, E-mail: gradsch@niu.edu. Website: http://www.chembio.niu.edu/

**Northwestern University,** The Graduate School, Interdisciplinary Biological Sciences Program (IBiS), Evanston, IL 60208. Offers biochemistry (PhD); bioengineering and biotechnology (PhD); biotechnology (PhD); cell and molecular biology (PhD); developmental and systems biology (PhD); nanotechnology (PhD); neurobiology (PhD); structural biology and biophysics (PhD). *Degree requirements:* For doctorate, thesis/dissertation, qualifying exam. *Entrance requirements:* For doctorate, GRE General Test. Additional exam requirements/recommendations for international students: required—TOEFL (minimum score 600 paper-based). Electronic applications accepted.

**The Ohio State University,** Graduate School, College of Arts and Sciences, Division of Natural and Mathematical Sciences, Biochemistry Program, Columbus, OH 43210. Offers PhD. Terminal master's awarded for partial completion of doctoral program. *Entrance requirements:* For doctorate, GRE General Test. Additional exam requirements/recommendations for international students: required—TOEFL (minimum score 620 paper-based; 105 iBT); recommended—IELTS (minimum score 8). Electronic applications accepted.

**The Ohio State University,** Graduate School, College of Arts and Sciences, Division of Natural and Mathematical Sciences, Department of Chemistry and Biochemistry, Columbus, OH 43210. Offers biochemistry (MS); chemistry (MS, PhD). *Entrance requirements:* For master's and doctorate, GRE General Test. Additional exam requirements/recommendations for international students: required—TOEFL (minimum score 550 paper-based; 79 iBT), Michigan English Language Assessment Battery (minimum score 82); recommended—IELTS (minimum score 7). Electronic applications accepted.

**Ohio University,** Graduate College, College of Arts and Sciences, Department of Chemistry and Biochemistry, Athens, OH 45701-2979. Offers MS, PhD. *Degree requirements:* For master's, comprehensive exam, thesis, exam; for doctorate, comprehensive exam, thesis/dissertation, exam. *Entrance requirements:* For master's and doctorate, GRE. Additional exam requirements/recommendations for international

students: required—TOEFL (minimum score 550 paper-based; 80 iBT) or IELTS (minimum score 6.5). Electronic applications accepted.

**Oklahoma State University,** College of Agricultural Science and Natural Resources, Department of Biochemistry and Molecular Biology, Stillwater, OK 74078. Offers MS, PhD. *Faculty:* 17 full-time (6 women). *Students:* 2 full-time (1 woman), 18 part-time (8 women); includes 2 minority (1 Asian, non-Hispanic/Latino; 1 Hispanic/Latino), 8 international. Average age 29. 18 applicants, 28% accepted, 5 enrolled. In 2019, 2 master's, 5 doctorates awarded. *Entrance requirements:* For master's and doctorate, GRE or GMAT. Additional exam requirements/recommendations for international students: required—TOEFL (minimum score 550 paper-based; 79 iBT). *Application deadline:* For fall admission, 3/1 priority date for international students; for spring admission, 8/1 priority date for international students. Applications are processed on a rolling basis. Application fee: $50 ($75 for international students). Electronic applications accepted. *Expenses: Tuition, area resident:* Full-time $4148.10; part-time $2765.40 per credit hour. *Tuition, state resident:* Full-time $4148.10; part-time $2765.40 per credit hour. *Tuition, nonresident:* full-time $15,775; part-time $10,516.80 per credit hour. *International tuition:* $15,775.20 full-time. *Required fees:* $2196.90; $122.05 per credit hour. Tuition and fees vary according to course load, campus/location and program. *Financial support:* In 2019–20, 12 research assistantships (averaging $1,812 per year), 8 teaching assistantships (averaging $1,863 per year) were awarded; career-related internships or fieldwork, Federal Work-Study, scholarships/grants, health care benefits, tuition waivers (partial), and unspecified assistantships also available. Support available to part-time students. Financial award application deadline: 3/1; financial award applicants required to submit FAFSA. *Unit head:* Dr. John Gustafson, Department Head, 405-744-6189, E-mail: john.gustafson@okstate.edu. *Application contact:* Dr. Sheryl Tucker, Dean, 405-744-6368, Fax: 405-744-0355, E-mail: gradi@okstate.edu. Website: http://biochemistry.okstate.edu/

**Old Dominion University,** College of Sciences, Program in Chemistry, Norfolk, VA 23529. Offers analytical chemistry (MS, PhD); biochemistry (MS, PhD); environmental chemistry (MS, PhD); inorganic chemistry (MS, PhD); organic chemistry (MS, PhD); physical chemistry (MS, PhD). *Program availability:* Part-time. Terminal master's awarded for partial completion of doctoral program. *Degree requirements:* For master's, comprehensive exam, thesis (for some programs); for doctorate, comprehensive exam, thesis/dissertation. *Entrance requirements:* For master's and doctorate, GRE General Test, minimum GPA of 3.0 in major, 2.5 overall, transcripts, essay, three letters of recommendation, resume. Additional exam requirements/recommendations for international students: required—TOEFL (minimum score 84 iBT). Electronic applications accepted. *Expenses:* Contact institution.

**Oregon Health & Science University,** School of Medicine, Graduate Programs in Medicine, Department of Environmental and Biomolecular Systems, Portland, OR 97239-3098. Offers biochemistry and molecular biology (MS, PhD); environmental science and engineering (MS, PhD). *Program availability:* Part-time. Terminal master's awarded for partial completion of doctoral program. *Degree requirements:* For master's, thesis (for some programs); for doctorate, comprehensive exam, thesis/dissertation, qualifying exam. *Entrance requirements:* For master's and doctorate, GRE General Test (minimum scores: 153 Verbal/148 Quantitative/4.5 Analytical) or MCAT (for some programs). Electronic applications accepted.

**Oregon Health & Science University,** School of Medicine, Graduate Programs in Medicine, Program in Molecular and Cellular Biosciences, Department of Biochemistry and Molecular Biology, Portland, OR 97239-3098. Offers PhD. *Degree requirements:* For doctorate, comprehensive exam, thesis/dissertation, qualifying exam. *Entrance requirements:* For doctorate, GRE General Test (minimum scores: 153 Verbal/148 Quantitative/4.5 Analytical). Electronic applications accepted.

**Oregon State University,** College of Agricultural Sciences, Program in Food Science and Technology, Corvallis, OR 97331. Offers brewing (MS, PhD); enology (MS, PhD); flavor chemistry (MS, PhD); food and seafood processing (MS, PhD); food chemistry/biochemistry (MS, PhD); food engineering (MS, PhD); food microbiology/biotechnology (MS, PhD); sensory evaluation (MS, PhD). *Entrance requirements:* For master's and doctorate, GRE (minimum Verbal and Quantitative scores of 300), minimum GPA of 3.0 in last 90 hours. Additional exam requirements/recommendations for international students: required—TOEFL (minimum score 80 iBT), IELTS (minimum score 6.5).

**Oregon State University,** College of Science, Program in Biochemistry and Biophysics, Corvallis, OR 97331. Offers MA, MS, PhD. Terminal master's awarded for partial completion of doctoral program. *Degree requirements:* For master's, thesis optional; for doctorate, thesis/dissertation, exams. *Entrance requirements:* For master's and doctorate, GRE, minimum GPA of 3.0. Additional exam requirements/recommendations for international students: required—TOEFL (minimum score 600 paper-based; 100 iBT), IELTS (minimum score 7). Electronic applications accepted.

**Oregon State University,** Interdisciplinary/Institutional Programs, Program in Environmental Sciences, Corvallis, OR 97331. Offers biogeochemistry (MA, MS, PSM, PhD); ecology (MA, MS, PSM, PhD); environmental education (MA, MS, PhD); quantitative analysis (PSM); social science (MA, MS, PSM, PhD); water resources (MA, MS, PhD). *Program availability:* Part-time. *Degree requirements:* For master's, variable foreign language requirement, thesis; for doctorate, thesis/dissertation. *Entrance requirements:* For master's and doctorate, GRE. Additional exam requirements/recommendations for international students: required—TOEFL (minimum score 80 iBT), IELTS (minimum score 6.5).

**Pace University,** Dyson College of Arts and Sciences, Program in Biochemistry and Molecular Biology, New York, NY 10038. Offers MS. *Program availability:* Part-time, evening/weekend. *Degree requirements:* For master's, thesis. *Entrance requirements:* For master's, official transcripts, two letters of recommendation, personal statement. Additional exam requirements/recommendations for international students: required—TOEFL (minimum score 88 iBT), IELTS (minimum score 7) or PTE (minimum score 60). Electronic applications accepted.

**Penn State Hershey Medical Center,** College of Medicine, Graduate School Programs in the Biomedical Sciences, Graduate Program in Biomedical Sciences, Hershey, PA 17033. Offers biochemistry and molecular genetics (MS, PhD); biomedical sciences (MS, PhD); cellular and integrative physiology (MS, PhD); translational therapeutics (MS, PhD); virology and immunology (MS, PhD); MD/PhD; PhD/MBA. Terminal master's awarded for partial completion of doctoral program. *Degree requirements:* For master's, thesis; for doctorate, comprehensive exam, thesis/dissertation, candidacy exam. *Entrance requirements:* For doctorate, GRE General Test. Additional exam requirements/recommendations for international students: required—TOEFL (minimum score 550 paper-based; 81 iBT). Electronic applications accepted.

**Penn State University Park,** Graduate School, Eberly College of Science, Department of Biochemistry and Molecular Biology, University Park, PA 16802. Offers biochemistry, microbiology, and molecular biology (MS, PhD); biotechnology (MBIOT).

**Purdue University,** College of Pharmacy and Graduate School, Graduate Programs in Pharmacy and Pharmacal Sciences, Department of Medicinal Chemistry and Molecular Pharmacology, West Lafayette, IN 47907. Offers biophysical and computational chemistry (PhD); cancer research (PhD); immunology and infectious disease (PhD);

medicinal biochemistry and molecular biology (PhD); medicinal chemistry and chemical biology (PhD); molecular pharmacology (PhD); neuropharmacology, neurodegeneration, and neurotoxicity (PhD); systems biology and functional genomics (PhD). *Faculty:* 20 full-time (5 women), 7 part-time/adjunct (2 women). *Students:* 80 full-time (40 women), 2 part-time (0 women); includes 9 minority (5 Asian, non-Hispanic/Latino; 2 Hispanic/Latino; 2 Two or more races, non-Hispanic/Latino), 44 international. Average age 26. 162 applicants, 20% accepted, 15 enrolled. In 2019, 11 doctorates awarded. *Degree requirements:* For doctorate, thesis/dissertation. *Entrance requirements:* For doctorate, GRE General Test; GRE Subject Test in biology, biochemistry, and chemistry (recommended), minimum undergraduate GPA of 3.0. Additional exam requirements/recommendations for international students: required—TOEFL (minimum score 550 paper-based; 77 iBT); recommended—TWE. *Application deadline:* For fall admission, 2/1 for domestic and international students. Applications are processed on a rolling basis. Application fee: $60 ($75 for international students). Electronic applications accepted. *Financial support:* Fellowships, research assistantships, teaching assistantships, and traineeships available. Support available to part-time students. Financial award applicants required to submit FAFSA. *Unit head:* Zhong-Yin Zhang, Head, 765-494-1403, E-mail: zhang-yn@purdue.edu. *Application contact:* Delayne Graham, Graduate Contact, 765-494-1362, E-mail: dkgraham@purdue.edu.

**Purdue University,** Graduate School, College of Agriculture, Department of Biochemistry, West Lafayette, IN 47907. Offers MS, PhD. *Faculty:* 19 full-time (8 women), 5 part-time/adjunct (2 women). *Students:* 50 full-time (22 women); includes 8 minority (3 Black or African American, non-Hispanic/Latino; 3 Asian, non-Hispanic/Latino; 1 Hispanic/Latino; 1 Two or more races, non-Hispanic/Latino), 20 international. Average age 27. 47 applicants, 38% accepted, 8 enrolled. In 2019, 1 master's, 7 doctorates awarded. Terminal master's awarded for partial completion of doctoral program. *Degree requirements:* For doctorate, thesis/dissertation, preliminary and qualifying exams. *Entrance requirements:* For doctorate, GRE General Test, minimum undergraduate GPA of 3.0 or equivalent. Additional exam requirements/recommendations for international students: required—TOEFL (minimum score 600 paper-based; 77 iBT). *Application deadline:* For fall admission, 1/15 priority date for domestic and international students; for spring admission, 9/30 for domestic and international students. Applications are processed on a rolling basis. Application fee: $60 ($75 for international students). Electronic applications accepted. *Financial support:* Fellowships, research assistantships, and teaching assistantships available. Support available to part-time students. Financial award application deadline: 4/15; financial award applicants required to submit FAFSA. *Unit head:* Andrew Mesecar, Head of the Graduate Program, 765-494-1607, E-mail: amesecar@purdue.edu. *Application contact:* Traci Jordan, Graduate Contact for Admissions, 765-496-7232, E-mail: tljordan@purdue.edu.
Website: https://ag.purdue.edu/biochem

**Purdue University,** Graduate School, PULSe - Purdue University Life Sciences Program, West Lafayette, IN 47907. Offers biomolecular structure and biophysics (PhD); biotechnology (PhD); chemical biology (PhD); chromatin and regulation of gene expression (PhD); integrative neuroscience (PhD); integrative plant sciences (PhD); membrane biology (PhD); microbiology (PhD); molecular evolutionary and cancer biology (PhD); molecular evolutionary genetics (PhD); molecular virology (PhD). *Students:* 37 full-time (23 women); includes 7 minority (1 Black or African American, non-Hispanic/Latino; 2 Asian, non-Hispanic/Latino; 4 Hispanic/Latino), 22 international. Average age 25. 162 applicants, 36% accepted, 19 enrolled. *Entrance requirements:* For doctorate, GRE, minimum undergraduate GPA of 3.0. Additional exam requirements/recommendations for international students: required—TOEFL (minimum score 550 paper-based; 77 iBT). *Application deadline:* For fall admission, 1/15 priority date for domestic and international students. Applications are processed on a rolling basis. Application fee: $60 ($75 for international students). Electronic applications accepted. *Financial support:* In 2019–20, research assistantships with tuition reimbursements (averaging $22,500 per year), teaching assistantships with tuition reimbursements (averaging $22,500 per year) were awarded. *Application contact:* Lindsey Springer, Graduate Contact for Admissions, 765-496-9667, E-mail: lbcampbe@purdue.edu.
Website: http://www.gradschool.purdue.edu/pulse

**Rensselaer Polytechnic Institute,** Graduate School, School of Science, Program in Biochemistry and Biophysics, Troy, NY 12180-3590. Offers MS, PhD. *Faculty:* 21 full-time (8 women), 2 part-time/adjunct (1 woman). *Students:* 12 full-time (6 women), 1 (woman) part-time; includes 3 minority (2 Asian, non-Hispanic/Latino; 1 Hispanic/Latino), 2 international. Average age 27. 38 applicants, 39% accepted, 4 enrolled. In 2019, 2 master's, 6 doctorates awarded. Terminal master's awarded for partial completion of doctoral program. *Degree requirements:* For master's, thesis optional; for doctorate, comprehensive exam, thesis/dissertation. *Entrance requirements:* For master's and doctorate, GRE. Additional exam requirements/recommendations for international students: required—TOEFL (minimum score 600 paper-based; 100 iBT), IELTS (minimum score 7), PTE (minimum score 68). *Application deadline:* For fall admission, 1/1 priority date for domestic and international students; for spring admission, 8/15 priority date for domestic and international students. Applications are processed on a rolling basis. Application fee: $75. Electronic applications accepted. *Financial support:* In 2019–20, research assistantships (averaging $23,000 per year), teaching assistantships (averaging $23,000 per year) were awarded; fellowships also available. Financial award application deadline: 1/1. *Unit head:* Dr. Cathy Royer, Graduate Program Director, 518-276-3796, E-mail: royerc@rpi.edu. *Application contact:* Jarron Decker, Director of Graduate Admissions, 518-276-6216, Fax: 518-276-4072, E-mail: gradadmissions@rpi.edu.
Website: https://science.rpi.edu/biology

**Rice University,** Graduate Programs, Wiess School of Natural Sciences, Department of Biochemistry and Cell Biology, Houston, TX 77251-1892. Offers MA, PhD. Terminal master's awarded for partial completion of doctoral program. *Degree requirements:* For master's, thesis; for doctorate, thesis/dissertation. *Entrance requirements:* For master's and doctorate, GRE. Additional exam requirements/recommendations for international students: required—TOEFL (minimum score 600 paper-based; 90 iBT). Electronic applications accepted. *Expenses:* Contact institution.

**Rosalind Franklin University of Medicine and Science,** School of Graduate and Postdoctoral Studies - Interdisciplinary Graduate Program in Biomedical Sciences, Department of Biochemistry and Molecular Biology, North Chicago, IL 60064-3095. Offers PhD, MD/PhD. Terminal master's awarded for partial completion of doctoral program. *Degree requirements:* For doctorate, comprehensive exam, thesis/dissertation. *Entrance requirements:* For doctorate, GRE General Test, minimum GPA of 3.0. Additional exam requirements/recommendations for international students: required—TOEFL, TWE. Electronic applications accepted.

**Rush University,** Graduate College, Division of Biochemistry, Chicago, IL 60612-3832. Offers MS, PhD, MD/PhD. *Degree requirements:* For doctorate, thesis/dissertation, preliminary exam. *Entrance requirements:* For doctorate, GRE General Test. Additional exam requirements/recommendations for international students: required—TOEFL. Electronic applications accepted.

**Rutgers University - Newark,** Graduate School of Biomedical Sciences, Department of Biochemistry and Molecular Biology, Newark, NJ 07107. Offers MS, PhD. *Degree requirements:* For master's, thesis; for doctorate, thesis/dissertation, qualifying exam. *Entrance requirements:* For master's and doctorate, GRE General Test. Additional exam requirements/recommendations for international students: required—TOEFL. Electronic applications accepted.

**Rutgers University - Newark,** Graduate School, Program in Chemistry, Newark, NJ 07102. Offers analytical chemistry (MS, PhD); biochemistry (MS, PhD); inorganic chemistry (MS, PhD); organic chemistry (MS, PhD); physical chemistry (MS, PhD). *Program availability:* Part-time, evening/weekend. Terminal master's awarded for partial completion of doctoral program. *Degree requirements:* For master's, thesis optional, cumulative exams; for doctorate, thesis/dissertation, exams, research proposal. *Entrance requirements:* For master's and doctorate, GRE General Test, minimum undergraduate B average. Additional exam requirements/recommendations for international students: required—TOEFL. Electronic applications accepted.

**Rutgers University - New Brunswick,** Graduate School-New Brunswick, Department of Chemistry and Chemical Biology, Piscataway, NJ 08854-8097. Offers biological chemistry (MS, PhD); inorganic chemistry (MS, PhD); organic chemistry (MS, PhD); physical chemistry (MS, PhD). *Program availability:* Part-time, evening/weekend. Terminal master's awarded for partial completion of doctoral program. *Degree requirements:* For master's, thesis or alternative, exam; for doctorate, thesis/dissertation, 1 year residency. *Entrance requirements:* For master's and doctorate, GRE General Test, GRE Subject Test. Additional exam requirements/recommendations for international students: required—TOEFL. Electronic applications accepted.

**Rutgers University - New Brunswick,** Graduate School-New Brunswick, Programs in the Molecular Biosciences, Piscataway, NJ 08854-8097. Offers biochemistry (PhD); cell and developmental biology (MS, PhD); microbiology and molecular genetics (MS, PhD), including applied microbiology, clinical microbiology, computational molecular biology (PhD), immunology, microbial biochemistry, molecular genetics, virology.

**Rutgers University - New Brunswick,** Graduate School of Biomedical Sciences, Program in Biochemistry, Piscataway, NJ 08854-5635. Offers MS, PhD, MD/PhD. Terminal master's awarded for partial completion of doctoral program. *Degree requirements:* For master's, thesis, qualifying exam; for doctorate, thesis/dissertation, qualifying exam. *Entrance requirements:* For master's and doctorate, GRE General Test. Additional exam requirements/recommendations for international students: required—TOEFL. Electronic applications accepted.

**Saint Louis University,** Graduate Programs, School of Medicine, Graduate Programs in Biomedical Sciences and Graduate Programs, Department of Biochemistry and Molecular Biology, St. Louis, MO 63103. Offers PhD. *Degree requirements:* For doctorate, comprehensive exam, thesis/dissertation, departmental qualifying exams. *Entrance requirements:* For doctorate, GRE General Test, GRE Subject Test (optional), letters of recommendation, resume, interview. Additional exam requirements/recommendations for international students: required—TOEFL (minimum score 525 paper-based). Electronic applications accepted.

**San Diego State University,** Graduate and Research Affairs, College of Sciences, Department of Chemistry and Biochemistry, San Diego, CA 92182. Offers MA, MS, PhD. Terminal master's awarded for partial completion of doctoral program. *Degree requirements:* For doctorate, thesis/dissertation. *Entrance requirements:* For master's, GRE General Test, bachelor's degree in related field, 3 letters of reference; for doctorate, GRE General Test, GRE Subject Test. Additional exam requirements/recommendations for international students: required—TOEFL. Electronic applications accepted.

**San Francisco State University,** Division of Graduate Studies, College of Science and Engineering, Department of Chemistry and Biochemistry, San Francisco, CA 94132-1722. Offers biochemistry (MS); chemistry (MS). *Program availability:* Part-time. *Application deadline:* Applications are processed on a rolling basis. Electronic applications accepted. *Expenses: Tuition, area resident:* Full-time $7176; part-time $4164 per year. Tuition, state resident: full-time $7176; part-time $4164 per year. Tuition, nonresident: full-time $16,680; part-time $396 per unit. *International tuition:* $16,680 full-time. *Required fees:* $1524; $1524 per unit. $762 per semester. Tuition and fees vary according to degree level and program. *Unit head:* Dr. Teaster Baird, Jr., Chair, 415-338-1288, Fax: 415-338-2384, E-mail: tbaird@sfsu.edu. *Application contact:* Dr. Andrew Ichimura, Graduate Coordinator, 415-405-0721, Fax: 415-338-2384, E-mail: ichimura@sfsu.edu.
Website: http://www.chembiochem.sfsu.edu/0home/0layout.php

**Seton Hall University,** College of Arts and Sciences, Department of Chemistry and Biochemistry, South Orange, NJ 07079-2697. Offers analytical chemistry (MS, PhD); biochemistry (MS, PhD); chemistry (MS); inorganic chemistry (MS, PhD); organic chemistry (MS, PhD); physical chemistry (MS, PhD). *Program availability:* Part-time, evening/weekend. Terminal master's awarded for partial completion of doctoral program. *Degree requirements:* For master's, thesis optional; for doctorate, comprehensive exam, thesis/dissertation. *Entrance requirements:* Additional exam requirements/recommendations for international students: required—TOEFL. Electronic applications accepted.

**Simon Fraser University,** Office of Graduate Studies and Postdoctoral Fellows, Faculty of Science, Department of Molecular Biology and Biochemistry, Burnaby, BC V5A 1S6, Canada. Offers bioinformatics (Graduate Diploma); molecular biology and biochemistry (M Sc, PhD). *Degree requirements:* For master's, thesis; for doctorate, thesis/dissertation; for Graduate Diploma, practicum. *Entrance requirements:* For master's, minimum GPA of 3.0 (on scale of 4.33) or 3.33 based on last 60 credits of undergraduate courses; for doctorate, minimum GPA of 3.5; for Graduate Diploma, minimum GPA of 2.5 (on scale of 4.33) or 2.67 based on last 60 credits of undergraduate courses. Additional exam requirements/recommendations for international students: recommended—TOEFL (minimum score 580 paper-based; 100 iBT), IELTS (minimum score 7.5), TWE (minimum score 5). Electronic applications accepted.

**Sonoma State University,** School of Science and Technology, Department of Biology, Rohnert Park, CA 94928. Offers biochemistry (MA). *Program availability:* Part-time. *Degree requirements:* For master's, thesis or alternative, oral exam. *Entrance requirements:* For master's, GRE General Test, GRE Subject Test, minimum GPA of 3.0. Additional exam requirements/recommendations for international students: required—TOEFL (minimum score 500 paper-based).

**South Dakota State University,** Graduate School, College of Natural Sciences, Department of Chemistry and Biochemistry, Brookings, SD 57007. Offers biochemistry (PhD); chemistry (MS, PhD). *Degree requirements:* For master's, thesis, oral exam; for doctorate, thesis/dissertation, preliminary oral and written exams, research tool. *Entrance requirements:* For master's and doctorate, bachelor's degree in chemistry or closely related discipline. Additional exam requirements/recommendations for international students: required—TOEFL (minimum score 580 paper-based; 92 iBT).

**Southern Illinois University Carbondale,** Graduate School, College of Science, Department of Chemistry and Biochemistry, Carbondale, IL 62901-4701. Offers MS,

PhD. *Program availability:* Part-time. Terminal master's awarded for partial completion of doctoral program. *Degree requirements:* For master's, one foreign language, thesis; for doctorate, variable foreign language requirement, thesis/dissertation. *Entrance requirements:* For master's, GRE, minimum GPA of 2.7; for doctorate, GRE General Test, minimum GPA of 3.25. Additional exam requirements/recommendations for international students: required—TOEFL.

**Southern Illinois University Carbondale,** Graduate School, College of Science, Program in Molecular Biology, Microbiology, and Biochemistry, Carbondale, IL 62901-4701. Offers MS, PhD. *Degree requirements:* For master's, thesis; for doctorate, thesis/dissertation. *Entrance requirements:* For master's, GRE, minimum GPA of 2.7; for doctorate, GRE, minimum GPA of 3.25. Additional exam requirements/recommendations for international students: required—TOEFL.

**Southern University and Agricultural and Mechanical College,** Graduate School, College of Sciences and Engineering, Program in Chemistry, Baton Rouge, LA 70813. Offers analytical chemistry (MS); biochemistry (MS); environmental sciences (MS); inorganic chemistry (MS); organic chemistry (MS); physical chemistry (MS). *Degree requirements:* For master's, thesis. *Entrance requirements:* For master's, GMAT or GRE General Test. Additional exam requirements/recommendations for international students: required—TOEFL (minimum score 525 paper-based).

**Stanford University,** School of Medicine, Graduate Programs in Medicine, Department of Biochemistry, Stanford, CA 94305-2004. Offers PhD. *Expenses: Tuition:* Full-time $52,479; part-time $34,110 per unit. *Required fees:* $672; $224 per quarter. Tuition and fees vary according to program and student level.
Website: http://cmgm.stanford.edu/biochem/

**Stanford University,** School of Medicine, Graduate Programs in Medicine, Department of Chemical and Systems Biology, Stanford, CA 94305-2004. Offers PhD. *Expenses: Tuition:* Full-time $52,479; part-time $34,110 per unit. *Required fees:* $672; $224 per quarter. Tuition and fees vary according to program and student level.

**State University of New York College of Environmental Science and Forestry,** Department of Chemistry, Syracuse, NY 13210-2779. Offers biochemistry (MPS, MS, PhD); environmental chemistry (MPS, MS, PhD); organic chemistry of natural products (MPS, MS, PhD); polymer chemistry (MPS, MS, PhD). *Program availability:* Part-time. *Faculty:* 14 full-time (1 woman), 1 part-time/adjunct (0 women). *Students:* 34 full-time (15 women), 4 part-time (2 women); includes 1 minority (Asian, non-Hispanic/Latino), 12 international. Average age 28. 32 applicants, 59% accepted, 6 enrolled. In 2019, 6 master's, 4 doctorates awarded. Terminal master's awarded for partial completion of doctoral program. *Degree requirements:* For master's, thesis; for doctorate, comprehensive exam, thesis/dissertation. *Entrance requirements:* For master's and doctorate, GRE General Test, GRE Subject Test, minimum GPA of 3.0. Additional exam requirements/recommendations for international students: required—TOEFL (minimum score 550 paper-based; 80 iBT), IELTS (minimum score 6). *Application deadline:* For fall admission, 2/1 priority date for domestic and international students; for spring admission, 11/1 priority date for domestic and international students. Applications are processed on a rolling basis. Application fee: $60. Electronic applications accepted. *Expenses:* Tuition, state resident: full-time $11,310; part-time $472 per credit hour. Tuition, nonresident: full-time $23,100; part-time $963 per credit hour. *Required fees:* $1890; $95.21 per credit hour. *Financial support:* In 2019–20, 12 students received support. Unspecified assistantships available. Financial award application deadline: 6/30; financial award applicants required to submit FAFSA. *Unit head:* Dr. Avik Chatterjee, Chair, 315-470-4747, Fax: 315-470-6855, E-mail: achatter@esf.edu. *Application contact:* Laura Payne, Administrative Assistant, Office of Instruction and Graduate Studies, 315-470-6599, Fax: 315-470-6978, E-mail: esfgrad@esf.edu.
Website: http://www.esf.edu/chemistry

**State University of New York Upstate Medical University,** College of Graduate Studies, Program in Biochemistry and Molecular Biology, Syracuse, NY 13210. Offers biochemistry (MS); biochemistry and molecular biology (PhD); MD/PhD. Terminal master's awarded for partial completion of doctoral program. *Degree requirements:* For master's, thesis; for doctorate, comprehensive exam, thesis/dissertation. *Entrance requirements:* For master's, GRE General Test, interview; for doctorate, GRE General Test, telephone interview. Additional exam requirements/recommendations for international students: required—TOEFL. Electronic applications accepted.

**Stevens Institute of Technology,** Graduate School, Charles V. Schaefer Jr. School of Engineering and Science, Department of Chemistry, Chemical Biology and Biomedical Engineering, Program in Chemical Biology, Hoboken, NJ 07030. Offers MS, PhD, Certificate. *Program availability:* Part-time, evening/weekend. *Faculty:* 12 full-time (4 women), 4 part-time/adjunct. *Students:* 26 full-time (14 women), 2 part-time (1 woman); includes 3 minority (1 Black or African American, non-Hispanic/Latino; 2 Asian, non-Hispanic/Latino), 18 international. Average age 26. In 2019, 6 master's awarded. Terminal master's awarded for partial completion of doctoral program. *Degree requirements:* For master's, thesis optional, minimum B average in major field and overall; for doctorate, comprehensive exam (for some programs), thesis/dissertation; for Certificate, minimum B average. *Entrance requirements:* For master's, International applicants must submit TOEFL/IELTS scores and fulfill the English Language Proficiency Requirement. Applicants to full-time programs who do not qualify for a score waiver are required to submit GRE/GMAT scores. Additional exam requirements/recommendations for international students: required—TOEFL (minimum score 74 iBT), IELTS (minimum score 6). *Application deadline:* For fall admission, 4/1 for domestic students, 4/15 for international students; for spring admission, 11/1 for domestic and international students; for summer admission, 5/1 for domestic students. Applications are processed on a rolling basis. Application fee: $60. Electronic applications accepted. *Expenses: Tuition:* Full-time $52,134. *Required fees:* $1880. Tuition and fees vary according to course load. *Financial support:* Fellowships, research assistantships, teaching assistantships, career-related internships or fieldwork, Federal Work-Study, scholarships/grants, and unspecified assistantships available. Financial award application deadline: 2/15; financial award applicants required to submit FAFSA. *Unit head:* Dr. Jean Zu, Dean of SES, 201-216.8233, Fax: 201-216.8372, E-mail: Jean.Zu@stevens.edu. *Application contact:* Graduate Admissions, 888-783-8367, Fax: 888-511-1306, E-mail: graduate@stevens.edu.

**Stony Brook University, State University of New York,** Graduate School, College of Arts and Sciences, Department of Biochemistry and Cell Biology, Biochemistry and Cell Biology Program, Stony Brook, NY 11794. Offers MS. *Program availability:* Part-time. *Students:* 19 full-time (14 women), 7 part-time (4 women); includes 8 minority (1 Black or African American, non-Hispanic/Latino; 5 Asian, non-Hispanic/Latino; 2 Hispanic/Latino), 6 international. Average age 26. 63 applicants, 46% accepted, 17 enrolled. In 2019, 11 master's awarded. *Entrance requirements:* For master's, three letters of recommendation, BS or BA in a life science related field with minimum B average, personal statement. Additional exam requirements/recommendations for international students: required—TOEFL (minimum score 550 paper-based; 90 iBT). *Application deadline:* For fall admission, 1/15 for domestic students; for summer admission, 10/1 for domestic students. Applications are processed on a rolling basis. Application fee: $100. Electronic applications accepted. *Expenses:* Contact institution. *Financial support:* Research assistantships available. *Unit head:* Prof. Aaron Neiman, Chair, 631-632-8550, Fax: 631-632-8575, E-mail: aaron.neiman@stonybrook.edu. *Application contact:* Pam Wolfskill, Coordinator, 631-632-8585, Fax: 631-632-8575, E-mail: carol.juliano@stonybrook.edu.
Website: https://www.stonybrook.edu/commcms/biochem/education/graduate/biochemistry-and-cell-biology-ms

**Stony Brook University, State University of New York,** Graduate School, College of Arts and Sciences, Department of Biochemistry and Cell Biology, Program in Biochemistry and Structural Biology, Stony Brook, NY 11794. Offers PhD. *Students:* 26 full-time (18 women); includes 3 minority (2 Black or African American, non-Hispanic/Latino; 1 Hispanic/Latino), 16 international. Average age 26. 31 applicants, 39% accepted, 3 enrolled. In 2019, 9 doctorates awarded. *Entrance requirements:* For doctorate, GRE. Additional exam requirements/recommendations for international students: required—TOEFL (minimum score 90 iBT). *Application deadline:* For fall admission, 1/15 for domestic students; for spring admission, 10/1 for domestic students. Application fee: $100. *Expenses:* Contact institution. *Financial support:* In 2019–20, 1 fellowship, 18 research assistantships, 3 teaching assistantships were awarded. *Unit head:* Prof. Aaron Neiman, Chair, 631-632-8550, Fax: 631-632-8575, E-mail: aaron.neiman@stonybrook.edu. *Application contact:* Amy Saas, Graduate Program Administrator, 631-632-8613, Fax: 631-632-9730, E-mail: amy.saas@stonybrook.edu.
Website: https://www.stonybrook.edu/bsb/

**Texas A&M University,** College of Agriculture and Life Sciences, Department of Biochemistry and Biophysics, College Station, TX 77843. Offers biochemistry (MS, PhD). *Faculty:* 49. *Students:* 132 full-time (62 women), 3 part-time (1 woman); includes 22 minority (6 Black or African American, non-Hispanic/Latino; 3 Asian, non-Hispanic/Latino; 10 Hispanic/Latino; 1 Native Hawaiian or other Pacific Islander, non-Hispanic/Latino; 2 Two or more races, non-Hispanic/Latino), 62 international. Average age 28. 103 applicants, 42% accepted, 28 enrolled. In 2019, 5 master's, 18 doctorates awarded. *Degree requirements:* For master's, thesis (for some programs); for doctorate, thesis/dissertation. *Entrance requirements:* For master's and doctorate, letters of recommendation, statement of purpose. Additional exam requirements/recommendations for international students: required—TOEFL (minimum score 550 paper-based; 80 iBT), IELTS (minimum score 6), PTE (minimum score 53). *Application deadline:* For fall admission, 12/1 priority date for domestic and international students. Applications are processed on a rolling basis. Application fee: $65 ($90 for international students). Electronic applications accepted. *Expenses:* Contact institution. *Financial support:* In 2019–20, 135 students received support, including 13 fellowships with tuition reimbursements available (averaging $10,044 per year), 109 research assistantships with tuition reimbursements available (averaging $20,228 per year), 47 teaching assistantships with tuition reimbursements available (averaging $15,610 per year); career-related internships or fieldwork, institutionally sponsored loans, scholarships/grants, traineeships, health care benefits, tuition waivers (full and partial), and unspecified assistantships also available. Support available to part-time students. Financial award application deadline: 3/15; financial award applicants required to submit FAFSA. *Unit head:* Joshua Wand, Professor and Department Head, 979-845-5032, E-mail: wand@tamu.edu. *Application contact:* Justine deGruyter, Graduate Advisor, 979-845-1779, E-mail: biobiograd@tamu.edu.
Website: http://biochemistry.tamu.edu/

**Texas Christian University,** College of Science and Engineering, Department of Chemistry and Biochemistry, Fort Worth, TX 76129-0002. Offers MA, MS, PhD. *Program availability:* Part-time. *Faculty:* 12 full-time (2 women). *Students:* 18 full-time (8 women); includes 3 minority (2 Asian, non-Hispanic/Latino; 1 Hispanic/Latino), 9 international. Average age 27. 11 applicants, 82% accepted, 4 enrolled. In 2019, 8 doctorates awarded. Terminal master's awarded for partial completion of doctoral program. *Degree requirements:* For master's, thesis; for doctorate, thesis/dissertation, literature seminar, cumulative exams, research progress report, independent research proposal, teaching of undergraduate labs. *Entrance requirements:* Additional exam requirements/recommendations for international students: required—TOEFL (minimum score 80 iBT). *Application deadline:* For fall admission, 3/1 for domestic and international students; for spring admission, 10/1 for domestic and international students. Applications are processed on a rolling basis. Application fee: $60. Electronic applications accepted. Full-time tuition and fees vary according to program. *Financial support:* In 2019–20, 18 students received support, including 18 fellowships with full tuition reimbursements available (averaging $21,000 per year); scholarships/grants, traineeships, health care benefits, tuition waivers, and unspecified assistantships also available. Support available to part-time students. Financial award application deadline: 4/1. *Unit head:* Dr. Eric Simanek, Chair/Professor, 817-257-5355, Fax: 817-257-5851, E-mail: e.simanek@tcu.edu. *Application contact:* Dr. Benjamin G. Janesko, Director of Graduate Studies/Associate Professor, 817-257-6202, Fax: 817-257-5851, E-mail: b.janesko@tcu.edu.
Website: http://www.chm.tcu.edu/

**Texas State University,** The Graduate College, College of Science and Engineering, Program in Biochemistry, San Marcos, TX 78666. Offers MS. *Program availability:* Part-time. *Degree requirements:* For master's, comprehensive exam, thesis. *Entrance requirements:* For master's, official GRE (general test only) required with competitive scores in the verbal reasoning and quantitative reasoning sections, baccalaureate degree in chemistry, biochemistry or closely-related field from regionally-accredited university with minimum GPA of 3.0 on last 60 undergraduate semester hours, 2 letters of recommendation, statement of purpose discussing career goals and undergraduate experiences. Additional exam requirements/recommendations for international students: required—TOEFL (minimum score 550 paper-based; 78 iBT), IELTS (minimum score 6.5). Electronic applications accepted.

**Thomas Jefferson University,** Jefferson College of Life Sciences, PhD Program in Biochemistry and Molecular Pharmacology, Philadelphia, PA 19107. Offers PhD. *Degree requirements:* For doctorate, comprehensive exam, thesis/dissertation. *Entrance requirements:* For doctorate, GRE General Test or MCAT, minimum GPA of 3.2. Additional exam requirements/recommendations for international students: required—TOEFL, IELTS (minimum score 7). Electronic applications accepted.

**Tufts University,** Graduate School of Biomedical Sciences, Cell, Molecular, and Developmental Biology Program, Medford, MA 02155. Offers cancer biology (PhD); developmental and regenerative biology (PhD); molecular and cellular medicine (PhD); structural and chemical biology (PhD). *Faculty:* 84 full-time (30 women). *Students:* 32 full-time (15 women); includes 10 minority (2 Black or African American, non-Hispanic/Latino; 4 Asian, non-Hispanic/Latino; 4 Hispanic/Latino), 4 international. Average age 28. 168 applicants, 5% accepted, 3 enrolled. In 2019, 5 doctorates awarded. Terminal master's awarded for partial completion of doctoral program. *Degree requirements:* For doctorate, comprehensive exam, thesis/dissertation. *Entrance requirements:* For doctorate, 3 letters of reference, resume, personal statement. *Application deadline:* For fall admission, 12/1 priority date for domestic and international students. Application fee: $90. Electronic applications accepted. *Expenses: Tuition:* Part-time $1799 per credit hour. Full-time tuition and fees vary according to degree level, program and student level. Part-time tuition and fees vary according to course load. *Financial support:* In 2019–20, 100 students received support, including 3 research assistantships with full tuition reimbursements available (averaging $40,000 per year); fellowships,

traineeships, and health care benefits also available. Financial award application deadline: 12/1. *Unit head:* Dr. Brent Cochran, Program Director, 617-636-0442. *Application contact:* Jeff Miller, Admissions Coordinator, 617-636-6767, Fax: 617-636-0375, E-mail: gsbs-admissions@tufts.edu.
Website: https://gsbs.tufts.edu/academics/CMDB

**Tulane University,** School of Medicine, Graduate Programs in Biomedical Sciences, Department of Biochemistry and Molecular Biology, New Orleans, LA 70118-5669. Offers MS. *Degree requirements:* For master's, thesis. *Entrance requirements:* For master's, GRE General Test, GRE Subject Test, minimum B average in undergraduate course work. Additional exam requirements/recommendations for international students: required—TOEFL. Electronic applications accepted. *Expenses: Tuition:* Full-time $57,004; part-time $3167 per credit hour. *Required fees:* $2086; $44.50 per credit hour. $80 per term. Tuition and fees vary according to course load, degree level and program.

**Universidad Central del Caribe,** School of Medicine, Program in Biomedical Sciences, Bayamón, PR 00960-6032. Offers anatomy and cell biology (MA, MS); biochemistry (MS); biomedical sciences (MA); cellular and molecular biology (PhD); microbiology and immunology (MA, MS); pharmacology (MS); physiology (MS).

**Université de Moncton,** Faculty of Sciences, Department of Chemistry and Biochemistry, Moncton, NB E1A 3E9, Canada. Offers biochemistry (M Sc); chemistry (M Sc). *Program availability:* Part-time. *Degree requirements:* For master's, one foreign language, thesis. *Entrance requirements:* For master's, minimum GPA of 3.0. Electronic applications accepted.

**Université de Montréal,** Faculty of Medicine, Department of Biochemistry, Montréal, QC H3C 3J7, Canada. Offers biochemistry (M Sc, PhD); clinical biochemistry (DEPD). Terminal master's awarded for partial completion of doctoral program. *Degree requirements:* For master's, thesis; for doctorate, thesis/dissertation, general exam. *Entrance requirements:* For master's and doctorate, proficiency in French, knowledge of English; for DEPD, proficiency in French. Electronic applications accepted.

**Université de Sherbrooke,** Faculty of Medicine and Health Sciences, Graduate Programs in Medicine, Department of Biochemistry, Sherbrooke, QC J1H 5N4, Canada. Offers M Sc, PhD. Terminal master's awarded for partial completion of doctoral program. *Degree requirements:* For master's, thesis; for doctorate, thesis/dissertation. Electronic applications accepted.

**University at Buffalo, the State University of New York,** Graduate School, Jacobs School of Medicine and Biomedical Sciences, Graduate Programs in Medicine and Biomedical Sciences, Department of Biochemistry, Buffalo, NY 14203. Offers MA, PhD. *Program availability:* Part-time. *Faculty:* 21 full-time (7 women), 1 (woman) part-time/adjunct. *Students:* 23 full-time (12 women); includes 5 minority (1 Black or African American, non-Hispanic/Latino; 1 American Indian or Alaska Native, non-Hispanic/Latino; 2 Asian, non-Hispanic/Latino; 1 Hispanic/Latino), 6 international. Average age 25. 17 applicants, 47% accepted, 6 enrolled. In 2019, 5 master's, 4 doctorates awarded. Terminal master's awarded for partial completion of doctoral program. *Degree requirements:* For master's, thesis optional; for doctorate, comprehensive exam, thesis/dissertation. *Entrance requirements:* For master's, GRE General Test; for doctorate, 3 letters of recommendation. Additional exam requirements/recommendations for international students: required—TOEFL (minimum score 79 iBT), IELTS. *Application deadline:* For fall admission, 2/1 priority date for domestic and international students. Applications are processed on a rolling basis. Application fee: $85. Electronic applications accepted. *Expenses:* Contact institution. *Financial support:* In 2019–20, 19 students received support, including 19 research assistantships with full tuition reimbursements available (averaging $27,000 per year); fellowships with full tuition reimbursements available, scholarships/grants, health care benefits, and unspecified assistantships also available. Financial award application deadline: 2/1; financial award applicants required to submit FAFSA. *Unit head:* Dr. Mark R. O'Brian, Chair, 716-829-3200, Fax: 716-829-2725, E-mail: mrobrian@buffalo.edu. *Application contact:* Dr. Satrajit Sinha, Director of Graduate Studies, 716-881-7994, Fax: 716-829-2725, E-mail: ssinha2@buffalo.edu.
Website: http://www.smbs.buffalo.edu/bch/

**The University of Alabama at Birmingham,** Joint Health Sciences, Biochemistry, Structural, and Stem Cell Biology Theme, Birmingham, AL 35294. Offers PhD. *Students:* 34 full-time (15 women); includes 9 minority (2 Black or African American, non-Hispanic/Latino; 1 American Indian or Alaska Native, non-Hispanic/Latino; 4 Asian, non-Hispanic/Latino; 2 Hispanic/Latino), 4 international. Average age 26. 41 applicants, 2% accepted, 1 enrolled. In 2019, 5 doctorates awarded. *Degree requirements:* For doctorate, comprehensive exam, thesis/dissertation. *Entrance requirements:* For doctorate, personal statement, resume or curriculum vitae, letters of recommendation, research experience, interview. Additional exam requirements/recommendations for international students: required—TOEFL (minimum score 80 iBT), IELTS (minimum score 6.5). *Application deadline:* For fall admission, 12/31 for domestic and international students. Applications are processed on a rolling basis. Electronic applications accepted. *Financial support:* In 2019–20, fellowships with full tuition reimbursements (averaging $30,000 per year), research assistantships with full tuition reimbursements (averaging $31,000 per year) were awarded; health care benefits also available. *Unit head:* Dr. Thomas Ryan, Theme Director, 205-996-2175, E-mail: tryan@uab.edu. *Application contact:* Alyssa Zasada, Admissions Manager for Graduate Biomedical Sciences, 205-934-3857, E-mail: grad-gbs@uab.edu.
Website: http://www.uab.edu/gbs/home/themes/bssb

**University of Alaska Fairbanks,** College of Natural Science and Mathematics, Department of Chemistry and Biochemistry, Fairbanks, AK 99775-6160. Offers biochemistry and neuroscience (PhD); chemistry (MA, MS), including chemistry (MS); environmental chemistry (PhD). *Program availability:* Part-time. *Degree requirements:* For master's, comprehensive exam, thesis (for some programs), oral defense of project or thesis; for doctorate, comprehensive exam, thesis/dissertation, oral defense of dissertation. *Entrance requirements:* For master's, GRE General Test (for MS), bachelor's degree from accredited institution with minimum cumulative undergraduate and major GPA of 3.0; for doctorate, GRE General Test, minimum cumulative GPA of 3.0. Additional exam requirements/recommendations for international students: required—TOEFL (minimum score 550 paper-based; 79 iBT), TWE. Electronic applications accepted.

**University of Alberta,** Faculty of Medicine and Dentistry and Faculty of Graduate Studies and Research, Graduate Programs in Medicine, Department of Biochemistry, Edmonton, AB T6G 2E1, Canada. Offers M Sc, PhD. Terminal master's awarded for partial completion of doctoral program. *Degree requirements:* For master's, thesis; for doctorate, thesis/dissertation. *Entrance requirements:* For master's and doctorate, minimum GPA of 3.3. Additional exam requirements/recommendations for international students: required—TOEFL (minimum score 550 paper-based).

**The University of Arizona,** College of Science, Biochemistry and Molecular and Cellular Biology Program, Tucson, AZ 85721. Offers PhD. *Program availability:* Evening/weekend. *Degree requirements:* For doctorate, thesis/dissertation. *Entrance requirements:* For doctorate, 3 letters of recommendation, statement of purpose. Additional exam requirements/recommendations for international students: required—TOEFL (minimum score 600 paper-based; 90 iBT), IELTS (minimum score 7). Electronic applications accepted.

**The University of Arizona,** College of Science, Department of Chemistry and Biochemistry, Tucson, AZ 85721. Offers biochemistry (PhD); chemistry (MA, MS, PhD). *Program availability:* Part-time. *Degree requirements:* For doctorate, comprehensive exam, thesis/dissertation. *Entrance requirements:* For doctorate, GRE General Test, 3 letters of recommendation, statement of purpose. Additional exam requirements/recommendations for international students: required—TOEFL (minimum score 550 paper-based; 79 iBT). Electronic applications accepted.

**University of Arkansas for Medical Sciences,** Graduate School, Little Rock, AR 72205. Offers biochemistry and molecular biology (MS, PhD); bioinformatics (MS, PhD); cellular physiology and molecular biophysics (MS, PhD); clinical nutrition (MS); interdisciplinary biomedical sciences (MS, PhD, Certificate); interdisciplinary toxicology (MS); microbiology and immunology (PhD); neurobiology and developmental sciences (PhD); pharmacology (PhD); MD/PhD. *Program availability:* Part-time. Terminal master's awarded for partial completion of doctoral program. *Degree requirements:* For master's, comprehensive exam (for some programs), thesis (for some programs); for doctorate, thesis/dissertation. *Entrance requirements:* For master's and doctorate, GRE. Additional exam requirements/recommendations for international students: required—TOEFL. Electronic applications accepted. *Expenses:* Contact institution.

**The University of British Columbia,** Faculty of Medicine, Department of Biochemistry and Molecular Biology, Vancouver, BC V6T 1Z3, Canada. Offers M Sc, PhD. *Degree requirements:* For master's, thesis; for doctorate, comprehensive exam, thesis/dissertation. *Entrance requirements:* For master's, first class B Sc; for doctorate, master's or first class honors bachelor's degree in biochemistry. Additional exam requirements/recommendations for international students: required—TOEFL (minimum score 625 paper-based). Electronic applications accepted. *Expenses:* Contact institution.

**University of Calgary,** Cumming School of Medicine and Faculty of Graduate Studies, Program in Biochemistry and Molecular Biology, Calgary, AB T2N 1N4, Canada. Offers M Sc, PhD. *Degree requirements:* For master's, thesis; for doctorate, thesis/dissertation, candidacy exam. *Entrance requirements:* For master's and doctorate, GRE General Test, minimum GPA of 3.2. Additional exam requirements/recommendations for international students: required—TOEFL. Electronic applications accepted.

**University of California, Berkeley,** Graduate Division, Group in Comparative Biochemistry, Berkeley, CA 94720. Offers PhD. *Degree requirements:* For doctorate, thesis/dissertation, qualifying exam. *Entrance requirements:* For doctorate, GRE General Test, GRE Subject Test, minimum GPA of 3.0, 3 letters of recommendation. Additional exam requirements/recommendations for international students: required—TOEFL. Electronic applications accepted.

**University of California, Davis,** Graduate Studies, Graduate Group in Biochemistry and Molecular Biology, Davis, CA 95616. Offers MS, PhD. Terminal master's awarded for partial completion of doctoral program. *Degree requirements:* For master's, comprehensive exam (for some programs), thesis (for some programs); for doctorate, thesis/dissertation. *Entrance requirements:* For master's and doctorate, GRE General Test, GRE Subject Test. Additional exam requirements/recommendations for international students: required—TOEFL (minimum score 550 paper-based). Electronic applications accepted.

**University of California, Irvine,** School of Biological Sciences, Department of Molecular Biology and Biochemistry, Irvine, CA 92697. Offers biological science (MS); biological sciences (PhD); biotechnology (MS); biotechnology management (MS); MD/PhD. *Students:* 46 full-time (24 women); includes 17 minority (2 Black or African American, non-Hispanic/Latino; 8 Asian, non-Hispanic/Latino; 7 Hispanic/Latino), 5 international. Average age 28. 5 applicants, 100% accepted, 4 enrolled. In 2019, 3 master's, 10 doctorates awarded. *Entrance requirements:* For master's, GRE, minimum GPA of 3.0; for doctorate, GRE General Test, GRE Subject Test, minimum GPA of 3.0. Additional exam requirements/recommendations for international students: required—TOEFL (minimum score 550 paper-based). *Application deadline:* For fall admission, 12/15 priority date for domestic students, 12/15 for international students. Applications are processed on a rolling basis. Application fee: $120 ($140 for international students). Electronic applications accepted. *Financial support:* Fellowships, research assistantships with full tuition reimbursements, teaching assistantships, institutionally sponsored loans, traineeships, health care benefits, and unspecified assistantships available. Financial award application deadline: 3/1; financial award applicants required to submit FAFSA. *Unit head:* Prof. Christopher Hughes, Chair, 949-824-8771, Fax: 949-824-8551, E-mail: cchughes@uci.edu. *Application contact:* Morgan Oldham, Student Affairs Assistant, 949-826-6034, Fax: 949-824-8551, E-mail: morgano@uci.edu.
Website: http://www.bio.uci.edu/

**University of California, Irvine,** School of Biological Sciences and School of Medicine, Interdisciplinary Graduate Program in Cellular and Molecular Biosciences, Irvine, CA 92697. Offers PhD. *Students:* 26 full-time (17 women); includes 13 minority (1 Black or African American, non-Hispanic/Latino; 6 Asian, non-Hispanic/Latino; 6 Hispanic/Latino). Average age 28. 448 applicants, 17% accepted, 26 enrolled. *Degree requirements:* For doctorate, thesis/dissertation, teaching assignment, preliminary exam. *Entrance requirements:* For doctorate, GRE General Test, three letters of recommendation, interview. Additional exam requirements/recommendations for international students: required—TOEFL or IELTS. *Application deadline:* For fall admission, 12/8 for domestic and international students. Application fee: $120 ($140 for international students). Electronic applications accepted. *Expenses:* Contact institution. *Financial support:* Fellowships with full tuition reimbursements, institutionally sponsored loans, scholarships/grants, tuition waivers (full), unspecified assistantships, and stipends available. Financial award application deadline: 1/1; financial award applicants required to submit FAFSA. *Unit head:* Melanie Cocco, Director, 949-824-4487, Fax: 949-824-1965, E-mail: mcocco@uci.edu. *Application contact:* Renee Frigo, Administrator, 949-824-8145, Fax: 949-824-1965, E-mail: rfrigo@uci.edu.
Website: http://cmb.uci.edu/

**University of California, Irvine,** School of Medicine and School of Biological Sciences, Department of Biological Chemistry, Irvine, CA 92697. Offers biological sciences (MS, PhD). *Students:* 23 full-time (12 women); includes 13 minority (1 Black or African American, non-Hispanic/Latino; 9 Asian, non-Hispanic/Latino; 3 Hispanic/Latino), 4 international. Average age 29. In 2019, 6 master's, 2 doctorates awarded. *Entrance requirements:* For master's, minimum GPA of 3.0; for doctorate, GRE General Test, GRE Subject Test, minimum GPA of 3.0. Additional exam requirements/recommendations for international students: required—TOEFL (minimum score 550 paper-based). *Application deadline:* For fall admission, 1/15 priority date for domestic students, 1/15 for international students. Application fee: $120 ($140 for international students). Electronic applications accepted. *Financial support:* Fellowships, research assistantships with full tuition reimbursements, teaching assistantships, institutionally sponsored loans, traineeships, health care benefits, and unspecified assistantships available. Financial award application deadline: 3/1; financial award applicants required to submit FAFSA. *Unit head:* Peter Kaiser, Chair/Professor, 949-824-9442, Fax: 949-824-2688, E-mail: pkaiser@uci.edu. *Application contact:* Andrew Komoto, Graduate

Coordinator, 949-824-6051, Fax: 949-824-2688, E-mail: akomoto@uci.edu. Website: http://www.biochem.uci.edu/

**University of California, Los Angeles,** David Geffen School of Medicine and Graduate Division, Graduate Programs in Medicine, Department of Biological Chemistry, Los Angeles, CA 90095. Offers MS, PhD. Terminal master's awarded for partial completion of doctoral program. *Degree requirements:* For master's, comprehensive exam or thesis; for doctorate, thesis/dissertation, oral and written qualifying exams; 2 quarters of teaching experience. *Entrance requirements:* For master's and doctorate, GRE General Test, bachelor's degree; minimum undergraduate GPA of 3.0 (or its equivalent if letter grade system not used). Additional exam requirements/recommendations for international students: required—TOEFL. Electronic applications accepted.

**University of California, Los Angeles,** Graduate Division, College of Letters and Science, Department of Chemistry and Biochemistry, Program in Biochemistry and Molecular Biology, Los Angeles, CA 90095. Offers MS, PhD. Terminal master's awarded for partial completion of doctoral program. *Degree requirements:* For master's, comprehensive exam or thesis; for doctorate, thesis/dissertation, oral and written qualifying exams; 3 quarters of teaching experience. *Entrance requirements:* For doctorate, GRE General Test, GRE Subject Test (recommended), bachelor's degree; minimum undergraduate GPA of 3.0 (or its equivalent if letter grade system not used). Additional exam requirements/recommendations for international students: required—TOEFL. Electronic applications accepted.

**University of California, Los Angeles,** Graduate Division, College of Letters and Science and David Geffen School of Medicine, UCLA ACCESS to Programs in the Molecular, Cellular and Integrative Life Sciences, Los Angeles, CA 90095. Offers biochemistry and molecular biology (PhD); biological chemistry (PhD); cellular and molecular pathology (PhD); human genetics (PhD); microbiology, immunology, and molecular genetics (PhD); molecular biology (PhD); molecular toxicology (PhD); molecular, cellular and integrative physiology (PhD); neurobiology (PhD); oral biology (PhD); physiology (PhD). *Degree requirements:* For doctorate, thesis/dissertation, oral and written qualifying exams. *Entrance requirements:* For doctorate, GRE General Test, bachelor's degree; minimum undergraduate GPA of 3.0 (or its equivalent if letter grade system not used). Additional exam requirements/recommendations for international students: required—TOEFL. Electronic applications accepted.

**University of California, Merced,** Graduate Division, School of Natural Sciences, Merced, CA 95343. Offers applied mathematics (MS, PhD); chemistry and chemical biology (MS, PhD); physics (MS, PhD); quantitative and systems biology (MS, PhD), including molecular and cellular biology (PhD). *Faculty:* 79 full-time (32 women). *Students:* 255 full-time (104 women), 1 (woman) part-time; includes 83 minority (5 Black or African American, non-Hispanic/Latino; 25 Asian, non-Hispanic/Latino; 44 Hispanic/Latino; 9 Two or more races, non-Hispanic/Latino), 77 international. Average age 28. 292 applicants, 43% accepted, 54 enrolled. In 2019, 13 master's, 23 doctorates awarded. Terminal master's awarded for partial completion of doctoral program. *Degree requirements:* For master's, variable foreign language requirement, comprehensive exam, thesis or alternative, oral defense; for doctorate, variable foreign language requirement, comprehensive exam, thesis/dissertation, oral defense. *Entrance requirements:* For master's and doctorate, GRE. Additional exam requirements/recommendations for international students: required—TOEFL (minimum score 550 paper-based; 80 iBT); recommended—IELTS (minimum score 6.5). *Application deadline:* For fall admission, 1/15 for domestic and international students. Application fee: $105 ($125 for international students). Electronic applications accepted. *Expenses: Tuition, area resident:* Full-time $11,442; part-time $5721 per semester. *Tuition, state resident:* full-time $11,442; part-time $5721 per semester. *Tuition, nonresident:* full-time $26,544; part-time $13,272 per semester. *International tuition:* $26,544 full-time. *Required fees:* $564 per semester. *Financial support:* In 2019–20, 233 students received support, including 9 fellowships with full tuition reimbursements available (averaging $22,005 per year), 56 research assistantships with full tuition reimbursements available (averaging $21,420 per year), 168 teaching assistantships with full tuition reimbursements available (averaging $21,911 per year); scholarships/grants, traineeships, and health care benefits also available. *Unit head:* Dr. Elizabeth Dumont, Dean, 209-228-4487, Fax: 209-228-4060, E-mail: edumont@ucmerced.edu. *Application contact:* Tsu Ya, Director of Graduate Admissions and Academic Services, 209-228-4521, Fax: 209-228-6906, E-mail: tya@ucmerced.edu.

**University of California, Riverside,** Graduate Division, Department of Biochemistry and Molecular Biology, Riverside, CA 92521-0102. Offers MS, PhD. *Program availability:* Part-time. Terminal master's awarded for partial completion of doctoral program. *Degree requirements:* For master's, comprehensive exam (for some programs), thesis (for some programs), comprehensive exam or thesis; for doctorate, comprehensive exam, thesis/dissertation, 2 quarters of teaching experience, written exam, oral qualifying exam. *Entrance requirements:* For master's, GRE General Test, minimum GPA of 3.0; for doctorate, GRE General Test, minimum GPA of 3.25. Additional exam requirements/recommendations for international students: required—TOEFL (minimum score 550 paper-based, 80 iBT) or IELTS. Electronic applications accepted.

**University of California, San Diego,** Graduate Division, Department of Chemistry and Biochemistry, La Jolla, CA 92093. Offers chemistry (MS, PhD). *Students:* 308 full-time (133 women), 7 part-time (2 women). 769 applicants, 31% accepted, 66 enrolled. In 2019, 60 master's, 32 doctorates awarded. *Degree requirements:* For master's, comprehensive exam (for some programs), thesis (for some programs); for doctorate, comprehensive exam, thesis/dissertation. *Entrance requirements:* For master's, GRE General Test, MS Thesis Agreement Form, letters of recommendation, statement of purpose; for doctorate, GRE General Test, GRE Subject Test, letters of recommendation, statement of purpose. Additional exam requirements/recommendations for international students: required—TOEFL (minimum score 550 paper-based; 80 iBT), IELTS (minimum score 7), PTE (minimum score 65). *Application deadline:* For fall admission, 3/19 for domestic students. Application fee: $105 ($125 for international students). Electronic applications accepted. *Financial support:* Fellowships, research assistantships, teaching assistantships, scholarships/grants, and traineeships available. Financial award applicants required to submit FAFSA. *Unit head:* Vicki Grassian, Chair, 858-534-2499, E-mail: vhgrassian@ucsd.edu. *Application contact:* Jeff Rances, Admissions Coordinator, 858-534-9728, E-mail: chemgradinfo@ucsd.edu. Website: http://chemistry.ucsd.edu

**University of California, San Francisco,** Graduate Division and School of Medicine, Tetrad Graduate Program, Biochemistry and Molecular Biology Track, San Francisco, CA 94143. Offers PhD, MD/PhD. *Degree requirements:* For doctorate, thesis/dissertation. *Entrance requirements:* For doctorate, GRE General Test, GRE Subject Test. Additional exam requirements/recommendations for international students: required—TOEFL. *Expenses:* Contact institution.

**University of California, San Francisco,** School of Pharmacy and Graduate Division, Chemistry and Chemical Biology Graduate Program, San Francisco, CA 94143. Offers PhD. *Degree requirements:* For doctorate, thesis/dissertation. *Entrance requirements:* For doctorate, GRE General Test, minimum GPA of 3.0, bachelor's degree. Additional

exam requirements/recommendations for international students: required—TOEFL (minimum score 550 paper-based; 80 iBT). Electronic applications accepted.

**University of California, Santa Barbara,** Graduate Division, College of Letters and Sciences, Division of Mathematics, Life, and Physical Sciences, Interdepartmental Graduate Program in Biomolecular Science and Engineering, Santa Barbara, CA 93106-2014. Offers biochemistry and molecular biology (PhD), including biochemistry and molecular biology, biophysics and bioengineering. Terminal master's awarded for partial completion of doctoral program. *Degree requirements:* For doctorate, thesis/dissertation. *Entrance requirements:* For doctorate, GRE General Test. Additional exam requirements/recommendations for international students: required—TOEFL (minimum score 630 paper-based; 109 iBT), IELTS (minimum score 7). Electronic applications accepted.

**University of California, Santa Cruz,** Division of Graduate Studies, Division of Physical and Biological Sciences, Department of Chemistry and Biochemistry, Santa Cruz, CA 95064. Offers MS, PhD. *Degree requirements:* For master's, thesis optional; for doctorate, one foreign language, thesis/dissertation, qualifying exam. *Entrance requirements:* For master's and doctorate, GRE General Test, GRE Subject Test. Additional exam requirements/recommendations for international students: required—TOEFL (minimum score 570 paper-based; 89 iBT); recommended—IELTS (minimum score 8). Electronic applications accepted.

**University of Cincinnati,** Graduate School, College of Medicine, Graduate Programs in Biomedical Sciences, Molecular Genetics, Biochemistry and Microbiology Graduate Program, Cincinnati, OH 45221. Offers MS, PhD. *Faculty:* 30 full-time (5 women). *Students:* 26 full-time (11 women), 4 part-time (2 women); includes 3 minority (1 Black or African American, non-Hispanic/Latino; 1 Asian, non-Hispanic/Latino; 1 Hispanic/Latino), 2 international. Average age 27. 40 applicants, 30% accepted, 6 enrolled. In 2019, 2 master's, 4 doctorates awarded. Terminal master's awarded for partial completion of doctoral program. *Degree requirements:* For master's, thesis or alternative; for doctorate, thesis/dissertation, qualifying exam. *Entrance requirements:* For master's and doctorate, GRE highly recommended but not required. Additional exam requirements/recommendations for international students: required—TOEFL (minimum score 600 paper-based; 100 iBT). *Application deadline:* For fall admission, 12/15 priority date for domestic and international students. Applications are processed on a rolling basis. Application fee: $40. Electronic applications accepted. *Financial support:* In 2019–20, 6 research assistantships with full tuition reimbursements (averaging $28,000 per year) were awarded; health care benefits also available. Financial award application deadline: 5/1. *Unit head:* Dr. Michael Lieberman, Professor and Chair, 513-558-5645, E-mail: michael.lieberman@uc.edu. *Application contact:* Dr. William Miller, Graduate Program Director, 513-558-0866, Fax: 513-558-8474, E-mail: william.miller@uc.edu. Website: http://med.uc.edu/molgen-graduate

**University of Cincinnati,** Graduate School, McMicken College of Arts and Sciences, Department of Chemistry, Cincinnati, OH 45221. Offers analytical chemistry (MS, PhD); biochemistry (MS, PhD); inorganic chemistry (MS, PhD); organic chemistry (MS, PhD); physical chemistry (MS, PhD); polymer chemistry (MS, PhD); sensors (PhD). *Program availability:* Part-time, evening/weekend. Terminal master's awarded for partial completion of doctoral program. *Degree requirements:* For master's, thesis optional; for doctorate, comprehensive exam, thesis/dissertation. *Entrance requirements:* For master's and doctorate, GRE General Test. Additional exam requirements/recommendations for international students: required—TOEFL (minimum score 580 paper-based). Electronic applications accepted.

**University of Colorado Boulder,** Graduate School, College of Arts and Sciences, Department of Chemistry, Boulder, CO 80309. Offers MS, PhD. Terminal master's awarded for partial completion of doctoral program. *Degree requirements:* For master's, comprehensive exam or thesis; for doctorate, comprehensive exam, thesis/dissertation, cumulative exam. *Entrance requirements:* For master's, GRE General Test, GRE Subject Test, minimum undergraduate GPA of 2.75; for doctorate, GRE General Test, GRE Subject Test, minimum GPA of 3.0. Electronic applications accepted. Application fee is waived when completed online.

**University of Colorado Denver,** School of Medicine, Biochemistry Program, Aurora, CO 80045. Offers biochemistry (PhD); biochemistry and molecular genetics (PhD). *Degree requirements:* For doctorate, comprehensive exam, thesis/dissertation, 30 credit hours each of coursework and thesis research. *Entrance requirements:* For doctorate, GRE, minimum of three letters of recommendation from qualified referees. Additional exam requirements/recommendations for international students: required—TOEFL (minimum score 550 paper-based; 80 iBT). Electronic applications accepted. Tuition and fees vary according to course load, program and reciprocity agreements.

**University of Connecticut Health Center,** Graduate School, Programs in Biomedical Sciences, Graduate Program in Molecular Biology and Biochemistry, Farmington, CT 06030. Offers PhD, DMD/PhD, MD/PhD. *Degree requirements:* For doctorate, comprehensive exam, thesis/dissertation. *Entrance requirements:* For doctorate, GRE General Test. Additional exam requirements/recommendations for international students: required—TOEFL (minimum score 600 paper-based). Electronic applications accepted.

**University of Dayton,** Department of Chemistry and Biochemistry, Dayton, OH 45469. Offers MS. *Program availability:* Part-time. *Degree requirements:* For master's, thesis, 30 credit hours. *Entrance requirements:* For master's, BS in chemistry or closely-related discipline. Additional exam requirements/recommendations for international students: required—TOEFL (minimum score 550 paper-based; 80 iBT), GRE; recommended—IELTS. Electronic applications accepted.

**University of Delaware,** College of Arts and Sciences, Department of Chemistry and Biochemistry, Newark, DE 19716. Offers biochemistry (MA, MS, PhD); chemistry (MA, MS, PhD). *Program availability:* Part-time. Terminal master's awarded for partial completion of doctoral program. *Degree requirements:* For master's, one foreign language, thesis (for some programs); for doctorate, one foreign language, thesis/dissertation, cumulative exam. *Entrance requirements:* For master's and doctorate, GRE General Test. Additional exam requirements/recommendations for international students: required—TOEFL (minimum score 600 paper-based). Electronic applications accepted.

**University of Florida,** College of Medicine and Graduate School, Interdisciplinary Program in Biomedical Sciences, Concentration in Biochemistry and Molecular Biology, Gainesville, FL 32611. Offers PhD. *Degree requirements:* For doctorate, thesis/dissertation. *Entrance requirements:* For doctorate, GRE General Test, minimum GPA of 3.0, biochemistry before enrollment. Additional exam requirements/recommendations for international students: required—TOEFL. Electronic applications accepted.

**University of Georgia,** Franklin College of Arts and Sciences, Department of Biochemistry and Molecular Biology, Athens, GA 30602. Offers MS, PhD. *Degree requirements:* For master's, one foreign language, thesis; for doctorate, one foreign language, thesis/dissertation. *Entrance requirements:* For master's and doctorate, GRE General Test. Additional exam requirements/recommendations for international students: required—TOEFL. Electronic applications accepted.

*Biochemistry*

**University of Guelph,** Office of Graduate and Postdoctoral Studies, College of Biological Science, Department of Molecular and Cellular Biology, Guelph, ON N1G 2W1, Canada. Offers biochemistry (M Sc, PhD); biophysics (M Sc, PhD); botany (M Sc, PhD); microbiology (M Sc, PhD); molecular biology and genetics (M Sc, PhD). *Degree requirements:* For master's, thesis, research proposal; for doctorate, comprehensive exam, thesis/dissertation, research proposal. *Entrance requirements:* For master's, minimum B-average during previous 2 years of coursework; for doctorate, minimum A-average. Additional exam requirements/recommendations for international students: required—TOEFL (minimum score 550 paper-based), IELTS (minimum score 6.5). Electronic applications accepted.

**University of Guelph,** Office of Graduate and Postdoctoral Studies, College of Physical and Engineering Science, Guelph-Waterloo Centre for Graduate Work in Chemistry and Biochemistry, Guelph, ON N1G 2W1, Canada. Offers M Sc, PhD. *Program availability:* Part-time. *Degree requirements:* For master's, thesis; for doctorate, thesis/dissertation.

**University of Houston,** College of Natural Sciences and Mathematics, Department of Biology and Biochemistry, Houston, TX 77204. Offers biochemistry (MA, PhD); biology (MA). Terminal master's awarded for partial completion of doctoral program. *Degree requirements:* For master's, comprehensive exam (for some programs), thesis optional; for doctorate, comprehensive exam (for some programs), thesis/dissertation. *Entrance requirements:* For master's and doctorate, GRE. Additional exam requirements/recommendations for international students: required—TOEFL (minimum score 550 paper-based; 79 iBT), IELTS (minimum score 6.5). Electronic applications accepted.

**University of Idaho,** College of Graduate Studies, College of Science, Department of Biological Sciences, Moscow, ID 83844-2282. Offers biology (MS, PhD); microbiology, molecular biology and biochemistry (PhD). *Faculty:* 18 full-time (7 women). *Students:* 27 full-time (14 women). Average age 27. In 2019, 2 master's, 2 doctorates awarded. *Degree requirements:* For master's, thesis; for doctorate, thesis/dissertation. *Entrance requirements:* For master's and doctorate, GRE, minimum GPA of 3.0. Additional exam requirements/recommendations for international students: required—TOEFL (minimum score 79 iBT). *Application deadline:* For fall admission, 12/1 for domestic students. Applications are processed on a rolling basis. Application fee: $60. Electronic applications accepted. *Expenses:* Tuition, state resident: full-time $7753.80; part-time $502 per credit hour. Tuition, nonresident: full-time $26,990; part-time $1571 per credit hour. *Required fees:* $2122.20; $47 per credit hour. *Financial support:* Research assistantships and teaching assistantships available. Financial award applicants required to submit FAFSA. *Unit head:* Dr. James J. Nagler, Chair, 208-885-6280, Fax: 208-885-7905, E-mail: biosci@uidaho.edu. *Application contact:* Dr. James J. Nagler, Chair, 208-885-6280, Fax: 208-885-7905, E-mail: biosci@uidaho.edu. Website: https://www.uidaho.edu/sci/biology

**University of Illinois at Chicago,** College of Medicine, Graduate Programs in Medicine, Department of Biochemistry and Molecular Genetics, Chicago, IL 60607-7128. Offers PhD, MD/PhD. Terminal master's awarded for partial completion of doctoral program. *Degree requirements:* For doctorate, thesis/dissertation. *Entrance requirements:* For doctorate, GRE General Test. Additional exam requirements/recommendations for international students: required—TOEFL. Electronic applications accepted.

**University of Illinois at Urbana-Champaign,** Graduate College, College of Liberal Arts and Sciences, School of Chemical Sciences, Champaign, IL 61820. Offers MA, MS, PhD, MS/JD, MS/MBA. *Expenses:* Contact institution.

**University of Illinois at Urbana-Champaign,** Graduate College, College of Liberal Arts and Sciences, School of Molecular and Cellular Biology, Department of Biochemistry, Champaign, IL 61820. Offers MS, PhD.

**The University of Iowa,** Roy J. and Lucille A. Carver College of Medicine and Graduate College, Graduate Programs in Medicine, Department of Biochemistry, Iowa City, IA 52242. Offers MS, PhD, MD/PhD. Terminal master's awarded for partial completion of doctoral program. *Degree requirements:* For master's, thesis; for doctorate, comprehensive exam, thesis/dissertation. *Entrance requirements:* For master's, GRE General Test. Additional exam requirements/recommendations for international students: required—TOEFL (minimum score 600 paper-based; 100 iBT). Electronic applications accepted.

**The University of Kansas,** Graduate Studies, College of Liberal Arts and Sciences, Department of Molecular Biosciences, Lawrence, KS 66044. Offers biochemistry and biophysics (PhD); microbiology (PhD); molecular, cellular, and developmental biology (PhD). *Program availability:* Part-time. *Students:* 66 full-time (39 women); includes 36 minority (1 Black or African American, non-Hispanic/Latino; 2 Asian, non-Hispanic/Latino; 31 Hispanic/Latino; 2 Two or more races, non-Hispanic/Latino), 31 international. Average age 28. 93 applicants, 30% accepted, 12 enrolled. In 2019, 3 doctorates awarded. Terminal master's awarded for partial completion of doctoral program. *Entrance requirements:* For doctorate, GRE General Test, 1-page statement of research interests and goals, 1-2 page curriculum vitae or resume, official transcript, 3 recommendation letters. Additional exam requirements/recommendations for international students: required—TOEFL, IELTS, TOEFL or IELTS. *Application deadline:* For fall admission, 12/1 for domestic and international students. Application fee: $65 ($85 for international students). Electronic applications accepted. *Expenses:* Tuition, state resident: full-time $9989. Tuition, nonresident: full-time $23,950. *International tuition:* $23,950 full-time. *Required fees:* $984; $81.99 per credit hour. Tuition and fees vary according to course load, campus/location and program. *Financial support:* Fellowships, research assistantships, teaching assistantships, scholarships/grants, health care benefits, and unspecified assistantships available. Financial award application deadline: 12/1. *Unit head:* Susan M. Egan, Chair, 785-864-4294, E-mail: sme@ku.edu. *Application contact:* John Connolly, Graduate Admissions Contact, 785-864-4311, E-mail: jconnolly@ku.edu. Website: http://www.molecularbiosciences.ku.edu/

**The University of Kansas,** University of Kansas Medical Center, School of Medicine, Department of Biochemistry and Molecular Biology, Kansas City, KS 66160. Offers PhD, MD/PhD. *Faculty:* 17. *Students:* 15 full-time (8 women); includes 1 minority (Black or African American, non-Hispanic/Latino), 3 international. Average age 29. Terminal master's awarded for partial completion of doctoral program. *Degree requirements:* For doctorate, comprehensive exam, thesis/dissertation, comprehensive oral and written exam. *Entrance requirements:* For doctorate, GRE. Additional exam requirements/recommendations for international students: required—TOEFL. *Application deadline:* For fall admission, 12/1 for domestic and international students. Applications are processed on a rolling basis. Application fee: $60. Electronic applications accepted. Application fee is waived when completed online. *Expenses:* Tuition, state resident: full-time $9989. Tuition, nonresident: full-time $23,950. *International tuition:* $23,950 full-time. *Required fees:* $984; $81.99 per credit hour. Tuition and fees vary according to course load, campus/location and program. *Financial support:* Fellowships, research assistantships with partial tuition reimbursements, teaching assistantships with partial tuition reimbursements, traineeships, health care benefits, and unspecified assistantships available. Financial award application deadline: 3/1; financial award applicants required to submit FAFSA. *Unit head:* Dr. Liskin Swint-Kruse, Professor and Chair, 913-588-0399, E-mail: lswint-kruse@kumc.edu. *Application contact:* Dr. Aron W.

Fenton, Professor and Director of Graduate Studies, 913-588-7033, E-mail: afenton@kumc.edu.
Website: http://www.kumc.edu/school-of-medicine/biochemistry-and-molecular-biology.html

**University of Kentucky,** Graduate School, Graduate School Programs from the College of Medicine, Program in Molecular and Cellular Biochemistry, Lexington, KY 40506-0032. Offers PhD, MD/PhD. *Degree requirements:* For doctorate, comprehensive exam, thesis/dissertation. *Entrance requirements:* For doctorate, GRE General Test, minimum undergraduate GPA of 2.75. Additional exam requirements/recommendations for international students: required—TOEFL (minimum score 550 paper-based). Electronic applications accepted.

**University of Lethbridge,** School of Graduate Studies, Lethbridge, AB T1K 3M4, Canada. Offers addictions counseling (M Sc); agricultural biotechnology (M Sc); agricultural studies (M Sc, MA); anthropology (MA); archaeology (M Sc, MA); art (MA, MFA); biochemistry (M Sc); biological sciences (M Sc); biomolecular science (PhD); biosystems and biodiversity (PhD); Canadian studies (MA); chemistry (M Sc); computer science (M Sc); computer science and geographical information science (M Sc); counseling (MC); counseling psychology (M Ed); dramatic arts (MA); earth, space, and physical science (PhD); economics (MA); education (MA, PhD); educational leadership (M Ed); English (MA); environmental science (M Sc); evolution and behavior (PhD); exercise science (M Sc); French (MA); French/German (MA); French/Spanish (MA); general education (M Ed); geography (M Sc, MA); German (MA); health sciences (M Sc); individualized multidisciplinary (M Sc, MA); kinesiology (M Sc, MA); management (M Sc), including accounting, finance, human resource management and labor relations, information systems, international management, marketing, policy and strategy; mathematics (M Sc); music (M Mus, MA); Native American studies (MA); neuroscience (M Sc, PhD); new media (MA, MFA); nursing (M Sc, MN); philosophy (MA); physics (M Sc); political science (MA); psychology (M Sc, MA); religious studies (MA); sociology (MA); theatre and dramatic arts (MFA); theoretical and computational science (PhD); urban and regional studies (MA); women and gender studies (MA). *Program availability:* Part-time, evening/weekend. *Degree requirements:* For master's, thesis (for some programs); for doctorate, comprehensive exam, thesis/dissertation. *Entrance requirements:* For master's, GMAT (for M Sc in management), bachelor's degree in related field, minimum GPA of 3.0 during previous 20 graded semester courses, 2 years' teaching or related experience (M Ed); for doctorate, master's degree, minimum graduate GPA of 3.5. Additional exam requirements/recommendations for international students: required—TOEFL (minimum score 580 paper-based; 93 iBT). Electronic applications accepted.

**University of Louisville,** Graduate School, College of Arts and Sciences, Department of Chemistry, Louisville, KY 40292-0001. Offers analytical chemistry (MS, PhD); biochemistry (MS, PhD); chemical physics (PhD); inorganic chemistry (MS, PhD); organic chemistry (MS, PhD); physical chemistry (MS, PhD). *Program availability:* Part-time. *Faculty:* 25 full-time (8 women), 4 part-time/adjunct (2 women). *Students:* 47 full-time (15 women), 13 part-time (4 women); includes 4 minority (all Asian, non-Hispanic/Latino), 45 international. Average age 31. 58 applicants, 34% accepted, 11 enrolled. In 2019, 11 master's, 6 doctorates awarded. Terminal master's awarded for partial completion of doctoral program. *Degree requirements:* For master's, thesis (for some programs), Literature Seminars; for doctorate, thesis/dissertation, Cumulative Exams, Literature Seminars; Research. *Entrance requirements:* For master's, 2 letters of reference, official transcripts, personal statement; for doctorate, GRE General Test, official transcripts, recommendation letters (minimum of 2), personal statement. Additional exam requirements/recommendations for international students: required—TOEFL (minimum score 550 paper-based; 79 iBT), IELTS can be taken in place of TOEFL; recommended—IELTS (minimum score 6.5). *Application deadline:* For fall admission, 1/15 priority date for domestic and international students; for spring admission, 9/15 priority date for domestic and international students. Applications are processed on a rolling basis. Application fee: $65. Electronic applications accepted. *Expenses: Tuition, area resident:* Full-time $13,000; part-time $723 per credit hour. Tuition, state resident: full-time $13,000; part-time $723 per credit hour. Tuition, nonresident: full-time $27,114; part-time $1507 per credit hour. *International tuition:* $27,114 full-time. *Required fees:* $196. Tuition and fees vary according to program and reciprocity agreements. *Financial support:* In 2019–20, 65 students received support, including 2 fellowships with full tuition reimbursements available (averaging $23,000 per year), 10 research assistantships with full tuition reimbursements available (averaging $23,000 per year), 41 teaching assistantships with full tuition reimbursements available (averaging $23,000 per year); scholarships/grants, health care benefits, and unspecified assistantships also available. Financial award application deadline: 1/15. *Unit head:* Dr. Pawel Kozlowski, Professor and Chair, 502-852-8148, Fax: 502-852-8149, E-mail: pawel@louisville.edu. *Application contact:* Sherry Nalley, Graduate Program Assistant, 502-852-6798, Fax: 502-852-8149, E-mail: sherry.nalley@louisville.edu. Website: http://louisville.edu/chemistry

**University of Louisville,** School of Medicine, Department of Biochemistry and Molecular Genetics, Louisville, KY 40292-0001. Offers MS, PhD, MD/PhD. *Program availability:* Part-time. *Faculty:* 12 full-time (3 women). *Students:* 21 full-time (11 women), 4 part-time (3 women); includes 6 minority (2 Black or African American, non-Hispanic/Latino; 3 Asian, non-Hispanic/Latino; 1 Hispanic/Latino), 4 international. Average age 30. 28 applicants, 21% accepted, 5 enrolled. In 2019, 5 master's, 6 doctorates awarded. Terminal master's awarded for partial completion of doctoral program. *Degree requirements:* For master's, thesis (for some programs); for doctorate, comprehensive exam, thesis/dissertation. *Entrance requirements:* For doctorate, minimum GPA of 3.0. Additional exam requirements/recommendations for international students: required—TOEFL, IELTS. *Application deadline:* For fall admission, 12/15 priority date for domestic and international students. Applications are processed on a rolling basis. Application fee: $60. Electronic applications accepted. *Expenses: Tuition, area resident:* Full-time $13,000; part-time $723 per credit hour. Tuition, state resident: full-time $13,000; part-time $723 per credit hour. Tuition, nonresident: full-time $27,114; part-time $1507 per credit hour. *International tuition:* $27,114 full-time. *Required fees:* $196. Tuition and fees vary according to program and reciprocity agreements. *Financial support:* In 2019–20, 20 students received support, including 5 fellowships with full tuition reimbursements available (averaging $26,000 per year); health care benefits also available. Financial award application deadline: 1/15. *Unit head:* Dr. Ronald Gregg, Professor and Chair, 502-852-5217, E-mail: ronald.gregg@louisville.edu. *Application contact:* Dr. Brian Clem, Associate Professor, 502-852-8427, E-mail: bfclem01@louisville.edu.

**The University of Manchester,** School of Biological Sciences, Manchester, United Kingdom. Offers adaptive organismal biology (M Phil, PhD); animal biology (M Phil, PhD); biochemistry (M Phil, PhD); bioinformatics (M Phil, PhD); biomolecular sciences (M Phil, PhD); biotechnology (M Phil, PhD); cell biology (M Phil, PhD); cell matrix research (M Phil, PhD); channels and transporters (M Phil, PhD); developmental biology (M Phil, PhD); environmental biology (M Phil, PhD); evolutionary biology (M Phil, PhD); gene expression (M Phil, PhD); genetics (M Phil, PhD); history of science, technology and medicine (M Phil, PhD); immunology (M Phil, PhD); integrative neurobiology and behavior (M Phil, PhD); membrane trafficking (M Phil, PhD); microbiology (M Phil, PhD);

molecular and cellular neuroscience (M Phil, PhD); molecular biology (M Phil, PhD); molecular cancer studies (M Phil, PhD); neuroscience (M Phil, PhD); ophthalmology (M Phil, PhD); optometry (M Phil, PhD); organelle function (M Phil, PhD); pharmacology (M Phil, PhD); physiology (M Phil, PhD); plant sciences (M Phil, PhD); stem cell research (M Phil, PhD); structural biology (M Phil, PhD); systems neuroscience (M Phil, PhD); toxicology (M Phil, PhD).

**The University of Manchester,** School of Chemistry, Manchester, United Kingdom. Offers biological chemistry (PhD); chemistry (M Ent, M Phil, M Sc, D Ent, PhD); inorganic chemistry (PhD); materials chemistry (PhD); nanoscience (PhD); nuclear fission (PhD); organic chemistry (PhD); physical chemistry (PhD); theoretical chemistry (PhD).

**University of Manitoba,** Max Rady College of Medicine and Faculty of Graduate Studies, Graduate Programs in Medicine, Department of Biochemistry and Medical Genetics, Winnipeg, MB R3T 2N2, Canada. Offers biochemistry and medical genetics (M Sc, PhD); genetic counseling (M Sc). Terminal master's awarded for partial completion of doctoral program. *Degree requirements:* For master's, thesis; for doctorate, thesis/dissertation.

**University of Maryland, Baltimore,** Graduate School, Graduate Program in Life Sciences, Program in Biochemistry and Molecular Biology, Baltimore, MD 21201. Offers biochemistry (MS, PhD); MD/PhD. *Degree requirements:* For doctorate, comprehensive exam, thesis/dissertation. *Entrance requirements:* For master's and doctorate, GRE General Test, minimum GPA of 3.0, curriculum vitae, essay, 3 letters of recommendation. Additional exam requirements/recommendations for international students: required—TOEFL (minimum score 80 iBT); recommended—IELTS (minimum score 7). Electronic applications accepted.

**University of Maryland, College Park,** Academic Affairs, College of Computer, Mathematical and Natural Sciences, Department of Chemistry and Biochemistry, Biochemistry Program, College Park, MD 20742. Offers MS, PhD. *Program availability:* Part-time, evening/weekend. Terminal master's awarded for partial completion of doctoral program. *Degree requirements:* For master's, thesis or alternative; for doctorate, thesis/dissertation, 2 seminar presentations, oral exam. *Entrance requirements:* For master's and doctorate, GRE General Test, GRE Subject Test (recommended), minimum GPA of 3.0, 3 letters of recommendation. Additional exam requirements/recommendations for international students: required—TOEFL. Electronic applications accepted.

**University of Massachusetts Amherst,** Graduate School, College of Natural Sciences, Department of Biochemistry and Molecular Biology, Amherst, MA 01003. Offers MS, PhD. *Program availability:* Part-time. Terminal master's awarded for partial completion of doctoral program. *Degree requirements:* For master's, thesis or alternative; for doctorate, comprehensive exam, thesis/dissertation. *Entrance requirements:* Additional exam requirements/recommendations for international students: required—TOEFL (minimum score 550 paper-based; 80 iBT), IELTS (minimum score 6.5). Electronic applications accepted.

**University of Massachusetts Amherst,** Graduate School, Interdisciplinary Programs, Program in Molecular and Cellular Biology, Amherst, MA 01003. Offers biological chemistry and molecular biophysics (PhD); biomedicine (PhD); cellular and developmental biology (PhD). *Program availability:* Part-time. Terminal master's awarded for partial completion of doctoral program. *Degree requirements:* For doctorate, comprehensive exam, thesis/dissertation. *Entrance requirements:* For doctorate, GRE General Test. Additional exam requirements/recommendations for international students: required—TOEFL (minimum score 550 paper-based; 80 iBT), IELTS (minimum score 6.5). Electronic applications accepted.

**University of Massachusetts Amherst,** Graduate School, Interdisciplinary Programs, Program in Plant Biology, Amherst, MA 01003. Offers biochemistry and metabolism (MS, PhD); cell biology and physiology (MS, PhD); environmental, ecological and integrative biology (MS, PhD); genetics and evolution (MS, PhD). *Degree requirements:* For master's, thesis; for doctorate, 2 foreign languages, comprehensive exam, thesis/dissertation. *Entrance requirements:* For master's and doctorate, GRE General Test. Additional exam requirements/recommendations for international students: required—TOEFL (minimum score 550 paper-based; 80 iBT), IELTS (minimum score 6.5). Electronic applications accepted.

**University of Massachusetts Dartmouth,** Graduate School, College of Arts and Sciences, Department of Chemistry and Biochemistry, North Dartmouth, MA 02747-2300. Offers chemistry (MS, PhD). *Program availability:* Part-time. *Faculty:* 19 full-time (6 women), 3 part-time/adjunct (2 women). *Students:* 15 full-time (8 women), 26 part-time (10 women); includes 6 minority (1 Black or African American, non-Hispanic/Latino; 5 Asian, non-Hispanic/Latino), 17 international. Average age 29. 18 applicants, 89% accepted, 6 enrolled. In 2019, 2 doctorates awarded. *Degree requirements:* For master's, thesis, Thesis or Project; for doctorate, comprehensive exam, thesis/dissertation, Dissertation. *Entrance requirements:* For master's and doctorate, GRE, statement of purpose (300-600 words), resume, official transcripts, 3 letters of recommendation. Additional exam requirements/recommendations for international students: required—TOEFL (minimum score 80 iBT). *Application deadline:* For fall admission, 8/15 for domestic students, 7/15 for international students; for spring admission, 11/1 for domestic students, 10/1 for international students. Application fee: $60. Electronic applications accepted. *Expenses: Tuition, area resident:* Full-time $16,390; part-time $682.92 per credit. Tuition, state resident: full-time $16,390; part-time $682.92 per credit. Tuition, nonresident: full-time $29,578; part-time $1232.42 per credit. *Required fees:* $575. *Financial support:* In 2019–20, 7 fellowships (averaging $8,857 per year), 10 research assistantships (averaging $9,973 per year), 28 teaching assistantships (averaging $8,363 per year) were awarded; tuition waivers (full and partial) and Doctoral Writing Support also available. Financial award application deadline: 3/1; financial award applicants required to submit FAFSA. *Unit head:* Yuegang Zuo, Graduate Program Director, Chemistry, 508-999-8959, Fax: 508-999-9167, E-mail: yzuo@umassd.edu. *Application contact:* Scott Webster, Director of Graduate Studies and Admissions, 508-999-8604, Fax: 508-999-8183, E-mail: graduate@umassd.edu. Website: http://www.umassd.edu/cas/chemistry

**University of Massachusetts Lowell,** College of Sciences, Department of Chemistry, Lowell, MA 01854. Offers analytical chemistry (PhD); biochemistry (PhD); chemistry (MS, PhD); environmental studies (PhD); green chemistry (PhD); inorganic chemistry (PhD); organic chemistry (PhD); polymer science (MS). Terminal master's awarded for partial completion of doctoral program. *Degree requirements:* For master's, thesis; for doctorate, 2 foreign languages, thesis/dissertation. *Entrance requirements:* For master's and doctorate, GRE General Test. Electronic applications accepted.

**University of Massachusetts Medical School,** Graduate School of Biomedical Sciences, Worcester, MA 01655. Offers biomedical sciences (PhD), including biochemistry and molecular pharmacology, bioinformatics and computational biology, cancer biology, immunology and microbiology, interdisciplinary, neuroscience, translational science; biomedical sciences (millennium program) (PhD); clinical and population health research (PhD); clinical investigation (MS). *Faculty:* 1,258 full-time (525 women), 372 part-time/adjunct (238 women). *Students:* 344 full-time (198 women), 1 (woman) part-time; includes 73 minority (12 Black or African American, non-Hispanic/

Latino; 1 American Indian or Alaska Native, non-Hispanic/Latino; 45 Asian, non-Hispanic/Latino; 15 Hispanic/Latino), 120 international. Average age 29. 581 applicants, 23% accepted, 56 enrolled. In 2019, 6 master's, 49 doctorates awarded. Terminal master's awarded for partial completion of doctoral program. *Degree requirements:* For master's, comprehensive exam, thesis; for doctorate, comprehensive exam, thesis/dissertation. *Entrance requirements:* For master's, MD, PhD, DVM, or PharmD; for doctorate, bachelor's degree. Additional exam requirements/recommendations for international students: required—TOEFL, IELTS, TOEFL (minimum score 100 IBT) or IELTS (minimum score 7.0). *Application deadline:* For fall admission, 12/1 for domestic and international students. Applications are processed on a rolling basis. Application fee: $80. Electronic applications accepted. Application fee is waived when completed online. *Expenses:* Contact institution. *Financial support:* In 2019–20, 22 fellowships with full tuition reimbursements (averaging $33,061 per year), 322 research assistantships with full tuition reimbursements (averaging $32,850 per year) were awarded; institutionally sponsored loans and scholarships/grants also available. Financial award application deadline: 5/15. *Unit head:* Dr. Mary Ellen Lane, Dean, 508-856-4018, E-mail: maryellen.lane@umassmed.edu. *Application contact:* Dr. Kendall Knight, Assistant Vice Provost for Admissions, 508-856-5628, Fax: 508-856-3659, E-mail: kendall.knight@umassmed.edu.
Website: http://www.umassmed.edu/gsbs/

**University of Miami,** Graduate School, Miller School of Medicine, Graduate Programs in Medicine, Department of Biochemistry and Molecular Biology, Coral Gables, FL 33124. Offers PhD, MD/PhD. *Faculty:* 36 full-time (10 women). *Students:* 64 full-time (38 women); includes 27 minority (5 Black or African American, non-Hispanic/Latino; 8 Asian, non-Hispanic/Latino; 10 Hispanic/Latino; 4 Two or more races, non-Hispanic/Latino), 11 international. Average age 29. 49 applicants, 55% accepted, 27 enrolled. In 2019, 4 doctorates awarded. *Degree requirements:* For doctorate, comprehensive exam, thesis/dissertation, proposition exams. *Entrance requirements:* Additional exam requirements/recommendations for international students: required—TOEFL, IELTS, Either TOEFL or the ITELS is accepted. *Financial support:* In 2019–20, 34 fellowships with full tuition reimbursements (averaging $25,500 per year) were awarded; research assistantships, scholarships/grants, and tuition waivers (full) also available. *Unit head:* Dr. Sylvia Daunert, Department Chair, 305-243-4005, Fax: 305-243-3955, E-mail: sdaunert@med.miami.edu. *Application contact:* Dr. Sapna Deo, Graduate Program Director, 305-243-4421, Fax: 305-243-3955, E-mail: sdeo@med.miami.edu.
Website: http://bm.med.miami.edu/

**University of Michigan,** Rackham Graduate School, College of Literature, Science, and the Arts, Department of Chemistry, Ann Arbor, MI 48109-1055. Offers analytical chemistry (PhD); chemical biology (PhD); chemical sciences (MS); inorganic chemistry (PhD); materials chemistry (PhD); organic chemistry (PhD); physical chemistry (PhD). *Program availability:* Part-time. *Degree requirements:* For doctorate, comprehensive exam, thesis/dissertation, oral defense of dissertation, organic cumulative proficiency exams. *Entrance requirements:* For master's, bachelor's degree, 3 letters of recommendation, personal statement; for doctorate, bachelor's degree, 3 letters of recommendation, personal statement, curriculum vitae/resume. Additional exam requirements/recommendations for international students: required—TOEFL (minimum score 560 paper-based; 84 iBT) or IELTS. Electronic applications accepted.

**University of Michigan,** Rackham Graduate School, Program in Biomedical Sciences (PIBS), Department of Biological Chemistry, Ann Arbor, MI 48109. Offers MS, PhD. Terminal master's awarded for partial completion of doctoral program. *Degree requirements:* For master's, written thesis (for research track); literature analysis project (for course track); for doctorate, comprehensive exam, thesis/dissertation, oral defense, written thesis. *Entrance requirements:* For master's, 3 letters of recommendation, undergraduate transcripts, bachelor's degree, research experience; for doctorate, 3 letters of recommendation, undergraduate transcripts, bachelor's degree, significance research experience. Additional exam requirements/recommendations for international students: required—TOEFL (minimum score 84 iBT). Electronic applications accepted. *Expenses:* Contact institution.

**University of Michigan,** Rackham Graduate School, Program in Chemical Biology, Ann Arbor, MI 48109. Offers cancer chemical biology (MS); chemical biology (PhD). *Program availability:* Part-time. *Degree requirements:* For doctorate, thesis/dissertation. *Entrance requirements:* Additional exam requirements/recommendations for international students: required—TOEFL (minimum score 600 paper-based; 102 iBT). Electronic applications accepted.

**University of Minnesota, Duluth,** Graduate School, Swenson College of Science and Engineering, Department of Chemistry and Biochemistry, Duluth, MN 55812-2496. Offers MS. *Program availability:* Part-time. *Degree requirements:* For master's, thesis. *Entrance requirements:* For master's, bachelor's degree in chemistry, minimum GPA of 3.0. Additional exam requirements/recommendations for international students: required—TOEFL (minimum score 550 paper-based; 79 iBT), IELTS (minimum score 6.5).

**University of Minnesota, Duluth,** Medical School, Department of Biochemistry, Molecular Biology and Biophysics, Duluth, MN 55812-2496. Offers biochemistry, molecular biology and biophysics (MS); biology and biophysics (PhD); social, administrative, and clinical pharmacy (MS, PhD); toxicology (MS, PhD). Terminal master's awarded for partial completion of doctoral program. *Degree requirements:* For master's, comprehensive exam, thesis; for doctorate, comprehensive exam, thesis/dissertation. *Entrance requirements:* For master's and doctorate, GRE General Test. Additional exam requirements/recommendations for international students: required—TOEFL. Electronic applications accepted.

**University of Minnesota, Twin Cities Campus,** Graduate School, College of Biological Sciences, Biochemistry, Molecular Biology and Biophysics Graduate Program, Minneapolis, MN 55455-0213. Offers PhD. *Degree requirements:* For doctorate, thesis/dissertation. *Entrance requirements:* For doctorate, GRE, 3 letters of recommendation, more than 1 semester of laboratory experience. Additional exam requirements/recommendations for international students: required—TOEFL (minimum score 625 paper-based; 108 iBT with writing subsection 25 and reading subsection 25) or IELTS (minimum score 7). Electronic applications accepted.

**University of Mississippi Medical Center,** School of Graduate Studies in Health Sciences, Department of Biochemistry, Jackson, MS 39216-4505. Offers PhD, MD/PhD. *Degree requirements:* For doctorate, thesis/dissertation, first authored publication. *Entrance requirements:* For doctorate, GRE General Test, minimum GPA of 3.0. Additional exam requirements/recommendations for international students: required—TOEFL.

**University of Missouri,** Office of Research and Graduate Studies, College of Agriculture, Food and Natural Resources, Department of Biochemistry, Columbia, MO 65211. Offers MS, PhD, PhD/MD. Terminal master's awarded for partial completion of doctoral program. *Entrance requirements:* For master's and doctorate, GRE, minimum GPA of 3.0; undergraduate research; 3 letters of reference; 500-word personal statement.

**University of Missouri–Kansas City,** School of Biological Sciences, Program in Molecular Biology and Biochemistry, Kansas City, MO 64110-2499. Offers PhD. *Degree*

*requirements:* For doctorate, comprehensive exam, thesis/dissertation. *Entrance requirements:* For doctorate, GRE General Test, bachelor's degree in chemistry, biology, or a related discipline; minimum GPA of 3.0. Additional exam requirements/recommendations for international students: required—TOEFL (minimum score 550 paper-based; 80 iBT).

**University of Missouri–St. Louis,** College of Arts and Sciences, Department of Chemistry and Biochemistry, St. Louis, MO 63121. Offers biochemistry and biotechnology (MS); chemistry (MS, PhD). *Program availability:* Part-time, evening/weekend. Terminal master's awarded for partial completion of doctoral program. *Degree requirements:* For master's, thesis optional; for doctorate, thesis/dissertation. *Entrance requirements:* For master's, 2 letters of recommendation; for doctorate, GRE General Test, 3 letters of recommendation. Additional exam requirements/recommendations for international students: required—TOEFL (minimum score 550 paper-based; 79 iBT), IELTS (minimum score 6.5). Electronic applications accepted. *Expenses: Tuition, area resident:* Full-time $9005.40; part-time $6003.60 per credit hour. Tuition, state resident: full-time $9005.40; part-time $6003.60 per credit hour. Tuition, nonresident: full-time $22,108; part-time $14,738.40 per credit hour. *International tuition:* $22,108 full-time. Tuition and fees vary according to course load.

**University of Montana,** Graduate School, College of Humanities and Sciences, Division of Biological Sciences, Program in Cellular, Molecular and Microbial Biology, Missoula, MT 59812. Offers cellular and developmental biology (PhD); microbial evolution and ecology (PhD); microbiology and immunology (PhD); molecular biology and biochemistry (PhD). Terminal master's awarded for partial completion of doctoral program. *Degree requirements:* For doctorate, variable foreign language requirement, thesis/dissertation. *Entrance requirements:* For doctorate, GRE General Test.

**University of Nebraska–Lincoln,** Graduate College, College of Agricultural Sciences and Natural Resources and College of Arts and Sciences, Department of Biochemistry, Lincoln, NE 68588. Offers MS, PhD. Terminal master's awarded for partial completion of doctoral program. *Degree requirements:* For master's, thesis optional; for doctorate, comprehensive exam, thesis/dissertation. *Entrance requirements:* For master's and doctorate, GRE General Test, GRE Subject Test. Additional exam requirements/recommendations for international students: required—TOEFL (minimum score 550 paper-based). Electronic applications accepted.

**University of Nebraska–Lincoln,** Graduate College, College of Arts and Sciences, Department of Chemistry, Lincoln, NE 68588. Offers analytical chemistry (PhD); biochemistry (PhD); chemistry (MS); inorganic chemistry (PhD); materials chemistry (PhD); organic chemistry (PhD); physical chemistry (PhD). *Degree requirements:* For master's, one foreign language, thesis optional, departmental qualifying exam; for doctorate, one foreign language, comprehensive exam, thesis/dissertation, departmental qualifying exams. *Entrance requirements:* For master's and doctorate, GRE. Additional exam requirements/recommendations for international students: required—TOEFL (minimum score 550 paper-based). Electronic applications accepted.

**University of Nebraska Medical Center,** Interdisciplinary Graduate Program in Biomedical Sciences, Department of Biochemistry and Molecular Biology, Omaha, NE 68198. Offers MS. Terminal master's awarded for partial completion of doctoral program. *Degree requirements:* For master's, comprehensive exam, thesis. *Entrance requirements:* For master's, GRE General Test. Additional exam requirements/recommendations for international students: required—TOEFL (minimum score 550 paper-based). Electronic applications accepted. Application fee is waived when completed online.

**University of Nevada, Las Vegas,** Graduate College, College of Sciences, Department of Chemistry and Biochemistry, Las Vegas, NV 89154-4003. Offers biochemistry (MS); chemistry (MS, PhD); radio chemistry (PhD). *Program availability:* Part-time. *Faculty:* 16 full-time (2 women), 1 part-time/adjunct (0 women). *Students:* 39 full-time (20 women), 3 part-time (0 women); includes 17 minority (1 Black or African American, non-Hispanic/Latino; 5 Asian, non-Hispanic/Latino; 7 Hispanic/Latino; 4 Two or more races, non-Hispanic/Latino), 2 international. Average age 30. 26 applicants, 35% accepted, 8 enrolled. In 2019, 4 doctorates awarded. Terminal master's awarded for partial completion of doctoral program. *Degree requirements:* For master's, thesis, departmental seminar; for doctorate, comprehensive exam (for some programs), thesis/dissertation, oral exam. *Entrance requirements:* For master's, GRE General Test, bachelor's degree; 2 letters of recommendation; for doctorate, GRE General Test, bachelor's degree/master's degree with minimum GPA of 3.0; statement of interest; 3 letters of recommendation. Additional exam requirements/recommendations for international students: required—TOEFL (minimum score 550 paper-based; 80 iBT), IELTS (minimum score 7). *Application deadline:* For fall admission, 2/1 for domestic and international students; for spring admission, 10/1 for domestic and international students. Application fee: $60 ($95 for international students). Electronic applications accepted. *Expenses:* Contact institution. *Financial support:* In 2019–20, 39 students received support, including 15 research assistantships with full tuition reimbursements available (averaging $21,232 per year), 24 teaching assistantships with full tuition reimbursements available (averaging $21,677 per year); institutionally sponsored loans, scholarships/grants, health care benefits, and unspecified assistantships also available. Financial award application deadline: 3/15; financial award applicants required to submit FAFSA. *Unit head:* Dr. Spencer Steinberg, Chair, 702-895-3599, Fax: 702-895-4072, E-mail: chemistry.chair@unlv.edu. *Application contact:* Dr. Dong-Chan Lee, Graduate Coordinator, 702-895-1486, Fax: 702-895-4072, E-mail: chemistry.gradcoord@unlv.edu.
Website: http://www.unlv.edu/chemistry

**University of Nevada, Reno,** Graduate School, College of Agriculture, Biotechnology and Natural Resources, Program in Biochemistry, Reno, NV 89557. Offers MS, PhD. Terminal master's awarded for partial completion of doctoral program. *Degree requirements:* For master's, thesis; for doctorate, thesis/dissertation. *Entrance requirements:* For master's, GRE General Test, minimum GPA of 2.75; for doctorate, GRE General Test, minimum GPA of 3.0. Additional exam requirements/recommendations for international students: required—TOEFL (minimum score 500 paper-based; 61 iBT), IELTS (minimum score 6). Electronic applications accepted.

**University of New Hampshire,** Graduate School, College of Life Sciences and Agriculture, Department of Molecular, Cellular and Biomedical Sciences, Program in Biochemistry, Durham, NH 03824. Offers MS, PhD. *Program availability:* Part-time. *Students:* 13 full-time (7 women), 6 part-time (1 woman), 7 international. Average age 30. 26 applicants, 27% accepted, 6 enrolled. In 2019, 3 master's awarded. Terminal master's awarded for partial completion of doctoral program. *Entrance requirements:* For master's and doctorate, GRE General Test. Additional exam requirements/recommendations for international students: required—TOEFL (minimum score 550 paper-based; 80 iBT), IELTS, PTE. *Application deadline:* For fall admission, 1/15 priority date for domestic students, 4/15 for international students. Application fee: $65. Electronic applications accepted. *Financial support:* In 2019–20, 14 students received support, including 1 fellowship, 5 research assistantships, 9 teaching assistantships; career-related internships or fieldwork, Federal Work-Study, scholarships/grants, and tuition waivers (full and partial) also available. Support available to part-time students. Financial award application deadline: 2/15. *Unit head:* Louis Tisa, Chair, 603-862-2458. *Application contact:* Paul Boisselle, Administrative Assistant, 603-862-4818, E-mail: paul.boisselle@unh.edu.
Website: https://colsa.unh.edu/molecular-cellular-biomedical-sciences

**University of New Mexico,** Graduate Studies, Health Sciences Center, Program in Biomedical Sciences, Albuquerque, NM 87131-5196. Offers biochemistry and molecular biology (MS, PhD); cell biology and physiology (MS, PhD); molecular genetics and microbiology (MS, PhD); neuroscience (MS, PhD); pathology (MS, PhD); toxicology (MS, PhD). *Program availability:* Part-time. Terminal master's awarded for partial completion of doctoral program. *Degree requirements:* For master's, thesis; for doctorate, comprehensive exam, thesis/dissertation, qualifying exam at the end of year 1/core curriculum. *Entrance requirements:* For master's and doctorate, GRE General Test, minimum undergraduate GPA of 3.0. Additional exam requirements/recommendations for international students: required—TOEFL. Electronic applications accepted. *Expenses:* Tuition, state resident: full-time $7633; part-time $972 per year. Tuition, nonresident: full-time $22,586; part-time $3840 per year. *International tuition:* $23,292 full-time. *Required fees:* $8608. Tuition and fees vary according to course level, course load, degree level, program and student level.

**The University of North Carolina at Chapel Hill,** School of Medicine and Graduate School, Biological and Biomedical Sciences Program, Department of Biochemistry and Biophysics, Chapel Hill, NC 27599. Offers MS, PhD. *Faculty:* 42 full-time (8 women). *Students:* 35 full-time (14 women); includes 10 minority (1 Black or African American, non-Hispanic/Latino; 1 American Indian or Alaska Native, non-Hispanic/Latino; 3 Asian, non-Hispanic/Latino; 3 Hispanic/Latino; 2 Two or more races, non-Hispanic/Latino). Average age 26. In 2019, 1 master's, 5 doctorates awarded. Terminal master's awarded for partial completion of doctoral program. *Degree requirements:* For doctorate, comprehensive exam, thesis/dissertation. *Entrance requirements:* Additional exam requirements/recommendations for international students: required—TOEFL. *Application deadline:* For fall admission, 12/3 priority date for domestic and international students. Applications are processed on a rolling basis. Application fee: $70. Electronic applications accepted. *Financial support:* In 2019–20, fellowships with full tuition reimbursements (averaging $32,000 per year), research assistantships with full tuition reimbursements (averaging $32,000 per year) were awarded; career-related internships or fieldwork, health care benefits, and tuition waivers (full) also available. *Unit head:* Dr. Leslie Parise, Chair, 919-962-8326, E-mail: parise@med.unc.edu. *Application contact:* Jeffrey Steinbach, Assistant Director of Admissions, 919-843-7129, E-mail: jsteinba@email.unc.edu.
Website: https://www.med.unc.edu/biochem/

**The University of North Carolina at Greensboro,** Graduate School, College of Arts and Sciences, Department of Chemistry and Biochemistry, Greensboro, NC 27412-5001. Offers biochemistry (MS); chemistry (MS). *Degree requirements:* For master's, one foreign language, thesis. *Entrance requirements:* For master's, GRE General Test. Additional exam requirements/recommendations for international students: required—TOEFL. Electronic applications accepted.

**University of North Texas,** Toulouse Graduate School, Denton, TX 76203-5459. Offers accounting (MS); applied anthropology (MA, MS); applied behavior analysis (Certificate); applied geography (MA); applied technology and performance improvement (M Ed, MS); art education (MA); art history (MA); arts leadership (Certificate); audiology (Au D); behavior analysis (MS); behavioral science (PhD); biochemistry and molecular biology (MS); biology (MA, MS); biomedical engineering (MS); business analysis (MS); chemistry (MS); clinical health psychology (PhD); communication studies (MA, MS); computer engineering (MS); computer science (MS); counseling (M Ed, MS), including clinical mental health counseling (MS), college and university counseling, elementary school counseling, secondary school counseling; creative writing (MA); criminal justice (MS); curriculum and instruction (M Ed); decision sciences (MBA); design (MA, MFA), including fashion design (MFA), innovation studies, interior design (MFA); early childhood studies (MS); economics (MS); educational leadership (M Ed, Ed D); educational psychology (MS, PhD), including family studies (MS), gifted and talented (MS), human development (MS), learning and cognition (MS), research, measurement and evaluation (MS); electrical engineering (MS); emergency management (MPA); engineering technology (MS); English (MA); English as a second language (MA); environmental science (MS); finance (MBA, MS); financial management (MPA); French (MA); health services management (MBA); higher education (M Ed, Ed D); history (MA, MS); hospitality management (MS); human resources management (MPA); information science (MS); information systems (PhD); information technologies (MBA); interdisciplinary studies (MA, MS); international studies (MA); international sustainable tourism (MS); jazz studies (MM); journalism (MA, MJ, Graduate Certificate), including interactive and virtual digital communication (Graduate Certificate), narrative journalism (Graduate Certificate), public relations (Graduate Certificate); kinesiology (MS); linguistics (MA); local government management (MPA); logistics (PhD); logistics and supply chain management (MBA); long-term care, senior housing, and aging services (MA); management (PhD); marketing (MBA); mathematics (MA, MS); mechanical and energy engineering (MS, PhD); music (MA), including ethnomusicology, music theory, musicology, performance; music composition (PhD); music education (MM Ed, PhD); nonprofit management (MPA); operations and supply chain management (MBA); performance (MM, DMA); philosophy (MA); political science (MA); professional and technical communication (MA); radio, television and film (MA, MFA); rehabilitation counseling (Certificate); sociology (MA); Spanish (MA); special education (M Ed); speech-language pathology (MA); strategic management (MBA); studio art (MFA); teaching (M Ed); MBA/MS. *Program availability:* Part-time, evening/weekend, online learning. Terminal master's awarded for partial completion of doctoral program. *Degree requirements:* For master's, variable foreign language requirement, comprehensive exam (for some programs), thesis (for some programs); for doctorate, variable foreign language requirement, comprehensive exam (for some programs), thesis/dissertation; for other advanced degree, variable foreign language requirement, comprehensive exam (for some programs). *Entrance requirements:* For master's and doctorate, GRE, GMAT. Additional exam requirements/recommendations for international students: required—TOEFL (minimum score 550 paper-based; 79 iBT). Electronic applications accepted.

**University of North Texas Health Science Center at Fort Worth,** Graduate School of Biomedical Sciences, Fort Worth, TX 76107-2699. Offers biochemistry and cancer biology (MS, PhD); biotechnology (MS); cell biology, immunology and microbiology (MS, PhD); clinical research management (MS); forensic genetics (MS); genetics (MS, PhD); integrative physiology (MS, PhD); medical sciences (MS); pharmaceutical sciences and pharmacotherapy (MS, PhD); pharmacology and neuroscience (MS, PhD); structural anatomy and rehabilitation sciences (MS, PhD); DO/MS; DO/PhD. Terminal master's awarded for partial completion of doctoral program. *Degree requirements:* For master's, thesis; for doctorate, thesis/dissertation. *Entrance requirements:* For master's and doctorate, GRE General Test. Additional exam requirements/recommendations for international students: required—TOEFL. *Expenses:* Contact institution.

**University of Notre Dame,** The Graduate School, College of Science, Department of Chemistry and Biochemistry, Notre Dame, IN 46556. Offers biochemistry (MS, PhD); inorganic chemistry (MS, PhD); organic chemistry (MS, PhD); physical chemistry (MS, PhD). Terminal master's awarded for partial completion of doctoral program. *Degree*

*requirements:* For master's, comprehensive exam, thesis; for doctorate, thesis/dissertation, qualifying exam. *Entrance requirements:* For master's and doctorate, GRE General Test, GRE Subject Test (strongly recommended). Additional exam requirements/recommendations for international students: required—TOEFL (minimum score 600 paper-based; 80 iBT). Electronic applications accepted.

**University of Oklahoma,** College of Arts and Sciences, Department of Chemistry and Biochemistry, Norman, OK 73019. Offers chemistry (MS, PhD), including analytical chemistry, biochemistry, chemical education, inorganic chemistry, inter-and/or multidisciplinary, organic chemistry, physical chemistry, structural biology. *Program availability:* Part-time. Terminal master's awarded for partial completion of doctoral program. *Degree requirements:* For master's, comprehensive exam (for some programs), thesis (for some programs); for doctorate, comprehensive exam, thesis/dissertation, general exam. *Entrance requirements:* For master's and doctorate, GRE. Additional exam requirements/recommendations for international students: required—TOEFL (minimum score 79 iBT) or IELTS (minimum score 6.5). Electronic applications accepted. *Expenses:* Tuition, state resident: full-time $6583.20; part-time $274.30 per credit hour. Tuition, nonresident: full-time $21,242; part-time $885.10 per credit hour. International tuition: $21,242.40 full-time. *Required fees:* $1994.20; $72.55 per credit hour. $126.50 per semester. Tuition and fees vary according to course load and degree level.

**University of Oklahoma Health Sciences Center,** College of Medicine and Graduate College, Graduate Programs in Medicine, Department of Biochemistry and Molecular Biology, Oklahoma City, OK 73190. Offers biochemistry (MS, PhD); molecular biology (MS, PhD). *Program availability:* Part-time. Terminal master's awarded for partial completion of doctoral program. *Degree requirements:* For master's, thesis; for doctorate, thesis/dissertation. *Entrance requirements:* For master's, GRE General Test, 2 letters of recommendation; for doctorate, GRE General Test, 3 letters of recommendation. Additional exam requirements/recommendations for international students: required—TOEFL.

**University of Oregon,** Graduate School, College of Arts and Sciences, Department of Chemistry, Eugene, OR 97403. Offers biochemistry (MA, MS, PhD); chemistry (MA, MS, PhD). Terminal master's awarded for partial completion of doctoral program. *Degree requirements:* For doctorate, thesis/dissertation. *Entrance requirements:* For master's and doctorate, GRE General Test, minimum GPA of 3.0. Additional exam requirements/recommendations for international students: required—TOEFL.

**University of Ottawa,** Faculty of Graduate and Postdoctoral Studies, Faculty of Medicine, Department of Biochemistry, Microbiology and Immunology, Ottawa, ON K1N 6N5, Canada. Offers biochemistry (M Sc, PhD); microbiology and immunology (M Sc, PhD). *Degree requirements:* For master's, thesis; for doctorate, comprehensive exam, thesis/dissertation, seminar. *Entrance requirements:* For master's, honors degree or equivalent, minimum B average; for doctorate, master's degree, minimum B+ average. Electronic applications accepted.

**University of Pennsylvania,** Perelman School of Medicine, Biomedical Graduate Studies, Graduate Group in Biochemistry and Molecular Biophysics, Philadelphia, PA 19104. Offers PhD, MD/PhD, VMD/PhD. *Faculty:* 107 full-time (24 women). *Students:* 105 full-time (65 women); includes 48 minority (2 Black or African American, non-Hispanic/Latino; 14 Asian, non-Hispanic/Latino; 30 Hispanic/Latino; 2 Two or more races, non-Hispanic/Latino), 7 international. 163 applicants, 20% accepted, 20 enrolled. In 2019, 11 doctorates awarded. *Unit head:* Dr. Kim Sharp, Chairperson, 215-573-3506. *Application contact:* Kelli McKenna, Coordinator, 215-898-4639.
Website: http://www.med.upenn.edu/bmbgrad/

**University of Puerto Rico - Medical Sciences Campus,** School of Medicine, Biomedical Sciences Graduate Program, Department of Biochemistry, San Juan, PR 00936-5067. Offers MS, PhD. *Degree requirements:* For master's, thesis; for doctorate, comprehensive exam, thesis/dissertation. *Entrance requirements:* For master's and doctorate, GRE General Test, GRE Subject Test, interview, minimum GPA of 3.0. Electronic applications accepted.

**University of Regina,** Faculty of Graduate Studies and Research, Faculty of Science, Department of Chemistry and Biochemistry, Regina, SK S4S 0A2, Canada. Offers biophysics of biological interfaces (M Sc, PhD); computational chemistry (M Sc, PhD); environmental analytical chemistry (M Sc, PhD); enzymology/chemical biology (M Sc, PhD); inorganic/organometallic chemistry (M Sc, PhD); signal transduction and mechanisms of cancer cell regulation (M Sc, PhD); supramolecular organic photochemistry and photophysics (M Sc, PhD); synthetic organic chemistry (M Sc, PhD). *Program availability:* Part-time. *Faculty:* 12 full-time (2 women), 6 part-time/adjunct (0 women). *Students:* 19 full-time (9 women), 1 (woman) part-time. Average age 30. 18 applicants, 17% accepted. In 2019, 3 master's, 1 doctorate awarded. *Degree requirements:* For master's, thesis; for doctorate, comprehensive exam, thesis/dissertation. *Entrance requirements:* For master's, 4 years Bachelor degree in Chemistry or related program; for doctorate, completion of Master's in Chemistry. Additional exam requirements/recommendations for international students: required—TOEFL (minimum score 580 paper-based; 80 iBT), IELTS (minimum score 6.5), PTE (minimum score 59), other options are CAEL, MELAB, Cantest and U of R ESL. *Application deadline:* Applications are processed on a rolling basis. Application fee: $100. Electronic applications accepted. *Expenses: Tuition:* Full-time $6684 Canadian dollars. *Required fees:* $100 Canadian dollars; $3351.45 Canadian dollars per trimester. $1117.15 Canadian dollars per semester. Tuition and fees vary according to course level, course load, degree level and program. *Financial support:* Fellowships, research assistantships, teaching assistantships, career-related internships or fieldwork, Federal Work-Study, scholarships/grants, unspecified assistantships, and travel award and Graduate Scholarship Base Funds available. Support available to part-time students. Financial award application deadline: 9/30. *Unit head:* Dr. Renata Raina-Fulton, Department Head, 306-585-4012, Fax: 306-337-2409, E-mail: renata.raina@uregina.ca. *Application contact:* Dr. Brian Sterenberg, Graduate Program Coordinator, 306-585-4106, Fax: 306-337-2409, E-mail: brian.sterenberg@uregina.ca.
Website: http://www.uregina.ca/science/chem-biochem/

**University of Rhode Island,** Graduate School, College of the Environment and Life Sciences, Department of Cell and Molecular Biology, Kingston, RI 02881. Offers biochemistry (MS, PhD); clinical laboratory sciences (MS), including biotechnology, clinical laboratory science, cytopathology; microbiology (MS, PhD); molecular genetics (MS, PhD). *Program availability:* Part-time. *Faculty:* 20 full-time (9 women). *Students:* 1 (woman) part-time. In 2019, 16 master's awarded. *Entrance requirements:* Additional exam requirements/recommendations for international students: required—TOEFL. *Application deadline:* For fall admission, 1/15 for domestic and international students. Application fee: $65. Electronic applications accepted. *Expenses: Tuition, area resident:* Full-time $13,734; part-time $763 per credit. Tuition, state resident: full-time $13,734; part-time $763 per credit. Tuition, nonresident: full-time $26,512; part-time $1473 per credit. International tuition: $26,512 full-time. *Required fees:* $1780; $52 per credit. $35 per term. One-time fee: $165. *Financial support:* In 2019–20, 11 teaching assistantships with tuition reimbursements (averaging $10,985 per year) were awarded; traineeships also available. Financial award application deadline: 1/15; financial award applicants required to submit FAFSA. *Unit head:* Dr. Joel Chandlee, Chair, E-mail: joelchandlee@

uri.edu. *Application contact:* Dr. Steven Gregory, Graduate Program Director, 401-874-5947, E-mail: stgregory@uri.edu.
Website: https://web.uri.edu/cmb/

**University of Rochester,** School of Medicine and Dentistry, Graduate Programs in Medicine and Dentistry, Department of Biochemistry and Biophysics, Programs in Biochemistry, Rochester, NY 14627. Offers biochemistry and molecular biology (PhD). Terminal master's awarded for partial completion of doctoral program. *Degree requirements:* For doctorate, thesis/dissertation, qualifying exam. *Entrance requirements:* For doctorate, GRE General Test.

**University of Saint Joseph,** Department of Chemistry, West Hartford, CT 06117-2700. Offers biochemistry (MS); chemistry (MS). *Program availability:* Part-time, evening/weekend, online learning. *Degree requirements:* For master's, comprehensive exam, thesis optional. *Entrance requirements:* For master's, 2 letters of recommendation, official undergraduate transcript. Electronic applications accepted. Application fee is waived when completed online.

**University of Saskatchewan,** College of Medicine, Department of Biochemistry, Microbiology and Immunology, Saskatoon, SK S7N 5A2, Canada. Offers biochemistry (M Sc, PhD); microbiology and immunology (M Sc, PhD). *Degree requirements:* For master's, thesis; for doctorate, thesis/dissertation. *Entrance requirements:* Additional exam requirements/recommendations for international students: required—TOEFL.

**The University of Scranton,** College of Arts and Sciences, Department of Chemistry, Program in Biochemistry, Scranton, PA 18510. Offers MS. *Program availability:* Part-time, evening/weekend. *Degree requirements:* For master's, comprehensive exam (for some programs), thesis (for some programs), capstone experience. *Entrance requirements:* For master's, minimum GPA of 3.0, three letters of reference. Additional exam requirements/recommendations for international students: required—TOEFL (minimum score 500 paper-based; 80 iBT), IELTS (minimum score 6.5). Electronic applications accepted.

**University of South Carolina,** The Graduate School, College of Arts and Sciences, Department of Chemistry and Biochemistry, Columbia, SC 29208. Offers IMA, MAT, MS, PhD. *Program availability:* Part-time. Terminal master's awarded for partial completion of doctoral program. *Degree requirements:* For master's, comprehensive exam, thesis; for doctorate, comprehensive exam, thesis/dissertation. *Entrance requirements:* For master's and doctorate, GRE General Test. Additional exam requirements/recommendations for international students: required—TOEFL. Electronic applications accepted.

**University of Southern California,** Keck School of Medicine and Graduate School, Graduate Programs in Medicine, Department of Biochemistry and Molecular Medicine, Los Angeles, CA 90089. Offers MS. *Program availability:* Part-time. *Faculty:* 36 full-time (10 women). *Students:* 34 full-time (21 women), 1 (woman) part-time; includes 34 minority (33 Asian, non-Hispanic/Latino; 1 Hispanic/Latino). Average age 24. 67 applicants, 58% accepted, 15 enrolled. In 2019, 19 master's awarded. Terminal master's awarded for partial completion of doctoral program. *Degree requirements:* For master's, thesis. *Entrance requirements:* For master's, GRE General Test, minimum GPA of 3.0. Additional exam requirements/recommendations for international students: required—TOEFL (minimum score 600 paper-based; 100 iBT), IELTS. *Application deadline:* For fall admission, 4/1 priority date for domestic and international students. Applications are processed on a rolling basis. Application fee: $90. Electronic applications accepted. *Financial support:* Application deadline: 5/4; applicants required to submit CSS PROFILE or FAFSA. *Unit head:* Dr. Peggy R. Farnham, Chair, 323-442-8015, E-mail: peggy.farnham@med.usc.edu. *Application contact:* Janet Stoeckert, Administrative Director, Basic Science Departments, 323-442-3568, Fax: 323-442-1610, E-mail: janet.stoeckert@usc.edu.
Website: https://keck.usc.edu/biochemistry-and-molecular-medicine/

**The University of Tennessee,** Graduate School, College of Arts and Sciences, Department of Biochemistry, Cellular and Molecular Biology, Knoxville, TN 37996. Offers MS, PhD. Terminal master's awarded for partial completion of doctoral program. *Degree requirements:* For master's, thesis; for doctorate, thesis/dissertation. *Entrance requirements:* For master's and doctorate, GRE General Test, minimum GPA of 2.7. Additional exam requirements/recommendations for international students: required—TOEFL. Electronic applications accepted.

**The University of Texas at Austin,** Graduate School, College of Natural Sciences, Department of Chemistry and Biochemistry, Program in Biochemistry, Austin, TX 78712-1111. Offers PhD. *Entrance requirements:* For doctorate, GRE General Test.

**The University of Texas at Dallas,** School of Natural Sciences and Mathematics, Department of Chemistry and Biochemistry, Richardson, TX 75080. Offers MS, PhD. *Program availability:* Part-time, evening/weekend. *Faculty:* 22 full-time (4 women), 1 part-time/adjunct (0 women). *Students:* 113 full-time (59 women), 4 part-time (1 woman); includes 20 minority (4 Black or African American, non-Hispanic/Latino; 7 Asian, non-Hispanic/Latino; 9 Hispanic/Latino), 68 international. Average age 29. 171 applicants, 19% accepted, 31 enrolled. In 2019, 3 master's, 12 doctorates awarded. *Degree requirements:* For master's, thesis or internship; for doctorate, comprehensive exam, thesis/dissertation, research practica. *Entrance requirements:* For master's and doctorate, GRE General Test, minimum GPA of 3.0 in upper-level course work in field. Additional exam requirements/recommendations for international students: required—TOEFL (minimum score 600 paper-based). *Application deadline:* For fall admission, 7/15 for domestic students, 5/1 priority date for international students; for spring admission, 11/15 for domestic students, 9/1 priority date for international students. Applications are processed on a rolling basis. Application fee: $50 ($100 for international students). Electronic applications accepted. *Expenses: Tuition, area resident:* Full-time $16,504. Tuition, state resident: full-time $16,504. Tuition, nonresident: full-time $34,266. Tuition and fees vary according to course load. *Financial support:* In 2019–20, 113 students received support, including 53 research assistantships with partial tuition reimbursements available (averaging $25,869 per year), 60 teaching assistantships with partial tuition reimbursements available (averaging $18,105 per year); fellowships, career-related internships or fieldwork, Federal Work-Study, institutionally sponsored loans, scholarships/grants, and unspecified assistantships also available. Support available to part-time students. Financial award application deadline: 4/30; financial award applicants required to submit FAFSA. *Unit head:* Dr. Kenneth Balkus, Department Head, 972-883-2659, Fax: 972-883-2925, E-mail: chemistry@utdallas.edu. *Application contact:* Dr. Steven Nielsen, Associate Professor, 972-883-5323, Fax: 972-883-2925, E-mail: steven.nielsen@utdallas.edu.
Website: https://chemistry.utdallas.edu/

**The University of Texas at El Paso,** Graduate School, College of Science, Department of Chemistry and Biochemistry, El Paso, TX 79968-0001. Offers MS, PhD. *Program availability:* Part-time, evening/weekend. *Degree requirements:* For master's, thesis; for doctorate, thesis/dissertation. *Entrance requirements:* For master's, GRE, minimum GPA of 3.0; for doctorate, GRE, letters of recommendation. Additional exam requirements/recommendations for international students: required—TOEFL; recommended—IELTS. Electronic applications accepted.

## Biochemistry

**The University of Texas Health Science Center at Houston,** MD Anderson UTHealth Graduate School, Houston, TX 77225-0036. Offers biochemistry and cell biology (PhD); biomedical sciences (MS); cancer biology (PhD); genetic counseling (MS); genetics and epigenetics (PhD); immunology (PhD); medical physics (MS, PhD); microbiology and infectious diseases (PhD); neuroscience (PhD); quantitative sciences (PhD); therapeutics and pharmacology (PhD); MD/PhD. Terminal master's awarded for partial completion of doctoral program. *Degree requirements:* For master's, thesis; for doctorate, thesis/dissertation. *Entrance requirements:* For master's and doctorate, GRE General Test. Additional exam requirements/recommendations for international students: required—TOEFL. Electronic applications accepted.

**The University of Texas Health Science Center at San Antonio,** Graduate School of Biomedical Sciences, Department of Biochemistry, San Antonio, TX 78229. Offers MS, PhD. *Degree requirements:* For master's, thesis; for doctorate, comprehensive exam, thesis/dissertation.

**The University of Texas Medical Branch,** Graduate School of Biomedical Sciences, Program in Biochemistry and Molecular Biology, Galveston, TX 77555. Offers biochemistry (PhD); bioinformatics (PhD); biophysics (PhD); cell biology (PhD); computational biology (PhD); structural biology (PhD). *Degree requirements:* For doctorate, thesis/dissertation. *Entrance requirements:* Additional exam requirements/recommendations for international students: required—TOEFL (minimum score 550 paper-based). Electronic applications accepted.

**The University of Texas Southwestern Medical Center,** Southwestern Graduate School of Biomedical Sciences, Division of Basic Science, Program in Biological Chemistry, Dallas, TX 75390. Offers PhD. *Degree requirements:* For doctorate, thesis/dissertation, qualifying exam. *Entrance requirements:* For doctorate, GRE General Test, minimum GPA of 3.0. Additional exam requirements/recommendations for international students: required—TOEFL. Electronic applications accepted.

**University of the Sciences,** Program in Chemistry, Biochemistry and Pharmacognosy, Philadelphia, PA 19104-4495. Offers biochemistry (MS, PhD); chemistry (MS, PhD); pharmacognosy (MS, PhD). *Program availability:* Part-time. *Degree requirements:* For master's, thesis, qualifying exams; for doctorate, comprehensive exam, thesis/dissertation, qualifying exams. *Entrance requirements:* For master's and doctorate, GRE General Test, GRE Subject Test. Additional exam requirements/recommendations for international students: required—TOEFL, TWE. *Expenses:* Contact institution.

**The University of Toledo,** College of Graduate Studies, College of Natural Sciences and Mathematics, Department of Chemistry, Toledo, OH 43606-3390. Offers analytical chemistry (MS, PhD); biological chemistry (MS, PhD); inorganic chemistry (MS, PhD); organic chemistry (MS, PhD); physical chemistry (MS, PhD). *Program availability:* Part-time. *Degree requirements:* For master's, thesis or alternative; for doctorate, thesis/dissertation. *Entrance requirements:* For master's and doctorate, GRE General Test, GRE Subject Test, minimum cumulative point-hour ratio of 2.7 for all previous academic work, three letters of recommendation, statement of purpose, transcripts from all prior institutions attended. Additional exam requirements/recommendations for international students: required—TOEFL (minimum score 550 paper-based; 80 iBT). Electronic applications accepted.

**The University of Toledo,** College of Graduate Studies, College of Pharmacy and Pharmaceutical Sciences, Program in Medicinal and Biological Chemistry, Toledo, OH 43606-3390. Offers MS, PhD. Terminal master's awarded for partial completion of doctoral program. *Degree requirements:* For master's, thesis; for doctorate, thesis/dissertation. *Entrance requirements:* For master's and doctorate, GRE General Test. Additional exam requirements/recommendations for international students: required—TOEFL (minimum score 550 paper-based; 80 iBT). Electronic applications accepted.

**University of Toronto,** Faculty of Medicine, Department of Biochemistry, Toronto, ON M5S 1A1, Canada. Offers M Sc, PhD. *Degree requirements:* For master's, thesis, oral examination of thesis; for doctorate, thesis/dissertation, oral defense of thesis. *Entrance requirements:* For master's, B Sc in biochemistry or molecular biology, minimum B+ average, letters of reference. Additional exam requirements/recommendations for international students: required—TOEFL (minimum score 580 paper-based; 93 iBT), TWE (minimum score 5). Electronic applications accepted.

**University of Utah,** School of Medicine and Graduate School, Graduate Programs in Medicine, Department of Biochemistry, Salt Lake City, UT 84112-1107. Offers MS, PhD. Terminal master's awarded for partial completion of doctoral program. *Degree requirements:* For master's, thesis; for doctorate, thesis/dissertation. *Entrance requirements:* For doctorate, GRE Subject Test, minimum GPA of 3.0. Additional exam requirements/recommendations for international students: required—TOEFL. Electronic applications accepted. *Expenses:* Tuition, state resident: full-time $7085; part-time $272.51 per credit hour. Tuition, nonresident: full-time $24,937; part-time $959.12 per credit hour. *Required fees:* $880.52; $880.52 per semester. Tuition and fees vary according to degree level, program and student level.

**University of Vermont,** The Robert Larner, MD College of Medicine and Graduate College, Graduate Programs in Medicine, Department of Biochemistry, Burlington, VT 05405. Offers MS, PhD. *Degree requirements:* For master's, thesis; for doctorate, thesis/dissertation. *Entrance requirements:* For master's and doctorate, GRE General Test. Additional exam requirements/recommendations for international students: required—TOEFL (minimum score 550 paper-based, 90 iBT) or IELTS (6.5). Electronic applications accepted.

**University of Victoria,** Faculty of Graduate Studies, Faculty of Science, Department of Biochemistry and Microbiology, Victoria, BC V8W 2Y2, Canada. Offers biochemistry (M Sc, PhD); microbiology (M Sc, PhD). *Degree requirements:* For master's, thesis, seminar; for doctorate, thesis/dissertation, seminar, candidacy exam. *Entrance requirements:* For master's, GRE General Test, minimum B+ average; for doctorate, GRE General Test, minimum B+ average, M Sc. Additional exam requirements/recommendations for international students: required—TOEFL (minimum score 600 paper-based). Electronic applications accepted.

**University of Virginia,** School of Medicine, Department of Biochemistry and Molecular Genetics, Charlottesville, VA 22903. Offers biochemistry (PhD); MD/PhD. *Degree requirements:* For doctorate, thesis/dissertation, written research proposal and defense. *Entrance requirements:* For doctorate, GRE General Test, 3 letters of recommendation. Additional exam requirements/recommendations for international students: recommended—TOEFL (minimum score 630 paper-based; 90 iBT). Electronic applications accepted.

**University of Washington,** Graduate School, School of Medicine, Graduate Programs in Medicine, Department of Biochemistry, Seattle, WA 98195. Offers PhD. *Degree requirements:* For doctorate, thesis/dissertation. *Entrance requirements:* For doctorate, GRE General Test, GRE Subject Test (biology, chemistry, biochemistry, or cell and molecular biology), minimum GPA of 3.0. Additional exam requirements/recommendations for international students: required—TOEFL. Electronic applications accepted.

**University of Waterloo,** Graduate Studies and Postdoctoral Affairs, Faculty of Science, Department of Chemistry, Waterloo, ON N2L 3G1, Canada. Offers M Sc, PhD. *Program availability:* Part-time. *Degree requirements:* For master's and doctorate, project or thesis. *Entrance requirements:* For master's, GRE, honors degree, minimum B average; for doctorate, GRE, master's degree, minimum B average. Additional exam requirements/recommendations for international students: required—TOEFL, IELTS, PTE. Electronic applications accepted.

**The University of Western Ontario,** Schulich School of Medicine and Dentistry, Department of Biochemistry, London, ON N6A 3K7, Canada. Offers M Sc, PhD. *Degree requirements:* For master's, thesis; for doctorate, thesis/dissertation. *Entrance requirements:* For master's, minimum B+ average in last 2 years of undergraduate study; for doctorate, M Sc or an external scholarship winner.

**University of Windsor,** Faculty of Graduate Studies, Faculty of Science, Department of Chemistry and Biochemistry, Windsor, ON N9B 3P4, Canada. Offers M Sc, PhD. *Program availability:* Part-time. *Degree requirements:* For master's, thesis; for doctorate, comprehensive exam, thesis/dissertation. *Entrance requirements:* For master's and doctorate, minimum B average. Additional exam requirements/recommendations for international students: required—TOEFL (minimum score 560 paper-based). Electronic applications accepted.

**University of Wisconsin–Madison,** Graduate School, College of Agricultural and Life Sciences, Department of Biochemistry, Madison, WI 53706. Offers PhD. Terminal master's awarded for partial completion of doctoral program. *Degree requirements:* For doctorate, thesis/dissertation. *Entrance requirements:* For doctorate, GRE General Test, GRE Subject Test (recommended). Additional exam requirements/recommendations for international students: required—TOEFL. Electronic applications accepted.

**University of Wisconsin–Madison,** Graduate School, College of Agricultural and Life Sciences, Integrated Program in Biochemistry, Madison, WI 53706. Offers MS, PhD.

**University of Wisconsin–Milwaukee,** Graduate School, College of Letters and Science, Department of Chemistry and Biochemistry, Milwaukee, WI 53201-0413. Offers MS, PhD. *Entrance requirements:* For doctorate, GRE General Test. Additional exam requirements/recommendations for international students: required—TOEFL (minimum score 600 paper-based; 79 iBT), IELTS (minimum score 6.5). Electronic applications accepted.

**Université Laval,** Faculty of Medicine, Post-Professional Programs in Medical Studies, Québec, QC G1K 7P4, Canada. Offers anatomy–pathology (DESS); anesthesiology (DESS); cardiology (DESS); care of older people (Diploma); clinical research (DESS); community health (DESS); dermatology (DESS); diagnostic radiology (DESS); emergency medicine (Diploma); family medicine (DESS); general surgery (DESS); geriatrics (DESS); hematology (DESS); internal medicine (DESS); maternal and fetal medicine (Diploma); medical biochemistry (DESS); medical microbiology and infectious diseases (DESS); medical oncology (DESS); nephrology (DESS); neurology (DESS); neurosurgery (DESS); obstetrics and gynecology (DESS); ophthalmology (DESS); orthopedic surgery (DESS); oto-rhino-laryngology (DESS); palliative medicine (Diploma); pediatrics (DESS); plastic surgery (DESS); psychiatry (DESS); pulmonary medicine (DESS); radiology–oncology (DESS); thoracic surgery (DESS); urology (DESS). *Degree requirements:* For other advanced degree, comprehensive exam. *Entrance requirements:* For degree, knowledge of French. Electronic applications accepted.

**Université Laval,** Faculty of Sciences and Engineering, Department of Biochemistry and Microbiology, Programs in Biochemistry, Québec, QC G1K 7P4, Canada. Offers M Sc, PhD. Terminal master's awarded for partial completion of doctoral program. *Degree requirements:* For master's, thesis; for doctorate, comprehensive exam, thesis/dissertation. *Entrance requirements:* For master's and doctorate, knowledge of French, comprehension of written English. Electronic applications accepted.

**Utah State University,** School of Graduate Studies, College of Science, Department of Chemistry and Biochemistry, Logan, UT 84322. Offers biochemistry (MS, PhD); chemistry (MS, PhD). *Program availability:* Part-time. Terminal master's awarded for partial completion of doctoral program. *Degree requirements:* For master's, thesis, oral and written exams; for doctorate, thesis/dissertation, oral and written exams. *Entrance requirements:* For master's and doctorate, GRE General Test, minimum GPA of 3.0. Additional exam requirements/recommendations for international students: required—TOEFL.

**Vanderbilt University,** School of Medicine, Department of Biochemistry, Nashville, TN 37240-1001. Offers MS, PhD, MD/PhD. *Faculty:* 23 full-time (5 women). *Students:* 38 full-time (24 women); includes 9 minority (2 Black or African American, non-Hispanic/Latino; 1 Asian, non-Hispanic/Latino; 5 Hispanic/Latino; 1 Two or more races, non-Hispanic/Latino), 7 international. Average age 27. In 2019, 7 doctorates awarded. Terminal master's awarded for partial completion of doctoral program. *Degree requirements:* For master's, thesis; for doctorate, thesis/dissertation, preliminary, qualifying, and final exams. *Entrance requirements:* For master's, GRE General Test; for doctorate, GRE General Test, GRE Subject Test (recommended). Additional exam requirements/recommendations for international students: required—TOEFL (minimum score 570 paper-based; 88 iBT). *Application deadline:* For fall admission, 1/15 for domestic and international students. Electronic applications accepted. *Expenses:* Tuition: Full-time $51,018; part-time $2087 per hour. *Required fees:* $542. Tuition and fees vary according to program. *Financial support:* Fellowships with full tuition reimbursements, research assistantships with full tuition reimbursements, Federal Work-Study, institutionally sponsored loans, scholarships/grants, traineeships, and tuition waivers (partial) available. Financial award application deadline: 1/15; financial award applicants required to submit CSS PROFILE or FAFSA. *Unit head:* Dr. John York, Chair, 615-322-3315, Fax: 615-322-4349. *Application contact:* Manual Ascano, Director of Graduate Studies, 615-875-8714, E-mail: manuel.ascano@vanderbilt.edu. Website: https://medschool.vanderbilt.edu/biochemistry/

**Vanderbilt University,** School of Medicine, Program in Chemical and Physical Biology, Nashville, TN 37240-1001. Offers PhD. *Faculty:* 71 full-time (9 women). *Students:* 48 full-time (20 women); includes 12 minority (2 Black or African American, non-Hispanic/Latino; 3 Asian, non-Hispanic/Latino; 7 Hispanic/Latino), 4 international. Average age 27. In 2019, 6 doctorates awarded. *Degree requirements:* For doctorate, comprehensive exam, thesis/dissertation, dissertation defense. *Entrance requirements:* For doctorate, GRE, 3 letters of recommendation, official transcripts. Additional exam requirements/recommendations for international students: required—TOEFL. *Application deadline:* For fall admission, 1/15 priority date for domestic students, 1/15 for international students. Applications are processed on a rolling basis. Electronic applications accepted. *Expenses: Tuition:* Full-time $51,018; part-time $2087 per hour. *Required fees:* $542. Tuition and fees vary according to program. *Financial support:* Fellowships with full tuition reimbursements, traineeships, health care benefits, and tuition waivers (full) available. *Unit head:* Dr. Bruce Damon, Director of Graduate Studies, 615-322-4235, Fax: 615-343-0490, E-mail: bruce.damon@vanderbilt.edu. *Application contact:* Patricia Mueller, Coordinator, 615-322-8727, E-mail: patricia.l.mueller@vanderbilt.edu.

**Virginia Commonwealth University,** Medical College of Virginia-Professional Programs, School of Medicine, Graduate Programs in Medicine, Department of Biochemistry and Molecular Biology, Richmond, VA 23284-9005. Offers MS, PhD, MD/PhD. *Degree requirements:* For master's, thesis; for doctorate, thesis/dissertation,

comprehensive oral and written exams. *Entrance requirements:* For master's and doctorate, GRE, MCAT or DAT. Electronic applications accepted.

**Virginia Polytechnic Institute and State University,** Graduate School, College of Agriculture and Life Sciences, Blacksburg, VA 24061. Offers agricultural and applied economics (MS, PhD); agricultural and life sciences (MS); agriculture, leadership, and community education (MS, PhD); animal and poultry science (MS, PhD); biochemistry (MS, PhD); crop and soil environmental sciences (MS, PhD); dairy science (MS, PhD); entomology (MS, PhD); food science and technology (MS, PhD); horticulture (PhD); human nutrition, foods and exercise (MS, PhD); plant pathology, physiology, and weed science (MS, PhD). *Faculty:* 246 full-time (83 women). *Students:* 364 full-time (213 women), 106 part-time (68 women); includes 79 minority (29 Black or African American, non-Hispanic/Latino; 1 American Indian or Alaska Native, non-Hispanic/Latino; 13 Asian, non-Hispanic/Latino; 16 Hispanic/Latino; 20 Two or more races, non-Hispanic/Latino), 106 international. Average age 28. 314 applicants, 57% accepted, 130 enrolled. In 2019, 92 master's, 59 doctorates awarded. *Degree requirements:* For master's, comprehensive exam (for some programs), thesis (for some programs); for doctorate, comprehensive exam (for some programs), thesis/dissertation (for some programs). *Entrance requirements:* For master's and doctorate, GRE/GMAT. Additional exam requirements/recommendations for international students: required—TOEFL (minimum score 90 iBT). *Application deadline:* For fall admission, 8/1 for domestic students, 4/1 for international students; for spring admission, 1/1 for domestic students, 9/1 for international students. Applications are processed on a rolling basis. Application fee: $75. Electronic applications accepted. *Expenses:* Tuition, state resident: full-time $13,700; part-time $761.25 per credit hour. Tuition, nonresident: full-time $27,614; part-time $1534 per credit hour. *Required fees:* $886.50 per term. Tuition and fees vary according to campus/location and program. *Financial support:* In 2019–20, 248 research assistantships with full tuition reimbursements (averaging $20,360 per year), 127 teaching assistantships with full tuition reimbursements (averaging $18,183 per year) were awarded; fellowships, scholarships/grants, and unspecified assistantships also available. Financial award application deadline: 3/1; financial award applicants required to submit FAFSA. *Unit head:* Dr. Alan L. Grant, Dean, 540-231-4152, Fax: 540-231-4163, E-mail: algrant@vt.edu. *Application contact:* Crystal Tawney, Administrative Assistant, 540-231-4152, Fax: 540-231-4163, E-mail: cdtawney@vt.edu. Website: http://www.cals.vt.edu/

**Wake Forest University,** School of Medicine and Graduate School of Arts and Sciences, Graduate Programs in Medicine, Department of Biochemistry, Winston-Salem, NC 27109. Offers PhD, MD/PhD. *Degree requirements:* For doctorate, thesis/dissertation. *Entrance requirements:* For doctorate, GRE General Test. Additional exam requirements/recommendations for international students: required—TOEFL. Electronic applications accepted.

**Washington State University,** College of Veterinary Medicine, School of Molecular Biosciences, Pullman, WA 99164-7520. Offers molecular biosciences (MS, PhD), including genetics (PhD). *Faculty:* 26 full-time (9 women), 15 part-time/adjunct (3 women). *Students:* 39 full-time (21 women), 1 (woman) part-time; includes 9 minority (1 Black or African American, non-Hispanic/Latino; 2 Asian, non-Hispanic/Latino; 6 Hispanic/Latino), 2 international. Average age 27. 60 applicants, 40% accepted, 13 enrolled. In 2019, 1 doctorate awarded. Terminal master's awarded for partial completion of doctoral program. *Degree requirements:* For master's, thesis (for some programs), oral defense; for doctorate, comprehensive exam, thesis/dissertation, oral defense. *Entrance requirements:* For master's and doctorate, GRE General Test for 2019-2020 entrance. Will be removed in the 2020-2021 recruiting year, minimum GPA of 3.0. Additional exam requirements/recommendations for international students: required—TOEFL (minimum score 600 paper-based; 100 iBT). *Application deadline:* For fall admission, 12/15 priority date for domestic and international students. Application fee: $75. Electronic applications accepted. *Expenses:* $6,997.58 In-State/Semester = $13,995.16 per academic year; $13,875.08 Out of State/Semester = $27,750.16 per academice year. Average 5 years to completion. *Financial support:* In 2019–20, 36 students received support, including 5 fellowships with full tuition reimbursements available (averaging $27,426 per year), 19 research assistantships with full tuition reimbursements available (averaging $29,700 per year), 14 teaching assistantships with full tuition reimbursements available (averaging $20,570 per year); scholarships/grants, traineeships, and health care benefits also available. Financial award application deadline: 4/15. *Unit head:* Dr. Michael D. Griswold, Director, 509-335-8724, Fax: 509-335-4159, E-mail: mgriswold@wsu.edu. *Application contact:* Tami Breske, Graduate Academic Coordinator, 509-335-4318, E-mail: tamara.breske@wsu.edu. Website: http://www.smb.wsu.edu

**Washington University in St. Louis,** The Graduate School, Division of Biology and Biomedical Sciences, Program in Biochemistry, St. Louis, MO 63130-4899. Offers PhD. *Degree requirements:* For doctorate, thesis/dissertation. *Entrance requirements:* For doctorate, GRE General Test, GRE Subject Test. Additional exam requirements/recommendations for international students: required—TOEFL. Electronic applications accepted.

**Weill Cornell Medicine,** Weill Cornell Graduate School of Medical Sciences, Biochemistry, Cell and Molecular Biology Allied Program, New York, NY 10065. Offers MS, PhD. Terminal master's awarded for partial completion of doctoral program. *Degree requirements:* For master's, comprehensive exam; for doctorate, thesis/dissertation, final exam. *Entrance requirements:* For doctorate, GRE General Test, background in genetics, molecular biology, chemistry, or biochemistry. Additional exam requirements/

recommendations for international students: required—TOEFL. Electronic applications accepted.

**Weill Cornell Medicine,** Weill Cornell Graduate School of Medical Sciences, Cornell/Rockefeller/Sloan Kettering Tri-Institutional PhD Program in Chemical Biology, New York, NY 10065. Offers PhD. *Degree requirements:* For doctorate, comprehensive exam, thesis/dissertation. *Entrance requirements:* For doctorate, GRE General Test; GRE Subject Test in chemistry (recommended), 3 letters of recommendation. Additional exam requirements/recommendations for international students: required—TOEFL (minimum score 600 paper-based; 90 iBT). Electronic applications accepted.

**Wesleyan University,** Graduate Studies, Department of Chemistry, Middletown, CT 06459. Offers biochemistry (PhD); chemical physics (PhD); inorganic chemistry (PhD); organic chemistry (PhD); physical chemistry (PhD); theoretical chemistry (PhD). Terminal master's awarded for partial completion of doctoral program. *Degree requirements:* For doctorate, thesis/dissertation. *Entrance requirements:* For doctorate, GRE General Test, 3 recommendations. Additional exam requirements/recommendations for international students: required—TOEFL, IELTS. Electronic applications accepted.

**Wesleyan University,** Graduate Studies, Department of Molecular Biology and Biochemistry, Middletown, CT 06459. Offers molecular biology and biochemistry (PhD); molecular biophysics (PhD). Terminal master's awarded for partial completion of doctoral program. *Degree requirements:* For doctorate, comprehensive exam, thesis/dissertation. *Entrance requirements:* For doctorate, GRE General Test, GRE Subject Test. Additional exam requirements/recommendations for international students: required—TOEFL. Electronic applications accepted.

**West Virginia University,** School of Medicine, Morgantown, WV 26506. Offers biochemistry and molecular biology (PhD); biomedical science (MS); cancer cell biology (PhD); cellular and integrative physiology (PhD); exercise physiology (MS, PhD); health sciences (MS); immunology (PhD); medicine (MD); occupational therapy (MOT); pathologists assistant' (MHS); physical therapy (DPT). *Accreditation:* AOTA; LCME/AMA. *Program availability:* Part-time, evening/weekend. *Entrance requirements:* Additional exam requirements/recommendations for international students: required—TOEFL. Electronic applications accepted. *Expenses:* Contact institution.

**Worcester Polytechnic Institute,** Graduate Admissions, Department of Chemistry and Biochemistry, Worcester, MA 01609-2280. Offers biochemistry (MS, PhD); chemistry (MS, PhD). *Program availability:* Part-time, evening/weekend. *Degree requirements:* For doctorate, comprehensive exam, thesis/dissertation. *Entrance requirements:* For master's and doctorate, GRE General Test, 3 letters of recommendation, statement of purpose. Additional exam requirements/recommendations for international students: required—TOEFL (minimum score 563 paper-based; 84 iBT), IELTS (minimum score 7). Electronic applications accepted.

**Wright State University,** Graduate School, College of Science and Mathematics, Department of Biochemistry and Molecular Biology, Dayton, OH 45435. Offers MS. *Degree requirements:* For master's, thesis. *Entrance requirements:* Additional exam requirements/recommendations for international students: required—TOEFL.

**Yale University,** Graduate School of Arts and Sciences, Department of Geology and Geophysics, New Haven, CT 06520. Offers biogeochemistry (PhD); climate dynamics (PhD); geochemistry (PhD); geophysics (PhD); meteorology (PhD); oceanography (PhD); paleontology (PhD); paleooceanography (PhD); petrology (PhD); tectonics (PhD). *Degree requirements:* For doctorate, thesis/dissertation. *Entrance requirements:* For doctorate, GRE General Test. Additional exam requirements/recommendations for international students: required—TOEFL.

**Yale University,** Graduate School of Arts and Sciences, Department of Molecular Biophysics and Biochemistry, New Haven, CT 06520. Offers PhD. *Degree requirements:* For doctorate, thesis/dissertation. *Entrance requirements:* For doctorate, GRE General Test, GRE Subject Test.

**Yale University,** Graduate School of Arts and Sciences, Department of Molecular, Cellular, and Developmental Biology, Program in Biochemistry, Molecular Biology and Chemical Biology, New Haven, CT 06520. Offers PhD. *Degree requirements:* For doctorate, thesis/dissertation. *Entrance requirements:* For doctorate, GRE General Test, GRE Subject Test.

**Yale University,** Yale School of Medicine and Graduate School of Arts and Sciences, Combined Program in Biological and Biomedical Sciences (BBS), Molecular Biophysics and Biochemistry Track, New Haven, CT 06520. Offers PhD, MD/PhD. *Degree requirements:* For doctorate, thesis/dissertation. *Entrance requirements:* For doctorate, GRE General Test. Additional exam requirements/recommendations for international students: required—TOEFL. Electronic applications accepted.

**Youngstown State University,** College of Graduate Studies, College of Science, Technology, Engineering and Mathematics, Department of Chemistry, Youngstown, OH 44555-0001. Offers analytical chemistry (MS); biochemistry (MS); chemistry education (MS); inorganic chemistry (MS); organic chemistry (MS); physical chemistry (MS). *Program availability:* Part-time. *Degree requirements:* For master's, thesis. *Entrance requirements:* For master's, bachelor's degree in chemistry, minimum GPA of 2.7. Additional exam requirements/recommendations for international students: required—TOEFL.

# Section 4
# Biophysics

This section contains a directory of institutions offering graduate work in biophysics, followed by an in-depth entry submitted by an institution that chose to prepare a detailed program description. Additional information about programs listed in the directory but not augmented by an in-depth entry may be obtained by writing directly to the dean of a graduate school or chair of a department at the address given in the directory.

For programs offering related work, see also in this book *Allied Health; Biochemistry; Biological and Biomedical Sciences; Cell, Molecular, and Structural Biology; Optometry and Vision Sciences; Neuroscience and Neurobiology; Physiology;* and *Public Health.* In the other guides in this series:

**Graduate Programs in the Physical Sciences, Mathematics, Agricultural Sciences, the Environment & Natural Resources**

See *Chemistry* and *Physics*

**Graduate Programs in Engineering & Applied Sciences**

See *Agricultural Engineering and Bioengineering* and *Biomedical Engineering and Biotechnology*

## CONTENTS

### Program Directories

# Biophysics

**Albert Einstein College of Medicine,** Graduate Programs in the Biomedical Sciences, Department of Physiology and Biophysics, Bronx, NY 10461. Offers PhD, MD/PhD. *Degree requirements:* For doctorate, thesis/dissertation. *Entrance requirements:* For doctorate, GRE General Test. Additional exam requirements/recommendations for international students: required—TOEFL.

**Baylor College of Medicine,** Graduate School of Biomedical Sciences, Department of Molecular Physiology and Biophysics, Houston, TX 77030-3498. Offers cardiovascular sciences (PhD); molecular physiology and biophysics (PhD); MD/PhD. *Degree requirements:* For doctorate, thesis/dissertation, public defense. *Entrance requirements:* For doctorate, GRE General Test, GRE Subject Test (strongly recommended), minimum GPA of 3.0. Additional exam requirements/recommendations for international students: required—TOEFL. Electronic applications accepted.

**Boston University,** School of Medicine, Graduate Medical Sciences, Department of Physiology and Biophysics, Boston, MA 02118. Offers MA, PhD, MD/PhD. *Program availability:* Part-time. Terminal master's awarded for partial completion of doctoral program. *Application deadline:* For fall admission, 1/15 for domestic students; for spring admission, 10/15 for domestic students. *Unit head:* Dr. David Atkinson, Chairman, E-mail: atkinson@bu.edu. *Application contact:* GMS Admissions Office, 617-358-9518, Fax: 617-358-2913, E-mail: gmsbusm@bu.edu. Website: http://www.bumc.bu.edu/phys-biophys/

**Brandeis University,** Graduate School of Arts and Sciences, Department of Biochemistry, Waltham, MA 02454. Offers biochemistry and biophysics (MS, PhD); biochemistry and biophysics and quantitative biology (PhD). *Program availability:* Part-time. *Faculty:* 11 full-time (6 women). *Students:* 39 full-time (19 women); includes 12 minority (5 Asian, non-Hispanic/Latino; 4 Hispanic/Latino; 3 Two or more races, non-Hispanic/Latino), 9 international. Average age 26. 72 applicants, 31% accepted, 8 enrolled. In 2019, 6 doctorates awarded. Terminal master's awarded for partial completion of doctoral program. *Degree requirements:* For master's, thesis; for doctorate, comprehensive exam, thesis/dissertation. *Entrance requirements:* For master's, transcripts, letters of recommendation, resume, statement of purpose; for doctorate, transcripts, letters of recommendation, resume, statement of purpose, program questions. Additional exam requirements/recommendations for international students: required—TOEFL, IELTS, PTE. *Application deadline:* For fall admission, 12/1 priority date for domestic students. Applications are processed on a rolling basis. Application fee: $75. Electronic applications accepted. *Financial support:* In 2019–20, 10 teaching assistantships (averaging $3,550 per year) were awarded; fellowships, research assistantships, scholarships/grants, and health care benefits also available. *Unit head:* Dr. Dagmar Ringe, Director of Graduate Studies, 781-736-4902, E-mail: ringe@brandeis.edu. *Application contact:* Maryanna Aldrich, Administrator, 781-736-2352, E-mail: scigradoffice@brandeis.edu. Website: http://www.brandeis.edu/gsas/programs/bio.html

**California Institute of Technology,** Division of Biology and Biological Engineering, Program in Cell Biology and Biophysics, Pasadena, CA 91125-0001. Offers PhD. *Degree requirements:* For doctorate, thesis/dissertation, qualifying exam. *Entrance requirements:* For doctorate, GRE General Test.

**Carnegie Mellon University,** Mellon College of Science, Department of Biological Sciences, Pittsburgh, PA 15213-3891. Offers biochemistry (PhD); biophysics (PhD); cell and developmental biology (PhD); computational biology (MS, PhD); genetics (PhD); molecular biology (PhD); neuroscience (PhD); structural biology (PhD). *Degree requirements:* For doctorate, comprehensive exam, thesis/dissertation. *Entrance requirements:* For doctorate, GRE General Test, GRE Subject Test, interview. Electronic applications accepted.

**Case Western Reserve University,** School of Medicine and School of Graduate Studies, Graduate Programs in Medicine, Department of Physiology and Biophysics, Cleveland, OH 44106. Offers medical physiology (MS); physiology and biophysics (PhD); MD/PhD. Terminal master's awarded for partial completion of doctoral program. *Degree requirements:* For master's, thesis; for doctorate, thesis/dissertation. *Entrance requirements:* For master's, GRE General Test, minimum GPA of 3.28; for doctorate, GRE General Test, minimum GPA of 3.6. Additional exam requirements/recommendations for international students: required—TOEFL. Electronic applications accepted.

**Columbia University,** College of Physicians and Surgeons, Department of Biochemistry and Molecular Biophysics, New York, NY 10032. Offers biochemistry and molecular biophysics (M Phil, PhD); biophysics (PhD); MD/PhD. *Degree requirements:* For doctorate, one foreign language, thesis/dissertation. *Entrance requirements:* For master's and doctorate, GRE General Test. Additional exam requirements/recommendations for international students: required—TOEFL. *Expenses: Tuition:* Full-time $47,600; part-time $1880 per credit. One-time fee: $105.

**Columbia University,** College of Physicians and Surgeons, Department of Physiology and Cellular Biophysics, New York, NY 10032. Offers M Phil, MA, PhD, MD/PhD. Terminal master's awarded for partial completion of doctoral program. *Degree requirements:* For doctorate, thesis/dissertation. *Entrance requirements:* For master's and doctorate, GRE General Test. Additional exam requirements/recommendations for international students: required—TOEFL. *Expenses: Tuition:* Full-time $47,600; part-time $1880 per credit. One-time fee: $105.

**Columbia University,** College of Physicians and Surgeons, Integrated Program in Cellular, Molecular, Structural and Genetic Studies, New York, NY 10032. Offers PhD. Terminal master's awarded for partial completion of doctoral program. *Degree requirements:* For doctorate, thesis/dissertation. *Entrance requirements:* For doctorate, GRE General Test, GRE Subject Test. Additional exam requirements/recommendations for international students: required—TOEFL. *Expenses:* Contact institution.

**Cornell University,** Graduate School, Graduate Fields of Agriculture and Life Sciences, Field of Biochemistry, Molecular and Cell Biology, Ithaca, NY 14853. Offers biochemistry (PhD); biophysics (PhD); cell biology (PhD); molecular biology (PhD). *Degree requirements:* For doctorate, comprehensive exam, thesis/dissertation, 2 semesters of teaching experience. *Entrance requirements:* For doctorate, GRE General Test, GRE Subject Test (biology, chemistry, physics, biochemistry, cell and molecular biology), 3 letters of recommendation. Additional exam requirements/recommendations for international students: required—TOEFL (minimum score 600 paper-based; 77 iBT). Electronic applications accepted.

**Cornell University,** Graduate School, Graduate Fields of Agriculture and Life Sciences, Field of Biophysics, Ithaca, NY 14853. Offers PhD. *Degree requirements:* For doctorate, comprehensive exam, thesis/dissertation. *Entrance requirements:* For doctorate, GRE General Test, GRE Subject Test (physics or chemistry preferred), 3 letters of recommendation. Additional exam requirements/recommendations for international

students: required—TOEFL (minimum score 550 paper-based; 77 iBT). Electronic applications accepted.

**Dalhousie University,** Faculty of Medicine, Department of Physiology and Biophysics, Halifax, NS B3H 1X5, Canada. Offers M Sc, PhD, M Sc/PhD. *Degree requirements:* For master's, thesis; for doctorate, thesis/dissertation. *Entrance requirements:* For master's and doctorate, GRE Subject Test (for international students). Additional exam requirements/recommendations for international students: required—1 of 5 approved tests: TOEFL, IELTS, CANTEST, CAEL, Michigan English Language Assessment Battery. Electronic applications accepted.

**East Carolina University,** Graduate School, Thomas Harriot College of Arts and Sciences, Department of Physics, Greenville, NC 27858-4353. Offers applied physics (MS); biomedical physics (PhD); health physics (MS); medical physics (MS). *Program availability:* Part-time. *Application deadline:* For fall admission, 3/1 priority date for domestic and international students. *Expenses: Tuition, area resident:* Full-time $4749; part-time $185 per credit hour. Tuition, state resident: full-time $4749; part-time $185 per credit hour. Tuition, nonresident: full-time $17,898; part-time $864 per credit hour. *International tuition:* $17,898 full-time. *Required fees:* $2787. *Financial support:* Application deadline: 3/1. *Unit head:* Dr. Jefferson Shinpaugh, Chair, 252-328-6739, E-mail: shinpaughj@ecu.edu. *Application contact:* Graduate School Admissions, 252-328-6012, Fax: 252-328-6071, E-mail: gradschool@ecu.edu. Website: https://physics.ecu.edu/

**Harvard University,** Graduate School of Arts and Sciences, Committee on Biophysics, Cambridge, MA 02138. Offers PhD. *Degree requirements:* For doctorate, thesis/dissertation, exam, qualifying paper. *Entrance requirements:* For doctorate, GRE General Test, GRE Subject Test (recommended). Additional exam requirements/recommendations for international students: required—TOEFL.

**Howard University,** Graduate School, Department of Physiology and Biophysics, Washington, DC 20059-0002. Offers biophysics (PhD); physiology (PhD). *Degree requirements:* For doctorate, comprehensive exam, thesis/dissertation. *Entrance requirements:* For doctorate, GRE General Test, minimum B average in field.

**Illinois State University,** Graduate School, College of Arts and Sciences, School of Biological Sciences, Normal, IL 61790. Offers animal behavior (MS); bacteriology (MS); biochemistry (MS); biological sciences (MS); biology (PhD); biophysics (MS); biotechnology (MS); botany (MS, PhD); cell biology (MS); conservation biology (MS); developmental biology (MS); ecology (MS, PhD); entomology (MS); evolutionary biology (MS); genetics (MS, PhD); immunology (MS); microbiology (MS, PhD); molecular biology (MS); molecular genetics (MS); neurobiology (MS); neuroscience (MS); parasitology (MS); physiology (MS, PhD); plant biology (MS); plant molecular biology (MS); plant sciences (MS); structural biology (MS); zoology (MS, PhD). *Program availability:* Part-time. *Faculty:* 26 full-time (6 women), 7 part-time/adjunct (2 women). *Students:* 51 full-time (33 women), 15 part-time (8 women). Average age 27. 71 applicants, 28% accepted, 9 enrolled. In 2019, 14 master's, 3 doctorates awarded. *Degree requirements:* For master's, thesis or alternative; for doctorate, variable foreign language requirement, thesis/dissertation, 2 terms of residency. *Entrance requirements:* For master's, GRE General Test, minimum GPA of 2.6 in last 60 hours of course work; for doctorate, GRE General Test. *Application deadline:* Applications are processed on a rolling basis. Application fee: $50. *Expenses: Tuition, area resident:* Full-time $7956; part-time $9767 per year. Tuition, nonresident: full-time $9233; part-time $17,592 per year. *Required fees:* $1797. *Financial support:* In 2019–20, 20 research assistantships, 41 teaching assistantships were awarded; Federal Work-Study, tuition waivers (full), and unspecified assistantships also available. Financial award application deadline: 4/1. *Unit head:* Dr. Craig Gatto, School Director, 309-438-3087, E-mail: cgatto@IllinoisState.edu. *Application contact:* Dr. Ben Sadd, Assistant Chair for Graduate Studies, 309-438-2651, E-mail: bmsadd@IllinoisState.edu. Website: http://www.bio.ilstu.edu/

**Iowa State University of Science and Technology,** Program in Biophysics, Ames, IA 50011. Offers MS, PhD. *Entrance requirements:* For master's, GRE. Additional exam requirements/recommendations for international students: required—TOEFL (minimum score 550 paper-based; 79 iBT), IELTS (minimum score 6.5). Electronic applications accepted.

**Johns Hopkins University,** National Institutes of Health Sponsored Programs, Baltimore, MD 21218. Offers biology (PhD), including biochemistry, biophysics, cell biology, developmental biology, genetic biology, molecular biology; cell, molecular, and developmental biology and biophysics (PhD). *Degree requirements:* For doctorate, comprehensive exam, thesis/dissertation. *Entrance requirements:* Additional exam requirements/recommendations for international students: required—TOEFL (minimum score 600 paper-based). Electronic applications accepted.

**Johns Hopkins University,** Zanvyl Krieger School of Arts and Sciences, Thomas C. Jenkins Department of Biophysics, Baltimore, MD 21218. Offers PhD. *Degree requirements:* For doctorate, comprehensive exam, thesis/dissertation. *Entrance requirements:* For doctorate, GRE General Test. Additional exam requirements/recommendations for international students: required—TOEFL (minimum score 600 paper-based), IELTS; recommended—TWE. Electronic applications accepted.

**Northwestern University,** The Graduate School, Interdisciplinary Biological Sciences Program (IBiS), Evanston, IL 60208. Offers biochemistry (PhD); bioengineering and biotechnology (PhD); biotechnology (PhD); cell and molecular biology (PhD); developmental and systems biology (PhD); nanotechnology (PhD); neurobiology (PhD); structural biology and biophysics (PhD). *Degree requirements:* For doctorate, thesis/dissertation, qualifying exam. *Entrance requirements:* For doctorate, GRE General Test. Additional exam requirements/recommendations for international students: required—TOEFL (minimum score 600 paper-based). Electronic applications accepted.

**The Ohio State University,** Graduate School, College of Arts and Sciences, Division of Natural and Mathematical Sciences, Program in Biophysics, Columbus, OH 43210. Offers MS, PhD. *Entrance requirements:* For master's and doctorate, GRE General Test (minimum 50th percentile on each section). Additional exam requirements/recommendations for international students: required—TOEFL (minimum score 600 paper-based; 100 iBT), Michigan English Language Assessment Battery (minimum score 86); recommended—IELTS (minimum score 8). Electronic applications accepted.

**Oregon State University,** College of Science, Program in Biochemistry and Biophysics, Corvallis, OR 97331. Offers MA, MS, PhD. Terminal master's awarded for partial completion of doctoral program. *Degree requirements:* For master's, thesis optional; for doctorate, thesis/dissertation, exams. *Entrance requirements:* For master's and doctorate, GRE, minimum GPA of 3.0. Additional exam requirements/recommendations for international students: required—TOEFL (minimum score 600 paper-based; 100 iBT), IELTS (minimum score 7). Electronic applications accepted.

**Purdue University,** Graduate School, PULSe - Purdue University Life Sciences Program, West Lafayette, IN 47907. Offers biomolecular structure and biophysics (PhD); biotechnology (PhD); chemical biology (PhD); chromatin and regulation of gene expression (PhD); integrative neuroscience (PhD); integrative plant sciences (PhD); membrane biology (PhD); microbiology (PhD); molecular evolutionary and cancer biology (PhD); molecular evolutionary genetics (PhD); molecular virology (PhD). *Students:* 37 full-time (23 women); includes 7 minority (1 Black or African American, non-Hispanic/Latino; 2 Asian, non-Hispanic/Latino; 4 Hispanic/Latino), 22 international. Average age 25. 162 applicants, 36% accepted, 19 enrolled. *Entrance requirements:* For doctorate, GRE, minimum undergraduate GPA of 3.0. Additional exam requirements/recommendations for international students: required—TOEFL (minimum score 550 paper-based; 77 iBT). *Application deadline:* For fall admission, 1/15 priority date for domestic and international students. Applications are processed on a rolling basis. Application fee: $60 ($75 for international students). Electronic applications accepted. *Financial support:* In 2019–20, research assistantships with tuition reimbursements (averaging $22,500 per year), teaching assistantships with tuition reimbursements (averaging $22,500 per year) were awarded. *Application contact:* Lindsey Springer, Graduate Contact for Admissions, 765-496-9667, E-mail: lbcampbe@purdue.edu.
Website: http://www.gradschool.purdue.edu/pulse

**Rensselaer Polytechnic Institute,** Graduate School, School of Science, Program in Biochemistry and Biophysics, Troy, NY 12180-3590. Offers MS, PhD. *Faculty:* 21 full-time (8 women), 2 part-time/adjunct (1 woman). *Students:* 12 full-time (6 women), 1 (woman) part-time; includes 3 minority (2 Asian, non-Hispanic/Latino; 1 Hispanic/Latino), 2 international. Average age 27. 38 applicants, 39% accepted, 4 enrolled. In 2019, 2 master's, 6 doctorates awarded. Terminal master's awarded for partial completion of doctoral program. *Degree requirements:* For master's, thesis optional; for doctorate, comprehensive exam, thesis/dissertation. *Entrance requirements:* For master's and doctorate, GRE. Additional exam requirements/recommendations for international students: required—TOEFL (minimum score 600 paper-based; 100 iBT), IELTS (minimum score 7), PTE (minimum score 68). *Application deadline:* For fall admission, 1/1 priority date for domestic and international students; for spring admission, 8/15 priority date for domestic and international students. Applications are processed on a rolling basis. Application fee: $75. Electronic applications accepted. *Financial support:* In 2019–20, research assistantships (averaging $23,000 per year), teaching assistantships (averaging $23,000 per year) were awarded; fellowships also available. Financial award application deadline: 1/1. *Unit head:* Dr. Cathy Royer, Graduate Program Director, 518-276-3796, E-mail: royerc@rpi.edu. *Application contact:* Jarron Decker, Director of Graduate Admissions, 518-276-6216, Fax: 518-276-4072, E-mail: gradadmissions@rpi.edu.
Website: https://science.rpi.edu/biology

**Rosalind Franklin University of Medicine and Science,** School of Graduate and Postdoctoral Studies - Interdisciplinary Graduate Program in Biomedical Sciences, Department of Physiology and Biophysics, North Chicago, IL 60064-3095. Offers MS, PhD, MD/PhD. Terminal master's awarded for partial completion of doctoral program. *Degree requirements:* For master's, comprehensive exam, thesis; for doctorate, comprehensive exam, thesis/dissertation. *Entrance requirements:* For master's and doctorate, GRE General Test. Additional exam requirements/recommendations for international students: required—TOEFL, TWE.

**Stanford University,** School of Humanities and Sciences, Program in Biophysics, Stanford, CA 94305-2004. Offers PhD. *Expenses: Tuition:* Full-time $52,479; part-time $34,110 per unit. *Required fees:* $672; $224 per quarter. Tuition and fees vary according to program and student level.

**Stony Brook University, State University of New York,** Stony Brook Medicine, Renaissance School of Medicine and Graduate School, Graduate Programs in Medicine, Department of Physiology and Biophysics, Stony Brook, NY 11794. Offers PhD. *Faculty:* 11 full-time (4 women), 2 part-time/adjunct (1 woman). *Students:* 22 full-time (14 women), 4 part-time (all women); includes 17 minority (7 Black or African American, non-Hispanic/Latino; 4 Asian, non-Hispanic/Latino; 6 Hispanic/Latino). Average age 23. 4 applicants, 25% accepted, 1 enrolled. *Degree requirements:* For doctorate, comprehensive exam, thesis/dissertation. *Entrance requirements:* For doctorate, GRE General Test, GRE Subject Test, BS in related field, minimum GPA of 3.0, recommendation. Additional exam requirements/recommendations for international students: required—TOEFL (minimum score 550 paper-based). *Application deadline:* For fall admission, 1/15 for domestic students; for spring admission, 10/1 for domestic students. Application fee: $100. *Expenses:* Contact institution. *Financial support:* In 2019–20, 3 research assistantships were awarded; fellowships, teaching assistantships, and Federal Work-Study also available. Financial award application deadline: 3/15. *Unit head:* Dr. Todd Miller, Chair, 631-444-3533, Fax: 631-444-3432, E-mail: todd.miller@stonybrook.edu. *Application contact:* Odalis Hernandez, Coordinator, 631-444-3057, Fax: 631-444-9749, E-mail: odalis.hernandez@stonybrook.edu.
Website: https://renaissance.stonybrookmedicine.edu/pnb

**Texas Christian University,** College of Science and Engineering, Department of Physics and Astronomy, Fort Worth, TX 76129-0002. Offers physics (MA, MS, PhD), including astrophysics (PhD); biophysics (PhD); PhD/MBA. *Program availability:* Part-time. *Faculty:* 8 full-time (3 women). *Students:* 16 full-time (7 women); includes 2 minority (1 Black or African American, non-Hispanic/Latino; 1 Hispanic/Latino), 6 international. Average age 26. 31 applicants, 32% accepted, 9 enrolled. In 2019, 11 master's, 3 doctorates awarded. Terminal master's awarded for partial completion of doctoral program. *Degree requirements:* For master's, one foreign language, comprehensive exam, thesis or alternative; for doctorate, comprehensive exam, thesis/dissertation. *Entrance requirements:* Additional exam requirements/recommendations for international students: required—TOEFL (minimum score 550 paper-based; 80 iBT), IELTS (minimum score 6.5). *Application deadline:* For fall admission, 1/1 priority date for domestic and international students; for spring admission, 9/1 priority date for domestic and international students. Applications are processed on a rolling basis. Application fee: $0 ($60 for international students). Electronic applications accepted. *Expenses:* Contact institution. *Financial support:* In 2019–20, 16 students received support, including 3 research assistantships with full tuition reimbursements available (averaging $24,000 per year), 13 teaching assistantships with full tuition reimbursements available (averaging $21,000 per year); scholarships/grants and unspecified assistantships also available. Financial award application deadline: 1/1. *Unit head:* Dr. Yuri M. Strzhemechny, Associate Professor/Chair, 817-257-5793, Fax: 817-257-7742, E-mail: y.strzhemechny@tcu.edu. *Application contact:* Dr. Peter M. Frinchaboy, III, Associate Professor, 817-257-6387, Fax: 817-257-7742, E-mail: p.frinchaboy@tcu.edu.
Website: http://physics.tcu.edu/

**Université de Sherbrooke,** Faculty of Medicine and Health Sciences, Graduate Programs in Medicine, Department of Physiology and Biophysics, Sherbrooke, QC J1H 5N4, Canada. Offers M Sc, PhD. Terminal master's awarded for partial completion of doctoral program. *Degree requirements:* For master's, thesis; for doctorate, thesis/dissertation. Electronic applications accepted.

**Université du Québec à Trois-Rivières,** Graduate Programs, Program in Biophysics and Cellular Biology, Trois-Rivières, QC G9A 5H7, Canada. Offers M Sc, PhD. *Program*

*availability:* Part-time. *Degree requirements:* For master's, thesis; for doctorate, thesis/dissertation. *Entrance requirements:* For master's, appropriate bachelor's degree, proficiency in French; for doctorate, appropriate master's degree, proficiency in French.

**University at Buffalo, the State University of New York,** Graduate School, Jacobs School of Medicine and Biomedical Sciences, Graduate Programs in Medicine and Biomedical Sciences, Department of Physiology and Biophysics, Buffalo, NY 14260. Offers biophysics (MS, PhD); physiology (MA, PhD). *Faculty:* 17 full-time (4 women). *Students:* 5 full-time (1 woman); includes 3 minority (1 Black or African American, non-Hispanic/Latino; 2 Asian, non-Hispanic/Latino). Average age 27. 10 applicants, 10% accepted, 1 enrolled. In 2019, 2 master's awarded. Terminal master's awarded for partial completion of doctoral program. *Degree requirements:* For master's, comprehensive exam, thesis or alternative, oral exam, project; for doctorate, comprehensive exam, thesis/dissertation, oral and written qualifying exam or 2 research proposals. *Entrance requirements:* For master's, GRE General Test, unofficial transcripts, 3 letters of recommendation, personal statement, curriculum vitae; for doctorate, GRE General Test or MCAT, unofficial transcripts, 3 letters of recommendation, personal statement, curriculum vitae. Additional exam requirements/recommendations for international students: required—TOEFL (minimum score 550 paper-based; 79 iBT). *Application deadline:* Applications are processed on a rolling basis. Application fee: $85. Electronic applications accepted. *Expenses: Tuition, area resident:* Full-time $11,310; part-time $471 per credit hour. Tuition, state resident: full-time $11,310; part-time $471 per credit hour. Tuition, nonresident: full-time $23,100; part-time $963 per credit hour. *International tuition:* $23,100 full-time. *Required fees:* $2820. *Financial support:* In 2019–20, 2 students received support, including 2 research assistantships with full tuition reimbursements available (averaging $27,000 per year); health care benefits also available. Financial award applicants required to submit FAFSA. *Unit head:* Dr. Perry M. Hogan, Chair, 716-829-2738, Fax: 716-829-2344, E-mail: phogan@buffalo.edu. *Application contact:* Kara M. Rickicki, Assistant Director of Academic Administration, 716-829-2417, Fax: 716-829-2801, E-mail: rickicki@buffalo.edu.
Website: https://medicine.buffalo.edu/departments/physiology.html

**University of California, Berkeley,** Graduate Division, College of Letters and Science, Group in Biophysics, Berkeley, CA 94720. Offers PhD. *Degree requirements:* For doctorate, thesis/dissertation, qualifying exam. *Entrance requirements:* For doctorate, GRE General Test, minimum GPA of 3.0, 3 letters of recommendation. Electronic applications accepted.

**University of California, Davis,** Graduate Studies, Graduate Group in Biophysics, Davis, CA 95616. Offers MS, PhD. *Degree requirements:* For doctorate, thesis/dissertation. *Entrance requirements:* For master's and doctorate, GRE General Test, GRE Subject Test. Additional exam requirements/recommendations for international students: required—TOEFL (minimum score 550 paper-based). Electronic applications accepted.

**University of California, Irvine,** School of Medicine and School of Biological Sciences, Department of Physiology and Biophysics, Irvine, CA 92697. Offers biological sciences (PhD); MD/PhD. *Students:* 20 full-time (8 women); includes 9 minority (1 American Indian or Alaska Native, non-Hispanic/Latino; 7 Asian, non-Hispanic/Latino; 1 Hispanic/Latino), 3 international. Average age 29. In 2019, 2 doctorates awarded. *Entrance requirements:* For doctorate, GRE General Test, GRE Subject Test, minimum GPA of 3.0. Additional exam requirements/recommendations for international students: required—TOEFL (minimum score 550 paper-based). *Application deadline:* For fall admission, 1/15 priority date for domestic students, 1/15 for international students. Application fee: $120 ($140 for international students). Electronic applications accepted. *Financial support:* Fellowships, research assistantships with full tuition reimbursements, teaching assistantships, institutionally sponsored loans, traineeships, health care benefits, and unspecified assistantships available. Financial award application deadline: 3/1; financial award applicants required to submit FAFSA. *Unit head:* Prof. Michael Cahalan, Chair, 949-824-7776, Fax: 949-824-3143, E-mail: mcahalan@uci.edu. *Application contact:* Janita Parpana, Chief Administrative Officer, 949-824-6833, Fax: 949-824-8540, E-mail: jparpana@uci.edu.
Website: http://www.physiology.uci.edu/

**University of California, San Diego,** Graduate Division, Department of Physics, La Jolla, CA 92093. Offers biophysics (PhD); computational neuroscience (PhD); computational science (PhD); multi-scale biology (PhD); physics (MS, PhD); quantitative biology (PhD). *Students:* 166 full-time (26 women), 2 part-time (1 woman). 566 applicants, 22% accepted, 22 enrolled. In 2019, 9 master's, 23 doctorates awarded. *Degree requirements:* For doctorate, comprehensive exam, thesis/dissertation, 1-quarter teaching assistantship. *Entrance requirements:* For doctorate, GRE General Test, GRE Subject Test, statement of purpose, three letters of reference. Additional exam requirements/recommendations for international students: required—TOEFL (minimum score 550 paper-based; 80 iBT), IELTS (minimum score 7). *Application deadline:* For fall admission, 12/18 for domestic students. Application fee: $105 ($125 for international students). Electronic applications accepted. *Financial support:* Fellowships, research assistantships, teaching assistantships, scholarships/grants, and unspecified assistantships available. Financial award applicants required to submit FAFSA. *Unit head:* Brian Maple, Chair, 858-534-6857, E-mail: chair@physics.ucsd.edu. *Application contact:* Saixious Dominguez-Kilday, Graduate Admissions Coordinator, 858-534-3293, E-mail: skilday@physics.ucsd.edu.
Website: http://physics.ucsd.edu/

**University of California, San Francisco,** School of Pharmacy and School of Medicine, Program in Biophysics, San Francisco, CA 94143. Offers PhD. *Degree requirements:* For doctorate, thesis/dissertation. *Entrance requirements:* For doctorate, GRE General Test; GRE Subject Test (recommended), bachelor's degree with minimum GPA of 3.0. Additional exam requirements/recommendations for international students: required—TOEFL. Electronic applications accepted.

**University of California, Santa Barbara,** Graduate Division, College of Letters and Sciences, Division of Mathematics, Life, and Physical Sciences, Interdepartmental Graduate Program in Biomolecular Science and Engineering, Santa Barbara, CA 93106-2014. Offers biochemistry and molecular biology (PhD), including biochemistry and molecular biology, biophysics and bioengineering. Terminal master's awarded for partial completion of doctoral program. *Degree requirements:* For doctorate, thesis/dissertation. *Entrance requirements:* For doctorate, GRE General Test. Additional exam requirements/recommendations for international students: required—TOEFL (minimum score 630 paper-based; 109 iBT), IELTS (minimum score 7). Electronic applications accepted.

**University of Chicago,** Division of the Physical Sciences, Graduate Program in Biophysical Sciences, Chicago, IL 60637. Offers PhD. *Degree requirements:* For doctorate, comprehensive exam, thesis/dissertation, ethics class, 2 teaching assistantships. *Entrance requirements:* For doctorate, GRE General Test, research statement, 3 letters of recommendation, transcripts for all previous degrees and institutions attended. Additional exam requirements/recommendations for international students: required—TOEFL (minimum score 600 paper-based; 104 iBT), IELTS (minimum score 7). Electronic applications accepted.

## Biophysics

**University of Cincinnati,** Graduate School, College of Medicine, Graduate Programs in Biomedical Sciences, Department of Pharmacology and Cell Biophysics, Cincinnati, OH 45221. Offers cell biophysics (PhD); pharmacology (PhD). *Degree requirements:* For doctorate, thesis/dissertation, qualifying exam. *Entrance requirements:* For doctorate, GRE General Test. Additional exam requirements/recommendations for international students: required—TOEFL. Electronic applications accepted.

**University of Colorado Denver,** School of Medicine, Graduate Program in Genetic Counseling, Aurora, CO 80045. Offers biophysics and genetics (MS). *Degree requirements:* For master's, 44 core semester hours, project or thesis. *Entrance requirements:* For master's, GRE, minimum undergraduate GPA of 3.0; 4 letters of recommendation; prerequisite coursework in biology, general chemistry, general biochemistry, general genetics, and general psychology; experience in counseling and laboratory settings and strong understanding of genetic counseling field (highly recommended). Additional exam requirements/recommendations for international students: required—TOEFL (minimum score 570 paper-based; 89 iBT). Electronic applications accepted. Tuition and fees vary according to course load, program and reciprocity agreements.

**University of Connecticut,** Graduate School, College of Liberal Arts and Sciences, Department of Molecular and Cell Biology, Storrs, CT 06269. Offers applied genomics (PSM); cell and developmental biology (MS, PhD); genetics and genomics (MS, PhD); microbial systems analysis (PSM); microbiology (MS, PhD); structural biology, biochemistry and biophysics (MS, PhD). Terminal master's awarded for partial completion of doctoral program. *Degree requirements:* For master's, comprehensive exam; for doctorate, thesis/dissertation. *Entrance requirements:* For master's and doctorate, GRE General Test, GRE Subject Test. Additional exam requirements/recommendations for international students: required—TOEFL (minimum score 550 paper-based). Electronic applications accepted.

**University of Guelph,** Office of Graduate and Postdoctoral Studies, Biophysics Interdepartmental Group, Guelph, ON N1G 2W1, Canada. Offers M Sc, PhD. *Degree requirements:* For master's, thesis; for doctorate, comprehensive exam, thesis/dissertation. *Entrance requirements:* For master's, minimum B average during previous 2 years of course work; for doctorate, minimum B+ average. Additional exam requirements/recommendations for international students: required—TOEFL (minimum score 550 paper-based). Electronic applications accepted.

**University of Guelph,** Office of Graduate and Postdoctoral Studies, College of Biological Science, Department of Molecular and Cellular Biology, Guelph, ON N1G 2W1, Canada. Offers biochemistry (M Sc, PhD); biophysics (M Sc, PhD); botany (M Sc, PhD); microbiology (M Sc, PhD); molecular biology and genetics (M Sc, PhD). *Degree requirements:* For master's, thesis, research proposal; for doctorate, comprehensive exam, thesis/dissertation, research proposal. *Entrance requirements:* For master's, minimum B-average during previous 2 years of coursework; for doctorate, minimum A-average. Additional exam requirements/recommendations for international students: required—TOEFL (minimum score 550 paper-based), IELTS (minimum score 6.5). Electronic applications accepted.

**University of Illinois at Chicago,** College of Medicine, Graduate Programs in Medicine, Department of Physiology and Biophysics, Chicago, IL 60607-7128. Offers MS, PhD. Terminal master's awarded for partial completion of doctoral program. *Degree requirements:* For master's, thesis; for doctorate, thesis/dissertation. *Entrance requirements:* For master's and doctorate, GRE General Test. Additional exam requirements/recommendations for international students: required—TOEFL. Electronic applications accepted.

**University of Illinois at Urbana-Champaign,** Graduate College, College of Liberal Arts and Sciences, School of Molecular and Cellular Biology, Center for Biophysics and Computational Biology, Champaign, IL 61820. Offers MS, PhD.

**The University of Iowa,** Roy J. and Lucille A. Carver College of Medicine and Graduate College, Graduate Programs in Medicine, Department of Molecular Physiology and Biophysics, Iowa City, IA 52242-1316. Offers MS, PhD. *Faculty:* 9 full-time (2 women). *Students:* 10 full-time (2 women); includes 3 minority (2 Asian, non-Hispanic/Latino; 1 Hispanic/Latino), 1 international. Average age 23. 5 applicants, 60% accepted, 3 enrolled. In 2019, 1 doctorate awarded. *Degree requirements:* For master's, comprehensive exam; for doctorate, comprehensive exam, thesis/dissertation. *Entrance requirements:* Additional exam requirements/recommendations for international students: required—TOEFL. *Application deadline:* For fall admission, 4/1 for domestic students, 3/1 for international students; for spring admission, 10/1 for domestic students, 9/1 for international students. Applications are processed on a rolling basis. Application fee: $60 ($80 for international students). Electronic applications accepted. *Financial support:* In 2019–20, 1 fellowship with full tuition reimbursement (averaging $26,000 per year), 14 research assistantships with full tuition reimbursements (averaging $26,000 per year) were awarded; traineeships also available. Financial award application deadline: 4/1. *Unit head:* Dr. Kevin P. Campbell, Chair and Department Executive Officer, 319-335-7800, Fax: 319-335-7330, E-mail: kevin-campbell@uiowa.edu. *Application contact:* Dr. Mark Stamnes, Director of Graduate Studies, 319-335-7858, Fax: 319-335-7330, E-mail: mark-stamnes@uiowa.edu. Website: http://www.physiology.uiowa.edu/

**The University of Kansas,** Graduate Studies, College of Liberal Arts and Sciences, Department of Molecular Biosciences, Lawrence, KS 66044. Offers biochemistry and biophysics (PhD); microbiology (PhD); molecular, cellular, and developmental biology (PhD). *Program availability:* Part-time. *Students:* 66 full-time (39 women); includes 36 minority (1 Black or African American, non-Hispanic/Latino; 2 Asian, non-Hispanic/Latino; 31 Hispanic/Latino; 2 Two or more races, non-Hispanic/Latino), 31 international. Average age 28. 93 applicants, 30% accepted, 12 enrolled. In 2019, 3 doctorates awarded. Terminal master's awarded for partial completion of doctoral program. *Entrance requirements:* For doctorate, GRE General Test, 1-page statement of research interests and goals, 1-2 page curriculum vitae or resume, official transcript, 3 recommendation letters. Additional exam requirements/recommendations for international students: required—TOEFL, IELTS, TOEFL or IELTS. *Application deadline:* For fall admission, 12/1 for domestic and international students. Application fee: $65 ($85 for international students). Electronic applications accepted. *Expenses:* Tuition, state resident: full-time $9989. Tuition, nonresident: full-time $23,950. International tuition: $23,950 full-time. *Required fees:* $984; $81.99 per credit hour. Tuition and fees vary according to course load, campus/location and program. *Financial support:* Fellowships, research assistantships, teaching assistantships, scholarships/grants, health care benefits, and unspecified assistantships available. Financial award application deadline: 12/1. *Unit head:* Susan M. Egan, Chair, 785-864-4294, E-mail: sme@ku.edu. *Application contact:* John Connolly, Graduate Admissions Contact, 785-864-4311, E-mail: jconnolly@ku.edu. Website: http://www.molecularbiosciences.ku.edu/

**The University of Manchester,** School of Physics and Astronomy, Manchester, United Kingdom. Offers astronomy and astrophysics (M Sc, PhD); biological physics (M Sc, PhD); condensed matter physics (M Sc, PhD); nonlinear and liquid crystals physics (M Sc, PhD); nuclear physics (M Sc, PhD); particle physics (M Sc, PhD); photon physics (M Sc, PhD); physics (M Sc, PhD); theoretical physics (M Sc, PhD).

**University of Maryland, College Park,** Academic Affairs, College of Computer, Mathematical and Natural Sciences, Department of Biology, PhD Program in Biological Sciences, College Park, MD 20742. Offers behavior, ecology, evolution, and systematics (PhD); computational biology, bioinformatics, and genomics (PhD); molecular and cellular biology (PhD); physiological systems (PhD). *Degree requirements:* For doctorate, comprehensive exam, thesis/dissertation, thesis work presentation in seminar. *Entrance requirements:* For doctorate, GRE General Test; GRE Subject Test in biology (recommended), academic transcripts, statement of purpose/research interests, 3 letters of recommendation. Additional exam requirements/recommendations for international students: required—TOEFL. Electronic applications accepted.

**University of Maryland, College Park,** Academic Affairs, College of Computer, Mathematical and Natural Sciences, Institute for Physical Science and Technology, Program in Biophysics, College Park, MD 20742. Offers PhD.

**University of Miami,** Graduate School, Miller School of Medicine, Graduate Programs in Medicine, Department of Physiology and Biophysics, Miami, FL 33124. Offers cellular physiology and molecular biophysics (MD/PhD); MD/PhD. *Faculty:* 12 full-time (3 women), 1 part-time/adjunct (0 women). *Students:* 7 full-time (5 women); includes 1 minority (Black or African American, non-Hispanic/Latino), 2 international. Average age 27. *Degree requirements:* For doctorate, thesis/dissertation, qualifying exam. *Entrance requirements:* For doctorate, GRE General Test, minimum GPA of 3.0 in sciences. Additional exam requirements/recommendations for international students: required—TOEFL (minimum score 80 paper-based), IELTS (minimum score 6.5). *Application deadline:* For fall admission, 12/1 priority date for domestic students, 12/1 for international students. Applications are processed on a rolling basis. Application fee: $100. Electronic applications accepted. *Financial support:* In 2019–20, 7 students received support, including 7 fellowships with full tuition reimbursements available (averaging $30,000 per year), 7 research assistantships with full tuition reimbursements available (averaging $30,000 per year); health care benefits and tuition waivers (full) also available. Financial award applicants required to submit FAFSA. *Unit head:* Dr. Karl Magleby, Chairman, 305-243-6236, Fax: 305-243-6898, E-mail: kmagleby@miami.edu. *Application contact:* Dr. Hans Peter Larsson, Graduate Program Director, 305-243-1021, E-mail: plarsson@miami.edu. Website: http://physiology-biophysics.med.miami.edu/

**University of Michigan,** Rackham Graduate School, College of Literature, Science, and the Arts, Department of Biophysics, Ann Arbor, MI 48109. Offers PhD. *Degree requirements:* For doctorate, thesis/dissertation, preliminary exam, oral defense of dissertation. *Entrance requirements:* Additional exam requirements/recommendations for international students: required—TOEFL (minimum score 84 iBT). Electronic applications accepted. Application fee is waived when completed online.

**University of Minnesota, Duluth,** Medical School, Department of Biochemistry, Molecular Biology and Biophysics, Duluth, MN 55812-2496. Offers biochemistry, molecular biology and biophysics (MS); biology and biophysics (PhD); social, administrative, and clinical pharmacy (MS, PhD); toxicology (MS, PhD). Terminal master's awarded for partial completion of doctoral program. *Degree requirements:* For master's, comprehensive exam, thesis; for doctorate, comprehensive exam, thesis/dissertation. *Entrance requirements:* For master's and doctorate, GRE General Test. Additional exam requirements/recommendations for international students: required—TOEFL. Electronic applications accepted.

**University of Minnesota, Twin Cities Campus,** Graduate School, College of Biological Sciences, Biochemistry, Molecular Biology and Biophysics Graduate Program, Minneapolis, MN 55455-0213. Offers PhD. *Degree requirements:* For doctorate, thesis/dissertation. *Entrance requirements:* For doctorate, GRE, 3 letters of recommendation, more than 1 semester of laboratory experience. Additional exam requirements/recommendations for international students: required—TOEFL (minimum score 625 paper-based; 108 iBT with writing subsection 25 and reading subsection 25) or IELTS (minimum score 7). Electronic applications accepted.

**University of Minnesota, Twin Cities Campus,** Graduate School, Program in Biophysical Sciences and Medical Physics, Minneapolis, MN 55455-0213. Offers MS, PhD. *Program availability:* Part-time. *Degree requirements:* For master's, thesis optional, research paper, oral exam; for doctorate, thesis/dissertation, oral/written preliminary exam, oral final exam.

**University of Mississippi Medical Center,** School of Graduate Studies in Health Sciences, Department of Physiology and Biophysics, Jackson, MS 39216-4505. Offers PhD, MD/PhD. *Degree requirements:* For doctorate, thesis/dissertation, first authored publication. *Entrance requirements:* For doctorate, GRE General Test, minimum GPA of 3.0.

**University of Missouri–Kansas City,** School of Biological Sciences, Program in Cell Biology and Biophysics, Kansas City, MO 64110-2499. Offers PhD. *Degree requirements:* For doctorate, comprehensive exam, thesis/dissertation. *Entrance requirements:* For doctorate, GRE General Test, bachelor's degree in chemistry, biology or related field; minimum GPA of 3.0. Additional exam requirements/recommendations for international students: required—TOEFL (minimum score 550 paper-based; 80 iBT). Electronic applications accepted.

**The University of North Carolina at Chapel Hill,** School of Medicine and Graduate School, Biological and Biomedical Sciences Program, Department of Biochemistry and Biophysics, Chapel Hill, NC 27599. Offers MS, PhD. *Faculty:* 42 full-time (8 women). *Students:* 35 full-time (14 women); includes 10 minority (1 Black or African American, non-Hispanic/Latino; 1 American Indian or Alaska Native, non-Hispanic/Latino; 3 Asian, non-Hispanic/Latino; 3 Hispanic/Latino; 2 Two or more races, non-Hispanic/Latino). Average age 26. In 2019, 1 master's, 5 doctorates awarded. Terminal master's awarded for partial completion of doctoral program. *Degree requirements:* For doctorate, comprehensive exam, thesis/dissertation. *Entrance requirements:* Additional exam requirements/recommendations for international students: required—TOEFL. *Application deadline:* For fall admission, 12/3 priority date for domestic and international students. Applications are processed on a rolling basis. Application fee: $70. Electronic applications accepted. *Financial support:* In 2019–20, fellowships with full tuition reimbursements (averaging $32,000 per year), research assistantships with full tuition reimbursements (averaging $32,000 per year) were awarded; career-related internships or fieldwork, health care benefits, and tuition waivers (full) also available. *Unit head:* Dr. Leslie Parise, Chair, 919-962-8326, E-mail: parise@med.unc.edu. *Application contact:* Jeffrey Steinbach, Assistant Director of Admissions, 919-843-7129, E-mail: jsteinba@email.unc.edu. Website: https://www.med.unc.edu/biochem/

**University of Regina,** Faculty of Graduate Studies and Research, Faculty of Science, Department of Chemistry and Biochemistry, Regina, SK S4S 0A2, Canada. Offers biophysics of biological interfaces (M Sc, PhD); computational chemistry (M Sc, PhD); environmental analytical chemistry (M Sc, PhD); enzymology/chemical biology (M Sc, PhD); inorganic/organometallic chemistry (M Sc, PhD); signal transduction and mechanisms of cancer cell regulation (M Sc, PhD); supramolecular organic photochemistry and photophysics (M Sc, PhD); synthetic organic chemistry (M Sc, PhD). *Program availability:* Part-time. *Faculty:* 12 full-time (2 women), 6 part-time/

adjunct (0 women). *Students:* 19 full-time (9 women), 1 (woman) part-time. Average age 30. 18 applicants, 17% accepted. In 2019, 3 master's, 1 doctorate awarded. *Degree requirements:* For master's, thesis; for doctorate, comprehensive exam, thesis/dissertation. *Entrance requirements:* For master's, 4 years Bachelor degree in Chemistry or related program; for doctorate, completion of Master's in Chemistry. Additional exam requirements/recommendations for international students: required—TOEFL (minimum score 580 paper-based; 80 iBT), IELTS (minimum score 6.5), PTE (minimum score 59), other options are CAEL, MELAB, Cantest and U of R ESL. *Application deadline:* Applications are processed on a rolling basis. Application fee: $100. Electronic applications accepted. *Expenses: Tuition:* Full-time $6684 Canadian dollars. *Required fees:* $100 Canadian dollars; $3351.45 Canadian dollars per trimester. $1117.15 Canadian dollars per semester. Tuition and fees vary according to course level, course load, degree level and program. *Financial support:* Fellowships, research assistantships, teaching assistantships, career-related internships or fieldwork, Federal Work-Study, scholarships/grants, unspecified assistantships, and travel award and Graduate Scholarship Base Funds available. Support available to part-time students. Financial award application deadline: 9/30. *Unit head:* Dr. Renata Raina-Fulton, Department Head, 306-585-4012, Fax: 306-337-2409, E-mail: renata.raina@uregina.ca. *Application contact:* Dr. Brian Sterenberg, Graduate Program Coordinator, 306-585-4106, Fax: 306-337-2409, E-mail: brian.sterenberg@uregina.ca.
Website: http://www.uregina.ca/science/chem-biochem/

**University of Rochester,** School of Medicine and Dentistry, Graduate Programs in Medicine and Dentistry, Department of Biochemistry and Biophysics, Programs in Biophysics, Rochester, NY 14627. Offers biophysics, structural and computational biology (PhD). Terminal master's awarded for partial completion of doctoral program. *Degree requirements:* For doctorate, thesis/dissertation, qualifying exam. *Entrance requirements:* For doctorate, GRE General Test.

**University of Southern California,** Keck School of Medicine and Graduate School, Graduate Programs in Medicine, Department of Physiology and Neuroscience, Los Angeles, CA 90089. Offers medical biophysics (MS); medical physiology (MS). *Program availability:* Part-time. *Faculty:* 13 full-time (2 women). *Students:* 2 full-time (both women); both minorities (both Asian, non-Hispanic/Latino). Average age 23. 10 applicants, 30% accepted, 2 enrolled. In 2019, 2 master's awarded. *Degree requirements:* For master's, thesis. *Entrance requirements:* For master's, GRE General Test, minimum GPA of 3.0. Additional exam requirements/recommendations for international students: required—TOEFL (minimum score 600 paper-based; 100 iBT). *Application deadline:* For fall admission, 4/15 priority date for domestic and international students. Applications are processed on a rolling basis. Application fee: $90. Electronic applications accepted. *Expenses:* Contact institution. *Financial support:* Application deadline: 4/15; applicants required to submit FAFSA. *Unit head:* Dr. Berislav Zlokavic, Chair, 323-442-2566, Fax: 323-442-2230, E-mail: zlokovic@usc.edu. *Application contact:* Monica Pan, Student Services Advisor, 323-442-0230, Fax: 323-442-1610, E-mail: monicap@med.usc.edu.
Website: https://keck.usc.edu/physiology-and-neuroscience/

**University of Southern California,** Keck School of Medicine and Graduate School, Graduate Programs in Medicine, Programs in Biomedical and Biological Sciences (PIBBS), Program in Medical Biophysics, Los Angeles, CA 90089. Offers PhD. *Faculty:* 23 full-time (6 women). *Students:* 7 full-time (3 women); includes 5 minority (1 Black or African American, non-Hispanic/Latino; 2 Asian, non-Hispanic/Latino; 2 Hispanic/Latino), 1 international. Average age 24. 3 applicants, 100% accepted, 3 enrolled. In 2019, 2 doctorates awarded. *Degree requirements:* For doctorate, comprehensive exam, thesis/dissertation. *Entrance requirements:* For doctorate, GRE, minimum GPA of 3.5. Additional exam requirements/recommendations for international students: required—TOEFL (minimum score 600 paper-based; 100 iBT), IELTS (minimum score 7), PTE. *Application deadline:* For fall admission, 12/1 priority date for domestic and international students. Application fee: $90. Electronic applications accepted. *Financial support:* In 2019–20, 4 students received support, including 1 fellowship with full tuition reimbursement available (averaging $35,000 per year), 6 research assistantships with full tuition reimbursements available (averaging $35,000 per year); institutionally sponsored loans, scholarships/grants, traineeships, health care benefits, and unspecified assistantships also available. Financial award application deadline: 4/15; financial award applicants required to submit CSS PROFILE or FAFSA. *Unit head:* Dr. Ralf Langen, Director, 323-442-1475, Fax: 323-442-1199, E-mail: langen@med.usc.edu. *Application contact:* Karina Recinos, Student Services Advisor, 323-442-1609, Fax: 323-442-1199, E-mail: karina.recinos@med.usc.edu.
Website: https://keck.usc.edu/pibbs/phd-programs/medical-biophysics

**The University of Texas Medical Branch,** Graduate School of Biomedical Sciences, Program in Biochemistry and Molecular Biology, Galveston, TX 77555. Offers biochemistry (PhD); bioinformatics (PhD); biophysics (PhD); cell biology (PhD); computational biology (PhD); structural biology (PhD). *Degree requirements:* For doctorate, thesis/dissertation. *Entrance requirements:* Additional exam requirements/recommendations for international students: required—TOEFL (minimum score 550 paper-based). Electronic applications accepted.

**University of Toronto,** Faculty of Medicine, Department of Medical Biophysics, Toronto, ON M5S 1A1, Canada. Offers M Sc, PhD. *Degree requirements:* For master's, thesis; for doctorate, thesis/dissertation. *Entrance requirements:* For master's and doctorate, resume, 2 letters of reference. Additional exam requirements/recommendations for international students: required—TOEFL (minimum score 620 paper-based), TWE (minimum score 5). Electronic applications accepted.

**University of Virginia,** School of Medicine, Department of Molecular Physiology and Biological Physics, Charlottesville, VA 22903. Offers biological and physical sciences (MS); physiology (PhD); MD/PhD. *Entrance requirements:* For doctorate, GRE General Test, GRE Subject Test. Additional exam requirements/recommendations for international students: required—TOEFL. Electronic applications accepted.

**University of Virginia,** School of Medicine, Interdisciplinary Program in Biophysics, Charlottesville, VA 22908. Offers PhD. *Degree requirements:* For doctorate, thesis/dissertation, research proposal, oral defense. *Entrance requirements:* For doctorate, GRE General Test, GRE Subject Test (recommended), 2 or more letters of recommendation. Additional exam requirements/recommendations for international students: required—TOEFL. Electronic applications accepted.

**University of Washington,** Graduate School, School of Medicine, Graduate Programs in Medicine, Department of Physiology and Biophysics, Seattle, WA 98195. Offers PhD. *Degree requirements:* For doctorate, thesis/dissertation. *Entrance requirements:* For doctorate, GRE General Test. Additional exam requirements/recommendations for international students: required—TOEFL (minimum score 580 paper-based; 70 iBT).

**The University of Western Ontario,** Schulich School of Medicine and Dentistry, Department of Medical Biophysics, London, ON N6A 3K7, Canada. Offers M Sc, PhD. *Degree requirements:* For master's, thesis; for doctorate, thesis/dissertation. *Entrance requirements:* Additional exam requirements/recommendations for international students: required—TOEFL.

**University of Wisconsin–Madison,** Graduate School, Program in Biophysics, Madison, WI 53706. Offers PhD. *Degree requirements:* For doctorate, comprehensive exam, thesis/dissertation. *Entrance requirements:* For doctorate, GRE General Test, minimum GPA of 3.0. Additional exam requirements/recommendations for international students: required—TOEFL (minimum score 580 paper-based; 92 iBT). Electronic applications accepted.

**Vanderbilt University,** School of Medicine, Department of Molecular Physiology and Biophysics, Nashville, TN 37240-1001. Offers MS, PhD, MD/PhD. *Faculty:* 23 full-time (2 women). *Students:* 26 full-time (16 women); includes 9 minority (4 Black or African American, non-Hispanic/Latino; 1 Asian, non-Hispanic/Latino; 3 Hispanic/Latino; 1 Two or more races, non-Hispanic/Latino), 5 international. Average age 26. In 2019, 12 doctorates awarded. *Degree requirements:* For doctorate, comprehensive exam, thesis/dissertation, preliminary, qualifying, and final exams. *Entrance requirements:* For doctorate, GRE General Test, GRE Subject Test (recommended). Additional exam requirements/recommendations for international students: required—TOEFL (minimum score 570 paper-based; 88 iBT). *Application deadline:* For fall admission, 1/15 for domestic and international students. Electronic applications accepted. *Expenses: Tuition:* Full-time $51,018; part-time $2087 per hour. *Required fees:* $542. Tuition and fees vary according to program. *Financial support:* Fellowships with full tuition reimbursements, research assistantships with full tuition reimbursements, Federal Work-Study, institutionally sponsored loans, scholarships/grants, traineeships, health care benefits, and tuition waivers (partial) available. Financial award application deadline: 1/15; financial award applicants required to submit CSS PROFILE or FAFSA. *Unit head:* Dr. Roger Cone, Acting Chair, 615-322-7000, Fax: 615-343-0490, E-mail: roger.cone@vanderbilt.edu. *Application contact:* Richard O'Brien, Director of Graduate Studies, 615-322-7000, E-mail: richard.obrien@vanderbilt.edu.
Website: http://www.mc.vanderbilt.edu/root/vumc.php?site-MPB

**Vanderbilt University,** School of Medicine, Program in Chemical and Physical Biology, Nashville, TN 37240-1001. Offers PhD. *Faculty:* 71 full-time (9 women). *Students:* 48 full-time (20 women); includes 12 minority (2 Black or African American, non-Hispanic/Latino; 3 Asian, non-Hispanic/Latino; 7 Hispanic/Latino), 4 international. Average age 27. In 2019, 6 doctorates awarded. *Degree requirements:* For doctorate, comprehensive exam, thesis/dissertation, dissertation defense. *Entrance requirements:* For doctorate, GRE, 3 letters of recommendation, official transcripts. Additional exam requirements/recommendations for international students: required—TOEFL. *Application deadline:* For fall admission, 1/15 priority date for domestic students, 1/15 for international students. Applications are processed on a rolling basis. Electronic applications accepted. *Expenses: Tuition:* Full-time $51,018; part-time $2087 per hour. *Required fees:* $542. Tuition and fees vary according to program. *Financial support:* Fellowships with full tuition reimbursements, traineeships, health care benefits, and tuition waivers (full) available. *Unit head:* Dr. Bruce Damon, Director of Graduate Studies, 615-322-4235, Fax: 615-343-0490, E-mail: bruce.damon@vanderbilt.edu. *Application contact:* Patricia Mueller, Coordinator, 615-322-8727, E-mail: patricia.l.mueller@vanderbilt.edu.

**Washington State University,** College of Veterinary Medicine, School of Molecular Biosciences, Pullman, WA 99164-7520. Offers molecular biosciences (MS, PhD), including genetics (PhD). *Faculty:* 26 full-time (9 women), 15 part-time/adjunct (3 women). *Students:* 39 full-time (21 women), 1 (woman) part-time; includes 9 minority (1 Black or African American, non-Hispanic/Latino; 2 Asian, non-Hispanic/Latino; 6 Hispanic/Latino), 2 international. Average age 27. 60 applicants, 40% accepted, 13 enrolled. In 2019, 1 doctorate awarded. Terminal master's awarded for partial completion of doctoral program. *Degree requirements:* For master's, thesis (for some programs), oral defense; for doctorate, comprehensive exam, thesis/dissertation, oral defense. *Entrance requirements:* For master's and doctorate, GRE General Test for 2019-2020 entrance. Will be removed in the 2020-2021 recruiting year, minimum GPA of 3.0. Additional exam requirements/recommendations for international students: required—TOEFL (minimum score 600 paper-based; 100 iBT). *Application deadline:* For fall admission, 12/15 priority date for domestic and international students. Application fee: $75. Electronic applications accepted. *Expenses:* $6,997.58 In-State/Semester = $13,995.16 per academic year; $13,875.08 Out of State/Semester = $27,750.16 per academice year. Average 5 years to completion. *Financial support:* In 2019–20, 36 students received support, including 5 fellowships with full tuition reimbursements available (averaging $27,426 per year), 19 research assistantships with full tuition reimbursements available (averaging $29,700 per year), 14 teaching assistantships with full tuition reimbursements available (averaging $20,570 per year); scholarships/grants, traineeships, and health care benefits also available. Financial award application deadline: 4/15. *Unit head:* Dr. Michael D. Griswold, Director, 509-335-8724, Fax: 509-335-4159, E-mail: mgriswold@wsu.edu. *Application contact:* Tami Breske, Graduate Academic Coordinator, 509-335-4318, E-mail: tamara.breske@wsu.edu.
Website: http://www.smb.wsu.edu

**Weill Cornell Medicine,** Weill Cornell Graduate School of Medical Sciences, Physiology, Biophysics and Systems Biology Program, New York, NY 10065. Offers MS, PhD. Terminal master's awarded for partial completion of doctoral program. *Degree requirements:* For master's, comprehensive exam; for doctorate, thesis/dissertation, final exam. *Entrance requirements:* For doctorate, GRE General Test, introductory courses in biology, inorganic and organic chemistry, physics, and mathematics. Additional exam requirements/recommendations for international students: required—TOEFL.

**Yale University,** Graduate School of Arts and Sciences, Department of Molecular Biophysics and Biochemistry, New Haven, CT 06520. Offers PhD. *Degree requirements:* For doctorate, thesis/dissertation. *Entrance requirements:* For doctorate, GRE General Test, GRE Subject Test.

# Molecular Biophysics

**Baylor College of Medicine,** Graduate School of Biomedical Sciences, Program in Structural and Computational Biology and Molecular Biophysics, Houston, TX 77030-3498. Offers PhD, MD/PhD. *Degree requirements:* For doctorate, thesis/dissertation, public defense. *Entrance requirements:* For doctorate, GRE General Test, GRE Subject Test (strongly recommended), minimum GPA of 3.0. Additional exam requirements/recommendations for international students: required—TOEFL. Electronic applications accepted.

**California Institute of Technology,** Division of Biology and Biological Engineering and Division of Chemistry and Chemical Engineering, Biochemistry and Molecular Biophysics Graduate Option, Pasadena, CA 91125-0001. Offers PhD. *Degree requirements:* For doctorate, thesis/dissertation, qualifying exam. *Entrance requirements:* For doctorate, GRE General Test. Additional exam requirements/recommendations for international students: required—TOEFL. Electronic applications accepted.

**California Institute of Technology,** Division of Chemistry and Chemical Engineering, Pasadena, CA 91125-0001. Offers biochemistry and molecular biophysics (MS, PhD); chemical engineering (MS, PhD); chemistry (MS, PhD). Terminal master's awarded for partial completion of doctoral program. *Degree requirements:* For master's, thesis; for doctorate, thesis/dissertation. *Entrance requirements:* For doctorate, GRE, BS. Additional exam requirements/recommendations for international students: required—TOEFL; recommended—IELTS, TWE. Electronic applications accepted. *Expenses:* Contact institution.

**Carnegie Mellon University,** Mellon College of Science, Joint Pitt + CMU Molecular Biophysics and Structural Biology Graduate Program, Pittsburgh, PA 15213-3891. Offers PhD. *Degree requirements:* For doctorate, comprehensive exam, thesis/dissertation. *Entrance requirements:* For doctorate, GRE General Test. Additional exam requirements/recommendations for international students: required—TOEFL (minimum score 600 paper-based; 100 iBT), IELTS (minimum score 7). Electronic applications accepted.

**Duke University,** Graduate School, University Program in Structural Biology and Biophysics, Durham, NC 27710. Offers Certificate. *Entrance requirements:* For degree, GRE General Test. Additional exam requirements/recommendations for international students: required—TOEFL (minimum score 577 paper-based; 90 iBT) or IELTS (minimum score 7).

**Florida State University,** The Graduate School, College of Arts and Sciences, Program in Molecular Biophysics, Tallahassee, FL 32304. Offers structural biology (PhD). *Faculty:* 33 full-time (6 women). *Students:* 18 full-time (8 women); includes 14 minority (11 Asian, non-Hispanic/Latino; 3 Two or more races, non-Hispanic/Latino), 1 international. Average age 27. 22 applicants, 36% accepted, 5 enrolled. In 2019, 2 doctorates awarded. *Degree requirements:* For doctorate, comprehensive exam, thesis/dissertation, teaching 1 term in professor's major department. *Entrance requirements:* For doctorate, GRE General Test (minimum score 153 Verbal portion, 154 Quantitative portion). Additional exam requirements/recommendations for international students: required—TOEFL (minimum score 550 paper-based; 90 iBT), IELTS (minimum score 6.5). *Application deadline:* For fall admission, 1/15 for domestic and international students. Applications are processed on a rolling basis. Application fee: $30. Electronic applications accepted. *Expenses:* Contact institution. *Financial support:* In 2019–20, 18 students received support, including 4 fellowships with partial tuition reimbursements available (averaging $34,000 per year), 15 research assistantships with partial tuition reimbursements available (averaging $24,200 per year), 2 teaching assistantships with partial tuition reimbursements available (averaging $24,200 per year); scholarships/grants, health care benefits, tuition waivers (full), and unspecified assistantships also available. Financial award application deadline: 1/15; financial award applicants required to submit FAFSA. *Unit head:* Dr. Hong Li, Director, 850-644-6785, Fax: 850-644-7244, E-mail: hongli@sb.fsu.edu. *Application contact:* Shaimaa Khanam, Academic Coordinator, Graduate Programs, 850-644-1012, Fax: 850-644-7244, E-mail: skhanam@fsu.edu.
Website: http://biophysics.fsu.edu/

**Illinois Institute of Technology,** Graduate College, College of Science, Department of Biology, Chicago, IL 60616. Offers applied life sciences (MS); biochemistry (MS); biology (MS, PhD); cell and molecular biology (MS); microbiology (MS); molecular biochemistry and biophysics (MS, PhD). *Program availability:* Part-time, evening/weekend, online learning. Terminal master's awarded for partial completion of doctoral program. *Degree requirements:* For master's, comprehensive exam, thesis (for some programs); for doctorate, comprehensive exam, thesis/dissertation. *Entrance requirements:* For master's, GRE General Test (minimum score 300 Quantitative and Verbal, 2.5 Analytical Writing), minimum undergraduate GPA of 3.0; for doctorate, GRE General Test (minimum score 310 Quantitative and Verbal, 3.0 Analytical Writing); GRE Subject Test (strongly recommended), minimum undergraduate GPA of 3.0. Additional exam requirements/recommendations for international students: required—TOEFL (minimum score 550 paper-based; 80 iBT). Electronic applications accepted.

**Johns Hopkins University,** Program in Molecular Biophysics, Baltimore, MD 21218. Offers PhD. *Degree requirements:* For doctorate, thesis/dissertation. *Entrance requirements:* For doctorate, GRE General Test, GRE Subject Test.

**Johns Hopkins University,** School of Medicine, Graduate Programs in Medicine, Program in Molecular Biophysics, Baltimore, MD 21218. Offers MS, PhD. *Degree requirements:* For doctorate, comprehensive exam, thesis/dissertation, oral exam, thesis defense. *Entrance requirements:* For doctorate, GRE. Additional exam requirements/recommendations for international students: required—TOEFL (minimum score 600 paper-based), IELTS; recommended—TWE. Electronic applications accepted.

**Johns Hopkins University,** Zanvyl Krieger School of Arts and Sciences, Program in Cell, Molecular, Developmental Biology, and Biophysics, Baltimore, MD 21218. Offers PhD. Terminal master's awarded for partial completion of doctoral program. *Degree requirements:* For doctorate, comprehensive exam, thesis/dissertation. *Entrance requirements:* For doctorate, GRE General Test. Additional exam requirements/recommendations for international students: required—TOEFL (minimum score 600 paper-based), IELTS, TWE. Electronic applications accepted.

**Rutgers University - New Brunswick,** Graduate School-New Brunswick, BioMaPS Institute for Quantitative Biology, Piscataway, NJ 08854-8097. Offers computational biology and molecular biophysics (PhD). *Degree requirements:* For doctorate, comprehensive exam, thesis/dissertation. *Entrance requirements:* For doctorate, GRE. Additional exam requirements/recommendations for international students: required—TOEFL. Electronic applications accepted.

**University at Buffalo, the State University of New York,** Graduate School, Graduate Programs in Cancer Research and Biomedical Sciences at Roswell Park Cancer Institute, Buffalo, NY 14260. Offers cancer pathology and prevention (PhD); cellular and molecular biology (PhD); immunology (PhD); interdisciplinary natural sciences (MS); molecular and cellular biophysics and biochemistry (PhD); molecular pharmacology and cancer therapeutics (PhD). Terminal master's awarded for partial completion of doctoral program. *Degree requirements:* For master's, thesis, oral defense of thesis; for doctorate, comprehensive exam, thesis/dissertation, oral defense of dissertation. *Entrance requirements:* For master's and doctorate, GRE General Test. Additional exam requirements/recommendations for international students: required—TOEFL (minimum score 79 iBT). Electronic applications accepted. *Expenses: Tuition, area resident:* Full-time $11,310; part-time $471 per credit hour. Tuition, state resident: full-time $11,310; part-time $471 per credit hour. Tuition, nonresident: full-time $23,100; part-time $963 per credit hour. *International tuition:* $23,100 full-time. *Required fees:* $2820.

**University of Arkansas for Medical Sciences,** Graduate School, Little Rock, AR 72205. Offers biochemistry and molecular biology (MS, PhD); bioinformatics (MS, PhD); cellular physiology and molecular biophysics (MS, PhD); clinical nutrition (MS); interdisciplinary biomedical sciences (MS, PhD, Certificate); interdisciplinary toxicology (MS); microbiology and immunology (PhD); neurobiology and developmental sciences (PhD); pharmacology (PhD); MD/PhD. *Program availability:* Part-time. Terminal master's awarded for partial completion of doctoral program. *Degree requirements:* For master's, comprehensive exam (for some programs), thesis (for some programs); for doctorate, thesis/dissertation. *Entrance requirements:* For master's and doctorate, GRE. Additional exam requirements/recommendations for international students: required—TOEFL. Electronic applications accepted. *Expenses:* Contact institution.

**University of Chicago,** Division of the Biological Sciences, Biochemistry and Molecular Biology Department, Chicago, IL 60637. Offers PhD, MD/PhD. *Degree requirements:* For doctorate, thesis/dissertation, ethics class, 2 teaching assistantships. *Entrance requirements:* For doctorate, GRE General Test, transcripts, statement of purpose, 3 letters of recommendation. Additional exam requirements/recommendations for international students: required—TOEFL (minimum score 600 paper-based; 104 iBT), IELTS (minimum score 7). Electronic applications accepted.

**University of Massachusetts Amherst,** Graduate School, Interdisciplinary Programs, Program in Molecular and Cellular Biology, Amherst, MA 01003. Offers biological chemistry and molecular biophysics (PhD); biomedicine (PhD); cellular and developmental biology (PhD). *Program availability:* Part-time. Terminal master's awarded for partial completion of doctoral program. *Degree requirements:* For doctorate, comprehensive exam, thesis/dissertation. *Entrance requirements:* For doctorate, GRE General Test. Additional exam requirements/recommendations for international students: required—TOEFL (minimum score 550 paper-based; 80 iBT), IELTS (minimum score 6.5). Electronic applications accepted.

**University of Pennsylvania,** Perelman School of Medicine, Biomedical Graduate Studies, Graduate Group in Biochemistry and Molecular Biophysics, Philadelphia, PA 19104. Offers PhD, MD/PhD, VMD/PhD. *Faculty:* 107 full-time (24 women). *Students:* 105 full-time (65 women); includes 48 minority (2 Black or African American, non-Hispanic/Latino; 14 Asian, non-Hispanic/Latino; 30 Hispanic/Latino; 2 Two or more races, non-Hispanic/Latino), 7 international. 163 applicants, 20% accepted, 20 enrolled. In 2019, 11 doctorates awarded. *Unit head:* Dr. Kim Sharp, Chairperson, 215-573-3506. *Application contact:* Kelli McKenna, Coordinator, 215-898-4639.
Website: http://www.med.upenn.edu/bmbgrad/

**University of Pittsburgh,** School of Medicine, Graduate Programs in Medicine and Kenneth P. Dietrich School of Arts and Sciences, Molecular Biophysics and Structural Biology Graduate Program, Pittsburgh, PA 15260. Offers PhD. *Degree requirements:* For doctorate, comprehensive exam, thesis/dissertation. *Entrance requirements:* For doctorate, GRE General Test. Additional exam requirements/recommendations for international students: required—TOEFL (minimum score 600 paper-based; 100 iBT), IELTS (minimum score 7). Electronic applications accepted. *Expenses:* Contact institution.

**The University of Texas Medical Branch,** Graduate School of Biomedical Sciences, Molecular Biophysics Educational Track, Galveston, TX 77555. Offers PhD.

**The University of Texas Southwestern Medical Center,** Southwestern Graduate School of Biomedical Sciences, Division of Basic Science, Program in Molecular Biophysics, Dallas, TX 75390. Offers PhD. *Degree requirements:* For doctorate, thesis/dissertation, qualifying exam. *Entrance requirements:* For doctorate, GRE General Test, minimum GPA of 3.0. Additional exam requirements/recommendations for international students: required—TOEFL. Electronic applications accepted.

**Washington University in St. Louis,** The Graduate School, Division of Biology and Biomedical Sciences, Program in Computational and Molecular Biophysics, St. Louis, MO 63130-4899. Offers PhD. *Degree requirements:* For doctorate, thesis/dissertation. *Entrance requirements:* For doctorate, GRE General Test, GRE Subject Test. Additional exam requirements/recommendations for international students: required—TOEFL. Electronic applications accepted.

**Wesleyan University,** Graduate Studies, Department of Molecular Biology and Biochemistry, Middletown, CT 06459. Offers molecular biology and biochemistry (PhD); molecular biophysics (PhD). Terminal master's awarded for partial completion of doctoral program. *Degree requirements:* For doctorate, comprehensive exam, thesis/dissertation. *Entrance requirements:* For doctorate, GRE General Test, GRE Subject Test. Additional exam requirements/recommendations for international students: required—TOEFL. Electronic applications accepted.

**Yale University,** Yale School of Medicine and Graduate School of Arts and Sciences, Combined Program in Biological and Biomedical Sciences (BBS), Molecular Biophysics and Biochemistry Track, New Haven, CT 06520. Offers PhD, MD/PhD. *Degree requirements:* For doctorate, thesis/dissertation. *Entrance requirements:* For doctorate, GRE General Test. Additional exam requirements/recommendations for international students: required—TOEFL. Electronic applications accepted.

# Radiation Biology

**Georgetown University,** Graduate School of Arts and Sciences, Department of Health Physics and Radiation Protection, Washington, DC 20057. Offers health physics (MS); nuclear nonproliferation (MS). *Degree requirements:* For master's, thesis. *Entrance requirements:* Additional exam requirements/recommendations for international students: required—TOEFL.

**Université de Sherbrooke,** Faculty of Medicine and Health Sciences, Graduate Programs in Medicine, Program in Radiobiology, Sherbrooke, QC J1H 5N4, Canada. Offers M Sc, PhD. Terminal master's awarded for partial completion of doctoral program. *Degree requirements:* For master's, thesis; for doctorate, thesis/dissertation. Electronic applications accepted.

**The University of Iowa,** Roy J. and Lucille A. Carver College of Medicine and Graduate College, Graduate Programs in Medicine, Program in Free Radical and Radiation Biology, Iowa City, IA 52242. Offers MS. *Faculty:* 8 full-time (2 women). *Students:* 11 full-time (5 women); includes 3 minority (all Asian, non-Hispanic/Latino). Average age 30. 11 applicants, 27% accepted, 3 enrolled. *Degree requirements:* For master's, thesis. *Entrance requirements:* Additional exam requirements/recommendations for international students: required—TOEFL (minimum score 81 paper-based). *Application deadline:* For fall admission, 12/1 priority date for domestic and international students; for spring admission, 4/15 for domestic and international students. Applications are processed on a rolling basis. Application fee: $60 ($100 for international students). Electronic applications accepted. *Financial support:* In 2019–20, 11 students received support, including 3 fellowships with full tuition reimbursements available (averaging $30,000 per year), 8 research assistantships with full tuition reimbursements available (averaging $30,000 per year); traineeships and health care benefits also available. Financial award application deadline: 4/15. *Unit head:* Dr. Douglas Spitz, Director, 319-335-8019, Fax: 319-335-8039. *Application contact:* Laura Hefley, Secretary III, 319-335-8019, Fax: 319-335-8039, E-mail: laura-hefley@uiowa.edu. Website: http://frrbp.medicine.uiowa.edu/

**University of Oklahoma Health Sciences Center,** College of Medicine and Graduate College, Graduate Programs in Medicine, Department of Radiological Sciences, Oklahoma City, OK 73190. Offers medical radiation physics (MS, PhD), including diagnostic radiology, nuclear medicine, radiation therapy, ultrasound. *Program availability:* Part-time. Terminal master's awarded for partial completion of doctoral program. *Degree requirements:* For master's, thesis; for doctorate, thesis/dissertation. *Entrance requirements:* For master's, GRE General Test; for doctorate, GRE General Test, 3 letters of recommendation. Additional exam requirements/recommendations for international students: required—TOEFL.

# Section 5
# Botany and Plant Biology

This section contains a directory of institutions offering graduate work in botany and plant biology. Additional information about programs listed in the directory may be obtained by writing directly to the dean of a graduate school or chair of a department at the address given in the directory.

For programs offering related work, see also in this book *Biochemistry; Biological and Biomedical Sciences; Cell, Molecular, and Structural Biology; Ecology, Environmental Biology, and Evolutionary Biology; Entomology; Genetics, Developmental Biology, and Reproductive Biology;* and *Microbiological Sciences.* In the other guides in this series:

**Graduate Programs in the Humanities, Arts & Social Sciences**

See *Architecture (Landscape Architecture)* and *Economics (Agricultural Economics and Agribusiness)*

**Graduate Programs in the Physical Sciences, Mathematics, Agricultural Sciences, the Environment & Natural Resources**

See *Agricultural and Food Sciences*

**Graduate Programs in Engineering & Applied Sciences**

See *Agricultural Engineering* and *Bioengineering*

## CONTENTS

**Program Directories**

# Botany

**Auburn University,** Graduate School, College of Sciences and Mathematics, Department of Biological Sciences, Auburn, AL 36849. Offers botany (MS); zoology (MS). *Program availability:* Part-time. *Faculty:* 44 full-time (22 women), 2 part-time/adjunct (1 woman). *Students:* 56 full-time (35 women), 70 part-time (39 women); includes 27 minority (10 Black or African American, non-Hispanic/Latino; 4 Asian, non-Hispanic/Latino; 5 Hispanic/Latino; 8 Two or more races, non-Hispanic/Latino), 23 international. Average age 28. 102 applicants, 48% accepted, 44 enrolled. In 2019, 26 master's, 6 doctorates awarded. *Degree requirements:* For master's, thesis (for some programs); for doctorate, thesis/dissertation. *Entrance requirements:* For master's and doctorate, GRE General Test. Additional exam requirements/recommendations for international students: required—iTEP; recommended—TOEFL (minimum score 550 paper-based; 79 iBT), IELTS (minimum score 6.5). *Application deadline:* Applications are processed on a rolling basis. Application fee: $60 ($70 for international students). Electronic applications accepted. *Expenses: Tuition, area resident:* Full-time $9828; part-time $546 per credit hour. Tuition, state resident: full-time $9828; part-time $546 per credit hour. Tuition, nonresident: full-time $29,484; part-time $1638 per credit hour. *International tuition:* $29,744 full-time. Tuition and fees vary according to course load, program and reciprocity agreements. *Financial support:* In 2019–20, 61 fellowships with tuition reimbursements, 28 research assistantships with tuition reimbursements (averaging $22,237 per year), 81 teaching assistantships with tuition reimbursements (averaging $27,166 per year) were awarded. Financial award application deadline: 3/15; financial award applicants required to submit FAFSA. *Unit head:* Dr. Scott R. Santos, Chair, 334-844-7410, Fax: 334-844-1645, E-mail: santos@auburn.edu. *Application contact:* Dr. George Flowers, Dean of the Graduate School, 334-844-2125.
Website: http://www.auburn.edu/cosam/departments/biology/

**Central Washington University,** School of Graduate Studies and Research, College of the Sciences, Department of Biological Sciences, Ellensburg, WA 98926. Offers botany (MS); microbiology and parasitology (MS); stream ecology and fisheries (MS); terrestrial ecology (MS). *Program availability:* Part-time. *Entrance requirements:* For master's, GRE General Test, minimum GPA of 3.0. Additional exam requirements/recommendations for international students: required—TOEFL (minimum score 550 paper-based; 79 iBT). Electronic applications accepted.

**Claremont Graduate University,** Graduate Programs, Program in Botany, Claremont, CA 91711-6160. Offers MS, PhD. *Program availability:* Part-time. Terminal master's awarded for partial completion of doctoral program. *Entrance requirements:* For master's and doctorate, GRE General Test. Additional exam requirements/recommendations for international students: required—TOEFL (minimum score 75 iBT). Electronic applications accepted.

**Colorado State University,** College of Natural Sciences, Department of Biology, Fort Collins, CO 80523-1878. Offers botany (MS, PhD). *Faculty:* 31 full-time (12 women), 2 part-time/adjunct (both women). *Students:* 12 full-time (6 women), 26 part-time (12 women); includes 6 minority (1 Asian, non-Hispanic/Latino; 4 Hispanic/Latino; 1 Two or more races, non-Hispanic/Latino), 3 international. Average age 30. 31 applicants, 32% accepted, 8 enrolled. In 2019, 5 master's, 5 doctorates awarded. Terminal master's awarded for partial completion of doctoral program. *Degree requirements:* For master's, thesis, defense; for doctorate, comprehensive exam, thesis/dissertation. *Entrance requirements:* For master's and doctorate, transcripts, minimum GPA of 3.0; recommendation letters. Additional exam requirements/recommendations for international students: required—TOEFL (minimum score 550 paper-based; 80 iBT), IELTS (minimum score 6.5). *Application deadline:* For fall admission, 1/1 for domestic and international students; for spring admission, 10/1 for domestic and international students. Application fee: $60 ($70 for international students). Electronic applications accepted. *Expenses:* Tuition, state resident: full-time $10,520; part-time $5844 per credit hour. Tuition, nonresident: full-time $25,791; part-time $14,328 per credit hour. *International tuition:* $25,791 full-time. *Required fees:* $2512.80. Part-time tuition and fees vary according to course level, course load, degree level, program and student level. *Financial support:* In 2019–20, 80 students received support, including 8 research assistantships with full and partial tuition reimbursements available (averaging $20,858 per year), 78 teaching assistantships with full and partial tuition reimbursements available (averaging $20,340 per year); fellowships with full and partial tuition reimbursements available, career-related internships or fieldwork, health care benefits, and unspecified assistantships also available. Financial award applicants required to submit FAFSA. *Unit head:* Dr. Deborah Garrity, Department Chair and Professor, 970-491-2513, Fax: 970-491-0649, E-mail: deborah.garrity@colostate.edu. *Application contact:* Dorothy Ramirez, Graduate Coordinator, 970-491-1923, Fax: 970-491-0649, E-mail: dramirez@colostate.edu.
Website: http://www.biology.colostate.edu/

**Dalhousie University,** Faculty of Agriculture, Halifax, NS B3H 4R2, Canada. Offers agriculture (M Sc), including air quality, animal behavior, animal molecular genetics, animal nutrition, animal technology, aquaculture, botany, crop management, crop physiology, ecology, environmental microbiology, food science, horticulture, nutrient management, pest management, physiology, plant biotechnology, plant pathology, soil chemistry, soil fertility, waste management and composting, water quality. *Program availability:* Part-time. *Degree requirements:* For master's, thesis, ATC Exam Teaching Assistantship. *Entrance requirements:* For master's, honors B Sc, minimum GPA of 3.0. Additional exam requirements/recommendations for international students: required—TOEFL (minimum score 580 paper-based; 92 iBT), IELTS, Michigan English Language Assessment Battery, CanTEST, CAEL.

**Emporia State University,** Department of Biological Sciences, Emporia, KS 66801-5415. Offers botany (MS); environmental biology (MS); forensic science (MS); general biology (MS); microbial and cellular biology (MS); zoology (MS). *Program availability:* Part-time. *Degree requirements:* For master's, comprehensive exam or thesis. *Entrance requirements:* For master's, GRE, appropriate undergraduate degree, interview, letters of reference. Additional exam requirements/recommendations for international students: required—TOEFL (minimum score 520 paper-based; 68 iBT). Electronic applications accepted. *Expenses: Tuition, area resident:* Full-time $6394; part-time $266.41 per credit hour. Tuition, state resident: full-time $6394; part-time $266.41 per credit hour. Tuition, nonresident: full-time $20,128; part-time $828.66 per credit hour. *International tuition:* $20,128 full-time. *Required fees:* $2183; $90.95 per credit hour. Tuition and fees vary according to campus/location and program.

**Illinois State University,** Graduate School, College of Arts and Sciences, School of Biological Sciences, Normal, IL 61790. Offers animal behavior (MS); bacteriology (MS); biochemistry (MS); biological sciences (MS); biology (PhD); biophysics (MS); biotechnology (MS); botany (MS, PhD); cell biology (MS); conservation biology (MS); developmental biology (MS); ecology (MS, PhD); entomology (MS); evolutionary biology (MS); genetics (MS, PhD); immunology (MS); microbiology (MS, PhD); molecular

biology (MS); molecular genetics (MS); neurobiology (MS); neuroscience (MS); parasitology (MS); physiology (MS, PhD); plant biology (MS); plant molecular biology (MS); plant sciences (MS); structural biology (MS); zoology (MS, PhD). *Program availability:* Part-time. *Faculty:* 26 full-time (6 women), 7 part-time/adjunct (2 women). *Students:* 51 full-time (33 women), 15 part-time (8 women). Average age 27. 71 applicants, 28% accepted, 9 enrolled. In 2019, 14 master's, 3 doctorates awarded. *Degree requirements:* For master's, thesis or alternative; for doctorate, variable foreign language requirement, thesis/dissertation, 2 terms of residency. *Entrance requirements:* For master's, GRE General Test, minimum GPA of 2.6 in last 60 hours of course work; for doctorate, GRE General Test. *Application deadline:* Applications are processed on a rolling basis. Application fee: $50. *Expenses: Tuition, area resident:* Full-time $7956; part-time $9767 per year. Tuition, nonresident: full-time $9233; part-time $17,592 per year. *Required fees:* $1797. *Financial support:* In 2019–20, 20 research assistantships, 41 teaching assistantships were awarded; Federal Work-Study, tuition waivers (full), and unspecified assistantships also available. Financial award application deadline: 4/1. *Unit head:* Dr. Craig Gatto, School Director, 309-438-3087, E-mail: cgatto@IllinoisState.edu. *Application contact:* Dr. Ben Sadd, Assistant Chair for Graduate Studies, 309-438-2651, E-mail: bmsadd@IllinoisState.edu.
Website: http://www.bio.ilstu.edu/

**Kent State University,** College of Arts and Sciences, Department of Biological Sciences, Kent, OH 44242. Offers biological sciences (MA, MS, PhD), including botany (MS, PhD), cell biology (MS, PhD), ecology (MS, PhD), physiology (MS, PhD). *Program availability:* Part-time. *Faculty:* 19 full-time (5 women), 2 part-time/adjunct (1 woman). *Students:* 51 full-time (35 women), 9 part-time (4 women); includes 1 minority (Two or more races, non-Hispanic/Latino), 10 international. Average age 29. 53 applicants, 38% accepted, 14 enrolled. In 2019, 8 master's, 9 doctorates awarded. Terminal master's awarded for partial completion of doctoral program. *Degree requirements:* For master's, thesis (for some programs), departmental seminar presentation about research (for MS); for doctorate, thesis/dissertation, departmental seminar presentation about research, admitted to doctoral candidacy following written and oral candidacy. *Entrance requirements:* For master's, GRE, minimum GPA of 3.0, official transcripts, goal statement, three letters of recommendation, list of up to five potential faculty advisors, undergraduate coursework roughly equivalent to a biology minor, acceptance of student by a faculty advisor; for doctorate, GRE; After completing the required coursework, students complete the doctoral program by being admitted to candidacy, by proposing a research project to the faculty, and by completing and defending that research with a written dissertation before a faculty committee, official transcripts, goal statement, three letters of recommendation, list of up to five potential faculty advisors, baccalaureate degree with strong background in biology and related subjects such as chemistry and mathematics, acceptance of the student by a faculty advisor. Additional exam requirements/recommendations for international students: required—TOEFL (minimum score 94 iBT), IELTS (minimum score 7), PTE (minimum score 65), Michigan English Language Assessment Battery (minimum score 82). *Application deadline:* For fall admission, 12/15 for domestic students, 12/5 for international students. Applications are processed on a rolling basis. Application fee: $45 ($70 for international students). Electronic applications accepted. *Financial support:* Research assistantships with full tuition reimbursements, teaching assistantships with full tuition reimbursements, Federal Work-Study, scholarships/grants, health care benefits, and unspecified assistantships available. Financial award application deadline: 12/15. *Unit head:* Dr. James L. Blank, Dean, 330-672-2650, E-mail: jblank@kent.edu. *Application contact:* Dr. Heather K. Caldwell, Associate Professor and Graduate Coordinator, 330-672-3636, E-mail: hcaldwel@kent.edu.
Website: http://www.kent.edu/biology

**North Dakota State University,** College of Graduate and Interdisciplinary Studies, College of Science and Mathematics, Department of Biological Sciences, Fargo, ND 58102. Offers biology (MS); botany (MS, PhD); zoology (MS, PhD). *Entrance requirements:* For master's and doctorate, GRE General Test. Additional exam requirements/recommendations for international students: required—TOEFL. Electronic applications accepted. Tuition and fees vary according to program and reciprocity agreements.

**Oklahoma State University,** College of Arts and Sciences, Department of Plant Biology, Ecology, and Evolution, Stillwater, OK 74078. Offers botany (MS); environmental science (PhD). *Faculty:* 8 full-time (2 women). *Students:* 13 part-time (4 women), 5 international. Average age 28. 4 applicants, 75% accepted, 2 enrolled. In 2019, 5 master's awarded. *Entrance requirements:* For master's and doctorate, GRE or GMAT. Additional exam requirements/recommendations for international students: required—TOEFL (minimum score 550 paper-based; 79 iBT). *Application deadline:* For fall admission, 3/1 priority date for international students; for spring admission, 8/1 priority date for international students. Applications are processed on a rolling basis. Application fee: $50 ($75 for international students). Electronic applications accepted. *Expenses: Tuition, area resident:* Full-time $4148.10; part-time $2765.40 per credit hour. Tuition, state resident: full-time $4148.10; part-time $2765.40 per credit hour. Tuition, nonresident: full-time $15,775; part-time $10,516.80 per credit hour. *International tuition:* $15,775.20 full-time. *Required fees:* $2196.90; $122.05 per credit hour. Tuition and fees vary according to course load, campus/location and program. *Financial support:* In 2019–20, 2 research assistantships (averaging $2,575 per year), 11 teaching assistantships (averaging $2,274 per year) were awarded; career-related internships or fieldwork, Federal Work-Study, scholarships/grants, health care benefits, tuition waivers (partial), and unspecified assistantships also available. Support available to part-time students. Financial award application deadline: 3/1; financial award applicants required to submit FAFSA. *Unit head:* Dr. Andrew Doust, Department Head, 405-744-2544, Fax: 405-744-7074, E-mail: andrew.doust@okstate.edu. *Application contact:* Dr. Sheryl Tucker, Dean, 405-744-6368, Fax: 405-744-0355, E-mail: gradi@okstate.edu.
Website: http://plantbio.okstate.edu

**Oregon State University,** College of Agricultural Sciences, Program in Botany and Plant Pathology, Corvallis, OR 97331. Offers applied systematics (MS); ecology (MS, PhD); genetics (MS, PhD); genomics and computational biology (MS, PhD); molecular and cellular biology (MS, PhD); mycology (MS, PhD); plant pathology (MS, PhD); plant physiology (MS, PhD). *Entrance requirements:* For master's and doctorate, GRE.

**Purdue University,** Graduate School, College of Agriculture, Department of Botany and Plant Pathology, West Lafayette, IN 47907. Offers MS, PhD. *Program availability:* Part-time. *Faculty:* 32 full-time (11 women), 1 part-time/adjunct (0 women). *Students:* 55 full-time (23 women), 3 part-time (0 women); includes 5 minority (all Hispanic/Latino), 33 international. Average age 27. 32 applicants, 25% accepted, 6 enrolled. In 2019, 5 master's, 7 doctorates awarded. Terminal master's awarded for partial completion of doctoral program. *Degree requirements:* For master's, thesis; for doctorate, thesis/

dissertation. *Entrance requirements:* For master's, GRE General Test, minimum undergraduate GPA of 3.0 or equivalent; for doctorate, GRE, minimum undergraduate GPA of 3.0 or equivalent. Additional exam requirements/recommendations for international students: required—TOEFL (minimum score 550 paper-based; 77 iBT); recommended—TWE. *Application deadline:* For fall admission, 4/15 priority date for domestic and international students; for spring admission, 12/15 for domestic students, 9/15 for international students; for summer admission, 4/15 for domestic students, 2/15 for international students. Applications are processed on a rolling basis. Application fee: $60 ($75 for international students). Electronic applications accepted. *Financial support:* In 2019–20, 30 students received support. Fellowships with full tuition reimbursements available, research assistantships with full tuition reimbursements available, teaching assistantships with full tuition reimbursements available, and career-related internships or fieldwork available. Support available to part-time students. Financial award application deadline: 3/1; financial award applicants required to submit FAFSA. *Unit head:* Christopher Staiger, Head of the Graduate Program, 765-494-4615, E-mail: staiger@purdue.edu. *Application contact:* Lisa Gross, Graduate Contact, 765-494-9871, E-mail: gross25@purdue.edu.
Website: https://ag.purdue.edu/btny

**The University of British Columbia,** Faculty of Science, Department of Botany, Vancouver, BC V6T 1Z4, Canada. Offers M Sc, PhD. *Degree requirements:* For master's, thesis; for doctorate, comprehensive exam, thesis/dissertation. *Entrance requirements:* Additional exam requirements/recommendations for international students: required—TOEFL. Electronic applications accepted. *Expenses:* Contact institution.

**University of California, Riverside,** Graduate Division, Department of Botany and Plant Sciences, Riverside, CA 92521-0102. Offers plant biology (MS, PhD), including plant cell, molecular, and developmental biology (PhD), plant ecology (PhD), plant genetics (PhD). *Program availability:* Part-time. Terminal master's awarded for partial completion of doctoral program. *Degree requirements:* For master's, comprehensive exams or thesis; for doctorate, thesis/dissertation, qualifying exams. *Entrance requirements:* For master's and doctorate, GRE General Test, minimum GPA of 3.2. Additional exam requirements/recommendations for international students: required—TOEFL (minimum score 550 paper-based, 80 iBT) or IELTS. Electronic applications accepted.

**University of Connecticut,** Graduate School, College of Liberal Arts and Sciences, Department of Ecology and Evolutionary Biology, Storrs, CT 06269. Offers botany (MS, PhD). Terminal master's awarded for partial completion of doctoral program. *Degree requirements:* For master's, comprehensive exam; for doctorate, thesis/dissertation. *Entrance requirements:* For master's and doctorate, GRE General Test, GRE Subject Test. Additional exam requirements/recommendations for international students: required—TOEFL (minimum score 550 paper-based). Electronic applications accepted.

**University of Florida,** Graduate School, College of Liberal Arts and Sciences, Department of Biology, Gainesville, FL 32611. Offers botany (MS, MST, PhD), including botany, tropical conservation and development, wetland sciences; zoology (MS, MST, PhD), including animal molecular and cellular biology (PhD), tropical conservation and development, wetland sciences, zoology. *Degree requirements:* For master's, comprehensive exam (for some programs), thesis; for doctorate, comprehensive exam, thesis/dissertation. *Entrance requirements:* For master's and doctorate, GRE General Test, minimum GPA of 3.0. Additional exam requirements/recommendations for international students: required—TOEFL (minimum score 550 paper-based; 80 iBT), IELTS (minimum score 6). Electronic applications accepted.

**University of Guelph,** Office of Graduate and Postdoctoral Studies, College of Biological Science, Department of Integrative Biology, Botany and Zoology, Guelph, ON N1G 2W1, Canada. Offers botany (M Sc, PhD); zoology (M Sc, PhD). *Program availability:* Part-time. *Degree requirements:* For master's, thesis, research proposal; for doctorate, thesis/dissertation, research proposal, qualifying exam. *Entrance requirements:* For master's, minimum B average during previous 2 years of course work. Additional exam requirements/recommendations for international students: required—TOEFL (minimum score 550 paper-based), IELTS (minimum score 6.5). Electronic applications accepted.

**University of Guelph,** Office of Graduate and Postdoctoral Studies, College of Biological Science, Department of Molecular and Cellular Biology, Guelph, ON N1G 2W1, Canada. Offers biochemistry (M Sc, PhD); biophysics (M Sc, PhD); botany (M Sc, PhD); microbiology (M Sc, PhD); molecular biology and genetics (M Sc, PhD). *Degree requirements:* For master's, thesis, research proposal; for doctorate, comprehensive exam, thesis/dissertation, research proposal. *Entrance requirements:* For master's, minimum B-average during previous 2 years of coursework; for doctorate, minimum A-average. Additional exam requirements/recommendations for international students: required—TOEFL (minimum score 550 paper-based), IELTS (minimum score 6.5). Electronic applications accepted.

**University of Hawaii at Manoa,** Office of Graduate Education, College of Natural Sciences, Department of Botany, Honolulu, HI 96822. Offers MS, PhD. *Program availability:* Part-time. Terminal master's awarded for partial completion of doctoral program. *Degree requirements:* For master's, one foreign language, thesis optional,

presentation; for doctorate, one foreign language, comprehensive exam, thesis/dissertation, presentation. *Entrance requirements:* For master's and doctorate, GRE General Test, GRE Subject Test (biology). Additional exam requirements/recommendations for international students: required—TOEFL (minimum score 540 paper-based; 76 iBT), IELTS (minimum score 5).

**University of Maine,** Graduate School, College of Natural Sciences, Forestry, and Agriculture, School of Biology and Ecology, Orono, ME 04469. Offers biological sciences (PhD); botany and plant pathology (MS); entomology (MS); zoology (MS, PhD). *Program availability:* Part-time. *Faculty:* 30 full-time (16 women), 2 part-time/adjunct (1 woman). *Students:* 84 full-time (54 women), 12 part-time (6 women); includes 9 minority (1 Black or African American, non-Hispanic/Latino; 1 American Indian or Alaska Native, non-Hispanic/Latino; 1 Asian, non-Hispanic/Latino; 5 Hispanic/Latino; 1 Two or more races, non-Hispanic/Latino), 21 international. Average age 30. 62 applicants, 40% accepted, 22 enrolled. In 2019, 12 master's, 12 doctorates awarded. Terminal master's awarded for partial completion of doctoral program. *Degree requirements:* For master's, thesis (for some programs); for doctorate, comprehensive exam, thesis/dissertation. *Entrance requirements:* For master's and doctorate, GRE General Test. Additional exam requirements/recommendations for international students: required—TOEFL (minimum score 80 iBT), IELTS (minimum score 6.5). *Application deadline:* For fall admission, 2/1 priority date for domestic students. Applications are processed on a rolling basis. Application fee: $65. Electronic applications accepted. *Expenses: Tuition, area resident:* Full-time $8100; part-time $450 per credit hour. Tuition, state resident: full-time $8100; part-time $450 per credit hour. Tuition, nonresident: full-time $26,388; part-time $1466 per credit hour. *International tuition:* $26,388 full-time. *Required fees:* $1257; $278 per semester. Tuition and fees vary according to course load. *Financial support:* In 2019–20, 108 students received support, including 1 fellowship with full tuition reimbursement available (averaging $25,000 per year), 79 research assistantships with full tuition reimbursements available (averaging $15,825 per year), 23 teaching assistantships with full tuition reimbursements available (averaging $15,825 per year); career-related internships or fieldwork, Federal Work-Study, institutionally sponsored loans, tuition waivers (full and partial), and unspecified assistantships also available. Financial award application deadline: 3/1; financial award applicants required to submit FAFSA. *Unit head:* Dr. Andrei Aloykhin, Director, 207-581-2977, Fax: 207-581-2537. *Application contact:* Scott G. Delcourt, Assistant Vice President for Graduate Studies and Senior Associate Dean, 207-581-3291, Fax: 207-581-3232, E-mail: graduate@maine.edu.
Website: http://sbe.umaine.edu.

**University of Manitoba,** Faculty of Graduate Studies, Faculty of Science, Department of Biological Sciences, Winnipeg, MB R3T 2N2, Canada. Offers botany (M Sc, PhD); ecology (M Sc, PhD); zoology (M Sc, PhD).

**The University of North Carolina at Chapel Hill,** Graduate School, College of Arts and Sciences, Department of Biology, Chapel Hill, NC 27599. Offers botany (MA, MS, PhD); cell biology, development, and physiology (MA, MS, PhD); cell motility and cytoskeleton (PhD); ecology and behavior (MA, MS, PhD); genetics and molecular biology (MA, MS, PhD); morphology, systematics, and evolution (MA, MS, PhD). Terminal master's awarded for partial completion of doctoral program. *Degree requirements:* For master's, comprehensive exam, thesis (for some programs); for doctorate, comprehensive exam, thesis/dissertation. *Entrance requirements:* For master's, GRE General Test, GRE Subject Test, 2 semesters of calculus or statistics; 2 semesters of physics, organic chemistry; 3 semesters of biology; for doctorate, GRE General Test, GRE Subject Test, 2 semesters calculus or statistics, 2 semesters physics, organic chemistry, 3 semesters of biology. Additional exam requirements/recommendations for international students: required—TOEFL (minimum score 550 paper-based). Electronic applications accepted.

**University of Wisconsin–Madison,** Graduate School, College of Letters and Science, Department of Botany, Madison, WI 53706-1380. Offers MS, PhD. *Program availability:* Part-time. Terminal master's awarded for partial completion of doctoral program. *Degree requirements:* For master's, thesis; for doctorate, one foreign language, thesis/dissertation. *Entrance requirements:* For master's and doctorate, GRE General Test. Electronic applications accepted.

**University of Wisconsin–Oshkosh,** Graduate Studies, College of Letters and Science, Department of Biology and Microbiology, Oshkosh, WI 54901. Offers biology (MS), including botany, microbiology, zoology. *Degree requirements:* For master's, comprehensive exam, thesis. *Entrance requirements:* For master's, GRE General Test, minimum GPA of 3.0, BS in biology. Additional exam requirements/recommendations for international students: required—TOEFL (minimum score 550 paper-based; 79 iBT). Electronic applications accepted.

**University of Wyoming,** College of Arts and Sciences, Department of Botany, Laramie, WY 82071. Offers botany (MS, PhD); botany/water resources (MS). *Program availability:* Part-time. Terminal master's awarded for partial completion of doctoral program. *Degree requirements:* For master's, thesis; for doctorate, thesis/dissertation. *Entrance requirements:* For master's and doctorate, GRE General Test, minimum GPA of 3.0. Additional exam requirements/recommendations for international students: required—TOEFL. Electronic applications accepted.

# Plant Biology

**Arizona State University at Tempe,** College of Liberal Arts and Sciences, School of Life Sciences, Tempe, AZ 85287-4601. Offers animal behavior (PhD); applied ethics (biomedical and health ethics) (MA); biology (MS, PhD), including biology, biology and society, complex adaptive systems science (PhD), plant biology and conservation (MS); environmental life sciences (PhD); evolutionary biology (PhD); history and philosophy of science (PhD); human and social dimensions of science and technology (PhD); microbiology (PhD); molecular and cellular biology (PhD); neuroscience (PhD). Terminal master's awarded for partial completion of doctoral program. *Degree requirements:* For master's, thesis (for some programs), interactive Program of Study (iPOS) submitted before completing 50 percent of required credit hours; for doctorate, variable foreign language requirement, comprehensive exam, thesis/dissertation, interactive Program of Study (iPOS) submitted before completing 50 percent of required credit hours. *Entrance requirements:* For master's and doctorate, GRE, minimum GPA of 3.0 or equivalent in last 2 years of work leading to bachelor's degree. Additional exam requirements/recommendations for international students: required—TOEFL (minimum score 600 paper-based; 100 iBT). Electronic applications accepted.

**Clemson University,** Graduate School, College of Agriculture, Forestry and Life Sciences, Department of Plant and Environmental Sciences, Clemson, SC 29634.

Offers entomology (MS, PhD); plant and environmental sciences (MS, PhD). *Faculty:* 46 full-time (11 women), 1 part-time/adjunct (0 women). *Students:* 74 full-time (31 women), 16 part-time (2 women); includes 2 minority (1 Asian, non-Hispanic/Latino; 1 Two or more races, non-Hispanic/Latino), 29 international. Average age 28. 56 applicants, 86% accepted, 32 enrolled. In 2019, 20 master's, 12 doctorates awarded. *Expenses:* Full-Time Student per Semester: Tuition: $4600 (in-state), $9525 (out-of-state), Fees: $598; Graduate Assistant Per Semester: $1144; Part-Time Student Per Credit Hour: $556 (in-state), $1106 (out-of-state), Fees: $617; other fees apply depending on program, credit hours, campus & residency. Doctoral Base Fee per Semester: $4938 (in-state), $10405 (out-of-state). *Financial support:* In 2019–20, 91 students received support, including 13 fellowships with full and partial tuition reimbursements available (averaging $10,923 per year), 70 research assistantships with full and partial tuition reimbursements available (averaging $19,437 per year), 8 teaching assistantships with full and partial tuition reimbursements available (averaging $16,729 per year); career-related internships or fieldwork also available. *Application contact:* Dr. Guido Schnabel, Graduate Program Coordinator, 864-656-6705, E-mail: schnabe@clemson.edu.
Website: http://www.clemson.edu/cafls/departments/plant-environmental-sciences/index.html

## Plant Biology

**Cornell University,** Graduate School, Graduate Fields of Agriculture and Life Sciences, Field of Plant Biology, Ithaca, NY 14853. Offers cytology (MS, PhD); paleobotany (MS, PhD); plant biochemistry (MS, PhD); plant cell biology (MS, PhD); plant ecology (MS, PhD); plant molecular biology (MS, PhD); plant morphology, anatomy and biomechanics (MS, PhD); plant physiology (MS, PhD); systematic botany (MS, PhD). *Degree requirements:* For doctorate, comprehensive exam, thesis/dissertation. *Entrance requirements:* For doctorate, GRE General Test, GRE Subject Test in biology (recommended), 3 letters of recommendation. Additional exam requirements/recommendations for international students: required—TOEFL (minimum score 610 paper-based; 77 iBT). Electronic applications accepted.

**Illinois State University,** Graduate School, College of Arts and Sciences, School of Biological Sciences, Normal, IL 61790. Offers animal behavior (MS); bacteriology (MS); biochemistry (MS); biological sciences (MS); biology (PhD); biophysics (MS); biotechnology (MS); botany (MS, PhD); cell biology (MS); conservation biology (MS); developmental biology (MS); ecology (MS, PhD); entomology (MS); evolutionary biology (MS); genetics (MS, PhD); immunology (MS); microbiology (MS, PhD); molecular biology (MS); molecular genetics (MS); neurobiology (MS); neuroscience (MS); parasitology (MS); physiology (MS, PhD); plant biology (MS); plant molecular biology (MS); plant sciences (MS); structural biology (MS); zoology (MS, PhD). *Program availability:* Part-time. *Faculty:* 26 full-time (6 women), 7 part-time/adjunct (2 women). *Students:* 51 full-time (33 women), 15 part-time (8 women). Average age 27. 71 applicants, 28% accepted, 9 enrolled. In 2019, 14 master's, 3 doctorates awarded. *Degree requirements:* For master's, thesis or alternative; for doctorate, variable foreign language requirement, thesis/dissertation, 2 terms of residency. *Entrance requirements:* For master's, GRE General Test, minimum GPA of 2.6 in last 60 hours of course work; for doctorate, GRE General Test. *Application deadline:* Applications are processed on a rolling basis. Application fee: $50. *Expenses: Tuition, area resident:* Full-time $7956; part-time $9767 per year. Tuition, nonresident: full-time $9233; part-time $17,592 per year. *Required fees:* $1797. *Financial support:* In 2019–20, 20 research assistantships, 41 teaching assistantships were awarded; Federal Work-Study, tuition waivers (full), and unspecified assistantships also available. Financial award application deadline: 4/1. *Unit head:* Dr. Craig Gatto, School Director, 309-438-3087, E-mail: cgatto@IllinoisState.edu. *Application contact:* Dr. Ben Sadd, Assistant Chair for Graduate Studies, 309-438-2651, E-mail: bmsadd@IllinoisState.edu.
Website: http://www.bio.ilstu.edu/

**Indiana University Bloomington,** University Graduate School, College of Arts and Sciences, Department of Biology, Bloomington, IN 47405. Offers biology teaching (MAT); biotechnology (MA); evolution, ecology, and behavior (MA, PhD); genetics (PhD); microbiology (MA, PhD); molecular, cellular, and developmental biology (PhD); plant sciences (MA, PhD); zoology (MA, PhD). Terminal master's awarded for partial completion of doctoral program. *Degree requirements:* For master's, thesis, oral defense; for doctorate, thesis/dissertation, oral defense. *Entrance requirements:* For master's and doctorate, GRE General Test. Additional exam requirements/recommendations for international students: required—TOEFL (minimum score 100 iBT). Electronic applications accepted.

**Iowa State University of Science and Technology,** Program in Plant Biology, Ames, IA 50011. Offers MS, PhD. *Degree requirements:* For master's, thesis; for doctorate, thesis/dissertation. *Entrance requirements:* For master's and doctorate, GRE General Test. Additional exam requirements/recommendations for international students: required—TOEFL (minimum score 550 paper-based; 79 iBT), IELTS (minimum score 6.5). Electronic applications accepted.

**Michigan State University,** The Graduate School, College of Natural Science, Department of Plant Biology, East Lansing, MI 48824. Offers plant biology (MS, PhD); plant breeding, genetics and biotechnology - plant biology (MS, PhD). *Entrance requirements:* Additional exam requirements/recommendations for international students: required—TOEFL. Electronic applications accepted.

**Michigan State University,** The Graduate School, College of Natural Science, MSU-DOE Plant Research Laboratory, East Lansing, MI 48824. Offers biochemistry and molecular biology (PhD); cellular and molecular biology (PhD); crop and soil sciences (PhD); genetics (PhD); microbiology and molecular genetics (PhD); plant biology (PhD); plant physiology (PhD). *Degree requirements:* For doctorate, comprehensive exam, thesis/dissertation, laboratory rotation, defense of dissertation. *Entrance requirements:* For doctorate, GRE General Test, acceptance into one of the affiliated department programs; 3 letters of recommendation; bachelor's degree or equivalent in life sciences, chemistry, biochemistry, or biophysics; research experience. Electronic applications accepted.

**New York University,** Graduate School of Arts and Science, Department of Biology, New York, NY 10012-1019. Offers biology (PhD); biomedical journalism (MS); cancer and molecular biology (PhD); computational biology (PhD); computers in biological research (MS); developmental genetics (PhD); general biology (MS); immunology and microbiology (PhD); molecular genetics (PhD); neurobiology (PhD); oral biology (MS); plant biology (PhD); recombinant DNA technology (MS); MS/MBA. *Program availability:* Part-time. Terminal master's awarded for partial completion of doctoral program. *Degree requirements:* For master's, thesis or alternative, qualifying paper; for doctorate, comprehensive exam, thesis/dissertation. *Entrance requirements:* For master's and doctorate, GRE General Test. Additional exam requirements/recommendations for international students: required—TOEFL, IELTS.

**North Carolina State University,** Graduate School, College of Agriculture and Life Sciences, Department of Plant and Microbial Biology, Raleigh, NC 27695. Offers microbiology (MS, PhD); plant biology (MS, PhD). *Program availability:* Part-time. Terminal master's awarded for partial completion of doctoral program. *Degree requirements:* For master's, thesis (for some programs); for doctorate, thesis/dissertation. *Entrance requirements:* For master's and doctorate, GRE. Additional exam requirements/recommendations for international students: required—TOEFL. Electronic applications accepted.

**Northwestern University,** The Graduate School, Judd A. and Marjorie Weinberg College of Arts and Sciences, Program in Plant Biology and Conservation, Evanston, IL 60208. Offers MA, PhD.

**Ohio University,** Graduate College, College of Arts and Sciences, Department of Environmental and Plant Biology, Athens, OH 45701-2979. Offers MS, PhD. *Program availability:* Part-time. *Degree requirements:* For master's, thesis, 2 terms of teaching experience; for doctorate, comprehensive exam, thesis/dissertation, 2 terms of teaching experience. *Entrance requirements:* For master's, GRE General Test, minimum GPA of 3.0; for doctorate, GRE General Test, minimum GPA of 3.2. Additional exam requirements/recommendations for international students: required—TOEFL (minimum score 620 paper-based; 105 iBT) or IELTS (minimum score 7.5). Electronic applications accepted.

**Oklahoma State University,** College of Arts and Sciences, Department of Plant Biology, Ecology, and Evolution, Stillwater, OK 74078. Offers botany (MS); environmental science (PhD). *Faculty:* 8 full-time (2 women). *Students:* 13 part-time (4 women), 5 international. Average age 28. 4 applicants, 75% accepted, 2 enrolled. In 2019, 5 master's awarded. *Entrance requirements:* For master's and doctorate, GRE or GMAT. Additional exam requirements/recommendations for international students: required—TOEFL (minimum score 550 paper-based; 79 iBT). *Application deadline:* For fall admission, 3/1 priority date for international students; for spring admission, 8/1 priority date for international students. Applications are processed on a rolling basis. Application fee: $50 ($75 for international students). Electronic applications accepted. *Expenses: Tuition, area resident:* Full-time $4148.10; part-time $2765.40 per credit hour. Tuition, state resident: full-time $4148.10; part-time $2765.40 per credit hour. Tuition, nonresident: full-time $15,775; part-time $10,516.80 per credit hour. *International tuition:* $15,775.20 full-time. *Required fees:* $2196.90; $122.05 per credit hour. Tuition and fees vary according to course load, campus/location and program. *Financial support:* In 2019–20, 2 research assistantships (averaging $2,575 per year), 11 teaching assistantships (averaging $2,274 per year) were awarded; career-related internships or fieldwork, Federal Work-Study, scholarships/grants, health care benefits, tuition waivers (partial), and unspecified assistantships also available. Support available to part-time students. Financial award application deadline: 3/1; financial award applicants required to submit FAFSA. *Unit head:* Dr. Andrew Doust, Department Head, 405-744-2544, Fax: 405-744-7074, E-mail: andrew.doust@okstate.edu. *Application contact:* Dr. Sheryl Tucker, Dean, 405-744-6368, Fax: 405-744-0355, E-mail: gradi@okstate.edu.
Website: http://plantbio.okstate.edu

**Penn State University Park,** Graduate School, Intercollege Graduate Programs, Intercollege Graduate Program in Plant Biology, University Park, PA 16802. Offers MS, PhD.

**Rutgers University - New Brunswick,** Graduate School-New Brunswick, Program in Plant Biology, Piscataway, NJ 08854-8097. Offers horticulture and plant technology (MS, PhD); molecular and cellular biology (MS, PhD); organismal and population biology (MS, PhD); plant pathology (MS, PhD). *Program availability:* Part-time. Terminal master's awarded for partial completion of doctoral program. *Degree requirements:* For master's, comprehensive exam, thesis or alternative; for doctorate, comprehensive exam, thesis/dissertation. *Entrance requirements:* For master's and doctorate, GRE General Test, GRE Subject Test (recommended). Additional exam requirements/recommendations for international students: required—TOEFL (minimum score 600 paper-based). Electronic applications accepted.

**Southern Illinois University Carbondale,** Graduate School, College of Science, Department of Plant Biology, Carbondale, IL 62901-4701. Offers MS, PhD. *Degree requirements:* For master's, thesis; for doctorate, one foreign language, thesis/dissertation. *Entrance requirements:* For master's, GRE General Test, minimum GPA of 2.7; for doctorate, GRE General Test, minimum GPA of 3.25. Additional exam requirements/recommendations for international students: required—TOEFL (minimum score 80 iBT).

**University of Alberta,** Faculty of Graduate Studies and Research, Department of Biological Sciences, Edmonton, AB T6G 2E1, Canada. Offers environmental biology and ecology (M Sc, PhD); microbiology and biotechnology (M Sc, PhD); molecular biology and genetics (M Sc, PhD); physiology and cell biology (M Sc, PhD); plant biology (M Sc, PhD); systematics and evolution (M Sc, PhD). Terminal master's awarded for partial completion of doctoral program. *Degree requirements:* For master's, thesis; for doctorate, thesis/dissertation. *Entrance requirements:* Additional exam requirements/recommendations for international students: required—TOEFL.

**University of California, Berkeley,** Graduate Division, College of Natural Resources, Department of Plant and Microbial Biology, Berkeley, CA 94720. Offers microbiology (PhD); plant biology (PhD). *Degree requirements:* For doctorate, thesis/dissertation, qualifying exam, seminar presentation. *Entrance requirements:* For doctorate, GRE General Test, minimum GPA of 3.0, 3 letters of recommendation. Electronic applications accepted.

**University of California, Davis,** Graduate Studies, Graduate Group in Plant Biology, Davis, CA 95616. Offers MS, PhD. *Degree requirements:* For master's, comprehensive exam (for some programs), thesis (for some programs); for doctorate, thesis/dissertation. *Entrance requirements:* For master's, GRE General Test, GRE Subject Test (biology), minimum GPA of 3.0; for doctorate, GRE General Test, GRE Subject Test (biology). Additional exam requirements/recommendations for international students: required—TOEFL (minimum score 550 paper-based). Electronic applications accepted.

**University of California, Riverside,** Graduate Division, Department of Botany and Plant Sciences, Riverside, CA 92521-0102. Offers plant biology (MS, PhD), including plant cell, molecular, and developmental biology (PhD), plant ecology (PhD), plant genetics (PhD). *Program availability:* Part-time. Terminal master's awarded for partial completion of doctoral program. *Degree requirements:* For master's, comprehensive exams or thesis; for doctorate, thesis/dissertation, qualifying exams. *Entrance requirements:* For master's and doctorate, GRE General Test, minimum GPA of 3.2. Additional exam requirements/recommendations for international students: required—TOEFL (minimum score 550 paper-based, 80 iBT) or IELTS. Electronic applications accepted.

**University of Florida,** Graduate School, College of Agricultural and Life Sciences, Program in Plant Molecular and Cellular Biology, Gainesville, FL 32611. Offers plant molecular and cellular biology (MS, PhD), including toxicology (PhD). *Degree requirements:* For master's, thesis; for doctorate, comprehensive exam, thesis/dissertation, first author peer-reviewed publication. *Entrance requirements:* For master's and doctorate, GRE General Test, minimum GPA of 3.0. Additional exam requirements/recommendations for international students: required—TOEFL (minimum score 550 paper-based; 80 iBT), IELTS (minimum score 6). Electronic applications accepted.

**University of Georgia,** Franklin College of Arts and Sciences, Department of Plant Biology, Athens, GA 30602. Offers MS, PhD. *Degree requirements:* For master's, thesis; for doctorate, one foreign language, thesis/dissertation. *Entrance requirements:* For master's and doctorate, GRE General Test. Electronic applications accepted.

**University of Illinois at Urbana-Champaign,** Graduate College, College of Liberal Arts and Sciences, School of Integrative Biology, Department of Plant Biology, Champaign, IL 61820. Offers plant biology (MS, PhD); plant biotechnology (PSM).

**University of Maryland, College Park,** Academic Affairs, College of Computer, Mathematical and Natural Sciences, Department of Cell Biology and Molecular Genetics, College Park, MD 20742. Offers cell biology and molecular genetics (MS, PhD); molecular and cellular biology (PhD); plant biology (MS, PhD). *Program availability:* Part-time, evening/weekend. Terminal master's awarded for partial completion of doctoral program. *Degree requirements:* For master's, thesis; for doctorate, thesis/dissertation. *Entrance requirements:* For master's, GRE General Test, minimum GPA of 3.0, 3 letters of recommendation; for doctorate, GRE General Test. Additional exam requirements/recommendations for international students: required—TOEFL. Electronic applications accepted.

**University of Massachusetts Amherst,** Graduate School, Interdisciplinary Programs, Program in Plant Biology, Amherst, MA 01003. Offers biochemistry and metabolism (MS, PhD); cell biology and physiology (MS, PhD); environmental, ecological and integrative biology (MS, PhD); genetics and evolution (MS, PhD). *Degree requirements:*

For master's, thesis; for doctorate, 2 foreign languages, comprehensive exam, thesis/dissertation. *Entrance requirements:* For master's and doctorate, GRE General Test. Additional exam requirements/recommendations for international students: required—TOEFL (minimum score 550 paper-based; 80 iBT), IELTS (minimum score 6.5). Electronic applications accepted.

**University of Minnesota, Twin Cities Campus,** Graduate School, College of Biological Sciences, Program in Plant Biological Sciences, Minneapolis, MN 55455-0213. Offers MS, PhD. *Program availability:* Part-time. Terminal master's awarded for partial completion of doctoral program. *Degree requirements:* For master's, thesis or alternative; for doctorate, thesis/dissertation, written and oral preliminary exams. *Entrance requirements:* For master's and doctorate, GRE General Test. Additional exam requirements/recommendations for international students: required—TOEFL. Electronic applications accepted.

**University of Missouri,** Office of Research and Graduate Studies, College of Agriculture, Food and Natural Resources, Division of Plant Sciences, Columbia, MO 65211. Offers crop, soil and pest management (MS, PhD); entomology (MS, PhD); horticulture (MS, PhD); plant breeding, genetics and genomics (MS, PhD); plant stress biology (MS, PhD). Terminal master's awarded for partial completion of doctoral program. *Degree requirements:* For master's, thesis; for doctorate, comprehensive exam, thesis/dissertation. *Entrance requirements:* For master's and doctorate, GRE General Test, minimum GPA of 3.0; bachelor's degree from accredited college. Additional exam requirements/recommendations for international students: required—TOEFL (minimum score 500 paper-based; 61 iBT), IELTS (minimum score 5.5). Electronic applications accepted.

**University of Oklahoma,** College of Arts and Sciences, Department of Microbiology and Plant Biology, Norman, OK 73019-0390. Offers microbiology (MS, PhD); plant biology (MS, PhD), including ecology and evolutionary biology (PhD), plant biology. Terminal master's awarded for partial completion of doctoral program. *Degree requirements:* For master's, comprehensive exam, thesis; for doctorate, comprehensive exam, thesis/dissertation. *Entrance requirements:* For master's and doctorate, GRE, 3 recommendation letters, letter of intent, bachelor's degree. Additional exam requirements/recommendations for international students: required—TOEFL (minimum score 80 iBT) or IELTS (minimum score 6.5). Electronic applications accepted. *Expenses:* Tuition, state resident: full-time $6583.20; part-time $274.30 per credit hour. Tuition, nonresident: full-time $21,242; part-time $885.10 per credit hour. *International*

tuition: $21,242.40 full-time. *Required fees:* $1994.20; $72.55 per credit hour. $126.50 per semester. Tuition and fees vary according to course load and degree level.

**The University of Texas at Austin,** Graduate School, College of Natural Sciences, School of Biological Sciences, Program in Plant Biology, Austin, TX 78712-1111. Offers MA, PhD. *Entrance requirements:* For master's and doctorate, GRE General Test, minimum GPA of 3.0. Additional exam requirements/recommendations for international students: required—TOEFL. Electronic applications accepted.

**University of Vermont,** Graduate College, College of Agriculture and Life Sciences, Field Naturalist Program, Burlington, VT 05405. Offers plant biology (MS), including field naturalist. *Degree requirements:* For master's, thesis, final exam, project. *Entrance requirements:* For master's, GRE General Test, interview. Additional exam requirements/recommendations for international students: required—TOEFL (minimum score 550 paper-based, 90 iBT) or IELTS (6.5). Electronic applications accepted.

**University of Vermont,** Graduate College, College of Agriculture and Life Sciences, Program in Plant Biology, Burlington, VT 05405. Offers plant biology (MS, PhD). *Entrance requirements:* For master's and doctorate, GRE. Additional exam requirements/recommendations for international students: required—TOEFL (minimum score 550 paper-based, 100 iBT) or IELTS (7). Electronic applications accepted.

**Université Laval,** Faculty of Agricultural and Food Sciences, Program in Plant Biology, Québec, QC G1K 7P4, Canada. Offers M Sc, PhD. Terminal master's awarded for partial completion of doctoral program. *Degree requirements:* For master's, thesis (for some programs); for doctorate, comprehensive exam, thesis/dissertation. *Entrance requirements:* For master's and doctorate, knowledge of French and English. Electronic applications accepted.

**Washington University in St. Louis,** The Graduate School, Division of Biology and Biomedical Sciences, Program in Plant and Microbial Biosciences, St. Louis, MO 63130-4899. Offers PhD. *Degree requirements:* For doctorate, thesis/dissertation. *Entrance requirements:* For doctorate, GRE General Test, GRE Subject Test. Additional exam requirements/recommendations for international students: required—TOEFL. Electronic applications accepted.

**Yale University,** Graduate School of Arts and Sciences, Department of Molecular, Cellular, and Developmental Biology, Program in Plant Sciences, New Haven, CT 06520. Offers PhD. *Degree requirements:* For doctorate, thesis/dissertation. *Entrance requirements:* For doctorate, GRE General Test, GRE Subject Test.

# Plant Molecular Biology

**Cornell University,** Graduate School, Graduate Fields of Agriculture and Life Sciences, Field of Plant Biology, Ithaca, NY 14853. Offers cytology (MS, PhD); paleobotany (MS, PhD); plant biochemistry (MS, PhD); plant cell biology (MS, PhD); plant ecology (MS, PhD); plant molecular biology (MS, PhD); plant morphology, anatomy and biomechanics (MS, PhD); plant physiology (MS, PhD); systematic botany (MS, PhD). *Degree requirements:* For doctorate, comprehensive exam, thesis/dissertation. *Entrance requirements:* For doctorate, GRE General Test, GRE Subject Test in biology (recommended), 3 letters of recommendation. Additional exam requirements/recommendations for international students: required—TOEFL (minimum score 610 paper-based; 77 iBT). Electronic applications accepted.

**Illinois State University,** Graduate School, College of Arts and Sciences, School of Biological Sciences, Normal, IL 61790. Offers animal behavior (MS); bacteriology (MS); biochemistry (MS); biological sciences (MS); biology (PhD); biophysics (MS); biotechnology (MS); botany (MS, PhD); cell biology (MS); conservation biology (MS); developmental biology (MS); ecology (MS, PhD); entomology (MS); evolutionary biology (MS); genetics (MS, PhD); immunology (MS); microbiology (MS, PhD); molecular biology (MS); molecular genetics (MS); neurobiology (MS); neuroscience (MS); parasitology (MS); physiology (MS, PhD); plant biology (MS); plant molecular biology (MS); plant sciences (MS); structural biology (MS); zoology (MS, PhD). *Program availability:* Part-time. *Faculty:* 26 full-time (6 women), 7 part-time/adjunct (2 women). *Students:* 51 full-time (33 women), 15 part-time (8 women). Average age 27. 71 applicants, 28% accepted, 9 enrolled. In 2019, 14 master's, 3 doctorates awarded. *Degree requirements:* For master's, thesis or alternative; for doctorate, variable foreign language requirement, thesis/dissertation, 2 terms of residency. *Entrance requirements:* For master's, GRE General Test, minimum GPA of 2.6 in last 60 hours of course work; for doctorate, GRE General Test. *Application deadline:* Applications are processed on a rolling basis. Application fee: $50. *Expenses: Tuition, area resident:* Full-time $7956; part-time $9767 per year. Tuition, nonresident: full-time $9233; part-time $17,592 per year. *Required fees:* $1797. *Financial support:* In 2019–20, 20 research assistantships, 41 teaching assistantships were awarded; Federal Work-Study, tuition waivers (full), and unspecified assistantships also available. Financial award application deadline: 4/1. *Unit head:* Dr. Craig Gatto, School Director, 309-438-3087, E-mail: cgatto@IllinoisState.edu. *Application contact:* Dr. Ben Sadd, Assistant Chair for Graduate Studies, 309-438-2651, E-mail: bmsadd@IllinoisState.edu.
Website: http://www.bio.ilstu.edu/

**Oregon State University,** Interdisciplinary/Institutional Programs, Program in Molecular and Cellular Biology, Corvallis, OR 97331. Offers bioinformatics (PhD); biotechnology (PhD); genome biology (PhD); molecular virology (PhD); plant molecular biology (PhD). *Degree requirements:* For doctorate, thesis/dissertation, oral and written qualifying exams. *Entrance requirements:* For doctorate, GRE. Additional exam requirements/

recommendations for international students: required—TOEFL (minimum score 80 iBT), IELTS (minimum score 6.5).

**Rutgers University - New Brunswick,** Graduate School-New Brunswick, Program in Plant Biology, Piscataway, NJ 08854-8097. Offers horticulture and plant technology (MS, PhD); molecular and cellular biology (MS, PhD); organismal and population biology (MS, PhD); plant pathology (MS, PhD). *Program availability:* Part-time. Terminal master's awarded for partial completion of doctoral program. *Degree requirements:* For master's, comprehensive exam, thesis or alternative; for doctorate, comprehensive exam, thesis/dissertation. *Entrance requirements:* For master's and doctorate, GRE General Test, GRE Subject Test (recommended). Additional exam requirements/recommendations for international students: required—TOEFL (minimum score 600 paper-based). Electronic applications accepted.

**University of California, Riverside,** Graduate Division, Department of Botany and Plant Sciences, Riverside, CA 92521-0102. Offers plant biology (MS, PhD), including plant cell, molecular, and developmental biology (PhD), plant ecology (PhD), plant genetics (PhD). *Program availability:* Part-time. Terminal master's awarded for partial completion of doctoral program. *Degree requirements:* For master's, comprehensive exams or thesis; for doctorate, thesis/dissertation, qualifying exams. *Entrance requirements:* For master's and doctorate, GRE General Test, minimum GPA of 3.2. Additional exam requirements/recommendations for international students: required—TOEFL (minimum score 550 paper-based, 80 iBT) or IELTS. Electronic applications accepted.

**University of Florida,** Graduate School, College of Agricultural and Life Sciences, Program in Plant Molecular and Cellular Biology, Gainesville, FL 32611. Offers plant molecular and cellular biology (MS, PhD), including toxicology (PhD). *Degree requirements:* For master's, thesis; for doctorate, comprehensive exam, thesis/dissertation, first author peer-reviewed publication. *Entrance requirements:* For master's and doctorate, GRE General Test, minimum GPA of 3.0. Additional exam requirements/recommendations for international students: required—TOEFL (minimum score 550 paper-based; 80 iBT), IELTS (minimum score 6). Electronic applications accepted.

**University of Massachusetts Amherst,** Graduate School, Interdisciplinary Programs, Program in Plant Biology, Amherst, MA 01003. Offers biochemistry and metabolism (MS, PhD); cell biology and physiology (MS, PhD); environmental, ecological and integrative biology (MS, PhD); genetics and evolution (MS, PhD). *Degree requirements:* For master's, thesis; for doctorate, 2 foreign languages, comprehensive exam, thesis/dissertation. *Entrance requirements:* For master's and doctorate, GRE General Test. Additional exam requirements/recommendations for international students: required—TOEFL (minimum score 550 paper-based; 80 iBT), IELTS (minimum score 6.5). Electronic applications accepted.

# Plant Pathology

**Auburn University,** Graduate School, College of Agriculture, Department of Entomology and Plant Pathology, Auburn, AL 36849. Offers entomology (M Ag, MS); plant pathology (M Ag, MS, PhD). *Program availability:* Part-time. *Faculty:* 20 full-time (9 women). *Students:* 37 full-time (17 women), 15 part-time (8 women); includes 6 minority (3 Asian, non-Hispanic/Latino; 2 Hispanic/Latino; 1 Two or more races, non-Hispanic/Latino), 28 international. Average age 28. 19 applicants, 68% accepted, 10 enrolled. In 2019, 10 master's, 2 doctorates awarded. *Degree requirements:* For master's, thesis (for some programs); for doctorate, one foreign language, thesis/dissertation. *Entrance*

*requirements:* For master's, GRE General Test; for doctorate, GRE General Test, GRE Subject Test, master's degree with thesis. Additional exam requirements/recommendations for international students: required—TOEFL (minimum score 550 paper-based; 79 iBT), iTEP; recommended—IELTS (minimum score 6.5). *Application deadline:* Applications are processed on a rolling basis. Application fee: $60 ($70 for international students). Electronic applications accepted. *Expenses: Tuition, area resident:* Full-time $9828; part-time $546 per credit hour. Tuition, state resident: full-time $9828; part-time $546 per credit hour. Tuition, nonresident: full-time $29,484; part-

time $1638 per credit hour. *International tuition:* $29,744 full-time. Tuition and fees vary according to course load, program and reciprocity agreements. *Financial support:* In 2019–20, 36 fellowships with tuition reimbursements (averaging $716 per year), 33 research assistantships with tuition reimbursements (averaging $19,392 per year) were awarded; Federal Work-Study also available. Support available to part-time students. Financial award application deadline: 3/15; financial award applicants required to submit FAFSA. *Unit head:* Dr. Nannan Liu, Chair, 334-844-4266. *Application contact:* Dr. George Flowers, Dean of the Graduate School, 334-844-2125.

**Colorado State University,** College of Agricultural Sciences, Department of Agricultural Biology, Fort Collins, CO 80523-1177. Offers entomology (MS, PhD); pest management (MS); plant pathology (MS, PhD); weed science (MS, PhD). *Faculty:* 24 full-time (11 women). *Students:* 22 full-time (12 women), 20 part-time (13 women); includes 5 minority (1 Asian, non-Hispanic/Latino; 2 Hispanic/Latino; 2 Two or more races, non-Hispanic/Latino), 12 international. Average age 29. 32 applicants, 41% accepted, 13 enrolled. In 2019, 7 master's, 3 doctorates awarded. Terminal master's awarded for partial completion of doctoral program. *Degree requirements:* For master's, thesis; for doctorate, thesis/dissertation. *Entrance requirements:* For master's and doctorate, minimum GPA of 3.0, three letters of recommendation, essay, transcripts, short essay outlining experience and career goals. Additional exam requirements/recommendations for international students: required—TOEFL (minimum score 550 paper-based). *Application deadline:* For fall admission, 1/15 priority date for domestic and international students; for spring admission, 9/1 priority date for domestic and international students. Application fee: $60 ($70 for international students). Electronic applications accepted. *Expenses:* Tuition, state resident: full-time $10,520; part-time $5844 per credit hour. Tuition, nonresident: full-time $25,791; part-time $14,328 per credit hour. *International tuition:* $25,791 full-time. *Required fees:* $2512.80. Part-time tuition and fees vary according to course level, course load, degree level, program and student level. *Financial support:* In 2019–20, 22 research assistantships with partial tuition reimbursements (averaging $22,683 per year), 10 teaching assistantships with partial tuition reimbursements (averaging $18,912 per year) were awarded; fellowships with partial tuition reimbursements and scholarships/grants also available. Financial award application deadline: 1/15. *Unit head:* Dr. Amy Charkowski, Department Head and Professor, 970-491-8586, E-mail: amy.charkowski@colostate.edu. *Application contact:* Janet Dill, Graduate Student Coordinator, 970-491-0402, Fax: 970-491-3862, E-mail: janet.dill@colostate.edu.
Website: http://bspm.agsci.colostate.edu/

**Cornell University,** Graduate School, Graduate Fields of Agriculture and Life Sciences, Field of Plant Pathology and Plant-Microbe Biology, Ithaca, NY 14853. Offers fungal and oomycete biology (MPS, MS, PhD); plant microbe pathology (MPS, MS, PhD); plant pathology (MPS, MS, PhD). *Degree requirements:* For master's, thesis (MS), project paper (MPS); for doctorate, comprehensive exam, thesis/dissertation. *Entrance requirements:* For master's and doctorate, GRE General Test, GRE Subject Test (biology recommended), 3 letters of recommendation. Additional exam requirements/recommendations for international students: required—TOEFL (minimum score 550 paper-based; 77 iBT). Electronic applications accepted.

**Dalhousie University,** Faculty of Agriculture, Halifax, NS B3H 4R2, Canada. Offers agriculture (M Sc), including air quality, animal behavior, animal molecular genetics, animal nutrition, animal technology, aquaculture, botany, crop management, crop physiology, ecology, environmental microbiology, food science, horticulture, nutrient management, pest management, physiology, plant biotechnology, plant pathology, soil chemistry, soil fertility, waste management and composting, water quality. *Program availability:* Part-time. *Degree requirements:* For master's, thesis, ATC Exam Teaching Assistantship. *Entrance requirements:* For master's, honors B Sc, minimum GPA of 3.0. Additional exam requirements/recommendations for international students: required—TOEFL (minimum score 580 paper-based; 92 iBT), IELTS, Michigan English Language Assessment Battery, CanTEST, CAEL.

**Iowa State University of Science and Technology,** Department of Plant Pathology, Ames, IA 50011. Offers MS, PhD. *Entrance requirements:* For master's and doctorate, GRE General Test, resume. Additional exam requirements/recommendations for international students: required—TOEFL (minimum score 550 paper-based; 79 iBT), IELTS (minimum score 6.5). Electronic applications accepted.

**Kansas State University,** Graduate School, College of Agriculture, Department of Plant Pathology, Manhattan, KS 66506. Offers genetics (MS, PhD); plant pathology (MS, PhD). Terminal master's awarded for partial completion of doctoral program. *Degree requirements:* For master's, thesis, oral exam; for doctorate, thesis/dissertation, preliminary exams, oral exam. *Entrance requirements:* For master's and doctorate, minimum undergraduate GPA of 3.0. Additional exam requirements/recommendations for international students: required—TOEFL (minimum score 550 paper-based; 79 iBT). Electronic applications accepted.

**Louisiana State University and Agricultural & Mechanical College,** Graduate School, College of Agriculture, Department of Plant Pathology and Crop Physiology, Baton Rouge, LA 70803. Offers plant health (MS, PhD).

**Michigan State University,** The Graduate School, College of Agriculture and Natural Resources, Department of Plant, Soil and Microbial Sciences, East Lansing, MI 48824. Offers crop and soil sciences (MS, PhD); crop and soil sciences-environmental toxicology (PhD); plant breeding and genetics-crop and soil sciences (MS); plant breeding, genetics and biotechnology-crop and soil sciences (PhD); plant pathology (MS, PhD). *Entrance requirements:* Additional exam requirements/recommendations for international students: required—TOEFL (minimum score 550 paper-based), Michigan State University ELT ( minimum score 85), Michigan Michigan English Language Assessment Battery (minimum score 83). Electronic applications accepted.

**Montana State University,** The Graduate School, College of Agriculture, Department of Plant Sciences and Plant Pathology, Bozeman, MT 59717. Offers plant pathology (MS); plant sciences (MS, PhD), including plant genetics (PhD), plant pathology (PhD). *Program availability:* Part-time. *Degree requirements:* For master's, comprehensive exam; for doctorate, comprehensive exam, thesis/dissertation. *Entrance requirements:* For master's, GRE General Test, minimum GPA of 3.0; for doctorate, GRE General Test. Additional exam requirements/recommendations for international students: required—TOEFL (minimum score 550 paper-based). Electronic applications accepted.

**New Mexico State University,** College of Agricultural, Consumer and Environmental Sciences, Department of Entomology, Plant Pathology and Weed Science, Las Cruces, NM 88003-8001. Offers MS. *Program availability:* Part-time. *Faculty:* 10 full-time (2 women). *Students:* 8 full-time (6 women), 2 part-time (1 woman); includes 3 minority (1 Black or African American, non-Hispanic/Latino; 2 Hispanic/Latino), 3 international. Average age 26. 9 applicants, 78% accepted, 4 enrolled. In 2019, 4 master's awarded. *Degree requirements:* For master's, comprehensive exam, thesis. *Entrance requirements:* For master's, GRE General Test. Additional exam requirements/recommendations for international students: required—TOEFL (minimum score 550 paper-based; 79 iBT), IELTS (minimum score 6.5). *Application deadline:* For fall admission, 7/1 priority date for domestic students; for spring admission, 11/1 priority date for domestic students. Applications are processed on a rolling basis. Application fee: $40 ($50 for international students). Electronic applications accepted. *Financial support:* In 2019–20, 8 students received support, including 8 research assistantships (averaging $23,169 per year), 5 teaching assistantships (averaging $17,716 per year); career-related internships or fieldwork, Federal Work-Study, scholarships/grants, traineeships, health care benefits, and unspecified assistantships also available. Support available to part-time students. Financial award application deadline: 3/1. *Unit head:* Dr. Gerald K. Sims, Department Head, 575-646-3225, Fax: 575-646-8087, E-mail: gksims@nmsu.edu. *Application contact:* Belinda Williams, Administrative Assistant, 575-646-3225, Fax: 575-646-8087.
Website: http://eppws.nmsu.edu/

**North Dakota State University,** College of Graduate and Interdisciplinary Studies, College of Agriculture, Food Systems, and Natural Resources, Department of Plant Pathology, Fargo, ND 58102. Offers MS, PhD. *Program availability:* Part-time. *Entrance requirements:* Additional exam requirements/recommendations for international students: required—TOEFL (minimum score 550 paper-based; 79 iBT). Electronic applications accepted. Tuition and fees vary according to program and reciprocity agreements.

**The Ohio State University,** Graduate School, College of Food, Agricultural, and Environmental Sciences, Department of Plant Pathology, Columbus, OH 43210. Offers MPHM, MS, PhD. *Entrance requirements:* For master's and doctorate, GRE General Test. Additional exam requirements/recommendations for international students: required—TOEFL (minimum score 550 paper-based; 79 iBT), Michigan English Language Assessment Battery (minimum score 82); recommended—IELTS (minimum score 7). Electronic applications accepted.

**Oklahoma State University,** College of Agricultural Science and Natural Resources, Department of Entomology and Plant Pathology, Stillwater, OK 74078. Offers entomology (PhD); entomology and plant pathology (MS). *Faculty:* 20 full-time (4 women). *Students:* 5 full-time (2 women), 19 part-time (10 women); includes 2 minority (1 Hispanic/Latino; 1 Two or more races, non-Hispanic/Latino), 13 international. Average age 28. 14 applicants, 57% accepted, 8 enrolled. In 2019, 9 master's, 2 doctorates awarded. *Entrance requirements:* For master's and doctorate, GRE or GMAT. Additional exam requirements/recommendations for international students: required—TOEFL (minimum score 550 paper-based; 79 iBT). *Application deadline:* For fall admission, 3/1 priority date for international students; for spring admission, 8/1 priority date for international students. Applications are processed on a rolling basis. Application fee: $50 ($75 for international students). Electronic applications accepted. *Expenses: Tuition, area resident:* Full-time $4148.10; part-time $2765.40 per credit hour. Tuition, state resident: full-time $4148.10; part-time $2765.40 per credit hour. Tuition, nonresident: full-time $15,775; part-time $10,516.80 per credit hour. *International tuition:* $15,775.20 full-time. *Required fees:* $2196.90; $122.05 per credit hour. Tuition and fees vary according to course load, campus/location and program. *Financial support:* In 2019–20, 23 research assistantships (averaging $1,557 per year), 2 teaching assistantships (averaging $1,511 per year) were awarded; career-related internships or fieldwork, Federal Work-Study, scholarships/grants, health care benefits, tuition waivers (partial), and unspecified assistantships also available. Support available to part-time students. Financial award application deadline: 3/1; financial award applicants required to submit FAFSA. *Unit head:* Dr. Phillip Mulder, Jr., Department Head, 405-744-5527, Fax: 405-744-6039, E-mail: phil.mulder@okstate.edu. *Application contact:* Dr. Sheryl Tucker, VICE PROVOST/DEAN/PROF, 405-744-6368, E-mail: igrad@okstate.edu.
Website: http://entoplp.okstate.edu

**Oregon State University,** College of Agricultural Sciences, Program in Botany and Plant Pathology, Corvallis, OR 97331. Offers applied systematics (MS); ecology (MS, PhD); genetics (MS, PhD); genomics and computational biology (MS, PhD); molecular and cellular biology (MS, PhD); mycology (MS, PhD); plant pathology (MS, PhD); plant physiology (MS, PhD). *Entrance requirements:* For master's and doctorate, GRE.

**Penn State University Park,** Graduate School, College of Agricultural Sciences, Department of Plant Pathology and Environmental Microbiology, University Park, PA 16802. Offers plant pathology (MS, PhD).

**Purdue University,** Graduate School, College of Agriculture, Department of Botany and Plant Pathology, West Lafayette, IN 47907. Offers MS, PhD. *Program availability:* Part-time. *Faculty:* 32 full-time (11 women), 1 part-time/adjunct (0 women). *Students:* 55 full-time (23 women), 3 part-time (0 women); includes 5 minority (all Hispanic/Latino), 33 international. Average age 27. 32 applicants, 25% accepted, 6 enrolled. In 2019, 5 master's, 7 doctorates awarded. Terminal master's awarded for partial completion of doctoral program. *Degree requirements:* For master's, thesis; for doctorate, thesis/dissertation. *Entrance requirements:* For master's, GRE General Test, minimum undergraduate GPA of 3.0 or equivalent; for doctorate, GRE, minimum undergraduate GPA of 3.0 or equivalent. Additional exam requirements/recommendations for international students: required—TOEFL (minimum score 550 paper-based; 77 iBT); recommended—TWE. *Application deadline:* For fall admission, 4/15 priority date for domestic and international students; for spring admission, 12/15 for domestic students, 9/15 for international students; for summer admission, 4/15 for domestic students, 2/15 for international students. Applications are processed on a rolling basis. Application fee: $60 ($75 for international students). Electronic applications accepted. *Financial support:* In 2019–20, 30 students received support. Fellowships with full tuition reimbursements available, research assistantships with full tuition reimbursements available, teaching assistantships with full tuition reimbursements available, and career-related internships or fieldwork available. Support available to part-time students. Financial award application deadline: 3/1; financial award applicants required to submit FAFSA. *Unit head:* Christopher Staiger, Head of the Graduate Program, 765-494-4615, E-mail: staiger@purdue.edu. *Application contact:* Lisa Gross, Graduate Contact, 765-494-9871, E-mail: gross25@purdue.edu.
Website: https://ag.purdue.edu/btny

**Rutgers University - New Brunswick,** Graduate School-New Brunswick, Program in Plant Biology, Piscataway, NJ 08854-8097. Offers horticulture and plant technology (MS, PhD); molecular and cellular biology (MS, PhD); organismal and population biology (MS, PhD); plant pathology (MS, PhD). *Program availability:* Part-time. Terminal master's awarded for partial completion of doctoral program. *Degree requirements:* For master's, comprehensive exam, thesis or alternative; for doctorate, comprehensive exam, thesis/dissertation. *Entrance requirements:* For master's and doctorate, GRE General Test, GRE Subject Test (recommended). Additional exam requirements/recommendations for international students: required—TOEFL (minimum score 600 paper-based). Electronic applications accepted.

**State University of New York College of Environmental Science and Forestry,** Department of Environmental and Forest Biology, Syracuse, NY 13210-2779. Offers applied ecology (MPS); chemical ecology (MPS, MS, PhD); conservation biology (MPS, MS, PhD); ecology (MPS, MS, PhD); entomology (MPS, MS, PhD); environmental interpretation (MPS, MS, PhD); environmental physiology (MPS, MS, PhD); fish and wildlife biology and management (MPS, MS, PhD); forest pathology and mycology (MPS, MS, PhD); plant biotechnology (MPS); plant science and biotechnology (MPS, MS, PhD). *Program availability:* Part-time. *Faculty:* 35 full-time (10 women), 4 part-time/adjunct (3 women). *Students:* 103 full-time (60 women), 17 part-time (7 women);

includes 7 minority (4 American Indian or Alaska Native, non-Hispanic/Latino; 2 Asian, non-Hispanic/Latino; 1 Hispanic/Latino), 13 international. Average age 29. 69 applicants, 45% accepted, 17 enrolled. In 2019, 28 master's, 6 doctorates awarded. Terminal master's awarded for partial completion of doctoral program. *Degree requirements:* For master's, thesis (for some programs), capstone seminar; for doctorate, comprehensive exam, thesis/dissertation, capstone seminar. *Entrance requirements:* For master's and doctorate, GRE General Test, minimum GPA of 3.0. Additional exam requirements/recommendations for international students: required—TOEFL (minimum score 550 paper-based; 80 iBT), IELTS (minimum score 6). *Application deadline:* For fall admission, 2/1 priority date for domestic and international students; for spring admission, 11/1 priority date for domestic and international students. Applications are processed on a rolling basis. Application fee: $60. Electronic applications accepted. *Expenses: Tuition,* state resident: full-time $11,310; part-time $472 per credit hour. Tuition, nonresident: full-time $23,100; part-time $963 per credit hour. *Required fees:* $1890; $95.21 per credit hour. *Financial support:* In 2019–20, 35 students received support. Unspecified assistantships available. Financial award application deadline: 6/30; financial award applicants required to submit FAFSA. *Unit head:* Dr. Melissa K. Fierke, Chair, 315-470-6809, Fax: 315-470-6743, E-mail: mkfierke@esf.edu. *Application contact:* Laura Payne, Administrative Assistant Office of Instruction & Graduate Studies, 315-470-6599, E-mail: esfgrad@esf.edu.
Website: http://www.esf.edu/efb/grad/default.asp

**Texas A&M University,** College of Agriculture and Life Sciences, Department of Plant Pathology and Microbiology, College Station, TX 77843. Offers plant pathology (MS). *Program availability:* Part-time, blended/hybrid learning. *Faculty:* 17. *Students:* 31 full-time (14 women), 1 part-time (0 women); includes 6 minority (1 Black or African American, non-Hispanic/Latino; 1 Asian, non-Hispanic/Latino; 3 Hispanic/Latino; 1 Two or more races, non-Hispanic/Latino), 12 international. Average age 28. 9 applicants, 100% accepted, 9 enrolled. In 2019, 2 master's, 5 doctorates awarded. *Degree requirements:* For master's, comprehensive exam (for some programs), thesis; for doctorate, comprehensive exam, thesis/dissertation. *Entrance requirements:* For master's and doctorate, GRE General Test, letters of recommendation, BS/BA in biological sciences. Additional exam requirements/recommendations for international students: required—TOEFL (minimum score 550 paper-based; 80 iBT), IELTS (minimum score 6), PTE (minimum score 53). *Application deadline:* Applications are processed on a rolling basis. Application fee: $65 ($90 for international students). Electronic applications accepted. *Expenses:* Contact institution. *Financial support:* In 2019–20, 35 students received support, including 3 fellowships with tuition reimbursements available (averaging $3,000 per year), 20 research assistantships with tuition reimbursements available (averaging $19,513 per year), 13 teaching assistantships with tuition reimbursements available (averaging $16,951 per year); career-related internships or fieldwork, institutionally sponsored loans, scholarships/grants, traineeships, health care benefits, tuition waivers (full and partial), and unspecified assistantships also available. Support available to part-time students. Financial award application deadline: 3/15; financial award applicants required to submit FAFSA. *Unit head:* Dr. Leland S. Pierson, III, Professor and Department Head, 979-845-8288, Fax: 979-845-6483, E-mail: lspierson@tamu.edu. *Application contact:* Dr. Won Bo Shim, Associate Department Head for Academic Affairs, 979-458-2190, E-mail: wbshim@tamu.edu.
Website: http://plantpathology.tamu.edu/

**The University of Arizona,** College of Agriculture and Life Sciences, School of Plant Sciences, Program in Plant Pathology, Tucson, AZ 85721. Offers MS, PhD. *Program availability:* Part-time. *Degree requirements:* For master's, thesis optional; for doctorate, thesis/dissertation. *Entrance requirements:* For master's, GRE (recommended), minimum GPA of 3.0, academic resume, 3 letters of recommendation; for doctorate, GRE (recommended), minimum GPA of 3.0, academic resume, statement of purpose, 3 letters of recommendation. Additional exam requirements/recommendations for international students: required—TOEFL (minimum score 550 paper-based; 79 iBT). Electronic applications accepted.

**University of Arkansas,** Graduate School, Dale Bumpers College of Agricultural, Food and Life Sciences, Department of Plant Pathology, Fayetteville, AR 72701. Offers MS. *Students:* 3 full-time (2 women), 4 part-time (all women); includes 2 minority (1 Hispanic/Latino; 1 Two or more races, non-Hispanic/Latino), 2 international. In 2019, 5 master's awarded. *Application deadline:* For fall admission, 8/1 for domestic students, 4/1 for international students; for spring admission, 12/1 for domestic students, 10/1 for international students; for summer admission, 4/15 for domestic students, 3/1 for international students. Applications are processed on a rolling basis. Application fee: $60. Electronic applications accepted. *Financial support:* In 2019–20, 10 research assistantships were awarded; fellowships, teaching assistantships, career-related internships or fieldwork, and Federal Work-Study also available. Support available to part-time students. Financial award application deadline: 4/1; financial award applicants required to submit FAFSA. *Unit head:* Dr. Kenneth Korth, Department Head, 479-575-2445, Fax: 479-575-7601, E-mail: kkorth@uark.edu. *Application contact:* Kenneth Korth, Professor, 479-575-2445, Fax: 479-575-7601, E-mail: kkorth@uark.edu.
Website: https://plant-pathology.uark.edu/

**University of California, Davis,** Graduate Studies, Program in Plant Pathology, Davis, CA 95616. Offers MS, PhD. Terminal master's awarded for partial completion of doctoral program. *Degree requirements:* For master's, comprehensive exam (for some programs), thesis (for some programs); for doctorate, thesis/dissertation. *Entrance requirements:* For master's and doctorate, GRE General Test. Additional exam requirements/recommendations for international students: required—TOEFL (minimum score 550 paper-based). Electronic applications accepted.

**University of California, Riverside,** Graduate Division, Department of Plant Pathology, Riverside, CA 92521-0102. Offers MS, PhD. Terminal master's awarded for partial completion of doctoral program. *Degree requirements:* For master's, comprehensive exams or thesis; for doctorate, thesis/dissertation, qualifying exams. *Entrance requirements:* For master's and doctorate, GRE General Test (minimum score 1100 or approximately 300 on new scoring scale), minimum GPA of 3.2. Additional exam requirements/recommendations for international students: required—TOEFL (minimum score 550 paper-based; 80 iBT). Electronic applications accepted.

**University of Florida,** Graduate School, College of Agricultural and Life Sciences, Department of Plant Pathology, Gainesville, FL 32611. Offers plant pathology (MS, PhD), including toxicology (PhD). *Program availability:* Part-time. Terminal master's awarded for partial completion of doctoral program. *Degree requirements:* For master's, comprehensive exam (for some programs), thesis optional; for doctorate, comprehensive exam, thesis/dissertation. *Entrance requirements:* For master's and doctorate, GRE General Test, minimum GPA of 3.0. Additional exam requirements/recommendations for international students: required—TOEFL (minimum score 550 paper-based; 80 iBT), IELTS (minimum score 6). Electronic applications accepted.

**University of Georgia,** College of Agricultural and Environmental Sciences, Department of Plant Pathology, Athens, GA 30602. Offers MS, PhD. *Degree requirements:* For master's, thesis (MS); for doctorate, one foreign language, thesis/dissertation. *Entrance requirements:* For master's and doctorate, GRE General Test. Electronic applications accepted.

**University of Guelph,** Office of Graduate and Postdoctoral Studies, Ontario Agricultural College, Department of Environmental Biology, Guelph, ON N1G 2W1, Canada. Offers entomology (M Sc, PhD); environmental microbiology and biotechnology (M Sc, PhD); environmental toxicology (M Sc, PhD); plant and forest systems (M Sc, PhD); plant pathology (M Sc, PhD). *Program availability:* Part-time. *Degree requirements:* For master's, thesis; for doctorate, comprehensive exam, thesis/dissertation. *Entrance requirements:* For master's, minimum 75% average during previous 2 years of course work; for doctorate, minimum 75% average. Additional exam requirements/recommendations for international students: required—TOEFL or IELTS. Electronic applications accepted.

**University of Hawaii at Manoa,** Office of Graduate Education, College of Tropical Agriculture and Human Resources, Department of Plant and Environmental Protection Sciences, Program in Tropical Plant Pathology, Honolulu, HI 96822. Offers MS, PhD. *Program availability:* Part-time. *Degree requirements:* For master's, thesis optional; for doctorate, comprehensive exam, thesis/dissertation. *Entrance requirements:* For master's and doctorate, GRE General Test. Additional exam requirements/recommendations for international students: required—TOEFL (minimum score 540 paper-based; 76 iBT), IELTS (minimum score 5).

**University of Idaho,** College of Graduate Studies, College of Agricultural and Life Sciences, Department of Entomology, Plant Pathology and Nematology, Moscow, ID 83844-2282. Offers plant science (MS). *Faculty:* 14 full-time (5 women). *Students:* 21. Average age 30. In 2019, 1 master's, 2 doctorates awarded. *Entrance requirements:* For master's and doctorate, minimum GPA of 3.0. Additional exam requirements/recommendations for international students: required—TOEFL (minimum score 550 paper-based; 79 iBT). *Application deadline:* For fall admission, 7/30 for domestic students; for spring admission, 12/1 for domestic students. Applications are processed on a rolling basis. Application fee: $60. Electronic applications accepted. *Expenses:* Tuition, state resident: full-time $7753.80; part-time $502 per credit hour. Tuition, nonresident: full-time $26,990; part-time $1571 per credit hour. *Required fees:* $2122.20; $47 per credit hour. *Financial support:* Research assistantships and teaching assistantships available. Financial award applicants required to submit FAFSA. *Unit head:* Dr. Edwin Lewis, Department Head, 208-885-3776, E-mail: eppn@uidaho.edu. *Application contact:* Dr. Edwin Lewis, Department Head, 208-885-3776, E-mail: eppn@uidaho.edu.
Website: https://www.uidaho.edu/cals/entomology-plant-pathology-and-nematology

**University of Kentucky,** Graduate School, College of Agriculture, Food and Environment, Program in Plant Pathology, Lexington, KY 40506-0032. Offers MS, PhD. *Degree requirements:* For master's, comprehensive exam, thesis; for doctorate, comprehensive exam, thesis/dissertation. *Entrance requirements:* For master's, GRE General Test, minimum undergraduate GPA of 2.75; for doctorate, GRE General Test, minimum graduate GPA of 3.0. Additional exam requirements/recommendations for international students: required—TOEFL (minimum score 550 paper-based). Electronic applications accepted.

**University of Maine,** Graduate School, College of Natural Sciences, Forestry, and Agriculture, School of Biology and Ecology, Orono, ME 04469. Offers biological sciences (PhD); botany and plant pathology (MS); entomology (MS); zoology (MS, PhD). *Program availability:* Part-time. *Faculty:* 30 full-time (16 women), 2 part-time/adjunct (1 woman). *Students:* 84 full-time (54 women), 12 part-time (6 women); includes 9 minority (1 Black or African American, non-Hispanic/Latino; 1 American Indian or Alaska Native, non-Hispanic/Latino; 1 Asian, non-Hispanic/Latino; 5 Hispanic/Latino; 1 Two or more races, non-Hispanic/Latino), 21 international. Average age 30. 62 applicants, 40% accepted, 22 enrolled. In 2019, 12 master's, 12 doctorates awarded. Terminal master's awarded for partial completion of doctoral program. *Degree requirements:* For master's, thesis (for some programs); for doctorate, comprehensive exam, thesis/dissertation. *Entrance requirements:* For master's and doctorate, GRE General Test. Additional exam requirements/recommendations for international students: required—TOEFL (minimum score 80 iBT), IELTS (minimum score 6.5). *Application deadline:* For fall admission, 2/1 priority date for domestic students. Applications are processed on a rolling basis. Application fee: $65. Electronic applications accepted. *Expenses: Tuition,* area resident: Full-time $8100; part-time $450 per credit hour. Tuition, state resident: full-time $8100; part-time $450 per credit hour. Tuition, nonresident: full-time $26,388; part-time $1466 per credit hour. *International tuition:* $26,388 full-time. *Required fees:* $1257; $278 per semester. Tuition and fees vary according to course load. *Financial support:* In 2019–20, 108 students received support, including 1 fellowship with full tuition reimbursement available (averaging $25,000 per year), 79 research assistantships with full tuition reimbursements available (averaging $15,825 per year), 23 teaching assistantships with full tuition reimbursements available (averaging $15,825 per year); career-related internships or fieldwork, Federal Work-Study, institutionally sponsored loans, tuition waivers (full and partial), and unspecified assistantships also available. Financial award application deadline: 3/1; financial award applicants required to submit FAFSA. *Unit head:* Dr. Andrei Aloykhin, Director, 207-581-2977, Fax: 207-581-2537. *Application contact:* Scott G. Delcourt, Assistant Vice President for Graduate Studies and Senior Associate Dean, 207-581-3291, Fax: 207-581-3232, E-mail: graduate@maine.edu.
Website: http://sbe.umaine.edu/

**University of Minnesota, Twin Cities Campus,** Graduate School, College of Food, Agricultural and Natural Resource Sciences, Department of Plant Pathology, St. Paul, MN 55108. Offers MS, PhD. *Program availability:* Part-time. Terminal master's awarded for partial completion of doctoral program. *Degree requirements:* For master's, comprehensive exam, thesis; for doctorate, comprehensive exam, thesis/dissertation. *Entrance requirements:* For master's and doctorate, GRE General Test. Additional exam requirements/recommendations for international students: required—TOEFL (minimum score 550 paper-based; 79 iBT), IELTS (minimum score 6.5). Electronic applications accepted.

**The University of Tennessee,** Graduate School, College of Agricultural Sciences and Natural Resources, Department of Entomology and Plant Pathology, Knoxville, TN 37996. Offers entomology (MS, PhD); integrated pest management and bioactive natural products (PhD); plant pathology (MS, PhD). *Program availability:* Part-time. *Degree requirements:* For master's, thesis, seminar. *Entrance requirements:* For master's, GRE General Test, minimum GPA of 2.7, 3 reference letters, letter of intent; for doctorate, GRE General Test, minimum GPA of 2.7, 3 reference letters, letter of intent, proposed dissertation research. Additional exam requirements/recommendations for international students: required—TOEFL. Electronic applications accepted.

**University of Vermont,** Graduate College, College of Agriculture and Life Sciences, Department of Plant and Soil Science, Burlington, VT 05405. Offers agroecology (Graduate Certificate); plant and soil science (MS, PhD), including agroecology, agronomy (MS), ecological landscape design, entomology, horticulture (MS), plant pathology (MS), soil science. *Degree requirements:* For master's, thesis; for doctorate, one foreign language, thesis/dissertation. *Entrance requirements:* For master's and doctorate, GRE General Test. Additional exam requirements/recommendations for international students: required—TOEFL (minimum score 550 paper-based; 90 iBT), IELTS (minimum score 6.5). Electronic applications accepted.

*Plant Pathology*

**University of Wisconsin–Madison,** Graduate School, College of Agricultural and Life Sciences, Department of Plant Pathology, Madison, WI 53706-1380. Offers MS, PhD. *Program availability:* Part-time. Terminal master's awarded for partial completion of doctoral program. *Degree requirements:* For master's, thesis; for doctorate, thesis/dissertation. *Entrance requirements:* For master's and doctorate, GRE. Additional exam requirements/recommendations for international students: required—TOEFL. Electronic applications accepted.

**Virginia Polytechnic Institute and State University,** Graduate School, College of Agriculture and Life Sciences, Blacksburg, VA 24061. Offers agricultural and applied economics (MS, PhD); agricultural and life sciences (MS); agriculture, leadership, and community education (MS, PhD); animal and poultry science (MS, PhD); biochemistry (MS, PhD); crop and soil environmental sciences (MS, PhD); dairy science (MS, PhD); entomology (MS, PhD); food science and technology (MS, PhD); horticulture (PhD); human nutrition, foods and exercise (MS, PhD); plant pathology, physiology, and weed science (MS, PhD). *Faculty:* 246 full-time (83 women). *Students:* 364 full-time (213 women), 106 part-time (68 women); includes 79 minority (29 Black or African American, non-Hispanic/Latino; 1 American Indian or Alaska Native, non-Hispanic/Latino; 13 Asian, non-Hispanic/Latino; 16 Hispanic/Latino; 20 Two or more races, non-Hispanic/Latino; 106 international. Average age 28. 314 applicants, 57% accepted, 130 enrolled. In 2019, 92 master's, 59 doctorates awarded. *Degree requirements:* For master's, comprehensive exam (for some programs), thesis (for some programs); for doctorate, comprehensive exam (for some programs), thesis/dissertation (for some programs). *Entrance requirements:* For master's and doctorate, GRE/GMAT. Additional exam requirements/recommendations for international students: required—TOEFL (minimum score 90 iBT). *Application deadline:* For fall admission, 8/1 for domestic students, 4/1 for international students; for spring admission, 1/1 for domestic students, 9/1 for international students. Applications are processed on a rolling basis. Application fee: $75. Electronic applications accepted. *Expenses:* Tuition, state resident: full-time $13,700; part-time $761.25 per credit hour. Tuition, nonresident: full-time $27,614; part-time $1534 per credit hour. *Required fees:* $886.50 per term. Tuition and fees vary according to campus/location and program. *Financial support:* In 2019–20, 248 research assistantships with full tuition reimbursements (averaging $20,360 per year), 127 teaching assistantships with full tuition reimbursements (averaging $18,183 per year) were awarded; fellowships, scholarships/grants, and unspecified assistantships also available. Financial award application deadline: 3/1; financial award applicants required to submit FAFSA. *Unit head:* Dr. Alan L. Grant, Dean, 540-231-4152, Fax: 540-231-4163, E-mail: algrant@vt.edu. *Application contact:* Crystal Tawney, Administrative Assistant, 540-231-4152, Fax: 540-231-4163, E-mail: cdtawney@vt.edu. Website: http://www.cals.vt.edu/

**Washington State University,** College of Agricultural, Human, and Natural Resource Sciences, Department of Plant Pathology, Pullman, WA 99164. Offers MS, PhD. Terminal master's awarded for partial completion of doctoral program. *Degree requirements:* For master's, comprehensive exam (for some programs), thesis (for some programs), oral exam; for doctorate, comprehensive exam, thesis/dissertation, oral exam. *Entrance requirements:* For master's and doctorate, GRE, statement of purpose. Additional exam requirements/recommendations for international students: required—TOEFL (minimum score 550 paper-based), IELTS. Electronic applications accepted.

**West Virginia University,** Davis College of Agriculture, Forestry and Consumer Sciences, Morgantown, WV 26506. Offers agricultural and extension education (MS, PhD); agriculture and resource management (MS); agriculture, natural resources and design (M Agr); agronomy (MS); animal and food science (MS); animal physiology (MS); applied and environmental microbiology (MS); design and merchandising (MS); entomology (MS); forest resource science (PhD); forestry (MSF); genetics and developmental biology (MS, PhD); horticulture (MS); human and community development (PhD); landscape architecture (MLA); natural resource economics (PhD); nutritional and food science (MS); plant and soil science (PhD); plant pathology (MS); recreation, parks and tourism resources (MS); reproductive physiology (MS, PhD); wildlife and fisheries resources (PhD). *Accreditation:* ASLA. *Program availability:* Part-time. *Degree requirements:* For master's, thesis; for doctorate, thesis/dissertation. *Entrance requirements:* Additional exam requirements/recommendations for international students: required—TOEFL (minimum score 550 paper-based). Electronic applications accepted.

# Plant Physiology

**Cornell University,** Graduate School, Graduate Fields of Agriculture and Life Sciences, Field of Plant Biology, Ithaca, NY 14853. Offers cytology (MS, PhD); paleobotany (MS, PhD); plant biochemistry (MS, PhD); plant cell biology (MS, PhD); plant ecology (MS, PhD); plant molecular biology (MS, PhD); plant morphology, anatomy and biomechanics (MS, PhD); plant physiology (MS, PhD); systematic botany (MS, PhD). *Degree requirements:* For doctorate, comprehensive exam, thesis/dissertation. *Entrance requirements:* For doctorate, GRE General Test, GRE Subject Test in biology (recommended), 3 letters of recommendation. Additional exam requirements/recommendations for international students: required—TOEFL (minimum score 610 paper-based; 77 iBT). Electronic applications accepted.

**Dalhousie University,** Faculty of Agriculture, Halifax, NS B3H 4R2, Canada. Offers agriculture (M Sc), including air quality, animal behavior, animal molecular genetics, animal nutrition, animal technology, aquaculture, botany, crop management, crop physiology, ecology, environmental microbiology, food science, horticulture, nutrient management, pest management, physiology, plant biotechnology, plant pathology, soil chemistry, soil fertility, waste management and composting, water quality. *Program availability:* Part-time. *Degree requirements:* For master's, thesis, ATC Exam Teaching Assistantship. *Entrance requirements:* For master's, honors B Sc, minimum GPA of 3.0. Additional exam requirements/recommendations for international students: required—TOEFL (minimum score 580 paper-based; 92 iBT), IELTS, Michigan English Language Assessment Battery, CanTEST, CAEL.

**Oregon State University,** College of Agricultural Sciences, Program in Botany and Plant Pathology, Corvallis, OR 97331. Offers applied systematics (MS); ecology (MS, PhD); genetics (MS, PhD); genomics and computational biology (MS, PhD); molecular and cellular biology (MS, PhD); mycology (MS, PhD); plant pathology (MS, PhD); plant physiology (MS, PhD). *Entrance requirements:* For master's and doctorate, GRE.

**University of Manitoba,** Faculty of Graduate Studies, Faculty of Agricultural and Food Sciences, Department of Plant Science, Winnipeg, MB R3T 2N2, Canada. Offers agronomy and plant protection (M Sc, PhD); horticulture (M Sc, PhD); plant breeding and genetics (M Sc, PhD); plant physiology-biochemistry (M Sc, PhD). *Degree requirements:* For master's, thesis; for doctorate, one foreign language, thesis/dissertation.

**University of Massachusetts Amherst,** Graduate School, Interdisciplinary Programs, Program in Plant Biology, Amherst, MA 01003. Offers biochemistry and metabolism (MS, PhD); cell biology and physiology (MS, PhD); environmental, ecological and integrative biology (MS, PhD); genetics and evolution (MS, PhD). *Degree requirements:* For master's, thesis; for doctorate, 2 foreign languages, comprehensive exam, thesis/dissertation. *Entrance requirements:* For master's and doctorate, GRE General Test. Additional exam requirements/recommendations for international students: required—TOEFL (minimum score 550 paper-based; 80 iBT), IELTS (minimum score 6.5). Electronic applications accepted.

**The University of Tennessee,** Graduate School, College of Arts and Sciences, Program in Life Sciences, Knoxville, TN 37996. Offers genome science and technology (MS, PhD); plant physiology and genetics (MS, PhD). *Degree requirements:* For doctorate, one foreign language, thesis/dissertation. *Entrance requirements:* For master's and doctorate, GRE General Test, minimum GPA of 2.7. Additional exam requirements/recommendations for international students: required—TOEFL. Electronic applications accepted.

**Virginia Polytechnic Institute and State University,** Graduate School, College of Agriculture and Life Sciences, Blacksburg, VA 24061. Offers agricultural and applied economics (MS, PhD); agricultural and life sciences (MS); agriculture, leadership, and community education (MS, PhD); animal and poultry science (MS, PhD); biochemistry (MS, PhD); crop and soil environmental sciences (MS, PhD); dairy science (MS, PhD); entomology (MS, PhD); food science and technology (MS, PhD); horticulture (PhD); human nutrition, foods and exercise (MS, PhD); plant pathology, physiology, and weed science (MS, PhD). *Faculty:* 246 full-time (83 women). *Students:* 364 full-time (213 women), 106 part-time (68 women); includes 79 minority (29 Black or African American, non-Hispanic/Latino; 1 American Indian or Alaska Native, non-Hispanic/Latino; 13 Asian, non-Hispanic/Latino; 16 Hispanic/Latino; 20 Two or more races, non-Hispanic/Latino; 106 international. Average age 28. 314 applicants, 57% accepted, 130 enrolled. In 2019, 92 master's, 59 doctorates awarded. *Degree requirements:* For master's, comprehensive exam (for some programs), thesis (for some programs); for doctorate, comprehensive exam (for some programs), thesis/dissertation (for some programs). *Entrance requirements:* For master's and doctorate, GRE/GMAT. Additional exam requirements/recommendations for international students: required—TOEFL (minimum score 90 iBT). *Application deadline:* For fall admission, 8/1 for domestic students, 4/1 for international students; for spring admission, 1/1 for domestic students, 9/1 for international students. Applications are processed on a rolling basis. Application fee: $75. Electronic applications accepted. *Expenses:* Tuition, state resident: full-time $13,700; part-time $761.25 per credit hour. Tuition, nonresident: full-time $27,614; part-time $1534 per credit hour. *Required fees:* $886.50 per term. Tuition and fees vary according to campus/location and program. *Financial support:* In 2019–20, 248 research assistantships with full tuition reimbursements (averaging $20,360 per year), 127 teaching assistantships with full tuition reimbursements (averaging $18,183 per year) were awarded; fellowships, scholarships/grants, and unspecified assistantships also available. Financial award application deadline: 3/1; financial award applicants required to submit FAFSA. *Unit head:* Dr. Alan L. Grant, Dean, 540-231-4152, Fax: 540-231-4163, E-mail: algrant@vt.edu. *Application contact:* Crystal Tawney, Administrative Assistant, 540-231-4152, Fax: 540-231-4163, E-mail: cdtawney@vt.edu. Website: http://www.cals.vt.edu/

# Section 6
# Cell, Molecular, and Structural Biology

This section contains a directory of institutions offering graduate work in cell, molecular, and structural biology, followed by in-depth entries submitted by institutions that chose to prepare detailed program descriptions. Additional information about programs listed in the directory but not augmented by an in-depth entry may be obtained by writing directly to the dean of a graduate school or chair of a department at the address given in the directory.

For programs offering related work, see also in this book *Anatomy; Biochemistry; Biological and Biomedical Sciences; Biophysics; Botany and Plant Biology; Genetics, Developmental Biology, and Reproductive Biology; Microbiological Sciences; Pathology and Pathobiology; Pharmacology and Toxicology; Pharmacy and Pharmaceutical Sciences; Physiology;* and *Veterinary Medicine and Sciences.* In the other guides in this series:

**Graduate Programs in the Physical Sciences, Mathematics, Agricultural Sciences, the Environment & Natural Resources**
See *Chemistry*
**Graduate Programs in Engineering & Applied Sciences**
See *Agricultural Engineering and Bioengineering* and *Biomedical Engineering and Biotechnology*

## CONTENTS

### Program Directories

# Cancer Biology/Oncology

**Augusta University,** Program in Biochemistry and Cancer Biology, Augusta, GA 30912. Offers PhD. *Degree requirements:* For doctorate, comprehensive exam, thesis/dissertation. *Entrance requirements:* For doctorate, GRE General Test. Additional exam requirements/recommendations for international students: required—TOEFL (minimum score 550 paper-based; 79 iBT). Electronic applications accepted.

**Baylor College of Medicine,** Graduate School of Biomedical Sciences, Program in Translational Biology and Molecular Medicine, Houston, TX 77030-3498. Offers PhD. *Degree requirements:* For doctorate, thesis/dissertation, public defense. *Entrance requirements:* For doctorate, GRE, minimum GPA of 3.0. Additional exam requirements/recommendations for international students: required—TOEFL. Electronic applications accepted.

**Case Western Reserve University,** School of Medicine and School of Graduate Studies, Graduate Programs in Medicine, Cancer Biology Training Program, Cleveland, OH 44106. Offers PhD, MD/PhD. *Degree requirements:* For doctorate, comprehensive exam, thesis/dissertation. *Entrance requirements:* For doctorate, GRE. Additional exam requirements/recommendations for international students: required—TOEFL (minimum score 550 paper-based).

**Duke University,** Graduate School, University Program in Molecular Cancer Biology, Durham, NC 27710. Offers PhD. *Degree requirements:* For doctorate, thesis/dissertation. *Entrance requirements:* For doctorate, GRE General Test, GRE Subject Test in biology or biochemistry, cell and molecular biology (recommended). Additional exam requirements/recommendations for international students: required—TOEFL (minimum score 577 paper-based; 90 iBT) or IELTS (minimum score 7). Electronic applications accepted.

**Emory University,** Laney Graduate School, Division of Biological and Biomedical Sciences, Program in Cancer Biology, Atlanta, GA 30322. Offers PhD. *Degree requirements:* For doctorate, comprehensive exam, thesis/dissertation. *Entrance requirements:* For doctorate, GRE General Test, minimum GPA of 3.0 in science course work (recommended). Additional exam requirements/recommendations for international students: required—TOEFL. Electronic applications accepted. *Expenses:* Contact institution.

**Gerstner Sloan Kettering Graduate School of Biomedical Sciences,** Program in Cancer Biology, New York, NY 10021. Offers PhD. *Degree requirements:* For doctorate, comprehensive exam, thesis/dissertation. *Entrance requirements:* For doctorate, transcripts, 3 letters of recommendation, GRE optional. Additional exam requirements/recommendations for international students: required—TOEFL. Electronic applications accepted.

**Grand Valley State University,** College of Health Professions, Medical Dosimetry Program, Allendale, MI 49401-9403. Offers MS. *Program availability:* Part-time. *Students:* 17 full-time (10 women); includes 1 minority (Black or African American, non-Hispanic/Latino). Average age 29. 20 applicants, 90% accepted, 17 enrolled. In 2019, 14 master's awarded. *Degree requirements:* For master's, thesis optional, project or thesis. *Entrance requirements:* For master's, minimum GPA of 3.0, resume, personal statement, 2 letters of recommendation, 16 hours of volunteer or paid health care experience or 2-3 hours of job shadow. Additional exam requirements/recommendations for international students: required—TOEFL (minimum iBT score of 80), IELTS (6.5), or Michigan English Language Assessment Battery (77). *Application deadline:* For fall admission, 3/1 for domestic students. Application fee: $30. Electronic applications accepted. *Expenses:* $702 per credit hour, 37 credit hours. *Financial support:* In 2019–20, 2 students received support, including 2 fellowships. *Unit head:* Kristen Vu, Director, 616-331-5753, Fax: 616-331-5600, E-mail: vukr@gvsu.edu. *Application contact:* Darlene Zwart, Student Services Coordinator, 616-331-3958, E-mail: zwartda@gvsu.edu.
Website: http://www.gvsu.edu/grad/dosimetry/

**Irell & Manella Graduate School of Biological Sciences,** Graduate Program, Duarte, CA 91010. Offers brain metastatic cancer (PhD); cancer and stem cell metabolism (PhD); cancer biology (PhD); cancer biology and developmental therapeutics (PhD); cell biology (PhD); chemical biology (PhD); chromosomal break repair (PhD); diabetes and pancreatic progenitor cell biology (PhD); DNA repair and cancer biology (PhD); germline epigenetic remodeling and endocrine disruptors (PhD); hematology and hematopoietic cell transplantation (PhD); hematology and immunology (PhD); inflammation and cancer (PhD); micrornas and gene regulation in cardiovascular disease (PhD); mixed chimerism for reversal of autoimmunity (PhD); molecular and cellular biology (PhD); molecular biology and genetics (PhD); nanoparticle mediated twist1 silencing in metastatic cancer (PhD); neuro-oncology and stem cell biology (PhD); neuroscience (PhD); RNA directed therapies for HIV-1 (PhD); small RNA-induced transcriptional gene activation (PhD); stem cell regulation by the microenvironment (PhD); translational oncology and pharmaceutical sciences (PhD); tumor biology (PhD). *Degree requirements:* For doctorate, comprehensive exam, thesis/dissertation, qualifying exams, two advanced courses. *Entrance requirements:* For doctorate, GRE General Test; GRE Subject Test (recommended), 2 years of course work in chemistry (general and organic); 1 year of course work each in biochemistry, general biology, and general physics; 2 semesters of course work in mathematics; significant research laboratory experience. Additional exam requirements/recommendations for international students: required—TOEFL. Electronic applications accepted.

**McMaster University,** Faculty of Health Sciences and School of Graduate Studies, Program in Medical Sciences, Genetics and Cancer Area, Hamilton, ON L8S 4M2, Canada. Offers M Sc, PhD, MD/PhD. *Degree requirements:* For master's, thesis; for doctorate, comprehensive exam, thesis/dissertation. *Entrance requirements:* For master's, honors B Sc, B+ average in related field; for doctorate, M Sc, minimum B+ average, students with proven research experience and an A average may be admitted with a B Sc degree. Additional exam requirements/recommendations for international students: required—TOEFL (minimum score 580 paper-based; 92 iBT).

**Medical University of South Carolina,** College of Graduate Studies, Program in Molecular and Cellular Biology and Pathobiology, Charleston, SC 29425. Offers cancer biology (PhD); cardiovascular biology (PhD); cardiovascular imaging (PhD); cell regulation (PhD); craniofacial biology (PhD); genetics and development (PhD); marine biomedicine (PhD); DMD/PhD; MD/PhD. *Degree requirements:* For doctorate, thesis/dissertation, oral and written exams. *Entrance requirements:* For doctorate, GRE General Test, interview, minimum GPA of 3.0. Additional exam requirements/recommendations for international students: required—TOEFL (minimum score 600 paper-based; 100 iBT). Electronic applications accepted.

**Meharry Medical College,** School of Graduate Studies, Program in Biomedical Sciences, Biochemistry and Cancer Biology Emphasis, Nashville, TN 37208-9989. Offers PhD, MD/PhD. *Degree requirements:* For doctorate, comprehensive exam, thesis/dissertation. *Entrance requirements:* For doctorate, GRE. *Application deadline:* For fall admission, 6/1 for domestic students. Applications are processed on a rolling basis. Application fee: $65. *Financial support:* Fellowships available. Financial award application deadline: 4/15. *Unit head:* Dr. Armandla Ramesh, Associate Professor, 615-327-6486, E-mail: aramesh@mmc.edu. *Application contact:* Dr. Armandla Ramesh, Associate Professor, 615-327-6486, E-mail: aramesh@mmc.edu.
Website: https://home.mmc.edu/school-of-graduate-studies-research/biochemistry-cancer-biology/

**Memorial University of Newfoundland,** Faculty of Medicine and School of Graduate Studies, Graduate Programs in Medicine, Division of Biomedical Sciences, St. John's, NL A1C 5S7, Canada. Offers cancer (M Sc, PhD); cardiovascular (M Sc, PhD); immunology (M Sc, PhD); neuroscience (M Sc, PhD). *Program availability:* Part-time. *Degree requirements:* For master's, thesis; for doctorate, comprehensive exam, thesis/dissertation, oral defense of thesis. *Entrance requirements:* For master's, MD or B Sc; for doctorate, MD or M Sc. Additional exam requirements/recommendations for international students: required—TOEFL.

**New York University,** Graduate School of Arts and Science, Department of Biology, New York, NY 10012-1019. Offers biology (PhD); biomedical journalism (MS); cancer and molecular biology (PhD); computational biology (PhD); computers in biological research (MS); developmental genetics (PhD); general biology (MS); immunology and microbiology (PhD); molecular genetics (PhD); neurobiology (PhD); oral biology (MS); plant biology (PhD); recombinant DNA technology (MS); MS/MBA. *Program availability:* Part-time. Terminal master's awarded for partial completion of doctoral program. *Degree requirements:* For master's, thesis or alternative, qualifying paper; for doctorate, comprehensive exam, thesis/dissertation. *Entrance requirements:* For master's and doctorate, GRE General Test. Additional exam requirements/recommendations for international students: required—TOEFL, IELTS.

**Oregon Health & Science University,** School of Medicine, Graduate Programs in Medicine, Program in Molecular and Cellular Biosciences, Cancer Biology Program, Portland, OR 97239-3098. Offers PhD. *Degree requirements:* For doctorate, comprehensive exam, thesis/dissertation, qualifying exam. *Entrance requirements:* For doctorate, GRE General Test (minimum scores: 158 Verbal/148 Quantitative/4.5 Analytical). Electronic applications accepted.

**Purdue University,** Graduate School, PULSe - Purdue University Life Sciences Program, West Lafayette, IN 47907. Offers biomolecular structure and biophysics (PhD); biotechnology (PhD); chemical biology (PhD); chromatin and regulation of gene expression (PhD); integrative neuroscience (PhD); integrative plant sciences (PhD); membrane biology (PhD); microbiology (PhD); molecular evolutionary and cancer biology (PhD); molecular evolutionary genetics (PhD); molecular virology (PhD). *Students:* 37 full-time (23 women); includes 7 minority (1 Black or African American, non-Hispanic/Latino; 2 Asian, non-Hispanic/Latino; 4 Hispanic/Latino), 22 international. Average age 25. 162 applicants, 36% accepted, 19 enrolled. *Entrance requirements:* For doctorate, GRE, minimum undergraduate GPA of 3.0. Additional exam requirements/recommendations for international students: required—TOEFL (minimum score 550 paper-based; 77 iBT). *Application deadline:* For fall admission, 1/15 priority date for domestic and international students. Applications are processed on a rolling basis. Application fee: $60 ($75 for international students). Electronic applications accepted. *Financial support:* In 2019–20, research assistantships with tuition reimbursements (averaging $22,500 per year), teaching assistantships with tuition reimbursements (averaging $22,500 per year) were awarded. *Application contact:* Lindsey Springer, Graduate Contact for Admissions, 765-496-9667, E-mail: lbcampbe@purdue.edu.
Website: http://www.gradschool.purdue.edu/pulse

**Rutgers University - New Brunswick,** Graduate School-New Brunswick, Program in Endocrinology and Animal Biosciences, Piscataway, NJ 08854-8097. Offers MS, PhD. Terminal master's awarded for partial completion of doctoral program. *Degree requirements:* For master's, thesis; for doctorate, comprehensive exam, thesis/dissertation. *Entrance requirements:* For master's and doctorate, GRE General Test. Additional exam requirements/recommendations for international students: required—TOEFL. Electronic applications accepted.

**Saint Francis University,** Cancer Care Program, Loretto, PA 15940-0600. Offers MS. *Faculty:* 10 full-time (5 women). *Students:* 10 full-time (2 women), 1 (woman) part-time. Average age 23. In 2019, 3 master's awarded. Terminal master's awarded for partial completion of doctoral program. *Degree requirements:* For master's, thesis. *Application deadline:* Applications are processed on a rolling basis. Application fee: $35. Electronic applications accepted. *Expenses:* 46 credits. 775 a credit. *Financial support:* Unspecified assistantships available. Financial award applicants required to submit FAFSA. *Unit head:* Dr. Stephen LoRusso, Coordinator, 814-472-3853, E-mail: slorusso@francis.edu. *Application contact:* Dr. Peter Raymond Skoner.
Website: https://www.francis.edu/master-of-cancer-care/

**Thomas Jefferson University,** Jefferson College of Life Sciences, PhD Program in Genetics, Genomics and Cancer Biology, Philadelphia, PA 19107. Offers PhD. *Degree requirements:* For doctorate, comprehensive exam, thesis/dissertation. *Entrance requirements:* For doctorate, GRE General Test, minimum GPA of 3.2. Additional exam requirements/recommendations for international students: required—TOEFL, IELTS (minimum score 7). Electronic applications accepted.

**Tufts University,** Graduate School of Biomedical Sciences, Cell, Molecular, and Developmental Biology Program, Medford, MA 02155. Offers cancer biology (PhD); developmental and regenerative biology (PhD); molecular and cellular medicine (PhD); structural and chemical biology (PhD). *Faculty:* 84 full-time (30 women). *Students:* 32 full-time (15 women); includes 10 minority (2 Black or African American, non-Hispanic/Latino; 4 Asian, non-Hispanic/Latino; 4 Hispanic/Latino), 4 international. Average age 28. 168 applicants, 5% accepted, 3 enrolled. In 2019, 5 doctorates awarded. Terminal master's awarded for partial completion of doctoral program. *Degree requirements:* For doctorate, comprehensive exam, thesis/dissertation. *Entrance requirements:* For doctorate, 3 letters of reference, resume, personal statement. *Application deadline:* For fall admission, 12/1 priority date for domestic and international students. Application fee: $90. Electronic applications accepted. *Expenses: Tuition:* Part-time $1799 per credit hour. Full-time tuition and fees vary according to degree level, program and student level. Part-time tuition and fees vary according to course load. *Financial support:* In 2019–20, 100 students received support, including 3 research assistantships with full tuition reimbursements available (averaging $40,000 per year); fellowships, traineeships, and health care benefits also available. Financial award application deadline: 12/1. *Unit head:* Dr. Brent Cochran, Program Director, 617-636-0442. *Application contact:* Jeff Miller, Admissions Coordinator, 617-636-6767, Fax: 617-636-

0375, E-mail: gsbs-admissions@tufts.edu.
Website: https://gsbs.tufts.edu/academics/CMDB

**University at Buffalo, the State University of New York,** Graduate School, Graduate Programs in Cancer Research and Biomedical Sciences at Roswell Park Cancer Institute, Interdisciplinary Master of Science Program at Roswell Park Cancer Institute, Buffalo, NY 14260. Offers MS. *Program availability:* Part-time. *Degree requirements:* For master's, thesis, oral defense of thesis based on research project. *Entrance requirements:* For master's, GRE General Test. Additional exam requirements/recommendations for international students: required—TOEFL (minimum score 79 iBT). Electronic applications accepted. *Expenses: Tuition, area resident:* Full-time $11,310; part-time $471 per credit hour. Tuition, state resident: full-time $11,310; part-time $471 per credit hour. Tuition, nonresident: full-time $23,100; part-time $963 per credit hour. *International tuition:* $23,100 full-time. *Required fees:* $2820.

**The University of Alabama at Birmingham,** Joint Health Sciences, Cancer Biology Theme, Birmingham, AL 35294. Offers PhD. *Students:* Average age 27. 81 applicants, 5% accepted, 3 enrolled. In 2019, 6 doctorates awarded. *Degree requirements:* For doctorate, comprehensive exam, thesis/dissertation. *Entrance requirements:* For doctorate, personal statement, resume or curriculum vitae, letters of recommendation, research experience, interview. Additional exam requirements/recommendations for international students: required—TOEFL (minimum score 80 iBT), IELTS (minimum score 6.5). *Application deadline:* For fall admission, 12/31 for domestic and international students. Applications are processed on a rolling basis. Electronic applications accepted. *Financial support:* In 2019–20, fellowships with full tuition reimbursements (averaging $30,000 per year), research assistantships with full tuition reimbursements (averaging $31,000 per year) were awarded; health care benefits also available. *Unit head:* Dr. Lalita Shevde-Samant, Theme Director, 205-975-6261, E-mail: lsamant@uab.edu. *Application contact:* Alyssa Zasada, Admissions Manager for Graduate Biomedical Sciences, 205-934-3857, E-mail: grad-gbs@uab.edu.
Website: http://www.uab.edu/gbs/home/themes/cancer

**University of Alberta,** Faculty of Medicine and Dentistry and Faculty of Graduate Studies and Research, Graduate Programs in Medicine, Department of Oncology, Edmonton, AB T6G 2E1, Canada. Offers M Sc, PhD. Terminal master's awarded for partial completion of doctoral program. *Degree requirements:* For master's, thesis; for doctorate, thesis/dissertation. *Entrance requirements:* For master's and doctorate, minimum GPA of 7.0 on a 9.0 scale, B SC. Additional exam requirements/recommendations for international students: required—TOEFL (minimum score 600 paper-based). Electronic applications accepted.

**The University of Arizona,** Graduate Interdisciplinary Programs, Graduate Interdisciplinary Program in Cancer Biology, Tucson, AZ 85721. Offers PhD. *Degree requirements:* For doctorate, comprehensive exam, thesis/dissertation. *Entrance requirements:* For doctorate, GRE General Test, 3 letters of recommendation. Additional exam requirements/recommendations for international students: required—TOEFL (minimum score 550 paper-based; 79 iBT). Electronic applications accepted.

**University of Calgary,** Cumming School of Medicine and Faculty of Graduate Studies, Program in Medical Science, Calgary, AB T2N 1N4, Canada. Offers cancer biology (M Sc, PhD); critical care medicine (M Sc, PhD); joint injury and arthritis (M Sc, PhD); molecular and medical genetics (M Sc, PhD); mountain medicine and high altitude physiology (M Sc, PhD); pathologists' assistant (M Sc, PhD). *Degree requirements:* For master's, thesis; for doctorate, thesis/dissertation, candidacy exam. *Entrance requirements:* For master's, minimum undergraduate GPA of 3.2; for doctorate, minimum graduate GPA of 3.2. Additional exam requirements/recommendations for international students: required—TOEFL (minimum score 600 paper-based). Electronic applications accepted.

**University of Chicago,** Division of the Biological Sciences, Committee on Cancer Biology, Chicago, IL 60637. Offers PhD. *Degree requirements:* For doctorate, thesis/dissertation, ethics class, 2 teaching assistantships, preliminary exam. *Entrance requirements:* For doctorate, GRE General Test, transcripts, statement of purpose, 3 letters of recommendation. Additional exam requirements/recommendations for international students: required—TOEFL (minimum score 600 paper-based; 104 iBT), IELTS (minimum score 7). Electronic applications accepted.

**University of Cincinnati,** Graduate School, College of Medicine, Graduate Programs in Biomedical Sciences, Cancer and Cell Biology Graduate Program, Cincinnati, OH 45267. Offers PhD. *Degree requirements:* For doctorate, thesis/dissertation, qualifying exam. *Entrance requirements:* For doctorate, GRE or MCAT, baccalaureate degree; strong background in biology, chemistry, and/or physics and mathematics; minimum overall GPA of 3.0; curriculum vitae or resume; transcripts; essay; letters of recommendation. Additional exam requirements/recommendations for international students: required—TOEFL (minimum score 600 paper-based; 100 iBT), IELTS (minimum score 7), PTE (minimum score 68). Electronic applications accepted. *Expenses:* Contact institution.

**University of Colorado Denver,** School of Medicine, Program in Cancer Biology, Aurora, CO 80045. Offers PhD. *Degree requirements:* For doctorate, comprehensive exam, thesis/dissertation, 3 laboratory rotations. *Entrance requirements:* For doctorate, GRE General Test, interview, minimum undergraduate GPA of 3.0. Additional exam requirements/recommendations for international students: required—TOEFL (minimum score 550 paper-based; 80 iBT). Tuition and fees vary according to course load, program and reciprocity agreements.

**University of Delaware,** College of Arts and Sciences, Department of Biological Sciences, Newark, DE 19716. Offers biotechnology (MS); cancer biology (MS, PhD); cell and extracellular matrix biology (MS, PhD); cell and systems physiology (MS, PhD); developmental biology (MS, PhD); ecology and evolution (MS, PhD); microbiology (MS, PhD); molecular biology and genetics (MS, PhD). Terminal master's awarded for partial completion of doctoral program. *Degree requirements:* For master's, thesis, preliminary exam; for doctorate, comprehensive exam, thesis/dissertation, preliminary exam. *Entrance requirements:* For master's and doctorate, GRE General Test. Additional exam requirements/recommendations for international students: required—TOEFL (minimum score 600 paper-based); recommended—TWE. Electronic applications accepted.

**The University of Kansas,** University of Kansas Medical Center, School of Medicine, Department of Cancer Biology, Kansas City, KS 66045. Offers MS, PhD. *Faculty:* 11. *Students:* 11 full-time (7 women), 3 international. Average age 28. In 2019, 1 master's awarded. *Degree requirements:* For master's, thesis; for doctorate, comprehensive exam, thesis/dissertation. *Entrance requirements:* For master's and doctorate, GRE. Additional exam requirements/recommendations for international students: required—TOEFL or IELTS. *Application deadline:* For fall admission, 12/1 priority date for domestic and international students. Applications are processed on a rolling basis. Application fee: $60. Electronic applications accepted. *Expenses: Tuition, state resident:* full-time $9989. Tuition, nonresident: full-time $23,950. *International tuition:* $23,950 full-time. *Required fees:* $984; $81.99 per credit hour. Tuition and fees vary according to course load, campus/location and program. *Financial support:* Fellowships with full tuition reimbursements and research assistantships with full tuition reimbursements available. Financial award application deadline: 3/1; financial award applicants required to submit FAFSA. *Unit head:* Dr. Shrikant Anant, Professor and Chair, E-mail: cancerbiology@

kumc.edu. *Application contact:* Dr. Joan Lewis-Wambi, Associate Professor and Graduate Program Director, 913-588 Ext. 4739, E-mail: jlewis-wambi@kumc.edu.
Website: http://www.kumc.edu/school-of-medicine/cancer-biology.html

**The University of Manchester,** School of Biological Sciences, Manchester, United Kingdom. Offers adaptive organismal biology (M Phil, PhD); animal biology (M Phil, PhD); biochemistry (M Phil, PhD); bioinformatics (M Phil, PhD); biomolecular sciences (M Phil, PhD); biotechnology (M Phil, PhD); cell biology (M Phil, PhD); cell matrix research (M Phil, PhD); channels and transporters (M Phil, PhD); developmental biology (M Phil, PhD); environmental biology (M Phil, PhD); evolutionary biology (M Phil, PhD); gene expression (M Phil, PhD); genetics (M Phil, PhD); history of science, technology and medicine (M Phil, PhD); immunology (M Phil, PhD); integrative neurobiology and behavior (M Phil, PhD); membrane trafficking (M Phil, PhD); microbiology (M Phil, PhD); molecular and cellular neuroscience (M Phil, PhD); molecular biology (M Phil, PhD); molecular cancer studies (M Phil, PhD); neuroscience (M Phil, PhD); ophthalmology (M Phil, PhD); optometry (M Phil, PhD); organelle function (M Phil, PhD); pharmacology (M Phil, PhD); physiology (M Phil, PhD); plant sciences (M Phil, PhD); stem cell research (M Phil, PhD); structural biology (M Phil, PhD); systems neuroscience (M Phil, PhD); toxicology (M Phil, PhD).

**The University of Manchester,** School of Dentistry, Manchester, United Kingdom. Offers basic dental sciences (cancer studies) (M Phil, PhD); basic dental sciences (molecular genetics) (M Phil, PhD); basic dental sciences (stem cell biology) (M Phil, PhD); biomaterials sciences and dental technology (M Phil, PhD); dental public health/community dentistry (M Phil, PhD); dental science (clinical) (PhD); endodontology (M Phil, PhD); fixed and removable prosthodontics (M Phil, PhD); operative dentistry (M Phil, PhD); oral and maxillofacial surgery (M Phil, PhD); oral radiology (M Phil, PhD); orthodontics (M Phil, PhD); restorative dentistry (M Phil, PhD).

**University of Manitoba,** Faculty of Graduate Studies, College of Nursing, Winnipeg, MB R3T 2N2, Canada. Offers cancer nursing (MN); nursing (MN). *Degree requirements:* For master's, thesis.

**University of Maryland, Baltimore,** Graduate School, Graduate Program in Life Sciences, Program in Molecular Medicine, Baltimore, MD 21201. Offers applied pharmacology and toxicology (PhD); cancer biology (PhD); genome biology (PhD); molecular and cellular physiology (PhD); MD/PhD. *Degree requirements:* For doctorate, comprehensive exam, thesis/dissertation. *Entrance requirements:* For doctorate, GRE, minimum GPA of 3.0, curriculum vitae, essay, 3 letters of recommendation. Additional exam requirements/recommendations for international students: required—TOEFL (minimum score 80 iBT); recommended—IELTS (minimum score 7). Electronic applications accepted.

**University of Massachusetts Medical School,** Graduate School of Biomedical Sciences, Worcester, MA 01655. Offers biomedical sciences (PhD), including biochemistry and molecular pharmacology, bioinformatics and computational biology, cancer biology, immunology and microbiology, interdisciplinary, neuroscience, translational science; biomedical sciences (millennium program) (PhD); clinical and population health research (PhD); clinical investigation (MS). *Faculty:* 1,258 full-time (525 women), 372 part-time/adjunct (238 women). *Students:* 344 full-time (198 women), 1 (woman) part-time; includes 73 minority (12 Black or African American, non-Hispanic/Latino; 1 American Indian or Alaska Native, non-Hispanic/Latino; 45 Asian, non-Hispanic/Latino; 15 Hispanic/Latino), 120 international. Average age 29. 581 applicants, 23% accepted, 56 enrolled. In 2019, 6 master's, 49 doctorates awarded. Terminal master's awarded for partial completion of doctoral program. *Degree requirements:* For master's, comprehensive exam, thesis; for doctorate, comprehensive exam, thesis/dissertation. *Entrance requirements:* For master's, MD, PhD, DVM, or PharmD; for doctorate, bachelor's degree. Additional exam requirements/recommendations for international students: required—TOEFL, IELTS, TOEFL (minimum score 100 IBT) or IELTS (minimum score 7.0). *Application deadline:* For fall admission, 12/1 for domestic and international students. Applications are processed on a rolling basis. Application fee: $80. Electronic applications accepted. Application fee is waived when completed online. *Expenses:* Contact institution. *Financial support:* In 2019–20, 22 fellowships with full tuition reimbursements (averaging $33,061 per year), 322 research assistantships with full tuition reimbursements (averaging $32,850 per year) were awarded; institutionally sponsored loans and scholarships/grants also available. Financial award application deadline: 5/15. *Unit head:* Dr. Mary Ellen Lane, Dean, 508-856-4018, E-mail: maryellen.lane@umassmed.edu. *Application contact:* Dr. Kendall Knight, Assistant Vice Provost for Admissions, 508-856-5628, Fax: 508-856-3659, E-mail: kendall.knight@umassmed.edu.
Website: http://www.umassmed.edu/gsbs/

**University of Miami,** Graduate School, Miller School of Medicine, Program in Cancer Biology, Coral Gables, FL 33124. Offers PhD, MD/PhD.
Website: http://www.biomed.miami.edu/graduate-programs/cancer-biology

**University of Michigan,** Rackham Graduate School, Program in Biomedical Sciences (PIBS), Doctoral Program in Cancer Biology, Ann Arbor, MI 48109. Offers PhD. *Degree requirements:* For doctorate, thesis/dissertation, preliminary examination, oral defense of dissertation. *Entrance requirements:* For doctorate, three letters of recommendation, research experience, personal and research statements. Additional exam requirements/recommendations for international students: required—TOEFL (minimum score 84 iBT). Electronic applications accepted. *Expenses:* Contact institution.

**University of Michigan,** Rackham Graduate School, Program in Chemical Biology, Ann Arbor, MI 48109. Offers cancer chemical biology (MS); chemical biology (PhD). *Program availability:* Part-time. *Degree requirements:* For doctorate, thesis/dissertation. *Entrance requirements:* Additional exam requirements/recommendations for international students: required—TOEFL (minimum score 600 paper-based; 102 iBT). Electronic applications accepted.

**University of Minnesota, Twin Cities Campus,** Graduate School, PhD Program in Microbiology, Immunology and Cancer Biology, Minneapolis, MN 55455-0213. Offers PhD. *Degree requirements:* For doctorate, thesis/dissertation. *Entrance requirements:* For doctorate, GRE General Test. Additional exam requirements/recommendations for international students: required—TOEFL (minimum score 600 paper-based). Electronic applications accepted.

**University of Nebraska Medical Center,** Interdisciplinary Graduate Program in Biomedical Sciences, Cancer Research Doctoral Program, Omaha, NE 68198. Offers PhD. Terminal master's awarded for partial completion of doctoral program. *Degree requirements:* For doctorate, comprehensive exam, thesis/dissertation. *Entrance requirements:* For doctorate, 3 letters of reference; course work in chemistry, biology, physics and mathematics. Additional exam requirements/recommendations for international students: required—TOEFL (minimum score 550 paper-based; 95 iBT). Electronic applications accepted. Application fee is waived when completed online.

**University of North Texas Health Science Center at Fort Worth,** Graduate School of Biomedical Sciences, Fort Worth, TX 76107-2699. Offers biochemistry and cancer biology (MS, PhD); biotechnology (MS); cell biology, immunology and microbiology (MS, PhD); clinical research management (MS); forensic genetics (MS); genetics (MS, PhD); integrative physiology (MS, PhD); medical sciences (MS); pharmaceutical sciences and

pharmacotherapy (MS, PhD); pharmacology and neuroscience (MS, PhD); structural anatomy and rehabilitation sciences (MS, PhD); DO/MS; DO/PhD. Terminal master's awarded for partial completion of doctoral program. *Degree requirements:* For master's, thesis; for doctorate, thesis/dissertation. *Entrance requirements:* For master's and doctorate, GRE General Test. Additional exam requirements/recommendations for international students: required—TOEFL. *Expenses:* Contact institution.

**University of Pennsylvania,** Perelman School of Medicine, Biomedical Graduate Studies, Graduate Group in Cell and Molecular Biology, Philadelphia, PA 19104. Offers cancer biology (PhD); cell biology, physiology, and metabolism (PhD); developmental stem cell regenerative biology (PhD); gene therapy and vaccines (PhD); genetics and gene regulation (PhD); microbiology, virology, and parasitology (PhD); MD/PhD; VMD/PhD. *Faculty:* 400 full-time (118 women). *Students:* 378 full-time (221 women); includes 134 minority (6 Black or African American, non-Hispanic/Latino; 56 Asian, non-Hispanic/Latino; 58 Hispanic/Latino; 2 Native Hawaiian or other Pacific Islander, non-Hispanic/Latino; 12 Two or more races, non-Hispanic/Latino), 52 international. 851 applicants, 14% accepted, 59 enrolled. In 2019, 43 doctorates awarded. *Unit head:* Dr. Daniel Kessler, Graduate Group Chair, 215-898-1478. *Application contact:* Meagan Schofer, Associate Director, 215-898-1478.
Website: http://www.med.upenn.edu/camb/

**University of Regina,** Faculty of Graduate Studies and Research, Faculty of Science, Department of Chemistry and Biochemistry, Regina, SK S4S 0A2, Canada. Offers biophysics of biological interfaces (M Sc, PhD); computational chemistry (M Sc, PhD); environmental analytical chemistry (M Sc, PhD); enzymology/chemical biology (M Sc, PhD); inorganic/organometallic chemistry (M Sc, PhD); signal transduction and mechanisms of cancer cell regulation (M Sc, PhD); supramolecular organic photochemistry and photophysics (M Sc, PhD); synthetic organic chemistry (M Sc, PhD). *Program availability:* Part-time. *Faculty:* 12 full-time (2 women), 6 part-time/adjunct (0 women). *Students:* 19 full-time (9 women), 1 (woman) part-time. Average age 30. 18 applicants, 17% accepted. In 2019, 3 master's, 1 doctorate awarded. *Degree requirements:* For master's, thesis; for doctorate, comprehensive exam, thesis/dissertation. *Entrance requirements:* For master's, 4 years Bachelor degree in Chemistry or related program; for doctorate, completion of Master's in Chemistry. Additional exam requirements/recommendations for international students: required—TOEFL (minimum score 580 paper-based; 80 iBT), IELTS (minimum score 6.5), PTE (minimum score 59), other options are CAEL, MELAB, Cantest and U of R ESL. *Application deadline:* Applications are processed on a rolling basis. Application fee: $100. Electronic applications accepted. *Expenses: Tuition:* Full-time $6684 Canadian dollars. *Required fees:* $100 Canadian dollars; $3351.45 Canadian dollars per trimester. $1117.15 Canadian dollars per semester. Tuition and fees vary according to course level, course load, degree level and program. *Financial support:* Fellowships, research assistantships, teaching assistantships, career-related internships or fieldwork, Federal Work-Study, scholarships/grants, unspecified assistantships, and travel award and Graduate Scholarship Base Funds available. Support available to part-time students. Financial award application deadline: 9/30. *Unit head:* Dr. Renata Raina-Fulton, Department Head, 306-585-4012, Fax: 306-337-2409, E-mail: renata.raina@uregina.ca. *Application contact:* Dr. Brian Sterenberg, Graduate Program Coordinator, 306-585-4106, Fax: 306-337-2409, E-mail: brian.sterenberg@uregina.ca.
Website: http://www.uregina.ca/science/chem-biochem/

**University of Southern California,** Keck School of Medicine and Graduate School, Graduate Programs in Medicine, Programs in Biomedical and Biological Sciences (PIBBS), Program in Cancer Biology and Genomics, Los Angeles, CA 90089. Offers PhD. *Faculty:* 43 full-time (10 women). *Students:* 26 full-time (17 women); includes 10 minority (5 Asian, non-Hispanic/Latino; 2 Hispanic/Latino; 2 Native Hawaiian or other Pacific Islander, non-Hispanic/Latino; 1 Two or more races, non-Hispanic/Latino), 9 international. Average age 28. 7 applicants, 100% accepted, 7 enrolled. In 2019, 4 doctorates awarded. *Degree requirements:* For doctorate, comprehensive exam, thesis/dissertation. *Entrance requirements:* For doctorate, GRE, minimum GPA of 3.0. Additional exam requirements/recommendations for international students: required—TOEFL (minimum score 600 paper-based; 100 iBT), IELTS (minimum score 7), PTE. *Application deadline:* For fall admission, 12/1 priority date for domestic and international students. Application fee: $90. Electronic applications accepted. *Financial support:* In 2019–20, 24 students received support, including 6 fellowships with full tuition reimbursements available (averaging $35,000 per year), 20 research assistantships with full tuition reimbursements available (averaging $35,000 per year); institutionally sponsored loans, scholarships/grants, traineeships, health care benefits, and unspecified assistantships also available. Financial award application deadline: 4/15; financial award applicants required to submit CSS PROFILE or FAFSA. *Unit head:* Dr. Josh Neman-Ebrahim, Director, 323-442-1475, Fax: 323-442-1199, E-mail: yebrahim@usc.edu. *Application contact:* Karina Recinos, Student Services Advisor, 323-442-1609, Fax: 323-442-1199, E-mail: karina.recinos@med.usc.edu.
Website: https://keck.usc.edu/pibbs/phd-programs/cancer-biology-and-genomics

**University of South Florida,** College of Arts and Sciences, Department of Cell Biology, Microbiology, and Molecular Biology, Tampa, FL 33620-9951. Offers biology (MS), including cell biology, microbiology and molecular biology; cancer biology (PhD); cancer chemical biology (PhD); cancer immunology and immunotherapy (PhD); cell and molecular biology (PhD); microbiology (MS). *Faculty:* 21 full-time (8 women). *Students:* 85 full-time (50 women), 4 part-time (all women); includes 10 minority (1 Black or African American, non-Hispanic/Latino; 3 Asian, non-Hispanic/Latino; 4 Hispanic/Latino; 2 Two or more races, non-Hispanic/Latino), 35 international. Average age 27. 178 applicants, 15% accepted, 20 enrolled. In 2019, 12 master's, 12 doctorates awarded. *Degree requirements:* For master's, thesis or alternative; for doctorate, comprehensive exam, thesis/dissertation. *Entrance requirements:* For master's and doctorate, GRE General Test, minimum GPA of 3.0, extensive background in biology or chemistry. Additional exam requirements/recommendations for international students: required—TOEFL (minimum score 570 paper-based; 79 iBT) or IELTS (minimum score 6.5). *Application deadline:* For fall admission, 11/30 priority date for domestic and international students; for spring admission, 7/1 priority date for domestic students, 7/1 for international students. Application fee: $30. *Financial support:* In 2019–20, 9 students received support. Career-related internships or fieldwork, health care benefits, and unspecified assistantships available. Financial award application deadline: 4/1. *Unit head:* Dr. James Garey, Professor/Chair, 813-974-7103, Fax: 813-974-1614, E-mail: garey@usf.edu. *Application contact:* Dr. Kenneth Wright, Associate Professor of Cancer Biology, H. Lee Moffitt Cancer Center and Research Institute, 813-745-3918, Fax: 813-974-1614, E-mail: ken.wright@moffitt.org.
Website: http://biology.usf.edu/cmmb/

**The University of Texas Health Science Center at Houston,** MD Anderson UTHealth Graduate School, Houston, TX 77225-0036. Offers biochemistry and cell biology (PhD); biomedical sciences (MS); cancer biology (PhD); genetic counseling (MS); genetics and epigenetics (PhD); immunology (PhD); medical physics (MS, PhD); microbiology and infectious diseases (PhD); neuroscience (PhD); quantitative sciences (PhD); therapeutics and pharmacology (PhD); MD/PhD. Terminal master's awarded for partial completion of doctoral program. *Degree requirements:* For master's, thesis; for doctorate, thesis/dissertation. *Entrance requirements:* For master's and doctorate, GRE General Test. Additional exam requirements/recommendations for international students: required—TOEFL. Electronic applications accepted.

**The University of Texas Southwestern Medical Center,** Southwestern Graduate School of Biomedical Sciences, Division of Basic Science, Program in Cancer Biology, Dallas, TX 75390. Offers PhD. *Degree requirements:* For doctorate, thesis/dissertation, qualifying examination.

**University of the District of Columbia,** College of Arts and Sciences, Program in Cancer Biology, Prevention and Control, Washington, DC 20008-1175. Offers MS.

**The University of Toledo,** College of Graduate Studies, College of Medicine and Life Sciences, Department of Biochemistry and Cancer Biology, Toledo, OH 43606-3390. Offers cancer biology (MSBS, PhD); MD/MSBS; MD/PhD. Terminal master's awarded for partial completion of doctoral program. *Degree requirements:* For master's, thesis, qualifying exam; for doctorate, thesis/dissertation, qualifying exam. *Entrance requirements:* For master's and doctorate, GRE, minimum undergraduate GPA of 3.0, three letters of recommendation, statement of purpose, transcripts from all prior institutions attended; resume. Additional exam requirements/recommendations for international students: required—TOEFL (minimum score 550 paper-based; 80 iBT). Electronic applications accepted.

**University of Utah,** School of Medicine and Graduate School, Graduate Programs in Medicine, Department of Oncological Sciences, Salt Lake City, UT 84112-1107. Offers M Phil, MS, PhD. Terminal master's awarded for partial completion of doctoral program. *Degree requirements:* For master's, thesis (for some programs); for doctorate, thesis/dissertation. *Entrance requirements:* For master's and doctorate, GRE General Test, GRE Subject Test, minimum GPA of 3.0. Additional exam requirements/recommendations for international students: required—TOEFL. *Expenses:* Tuition, state resident: full-time $7085; part-time $272.51 per credit hour. Tuition, nonresident: full-time $24,937; part-time $959.12 per credit hour. *Required fees:* $880.52; $880.52 per semester. Tuition and fees vary according to degree level, program and student level.

**University of Wisconsin–La Crosse,** College of Science and Health, Department of Health Professions, Program in Medical Dosimetry, La Crosse, WI 54601-3742. Offers MS. *Program availability:* Online learning. *Faculty:* 2 part-time/adjunct (both women). *Students:* 51 full-time (29 women), 7 part-time (2 women); includes 12 minority (2 Black or African American, non-Hispanic/Latino; 6 Asian, non-Hispanic/Latino; 2 Hispanic/Latino; 2 Two or more races, non-Hispanic/Latino). Average age 32. 60 applicants, 45% accepted, 26 enrolled. In 2019, 29 master's awarded. *Entrance requirements:* For master's, American Registry of Radiologic Technologists test, Medical Dosimetrist Certification Board Exam. Additional exam requirements/recommendations for international students: required—TOEFL (minimum score 600 paper-based; 100 iBT). *Application deadline:* For fall admission, 12/1 priority date for domestic students, 11/1 priority date for international students. Application fee: $50. Electronic applications accepted. *Expenses:* Contact institution. *Financial support:* Federal Work-Study and scholarships/grants available. Support available to part-time students. Financial award applicants required to submit FAFSA. *Unit head:* Dr. Nishele Lenards, Program Director, 608-785-8470, E-mail: nlenards@uwlax.edu. *Application contact:* Peter Amann, Senior Graduate Student Status Examiner, 608-785-6622, E-mail: pamann@uwlax.edu.
Website: http://www.uwlax.edu/md/

**University of Wisconsin–Madison,** School of Medicine and Public Health, Cancer Biology Graduate Program, Madison, WI 53706. Offers PhD. *Degree requirements:* For doctorate, comprehensive exam, thesis/dissertation. *Entrance requirements:* For doctorate, GRE General Test. Additional exam requirements/recommendations for international students: required—TOEFL (minimum score 580 paper-based; 92 iBT). Electronic applications accepted.

**Université Laval,** Faculty of Medicine, Post-Professional Programs in Medical Studies, Québec, QC G1K 7P4, Canada. Offers anatomy–pathology (DESS); anesthesiology (DESS); cardiology (DESS); care of older people (Diploma); clinical research (DESS); community health (DESS); dermatology (DESS); diagnostic radiology (DESS); emergency medicine (Diploma); family medicine (DESS); general surgery (DESS); geriatrics (DESS); hematology (DESS); internal medicine (DESS); maternal and fetal medicine (Diploma); medical biochemistry (DESS); medical microbiology and infectious diseases (DESS); medical oncology (DESS); nephrology (DESS); neurology (DESS); neurosurgery (DESS); obstetrics and gynecology (DESS); ophthalmology (DESS); orthopedic surgery (DESS); oto-rhino-laryngology (DESS); palliative medicine (Diploma); pediatrics (DESS); plastic surgery (DESS); psychiatry (DESS); pulmonary medicine (DESS); radiology–oncology (DESS); thoracic surgery (DESS); urology (DESS). *Degree requirements:* For other advanced degree, comprehensive exam. *Entrance requirements:* For degree, knowledge of French. Electronic applications accepted.

**Wake Forest University,** School of Medicine and Graduate School of Arts and Sciences, Graduate Programs in Medicine, Department of Cancer Biology, Winston-Salem, NC 27109. Offers PhD, MD/PhD. *Degree requirements:* For doctorate, thesis/dissertation. *Entrance requirements:* For doctorate, GRE General Test. Additional exam requirements/recommendations for international students: required—TOEFL. Electronic applications accepted.

**West Virginia University,** School of Medicine, Morgantown, WV 26506. Offers biochemistry and molecular biology (PhD); biomedical science (MS); cancer cell biology (PhD); cellular and integrative physiology (PhD); exercise physiology (MS, PhD); health sciences (MS); immunology (PhD); medicine (MD); occupational therapy (MOT); pathologists assistant' (MHS); physical therapy (DPT). *Accreditation:* AOTA; LCME/AMA. *Program availability:* Part-time, evening/weekend. *Entrance requirements:* Additional exam requirements/recommendations for international students: required—TOEFL. Electronic applications accepted. *Expenses:* Contact institution.

# Cell Biology

**Albany College of Pharmacy and Health Sciences,** School of Arts and Sciences, Albany, NY 12208. Offers clinical laboratory sciences (MS); cytotechnology and molecular cytology (MS); health outcomes research (MS); molecular biosciences (MS). *Degree requirements:* For master's, thesis. *Entrance requirements:* For master's, GRE, minimum GPA of 3.0. Additional exam requirements/recommendations for international students: required—TOEFL (minimum score 84 iBT). Electronic applications accepted.

**Albany Medical College,** Center for Cell Biology and Cancer Research, Albany, NY 12208-3479. Offers MS, PhD. *Program availability:* Part-time. Terminal master's awarded for partial completion of doctoral program. *Degree requirements:* For master's, thesis; for doctorate, comprehensive exam, thesis/dissertation. *Entrance requirements:* For master's and doctorate, GRE General Test, all transcripts, letters of recommendation. Additional exam requirements/recommendations for international students: required—TOEFL.

**Albert Einstein College of Medicine,** Graduate Programs in the Biomedical Sciences, Department of Cell Biology, Bronx, NY 10461. Offers PhD, MD/PhD. *Degree requirements:* For doctorate, thesis/dissertation. *Entrance requirements:* For doctorate, GRE General Test. Additional exam requirements/recommendations for international students: required—TOEFL.

**Appalachian State University,** Cratis D. Williams School of Graduate Studies, Department of Biology, Boone, NC 28608. Offers cell and molecular biology (MS). *Program availability:* Part-time. *Degree requirements:* For master's, comprehensive exam, thesis. *Entrance requirements:* For master's, GRE General Test, 3 letters of recommendation. Additional exam requirements/recommendations for international students: required—TOEFL (minimum score 570 paper-based; 79 iBT), IELTS (minimum score 6.5). Electronic applications accepted.

**Arizona State University at Tempe,** College of Liberal Arts and Sciences, School of Life Sciences, Tempe, AZ 85287-4601. Offers animal behavior (PhD); applied ethics (biomedical and health ethics) (MA); biology (MS, PhD), including biology, biology and society, complex adaptive systems science (PhD), plant biology and conservation (MS); environmental life sciences (PhD); evolutionary biology (PhD); history and philosophy of science (PhD); human and social dimensions of science and technology (PhD); microbiology (PhD); molecular and cellular biology (PhD); neuroscience (PhD). Terminal master's awarded for partial completion of doctoral program. *Degree requirements:* For master's, thesis (for some programs), interactive Program of Study (iPOS) submitted before completing 50 percent of required credit hours; for doctorate, variable foreign language requirement, comprehensive exam, thesis/dissertation, interactive Program of Study (iPOS) submitted before completing 50 percent of required credit hours. *Entrance requirements:* For master's and doctorate, GRE, minimum GPA of 3.0 or equivalent in last 2 years of work leading to bachelor's degree. Additional exam requirements/recommendations for international students: required—TOEFL (minimum score 600 paper-based; 100 iBT). Electronic applications accepted.

**Auburn University,** Graduate School, Interdepartmental Programs, Auburn University, AL 36849. Offers applied economics (PhD); cell and molecular biology (PhD); real estate development (MRED); sociology and rural sociology (MA, MS). *Program availability:* Part-time. *Students:* 16 full-time (9 women), 6 part-time (4 women); includes 1 minority (Hispanic/Latino), 3 international. Average age 30. 53 applicants, 75% accepted, 27 enrolled. In 2019, 10 master's, 4 doctorates awarded. *Entrance requirements:* For master's, GRE General Test. Additional exam requirements/recommendations for international students: required—TOEFL (minimum score 550 paper-based; 79 iBT), iTEP; recommended—IELTS (minimum score 6.5). *Application deadline:* Applications are processed on a rolling basis. Application fee: $60 ($70 for international students). Electronic applications accepted. *Expenses: Tuition, area resident:* Full-time $9828; part-time $546 per credit hour. Tuition, state resident: full-time $9828; part-time $546 per credit hour. Tuition, nonresident: full-time $29,484; part-time $1638 per credit hour. *International tuition:* $29,744 full-time. Tuition and fees vary according to course load, program and reciprocity agreements. *Financial support:* In 2019–20, 2 fellowships (averaging $3,600 per year) were awarded; research assistantships, teaching assistantships, and Federal Work-Study also available. Support available to part-time students. Financial award application deadline: 3/15; financial award applicants required to submit FAFSA. *Application contact:* Dr. George Flowers, Dean of the Graduate School, 334-844-2125.

**Augusta University,** Program in Cellular Biology and Anatomy, Augusta, GA 30912. Offers PhD. *Degree requirements:* For doctorate, comprehensive exam, thesis/dissertation. *Entrance requirements:* For doctorate, GRE General Test. Additional exam requirements/recommendations for international students: required—TOEFL (minimum score 550 paper-based; 79 iBT).

**Baylor College of Medicine,** Graduate School of Biomedical Sciences, Department of Molecular and Cellular Biology, Houston, TX 77030-3498. Offers PhD, MD/PhD. *Degree requirements:* For doctorate, thesis/dissertation, public defense, qualifying exam. *Entrance requirements:* For doctorate, GRE General Test, GRE Subject Test (strongly recommended), minimum GPA of 3.0. Additional exam requirements/recommendations for international students: required—TOEFL. Electronic applications accepted.

**Baylor College of Medicine,** Graduate School of Biomedical Sciences, Interdepartmental Program in Cell and Molecular Biology, Houston, TX 77030-3498. Offers biochemistry (PhD); cell and molecular biology (PhD); genetics (PhD); human genetics (PhD); immunology (PhD); microbiology (PhD); virology (PhD); MD/PhD. *Degree requirements:* For doctorate, thesis/dissertation, public defense. *Entrance requirements:* For doctorate, GRE General Test, GRE Subject Test (strongly recommended), minimum GPA of 3.0. Additional exam requirements/recommendations for international students: required—TOEFL. Electronic applications accepted.

**Boston University,** Graduate School of Arts and Sciences, Molecular Biology, Cell Biology, and Biochemistry Program (MCBB), Boston, MA 02215. Offers MA, PhD. *Students:* 34 full-time (19 women), 2 part-time (both women); includes 7 minority (3 Black or African American, non-Hispanic/Latino; 3 Hispanic/Latino; 1 Two or more races, non-Hispanic/Latino), 9 international. Average age 27. 220 applicants, 9% accepted, 5 enrolled. In 2019, 10 master's, 4 doctorates awarded. Terminal master's awarded for partial completion of doctoral program. *Degree requirements:* For master's, thesis (for some programs); for doctorate, comprehensive exam, thesis/dissertation, teaching requirement. *Entrance requirements:* For master's and doctorate, 3 letters of recommendation, transcripts, personal statement. Additional exam requirements/recommendations for international students: required—TOEFL (minimum score 550 paper-based; 84 iBT). *Application deadline:* For fall admission, 12/10 for domestic and international students. Application fee: $95. Electronic applications accepted. *Financial support:* In 2019–20, 31 students received support, including 3 fellowships with full tuition reimbursements available (averaging $23,340 per year), 5 research assistantships with full tuition reimbursements available (averaging $23,340 per year), 5 teaching assistantships with full tuition reimbursements available (averaging $23,440 per year); Federal Work-Study, scholarships/grants, traineeships, and health care benefits also available. Financial award application deadline: 12/10; financial award applicants required to submit FAFSA. *Unit head:* Thomas Gilmore, Director, 617-353-2432, Fax: 617-353-6340, E-mail: gilmore@bu.edu. *Application contact:* Christina Honeycutt, Academic Administrator, 617-353-2432, Fax: 617-353-6340, E-mail: cjhoney@bu.edu.
Website: http://www.bu.edu/mcbb/

**Brandeis University,** Graduate School of Arts and Sciences, Department of Biology, Waltham, MA 02454-9110. Offers genetics (PhD); microbiology (PhD); molecular and cell biology (MS, PhD); molecular biology (PhD); neurobiology (PhD); quantitative biology (PhD). *Program availability:* Part-time. *Faculty:* 28 full-time (14 women), 1 part-time/adjunct (0 women). *Students:* 44 full-time (26 women), 1 (woman) part-time; includes 15 minority (1 American Indian or Alaska Native, non-Hispanic/Latino; 7 Asian, non-Hispanic/Latino; 7 Hispanic/Latino), 10 international. Average age 27. 202 applicants, 22% accepted, 12 enrolled. In 2019, 9 master's, 6 doctorates awarded. Terminal master's awarded for partial completion of doctoral program. *Degree requirements:* For master's, thesis optional; for doctorate, comprehensive exam, thesis/dissertation. *Entrance requirements:* For master's, transcripts, letters of recommendation, resume, statement of purpose; for doctorate, transcripts, letters of recommendation, resume, program questions, statement of purpose. Additional exam requirements/recommendations for international students: required—TOEFL, IELTS, PTE. *Application deadline:* For fall admission, 12/1 priority date for domestic and international students; for spring admission, 10/15 for domestic students, 11/15 for international students. Applications are processed on a rolling basis. Application fee: $75. Electronic applications accepted. *Financial support:* In 2019–20, 50 fellowships with full tuition reimbursements (averaging $35,000 per year), 21 teaching assistantships (averaging $3,550 per year) were awarded; research assistantships, scholarships/grants, health care benefits, and tuition waivers also available. Support available to part-time students. *Unit head:* Dr. Michael Marr, Director of Graduate Studies, 781-736-2481, E-mail: mmarr@brandeis.edu. *Application contact:* Maryanna Aldrich, Administrator, 781-736-2352, E-mail: scigradoffice@brandeis.edu.
Website: http://www.brandeis.edu/gsas/programs/mcbio.html

**Brown University,** Graduate School, Division of Biology and Medicine, Department of Molecular Biology, Cell Biology, and Biochemistry, Providence, RI 02912. Offers MA, PhD. *Program availability:* Part-time. Terminal master's awarded for partial completion of doctoral program. *Degree requirements:* For master's, thesis (for some programs); for doctorate, one foreign language, thesis/dissertation, preliminary exam. *Entrance requirements:* For master's and doctorate, GRE General Test, GRE Subject Test. Additional exam requirements/recommendations for international students: required—TOEFL. Electronic applications accepted.

**California Institute of Technology,** Division of Biology and Biological Engineering, Program in Cell Biology and Biophysics, Pasadena, CA 91125-0001. Offers PhD. *Degree requirements:* For doctorate, thesis/dissertation, qualifying exam. *Entrance requirements:* For doctorate, GRE General Test.

**California State University, Sacramento,** College of Natural Sciences and Mathematics, Department of Biological Sciences, Sacramento, CA 95819. Offers biological conservation (MS); molecular and cellular biology (MS); stem cell (MA). *Program availability:* Part-time. *Students:* 38 full-time (12 women), 24 part-time (8 women); includes 19 minority (14 Asian, non-Hispanic/Latino; 4 Hispanic/Latino; 1 Native Hawaiian or other Pacific Islander, non-Hispanic/Latino), 1 international. Average age 29. 68 applicants, 44% accepted, 23 enrolled. In 2019, 13 master's awarded. *Degree requirements:* For master's, comprehensive exam (for some programs), thesis (for some programs), thesis or project; writing proficiency exam. *Entrance requirements:* For master's, GRE, bachelor's degree in biology or equivalent; minimum GPA of 2.75 in all biology courses, 3.0 in all upper-division biology courses. Additional exam requirements/recommendations for international students: required—TOEFL (minimum score 550 paper-based; 80 iBT); recommended—IELTS (minimum score 7). *Application deadline:* For fall admission, 2/1 for domestic students, 1/1 for international students. Applications are processed on a rolling basis. Application fee: $70. Electronic applications accepted. *Expenses:* Contact institution. *Financial support:* Teaching assistantships, career-related internships or fieldwork, Federal Work-Study, and scholarships/grants available. Support available to part-time students. Financial award application deadline: 3/1; financial award applicants required to submit FAFSA. *Unit head:* Dr. Shannon Datwyler, Chair, 916-278-6535, Fax: 916-278-6993, E-mail: datwyler@csus.edu. *Application contact:* Jose Martinez, Graduate Admissions Supervisor, 916-278-7871, E-mail: martinj@skymail.csus.edu.
Website: http://www.csus.edu/bios

**Carnegie Mellon University,** Mellon College of Science, Department of Biological Sciences, Pittsburgh, PA 15213-3891. Offers biochemistry (PhD); biophysics (PhD); cell and developmental biology (PhD); computational biology (MS, PhD); genetics (PhD); molecular biology (PhD); neuroscience (PhD); structural biology (PhD). *Degree requirements:* For doctorate, comprehensive exam, thesis/dissertation. *Entrance requirements:* For doctorate, GRE General Test, GRE Subject Test, interview. Electronic applications accepted.

**Case Western Reserve University,** School of Medicine and School of Graduate Studies, Graduate Programs in Medicine, Department of Molecular Biology and Microbiology, Program in Cell Biology, Cleveland, OH 44106. Offers PhD. *Degree requirements:* For doctorate, thesis/dissertation. *Entrance requirements:* For doctorate, GRE General Test, GRE Subject Test, previous course work in biochemistry. Additional exam requirements/recommendations for international students: required—TOEFL. Electronic applications accepted.

**The Catholic University of America,** School of Arts and Sciences, Department of Biology, Washington, DC 20064. Offers biotechnology (MS); cell and microbial biology (MS, PhD), including cell biology; clinical laboratory science (MS, PhD); MSLS/MS. *Program availability:* Part-time. *Faculty:* 10 full-time (4 women), 3 part-time/adjunct (1 woman). *Students:* 16 full-time (13 women), 36 part-time (19 women); includes 11 minority (4 Black or African American, non-Hispanic/Latino; 3 Asian, non-Hispanic/Latino; 4 Two or more races, non-Hispanic/Latino), 33 international. Average age 31. 46 applicants, 65% accepted, 12 enrolled. In 2019, 15 master's, 8 doctorates awarded. Terminal master's awarded for partial completion of doctoral program. *Degree requirements:* For master's and doctorate, comprehensive exam. *Entrance requirements:* For master's and doctorate, GRE General Test, GRE Subject Test, statement of purpose, official copies of academic transcripts, three letters of recommendation. Additional exam requirements/recommendations for international

students: required—TOEFL (minimum score 550 paper-based; 80 iBT). *Application deadline:* For fall admission, 7/15 priority date for domestic students, 7/1 for international students; for spring admission, 11/15 priority date for domestic students, 11/1 for international students. Applications are processed on a rolling basis. Application fee: $55. Electronic applications accepted. *Expenses:* Contact institution. *Financial support:* Fellowships, research assistantships, teaching assistantships, Federal Work-Study, scholarships/grants, tuition waivers (full and partial), and unspecified assistantships available. Financial award application deadline: 2/1; financial award applicants required to submit FAFSA. *Unit head:* Dr. Venigalla Rao, Chair, 202-319-5271, Fax: 202-319-5721, E-mail: rao@cua.edu. *Application contact:* Dr. Steven Brown, Director of Graduate Admissions, 202-319-5057, Fax: 202-319-6533, E-mail: cua-admissions@cua.edu.
Website: http://biology.cua.edu/

**Columbia University,** College of Physicians and Surgeons, Department of Anatomy and Cell Biology, New York, NY 10032. Offers anatomy (M Phil, MA, PhD); anatomy and cell biology (PhD); MD/PhD. Terminal master's awarded for partial completion of doctoral program. *Degree requirements:* For doctorate, thesis/dissertation, oral exam. *Entrance requirements:* For master's and doctorate, GRE General Test. Additional exam requirements/recommendations for international students: required—TOEFL. *Expenses: Tuition:* Full-time $47,600; part-time $1880 per credit. One-time fee: $105.

**Columbia University,** College of Physicians and Surgeons, Integrated Program in Cellular, Molecular, Structural and Genetic Studies, New York, NY 10032. Offers PhD. Terminal master's awarded for partial completion of doctoral program. *Degree requirements:* For doctorate, thesis/dissertation. *Entrance requirements:* For doctorate, GRE General Test, GRE Subject Test. Additional exam requirements/recommendations for international students: required—TOEFL. *Expenses:* Contact institution.

**Cornell University,** Graduate School, Graduate Fields of Agriculture and Life Sciences, Field of Biochemistry, Molecular and Cell Biology, Ithaca, NY 14853. Offers biochemistry (PhD); biophysics (PhD); cell biology (PhD); molecular biology (PhD). *Degree requirements:* For doctorate, comprehensive exam, thesis/dissertation, 2 semesters of teaching experience. *Entrance requirements:* For doctorate, GRE General Test, GRE Subject Test (biology, chemistry, physics, biochemistry, cell and molecular biology), 3 letters of recommendation. Additional exam requirements/recommendations for international students: required—TOEFL (minimum score 600 paper-based; 77 iBT). Electronic applications accepted.

**Cornell University,** Graduate School, Graduate Fields of Agriculture and Life Sciences, Field of Computational Biology, Ithaca, NY 14853. Offers computational behavioral biology (PhD); computational biology (PhD); computational cell biology (PhD); computational ecology (PhD); computational genetics (PhD); computational macromolecular biology (PhD); computational organismal biology (PhD). *Degree requirements:* For doctorate, comprehensive exam, thesis/dissertation, 2 semesters of teaching experience. *Entrance requirements:* For doctorate, GRE General Test, GRE Subject Test (biology), 2 letters of recommendation. Additional exam requirements/recommendations for international students: required—TOEFL (minimum score 550 paper-based; 77 iBT). Electronic applications accepted.

**Dartmouth College,** Guarini School of Graduate and Advanced Studies, Graduate Programs in Biological Sciences, Graduate Program in Molecular and Cellular Biology, Hanover, NH 03755. Offers PhD, MBA/PhD, MD/PhD. *Entrance requirements:* For doctorate, GRE General Test, letters of recommendation, minimum GPA of 3.0. Electronic applications accepted.

**Drexel University,** College of Medicine, Biomedical Graduate Programs, Interdisciplinary Program in Molecular and Cell Biology and Genetics, Philadelphia, PA 19104-2875. Offers MS, PhD, MD/PhD. Terminal master's awarded for partial completion of doctoral program. *Degree requirements:* For master's, comprehensive exam, thesis; for doctorate, thesis/dissertation, qualifying exam. *Entrance requirements:* For master's, GRE General Test, minimum GPA of 2.75; for doctorate, GRE General Test, minimum GPA of 3.0. Additional exam requirements/recommendations for international students: required—TOEFL. Electronic applications accepted.

**Duke University,** Graduate School, Department of Cell Biology, Durham, NC 27710. Offers PhD. *Degree requirements:* For doctorate, thesis/dissertation. *Entrance requirements:* For doctorate, GRE General Test, GRE Subject Test in biology, chemistry, cell and molecular biology (recommended). Additional exam requirements/recommendations for international students: required—TOEFL (minimum score 577 paper-based; 90 iBT) or IELTS (minimum score 7). Electronic applications accepted.

**Duke University,** Graduate School, Department of Evolutionary Anthropology, Durham, NC 27708. Offers cellular and molecular biology (PhD); gross anatomy and physical anthropology (PhD), including comparative morphology of human and non-human primates, primate social behavior, vertebrate paleontology; neuroanatomy (PhD). *Degree requirements:* For doctorate, one foreign language, thesis/dissertation. *Entrance requirements:* For doctorate, GRE General Test. Additional exam requirements/recommendations for international students: required—TOEFL (minimum score 577 paper-based; 90 iBT) or IELTS (minimum score 7). Electronic applications accepted.

**Duke University,** Graduate School, Program in Cell and Molecular Biology, Durham, NC 27710. Offers Certificate. *Entrance requirements:* Additional exam requirements/recommendations for international students: required—TOEFL (minimum score 577 paper-based; 90 iBT) or IELTS (minimum score 7). Electronic applications accepted.

**East Carolina University,** Brody School of Medicine, Office of Research and Graduate Studies, Greenville, NC 27858-4353. Offers anatomy and cell biology (PhD); biochemistry and molecular biology (PhD); biomedical science (MS); microbiology and immunology (PhD); pharmacology and toxicology (PhD); physiology (PhD). *Students:* 102 full-time (44 women), 1 part-time (0 women); includes 16 minority (4 Black or African American, non-Hispanic/Latino; 7 Asian, non-Hispanic/Latino; 4 Hispanic/Latino; 1 Two or more races, non-Hispanic/Latino), 13 international. Average age 28. 83 applicants, 40% accepted, 20 enrolled. In 2019, 3 master's, 10 doctorates awarded. *Degree requirements:* For doctorate, comprehensive exam, thesis/dissertation. *Entrance requirements:* For doctorate, GRE General Test. Additional exam requirements/recommendations for international students: required—some international applicants may be required to demonstrate English proficiency via the TOEFL, IELTS, or PTE exam.; recommended—TOEFL (minimum score 78 iBT), IELTS (minimum score 6.5), TSE (minimum score 65). *Application deadline:* For fall admission, 8/15 for domestic students; for spring admission, 12/20 for domestic students. Applications are processed on a rolling basis. Application fee: $75. Electronic applications accepted. *Expenses: Tuition, area resident:* Full-time $4749; part-time $185 per credit hour. Tuition, state resident: full-time $4749; part-time $185 per credit hour. Tuition, nonresident: full-time $17,898; part-time $864 per credit hour. *International tuition:* $17,898 full-time. *Required fees:* $2787. *Financial support:* Fellowships available. Financial award application deadline: 6/1. *Unit head:* Dr. Russ Price, Associate Dean, 252-744-9346, E-mail: pricest17@ecu.edu. *Application contact:* Dr. Russ Price, Associate Dean, 252-744-9346, E-mail: pricest17@ecu.edu.
Website: http://www.ecu.edu/cs-dhs/bsomresearchgradstudies/index.cfm

**Emory University,** Laney Graduate School, Division of Biological and Biomedical Sciences, Program in Biochemistry, Cell and Developmental Biology, Atlanta, GA 30322. Offers PhD. *Degree requirements:* For doctorate, comprehensive exam, thesis/dissertation. *Entrance requirements:* For doctorate, GRE General Test, minimum GPA of 3.0 in science course work (recommended). Additional exam requirements/recommendations for international students: required—TOEFL. Electronic applications accepted.

**Emporia State University,** Department of Biological Sciences, Emporia, KS 66801-5415. Offers botany (MS); environmental biology (MS); forensic science (MS); general biology (MS); microbial and cellular biology (MS); zoology (MS). *Program availability:* Part-time. *Degree requirements:* For master's, comprehensive exam or thesis. *Entrance requirements:* For master's, GRE, appropriate undergraduate degree, interview, letters of reference. Additional exam requirements/recommendations for international students: required—TOEFL (minimum score 520 paper-based; 68 iBT). Electronic applications accepted. *Expenses: Tuition, area resident:* Full-time $6394; part-time $266.41 per credit hour. Tuition, state resident: full-time $6394; part-time $266.41 per credit hour. Tuition, nonresident: full-time $20,128; part-time $828.66 per credit hour. *International tuition:* $20,128 full-time. *Required fees:* $2183; $90.95 per credit hour. Tuition and fees vary according to campus/location and program.

**Florida Institute of Technology,** College of Engineering and Science, Program in Cell and Molecular Biology, Melbourne, FL 32901-6975. Offers MS. *Program availability:* Part-time. *Degree requirements:* For master's, thesis. *Entrance requirements:* For master's, GRE General Test, 3 letters of recommendation, minimum GPA of 3.0, statement of objectives. Additional exam requirements/recommendations for international students: required—TOEFL (minimum score 550 paper-based; 79 iBT). Electronic applications accepted.

**Florida State University,** The Graduate School, College of Arts and Sciences, Department of Biological Science, Specialization in Cell and Molecular Biology, Tallahassee, FL 32306-4295. Offers MS, PhD. Terminal master's awarded for partial completion of doctoral program. *Degree requirements:* For master's, comprehensive exam (for some programs), thesis, teaching experience, seminar presentation; for doctorate, comprehensive exam, thesis/dissertation, teaching experience; seminar presentation. *Entrance requirements:* For master's and doctorate, GRE General Test, minimum upper-division GPA of 3.0. Additional exam requirements/recommendations for international students: required—TOEFL (minimum score 600 paper-based; 92 iBT). Electronic applications accepted.

**Georgia State University,** College of Arts and Sciences, Department of Biology, Program in Cellular and Molecular Biology and Physiology, Atlanta, GA 30302-3083. Offers bioinformatics (MS); cellular and molecular biology and physiology (MS, PhD). *Program availability:* Part-time. Terminal master's awarded for partial completion of doctoral program. *Entrance requirements:* For master's and doctorate, GRE. *Application deadline:* Applications are processed on a rolling basis. Application fee: $50. Electronic applications accepted. *Expenses: Tuition, area resident:* Full-time $7164; part-time $398 per credit hour. Tuition, state resident: full-time $7164; part-time $398 per credit hour. Tuition, nonresident: full-time $22,662; part-time $1259 per credit hour. *International tuition:* $22,662 full-time. *Required fees:* $2128; $312 per credit hour. Tuition and fees vary according to course load and program. *Financial support:* Fellowships and research assistantships available. Financial award application deadline: 12/3. *Unit head:* Dr. Charles Derby, Director of Graduate Studies, 404-413-5393, Fax: 404-413-5446, E-mail: cderby@gsu.edu. *Application contact:* Dr. Charles Derby, Director of Graduate Studies, 404-413-5393, Fax: 404-413-5446, E-mail: cderby@gsu.edu.
Website: http://biology.gsu.edu/

**Grand Valley State University,** College of Liberal Arts and Sciences, Program in Cell and Molecular Biology, Allendale, MI 49401-9403. Offers MS. *Faculty:* 8 full-time (5 women), 2 part-time/adjunct (1 woman). *Students:* 22 full-time (8 women), 16 part-time (9 women); includes 5 minority (2 Black or African American, non-Hispanic/Latino; 1 Hispanic/Latino; 2 Two or more races, non-Hispanic/Latino), 10 international. Average age 25. 30 applicants, 93% accepted, 15 enrolled. In 2019, 9 master's awarded. *Degree requirements:* For master's, thesis, thesis. *Entrance requirements:* For master's, GRE, minimum GPA of 3.0, resume or curriculum vitae, personal statement, minimum of 2 letters of recommendation, interview. Additional exam requirements/recommendations for international students: required—TOEFL (minimum iBT score of 80), IELTS (6.5), or Michigan English Language Assessment Battery (77). *Application deadline:* Applications are processed on a rolling basis. Application fee: $30. Electronic applications accepted. *Expenses:* $702 per credit hour, 36 credit hours. *Financial support:* In 2019–20, 15 students received support, including 14 research assistantships with full and partial tuition reimbursements available (averaging $4,000 per year); fellowships and unspecified assistantships also available. *Unit head:* Dr. Mark Staves, Department Chair, 616-331-2473, Fax: 616-331-3446, E-mail: stavesm@gvsu.edu. *Application contact:* Anirudh Chowdhary, PSM Coordinator/Student Recruiting Contact, 616-331-6297, Fax: 616-331-6770, E-mail: chowdhan@gvsu.edu.
Website: https://www.gvsu.edu/grad/cellbio/

**Harvard University,** Graduate School of Arts and Sciences, Department of Molecular and Cellular Biology, Cambridge, MA 02138. Offers PhD. *Degree requirements:* For doctorate, thesis/dissertation, oral exam. *Entrance requirements:* For doctorate, GRE General Test, GRE Subject Test (recommended). Additional exam requirements/recommendations for international students: required—TOEFL.

**Harvard University,** Graduate School of Arts and Sciences, Division of Medical Sciences, Boston, MA 02115. Offers biological chemistry and molecular pharmacology (PhD); cell biology (PhD); genetics (PhD); microbiology and molecular genetics (PhD); pathology (PhD), including experimental pathology. *Degree requirements:* For doctorate, thesis/dissertation. *Entrance requirements:* For doctorate, GRE General Test, GRE Subject Test. Additional exam requirements/recommendations for international students: required—TOEFL.

**Illinois Institute of Technology,** Graduate College, College of Science, Department of Biology, Chicago, IL 60616. Offers applied life sciences (MS); biochemistry (MS); biology (MS, PhD); cell and molecular biology (MS); microbiology (MS); molecular biochemistry and biophysics (MS, PhD). *Program availability:* Part-time, evening/weekend, online learning. Terminal master's awarded for partial completion of doctoral program. *Degree requirements:* For master's, comprehensive exam, thesis (for some programs); for doctorate, comprehensive exam, thesis/dissertation. *Entrance requirements:* For master's, GRE General Test (minimum score 300 Quantitative and Verbal, 2.5 Analytical Writing), minimum undergraduate GPA of 3.0; for doctorate, GRE General Test (minimum score 310 Quantitative and Verbal, 3.0 Analytical Writing); GRE Subject Test (strongly recommended), minimum undergraduate GPA of 3.0. Additional exam requirements/recommendations for international students: required—TOEFL (minimum score 550 paper-based; 80 iBT). Electronic applications accepted.

**Illinois State University,** Graduate School, College of Arts and Sciences, School of Biological Sciences, Normal, IL 61790. Offers animal behavior (MS); bacteriology (MS); biochemistry (MS); biological sciences (MS); biology (PhD); biophysics (MS); biotechnology (MS); botany (MS, PhD); cell biology (MS); conservation biology (MS); developmental biology (MS); ecology (MS, PhD); entomology (MS); evolutionary biology

(MS); genetics (MS, PhD); immunology (MS); microbiology (MS, PhD); molecular biology (MS); molecular genetics (MS); neurobiology (MS); neuroscience (MS); parasitology (MS); physiology (MS, PhD); plant biology (MS); plant molecular biology (MS); plant sciences (MS); structural biology (MS); zoology (MS, PhD). *Program availability:* Part-time. *Faculty:* 26 full-time (6 women), 7 part-time/adjunct (2 women). *Students:* 51 full-time (33 women), 15 part-time (8 women). Average age 27. 71 applicants, 28% accepted, 9 enrolled. In 2019, 14 master's, 3 doctorates awarded. *Degree requirements:* For master's, thesis or alternative; for doctorate, variable foreign language requirement, thesis/dissertation, 2 terms of residency. *Entrance requirements:* For master's, GRE General Test, minimum GPA of 2.6 in last 60 hours of course work; for doctorate, GRE General Test. *Application deadline:* Applications are processed on a rolling basis. Application fee: $50. *Expenses: Tuition, area resident:* Full-time $7956; part-time $9767 per year. Tuition, nonresident: full-time $9233; part-time $17,592 per year. *Required fees:* $1797. *Financial support:* In 2019–20, 20 research assistantships, 41 teaching assistantships were awarded; Federal Work-Study, tuition waivers (full), and unspecified assistantships also available. Financial award application deadline: 4/1. *Unit head:* Dr. Craig Gatto, School Director, 309-438-3087, E-mail: cgatto@IllinoisState.edu. *Application contact:* Dr. Ben Sadd, Assistant Chair for Graduate Studies, 309-438-2651, E-mail: bmsadd@IllinoisState.edu.
Website: http://www.bio.ilstu.edu/

**Indiana State University,** College of Graduate and Professional Studies, College of Arts and Sciences, Department of Biology, Terre Haute, IN 47809. Offers cellular and molecular biology (PhD); ecology, systematics and evolution (PhD); life sciences (MS); physiology (PhD); science education (MS). *Degree requirements:* For master's, thesis optional; for doctorate, comprehensive exam, thesis/dissertation. *Entrance requirements:* For master's and doctorate, GRE General Test. Electronic applications accepted.

**Indiana University Bloomington,** University Graduate School, College of Arts and Sciences, Department of Biology, Bloomington, IN 47405. Offers biology teaching (MAT); biotechnology (MA); evolution, ecology, and behavior (MA, PhD); genetics (PhD); microbiology (MA, PhD); molecular, cellular, and developmental biology (PhD); plant sciences (MA, PhD); zoology (MA, PhD). Terminal master's awarded for partial completion of doctoral program. *Degree requirements:* For master's, thesis, oral defense; for doctorate, thesis/dissertation, oral defense. *Entrance requirements:* For master's and doctorate, GRE General Test. Additional exam requirements/recommendations for international students: required—TOEFL (minimum score 100 iBT). Electronic applications accepted.

**Indiana University-Purdue University Indianapolis,** Indiana University School of Medicine, Department of Anatomy and Cell Biology, Indianapolis, IN 46202. Offers MS, PhD, MD/PhD. *Degree requirements:* For master's, thesis or alternative; for doctorate, thesis/dissertation. *Entrance requirements:* For master's and doctorate, GRE General Test. Additional exam requirements/recommendations for international students: required—TOEFL. Electronic applications accepted. *Expenses:* Contact institution.

**Iowa State University of Science and Technology,** Program in Molecular, Cellular, and Developmental Biology, Ames, IA 50011. Offers MS, PhD. *Entrance requirements:* For master's and doctorate, GRE General Test. Additional exam requirements/recommendations for international students: required—TOEFL (minimum score 580 paper-based; 85 iBT), IELTS (minimum score 7). Electronic applications accepted.

**Irell & Manella Graduate School of Biological Sciences,** Graduate Program, Duarte, CA 91010. Offers brain metastatic cancer (PhD); cancer and stem cell metabolism (PhD); cancer biology (PhD); cancer biology and developmental therapeutics (PhD); cell biology (PhD); chemical biology (PhD); chromosomal break repair (PhD); diabetes and pancreatic progenitor cell biology (PhD); DNA repair and cancer biology (PhD); germline epigenetic remodeling and endocrine disruptors (PhD); hematology and hematopoietic cell transplantation (PhD); hematology and immunology (PhD); inflammation and cancer (PhD); micrornas and gene regulation in cardiovascular disease (PhD); mixed chimerism for reversal of autoimmunity (PhD); molecular and cellular biology (PhD); molecular biology and genetics (PhD); nanoparticle mediated twist1 silencing in metastatic cancer (PhD); neuro-oncology and stem cell biology (PhD); neuroscience (PhD); RNA directed therapies for HIV-1 (PhD); small RNA-induced transcriptional gene activation (PhD); stem cell regulation by the microenvironment (PhD); translational oncology and pharmaceutical sciences (PhD); tumor biology (PhD). *Degree requirements:* For doctorate, comprehensive exam, thesis/dissertation, qualifying exams, two advanced courses. *Entrance requirements:* For doctorate, GRE General Test; GRE Subject Test (recommended), 2 years of course work in chemistry (general and organic); 1 year of course work each in biochemistry, general biology, and general physics; 2 semesters of course work in mathematics; significant research laboratory experience. Additional exam requirements/recommendations for international students: required—TOEFL. Electronic applications accepted.

**Johns Hopkins University,** National Institutes of Health Sponsored Programs, Baltimore, MD 21218. Offers biology (PhD), including biochemistry, biophysics, cell biology, developmental biology, genetic biology, molecular biology; cell, molecular, and developmental biology and biophysics (PhD). *Degree requirements:* For doctorate, comprehensive exam, thesis/dissertation. *Entrance requirements:* Additional exam requirements/recommendations for international students: required—TOEFL (minimum score 600 paper-based). Electronic applications accepted.

**Johns Hopkins University,** School of Medicine, Graduate Programs in Medicine, Graduate Program in Cellular and Molecular Medicine, Baltimore, MD 21218. Offers PhD. *Degree requirements:* For doctorate, comprehensive exam, thesis/dissertation, oral exam, thesis defense. *Entrance requirements:* For doctorate, GRE. Electronic applications accepted. *Expenses:* Contact institution.

**Johns Hopkins University,** School of Medicine, Graduate Programs in Medicine, Program in Biochemistry, Cellular and Molecular Biology, Baltimore, MD 21205. Offers PhD. *Degree requirements:* For doctorate, comprehensive exam, thesis/dissertation. *Entrance requirements:* Additional exam requirements/recommendations for international students: required—TOEFL. Electronic applications accepted.

**Johns Hopkins University,** Zanvyl Krieger School of Arts and Sciences, Program in Cell, Molecular, Developmental Biology, and Biophysics, Baltimore, MD 21218. Offers PhD. Terminal master's awarded for partial completion of doctoral program. *Degree requirements:* For doctorate, comprehensive exam, thesis/dissertation. *Entrance requirements:* For doctorate, GRE General Test. Additional exam requirements/recommendations for international students: required—TOEFL (minimum score 600 paper-based), IELTS, TWE. Electronic applications accepted.

**Kent State University,** College of Arts and Sciences, Department of Biological Sciences, Kent, OH 44242. Offers biological sciences (MA, MS, PhD), including botany (MS, PhD), cell biology (MS, PhD), ecology (MS, PhD), physiology (MS, PhD). *Program availability:* Part-time. *Faculty:* 19 full-time (5 women), 2 part-time/adjunct (1 woman). *Students:* 51 full-time (35 women), 9 part-time (4 women); includes 1 minority (Two or more races, non-Hispanic/Latino), 10 international. Average age 29. 53 applicants, 38% accepted, 14 enrolled. In 2019, 8 master's, 9 doctorates awarded. Terminal master's awarded for partial completion of doctoral program. *Degree requirements:* For master's, thesis (for some programs), departmental seminar presentation about research (for MS); for doctorate, thesis/dissertation, departmental seminar presentation about research, admitted to doctoral candidacy following written and oral candidacy. *Entrance requirements:* For master's, GRE, minimum GPA of 3.0, official transcripts, goal statement, three letters of recommendation, list of up to five potential faculty advisors, undergraduate coursework roughly equivalent to a biology minor, acceptance of student by a faculty advisor; for doctorate, GRE; After completing the required coursework, students complete the doctoral program by being admitted to candidacy, by proposing a research project to the faculty, and by completing and defending that research with a written dissertation before a faculty committee, official transcripts, goal statement, three letters of recommendation, list of up to five potential faculty advisors, baccalaureate degree with strong background in biology and related subjects such as chemistry and mathematics, acceptance of the student by a faculty advisor. Additional exam requirements/recommendations for international students: required—TOEFL (minimum score 94 iBT), IELTS (minimum score 7), PTE (minimum score 65), Michigan English Language Assessment Battery (minimum score 82). *Application deadline:* For fall admission, 12/15 for domestic students, 12/5 for international students. Applications are processed on a rolling basis. Application fee: $45 ($70 for international students). Electronic applications accepted. *Financial support:* Research assistantships with full tuition reimbursements, teaching assistantships with full tuition reimbursements, Federal Work-Study, scholarships/grants, health care benefits, and unspecified assistantships available. Financial award application deadline: 12/15. *Unit head:* Dr. James L. Blank, Dean, 330-672-2650, E-mail: jblank@kent.edu. *Application contact:* Dr. Heather K. Caldwell, Associate Professor and Graduate Coordinator, 330-672-3636, E-mail: hcaldwel@kent.edu.
Website: http://www.kent.edu/biology

**Kent State University,** College of Arts and Sciences, School of Biomedical Sciences, Kent, OH 44242-0001. Offers biological anthropology (PhD); biomedical mathematics (MS, PhD); cellular and molecular biology (MS, PhD), including cellular biology and structures, molecular biology and genetics; neurosciences (MS, PhD); pharmacology (MS, PhD); physiology (MS, PhD). *Faculty:* 17 full-time (8 women). *Students:* 73 full-time (48 women), 2 part-time (1 woman); includes 9 minority (2 Black or African American, non-Hispanic/Latino; 1 Asian, non-Hispanic/Latino; 3 Hispanic/Latino; 3 Two or more races, non-Hispanic/Latino), 53 international. Average age 29. 78 applicants, 17% accepted, 9 enrolled. In 2019, 2 master's, 5 doctorates awarded. *Degree requirements:* For master's, thesis; for doctorate, comprehensive exam, thesis/dissertation. *Entrance requirements:* For master's, GRE, bachelor's degree, transcripts, minimum GPA of 3.0 undergraduate GPA, goal statement, three letters of recommendation, academic preparation adequate to perform graduate work in the desired field (typically two years of chemistry, one year of mathematics, one year of physics and courses in anthropology, biology and psychology); for doctorate, GRE, master's degree, minimum GPA of 3.0, transcripts, goal statement, three letters of recommendation. Additional exam requirements/recommendations for international students: required—TOEFL (minimum score 100 iBT), IELTS (minimum score 7), PTE (minimum score 68), Michigan English Language Assessment Battery (minimum score 85). *Application deadline:* For fall admission, 1/1 for domestic students, 12/15 for international students. Applications are processed on a rolling basis. Application fee: $45 ($70 for international students). Electronic applications accepted. *Financial support:* Research assistantships with full tuition reimbursements, teaching assistantships, health care benefits, and unspecified assistantships available. Financial award application deadline: 1/1. *Unit head:* Dr. Ernest J. Freeman, Director, School of Biomedical Sciences, 330-672-2363, E-mail: efreema2@kent.edu. *Application contact:* School of Biomedical Sciences, 330-6722263, Fax: 330-6729391.
Website: http://www.kent.edu/biomedical/

**Lehigh University,** College of Arts and Sciences, Department of Biological Sciences, Bethlehem, PA 18015. Offers biochemistry (PhD); cell and molecular biology (PhD); integrative biology (PhD); molecular biology (MS). *Program availability:* 100% online, MS MBio Program Only. *Faculty:* 24 full-time (11 women), 1 (woman) part-time/adjunct. *Students:* 36 full-time (18 women), 23 part-time (16 women); includes 12 minority (1 Black or African American, non-Hispanic/Latino; 1 American Indian or Alaska Native, non-Hispanic/Latino; 2 Asian, non-Hispanic/Latino; 7 Hispanic/Latino; 1 Two or more races, non-Hispanic/Latino), 9 international. Average age 28. 53 applicants, 57% accepted, 22 enrolled. In 2019, 9 master's, 7 doctorates awarded. Terminal master's awarded for partial completion of doctoral program. *Degree requirements:* For master's, thesis optional; for doctorate, comprehensive exam, thesis/dissertation. *Entrance requirements:* For master's, bachelor's degree in a life science or chemistry with a GPA of 3.0 or higher, 2 letters of recommendation, official transcripts of previous educational experience; for doctorate, GRE General Test, Three letters of recommendation, curriculum vitae, official transcripts, minimum Bachelor's degree or equivalent, personal statement. Additional exam requirements/recommendations for international students: required—TOEFL (minimum score 85 iBT). *Application deadline:* For fall admission, 7/15 for domestic and international students; for spring admission, 12/1 for domestic and international students; for summer admission, 4/30 for domestic and international students. Application fee: $75. Electronic applications accepted. *Financial support:* In 2019–20, 39 students received support, including 2 fellowships with full tuition reimbursements available (averaging $29,000 per year), 14 research assistantships with full tuition reimbursements available (averaging $29,000 per year), 18 teaching assistantships with full tuition reimbursements available (averaging $29,000 per year); tuition waivers (full and partial) and partially reimbursed health care benefits also available. Financial award application deadline: 1/1. *Unit head:* Dr. Linda Lowe-Krentz, Chairperson, 610-758-5084, Fax: 610-758-4004, E-mail: lij0@lehigh.edu. *Application contact:* Dr. Amber Rice, Graduate Coordinator, 610-758-5509, Fax: 610-758-4004, E-mail: amr511@lehigh.edu.
Website: http://www.lehigh.edu/~inbios/

**Liberty University,** School of Health Sciences, Lynchburg, VA 24515. Offers anatomy and cell biology (PhD); biomedical sciences (MS); epidemiology (MPH); exercise science (MS), including clinical, community physical activity, human performance, nutrition; global health (MPH); health promotion (MPH); medical sciences (MA), including biopsychology, business management, health informatics, molecular medicine, public health; nutrition (MPH). *Program availability:* Part-time, online learning. *Students:* 820 full-time (588 women), 889 part-time (612 women); includes 611 minority (402 Black or African American, non-Hispanic/Latino; 10 American Indian or Alaska Native, non-Hispanic/Latino; 43 Asian, non-Hispanic/Latino; 85 Hispanic/Latino; 1 Native Hawaiian or other Pacific Islander, non-Hispanic/Latino; 70 Two or more races, non-Hispanic/Latino), 67 international. Average age 32. 2,610 applicants, 33% accepted, 406 enrolled. In 2019, 445 master's awarded. *Degree requirements:* For master's, thesis (for some programs); for doctorate, thesis/dissertation. *Entrance requirements:* For doctorate, MAT or GRE, minimum GPA of 3.25 in master's program, 2-3 recommendations, writing samples (for some programs), letter of intent, professional vitae. Additional exam requirements/recommendations for international students: required—TOEFL (minimum score 600 paper-based; 100 iBT). Application fee: $50. *Expenses: Tuition:* Full-time $545; part-time $410 per credit hour. One-time fee: $50. *Financial support:* In 2019–20, 918 students received support. Federal Work-Study available. Financial award applicants required to submit FAFSA. *Unit head:* Dr. Ralph Linstra, Dean. *Application contact:* Jay Bridge, Director of Admissions, 800-424-9595, Fax: 800-628-7977, E-mail:

gradadmissions@liberty.edu.
Website: https://www.liberty.edu/health-sciences/

**Louisiana State University Health Sciences Center,** School of Graduate Studies in New Orleans, Department of Cell Biology and Anatomy, New Orleans, LA 70112-2223. Offers cell biology and anatomy (PhD), including clinical anatomy, development, cell, and neurobiology; MD/PhD. *Degree requirements:* For doctorate, comprehensive exam, thesis/dissertation. *Entrance requirements:* For doctorate, GRE General Test, minimum undergraduate GPA of 3.0. Additional exam requirements/recommendations for international students: recommended—TOEFL, IELTS.

**Louisiana State University Health Sciences Center at Shreveport,** Department of Cellular Biology and Anatomy, Shreveport, LA 71130-3932. Offers MS, PhD, MD/PhD. Terminal master's awarded for partial completion of doctoral program. *Degree requirements:* For master's, thesis; for doctorate, thesis/dissertation. *Entrance requirements:* For master's and doctorate, GRE General Test. Additional exam requirements/recommendations for international students: required—TOEFL.

**Loyola University Chicago,** Graduate School, Integrated Program in Biomedical Sciences, Maywood, IL 60660. Offers biochemistry and molecular biology (MS, PhD); cell and molecular physiology (MS, PhD); infectious disease and immunology (MS); integrative cell biology (MS, PhD); microbiology and immunology (MS, PhD); molecular pharmacology and therapeutics (MS, PhD); neuroscience (MS, PhD). *Students:* Average age 25. 773 applicants, 34% accepted, 122 enrolled. In 2019, 46 master's, 12 doctorates awarded. *Degree requirements:* For master's, thesis; for doctorate, comprehensive exam, thesis/dissertation. *Entrance requirements:* For doctorate, GRE. Additional exam requirements/recommendations for international students: required—TOEFL (minimum score 94 iBT), IELTS (minimum score 7.5). *Application deadline:* For fall admission, 2/7 for domestic students. Applications are processed on a rolling basis. Electronic applications accepted. *Expenses:* Contact institution. *Financial support:* In 2019–20, 20 students received support. Schmitt Fellowships and yearly tuition scholarships (averaging $25,032) available. Financial award application deadline: 6/15; financial award applicants required to submit FAFSA. *Unit head:* Dr. Leanne L. Cribbs, Associate Dean, Graduate Education, 708-327-2817, Fax: 708-216-8216, E-mail: lcribbs@luc.edu. *Application contact:* Margarita Quesada, Graduate Program Secretary, 708-216-3532, Fax: 708-216-8216, E-mail: mquesad@luc.edu.
Website: http://ssom.luc.edu/graduate_school/degree-programs/ipbsphd/

**Marquette University,** Graduate School, College of Arts and Sciences, Department of Biological Sciences, Milwaukee, WI 53201-1881. Offers cell biology (MS, PhD); developmental biology (MS, PhD); ecology (MS, PhD); epithelial physiology (MS, PhD); genetics (MS, PhD); microbiology (MS, PhD); molecular biology (MS, PhD); muscle and exercise physiology (MS, PhD); neuroscience (PhD). Terminal master's awarded for partial completion of doctoral program. *Degree requirements:* For master's, comprehensive exam, thesis, 1 year of teaching experience or equivalent; for doctorate, thesis/dissertation, 1 year of teaching experience or equivalent, qualifying exam. *Entrance requirements:* For master's and doctorate, GRE General Test, GRE Subject Test, official transcripts from all current and previous colleges/universities except Marquette, statement of professional goals and aspirations, three letters of recommendation. Additional exam requirements/recommendations for international students: required—TOEFL (minimum score 530 paper-based). Electronic applications accepted.

**Massachusetts Institute of Technology,** School of Science, Department of Biology, Cambridge, MA 02139. Offers biochemistry (PhD); biological oceanography (PhD); biology (PhD); biophysical chemistry and molecular structure (PhD); cell biology (PhD); computational and systems biology (PhD); developmental biology (PhD); genetics (PhD); immunology (PhD); microbiology (PhD); molecular biology (PhD); neurobiology (PhD). *Degree requirements:* For doctorate, comprehensive exam, thesis/dissertation, teaching assistantship during two semesters. *Entrance requirements:* For doctorate, GRE General Test. Additional exam requirements/recommendations for international students: required—TOEFL, IELTS. Electronic applications accepted.

**McGill University,** Faculty of Graduate and Postdoctoral Studies, Faculty of Medicine, Department of Anatomy and Cell Biology, Montréal, QC H3A 2T5, Canada. Offers M Sc, PhD.

**McMaster University,** Faculty of Health Sciences and School of Graduate Studies, Program in Medical Sciences, Metabolism and Nutrition Area, Hamilton, ON L8S 4M2, Canada. Offers M Sc, PhD, MD/PhD. *Degree requirements:* For master's, thesis; for doctorate, comprehensive exam, thesis/dissertation. *Entrance requirements:* For master's, honors B Sc, B+ average in related field; for doctorate, M Sc, minimum B+ average, students with proven research experience and an A average may be admitted with a B Sc degree. Additional exam requirements/recommendations for international students: required—TOEFL (minimum score 580 paper-based; 92 iBT).

**Medical University of South Carolina,** College of Graduate Studies, Program in Molecular and Cellular Biology and Pathobiology, Charleston, SC 29425. Offers cancer biology (PhD); cardiovascular biology (PhD); cardiovascular imaging (PhD); cell regulation (PhD); craniofacial biology (PhD); genetics and development (PhD); marine biomedicine (PhD); DMD/PhD; MD/PhD. *Degree requirements:* For doctorate, thesis/dissertation, oral and written exams. *Entrance requirements:* For doctorate, GRE General Test, interview, minimum GPA of 3.0. Additional exam requirements/recommendations for international students: required—TOEFL (minimum score 600 paper-based; 100 iBT). Electronic applications accepted.

**Michigan State University,** The Graduate School, College of Natural Science, MSU-DOE Plant Research Laboratory, East Lansing, MI 48824. Offers biochemistry and molecular biology (PhD); cellular and molecular biology (PhD); crop and soil sciences (PhD); genetics (PhD); microbiology and molecular genetics (PhD); plant biology (PhD); plant physiology (PhD). *Degree requirements:* For doctorate, comprehensive exam, thesis/dissertation, laboratory rotation, defense of dissertation. *Entrance requirements:* For doctorate, GRE General Test, acceptance into one of the affiliated department programs; 3 letters of recommendation; bachelor's degree or equivalent in life sciences, chemistry, biochemistry, or biophysics; research experience. Electronic applications accepted.

**Michigan State University,** The Graduate School, College of Natural Science, Program in Cell and Molecular Biology, East Lansing, MI 48824. Offers cell and molecular biology (MS, PhD); cell and molecular biology/environmental toxicology (PhD). *Entrance requirements:* Additional exam requirements/recommendations for international students: required—TOEFL. Electronic applications accepted.

**Missouri State University,** Graduate College, College of Health and Human Services, Department of Biomedical Sciences, Program in Cell and Molecular Biology, Springfield, MO 65897. Offers MS. *Program availability:* Part-time. *Degree requirements:* For master's, thesis or alternative, oral and written exams. *Entrance requirements:* For master's, GRE General Test, 2 semesters of course work in organic chemistry and physics, 1 semester of course work in calculus, minimum GPA of 3.0 in last 60 hours of course work. Additional exam requirements/recommendations for international students: required—TOEFL (minimum score 550 paper-based; 79 iBT), IELTS (minimum score 6). Electronic applications accepted. *Expenses: Tuition, area resident:* Full-time $2600;

part-time $1735 per credit hour. Tuition, nonresident: full-time $5240; part-time $3495 per credit hour. *International tuition:* $5240 full-time. *Required fees:* $530; $438 per credit hour. Tuition and fees vary according to class time, course level, course load, degree level, campus/location and program.

**New York Medical College,** Graduate School of Basic Medical Sciences, Valhalla, NY 10595. Offers biochemistry and molecular biology (MS, PhD); cell biology (MS, PhD); microbiology and immunology (MS, PhD); pathology (MS, PhD); pharmacology (MS, PhD); physiology (MS, PhD); MD/PhD. *Program availability:* Part-time, evening/weekend. *Faculty:* 98 full-time (24 women). *Students:* 141 full-time (90 women), 17 part-time (3 women); includes 68 minority (16 Black or African American, non-Hispanic/Latino; 32 Asian, non-Hispanic/Latino; 15 Hispanic/Latino; 1 Native Hawaiian or other Pacific Islander, non-Hispanic/Latino; 4 Two or more races, non-Hispanic/Latino), 19 international. Average age 26. 351 applicants, 62% accepted, 86 enrolled. In 2019, 28 master's, 5 doctorates awarded. Terminal master's awarded for partial completion of doctoral program. *Degree requirements:* For master's, thesis; for doctorate, comprehensive exam, thesis/dissertation. *Entrance requirements:* For master's, GRE General Test, MCAT, or DAT, OAT. Additional exam requirements/recommendations for international students: required—TOEFL (minimum score 90 iBT), TOEFL or IELTS; one of the two exams are required. *Application deadline:* For fall admission, 6/1 priority date for domestic students, 5/1 priority date for international students. Applications are processed on a rolling basis. Application fee: $75 ($100 for international students). Electronic applications accepted. *Expenses:* $1200 credit and $620 fees. *Financial support:* In 2019–20, 400 students received support. Federal Work-Study, scholarships/grants, unspecified assistantships, and Student Federal Loans available. Financial award application deadline: 4/30; financial award applicants required to submit FAFSA. *Unit head:* Dr. Marina K Holz, Dean, 914-594-4110, Fax: 914-594-4944, E-mail: mholz@nymc.edu. *Application contact:* Valerie Romeo-Messana, Director of Admissions, 914-594-4110, Fax: 914-594-4944, E-mail: v_romeomessana@nymc.edu.
Website: https://www.nymc.edu/graduate-school-of-basic-medical-sciences-gsbms/gsbms-academics/

**North Carolina State University,** College of Veterinary Medicine, Program in Comparative Biomedical Sciences, Raleigh, NC 27695. Offers cell biology (MS, PhD); infectious disease (MS, PhD); pathology (MS, PhD); pharmacology (MS, PhD); population medicine (MS, PhD). *Program availability:* Part-time. *Degree requirements:* For master's, thesis; for doctorate, thesis/dissertation. *Entrance requirements:* For master's and doctorate, GRE General Test. Additional exam requirements/recommendations for international students: required—TOEFL (minimum score 550 paper-based). Electronic applications accepted. *Expenses:* Contact institution.

**North Dakota State University,** College of Graduate and Interdisciplinary Studies, Interdisciplinary Program in Cellular and Molecular Biology, Fargo, ND 58102. Offers PhD. *Degree requirements:* For doctorate, thesis/dissertation. *Entrance requirements:* Additional exam requirements/recommendations for international students: required—TOEFL. Electronic applications accepted. Tuition and fees vary according to program and reciprocity agreements.

**Northeastern Illinois University,** College of Graduate Studies and Research, College of Arts and Sciences, Program in Biology, Chicago, IL 60625. Offers biology (MS), including cell biology, ecology, molecular biology, organismal biology. *Program availability:* Part-time, evening/weekend. *Degree requirements:* For master's, comprehensive exam, thesis optional. *Entrance requirements:* For master's, minimum GPA of 2.75. Additional exam requirements/recommendations for international students: required—TOEFL (minimum score 550 paper-based; 79 iBT). Electronic applications accepted.

**Northwestern University,** The Graduate School, Interdisciplinary Biological Sciences Program (IBiS), Evanston, IL 60208. Offers biochemistry (PhD); bioengineering and biotechnology (PhD); biotechnology (PhD); cell and molecular biology (PhD); developmental and systems biology (PhD); nanotechnology (PhD); neurobiology (PhD); structural biology and biophysics (PhD). *Degree requirements:* For doctorate, thesis/dissertation, qualifying exam. *Entrance requirements:* For doctorate, GRE General Test. Additional exam requirements/recommendations for international students: required—TOEFL (minimum score 600 paper-based). Electronic applications accepted.

**The Ohio State University,** Graduate School, College of Arts and Sciences, Division of Natural and Mathematical Sciences, Department of Molecular Genetics, Columbus, OH 43210. Offers cell and developmental biology (MS, PhD); genetics (MS, PhD); molecular biology (MS, PhD). *Entrance requirements:* For doctorate, GRE General Test, GRE Subject Test in biology or chemistry (recommended). Additional exam requirements/recommendations for international students: required—TOEFL (minimum score 550 paper-based; 79 iBT), Michigan English Language Assessment Battery (minimum score 82); recommended—IELTS (minimum score 7). Electronic applications accepted.

**The Ohio State University,** Graduate School, College of Arts and Sciences, Division of Natural and Mathematical Sciences, Program in Molecular, Cellular and Developmental Biology, Columbus, OH 43210. Offers MS, PhD. Terminal master's awarded for partial completion of doctoral program. *Entrance requirements:* For doctorate, GRE General Test, GRE Subject Test in any science (desired, preferably biology or chemistry, biochemistry or cell and molecular biology). Additional exam requirements/recommendations for international students: required—TOEFL (minimum score 600 paper-based; 85 iBT); recommended—IELTS (minimum score 8). Electronic applications accepted.

**Ohio University,** Graduate College, College of Arts and Sciences, Department of Biological Sciences, Athens, OH 45701-2979. Offers biological sciences (MS, PhD); cell biology and physiology (MS, PhD); ecology and evolutionary biology (MS, PhD); exercise physiology and muscle biology (MS, PhD); microbiology (MS, PhD); neuroscience (MS, PhD). Terminal master's awarded for partial completion of doctoral program. *Degree requirements:* For master's, comprehensive exam, thesis, 1 quarter of teaching experience; for doctorate, comprehensive exam, thesis/dissertation, 2 quarters of teaching experience. *Entrance requirements:* For master's, GRE General Test, names of three faculty members whose research interests most closely match the applicant's interest; for doctorate, GRE General Test, essay concerning prior training, research interest and career goals, plus names of three faculty members whose research interests most closely match the applicant's interest. Additional exam requirements/recommendations for international students: required—TOEFL (minimum score 620 paper-based; 105 iBT) or IELTS (minimum score 7.5). Electronic applications accepted.

**Ohio University,** Graduate College, College of Arts and Sciences, Interdisciplinary Graduate Program in Molecular and Cellular Biology, Athens, OH 45701-2979. Offers PhD. *Degree requirements:* For doctorate, comprehensive exam, thesis/dissertation, research proposal, teaching experience. *Entrance requirements:* For doctorate, GRE General Test. Additional exam requirements/recommendations for international students: required—TOEFL (minimum score 620 paper-based; 105 iBT); recommended—TWE. Electronic applications accepted.

**Oregon Health & Science University,** School of Medicine, Graduate Programs in Medicine, Program in Molecular and Cellular Biosciences, Cell and Developmental Biology Graduate Program, Portland, OR 97239-3098. Offers PhD. *Degree*

*requirements:* For doctorate, comprehensive exam, thesis/dissertation, qualifying exam. *Entrance requirements:* For doctorate, GRE General Test (minimum scores: 153 Verbal/ 148 Quantitative/4.5 Analytical) or MCAT.

**Oregon State University,** College of Agricultural Sciences, Program in Botany and Plant Pathology, Corvallis, OR 97331. Offers applied systematics (MS); ecology (MS, PhD); genetics (MS, PhD); genomics and computational biology (MS, PhD); molecular and cellular biology (MS, PhD); mycology (MS, PhD); plant pathology (MS, PhD); plant physiology (MS, PhD). *Entrance requirements:* For master's and doctorate, GRE.

**Oregon State University,** Interdisciplinary/Institutional Programs, Program in Molecular and Cellular Biology, Corvallis, OR 97331. Offers bioinformatics (PhD); biotechnology (PhD); genome biology (PhD); molecular virology (PhD); plant molecular biology (PhD). *Degree requirements:* For doctorate, thesis/dissertation, oral and written qualifying exams. *Entrance requirements:* For doctorate, GRE. Additional exam requirements/ recommendations for international students: required—TOEFL (minimum score 80 iBT), IELTS (minimum score 6.5).

**Penn State Hershey Medical Center,** College of Medicine, Graduate School Programs in the Biomedical Sciences, Huck Institutes of the Life Sciences, Intercollege Graduate Program in Molecular Cellular and Integrative Biosciences, Hershey, PA 17033. Offers cell and developmental biology (PhD); molecular medicine (PhD); molecular toxicology (PhD); neurobiology (PhD). *Degree requirements:* For doctorate, comprehensive exam, thesis/dissertation, oral exam. *Entrance requirements:* For doctorate, GRE, minimum GPA of 3.0. Additional exam requirements/recommendations for international students: required—TOEFL (minimum score 500 paper-based). Electronic applications accepted.

**Penn State University Park,** Graduate School, Intercollege Graduate Programs, Program in Molecular, Cellular, and Integrative Biosciences, University Park, PA 16802. Offers MS, PhD.

**Purdue University,** Graduate School, College of Science, Department of Biological Sciences, West Lafayette, IN 47907. Offers cell and developmental biology (PhD); genetics (MS); microbiology (MS, PhD); neurobiology (MS, PhD). *Faculty:* 43 full-time (14 women), 6 part-time/adjunct (1 woman). *Students:* 117 full-time (58 women), 10 part-time (6 women); includes 24 minority (5 Black or African American, non-Hispanic/ Latino; 12 Asian, non-Hispanic/Latino; 4 Hispanic/Latino; 3 Two or more races, non-Hispanic/Latino), 56 international. Average age 27. 146 applicants, 32% accepted, 27 enrolled. In 2019, 7 master's, 18 doctorates awarded. Terminal master's awarded for partial completion of doctoral program. *Degree requirements:* For master's, thesis (for some programs); for doctorate, thesis/dissertation, seminars, teaching experience. *Entrance requirements:* For master's, GRE General Test (minimum analytical writing score of 3.5), minimum undergraduate GPA of 3.0; for doctorate, GRE General Test (minimum analytical writing score of 3.5), minimum undergraduate GPA of 3.5. Additional exam requirements/recommendations for international students: required— TOEFL minimum score 600 paper-based; 107 iBT (for MS), 80 iBT (for PhD). *Application deadline:* For fall admission, 12/7 for domestic and international students. Applications are processed on a rolling basis. Application fee: $60 ($75 for international students). Electronic applications accepted. *Financial support:* Fellowships, research assistantships, and teaching assistantships available. Support available to part-time students. Financial award application deadline: 2/15; financial award applicants required to submit FAFSA. *Unit head:* Janice P. Evans, Head, 765-494-4407, E-mail: janiceevans@purdue.edu. *Application contact:* Georgina E. Rupp, Graduate Coordinator, 765-494-8142, E-mail: ruppg@purdue.edu. Website: http://www.bio.purdue.edu/

**Quinnipiac University,** College of Arts and Sciences, Program in Molecular and Cell Biology, Hamden, CT 06518-1940. Offers MS. *Program availability:* Part-time, evening/ weekend. *Degree requirements:* For master's, thesis optional. *Entrance requirements:* For master's, bachelor's degree in biological, medical, or health sciences. Additional exam requirements/recommendations for international students: required—TOEFL (minimum score 575 paper-based; 90 iBT), IELTS (minimum score 6.5). Electronic applications accepted. *Expenses: Tuition:* Part-time $1055 per credit. *Required fees:* $945 per semester. Tuition and fees vary according to course load and program.

**Rice University,** Graduate Programs, Wiess School of Natural Sciences, Department of Biochemistry and Cell Biology, Houston, TX 77251-1892. Offers MA, PhD. Terminal master's awarded for partial completion of doctoral program. *Degree requirements:* For master's, thesis; for doctorate, thesis/dissertation. *Entrance requirements:* For master's and doctorate, GRE. Additional exam requirements/recommendations for international students: required—TOEFL (minimum score 600 paper-based; 90 iBT). Electronic applications accepted. *Expenses:* Contact institution.

**Rosalind Franklin University of Medicine and Science,** School of Graduate and Postdoctoral Studies - Interdisciplinary Graduate Program in Biomedical Sciences, Department of Cell Biology and Anatomy, North Chicago, IL 60064-3095. Offers PhD, MD/PhD. Terminal master's awarded for partial completion of doctoral program. *Degree requirements:* For doctorate, comprehensive exam, thesis/dissertation, original research project. *Entrance requirements:* For doctorate, GRE General Test, minimum GPA of 3.0. Additional exam requirements/recommendations for international students: required— TOEFL, TWE.

**Rush University,** Graduate College, Division of Anatomy and Cell Biology, Chicago, IL 60612-3832. Offers MS, PhD, MD/MS, MD/PhD. Terminal master's awarded for partial completion of doctoral program. *Degree requirements:* For master's, thesis; for doctorate, comprehensive exam, thesis/dissertation, preliminary exam, dissertation proposal. *Entrance requirements:* For master's, GRE General Test, minimum GPA of 3.0, bachelor's degree in biology or chemistry (preferred), interview; for doctorate, GRE General Test, minimum GPA of 3.0, interview. Additional exam requirements/ recommendations for international students: required—TOEFL. Electronic applications accepted.

**Rutgers University - Newark,** Graduate School of Biomedical Sciences, Department of Cell Biology and Molecular Medicine, Newark, NJ 07107. Offers PhD. *Degree requirements:* For doctorate, thesis/dissertation, qualifying exam. *Entrance requirements:* For doctorate, GRE General Test. Additional exam requirements/ recommendations for international students: required—TOEFL. Electronic applications accepted.

**Rutgers University - New Brunswick,** Graduate School-New Brunswick, Programs in the Molecular Biosciences, Program in Cell and Developmental Biology, Piscataway, NJ 08854-8097. Offers MS, PhD. *Program availability:* Part-time. Terminal master's awarded for partial completion of doctoral program. *Degree requirements:* For master's, thesis; for doctorate, thesis/dissertation, written qualifying exam. *Entrance requirements:* For master's, GRE General Test; for doctorate, GRE General Test, GRE Subject Test (recommended), minimum GPA of 3.0. Additional exam requirements/recommendations for international students: required—TOEFL. Electronic applications accepted.

**San Diego State University,** Graduate and Research Affairs, College of Sciences, Department of Biology, San Diego, CA 92182. Offers biology (MA, MS), including ecology (MS); molecular biology (MS); physiology (MS); systematics/evolution (MS); cell and molecular biology (PhD); ecology (MS, PhD); microbiology (MS). Terminal master's awarded for partial completion of doctoral program. *Degree requirements:* For master's,

thesis; for doctorate, thesis/dissertation. *Entrance requirements:* For master's, GRE General Test, GRE Subject Test, resume or curriculum vitae, 2 letters of recommendation. Additional exam requirements/recommendations for international students: required—TOEFL. Electronic applications accepted.

**San Diego State University,** Graduate and Research Affairs, College of Sciences, Molecular Biology Institute, Program in Cell and Molecular Biology, San Diego, CA 92182. Offers PhD. *Degree requirements:* For doctorate, thesis/dissertation, oral comprehensive qualifying exam. *Entrance requirements:* For doctorate, GRE General Test, GRE Subject Test, resumé or curriculum vitae, 3 letters of recommendation. Electronic applications accepted.

**San Francisco State University,** Division of Graduate Studies, College of Science and Engineering, Department of Biology, Program in Cell and Molecular Biology, San Francisco, CA 94132-1722. Offers MS. *Application deadline:* Applications are processed on a rolling basis. *Expenses:* Tuition, area resident: Full-time $7176; part-time $4164 per year. Tuition, state resident: full-time $7176; part-time $4164 per year. Tuition, nonresident: full-time $16,680; part-time $396 per unit. *International tuition:* $16,680 full-time. *Required fees:* $1524; $1524 per unit. $762 per semester. Tuition and fees vary according to degree level and program. *Unit head:* Dr. Diana Chu, Program Coordinator, 415-405-3487, Fax: 415-338-2295, E-mail: chud@sfsu.edu. *Application contact:* Dr. Diana Chu, Program Coordinator, 415-405-3487, Fax: 415-338-2295, E-mail: chud@sfsu.edu. Website: http://biology.sfsu.edu/graduate/cell-and-molecular-biology

**Southern Methodist University,** Dedman College of Humanities and Sciences, Department of Biological Sciences, Dallas, TX 75275. Offers molecular and cellular biology (MA, MS, PhD). Terminal master's awarded for partial completion of doctoral program. *Degree requirements:* For master's, thesis (for MS), oral exam; for doctorate, thesis/dissertation, qualifying exam. *Entrance requirements:* For master's and doctorate, GRE General Test (minimum score 1200), minimum GPA of 3.0. Additional exam requirements/recommendations for international students: required—TOEFL (minimum score 550 paper-based). Electronic applications accepted.

**State University of New York Downstate Medical Center,** School of Graduate Studies, Program in Molecular and Cellular Biology, Brooklyn, NY 11203-2098. Offers PhD, MD/PhD. *Degree requirements:* For doctorate, comprehensive exam, thesis/ dissertation. *Entrance requirements:* For doctorate, GRE General Test. Additional exam requirements/recommendations for international students: recommended—TOEFL.

**State University of New York Upstate Medical University,** College of Graduate Studies, Program in Cell and Developmental Biology, Syracuse, NY 13210. Offers anatomy (MS, PhD); MD/PhD. Terminal master's awarded for partial completion of doctoral program. *Degree requirements:* For master's, thesis; for doctorate, comprehensive exam, thesis/dissertation. *Entrance requirements:* For master's, GRE General Test, interview; for doctorate, GRE General Test, telephone interview. Additional exam requirements/recommendations for international students: required— TOEFL. Electronic applications accepted.

**Stony Brook University, State University of New York,** Graduate School, College of Arts and Sciences, Department of Biochemistry and Cell Biology, Biochemistry and Cell Biology Program, Stony Brook, NY 11794. Offers MS. *Program availability:* Part-time. *Students:* 19 full-time (14 women), 7 part-time (4 women); includes 8 minority (1 Black or African American, non-Hispanic/Latino; 5 Asian, non-Hispanic/Latino; 2 Hispanic/ Latino), 6 international. Average age 26. 63 applicants, 46% accepted, 17 enrolled. In 2019, 11 master's awarded. *Entrance requirements:* For master's, three letters of recommendation, BS or BA in a life science related field with minimum B average, personal statement. Additional exam requirements/recommendations for international students: required—TOEFL (minimum score 550 paper-based; 90 iBT). *Application deadline:* For fall admission, 1/15 for domestic students; for summer admission, 10/1 for domestic students. Applications are processed on a rolling basis. Application fee: $100. Electronic applications accepted. *Expenses:* Contact institution. *Financial support:* Research assistantships available. *Unit head:* Prof. Aaron Neiman, Chair, 631-632-8550, Fax: 631-632-8575, E-mail: aaron.neiman@stonybrook.edu. *Application contact:* Pam Wolfskill, Coordinator, 631-632-8585, Fax: 631-632-8575, E-mail: carol.juliano@stonybrook.edu. Website: https://www.stonybrook.edu/commcms/biochem/education/graduate/biochemistry-and-cell-biology-ms

**Stony Brook University, State University of New York,** Graduate School, College of Arts and Sciences, Department of Biochemistry and Cell Biology, Molecular and Cellular Biology Program, Stony Brook, NY 11794. Offers MA, PhD. *Students:* 59 full-time (29 women); includes 17 minority (3 Black or African American, non-Hispanic/Latino; 10 Asian, non-Hispanic/Latino; 4 Hispanic/Latino), 26 international. Average age 26. 111 applicants, 32% accepted, 15 enrolled. In 2019, 8 doctorates awarded. *Degree requirements:* For doctorate, comprehensive exam, thesis/dissertation, teaching experience. *Entrance requirements:* For doctorate, GRE General Test, GRE Subject Test. Additional exam requirements/recommendations for international students: required—TOEFL. *Application deadline:* For fall admission, 1/15 for domestic students; for spring admission, 10/1 for domestic students. Application fee: $100. Electronic applications accepted. *Expenses:* Contact institution. *Financial support:* In 2019–20, 4 fellowships, 23 research assistantships, 14 teaching assistantships were awarded; Federal Work-Study also available. *Unit head:* Prof. Aaron Neiman, Chair, 631-632-8550, Fax: 631-632-8575, E-mail: aaron.neiman@stonybrook.edu. *Application contact:* Amy Saas, Graduate Program Administrator, 631-632-8613, Fax: 631-632-9730, E-mail: mcbgraduateprogram@stonybrook.edu. Website: https://www.stonybrook.edu/mcb/

**Texas Tech University Health Sciences Center,** Graduate School of Biomedical Sciences, Program in Biomedical Sciences, Lubbock, TX 79430. Offers MS, PhD, MD/ PhD, MS/PhD. Terminal master's awarded for partial completion of doctoral program. *Degree requirements:* For master's, comprehensive exam, thesis; for doctorate, comprehensive exam, thesis/dissertation. *Entrance requirements:* For master's and doctorate, GRE General Test, minimum GPA of 3.0. Additional exam requirements/ recommendations for international students: required—TOEFL (minimum score 550 paper-based). Electronic applications accepted.

**Thomas Jefferson University,** Jefferson College of Life Sciences, MS Program in Cell and Developmental Biology, Philadelphia, PA 19107. Offers MS. *Program availability:* Part-time, evening/weekend. *Degree requirements:* For master's, thesis, clerkship. *Entrance requirements:* For master's, GRE General Test or MCAT, minimum GPA of 3.0. Additional exam requirements/recommendations for international students: required—TOEFL, IELTS (minimum score 7). Electronic applications accepted.

**Thomas Jefferson University,** Jefferson College of Life Sciences, PhD Program in Cell Biology and Regenerative Medicine, Philadelphia, PA 19107. Offers PhD. *Degree requirements:* For doctorate, comprehensive exam, thesis/dissertation. *Entrance requirements:* For doctorate, GRE General Test, minimum GPA of 3.2. Additional exam requirements/recommendations for international students: required—TOEFL (minimum score 100 iBT), IELTS (minimum score 7). Electronic applications accepted.

## Cell Biology

**Tufts University,** Graduate School of Biomedical Sciences, Cell, Molecular, and Developmental Biology Program, Medford, MA 02155. Offers cancer biology (PhD); developmental and regenerative biology (PhD); molecular and cellular medicine (PhD); structural and chemical biology (PhD). *Faculty:* 84 full-time (30 women). *Students:* 32 full-time (15 women); includes 10 minority (2 Black or African American, non-Hispanic/Latino; 4 Asian, non-Hispanic/Latino; 4 Hispanic/Latino), 4 international. Average age 28. 168 applicants, 5% accepted, 3 enrolled. In 2019, 5 doctorates awarded. Terminal master's awarded for partial completion of doctoral program. *Degree requirements:* For doctorate, comprehensive exam, thesis/dissertation. *Entrance requirements:* For doctorate, 3 letters of reference, resume, personal statement. *Application deadline:* For fall admission, 12/1 priority date for domestic and international students. Application fee: $90. Electronic applications accepted. *Expenses: Tuition:* Part-time $1799 per credit hour. Full-time tuition and fees vary according to degree level, program and student level. Part-time tuition and fees vary according to course load. *Financial support:* In 2019–20, 100 students received support, including 3 research assistantships with full tuition reimbursements available (averaging $40,000 per year); fellowships, traineeships, and health care benefits also available. Financial award application deadline: 12/1. *Unit head:* Dr. Brent Cochran, Program Director, 617-636-0442. *Application contact:* Jeff Miller, Admissions Coordinator, 617-636-6767, Fax: 617-636-0375, E-mail: gsbs-admissions@tufts.edu.
Website: https://gsbs.tufts.edu/academics/CMDB

**Tulane University,** School of Medicine, Graduate Programs in Biomedical Sciences, Department of Structural and Cellular Biology, New Orleans, LA 70118-5669. Offers MS, PhD, MD/PhD. *Degree requirements:* For master's, one foreign language, thesis; for doctorate, 2 foreign languages, thesis/dissertation. *Entrance requirements:* For master's, GRE General Test, minimum B average in undergraduate course work; for doctorate, GRE General Test. Additional exam requirements/recommendations for international students: required—TOEFL. Electronic applications accepted. *Expenses: Tuition:* Full-time $57,004; part-time $3167 per credit hour. *Required fees:* $2086; $44.50 per credit hour. $80 per term. Tuition and fees vary according to course load, degree level and program.

**Tulane University,** School of Medicine, Graduate Programs in Biomedical Sciences, Interdisciplinary Graduate Program in Molecular and Cellular Biology, New Orleans, LA 70118-5669. Offers PhD, MD/PhD. *Degree requirements:* For doctorate, thesis/dissertation. *Entrance requirements:* For doctorate, GRE General Test, GRE Subject Test. Additional exam requirements/recommendations for international students: required—TOEFL. Electronic applications accepted. *Expenses: Tuition:* Full-time $57,004; part-time $3167 per credit hour. *Required fees:* $2086; $44.50 per credit hour. $80 per term. Tuition and fees vary according to course load, degree level and program.

**Tulane University,** School of Science and Engineering, Department of Cell and Molecular Biology, New Orleans, LA 70118-5669. Offers MS, PhD. Terminal master's awarded for partial completion of doctoral program. *Degree requirements:* For doctorate, thesis/dissertation. *Entrance requirements:* For master's, GRE General Test, minimum B average in undergraduate course work; for doctorate, GRE General Test. Additional exam requirements/recommendations for international students: required—TOEFL. Electronic applications accepted. *Expenses: Tuition:* Full-time $57,004; part-time $3167 per credit hour. *Required fees:* $2086; $44.50 per credit hour. $80 per term. Tuition and fees vary according to course load, degree level and program.

**Uniformed Services University of the Health Sciences,** F. Edward Hebert School of Medicine, Graduate Programs in the Biomedical Sciences and Public Health, Graduate Program in Molecular and Cell Biology, Bethesda, MD 20814-4799. Offers MS, PhD. *Degree requirements:* For doctorate, comprehensive exam, thesis/dissertation, qualifying exam. *Entrance requirements:* For doctorate, GRE General Test, minimum GPA of 3.0. Electronic applications accepted. Application fee is waived when completed online.

**Universidad Central del Caribe,** School of Medicine, Program in Biomedical Sciences, Bayamón, PR 00960-6032. Offers anatomy and cell biology (MA, MS); biochemistry (MS); biomedical sciences (MA); cellular and molecular biology (PhD); microbiology and immunology (MA, MS); pharmacology (MS); physiology (MS).

**Université de Montréal,** Faculty of Medicine, Department of Pathology and Cellular Biology, Montréal, QC H3C 3J7, Canada. Offers M Sc, PhD. Terminal master's awarded for partial completion of doctoral program. *Degree requirements:* For master's, thesis; for doctorate, thesis/dissertation, general exam. *Entrance requirements:* For master's and doctorate, proficiency in French, knowledge of English. Electronic applications accepted.

**Université de Sherbrooke,** Faculty of Medicine and Health Sciences, Graduate Programs in Medicine, Department of Anatomy and Cell Biology, Sherbrooke, QC J1H 5N4, Canada. Offers cell biology (M Sc, PhD). Terminal master's awarded for partial completion of doctoral program. *Degree requirements:* For master's, thesis; for doctorate, thesis/dissertation. Electronic applications accepted.

**University at Buffalo, the State University of New York,** Graduate School, Graduate Programs in Cancer Research and Biomedical Sciences at Roswell Park Cancer Institute, Buffalo, NY 14260. Offers cancer pathology and prevention (PhD); cellular and molecular biology (PhD); immunology (PhD); interdisciplinary natural sciences (MS); molecular and cellular biophysics and biochemistry (PhD); molecular pharmacology and cancer therapeutics (PhD). Terminal master's awarded for partial completion of doctoral program. *Degree requirements:* For master's, thesis, oral defense of thesis; for doctorate, comprehensive exam, thesis/dissertation, oral defense of dissertation. *Entrance requirements:* For master's and doctorate, GRE General Test. Additional exam requirements/recommendations for international students: required—TOEFL (minimum score 79 iBT). Electronic applications accepted. *Expenses: Tuition, area resident:* Full-time $11,310; part-time $471 per credit hour. Tuition, state resident: full-time $11,310; part-time $471 per credit hour. Tuition, nonresident: full-time $23,100; part-time $963 per credit hour. *International tuition:* $23,100 full-time. *Required fees:* $2820.

**University at Buffalo, the State University of New York,** Graduate School, Jacobs School of Medicine and Biomedical Sciences, Graduate Programs in Medicine and Biomedical Sciences, Department of Pathology and Anatomical Sciences, Buffalo, NY 14203. Offers anatomical sciences (MA, PhD); computational cell biology, anatomy, and pathology (PhD); pathology (MA, PhD). *Faculty:* 14 full-time (2 women). *Students:* 16 full-time (6 women); includes 2 minority (1 American Indian or Alaska Native, non-Hispanic/Latino; 1 Asian, non-Hispanic/Latino), 1 international. Average age 29. 26 applicants, 27% accepted, 3 enrolled. In 2019, 2 master's, 2 doctorates awarded. *Degree requirements:* For master's, thesis; for doctorate, thesis/dissertation. *Entrance requirements:* For master's and doctorate, 3 letters of recommendation. Additional exam requirements/recommendations for international students: required—TOEFL (minimum score 600 paper-based; 100 iBT). *Application deadline:* For fall admission, 5/1 priority date for domestic students, 3/1 priority date for international students. Applications are processed on a rolling basis. Application fee: $85. Electronic applications accepted. *Expenses:* Contact institution. *Financial support:* In 2019–20, 7 students received support, including 1 research assistantship with full tuition reimbursement available (averaging $24,900 per year), 1 teaching assistantship with full tuition reimbursement available (averaging $24,900 per year); Federal Work-Study, scholarships/grants, health care benefits, and unspecified assistantships also available. Financial award application deadline: 2/1; financial award applicants required to submit FAFSA. *Unit head:* Dr. John E. Tomaszewski, Department Chair, 716-829-2846, Fax: 716-829-2911, E-mail: johntoma@buffalo.edu. *Application contact:* Lannette M. Garcia, Assistant for Academic Activity, 716-829-5204, E-mail: ubpathad@buffalo.edu.
Website: http://medicine.buffalo.edu/departments/pathology.html

**The University of Alabama at Birmingham,** Joint Health Sciences, Biochemistry, Structural, and Stem Cell Biology Theme, Birmingham, AL 35294. Offers PhD. *Students:* 34 full-time (15 women); includes 9 minority (2 Black or African American, non-Hispanic/Latino; 1 American Indian or Alaska Native, non-Hispanic/Latino; 4 Asian, non-Hispanic/Latino; 2 Hispanic/Latino), 4 international. Average age 26. 41 applicants, 2% accepted, 1 enrolled. In 2019, 5 doctorates awarded. *Degree requirements:* For doctorate, comprehensive exam, thesis/dissertation. *Entrance requirements:* For doctorate, personal statement, resume or curriculum vitae, letters of recommendation, research experience, interview. Additional exam requirements/recommendations for international students: required—TOEFL (minimum score 80 iBT), IELTS (minimum score 6.5). *Application deadline:* For fall admission, 12/31 for domestic and international students. Applications are processed on a rolling basis. Electronic applications accepted. *Financial support:* In 2019–20, fellowships with full tuition reimbursements (averaging $30,000 per year), research assistantships with full tuition reimbursements (averaging $31,000 per year) were awarded; health care benefits also available. *Unit head:* Dr. Thomas Ryan, Theme Director, 205-996-2175, E-mail: tryan@uab.edu. *Application contact:* Alyssa Zasada, Admissions Manager for Graduate Biomedical Sciences, 205-934-3857, E-mail: grad-gbs@uab.edu.
Website: http://www.uab.edu/gbs/home/themes/bssb

**The University of Alabama at Birmingham,** Joint Health Sciences, Cell, Molecular, and Developmental Biology Theme, Birmingham, AL 35294. Offers PhD. *Students:* Average age 27. 32 applicants, 28% accepted, 3 enrolled. In 2019, 7 doctorates awarded. *Degree requirements:* For doctorate, comprehensive exam, thesis/dissertation. *Entrance requirements:* For doctorate, personal statement, resume or curriculum vitae, letters of recommendation, research experience, interview. Additional exam requirements/recommendations for international students: required—TOEFL (minimum score 80 iBT), IELTS (minimum score 6.5). *Application deadline:* For fall admission, 12/31 for domestic and international students. Applications are processed on a rolling basis. Electronic applications accepted. *Financial support:* In 2019–20, fellowships with full tuition reimbursements (averaging $30,000 per year), research assistantships with full tuition reimbursements (averaging $31,000 per year) were awarded; health care benefits also available. *Unit head:* Dr. Alecia K. Gross, Theme Director, 205-975-8396, E-mail: agross@uab.edu. *Application contact:* Alyssa Zasada, Admissions Manager for Graduate Biomedical Sciences, 205-934-3857, E-mail: grad-gbs@uab.edu.
Website: http://www.uab.edu/gbs/home/themes/cmdb

**University of Alberta,** Faculty of Graduate Studies and Research, Department of Biological Sciences, Edmonton, AB T6G 2E1, Canada. Offers environmental biology and ecology (M Sc, PhD); microbiology and biotechnology (M Sc, PhD); molecular biology and genetics (M Sc, PhD); physiology and cell biology (M Sc, PhD); plant biology (M Sc, PhD); systematics and evolution (M Sc, PhD). Terminal master's awarded for partial completion of doctoral program. *Degree requirements:* For master's, thesis; for doctorate, thesis/dissertation. *Entrance requirements:* Additional exam requirements/recommendations for international students: required—TOEFL.

**University of Alberta,** Faculty of Medicine and Dentistry and Faculty of Graduate Studies and Research, Graduate Programs in Medicine, Department of Cell Biology, Edmonton, AB T6G 2E1, Canada. Offers cell and molecular biology (M Sc, PhD). Terminal master's awarded for partial completion of doctoral program. *Degree requirements:* For master's, thesis; for doctorate, thesis/dissertation. *Entrance requirements:* For master's and doctorate, 3 letters of reference, curriculum vitae. Additional exam requirements/recommendations for international students: required—TOEFL (minimum score 600 paper-based).

**The University of Arizona,** College of Science, Biochemistry and Molecular and Cellular Biology Program, Tucson, AZ 85721. Offers PhD. *Program availability:* Evening/weekend. *Degree requirements:* For doctorate, thesis/dissertation. *Entrance requirements:* For doctorate, 3 letters of recommendation, statement of purpose. Additional exam requirements/recommendations for international students: required—TOEFL (minimum score 600 paper-based; 90 iBT), IELTS (minimum score 7). Electronic applications accepted.

**University of Arkansas,** Graduate School, Interdisciplinary Program in Cell and Molecular Biology, Fayetteville, AR 72701. Offers MS, PhD. *Students:* 64 full-time (40 women), 32 part-time (16 women); includes 8 minority (2 Black or African American, non-Hispanic/Latino; 1 American Indian or Alaska Native, non-Hispanic/Latino; 4 Hispanic/Latino; 1 Two or more races, non-Hispanic/Latino), 63 international. 20 applicants, 100% accepted. In 2019, 6 master's, 10 doctorates awarded. *Application deadline:* For fall admission, 8/1 for domestic students, 4/1 for international students; for spring admission, 12/1 for domestic students, 10/1 for international students; for summer admission, 4/15 for domestic students, 3/1 for international students. Applications are processed on a rolling basis. Application fee: $60. Electronic applications accepted. *Financial support:* In 2019–20, 31 research assistantships, 12 teaching assistantships were awarded; fellowships with tuition reimbursements also available. Financial award application deadline: 4/1; financial award applicants required to submit FAFSA. *Unit head:* Dr. Douglas Rhoads, Program Director, 479-575-3251, Fax: 479-575-4010, E-mail: drhoads@uark.edu. *Application contact:* Dr. Adnan Alrubaye, Program Associate Director, 479-575-3251, Fax: 479-575-4010, E-mail: aakhalaf@uark.edu.
Website: https://cell.uark.edu/

**The University of British Columbia,** Faculty of Medicine, Department of Cellular and Physiological Sciences, Vancouver, BC V6T 1Z3, Canada. Offers bioinformatics (M Sc, PhD); cell and developmental biology (M Sc, PhD); genome science and technology (M Sc, PhD); neuroscience (M Sc, PhD). *Degree requirements:* For master's, thesis, oral defense; for doctorate, comprehensive exam, thesis/dissertation, oral defense. *Entrance requirements:* For master's, minimum overall B+ average in third- and fourth-year courses; for doctorate, minimum overall B+ average in master's degree (or equivalent) from approved institution with clear evidence of research ability or potential. Additional exam requirements/recommendations for international students: required—TOEFL, IELTS. *Expenses:* Contact institution.

**University of California, Berkeley,** Graduate Division, College of Letters and Science, Department of Molecular and Cell Biology, Berkeley, CA 94720. Offers PhD. *Degree requirements:* For doctorate, comprehensive exam, thesis/dissertation, qualifying exam, 2 semesters of teaching. *Entrance requirements:* For doctorate, GRE General Test, GRE Subject Test (recommended), minimum GPA of 3.0. Additional exam requirements/recommendations for international students: required—TOEFL (minimum score 570 paper-based; 68 iBT), IELTS (minimum score 7). Electronic applications accepted.

**University of California, Davis,** Graduate Studies, Graduate Group in Cell and Developmental Biology, Davis, CA 95616. Offers MS, PhD. *Degree requirements:* For

integrative biology (MS, PhD); genetics and evolution (MS, PhD). *Degree requirements:* For master's, thesis; for doctorate, 2 foreign languages, comprehensive exam, thesis/dissertation. *Entrance requirements:* For master's and doctorate, GRE General Test. Additional exam requirements/recommendations for international students: required—TOEFL (minimum score 550 paper-based; 80 iBT), IELTS (minimum score 6.5). Electronic applications accepted.

**University of Miami,** Graduate School, Miller School of Medicine, Graduate Programs in Medicine, Department of Cell Biology, Miami, FL 33124. Offers molecular cell and developmental biology (PhD); MD/PhD. *Faculty:* 29 full-time (3 women). *Students:* 13 full-time (4 women); includes 7 minority (1 Black or African American, non-Hispanic/Latino; 3 Asian, non-Hispanic/Latino; 2 Hispanic/Latino; 1 Two or more races, non-Hispanic/Latino), 3 international. Average age 29. 2 applicants, 100% accepted, 1 enrolled. In 2019, 1 doctorate awarded. *Degree requirements:* For doctorate, thesis/dissertation, Qualifying Exam. *Entrance requirements:* For doctorate, GRE General Test, GRE Subject Test. Additional exam requirements/recommendations for international students: required—TOEFL. *Application deadline:* For fall admission, 3/1 priority date for domestic students. Applications are processed on a rolling basis. Application fee: $95. Electronic applications accepted. *Financial support:* In 2019–20, 8 fellowships (averaging $29,500 per year), 8 research assistantships (averaging $29,500 per year) were awarded; teaching assistantships also available. *Unit head:* Dr. Glen Barber, Chair, 305-243-5914, Fax: 305-243-7020, E-mail: gbarber@miami.edu. *Application contact:* Dr. Xiangxi Mike Xu, Program Director, 305-243-1750, E-mail: xxu2@miami.edu.
Website: http://cellbiology.med.miami.edu/

**University of Michigan,** Rackham Graduate School, College of Literature, Science, and the Arts, Department of Molecular, Cellular, and Developmental Biology, Ann Arbor, MI 48109. Offers MS, PhD. *Program availability:* Part-time. Terminal master's awarded for partial completion of doctoral program. *Degree requirements:* For master's, thesis (for some programs), 24 credits with at least 16 in molecular, cellular, and developmental biology and 4 in a cognate field; for doctorate, comprehensive exam, thesis/dissertation, preliminary exam, oral defense. *Entrance requirements:* Additional exam requirements/recommendations for international students: required—TOEFL (minimum score 600 paper-based; 100 iBT). Electronic applications accepted. *Expenses:* Contact institution.

**University of Michigan,** Rackham Graduate School, Program in Biomedical Sciences (PIBS), Department of Cell and Developmental Biology, Ann Arbor, MI 48109. Offers PhD. *Degree requirements:* For doctorate, thesis/dissertation, oral defense of dissertation, preliminary exam. *Entrance requirements:* For doctorate, GRE General Test, 3 letters of recommendation, research experience. Additional exam requirements/recommendations for international students: required—TOEFL (minimum score 84 iBT). Electronic applications accepted.

**University of Michigan,** Rackham Graduate School, Program in Biomedical Sciences (PIBS), Interdisciplinary Program in Cellular and Molecular Biology, Ann Arbor, MI 48109. Offers PhD. *Degree requirements:* For doctorate, comprehensive exam, thesis/dissertation, preliminary exam; oral defense of dissertation. *Entrance requirements:* For doctorate, GRE General Test. Additional exam requirements/recommendations for international students: required—TOEFL (minimum score 560 paper-based; 84 iBT), IELTS (minimum score 6.5), Michigan English Language Assessment Battery. Electronic applications accepted. *Expenses:* Contact institution.

**University of Minnesota, Twin Cities Campus,** Graduate School, Program in Molecular, Cellular, Developmental Biology and Genetics, Minneapolis, MN 55455-0213. Offers genetic counseling (MS); molecular, cellular, developmental biology and genetics (PhD). Terminal master's awarded for partial completion of doctoral program. *Degree requirements:* For master's, thesis optional; for doctorate, thesis/dissertation. *Entrance requirements:* For master's and doctorate, GRE General Test. Additional exam requirements/recommendations for international students: required—TOEFL (minimum score 625 paper-based; 80 iBT). Electronic applications accepted.

**University of Minnesota, Twin Cities Campus,** Graduate School, Stem Cell Biology Graduate Program, Minneapolis, MN 55455-3007. Offers MS. *Degree requirements:* For master's, thesis. *Entrance requirements:* For master's, GRE, BS, BA, or foreign equivalent in biological sciences or related field; minimum undergraduate GPA of 3.2. Additional exam requirements/recommendations for international students: required—TOEFL (minimum score 580 paper-based, with a minimum score of 4 in the TWE, or 94 Internet-based, with a minimum score of 22 on each of the reading and listening, 26 on the speaking, and 26 on the writing section.

**University of Missouri–Kansas City,** School of Biological Sciences, Program in Cell Biology and Biophysics, Kansas City, MO 64110-2499. Offers PhD. *Degree requirements:* For doctorate, comprehensive exam, thesis/dissertation. *Entrance requirements:* For doctorate, GRE General Test, bachelor's degree in chemistry, biology or related field; minimum GPA of 3.0. Additional exam requirements/recommendations for international students: required—TOEFL (minimum score 550 paper-based; 80 iBT). Electronic applications accepted.

**University of Montana,** Graduate School, College of Humanities and Sciences, Division of Biological Sciences, Program in Cellular, Molecular and Microbial Biology, Missoula, MT 59812. Offers cellular and developmental biology (PhD); microbial evolution and ecology (PhD); microbiology and immunology (PhD); molecular biology and biochemistry (PhD). Terminal master's awarded for partial completion of doctoral program. *Degree requirements:* For doctorate, variable foreign language requirement, thesis/dissertation. *Entrance requirements:* For doctorate, GRE General Test.

**University of Nebraska Medical Center,** Interdisciplinary Graduate Program in Biomedical Sciences, Department of Genetics, Cell Biology and Anatomy, Omaha, NE 68198. Offers genetics, cell biology and anatomy (PhD); medical anatomy (MS); molecular genetics and cell biology (MS). Terminal master's awarded for partial completion of doctoral program. *Degree requirements:* For master's, comprehensive exam, thesis (for some programs); for doctorate, comprehensive exam, thesis/dissertation. *Entrance requirements:* For master's, GRE General Test (MCAT or DAT acceptable for MS in medical anatomy); for doctorate, GRE General Test. Additional exam requirements/recommendations for international students: required—TOEFL (minimum score 550 paper-based; 80 iBT). Electronic applications accepted. *Expenses:* Contact institution.

**University of Nevada, Reno,** Graduate School, Interdisciplinary Program in Cell and Molecular Biology, Reno, NV 89557. Offers MS, PhD. Terminal master's awarded for partial completion of doctoral program. *Degree requirements:* For master's, thesis; for doctorate, thesis/dissertation. *Entrance requirements:* For master's, GRE Subject Test (recommended), minimum GPA of 2.75; for doctorate, GRE Subject Test (recommended), minimum GPA of 3.0. Additional exam requirements/recommendations for international students: required—TOEFL (minimum score 500 paper-based; 61 iBT), IELTS (minimum score 6). Electronic applications accepted.

**University of New Haven,** Graduate School, College of Arts and Sciences, Program in Cellular and Molecular Biology, West Haven, CT 06516. Offers MS. *Program availability:* Part-time, evening/weekend. *Students:* 42 full-time (30 women), 5 part-time (4 women); includes 7 minority (1 Black or African American, non-Hispanic/Latino; 2 Asian, non-Hispanic/Latino; 4 Hispanic/Latino), 21 international. Average age 25. 65 applicants, 82% accepted, 19 enrolled. In 2019, 17 master's awarded. *Entrance requirements:* Additional exam requirements/recommendations for international students: required—TOEFL (minimum score 80 iBT), IELTS, PTE. *Application deadline:* Applications are processed on a rolling basis. Application fee: $50. Electronic applications accepted. Application fee is waived when completed online. *Financial support:* Research assistantships with partial tuition reimbursements, teaching assistantships with partial tuition reimbursements, Federal Work-Study, scholarships/grants, and unspecified assistantships available. Support available to part-time students. Financial award application deadline: 5/1; financial award applicants required to submit FAFSA. *Unit head:* Dr. Eva Sapi, Professor, 203-479-4552, E-mail: esapi@newhaven.edu. *Application contact:* Selina O'Toole, Senior Associate Director of Graduate Admissions, 203-932-7337, E-mail: SOToole@newhaven.edu.
Website: https://www.newhaven.edu/arts-sciences/graduate-programs/cellular-molecular-biology/

**University of New Mexico,** Graduate Studies, Health Sciences Center, Program in Biomedical Sciences, Albuquerque, NM 87131-5196. Offers biochemistry and molecular biology (MS, PhD); cell biology and physiology (MS, PhD); molecular genetics and microbiology (MS, PhD); neuroscience (MS, PhD); pathology (MS, PhD); toxicology (MS, PhD). *Program availability:* Part-time. Terminal master's awarded for partial completion of doctoral program. *Degree requirements:* For master's, thesis; for doctorate, comprehensive exam, thesis/dissertation, qualifying exam at the end of year 1/core curriculum. *Entrance requirements:* For master's and doctorate, GRE General Test, minimum undergraduate GPA of 3.0. Additional exam requirements/recommendations for international students: required—TOEFL. Electronic applications accepted. *Expenses:* Tuition, state resident: full-time $7633; part-time $972 per year. Tuition, nonresident: full-time $22,586; part-time $3840 per year. *International tuition:* $23,292 full-time. *Required fees:* $8608. Tuition and fees vary according to course level, course load, degree level, program and student level.

**The University of North Carolina at Chapel Hill,** Graduate School, College of Arts and Sciences, Department of Biology, Chapel Hill, NC 27599. Offers botany (MA, MS, PhD); cell biology, development, and physiology (MA, MS, PhD); cell motility and cytoskeleton (PhD); ecology and behavior (MA, MS, PhD); genetics and molecular biology (MA, MS, PhD); morphology, systematics, and evolution (MA, MS, PhD). Terminal master's awarded for partial completion of doctoral program. *Degree requirements:* For master's, comprehensive exam, thesis (for some programs); for doctorate, comprehensive exam, thesis/dissertation. *Entrance requirements:* For master's, GRE General Test, GRE Subject Test, 2 semesters of calculus or statistics; 2 semesters of physics, organic chemistry; 3 semesters of biology; for doctorate, GRE General Test, GRE Subject Test, 2 semesters calculus or statistics, 2 semesters physics, organic chemistry, 3 semesters of biology. Additional exam requirements/recommendations for international students: required—TOEFL (minimum score 550 paper-based). Electronic applications accepted.

**The University of North Carolina at Chapel Hill,** School of Medicine and Graduate School, Biological and Biomedical Sciences Program, Molecular, Cellular & Developmental Biology, Chapel Hill, NC 27599. Offers PhD. *Faculty:* 16 full-time (2 women). *Students:* 3 full-time (1 woman). Average age 26. In 2019, 1 doctorate awarded. *Degree requirements:* For doctorate, comprehensive exam, thesis/dissertation. *Entrance requirements:* Additional exam requirements/recommendations for international students: required—TOEFL. *Application deadline:* For fall admission, 12/3 priority date for domestic and international students. Applications are processed on a rolling basis. Application fee: $73. Electronic applications accepted. *Financial support:* In 2019–20, 6 fellowships with tuition reimbursements (averaging $32,000 per year), 29 research assistantships with full tuition reimbursements (averaging $32,000 per year) were awarded; teaching assistantships with full tuition reimbursements, career-related internships or fieldwork, health care benefits, and tuition waivers (full) also available. *Unit head:* Dr. Christopher Willett, Director, E-mail: willett4@email.unc.edu. *Application contact:* Jeffrey Steinbach, Assistant Director of Admissions, 919-843-7129, E-mail: jsteinba@email.unc.edu.
Website: https://bio.unc.edu/graduate/mcdb/

**University of Notre Dame,** The Graduate School, College of Science, Department of Biological Sciences, Notre Dame, IN 46556. Offers aquatic ecology, evolution and environmental biology (MS, PhD); cellular and molecular biology (MS, PhD); genetics (MS, PhD); physiology (MS, PhD); vector biology and parasitology (MS, PhD). Terminal master's awarded for partial completion of doctoral program. *Degree requirements:* For master's, comprehensive exam, thesis; for doctorate, comprehensive exam, thesis/dissertation, candidacy exam. *Entrance requirements:* For master's and doctorate, GRE General Test. Additional exam requirements/recommendations for international students: required—TOEFL (minimum score 600 paper-based; 80 iBT). Electronic applications accepted.

**University of Oklahoma Health Sciences Center,** College of Medicine and Graduate College, Graduate Programs in Medicine, Department of Cell Biology, Oklahoma City, OK 73190. Offers MS, PhD. *Degree requirements:* For master's, thesis; for doctorate, thesis/dissertation. *Entrance requirements:* For doctorate, GRE General Test, GRE Subject Test, 3 letters of recommendation. Additional exam requirements/recommendations for international students: required—TOEFL.

**University of Ottawa,** Faculty of Graduate and Postdoctoral Studies, Faculty of Medicine, Department of Cellular and Molecular Medicine, Ottawa, ON K1H 8M5, Canada. Offers M Sc, PhD. *Degree requirements:* For master's, thesis, seminar; for doctorate, comprehensive exam, thesis/dissertation, seminar. *Entrance requirements:* For master's, honors degree or equivalent, minimum B average; for doctorate, master's degree, minimum B+ average. Electronic applications accepted.

**University of Pennsylvania,** Perelman School of Medicine, Biomedical Graduate Studies, Graduate Group in Cell and Molecular Biology, Philadelphia, PA 19104. Offers cancer biology (PhD); cell biology, physiology, and metabolism (PhD); developmental stem cell regenerative biology (PhD); gene therapy and vaccines (PhD); genetics and gene regulation (PhD); microbiology, virology, and parasitology (PhD); MD/PhD; VMD/PhD. *Faculty:* 400 full-time (118 women). *Students:* 378 full-time (221 women); includes 134 minority (6 Black or African American, non-Hispanic/Latino; 56 Asian, non-Hispanic/Latino; 58 Hispanic/Latino; 2 Native Hawaiian or other Pacific Islander, non-Hispanic/Latino; 12 Two or more races, non-Hispanic/Latino), 52 international. 851 applicants, 14% accepted, 59 enrolled. In 2019, 43 doctorates awarded. *Unit head:* Dr. Daniel Kessler, Graduate Group Chair, 215-898-1478. *Application contact:* Meagan Schofer, Associate Director, 215-898-1478.
Website: http://www.med.upenn.edu/camb/

**University of Pittsburgh,** Kenneth P. Dietrich School of Arts and Sciences, Department of Biological Sciences, Program in Molecular, Cellular, and Developmental Biology, Pittsburgh, PA 15260. Offers PhD. *Faculty:* 27 full-time (9 women). *Students:* 52 full-time (31 women); includes 7 minority (4 Black or African American, non-Hispanic/Latino; 1 Hispanic/Latino; 2 Two or more races, non-Hispanic/Latino), 8 international. Average age 23. In 2019, 6 doctorates awarded. *Degree requirements:* For doctorate, comprehensive exam, thesis/dissertation, completion of research integrity module.

## Cell Biology

*Entrance requirements:* Additional exam requirements/recommendations for international students: required—TOEFL (minimum score 90 paper-based), IELTS (minimum score 7). *Application deadline:* For fall admission, 12/2 priority date for domestic and international students. Applications are processed on a rolling basis. Application fee: $0 ($75 for international students). Electronic applications accepted. *Financial support:* In 2019–20, 37 fellowships with full tuition reimbursements (averaging $36,108 per year), 94 research assistantships with full tuition reimbursements (averaging $30,840 per year), 19 teaching assistantships with full tuition reimbursements (averaging $30,375 per year) were awarded; Federal Work-Study, traineeships, and health care benefits also available. *Unit head:* Dr. Jeffrey G. Lawrence, Professor and Chair, 412-624-4350, Fax: 412-624-4759, E-mail: jlawrence@pitt.edu. *Application contact:* Cathleen M. Barr, Graduate Administrator, 412-624-4268, Fax: 412-624-4349, E-mail: cbarr@pitt.edu.
Website: http://www.biology.pitt.edu

**University of Puerto Rico at Rio Piedras,** College of Natural Sciences, Department of Biology, San Juan, PR 00931-3300. Offers ecology/systematics (MS, PhD); evolution/genetics (MS, PhD); molecular/cellular biology (MS, PhD); neuroscience (MS, PhD). *Program availability:* Part-time. *Degree requirements:* For master's, one foreign language, comprehensive exam, thesis; for doctorate, one foreign language, comprehensive exam, thesis/dissertation. *Entrance requirements:* For master's, GRE Subject Test, interview, minimum GPA of 3.0, letter of recommendation; for doctorate, GRE Subject Test, interview, master's degree, minimum GPA of 3.0, letter of recommendation.

**University of Rhode Island,** Graduate School, College of the Environment and Life Sciences, Department of Biological Sciences, Kingston, RI 02881. Offers cell and molecular biology (MS, PhD); earth and environmental sciences (MS, PhD); ecology and ecosystem sciences (MS, PhD); evolutionary and marine biology (MS, PhD); sustainable agriculture and food systems (MS, PhD). *Program availability:* Part-time. *Faculty:* 20 full-time (10 women). *Students:* 108 full-time (68 women), 22 part-time (15 women); includes 12 minority (6 Black or African American, non-Hispanic/Latino; 4 Asian, non-Hispanic/Latino; 1 Hispanic/Latino; 1 Two or more races, non-Hispanic/Latino), 22 international. In 2019, 12 master's, 10 doctorates awarded. *Entrance requirements:* Additional exam requirements/recommendations for international students: required—TOEFL. *Application deadline:* For fall admission, 1/15 for domestic and international students. Application fee: $65. Electronic applications accepted. *Expenses: Tuition, area resident:* Full-time $13,734; part-time $763 per credit. Tuition, state resident: full-time $13,734; part-time $763 per credit. Tuition, nonresident: full-time $26,512; part-time $1473 per credit. *International tuition:* $26,512 full-time. *Required fees:* $1780; $52 per credit. $35 per term. One-time fee: $165. *Financial support:* In 2019–20, 24 research assistantships with tuition reimbursements (averaging $9,961 per year), 1 teaching assistantship with tuition reimbursement (averaging $7,521 per year) were awarded. Financial award application deadline: 1/15; financial award applicants required to submit FAFSA. *Unit head:* Dr. Alison Roberts, Chair, E-mail: bio_chair@etal.uri.edu. *Application contact:* Bethany Jenkins, Graduate Program Director, 401-874-7551, E-mail: bdjenkins@uri.edu.
Website: http://web.uri.edu/bio/

**University of Rhode Island,** Graduate School, College of the Environment and Life Sciences, Department of Cell and Molecular Biology, Kingston, RI 02881. Offers biochemistry (MS, PhD); clinical laboratory sciences (MS), including biotechnology, clinical laboratory science, cytopathology; microbiology (MS, PhD); molecular genetics (MS, PhD). *Program availability:* Part-time. *Faculty:* 20 full-time (9 women). *Students:* 1 (woman) part-time. In 2019, 16 master's awarded. *Entrance requirements:* Additional exam requirements/recommendations for international students: required—TOEFL. *Application deadline:* For fall admission, 1/15 for domestic and international students. Application fee: $65. Electronic applications accepted. *Expenses: Tuition, area resident:* Full-time $13,734; part-time $763 per credit. Tuition, state resident: full-time $13,734; part-time $763 per credit. Tuition, nonresident: full-time $26,512; part-time $1473 per credit. *International tuition:* $26,512 full-time. *Required fees:* $1780; $52 per credit. $35 per term. One-time fee: $165. *Financial support:* In 2019–20, 11 teaching assistantships with tuition reimbursements (averaging $10,985 per year) were awarded; traineeships also available. Financial award application deadline: 1/15; financial award applicants required to submit FAFSA. *Unit head:* Dr. Joel Chandlee, Chair, E-mail: joelchandlee@uri.edu. *Application contact:* Dr. Steven Gregory, Graduate Program Director, 401-874-5947, E-mail: stgregory@uri.edu.
Website: https://web.uri.edu/cmb/

**University of Saskatchewan,** College of Medicine, Department of Anatomy, Physiology and Pharmacology, Saskatoon, SK S7N 5A2, Canada. Offers anatomy and cell biology (M Sc, PhD); pharmacology (M Sc, PhD); physiology (M Sc, PhD). *Degree requirements:* For master's, thesis; for doctorate, thesis/dissertation. *Entrance requirements:* Additional exam requirements/recommendations for international students: required—TOEFL.

**University of South Carolina,** The Graduate School, College of Arts and Sciences, Department of Biological Sciences, Graduate Training Program in Molecular, Cellular, and Developmental Biology, Columbia, SC 29208. Offers MS, PhD. *Degree requirements:* For master's, one foreign language, thesis; for doctorate, one foreign language, thesis/dissertation. *Entrance requirements:* For master's and doctorate, GRE General Test, minimum GPA of 3.0 in science. Electronic applications accepted.

**University of South Dakota,** Graduate School, Sanford School of Medicine and Graduate School, Biomedical Sciences Graduate Program, Cellular and Molecular Biology Group, Vermillion, SD 57069. Offers MS, PhD. Terminal master's awarded for partial completion of doctoral program. *Degree requirements:* For master's, thesis; for doctorate, comprehensive exam, thesis/dissertation. *Entrance requirements:* For master's and doctorate, GRE General Test, GRE Subject Test, minimum GPA of 3.0. Additional exam requirements/recommendations for international students: required—TOEFL (minimum score 550 paper-based; 80 iBT), IELTS (minimum score 6). Electronic applications accepted. *Expenses:* Contact institution.

**University of Southern California,** Keck School of Medicine and Graduate School, Graduate Programs in Medicine, Master of Science Program in Stem Cell Biology and Regenerative Medicine, Los Angeles, CA 90089. Offers MS. *Program availability:* Part-time. *Faculty:* 27 full-time (9 women). *Students:* 27 full-time (14 women), 6 part-time (all women); includes 17 minority (1 Black or African American, non-Hispanic/Latino; 14 Asian, non-Hispanic/Latino; 2 Hispanic/Latino). Average age 23. 77 applicants, 62% accepted, 22 enrolled. In 2019, 26 master's awarded. *Entrance requirements:* For master's, GRE, MCAT, or DAT. Additional exam requirements/recommendations for international students: required—TOEFL (minimum score 90 iBT), IELTS (minimum score 6.5). *Application deadline:* For fall admission, 4/30 for domestic and international students. Applications are processed on a rolling basis. Application fee: $90. Electronic applications accepted. *Financial support:* Federal Work-Study, institutionally sponsored loans, and scholarships/grants available. Financial award applicants required to submit FAFSA. *Unit head:* Dr. Francesca Mariani, Program Director, 323-442-7855, Fax: 323-442-2230, E-mail: fmariani@usc.edu. *Application contact:* Belen Lopez, Program Assistant, 323-865-1266, Fax: 323-442-8067, E-mail: belen.lopez@med.usc.edu.
Website: http://scrm.usc.edu/

**University of Southern California,** Keck School of Medicine and Graduate School, Graduate Programs in Medicine, Programs in Biomedical and Biological Sciences (PIBBS), Program in Development, Stem Cell and Regenerative Medicine, Los Angeles, CA 90089. Offers PhD. *Faculty:* 36 full-time (15 women). *Students:* 57 full-time (26 women); includes 15 minority (1 American Indian or Alaska Native, non-Hispanic/Latino; 6 Asian, non-Hispanic/Latino; 6 Hispanic/Latino; 1 Native Hawaiian or other Pacific Islander, non-Hispanic/Latino; 1 Two or more races, non-Hispanic/Latino), 27 international. Average age 26. 16 applicants, 100% accepted, 16 enrolled. In 2019, 8 doctorates awarded. *Degree requirements:* For doctorate, comprehensive exam, thesis/dissertation. *Entrance requirements:* For doctorate, GRE, minimum GPA of 3.5. Additional exam requirements/recommendations for international students: required—TOEFL (minimum score 600 paper-based; 100 iBT), IELTS (minimum score 7), PTE. *Application deadline:* For fall admission, 12/1 priority date for domestic and international students. Application fee: $90. Electronic applications accepted. *Financial support:* In 2019–20, 50 students received support, including 11 fellowships with full tuition reimbursements available (averaging $35,000 per year), 41 research assistantships with full tuition reimbursements available (averaging $35,000 per year), 5 teaching assistantships with full tuition reimbursements available (averaging $35,000 per year); institutionally sponsored loans, scholarships/grants, traineeships, health care benefits, and unspecified assistantships also available. Financial award application deadline: 4/15; financial award applicants required to submit CSS PROFILE or FAFSA. *Unit head:* Dr. Gage Crump, Director, 323-442-1475, Fax: 323-442-1199, E-mail: gcrump@med.usc.edu. *Application contact:* Karina Recinos, Student Services Advisor, 323-442-1609, Fax: 323-442-1199, E-mail: karina.recinos@med.usc.edu.
Website: http://keck.usc.edu/pibbs/phd-programs/development-stem-cell-and-regenerative-medicine

**University of South Florida,** College of Arts and Sciences, Department of Cell Biology, Microbiology, and Molecular Biology, Tampa, FL 33620-9951. Offers biology (MS), including cell biology, microbiology and molecular biology; cancer biology (PhD); cancer chemical biology (PhD); cancer immunology and immunotherapy (PhD); cell and molecular biology (PhD); microbiology (MS). *Faculty:* 21 full-time (8 women). *Students:* 85 full-time (50 women), 4 part-time (all women); includes 10 minority (1 Black or African American, non-Hispanic/Latino; 3 Asian, non-Hispanic/Latino; 4 Hispanic/Latino; 2 Two or more races, non-Hispanic/Latino), 35 international. Average age 27. 178 applicants, 15% accepted, 20 enrolled. In 2019, 12 master's, 12 doctorates awarded. *Degree requirements:* For master's, thesis or alternative; for doctorate, comprehensive exam, thesis/dissertation. *Entrance requirements:* For master's and doctorate, GRE General Test, minimum GPA of 3.0, extensive background in biology or chemistry. Additional exam requirements/recommendations for international students: required—TOEFL (minimum score 570 paper-based; 79 iBT) or IELTS (minimum score 6.5). *Application deadline:* For fall admission, 11/30 priority date for domestic and international students; for spring admission, 7/1 priority date for domestic students, 7/1 for international students. Application fee: $30. *Financial support:* In 2019–20, 9 students received support. Career-related internships or fieldwork, health care benefits, and unspecified assistantships available. Financial award application deadline: 4/1. *Unit head:* Dr. James Garey, Professor/Chair, 813-974-7103, Fax: 813-974-1614, E-mail: garey@usf.edu. *Application contact:* Dr. Kenneth Wright, Associate Professor of Cancer Biology, H. Lee Moffitt Cancer Center and Research Institute, 813-745-3918, Fax: 813-974-1614, E-mail: ken.wright@moffitt.org.
Website: http://biology.usf.edu/cmmb/

**The University of Texas at Austin,** Graduate School, Institute for Cellular and Molecular Biology, Austin, TX 78712-1111. Offers PhD.

**The University of Texas at Dallas,** School of Natural Sciences and Mathematics, Department of Biological Sciences, Richardson, TX 75080. Offers bioinformatics and computational biology (MS); biotechnology (MS); molecular and cell biology (MS, PhD). *Program availability:* Part-time, evening/weekend. *Faculty:* 20 full-time (5 women), 6 part-time/adjunct (4 women). *Students:* 128 full-time (81 women), 12 part-time (7 women); includes 29 minority (1 Black or African American, non-Hispanic/Latino; 19 Asian, non-Hispanic/Latino; 7 Hispanic/Latino; 2 Two or more races, non-Hispanic/Latino), 77 international. Average age 28. 309 applicants, 25% accepted, 38 enrolled. In 2019, 36 master's, 7 doctorates awarded. *Degree requirements:* For master's, thesis optional; for doctorate, thesis/dissertation, publishable paper. *Entrance requirements:* For master's and doctorate, GRE (minimum combined score of 1000 on verbal and quantitative). Additional exam requirements/recommendations for international students: required—TOEFL (minimum score 550 paper-based; 80 iBT). *Application deadline:* For fall admission, 7/15 for domestic students, 5/1 priority date for international students; for spring admission, 11/15 for domestic students, 9/1 priority date for international students. Applications are processed on a rolling basis. Application fee: $50 ($100 for international students). Electronic applications accepted. *Expenses: Tuition, area resident:* Full-time $16,504. Tuition, state resident: full-time $16,504. Tuition, nonresident: full-time $34,266. Tuition and fees vary according to course load. *Financial support:* In 2019–20, 86 students received support, including 1 fellowship with partial tuition reimbursement available (averaging $500 per year), 16 research assistantships with partial tuition reimbursements available (averaging $25,200 per year), 69 teaching assistantships with partial tuition reimbursements available (averaging $18,173 per year); career-related internships or fieldwork, Federal Work-Study, institutionally sponsored loans, scholarships/grants, and unspecified assistantships also available. Support available to part-time students. Financial award application deadline: 4/30; financial award applicants required to submit FAFSA. *Unit head:* Dr. Tae Hoon Kim, Department Head, 972-883-6032, Fax: 972-883-4551, E-mail: biology@utdallas.edu. *Application contact:* Nancy Yu, Graduate Support Assistant, 972-883-4794, Fax: 972-883-4551, E-mail: biology@utdallas.edu.
Website: https://biology.utdallas.edu/

**The University of Texas at San Antonio,** College of Sciences, Department of Biology, San Antonio, TX 78249-0617. Offers biology (MS); biotechnology (MS); cell and molecular biology (PhD); neurobiology (PhD). Terminal master's awarded for partial completion of doctoral program. *Degree requirements:* For master's, comprehensive exam, thesis or alternative; for doctorate, comprehensive exam, thesis/dissertation. *Entrance requirements:* For master's, GRE General Test, bachelor's degree with 18 credit hours in field of study or in another appropriate field of study; for doctorate, GRE General Test, 3 letters of recommendation, statement of purpose, resume. Additional exam requirements/recommendations for international students: required—TOEFL (minimum score 500 paper-based; 100 iBT), IELTS (minimum score 5). Electronic applications accepted.

**The University of Texas Health Science Center at Houston,** MD Anderson UTHealth Graduate School, Houston, TX 77225-0036. Offers biochemistry and cell biology (PhD); biomedical sciences (MS); cancer biology (PhD); genetic counseling (MS); genetics and epigenetics (PhD); immunology (PhD); medical physics (MS, PhD); microbiology and infectious diseases (PhD); neuroscience (PhD); quantitative sciences (PhD); therapeutics and pharmacology (PhD); MD/PhD. Terminal master's awarded for partial completion of doctoral program. *Degree requirements:* For master's, thesis; for doctorate, thesis/dissertation. *Entrance requirements:* For master's and doctorate, GRE

General Test. Additional exam requirements/recommendations for international students: required—TOEFL. Electronic applications accepted.

**The University of Texas Health Science Center at San Antonio,** Graduate School of Biomedical Sciences, Department of Cellular and Structural Biology, San Antonio, TX 78229-3900. Offers MS, PhD. *Degree requirements:* For master's, thesis; for doctorate, comprehensive exam, thesis/dissertation.

**The University of Texas Medical Branch,** Graduate School of Biomedical Sciences, Program in Biochemistry and Molecular Biology, Galveston, TX 77555. Offers biochemistry (PhD); bioinformatics (PhD); biophysics (PhD); cell biology (PhD); computational biology (PhD); structural biology (PhD). *Degree requirements:* For doctorate, thesis/dissertation. *Entrance requirements:* Additional exam requirements/recommendations for international students: required—TOEFL (minimum score 550 paper-based). Electronic applications accepted.

**The University of Texas Medical Branch,** Graduate School of Biomedical Sciences, Program in Cell Biology, Galveston, TX 77555. Offers MS, PhD. *Degree requirements:* For doctorate, thesis/dissertation. *Entrance requirements:* For doctorate, GRE General Test. Additional exam requirements/recommendations for international students: required—TOEFL (minimum score 550 paper-based). Electronic applications accepted.

**The University of Texas Southwestern Medical Center,** Southwestern Graduate School of Biomedical Sciences, Division of Basic Science, Program in Cell Regulation, Dallas, TX 75390. Offers PhD. *Degree requirements:* For doctorate, thesis/dissertation, qualifying exam. *Entrance requirements:* For doctorate, GRE General Test, minimum GPA of 3.0. Additional exam requirements/recommendations for international students: required—TOEFL. Electronic applications accepted.

**University of the Sciences,** Program in Cell Biology and Biotechnology, Philadelphia, PA 19104-4495. Offers MS. *Program availability:* Part-time, evening/weekend. *Degree requirements:* For master's, thesis optional. *Entrance requirements:* For master's, GRE General Test. Additional exam requirements/recommendations for international students: required—TOEFL, TWE. *Expenses:* Contact institution.

**University of Toronto,** School of Graduate Studies, Faculty of Arts and Science, Department of Cell and Systems Biology, Toronto, ON M5S 1A1, Canada. Offers M Sc, PhD. *Degree requirements:* For master's, thesis, thesis defense; for doctorate, thesis/dissertation, thesis defense, oral thesis examination. *Entrance requirements:* For master's, minimum B+ average in final year, B overall, 3 letters of reference. Additional exam requirements/recommendations for international students: required—TOEFL (minimum score 580 paper-based; 93 iBT), TWE (minimum score 5). Electronic applications accepted.

**University of Vermont,** Graduate College, Cross-College Interdisciplinary Program, Cellular, Molecular and Biomedical Sciences Program, Burlington, VT 05405. Offers PhD. *Degree requirements:* For doctorate, thesis/dissertation. *Entrance requirements:* For doctorate, GRE General Test. Additional exam requirements/recommendations for international students: required—TOEFL (minimum score 550 paper-based; 100 iBT), IELTS (minimum score 7). Electronic applications accepted.

**University of Virginia,** School of Medicine, Department of Cell Biology, Charlottesville, VA 22903. Offers PhD, MD/PhD. *Degree requirements:* For doctorate, one foreign language, thesis/dissertation. *Entrance requirements:* For doctorate, GRE General Test, GRE Subject Test (recommended), 2 letters of recommendation. Additional exam requirements/recommendations for international students: required—TOEFL. Electronic applications accepted.

**University of Washington,** Graduate School, School of Medicine, Graduate Programs in Medicine, Program in Molecular and Cellular Biology, Seattle, WA 98195. Offers PhD. *Degree requirements:* For doctorate, thesis/dissertation. *Entrance requirements:* For doctorate, GRE General Test. Additional exam requirements/recommendations for international students: required—TOEFL. Electronic applications accepted.

**The University of Western Ontario,** Schulich School of Medicine and Dentistry, Department of Anatomy and Cell Biology, London, ON N6A 3K7, Canada. Offers anatomy and cell biology (M Sc, PhD); clinical anatomy (M Sc). *Degree requirements:* For master's, thesis; for doctorate, comprehensive exam, thesis/dissertation. *Entrance requirements:* For master's, honors degree or equivalent in biological sciences; for doctorate, master's degree. Additional exam requirements/recommendations for international students: required—TOEFL.

**University of Wisconsin–La Crosse,** College of Science and Health, Department of Biology, La Crosse, WI 54601. Offers aquatic sciences (MS); biology (MS); cellular and molecular biology (MS); clinical microbiology (MS); microbiology (MS); nurse anesthesia (MS); physiology (MS). *Accreditation:* AANA/CANAEP. *Program availability:* Part-time. *Faculty:* 19 full-time (7 women). *Students:* 12 full-time (6 women), 39 part-time (15 women); includes 2 minority (1 Black or African American, non-Hispanic/Latino; 1 Asian, non-Hispanic/Latino). Average age 28. 37 applicants, 68% accepted, 19 enrolled. In 2019, 19 master's awarded. *Degree requirements:* For master's, comprehensive exam, thesis. *Entrance requirements:* For master's, GRE General Test, minimum GPA of 2.85. Additional exam requirements/recommendations for international students: required—TOEFL (minimum score 550 paper-based; 79 iBT). *Application deadline:* For fall admission, 2/1 priority date for domestic and international students; for spring admission, 1/4 priority date for domestic and international students. Applications are processed on a rolling basis. Electronic applications accepted. *Financial support:* Research assistantships with partial tuition reimbursements, Federal Work-Study, scholarships/grants, health care benefits, and tuition waivers (partial) available. Support available to part-time students. Financial award application deadline: 3/15; financial award applicants required to submit FAFSA. *Unit head:* Dr. Michael Abler, Department Chair, 608-785-6962, E-mail: mabler@uwlax.edu. *Application contact:* Jennifer Weber, Senior Student Services Coordinator Graduate Admissions, 608-785-8939, E-mail: admissions@uwlax.edu.
Website: http://uwlax.edu/biology/

**University of Wisconsin–Madison,** Graduate School, Program in Cellular and Molecular Biology, Madison, WI 53706-1596. Offers PhD. *Degree requirements:* For doctorate, comprehensive exam, thesis/dissertation. *Entrance requirements:* For doctorate, minimum GPA of 3.0, lab experience. Additional exam requirements/recommendations for international students: required—TOEFL (minimum score 580 paper-based; 92 iBT). Electronic applications accepted.

**University of Wisconsin–Milwaukee,** Graduate School, College of Letters and Science, Department of Biological Sciences, Milwaukee, WI 53201-0413. Offers cellular and molecular biology (MS, PhD); microbiology (MS, PhD). *Degree requirements:* For master's, thesis; for doctorate, thesis/dissertation, 1 foreign language or data analysis proficiency. *Entrance requirements:* For master's and doctorate, GRE General Test. Additional exam requirements/recommendations for international students: required—TOEFL (minimum score 550 paper-based; 79 iBT), IELTS (minimum score 6.5). Electronic applications accepted.

**University of Wyoming,** Graduate Program in Molecular and Cellular Life Sciences, Laramie, WY 82071. Offers PhD. *Degree requirements:* For doctorate, thesis/dissertation, four eight-week laboratory rotations, comprehensive basic practical exam, two-part qualifying exam, seminars, symposium.

**Université Laval,** Faculty of Medicine, Graduate Programs in Medicine, Programs in Cellular and Molecular Biology, Québec, QC G1K 7P4, Canada. Offers M Sc, PhD. Terminal master's awarded for partial completion of doctoral program. *Degree requirements:* For master's, thesis; for doctorate, comprehensive exam, thesis/dissertation. *Entrance requirements:* For master's and doctorate, knowledge of French, comprehension of written English. Electronic applications accepted.

**Vanderbilt University,** School of Medicine, Department of Cell and Developmental Biology, Nashville, TN 37240-1001. Offers MS, PhD, MD/PhD. *Faculty:* 22 full-time (9 women). *Students:* 57 full-time (39 women); includes 10 minority (2 Black or African American, non-Hispanic/Latino; 1 Asian, non-Hispanic/Latino; 5 Hispanic/Latino; 2 Two or more races, non-Hispanic/Latino), 12 international. Average age 27. In 2019, 1 master's, 10 doctorates awarded. Terminal master's awarded for partial completion of doctoral program. *Degree requirements:* For master's, thesis or alternative; for doctorate, thesis/dissertation, preliminary, qualifying, and final exams. *Entrance requirements:* For master's, GRE General Test; for doctorate, GRE General Test, GRE Subject Test (recommended). Additional exam requirements/recommendations for international students: required—TOEFL (minimum score 570 paper-based; 88 iBT). *Application deadline:* For fall admission, 1/15 for domestic and international students. Electronic applications accepted. *Expenses:* Tuition: Full-time $51,018; part-time $2087 per hour. *Required fees:* $542. Tuition and fees vary according to program. *Financial support:* Fellowships, research assistantships, career-related internships or fieldwork, Federal Work-Study, institutionally sponsored loans, scholarships/grants, traineeships, health care benefits, and tuition waivers (partial) available. Financial award application deadline: 1/15; financial award applicants required to submit CSS PROFILE or FAFSA. *Unit head:* Ian Macara, Chair, 615-875-5565, Fax: 615-343-4539, E-mail: ian.macara@vanderbilt.edu. *Application contact:* Kristi Hargrove, Program Coordinator, 615-322-2294, Fax: 615-343-4539, E-mail: kristi.l.hargrove@vanderbilt.edu.
Website: http://www.mc.vanderbilt.edu/cdb/

**Washington University in St. Louis,** The Graduate School, Division of Biology and Biomedical Sciences, Program in Molecular Cell Biology, St. Louis, MO 63130-4899. Offers PhD. *Degree requirements:* For doctorate, thesis/dissertation. *Entrance requirements:* For doctorate, GRE General Test, GRE Subject Test. Additional exam requirements/recommendations for international students: required—TOEFL. Electronic applications accepted.

**Weill Cornell Medicine,** Weill Cornell Graduate School of Medical Sciences, Biochemistry, Cell and Molecular Biology Allied Program, New York, NY 10065. Offers MS, PhD. Terminal master's awarded for partial completion of doctoral program. *Degree requirements:* For master's, comprehensive exam; for doctorate, thesis/dissertation, final exam. *Entrance requirements:* For doctorate, GRE General Test, background in genetics, molecular biology, chemistry, or biochemistry. Additional exam requirements/recommendations for international students: required—TOEFL. Electronic applications accepted.

**Wesleyan University,** Graduate Studies, Department of Biology, Middletown, CT 06459. Offers cell and developmental biology (PhD); evolution and ecology (PhD); genetics and genomics (PhD), including bioinformatics; neurobiology and behavior (PhD). Terminal master's awarded for partial completion of doctoral program. *Degree requirements:* For doctorate, comprehensive exam, thesis/dissertation, public seminar. *Entrance requirements:* For doctorate, GRE, official transcripts, three recommendation letters, essay. Additional exam requirements/recommendations for international students: required—TOEFL. Electronic applications accepted.

**Yale University,** Graduate School of Arts and Sciences, Department of Cell Biology, New Haven, CT 06520. Offers PhD. *Degree requirements:* For doctorate, thesis/dissertation. *Entrance requirements:* For doctorate, GRE General Test. *Expenses:* Contact institution.

**Yale University,** Graduate School of Arts and Sciences, Department of Molecular, Cellular, and Developmental Biology, Program in Cellular and Developmental Biology, New Haven, CT 06520. Offers PhD. *Degree requirements:* For doctorate, thesis/dissertation. *Entrance requirements:* For doctorate, GRE General Test, GRE Subject Test.

**Yale University,** Yale School of Medicine and Graduate School of Arts and Sciences, Combined Program in Biological and Biomedical Sciences (BBS), Molecular Cell Biology, Genetics, and Development Track, New Haven, CT 06520. Offers PhD, MD/PhD. *Entrance requirements:* Additional exam requirements/recommendations for international students: required—TOEFL.

# Molecular Biology

**Albany College of Pharmacy and Health Sciences,** School of Arts and Sciences, Albany, NY 12208. Offers clinical laboratory sciences (MS); cytotechnology and molecular cytology (MS); health outcomes research (MS); molecular biosciences (MS). *Degree requirements:* For master's, thesis. *Entrance requirements:* For master's, GRE, minimum GPA of 3.0. Additional exam requirements/recommendations for international students: required—TOEFL (minimum score 84 iBT). Electronic applications accepted.

**Albany Medical College,** Center for Cell Biology and Cancer Research, Albany, NY 12208-3479. Offers MS, PhD. *Program availability:* Part-time. Terminal master's awarded for partial completion of doctoral program. *Degree requirements:* For master's, thesis; for doctorate, comprehensive exam, thesis/dissertation. *Entrance requirements:* For master's and doctorate, GRE General Test, all transcripts, letters of recommendation. Additional exam requirements/recommendations for international students: required—TOEFL.

**Albert Einstein College of Medicine,** Graduate Programs in the Biomedical Sciences, Department of Developmental and Molecular Biology, Bronx, NY 10461. Offers PhD, MD/PhD. *Degree requirements:* For doctorate, thesis/dissertation. *Entrance*

*requirements:* For doctorate, GRE General Test. Additional exam requirements/recommendations for international students: required—TOEFL.

**Appalachian State University,** Cratis D. Williams School of Graduate Studies, Department of Biology, Boone, NC 28608. Offers cell and molecular biology (MS). *Program availability:* Part-time. *Degree requirements:* For master's, comprehensive exam, thesis. *Entrance requirements:* For master's, GRE General Test, 3 letters of recommendation. Additional exam requirements/recommendations for international students: required—TOEFL (minimum score 570 paper-based; 79 iBT), IELTS (minimum score 6.5). Electronic applications accepted.

**Arizona State University at Tempe,** College of Liberal Arts and Sciences, School of Life Sciences, Tempe, AZ 85287-4601. Offers animal behavior (PhD); applied ethics (biomedical and health ethics) (MA); biology (MS, PhD), including biology, biology and society, complex adaptive systems science (PhD), plant biology and conservation (MS); environmental life sciences (PhD); evolutionary biology (PhD); history and philosophy of science (PhD); human and social dimensions of science and technology (PhD); microbiology (PhD); molecular and cellular biology (PhD); neuroscience (PhD). Terminal master's awarded for partial completion of doctoral program. *Degree requirements:* For master's, thesis (for some programs), interactive Program of Study (iPOS) submitted before completing 50 percent of required credit hours; for doctorate, variable foreign language requirement, comprehensive exam, thesis/dissertation, interactive Program of Study (iPOS) submitted before completing 50 percent of required credit hours. *Entrance requirements:* For master's and doctorate, GRE, minimum GPA of 3.0 or equivalent in last 2 years of work leading to bachelor's degree. Additional exam requirements/recommendations for international students: required—TOEFL (minimum score 600 paper-based; 100 iBT). Electronic applications accepted.

**Arkansas State University,** Graduate School, College of Sciences and Mathematics, Program in Molecular Biosciences, State University, AR 72467. Offers molecular biosciences (MS, PhD). *Program availability:* Part-time. *Degree requirements:* For master's, comprehensive exam, thesis; for doctorate, comprehensive exam, thesis/dissertation. *Entrance requirements:* For master's, GRE, appropriate bachelor's degree, official transcripts, immunization records, letters of reference, autobiography; for doctorate, GRE, appropriate bachelor's or master's degree, interview, letters of recommendation, official transcripts, personal statement, immunization records. Additional exam requirements/recommendations for international students: required—TOEFL (minimum score 550 paper-based; 79 iBT), IELTS (minimum score 6), PTE (minimum score 56). Electronic applications accepted.

**Auburn University,** Graduate School, Interdepartmental Programs, Auburn University, AL 36849. Offers applied economics (PhD); cell and molecular biology (PhD); real estate development (MRED); sociology and rural sociology (MA, MS). *Program availability:* Part-time. *Students:* 16 full-time (9 women), 6 part-time (4 women); includes 1 minority (Hispanic/Latino), 3 international. Average age 30. 53 applicants, 75% accepted, 27 enrolled. In 2019, 10 master's, 4 doctorates awarded. *Entrance requirements:* For master's, GRE General Test. Additional exam requirements/recommendations for international students: required—TOEFL (minimum score 550 paper-based; 79 iBT), iTEP; recommended—IELTS (minimum score 6.5). *Application deadline:* Applications are processed on a rolling basis. Application fee: $60 ($70 for international students). Electronic applications accepted. *Expenses:* Tuition, area resident: Full-time $9828; part-time $546 per credit hour. Tuition, state resident: full-time $9828; part-time $546 per credit hour. Tuition, nonresident: full-time $29,484; part-time $1638 per credit hour. *International tuition:* $29,744 full-time. Tuition and fees vary according to course load, program and reciprocity agreements. *Financial support:* In 2019–20, 2 fellowships (averaging $3,600 per year) were awarded; research assistantships, teaching assistantships, and Federal Work-Study also available. Support available to part-time students. Financial award application deadline: 3/15; financial award applicants required to submit FAFSA. *Application contact:* Dr. George Flowers, Dean of the Graduate School, 334-844-2125.

**Baylor College of Medicine,** Graduate School of Biomedical Sciences, Department of Biochemistry and Molecular Biology, Houston, TX 77030-3498. Offers PhD; MD/PhD. *Degree requirements:* For doctorate, thesis/dissertation, public defense. *Entrance requirements:* For doctorate, GRE General Test, GRE Subject Test (strongly recommended), minimum GPA of 3.0. Additional exam requirements/recommendations for international students: required—TOEFL. Electronic applications accepted.

**Baylor College of Medicine,** Graduate School of Biomedical Sciences, Department of Molecular and Cellular Biology, Houston, TX 77030-3498. Offers PhD; MD/PhD. *Degree requirements:* For doctorate, thesis/dissertation, public defense, qualifying exam. *Entrance requirements:* For doctorate, GRE General Test, GRE Subject Test (strongly recommended), minimum GPA of 3.0. Additional exam requirements/recommendations for international students: required—TOEFL. Electronic applications accepted.

**Baylor College of Medicine,** Graduate School of Biomedical Sciences, Interdepartmental Program in Cell and Molecular Biology, Houston, TX 77030-3498. Offers biochemistry (PhD); cell and molecular biology (PhD); genetics (PhD); human genetics (PhD); immunology (PhD); microbiology (PhD); virology (PhD); MD/PhD. *Degree requirements:* For doctorate, thesis/dissertation, public defense. *Entrance requirements:* For doctorate, GRE General Test, GRE Subject Test (strongly recommended), minimum GPA of 3.0. Additional exam requirements/recommendations for international students: required—TOEFL. Electronic applications accepted.

**Boise State University,** College of Arts and Sciences, Department of Biological Sciences, Boise, ID 83725-1515. Offers biology (MA, MS); biomolecular sciences (PhD); raptor biology (MS). *Program availability:* Part-time. *Students:* 50 full-time (36 women), 10 part-time (5 women); includes 6 minority (4 Hispanic/Latino; 1 Native Hawaiian or other Pacific Islander, non-Hispanic/Latino; 1 Two or more races, non-Hispanic/Latino), 4 international. *Degree requirements:* For master's, thesis. *Entrance requirements:* For master's, GRE General Test, minimum GPA of 3.0. Additional exam requirements/recommendations for international students: required—TOEFL, IELTS. Electronic applications accepted. *Expenses: Tuition, area resident:* Full-time $7110; part-time $470 per credit hour. Tuition, state resident: full-time $7110; part-time $470 per credit hour. Tuition, nonresident: full-time $24,030; part-time $827 per credit hour. *International tuition:* $24,030 full-time. *Required fees:* $2536. Tuition and fees vary according to course load and program. *Financial support:* Research assistantships, teaching assistantships, institutionally sponsored loans, and unspecified assistantships available. Financial award application deadline: 1/15; financial award applicants required to submit FAFSA. *Unit head:* Dr. Kevin Feris, Chair, 208-426-4267, E-mail: kevinferis@boisestate.edu. *Application contact:* Dr. Ian Roberts, Graduate Coordinator, 208-426-3208, E-mail: iroberts@boisestate.edu.
Website: https://www.boisestate.edu/biology/

**Boston University,** Graduate School of Arts and Sciences, Molecular Biology, Cell Biology, and Biochemistry Program (MCBB), Boston, MA 02215. Offers MA, PhD. *Students:* 34 full-time (19 women), 2 part-time (both women); includes 7 minority (3 Black or African American, non-Hispanic/Latino; 3 Hispanic/Latino; 1 Two or more races, non-Hispanic/Latino), 9 international. Average age 27. 220 applicants, 9% accepted, 5 enrolled. In 2019, 10 master's, 4 doctorates awarded. Terminal master's awarded for partial completion of doctoral program. *Degree requirements:* For master's, thesis (for some programs); for doctorate, comprehensive exam, thesis/dissertation, teaching requirement. *Entrance requirements:* For master's and doctorate, 3 letters of recommendation, transcripts, personal statement. Additional exam requirements/recommendations for international students: required—TOEFL (minimum score 550 paper-based; 84 iBT). *Application deadline:* For fall admission, 12/10 for domestic and international students. Application fee: $95. Electronic applications accepted. *Financial support:* In 2019–20, 31 students received support, including 3 fellowships with full tuition reimbursements available (averaging $23,340 per year), 5 research assistantships with full tuition reimbursements available (averaging $23,340 per year), 5 teaching assistantships with full tuition reimbursements available (averaging $23,440 per year); Federal Work-Study, scholarships/grants, traineeships, and health care benefits also available. Financial award application deadline: 12/10; financial award applicants required to submit FAFSA. *Unit head:* Thomas Gilmore, Director, 617-353-2432, Fax: 617-353-6340, E-mail: gilmore@bu.edu. *Application contact:* Christina Honeycutt, Academic Administrator, 617-353-2432, Fax: 617-353-6340, E-mail: cjhoney@bu.edu.
Website: http://www.bu.edu/mcbb/

**Brandeis University,** Graduate School of Arts and Sciences, Department of Biology, Waltham, MA 02454-9110. Offers genetics (PhD); microbiology (PhD); molecular and cell biology (MS, PhD); molecular biology (PhD); neurobiology (PhD); quantitative biology (PhD). *Program availability:* Part-time. *Faculty:* 28 full-time (14 women), 1 part-time/adjunct (0 women). *Students:* 44 full-time (26 women), 1 (woman) part-time; includes 15 minority (1 American Indian or Alaska Native, non-Hispanic/Latino; 7 Asian, non-Hispanic/Latino; 7 Hispanic/Latino), 10 international. Average age 27. 202 applicants, 22% accepted, 12 enrolled. In 2019, 9 master's, 6 doctorates awarded. Terminal master's awarded for partial completion of doctoral program. *Degree requirements:* For master's, thesis optional; for doctorate, comprehensive exam, thesis/dissertation. *Entrance requirements:* For master's, transcripts, letters of recommendation, resume, statement of purpose; for doctorate, transcripts, letters of recommendation, resume, program questions, statement of purpose. Additional exam requirements/recommendations for international students: required—TOEFL, IELTS, PTE. *Application deadline:* For fall admission, 12/1 priority date for domestic and international students; for spring admission, 10/15 for domestic students, 11/15 for international students. Applications are processed on a rolling basis. Application fee: $75. Electronic applications accepted. *Financial support:* In 2019–20, 50 fellowships with full tuition reimbursements (averaging $35,000 per year), 21 teaching assistantships (averaging $3,550 per year) were awarded; research assistantships, scholarships/grants, health care benefits, and tuition waivers also available. Support available to part-time students. *Unit head:* Dr. Michael Marr, Director of Graduate Studies, 781-736-2481, E-mail: mmarr@brandeis.edu. *Application contact:* Maryanna Aldrich, Administrator, 781-736-2352, E-mail: scigradoffice@brandeis.edu.
Website: http://www.brandeis.edu/gsas/programs/mcbio.html

**Brigham Young University,** Graduate Studies, College of Life Sciences, Department of Microbiology and Molecular Biology, Provo, UT 84602-1001. Offers MS, PhD. *Faculty:* 19 full-time (3 women), 8 part-time/adjunct (6 women). *Students:* 30 full-time (15 women); includes 9 minority (1 Black or African American, non-Hispanic/Latino; 2 Asian, non-Hispanic/Latino; 5 Hispanic/Latino; 1 Native Hawaiian or other Pacific Islander, non-Hispanic/Latino), 7 international. Average age 29. 19 applicants, 79% accepted, 8 enrolled. In 2019, 7 master's, 3 doctorates awarded. Terminal master's awarded for partial completion of doctoral program. *Degree requirements:* For master's, comprehensive exam, thesis, Completion of research and didactic credits; for doctorate, comprehensive exam, thesis/dissertation, Published in a scientific journal, completion of research and didactic credits. *Entrance requirements:* For master's, GRE General Test, minimum GPA of 3.0 during previous 2 years; for doctorate, GRE General Test, minimum GPA of 3.0. Additional exam requirements/recommendations for international students: required—TOEFL (minimum score 580 paper-based; 85 iBT), IELTS (minimum score 7), PTE. *Application deadline:* For fall admission, 1/15 for domestic and international students. Application fee: $50. Electronic applications accepted. *Expenses:* LDS $430 per credit, Non-LDS $860 per credit. *Financial support:* Fellowships, institutionally sponsored loans, scholarships/grants, health care benefits, and unspecified assistantships available. Financial award application deadline: 2/1; financial award applicants required to submit FAFSA. *Unit head:* Dr. Richard Robison, Chair, 801-422-2416, Fax: 801-422-0004, E-mail: richard_robison@byu.edu. *Application contact:* Dr. Kevin Ornal Johnson, Graduate Coordinator, 801-422-4293, Fax: 801-422-0004, E-mail: kevin_johnson@byu.edu.
Website: http://mmbio.byu.edu/

**Brown University,** Graduate School, Division of Biology and Medicine, Department of Molecular Biology, Cell Biology, and Biochemistry, Providence, RI 02912. Offers MA, PhD. *Program availability:* Part-time. Terminal master's awarded for partial completion of doctoral program. *Degree requirements:* For master's, thesis (for some programs); for doctorate, one foreign language, thesis/dissertation, preliminary exam. *Entrance requirements:* For master's and doctorate, GRE General Test, GRE Subject Test. Additional exam requirements/recommendations for international students: required—TOEFL. Electronic applications accepted.

**California Institute of Technology,** Division of Biology and Biological Engineering, Program in Molecular Biology, Pasadena, CA 91125-0001. Offers PhD. *Degree requirements:* For doctorate, thesis/dissertation, qualifying exam. *Entrance requirements:* For doctorate, GRE General Test.

**California State University, Sacramento,** College of Natural Sciences and Mathematics, Department of Biological Sciences, Sacramento, CA 95819. Offers biological conservation (MS); molecular and cellular biology (MS); stem cell (MA). *Program availability:* Part-time. *Students:* 38 full-time (12 women), 24 part-time (8 women); includes 19 minority (14 Asian, non-Hispanic/Latino; 4 Hispanic/Latino; 1 Native Hawaiian or other Pacific Islander, non-Hispanic/Latino), 1 international. Average age 29. 68 applicants, 44% accepted, 23 enrolled. In 2019, 13 master's awarded. *Degree requirements:* For master's, comprehensive exam (for some programs), thesis (for some programs), thesis or project; writing proficiency exam. *Entrance requirements:* For master's, GRE, bachelor's degree in biology or equivalent; minimum GPA of 2.75 in all biology courses, 3.0 in all upper-division biology courses. Additional exam requirements/recommendations for international students: required—TOEFL (minimum score 550 paper-based; 80 iBT); recommended—IELTS (minimum score 7). *Application deadline:* For fall admission, 2/1 for domestic students, 1/1 for international students. Applications are processed on a rolling basis. Application fee: $70. Electronic applications accepted. *Expenses:* Contact institution. *Financial support:* Teaching assistantships, career-related internships or fieldwork, Federal Work-Study, and scholarships/grants available. Support available to part-time students. Financial award application deadline: 3/1; financial award applicants required to submit FAFSA. *Unit head:* Dr. Shannon Datwyler, Chair, 916-278-6535, Fax: 916-278-6993, E-mail: datwyler@csus.edu. *Application contact:* Jose Martinez, Graduate Admissions Supervisor, 916-278-7871, E-mail: martinj@skymail.csus.edu.
Website: http://www.csus.edu/bios

**Carnegie Mellon University,** Mellon College of Science, Department of Biological Sciences, Pittsburgh, PA 15213-3891. Offers biochemistry (PhD); biophysics (PhD); cell

and developmental biology (PhD); computational biology (MS, PhD); genetics (PhD); molecular biology (PhD); neuroscience (PhD); structural biology (PhD). *Degree requirements:* For doctorate, comprehensive exam, thesis/dissertation. *Entrance requirements:* For doctorate, GRE General Test, GRE Subject Test, interview. Electronic applications accepted.

**Case Western Reserve University,** School of Medicine and School of Graduate Studies, Graduate Programs in Medicine, Department of Molecular Biology and Microbiology, Cleveland, OH 44106-4960. Offers cell biology (PhD); molecular biology (PhD); molecular virology (PhD); MD/PhD. *Degree requirements:* For doctorate, thesis/dissertation. *Entrance requirements:* For doctorate, GRE General Test, GRE Subject Test. Additional exam requirements/recommendations for international students: required—TOEFL. Electronic applications accepted.

**Central Connecticut State University,** School of Graduate Studies, School of Engineering, Science and Technology, Department of Biomolecular Sciences, New Britain, CT 06050-4010. Offers MS, Certificate. *Program availability:* Part-time, evening/weekend. *Degree requirements:* For master's, comprehensive exam, thesis or alternative; for Certificate, qualifying exam. *Entrance requirements:* For master's, minimum undergraduate GPA of 2.7, essay; for Certificate, essay. Additional exam requirements/recommendations for international students: required—TOEFL (minimum score 550 paper-based; 79 iBT); recommended—IELTS (minimum score 6.5). Electronic applications accepted.

**Clemson University,** Graduate School, College of Science, Department of Genetics and Biochemistry, Clemson, SC 29634. Offers biochemistry and molecular biology (PhD); genetics (PhD). *Degree requirements:* For doctorate, comprehensive exam, thesis/dissertation. *Entrance requirements:* For doctorate, GRE General Test, unofficial transcripts, letters of recommendation. Additional exam requirements/recommendations for international students: required—TOEFL (minimum score 80 paper-based; 80 iBT); recommended—IELTS (minimum score 6.5), TSE (minimum score 54). Electronic applications accepted. *Expenses:* Contact institution.

**Columbia University,** College of Physicians and Surgeons, Integrated Program in Cellular, Molecular, Structural and Genetic Studies, New York, NY 10032. Offers PhD. Terminal master's awarded for partial completion of doctoral program. *Degree requirements:* For doctorate, thesis/dissertation. *Entrance requirements:* For doctorate, GRE General Test, GRE Subject Test. Additional exam requirements/recommendations for international students: required—TOEFL. *Expenses:* Contact institution.

**Cornell University,** Graduate School, Graduate Fields of Agriculture and Life Sciences, Field of Biochemistry, Molecular and Cell Biology, Ithaca, NY 14853. Offers biochemistry (PhD); biophysics (PhD); cell biology (PhD); molecular biology (PhD). *Degree requirements:* For doctorate, comprehensive exam, thesis/dissertation, 2 semesters of teaching experience. *Entrance requirements:* For doctorate, GRE General Test, GRE Subject Test (biology, chemistry, physics, biochemistry, cell and molecular biology), 3 letters of recommendation. Additional exam requirements/recommendations for international students: required—TOEFL (minimum score 600 paper-based; 77 iBT). Electronic applications accepted.

**Cornell University,** Graduate School, Graduate Fields of Agriculture and Life Sciences and Graduate Fields of Human Ecology, Field of Nutrition, Ithaca, NY 14853. Offers animal nutrition (MPS, PhD); community nutrition (MPS, PhD); human nutrition (MPS, PhD); international nutrition (MPS, PhD); molecular biochemistry (MPS, PhD). *Degree requirements:* For master's, thesis (MS), project papers (MPS); for doctorate, comprehensive exam, thesis/dissertation. *Entrance requirements:* For master's and doctorate, GRE General Test, previous course work in organic chemistry (with laboratory) and biochemistry; 2 letters of recommendation. Additional exam requirements/recommendations for international students: required—TOEFL (minimum score 550 paper-based; 77 iBT). Electronic applications accepted.

**Dartmouth College,** Guarini School of Graduate and Advanced Studies, Graduate Programs in Biological Sciences, Graduate Program in Molecular and Cellular Biology, Hanover, NH 03755. Offers PhD, MBA/PhD, MD/PhD. *Entrance requirements:* For doctorate, GRE General Test, letters of recommendation, minimum GPA of 3.0. Electronic applications accepted.

**Drexel University,** College of Medicine, Biomedical Graduate Programs, Interdisciplinary Program in Molecular and Cell Biology and Genetics, Philadelphia, PA 19104-2875. Offers MS, PhD, MD/PhD. Terminal master's awarded for partial completion of doctoral program. *Degree requirements:* For master's, comprehensive exam, thesis; for doctorate, thesis/dissertation, qualifying exam. *Entrance requirements:* For master's, GRE General Test, minimum GPA of 2.75; for doctorate, GRE General Test, minimum GPA of 3.0. Additional exam requirements/recommendations for international students: required—TOEFL. Electronic applications accepted.

**Duke University,** Graduate School, Department of Evolutionary Anthropology, Durham, NC 27708. Offers cellular and molecular biology (PhD); gross anatomy and physical anthropology (PhD), including comparative morphology of human and non-human primates, primate social behavior, vertebrate paleontology; neuroanatomy (PhD). *Degree requirements:* For doctorate, one foreign language, thesis/dissertation. *Entrance requirements:* For doctorate, GRE General Test. Additional exam requirements/recommendations for international students: required—TOEFL (minimum score 577 paper-based; 90 iBT) or IELTS (minimum score 7). Electronic applications accepted.

**Duke University,** Graduate School, Program in Cell and Molecular Biology, Durham, NC 27710. Offers Certificate. *Entrance requirements:* Additional exam requirements/recommendations for international students: required—TOEFL (minimum score 577 paper-based; 90 iBT) or IELTS (minimum score 7). Electronic applications accepted.

**East Carolina University,** Brody School of Medicine, Office of Research and Graduate Studies, Greenville, NC 27858-4353. Offers anatomy and cell biology (PhD); biochemistry and molecular biology (PhD); biomedical science (MS); microbiology and immunology (PhD); pharmacology and toxicology (PhD); physiology (PhD). *Students:* 102 full-time (44 women), 1 part-time (0 women); includes 16 minority (4 Black or African American, non-Hispanic/Latino; 7 Asian, non-Hispanic/Latino; 4 Hispanic/Latino; 1 Two or more races, non-Hispanic/Latino), 13 international. Average age 28. 83 applicants, 40% accepted, 20 enrolled. In 2019, 3 master's, 10 doctorates awarded. *Degree requirements:* For doctorate, comprehensive exam, thesis/dissertation. *Entrance requirements:* For doctorate, GRE General Test. Additional exam requirements/recommendations for international students: required—some international applicants may be required to demonstrate English proficiency via the TOEFL, IELTS, or PTE exam.; recommended—TOEFL (minimum score 78 iBT), IELTS (minimum score 6.5), TSE (minimum score 65). *Application deadline:* For fall admission, 8/15 for domestic students; for spring admission, 12/20 for domestic students. Applications are processed on a rolling basis. Application fee: $75. Electronic applications accepted. *Expenses: Tuition, area resident:* Full-time $4749; part-time $185 per credit hour. Tuition, state resident: full-time $4749; part-time $185 per credit hour. Tuition, nonresident: full-time $17,898; part-time $864 per credit hour. *International tuition:* $17,898 full-time. *Required fees:* $2787. *Financial support:* Fellowships available. Financial award application deadline: 6/1. *Unit head:* Dr. Russ Price, Associate Dean, 252-744-9346, E-mail: pricest17@ecu.edu. *Application contact:* Dr. Russ Price, Associate Dean, 252-744-9346, E-mail: pricest17@ecu.edu.
Website: http://www.ecu.edu/cs-dhs/bsomresearchgradstudies/index.cfm

**East Carolina University,** Graduate School, Thomas Harriot College of Arts and Sciences, Department of Biology, Greenville, NC 27858-4353. Offers biology (MS); molecular biology and biotechnology (MS). *Program availability:* Part-time. *Application deadline:* For fall admission, 6/1 priority date for domestic students, 3/1 priority date for international students; for spring admission, 10/15 priority date for domestic students. *Expenses: Tuition, area resident:* Full-time $4749; part-time $185 per credit hour. Tuition, state resident: full-time $4749; part-time $185 per credit hour. Tuition, nonresident: full-time $17,898; part-time $864 per credit hour. *International tuition:* $17,898 full-time. *Required fees:* $2787. *Financial support:* Application deadline: 3/1. *Unit head:* Dr. David Chalcraft, Chair, 252-328-2797, E-mail: chalcraftd@ecu.edu. *Application contact:* graduate School Admissions, 252-328-6012, Fax: 252-328-6071, E-mail: gradschool@ecu.edu.
Website: https://biology.ecu.edu/

**Emory University,** Laney Graduate School, Division of Biological and Biomedical Sciences, Program in Genetics and Molecular Biology, Atlanta, GA 30322-1100. Offers PhD. *Degree requirements:* For doctorate, comprehensive exam, thesis/dissertation. *Entrance requirements:* For doctorate, GRE General Test, minimum GPA of 3.0 in science course work (recommended). Additional exam requirements/recommendations for international students: required—TOEFL. Electronic applications accepted.

**Florida Institute of Technology,** College of Engineering and Science, Program in Cell and Molecular Biology, Melbourne, FL 32901-6975. Offers MS. *Program availability:* Part-time. *Degree requirements:* For master's, thesis. *Entrance requirements:* For master's, GRE General Test, 3 letters of recommendation, minimum GPA of 3.0, statement of objectives. Additional exam requirements/recommendations for international students: required—TOEFL (minimum score 550 paper-based; 79 iBT). Electronic applications accepted.

**Florida State University,** The Graduate School, College of Arts and Sciences, Department of Biological Science, Specialization in Cell and Molecular Biology, Tallahassee, FL 32306-4295. Offers MS, PhD. Terminal master's awarded for partial completion of doctoral program. *Degree requirements:* For master's, comprehensive exam (for some programs), thesis, teaching experience, seminar presentation; for doctorate, comprehensive exam, thesis/dissertation, teaching experience; seminar presentation. *Entrance requirements:* For master's and doctorate, GRE General Test, minimum upper-division GPA of 3.0. Additional exam requirements/recommendations for international students: required—TOEFL (minimum score 600 paper-based; 92 iBT). Electronic applications accepted.

**Georgetown University,** Graduate School of Arts and Sciences, Department of Biochemistry and Molecular and Cellular Biology, Washington, DC 20057. Offers MS, PhD. *Degree requirements:* For doctorate, comprehensive exam, thesis/dissertation. *Entrance requirements:* For doctorate, GRE General Test. Additional exam requirements/recommendations for international students: required—TOEFL.

**Georgia State University,** College of Arts and Sciences, Department of Biology, Program in Cellular and Molecular Biology and Physiology, Atlanta, GA 30302-3083. Offers bioinformatics (MS); cellular and molecular biology and physiology (MS, PhD). *Program availability:* Part-time. Terminal master's awarded for partial completion of doctoral program. *Entrance requirements:* For master's and doctorate, GRE. *Application deadline:* Applications are processed on a rolling basis. Application fee: $50. Electronic applications accepted. *Expenses: Tuition, area resident:* Full-time $7164; part-time $398 per credit hour. Tuition, state resident: full-time $7164; part-time $398 per credit hour. Tuition, nonresident: full-time $22,662; part-time $1259 per credit hour. *International tuition:* $22,662 full-time. *Required fees:* $2128; $312 per credit hour. Tuition and fees vary according to course load and program. *Financial support:* Fellowships and research assistantships available. Financial award application deadline: 12/3. *Unit head:* Dr. Charles Derby, Director of Graduate Studies, 404-413-5393, Fax: 404-413-5446, E-mail: cderby@gsu.edu. *Application contact:* Dr. Charles Derby, Director of Graduate Studies, 404-413-5393, Fax: 404-413-5446, E-mail: cderby@gsu.edu.
Website: http://biology.gsu.edu/

**Grand Valley State University,** College of Liberal Arts and Sciences, Program in Cell and Molecular Biology, Allendale, MI 49401-9403. Offers MS. *Faculty:* 8 full-time (5 women), 2 part-time/adjunct (1 woman). *Students:* 22 full-time (8 women), 16 part-time (9 women); includes 5 minority (2 Black or African American, non-Hispanic/Latino; 1 Hispanic/Latino; 2 Two or more races, non-Hispanic/Latino), 10 international. Average age 25. 30 applicants, 93% accepted, 15 enrolled. In 2019, 9 master's awarded. *Degree requirements:* For master's, thesis, thesis. *Entrance requirements:* For master's, GRE, minimum GPA of 3.0, resume or curriculum vitae, personal statement, minimum of 2 letters of recommendation, interview. Additional exam requirements/recommendations for international students: required—TOEFL (minimum iBT score of 80), IELTS (6.5), or Michigan English Language Assessment Battery (77). *Application deadline:* Applications are processed on a rolling basis. Application fee: $30. Electronic applications accepted. *Expenses:* $702 per credit hour, 36 credit hours. *Financial support:* In 2019–20, 15 students received support, including 14 research assistantships with full and partial tuition reimbursements available (averaging $4,000 per year); fellowships and unspecified assistantships also available. *Unit head:* Dr. Mark Staves, Department Chair, 616-331-2473, Fax: 616-331-3446, E-mail: stavesm@gvsu.edu. *Application contact:* Anirudh Chowdhary, PSM Coordinator/Student Recruiting Contact, 616-331-6297, Fax: 616-331-6770, E-mail: chowdhan@gvsu.edu.
Website: https://www.gvsu.edu/grad/cellbio/

**Harvard University,** Graduate School of Arts and Sciences, Department of Molecular and Cellular Biology, Cambridge, MA 02138. Offers PhD. *Degree requirements:* For doctorate, thesis/dissertation, oral exam. *Entrance requirements:* For doctorate, GRE General Test, GRE Subject Test (recommended). Additional exam requirements/recommendations for international students: required—TOEFL.

**Harvard University,** Graduate School of Arts and Sciences, Program in Chemical Biology, Cambridge, MA 02138. Offers PhD.

**Howard University,** College of Medicine, Department of Biochemistry and Molecular Biology, Washington, DC 20059-0002. Offers biochemistry and molecular biology (PhD); biotechnology (MS); MD/PhD. *Program availability:* Part-time. *Degree requirements:* For master's, externship; for doctorate, comprehensive exam, thesis/dissertation. *Entrance requirements:* For master's and doctorate, GRE General Test, minimum GPA of 3.0.

**Illinois Institute of Technology,** Graduate College, College of Science, Department of Biology, Chicago, IL 60616. Offers applied life sciences (MS); biochemistry (MS); biology (MS, PhD); cell and molecular biology (MS); microbiology (MS); molecular biochemistry and biophysics (MS, PhD). *Program availability:* Part-time, evening/weekend, online learning. Terminal master's awarded for partial completion of doctoral program. *Degree requirements:* For master's, comprehensive exam, thesis (for some programs); for doctorate, comprehensive exam, thesis/dissertation. *Entrance requirements:* For master's, GRE General Test (minimum score 300 Quantitative and Verbal, 2.5 Analytical Writing), minimum undergraduate GPA of 3.0; for doctorate, GRE General Test (minimum score 310 Quantitative and Verbal, 3.0 Analytical Writing); GRE

Subject Test (strongly recommended), minimum undergraduate GPA of 3.0. Additional exam requirements/recommendations for international students: required—TOEFL (minimum score 550 paper-based; 80 iBT). Electronic applications accepted.

**Illinois State University,** Graduate School, College of Arts and Sciences, School of Biological Sciences, Normal, IL 61790. Offers animal behavior (MS); bacteriology (MS); biochemistry (MS); biological sciences (MS); biology (PhD); biophysics (MS); biotechnology (MS); botany (MS, PhD); cell biology (MS); conservation biology (MS); developmental biology (MS); ecology (MS, PhD); entomology (MS); evolutionary biology (MS); genetics (MS, PhD); immunology (MS); microbiology (MS, PhD); molecular biology (MS); molecular genetics (MS); neurobiology (MS); neuroscience (MS); parasitology (MS); physiology (MS, PhD); plant biology (MS); plant molecular biology (MS); plant sciences (MS); structural biology (MS); zoology (MS, PhD). *Program availability:* Part-time. *Faculty:* 26 full-time (6 women), 7 part-time/adjunct (2 women). *Students:* 51 full-time (33 women), 15 part-time (8 women). Average age 27. 71 applicants, 28% accepted, 9 enrolled. In 2019, 14 master's, 3 doctorates awarded. *Degree requirements:* For master's, thesis or alternative; for doctorate, variable foreign language requirement, thesis/dissertation, 2 terms of residency. *Entrance requirements:* For master's, GRE General Test, minimum GPA of 2.6 in last 60 hours of course work; for doctorate, GRE General Test. *Application deadline:* Applications are processed on a rolling basis. Application fee: $50. *Expenses: Tuition, area resident:* Full-time $7956; part-time $9767 per year. Tuition, nonresident: full-time $9233; part-time $17,592 per year. *Required fees:* $1797. *Financial support:* In 2019–20, 20 research assistantships, 41 teaching assistantships were awarded; Federal Work-Study, tuition waivers (full), and unspecified assistantships also available. Financial award application deadline: 4/1. *Unit head:* Dr. Craig Gatto, School Director, 309-438-3087, E-mail: cgatto@IllinoisState.edu. *Application contact:* Dr. Ben Sadd, Assistant Chair for Graduate Studies, 309-438-2651, E-mail: bmsadd@IllinoisState.edu.
Website: http://www.bio.ilstu.edu/

**Indiana State University,** College of Graduate and Professional Studies, College of Arts and Sciences, Department of Biology, Terre Haute, IN 47809. Offers cellular and molecular biology (PhD); ecology, systematics and evolution (PhD); life sciences (MS); physiology (PhD); science education (MS). *Degree requirements:* For master's, thesis optional; for doctorate, comprehensive exam, thesis/dissertation. *Entrance requirements:* For master's and doctorate, GRE General Test. Electronic applications accepted.

**Indiana University Bloomington,** University Graduate School, College of Arts and Sciences, Department of Biology, Bloomington, IN 47405. Offers biology teaching (MAT); biotechnology (MA); evolution, ecology, and behavior (MA, PhD); genetics (PhD); microbiology (MA, PhD); molecular, cellular, and developmental biology (PhD); plant sciences (MA, PhD); zoology (MA, PhD). Terminal master's awarded for partial completion of doctoral program. *Degree requirements:* For master's, thesis, oral defense; for doctorate, thesis/dissertation, oral defense. *Entrance requirements:* For master's and doctorate, GRE General Test. Additional exam requirements/recommendations for international students: required—TOEFL (minimum score 100 iBT). Electronic applications accepted.

**Indiana University-Purdue University Indianapolis,** Indiana University School of Medicine, Department of Biochemistry and Molecular Biology, Indianapolis, IN 46202. Offers MS, PhD, MD/MS, MD/PhD. Terminal master's awarded for partial completion of doctoral program. *Degree requirements:* For master's, thesis; for doctorate, thesis/dissertation. *Entrance requirements:* For master's and doctorate, GRE General Test, GRE Subject Test (recommended), previous course work in organic chemistry. Additional exam requirements/recommendations for international students: required—TOEFL. Electronic applications accepted.

**Inter American University of Puerto Rico, Metropolitan Campus,** Graduate Programs, Program in Medical Technology, San Juan, PR 00919-1293. Offers administration of clinical laboratories (MS); molecular microbiology (MS). *Accreditation:* NAACLS. *Program availability:* Part-time. *Degree requirements:* For master's, comprehensive exam. *Entrance requirements:* For master's, BS in medical technology, minimum GPA of 2.5. Electronic applications accepted.

**Iowa State University of Science and Technology,** Bioinformatics and Computational Biology Program, Ames, IA 50011. Offers MS, PhD. *Degree requirements:* For doctorate, thesis/dissertation. *Entrance requirements:* For master's and doctorate, GRE General Test. Additional exam requirements/recommendations for international students: recommended—TOEFL, IELTS. Electronic applications accepted.

**Iowa State University of Science and Technology,** Program in Molecular, Cellular, and Developmental Biology, Ames, IA 50011. Offers MS, PhD. *Entrance requirements:* For master's and doctorate, GRE General Test. Additional exam requirements/recommendations for international students: required—TOEFL (minimum score 580 paper-based; 85 iBT), IELTS (minimum score 7). Electronic applications accepted.

**Irell & Manella Graduate School of Biological Sciences,** Graduate Program, Duarte, CA 91010. Offers brain metastatic cancer (PhD); cancer and stem cell metabolism (PhD); cancer biology (PhD); cancer biology and developmental therapeutics (PhD); cell biology (PhD); chemical biology (PhD); chromosomal break repair (PhD); diabetes and pancreatic progenitor cell biology (PhD); DNA repair and cancer biology (PhD); germline epigenetic remodeling and endocrine disruptors (PhD); hematology and hematopoietic cell transplantation (PhD); hematology and immunology (PhD); inflammation and cancer (PhD); micrornas and gene regulation in cardiovascular disease (PhD); mixed chimerism for reversal of autoimmunity (PhD); molecular and cellular biology (PhD); molecular biology and genetics (PhD); nanoparticle mediated twist1 silencing in metastatic cancer (PhD); neuro-oncology and stem cell biology (PhD); neuroscience (PhD); RNA directed therapies for HIV-1 (PhD); small RNA-induced transcriptional gene activation (PhD); stem cell regulation by the microenvironment (PhD); translational oncology and pharmaceutical sciences (PhD); tumor biology (PhD). *Degree requirements:* For doctorate, comprehensive exam, thesis/dissertation, qualifying exams, two advanced courses. *Entrance requirements:* For doctorate, GRE General Test; GRE Subject Test (recommended), 2 years of course work in chemistry (general and organic); 1 year of course work each in biochemistry, general biology, and general physics; 2 semesters of course work in mathematics; significant research laboratory experience. Additional exam requirements/recommendations for international students: required—TOEFL. Electronic applications accepted.

**Johns Hopkins University,** Bloomberg School of Public Health, Department of Biochemistry and Molecular Biology, Baltimore, MD 21205. Offers MHS, Sc M, PhD. *Program availability:* Part-time. *Degree requirements:* For master's, thesis; for doctorate, comprehensive exam, thesis/dissertation, oral and written exams. *Entrance requirements:* For master's, MCAT or GRE, 3 letters of recommendation, curriculum vitae; for doctorate, GRE General Test, 3 letters of recommendation, curriculum vitae. Electronic applications accepted.

**Johns Hopkins University,** National Institutes of Health Sponsored Programs, Baltimore, MD 21218. Offers biology (PhD), including biochemistry, biophysics, cell biology, developmental biology, genetic biology, molecular biology; cell, molecular, and developmental biology and biophysics (PhD). *Degree requirements:* For doctorate, comprehensive exam, thesis/dissertation. *Entrance requirements:* Additional exam requirements/recommendations for international students: required—TOEFL (minimum score 600 paper-based). Electronic applications accepted.

**Johns Hopkins University,** School of Medicine, Graduate Programs in Medicine, Department of Pharmacology and Molecular Sciences, Baltimore, MD 21205. Offers PhD. *Degree requirements:* For doctorate, comprehensive exam, thesis/dissertation, departmental seminar. *Entrance requirements:* Additional exam requirements/recommendations for international students: required—TOEFL. Electronic applications accepted.

**Johns Hopkins University,** School of Medicine, Graduate Programs in Medicine, Program in Biochemistry, Cellular and Molecular Biology, Baltimore, MD 21205. Offers PhD. *Degree requirements:* For doctorate, comprehensive exam, thesis/dissertation. *Entrance requirements:* Additional exam requirements/recommendations for international students: required—TOEFL. Electronic applications accepted.

**Kent State University,** College of Arts and Sciences, School of Biomedical Sciences, Kent, OH 44242-0001. Offers biological anthropology (PhD); biomedical mathematics (MS, PhD); cellular and molecular biology (MS, PhD), including cellular biology and structures, molecular biology and genetics; neurosciences (MS, PhD); pharmacology (MS, PhD); physiology (MS, PhD). *Faculty:* 17 full-time (8 women). *Students:* 73 full-time (48 women), 2 part-time (1 woman); includes 9 minority (2 Black or African American, non-Hispanic/Latino; 1 Asian, non-Hispanic/Latino; 3 Hispanic/Latino; 3 Two or more races, non-Hispanic/Latino), 53 international. Average age 29. 78 applicants, 17% accepted, 9 enrolled. In 2019, 2 master's, 5 doctorates awarded. *Degree requirements:* For master's, thesis; for doctorate, comprehensive exam, thesis/dissertation. *Entrance requirements:* For master's, GRE, bachelor's degree, transcripts, minimum GPA of 3.0 undergraduate GPA, goal statement, three letters of recommendation, academic preparation adequate to perform graduate work in the desired field (typically two years of chemistry, one year of mathematics, one year of physics and courses in anthropology, biology and psychology); for doctorate, GRE, master's degree, minimum GPA of 3.0, transcripts, goal statement, three letters of recommendation. Additional exam requirements/recommendations for international students: required—TOEFL (minimum score 100 iBT), IELTS (minimum score 7), PTE (minimum score 68), Michigan English Language Assessment Battery (minimum score 85). *Application deadline:* For fall admission, 1/1 for domestic students, 12/15 for international students. Applications are processed on a rolling basis. Application fee: $45 ($70 for international students). Electronic applications accepted. *Financial support:* Research assistantships with full tuition reimbursements, teaching assistantships, health care benefits, and unspecified assistantships available. Financial award application deadline: 1/1. *Unit head:* Dr. Ernest J. Freeman, Director, School of Biomedical Sciences, 330-672-2363, E-mail: efreema2@kent.edu. *Application contact:* School of Biomedical Sciences, 330-6722263, Fax: 330-6729391.
Website: http://www.kent.edu/biomedical/

**Lehigh University,** College of Arts and Sciences, Department of Biological Sciences, Bethlehem, PA 18015. Offers biochemistry (PhD); cell and molecular biology (PhD); integrative biology (PhD); molecular biology (MS). *Program availability:* 100% online, MS MBio Program Only. *Faculty:* 24 full-time (11 women), 1 (woman) part-time/adjunct. *Students:* 36 full-time (18 women), 23 part-time (16 women); includes 12 minority (1 Black or African American, non-Hispanic/Latino; 1 American Indian or Alaska Native, non-Hispanic/Latino; 2 Asian, non-Hispanic/Latino; 7 Hispanic/Latino; 1 Two or more races, non-Hispanic/Latino), 9 international. Average age 28. 53 applicants, 57% accepted, 22 enrolled. In 2019, 9 master's, 7 doctorates awarded. Terminal master's awarded for partial completion of doctoral program. *Degree requirements:* For master's, thesis optional; for doctorate, comprehensive exam, thesis/dissertation. *Entrance requirements:* For master's, bachelor's degree in a life science or chemistry with a GPA of 3.0 or higher, 2 letters of recommendation, official transcripts of previous educational experience; for doctorate, GRE General Test, Three letters of recommendation, curriculum vitae, official transcripts, minimum Bachelor's degree or equivalent, personal statement. Additional exam requirements/recommendations for international students: required—TOEFL (minimum score 85 iBT). *Application deadline:* For fall admission, 7/15 for domestic and international students; for spring admission, 12/1 for domestic and international students; for summer admission, 4/30 for domestic and international students. Application fee: $75. Electronic applications accepted. *Financial support:* In 2019–20, 39 students received support, including 2 fellowships with full tuition reimbursements available (averaging $29,000 per year), 14 research assistantships with full tuition reimbursements available (averaging $29,000 per year), 18 teaching assistantships with full tuition reimbursements available (averaging $29,000 per year); tuition waivers (full and partial) and partially reimbursed health care benefits also available. Financial award application deadline: 1/1. *Unit head:* Dr. Linda Lowe-Krentz, Chairperson, 610-758-5084, Fax: 610-758-4004, E-mail: lij0@lehigh.edu. *Application contact:* Dr. Amber Rice, Graduate Coordinator, 610-758-5509, Fax: 610-758-4004, E-mail: amr511@lehigh.edu.
Website: http://www.lehigh.edu/~inbios/

**Lipscomb University,** Program in Biomolecular Science, Nashville, TN 37204-3951. Offers human disease (MS); laboratory research (MS). *Program availability:* Part-time, evening/weekend. *Degree requirements:* For master's, capstone project. *Entrance requirements:* For master's, GRE (minimum score of 300/1000 on prior scoring system), MCAT (minimum score of 24), DAT (minimum score of 17), BS in related field, transcripts, minimum undergraduate GPA of 3.0, 2 letters of recommendation, resume. Additional exam requirements/recommendations for international students: required—TOEFL (minimum score 570 paper-based). Electronic applications accepted. *Expenses:* Contact institution.

**Louisiana State University Health Sciences Center at Shreveport,** Department of Biochemistry and Molecular Biology, Shreveport, LA 71130-3932. Offers MS, PhD, MD/PhD. *Degree requirements:* For master's, thesis; for doctorate, thesis/dissertation. *Entrance requirements:* For master's and doctorate, GRE General Test. Additional exam requirements/recommendations for international students: required—TOEFL (minimum score 100 iBT), IELTS (minimum score 7). Electronic applications accepted. *Expenses:* Contact institution.

**Louisiana Tech University,** Graduate School, College of Applied and Natural Sciences, Ruston, LA 71272. Offers biology (MS); dietetics (Graduate Certificate); health informatics (MHI); molecular science and nanotechnology (MS, PhD). *Program availability:* Part-time. *Degree requirements:* For master's, comprehensive exam (for some programs), thesis (for some programs); for doctorate, comprehensive exam, thesis/dissertation. *Entrance requirements:* For master's and doctorate, GRE General Test, transcript with bachelor's degree awarded; for Graduate Certificate, transcript with bachelor's degree awarded. Additional exam requirements/recommendations for international students: required—TOEFL (minimum score 550 paper-based; 80 iBT), IELTS (minimum score 6.5). Electronic applications accepted. *Expenses: Tuition, area resident:* Full-time $6592; part-time $400 per credit. Tuition, state resident: full-time $6592; part-time $400 per credit. Tuition, nonresident: full-time $13,333; part-time $681 per credit. *International tuition:* $13,333 full-time. *Required fees:* $3011; $3011 per unit.

**Loyola University Chicago,** Graduate School, Integrated Program in Biomedical Sciences, Maywood, IL 60660. Offers biochemistry and molecular biology (MS, PhD);

cell and molecular physiology (MS, PhD); infectious disease and immunology (MS); integrative cell biology (MS, PhD); microbiology and immunology (MS, PhD); molecular pharmacology and therapeutics (MS, PhD); neuroscience (MS, PhD). *Students:* Average age 25. 773 applicants, 34% accepted, 122 enrolled. In 2019, 46 master's, 12 doctorates awarded. *Degree requirements:* For master's, thesis; for doctorate, comprehensive exam, thesis/dissertation. *Entrance requirements:* For doctorate, GRE. Additional exam requirements/recommendations for international students: required— TOEFL (minimum score 94 iBT), IELTS (minimum score 7.5). *Application deadline:* For fall admission, 2/7 for domestic students. Applications are processed on a rolling basis. Electronic applications accepted. *Expenses:* Contact institution. *Financial support:* In 2019–20, 20 students received support. Schmitt Fellowships and yearly tuition scholarships (averaging $25,032) available. Financial award application deadline: 6/15; financial award applicants required to submit FAFSA. *Unit head:* Dr. Leanne L. Cribbs, Associate Dean, Graduate Education, 708-327-2817, Fax: 708-216-8216, E-mail: lcribbs@luc.edu. *Application contact:* Margarita Quesada, Graduate Program Secretary, 708-216-3532, Fax: 708-216-8216, E-mail: mquesad@luc.edu. Website: http://ssom.luc.edu/graduate_school/degree-programs/ipbsphd/

**Marquette University,** Graduate School, College of Arts and Sciences, Department of Biological Sciences, Milwaukee, WI 53201-1881. Offers cell biology (MS, PhD); developmental biology (MS, PhD); ecology (MS, PhD); epithelial physiology (MS, PhD); genetics (MS, PhD); microbiology (MS, PhD); molecular biology (MS, PhD); muscle and exercise physiology (MS, PhD); neuroscience (PhD). Terminal master's awarded for partial completion of doctoral program. *Degree requirements:* For master's, comprehensive exam, thesis, 1 year of teaching experience or equivalent; for doctorate, thesis/dissertation, 1 year of teaching experience or equivalent, qualifying exam. *Entrance requirements:* For master's and doctorate, GRE General Test, GRE Subject Test, official transcripts from all current and previous colleges/universities except Marquette, statement of professional goals and aspirations, three letters of recommendation. Additional exam requirements/recommendations for international students: required—TOEFL (minimum score 530 paper-based). Electronic applications accepted.

**Massachusetts Institute of Technology,** School of Engineering, Department of Electrical Engineering and Computer Science, Cambridge, MA 02139. Offers computer science (PhD, Sc D, ECS); computer science and engineering (PhD, Sc D); computer science and molecular biology (M Eng); electrical engineering (PhD, Sc D, EE); electrical engineering and computer science (M Eng, SM, PhD, Sc D); SM/MBA. *Degree requirements:* For master's and other advanced degree, thesis; for doctorate, comprehensive exam, thesis/dissertation. *Entrance requirements:* Additional exam requirements/recommendations for international students: required—TOEFL, IELTS. Electronic applications accepted.

**Massachusetts Institute of Technology,** School of Science, Department of Biology, Cambridge, MA 02139. Offers biochemistry (PhD); biological oceanography (PhD); biology (PhD); biophysical chemistry and molecular structure (PhD); cell biology (PhD); computational and systems biology (PhD); developmental biology (PhD); genetics (PhD); immunology (PhD); microbiology (PhD); molecular biology (PhD); neurobiology (PhD). *Degree requirements:* For doctorate, comprehensive exam, thesis/dissertation, teaching assistantship during two semesters. *Entrance requirements:* For doctorate, GRE General Test. Additional exam requirements/recommendations for international students: required—TOEFL, IELTS. Electronic applications accepted.

**Mayo Clinic Graduate School of Biomedical Sciences,** Program in Biochemistry and Molecular Biology, Rochester, MN 55905. Offers MS, PhD. Terminal master's awarded for partial completion of doctoral program. *Degree requirements:* For master's, thesis; for doctorate, comprehensive exam, thesis/dissertation, oral defense of dissertation, qualifying oral and written exam. *Entrance requirements:* For doctorate, GRE, 1 year of chemistry, biology, calculus, and physics. Additional exam requirements/recommendations for international students: required—TOEFL. Electronic applications accepted.

**McMaster University,** Faculty of Health Sciences and School of Graduate Studies, Program in Medical Sciences, Hamilton, ON L8S 4M2, Canada. Offers blood and vascular (M Sc, PhD); genetics and cancer (M Sc, PhD); immunity and infection (M Sc, PhD); metabolism and nutrition (M Sc, PhD); neurosciences and behavioral sciences (M Sc, PhD); physiology/pharmacology (M Sc, PhD); MD/PhD. *Degree requirements:* For master's, thesis; for doctorate, comprehensive exam, thesis/dissertation. *Entrance requirements:* For master's, honors B Sc, B+ average in related field; for doctorate, M Sc, minimum B+ average. Additional exam requirements/recommendations for international students: required—TOEFL (minimum score 580 paper-based; 92 iBT).

**Medical University of South Carolina,** College of Graduate Studies, Department of Biochemistry and Molecular Biology, Charleston, SC 29425. Offers MS, PhD, MD/PhD. Terminal master's awarded for partial completion of doctoral program. *Degree requirements:* For master's, thesis, oral exam/thesis defense; for doctorate, thesis/dissertation, oral and written exams/dissertation defense. *Entrance requirements:* For master's, GRE General Test; for doctorate, GRE General Test, interview, minimum GPA of 3.0. Additional exam requirements/recommendations for international students: required—TOEFL (minimum score 600 paper-based; 100 iBT). Electronic applications accepted.

**Medical University of South Carolina,** College of Graduate Studies, Program in Molecular and Cellular Biology and Pathobiology, Charleston, SC 29425. Offers cancer biology (PhD); cardiovascular biology (PhD); cardiovascular imaging (PhD); cell regulation (PhD); craniofacial biology (PhD); genetics and development (PhD); marine biomedicine (PhD); DMD/PhD; MD/PhD. *Degree requirements:* For doctorate, thesis/ dissertation, oral and written exams. *Entrance requirements:* For doctorate, GRE General Test, interview, minimum GPA of 3.0. Additional exam requirements/ recommendations for international students: required—TOEFL (minimum score 600 paper-based; 100 iBT). Electronic applications accepted.

**Michigan State University,** The Graduate School, College of Natural Science, Department of Biochemistry and Molecular Biology, East Lansing, MI 48824. Offers biochemistry and molecular biology (MS, PhD); biochemistry and molecular biology/ environmental toxicology (PhD). *Entrance requirements:* Additional exam requirements/ recommendations for international students: required—TOEFL. Electronic applications accepted.

**Michigan State University,** The Graduate School, College of Natural Science, MSU-DOE Plant Research Laboratory, East Lansing, MI 48824. Offers biochemistry and molecular biology (PhD); cellular and molecular biology (PhD); crop and soil sciences (PhD); genetics (PhD); microbiology and molecular genetics (PhD); plant biology (PhD); plant physiology (PhD). *Degree requirements:* For doctorate, comprehensive exam, thesis/dissertation, laboratory rotation, defense of dissertation. *Entrance requirements:* For doctorate, GRE General Test, acceptance into one of the affiliated department programs; 3 letters of recommendation; bachelor's degree or equivalent in life sciences, chemistry, biochemistry, or biophysics; research experience. Electronic applications accepted.

**Michigan State University,** The Graduate School, College of Natural Science, Program in Cell and Molecular Biology, East Lansing, MI 48824. Offers cell and molecular biology (MS, PhD); cell and molecular biology/environmental toxicology (PhD). *Entrance requirements:* Additional exam requirements/recommendations for international students: required—TOEFL. Electronic applications accepted.

**Michigan Technological University,** Graduate School, Interdisciplinary Programs, Houghton, MI 49931. Offers automotive systems and controls (Graduate Certificate); biochemistry and molecular biology (PhD); computational science and engineering (PhD); data science (Graduate Certificate); sustainability (Graduate Certificate). *Program availability:* Part-time. *Faculty:* 132 full-time, 6 part-time/adjunct. *Students:* 57 full-time (20 women), 19 part-time; includes 7 minority (3 Black or African American, non-Hispanic/Latino; 1 American Indian or Alaska Native, non-Hispanic/Latino; 1 Asian, non-Hispanic/Latino; 2 Two or more races, non-Hispanic/Latino), 42 international. Average age 30. 475 applicants, 29% accepted, 25 enrolled. In 2019, 23 master's, 10 doctorates, 36 other advanced degrees awarded. Terminal master's awarded for partial completion of doctoral program. *Degree requirements:* For master's, comprehensive exam (for some programs), thesis (for some programs); for doctorate, comprehensive exam, thesis/dissertation. *Entrance requirements:* For master's, doctorate, and Graduate Certificate, GRE, statement of purpose, personal statement, official transcripts, 2-3 letters of recommendation. Additional exam requirements/ recommendations for international students: required—TOEFL or IELTS. *Application deadline:* Applications are processed on a rolling basis. Electronic applications accepted. *Expenses: Tuition, area resident:* Full-time $19,206; part-time $1067 per credit. Tuition, state resident: full-time $19,206; part-time $1067 per credit. Tuition, nonresident: full-time $19,206; part-time $1067 per credit. *International tuition:* $19,206 full-time. *Required fees:* $248; $248 per unit. $124 per semester. Tuition and fees vary according to course load and program. *Financial support:* In 2019–20, 54 students received support, including 9 fellowships with tuition reimbursements available (averaging $16,590 per year), 14 research assistantships with tuition reimbursements available (averaging $16,590 per year), 10 teaching assistantships with tuition reimbursements available (averaging $16,590 per year); career-related internships or fieldwork, Federal Work-Study, scholarships/grants, health care benefits, unspecified assistantships, and cooperative program also available. Financial award applicants required to submit FAFSA. *Unit head:* Dr. Will H Cantrell, Dean of the Graduate School, 906-487-3007, Fax: 906-487-2284, E-mail: cantrell@mtu.edu. *Application contact:* Ashli Wells, Assistant Director of Graduate Enrollment Services, 906-487-3513, Fax: 906-487-2284, E-mail: aesniego@mtu.edu.

**Middle Tennessee State University,** College of Graduate Studies, College of Basic and Applied Sciences, Interdisciplinary Program in Molecular Biosciences, Murfreesboro, TN 37132. Offers PhD. *Degree requirements:* For doctorate, comprehensive exam, thesis/dissertation. *Entrance requirements:* For doctorate, GRE. Additional exam requirements/recommendations for international students: required— TOEFL (minimum score 525 paper-based; 71 iBT) or IELTS (minimum score 6). Electronic applications accepted.

**Mississippi State University,** College of Agriculture and Life Sciences, Department of Biochemistry, Molecular Biology, Entomology and Plant Pathology, Mississippi State, MS 39762. Offers biochemistry (MS, PhD); entomology (MS, PhD); plant pathology (MS, PhD). *Faculty:* 36 full-time (9 women). *Students:* 39 full-time (19 women), 8 part-time (4 women); includes 4 minority (1 Black or African American, non-Hispanic/Latino; 1 Asian, non-Hispanic/Latino; 2 Hispanic/Latino), 14 international. Average age 31. 24 applicants, 33% accepted, 3 enrolled. In 2019, 3 master's, 4 doctorates awarded. Terminal master's awarded for partial completion of doctoral program. *Degree requirements:* For master's, thesis (for some programs), final oral exam; for doctorate, thesis/dissertation, preliminary oral and written exam. *Entrance requirements:* For master's, GRE General Test, minimum GPA of 2.75; for doctorate, GRE. Additional exam requirements/recommendations for international students: required—TOEFL (minimum score 500 paper-based; 61 iBT); recommended—IELTS (minimum score 5.5). *Application deadline:* For fall admission, 7/1 for domestic students, 5/1 for international students; for spring admission, 11/1 for domestic students, 9/1 for international students. Applications are processed on a rolling basis. Application fee: $60 ($80 for international students). Electronic applications accepted. *Expenses: Tuition, area resident:* Full-time $8880; part-time $456 per credit hour. Tuition, state resident: full-time $8880. Tuition, nonresident: full-time $23,840; part-time $1236 per credit hour. *Required fees:* $110; $11.12 per credit hour. Tuition and fees vary according to course load. *Financial support:* In 2019–20, 29 research assistantships with full tuition reimbursements (averaging $16,492 per year) were awarded; Federal Work-Study, institutionally sponsored loans, and unspecified assistantships also available. Financial award application deadline: 4/1; financial award applicants required to submit FAFSA. *Unit head:* Dr. Jeffrey Dean, Professor and Head, 662-325-2640, Fax: 662-325-8664, E-mail: jd1891@msstate.edu. *Application contact:* Ryan King, Admissions and Enrollment Assistant, 662-325-8951, E-mail: rjk101@grad.msstate.edu. Website: http://www.biochemistry.msstate.edu

**Missouri State University,** Graduate College, College of Health and Human Services, Department of Biomedical Sciences, Program in Cell and Molecular Biology, Springfield, MO 65897. Offers MS. *Program availability:* Part-time. *Degree requirements:* For master's, thesis or alternative, oral and written exams. *Entrance requirements:* For master's, GRE General Test, 2 semesters of course work in organic chemistry and physics, 1 semester of course work in calculus, minimum GPA of 3.0 in last 60 hours of course work. Additional exam requirements/recommendations for international students: required—TOEFL (minimum score 550 paper-based; 79 iBT), IELTS (minimum score 6). Electronic applications accepted. *Expenses: Tuition, area resident:* Full-time $2600; part-time $1735 per credit hour. Tuition, nonresident: full-time $5240; part-time $3495 per credit hour. *International tuition:* $5240 full-time. *Required fees:* $530; $438 per credit hour. Tuition and fees vary according to class time, course level, course load, degree level, campus/location and program.

**Montclair State University,** The Graduate School, College of Science and Mathematics, Molecular Biology Certificate Program, Montclair, NJ 07043-1624. Offers Certificate. *Degree requirements:* For Certificate, thesis optional.

**Montclair State University,** The Graduate School, College of Science and Mathematics, MS Program in Molecular Biology, Montclair, NJ 07043-1624. Offers MS. *Degree requirements:* For master's, thesis optional.

**New Mexico State University,** Graduate School, Program in Molecular Biology, Las Cruces, NM 88003-8001. Offers MS, PhD. *Program availability:* Part-time. *Students:* 12 full-time (9 women); includes 3 minority (2 Asian, non-Hispanic/Latino; 1 Hispanic/ Latino), 7 international. Average age 31. 5 applicants, 80% accepted. In 2019, 1 doctorate awarded. *Degree requirements:* For master's, thesis, oral seminars; for doctorate, comprehensive exam, thesis/dissertation, oral seminars. *Entrance requirements:* For master's and doctorate, GRE General Test: 300, minimum GPA of 3.3. Additional exam requirements/recommendations for international students: required—TOEFL (minimum score 550 paper-based; 79 iBT), IELTS (minimum score 6.5). *Application deadline:* For fall admission, 12/15 for domestic and international students; for spring admission, 10/15 for domestic and international students. Applications are processed on a rolling basis. Application fee: $40 ($50 for international students). Electronic applications accepted. *Financial support:* In 2019–20, 12 students received support, including 2 fellowships (averaging $4,844 per year), 1 research

assistantship (averaging $20,592 per year), 3 teaching assistantships (averaging $18,302 per year); career-related internships or fieldwork, Federal Work-Study, scholarships/grants, health care benefits, and unspecified assistantships also available. Financial award application deadline: 3/1. *Unit head:* Dr. Jennifer J. Randall, Director, 575-646-2920, Fax: 575-646-8087, E-mail: jrandall@nmsu.edu. *Application contact:* Nancy Treffler-McDow, Administrative Assistant, 575-646-3437, Fax: 575-646-8087, E-mail: nancyt@nmsu.edu.
Website: http://molb.research.nmsu.edu

**New York Medical College,** Graduate School of Basic Medical Sciences, Valhalla, NY 10595. Offers biochemistry and molecular biology (MS, PhD); cell biology (MS, PhD); microbiology and immunology (MS, PhD); pathology (MS, PhD); pharmacology (MS, PhD); physiology (MS, PhD); MD/PhD. *Program availability:* Part-time, evening/weekend. *Faculty:* 98 full-time (24 women). *Students:* 141 full-time (90 women), 17 part-time (3 women); includes 68 minority (16 Black or African American, non-Hispanic/Latino; 32 Asian, non-Hispanic/Latino; 15 Hispanic/Latino; 1 Native Hawaiian or other Pacific Islander, non-Hispanic/Latino; 4 Two or more races, non-Hispanic/Latino), 19 international. Average age 26. 351 applicants, 62% accepted, 86 enrolled. In 2019, 28 master's, 5 doctorates awarded. Terminal master's awarded for partial completion of doctoral program. *Degree requirements:* For master's, thesis; for doctorate, comprehensive exam, thesis/dissertation. *Entrance requirements:* For master's, GRE General Test, MCAT, or DAT, OAT. Additional exam requirements/recommendations for international students: required—TOEFL (minimum score 90 iBT), TOEFL or IELTS; one of the two exams are required. *Application deadline:* For fall admission, 6/1 priority date for domestic students, 5/1 priority date for international students. Applications are processed on a rolling basis. Application fee: $75 ($100 for international students). Electronic applications accepted. *Expenses:* $1200 credit and $620 fees. *Financial support:* In 2019–20, 400 students received support. Federal Work-Study, scholarships/grants, unspecified assistantships, and Student Federal Loans available. Financial award application deadline: 4/30; financial award applicants required to submit FAFSA. *Unit head:* Dr. Marina K Holz, Dean, 914-594-4110, Fax: 914-594-4944, E-mail: mholz@nymc.edu. *Application contact:* Valerie Romeo-Messana, Director of Admissions, 914-594-4110, Fax: 914-594-4944, E-mail: v_romeomessana@nymc.edu.
Website: https://www.nymc.edu/graduate-school-of-basic-medical-sciences-gsbms/gsbms-academics/

**New York University,** Graduate School of Arts and Science, Department of Biology, New York, NY 10012-1019. Offers biology (PhD); biomedical journalism (MS); cancer and molecular biology (PhD); computational biology (PhD); computers in biological research (MS); developmental genetics (PhD); general biology (MS); immunology and microbiology (PhD); molecular genetics (PhD); neurobiology (PhD); oral biology (MS); plant biology (PhD); recombinant DNA technology (MS); MS/MBA. *Program availability:* Part-time. Terminal master's awarded for partial completion of doctoral program. *Degree requirements:* For master's, thesis or alternative, qualifying paper; for doctorate, comprehensive exam, thesis/dissertation. *Entrance requirements:* For master's and doctorate, GRE General Test. Additional exam requirements/recommendations for international students: required—TOEFL, IELTS.

**North Dakota State University,** College of Graduate and Interdisciplinary Studies, Interdisciplinary Program in Cellular and Molecular Biology, Fargo, ND 58102. Offers PhD. *Degree requirements:* For doctorate, thesis/dissertation. *Entrance requirements:* Additional exam requirements/recommendations for international students: required—TOEFL. Electronic applications accepted. Tuition and fees vary according to program and reciprocity agreements.

**Northeastern Illinois University,** College of Graduate Studies and Research, College of Arts and Sciences, Program in Biology, Chicago, IL 60625. Offers biology (MS), including cell biology, ecology, molecular biology, organismal biology. *Program availability:* Part-time, evening/weekend. *Degree requirements:* For master's, comprehensive exam, thesis optional. *Entrance requirements:* For master's, minimum GPA of 2.75. Additional exam requirements/recommendations for international students: required—TOEFL (minimum score 550 paper-based; 79 iBT). Electronic applications accepted.

**Northwestern University,** The Graduate School, Interdisciplinary Biological Sciences Program (IBiS), Evanston, IL 60208. Offers biochemistry (PhD); bioengineering and biotechnology (PhD); biotechnology (PhD); cell and molecular biology (PhD); developmental and systems biology (PhD); nanotechnology (PhD); neurobiology (PhD); structural biology and biophysics (PhD). *Degree requirements:* For doctorate, thesis/dissertation, qualifying exam. *Entrance requirements:* For doctorate, GRE General Test. Additional exam requirements/recommendations for international students: required—TOEFL (minimum score 600 paper-based). Electronic applications accepted.

**The Ohio State University,** Graduate School, College of Arts and Sciences, Division of Natural and Mathematical Sciences, Department of Molecular Genetics, Columbus, OH 43210. Offers cell and developmental biology (MS, PhD); genetics (MS, PhD); molecular biology (MS, PhD). *Entrance requirements:* For doctorate, GRE General Test, GRE Subject Test in biology or chemistry (recommended). Additional exam requirements/recommendations for international students: required—TOEFL (minimum score 550 paper-based; 79 iBT), Michigan English Language Assessment Battery (minimum score 82); recommended—IELTS (minimum score 7). Electronic applications accepted.

**The Ohio State University,** Graduate School, College of Arts and Sciences, Division of Natural and Mathematical Sciences, Program in Molecular, Cellular and Developmental Biology, Columbus, OH 43210. Offers MS, PhD. Terminal master's awarded for partial completion of doctoral program. *Entrance requirements:* For doctorate, GRE General Test, GRE Subject Test in any science (desired, preferably biology or chemistry, biochemistry or cell and molecular biology). Additional exam requirements/recommendations for international students: required—TOEFL (minimum score 600 paper-based; 85 iBT); recommended—IELTS (minimum score 8). Electronic applications accepted.

**Ohio University,** Graduate College, College of Arts and Sciences, Interdisciplinary Graduate Program in Molecular and Cellular Biology, Athens, OH 45701-2979. Offers PhD. *Degree requirements:* For doctorate, comprehensive exam, thesis/dissertation, research proposal, teaching experience. *Entrance requirements:* For doctorate, GRE General Test. Additional exam requirements/recommendations for international students: required—TOEFL (minimum score 620 paper-based; 105 iBT); recommended—TWE. Electronic applications accepted.

**Oklahoma State University,** College of Agricultural Science and Natural Resources, Department of Biochemistry and Molecular Biology, Stillwater, OK 74078. Offers MS, PhD. *Faculty:* 17 full-time (6 women). *Students:* 2 full-time (1 woman), 18 part-time (8 women); includes 2 minority (1 Asian, non-Hispanic/Latino; 1 Hispanic/Latino), 8 international. Average age 29. 18 applicants, 28% accepted, 5 enrolled. In 2019, 2 master's, 5 doctorates awarded. *Entrance requirements:* For master's and doctorate, GRE or GMAT. Additional exam requirements/recommendations for international students: required—TOEFL (minimum score 550 paper-based; 79 iBT). *Application deadline:* For fall admission, 3/1 priority date for international students; for spring admission, 8/1 priority date for international students. Applications are processed on a rolling basis. Application fee: $50 ($75 for international students). Electronic applications accepted. *Expenses: Tuition, area resident:* Full-time $4148.10; part-time $2765.40 per credit hour. Tuition, state resident: full-time $4148.10; part-time $2765.40 per credit hour. Tuition, nonresident: full-time $15,775; part-time $10,516.80 per credit hour. *International tuition:* $15,775.20 full-time. *Required fees:* $2196.90; $122.05 per credit hour. Tuition and fees vary according to course load, campus/location and program. *Financial support:* In 2019–20, 12 research assistantships (averaging $1,812 per year), 8 teaching assistantships (averaging $1,863 per year) were awarded; career-related internships or fieldwork, Federal Work-Study, scholarships/grants, health care benefits, tuition waivers (partial), and unspecified assistantships also available. Support available to part-time students. Financial award application deadline: 3/1; financial award applicants required to submit FAFSA. *Unit head:* Dr. John Gustafson, Department Head, 405-744-6189, E-mail: john.gustafson@okstate.edu. *Application contact:* Dr. Sheryl Tucker, Dean, 405-744-6368, Fax: 405-744-0355, E-mail: gradi@okstate.edu.
Website: http://biochemistry.okstate.edu/

**Oregon Health & Science University,** School of Medicine, Graduate Programs in Medicine, Department of Environmental and Biomolecular Systems, Portland, OR 97239-3098. Offers biochemistry and molecular biology (MS, PhD); environmental science and engineering (MS, PhD). *Program availability:* Part-time. Terminal master's awarded for partial completion of doctoral program. *Degree requirements:* For master's, thesis (for some programs); for doctorate, comprehensive exam, thesis/dissertation, qualifying exam. *Entrance requirements:* For master's and doctorate, GRE General Test (minimum scores: 153 Verbal/148 Quantitative/4.5 Analytical) or MCAT (for some programs). Electronic applications accepted.

**Oregon Health & Science University,** School of Medicine, Graduate Programs in Medicine, Program in Molecular and Cellular Biosciences, Department of Biochemistry and Molecular Biology, Portland, OR 97239-3098. Offers PhD. *Degree requirements:* For doctorate, comprehensive exam, thesis/dissertation, qualifying exam. *Entrance requirements:* For doctorate, GRE General Test (minimum scores: 153 Verbal/148 Quantitative/4.5 Analytical). Electronic applications accepted.

**Oregon State University,** College of Agricultural Sciences, Program in Botany and Plant Pathology, Corvallis, OR 97331. Offers applied systematics (MS); ecology (MS, PhD); genetics (MS, PhD); genomics and computational biology (MS, PhD); molecular and cellular biology (MS, PhD); mycology (MS, PhD); plant pathology (MS, PhD); plant physiology (MS, PhD). *Entrance requirements:* For master's and doctorate, GRE.

**Oregon State University,** Interdisciplinary/Institutional Programs, Program in Molecular and Cellular Biology, Corvallis, OR 97331. Offers bioinformatics (PhD); biotechnology (PhD); genome biology (PhD); molecular virology (PhD); plant molecular biology (PhD). *Degree requirements:* For doctorate, thesis/dissertation, oral and written qualifying exams. *Entrance requirements:* For doctorate, GRE. Additional exam requirements/recommendations for international students: required—TOEFL (minimum score 80 iBT), IELTS (minimum score 6.5).

**Pace University,** Dyson College of Arts and Sciences, Program in Biochemistry and Molecular Biology, New York, NY 10038. Offers MS. *Program availability:* Part-time, evening/weekend. *Degree requirements:* For master's, thesis. *Entrance requirements:* For master's, official transcripts, two letters of recommendation, personal statement. Additional exam requirements/recommendations for international students: required—TOEFL (minimum score 88 iBT), IELTS (minimum score 7) or PTE (minimum score 60). Electronic applications accepted.

**Penn State University Park,** Graduate School, Eberly College of Science, Department of Biochemistry and Molecular Biology, University Park, PA 16802. Offers biochemistry, microbiology, and molecular biology (MS, PhD); biotechnology (MBIOT).

**Penn State University Park,** Graduate School, Intercollege Graduate Programs, Program in Molecular, Cellular, and Integrative Biosciences, University Park, PA 16802. Offers MS, PhD.

**Princeton University,** Graduate School, Department of Molecular Biology, Princeton, NJ 08544-1019. Offers PhD. *Degree requirements:* For doctorate, thesis/dissertation. *Entrance requirements:* For doctorate, GRE General Test. Additional exam requirements/recommendations for international students: required—TOEFL (minimum score 600 paper-based). Electronic applications accepted.

**Purdue University,** College of Pharmacy and Graduate School, Graduate Programs in Pharmacy and Pharmacal Sciences, Department of Medicinal Chemistry and Molecular Pharmacology, West Lafayette, IN 47907. Offers biophysical and computational chemistry (PhD); cancer research (PhD); immunology and infectious disease (PhD); medicinal biochemistry and molecular biology (PhD); medicinal chemistry and chemical biology (PhD); molecular pharmacology (PhD); neuropharmacology, neurodegeneration, and neurotoxicity (PhD); systems biology and functional genomics (PhD). *Faculty:* 20 full-time (5 women), 7 part-time/adjunct (2 women). *Students:* 80 full-time (40 women), 2 part-time (0 women); includes 9 minority (5 Asian, non-Hispanic/Latino; 2 Hispanic/Latino; 2 Two or more races, non-Hispanic/Latino), 44 international. Average age 26. 162 applicants, 20% accepted, 15 enrolled. In 2019, 11 doctorates awarded. *Degree requirements:* For doctorate, thesis/dissertation. *Entrance requirements:* For doctorate, GRE General Test; GRE Subject Test in biology, biochemistry, and chemistry (recommended), minimum undergraduate GPA of 3.0. Additional exam requirements/recommendations for international students: required—TOEFL (minimum score 550 paper-based; 77 iBT); recommended—TWE. *Application deadline:* For fall admission, 2/1 for domestic and international students. Applications are processed on a rolling basis. Application fee: $60 ($75 for international students). Electronic applications accepted. *Financial support:* Fellowships, research assistantships, teaching assistantships, and traineeships available. Support available to part-time students. Financial award applicants required to submit FAFSA. *Unit head:* Zhong-Yin Zhang, Head, 765-494-1403, E-mail: zhang-yn@purdue.edu. *Application contact:* Delayne Graham, Graduate Contact, 765-494-1362, E-mail: dkgraham@purdue.edu.

**Purdue University,** Graduate School, PULSe - Purdue University Life Sciences Program, West Lafayette, IN 47907. Offers biomolecular structure and biophysics (PhD); biotechnology (PhD); chemical biology (PhD); chromatin and regulation of gene expression (PhD); integrative neuroscience (PhD); integrative plant sciences (PhD); membrane biology (PhD); microbiology (PhD); molecular evolutionary and cancer biology (PhD); molecular evolutionary genetics (PhD); molecular virology (PhD). *Students:* 37 full-time (23 women); includes 7 minority (1 Black or African American, non-Hispanic/Latino; 2 Asian, non-Hispanic/Latino; 4 Hispanic/Latino), 22 international. Average age 25. 162 applicants, 36% accepted, 19 enrolled. *Entrance requirements:* For doctorate, GRE, minimum undergraduate GPA of 3.0. Additional exam requirements/recommendations for international students: required—TOEFL (minimum score 550 paper-based; 77 iBT). *Application deadline:* For fall admission, 1/15 priority date for domestic and international students. Applications are processed on a rolling basis. Application fee: $60 ($75 for international students). Electronic applications accepted. *Financial support:* In 2019–20, research assistantships with tuition reimbursements (averaging $22,500 per year), teaching assistantships with tuition reimbursements (averaging $22,500 per year) were awarded. *Application contact:* Lindsey Springer, Graduate Contact for Admissions, 765-496-9667, E-mail: lbcampbe@

purdue.edu.
Website: http://www.gradschool.purdue.edu/pulse

**Quinnipiac University,** College of Arts and Sciences, Program in Molecular and Cell Biology, Hamden, CT 06518-1940. Offers MS. *Program availability:* Part-time, evening/weekend. *Degree requirements:* For master's, thesis optional. *Entrance requirements:* For master's, bachelor's degree in biological, medical, or health sciences. Additional exam requirements/recommendations for international students: required—TOEFL (minimum score 575 paper-based; 90 iBT), IELTS (minimum score 6.5). Electronic applications accepted. *Expenses: Tuition:* Part-time $1055 per credit. *Required fees:* $945 per semester. Tuition and fees vary according to course load and program.

**Rosalind Franklin University of Medicine and Science,** School of Graduate and Postdoctoral Studies - Interdisciplinary Graduate Program in Biomedical Sciences, Department of Biochemistry and Molecular Biology, North Chicago, IL 60064-3095. Offers PhD, MD/PhD. Terminal master's awarded for partial completion of doctoral program. *Degree requirements:* For doctorate, comprehensive exam, thesis/dissertation. *Entrance requirements:* For doctorate, GRE General Test, minimum GPA of 3.0. Additional exam requirements/recommendations for international students: required—TOEFL, TWE. Electronic applications accepted.

**Rutgers University - Newark,** Graduate School of Biomedical Sciences, Department of Biochemistry and Molecular Biology, Newark, NJ 07107. Offers MS, PhD. *Degree requirements:* For master's, thesis; for doctorate, thesis/dissertation, qualifying exam. *Entrance requirements:* For master's and doctorate, GRE General Test. Additional exam requirements/recommendations for international students: required—TOEFL. Electronic applications accepted.

**Rutgers University - New Brunswick,** Graduate School-New Brunswick, Programs in the Molecular Biosciences, Piscataway, NJ 08854-8097. Offers biochemistry (PhD); cell and developmental biology (MS, PhD); microbiology and molecular genetics (MS, PhD), including applied microbiology, clinical microbiology, computational molecular biology (PhD), immunology, microbial biochemistry, molecular genetics, virology.

**Rutgers University - New Brunswick,** Graduate School of Biomedical Sciences, Piscataway, NJ 08854-5635. Offers biochemistry and molecular biology (MS, PhD); biomedical engineering (MS, PhD); biomedical science (MS); cellular and molecular pharmacology (MS, PhD); clinical and translational science (MS); environmental sciences/exposure assessment (PhD); molecular genetics, microbiology and immunology (MS, PhD); neuroscience (MS, PhD); physiology and integrative biology (MS, PhD); toxicology (PhD); MD/PhD. Terminal master's awarded for partial completion of doctoral program. *Degree requirements:* For master's, thesis (for some programs), ethics training; for doctorate, comprehensive exam, thesis/dissertation, ethics training. *Entrance requirements:* For master's, GRE General Test, MCAT, DAT; for doctorate, GRE General Test. Additional exam requirements/recommendations for international students: required—TOEFL. Electronic applications accepted.

**Sacred Heart University,** Graduate Programs, College of Arts and Sciences, Department of Chemistry, Fairfield, CT 06825. Offers bioinformatics (MS); chemistry (MS); molecular biology (MS). *Program availability:* Part-time, evening/weekend. *Degree requirements:* For master's, thesis optional. *Entrance requirements:* For master's, bachelor's degree in related area (natural science with a heavy concentration in chemistry), minimum GPA of 2.75. Additional exam requirements/recommendations for international students: required—TOEFL (minimum score 570 paper-based, 80 iBT), TWE, or IELTS (6.5); recommended—TSE. Electronic applications accepted. *Expenses:* Contact institution.

**Saint Louis University,** Graduate Programs, School of Medicine, Graduate Programs in Biomedical Sciences and Graduate Programs, Department of Biochemistry and Molecular Biology, St. Louis, MO 63103. Offers PhD. *Degree requirements:* For doctorate, comprehensive exam, thesis/dissertation, departmental qualifying exams. *Entrance requirements:* For doctorate, GRE General Test, GRE Subject Test (optional), letters of recommendation, resume, interview. Additional exam requirements/recommendations for international students: required—TOEFL (minimum score 525 paper-based). Electronic applications accepted.

**San Diego State University,** Graduate and Research Affairs, College of Sciences, Department of Biology, San Diego, CA 92182. Offers biology (MA, MS), including ecology (MS), molecular biology (MS), physiology (MS), systematics/evolution (MS); cell and molecular biology (PhD); ecology (MS, PhD); microbiology (MS). Terminal master's awarded for partial completion of doctoral program. *Degree requirements:* For master's, thesis; for doctorate, thesis/dissertation. *Entrance requirements:* For master's, GRE General Test, GRE Subject Test, resume or curriculum vitae, 2 letters of recommendation. Additional exam requirements/recommendations for international students: required—TOEFL. Electronic applications accepted.

**San Diego State University,** Graduate and Research Affairs, College of Sciences, Molecular Biology Institute, Program in Cell and Molecular Biology, San Diego, CA 92182. Offers PhD. *Degree requirements:* For doctorate, thesis/dissertation, oral comprehensive qualifying exam. *Entrance requirements:* For doctorate, GRE General Test, GRE Subject Test, resumé or curriculum vitae, 3 letters of recommendation. Electronic applications accepted.

**San Francisco State University,** Division of Graduate Studies, College of Science and Engineering, Department of Biology, Program in Cell and Molecular Biology, San Francisco, CA 94132-1722. Offers MS. *Application deadline:* Applications are processed on a rolling basis. *Expenses: Tuition, area resident:* Full-time $7176; part-time $4164 per year. Tuition, state resident: full-time $7176; part-time $4164 per year. Tuition, nonresident: full-time $16,680; part-time $396 per unit. *International tuition:* $16,680 full-time. *Required fees:* $1524; $1524 per unit. $762 per semester. Tuition and fees vary according to degree level and program. *Unit head:* Dr. Diana Chu, Program Coordinator, 415-405-3487, Fax: 415-338-2295, E-mail: chud@sfsu.edu. *Application contact:* Dr. Diana Chu, Program Coordinator, 415-405-3487, Fax: 415-338-2295, E-mail: chud@sfsu.edu.
Website: http://biology.sfsu.edu/graduate/cell-and-molecular-biology

**San Jose State University,** Program in Biological Sciences, San Jose, CA 95192-0001. Offers biological sciences (MA, MS); molecular biology and microbiology (MS); organismal biology, conservation and ecology (MS); physiology (MS). *Program availability:* Part-time. *Entrance requirements:* For master's, GRE. Electronic applications accepted. *Expenses: Tuition, area resident:* Full-time $7176; part-time $4164 per credit hour. Tuition, state resident: full-time $7176; part-time $4164 per credit hour. Tuition, nonresident: full-time $7176; part-time $4165 per credit hour. *International tuition:* $7176 full-time. *Required fees:* $2110; $2110.

**Seton Hall University,** College of Arts and Sciences, Department of Biological Sciences, South Orange, NJ 07079-2697. Offers biology (MS); biology/business administration (MS); microbiology (MS); molecular bioscience (PhD); molecular bioscience/neuroscience (PhD). *Program availability:* Part-time, evening/weekend. *Degree requirements:* For master's, thesis optional; for doctorate, comprehensive exam, thesis/dissertation. *Entrance requirements:* For master's, GRE or undergraduate degree (BS in biological sciences) with minimum GPA of 3.0 from accredited U.S. institution; for doctorate, GRE. Additional exam requirements/recommendations for international students: required—TOEFL. Electronic applications accepted.

**Simon Fraser University,** Office of Graduate Studies and Postdoctoral Fellows, Faculty of Science, Department of Molecular Biology and Biochemistry, Burnaby, BC V5A 1S6, Canada. Offers bioinformatics (Graduate Diploma); molecular biology and biochemistry (M Sc, PhD). *Degree requirements:* For master's, thesis; for doctorate, thesis/dissertation; for Graduate Diploma, practicum. *Entrance requirements:* For master's, minimum GPA of 3.0 (on scale of 4.33) or 3.33 based on last 60 credits of undergraduate courses; for doctorate, minimum GPA of 3.5; for Graduate Diploma, minimum GPA of 2.5 (on scale of 4.33) or 2.67 based on last 60 credits of undergraduate courses. Additional exam requirements/recommendations for international students: recommended—TOEFL (minimum score 580 paper-based; 100 iBT), IELTS (minimum score 7.5), TWE (minimum score 5). Electronic applications accepted.

**Southern Illinois University Carbondale,** Graduate School, College of Science, Program in Molecular Biology, Microbiology, and Biochemistry, Carbondale, IL 62901-4701. Offers MS, PhD. *Degree requirements:* For master's, thesis; for doctorate, thesis/dissertation. *Entrance requirements:* For master's, GRE, minimum GPA of 2.7; for doctorate, GRE, minimum GPA of 3.25. Additional exam requirements/recommendations for international students: required—TOEFL.

**Southern Methodist University,** Dedman College of Humanities and Sciences, Department of Biological Sciences, Dallas, TX 75275. Offers molecular and cellular biology (MA, MS, PhD). Terminal master's awarded for partial completion of doctoral program. *Degree requirements:* For master's, thesis (for MS), oral exam; for doctorate, thesis/dissertation, qualifying exam. *Entrance requirements:* For master's and doctorate, GRE General Test (minimum score 1200), minimum GPA of 3.0. Additional exam requirements/recommendations for international students: required—TOEFL (minimum score 550 paper-based). Electronic applications accepted.

**State University of New York Downstate Medical Center,** School of Graduate Studies, Program in Molecular and Cellular Biology, Brooklyn, NY 11203-2098. Offers PhD, MD/PhD. *Degree requirements:* For doctorate, comprehensive exam, thesis/dissertation. *Entrance requirements:* For doctorate, GRE General Test. Additional exam requirements/recommendations for international students: recommended—TOEFL.

**State University of New York Upstate Medical University,** College of Graduate Studies, Program in Biochemistry and Molecular Biology, Syracuse, NY 13210. Offers biochemistry (MS); biochemistry and molecular biology (PhD); MD/PhD. Terminal master's awarded for partial completion of doctoral program. *Degree requirements:* For master's, thesis; for doctorate, comprehensive exam, thesis/dissertation. *Entrance requirements:* For master's, GRE General Test, interview; for doctorate, GRE General Test, telephone interview. Additional exam requirements/recommendations for international students: required—TOEFL. Electronic applications accepted.

**Stony Brook University, State University of New York,** Graduate School, College of Arts and Sciences, Department of Biochemistry and Cell Biology, Molecular and Cellular Biology Program, Stony Brook, NY 11794. Offers MA, PhD. *Students:* 59 full-time (29 women); includes 17 minority (3 Black or African American, non-Hispanic/Latino; 10 Asian, non-Hispanic/Latino; 4 Hispanic/Latino), 26 international. Average age 26. 111 applicants, 32% accepted, 15 enrolled. In 2019, 8 doctorates awarded. *Degree requirements:* For doctorate, comprehensive exam, thesis/dissertation, teaching experience. *Entrance requirements:* For doctorate, GRE General Test, GRE Subject Test. Additional exam requirements/recommendations for international students: required—TOEFL. *Application deadline:* For fall admission, 1/15 for domestic students; for spring admission, 10/1 for domestic students. Application fee: $100. Electronic applications accepted. *Expenses:* Contact institution. *Financial support:* In 2019–20, 4 fellowships, 23 research assistantships, 14 teaching assistantships were awarded; Federal Work-Study also available. *Unit head:* Prof. Aaron Neiman, Chair, 631-632-8550, Fax: 631-632-8575, E-mail: aaron.neiman@stonybrook.edu. *Application contact:* Amy Saas, Graduate Program Administrator, 631-632-8613, Fax: 631-632-9730, E-mail: mcbgraduateprogram@stonybrook.edu.
Website: https://www.stonybrook.edu/mcb/

**Texas Woman's University,** Graduate School, College of Arts and Sciences, Department of Biology, Denton, TX 76204. Offers biology (MS); molecular biology (PhD). *Program availability:* Part-time. *Faculty:* 14 full-time (10 women). *Students:* 2 full-time (both women), 29 part-time (21 women); includes 3 minority (1 Asian, non-Hispanic/Latino; 2 Hispanic/Latino), 20 international. Average age 34. 18 applicants, 11% accepted, 1 enrolled. In 2019, 16 master's, 3 doctorates awarded. Terminal master's awarded for partial completion of doctoral program. *Degree requirements:* For master's, thesis or alternative, professional paper or thesis; oral defense of thesis or professional paper; for doctorate, comprehensive exam, thesis/dissertation, 1-year residency; dissertation defense and oral exam by the dissertation committee. *Entrance requirements:* For master's, 3 letters of reference; letter of interest; for doctorate, 3 letters of reference, letter of interest, bachelor's degree in Biology. Additional exam requirements/recommendations for international students: required—TOEFL (minimum score 79 iBT); recommended—IELTS (minimum score 7.5), TSE (minimum score 53). *Application deadline:* For fall admission, 4/1 for domestic and international students; for spring admission, 11/1 for domestic and international students. Application fee: $50 ($75 for international students). Electronic applications accepted. *Expenses:* All are estimates. Tuition for 10 hours = $2,763; Fees for 10 hours = $1,342. Biology courses require an additional $25/SCH not included in the estimates above. *Financial support:* In 2019–20, 21 students received support, including 7 research assistantships (averaging $15,715 per year), 12 teaching assistantships (averaging $12,657 per year); career-related internships or fieldwork, health care benefits, and unspecified assistantships also available. Support available to part-time students. Financial award application deadline: 3/1; financial award applicants required to submit FAFSA. *Unit head:* Dr. Juliet Spencer, Chair, 940-898-2351, Fax: 940-898-2382, E-mail: biology@twu.edu. *Application contact:* Korie Hawkins, Associate Director of Admissions, Graduate Recruitment, 940-898-3188, Fax: 940-898-3081, E-mail: admissions@twu.edu.
Website: http://www.twu.edu/biology

**Tufts University,** Graduate School of Biomedical Sciences, Cell, Molecular, and Developmental Biology Program, Medford, MA 02155. Offers cancer biology (PhD); developmental and regenerative biology (PhD); molecular and cellular medicine (PhD); structural and chemical biology (PhD). *Faculty:* 84 full-time (30 women). *Students:* 32 full-time (15 women); includes 10 minority (2 Black or African American, non-Hispanic/Latino; 4 Asian, non-Hispanic/Latino; 4 Hispanic/Latino), 4 international. Average age 28. 168 applicants, 5% accepted, 3 enrolled. In 2019, 5 doctorates awarded. Terminal master's awarded for partial completion of doctoral program. *Degree requirements:* For doctorate, comprehensive exam, thesis/dissertation. *Entrance requirements:* For doctorate, 3 letters of reference, resume, personal statement. *Application deadline:* For fall admission, 12/1 priority date for domestic and international students. Application fee: $90. Electronic applications accepted. *Expenses: Tuition:* Part-time $1799 per credit hour. Full-time tuition and fees vary according to degree level, program and student level. Part-time tuition and fees vary according to course load. *Financial support:* In 2019–20, 100 students received support, including 3 research assistantships with full

tuition reimbursements available (averaging $40,000 per year); fellowships, traineeships, and health care benefits also available. Financial award application deadline: 12/1. *Unit head:* Dr. Brent Cochran, Program Director, 617-636-0442. *Application contact:* Jeff Miller, Admissions Coordinator, 617-636-6767, Fax: 617-636-0375, E-mail: gsbs-admissions@tufts.edu.
Website: https://gsbs.tufts.edu/academics/CMDB

**Tufts University,** Graduate School of Biomedical Sciences, Molecular Microbiology Program, Medford, MA 02155. Offers medically-oriented research in graduate education (PhD); molecular microbiology (PhD). *Faculty:* 23 full-time (10 women). *Students:* 42 full-time (23 women); includes 14 minority (2 Black or African American, non-Hispanic/Latino; 4 Asian, non-Hispanic/Latino; 4 Hispanic/Latino; 4 Two or more races, non-Hispanic/Latino), 3 international. Average age 30. 66 applicants, 30% accepted, 6 enrolled. In 2019, 2 doctorates awarded. Terminal master's awarded for partial completion of doctoral program. *Degree requirements:* For doctorate, comprehensive exam, thesis/dissertation. *Entrance requirements:* For doctorate, 3 letters of reference, resume, personal statement. *Application deadline:* For fall admission, 12/1 priority date for domestic and international students. Application fee: $90. Electronic applications accepted. *Expenses: Tuition:* Part-time $1799 per credit hour. Full-time tuition and fees vary according to degree level, program and student level. Part-time tuition and fees vary according to course load. *Financial support:* Application deadline: 12/1. *Unit head:* Dr. Katya Heldwein, Director, 617-636-6750, Fax: 617-636-0337, E-mail: katya.heldwein@tufts.edu. *Application contact:* Jeff Miller, 617-636-6767, Fax: 617-636-0375, E-mail: GSBS-Admissions@tufts.edu.
Website: https://gsbs.tufts.edu/academics/molecularMicrobiology

**Tulane University,** School of Medicine, Graduate Programs in Biomedical Sciences, Interdisciplinary Graduate Program in Molecular and Cellular Biology, New Orleans, LA 70118-5669. Offers PhD, MD/PhD. *Degree requirements:* For doctorate, thesis/dissertation. *Entrance requirements:* For doctorate, GRE General Test, GRE Subject Test. Additional exam requirements/recommendations for international students: required—TOEFL. Electronic applications accepted. *Expenses: Tuition:* Full-time $57,004; part-time $3167 per credit hour. *Required fees:* $2086; $44.50 per credit hour. $80 per term. Tuition and fees vary according to course load, degree level and program.

**Tulane University,** School of Science and Engineering, Department of Cell and Molecular Biology, New Orleans, LA 70118-5669. Offers MS, PhD. Terminal master's awarded for partial completion of doctoral program. *Degree requirements:* For doctorate, thesis/dissertation. *Entrance requirements:* For master's, GRE General Test, minimum B average in undergraduate course work; for doctorate, GRE General Test. Additional exam requirements/recommendations for international students: required—TOEFL. Electronic applications accepted. *Expenses: Tuition:* Full-time $57,004; part-time $3167 per credit hour. *Required fees:* $2086; $44.50 per credit hour. $80 per term. Tuition and fees vary according to course load, degree level and program.

**Uniformed Services University of the Health Sciences,** F. Edward Hebert School of Medicine, Graduate Programs in the Biomedical Sciences and Public Health, Graduate Program in Molecular and Cell Biology, Bethesda, MD 20814-4799. Offers MS, PhD. *Degree requirements:* For doctorate, comprehensive exam, thesis/dissertation, qualifying exam. *Entrance requirements:* For doctorate, GRE General Test, minimum GPA of 3.0. Electronic applications accepted. Application fee is waived when completed online.

**Universidad Central del Caribe,** School of Medicine, Program in Biomedical Sciences, Bayamón, PR 00960-6032. Offers anatomy and cell biology (MA, MS); biochemistry (MS); biomedical sciences (MA); cellular and molecular biology (PhD); microbiology and immunology (MA, MS); pharmacology (MS); physiology (MS).

**Université de Montréal,** Faculty of Medicine, Program in Molecular Biology, Montréal, QC H3C 3J7, Canada. Offers M Sc, PhD. Terminal master's awarded for partial completion of doctoral program. *Degree requirements:* For master's, thesis; for doctorate, thesis/dissertation, general exam. *Entrance requirements:* For master's and doctorate, proficiency in French, knowledge of English. Electronic applications accepted.

**University at Buffalo, the State University of New York,** Graduate School, Graduate Programs in Cancer Research and Biomedical Sciences at Roswell Park Cancer Institute, Buffalo, NY 14260. Offers cancer pathology and prevention (PhD); cellular and molecular biology (PhD); immunology (PhD); interdisciplinary natural sciences (MS); molecular and cellular biophysics and biochemistry (PhD); molecular pharmacology and cancer therapeutics (PhD). Terminal master's awarded for partial completion of doctoral program. *Degree requirements:* For master's, thesis, oral defense of thesis; for doctorate, comprehensive exam, thesis/dissertation, oral defense of dissertation. *Entrance requirements:* For master's and doctorate, GRE General Test. Additional exam requirements/recommendations for international students: required—TOEFL (minimum score 79 iBT). Electronic applications accepted. *Expenses: Tuition, area resident:* Full-time $11,310; part-time $471 per credit hour. Tuition, state resident: full-time $11,310; part-time $471 per credit hour. Tuition, nonresident: full-time $23,100; part-time $963 per credit hour. *International tuition:* $23,100 full-time. *Required fees:* $2820.

**The University of Alabama at Birmingham,** Joint Health Sciences, Cell, Molecular, and Developmental Biology Theme, Birmingham, AL 35294. Offers PhD. *Students:* Average age 27. 32 applicants, 28% accepted, 3 enrolled. In 2019, 7 doctorates awarded. *Degree requirements:* For doctorate, comprehensive exam, thesis/dissertation. *Entrance requirements:* For doctorate, personal statement, resume or curriculum vitae, letters of recommendation, research experience, interview. Additional exam requirements/recommendations for international students: required—TOEFL (minimum score 80 iBT), IELTS (minimum score 6.5). *Application deadline:* For fall admission, 12/31 for domestic and international students. Applications are processed on a rolling basis. Electronic applications accepted. *Financial support:* In 2019–20, fellowships with full tuition reimbursements (averaging $30,000 per year), research assistantships with full tuition reimbursements (averaging $31,000 per year) were awarded; health care benefits also available. *Unit head:* Dr. Alecia K. Gross, Theme Director, 205-975-8396, E-mail: agross@uab.edu. *Application contact:* Alyssa Zasada, Admissions Manager for Graduate Biomedical Sciences, 205-934-3857, E-mail: grad-gbs@uab.edu.
Website: http://www.uab.edu/gbs/home/themes/cmdb

**University of Alberta,** Faculty of Graduate Studies and Research, Department of Biological Sciences, Edmonton, AB T6G 2E1, Canada. Offers environmental biology and ecology (M Sc, PhD); microbiology and biotechnology (M Sc, PhD); molecular biology and genetics (M Sc, PhD); physiology and cell biology (M Sc, PhD); plant biology (M Sc, PhD); systematics and evolution (M Sc, PhD). Terminal master's awarded for partial completion of doctoral program. *Degree requirements:* For master's, thesis; for doctorate, thesis/dissertation. *Entrance requirements:* Additional exam requirements/recommendations for international students: required—TOEFL.

**University of Alberta,** Faculty of Medicine and Dentistry and Faculty of Graduate Studies and Research, Graduate Programs in Medicine, Department of Cell Biology, Edmonton, AB T6G 2E1, Canada. Offers cell and molecular biology (M Sc, PhD). Terminal master's awarded for partial completion of doctoral program. *Degree requirements:* For master's, thesis; for doctorate, thesis/dissertation. *Entrance requirements:* For master's and doctorate, 3 letters of reference, curriculum vitae. Additional exam requirements/recommendations for international students: required—TOEFL (minimum score 600 paper-based).

**The University of Arizona,** College of Science, Biochemistry and Molecular and Cellular Biology Program, Tucson, AZ 85721. Offers PhD. *Program availability:* Evening/weekend. *Degree requirements:* For doctorate, thesis/dissertation. *Entrance requirements:* For doctorate, 3 letters of recommendation, statement of purpose. Additional exam requirements/recommendations for international students: required—TOEFL (minimum score 600 paper-based; 90 iBT), IELTS (minimum score 7). Electronic applications accepted.

**University of Arkansas,** Graduate School, Interdisciplinary Program in Cell and Molecular Biology, Fayetteville, AR 72701. Offers MS, PhD. *Students:* 64 full-time (40 women), 32 part-time (16 women); includes 8 minority (2 Black or African American, non-Hispanic/Latino; 1 American Indian or Alaska Native, non-Hispanic/Latino; 4 Hispanic/Latino; 1 Two or more races, non-Hispanic/Latino), 63 international. 20 applicants, 100% accepted. In 2019, 6 master's, 10 doctorates awarded. *Application deadline:* For fall admission, 8/1 for domestic students, 4/1 for international students; for spring admission, 12/1 for domestic students, 10/1 for international students; for summer admission, 4/15 for domestic students, 3/1 for international students. Applications are processed on a rolling basis. Application fee: $60. Electronic applications accepted. *Financial support:* In 2019–20, 31 research assistantships, 12 teaching assistantships were awarded; fellowships with tuition reimbursements also available. Financial award application deadline: 4/1; financial award applicants required to submit FAFSA. *Unit head:* Dr. Douglas Rhoads, Program Director, 479-575-3251, Fax: 479-575-4010, E-mail: drhoads@uark.edu. *Application contact:* Dr. Adnan Alrubaye, Program Associate Director, 479-575-3251, Fax: 479-575-4010, E-mail: aakhalaf@uark.edu.
Website: https://cell.uark.edu/

**University of Arkansas for Medical Sciences,** Graduate School, Little Rock, AR 72205. Offers biochemistry and molecular biology (MS, PhD); bioinformatics (MS, PhD); cellular physiology and molecular biophysics (MS, PhD); clinical nutrition (MS); interdisciplinary biomedical sciences (MS, PhD, Certificate); interdisciplinary toxicology (MS); microbiology and immunology (PhD); neurobiology and developmental sciences (PhD); pharmacology (PhD); MD/PhD. *Program availability:* Part-time. Terminal master's awarded for partial completion of doctoral program. *Degree requirements:* For master's, comprehensive exam (for some programs), thesis (for some programs); for doctorate, thesis/dissertation. *Entrance requirements:* For master's and doctorate, GRE. Additional exam requirements/recommendations for international students: required—TOEFL. Electronic applications accepted. *Expenses:* Contact institution.

**The University of British Columbia,** Faculty of Medicine, Department of Biochemistry and Molecular Biology, Vancouver, BC V6T 1Z3, Canada. Offers M Sc, PhD. *Degree requirements:* For master's, thesis; for doctorate, comprehensive exam, thesis/dissertation. *Entrance requirements:* For master's, first class B Sc; for doctorate, master's or first class honors bachelor's degree in biochemistry. Additional exam requirements/recommendations for international students: required—TOEFL (minimum score 625 paper-based). Electronic applications accepted. *Expenses:* Contact institution.

**University of Calgary,** Cumming School of Medicine and Faculty of Graduate Studies, Program in Biochemistry and Molecular Biology, Calgary, AB T2N 1N4, Canada. Offers M Sc, PhD. *Degree requirements:* For master's, thesis; for doctorate, thesis/dissertation, candidacy exam. *Entrance requirements:* For master's and doctorate, GRE General Test, minimum GPA of 3.2. Additional exam requirements/recommendations for international students: required—TOEFL. Electronic applications accepted.

**University of California, Berkeley,** Graduate Division, College of Letters and Science, Department of Molecular and Cell Biology, Berkeley, CA 94720. Offers PhD. *Degree requirements:* For doctorate, comprehensive exam, thesis/dissertation, qualifying exam, 2 semesters of teaching. *Entrance requirements:* For doctorate, GRE General Test, GRE Subject Test (recommended), minimum GPA of 3.0. Additional exam requirements/recommendations for international students: required—TOEFL (minimum score 570 paper-based; 68 iBT), IELTS (minimum score 7). Electronic applications accepted.

**University of California, Davis,** Graduate Studies, Graduate Group in Biochemistry and Molecular Biology, Davis, CA 95616. Offers MS, PhD. Terminal master's awarded for partial completion of doctoral program. *Degree requirements:* For master's, comprehensive exam (for some programs), thesis (for some programs); for doctorate, thesis/dissertation. *Entrance requirements:* For master's and doctorate, GRE General Test, GRE Subject Test. Additional exam requirements/recommendations for international students: required—TOEFL (minimum score 550 paper-based). Electronic applications accepted.

**University of California, Irvine,** School of Biological Sciences, Department of Molecular Biology and Biochemistry, Irvine, CA 92697. Offers biological science (MS); biological sciences (PhD); biotechnology (MS); biotechnology management (MS); MD/PhD. *Students:* 46 full-time (24 women); includes 17 minority (2 Black or African American, non-Hispanic/Latino; 8 Asian, non-Hispanic/Latino; 7 Hispanic/Latino), 5 international. Average age 28. 5 applicants, 100% accepted, 4 enrolled. In 2019, 3 master's, 10 doctorates awarded. *Entrance requirements:* For master's, GRE, minimum GPA of 3.0; for doctorate, GRE General Test, GRE Subject Test, minimum GPA of 3.0. Additional exam requirements/recommendations for international students: required—TOEFL (minimum score 550 paper-based). *Application deadline:* For fall admission, 12/15 priority date for domestic students, 12/15 for international students. Applications are processed on a rolling basis. Application fee: $120 ($140 for international students). Electronic applications accepted. *Financial support:* Fellowships, research assistantships with full tuition reimbursements, teaching assistantships, institutionally sponsored loans, traineeships, health care benefits, and unspecified assistantships available. Financial award application deadline: 3/1; financial award applicants required to submit FAFSA. *Unit head:* Prof. Christopher Hughes, Chair, 949-824-8771, Fax: 949-824-8551, E-mail: cchughes@uci.edu. *Application contact:* Morgan Oldham, Student Affairs Assistant, 949-826-6034, Fax: 949-824-8551, E-mail: morgano@uci.edu.
Website: http://www.bio.uci.edu/

**University of California, Irvine,** School of Biological Sciences and School of Medicine, Interdisciplinary Graduate Program in Cellular and Molecular Biosciences, Irvine, CA 92697. Offers PhD. *Students:* 26 full-time (17 women); includes 13 minority (1 Black or African American, non-Hispanic/Latino; 6 Asian, non-Hispanic/Latino; 6 Hispanic/Latino). Average age 28. 448 applicants, 17% accepted, 26 enrolled. *Degree requirements:* For doctorate, thesis/dissertation, teaching assignment, preliminary exam. *Entrance requirements:* For doctorate, GRE General Test, three letters of recommendation, interview. Additional exam requirements/recommendations for international students: required—TOEFL or IELTS. *Application deadline:* For fall admission, 12/8 for domestic and international students. Application fee: $120 ($140 for international students). Electronic applications accepted. *Expenses:* Contact institution. *Financial support:* Fellowships with full tuition reimbursements, institutionally sponsored loans, scholarships/grants, tuition waivers (full), unspecified assistantships, and stipends available. Financial award application deadline: 1/1; financial award applicants required to submit FAFSA. *Unit head:* Melanie Cocco, Director, 949-824-4487, Fax: 949-

824-1965, E-mail: mcocco@uci.edu. *Application contact:* Renee Frigo, Administrator, 949-824-8145, Fax: 949-824-1965, E-mail: rfrigo@uci.edu. Website: http://cmb.uci.edu/

**University of California, Los Angeles,** Graduate Division, College of Letters and Science, Department of Chemistry and Biochemistry, Program in Biochemistry and Molecular Biology, Los Angeles, CA 90095. Offers MS, PhD. Terminal master's awarded for partial completion of doctoral program. *Degree requirements:* For master's, comprehensive exam or thesis; for doctorate, thesis/dissertation, oral and written qualifying exams; 3 quarters of teaching experience. *Entrance requirements:* For doctorate, GRE General Test, GRE Subject Test (recommended), bachelor's degree; minimum undergraduate GPA of 3.0 (or its equivalent if letter grade system not used). Additional exam requirements/recommendations for international students: required—TOEFL. Electronic applications accepted.

**University of California, Los Angeles,** Graduate Division, College of Letters and Science, Department of Molecular, Cell and Developmental Biology, Los Angeles, CA 90095. Offers MA, PhD. Terminal master's awarded for partial completion of doctoral program. *Degree requirements:* For master's, comprehensive exam, thesis; for doctorate, thesis/dissertation, oral and written qualifying exams; 2 quarters of teaching experience. *Entrance requirements:* For doctorate, GRE General Test. Additional exam requirements/recommendations for international students: required—TOEFL. Electronic applications accepted.

**University of California, Los Angeles,** Graduate Division, College of Letters and Science, Program in Molecular Biology, Los Angeles, CA 90095. Offers PhD, MD/PhD. *Degree requirements:* For doctorate, thesis/dissertation, oral and written qualifying exams. *Entrance requirements:* For doctorate, GRE General Test; GRE Subject Test (biochemistry, chemistry, biology, or physics), bachelor's degree; minimum undergraduate GPA of 3.0 (or its equivalent if letter grade system not used). Additional exam requirements/recommendations for international students: required—TOEFL. Electronic applications accepted.

**University of California, Los Angeles,** Graduate Division, College of Letters and Science and David Geffen School of Medicine, UCLA ACCESS to Programs in the Molecular, Cellular and Integrative Life Sciences, Los Angeles, CA 90095. Offers biochemistry and molecular biology (PhD); biological chemistry (PhD); cellular and molecular pathology (PhD); human genetics (PhD); microbiology, immunology, and molecular genetics (PhD); molecular biology (PhD); molecular toxicology (PhD); molecular, cellular and integrative physiology (PhD); neurobiology (PhD); oral biology (PhD); physiology (PhD). *Degree requirements:* For doctorate, thesis/dissertation, oral and written qualifying exams. *Entrance requirements:* For doctorate, GRE General Test, bachelor's degree; minimum undergraduate GPA of 3.0 (or its equivalent if letter grade system not used). Additional exam requirements/recommendations for international students: required—TOEFL. Electronic applications accepted.

**University of California, Riverside,** Graduate Division, Department of Biochemistry and Molecular Biology, Riverside, CA 92521-0102. Offers MS, PhD. *Program availability:* Part-time. Terminal master's awarded for partial completion of doctoral program. *Degree requirements:* For master's, comprehensive exam (for some programs), thesis (for some programs), comprehensive exam or thesis; for doctorate, comprehensive exam, thesis/dissertation, 2 quarters of teaching experience, written exam, oral qualifying exam. *Entrance requirements:* For master's, GRE General Test, minimum GPA of 3.0; for doctorate, GRE General Test, minimum GPA of 3.25. Additional exam requirements/recommendations for international students: required—TOEFL (minimum score 550 paper-based, 80 iBT) or IELTS. Electronic applications accepted.

**University of California, Riverside,** Graduate Division, Program in Cell, Molecular, and Developmental Biology, Riverside, CA 92521-0102. Offers MS, PhD. Terminal master's awarded for partial completion of doctoral program. *Degree requirements:* For master's, thesis, oral defense of thesis; for doctorate, thesis/dissertation, oral defense of thesis, qualifying exams, 2 quarters of teaching experience. *Entrance requirements:* For master's and doctorate, GRE General Test, minimum GPA of 3.2. Additional exam requirements/recommendations for international students: required—TOEFL (minimum score 550 paper-based; 80 iBT). Electronic applications accepted.

**University of California, San Francisco,** Graduate Division and School of Medicine, Tetrad Graduate Program, Biochemistry and Molecular Biology Track, San Francisco, CA 94143. Offers PhD, MD/PhD. *Degree requirements:* For doctorate, thesis/dissertation. *Entrance requirements:* For doctorate, GRE General Test, GRE Subject Test. Additional exam requirements/recommendations for international students: required—TOEFL. *Expenses:* Contact institution.

**University of California, Santa Barbara,** Graduate Division, College of Letters and Sciences, Division of Mathematics, Life, and Physical Sciences, Department of Molecular, Cellular, and Developmental Biology, Santa Barbara, CA 93106-9625. Offers MA, PhD, MA/PhD. Terminal master's awarded for partial completion of doctoral program. *Degree requirements:* For master's, comprehensive exam (for some programs), thesis (for some programs); for doctorate, comprehensive exam, thesis/dissertation. *Entrance requirements:* For master's and doctorate, GRE General Test, 3 letters of recommendation, statement of purpose, personal achievements/contributions statement, resume/curriculum vitae, transcripts for post-secondary institutions attended. Additional exam requirements/recommendations for international students: required—TOEFL (minimum score 550 paper-based; 80 iBT), IELTS (minimum score 7). Electronic applications accepted.

**University of California, Santa Barbara,** Graduate Division, College of Letters and Sciences, Division of Mathematics, Life, and Physical Sciences, Interdepartmental Graduate Program in Biomolecular Science and Engineering, Santa Barbara, CA 93106-2014. Offers biochemistry and molecular biology (PhD), including biochemistry and molecular biology, biophysics and bioengineering. Terminal master's awarded for partial completion of doctoral program. *Degree requirements:* For doctorate, thesis/dissertation. *Entrance requirements:* For doctorate, GRE General Test. Additional exam requirements/recommendations for international students: required—TOEFL (minimum score 630 paper-based; 109 iBT), IELTS (minimum score 7). Electronic applications accepted.

**University of California, Santa Cruz,** Division of Graduate Studies, Division of Physical and Biological Sciences, Program in Molecular, Cellular, and Developmental Biology, Santa Cruz, CA 95064. Offers MA, PhD. Terminal master's awarded for partial completion of doctoral program. *Degree requirements:* For master's, thesis; for doctorate, thesis/dissertation, qualifying exam. *Entrance requirements:* For master's and doctorate, GRE General Test, 3 letters of recommendation, interview. Additional exam requirements/recommendations for international students: required—TOEFL (minimum score 550 paper-based; 83 iBT); recommended—IELTS (minimum score 8). Electronic applications accepted.

**University of Chicago,** Division of the Biological Sciences, Program in Cell and Molecular Biology, Chicago, IL 60637. Offers PhD. *Degree requirements:* For doctorate, thesis/dissertation, ethics class, 2 teaching assistantships. *Entrance requirements:* For doctorate, GRE General Test, transcripts, statement of purpose, 3 letters of

recommendation. Additional exam requirements/recommendations for international students: required—TOEFL (minimum score 600 paper-based; 104 iBT), IELTS (minimum score 7). Electronic applications accepted.

**University of Cincinnati,** Graduate School, College of Medicine, Graduate Programs in Biomedical Sciences, Department of Environmental Health, Programs in Environmental Genetics and Molecular Toxicology, Cincinnati, OH 45221. Offers MS, PhD. *Degree requirements:* For doctorate, thesis/dissertation. *Entrance requirements:* For master's, GRE, minimum GPA of 3.0, 3 letters of recommendation. Additional exam requirements/recommendations for international students: required—TOEFL (minimum score 520 paper-based).

**University of Cincinnati,** Graduate School, College of Medicine, Graduate Programs in Biomedical Sciences, Department of Pediatrics, Program in Molecular and Developmental Biology, Cincinnati, OH 45221. Offers PhD. *Degree requirements:* For doctorate, thesis/dissertation, qualifying exam. *Entrance requirements:* For doctorate, GRE General Test, minimum GPA of 3.2. Additional exam requirements/recommendations for international students: required—TOEFL (minimum score 520 paper-based). Electronic applications accepted.

**University of Cincinnati,** Graduate School, College of Medicine, Graduate Programs in Biomedical Sciences, Molecular Genetics, Biochemistry and Microbiology Graduate Program, Cincinnati, OH 45221. Offers MS, PhD. *Faculty:* 30 full-time (5 women). *Students:* 26 full-time (11 women), 4 part-time (2 women); includes 3 minority (1 Black or African American, non-Hispanic/Latino; 1 Asian, non-Hispanic/Latino; 1 Hispanic/Latino), 2 international. Average age 27. 40 applicants, 30% accepted, 6 enrolled. In 2019, 2 master's, 4 doctorates awarded. Terminal master's awarded for partial completion of doctoral program. *Degree requirements:* For master's, thesis or alternative; for doctorate, thesis/dissertation, qualifying exam. *Entrance requirements:* For master's and doctorate, GRE highly recommended but not required. Additional exam requirements/recommendations for international students: required—TOEFL (minimum score 600 paper-based; 100 iBT). *Application deadline:* For fall admission, 12/15 priority date for domestic and international students. Applications are processed on a rolling basis. Application fee: $40. Electronic applications accepted. *Financial support:* In 2019–20, 6 research assistantships with full tuition reimbursements (averaging $28,000 per year) were awarded; health care benefits also available. Financial award application deadline: 5/1. *Unit head:* Dr. Michael Lieberman, Professor and Chair, 513-558-5645, E-mail: michael.lieberman@uc.edu. *Application contact:* Dr. William Miller, Graduate Program Director, 513-558-0866, Fax: 513-558-8474, E-mail: william.miller@uc.edu. Website: http://med.uc.edu/molgen-graduate

**University of Colorado Boulder,** Graduate School, College of Arts and Sciences, Department of Molecular, Cellular, and Developmental Biology, Boulder, CO 80309. Offers cellular structure and function (MA, PhD); developmental biology (PhD); molecular biology (PhD). Terminal master's awarded for partial completion of doctoral program. *Degree requirements:* For master's, comprehensive exam, thesis or alternative; for doctorate, comprehensive exam, thesis/dissertation. *Entrance requirements:* For master's, GRE General Test, GRE Subject Test, minimum undergraduate GPA of 3.0; for doctorate, GRE General Test, GRE Subject Test. Electronic applications accepted. Application fee is waived when completed online.

**University of Colorado Denver,** School of Medicine, Program in Molecular Biology, Aurora, CO 80045. Offers biomolecular structure (PhD). *Degree requirements:* For doctorate, comprehensive exam, thesis/dissertation, 2 years of structured didactic courses, 2-3 years of research, laboratory work, thesis project. *Entrance requirements:* For doctorate, GRE, organic chemistry (2 semesters, including 1 semester of laboratory), biology, general physics, college-level mathematics through calculus, three letters of reference. Additional exam requirements/recommendations for international students: required—TOEFL (minimum score 550 paper-based; 80 iBT). Electronic applications accepted. Tuition and fees vary according to course load, program and reciprocity agreements.

**University of Colorado Denver,** School of Medicine, Program in Pharmacology, Aurora, CO 80206. Offers bioinformatics (PhD); biomolecular structure (PhD). *Degree requirements:* For doctorate, comprehensive exam, thesis/dissertation, major seminar, 3 research rotations in the first year, 30 hours each of course work and thesis. *Entrance requirements:* For doctorate, GRE General Test, three letters of recommendation, personal statement. Additional exam requirements/recommendations for international students: required—TOEFL (minimum score 550 paper-based; 80 iBT). Electronic applications accepted. Tuition and fees vary according to course load, program and reciprocity agreements.

**University of Connecticut,** Graduate School, College of Liberal Arts and Sciences, Department of Molecular and Cell Biology, Storrs, CT 06269. Offers applied genomics (PSM); cell and developmental biology (MS, PhD); genetics and genomics (MS, PhD); microbial systems analysis (PSM); microbiology (MS, PhD); structural biology, biochemistry and biophysics (MS, PhD). Terminal master's awarded for partial completion of doctoral program. *Degree requirements:* For master's, comprehensive exam; for doctorate, thesis/dissertation. *Entrance requirements:* For master's and doctorate, GRE General Test, GRE Subject Test. Additional exam requirements/recommendations for international students: required—TOEFL (minimum score 550 paper-based). Electronic applications accepted.

**University of Connecticut Health Center,** Graduate School, Programs in Biomedical Sciences, Graduate Program in Molecular Biology and Biochemistry, Farmington, CT 06030. Offers PhD, DMD/PhD, MD/PhD. *Degree requirements:* For doctorate, comprehensive exam, thesis/dissertation. *Entrance requirements:* For doctorate, GRE General Test. Additional exam requirements/recommendations for international students: required—TOEFL (minimum score 600 paper-based). Electronic applications accepted.

**University of Delaware,** College of Arts and Sciences, Department of Biological Sciences, Newark, DE 19716. Offers biotechnology (MS); cancer biology (MS, PhD); cell and extracellular matrix biology (MS, PhD); cell and systems physiology (MS, PhD); developmental biology (MS, PhD); ecology and evolution (MS, PhD); microbiology (MS, PhD); molecular biology and genetics (MS, PhD). Terminal master's awarded for partial completion of doctoral program. *Degree requirements:* For master's, thesis, preliminary exam; for doctorate, comprehensive exam, thesis/dissertation, preliminary exam. *Entrance requirements:* For master's and doctorate, GRE General Test. Additional exam requirements/recommendations for international students: required—TOEFL (minimum score 600 paper-based); recommended—TWE. Electronic applications accepted.

**University of Denver,** Division of Natural Sciences and Mathematics, Department of Biological Sciences, Denver, CO 80208. Offers biology, ecology and evolution (MS, PhD); biomedical sciences (PSM); cell and molecular biology (MS, PhD). *Program availability:* Part-time. *Faculty:* 23 full-time (10 women), 2 part-time/adjunct (both women). *Students:* 12 full-time (7 women), 31 part-time (18 women); includes 6 minority (4 Hispanic/Latino; 2 Two or more races, non-Hispanic/Latino), 3 international. Average age 25. 100 applicants, 34% accepted, 18 enrolled. In 2019, 9 master's, 6 doctorates awarded. Terminal master's awarded for partial completion of doctoral program. *Degree requirements:* For master's, thesis; for doctorate, comprehensive exam, thesis/

dissertation. *Entrance requirements:* For master's and doctorate, GRE General Test, bachelor's degree in biology or related field, transcripts, personal statement, three letters of recommendation. Additional exam requirements/recommendations for international students: required—TOEFL (minimum score 550 paper-based; 80 iBT). *Application deadline:* For fall admission, 1/2 priority date for domestic and international students. Applications are processed on a rolling basis. Application fee: $65. Electronic applications accepted. *Expenses:* Contact institution. *Financial support:* In 2019–20, 43 students received support, including 9 research assistantships with tuition reimbursements available (averaging $16,589 per year), 26 teaching assistantships with tuition reimbursements available (averaging $18,869 per year); Federal Work-Study, institutionally sponsored loans, scholarships/grants, and unspecified assistantships also available. Support available to part-time students. Financial award application deadline: 2/15; financial award applicants required to submit FAFSA. *Unit head:* Dr. Joe Angleson, Associate Professor and Chair, 303-871-3463, E-mail: jangleso@du.edu. *Application contact:* Randi Flageolle, Assistant to the Chair, 303-871-3457, E-mail: rflageol@du.edu.
Website: http://www.du.edu/nsm/departments/biologicalsciences

**University of Florida,** College of Medicine and Graduate School, Interdisciplinary Program in Biomedical Sciences, Concentration in Biochemistry and Molecular Biology, Gainesville, FL 32611. Offers PhD. *Degree requirements:* For doctorate, thesis/dissertation. *Entrance requirements:* For doctorate, GRE General Test, minimum GPA of 3.0, biochemistry before enrollment. Additional exam requirements/recommendations for international students: required—TOEFL. Electronic applications accepted.

**University of Florida,** Graduate School, College of Agricultural and Life Sciences, Department of Animal Sciences, Interdisciplinary Concentration in Animal Molecular and Cellular Biology, Gainesville, FL 32611. Offers MS, PhD. *Entrance requirements:* For master's and doctorate, GRE General Test, minimum GPA of 3.0. Additional exam requirements/recommendations for international students: required—TOEFL (minimum score 550 paper-based; 80 iBT), IELTS (minimum score 6). Electronic applications accepted.

**University of Florida,** Graduate School, College of Liberal Arts and Sciences, Department of Biology, Gainesville, FL 32611. Offers botany (MS, MST, PhD), including botany, tropical conservation and development, wetland sciences; zoology (MS, MST, PhD), including animal molecular and cellular biology (PhD), tropical conservation and development, wetland sciences, zoology. *Degree requirements:* For master's, comprehensive exam (for some programs), thesis; for doctorate, comprehensive exam, thesis/dissertation. *Entrance requirements:* For master's and doctorate, GRE General Test, minimum GPA of 3.0. Additional exam requirements/recommendations for international students: required—TOEFL (minimum score 550 paper-based; 80 iBT), IELTS (minimum score 6). Electronic applications accepted.

**University of Georgia,** Franklin College of Arts and Sciences, Department of Biochemistry and Molecular Biology, Athens, GA 30602. Offers MS, PhD. *Degree requirements:* For master's, one foreign language, thesis; for doctorate, one foreign language, thesis/dissertation. *Entrance requirements:* For master's and doctorate, GRE General Test. Additional exam requirements/recommendations for international students: required—TOEFL. Electronic applications accepted.

**University of Guelph,** Office of Graduate and Postdoctoral Studies, College of Biological Science, Department of Molecular and Cellular Biology, Guelph, ON N1G 2W1, Canada. Offers biochemistry (M Sc, PhD); biophysics (M Sc, PhD); botany (M Sc, PhD); microbiology (M Sc, PhD); molecular biology and genetics (M Sc, PhD). *Degree requirements:* For master's, thesis, research proposal; for doctorate, comprehensive exam, thesis/dissertation, research proposal. *Entrance requirements:* For master's, minimum B-average during previous 2 years of coursework; for doctorate, minimum A-average. Additional exam requirements/recommendations for international students: required—TOEFL (minimum score 550 paper-based), IELTS (minimum score 6.5). Electronic applications accepted.

**University of Hawaii at Manoa,** John A. Burns School of Medicine, Program in Cell and Molecular Biology, Honolulu, HI 96813. Offers MS, PhD. *Program availability:* Part-time. Terminal master's awarded for partial completion of doctoral program. *Degree requirements:* For master's, thesis optional; for doctorate, comprehensive exam, thesis/dissertation. *Entrance requirements:* For master's and doctorate, GRE General Test, minimum GPA of 3.0. Additional exam requirements/recommendations for international students: required—TOEFL (minimum score 500 paper-based; 61 iBT), IELTS (minimum score 5).

**University of Hawaii at Manoa,** Office of Graduate Education, College of Tropical Agriculture and Human Resources, Department of Molecular Biosciences and Bioengineering, Honolulu, HI 96822. Offers bioengineering (MS); molecular bioscience and bioengineering (MS); molecular biosciences and bioengineering (PhD). *Program availability:* Part-time. *Degree requirements:* For master's, thesis optional; for doctorate, comprehensive exam, thesis/dissertation. *Entrance requirements:* For master's and doctorate, GRE General Test. Additional exam requirements/recommendations for international students: required—TOEFL (minimum score 550 paper-based; 79 iBT), IELTS (minimum score 5).

**University of Illinois at Chicago,** College of Medicine, Graduate Programs in Medicine, Department of Biochemistry and Molecular Genetics, Chicago, IL 60607-7128. Offers PhD, MD/PhD. Terminal master's awarded for partial completion of doctoral program. *Degree requirements:* For doctorate, thesis/dissertation. *Entrance requirements:* For doctorate, GRE General Test. Additional exam requirements/recommendations for international students: required—TOEFL. Electronic applications accepted.

**The University of Iowa,** Graduate College, Program in Molecular and Cellular Biology, Iowa City, IA 52242-1316. Offers PhD. *Degree requirements:* For doctorate, comprehensive exam, thesis/dissertation. *Entrance requirements:* For doctorate, GRE General Test, minimum GPA of 3.0. Additional exam requirements/recommendations for international students: required—TOEFL (minimum score 600 paper-based; 100 iBT). Electronic applications accepted.

**The University of Kansas,** Graduate Studies, College of Liberal Arts and Sciences, Department of Molecular Biosciences, Lawrence, KS 66044. Offers biochemistry and biophysics (PhD); microbiology (PhD); molecular, cellular, and developmental biology (PhD). *Program availability:* Part-time. *Students:* 66 full-time (39 women); includes 36 minority (1 Black or African American, non-Hispanic/Latino; 2 Asian, non-Hispanic/Latino; 31 Hispanic/Latino; 2 Two or more races, non-Hispanic/Latino), 31 international. Average age 28. 93 applicants, 30% accepted, 12 enrolled. In 2019, 3 doctorates awarded. Terminal master's awarded for partial completion of doctoral program. *Entrance requirements:* For doctorate, GRE General Test, 1-page statement of research interests and goals, 1-2 page curriculum vitae or resume, official transcript, 3 recommendation letters. Additional exam requirements/recommendations for international students: required—TOEFL, IELTS, TOEFL or IELTS. *Application deadline:* For fall admission, 12/1 for domestic and international students. Application fee: $65 ($85 for international students). Electronic applications accepted. *Expenses:* Tuition, state resident: full-time $9989. Tuition, nonresident: full-time $23,950. *International tuition:* $23,950 full-time. *Required fees:* $984; $81.99 per credit hour. Tuition and fees vary according to course load, campus/location and program. *Financial support:* Fellowships, research assistantships, teaching assistantships, scholarships/grants, health care benefits, and unspecified assistantships available. Financial award application deadline: 12/1. *Unit head:* Susan M. Egan, Chair, 785-864-4294, E-mail: sme@ku.edu. *Application contact:* John Connolly, Graduate Admissions Contact, 785-864-4311, E-mail: jconnolly@ku.edu.
Website: http://www.molecularbiosciences.ku.edu/

**The University of Kansas,** University of Kansas Medical Center, School of Medicine, Department of Biochemistry and Molecular Biology, Kansas City, KS 66160. Offers PhD, MD/PhD. *Faculty:* 17. *Students:* 15 full-time (8 women); includes 1 minority (Black or African American, non-Hispanic/Latino), 3 international. Average age 29. Terminal master's awarded for partial completion of doctoral program. *Degree requirements:* For doctorate, comprehensive exam, thesis/dissertation, comprehensive oral and written exam. *Entrance requirements:* For doctorate, GRE. Additional exam requirements/recommendations for international students: required—TOEFL. *Application deadline:* For fall admission, 12/1 for domestic and international students. Applications are processed on a rolling basis. Application fee: $60. Electronic applications accepted. Application fee is waived when completed online. *Expenses:* Tuition, state resident: full-time $9989. Tuition, nonresident: full-time $23,950. *International tuition:* $23,950 full-time. *Required fees:* $984; $81.99 per credit hour. Tuition and fees vary according to course load, campus/location and program. *Financial support:* Fellowships, research assistantships with partial tuition reimbursements, teaching assistantships with partial tuition reimbursements, traineeships, health care benefits, and unspecified assistantships available. Financial award application deadline: 3/1; financial award applicants required to submit FAFSA. *Unit head:* Dr. Liskin Swint-Kruse, Professor and Chair, 913-588-0399, E-mail: lswint-kruse@kumc.edu. *Application contact:* Dr. Aron W. Fenton, Professor and Director of Graduate Studies, 913-588-7033, E-mail: afenton@kumc.edu.
Website: http://www.kumc.edu/school-of-medicine/biochemistry-and-molecular-biology.html

**University of Lethbridge,** School of Graduate Studies, Lethbridge, AB T1K 3M4, Canada. Offers addictions counseling (M Sc); agricultural biotechnology (M Sc); agricultural studies (M Sc, MA); anthropology (MA); archaeology (M Sc, MA); art (MA, MFA); biochemistry (M Sc); biological sciences (M Sc); biomolecular science (PhD); biosystems and biodiversity (PhD); Canadian studies (MA); chemistry (M Sc); computer science (M Sc); computer science and geographical information science (M Sc); counseling (MC); counseling psychology (M Ed); dramatic arts (MA); earth, space, and physical science (PhD); economics (MA); education (MA, PhD); educational leadership (M Ed); English (MA); environmental science (M Sc); evolution and behavior (PhD); exercise science (M Sc); French (MA); French/German (MA); French/Spanish (MA); general education (M Ed); geography (M Sc, MA); German (MA); health sciences (M Sc); individualized multidisciplinary (M Sc, MA); kinesiology (M Sc, MA); management (M Sc), including accounting, finance, human resource management and labor relations, information systems, international management, marketing, policy and strategy; mathematics (M Sc); music (M Mus, MA); Native American studies (MA); neuroscience (M Sc, PhD); new media (MA, MFA); nursing (M Sc, MN); philosophy (MA); physics (M Sc); political science (MA); psychology (M Sc, MA); religious studies (MA); sociology (MA); theatre and dramatic arts (MFA); theoretical and computational science (PhD); urban and regional studies (MA); women and gender studies (MA). *Program availability:* Part-time, evening/weekend. *Degree requirements:* For master's, thesis (for some programs); for doctorate, comprehensive exam, thesis/dissertation. *Entrance requirements:* For master's, GMAT (for M Sc in management), bachelor's degree in related field, minimum GPA of 3.0 during previous 20 graded semester courses, 2 years' teaching or related experience (M Ed); for doctorate, master's degree, minimum graduate GPA of 3.5. Additional exam requirements/recommendations for international students: required—TOEFL (minimum score 580 paper-based; 93 iBT). Electronic applications accepted.

**University of Maine,** Graduate School, College of Natural Sciences, Forestry, and Agriculture, Department of Molecular and Biomedical Sciences, Orono, ME 04469. Offers microbiology (PhD). *Faculty:* 10 full-time (5 women). *Students:* 24 full-time (14 women), 6 part-time (5 women); includes 3 minority (1 Black or African American, non-Hispanic/Latino; 1 Asian, non-Hispanic/Latino; 1 Two or more races, non-Hispanic/Latino), 7 international. Average age 29. 41 applicants, 46% accepted, 8 enrolled. In 2019, 2 master's, 3 doctorates awarded. *Degree requirements:* For master's, thesis (for some programs); for doctorate, comprehensive exam, thesis/dissertation. *Entrance requirements:* For master's and doctorate, GRE General Test. Additional exam requirements/recommendations for international students: required—TOEFL (minimum score 580 paper-based; 92 iBT), IELTS (minimum score 7). *Application deadline:* For fall admission, 1/15 for domestic and international students; for spring admission, 9/15 for domestic and international students. Applications are processed on a rolling basis. Application fee: $65. Electronic applications accepted. *Expenses: Tuition, area resident:* Full-time $8100; part-time $450 per credit hour. Tuition, state resident: full-time $8100; part-time $450 per credit hour. Tuition, nonresident: full-time $26,388; part-time $1466 per credit hour. *International tuition:* $26,388 full-time. *Required fees:* $1257; $278 per semester. Tuition and fees vary according to course load. *Financial support:* In 2019–20, 60 students received support, including 1 fellowship with full tuition reimbursement available (averaging $34,000 per year), 49 research assistantships with full tuition reimbursements available (averaging $22,000 per year), 10 teaching assistantships with full tuition reimbursements available (averaging $15,850 per year); tuition waivers (full and partial) also available. Financial award application deadline: 3/1; financial award applicants required to submit FAFSA. *Unit head:* Dr. Robert Gundersen, Chair, 207-581-2802, Fax: 207-581-2801. *Application contact:* Scott G. Delcourt, Assistant Vice President for Graduate Studies and Senior Associate Dean, 207-581-3291, Fax: 207-581-3232, E-mail: graduate@maine.edu.
Website: http://umaine.edu/biomed/

**The University of Manchester,** School of Biological Sciences, Manchester, United Kingdom. Offers adaptive organismal biology (M Phil, PhD); animal biology (M Phil, PhD); biochemistry (M Phil, PhD); bioinformatics (M Phil, PhD); biomolecular sciences (M Phil, PhD); biotechnology (M Phil, PhD); cell biology (M Phil, PhD); cell matrix research (M Phil, PhD); channels and transporters (M Phil, PhD); developmental biology (M Phil, PhD); environmental biology (M Phil, PhD); evolutionary biology (M Phil, PhD); gene expression (M Phil, PhD); genetics (M Phil, PhD); history of science, technology and medicine (M Phil, PhD); immunology (M Phil, PhD); integrative neurobiology and behavior (M Phil, PhD); membrane trafficking (M Phil, PhD); microbiology (M Phil, PhD); molecular and cellular neuroscience (M Phil, PhD); molecular biology (M Phil, PhD); molecular cancer studies (M Phil, PhD); neuroscience (M Phil, PhD); ophthalmology (M Phil, PhD); optometry (M Phil, PhD); organelle function (M Phil, PhD); pharmacology (M Phil, PhD); physiology (M Phil, PhD); plant sciences (M Phil, PhD); stem cell research (M Phil, PhD); structural biology (M Phil, PhD); systems neuroscience (M Phil, PhD); toxicology (M Phil, PhD).

**The University of Manchester,** School of Dentistry, Manchester, United Kingdom. Offers basic dental sciences (cancer studies) (M Phil, PhD); basic dental sciences (molecular genetics) (M Phil, PhD); basic dental sciences (stem cell biology) (M Phil,

PhD); biomaterials sciences and dental technology (M Phil, PhD); dental public health/community dentistry (M Phil, PhD); dental science (clinical) (PhD); endodontology (M Phil, PhD); fixed and removable prosthodontics (M Phil, PhD); operative dentistry (M Phil, PhD); oral and maxillofacial surgery (M Phil, PhD); oral radiology (M Phil, PhD); orthodontics (M Phil, PhD); restorative dentistry (M Phil, PhD).

**University of Maryland, Baltimore,** Graduate School, Graduate Program in Life Sciences, Program in Biochemistry and Molecular Biology, Baltimore, MD 21201. Offers biochemistry (MS, PhD); MD/PhD. *Degree requirements:* For doctorate, comprehensive exam, thesis/dissertation. *Entrance requirements:* For master's and doctorate, GRE General Test, minimum GPA of 3.0, curriculum vitae, essay, 3 letters of recommendation. Additional exam requirements/recommendations for international students: required—TOEFL (minimum score 80 iBT); recommended—IELTS (minimum score 7). Electronic applications accepted.

**University of Maryland, Baltimore,** Graduate School, Graduate Program in Life Sciences, Program in Cellular and Molecular Biomedical Science, Baltimore, MD 21201. Offers MS. *Program availability:* Part-time. *Degree requirements:* For master's, thesis (for some programs). *Entrance requirements:* For master's, GRE General Test, minimum GPA of 3.0, curriculum vitae, essay, 3 letters of recommendation. Additional exam requirements/recommendations for international students: required—TOEFL (minimum score 80 iBT); recommended—IELTS (minimum score 7). Electronic applications accepted.

**University of Maryland, Baltimore,** Graduate School, Graduate Program in Life Sciences, Program in Molecular Medicine, Baltimore, MD 21201. Offers applied pharmacology and toxicology (PhD); cancer biology (PhD); genome biology (PhD); molecular and cellular physiology (PhD); MD/PhD. *Degree requirements:* For doctorate, comprehensive exam, thesis/dissertation. *Entrance requirements:* For doctorate, GRE, minimum GPA of 3.0, curriculum vitae, essay, 3 letters of recommendation. Additional exam requirements/recommendations for international students: required—TOEFL (minimum score 80 iBT); recommended—IELTS (minimum score 7). Electronic applications accepted.

**University of Maryland, Baltimore County,** The Graduate School, College of Natural and Mathematical Sciences, Department of Biological Sciences, Program in Applied Molecular Biology, Baltimore, MD 21250. Offers MS. *Faculty:* 26 full-time (11 women). *Students:* 6 full-time (2 women), 4 part-time (3 women); includes 2 minority (1 Black or African American, non-Hispanic/Latino; 1 Hispanic/Latino), 1 international. Average age 25. 30 applicants, 37% accepted, 10 enrolled. In 2019, 9 master's awarded. *Entrance requirements:* For master's, GRE General Test, GRE Subject Test (recommended), minimum GPA of 3.0. Additional exam requirements/recommendations for international students: required—TOEFL (minimum score 600 paper-based; 80 iBT), IELTS (minimum score 6.5). *Application deadline:* For fall admission, 2/1 priority date for domestic and international students. Applications are processed on a rolling basis. Application fee: $50. Electronic applications accepted. *Expenses: Tuition, area resident:* Full-time $659. Tuition, state resident: full-time $659. Tuition, nonresident: full-time $1132. *International tuition:* $1132 full-time. *Required fees:* $140; $140 per credit hour. *Financial support:* Applicants required to submit FAFSA. *Unit head:* Dr. Michelle Starz-Gaiano, Director, Applied Molecular Biology Graduate Program, 410-455-2217, Fax: 410-455-3875, E-mail: biograd@umbc.edu. *Application contact:* Brandy Darcey, Graduate Program Coordinator, 410-455-3669, Fax: 410-455-3875, E-mail: bdarcey@umbc.edu.
Website: http://biology.umbc.edu/grad/graduate-programs/apmb/

**University of Maryland, Baltimore County,** The Graduate School, College of Natural and Mathematical Sciences, Department of Biological Sciences, Program in Molecular and Cell Biology, Baltimore, MD 21250. Offers PhD. *Faculty:* 26 full-time (11 women). *Students:* 3 full-time (1 woman), 2 international. Average age 25. 16 applicants, 13% accepted, 1 enrolled. *Degree requirements:* For doctorate, thesis/dissertation. *Entrance requirements:* For doctorate, GRE General Test, GRE Subject Test, minimum GPA of 3.0. Additional exam requirements/recommendations for international students: required—TOEFL (minimum score 80 iBT), IELTS (minimum score 6.5). *Application deadline:* For fall admission, 4/15 priority date for domestic and international students. Application fee: $50. Electronic applications accepted. *Expenses: Tuition, area resident:* Full-time $659. Tuition, state resident: full-time $659. Tuition, nonresident: full-time $1132. *International tuition:* $1132 full-time. *Required fees:* $140; $140 per credit hour. *Financial support:* In 2019–20, 3 students received support, including 1 research assistantship with full tuition reimbursement available (averaging $24,600 per year), 2 teaching assistantships with full tuition reimbursements available (averaging $24,600 per year); Federal Work-Study and unspecified assistantships also available. *Unit head:* Dr. Michelle Starz-Gaiano, Director, 410-455-2217, Fax: 410-455-3875, E-mail: biograd@umbc.edu. *Application contact:* Brandy Darcey, Graduate Program Coordinator, 410-4553669, E-mail: bdarcey@umbc.edu.
Website: http://biology.umbc.edu/grad/graduate-programs/mocb/

**University of Maryland, College Park,** Academic Affairs, College of Computer, Mathematical and Natural Sciences, Department of Biology, PhD Program in Biological Sciences, College Park, MD 20742. Offers behavior, ecology, evolution, and systematics (PhD); computational biology, bioinformatics, and genomics (PhD); molecular and cellular biology (PhD); physiological systems (PhD). *Degree requirements:* For doctorate, comprehensive exam, thesis/dissertation, thesis work presentation in seminar. *Entrance requirements:* For doctorate, GRE General Test; GRE Subject Test in biology (recommended), academic transcripts, statement of purpose/research interests, 3 letters of recommendation. Additional exam requirements/recommendations for international students: required—TOEFL. Electronic applications accepted.

**University of Maryland, College Park,** Academic Affairs, College of Computer, Mathematical and Natural Sciences, Department of Cell Biology and Molecular Genetics, Program in Molecular and Cellular Biology, College Park, MD 20742. Offers PhD. *Program availability:* Part-time, evening/weekend. *Degree requirements:* For doctorate, thesis/dissertation, exam, public service.

**University of Miami,** Graduate School, Miller School of Medicine, Graduate Programs in Medicine, Department of Biochemistry and Molecular Biology, Coral Gables, FL 33124. Offers PhD, MD/PhD. *Faculty:* 36 full-time (10 women). *Students:* 64 full-time (38 women); includes 27 minority (5 Black or African American, non-Hispanic/Latino; 8 Asian, non-Hispanic/Latino; 10 Hispanic/Latino; 4 Two or more races, non-Hispanic/Latino), 11 international. Average age 29. 49 applicants, 55% accepted, 27 enrolled. In 2019, 4 doctorates awarded. *Degree requirements:* For doctorate, comprehensive exam, thesis/dissertation, proposition exams. *Entrance requirements:* Additional exam requirements/recommendations for international students: required—TOEFL, IELTS, Either TOEFL or the ITELS is accepted. *Financial support:* In 2019–20, 34 fellowships with full tuition reimbursements (averaging $25,500 per year) were awarded; research assistantships, scholarships/grants, and tuition waivers (full) also available. *Unit head:* Dr. Sylvia Daunert, Department Chair, 305-243-4005, Fax: 305-243-3955, E-mail: sdaunert@med.miami.edu. *Application contact:* Dr. Sapna Deo, Graduate Program Director, 305-243-4421, Fax: 305-243-3955, E-mail: sdeo@med.miami.edu.
Website: http://bm.med.miami.edu/

**University of Miami,** Graduate School, Miller School of Medicine, Graduate Programs in Medicine, Department of Cell Biology, Miami, FL 33124. Offers molecular cell and developmental biology (PhD); MD/PhD. *Faculty:* 29 full-time (3 women). *Students:* 13 full-time (4 women); includes 7 minority (1 Black or African American, non-Hispanic/Latino; 3 Asian, non-Hispanic/Latino; 2 Hispanic/Latino; 1 Two or more races, non-Hispanic/Latino), 3 international. Average age 29. 2 applicants, 100% accepted, 1 enrolled. In 2019, 1 doctorate awarded. *Degree requirements:* For doctorate, thesis/dissertation, Qualifying Exam. *Entrance requirements:* For doctorate, GRE General Test, GRE Subject Test. Additional exam requirements/recommendations for international students: required—TOEFL. *Application deadline:* For fall admission, 3/1 priority date for domestic students. Applications are processed on a rolling basis. Application fee: $95. Electronic applications accepted. *Financial support:* In 2019–20, 8 fellowships (averaging $29,500 per year), 8 research assistantships (averaging $29,500 per year) were awarded; teaching assistantships also available. *Unit head:* Dr. Glen Barber, Chair, 305-243-5914, Fax: 305-243-7020, E-mail: gbarber@miami.edu. *Application contact:* Dr. Xiangxi Mike Xu, Program Director, 305-243-1750, E-mail: xxu2@miami.edu.
Website: http://cellbiology.med.miami.edu/

**University of Michigan,** Rackham Graduate School, College of Literature, Science, and the Arts, Department of Molecular, Cellular, and Developmental Biology, Ann Arbor, MI 48109. Offers MS, PhD. *Program availability:* Part-time. Terminal master's awarded for partial completion of doctoral program. *Degree requirements:* For master's, thesis (for some programs), 24 credits with at least 16 in molecular, cellular, and developmental biology and 4 in a cognate field; for doctorate, comprehensive exam, thesis/dissertation, preliminary exam, oral defense. *Entrance requirements:* Additional exam requirements/recommendations for international students: required—TOEFL (minimum score 600 paper-based; 100 iBT). Electronic applications accepted. *Expenses:* Contact institution.

**University of Michigan,** Rackham Graduate School, Program in Biomedical Sciences (PIBS), Interdisciplinary Program in Cellular and Molecular Biology, Ann Arbor, MI 48109. Offers PhD. *Degree requirements:* For doctorate, comprehensive exam, thesis/dissertation, preliminary exam; oral defense of dissertation. *Entrance requirements:* For doctorate, GRE General Test. Additional exam requirements/recommendations for international students: required—TOEFL (minimum score 560 paper-based; 84 iBT), IELTS (minimum score 6.5), Michigan English Language Assessment Battery. Electronic applications accepted. *Expenses:* Contact institution.

**University of Minnesota, Duluth,** Medical School, Department of Biochemistry, Molecular Biology and Biophysics, Duluth, MN 55812-2496. Offers biochemistry, molecular biology and biophysics (MS); biology and biophysics (PhD); social, administrative, and clinical pharmacy (MS, PhD); toxicology (MS, PhD). Terminal master's awarded for partial completion of doctoral program. *Degree requirements:* For master's, comprehensive exam, thesis; for doctorate, comprehensive exam, thesis/dissertation. *Entrance requirements:* For master's and doctorate, GRE General Test. Additional exam requirements/recommendations for international students: required—TOEFL. Electronic applications accepted.

**University of Minnesota, Twin Cities Campus,** Graduate School, College of Biological Sciences, Biochemistry, Molecular Biology and Biophysics Graduate Program, Minneapolis, MN 55455-0213. Offers PhD. *Degree requirements:* For doctorate, thesis/dissertation. *Entrance requirements:* For doctorate, GRE, 3 letters of recommendation, more than 1 semester of laboratory experience. Additional exam requirements/recommendations for international students: required—TOEFL (minimum score 625 paper-based; 108 iBT with writing subsection 25 and reading subsection 25) or IELTS (minimum score 7). Electronic applications accepted.

**University of Minnesota, Twin Cities Campus,** Graduate School, Program in Molecular, Cellular, Developmental Biology and Genetics, Minneapolis, MN 55455-0213. Offers genetic counseling (MS); molecular, cellular, developmental biology and genetics (PhD). Terminal master's awarded for partial completion of doctoral program. *Degree requirements:* For master's, thesis optional; for doctorate, thesis/dissertation. *Entrance requirements:* For master's and doctorate, GRE General Test. Additional exam requirements/recommendations for international students: required—TOEFL (minimum score 625 paper-based; 80 iBT). Electronic applications accepted.

**University of Missouri–Kansas City,** School of Biological Sciences, Program in Molecular Biology and Biochemistry, Kansas City, MO 64110-2499. Offers PhD. *Degree requirements:* For doctorate, comprehensive exam, thesis/dissertation. *Entrance requirements:* For doctorate, GRE General Test, bachelor's degree in chemistry, biology, or a related discipline; minimum GPA of 3.0. Additional exam requirements/recommendations for international students: required—TOEFL (minimum score 550 paper-based; 80 iBT).

**University of Montana,** Graduate School, College of Humanities and Sciences, Division of Biological Sciences, Program in Cellular, Molecular and Microbial Biology, Missoula, MT 59812. Offers cellular and developmental biology (PhD); microbial evolution and ecology (PhD); microbiology and immunology (PhD); molecular biology and biochemistry (PhD). Terminal master's awarded for partial completion of doctoral program. *Degree requirements:* For doctorate, variable foreign language requirement, thesis/dissertation. *Entrance requirements:* For doctorate, GRE General Test.

**University of Nebraska Medical Center,** Interdisciplinary Graduate Program in Biomedical Sciences, Department of Biochemistry and Molecular Biology, Omaha, NE 68198. Offers MS. Terminal master's awarded for partial completion of doctoral program. *Degree requirements:* For master's, comprehensive exam, thesis. *Entrance requirements:* For master's, GRE General Test. Additional exam requirements/recommendations for international students: required—TOEFL (minimum score 550 paper-based). Electronic applications accepted. Application fee is waived when completed online.

**University of Nevada, Reno,** Graduate School, Interdisciplinary Program in Cell and Molecular Biology, Reno, NV 89557. Offers MS, PhD. Terminal master's awarded for partial completion of doctoral program. *Degree requirements:* For master's, thesis; for doctorate, thesis/dissertation. *Entrance requirements:* For master's, GRE Subject Test (recommended), minimum GPA of 2.75; for doctorate, GRE Subject Test (recommended), minimum GPA of 3.0. Additional exam requirements/recommendations for international students: required—TOEFL (minimum score 500 paper-based; 61 iBT), IELTS (minimum score 6). Electronic applications accepted.

**University of New Haven,** Graduate School, College of Arts and Sciences, Program in Cellular and Molecular Biology, West Haven, CT 06516. Offers MS. *Program availability:* Part-time, evening/weekend. *Students:* 42 full-time (30 women), 5 part-time (4 women); includes 7 minority (1 Black or African American, non-Hispanic/Latino; 2 Asian, non-Hispanic/Latino; 4 Hispanic/Latino), 21 international. Average age 25. 65 applicants, 82% accepted, 19 enrolled. In 2019, 17 master's awarded. *Entrance requirements:* Additional exam requirements/recommendations for international students: required—TOEFL (minimum score 80 iBT), IELTS, PTE. *Application deadline:* Applications are processed on a rolling basis. Application fee: $50. Electronic applications accepted. Application fee is waived when completed online. *Financial support:* Research assistantships with partial tuition reimbursements, teaching assistantships with partial

tuition reimbursements, Federal Work-Study, scholarships/grants, and unspecified assistantships available. Support available to part-time students. Financial award application deadline: 5/1; financial award applicants required to submit FAFSA. *Unit head:* Dr. Eva Sapi, Professor, 203-479-4552, E-mail: esapi@newhaven.edu. *Application contact:* Selina O'Toole, Senior Associate Director of Graduate Admissions, 203-932-7337, E-mail: SOToole@newhaven.edu.
Website: https://www.newhaven.edu/arts-sciences/graduate-programs/cellular-molecular-biology/

**University of New Mexico,** Graduate Studies, Health Sciences Center, Program in Biomedical Sciences, Albuquerque, NM 87131-5196. Offers biochemistry and molecular biology (MS, PhD); cell biology and physiology (MS, PhD); molecular genetics and microbiology (MS, PhD); neuroscience (MS, PhD); pathology (MS, PhD); toxicology (MS, PhD). *Program availability:* Part-time. Terminal master's awarded for partial completion of doctoral program. *Degree requirements:* For master's, thesis; for doctorate, comprehensive exam, thesis/dissertation, qualifying exam at the end of year 1/core curriculum. *Entrance requirements:* For master's and doctorate, GRE General Test, minimum undergraduate GPA of 3.0. Additional exam requirements/recommendations for international students: required—TOEFL. Electronic applications accepted. *Expenses:* Tuition, state resident: full-time $7633; part-time $972 per year. Tuition, nonresident: full-time $22,586; part-time $3840 per year. *International tuition:* $23,292 full-time. *Required fees:* $8608. Tuition and fees vary according to course level, course load, degree level, program and student level.

**The University of North Carolina at Chapel Hill,** Graduate School, College of Arts and Sciences, Department of Biology, Chapel Hill, NC 27599. Offers botany (MA, MS, PhD); cell biology, development, and physiology (MA, MS, PhD); cell motility and cytoskeleton (PhD); ecology and behavior (MA, MS, PhD); genetics and molecular biology (MA, MS, PhD); morphology, systematics, and evolution (MA, MS, PhD). Terminal master's awarded for partial completion of doctoral program. *Degree requirements:* For master's, comprehensive exam, thesis (for some programs); for doctorate, comprehensive exam, thesis/dissertation. *Entrance requirements:* For master's, GRE General Test, GRE Subject Test, 2 semesters of calculus or statistics; 2 semesters of physics, organic chemistry; 3 semesters of biology; for doctorate, GRE General Test, GRE Subject Test, 2 semesters calculus or statistics, 2 semesters physics, organic chemistry, 3 semesters of biology. Additional exam requirements/recommendations for international students: required—TOEFL (minimum score 550 paper-based). Electronic applications accepted.

**The University of North Carolina at Chapel Hill,** School of Medicine and Graduate School, Biological and Biomedical Sciences Program, Curriculum in Genetics and Molecular Biology, Chapel Hill, NC 27599. Offers MS, PhD. *Faculty:* 82 full-time (26 women). *Students:* 65 full-time (41 women); includes 12 minority (5 Black or African American, non-Hispanic/Latino; 1 Asian, non-Hispanic/Latino; 4 Hispanic/Latino; 2 Two or more races, non-Hispanic/Latino), 6 international. Average age 26. In 2019, 7 doctorates awarded. *Degree requirements:* For doctorate, comprehensive exam, thesis/dissertation. *Entrance requirements:* Additional exam requirements/recommendations for international students: required—TOEFL. *Application deadline:* For fall admission, 12/3 priority date for domestic and international students. Applications are processed on a rolling basis. Application fee: $77. Electronic applications accepted. *Financial support:* In 2019–20, 8 fellowships with full tuition reimbursements (averaging $32,000 per year), 15 research assistantships with full tuition reimbursements (averaging $32,000 per year), 6 teaching assistantships with full tuition reimbursements (averaging $32,000 per year) were awarded; career-related internships or fieldwork, traineeships, health care benefits, and tuition waivers (full) also available. *Unit head:* Dr. Robert J. Duronio, Director, 919-962-7749, E-mail: duronio@med.unc.edu. *Application contact:* Jeffrey Steinbach, Assistant Director of Admission, 919-843-7129, E-mail: jsteinba@email.unc.edu.
Website: http://gmb.unc.edu/

**University of North Texas,** Toulouse Graduate School, Denton, TX 76203-5459. Offers accounting (MS); applied anthropology (MA, MS); applied behavior analysis (Certificate); applied geography (MA); applied technology and performance improvement (M Ed, MS); art education (MA); art history (MA); arts leadership (Certificate); audiology (Au D); behavior analysis (MS); behavioral science (PhD); biochemistry and molecular biology (MS); biology (MA, MS); biomedical engineering (MS); business analysis (MS); chemistry (MS); clinical health psychology (PhD); communication studies (MA, MS); computer engineering (MS); computer science (MS); counseling (M Ed, MS), including clinical mental health counseling (MS), college and university counseling, elementary school counseling, secondary school counseling; creative writing (MA); criminal justice (MS); curriculum and instruction (M Ed); decision sciences (MBA); design (MA, MFA), including fashion design (MFA), innovation studies, interior design (MFA); early childhood studies (MS); economics (MS); educational leadership (M Ed, Ed D); educational psychology (MS, PhD), including family studies (MS), gifted and talented (MS), human development (MS), learning and cognition (MS), research, measurement and evaluation (MS); electrical engineering (MS); emergency management (MPA); engineering technology (MS); English (MA); English as a second language (MA); environmental science (MS); finance (MBA, MS); financial management (MPA); French (MA); health services management (MBA); higher education (M Ed, Ed D); history (MA, MS); hospitality management (MS); human resources management (MPA); information science (MS); information systems (PhD); information technologies (MBA); interdisciplinary studies (MA, MS); international studies (MA); international sustainable tourism (MS); jazz studies (MM); journalism (MA, MJ, Graduate Certificate), including interactive and virtual digital communication (Graduate Certificate), narrative journalism (Graduate Certificate), public relations (Graduate Certificate); kinesiology (MS); linguistics (MA); local government management (MPA); logistics (PhD); logistics and supply chain management (MBA); long-term care, senior housing, and aging services (MA); management (PhD); marketing (MBA); mathematics (MA, MS); mechanical and energy engineering (MS, PhD); music (MA), including ethnomusicology, music theory, musicology, performance; music composition (PhD); music education (MM Ed, PhD); nonprofit management (MPA); operations and supply chain management (MBA); performance (MM, DMA); philosophy (MA); political science (MA); professional and technical communication (MA); radio, television and film (MA, MFA); rehabilitation counseling (Certificate); sociology (MA); Spanish (MA); special education (M Ed); speech-language pathology (MA); strategic management (MBA); studio art (MFA); teaching (M Ed); MBA/MS. *Program availability:* Part-time, evening/weekend, online learning. Terminal master's awarded for partial completion of doctoral program. *Degree requirements:* For master's, variable foreign language requirement, comprehensive exam (for some programs), thesis (for some programs); for doctorate, variable foreign language requirement, comprehensive exam (for some programs), thesis/dissertation; for other advanced degree, variable foreign language requirement, comprehensive exam (for some programs). *Entrance requirements:* For master's and doctorate, GRE, GMAT. Additional exam requirements/recommendations for international students: required—TOEFL (minimum score 550 paper-based; 79 iBT). Electronic applications accepted.

**University of Notre Dame,** The Graduate School, College of Science, Department of Biological Sciences, Notre Dame, IN 46556. Offers aquatic ecology, evolution and environmental biology (MS, PhD); cellular and molecular biology (MS, PhD); genetics (MS, PhD); physiology (MS, PhD); vector biology and parasitology (MS, PhD). Terminal master's awarded for partial completion of doctoral program. *Degree requirements:* For master's, comprehensive exam, thesis; for doctorate, comprehensive exam, thesis/dissertation, candidacy exam. *Entrance requirements:* For master's and doctorate, GRE General Test. Additional exam requirements/recommendations for international students: required—TOEFL (minimum score 600 paper-based; 80 iBT). Electronic applications accepted.

**University of Oklahoma Health Sciences Center,** College of Medicine and Graduate College, Graduate Programs in Medicine, Department of Biochemistry and Molecular Biology, Oklahoma City, OK 73190. Offers biochemistry (MS, PhD); molecular biology (MS, PhD). *Program availability:* Part-time. Terminal master's awarded for partial completion of doctoral program. *Degree requirements:* For master's, thesis; for doctorate, thesis/dissertation. *Entrance requirements:* For master's, GRE General Test, 2 letters of recommendation; for doctorate, GRE General Test, 3 letters of recommendation. Additional exam requirements/recommendations for international students: required—TOEFL.

**University of Oregon,** Graduate School, College of Arts and Sciences, Department of Biology, Eugene, OR 97403. Offers ecology and evolution (MA, MS, PhD); marine biology (MA, MS, PhD); molecular, cellular and genetic biology (PhD); neuroscience and development (PhD). Terminal master's awarded for partial completion of doctoral program. *Degree requirements:* For master's, thesis (for some programs); for doctorate, thesis/dissertation. *Entrance requirements:* For master's and doctorate, GRE General Test, minimum GPA of 3.2. Additional exam requirements/recommendations for international students: required—TOEFL.

**University of Ottawa,** Faculty of Graduate and Postdoctoral Studies, Faculty of Medicine, Department of Cellular and Molecular Medicine, Ottawa, ON K1H 8M5, Canada. Offers M Sc, PhD. *Degree requirements:* For master's, thesis, seminar; for doctorate, comprehensive exam, thesis/dissertation, seminar. *Entrance requirements:* For master's, honors degree or equivalent, minimum B average; for doctorate, master's degree, minimum B+ average. Electronic applications accepted.

**University of Pennsylvania,** Perelman School of Medicine, Biomedical Graduate Studies, Graduate Group in Cell and Molecular Biology, Philadelphia, PA 19104. Offers cancer biology (PhD); cell biology, physiology, and metabolism (PhD); developmental stem cell regenerative biology (PhD); gene therapy and vaccines (PhD); genetics and gene regulation (PhD); microbiology, virology, and parasitology (PhD); MD/PhD; VMD/PhD. *Faculty:* 400 full-time (118 women). *Students:* 378 full-time (221 women); includes 134 minority (6 Black or African American, non-Hispanic/Latino; 56 Asian, non-Hispanic/Latino; 58 Hispanic/Latino; 2 Native Hawaiian or other Pacific Islander, non-Hispanic/Latino; 12 Two or more races, non-Hispanic/Latino), 52 international. 851 applicants, 14% accepted, 59 enrolled. In 2019, 43 doctorates awarded. *Unit head:* Dr. Daniel Kessler, Graduate Group Chair, 215-898-1478. *Application contact:* Meagan Schofer, Associate Director, 215-898-1478.
Website: http://www.med.upenn.edu/camb/

**University of Pittsburgh,** Kenneth P. Dietrich School of Arts and Sciences, Department of Biological Sciences, Program in Molecular, Cellular, and Developmental Biology, Pittsburgh, PA 15260. Offers PhD. *Faculty:* 27 full-time (9 women). *Students:* 52 full-time (31 women); includes 7 minority (4 Black or African American, non-Hispanic/Latino; 1 Hispanic/Latino; 2 Two or more races, non-Hispanic/Latino), 8 international. Average age 23. In 2019, 6 doctorates awarded. *Degree requirements:* For doctorate, comprehensive exam, thesis/dissertation, completion of research integrity module. *Entrance requirements:* Additional exam requirements/recommendations for international students: required—TOEFL (minimum score 90 paper-based), IELTS (minimum score 7). *Application deadline:* For fall admission, 12/2 priority date for domestic and international students. Applications are processed on a rolling basis. Application fee: $0 ($75 for international students). Electronic applications accepted. *Financial support:* In 2019–20, 37 fellowships with full tuition reimbursements (averaging $36,108 per year), 94 research assistantships with full tuition reimbursements (averaging $30,840 per year), 19 teaching assistantships with full tuition reimbursements (averaging $30,375 per year) were awarded; Federal Work-Study, traineeships, and health care benefits also available. *Unit head:* Dr. Jeffrey G. Lawrence, Professor and Chair, 412-624-4350, Fax: 412-624-4759, E-mail: jlawrence@pitt.edu. *Application contact:* Cathleen M. Barr, Graduate Administrator, 412-624-4268, Fax: 412-624-4349, E-mail: cbarr@pitt.edu.
Website: http://www.biology.pitt.edu

**University of Puerto Rico at Rio Piedras,** College of Natural Sciences, Department of Biology, San Juan, PR 00931-3300. Offers ecology/systematics (MS, PhD); evolution/genetics (MS, PhD); molecular/cellular biology (MS, PhD); neuroscience (MS, PhD). *Program availability:* Part-time. *Degree requirements:* For master's, one foreign language, comprehensive exam, thesis; for doctorate, one foreign language, comprehensive exam, thesis/dissertation. *Entrance requirements:* For master's, GRE Subject Test, interview, minimum GPA of 3.0, letter of recommendation; for doctorate, GRE Subject Test, interview, master's degree, minimum GPA of 3.0, letter of recommendation.

**University of Rhode Island,** Graduate School, College of the Environment and Life Sciences, Department of Biological Sciences, Kingston, RI 02881. Offers cell and molecular biology (MS, PhD); earth and environmental sciences (MS, PhD); ecology and ecosystem sciences (MS, PhD); evolutionary and marine biology (MS, PhD); sustainable agriculture and food systems (MS, PhD). *Program availability:* Part-time. *Faculty:* 20 full-time (10 women). *Students:* 108 full-time (68 women), 22 part-time (15 women); includes 12 minority (6 Black or African American, non-Hispanic/Latino; 4 Asian, non-Hispanic/Latino; 1 Hispanic/Latino; 1 Two or more races, non-Hispanic/Latino), 22 international. In 2019, 12 master's, 10 doctorates awarded. *Entrance requirements:* Additional exam requirements/recommendations for international students: required—TOEFL. *Application deadline:* For fall admission, 1/15 for domestic and international students. Application fee: $65. Electronic applications accepted. *Expenses: Tuition, area resident:* Full-time $13,734; part-time $763 per credit. Tuition, state resident: full-time $13,734; part-time $763 per credit. Tuition, nonresident: full-time $26,512; part-time $1473 per credit. *International tuition:* $26,512 full-time. *Required fees:* $1780; $52 per credit. $35 per term. One-time fee: $165. *Financial support:* In 2019–20, 24 research assistantships with tuition reimbursements (averaging $9,961 per year), 1 teaching assistantship with tuition reimbursement (averaging $7,521 per year) were awarded. Financial award application deadline: 1/15; financial award applicants required to submit FAFSA. *Unit head:* Dr. Alison Roberts, Chair, E-mail: bio_chair@etal.uri.edu. *Application contact:* Bethany Jenkins, Graduate Program Director, 401-874-7551, E-mail: bdjenkins@uri.edu.
Website: http://web.uri.edu/bio/

**University of Rhode Island,** Graduate School, College of the Environment and Life Sciences, Department of Cell and Molecular Biology, Kingston, RI 02881. Offers biochemistry (MS, PhD); clinical laboratory sciences (MS), including biotechnology, clinical laboratory science, cytopathology; microbiology (MS, PhD); molecular genetics (MS, PhD). *Program availability:* Part-time. *Faculty:* 20 full-time (9 women). *Students:* 1 (woman) part-time. In 2019, 16 master's awarded. *Entrance requirements:* Additional

exam requirements/recommendations for international students: required—TOEFL. *Application deadline:* For fall admission, 1/15 for domestic and international students. Application fee: $65. Electronic applications accepted. *Expenses: Tuition, area resident:* Full-time $13,734; part-time $763 per credit. Tuition, state resident: full-time $13,734; part-time $763 per credit. Tuition, nonresident: full-time $26,512; part-time $1473 per credit. *International tuition:* $26,512 full-time. *Required fees:* $1780; $52 per credit. $35 per term. One-time fee: $165. *Financial support:* In 2019–20, 11 teaching assistantships with tuition reimbursements (averaging $10,985 per year) were awarded; traineeships also available. Financial award application deadline: 1/15; financial award applicants required to submit FAFSA. *Unit head:* Dr. Joel Chandlee, Chair, E-mail: joelchandlee@uri.edu. *Application contact:* Dr. Steven Gregory, Graduate Program Director, 401-874-5947, E-mail: stgregory@uri.edu.
Website: https://web.uri.edu/cmb/

**University of Rochester,** School of Arts and Sciences, Department of Biology, Rochester, NY 14627. Offers biology (MS); ecology, genetics, and genomics (PhD); molecular, cellular, and developmental biology evolution (PhD). *Program availability:* Part-time. *Faculty:* 24 full-time (8 women). *Students:* 47 full-time (22 women), 1 (woman) part-time; includes 6 minority (1 Black or African American, non-Hispanic/Latino; 2 Asian, non-Hispanic/Latino; 3 Hispanic/Latino; 20 international. Average age 27. 98 applicants, 34% accepted, 12 enrolled. In 2019, 8 master's, 8 doctorates awarded. Terminal master's awarded for partial completion of doctoral program. *Degree requirements:* For master's, comprehensive exam (for some programs), thesis (for some programs); for doctorate, thesis/dissertation, qualifying exam. *Entrance requirements:* For master's and doctorate, personal statement, transcripts, three letters of recommendation. Additional exam requirements/recommendations for international students: required—TOEFL (minimum score 600 paper-based; 100 iBT), IELTS. *Application deadline:* For fall admission, 12/1 for domestic and international students. Application fee: $60. Electronic applications accepted. *Financial support:* In 2019–20, 40 students received support, including 5 fellowships (averaging $30,080 per year), 20 research assistantships (averaging $28,000 per year), 15 teaching assistantships (averaging $28,000 per year); health care benefits and tuition waivers (full) also available. Financial award application deadline: 12/1. *Unit head:* Michael Welte, Professor and Chair, 585-276-3897, E-mail: michael.welte@rochester.edu. *Application contact:* Cynthia Landry, Administrative Assistant, 585-275-7991, E-mail: cynthia.landry@rochester.edu.
Website: https://www.sas.rochester.edu/bio/graduate/index.html

**University of Rochester,** School of Medicine and Dentistry, Graduate Programs in Medicine and Dentistry, Department of Biochemistry and Biophysics, Programs in Biochemistry, Rochester, NY 14627. Offers biochemistry and molecular biology (PhD). Terminal master's awarded for partial completion of doctoral program. *Degree requirements:* For doctorate, thesis/dissertation, qualifying exam. *Entrance requirements:* For doctorate, GRE General Test.

**University of South Carolina,** The Graduate School, College of Arts and Sciences, Department of Biological Sciences, Graduate Training Program in Molecular, Cellular, and Developmental Biology, Columbia, SC 29208. Offers MS, PhD. *Degree requirements:* For master's, one foreign language, thesis; for doctorate, one foreign language, thesis/dissertation. *Entrance requirements:* For master's and doctorate, GRE General Test, minimum GPA of 3.0 in science. Electronic applications accepted.

**University of South Dakota,** Graduate School, Sanford School of Medicine and Graduate School, Biomedical Sciences Graduate Program, Cellular and Molecular Biology Group, Vermillion, SD 57069. Offers MS, PhD. Terminal master's awarded for partial completion of doctoral program. *Degree requirements:* For master's, thesis; for doctorate, comprehensive exam, thesis/dissertation. *Entrance requirements:* For master's and doctorate, GRE General Test, GRE Subject Test, minimum GPA of 3.0. Additional exam requirements/recommendations for international students: required—TOEFL (minimum score 550 paper-based; 80 iBT), IELTS (minimum score 6). Electronic applications accepted. *Expenses:* Contact institution.

**University of Southern California,** Graduate School, Dana and David Dornsife College of Letters, Arts and Sciences, Department of Biological Sciences, Program in Molecular and Computational Biology, Los Angeles, CA 90089. Offers computational biology and bioinformatics (PhD); molecular biology (PhD). *Degree requirements:* For doctorate, comprehensive exam, thesis/dissertation, qualifying examination, dissertation defense. *Entrance requirements:* For doctorate, GRE, 3 letters of recommendation, personal statement, resume, minimum GPA of 3.0. Additional exam requirements/recommendations for international students: required—TOEFL (minimum score 600 paper-based; 100 iBT). Electronic applications accepted.

**University of South Florida,** College of Arts and Sciences, Department of Cell Biology, Microbiology, and Molecular Biology, Tampa, FL 33620-9951. Offers biology (MS), including cell biology, microbiology and molecular biology; cancer biology (PhD); cancer chemical biology (PhD); cancer immunology and immunotherapy (PhD); cell and molecular biology (PhD); microbiology (MS). *Faculty:* 21 full-time (8 women). *Students:* 85 full-time (50 women), 4 part-time (all women); includes 10 minority (1 Black or African American, non-Hispanic/Latino; 3 Asian, non-Hispanic/Latino; 4 Hispanic/Latino; 2 Two or more races, non-Hispanic/Latino), 35 international. Average age 27. 178 applicants, 15% accepted, 20 enrolled. In 2019, 12 master's, 12 doctorates awarded. *Degree requirements:* For master's, thesis or alternative; for doctorate, comprehensive exam, thesis/dissertation. *Entrance requirements:* For master's and doctorate, GRE General Test, minimum GPA of 3.0, extensive background in biology or chemistry. Additional exam requirements/recommendations for international students: required—TOEFL (minimum score 570 paper-based; 79 iBT) or IELTS (minimum score 6.5). *Application deadline:* For fall admission, 11/30 priority date for domestic and international students; for spring admission, 7/1 priority date for domestic students, 7/1 for international students. Application fee: $30. *Financial support:* In 2019–20, 9 students received support. Career-related internships or fieldwork, health care benefits, and unspecified assistantships available. Financial award application deadline: 4/1. *Unit head:* Dr. James Garey, Professor/Chair, 813-974-7103, Fax: 813-974-1614, E-mail: garey@usf.edu. *Application contact:* Dr. Kenneth Wright, Associate Professor of Cancer Biology, H. Lee Moffitt Cancer Center and Research Institute, 813-745-3918, Fax: 813-974-1614, E-mail: ken.wright@moffitt.org.
Website: http://biology.usf.edu/cmmb/

**The University of Texas at Austin,** Graduate School, Institute for Cellular and Molecular Biology, Austin, TX 78712-1111. Offers PhD.

**The University of Texas at Dallas,** School of Natural Sciences and Mathematics, Department of Biological Sciences, Richardson, TX 75080. Offers bioinformatics and computational biology (MS); biotechnology (MS); molecular and cell biology (MS, PhD). *Program availability:* Part-time, evening/weekend. *Faculty:* 20 full-time (5 women), 6 part-time/adjunct (4 women). *Students:* 128 full-time (81 women), 12 part-time (7 women); includes 29 minority (1 Black or African American, non-Hispanic/Latino; 19 Asian, non-Hispanic/Latino; 7 Hispanic/Latino; 2 Two or more races, non-Hispanic/Latino), 77 international. Average age 28. 309 applicants, 25% accepted, 38 enrolled. In 2019, 36 master's, 7 doctorates awarded. *Degree requirements:* For master's, thesis optional; for doctorate, thesis/dissertation, publishable paper. *Entrance requirements:*

For master's and doctorate, GRE (minimum combined score of 1000 on verbal and quantitative). Additional exam requirements/recommendations for international students: required—TOEFL (minimum score 550 paper-based; 80 iBT). *Application deadline:* For fall admission, 7/15 for domestic students, 5/1 priority date for international students; for spring admission, 11/15 for domestic students, 9/1 priority date for international students. Applications are processed on a rolling basis. Application fee: $50 ($100 for international students). Electronic applications accepted. *Expenses: Tuition, area resident:* Full-time $16,504. Tuition, state resident: full-time $16,504. Tuition, nonresident: full-time $34,266. Tuition and fees vary according to course load. *Financial support:* In 2019–20, 86 students received support, including 1 fellowship with partial tuition reimbursement available (averaging $500 per year), 16 research assistantships with partial tuition reimbursements available (averaging $25,200 per year), 69 teaching assistantships with partial tuition reimbursements available (averaging $18,173 per year); career-related internships or fieldwork, Federal Work-Study, institutionally sponsored loans, scholarships/grants, and unspecified assistantships also available. Support available to part-time students. Financial award application deadline: 4/30; financial award applicants required to submit FAFSA. *Unit head:* Dr. Tae Hoon Kim, Department Head, 972-883-6032, Fax: 972-883-4551, E-mail: biology@utdallas.edu. *Application contact:* Nancy Yu, Graduate Support Assistant, 972-883-4794, Fax: 972-883-4551, E-mail: biology@utdallas.edu.
Website: https://biology.utdallas.edu/

**The University of Texas at San Antonio,** College of Sciences, Department of Biology, San Antonio, TX 78249-0617. Offers biology (MS); biotechnology (MS); cell and molecular biology (PhD); neurobiology (PhD). Terminal master's awarded for partial completion of doctoral program. *Degree requirements:* For master's, comprehensive exam, thesis or alternative; for doctorate, comprehensive exam, thesis/dissertation. *Entrance requirements:* For master's, GRE General Test, bachelor's degree with 18 credit hours in field of study or in another appropriate field of study; for doctorate, GRE General Test, 3 letters of recommendation, statement of purpose, resume. Additional exam requirements/recommendations for international students: required—TOEFL (minimum score 500 paper-based; 100 iBT), IELTS (minimum score 5). Electronic applications accepted.

**University of Utah,** School of Medicine, Program in Molecular Biology, Salt Lake City, UT 84132. Offers PhD. *Degree requirements:* For doctorate, thesis/dissertation, preliminary exams. *Entrance requirements:* For doctorate, GRE General Test, personal statement, transcripts, letters of recommendation. Additional exam requirements/recommendations for international students: required—TOEFL (minimum score 500 paper-based; 60 iBT). Electronic applications accepted. *Expenses:* Tuition, state resident: full-time $7085; part-time $272.51 per credit hour. Tuition, nonresident: full-time $24,937; part-time $959.12 per credit hour. *Required fees:* $880.52; $880.52 per semester. Tuition and fees vary according to degree level, program and student level.

**University of Vermont,** Graduate College, Cross-College Interdisciplinary Program, Cellular, Molecular and Biomedical Sciences Program, Burlington, VT 05405. Offers PhD. *Degree requirements:* For doctorate, thesis/dissertation. *Entrance requirements:* For doctorate, GRE General Test. Additional exam requirements/recommendations for international students: required—TOEFL (minimum score 550 paper-based; 100 iBT), IELTS (minimum score 7). Electronic applications accepted.

**University of Washington,** Graduate School, School of Medicine, Graduate Programs in Medicine, Program in Molecular and Cellular Biology, Seattle, WA 98195. Offers PhD. *Degree requirements:* For doctorate, thesis/dissertation. *Entrance requirements:* For doctorate, GRE General Test. Additional exam requirements/recommendations for international students: required—TOEFL. Electronic applications accepted.

**University of Wisconsin–La Crosse,** College of Science and Health, Department of Biology, La Crosse, WI 54601. Offers aquatic sciences (MS); biology (MS); cellular and molecular biology (MS); clinical microbiology (MS); microbiology (MS); nurse anesthesia (MS); physiology (MS). *Accreditation:* AANA/CANAEP. *Program availability:* Part-time. *Faculty:* 19 full-time (7 women). *Students:* 12 full-time (6 women), 39 part-time (15 women); includes 2 minority (1 Black or African American, non-Hispanic/Latino; 1 Asian, non-Hispanic/Latino). Average age 28. 37 applicants, 68% accepted, 19 enrolled. In 2019, 19 master's awarded. *Degree requirements:* For master's, comprehensive exam, thesis. *Entrance requirements:* For master's, GRE General Test, minimum GPA of 2.85. Additional exam requirements/recommendations for international students: required—TOEFL (minimum score 550 paper-based; 79 iBT). *Application deadline:* For fall admission, 2/1 priority date for domestic and international students; for spring admission, 1/4 priority date for domestic and international students. Applications are processed on a rolling basis. Electronic applications accepted. *Financial support:* Research assistantships with partial tuition reimbursements, Federal Work-Study, scholarships/grants, health care benefits, and tuition waivers (partial) available. Support available to part-time students. Financial award application deadline: 3/15; financial award applicants required to submit FAFSA. *Unit head:* Dr. Michael Abler, Department Chair, 608-785-6962, E-mail: mabler@uwlax.edu. *Application contact:* Jennifer Weber, Senior Student Services Coordinator Graduate Admissions, 608-785-8939, E-mail: admissions@uwlax.edu.
Website: http://uwlax.edu/biology/

**University of Wisconsin–Madison,** Graduate School, Program in Cellular and Molecular Biology, Madison, WI 53706-1596. Offers PhD. *Degree requirements:* For doctorate, comprehensive exam, thesis/dissertation. *Entrance requirements:* For doctorate, minimum GPA of 3.0, lab experience. Additional exam requirements/recommendations for international students: required—TOEFL (minimum score 580 paper-based; 92 iBT). Electronic applications accepted.

**University of Wisconsin–Milwaukee,** Graduate School, College of Letters and Science, Department of Biological Sciences, Milwaukee, WI 53201-0413. Offers cellular and molecular biology (MS, PhD); microbiology (MS, PhD). *Degree requirements:* For master's, thesis; for doctorate, thesis/dissertation, 1 foreign language or data analysis proficiency. *Entrance requirements:* For master's and doctorate, GRE General Test. Additional exam requirements/recommendations for international students: required—TOEFL (minimum score 550 paper-based; 79 iBT), IELTS (minimum score 6.5). Electronic applications accepted.

**University of Wisconsin–Parkside,** College of Natural and Health Sciences, Program in Applied Molecular Biology, Kenosha, WI 53141. Offers MSBS. *Program availability:* Part-time. *Degree requirements:* For master's, thesis. *Entrance requirements:* For master's, GRE General Test, BS or BA from regionally-accredited institution; minimum GPA of 3.0; 2 semesters each of general chemistry, organic chemistry, introduction to biology with laboratory, and physics; 1 semester each of genetics, biochemistry, molecular biology, and calculus. Additional exam requirements/recommendations for international students: required—TOEFL (minimum score 525 paper-based; 71 iBT). Electronic applications accepted. *Expenses: Tuition, area resident:* Full-time $9173; part-time $509.64 per credit. Tuition, state resident: full-time $9173; part-time $509.64 per credit. Tuition, nonresident: full-time $18,767; part-time $1042.64 per credit. *International tuition:* $18,767 full-time. *Required fees:* $1123.20; $63.64 per credit. Tuition and fees vary according to campus/location, program and reciprocity agreements.

**University of Wyoming,** College of Agriculture and Natural Resources, Department of Molecular Biology, Laramie, WY 82071. Offers MA, MS, PhD. Terminal master's awarded for partial completion of doctoral program. *Degree requirements:* For master's, comprehensive exam (for some programs), thesis; for doctorate, comprehensive exam, thesis/dissertation. *Entrance requirements:* For master's and doctorate, GRE General Test, GRE Subject Test (recommended), minimum GPA of 3.0. Additional exam requirements/recommendations for international students: required—TOEFL. Electronic applications accepted.

**University of Wyoming,** Graduate Program in Molecular and Cellular Life Sciences, Laramie, WY 82071. Offers PhD. *Degree requirements:* For doctorate, thesis/dissertation, four eight-week laboratory rotations, comprehensive basic practical exam, two-part qualifying exam, seminars, symposium.

**Université Laval,** Faculty of Medicine, Graduate Programs in Medicine, Programs in Cellular and Molecular Biology, Québec, QC G1K 7P4, Canada. Offers M Sc, PhD. Terminal master's awarded for partial completion of doctoral program. *Degree requirements:* For master's, thesis; for doctorate, comprehensive exam, thesis/dissertation. *Entrance requirements:* For master's and doctorate, knowledge of French, comprehension of written English. Electronic applications accepted.

**Vanderbilt University,** School of Medicine, Department of Molecular Physiology and Biophysics, Nashville, TN 37240-1001. Offers MS, PhD, MD/PhD. *Faculty:* 23 full-time (2 women). *Students:* 26 full-time (16 women); includes 9 minority (4 Black or African American, non-Hispanic/Latino; 1 Asian, non-Hispanic/Latino; 3 Hispanic/Latino; 1 Two or more races, non-Hispanic/Latino), 5 international. Average age 26. In 2019, 12 doctorates awarded. *Degree requirements:* For doctorate, comprehensive exam, thesis/dissertation, preliminary, qualifying, and final exams. *Entrance requirements:* For doctorate, GRE General Test, GRE Subject Test (recommended). Additional exam requirements/recommendations for international students: required—TOEFL (minimum score 570 paper-based; 88 iBT). *Application deadline:* For fall admission, 1/15 for domestic and international students. Electronic applications accepted. *Expenses: Tuition:* Full-time $51,018; part-time $2087 per hour. *Required fees:* $542. Tuition and fees vary according to program. *Financial support:* Fellowships with full tuition reimbursements, research assistantships with full tuition reimbursements, Federal Work-Study, institutionally sponsored loans, scholarships/grants, traineeships, health care benefits, and tuition waivers (partial) available. Financial award application deadline: 1/15; financial award applicants required to submit CSS PROFILE or FAFSA. *Unit head:* Dr. Roger Cone, Acting Chair, 615-322-7000, Fax: 615-343-0490, E-mail: roger.cone@vanderbilt.edu. *Application contact:* Richard O'Brien, Director of Graduate Studies, 615-322-7000, E-mail: richard.obrien@vanderbilt.edu.
Website: http://www.mc.vanderbilt.edu/root/vumc.php?site-MPB

**Virginia Commonwealth University,** Medical College of Virginia-Professional Programs, School of Medicine, Graduate Programs in Medicine, Department of Biochemistry and Molecular Biology, Richmond, VA 23284-9005. Offers MS, PhD, MD/PhD. *Degree requirements:* For master's, thesis; for doctorate, thesis/dissertation, comprehensive oral and written exams. *Entrance requirements:* For master's and doctorate, GRE, MCAT or DAT. Electronic applications accepted.

**Virginia Commonwealth University,** Medical College of Virginia-Professional Programs, School of Medicine, Graduate Programs in Medicine, Department of Physiology and Biophysics, Richmond, VA 23284-9005. Offers molecular biology and genetics (MS); physical therapy (PhD); physiology (MS, PhD); MD/PhD. Terminal master's awarded for partial completion of doctoral program. *Degree requirements:* For master's, thesis; for doctorate, thesis/dissertation, comprehensive oral and written exams. *Entrance requirements:* For master's, GRE General Test, MCAT, or DAT; for doctorate, GRE, MCAT or DAT. Additional exam requirements/recommendations for international students: required—TOEFL (minimum score 600 paper-based; 100 iBT). Electronic applications accepted.

**Washington University in St. Louis,** The Graduate School, Division of Biology and Biomedical Sciences, Program in Molecular Cell Biology, St. Louis, MO 63130-4899. Offers PhD. *Degree requirements:* For doctorate, thesis/dissertation. *Entrance requirements:* For doctorate, GRE General Test, GRE Subject Test. Additional exam requirements/recommendations for international students: required—TOEFL. Electronic applications accepted.

**Weill Cornell Medicine,** Weill Cornell Graduate School of Medical Sciences, Biochemistry, Cell and Molecular Biology Allied Program, New York, NY 10065. Offers MS, PhD. Terminal master's awarded for partial completion of doctoral program. *Degree requirements:* For master's, comprehensive exam; for doctorate, thesis/dissertation, final exam. *Entrance requirements:* For doctorate, GRE General Test, background in genetics, molecular biology, chemistry, or biochemistry. Additional exam requirements/recommendations for international students: required—TOEFL. Electronic applications accepted.

**Wesleyan University,** Graduate Studies, Department of Molecular Biology and Biochemistry, Middletown, CT 06459. Offers molecular biology and biochemistry (PhD); molecular biophysics (PhD). Terminal master's awarded for partial completion of doctoral program. *Degree requirements:* For doctorate, comprehensive exam, thesis/dissertation. *Entrance requirements:* For doctorate, GRE General Test, GRE Subject Test. Additional exam requirements/recommendations for international students: required—TOEFL. Electronic applications accepted.

**West Virginia University,** School of Medicine, Morgantown, WV 26506. Offers biochemistry and molecular biology (PhD); biomedical science (MS); cancer cell biology (PhD); cellular and integrative physiology (PhD); exercise physiology (MS, PhD); health sciences (MS); immunology (PhD); medicine (MD); occupational therapy (MOT); pathologists assistant' (MHS); physical therapy (DPT). *Accreditation:* AOTA; LCME/AMA. *Program availability:* Part-time, evening/weekend. *Entrance requirements:* Additional exam requirements/recommendations for international students: required—TOEFL. Electronic applications accepted. *Expenses:* Contact institution.

**Wright State University,** Graduate School, College of Science and Mathematics, Department of Biochemistry and Molecular Biology, Dayton, OH 45435. Offers MS. *Degree requirements:* For master's, thesis. *Entrance requirements:* Additional exam requirements/recommendations for international students: required—TOEFL.

**Yale University,** Graduate School of Arts and Sciences, Department of Molecular, Cellular, and Developmental Biology, Program in Biochemistry, Molecular Biology and Chemical Biology, New Haven, CT 06520. Offers PhD. *Degree requirements:* For doctorate, thesis/dissertation. *Entrance requirements:* For doctorate, GRE General Test, GRE Subject Test.

**Yale University,** Yale School of Medicine and Graduate School of Arts and Sciences, Combined Program in Biological and Biomedical Sciences (BBS), Molecular Cell Biology, Genetics, and Development Track, New Haven, CT 06520. Offers PhD, MD/PhD. *Entrance requirements:* Additional exam requirements/recommendations for international students: required—TOEFL.

**Youngstown State University,** College of Graduate Studies, College of Science, Technology, Engineering and Mathematics, Department of Biological Sciences, Youngstown, OH 44555-0001. Offers environmental biology (MS); molecular biology, microbiology, and genetics (MS); physiology and anatomy (MS). *Program availability:* Part-time. *Degree requirements:* For master's, comprehensive exam, thesis, oral review. *Entrance requirements:* For master's, GRE General Test, minimum GPA of 2.7. Additional exam requirements/recommendations for international students: required—TOEFL.

# Molecular Medicine

**Augusta University,** Program in Molecular Medicine, Augusta, GA 30912. Offers PhD. *Degree requirements:* For doctorate, comprehensive exam, thesis/dissertation. *Entrance requirements:* For doctorate, GRE General Test. Additional exam requirements/recommendations for international students: required—TOEFL (minimum score 550 paper-based; 79 iBT). Electronic applications accepted.

**Baylor College of Medicine,** Graduate School of Biomedical Sciences, Program in Translational Biology and Molecular Medicine, Houston, TX 77030-3498. Offers PhD. *Degree requirements:* For doctorate, thesis/dissertation, public defense. *Entrance requirements:* For doctorate, GRE, minimum GPA of 3.0. Additional exam requirements/recommendations for international students: required—TOEFL. Electronic applications accepted.

**Boston University,** School of Medicine, Graduate Medical Sciences, Program in Molecular and Translational Medicine, Boston, MA 02215. Offers PhD, MD/PhD. *Application deadline:* For fall admission, 1/15 for domestic students; for spring admission, 10/15 for domestic students. *Unit head:* Dr. Matt Jones, Director, E-mail: mattj@bu.edu. *Application contact:* Cassandra Kocek, Program Administrator, 617-358-0285, E-mail: gmsbusm@bu.edu.
Website: http://www.bumc.bu.edu/gms/mtm/

**Case Western Reserve University,** School of Medicine and School of Graduate Studies, Graduate Programs in Medicine, Cleveland Clinic Lerner Research Institute–Molecular Medicine PhD Program, Cleveland, OH 44106. Offers PhD. *Degree requirements:* For doctorate, comprehensive exam, thesis/dissertation, seminar. *Entrance requirements:* For doctorate, GRE, 3 letters of reference, prior research experience, interview. Additional exam requirements/recommendations for international students: required—TOEFL (minimum score 577 paper-based; 90 iBT); recommended—IELTS (minimum score 7). Electronic applications accepted.

**Cleveland State University,** College of Graduate Studies, College of Sciences and Health Professions, Department of Chemistry, Cleveland, OH 44115. Offers clinical chemistry (PhD), including cellular and molecular medicine, clinical/bioanalytical chemistry; organic chemistry (MS); physical chemistry (MS). *Program availability:* Part-time, evening/weekend. *Faculty:* 17 full-time (3 women). *Students:* 45 full-time (24 women), 17 part-time (8 women); includes 5 minority (3 Black or African American, non-Hispanic/Latino; 2 Asian, non-Hispanic/Latino), 35 international. Average age 30. 63 applicants, 63% accepted, 11 enrolled. In 2019, 9 master's, 12 doctorates awarded. *Entrance requirements:* For master's and doctorate, GRE General Test. Additional exam requirements/recommendations for international students: required—TOEFL (minimum score 550 paper-based; 78 iBT). *Application deadline:* Applications are processed on a rolling basis. Application fee: $40. Electronic applications accepted. *Expenses:* Tuition, state resident: full-time $10,215; part-time $6810 per credit hour. Tuition, nonresident: full-time $17,496; part-time $11,664 per credit hour. *International tuition:* $19,316 full-time. Tuition and fees vary according to degree level and program. *Financial support:* In 2019–20, 44 students received support. Fellowships, research assistantships, teaching assistantships, scholarships/grants, and unspecified assistantships available. Financial award application deadline: 1/15; financial award applicants required to submit FAFSA. *Unit head:* Dr. David W. Ball, Chair, 216-687-2467, Fax: 216-687-9298, E-mail: d.ball@csuohio.edu. *Application contact:* Richelle P. Emery, Administrative Coordinator, 216-687-2457, Fax: 216-687-9298, E-mail: r.emery@csuohio.edu.
Website: http://www.csuohio.edu/sciences/chemistry

**Dartmouth College,** Program in Experimental and Molecular Medicine, Hanover, NH 03755. Offers biomedical physiology (PhD); cancer biology and molecular therapeutics (PhD); cardiovascular diseases (PhD); molecular pharmacology, toxicology and experimental therapeutics (PhD); neuroscience (PhD); MD/PhD. *Degree requirements:* For doctorate, comprehensive exam, thesis/dissertation. *Entrance requirements:* For doctorate, GRE, 3 letters of recommendation, interview, minimum GPA of 3.0. Additional exam requirements/recommendations for international students: required—TOEFL (minimum score 620 paper-based; 105 iBT). Electronic applications accepted.

**Drexel University,** College of Medicine, Biomedical Graduate Programs, Molecular Medicine Program, Philadelphia, PA 19104-2875. Offers MS.

**Elmezzi Graduate School of Molecular Medicine,** Graduate Program, Manhasset, NY 11030. Offers PhD. *Degree requirements:* For doctorate, comprehensive exam, thesis/dissertation. *Entrance requirements:* For doctorate, MCAT or GRE, MD or equivalent, current curriculum vitae, official transcripts, three letters of recommendation, interview.

**The George Washington University,** Columbian College of Arts and Sciences, Institute for Biomedical Sciences, Program in Molecular Medicine, Washington, DC 20037. Offers molecular and cellular oncology (PhD); neurosciences (PhD); pharmacology and physiology (PhD). *Degree requirements:* For doctorate, comprehensive exam, thesis/dissertation, general exams. *Entrance requirements:* For doctorate, GRE General Test, interview, minimum GPA of 3.0. Additional exam requirements/recommendations for international students: required—TOEFL (minimum score 600 paper-based). Electronic applications accepted.

**Hofstra University,** Donald and Barbara Zucker School of Medicine at Hofstra/Northwell, Hempstead, NY 11549. Offers medicine (MD); molecular basis of medicine (PhD); MD/MPH; MD/PhD. *Accreditation:* LCME/AMA. *Faculty:* 20 full-time (13 women), 15 part-time/adjunct (10 women). *Students:* 429 full-time (197 women); includes 195 minority (26 Black or African American, non-Hispanic/Latino; 108 Asian, non-Hispanic/

Latino; 46 Hispanic/Latino; 4 Native Hawaiian or other Pacific Islander, non-Hispanic/Latino; 11 Two or more races, non-Hispanic/Latino), 2 international. Average age 25. 5,330 applicants, 7% accepted, 104 enrolled. In 2019, 98 doctorates awarded. *Entrance requirements:* For doctorate, MCAT, CASPER, Pre-med committee letter or 3 letters of recommendation. *Application deadline:* For fall admission, 12/1 priority date for domestic students. Applications are processed on a rolling basis. Application fee: $100. Electronic applications accepted. *Expenses:* $26,595 per term (tuition and fees) for MD rate. $13,250 per term (tuition and fees) for PHD rate. *Financial support:* In 2019–20, 352 students received support, including 347 fellowships with full and partial tuition reimbursements available (averaging $26,261 per year); research assistantships with full and partial tuition reimbursements available, career-related internships or fieldwork, Federal Work-Study, institutionally sponsored loans, scholarships/grants, tuition waivers (full and partial), unspecified assistantships, and scholarships and endowed scholarships also available. Support available to part-time students. Financial award applicants required to submit FAFSA. *Unit head:* Dr. Lawrence Smith, Dean, 516-463-7517, Fax: 516-463-7543, E-mail: lawrence.smith@hofstra.edu. *Application contact:* Sunil Samuel, Assistant Vice President of Admissions, 516-463-4723, Fax: 516-463-4664.
Website: http://medicine.hofstra.edu/index.html

**Johns Hopkins University,** School of Medicine, Graduate Programs in Medicine, Graduate Program in Cellular and Molecular Medicine, Baltimore, MD 21218. Offers PhD. *Degree requirements:* For doctorate, comprehensive exam, thesis/dissertation, oral exam, thesis defense. *Entrance requirements:* For doctorate, GRE. Electronic applications accepted. *Expenses:* Contact institution.

**Liberty University,** School of Health Sciences, Lynchburg, VA 24515. Offers anatomy and cell biology (PhD); biomedical sciences (MS); epidemiology (MPH); exercise science (MS), including clinical, community physical activity, human performance, nutrition; global health (MPH); health promotion (MPH); medical sciences (MA), including biopsychology, business management, health informatics, molecular medicine, public health; nutrition (MPH). *Program availability:* Part-time, online learning. *Students:* 820 full-time (588 women), 889 part-time (612 women); includes 611 minority (402 Black or African American, non-Hispanic/Latino; 10 American Indian or Alaska Native, non-Hispanic/Latino; 43 Asian, non-Hispanic/Latino; 85 Hispanic/Latino; 1 Native Hawaiian or other Pacific Islander, non-Hispanic/Latino; 70 Two or more races, non-Hispanic/Latino), 67 international. Average age 32. 2,610 applicants, 33% accepted, 406 enrolled. In 2019, 445 master's awarded. *Degree requirements:* For master's, thesis (for some programs); for doctorate, thesis/dissertation. *Entrance requirements:* For doctorate, MAT or GRE, minimum GPA of 3.25 in master's program, 2-3 recommendations, writing samples (for some programs), letter of intent, professional vitae. Additional exam requirements/recommendations for international students: required—TOEFL (minimum score 600 paper-based; 100 iBT). Application fee: $50. *Expenses: Tuition:* Full-time $545; part-time $410 per credit hour. One-time fee: $50. *Financial support:* In 2019–20, 918 students received support. Federal Work-Study available. Financial award applicants required to submit FAFSA. *Unit head:* Dr. Ralph Linstra, Dean. *Application contact:* Jay Bridge, Director of Admissions, 800-424-9595, Fax: 800-628-7977, E-mail: gradadmissions@liberty.edu.
Website: https://www.liberty.edu/health-sciences/

**Oregon Health & Science University,** School of Medicine, Graduate Programs in Medicine, Department of Environmental and Biomolecular Systems, Portland, OR 97239-3098. Offers biochemistry and molecular biology (MS, PhD); environmental science and engineering (MS, PhD). *Program availability:* Part-time. Terminal master's awarded for partial completion of doctoral program. *Degree requirements:* For master's, thesis (for some programs); for doctorate, comprehensive exam, thesis/dissertation, qualifying exam. *Entrance requirements:* For master's and doctorate, GRE General Test (minimum scores: 153 Verbal/148 Quantitative/4.5 Analytical) or MCAT (for some programs). Electronic applications accepted.

**Penn State Hershey Medical Center,** College of Medicine, Graduate School Programs in the Biomedical Sciences, Huck Institutes of the Life Sciences, Intercollege Graduate Program in Molecular Cellular and Integrative Biosciences, Hershey, PA 17033. Offers cell and developmental biology (PhD); molecular medicine (PhD); molecular toxicology (PhD); neurobiology (PhD). *Degree requirements:* For doctorate, comprehensive exam, thesis/dissertation, oral exam. *Entrance requirements:* For doctorate, GRE, minimum GPA of 3.0. Additional exam requirements/recommendations for international students: required—TOEFL (minimum score 500 paper-based). Electronic applications accepted.

**Queen's University at Kingston,** School of Graduate Studies, Faculty of Health Sciences, Department of Pathology and Molecular Medicine, Kingston, ON K7L 3N6, Canada. Offers M Sc, PhD. *Program availability:* Part-time. *Degree requirements:* For master's, thesis; for doctorate, comprehensive exam, thesis/dissertation. *Entrance requirements:* Additional exam requirements/recommendations for international students: required—TOEFL.

**Rutgers University - Newark,** Graduate School of Biomedical Sciences, Department of Cell Biology and Molecular Medicine, Newark, NJ 07107. Offers PhD. *Degree requirements:* For doctorate, thesis/dissertation, qualifying exam. *Entrance requirements:* For doctorate, GRE General Test. Additional exam requirements/recommendations for international students: required—TOEFL. Electronic applications accepted.

**Tufts University,** Graduate School of Biomedical Sciences, Cell, Molecular, and Developmental Biology Program, Medford, MA 02155. Offers cancer biology (PhD); developmental and regenerative biology (PhD); molecular and cellular medicine (PhD); structural and chemical biology (PhD). *Faculty:* 84 full-time (30 women). *Students:* 32 full-time (15 women); includes 10 minority (2 Black or African American, non-Hispanic/Latino; 4 Asian, non-Hispanic/Latino; 4 Hispanic/Latino), 4 international. Average age 28. 168 applicants, 5% accepted, 3 enrolled. In 2019, 5 doctorates awarded. Terminal master's awarded for partial completion of doctoral program. *Degree requirements:* For doctorate, comprehensive exam, thesis/dissertation. *Entrance requirements:* For doctorate, 3 letters of reference, resume, personal statement. *Application deadline:* For fall admission, 12/1 priority date for domestic and international students. Application fee: $90. Electronic applications accepted. *Expenses: Tuition:* Part-time $1799 per credit hour. Full-time tuition and fees vary according to degree level, program and student level. Part-time tuition and fees vary according to course load. *Financial support:* In 2019–20, 100 students received support, including 3 research assistantships with full tuition reimbursements available (averaging $40,000 per year); fellowships, traineeships, and health care benefits also available. Financial award application deadline: 12/1. *Unit head:* Dr. Brent Cochran, Program Director, 617-636-0442. *Application contact:* Jeff Miller, Admissions Coordinator, 617-636-6767, Fax: 617-636-0375, E-mail: gsbs-admissions@tufts.edu.
Website: https://gsbs.tufts.edu/academics/CMDB

**The University of Alabama at Birmingham,** Joint Health Sciences, Pathobiology and Molecular Medicine Theme, Birmingham, AL 35294. Offers PhD. *Students:* Average age 28. 41 applicants, 15% accepted, 4 enrolled. In 2019, 9 doctorates awarded. *Degree requirements:* For doctorate, comprehensive exam, thesis/dissertation. *Entrance requirements:* For doctorate, personal statement, resume or curriculum vitae, letters of recommendation, research experience, interview. Additional exam requirements/recommendations for international students: required—TOEFL (minimum score 80 iBT), IELTS (minimum score 6.5). *Application deadline:* For fall admission, 12/31 for domestic and international students. Applications are processed on a rolling basis. Electronic applications accepted. *Financial support:* In 2019–20, fellowships with full tuition reimbursements (averaging $30,000 per year), research assistantships with full tuition reimbursements (averaging $31,000 per year) were awarded; health care benefits also available. *Unit head:* Dr. Yabing Chen, Theme Director, 205-996-6293, E-mail: ybchen@uab.edu. *Application contact:* Alyssa Zasada, Admissions Manager for Graduate Biomedical Sciences, 205-934-3857, E-mail: grad-gbs@uab.edu.
Website: http://www.uab.edu/gbs/home/themes/pbmm

**The University of Arizona,** College of Medicine, Department of Cellular and Molecular Medicine, Tucson, AZ 85721. Offers MS, PhD. *Degree requirements:* For doctorate, comprehensive exam. *Entrance requirements:* Additional exam requirements/recommendations for international students: required—TOEFL, IELTS. Electronic applications accepted.

**University of Cincinnati,** Graduate School, College of Medicine, Graduate Programs in Biomedical Sciences, Program in Pathobiology and Molecular Medicine, Cincinnati, OH 45267-0529. Offers pathology (PhD), including anatomic pathology, laboratory medicine, pathobiology and molecular medicine. *Degree requirements:* For doctorate, thesis/dissertation, qualifying exam. *Entrance requirements:* For doctorate, GRE General Test. Additional exam requirements/recommendations for international students: required—TOEFL. Electronic applications accepted.

**University of Maryland, Baltimore,** Graduate School, Graduate Program in Life Sciences, Program in Molecular Medicine, Baltimore, MD 21201. Offers applied pharmacology and toxicology (PhD); cancer biology (PhD); genome biology (PhD); molecular and cellular physiology (PhD); MD/PhD. *Degree requirements:* For doctorate, comprehensive exam, thesis/dissertation. *Entrance requirements:* For doctorate, GRE, minimum GPA of 3.0, curriculum vitae, essay, 3 letters of recommendation. Additional exam requirements/recommendations for international students: required—TOEFL (minimum score 80 iBT); recommended—IELTS (minimum score 7). Electronic applications accepted.

**University of Nebraska Medical Center,** Interdisciplinary Graduate Program in Biomedical Sciences, Integrative Physiology and Molecular Medicine Doctoral Program, Omaha, NE 68198. Offers PhD. *Program availability:* Part-time. *Degree requirements:* For doctorate, comprehensive exam, thesis/dissertation, at least one first-author research publication. *Entrance requirements:* For doctorate, GRE General Test or MCAT, course work in biology, chemistry, mathematics, and physics; minimum GPA of 3.25. Additional exam requirements/recommendations for international students: required—TOEFL (minimum score 600 paper-based; 95 iBT), IELTS (minimum score 7). Electronic applications accepted.

**University of Southern California,** Keck School of Medicine and Graduate School, Graduate Programs in Medicine, Department of Biochemistry and Molecular Medicine, Los Angeles, CA 90089. Offers MS. *Program availability:* Part-time. *Faculty:* 36 full-time (10 women). *Students:* 34 full-time (21 women), 1 (woman) part-time; includes 34 minority (33 Asian, non-Hispanic/Latino; 1 Hispanic/Latino). Average age 24. 67 applicants, 58% accepted, 15 enrolled. In 2019, 19 master's awarded. Terminal master's awarded for partial completion of doctoral program. *Degree requirements:* For master's, thesis. *Entrance requirements:* For master's, GRE General Test, minimum GPA of 3.0. Additional exam requirements/recommendations for international students: required—TOEFL (minimum score 600 paper-based; 100 iBT), IELTS. *Application deadline:* For fall admission, 4/1 priority date for domestic and international students. Applications are processed on a rolling basis. Application fee: $90. Electronic applications accepted. *Financial support:* Application deadline: 5/4; applicants required to submit CSS PROFILE or FAFSA. *Unit head:* Dr. Peggy R. Farnham, Chair, 323-442-8015, E-mail: peggy.farnham@med.usc.edu. *Application contact:* Janet Stoeckert, Administrative Director, Basic Science Departments, 323-442-3568, Fax: 323-442-1610, E-mail: janet.stoeckert@usc.edu.
Website: https://keck.usc.edu/biochemistry-and-molecular-medicine/

**The University of Texas Health Science Center at San Antonio,** Graduate School of Biomedical Sciences, Department of Molecular Medicine, San Antonio, TX 78245-3207. Offers MS, PhD. Terminal master's awarded for partial completion of doctoral program. *Degree requirements:* For master's, comprehensive exam, thesis; for doctorate, comprehensive exam, thesis/dissertation.

**University of Washington,** Graduate School, School of Medicine, Graduate Programs in Medicine, Department of Pathology, Seattle, WA 98195. Offers molecular medicine and mechanisms of disease (PhD). *Degree requirements:* For doctorate, thesis/dissertation. *Entrance requirements:* For doctorate, GRE General Test.

**Wake Forest University,** School of Medicine and Graduate School of Arts and Sciences, Graduate Programs in Medicine, Program in Molecular Medicine and Translational Science, Winston-Salem, NC 27109. Offers MS, PhD, MD/PhD. *Degree requirements:* For master's, thesis; for doctorate, thesis/dissertation. *Entrance requirements:* For master's and doctorate, GRE General Test. Additional exam requirements/recommendations for international students: required—TOEFL. Electronic applications accepted.

**Yale University,** Yale School of Medicine and Graduate School of Arts and Sciences, Combined Program in Biological and Biomedical Sciences (BBS), Pharmacological Sciences and Molecular Medicine Track, New Haven, CT 06520. Offers PhD, MD/PhD. *Degree requirements:* For doctorate, thesis/dissertation. *Entrance requirements:* For doctorate, GRE General Test. Additional exam requirements/recommendations for international students: required—TOEFL. Electronic applications accepted.

# Structural Biology

**Albert Einstein College of Medicine,** Graduate Programs in the Biomedical Sciences, Department of Anatomy and Structural Biology, Bronx, NY 10461. Offers anatomy (PhD); MD/PhD. *Degree requirements:* For doctorate, thesis/dissertation. *Entrance requirements:* For doctorate, GRE General Test. Additional exam requirements/ recommendations for international students: required—TOEFL. Electronic applications accepted.

**Baylor College of Medicine,** Graduate School of Biomedical Sciences, Program in Structural and Computational Biology and Molecular Biophysics, Houston, TX 77030- 3498. Offers PhD, MD/PhD. *Degree requirements:* For doctorate, thesis/dissertation, public defense. *Entrance requirements:* For doctorate, GRE General Test, GRE Subject Test (strongly recommended), minimum GPA of 3.0. Additional exam requirements/ recommendations for international students: required—TOEFL. Electronic applications accepted.

**Carnegie Mellon University,** Mellon College of Science, Department of Biological Sciences, Pittsburgh, PA 15213-3891. Offers biochemistry (PhD); biophysics (PhD); cell and developmental biology (PhD); computational biology (MS, PhD); genetics (PhD); molecular biology (PhD); neuroscience (PhD); structural biology (PhD). *Degree requirements:* For doctorate, comprehensive exam, thesis/dissertation. *Entrance requirements:* For doctorate, GRE General Test, GRE Subject Test, interview. Electronic applications accepted.

**Carnegie Mellon University,** Mellon College of Science, Joint Pitt + CMU Molecular Biophysics and Structural Biology Graduate Program, Pittsburgh, PA 15213-3891. Offers PhD. *Degree requirements:* For doctorate, comprehensive exam, thesis/ dissertation. *Entrance requirements:* For doctorate, GRE General Test. Additional exam requirements/recommendations for international students: required—TOEFL (minimum score 600 paper-based; 100 iBT), IELTS (minimum score 7). Electronic applications accepted.

**Columbia University,** College of Physicians and Surgeons, Integrated Program in Cellular, Molecular, Structural and Genetic Studies, New York, NY 10032. Offers PhD. Terminal master's awarded for partial completion of doctoral program. *Degree requirements:* For doctorate, thesis/dissertation. *Entrance requirements:* For doctorate, GRE General Test, GRE Subject Test. Additional exam requirements/recommendations for international students: required—TOEFL. *Expenses:* Contact institution.

**Duke University,** Graduate School, University Program in Structural Biology and Biophysics, Durham, NC 27710. Offers Certificate. *Entrance requirements:* For degree, GRE General Test. Additional exam requirements/recommendations for international students: required—TOEFL (minimum score 577 paper-based; 90 iBT) or IELTS (minimum score 7).

**Florida State University,** The Graduate School, College of Arts and Sciences, Program in Molecular Biophysics, Tallahassee, FL 32304. Offers structural biology (PhD). *Faculty:* 33 full-time (6 women). *Students:* 18 full-time (8 women); includes 14 minority (11 Asian, non-Hispanic/Latino; 3 Two or more races, non-Hispanic/Latino), 1 international. Average age 27. 22 applicants, 36% accepted, 5 enrolled. In 2019, 2 doctorates awarded. *Degree requirements:* For doctorate, comprehensive exam, thesis/ dissertation, teaching 1 term in professor's major department. *Entrance requirements:* For doctorate, GRE General Test (minimum score 153 Verbal portion, 154 Quantitative portion). Additional exam requirements/recommendations for international students: required—TOEFL (minimum score 550 paper-based; 90 iBT), IELTS (minimum score 6.5). *Application deadline:* For fall admission, 1/15 for domestic and international students. Applications are processed on a rolling basis. Application fee: $30. Electronic applications accepted. *Expenses:* Contact institution. *Financial support:* In 2019–20, 18 students received support, including 4 fellowships with partial tuition reimbursements available (averaging $34,000 per year), 15 research assistantships with partial tuition reimbursements available (averaging $24,200 per year), 2 teaching assistantships with partial tuition reimbursements available (averaging $24,200 per year); scholarships/ grants, health care benefits, tuition waivers (full), and unspecified assistantships also available. Financial award application deadline: 1/15; financial award applicants required to submit FAFSA. *Unit head:* Dr. Hong Li, Director, 850-644-6785, Fax: 850-644-7244, E-mail: hongli@sb.fsu.edu. *Application contact:* Shaimaa Khanam, Academic Coordinator, Graduate Programs, 850-644-1012, Fax: 850-644-7244, E-mail: skhanam@fsu.edu.
Website: http://biophysics.fsu.edu/

**Illinois State University,** Graduate School, College of Arts and Sciences, School of Biological Sciences, Normal, IL 61790. Offers animal behavior (MS); bacteriology (MS); biochemistry (MS); biological sciences (MS); biology (PhD); biophysics (MS); biotechnology (MS); botany (MS, PhD); cell biology (MS); conservation biology (MS); developmental biology (MS); ecology (MS, PhD); entomology (MS); evolutionary biology (MS); genetics (MS, PhD); immunology (MS); microbiology (MS, PhD); molecular biology (MS); molecular genetics (MS); neurobiology (MS); neuroscience (MS); parasitology (MS); physiology (MS, PhD); plant biology (MS); plant molecular biology (MS); plant sciences (MS); structural biology (MS); zoology (MS, PhD). *Program availability:* Part-time. *Faculty:* 26 full-time (6 women), 7 part-time/adjunct (2 women). *Students:* 51 full-time (33 women), 15 part-time (8 women). Average age 27. 71 applicants, 28% accepted, 9 enrolled. In 2019, 14 master's, 3 doctorates awarded. *Degree requirements:* For master's, thesis or alternative; for doctorate, variable foreign language requirement, thesis/dissertation, 2 terms of residency. *Entrance requirements:* For master's, GRE General Test, minimum GPA of 2.6 in last 60 hours of course work; for doctorate, GRE General Test. *Application deadline:* Applications are processed on a rolling basis. Application fee: $50. *Expenses: Tuition, area resident:* Full-time $7956; part-time $9767 per year. Tuition, nonresident: full-time $9233; part-time $17,592 per year. *Required fees:* $1797. *Financial support:* In 2019–20, 20 research assistantships, 41 teaching assistantships were awarded; Federal Work-Study, tuition waivers (full), and unspecified assistantships also available. Financial award application deadline: 4/1. *Unit head:* Dr. Craig Gatto, School Director, 309-438-3087, E-mail: cgatto@IllinoisState.edu. *Application contact:* Dr. Ben Sadd, Assistant Chair for Graduate Studies, 309-438-2651, E-mail: bmsadd@IllinoisState.edu.
Website: http://www.bio.ilstu.edu/

**Iowa State University of Science and Technology,** Bioinformatics and Computational Biology Program, Ames, IA 50011. Offers MS, PhD. *Degree requirements:* For doctorate, thesis/dissertation. *Entrance requirements:* For master's and doctorate, GRE General Test. Additional exam requirements/recommendations for international students: recommended—TOEFL, IELTS. Electronic applications accepted.

**Massachusetts Institute of Technology,** School of Science, Department of Biology, Cambridge, MA 02139. Offers biochemistry (PhD); biological oceanography (PhD); biology (PhD); biophysical chemistry and molecular structure (PhD); cell biology (PhD);

computational and systems biology (PhD); developmental biology (PhD); genetics (PhD); immunology (PhD); microbiology (PhD); molecular biology (PhD); neurobiology (PhD). *Degree requirements:* For doctorate, comprehensive exam, thesis/dissertation, teaching assistantship during two semesters. *Entrance requirements:* For doctorate, GRE General Test. Additional exam requirements/recommendations for international students: required—TOEFL, IELTS. Electronic applications accepted.

**Michigan State University,** The Graduate School, College of Natural Science, Quantitative Biology Program, East Lansing, MI 48824. Offers PhD.

**Northwestern University,** The Graduate School, Interdisciplinary Biological Sciences Program (IBiS), Evanston, IL 60208. Offers biochemistry (PhD); bioengineering and biotechnology (PhD); biotechnology (PhD); cell and molecular biology (PhD); developmental and systems biology (PhD); nanotechnology (PhD); neurobiology (PhD); structural biology and biophysics (PhD). *Degree requirements:* For doctorate, thesis/ dissertation, qualifying exam. *Entrance requirements:* For doctorate, GRE General Test. Additional exam requirements/recommendations for international students: required— TOEFL (minimum score 600 paper-based). Electronic applications accepted.

**Stanford University,** School of Medicine, Graduate Programs in Medicine, Department of Structural Biology, Stanford, CA 94305-2004. Offers PhD. *Expenses: Tuition:* Full-time $52,479; part-time $34,110 per unit. *Required fees:* $672; $224 per quarter. Tuition and fees vary according to program and student level.
Website: http://structuralbio.stanford.edu/

**Stony Brook University, State University of New York,** Graduate School, College of Arts and Sciences, Department of Biochemistry and Cell Biology, Program in Biochemistry and Structural Biology, Stony Brook, NY 11794. Offers PhD. *Students:* 26 full-time (18 women); includes 3 minority (2 Black or African American, non-Hispanic/ Latino; 1 Hispanic/Latino), 16 international. Average age 26. 31 applicants, 39% accepted, 3 enrolled. In 2019, 9 doctorates awarded. *Entrance requirements:* For doctorate, GRE. Additional exam requirements/recommendations for international students: required—TOEFL (minimum score 90 iBT). *Application deadline:* For fall admission, 1/15 for domestic students; for spring admission, 10/1 for domestic students. Application fee: $100. *Expenses:* Contact institution. *Financial support:* In 2019–20, 1 fellowship, 18 research assistantships, 3 teaching assistantships were awarded. *Unit head:* Prof. Aaron Neiman, Chair, 631-632-8550, Fax: 631-632-8575, E-mail: aaron.neiman@stonybrook.edu. *Application contact:* Amy Saas, Graduate Program Administrator, 631-632-8613, Fax: 631-632-9730, E-mail: amy.saas@stonybrook.edu.
Website: https://www.stonybrook.edu/bsb/

**Tufts University,** Graduate School of Biomedical Sciences, Cell, Molecular, and Developmental Biology Program, Medford, MA 02155. Offers cancer biology (PhD); developmental and regenerative biology (PhD); molecular and cellular medicine (PhD); structural and chemical biology (PhD). *Faculty:* 84 full-time (30 women). *Students:* 32 full-time (15 women); includes 10 minority (2 Black or African American, non-Hispanic/ Latino; 4 Asian, non-Hispanic/Latino; 4 Hispanic/Latino), 4 international. Average age 28. 168 applicants, 5% accepted, 3 enrolled. In 2019, 5 doctorates awarded. Terminal master's awarded for partial completion of doctoral program. *Degree requirements:* For doctorate, comprehensive exam, thesis/dissertation. *Entrance requirements:* For doctorate, 3 letters of reference, resume, personal statement. *Application deadline:* For fall admission, 12/1 priority date for domestic and international students. Application fee: $90. Electronic applications accepted. *Expenses: Tuition:* Part-time $1799 per credit hour. Full-time tuition and fees vary according to degree level, program and student level. Part-time tuition and fees vary according to course load. *Financial support:* In 2019–20, 100 students received support, including 3 research assistantships with full tuition reimbursements available (averaging $40,000 per year); fellowships, traineeships, and health care benefits also available. Financial award application deadline: 12/1. *Unit head:* Dr. Brent Cochran, Program Director, 617-636-0442. *Application contact:* Jeff Miller, Admissions Coordinator, 617-636-6767, Fax: 617-636- 0375, E-mail: gsbs-admissions@tufts.edu.
Website: https://gsbs.tufts.edu/academics/CMDB

**Tulane University,** School of Medicine, Graduate Programs in Biomedical Sciences, Department of Structural and Cellular Biology, New Orleans, LA 70118-5669. Offers MS, PhD, MD/PhD. *Degree requirements:* For master's, one foreign language, thesis; for doctorate, 2 foreign languages, thesis/dissertation. *Entrance requirements:* For master's, GRE General Test, minimum B average in undergraduate course work; for doctorate, GRE General Test. Additional exam requirements/recommendations for international students: required—TOEFL. Electronic applications accepted. *Expenses: Tuition:* Full-time $57,004; part-time $3167 per credit hour. *Required fees:* $2086; $44.50 per credit hour. $80 per term. Tuition and fees vary according to course load, degree level and program.

**University at Buffalo, the State University of New York,** Graduate School, Jacobs School of Medicine and Biomedical Sciences, Graduate Programs in Medicine and Biomedical Sciences, Department of Structural Biology, Buffalo, NY 14260. Offers MS, PhD. *Faculty:* 4 full-time (1 woman), 2 part-time/adjunct (0 women). *Students:* 1 full-time (0 women). Average age 27. In 2019, 1 doctorate awarded. Terminal master's awarded for partial completion of doctoral program. *Degree requirements:* For master's, comprehensive exam, thesis; for doctorate, comprehensive exam, thesis/dissertation. *Entrance requirements:* For master's, BS or BA in science, engineering, or math; for doctorate, GRE General Test, BS or BA in science, engineering, or math. Additional exam requirements/recommendations for international students: required—TOEFL (minimum score 600 paper-based; 100 iBT). *Application deadline:* For fall admission, 2/ 1 priority date for domestic and international students. Applications are processed on a rolling basis. Application fee: $50. Electronic applications accepted. *Expenses: Tuition, area resident:* Full-time $11,310; part-time $471 per credit hour. Tuition, state resident: full-time $11,310; part-time $471 per credit hour. Tuition, nonresident: full-time $23,100; part-time $963 per credit hour. *International tuition:* $23,100 full-time. *Required fees:* $2820. *Financial support:* Application deadline: 2/1; applicants required to submit FAFSA. *Unit head:* Dr. Michael G. Malkowski, Professor and Chair, 716-829-3698, E-mail: mgm22@buffalo.edu. *Application contact:* Elizabeth A. White, Administrative Director, 716-829-3399, Fax: 716-829-2437, E-mail: bethw@buffalo.edu.
Website: http://medicine.buffalo.edu/departments/structural-biology.html

**The University of Alabama at Birmingham,** Joint Health Sciences, Biochemistry, Structural, and Stem Cell Biology Theme, Birmingham, AL 35294. Offers PhD. *Students:* 34 full-time (15 women); includes 9 minority (2 Black or African American, non-Hispanic/ Latino; 1 American Indian or Alaska Native, non-Hispanic/Latino; 4 Asian, non-Hispanic/ Latino; 2 Hispanic/Latino), 4 international. Average age 26. 41 applicants, 2% accepted, 1 enrolled. In 2019, 5 doctorates awarded. *Degree requirements:* For doctorate, comprehensive exam, thesis/dissertation. *Entrance requirements:* For doctorate, personal statement, resume or curriculum vitae, letters of recommendation, research

experience, interview. Additional exam requirements/recommendations for international students: required—TOEFL (minimum score 80 iBT), IELTS (minimum score 6.5). *Application deadline:* For fall admission, 12/31 for domestic and international students. Applications are processed on a rolling basis. Electronic applications accepted. *Financial support:* In 2019–20, fellowships with full tuition reimbursements (averaging $30,000 per year), research assistantships with full tuition reimbursements (averaging $31,000 per year) were awarded; health care benefits also available. *Unit head:* Dr. Thomas Ryan, Theme Director, 205-996-2175, E-mail: tryan@uab.edu. *Application contact:* Alyssa Zasada, Admissions Manager for Graduate Biomedical Sciences, 205-934-3857, E-mail: grad-gbs@uab.edu.
Website: http://www.uab.edu/gbs/home/themes/bssb

**University of Connecticut,** Graduate School, College of Liberal Arts and Sciences, Department of Molecular and Cell Biology, Storrs, CT 06269. Offers applied genomics (PSM); cell and developmental biology (MS, PhD); genetics and genomics (MS, PhD); microbial systems analysis (PSM); microbiology (MS, PhD); structural biology, biochemistry and biophysics (MS, PhD). Terminal master's awarded for partial completion of doctoral program. *Degree requirements:* For master's, comprehensive exam; for doctorate, thesis/dissertation. *Entrance requirements:* For master's and doctorate, GRE General Test, GRE Subject Test. Additional exam requirements/recommendations for international students: required—TOEFL (minimum score 550 paper-based). Electronic applications accepted.

**The University of Manchester,** School of Biological Sciences, Manchester, United Kingdom. Offers adaptive organismal biology (M Phil, PhD); animal biology (M Phil, PhD); biochemistry (M Phil, PhD); bioinformatics (M Phil, PhD); biomolecular sciences (M Phil, PhD); biotechnology (M Phil, PhD); cell biology (M Phil, PhD); cell matrix research (M Phil, PhD); channels and transporters (M Phil, PhD); developmental biology (M Phil, PhD); environmental biology (M Phil, PhD); evolutionary biology (M Phil, PhD); gene expression (M Phil, PhD); genetics (M Phil, PhD); history of science, technology and medicine (M Phil, PhD); immunology (M Phil, PhD); integrative neurobiology and behavior (M Phil, PhD); membrane trafficking (M Phil, PhD); microbiology (M Phil, PhD); molecular and cellular neuroscience (M Phil, PhD); molecular biology (M Phil, PhD); molecular cancer studies (M Phil, PhD); neuroscience (M Phil, PhD); ophthalmology (M Phil, PhD); optometry (M Phil, PhD); organelle function (M Phil, PhD); pharmacology (M Phil, PhD); physiology (M Phil, PhD); plant sciences (M Phil, PhD); stem cell research (M Phil, PhD); structural biology (M Phil, PhD); systems neuroscience (M Phil, PhD); toxicology (M Phil, PhD).

**University of Minnesota, Twin Cities Campus,** Graduate School, College of Biological Sciences, Biochemistry, Molecular Biology and Biophysics Graduate Program, Minneapolis, MN 55455-0213. Offers PhD. *Degree requirements:* For doctorate, thesis/dissertation. *Entrance requirements:* For doctorate, GRE, 3 letters of recommendation, more than 1 semester of laboratory experience. Additional exam requirements/recommendations for international students: required—TOEFL (minimum score 625 paper-based; 108 iBT with writing subsection 25 and reading subsection 25) or IELTS (minimum score 7). Electronic applications accepted.

**University of Oklahoma,** College of Arts and Sciences, Department of Chemistry and Biochemistry, Norman, OK 73019. Offers chemistry (MS, PhD), including analytical chemistry, biochemistry, chemical education, inorganic chemistry, inter-and/or multidisciplinary, organic chemistry, physical chemistry, structural biology. *Program availability:* Part-time. Terminal master's awarded for partial completion of doctoral

program. *Degree requirements:* For master's, comprehensive exam (for some programs), thesis (for some programs); for doctorate, comprehensive exam, thesis/dissertation, general exam. *Entrance requirements:* For master's and doctorate, GRE. Additional exam requirements/recommendations for international students: required—TOEFL (minimum score 79 iBT) or IELTS (minimum score 6.5). Electronic applications accepted. *Expenses:* Tuition, state resident: full-time $6583.20; part-time $274.30 per credit hour. Tuition, nonresident: full-time $21,242; part-time $885.10 per credit hour. *International tuition:* $21,242.40 full-time. *Required fees:* $1994.20; $72.55 per credit hour. $126.50 per semester. Tuition and fees vary according to course load and degree level.

**University of Pittsburgh,** School of Medicine, Graduate Programs in Medicine and Kenneth P. Dietrich School of Arts and Sciences, Molecular Biophysics and Structural Biology Graduate Program, Pittsburgh, PA 15260. Offers PhD. *Degree requirements:* For doctorate, comprehensive exam, thesis/dissertation. *Entrance requirements:* For doctorate, GRE General Test. Additional exam requirements/recommendations for international students: required—TOEFL (minimum score 600 paper-based; 100 iBT), IELTS (minimum score 7). Electronic applications accepted. *Expenses:* Contact institution.

**University of Rochester,** School of Medicine and Dentistry, Graduate Programs in Medicine and Dentistry, Department of Biochemistry and Biophysics, Programs in Biophysics, Rochester, NY 14627. Offers biophysics, structural and computational biology (PhD). Terminal master's awarded for partial completion of doctoral program. *Degree requirements:* For doctorate, thesis/dissertation, qualifying exam. *Entrance requirements:* For doctorate, GRE General Test.

**The University of Texas Health Science Center at San Antonio,** Graduate School of Biomedical Sciences, Department of Cellular and Structural Biology, San Antonio, TX 78229-3900. Offers MS, PhD. *Degree requirements:* For master's, thesis; for doctorate, comprehensive exam, thesis/dissertation.

**The University of Texas Medical Branch,** Graduate School of Biomedical Sciences, Program in Biochemistry and Molecular Biology, Galveston, TX 77555. Offers biochemistry (PhD); bioinformatics (PhD); biophysics (PhD); cell biology (PhD); computational biology (PhD); structural biology (PhD). *Degree requirements:* For doctorate, thesis/dissertation. *Entrance requirements:* Additional exam requirements/recommendations for international students: required—TOEFL (minimum score 550 paper-based). Electronic applications accepted.

**University of Washington,** Graduate School, School of Medicine, Graduate Programs in Medicine, Department of Biological Structure, Seattle, WA 98195. Offers PhD. *Degree requirements:* For doctorate, thesis/dissertation.

**Weill Cornell Medicine,** Weill Cornell Graduate School of Medical Sciences, Biochemistry, Cell and Molecular Biology Allied Program, New York, NY 10065. Offers MS, PhD. Terminal master's awarded for partial completion of doctoral program. *Degree requirements:* For master's, comprehensive exam; for doctorate, thesis/dissertation, final exam. *Entrance requirements:* For doctorate, GRE General Test, background in genetics, molecular biology, chemistry, or biochemistry. Additional exam requirements/recommendations for international students: required—TOEFL. Electronic applications accepted.

# Section 7
# Computational, Systems, and Translational Biology

This section contains a directory of institutions offering graduate work in computational, systems, and translational biology. Additional information about programs listed in the directory may be obtained by writing directly to the dean of a graduate school or chair of a department at the address given in the directory.

## CONTENTS

**Program Directories**

# Computational Biology

**Albert Einstein College of Medicine,** Graduate Programs in the Biomedical Sciences, Department of Systems and Computational Biology, Bronx, NY 10461. Offers PhD.

**Baylor College of Medicine,** Graduate School of Biomedical Sciences, Program in Structural and Computational Biology and Molecular Biophysics, Houston, TX 77030-3498. Offers PhD, MD/PhD. *Degree requirements:* For doctorate, thesis/dissertation, public defense. *Entrance requirements:* For doctorate, GRE General Test, GRE Subject Test (strongly recommended), minimum GPA of 3.0. Additional exam requirements/recommendations for international students: required—TOEFL. Electronic applications accepted.

**Carnegie Mellon University,** Joint CMU-Pitt PhD Program in Computational Biology, Pittsburgh, PA 15213-3891. Offers PhD.

**Carnegie Mellon University,** Mellon College of Science, Department of Biological Sciences, Program in Computational Biology, Pittsburgh, PA 15213-3891. Offers MS. *Entrance requirements:* For master's, GRE General Test, GRE Subject Test, interview.

**Claremont Graduate University,** Graduate Programs, Institute of Mathematical Sciences, Claremont, CA 91711-6160. Offers computational and systems biology (PhD); computational mathematics and numerical analysis (MA, MS); computational science (PhD); engineering and industrial applied mathematics (PhD); mathematics (PhD); operations research and statistics (MA, MS); physical applied mathematics (MA, MS); pure mathematics (MA, MS); scientific computing (MA, MS); systems and control theory (MA, MS). *Program availability:* Part-time. Terminal master's awarded for partial completion of doctoral program. *Entrance requirements:* For master's and doctorate, GRE General Test. Additional exam requirements/recommendations for international students: required—TOEFL (minimum score 75 iBT). Electronic applications accepted.

**Cornell University,** Graduate School, Graduate Fields of Agriculture and Life Sciences, Field of Computational Biology, Ithaca, NY 14853. Offers computational behavioral biology (PhD); computational biology (PhD); computational cell biology (PhD); computational ecology (PhD); computational genetics (PhD); computational macromolecular biology (PhD); computational organismal biology (PhD). *Degree requirements:* For doctorate, comprehensive exam, thesis/dissertation, 2 semesters of teaching experience. *Entrance requirements:* For doctorate, GRE General Test, GRE Subject Test (biology), 2 letters of recommendation. Additional exam requirements/recommendations for international students: required—TOEFL (minimum score 550 paper-based; 77 iBT). Electronic applications accepted.

**Duke University,** Graduate School, Department of Computational Biology and Bioinformatics, Durham, NC 27708. Offers PhD, Certificate. *Degree requirements:* For doctorate, thesis/dissertation. *Entrance requirements:* For doctorate, GRE General Test. Additional exam requirements/recommendations for international students: required—TOEFL (minimum score 577 paper-based; 90 iBT) or IELTS (minimum score 7). Electronic applications accepted.

**George Mason University,** College of Science, School of Systems Biology, Manassas, VA 22030. Offers bioinformatics and computational biology (MS, PhD, Certificate); bioinformatics management (MS); biology (MS); biosciences (PhD). *Degree requirements:* For master's, comprehensive exam (for some programs), research project or thesis; for doctorate, comprehensive exam, thesis/dissertation. *Entrance requirements:* For master's, GRE, resume; 3 letters of recommendation; expanded goals statement; 2 copies of official transcripts; bachelor's degree in related field with minimum GPA of 3.0 in last 60 hours; for doctorate, GRE, self-assessment form; resume; 3 letters of recommendation; expanded goals statement; 2 copies of official transcripts; bachelor's degree in related field with minimum GPA of 3.0 in last 60 hours; for Certificate, resume; 2 copies of official transcripts. Additional exam requirements/recommendations for international students: required—TOEFL (minimum score 575 paper-based; 88 iBT), IELTS (minimum score 6.5), PTE (minimum score 59). Electronic applications accepted.

**Harvard University,** Harvard T.H. Chan School of Public Health, Master of Science Program in Computational Biology and Quantitative Genetics, Cambridge, MA 02138. Offers SM. *Students:* 23 full-time (14 women), 1 part-time (0 women); includes 4 minority (3 Asian, non-Hispanic/Latino; 1 Two or more races, non-Hispanic/Latino), 18 international. Average age 29. 59 applicants, 32% accepted, 13 enrolled. In 2019, 16 master's awarded. *Entrance requirements:* For master's, GRE. Additional exam requirements/recommendations for international students: recommended—TOEFL (minimum score 600 paper-based; 100 iBT), IELTS (minimum score 7). *Application deadline:* For fall admission, 12/1 for domestic and international students. Application fee: $140. Electronic applications accepted. *Financial support:* Application deadline: 2/15; applicants required to submit FAFSA. *Unit head:* Dr. John Quackenbush, Director, 617-582-8163. *Application contact:* Vincent W. James, Director of Admissions, 617-432-1031, Fax: 617-432-7080, E-mail: admissions@hsph.harvard.edu.
Website: http://www.hsph.harvard.edu/sm-computational-biology/

**Iowa State University of Science and Technology,** Bioinformatics and Computational Biology Program, Ames, IA 50011. Offers MS, PhD. *Degree requirements:* For doctorate, thesis/dissertation. *Entrance requirements:* For master's and doctorate, GRE General Test. Additional exam requirements/recommendations for international students: recommended—TOEFL, IELTS. Electronic applications accepted.

**Lewis University,** College of Aviation, Science and Technology, Program in Data Science, Romeoville, IL 60446. Offers computational biology and bioinformatics (MS); computer science (MS). *Program availability:* Part-time, evening/weekend, 100% online, blended/hybrid learning. *Students:* 22 full-time (6 women), 95 part-time (35 women); includes 33 minority (5 Black or African American, non-Hispanic/Latino; 11 Asian, non-Hispanic/Latino; 9 Hispanic/Latino; 2 Native Hawaiian or other Pacific Islander, non-Hispanic/Latino; 6 Two or more races, non-Hispanic/Latino), 10 international. Average age 33. *Entrance requirements:* For master's, bachelor's degree, undergraduate coursework in calculus, minimum undergraduate GPA of 3.0, resume, statement of purpose, two letters of recommendation. Additional exam requirements/recommendations for international students: required—TOEFL (minimum score 550 paper-based; 79 iBT), IELTS (minimum score 6). *Application deadline:* For fall admission, 5/1 priority date for international students; for winter admission, 11/1 priority date for international students. Applications are processed on a rolling basis. Application fee: $40. Electronic applications accepted. *Financial support:* Federal Work-Study and unspecified assistantships available. Financial award application deadline: 5/1; financial award applicants required to submit FAFSA. *Unit head:* Dr. Piotr Szczurek, Program Director. *Application contact:* Sheri Vilcek, Graduate Admissions Counselor, 815-836-5610, E-mail: grad@lewisu.edu.
Website: http://www.lewisu.edu/academics/data-science/index.htm

**Massachusetts Institute of Technology,** School of Engineering and School of Science, Program in Computational and Systems Biology, Cambridge, MA 02139. Offers PhD. *Degree requirements:* For doctorate, comprehensive exam, thesis/dissertation, teaching assistantship during one semester; training in the ethical conduct of research. *Entrance requirements:* For doctorate, GRE General Test. Additional exam requirements/recommendations for international students: required—TOEFL, IELTS. Electronic applications accepted.

**Massachusetts Institute of Technology,** School of Science, Department of Biology, Cambridge, MA 02139. Offers biochemistry (PhD); biological oceanography (PhD); biology (PhD); biophysical chemistry and molecular structure (PhD); cell biology (PhD); computational and systems biology (PhD); developmental biology (PhD); genetics (PhD); immunology (PhD); microbiology (PhD); molecular biology (PhD); neurobiology (PhD). *Degree requirements:* For doctorate, comprehensive exam, thesis/dissertation, teaching assistantship during two semesters. *Entrance requirements:* For doctorate, GRE General Test. Additional exam requirements/recommendations for international students: required—TOEFL, IELTS. Electronic applications accepted.

**New York University,** Graduate School of Arts and Science, Department of Biology, Program in Computational Biology, New York, NY 10012-1019. Offers PhD. *Entrance requirements:* For doctorate, GRE. Additional exam requirements/recommendations for international students: required—TOEFL, IELTS.

**Oregon Health & Science University,** School of Medicine, Graduate Programs in Medicine, Department of Medical Informatics and Clinical Epidemiology, Portland, OR 97239-3098. Offers bioinformatics and computational biology (MS, PhD); clinical informatics (MBI, MS, PhD, Certificate); health information management (Certificate). *Program availability:* Part-time, online learning. Terminal master's awarded for partial completion of doctoral program. *Degree requirements:* For master's, thesis or capstone project; for doctorate, comprehensive exam, thesis/dissertation, qualifying exam. *Entrance requirements:* For master's and doctorate, GRE General Test (minimum scores: 153 Verbal/148 Quantitative/4.5 Analytical), coursework in computer programming, human anatomy and physiology. Electronic applications accepted. *Expenses:* Contact institution.

**Oregon State University,** College of Agricultural Sciences, Program in Botany and Plant Pathology, Corvallis, OR 97331. Offers applied systematics (MS); ecology (MS, PhD); genetics (MS, PhD); genomics and computational biology (MS, PhD); molecular and cellular biology (MS, PhD); mycology (MS, PhD); plant pathology (MS, PhD); plant physiology (MS, PhD). *Entrance requirements:* For master's and doctorate, GRE.

**Oregon State University,** College of Engineering, Program in Bioengineering, Corvallis, OR 97331. Offers biomaterials (M Eng, MS, PhD); biomedical devices and instrumentation (M Eng, MS, PhD); human performance engineering (M Eng, MS, PhD); medical imaging (M Eng, MS, PhD); systems and computational biology (M Eng, MS, PhD). Electronic applications accepted. *Expenses:* Contact institution.

**Princeton University,** Graduate School, Department of Molecular Biology, Princeton, NJ 08544-1019. Offers PhD. *Degree requirements:* For doctorate, thesis/dissertation. *Entrance requirements:* For doctorate, GRE General Test. Additional exam requirements/recommendations for international students: required—TOEFL (minimum score 600 paper-based). Electronic applications accepted.

**Rutgers University - Camden,** Graduate School of Arts and Sciences, Program in Computational and Integrative Biology, Camden, NJ 08102-1401. Offers MS, PhD. *Degree requirements:* For doctorate, original research, oral defense. *Entrance requirements:* For master's and doctorate, GRE General Test; GRE Subject Test (recommended), transcripts, personal statement, three letters of recommendation. Additional exam requirements/recommendations for international students: required—TOEFL. Electronic applications accepted.

**Rutgers University - Newark,** Graduate School, Program in Computational Biology, Newark, NJ 07102. Offers MS. *Entrance requirements:* For master's, GRE, minimum undergraduate B average. Additional exam requirements/recommendations for international students: required—TOEFL.

**Rutgers University - New Brunswick,** Graduate School-New Brunswick, BioMaPS Institute for Quantitative Biology, Piscataway, NJ 08854-8097. Offers computational biology and molecular biophysics (PhD). *Degree requirements:* For doctorate, comprehensive exam, thesis/dissertation. *Entrance requirements:* For doctorate, GRE. Additional exam requirements/recommendations for international students: required—TOEFL. Electronic applications accepted.

**Saint Louis University,** Graduate Programs, College of Arts and Sciences, Department of Computer Science, St. Louis, MO 63103. Offers bioinformatics and computational biology (MS); computer science (MS); software engineering (MS).

**University of California, Irvine,** School of Biological Sciences, Program in Mathematical, Computational and Systems Biology, Irvine, CA 92697. Offers PhD. *Students:* 49 full-time (20 women); includes 12 minority (8 Asian, non-Hispanic/Latino; 4 Hispanic/Latino), 17 international. Average age 27. 139 applicants, 22% accepted, 12 enrolled. In 2019, 1 doctorate awarded. Application fee: $120 ($140 for international students). *Unit head:* Prof. John Lowengrub, Director, 949-824-8456, Fax: 949-824-7993, E-mail: jlowengr@uci.edu. *Application contact:* Aracely Dean, Assistant Administrative Analyst, 949-824-4120, Fax: 949-824-6444, E-mail: mcsb@uci.edu.
Website: http://mcsb.bio.uci.edu/

**University of Colorado Denver,** College of Liberal Arts and Sciences, Department of Mathematical and Statistical Sciences, Denver, CO 80217. Offers applied mathematics (MS, PhD), including applied mathematics, applied probability (MS), applied statistics (MS), computational biology (PhD), computational mathematics (PhD), discrete mathematics, finite geometry (PhD), mathematics education (PhD), mathematics of engineering and science (MS), numerical analysis, operations research (MS), optimization and operations research (PhD), probability (PhD), statistics (PhD). *Program availability:* Part-time. *Degree requirements:* For master's, comprehensive exam, thesis optional, 30 hours of course work with minimum GPA of 3.0; for doctorate, comprehensive exam, thesis/dissertation, 42 hours of course work with minimum GPA of 3.25. *Entrance requirements:* For master's, GRE General Test; GRE Subject Test in math (recommended), 30 hours of course work in mathematics (24 of which must be upper-division mathematics), bachelor's degree with minimum GPA of 3.0; for doctorate, GRE General Test; GRE Subject Test in math (recommended), 30 hours of course work in mathematics (24 of which must be upper-division mathematics), master's degree with minimum GPA of 3.25. Additional exam requirements/recommendations for international students: required—TOEFL (minimum score 537 paper-based; 75 iBT); recommended—IELTS (minimum score 6.5). Electronic applications accepted. Tuition and fees vary according to course load, program and reciprocity agreements.

**University of Colorado Denver,** School of Medicine, Program in Computational Bioscience, Aurora, CO 80045-0511. Offers PhD. *Program availability:* Part-time.

*Degree requirements:* For doctorate, comprehensive exam, thesis/dissertation, minimum of 30 semester credit hours each of course work and dissertation research. *Entrance requirements:* For doctorate, GRE General Test, GRE Subject Test in computer science (recommended), demonstrated adequate computational and biological backgrounds, interviews. Additional exam requirements/recommendations for international students: required—TOEFL (minimum score 550 paper-based; 80 iBT). Electronic applications accepted. Tuition and fees vary according to course load, program and reciprocity agreements.

**University of Idaho,** College of Graduate Studies, College of Science, Department of Bioinformatics and Computational Biology, Moscow, ID 83844-2282. Offers MS, PhD. *Faculty:* 15. *Students:* 18. Average age 29. In 2019, 3 master's, 4 doctorates awarded. *Degree requirements:* For master's, thesis; for doctorate, thesis/dissertation. *Entrance requirements:* For master's, GRE, minimum GPA of 3.0. Additional exam requirements/recommendations for international students: required—TOEFL (minimum score 100 iBT). *Application deadline:* For fall admission, 1/6 for domestic students; for spring admission, 9/1 for domestic students. Applications are processed on a rolling basis. Application fee: $60. Electronic applications accepted. *Expenses:* Tuition, state resident: full-time $7753.80; part-time $502 per credit hour. Tuition, nonresident: full-time $26,990; part-time $1571 per credit hour. *Required fees:* $2122.20; $47 per credit hour. *Financial support:* Applicants required to submit FAFSA. *Unit head:* Dr. David Tank, Director, 208-885-6010, E-mail: bcb@uidaho.edu. *Application contact:* Dr. David Tank, Director, 208-885-6010, E-mail: bcb@uidaho.edu.
Website: https://www.uidaho.edu/sci/bcb

**University of Illinois at Urbana-Champaign,** Graduate College, College of Liberal Arts and Sciences, School of Molecular and Cellular Biology, Center for Biophysics and Computational Biology, Champaign, IL 61820. Offers MS, PhD.

**The University of Iowa,** Graduate College, Program in Informatics, Iowa City, IA 52242-1316. Offers bioinformatics (MS, PhD); bioinformatics and computational biology (Certificate); geoinformatics (MS, PhD, Certificate); health informatics (MS, PhD, Certificate); information science (MS, PhD, Certificate). *Degree requirements:* For master's, thesis optional; for doctorate, comprehensive exam, thesis/dissertation. *Entrance requirements:* For master's and doctorate, GRE General Test, minimum GPA of 3.0. Additional exam requirements/recommendations for international students: required—TOEFL (minimum score 550 paper-based; 81 iBT). Electronic applications accepted.

**The University of Kansas,** Graduate Studies, College of Liberal Arts and Sciences, Department of Computational Biology, Lawrence, KS 66045. Offers PhD. *Students:* 15 full-time (5 women); includes 1 minority (Black or African American, non-Hispanic/Latino), 7 international. Average age 27. 12 applicants, 50% accepted, 4 enrolled. In 2019, 4 doctorates awarded. *Entrance requirements:* For doctorate, GRE, official transcripts of all undergraduate and graduate study completed, three letters of recommendation received directly from the persons writing them, resume or curriculum vitae, personal statement. Additional exam requirements/recommendations for international students: required—TOEFL. *Application deadline:* For fall admission, 6/1 for domestic and international students. Application fee: $65 ($85 for international students). Electronic applications accepted. *Expenses:* Tuition, state resident: full-time $9989. Tuition, nonresident: full-time $23,950. *International tuition:* $23,950 full-time. *Required fees:* $984; $81.99 per credit hour. Tuition and fees vary according to course load, campus/location and program. *Financial support:* Research assistantships, teaching assistantships, scholarships/grants, and unspecified assistantships available. *Unit head:* Susan Egan, Department Chair, 785-864-4294, E-mail: sme@ku.edu. *Application contact:* Debbie Douglass-Metsker, Office Manager, 785-864-1057, E-mail: douglass@ku.edu.
Website: http://www.bioinformatics.ku.edu/

**University of Maryland, College Park,** Academic Affairs, College of Computer, Mathematical and Natural Sciences, Department of Biology, PhD Program in Biological Sciences, College Park, MD 20742. Offers behavior, ecology, evolution, and systematics (PhD); computational biology, bioinformatics, and genomics (PhD); molecular and cellular biology (PhD); physiological systems (PhD). *Degree requirements:* For doctorate, comprehensive exam, thesis/dissertation, thesis work presentation in seminar. *Entrance requirements:* For doctorate, GRE General Test; GRE Subject Test in biology (recommended), academic transcripts, statement of purpose/research interests, 3 letters of recommendation. Additional exam requirements/recommendations for international students: required—TOEFL. Electronic applications accepted.

**University of Massachusetts Medical School,** Graduate School of Biomedical Sciences, Worcester, MA 01655. Offers biomedical sciences (PhD), including biochemistry and molecular pharmacology, bioinformatics and computational biology, cancer biology, immunology and microbiology, interdisciplinary, neuroscience, translational science; biomedical sciences (millennium program) (PhD); clinical and population health research (PhD); clinical investigation (MS). *Faculty:* 1,258 full-time (525 women), 372 part-time/adjunct (238 women). *Students:* 344 full-time (198 women), 1 (woman) part-time; includes 73 minority (12 Black or African American, non-Hispanic/Latino; 1 American Indian or Alaska Native, non-Hispanic/Latino; 45 Asian, non-Hispanic/Latino; 15 Hispanic/Latino), 120 international. Average age 29. 581 applicants, 23% accepted, 56 enrolled. In 2019, 6 master's, 49 doctorates awarded. Terminal master's awarded for partial completion of doctoral program. *Degree requirements:* For master's, comprehensive exam, thesis; for doctorate, comprehensive exam, thesis/dissertation. *Entrance requirements:* For master's, MD, PhD, DVM, or PharmD; for doctorate, bachelor's degree. Additional exam requirements/recommendations for international students: required—TOEFL, IELTS, TOEFL (minimum score 100 IBT) or IELTS (minimum score 7.0). *Application deadline:* For fall admission, 12/1 for domestic and international students. Applications are processed on a rolling basis. Application fee: $80. Electronic applications accepted. Application fee is waived when completed online. *Expenses:* Contact institution. *Financial support:* In 2019–20, 22 fellowships with full tuition reimbursements (averaging $33,061 per year), 322 research assistantships with full tuition reimbursements (averaging $32,850 per year) were awarded; institutionally sponsored loans and scholarships/grants also available. Financial award application deadline: 5/15. *Unit head:* Dr. Mary Ellen Lane, Dean, 508-856-4018, E-mail: maryellen.lane@umassmed.edu. *Application contact:* Dr. Kendall Knight, Assistant Vice Provost for Admissions, 508-856-5628, Fax: 508-856-3659, E-mail: kendall.knight@umassmed.edu.
Website: http://www.umassmed.edu/gsbs/

**University of Minnesota Rochester,** Graduate Programs, Rochester, MN 55904. Offers bioinformatics and computational biology (MS, PhD); business administration (MBA); occupational therapy (MOT). *Accreditation:* AOTA.

**The University of North Carolina at Chapel Hill,** School of Medicine and Graduate School, Biological and Biomedical Sciences Program, Curriculum in Bioinformatics and Computational Biology, Chapel Hill, NC 27599. Offers PhD. *Faculty:* 40 full-time (6 women). *Students:* 11 full-time (6 women); includes 2 minority (1 Black or African American, non-Hispanic/Latino; 1 Asian, non-Hispanic/Latino), 3 international. Average age 27. In 2019, 6 doctorates awarded. *Degree requirements:* For doctorate, comprehensive exam, thesis/dissertation. *Entrance requirements:* Additional exam requirements/recommendations for international students: required—TOEFL. *Application deadline:* For fall admission, 12/3 for domestic and international students. Applications are processed on a rolling basis. Application fee: $77. Electronic applications accepted. *Financial support:* In 2019–20, 2 fellowships with full tuition reimbursements (averaging $32,000 per year), 9 research assistantships with full tuition reimbursements (averaging $32,000 per year) were awarded; career-related internships or fieldwork, health care benefits, and tuition waivers (full) also available. *Unit head:* Dr. Will Valdar, Director, 919-843-2833, E-mail: william.valdar@unc.edu. *Application contact:* Jeffrey Steinbach, Assistant Director of Admissions, 919-843-7129, E-mail: jsteinba@email.unc.edu.
Website: http://bcb.unc.edu/

**University of Pennsylvania,** Perelman School of Medicine, Biomedical Graduate Studies, Graduate Group in Genomics and Computational Biology, Philadelphia, PA 19104. Offers PhD, MD/PhD, VMD/PhD. *Faculty:* 83 full-time (25 women). *Students:* 55 full-time (22 women); includes 22 minority (3 Black or African American, non-Hispanic/Latino; 18 Asian, non-Hispanic/Latino; 1 Two or more races, non-Hispanic/Latino), 12 international. 198 applicants, 11% accepted, 9 enrolled. In 2019, 6 doctorates awarded. *Unit head:* Dr. Ben Voight, Chairperson, 215-746-7015. *Application contact:* Maureen Kirsch, Graduate Coordinator, 215-746-2807.
Website: http://www.med.upenn.edu/gcb/

**University of Rochester,** School of Medicine and Dentistry, Graduate Programs in Medicine and Dentistry, Department of Biochemistry and Biophysics, Programs in Biophysics, Rochester, NY 14627. Offers biophysics, structural and computational biology (PhD). Terminal master's awarded for partial completion of doctoral program. *Degree requirements:* For doctorate, thesis/dissertation, qualifying exam. *Entrance requirements:* For doctorate, GRE General Test.

**University of Rochester,** School of Medicine and Dentistry, Graduate Programs in Medicine and Dentistry, Department of Biostatistics and Computational Biology, Programs in Statistics, Rochester, NY 14642. Offers bioinformatics and computational biology (PhD).

**University of Southern California,** Graduate School, Dana and David Dornsife College of Letters, Arts and Sciences, Department of Biological Sciences, Program in Molecular and Computational Biology, Los Angeles, CA 90089. Offers computational biology and bioinformatics (PhD); molecular biology (PhD). *Degree requirements:* For doctorate, comprehensive exam, thesis/dissertation, qualifying examination, dissertation defense. *Entrance requirements:* For doctorate, GRE, 3 letters of recommendation, personal statement, resume, minimum GPA of 3.0. Additional exam requirements/recommendations for international students: required—TOEFL (minimum score 600 paper-based; 100 iBT). Electronic applications accepted.

**University of South Florida,** Morsani College of Medicine and College of Graduate Studies, Graduate Programs in Medical Sciences, Tampa, FL 33620-9951. Offers bioinformatics and computational biology (MSBCB). *Faculty:* 1 (woman) full-time. *Students:* 355 full-time (207 women), 229 part-time (145 women); includes 283 minority (71 Black or African American, non-Hispanic/Latino; 2 American Indian or Alaska Native, non-Hispanic/Latino; 89 Asian, non-Hispanic/Latino; 103 Hispanic/Latino; 2 Native Hawaiian or other Pacific Islander, non-Hispanic/Latino; 16 Two or more races, non-Hispanic/Latino), 48 international. Average age 28. 898 applicants, 57% accepted, 323 enrolled. In 2019, 227 master's, 13 doctorates awarded. Terminal master's awarded for partial completion of doctoral program. *Degree requirements:* For master's, comprehensive exam, thesis; for doctorate, comprehensive exam, thesis/dissertation. *Entrance requirements:* For master's, GRE General Test or GMAT, bachelor's degree or equivalent from regionally-accredited university with minimum GPA of 3.0 in upper-division sciences coursework; prerequisites in general biology, general chemistry, general physics, organic chemistry, quantitative analysis, and integral and differential calculus; for doctorate, GRE General Test, bachelor's degree from regionally-accredited university with minimum GPA of 3.0 in upper-division sciences coursework; 3 letters of recommendation; personal interview; 1-2 page personal statement; prerequisites in biology, chemistry, physics, organic chemistry, quantitative analysis, and integral/differential calculus. Additional exam requirements/recommendations for international students: required—TOEFL (minimum score 550 paper-based; 79 iBT) or IELTS (minimum score 6.5). *Application deadline:* For fall admission, 2/1 priority date for domestic students, 2/1 for international students. Application fee: $30. Electronic applications accepted. *Expenses:* Contact institution. *Financial support:* In 2019–20, 106 students received support. *Unit head:* Dr. Michael Barber, Professor/Associate Dean for Graduate and Postdoctoral Affairs, 813-974-9908, Fax: 813-974-4317, E-mail: mbarber@health.usf.edu. *Application contact:* Dr. Eric Bennett, Graduate Director, PhD Program in Medical Sciences, 813-974-1545, Fax: 813-974-4317, E-mail: esbennet@health.usf.edu.
Website: http://health.usf.edu/nocms/medicine/graduatestudies/

**The University of Texas Medical Branch,** Graduate School of Biomedical Sciences, Program in Biochemistry and Molecular Biology, Galveston, TX 77555. Offers biochemistry (PhD); bioinformatics (PhD); biophysics (PhD); cell biology (PhD); computational biology (PhD); structural biology (PhD). *Degree requirements:* For doctorate, thesis/dissertation. *Entrance requirements:* Additional exam requirements/recommendations for international students: required—TOEFL (minimum score 550 paper-based). Electronic applications accepted.

**University of Wyoming,** Graduate Program in Molecular and Cellular Life Sciences, Laramie, WY 82071. Offers PhD. *Degree requirements:* For doctorate, thesis/dissertation, four eight-week laboratory rotations, comprehensive basic practical exam, two-part qualifying exam, seminars, symposium.

**Washington University in St. Louis,** The Graduate School, Division of Biology and Biomedical Sciences, Program in Computational and Systems Biology, St. Louis, MO 63130-4899. Offers PhD. *Degree requirements:* For doctorate, thesis/dissertation. *Entrance requirements:* For doctorate, GRE General Test, GRE Subject Test. Additional exam requirements/recommendations for international students: required—TOEFL. Electronic applications accepted.

**Wayne State University,** College of Engineering, Department of Computer Science, Detroit, MI 48202. Offers computer science (MS, PhD), including bioinformatics and computational biology (PhD); data science and business analytics (MS). *Faculty:* 23. *Students:* 97 full-time (41 women), 42 part-time (10 women); includes 15 minority (3 Black or African American, non-Hispanic/Latino; 9 Asian, non-Hispanic/Latino; 2 Hispanic/Latino; 1 Two or more races, non-Hispanic/Latino), 94 international. Average age 30. 276 applicants, 31% accepted, 30 enrolled. In 2019, 42 master's, 10 doctorates awarded. *Degree requirements:* For master's, thesis (for some programs), practicum (for MS in data science and business analytics); for doctorate, thesis/dissertation. *Entrance requirements:* For master's, GRE only for Data Science and Business Analytics degree, minimum GPA of 3.0, three letters of recommendation, adequate preparation in computer science and mathematics courses, personal statement, resume (for MS in data science and business analytics); for doctorate, GRE, bachelor's or master's degree in computer science or related field; minimum GPA of 3.3 in most recent degree; three letters of recommendation; personal statement; adequate preparation in computer

science and mathematics courses. Additional exam requirements/recommendations for international students: required—TOEFL (minimum score 550 paper-based; 79 iBT), TWE (minimum score 5.5); recommended—IELTS (minimum score 6.5). *Application deadline:* For fall admission, 6/1 priority date for domestic students, 5/1 priority date for international students; for winter admission, 10/1 priority date for domestic students, 9/1 priority date for international students; for spring admission, 2/1 priority date for domestic students, 1/2 priority date for international students. Applications are processed on a rolling basis. Application fee: $50. Electronic applications accepted. *Expenses:* In-state tuition: $790/credit hour; Out-of-state tuition: $1579/credit hour. MS degree is 30 credits; PhD degree is 90 credits. *Financial support:* In 2019–20, 92 students received support, including 4 fellowships with tuition reimbursements available (averaging $20,000 per year), 18 research assistantships with tuition reimbursements available (averaging $20,693 per year), 32 teaching assistantships with tuition reimbursements available (averaging $20,760 per year); scholarships/grants, health care benefits, and unspecified assistantships also available. Financial award application deadline: 2/17; financial award applicants required to submit FAFSA. *Unit head:* Dr. Loren Schwiebert, Chair, 313-577-5474, E-mail: loren@wayne.edu. *Application contact:* Robert Reynolds, Graduate Program Director, 313-577-0726, E-mail: csgradadvisor@cs.wayne.edu.
Website: http://engineering.wayne.edu/cs/

**Weill Cornell Medicine,** Weill Cornell Graduate School of Medical Sciences, Cornell/Weill Cornell/Sloan Kettering Tri-Institutional PhD Program in Computational Biology and Medicine, New York, NY 10065. Offers PhD. Terminal master's awarded for partial completion of doctoral program. *Degree requirements:* For doctorate, comprehensive exam, thesis/dissertation. *Entrance requirements:* For doctorate, GRE General Test, three letters of recommendation. Additional exam requirements/recommendations for international students: required—TOEFL. Electronic applications accepted.

**Worcester Polytechnic Institute,** Graduate Admissions, Program in Bioinformatics and Computational Biology, Worcester, MA 01609-2280. Offers bioinformatics & computational biology (PhD). *Program availability:* Evening/weekend. *Entrance requirements:* For master's and doctorate, GRE, 3 letters of recommendation, statement of purpose. Additional exam requirements/recommendations for international students: required—TOEFL (minimum score 563 paper-based; 84 iBT), IELTS (minimum score 7). Electronic applications accepted.

**Yale University,** Yale School of Medicine and Graduate School of Arts and Sciences, Combined Program in Biological and Biomedical Sciences (BBS), Computational Biology and Bioinformatics Track, New Haven, CT 06520. Offers PhD, MD/PhD. *Entrance requirements:* Additional exam requirements/recommendations for international students: required—TOEFL.

# Systems Biology

**Albert Einstein College of Medicine,** Graduate Programs in the Biomedical Sciences, Department of Systems and Computational Biology, Bronx, NY 10461. Offers PhD.

**George Mason University,** College of Science, School of Systems Biology, Manassas, VA 22030. Offers bioinformatics and computational biology (MS, PhD, Certificate); bioinformatics management (MS); biology (MS); biosciences (PhD). *Degree requirements:* For master's, comprehensive exam (for some programs), research project or thesis; for doctorate, comprehensive exam, thesis/dissertation. *Entrance requirements:* For master's, GRE, resume; 3 letters of recommendation; expanded goals statement; 2 copies of official transcripts; bachelor's degree in related field with minimum GPA of 3.0 in last 60 hours; for doctorate, GRE, self-assessment form; resume; 3 letters of recommendation; expanded goals statement; 2 copies of official transcripts; bachelor's degree in related field with minimum GPA of 3.0 in last 60 hours; for Certificate, resume; 2 copies of official transcripts. Additional exam requirements/recommendations for international students: required—TOEFL (minimum score 575 paper-based; 88 iBT), IELTS (minimum score 6.5), PTE (minimum score 59). Electronic applications accepted.

**The George Washington University,** Columbian College of Arts and Sciences, Institute for Biomedical Sciences, Program in Biochemistry and Systems Biology, Washington, DC 20037. Offers PhD. Terminal master's awarded for partial completion of doctoral program. *Degree requirements:* For doctorate, thesis/dissertation, general exam. *Entrance requirements:* For doctorate, GRE General Test, interview, minimum GPA of 3.0. Additional exam requirements/recommendations for international students: required—TOEFL (minimum score 600 paper-based). Electronic applications accepted.

**Harvard University,** Graduate School of Arts and Sciences, Department of Systems Biology, Cambridge, MA 02138. Offers PhD. *Degree requirements:* For doctorate, thesis/dissertation, lab rotation, qualifying examination. *Entrance requirements:* For doctorate, GRE. Additional exam requirements/recommendations for international students: required—TOEFL. Electronic applications accepted.

**Massachusetts Institute of Technology,** School of Engineering and School of Science, Program in Computational and Systems Biology, Cambridge, MA 02139. Offers PhD. *Degree requirements:* For doctorate, comprehensive exam, thesis/dissertation, teaching assistantship during one semester; training in the ethical conduct of research. *Entrance requirements:* For doctorate, GRE General Test. Additional exam requirements/recommendations for international students: required—TOEFL, IELTS. Electronic applications accepted.

**Michigan State University,** The Graduate School, College of Natural Science, Quantitative Biology Program, East Lansing, MI 48824. Offers PhD.

**Northwestern University,** The Graduate School, Interdisciplinary Biological Sciences Program (IBiS), Evanston, IL 60208. Offers biochemistry (PhD); bioengineering and biotechnology (PhD); biotechnology (PhD); cell and molecular biology (PhD); developmental and systems biology (PhD); nanotechnology (PhD); neurobiology (PhD); structural biology and biophysics (PhD). *Degree requirements:* For doctorate, thesis/dissertation, qualifying exam. *Entrance requirements:* For doctorate, GRE General Test. Additional exam requirements/recommendations for international students: required—TOEFL (minimum score 600 paper-based). Electronic applications accepted.

**Oregon State University,** College of Engineering, Program in Bioengineering, Corvallis, OR 97331. Offers biomaterials (M Eng, MS, PhD); biomedical devices and instrumentation (M Eng, MS, PhD); human performance engineering (M Eng, MS, PhD); medical imaging (M Eng, MS, PhD); systems and computational biology (M Eng, MS, PhD). Electronic applications accepted. *Expenses:* Contact institution.

**Purdue University,** College of Pharmacy and Graduate School, Graduate Programs in Pharmacy and Pharmacal Sciences, Department of Medicinal Chemistry and Molecular Pharmacology, West Lafayette, IN 47907. Offers biophysical and computational chemistry (PhD); cancer research (PhD); immunology and infectious disease (PhD); medicinal biochemistry and molecular biology (PhD); medicinal chemistry and chemical biology (PhD); molecular pharmacology (PhD); neuropharmacology, neurodegeneration, and neurotoxicity (PhD); systems biology and functional genomics (PhD). *Faculty:* 20 full-time (5 women), 7 part-time/adjunct (2 women). *Students:* 80 full-time (40 women), 2 part-time (0 women); includes 9 minority (5 Asian, non-Hispanic/Latino; 2 Hispanic/Latino; 2 Two or more races, non-Hispanic/Latino), 44 international. Average age 26. 162 applicants, 20% accepted, 15 enrolled. In 2019, 11 doctorates awarded. *Degree requirements:* For doctorate, thesis/dissertation. *Entrance requirements:* For doctorate, GRE General Test; GRE Subject Test in biology, biochemistry, and chemistry (recommended), minimum undergraduate GPA of 3.0. Additional exam requirements/recommendations for international students: required—TOEFL (minimum score 550 paper-based; 77 iBT); recommended—TWE. *Application deadline:* For fall admission, 2/1 for domestic and international students. Applications are processed on a rolling basis. Application fee: $60 ($75 for international students). Electronic applications accepted. *Financial support:* Fellowships, research assistantships, teaching assistantships, and traineeships available. Support available to part-time students. Financial award applicants required to submit FAFSA. *Unit head:* Zhong-Yin Zhang, Head, 765-494-1403, E-mail: zhang-yn@purdue.edu. *Application contact:* Delayne Graham, Graduate Contact, 765-494-1362, E-mail: dkgraham@purdue.edu.

**Rutgers University - New Brunswick,** Graduate School-New Brunswick, BioMaPS Institute for Quantitative Biology, Piscataway, NJ 08854-8097. Offers computational biology and molecular biophysics (PhD). *Degree requirements:* For doctorate, comprehensive exam, thesis/dissertation. *Entrance requirements:* For doctorate, GRE. Additional exam requirements/recommendations for international students: required—TOEFL. Electronic applications accepted.

**Stanford University,** School of Medicine, Graduate Programs in Medicine, Department of Chemical and Systems Biology, Stanford, CA 94305-2004. Offers PhD. *Expenses: Tuition:* Full-time $52,479; part-time $34,110 per unit. *Required fees:* $672; $224 per quarter. Tuition and fees vary according to program and student level.

**University of California, Irvine,** School of Biological Sciences, Program in Mathematical, Computational and Systems Biology, Irvine, CA 92697. Offers PhD. *Students:* 49 full-time (20 women); includes 12 minority (8 Asian, non-Hispanic/Latino; 4 Hispanic/Latino), 17 international. Average age 27. 139 applicants, 22% accepted, 12 enrolled. In 2019, 1 doctorate awarded. Application fee: $120 ($140 for international students). *Unit head:* Prof. John Lowengrub, Director, 949-824-8456, Fax: 949-824-7993, E-mail: jlowengr@uci.edu. *Application contact:* Aracely Dean, Assistant Administrative Analyst, 949-824-4120, Fax: 949-824-6444, E-mail: mcsb@uci.edu.
Website: http://mcsb.bio.uci.edu/

**University of California, Merced,** Graduate Division, School of Natural Sciences, Merced, CA 95343. Offers applied mathematics (MS, PhD); chemistry and chemical biology (MS, PhD); physics (MS, PhD); quantitative and systems biology (MS, PhD), including molecular and cellular biology (PhD). *Faculty:* 79 full-time (32 women). *Students:* 255 full-time (104 women), 1 (woman) part-time; includes 83 minority (5 Black or African American, non-Hispanic/Latino; 25 Asian, non-Hispanic/Latino; 44 Hispanic/Latino; 9 Two or more races, non-Hispanic/Latino), 77 international. Average age 28. 292 applicants, 43% accepted, 54 enrolled. In 2019, 13 master's, 23 doctorates awarded. Terminal master's awarded for partial completion of doctoral program. *Degree requirements:* For master's, variable foreign language requirement, comprehensive exam, thesis or alternative, oral defense; for doctorate, variable foreign language requirement, comprehensive exam, thesis/dissertation, oral defense. *Entrance requirements:* For master's and doctorate, GRE. Additional exam requirements/recommendations for international students: required—TOEFL (minimum score 550 paper-based; 80 iBT); recommended—IELTS (minimum score 6.5). *Application deadline:* For fall admission, 1/15 for domestic and international students. Application fee: $105 ($125 for international students). Electronic applications accepted. *Expenses: Tuition, area resident:* Full-time $11,442; part-time $5721 per semester. Tuition, state resident: full-time $11,442; part-time $5721 per semester. Tuition, nonresident: full-time $26,544; part-time $13,272 per semester. *International tuition:* $26,544 full-time. *Required fees:* $564 per semester. *Financial support:* In 2019–20, 233 students received support, including 9 fellowships with full tuition reimbursements available (averaging $22,005 per year), 56 research assistantships with full tuition reimbursements available (averaging $21,420 per year), 168 teaching assistantships with full tuition reimbursements available (averaging $21,911 per year); scholarships/grants, traineeships, and health care benefits also available. *Unit head:* Dr. Elizabeth Dumont, Dean, 209-228-4487, Fax: 209-228-4060, E-mail: edumont@ucmerced.edu. *Application contact:* Tsu Ya, Director of Graduate Admissions and Academic Services, 209-228-4521, Fax: 209-228-6906, E-mail: tya@ucmerced.edu.

**University of California, San Diego,** Graduate Division, Program in Bioinformatics and Systems Biology, La Jolla, CA 92093. Offers PhD. *Students:* 67 full-time (23 women), 1 part-time (0 women). 296 applicants, 10% accepted, 13 enrolled. In 2019, 10 doctorates awarded. *Degree requirements:* For doctorate, comprehensive exam, thesis/dissertation, two quarters as teaching assistant. *Entrance requirements:* For doctorate, GRE General Test. Additional exam requirements/recommendations for international students: required—TOEFL (minimum score 550 paper-based; 80 iBT), IELTS (minimum score 7). *Application deadline:* For fall admission, 12/10 for domestic students. Application fee: $105 ($125 for international students). Electronic applications accepted. *Financial support:* Fellowships, research assistantships, teaching assistantships, scholarships/grants, and traineeships available. Financial award applicants required to submit FAFSA. *Unit head:* Trey Ideker, Director, 858-822-4558, E-mail: tideker@ucsd.edu. *Application contact:* Savannah Orosco, Graduate Coordinator, 858-822-0831, E-mail: bioinfo@ucsd.edu.
Website: http://bioinformatics.ucsd.edu/

**University of Chicago,** Division of the Biological Sciences, Committee on Genetics, Genomics and Systems Biology, Chicago, IL 60637. Offers PhD. *Degree requirements:* For doctorate, thesis/dissertation, ethics class, 2 teaching assistantships, preliminary exam. *Entrance requirements:* For doctorate, GRE General Test, transcripts, statement of purpose, 3 letters of recommendation. Additional exam requirements/recommendations for international students: required—TOEFL (minimum score 600 paper-based; 104 iBT), IELTS (minimum score 7). Electronic applications accepted.

**University of Cincinnati,** Graduate School, College of Medicine, Systems Biology and Physiology Graduate Program, Cincinnati, OH 45221. Offers PhD. *Entrance requirements:* Additional exam requirements/recommendations for international students: required—TOEFL (minimum score 80 iBT) or IELTS (minimum score 6.5).

**University of Colorado Denver,** College of Liberal Arts and Sciences, Department of Integrative Biology, Denver, CO 80217. Offers biology (MS); integrative and systems biology (PhD). *Program availability:* Part-time. *Degree requirements:* For master's, comprehensive exam, thesis, 30-32 credit hours; for doctorate, comprehensive exam, thesis/dissertation. *Entrance requirements:* For master's, GRE General Test (minimum score in 50th percentile in each section), BA/BS from accredited institution awarded within the last 10 years; minimum undergraduate GPA of 3.0; prerequisite courses: 1 year each of general biology and general chemistry; 1 semester each of general genetics, general ecology, and cell biology; and a structure/function course; for doctorate, GRE, minimum undergraduate GPA of 3.2, three letters of recommendation, official transcripts from all universities and colleges attended. Additional exam requirements/recommendations for international students: required—TOEFL (minimum score 537 paper-based; 75 iBT); recommended—IELTS (minimum score 6.5). Electronic applications accepted. Tuition and fees vary according to course load, program and reciprocity agreements.

**University of Pittsburgh,** School of Medicine, Graduate Programs in Medicine and Kenneth P. Dietrich School of Arts and Sciences, Integrative Systems Biology Program, Pittsburgh, PA 15260. Offers PhD. *Degree requirements:* For doctorate, comprehensive exam, thesis/dissertation. *Entrance requirements:* For doctorate, GRE, minimum GPA of 3.7, 3 letters of recommendation, baccalaureate degree in natural or physical science or engineering program, personal statement. Additional exam requirements/recommendations for international students: required—TOEFL (minimum score 700 paper-based; 100 iBT), IELTS (minimum score 7). Electronic applications accepted. *Expenses:* Contact institution.

**University of Toronto,** School of Graduate Studies, Faculty of Arts and Science, Department of Cell and Systems Biology, Toronto, ON M5S 1A1, Canada. Offers M Sc, PhD. *Degree requirements:* For master's, thesis, thesis defense; for doctorate, thesis/dissertation, thesis defense, oral thesis examination. *Entrance requirements:* For master's, minimum B+ average in final year, B overall, 3 letters of reference. Additional exam requirements/recommendations for international students: required—TOEFL (minimum score 580 paper-based; 93 iBT), TWE (minimum score 5). Electronic applications accepted.

**Virginia Commonwealth University,** Graduate School, School of Life Sciences, Doctoral Program in Integrative Life Sciences, Richmond, VA 23284-9005. Offers PhD. *Entrance requirements:* For doctorate, GRE, minimum GPA of 3.0 in last 60 credits of undergraduate work or in graduate degree, 3 letters of recommendation. Additional exam requirements/recommendations for international students: required—TOEFL (minimum score 600 paper-based; 100 iBT). Electronic applications accepted.

**Washington University in St. Louis,** The Graduate School, Division of Biology and Biomedical Sciences, Program in Computational and Systems Biology, St. Louis, MO 63130-4899. Offers PhD. *Degree requirements:* For doctorate, thesis/dissertation. *Entrance requirements:* For doctorate, GRE General Test, GRE Subject Test. Additional exam requirements/recommendations for international students: required—TOEFL. Electronic applications accepted.

**Weill Cornell Medicine,** Weill Cornell Graduate School of Medical Sciences, Physiology, Biophysics and Systems Biology Program, New York, NY 10065. Offers MS, PhD. Terminal master's awarded for partial completion of doctoral program. *Degree requirements:* For master's, comprehensive exam; for doctorate, thesis/dissertation, final exam. *Entrance requirements:* For doctorate, GRE General Test, introductory courses in biology, inorganic and organic chemistry, physics, and mathematics. Additional exam requirements/recommendations for international students: required—TOEFL.

# Translational Biology

**Baylor College of Medicine,** Graduate School of Biomedical Sciences, Program in Translational Biology and Molecular Medicine, Houston, TX 77030-3498. Offers PhD. *Degree requirements:* For doctorate, thesis/dissertation, public defense. *Entrance requirements:* For doctorate, GRE, minimum GPA of 3.0. Additional exam requirements/recommendations for international students: required—TOEFL. Electronic applications accepted.

**Boston University,** School of Medicine, Graduate Medical Sciences, Program in Molecular and Translational Medicine, Boston, MA 02215. Offers PhD, MD/PhD. *Application deadline:* For fall admission, 1/15 for domestic students; for spring admission, 10/15 for domestic students. *Unit head:* Dr. Matt Jones, Director, E-mail: mattj@bu.edu. *Application contact:* Cassandra Kocek, Program Administrator, 617-358-0285, E-mail: gmsbusm@bu.edu. Website: http://www.bumc.bu.edu/gms/mtm/

**Cedars-Sinai Medical Center,** Graduate Programs, Los Angeles, CA 90048. Offers biomedical and translational sciences (PhD); magnetic resonance in medicine (MS). *Degree requirements:* For doctorate, comprehensive exam, thesis/dissertation. *Entrance requirements:* For doctorate, GRE, 3 letters of recommendation. Additional exam requirements/recommendations for international students: required—TOEFL (minimum score 550 paper-based; 80 iBT), IELTS (minimum score 6.5). Electronic applications accepted.

**Rutgers University - New Brunswick,** Graduate School of Biomedical Sciences, Program in Clinical and Translational Science, Piscataway, NJ 08854-8097. Offers MS. *Program availability:* Part-time. *Degree requirements:* For master's, thesis.

**University of California, Irvine,** School of Medicine, Program in Biomedical and Translational Science, Irvine, CA 92697. Offers MS. *Students:* 14 full-time (7 women); includes 7 minority (1 Black or African American, non-Hispanic/Latino; 5 Asian, non-Hispanic/Latino; 1 Hispanic/Latino), 2 international. Average age 30. 24 applicants, 58% accepted, 11 enrolled. In 2019, 10 master's awarded. *Entrance requirements:* For master's, curriculum vitae. *Application deadline:* For fall admission, 1/15 priority date for domestic students. Application fee: $120 ($140 for international students). *Unit head:* Dr. Sherrie Kaplan, Director, 949-824-0095. *Application contact:* Dr. Sherrie Kaplan, Director, 949-824-0095. Website: http://www.som.uci.edu/bats/education/ms-degree.asp

**The University of Iowa,** Graduate College, Program in Translational Biomedicine, Iowa City, IA 52242-1316. Offers MS, PhD. Terminal master's awarded for partial completion of doctoral program. *Degree requirements:* For master's, comprehensive exam; for doctorate, comprehensive exam, thesis/dissertation. *Entrance requirements:* For master's and doctorate, minimum GPA of 3.0. Additional exam requirements/recommendations for international students: required—TOEFL (minimum score 550 paper-based; 81 iBT). Electronic applications accepted.

**University of Massachusetts Medical School,** Graduate School of Biomedical Sciences, Worcester, MA 01655. Offers biomedical sciences (PhD), including biochemistry and molecular pharmacology, bioinformatics and computational biology, cancer biology, immunology and microbiology, interdisciplinary, neuroscience, translational science; biomedical sciences (millennium program) (PhD); clinical and population health research (PhD); clinical investigation (MS). *Faculty:* 1,258 full-time (525 women), 372 part-time/adjunct (238 women). *Students:* 344 full-time (198 women), 1 (woman) part-time; includes 73 minority (12 Black or African American, non-Hispanic/Latino; 1 American Indian or Alaska Native, non-Hispanic/Latino; 45 Asian, non-Hispanic/Latino; 15 Hispanic/Latino), 120 international. Average age 29. 581 applicants, 23% accepted, 56 enrolled. In 2019, 6 master's, 49 doctorates awarded. Terminal master's awarded for partial completion of doctoral program. *Degree requirements:* For master's, comprehensive exam, thesis; for doctorate, comprehensive exam, thesis/dissertation. *Entrance requirements:* For master's, MD, PhD, DVM, or PharmD; for doctorate, bachelor's degree. Additional exam requirements/recommendations for international students: required—TOEFL, IELTS, TOEFL (minimum score 100 IBT) or IELTS (minimum score 7.0). *Application deadline:* For fall admission, 12/1 for domestic and international students. Applications are processed on a rolling basis. Application fee: $80. Electronic applications accepted. Application fee is waived when completed online. *Expenses:* Contact institution. *Financial support:* In 2019–20, 22 fellowships with full tuition reimbursements (averaging $33,061 per year), 322 research assistantships with full tuition reimbursements (averaging $32,850 per year) were awarded; institutionally sponsored loans and scholarships/grants also available. Financial award application deadline: 5/15. *Unit head:* Dr. Mary Ellen Lane, Dean, 508-856-4018, E-mail: maryellen.lane@umassmed.edu. *Application contact:* Dr. Kendall Knight, Assistant Vice Provost for Admissions, 508-856-5628, Fax: 508-856-3659, E-mail: kendall.knight@umassmed.edu. Website: http://www.umassmed.edu/gsbs/

**The University of Texas at San Antonio,** Joint PhD Program in Translational Science, San Antonio, TX 78249-0617. Offers PhD. *Program availability:* Part-time. *Degree requirements:* For doctorate, comprehensive exam, thesis/dissertation. *Entrance requirements:* For doctorate, GRE General Test, official transcripts, copy of U.S. medical license/certificate, criminal background check, resume or curriculum vitae, 3 letters of recommendation, statement of purpose. Additional exam requirements/recommendations for international students: required—TOEFL (minimum score 565 paper-based; 86 iBT), IELTS (minimum score 6.5). Electronic applications accepted. *Expenses:* Contact institution.

**The University of Texas Medical Branch,** Graduate School of Biomedical Sciences, Program in Human Pathophysiology and Translational Medicine, Galveston, TX 77555. Offers MS, PhD. *Degree requirements:* For master's, thesis or alternative; for doctorate, thesis/dissertation. *Entrance requirements:* For master's and doctorate, GRE General Test. Additional exam requirements/recommendations for international students: required—TOEFL (minimum score 550 paper-based). Electronic applications accepted.

**Virginia Polytechnic Institute and State University,** Graduate School, Intercollege, Blacksburg, VA 24061. Offers genetics, bioinformatics, and computational biology (PhD); information technology (MIT); macromolecular science and engineering (MS, PhD); translational biology, medicine, and health (PhD). *Students:* 203 full-time (86 women), 745 part-time (218 women); includes 278 minority (64 Black or African American, non-Hispanic/Latino; 119 Asian, non-Hispanic/Latino; 59 Hispanic/Latino; 1 Native Hawaiian or other Pacific Islander, non-Hispanic/Latino; 35 Two or more races, non-Hispanic/Latino), 93 international. Average age 33. 603 applicants, 78% accepted, 327 enrolled. In 2019, 138 master's, 20 doctorates awarded. *Degree requirements:* For master's, comprehensive exam (for some programs), thesis (for some programs); for doctorate, comprehensive exam (for some programs), thesis/dissertation (for some programs). *Entrance requirements:* For master's and doctorate, GRE/GMAT. Additional exam requirements/recommendations for international students: required—TOEFL (minimum score 90 iBT). *Application deadline:* For fall admission, 8/1 for domestic students, 4/1 for international students; for spring admission, 1/1 for domestic students, 9/1 for international students. Applications are processed on a rolling basis. Application fee: $75. Electronic applications accepted. *Expenses:* Tuition, state resident: full-time $13,700; part-time $761.25 per credit hour. Tuition, nonresident: full-time $27,614; part-time $1534 per credit hour. *Required fees:* $886.50 per term. Tuition and fees vary according to campus/location and program. *Financial support:* In 2019–20, 4 fellowships with full and partial tuition reimbursements (averaging $17,088 per year), 153 research assistantships with full tuition reimbursements (averaging $23,076 per year), 27 teaching assistantships with full tuition reimbursements (averaging $19,900 per year) were awarded; scholarships/grants also available. Financial award application deadline: 3/1; financial award applicants required to submit FAFSA. *Unit head:* Dr. Karen P. DePauw, Vice President and Dean for Graduate Education, 540-231-7581, Fax: 540-231-1670, E-mail: kpdepauw@vt.edu. *Application contact:* Dr. Janice Austin, 540-231-6691, E-mail: grads@vt.edu.

**Wake Forest University,** School of Medicine and Graduate School of Arts and Sciences, Graduate Programs in Medicine, Program in Molecular Medicine and Translational Science, Winston-Salem, NC 27109. Offers MS, PhD, MD/PhD. *Degree requirements:* For master's, thesis; for doctorate, thesis/dissertation. *Entrance requirements:* For master's and doctorate, GRE General Test. Additional exam requirements/recommendations for international students: required—TOEFL. Electronic applications accepted.

# Section 8
# Ecology, Environmental Biology, and Evolutionary Biology

This section contains a directory of institutions offering graduate work in ecology, environmental biology. Additional information about programs listed in the directory may be obtained by writing directly to the dean of a graduate school or chair of a department at the address given in the directory.

For programs offering related work, see also in this book *Biological and Biomedical Sciences; Botany and Plant Biology; Entomology; Genetics, Developmental Biology, and Reproductive Biology; Microbiological Sciences; Pharmacology and Toxicology; Public Health;* and *Zoology.* In the other guides in this series:

**Graduate Programs in the Humanities, Arts & Social Sciences**

See *Sociology, Anthropology, and Archaeology*

**Graduate Programs in the Physical Sciences, Mathematics, Agricultural Sciences, the Environment & Natural Resources**

See *Agricultural and Food Sciences, Geosciences, Marine Sciences and Oceanography,* and *Mathematical Sciences*

**Graduate Programs in Engineering & Applied Sciences**

See *Civil and Environmental Engineering, Management of Engineering and Technology,* and *Ocean Engineering*

## CONTENTS

# Conservation Biology

**Antioch University New England,** Graduate School, Department of Environmental Studies, Keene, NH 03431-3552. Offers advocacy for social justice and sustainability (MS); conservation biology (MS); environmental education (MS); environmental studies (PhD); resource management and conservation (MS); science teacher certification (MS); self-designed studies (MS); sustainable development and climate change (MS). *Faculty:* 3 full-time (1 woman), 6 part-time/adjunct (3 women). *Students:* 120 full-time (88 women), 75 part-time (49 women); includes 21 minority (3 Black or African American, non-Hispanic/Latino; 6 Asian, non-Hispanic/Latino; 10 Hispanic/Latino; 1 Native Hawaiian or other Pacific Islander, non-Hispanic/Latino; 1 Two or more races, non-Hispanic/Latino), 7 international. Average age 36. 81 applicants, 98% accepted, 54 enrolled. In 2019, 108 master's, 10 doctorates awarded. *Degree requirements:* For master's, practicum; for doctorate, thesis/dissertation, practicum. *Entrance requirements:* Additional exam requirements/recommendations for international students: required—TOEFL (minimum score 550 paper-based). *Application deadline:* For fall admission, 7/1 for domestic students, 6/1 for international students; for spring admission, 12/1 for domestic and international students. Applications are processed on a rolling basis. Application fee: $50. Electronic applications accepted. *Expenses:* Contact institution. *Financial support:* Applicants required to submit FAFSA. *Unit head:* Dr. Michael Simpson, Chairperson, 603-283-2331, Fax: 603-357-0718, E-mail: msimpson@antioch.edu. *Application contact:* Jennifer Fritz, Director of Admissions, 800-552-8380, Fax: 603-357-0718, E-mail: admissions.ane@antioch.edu. Website: http://www.antiochne.edu/environmental-studies/

**Arizona State University at Tempe,** College of Liberal Arts and Sciences, School of Life Sciences, Tempe, AZ 85287-4601. Offers animal behavior (PhD); applied ethics (biomedical and health ethics) (MA); biology (MS, PhD), including biology, biology and society, complex adaptive systems science (PhD), plant biology and conservation (MS); environmental life sciences (PhD); evolutionary biology (PhD); history and philosophy of science (PhD); human and social dimensions of science and technology (PhD); microbiology (PhD); molecular and cellular biology (PhD); neuroscience (PhD). Terminal master's awarded for partial completion of doctoral program. *Degree requirements:* For master's, thesis (for some programs), interactive Program of Study (iPOS) submitted before completing 50 percent of required credit hours; for doctorate, variable foreign language requirement, comprehensive exam, thesis/dissertation, interactive Program of Study (iPOS) submitted before completing 50 percent of required credit hours. *Entrance requirements:* For master's and doctorate, GRE, minimum GPA of 3.0 or equivalent in last 2 years of work leading to bachelor's degree. Additional exam requirements/recommendations for international students: required—TOEFL (minimum score 600 paper-based; 100 iBT). Electronic applications accepted.

**California State University, Sacramento,** College of Natural Sciences and Mathematics, Department of Biological Sciences, Sacramento, CA 95819. Offers biological conservation (MS); molecular and cellular biology (MS); stem cell (MA). *Program availability:* Part-time. *Students:* 38 full-time (12 women), 24 part-time (8 women); includes 19 minority (14 Asian, non-Hispanic/Latino; 4 Hispanic/Latino; 1 Native Hawaiian or other Pacific Islander, non-Hispanic/Latino), 1 international. Average age 29. 68 applicants, 44% accepted, 23 enrolled. In 2019, 13 master's awarded. *Degree requirements:* For master's, comprehensive exam (for some programs), thesis (for some programs), thesis or project; writing proficiency exam. *Entrance requirements:* For master's, GRE, bachelor's degree in biology or equivalent; minimum GPA of 2.75 in all biology courses, 3.0 in all upper-division biology courses. Additional exam requirements/recommendations for international students: required—TOEFL (minimum score 550 paper-based; 80 iBT); recommended—IELTS (minimum score 7). *Application deadline:* For fall admission, 2/1 for domestic students, 1/1 for international students. Applications are processed on a rolling basis. Application fee: $70. Electronic applications accepted. *Expenses:* Contact institution. *Financial support:* Teaching assistantships, career-related internships or fieldwork, Federal Work-Study, and scholarships/grants available. Support available to part-time students. Financial award application deadline: 3/1; financial award applicants required to submit FAFSA. *Unit head:* Dr. Shannon Datwyler, Chair, 916-278-6535, Fax: 916-278-6993, E-mail: datwyler@csus.edu. *Application contact:* Jose Martinez, Graduate Admissions Supervisor, 916-278-7871, E-mail: martinj@skymail.csus.edu. Website: http://www.csus.edu/bios

**California State University, Stanislaus,** College of Natural Sciences, MS Program in Ecology and Sustainability, Turlock, CA 95382. Offers ecological conservation (MS). *Program availability:* Part-time. *Degree requirements:* For master's, thesis. *Entrance requirements:* For master's, GRE, minimum GPA of 3.0, 3 letters of recommendation, personal statement. Additional exam requirements/recommendations for international students: required—TOEFL (minimum score 550 paper-based). Electronic applications accepted.

**Central Michigan University,** College of Graduate Studies, College of Science and Engineering, Department of Biology, Mount Pleasant, MI 48859. Offers biology (MS); conservation biology (MS). *Faculty:* 42 full-time (17 women). *Students:* 8 full-time (6 women), 40 part-time (19 women); includes 5 minority (2 Hispanic/Latino; 3 Two or more races, non-Hispanic/Latino), 7 international. Average age 26. 53 applicants, 62% accepted, 20 enrolled. In 2019, 24 master's awarded. *Degree requirements:* For master's, thesis optional, Plan A requires 30 credits and a thesis. *Entrance requirements:* Additional exam requirements/recommendations for international students: required—This section should be directed towards Admissions Processing as these are their requirements. *Application deadline:* For fall admission, 2/1 for domestic and international students; for spring admission, 10/1 for domestic and international students. Applications are processed on a rolling basis. Application fee: $50. *Expenses: Tuition, area resident:* Full-time $12,267; part-time $8178 per year. *Tuition, state resident:* full-time $12,267; part-time $8178 per year. *Tuition, nonresident:* full-time $12,267; part-time $8178 per year. *International tuition:* $16,110 full-time. *Required fees:* $225 per semester. Tuition and fees vary according to degree level and program. *Financial support:* In 2019–20, 32 students received support, including 18 research assistantships with full tuition reimbursements available (averaging $13,900 per year), 21 teaching assistantships with full tuition reimbursements available (averaging $13,900 per year). Financial award application deadline: 2/1. *Unit head:* Dr. Tracy Galarowicz, 989-774-3227, Fax: 989-774-3462, E-mail: galar1tl@cmich.edu. *Application contact:* Dr. Tom Gehring, 989-774-3227, Fax: 989-774-3462, E-mail: gehri1tm@cmich.edu. Website: www.cmich.edu

**Colorado State University,** Warner College of Natural Resources, Department of Fish, Wildlife, and Conservation Biology, Fort Collins, CO 80523-1474. Offers MFWCB, MS, PhD. *Program availability:* 100% online. *Degree requirements:* For master's, comprehensive exam, thesis (for some programs); for doctorate, comprehensive exam, thesis/dissertation. *Entrance requirements:* For master's, GRE, minimum cumulative undergraduate GPA of 3.0; faculty advisor; statement of purpose; related degree; 2

years of relevant employment (for online program); for doctorate, GRE, minimum cumulative undergraduate GPA of 3.0; faculty advisor; statement of purpose; related degree. Additional exam requirements/recommendations for international students: required—TOEFL (minimum score 550 paper-based; 79 iBT), IELTS (minimum score 6.5). Electronic applications accepted. *Expenses:* Contact institution.

**Columbia University,** Graduate School of Arts and Sciences, New York, NY 10027. Offers African-American studies (MA); American studies (MA); anthropology (MA, PhD); art history and archaeology (MA, PhD); astronomy (PhD); biological sciences (PhD); biotechnology (MA); chemical physics (PhD); chemistry (PhD); classical studies (MA, PhD); classics (MA, PhD); climate and society (MA); conservation biology (MA); earth and environmental sciences (PhD); East Asia: regional studies (MA); East Asian languages and cultures (MA, PhD); ecology, evolution and environmental biology (MA), including conservation biology; ecology, evolution, and environmental biology (PhD), including ecology and evolutionary biology, evolutionary primatology; economics (MA, PhD); English and comparative literature (MA, PhD); French and Romance philology (MA, PhD); Germanic languages (MA, PhD); global French studies (MA); global thought (MA); Hispanic cultural studies (MA); history (PhD); history and literature (MA); human rights studies (MA); Islamic studies (MA); Italian (MA, PhD); Japanese pedagogy (MA); Jewish studies (MA); Latin America and the Caribbean: regional studies (MA); Latin American and Iberian cultures (PhD); mathematics (MA, PhD), including finance (MA); medieval and Renaissance studies (MA); Middle Eastern, South Asian, and African studies (MA, PhD); modern art: critical and curatorial studies (MA); modern European studies (MA); museum anthropology (MA); music (DMA, PhD); oral history (MA); philosophical foundations of physics (MA); philosophy (MA, PhD); physics (PhD); political science (MA, PhD); psychology (PhD); quantitative methods in the social sciences (MA); religion (MA, PhD); Russia, Eurasia and East Europe: regional studies (MA); Russian translation (MA); Slavic cultures (MA); Slavic languages (MA, PhD); sociology (MA, PhD); South Asian studies (MA); statistics (MA, PhD); theatre (PhD). *Program availability:* Part-time. *Students:* 3,506 full-time (1,844 women), 208 part-time (121 women); includes 864 minority (110 Black or African American, non-Hispanic/Latino; 5 American Indian or Alaska Native, non-Hispanic/Latino; 416 Asian, non-Hispanic/Latino; 147 Hispanic/Latino; 6 Native Hawaiian or other Pacific Islander, non-Hispanic/Latino; 180 Two or more races, non-Hispanic/Latino), 2,065 international. 14,545 applicants, 25% accepted, 1,429 enrolled. In 2019, 1,262 master's, 363 doctorates awarded. Terminal master's awarded for partial completion of doctoral program. *Degree requirements:* For master's, variable foreign language requirement, comprehensive exam (for some programs), thesis (for some programs); for doctorate, variable foreign language requirement, comprehensive exam (for some programs), thesis/dissertation. *Entrance requirements:* For master's and doctorate, GRE General Test, GRE Subject Test (for some programs). Additional exam requirements/recommendations for international students: required—TOEFL (minimum score 600 paper-based; 100 iBT), IELTS (minimum score 7.5). Application fee: $115. Electronic applications accepted. *Expenses:* Tuition: Full-time $47,600; part-time $1880 per credit. One-time fee: $105. *Financial support:* Fellowships, research assistantships, teaching assistantships, career-related internships or fieldwork, Federal Work-Study, institutionally sponsored loans, scholarships/grants, traineeships, health care benefits, tuition waivers, and unspecified assistantships available. Support available to part-time students. Financial award application deadline: 12/15. *Unit head:* Dr. Carlos J. Alonso, Dean of the Graduate School of Arts and Sciences and Vice President for Graduate Education, 212-854-2861, E-mail: gsas-dean@columbia.edu. *Application contact:* GSAS Office of Admissions, 212-854-6729, E-mail: gsas-admissions@columbia.edu. Website: http://gsas.columbia.edu/

**Cornell University,** Graduate School, Graduate Fields of Agriculture and Life Sciences, Field of Natural Resources, Ithaca, NY 14853. Offers community-based natural resources management (MS, PhD); conservation biology (MS, PhD); ecosystem biology and biogeochemistry (MPS, MS, PhD); environmental management (MPS); fishery and aquatic science (MPS, MS, PhD); forest science (MPS, MS, PhD); human dimensions of natural resources management (MPS, MS, PhD); policy and institutional analysis (MS, PhD); program development and evaluation (MPS, MS, PhD); quantitative ecology (MS, PhD); wildlife science (MPS, MS, PhD). *Degree requirements:* For master's, thesis (MS), project paper (MPS); for doctorate, comprehensive exam, thesis/dissertation. *Entrance requirements:* For master's and doctorate, GRE General Test, 2 letters of recommendation. Additional exam requirements/recommendations for international students: required—TOEFL (minimum score 550 paper-based; 77 iBT). Electronic applications accepted.

**Florida Institute of Technology,** College of Engineering and Science, Program in Conservation Technology, Melbourne, FL 32901-6975. Offers MS. *Program availability:* Part-time. *Degree requirements:* For master's, thesis or alternative. *Entrance requirements:* For master's, GRE General Test, 3 letters of recommendation, statement of objectives. Additional exam requirements/recommendations for international students: required—TOEFL (minimum score 550 paper-based; 79 iBT). Electronic applications accepted.

**Fordham University,** Graduate School of Arts and Sciences, Department of Biological Sciences, New York, NY 10458. Offers biological sciences (MS, PhD); conservation biology (Graduate Certificate). *Program availability:* Part-time, evening/weekend. *Students:* 40 full-time (27 women), 6 part-time (4 women); includes 5 minority (4 Asian, non-Hispanic/Latino; 1 Hispanic/Latino), 6 international. Average age 29. 88 applicants, 26% accepted, 15 enrolled. In 2019, 5 master's, 10 doctorates, 1 other advanced degree awarded. Terminal master's awarded for partial completion of doctoral program. *Degree requirements:* For master's, one foreign language, comprehensive exam, thesis optional; for doctorate, one foreign language, comprehensive exam, thesis/dissertation. *Entrance requirements:* For master's and doctorate, GRE General Test, GRE Subject Test (recommended). Additional exam requirements/recommendations for international students: required—TOEFL (minimum score 550 paper-based). *Application deadline:* For fall admission, 1/4 priority date for domestic students; for spring admission, 11/1 for domestic students. Application fee: $70. Electronic applications accepted. *Financial support:* In 2019–20, 15 students received support, including 4 fellowships with tuition reimbursements available (averaging $31,000 per year), 42 teaching assistantships with tuition reimbursements available (averaging $29,270 per year); research assistantships, Federal Work-Study, scholarships/grants, tuition waivers (full and partial), and unspecified assistantships also available. Financial award application deadline: 1/4; financial award applicants required to submit FAFSA. *Unit head:* Dr. Silvia Finnemann, Ph.D., Associate Chair of Graduate Studies, 718-817-3630, E-mail: finnemann@fordham.edu. *Application contact:* Garrett Marino, Director of Graduate Admissions, 718-817-4419, Fax: 718-817-3566, E-mail: gmarino10@fordham.edu.

**Frostburg State University,** College of Liberal Arts and Sciences, Department of Biology, Program in Applied Ecology and Conservation Biology, Frostburg, MD 21532-

1099. Offers MS. *Degree requirements:* For master's, thesis. *Entrance requirements:* For master's, GRE General Test, resume. Additional exam requirements/recommendations for international students: required—TOEFL. Electronic applications accepted.

**Illinois State University,** Graduate School, College of Arts and Sciences, School of Biological Sciences, Normal, IL 61790. Offers animal behavior (MS); bacteriology (MS); biochemistry (MS); biological sciences (MS); biology (PhD); biophysics (MS); biotechnology (MS); botany (MS, PhD); cell biology (MS); conservation biology (MS); developmental biology (MS); ecology (MS, PhD); entomology (MS); evolutionary biology (MS); genetics (MS, PhD); immunology (MS); microbiology (MS, PhD); molecular biology (MS); molecular genetics (MS); neurobiology (MS); neuroscience (MS); parasitology (MS); physiology (MS, PhD); plant biology (MS); plant molecular biology (MS); plant sciences (MS); structural biology (MS); zoology (MS, PhD). *Program availability:* Part-time. *Faculty:* 26 full-time (6 women), 7 part-time/adjunct (2 women). *Students:* 51 full-time (33 women), 15 part-time (8 women). Average age 27. 71 applicants, 28% accepted, 9 enrolled. In 2019, 14 master's, 3 doctorates awarded. *Degree requirements:* For master's, thesis or alternative; for doctorate, variable foreign language requirement, thesis/dissertation, 2 terms of residency. *Entrance requirements:* For master's, GRE General Test, minimum GPA of 2.6 in last 60 hours of course work; for doctorate, GRE General Test. *Application deadline:* Applications are processed on a rolling basis. Application fee: $50. *Expenses: Tuition, area resident:* Full-time $7956; part-time $9767 per year. Tuition, nonresident: full-time $9233; part-time $17,592 per year. *Required fees:* $1797. *Financial support:* In 2019–20, 20 research assistantships, 41 teaching assistantships were awarded; Federal Work-Study, tuition waivers (full), and unspecified assistantships also available. Financial award application deadline: 4/1. *Unit head:* Dr. Craig Gatto, School Director, 309-438-3087, E-mail: cgatto@IllinoisState.edu. *Application contact:* Dr. Ben Sadd, Assistant Chair for Graduate Studies, 309-438-2651, E-mail: bmsadd@IllinoisState.edu.
Website: http://www.bio.ilstu.edu/

**North Dakota State University,** College of Graduate and Interdisciplinary Studies, Interdisciplinary Program in Environmental and Conservation Sciences, Fargo, ND 58102. Offers MS, PhD. *Entrance requirements:* Additional exam requirements/recommendations for international students: required—TOEFL. Tuition and fees vary according to program and reciprocity agreements.

**Oregon State University,** College of Agricultural Sciences, Program in Fisheries Science, Corvallis, OR 97331. Offers aquaculture (MS); conservation biology (MS, PhD); fish genetics (MS, PhD); ichthyology (MS, PhD); limnology (MS, PhD); parasites and diseases (MS, PhD); physiology and ecology of marine and freshwater fishes (MS, PhD); stream ecology (MS, PhD); toxicology (MS, PhD); water pollution biology (MS, PhD). *Program availability:* Part-time. *Entrance requirements:* For master's and doctorate, GRE, minimum GPA of 3.0 in last 90 hours. Additional exam requirements/recommendations for international students: required—TOEFL (minimum score 80 iBT), IELTS (minimum score 6.5).

**State University of New York College of Environmental Science and Forestry,** Department of Environmental and Forest Biology, Syracuse, NY 13210-2779. Offers applied ecology (MPS); chemical ecology (MPS, MS, PhD); conservation biology (MPS, MS, PhD); ecology (MPS, MS, PhD); entomology (MPS, MS, PhD); environmental interpretation (MPS, MS, PhD); environmental physiology (MPS, MS, PhD); fish and wildlife biology and management (MPS, MS, PhD); forest pathology and mycology (MPS, MS, PhD); plant biotechnology (MPS); plant science and biotechnology (MPS, MS, PhD). *Program availability:* Part-time. *Faculty:* 35 full-time (10 women), 4 part-time/adjunct (3 women). *Students:* 103 full-time (60 women), 17 part-time (7 women); includes 7 minority (4 American Indian or Alaska Native, non-Hispanic/Latino; 2 Asian, non-Hispanic/Latino; 1 Hispanic/Latino), 13 international. Average age 29. 69 applicants, 45% accepted, 17 enrolled. In 2019, 28 master's, 6 doctorates awarded. Terminal master's awarded for partial completion of doctoral program. *Degree requirements:* For master's, thesis (for some programs), capstone seminar; for doctorate, comprehensive exam, thesis/dissertation, capstone seminar. *Entrance requirements:* For master's and doctorate, GRE General Test, minimum GPA of 3.0. Additional exam requirements/recommendations for international students: required—TOEFL (minimum score 550 paper-based; 80 iBT), IELTS (minimum score 6). *Application deadline:* For fall admission, 2/1 priority date for domestic and international students; for spring admission, 11/1 priority date for domestic and international students. Applications are processed on a rolling basis. Application fee: $60. Electronic applications accepted. *Expenses:* Tuition, state resident: full-time $11,310; part-time $472 per credit hour. Tuition, nonresident: full-time $23,100; part-time $963 per credit hour. *Required fees:* $1890; $95.21 per credit hour. *Financial support:* In 2019–20, 35 students received support. Unspecified assistantships available. Financial award application deadline: 6/30; financial award applicants required to submit FAFSA. *Unit head:* Dr. Melissa K. Fierke, Chair, 315-470-6809, Fax: 315-470-6743, E-mail: mkfierke@esf.edu. *Application contact:* Laura Payne, Administrative Assistant Office of Instruction & Graduate Studies, 315-470-6599, E-mail: esfgrad@esf.edu.
Website: http://www.esf.edu/efb/grad/default.asp

**Texas State University,** The Graduate College, College of Science and Engineering, Program in Population and Conservation Biology, San Marcos, TX 78666. Offers MS. *Degree requirements:* For master's, comprehensive exam, thesis. *Entrance requirements:* For master's, official GRE (general test only) required with competitive scores in the verbal reasoning and quantitative reasoning sections, baccalaureate degree in biology or related discipline from regionally-accredited university with minimum GPA of 3.0 on last 60 undergraduate semester hours, statement of purpose, current curriculum vitae, 3 letters of recommendation, letter of intent to mentor from faculty member of Biology Department. Additional exam requirements/recommendations for international students: required—TOEFL (minimum score 550 paper-based; 78 iBT), IELTS (minimum score 6.5). Electronic applications accepted.

**Tropical Agriculture Research and Higher Education Center,** Graduate School, Turrialba, Costa Rica. Offers agribusiness management (MS); agroforestry systems (PhD); development practices (MS); ecological agriculture (MS); environmental socioeconomics (MS); forestry in tropical and subtropical zones (PhD); integrated watershed management (MS); international sustainable tourism (MS); management and conservation of tropical rainforests and biodiversity (MS); tropical agriculture (PhD); tropical agroforestry (MS). *Entrance requirements:* For master's, GRE, 2 years of related professional experience, letters of recommendation; for doctorate, GRE, 4 letters of recommendation, letter of support from employing organization, master's degree in agronomy, biological sciences, forestry, natural resources or related field. Additional exam requirements/recommendations for international students: required—TOEFL (minimum score 550 paper-based). Electronic applications accepted.

**University of Alberta,** Faculty of Graduate Studies and Research, Department of Renewable Resources, Edmonton, AB T6G 2E1, Canada. Offers agroforestry (M Ag, M Sc, MF); conservation biology (M Sc, PhD); forest biology and management (M Sc, PhD); land reclamation and remediation (M Sc, PhD); protected areas and wildlands management (M Sc, PhD); soil science (M Ag, M Sc, PhD); water and land resources (M Ag, M Sc, PhD); wildlife ecology and management (M Sc, PhD); MBA/M Ag; MBA/MF. *Program availability:* Part-time. *Degree requirements:* For master's, thesis (for some programs); for doctorate, comprehensive exam, thesis/dissertation. *Entrance requirements:* For master's, minimum 2 years of relevant professional experiences, minimum GPA of 3.0; for doctorate, minimum GPA of 3.0. Additional exam requirements/recommendations for international students: required—TOEFL (minimum score 550 paper-based). Electronic applications accepted.

**University of Central Florida,** College of Sciences, Department of Biology, Orlando, FL 32816. Offers conservation biology (Certificate). *Program availability:* Part-time, evening/weekend. *Students:* 55 full-time (27 women), 6 part-time (2 women); includes 6 minority (1 Black or African American, non-Hispanic/Latino; 2 Asian, non-Hispanic/Latino; 1 Hispanic/Latino; 2 Two or more races, non-Hispanic/Latino), 9 international. Average age 29. 38 applicants, 34% accepted, 12 enrolled. In 2019, 8 master's, 4 doctorates awarded. *Degree requirements:* For master's, comprehensive exam, thesis or alternative, field exam. *Entrance requirements:* For master's, GRE General Test, minimum GPA of 3.0 in last 60 hours, letters of recommendation, resume, personal/professional statement; for doctorate, GRE General Test, letters of recommendation, resume, personal/professional statement. Additional exam requirements/recommendations for international students: required—TOEFL. *Application deadline:* For fall admission, 1/15 priority date for domestic students. Application fee: $30. Electronic applications accepted. *Financial support:* In 2019–20, 54 students received support, including 20 fellowships with partial tuition reimbursements available (averaging $9,210 per year), 7 research assistantships with partial tuition reimbursements available (averaging $6,146 per year), 51 teaching assistantships with partial tuition reimbursements available (averaging $8,061 per year); career-related internships or fieldwork, Federal Work-Study, institutionally sponsored loans, health care benefits, tuition waivers (partial), and unspecified assistantships also available. Financial award application deadline: 3/1; financial award applicants required to submit FAFSA. *Unit head:* Dr. Graham Worthy, Chair, 407-823-2141, Fax: 407-823-5769, E-mail: graham.worthy@ucf.edu. *Application contact:* Associate Director, Graduate Admissions, 407-823-2766, Fax: 407-823-6442, E-mail: gradadmissions@ucf.edu.
Website: https://sciences.ucf.edu/biology/

**University of Hawaii at Hilo,** Program in Tropical Conservation Biology and Environmental Science, Hilo, HI 96720-4091. Offers MS. *Entrance requirements:* Additional exam requirements/recommendations for international students: required—TOEFL, IELTS. Electronic applications accepted.

**University of Illinois at Urbana-Champaign,** Graduate College, College of Liberal Arts and Sciences, School of Integrative Biology, Program in Ecology, Evolution and Conservation Biology, Champaign, IL 61820. Offers MS, PhD.

**University of Maryland, College Park,** Academic Affairs, College of Computer, Mathematical and Natural Sciences, Department of Biology, Program in Sustainable Development and Conservation Biology, College Park, MD 20742. Offers MS. *Program availability:* Part-time, evening/weekend. *Degree requirements:* For master's, internship, scholarly paper. *Entrance requirements:* For master's, GRE General Test, minimum GPA of 3.0, 3 letters of recommendation. Electronic applications accepted.

**University of Minnesota, Twin Cities Campus,** Graduate School, College of Food, Agricultural and Natural Resource Sciences, Program in Conservation Sciences, St. Paul, MN 55108. Offers conservation sciences (MS), including conservation science, fisheries & aquatic biology, wildlife ecology & management. *Program availability:* Part-time. Terminal master's awarded for partial completion of doctoral program. *Degree requirements:* For master's, comprehensive exam, thesis; for doctorate, comprehensive exam, thesis/dissertation. *Entrance requirements:* For master's and doctorate, GRE, advanced ecology course. Additional exam requirements/recommendations for international students: required—TOEFL (minimum score 550 paper-based; 79 iBT), IELTS (minimum score 6.5). Electronic applications accepted.

**University of Missouri,** Office of Research and Graduate Studies, College of Agriculture, Food and Natural Resources, School of Natural Resources, Columbia, MO 65211. Offers agroforestry (MS, Certificate); conservation biology (Certificate); fisheries and wildlife sciences (MS, PhD); forestry (MS, PhD); geographical information science (Certificate); human dimensions of natural resources (MS, PhD); parks, recreation and tourism (MS); society and ecosystems (Certificate); soil, environmental and atmospheric sciences (MS, PhD); water resources (MS, PhD). *Program availability:* Part-time. *Degree requirements:* For doctorate, thesis/dissertation. *Entrance requirements:* For master's and doctorate, GRE General Test (minimum score 1200 Verbal and Quantitative), minimum GPA of 3.2. Additional exam requirements/recommendations for international students: required—TOEFL (minimum score 550 paper-based; 80 iBT), IELTS (minimum score 6.5). Electronic applications accepted.

**University of Nevada, Reno,** Graduate School, Interdisciplinary Program in Ecology, Evolution, and Conservation Biology, Reno, NV 89557. Offers PhD. *Degree requirements:* For doctorate, thesis/dissertation. *Entrance requirements:* For doctorate, GRE General Test, GRE Subject Test, minimum GPA of 3.0. Additional exam requirements/recommendations for international students: required—TOEFL (minimum score 500 paper-based; 61 iBT), IELTS (minimum score 6). Electronic applications accepted.

**University of New Hampshire,** Graduate School, College of Life Sciences and Agriculture, Department of Natural Resources and the Environment, Durham, NH 03824. Offers environmental conservation (MS); environmental economics (MS); forestry (MS); natural resources (MS); resource administration and management (MS); soil and water resource management (MS); wildlife and conservation biology (MS). *Program availability:* Part-time. *Students:* 58 full-time (33 women), 33 part-time (21 women); includes 7 minority (2 Black or African American, non-Hispanic/Latino; 1 Asian, non-Hispanic/Latino; 2 Hispanic/Latino; 2 Two or more races, non-Hispanic/Latino), 5 international. Average age 31. 44 applicants, 48% accepted, 19 enrolled. In 2019, 17 master's awarded. *Entrance requirements:* For master's, GRE General Test. Additional exam requirements/recommendations for international students: required—TOEFL (minimum score 550 paper-based; 80 iBT), IELTS, PTE. *Application deadline:* For fall admission, 2/15 priority date for domestic students, 4/1 for international students; for spring admission, 12/1 for domestic students. Application fee: $65. Electronic applications accepted. *Financial support:* In 2019–20, 61 students received support, including 5 fellowships, 21 research assistantships, 31 teaching assistantships; career-related internships or fieldwork, Federal Work-Study, scholarships/grants, and tuition waivers (full and partial) also available. Support available to part-time students. Financial award application deadline: 2/15. *Unit head:* Mark Ducey, Chair, 603-862-1017, E-mail: natural.resources@unh.edu. *Application contact:* Wendy Rose, Administrative Assistant, 603-862-3933, E-mail: natural.resources@unh.edu.
Website: http://colsa.unh.edu/nren

**The University of West Alabama,** School of Graduate Studies, College of Natural Sciences and Mathematics, Program in Conservation Biology, Livingston, AL 35470. Offers MS. *Program availability:* Part-time, evening/weekend, 100% online. *Faculty:* 6 full-time (1 woman), 3 part-time/adjunct (0 women). *Students:* 25 full-time (20 women), 3 part-time (0 women); includes 2 minority (1 Black or African American, non-Hispanic/Latino; 1 Hispanic/Latino). Average age 27. 11 applicants, 100% accepted, 10 enrolled. In 2019, 13 master's awarded. *Degree requirements:* For master's, thesis optional. *Entrance requirements:* For master's, GRE, Bachelor's degree with minimum GPA of

2.5; Official transcripts; Statement of Purpose; Three Academic references. Additional exam requirements/recommendations for international students: required—TOEFL (minimum score 500 paper-based; 61 iBT). *Application deadline:* Applications are processed on a rolling basis. Application fee: $40. Electronic applications accepted. *Expenses: Required fees:* $380; $130. *Financial support:* In 2019–20, 5 teaching assistantships (averaging $7,344 per year) were awarded; Federal Work-Study, scholarships/grants, and unspecified assistantships also available. Support available to part-time students. Financial award application deadline: 3/1; financial award applicants required to submit FAFSA. *Unit head:* Dr. John McCall, Dean, 205-652-3412, Fax: 205-652-3831, E-mail: jmccall@uwa.edu. *Application contact:* Dr. John McCall, Dean, 205-652-3412, Fax: 205-652-3831, E-mail: jmccall@uwa.edu.
Website: http://www.uwa.edu/nsm/

**University of Wisconsin–Madison,** Graduate School, Gaylord Nelson Institute for Environmental Studies, Environmental Conservation Program, Madison, WI 53706-1380. Offers MS. *Degree requirements:* For master's, thesis or alternative, spring/summer leadership (internship) experience. *Entrance requirements:* For master's, GRE General Test (recommended for potential scholarship consideration). Additional exam requirements/recommendations for international students: required—TOEFL (minimum score 550 paper-based, 80 iBT) or IELTS (6.5). Electronic applications accepted. *Expenses:* Contact institution.

**University of Wisconsin–Stout,** Graduate School, College of Science, Technology, Engineering and Mathematics, Program in Conservation Biology, Menomonie, WI 54751. Offers PSM. *Program availability:* Online learning.

# Ecology

**Baylor University,** Graduate School, College of Arts and Sciences, The Institute of Ecological, Earth and Environmental Sciences, Waco, TX 76798. Offers PhD. *Degree requirements:* For doctorate, comprehensive exam, thesis/dissertation. *Entrance requirements:* For doctorate, GRE. Additional exam requirements/recommendations for international students: required—TOEFL (minimum score 550 paper-based; 80 iBT); recommended—IELTS (minimum score 6.5). Electronic applications accepted. *Expenses:* Contact institution.

**Brown University,** Graduate School, Division of Biology and Medicine, Department of Ecology and Evolutionary Biology, Providence, RI 02912. Offers PhD. *Degree requirements:* For doctorate, thesis/dissertation, preliminary exam. *Entrance requirements:* For doctorate, GRE General Test, GRE Subject Test. Additional exam requirements/recommendations for international students: required—TOEFL. Electronic applications accepted.

**California State University, Stanislaus,** College of Natural Sciences, MS Program in Ecology and Sustainability, Turlock, CA 95382. Offers ecological conservation (MS). *Program availability:* Part-time. *Degree requirements:* For master's, thesis. *Entrance requirements:* For master's, GRE, minimum GPA of 3.0, 3 letters of recommendation, personal statement. Additional exam requirements/recommendations for international students: required—TOEFL (minimum score 550 paper-based). Electronic applications accepted.

**Central Washington University,** School of Graduate Studies and Research, College of the Sciences, Department of Biological Sciences, Ellensburg, WA 98926. Offers botany (MS); microbiology and parasitology (MS); stream ecology and fisheries (MS); terrestrial ecology (MS). *Program availability:* Part-time. *Entrance requirements:* For master's, GRE General Test, minimum GPA of 3.0. Additional exam requirements/recommendations for international students: required—TOEFL (minimum score 550 paper-based; 79 iBT). Electronic applications accepted.

**Columbia University,** Graduate School of Arts and Sciences, New York, NY 10027. Offers African-American studies (MA); American studies (MA); anthropology (MA, PhD); art history and archaeology (MA, PhD); astronomy (PhD); biological sciences (PhD); biotechnology (MA); chemical physics (PhD); chemistry (PhD); classical studies (MA, PhD); classics (MA, PhD); climate and society (MA); conservation biology (MA); earth and environmental sciences (PhD); East Asia: regional studies (MA); East Asian languages and cultures (MA, PhD); ecology, evolution and environmental biology (MA), including conservation biology; ecology, evolution, and environmental biology (PhD), including ecology and evolutionary biology, evolutionary primatology; economics (MA, PhD); English and comparative literature (MA, PhD); French and Romance philology (MA, PhD); Germanic languages (MA, PhD); global French studies (MA); global thought (MA); Hispanic cultural studies (MA); history (PhD); history and literature (MA); human rights studies (MA); Islamic studies (MA); Italian (MA, PhD); Japanese pedagogy (MA); Jewish studies (MA); Latin America and the Caribbean: regional studies (MA); Latin American and Iberian cultures (PhD); mathematics (MA, PhD), including finance (MA); medieval and Renaissance studies (MA); Middle Eastern, South Asian, and African studies (MA, PhD); modern art: critical and curatorial studies (MA); modern European studies (MA); museum anthropology (MA); music (DMA, PhD); oral history (MA); philosophical foundations of physics (MA); philosophy (MA, PhD); physics (PhD); political science (MA, PhD); psychology (PhD); quantitative methods in the social sciences (MA); religion (MA, PhD); Russia, Eurasia and East Europe: regional studies (MA); Russian translation (MA); Slavic cultures (MA); Slavic languages (MA, PhD); sociology (MA, PhD); South Asian studies (MA); statistics (MA, PhD); theatre (PhD). *Program availability:* Part-time. *Students:* 3,506 full-time (1,844 women), 208 part-time (121 women); includes 864 minority (110 Black or African American, non-Hispanic/Latino; 5 American Indian or Alaska Native, non-Hispanic/Latino; 416 Asian, non-Hispanic/Latino; 147 Hispanic/Latino; 6 Native Hawaiian or other Pacific Islander, non-Hispanic/Latino; 180 Two or more races, non-Hispanic/Latino), 2,065 international. 14,545 applicants, 25% accepted, 1,429 enrolled. In 2019, 1,262 master's, 363 doctorates awarded. Terminal master's awarded for partial completion of doctoral program. *Degree requirements:* For master's, variable foreign language requirement, comprehensive exam (for some programs), thesis (for some programs); for doctorate, variable foreign language requirement, comprehensive exam (for some programs), thesis/dissertation. *Entrance requirements:* For master's and doctorate, GRE General Test, GRE Subject Test (for some programs). Additional exam requirements/recommendations for international students: required—TOEFL (minimum score 600 paper-based; 100 iBT), IELTS (minimum score 7.5). Application fee: $115. Electronic applications accepted. *Expenses: Tuition:* Full-time $47,600; part-time $1880 per credit. One-time fee: $105. *Financial support:* Fellowships, research assistantships, teaching assistantships, career-related internships or fieldwork, Federal Work-Study, institutionally sponsored loans, scholarships/grants, traineeships, health care benefits, tuition waivers, and unspecified assistantships available. Support available to part-time students. Financial award application deadline: 12/15. *Unit head:* Dr. Carlos J. Alonso, Dean of the Graduate School of Arts and Sciences and Vice President for Graduate Education, 212-854-2861, E-mail: gsas-dean@columbia.edu. *Application contact:* GSAS Office of Admissions, 212-854-6729, E-mail: gsas-admissions@columbia.edu.
Website: http://gsas.columbia.edu/

**Cornell University,** Graduate School, Graduate Fields of Agriculture and Life Sciences, Field of Computational Biology, Ithaca, NY 14853. Offers computational behavioral biology (PhD); computational biology (PhD); computational cell biology (PhD); computational ecology (PhD); computational genetics (PhD); computational macromolecular biology (PhD); computational organismal biology (PhD). *Degree requirements:* For doctorate, comprehensive exam, thesis/dissertation, 2 semesters of teaching experience. *Entrance requirements:* For doctorate, GRE General Test, GRE Subject Test (biology), 2 letters of recommendation. Additional exam requirements/recommendations for international students: required—TOEFL (minimum score 550 paper-based; 77 iBT). Electronic applications accepted.

**Cornell University,** Graduate School, Graduate Fields of Agriculture and Life Sciences, Field of Ecology and Evolutionary Biology, Ithaca, NY 14853. Offers ecology (PhD), including animal ecology, applied ecology, biogeochemistry, community and ecosystem ecology, limnology, oceanography, physiological ecology, plant ecology, population ecology, theoretical ecology, vertebrate zoology; evolutionary biology (PhD), including ecological genetics, paleobiology, population biology, systematics. *Degree requirements:* For doctorate, comprehensive exam, thesis/dissertation, 2 semesters of teaching experience. *Entrance requirements:* For doctorate, GRE General Test, GRE Subject Test (biology), 2 letters of recommendation. Additional exam requirements/recommendations for international students: required—TOEFL (minimum score 550 paper-based; 77 iBT). Electronic applications accepted.

**Cornell University,** Graduate School, Graduate Fields of Agriculture and Life Sciences, Field of Horticulture, Ithaca, NY 14853. Offers breeding of horticultural crops (MPS); horticultural crop management systems (MPS); human-plant interactions (MPS, PhD); physiology and ecology of horticultural crops (MPS, MS, PhD). *Degree requirements:* For master's, thesis (MS); for doctorate, comprehensive exam, thesis/dissertation. *Entrance requirements:* For master's and doctorate, GRE General Test, 3 letters of recommendation. Additional exam requirements/recommendations for international students: required—TOEFL (minimum score 550 paper-based; 77 iBT). Electronic applications accepted.

**Cornell University,** Graduate School, Graduate Fields of Agriculture and Life Sciences, Field of Natural Resources, Ithaca, NY 14853. Offers community-based natural resources management (MS, PhD); conservation biology (MS, PhD); ecosystem biology and biogeochemistry (MPS, MS, PhD); environmental management (MPS); fishery and aquatic science (MPS, MS, PhD); forest science (MPS, MS, PhD); human dimensions of natural resources management (MPS, MS, PhD); policy and institutional analysis (MS, PhD); program development and evaluation (MPS, MS, PhD); quantitative ecology (MS, PhD); wildlife science (MPS, MS, PhD). *Degree requirements:* For master's, thesis (MS), project paper (MPS); for doctorate, comprehensive exam, thesis/dissertation. *Entrance requirements:* For master's and doctorate, GRE General Test, 2 letters of recommendation. Additional exam requirements/recommendations for international students: required—TOEFL (minimum score 550 paper-based; 77 iBT). Electronic applications accepted.

**Dalhousie University,** Faculty of Agriculture, Halifax, NS B3H 4R2, Canada. Offers agriculture (M Sc), including air quality, animal behavior, animal molecular genetics, animal nutrition, animal technology, aquaculture, botany, crop management, crop physiology, ecology, environmental microbiology, food science, horticulture, nutrient management, pest management, physiology, plant biotechnology, plant pathology, soil chemistry, soil fertility, waste management and composting, water quality. *Program availability:* Part-time. *Degree requirements:* For master's, thesis, ATC Exam Teaching Assistantship. *Entrance requirements:* For master's, honors B Sc, minimum GPA of 3.0. Additional exam requirements/recommendations for international students: required—TOEFL (minimum score 580 paper-based; 92 iBT), IELTS, Michigan English Language Assessment Battery, CanTEST, CAEL.

**Dartmouth College,** Guarini School of Graduate and Advanced Studies, Graduate Programs in Biological Sciences, Program in Ecology, Evolution, Ecosystems, and Society, Hanover, NH 03755. Offers ecology and evolutionary biology (PhD); sustainability, ecosystems, and environment (PhD). *Entrance requirements:* For doctorate, GRE General Test, GRE Subject Test in biology (highly recommended). Additional exam requirements/recommendations for international students: required—TOEFL. Electronic applications accepted.

**Duke University,** Graduate School, Department of Ecology, Durham, NC 27708-0329. Offers PhD, Certificate. *Degree requirements:* For doctorate, thesis/dissertation. *Entrance requirements:* For doctorate, GRE General Test. Additional exam requirements/recommendations for international students: required—TOEFL (minimum score 577 paper-based; 90 iBT) or IELTS (minimum score 7). Electronic applications accepted.

**Eastern Kentucky University,** The Graduate School, College of Arts and Sciences, Department of Biological Sciences, Richmond, KY 40475-3102. Offers biological sciences (MS); ecology (MS). *Program availability:* Part-time. *Degree requirements:* For master's, thesis. *Entrance requirements:* For master's, GRE General Test, minimum GPA of 2.5.

**Emory University,** Laney Graduate School, Division of Biological and Biomedical Sciences, Program in Population Biology, Ecology and Evolution, Atlanta, GA 30322-1100. Offers PhD. *Degree requirements:* For doctorate, comprehensive exam, thesis/dissertation. *Entrance requirements:* For doctorate, GRE General Test, minimum GPA of 3.0 in science course work (recommended). Additional exam requirements/recommendations for international students: required—TOEFL. Electronic applications accepted.

**Florida Institute of Technology,** College of Engineering and Science, Program in Biological Sciences, Melbourne, FL 32901-6975. Offers biological sciences (PhD); biotechnology (MS); ecology (MS). *Program availability:* Part-time. *Degree requirements:* For doctorate, comprehensive exam, thesis/dissertation, dissertations seminar, publications. *Entrance requirements:* For doctorate, GRE General Test, resume, 3 letters of recommendation, minimum GPA of 3.2, statement of objectives. Additional exam requirements/recommendations for international students: required—TOEFL (minimum score 550 paper-based; 79 iBT). Electronic applications accepted.

**Florida State University,** The Graduate School, College of Arts and Sciences, Department of Biological Science, Specialization in Ecology and Evolutionary Biology, Tallahassee, FL 32306-4295. Offers MS, PhD. Terminal master's awarded for partial completion of doctoral program. *Degree requirements:* For master's, comprehensive exam (for some programs), thesis (for some programs), teaching experience, seminar presentation; for doctorate, comprehensive exam, thesis/dissertation, teaching experience; seminar presentation. *Entrance requirements:* For master's and doctorate, GRE General Test, minimum upper-division GPA of 3.0. Additional exam requirements/recommendations for international students: required—TOEFL (minimum score 600 paper-based; 92 iBT). Electronic applications accepted.

**Frostburg State University,** College of Liberal Arts and Sciences, Department of Biology, Program in Applied Ecology and Conservation Biology, Frostburg, MD 21532-1099. Offers MS. *Degree requirements:* For master's, thesis. *Entrance requirements:* For master's, GRE General Test, resume. Additional exam requirements/recommendations for international students: required—TOEFL. Electronic applications accepted.

**Illinois State University,** Graduate School, College of Arts and Sciences, School of Biological Sciences, Normal, IL 61790. Offers animal behavior (MS); bacteriology (MS); biochemistry (MS); biological sciences (MS); biology (PhD); biophysics (MS); biotechnology (MS); botany (MS, PhD); cell biology (MS); conservation biology (MS); developmental biology (MS); ecology (MS, PhD); entomology (MS); evolutionary biology (MS); genetics (MS, PhD); immunology (MS); microbiology (MS, PhD); molecular biology (MS); molecular genetics (MS); neurobiology (MS); neuroscience (MS); parasitology (MS); physiology (MS, PhD); plant biology (MS); plant molecular biology (MS); plant sciences (MS); structural biology (MS); zoology (MS, PhD). *Program availability:* Part-time. *Faculty:* 26 full-time (6 women), 7 part-time/adjunct (2 women). *Students:* 51 full-time (33 women), 15 part-time (8 women). Average age 27. 71 applicants, 28% accepted, 9 enrolled. In 2019, 14 master's, 3 doctorates awarded. *Degree requirements:* For master's, thesis or alternative; for doctorate, variable foreign language requirement, thesis/dissertation, 2 terms of residency. *Entrance requirements:* For master's, GRE General Test, minimum GPA of 2.6 in last 60 hours of course work; for doctorate, GRE General Test. *Application deadline:* Applications are processed on a rolling basis. Application fee: $50. *Expenses: Tuition,* area resident: Full-time $7956; part-time $9767 per year. Tuition, nonresident: full-time $9233; part-time $17,592 per year. *Required fees:* $1797. *Financial support:* In 2019–20, 20 research assistantships, 41 teaching assistantships were awarded; Federal Work-Study, tuition waivers (full), and unspecified assistantships also available. Financial award application deadline: 4/1. *Unit head:* Dr. Craig Gatto, School Director, 309-438-3087, E-mail: cgatto@IllinoisState.edu. *Application contact:* Dr. Ben Sadd, Assistant Chair for Graduate Studies, 309-438-2651, E-mail: bmsadd@IllinoisState.edu.
Website: http://www.bio.ilstu.edu/

**Indiana State University,** College of Graduate and Professional Studies, College of Arts and Sciences, Department of Biology, Terre Haute, IN 47809. Offers cellular and molecular biology (PhD); ecology, systematics and evolution (PhD); life sciences (MS); physiology (PhD); science education (MS). *Degree requirements:* For master's, thesis optional; for doctorate, comprehensive exam, thesis/dissertation. *Entrance requirements:* For master's and doctorate, GRE General Test. Electronic applications accepted.

**Indiana University Bloomington,** School of Public and Environmental Affairs, Environmental Science Programs, Bloomington, IN 47405. Offers applied ecology (MSES); energy (MSES); environmental chemistry, toxicology, and risk assessment (MSES); environmental science (PhD); hazardous materials management (Certificate); specialized environmental science (MSES); water resources (MSES); JD/MSES; MSES/MA; MSES/MPA; MSES/MS. *Program availability:* Part-time. Terminal master's awarded for partial completion of doctoral program. *Degree requirements:* For master's, capstone or thesis; internship; for doctorate, comprehensive exam, thesis/dissertation. *Entrance requirements:* For master's, GRE General Test or GMAT, official transcripts, 3 letters of recommendation, resume, personal statement; for doctorate, GRE General Test or LSAT, official transcripts, 3 letters of recommendation, resume or curriculum vitae, statement of purpose. Additional exam requirements/recommendations for international students: required—TOEFL (minimum score 600 paper-based; 96 iBT); recommended—IELTS (minimum score 7). Electronic applications accepted.

**Indiana University Bloomington,** University Graduate School, College of Arts and Sciences, Department of Biology, Bloomington, IN 47405. Offers biology teaching (MAT); biotechnology (MA); evolution, ecology, and behavior (MA, PhD); genetics (PhD); microbiology (MA, PhD); molecular, cellular, and developmental biology (PhD); plant sciences (MA, PhD); zoology (MA, PhD). Terminal master's awarded for partial completion of doctoral program. *Degree requirements:* For master's, thesis, oral defense; for doctorate, thesis/dissertation, oral defense. *Entrance requirements:* For master's and doctorate, GRE General Test. Additional exam requirements/recommendations for international students: required—TOEFL (minimum score 100 iBT). Electronic applications accepted.

**Inter American University of Puerto Rico, Bayamón Campus,** Graduate School, Bayamón, PR 00957. Offers biology (MS), including environmental sciences and ecology, molecular biotechnology; electrical engineering (ME), including control system, potence system; human resources (MBA); mechanical engineering (ME, MS), including aerospace, energy. *Program availability:* Part-time, evening/weekend. *Degree requirements:* For master's, comprehensive exam, research project. *Entrance requirements:* For master's, EXADEP, GRE General Test, letters of recommendation. *Expenses: Tuition:* Full-time $3870; part-time $1935 per year. *Required fees:* $735; $642 per unit.

**Iowa State University of Science and Technology,** Program in Ecology and Evolutionary Biology, Ames, IA 50011. Offers MS, PhD. *Degree requirements:* For master's, thesis or alternative; for doctorate, thesis/dissertation. *Entrance requirements:* For master's and doctorate, GRE General Test. Additional exam requirements/recommendations for international students: required—TOEFL (minimum score 550 paper-based; 79 iBT), IELTS (minimum score 6.5). Electronic applications accepted.

**Kent State University,** College of Arts and Sciences, Department of Biological Sciences, Kent, OH 44242. Offers biological sciences (MA, MS, PhD), including botany (MS, PhD), cell biology (MS, PhD), ecology (MS, PhD), physiology (MS, PhD). *Program availability:* Part-time. *Faculty:* 19 full-time (5 women), 2 part-time/adjunct (1 woman). *Students:* 51 full-time (35 women), 9 part-time (4 women); includes 1 minority (Two or more races, non-Hispanic/Latino), 10 international. Average age 29. 53 applicants, 38% accepted, 14 enrolled. In 2019, 8 master's, 9 doctorates awarded. Terminal master's awarded for partial completion of doctoral program. *Degree requirements:* For master's, thesis (for some programs), departmental seminar presentation about research (for MS); for doctorate, thesis/dissertation, departmental seminar presentation about research, admitted to doctoral candidacy following written and oral candidacy. *Entrance requirements:* For master's, GRE, minimum GPA of 3.0, official transcripts, goal statement, three letters of recommendation, list of up to five potential faculty advisors, undergraduate coursework roughly equivalent to a biology minor, acceptance of student by a faculty advisor; for doctorate, GRE; After completing the required coursework,

students complete the doctoral program by being admitted to candidacy, by proposing a research project to the faculty, and by completing and defending that research with a written dissertation before a faculty committee, official transcripts, goal statement, three letters of recommendation, list of up to five potential faculty advisors, baccalaureate degree with strong background in biology and related subjects such as chemistry and mathematics, acceptance of the student by a faculty advisor. Additional exam requirements/recommendations for international students: required—TOEFL (minimum score 94 iBT), IELTS (minimum score 7), PTE (minimum score 65), Michigan English Language Assessment Battery (minimum score 82). *Application deadline:* For fall admission, 12/15 for domestic students, 12/5 for international students. Applications are processed on a rolling basis. Application fee: $45 ($70 for international students). Electronic applications accepted. *Financial support:* Research assistantships with full tuition reimbursements, teaching assistantships with full tuition reimbursements, Federal Work-Study, scholarships/grants, health care benefits, and unspecified assistantships available. Financial award application deadline: 12/15. *Unit head:* Dr. James L. Blank, Dean, 330-672-2650, E-mail: jblank@kent.edu. *Application contact:* Dr. Heather K. Caldwell, Associate Professor and Graduate Coordinator, 330-672-3636, E-mail: hcaldwel@kent.edu.
Website: http://www.kent.edu/biology

**Laurentian University,** School of Graduate Studies and Research, Programme in Biology, Sudbury, ON P3E 2C6, Canada. Offers biology (M Sc); boreal ecology (PhD). *Program availability:* Part-time. *Degree requirements:* For master's, thesis. *Entrance requirements:* For master's, honors degree with second class or better.

**Lesley University,** Graduate School of Education, Cambridge, MA 02138-2790. Offers arts, community, and education (M Ed); autism studies (Certificate); curriculum and instruction (M Ed, CAGS); early childhood education (M Ed); ecological teaching and learning (MS); educational studies (PhD), including adult learning, educational leadership, individually designed; elementary education (M Ed); emergent technologies for educators (Certificate); ESLArts: language learning through the arts (M Ed); high school education (M Ed); individually designed (M Ed); integrated teaching through the arts (M Ed); literacy for K-8 classroom teachers (M Ed); mathematics education (M Ed); middle school education (M Ed); moderate disabilities (M Ed); online learning (Certificate); reading (CAGS); science in education (M Ed); severe disabilities (M Ed); special needs (CAGS); specialist teacher of reading (M Ed); teacher of visual art (M Ed); technology in education (M Ed, CAGS). *Accreditation:* TEAC. *Program availability:* Part-time, evening/weekend, online learning. *Degree requirements:* For master's, practicum; for doctorate, thesis/dissertation. *Entrance requirements:* For master's, Massachusetts Tests for Educator Licensure (MTEL), transcripts, statement of purpose, recommendations; interview (for special education); for doctorate, GRE General Test, transcripts, statement of purpose, recommendations, interview, master's degree, resume; for other advanced degree, interview, master's degree. Additional exam requirements/recommendations for international students: required—TOEFL (minimum score 550 paper-based; 80 iBT). Electronic applications accepted.

**Marquette University,** Graduate School, College of Arts and Sciences, Department of Biological Sciences, Milwaukee, WI 53201-1881. Offers cell biology (MS, PhD); developmental biology (MS, PhD); ecology (MS, PhD); epithelial physiology (MS, PhD); genetics (MS, PhD); microbiology (MS, PhD); molecular biology (MS, PhD); muscle and exercise physiology (MS, PhD); neuroscience (PhD). Terminal master's awarded for partial completion of doctoral program. *Degree requirements:* For master's, comprehensive exam, thesis, 1 year of teaching experience or equivalent; for doctorate, thesis/dissertation, 1 year of teaching experience or equivalent, qualifying exam. *Entrance requirements:* For master's and doctorate, GRE General Test, GRE Subject Test, official transcripts from all current and previous colleges/universities except Marquette, statement of professional goals and aspirations, three letters of recommendation. Additional exam requirements/recommendations for international students: required—TOEFL (minimum score 530 paper-based). Electronic applications accepted.

**Michigan State University,** The Graduate School, College of Natural Science, Interdepartmental Program in Ecology, Evolutionary Biology and Behavior, East Lansing, MI 48824. Offers PhD. *Entrance requirements:* Additional exam requirements/recommendations for international students: required—TOEFL. Electronic applications accepted.

**Montana State University,** The Graduate School, College of Letters and Science, Department of Ecology, Bozeman, MT 59717. Offers ecological and environmental statistics (MS); ecology and environmental sciences (PhD); fish and wildlife biology (PhD); fish and wildlife management (MS). *Program availability:* Part-time. *Degree requirements:* For master's, comprehensive exam, thesis (for some programs); for doctorate, comprehensive exam, thesis/dissertation. *Entrance requirements:* For master's and doctorate, GRE, minimum GPA of 3.0, letters of recommendation, essay. Additional exam requirements/recommendations for international students: required—TOEFL (minimum score 550 paper-based). Electronic applications accepted.

**Montclair State University,** The Graduate School, College of Science and Mathematics, Program in Biology, Montclair, NJ 07043-1624. Offers biological science/education (MS); biology (MS); ecology and evolution (MS); physiology (MS).

**Naropa University,** Graduate Programs, Program in Ecopsychology, Boulder, CO 80302-6697. Offers MA. *Program availability:* Part-time, blended/hybrid learning. *Degree requirements:* For master's, thesis, service learning. *Entrance requirements:* For master's, curriculum vitae/resume with pertinent academic, employment and volunteer activities; 2 letters of recommendation; transcripts; letter of interest. Additional exam requirements/recommendations for international students: required—TOEFL (minimum score 550 paper-based; 80 iBT). Electronic applications accepted. *Expenses:* Contact institution.

**Northeastern Illinois University,** College of Graduate Studies and Research, College of Arts and Sciences, Program in Biology, Chicago, IL 60625. Offers biology (MS), including cell biology, ecology, molecular biology, organismal biology. *Program availability:* Part-time, evening/weekend. *Degree requirements:* For master's, comprehensive exam, thesis optional. *Entrance requirements:* For master's, minimum GPA of 2.75. Additional exam requirements/recommendations for international students: required—TOEFL (minimum score 550 paper-based; 79 iBT). Electronic applications accepted.

**The Ohio State University,** Graduate School, College of Arts and Sciences, Division of Natural and Mathematical Sciences, Department of Evolution, Ecology, and Organismal Biology, Columbus, OH 43210. Offers MS, PhD. *Entrance requirements:* For master's and doctorate, GRE General Test. Additional exam requirements/recommendations for international students: required—TOEFL (minimum score 550 paper-based; 79 iBT), Michigan English Language Assessment Battery (minimum score 86); recommended—IELTS (minimum score 7). Electronic applications accepted.

**The Ohio State University,** Graduate School, College of Food, Agricultural, and Environmental Sciences, School of Environment and Natural Resources, Columbus, OH 43210. Offers ecological restoration (MS, PhD); ecosystem science (MS, PhD); environment and natural resources (MENR); environmental social sciences (MS, PhD); fisheries and wildlife science (MS, PhD); forest science (MS, PhD); rural sociology (MS,

*Ecology*

PhD); soil science (MS, PhD). *Entrance requirements:* For master's and doctorate, GRE. Additional exam requirements/recommendations for international students: required—TOEFL (minimum score 550 paper-based; 79 iBT), Michigan English Language Assessment Battery (minimum score 82); recommended—IELTS (minimum score 7). Electronic applications accepted.

**Ohio University,** Graduate College, College of Arts and Sciences, Department of Biological Sciences, Athens, OH 45701-2979. Offers biological sciences (MS, PhD); cell biology and physiology (MS, PhD); ecology and evolutionary biology (MS, PhD); exercise physiology and muscle biology (MS, PhD); microbiology (MS, PhD); neuroscience (MS, PhD). Terminal master's awarded for partial completion of doctoral program. *Degree requirements:* For master's, comprehensive exam, thesis, 1 quarter of teaching experience; for doctorate, comprehensive exam, thesis/dissertation, 2 quarters of teaching experience. *Entrance requirements:* For master's, GRE General Test, names of three faculty members whose research interests most closely match the applicant's interest; for doctorate, GRE General Test, essay concerning prior training, research interest and career goals, plus names of three faculty members whose research interests most closely match the applicant's interest. Additional exam requirements/recommendations for international students: required—TOEFL (minimum score 620 paper-based; 105 iBT) or IELTS (minimum score 7.5). Electronic applications accepted.

**Oklahoma State University,** College of Arts and Sciences, Department of Plant Biology, Ecology, and Evolution, Stillwater, OK 74078. Offers botany (MS); environmental science.(PhD). *Faculty:* 8 full-time (2 women). *Students:* 13 part-time (4 women), 5 international. Average age 28. 4 applicants, 75% accepted, 2 enrolled. In 2019, 5 master's awarded. *Entrance requirements:* For master's and doctorate, GRE or GMAT. Additional exam requirements/recommendations for international students: required—TOEFL (minimum score 550 paper-based; 79 iBT). *Application deadline:* For fall admission, 3/1 priority date for international students; for spring admission, 8/1 priority date for international students. Applications are processed on a rolling basis. Application fee: $50 ($75 for international students). Electronic applications accepted. *Expenses:* Tuition, area resident: Full-time $4148.10; part-time $2765.40 per credit hour. Tuition, state resident: full-time $4148.10; part-time $2765.40 per credit hour. Tuition, nonresident: full-time $15,775; part-time $10,516.80 per credit hour. *International tuition:* $15,775.20 full-time. *Required fees:* $2196.90; $122.05 per credit hour. Tuition and fees vary according to course load, campus/location and program. *Financial support:* In 2019–20, 2 research assistantships (averaging $2,575 per year), 11 teaching assistantships (averaging $2,274 per year) were awarded; career-related internships or fieldwork, Federal Work-Study, scholarships/grants, health care benefits, tuition waivers (partial), and unspecified assistantships also available. Support available to part-time students. Financial award application deadline: 3/1; financial award applicants required to submit FAFSA. *Unit head:* Dr. Andrew Doust, Department Head, 405-744-2544, Fax: 405-744-7074, E-mail: andrew.doust@okstate.edu. *Application contact:* Dr. Sheryl Tucker, Dean, 405-744-6368, Fax: 405-744-0355, E-mail: gradi@okstate.edu.
Website: http://plantbio.okstate.edu

**Old Dominion University,** College of Sciences, Program in Ecological Sciences, Norfolk, VA 23529. Offers PhD. *Degree requirements:* For doctorate, one foreign language, comprehensive exam, thesis/dissertation. *Entrance requirements:* For doctorate, GRE General Test, 3 letters of recommendation. Additional exam requirements/recommendations for international students: required—TOEFL (minimum score 550 paper-based; 79 iBT). Electronic applications accepted.

**Oregon State University,** College of Agricultural Sciences, Program in Botany and Plant Pathology, Corvallis, OR 97331. Offers applied systematics (MS); ecology (MS, PhD); genetics (MS, PhD); genomics and computational biology (MS, PhD); molecular and cellular biology (MS, PhD); mycology (MS, PhD); plant pathology (MS, PhD); plant physiology (MS, PhD). *Entrance requirements:* For master's and doctorate, GRE.

**Oregon State University,** Interdisciplinary/Institutional Programs, Program in Environmental Sciences, Corvallis, OR 97331. Offers biogeochemistry (MA, MS, PSM, PhD); ecology (MA, MS, PSM, PhD); environmental education (MA, MS, PhD); quantitative analysis (PSM); social science (MA, MS, PSM, PhD); water resources (MA, MS, PhD). *Program availability:* Part-time. *Degree requirements:* For master's, variable foreign language requirement, thesis; for doctorate, thesis/dissertation. *Entrance requirements:* For master's and doctorate, GRE. Additional exam requirements/recommendations for international students: required—TOEFL (minimum score 80 iBT), IELTS (minimum score 6.5).

**Penn State University Park,** Graduate School, Intercollege Graduate Programs, Intercollege Graduate Program in Ecology, University Park, PA 16802. Offers MS, PhD.

**Princeton University,** Graduate School, Department of Ecology and Evolutionary Biology, Princeton, NJ 08544-1019. Offers PhD. *Degree requirements:* For doctorate, thesis/dissertation. *Entrance requirements:* For doctorate, GRE General Test, GRE Subject Test. Additional exam requirements/recommendations for international students: required—TOEFL (minimum score 600 paper-based). Electronic applications accepted.

**Purdue University,** College of Engineering, Division of Environmental and Ecological Engineering, West Lafayette, IN 47907. Offers MS, PhD. *Faculty:* 1. *Students:* 54. *Degree requirements:* For master's, thesis optional; for doctorate, thesis/dissertation. *Application deadline:* For fall admission, 12/15 for domestic and international students; for spring admission, 9/15 for domestic and international students. Application fee: $60 ($75 for international students). *Financial support:* Fellowships with full and partial tuition reimbursements, research assistantships with full and partial tuition reimbursements, teaching assistantships with full and partial tuition reimbursements, career-related internships or fieldwork, scholarships/grants, health care benefits, and unspecified assistantships available. *Unit head:* Dr. John W. Sutherland, Professor/Head of Environmental and Ecological Engineering, 765-496-9697, E-mail: jwsuther@purdue.edu. *Application contact:* Cresta Cates, Graduate Administrative Assistant, 765-496-0545, E-mail: eeegrad@purdue.edu.
Website: https://engineering.purdue.edu/EEE

**Purdue University,** Graduate School, College of Agriculture, Department of Forestry and Natural Resources, West Lafayette, IN 47907. Offers fisheries and aquatic sciences (MS, MSF, PhD); forest biology (MS, MSF, PhD); natural resource social science (MS, PhD); natural resources social science (MSF); quantitative ecology (MS, MSF, PhD); wildlife science (MS, MSF, PhD); wood products and wood products manufacturing (MS, MSF, PhD). *Faculty:* 29 full-time (7 women), 3 part-time/adjunct (1 woman). *Students:* 62 full-time (38 women), 13 part-time (7 women); includes 15 minority (1 Black or African American, non-Hispanic/Latino; 1 American Indian or Alaska Native, non-Hispanic/Latino; 2 Asian, non-Hispanic/Latino; 5 Hispanic/Latino; 1 Native Hawaiian or other Pacific Islander, non-Hispanic/Latino; 5 Two or more races, non-Hispanic/Latino), 12 international. Average age 28. 56 applicants, 32% accepted, 17 enrolled. In 2019, 18 master's, 11 doctorates awarded. *Degree requirements:* For master's, thesis; for doctorate, thesis/dissertation. *Entrance requirements:* For master's and doctorate, GRE General Test (minimum score: verbal 50th percentile; quantitative 50th percentile; analytical writing 4.0), minimum undergraduate GPA of 3.2 or equivalent. Additional

exam requirements/recommendations for international students: required—TOEFL (minimum score 550 paper-based; 77 iBT). *Application deadline:* For fall admission, 1/5 for domestic students, 1/15 for international students; for spring admission, 9/15 for domestic and international students. Applications are processed on a rolling basis. Application fee: $60 ($75 for international students). Electronic applications accepted. *Financial support:* In 2019–20, 10 research assistantships (averaging $15,259 per year) were awarded; fellowships, teaching assistantships, career-related internships or fieldwork, and scholarships/grants also available. Support available to part-time students. Financial award application deadline: 1/5; financial award applicants required to submit FAFSA. *Unit head:* Robert G. Wagner, Head of the Graduate Program, 765-494-3590, E-mail: rgwagner@purdue.edu. *Application contact:* Jacqueline Getson, Graduate Contact, 765-494-3572, E-mail: jgetson@purdue.edu.
Website: https://ag.purdue.edu/fnr

**Purdue University,** Graduate School, Interdisciplinary Graduate Program in Ecological Sciences and Engineering, West Lafayette, IN 47907. Offers MS, PhD. *Students:* 23 full-time (17 women), 2 part-time (1 woman); includes 5 minority (1 Black or African American, non-Hispanic/Latino; 3 Hispanic/Latino; 1 Two or more races, non-Hispanic/Latino), 8 international. Average age 27. 20 applicants, 65% accepted, 7 enrolled. *Degree requirements:* For master's, thesis optional; for doctorate, thesis/dissertation, written and oral preliminary exam. *Entrance requirements:* For master's and doctorate, GRE (minimum old score Verbal and Quantitative combined 1200, new score 300; Analytical Writing 4.0), previous research or environmental project experience; minimum GPA of 3.3. Additional exam requirements/recommendations for international students: required—TOEFL (minimum score 550 paper-based; 77 iBT), IELTS (minimum score 6.5); recommended—TWE. *Application deadline:* For fall admission, 12/15 for domestic and international students. Applications are processed on a rolling basis. Application fee: $65 ($70 for international students). Electronic applications accepted. *Financial support:* Fellowships and research assistantships available. *Unit head:* Dr. Linda S. Lee, Head of the Graduate Program, 765-494-8612, E-mail: lslee@purdue.edu. *Application contact:* Deirdre Carmicheal, Graduate Contact, 765-494-0379, E-mail: dnolan@purdue.edu.
Website: http://www.gradschool.purdue.edu/ese/

**Rice University,** Graduate Programs, Wiess School of Natural Sciences, Department of Ecology and Evolutionary Biology, Houston, TX 77251-1892. Offers MA, MS, PhD. Terminal master's awarded for partial completion of doctoral program. *Degree requirements:* For master's, comprehensive exam (for some programs), thesis (for some programs); for doctorate, comprehensive exam, thesis/dissertation. *Entrance requirements:* For master's and doctorate, GRE General Test, GRE Subject Test. Additional exam requirements/recommendations for international students: required—TOEFL (minimum score 600 paper-based; 90 iBT). Electronic applications accepted.

**Rutgers University - New Brunswick,** Graduate School-New Brunswick, Program in Ecology and Evolution, Piscataway, NJ 08854-8097. Offers MS, PhD. *Program availability:* Part-time. Terminal master's awarded for partial completion of doctoral program. *Degree requirements:* For master's, comprehensive exam; for doctorate, comprehensive exam, thesis/dissertation. *Entrance requirements:* For master's and doctorate, GRE General Test, minimum GPA of 3.0. Additional exam requirements/recommendations for international students: required—TOEFL (minimum score 550 paper-based). Electronic applications accepted.

**San Diego State University,** Graduate and Research Affairs, College of Sciences, Department of Biology, Program in Ecology, San Diego, CA 92182. Offers MS, PhD. *Degree requirements:* For master's, thesis; for doctorate, thesis/dissertation. *Entrance requirements:* For master's, GRE General Test, resumé or curriculum vitae, 2 letters of recommendation; for doctorate, GRE General Test, GRE Subject Test, resume or curriculum vitae, 3 letters of recommendation. Electronic applications accepted.

**San Francisco State University,** Division of Graduate Studies, College of Science and Engineering, Department of Biology, Program in Integrative Biology, San Francisco, CA 94132-1722. Offers MS. *Application deadline:* Applications are processed on a rolling basis. *Expenses:* Tuition, area resident: Full-time $7176; part-time $4164 per year. Tuition, state resident: full-time $7176; part-time $4164 per year. Tuition, nonresident: full-time $16,680; part-time $396 per unit. *International tuition:* $16,680 full-time. *Required fees:* $1524; $1524 per unit. $762 per semester. Tuition and fees vary according to degree level and program. *Unit head:* Dr. Andrew Zink, Coordinator, 415-405-2761, Fax: 415-338-6136, E-mail: zink@sfsu.edu. *Application contact:* Dr. Andrew Zink, Coordinator, 415-405-2761, Fax: 415-338-6136, E-mail: zink@sfsu.edu.
Website: http://biology.sfsu.edu/graduate/ecology-evolution-and-conservation-biology-eecb-0

**San Jose State University,** Program in Biological Sciences, San Jose, CA 95192-0001. Offers biological sciences (MA, MS); molecular biology and microbiology (MS); organismal biology, conservation and ecology (MS); physiology (MS). *Program availability:* Part-time. *Entrance requirements:* For master's, GRE. Electronic applications accepted. *Expenses:* Tuition, area resident: Full-time $7176; part-time $4164 per credit hour. Tuition, state resident: full-time $7176; part-time $4164 per credit hour. Tuition, nonresident: full-time $7176; part-time $4165 per credit hour. *International tuition:* $7176 full-time. *Required fees:* $2110; $2110.

**Stanford University,** School of Humanities and Sciences, Department of Anthropology, Stanford, CA 94305-2004. Offers anthropology (MA); archaeology (PhD); culture and society (PhD); ecology and environment (PhD). *Expenses:* Tuition: Full-time $52,479; part-time $34,110 per unit. *Required fees:* $672; $224 per quarter. Tuition and fees vary according to program and student level.
Website: http://www.stanford.edu/dept/anthsci/

**State University of New York College of Environmental Science and Forestry,** Department of Environmental and Forest Biology, Syracuse, NY 13210-2779. Offers applied ecology (MPS); chemical ecology (MPS, MS, PhD); conservation biology (MPS, MS, PhD); ecology (MPS, MS, PhD); entomology (MPS, MS, PhD); environmental interpretation (MPS, MS, PhD); environmental physiology (MPS, MS, PhD); fish and wildlife biology and management (MPS, MS, PhD); forest pathology and mycology (MPS, MS, PhD); plant biotechnology (MPS); plant science and biotechnology (MPS, MS, PhD). *Program availability:* Part-time. *Faculty:* 35 full-time (10 women), 4 part-time/adjunct (3 women). *Students:* 103 full-time (60 women), 17 part-time (7 women); includes 7 minority (4 American Indian or Alaska Native, non-Hispanic/Latino; 2 Asian, non-Hispanic/Latino; 1 Hispanic/Latino), 13 international. Average age 29. 69 applicants, 45% accepted, 17 enrolled. In 2019, 28 master's, 6 doctorates awarded. Terminal master's awarded for partial completion of doctoral program. *Degree requirements:* For master's, thesis (for some programs), capstone seminar; for doctorate, comprehensive exam, thesis/dissertation, capstone seminar. *Entrance requirements:* For master's and doctorate, GRE General Test, minimum GPA of 3.0. Additional exam requirements/recommendations for international students: required—TOEFL (minimum score 550 paper-based; 80 iBT), IELTS (minimum score 6). *Application deadline:* For fall admission, 2/1 priority date for domestic and international students; for spring admission, 11/1 priority date for domestic and international students. Applications are processed on a rolling basis. Application fee: $60. Electronic applications accepted. *Expenses:* Tuition, state resident: full-time $11,310; part-time

$472 per credit hour. Tuition, nonresident: full-time $23,100; part-time $963 per credit hour. *Required fees:* $1890; $95.21 per credit hour. *Financial support:* In 2019–20, 35 students received support. Unspecified assistantships available. Financial award application deadline: 6/30; financial award applicants required to submit FAFSA. *Unit head:* Dr. Melissa K. Fierke, Chair, 315-470-6809, Fax: 315-470-6743, E-mail: mkfierke@esf.edu. *Application contact:* Laura Payne, Administrative Assistant Office of Instruction & Graduate Studies, 315-470-6599, E-mail: esfgrad@esf.edu.
Website: http://www.esf.edu/efb/grad/default.asp

**State University of New York College of Environmental Science and Forestry,** Department of Sustainable Resources Management, Syracuse, NY 13210-2779. Offers ecology and ecosystems (MPS, MS, PhD); economics, governance and human dimensions (MPS, MS, PhD); forest and natural resources management (MPS, MS, PhD); forest resources management (MF); monitoring, analysis and modeling (MPS, MS, PhD). *Accreditation:* SAF. *Program availability:* Part-time. *Faculty:* 33 full-time (8 women), 7 part-time/adjunct (0 women). *Students:* 106 full-time (67 women), 18 part-time (12 women); includes 10 minority (2 Black or African American, non-Hispanic/Latino; 4 American Indian or Alaska Native, non-Hispanic/Latino; 3 Asian, non-Hispanic/Latino; 1 Hispanic/Latino), 40 international. Average age 30. 96 applicants, 83% accepted, 39 enrolled. In 2019, 13 master's, 3 doctorates awarded. Terminal master's awarded for partial completion of doctoral program. *Degree requirements:* For master's, thesis (for some programs); for doctorate, comprehensive exam, thesis/dissertation. *Entrance requirements:* For master's and doctorate, GRE General Test, minimum GPA of 3.0. Additional exam requirements/recommendations for international students: required—TOEFL (minimum score 550 paper-based; 80 iBT), IELTS (minimum score 6). *Application deadline:* For fall admission, 2/1 priority date for domestic and international students; for spring admission, 11/1 priority date for domestic and international students. Applications are processed on a rolling basis. Application fee: $60. *Expenses:* Tuition, state resident: full-time $11,310; part-time $472 per credit hour. Tuition, nonresident: full-time $23,100; part-time $963 per credit hour. *Required fees:* $1890; $95.21 per credit hour. *Financial support:* In 2019–20, 21 students received support. Unspecified assistantships available. Financial award application deadline: 6/30; financial award applicants required to submit FAFSA. *Unit head:* Dr. Christopher Nowak, Chair, 315-470-6575, Fax: 315-470-6536, E-mail: canowak@esf.edu. *Application contact:* Laura Payne, Office of Instruction & Graduate Studies, 315-470-6599, Fax: 315-470-6978, E-mail: esfgrad@esf.edu.
Website: http://www.esf.edu/fnrm/

**Stony Brook University, State University of New York,** Graduate School, College of Arts and Sciences, Department of Ecology and Evolution, Stony Brook, NY 11794. Offers applied ecology (MA); ecology and evolution (PhD). *Faculty:* 15 full-time (5 women), 1 part-time/adjunct (0 women). *Students:* 37 full-time (16 women); includes 4 minority (2 Asian, non-Hispanic/Latino; 2 Hispanic/Latino), 9 international. Average age 27. 23 applicants, 30% accepted, 4 enrolled. In 2019, 8 doctorates awarded. *Degree requirements:* For doctorate, one foreign language, comprehensive exam, thesis/dissertation, teaching experience. *Entrance requirements:* For doctorate, GRE General Test, GRE Subject Test. Additional exam requirements/recommendations for international students: required—TOEFL. *Application deadline:* For fall admission, 1/15 for domestic students; for spring admission, 10/1 for domestic students. Application fee: $100. Electronic applications accepted. *Expenses:* Contact institution. *Financial support:* In 2019–20, 4 fellowships, 8 research assistantships, 21 teaching assistantships were awarded; Federal Work-Study also available. *Unit head:* Dr. Robert W. Thacker, Chair, 631-632-8590, E-mail: robert.thacker@stonybrook.edu. *Application contact:* Melissa Cohen, Coordinator, 631-246-8604, Fax: 631-632-7626, E-mail: melissa.j.cohen@stonybrook.edu.
Website: http://life.bio.sunysb.edu/ee/

**Tulane University,** School of Science and Engineering, Department of Ecology and Evolutionary Biology, New Orleans, LA 70118-5669. Offers MS, PhD. Terminal master's awarded for partial completion of doctoral program. *Degree requirements:* For master's, thesis or alternative; for doctorate, thesis/dissertation. *Entrance requirements:* For master's, GRE General Test, minimum B average in undergraduate course work; for doctorate, GRE General Test. Additional exam requirements/recommendations for international students: required—TOEFL. Electronic applications accepted. *Expenses: Tuition:* Full-time $57,004; part-time $3167 per credit hour. *Required fees:* $2086; $44.50 per credit hour. $80 per term. Tuition and fees vary according to course load, degree level and program.

**Universidad Nacional Pedro Henriquez Urena,** Graduate School, Santo Domingo, Dominican Republic. Offers agricultural diversity (MS), including horticultural/fruit production, tropical animal production; conservation of monuments and cultural assets (M Arch); ecology and environment (MS); environmental engineering (MEE); international relations (MA); natural resource management (MS); political science (MA); project feasibility (MPM); project management (MPM); project optimization (MPM); sanitation engineering (ME); science for teachers (MS); tropical Caribbean architecture (M Arch).

**University at Buffalo, the State University of New York,** Graduate School, College of Arts and Sciences, Program in Evolution, Ecology and Behavior, Buffalo, NY 14260. Offers MS, PhD, Certificate. Terminal master's awarded for partial completion of doctoral program. *Degree requirements:* For master's, project; for doctorate, comprehensive exam, thesis/dissertation. *Entrance requirements:* For master's, GRE, minimum undergraduate GPA of 3.0; for doctorate, GRE, minimum GPA of 3.0. Additional exam requirements/recommendations for international students: required—TOEFL (minimum score 550 paper-based; 79 iBT). Electronic applications accepted. *Expenses: Tuition, area resident:* Full-time $11,310; part-time $471 per credit hour. Tuition, state resident: full-time $11,310; part-time $471 per credit hour. Tuition, nonresident: full-time $23,100; part-time $963 per credit hour. *International tuition:* $23,100 full-time. *Required fees:* $2820.

**University at Buffalo, the State University of New York,** Graduate School, School of Architecture and Planning, Department of Architecture, Buffalo, NY 14260. Offers architecture (M Arch); ecological practices, inclusive design, situated technologies, historic preservation (MS Arch); M Arch/MBA; M Arch/MFA; M Arch/MUP. *Program availability:* Part-time. *Faculty:* 30 full-time (10 women), 7 part-time/adjunct (4 women). *Students:* 122 full-time (55 women), 9 part-time (6 women); includes 25 minority (6 Black or African American, non-Hispanic/Latino; 11 Asian, non-Hispanic/Latino; 7 Hispanic/Latino; 1 Two or more races, non-Hispanic/Latino), 32 international. Average age 25. 170 applicants, 43% accepted, 57 enrolled. In 2019, 45 master's awarded. *Degree requirements:* For master's, thesis or alternative, project, portfolio. *Entrance requirements:* For master's, portfolio, two letters of recommendation, transcripts, personal statement. Additional exam requirements/recommendations for international students: required—TOEFL (minimum score 79 iBT), IELTS (minimum score 6.5). *Application deadline:* For fall admission, 1/1 priority date for domestic and international students. Application fee: $75. Electronic applications accepted. *Expenses:* Contact institution. *Financial support:* In 2019–20, 86 students received support, including 4 fellowships with full tuition reimbursements available (averaging $15,600 per year), 2 research assistantships with partial tuition reimbursements available (averaging $15,814 per year), 40 teaching assistantships with partial tuition reimbursements available (averaging $5,756 per year); career-related internships or fieldwork, Federal Work-Study, scholarships/grants, health care benefits, tuition waivers (full and partial), and unspecified assistantships also available. Financial award application deadline: 3/1; financial award applicants required to submit FAFSA. *Unit head:* Dr. Korydon Smith, Professor and Chair, 716-829-5908, Fax: 716-829-3256, E-mail: khsmith@buffalo.edu. *Application contact:* Stacey Komendat, Graduate Programs Coordinator, 716-829-3671, Fax: 716-829-3256, E-mail: staceyga@buffalo.edu.
Website: http://www.ap.buffalo.edu/architecture/

**University of Alberta,** Faculty of Graduate Studies and Research, Department of Biological Sciences, Edmonton, AB T6G 2E1, Canada. Offers environmental biology and ecology (M Sc, PhD); microbiology and biotechnology (M Sc, PhD); molecular biology and genetics (M Sc, PhD); physiology and cell biology (M Sc, PhD); plant biology (M Sc, PhD); systematics and evolution (M Sc, PhD). Terminal master's awarded for partial completion of doctoral program. *Degree requirements:* For master's, thesis; for doctorate, thesis/dissertation. *Entrance requirements:* Additional exam requirements/recommendations for international students: required—TOEFL.

**The University of Arizona,** College of Science, Department of Ecology and Evolutionary Biology, Tucson, AZ 85721. Offers MS, PhD. Terminal master's awarded for partial completion of doctoral program. *Degree requirements:* For master's, thesis optional; for doctorate, one foreign language, comprehensive exam, thesis/dissertation. *Entrance requirements:* For master's, GRE General Test, GRE Subject Test, statement of purpose, curriculum vitae, 3 letters of recommendation; for doctorate, GRE General Test, GRE Subject Test, curriculum vitae, 3 letters of recommendation. Additional exam requirements/recommendations for international students: required—TOEFL (minimum score 550 paper-based; 79 iBT).

**University of California, Davis,** Graduate Studies, Graduate Group in Ecology, Davis, CA 95616. Offers MS, PhD. *Degree requirements:* For master's, comprehensive exam (for some programs), thesis (for some programs); for doctorate, thesis/dissertation. *Entrance requirements:* For master's and doctorate, GRE General Test. Additional exam requirements/recommendations for international students: required—TOEFL (minimum score 550 paper-based). Electronic applications accepted.

**University of California, Irvine,** School of Biological Sciences, Department of Ecology and Evolutionary Biology, Irvine, CA 92697. Offers biological sciences (MS, PhD). *Students:* 85 full-time (50 women); includes 36 minority (2 Black or African American, non-Hispanic/Latino; 9 Asian, non-Hispanic/Latino; 23 Hispanic/Latino; 2 Two or more races, non-Hispanic/Latino), 7 international. Average age 28. 107 applicants, 35% accepted, 25 enrolled. In 2019, 19 master's, 14 doctorates awarded. *Entrance requirements:* For master's and doctorate, GRE General Test, GRE Subject Test, minimum GPA of 3.0. Additional exam requirements/recommendations for international students: required—TOEFL (minimum score 550 paper-based). *Application deadline:* For fall admission, 1/15 priority date for domestic students, 1/15 for international students. Applications are processed on a rolling basis. Application fee: $120 ($140 for international students). Electronic applications accepted. *Financial support:* Fellowships, research assistantships with full tuition reimbursements, teaching assistantships, career-related internships or fieldwork, institutionally sponsored loans, traineeships, health care benefits, and unspecified assistantships available. Financial award application deadline: 3/1; financial award applicants required to submit FAFSA. *Unit head:* James W. Hicks, Department Chair, 949-824-6386, Fax: 949-824-2181, E-mail: jhicks@uci.edu. *Application contact:* Pam McDonald, Student Affairs Coordinator, 949-824-4743, Fax: 949-824-2181, E-mail: pmcdonal@uci.edu.
Website: http://ecoevo.bio.uci.edu/

**University of California, Los Angeles,** Graduate Division, College of Letters and Science, Department of Ecology and Evolutionary Biology, Los Angeles, CA 90095. Offers MA, PhD. Terminal master's awarded for partial completion of doctoral program. *Degree requirements:* For master's, comprehensive exam or thesis; for doctorate, thesis/dissertation, oral and written qualifying exams; 3 quarters of teaching experience. *Entrance requirements:* For master's and doctorate, GRE General Test, GRE Subject Test (biology), bachelor's degree; minimum undergraduate GPA of 3.0 (or its equivalent if letter grade system not used). Additional exam requirements/recommendations for international students: required—TOEFL. Electronic applications accepted.

**University of California, Santa Barbara,** Graduate Division, College of Letters and Sciences, Division of Mathematics, Life, and Physical Sciences, Department of Ecology, Evolution, and Marine Biology, Santa Barbara, CA 93106-9620. Offers MA, PhD, MA/PhD. *Degree requirements:* For master's, comprehensive exam (for some programs), thesis (for some programs); for doctorate, comprehensive exam, thesis/dissertation. *Entrance requirements:* For master's and doctorate, GRE General Test. Additional exam requirements/recommendations for international students: required—TOEFL (minimum score 550 paper-based; 80 iBT), IELTS. Electronic applications accepted.

**University of California, Santa Cruz,** Division of Graduate Studies, Division of Physical and Biological Sciences, Department of Ecology and Evolutionary Biology, Santa Cruz, CA 95064. Offers MA, PhD. *Degree requirements:* For master's, thesis; for doctorate, comprehensive exam, thesis/dissertation. *Entrance requirements:* For master's and doctorate, GRE General Test, GRE Subject Test, 3 letters of recommendation. Additional exam requirements/recommendations for international students: required—TOEFL (minimum score 550 paper-based; 83 iBT); recommended—IELTS (minimum score 8). Electronic applications accepted.

**University of Chicago,** Division of the Biological Sciences, Department of Ecology and Evolution, Chicago, IL 60637. Offers PhD. *Degree requirements:* For doctorate, comprehensive exam, thesis/dissertation, ethics class, 2 teaching assistantships. *Entrance requirements:* For doctorate, GRE General Test, transcripts, statement of purpose, 3 letters of recommendation. Additional exam requirements/recommendations for international students: required—TOEFL (minimum score 600 paper-based; 104 iBT), IELTS (minimum score 7). Electronic applications accepted.

**University of Colorado Boulder,** Graduate School, College of Arts and Sciences, Department of Ecology and Evolutionary Biology, Boulder, CO 80309. Offers population biology (MA). Terminal master's awarded for partial completion of doctoral program. *Degree requirements:* For master's, comprehensive exam, thesis or alternative; for doctorate, comprehensive exam, thesis/dissertation. *Entrance requirements:* For master's, GRE General Test, GRE Subject Test, minimum undergraduate GPA of 3.0; for doctorate, GRE General Test, GRE Subject Test. Electronic applications accepted. Application fee is waived when completed online.

**University of Colorado Denver,** College of Liberal Arts and Sciences, Department of Geography and Environmental Sciences, Denver, CO 80217. Offers environmental sciences (MS), including air quality, ecosystems, environmental health, geospatial analysis, hazardous waste, water quality. *Program availability:* Part-time, evening/weekend. *Degree requirements:* For master's, thesis or alternative, 30 credits including 21 of core requirements and 9 of environmental science electives. *Entrance requirements:* For master's, GRE General Test, BA in one of the natural/physical sciences or engineering (or equivalent background); prerequisite coursework in calculus and physics (one semester each); general chemistry with lab and general biology with lab (two semesters each); three letters of recommendation. Additional exam requirements/recommendations for international students: required—TOEFL (minimum

score 537 paper-based; 75 iBT); recommended—IELTS (minimum score 6.5). Electronic applications accepted. Tuition and fees vary according to course load, program and reciprocity agreements.

**University of Connecticut,** Graduate School, College of Liberal Arts and Sciences, Department of Psychological Sciences, Storrs, CT 06269. Offers behavioral neuroscience (PhD); biopsychology (PhD); clinical psychology (MA, PhD); cognition and instruction (PhD); developmental psychology (MA, PhD); ecological psychology (PhD); experimental psychology (PhD); general psychology (MA, PhD); industrial/organizational psychology (PhD); language and cognition (PhD); neuroscience (PhD); social psychology (MA, PhD). *Accreditation:* APA. Terminal master's awarded for partial completion of doctoral program. *Degree requirements:* For master's, comprehensive exam; for doctorate, thesis/dissertation. *Entrance requirements:* For master's and doctorate, GRE General Test, GRE Subject Test. Additional exam requirements/recommendations for international students: required—TOEFL (minimum score 550 paper-based). Electronic applications accepted.

**University of Delaware,** College of Agriculture and Natural Resources, Department of Entomology and Wildlife Ecology, Newark, DE 19716. Offers entomology and applied ecology (MS, PhD), including avian ecology, evolution and taxonomy, insect biological control, insect ecology and behavior (MS), insect genetics, pest management, plant-insect interactions, wildlife ecology and management. *Program availability:* Part-time. *Degree requirements:* For master's, comprehensive exam, thesis, oral exam, seminar; for doctorate, comprehensive exam, thesis/dissertation, qualifying exam, seminar. *Entrance requirements:* For master's, GRE General Test, minimum GPA of 3.0 in field, 2.8 overall; for doctorate, GRE General Test, GRE Subject Test (biology), minimum GPA of 3.0 in field, 2.8 overall. Additional exam requirements/recommendations for international students: required—TOEFL. Electronic applications accepted.

**University of Delaware,** College of Arts and Sciences, Department of Biological Sciences, Newark, DE 19716. Offers biotechnology (MS); cancer biology (MS, PhD); cell and extracellular matrix biology (MS, PhD); cell and systems physiology (MS, PhD); developmental biology (MS, PhD); ecology and evolution (MS, PhD); microbiology (MS, PhD); molecular biology and genetics (MS, PhD). Terminal master's awarded for partial completion of doctoral program. *Degree requirements:* For master's, thesis, preliminary exam; for doctorate, comprehensive exam, thesis/dissertation, preliminary exam. *Entrance requirements:* For master's and doctorate, GRE General Test. Additional exam requirements/recommendations for international students: required—TOEFL (minimum score 600 paper-based); recommended—TWE. Electronic applications accepted.

**University of Denver,** Division of Natural Sciences and Mathematics, Department of Biological Sciences, Denver, CO 80208. Offers biology, ecology and evolution (MS, PhD); biomedical sciences (PSM); cell and molecular biology (MS, PhD). *Program availability:* Part-time. *Faculty:* 23 full-time (10 women), 2 part-time/adjunct (both women). *Students:* 12 full-time (7 women), 31 part-time (18 women); includes 6 minority (4 Hispanic/Latino; 2 Two or more races, non-Hispanic/Latino), 3 international. Average age 25. 100 applicants, 34% accepted, 18 enrolled. In 2019, 9 master's, 6 doctorates awarded. Terminal master's awarded for partial completion of doctoral program. *Degree requirements:* For master's, thesis; for doctorate, comprehensive exam, thesis/dissertation. *Entrance requirements:* For master's and doctorate, GRE General Test, bachelor's degree in biology or related field, transcripts, personal statement, three letters of recommendation. Additional exam requirements/recommendations for international students: required—TOEFL (minimum score 550 paper-based; 80 iBT). *Application deadline:* For fall admission, 1/2 priority date for domestic and international students. Applications are processed on a rolling basis. Application fee: $65. Electronic applications accepted. *Expenses:* Contact institution. *Financial support:* In 2019–20, 43 students received support, including 9 research assistantships with tuition reimbursements available (averaging $16,589 per year), 26 teaching assistantships with tuition reimbursements available (averaging $18,869 per year); Federal Work-Study, institutionally sponsored loans, scholarships/grants, and unspecified assistantships also available. Support available to part-time students. Financial award application deadline: 2/15; financial award applicants required to submit FAFSA. *Unit head:* Dr. Joe Angleson, Associate Professor and Chair, 303-871-3463, E-mail: jangleso@du.edu. *Application contact:* Randi Flageolle, Assistant to the Chair, 303-871-3457, E-mail: rflageol@du.edu.
Website: http://www.du.edu/nsm/departments/biologicalsciences

**University of Florida,** Graduate School, College of Agricultural and Life Sciences, Department of Wildlife Ecology and Conservation, Gainesville, FL 32611. Offers environmental education and communications (Certificate); wildlife ecology and conservation (MS, PhD), including geographic information systems, tropical conservation and development, wetland sciences. *Degree requirements:* For master's, comprehensive exam, thesis optional; for doctorate, comprehensive exam, thesis/dissertation. *Entrance requirements:* For master's and doctorate, GRE General Test (minimum 34th percentile for Quantitative), minimum GPA of 3.3. Additional exam requirements/recommendations for international students: required—TOEFL (minimum score 550 paper-based; 80 iBT), IELTS (minimum score 6). Electronic applications accepted.

**University of Florida,** Graduate School, School of Natural Resources and Environment, Gainesville, FL 32611. Offers interdisciplinary ecology (MS, PhD). *Degree requirements:* For master's, comprehensive exam, thesis; for doctorate, comprehensive exam, thesis/dissertation. *Entrance requirements:* For master's and doctorate, GRE General Test, minimum GPA of 3.0. Additional exam requirements/recommendations for international students: required—TOEFL (minimum score 550 paper-based; 80 iBT), IELTS (minimum score 6). Electronic applications accepted.

**University of Georgia,** Eugene P. Odum School of Ecology, Athens, GA 30602. Offers conservation ecology and sustainable development (MS); ecology (PhD). *Degree requirements:* For master's, thesis; for doctorate, one foreign language, thesis/dissertation. *Entrance requirements:* For master's and doctorate, GRE General Test. Electronic applications accepted.

**University of Guelph,** Office of Graduate and Postdoctoral Studies, College of Biological Science, Department of Integrative Biology, Botany and Zoology, Guelph, ON N1G 2W1, Canada. Offers botany (M Sc, PhD); zoology (M Sc, PhD). *Program availability:* Part-time. *Degree requirements:* For master's, thesis, research proposal; for doctorate, thesis/dissertation, research proposal, qualifying exam. *Entrance requirements:* For master's, minimum B average during previous 2 years of course work. Additional exam requirements/recommendations for international students: required—TOEFL (minimum score 550 paper-based), IELTS (minimum score 6.5). Electronic applications accepted.

**University of Illinois at Urbana-Champaign,** Graduate College, College of Liberal Arts and Sciences, School of Integrative Biology, Department of Animal Biology, Champaign, IL 61820. Offers animal biology (ecology, ethology and evolution) (MS, PhD).

**University of Illinois at Urbana-Champaign,** Graduate College, College of Liberal Arts and Sciences, School of Integrative Biology, Program in Ecology, Evolution and Conservation Biology, Champaign, IL 61820. Offers MS, PhD.

**The University of Kansas,** Graduate Studies, College of Liberal Arts and Sciences, Department of Ecology and Evolutionary Biology, Lawrence, KS 66045. Offers MA, PhD. *Program availability:* Part-time. *Students:* 80 full-time (43 women); includes 9 minority (1 Black or African American, non-Hispanic/Latino; 2 Asian, non-Hispanic/Latino; 3 Hispanic/Latino; 3 Two or more races, non-Hispanic/Latino), 21 international. Average age 30. 62 applicants, 47% accepted, 22 enrolled. In 2019, 5 master's, 9 doctorates awarded. Terminal master's awarded for partial completion of doctoral program. *Degree requirements:* For master's, comprehensive exam, thesis (for some programs), 30-36 credits, thesis presentation; for doctorate, comprehensive exam, thesis/dissertation, residency, final exam, dissertation defense. *Entrance requirements:* For master's and doctorate, GRE General Test, curriculum vitae, personal statement, three letters of recommendation, official transcripts. Additional exam requirements/recommendations for international students: required—TOEFL, IELTS, TOEFL or IELTS. *Application deadline:* For fall admission, 12/1 for domestic and international students. Application fee: $65 ($85 for international students). Electronic applications accepted. *Expenses:* Tuition, state resident: full-time $9989. Tuition, nonresident: full-time $23,950. *International tuition:* $23,950 full-time. *Required fees:* $984; $81.99 per credit hour. Tuition and fees vary according to course load, campus/location and program. *Financial support:* Fellowships, research assistantships, teaching assistantships, scholarships/grants, traineeships, health care benefits, and unspecified assistantships available. Financial award application deadline: 12/1. *Unit head:* Dr. Christopher Haufler, Chair, 785-864-3255, E-mail: vulgare@ku.edu. *Application contact:* Aagje Ashe, Graduate Coordinator, 785-864-2362, Fax: 785-864-5860, E-mail: a4ashe@ku.edu.
Website: http://eeb.ku.edu/

**The University of Manchester,** School of Biological Sciences, Manchester, United Kingdom. Offers adaptive organismal biology (M Phil, PhD); animal biology (M Phil, PhD); biochemistry (M Phil, PhD); bioinformatics (M Phil, PhD); biomolecular sciences (M Phil, PhD); biotechnology (M Phil, PhD); cell biology (M Phil, PhD); cell matrix research (M Phil, PhD); channels and transporters (M Phil, PhD); developmental biology (M Phil, PhD); environmental biology (M Phil, PhD); evolutionary biology (M Phil, PhD); gene expression (M Phil, PhD); genetics (M Phil, PhD); history of science, technology and medicine (M Phil, PhD); immunology (M Phil, PhD); integrative neurobiology and behavior (M Phil, PhD); membrane trafficking (M Phil, PhD); microbiology (M Phil, PhD); molecular and cellular neuroscience (M Phil, PhD); molecular biology (M Phil, PhD); molecular cancer studies (M Phil, PhD); neuroscience (M Phil, PhD); ophthalmology (M Phil, PhD); optometry (M Phil, PhD); organelle function (M Phil, PhD); pharmacology (M Phil, PhD); physiology (M Phil, PhD); plant sciences (M Phil, PhD); stem cell research (M Phil, PhD); structural biology (M Phil, PhD); systems neuroscience (M Phil, PhD); toxicology (M Phil, PhD).

**University of Manitoba,** Faculty of Graduate Studies, Faculty of Science, Department of Biological Sciences, Winnipeg, MB R3T 2N2, Canada. Offers botany (M Sc, PhD); ecology (M Sc, PhD); zoology (M Sc, PhD).

**University of Maryland, College Park,** Academic Affairs, College of Computer, Mathematical and Natural Sciences, Department of Biology, Behavior, Ecology, Evolution, and Systematics Program, College Park, MD 20742. Offers MS, PhD. *Degree requirements:* For master's, thesis, oral defense, seminar; for doctorate, thesis/dissertation, exam, 4 seminars. *Entrance requirements:* For master's and doctorate, GRE General Test, GRE Subject Test (biology), 3 letters of recommendation. Additional exam requirements/recommendations for international students: required—TOEFL.

**University of Maryland, College Park,** Academic Affairs, College of Computer, Mathematical and Natural Sciences, Department of Biology, PhD Program in Biological Sciences, College Park, MD 20742. Offers behavior, ecology, evolution, and systematics (PhD); computational biology, bioinformatics, and genomics (PhD); molecular and cellular biology (PhD); physiological systems (PhD). *Degree requirements:* For doctorate, comprehensive exam, thesis/dissertation, thesis work presentation in seminar. *Entrance requirements:* For doctorate, GRE General Test; GRE Subject Test in biology (recommended), academic transcripts, statement of purpose/research interests, 3 letters of recommendation. Additional exam requirements/recommendations for international students: required—TOEFL. Electronic applications accepted.

**University of Michigan,** Rackham Graduate School, College of Literature, Science, and the Arts, Department of Ecology and Evolutionary Biology, Ann Arbor, MI 48109. Offers MS, PhD. Terminal master's awarded for partial completion of doctoral program. *Degree requirements:* For master's, thesis (for some programs); for doctorate, comprehensive exam, thesis/dissertation, 2 semesters of teaching. *Entrance requirements:* For master's and doctorate, GRE. Additional exam requirements/recommendations for international students: required—TOEFL (minimum score 84 iBT). Electronic applications accepted.

**University of Michigan,** School for Environment and Sustainability, Program in Environment and Sustainability, Ann Arbor, MI 48109. Offers behavior, education and communication (MS); conservation ecology (MS); environment and sustainability (PhD); environmental informatics (MS); environmental justice (MS); environmental policy and planning (MS); sustainable systems (MS); MS/JD; MS/MBA; MS/MPH; MS/MPP; MS/MSE; MS/MURP. Terminal master's awarded for partial completion of doctoral program. *Degree requirements:* For master's, thesis, practicum, or group project; for doctorate, comprehensive exam, thesis/dissertation, oral defense of dissertation, preliminary exam. *Entrance requirements:* For master's, GRE General Test (must be taken within 5 years of application submission); for doctorate, GRE General Test (must be taken within 5 years of application submission), Master's Degree. Additional exam requirements/recommendations for international students: required—TOEFL (minimum score 560 paper-based; 84 iBT). Electronic applications accepted.

**University of Minnesota, Twin Cities Campus,** Graduate School, College of Biological Sciences, Department of Ecology, Evolution, and Behavior, St. Paul, MN 55418. Offers MS, PhD. Terminal master's awarded for partial completion of doctoral program. *Degree requirements:* For master's, comprehensive exam, thesis or projects; for doctorate, comprehensive exam, thesis/dissertation. *Entrance requirements:* For master's and doctorate, GRE General Test, minimum GPA of 3.0. Additional exam requirements/recommendations for international students: required—TOEFL (minimum score 550 paper-based; 79 iBT), Michigan English Language Assessment Battery. Electronic applications accepted.

**University of Missouri,** Office of Research and Graduate Studies, College of Arts and Science, Division of Biological Sciences, Columbia, MO 65211. Offers evolutionary biology and ecology (MA, PhD). Terminal master's awarded for partial completion of doctoral program. *Entrance requirements:* For master's and doctorate, GRE General Test (minimum score 1200 verbal and quantitative), minimum GPA of 3.0. Additional exam requirements/recommendations for international students: required—TOEFL.

**University of Montana,** Graduate School, College of Forestry and Conservation, Missoula, MT 59812. Offers fish and wildlife biology (PhD); forest and conservation sciences (PhD); forestry (MS); recreation management (MS); resource conservation (MS); systems ecology (MS, PhD); wildlife biology (MS). *Degree requirements:* For doctorate, thesis/dissertation. *Entrance requirements:* For master's and doctorate, GRE

General Test. Additional exam requirements/recommendations for international students: required—TOEFL (minimum score 575 paper-based).

**University of Montana,** Graduate School, College of Humanities and Sciences, Division of Biological Sciences, Interdisciplinary Program in Systems Ecology, Missoula, MT 59812. Offers MS, PhD.

**University of Montana,** Graduate School, College of Humanities and Sciences, Division of Biological Sciences, Program in Organismal Biology and Ecology, Missoula, MT 59812. Offers MS, PhD. Terminal master's awarded for partial completion of doctoral program. *Degree requirements:* For master's, one foreign language, thesis; for doctorate, 2 foreign languages, thesis/dissertation. *Entrance requirements:* For master's and doctorate, GRE General Test.

**University of Nevada, Reno,** Graduate School, Interdisciplinary Program in Ecology, Evolution, and Conservation Biology, Reno, NV 89557. Offers PhD. *Degree requirements:* For doctorate, thesis/dissertation. *Entrance requirements:* For doctorate, GRE General Test, GRE Subject Test, minimum GPA of 3.0. Additional exam requirements/recommendations for international students: required—TOEFL (minimum score 500 paper-based; 61 iBT), IELTS (minimum score 6). Electronic applications accepted.

**University of New Haven,** Graduate School, College of Arts and Sciences, Program in Environmental Science, West Haven, CT 06516. Offers environmental ecology (MS); environmental geoscience (MS); environmental health and management (MS); environmental science (MS); geographical information systems (MS). *Program availability:* Part-time, evening/weekend. *Students:* 14 full-time (8 women), 13 part-time (6 women); includes 7 minority (3 Black or African American, non-Hispanic/Latino; 3 Hispanic/Latino; 1 Native Hawaiian or other Pacific Islander, non-Hispanic/Latino), 4 international. Average age 29. 59 applicants, 86% accepted, 10 enrolled. In 2019, 17 master's awarded. *Entrance requirements:* Additional exam requirements/recommendations for international students: required—TOEFL (minimum score 80 iBT), IELTS, PTE. *Application deadline:* Applications are processed on a rolling basis. Application fee: $50. Electronic applications accepted. Application fee is waived when completed online. *Financial support:* Research assistantships with partial tuition reimbursements, teaching assistantships with partial tuition reimbursements, Federal Work-Study, scholarships/grants, and unspecified assistantships available. Support available to part-time students. Financial award applicants required to submit FAFSA. *Unit head:* Dr. Christian Conroy, Assistant Professor, 203-932-7436, E-mail: CWConroy@newhaven.edu. *Application contact:* Selina O'Toole, Senior Associate Director of Graduate Admissions, 203-932-7337, E-mail: SOToole@newhaven.edu.
Website: https://www.newhaven.edu/arts-sciences/graduate-programs/environmental-science/

**The University of North Carolina at Chapel Hill,** Graduate School, College of Arts and Sciences, Curriculum in Ecology, Chapel Hill, NC 27599. Offers MA, MS, PhD. *Degree requirements:* For master's, comprehensive exam, thesis (for some programs), oral defense of thesis; for doctorate, comprehensive exam, thesis/dissertation, oral exams, oral defense of dissertation. *Entrance requirements:* For master's and doctorate, GRE General Test. Additional exam requirements/recommendations for international students: required—TOEFL (minimum score 550 paper-based). Electronic applications accepted.

**The University of North Carolina at Chapel Hill,** Graduate School, College of Arts and Sciences, Department of Biology, Chapel Hill, NC 27599. Offers botany (MA, MS, PhD); cell biology, development, and physiology (MA, MS, PhD); cell motility and cytoskeleton (PhD); ecology and behavior (MA, MS, PhD); genetics and molecular biology (MA, MS, PhD); morphology, systematics, and evolution (MA, MS, PhD). Terminal master's awarded for partial completion of doctoral program. *Degree requirements:* For master's, comprehensive exam, thesis (for some programs); for doctorate, comprehensive exam, thesis/dissertation. *Entrance requirements:* For master's, GRE General Test, GRE Subject Test, 2 semesters of calculus or statistics; 2 semesters of physics, organic chemistry; 3 semesters of biology; for doctorate, GRE General Test, GRE Subject Test, 2 semesters calculus or statistics, 2 semesters physics, organic chemistry, 3 semesters of biology. Additional exam requirements/recommendations for international students: required—TOEFL (minimum score 550 paper-based). Electronic applications accepted.

**University of Notre Dame,** The Graduate School, College of Science, Department of Biological Sciences, Notre Dame, IN 46556. Offers aquatic ecology, evolution and environmental biology (MS, PhD); cellular and molecular biology (MS, PhD); genetics (MS, PhD); physiology (MS, PhD); vector biology and parasitology (MS, PhD). Terminal master's awarded for partial completion of doctoral program. *Degree requirements:* For master's, comprehensive exam, thesis; for doctorate, comprehensive exam, thesis/dissertation, candidacy exam. *Entrance requirements:* For master's and doctorate, GRE General Test. Additional exam requirements/recommendations for international students: required—TOEFL (minimum score 600 paper-based; 80 iBT). Electronic applications accepted.

**University of Oklahoma,** College of Arts and Sciences, Department of Biology, Norman, OK 73019. Offers biology (MS, PhD); cellular and behavioral neurobiology (PhD), including biology; ecology and evolutionary biology (PhD), including biology. *Degree requirements:* For master's, thesis, course in biostatistics; for doctorate, comprehensive exam, thesis/dissertation, course in biostatistics, 2 semesters as teaching assistant. *Entrance requirements:* For master's and doctorate, GRE General Test, transcripts, 3 letters of recommendation, personal statement, curriculum vitae. Additional exam requirements/recommendations for international students: required—TOEFL (minimum score 79 iBT) or IELTS (minimum score 6.5). Electronic applications accepted. *Expenses:* Tuition, state resident: full-time $6583.20; part-time $274.30 per credit hour. Tuition, nonresident: full-time $21,242; part-time $885.10 per credit hour. *International tuition:* $21,242.40 full-time. *Required fees:* $1994.20; $72.55 per credit hour. $126.50 per semester. Tuition and fees vary according to course load and degree level.

**University of Oklahoma,** College of Arts and Sciences, Department of Microbiology and Plant Biology, Norman, OK 73019-0390. Offers microbiology (MS, PhD); plant biology (MS, PhD), including ecology and evolutionary biology (PhD), plant biology. Terminal master's awarded for partial completion of doctoral program. *Degree requirements:* For master's, comprehensive exam, thesis; for doctorate, comprehensive exam, thesis/dissertation. *Entrance requirements:* For master's and doctorate, GRE, 3 recommendation letters, letter of intent, bachelor's degree. Additional exam requirements/recommendations for international students: required—TOEFL (minimum score 80 iBT) or IELTS (minimum score 6.5). Electronic applications accepted. *Expenses:* Tuition, state resident: full-time $6583.20; part-time $274.30 per credit hour. Tuition, nonresident: full-time $21,242; part-time $885.10 per credit hour. *International tuition:* $21,242.40 full-time. *Required fees:* $1994.20; $72.55 per credit hour. $126.50 per semester. Tuition and fees vary according to course load and degree level.

**University of Oregon,** Graduate School, College of Arts and Sciences, Department of Biology, Eugene, OR 97403. Offers ecology and evolution (MA, MS, PhD); marine biology (MA, MS, PhD); molecular, cellular and genetic biology (PhD); neuroscience and development (PhD). Terminal master's awarded for partial completion of doctoral program. *Degree requirements:* For master's, thesis (for some programs); for doctorate, thesis/dissertation. *Entrance requirements:* For master's and doctorate, GRE General Test, minimum GPA of 3.2. Additional exam requirements/recommendations for international students: required—TOEFL.

**University of Pittsburgh,** Kenneth P. Dietrich School of Arts and Sciences, Department of Biological Sciences, Program in Ecology and Evolution, Pittsburgh, PA 15260. Offers PhD. *Faculty:* 9 full-time (5 women). *Students:* 17 full-time (12 women); includes 2 minority (both Hispanic/Latino), 1 international. Average age 23. In 2019, 2 doctorates awarded. *Degree requirements:* For doctorate, comprehensive exam, thesis/dissertation, Completion of Research Integrity Module. *Entrance requirements:* Additional exam requirements/recommendations for international students: required—TOEFL (minimum score 90 paper-based), IELTS. *Application deadline:* For fall admission, 12/2 priority date for domestic and international students. Applications are processed on a rolling basis. Application fee: $0 ($75 for international students). Electronic applications accepted. *Financial support:* In 2019–20, 19 fellowships with full tuition reimbursements (averaging $36,108 per year), 15 research assistantships with full tuition reimbursements (averaging $30,840 per year), 14 teaching assistantships with full tuition reimbursements (averaging $30,375 per year) were awarded; Federal Work-Study, traineeships, and health care benefits also available. *Unit head:* Dr. Jeffrey G. Lawrence, Professor and Chair, 412-624-4350, Fax: 412-624-4759, E-mail: jlawrenc@pitt.edu. *Application contact:* Cathleen M. Barr, Graduate Administrator, 412-624-4268, Fax: 412-624-4349, E-mail: cbarr@pitt.edu.
Website: http://www.biology.pitt.edu

**University of Puerto Rico at Rio Piedras,** College of Natural Sciences, Department of Biology, San Juan, PR 00931-3300. Offers ecology/systematics (MS, PhD); evolution/genetics (MS, PhD); molecular/cellular biology (MS, PhD); neuroscience (MS, PhD). *Program availability:* Part-time. *Degree requirements:* For master's, one foreign language, comprehensive exam, thesis; for doctorate, one foreign language, comprehensive exam, thesis/dissertation. *Entrance requirements:* For master's, GRE Subject Test, interview, minimum GPA of 3.0, letter of recommendation; for doctorate, GRE Subject Test, interview, master's degree, minimum GPA of 3.0, letter of recommendation.

**University of Rhode Island,** Graduate School, College of the Environment and Life Sciences, Department of Biological Sciences, Kingston, RI 02881. Offers cell and molecular biology (MS, PhD); earth and environmental sciences (MS, PhD); ecology and ecosystem sciences (MS, PhD); evolutionary and marine biology (MS, PhD); sustainable agriculture and food systems (MS, PhD). *Program availability:* Part-time. *Faculty:* 20 full-time (10 women). *Students:* 108 full-time (68 women), 22 part-time (15 women); includes 12 minority (6 Black or African American, non-Hispanic/Latino; 4 Asian, non-Hispanic/Latino; 1 Hispanic/Latino; 1 Two or more races, non-Hispanic/Latino), 22 international. In 2019, 12 master's, 10 doctorates awarded. *Entrance requirements:* Additional exam requirements/recommendations for international students: required—TOEFL. *Application deadline:* For fall admission, 1/15 for domestic and international students. Application fee: $65. Electronic applications accepted. *Expenses: Tuition, area resident:* Full-time $13,734; part-time $763 per credit. Tuition, state resident: full-time $13,734; part-time $763 per credit. Tuition, nonresident: full-time $26,512; part-time $1473 per credit. *International tuition:* $26,512 full-time. *Required fees:* $1780; $52 per credit. $35 per term. One-time fee: $165. *Financial support:* In 2019–20, 24 research assistantships with tuition reimbursements (averaging $9,961 per year), 1 teaching assistantship with tuition reimbursement (averaging $7,521 per year) were awarded. Financial award application deadline: 1/15; financial award applicants required to submit FAFSA. *Unit head:* Dr. Alison Roberts, Chair, E-mail: bio_chair@etal.uri.edu. *Application contact:* Bethany Jenkins, Graduate Program Director, 401-874-7551, E-mail: bdjenkins@uri.edu.
Website: http://web.uri.edu/bio/

**University of Rochester,** School of Arts and Sciences, Department of Biology, Rochester, NY 14627. Offers biology (MS); ecology, genetics, and genomics (PhD); molecular, cellular, and developmental biology evolution (PhD). *Program availability:* Part-time. *Faculty:* 24 full-time (8 women). *Students:* 47 full-time (22 women), 1 (woman) part-time; includes 6 minority (1 Black or African American, non-Hispanic/Latino; 2 Asian, non-Hispanic/Latino; 3 Hispanic/Latino), 20 international. Average age 27. 98 applicants, 34% accepted, 12 enrolled. In 2019, 8 master's, 8 doctorates awarded. Terminal master's awarded for partial completion of doctoral program. *Degree requirements:* For master's, comprehensive exam (for some programs), thesis (for some programs); for doctorate, thesis/dissertation, qualifying exam. *Entrance requirements:* For master's and doctorate, personal statement, transcripts, three letters of recommendation. Additional exam requirements/recommendations for international students: required—TOEFL (minimum score 600 paper-based; 100 iBT), IELTS. *Application deadline:* For fall admission, 12/1 for domestic and international students. Application fee: $60. Electronic applications accepted. *Financial support:* In 2019–20, 40 students received support, including 5 fellowships (averaging $30,080 per year), 20 research assistantships (averaging $28,000 per year), 15 teaching assistantships (averaging $28,000 per year); health care benefits and tuition waivers (full) also available. Financial award application deadline: 12/1. *Unit head:* Michael Welte, Professor and Chair, 585-276-3897, E-mail: michael.welte@rochester.edu. *Application contact:* Cynthia Landry, Administrative Assistant, 585-275-7991, E-mail: cynthia.landry@rochester.edu.
Website: https://www.sas.rochester.edu/bio/graduate/index.html

**University of South Carolina,** The Graduate School, College of Arts and Sciences, Department of Biological Sciences, Graduate Training Program in Ecology, Evolution, and Organismal Biology, Columbia, SC 29208. Offers MS, PhD. *Degree requirements:* For master's, one foreign language, comprehensive exam, thesis; for doctorate, one foreign language, comprehensive exam, thesis/dissertation. *Entrance requirements:* For master's and doctorate, GRE General Test, minimum GPA of 3.0 in science. Additional exam requirements/recommendations for international students: required—TOEFL (minimum score 570 paper-based). Electronic applications accepted.

**University of South Florida,** College of Arts and Sciences, Department of Integrative Biology, Tampa, FL 33620-9951. Offers biology (MS), including ecology and evolution, environmental and ecological microbiology, physiology and morphology. *Program availability:* Part-time. *Faculty:* 12 full-time (4 women). *Students:* 27 full-time (15 women), 3 part-time (all women); includes 5 minority (1 Black or African American, non-Hispanic/Latino; 2 Asian, non-Hispanic/Latino; 2 Hispanic/Latino), 3 international. Average age 32. 37 applicants, 24% accepted, 6 enrolled. In 2019, 4 master's, 3 doctorates awarded. *Degree requirements:* For master's, comprehensive exam, thesis (for some programs); for doctorate, comprehensive exam, thesis/dissertation. *Entrance requirements:* For master's, GRE: Preferred scores of 155V (69th percentile), 150Q (38th percentile), 4.5AW, minimum GPA of 3.0; Acceptance by faculty member; 3 letters of recommendation (see student recommendation form on department website); statement of research and professional goals; TA application; It is expected that candidates will have completed courses equivalent to those required for the BS in Biology at USF; for doctorate, GRE: 155+ (70%)V, 150+ (70%)Q, 4.5 (70%) AW, Bachelor of Science required. It is expected that candidates for the Ph.D. degree will have completed courses equivalent to those required for the B.S. in Biology at U.S.F. Acceptance by a faculty member in the Department of Integrative Biology is mandatory.

Additional exam requirements/recommendations for international students: required—TOEFL. *Application deadline:* For fall admission, 11/30 priority date for domestic and international students; for spring admission, 7/1 priority date for domestic and international students. Application fee: $30. Electronic applications accepted. *Financial support:* In 2019–20, 11 students received support. Research assistantships, teaching assistantships, and unspecified assistantships available. Financial award application deadline: 6/30; financial award applicants required to submit FAFSA. *Unit head:* Dr. Valerie Harwood, Professor and Chair, 813-974-1524, Fax: 813-974-3263, E-mail: vharwood@usf.edu. *Application contact:* Dr. Stephen Deban, Associate Professor and Graduate Program Director, 813-974-2242, E-mail: sdeban@usf.edu. Website: http://biology.usf.edu/ib/grad/

**The University of Tennessee,** Graduate School, College of Arts and Sciences, Department of Ecology and Evolutionary Biology, Knoxville, TN 37996. Offers behavior (MS, PhD); ecology (MS, PhD); evolutionary biology (MS, PhD). *Program availability:* Part-time. *Degree requirements:* For master's, thesis; for doctorate, thesis/dissertation. *Entrance requirements:* For master's and doctorate, GRE General Test, minimum GPA of 2.7. Additional exam requirements/recommendations for international students: required—TOEFL. Electronic applications accepted.

**The University of Tennessee,** Graduate School, College of Arts and Sciences, Department of Mathematics, Knoxville, TN 37996. Offers applied mathematics (MS); mathematical ecology (PhD); mathematics (M Math, MS, PhD). *Program availability:* Part-time. *Degree requirements:* For master's, thesis or alternative; for doctorate, one foreign language, thesis/dissertation. *Entrance requirements:* For master's and doctorate, minimum GPA of 2.7. Additional exam requirements/recommendations for international students: required—TOEFL. Electronic applications accepted.

**The University of Texas at Austin,** Graduate School, College of Natural Sciences, School of Biological Sciences, Program in Ecology, Evolution and Behavior, Austin, TX 78712-1111. Offers PhD. *Entrance requirements:* For doctorate, GRE General Test. Additional exam requirements/recommendations for international students: required—TOEFL. Electronic applications accepted.

**The University of Texas at San Antonio,** College of Sciences, Department of Environmental Science and Ecology, San Antonio, TX 78249-0617. Offers MS. *Entrance requirements:* For master's, GRE, bachelor's degree in biology, ecology, environmental science, chemistry, geology, engineering, or some other related scientific discipline; one semester each of general statistics, organic chemistry, and environmental science or ecology; undergraduate transcripts; resume; two recommendation letters; statement of purpose. Additional exam requirements/recommendations for international students: required—TOEFL (minimum score 550 paper-based; 79 iBT), IELTS (minimum score 6.5). Electronic applications accepted.

**The University of Toledo,** College of Graduate Studies, College of Natural Sciences and Mathematics, Department of Environmental Sciences, Toledo, OH 43606-3390. Offers biology (MS, PhD), including ecology; geology (MS), including earth surface processes. *Program availability:* Part-time. *Degree requirements:* For master's, thesis or alternative. *Entrance requirements:* For master's, GRE General Test, minimum cumulative point-hour ratio of 2.7 for all previous academic work, three letters of recommendation, statement of purpose, transcripts from all prior institutions attended. Additional exam requirements/recommendations for international students: required—TOEFL (minimum score 550 paper-based; 80 iBT). Electronic applications accepted.

**University of Toronto,** School of Graduate Studies, Faculty of Arts and Science, Department of Ecology and Evolutionary Biology, Toronto, ON M5S 1A1, Canada. Offers M Sc, PhD. *Degree requirements:* For master's, thesis, thesis defense; for doctorate, thesis/dissertation, thesis defense. *Entrance requirements:* For master's, minimum B average in last 2 years; knowledge of physics, chemistry, and biology. Additional exam requirements/recommendations for international students: required—TOEFL (minimum score 580 paper-based; 93 iBT), TWE (minimum score 5). Electronic applications accepted.

**University of Washington,** Graduate School, College of the Environment, School of Environmental and Forest Sciences, Seattle, WA 98195. Offers bioresource science and engineering (MS, PhD); environmental horticulture (MEH); forest ecology (MS, PhD); forest management (MFR); forest soils (MS, PhD); restoration ecology (MS, PhD); restoration ecology and environmental horticulture (MS, PhD); social sciences (MS, PhD); sustainable resource management (MS, PhD); wildlife science (MS, PhD); MFR/MAIS; MPA/MS. *Accreditation:* SAF. *Program availability:* Part-time. *Degree requirements:* For master's, thesis; for doctorate, comprehensive exam, thesis/

dissertation. *Entrance requirements:* For master's and doctorate, GRE, minimum GPA of 3.0. Additional exam requirements/recommendations for international students: required—TOEFL. Electronic applications accepted.

**University of Wisconsin–Madison,** Graduate School, College of Agricultural and Life Sciences, Agroecology Program, Madison, WI 53706-1380. Offers MS. *Degree requirements:* For master's, thesis (for some programs). *Entrance requirements:* For master's, GRE. Additional exam requirements/recommendations for international students: required—TOEFL (minimum score 580 paper-based; 92 iBT), IELTS (minimum score 7). Electronic applications accepted.

**University of Wyoming,** Program in Ecology, Laramie, WY 82071. Offers MS, PhD. *Entrance requirements:* For master's and doctorate, GRE.

**Utah State University,** School of Graduate Studies, College of Science, Department of Biology, Logan, UT 84322. Offers biology (MS, PhD); ecology (MS, PhD). *Program availability:* Part-time. *Degree requirements:* For master's, thesis; for doctorate, thesis/dissertation. *Entrance requirements:* For master's and doctorate, GRE General Test, minimum GPA of 3.0. Additional exam requirements/recommendations for international students: required—TOEFL (minimum score 575 paper-based).

**Utah State University,** School of Graduate Studies, S.J. and Jessie E. Quinney College of Natural Resources, Department of Environment and Society, Logan, UT 84322. Offers bioregional planning (MS); geography (MA, MS); human dimensions of ecosystem science and management (MS, PhD); recreation resource management (MS, PhD). *Degree requirements:* For master's, comprehensive exam, thesis (for some programs). *Entrance requirements:* For master's and doctorate, GRE General Test, minimum GPA of 3.0. Additional exam requirements/recommendations for international students: required—TOEFL. Electronic applications accepted.

**Utah State University,** School of Graduate Studies, S.J. and Jessie E. Quinney College of Natural Resources, Department of Watershed Sciences, Logan, UT 84322. Offers ecology (MS, PhD); fisheries biology (MS, PhD); watershed science (MS, PhD). *Degree requirements:* For master's, thesis (for some programs); for doctorate, thesis/dissertation. *Entrance requirements:* For master's and doctorate, GRE General Test, minimum GPA of 3.2. Additional exam requirements/recommendations for international students: required—TOEFL. Electronic applications accepted.

**Utah State University,** School of Graduate Studies, S.J. and Jessie E. Quinney College of Natural Resources, Department of Wildland Resources, Logan, UT 84322. Offers ecology (MS, PhD); forestry (MS, PhD); range science (MS, PhD); wildlife biology (MS, PhD). *Program availability:* Part-time. *Degree requirements:* For master's, thesis; for doctorate, comprehensive exam, thesis/dissertation. *Entrance requirements:* For master's and doctorate, GRE General Test, minimum GPA of 3.0. Additional exam requirements/recommendations for international students: required—TOEFL.

**Washington University in St. Louis,** The Graduate School, Division of Biology and Biomedical Sciences, Program in Evolution, Ecology and Population Biology, St. Louis, MO 63130-4899. Offers ecology (PhD). *Degree requirements:* For doctorate, thesis/dissertation. *Entrance requirements:* For doctorate, GRE General Test, GRE Subject Test. Additional exam requirements/recommendations for international students: required—TOEFL. Electronic applications accepted.

**Wesleyan University,** Graduate Studies, Department of Biology, Middletown, CT 06459. Offers cell and developmental biology (PhD); evolution and ecology (PhD); genetics and genomics (PhD), including bioinformatics; neurobiology and behavior (PhD). Terminal master's awarded for partial completion of doctoral program. *Degree requirements:* For doctorate, comprehensive exam, thesis/dissertation, public seminar. *Entrance requirements:* For doctorate, GRE, official transcripts, three recommendation letters, essay. Additional exam requirements/recommendations for international students: required—TOEFL. Electronic applications accepted.

**Western Illinois University,** School of Graduate Studies, College of Arts and Sciences, Program in Environmental Science: Large River Ecosystems, Macomb, IL 61455-1390. Offers PhD. *Entrance requirements:* For doctorate, GRE, three letters of recommendation, official transcripts, statement of research intent, curriculum vitae. Additional exam requirements/recommendations for international students: required—TOEFL.

**Yale University,** Graduate School of Arts and Sciences, Department of Ecology and Evolutionary Biology, New Haven, CT 06520. Offers PhD. *Entrance requirements:* For doctorate, GRE General Test, GRE Subject Test (biology).

# Environmental Biology

**Chatham University,** Program in Biology, Pittsburgh, PA 15232-2826. Offers environmental biology (MS); human biology (MS). *Program availability:* Part-time. *Degree requirements:* For master's, thesis optional. *Entrance requirements:* For master's, 3 letters of recommendation. Additional exam requirements/recommendations for international students: required—TOEFL (minimum score 600 paper-based; 100 iBT), IELTS (minimum score 7), TWE. Electronic applications accepted. Application fee is waived when completed online. *Expenses: Tuition:* Part-time $1017 per credit. *Required fees:* $30 per credit. Tuition and fees vary according to program.

**Dalhousie University,** Faculty of Agriculture, Halifax, NS B3H 4R2, Canada. Offers agriculture (M Sc), including air quality, animal behavior, animal molecular genetics, animal nutrition, animal technology, aquaculture, botany, crop management, crop physiology, ecology, environmental microbiology, food science, horticulture, nutrient management, pest management, physiology, plant biotechnology, plant pathology, soil chemistry, soil fertility, waste management and composting, water quality. *Program availability:* Part-time. *Degree requirements:* For master's, thesis, ATC Exam Teaching Assistantship. *Entrance requirements:* For master's, honors B Sc, minimum GPA of 3.0. Additional exam requirements/recommendations for international students: required—TOEFL (minimum score 580 paper-based; 92 iBT), IELTS, Michigan English Language Assessment Battery, CanTEST, CAEL.

**Dartmouth College,** Guarini School of Graduate and Advanced Studies, Graduate Programs in Biological Sciences, Program in Ecology, Evolution, Ecosystems, and Society, Hanover, NH 03755. Offers ecology and evolutionary biology (PhD); sustainability, ecosystems, and environment (PhD). *Entrance requirements:* For doctorate, GRE General Test, GRE Subject Test in biology (highly recommended). Additional exam requirements/recommendations for international students: required—TOEFL. Electronic applications accepted.

**Emporia State University,** Department of Biological Sciences, Emporia, KS 66801-5415. Offers botany (MS); environmental biology (MS); forensic science (MS); general biology (MS); microbial and cellular biology (MS); zoology (MS). *Program availability:* Part-time. *Degree requirements:* For master's, comprehensive exam or thesis. *Entrance requirements:* For master's, GRE, appropriate undergraduate degree, interview, letters of reference. Additional exam requirements/recommendations for international students: required—TOEFL (minimum score 520 paper-based; 68 iBT). Electronic applications accepted. *Expenses: Tuition, area resident:* Full-time $6394; part-time $266.41 per credit hour. Tuition, state resident: full-time $6394; part-time $266.41 per credit hour. Tuition, nonresident: full-time $20,128; part-time $828.66 per credit hour. *International tuition:* $20,128 full-time. *Required fees:* $2183; $90.95 per credit hour. Tuition and fees vary according to campus/location and program.

**Georgia State University,** College of Arts and Sciences, Department of Biology, Program in Applied and Environmental Microbiology, Atlanta, GA 30302-3083. Offers applied and environmental microbiology (MS, PhD); bioinformatics (MS). *Program availability:* Part-time. Terminal master's awarded for partial completion of doctoral program. *Degree requirements:* For master's, comprehensive exam (for some programs), thesis optional; for doctorate, comprehensive exam, thesis/dissertation. *Entrance requirements:* For master's and doctorate, GRE. *Application deadline:* For fall admission, 7/1 priority date for domestic students, 6/1 priority date for international students; for spring admission, 11/15 priority date for domestic students, 10/15 priority date for international students. Applications are processed on a rolling basis. Application fee: $50. Electronic applications accepted. *Expenses: Tuition, area resident:* Full-time $7164; part-time $398 per credit hour. Tuition, state resident: full-time $7164; part-time $398 per credit hour. Tuition, nonresident: full-time $22,662; part-time $1259 per credit hour. *International tuition:* $22,662 full-time. *Required fees:* $2128; $312 per credit hour. Tuition and fees vary according to course load and program. *Financial support:* In 2019–20, fellowships with full tuition reimbursements (averaging $22,000 per year),

research assistantships with full tuition reimbursements (averaging $20,000 per year) were awarded. Financial award application deadline: 12/3. *Unit head:* Dr. Charles Derby, Director of Graduate Studies, 404-413-5393, Fax: 404-413-5446, E-mail: cderby@gsu.edu. *Application contact:* Dr. Charles Derby, Director of Graduate Studies, 404-413-5393, Fax: 404-413-5446, E-mail: cderby@gsu.edu.
Website: http://biology.gsu.edu/

**Governors State University,** College of Arts and Sciences, Program in Environmental Biology, University Park, IL 60484. Offers MS. *Program availability:* Part-time. *Faculty:* 39 full-time (14 women), 25 part-time/adjunct (12 women). *Students:* 1 full-time (0 women), 8 part-time (5 women); includes 4 minority (2 Black or African American, non-Hispanic/Latino; 1 Hispanic/Latino; 1 Two or more races, non-Hispanic/Latino). Average age 34. 7 applicants, 57% accepted, 2 enrolled. In 2019, 1 master's awarded. *Application deadline:* For fall admission, 4/1 for domestic students. Applications are processed on a rolling basis. Application fee: $50. Electronic applications accepted. *Expenses: Tuition, area resident:* Full-time $8472; part-time $353 per credit hour. Tuition, state resident: full-time $8472; part-time $353 per credit hour. Tuition, nonresident: full-time $16,944; part-time $706 per credit hour. *International tuition:* $16,944 full-time. *Required fees:* $2520; $105 per credit hour. $38 per term. Tuition and fees vary according to course load, degree level and program. *Financial support:* Application deadline: 5/1; applicants required to submit FAFSA. *Unit head:* Mary Carrington, Chair, Division of Science, Mathematics, and Technology, 708-534-5000 Ext. 4532, E-mail: mcarrington@govst.edu. *Application contact:* Mary Carrington, Chair, Division of Science, Mathematics, and Technology, 708-534-5000 Ext. 4532, E-mail: mcarrington@govst.edu.

**Hampton University,** School of Science, Department of Biological Sciences, Hampton, VA 23668. Offers biology (MS); environmental science (MS). *Program availability:* Part-time. *Students:* 7 full-time (6 women); includes 5 minority (all Black or African American, non-Hispanic/Latino), 1 international. Average age 24. 15 applicants, 40% accepted, 5 enrolled. In 2019, 1 master's awarded. *Degree requirements:* For master's, comprehensive exam (for some programs), thesis optional. *Entrance requirements:* For master's, GRE General Test. *Application deadline:* For fall admission, 6/1 priority date for domestic students, 6/1 for international students; for spring admission, 11/1 priority date for domestic students, 11/1 for international students; for summer admission, 4/1 priority date for domestic students, 2/1 priority date for international students. Applications are processed on a rolling basis. Application fee: $35. Electronic applications accepted. *Financial support:* Fellowships, research assistantships, teaching assistantships, career-related internships or fieldwork, Federal Work-Study, institutionally sponsored loans, scholarships/grants, and stipends available. Support available to part-time students. Financial award application deadline: 6/30; financial award applicants required to submit FAFSA. *Unit head:* Dr. Jermel Watkins, Chair, 757-727-5267, E-mail: jermel.watkins@hamptonu.edu. *Application contact:* Dr. Jermel Watkins, Chair, 757-727-5267, E-mail: jermel.watkins@hamptonu.edu.

**Hood College,** Graduate School, Program in Environmental Biology, Frederick, MD 21701-8575. Offers environmental biology (MS); geographic information systems (Certificate). *Program availability:* Part-time, evening/weekend. *Degree requirements:* For master's, thesis or alternative, independent project (A); internship (A); capstone (A). *Entrance requirements:* For master's, minimum GPA of 2.75, 3.0 preferred; official transcripts; essay; completed and earned at least a B in the following five courses: two college-level biology courses (with lab), two college-level chemistry courses (with lab), and one college-level math course (e.g., statistics, algebra, pre-calculus, calculus). Additional exam requirements/recommendations for international students: required—TOEFL (minimum score 575 paper-based; 89 iBT), IELTS (minimum score 6.5). Electronic applications accepted.

**Massachusetts Institute of Technology,** School of Engineering, Department of Civil and Environmental Engineering, Cambridge, MA 02139. Offers biological oceanography (PhD, Sc D); chemical oceanography (PhD, Sc D); civil and environmental engineering (M Eng, SM, PhD, Sc D); civil and environmental systems (PhD, Sc D); civil engineering (PhD, Sc D, CE); civil engineering and computation (PhD); coastal engineering (PhD, Sc D); construction engineering and management (PhD, Sc D); environmental biology (PhD, Sc D); environmental chemistry (PhD, Sc D); environmental engineering (PhD, Sc D); environmental engineering and computation (PhD); environmental fluid mechanics (PhD, Sc D); geotechnical and geoenvironmental engineering (PhD, Sc D); hydrology (PhD, Sc D); information technology (PhD, Sc D); oceanographic engineering (PhD, Sc D); structures and materials (PhD, Sc D); transportation (PhD, Sc D); SM/MBA. *Degree requirements:* For master's, thesis; for doctorate, comprehensive exam, thesis/dissertation; for CE, comprehensive exam, thesis. *Entrance requirements:* For master's, doctorate, and CE, GRE General Test. Additional exam requirements/recommendations for international students: required—TOEFL, IELTS. Electronic applications accepted.

**Missouri University of Science and Technology,** Department of Biological Sciences, Rolla, MO 65409. Offers applied and environmental biology (MS). *Faculty:* 10 full-time (3 women). *Students:* 10 full-time (6 women), 6 part-time (5 women); includes 1 minority (Hispanic/Latino), 6 international. Average age 28. 19 applicants, 68% accepted, 7 enrolled. In 2019, 8 master's awarded. *Entrance requirements:* For master's, GRE (minimum score 600 quantitative, 4 writing). Additional exam requirements/recommendations for international students: required—TOEFL (minimum score 570 paper-based). Application fee: $50. *Expenses:* Tuition, state resident: full-time $7839; part-time $435.50 per credit hour. Tuition, nonresident: full-time $22,169; part-time $1231.60 per credit hour. *International tuition:* $22,169 full-time. *Required fees:* $649.76. One-time fee: $119. Tuition and fees vary according to course load and program. *Financial support:* In 2019–20, 6 research assistantships (averaging $1,810 per year), 1 teaching assistantship (averaging $1,814 per year) were awarded; institutionally sponsored loans and unspecified assistantships also available. *Unit head:* Dr. David Duvernell, Chair, 573-341-6988, Fax: 573-341-4821, E-mail: duvernelld@mst.edu. *Application contact:* Debbie Schwertz, Admissions Coordinator, 573-341-6013, Fax: 573-341-6271, E-mail: schwertz@mst.edu.
Website: http://biosci.mst.edu/

**Morgan State University,** School of Graduate Studies, School of Computer, Mathematical, and Natural Sciences, Department of Biology, Program in Bioenvironmental Science, Baltimore, MD 21251. Offers PhD. *Program availability:* Part-time, evening/weekend. *Faculty:* 26 full-time (11 women), 2 part-time/adjunct (1 woman). *Students:* 21 full-time (12 women), 3 part-time (0 women); includes 13 minority (8 Black or African American, non-Hispanic/Latino; 3 Asian, non-Hispanic/Latino; 1 Hispanic/Latino; 1 Two or more races, non-Hispanic/Latino). Average age 36. 12 applicants, 58% accepted, 1 enrolled. In 2019, 1 doctorate awarded. *Degree requirements:* For doctorate, comprehensive exam, thesis/dissertation, oral defense of dissertation. *Entrance requirements:* For doctorate, GRE General Test, GRE Subject Test (biology, chemistry, or related science), bachelor's or master's degree in biology, chemistry, physics or related field; minimum GPA of 3.0. Additional exam requirements/recommendations for international students: required—TOEFL (minimum score 550 paper-based; 70 iBT). *Application deadline:* For fall admission, 2/1 priority date for domestic students, 4/15 for international students; for spring admission, 10/1 priority date for domestic students, 10/1 for international students. Applications are processed

on a rolling basis. Application fee: $50 ($70 for international students). Electronic applications accepted. *Expenses:* Tuition, state resident: full-time $455; part-time $455 per credit hour. Tuition, nonresident: full-time $894; part-time $894 per credit hour. *Required fees:* $82; $82 per credit hour. *Financial support:* In 2019–20, 13 students received support. Fellowships with full and partial tuition reimbursements available, research assistantships with full and partial tuition reimbursements available, teaching assistantships with full and partial tuition reimbursements available, career-related internships or fieldwork, scholarships/grants, tuition waivers (full and partial), and unspecified assistantships available. Support available to part-time students. Financial award application deadline: 2/1. *Unit head:* Dr. Chunlei Fan, Program Coordinator, 443-885-5933, E-mail: chunlei.fan@morgan.edu. *Application contact:* Dr. Jahmaine Smith, Director of Admissions, 443-885-3185, Fax: 443-885-8226, E-mail: dean.campbell@morgan.edu.
Website: https://www.morgan.edu/school_of_computer_mathematical_and_natural_sciences/graduate_programs/phd_in_bioenvironmental_science.html

**Nicholls State University,** Graduate Studies, College of Arts and Sciences, Department of Biological Sciences, Thibodaux, LA 70310. Offers marine and environmental biology (MS). *Program availability:* Part-time. *Degree requirements:* For master's, comprehensive exam, thesis. *Entrance requirements:* For master's, GRE. Additional exam requirements/recommendations for international students: required—TOEFL (minimum score 600 paper-based).

**Ohio University,** Graduate College, College of Arts and Sciences, Department of Environmental and Plant Biology, Athens, OH 45701-2979. Offers MS, PhD. *Program availability:* Part-time. *Degree requirements:* For master's, thesis, 2 terms of teaching experience; for doctorate, comprehensive exam, thesis/dissertation, 2 terms of teaching experience. *Entrance requirements:* For master's, GRE General Test, minimum GPA of 3.0; for doctorate, GRE General Test, minimum GPA of 3.2. Additional exam requirements/recommendations for international students: required—TOEFL (minimum score 620 paper-based; 105 iBT) or IELTS (minimum score 7.5). Electronic applications accepted.

**Oregon State University,** College of Science, Program in Microbiology, Corvallis, OR 97331. Offers environmental microbiology (MA, MS, PhD); food microbiology (MA, MS, PhD); genomics (MA, MS, PhD); immunology (MA, MS, PhD); microbial ecology (MA, MS, PhD); microbial evolution (MA, MS, PhD); parasitology (MA, MS, PhD); pathogenic microbiology (MA, MS, PhD); virology (MA). Terminal master's awarded for partial completion of doctoral program. *Entrance requirements:* For master's and doctorate, GRE. Additional exam requirements/recommendations for international students: required—TOEFL (minimum score 600 paper-based; 100 iBT).

**Regis University,** Regis College, Denver, CO 80221-1099. Offers biomedical sciences (MS); developmental practice (MDP); education (MA); environmental biology (MS). *Accreditation:* TEAC. *Program availability:* Part-time. *Degree requirements:* For master's, thesis (for some programs), capstone presentation. *Entrance requirements:* For master's, official transcript reflecting baccalaureate degree awarded from U.S.-based regionally-accredited college or university. Additional exam requirements/recommendations for international students: required—TOEFL (minimum score 550 paper-based; 82 iBT). Electronic applications accepted. *Expenses:* Contact institution.

**Rutgers University - New Brunswick,** Graduate School-New Brunswick, Department of Environmental Sciences, Piscataway, NJ 08854-8097. Offers air pollution and resources (MS, PhD); aquatic biology (MS, PhD); aquatic chemistry (MS, PhD); atmospheric science (MS, PhD); chemistry and physics of aerosol and hydrosol systems (MS, PhD); environmental chemistry (MS, PhD); environmental microbiology (MS, PhD); environmental toxicology (PhD); exposure assessment (PhD); fate and effects of pollutants (MS, PhD); pollution prevention and control (MS, PhD); water and wastewater treatment (MS, PhD); water resources (MS, PhD). Terminal master's awarded for partial completion of doctoral program. *Degree requirements:* For master's, comprehensive exam, thesis or alternative, oral final exam; for doctorate, comprehensive exam, thesis/dissertation, thesis defense, qualifying exam. *Entrance requirements:* For master's and doctorate, GRE General Test. Additional exam requirements/recommendations for international students: required—TOEFL. Electronic applications accepted.

**State University of New York College of Environmental Science and Forestry,** Department of Environmental and Forest Biology, Syracuse, NY 13210-2779. Offers applied ecology (MPS); chemical ecology (MPS, MS, PhD); conservation biology (MPS, MS, PhD); ecology (MPS, MS, PhD); entomology (MPS, MS, PhD); environmental interpretation (MPS, MS, PhD); environmental physiology (MPS, MS, PhD); fish and wildlife biology and management (MPS, MS, PhD); forest pathology and mycology (MPS, MS, PhD); plant biotechnology (MPS); plant science and biotechnology (MPS, MS, PhD). *Program availability:* Part-time. *Faculty:* 35 full-time (10 women), 4 part-time/adjunct (3 women). *Students:* 103 full-time (60 women), 17 part-time (7 women); includes 7 minority (4 American Indian or Alaska Native, non-Hispanic/Latino; 2 Asian, non-Hispanic/Latino; 1 Hispanic/Latino), 13 international. Average age 29. 69 applicants, 45% accepted, 17 enrolled. In 2019, 28 master's, 6 doctorates awarded. Terminal master's awarded for partial completion of doctoral program. *Degree requirements:* For master's, thesis (for some programs), capstone seminar; for doctorate, comprehensive exam, thesis/dissertation, capstone seminar. *Entrance requirements:* For master's and doctorate, GRE General Test, minimum GPA of 3.0. Additional exam requirements/recommendations for international students: required—TOEFL (minimum score 550 paper-based; 80 iBT), IELTS (minimum score 6). *Application deadline:* For fall admission, 2/1 priority date for domestic and international students; for spring admission, 11/1 priority date for domestic and international students. Applications are processed on a rolling basis. Application fee: $60. Electronic applications accepted. *Expenses:* Tuition, state resident: full-time $11,310; part-time $472 per credit hour. Tuition, nonresident: full-time $23,100; part-time $963 per credit hour. *Required fees:* $1890; $95.21 per credit hour. *Financial support:* In 2019–20, 35 students received support. Unspecified assistantships available. Financial award application deadline: 6/30; financial award applicants required to submit FAFSA. *Unit head:* Dr. Melissa K. Fierke, Chair, 315-470-6809, Fax: 315-470-6743, E-mail: mkfierke@esf.edu. *Application contact:* Laura Payne, Administrative Assistant Office of Instruction & Graduate Studies, 315-470-6599, E-mail: esfgrad@esf.edu.
Website: http://www.esf.edu/efb/grad/default.asp

**Universidad del Turabo,** Graduate Programs, Programs in Science and Technology, Gurabo, PR 00778-3030. Offers environmental analysis (MSE), including environmental chemistry; environmental management (MSE), including pollution management; environmental science (D Sc), including environmental biology. *Entrance requirements:* For master's, GRE, EXADEP, GMAT, interview, official transcript, essay, recommendation letters; for doctorate, GRE, EXADEP, GMAT, official transcript, recommendation letters, essay, curriculum vitae, interview. Electronic applications accepted.

**University of Alberta,** Faculty of Graduate Studies and Research, Department of Biological Sciences, Edmonton, AB T6G 2E1, Canada. Offers environmental biology and ecology (M Sc, PhD); microbiology and biotechnology (M Sc, PhD); molecular biology and genetics (M Sc, PhD); physiology and cell biology (M Sc, PhD); plant

biology (M Sc, PhD); systematics and evolution (M Sc, PhD). Terminal master's awarded for partial completion of doctoral program. *Degree requirements:* For master's, thesis; for doctorate, thesis/dissertation. *Entrance requirements:* Additional exam requirements/recommendations for international students: required—TOEFL.

**University of California, Santa Cruz,** Division of Graduate Studies, Division of Physical and Biological Sciences, Department of Microbiology and Environmental Toxicology, Santa Cruz, CA 95064. Offers MS, PhD. Terminal master's awarded for partial completion of doctoral program. *Degree requirements:* For master's, comprehensive exam, thesis; for doctorate, thesis/dissertation, qualifying exams. *Entrance requirements:* For master's and doctorate, GRE. Additional exam requirements/recommendations for international students: required—TOEFL (minimum score 550 paper-based; 83 iBT); recommended—IELTS (minimum score 8). Electronic applications accepted.

**University of Guelph,** Office of Graduate and Postdoctoral Studies, Ontario Agricultural College, Department of Environmental Biology, Guelph, ON N1G 2W1, Canada. Offers entomology (M Sc, PhD); environmental microbiology and biotechnology (M Sc, PhD); environmental toxicology (M Sc, PhD); plant and forest systems (M Sc, PhD); plant pathology (M Sc, PhD). *Program availability:* Part-time. *Degree requirements:* For master's, thesis; for doctorate, comprehensive exam, thesis/dissertation. *Entrance requirements:* For master's, minimum 75% average during previous 2 years of course work; for doctorate, minimum 75% average. Additional exam requirements/recommendations for international students: required—TOEFL or IELTS. Electronic applications accepted.

**University of Louisiana at Lafayette,** College of Sciences, Department of Biology, Lafayette, LA 70504. Offers biology (MS); environmental and evolutionary biology (PhD). Terminal master's awarded for partial completion of doctoral program. *Degree requirements:* For master's, thesis; for doctorate, 2 foreign languages, comprehensive exam, thesis/dissertation. *Entrance requirements:* For master's, GRE General Test, minimum GPA of 2.75; for doctorate, GRE General Test, GRE Subject Test, minimum GPA of 3.0. Additional exam requirements/recommendations for international students: required—TOEFL (minimum score 550 paper-based). Electronic applications accepted. *Expenses: Tuition, area resident:* Full-time $5511; part-time $1630 per credit hour. Tuition, state resident: full-time $5511; part-time $1630 per credit hour. Tuition, nonresident: full-time $19,239; part-time $2409 per credit hour. *Required fees:* $46,637.

**University of Louisville,** Graduate School, College of Arts and Sciences, Department of Biology, Louisville, KY 40292-0001. Offers biology (MS); environmental biology (PhD). *Program availability:* Part-time. *Faculty:* 22 full-time (8 women), 7 part-time/adjunct (3 women). *Students:* 37 full-time (18 women), 7 part-time (4 women); includes 11 minority (2 Asian, non-Hispanic/Latino; 5 Hispanic/Latino; 4 Two or more races, non-Hispanic/Latino), 8 international. Average age 30. 25 applicants, 36% accepted, 7 enrolled. In 2019, 7 master's, 5 doctorates awarded. Terminal master's awarded for partial completion of doctoral program. *Degree requirements:* For master's, comprehensive exam, thesis (for some programs); for doctorate, comprehensive exam, thesis/dissertation. *Entrance requirements:* For master's, GRE, MCAT, or DAT, Two letters of reference, official transcripts; for doctorate, GRE, Two letters of reference, official transcripts. Additional exam requirements/recommendations for international students: required—TOEFL (minimum score 550 paper-based; 79 iBT), IELTS can be used in place of the TOEFL; recommended—IELTS (minimum score 6.5). *Application deadline:* For fall admission, 1/15 priority date for domestic and international students; for spring admission, 12/1 for domestic and international students; for summer admission, 4/15 for domestic and international students. Applications are processed on a rolling basis. Application fee: $65. Electronic applications accepted. *Expenses: Tuition, area resident:* Full-time $13,000; part-time $723 per credit hour. Tuition, state resident: full-time $13,000; part-time $723 per credit hour. Tuition, nonresident: full-time $27,114; part-time $1507 per credit hour. *International tuition:* $27,114 full-time. *Required fees:* $196. Tuition and fees vary according to program and reciprocity agreements. *Financial support:* In 2019–20, 43 students received support, including 5 fellowships with full tuition reimbursements available (averaging $22,000 per year), 2 research assistantships with full tuition reimbursements available (averaging $22,000 per year), 28 teaching assistantships with full tuition reimbursements available (averaging $22,000 per year); health care benefits and unspecified assistantships also available. Financial award application deadline: 1/15. *Unit head:* Dr. Perri Eason, Professor and Chair, 502-852-6771, Fax: 502-852-0725, E-mail: perri.eason@louisville.edu. *Application contact:* Dr. Sarah Emery, Professor and Director of Graduate Studies, 502-852-5940, E-mail: sarah.emery@louisville.edu.
Website: http://louisville.edu/biology

**The University of Manchester,** School of Biological Sciences, Manchester, United Kingdom. Offers adaptive organismal biology (M Phil, PhD); animal biology (M Phil, PhD); biochemistry (M Phil, PhD); bioinformatics (M Phil, PhD); biomolecular sciences (M Phil, PhD); biotechnology (M Phil, PhD); cell biology (M Phil, PhD); cell matrix research (M Phil, PhD); channels and transporters (M Phil, PhD); developmental biology (M Phil, PhD); environmental biology (M Phil, PhD); evolutionary biology (M Phil, PhD); gene expression (M Phil, PhD); genetics (M Phil, PhD); history of science, technology and medicine (M Phil, PhD); immunology (M Phil, PhD); integrative neurobiology and behavior (M Phil, PhD); membrane trafficking (M Phil, PhD); microbiology (M Phil, PhD); molecular and cellular neuroscience (M Phil, PhD); molecular biology (M Phil, PhD); molecular cancer studies (M Phil, PhD); neuroscience (M Phil, PhD); ophthalmology (M Phil, PhD); optometry (M Phil, PhD); organelle function (M Phil, PhD); pharmacology (M Phil, PhD); physiology (M Phil, PhD); plant sciences (M Phil, PhD); stem cell research (M Phil, PhD); structural biology (M Phil, PhD); systems neuroscience (M Phil, PhD); toxicology (M Phil, PhD).

**University of Massachusetts Amherst,** Graduate School, College of Natural Sciences, Department of Environmental Conservation, Amherst, MA 01003. Offers building systems (MS, PhD); environmental policy and human dimensions (MS, PhD); forest resources (MS, PhD); sustainability science (MS); water, wetlands and watersheds (MS, PhD); wildlife and fisheries conservation (MS, PhD). *Program availability:* Part-time. Terminal master's awarded for partial completion of doctoral program. *Degree requirements:* For master's, thesis or alternative; for doctorate, comprehensive exam, thesis/dissertation. *Entrance requirements:* For master's and doctorate, GRE General Test. Additional exam requirements/recommendations for international students: required—TOEFL (minimum score 550 paper-based; 80 iBT), IELTS (minimum score 6.5). Electronic applications accepted.

**University of Southern California,** Graduate School, Dana and David Dornsife College of Letters, Arts and Sciences, Department of Biological Sciences, Program in Marine Biology and Biological Oceanography, Los Angeles, CA 90089. Offers marine and environmental biology (MS); marine biology and biological oceanography (PhD). Terminal master's awarded for partial completion of doctoral program. *Degree requirements:* For master's, research paper; for doctorate, comprehensive exam, thesis/dissertation, qualifying examination, dissertation defense. *Entrance requirements:* For master's and doctorate, GRE, 3 letters of recommendation, personal statement, resume, minimum GPA of 3.0. Additional exam requirements/recommendations for international students: required—TOEFL (minimum score 600 paper-based; 100 iBT). Electronic applications accepted.

**University of South Florida,** College of Arts and Sciences, Department of Integrative Biology, Tampa, FL 33620-9951. Offers biology (MS), including ecology and evolution, environmental and ecological microbiology, physiology and morphology. *Program availability:* Part-time. *Faculty:* 12 full-time (4 women). *Students:* 27 full-time (15 women), 3 part-time (all women); includes 5 minority (1 Black or African American, non-Hispanic/Latino; 2 Asian, non-Hispanic/Latino; 2 Hispanic/Latino), 3 international. Average age 32. 37 applicants, 24% accepted, 6 enrolled. In 2019, 4 master's, 3 doctorates awarded. *Degree requirements:* For master's, comprehensive exam, thesis (for some programs); for doctorate, comprehensive exam, thesis/dissertation. *Entrance requirements:* For master's, GRE: Preferred scores of 155V (69th percentile), 150Q (38th percentile), 4.5AW, minimum GPA of 3.0; Acceptance by faculty member; 3 letters of recommendation (see student recommendation form on department website); statement of research and professional goals; TA application; It is expected that candidates will have completed courses equivalent to those required for the BS in Biology at USF; for doctorate, GRE: 155+ (70%)V, 150+ (70%)Q, 4.5 (70%) AW, Bachelor of Science required. It is expected that candidates for the Ph.D. degree will have completed courses equivalent to those required for the B.S. in Biology at U.S.F. Acceptance by a faculty member in the Department of Integrative Biology is mandatory. Additional exam requirements/recommendations for international students: required—TOEFL. *Application deadline:* For fall admission, 11/30 priority date for domestic and international students; for spring admission, 7/1 priority date for domestic and international students. Application fee: $30. Electronic applications accepted. *Financial support:* In 2019–20, 11 students received support. Research assistantships, teaching assistantships, and unspecified assistantships available. Financial award application deadline: 6/30; financial award applicants required to submit FAFSA. *Unit head:* Dr. Valerie Harwood, Professor and Chair, 813-974-1524, Fax: 813-974-3263, E-mail: vharwood@usf.edu. *Application contact:* Dr. Stephen Deban, Associate Professor and Graduate Program Director, 813-974-2242, E-mail: sdeban@usf.edu.
Website: http://biology.usf.edu/ib/grad/

**University of Wisconsin–Madison,** School of Medicine and Public Health, Molecular and Environmental Toxicology Graduate Program, Madison, WI 53706. Offers MS, PhD.

**Washington University in St. Louis,** The Graduate School, Division of Biology and Biomedical Sciences, St. Louis, MO 63130-4899. Offers biochemistry (PhD); computational and molecular biophysics (PhD); computational and systems biology (PhD); developmental, regenerative, and stem cell biology (PhD); evolution, ecology and population biology (PhD), including ecology, environmental biology, evolutionary biology, genetics; human and statistical genetics (PhD); immunology (PhD); molecular cell biology (PhD); molecular genetics and genomics (PhD); molecular microbiology and microbial pathogenesis (PhD); neurosciences (PhD); plant and microbial biosciences (PhD); MD/PhD. *Degree requirements:* For doctorate, thesis/dissertation. *Entrance requirements:* For doctorate, GRE General Test, GRE Subject Test. Additional exam requirements/recommendations for international students: required—TOEFL. Electronic applications accepted.

**Youngstown State University,** College of Graduate Studies, College of Science, Technology, Engineering and Mathematics, Department of Biological Sciences, Youngstown, OH 44555-0001. Offers environmental biology (MS); molecular biology, microbiology, and genetics (MS); physiology and anatomy (MS). *Program availability:* Part-time. *Degree requirements:* For master's, comprehensive exam, thesis, oral review. *Entrance requirements:* For master's, GRE General Test, minimum GPA of 2.7. Additional exam requirements/recommendations for international students: required—TOEFL.

# Evolutionary Biology

**Arizona State University at Tempe,** College of Liberal Arts and Sciences, School of Life Sciences, Tempe, AZ 85287-4601. Offers animal behavior (PhD); applied ethics (biomedical and health ethics) (MA); biology (MS, PhD), including biology, biology and society, complex adaptive systems science (PhD), plant biology and conservation (MS); environmental life sciences (PhD); evolutionary biology (PhD); history and philosophy of science (PhD); human and social dimensions of science and technology (PhD); microbiology (PhD); molecular and cellular biology (PhD); neuroscience (PhD). Terminal master's awarded for partial completion of doctoral program. *Degree requirements:* For master's, thesis (for some programs), interactive Program of Study (iPOS) submitted before completing 50 percent of required credit hours; for doctorate, variable foreign language requirement, comprehensive exam, thesis/dissertation, interactive Program of Study (iPOS) submitted before completing 50 percent of required credit hours. *Entrance requirements:* For master's and doctorate, GRE, minimum GPA of 3.0 or equivalent in last 2 years of work leading to bachelor's degree. Additional exam requirements/recommendations for international students: required—TOEFL (minimum score 600 paper-based; 100 iBT). Electronic applications accepted.

**Brown University,** Graduate School, Division of Biology and Medicine, Department of Ecology and Evolutionary Biology, Providence, RI 02912. Offers PhD. *Degree requirements:* For doctorate, thesis/dissertation, preliminary exam. *Entrance requirements:* For doctorate, GRE General Test, GRE Subject Test. Additional exam requirements/recommendations for international students: required—TOEFL. Electronic applications accepted.

**Columbia University,** Graduate School of Arts and Sciences, New York, NY 10027. Offers African-American studies (MA); American studies (MA); anthropology (MA, PhD); art history and archaeology (MA, PhD); astronomy (PhD); biological sciences (PhD); biotechnology (MA); chemical physics (PhD); chemistry (PhD); classical studies (MA, PhD); classics (MA, PhD); climate and society (MA); conservation biology (MA); earth and environmental sciences (PhD); East Asia: regional studies (MA); East Asian

languages and cultures (MA, PhD); ecology, evolution and environmental biology (MA), including conservation biology; ecology, evolution, and environmental biology (PhD), including ecology and evolutionary biology, evolutionary primatology; economics (MA, PhD); English and comparative literature (MA, PhD); French and Romance philology (MA, PhD); Germanic languages (MA, PhD); global French studies (MA); global thought (MA); Hispanic cultural studies (MA); history (PhD); history and literature (MA); human rights studies (MA); Islamic studies (MA); Italian (MA, PhD); Japanese pedagogy (MA); Jewish studies (MA); Latin America and the Caribbean: regional studies (MA); Latin American and Iberian cultures (PhD); mathematics (MA, PhD), including finance (MA); medieval and Renaissance studies (MA); Middle Eastern, South Asian, and African studies (MA, PhD); modern art: critical and curatorial studies (MA); modern European studies (MA); museum anthropology (MA); music (DMA, PhD); oral history (MA); philosophical foundations of physics (MA); philosophy (MA, PhD); physics (PhD); political science (MA, PhD); psychology (PhD); quantitative methods in the social sciences (MA); religion (MA, PhD); Russia, Eurasia and East Europe: regional studies (MA); Russian translation (MA); Slavic cultures (MA); Slavic languages (MA, PhD); sociology (MA, PhD); South Asian studies (MA); statistics (MA, PhD); theatre (PhD). *Program availability:* Part-time. *Students:* 3,506 full-time (1,844 women), 208 part-time (121 women); includes 864 minority (110 Black or African American, non-Hispanic/Latino; 5 American Indian or Alaska Native, non-Hispanic/Latino; 416 Asian, non-Hispanic/Latino; 147 Hispanic/Latino; 6 Native Hawaiian or other Pacific Islander, non-Hispanic/Latino; 180 Two or more races, non-Hispanic/Latino), 2,065 international. 14,545 applicants, 25% accepted, 1,429 enrolled. In 2019, 1,262 master's, 363 doctorates awarded. Terminal master's awarded for partial completion of doctoral program. *Degree requirements:* For master's, variable foreign language requirement, comprehensive exam (for some programs), thesis (for some programs); for doctorate, variable foreign language requirement, comprehensive exam (for some programs), thesis/dissertation. *Entrance requirements:* For master's and doctorate, GRE General Test, GRE Subject Test (for some programs). Additional exam requirements/recommendations for international students: required—TOEFL (minimum score 600 paper-based; 100 iBT), IELTS (minimum score 7.5). Application fee: $115. Electronic applications accepted. *Expenses: Tuition:* Full-time $47,600; part-time $1880 per credit. One-time fee: $105. *Financial support:* Fellowships, research assistantships, teaching assistantships, career-related internships or fieldwork, Federal Work-Study, institutionally sponsored loans, scholarships/grants, traineeships, health care benefits, tuition waivers, and unspecified assistantships available. Support available to part-time students. Financial award application deadline: 12/15. *Unit head:* Dr. Carlos J. Alonso, Dean of the Graduate School of Arts and Sciences and Vice President for Graduate Education, 212-854-2861, E-mail: gsas-dean@columbia.edu. *Application contact:* GSAS Office of Admissions, 212-854-6729, E-mail: gsas-admissions@columbia.edu.
Website: http://gsas.columbia.edu/

**Cornell University,** Graduate School, Graduate Fields of Agriculture and Life Sciences, Field of Ecology and Evolutionary Biology, Ithaca, NY 14853. Offers ecology (PhD), including animal ecology, applied ecology, biogeochemistry, community and ecosystem ecology, limnology, oceanography, physiological ecology, plant ecology, population ecology, theoretical ecology, vertebrate zoology; evolutionary biology (PhD), including ecological genetics, paleobiology, population biology, systematics. *Degree requirements:* For doctorate, comprehensive exam, thesis/dissertation, 2 semesters of teaching experience. *Entrance requirements:* For doctorate, GRE General Test, GRE Subject Test (biology), 2 letters of recommendation. Additional exam requirements/recommendations for international students: required—TOEFL (minimum score 550 paper-based; 77 iBT). Electronic applications accepted.

**Dartmouth College,** Guarini School of Graduate and Advanced Studies, Graduate Programs in Biological Sciences, Program in Ecology, Evolution, Ecosystems, and Society, Hanover, NH 03755. Offers ecology and evolutionary biology (PhD); sustainability, ecosystems, and environment (PhD). *Entrance requirements:* For doctorate, GRE General Test, GRE Subject Test in biology (highly recommended). Additional exam requirements/recommendations for international students: required—TOEFL. Electronic applications accepted.

**Emory University,** Laney Graduate School, Division of Biological and Biomedical Sciences, Program in Population Biology, Ecology and Evolution, Atlanta, GA 30322-1100. Offers PhD. *Degree requirements:* For doctorate, comprehensive exam, thesis/dissertation. *Entrance requirements:* For doctorate, GRE General Test, minimum GPA of 3.0 in science course work (recommended). Additional exam requirements/recommendations for international students: required—TOEFL. Electronic applications accepted.

**Florida State University,** The Graduate School, College of Arts and Sciences, Department of Biological Science, Specialization in Ecology and Evolutionary Biology, Tallahassee, FL 32306-4295. Offers MS, PhD. Terminal master's awarded for partial completion of doctoral program. *Degree requirements:* For master's, comprehensive exam (for some programs), thesis (for some programs), teaching experience, seminar presentation; for doctorate, comprehensive exam, thesis/dissertation, teaching experience; seminar presentation. *Entrance requirements:* For master's and doctorate, GRE General Test, minimum upper-division GPA of 3.0. Additional exam requirements/recommendations for international students: required—TOEFL (minimum score 600 paper-based; 92 iBT). Electronic applications accepted.

**Harvard University,** Graduate School of Arts and Sciences, Department of Organismic and Evolutionary Biology, Cambridge, MA 02138. Offers biology (PhD). *Degree requirements:* For doctorate, 2 foreign languages, public presentation of thesis research, exam. *Entrance requirements:* For doctorate, GRE General Test, GRE Subject Test (recommended), 7 courses in biology, chemistry, physics, mathematics, computer science, or geology. Additional exam requirements/recommendations for international students: required—TOEFL.

**Illinois State University,** Graduate School, College of Arts and Sciences, School of Biological Sciences, Normal, IL 61790. Offers animal behavior (MS); bacteriology (MS); biochemistry (MS); biological sciences (MS); biology (PhD); biophysics (MS); biotechnology (MS); botany (MS, PhD); cell biology (MS); conservation biology (MS); developmental biology (MS); ecology (MS, PhD); entomology (MS); evolutionary biology (MS); genetics (MS, PhD); immunology (MS); microbiology (MS, PhD); molecular biology (MS); molecular genetics (MS); neurobiology (MS); neuroscience (MS); parasitology (MS); physiology (MS, PhD); plant biology (MS); plant molecular biology (MS); plant sciences (MS); structural biology (MS); zoology (MS, PhD). *Program availability:* Part-time. *Faculty:* 26 full-time (6 women), 7 part-time/adjunct (2 women). *Students:* 51 full-time (33 women), 15 part-time (8 women). Average age 27. 71 applicants, 28% accepted, 9 enrolled. In 2019, 14 master's, 3 doctorates awarded. *Degree requirements:* For master's, thesis or alternative; for doctorate, variable foreign language requirement, thesis/dissertation, 2 terms of residency. *Entrance requirements:* For master's, GRE General Test, minimum GPA of 2.6 in last 60 hours of course work; for doctorate, GRE General Test. *Application deadline:* Applications are processed on a rolling basis. Application fee: $50. *Expenses: Tuition, area resident:* Full-time $7956; part-time $9767 per year. Tuition, nonresident: full-time $9233; part-time $17,592 per year. *Required fees:* $1797. *Financial support:* In 2019–20, 20 research assistantships, 41 teaching assistantships were awarded; Federal Work-Study, tuition waivers (full), and unspecified assistantships also available. Financial award application deadline: 4/1. *Unit head:* Dr. Craig Gatto, School Director, 309-438-3087, E-mail: cgatto@IllinoisState.edu. *Application contact:* Dr. Ben Sadd, Assistant Chair for Graduate Studies, 309-438-2651, E-mail: bmsadd@IllinoisState.edu.
Website: http://www.bio.ilstu.edu/

**Indiana State University,** College of Graduate and Professional Studies, College of Arts and Sciences, Department of Biology, Terre Haute, IN 47809. Offers cellular and molecular biology (PhD); ecology, systematics and evolution (PhD); life sciences (MS); physiology (PhD); science education (MS). *Degree requirements:* For master's, thesis optional; for doctorate, comprehensive exam, thesis/dissertation. *Entrance requirements:* For master's and doctorate, GRE General Test. Electronic applications accepted.

**Indiana University Bloomington,** University Graduate School, College of Arts and Sciences, Department of Biology, Bloomington, IN 47405. Offers biology teaching (MAT); biotechnology (MA); evolution, ecology, and behavior (MA, PhD); genetics (PhD); microbiology (MA, PhD); molecular, cellular, and developmental biology (PhD); plant sciences (MA, PhD); zoology (MA, PhD). Terminal master's awarded for partial completion of doctoral program. *Degree requirements:* For master's, thesis, oral defense; for doctorate, thesis/dissertation, oral defense. *Entrance requirements:* For master's and doctorate, GRE General Test. Additional exam requirements/recommendations for international students: required—TOEFL (minimum score 100 iBT). Electronic applications accepted.

**Iowa State University of Science and Technology,** Program in Ecology and Evolutionary Biology, Ames, IA 50011. Offers MS, PhD. *Degree requirements:* For master's, thesis or alternative; for doctorate, thesis/dissertation. *Entrance requirements:* For master's and doctorate, GRE General Test. Additional exam requirements/recommendations for international students: required—TOEFL (minimum score 550 paper-based; 79 iBT), IELTS (minimum score 6.5). Electronic applications accepted.

**Johns Hopkins University,** School of Medicine, Graduate Programs in Medicine, Center for Functional Anatomy and Evolution, Baltimore, MD 21218. Offers PhD. *Degree requirements:* For doctorate, comprehensive exam, thesis/dissertation, oral exams. *Entrance requirements:* For doctorate, GRE. Additional exam requirements/recommendations for international students: required—TOEFL. Electronic applications accepted.

**Michigan State University,** The Graduate School, College of Natural Science, Interdepartmental Program in Ecology, Evolutionary Biology and Behavior, East Lansing, MI 48824. Offers PhD. *Entrance requirements:* Additional exam requirements/recommendations for international students: required—TOEFL. Electronic applications accepted.

**Montclair State University,** The Graduate School, College of Science and Mathematics, Program in Biology, Montclair, NJ 07043-1624. Offers biological science/education (MS); biology (MS); ecology and evolution (MS); physiology (MS).

**The Ohio State University,** Graduate School, College of Arts and Sciences, Division of Natural and Mathematical Sciences, Department of Evolution, Ecology, and Organismal Biology, Columbus, OH 43210. Offers MS, PhD. *Entrance requirements:* For master's and doctorate, GRE General Test. Additional exam requirements/recommendations for international students: required—TOEFL (minimum score 550 paper-based; 79 iBT), Michigan English Language Assessment Battery (minimum score 86); recommended—IELTS (minimum score 7). Electronic applications accepted.

**Ohio University,** Graduate College, College of Arts and Sciences, Department of Biological Sciences, Athens, OH 45701-2979. Offers biological sciences (MS, PhD); cell biology and physiology (MS, PhD); ecology and evolutionary biology (MS, PhD); exercise physiology and muscle biology (MS, PhD); microbiology (MS, PhD); neuroscience (MS, PhD). Terminal master's awarded for partial completion of doctoral program. *Degree requirements:* For master's, comprehensive exam, thesis, 1 quarter of teaching experience; for doctorate, comprehensive exam, thesis/dissertation, 2 quarters of teaching experience. *Entrance requirements:* For master's, GRE General Test, names of three faculty members whose research interests most closely match the applicant's interest; for doctorate, GRE General Test, essay concerning prior training, research interest and career goals, plus names of three faculty members whose research interests most closely match the applicant's interest. Additional exam requirements/recommendations for international students: required—TOEFL (minimum score 620 paper-based; 105 iBT) or IELTS (minimum score 7.5). Electronic applications accepted.

**Oklahoma State University,** College of Arts and Sciences, Department of Plant Biology, Ecology, and Evolution, Stillwater, OK 74078. Offers botany (MS); environmental science (PhD). *Faculty:* 8 full-time (2 women). *Students:* 13 part-time (4 women), 5 international. Average age 28. 4 applicants, 75% accepted, 2 enrolled. In 2019, 5 master's awarded. *Entrance requirements:* For master's and doctorate, GRE or GMAT. Additional exam requirements/recommendations for international students: required—TOEFL (minimum score 550 paper-based; 79 iBT). *Application deadline:* For fall admission, 3/1 priority date for international students; for spring admission, 8/1 priority date for international students. Applications are processed on a rolling basis. Application fee: $50 ($75 for international students). Electronic applications accepted. *Expenses: Tuition, area resident:* Full-time $4148.10; part-time $2765.40 per credit hour. Tuition, state resident: full-time $4148.10; part-time $2765.40 per credit hour. Tuition, nonresident: full-time $15,775; part-time $10,516.80 per credit hour. *International tuition:* $15,775.20 full-time. *Required fees:* $2196.90; $122.05 per credit hour. Tuition and fees vary according to course load, campus/location and program. *Financial support:* In 2019–20, 2 research assistantships (averaging $2,575 per year), 11 teaching assistantships (averaging $2,274 per year) were awarded; career-related internships or fieldwork, Federal Work-Study, scholarships/grants, health care benefits, tuition waivers (partial), and unspecified assistantships also available. Support available to part-time students. Financial award application deadline: 3/1; financial award applicants required to submit FAFSA. *Unit head:* Dr. Andrew Doust, Department Head, 405-744-2544, Fax: 405-744-7074, E-mail: andrew.doust@okstate.edu. *Application contact:* Dr. Sheryl Tucker, Dean, 405-744-6368, Fax: 405-744-0355, E-mail: gradi@okstate.edu.
Website: http://plantbio.okstate.edu

**Princeton University,** Graduate School, Department of Ecology and Evolutionary Biology, Princeton, NJ 08544-1019. Offers PhD. *Degree requirements:* For doctorate, thesis/dissertation. *Entrance requirements:* For doctorate, GRE General Test, GRE Subject Test. Additional exam requirements/recommendations for international students: required—TOEFL (minimum score 600 paper-based). Electronic applications accepted.

**Purdue University,** Graduate School, PULSe - Purdue University Life Sciences Program, West Lafayette, IN 47907. Offers biomolecular structure and biophysics (PhD); biotechnology (PhD); chemical biology (PhD); chromatin and regulation of gene expression (PhD); integrative neuroscience (PhD); integrative plant sciences (PhD); membrane biology (PhD); microbiology (PhD); molecular evolutionary and cancer biology (PhD); molecular evolutionary genetics (PhD); molecular virology (PhD).

*Students:* 37 full-time (23 women); includes 7 minority (1 Black or African American, non-Hispanic/Latino; 2 Asian, non-Hispanic/Latino; 4 Hispanic/Latino), 22 international. Average age 25. 162 applicants, 36% accepted, 19 enrolled. *Entrance requirements:* For doctorate, GRE, minimum undergraduate GPA of 3.0. Additional exam requirements/recommendations for international students: required—TOEFL (minimum score 550 paper-based; 77 iBT). *Application deadline:* For fall admission, 1/15 priority date for domestic and international students. Applications are processed on a rolling basis. Application fee: $60 ($75 for international students). Electronic applications accepted. *Financial support:* In 2019–20, research assistantships with tuition reimbursements (averaging $22,500 per year), teaching assistantships with tuition reimbursements (averaging $22,500 per year) were awarded. *Application contact:* Lindsey Springer, Graduate Contact for Admissions, 765-496-9667, E-mail: lbcampbe@purdue.edu.
Website: http://www.gradschool.purdue.edu/pulse

**Rice University,** Graduate Programs, Wiess School of Natural Sciences, Department of Ecology and Evolutionary Biology, Houston, TX 77251-1892. Offers MA, MS, PhD. Terminal master's awarded for partial completion of doctoral program. *Degree requirements:* For master's, comprehensive exam (for some programs), thesis (for some programs); for doctorate, comprehensive exam, thesis/dissertation. *Entrance requirements:* For master's and doctorate, GRE General Test, GRE Subject Test. Additional exam requirements/recommendations for international students: required—TOEFL (minimum score 600 paper-based; 90 iBT). Electronic applications accepted.

**Rutgers University - New Brunswick,** Graduate School-New Brunswick, Program in Ecology and Evolution, Piscataway, NJ 08854-8097. Offers MS, PhD. *Program availability:* Part-time. Terminal master's awarded for partial completion of doctoral program. *Degree requirements:* For master's, comprehensive exam; for doctorate, comprehensive exam, thesis/dissertation. *Entrance requirements:* For master's and doctorate, GRE General Test, minimum GPA of 3.0. Additional exam requirements/recommendations for international students: required—TOEFL (minimum score 550 paper-based). Electronic applications accepted.

**Rutgers University - New Brunswick,** Graduate School-New Brunswick, Program in Plant Biology, Piscataway, NJ 08854-8097. Offers horticulture and plant technology (MS, PhD); molecular and cellular biology (MS, PhD); organismal and population biology (MS, PhD); plant pathology (MS, PhD). *Program availability:* Part-time. Terminal master's awarded for partial completion of doctoral program. *Degree requirements:* For master's, comprehensive exam, thesis or alternative; for doctorate, comprehensive exam, thesis/dissertation. *Entrance requirements:* For master's and doctorate, GRE General Test, GRE Subject Test (recommended). Additional exam requirements/recommendations for international students: required—TOEFL (minimum score 600 paper-based). Electronic applications accepted.

**Stony Brook University, State University of New York,** Graduate School, College of Arts and Sciences, Department of Ecology and Evolution, Stony Brook, NY 11794. Offers applied ecology (MA); ecology and evolution (PhD). *Faculty:* 15 full-time (5 women), 1 part-time/adjunct (0 women). *Students:* 37 full-time (16 women); includes 4 minority (2 Asian, non-Hispanic/Latino; 2 Hispanic/Latino), 9 international. Average age 27. 23 applicants, 30% accepted, 4 enrolled. In 2019, 8 doctorates awarded. *Degree requirements:* For doctorate, one foreign language, comprehensive exam, thesis/dissertation, teaching experience. *Entrance requirements:* For doctorate, GRE General Test, GRE Subject Test. Additional exam requirements/recommendations for international students: required—TOEFL. *Application deadline:* For fall admission, 1/15 for domestic students; for spring admission, 10/1 for domestic students. Application fee: $100. Electronic applications accepted. *Expenses:* Contact institution. *Financial support:* In 2019–20, 4 fellowships, 8 research assistantships, 21 teaching assistantships were awarded; Federal Work-Study also available. *Unit head:* Dr. Robert W. Thacker, Chair, 631-632-8590, E-mail: robert.thacker@stonybrook.edu. *Application contact:* Melissa Cohen, Coordinator, 631-246-8604, Fax: 631-632-7626, E-mail: melissa.j.cohen@stonybrook.edu.
Website: http://life.bio.sunysb.edu/ee/

**Tulane University,** School of Science and Engineering, Department of Ecology and Evolutionary Biology, New Orleans, LA 70118-5669. Offers MS, PhD. Terminal master's awarded for partial completion of doctoral program. *Degree requirements:* For master's, thesis or alternative; for doctorate, thesis/dissertation. *Entrance requirements:* For master's, GRE General Test, minimum B average in undergraduate course work; for doctorate, GRE General Test. Additional exam requirements/recommendations for international students: required—TOEFL. Electronic applications accepted. *Expenses: Tuition:* Full-time $57,004; part-time $3167 per credit hour. *Required fees:* $2086; $44.50 per credit hour. $80 per term. Tuition and fees vary according to course load, degree level and program.

**University at Buffalo, the State University of New York,** Graduate School, College of Arts and Sciences, Program in Evolution, Ecology and Behavior, Buffalo, NY 14260. Offers MS, PhD, Certificate. Terminal master's awarded for partial completion of doctoral program. *Degree requirements:* For master's, project; for doctorate, comprehensive exam, thesis/dissertation. *Entrance requirements:* For master's, GRE, minimum undergraduate GPA of 3.0; for doctorate, GRE, minimum GPA of 3.0. Additional exam requirements/recommendations for international students: required—TOEFL (minimum score 550 paper-based; 79 iBT). Electronic applications accepted. *Expenses: Tuition, area resident:* Full-time $11,310; part-time $471 per credit hour. Tuition, state resident: full-time $11,310; part-time $471 per credit hour. Tuition, nonresident: full-time $23,100; part-time $963 per credit hour. *International tuition:* $23,100 full-time. *Required fees:* $2820.

**University of Alberta,** Faculty of Graduate Studies and Research, Department of Biological Sciences, Edmonton, AB T6G 2E1, Canada. Offers environmental biology and ecology (M Sc, PhD); microbiology and biotechnology (M Sc, PhD); molecular biology and genetics (M Sc, PhD); physiology and cell biology (M Sc, PhD); plant biology (M Sc, PhD); systematics and evolution (M Sc, PhD). Terminal master's awarded for partial completion of doctoral program. *Degree requirements:* For master's, thesis; for doctorate, thesis/dissertation. *Entrance requirements:* Additional exam requirements/recommendations for international students: required—TOEFL.

**The University of Arizona,** College of Science, Department of Ecology and Evolutionary Biology, Tucson, AZ 85721. Offers MS, PhD. Terminal master's awarded for partial completion of doctoral program. *Degree requirements:* For master's, thesis optional; for doctorate, one foreign language, comprehensive exam, thesis/dissertation. *Entrance requirements:* For master's, GRE General Test, GRE Subject Test, statement of purpose, curriculum vitae, 3 letters of recommendation; for doctorate, GRE General Test, GRE Subject Test, curriculum vitae, 3 letters of recommendation. Additional exam requirements/recommendations for international students: required—TOEFL (minimum score 550 paper-based; 79 iBT).

**University of California, Davis,** Graduate Studies, Graduate Group in Population Biology, Davis, CA 95616. Offers PhD. *Degree requirements:* For doctorate, thesis/dissertation. *Entrance requirements:* For doctorate, GRE General Test, GRE Subject Test. Additional exam requirements/recommendations for international students: required—TOEFL (minimum score 550 paper-based). Electronic applications accepted.

**University of California, Irvine,** School of Biological Sciences, Department of Ecology and Evolutionary Biology, Irvine, CA 92697. Offers biological sciences (MS, PhD). *Students:* 85 full-time (50 women); includes 36 minority (2 Black or African American, non-Hispanic/Latino; 9 Asian, non-Hispanic/Latino; 23 Hispanic/Latino; 2 Two or more races, non-Hispanic/Latino), 7 international. Average age 28. 107 applicants, 35% accepted, 25 enrolled. In 2019, 19 master's, 14 doctorates awarded. *Entrance requirements:* For master's and doctorate, GRE General Test, GRE Subject Test, minimum GPA of 3.0. Additional exam requirements/recommendations for international students: required—TOEFL (minimum score 550 paper-based). *Application deadline:* For fall admission, 1/15 priority date for domestic students, 1/15 for international students. Applications are processed on a rolling basis. Application fee: $120 ($140 for international students). Electronic applications accepted. *Financial support:* Fellowships, research assistantships with full tuition reimbursements, teaching assistantships, career-related internships or fieldwork, institutionally sponsored loans, traineeships, health care benefits, and unspecified assistantships available. Financial award application deadline: 3/1; financial award applicants required to submit FAFSA. *Unit head:* James W. Hicks, Department Chair, 949-824-6386, Fax: 949-824-2181, E-mail: jhicks@uci.edu. *Application contact:* Pam McDonald, Student Affairs Coordinator, 949-824-4743, Fax: 949-824-2181, E-mail: pmcdonal@uci.edu.
Website: http://ecoevo.bio.uci.edu/

**University of California, Los Angeles,** Graduate Division, College of Letters and Science, Department of Ecology and Evolutionary Biology, Los Angeles, CA 90095. Offers MA, PhD. Terminal master's awarded for partial completion of doctoral program. *Degree requirements:* For master's, comprehensive exam or thesis; for doctorate, thesis/dissertation, oral and written qualifying exams; 3 quarters of teaching experience. *Entrance requirements:* For master's and doctorate, GRE General Test, GRE Subject Test (biology), bachelor's degree; minimum undergraduate GPA of 3.0 (or its equivalent if letter grade system not used). Additional exam requirements/recommendations for international students: required—TOEFL. Electronic applications accepted.

**University of California, Riverside,** Graduate Division, Department of Evolution, Ecology, and Organismal Biology, Riverside, CA 92521-0102. Offers evolution, ecology and organismal biology (MS, PhD). Terminal master's awarded for partial completion of doctoral program. *Degree requirements:* For master's, thesis, oral defense of thesis; for doctorate, comprehensive exam, thesis/dissertation, 3 quarters of teaching experience, qualifying exams. *Entrance requirements:* For master's and doctorate, GRE General Test, minimum GPA of 3.2. Additional exam requirements/recommendations for international students: required—TOEFL (minimum score 550 paper-based, 80 iBT) or IELTS; recommended—TWE. Electronic applications accepted.

**University of California, Santa Barbara,** Graduate Division, College of Letters and Sciences, Division of Mathematics, Life, and Physical Sciences, Department of Ecology, Evolution, and Marine Biology, Santa Barbara, CA 93106-9620. Offers MA, PhD, MA/PhD. *Degree requirements:* For master's, comprehensive exam (for some programs), thesis (for some programs); for doctorate, comprehensive exam, thesis/dissertation. *Entrance requirements:* For master's and doctorate, GRE General Test. Additional exam requirements/recommendations for international students: required—TOEFL (minimum score 550 paper-based; 80 iBT), IELTS. Electronic applications accepted.

**University of California, Santa Cruz,** Division of Graduate Studies, Division of Physical and Biological Sciences, Department of Ecology and Evolutionary Biology, Santa Cruz, CA 95064. Offers MA, PhD. *Degree requirements:* For master's, thesis; for doctorate, comprehensive exam, thesis/dissertation. *Entrance requirements:* For master's and doctorate, GRE General Test, GRE Subject Test, 3 letters of recommendation. Additional exam requirements/recommendations for international students: required—TOEFL (minimum score 550 paper-based; 83 iBT); recommended—IELTS (minimum score 8). Electronic applications accepted.

**University of Chicago,** Division of the Biological Sciences, Committee on Evolutionary Biology, Chicago, IL 60637. Offers PhD. Terminal master's awarded for partial completion of doctoral program. *Degree requirements:* For doctorate, thesis/dissertation, ethics class, 2 teaching assistantships. *Entrance requirements:* For doctorate, GRE General Test, transcripts, statement of purpose, 3 letters of recommendation. Additional exam requirements/recommendations for international students: required—TOEFL (minimum score 600 paper-based; 104 iBT), IELTS (minimum score 7). Electronic applications accepted.

**University of Colorado Boulder,** Graduate School, College of Arts and Sciences, Department of Ecology and Evolutionary Biology, Boulder, CO 80309. Offers population biology (MA). Terminal master's awarded for partial completion of doctoral program. *Degree requirements:* For master's, comprehensive exam, thesis or alternative; for doctorate, comprehensive exam, thesis/dissertation. *Entrance requirements:* For master's, GRE General Test, GRE Subject Test, minimum undergraduate GPA of 3.0; for doctorate, GRE General Test, GRE Subject Test. Electronic applications accepted. Application fee is waived when completed online.

**University of Delaware,** College of Arts and Sciences, Department of Biological Sciences, Newark, DE 19716. Offers biotechnology (MS); cancer biology (MS, PhD); cell and extracellular matrix biology (MS, PhD); cell and systems physiology (MS, PhD); developmental biology (MS, PhD); ecology and evolution (MS, PhD); microbiology (MS, PhD); molecular biology and genetics (MS, PhD). Terminal master's awarded for partial completion of doctoral program. *Degree requirements:* For master's, thesis, preliminary exam; for doctorate, comprehensive exam, thesis/dissertation, preliminary exam. *Entrance requirements:* For master's and doctorate, GRE General Test. Additional exam requirements/recommendations for international students: required—TOEFL (minimum score 600 paper-based); recommended—TWE. Electronic applications accepted.

**University of Denver,** Division of Natural Sciences and Mathematics, Department of Biological Sciences, Denver, CO 80208. Offers biology, ecology and evolution (MS, PhD); biomedical sciences (PSM); cell and molecular biology (MS, PhD). *Program availability:* Part-time. *Faculty:* 23 full-time (10 women), 2 part-time/adjunct (both women). *Students:* 12 full-time (7 women), 31 part-time (18 women); includes 6 minority (4 Hispanic/Latino; 2 Two or more races, non-Hispanic/Latino), 3 international. Average age 25. 100 applicants, 34% accepted, 18 enrolled. In 2019, 9 master's, 6 doctorates awarded. Terminal master's awarded for partial completion of doctoral program. *Degree requirements:* For master's, thesis; for doctorate, comprehensive exam, thesis/dissertation. *Entrance requirements:* For master's and doctorate, GRE General Test, bachelor's degree in biology or related field, transcripts, personal statement, three letters of recommendation. Additional exam requirements/recommendations for international students: required—TOEFL (minimum score 550 paper-based; 80 iBT). *Application deadline:* For fall admission, 1/2 priority date for domestic and international students. Applications are processed on a rolling basis. Application fee: $65. Electronic applications accepted. *Expenses:* Contact institution. *Financial support:* In 2019–20, 43 students received support, including 9 research assistantships with tuition reimbursements available (averaging $16,589 per year), 26 teaching assistantships with tuition reimbursements available (averaging $18,869 per year); Federal Work-Study, institutionally sponsored loans, scholarships/grants, and unspecified assistantships also available. Support available to part-time students. Financial award application deadline: 2/15; financial award applicants required to submit FAFSA. *Unit head:* Dr. Joe Angleson,

Associate Professor and Chair, 303-871-3463, E-mail: jangleso@du.edu. *Application contact:* Randi Flageolle, Assistant to the Chair, 303-871-3457, E-mail: rflageol@du.edu.
Website: http://www.du.edu/nsm/departments/biologicalsciences

**University of Guelph,** Office of Graduate and Postdoctoral Studies, College of Biological Science, Department of Integrative Biology, Botany and Zoology, Guelph, ON N1G 2W1, Canada. Offers botany (M Sc, PhD); zoology (M Sc, PhD). *Program availability:* Part-time. *Degree requirements:* For master's, thesis, research proposal; for doctorate, thesis/dissertation, research proposal, qualifying exam. *Entrance requirements:* For master's, minimum B average during previous 2 years of course work. Additional exam requirements/recommendations for international students: required—TOEFL (minimum score 550 paper-based), IELTS (minimum score 6.5). Electronic applications accepted.

**University of Illinois at Urbana-Champaign,** Graduate College, College of Liberal Arts and Sciences, School of Integrative Biology, Department of Animal Biology, Champaign, IL 61820. Offers animal biology (ecology, ethology and evolution) (MS, PhD).

**University of Illinois at Urbana-Champaign,** Graduate College, College of Liberal Arts and Sciences, School of Integrative Biology, Program in Ecology, Evolution and Conservation Biology, Champaign, IL 61820. Offers MS, PhD.

**The University of Iowa,** Graduate College, College of Liberal Arts and Sciences, Department of Biology, Iowa City, IA 52242-1324. Offers biology (MS, PhD); cell and developmental biology (MS, PhD); evolution (MS, PhD); genetics (MS, PhD); neurobiology (MS, PhD). Terminal master's awarded for partial completion of doctoral program. *Degree requirements:* For master's, thesis optional, exam; for doctorate, comprehensive exam, thesis/dissertation. *Entrance requirements:* For master's and doctorate, GRE General Test, minimum GPA of 3.0. Additional exam requirements/recommendations for international students: required—TOEFL (minimum score 600 paper-based; 100 iBT). Electronic applications accepted.

**The University of Kansas,** Graduate Studies, College of Liberal Arts and Sciences, Department of Ecology and Evolutionary Biology, Lawrence, KS 66045. Offers MA, PhD. *Program availability:* Part-time. *Students:* 80 full-time (43 women); includes 9 minority (1 Black or African American, non-Hispanic/Latino; 2 Asian, non-Hispanic/Latino; 3 Hispanic/Latino; 3 Two or more races, non-Hispanic/Latino), 21 international. Average age 30. 62 applicants, 47% accepted, 22 enrolled. In 2019, 5 master's, 9 doctorates awarded. Terminal master's awarded for partial completion of doctoral program. *Degree requirements:* For master's, comprehensive exam, thesis (for some programs), 30-36 credits, thesis presentation; for doctorate, comprehensive exam, thesis/dissertation, residency, final exam, dissertation defense. *Entrance requirements:* For master's and doctorate, GRE General Test, curriculum vitae, personal statement, three letters of recommendation, official transcripts. Additional exam requirements/recommendations for international students: required—TOEFL, IELTS, TOEFL or IELTS. *Application deadline:* For fall admission, 12/1 for domestic and international students. Application fee: $65 ($85 for international students). Electronic applications accepted. *Expenses:* Tuition, state resident: full-time $9989. Tuition, nonresident: full-time $23,950. *International tuition:* $23,950 full-time. *Required fees:* $984; $81.99 per credit hour. Tuition and fees vary according to course load, campus/location and program. *Financial support:* Fellowships, research assistantships, teaching assistantships, scholarships/grants, traineeships, health care benefits, and unspecified assistantships available. Financial award application deadline: 12/1. *Unit head:* Dr. Christopher Haufler, Chair, 785-864-3255, E-mail: vulgare@ku.edu. *Application contact:* Aagje Ashe, Graduate Coordinator, 785-864-2362, Fax: 785-864-5860, E-mail: a4ashe@ku.edu.
Website: http://eeb.ku.edu/

**University of Louisiana at Lafayette,** College of Sciences, Department of Biology, Lafayette, LA 70504. Offers biology (MS); environmental and evolutionary biology (PhD). Terminal master's awarded for partial completion of doctoral program. *Degree requirements:* For master's, thesis; for doctorate, 2 foreign languages, comprehensive exam, thesis/dissertation. *Entrance requirements:* For master's, GRE General Test, minimum GPA of 2.75; for doctorate, GRE General Test, GRE Subject Test, minimum GPA of 3.0. Additional exam requirements/recommendations for international students: required—TOEFL (minimum score 550 paper-based). Electronic applications accepted. *Expenses:* Tuition, area resident: Full-time $5511; part-time $1630 per credit hour. Tuition, state resident: full-time $5511; part-time $1630 per credit hour. Tuition, nonresident: full-time $19,239; part-time $2409 per credit hour. *Required fees:* $46,637.

**The University of Manchester,** School of Biological Sciences, Manchester, United Kingdom. Offers adaptive organismal biology (M Phil, PhD); animal biology (M Phil, PhD); biochemistry (M Phil, PhD); bioinformatics (M Phil, PhD); biomolecular sciences (M Phil, PhD); biotechnology (M Phil, PhD); cell biology (M Phil, PhD); cell matrix research (M Phil, PhD); channels and transporters (M Phil, PhD); developmental biology (M Phil, PhD); environmental biology (M Phil, PhD); evolutionary biology (M Phil, PhD); gene expression (M Phil, PhD); genetics (M Phil, PhD); history of science, technology and medicine (M Phil, PhD); immunology (M Phil, PhD); integrative neurobiology and behavior (M Phil, PhD); membrane trafficking (M Phil, PhD); microbiology (M Phil, PhD); molecular and cellular neuroscience (M Phil, PhD); molecular biology (M Phil, PhD); molecular cancer studies (M Phil, PhD); neuroscience (M Phil, PhD); ophthalmology (M Phil, PhD); optometry (M Phil, PhD); organelle function (M Phil, PhD); pharmacology (M Phil, PhD); physiology (M Phil, PhD); plant sciences (M Phil, PhD); stem cell research (M Phil, PhD); structural biology (M Phil, PhD); systems neuroscience (M Phil, PhD); toxicology (M Phil, PhD).

**University of Maryland, College Park,** Academic Affairs, College of Computer, Mathematical and Natural Sciences, Department of Biology, Behavior, Ecology, Evolution, and Systematics Program, College Park, MD 20742. Offers MS, PhD. *Degree requirements:* For master's, thesis, oral defense, seminar; for doctorate, thesis/dissertation, exam, 4 seminars. *Entrance requirements:* For master's and doctorate, GRE General Test, GRE Subject Test (biology), 3 letters of recommendation. Additional exam requirements/recommendations for international students: required—TOEFL.

**University of Maryland, College Park,** Academic Affairs, College of Computer, Mathematical and Natural Sciences, Department of Biology, PhD Program in Biological Sciences, College Park, MD 20742. Offers behavior, ecology, evolution, and systematics (PhD); computational biology, bioinformatics, and genomics (PhD); molecular and cellular biology (PhD); physiological systems (PhD). *Degree requirements:* For doctorate, comprehensive exam, thesis/dissertation, thesis work presentation in seminar. *Entrance requirements:* For doctorate, GRE General Test; GRE Subject Test in biology (recommended), academic transcripts, statement of purpose, research interests, 3 letters of recommendation. Additional exam requirements/recommendations for international students: required—TOEFL. Electronic applications accepted.

**University of Massachusetts Amherst,** Graduate School, Interdisciplinary Programs, Program in Organismic and Evolutionary Biology, Amherst, MA 01003. Offers MS, PhD. *Program availability:* Part-time. Terminal master's awarded for partial completion of doctoral program. *Degree requirements:* For master's, thesis or alternative; for doctorate, comprehensive exam, thesis/dissertation. *Entrance requirements:* For master's and doctorate, GRE General Test, 3 letters of recommendation. Additional

exam requirements/recommendations for international students: required—TOEFL (minimum score 550 paper-based; 80 iBT), IELTS (minimum score 6.5). Electronic applications accepted.

**University of Massachusetts Amherst,** Graduate School, Interdisciplinary Programs, Program in Plant Biology, Amherst, MA 01003. Offers biochemistry and metabolism (MS, PhD); cell biology and physiology (MS, PhD); environmental, ecological and integrative biology (MS, PhD); genetics and evolution (MS, PhD). *Degree requirements:* For master's, thesis; for doctorate, 2 foreign languages, comprehensive exam, thesis/dissertation. *Entrance requirements:* For master's and doctorate, GRE General Test. Additional exam requirements/recommendations for international students: required—TOEFL (minimum score 550 paper-based; 80 iBT), IELTS (minimum score 6.5). Electronic applications accepted.

**University of Miami,** Graduate School, College of Arts and Sciences, Department of Biology, Coral Gables, FL 33124. Offers biology (MS, PhD); genetics and evolution (MS, PhD). Terminal master's awarded for partial completion of doctoral program. *Degree requirements:* For master's, comprehensive exam (for some programs), thesis (for some programs); for doctorate, thesis/dissertation, oral and written qualifying exam. *Entrance requirements:* For master's, GRE General Test, 3 letters of recommendation, research papers; for doctorate, GRE General Test, 3 letters of recommendation, research papers, sponsor letter. Additional exam requirements/recommendations for international students: required—TOEFL (minimum score 550 paper-based; 59 iBT). Electronic applications accepted.

**University of Michigan,** Rackham Graduate School, College of Literature, Science, and the Arts, Department of Ecology and Evolutionary Biology, Ann Arbor, MI 48109. Offers MS, PhD. Terminal master's awarded for partial completion of doctoral program. *Degree requirements:* For master's, thesis (for some programs); for doctorate, comprehensive exam, thesis/dissertation, 2 semesters of teaching. *Entrance requirements:* For master's and doctorate, GRE. Additional exam requirements/recommendations for international students: required—TOEFL (minimum score 84 iBT). Electronic applications accepted.

**University of Minnesota, Twin Cities Campus,** Graduate School, College of Biological Sciences, Department of Ecology, Evolution, and Behavior, St. Paul, MN 55418. Offers MS, PhD. Terminal master's awarded for partial completion of doctoral program. *Degree requirements:* For master's, comprehensive exam, thesis or projects; for doctorate, comprehensive exam, thesis/dissertation. *Entrance requirements:* For master's and doctorate, GRE General Test, minimum GPA of 3.0. Additional exam requirements/recommendations for international students: required—TOEFL (minimum score 550 paper-based; 79 iBT), Michigan English Language Assessment Battery. Electronic applications accepted.

**University of Missouri,** Office of Research and Graduate Studies, College of Arts and Science, Division of Biological Sciences, Columbia, MO 65211. Offers evolutionary biology and ecology (MA, PhD). Terminal master's awarded for partial completion of doctoral program. *Entrance requirements:* For master's and doctorate, GRE General Test (minimum score 1200 verbal and quantitative), minimum GPA of 3.0. Additional exam requirements/recommendations for international students: required—TOEFL.

**University of Nevada, Reno,** Graduate School, Interdisciplinary Program in Ecology, Evolution, and Conservation Biology, Reno, NV 89557. Offers PhD. *Degree requirements:* For doctorate, thesis/dissertation. *Entrance requirements:* For doctorate, GRE General Test, GRE Subject Test, minimum GPA of 3.0. Additional exam requirements/recommendations for international students: required—TOEFL (minimum score 500 paper-based; 61 iBT), IELTS (minimum score 6). Electronic applications accepted.

**University of New Hampshire,** Graduate School, College of Life Sciences and Agriculture, Department of Molecular, Cellular and Biomedical Sciences, Program in Molecular and Evolutionary Systems Biology, Durham, NH 03824. Offers PhD. *Program availability:* Part-time. *Students:* 10 full-time (6 women), 4 part-time (2 women); includes 1 minority (Hispanic/Latino), 4 international. Average age 28. 9 applicants, 56% accepted, 3 enrolled. *Entrance requirements:* For doctorate, GRE General Test. Additional exam requirements/recommendations for international students: required—TOEFL (minimum score 550 paper-based; 80 iBT), IELTS, PTE. *Application deadline:* For fall admission, 1/15 priority date for domestic students, 4/1 for international students. Application fee: $65. Electronic applications accepted. *Financial support:* In 2019–20, 13 students received support, including 1 fellowship, 4 research assistantships, 8 teaching assistantships; Federal Work-Study, scholarships/grants, and tuition waivers (full and partial) also available. Support available to part-time students. Financial award application deadline: 2/15. *Unit head:* Louis Tisa, Chair, 603-862-2442. *Application contact:* Paul Boisselle, Administrative Assistant, 603-862-4814, E-mail: paul.boisselle@unh.edu.
Website: https://colsa.unh.edu/molecular-cellular-biomedical-sciences

**The University of North Carolina at Chapel Hill,** Graduate School, College of Arts and Sciences, Department of Biology, Chapel Hill, NC 27599. Offers botany (MA, MS, PhD); cell biology, development, and physiology (MA, MS, PhD); cell motility and cytoskeleton (PhD); ecology and behavior (MA, MS, PhD); genetics and molecular biology (MA, MS, PhD); morphology, systematics, and evolution (MA, MS, PhD). Terminal master's awarded for partial completion of doctoral program. *Degree requirements:* For master's, comprehensive exam, thesis (for some programs); for doctorate, comprehensive exam, thesis/dissertation. *Entrance requirements:* For master's, GRE General Test, GRE Subject Test, 2 semesters of calculus or statistics; 2 semesters of physics, organic chemistry; 3 semesters of biology; for doctorate, GRE General Test, GRE Subject Test, 2 semesters calculus or statistics, 2 semesters physics, organic chemistry, 3 semesters of biology. Additional exam requirements/recommendations for international students: required—TOEFL (minimum score 550 paper-based). Electronic applications accepted.

**University of Notre Dame,** The Graduate School, College of Science, Department of Biological Sciences, Notre Dame, IN 46556. Offers aquatic ecology, evolution and environmental biology (MS, PhD); cellular and molecular biology (MS, PhD); genetics (MS, PhD); physiology (MS, PhD); vector biology and parasitology (MS, PhD). Terminal master's awarded for partial completion of doctoral program. *Degree requirements:* For master's, comprehensive exam, thesis; for doctorate, comprehensive exam, thesis/dissertation, candidacy exam. *Entrance requirements:* For master's and doctorate, GRE General Test. Additional exam requirements/recommendations for international students: required—TOEFL (minimum score 600 paper-based; 80 iBT). Electronic applications accepted.

**University of Oklahoma,** College of Arts and Sciences, Department of Biology, Norman, OK 73019. Offers biology (MS, PhD); cellular and behavioral neurobiology (PhD), including biology; ecology and evolutionary biology (PhD), including biology. *Degree requirements:* For master's, thesis, course in biostatistics; for doctorate, comprehensive exam, thesis/dissertation, course in biostatistics, 2 semesters as teaching assistant. *Entrance requirements:* For master's and doctorate, GRE General Test, transcripts, 3 letters of recommendation, personal statement, curriculum vitae. Additional exam requirements/recommendations for international students: required—TOEFL (minimum score 79 iBT) or IELTS (minimum score 6.5). Electronic applications accepted. *Expenses:* Tuition, state resident: full-time $6583.20; part-time $274.30 per

credit hour. Tuition, nonresident: full-time $21,242; part-time $885.10 per credit hour. *International tuition:* $21,242.40 full-time. *Required fees:* $1994.20; $72.55 per credit hour. $126.50 per semester. Tuition and fees vary according to course load and degree level.

**University of Oklahoma,** College of Arts and Sciences, Department of Microbiology and Plant Biology, Norman, OK 73019-0390. Offers microbiology (MS, PhD); plant biology (MS, PhD), including ecology and evolutionary biology (PhD), plant biology. Terminal master's awarded for partial completion of doctoral program. *Degree requirements:* For master's, comprehensive exam, thesis; for doctorate, comprehensive exam, thesis/dissertation. *Entrance requirements:* For master's and doctorate, GRE, 3 recommendation letters, letter of intent, bachelor's degree. Additional exam requirements/recommendations for international students: required—TOEFL (minimum score 80 iBT) or IELTS (minimum score 6.5). Electronic applications accepted. *Expenses:* Tuition, state resident: full-time $6583.20; part-time $274.30 per credit hour. Tuition, nonresident: full-time $21,242; part-time $885.10 per credit hour. *International tuition:* $21,242.40 full-time. *Required fees:* $1994.20; $72.55 per credit hour. $126.50 per semester. Tuition and fees vary according to course load and degree level.

**University of Oregon,** Graduate School, College of Arts and Sciences, Department of Biology, Eugene, OR 97403. Offers ecology and evolution (MA, MS, PhD); marine biology (MA, MS, PhD); molecular, cellular and genetic biology (PhD); neuroscience and development (PhD). Terminal master's awarded for partial completion of doctoral program. *Degree requirements:* For master's, thesis (for some programs); for doctorate, thesis/dissertation. *Entrance requirements:* For master's and doctorate, GRE General Test, minimum GPA of 3.2. Additional exam requirements/recommendations for international students: required—TOEFL.

**University of Pittsburgh,** Kenneth P. Dietrich School of Arts and Sciences, Department of Biological Sciences, Program in Ecology and Evolution, Pittsburgh, PA 15260. Offers PhD. *Faculty:* 9 full-time (5 women). *Students:* 17 full-time (12 women); includes 2 minority (both Hispanic/Latino), 1 international. Average age 23. In 2019, 2 doctorates awarded. *Degree requirements:* For doctorate, comprehensive exam, thesis/dissertation, Completion of Research Integrity Module. *Entrance requirements:* Additional exam requirements/recommendations for international students: required—TOEFL (minimum score 90 paper-based), IELTS. *Application deadline:* For fall admission, 12/2 priority date for domestic and international students. Applications are processed on a rolling basis. Application fee: $0 ($75 for international students). Electronic applications accepted. *Financial support:* In 2019–20, 19 fellowships with full tuition reimbursements (averaging $36,108 per year), 15 research assistantships with full tuition reimbursements (averaging $30,840 per year), 14 teaching assistantships with full tuition reimbursements (averaging $30,375 per year) were awarded; Federal Work-Study, traineeships, and health care benefits also available. *Unit head:* Dr. Jeffrey G. Lawrence, Professor and Chair, 412-624-4350, Fax: 412-624-4759, E-mail: jlawrenc@pitt.edu. *Application contact:* Cathleen M. Barr, Graduate Administrator, 412-624-4268, Fax: 412-624-4349, E-mail: cbarr@pitt.edu.
Website: http://www.biology.pitt.edu

**University of Puerto Rico at Rio Piedras,** College of Natural Sciences, Department of Biology, San Juan, PR 00931-3300. Offers ecology/systematics (MS, PhD); evolution/genetics (MS, PhD); molecular/cellular biology (MS, PhD); neuroscience (MS, PhD). *Program availability:* Part-time. *Degree requirements:* For master's, one foreign language, comprehensive exam, thesis; for doctorate, one foreign language, comprehensive exam, thesis/dissertation. *Entrance requirements:* For master's, GRE Subject Test, interview, minimum GPA of 3.0, letter of recommendation; for doctorate, GRE Subject Test, interview, master's degree, minimum GPA of 3.0, letter of recommendation.

**University of Rhode Island,** Graduate School, College of the Environment and Life Sciences, Department of Biological Sciences, Kingston, RI 02881. Offers cell and molecular biology (MS, PhD); earth and environmental sciences (MS, PhD); ecology and ecosystem sciences (MS, PhD); evolutionary and marine biology (MS, PhD); sustainable agriculture and food systems (MS, PhD). *Program availability:* Part-time. *Faculty:* 20 full-time (10 women). *Students:* 108 full-time (68 women), 22 part-time (15 women); includes 12 minority (6 Black or African American, non-Hispanic/Latino; 4 Asian, non-Hispanic/Latino; 1 Hispanic/Latino; 1 Two or more races, non-Hispanic/Latino), 22 international. In 2019, 12 master's, 10 doctorates awarded. *Entrance requirements:* Additional exam requirements/recommendations for international students: required—TOEFL. *Application deadline:* For fall admission, 1/15 for domestic and international students. Application fee: $65. Electronic applications accepted. *Expenses: Tuition, area resident:* Full-time $13,734; part-time $763 per credit. Tuition, state resident: full-time $13,734; part-time $763 per credit. Tuition, nonresident: full-time $26,512; part-time $1473 per credit. *International tuition:* $26,512 full-time. *Required fees:* $1780; $52 per credit. $35 per term. One-time fee: $165. *Financial support:* In 2019–20, 24 research assistantships with tuition reimbursements (averaging $9,961 per year), 1 teaching assistantship with tuition reimbursement (averaging $7,521 per year) were awarded. Financial award application deadline: 1/15; financial award applicants required to submit FAFSA. *Unit head:* Dr. Alison Roberts, Chair, E-mail: bio_chair@etal.uri.edu. *Application contact:* Bethany Jenkins, Graduate Program Director, 401-874-7551, E-mail: bdjenkins@uri.edu.
Website: http://web.uri.edu/bio/

**University of South Carolina,** The Graduate School, College of Arts and Sciences, Department of Biological Sciences, Graduate Training Program in Ecology, Evolution, and Organismal Biology, Columbia, SC 29208. Offers MS, PhD. *Degree requirements:* For master's, one foreign language, comprehensive exam, thesis; for doctorate, one foreign language, comprehensive exam, thesis/dissertation. *Entrance requirements:* For master's and doctorate, GRE General Test, minimum GPA of 3.0 in science. Additional exam requirements/recommendations for international students: required—TOEFL (minimum score 570 paper-based). Electronic applications accepted.

**University of Southern California,** Graduate School, Dana and David Dornsife College of Letters, Arts and Sciences, Department of Biological Sciences, Program in Integrative and Evolutionary Biology, Los Angeles, CA 90089. Offers PhD. Terminal master's awarded for partial completion of doctoral program. *Degree requirements:* For doctorate, comprehensive exam, thesis/dissertation, qualifying examination, dissertation defense. *Entrance requirements:* For doctorate, GRE, 3 letters of recommendation, personal statement, resume, minimum GPA of 3.0. Additional exam requirements/recommendations for international students: required—TOEFL (minimum score 600 paper-based; 100 iBT). Electronic applications accepted.

**University of South Florida,** College of Arts and Sciences, Department of Integrative Biology, Tampa, FL 33620-9951. Offers biology (MS), including ecology and evolution, environmental and ecological microbiology, physiology and morphology. *Program availability:* Part-time. *Faculty:* 12 full-time (4 women). *Students:* 27 full-time (15 women), 3 part-time (all women); includes 5 minority (1 Black or African American, non-Hispanic/Latino; 2 Asian, non-Hispanic/Latino; 2 Hispanic/Latino), 3 international. Average age 32. 37 applicants, 24% accepted, 6 enrolled. In 2019, 4 master's, 3 doctorates awarded. *Degree requirements:* For master's, comprehensive exam, thesis (for some programs); for doctorate, comprehensive exam, thesis/dissertation. *Entrance requirements:* For master's, GRE: Preferred scores of 155V (69th percentile), 150Q (38th percentile), 4.5AW, minimum GPA of 3.0; Acceptance by faculty member; 3 letters of recommendation (see student recommendation form on department website); statement of research and professional goals; TA application; It is expected that candidates will have completed courses equivalent to those required for the BS in Biology at USF; for doctorate, GRE: 155+ (70%)V, 150+ (70%)Q, 4.5 (70%) AW, Bachelor of Science required. It is expected that candidates for the Ph.D. degree will have completed courses equivalent to those required for the B.S. in Biology at U.S.F. Acceptance by a faculty member in the Department of Integrative Biology is mandatory. Additional exam requirements/recommendations for international students: required—TOEFL. *Application deadline:* For fall admission, 11/30 priority date for domestic and international students; for spring admission, 7/1 priority date for domestic and international students. Application fee: $30. Electronic applications accepted. *Financial support:* In 2019–20, 11 students received support. Research assistantships, teaching assistantships, and unspecified assistantships available. Financial award application deadline: 6/30; financial award applicants required to submit FAFSA. *Unit head:* Dr. Valerie Harwood, Professor and Chair, 813-974-1524, Fax: 813-974-3263, E-mail: vharwood@usf.edu. *Application contact:* Dr. Stephen Deban, Associate Professor and Graduate Program Director, 813-974-2242, E-mail: sdeban@usf.edu.
Website: http://biology.usf.edu/ib/grad/

**The University of Tennessee,** Graduate School, College of Arts and Sciences, Department of Ecology and Evolutionary Biology, Knoxville, TN 37996. Offers behavior (MS, PhD); ecology (MS, PhD); evolutionary biology (MS, PhD). *Program availability:* Part-time. *Degree requirements:* For master's, thesis; for doctorate, thesis/dissertation. *Entrance requirements:* For master's and doctorate, GRE General Test, minimum GPA of 2.7. Additional exam requirements/recommendations for international students: required—TOEFL. Electronic applications accepted.

**The University of Texas at Austin,** Graduate School, College of Natural Sciences, School of Biological Sciences, Program in Ecology, Evolution and Behavior, Austin, TX 78712-1111. Offers PhD. *Entrance requirements:* For doctorate, GRE General Test. Additional exam requirements/recommendations for international students: required—TOEFL. Electronic applications accepted.

**University of Toronto,** School of Graduate Studies, Faculty of Arts and Science, Department of Ecology and Evolutionary Biology, Toronto, ON M5S 1A1, Canada. Offers M Sc, PhD. *Degree requirements:* For master's, thesis, thesis defense; for doctorate, thesis/dissertation, thesis defense. *Entrance requirements:* For master's, minimum B average in last 2 years; knowledge of physics, chemistry, and biology. Additional exam requirements/recommendations for international students: required—TOEFL (minimum score 580 paper-based; 93 iBT), TWE (minimum score 5). Electronic applications accepted.

**Washington University in St. Louis,** The Graduate School, Division of Biology and Biomedical Sciences, Program in Evolution, Ecology and Population Biology, St. Louis, MO 63130-4899. Offers ecology (PhD). *Degree requirements:* For doctorate, thesis/dissertation. *Entrance requirements:* For doctorate, GRE General Test, GRE Subject Test. Additional exam requirements/recommendations for international students: required—TOEFL. Electronic applications accepted.

**Wesleyan University,** Graduate Studies, Department of Biology, Middletown, CT 06459. Offers cell and developmental biology (PhD); evolution and ecology (PhD); genetics and genomics (PhD), including bioinformatics; neurobiology and behavior (PhD). Terminal master's awarded for partial completion of doctoral program. *Degree requirements:* For doctorate, comprehensive exam, thesis/dissertation, public seminar. *Entrance requirements:* For doctorate, GRE, official transcripts, three recommendation letters, essay. Additional exam requirements/recommendations for international students: required—TOEFL. Electronic applications accepted.

**Yale University,** Graduate School of Arts and Sciences, Department of Ecology and Evolutionary Biology, New Haven, CT 06520. Offers PhD. *Entrance requirements:* For doctorate, GRE General Test, GRE Subject Test (biology).

# Section 9
# Entomology

This section contains a directory of institutions offering graduate work in entomology. Additional information about programs listed in the directory may be obtained by writing directly to the dean of a graduate school or chair of a department at the address given in the directory.

For programs offering related work, see also in this book *Biochemistry; Biological and Biomedical Sciences; Botany and Plant Biology; Ecology, Environmental Biology, and Evolutionary Biology; Genetics, Developmental Biology, and Reproductive Biology; Microbiological Sciences; Physiology;* and *Zoology.* In the other guides in this series:

**Graduate Programs in the Humanities, Arts & Social Sciences**
See *Economics (Agricultural Economics and Agribusiness)*

**Graduate Programs in the Physical Sciences, Mathematics, Agricultural Sciences, the Environment & Natural Resources**
See *Agricultural and Food Sciences* and *Environmental Sciences and Management*

**Graduate Programs in Engineering & Applied Sciences**
See *Agricultural Engineering* and *Bioengineering*

## CONTENTS

## Program Directory

# Entomology

**Auburn University,** Graduate School, College of Agriculture, Department of Entomology and Plant Pathology, Auburn, AL 36849. Offers entomology (M Ag, MS); plant pathology (M Ag, MS, PhD). *Program availability:* Part-time. *Faculty:* 20 full-time (9 women). *Students:* 37 full-time (17 women), 15 part-time (8 women); includes 6 minority (3 Asian, non-Hispanic/Latino; 2 Hispanic/Latino; 1 Two or more races, non-Hispanic/Latino), 28 international. Average age 28. 19 applicants, 68% accepted, 10 enrolled. In 2019, 10 master's, 2 doctorates awarded. *Degree requirements:* For master's, thesis (for some programs); for doctorate, one foreign language, thesis/dissertation. *Entrance requirements:* For master's, GRE General Test; for doctorate, GRE General Test, GRE Subject Test, master's degree with thesis. Additional exam requirements/recommendations for international students: required—TOEFL (minimum score 550 paper-based; 79 iBT), iTEP; recommended—IELTS (minimum score 6.5). *Application deadline:* Applications are processed on a rolling basis. Application fee: $60 ($70 for international students). Electronic applications accepted. *Expenses: Tuition, area resident:* Full-time $9828; part-time $546 per credit hour. Tuition, state resident: full-time $9828; part-time $546 per credit hour. Tuition, nonresident: full-time $29,484; part-time $1638 per credit hour. *International tuition:* $29,744 full-time. Tuition and fees vary according to course load, program and reciprocity agreements. *Financial support:* In 2019–20, 36 fellowships with tuition reimbursements (averaging $716 per year), 33 research assistantships with tuition reimbursements (averaging $19,392 per year) were awarded; Federal Work-Study also available. Support available to part-time students. Financial award application deadline: 3/15; financial award applicants required to submit FAFSA. *Unit head:* Dr. Nannan Liu, Chair, 334-844-4266. *Application contact:* Dr. George Flowers, Dean of the Graduate School, 334-844-2125.

**Clemson University,** Graduate School, College of Agriculture, Forestry and Life Sciences, Department of Plant and Environmental Sciences, Clemson, SC 29634. Offers entomology (MS, PhD); plant and environmental sciences (MS, PhD). *Faculty:* 46 full-time (11 women), 1 part-time/adjunct (0 women). *Students:* 74 full-time (31 women), 16 part-time (2 women); includes 2 minority (1 Asian, non-Hispanic/Latino; 1 Two or more races, non-Hispanic/Latino), 29 international. Average age 28. 56 applicants, 86% accepted, 32 enrolled. In 2019, 20 master's, 12 doctorates awarded. *Expenses:* Full-Time Student per Semester: Tuition: $4600 (in-state), $9525 (out-of-state); Fees: $598; Graduate Assistant Per Semester: $1144; Part-Time Student Per Credit Hour: $556 (in-state), $1106 (out-of-state), Fees: $617; other fees apply depending on program, credit hours, campus & residency. Doctoral Base Fee per Semester: $4938 (in-state), $10405 (out-of-state). *Financial support:* In 2019–20, 91 students received support, including 13 fellowships with full and partial tuition reimbursements available (averaging $10,923 per year), 70 research assistantships with full and partial tuition reimbursements available (averaging $19,437 per year), 8 teaching assistantships with full and partial tuition reimbursements available (averaging $16,729 per year); career-related internships or fieldwork also available. *Application contact:* Dr. Guido Schnabel, Graduate Program Coordinator, 864-656-6705, E-mail: schnabe@clemson.edu.
Website: http://www.clemson.edu/cafls/departments/plant-environmental-sciences/index.html

**Colorado State University,** College of Agricultural Sciences, Department of Agricultural Biology, Fort Collins, CO 80523-1177. Offers entomology (MS, PhD); pest management (MS); plant pathology (MS, PhD); weed science (MS, PhD). *Faculty:* 24 full-time (11 women). *Students:* 22 full-time (12 women), 20 part-time (13 women); includes 5 minority (1 Asian, non-Hispanic/Latino; 2 Hispanic/Latino; 2 Two or more races, non-Hispanic/Latino), 12 international. Average age 29. 32 applicants, 41% accepted, 13 enrolled. In 2019, 7 master's, 3 doctorates awarded. Terminal master's awarded for partial completion of doctoral program. *Degree requirements:* For master's, thesis; for doctorate, thesis/dissertation. *Entrance requirements:* For master's and doctorate, minimum GPA of 3.0, three letters of recommendation, essay, transcripts, short essay outlining experience and career goals. Additional exam requirements/recommendations for international students: required—TOEFL (minimum score 550 paper-based). *Application deadline:* For fall admission, 1/15 priority date for domestic and international students; for spring admission, 9/1 priority date for domestic and international students. Application fee: $60 ($70 for international students). Electronic applications accepted. *Expenses:* Tuition, state resident: full-time $10,520; part-time $5844 per credit hour. Tuition, nonresident: full-time $25,791; part-time $14,328 per credit hour. *International tuition:* $25,791 full-time. *Required fees:* $2512.80. Part-time tuition and fees vary according to course level, course load, degree level, program and student level. *Financial support:* In 2019–20, 22 research assistantships with partial tuition reimbursements (averaging $22,683 per year), 10 teaching assistantships with partial tuition reimbursements (averaging $18,912 per year) were awarded; fellowships with partial tuition reimbursements and scholarships/grants also available. Financial award application deadline: 1/15. *Unit head:* Dr. Amy Charkowski, Department Head and Professor, 970-491-8586, E-mail: amy.charkowski@colostate.edu. *Application contact:* Janet Dill, Graduate Student Coordinator, 970-491-0402, Fax: 970-491-3862, E-mail: janet.dill@colostate.edu.
Website: http://bspm.agsci.colostate.edu/

**Cornell University,** Graduate School, Graduate Fields of Agriculture and Life Sciences, Field of Entomology, Ithaca, NY 14853. Offers acarology (MS, PhD); apiculture (MS, PhD); applied entomology (MS, PhD); aquatic entomology (MS, PhD); biological control (MS, PhD); insect behavior (MS, PhD); insect biochemistry (MS, PhD); insect ecology (MS, PhD); insect genetics (MS, PhD); insect morphology (MS, PhD); insect pathology (MS, PhD); insect physiology (MS, PhD); insect systematics (MS, PhD); insect toxicology and insecticide chemistry (MS, PhD); integrated pest management (MS, PhD); medical and veterinary entomology (MS, PhD). *Degree requirements:* For master's, thesis; for doctorate, comprehensive exam, thesis/dissertation. *Entrance requirements:* For master's and doctorate, GRE General Test, GRE Subject Test (biology), 3 letters of recommendation. Additional exam requirements/recommendations for international students: required—TOEFL (minimum score 550 paper-based; 77 iBT). Electronic applications accepted.

**Illinois State University,** Graduate School, College of Arts and Sciences, School of Biological Sciences, Normal, IL 61790. Offers animal behavior (MS); bacteriology (MS); biochemistry (MS); biological sciences (MS); biology (PhD); biophysics (MS); biotechnology (MS); botany (MS, PhD); cell biology (MS); conservation biology (MS); developmental biology (MS); ecology (MS, PhD); entomology (MS); evolutionary biology (MS); genetics (MS, PhD); immunology (MS); microbiology (MS, PhD); molecular biology (MS); molecular genetics (MS); neurobiology (MS); neuroscience (MS); parasitology (MS); physiology (MS, PhD); plant biology (MS); plant molecular biology (MS); plant sciences (MS); structural biology (MS); zoology (MS, PhD). *Program availability:* Part-time. *Faculty:* 26 full-time (6 women), 7 part-time/adjunct (2 women). *Students:* 51 full-time (33 women), 15 part-time (8 women). Average age 27. 71 applicants, 28% accepted, 9 enrolled. In 2019, 14 master's, 3 doctorates awarded.

*Degree requirements:* For master's, thesis or alternative; for doctorate, variable foreign language requirement, thesis/dissertation, 2 terms of residency. *Entrance requirements:* For master's, GRE General Test, minimum GPA of 2.6 in last 60 hours of course work; for doctorate, GRE General Test. *Application deadline:* Applications are processed on a rolling basis. Application fee: $50. *Expenses: Tuition, area resident:* Full-time $7956; part-time $9767 per year. Tuition, nonresident: full-time $9233; part-time $17,592 per year. *Required fees:* $1797. *Financial support:* In 2019–20, 20 research assistantships, 41 teaching assistantships were awarded; Federal Work-Study, tuition waivers (full), and unspecified assistantships also available. Financial award application deadline: 4/1. *Unit head:* Dr. Craig Gatto, School Director, 309-438-3087, E-mail: cgatto@IllinoisState.edu. *Application contact:* Dr. Ben Sadd, Assistant Chair for Graduate Studies, 309-438-2651, E-mail: bmsadd@IllinoisState.edu.
Website: http://www.bio.ilstu.edu/

**Iowa State University of Science and Technology,** Department of Entomology, Ames, IA 50011. Offers MS, PhD. *Degree requirements:* For master's, thesis; for doctorate, thesis/dissertation. *Entrance requirements:* For master's and doctorate, GRE General Test, GRE Subject Test (biology). Additional exam requirements/recommendations for international students: required—TOEFL (minimum score 550 paper-based; 79 iBT), IELTS (minimum score 6.5). Electronic applications accepted.

**Kansas State University,** Graduate School, College of Agriculture, Department of Entomology, Manhattan, KS 66506. Offers MS, PhD. *Degree requirements:* For master's, thesis, oral exam; for doctorate, comprehensive exam, thesis/dissertation, written and oral exams. *Entrance requirements:* Additional exam requirements/recommendations for international students: required—TOEFL (minimum score 550 paper-based; 79 iBT). Electronic applications accepted.

**Louisiana State University and Agricultural & Mechanical College,** Graduate School, College of Agriculture, Department of Entomology, Baton Rouge, LA 70803. Offers MS, PhD.

**McGill University,** Faculty of Graduate and Postdoctoral Studies, Faculty of Agricultural and Environmental Sciences, Department of Natural Resource Sciences, Montréal, QC H3A 2T5, Canada. Offers entomology (M Sc, PhD); environmental assessment (M Sc); forest science (M Sc, PhD); microbiology (M Sc, PhD); micrometeorology (M Sc, PhD); neotropical environment (M Sc, PhD); soil science (M Sc, PhD); wildlife biology (M Sc, PhD).

**Michigan State University,** The Graduate School, College of Agriculture and Natural Resources, Department of Entomology, East Lansing, MI 48824. Offers entomology (MS, PhD); integrated pest management (MS). *Entrance requirements:* Additional exam requirements/recommendations for international students: required—TOEFL (minimum score 550 paper-based), Michigan State University ELT ( minimum score 85), Michigan English Language Assessment Battery (minimum score 83). Electronic applications accepted.

**New Mexico State University,** College of Agricultural, Consumer and Environmental Sciences, Department of Entomology, Plant Pathology and Weed Science, Las Cruces, NM 88003-8001. Offers MS. *Program availability:* Part-time. *Faculty:* 10 full-time (2 women). *Students:* 8 full-time (6 women), 2 part-time (1 woman); includes 3 minority (1 Black or African American, non-Hispanic/Latino; 2 Hispanic/Latino), 3 international. Average age 26. 9 applicants, 78% accepted, 4 enrolled. In 2019, 4 master's awarded. *Degree requirements:* For master's, comprehensive exam, thesis. *Entrance requirements:* For master's, GRE General Test. Additional exam requirements/recommendations for international students: required—TOEFL (minimum score 550 paper-based; 79 iBT), IELTS (minimum score 6.5). *Application deadline:* For fall admission, 7/1 priority date for domestic students; for spring admission, 11/1 priority date for domestic students. Applications are processed on a rolling basis. Application fee: $40 ($50 for international students). Electronic applications accepted. *Financial support:* In 2019–20, 8 students received support, including 8 research assistantships (averaging $23,169 per year), 5 teaching assistantships (averaging $17,716 per year); career-related internships or fieldwork, Federal Work-Study, scholarships/grants, traineeships, health care benefits, and unspecified assistantships also available. Support available to part-time students. Financial award application deadline: 3/1. *Unit head:* Dr. Gerald K. Sims, Department Head, 575-646-3225, Fax: 575-646-8087, E-mail: gksims@nmsu.edu. *Application contact:* Belinda Williams, Administrative Assistant, 575-646-3225, Fax: 575-646-8087.
Website: http://eppws.nmsu.edu/

**North Carolina State University,** Graduate School, College of Agriculture and Life Sciences, Department of Entomology, Raleigh, NC 27695. Offers MS, PhD. Terminal master's awarded for partial completion of doctoral program. *Degree requirements:* For master's, thesis (for some programs); for doctorate, thesis/dissertation. *Entrance requirements:* For master's and doctorate, GRE General Test. Electronic applications accepted.

**North Dakota State University,** College of Graduate and Interdisciplinary Studies, College of Agriculture, Food Systems, and Natural Resources, Department of Entomology, Fargo, ND 58102. Offers MS, PhD. *Program availability:* Part-time. *Degree requirements:* For master's, thesis; for doctorate, comprehensive exam, thesis/dissertation. *Entrance requirements:* For master's and doctorate, minimum GPA of 3.0. Additional exam requirements/recommendations for international students: required—TOEFL (minimum score 550 paper-based; 79 iBT). Electronic applications accepted. Tuition and fees vary according to program and reciprocity agreements.

**The Ohio State University,** Graduate School, College of Food, Agricultural, and Environmental Sciences, Department of Entomology, Columbus, OH 43210. Offers MPHM, MS, PhD. *Degree requirements:* For master's, variable foreign language requirement, thesis optional; for doctorate, variable foreign language requirement, thesis/dissertation. *Entrance requirements:* For master's and doctorate, GRE General Test. Additional exam requirements/recommendations for international students: required—TOEFL (minimum score 550 paper-based; 79 iBT), Michigan English Language Assessment Battery (minimum score 82); recommended—IELTS (minimum score 7). Electronic applications accepted.

**Oklahoma State University,** College of Agricultural Science and Natural Resources, Department of Entomology and Plant Pathology, Stillwater, OK 74078. Offers entomology (PhD); entomology and plant pathology (MS). *Faculty:* 20 full-time (4 women). *Students:* 5 full-time (2 women), 19 part-time (10 women); includes 2 minority (1 Hispanic/Latino; 1 Two or more races, non-Hispanic/Latino), 13 international. Average age 28. 14 applicants, 57% accepted, 8 enrolled. In 2019, 9 master's, 2 doctorates awarded. *Entrance requirements:* For master's and doctorate, GRE or GMAT. Additional exam requirements/recommendations for international students: required—TOEFL (minimum score 550 paper-based; 79 iBT). *Application deadline:* For

fall admission, 3/1 priority date for international students; for spring admission, 8/1 priority date for international students. Applications are processed on a rolling basis. Application fee: $50 ($75 for international students). Electronic applications accepted. *Expenses: Tuition, area resident:* Full-time $4148.10; part-time $2765.40 per credit hour. Tuition, state resident: full-time $4148.10; part-time $2765.40 per credit hour. Tuition, nonresident: full-time $15,775; part-time $10,516.80 per credit hour. *International tuition:* $15,775.20 full-time. *Required fees:* $2196.90; $122.05 per credit hour. Tuition and fees vary according to course load, campus/location and program. *Financial support:* In 2019–20, 23 research assistantships (averaging $1,557 per year), 2 teaching assistantships (averaging $1,511 per year) were awarded; career-related internships or fieldwork, Federal Work-Study, scholarships/grants, health care benefits, tuition waivers (partial), and unspecified assistantships also available. Support available to part-time students. Financial award application deadline: 3/1; financial award applicants required to submit FAFSA. *Unit head:* Dr. Phillip Mulder, Jr., Department Head, 405-744-5527, Fax: 405-744-6039, E-mail: phil.mulder@okstate.edu. *Application contact:* Dr. Sheryl Tucker, VICE PROVOST/DEAN/PROF, 405-744-6368, E-mail: igrad@okstate.edu.
Website: http://entoplp.okstate.edu

**Penn State University Park,** Graduate School, College of Agricultural Sciences, Department of Entomology, University Park, PA 16802. Offers MS, PhD.

**Purdue University,** Graduate School, College of Agriculture, Department of Entomology, West Lafayette, IN 47907. Offers MS, PhD. *Program availability:* Part-time. *Faculty:* 21 full-time (4 women), 3 part-time/adjunct (0 women). *Students:* 40 full-time (19 women), 2 part-time (1 woman); includes 11 minority (2 Black or African American, non-Hispanic/Latino; 1 Asian, non-Hispanic/Latino; 5 Hispanic/Latino; 3 Two or more races, non-Hispanic/Latino), 8 international. Average age 27. 28 applicants, 54% accepted, 15 enrolled. In 2019, 2 master's, 5 doctorates awarded. *Degree requirements:* For master's, thesis (for some programs), seminar; for doctorate, thesis/dissertation, seminar. *Entrance requirements:* For master's, GRE General Test, minimum undergraduate GPA of 3.0 or equivalent; for doctorate, GRE, minimum undergraduate GPA of 3.0 or equivalent; master's degree (highly recommended). Additional exam requirements/recommendations for international students: required—TOEFL (minimum score 550 paper-based; 77 iBT). *Application deadline:* For fall admission, 7/1 priority date for domestic students, 3/15 for international students; for spring admission, 11/1 for domestic students, 8/15 for international students. Applications are processed on a rolling basis. Application fee: $60 ($75 for international students). Electronic applications accepted. *Financial support:* Fellowships with tuition reimbursements, research assistantships with tuition reimbursements, teaching assistantships with tuition reimbursements, and career-related internships or fieldwork available. Support available to part-time students. Financial award application deadline: 3/1; financial award applicants required to submit FAFSA. *Unit head:* Stephen Cameron, Head, 765-494-4554, E-mail: cameros@purdue.edu. *Application contact:* Amanda L. Wilson, Graduate Contact, 765-494-9061, E-mail: apendle@purdue.edu.
Website: https://ag.purdue.edu/entm

**Rutgers University - New Brunswick,** Graduate School-New Brunswick, Program in Entomology, Piscataway, NJ 08854-8097. Offers MS, PhD. *Degree requirements:* For master's, thesis or alternative; for doctorate, thesis/dissertation. *Entrance requirements:* For master's and doctorate, GRE General Test, GRE Subject Test (recommended). Additional exam requirements/recommendations for international students: required—TOEFL. Electronic applications accepted.

**Simon Fraser University,** Office of Graduate Studies and Postdoctoral Fellows, Faculty of Science, Department of Biological Sciences, Burnaby, BC V5A 1S6, Canada. Offers bioinformatics (Graduate Diploma); biological sciences (M Sc, PhD); environmental toxicology (MET); pest management (MPM). *Degree requirements:* For master's, thesis; for doctorate, thesis/dissertation, candidacy exam; for Graduate Diploma, practicum. *Entrance requirements:* For master's, minimum GPA of 3.0 (on scale of 4.33) or 3.33 based on last 60 credits of undergraduate courses; for doctorate, minimum GPA of 3.5 (on scale of 4.33); for Graduate Diploma, minimum GPA of 2.5 (on scale of 4.33) or 2.67 based on last 60 credits of undergraduate courses. Additional exam requirements/recommendations for international students: recommended—TOEFL (minimum score 580 paper-based; 93 iBT), IELTS (minimum score 7), TWE (minimum score 5). Electronic applications accepted.

**State University of New York College of Environmental Science and Forestry,** Department of Environmental and Forest Biology, Syracuse, NY 13210-2779. Offers applied ecology (MPS); chemical ecology (MPS, MS, PhD); conservation biology (MPS, MS, PhD); ecology (MPS, MS, PhD); entomology (MPS, MS, PhD); environmental interpretation (MPS, MS, PhD); environmental physiology (MPS, MS, PhD); fish and wildlife biology and management (MPS, MS, PhD); forest pathology and mycology (MPS, MS, PhD); plant biotechnology (MPS); plant science and biotechnology (MPS, MS, PhD). *Program availability:* Part-time. *Faculty:* 35 full-time (10 women), 4 part-time/adjunct (3 women). *Students:* 103 full-time (60 women), 17 part-time (7 women); includes 7 minority (4 American Indian or Alaska Native, non-Hispanic/Latino; 2 Asian, non-Hispanic/Latino; 1 Hispanic/Latino), 13 international. Average age 29. 69 applicants, 45% accepted, 17 enrolled. In 2019, 28 master's, 6 doctorates awarded. Terminal master's awarded for partial completion of doctoral program. *Degree requirements:* For master's, thesis (for some programs), capstone seminar; for doctorate, comprehensive exam, thesis/dissertation, capstone seminar. *Entrance requirements:* For master's and doctorate, GRE General Test, minimum GPA of 3.0. Additional exam requirements/recommendations for international students: required—TOEFL (minimum score 550 paper-based; 80 iBT), IELTS (minimum score 6). *Application deadline:* For fall admission, 2/1 priority date for domestic and international students; for spring admission, 11/1 priority date for domestic and international students. Applications are processed on a rolling basis. Application fee: $60. Electronic applications accepted. *Expenses:* Tuition, state resident: full-time $11,310; part-time $472 per credit hour. Tuition, nonresident: full-time $23,100; part-time $963 per credit hour. *Required fees:* $1890; $95.21 per credit hour. *Financial support:* In 2019–20, 35 students received support. Unspecified assistantships available. Financial award application deadline: 6/30; financial award applicants required to submit FAFSA. *Unit head:* Dr. Melissa K. Fierke, Chair, 315-470-6809, Fax: 315-470-6743, E-mail: mkfierke@esf.edu. *Application contact:* Laura Payne, Administrative Assistant Office of Instruction & Graduate Studies, 315-470-6599, E-mail: esfgrad@esf.edu.
Website: http://www.esf.edu/efb/grad/default.asp

**Texas A&M University,** College of Agriculture and Life Sciences, Department of Entomology, College Station, TX 77843. Offers entomology (MS). *Faculty:* 26. *Students:* 67 full-time (35 women), 12 part-time (6 women); includes 18 minority (4 Black or African American, non-Hispanic/Latino; 2 Asian, non-Hispanic/Latino; 10 Hispanic/Latino; 2 Two or more races, non-Hispanic/Latino), 17 international. Average age 29. 24 applicants, 46% accepted, 10 enrolled. In 2019, 3 master's, 12 doctorates awarded. *Degree requirements:* For master's, comprehensive exam, thesis (for some programs); for doctorate, comprehensive exam, thesis/dissertation. *Entrance requirements:* For master's and doctorate, GRE General Test. Additional exam requirements/recommendations for international students: required—TOEFL (minimum score 550 paper-based; 80 iBT), IELTS (minimum score 6), PTE (minimum score 53). *Application deadline:* For fall admission, 6/1 priority date for domestic students; for spring admission, 11/1 for domestic students; for summer admission, 3/1 for domestic students. Applications are processed on a rolling basis. Application fee: $65 ($90 for international students). Electronic applications accepted. *Expenses:* Contact institution. *Financial support:* In 2019–20, 77 students received support, including 10 fellowships with tuition reimbursements available (averaging $22,575 per year), 50 research assistantships with tuition reimbursements available (averaging $12,899 per year), 30 teaching assistantships with tuition reimbursements available (averaging $13,757 per year); career-related internships or fieldwork, institutionally sponsored loans, scholarships/grants, traineeships, health care benefits, tuition waivers (full and partial), and unspecified assistantships also available. Support available to part-time students. Financial award application deadline: 3/15; financial award applicants required to submit FAFSA. *Unit head:* Phillip Kaufman, Professor and Head, 979-845-2510, E-mail: pkaufman@tamu.edu. *Application contact:* Rebecca Hapes, Academic Advisor IV, 979-845-9733, E-mail: rhapes@tamu.edu.
Website: http://entomology.tamu.edu

**The University of Arizona,** Graduate Interdisciplinary Programs, Graduate Interdisciplinary Program in Entomology and Insect Science, Tucson, AZ 85721. Offers MS, PhD. *Program availability:* Part-time. *Degree requirements:* For master's, thesis; for doctorate, comprehensive exam, thesis/dissertation. *Entrance requirements:* For master's, GRE General Test, GRE Subject Test, minimum GPA of 3.0, 3 letters of recommendation; for doctorate, GRE General Test, GRE Subject Test, minimum GPA of 3.0, 3 letters of recommendation, statement of purpose. Additional exam requirements/recommendations for international students: required—TOEFL (minimum score 550 paper-based).

**University of Arkansas,** Graduate School, Dale Bumpers College of Agricultural, Food and Life Sciences, Department of Entomology, Fayetteville, AR 72701. Offers MS, PhD. *Students:* 10 full-time (6 women), 5 part-time (2 women), 3 international. 5 applicants, 80% accepted. In 2019, 4 master's, 4 doctorates awarded. *Degree requirements:* For master's, thesis; for doctorate, one foreign language, thesis/dissertation. *Entrance requirements:* For master's, GRE, minimum GPA of 3.0; for doctorate, GRE, minimum GPA of 3.25. *Application deadline:* For fall admission, 8/1 for domestic students, 4/1 for international students; for spring admission, 12/1 for domestic students, 10/1 for international students; for summer admission, 4/15 for domestic students, 3/1 for international students. Applications are processed on a rolling basis. Application fee: $60. Electronic applications accepted. *Financial support:* In 2019–20, 19 research assistantships were awarded; fellowships with tuition reimbursements, teaching assistantships, career-related internships or fieldwork, and Federal Work-Study also available. Support available to part-time students. Financial award application deadline: 4/1; financial award applicants required to submit FAFSA. *Unit head:* Dr. Kenneth Korth, Department Head, 479-575-2451, E-mail: kkorth@uark.edu. *Application contact:* Dr. Ashley Dowling, Coordinator, 479-575-2451, E-mail: adowling@uark.edu.
Website: https://entomology.uark.edu/index.php

**University of California, Davis,** Graduate Studies, Graduate Group in Integrated Pest Management, Davis, CA 95616. Offers MS. *Degree requirements:* For master's, comprehensive exam (for some programs), thesis (for some programs). *Entrance requirements:* For master's, GRE General Test, GRE Subject Test (biology), minimum GPA of 3.0. Additional exam requirements/recommendations for international students: required—TOEFL (minimum score 550 paper-based). Electronic applications accepted.

**University of California, Davis,** Graduate Studies, Program in Entomology, Davis, CA 95616. Offers MS, PhD. Terminal master's awarded for partial completion of doctoral program. *Degree requirements:* For master's, comprehensive exam (for some programs), thesis (for some programs); for doctorate, thesis/dissertation. *Entrance requirements:* For master's and doctorate, GRE General Test, GRE Subject Test (biology). Additional exam requirements/recommendations for international students: required—TOEFL (minimum score 550 paper-based). Electronic applications accepted.

**University of California, Riverside,** Graduate Division, Department of Entomology, Riverside, CA 92521-0102. Offers MS, PhD. *Program availability:* Part-time. Terminal master's awarded for partial completion of doctoral program. *Degree requirements:* For master's, thesis; for doctorate, thesis/dissertation, qualifying exams. *Entrance requirements:* For master's and doctorate, GRE General Test, minimum GPA of 3.2. Additional exam requirements/recommendations for international students: required—TOEFL (minimum score 550 paper-based; 80 iBT) or IELTS. Electronic applications accepted.

**University of Delaware,** College of Agriculture and Natural Resources, Department of Entomology and Wildlife Ecology, Newark, DE 19716. Offers entomology and applied ecology (MS, PhD), including avian ecology, evolution and taxonomy, insect biological control, insect ecology and behavior (MS), insect genetics, pest management, plant-insect interactions, wildlife ecology and management. *Program availability:* Part-time. *Degree requirements:* For master's, comprehensive exam, thesis, oral exam, seminar; for doctorate, comprehensive exam, thesis/dissertation, qualifying exam, seminar. *Entrance requirements:* For master's, GRE General Test, minimum GPA of 3.0 in field, 2.8 overall; for doctorate, GRE General Test, GRE Subject Test (biology), minimum GPA of 3.0 in field, 2.8 overall. Additional exam requirements/recommendations for international students: required—TOEFL. Electronic applications accepted.

**University of Georgia,** College of Agricultural and Environmental Sciences, Department of Entomology, Athens, GA 30602. Offers entomology (MS, PhD). *Degree requirements:* For master's, thesis (MS); for doctorate, one foreign language, thesis/dissertation. *Entrance requirements:* For master's and doctorate, GRE General Test. Electronic applications accepted.

**University of Guelph,** Office of Graduate and Postdoctoral Studies, Ontario Agricultural College, Department of Environmental Biology, Guelph, ON N1G 2W1, Canada. Offers entomology (M Sc, PhD); environmental microbiology and biotechnology (M Sc, PhD); environmental toxicology (M Sc, PhD); plant and forest systems (M Sc, PhD); plant pathology (M Sc, PhD). *Program availability:* Part-time. *Degree requirements:* For master's, thesis; for doctorate, comprehensive exam, thesis/dissertation. *Entrance requirements:* For master's, minimum 75% average during previous 2 years of course work; for doctorate, minimum 75% average. Additional exam requirements/recommendations for international students: required—TOEFL or IELTS. Electronic applications accepted.

**University of Hawaii at Manoa,** Office of Graduate Education, College of Tropical Agriculture and Human Resources, Department of Plant and Environmental Protection Sciences, Program in Entomology, Honolulu, HI 96822. Offers MS, PhD. *Program availability:* Part-time. *Degree requirements:* For master's, thesis optional; for doctorate, comprehensive exam, thesis/dissertation. *Entrance requirements:* For master's and doctorate, GRE General Test, GRE Subject Test (biology). Additional exam requirements/recommendations for international students: required—TOEFL (minimum score 500 paper-based; 61 iBT), IELTS (minimum score 5).

**University of Idaho,** College of Graduate Studies, College of Agricultural and Life Sciences, Department of Entomology, Plant Pathology and Nematology, Moscow, ID 83844-2282. Offers plant science (MS). *Faculty:* 14 full-time (5 women). *Students:* 21. Average age 30. In 2019, 1 master's, 2 doctorates awarded. *Entrance requirements:* For

master's and doctorate, minimum GPA of 3.0. Additional exam requirements/recommendations for international students: required—TOEFL (minimum score 550 paper-based; 79 iBT). *Application deadline:* For fall admission, 7/30 for domestic students; for spring admission, 12/1 for domestic students. Applications are processed on a rolling basis. Application fee: $60. Electronic applications accepted. *Expenses:* Tuition, state resident: full-time $7753.80; part-time $502 per credit hour. Tuition, nonresident: full-time $26,990; part-time $1571 per credit hour. *Required fees:* $2122.20; $47 per credit hour. *Financial support:* Research assistantships and teaching assistantships available. Financial award applicants required to submit FAFSA. *Unit head:* Dr. Edwin Lewis, Department Head, 208-885-3776, E-mail: eppn@uidaho.edu. *Application contact:* Dr. Edwin Lewis, Department Head, 208-885-3776, E-mail: eppn@uidaho.edu.
Website: https://www.uidaho.edu/cals/entomology-plant-pathology-and-nematology

**University of Illinois at Urbana-Champaign,** Graduate College, College of Liberal Arts and Sciences, School of Integrative Biology, Department of Entomology, Champaign, IL 61820. Offers MS, PhD. Terminal master's awarded for partial completion of doctoral program.

**University of Kentucky,** Graduate School, College of Agriculture, Food and Environment, Program in Entomology, Lexington, KY 40506-0032. Offers MS, PhD. *Degree requirements:* For master's, comprehensive exam, thesis optional; for doctorate, comprehensive exam, thesis/dissertation. *Entrance requirements:* For master's, GRE General Test, minimum undergraduate GPA of 2.75; for doctorate, GRE General Test, minimum graduate GPA of 3.0. Additional exam requirements/recommendations for international students: required—TOEFL (minimum score 550 paper-based). Electronic applications accepted.

**University of Maine,** Graduate School, College of Natural Sciences, Forestry, and Agriculture, School of Biology and Ecology, Orono, ME 04469. Offers biological sciences (PhD); botany and plant pathology (MS); entomology (MS); zoology (MS, PhD). *Program availability:* Part-time. *Faculty:* 30 full-time (16 women), 2 part-time/adjunct (1 woman). *Students:* 84 full-time (54 women), 12 part-time (6 women); includes 9 minority (1 Black or African American, non-Hispanic/Latino; 1 American Indian or Alaska Native, non-Hispanic/Latino; 1 Asian, non-Hispanic/Latino; 5 Hispanic/Latino; 1 Two or more races, non-Hispanic/Latino), 21 international. Average age 30. 62 applicants, 40% accepted, 22 enrolled. In 2019, 12 master's, 12 doctorates awarded. Terminal master's awarded for partial completion of doctoral program. *Degree requirements:* For master's, thesis (for some programs); for doctorate, comprehensive exam, thesis/dissertation. *Entrance requirements:* For master's and doctorate, GRE General Test. Additional exam requirements/recommendations for international students: required—TOEFL (minimum score 80 iBT), IELTS (minimum score 6.5). *Application deadline:* For fall admission, 2/1 priority date for domestic students. Applications are processed on a rolling basis. Application fee: $65. Electronic applications accepted. *Expenses: Tuition, area resident:* Full-time $8100; part-time $450 per credit hour. Tuition, state resident: full-time $8100; part-time $450 per credit hour. Tuition, nonresident: full-time $26,388; part-time $1466 per credit hour. *International tuition:* $26,388 full-time. *Required fees:* $1257; $278 per semester. Tuition and fees vary according to course load. *Financial support:* In 2019–20, 108 students received support, including 1 fellowship with full tuition reimbursement available (averaging $25,000 per year), 79 research assistantships with full tuition reimbursements available (averaging $15,825 per year), 23 teaching assistantships with full tuition reimbursements available (averaging $15,825 per year); career-related internships or fieldwork, Federal Work-Study, institutionally sponsored loans, tuition waivers (full and partial), and unspecified assistantships also available. Financial award application deadline: 3/1; financial award applicants required to submit FAFSA. *Unit head:* Dr. Andrei Aloykhin, Director, 207-581-2977, Fax: 207-581-2537. *Application contact:* Scott G. Delcourt, Assistant Vice President for Graduate Studies and Senior Associate Dean, 207-581-3291, Fax: 207-581-3232, E-mail: graduate@maine.edu.
Website: http://sbe.umaine.edu/

**University of Manitoba,** Faculty of Graduate Studies, Faculty of Agricultural and Food Sciences, Department of Entomology, Winnipeg, MB R3T 2N2, Canada. Offers M Sc, PhD. *Degree requirements:* For master's, thesis; for doctorate, one foreign language, thesis/dissertation.

**University of Maryland, College Park,** Academic Affairs, College of Computer, Mathematical and Natural Sciences, Department of Entomology, College Park, MD 20742. Offers MS, PhD. *Program availability:* Part-time, evening/weekend. Terminal master's awarded for partial completion of doctoral program. *Degree requirements:* For master's, thesis; for doctorate, thesis/dissertation, oral qualifying exam. *Entrance requirements:* For master's and doctorate, GRE General Test, minimum GPA of 3.0, 3 letters of recommendation. Electronic applications accepted.

**University of Minnesota, Twin Cities Campus,** Graduate School, College of Food, Agricultural and Natural Resource Sciences, Entomology Graduate Program, Saint Paul, MN 55108. Offers MS, PhD. *Program availability:* Part-time. Terminal master's awarded for partial completion of doctoral program. *Degree requirements:* For master's, comprehensive exam, thesis; for doctorate, comprehensive exam, thesis/dissertation. *Entrance requirements:* For master's, GRE, minimum undergraduate GPA of 3.0; for doctorate, GRE, minimum undergraduate GPA of 3.0, graduate 3.5. Additional exam requirements/recommendations for international students: required—TOEFL (minimum score 550 paper-based; 79 iBT), IELTS (minimum score 6.5). Electronic applications accepted.

**University of Missouri,** Office of Research and Graduate Studies, College of Agriculture, Food and Natural Resources, Division of Plant Sciences, Columbia, MO 65211. Offers crop, soil and pest management (MS, PhD); entomology (MS, PhD); horticulture (MS, PhD); plant breeding, genetics and genomics (MS, PhD); plant stress biology (MS, PhD). Terminal master's awarded for partial completion of doctoral program. *Degree requirements:* For master's, thesis; for doctorate, comprehensive exam, thesis/dissertation. *Entrance requirements:* For master's and doctorate, GRE General Test, minimum GPA of 3.0; bachelor's degree from accredited college. Additional exam requirements/recommendations for international students: required—TOEFL (minimum score 500 paper-based; 61 iBT), IELTS (minimum score 5.5). Electronic applications accepted.

**University of Nebraska–Lincoln,** Graduate College, College of Agricultural Sciences and Natural Resources, Department of Entomology, Lincoln, NE 68588. Offers MS, PhD. *Program availability:* Online learning. *Degree requirements:* For master's, thesis optional; for doctorate, comprehensive exam, thesis/dissertation. *Entrance requirements:* For master's and doctorate, GRE General Test. Additional exam requirements/recommendations for international students: required—TOEFL (minimum score 550 paper-based). Electronic applications accepted.

**The University of Tennessee,** Graduate School, College of Agricultural Sciences and Natural Resources, Department of Entomology and Plant Pathology, Knoxville, TN 37996. Offers entomology (MS, PhD); integrated pest management and bioactive natural products (PhD); plant pathology (MS, PhD). *Program availability:* Part-time. *Degree requirements:* For master's, thesis, seminar. *Entrance requirements:* For master's, GRE General Test, minimum GPA of 2.7, 3 reference letters, letter of intent; for doctorate, GRE General Test, minimum GPA of 2.7, 3 reference letters, letter of intent, proposed dissertation research. Additional exam requirements/recommendations for international students: required—TOEFL. Electronic applications accepted.

**University of Vermont,** Graduate College, College of Agriculture and Life Sciences, Department of Plant and Soil Science, Burlington, VT 05405. Offers agroecology (Graduate Certificate); plant and soil science (MS, PhD), including agroecology, agronomy (MS), ecological landscape design, entomology, horticulture (MS), plant pathology (MS), soil science. *Degree requirements:* For master's, thesis; for doctorate, one foreign language, thesis/dissertation. *Entrance requirements:* For master's and doctorate, GRE General Test. Additional exam requirements/recommendations for international students: required—TOEFL (minimum score 550 paper-based; 90 iBT), IELTS (minimum score 6.5). Electronic applications accepted.

**University of Wisconsin–Madison,** Graduate School, College of Agricultural and Life Sciences, Department of Entomology, Madison, WI 53706-1380. Offers MS, PhD. *Degree requirements:* For master's, thesis; for doctorate, thesis/dissertation. *Entrance requirements:* For master's and doctorate, GRE General Test, minimum GPA of 3.0. Additional exam requirements/recommendations for international students: required—TOEFL. Electronic applications accepted.

**University of Wyoming,** College of Agriculture and Natural Resources, Department of Ecosystem Science and Management, Program in Entomology, Laramie, WY 82071. Offers MS, PhD. *Degree requirements:* For master's, thesis; for doctorate, thesis/dissertation. *Entrance requirements:* For master's and doctorate, GRE General Test, minimum GPA of 3.0. Additional exam requirements/recommendations for international students: required—TOEFL. Electronic applications accepted.

**Virginia Polytechnic Institute and State University,** Graduate School, College of Agriculture and Life Sciences, Blacksburg, VA 24061. Offers agricultural and applied economics (MS, PhD); agricultural and life sciences (MS); agriculture, leadership, and community education (MS, PhD); animal and poultry science (MS, PhD); biochemistry (MS, PhD); crop and soil environmental sciences (MS, PhD); dairy science (MS, PhD); entomology (MS, PhD); food science and technology (MS, PhD); horticulture (PhD); human nutrition, foods and exercise (MS, PhD); plant pathology, physiology, and weed science (MS, PhD). *Faculty:* 246 full-time (83 women). *Students:* 364 full-time (213 women), 106 part-time (68 women); includes 79 minority (29 Black or African American, non-Hispanic/Latino; 1 American Indian or Alaska Native, non-Hispanic/Latino; 13 Asian, non-Hispanic/Latino; 16 Hispanic/Latino; 20 Two or more races, non-Hispanic/Latino), 106 international. Average age 28. 314 applicants, 57% accepted, 130 enrolled. In 2019, 92 master's, 59 doctorates awarded. *Degree requirements:* For master's, comprehensive exam (for some programs), thesis (for some programs); for doctorate, comprehensive exam (for some programs), thesis/dissertation (for some programs). *Entrance requirements:* For master's and doctorate, GRE/GMAT. Additional exam requirements/recommendations for international students: required—TOEFL (minimum score 90 iBT). *Application deadline:* For fall admission, 8/1 for domestic students, 4/1 for international students; for spring admission, 1/1 for domestic students, 9/1 for international students. Applications are processed on a rolling basis. Application fee: $75. Electronic applications accepted. *Expenses:* Tuition, state resident: full-time $13,700; part-time $761.25 per credit hour. Tuition, nonresident: full-time $27,614; part-time $1534 per credit hour. *Required fees:* $886.50 per term. Tuition and fees vary according to campus/location and program. *Financial support:* In 2019–20, 248 research assistantships with full tuition reimbursements (averaging $20,360 per year), 127 teaching assistantships with full tuition reimbursements (averaging $18,183 per year) were awarded; fellowships, scholarships/grants, and unspecified assistantships also available. Financial award application deadline: 3/1; financial award applicants required to submit FAFSA. *Unit head:* Dr. Alan L. Grant, Dean, 540-231-4152, Fax: 540-231-4163, E-mail: algrant@vt.edu. *Application contact:* Crystal Tawney, Administrative Assistant, 540-231-4152, Fax: 540-231-4163, E-mail: cdtawney@vt.edu.
Website: http://www.cals.vt.edu/

**Washington State University,** College of Agricultural, Human, and Natural Resource Sciences, Department of Entomology, Pullman, WA 99164. Offers MS, PhD. Terminal master's awarded for partial completion of doctoral program. *Degree requirements:* For master's, comprehensive exam, thesis, oral exam; for doctorate, comprehensive exam, thesis/dissertation, oral exam, written exam. *Entrance requirements:* For master's, GRE General Test, GRE Subject Test in advanced biology (recommended), undergraduate degree in biology, ecology or related area; minimum GPA of 3.0; 3 letters of recommendation; for doctorate, GRE General Test, MS in entomology, biology, ecology or related area; minimum GPA of 3.0; 3 letters of recommendation. Additional exam requirements/recommendations for international students: required—TOEFL (minimum score 550 paper-based), IELTS. Electronic applications accepted.

**West Virginia University,** Davis College of Agriculture, Forestry and Consumer Sciences, Morgantown, WV 26506. Offers agricultural and extension education (MS, PhD); agriculture and resource management (MS); agriculture, natural resources and design (M Agr); agronomy (MS); animal and food science (PhD); animal physiology (MS); applied and environmental microbiology (MS); design and merchandising (MS); entomology (MS); forest resource science (PhD); forestry (MSF); genetics and developmental biology (MS, PhD); horticulture (MS); human and community development (PhD); landscape architecture (MLA); natural resource economics (PhD); nutritional and food science (MS); plant and soil science (PhD); plant pathology (MS); recreation, parks and tourism resources (MS); reproductive physiology (MS, PhD); wildlife and fisheries resources (PhD). *Accreditation:* ASLA. *Program availability:* Part-time. *Degree requirements:* For master's, thesis; for doctorate, thesis/dissertation. *Entrance requirements:* Additional exam requirements/recommendations for international students: required—TOEFL (minimum score 550 paper-based). Electronic applications accepted.

# Section 10
# Genetics, Developmental Biology, and Reproductive Biology

This section contains a directory of institutions offering graduate work in genetics, developmental biology, and reproductive biology, followed by in-depth entries submitted by institutions that chose to prepare detailed program descriptions. Additional information about programs listed in the directory but not augmented by an in-depth entry may be obtained by writing directly to the dean of a graduate school or chair of a department at the address given in the directory.

For programs offering related work, see also all other sections of this book. In the other guides in this series:

**Graduate Programs in the Physical Sciences, Mathematics, Agricultural Sciences, the Environment & Natural Resources**

See *Agricultural and Food Sciences, Chemistry,* and *Environmental Sciences and Management*

**Graduate Programs in Engineering & Applied Sciences**

See *Agricultural Engineering and Bioengineering* and *Biomedical Engineering and Biotechnology*

## CONTENTS

### Program Directories

# Developmental Biology

**Albert Einstein College of Medicine,** Graduate Programs in the Biomedical Sciences, Department of Developmental and Molecular Biology, Bronx, NY 10461. Offers PhD, MD/PhD. *Degree requirements:* For doctorate, thesis/dissertation. *Entrance requirements:* For doctorate, GRE General Test. Additional exam requirements/recommendations for international students: required—TOEFL.

**Baylor College of Medicine,** Graduate School of Biomedical Sciences, Program in Developmental Biology, Houston, TX 77030-3498. Offers PhD, MD/PhD. *Degree requirements:* For doctorate, thesis/dissertation, public defense. *Entrance requirements:* For doctorate, GRE General Test, GRE Subject Test (strongly recommended), minimum GPA of 3.0. Additional exam requirements/recommendations for international students: required—TOEFL. Electronic applications accepted.

**Brigham Young University,** Graduate Studies, College of Life Sciences, Department of Physiology and Developmental Biology, Provo, UT 84602. Offers neuroscience (MS, PhD); physiology and developmental biology (MS, PhD). *Program availability:* Part-time. *Faculty:* 22 full-time (1 woman). *Students:* 15 full-time (7 women); includes 5 minority (all Asian, non-Hispanic/Latino). Average age 31. 7 applicants, 29% accepted. In 2019, 5 master's, 1 doctorate awarded. Terminal master's awarded for partial completion of doctoral program. *Degree requirements:* For master's, thesis, Coursework Oral Exam; for doctorate, comprehensive exam, thesis/dissertation. *Entrance requirements:* For master's, GRE General Test, MCAT, or DAT, minimum GPA of 3.0 during previous 2 years; for doctorate, GRE General Test, minimum GPA of 3.0 overall. Additional exam requirements/recommendations for international students: required—TOEFL (minimum score 580 paper-based; 85 iBT), E3PT; recommended—IELTS. *Application deadline:* For fall admission, 1/15 priority date for domestic and international students. Application fee: $50. Electronic applications accepted. *Financial support:* In 2019–20, 16 students received support, including 1 fellowship with full tuition reimbursement available (averaging $7,200 per year), 12 research assistantships with full tuition reimbursements available (averaging $6,400 per year), 2 teaching assistantships with partial tuition reimbursements available (averaging $6,000 per year); career-related internships or fieldwork, institutionally sponsored loans, scholarships/grants, tuition waivers (full and partial), unspecified assistantships, and tuition awards also available. Financial award application deadline: 2/1; financial award applicants required to submit FAFSA. *Unit head:* Dr. Michael R. Stark, Chair, 801-422-9498, Fax: 801-422-0004, E-mail: michael_stark@byu.edu. *Application contact:* Connie L. Provost, Graduate Program Manager, 801-422-3706, Fax: 801-422-0004, E-mail: connie_provost@byu.edu.
Website: http://pdbio.byu.edu

**California Institute of Technology,** Division of Biology and Biological Engineering, Program in Developmental Biology, Pasadena, CA 91125-0001. Offers PhD. *Degree requirements:* For doctorate, thesis/dissertation, qualifying exam. *Entrance requirements:* For doctorate, GRE General Test.

**California State University, Sacramento,** College of Natural Sciences and Mathematics, Department of Biological Sciences, Sacramento, CA 95819. Offers biological conservation (MS); molecular and cellular biology (MS); stem cell (MA). *Program availability:* Part-time. *Students:* 38 full-time (12 women), 24 part-time (8 women); includes 19 minority (14 Asian, non-Hispanic/Latino; 4 Hispanic/Latino; 1 Native Hawaiian or other Pacific Islander, non-Hispanic/Latino), 1 international. Average age 29. 68 applicants, 44% accepted, 23 enrolled. In 2019, 13 master's awarded. *Degree requirements:* For master's, comprehensive exam (for some programs), thesis (for some programs), thesis or project; writing proficiency exam. *Entrance requirements:* For master's, GRE, bachelor's degree in biology or equivalent; minimum GPA of 2.75 in all biology courses, 3.0 in all upper-division biology courses. Additional exam requirements/recommendations for international students: required—TOEFL (minimum score 550 paper-based; 80 iBT); recommended—IELTS (minimum score 7). *Application deadline:* For fall admission, 2/1 for domestic students, 1/1 for international students. Applications are processed on a rolling basis. Application fee: $70. Electronic applications accepted. *Expenses:* Contact institution. *Financial support:* Teaching assistantships, career-related internships or fieldwork, Federal Work-Study, and scholarships/grants available. Support available to part-time students. Financial award application deadline: 3/1; financial award applicants required to submit FAFSA. *Unit head:* Dr. Shannon Datwyler, Chair, 916-278-6535, Fax: 916-278-6993, E-mail: datwyler@csus.edu. *Application contact:* Jose Martinez, Graduate Admissions Supervisor, 916-278-7871, E-mail: martinj@skymail.csus.edu.
Website: http://www.csus.edu/bios

**Carnegie Mellon University,** Mellon College of Science, Department of Biological Sciences, Pittsburgh, PA 15213-3891. Offers biochemistry (PhD); biophysics (PhD); cell and developmental biology (PhD); computational biology (MS, PhD); genetics (PhD); molecular biology (PhD); neuroscience (PhD); structural biology (PhD). *Degree requirements:* For doctorate, comprehensive exam, thesis/dissertation. *Entrance requirements:* For doctorate, GRE General Test, GRE Subject Test, interview. Electronic applications accepted.

**Columbia University,** College of Physicians and Surgeons, Department of Genetics and Development, New York, NY 10032. Offers genetics (M Phil, MA, PhD); MD/PhD. Terminal master's awarded for partial completion of doctoral program. *Degree requirements:* For doctorate, thesis/dissertation. *Entrance requirements:* For master's and doctorate, GRE General Test. Additional exam requirements/recommendations for international students: required—TOEFL. *Expenses: Tuition:* Full-time $47,600; part-time $1880 per credit. One-time fee: $105.

**Cornell University,** Graduate School, Graduate Fields of Agriculture and Life Sciences, Field of Genetics, Genomics and Development, Ithaca, NY 14853. Offers developmental biology (PhD); genetics (PhD); genomics (PhD). *Degree requirements:* For doctorate, comprehensive exam, thesis/dissertation, 2 semesters of teaching experience. *Entrance requirements:* For doctorate, GRE General Test, GRE Subject Test in biology or biochemistry (recommended), 2 letters of recommendation. Additional exam requirements/recommendations for international students: required—TOEFL (minimum score 550 paper-based; 77 iBT). Electronic applications accepted.

**Dalhousie University,** Faculty of Graduate Studies, Department of Medical Neuroscience, Halifax, NS B3H 4H7, Canada. Offers anatomy and neuroscience (M Sc, PhD). *Degree requirements:* For doctorate, thesis/dissertation. *Entrance requirements:* For master's and doctorate, 4 year honors degree or equivalent, minimum A- average. Additional exam requirements/recommendations for international students: required—1 of 5 approved tests: TOEFL, IELTS, CANTEST, CAEL, Michigan English Language Assessment Battery. Electronic applications accepted.

**Duke University,** Graduate School, Program in Developmental and Stem Cell Biology, Durham, NC 27710. Offers Certificate. *Entrance requirements:* For degree, GRE General Test. Additional exam requirements/recommendations for international students: required—TOEFL (minimum score 577 paper-based; 90 iBT) or IELTS (minimum score 7).

**Emory University,** Laney Graduate School, Division of Biological and Biomedical Sciences, Program in Biochemistry, Cell and Developmental Biology, Atlanta, GA 30322. Offers PhD. *Degree requirements:* For doctorate, comprehensive exam, thesis/dissertation. *Entrance requirements:* For doctorate, GRE General Test, minimum GPA of 3.0 in science course work (recommended). Additional exam requirements/recommendations for international students: required—TOEFL. Electronic applications accepted.

**Illinois State University,** Graduate School, College of Arts and Sciences, School of Biological Sciences, Normal, IL 61790. Offers animal behavior (MS); bacteriology (MS); biochemistry (MS); biological sciences (MS); biology (PhD); biophysics (MS); biotechnology (MS); botany (MS, PhD); cell biology (MS); conservation biology (MS); developmental biology (MS); ecology (MS, PhD); entomology (MS); evolutionary biology (MS); genetics (MS, PhD); immunology (MS); microbiology (MS, PhD); molecular biology (MS); molecular genetics (MS); neurobiology (MS); neuroscience (MS); parasitology (MS); physiology (MS, PhD); plant biology (MS); plant molecular biology (MS); plant sciences (MS); structural biology (MS); zoology (MS, PhD). *Program availability:* Part-time. *Faculty:* 26 full-time (6 women), 7 part-time/adjunct (2 women). *Students:* 51 full-time (33 women), 15 part-time (8 women). Average age 27. 71 applicants, 28% accepted, 9 enrolled. In 2019, 14 master's, 3 doctorates awarded. *Degree requirements:* For master's, thesis or alternative; for doctorate, variable foreign language requirement, thesis/dissertation, 2 terms of residency. *Entrance requirements:* For master's, GRE General Test, minimum GPA of 2.6 in last 60 hours of course work; for doctorate, GRE General Test. *Application deadline:* Applications are processed on a rolling basis. Application fee: $50. *Expenses: Tuition, area resident:* Full-time $7956; part-time $9767 per year. Tuition, nonresident: full-time $9233; part-time $17,592 per year. *Required fees:* $1797. *Financial support:* In 2019–20, 20 research assistantships, 41 teaching assistantships were awarded; Federal Work-Study, tuition waivers (full), and unspecified assistantships also available. Financial award application deadline: 4/1. *Unit head:* Dr. Craig Gatto, School Director, 309-438-3087, E-mail: cgatto@IllinoisState.edu. *Application contact:* Dr. Ben Sadd, Assistant Chair for Graduate Studies, 309-438-2651, E-mail: bmsadd@IllinoisState.edu.
Website: http://www.bio.ilstu.edu/

**Iowa State University of Science and Technology,** Program in Molecular, Cellular, and Developmental Biology, Ames, IA 50011. Offers MS, PhD. *Entrance requirements:* For master's and doctorate, GRE General Test. Additional exam requirements/recommendations for international students: required—TOEFL (minimum score 580 paper-based; 85 iBT), IELTS (minimum score 7). Electronic applications accepted.

**Irell & Manella Graduate School of Biological Sciences,** Graduate Program, Duarte, CA 91010. Offers brain metastatic cancer (PhD); cancer and stem cell metabolism (PhD); cancer biology (PhD); cancer biology and developmental therapeutics (PhD); cell biology (PhD); chemical biology (PhD); chromosomal break repair (PhD); diabetes and pancreatic progenitor cell biology (PhD); DNA repair and cancer biology (PhD); germline epigenetic remodeling and endocrine disruptors (PhD); hematology and hematopoietic cell transplantation (PhD); hematology and immunology (PhD); inflammation and cancer (PhD); micrornas and gene regulation in cardiovascular disease (PhD); mixed chimerism for reversal of autoimmunity (PhD); molecular and cellular biology (PhD); molecular biology and genetics (PhD); nanoparticle mediated twist1 silencing in metastatic cancer (PhD); neuro-oncology and stem cell biology (PhD); neuroscience (PhD); RNA directed therapies for HIV-1 (PhD); small RNA-induced transcriptional gene activation (PhD); stem cell regulation by the microenvironment (PhD); translational oncology and pharmaceutical sciences (PhD); tumor biology (PhD). *Degree requirements:* For doctorate, comprehensive exam, thesis/dissertation, qualifying exams, two advanced courses. *Entrance requirements:* For doctorate, GRE General Test; GRE Subject Test (recommended), 2 years of course work in chemistry (general and organic); 1 year of course work each in biochemistry, general biology, and general physics; 2 semesters of course work in mathematics; significant research laboratory experience. Additional exam requirements/recommendations for international students: required—TOEFL. Electronic applications accepted.

**Johns Hopkins University,** National Institutes of Health Sponsored Programs, Baltimore, MD 21218. Offers biology (PhD), including biochemistry, biophysics, cell biology, developmental biology, genetic biology, molecular biology; cell, molecular, and developmental biology and biophysics (PhD). *Degree requirements:* For doctorate, comprehensive exam, thesis/dissertation. *Entrance requirements:* Additional exam requirements/recommendations for international students: required—TOEFL (minimum score 600 paper-based). Electronic applications accepted.

**Johns Hopkins University,** Zanvyl Krieger School of Arts and Sciences, Program in Cell, Molecular, Developmental Biology, and Biophysics, Baltimore, MD 21218. Offers PhD. Terminal master's awarded for partial completion of doctoral program. *Degree requirements:* For doctorate, comprehensive exam, thesis/dissertation. *Entrance requirements:* For doctorate, GRE General Test. Additional exam requirements/recommendations for international students: required—TOEFL (minimum score 600 paper-based), IELTS, TWE. Electronic applications accepted.

**Louisiana State University Health Sciences Center,** School of Graduate Studies in New Orleans, Department of Cell Biology and Anatomy, New Orleans, LA 70112-2223. Offers cell biology and anatomy (PhD), including clinical anatomy, development, cell, and neurobiology; MD/PhD. *Degree requirements:* For doctorate, comprehensive exam, thesis/dissertation. *Entrance requirements:* For doctorate, GRE General Test, minimum undergraduate GPA of 3.0. Additional exam requirements/recommendations for international students: recommended—TOEFL, IELTS.

**Marquette University,** Graduate School, College of Arts and Sciences, Department of Biological Sciences, Milwaukee, WI 53201-1881. Offers cell biology (MS, PhD); developmental biology (MS, PhD); ecology (MS, PhD); epithelial physiology (MS, PhD); genetics (MS, PhD); microbiology (MS, PhD); molecular biology (MS, PhD); muscle and exercise physiology (MS, PhD); neuroscience (PhD). Terminal master's awarded for partial completion of doctoral program. *Degree requirements:* For master's, comprehensive exam, thesis, 1 year of teaching experience or equivalent; for doctorate, thesis/dissertation, 1 year of teaching experience or equivalent, qualifying exam. *Entrance requirements:* For master's and doctorate, GRE General Test, GRE Subject Test, official transcripts from all current and previous colleges/universities except Marquette, statement of professional goals and aspirations, three letters of recommendation. Additional exam requirements/recommendations for international students: required—TOEFL (minimum score 530 paper-based). Electronic applications accepted.

**Massachusetts Institute of Technology,** School of Science, Department of Biology, Cambridge, MA 02139. Offers biochemistry (PhD); biological oceanography (PhD); biology (PhD); biophysical chemistry and molecular structure (PhD); cell biology (PhD); computational and systems biology (PhD); developmental biology (PhD); genetics (PhD); immunology (PhD); microbiology (PhD); molecular biology (PhD); neurobiology (PhD). *Degree requirements:* For doctorate, comprehensive exam, thesis/dissertation, teaching assistantship during two semesters. *Entrance requirements:* For doctorate, GRE General Test. Additional exam requirements/recommendations for international students: required—TOEFL, IELTS. Electronic applications accepted.

**Medical University of South Carolina,** College of Graduate Studies, Program in Molecular and Cellular Biology and Pathobiology, Charleston, SC 29425. Offers cancer biology (PhD); cardiovascular biology (PhD); cardiovascular imaging (PhD); cell regulation (PhD); craniofacial biology (PhD); genetics and development (PhD); marine biomedicine (PhD); DMD/PhD; MD/PhD. *Degree requirements:* For doctorate, thesis/dissertation, oral and written exams. *Entrance requirements:* For doctorate, GRE General Test, interview, minimum GPA of 3.0. Additional exam requirements/recommendations for international students: required—TOEFL (minimum score 600 paper-based; 100 iBT). Electronic applications accepted.

**New York University,** Graduate School of Arts and Science, Department of Biology, New York, NY 10012-1019. Offers biology (PhD); biomedical journalism (MS); cancer and molecular biology (PhD); computational biology (PhD); computers in biological research (MS); developmental genetics (PhD); general biology (MS); immunology and microbiology (PhD); molecular genetics (PhD); neurobiology (PhD); oral biology (MS); plant biology (PhD); recombinant DNA technology (MS); MS/MBA. *Program availability:* Part-time. Terminal master's awarded for partial completion of doctoral program. *Degree requirements:* For master's, thesis or alternative, qualifying paper; for doctorate, comprehensive exam, thesis/dissertation. *Entrance requirements:* For master's and doctorate, GRE General Test. Additional exam requirements/recommendations for international students: required—TOEFL, IELTS.

**Northwestern University,** The Graduate School, Interdisciplinary Biological Sciences Program (IBiS), Evanston, IL 60208. Offers biochemistry (PhD); bioengineering and biotechnology (PhD); biotechnology (PhD); cell and molecular biology (PhD); developmental and systems biology (PhD); nanotechnology (PhD); neurobiology (PhD); structural biology and biophysics (PhD). *Degree requirements:* For doctorate, thesis/dissertation, qualifying exam. *Entrance requirements:* For doctorate, GRE General Test. Additional exam requirements/recommendations for international students: required—TOEFL (minimum score 600 paper-based). Electronic applications accepted.

**The Ohio State University,** Graduate School, College of Arts and Sciences, Division of Natural and Mathematical Sciences, Department of Molecular Genetics, Columbus, OH 43210. Offers cell and developmental biology (MS, PhD); genetics (MS, PhD); molecular biology (MS, PhD). *Entrance requirements:* For doctorate, GRE General Test, GRE Subject Test in biology or chemistry (recommended). Additional exam requirements/recommendations for international students: required—TOEFL (minimum score 550 paper-based; 79 iBT), Michigan English Language Assessment Battery (minimum score 82); recommended—IELTS (minimum score 7). Electronic applications accepted.

**The Ohio State University,** Graduate School, College of Arts and Sciences, Division of Natural and Mathematical Sciences, Program in Molecular, Cellular and Developmental Biology, Columbus, OH 43210. Offers MS, PhD. Terminal master's awarded for partial completion of doctoral program. *Entrance requirements:* For doctorate, GRE General Test, GRE Subject Test in any science (desired, preferably biology or chemistry, biochemistry or cell and molecular biology). Additional exam requirements/recommendations for international students: required—TOEFL (minimum score 600 paper-based; 85 iBT); recommended—IELTS (minimum score 8). Electronic applications accepted.

**Oregon Health & Science University,** School of Medicine, Graduate Programs in Medicine, Program in Molecular and Cellular Biosciences, Cell and Developmental Biology Graduate Program, Portland, OR 97239-3098. Offers PhD. *Degree requirements:* For doctorate, comprehensive exam, thesis/dissertation, qualifying exam. *Entrance requirements:* For doctorate, GRE General Test (minimum scores: 153 Verbal/148 Quantitative/4.5 Analytical) or MCAT.

**Penn State Hershey Medical Center,** College of Medicine, Graduate School Programs in the Biomedical Sciences, Huck Institutes of the Life Sciences, Intercollege Graduate Program in Molecular Cellular and Integrative Biosciences, Hershey, PA 17033. Offers cell and developmental biology (PhD); molecular medicine (PhD); molecular toxicology (PhD); neurobiology (PhD). *Degree requirements:* For doctorate, comprehensive exam, thesis/dissertation, oral exam. *Entrance requirements:* For doctorate, GRE, minimum GPA of 3.0. Additional exam requirements/recommendations for international students: required—TOEFL (minimum score 500 paper-based). Electronic applications accepted.

**Purdue University,** Graduate School, College of Science, Department of Biological Sciences, West Lafayette, IN 47907. Offers cell and developmental biology (PhD); genetics (MS); microbiology (MS, PhD); neurobiology (MS, PhD). *Faculty:* 43 full-time (14 women), 6 part-time/adjunct (1 woman). *Students:* 117 full-time (58 women), 10 part-time (6 women); includes 24 minority (5 Black or African American, non-Hispanic/Latino; 12 Asian, non-Hispanic/Latino; 4 Hispanic/Latino; 3 Two or more races, non-Hispanic/Latino), 56 international. Average age 27. 146 applicants, 32% accepted, 27 enrolled. In 2019, 7 master's, 18 doctorates awarded. Terminal master's awarded for partial completion of doctoral program. *Degree requirements:* For master's, thesis (for some programs); for doctorate, thesis/dissertation, seminars, teaching experience. *Entrance requirements:* For master's, GRE General Test (minimum analytical writing score of 3.5), minimum undergraduate GPA of 3.0; for doctorate, GRE General Test (minimum analytical writing score of 3.5), minimum undergraduate GPA of 3.5. Additional exam requirements/recommendations for international students: required—TOEFL minimum score 600 paper-based; 107 iBT (for MS), 80 iBT (for PhD). *Application deadline:* For fall admission, 12/7 for domestic and international students. Applications are processed on a rolling basis. Application fee: $60 ($75 for international students). Electronic applications accepted. *Financial support:* Fellowships, research assistantships, and teaching assistantships available. Support available to part-time students. Financial award application deadline: 2/15; financial award applicants required to submit FAFSA. *Unit head:* Janice P. Evans, Head, 765-494-4407, E-mail: janiceevans@purdue.edu. *Application contact:* Georgina E. Rupp, Graduate Coordinator, 765-494-8142, E-mail: ruppg@purdue.edu.
Website: http://www.bio.purdue.edu/

**Rutgers University - New Brunswick,** Graduate School-New Brunswick, Programs in the Molecular Biosciences, Program in Cell and Developmental Biology, Piscataway, NJ 08854-8097. Offers MS, PhD. *Program availability:* Part-time. Terminal master's awarded for partial completion of doctoral program. *Degree requirements:* For master's, thesis; for doctorate, thesis/dissertation, written qualifying exam. *Entrance requirements:* For master's, GRE General Test; for doctorate, GRE General Test, GRE Subject Test (recommended), minimum GPA of 3.0. Additional exam requirements/recommendations for international students: required—TOEFL. Electronic applications accepted.

**San Francisco State University,** Division of Graduate Studies, College of Science and Engineering, Department of Biology, Professional Science Master's Program, San Francisco, CA 94132-1722. Offers biotechnology (PSM); stem cell science (PSM). *Expenses: Tuition, area resident:* Full-time $7176; part-time $4164 per year. Tuition, state resident: full-time $7176; part-time $4164 per year. Tuition, nonresident: full-time $16,680; part-time $396 per unit. *International tuition:* $16,680 full-time. *Required fees:* $1524; $1524 per unit. $762 per semester. Tuition and fees vary according to degree level and program. *Unit head:* Dr. Lily Chen, Director, 415-338-6763, Fax: 415-338-2295, E-mail: lilychen@sfsu.edu. *Application contact:* Dr. Linda H. Chen, Associate Director and Program Coordinator, 415-338-1696, Fax: 415-338-2295, E-mail: psm@sfsu.edu.
Website: http://psm.sfsu.edu/

**Stanford University,** School of Medicine, Graduate Programs in Medicine, Department of Developmental Biology, Stanford, CA 94305-2004. Offers MS, PhD. *Expenses: Tuition:* Full-time $52,479; part-time $34,110 per unit. *Required fees:* $672; $224 per quarter. Tuition and fees vary according to program and student level.
Website: http://devbio.stanford.edu/

**Stony Brook University, State University of New York,** Graduate School, College of Arts and Sciences, Department of Biochemistry and Cell Biology, Stony Brook, NY 11794. Offers biochemistry and structural biology (PhD); molecular and cellular biology (MA, PhD), including biochemistry and molecular biology (PhD), biological sciences (MA), cellular and developmental biology (PhD), immunology and pathology (PhD), molecular and cellular biology (PhD). *Faculty:* 18 full-time (5 women), 1 part-time/adjunct (0 women). *Students:* 104 full-time (61 women), 7 part-time (4 women); includes 28 minority (6 Black or African American, non-Hispanic/Latino; 15 Asian, non-Hispanic/Latino; 7 Hispanic/Latino), 48 international. Average age 26. 205 applicants, 37% accepted, 35 enrolled. In 2019, 11 master's, 17 doctorates awarded. *Degree requirements:* For doctorate, comprehensive exam, thesis/dissertation, teaching experience. *Entrance requirements:* For doctorate, GRE General Test, GRE Subject Test. Additional exam requirements/recommendations for international students: required—TOEFL (minimum score 90 iBT). *Application deadline:* For fall admission, 1/15 for domestic students; for spring admission, 10/15 for domestic students. Application fee: $100. *Expenses:* Contact institution. *Financial support:* In 2019–20, 6 fellowships, 41 research assistantships, 17 teaching assistantships were awarded; Federal Work-Study also available. *Unit head:* Prof. Aaron Neiman, Chair, 631-632-1543, Fax: 631-632-8575, E-mail: aaron.neiman@stonybrook.edu. *Application contact:* Amy Saas, Coordinator, 631-632-8613, Fax: 631-632-9730, E-mail: Amy.Saas@stonybrook.edu.
Website: http://www.sunysb.edu/biochem/

**Thomas Jefferson University,** Jefferson College of Life Sciences, MS Program in Cell and Developmental Biology, Philadelphia, PA 19107. Offers MS. *Program availability:* Part-time, evening/weekend. *Degree requirements:* For master's, thesis, clerkship. *Entrance requirements:* For master's, GRE General Test or MCAT, minimum GPA of 3.0. Additional exam requirements/recommendations for international students: required—TOEFL, IELTS (minimum score 7). Electronic applications accepted.

**Tufts University,** Graduate School of Biomedical Sciences, Cell, Molecular, and Developmental Biology Program, Medford, MA 02155. Offers cancer biology (PhD); developmental and regenerative biology (PhD); molecular and cellular medicine (PhD); structural and chemical biology (PhD). *Faculty:* 84 full-time (30 women). *Students:* 32 full-time (15 women); includes 10 minority (2 Black or African American, non-Hispanic/Latino; 4 Asian, non-Hispanic/Latino; 4 Hispanic/Latino), 4 international. Average age 28. 168 applicants, 5% accepted, 3 enrolled. In 2019, 5 doctorates awarded. Terminal master's awarded for partial completion of doctoral program. *Degree requirements:* For doctorate, comprehensive exam, thesis/dissertation. *Entrance requirements:* For doctorate, 3 letters of reference, resume, personal statement. *Application deadline:* For fall admission, 12/1 priority date for domestic and international students. Application fee: $90. Electronic applications accepted. *Expenses: Tuition:* Part-time $1799 per credit hour. Full-time tuition and fees vary according to degree level, program and student level. Part-time tuition and fees vary according to course load. *Financial support:* In 2019–20, 100 students received support, including 3 research assistantships with full tuition reimbursements available (averaging $40,000 per year); fellowships, traineeships, and health care benefits also available. Financial award application deadline: 12/1. *Unit head:* Dr. Brent Cochran, Program Director, 617-636-0442. *Application contact:* Jeff Miller, Admissions Coordinator, 617-636-6767, Fax: 617-636-0375, E-mail: gsbs-admissions@tufts.edu.
Website: https://gsbs.tufts.edu/academics/CMDB

**The University of Alabama at Birmingham,** Joint Health Sciences, Cell, Molecular, and Developmental Biology Theme, Birmingham, AL 35294. Offers PhD. *Students:* Average age 27. 32 applicants, 28% accepted, 3 enrolled. In 2019, 7 doctorates awarded. *Degree requirements:* For doctorate, comprehensive exam, thesis/dissertation. *Entrance requirements:* For doctorate, personal statement, resume or curriculum vitae, letters of recommendation, research experience, interview. Additional exam requirements/recommendations for international students: required—TOEFL (minimum score 80 iBT), IELTS (minimum score 6.5). *Application deadline:* For fall admission, 12/31 for domestic and international students. Applications are processed on a rolling basis. Electronic applications accepted. *Financial support:* In 2019–20, fellowships with full tuition reimbursements (averaging $30,000 per year), research assistantships with full tuition reimbursements (averaging $31,000 per year) were awarded; health care benefits also available. *Unit head:* Dr. Alecia K. Gross, Theme Director, 205-975-8396, E-mail: agross@uab.edu. *Application contact:* Alyssa Zasada, Admissions Manager for Graduate Biomedical Sciences, 205-934-3857, E-mail: grad-gbs@uab.edu.
Website: http://www.uab.edu/gbs/home/themes/cmdb

**The University of British Columbia,** Faculty of Medicine, Department of Cellular and Physiological Sciences, Vancouver, BC V6T 1Z3, Canada. Offers bioinformatics (M Sc, PhD); cell and developmental biology (M Sc, PhD); genome science and technology (M Sc, PhD); neuroscience (M Sc, PhD). *Degree requirements:* For master's, thesis, oral defense; for doctorate, comprehensive exam, thesis/dissertation, oral defense. *Entrance requirements:* For master's, minimum overall B+ average in third- and fourth-year courses; for doctorate, minimum overall B+ average in master's degree (or equivalent) from approved institution with clear evidence of research ability or potential. Additional exam requirements/recommendations for international students: required—TOEFL, IELTS. *Expenses:* Contact institution.

**University of California, Davis,** Graduate Studies, Graduate Group in Cell and Developmental Biology, Davis, CA 95616. Offers MS, PhD. *Degree requirements:* For master's, comprehensive exam (for some programs), thesis (for some programs); for doctorate, thesis/dissertation. *Entrance requirements:* For doctorate, GRE General Test, GRE Subject Test. Additional exam requirements/recommendations for international students: required—TOEFL (minimum score 550 paper-based). Electronic applications accepted.

**University of California, Irvine,** School of Biological Sciences, Department of Developmental and Cell Biology, Irvine, CA 92697. Offers biological sciences (MS, PhD). *Students:* 32 full-time (24 women), 2 part-time (1 woman); includes 18 minority (1 Black or African American, non-Hispanic/Latino; 10 Asian, non-Hispanic/Latino; 7 Hispanic/Latino), 1 international. Average age 27. In 2019, 9 master's, 9 doctorates

awarded. *Entrance requirements:* For master's and doctorate, GRE General Test, GRE Subject Test, minimum GPA of 3.0. Additional exam requirements/recommendations for international students: required—TOEFL (minimum score 550 paper-based). *Application deadline:* For fall admission, 12/15 priority date for domestic and international students. Application fee: $120 ($140 for international students). Electronic applications accepted. *Financial support:* Fellowships, research assistantships with full tuition reimbursements, teaching assistantships, institutionally sponsored loans, traineeships, health care benefits, and unspecified assistantships available. Financial award application deadline: 3/1; financial award applicants required to submit FAFSA. *Unit head:* Prof. Thomas F. Schilling, Chair, 949-824-4562, Fax: 949-824-1105, E-mail: dkodowd@uci.edu. *Application contact:* Prof. Aimee Edinger, Graduate Advisor, 949-824-1921, Fax: 949-824-4709, E-mail: aedinger@uci.edu.
Website: http://devcell.bio.uci.edu/

**University of California, Los Angeles,** Graduate Division, College of Letters and Science, Department of Molecular, Cell and Developmental Biology, Los Angeles, CA 90095. Offers MA, PhD. Terminal master's awarded for partial completion of doctoral program. *Degree requirements:* For master's, comprehensive exam, thesis; for doctorate, thesis/dissertation, oral and written qualifying exams; 2 quarters of teaching experience. *Entrance requirements:* For doctorate, GRE General Test. Additional exam requirements/recommendations for international students: required—TOEFL. Electronic applications accepted.

**University of California, Riverside,** Graduate Division, Program in Cell, Molecular, and Developmental Biology, Riverside, CA 92521-0102. Offers MS, PhD. Terminal master's awarded for partial completion of doctoral program. *Degree requirements:* For master's, thesis, oral defense of thesis; for doctorate, thesis/dissertation, oral defense of thesis, qualifying exams, 2 quarters of teaching experience. *Entrance requirements:* For master's and doctorate, GRE General Test, minimum GPA of 3.2. Additional exam requirements/recommendations for international students: required—TOEFL (minimum score 550 paper-based; 80 iBT). Electronic applications accepted.

**University of California, San Francisco,** Graduate Division and School of Medicine, Tetrad Graduate Program, San Francisco, CA 94143. Offers biochemistry and molecular biology (PhD); cell biology (PhD); developmental biology (PhD); genetics (PhD); MD/PhD. *Degree requirements:* For doctorate, thesis/dissertation. *Entrance requirements:* For doctorate, GRE General Test, GRE Subject Test. Additional exam requirements/recommendations for international students: required—TOEFL. *Expenses:* Contact institution.

**University of California, Santa Barbara,** Graduate Division, College of Letters and Sciences, Division of Mathematics, Life, and Physical Sciences, Department of Molecular, Cellular, and Developmental Biology, Santa Barbara, CA 93106-9625. Offers MA, PhD, MA/PhD. Terminal master's awarded for partial completion of doctoral program. *Degree requirements:* For master's, comprehensive exam (for some programs), thesis (for some programs); for doctorate, comprehensive exam, thesis/dissertation. *Entrance requirements:* For master's and doctorate, GRE General Test, 3 letters of recommendation, statement of purpose, personal achievements/contributions statement, resume/curriculum vitae, transcripts for post-secondary institutions attended. Additional exam requirements/recommendations for international students: required—TOEFL (minimum score 550 paper-based; 80 iBT), IELTS (minimum score 7). Electronic applications accepted.

**University of California, Santa Cruz,** Division of Graduate Studies, Division of Physical and Biological Sciences, Program in Molecular, Cellular, and Developmental Biology, Santa Cruz, CA 95064. Offers MA, PhD. Terminal master's awarded for partial completion of doctoral program. *Degree requirements:* For master's, thesis; for doctorate, thesis/dissertation, qualifying exam. *Entrance requirements:* For master's and doctorate, GRE General Test, 3 letters of recommendation, interview. Additional exam requirements/recommendations for international students: required—TOEFL (minimum score 550 paper-based; 83 iBT); recommended—IELTS (minimum score 8). Electronic applications accepted.

**University of Chicago,** Division of the Biological Sciences, Committee on Development, Regeneration, and Stem Cell Biology, Chicago, IL 60637-1513. Offers PhD. *Degree requirements:* For doctorate, thesis/dissertation, ethics class, 2 teaching assistantships, preliminary exams. *Entrance requirements:* For doctorate, GRE General Test, transcripts, statement of purpose, 3 letters of recommendation. Additional exam requirements/recommendations for international students: required—TOEFL (minimum score 600 paper-based; 104 iBT), IELTS (minimum score 7). Electronic applications accepted.

**University of Cincinnati,** Graduate School, College of Medicine, Graduate Programs in Biomedical Sciences, Department of Pediatrics, Program in Molecular and Developmental Biology, Cincinnati, OH 45221. Offers PhD. *Degree requirements:* For doctorate, thesis/dissertation, qualifying exam. *Entrance requirements:* For doctorate, GRE General Test, minimum GPA of 3.2. Additional exam requirements/recommendations for international students: required—TOEFL (minimum score 520 paper-based). Electronic applications accepted.

**University of Colorado Boulder,** Graduate School, College of Arts and Sciences, Department of Molecular, Cellular, and Developmental Biology, Boulder, CO 80309. Offers cellular structure and function (MA, PhD); developmental biology (PhD); molecular biology (PhD). Terminal master's awarded for partial completion of doctoral program. *Degree requirements:* For master's, comprehensive exam, thesis or alternative; for doctorate, comprehensive exam, thesis/dissertation. *Entrance requirements:* For master's, GRE General Test, GRE Subject Test, minimum undergraduate GPA of 3.0; for doctorate, GRE General Test, GRE Subject Test. Electronic applications accepted. Application fee is waived when completed online.

**University of Colorado Denver,** School of Medicine, Program in Cell Biology, Stem Cells, and Development, Aurora, CO 80045. Offers cell biology, stem cells, and developmental biology (PhD); modern human anatomy (MS). *Degree requirements:* For doctorate, comprehensive exam, thesis/dissertation, at least 30 credit hours of coursework and 30 credit hours of thesis research; laboratory rotations. *Entrance requirements:* For doctorate, GRE, minimum GPA of 3.0; 3 letters of reference; prerequisite coursework in organic chemistry, biology, biochemistry, physics and calculus; research experience (highly recommended). Additional exam requirements/recommendations for international students: required—TOEFL (minimum score 550 paper-based; 80 iBT). Tuition and fees vary according to course load, program and reciprocity agreements.

**University of Connecticut,** Graduate School, College of Liberal Arts and Sciences, Department of Molecular and Cell Biology, Storrs, CT 06269. Offers applied genomics (PSM); cell and developmental biology (MS, PhD); genetics and genomics (MS, PhD); microbial systems analysis (PSM); microbiology (MS, PhD); structural biology, biochemistry and biophysics (MS, PhD). Terminal master's awarded for partial completion of doctoral program. *Degree requirements:* For master's, comprehensive exam; for doctorate, thesis/dissertation. *Entrance requirements:* For master's and doctorate, GRE General Test, GRE Subject Test. Additional exam requirements/recommendations for international students: required—TOEFL (minimum score 550 paper-based). Electronic applications accepted.

**University of Connecticut Health Center,** Graduate School, Programs in Biomedical Sciences, Program in Genetics and Developmental Biology, Farmington, CT 06030. Offers PhD, DMD/PhD, MD/PhD. *Degree requirements:* For doctorate, comprehensive exam, thesis/dissertation. *Entrance requirements:* For doctorate, GRE General Test, GRE Subject Test. Additional exam requirements/recommendations for international students: required—TOEFL (minimum score 600 paper-based). Electronic applications accepted.

**University of Delaware,** College of Arts and Sciences, Department of Biological Sciences, Newark, DE 19716. Offers biotechnology (MS); cancer biology (MS, PhD); cell and extracellular matrix biology (MS, PhD); cell and systems physiology (MS, PhD); developmental biology (MS, PhD); ecology and evolution (MS, PhD); microbiology (MS, PhD); molecular biology and genetics (MS, PhD). Terminal master's awarded for partial completion of doctoral program. *Degree requirements:* For master's, thesis, preliminary exam; for doctorate, comprehensive exam, thesis/dissertation, preliminary exam. *Entrance requirements:* For master's and doctorate, GRE General Test. Additional exam requirements/recommendations for international students: required—TOEFL (minimum score 600 paper-based); recommended—TWE. Electronic applications accepted.

**University of Hawaii at Manoa,** John A. Burns School of Medicine, Program in Developmental and Reproductive Biology, Honolulu, HI 96813. Offers MS, PhD. *Program availability:* Part-time. *Degree requirements:* For doctorate, thesis/dissertation. *Entrance requirements:* For doctorate, GRE General Test, GRE Subject Test. Additional exam requirements/recommendations for international students: recommended—TOEFL (minimum score 560 paper-based), IELTS (minimum score 5).

**University of Illinois at Urbana-Champaign,** Graduate College, College of Liberal Arts and Sciences, School of Molecular and Cellular Biology, Department of Cell and Developmental Biology, Champaign, IL 61820. Offers PhD.

**The University of Kansas,** Graduate Studies, College of Liberal Arts and Sciences, Department of Molecular Biosciences, Lawrence, KS 66044. Offers biochemistry and biophysics (PhD); microbiology (PhD); molecular, cellular, and developmental biology (PhD). *Program availability:* Part-time. *Students:* 66 full-time (39 women); includes 36 minority (1 Black or African American, non-Hispanic/Latino; 2 Asian, non-Hispanic/Latino; 31 Hispanic/Latino; 2 Two or more races, non-Hispanic/Latino), 31 international. Average age 28. 93 applicants, 30% accepted, 12 enrolled. In 2019, 3 doctorates awarded. Terminal master's awarded for partial completion of doctoral program. *Entrance requirements:* For doctorate, GRE General Test, 1-page statement of research interests and goals, 1-2 page curriculum vitae or resume, official transcript, 3 recommendation letters. Additional exam requirements/recommendations for international students: required—TOEFL, IELTS, TOEFL or IELTS. *Application deadline:* For fall admission, 12/1 for domestic and international students. Application fee: $65 ($85 for international students). Electronic applications accepted. *Expenses:* Tuition, state resident: full-time $9989. Tuition, nonresident: full-time $23,950. *International tuition:* $23,950 full-time. *Required fees:* $984; $81.99 per credit hour. Tuition and fees vary according to course load, campus/location and program. *Financial support:* Fellowships, research assistantships, teaching assistantships, scholarships/grants, health care benefits, and unspecified assistantships available. Financial award application deadline: 12/1. *Unit head:* Susan M. Egan, Chair, 785-864-4294, E-mail: sme@ku.edu. *Application contact:* John Connolly, Graduate Admissions Contact, 785-864-4311, E-mail: jconnolly@ku.edu.
Website: http://www.molecularbiosciences.ku.edu/

**The University of Manchester,** School of Biological Sciences, Manchester, United Kingdom. Offers adaptive organismal biology (M Phil, PhD); animal biology (M Phil, PhD); biochemistry (M Phil, PhD); bioinformatics (M Phil, PhD); biomolecular sciences (M Phil, PhD); biotechnology (M Phil, PhD); cell biology (M Phil, PhD); cell matrix research (M Phil, PhD); channels and transporters (M Phil, PhD); developmental biology (M Phil, PhD); environmental biology (M Phil, PhD); evolutionary biology (M Phil, PhD); gene expression (M Phil, PhD); genetics (M Phil, PhD); history of science, technology and medicine (M Phil, PhD); immunology (M Phil, PhD); integrative neurobiology and behavior (M Phil, PhD); membrane trafficking (M Phil, PhD); microbiology (M Phil, PhD); molecular and cellular neuroscience (M Phil, PhD); molecular biology (M Phil, PhD); molecular cancer studies (M Phil, PhD); neuroscience (M Phil, PhD); ophthalmology (M Phil, PhD); optometry (M Phil, PhD); organelle function (M Phil, PhD); pharmacology (M Phil, PhD); physiology (M Phil, PhD); plant sciences (M Phil, PhD); stem cell research (M Phil, PhD); structural biology (M Phil, PhD); systems neuroscience (M Phil, PhD); toxicology (M Phil, PhD).

**The University of Manchester,** School of Dentistry, Manchester, United Kingdom. Offers basic dental sciences (cancer studies) (M Phil, PhD); basic dental sciences (molecular genetics) (M Phil, PhD); basic dental sciences (stem cell biology) (M Phil, PhD); biomaterials sciences and dental technology (M Phil, PhD); dental public health/community dentistry (M Phil, PhD); dental science (clinical) (PhD); endodontology (M Phil, PhD); fixed and removable prosthodontics (M Phil, PhD); operative dentistry (M Phil, PhD); oral and maxillofacial surgery (M Phil, PhD); oral radiology (M Phil, PhD); orthodontics (M Phil, PhD); restorative dentistry (M Phil, PhD).

**University of Massachusetts Amherst,** Graduate School, Interdisciplinary Programs, Program in Molecular and Cellular Biology, Amherst, MA 01003. Offers biological chemistry and molecular biophysics (PhD); biomedicine (PhD); cellular and developmental biology (PhD). *Program availability:* Part-time. Terminal master's awarded for partial completion of doctoral program. *Degree requirements:* For doctorate, comprehensive exam, thesis/dissertation. *Entrance requirements:* For doctorate, GRE General Test. Additional exam requirements/recommendations for international students: required—TOEFL (minimum score 550 paper-based; 80 iBT), IELTS (minimum score 6.5). Electronic applications accepted.

**University of Miami,** Graduate School, Miller School of Medicine, Graduate Programs in Medicine, Department of Cell Biology, Miami, FL 33124. Offers molecular cell and developmental biology (PhD); MD/PhD. *Faculty:* 29 full-time (3 women). *Students:* 13 full-time (4 women); includes 7 minority (1 Black or African American, non-Hispanic/Latino; 3 Asian, non-Hispanic/Latino; 2 Hispanic/Latino; 1 Two or more races, non-Hispanic/Latino), 3 international. Average age 29. 2 applicants, 100% accepted, 1 enrolled. In 2019, 1 doctorate awarded. *Degree requirements:* For doctorate, thesis/dissertation, Qualifying Exam. *Entrance requirements:* For doctorate, GRE General Test, GRE Subject Test. Additional exam requirements/recommendations for international students: required—TOEFL. *Application deadline:* For fall admission, 3/1 priority date for domestic students. Applications are processed on a rolling basis. Application fee: $95. Electronic applications accepted. *Financial support:* In 2019–20, 8 fellowships (averaging $29,500 per year), 8 research assistantships (averaging $29,500 per year) were awarded; teaching assistantships also available. *Unit head:* Dr. Glen Barber, Chair, 305-243-5914, Fax: 305-243-7020, E-mail: gbarber@miami.edu. *Application contact:* Dr. Xiangxi Mike Xu, Program Director, 305-243-1750, E-mail: xxu2@miami.edu.
Website: http://cellbiology.med.miami.edu/

**University of Michigan,** Rackham Graduate School, College of Literature, Science, and the Arts, Department of Molecular, Cellular, and Developmental Biology, Ann Arbor, MI 48109. Offers MS, PhD. *Program availability:* Part-time. Terminal master's awarded

for partial completion of doctoral program. *Degree requirements:* For master's, thesis (for some programs), 24 credits with at least 16 in molecular, cellular, and developmental biology and 4 in a cognate field; for doctorate, comprehensive exam, thesis/dissertation, preliminary exam, oral defense. *Entrance requirements:* Additional exam requirements/recommendations for international students: required—TOEFL (minimum score 600 paper-based; 100 iBT). Electronic applications accepted. *Expenses:* Contact institution.

**University of Michigan,** Rackham Graduate School, Program in Biomedical Sciences (PIBS), Department of Cell and Developmental Biology, Ann Arbor, MI 48109. Offers PhD. *Degree requirements:* For doctorate, thesis/dissertation, oral defense of dissertation, preliminary exam. *Entrance requirements:* For doctorate, GRE General Test, 3 letters of recommendation, research experience. Additional exam requirements/ recommendations for international students: required—TOEFL (minimum score 84 iBT). Electronic applications accepted.

**University of Minnesota, Twin Cities Campus,** Graduate School, Program in Molecular, Cellular, Developmental Biology and Genetics, Minneapolis, MN 55455-0213. Offers genetic counseling (MS); molecular, cellular, developmental biology and genetics (PhD). Terminal master's awarded for partial completion of doctoral program. *Degree requirements:* For master's, thesis optional; for doctorate, thesis/dissertation. *Entrance requirements:* For master's and doctorate, GRE General Test. Additional exam requirements/recommendations for international students: required—TOEFL (minimum score 625 paper-based; 80 iBT). Electronic applications accepted.

**University of Montana,** Graduate School, College of Humanities and Sciences, Division of Biological Sciences, Program in Cellular, Molecular and Microbial Biology, Missoula, MT 59812. Offers cellular and developmental biology (PhD); microbial evolution and ecology (PhD); microbiology and immunology (PhD); molecular biology and biochemistry (PhD). Terminal master's awarded for partial completion of doctoral program. *Degree requirements:* For doctorate, variable foreign language requirement, thesis/dissertation. *Entrance requirements:* For doctorate, GRE General Test.

**The University of North Carolina at Chapel Hill,** Graduate School, College of Arts and Sciences, Department of Biology, Chapel Hill, NC 27599. Offers botany (MA, MS, PhD); cell biology, development, and physiology (MA, MS, PhD); cell motility and cytoskeleton (PhD); ecology and behavior (MA, MS, PhD); genetics and molecular biology (MA, MS, PhD); morphology, systematics, and evolution (MA, MS, PhD). Terminal master's awarded for partial completion of doctoral program. *Degree requirements:* For master's, comprehensive exam, thesis (for some programs); for doctorate, comprehensive exam, thesis/dissertation. *Entrance requirements:* For master's, GRE General Test, GRE Subject Test, 2 semesters of calculus or statistics; 2 semesters of physics, organic chemistry; 3 semesters of biology; for doctorate, GRE General Test, GRE Subject Test, 2 semesters calculus or statistics, 2 semesters physics, organic chemistry, 3 semesters of biology. Additional exam requirements/recommendations for international students: required—TOEFL (minimum score 550 paper-based). Electronic applications accepted.

**The University of North Carolina at Chapel Hill,** School of Medicine and Graduate School, Biological and Biomedical Sciences Program, Molecular, Cellular & Developmental Biology, Chapel Hill, NC 27599. Offers PhD. *Faculty:* 16 full-time (2 women). *Students:* 3 full-time (1 woman). Average age 26. In 2019, 1 doctorate awarded. *Degree requirements:* For doctorate, comprehensive exam, thesis/ dissertation. *Entrance requirements:* Additional exam requirements/recommendations for international students: required—TOEFL. *Application deadline:* For fall admission, 12/3 priority date for domestic and international students. Applications are processed on a rolling basis. Application fee: $73. Electronic applications accepted. *Financial support:* In 2019–20, 6 fellowships with tuition reimbursements (averaging $32,000 per year), 29 research assistantships with full tuition reimbursements (averaging $32,000 per year) were awarded; teaching assistantships with full tuition reimbursements, career-related internships or fieldwork, health care benefits, and tuition waivers (full) also available. *Unit head:* Dr. Christopher Willett, Director, E-mail: willett4@email.unc.edu. *Application contact:* Jeffrey Steinbach, Assistant Director of Admissions, 919-843-7129, E-mail: jsteinba@email.unc.edu.
Website: https://bio.unc.edu/graduate/mcdb/

**University of Pennsylvania,** Perelman School of Medicine, Biomedical Graduate Studies, Graduate Group in Cell and Molecular Biology, Philadelphia, PA 19104. Offers cancer biology (PhD); cell biology, physiology, and metabolism (PhD); developmental stem cell regenerative biology (PhD); gene therapy and vaccines (PhD); genetics and gene regulation (PhD); microbiology, virology, and parasitology (PhD); MD/PhD; VMD/ PhD. *Faculty:* 400 full-time (118 women). *Students:* 378 full-time (221 women); includes 134 minority (6 Black or African American, non-Hispanic/Latino; 56 Asian, non-Hispanic/ Latino; 58 Hispanic/Latino; 2 Native Hawaiian or other Pacific Islander, non-Hispanic/ Latino; 12 Two or more races, non-Hispanic/Latino), 52 international. 851 applicants, 14% accepted, 59 enrolled. In 2019, 43 doctorates awarded. *Unit head:* Dr. Daniel Kessler, Graduate Group Chair, 215-898-1478. *Application contact:* Meagan Schofer, Associate Director, 215-898-1478.
Website: http://www.med.upenn.edu/camb/

**University of Pittsburgh,** Kenneth P. Dietrich School of Arts and Sciences, Department of Biological Sciences, Program in Molecular, Cellular, and Developmental Biology, Pittsburgh, PA 15260. Offers PhD. *Faculty:* 27 full-time (9 women). *Students:* 52 full-time (31 women); includes 7 minority (4 Black or African American, non-Hispanic/Latino; 1 Hispanic/Latino; 2 Two or more races, non-Hispanic/Latino), 8 international. Average age 23. In 2019, 6 doctorates awarded. *Degree requirements:* For doctorate, comprehensive exam, thesis/dissertation, completion of research integrity module. *Entrance requirements:* Additional exam requirements/recommendations for international students: required—TOEFL (minimum score 90 paper-based), IELTS (minimum score 7). *Application deadline:* For fall admission, 12/2 priority date for domestic and international students. Applications are processed on a rolling basis. Application fee: $0 ($75 for international students). Electronic applications accepted. *Financial support:* In 2019–20, 37 fellowships with full tuition reimbursements (averaging $36,108 per year), 94 research assistantships with full tuition reimbursements (averaging $30,840 per year), 19 teaching assistantships with full tuition reimbursements (averaging $30,375 per year) were awarded; Federal Work-Study, traineeships, and health care benefits also available. *Unit head:* Dr. Jeffrey G. Lawrence, Professor and Chair, 412-624-4350, Fax: 412-624-4759, E-mail: jlawrence@ pitt.edu. *Application contact:* Cathleen M. Barr, Graduate Administrator, 412-624-4268, Fax: 412-624-4349, E-mail: cbarr@pitt.edu.
Website: http://www.biology.pitt.edu

**University of South Carolina,** The Graduate School, College of Arts and Sciences, Department of Biological Sciences, Graduate Training Program in Molecular, Cellular, and Developmental Biology, Columbia, SC 29208. Offers MS, PhD. *Degree requirements:* For master's, one foreign language, thesis; for doctorate, one foreign language, thesis/dissertation. *Entrance requirements:* For master's and doctorate, GRE General Test, minimum GPA of 3.0 in science. Electronic applications accepted.

**University of Southern California,** Keck School of Medicine and Graduate School, Graduate Programs in Medicine, Programs in Biomedical and Biological Sciences (PIBBS), Program in Development, Stem Cell and Regenerative Medicine, Los Angeles, CA 90089. Offers PhD. *Faculty:* 36 full-time (15 women). *Students:* 57 full-time (26 women); includes 15 minority (1 American Indian or Alaska Native, non-Hispanic/Latino; 6 Asian, non-Hispanic/Latino; 6 Hispanic/Latino; 1 Native Hawaiian or other Pacific Islander, non-Hispanic/Latino; 1 Two or more races, non-Hispanic/Latino), 27 international. Average age 26. 16 applicants, 100% accepted, 16 enrolled. In 2019, 8 doctorates awarded. *Degree requirements:* For doctorate, comprehensive exam, thesis/ dissertation. *Entrance requirements:* For doctorate, GRE, minimum GPA of 3.5. Additional exam requirements/recommendations for international students: required— TOEFL (minimum score 600 paper-based; 100 iBT), IELTS (minimum score 7), PTE. *Application deadline:* For fall admission, 12/1 priority date for domestic and international students. Application fee: $90. Electronic applications accepted. *Financial support:* In 2019–20, 50 students received support, including 11 fellowships with full tuition reimbursements available (averaging $35,000 per year), 41 research assistantships with full tuition reimbursements available (averaging $35,000 per year), 5 teaching assistantships with full tuition reimbursements available (averaging $35,000 per year); institutionally sponsored loans, scholarships/grants, traineeships, health care benefits, and unspecified assistantships also available. Financial award application deadline: 4/ 15; financial award applicants required to submit CSS PROFILE or FAFSA. *Unit head:* Dr. Gage Crump, Director, 323-442-1475, Fax: 323-442-1199, E-mail: gcrump@ med.usc.edu. *Application contact:* Karina Recinos, Student Services Advisor, 323-442-1609, Fax: 323-442-1199, E-mail: karina.recinos@med.usc.edu.
Website: http://keck.usc.edu/pibbs/phd-programs/development-stem-cell-and-regenerative-medicine

**The University of Texas Southwestern Medical Center,** Southwestern Graduate School of Biomedical Sciences, Division of Basic Science, Program in Genetics and Development, Dallas, TX 75390. Offers PhD. *Degree requirements:* For doctorate, thesis/dissertation, qualifying exam. *Entrance requirements:* For doctorate, GRE General Test, minimum GPA of 3.0. Additional exam requirements/recommendations for international students: required—TOEFL. Electronic applications accepted.

**Vanderbilt University,** School of Medicine, Department of Cell and Developmental Biology, Nashville, TN 37240-1001. Offers MS, PhD, MD/PhD. *Faculty:* 22 full-time (9 women). *Students:* 57 full-time (39 women); includes 10 minority (2 Black or African American, non-Hispanic/Latino; 1 Asian, non-Hispanic/Latino; 5 Hispanic/Latino; 2 Two or more races, non-Hispanic/Latino), 12 international. Average age 27. In 2019, 1 master's, 10 doctorates awarded. Terminal master's awarded for partial completion of doctoral program. *Degree requirements:* For master's, thesis or alternative; for doctorate, thesis/dissertation, preliminary, qualifying, and final exams. *Entrance requirements:* For master's, GRE General Test; for doctorate, GRE General Test, GRE Subject Test (recommended). Additional exam requirements/recommendations for international students: required—TOEFL (minimum score 570 paper-based; 88 iBT). *Application deadline:* For fall admission, 1/15 for domestic and international students. Electronic applications accepted. *Expenses: Tuition:* Full-time $51,018; part-time $2087 per hour. *Required fees:* $542. Tuition and fees vary according to program. *Financial support:* Fellowships, research assistantships, career-related internships or fieldwork, Federal Work-Study, institutionally sponsored loans, scholarships/grants, traineeships, health care benefits, and tuition waivers (partial) available. Financial award application deadline: 1/15; financial award applicants required to submit CSS PROFILE or FAFSA. *Unit head:* Ian Macara, Chair, 615-875-5565, Fax: 615-343-4539, E-mail: ian.macara@ vanderbilt.edu. *Application contact:* Kristi Hargrove, Program Coordinator, 615-322-2294, Fax: 615-343-4539, E-mail: kristi.l.hargrove@vanderbilt.edu.
Website: http://www.mc.vanderbilt.edu/cdb/

**Washington University in St. Louis,** The Graduate School, Division of Biology and Biomedical Sciences, Program in Developmental, Regenerative, and Stem Cell Biology, St. Louis, MO 63130-4899. Offers PhD. *Degree requirements:* For doctorate, thesis/ dissertation. *Entrance requirements:* For doctorate, GRE General Test, GRE Subject Test. Additional exam requirements/recommendations for international students: required—TOEFL. Electronic applications accepted.

**Wesleyan University,** Graduate Studies, Department of Biology, Middletown, CT 06459. Offers cell and developmental biology (PhD); evolution and ecology (PhD); genetics and genomics (PhD), including bioinformatics; neurobiology and behavior (PhD). Terminal master's awarded for partial completion of doctoral program. *Degree requirements:* For doctorate, comprehensive exam, thesis/dissertation, public seminar. *Entrance requirements:* For doctorate, GRE, official transcripts, three recommendation letters, essay. Additional exam requirements/recommendations for international students: required—TOEFL. Electronic applications accepted.

**West Virginia University,** Davis College of Agriculture, Forestry and Consumer Sciences, Morgantown, WV 26506. Offers agricultural and extension education (MS, PhD); agriculture and resource management (MS); agriculture, natural resources and design (M Agr); agronomy (MS); animal and food science (PhD); animal physiology (MS); applied and environmental microbiology (MS); design and merchandising (MS); entomology (MS); forest resource science (PhD); forestry (MSF); genetics and developmental biology (MS, PhD); horticulture (MS); human and community development (PhD); landscape architecture (MLA); natural resource economics (PhD); nutritional and food science (MS); plant and soil science (PhD); plant pathology (MS); recreation, parks and tourism resources (MS); reproductive physiology (MS, PhD); wildlife and fisheries resources (PhD). *Accreditation:* ASLA. *Program availability:* Part-time. *Degree requirements:* For master's, thesis; for doctorate, thesis/dissertation. *Entrance requirements:* Additional exam requirements/recommendations for international students: required—TOEFL (minimum score 550 paper-based). Electronic applications accepted.

**Yale University,** Graduate School of Arts and Sciences, Department of Molecular, Cellular, and Developmental Biology, New Haven, CT 06520. Offers biochemistry, molecular biology and chemical biology (PhD); cellular and developmental biology (PhD); genetics (PhD); neurobiology (PhD); plant sciences (PhD). *Degree requirements:* For doctorate, thesis/dissertation. *Entrance requirements:* For doctorate, GRE General Test, GRE Subject Test.

# Genetics

**Albert Einstein College of Medicine,** Graduate Programs in the Biomedical Sciences, Department of Genetics, Bronx, NY 10461. Offers computational genetics (PhD); molecular genetics (PhD); translational genetics (PhD); MD/PhD. *Degree requirements:* For doctorate, thesis/dissertation. *Entrance requirements:* For doctorate, GRE General Test. Additional exam requirements/recommendations for international students: required—TOEFL.

**Baylor College of Medicine,** Graduate School of Biomedical Sciences, Department of Molecular and Human Genetics, Houston, TX 77030-3498. Offers PhD, MD/PhD. *Degree requirements:* For doctorate, thesis/dissertation, public defense. *Entrance requirements:* For doctorate, GRE General Test, GRE Subject Test (strongly recommended), minimum GPA of 3.0. Additional exam requirements/recommendations for international students: required—TOEFL. Electronic applications accepted.

**Baylor College of Medicine,** Graduate School of Biomedical Sciences, Interdepartmental Program in Cell and Molecular Biology, Houston, TX 77030-3498. Offers biochemistry (PhD); cell and molecular biology (PhD); genetics (PhD); human genetics (PhD); immunology (PhD); microbiology (PhD); virology (PhD); MD/PhD. *Degree requirements:* For doctorate, thesis/dissertation, public defense. *Entrance requirements:* For doctorate, GRE General Test, GRE Subject Test (strongly recommended), minimum GPA of 3.0. Additional exam requirements/recommendations for international students: required—TOEFL. Electronic applications accepted.

**Baylor College of Medicine,** Graduate School of Biomedical Sciences, Program in Translational Biology and Molecular Medicine, Houston, TX 77030-3498. Offers PhD. *Degree requirements:* For doctorate, thesis/dissertation, public defense. *Entrance requirements:* For doctorate, GRE, minimum GPA of 3.0. Additional exam requirements/recommendations for international students: required—TOEFL. Electronic applications accepted.

**Boston University,** School of Medicine, Graduate Medical Sciences, Program in Genetics and Genomics, Boston, MA 02215. Offers PhD. *Application deadline:* For fall admission, 1/15 for domestic students; for spring admission, 10/15 for domestic students. *Unit head:* Dr. Shoumita Dasgupta, Director, 617-414-1369, E-mail: gpgg@bu.edu. *Application contact:* GMS Admissions Office, 617-358-9518, Fax: 617-358-2913, E-mail: gpgg@bu.edu.
Website: https://www.bumc.bu.edu/gpgg/

**Brandeis University,** Graduate School of Arts and Sciences, Department of Biology, Waltham, MA 02454-9110. Offers genetics (PhD); microbiology (PhD); molecular and cell biology (MS, PhD); molecular biology (PhD); neurobiology (PhD); quantitative biology (PhD). *Program availability:* Part-time. *Faculty:* 28 full-time (14 women), 1 part-time/adjunct (0 women). *Students:* 44 full-time (26 women), 1 (woman) part-time; includes 15 minority (1 American Indian or Alaska Native, non-Hispanic/Latino; 7 Asian, non-Hispanic/Latino; 7 Hispanic/Latino), 10 international. Average age 27. 202 applicants, 22% accepted, 12 enrolled. In 2019, 9 master's, 6 doctorates awarded. Terminal master's awarded for partial completion of doctoral program. *Degree requirements:* For master's, thesis optional; for doctorate, comprehensive exam, thesis/dissertation. *Entrance requirements:* For master's, transcripts, letters of recommendation, resume, statement of purpose; for doctorate, transcripts, letters of recommendation, resume, program questions, statement of purpose. Additional exam requirements/recommendations for international students: required—TOEFL, IELTS, PTE. *Application deadline:* For fall admission, 12/1 priority date for domestic and international students; for spring admission, 10/15 for domestic students, 11/15 for international students. Applications are processed on a rolling basis. Application fee: $75. Electronic applications accepted. *Financial support:* In 2019–20, 50 fellowships with full tuition reimbursements (averaging $35,000 per year), 21 teaching assistantships (averaging $3,550 per year) were awarded; research assistantships, scholarships/grants, health care benefits, and tuition waivers also available. Support available to part-time students. *Unit head:* Dr. Michael Marr, Director of Graduate Studies, 781-736-2481, E-mail: mmarr@brandeis.edu. *Application contact:* Maryanna Aldrich, Administrator, 781-736-2352, E-mail: scigradoffice@brandeis.edu.
Website: http://www.brandeis.edu/gsas/programs/mcbio.html

**California Institute of Technology,** Division of Biology and Biological Engineering, Program in Genetics, Pasadena, CA 91125-0001. Offers PhD. *Degree requirements:* For doctorate, thesis/dissertation, qualifying exam. *Entrance requirements:* For doctorate, GRE General Test.

**Carnegie Mellon University,** Mellon College of Science, Department of Biological Sciences, Pittsburgh, PA 15213-3891. Offers biochemistry (PhD); biophysics (PhD); cell and developmental biology (PhD); computational biology (MS, PhD); genetics (PhD); molecular biology (PhD); neuroscience (PhD); structural biology (PhD). *Degree requirements:* For doctorate, comprehensive exam, thesis/dissertation. *Entrance requirements:* For doctorate, GRE General Test, GRE Subject Test, interview. Electronic applications accepted.

**Clemson University,** Graduate School, College of Behavioral, Social and Health Sciences, School of Nursing, Clemson, SC 29634. Offers clinical and translational research (PhD); global health (Certificate), including low resource countries; healthcare genetics (PhD); nursing (MS, DNP), including adult/gerontology nurse practitioner (MS); family nurse practitioner (MS). *Accreditation:* AACN. *Program availability:* Part-time, 100% online, blended/hybrid learning. *Faculty:* 47 full-time (45 women), 1 (woman) part-time/adjunct. *Students:* 67 full-time (59 women), 66 part-time (49 women); includes 18 minority (10 Black or African American, non-Hispanic/Latino; 4 Asian, non-Hispanic/Latino; 4 Two or more races, non-Hispanic/Latino), 7 international. Average age 35. 109 applicants, 62% accepted, 49 enrolled. In 2019, 56 master's, 8 doctorates awarded. *Degree requirements:* For master's, comprehensive exam, thesis or alternative; for doctorate, comprehensive exam, thesis/dissertation. *Entrance requirements:* For master's, GRE General Test, South Carolina RN license, unofficial transcripts, resume, letters of recommendation; for doctorate, GRE General Test, unofficial transcripts, MS/MA thesis or publications, curriculum vitae, statement of career goals, letters of recommendation. Additional exam requirements/recommendations for international students: required—TOEFL (minimum score 80 paper-based; 80 iBT); recommended—IELTS (minimum score 6.5), TSE (minimum score 54). *Application deadline:* For fall admission, 4/15 priority date for international students; for spring admission, 10/15 priority date for international students. Applications are processed on a rolling basis. Application fee: $80 ($90 for international students). Electronic applications accepted. *Expenses:* MS Nursing Full-Time Student per Semester: Tuition: $9075 (in-state), $16051 (out-of-state), Fees: $598; Graduate Assistant Per Semester: $1144; Part-Time Student Per Credit Hour: $1009 (in-state), $1784 (out-of-state), Fees: $46; other fees apply depending on program, credit hours, campus & residency. Doctoral Base Fee per Semester: $4938 (in-state), $10405 (out-of-state). *Financial support:* In 2019–20, 47 students received support, including 46 teaching assistantships with full and partial

tuition reimbursements available (averaging $6,766 per year); career-related internships or fieldwork and unspecified assistantships also available. *Unit head:* Dr. Kathleen Valentine, Chief Academic Nursing Officer & Director, 864-656-4758, E-mail: klvalen@clemson.edu. *Application contact:* Dr. Stephanie Davis, Director of Graduate Programs, 864-656-2588, E-mail: stephad@clemson.edu.
Website: http://www.clemson.edu/cbshs/departments/nursing/

**Clemson University,** Graduate School, College of Science, Department of Genetics and Biochemistry, Clemson, SC 29634. Offers biochemistry and molecular biology (PhD); genetics (PhD). *Degree requirements:* For doctorate, comprehensive exam, thesis/dissertation. *Entrance requirements:* For doctorate, GRE General Test, unofficial transcripts, letters of recommendation. Additional exam requirements/recommendations for international students: required—TOEFL (minimum score 80 paper-based; 80 iBT); recommended—IELTS (minimum score 6.5), TSE (minimum score 54). Electronic applications accepted. *Expenses:* Contact institution.

**Columbia University,** College of Physicians and Surgeons, Department of Genetics and Development, New York, NY 10032. Offers genetics (M Phil, MA, PhD); MD/PhD. Terminal master's awarded for partial completion of doctoral program. *Degree requirements:* For doctorate, thesis/dissertation. *Entrance requirements:* For master's and doctorate, GRE General Test. Additional exam requirements/recommendations for international students: required—TOEFL. *Expenses: Tuition:* Full-time $47,600; part-time $1880 per credit. One-time fee: $105.

**Columbia University,** College of Physicians and Surgeons, Integrated Program in Cellular, Molecular, Structural and Genetic Studies, New York, NY 10032. Offers PhD. Terminal master's awarded for partial completion of doctoral program. *Degree requirements:* For doctorate, thesis/dissertation. *Entrance requirements:* For doctorate, GRE General Test, GRE Subject Test. Additional exam requirements/recommendations for international students: required—TOEFL. *Expenses:* Contact institution.

**Cornell University,** Graduate School, Graduate Fields of Agriculture and Life Sciences, Field of Computational Biology, Ithaca, NY 14853. Offers computational behavioral biology (PhD); computational biology (PhD); computational cell biology (PhD); computational ecology (PhD); computational genetics (PhD); computational macromolecular biology (PhD); computational organismal biology (PhD). *Degree requirements:* For doctorate, comprehensive exam, thesis/dissertation, 2 semesters of teaching experience. *Entrance requirements:* For doctorate, GRE General Test, GRE Subject Test (biology), 2 letters of recommendation. Additional exam requirements/recommendations for international students: required—TOEFL (minimum score 550 paper-based; 77 iBT). Electronic applications accepted.

**Cornell University,** Graduate School, Graduate Fields of Agriculture and Life Sciences, Field of Genetics, Genomics and Development, Ithaca, NY 14853. Offers developmental biology (PhD); genetics (PhD); genomics (PhD). *Degree requirements:* For doctorate, comprehensive exam, thesis/dissertation, 2 semesters of teaching experience. *Entrance requirements:* For doctorate, GRE General Test, GRE Subject Test in biology or biochemistry (recommended), 2 letters of recommendation. Additional exam requirements/recommendations for international students: required—TOEFL (minimum score 550 paper-based; 77 iBT). Electronic applications accepted.

**Drexel University,** College of Medicine, Biomedical Graduate Programs, Interdisciplinary Program in Molecular and Cell Biology and Genetics, Philadelphia, PA 19104-2875. Offers MS, PhD, MD/PhD. Terminal master's awarded for partial completion of doctoral program. *Degree requirements:* For master's, comprehensive exam, thesis; for doctorate, thesis/dissertation, qualifying exam. *Entrance requirements:* For master's, GRE General Test, minimum GPA of 2.75; for doctorate, GRE General Test, minimum GPA of 3.0. Additional exam requirements/recommendations for international students: required—TOEFL. Electronic applications accepted.

**Duke University,** Graduate School, Department of Biochemistry, Durham, NC 27710. Offers crystallography of macromolecules (PhD); enzyme mechanisms (PhD); lipid biochemistry (PhD); membrane structure and function (PhD); molecular genetics (PhD); neurochemistry (PhD); nucleic acid structure and function (PhD); protein structure and function (PhD). *Degree requirements:* For doctorate, thesis/dissertation. *Entrance requirements:* For doctorate, GRE General Test, GRE Subject Test (recommended). Additional exam requirements/recommendations for international students: required—TOEFL (minimum score 577 paper-based; 90 iBT) or IELTS (minimum score 7). Electronic applications accepted.

**Duke University,** Graduate School, University Program in Genetics and Genomics, Durham, NC 27710. Offers PhD. *Degree requirements:* For doctorate, variable foreign language requirement, thesis/dissertation. *Entrance requirements:* For doctorate, GRE General Test. Additional exam requirements/recommendations for international students: required—TOEFL (minimum score 577 paper-based; 90 iBT) or IELTS (minimum score 7).

**Emory University,** Laney Graduate School, Division of Biological and Biomedical Sciences, Program in Genetics and Molecular Biology, Atlanta, GA 30322-1100. Offers PhD. *Degree requirements:* For doctorate, comprehensive exam, thesis/dissertation. *Entrance requirements:* For doctorate, GRE General Test, minimum GPA of 3.0 in science course work (recommended). Additional exam requirements/recommendations for international students: required—TOEFL. Electronic applications accepted.

**Harvard University,** Graduate School of Arts and Sciences, Division of Medical Sciences, Boston, MA 02115. Offers biological chemistry and molecular pharmacology (PhD); cell biology (PhD); genetics (PhD); microbiology and molecular genetics (PhD); pathology (PhD), including experimental pathology. *Degree requirements:* For doctorate, thesis/dissertation. *Entrance requirements:* For doctorate, GRE General Test, GRE Subject Test. Additional exam requirements/recommendations for international students: required—TOEFL.

**Harvard University,** Harvard T.H. Chan School of Public Health, Master of Science Program in Computational Biology and Quantitative Genetics, Cambridge, MA 02138. Offers SM. *Students:* 23 full-time (14 women), 1 part-time (0 women); includes 4 minority (3 Asian, non-Hispanic/Latino; 1 Two or more races, non-Hispanic/Latino), 18 international. Average age 29. 59 applicants, 32% accepted, 13 enrolled. In 2019, 16 master's awarded. *Entrance requirements:* For master's, GRE. Additional exam requirements/recommendations for international students: recommended—TOEFL (minimum score 600 paper-based; 100 iBT), IELTS (minimum score 7). *Application deadline:* For fall admission, 12/1 for domestic and international students. Application fee: $140. Electronic applications accepted. *Financial support:* Application deadline: 2/15; applicants required to submit FAFSA. *Unit head:* Dr. John Quackenbush, Director, 617-582-8163. *Application contact:* Vincent W. James, Director of Admissions, 617-432-1031, Fax: 617-432-7080, E-mail: admissions@hsph.harvard.edu.
Website: http://www.hsph.harvard.edu/sm-computational-biology/

**Illinois State University,** Graduate School, College of Arts and Sciences, School of Biological Sciences, Normal, IL 61790. Offers animal behavior (MS); bacteriology (MS); biochemistry (MS); biological sciences (MS); biology (PhD); biophysics (MS); biotechnology (MS); botany (MS, PhD); cell biology (MS); conservation biology (MS); developmental biology (MS); ecology (MS, PhD); entomology (MS); evolutionary biology (MS); genetics (MS, PhD); immunology (MS); microbiology (MS, PhD); molecular biology (MS); molecular genetics (MS); neurobiology (MS); neuroscience (MS); parasitology (MS); physiology (MS, PhD); plant biology (MS); plant molecular biology (MS); plant sciences (MS); structural biology (MS); zoology (MS, PhD). *Program availability:* Part-time. *Faculty:* 26 full-time (6 women), 7 part-time/adjunct (2 women). *Students:* 51 full-time (33 women), 15 part-time (8 women). Average age 27. 71 applicants, 28% accepted, 9 enrolled. In 2019, 14 master's, 3 doctorates awarded. *Degree requirements:* For master's, thesis or alternative; for doctorate, variable foreign language requirement, thesis/dissertation, 2 terms of residency. *Entrance requirements:* For master's, GRE General Test, minimum GPA of 2.6 in last 60 hours of course work; for doctorate, GRE General Test. *Application deadline:* Applications are processed on a rolling basis. Application fee: $50. *Expenses: Tuition, area resident:* Full-time $7956; part-time $9767 per year. Tuition, nonresident: full-time $9233; part-time $17,592 per year. *Required fees:* $1797. *Financial support:* In 2019–20, 20 research assistantships, 41 teaching assistantships were awarded; Federal Work-Study, tuition waivers (full), and unspecified assistantships also available. Financial award application deadline: 4/1. *Unit head:* Dr. Craig Gatto, School Director, 309-438-3087, E-mail: cgatto@IllinoisState.edu. *Application contact:* Dr. Ben Sadd, Assistant Chair for Graduate Studies, 309-438-2651, E-mail: bmsadd@IllinoisState.edu.
Website: http://www.bio.ilstu.edu/

**Indiana University Bloomington,** University Graduate School, College of Arts and Sciences, Department of Biology, Bloomington, IN 47405. Offers biology teaching (MAT); biotechnology (MA); evolution, ecology, and behavior (MA, PhD); genetics (PhD); microbiology (MA, PhD); molecular, cellular, and developmental biology (PhD); plant sciences (MA, PhD); zoology (MA, PhD). Terminal master's awarded for partial completion of doctoral program. *Degree requirements:* For master's, thesis, oral defense; for doctorate, thesis/dissertation, oral defense. *Entrance requirements:* For master's and doctorate, GRE General Test. Additional exam requirements/recommendations for international students: required—TOEFL (minimum score 100 iBT). Electronic applications accepted.

**Iowa State University of Science and Technology,** Bioinformatics and Computational Biology Program, Ames, IA 50011. Offers MS, PhD. *Degree requirements:* For doctorate, thesis/dissertation. *Entrance requirements:* For master's and doctorate, GRE General Test. Additional exam requirements/recommendations for international students: recommended—TOEFL, IELTS. Electronic applications accepted.

**Iowa State University of Science and Technology,** Program in Genetics, Ames, IA 50011. Offers MS, PhD. *Entrance requirements:* For master's and doctorate, GRE General Test. Additional exam requirements/recommendations for international students: required—TOEFL (minimum score 550 paper-based; 79 iBT), IELTS (minimum score 6.5). Electronic applications accepted.

**Irell & Manella Graduate School of Biological Sciences,** Graduate Program, Duarte, CA 91010. Offers brain metastatic cancer (PhD); cancer and stem cell metabolism (PhD); cancer biology (PhD); cancer biology and developmental therapeutics (PhD); cell biology (PhD); chemical biology (PhD); chromosomal break repair (PhD); diabetes and pancreatic progenitor cell biology (PhD); DNA repair and cancer biology (PhD); germline epigenetic remodeling and endocrine disruptors (PhD); hematology and hematopoietic cell transplantation (PhD); hematology and immunology (PhD); inflammation and cancer (PhD); micrornas and gene regulation in cardiovascular disease (PhD); mixed chimerism for reversal of autoimmunity (PhD); molecular and cellular biology (PhD); molecular biology and genetics (PhD); nanoparticle mediated twist1 silencing in metastatic cancer (PhD); neuro-oncology and stem cell biology (PhD); neuroscience (PhD); RNA directed therapies for HIV-1 (PhD); small RNA-induced transcriptional gene activation (PhD); stem cell regulation by the microenvironment (PhD); translational oncology and pharmaceutical sciences (PhD); tumor biology (PhD). *Degree requirements:* For doctorate, comprehensive exam, thesis/dissertation, qualifying exams, two advanced courses. *Entrance requirements:* For doctorate, GRE General Test; GRE Subject Test (recommended), 2 years of course work in chemistry (general and organic); 1 year of course work each in biochemistry, general biology, and general physics; 2 semesters of course work in mathematics; significant research laboratory experience. Additional exam requirements/recommendations for international students: required—TOEFL. Electronic applications accepted.

**Johns Hopkins University,** Bloomberg School of Public Health, Department of Epidemiology, Baltimore, MD 21205. Offers cancer epidemiology (MHS, Sc M, PhD, Sc D); cardiovascular disease and clinical epidemiology (MHS, Sc M, PhD, Sc D); clinical trials (PhD, Sc D); clinical trials and evidence synthesis (MHS, Sc M, PhD, Sc D); environmental epidemiology (MHS, Sc M, PhD, Sc D); epidemiology of aging (MHS, Sc M, PhD, Sc D); general epidemiology and methodology (MHS, Sc M); genetic epidemiology (MHS, Sc M, PhD, Sc D); infectious disease epidemiology (MHS, Sc M, PhD, Sc D). *Degree requirements:* For master's, comprehensive exam, thesis, 1-year full-time residency; for doctorate, comprehensive exam, thesis/dissertation, 2 years' full-time residency, oral and written exams, student teaching. *Entrance requirements:* For master's, GRE General Test or MCAT, 3 letters of recommendation, curriculum vitae; for doctorate, GRE General Test, minimum 1 year of work experience, 3 letters of recommendation, curriculum vitae, academic records from all schools. Additional exam requirements/recommendations for international students: required—TOEFL (minimum score 100 iBT), IELTS (minimum score 7.5). Electronic applications accepted.

**Johns Hopkins University,** National Institutes of Health Sponsored Programs, Baltimore, MD 21218. Offers biology (PhD), including biochemistry, biophysics, cell biology, developmental biology, genetic biology, molecular biology; cell, molecular, and developmental biology and biophysics (PhD). *Degree requirements:* For doctorate, comprehensive exam, thesis/dissertation. *Entrance requirements:* Additional exam requirements/recommendations for international students: required—TOEFL (minimum score 600 paper-based). Electronic applications accepted.

**Kansas State University,** Graduate School, College of Agriculture, Department of Animal Sciences and Industry, Manhattan, KS 66506. Offers genetics (MS, PhD); meat science (MS, PhD); monogastric nutrition (MS, PhD); physiology (MS, PhD); ruminant nutrition (MS, PhD). *Degree requirements:* For master's, comprehensive exam, thesis, oral exam; for doctorate, comprehensive exam, thesis/dissertation, preliminary exams. *Entrance requirements:* Additional exam requirements/recommendations for international students: required—TOEFL (minimum score 550 paper-based; 79 iBT). Electronic applications accepted.

**Kansas State University,** Graduate School, College of Agriculture, Department of Plant Pathology, Manhattan, KS 66506. Offers genetics (MS, PhD); plant pathology (MS, PhD). Terminal master's awarded for partial completion of doctoral program. *Degree requirements:* For master's, thesis, oral exam; for doctorate, thesis/dissertation, preliminary exams, oral exam. *Entrance requirements:* For master's and doctorate, minimum undergraduate GPA of 3.0. Additional exam requirements/recommendations

for international students: required—TOEFL (minimum score 550 paper-based; 79 iBT). Electronic applications accepted.

**Kent State University,** College of Arts and Sciences, School of Biomedical Sciences, Kent, OH 44242-0001. Offers biological anthropology (PhD); biomedical mathematics (MS, PhD); cellular and molecular biology (MS, PhD), including cellular biology and structures, molecular biology and genetics; neurosciences (MS, PhD); pharmacology (MS, PhD); physiology (MS, PhD). *Faculty:* 17 full-time (8 women). *Students:* 73 full-time (48 women), 2 part-time (1 woman); includes 9 minority (2 Black or African American, non-Hispanic/Latino; 1 Asian, non-Hispanic/Latino; 3 Hispanic/Latino; 3 Two or more races, non-Hispanic/Latino), 53 international. Average age 29. 78 applicants, 17% accepted, 9 enrolled. In 2019, 2 master's, 5 doctorates awarded. *Degree requirements:* For master's, thesis; for doctorate, comprehensive exam, thesis/dissertation. *Entrance requirements:* For master's, GRE, bachelor's degree, transcripts, minimum GPA of 3.0 undergraduate GPA, goal statement, three letters of recommendation, academic preparation adequate to perform graduate work in the desired field (typically two years of chemistry, one year of mathematics, one year of physics and courses in anthropology, biology and psychology); for doctorate, GRE, master's degree, minimum GPA of 3.0, transcripts, goal statement, three letters of recommendation. Additional exam requirements/recommendations for international students: required—TOEFL (minimum score 100 iBT), IELTS (minimum score 7), PTE (minimum score 68), Michigan English Language Assessment Battery (minimum score 85). *Application deadline:* For fall admission, 1/1 for domestic students, 12/15 for international students. Applications are processed on a rolling basis. Application fee: $45 ($70 for international students). Electronic applications accepted. *Financial support:* Research assistantships with full tuition reimbursements, teaching assistantships, health care benefits, and unspecified assistantships available. Financial award application deadline: 1/1. *Unit head:* Dr. Ernest J. Freeman, Director, School of Biomedical Sciences, 330-672-2363, E-mail: efreema2@kent.edu. *Application contact:* School of Biomedical Sciences, 330-6722263, Fax: 330-6729391.
Website: http://www.kent.edu/biomedical/

**Marquette University,** Graduate School, College of Arts and Sciences, Department of Biological Sciences, Milwaukee, WI 53201-1881. Offers cell biology (MS, PhD); developmental biology (MS, PhD); ecology (MS, PhD); epithelial physiology (MS, PhD); genetics (MS, PhD); microbiology (MS, PhD); molecular biology (MS, PhD); muscle and exercise physiology (MS, PhD); neuroscience (PhD). Terminal master's awarded for partial completion of doctoral program. *Degree requirements:* For master's, comprehensive exam, thesis, 1 year of teaching experience or equivalent; for doctorate, thesis/dissertation, 1 year of teaching experience or equivalent, qualifying exam. *Entrance requirements:* For master's and doctorate, GRE General Test, GRE Subject Test, official transcripts from all current and previous colleges/universities except Marquette, statement of professional goals and aspirations, three letters of recommendation. Additional exam requirements/recommendations for international students: required—TOEFL (minimum score 530 paper-based). Electronic applications accepted.

**Massachusetts Institute of Technology,** School of Science, Department of Biology, Cambridge, MA 02139. Offers biochemistry (PhD); biological oceanography (PhD); biology (PhD); biophysical chemistry and molecular structure (PhD); cell biology (PhD); computational and systems biology (PhD); developmental biology (PhD); genetics (PhD); immunology (PhD); microbiology (PhD); molecular biology (PhD); neurobiology (PhD). *Degree requirements:* For doctorate, comprehensive exam, thesis/dissertation, teaching assistantship during two semesters. *Entrance requirements:* For doctorate, GRE General Test. Additional exam requirements/recommendations for international students: required—TOEFL, IELTS. Electronic applications accepted.

**Mayo Clinic Graduate School of Biomedical Sciences,** Program in Virology and Gene Therapy, Rochester, MN 55905. Offers PhD. *Degree requirements:* For doctorate, comprehensive exam, thesis/dissertation. *Entrance requirements:* Additional exam requirements/recommendations for international students: required—TOEFL. Electronic applications accepted.

**McMaster University,** Faculty of Health Sciences and School of Graduate Studies, Program in Medical Sciences, Genetics and Cancer Area, Hamilton, ON L8S 4M2, Canada. Offers M Sc, PhD, MD/PhD. *Degree requirements:* For master's, thesis; for doctorate, comprehensive exam, thesis/dissertation. *Entrance requirements:* For master's, honors B Sc, B+ average in related field; for doctorate, M Sc, minimum B+ average, students with proven research experience and an A average may be admitted with a B Sc degree. Additional exam requirements/recommendations for international students: required—TOEFL (minimum score 580 paper-based; 92 iBT).

**Medical University of South Carolina,** College of Graduate Studies, Program in Molecular and Cellular Biology and Pathobiology, Charleston, SC 29425. Offers cancer biology (PhD); cardiovascular biology (PhD); cardiovascular imaging (PhD); cell regulation (PhD); craniofacial biology (PhD); genetics and development (PhD); marine biomedicine (PhD); DMD/PhD; MD/PhD. *Degree requirements:* For doctorate, thesis/dissertation, oral and written exams. *Entrance requirements:* For doctorate, GRE General Test, interview, minimum GPA of 3.0. Additional exam requirements/recommendations for international students: required—TOEFL (minimum score 600 paper-based; 100 iBT). Electronic applications accepted.

**Michigan State University,** College of Veterinary Medicine and The Graduate School, Graduate Programs in Veterinary Medicine, East Lansing, MI 48824. Offers comparative medicine and integrative biology (MS, PhD), including comparative medicine and integrative biology, comparative medicine and integrative biology–environmental toxicology (PhD); food safety and toxicology (MS), including food safety; integrative toxicology (PhD), including animal science–environmental toxicology, biochemistry and molecular biology–environmental toxicology, chemistry–environmental toxicology, crop and soil sciences–environmental toxicology, environmental engineering–environmental toxicology, environmental geosciences–environmental toxicology, fisheries and wildlife–environmental toxicology, food science–environmental toxicology, forestry–environmental toxicology, genetics–environmental toxicology, human nutrition–environmental toxicology, microbiology–environmental toxicology, pharmacology and toxicology–environmental toxicology, zoology–environmental toxicology; large animal clinical sciences (MS, PhD); microbiology and molecular genetics (MS, PhD), including industrial microbiology, microbiology, microbiology and molecular genetics, microbiology–environmental toxicology (PhD); pathobiology and diagnostic investigation (MS, PhD), including pathology, pathology–environmental toxicology (PhD); pharmacology and toxicology (MS, PhD); pharmacology and toxicology–environmental toxicology (PhD); physiology (MS, PhD); small animal clinical sciences (MS). Electronic applications accepted.

**Michigan State University,** The Graduate School, College of Natural Science, Department of Microbiology and Molecular Genetics, East Lansing, MI 48824. Offers industrial microbiology (MS, PhD); microbiology (MS, PhD); microbiology and molecular genetics (MS, PhD); microbiology–environmental toxicology (PhD). *Entrance requirements:* For master's, GRE General Test. Additional exam requirements/recommendations for international students: required—TOEFL (minimum score 550

paper-based), Michigan State University ELT ( minimum score 85), Michigan English Language Assessment Battery (minimum score 83). Electronic applications accepted.

**Michigan State University,** The Graduate School, College of Natural Science, MSU-DOE Plant Research Laboratory, East Lansing, MI 48824. Offers biochemistry and molecular biology (PhD); cellular and molecular biology (PhD); crop and soil sciences (PhD); genetics (PhD); microbiology and molecular genetics (PhD); plant biology (PhD); plant physiology (PhD). *Degree requirements:* For doctorate, comprehensive exam, thesis/dissertation, laboratory rotation, defense of dissertation. *Entrance requirements:* For doctorate, GRE General Test, acceptance into one of the affiliated department programs; 3 letters of recommendation; bachelor's degree or equivalent in life sciences, chemistry, biochemistry, or biophysics; research experience. Electronic applications accepted.

**Michigan State University,** The Graduate School, College of Natural Science, Program in Genetics, East Lansing, MI 48824. Offers genetics (MS, PhD); genetics–environmental toxicology (PhD). *Entrance requirements:* Additional exam requirements/recommendations for international students: required—TOEFL. Electronic applications accepted.

**Mississippi State University,** College of Agriculture and Life Sciences, Department of Animal and Dairy Sciences, Mississippi State, MS 39762. Offers agricultural life sciences (MS), including animal physiology (MS, PhD), genetics (MS, PhD); agricultural science (PhD), including animal dairy sciences, animal nutrition (MS, PhD); agriculture (MS), including animal nutrition (MS, PhD), animal science; life sciences (PhD), including animal physiology (MS, PhD), genetics (MS, PhD). *Faculty:* 19 full-time (6 women). *Students:* 21 full-time (18 women), 13 part-time (6 women); includes 3 minority (1 American Indian or Alaska Native, non-Hispanic/Latino; 2 Hispanic/Latino), 7 international. Average age 27. 15 applicants, 60% accepted, 6 enrolled. In 2019, 5 master's, 2 doctorates awarded. *Degree requirements:* For master's, comprehensive exam (for some programs), thesis, written proposal of intended research area; for doctorate, comprehensive exam, thesis/dissertation, written proposal of intended research area. *Entrance requirements:* For master's, GRE General Test, minimum GPA of 3.0; for doctorate, GRE General Test. Additional exam requirements/recommendations for international students: required—TOEFL (minimum score 575 paper-based; 84 iBT), IELTS (minimum score 7). *Application deadline:* For fall admission, 7/1 for domestic students, 5/1 for international students; for spring admission, 11/1 for domestic students, 9/1 for international students. Applications are processed on a rolling basis. Application fee: $60 ($80 for international students). Electronic applications accepted. *Expenses: Tuition, area resident:* Full-time $8880; part-time $456 per credit hour. Tuition, state resident: full-time $8880. Tuition, nonresident: full-time $23,840; part-time $1236 per credit hour. *Required fees:* $110; $11.12 per credit hour. Tuition and fees vary according to course load. *Financial support:* In 2019–20, 12 research assistantships (averaging $12,628 per year) were awarded; Federal Work-Study, institutionally sponsored loans, and unspecified assistantships also available. Financial award application deadline: 4/1; financial award applicants required to submit FAFSA. *Unit head:* Dr. John Blanton, Professor and Head, 662-325-2802, Fax: 662-325-8873, E-mail: john.blanton@msstate.edu. *Application contact:* Ryan King, Admissions and Enrollment Assistant, 662-325-8951, E-mail: rjk101@grad.msstate.edu.
Website: http://www.ads.msstate.edu/

**New York University,** Graduate School of Arts and Science, Department of Biology, New York, NY 10012-1019. Offers biology (PhD); biomedical journalism (MS); cancer and molecular biology (PhD); computational biology (PhD); computers in biological research (MS); developmental genetics (PhD); general biology (MS); immunology and microbiology (PhD); molecular genetics (PhD); neurobiology (PhD); oral biology (MS); plant biology (PhD); recombinant DNA technology (MS); MS/MBA. *Program availability:* Part-time. Terminal master's awarded for partial completion of doctoral program. *Degree requirements:* For master's, thesis or alternative, qualifying paper; for doctorate, comprehensive exam, thesis/dissertation. *Entrance requirements:* For master's and doctorate, GRE General Test. Additional exam requirements/recommendations for international students: required—TOEFL, IELTS.

**The Ohio State University,** Graduate School, College of Arts and Sciences, Division of Natural and Mathematical Sciences, Department of Molecular Genetics, Columbus, OH 43210. Offers cell and developmental biology (MS, PhD); genetics (MS, PhD); molecular biology (MS, PhD). *Entrance requirements:* For doctorate, GRE General Test, GRE Subject Test in biology or chemistry (recommended). Additional exam requirements/recommendations for international students: required—TOEFL (minimum score 550 paper-based; 79 iBT), Michigan English Language Assessment Battery (minimum score 82); recommended—IELTS (minimum score 7). Electronic applications accepted.

**Oregon Health & Science University,** School of Medicine, Graduate Programs in Medicine, Program in Molecular and Cellular Biosciences, Department of Molecular and Medical Genetics, Portland, OR 97239-3098. Offers PhD. Terminal master's awarded for partial completion of doctoral program. *Degree requirements:* For doctorate, comprehensive exam, thesis/dissertation. *Entrance requirements:* For doctorate, GRE General Test (minimum scores: 153 Verbal/148 Quantitative/4.5 Analytical) or MCAT (for some programs). Electronic applications accepted.

**Oregon State University,** College of Agricultural Sciences, Program in Botany and Plant Pathology, Corvallis, OR 97331. Offers applied systematics (MS); ecology (MS, PhD); genetics (MS, PhD); genomics and computational biology (MS, PhD); molecular and cellular biology (MS, PhD); mycology (MS, PhD); plant pathology (MS, PhD); plant physiology (MS, PhD). *Entrance requirements:* For master's and doctorate, GRE.

**Oregon State University,** College of Agricultural Sciences, Program in Horticulture, Corvallis, OR 97331. Offers breeding, genetics, and biotechnology (MS, PhD); community and landscape horticultural systems (MS, PhD); sustainable crop production (MS, PhD). *Degree requirements:* For master's, thesis (for some programs); for doctorate, thesis/dissertation. *Entrance requirements:* For master's and doctorate, GRE General Test, minimum GPA of 3.0 in last 90 hours. Additional exam requirements/recommendations for international students: required—TOEFL (minimum score 80 iBT), IELTS (minimum score 6.5).

**Purdue University,** Graduate School, College of Science, Department of Biological Sciences, West Lafayette, IN 47907. Offers cell and developmental biology (PhD); genetics (MS); microbiology (MS, PhD); neurobiology (MS, PhD). *Faculty:* 43 full-time (14 women), 6 part-time/adjunct (1 woman). *Students:* 117 full-time (58 women), 10 part-time (6 women); includes 24 minority (5 Black or African American, non-Hispanic/Latino; 12 Asian, non-Hispanic/Latino; 4 Hispanic/Latino; 3 Two or more races, non-Hispanic/Latino), 56 international. Average age 27. 146 applicants, 32% accepted, 27 enrolled. In 2019, 7 master's, 18 doctorates awarded. Terminal master's awarded for partial completion of doctoral program. *Degree requirements:* For master's, thesis (for some programs); for doctorate, thesis/dissertation, seminars, teaching experience. *Entrance requirements:* For master's, GRE General Test (minimum analytical writing score of 3.5), minimum undergraduate GPA of 3.0; for doctorate, GRE General Test (minimum analytical writing score of 3.5), minimum undergraduate GPA of 3.5. Additional exam requirements/recommendations for international students: required—TOEFL minimum score 600 paper-based; 107 iBT (for MS), 80 iBT (for PhD). *Application deadline:* For fall admission, 12/7 for domestic and international students. Applications are processed on a rolling basis. Application fee: $60 ($75 for international students). Electronic applications accepted. *Financial support:* Fellowships, research assistantships, and teaching assistantships available. Support available to part-time students. Financial award application deadline: 2/15; financial award applicants required to submit FAFSA. *Unit head:* Janice P. Evans, Head, 765-494-4407, E-mail: janiceevans@purdue.edu. *Application contact:* Georgina E. Rupp, Graduate Coordinator, 765-494-8142, E-mail: ruppg@purdue.edu.
Website: http://www.bio.purdue.edu/

**Purdue University,** Graduate School, PULSe - Purdue University Life Sciences Program, West Lafayette, IN 47907. Offers biomolecular structure and biophysics (PhD); biotechnology (PhD); chemical biology (PhD); chromatin and regulation of gene expression (PhD); integrative neuroscience (PhD); integrative plant sciences (PhD); membrane biology (PhD); microbiology (PhD); molecular evolutionary and cancer biology (PhD); molecular evolutionary genetics (PhD); molecular virology (PhD). *Students:* 37 full-time (23 women); includes 7 minority (1 Black or African American, non-Hispanic/Latino; 2 Asian, non-Hispanic/Latino; 4 Hispanic/Latino), 22 international. Average age 25. 162 applicants, 36% accepted, 19 enrolled. *Entrance requirements:* For doctorate, GRE, minimum undergraduate GPA of 3.0. Additional exam requirements/recommendations for international students: required—TOEFL (minimum score 550 paper-based; 77 iBT). *Application deadline:* For fall admission, 1/15 priority date for domestic and international students. Applications are processed on a rolling basis. Application fee: $60 ($75 for international students). Electronic applications accepted. *Financial support:* In 2019–20, research assistantships with tuition reimbursements (averaging $22,500 per year), teaching assistantships with tuition reimbursements (averaging $22,500 per year) were awarded. *Application contact:* Lindsey Springer, Graduate Contact for Admissions, 765-496-9667, E-mail: lbcampbe@purdue.edu.
Website: http://www.gradschool.purdue.edu/pulse

**Rutgers University - New Brunswick,** Graduate School-New Brunswick, Programs in the Molecular Biosciences, Piscataway, NJ 08854-8097. Offers biochemistry (PhD); cell and developmental biology (MS, PhD); microbiology and molecular genetics (MS, PhD), including applied microbiology, clinical microbiology, computational molecular biology (PhD), immunology, microbial biochemistry, molecular genetics, virology.

**Stanford University,** School of Medicine, Graduate Programs in Medicine, Department of Genetics, Stanford, CA 94305-2004. Offers PhD. *Expenses: Tuition:* Full-time $52,479; part-time $34,110 per unit. *Required fees:* $672; $224 per quarter. Tuition and fees vary according to program and student level.
Website: http://genetics.stanford.edu/

**Stony Brook University, State University of New York,** Graduate School, College of Arts and Sciences, Graduate Program in Genetics, Stony Brook, NY 11794. Offers PhD. *Students:* 36 full-time (17 women); includes 8 minority (3 Asian, non-Hispanic/Latino; 3 Hispanic/Latino; 2 Two or more races, non-Hispanic/Latino), 14 international. Average age 27. 33 applicants, 42% accepted, 10 enrolled. In 2019, 3 doctorates awarded. *Degree requirements:* For doctorate, comprehensive exam, thesis/dissertation, teaching experience. *Entrance requirements:* For doctorate, GRE General Test, GRE Subject Test. Additional exam requirements/recommendations for international students: required—TOEFL (minimum score 90 iBT). *Application deadline:* For fall admission, 1/15 for domestic students; for spring admission, 10/1 for domestic students. Application fee: $100. *Expenses:* Contact institution. *Financial support:* In 2019–20, 9 fellowships, 11 research assistantships, 7 teaching assistantships were awarded; Federal Work-Study also available. *Unit head:* Dr. Martha B. Furie, Program Director, 631-632-4232, Fax: 631-632-4294, E-mail: martha.furie@stonybrook.edu. *Application contact:* Jennifer Jokinen, Coordinator, 631-632-8812, Fax: 631-632-9797, E-mail: jennifer.jokinen@stonybrook.edu.
Website: http://life.bio.sunysb.edu/gen/

**Thomas Jefferson University,** Jefferson College of Life Sciences, PhD Program in Genetics, Genomics and Cancer Biology, Philadelphia, PA 19107. Offers PhD. *Degree requirements:* For doctorate, comprehensive exam, thesis/dissertation. *Entrance requirements:* For doctorate, GRE General Test, minimum GPA of 3.2. Additional exam requirements/recommendations for international students: required—TOEFL, IELTS (minimum score 7). Electronic applications accepted.

**Tufts University,** Graduate School of Biomedical Sciences, Genetics Program, Medford, MA 02155. Offers genetics (PhD); mammalian genetics (PhD). *Faculty:* 55 full-time (17 women). *Students:* 27 full-time (15 women); includes 1 minority (Asian, non-Hispanic/Latino), 1 international. Average age 29. 43 applicants, 21% accepted, 5 enrolled. In 2019, 4 doctorates awarded. Terminal master's awarded for partial completion of doctoral program. *Degree requirements:* For doctorate, comprehensive exam, thesis/dissertation. *Entrance requirements:* For doctorate, 3 letters of reference, resume, personal statement. *Application deadline:* For fall admission, 12/1 priority date for domestic and international students. Application fee: $90. Electronic applications accepted. *Expenses: Tuition:* Part-time $1799 per credit hour. Full-time tuition and fees vary according to degree level, program and student level. Part-time tuition and fees vary according to course load. *Financial support:* Research assistantships with full tuition reimbursements and health care benefits available. Financial award application deadline: 12/1. *Unit head:* Dr. Pamela Yelick, Program Director, 617-636-6836. *Application contact:* Jeff Miller, Admissions Coordinator, 617-636-6767, E-mail: GSBS-Admissions@tufts.edu.
Website: https://gsbs.tufts.edu/academics/genetics

**Université de Montréal,** Faculty of Medicine, Program in Medical Genetics, Montréal, QC H3C 3J7, Canada. Offers DESS.

**Université du Québec à Chicoutimi,** Graduate Programs, Program in Experimental Medicine, Chicoutimi, QC G7H 2B1, Canada. Offers genetics (M Sc). *Degree requirements:* For master's, thesis. *Entrance requirements:* For master's, appropriate bachelor's degree, proficiency in French.

**University at Buffalo, the State University of New York,** Graduate School, Jacobs School of Medicine and Biomedical Sciences, Graduate Programs in Medicine and Biomedical Sciences, Program in Genetics, Genomics and Bioinformatics, Buffalo, NY 14203. Offers MS, PhD, MD/PhD. *Faculty:* 59 full-time (16 women). *Students:* 12 full-time (6 women); includes 5 minority (all Asian, non-Hispanic/Latino). Average age 25. 9 applicants, 89% accepted, 3 enrolled. In 2019, 6 master's awarded. Terminal master's awarded for partial completion of doctoral program. *Degree requirements:* For master's, thesis or alternative; for doctorate, thesis/dissertation. *Entrance requirements:* For master's and doctorate, GRE. Additional exam requirements/recommendations for international students: required—TOEFL (minimum score 100 iBT); recommended—IELTS (minimum score 6.5). *Application deadline:* For fall admission, 3/1 for domestic and international students. Application fee: $85. Electronic applications accepted. *Expenses: Tuition, area resident:* Full-time $11,310; part-time $471 per credit hour. Tuition, state resident: full-time $11,310; part-time $471 per credit hour. Tuition, nonresident: full-time $23,100; part-time $963 per credit hour. *International tuition:* $23,100 full-time. *Required fees:* $2820. *Unit head:* Dr. Richard Gronostajski, Director, 716-829-3471, Fax: 716-849-6655, E-mail: rgron@buffalo.edu. *Application contact:* M.

Sara Thomas, Program Administrator, 716-829-3890, E-mail: msthomas@buffalo.edu.
Website: http://medicine.buffalo.edu/education/ggb.html

**The University of Alabama at Birmingham,** Joint Health Sciences, Genetics, Genomics, and Bioinformatics Theme, Birmingham, AL 35294. Offers PhD. *Students:* Average age 27. 39 applicants, 18% accepted, 4 enrolled. In 2019, 4 doctorates awarded. *Degree requirements:* For doctorate, comprehensive exam, thesis/dissertation. *Entrance requirements:* For doctorate, personal statement, resume or curriculum vitae, letters of recommendation, research experience, interview. Additional exam requirements/recommendations for international students: required—TOEFL (minimum score 80 iBT), IELTS (minimum score 6.5). *Application deadline:* For fall admission, 12/31 for domestic and international students. Applications are processed on a rolling basis. Electronic applications accepted. *Financial support:* In 2019–20, fellowships with full tuition reimbursements (averaging $30,000 per year), research assistantships with full tuition reimbursements (averaging $31,000 per year) were awarded; health care benefits also available. *Unit head:* Dr. Kevin Dybvig, Theme Director, 205-934-9327, E-mail: dybvig@uab.edu. *Application contact:* Alyssa Zasada, Admissions Manager for Graduate Biomedical Sciences, 205-934-3857, E-mail: gradgbs@uab.edu.
Website: http://www.uab.edu/gbs/home/themes/ggb

**University of Alberta,** Faculty of Graduate Studies and Research, Department of Biological Sciences, Edmonton, AB T6G 2E1, Canada. Offers environmental biology and ecology (M Sc, PhD); microbiology and biotechnology (M Sc, PhD); molecular biology and genetics (M Sc, PhD); physiology and cell biology (M Sc, PhD); plant biology (M Sc, PhD); systematics and evolution (M Sc, PhD). Terminal master's awarded for partial completion of doctoral program. *Degree requirements:* For master's, thesis; for doctorate, thesis/dissertation. *Entrance requirements:* Additional exam requirements/recommendations for international students: required—TOEFL.

**University of Alberta,** Faculty of Medicine and Dentistry and Faculty of Graduate Studies and Research, Graduate Programs in Medicine, Department of Medical Genetics, Edmonton, AB T6G 2E1, Canada. Offers M Sc, PhD. *Degree requirements:* For master's, comprehensive exam, thesis; for doctorate, comprehensive exam, thesis/dissertation. *Entrance requirements:* For master's and doctorate, minimum GPA of 3.2.

**The University of Arizona,** Graduate Interdisciplinary Programs, Graduate Interdisciplinary Program in Genetics, Tucson, AZ 85719. Offers MS, PhD. Terminal master's awarded for partial completion of doctoral program. *Degree requirements:* For master's, thesis; for doctorate, one foreign language, comprehensive exam, thesis/dissertation. *Entrance requirements:* For master's, GRE General Test, 3 letters of recommendation; for doctorate, GRE General Test, statement of purpose, 3 letters of recommendation. Additional exam requirements/recommendations for international students: required—TOEFL (minimum score 550 paper-based; 79 iBT). Electronic applications accepted.

**The University of British Columbia,** Faculty of Medicine, Department of Medical Genetics, Medical Genetics Graduate Program, Vancouver, BC V6T 1Z1, Canada. Offers M Sc, PhD. *Degree requirements:* For master's, thesis, 18 credits of coursework; for doctorate, comprehensive exam, thesis/dissertation, 18 credits of coursework. Electronic applications accepted. *Expenses:* Contact institution.

**University of Calgary,** Cumming School of Medicine and Faculty of Graduate Studies, Program in Medical Science, Calgary, AB T2N 1N4, Canada. Offers cancer biology (M Sc, PhD); critical care medicine (M Sc, PhD); joint injury and arthritis (M Sc, PhD); molecular and medical genetics (M Sc, PhD); mountain medicine and high altitude physiology (M Sc, PhD); pathologists' assistant (M Sc, PhD). *Degree requirements:* For master's, thesis; for doctorate, thesis/dissertation, candidacy exam. *Entrance requirements:* For master's, minimum undergraduate GPA of 3.2; for doctorate, minimum graduate GPA of 3.2. Additional exam requirements/recommendations for international students: required—TOEFL (minimum score 600 paper-based). Electronic applications accepted.

**University of California, Davis,** Graduate Studies, Graduate Group in Genetics, Davis, CA 95616. Offers MS, PhD. Terminal master's awarded for partial completion of doctoral program. *Degree requirements:* For master's, comprehensive exam (for some programs), thesis (for some programs); for doctorate, thesis/dissertation. *Entrance requirements:* For master's and doctorate, GRE General Test, GRE Subject Test. Additional exam requirements/recommendations for international students: required—TOEFL (minimum score 550 paper-based). Electronic applications accepted.

**University of California, Irvine,** School of Biological Sciences and School of Medicine, Interdisciplinary Graduate Program in Cellular and Molecular Biosciences, Irvine, CA 92697. Offers PhD. *Students:* 26 full-time (17 women); includes 13 minority (1 Black or African American, non-Hispanic/Latino; 6 Asian, non-Hispanic/Latino; 6 Hispanic/Latino). Average age 28. 448 applicants, 17% accepted, 26 enrolled. *Degree requirements:* For doctorate, thesis/dissertation, teaching assignment, preliminary exam. *Entrance requirements:* For doctorate, GRE General Test, three letters of recommendation, interview. Additional exam requirements/recommendations for international students: required—TOEFL or IELTS. *Application deadline:* For fall admission, 12/8 for domestic and international students. Application fee: $120 ($140 for international students). Electronic applications accepted. *Expenses:* Contact institution. *Financial support:* Fellowships with full tuition reimbursements, institutionally sponsored loans, scholarships/grants, tuition waivers (full), unspecified assistantships, and stipends available. Financial award application deadline: 1/1; financial award applicants required to submit FAFSA. *Unit head:* Melanie Cocco, Director, 949-824-4487, Fax: 949-824-1965, E-mail: mcocco@uci.edu. *Application contact:* Renee Frigo, Administrator, 949-824-8145, Fax: 949-824-1965, E-mail: rfrigo@uci.edu.
Website: http://cmb.uci.edu/

**University of California, Riverside,** Graduate Division, Graduate Program in Genetics, Genomics, and Bioinformatics, Riverside, CA 92521-0102. Offers PhD. *Degree requirements:* For doctorate, thesis/dissertation, qualifying exams, teaching experience. *Entrance requirements:* For doctorate, GRE General Test, minimum GPA of 3.2. Additional exam requirements/recommendations for international students: required—TOEFL (minimum score 550 paper-based, 80 iBT) or IELTS. Electronic applications accepted.

**University of California, San Francisco,** Graduate Division and School of Medicine, Tetrad Graduate Program, Genetics Track, San Francisco, CA 94143. Offers PhD, MD/PhD. *Degree requirements:* For doctorate, thesis/dissertation. *Entrance requirements:* For doctorate, GRE General Test, GRE Subject Test. Additional exam requirements/recommendations for international students: required—TOEFL. *Expenses:* Contact institution.

**University of Chicago,** Division of the Biological Sciences, Committee on Genetics, Genomics and Systems Biology, Chicago, IL 60637. Offers PhD. *Degree requirements:* For doctorate, thesis/dissertation, ethics class, 2 teaching assistantships, preliminary exam. *Entrance requirements:* For doctorate, GRE General Test, transcripts, statement of purpose, 3 letters of recommendation. Additional exam requirements/recommendations for international students: required—TOEFL (minimum score 600 paper-based; 104 iBT), IELTS (minimum score 7). Electronic applications accepted.

**University of Colorado Denver,** School of Medicine, Program in Human Medical Genetics and Genomics, Aurora, CO 80206. Offers PhD. *Degree requirements:* For doctorate, comprehensive exam, thesis/dissertation, at least 30 semester hours in course work (rotations and research courses taken prior to the completion of the comprehensive examination) and 30 semester hours of thesis/didactic credits prior to defending. *Entrance requirements:* For doctorate, GRE General Test (minimum combined score of 1205), minimum GPA of 3.0, 4 letters of recommendation; prerequisite courses in biology, chemistry (general and organic), physics, genetics, calculus, and statistics (recommended). Additional exam requirements/recommendations for international students: required—TOEFL (minimum score 570 paper-based; 80 iBT). Electronic applications accepted. Tuition and fees vary according to course load, program and reciprocity agreements.

**University of Connecticut,** Graduate School, College of Liberal Arts and Sciences, Department of Molecular and Cell Biology, Storrs, CT 06269. Offers applied genomics (PSM); cell and developmental biology (MS, PhD); genetics and genomics (MS, PhD); microbial systems analysis (PSM); microbiology (MS, PhD); structural biology, biochemistry and biophysics (MS, PhD). Terminal master's awarded for partial completion of doctoral program. *Degree requirements:* For master's, comprehensive exam; for doctorate, thesis/dissertation. *Entrance requirements:* For master's and doctorate, GRE General Test, GRE Subject Test. Additional exam requirements/recommendations for international students: required—TOEFL (minimum score 550 paper-based). Electronic applications accepted.

**University of Connecticut Health Center,** Graduate School, Programs in Biomedical Sciences, Program in Genetics and Developmental Biology, Farmington, CT 06030. Offers PhD, DMD/PhD, MD/PhD. *Degree requirements:* For doctorate, comprehensive exam, thesis/dissertation. *Entrance requirements:* For doctorate, GRE General Test, GRE Subject Test. Additional exam requirements/recommendations for international students: required—TOEFL (minimum score 600 paper-based). Electronic applications accepted.

**University of Delaware,** College of Arts and Sciences, Department of Biological Sciences, Newark, DE 19716. Offers biotechnology (MS); cancer biology (MS, PhD); cell and extracellular matrix biology (MS, PhD); cell and systems physiology (MS, PhD); developmental biology (MS, PhD); ecology and evolution (MS, PhD); microbiology (MS, PhD); molecular biology and genetics (MS, PhD). Terminal master's awarded for partial completion of doctoral program. *Degree requirements:* For master's, thesis, preliminary exam; for doctorate, comprehensive exam, thesis/dissertation, preliminary exam. *Entrance requirements:* For master's and doctorate, GRE General Test. Additional exam requirements/recommendations for international students: required—TOEFL (minimum score 600 paper-based); recommended—TWE. Electronic applications accepted.

**University of Florida,** College of Medicine and Graduate School, Interdisciplinary Program in Biomedical Sciences, Concentration in Genetics, Gainesville, FL 32611. Offers PhD. *Degree requirements:* For doctorate, thesis/dissertation. *Entrance requirements:* For doctorate, GRE General Test, minimum GPA of 3.0, biochemistry before enrollment. Additional exam requirements/recommendations for international students: required—TOEFL, IELTS. Electronic applications accepted.

**University of Georgia,** College of Agricultural and Environmental Sciences, Institute of Plant Breeding, Genetics and Genomics, Athens, GA 30602. Offers MS, PhD.

**University of Georgia,** Franklin College of Arts and Sciences, Department of Genetics, Athens, GA 30602. Offers MS, PhD. Terminal master's awarded for partial completion of doctoral program. *Degree requirements:* For master's, thesis; for doctorate, comprehensive exam, thesis/dissertation. *Entrance requirements:* For master's and doctorate, GRE General Test. Additional exam requirements/recommendations for international students: required—TOEFL. Electronic applications accepted.

**University of Hawaii at Manoa,** John A. Burns School of Medicine, Program in Cell and Molecular Biology, Honolulu, HI 96813. Offers MS, PhD. *Program availability:* Part-time. Terminal master's awarded for partial completion of doctoral program. *Degree requirements:* For master's, thesis optional; for doctorate, comprehensive exam, thesis/dissertation. *Entrance requirements:* For master's and doctorate, GRE General Test, minimum GPA of 3.0. Additional exam requirements/recommendations for international students: required—TOEFL (minimum score 500 paper-based; 61 iBT), IELTS (minimum score 5).

**University of Illinois at Chicago,** College of Medicine, Graduate Programs in Medicine, Department of Biochemistry and Molecular Genetics, Chicago, IL 60607-7128. Offers PhD, MD/PhD. Terminal master's awarded for partial completion of doctoral program. *Degree requirements:* For doctorate, thesis/dissertation. *Entrance requirements:* For doctorate, GRE General Test. Additional exam requirements/recommendations for international students: required—TOEFL. Electronic applications accepted.

**The University of Iowa,** Graduate College, College of Liberal Arts and Sciences, Department of Biology, Iowa City, IA 52242-1324. Offers biology (MS, PhD); cell and developmental biology (MS, PhD); evolution (MS, PhD); genetics (MS, PhD); neurobiology (MS, PhD). Terminal master's awarded for partial completion of doctoral program. *Degree requirements:* For master's, thesis optional, exam; for doctorate, comprehensive exam, thesis/dissertation. *Entrance requirements:* For master's and doctorate, GRE General Test, minimum GPA of 3.0. Additional exam requirements/recommendations for international students: required—TOEFL (minimum score 600 paper-based; 100 iBT). Electronic applications accepted.

**The University of Iowa,** Graduate College, Program in Genetics, Iowa City, IA 52242-1316. Offers PhD. *Degree requirements:* For doctorate, comprehensive exam, thesis/dissertation. *Entrance requirements:* For doctorate, GRE General Test, minimum GPA of 3.0. Additional exam requirements/recommendations for international students: required—TOEFL (minimum score 600 paper-based; 100 iBT). Electronic applications accepted. *Expenses:* Contact institution.

**The University of Iowa,** Roy J. and Lucille A. Carver College of Medicine and Graduate College, Graduate Programs in Medicine, Department of Microbiology, Iowa City, IA 52242-1316. Offers general microbiology and microbial physiology (MS, PhD); immunology (MS, PhD); microbial genetics (MS, PhD); pathogenic bacteriology (MS, PhD); virology (MS, PhD). *Degree requirements:* For master's, thesis; for doctorate, comprehensive exam, thesis/dissertation. *Entrance requirements:* For master's and doctorate, GRE General Test. Additional exam requirements/recommendations for international students: required—TOEFL (minimum score 600 paper-based). Electronic applications accepted.

**The University of Manchester,** School of Biological Sciences, Manchester, United Kingdom. Offers adaptive organismal biology (M Phil, PhD); animal biology (M Phil, PhD); biochemistry (M Phil, PhD); bioinformatics (M Phil, PhD); biomolecular sciences (M Phil, PhD); biotechnology (M Phil, PhD); cell biology (M Phil, PhD); cell matrix research (M Phil, PhD); channels and transporters (M Phil, PhD); developmental biology (M Phil, PhD); environmental biology (M Phil, PhD); evolutionary biology (M Phil, PhD); gene expression (M Phil, PhD); genetics (M Phil, PhD); history of science, technology and medicine (M Phil, PhD); immunology (M Phil, PhD); integrative neurobiology and behavior (M Phil, PhD); membrane trafficking (M Phil, PhD); microbiology (M Phil, PhD);

molecular and cellular neuroscience (M Phil, PhD); molecular biology (M Phil, PhD); molecular cancer studies (M Phil, PhD); neuroscience (M Phil, PhD); ophthalmology (M Phil, PhD); optometry (M Phil, PhD); organelle function (M Phil, PhD); pharmacology (M Phil, PhD); physiology (M Phil, PhD); plant sciences (M Phil, PhD); stem cell research (M Phil, PhD); structural biology (M Phil, PhD); systems neuroscience (M Phil, PhD); toxicology (M Phil, PhD).

**University of Massachusetts Amherst,** Graduate School, Interdisciplinary Programs, Program in Plant Biology, Amherst, MA 01003. Offers biochemistry and metabolism (MS, PhD); cell biology and physiology (MS, PhD); environmental, ecological and integrative biology (MS, PhD); genetics and evolution (MS, PhD). *Degree requirements:* For master's, thesis; for doctorate, 2 foreign languages, comprehensive exam, thesis/ dissertation. *Entrance requirements:* For master's and doctorate, GRE General Test. Additional exam requirements/recommendations for international students: required— TOEFL (minimum score 550 paper-based; 80 iBT), IELTS (minimum score 6.5). Electronic applications accepted.

**University of Miami,** Graduate School, College of Arts and Sciences, Department of Biology, Coral Gables, FL 33124. Offers biology (MS, PhD); genetics and evolution (MS, PhD). Terminal master's awarded for partial completion of doctoral program. *Degree requirements:* For master's, comprehensive exam (for some programs), thesis (for some programs); for doctorate, thesis/dissertation, oral and written qualifying exam. *Entrance requirements:* For master's, GRE General Test, 3 letters of recommendation, research papers; for doctorate, GRE General Test, 3 letters of recommendation, research papers, sponsor letter. Additional exam requirements/recommendations for international students: required—TOEFL (minimum score 550 paper-based; 59 iBT). Electronic applications accepted.

**University of Minnesota, Twin Cities Campus,** Graduate School, Program in Molecular, Cellular, Developmental Biology and Genetics, Minneapolis, MN 55455-0213. Offers genetic counseling (MS); molecular, cellular, developmental biology and genetics (PhD). Terminal master's awarded for partial completion of doctoral program. *Degree requirements:* For master's, thesis optional; for doctorate, thesis/dissertation. *Entrance requirements:* For master's and doctorate, GRE General Test. Additional exam requirements/recommendations for international students: required—TOEFL (minimum score 625 paper-based; 80 iBT). Electronic applications accepted.

**University of Nebraska Medical Center,** Interdisciplinary Graduate Program in Biomedical Sciences, Department of Genetics, Cell Biology and Anatomy, Omaha, NE 68198. Offers genetics, cell biology and anatomy (PhD); medical anatomy (MS); molecular genetics and cell biology (MS). Terminal master's awarded for partial completion of doctoral program. *Degree requirements:* For master's, comprehensive exam, thesis (for some programs); for doctorate, comprehensive exam, thesis/ dissertation. *Entrance requirements:* For master's, GRE General Test (MCAT or DAT acceptable for MS in medical anatomy); for doctorate, GRE General Test. Additional exam requirements/recommendations for international students: required—TOEFL (minimum score 550 paper-based; 80 iBT). Electronic applications accepted. *Expenses:* Contact institution.

**University of New Hampshire,** Graduate School, College of Life Sciences and Agriculture, Department of Molecular, Cellular and Biomedical Sciences, Program in Genetics, Durham, NH 03824. Offers MS, PhD. *Program availability:* Part-time. *Students:* 9 full-time (6 women), 4 part-time (1 woman); includes 2 minority (both Hispanic/Latino), 2 international. Average age 28. 18 applicants, 11% accepted, 2 enrolled. In 2019, 2 master's, 3 doctorates awarded. *Entrance requirements:* For master's and doctorate, GRE General Test, GRE Subject Test. Additional exam requirements/recommendations for international students: required—TOEFL (minimum score 550 paper-based; 80 iBT), IELTS, PTE. *Application deadline:* For fall admission, 1/15 priority date for domestic students, 4/1 for international students. Application fee: $65. Electronic applications accepted. *Financial support:* In 2019–20, 13 students received support, including 2 research assistantships, 11 teaching assistantships; fellowships, career-related internships or fieldwork, Federal Work-Study, and scholarships/grants also available. Support available to part-time students. Financial award application deadline: 2/15. *Unit head:* Louis Tisa, Chair, 603-862-2442. *Application contact:* Paul Boisselle, Administrative Assistant, 603-862-4814, E-mail: genetics.dept@unh.edu.
Website: https://colsa.unh.edu/molecular-cellular-biomedical-sciences

**University of New Mexico,** Graduate Studies, Health Sciences Center, Program in Biomedical Sciences, Albuquerque, NM 87131-5196. Offers biochemistry and molecular biology (MS, PhD); cell biology and physiology (MS, PhD); molecular genetics and microbiology (MS, PhD); neuroscience (MS, PhD); pathology (MS, PhD); toxicology (MS, PhD). *Program availability:* Part-time. Terminal master's awarded for partial completion of doctoral program. *Degree requirements:* For master's, thesis; for doctorate, comprehensive exam, thesis/dissertation, qualifying exam at the end of year 1/core curriculum. *Entrance requirements:* For master's and doctorate, GRE General Test, minimum undergraduate GPA of 3.0. Additional exam requirements/ recommendations for international students: required—TOEFL. Electronic applications accepted. *Expenses:* Tuition, state resident: full-time $7633; part-time $972 per year. Tuition, nonresident: full-time $22,586; part-time $3840 per year. *International tuition:* $23,292 full-time. *Required fees:* $8608. Tuition and fees vary according to course level, course load, degree level, program and student level.

**The University of North Carolina at Chapel Hill,** Graduate School, College of Arts and Sciences, Department of Biology, Chapel Hill, NC 27599. Offers botany (MA, MS, PhD); cell biology, development, and physiology (MA, MS, PhD); cell motility and cytoskeleton (PhD); ecology and behavior (MA, MS, PhD); genetics and molecular biology (MA, MS, PhD); morphology, systematics, and evolution (MA, MS, PhD). Terminal master's awarded for partial completion of doctoral program. *Degree requirements:* For master's, comprehensive exam, thesis (for some programs); for doctorate, comprehensive exam, thesis/dissertation. *Entrance requirements:* For master's, GRE General Test, GRE Subject Test, 2 semesters of calculus or statistics; 2 semesters of physics, organic chemistry; 3 semesters of biology; for doctorate, GRE General Test, GRE Subject Test, 2 semesters calculus or statistics, 2 semesters physics, organic chemistry, 3 semesters of biology. Additional exam requirements/recommendations for international students: required—TOEFL (minimum score 550 paper-based). Electronic applications accepted.

**The University of North Carolina at Chapel Hill,** School of Medicine and Graduate School, Biological and Biomedical Sciences Program, Curriculum in Genetics and Molecular Biology, Chapel Hill, NC 27599. Offers MS, PhD. *Faculty:* 82 full-time (26 women). *Students:* 65 full-time (41 women); includes 12 minority (5 Black or African American, non-Hispanic/Latino; 1 Asian, non-Hispanic/Latino; 4 Hispanic/Latino; 2 Two or more races, non-Hispanic/Latino), 6 international. Average age 26. In 2019, 7 doctorates awarded. *Degree requirements:* For doctorate, comprehensive exam, thesis/ dissertation. *Entrance requirements:* Additional exam requirements/recommendations for international students: required—TOEFL. *Application deadline:* For fall admission, 12/3 priority date for domestic and international students. Applications are processed on a rolling basis. Application fee: $77. Electronic applications accepted. *Financial support:* In 2019–20, 8 fellowships with full tuition reimbursements (averaging $32,000 per year), 15 research assistantships with full tuition reimbursements (averaging $32,000 per

year), 6 teaching assistantships with full tuition reimbursements (averaging $32,000 per year) were awarded; career-related internships or fieldwork, traineeships, health care benefits, and tuition waivers (full) also available. *Unit head:* Dr. Robert J. Duronio, Director, 919-962-7749, E-mail: duronio@med.unc.edu. *Application contact:* Jeffrey Steinbach, Assistant Director of Admission, 919-843-7129, E-mail: jsteinba@ email.unc.edu.
Website: http://gmb.unc.edu/

**University of North Dakota,** Graduate School, College of Arts and Sciences, Department of Biology, Grand Forks, ND 58202. Offers biology (MS); fisheries/wildlife (PhD); genetics (PhD); zoology (PhD). Terminal master's awarded for partial completion of doctoral program. *Degree requirements:* For master's, thesis, final exam; for doctorate, comprehensive exam, thesis/dissertation, final exam. *Entrance requirements:* For master's, GRE General Test, GRE Subject Test, minimum GPA of 3.0; for doctorate, GRE General Test, GRE Subject Test, minimum GPA of 3.5. Additional exam requirements/recommendations for international students: required—TOEFL (minimum score 550 paper-based; 79 iBT), IELTS (minimum score 6.5). Electronic applications accepted.

**University of North Texas Health Science Center at Fort Worth,** Graduate School of Biomedical Sciences, Fort Worth, TX 76107-2699. Offers biochemistry and cancer biology (MS, PhD); biotechnology (MS); cell biology, immunology and microbiology (MS, PhD); clinical research management (MS); forensic genetics (MS); genetics (MS, PhD); integrative physiology (MS, PhD); medical sciences (MS); pharmaceutical sciences and pharmacotherapy (MS, PhD); pharmacology and neuroscience (MS, PhD); structural anatomy and rehabilitation sciences (MS, PhD); DO/MS; DO/PhD. Terminal master's awarded for partial completion of doctoral program. *Degree requirements:* For master's, thesis; for doctorate, thesis/dissertation. *Entrance requirements:* For master's and doctorate, GRE General Test. Additional exam requirements/recommendations for international students: required—TOEFL. *Expenses:* Contact institution.

**University of Notre Dame,** The Graduate School, College of Science, Department of Biological Sciences, Notre Dame, IN 46556. Offers aquatic ecology, evolution and environmental biology (MS, PhD); cellular and molecular biology (MS, PhD); genetics (MS, PhD); physiology (MS, PhD); vector biology and parasitology (MS, PhD). Terminal master's awarded for partial completion of doctoral program. *Degree requirements:* For master's, comprehensive exam, thesis; for doctorate, comprehensive exam, thesis/ dissertation, candidacy exam. *Entrance requirements:* For master's and doctorate, GRE General Test. Additional exam requirements/recommendations for international students: required—TOEFL (minimum score 600 paper-based; 80 iBT). Electronic applications accepted.

**University of Oregon,** Graduate School, College of Arts and Sciences, Department of Biology, Eugene, OR 97403. Offers ecology and evolution (MA, MS, PhD); marine biology (MA, MS, PhD); molecular, cellular and genetic biology (PhD); neuroscience and development (PhD). Terminal master's awarded for partial completion of doctoral program. *Degree requirements:* For master's, thesis (for some programs); for doctorate, thesis/dissertation. *Entrance requirements:* For master's and doctorate, GRE General Test, minimum GPA of 3.2. Additional exam requirements/recommendations for international students: required—TOEFL.

**University of Pennsylvania,** Perelman School of Medicine, Biomedical Graduate Studies, Graduate Group in Cell and Molecular Biology, Philadelphia, PA 19104. Offers cancer biology (PhD); cell biology, physiology, and metabolism (PhD); developmental stem cell regenerative biology (PhD); gene therapy and vaccines (PhD); genetics and gene regulation (PhD); microbiology, virology, and parasitology (PhD); MD/PhD; VMD/ PhD. *Faculty:* 400 full-time (118 women). *Students:* 378 full-time (221 women); includes 134 minority (6 Black or African American, non-Hispanic/Latino; 56 Asian, non-Hispanic/ Latino; 58 Hispanic/Latino; 2 Native Hawaiian or other Pacific Islander, non-Hispanic/ Latino; 12 Two or more races, non-Hispanic/Latino), 52 international. 851 applicants, 14% accepted, 59 enrolled. In 2019, 43 doctorates awarded. *Unit head:* Dr. Daniel Kessler, Graduate Group Chair, 215-898-1478. *Application contact:* Meagan Schofer, Associate Director, 215-898-1478.
Website: http://www.med.upenn.edu/camb/

**University of Puerto Rico at Rio Piedras,** College of Natural Sciences, Department of Biology, San Juan, PR 00931-3300. Offers ecology/systematics (MS, PhD); evolution/ genetics (MS, PhD); molecular/cellular biology (MS, PhD); neuroscience (MS, PhD). *Program availability:* Part-time. *Degree requirements:* For master's, one foreign language, comprehensive exam, thesis; for doctorate, one foreign language, comprehensive exam, thesis/dissertation. *Entrance requirements:* For master's, GRE Subject Test, interview, minimum GPA of 3.0, letter of recommendation; for doctorate, GRE Subject Test, interview, master's degree, minimum GPA of 3.0, letter of recommendation.

**University of Rochester,** School of Arts and Sciences, Department of Biology, Rochester, NY 14627. Offers biology (MS); ecology, genetics, and genomics (PhD); molecular, cellular, and developmental biology evolution (PhD). *Program availability:* Part-time. *Faculty:* 24 full-time (8 women). *Students:* 47 full-time (22 women), 1 (woman) part-time; includes 6 minority (1 Black or African American, non-Hispanic/Latino; 2 Asian, non-Hispanic/Latino; 3 Hispanic/Latino), 20 international. Average age 27. 98 applicants, 34% accepted, 12 enrolled. In 2019, 8 master's, 8 doctorates awarded. Terminal master's awarded for partial completion of doctoral program. *Degree requirements:* For master's, comprehensive exam (for some programs), thesis (for some programs); for doctorate, thesis/dissertation, qualifying exam. *Entrance requirements:* For master's and doctorate, personal statement, transcripts, three letters of recommendation. Additional exam requirements/recommendations for international students: required—TOEFL (minimum score 600 paper-based; 100 iBT), IELTS. *Application deadline:* For fall admission, 12/1 for domestic and international students. Application fee: $60. Electronic applications accepted. *Financial support:* In 2019–20, 40 students received support, including 5 fellowships (averaging $30,080 per year), 20 research assistantships (averaging $28,000 per year), 15 teaching assistantships (averaging $28,000 per year); health care benefits and tuition waivers (full) also available. Financial award application deadline: 12/1. *Unit head:* Michael Welte, Professor and Chair, 585-276-3897, E-mail: michael.welte@rochester.edu. *Application contact:* Cynthia Landry, Administrative Assistant, 585-275-7991, E-mail: cynthia.landry@rochester.edu.
Website: https://www.sas.rochester.edu/bio/graduate/index.html

**University of Rochester,** School of Medicine and Dentistry, Graduate Programs in Medicine and Dentistry, Department of Biomedical Genetics, Rochester, NY 14627. Offers genetics, genomics and development (PhD). *Degree requirements:* For doctorate, thesis/dissertation, qualifying exam. *Entrance requirements:* For doctorate, GRE General Test.

**The University of Tennessee,** Graduate School, College of Arts and Sciences, Program in Life Sciences, Knoxville, TN 37996. Offers genome science and technology (MS, PhD); plant physiology and genetics (MS, PhD). *Degree requirements:* For doctorate, one foreign language, thesis/dissertation. *Entrance requirements:* For master's and doctorate, GRE General Test, minimum GPA of 2.7. Additional exam

requirements/recommendations for international students: required—TOEFL. Electronic applications accepted.

**The University of Texas Health Science Center at Houston,** MD Anderson UTHealth Graduate School, Houston, TX 77225-0036. Offers biochemistry and cell biology (PhD); biomedical sciences (MS); cancer biology (PhD); genetic counseling (MS); genetics and epigenetics (PhD); immunology (PhD); medical physics (MS, PhD); microbiology and infectious diseases (PhD); neuroscience (PhD); quantitative sciences (PhD); therapeutics and pharmacology (PhD); MD/PhD. Terminal master's awarded for partial completion of doctoral program. *Degree requirements:* For master's, thesis; for doctorate, thesis/dissertation. *Entrance requirements:* For master's and doctorate, GRE General Test. Additional exam requirements/recommendations for international students: required—TOEFL. Electronic applications accepted.

**The University of Texas MD Anderson Cancer Center,** School of Health Professions, Houston, TX 77030. Offers diagnostic genetics (MS). *Degree requirements:* For master's, successful defense of a written applied research project. *Entrance requirements:* For master's, bachelor's degree, minimum GPA of 3.0, clinical certification, three reference letters, personal interview. Additional exam requirements/ recommendations for international students: required—TOEFL.

**The University of Texas Southwestern Medical Center,** Southwestern Graduate School of Biomedical Sciences, Division of Basic Science, Program in Genetics and Development, Dallas, TX 75390. Offers PhD. *Degree requirements:* For doctorate, thesis/dissertation, qualifying exam. *Entrance requirements:* For doctorate, GRE General Test, minimum GPA of 3.0. Additional exam requirements/recommendations for international students: required—TOEFL. Electronic applications accepted.

**University of Washington,** Graduate School, School of Public Health, Institute for Public Health Genetics, Seattle, WA 98195. Offers genetic epidemiology (MS); public health genetics (MPH, PhD, Graduate Certificate). *Program availability:* Part-time, evening/weekend, online learning. *Students:* 18 full-time (14 women), 2 part-time (both women); includes 8 minority (6 Asian, non-Hispanic/Latino; 2 Hispanic/Latino), 1 international. Average age 28. 26 applicants, 62% accepted, 7 enrolled. In 2019, 2 master's, 2 doctorates awarded. Terminal master's awarded for partial completion of doctoral program. *Degree requirements:* For master's, thesis; for doctorate, comprehensive exam, thesis/dissertation, Preliminary exam. *Entrance requirements:* For master's and doctorate, TOEFL for international students, Statement of Purpose, CV or Resume, transcripts, minimum 3 recommendations, supplemental question (optional), Personal History Statement (optional); for Graduate Certificate, Certificate application, transcript, CV or Resume. Additional exam requirements/recommendations for international students: required—TOEFL (minimum score 500 paper-based; 80 iBT). Electronic applications accepted. *Financial support:* In 2019–20, 2 research assistantships (averaging $33,250 per year), 6 teaching assistantships with full and partial tuition reimbursements (averaging $33,250 per year) were awarded. Financial award application deadline: 1/3; financial award applicants required to submit FAFSA. *Unit head:* Dr. Bruce S. Weir, Director of the Institute for Public Health Genetics, 206-221-7947, E-mail: bsweir@uw.edu. *Application contact:* Annique Atwater, Program Manager, 206-616-9286, E-mail: phginfo@uw.edu. Website: http://iphg.biostat.washington.edu/

**University of Wisconsin–Madison,** Graduate School, College of Agricultural and Life Sciences and School of Medicine and Public Health, Department of Genetics, Madison, WI 53706-1380. Offers genetic counseling (MS); genetics (PhD). *Degree requirements:* For doctorate, thesis/dissertation.

**University of Wyoming,** Graduate Program in Molecular and Cellular Life Sciences, Laramie, WY 82071. Offers PhD. *Degree requirements:* For doctorate, thesis/dissertation, four eight-week laboratory rotations, comprehensive basic practical exam, two-part qualifying exam, seminars, symposium.

**Van Andel Institute Graduate School,** PhD Program, Grand Rapids, MI 49503. Offers cell and molecular genetics (PhD). *Degree requirements:* For doctorate, comprehensive exam, thesis/dissertation. *Entrance requirements:* For doctorate, GRE, personal statement, 3 letters of recommendation, official transcripts from all institutions attended, sample of scientific writing (research paper). Additional exam requirements/ recommendations for international students: required—TOEFL. Electronic applications accepted. *Expenses:* Contact institution.

**Virginia Polytechnic Institute and State University,** Graduate School, Intercollege, Blacksburg, VA 24061. Offers genetics, bioinformatics, and computational biology (PhD); information technology (MIT); macromolecular science and engineering (MS, PhD); translational biology, medicine, and health (PhD). *Students:* 203 full-time (86 women), 745 part-time (218 women); includes 278 minority (64 Black or African American, non-Hispanic/Latino; 119 Asian, non-Hispanic/Latino; 59 Hispanic/Latino; 1 Native Hawaiian or other Pacific Islander, non-Hispanic/Latino; 35 Two or more races, non-Hispanic/Latino), 93 international. Average age 33. 603 applicants, 78% accepted, 327 enrolled. In 2019, 138 master's, 20 doctorates awarded. *Degree requirements:* For master's, comprehensive exam (for some programs), thesis (for some programs); for doctorate, comprehensive exam (for some programs), thesis/dissertation (for some programs). *Entrance requirements:* For master's and doctorate, GRE/GMAT. Additional exam requirements/recommendations for international students: required—TOEFL (minimum score 90 iBT). *Application deadline:* For fall admission, 8/1 for domestic students, 4/1 for international students; for spring admission, 1/1 for domestic students, 9/1 for international students. Applications are processed on a rolling basis. Application fee: $75. Electronic applications accepted. *Expenses:* Tuition, state resident: full-time $13,700; part-time $761.25 per credit hour. Tuition, nonresident: full-time $27,614; part-time $1534 per credit hour. *Required fees:* $886.50 per term. Tuition and fees vary according to campus/location and program. *Financial support:* In 2019–20, 4 fellowships with full and partial tuition reimbursements (averaging $17,088 per year), 153 research assistantships with full tuition reimbursements (averaging $23,076 per year), 27 teaching assistantships with full tuition reimbursements (averaging $19,900 per year) were awarded; scholarships/grants also available. Financial award application

deadline: 3/1; financial award applicants required to submit FAFSA. *Unit head:* Dr. Karen P. DePauw, Vice President and Dean for Graduate Education, 540-231-7581, Fax: 540-231-1670, E-mail: kpdepauw@vt.edu. *Application contact:* Dr. Janice Austin, 540-231-6691, E-mail: grads@vt.edu.

**Washington State University,** College of Veterinary Medicine, School of Molecular Biosciences, Pullman, WA 99164-7520. Offers molecular biosciences (MS, PhD), including genetics (PhD). *Faculty:* 26 full-time (9 women), 15 part-time/adjunct (3 women). *Students:* 39 full-time (21 women), 1 (woman) part-time; includes 9 minority (1 Black or African American, non-Hispanic/Latino; 2 Asian, non-Hispanic/Latino; 6 Hispanic/Latino), 2 international. Average age 27. 60 applicants, 40% accepted, 13 enrolled. In 2019, 1 doctorate awarded. Terminal master's awarded for partial completion of doctoral program. *Degree requirements:* For master's, thesis (for some programs), oral defense; for doctorate, comprehensive exam, thesis/dissertation, oral defense. *Entrance requirements:* For master's and doctorate, GRE General Test for 2019-2020 entrance. Will be removed in the 2020-2021 recruiting year, minimum GPA of 3.0. Additional exam requirements/recommendations for international students: required—TOEFL (minimum score 600 paper-based; 100 iBT). *Application deadline:* For fall admission, 12/15 priority date for domestic and international students. Application fee: $75. Electronic applications accepted. *Expenses:* $6,997.58 In-State/Semester = $13,995.16 per academic year; $13,875.08 Out of State/Semester = $27,750.16 per academic year. Average 5 years to completion. *Financial support:* In 2019–20, 36 students received support, including 5 fellowships with full tuition reimbursements available (averaging $27,426 per year), 19 research assistantships with full tuition reimbursements available (averaging $29,700 per year), 14 teaching assistantships with full tuition reimbursements available (averaging $20,570 per year); scholarships/grants, traineeships, and health care benefits also available. Financial award application deadline: 4/15. *Unit head:* Dr. Michael D. Griswold, Director, 509-335-8724, Fax: 509-335-4159, E-mail: mgriswold@wsu.edu. *Application contact:* Tami Breske, Graduate Academic Coordinator, 509-335-4318, E-mail: tamara.breske@wsu.edu. Website: http://www.smb.wsu.edu

**Washington University in St. Louis,** The Graduate School, Division of Biology and Biomedical Sciences, St. Louis, MO 63130-4899. Offers biochemistry (PhD); computational and molecular biophysics (PhD); computational and systems biology (PhD); developmental, regenerative, and stem cell biology (PhD); evolution, ecology and population biology (PhD), including ecology, environmental biology, evolutionary biology, genetics; human and statistical genetics (PhD); immunology (PhD); molecular cell biology (PhD); molecular genetics and genomics (PhD); molecular microbiology and microbial pathogenesis (PhD); neurosciences (PhD); plant and microbial biosciences (PhD); MD/PhD. *Degree requirements:* For doctorate, thesis/dissertation. *Entrance requirements:* For doctorate, GRE General Test, GRE Subject Test. Additional exam requirements/recommendations for international students: required—TOEFL. Electronic applications accepted.

**Washington University in St. Louis,** School of Medicine, Program in Clinical Investigation, St. Louis, MO 63130-4899. Offers clinical investigation (MS), including bioethics, entrepreneurship, genetics/genomics, translational medicine. *Program availability:* Part-time, evening/weekend. *Degree requirements:* For master's, thesis. *Entrance requirements:* For master's, doctoral-level degree or in process of obtaining doctoral-level degree. Electronic applications accepted.

**Wesleyan University,** Graduate Studies, Department of Biology, Middletown, CT 06459. Offers cell and developmental biology (PhD); evolution and ecology (PhD); genetics and genomics (PhD), including bioinformatics; neurobiology and behavior (PhD). Terminal master's awarded for partial completion of doctoral program. *Degree requirements:* For doctorate, comprehensive exam, thesis/dissertation, public seminar. *Entrance requirements:* For doctorate, GRE, official transcripts, three recommendation letters, essay. Additional exam requirements/recommendations for international students: required—TOEFL. Electronic applications accepted.

**West Virginia University,** Davis College of Agriculture, Forestry and Consumer Sciences, Morgantown, WV 26506. Offers agricultural and extension education (MS, PhD); agriculture and resource management (MS); agriculture, natural resources and design (M Agr); agronomy (MS); animal and food science (PhD); animal physiology (MS); applied and environmental microbiology (MS); design and merchandising (MS); entomology (MS); forest resource science (PhD); forestry (MSF); genetics and developmental biology (MS, PhD); horticulture (MS); human and community development (PhD); landscape architecture (MLA); natural resource economics (PhD); nutritional and food science (MS); plant and soil science (PhD); plant pathology (MS); recreation, parks and tourism resources (MS); reproductive physiology (MS, PhD); wildlife and fisheries resources (PhD). *Accreditation:* ASLA. *Program availability:* Part-time. *Degree requirements:* For master's, thesis; for doctorate, thesis/dissertation. *Entrance requirements:* Additional exam requirements/recommendations for international students: required—TOEFL (minimum score 550 paper-based). Electronic applications accepted.

**Yale University,** Graduate School of Arts and Sciences, Department of Genetics, New Haven, CT 06520. Offers PhD, MD/PhD. *Degree requirements:* For doctorate, thesis/dissertation. *Entrance requirements:* For doctorate, GRE General Test, GRE Subject Test.

**Yale University,** Graduate School of Arts and Sciences, Department of Molecular, Cellular, and Developmental Biology, Program in Genetics, New Haven, CT 06520. Offers PhD. *Degree requirements:* For doctorate, thesis/dissertation. *Entrance requirements:* For doctorate, GRE General Test, GRE Subject Test.

**Yale University,** Yale School of Medicine and Graduate School of Arts and Sciences, Combined Program in Biological and Biomedical Sciences (BBS), Molecular Cell Biology, Genetics, and Development Track, New Haven, CT 06520. Offers PhD, MD/PhD. *Entrance requirements:* Additional exam requirements/recommendations for international students: required—TOEFL.

# Genomic Sciences

**Albert Einstein College of Medicine,** Graduate Programs in the Biomedical Sciences, Department of Genetics, Bronx, NY 10461. Offers computational genetics (PhD); molecular genetics (PhD); translational genetics (PhD); MD/PhD. *Degree requirements:* For doctorate, thesis/dissertation. *Entrance requirements:* For doctorate, GRE General Test. Additional exam requirements/recommendations for international students: required—TOEFL.

**Augusta University,** Program in Genomic Medicine, Augusta, GA 30912. Offers PhD. *Degree requirements:* For doctorate, comprehensive exam, thesis/dissertation. *Entrance requirements:* For doctorate, GRE General Test. Additional exam requirements/recommendations for international students: required—TOEFL (minimum score 550 paper-based; 79 iBT). Electronic applications accepted.

**Black Hills State University,** Graduate Studies, Program in Integrative Genomics, Spearfish, SD 57799. Offers MS. *Entrance requirements:* Additional exam

requirements/recommendations for international students: required—TOEFL (minimum score 500 paper-based; 60 iBT).

**Boston University,** School of Medicine, Graduate Medical Sciences, Program in Genetics and Genomics, Boston, MA 02215. Offers PhD. *Application deadline:* For fall admission, 1/15 for domestic students; for spring admission, 10/15 for domestic students. *Unit head:* Dr. Shoumita Dasgupta, Director, 617-414-1369, E-mail: gpgg@bu.edu. *Application contact:* GMS Admissions Office, 617-358-9518, Fax: 617-358-2913, E-mail: gpgg@bu.edu.
Website: https://www.bumc.bu.edu/gpgg/

**Case Western Reserve University,** School of Medicine and School of Graduate Studies, Graduate Programs in Medicine, Department of Genetics and Genome Sciences, Cleveland, OH 44106. Offers genetic counseling (MS); genetics and genome sciences (PhD); MD/PhD. Terminal master's awarded for partial completion of doctoral program. *Degree requirements:* For master's, thesis; for doctorate, comprehensive exam, thesis/dissertation. *Entrance requirements:* For master's, GRE General Test; for doctorate, GRE General Test, GRE Subject Test. Additional exam requirements/recommendations for international students: required—TOEFL.

**Concordia University,** School of Graduate Studies, Faculty of Arts and Science, Department of Biology, Montréal, QC H3G 1M8, Canada. Offers biology (M Sc, PhD); biotechnology and genomics (Diploma). *Degree requirements:* For master's, thesis; for doctorate, thesis/dissertation, pedagogical training. *Entrance requirements:* For master's, honors degree in biology; for doctorate, M Sc in life science.

**Cornell University,** Graduate School, Graduate Fields of Agriculture and Life Sciences, Field of Genetics, Genomics and Development, Ithaca, NY 14853. Offers developmental biology (PhD); genetics (PhD); genomics (PhD). *Degree requirements:* For doctorate, comprehensive exam, thesis/dissertation, 2 semesters of teaching experience. *Entrance requirements:* For doctorate, GRE General Test, GRE Subject Test in biology or biochemistry (recommended), 2 letters of recommendation. Additional exam requirements/recommendations for international students: required—TOEFL (minimum score 550 paper-based; 77 iBT). Electronic applications accepted.

**Duke University,** Graduate School, University Program in Genetics and Genomics, Durham, NC 27710. Offers PhD. *Degree requirements:* For doctorate, variable foreign language requirement, thesis/dissertation. *Entrance requirements:* For doctorate, GRE General Test. Additional exam requirements/recommendations for international students: required—TOEFL (minimum score 577 paper-based; 90 iBT) or IELTS (minimum score 7).

**Manchester University,** Master of Science in Pharmacogenomics Program, Fort Wayne, IN 46962-1225. Offers MS. *Program availability:* Part-time, 100% online, blended/hybrid learning. *Degree requirements:* For master's, minimum cumulative GPA of 3.0 at end of third semester; completion of all required didactic and clinical courses with grade of C or better. *Entrance requirements:* For master's, minimum of a bachelor's degree (chemistry, biology, medical technician, etc.); minimum GPA of 3.0 (preferred), science 2.7; official transcripts from all undergraduate and graduate schools attended; 2 letters of reference submitted on the applicant's behalf. Electronic applications accepted. *Expenses:* Contact institution.

**Massachusetts Institute of Technology,** School of Engineering, Harvard-MIT Health Sciences and Technology Program, Cambridge, MA 02139. Offers health sciences and technology (SM, PhD, Sc D), including bioastronautics (PhD, Sc D), bioinformatics and integrative genomics (PhD, Sc D), medical engineering and medical physics (PhD, Sc D), speech and hearing bioscience and technology (PhD, Sc D). Terminal master's awarded for partial completion of doctoral program. *Degree requirements:* For doctorate, comprehensive exam, thesis/dissertation. *Entrance requirements:* For doctorate, GRE General Test. Additional exam requirements/recommendations for international students: required—TOEFL, IELTS. Electronic applications accepted.

**North Carolina State University,** Graduate School, College of Agriculture and Life Sciences, Program in Functional Genomics, Raleigh, NC 27695. Offers MFG, MS, PhD. *Degree requirements:* For master's, thesis (for some programs); for doctorate, thesis/dissertation. *Entrance requirements:* For master's and doctorate, GRE, minimum B average. Additional exam requirements/recommendations for international students: required—TOEFL. Electronic applications accepted.

**North Dakota State University,** College of Graduate and Interdisciplinary Studies, Interdisciplinary Program in Genomics and Bioinformatics, Fargo, ND 58102. Offers MS, PhD. *Program availability:* Part-time. *Degree requirements:* For master's, thesis; for doctorate, comprehensive exam, thesis/dissertation. *Entrance requirements:* For master's and doctorate, minimum GPA of 3.0. Additional exam requirements/recommendations for international students: required—TOEFL. Electronic applications accepted. Tuition and fees vary according to program and reciprocity agreements.

**Oregon State University,** College of Agricultural Sciences, Program in Botany and Plant Pathology, Corvallis, OR 97331. Offers applied systematics (MS); ecology (MS, PhD); genetics (MS, PhD); genomics and computational biology (MS, PhD); molecular and cellular biology (MS, PhD); mycology (MS, PhD); plant pathology (MS, PhD); plant physiology (MS, PhD). *Entrance requirements:* For master's and doctorate, GRE.

**Oregon State University,** College of Science, Program in Microbiology, Corvallis, OR 97331. Offers environmental microbiology (MA, MS, PhD); food microbiology (MA, MS, PhD); genomics (MA, MS, PhD); immunology (MA, MS, PhD); microbial ecology (MA, MS, PhD); microbial evolution (MA, MS, PhD); parasitology (MA, MS, PhD); pathogenic microbiology (MA, MS, PhD); virology (MA). Terminal master's awarded for partial completion of doctoral program. *Entrance requirements:* For master's and doctorate, GRE. Additional exam requirements/recommendations for international students: required—TOEFL (minimum score 600 paper-based; 100 iBT).

**Penn State Hershey Medical Center,** College of Medicine, Graduate School Programs in the Biomedical Sciences, Huck Institutes of the Life Sciences, Intercollege Graduate Program in Bioinformatics and Genomics, Hershey, PA 17033-2360. Offers MS, PhD.

**Purdue University,** College of Pharmacy and Graduate School, Graduate Programs in Pharmacy and Pharmacal Sciences, Department of Medicinal Chemistry and Molecular Pharmacology, West Lafayette, IN 47907. Offers biophysical and computational chemistry (PhD); cancer research (PhD); immunology and infectious disease (PhD); medicinal biochemistry and molecular biology (PhD); medicinal chemistry and chemical biology (PhD); molecular pharmacology (PhD); neuropharmacology, neurodegeneration, and neurotoxicity (PhD); systems biology and functional genomics (PhD). *Faculty:* 20 full-time (5 women), 7 part-time/adjunct (2 women). *Students:* 80 full-time (40 women), 2 part-time (0 women); includes 9 minority (5 Asian, non-Hispanic/Latino; 2 Hispanic/Latino; 2 Two or more races, non-Hispanic/Latino), 44 international. Average age 26. 162 applicants, 20% accepted, 15 enrolled. In 2019, 11 doctorates awarded. *Degree requirements:* For doctorate, thesis/dissertation. *Entrance requirements:* For doctorate, GRE General Test; GRE Subject Test in biology, biochemistry, and chemistry (recommended), minimum undergraduate GPA of 3.0. Additional exam requirements/recommendations for international students: required—TOEFL (minimum score 550 paper-based; 77 iBT); recommended—TWE. *Application deadline:* For fall admission, 2/1 for domestic and international students. Applications are processed on a rolling basis. Application fee: $60 ($75 for international students).

Electronic applications accepted. *Financial support:* Fellowships, research assistantships, teaching assistantships, and traineeships available. Support available to part-time students. Financial award applicants required to submit FAFSA. *Unit head:* Zhong-Yin Zhang, Head, 765-494-1403, E-mail: zhang-yn@purdue.edu. *Application contact:* Delayne Graham, Graduate Contact, 765-494-1362, E-mail: dkgraham@purdue.edu.

**Thomas Jefferson University,** Jefferson College of Life Sciences, PhD Program in Genetics, Genomics and Cancer Biology, Philadelphia, PA 19107. Offers PhD. *Degree requirements:* For doctorate, comprehensive exam, thesis/dissertation. *Entrance requirements:* For doctorate, GRE General Test, minimum GPA of 3.2. Additional exam requirements/recommendations for international students: required—TOEFL, IELTS (minimum score 7). Electronic applications accepted.

**University at Buffalo, the State University of New York,** Graduate School, Jacobs School of Medicine and Biomedical Sciences, Graduate Programs in Medicine and Biomedical Sciences, Program in Genetics, Genomics and Bioinformatics, Buffalo, NY 14203. Offers MS, PhD, MD/PhD. *Faculty:* 59 full-time (16 women). *Students:* 12 full-time (6 women); includes 5 minority (all Asian, non-Hispanic/Latino). Average age 25. 9 applicants, 89% accepted, 3 enrolled. In 2019, 6 master's awarded. Terminal master's awarded for partial completion of doctoral program. *Degree requirements:* For master's, thesis or alternative; for doctorate, thesis/dissertation. *Entrance requirements:* For master's and doctorate, GRE. Additional exam requirements/recommendations for international students: required—TOEFL (minimum score 100 iBT); recommended—IELTS (minimum score 6.5). *Application deadline:* For fall admission, 3/1 for domestic and international students. Application fee: $85. Electronic applications accepted. *Expenses: Tuition, area resident:* Full-time $11,310; part-time $471 per credit hour. Tuition, state resident: full-time $11,310; part-time $471 per credit hour. Tuition, nonresident: full-time $23,100; part-time $963 per credit hour. *International tuition:* $23,100 full-time. *Required fees:* $2820. *Unit head:* Dr. Richard Gronostajski, Director, 716-829-3471, Fax: 716-849-6655, E-mail: rgron@buffalo.edu. *Application contact:* M. Sara Thomas, Program Administrator, 716-829-3890, E-mail: msthomas@buffalo.edu.
Website: http://medicine.buffalo.edu/education/ggb.html

**The University of Alabama at Birmingham,** Joint Health Sciences, Genetics, Genomics, and Bioinformatics Theme, Birmingham, AL 35294. Offers PhD. *Students:* Average age 27. 39 applicants, 18% accepted, 4 enrolled. In 2019, 4 doctorates awarded. *Degree requirements:* For doctorate, comprehensive exam, thesis/dissertation. *Entrance requirements:* For doctorate, personal statement, resume or curriculum vitae, letters of recommendation, research experience, interview. Additional exam requirements/recommendations for international students: required—TOEFL (minimum score 80 iBT), IELTS (minimum score 6.5). *Application deadline:* For fall admission, 12/31 for domestic and international students. Applications are processed on a rolling basis. Electronic applications accepted. *Financial support:* In 2019–20, fellowships with full tuition reimbursements (averaging $30,000 per year), research assistantships with full tuition reimbursements (averaging $31,000 per year) were awarded; health care benefits also available. *Unit head:* Dr. Kevin Dybvig, Theme Director, 205-934-9327, E-mail: dybvig@uab.edu. *Application contact:* Alyssa Zasada, Admissions Manager for Graduate Biomedical Sciences, 205-934-3857, E-mail: gradgbs@uab.edu.
Website: http://www.uab.edu/gbs/home/themes/ggb

**University of California, Riverside,** Graduate Division, Graduate Program in Genetics, Genomics, and Bioinformatics, Riverside, CA 92521-0102. Offers PhD. *Degree requirements:* For doctorate, thesis/dissertation, qualifying exams, teaching experience. *Entrance requirements:* For doctorate, GRE General Test, minimum GPA of 3.2. Additional exam requirements/recommendations for international students: required—TOEFL (minimum score 550 paper-based, 80 iBT) or IELTS. Electronic applications accepted.

**University of California, San Francisco,** School of Pharmacy and Graduate Division, Pharmaceutical Sciences and Pharmacogenomics Program, San Francisco, CA 94158-0775. Offers PhD. *Degree requirements:* For doctorate, comprehensive exam, thesis/dissertation. *Entrance requirements:* For doctorate, GRE General Test, bachelor's degree, 3 letters of recommendation, personal statement. Additional exam requirements/recommendations for international students: required—TOEFL. Electronic applications accepted.

**University of Chicago,** Division of the Biological Sciences, Committee on Genetics, Genomics and Systems Biology, Chicago, IL 60637. Offers PhD. *Degree requirements:* For doctorate, thesis/dissertation, ethics class, 2 teaching assistantships, preliminary exam. *Entrance requirements:* For doctorate, GRE General Test, transcripts, statement of purpose, 3 letters of recommendation. Additional exam requirements/recommendations for international students: required—TOEFL (minimum score 600 paper-based; 104 iBT), IELTS (minimum score 7). Electronic applications accepted.

**University of Cincinnati,** Graduate School, College of Medicine, Graduate Programs in Biomedical Sciences, Department of Environmental Health, Programs in Environmental Genetics and Molecular Toxicology, Cincinnati, OH 45221. Offers MS, PhD. *Degree requirements:* For doctorate, thesis/dissertation. *Entrance requirements:* For master's, GRE, minimum GPA of 3.0, 3 letters of recommendation. Additional exam requirements/recommendations for international students: required—TOEFL (minimum score 520 paper-based).

**University of Colorado Denver,** School of Medicine, Program in Human Medical Genetics and Genomics, Aurora, CO 80206. Offers PhD. *Degree requirements:* For doctorate, comprehensive exam, thesis/dissertation, at least 30 semester hours in course work (rotations and research courses taken prior to the completion of the comprehensive examination) and 30 semester hours of thesis/didactic credits prior to defending. *Entrance requirements:* For doctorate, GRE General Test (minimum combined score of 1205), minimum GPA of 3.0, 4 letters of recommendation; prerequisite courses in biology, chemistry (general and organic), physics, genetics, calculus, and statistics (recommended). Additional exam requirements/recommendations for international students: required—TOEFL (minimum score 570 paper-based; 80 iBT). Electronic applications accepted. Tuition and fees vary according to course load, program and reciprocity agreements.

**University of Connecticut,** Graduate School, College of Liberal Arts and Sciences, Department of Molecular and Cell Biology, Storrs, CT 06269. Offers applied genomics (PSM); cell and developmental biology (MS, PhD); genetics and genomics (MS, PhD); microbial systems analysis (PSM); microbiology (MS, PhD); structural biology, biochemistry and biophysics (MS, PhD). Terminal master's awarded for partial completion of doctoral program. *Degree requirements:* For master's, comprehensive exam; for doctorate, thesis/dissertation. *Entrance requirements:* For master's and doctorate, GRE General Test, GRE Subject Test. Additional exam requirements/recommendations for international students: required—TOEFL (minimum score 550 paper-based). Electronic applications accepted.

**University of Georgia,** College of Agricultural and Environmental Sciences, Institute of Plant Breeding, Genetics and Genomics, Athens, GA 30602. Offers MS, PhD.

**University of Maryland, Baltimore,** Graduate School, Graduate Program in Life Sciences, Program in Molecular Medicine, Baltimore, MD 21201. Offers applied pharmacology and toxicology (PhD); cancer biology (PhD); genome biology (PhD); molecular and cellular physiology (PhD); MD/PhD. *Degree requirements:* For doctorate, comprehensive exam, thesis/dissertation. *Entrance requirements:* For doctorate, GRE, minimum GPA of 3.0, curriculum vitae, essay, 3 letters of recommendation. Additional exam requirements/recommendations for international students: required—TOEFL (minimum score 80 iBT); recommended—IELTS (minimum score 7). Electronic applications accepted.

**University of Maryland, Baltimore,** School of Medicine, Department of Epidemiology and Public Health, Baltimore, MD 21201. Offers biostatistics (MS); clinical research (MS); epidemiology and preventive medicine (MPH, MS, PhD); gerontology (PhD); human genetics and genomic medicine (MS, PhD); molecular epidemiology (MS, PhD); toxicology (MS, PhD); JD/MS; MD/PhD; MS/PhD. *Accreditation:* CEPH. *Program availability:* Part-time. *Students:* 75 full-time (51 women), 32 part-time (28 women); includes 29 minority (11 Black or African American, non-Hispanic/Latino; 11 Asian, non-Hispanic/Latino; 5 Hispanic/Latino; 2 Two or more races, non-Hispanic/Latino), 24 international. Average age 31. In 2019, 27 master's, 9 doctorates awarded. *Degree requirements:* For doctorate, comprehensive exam, thesis/dissertation. *Entrance requirements:* For master's and doctorate, GRE General Test. Additional exam requirements/recommendations for international students: required—TOEFL (minimum score 550 paper-based; 80 iBT); recommended—IELTS (minimum score 7). *Application deadline:* For fall admission, 1/15 for domestic and international students. Application fee: $75. Electronic applications accepted. *Expenses:* Contact institution. *Financial support:* In 2019–20, research assistantships with partial tuition reimbursements (averaging $26,000 per year) were awarded; fellowships, Federal Work-Study, scholarships/grants, and unspecified assistantships also available. Financial award application deadline: 3/1; financial award applicants required to submit FAFSA. *Unit head:* Dr. Laura Hungerford, Program Director, 410-706-8492, Fax: 410-706-4225. *Application contact:* Jessica Kelley, Program Coordinator, 410-706-8492, Fax: 410-706-4225, E-mail: jkelley@som.umaryland.edu. Website: http://lifesciences.umaryland.edu/epidemiology/

**University of Maryland, College Park,** Academic Affairs, College of Computer, Mathematical and Natural Sciences, Department of Biology, PhD Program in Biological Sciences, College Park, MD 20742. Offers behavior, ecology, evolution, and systematics (PhD); computational biology, bioinformatics, and genomics (PhD); molecular and cellular biology (PhD); physiological systems (PhD). *Degree requirements:* For doctorate, comprehensive exam, thesis/dissertation, thesis work presentation in seminar. *Entrance requirements:* For doctorate, GRE General Test; GRE Subject Test in biology (recommended), academic transcripts, statement of purpose/research interests, 3 letters of recommendation. Additional exam requirements/recommendations for international students: required—TOEFL. Electronic applications accepted.

**University of Pennsylvania,** Perelman School of Medicine, Biomedical Graduate Studies, Graduate Group in Genomics and Computational Biology, Philadelphia, PA 19104. Offers PhD, MD/PhD, VMD/PhD. *Faculty:* 83 full-time (25 women). *Students:* 55 full-time (22 women); includes 22 minority (3 Black or African American, non-Hispanic/Latino; 18 Asian, non-Hispanic/Latino; 1 Two or more races, non-Hispanic/Latino), 12 international. 198 applicants, 11% accepted, 9 enrolled. In 2019, 6 doctorates awarded. *Unit head:* Dr. Ben Voight, Chairperson, 215-746-7015. *Application contact:* Maureen Kirsch, Graduate Coordinator, 215-746-2807. Website: http://www.med.upenn.edu/gcb/

**University of Rochester,** School of Medicine and Dentistry, Graduate Programs in Medicine and Dentistry, Department of Biomedical Genetics, Rochester, NY 14627. Offers genetics, genomics and development (PhD). *Degree requirements:* For doctorate, thesis/dissertation, qualifying exam. *Entrance requirements:* For doctorate, GRE General Test.

**University of Southern California,** Keck School of Medicine and Graduate School, Graduate Programs in Medicine, Programs in Biomedical and Biological Sciences (PIBBS), Program in Cancer Biology and Genomics, Los Angeles, CA 90089. Offers PhD. *Faculty:* 43 full-time (10 women). *Students:* 26 full-time (17 women); includes 10 minority (5 Asian, non-Hispanic/Latino; 2 Hispanic/Latino; 2 Native Hawaiian or other Pacific Islander, non-Hispanic/Latino; 1 Two or more races, non-Hispanic/Latino), 9 international. Average age 28. 7 applicants, 100% accepted, 7 enrolled. In 2019, 4 doctorates awarded. *Degree requirements:* For doctorate, comprehensive exam, thesis/dissertation. *Entrance requirements:* For doctorate, GRE, minimum GPA of 3.0. Additional exam requirements/recommendations for international students: required—TOEFL (minimum score 600 paper-based; 100 iBT), IELTS (minimum score 7), PTE. *Application deadline:* For fall admission, 12/1 priority date for domestic and international students. Application fee: $90. Electronic applications accepted. *Financial support:* In 2019–20, 24 students received support, including 6 fellowships with full tuition reimbursements available (averaging $35,000 per year), 20 research assistantships with full tuition reimbursements available (averaging $35,000 per year); institutionally sponsored loans, scholarships/grants, traineeships, health care benefits, and unspecified assistantships also available. Financial award application deadline: 4/15; financial award applicants required to submit CSS PROFILE or FAFSA. *Unit head:* Dr.

Josh Neman-Ebrahim, Director, 323-442-1475, Fax: 323-442-1199, E-mail: yebrahim@usc.edu. *Application contact:* Karina Recinos, Student Services Advisor, 323-442-1609, Fax: 323-442-1199, E-mail: karina.recinos@med.usc.edu. Website: https://keck.usc.edu/pibbs/phd-programs/cancer-biology-and-genomics

**The University of Tennessee,** Graduate School, College of Arts and Sciences, Program in Life Sciences, Knoxville, TN 37996. Offers genome science and technology (MS, PhD); plant physiology and genetics (MS, PhD). *Degree requirements:* For doctorate, one foreign language, thesis/dissertation. *Entrance requirements:* For master's and doctorate, GRE General Test, minimum GPA of 2.7. Additional exam requirements/recommendations for international students: required—TOEFL. Electronic applications accepted.

**The University of Tennessee–Oak Ridge National Laboratory,** Graduate Program in Genome Science and Technology, Knoxville, TN 37966. Offers life sciences (MS, PhD). *Degree requirements:* For master's, thesis; for doctorate, comprehensive exam, thesis/dissertation. *Entrance requirements:* For master's and doctorate, GRE General Test. Additional exam requirements/recommendations for international students: required—TOEFL. Electronic applications accepted.

**The University of Texas Health Science Center at Houston,** School of Public Health, Houston, TX 77030. Offers behavioral science (PhD); biostatistics (MPH, MS, PhD); environmental health (MPH); epidemiology (MPH, MS, PhD); general public health (Certificate); genomics and bioinformatics (Certificate); health disparities (Certificate); health promotion/health education (MPH, Dr PH); healthcare management (Certificate); management, policy and community health (MPH, Dr PH, PhD); maternal and child health (Certificate); public health informatics (Certificate); DDS/MPH; JD/MPH; MBA/MPH; MD/MPH; MGPS/MPH; MP Aff/MPH; MS/MPH; MSN/MPH; MSW/MPH; PhD/MPH. *Accreditation:* CAHME; CEPH. *Program availability:* Part-time. *Degree requirements:* For master's, thesis (for some programs); for doctorate, comprehensive exam, thesis/dissertation. *Entrance requirements:* For master's and doctorate, GRE General Test. Additional exam requirements/recommendations for international students: required—TOEFL (minimum score 600 paper-based, 100 iBT) or IELTS (7.5). Electronic applications accepted. *Expenses:* Contact institution.

**The University of Toledo,** College of Graduate Studies, College of Medicine and Life Sciences, Interdepartmental Programs, Toledo, OH 43606-3390. Offers bioinformatics and proteomics/genomics (MSBS); biomarkers and bioinformatics (Certificate); biomarkers and diagnostics (PSM); human donation sciences (MSBS); medical sciences (MSBS); MD/MSBS. *Degree requirements:* For master's, thesis or alternative. *Entrance requirements:* For master's, GRE, minimum undergraduate GPA of 3.0, three letters of recommendation, statement of purpose, transcripts from all prior institutions attended, resume; for Certificate, minimum undergraduate GPA of 3.0, three letters of recommendation, statement of purpose, transcripts from all prior institutions attended, resume. Additional exam requirements/recommendations for international students: required—TOEFL (minimum score 550 paper-based; 80 iBT). Electronic applications accepted.

**University of Washington,** Graduate School, School of Medicine, Graduate Programs in Medicine, Department of Genome Sciences, Seattle, WA 98195. Offers PhD. *Degree requirements:* For doctorate, thesis/dissertation, general exam. *Entrance requirements:* For doctorate, GRE General Test, minimum GPA of 3.0. Additional exam requirements/recommendations for international students: required—TOEFL. Electronic applications accepted.

**Wake Forest University,** School of Medicine and Graduate School of Arts and Sciences, Graduate Programs in Medicine, Molecular Genetics and Genomics Program, Winston-Salem, NC 27109. Offers PhD, MD/PhD. *Degree requirements:* For doctorate, thesis/dissertation. *Entrance requirements:* For doctorate, GRE General Test. Additional exam requirements/recommendations for international students: required—TOEFL. Electronic applications accepted.

**Washington University in St. Louis,** School of Medicine, Program in Clinical Investigation, St. Louis, MO 63130-4899. Offers clinical investigation (MS), including bioethics, entrepreneurship, genetics/genomics, translational medicine. *Program availability:* Part-time, evening/weekend. *Degree requirements:* For master's, thesis. *Entrance requirements:* For master's, doctoral-level degree or in process of obtaining doctoral-level degree. Electronic applications accepted.

**Wesleyan University,** Graduate Studies, Department of Biology, Middletown, CT 06459. Offers cell and developmental biology (PhD); evolution and ecology (PhD); genetics and genomics (PhD), including bioinformatics; neurobiology and behavior (PhD). Terminal master's awarded for partial completion of doctoral program. *Degree requirements:* For doctorate, comprehensive exam, thesis/dissertation, public seminar. *Entrance requirements:* For doctorate, GRE, official transcripts, three recommendation letters, essay. Additional exam requirements/recommendations for international students: required—TOEFL. Electronic applications accepted.

**Yale University,** Yale School of Medicine and Graduate School of Arts and Sciences, Combined Program in Biological and Biomedical Sciences (BBS), Computational Biology and Bioinformatics Track, New Haven, CT 06520. Offers PhD, MD/PhD. *Entrance requirements:* Additional exam requirements/recommendations for international students: required—TOEFL.

# Human Genetics

**Baylor College of Medicine,** Graduate School of Biomedical Sciences, Department of Molecular and Human Genetics, Houston, TX 77030-3498. Offers PhD, MD/PhD. *Degree requirements:* For doctorate, thesis/dissertation, public defense. *Entrance requirements:* For doctorate, GRE General Test, GRE Subject Test (strongly recommended), minimum GPA of 3.0. Additional exam requirements/recommendations for international students: required—TOEFL. Electronic applications accepted.

**Baylor College of Medicine,** Graduate School of Biomedical Sciences, Interdepartmental Program in Cell and Molecular Biology, Houston, TX 77030-3498. Offers biochemistry (PhD); cell and molecular biology (PhD); genetics (PhD); human genetics (PhD); immunology (PhD); microbiology (PhD); virology (PhD); MD/PhD. *Degree requirements:* For doctorate, thesis/dissertation, public defense. *Entrance requirements:* For doctorate, GRE General Test, GRE Subject Test (strongly recommended), minimum GPA of 3.0. Additional exam requirements/recommendations for international students: required—TOEFL. Electronic applications accepted.

**Case Western Reserve University,** School of Medicine and School of Graduate Studies, Graduate Programs in Medicine, Department of Genetics and Genome

Sciences, Cleveland, OH 44106. Offers genetic counseling (MS); genetics and genome sciences (PhD); MD/PhD. Terminal master's awarded for partial completion of doctoral program. *Degree requirements:* For master's, thesis; for doctorate, comprehensive exam, thesis/dissertation. *Entrance requirements:* For master's, GRE General Test; for doctorate, GRE General Test, GRE Subject Test. Additional exam requirements/recommendations for international students: required—TOEFL.

**Emory University,** School of Medicine, Programs in Allied Health Professions, Genetic Counseling Training Program, Atlanta, GA 30322. Offers MM Sc. *Degree requirements:* For master's, thesis, capstone project. *Entrance requirements:* For master's, GRE General Test, minimum GPA of 3.0; prerequisites: genetics, statistics, psychology, and biochemistry. Additional exam requirements/recommendations for international students: required—TOEFL.

**Louisiana State University Health Sciences Center,** School of Graduate Studies in New Orleans, Department of Human Genetics, New Orleans, LA 70112-2223. Offers PhD, MD/PhD. Terminal master's awarded for partial completion of doctoral program. *Degree requirements:* For doctorate, comprehensive exam, thesis/dissertation.

*Entrance requirements:* For doctorate, GRE General Test. Additional exam requirements/recommendations for international students: recommended—TOEFL, IELTS.

**McGill University,** Faculty of Graduate and Postdoctoral Studies, Faculty of Medicine, Department of Human Genetics, Montréal, QC H3A 2T5, Canada. Offers genetic counseling (M Sc); human genetics (M Sc, PhD).

**Memorial University of Newfoundland,** Faculty of Medicine and School of Graduate Studies, Graduate Programs in Medicine, Division of Human Genetics, St. John's, NL A1C 5S7, Canada. Offers M Sc, PhD, MD/PhD. *Program availability:* Part-time. *Degree requirements:* For master's, thesis; for doctorate, comprehensive exam, thesis/dissertation, oral defense of thesis. *Entrance requirements:* For master's, MD or B Sc; for doctorate, MD or M Sc. Additional exam requirements/recommendations for international students: required—TOEFL.

**Sarah Lawrence College,** Graduate Studies, Joan H. Marks Graduate Program in Human Genetics, Bronxville, NY 10708-5999. Offers MS. *Program availability:* Part-time. *Degree requirements:* For master's, thesis, fieldwork. *Entrance requirements:* For master's, previous course work in biology, chemistry, developmental biology, genetics, probability and statistics. Additional exam requirements/recommendations for international students: required—TOEFL (minimum score 600 paper-based). Electronic applications accepted. *Expenses:* Contact institution.

**Thomas Jefferson University,** Jefferson College of Life Sciences, MS Program in Human Genetics and Genetic Counseling, Philadelphia, PA 19107. Offers MS. *Entrance requirements:* For master's, BA, personal statement, official transcripts, recommendation letters. Additional exam requirements/recommendations for international students: required—TOEFL, IELTS (minimum score 7). Electronic applications accepted.

**Tulane University,** School of Medicine, Graduate Programs in Biomedical Sciences, Program in Human Genetics, New Orleans, LA 70118-5669. Offers MS. *Degree requirements:* For master's, thesis. *Entrance requirements:* For master's, GRE, MCAT. Additional exam requirements/recommendations for international students: required—TOEFL. Electronic applications accepted. *Expenses: Tuition:* Full-time $57,004; part-time $3167 per credit hour. *Required fees:* $2086; $44.50 per credit hour. $80 per term. Tuition and fees vary according to course load, degree level and program.

**University of California, Los Angeles,** David Geffen School of Medicine and Graduate Division, Graduate Programs in Medicine, Department of Human Genetics, Los Angeles, CA 90095. Offers MS, PhD. *Degree requirements:* For master's, thesis; for doctorate, thesis/dissertation, written and oral qualifying examination; 2 quarters of teaching experience. *Entrance requirements:* For master's and doctorate, GRE General Test; GRE Subject Test (recommended), bachelor's degree; minimum undergraduate GPA of 3.0 (or its equivalent if letter grade system not used). Additional exam requirements/recommendations for international students: required—TOEFL. Electronic applications accepted.

**University of California, Los Angeles,** Graduate Division, College of Letters and Science and David Geffen School of Medicine, UCLA ACCESS to Programs in the Molecular, Cellular and Integrative Life Sciences, Los Angeles, CA 90095. Offers biochemistry and molecular biology (PhD); biological chemistry (PhD); cellular and molecular pathology (PhD); human genetics (PhD); microbiology, immunology, and molecular genetics (PhD); molecular biology (PhD); molecular toxicology (PhD); molecular, cellular and integrative physiology (PhD); neurobiology (PhD); oral biology (PhD); physiology (PhD). *Degree requirements:* For doctorate, thesis/dissertation, oral and written qualifying exams. *Entrance requirements:* For doctorate, GRE General Test, bachelor's degree; minimum undergraduate GPA of 3.0 (or its equivalent if letter grade system not used). Additional exam requirements/recommendations for international students: required—TOEFL. Electronic applications accepted.

**University of Chicago,** Division of the Biological Sciences, Department of Human Genetics, Chicago, IL 60637. Offers PhD. *Degree requirements:* For doctorate, comprehensive exam, thesis/dissertation, ethics class, 2 teaching assistantships. *Entrance requirements:* For doctorate, GRE General Test, transcripts, statement of purpose, 3 letters of recommendation. Additional exam requirements/recommendations for international students: required—TOEFL (minimum score 600 paper-based; 104 iBT), IELTS (minimum score 7). Electronic applications accepted.

**University of Manitoba,** Max Rady College of Medicine and Faculty of Graduate Studies, Graduate Programs in Medicine, Department of Biochemistry and Medical Genetics, Winnipeg, MB R3T 2N2, Canada. Offers biochemistry and medical genetics (M Sc, PhD); genetic counseling (M Sc). Terminal master's awarded for partial completion of doctoral program. *Degree requirements:* For master's, thesis; for doctorate, thesis/dissertation.

**University of Maryland, Baltimore,** School of Medicine, Department of Epidemiology and Public Health, Baltimore, MD 21201. Offers biostatistics (MS); clinical research (MS); epidemiology and preventive medicine (MPH, MS, PhD); gerontology (PhD); human genetics and genomic medicine (MS, PhD); molecular epidemiology (MS, PhD); toxicology (MS, PhD); JD/MS; MD/PhD; MS/PhD. *Accreditation:* CEPH. *Program availability:* Part-time. *Students:* 75 full-time (51 women), 32 part-time (28 women); includes 29 minority (11 Black or African American, non-Hispanic/Latino; 11 Asian, non-Hispanic/Latino; 5 Hispanic/Latino; 2 Two or more races, non-Hispanic/Latino), 24 international. Average age 31. In 2019, 27 master's, 9 doctorates awarded. *Degree requirements:* For doctorate, comprehensive exam, thesis/dissertation. *Entrance requirements:* For master's and doctorate, GRE General Test. Additional exam requirements/recommendations for international students: required—TOEFL (minimum score 550 paper-based; 80 iBT); recommended—IELTS (minimum score 7). *Application deadline:* For fall admission, 1/15 for domestic and international students. Application fee: $75. Electronic applications accepted. *Expenses:* Contact institution. *Financial support:* In 2019–20, research assistantships with partial tuition reimbursements (averaging $26,000 per year) were awarded; fellowships, Federal Work-Study, scholarships/grants, and unspecified assistantships also available. Financial award application deadline: 3/1; financial award applicants required to submit FAFSA. *Unit head:* Dr. Laura Hungerford, Program Director, 410-706-8492, Fax: 410-706-4225. *Application contact:* Jessica Kelley, Program Coordinator, 410-706-8492, Fax: 410-706-4225, E-mail: jkelley@som.umaryland.edu.
Website: http://lifesciences.umaryland.edu/epidemiology/

**University of Michigan,** Rackham Graduate School, Program in Biomedical Sciences (PIBS), Department of Human Genetics, Ann Arbor, MI 48109. Offers genetic counseling (MS); human genetics (MS, PhD). Terminal master's awarded for partial completion of doctoral program. *Degree requirements:* For master's, thesis optional, research project (for MS in genetic counseling); for doctorate, thesis/dissertation, oral preliminary exam, oral defense of dissertation. *Entrance requirements:* For master's, GRE General Test, bachelor's degree; 3 letters of recommendation; advocacy experience (for the MS in genetic counseling); for doctorate, bachelor's degree; 3 letters of recommendation. Additional exam requirements/recommendations for international students: required—TOEFL (minimum score 84 iBT). Electronic applications accepted.

**University of Pennsylvania,** Perelman School of Medicine, Center for Clinical Epidemiology and Biostatistics, Philadelphia, PA 19104. Offers clinical epidemiology (MSCE), including bioethics, clinical trials, human genetics, patient centered outcome research, pharmacoepidemiology. *Program availability:* Part-time. *Faculty:* 102 full-time (49 women), 39 part-time/adjunct (25 women). *Students:* 92 full-time (59 women), 2 part-time (1 woman); includes 42 minority (15 Black or African American, non-Hispanic/Latino; 21 Asian, non-Hispanic/Latino; 5 Hispanic/Latino; 1 Two or more races, non-Hispanic/Latino). Average age 35. 40 applicants, 90% accepted, 31 enrolled. In 2019, 27 master's awarded. *Degree requirements:* For master's, comprehensive exam, thesis. *Entrance requirements:* For master's, GRE or MCAT, advanced degree in medicine or another health field, clinical experience (MD, DO,PharmD, DMD, DDS, VMD). Additional exam requirements/recommendations for international students: required—TOEFL. *Application deadline:* For fall admission, 12/1 priority date for domestic students, 12/1 for international students. Electronic applications accepted. *Expenses:* Contact institution. *Financial support:* In 2019–20, 50 students received support, including 50 fellowships with tuition reimbursements available (averaging $57,000 per year); research assistantships, teaching assistantships, and tuition waivers also available. Financial award application deadline: 12/1. *Unit head:* Dr. Harold Feldman, Director, 215-573-0901. *Application contact:* Jennifer Kuklinski, Program Coordinator, 215-573-2382, E-mail: jkuklins@pennmedicine.upenn.edu.
Website: http://www.cceb.med.upenn.edu/

**University of Pittsburgh,** Graduate School of Public Health, Department of Human Genetics, Pittsburgh, PA 15261. Offers genetic counseling (MS); human genetics (MS, PhD); public health genetics (MPH, Certificate); MD/PhD; MS/MPH. *Program availability:* Part-time. *Faculty:* 17 full-time (7 women), 91 part-time/adjunct (64 women). *Students:* 63 full-time (52 women), 15 part-time (13 women); includes 13 minority (2 Black or African American, non-Hispanic/Latino; 5 Asian, non-Hispanic/Latino; 3 Hispanic/Latino; 1 Native Hawaiian or other Pacific Islander, non-Hispanic/Latino; 2 Two or more races, non-Hispanic/Latino), 19 international. Average age 26. 251 applicants, 31% accepted, 32 enrolled. In 2019, 26 master's, 7 doctorates awarded. *Degree requirements:* For master's, comprehensive exam, thesis; for doctorate, comprehensive exam, thesis/dissertation, Qualifying Exam (Required). *Entrance requirements:* For master's, GRE (Domestic and International)/Will accept MCAT in Lieu of GRE; TOEFL or IELTS (International ONLY); for doctorate, GRE (Domestic and International)/Will accept MCAT in Lieu of GRE; TOEFL or IELTS (International ONLY). Additional exam requirements/recommendations for international students: required—TOEFL (minimum score 550 paper-based; 80 iBT), IELTS (minimum score 6.5), GRE, WES Evaluation for foreign education. *Application deadline:* For fall admission, 7/15 priority date for domestic students, 4/1 priority date for international students; for spring admission, 10/15 priority date for domestic students, 8/1 priority date for international students. Applications are processed on a rolling basis. Application fee: $135. Electronic applications accepted. *Expenses:* $13,379 per term full-time in-state, $23,407 per term full-time out-of-state; $1122 per credit part-time in-state, $1916 per credit part-time out-of-state; $500 per term for full-time dissertation research; $475 per term full-time fees; $295 per term part-time fees. *Financial support:* In 2019–20, 8 students received support. Career-related internships or fieldwork, scholarships/grants, and unspecified assistantships available. Financial award application deadline: 4/15; financial award applicants required to submit CSS PROFILE or FAFSA. *Unit head:* Jennifer Heinemann Palaski, MBA, Department Administrator, Human Genetics and Biostatistics, 412-648-1560, Fax: 412-624-3020, E-mail: JDH150@pitt.edu. *Application contact:* Noel C. Harrie, Recruitment and Academic Affairs Administrator, 412-624-3066, Fax: 412-624-3020, E-mail: nce1@pitt.edu.
Website: http://www.publichealth.pitt.edu/hugen

**University of Utah,** School of Medicine and Graduate School, Graduate Programs in Medicine, Department of Human Genetics, Salt Lake City, UT 84112-1107. Offers MS, PhD. Terminal master's awarded for partial completion of doctoral program. *Degree requirements:* For master's, comprehensive exam, thesis optional; for doctorate, comprehensive exam, thesis/dissertation. Electronic applications accepted. *Expenses:* Tuition, state resident: full-time $7085; part-time $272.51 per credit hour. Tuition, nonresident: full-time $24,937; part-time $959.12 per credit hour. *Required fees:* $880.52; $880.52 per semester. Tuition and fees vary according to degree level, program and student level.

**Vanderbilt University,** Program in Human Genetics, Nashville, TN 37240-1001. Offers PhD. *Faculty:* 32 full-time (10 women). *Students:* 19 full-time (14 women); includes 3 minority (2 Asian, non-Hispanic/Latino; 1 Two or more races, non-Hispanic/Latino), 5 international. Average age 26. In 2019, 3 doctorates awarded. *Degree requirements:* For doctorate, comprehensive exam, thesis/dissertation. *Entrance requirements:* For doctorate, GRE General Test. Additional exam requirements/recommendations for international students: required—TOEFL (minimum score 570 paper-based; 88 iBT). *Application deadline:* For fall admission, 1/15 for domestic and international students. Electronic applications accepted. *Expenses: Tuition:* Full-time $51,018; part-time $2087 per hour. *Required fees:* $542. Tuition and fees vary according to program. *Financial support:* Fellowships, research assistantships, Federal Work-Study, institutionally sponsored loans, traineeships, and health care benefits available. Financial award application deadline: 1/15; financial award applicants required to submit CSS PROFILE or FAFSA. *Unit head:* Dr. David Samuels, Director, 615-343-7870, Fax: 615-322-1453, E-mail: david.c.samuels@vanderbilt.edu. *Application contact:* Todd Edwards, Director of Graduate Studies, 615-322-3652, E-mail: todd.l.edwards@vanderbilt.edu.
Website: https://medschool.vanderbilt.edu/igp/human-genetics

**Virginia Commonwealth University,** Medical College of Virginia-Professional Programs, School of Medicine, Graduate Programs in Medicine, Department of Human and Molecular Genetics, Richmond, VA 23284-9005. Offers genetic counseling (MS); human genetics (PhD); MD/PhD. *Degree requirements:* For master's, thesis; for doctorate, thesis/dissertation, comprehensive oral and written exams. *Entrance requirements:* For master's, GRE; for doctorate, GRE General Test. Additional exam requirements/recommendations for international students: required—TOEFL (minimum score 600 paper-based; 100 iBT). Electronic applications accepted.

**Washington University in St. Louis,** The Graduate School, Division of Biology and Biomedical Sciences, Program in Human and Statistical Genetics, St. Louis, MO 63130-4899. Offers PhD. *Degree requirements:* For doctorate, thesis/dissertation. *Entrance requirements:* For doctorate, GRE General Test, GRE Subject Test. Additional exam requirements/recommendations for international students: required—TOEFL. Electronic applications accepted.

# Molecular Genetics

**Albert Einstein College of Medicine,** Graduate Programs in the Biomedical Sciences, Department of Genetics, Bronx, NY 10461. Offers computational genetics (PhD); molecular genetics (PhD); translational genetics (PhD); MD/PhD. *Degree requirements:* For doctorate, thesis/dissertation. *Entrance requirements:* For doctorate, GRE General Test. Additional exam requirements/recommendations for international students: required—TOEFL.

**Duke University,** Graduate School, Department of Molecular Genetics and Microbiology, Durham, NC 27710. Offers PhD. *Degree requirements:* For doctorate, thesis/dissertation. *Entrance requirements:* For doctorate, GRE General Test, GRE Subject Test in biology, chemistry, or biochemistry, cell and molecular biology (recommended). Additional exam requirements/recommendations for international students: required—TOEFL (minimum score 577 paper-based; 90 iBT) or IELTS (minimum score 7). Electronic applications accepted.

**Emory University,** Laney Graduate School, Division of Biological and Biomedical Sciences, Program in Microbiology and Molecular Genetics, Atlanta, GA 30322-1100. Offers PhD. *Degree requirements:* For doctorate, comprehensive exam, thesis/dissertation. *Entrance requirements:* For doctorate, GRE General Test, minimum GPA of 3.0 in science course work (recommended). Additional exam requirements/recommendations for international students: required—TOEFL. Electronic applications accepted.

**Georgia State University,** College of Arts and Sciences, Department of Biology, Program in Molecular Genetics and Biochemistry, Atlanta, GA 30302-3083. Offers bioinformatics (MS); molecular genetics and biochemistry (MS, PhD). *Program availability:* Part-time. Terminal master's awarded for partial completion of doctoral program. *Entrance requirements:* For master's and doctorate, GRE. *Application deadline:* Applications are processed on a rolling basis. Application fee: $50. Electronic applications accepted. *Expenses: Tuition, area resident:* Full-time $7164; part-time $398 per credit hour. Tuition, state resident: full-time $7164; part-time $398 per credit hour. Tuition, nonresident: full-time $22,662; part-time $1259 per credit hour. *International tuition:* $22,662 full-time. *Required fees:* $2128; $312 per credit hour. Tuition and fees vary according to course load and program. *Financial support:* Fellowships and research assistantships available. Financial award application deadline: 12/3. *Unit head:* Dr. Geert de Vries, Chair, 404-413-5658, Fax: 404-413-3518, E-mail: devries@gsu.edu. *Application contact:* Dr. Geert de Vries, Chair, 404-413-5658, Fax: 404-413-3518, E-mail: devries@gsu.edu.
Website: http://biology.gsu.edu/

**Harvard University,** Graduate School of Arts and Sciences, Division of Medical Sciences, Boston, MA 02115. Offers biological chemistry and molecular pharmacology (PhD); cell biology (PhD); genetics (PhD); microbiology and molecular genetics (PhD); pathology (PhD), including experimental pathology. *Degree requirements:* For doctorate, thesis/dissertation. *Entrance requirements:* For doctorate, GRE General Test, GRE Subject Test. Additional exam requirements/recommendations for international students: required—TOEFL.

**Illinois State University,** Graduate School, College of Arts and Sciences, School of Biological Sciences, Normal, IL 61790. Offers animal behavior (MS); bacteriology (MS); biochemistry (MS); biological sciences (MS); biology (PhD); biophysics (MS); biotechnology (MS); botany (MS, PhD); cell biology (MS); conservation biology (MS); developmental biology (MS); ecology (MS, PhD); entomology (MS); evolutionary biology (MS); genetics (MS, PhD); immunology (MS); microbiology (MS, PhD); molecular biology (MS); molecular genetics (MS); neurobiology (MS); neuroscience (MS); parasitology (MS); physiology (MS, PhD); plant biology (MS); plant molecular biology (MS); plant sciences (MS); structural biology (MS); zoology (MS, PhD). *Program availability:* Part-time. *Faculty:* 26 full-time (6 women), 7 part-time/adjunct (2 women). *Students:* 51 full-time (33 women), 15 part-time (8 women). Average age 27. 71 applicants, 28% accepted, 9 enrolled. In 2019, 14 master's, 3 doctorates awarded. *Degree requirements:* For master's, thesis or alternative; for doctorate, variable foreign language requirement, thesis/dissertation, 2 terms of residency. *Entrance requirements:* For master's, GRE General Test, minimum GPA of 2.6 in last 60 hours of course work; for doctorate, GRE General Test. *Application deadline:* Applications are processed on a rolling basis. Application fee: $50. *Expenses: Tuition, area resident:* Full-time $7956; part-time $9767 per year. Tuition, nonresident: full-time $9233; part-time $17,592 per year. *Required fees:* $1797. *Financial support:* In 2019–20, 20 research assistantships, 41 teaching assistantships were awarded; Federal Work-Study, tuition waivers (full), and unspecified assistantships also available. Financial award application deadline: 4/1. *Unit head:* Dr. Craig Gatto, School Director, 309-438-3087, E-mail: cgatto@IllinoisState.edu. *Application contact:* Dr. Ben Sadd, Assistant Chair for Graduate Studies, 309-438-2651, E-mail: bmsadd@IllinoisState.edu.
Website: http://www.bio.ilstu.edu/

**Indiana University-Purdue University Indianapolis,** Indiana University School of Medicine, Department of Medical and Molecular Genetics, Indianapolis, IN 46202. Offers genetic counseling (MS); medical and molecular genetics (MS, PhD); MD/MS; MD/PhD. *Program availability:* Part-time. Terminal master's awarded for partial completion of doctoral program. *Degree requirements:* For master's, thesis optional; for doctorate, thesis/dissertation, research ethics. *Entrance requirements:* For master's and doctorate, GRE General Test, minimum GPA of 3.0. Additional exam requirements/recommendations for international students: required—TOEFL (minimum score 79 iBT), IELTS (minimum score 6.5). *Expenses:* Contact institution.

**Iowa State University of Science and Technology,** Program in Animal Breeding and Genetics, Ames, IA 50011. Offers animal breeding and genetics (MS); immunogenetics (PhD); molecular genetics (PhD); quantitative genetics (PhD). *Entrance requirements:* For master's and doctorate, GRE. Additional exam requirements/recommendations for international students: required—TOEFL (minimum score 550 paper-based; 80 iBT), IELTS (minimum score 6.5). Electronic applications accepted.

**Michigan State University,** College of Human Medicine and The Graduate School, Graduate Programs in Human Medicine, East Lansing, MI 48824. Offers biochemistry and molecular biology (MS, PhD); epidemiology (MS, PhD); microbiology (MS); microbiology and molecular genetics (PhD); pharmacology and toxicology (MS, PhD); physiology (MS, PhD); public health (MPH). *Entrance requirements:* Additional exam requirements/recommendations for international students: required—TOEFL.

**Michigan State University,** College of Osteopathic Medicine and The Graduate School, Graduate Studies in Osteopathic Medicine, East Lansing, MI 48824. Offers biochemistry and molecular biology (MS, PhD); microbiology (MS); microbiology and molecular genetics (PhD); pharmacology and toxicology (MS, PhD), including integrative pharmacology (MS), pharmacology and toxicology, pharmacology and toxicology-environmental toxicology (PhD); physiology (MS, PhD).

**New York University,** Graduate School of Arts and Science, Department of Biology, New York, NY 10012-1019. Offers biology (PhD); biomedical journalism (MS); cancer and molecular biology (PhD); computational biology (PhD); computers in biological research (MS); developmental genetics (PhD); general biology (MS); immunology and microbiology (PhD); molecular genetics (PhD); neurobiology (PhD); oral biology (MS); plant biology (PhD); recombinant DNA technology (MS); MS/MBA. *Program availability:* Part-time. Terminal master's awarded for partial completion of doctoral program. *Degree requirements:* For master's, thesis or alternative, qualifying paper; for doctorate, comprehensive exam, thesis/dissertation. *Entrance requirements:* For master's and doctorate, GRE General Test. Additional exam requirements/recommendations for international students: required—TOEFL, IELTS.

**Northern Michigan University,** Office of Graduate Education and Research, College of Health Sciences and Professional Studies, School of Clinical Sciences, Marquette, MI 49855-5301. Offers clinical molecular genetics (MS). *Accreditation:* NAACLS. *Program availability:* Part-time. *Degree requirements:* For master's, thesis or project to be presented as a seminar at the conclusion of the program. *Entrance requirements:* For master's, minimum undergraduate GPA of 3.0; bachelor's degree in clinical laboratory science or biology; laboratory experience; statement of intent that includes lab skills and experiences along with reason for pursuing this degree; 3 letters of recommendation (instructors or professional references). Additional exam requirements/recommendations for international students: required—TOEFL (minimum score 500 paper-based; 61 iBT), IELTS (minimum score 6). *Application deadline:* For fall admission, 7/1 for domestic students; for winter admission, 12/1 for domestic students; for summer admission, 4/1 for domestic students. Applications are processed on a rolling basis. Application fee: $50. Electronic applications accepted. *Financial support:* Application deadline: 3/1; applicants required to submit FAFSA. *Unit head:* Dr. Paul Mann, Associate Dean/Director, 906-227-2338, E-mail: pmann@nmu.edu. *Application contact:* Dr. Matthew Jennings, Assistant Professor, 906-227-1661, E-mail: majennin@nmu.edu.
Website: http://www.nmu.edu/clinicalsciences/

**The Ohio State University,** Graduate School, College of Arts and Sciences, Division of Natural and Mathematical Sciences, Department of Molecular Genetics, Columbus, OH 43210. Offers cell and developmental biology (MS, PhD); genetics (MS, PhD); molecular biology (MS, PhD). *Entrance requirements:* For doctorate, GRE General Test, GRE Subject Test in biology or chemistry (recommended). Additional exam requirements/recommendations for international students: required—TOEFL (minimum score 550 paper-based; 79 iBT), Michigan English Language Assessment Battery (minimum score 82); recommended—IELTS (minimum score 7). Electronic applications accepted.

**Oklahoma State University,** College of Arts and Sciences, Department of Microbiology and Molecular Genetics, Stillwater, OK 74078. Offers MS, PhD. *Faculty:* 13 full-time (4 women). *Students:* 12 full-time (8 women), 32 part-time (18 women); includes 14 minority (2 Black or African American, non-Hispanic/Latino; 1 American Indian or Alaska Native, non-Hispanic/Latino; 1 Asian, non-Hispanic/Latino; 4 Hispanic/Latino; 6 Two or more races, non-Hispanic/Latino), 13 international. Average age 26. 49 applicants, 37% accepted, 15 enrolled. In 2019, 5 master's, 4 doctorates awarded. *Entrance requirements:* For master's and doctorate, GRE General Test. Additional exam requirements/recommendations for international students: required—TOEFL (minimum score 550 paper-based; 79 iBT). *Application deadline:* For fall admission, 3/1 priority date for international students; for spring admission, 8/1 priority date for international students. Applications are processed on a rolling basis. Application fee: $50 ($75 for international students). Electronic applications accepted. *Expenses: Tuition, area resident:* Full-time $4148.10; part-time $2765.40 per credit hour. Tuition, state resident: full-time $4148.10; part-time $2765.40 per credit hour. Tuition, nonresident: full-time $15,775; part-time $10,516.80 per credit hour. *International tuition:* $15,775.20 full-time. *Required fees:* $2196.90; $122.05 per credit hour. Tuition and fees vary according to course load, campus/location and program. *Financial support:* In 2019–20, 14 research assistantships (averaging $2,163 per year), 17 teaching assistantships (averaging $2,341 per year) were awarded; career-related internships or fieldwork, Federal Work-Study, scholarships/grants, health care benefits, tuition waivers (partial), and unspecified assistantships also available. Support available to part-time students. Financial award application deadline: 3/1; financial award applicants required to submit FAFSA. *Unit head:* Dr. Tyrrell Conway, Professor and Department Head, 405-744-6243, Fax: 405-744-6790, E-mail: tconway@okstate.edu. *Application contact:* Dr. Sheryl Tucker, Dean, 405-744-6368, Fax: 405-744-0355, E-mail: gradi@okstate.edu.
Website: http://microbiology.okstate.edu

**Penn State Hershey Medical Center,** College of Medicine, Graduate School Programs in the Biomedical Sciences, Graduate Program in Biomedical Sciences, Hershey, PA 17033. Offers biochemistry and molecular genetics (MS, PhD); biomedical sciences (MS, PhD); cellular and integrative physiology (MS, PhD); translational therapeutics (MS, PhD); virology and immunology (MS, PhD); MD/PhD; PhD/MBA. Terminal master's awarded for partial completion of doctoral program. *Degree requirements:* For master's, thesis; for doctorate, comprehensive exam, thesis/dissertation, candidacy exam. *Entrance requirements:* For doctorate, GRE General Test. Additional exam requirements/recommendations for international students: required—TOEFL (minimum score 550 paper-based; 81 iBT). Electronic applications accepted.

**Rutgers University - Newark,** Graduate School of Biomedical Sciences, Department of Microbiology and Molecular Genetics, Newark, NJ 07107. Offers PhD. *Degree requirements:* For doctorate, thesis/dissertation, qualifying exam. *Entrance requirements:* For doctorate, GRE General Test. Additional exam requirements/recommendations for international students: required—TOEFL. Electronic applications accepted.

**Rutgers University - New Brunswick,** Graduate School-New Brunswick, Programs in the Molecular Biosciences, Piscataway, NJ 08854-8097. Offers biochemistry (PhD); cell and developmental biology (MS, PhD); microbiology and molecular genetics (MS, PhD), including applied microbiology, clinical microbiology, computational molecular biology (PhD), immunology, microbial biochemistry, molecular genetics, virology.

**Rutgers University - New Brunswick,** Graduate School of Biomedical Sciences, Program in Microbiology and Molecular Genetics, Piscataway, NJ 08854-5635. Offers MS, PhD, MD/PhD. Terminal master's awarded for partial completion of doctoral program. *Degree requirements:* For master's, thesis, qualifying exam; for doctorate, thesis/dissertation, qualifying exam. *Entrance requirements:* For master's and doctorate, GRE General Test. Additional exam requirements/recommendations for international students: required—TOEFL. Electronic applications accepted.

**Stony Brook University, State University of New York,** Stony Brook Medicine, Renaissance School of Medicine and Graduate School, Graduate Programs in Medicine, Department of Microbiology and Immunology, Stony Brook, NY 11794-5222.

Offers PhD. *Faculty:* 15 full-time (3 women), 2 part-time/adjunct (1 woman). *Students:* 27 full-time (14 women); includes 8 minority (3 Asian, non-Hispanic/Latino; 4 Hispanic/Latino; 1 Two or more races, non-Hispanic/Latino), 5 international. Average age 26. 50 applicants, 26% accepted, 9 enrolled. In 2019, 3 doctorates awarded. *Degree requirements:* For doctorate, comprehensive exam, thesis/dissertation. *Entrance requirements:* For doctorate, GRE General Test, GRE Subject Test, undergraduate training in biochemistry, genetics, and cell biology; recommendations; personal statement. Additional exam requirements/recommendations for international students: required—TOEFL (minimum score 550 paper-based; 90 iBT). *Application deadline:* For fall admission, 1/15 for domestic students; for spring admission, 10/1 for domestic students. Application fee: $100. *Expenses:* Contact institution. *Financial support:* In 2019–20, 5 fellowships, 13 research assistantships were awarded; teaching assistantships and Federal Work-Study also available. Financial award application deadline: 3/15. *Unit head:* Dr. David G. Thanassi, Chair, 631-632-4549, Fax: 631-632-9797, E-mail: david.thanassi@stonybrook.edu. *Application contact:* Jennifer Jokinen, Graduate Program Coordinator, 631-632-8812, Fax: 631-632-9797, E-mail: jennifer.jokinen@stonybrook.edu.
Website: https://renaissance.stonybrookmedicine.edu/mi

**University of Calgary,** Cumming School of Medicine and Faculty of Graduate Studies, Program in Medical Science, Calgary, AB T2N 1N4, Canada. Offers cancer biology (M Sc, PhD); critical care medicine (M Sc, PhD); joint injury and arthritis (M Sc, PhD); molecular and medical genetics (M Sc, PhD); mountain medicine and high altitude physiology (M Sc, PhD); pathologists' assistant (M Sc, PhD). *Degree requirements:* For master's, thesis; for doctorate, thesis/dissertation, candidacy exam. *Entrance requirements:* For master's, minimum undergraduate GPA of 3.2; for doctorate, minimum graduate GPA of 3.2. Additional exam requirements/recommendations for international students: required—TOEFL (minimum score 600 paper-based). Electronic applications accepted.

**University of California, Irvine,** School of Medicine and School of Biological Sciences, Department of Microbiology and Molecular Genetics, Irvine, CA 92697. Offers biological sciences (MS, PhD); MD/PhD. *Students:* 14 full-time (6 women); includes 6 minority (5 Asian, non-Hispanic/Latino; 1 Hispanic/Latino), 1 international. Average age 28. In 2019, 7 doctorates awarded. *Entrance requirements:* For doctorate, GRE General Test, GRE Subject Test, minimum GPA of 3.0. Additional exam requirements/recommendations for international students: required—TOEFL (minimum score 550 paper-based). *Application deadline:* For fall admission, 12/15 priority date for domestic students, 12/15 for international students. Application fee: $120 ($140 for international students). Electronic applications accepted. *Financial support:* Fellowships, research assistantships with full tuition reimbursements, teaching assistantships, institutionally sponsored loans, traineeships, health care benefits, and unspecified assistantships available. Financial award applicants required to submit FAFSA. *Unit head:* Rozanne M. Sandri-Goldin, Chair, 949-824-7570, Fax: 949-824-8598, E-mail: rmsandri@uci.edu. *Application contact:* Janet Horwitz, Graduate Student Coordinator, 949-824-7669, E-mail: horwitz@uci.edu.
Website: http://www.microbiology.uci.edu/graduate-students.asp

**University of California, Los Angeles,** David Geffen School of Medicine and Graduate Division, Graduate Programs in Medicine, Department of Microbiology, Immunology and Molecular Genetics, Los Angeles, CA 90095. Offers MS, PhD. *Degree requirements:* For master's, thesis; for doctorate, thesis/dissertation, oral and written qualifying exams; 2 quarters of teaching experience. *Entrance requirements:* For master's and doctorate, GRE General Test, bachelor's degree; minimum undergraduate GPA of 3.0 (or its equivalent if letter grade system not used). Additional exam requirements/recommendations for international students: required—TOEFL. Electronic applications accepted.

**University of Cincinnati,** Graduate School, College of Medicine, Graduate Programs in Biomedical Sciences, Molecular Genetics, Biochemistry and Microbiology Graduate Program, Cincinnati, OH 45221. Offers MS, PhD. *Faculty:* 30 full-time (5 women). *Students:* 26 full-time (11 women), 4 part-time (2 women); includes 3 minority (1 Black or African American, non-Hispanic/Latino; 1 Asian, non-Hispanic/Latino; 1 Hispanic/Latino), 2 international. Average age 27. 40 applicants, 30% accepted, 6 enrolled. In 2019, 2 master's, 4 doctorates awarded. Terminal master's awarded for partial completion of doctoral program. *Degree requirements:* For master's, thesis or alternative; for doctorate, thesis/dissertation, qualifying exam. *Entrance requirements:* For master's and doctorate, GRE highly recommended but not required. Additional exam requirements/recommendations for international students: required—TOEFL (minimum score 600 paper-based; 100 iBT). *Application deadline:* For fall admission, 12/15 priority date for domestic and international students. Applications are processed on a rolling basis. Application fee: $40. Electronic applications accepted. *Financial support:* In 2019–20, 6 research assistantships with full tuition reimbursements (averaging $28,000 per year) were awarded; health care benefits also available. Financial award application deadline: 5/1. *Unit head:* Dr. Michael Lieberman, Professor and Chair, 513-558-5645, E-mail: michael.lieberman@uc.edu. *Application contact:* Dr. William Miller, Graduate Program Director, 513-558-0866, Fax: 513-558-8474, E-mail: william.miller@uc.edu.
Website: http://med.uc.edu/molgen-graduate

**University of Colorado Denver,** School of Medicine, Biochemistry Program, Aurora, CO 80045. Offers biochemistry (PhD); biochemistry and molecular genetics (PhD). *Degree requirements:* For doctorate, comprehensive exam, thesis/dissertation, 30 credit hours each of coursework and thesis research. *Entrance requirements:* For doctorate, GRE, minimum of three letters of recommendation from qualified referees. Additional exam requirements/recommendations for international students: required—TOEFL (minimum score 550 paper-based; 80 iBT). Electronic applications accepted. Tuition and fees vary according to course load, program and reciprocity agreements.

**University of Florida,** College of Medicine, Department of Molecular Genetics and Microbiology, Gainesville, FL 32610-0266. Offers MS. Terminal master's awarded for partial completion of doctoral program. *Degree requirements:* For master's, thesis. *Entrance requirements:* For master's, GRE General Test, minimum GPA of 3.0. Additional exam requirements/recommendations for international students: required—TOEFL, IELTS. Electronic applications accepted.

**University of Guelph,** Office of Graduate and Postdoctoral Studies, College of Biological Science, Department of Molecular and Cellular Biology, Guelph, ON N1G 2W1, Canada. Offers biochemistry (M Sc, PhD); biophysics (M Sc, PhD); botany (M Sc, PhD); microbiology (M Sc, PhD); molecular biology and genetics (M Sc, PhD). *Degree requirements:* For master's, thesis, research proposal; for doctorate, comprehensive exam, thesis/dissertation, research proposal. *Entrance requirements:* For master's, minimum B-average during previous 2 years of coursework; for doctorate, minimum A-average. Additional exam requirements/recommendations for international students: required—TOEFL (minimum score 550 paper-based), IELTS (minimum score 6.5). Electronic applications accepted.

**University of Illinois at Chicago,** College of Medicine, Graduate Programs in Medicine, Department of Biochemistry and Molecular Genetics, Chicago, IL 60607-7128. Offers PhD, MD/PhD. Terminal master's awarded for partial completion of doctoral program. *Degree requirements:* For doctorate, thesis/dissertation. *Entrance requirements:* For doctorate, GRE General Test. Additional exam requirements/recommendations for international students: required—TOEFL. Electronic applications accepted.

**University of Louisville,** School of Medicine, Department of Biochemistry and Molecular Genetics, Louisville, KY 40292-0001. Offers MS, PhD, MD/PhD. *Program availability:* Part-time. *Faculty:* 12 full-time (3 women). *Students:* 21 full-time (11 women), 4 part-time (3 women); includes 6 minority (2 Black or African American, non-Hispanic/Latino; 3 Asian, non-Hispanic/Latino; 1 Hispanic/Latino), 4 international. Average age 30. 28 applicants, 21% accepted, 5 enrolled. In 2019, 5 master's, 6 doctorates awarded. Terminal master's awarded for partial completion of doctoral program. *Degree requirements:* For master's, thesis (for some programs); for doctorate, comprehensive exam, thesis/dissertation. *Entrance requirements:* For doctorate, minimum GPA of 3.0. Additional exam requirements/recommendations for international students: required—TOEFL, IELTS. *Application deadline:* For fall admission, 12/15 priority date for domestic and international students. Applications are processed on a rolling basis. Application fee: $60. Electronic applications accepted. *Expenses: Tuition, area resident:* Full-time $13,000; part-time $723 per credit hour. Tuition, state resident: full-time $13,000; part-time $723 per credit hour. Tuition, nonresident: full-time $27,114; part-time $1507 per credit hour. *International tuition:* $27,114 full-time. *Required fees:* $196. Tuition and fees vary according to program and reciprocity agreements. *Financial support:* In 2019–20, 20 students received support, including 5 fellowships with full tuition reimbursements available (averaging $26,000 per year); health care benefits also available. Financial award application deadline: 1/15. *Unit head:* Dr. Ronald Gregg, Professor and Chair, 502-852-5217, E-mail: ronald.gregg@louisville.edu. *Application contact:* Dr. Brian Clem, Associate Professor, 502-852-8427, E-mail: bfclem01@louisville.edu.

**The University of Manchester,** School of Biological Sciences, Manchester, United Kingdom. Offers adaptive organismal biology (M Phil, PhD); animal biology (M Phil, PhD); biochemistry (M Phil, PhD); bioinformatics (M Phil, PhD); biomolecular sciences (M Phil, PhD); biotechnology (M Phil, PhD); cell biology (M Phil, PhD); cell matrix research (M Phil, PhD); channels and transporters (M Phil, PhD); developmental biology (M Phil, PhD); environmental biology (M Phil, PhD); evolutionary biology (M Phil, PhD); gene expression (M Phil, PhD); genetics (M Phil, PhD); history of science, technology and medicine (M Phil, PhD); immunology (M Phil, PhD); integrative neurobiology and behavior (M Phil, PhD); membrane trafficking (M Phil, PhD); microbiology (M Phil, PhD); molecular and cellular neuroscience (M Phil, PhD); molecular biology (M Phil, PhD); molecular cancer studies (M Phil, PhD); neuroscience (M Phil, PhD); ophthalmology (M Phil, PhD); optometry (M Phil, PhD); organelle function (M Phil, PhD); pharmacology (M Phil, PhD); physiology (M Phil, PhD); plant sciences (M Phil, PhD); stem cell research (M Phil, PhD); structural biology (M Phil, PhD); systems neuroscience (M Phil, PhD); toxicology (M Phil, PhD).

**University of Maryland, College Park,** Academic Affairs, College of Computer, Mathematical and Natural Sciences, Department of Cell Biology and Molecular Genetics, Program in Cell Biology and Molecular Genetics, College Park, MD 20742. Offers MS, PhD. *Degree requirements:* For master's, thesis; for doctorate, thesis/dissertation, exams.

**University of Nebraska Medical Center,** Interdisciplinary Graduate Program in Biomedical Sciences, Department of Genetics, Cell Biology and Anatomy, Omaha, NE 68198. Offers genetics, cell biology and anatomy (PhD); medical anatomy (MS); molecular genetics and cell biology (MS). Terminal master's awarded for partial completion of doctoral program. *Degree requirements:* For master's, comprehensive exam, thesis (for some programs); for doctorate, comprehensive exam, thesis/dissertation. *Entrance requirements:* For master's, GRE General Test (MCAT or DAT acceptable for MS in medical anatomy); for doctorate, GRE General Test. Additional exam requirements/recommendations for international students: required—TOEFL (minimum score 550 paper-based; 80 iBT). Electronic applications accepted. *Expenses:* Contact institution.

**University of Rhode Island,** Graduate School, College of the Environment and Life Sciences, Department of Cell and Molecular Biology, Kingston, RI 02881. Offers biochemistry (MS, PhD); clinical laboratory sciences (MS), including biotechnology, clinical laboratory science, cytopathology; microbiology (MS, PhD); molecular genetics (MS, PhD). *Program availability:* Part-time. *Faculty:* 20 full-time (9 women). *Students:* 1 (woman) part-time. In 2019, 16 master's awarded. *Entrance requirements:* Additional exam requirements/recommendations for international students: required—TOEFL. *Application deadline:* For fall admission, 1/15 for domestic and international students. Application fee: $65. Electronic applications accepted. *Expenses: Tuition, area resident:* Full-time $13,734; part-time $763 per credit. Tuition, state resident: full-time $13,734; part-time $763 per credit. Tuition, nonresident: full-time $26,512; part-time $1473 per credit. *International tuition:* $26,512 full-time. *Required fees:* $1780; $52 per credit. $35 per term. One-time fee: $165. *Financial support:* In 2019–20, 11 teaching assistantships with tuition reimbursements (averaging $10,985 per year) were awarded; traineeships also available. Financial award application deadline: 1/15; financial award applicants required to submit FAFSA. *Unit head:* Dr. Joel Chandlee, Chair, E-mail: joelchandlee@uri.edu. *Application contact:* Dr. Steven Gregory, Graduate Program Director, 401-874-5947, E-mail: stgregory@uri.edu.
Website: https://web.uri.edu/cmb/

**University of Toronto,** Faculty of Medicine, Department of Molecular Genetics, Toronto, ON M5S 1A1, Canada. Offers genetic counseling (M Sc); molecular genetics (M Sc, PhD). *Degree requirements:* For master's, thesis; for doctorate, thesis/dissertation. *Entrance requirements:* For master's, B Sc or equivalent; for doctorate, M Sc or equivalent, minimum B+ average. Additional exam requirements/recommendations for international students: required—TOEFL, IELTS (minimum score 7), Michigan English Language Assessment Battery (minimum score 85), or COPE (minimum score 4). Electronic applications accepted.

**University of Virginia,** School of Medicine, Department of Biochemistry and Molecular Genetics, Charlottesville, VA 22903. Offers biochemistry (PhD); MD/PhD. *Degree requirements:* For doctorate, thesis/dissertation, written research proposal and defense. *Entrance requirements:* For doctorate, GRE General Test, 3 letters of recommendation. Additional exam requirements/recommendations for international students: recommended—TOEFL (minimum score 630 paper-based; 90 iBT). Electronic applications accepted.

**Van Andel Institute Graduate School,** PhD Program, Grand Rapids, MI 49503. Offers cell and molecular genetics (PhD). *Degree requirements:* For doctorate, comprehensive exam, thesis/dissertation. *Entrance requirements:* For doctorate, GRE, personal statement, 3 letters of recommendation, official transcripts from all institutions attended, sample of scientific writing (research paper). Additional exam requirements/recommendations for international students: required—TOEFL. Electronic applications accepted. *Expenses:* Contact institution.

**Virginia Commonwealth University,** Medical College of Virginia-Professional Programs, School of Medicine, Graduate Programs in Medicine, Department of Physiology and Biophysics, Richmond, VA 23284-9005. Offers molecular biology and

genetics (MS); physical therapy (PhD); physiology (MS, PhD); MD/PhD. Terminal master's awarded for partial completion of doctoral program. *Degree requirements:* For master's, thesis; for doctorate, thesis/dissertation, comprehensive oral and written exams. *Entrance requirements:* For master's, GRE General Test, MCAT, or DAT; for doctorate, GRE, MCAT or DAT. Additional exam requirements/recommendations for international students: required—TOEFL (minimum score 600 paper-based; 100 iBT). Electronic applications accepted.

**Wake Forest University,** School of Medicine and Graduate School of Arts and Sciences, Graduate Programs in Medicine, Molecular Genetics and Genomics Program, Winston-Salem, NC 27109. Offers PhD, MD/PhD. *Degree requirements:* For doctorate, thesis/dissertation. *Entrance requirements:* For doctorate, GRE General Test. Additional exam requirements/recommendations for international students: required—TOEFL. Electronic applications accepted.

**Washington University in St. Louis,** The Graduate School, Division of Biology and Biomedical Sciences, Program in Molecular Genetics and Genomics, St. Louis, MO 63130-4899. Offers PhD. *Degree requirements:* For doctorate, thesis/dissertation. *Entrance requirements:* For doctorate, GRE General Test, GRE Subject Test. Additional exam requirements/recommendations for international students: required—TOEFL. Electronic applications accepted.

# Reproductive Biology

**Eastern Virginia Medical School,** Master's Program in Clinical Embryology and Andrology, Norfolk, VA 23501-1980. Offers MS. *Program availability:* Online learning. *Entrance requirements:* Additional exam requirements/recommendations for international students: required—TOEFL (minimum score 550 paper-based; 80 iBT). Electronic applications accepted. *Expenses:* Contact institution.

**Rutgers University - New Brunswick,** Graduate School-New Brunswick, Program in Endocrinology and Animal Biosciences, Piscataway, NJ 08854-8097. Offers MS, PhD. Terminal master's awarded for partial completion of doctoral program. *Degree requirements:* For master's, thesis; for doctorate, comprehensive exam, thesis/dissertation. *Entrance requirements:* For master's and doctorate, GRE General Test. Additional exam requirements/recommendations for international students: required—TOEFL. Electronic applications accepted.

**Tufts University,** Cummings School of Veterinary Medicine, North Grafton, MA 01536. Offers animals and public policy (MS); biomedical sciences (PhD), including digestive diseases, infectious diseases, neuroscience and reproductive biology, pathology; conservation medicine (MS); veterinary medicine (DVM); DVM/MPH; DVM/MS. *Accreditation:* AVMA (one or more programs are accredited). *Degree requirements:* For master's, thesis (for some programs); for doctorate, comprehensive exam, thesis/dissertation (for some programs). *Entrance requirements:* For master's and doctorate, GRE General Test. Additional exam requirements/recommendations for international students: required—TOEFL or IELTS. Electronic applications accepted. *Expenses:* Contact institution.

**The University of British Columbia,** Faculty of Medicine, Department of Obstetrics and Gynecology, Program in Reproductive and Developmental Sciences, Vancouver, BC V6H 3N1, Canada. Offers M Sc, PhD. *Program availability:* Part-time. Terminal master's awarded for partial completion of doctoral program. *Degree requirements:* For master's, thesis; for doctorate, thesis/dissertation. *Entrance requirements:* For master's, B Sc or equivalent, MD, DVM, DDS; for doctorate, B Sc with first class honors, M Sc, MD, DVM, DDS. Additional exam requirements/recommendations for international students: required—TOEFL, IELTS. Electronic applications accepted. *Expenses:* Contact institution.

**University of Hawaii at Manoa,** John A. Burns School of Medicine, Program in Developmental and Reproductive Biology, Honolulu, HI 96813. Offers MS, PhD. *Program availability:* Part-time. *Degree requirements:* For doctorate, thesis/dissertation. *Entrance requirements:* For doctorate, GRE General Test, GRE Subject Test. Additional exam requirements/recommendations for international students: recommended—TOEFL (minimum score 560 paper-based), IELTS (minimum score 5).

**University of Saskatchewan,** College of Medicine, Department of Obstetrics and Gynecology, Saskatoon, SK S7N 5A2, Canada. Offers M Sc, PhD. *Degree requirements:* For master's, thesis; for doctorate, thesis/dissertation. *Entrance requirements:* Additional exam requirements/recommendations for international students: required—TOEFL.

**University of Wyoming,** College of Agriculture and Natural Resources, Department of Animal Science, Program in Reproductive Biology, Laramie, WY 82071. Offers MS, PhD. *Degree requirements:* For master's, thesis; for doctorate, thesis/dissertation. *Entrance requirements:* For master's, GRE General Test, minimum GPA of 3.0; for doctorate, GRE General Test, minimum GPA of 3.0 or MS degree. Additional exam requirements/recommendations for international students: required—TOEFL.

# Section 11
# Marine Biology

This section contains a directory of institutions offering graduate work in marine biology. Additional information about programs listed in the directory may be obtained by writing directly to the dean of a graduate school or chair of a department at the address given in the directory.

For programs offering related work, see also in this book *Biological and Biomedical Sciences* and *Zoology*. In another guide in this series:

**Graduate Programs in the Physical Sciences, Mathematics, Agricultural Sciences, the Environment & Natural Resources**

See *Marine Sciences and Oceanography*

## CONTENTS

## Program Directory

# Marine Biology

**College of Charleston,** Graduate School, School of Sciences and Mathematics, Program in Marine Biology, Charleston, SC 29412. Offers MS. *Degree requirements:* For master's, comprehensive exam, thesis. *Entrance requirements:* For master's, GRE General Test, 3 letters of recommendation. Additional exam requirements/recommendations for international students: required—TOEFL (minimum score 81 iBT). Electronic applications accepted.

**Florida Institute of Technology,** College of Engineering and Science, Program in Biological Sciences, Melbourne, FL 32901-6975. Offers biological sciences (PhD); biotechnology (MS); ecology (MS). *Program availability:* Part-time. *Degree requirements:* For doctorate, comprehensive exam, thesis/dissertation, dissertations seminar, publications. *Entrance requirements:* For doctorate, GRE General Test, resume, 3 letters of recommendation, minimum GPA of 3.2, statement of objectives. Additional exam requirements/recommendations for international students: required—TOEFL (minimum score 550 paper-based; 79 iBT). Electronic applications accepted.

**Florida Institute of Technology,** College of Engineering and Science, Program in Marine Biology, Melbourne, FL 32901-6975. Offers MS. *Program availability:* Part-time. *Degree requirements:* For master's, thesis optional. *Entrance requirements:* For master's, GRE General Test, 3 letters of recommendation, objectives, résumé. Additional exam requirements/recommendations for international students: required—TOEFL (minimum score 550 paper-based; 79 iBT). Electronic applications accepted.

**Montclair State University,** The Graduate School, College of Science and Mathematics, Program in Marine Biology and Coastal Sciences, Montclair, NJ 07043-1624. Offers MS. *Degree requirements:* For master's, thesis.

**Nicholls State University,** Graduate Studies, College of Arts and Sciences, Department of Biological Sciences, Thibodaux, LA 70310. Offers marine and environmental biology (MS). *Program availability:* Part-time. *Degree requirements:* For master's, comprehensive exam, thesis. *Entrance requirements:* For master's, GRE. Additional exam requirements/recommendations for international students: required—TOEFL (minimum score 600 paper-based).

**Northeastern University,** College of Science, Boston, MA 02115-5096. Offers applied mathematics (MS); bioinformatics (MS); biology (PhD); biotechnology (MS); chemistry and chemical biology (MS, PhD); environmental science and policy (MS); marine and environmental sciences (PhD); marine biology (MS); mathematics (MS, PhD); operations research (MSOR); physics (MS, PhD); psychology (PhD). *Program availability:* Part-time. Terminal master's awarded for partial completion of doctoral program. *Degree requirements:* For master's, comprehensive exam (for some programs), thesis; for doctorate, comprehensive exam (for some programs), thesis/dissertation. *Entrance requirements:* For master's, GRE General Test. Electronic applications accepted. *Expenses:* Contact institution.

**Nova Southeastern University,** Halmos College of Natural Sciences and Oceanography, Fort Lauderdale, FL 33314-7796. Offers biological sciences (MS), including health studies; marine biology and oceanography (PhD), including marine biology, oceanography. *Program availability:* Part-time, evening/weekend, blended/hybrid learning. *Faculty:* 63 full-time (16 women), 60 part-time/adjunct (27 women). *Students:* 39 full-time (25 women), 118 part-time (88 women); includes 33 minority (11 Black or African American, non-Hispanic/Latino; 6 Asian, non-Hispanic/Latino; 12 Hispanic/Latino; 4 Two or more races, non-Hispanic/Latino), 10 international. Average age 27. 86 applicants, 49% accepted, 26 enrolled. In 2019, 48 master's, 2 doctorates awarded. *Degree requirements:* For master's, thesis; for doctorate, comprehensive exam, thesis/dissertation, departmental qualifying exam. *Entrance requirements:* For master's, GRE General Test, 3 letters of recommendation; BS/BA in natural science (for marine biology program); BS/BA in biology (for biological sciences program); minor in the natural sciences or equivalent (for coastal zone management and marine environmental sciences); for doctorate, GRE General Test, master's degree. Additional exam requirements/recommendations for international students: required—TOEFL (minimum score 550 paper-based); recommended—IELTS. *Application deadline:* Applications are processed on a rolling basis. Application fee: $50. Electronic applications accepted. *Expenses:* Contact institution. *Financial support:* In 2019–20, 101 students received support, including 6 fellowships with full and partial tuition reimbursements available (averaging $25,000 per year), 40 research assistantships with full and partial tuition reimbursements available (averaging $20,000 per year), 8 teaching assistantships with tuition reimbursements available (averaging $15,000 per year); career-related internships or fieldwork, Federal Work-Study, scholarships/grants, health care benefits, tuition waivers (full and partial), and unspecified assistantships also available. Support available to part-time students. Financial award application deadline: 4/15; financial award applicants required to submit FAFSA. *Unit head:* Dr. Richard Dodge, Dean, 954-262-3600, Fax: 954-262-4020, E-mail: dodge@nsu.nova.edu. *Application contact:* Dr. Bernhard Riegl, Chair, Department of Marine and Environmental Sciences, 954-262-3600, Fax: 954-262-4020, E-mail: rieglb@nova.edu. Website: http://cnso.nova.edu

**Princeton University,** Graduate School, Department of Geosciences, Princeton, NJ 80544. Offers atmospheric and oceanic sciences (PhD); geosciences (PhD); ocean sciences and marine biology (PhD). *Faculty:* 17 full-time (3 women). *Students:* 43 full-time (27 women); includes 5 minority (4 Asian, non-Hispanic/Latino; 1 Hispanic/Latino), 15 international. Average age 24. 58 applicants, 21% accepted, 7 enrolled. In 2019, 9 doctorates awarded. Terminal master's awarded for partial completion of doctoral program. *Degree requirements:* For doctorate, one foreign language, thesis/dissertation, General Qualifying Exam. *Entrance requirements:* Additional exam requirements/recommendations for international students: required—TOEFL (minimum score 600 paper-based). *Application deadline:* For fall admission, 12/31 for domestic and international students. Application fee: $95. Electronic applications accepted. *Financial support:* In 2019–20, 43 students received support, including 30 research assistantships with full tuition reimbursements available (averaging $30,000 per year), 20 teaching assistantships with full tuition reimbursements available (averaging $16,000 per year); fellowships with full tuition reimbursements available, Federal Work-Study, institutionally sponsored loans, and scholarships/grants also available. Financial award application deadline: 12/31. *Unit head:* Bess B Ward, Department Chair, 609-258-5150, Fax: 609-258-1274, E-mail: bbw@princeton.edu. *Application contact:* Graduate Admissions Office, 609-258-3034, Fax: 609-258-7262, E-mail: gsadmit@princeton.edu. Website: https://geosciences.princeton.edu/

**Rutgers University - New Brunswick,** Graduate School-New Brunswick, Department of Environmental Sciences, Piscataway, NJ 08854-8097. Offers air pollution and resources (MS, PhD); aquatic biology (MS, PhD); aquatic chemistry (MS, PhD); atmospheric science (MS, PhD); chemistry and physics of aerosol and hydrosol systems (MS, PhD); environmental chemistry (MS, PhD); environmental microbiology (MS, PhD); environmental toxicology (PhD); exposure assessment (PhD); fate and effects of pollutants (MS, PhD); pollution prevention and control (MS, PhD); water and wastewater treatment (MS, PhD); water resources (MS, PhD). Terminal master's awarded for partial completion of doctoral program. *Degree requirements:* For master's, comprehensive exam, thesis or alternative, oral final exam; for doctorate, comprehensive exam, thesis/dissertation, thesis defense, qualifying exam. *Entrance requirements:* For master's and doctorate, GRE General Test. Additional exam requirements/recommendations for international students: required—TOEFL. Electronic applications accepted.

**San Francisco State University,** Division of Graduate Studies, College of Science and Engineering, Department of Biology, San Francisco, CA 94132-1722. Offers cell and molecular biology (MS); ecology, evolution, and conservation biology (MS); interdisciplinary marine and estuarine science (MS); marine biology (MS); microbiology (MS); physiology and behavioral biology (MS); science (PSM), including biotechnology, stem cell science. *Application deadline:* Applications are processed on a rolling basis. *Expenses: Tuition, area resident:* Full-time $7176; part-time $4164 per year. Tuition, state resident: full-time $7176; part-time $4164 per year. Tuition, nonresident: full-time $16,680; part-time $396 per unit. *International tuition:* $16,680 full-time. *Required fees:* $1524; $1524 per unit. $762 per semester. Tuition and fees vary according to degree level and program. *Unit head:* Dr. Laura Burrus, Chair, 415-338-7680, Fax: 415-338-6136, E-mail: lburrus@sfsu.edu. *Application contact:* Giovanna Tuccori, Graduate Program Assistant, 415-405-3591, Fax: 415-338-6136. Website: http://biology.sfsu.edu/

**Texas A&M University,** Galveston Campus, Department of Marine Biology, College Station, TX 77843. Offers marine biology (MS). *Faculty:* 18. *Students:* 55 full-time (32 women), 11 part-time (5 women); includes 15 minority (4 Black or African American, non-Hispanic/Latino; 3 Asian, non-Hispanic/Latino; 6 Hispanic/Latino; 2 Two or more races, non-Hispanic/Latino), 7 international. Average age 29. 29 applicants, 62% accepted, 13 enrolled. In 2019, 6 master's awarded. Terminal master's awarded for partial completion of doctoral program. *Degree requirements:* For master's, comprehensive exam (for some programs), thesis (for some programs); for doctorate, comprehensive exam, thesis/dissertation. *Entrance requirements:* For master's and doctorate, GRE, letters of recommendation. Additional exam requirements/recommendations for international students: required—TOEFL (minimum score 550 paper-based; 80 iBT), IELTS (minimum score 6). *Application deadline:* For fall admission, 5/1 for domestic and international students; for spring admission, 10/15 for domestic students, 10/1 for international students. Application fee: $65. Electronic applications accepted. *Expenses:* Contact institution. *Financial support:* In 2019–20, 59 students received support, including 2 fellowships (averaging $24,070 per year), 39 research assistantships (averaging $10,155 per year), 35 teaching assistantships (averaging $5,611 per year); scholarships/grants, health care benefits, and unspecified assistantships also available. Financial award application deadline: 3/1; financial award applicants required to submit FAFSA. *Unit head:* Dr. Daniel Roelke, Department Head, 409-740-4750, E-mail: droelke@tamu.edu. *Application contact:* Dr. Daniel Roelke, Department Head, 409-740-4750, E-mail: droelke@tamu.edu. Website: http://www.tamug.edu/marb/

**Texas A&M University–Corpus Christi,** College of Graduate Studies, College of Science and Engineering, Corpus Christi, TX 78412. Offers biology (MS, PhD); chemistry (MS); coastal and marine system science (MS, PhD); computer science (MS); environmental science (MS); fisheries and mariculture (MS); geospatial computing sciences (PhD); geospatial surveying engineering (MS); marine biology (MS, PhD); mathematics (MS). *Program availability:* Part-time, evening/weekend. *Degree requirements:* For master's, comprehensive exam, thesis. *Entrance requirements:* For master's, GRE General Test. Additional exam requirements/recommendations for international students: required—TOEFL (minimum score 550 paper-based; 69 iBT), IELTS (minimum score 6.5). Electronic applications accepted.

**Texas State University,** The Graduate College, College of Science and Engineering, Aquatic Resources and Integrative Biology, San Marcos, TX 78666. Offers MS, PhD. *Degree requirements:* For master's, comprehensive exam, thesis, 3 seminars; for doctorate, comprehensive exam, thesis/dissertation. *Entrance requirements:* For master's, official GRE (general test only) required with competitive scores in the verbal reasoning and quantitative reasoning sections, baccalaureate degree in biology or related discipline from regionally-accredited university with minimum GPA of 3.0 on last 60 undergraduate semester hours; intent to mentor letter from biology faculty member; resume; statement of purpose describing professional aspirations and academic goals; 3 letters of recommendation. Additional exam requirements/recommendations for international students: required—TOEFL (minimum score 550 paper-based; 78 iBT), IELTS (minimum score 6.5). Electronic applications accepted.

**University of Alaska Fairbanks,** College of Fisheries and Ocean Sciences, Department of Marine Biology, Fairbanks, AK 99775-7220. Offers marine biology (MS, PhD); oceanography (MS, PhD). *Program availability:* Part-time. *Degree requirements:* For master's, comprehensive exam, thesis, oral defense of thesis; for doctorate, comprehensive exam, thesis/dissertation, oral defense of dissertation. *Entrance requirements:* For master's, GRE General Test, bachelor's degree from accredited institution with minimum cumulative undergraduate and major GPA of 3.0; for doctorate, GRE General Test, minimum cumulative GPA of 3.0. Additional exam requirements/recommendations for international students: required—TOEFL (minimum score 550 paper-based; 79 iBT), IELTS (minimum score 6.5). Electronic applications accepted.

**University of California, Santa Barbara,** Graduate Division, College of Letters and Sciences, Division of Mathematics, Life, and Physical Sciences, Department of Ecology, Evolution, and Marine Biology, Santa Barbara, CA 93106-9620. Offers MA, PhD, MA/PhD. *Degree requirements:* For master's, comprehensive exam (for some programs), thesis (for some programs); for doctorate, comprehensive exam, thesis/dissertation. *Entrance requirements:* For master's and doctorate, GRE General Test. Additional exam requirements/recommendations for international students: required—TOEFL (minimum score 550 paper-based; 80 iBT), IELTS. Electronic applications accepted.

**University of Guam,** Office of Graduate Studies, College of Natural and Applied Sciences, Program in Biology, Mangilao, GU 96923. Offers tropical marine biology (MS). *Degree requirements:* For master's, comprehensive exam, thesis. *Entrance requirements:* For master's, GRE General Test, GRE Subject Test. Additional exam requirements/recommendations for international students: required—TOEFL.

**University of Hawaii at Hilo,** Program in Tropical Conservation Biology and Environmental Science, Hilo, HI 96720-4091. Offers MS. *Entrance requirements:* Additional exam requirements/recommendations for international students: required—TOEFL, IELTS. Electronic applications accepted.

**University of Hawaii at Manoa,** Office of Graduate Education, School of Ocean and Earth Science and Technology, Program in Marine Biology, Honolulu, HI 96822. Offers

MS, PhD. *Degree requirements:* For master's, thesis, research project; for doctorate, thesis/dissertation, research project. *Entrance requirements:* For master's and doctorate, GRE. Additional exam requirements/recommendations for international students: required—TOEFL. *Expenses:* Contact institution.

**University of Massachusetts Dartmouth,** Graduate School, College of Arts and Sciences, Department of Biology, North Dartmouth, MA 02747-2300. Offers biology (MS); integrative biology (PhD); marine biology (MS). *Program availability:* Part-time. *Faculty:* 20 full-time (9 women), 2 part-time/adjunct (both women). *Students:* 13 full-time (8 women), 13 part-time (6 women); includes 4 minority (1 Asian, non-Hispanic/Latino; 2 Hispanic/Latino; 1 Two or more races, non-Hispanic/Latino), 1 international. Average age 29. 16 applicants, 50% accepted, 4 enrolled. In 2019, 6 master's awarded. *Degree requirements:* For master's, comprehensive exam, thesis; for doctorate, comprehensive exam, thesis/dissertation. *Entrance requirements:* For master's and doctorate, GRE, statement of purpose (300-600 words), resume, official transcripts, 3 letters of recommendation. Additional exam requirements/recommendations for international students: required—TOEFL (minimum score 80 iBT). *Application deadline:* For fall admission, 8/15 for domestic students, 7/15 for international students. Application fee: $60. Electronic applications accepted. *Expenses: Tuition, area resident:* Full-time $16,390; part-time $682.92 per credit. Tuition, state resident: full-time $16,390; part-time $682.92 per credit. Tuition, nonresident: full-time $29,578; part-time $1232.42 per credit. *Required fees:* $575. *Financial support:* In 2019–20, 8 research assistantships (averaging $8,993 per year), 10 teaching assistantships (averaging $13,875 per year) were awarded; tuition waivers (full) also available. Financial award application deadline: 3/1; financial award applicants required to submit FAFSA. *Unit head:* Whitney Hable, Graduate Program Director, Biology/Marine Biology, 508-999-8206, E-mail: whable@umassd.edu. *Application contact:* Scott Webster, Director of Graduate Studies and Admissions, 508-999-8604, Fax: 508-999-8183, E-mail: graduate@umassd.edu. Website: http://www.umassd.edu/cas/biology

**University of Miami,** Graduate School, Rosenstiel School of Marine and Atmospheric Science, Division of Marine Biology and Fisheries, Coral Gables, FL 33124. Offers MA, MS, PhD. Terminal master's awarded for partial completion of doctoral program. *Degree requirements:* For master's, comprehensive exam, thesis; for doctorate, comprehensive exam, thesis/dissertation. *Entrance requirements:* For master's and doctorate, GRE General Test. Additional exam requirements/recommendations for international students: required—TOEFL (minimum score 550 paper-based). Electronic applications accepted.

**University of New Hampshire,** Graduate School, College of Life Sciences and Agriculture, Department of Biological Sciences, Durham, NH 03824. Offers integrative and organismal biology (MS, PhD); marine biology (MS, PhD). *Program availability:* Part-time. *Students:* 14 full-time (7 women), 17 part-time (9 women); includes 4 minority (1 Asian, non-Hispanic/Latino; 1 Hispanic/Latino; 2 Two or more races, non-Hispanic/Latino), 2 international. Average age 27. 36 applicants, 25% accepted, 7 enrolled. In 2019, 8 master's awarded. *Entrance requirements:* For master's and doctorate, GRE General Test. Additional exam requirements/recommendations for international students: required—TOEFL (minimum score 550 paper-based; 80 iBT), IELTS, PTE. *Application deadline:* For fall admission, 1/15 priority date for domestic students, 8/1 for international students. Application fee: $65. Electronic applications accepted. *Financial support:* In 2019–20, 26 students received support, including 1 fellowship, 2 research assistantships, 23 teaching assistantships. Financial award application deadline: 2/15. *Unit head:* Bonnie Brown, Chair, 603-862-2100. *Application contact:* Diane Lavalliere, Senior Academic and Student Support Assistant, 603-862-2100, E-mail: diane.lavalliere@unh.edu.
Website: http://www.colsa.unh.edu/dbs

**The University of North Carolina Wilmington,** College of Arts and Sciences, Department of Biology and Marine Biology, Wilmington, NC 28403-3297. Offers biology (MS); marine biology (MS, PhD). *Program availability:* Part-time. *Faculty:* 37 full-time (11 women). *Students:* 16 full-time (15 women), 59 part-time (36 women); includes 7 minority (2 Black or African American, non-Hispanic/Latino; 1 Asian, non-Hispanic/Latino; 3 Hispanic/Latino; 1 Two or more races, non-Hispanic/Latino), 5 international. Average age 28. 70 applicants, 33% accepted, 18 enrolled. In 2019, 8 master's, 2 doctorates awarded. *Degree requirements:* For master's, comprehensive exam, thesis; for doctorate, comprehensive exam, thesis/dissertation. *Entrance requirements:* For master's, GRE General Test, 3 recommendations, research interests form and statement, resume or curriculum vitae, baccalaureate degree from biology-related field; for doctorate, GRE General Test, 3 recommendations, resume or curriculum vitae, summary of MS thesis research, statement of PhD research interests, copies of publications, master's degree or BS and 1 year of completed work in the MS in biology program. Additional exam requirements/recommendations for international students: required—TOEFL (minimum score 79 iBT), IELTS (minimum score 6.5). *Application deadline:* For fall admission, 5/15 for domestic students; for spring admission, 11/15 for

domestic students. Applications are processed on a rolling basis. Application fee: $75. Electronic applications accepted. *Expenses: Tuition, area resident:* Full-time $4719; part-time $326 per credit hour. Tuition, state resident: full-time $4719; part-time $326 per credit hour. Tuition, nonresident: full-time $18,548; part-time $1099 per credit hour. *Required fees:* $2738. Tuition and fees vary according to program. *Financial support:* Research assistantships with tuition reimbursements, teaching assistantships with tuition reimbursements, and scholarships/grants available. Support available to part-time students. Financial award application deadline: 1/1; financial award applicants required to submit FAFSA. *Unit head:* Dr. Heather Koopman, Chair, 910-962-7199, E-mail: koopmanh@uncw.edu. *Application contact:* Lisa Noah, Graduate Administrative Assistant, 910-962-3489, E-mail: noahl@uncw.edu.
Website: http://www.uncw.edu/bio/graduate.html

**University of Oregon,** Graduate School, College of Arts and Sciences, Department of Biology, Eugene, OR 97403. Offers ecology and evolution (MA, MS, PhD); marine biology (MA, MS, PhD); molecular, cellular and genetic biology (PhD); neuroscience and development (PhD). Terminal master's awarded for partial completion of doctoral program. *Degree requirements:* For master's, thesis (for some programs); for doctorate, thesis/dissertation. *Entrance requirements:* For master's and doctorate, GRE General Test, minimum GPA of 3.2. Additional exam requirements/recommendations for international students: required—TOEFL.

**University of Rhode Island,** Graduate School, College of the Environment and Life Sciences, Department of Biological Sciences, Kingston, RI 02881. Offers cell and molecular biology (MS, PhD); earth and environmental sciences (MS, PhD); ecology and ecosystem sciences (MS, PhD); evolutionary and marine biology (MS, PhD); sustainable agriculture and food systems (MS, PhD). *Program availability:* Part-time. *Faculty:* 20 full-time (10 women). *Students:* 108 full-time (68 women), 22 part-time (15 women); includes 12 minority (6 Black or African American, non-Hispanic/Latino; 4 Asian, non-Hispanic/Latino; 1 Hispanic/Latino; 1 Two or more races, non-Hispanic/Latino), 22 international. In 2019, 12 master's, 10 doctorates awarded. *Entrance requirements:* Additional exam requirements/recommendations for international students: required—TOEFL. *Application deadline:* For fall admission, 1/15 for domestic and international students. Application fee: $65. Electronic applications accepted. *Expenses: Tuition, area resident:* Full-time $13,734; part-time $763 per credit. Tuition, state resident: full-time $13,734; part-time $763 per credit. Tuition, nonresident: full-time $26,512; part-time $1473 per credit. *International tuition:* $26,512 full-time. *Required fees:* $1780; $52 per credit. $35 per term. One-time fee: $165. *Financial support:* In 2019–20, 24 research assistantships with tuition reimbursements (averaging $9,961 per year), 1 teaching assistantship with tuition reimbursement (averaging $7,521 per year) were awarded. Financial award application deadline: 1/15; financial award applicants required to submit FAFSA. *Unit head:* Dr. Alison Roberts, Chair, E-mail: bio_chair@etal.uri.edu. *Application contact:* Bethany Jenkins, Graduate Program Director, 401-874-7551, E-mail: bdjenkins@uri.edu.
Website: http://web.uri.edu/bio/

**University of Southern California,** Graduate School, Dana and David Dornsife College of Letters, Arts and Sciences, Department of Biological Sciences, Program in Marine Biology and Biological Oceanography, Los Angeles, CA 90089. Offers marine and environmental biology (MS); marine biology and biological oceanography (PhD). Terminal master's awarded for partial completion of doctoral program. *Degree requirements:* For master's, research paper; for doctorate, comprehensive exam, thesis/dissertation, qualifying examination, dissertation defense. *Entrance requirements:* For master's and doctorate, GRE, 3 letters of recommendation, personal statement, resume, minimum GPA of 3.0. Additional exam requirements/recommendations for international students: required—TOEFL (minimum score 600 paper-based; 100 iBT). Electronic applications accepted.

**Western Illinois University,** School of Graduate Studies, College of Arts and Sciences, Department of Biological Sciences, Macomb, IL 61455-1390. Offers biology (MS); environmental GIS (Certificate); zoo and aquarium studies (Certificate). *Program availability:* Part-time. *Entrance requirements:* Additional exam requirements/recommendations for international students: required—TOEFL (minimum score 550 paper-based; 80 iBT); recommended—IELTS. Electronic applications accepted.

**Woods Hole Oceanographic Institution,** MIT/WHOI Joint Program in Oceanography/Applied Ocean Science and Engineering, Woods Hole, MA 02543-1541. Offers applied ocean science and engineering (PhD); biological oceanography (PhD); chemical oceanography (PhD); marine geology and geophysics (PhD); physical oceanography (PhD). *Degree requirements:* For doctorate, thesis/dissertation. *Entrance requirements:* For doctorate, GRE General Test. Additional exam requirements/recommendations for international students: required—TOEFL or IELTS. Electronic applications accepted.

# Section 12
# Microbiological Sciences

This section contains a directory of institutions offering graduate work in microbiological sciences, followed by in-depth entries submitted by institutions that chose to prepare detailed program descriptions. Additional information about programs listed in the directory but not augmented by an in-depth entry may be obtained by writing directly to the dean of a graduate school or chair of a department at the address given in the directory.

For programs offering related work, see also in this book *Allied Health; Biochemistry; Biological and Biomedical Sciences; Botany and Plant Biology; Cell, Molecular, and Structural Biology; Dentistry and Dental Sciences; Ecology, Environmental Biology, and Evolutionary Biology; Entomology; Genetics, Developmental Biology, and Reproductive Biology; Parasitology; Pathology and Pathobiology; Pharmacy and Pharmaceutical Sciences; Public Health; Physiology; Veterinary Medicine and Sciences;* and *Zoology.* In the other guides in this series:

**Graduate Programs in the Physical Sciences, Mathematics, Agricultural Sciences, the Environment & Natural Resources**
See *Agricultural and Food Sciences* and *Chemistry*

**Graduate Programs in Engineering & Applied Sciences**
See *Agricultural Engineering and Bioengineering* and *Biomedical Engineering and Biotechnology*

## CONTENTS

### Program Directories

# Bacteriology

**Illinois State University,** Graduate School, College of Arts and Sciences, School of Biological Sciences, Normal, IL 61790. Offers animal behavior (MS); bacteriology (MS); biochemistry (MS); biological sciences (MS); biology (PhD); biophysics (MS); biotechnology (MS); botany (MS, PhD); cell biology (MS); conservation biology (MS); developmental biology (MS); ecology (MS, PhD); entomology (MS); evolutionary biology (MS); genetics (MS, PhD); immunology (MS); microbiology (MS, PhD); molecular biology (MS); molecular genetics (MS); neurobiology (MS); neuroscience (MS); parasitology (MS); physiology (MS, PhD); plant biology (MS); plant molecular biology (MS); plant sciences (MS); structural biology (MS); zoology (MS, PhD). *Program availability:* Part-time. *Faculty:* 26 full-time (6 women), 7 part-time/adjunct (2 women). *Students:* 51 full-time (33 women), 15 part-time (8 women). Average age 27. 71 applicants, 28% accepted, 9 enrolled. In 2019, 14 master's, 3 doctorates awarded. *Degree requirements:* For master's, thesis or alternative; for doctorate, variable foreign language requirement, thesis/dissertation, 2 terms of residency. *Entrance requirements:* For master's, GRE General Test, minimum GPA of 2.6 in last 60 hours of course work; for doctorate, GRE General Test. *Application deadline:* Applications are processed on a rolling basis. Application fee: $50. *Expenses: Tuition, area resident:* Full-time $7956; part-time $9767 per year. Tuition, nonresident: full-time $9233; part-time $17,592 per year. *Required fees:* $1797. *Financial support:* In 2019–20, 20 research assistantships, 41 teaching assistantships were awarded; Federal Work-Study, tuition waivers (full), and unspecified assistantships also available. Financial award application deadline: 4/1. *Unit head:* Dr. Craig Gatto, School Director, 309-438-3087, E-mail: cgatto@IllinoisState.edu. *Application contact:* Dr. Ben Sadd, Assistant Chair for Graduate Studies, 309-438-2651, E-mail: bmsadd@IllinoisState.edu.
Website: http://www.bio.ilstu.edu/

**The University of Iowa,** Roy J. and Lucille A. Carver College of Medicine and Graduate College, Graduate Programs in Medicine, Department of Microbiology, Iowa City, IA 52242-1316. Offers general microbiology and microbial physiology (MS, PhD); immunology (MS, PhD); microbial genetics (MS, PhD); pathogenic bacteriology (MS, PhD); virology (MS, PhD). *Degree requirements:* For master's, thesis; for doctorate, comprehensive exam, thesis/dissertation. *Entrance requirements:* For master's and doctorate, GRE General Test. Additional exam requirements/recommendations for international students: required—TOEFL (minimum score 600 paper-based). Electronic applications accepted.

**University of Prince Edward Island,** Atlantic Veterinary College, Graduate Program in Veterinary Medicine, Charlottetown, PE C1A 4P3, Canada. Offers anatomy (M Sc, PhD); bacteriology (M Sc, PhD); clinical pharmacology (M Sc, PhD); clinical sciences (M Sc, PhD); epidemiology (M Sc, PhD), including reproduction; fish health (M Sc, PhD); food animal nutrition (M Sc, PhD); immunology (M Sc, PhD); microanatomy (M Sc, PhD); parasitology (M Sc, PhD); pathology (M Sc, PhD); pharmacology (M Sc, PhD); physiology (M Sc, PhD); toxicology (M Sc, PhD); veterinary science (M Vet Sc); virology (M Sc, PhD). *Program availability:* Part-time. *Degree requirements:* For master's, thesis; for doctorate, thesis/dissertation. *Entrance requirements:* For master's, DVM, B Sc honors degree, or equivalent; for doctorate, M Sc. Additional exam requirements/ recommendations for international students: required—TOEFL (minimum score 550 paper-based; 80 iBT). *Expenses:* Contact institution.

**University of Wisconsin–Madison,** Graduate School, College of Agricultural and Life Sciences, Department of Bacteriology, Madison, WI 53706-1380. Offers MS. *Program availability:* Part-time. *Entrance requirements:* Additional exam requirements/ recommendations for international students: required—TOEFL. Electronic applications accepted.

# Immunology

**Albany Medical College,** Center for Immunology and Microbial Disease, Albany, NY 12208-3479. Offers MS, PhD. *Program availability:* Part-time. Terminal master's awarded for partial completion of doctoral program. *Degree requirements:* For master's, thesis; for doctorate, comprehensive exam, thesis/dissertation, oral qualifying exam, written preliminary exam, 1 published paper-peer review. *Entrance requirements:* For master's, GRE General Test, all transcripts, letters of recommendation; for doctorate, GRE General Test, letters of recommendation. Additional exam requirements/ recommendations for international students: required—TOEFL.

**Albert Einstein College of Medicine,** Graduate Programs in the Biomedical Sciences, Department of Microbiology and Immunology, Bronx, NY 10461. Offers PhD, MD/PhD. *Degree requirements:* For doctorate, thesis/dissertation. *Entrance requirements:* For doctorate, GRE General Test. Additional exam requirements/recommendations for international students: required—TOEFL.

**Baylor College of Medicine,** Graduate School of Biomedical Sciences, Department of Immunology, Houston, TX 77030-3498. Offers PhD, MD/PhD. *Degree requirements:* For doctorate, thesis/dissertation, public defense. *Entrance requirements:* For doctorate, GRE General Test, GRE Subject Test (strongly recommended), minimum GPA of 3.0. Additional exam requirements/recommendations for international students: required—TOEFL. Electronic applications accepted.

**Baylor College of Medicine,** Graduate School of Biomedical Sciences, Interdepartmental Program in Cell and Molecular Biology, Houston, TX 77030-3498. Offers biochemistry (PhD); cell and molecular biology (PhD); genetics (PhD); human genetics (PhD); immunology (PhD); microbiology (PhD); virology (PhD); MD/PhD. *Degree requirements:* For doctorate, thesis/dissertation, public defense. *Entrance requirements:* For doctorate, GRE General Test, GRE Subject Test (strongly recommended), minimum GPA of 3.0. Additional exam requirements/recommendations for international students: required—TOEFL. Electronic applications accepted.

**Boston University,** School of Medicine, Graduate Medical Sciences, Immunology Training Program, Boston, MA 02215. Offers PhD, MD/PhD. *Application deadline:* For fall admission, 1/15 for domestic students; for spring admission, 10/15 for domestic students. *Unit head:* Dr. Tom Kepler, Director, E-mail: itp@bu.edu. *Application contact:* GMS Admissions Office, 617-358-9518, Fax: 617-358-2913, E-mail: gmsbusm@bu.edu. Website: http://www.bumc.bu.edu/immunology/

**California Institute of Technology,** Division of Biology and Biological Engineering, Program in Immunology, Pasadena, CA 91125-0001. Offers PhD. *Degree requirements:* For doctorate, thesis/dissertation, qualifying exam. *Entrance requirements:* For doctorate, GRE General Test.

**Colorado State University,** College of Veterinary Medicine and Biomedical Sciences, Department of Microbiology, Immunology and Pathology, Fort Collins, CO 80523. Offers microbiology, immunology and pathology (MS, PhD); pathology (PhD). *Faculty:* 76 full-time (35 women), 12 part-time/adjunct (8 women). *Students:* 64 full-time (46 women), 39 part-time (30 women); includes 10 minority (1 Black or African American, non-Hispanic/Latino; 1 American Indian or Alaska Native, non-Hispanic/Latino; 4 Hispanic/Latino; 4 Two or more races, non-Hispanic/Latino), 3 international. Average age 28. 187 applicants, 30% accepted, 45 enrolled. In 2019, 28 master's, 9 doctorates awarded. Terminal master's awarded for partial completion of doctoral program. *Degree requirements:* For master's, thesis (for some programs); for doctorate, comprehensive exam, thesis/dissertation. *Entrance requirements:* Additional exam requirements/ recommendations for international students: required—TOEFL (minimum score 550 paper-based; 80 iBT), IELTS (minimum score 6.5), PTE (minimum score 58). *Application deadline:* For fall admission, 12/15 for domestic and international students. Application fee: $60 ($70 for international students). *Expenses:* For non-thesis MS, addition fee of $120 per credit. *Financial support:* In 2019–20, 27 students received support, including 24 research assistantships with full and partial tuition reimbursements available (averaging $25,025 per year), 6 teaching assistantships with full and partial tuition reimbursements available (averaging $18,612 per year); health care benefits also available. Financial award application deadline: 12/15. *Unit head:* Dr. Gregg Dean, Department Head, 970-491-6144, E-mail: Gregg.Dean@colostate.edu. *Application contact:* Heidi Runge, Academic Support Coordinator for Graduate Studies, 970-491-

1630, Fax: 970-491-1815, E-mail: heidi.runge@colostate.edu.
Website: https://vetmedbiosci.colostate.edu/mip/

**Creighton University,** School of Medicine and Graduate School, Graduate Programs in Medicine, Omaha, NE 68178-0001. Offers biomedical sciences (MS, PhD); clinical anatomy (MS); medical microbiology and immunology (MS, PhD); pharmacology (MS, PhD), including pharmaceutical sciences (MS), pharmacology; MD/PhD; Pharm D/MS. Terminal master's awarded for partial completion of doctoral program. *Degree requirements:* For master's, thesis; for doctorate, thesis/dissertation. *Entrance requirements:* For master's and doctorate, GRE General Test. Additional exam requirements/recommendations for international students: required—TOEFL (minimum score 550 paper-based; 80 iBT). Electronic applications accepted. *Expenses:* Contact institution.

**Dalhousie University,** Faculty of Medicine, Department of Microbiology and Immunology, Halifax, NS B3H 4R2, Canada. Offers M Sc, PhD. *Degree requirements:* For master's, thesis; for doctorate, comprehensive exam, thesis/dissertation. *Entrance requirements:* For master's, GRE General Test, honors B Sc; for doctorate, GRE General Test, honors B Sc in microbiology, M Sc in discipline or transfer after 1 year in master's program. Additional exam requirements/recommendations for international students: required—1 of 5 approved tests: TOEFL, IELTS, CANTEST, CAEL, Michigan English Language Assessment Battery. Electronic applications accepted.

**Drexel University,** College of Medicine, Biomedical Graduate Programs, Program in Microbiology and Immunology, Philadelphia, PA 19104-2875. Offers MS, PhD, MD/PhD. Terminal master's awarded for partial completion of doctoral program. *Degree requirements:* For master's, comprehensive exam, thesis; for doctorate, thesis/ dissertation, qualifying exam. *Entrance requirements:* For master's, GRE General Test, minimum GPA of 2.75; for doctorate, GRE General Test, minimum GPA of 3.0. Additional exam requirements/recommendations for international students: required— TOEFL. Electronic applications accepted.

**Duke University,** Graduate School, Department of Immunology, Durham, NC 27710. Offers PhD. *Degree requirements:* For doctorate, thesis/dissertation. *Entrance requirements:* For doctorate, GRE General Test, GRE Subject Test in biology or biochemistry, cell and molecular biology (strongly recommended). Additional exam requirements/recommendations for international students: required—TOEFL (minimum score 577 paper-based; 90 iBT) or IELTS (minimum score 7). Electronic applications accepted.

**East Carolina University,** Brody School of Medicine, Office of Research and Graduate Studies, Greenville, NC 27858-4353. Offers anatomy and cell biology (PhD); biochemistry and molecular biology (PhD); biomedical science (MS); microbiology and immunology (PhD); pharmacology and toxicology (PhD); physiology (PhD). *Students:* 102 full-time (44 women), 1 part-time (0 women); includes 16 minority (4 Black or African American, non-Hispanic/Latino; 7 Asian, non-Hispanic/Latino; 4 Hispanic/Latino; 1 Two or more races, non-Hispanic/Latino), 13 international. Average age 28. 83 applicants, 40% accepted, 20 enrolled. In 2019, 3 master's, 10 doctorates awarded. *Degree requirements:* For doctorate, comprehensive exam, thesis/dissertation. *Entrance requirements:* For doctorate, GRE General Test. Additional exam requirements/ recommendations for international students: required—some international applicants may be required to demonstrate English proficiency via the TOEFL, IELTS, or PTE exam.; recommended—TOEFL (minimum score 78 iBT), IELTS (minimum score 6.5), TSE (minimum score 65). *Application deadline:* For fall admission, 8/15 for domestic students; for spring admission, 12/20 for domestic students. Applications are processed on a rolling basis. Application fee: $75. Electronic applications accepted. *Expenses: Tuition, area resident:* Full-time $4749; part-time $185 per credit hour. Tuition, state resident: full-time $4749; part-time $185 per credit hour. Tuition, nonresident: full-time $17,898; part-time $864 per credit hour. International tuition: $17,898 full-time. *Required fees:* $2787. *Financial support:* Fellowships available. Financial award application deadline: 6/1. *Unit head:* Dr. Russ Price, Associate Dean, 252-744-9346, E-mail: pricest17@ecu.edu. *Application contact:* Dr. Russ Price, Associate Dean, 252-744-9346, E-mail: pricest17@ecu.edu.
Website: http://www.ecu.edu/cs-dhs/bsomresearchgradstudies/index.cfm

**Emory University,** Laney Graduate School, Division of Biological and Biomedical Sciences, Program in Immunology and Molecular Pathogenesis, Atlanta, GA 30322-1100. Offers PhD. *Degree requirements:* For doctorate, comprehensive exam, thesis/dissertation. *Entrance requirements:* For doctorate, GRE General Test, minimum GPA of 3.0 in science course work (recommended). Additional exam requirements/recommendations for international students: required—TOEFL. Electronic applications accepted.

**Georgetown University,** Graduate School of Arts and Sciences, Department of Microbiology and Immunology, Washington, DC 20057. Offers biohazardous threat agents and emerging infectious diseases (MS); biomedical science policy and advocacy (MS); general microbiology and immunology (MS); global infectious diseases (PhD); microbiology and immunology (PhD). *Program availability:* Part-time. *Degree requirements:* For master's, 30 credit hours of coursework; for doctorate, comprehensive exam, thesis/dissertation. *Entrance requirements:* For master's, GRE General Test, 3 letters of reference, bachelor's degree in related field; for doctorate, GRE General Test, 3 letters of reference, MS/BS in related field. Additional exam requirements/recommendations for international students: required—TOEFL (minimum score 505 paper-based). Electronic applications accepted.

**The George Washington University,** Columbian College of Arts and Sciences, Institute for Biomedical Sciences, Program in Microbiology and Immunology, Washington, DC 20037. Offers PhD. *Entrance requirements:* For doctorate, GRE General Test, minimum GPA of 3.0. Additional exam requirements/recommendations for international students: required—TOEFL (minimum score 600 paper-based). Electronic applications accepted.

**Illinois State University,** Graduate School, College of Arts and Sciences, School of Biological Sciences, Normal, IL 61790. Offers animal behavior (MS); bacteriology (MS); biochemistry (MS); biological sciences (MS); biology (PhD); biophysics (MS); biotechnology (MS); botany (MS, PhD); cell biology (MS); conservation biology (MS); developmental biology (MS); ecology (MS, PhD); entomology (MS); evolutionary biology (MS); genetics (MS, PhD); immunology (MS); microbiology (MS, PhD); molecular biology (MS); molecular genetics (MS); neurobiology (MS); neuroscience (MS); parasitology (MS); physiology (MS, PhD); plant biology (MS); plant molecular biology (MS); plant sciences (MS); structural biology (MS); zoology (MS, PhD). *Program availability:* Part-time. *Faculty:* 26 full-time (6 women), 7 part-time/adjunct (2 women). *Students:* 51 full-time (33 women), 15 part-time (8 women). Average age 27. 71 applicants, 28% accepted, 9 enrolled. In 2019, 14 master's, 3 doctorates awarded. *Degree requirements:* For master's, thesis or alternative; for doctorate, variable foreign language requirement, thesis/dissertation, 2 terms of residency. *Entrance requirements:* For master's, GRE General Test, minimum GPA of 2.6 in last 60 hours of course work; for doctorate, GRE General Test. *Application deadline:* Applications are processed on a rolling basis. Application fee: $50. *Expenses: Tuition, area resident:* Full-time $7956; part-time $9767 per year. Tuition, nonresident: full-time $9233; part-time $17,592 per year. *Required fees:* $1797. *Financial support:* In 2019–20, 20 research assistantships, 41 teaching assistantships were awarded; Federal Work-Study, tuition waivers (full), and unspecified assistantships also available. Financial award application deadline: 4/1. *Unit head:* Dr. Craig Gatto, School Director, 309-438-3087, E-mail: cgatto@IllinoisState.edu. *Application contact:* Dr. Ben Sadd, Assistant Chair for Graduate Studies, 309-438-2651, E-mail: bmsadd@IllinoisState.edu.
Website: http://www.bio.ilstu.edu/

**Indiana University-Purdue University Indianapolis,** Indiana University School of Medicine, Department of Microbiology and Immunology, Indianapolis, IN 46202. Offers MS, PhD, MD/MS, MD/PhD. Terminal master's awarded for partial completion of doctoral program. *Degree requirements:* For master's, thesis; for doctorate, thesis/dissertation. *Entrance requirements:* For master's and doctorate, GRE General Test, previous course work in calculus, cell biology, chemistry, genetics, physics, and biochemistry.

**Iowa State University of Science and Technology,** Program in Immunobiology, Ames, IA 50011. Offers MS, PhD. *Entrance requirements:* For master's and doctorate, GRE General Test, resume. Additional exam requirements/recommendations for international students: required—TOEFL (minimum score 600 paper-based; 85 iBT), IELTS (minimum score 7). Electronic applications accepted.

**Irell & Manella Graduate School of Biological Sciences,** Graduate Program, Duarte, CA 91010. Offers brain metastatic cancer (PhD); cancer and stem cell metabolism (PhD); cancer biology (PhD); cancer biology and developmental therapeutics (PhD); cell biology (PhD); chemical biology (PhD); chromosomal break repair (PhD); diabetes and pancreatic progenitor cell biology (PhD); DNA repair and cancer biology (PhD); germline epigenetic remodeling and endocrine disruptors (PhD); hematology and hematopoietic cell transplantation (PhD); hematology and immunology (PhD); inflammation and cancer (PhD); micrornas and gene regulation in cardiovascular disease (PhD); mixed chimerism for reversal of autoimmunity (PhD); molecular and cellular biology (PhD); molecular biology and genetics (PhD); nanoparticle mediated twist1 silencing in metastatic cancer (PhD); neuro-oncology and stem cell biology (PhD); neuroscience (PhD); RNA directed therapies for HIV-1 (PhD); small RNA-induced transcriptional gene activation (PhD); stem cell regulation by the microenvironment (PhD); translational oncology and pharmaceutical sciences (PhD); tumor biology (PhD). *Degree requirements:* For doctorate, comprehensive exam, thesis/dissertation, qualifying exams, two advanced courses. *Entrance requirements:* For doctorate, GRE General Test; GRE Subject Test (recommended), 2 years of course work in chemistry (general and organic); 1 year of course work each in biochemistry, general biology, and general physics; 2 semesters of course work in mathematics; significant research laboratory experience. Additional exam requirements/recommendations for international students: required—TOEFL. Electronic applications accepted.

**Johns Hopkins University,** Bloomberg School of Public Health, W. Harry Feinstone Department of Molecular Microbiology and Immunology, Baltimore, MD 21218. Offers MHS, Sc M, PhD. *Degree requirements:* For master's, comprehensive exam, thesis (for some programs), essay, written exams; for doctorate, comprehensive exam, thesis/dissertation, 1-year full-time residency, oral and written exams. *Entrance requirements:* For master's, GRE General Test or MCAT, 3 letters of recommendation, curriculum vitae; for doctorate, GRE General Test, 3 letters of recommendation, transcripts, curriculum vitae. Additional exam requirements/recommendations for international students: required—TOEFL (minimum score 600 paper-based). Electronic applications accepted.

**Johns Hopkins University,** School of Medicine, Graduate Programs in Medicine, Immunology Program, Baltimore, MD 21218. Offers PhD. *Degree requirements:* For doctorate, comprehensive exam, thesis/dissertation, oral exam, final thesis seminar. *Entrance requirements:* For doctorate, GRE General Test, 2 letters of recommendation. Additional exam requirements/recommendations for international students: required—TOEFL (minimum score 550 paper-based). Electronic applications accepted.

**London Metropolitan University,** Graduate Programs, London, United Kingdom. Offers applied psychology (M Sc); architecture (MA); biomedical science (M Sc); blood science (M Sc); cancer pharmacology (M Sc); computer networking and cyber security (M Sc); computing and information systems (M Sc); conference interpreting (MA); counter-terrorism studies (M Sc); creative, digital and professional writing (MA); crime, violence and prevention (M Sc); criminology (M Sc); curating contemporary art (MA); data analytics (M Sc); digital media (MA); early childhood studies (MA); education (MA, Ed D); financial services law, regulation and compliance (LL M); food science (M Sc); forensic psychology (M Sc); health and social care management and policy (M Sc); human nutrition (M Sc); human resource management (MA); human rights and international conflict (MA); information technology (M Sc); intelligence and security studies (M Sc); international oil, gas and energy law (LL M); international relations (MA); interpreting (MA); learning and teaching in higher education (MA); legal practice (LL M); media and entertainment law (LL M); organizational and consumer psychology (M Sc); psychological therapy (M Sc); psychology of mental health (M Sc); public health (M Sc); public policy and management (MPA); security studies (M Sc); social work (M Sc); spatial planning and urban design (MA); sports therapy (M Sc); supporting older children and young people with dyslexia (MA); teaching languages (MA), including Arabic, English; translation (MA); woman and child abuse (MA).

**Louisiana State University Health Sciences Center,** School of Graduate Studies in New Orleans, Department of Microbiology, Immunology, and Parasitology, New Orleans, LA 70112-1393. Offers microbiology and immunology (PhD); MD/PhD. *Degree requirements:* For doctorate, comprehensive exam, thesis/dissertation, preliminary exam, qualifying exam. *Entrance requirements:* For doctorate, GRE General Test. Additional exam requirements/recommendations for international students: recommended—TOEFL, IELTS.

**Louisiana State University Health Sciences Center at Shreveport,** Department of Microbiology and Immunology, Shreveport, LA 71130-3932. Offers MS, PhD, MD/PhD. Terminal master's awarded for partial completion of doctoral program. *Degree requirements:* For master's, comprehensive exam, thesis; for doctorate, comprehensive exam, thesis/dissertation, research proposal. *Entrance requirements:* For master's and doctorate, GRE General Test. Additional exam requirements/recommendations for international students: required—TOEFL. Electronic applications accepted. *Expenses:* Contact institution.

**Loyola University Chicago,** Graduate School, Integrated Program in Biomedical Sciences, Maywood, IL 60660. Offers biochemistry and molecular biology (MS, PhD); cell and molecular physiology (MS, PhD); infectious disease and immunology (MS); integrative cell biology (MS, PhD); microbiology and immunology (MS, PhD); molecular pharmacology and therapeutics (MS, PhD); neuroscience (MS, PhD). *Students:* Average age 25. 773 applicants, 34% accepted, 122 enrolled. In 2019, 46 master's, 12 doctorates awarded. *Degree requirements:* For master's, thesis; for doctorate, comprehensive exam, thesis/dissertation. *Entrance requirements:* For doctorate, GRE. Additional exam requirements/recommendations for international students: required—TOEFL (minimum score 94 iBT), IELTS (minimum score 7.5). *Application deadline:* For fall admission, 2/7 for domestic students. Applications are processed on a rolling basis. Electronic applications accepted. *Expenses:* Contact institution. *Financial support:* In 2019–20, 20 students received support. Schmitt Fellowships and yearly tuition scholarships (averaging $25,032) available. Financial award application deadline: 6/15; financial award applicants required to submit FAFSA. *Unit head:* Dr. Leanne L. Cribbs, Associate Dean, Graduate Education, 708-327-2817, Fax: 708-216-8216, E-mail: lcribbs@luc.edu. *Application contact:* Margarita Quesada, Graduate Program Secretary, 708-216-3532, Fax: 708-216-8216, E-mail: mquesad@luc.edu.
Website: http://ssom.luc.edu/graduate_school/degree-programs/ipbsphd/

**Massachusetts Institute of Technology,** School of Science, Department of Biology, Cambridge, MA 02139. Offers biochemistry (PhD); biological oceanography (PhD); biology (PhD); biophysical chemistry and molecular structure (PhD); cell biology (PhD); computational and systems biology (PhD); developmental biology (PhD); genetics (PhD); immunology (PhD); microbiology (PhD); molecular biology (PhD); neurobiology (PhD). *Degree requirements:* For doctorate, comprehensive exam, thesis/dissertation, teaching assistantship during two semesters. *Entrance requirements:* For doctorate, GRE General Test. Additional exam requirements/recommendations for international students: required—TOEFL, IELTS. Electronic applications accepted.

**Mayo Clinic Graduate School of Biomedical Sciences,** Program in Immunology, Rochester, MN 55905. Offers PhD. Terminal master's awarded for partial completion of doctoral program. *Degree requirements:* For doctorate, comprehensive exam, thesis/dissertation, oral defense of dissertation, qualifying oral and written exam. *Entrance requirements:* For doctorate, GRE, 1 year of chemistry, biology, calculus, and physics. Additional exam requirements/recommendations for international students: required—TOEFL. Electronic applications accepted.

**McGill University,** Faculty of Graduate and Postdoctoral Studies, Faculty of Medicine, Department of Microbiology and Immunology, Montréal, QC H3A 2T5, Canada. Offers M Sc, M Sc A, PhD.

**McMaster University,** Faculty of Health Sciences and School of Graduate Studies, Program in Medical Sciences, Immunity and Infection Area, Hamilton, ON L8S 4M2, Canada. Offers M Sc, PhD, MD/PhD. *Degree requirements:* For master's, thesis; for doctorate, comprehensive exam, thesis/dissertation. *Entrance requirements:* For master's, honors B Sc, B+ average in related field; for doctorate, M Sc, minimum B+ average, students with proven research experience and an A average may be admitted with a B Sc degree. Additional exam requirements/recommendations for international students: required—TOEFL (minimum score 580 paper-based; 92 iBT).

**Medical University of South Carolina,** College of Graduate Studies, Department of Microbiology and Immunology, Charleston, SC 29425. Offers MS, PhD, DMD/PhD, MD/PhD. Terminal master's awarded for partial completion of doctoral program. *Degree requirements:* For master's, thesis; for doctorate, thesis/dissertation, oral and written exams. *Entrance requirements:* For master's, GRE General Test, MCAT, or DAT, minimum GPA of 3.0; for doctorate, GRE General Test, interview, minimum GPA of 3.0, research experience. Additional exam requirements/recommendations for international students: required—TOEFL (minimum score 600 paper-based; 100 iBT). Electronic applications accepted.

**Meharry Medical College,** School of Graduate Studies, Program in Biomedical Sciences, Microbiology and Immunology Emphasis, Nashville, TN 37208-9989. Offers PhD, MD/PhD. *Degree requirements:* For doctorate, comprehensive exam, thesis/dissertation. *Entrance requirements:* For doctorate, GRE General Test, GRE Subject Test, undergraduate degree in related science. Additional exam requirements/recommendations for international students: required—TOEFL. *Application deadline:* For fall admission, 6/1 for domestic students. Applications are processed on a rolling basis. Application fee: $65. *Financial support:* Fellowships, research assistantships, and Federal Work-Study available. Financial award application deadline: 4/15. *Unit head:* Dr. Minu Chaudhuri, Professor, 615-327-5726, E-mail: mchaudhuri@mmc.edu. *Application contact:* Dr. Minu Chaudhuri, Professor, 615-327-5726, E-mail: mchaudhuri@mmc.edu.
Website: https://home.mmc.edu/school-of-graduate-studies-research/microbiology-immunology/

**Memorial University of Newfoundland,** Faculty of Medicine and School of Graduate Studies, Graduate Programs in Medicine, Division of Biomedical Sciences, St. John's, NL A1C 5S7, Canada. Offers cancer (M Sc, PhD); cardiovascular (M Sc, PhD);

immunology (M Sc, PhD); neuroscience (M Sc, PhD). *Program availability:* Part-time. *Degree requirements:* For master's, thesis; for doctorate, comprehensive exam, thesis/dissertation, oral defense of thesis. *Entrance requirements:* For master's, MD or B Sc; for doctorate, MD or M Sc. Additional exam requirements/recommendations for international students: required—TOEFL.

**Montana State University,** The Graduate School, College of Agriculture, Department of Immunology and Infectious Diseases, Bozeman, MT 59717. Offers MS, PhD. *Program availability:* Part-time. *Degree requirements:* For master's, comprehensive exam; for doctorate, comprehensive exam, thesis/dissertation. *Entrance requirements:* For master's and doctorate, GRE General Test. Additional exam requirements/recommendations for international students: required—TOEFL (minimum score 550 paper-based). Electronic applications accepted.

**New York Medical College,** Graduate School of Basic Medical Sciences, Valhalla, NY 10595. Offers biochemistry and molecular biology (MS, PhD); cell biology (MS, PhD); microbiology and immunology (MS, PhD); pathology (MS, PhD); pharmacology (MS, PhD); physiology (MS, PhD); MD/PhD. *Program availability:* Part-time, evening/weekend. *Faculty:* 98 full-time (24 women). *Students:* 141 full-time (90 women), 17 part-time (3 women); includes 68 minority (16 Black or African American, non-Hispanic/Latino; 32 Asian, non-Hispanic/Latino; 15 Hispanic/Latino; 1 Native Hawaiian or other Pacific Islander, non-Hispanic/Latino; 4 Two or more races, non-Hispanic/Latino), 19 international. Average age 26. 351 applicants, 62% accepted, 86 enrolled. In 2019, 28 master's, 5 doctorates awarded. Terminal master's awarded for partial completion of doctoral program. *Degree requirements:* For master's, thesis; for doctorate, comprehensive exam, thesis/dissertation. *Entrance requirements:* For master's, GRE General Test, MCAT, or DAT, OAT. Additional exam requirements/recommendations for international students: required—TOEFL (minimum score 90 iBT), TOEFL or IELTS; one of the two exams are required. *Application deadline:* For fall admission, 6/1 priority date for domestic students, 5/1 priority date for international students. Applications are processed on a rolling basis. Application fee: $75 ($100 for international students). Electronic applications accepted. *Expenses:* $1200 credit and $620 fees. *Financial support:* In 2019–20, 400 students received support. Federal Work-Study, scholarships/grants, unspecified assistantships, and Student Federal Loans available. Financial award application deadline: 4/30; financial award applicants required to submit FAFSA. *Unit head:* Dr. Marina K Holz, Dean, 914-594-4110, Fax: 914-594-4944, E-mail: mholz@nymc.edu. *Application contact:* Valerie Romeo-Messana, Director of Admissions, 914-594-4110, Fax: 914-594-4944, E-mail: v_romeomessana@nymc.edu.
Website: https://www.nymc.edu/graduate-school-of-basic-medical-sciences-gsbms/gsbms-academics/

**New York University,** Graduate School of Arts and Science, Department of Biology, New York, NY 10012-1019. Offers biology (PhD); biomedical journalism (MS); cancer and molecular biology (PhD); computational biology (PhD); computers in biological research (MS); developmental genetics (PhD); general biology (MS); immunology and microbiology (PhD); molecular genetics (PhD); neurobiology (PhD); oral biology (MS); plant biology (PhD); recombinant DNA technology (MS); MS/MBA. *Program availability:* Part-time. Terminal master's awarded for partial completion of doctoral program. *Degree requirements:* For master's, thesis or alternative, qualifying paper; for doctorate, comprehensive exam, thesis/dissertation. *Entrance requirements:* For master's and doctorate, GRE General Test. Additional exam requirements/recommendations for international students: required—TOEFL, IELTS.

**Old Dominion University,** College of Sciences, Master of Science in Biology Program, Norfolk, VA 23529. Offers biology (MS); microbiology and immunology (MS). *Program availability:* Part-time. *Degree requirements:* For master's, comprehensive exam, thesis optional, 31 credits. *Entrance requirements:* For master's, GRE General Test, MCAT, minimum GPA of 3.0. Additional exam requirements/recommendations for international students: required—TOEFL (minimum score 550 paper-based; 79 iBT). Electronic applications accepted.

**Oregon Health & Science University,** School of Medicine, Graduate Programs in Medicine, Program in Molecular and Cellular Biosciences, Department of Molecular Microbiology and Immunology, Portland, OR 97239-3098. Offers PhD. Terminal master's awarded for partial completion of doctoral program. *Degree requirements:* For doctorate, comprehensive exam, thesis/dissertation, qualifying exam. *Entrance requirements:* For doctorate, GRE General Test (minimum scores: 153 Verbal/148 Quantitative/4.5 Analytical) or MCAT (for some programs). Electronic applications accepted.

**Oregon State University,** College of Science; Program in Microbiology, Corvallis, OR 97331. Offers environmental microbiology (MA, MS, PhD); food microbiology (MA, MS, PhD); genomics (MA, MS, PhD); immunology (MA, MS, PhD); microbial ecology (MA, MS, PhD); microbial evolution (MA, MS, PhD); parasitology (MA, MS, PhD); pathogenic microbiology (MA, MS, PhD); virology (MA). Terminal master's awarded for partial completion of doctoral program. *Entrance requirements:* For master's and doctorate, GRE. Additional exam requirements/recommendations for international students: required—TOEFL (minimum score 600 paper-based; 100 iBT).

**Penn State Hershey Medical Center,** College of Medicine, Graduate School Programs in the Biomedical Sciences, Graduate Program in Biomedical Sciences, Hershey, PA 17033. Offers biochemistry and molecular genetics (MS, PhD); biomedical sciences (MS, PhD); cellular and integrative physiology (MS, PhD); translational therapeutics (MS, PhD); virology and immunology (MS, PhD); MD/PhD; PhD/MBA. Terminal master's awarded for partial completion of doctoral program. *Degree requirements:* For master's, thesis; for doctorate, comprehensive exam, thesis/dissertation, candidacy exam. *Entrance requirements:* For doctorate, GRE General Test. Additional exam requirements/recommendations for international students: required—TOEFL (minimum score 550 paper-based; 81 iBT). Electronic applications accepted.

**Purdue University,** College of Pharmacy and Graduate School, Graduate Programs in Pharmacy and Pharmacal Sciences, Department of Medicinal Chemistry and Molecular Pharmacology, West Lafayette, IN 47907. Offers biophysical and computational chemistry (PhD); cancer research (PhD); immunology and infectious disease (PhD); medicinal biochemistry and molecular biology (PhD); medicinal chemistry and chemical biology (PhD); molecular pharmacology (PhD); neuropharmacology, neurodegeneration, and neurotoxicity (PhD); systems biology and functional genomics (PhD). *Faculty:* 20 full-time (5 women), 7 part-time/adjunct (2 women). *Students:* 80 full-time (40 women), 2 part-time (0 women); includes 9 minority (5 Asian, non-Hispanic/Latino; 2 Hispanic/Latino; 2 Two or more races, non-Hispanic/Latino), 44 international. Average age 26. 162 applicants, 20% accepted, 15 enrolled. In 2019, 11 doctorates awarded. *Degree requirements:* For doctorate, thesis/dissertation. *Entrance requirements:* For doctorate, GRE General Test; GRE Subject Test in biology, biochemistry, and chemistry (recommended), minimum undergraduate GPA of 3.0. Additional exam requirements/recommendations for international students: required—TOEFL (minimum score 550 paper-based; 77 iBT); recommended—TWE. *Application deadline:* For fall admission, 2/1 for domestic and international students. Applications are processed on a rolling basis. Application fee: $60 ($75 for international students). Electronic applications accepted. *Financial support:* Fellowships, research assistantships, teaching assistantships, and traineeships available. Support available to

part-time students. Financial award applicants required to submit FAFSA. *Unit head:* Zhong-Yin Zhang, Head, 765-494-1403, E-mail: zhang-yn@purdue.edu. *Application contact:* Delayne Graham, Graduate Contact, 765-494-1362, E-mail: dkgraham@purdue.edu.

**Purdue University,** School of Veterinary Medicine and Graduate School, Graduate Programs in Veterinary Medicine, Department of Comparative Pathobiology, West Lafayette, IN 47907-2027. Offers comparative epidemiology and public health (MS); comparative epidemiology and public heath (PhD); comparative microbiology and immunology (MS, PhD); comparative pathobiology (MS, PhD); interdisciplinary studies (PhD), including microbial pathogenesis, molecular signaling and cancer biology, molecular virology; lab animal medicine (MS); veterinary anatomic pathology (MS); veterinary clinical pathology (MS). Terminal master's awarded for partial completion of doctoral program. *Degree requirements:* For master's, thesis (for some programs); for doctorate, thesis/dissertation. *Entrance requirements:* For master's and doctorate, GRE General Test. Additional exam requirements/recommendations for international students: required—TOEFL (minimum score 575 paper-based), IELTS (minimum score 6.5), TWE (minimum score 4). Electronic applications accepted.

**Rosalind Franklin University of Medicine and Science,** School of Graduate and Postdoctoral Studies - Interdisciplinary Graduate Program in Biomedical Sciences, Department of Microbiology and Immunology, North Chicago, IL 60064-3095. Offers PhD, MD/PhD. Terminal master's awarded for partial completion of doctoral program. *Degree requirements:* For doctorate, comprehensive exam, thesis/dissertation. *Entrance requirements:* For doctorate, GRE General Test. Additional exam requirements/recommendations for international students: required—TOEFL, TWE.

**Rush University,** Graduate College, Division of Immunology and Microbiology, Program in Immunology/Microbiology, Chicago, IL 60612-3832. Offers immunology (MS, PhD); virology (MS, PhD); MD/PhD. *Program availability:* Part-time. Terminal master's awarded for partial completion of doctoral program. *Degree requirements:* For master's, thesis; for doctorate, thesis/dissertation, comprehensive preliminary exam. *Entrance requirements:* For master's, GRE General Test; for doctorate, GRE General Test, interview, minimum GPA of 3.0. Additional exam requirements/recommendations for international students: required—TOEFL. Electronic applications accepted.

**Rutgers University - Newark,** Graduate School of Biomedical Sciences, Program in Molecular Pathology and Immunology, Newark, NJ 07107. Offers PhD. *Entrance requirements:* Additional exam requirements/recommendations for international students: required—TOEFL. Electronic applications accepted.

**Rutgers University - New Brunswick,** Graduate School-New Brunswick, Programs in the Molecular Biosciences, Piscataway, NJ 08854-8097. Offers biochemistry (PhD); cell and developmental biology (MS, PhD); microbiology and molecular genetics (MS, PhD), including applied microbiology, clinical microbiology, computational molecular biology (PhD), immunology, microbial biochemistry, molecular genetics, virology.

**Saint Louis University,** Graduate Programs, School of Medicine, Graduate Programs in Biomedical Sciences, Department of Molecular Microbiology and Immunology, St. Louis, MO 63103. Offers PhD. *Degree requirements:* For doctorate, comprehensive exam, thesis/dissertation, qualifying exams. *Entrance requirements:* For doctorate, GRE General Test (GRE Subject Test optional), letters of recommendation, resume, interview. Additional exam requirements/recommendations for international students: required—TOEFL (minimum score 525 paper-based). Electronic applications accepted.

**Stanford University,** School of Medicine, Graduate Programs in Medicine, Department of Microbiology and Immunology, Stanford, CA 94305-2004. Offers PhD. *Expenses:* Tuition: Full-time $52,479; part-time $34,110 per unit. *Required fees:* $672; $224 per quarter. Tuition and fees vary according to program and student level.
Website: http://cmgm.stanford.edu/micro/

**State University of New York Upstate Medical University,** College of Graduate Studies, Program in Microbiology and Immunology, Syracuse, NY 13210. Offers microbiology (MS); microbiology and immunology (PhD); MD/PhD. Terminal master's awarded for partial completion of doctoral program. *Degree requirements:* For master's, thesis; for doctorate, comprehensive exam, thesis/dissertation. *Entrance requirements:* For master's, GRE General Test, interview; for doctorate, GRE General Test, telephone interview. Additional exam requirements/recommendations for international students: required—TOEFL. Electronic applications accepted.

**Stony Brook University, State University of New York,** Graduate School, College of Arts and Sciences, Department of Biochemistry and Cell Biology, Stony Brook, NY 11794. Offers biochemistry and structural biology (PhD); molecular and cellular biology (MA, PhD), including biochemistry and molecular biology (PhD), biological sciences (MA), cellular and developmental biology (PhD), immunology and pathology (PhD), molecular and cellular biology (PhD). *Faculty:* 18 full-time (5 women), 1 part-time/adjunct (0 women). *Students:* 104 full-time (61 women), 7 part-time (4 women); includes 28 minority (6 Black or African American, non-Hispanic/Latino; 15 Asian, non-Hispanic/Latino; 7 Hispanic/Latino), 48 international. Average age 26. 205 applicants, 37% accepted, 35 enrolled. In 2019, 11 master's, 17 doctorates awarded. *Degree requirements:* For doctorate, comprehensive exam, thesis/dissertation, teaching experience. *Entrance requirements:* For doctorate, GRE General Test, GRE Subject Test. Additional exam requirements/recommendations for international students: required—TOEFL (minimum score 90 iBT). *Application deadline:* For fall admission, 1/15 for domestic students; for spring admission, 10/15 for domestic students. Application fee: $100. *Expenses:* Contact institution. *Financial support:* In 2019–20, 6 fellowships, 41 research assistantships, 17 teaching assistantships were awarded; Federal Work-Study also available. *Unit head:* Prof. Aaron Neiman, Chair, 631-632-1543, Fax: 631-632-8575, E-mail: aaron.neiman@stonybrook.edu. *Application contact:* Amy Saas, Coordinator, 631-632-8613, Fax: 631-632-9730, E-mail: Amy.Saas@stonybrook.edu. Website: http://www.sunysb.edu/biochem/

**Thomas Jefferson University,** Jefferson College of Life Sciences, PhD Program in Immunology and Microbial Pathogenesis, Philadelphia, PA 19107. Offers PhD. *Degree requirements:* For doctorate, comprehensive exam, thesis/dissertation. *Entrance requirements:* For doctorate, GRE General Test, minimum GPA of 3.2. Additional exam requirements/recommendations for international students: required—TOEFL, IELTS (minimum score 7). Electronic applications accepted.

**Tufts University,** Graduate School of Biomedical Sciences, Immunology Program, Medford, MA 02155. Offers PhD. *Faculty:* 28 full-time (13 women), 10 part-time/adjunct (5 women). *Students:* 22 full-time (12 women); includes 6 minority (2 Black or African American, non-Hispanic/Latino; 2 Asian, non-Hispanic/Latino; 1 Hispanic/Latino; 1 Two or more races, non-Hispanic/Latino), 2 international. Average age 30. 58 applicants, 12% accepted, 3 enrolled. In 2019, 2 doctorates awarded. Terminal master's awarded for partial completion of doctoral program. *Degree requirements:* For doctorate, comprehensive exam, thesis/dissertation. *Entrance requirements:* For doctorate, 3 letters of reference, resume, personal statement. *Application deadline:* For fall admission, 12/1 priority date for domestic and international students. Application fee: $90. Electronic applications accepted. *Expenses:* Tuition: Part-time $1799 per credit hour. Full-time tuition and fees vary according to degree level, program and student level. Part-time tuition and fees vary according to course load. *Financial support:*

Fellowships, research assistantships, and traineeships available. Financial award application deadline: 12/1. *Unit head:* Dr. Pilar Alcaide, Director, 617-636-6836, E-mail: Pilar.Alcaide@tufts.edu. *Application contact:* Jeff Miller, 617-636-6767, Fax: 617-636-0375, E-mail: GSBS-Admissions@tufts.edu.
Website: https://gsbs.tufts.edu/academics/immunology

**Tulane University,** School of Medicine, Graduate Programs in Biomedical Sciences, Department of Microbiology and Immunology, New Orleans, LA 70118-5669. Offers MS. *Degree requirements:* For master's, thesis. *Entrance requirements:* For master's, GRE General Test, minimum B average in undergraduate course work. Additional exam requirements/recommendations for international students: required—TOEFL. Electronic applications accepted. *Expenses: Tuition:* Full-time $57,004; part-time $3167 per credit hour. *Required fees:* $2086; $44.50 per credit hour. $80 per term. Tuition and fees vary according to course load, degree level and program.

**Uniformed Services University of the Health Sciences,** F. Edward Hebert School of Medicine, Graduate Programs in the Biomedical Sciences and Public Health, Graduate Program in Emerging Infectious Diseases, Bethesda, MD 20814-4799. Offers PhD. *Degree requirements:* For doctorate, comprehensive exam, thesis/dissertation, qualifying exam. *Entrance requirements:* For doctorate, GRE General Test. Electronic applications accepted.

**Universidad Central del Caribe,** School of Medicine, Program in Biomedical Sciences, Bayamón, PR 00960-6032. Offers anatomy and cell biology (MA, MS); biochemistry (MS); biomedical sciences (MA); cellular and molecular biology (PhD); microbiology and immunology (MA, MS); pharmacology (MS); physiology (MS).

**Université de Montréal,** Faculty of Medicine, Department of Microbiology and Immunology, Montréal, QC H3C 3J7, Canada. Offers M Sc, PhD. Terminal master's awarded for partial completion of doctoral program. *Degree requirements:* For master's, thesis; for doctorate, thesis/dissertation, general exam. *Entrance requirements:* For master's and doctorate, proficiency in French, knowledge of English. Electronic applications accepted.

**Université de Montréal,** Faculty of Veterinary Medicine, Program in Virology and Immunology, Montréal, QC H3C 3J7, Canada. Offers PhD. *Degree requirements:* For doctorate, thesis/dissertation, general exam. *Entrance requirements:* For doctorate, proficiency in French, knowledge of English. Electronic applications accepted.

**Université de Sherbrooke,** Faculty of Medicine and Health Sciences, Graduate Programs in Medicine, Program in Immunology, Sherbrooke, QC J1H 5N4, Canada. Offers M Sc, PhD. Electronic applications accepted.

**Université du Québec, Institut National de la Recherche Scientifique,** Graduate Programs, Armand-Frappier Santé Biotechnologie, Laval, QC H7V 1B7, Canada. Offers applied microbiology (M Sc); biology (PhD); experimental health sciences (M Sc); virology and immunology (M Sc, PhD). *Program availability:* Part-time. *Faculty:* 46 full-time. *Students:* 157 full-time (94 women), 9 part-time (4 women), 100 international. Average age 30. 23 applicants, 96% accepted, 21 enrolled. In 2019, 19 master's, 20 doctorates awarded. *Degree requirements:* For master's, thesis; for doctorate, thesis/dissertation. *Entrance requirements:* For master's, appropriate bachelor's degree, proficiency in French; for doctorate, appropriate master's degree, proficiency in French. *Application deadline:* For fall admission, 3/30 for domestic and international students; for winter admission, 11/1 for domestic and international students; for spring admission, 3/1 for domestic and international students. Application fee: $45 Canadian dollars. Electronic applications accepted. *Financial support:* In 2019-20, fellowships (averaging $16,500 per year) were awarded; research assistantships also available. *Unit head:* Claude Guertin, Director, 450-687-5010, Fax: 450-686-5501, E-mail: claude.guertin@iaf.inrs.ca. *Application contact:* Sean Otto, Registrar, 418-654-2518, Fax: 418-654-3858, E-mail: sean.otto@inrs.ca.
Website: http://www.iaf.inrs.ca

**University at Buffalo, the State University of New York,** Graduate School, Graduate Programs in Cancer Research and Biomedical Sciences at Roswell Park Cancer Institute, Buffalo, NY 14260. Offers cancer pathology and prevention (PhD); cellular and molecular biology (PhD); immunology (PhD); interdisciplinary natural sciences (MS); molecular and cellular biophysics and biochemistry (PhD); molecular pharmacology and cancer therapeutics (PhD). Terminal master's awarded for partial completion of doctoral program. *Degree requirements:* For master's, thesis, oral defense of thesis; for doctorate, comprehensive exam, thesis/dissertation, oral defense of dissertation. *Entrance requirements:* For master's and doctorate, GRE General Test. Additional exam requirements/recommendations for international students: required—TOEFL (minimum score 79 iBT). Electronic applications accepted. *Expenses: Tuition:* area resident: Full-time $11,310; part-time $471 per credit hour. Tuition, state resident: full-time $11,310; part-time $471 per credit hour. Tuition, nonresident: full-time $23,100; part-time $963 per credit hour. *International tuition:* $23,100 full-time. *Required fees:* $2820.

**University at Buffalo, the State University of New York,** Graduate School, Jacobs School of Medicine and Biomedical Sciences, Graduate Programs in Medicine and Biomedical Sciences, Department of Microbiology and Immunology, Buffalo, NY 14260. Offers MS, PhD. *Program availability:* Part-time. *Faculty:* 16 full-time (5 women), 1 part-time/adjunct (0 women). *Students:* 19 full-time (13 women), 10 part-time (8 women); includes 2 minority (1 Black or African American, non-Hispanic/Latino; 1 American Indian or Alaska Native, non-Hispanic/Latino), 9 international. Average age 26. 39 applicants, 31% accepted, 11 enrolled. In 2019, 4 master's, 4 doctorates awarded. Terminal master's awarded for partial completion of doctoral program. *Degree requirements:* For master's, comprehensive exam, thesis or alternative; for doctorate, thesis/dissertation, departmental qualifying exam. *Entrance requirements:* For master's, GRE General Test, 3 letters of recommendation, personal statement, curriculum vitae/resume, transcripts; for doctorate, 3 letters of recommendation, personal statement, curriculum vitae/resume, transcripts. Additional exam requirements/recommendations for international students: required—TOEFL (minimum score 79 iBT), IELTS (minimum score 6.5), TOEFL (minimum score 79 iBT) or IELTS (minimum score 6.0). *Application deadline:* For fall admission, 4/1 priority date for international students. Applications are processed on a rolling basis. Application fee: $85. Electronic applications accepted. *Expenses:* Contact institution. *Financial support:* In 2019-20, 4 students received support, including 3 teaching assistantships (averaging $3,500 per year). Financial award application deadline: 2/1; financial award applicants required to submit FAFSA. *Unit head:* Dr. James Bangs, Chair/Professor, 716-829-2907, Fax: 716-829-2158. *Application contact:* Dr. Laurie Read, Director of Graduate Studies, 716-829-3307, Fax: 716-829-2158, E-mail: lread@buffalo.edu.
Website: http://medicine.buffalo.edu/departments/micro.html

**The University of Alabama at Birmingham,** Joint Health Sciences, Immunology Theme, Birmingham, AL 35294. Offers PhD. *Students:* 43 full-time (18 women); includes 18 minority (4 Black or African American, non-Hispanic/Latino; 10 Asian, non-Hispanic/Latino; 4 Hispanic/Latino). Average age 27. 59 applicants, 17% accepted, 9 enrolled. In 2019, 8 doctorates awarded. *Degree requirements:* For doctorate, comprehensive exam, thesis/dissertation. *Entrance requirements:* For doctorate, personal statement, resume or curriculum vitae, letters of recommendation, research experience, interview. Additional exam requirements/recommendations for international students: required—TOEFL (minimum score 80 iBT), IELTS (minimum score 6.5). *Application deadline:* For

fall admission, 12/31 for domestic and international students. Applications are processed on a rolling basis. Electronic applications accepted. *Financial support:* In 2019-20, fellowships with full tuition reimbursements (averaging $29,000 per year), research assistantships with full tuition reimbursements (averaging $30,000 per year) were awarded; health care benefits also available. *Unit head:* Dr. Louis Justement, Theme Director, 205-934-1429, E-mail: lbjust@uab.edu. *Application contact:* Alyssa Zasada, Admissions Manager for Graduate Biomedical Sciences, 205-934-3857, E-mail: grad-gbs@uab.edu.
Website: http://www.uab.edu/gbs/home/themes/imm

**University of Alberta,** Faculty of Medicine and Dentistry and Faculty of Graduate Studies and Research, Graduate Programs in Medicine, Department of Medical Microbiology and Immunology, Edmonton, AB T6G 2E1, Canada. Offers M Sc, PhD. Terminal master's awarded for partial completion of doctoral program. *Degree requirements:* For master's, thesis; for doctorate, thesis/dissertation. *Entrance requirements:* For master's and doctorate, minimum GPA of 3.3. Additional exam requirements/recommendations for international students: required—TOEFL (minimum score 600 paper-based; 96 iBT).

**The University of Arizona,** College of Medicine, Department of Immunobiology, Tucson, AZ 85721. Offers PhD. *Degree requirements:* For doctorate, thesis/dissertation. *Entrance requirements:* For doctorate, GRE General Test, minimum GPA of 3.0.

**University of Arkansas for Medical Sciences,** Graduate School, Little Rock, AR 72205. Offers biochemistry and molecular biology (MS, PhD); bioinformatics (MS, PhD); cellular physiology and molecular biophysics (MS, PhD); clinical nutrition (MS); interdisciplinary biomedical sciences (MS, PhD, Certificate); interdisciplinary toxicology (MS); microbiology and immunology (PhD); neurobiology and developmental sciences (PhD); pharmacology (PhD); MD/PhD. *Program availability:* Part-time. Terminal master's awarded for partial completion of doctoral program. *Degree requirements:* For master's, comprehensive exam (for some programs), thesis (for some programs); for doctorate, thesis/dissertation. *Entrance requirements:* For master's and doctorate, GRE. Additional exam requirements/recommendations for international students: required—TOEFL. Electronic applications accepted. *Expenses:* Contact institution.

**The University of British Columbia,** Faculty of Science, Department of Microbiology and Immunology, Vancouver, BC V6T 1Z3, Canada. Offers M Sc, PhD. *Degree requirements:* For master's, thesis; for doctorate, comprehensive exam, thesis/dissertation. *Entrance requirements:* For master's and doctorate, GRE General Test. Additional exam requirements/recommendations for international students: required—TOEFL. Electronic applications accepted. *Expenses:* Contact institution.

**University of Calgary,** Cumming School of Medicine and Faculty of Graduate Studies, Program in Microbiology and infectious Disease, Calgary, AB T2N 1N4, Canada. Offers M Sc, PhD. *Degree requirements:* For master's, thesis, oral thesis exam; for doctorate, thesis/dissertation, candidacy exam, oral thesis exam. *Entrance requirements:* For master's and doctorate, minimum GPA of 3.2. Additional exam requirements/recommendations for international students: required—TOEFL (minimum score 580 paper-based). Electronic applications accepted.

**University of California, Berkeley,** Graduate Division, School of Public Health, Group in Infectious Diseases and Immunity, Berkeley, CA 94720. Offers PhD. *Entrance requirements:* For doctorate, GRE General Test, minimum GPA of 3.0, 3 letters of recommendation. Electronic applications accepted.

**University of California, Davis,** Graduate Studies, Graduate Group in Immunology, Davis, CA 95616. Offers MS, PhD. Terminal master's awarded for partial completion of doctoral program. *Degree requirements:* For master's, comprehensive exam (for some programs), thesis (for some programs); for doctorate, thesis/dissertation. *Entrance requirements:* For master's and doctorate, GRE General Test. Additional exam requirements/recommendations for international students: required—TOEFL (minimum score 550 paper-based). Electronic applications accepted.

**University of California, Los Angeles,** David Geffen School of Medicine and Graduate Division, Graduate Programs in Medicine, Department of Microbiology, Immunology and Molecular Genetics, Los Angeles, CA 90095. Offers MS, PhD. *Degree requirements:* For master's, thesis; for doctorate, thesis/dissertation, oral and written qualifying exams; 2 quarters of teaching experience. *Entrance requirements:* For master's and doctorate, GRE General Test, bachelor's degree; minimum undergraduate GPA of 3.0 (or its equivalent if letter grade system not used). Additional exam requirements/recommendations for international students: required—TOEFL. Electronic applications accepted.

**University of California, Los Angeles,** Graduate Division, College of Letters and Science and David Geffen School of Medicine, UCLA ACCESS to Programs in the Molecular, Cellular and Integrative Life Sciences, Los Angeles, CA 90095. Offers biochemistry and molecular biology (PhD); biological chemistry (PhD); cellular and molecular pathology (PhD); human genetics (PhD); microbiology, immunology, and molecular genetics (PhD); molecular biology (PhD); molecular toxicology (PhD); molecular, cellular and integrative physiology (PhD); neurobiology (PhD); oral biology (PhD); physiology (PhD). *Degree requirements:* For doctorate, thesis/dissertation, oral and written qualifying exams. *Entrance requirements:* For doctorate, GRE General Test, bachelor's degree; minimum undergraduate GPA of 3.0 (or its equivalent if letter grade system not used). Additional exam requirements/recommendations for international students: required—TOEFL. Electronic applications accepted.

**University of Chicago,** Division of the Biological Sciences, Committee on Immunology, Chicago, IL 60637. Offers PhD. *Degree requirements:* For doctorate, thesis/dissertation, ethics class, 2 teaching assistantships, preliminary exams. *Entrance requirements:* For doctorate, GRE General Test, transcripts, statement of purpose, 3 letters of recommendation. Additional exam requirements/recommendations for international students: required—TOEFL (minimum score 600 paper-based; 104 iBT), IELTS (minimum score 7). Electronic applications accepted.

**University of Cincinnati,** Graduate School, College of Medicine, Graduate Programs in Biomedical Sciences, Department of Pediatrics, Cincinnati, OH 45221. Offers immunobiology (PhD); molecular and developmental biology (PhD). *Degree requirements:* For doctorate, thesis/dissertation, qualifying exam. *Entrance requirements:* For doctorate, GRE General Test, minimum GPA of 3.0. Additional exam requirements/recommendations for international students: required—TOEFL (minimum score 600 paper-based; 100 iBT). Electronic applications accepted.

**University of Cincinnati,** Graduate School, College of Medicine, Graduate Programs in Biomedical Sciences, Immunology Graduate Program, Cincinnati, OH 45229. Offers MS, PhD. *Program availability:* Part-time. Terminal master's awarded for partial completion of doctoral program. *Degree requirements:* For master's, thesis, seminar, thesis with oral defense; for doctorate, thesis/dissertation, seminar, dissertation with oral defense, written and oral candidacy exams. *Entrance requirements:* For master's, bachelor's degree in biology-related field or bachelor's degree in any field and work experience in biology-related field; for doctorate, 3.0 minimum in a bachelor's degree in biology-related field, some research experience. Additional exam requirements/recommendations for international students: required—TOEFL (minimum score 100 paper-based; 100 iBT). Electronic applications accepted. *Expenses:* Contact institution.

*Immunology*

**University of Colorado Denver,** School of Medicine, Integrated Department of Immunology, Aurora, CO 80206. Offers PhD. *Degree requirements:* For doctorate, thesis/dissertation, 30 credit hours of formal course work, three laboratory rotations, oral comprehensive examination, 30 credit hours of dissertation research, final defense of the dissertation. *Entrance requirements:* For doctorate, GRE, letters of recommendation, statement of purpose, interview. Additional exam requirements/recommendations for international students: required—TOEFL (minimum score 550 paper-based; 89 iBT). Electronic applications accepted. Tuition and fees vary according to course load, program and reciprocity agreements.

**University of Colorado Denver,** School of Medicine, Program in Microbiology, Aurora, CO 80206. Offers microbiology (PhD); microbiology and immunology (PhD). *Entrance requirements:* For doctorate, GRE, three letters of reference, two copies of official transcripts, minimum GPA of 3.0. Tuition and fees vary according to course load, program and reciprocity agreements.

**University of Connecticut Health Center,** Graduate School, Programs in Biomedical Sciences, Graduate Program in Immunology, Farmington, CT 06030. Offers PhD, DMD/PhD, MD/PhD. *Degree requirements:* For doctorate, comprehensive exam, thesis/dissertation. *Entrance requirements:* For doctorate, GRE General Test. Additional exam requirements/recommendations for international students: required—TOEFL (minimum score 600 paper-based). Electronic applications accepted.

**University of Florida,** College of Medicine and Graduate School, Interdisciplinary Program in Biomedical Sciences, Concentration in Immunology and Microbiology, Gainesville, FL 32611. Offers PhD. *Degree requirements:* For doctorate, thesis/dissertation. *Entrance requirements:* For doctorate, GRE General Test, minimum GPA of 3.0, biochemistry before enrollment. Additional exam requirements/recommendations for international students: required—TOEFL. Electronic applications accepted.

**University of Guelph,** Ontario Veterinary College and Office of Graduate and Postdoctoral Studies, Graduate Programs in Veterinary Sciences, Department of Pathobiology, Guelph, ON N1G 2W1, Canada. Offers anatomic pathology (DV Sc, Diploma); clinical pathology (Diploma); comparative pathology (M Sc, PhD); immunology (M Sc, PhD); laboratory animal science (DV Sc); pathology (M Sc, PhD, Diploma); veterinary infectious diseases (M Sc, PhD); zoo animal/wildlife medicine (DV Sc). *Degree requirements:* For master's, thesis; for doctorate, thesis/dissertation. *Entrance requirements:* For master's, DVM with B average or an honours degree in biological sciences; for doctorate, DVM or MSC degree, minimum B+ average. Additional exam requirements/recommendations for international students: required—TOEFL (minimum score 550 paper-based).

**University of Illinois at Chicago,** College of Medicine, Graduate Programs in Medicine, Department of Microbiology and Immunology, Chicago, IL 60607-7128. Offers PhD, MD/PhD. *Degree requirements:* For doctorate, thesis/dissertation. *Entrance requirements:* For doctorate, GRE General Test, minimum GPA of 2.75. Additional exam requirements/recommendations for international students: required—TOEFL.

**The University of Iowa,** Graduate College, Program in Immunology, Iowa City, IA 52242-1316. Offers PhD. *Degree requirements:* For doctorate, comprehensive exam, thesis/dissertation. *Entrance requirements:* For doctorate, GRE General Test, minimum GPA of 3.0. Additional exam requirements/recommendations for international students: required—TOEFL (minimum score 600 paper-based; 100 iBT). Electronic applications accepted.

**The University of Iowa,** Roy J. and Lucille A. Carver College of Medicine and Graduate College, Graduate Programs in Medicine, Department of Microbiology, Iowa City, IA 52242-1316. Offers general microbiology and microbial physiology (MS, PhD); immunology (MS, PhD); microbial genetics (MS, PhD); pathogenic bacteriology (MS, PhD); virology (MS, PhD). *Degree requirements:* For master's, thesis; for doctorate, comprehensive exam, thesis/dissertation. *Entrance requirements:* For master's and doctorate, GRE General Test. Additional exam requirements/recommendations for international students: required—TOEFL (minimum score 600 paper-based). Electronic applications accepted.

**University of Kentucky,** Graduate School, Graduate School Programs from the College of Medicine, Program in Microbiology and Immunology, Lexington, KY 40506-0032. Offers PhD. *Degree requirements:* For doctorate, comprehensive exam, thesis/dissertation. *Entrance requirements:* For doctorate, GRE General Test, minimum undergraduate GPA of 2.75. Additional exam requirements/recommendations for international students: required—TOEFL (minimum score 550 paper-based). Electronic applications accepted.

**University of Louisville,** School of Medicine, Department of Microbiology and Immunology, Louisville, KY 40292-0001. Offers MS, PhD, MD/PhD. *Program availability:* Part-time. *Faculty:* 16 full-time (4 women). *Students:* 33 full-time (18 women), 3 part-time (2 women); includes 8 minority (2 Black or African American, non-Hispanic/Latino; 3 Hispanic/Latino; 3 Two or more races, non-Hispanic/Latino), 8 international. Average age 30. 34 applicants, 18% accepted, 5 enrolled. In 2019, 9 master's, 3 doctorates awarded. Terminal master's awarded for partial completion of doctoral program. *Degree requirements:* For master's, comprehensive exam, thesis or alternative; for doctorate, comprehensive exam, thesis/dissertation. *Entrance requirements:* For master's, GRE, GPA >3.0; 1 year of course work in biology and organic chemistry; 1 semester of course work in introductory calculus and biochemistry; for doctorate, GRE, GPA > 3.0; 1 year of course work in biology and organic chemistry; 1 semester of course work in introductory calculus and biochemistry. Additional exam requirements/recommendations for international students: required—TOEFL (minimum score 550 paper-based; 79 iBT); recommended—IELTS (minimum score 6.5). *Application deadline:* For fall admission, 1/15 priority date for domestic and international students. Application fee: $60. Electronic applications accepted. *Expenses: Tuition, area resident:* Full-time $13,000; part-time $723 per credit hour. Tuition, state resident: full-time $13,000; part-time $723 per credit hour. Tuition, nonresident: full-time $27,114; part-time $1507 per credit hour. *International tuition:* $27,114 full-time. *Required fees:* $196. Tuition and fees vary according to program and reciprocity agreements. *Financial support:* In 2019–20, 34 students received support, including 5 fellowships with full tuition reimbursements available (averaging $25,000 per year); research assistantships also available. *Unit head:* Dr. Nejat Egilmez, Chair, 502-852-5351, Fax: 502-852-7531, E-mail: nejat.egilmez@louisville.edu. *Application contact:* Dr. Pascale Alard, Graduate Admissions Committee, Chair, 502-852-5364, Fax: 502-852-7531, E-mail: p0alar01@louisville.edu.
Website: http://louisville.edu/medicine/departments/microbiology

**The University of Manchester,** School of Biological Sciences, Manchester, United Kingdom. Offers adaptive organismal biology (M Phil, PhD); animal biology (M Phil, PhD); biochemistry (M Phil, PhD); bioinformatics (M Phil, PhD); biomolecular sciences (M Phil, PhD); biotechnology (M Phil, PhD); cell biology (M Phil, PhD); cell matrix research (M Phil, PhD); channels and transporters (M Phil, PhD); developmental biology (M Phil, PhD); environmental biology (M Phil, PhD); evolutionary biology (M Phil, PhD); gene expression (M Phil, PhD); genetics (M Phil, PhD); history of science, technology and medicine (M Phil, PhD); immunology (M Phil, PhD); integrative neurobiology and behavior (M Phil, PhD); membrane trafficking (M Phil, PhD); microbiology (M Phil, PhD); molecular and cellular neuroscience (M Phil, PhD); molecular biology (M Phil, PhD); molecular cancer studies (M Phil, PhD); neuroscience (M Phil, PhD); ophthalmology (M Phil, PhD); optometry (M Phil, PhD); organelle function (M Phil, PhD); pharmacology (M Phil, PhD); physiology (M Phil, PhD); plant sciences (M Phil, PhD); stem cell research (M Phil, PhD); structural biology (M Phil, PhD); systems neuroscience (M Phil, PhD); toxicology (M Phil, PhD).

**University of Manitoba,** Max Rady College of Medicine and Faculty of Graduate Studies, Graduate Programs in Medicine, Department of Immunology, Winnipeg, MB R3T 2N2, Canada. Offers M Sc, PhD. Terminal master's awarded for partial completion of doctoral program. *Degree requirements:* For master's, thesis; for doctorate, one foreign language, thesis/dissertation.

**University of Maryland, Baltimore,** Graduate School, Graduate Program in Life Sciences, Program in Molecular Microbiology and Immunology, Baltimore, MD 21201. Offers PhD, MD/PhD. *Degree requirements:* For doctorate, comprehensive exam, thesis/dissertation. *Entrance requirements:* For doctorate, GRE General Test, minimum GPA of 3.0, curriculum vitae, essay, 3 letters of recommendation. Additional exam requirements/recommendations for international students: required—TOEFL (minimum score 80 iBT); recommended—IELTS (minimum score 7). Electronic applications accepted.

**University of Massachusetts Medical School,** Graduate School of Biomedical Sciences, Worcester, MA 01655. Offers biomedical sciences (PhD), including biochemistry and molecular pharmacology, bioinformatics and computational biology, cancer biology, immunology and microbiology, interdisciplinary, neuroscience, translational science; biomedical sciences (millennium program) (PhD); clinical and population health research (PhD); clinical investigation (MS). *Faculty:* 1,258 full-time (525 women), 372 part-time/adjunct (238 women). *Students:* 344 full-time (198 women), 1 (woman) part-time; includes 73 minority (12 Black or African American, non-Hispanic/Latino; 1 American Indian or Alaska Native, non-Hispanic/Latino; 45 Asian, non-Hispanic/Latino; 15 Hispanic/Latino), 120 international. Average age 29. 581 applicants, 23% accepted, 56 enrolled. In 2019, 6 master's, 49 doctorates awarded. Terminal master's awarded for partial completion of doctoral program. *Degree requirements:* For master's, comprehensive exam, thesis; for doctorate, comprehensive exam, thesis/dissertation. *Entrance requirements:* For master's, MD, PhD, DVM, or PharmD; for doctorate, bachelor's degree. Additional exam requirements/recommendations for international students: required—TOEFL, IELTS, TOEFL (minimum score 100 IBT) or IELTS (minimum score 7.0). *Application deadline:* For fall admission, 12/1 for domestic and international students. Applications are processed on a rolling basis. Application fee: $80. Electronic applications accepted. Application fee is waived when completed online. *Expenses:* Contact institution. *Financial support:* In 2019–20, 22 fellowships with full tuition reimbursements (averaging $33,061 per year), 322 research assistantships with full tuition reimbursements (averaging $32,850 per year) were awarded; institutionally sponsored loans and scholarships/grants also available. Financial award application deadline: 5/15. *Unit head:* Dr. Mary Ellen Lane, Dean, 508-856-4018, E-mail: maryellen.lane@umassmed.edu. *Application contact:* Dr. Kendall Knight, Assistant Vice Provost for Admissions, 508-856-5628, Fax: 508-856-3659, E-mail: kendall.knight@umassmed.edu.
Website: http://www.umassmed.edu/gsbs/

**University of Miami,** Graduate School, Miller School of Medicine, Graduate Programs in Medicine, Department of Microbiology and Immunology, Miami, FL 33124. Offers PhD, MD/PhD. *Faculty:* 22 full-time (6 women). *Students:* 24 full-time (19 women); includes 14 minority (4 Black or African American, non-Hispanic/Latino; 3 Asian, non-Hispanic/Latino; 6 Hispanic/Latino; 1 Two or more races, non-Hispanic/Latino). Average age 27. In 2019, 4 doctorates awarded. *Degree requirements:* For doctorate, thesis/dissertation, oral and written qualifying exams. *Entrance requirements:* For doctorate, GRE General Test. Additional exam requirements/recommendations for international students: required—TOEFL. *Application deadline:* For fall admission, 12/31 for domestic students. Applications are processed on a rolling basis. Application fee: $50. Electronic applications accepted. *Financial support:* In 2019–20, 22 students received support, including 22 fellowships with full tuition reimbursements available (averaging $30,000 per year), 22 research assistantships with full tuition reimbursements available (averaging $30,000 per year); institutionally sponsored loans also available. *Unit head:* Dr. Thomas Malek, Chairman, 305-243-5627, Fax: 305-243-5522, E-mail: tmalek@miami.edu. *Application contact:* Dr. Zhibin Chen, Director, Graduate Program, 305-243-8348, Fax: 305-243-5522, E-mail: zchen@med.miami.edu.
Website: http://micro.med.miami.edu/

**University of Michigan,** Rackham Graduate School, Program in Biomedical Sciences (PIBS), Department of Microbiology and Immunology, Ann Arbor, MI 48109-5620. Offers MS, PhD. *Program availability:* Part-time. Terminal master's awarded for partial completion of doctoral program. *Degree requirements:* For master's, thesis optional; for doctorate, comprehensive exam, thesis/dissertation, oral defense of dissertation, preliminary exam. *Entrance requirements:* For master's and doctorate, GRE General Test. Additional exam requirements/recommendations for international students: required—TOEFL (minimum score 600 paper-based; 84 iBT), TWE. Electronic applications accepted.

**University of Michigan,** Rackham Graduate School, Program in Biomedical Sciences (PIBS), Program in Immunology, Ann Arbor, MI 48109-5619. Offers PhD. *Degree requirements:* For doctorate, thesis/dissertation, oral defense of dissertation, preliminary exam, first-author publication, coursework. *Entrance requirements:* For doctorate, 3 letters of recommendation, research experience, personal statement, transcripts. Additional exam requirements/recommendations for international students: required—TOEFL (minimum score 84 iBT). Electronic applications accepted.

**University of Minnesota, Duluth,** Medical School, Microbiology, Immunology and Molecular Pathobiology Section, Duluth, MN 55812-2496. Offers MS, PhD. Terminal master's awarded for partial completion of doctoral program. *Degree requirements:* For master's, thesis, final oral exam; for doctorate, thesis/dissertation, final exam, oral and written preliminary exams. *Entrance requirements:* For master's and doctorate, GRE General Test. Additional exam requirements/recommendations for international students: required—TOEFL.

**University of Minnesota, Twin Cities Campus,** Graduate School, PhD Program in Microbiology, Immunology and Cancer Biology, Minneapolis, MN 55455-0213. Offers PhD. *Degree requirements:* For doctorate, thesis/dissertation. *Entrance requirements:* For doctorate, GRE General Test. Additional exam requirements/recommendations for international students: required—TOEFL (minimum score 600 paper-based). Electronic applications accepted.

**University of Missouri,** School of Medicine and Office of Research and Graduate Studies, Graduate Programs in Medicine, Department of Molecular Microbiology and Immunology, Columbia, MO 65211. Offers PhD. Terminal master's awarded for partial completion of doctoral program. *Degree requirements:* For doctorate, thesis/dissertation. *Entrance requirements:* For doctorate, GRE General Test, minimum GPA of 3.0. Additional exam requirements/recommendations for international students: required—TOEFL.

**University of Montana,** Graduate School, College of Humanities and Sciences, Division of Biological Sciences, Program in Cellular, Molecular and Microbial Biology,

Missoula, MT 59812. Offers cellular and developmental biology (PhD); microbial evolution and ecology (PhD); microbiology and immunology (PhD); molecular biology and biochemistry (PhD). Terminal master's awarded for partial completion of doctoral program. *Degree requirements:* For doctorate, variable foreign language requirement, thesis/dissertation. *Entrance requirements:* For doctorate, GRE General Test.

**University of Nebraska Medical Center,** Interdisciplinary Graduate Program in Biomedical Sciences, Immunology, Pathology and Infectious Disease Graduate Program, Omaha, NE 68198. Offers MS, PhD. *Program availability:* Part-time. Terminal master's awarded for partial completion of doctoral program. *Degree requirements:* For master's, comprehensive exam, thesis; for doctorate, comprehensive exam, thesis/dissertation. *Entrance requirements:* For master's and doctorate, previous course work in biology, chemistry, mathematics, and physics. Additional exam requirements/recommendations for international students: required—TOEFL (minimum score 550 paper-based; 90 iBT), IELTS (minimum score 6.5). Electronic applications accepted. Application fee is waived when completed online.

**The University of North Carolina at Chapel Hill,** School of Medicine and Graduate School, Biological and Biomedical Sciences Program, Department of Microbiology and Immunology, Chapel Hill, NC 27599-7290. Offers immunology (MS, PhD); microbiology (MS, PhD). *Faculty:* 65 full-time (20 women). *Students:* 55 full-time (39 women); includes 4 minority (3 Asian, non-Hispanic/Latino; 1 Two or more races, non-Hispanic/Latino), 5 international. Average age 26. In 2019, 2 master's, 5 doctorates awarded. Terminal master's awarded for partial completion of doctoral program. *Degree requirements:* For doctorate, comprehensive exam, thesis/dissertation. *Entrance requirements:* Additional exam requirements/recommendations for international students: required—TOEFL. *Application deadline:* For fall admission, 12/3 priority date for domestic and international students. Applications are processed on a rolling basis. Electronic applications accepted. *Financial support:* In 2019–20, 3 fellowships with full tuition reimbursements (averaging $32,000 per year), 69 research assistantships with full tuition reimbursements (averaging $32,000 per year) were awarded; career-related internships or fieldwork, health care benefits, and tuition waivers (full) also available. *Unit head:* Dr. Bob Bourret, Director of Graduate Studies, E-mail: bourrett@med.unc.edu. *Application contact:* Jeffrey Steinbach, Assistant Director of Admissions, 919-843-7129, E-mail: jsteinba@email.unc.edu.
Website: http://www.med.unc.edu/microimm/

**University of North Texas Health Science Center at Fort Worth,** Graduate School of Biomedical Sciences, Fort Worth, TX 76107-2699. Offers biochemistry and cancer biology (MS, PhD); biotechnology (MS); cell biology, immunology and microbiology (MS, PhD); clinical research management (MS); forensic genetics (MS); genetics (MS, PhD); integrative physiology (MS, PhD); medical sciences (MS); pharmaceutical sciences and pharmacotherapy (MS, PhD); pharmacology and neuroscience (MS, PhD); structural anatomy and rehabilitation sciences (MS, PhD); DO/MS; DO/PhD. Terminal master's awarded for partial completion of doctoral program. *Degree requirements:* For master's, thesis; for doctorate, thesis/dissertation. *Entrance requirements:* For master's and doctorate, GRE General Test. Additional exam requirements/recommendations for international students: required—TOEFL. *Expenses:* Contact institution.

**University of Oklahoma Health Sciences Center,** College of Medicine and Graduate College, Graduate Programs in Medicine, Department of Microbiology and Immunology, Oklahoma City, OK 73190. Offers immunology (MS, PhD); microbiology (MS, PhD). *Program availability:* Part-time. Terminal master's awarded for partial completion of doctoral program. *Degree requirements:* For master's, thesis or alternative; for doctorate, one foreign language, thesis/dissertation. *Entrance requirements:* For doctorate, GRE General Test, 3 letters of recommendation. Additional exam requirements/recommendations for international students: required—TOEFL.

**University of Ottawa,** Faculty of Graduate and Postdoctoral Studies, Faculty of Medicine, Department of Biochemistry, Microbiology and Immunology, Ottawa, ON K1N 6N5, Canada. Offers biochemistry (M Sc, PhD); microbiology and immunology (M Sc, PhD). *Degree requirements:* For master's, thesis; for doctorate, comprehensive exam, thesis/dissertation, seminar. *Entrance requirements:* For master's, honors degree or equivalent, minimum B average; for doctorate, master's degree, minimum B+ average. Electronic applications accepted.

**University of Pennsylvania,** Perelman School of Medicine, Biomedical Graduate Studies, Graduate Group in Immunology, Philadelphia, PA 19104. Offers PhD, MD/PhD, VMD/PhD. *Faculty:* 132 full-time (33 women). *Students:* 74 full-time (41 women); includes 33 minority (5 Black or African American, non-Hispanic/Latino; 14 Asian, non-Hispanic/Latino; 7 Hispanic/Latino; 7 Two or more races, non-Hispanic/Latino), 2 international. 271 applicants, 10% accepted, 13 enrolled. In 2019, 8 doctorates awarded. *Unit head:* Dr. David Allman, Chair, 215-746-5547. *Application contact:* Mary Taylor, Graduate Coordinator, 215-573-4394.
Website: http://www.med.upenn.edu/immun/

**University of Pittsburgh,** School of Medicine, Graduate Programs in Medicine, Microbiology and Immunology Program, Pittsburgh, PA 15260. Offers PhD. *Degree requirements:* For doctorate, comprehensive exam, thesis/dissertation, 34 course credits, 38 dissertation credits, published paper. *Entrance requirements:* For doctorate, GRE General Test. Additional exam requirements/recommendations for international students: required—TOEFL (minimum score 600 paper-based; 100 iBT), IELTS (minimum score 7). Electronic applications accepted. *Expenses:* Contact institution.

**University of Prince Edward Island,** Atlantic Veterinary College, Graduate Program in Veterinary Medicine, Charlottetown, PE C1A 4P3, Canada. Offers anatomy (M Sc, PhD); bacteriology (M Sc, PhD); clinical pharmacology (M Sc, PhD); clinical sciences (M Sc, PhD); epidemiology (M Sc, PhD), including reproduction; fish health (M Sc, PhD); food animal nutrition (M Sc, PhD); immunology (M Sc, PhD); microanatomy (M Sc, PhD); parasitology (M Sc, PhD); pathology (M Sc, PhD); pharmacology (M Sc, PhD); physiology (M Sc, PhD); toxicology (M Sc, PhD); veterinary science (M Vet Sc); virology (M Sc, PhD). *Program availability:* Part-time. *Degree requirements:* For master's, thesis; for doctorate, thesis/dissertation. *Entrance requirements:* For master's, DVM, B Sc honors degree, or equivalent; for doctorate, M Sc. Additional exam requirements/recommendations for international students: required—TOEFL (minimum score 550 paper-based; 80 iBT). *Expenses:* Contact institution.

**University of Rochester,** School of Medicine and Dentistry, Graduate Programs in Medicine and Dentistry, Department of Microbiology and Immunology, Program in Microbiology and Immunology, Rochester, NY 14627. Offers MS, PhD.

**University of Saskatchewan,** College of Medicine, Department of Biochemistry, Microbiology and Immunology, Saskatoon, SK S7N 5A2, Canada. Offers biochemistry (M Sc, PhD); microbiology and immunology (M Sc, PhD). *Degree requirements:* For master's, thesis; for doctorate, thesis/dissertation. *Entrance requirements:* Additional exam requirements/recommendations for international students: required—TOEFL.

**University of South Dakota,** Graduate School, Sanford School of Medicine and Graduate School, Biomedical Sciences Graduate Program, Molecular Microbiology and Immunology Group, Vermillion, SD 57069. Offers MS, PhD. Terminal master's awarded for partial completion of doctoral program. *Degree requirements:* For master's, thesis; for doctorate, comprehensive exam, thesis/dissertation. *Entrance requirements:* For master's and doctorate, GRE General Test, minimum GPA of 3.0. Additional exam requirements/recommendations for international students: required—TOEFL (minimum score 550 paper-based; 80 iBT), IELTS (minimum score 6). Electronic applications accepted. *Expenses:* Contact institution.

**University of Southern California,** Keck School of Medicine and Graduate School, Graduate Programs in Medicine, Department of Molecular Microbiology and Immunology, Los Angeles, CA 90089. Offers MS. *Program availability:* Part-time. *Faculty:* 19 full-time (4 women). *Students:* 41 full-time (24 women); includes 31 minority (1 Black or African American, non-Hispanic/Latino; 26 Asian, non-Hispanic/Latino; 4 Hispanic/Latino). Average age 26. 72 applicants, 76% accepted, 20 enrolled. In 2019, 15 master's awarded. Terminal master's awarded for partial completion of doctoral program. *Degree requirements:* For master's, comprehensive exam (for some programs), thesis optional. *Entrance requirements:* For master's, GRE General Test preferred (Verbal and Quantitative), MCAT (on a case-by-case basis). Additional exam requirements/recommendations for international students: required—TOEFL (minimum score 100 iBT), IELTS (minimum score 6.5). *Application deadline:* For fall admission, 6/1 for domestic students, 5/1 for international students; for spring admission, 11/1 for domestic students, 10/1 for international students. Applications are processed on a rolling basis. Application fee: $90. Electronic applications accepted. *Financial support:* Career-related internships or fieldwork, Federal Work-Study, institutionally sponsored loans, scholarships/grants, and health care benefits available. Financial award application deadline: 3/1; financial award applicants required to submit FAFSA. *Unit head:* Dr. Axel H. Schonthal, Associate Professor/Program Director, 323-442-1730, Fax: 323-442-1721, E-mail: schontha@usc.edu. *Application contact:* Monica C. Pan, Program Administrator, E-mail: monicap@med.usc.edu.
Website: http://keck.usc.edu/molecular-microbiology-and-immunology/

**The University of Texas Health Science Center at Houston,** MD Anderson UTHealth Graduate School, Houston, TX 77225-0036. Offers biochemistry and cell biology (PhD); biomedical sciences (MS); cancer biology (PhD); genetic counseling (MS); genetics and epigenetics (PhD); immunology (PhD); medical physics (MS, PhD); microbiology and infectious diseases (PhD); neuroscience (PhD); quantitative sciences (PhD); therapeutics and pharmacology (PhD); MD/PhD. Terminal master's awarded for partial completion of doctoral program. *Degree requirements:* For master's, thesis; for doctorate, thesis/dissertation. *Entrance requirements:* For master's and doctorate, GRE General Test. Additional exam requirements/recommendations for international students: required—TOEFL. Electronic applications accepted.

**The University of Texas Health Science Center at San Antonio,** Graduate School of Biomedical Sciences, Department of Microbiology and Immunology, San Antonio, TX 78229-3900. Offers MS, PhD. *Degree requirements:* For master's, thesis; for doctorate, comprehensive exam, thesis/dissertation.

**The University of Texas Medical Branch,** Graduate School of Biomedical Sciences, Program in Microbiology and Immunology, Galveston, TX 77555. Offers MS, PhD. Terminal master's awarded for partial completion of doctoral program. *Degree requirements:* For master's, thesis or alternative; for doctorate, thesis/dissertation. *Entrance requirements:* For doctorate, GRE General Test, minimum GPA of 3.0. Additional exam requirements/recommendations for international students: required—TOEFL (minimum score 550 paper-based). Electronic applications accepted.

**The University of Texas Southwestern Medical Center,** Southwestern Graduate School of Biomedical Sciences, Division of Basic Science, Program in Immunology, Dallas, TX 75390. Offers PhD. *Degree requirements:* For doctorate, thesis/dissertation, qualifying exam. *Entrance requirements:* For doctorate, GRE General Test, minimum GPA of 3.0. Additional exam requirements/recommendations for international students: required—TOEFL. Electronic applications accepted.

**The University of Toledo,** College of Graduate Studies, College of Medicine and Life Sciences, Department of Medical Microbiology and Immunology, Toledo, OH 43606-3390. Offers infection, immunity, and transplantation (MSBS, PhD); MD/MSBS; MD/PhD. Terminal master's awarded for partial completion of doctoral program. *Degree requirements:* For master's, thesis, qualifying exam; for doctorate, thesis/dissertation, qualifying exam. *Entrance requirements:* For master's and doctorate, GRE, minimum undergraduate GPA of 3.0, three letters of recommendation, statement of purpose, transcripts from all prior institutions attended, resume. Additional exam requirements/recommendations for international students: required—TOEFL (minimum score 550 paper-based; 80 iBT). Electronic applications accepted.

**University of Toronto,** Faculty of Medicine, Department of Immunology, Toronto, ON M5S 1A1, Canada. Offers M Sc, PhD, MD/PhD. *Degree requirements:* For master's, thesis, thesis defense; for doctorate, thesis/dissertation, thesis defense. *Entrance requirements:* For master's, resume, 3 letters of reference. Additional exam requirements/recommendations for international students: required—TOEFL (minimum score 580 paper-based; 93 iBT), TWE (minimum score 5). Electronic applications accepted.

**University of Washington,** Graduate School, School of Medicine, Graduate Programs in Medicine, Department of Immunology, Seattle, WA 98109-8059. Offers PhD. *Degree requirements:* For doctorate, thesis/dissertation, 1st-authored paper, accepted for publication. *Entrance requirements:* For doctorate, GRE General Test, BA or BS in related field. Additional exam requirements/recommendations for international students: required—TOEFL (minimum score 600 paper-based; 100 iBT). Electronic applications accepted.

**The University of Western Ontario,** Schulich School of Medicine and Dentistry, Department of Microbiology and Immunology, London, ON N6A 3K7, Canada. Offers M Sc, PhD. *Degree requirements:* For master's, thesis, oral and written exam; for doctorate, thesis/dissertation, oral and written exam. *Entrance requirements:* For master's, honors degree or equivalent in microbiology, immunology, or other biological science; minimum B average; for doctorate, M Sc in microbiology and immunology. Additional exam requirements/recommendations for international students: required—TOEFL.

**Université Laval,** Faculty of Medicine, Graduate Programs in Medicine, Programs in Microbiology-Immunology, Québec, QC G1K 7P4, Canada. Offers M Sc, PhD. Terminal master's awarded for partial completion of doctoral program. *Degree requirements:* For master's, thesis; for doctorate, comprehensive exam, thesis/dissertation. *Entrance requirements:* For master's and doctorate, knowledge of French, comprehension of written English. Electronic applications accepted.

**Vanderbilt University,** School of Medicine, Department of Molecular Pathology and Immunology, Nashville, TN 37240-1001. Offers PhD, MD/PhD. *Faculty:* 35 full-time (13 women), 1 (woman) part-time/adjunct. *Students:* 26 full-time (16 women); includes 5 minority (1 Black or African American, non-Hispanic/Latino; 1 Asian, non-Hispanic/Latino; 3 Hispanic/Latino), 4 international. Average age 26. In 2019, 1 doctorate awarded. *Degree requirements:* For doctorate, thesis/dissertation, qualifying and final exams. *Entrance requirements:* For doctorate, GRE General Test. Additional exam requirements/recommendations for international students: required—TOEFL (minimum score 570 paper-based; 88 iBT). *Application deadline:* For fall admission, 1/15 for domestic and international students. Electronic applications accepted. *Expenses:*

*Tuition:* Full-time $51,018; part-time $2087 per hour. *Required fees:* $542. Tuition and fees vary according to program. *Financial support:* Fellowships with full tuition reimbursements, research assistantships with full tuition reimbursements, Federal Work-Study, institutionally sponsored loans, traineeships, health care benefits, and tuition waivers (partial) available. Financial award application deadline: 1/15; financial award applicants required to submit CSS PROFILE or FAFSA. *Unit head:* Jay Jerome, Director of Graduate Studies, 615-322-2123, Fax: 615-322-0576, E-mail: jay.jerome@vanderbilt.edu. *Application contact:* Kristi Hargrove, Program Manager, 615-322-2294, E-mail: kristi.l.hargrove@vanderbilt.edu.
Website: https://medschool.vanderbilt.edu/igp/molecular-pathology-immunology

**Vanderbilt University,** School of Medicine, Microbe Host Interactions, Nashville, TN 37240-1001. Offers MS, PhD, MD/PhD. *Faculty:* 35 full-time (13 women). *Students:* 51 full-time (30 women); includes 17 minority (3 Black or African American, non-Hispanic/Latino; 6 Asian, non-Hispanic/Latino; 4 Hispanic/Latino; 4 Two or more races, non-Hispanic/Latino), 1 international. Average age 26. In 2019, 2 master's, 12 doctorates awarded. Terminal master's awarded for partial completion of doctoral program. *Degree requirements:* For master's, thesis; for doctorate, thesis/dissertation, final and qualifying exams. *Entrance requirements:* For master's and doctorate, GRE General Test, GRE Subject Test (recommended). Additional exam requirements/recommendations for international students: required—TOEFL (minimum score 570 paper-based; 88 iBT). *Application deadline:* For fall admission, 1/15 for domestic and international students. Electronic applications accepted. *Expenses: Tuition:* Full-time $51,018; part-time $2087 per hour. *Required fees:* $542. Tuition and fees vary according to program. *Financial support:* Fellowships with full tuition reimbursements, research assistantships with full tuition reimbursements, Federal Work-Study, institutionally sponsored loans, scholarships/grants, traineeships, health care benefits, and tuition waivers (partial) available. Financial award application deadline: 1/15; financial award applicants required to submit CSS PROFILE or FAFSA. *Unit head:* Dr. Roger Cone, Acting Chair, 615-322-7000, Fax: 615-322-5551, E-mail: roger.cone@vanderbilt.edu. *Application contact:* Jay Jerome, Director of Graduate Studies, 615-322-2123, E-mail: jay.jerome@vanderbilt.edu.
Website: http://www.mc.vanderbilt.edu/root/vumc.php?site-vmcpathology

**Virginia Commonwealth University,** Medical College of Virginia-Professional Programs, School of Medicine, Graduate Programs in Medicine, Department of Microbiology and Immunology, Richmond, VA 23284-9005. Offers microbiology and immunology (MS, PhD); MD/PhD. *Degree requirements:* For master's, thesis; for doctorate, thesis/dissertation, comprehensive oral and written exams. *Entrance requirements:* For master's and doctorate, GRE General Test or MCAT. Additional exam requirements/recommendations for international students: required—TOEFL (minimum score 600 paper-based; 100 iBT). Electronic applications accepted.

**Wake Forest University,** School of Medicine and Graduate School of Arts and Sciences, Graduate Programs in Medicine, Department of Microbiology and Immunology, Winston-Salem, NC 27109. Offers PhD, MD/PhD. *Degree requirements:* For doctorate, thesis/dissertation. *Entrance requirements:* For doctorate, GRE General Test. Additional exam requirements/recommendations for international students: required—TOEFL. Electronic applications accepted.

**Washington State University,** College of Veterinary Medicine, Program in Immunology and Infectious Diseases, Pullman, WA 99164. Offers MS, PhD. *Faculty:* 46 full-time (33 women). *Students:* 43 full-time (30 women); includes 13 minority (1 Black or African American, non-Hispanic/Latino; 5 Asian, non-Hispanic/Latino; 7 Hispanic/Latino), 7 international. Average age 30. 29 applicants, 24% accepted, 7 enrolled. In 2019, 3 master's, 6 doctorates awarded. Terminal master's awarded for partial completion of doctoral program. *Degree requirements:* For master's, thesis, oral exam; for doctorate, thesis/dissertation, oral exam. *Entrance requirements:* For master's and doctorate, minimum GPA of 3.0. Additional exam requirements/recommendations for international students: required—TOEFL (minimum score 550 paper-based; 80 iBT). *Application deadline:* For fall admission, 12/15 priority date for domestic and international students. Applications are processed on a rolling basis. Application fee: $75. Electronic applications accepted. *Financial support:* In 2019–20, 43 students received support, including 4 fellowships, 39 research assistantships, 1 teaching assistantship; institutionally sponsored loans, scholarships/grants, traineeships, and unspecified assistantships also available. Financial award application deadline: 3/1; financial award applicants required to submit FAFSA. *Unit head:* Dr. Anthony Nicola, Interim Chair, 509-335-6030, Fax: 509-335-8529, E-mail: anthony.nicola@wsu.edu. *Application contact:* Sue Zumwalt, Graduate Coordinator, 509-335-6027, Fax: 509-335-8529, E-mail: szumwalt@wsu.edu.
Website: http://vmp.vetmed.wsu.edu/graduate-programs

**Washington University in St. Louis,** The Graduate School, Division of Biology and Biomedical Sciences, Program in Immunology, St. Louis, MO 63130-4899. Offers PhD. *Degree requirements:* For doctorate, thesis/dissertation. *Entrance requirements:* For doctorate, GRE General Test, GRE Subject Test. Additional exam requirements/recommendations for international students: required—TOEFL. Electronic applications accepted.

**Weill Cornell Medicine,** Weill Cornell Graduate School of Medical Sciences, Immunology and Microbial Pathogenesis Program, New York, NY 10065. Offers immunology (MS, PhD), including immunology, microbiology, pathology. Terminal master's awarded for partial completion of doctoral program. *Degree requirements:* For master's, comprehensive exam; for doctorate, thesis/dissertation, final exam. *Entrance requirements:* For doctorate, GRE General Test, laboratory research experience, course work in biological sciences. Additional exam requirements/recommendations for international students: required—TOEFL. Electronic applications accepted.

**West Virginia University,** School of Medicine, Morgantown, WV 26506. Offers biochemistry and molecular biology (PhD); biomedical science (MS); cancer cell biology (PhD); cellular and integrative physiology (PhD); exercise physiology (MS, PhD); health sciences (MS); immunology (PhD); medicine (MD); occupational therapy (MOT); pathologists assistant' (MHS); physical therapy (DPT). *Accreditation:* AOTA; LCME/AMA. *Program availability:* Part-time, evening/weekend. *Entrance requirements:* Additional exam requirements/recommendations for international students: required—TOEFL. Electronic applications accepted. *Expenses:* Contact institution.

**Wright State University,** Graduate School, College of Science and Mathematics, Program in Microbiology and Immunology, Dayton, OH 45435. Offers MS. *Program availability:* Part-time. *Degree requirements:* For master's, thesis. *Entrance requirements:* Additional exam requirements/recommendations for international students: required—TOEFL.

**Yale University,** Graduate School of Arts and Sciences, Department of Immunobiology, New Haven, CT 06520. Offers PhD. *Degree requirements:* For doctorate, thesis/dissertation. *Entrance requirements:* For doctorate, GRE General Test.

**Yale University,** Yale School of Medicine and Graduate School of Arts and Sciences, Combined Program in Biological and Biomedical Sciences (BBS), Immunology Track, New Haven, CT 06520. Offers PhD, MD/PhD. *Degree requirements:* For doctorate, thesis/dissertation. *Entrance requirements:* For doctorate, GRE General Test. Additional exam requirements/recommendations for international students: required—TOEFL. Electronic applications accepted.

# Infectious Diseases

**Georgetown University,** Graduate School of Arts and Sciences, Department of Microbiology and Immunology, Washington, DC 20057. Offers biohazardous threat agents and emerging infectious diseases (MS); biomedical science policy and advocacy (MS); general microbiology and immunology (MS); global infectious diseases (PhD); microbiology and immunology (PhD). *Program availability:* Part-time. *Degree requirements:* For master's, 30 credit hours of coursework; for doctorate, comprehensive exam, thesis/dissertation. *Entrance requirements:* For master's, GRE General Test, 3 letters of reference, bachelor's degree in related field; for doctorate, GRE General Test, 3 letters of reference, MS/BS in related field. Additional exam requirements/recommendations for international students: required—TOEFL (minimum score 505 paper-based). Electronic applications accepted.

**The George Washington University,** Milken Institute School of Public Health, Department of Epidemiology and Biostatistics, Washington, DC 20052. Offers biostatistics (MPH); epidemiology (MPH); microbiology and emerging infectious diseases (MSPH). *Entrance requirements:* For master's, GMAT, GRE General Test, or MCAT. Additional exam requirements/recommendations for international students: required—TOEFL.

**The George Washington University,** School of Medicine and Health Sciences, Health Sciences Programs, Washington, DC 20052. Offers clinical practice management (MSHS); clinical research administration (MSHS); emergency services management (MSHS); end-of-life care (MSHS); immunohematology (MSHS); immunohematology and biotechnology (MSHS); physical therapy (DPT); physician assistant (MSHS). *Program availability:* Online learning. *Entrance requirements:* Additional exam requirements/recommendations for international students: required—TOEFL (minimum score 550 paper-based). *Expenses:* Contact institution.

**Johns Hopkins University,** Bloomberg School of Public Health, Department of Epidemiology, Baltimore, MD 21205. Offers cancer epidemiology (MHS, Sc M, PhD, Sc D); cardiovascular disease and clinical epidemiology (MHS, Sc M, PhD, Sc D); clinical trials (PhD, Sc D); clinical trials and evidence synthesis (MHS, Sc M, PhD, Sc D); environmental epidemiology (MHS, Sc M, PhD, Sc D); epidemiology of aging (MHS, Sc M, PhD, Sc D); general epidemiology and methodology (MHS, Sc M); genetic epidemiology (MHS, Sc M, PhD, Sc D); infectious disease epidemiology (MHS, Sc M, PhD, Sc D). *Degree requirements:* For master's, comprehensive exam, thesis, 1-year full-time residency; for doctorate, comprehensive exam, thesis/dissertation, 2 years' full-time residency, oral and written exams, student teaching. *Entrance requirements:* For master's, GRE General Test or MCAT, 3 letters of recommendation, curriculum vitae; for doctorate, GRE General Test, minimum 1 year of work experience, 3 letters of recommendation, curriculum vitae, academic records from all schools. Additional exam requirements/recommendations for international students: required—TOEFL (minimum score 100 iBT), IELTS (minimum score 7.5). Electronic applications accepted.

**Loyola University Chicago,** Graduate School, Integrated Program in Biomedical Sciences, Maywood, IL 60660. Offers biochemistry and molecular biology (MS, PhD); cell and molecular physiology (MS, PhD); infectious disease and immunology (MS); integrative cell biology (MS, PhD); microbiology and immunology (MS, PhD); molecular pharmacology and therapeutics (MS, PhD); neuroscience (MS, PhD). *Students:* Average age 25. 773 applicants, 34% accepted, 122 enrolled. In 2019, 46 master's, 12 doctorates awarded. *Degree requirements:* For master's, thesis; for doctorate, comprehensive exam, thesis/dissertation. *Entrance requirements:* For doctorate, GRE. Additional exam requirements/recommendations for international students: required—TOEFL (minimum score 94 iBT), IELTS (minimum score 7.5). *Application deadline:* For fall admission, 2/7 for domestic students. Applications are processed on a rolling basis. Electronic applications accepted. *Expenses:* Contact institution. *Financial support:* In 2019–20, 20 students received support. Schmitt Fellowships and yearly tuition scholarships (averaging $25,032) available. Financial award application deadline: 6/15; financial award applicants required to submit FAFSA. *Unit head:* Dr. Leanne L. Cribbs, Associate Dean, Graduate Education, 708-327-2817, Fax: 708-216-8216, E-mail: lcribbs@luc.edu. *Application contact:* Margarita Quesada, Graduate Program Secretary, 708-216-3532, Fax: 708-216-8216, E-mail: mquesad@luc.edu.
Website: http://ssom.luc.edu/graduate_school/degree-programs/ipbsphd/

**Loyola University Chicago,** Graduate School, Marcella Niehoff School of Nursing, Maywood, IL 60153. Offers adult clinical nurse specialist (MSN, Certificate); adult nurse practitioner (Certificate); dietetics (MS); family nurse practitioner (Certificate); family, adult, and women's health nurse practitioner (MSN); health systems leadership (MSN); healthcare quality using education in safety and technology (DNP); infection prevention (MSN, DNP); nursing science (PhD); women's health clinical nurse specialist (Certificate). *Accreditation:* AACN. *Program availability:* Part-time, blended/hybrid learning. *Faculty:* 36 full-time (32 women), 18 part-time/adjunct (16 women). *Students:* 182 full-time (168 women), 198 part-time (175 women); includes 95 minority (26 Black or African American, non-Hispanic/Latino; 29 Asian, non-Hispanic/Latino; 37 Hispanic/Latino; 3 Two or more races, non-Hispanic/Latino), 7 international. Average age 35. 148 applicants, 59% accepted, 54 enrolled. In 2019, 84 master's, 16 doctorates, 27 other advanced degrees awarded. *Degree requirements:* For master's, comprehensive exam; for doctorate, thesis/dissertation, qualifying examination (for PhD); project (for DNP). *Entrance requirements:* For master's, BSN, minimum nursing GPA of 3.0, Illinois RN license, 3 letters of recommendation, 1000 hours of experience in area of specialty prior to starting clinical rotations, personal statement; for doctorate, BSN or MSN, minimum GPA of 3.0, professional nursing license, 3 letters of recommendation, personal statement. Additional exam requirements/recommendations for international students: required—TOEFL (minimum score 550 paper-based; 79 iBT), IELTS (minimum score 6), PTE (minimum score 53). *Application deadline:* For fall admission, 7/1 priority date for domestic and international students; for spring admission, 12/1 priority date for domestic

and international students; for summer admission, 4/1 priority date for domestic and international students. Applications are processed on a rolling basis. Electronic applications accepted. Application fee is waived when completed online. *Expenses:* Contact institution. *Financial support:* In 2019–20, 53 students received support, including 3 research assistantships with full tuition reimbursements available (averaging $18,000 per year), 1 teaching assistantship with full tuition reimbursement available (averaging $18,000 per year); scholarships/grants, unspecified assistantships, and Nurse Faculty Loan Program also available. Financial award application deadline: 5/1; financial award applicants required to submit FAFSA. *Unit head:* Dr. Lorna Finnegan, Dean and Professor, 708-216-5448, Fax: 708-216-9555, E-mail: lornaf@luc.edu. *Application contact:* Glenda Runnels, Enrollment Advisor, 708-216-3751, Fax: 708-216-9555, E-mail: grunnels@luc.edu.
Website: http://www.luc.edu/nursing/

**Montana State University,** The Graduate School, College of Agriculture, Department of Immunology and Infectious Diseases, Bozeman, MT 59717. Offers MS, PhD. *Program availability:* Part-time. *Degree requirements:* For master's, comprehensive exam; for doctorate, comprehensive exam, thesis/dissertation. *Entrance requirements:* For master's and doctorate, GRE General Test. Additional exam requirements/recommendations for international students: required—TOEFL (minimum score 550 paper-based). Electronic applications accepted.

**North Carolina State University,** College of Veterinary Medicine, Program in Comparative Biomedical Sciences, Raleigh, NC 27695. Offers cell biology (MS, PhD); infectious disease (MS, PhD); pathology (MS, PhD); pharmacology (MS, PhD); population medicine (MS, PhD). *Program availability:* Part-time. *Degree requirements:* For master's, thesis; for doctorate, thesis/dissertation. *Entrance requirements:* For master's and doctorate, GRE General Test. Additional exam requirements/recommendations for international students: required—TOEFL (minimum score 550 paper-based). Electronic applications accepted. *Expenses:* Contact institution.

**North Dakota State University,** College of Graduate and Interdisciplinary Studies, College of Health Professions, Department of Public Health, Fargo, ND 58102. Offers American Indian public health (MPH); community health sciences (MPH); management of infectious diseases (MPH); Pharm D/MPH. *Accreditation:* CEPH. *Program availability:* Online learning. Tuition and fees vary according to program and reciprocity agreements.

**Thomas Jefferson University,** Jefferson College of Life Sciences, Certificate Program in Infectious Disease Control, Philadelphia, PA 19107. Offers Certificate. *Program availability:* Part-time. *Entrance requirements:* For degree, GRE General Test (recommended). Additional exam requirements/recommendations for international students: required—TOEFL, IELTS (minimum score 7).

**Tufts University,** Cummings School of Veterinary Medicine, North Grafton, MA 01536. Offers animals and public policy (MS); biomedical sciences (PhD), including digestive diseases, infectious diseases, neuroscience and reproductive biology, pathology; conservation medicine (MS); veterinary medicine (DVM); DVM/MPH; DVM/MS. *Accreditation:* AVMA (one or more programs are accredited). *Degree requirements:* For master's, thesis (for some programs); for doctorate, comprehensive exam, thesis/dissertation (for some programs). *Entrance requirements:* For master's and doctorate, GRE General Test. Additional exam requirements/recommendations for international students: required—TOEFL or IELTS. Electronic applications accepted. *Expenses:* Contact institution.

**Uniformed Services University of the Health Sciences,** F. Edward Hebert School of Medicine, Graduate Programs in the Biomedical Sciences and Public Health, Graduate Program in Emerging Infectious Diseases, Bethesda, MD 20814-4799. Offers PhD. *Degree requirements:* For doctorate, comprehensive exam, thesis/dissertation, qualifying exam. *Entrance requirements:* For doctorate, GRE General Test. Electronic applications accepted.

**The University of British Columbia,** Faculty of Medicine, Experimental Medicine Program, Vancouver, BC V5Z 1M9, Canada. Offers M Sc, PhD. *Degree requirements:* For master's, thesis; for doctorate, comprehensive exam, thesis/dissertation. *Entrance requirements:* For master's, minimum GPA of 75% or B+ standing, B Sc or MD; for doctorate, minimum GPA of 75% or B+ standing, M Sc. Additional exam requirements/recommendations for international students: required—TOEFL (minimum score 590 paper-based, 96 iBT), IELTS (minimum score 7.0) or Michigan English Language Assessment Battery (minimum score 84). Electronic applications accepted. *Expenses:* Contact institution.

**University of Calgary,** Cumming School of Medicine and Faculty of Graduate Studies, Program in Microbiology and infectious Disease, Calgary, AB T2N 1N4, Canada. Offers M Sc, PhD. *Degree requirements:* For master's, thesis, oral thesis exam; for doctorate, thesis/dissertation, candidacy exam, oral thesis exam. *Entrance requirements:* For master's and doctorate, minimum GPA of 3.2. Additional exam requirements/recommendations for international students: required—TOEFL (minimum score 580 paper-based). Electronic applications accepted.

**University of California, Berkeley,** Graduate Division, School of Public Health, Group in Epidemiology, Berkeley, CA 94720. Offers epidemiology (MS, PhD); infectious diseases (PhD). *Degree requirements:* For master's, comprehensive exam; for doctorate, thesis/dissertation, oral and written exam. *Entrance requirements:* For master's, GRE General Test, minimum GPA of 3.0; MD, DDS, DVM, or PhD in biomedical science (MPH); for doctorate, GRE General Test, minimum GPA of 3.0. Electronic applications accepted.

**University of California, Berkeley,** Graduate Division, School of Public Health, Group in Infectious Diseases and Immunity, Berkeley, CA 94720. Offers PhD. *Entrance requirements:* For doctorate, GRE General Test, minimum GPA of 3.0, 3 letters of recommendation. Electronic applications accepted.

**University of Georgia,** College of Veterinary Medicine, Department of Infectious Diseases, Athens, GA 30602. Offers PhD. *Degree requirements:* For doctorate, one foreign language, thesis/dissertation. *Entrance requirements:* For doctorate, GRE General Test. Electronic applications accepted.

**University of Guelph,** Ontario Veterinary College and Office of Graduate and Postdoctoral Studies, Graduate Programs in Veterinary Sciences, Department of Pathobiology, Guelph, ON N1G 2W1, Canada. Offers anatomic pathology (DV Sc, Diploma); clinical pathology (Diploma); comparative pathology (M Sc, PhD); immunology (M Sc, PhD); laboratory animal science (DV Sc); pathology (M Sc, PhD, Diploma); veterinary infectious diseases (M Sc, PhD); zoo animal/wildlife medicine (DV Sc). *Degree requirements:* For master's, thesis; for doctorate, thesis/dissertation. *Entrance requirements:* For master's, DVM with B average or an honours degree in biological sciences; for doctorate, DVM or MSC degree, minimum B+ average. Additional exam requirements/recommendations for international students: required—TOEFL (minimum score 550 paper-based).

**University of Manitoba,** Max Rady College of Medicine and Faculty of Graduate Studies, Graduate Programs in Medicine, Department of Medical Microbiology and Infectious Diseases, Winnipeg, MB R3T 2N2, Canada. Offers M Sc, PhD. *Program availability:* Part-time. Terminal master's awarded for partial completion of doctoral program. *Degree requirements:* For master's, thesis; for doctorate, one foreign

language, thesis/dissertation. *Entrance requirements:* For master's and doctorate, minimum GPA of 3.0. Electronic applications accepted.

**University of Minnesota, Twin Cities Campus,** School of Public Health, Division of Environmental Health Sciences, Area in Environmental Infectious Diseases, Minneapolis, MN 55455-0213. Offers MPH, MS, PhD. *Degree requirements:* For doctorate, thesis/dissertation. *Entrance requirements:* For master's and doctorate, GRE General Test. Electronic applications accepted.

**University of Nebraska Medical Center,** Interdisciplinary Graduate Program in Biomedical Sciences, Immunology, Pathology and Infectious Disease Graduate Program, Omaha, NE 68198. Offers MS, PhD. *Program availability:* Part-time. Terminal master's awarded for partial completion of doctoral program. *Degree requirements:* For master's, comprehensive exam, thesis; for doctorate, comprehensive exam, thesis/dissertation. *Entrance requirements:* For master's and doctorate, previous course work in biology, chemistry, mathematics, and physics. Additional exam requirements/recommendations for international students: required—TOEFL (minimum score 550 paper-based; 90 iBT), IELTS (minimum score 6.5). Electronic applications accepted. Application fee is waived when completed online.

**University of Pittsburgh,** Graduate School of Public Health, Department of Infectious Diseases and Microbiology, Pittsburgh, PA 15261. Offers infectious diseases and microbiology (MS, PhD); management, intervention, and community practice (MPH); pathogenesis, eradication, and laboratory practice (MPH). *Program availability:* Part-time. *Faculty:* 17 full-time (7 women), 4 part-time/adjunct (0 women). *Students:* 56 full-time (44 women), 20 part-time (10 women); includes 19 minority (6 Black or African American, non-Hispanic/Latino; 5 Asian, non-Hispanic/Latino; 3 Hispanic/Latino; 5 Two or more races, non-Hispanic/Latino), 6 international. Average age 26. 146 applicants, 80% accepted, 38 enrolled. In 2019, 24 master's, 2 doctorates awarded. Terminal master's awarded for partial completion of doctoral program. *Degree requirements:* For master's, comprehensive exam (for some programs), thesis; for doctorate, comprehensive exam, thesis/dissertation, preliminary exam, dissertation defense. *Entrance requirements:* Additional exam requirements/recommendations for international students: required—TOEFL (minimum score 550 paper-based; 80 iBT), IELTS (minimum score 6.5), TOEFL or IELTS, WES evaluation for foreign education. *Application deadline:* For fall admission, 1/15 for domestic students, 3/15 priority date for international students. Applications are processed on a rolling basis. Application fee: $135. Electronic applications accepted. *Expenses:* $13,379 state resident per term full-time, $23,407 non-state resident per term full-time, $1122 state resident per credit part-time, $1916 non-state resident per credit part-time, $500 per term for full-time dissertation research, $475 per term full-time fees, $295 per term part-time fees. *Financial support:* In 2019–20, 38 students received support. Scholarships/grants, traineeships, health care benefits, and unspecified assistantships available. Financial award applicants required to submit FAFSA. *Unit head:* Robin Tierno, Department Administrator, 412-624-3105, Fax: 412-624-4953, E-mail: rtierno@pitt.edu. *Application contact:* Chelsea Yonash, Student Services Coordinator, 412-624-3331, E-mail: cry8@pitt.edu.
Website: http://www.publichealth.pitt.edu/idm

**The University of Texas Health Science Center at Houston,** MD Anderson UTHealth Graduate School, Houston, TX 77225-0036. Offers biochemistry and cell biology (PhD); biomedical sciences (MS); cancer biology (PhD); genetic counseling (MS); genetics and epigenetics (PhD); immunology (PhD); medical physics (MS, PhD); microbiology and infectious diseases (PhD); neuroscience (PhD); quantitative sciences (PhD); therapeutics and pharmacology (PhD); MD/PhD. Terminal master's awarded for partial completion of doctoral program. *Degree requirements:* For master's, thesis; for doctorate, thesis/dissertation. *Entrance requirements:* For master's and doctorate, GRE General Test. Additional exam requirements/recommendations for international students: required—TOEFL. Electronic applications accepted.

**University of Washington,** Graduate School, School of Medicine, Graduate Programs in Medicine, Department of Pathology, Seattle, WA 98195. Offers molecular medicine and mechanisms of disease (PhD). *Degree requirements:* For doctorate, thesis/dissertation. *Entrance requirements:* For doctorate, GRE General Test.

**Université Laval,** Faculty of Medicine, Post-Professional Programs in Medical Studies, Québec, QC G1K 7P4, Canada. Offers anatomy–pathology (DESS); anesthesiology (DESS); cardiology (DESS); care of older people (Diploma); clinical research (DESS); community health (DESS); dermatology (DESS); diagnostic radiology (DESS); emergency medicine (Diploma); family medicine (DESS); general surgery (DESS); geriatrics (DESS); hematology (DESS); internal medicine (DESS); maternal and fetal medicine (Diploma); medical biochemistry (DESS); medical microbiology and infectious diseases (DESS); medical oncology (DESS); nephrology (DESS); neurology (DESS); neurosurgery (DESS); obstetrics and gynecology (DESS); ophthalmology (DESS); orthopedic surgery (DESS); oto-rhino-laryngology (DESS); palliative medicine (Diploma); pediatrics (DESS); plastic surgery (DESS); psychiatry (DESS); pulmonary medicine (DESS); radiology–oncology (DESS); thoracic surgery (DESS); urology (DESS). *Degree requirements:* For other advanced degree, comprehensive exam. *Entrance requirements:* For degree, knowledge of French. Electronic applications accepted.

**Washington State University,** College of Veterinary Medicine, Program in Immunology and Infectious Diseases, Pullman, WA 99164. Offers MS, PhD. *Faculty:* 46 full-time (33 women). *Students:* 43 full-time (30 women); includes 13 minority (1 Black or African American, non-Hispanic/Latino; 5 Asian, non-Hispanic/Latino; 7 Hispanic/Latino), 7 international. Average age 30. 29 applicants, 24% accepted, 7 enrolled. In 2019, 3 master's, 6 doctorates awarded. Terminal master's awarded for partial completion of doctoral program. *Degree requirements:* For master's, thesis, oral exam; for doctorate, thesis/dissertation, oral exam. *Entrance requirements:* For master's and doctorate, minimum GPA of 3.0. Additional exam requirements/recommendations for international students: required—TOEFL (minimum score 550 paper-based; 80 iBT). *Application deadline:* For fall admission, 12/15 priority date for domestic and international students. Applications are processed on a rolling basis. Application fee: $75. Electronic applications accepted. *Financial support:* In 2019–20, 43 students received support, including 4 fellowships, 39 research assistantships, 1 teaching assistantship; institutionally sponsored loans, scholarships/grants, traineeships, and unspecified assistantships also available. Financial award application deadline: 3/1; financial award applicants required to submit FAFSA. *Unit head:* Dr. Anthony Nicola, Interim Chair, 509-335-6030, Fax: 509-335-8529, E-mail: anthony.nicola@wsu.edu. *Application contact:* Sue Zumwalt, Graduate Coordinator, 509-335-6027, Fax: 509-335-8529, E-mail: szumwalt@wsu.edu.
Website: http://vmp.vetmed.wsu.edu/graduate-programs

**Yale University,** Yale School of Medicine and Graduate School of Arts and Sciences, Combined Program in Biological and Biomedical Sciences (BBS), Microbiology Track, New Haven, CT 06520. Offers PhD, MD/PhD. *Degree requirements:* For doctorate, thesis/dissertation. *Entrance requirements:* For doctorate, GRE General Test, GRE Subject Test. Additional exam requirements/recommendations for international students: required—TOEFL. Electronic applications accepted.

# Medical Microbiology

**The Citadel, The Military College of South Carolina,** Citadel Graduate College, School of Humanities and Social Sciences, Department of History, Charleston, SC 29409. Offers history (MA); history and teaching content (Graduate Certificate). *Program availability:* Part-time, evening/weekend, 100% online, blended/hybrid learning. *Faculty:* 14 full-time (6 women), 6 part-time/adjunct (1 woman). *Students:* 13 part-time (3 women); includes 1 minority (Hispanic/Latino). In 2019, 2 master's awarded. *Degree requirements:* For master's, thesis optional. *Entrance requirements:* For master's, MA History: GRE; MA Military History: GRE or MAT, Official transcript reflecting the highest degree earned from a regionally accredited college or university, UG cumulative GPA of 2.5 and major GPA of 3.0, 3 letters of recommendation, and a writing sample; for Graduate Certificate, Official transcript reflecting the highest degree earned from a regionally accredited college or university, letter of intent, 3 references, and either a Baccalaureate degree in Elementary Education, Social Studies, Education or History or a Baccalaureate degree in a related Social Studies. Additional exam requirements/recommendations for international students: required—TOEFL (minimum score 550 paper-based; 79 iBT). Application fee: $40. Electronic applications accepted. *Expenses:* MA Military History: $695 per credit hour. $165 per semester in fees ($75 Technology Fee + $75 Infrastructure Fee + $15 Registration Fee). *Financial support:* Federal Work-Study, scholarships/grants, tuition waivers (partial), and Athletics available. Financial award applicants required to submit FAFSA. *Unit head:* Joelle Neulander, Department Head of History, 843-953-5073, Fax: 843-953-1663, E-mail: neulanderj1@citadel.edu. *Application contact:* Caroline Schlatt, Assistant Director of Enrollment Management, 843-953-5073, Fax: 843-953-7630, E-mail: cschlatt@citadel.edu. Website: http://www.citadel.edu/root/history-masters-program

**Creighton University,** School of Medicine and Graduate School, Graduate Programs in Medicine, Omaha, NE 68178-0001. Offers biomedical sciences (MS, PhD); clinical anatomy (MS); medical microbiology and immunology (MS, PhD); pharmacology (MS, PhD), including pharmaceutical sciences (MS); pharmacology; MD/PhD; Pharm D/MS. Terminal master's awarded for partial completion of doctoral program. *Degree requirements:* For master's, thesis; for doctorate, thesis/dissertation. *Entrance requirements:* For master's and doctorate, GRE General Test. Additional exam requirements/recommendations for international students: required—TOEFL (minimum score 550 paper-based; 80 iBT). Electronic applications accepted. *Expenses:* Contact institution.

**HEC Montreal,** School of Business Administration, Doctoral Program in Administration, Montréal, QC H3T 2A7, Canada. Offers accounting (PhD); applied economics (PhD); data science (PhD); finance (PhD); financial engineering (PhD); information technology (PhD); international business (PhD); logistics and operations management (PhD); management science (PhD); management, strategy and organizations (PhD); marketing (PhD); organizational behaviour and human resources (PhD). *Accreditation:* AACSB. *Entrance requirements:* For doctorate, TAGE MAGE, GMAT, or GRE, master's degree in administration or related field. Electronic applications accepted.

**Idaho State University,** Graduate School, College of Science and Engineering, Department of Biological Sciences, Pocatello, ID 83209-8007. Offers biology (MNS, MS, DA, PhD); clinical laboratory science (MS); microbiology (MS). *Accreditation:* NAACLS. *Program availability:* Part-time. *Degree requirements:* For master's, comprehensive exam, thesis; for doctorate, comprehensive exam, thesis/dissertation, 9 credits of internship (for DA). *Entrance requirements:* For master's, GRE General Test, minimum GPA of 3.0 in all upper division classes; for doctorate, GRE General Test, GRE Subject Test (biology), diagnostic exam (DA), minimum GPA of 3.0 in all upper division classes. Additional exam requirements/recommendations for international students: required—TOEFL (minimum score 550 paper-based; 80 iBT). Electronic applications accepted.

**Rutgers University - New Brunswick,** Graduate School-New Brunswick, Programs in the Molecular Biosciences, Piscataway, NJ 08854-8097. Offers biochemistry (PhD); cell and developmental biology (MS, PhD); microbiology and molecular genetics (MS, PhD), including applied microbiology, clinical microbiology, computational molecular biology (PhD), immunology, microbial biochemistry, molecular genetics, virology.

**Université du Québec, Institut National de la Recherche Scientifique,** Graduate Programs, Armand-Frappier Santé Biotechnologie, Laval, QC H7V 1B7, Canada. Offers applied microbiology (M Sc); biology (PhD); experimental health sciences (M Sc); virology and immunology (M Sc, PhD). *Program availability:* Part-time. *Faculty:* 46 full-time. *Students:* 157 full-time (94 women), 9 part-time (4 women), 100 international. Average age 30. 23 applicants, 96% accepted, 21 enrolled. In 2019, 19 master's, 20 doctorates awarded. *Degree requirements:* For master's, thesis; for doctorate, thesis/dissertation. *Entrance requirements:* For master's, appropriate bachelor's degree, proficiency in French; for doctorate, appropriate master's degree, proficiency in French. *Application deadline:* For fall admission, 3/30 for domestic and international students; for winter admission, 11/1 for domestic and international students; for spring admission, 3/1 for domestic and international students. Application fee: $45 Canadian dollars. Electronic applications accepted. *Financial support:* In 2019–20, fellowships (averaging $16,500 per year) were awarded; research assistantships also available. *Unit head:* Claude Guertin, Director, 450-687-5010, Fax: 450-686-5501, E-mail: claude.guertin@iaf.inrs.ca. *Application contact:* Sean Otto, Registrar, 418-654-2518, Fax: 418-654-3858, E-mail: sean.otto@inrs.ca. Website: http://www.iaf.inrs.ca

**University of Alberta,** Faculty of Medicine and Dentistry and Faculty of Graduate Studies and Research, Graduate Programs in Medicine, Department of Medical Microbiology and Immunology, Edmonton, AB T6G 2E1, Canada. Offers M Sc, PhD. Terminal master's awarded for partial completion of doctoral program. *Degree requirements:* For master's, thesis; for doctorate, thesis/dissertation. *Entrance requirements:* For master's and doctorate, minimum GPA of 3.3. Additional exam

requirements/recommendations for international students: required—TOEFL (minimum score 600 paper-based; 96 iBT).

**University of Hawaii at Manoa,** John A. Burns School of Medicine and Office of Graduate Education, Graduate Programs in Biomedical Sciences, Department of Tropical Medicine, Medical Microbiology and Pharmacology, Honolulu, HI 96822. Offers tropical medicine (MS, PhD). *Program availability:* Part-time. Terminal master's awarded for partial completion of doctoral program. *Degree requirements:* For master's, thesis optional; for doctorate, comprehensive exam, thesis/dissertation. *Entrance requirements:* For master's and doctorate, GRE General Test. Additional exam requirements/recommendations for international students: required—TOEFL (minimum score 580 paper-based; 92 iBT), IELTS (minimum score 5).

**University of Manitoba,** Max Rady College of Medicine and Faculty of Graduate Studies, Graduate Programs in Medicine, Department of Medical Microbiology and Infectious Diseases, Winnipeg, MB R3T 2N2, Canada. Offers M Sc, PhD. *Program availability:* Part-time. Terminal master's awarded for partial completion of doctoral program. *Degree requirements:* For master's, thesis; for doctorate, one foreign language, thesis/dissertation. *Entrance requirements:* For master's and doctorate, minimum GPA of 3.0. Electronic applications accepted.

**University of Minnesota, Duluth,** Medical School, Microbiology, Immunology and Molecular Pathobiology Section, Duluth, MN 55812-2496. Offers MS, PhD. Terminal master's awarded for partial completion of doctoral program. *Degree requirements:* For master's, thesis, final oral exam; for doctorate, thesis/dissertation, final exam, oral and written preliminary exams. *Entrance requirements:* For master's and doctorate, GRE General Test. Additional exam requirements/recommendations for international students: required—TOEFL.

**University of Southern California,** Keck School of Medicine and Graduate School, Graduate Programs in Medicine, Programs in Biomedical and Biological Sciences (PIBBS), Program in Medical Biology, Los Angeles, CA 90089. Offers PhD. *Faculty:* 46 full-time (13 women). *Students:* 31 full-time (17 women); includes 9 minority (1 Black or African American, non-Hispanic/Latino; 4 Asian, non-Hispanic/Latino; 4 Hispanic/Latino), 13 international. Average age 26. 4 applicants, 100% accepted, 4 enrolled. *Degree requirements:* For doctorate, comprehensive exam, thesis/dissertation. *Entrance requirements:* For doctorate, GRE, minimum GPA of 3.5. Additional exam requirements/recommendations for international students: required—TOEFL (minimum score 600 paper-based; 100 iBT), IELTS (minimum score 7), PTE. *Application deadline:* For fall admission, 12/1 priority date for domestic and international students. Application fee: $90. Electronic applications accepted. *Financial support:* In 2019–20, 28 students received support, including 2 fellowships with full tuition reimbursements available (averaging $35,000 per year), 26 research assistantships with full tuition reimbursements available (averaging $35,000 per year), 2 teaching assistantships with full tuition reimbursements available (averaging $35,000 per year); institutionally sponsored loans, scholarships/grants, traineeships, health care benefits, unspecified assistantships, and Leave of Absence also available. Financial award application deadline: 4/15; financial award applicants required to submit CSS PROFILE or FAFSA. *Unit head:* Dr. W. Martin Kast, Director, 323-442-1645, Fax: 323-442-1199, E-mail: mkast@usc.edu. *Application contact:* Karina Recinos, Student Services Advisor, 323-442-1609, Fax: 323-442-1199, E-mail: karina.recinos@med.usc.edu. Website: https://keck.usc.edu/pibbs/phd-programs/medical-biology

**University of Wisconsin–La Crosse,** College of Science and Health, Department of Biology, La Crosse, WI 54601. Offers aquatic sciences (MS); biology (MS); cellular and molecular biology (MS); clinical microbiology (MS); microbiology (MS); nurse anesthesia (MS); physiology (MS). *Accreditation:* AANA/CANAEP. *Program availability:* Part-time. *Faculty:* 19 full-time (7 women). *Students:* 12 full-time (6 women), 39 part-time (15 women); includes 2 minority (1 Black or African American, non-Hispanic/Latino; 1 Asian, non-Hispanic/Latino). Average age 28. 37 applicants, 68% accepted, 19 enrolled. In 2019, 19 master's awarded. *Degree requirements:* For master's, comprehensive exam, thesis. *Entrance requirements:* For master's, GRE General Test, minimum GPA of 2.85. Additional exam requirements/recommendations for international students: required—TOEFL (minimum score 550 paper-based; 79 iBT). *Application deadline:* For fall admission, 2/1 priority date for domestic and international students; for spring admission, 1/4 priority date for domestic and international students. Applications are processed on a rolling basis. Electronic applications accepted. *Financial support:* Research assistantships with partial tuition reimbursements, Federal Work-Study, scholarships/grants, health care benefits, and tuition waivers (partial) available. Support available to part-time students. Financial award application deadline: 3/15; financial award applicants required to submit FAFSA. *Unit head:* Dr. Michael Abler, Department Chair, 608-785-6962, E-mail: mabler@uwlax.edu. *Application contact:* Jennifer Weber, Senior Student Services Coordinator Graduate Admissions, 608-785-8939, E-mail: admissions@uwlax.edu. Website: http://uwlax.edu/biology/

**University of Wisconsin–La Crosse,** College of Science and Health, Department of Microbiology, La Crosse, WI 54601-3742. Offers clinical microbiology (MS); microbiology (MS). *Faculty:* 7 full-time (2 women). *Students:* 9 full-time (4 women), 12 part-time (6 women); includes 1 minority (Two or more races, non-Hispanic/Latino), 1 international. Average age 26. 9 applicants, 89% accepted, 6 enrolled. In 2019, 7 master's awarded. *Unit head:* Dr. Michael Hoffman, Chair/Program Director, 608-785-6984, E-mail: mhoffman@uwlax.edu. *Application contact:* Jennifer Weber, Senior Student Service Coordinator Graduate Admissions, 608-785-8939, E-mail: admissions@uwlax.edu. Website: http://www.uwlax.edu/microbiology/

**University of Wisconsin–Madison,** Graduate School, College of Agricultural and Life Sciences, Microbiology Doctoral Training Program, Madison, WI 53706. Offers PhD.

# Microbiology

**Alabama State University,** College of Science, Mathematics and Technology, Department of Biological Sciences, Montgomery, AL 36101-0271. Offers biology (MS); microbiology (PhD). *Faculty:* 13 full-time (4 women), 7 part-time/adjunct (4 women). *Students:* 8 full-time (3 women), 11 part-time (7 women); includes 13 minority (12 Black or African American, non-Hispanic/Latino; 1 Asian, non-Hispanic/Latino), 4 international. Average age 29. 17 applicants, 41% accepted, 4 enrolled. In 2019, 3 master's, 1 doctorate awarded. *Degree requirements:* For master's, one foreign language, comprehensive exam, thesis; for doctorate, 3 foreign languages, thesis/dissertation.

*Entrance requirements:* For master's, GRE General Test, GRE Subject Test, writing competency test. Additional exam requirements/recommendations for international students: required—TOEFL (minimum score 500 paper-based). *Application deadline:* For fall admission, 4/15 for domestic and international students; for spring admission, 11/15 for domestic and international students; for summer admission, 3/15 for domestic and international students. Applications are processed on a rolling basis. Application fee: $25. Electronic applications accepted. Application fee is waived when completed online. *Financial support:* Fellowships, research assistantships, scholarships/grants, tuition waivers (partial), and unspecified assistantships available. Financial award application deadline: 6/30; financial award applicants required to submit FAFSA. *Unit head:* Dr. Boakai K. Robertson, Chair, 334-229-4467, Fax: 334-229-1007, E-mail: bkrobertson@alasu.edu. *Application contact:* Dr. Ed Brown, Dean of Graduate Studies, 334-229-4274, Fax: 334-229-4928, E-mail: wperson@alasu.edu.
Website: http://www.alasu.edu/academics/colleges—departments/science-mathematics-technology/biological-sciences-department/index.aspx

**Albany Medical College,** Center for Immunology and Microbial Disease, Albany, NY 12208-3479. Offers MS, PhD. *Program availability:* Part-time. Terminal master's awarded for partial completion of doctoral program. *Degree requirements:* For master's, thesis; for doctorate, comprehensive exam, thesis/dissertation, oral qualifying exam, written preliminary exam, 1 published paper-peer review. *Entrance requirements:* For master's, GRE General Test, all transcripts, letters of recommendation; for doctorate, GRE General Test, letters of recommendation. Additional exam requirements/recommendations for international students: required—TOEFL.

**Albert Einstein College of Medicine,** Graduate Programs in the Biomedical Sciences, Department of Microbiology and Immunology, Bronx, NY 10461. Offers PhD, MD/PhD. *Degree requirements:* For doctorate, thesis/dissertation. *Entrance requirements:* For doctorate, GRE General Test. Additional exam requirements/recommendations for international students: required—TOEFL.

**Arizona State University at Tempe,** College of Liberal Arts and Sciences, School of Life Sciences, Tempe, AZ 85287-4601. Offers animal behavior (PhD); applied ethics (biomedical and health ethics) (MA); biology (MS, PhD), including biology, biology and society, complex adaptive systems science (PhD), plant biology and conservation (MS); environmental life sciences (PhD); evolutionary biology (PhD); history and philosophy of science (PhD); human and social dimensions of science and technology (PhD); microbiology (PhD); molecular and cellular biology (PhD); neuroscience (PhD). Terminal master's awarded for partial completion of doctoral program. *Degree requirements:* For master's, thesis (for some programs), interactive Program of Study (iPOS) submitted before completing 50 percent of required credit hours; for doctorate, variable foreign language requirement, comprehensive exam, thesis/dissertation, interactive Program of Study (iPOS) submitted before completing 50 percent of required credit hours. *Entrance requirements:* For master's and doctorate, GRE, minimum GPA of 3.0 or equivalent in last 2 years of work leading to bachelor's degree. Additional exam requirements/recommendations for international students: required—TOEFL (minimum score 600 paper-based; 100 iBT). Electronic applications accepted.

**Baylor College of Medicine,** Graduate School of Biomedical Sciences, Department of Molecular Virology and Microbiology, Houston, TX 77030-3498. Offers PhD, MD/PhD. *Degree requirements:* For doctorate, thesis/dissertation, public defense. *Entrance requirements:* For doctorate, GRE General Test, GRE Subject Test (strongly recommended), minimum GPA of 3.0. Additional exam requirements/recommendations for international students: required—TOEFL. Electronic applications accepted.

**Baylor College of Medicine,** Graduate School of Biomedical Sciences, Interdepartmental Program in Cell and Molecular Biology, Houston, TX 77030-3498. Offers biochemistry (PhD); cell and molecular biology (PhD); genetics (PhD); human genetics (PhD); immunology (PhD); microbiology (PhD); virology (PhD); MD/PhD. *Degree requirements:* For doctorate, thesis/dissertation, public defense. *Entrance requirements:* For doctorate, GRE General Test, GRE Subject Test (strongly recommended), minimum GPA of 3.0. Additional exam requirements/recommendations for international students: required—TOEFL. Electronic applications accepted.

**Boston University,** School of Medicine, Graduate Medical Sciences, Department of Microbiology, Boston, MA 02118. Offers PhD, MD/PhD. Terminal master's awarded for partial completion of doctoral program. *Degree requirements:* For doctorate, comprehensive exam, thesis/dissertation. *Entrance requirements:* Additional exam requirements/recommendations for international students: required—TOEFL. *Application deadline:* For fall admission, 1/15 for domestic students; for spring admission, 10/15 for domestic students. *Unit head:* Dr. Ronald B. Corley, Chairman, E-mail: rbcorley@bu.edu. *Application contact:* GMS Admissions Office, 617-358-9518, Fax: 617-358-2913, E-mail: gmsbusm@bu.edu.
Website: http://www.bumc.bu.edu/microbiology/

**Brandeis University,** Graduate School of Arts and Sciences, Department of Biology, Waltham, MA 02454-9110. Offers genetics (PhD); microbiology (PhD); molecular and cell biology (MS, PhD); molecular biology (PhD); neurobiology (PhD); quantitative biology (PhD). *Program availability:* Part-time. *Faculty:* 28 full-time (14 women), 1 part-time/adjunct (0 women). *Students:* 44 full-time (26 women), 1 (woman) part-time; includes 15 minority (1 American Indian or Alaska Native, non-Hispanic/Latino; 7 Asian, non-Hispanic/Latino; 7 Hispanic/Latino), 10 international. Average age 27. 202 applicants, 22% accepted, 12 enrolled. In 2019, 9 master's, 6 doctorates awarded. Terminal master's awarded for partial completion of doctoral program. *Degree requirements:* For master's, thesis optional; for doctorate, comprehensive exam, thesis/dissertation. *Entrance requirements:* For master's, transcripts, letters of recommendation, resume, statement of purpose; for doctorate, transcripts, letters of recommendation, resume, program questions, statement of purpose. Additional exam requirements/recommendations for international students: required—TOEFL, IELTS, PTE. *Application deadline:* For fall admission, 12/1 priority date for domestic and international students; for spring admission, 10/15 for domestic students, 11/15 for international students. Applications are processed on a rolling basis. Application fee: $75. Electronic applications accepted. *Financial support:* In 2019–20, 50 fellowships with full tuition reimbursements (averaging $35,000 per year), 21 teaching assistantships (averaging $3,550 per year) were awarded; research assistantships, scholarships/grants, health care benefits, and tuition waivers also available. Support available to part-time students. *Unit head:* Dr. Michael Marr, Director of Graduate Studies, 781-736-2481, E-mail: mmarr@brandeis.edu. *Application contact:* Maryanna Aldrich, Administrator, 781-736-2352, E-mail: scigradoffice@brandeis.edu.
Website: http://www.brandeis.edu/gsas/programs/mcbio.html

**Brigham Young University,** Graduate Studies, College of Life Sciences, Department of Microbiology and Molecular Biology, Provo, UT 84602-1001. Offers MS, PhD. *Faculty:* 19 full-time (3 women), 8 part-time/adjunct (6 women). *Students:* 30 full-time (15 women); includes 9 minority (1 Black or African American, non-Hispanic/Latino; 2 Asian, non-Hispanic/Latino; 5 Hispanic/Latino; 1 Native Hawaiian or other Pacific Islander, non-Hispanic/Latino), 7 international. Average age 29. 19 applicants, 79% accepted, 8 enrolled. In 2019, 7 master's, 3 doctorates awarded. Terminal master's awarded for partial completion of doctoral program. *Degree requirements:* For master's, comprehensive exam, thesis, Completion of research and didactic credits; for doctorate, comprehensive exam, thesis/dissertation, Published in a scientific journal, completion of research and didactic credits. *Entrance requirements:* For master's, GRE General Test, minimum GPA of 3.0 during previous 2 years; for doctorate, GRE General Test, minimum GPA of 3.0. Additional exam requirements/recommendations for international students: required—TOEFL (minimum score 580 paper-based; 85 iBT), IELTS (minimum score 7), PTE. *Application deadline:* For fall admission, 1/15 for domestic and international students. Application fee: $50. Electronic applications accepted. *Expenses:* LDS $430 per credit, Non-LDS $860 per credit. *Financial support:* Fellowships, institutionally sponsored loans, scholarships/grants, health care benefits, and unspecified assistantships available. Financial award application deadline: 2/1; financial award applicants required to submit FAFSA. *Unit head:* Dr. Richard Robison, Chair, 801-422-2416, Fax: 801-422-0004, E-mail: richard_robison@byu.edu. *Application contact:* Dr. Kevin Ornal Johnson, Graduate Coordinator, 801-422-4293, Fax: 801-422-0004, E-mail: kevin_johnson@byu.edu.
Website: http://mmbio.byu.edu/

**California State University, Long Beach,** Graduate Studies, College of Natural Sciences and Mathematics, Department of Biological Sciences, Long Beach, CA 90840. Offers biology (MS); microbiology (MS). *Program availability:* Part-time. *Entrance requirements:* For master's, GRE Subject Test, minimum GPA of 3.0. Electronic applications accepted.

**Case Western Reserve University,** School of Medicine and School of Graduate Studies, Graduate Programs in Medicine, Department of Molecular Biology and Microbiology, Cleveland, OH 44106-4960. Offers cell biology (PhD); molecular biology (PhD); molecular virology (PhD); MD/PhD. *Degree requirements:* For doctorate, thesis/dissertation. *Entrance requirements:* For doctorate, GRE General Test, GRE Subject Test. Additional exam requirements/recommendations for international students: required—TOEFL. Electronic applications accepted.

**The Catholic University of America,** School of Arts and Sciences, Department of Biology, Washington, DC 20064. Offers biotechnology (MS); cell and microbial biology (MS, PhD), including cell biology; clinical laboratory science (MS, PhD); MSLS/MS. *Program availability:* Part-time. *Faculty:* 10 full-time (4 women), 3 part-time/adjunct (1 woman). *Students:* 16 full-time (13 women), 36 part-time (19 women); includes 11 minority (4 Black or African American, non-Hispanic/Latino; 3 Asian, non-Hispanic/Latino; 4 Two or more races, non-Hispanic/Latino), 33 international. Average age 31. 46 applicants, 65% accepted, 12 enrolled. In 2019, 15 master's, 8 doctorates awarded. Terminal master's awarded for partial completion of doctoral program. *Degree requirements:* For master's and doctorate, comprehensive exam. *Entrance requirements:* For master's and doctorate, GRE General Test, GRE Subject Test, statement of purpose, official copies of academic transcripts, three letters of recommendation. Additional exam requirements/recommendations for international students: required—TOEFL (minimum score 550 paper-based; 80 iBT). *Application deadline:* For fall admission, 7/15 priority date for domestic students, 7/1 for international students; for spring admission, 11/15 priority date for domestic students, 11/1 for international students. Applications are processed on a rolling basis. Application fee: $55. Electronic applications accepted. *Expenses:* Contact institution. *Financial support:* Fellowships, research assistantships, teaching assistantships, Federal Work-Study, scholarships/grants, tuition waivers (full and partial), and unspecified assistantships available. Financial award application deadline: 2/1; financial award applicants required to submit FAFSA. *Unit head:* Dr. Venigalla Rao, Chair, 202-319-5271, Fax: 202-319-5721, E-mail: rao@cua.edu. *Application contact:* Dr. Steven Brown, Director of Graduate Admissions, 202-319-5057, Fax: 202-319-6533, E-mail: cua-admissions@cua.edu.
Website: http://biology.cua.edu/

**Central Washington University,** School of Graduate Studies and Research, College of the Sciences, Department of Biological Sciences, Ellensburg, WA 98926. Offers botany (MS); microbiology and parasitology (MS); stream ecology and fisheries (MS); terrestrial ecology (MS). *Program availability:* Part-time. *Entrance requirements:* For master's, GRE General Test, minimum GPA of 3.0. Additional exam requirements/recommendations for international students: required—TOEFL (minimum score 550 paper-based; 79 iBT). Electronic applications accepted.

**Clemson University,** Graduate School, College of Science, Department of Biological Sciences, Clemson, SC 29634. Offers biological sciences (MS, PhD); biological sciences for science educators (MBS); environmental toxicology (MS, PhD); microbiology (MS, PhD). *Program availability:* Part-time, 100% online. *Faculty:* 48 full-time (22 women), 5 part-time/adjunct (0 women). *Students:* 72 full-time (40 women), 221 part-time (148 women); includes 39 minority (7 Black or African American, non-Hispanic/Latino; 2 American Indian or Alaska Native, non-Hispanic/Latino; 4 Asian, non-Hispanic/Latino; 14 Hispanic/Latino; 1 Native Hawaiian or other Pacific Islander, non-Hispanic/Latino; 11 Two or more races, non-Hispanic/Latino), 11 international. Average age 34. 206 applicants, 76% accepted, 122 enrolled. In 2019, 111 master's, 8 doctorates awarded. *Degree requirements:* For master's, comprehensive exam (for some programs), thesis (for some programs); for doctorate, comprehensive exam, thesis/dissertation. *Entrance requirements:* For master's and doctorate, GRE General Test, unofficial transcripts, letters of recommendation. Additional exam requirements/recommendations for international students: required—TOEFL (minimum score 102 paper-based; 102 iBT); recommended—IELTS (minimum score 7.5), TSE (minimum score 72). *Application deadline:* For fall admission, 12/10 priority date for domestic and international students. Applications are processed on a rolling basis. Application fee: $80 ($90 for international students). Electronic applications accepted. *Expenses:* Full-Time Student per Semester: Tuition: $4600 (in-state), $9525 (out-of-state), Fees: $598; Graduate Assistant Per Semester: $1144; Part-Time Student Per Credit Hour: $556 (in-state), $1106 (out-of-state), Fees: $617; other fees apply depending on program, credit hours, campus & residency. Doctoral Base Fee per Semester: $4938 (in-state), $10405 (out-of-state). *Financial support:* In 2019–20, 59 students received support, including 5 fellowships with full and partial tuition reimbursements available (averaging $3,622 per year), 11 research assistantships with full and partial tuition reimbursements available (averaging $23,227 per year), 43 teaching assistantships with full and partial tuition reimbursements available (averaging $22,326 per year); unspecified assistantships also available. Financial award application deadline: 12/10. *Unit head:* Dr. Saara Dewalt, Department Chair, 864-656-1112, E-mail: saarad@clemson.edu. *Application contact:* Jay Lyn Martin, Graduate Student Services Coordinator, 864-656-3587, E-mail: jaylyn@clemson.edu.
Website: http://www.clemson.edu/science/departments/biosci/

**Colorado State University,** College of Veterinary Medicine and Biomedical Sciences, Department of Microbiology, Immunology and Pathology, Fort Collins, CO 80523. Offers microbiology, immunology and pathology (MS, PhD); pathology (PhD). *Faculty:* 76 full-time (35 women), 12 part-time/adjunct (8 women). *Students:* 64 full-time (46 women), 39 part-time (30 women); includes 10 minority (1 Black or African American, non-Hispanic/Latino; 1 American Indian or Alaska Native, non-Hispanic/Latino; 4 Hispanic/Latino; 4 Two or more races, non-Hispanic/Latino), 3 international. Average age 28. 187 applicants, 30% accepted, 45 enrolled. In 2019, 28 master's, 9 doctorates awarded. Terminal master's awarded for partial completion of doctoral program. *Degree requirements:* For master's, thesis (for some programs); for doctorate, comprehensive

exam, thesis/dissertation. *Entrance requirements:* Additional exam requirements/recommendations for international students: required—TOEFL (minimum score 550 paper-based; 80 iBT), IELTS (minimum score 6.5), PTE (minimum score 58). *Application deadline:* For fall admission, 12/15 for domestic and international students. Application fee: $60 ($70 for international students). *Expenses:* For non-thesis MS, addition fee of $120 per credit. *Financial support:* In 2019–20, 27 students received support, including 24 research assistantships with full and partial tuition reimbursements available (averaging $25,025 per year), 6 teaching assistantships with full and partial tuition reimbursements available (averaging $18,612 per year); health care benefits also available. Financial award application deadline: 12/15. *Unit head:* Dr. Gregg Dean, Department Head, 970-491-6144, E-mail: Gregg.Dean@colostate.edu. *Application contact:* Heidi Runge, Academic Support Coordinator for Graduate Studies, 970-491-1630, Fax: 970-491-1815, E-mail: heidi.runge@colostate.edu.
Website: https://vetmedbiosci.colostate.edu/mip/

**Columbia University,** College of Physicians and Surgeons, Department of Microbiology, New York, NY 10032. Offers biomedical sciences (M Phil, MA, PhD); MD/PhD. Terminal master's awarded for partial completion of doctoral program. *Degree requirements:* For doctorate, thesis/dissertation. *Entrance requirements:* For master's, GRE General Test; for doctorate, GRE. Additional exam requirements/recommendations for international students: required—TOEFL. *Expenses: Tuition:* Full-time $47,600; part-time $1880 per credit. One-time fee: $105.

**Cornell University,** Graduate School, Graduate Fields of Agriculture and Life Sciences, Field of Microbiology, Ithaca, NY 14853. Offers PhD. *Degree requirements:* For doctorate, comprehensive exam, thesis/dissertation, 2 semesters of teaching experience. *Entrance requirements:* For doctorate, GRE General Test, 3 letters of recommendation. Additional exam requirements/recommendations for international students: required—TOEFL (minimum score 550 paper-based; 77 iBT). Electronic applications accepted.

**Dalhousie University,** Faculty of Medicine, Department of Microbiology and Immunology, Halifax, NS B3H 4R2, Canada. Offers M Sc, PhD. *Degree requirements:* For master's, thesis; for doctorate, comprehensive exam, thesis/dissertation. *Entrance requirements:* For master's, GRE General Test, honors B Sc; for doctorate, GRE General Test, honors B Sc in microbiology, M Sc in discipline or transfer after 1 year in master's program. Additional exam requirements/recommendations for international students: required—1 of 5 approved tests: TOEFL, IELTS, CANTEST, CAEL, Michigan English Language Assessment Battery. Electronic applications accepted.

**Dartmouth College,** Guarini School of Graduate and Advanced Studies, Graduate Programs in Biological Sciences, Graduate Program in Molecular and Cellular Biology, Department of Microbiology and Immunology, Hanover, NH 03755. Offers microbiology and molecular pathogenesis (PhD); MBA/PhD; MD/PhD. *Entrance requirements:* For doctorate, GRE General Test, letters of recommendation, minimum GPA of 3.0. Electronic applications accepted.

**Drexel University,** College of Medicine, Biomedical Graduate Programs, Program in Microbiology and Immunology, Philadelphia, PA 19104-2875. Offers MS, PhD, MD/PhD. Terminal master's awarded for partial completion of doctoral program. *Degree requirements:* For master's, comprehensive exam, thesis; for doctorate, thesis/dissertation, qualifying exam. *Entrance requirements:* For master's, GRE General Test, minimum GPA of 2.75; for doctorate, GRE General Test, minimum GPA of 3.0. Additional exam requirements/recommendations for international students: required—TOEFL. Electronic applications accepted.

**Duke University,** Graduate School, Department of Molecular Genetics and Microbiology, Durham, NC 27710. Offers PhD. *Degree requirements:* For doctorate, thesis/dissertation. *Entrance requirements:* For doctorate, GRE General Test, GRE Subject Test in biology, chemistry, or biochemistry, cell and molecular biology (recommended). Additional exam requirements/recommendations for international students: required—TOEFL (minimum score 577 paper-based; 90 iBT) or IELTS (minimum score 7). Electronic applications accepted.

**East Carolina University,** Brody School of Medicine, Office of Research and Graduate Studies, Greenville, NC 27858-4353. Offers anatomy and cell biology (PhD); biochemistry and molecular biology (PhD); biomedical science (MS); microbiology and immunology (PhD); pharmacology and toxicology (PhD); physiology (PhD). *Students:* 102 full-time (44 women), 1 part-time (0 women); includes 16 minority (4 Black or African American, non-Hispanic/Latino; 7 Asian, non-Hispanic/Latino; 4 Hispanic/Latino; 1 Two or more races, non-Hispanic/Latino), 13 international. Average age 28. 83 applicants, 40% accepted, 20 enrolled. In 2019, 3 master's, 10 doctorates awarded. *Degree requirements:* For doctorate, comprehensive exam, thesis/dissertation. *Entrance requirements:* For doctorate, GRE General Test. Additional exam requirements/recommendations for international students: required—some international applicants may be required to demonstrate English proficiency via the TOEFL, IELTS, or PTE exam.; recommended—TOEFL (minimum score 78 iBT), IELTS (minimum score 6.5), TSE (minimum score 65). *Application deadline:* For fall admission, 8/15 for domestic students; for spring admission, 12/20 for domestic students. Applications are processed on a rolling basis. Application fee: $75. Electronic applications accepted. *Expenses: Tuition, area resident:* Full-time $4749; part-time $185 per credit hour. Tuition, state resident: full-time $4749; part-time $185 per credit hour. Tuition, nonresident: full-time $17,898; part-time $864 per credit hour. *International tuition:* $17,898 full-time. *Required fees:* $2787. *Financial support:* Fellowships available. Financial award application deadline: 6/1. *Unit head:* Dr. Russ Price, Associate Dean, 252-744-9346, E-mail: pricest17@ecu.edu. *Application contact:* Dr. Russ Price, Associate Dean, 252-744-9346, E-mail: pricest17@ecu.edu.
Website: http://www.ecu.edu/cs-dhs/bsomresearchgradstudies/index.cfm

**East Tennessee State University,** College of Graduate and Continuing Studies, College of Arts and Sciences, Department of Biological Sciences, Johnson City, TN 37614. Offers biology (MS); biomedical sciences (MS); microbiology (MS). *Degree requirements:* For master's, comprehensive exam, thesis. *Entrance requirements:* For master's, GRE General Test or GRE Subject Test, minimum GPA of 3.0, undergraduate degree in life or physical sciences, two letters of recommendation; course in calculus and/or course in probability and statistics (recommended). Additional exam requirements/recommendations for international students: required—TOEFL (minimum score 550 paper-based; 79 iBT). Electronic applications accepted.

**East Tennessee State University,** Quillen College of Medicine, Department of Biomedical Sciences, Johnson City, TN 37614. Offers anatomy (PhD); biochemistry (PhD); microbiology (PhD); pharmaceutical sciences (PhD); pharmacology (PhD); physiology (PhD); quantitative biosciences (PhD). *Degree requirements:* For doctorate, comprehensive exam, thesis/dissertation, comprehensive qualifying exam; one-year residency. *Entrance requirements:* For doctorate, GRE General Test, GRE Subject Test, 3 letters of recommendation, minimum of 60 credit hours beyond the baccalaureate degree. Additional exam requirements/recommendations for international students: required—TOEFL (minimum score 550 paper-based; 79 iBT). Electronic applications accepted. *Expenses:* Contact institution.

**Emory University,** Laney Graduate School, Division of Biological and Biomedical Sciences, Program in Microbiology and Molecular Genetics, Atlanta, GA 30322-1100. Offers PhD. *Degree requirements:* For doctorate, comprehensive exam, thesis/dissertation. *Entrance requirements:* For doctorate, GRE General Test, minimum GPA of 3.0 in science course work (recommended). Additional exam requirements/recommendations for international students: required—TOEFL. Electronic applications accepted.

**Emporia State University,** Department of Biological Sciences, Emporia, KS 66801-5415. Offers botany (MS); environmental biology (MS); forensic science (MS); general biology (MS); microbial and cellular biology (MS); zoology (MS). *Program availability:* Part-time. *Degree requirements:* For master's, comprehensive exam or thesis. *Entrance requirements:* For master's, GRE, appropriate undergraduate degree, interview, letters of reference. Additional exam requirements/recommendations for international students: required—TOEFL (minimum score 520 paper-based; 68 iBT). Electronic applications accepted. *Expenses: Tuition, area resident:* Full-time $6394; part-time $266.41 per credit hour. Tuition, state resident: full-time $6394; part-time $266.41 per credit hour. Tuition, nonresident: full-time $20,128; part-time $828.66 per credit hour. *International tuition:* $20,128 full-time. *Required fees:* $2183; $90.95 per credit hour. Tuition and fees vary according to campus/location and program.

**Georgetown University,** Graduate School of Arts and Sciences, Department of Microbiology and Immunology, Washington, DC 20057. Offers biohazardous threat agents and emerging infectious diseases (MS); biomedical science policy and advocacy (MS); general microbiology and immunology (MS); global infectious diseases (PhD); microbiology and immunology (PhD). *Program availability:* Part-time. *Degree requirements:* For master's, 30 credit hours of coursework; for doctorate, comprehensive exam, thesis/dissertation. *Entrance requirements:* For master's, GRE General Test, 3 letters of reference, bachelor's degree in related field; for doctorate, GRE General Test, 3 letters of reference, MS/BS in related field. Additional exam requirements/recommendations for international students: required—TOEFL (minimum score 505 paper-based). Electronic applications accepted.

**The George Washington University,** Columbian College of Arts and Sciences, Institute for Biomedical Sciences, Program in Microbiology and Immunology, Washington, DC 20037. Offers PhD. *Entrance requirements:* For doctorate, GRE General Test, minimum GPA of 3.0. Additional exam requirements/recommendations for international students: required—TOEFL (minimum score 600 paper-based). Electronic applications accepted.

**The George Washington University,** Milken Institute School of Public Health, Department of Epidemiology and Biostatistics, Washington, DC 20052. Offers biostatistics (MPH); epidemiology (MPH); microbiology and emerging infectious diseases (MSPH). *Entrance requirements:* For master's, GMAT, GRE General Test, or MCAT. Additional exam requirements/recommendations for international students: required—TOEFL.

**The George Washington University,** School of Medicine and Health Sciences, Health Sciences Programs, Washington, DC 20052. Offers clinical practice management (MSHS); clinical research administration (MSHS); emergency services management (MSHS); end-of-life care (MSHS); immunohematology (MSHS); immunohematology and biotechnology (MSHS); physical therapy (DPT); physician assistant (MSHS). *Program availability:* Online learning. *Entrance requirements:* Additional exam requirements/recommendations for international students: required—TOEFL (minimum score 550 paper-based). *Expenses:* Contact institution.

**Georgia State University,** College of Arts and Sciences, Department of Biology, Program in Applied and Environmental Microbiology, Atlanta, GA 30302-3083. Offers applied and environmental microbiology (MS, PhD); bioinformatics (MS). *Program availability:* Part-time. Terminal master's awarded for partial completion of doctoral program. *Degree requirements:* For master's, comprehensive exam (for some programs), thesis optional; for doctorate, comprehensive exam, thesis/dissertation. *Entrance requirements:* For master's and doctorate, GRE. *Application deadline:* For fall admission, 7/1 priority date for domestic students, 6/1 priority date for international students; for spring admission, 11/15 priority date for domestic students, 10/15 priority date for international students. Applications are processed on a rolling basis. Application fee: $50. Electronic applications accepted. *Expenses: Tuition, area resident:* Full-time $7164; part-time $398 per credit hour. Tuition, state resident: full-time $7164; part-time $398 per credit hour. Tuition, nonresident: full-time $22,662; part-time $1259 per credit hour. *International tuition:* $22,662 full-time. *Required fees:* $2128; $312 per credit hour. Tuition and fees vary according to course load and program. *Financial support:* In 2019–20, fellowships with full tuition reimbursements (averaging $22,000 per year), research assistantships with full tuition reimbursements (averaging $20,000 per year) were awarded. Financial award application deadline: 12/3. *Unit head:* Dr. Charles Derby, Director of Graduate Studies, 404-413-5393, Fax: 404-413-5446, E-mail: cderby@gsu.edu. *Application contact:* Dr. Charles Derby, Director of Graduate Studies, 404-413-5393, Fax: 404-413-5446, E-mail: cderby@gsu.edu.
Website: http://biology.gsu.edu/

**Harvard University,** Graduate School of Arts and Sciences, Division of Medical Sciences, Boston, MA 02115. Offers biological chemistry and molecular pharmacology (PhD); cell biology (PhD); genetics (PhD); microbiology and molecular genetics (PhD); pathology (PhD), including experimental pathology. *Degree requirements:* For doctorate, thesis/dissertation. *Entrance requirements:* For doctorate, GRE General Test, GRE Subject Test. Additional exam requirements/recommendations for international students: required—TOEFL.

**Howard University,** College of Medicine, Department of Microbiology, Washington, DC 20059-0002. Offers PhD. *Degree requirements:* For doctorate, one foreign language, comprehensive exam, thesis/dissertation, qualifying exam, teaching experience. *Entrance requirements:* For doctorate, GRE General Test, minimum GPA of 3.0 in sciences. Additional exam requirements/recommendations for international students: required—TOEFL.

**Idaho State University,** Graduate School, College of Science and Engineering, Department of Biological Sciences, Pocatello, ID 83209-8007. Offers biology (MNS, MS, DA, PhD); clinical laboratory science (MS); microbiology (MS). *Accreditation:* NAACLS. *Program availability:* Part-time. *Degree requirements:* For master's, comprehensive exam, thesis; for doctorate, comprehensive exam, thesis/dissertation, 9 credits of internship (for DA). *Entrance requirements:* For master's, GRE General Test, minimum GPA of 3.0 in all upper division classes; for doctorate, GRE General Test, GRE Subject Test (biology), diagnostic exam (DA), minimum GPA of 3.0 in all upper division classes. Additional exam requirements/recommendations for international students: required—TOEFL (minimum score 550 paper-based; 80 iBT). Electronic applications accepted.

**Illinois Institute of Technology,** Graduate College, College of Science, Department of Biology, Chicago, IL 60616. Offers applied life sciences (MS); biochemistry (MS); biology (MS, PhD); cell and molecular biology (MS); microbiology (MS); molecular biochemistry and biophysics (MS, PhD). *Program availability:* Part-time, evening/weekend, online learning. Terminal master's awarded for partial completion of doctoral program. *Degree requirements:* For master's, comprehensive exam, thesis (for some programs); for doctorate, comprehensive exam, thesis/dissertation. *Entrance requirements:* For master's, GRE General Test (minimum score 300 Quantitative and Verbal, 2.5 Analytical Writing), minimum undergraduate GPA of 3.0; for doctorate, GRE

General Test (minimum score 310 Quantitative and Verbal, 3.0 Analytical Writing); GRE Subject Test (strongly recommended), minimum undergraduate GPA of 3.0. Additional exam requirements/recommendations for international students: required—TOEFL (minimum score 550 paper-based; 80 iBT). Electronic applications accepted.

**Illinois State University,** Graduate School, College of Arts and Sciences, School of Biological Sciences, Normal, IL 61790. Offers animal behavior (MS); bacteriology (MS); biochemistry (MS); biological sciences (MS); biology (PhD); biophysics (MS); biotechnology (MS); botany (MS, PhD); cell biology (MS); conservation biology (MS); developmental biology (MS); ecology (MS, PhD); entomology (MS); evolutionary biology (MS); genetics (MS, PhD); immunology (MS); microbiology (MS, PhD); molecular biology (MS); molecular genetics (MS); neurobiology (MS); neuroscience (MS); parasitology (MS); physiology (MS, PhD); plant biology (MS); plant molecular biology (MS); plant sciences (MS); structural biology (MS); zoology (MS, PhD). *Program availability:* Part-time. *Faculty:* 26 full-time (6 women), 7 part-time/adjunct (2 women). *Students:* 51 full-time (33 women), 15 part-time (8 women). Average age 27. 71 applicants, 28% accepted, 9 enrolled. In 2019, 14 master's, 3 doctorates awarded. *Degree requirements:* For master's, thesis or alternative; for doctorate, variable foreign language requirement, thesis/dissertation, 2 terms of residency. *Entrance requirements:* For master's, GRE General Test, minimum GPA of 2.6 in last 60 hours of course work; for doctorate, GRE General Test. *Application deadline:* Applications are processed on a rolling basis. Application fee: $50. *Expenses: Tuition, area resident:* Full-time $7956; part-time $9767 per year. Tuition, nonresident: full-time $9233; part-time $17,592 per year. *Required fees:* $1797. *Financial support:* In 2019–20, 20 research assistantships, 41 teaching assistantships were awarded; Federal Work-Study, tuition waivers (full), and unspecified assistantships also available. Financial award application deadline: 4/1. *Unit head:* Dr. Craig Gatto, School Director, 309-438-3087, E-mail: cgatto@IllinoisState.edu. *Application contact:* Dr. Ben Sadd, Assistant Chair for Graduate Studies, 309-438-2651, E-mail: bmsadd@IllinoisState.edu.
Website: http://www.bio.ilstu.edu/

**Indiana University Bloomington,** University Graduate School, College of Arts and Sciences, Department of Biology, Bloomington, IN 47405. Offers biology teaching (MAT); biotechnology (MA); evolution, ecology, and behavior (MA, PhD); genetics (PhD); microbiology (MA, PhD); molecular, cellular, and developmental biology (PhD); plant sciences (MA, PhD); zoology (MA, PhD). Terminal master's awarded for partial completion of doctoral program. *Degree requirements:* For master's, thesis, oral defense; for doctorate, thesis/dissertation, oral defense. *Entrance requirements:* For master's and doctorate, GRE General Test. Additional exam requirements/ recommendations for international students: required—TOEFL (minimum score 100 iBT). Electronic applications accepted.

**Indiana University-Purdue University Indianapolis,** Indiana University School of Medicine, Department of Microbiology and Immunology, Indianapolis, IN 46202. Offers MS, PhD, MD/MS, MD/PhD. Terminal master's awarded for partial completion of doctoral program. *Degree requirements:* For master's, thesis; for doctorate, thesis/ dissertation. *Entrance requirements:* For master's and doctorate, GRE General Test, previous course work in calculus, cell biology, chemistry, genetics, physics, and biochemistry.

**Inter American University of Puerto Rico, Metropolitan Campus,** Graduate Programs, Program in Medical Technology, San Juan, PR 00919-1293. Offers administration of clinical laboratories (MS); molecular microbiology (MS). *Accreditation:* NAACLS. *Program availability:* Part-time. *Degree requirements:* For master's, comprehensive exam. *Entrance requirements:* For master's, BS in medical technology, minimum GPA of 2.5. Electronic applications accepted.

**Iowa State University of Science and Technology,** Department of Veterinary Microbiology and Preventive Medicine, Ames, IA 50011. Offers veterinary microbiology (MS, PhD). *Entrance requirements:* For master's and doctorate, GRE General Test. Additional exam requirements/recommendations for international students: required—TOEFL (minimum score 550 paper-based; 79 iBT), IELTS (minimum score 6.5). Electronic applications accepted.

**Iowa State University of Science and Technology,** Program in Microbiology, Ames, IA 50011. Offers MS, PhD. *Entrance requirements:* For master's and doctorate, GRE General Test. Additional exam requirements/recommendations for international students: required—TOEFL (minimum score 550 paper-based; 79 iBT), IELTS (minimum score 6.5). Electronic applications accepted.

**Johns Hopkins University,** Bloomberg School of Public Health, W. Harry Feinstone Department of Molecular Microbiology and Immunology, Baltimore, MD 21218. Offers MHS, Sc M, PhD. *Degree requirements:* For master's, comprehensive exam, thesis (for some programs), essay, written exams; for doctorate, comprehensive exam, thesis/ dissertation, 1-year full-time residency, oral and written exams. *Entrance requirements:* For master's, GRE General Test or MCAT, 3 letters of recommendation, curriculum vitae; for doctorate, GRE General Test, 3 letters of recommendation, transcripts, curriculum vitae. Additional exam requirements/recommendations for international students: required—TOEFL (minimum score 600 paper-based). Electronic applications accepted.

**Loma Linda University,** School of Medicine, Programs in Biochemistry and Microbiology, Loma Linda, CA 92350. Offers biochemistry (MS, PhD); microbiology (PhD). *Program availability:* Part-time. *Degree requirements:* For master's, thesis or alternative; for doctorate, thesis/dissertation. *Entrance requirements:* For master's and doctorate, GRE General Test. Additional exam requirements/recommendations for international students: required—TOEFL (minimum score 550 paper-based).

**Louisiana State University Health Sciences Center,** School of Graduate Studies in New Orleans, Department of Microbiology, Immunology, and Parasitology, New Orleans, LA 70112-1393. Offers microbiology and immunology (PhD); MD/PhD. *Degree requirements:* For doctorate, comprehensive exam, thesis/dissertation, preliminary exam, qualifying exam. *Entrance requirements:* For doctorate, GRE General Test. Additional exam requirements/recommendations for international students: recommended—TOEFL, IELTS.

**Louisiana State University Health Sciences Center at Shreveport,** Department of Microbiology and Immunology, Shreveport, LA 71130-3932. Offers MS, PhD, MD/PhD. Terminal master's awarded for partial completion of doctoral program. *Degree requirements:* For master's, comprehensive exam, thesis; for doctorate, comprehensive exam, thesis/dissertation, research proposal. *Entrance requirements:* For master's and doctorate, GRE General Test. Additional exam requirements/recommendations for international students: required—TOEFL. Electronic applications accepted. *Expenses:* Contact institution.

**Loyola University Chicago,** Graduate School, Integrated Program in Biomedical Sciences, Maywood, IL 60660. Offers biochemistry and molecular biology (MS, PhD); cell and molecular physiology (MS, PhD); infectious disease and immunology (MS); integrative cell biology (MS, PhD); microbiology and immunology (MS, PhD); molecular pharmacology and therapeutics (MS, PhD); neuroscience (MS, PhD). *Students:* Average age 25. 773 applicants, 34% accepted, 122 enrolled. In 2019, 46 master's, 12 doctorates awarded. *Degree requirements:* For master's, thesis; for doctorate, comprehensive exam, thesis/dissertation. *Entrance requirements:* For doctorate, GRE. Additional exam requirements/recommendations for international students: required—TOEFL (minimum score 94 iBT), IELTS (minimum score 7.5). *Application deadline:* For fall admission, 2/7 for domestic students. Applications are processed on a rolling basis. Electronic applications accepted. *Expenses:* Contact institution. *Financial support:* In 2019–20, 20 students received support. Schmitt Fellowships and yearly tuition scholarships (averaging $25,032) available. Financial award application deadline: 6/15; financial award applicants required to submit FAFSA. *Unit head:* Dr. Leanne L. Cribbs, Associate Dean, Graduate Education, 708-327-2817, Fax: 708-216-8216, E-mail: lcribbs@luc.edu. *Application contact:* Margarita Quesada, Graduate Program Secretary, 708-216-3532, Fax: 708-216-8216, E-mail: mquesad@luc.edu.
Website: http://ssom.luc.edu/graduate_school/degree-programs/ipbsphd/

**Marquette University,** Graduate School, College of Arts and Sciences, Department of Biological Sciences, Milwaukee, WI 53201-1881. Offers cell biology (MS, PhD); developmental biology (MS, PhD); ecology (MS, PhD); epithelial physiology (MS, PhD); genetics (MS, PhD); microbiology (MS, PhD); molecular biology (MS, PhD); muscle and exercise physiology (MS, PhD); neuroscience (PhD). Terminal master's awarded for partial completion of doctoral program. *Degree requirements:* For master's, comprehensive exam, thesis, 1 year of teaching experience or equivalent; for doctorate, thesis/dissertation, 1 year of teaching experience or equivalent, qualifying exam. *Entrance requirements:* For master's and doctorate, GRE General Test, GRE Subject Test, official transcripts from all current and previous colleges/universities except Marquette, statement of professional goals and aspirations, three letters of recommendation. Additional exam requirements/recommendations for international students: required—TOEFL (minimum score 530 paper-based). Electronic applications accepted.

**Massachusetts Institute of Technology,** School of Science, Department of Biology, Cambridge, MA 02139. Offers biochemistry (PhD); biological oceanography (PhD); biology (PhD); biophysical chemistry and molecular structure (PhD); cell biology (PhD); computational and systems biology (PhD); developmental biology (PhD); genetics (PhD); immunology (PhD); microbiology (PhD); molecular biology (PhD); neurobiology (PhD). *Degree requirements:* For doctorate, comprehensive exam, thesis/dissertation, teaching assistantship during two semesters. *Entrance requirements:* For doctorate, GRE General Test. Additional exam requirements/recommendations for international students: required—TOEFL, IELTS. Electronic applications accepted.

**McGill University,** Faculty of Graduate and Postdoctoral Studies, Faculty of Agricultural and Environmental Sciences, Department of Natural Resource Sciences, Montréal, QC H3A 2T5, Canada. Offers entomology (M Sc, PhD); environmental assessment (M Sc); forest science (M Sc, PhD); microbiology (M Sc, PhD); micrometeorology (M Sc, PhD); neotropical environment (M Sc, PhD); soil science (M Sc, PhD); wildlife biology (M Sc, PhD).

**McGill University,** Faculty of Graduate and Postdoctoral Studies, Faculty of Medicine, Department of Microbiology and Immunology, Montréal, QC H3A 2T5, Canada. Offers M Sc, M Sc A, PhD.

**Medical University of South Carolina,** College of Graduate Studies, Department of Microbiology and Immunology, Charleston, SC 29425. Offers MS, PhD, DMD/PhD, MD/ PhD. Terminal master's awarded for partial completion of doctoral program. *Degree requirements:* For master's, thesis; for doctorate, thesis/dissertation, oral and written exams. *Entrance requirements:* For master's, GRE General Test, MCAT, or DAT, minimum GPA of 3.0; for doctorate, GRE General Test, interview, minimum GPA of 3.0, research experience. Additional exam requirements/recommendations for international students: required—TOEFL (minimum score 600 paper-based; 100 iBT). Electronic applications accepted.

**Meharry Medical College,** School of Graduate Studies, Program in Biomedical Sciences, Microbiology and Immunology Emphasis, Nashville, TN 37208-9989. Offers PhD, MD/PhD. *Degree requirements:* For doctorate, comprehensive exam, thesis/ dissertation. *Entrance requirements:* For doctorate, GRE General Test, GRE Subject Test, undergraduate degree in related science. Additional exam requirements/ recommendations for international students: required—TOEFL. *Application deadline:* For fall admission, 6/1 for domestic students. Applications are processed on a rolling basis. Application fee: $65. *Financial support:* Fellowships, research assistantships, and Federal Work-Study available. Financial award application deadline: 4/15. *Unit head:* Dr. Minu Chaudhuri, Professor, 615-327-5726, E-mail: mchaudhuri@mmc.edu. *Application contact:* Dr. Minu Chaudhuri, Professor, 615-327-5726, E-mail: mchaudhuri@mmc.edu.
Website: https://home.mmc.edu/school-of-graduate-studies-research/microbiology-immunology/

**Miami University,** College of Arts and Science, Department of Microbiology, Oxford, OH 45056. Offers MS, PhD.

**Michigan State University,** College of Human Medicine and The Graduate School, Graduate Programs in Human Medicine, East Lansing, MI 48824. Offers biochemistry and molecular biology (MS, PhD); epidemiology (MS, PhD); microbiology (MS); microbiology and molecular genetics (PhD); pharmacology and toxicology (MS, PhD); physiology (MS, PhD); public health (MPH). *Entrance requirements:* Additional exam requirements/recommendations for international students: required—TOEFL.

**Michigan State University,** College of Osteopathic Medicine and The Graduate School, Graduate Studies in Osteopathic Medicine, East Lansing, MI 48824. Offers biochemistry and molecular biology (MS, PhD); microbiology (MS); microbiology and molecular genetics (PhD); pharmacology and toxicology (MS, PhD), including integrative pharmacology (MS), pharmacology and toxicology, pharmacology and toxicology-environmental toxicology (PhD); physiology (MS, PhD).

**Michigan State University,** College of Veterinary Medicine and The Graduate School, Graduate Programs in Veterinary Medicine, East Lansing, MI 48824. Offers comparative medicine and integrative biology (MS, PhD), including comparative medicine and integrative biology, comparative medicine and integrative biology–environmental toxicology (PhD); food safety and toxicology (MS), including food safety; integrative toxicology (PhD), including animal science–environmental toxicology, biochemistry and molecular biology–environmental toxicology, chemistry–environmental toxicology, crop and soil sciences–environmental toxicology, environmental engineering–environmental toxicology, environmental geosciences–environmental toxicology, fisheries and wildlife–environmental toxicology, food science–environmental toxicology, forestry–environmental toxicology, genetics–environmental toxicology, human nutrition–environmental toxicology, microbiology–environmental toxicology, pharmacology and toxicology–environmental toxicology, zoology–environmental toxicology; large animal clinical sciences (MS, PhD); microbiology and molecular genetics (MS, PhD), including industrial microbiology, microbiology, microbiology and molecular genetics, microbiology–environmental toxicology (PhD); pathobiology and diagnostic investigation (MS, PhD), including pathology, pathology–environmental toxicology (PhD); pharmacology and toxicology (MS, PhD); pharmacology and toxicology–environmental toxicology (PhD); physiology (MS, PhD); small animal clinical sciences (MS). Electronic applications accepted.

*Microbiology*

**Michigan State University,** The Graduate School, College of Natural Science, Department of Microbiology and Molecular Genetics, East Lansing, MI 48824. Offers industrial microbiology (MS, PhD); microbiology (MS, PhD); microbiology and molecular genetics (MS, PhD); microbiology–environmental toxicology (PhD). *Entrance requirements:* For master's, GRE General Test. Additional exam requirements/recommendations for international students: required—TOEFL (minimum score 550 paper-based), Michigan State University ELT ( minimum score 85), Michigan English Language Assessment Battery (minimum score 83). Electronic applications accepted.

**Michigan State University,** The Graduate School, College of Natural Science, MSU-DOE Plant Research Laboratory, East Lansing, MI 48824. Offers biochemistry and molecular biology (PhD); cellular and molecular biology (PhD); crop and soil sciences (PhD); genetics (PhD); microbiology and molecular genetics (PhD); plant biology (PhD); plant physiology (PhD). *Degree requirements:* For doctorate, comprehensive exam, thesis/dissertation, laboratory rotation, defense of dissertation. *Entrance requirements:* For doctorate, GRE General Test, acceptance into one of the affiliated department programs; 3 letters of recommendation; bachelor's degree or equivalent in life sciences, chemistry, biochemistry, or biophysics; research experience. Electronic applications accepted.

**Montana State University,** The Graduate School, College of Letters and Science, Department of Microbiology, Bozeman, MT 59717. Offers MS, PhD. *Program availability:* Part-time. *Degree requirements:* For master's, comprehensive exam; for doctorate, comprehensive exam, thesis/dissertation. *Entrance requirements:* For master's and doctorate, GRE General Test. Additional exam requirements/recommendations for international students: required—TOEFL (minimum score 550 paper-based). Electronic applications accepted.

**New York Medical College,** Graduate School of Basic Medical Sciences, Valhalla, NY 10595. Offers biochemistry and molecular biology (MS, PhD); cell biology (MS, PhD); microbiology and immunology (MS, PhD); pathology (MS, PhD); pharmacology (MS, PhD); physiology (MS, PhD); MD/PhD. *Program availability:* Part-time, evening/weekend. *Faculty:* 98 full-time (24 women). *Students:* 141 full-time (90 women), 17 part-time (3 women); includes 68 minority (16 Black or African American, non-Hispanic/Latino; 32 Asian, non-Hispanic/Latino; 15 Hispanic/Latino; 1 Native Hawaiian or other Pacific Islander, non-Hispanic/Latino; 4 Two or more races, non-Hispanic/Latino), 19 international. Average age 26. 351 applicants, 62% accepted, 86 enrolled. In 2019, 28 master's, 5 doctorates awarded. Terminal master's awarded for partial completion of doctoral program. *Degree requirements:* For master's, thesis; for doctorate, comprehensive exam, thesis/dissertation. *Entrance requirements:* For master's, GRE General Test, MCAT, or DAT, OAT. Additional exam requirements/recommendations for international students: required—TOEFL (minimum score 90 iBT), TOEFL or IELTS; one of the two exams are required. *Application deadline:* For fall admission, 6/1 priority date for domestic students, 5/1 priority date for international students. Applications are processed on a rolling basis. Application fee: $75 ($100 for international students). Electronic applications accepted. *Expenses:* $1200 credit and $620 fees. *Financial support:* In 2019–20, 400 students received support. Federal Work-Study, scholarships/grants, unspecified assistantships, and Student Federal Loans available. Financial award application deadline: 4/30; financial award applicants required to submit FAFSA. *Unit head:* Dr. Marina K Holz, Dean, 914-594-4110, Fax: 914-594-4944, E-mail: mholz@nymc.edu. *Application contact:* Valerie Romeo-Messana, Director of Admissions, 914-594-4110, Fax: 914-594-4944, E-mail: v_romeomessana@nymc.edu.
Website: https://www.nymc.edu/graduate-school-of-basic-medical-sciences-gsbms/gsbms-academics/

**New York University,** Graduate School of Arts and Science, Department of Biology, New York, NY 10012-1019. Offers biology (PhD); biomedical journalism (MS); cancer and molecular biology (PhD); computational biology (PhD); computers in biological research (MS); developmental genetics (PhD); general biology (MS); immunology and microbiology (PhD); molecular genetics (PhD); neurobiology (PhD); oral biology (MS); plant biology (PhD); recombinant DNA technology (MS); MS/MBA. *Program availability:* Part-time. Terminal master's awarded for partial completion of doctoral program. *Degree requirements:* For master's, thesis or alternative, qualifying paper; for doctorate, comprehensive exam, thesis/dissertation. *Entrance requirements:* For master's and doctorate, GRE General Test. Additional exam requirements/recommendations for international students: required—TOEFL, IELTS.

**North Carolina State University,** Graduate School, College of Agriculture and Life Sciences, Department of Plant and Microbial Biology, Raleigh, NC 27695. Offers microbiology (MS, PhD); plant biology (MS, PhD). *Program availability:* Part-time. Terminal master's awarded for partial completion of doctoral program. *Degree requirements:* For master's, thesis (for some programs); for doctorate, thesis/dissertation. *Entrance requirements:* For master's and doctorate, GRE. Additional exam requirements/recommendations for international students: required—TOEFL. Electronic applications accepted.

**North Dakota State University,** College of Graduate and Interdisciplinary Studies, College of Agriculture, Food Systems, and Natural Resources, Department of Microbiological Sciences, Fargo, ND 58102. Offers microbiology (MS); molecular pathogenesis (PhD). *Program availability:* Part-time. *Degree requirements:* For master's, thesis; for doctorate, thesis/dissertation, oral and written preliminary exams. *Entrance requirements:* For master's and doctorate, GRE. Additional exam requirements/recommendations for international students: required—TOEFL (minimum score 525 paper-based; 71 iBT). Tuition and fees vary according to program and reciprocity agreements.

**The Ohio State University,** Graduate School, College of Arts and Sciences, Division of Natural and Mathematical Sciences, Department of Microbiology, Columbus, OH 43210. Offers MS, PhD. Terminal master's awarded for partial completion of doctoral program. *Entrance requirements:* For doctorate, GRE General Test. Additional exam requirements/recommendations for international students: required—TOEFL (minimum score 600 paper-based; 100 iBT), Michigan English Language Assessment Battery (minimum score 82); recommended—IELTS (minimum score 8). Electronic applications accepted.

**Ohio University,** Graduate College, College of Arts and Sciences, Department of Biological Sciences, Athens, OH 45701-2979. Offers biological sciences (MS, PhD); cell biology and physiology (MS, PhD); ecology and evolutionary biology (MS, PhD); exercise physiology and muscle biology (MS, PhD); microbiology (MS, PhD); neuroscience (MS, PhD). Terminal master's awarded for partial completion of doctoral program. *Degree requirements:* For master's, comprehensive exam, thesis, 1 quarter of teaching experience; for doctorate, comprehensive exam, thesis/dissertation, 2 quarters of teaching experience. *Entrance requirements:* For master's, GRE General Test, names of three faculty members whose research interests most closely match the applicant's interest; for doctorate, GRE General Test, essay concerning prior training, research interest and career goals, plus names of three faculty members whose research interests most closely match the applicant's interest. Additional exam requirements/recommendations for international students: required—TOEFL (minimum score 620 paper-based; 105 iBT) or IELTS (minimum score 7.5). Electronic applications accepted.

**Oklahoma State University,** College of Arts and Sciences, Department of Microbiology and Molecular Genetics, Stillwater, OK 74078. Offers MS, PhD. *Faculty:* 13 full-time (4 women). *Students:* 12 full-time (8 women), 32 part-time (18 women); includes 14 minority (2 Black or African American, non-Hispanic/Latino; 1 American Indian or Alaska Native, non-Hispanic/Latino; 1 Asian, non-Hispanic/Latino; 4 Hispanic/Latino; 6 Two or more races, non-Hispanic/Latino), 13 international. Average age 26. 49 applicants, 37% accepted, 15 enrolled. In 2019, 5 master's, 4 doctorates awarded. *Entrance requirements:* For master's and doctorate, GRE General Test. Additional exam requirements/recommendations for international students: required—TOEFL (minimum score 550 paper-based; 79 iBT). *Application deadline:* For fall admission, 3/1 priority date for international students; for spring admission, 8/1 priority date for international students. Applications are processed on a rolling basis. Application fee: $50 ($75 for international students). Electronic applications accepted. *Expenses: Tuition, area resident:* Full-time $4148.10; part-time $2765.40 per credit hour. Tuition, state resident: full-time $4148.10; part-time $2765.40 per credit hour. Tuition, nonresident: full-time $15,775; part-time $10,516.80 per credit hour. *International tuition:* $15,775.20 full-time. *Required fees:* $2196.90; $122.05 per credit hour. Tuition and fees vary according to course load, campus/location and program. *Financial support:* In 2019–20, 14 research assistantships (averaging $2,163 per year), 17 teaching assistantships (averaging $2,341 per year) were awarded; career-related internships or fieldwork, Federal Work-Study, scholarships/grants, health care benefits, tuition waivers (partial), and unspecified assistantships also available. Support available to part-time students. Financial award application deadline: 3/1; financial award applicants required to submit FAFSA. *Unit head:* Dr. Tyrrell Conway, Professor and Department Head, 405-744-6243, Fax: 405-744-6790, E-mail: tconway@okstate.edu. *Application contact:* Dr. Sheryl Tucker, Dean, 405-744-6368, Fax: 405-744-0355, E-mail: gradi@okstate.edu.
Website: http://microbiology.okstate.edu

**Old Dominion University,** College of Sciences, Master of Science in Biology Program, Norfolk, VA 23529. Offers biology (MS); microbiology and immunology (MS). *Program availability:* Part-time. *Degree requirements:* For master's, comprehensive exam, thesis optional, 31 credits. *Entrance requirements:* For master's, GRE General Test, MCAT, minimum GPA of 3.0. Additional exam requirements/recommendations for international students: required—TOEFL (minimum score 550 paper-based; 79 iBT). Electronic applications accepted.

**Oregon Health & Science University,** School of Medicine, Graduate Programs in Medicine, Program in Molecular and Cellular Biosciences, Department of Molecular Microbiology and Immunology, Portland, OR 97239-3098. Offers PhD. Terminal master's awarded for partial completion of doctoral program. *Degree requirements:* For doctorate, comprehensive exam, thesis/dissertation, qualifying exam. *Entrance requirements:* For doctorate, GRE General Test (minimum scores: 153 Verbal/148 Quantitative/4.5 Analytical) or MCAT (for some programs). Electronic applications accepted.

**Oregon State University,** College of Science, Program in Microbiology, Corvallis, OR 97331. Offers environmental microbiology (MA, MS, PhD); food microbiology (MA, MS, PhD); genomics (MA, MS, PhD); immunology (MA, MS, PhD); microbial ecology (MA, MS, PhD); microbial evolution (MA, MS, PhD); parasitology (MA, MS, PhD); pathogenic microbiology (MA, MS, PhD); virology (MA). Terminal master's awarded for partial completion of doctoral program. *Entrance requirements:* For master's and doctorate, GRE. Additional exam requirements/recommendations for international students: required—TOEFL (minimum score 600 paper-based; 100 iBT).

**Purdue University,** Graduate School, College of Science, Department of Biological Sciences, West Lafayette, IN 47907. Offers cell and developmental biology (PhD); genetics (MS); microbiology (MS, PhD); neurobiology (MS, PhD). *Faculty:* 43 full-time (14 women), 6 part-time/adjunct (1 woman). *Students:* 117 full-time (58 women), 10 part-time (6 women); includes 24 minority (5 Black or African American, non-Hispanic/Latino; 12 Asian, non-Hispanic/Latino; 4 Hispanic/Latino; 3 Two or more races, non-Hispanic/Latino), 56 international. Average age 27. 146 applicants, 32% accepted, 27 enrolled. In 2019, 7 master's, 18 doctorates awarded. Terminal master's awarded for partial completion of doctoral program. *Degree requirements:* For master's, thesis (for some programs); for doctorate, thesis/dissertation, seminars, teaching experience. *Entrance requirements:* For master's, GRE General Test (minimum analytical writing score of 3.5), minimum undergraduate GPA of 3.0; for doctorate, GRE General Test (minimum analytical writing score of 3.5), minimum undergraduate GPA of 3.5. Additional exam requirements/recommendations for international students: required—TOEFL minimum score 600 paper-based; 107 iBT (for MS), 80 iBT (for PhD). *Application deadline:* For fall admission, 12/7 for domestic and international students. Applications are processed on a rolling basis. Application fee: $60 ($75 for international students). Electronic applications accepted. *Financial support:* Fellowships, research assistantships, and teaching assistantships available. Support available to part-time students. Financial award application deadline: 2/15; financial award applicants required to submit FAFSA. *Unit head:* Janice P. Evans, Head, 765-494-4407, E-mail: janiceevans@purdue.edu. *Application contact:* Georgina E. Rupp, Graduate Coordinator, 765-494-8142, E-mail: ruppg@purdue.edu.
Website: http://www.bio.purdue.edu/

**Purdue University,** Graduate School, PULSe - Purdue University Life Sciences Program, West Lafayette, IN 47907. Offers biomolecular structure and biophysics (PhD); biotechnology (PhD); chemical biology (PhD); chromatin and regulation of gene expression (PhD); integrative neuroscience (PhD); integrative plant sciences (PhD); membrane biology (PhD); microbiology (PhD); molecular evolutionary and cancer biology (PhD); molecular evolutionary genetics (PhD); molecular virology (PhD). *Students:* 37 full-time (23 women); includes 7 minority (1 Black or African American, non-Hispanic/Latino; 2 Asian, non-Hispanic/Latino; 4 Hispanic/Latino), 22 international. Average age 25. 162 applicants, 36% accepted, 19 enrolled. *Entrance requirements:* For doctorate, GRE, minimum undergraduate GPA of 3.0. Additional exam requirements/recommendations for international students: required—TOEFL (minimum score 550 paper-based; 77 iBT). *Application deadline:* For fall admission, 1/15 priority date for domestic and international students. Applications are processed on a rolling basis. Application fee: $60 ($75 for international students). Electronic applications accepted. *Financial support:* In 2019–20, research assistantships with tuition reimbursements (averaging $22,500 per year), teaching assistantships with tuition reimbursements (averaging $22,500 per year) were awarded. *Application contact:* Lindsey Springer, Graduate Contact for Admissions, 765-496-9667, E-mail: lbcampbe@purdue.edu.
Website: http://www.gradschool.purdue.edu/pulse

**Purdue University,** School of Veterinary Medicine and Graduate School, Graduate Programs in Veterinary Medicine, Department of Comparative Pathobiology, West Lafayette, IN 47907-2027. Offers comparative epidemiology and public health (MS); comparative epidemiology and public heath (PhD); comparative microbiology and immunology (MS, PhD); comparative pathobiology (MS, PhD); interdisciplinary studies (PhD), including microbial pathogenesis, molecular signaling and cancer biology, molecular virology; lab animal medicine (MS); veterinary anatomic pathology (MS); veterinary clinical pathology (MS). Terminal master's awarded for partial completion of doctoral program. *Degree requirements:* For master's, thesis (for some programs); for

doctorate, thesis/dissertation. *Entrance requirements:* For master's and doctorate, GRE General Test. Additional exam requirements/recommendations for international students: required—TOEFL (minimum score 575 paper-based), IELTS (minimum score 6.5), TWE (minimum score 4). Electronic applications accepted.

**Rosalind Franklin University of Medicine and Science,** School of Graduate and Postdoctoral Studies - Interdisciplinary Graduate Program in Biomedical Sciences, Department of Microbiology and Immunology, North Chicago, IL 60064-3095. Offers PhD, MD/PhD. Terminal master's awarded for partial completion of doctoral program. *Degree requirements:* For doctorate, comprehensive exam, thesis/dissertation. *Entrance requirements:* For doctorate, GRE General Test. Additional exam requirements/recommendations for international students: required—TOEFL, TWE.

**Rush University,** Graduate College, Division of Immunology and Microbiology, Chicago, IL 60612-3832. Offers microbiology (PhD); virology (MS, PhD), including immunology, virology; MD/PhD. *Degree requirements:* For doctorate, thesis/dissertation, comprehensive preliminary exam. *Entrance requirements:* For doctorate, GRE General Test, interview, minimum GPA of 3.0. Additional exam requirements/recommendations for international students: required—TOEFL.

**Rutgers University - Newark,** Graduate School of Biomedical Sciences, Department of Microbiology and Molecular Genetics, Newark, NJ 07107. Offers PhD. *Degree requirements:* For doctorate, thesis/dissertation, qualifying exam. *Entrance requirements:* For doctorate, GRE General Test. Additional exam requirements/recommendations for international students: required—TOEFL. Electronic applications accepted.

**Rutgers University - New Brunswick,** Graduate School-New Brunswick, Programs in the Molecular Biosciences, Piscataway, NJ 08854-8097. Offers biochemistry (PhD); cell and developmental biology (MS, PhD); microbiology and molecular genetics (MS, PhD), including applied microbiology, clinical microbiology, computational molecular biology (PhD), immunology, microbial biochemistry, molecular genetics, virology.

**Rutgers University - New Brunswick,** Graduate School of Biomedical Sciences, Program in Microbiology and Molecular Genetics, Piscataway, NJ 08854-5635. Offers MS, PhD, MD/PhD. Terminal master's awarded for partial completion of doctoral program. *Degree requirements:* For master's, thesis, qualifying exam; for doctorate, thesis/dissertation, qualifying exam. *Entrance requirements:* For master's and doctorate, GRE General Test. Additional exam requirements/recommendations for international students: required—TOEFL. Electronic applications accepted.

**Saint Louis University,** Graduate Programs, School of Medicine, Graduate Programs in Biomedical Sciences, Department of Molecular Microbiology and Immunology, St. Louis, MO 63103. Offers PhD. *Degree requirements:* For doctorate, comprehensive exam, thesis/dissertation, qualifying exams. *Entrance requirements:* For doctorate, GRE General Test (GRE Subject Test optional), letters of recommendation, resume, interview. Additional exam requirements/recommendations for international students: required—TOEFL (minimum score 525 paper-based). Electronic applications accepted.

**San Diego State University,** Graduate and Research Affairs, College of Sciences, Department of Biology, Program in Microbiology, San Diego, CA 92182. Offers MS. *Degree requirements:* For master's, thesis, oral exam. *Entrance requirements:* For master's, GRE General Test, GRE Subject Test, resume or curriculum vitae, 2 letters of recommendation. Additional exam requirements/recommendations for international students: required—TOEFL. Electronic applications accepted.

**San Francisco State University,** Division of Graduate Studies, College of Science and Engineering, Department of Biology, San Francisco, CA 94132-1722. Offers cell and molecular biology (MS); ecology, evolution, and conservation biology (MS); interdisciplinary marine and estuarine science (MS); marine biology (MS); microbiology (MS); physiology and behavioral biology (MS); science (PSM), including biotechnology, stem cell science. *Application deadline:* Applications are processed on a rolling basis. *Expenses: Tuition, area resident:* Full-time $7176; part-time $4164 per year. Tuition, state resident: full-time $7176; part-time $4164 per year. Tuition, nonresident: full-time $16,680; part-time $396 per unit. *International tuition:* $16,680 full-time. *Required fees:* $1524; $1524 per unit. $762 per semester. Tuition and fees vary according to degree level and program. *Unit head:* Dr. Laura Burrus, Chair, 415-338-7680, Fax: 415-338-6136, E-mail: lburrus@sfsu.edu. *Application contact:* Giovanna Tuccori, Graduate Program Assistant, 415-405-3591, Fax: 415-338-6136.
Website: http://biology.sfsu.edu/

**San Jose State University,** Program in Biological Sciences, San Jose, CA 95192-0001. Offers biological sciences (MA, MS); molecular biology and microbiology (MS); organismal biology, conservation and ecology (MS); physiology (MS). *Program availability:* Part-time. *Entrance requirements:* For master's, GRE. Electronic applications accepted. *Expenses: Tuition, area resident:* Full-time $7176; part-time $4164 per credit hour. Tuition, state resident: full-time $7176; part-time $4164 per credit hour. Tuition, nonresident: full-time $7176; part-time $4165 per credit hour. *International tuition:* $7176 full-time. *Required fees:* $2110; $2110.

**Seton Hall University,** College of Arts and Sciences, Department of Biological Sciences, South Orange, NJ 07079-2697. Offers biology (MS); biology/business administration (MS); microbiology (MS); molecular bioscience (PhD); molecular bioscience/neuroscience (PhD). *Program availability:* Part-time, evening/weekend. *Degree requirements:* For master's, thesis optional; for doctorate, comprehensive exam, thesis/dissertation. *Entrance requirements:* For master's, GRE or undergraduate degree (BS in biological sciences) with minimum GPA of 3.0 from accredited U.S. institution; for doctorate, GRE. Additional exam requirements/recommendations for international students: required—TOEFL. Electronic applications accepted.

**South Dakota State University,** Graduate School, College of Natural Sciences, Department of Biology and Microbiology, Brookings, SD 57007. Offers biological sciences (MS, PhD). *Program availability:* Part-time. *Degree requirements:* For master's, thesis (for some programs), oral exam; for doctorate, comprehensive exam, thesis/dissertation, oral exam. *Entrance requirements:* For master's and doctorate, GRE General Test. Additional exam requirements/recommendations for international students: required—TOEFL (minimum score 600 paper-based; 100 iBT).

**Southern Illinois University Carbondale,** Graduate School, College of Science, Program in Molecular Biology, Microbiology, and Biochemistry, Carbondale, IL 62901-4701. Offers MS, PhD. *Degree requirements:* For master's, thesis; for doctorate, thesis/dissertation. *Entrance requirements:* For master's, GRE, minimum GPA of 2.7; for doctorate, GRE, minimum GPA of 3.25. Additional exam requirements/recommendations for international students: required—TOEFL.

**Southwestern Oklahoma State University,** College of Professional and Graduate Studies, School of Behavioral Sciences and Education, Specialization in Biomedical Science and Microbiology, Weatherford, OK 73096-3098. Offers M Ed. *Entrance requirements:* Additional exam requirements/recommendations for international students: required—TOEFL (minimum score 550 paper-based), IELTS (minimum score 6.5).

**Stanford University,** School of Medicine, Graduate Programs in Medicine, Department of Microbiology and Immunology, Stanford, CA 94305-2004. Offers PhD. *Expenses: Tuition:* Full-time $52,479; part-time $34,110 per unit. *Required fees:* $672; $224 per quarter. Tuition and fees vary according to program and student level.
Website: http://cmgm.stanford.edu/micro/

**State University of New York Upstate Medical University,** College of Graduate Studies, Program in Microbiology and Immunology, Syracuse, NY 13210. Offers microbiology (MS); microbiology and immunology (PhD); MD/PhD. Terminal master's awarded for partial completion of doctoral program. *Degree requirements:* For master's, thesis; for doctorate, comprehensive exam, thesis/dissertation. *Entrance requirements:* For master's, GRE General Test, interview; for doctorate, GRE General Test, telephone interview. Additional exam requirements/recommendations for international students: required—TOEFL. Electronic applications accepted.

**Stony Brook University, State University of New York,** Stony Brook Medicine, Renaissance School of Medicine and Graduate School, Graduate Programs in Medicine, Department of Microbiology and Immunology, Stony Brook, NY 11794-5222. Offers PhD. *Faculty:* 15 full-time (3 women), 2 part-time/adjunct (1 woman). *Students:* 27 full-time (14 women); includes 8 minority (3 Asian, non-Hispanic/Latino; 4 Hispanic/Latino; 1 Two or more races, non-Hispanic/Latino), 5 international. Average age 26. 50 applicants, 26% accepted, 9 enrolled. In 2019, 3 doctorates awarded. *Degree requirements:* For doctorate, comprehensive exam, thesis/dissertation. *Entrance requirements:* For doctorate, GRE General Test, GRE Subject Test, undergraduate training in biochemistry, genetics, and cell biology; recommendations; personal statement. Additional exam requirements/recommendations for international students: required—TOEFL (minimum score 550 paper-based; 90 iBT). *Application deadline:* For fall admission, 1/15 for domestic students; for spring admission, 10/1 for domestic students. Application fee: $100. *Expenses:* Contact institution. *Financial support:* In 2019–20, 5 fellowships, 13 research assistantships were awarded; teaching assistantships and Federal Work-Study also available. Financial award application deadline: 3/15. *Unit head:* Dr. David G. Thanassi, Chair, 631-632-4549, Fax: 631-632-9797, E-mail: david.thanassi@stonybrook.edu. *Application contact:* Jennifer Jokinen, Graduate Program Coordinator, 631-632-8812, Fax: 631-632-9797, E-mail: jennifer.jokinen@stonybrook.edu.
Website: https://renaissance.stonybrookmedicine.edu/mi

**Texas A&M University,** College of Science, Department of Biology, College Station, TX 77843. Offers biology (PhD); microbiology (MS, PhD). *Faculty:* 36. *Students:* 124 full-time (64 women), 7 part-time (3 women); includes 20 minority (3 Black or African American, non-Hispanic/Latino; 1 American Indian or Alaska Native, non-Hispanic/Latino; 5 Asian, non-Hispanic/Latino; 10 Hispanic/Latino; 1 Two or more races, non-Hispanic/Latino), 44 international. Average age 28. 91 applicants, 57% accepted, 40 enrolled. In 2019, 4 master's, 9 doctorates awarded. *Degree requirements:* For master's, comprehensive exam (for some programs), thesis optional; for doctorate, comprehensive exam, thesis/dissertation. *Entrance requirements:* For master's and doctorate, statement of purpose, letters of recommendation, curriculum vitae. Additional exam requirements/recommendations for international students: required—TOEFL. *Application deadline:* For fall admission, 12/1 for domestic students. Application fee: $65 ($90 for international students). Electronic applications accepted. *Expenses:* Contact institution. *Financial support:* In 2019–20, 126 students received support, including 12 fellowships with tuition reimbursements available (averaging $25,944 per year), 60 research assistantships with tuition reimbursements available (averaging $14,952 per year), 80 teaching assistantships with tuition reimbursements available (averaging $6,789 per year); career-related internships or fieldwork, institutionally sponsored loans, scholarships/grants, traineeships, health care benefits, tuition waivers (full and partial), and unspecified assistantships also available. Support available to part-time students. Financial award application deadline: 4/1; financial award applicants required to submit FAFSA. *Unit head:* Dr. Tom McKnight, Department Head, 979-845-3896, Fax: 979-845-2891, E-mail: mcknight@bio.tamu.edu. *Application contact:* Dr. Rene Garcia, Professor & Graduate Advisor, 979-845-2989, E-mail: gradadvising@bio.tamu.edu.
Website: http://www.bio.tamu.edu/

**Texas Tech University,** Graduate School, College of Arts and Sciences, Department of Biological Sciences, Lubbock, TX 79409-3131. Offers biology (MS, PhD); environmental sustainability and natural resource management (PSM); microbiology (MS); zoology (MS, PhD). *Program availability:* Part-time, blended/hybrid learning. *Faculty:* 45 full-time (16 women). *Students:* 131 full-time (71 women), 21 part-time (12 women); includes 22 minority (4 Black or African American, non-Hispanic/Latino; 1 Asian, non-Hispanic/Latino; 11 Hispanic/Latino; 6 Two or more races, non-Hispanic/Latino), 66 international. Average age 29. 80 applicants, 48% accepted, 34 enrolled. In 2019, 13 master's, 6 doctorates awarded. *Degree requirements:* For master's, comprehensive exam, thesis or alternative; for doctorate, comprehensive exam, thesis/dissertation. *Entrance requirements:* For master's and doctorate, GRE General Test. Additional exam requirements/recommendations for international students: required—TOEFL (minimum score 550 paper-based; 79 iBT). *Application deadline:* For fall admission, 6/1 priority date for domestic students, 1/15 priority date for international students; for spring admission, 9/1 priority date for domestic students, 6/15 priority date for international students. Applications are processed on a rolling basis. Application fee: $65. Electronic applications accepted. *Expenses:* Contact institution. *Financial support:* In 2019–20, 140 students received support, including 114 fellowships (averaging $1,560 per year), 22 research assistantships (averaging $19,738 per year), 114 teaching assistantships (averaging $17,489 per year); Federal Work-Study and health care benefits also available. Financial award application deadline: 2/15; financial award applicants required to submit FAFSA. *Unit head:* Dr. John Zak, Professor, Chair and Associate Dean, 806-834-2682, Fax: 806-742-2963, E-mail: john.zak@ttu.edu. *Application contact:* Dr. Lou Densmore, Graduate Adviser, 806-834-6479, Fax: 806-742-2963, E-mail: lou.densmore@ttu.edu.
Website: www.depts.ttu.edu/biology/

**Thomas Jefferson University,** Jefferson College of Life Sciences, MS Program in Microbiology, Philadelphia, PA 19107. Offers MS. *Program availability:* Part-time, evening/weekend. *Degree requirements:* For master's, thesis, clerkship. *Entrance requirements:* For master's, GRE General Test or MCAT, minimum GPA of 3.0. Additional exam requirements/recommendations for international students: required—TOEFL, IELTS (minimum score 7). Electronic applications accepted.

**Thomas Jefferson University,** Jefferson College of Life Sciences, PhD Program in Immunology and Microbial Pathogenesis, Philadelphia, PA 19107. Offers PhD. *Degree requirements:* For doctorate, comprehensive exam, thesis/dissertation. *Entrance requirements:* For doctorate, GRE General Test, minimum GPA of 3.2. Additional exam requirements/recommendations for international students: required—TOEFL, IELTS (minimum score 7). Electronic applications accepted.

**Tufts University,** Graduate School of Biomedical Sciences, Molecular Microbiology Program, Medford, MA 02155. Offers medically-oriented research in graduate education (PhD); molecular microbiology (PhD). *Faculty:* 23 full-time (10 women). *Students:* 42 full-time (23 women); includes 14 minority (2 Black or African American, non-Hispanic/Latino; 4 Asian, non-Hispanic/Latino; 4 Hispanic/Latino; 4 Two or more races, non-Hispanic/Latino), 3 international. Average age 30. 66 applicants, 30% accepted, 6 enrolled. In 2019, 2 doctorates awarded. Terminal master's awarded for partial completion of doctoral program. *Degree requirements:* For doctorate, comprehensive

exam, thesis/dissertation. *Entrance requirements:* For doctorate, 3 letters of reference, resume, personal statement. *Application deadline:* For fall admission, 12/1 priority date for domestic and international students. Application fee: $90. Electronic applications accepted. *Expenses: Tuition:* Part-time $1799 per credit hour. Full-time tuition and fees vary according to degree level, program and student level. Part-time tuition and fees vary according to course load. *Financial support:* Application deadline: 12/1. *Unit head:* Dr. Katya Heldwein, Director, 617-636-6750, Fax: 617-636-0337, E-mail: katya.heldwein@tufts.edu. *Application contact:* Jeff Miller, 617-636-6767, Fax: 617-636-0375, E-mail: GSBS-Admissions@tufts.edu.
Website: https://gsbs.tufts.edu/academics/molecularMicrobiology

**Tulane University,** School of Medicine, Graduate Programs in Biomedical Sciences, Department of Microbiology and Immunology, New Orleans, LA 70118-5669. Offers MS. *Degree requirements:* For master's, thesis. *Entrance requirements:* For master's, GRE General Test, minimum B average in undergraduate course work. Additional exam requirements/recommendations for international students: required—TOEFL. Electronic applications accepted. *Expenses: Tuition:* Full-time $57,004; part-time $3167 per credit hour. *Required fees:* $2086; $44.50 per credit hour. $80 per term. Tuition and fees vary according to course load, degree level and program.

**Universidad Central del Caribe,** School of Medicine, Program in Biomedical Sciences, Bayamón, PR 00960-6032. Offers anatomy and cell biology (MA, MS); biochemistry (MS); biomedical sciences (MA); cellular and molecular biology (PhD); microbiology and immunology (MA, MS); pharmacology (MS); physiology (MS).

**Université de Montréal,** Faculty of Medicine, Department of Microbiology and Immunology, Montréal, QC H3C 3J7, Canada. Offers M Sc, PhD. Terminal master's awarded for partial completion of doctoral program. *Degree requirements:* For master's, thesis; for doctorate, thesis/dissertation, general exam. *Entrance requirements:* For master's and doctorate, proficiency in French, knowledge of English. Electronic applications accepted.

**Université de Sherbrooke,** Faculty of Medicine and Health Sciences, Graduate Programs in Medicine, Program in Microbiology, Sherbrooke, QC J1H 5N4, Canada. Offers M Sc, PhD. Terminal master's awarded for partial completion of doctoral program. *Degree requirements:* For master's, thesis; for doctorate, thesis/dissertation. Electronic applications accepted.

**Université du Québec, Institut National de la Recherche Scientifique,** Graduate Programs, Armand-Frappier Santé Biotechnologie, Laval, QC H7V 1B7, Canada. Offers applied microbiology (M Sc); biology (PhD); experimental health sciences (M Sc); virology and immunology (M Sc, PhD). *Program availability:* Part-time. *Faculty:* 46 full-time. *Students:* 157 full-time (94 women), 9 part-time (4 women), 100 international. Average age 30. 23 applicants, 96% accepted, 21 enrolled. In 2019, 19 master's, 20 doctorates awarded. *Degree requirements:* For master's, thesis; for doctorate, thesis/dissertation. *Entrance requirements:* For master's, appropriate bachelor's degree, proficiency in French; for doctorate, appropriate master's degree, proficiency in French. *Application deadline:* For fall admission, 3/30 for domestic and international students; for winter admission, 11/1 for domestic and international students; for spring admission, 3/1 for domestic and international students. Application fee: $45 Canadian dollars. Electronic applications accepted. *Financial support:* In 2019–20, fellowships (averaging $16,500 per year) were awarded; research assistantships also available. *Unit head:* Claude Guertin, Director, 450-687-5010, Fax: 450-686-5501, E-mail: claude.guertin@iaf.inrs.ca. *Application contact:* Sean Otto, Registrar, 418-654-2518, Fax: 418-654-3858, E-mail: sean.otto@inrs.ca.
Website: http://www.iaf.inrs.ca

**University at Buffalo, the State University of New York,** Graduate School, Jacobs School of Medicine and Biomedical Sciences, Graduate Programs in Medicine and Biomedical Sciences, Department of Microbiology and Immunology, Buffalo, NY 14260. Offers MS, PhD. *Program availability:* Part-time. *Faculty:* 16 full-time (5 women), 1 part-time/adjunct (0 women). *Students:* 19 full-time (13 women), 10 part-time (8 women); includes 2 minority (1 Black or African American, non-Hispanic/Latino; 1 American Indian or Alaska Native, non-Hispanic/Latino), 9 international. Average age 26. 39 applicants, 31% accepted, 11 enrolled. In 2019, 4 master's, 4 doctorates awarded. Terminal master's awarded for partial completion of doctoral program. *Degree requirements:* For master's, comprehensive exam, thesis or alternative; for doctorate, thesis/dissertation, departmental qualifying exam. *Entrance requirements:* For master's, GRE General Test, 3 letters of recommendation, personal statement, curriculum vitae/resume, transcripts; for doctorate, 3 letters of recommendation, personal statement, curriculum vitae/resume, transcripts. Additional exam requirements/recommendations for international students: required—TOEFL (minimum score 79 iBT), IELTS (minimum score 6.5), TOEFL (minimum score 79 iBT) or IELTS (minimum score 6.0). *Application deadline:* For fall admission, 4/1 priority date for international students. Applications are processed on a rolling basis. Application fee: $85. Electronic applications accepted. *Expenses:* Contact institution. *Financial support:* In 2019–20, 4 students received support, including 3 teaching assistantships (averaging $3,500 per year). Financial award application deadline: 2/1; financial award applicants required to submit FAFSA. *Unit head:* Dr. James Bangs, Chair/Professor, 716-829-2907, Fax: 716-829-2158. *Application contact:* Dr. Laurie Read, Director of Graduate Studies, 716-829-3307, Fax: 716-829-2158, E-mail: lread@buffalo.edu.
Website: http://medicine.buffalo.edu/departments/micro.html

**The University of Alabama at Birmingham,** Joint Health Sciences, Microbiology Theme, Birmingham, AL 35294. Offers PhD. *Students:* Average age 26. 62 applicants, 13% accepted, 7 enrolled. In 2019, 8 doctorates awarded. *Degree requirements:* For doctorate, comprehensive exam, thesis/dissertation. *Entrance requirements:* For doctorate, personal statement, resume or curriculum vitae, letters of recommendation, research experience, interview. Additional exam requirements/recommendations for international students: required—TOEFL (minimum score 80 iBT), IELTS (minimum score 6.5). *Application deadline:* For fall admission, 12/31 priority date for domestic students, 12/31 for international students. Applications are processed on a rolling basis. Electronic applications accepted. *Financial support:* In 2019–20, fellowships with full tuition reimbursements (averaging $30,000 per year), research assistantships with full tuition reimbursements (averaging $31,000 per year) were awarded; health care benefits also available. *Unit head:* Dr. Janet Yother, Theme Director, 205-934-9531, E-mail: jyother@uab.edu. *Application contact:* Alyssa Zasada, Admissions Manager for Graduate Biomedical Sciences, 205-934-3857, E-mail: grad-gbs@uab.edu.
Website: http://www.uab.edu/gbs/home/themes/mic

**University of Alberta,** Faculty of Graduate Studies and Research, Department of Biological Sciences, Edmonton, AB T6G 2E1, Canada. Offers environmental biology and ecology (M Sc, PhD); microbiology and biotechnology (M Sc, PhD); molecular biology and genetics (M Sc, PhD); physiology and cell biology (M Sc, PhD); plant biology (M Sc, PhD); systematics and evolution (M Sc, PhD). Terminal master's awarded for partial completion of doctoral program. *Degree requirements:* For master's, thesis; for doctorate, thesis/dissertation. *Entrance requirements:* Additional exam requirements/recommendations for international students: required—TOEFL.

**The University of Arizona,** College of Medicine, Department of Immunobiology, Tucson, AZ 85721. Offers PhD. *Degree requirements:* For doctorate, thesis/dissertation. *Entrance requirements:* For doctorate, GRE General Test, minimum GPA of 3.0.

**University of Arkansas for Medical Sciences,** Graduate School, Little Rock, AR 72205. Offers biochemistry and molecular biology (MS, PhD); bioinformatics (MS, PhD); cellular physiology and molecular biophysics (MS, PhD); clinical nutrition (MS); interdisciplinary biomedical sciences (MS, PhD, Certificate); interdisciplinary toxicology (MS); microbiology and immunology (PhD); neurobiology and developmental sciences (PhD); pharmacology (PhD); MD/PhD. *Program availability:* Part-time. Terminal master's awarded for partial completion of doctoral program. *Degree requirements:* For master's, comprehensive exam (for some programs), thesis (for some programs); for doctorate, thesis/dissertation. *Entrance requirements:* For master's and doctorate, GRE. Additional exam requirements/recommendations for international students: required—TOEFL. Electronic applications accepted. *Expenses:* Contact institution.

**The University of British Columbia,** Faculty of Science, Department of Microbiology and Immunology, Vancouver, BC V6T 1Z3, Canada. Offers M Sc, PhD. *Degree requirements:* For master's, thesis; for doctorate, comprehensive exam, thesis/dissertation. *Entrance requirements:* For master's and doctorate, GRE General Test. Additional exam requirements/recommendations for international students: required—TOEFL. Electronic applications accepted. *Expenses:* Contact institution.

**University of Calgary,** Cumming School of Medicine and Faculty of Graduate Studies, Program in Microbiology and Infectious Disease, Calgary, AB T2N 1N4, Canada. Offers M Sc, PhD. *Degree requirements:* For master's, thesis, oral thesis exam; for doctorate, thesis/dissertation, candidacy exam, oral thesis exam. *Entrance requirements:* For master's and doctorate, minimum GPA of 3.2. Additional exam requirements/recommendations for international students: required—TOEFL (minimum score 580 paper-based). Electronic applications accepted.

**University of California, Berkeley,** Graduate Division, College of Natural Resources, Department of Plant and Microbial Biology, Berkeley, CA 94720. Offers microbiology (PhD); plant biology (PhD). *Degree requirements:* For doctorate, thesis/dissertation, qualifying exam, seminar presentation. *Entrance requirements:* For doctorate, GRE General Test, minimum GPA of 3.0, 3 letters of recommendation. Electronic applications accepted.

**University of California, Davis,** Graduate Studies, Graduate Group in Microbiology, Davis, CA 95616. Offers MS, PhD. Terminal master's awarded for partial completion of doctoral program. *Degree requirements:* For master's, thesis; for doctorate, thesis/dissertation. *Entrance requirements:* For master's and doctorate, GRE General Test, minimum GPA of 3.0. Additional exam requirements/recommendations for international students: required—TOEFL (minimum score 550 paper-based). Electronic applications accepted.

**University of California, Irvine,** School of Medicine and School of Biological Sciences, Department of Microbiology and Molecular Genetics, Irvine, CA 92697. Offers biological sciences (MS, PhD); MD/PhD. *Students:* 14 full-time (6 women); includes 6 minority (5 Asian, non-Hispanic/Latino; 1 Hispanic/Latino), 1 international. Average age 28. In 2019, 7 doctorates awarded. *Entrance requirements:* For doctorate, GRE General Test, GRE Subject Test, minimum GPA of 3.0. Additional exam requirements/recommendations for international students: required—TOEFL (minimum score 550 paper-based). *Application deadline:* For fall admission, 12/15 priority date for domestic students, 12/15 for international students. Application fee: $120 ($140 for international students). Electronic applications accepted. *Financial support:* Fellowships, research assistantships with full tuition reimbursements, teaching assistantships, institutionally sponsored loans, traineeships, health care benefits, and unspecified assistantships available. Financial award applicants required to submit FAFSA. *Unit head:* Rozanne M. Sandri-Goldin, Chair, 949-824-7570, Fax: 949-824-8598, E-mail: rmsandri@uci.edu. *Application contact:* Janet Horwitz, Graduate Student Coordinator, 949-824-7669, E-mail: horwitz@uci.edu.
Website: http://www.microbiology.uci.edu/graduate-students.asp

**University of California, Los Angeles,** David Geffen School of Medicine and Graduate Division, Graduate Programs in Medicine, Department of Microbiology, Immunology and Molecular Genetics, Los Angeles, CA 90095. Offers MS, PhD. *Degree requirements:* For master's, thesis; for doctorate, thesis/dissertation, oral and written qualifying exams; 2 quarters of teaching experience. *Entrance requirements:* For master's and doctorate, GRE General Test, bachelor's degree; minimum undergraduate GPA of 3.0 (or its equivalent if letter grade system not used). Additional exam requirements/recommendations for international students: required—TOEFL. Electronic applications accepted.

**University of California, Riverside,** Graduate Division, Program in Microbiology, Riverside, CA 92521-0102. Offers MS, PhD. *Program availability:* Part-time. Terminal master's awarded for partial completion of doctoral program. *Degree requirements:* For master's, thesis; for doctorate, thesis/dissertation, qualifying exams. *Entrance requirements:* For master's and doctorate, GRE General Test, minimum GPA of 3.2. Additional exam requirements/recommendations for international students: required—TOEFL (minimum score 550 paper-based; 80 iBT). Electronic applications accepted.

**University of California, Santa Cruz,** Division of Graduate Studies, Division of Physical and Biological Sciences, Department of Microbiology and Environmental Toxicology, Santa Cruz, CA 95064. Offers MS, PhD. Terminal master's awarded for partial completion of doctoral program. *Degree requirements:* For master's, comprehensive exam, thesis; for doctorate, thesis/dissertation, qualifying exams. *Entrance requirements:* For master's and doctorate, GRE. Additional exam requirements/recommendations for international students: required—TOEFL (minimum score 550 paper-based; 83 iBT); recommended—IELTS (minimum score 8). Electronic applications accepted.

**University of Chicago,** Division of the Biological Sciences, Committee on Microbiology, Chicago, IL 60637. Offers PhD. *Degree requirements:* For doctorate, thesis/dissertation, ethics class, 2 teaching assistantships. *Entrance requirements:* For doctorate, GRE General Test, transcripts, statement of purpose, 3 letters of recommendation. Additional exam requirements/recommendations for international students: required—TOEFL (minimum score 600 paper-based; 104 iBT), IELTS (minimum score 7). Electronic applications accepted.

**University of Cincinnati,** Graduate School, College of Medicine, Graduate Programs in Biomedical Sciences, Molecular Genetics, Biochemistry and Microbiology Graduate Program, Cincinnati, OH 45221. Offers MS, PhD. *Faculty:* 30 full-time (5 women). *Students:* 26 full-time (11 women), 4 part-time (2 women); includes 3 minority (1 Black or African American, non-Hispanic/Latino; 1 Asian, non-Hispanic/Latino; 1 Hispanic/Latino), 2 international. Average age 27. 40 applicants, 30% accepted, 6 enrolled. In 2019, 2 master's, 4 doctorates awarded. Terminal master's awarded for partial completion of doctoral program. *Degree requirements:* For master's, thesis or alternative; for doctorate, thesis/dissertation, qualifying exam. *Entrance requirements:* For master's and doctorate, GRE highly recommended but not required. Additional exam requirements/recommendations for international students: required—TOEFL (minimum score 600 paper-based; 100 iBT). *Application deadline:* For fall admission, 12/

15 priority date for domestic and international students. Applications are processed on a rolling basis. Application fee: $40. Electronic applications accepted. *Financial support:* In 2019–20, 6 research assistantships with full tuition reimbursements (averaging $28,000 per year) were awarded; health care benefits also available. Financial award application deadline: 5/1. *Unit head:* Dr. Michael Lieberman, Professor and Chair, 513-558-5645, E-mail: michael.lieberman@uc.edu. *Application contact:* Dr. William Miller, Graduate Program Director, 513-558-0866, Fax: 513-558-8474, E-mail: william.miller@uc.edu.
Website: http://med.uc.edu/molgen-graduate

**University of Colorado Denver,** School of Medicine, Program in Microbiology, Aurora, CO 80206. Offers microbiology (PhD); microbiology and immunology (PhD). *Entrance requirements:* For doctorate, GRE, three letters of reference, two copies of official transcripts, minimum GPA of 3.0. Tuition and fees vary according to course load, program and reciprocity agreements.

**University of Connecticut,** Graduate School, College of Liberal Arts and Sciences, Department of Molecular and Cell Biology, Storrs, CT 06269. Offers applied genomics (PSM); cell and developmental biology (MS, PhD); genetics and genomics (MS, PhD); microbial systems analysis (PSM); microbiology (MS, PhD); structural biology, biochemistry and biophysics (MS, PhD). Terminal master's awarded for partial completion of doctoral program. *Degree requirements:* For master's, comprehensive exam; for doctorate, thesis/dissertation. *Entrance requirements:* For master's and doctorate, GRE General Test, GRE Subject Test. Additional exam requirements/recommendations for international students: required—TOEFL (minimum score 550 paper-based). Electronic applications accepted.

**University of Delaware,** College of Arts and Sciences, Department of Biological Sciences, Newark, DE 19716. Offers biotechnology (MS); cancer biology (MS, PhD); cell and extracellular matrix biology (MS, PhD); cell and systems physiology (MS, PhD); developmental biology (MS, PhD); ecology and evolution (MS, PhD); microbiology (MS, PhD); molecular biology and genetics (MS, PhD). Terminal master's awarded for partial completion of doctoral program. *Degree requirements:* For master's, thesis, preliminary exam; for doctorate, comprehensive exam, thesis/dissertation, preliminary exam. *Entrance requirements:* For master's and doctorate, GRE General Test. Additional exam requirements/recommendations for international students: required—TOEFL (minimum score 600 paper-based); recommended—TWE. Electronic applications accepted.

**University of Florida,** College of Medicine, Department of Molecular Genetics and Microbiology, Gainesville, FL 32610-0266. Offers MS. Terminal master's awarded for partial completion of doctoral program. *Degree requirements:* For master's, thesis. *Entrance requirements:* For master's, GRE General Test, minimum GPA of 3.0. Additional exam requirements/recommendations for international students: required—TOEFL, IELTS. Electronic applications accepted.

**University of Florida,** College of Medicine and Graduate School, Interdisciplinary Program in Biomedical Sciences, Concentration in Immunology and Microbiology, Gainesville, FL 32611. Offers PhD. *Degree requirements:* For doctorate, thesis/dissertation. *Entrance requirements:* For doctorate, GRE General Test, minimum GPA of 3.0, biochemistry before enrollment. Additional exam requirements/recommendations for international students: required—TOEFL. Electronic applications accepted.

**University of Florida,** Graduate School, College of Agricultural and Life Sciences, Department of Microbiology and Cell Science, Gainesville, FL 32611. Offers microbiology and cell science (MS, PhD), including medical microbiology and biochemistry (MS), toxicology (PhD). *Degree requirements:* For master's, comprehensive exam, thesis (for some programs); for doctorate, comprehensive exam, thesis/dissertation. *Entrance requirements:* For master's and doctorate, GRE General Test, minimum GPA of 3.0. Additional exam requirements/recommendations for international students: required—TOEFL (minimum score 550 paper-based; 80 iBT), IELTS (minimum score 6). Electronic applications accepted.

**University of Georgia,** Franklin College of Arts and Sciences, Department of Microbiology, Athens, GA 30602. Offers MS, PhD. *Degree requirements:* For master's, thesis; for doctorate, one foreign language, thesis/dissertation. *Entrance requirements:* For master's and doctorate, GRE General Test. Additional exam requirements/recommendations for international students: required—TOEFL (minimum score 550 paper-based). Electronic applications accepted.

**University of Guelph,** Office of Graduate and Postdoctoral Studies, College of Biological Science, Department of Molecular and Cellular Biology, Guelph, ON N1G 2W1, Canada. Offers biochemistry (M Sc, PhD); biophysics (M Sc, PhD); botany (M Sc, PhD); microbiology (M Sc, PhD); molecular biology and genetics (M Sc, PhD). *Degree requirements:* For master's, thesis, research proposal; for doctorate, comprehensive exam, thesis/dissertation, research proposal. *Entrance requirements:* For master's, minimum B-average during previous 2 years of coursework; for doctorate, minimum A-average. Additional exam requirements/recommendations for international students: required—TOEFL (minimum score 550 paper-based), IELTS (minimum score 6.5). Electronic applications accepted.

**University of Hawaii at Manoa,** Office of Graduate Education, College of Natural Sciences, Department of Microbiology, Honolulu, HI 96822. Offers MS, PhD. *Program availability:* Part-time. *Degree requirements:* For master's, thesis optional; for doctorate, comprehensive exam, thesis/dissertation. *Entrance requirements:* For master's and doctorate, GRE General Test. Additional exam requirements/recommendations for international students: required—TOEFL (minimum score 580 paper-based; 92 iBT), IELTS (minimum score 5).

**University of Idaho,** College of Graduate Studies, College of Science, Department of Biological Sciences, Moscow, ID 83844-2282. Offers biology (MS, PhD); microbiology, molecular biology and biochemistry (PhD). *Faculty:* 18 full-time (7 women). *Students:* 27 full-time (14 women). Average age 27. In 2019, 2 master's, 2 doctorates awarded. *Degree requirements:* For master's, thesis; for doctorate, thesis/dissertation. *Entrance requirements:* For master's and doctorate, GRE, minimum GPA of 3.0. Additional exam requirements/recommendations for international students: required—TOEFL (minimum score 79 iBT). *Application deadline:* For fall admission, 12/1 for domestic students. Applications are processed on a rolling basis. Application fee: $60. Electronic applications accepted. *Expenses:* Tuition, state resident: full-time $7753.80; part-time $502 per credit hour. Tuition, nonresident: full-time $26,990; part-time $1571 per credit hour. *Required fees:* $2122.20; $47 per credit hour. *Financial support:* Research assistantships and teaching assistantships available. Financial award applicants required to submit FAFSA. *Unit head:* Dr. James J. Nagler, Chair, 208-885-6280, Fax: 208-885-7905, E-mail: biosci@uidaho.edu. *Application contact:* Dr. James J. Nagler, Chair, 208-885-6280, Fax: 208-885-7905, E-mail: biosci@uidaho.edu.
Website: https://www.uidaho.edu/sci/biology

**University of Illinois at Chicago,** College of Medicine, Graduate Programs in Medicine, Department of Microbiology and Immunology, Chicago, IL 60607-7128. Offers PhD, MD/PhD. *Degree requirements:* For doctorate, thesis/dissertation. *Entrance requirements:* For doctorate, GRE General Test, minimum GPA of 2.75. Additional exam requirements/recommendations for international students: required—TOEFL.

**University of Illinois at Urbana-Champaign,** Graduate College, College of Liberal Arts and Sciences, School of Molecular and Cellular Biology, Department of Microbiology, Champaign, IL 61820. Offers MS, PhD.

**The University of Iowa,** Roy J. and Lucille A. Carver College of Medicine and Graduate College, Graduate Programs in Medicine, Department of Microbiology, Iowa City, IA 52242-1316. Offers general microbiology and microbial physiology (MS, PhD); immunology (MS, PhD); microbial genetics (MS, PhD); pathogenic bacteriology (MS, PhD); virology (MS, PhD). *Degree requirements:* For master's, thesis; for doctorate, comprehensive exam, thesis/dissertation. *Entrance requirements:* For master's and doctorate, GRE General Test. Additional exam requirements/recommendations for international students: required—TOEFL (minimum score 600 paper-based). Electronic applications accepted.

**The University of Kansas,** Graduate Studies, College of Liberal Arts and Sciences, Department of Molecular Biosciences, Lawrence, KS 66044. Offers biochemistry and biophysics (PhD); microbiology (PhD); molecular, cellular, and developmental biology (PhD). *Program availability:* Part-time. *Students:* 66 full-time (39 women); includes 36 minority (1 Black or African American, non-Hispanic/Latino; 2 Asian, non-Hispanic/Latino; 31 Hispanic/Latino; 2 Two or more races, non-Hispanic/Latino), 31 international. Average age 28. 93 applicants, 30% accepted, 12 enrolled. In 2019, 3 doctorates awarded. Terminal master's awarded for partial completion of doctoral program. *Entrance requirements:* For doctorate, GRE General Test, 1-page statement of research interests and goals, 1-2 page curriculum vitae or resume, official transcript, 3 recommendation letters. Additional exam requirements/recommendations for international students: required—TOEFL, IELTS, TOEFL or IELTS. *Application deadline:* For fall admission, 12/1 for domestic and international students. Application fee: $65 ($85 for international students). Electronic applications accepted. *Expenses:* Tuition, state resident: full-time $9989. Tuition, nonresident: full-time $23,950. *International tuition:* $23,950 full-time. *Required fees:* $984; $81.99 per credit hour. Tuition and fees vary according to course load, campus/location and program. *Financial support:* Fellowships, research assistantships, teaching assistantships, scholarships/grants, health care benefits, and unspecified assistantships available. Financial award application deadline: 12/1. *Unit head:* Susan M. Egan, Chair, 785-864-4294, E-mail: sme@ku.edu. *Application contact:* John Connolly, Graduate Admissions Contact, 785-864-4311, E-mail: jconnolly@ku.edu.
Website: http://www.molecularbiosciences.ku.edu/

**The University of Kansas,** University of Kansas Medical Center, School of Medicine, Department of Microbiology, Molecular Genetics and Immunology, Kansas City, KS 66160. Offers MS, PhD, MD/PhD. *Faculty:* 12. *Students:* 15 full-time (6 women); includes 2 minority (1 Asian, non-Hispanic/Latino; 1 Two or more races, non-Hispanic/Latino), 6 international. Average age 27. In 2019, 1 doctorate awarded. Terminal master's awarded for partial completion of doctoral program. *Degree requirements:* For master's, thesis; for doctorate, comprehensive exam, thesis/dissertation. *Entrance requirements:* For doctorate, GRE General Test, B Sc. Additional exam requirements/recommendations for international students: required—TOEFL or IELTS. *Application deadline:* For fall admission, 12/1 priority date for domestic and international students. Applications are processed on a rolling basis. Application fee: $60. Electronic applications accepted. *Expenses:* Tuition, state resident: full-time $9989. Tuition, nonresident: full-time $23,950. *International tuition:* $23,950 full-time. *Required fees:* $984; $81.99 per credit hour. Tuition and fees vary according to course load, campus/location and program. *Financial support:* Research assistantships with full tuition reimbursements, teaching assistantships with full tuition reimbursements, and unspecified assistantships available. Financial award application deadline: 3/1; financial award applicants required to submit FAFSA. *Unit head:* Dr. Joseph Lutkenhaus, University Distinguished Professor and Chair, 913-588-7054, Fax: 913-588-7295, E-mail: jlutkenh@kumc.edu. *Application contact:* Dr. Jianming Qiu, Professor and Director of Graduate Studies, 913-588-4329, Fax: 913-588-7295, E-mail: jqiu@kumc.edu.
Website: http://www.kumc.edu/school-of-medicine/microbiology-molecular-genetics-and-immunology.html

**University of Kentucky,** Graduate School, Graduate School Programs from the College of Medicine, Program in Microbiology and Immunology, Lexington, KY 40506-0032. Offers PhD. *Degree requirements:* For doctorate, comprehensive exam, thesis/dissertation. *Entrance requirements:* For doctorate, GRE General Test, minimum undergraduate GPA of 2.75. Additional exam requirements/recommendations for international students: required—TOEFL (minimum score 550 paper-based). Electronic applications accepted.

**University of Louisville,** School of Medicine, Department of Microbiology and Immunology, Louisville, KY 40292-0001. Offers MS, PhD, MD/PhD. *Program availability:* Part-time. *Faculty:* 16 full-time (4 women). *Students:* 33 full-time (18 women), 3 part-time (2 women); includes 8 minority (2 Black or African American, non-Hispanic/Latino; 3 Hispanic/Latino; 3 Two or more races, non-Hispanic/Latino), 8 international. Average age 30. 34 applicants, 18% accepted, 5 enrolled. In 2019, 9 master's, 3 doctorates awarded. Terminal master's awarded for partial completion of doctoral program. *Degree requirements:* For master's, comprehensive exam, thesis or alternative; for doctorate, comprehensive exam, thesis/dissertation. *Entrance requirements:* For master's, GRE, GPA &gt;3.0; 1 year of course work in biology and organic chemistry; 1 semester of course work in introductory calculus and biochemistry; for doctorate, GRE, GPA &gt; 3.0; 1 year of course work in biology and organic chemistry; 1 semester of course work in introductory calculus and biochemistry. Additional exam requirements/recommendations for international students: required—TOEFL (minimum score 550 paper-based; 79 iBT); recommended—IELTS (minimum score 6.5). *Application deadline:* For fall admission, 1/15 priority date for domestic and international students. Application fee: $60. Electronic applications accepted. *Expenses: Tuition, area resident:* Full-time $13,000; part-time $723 per credit hour. Tuition, state resident: full-time $13,000; part-time $723 per credit hour. Tuition, nonresident: full-time $27,114; part-time $1507 per credit hour. *International tuition:* $27,114 full-time. *Required fees:* $196. Tuition and fees vary according to program and reciprocity agreements. *Financial support:* In 2019–20, 34 students received support, including 5 fellowships with full tuition reimbursements available (averaging $25,000 per year); research assistantships also available. *Unit head:* Dr. Nejat Egilmez, Chair, 502-852-5351, Fax: 502-852-7531, E-mail: nejat.egilmez@louisville.edu. *Application contact:* Dr. Pascale Alard, Graduate Admissions Committee, Chair, 502-852-5364, Fax: 502-852-7531, E-mail: p0alar01@louisville.edu.
Website: http://louisville.edu/medicine/departments/microbiology

**University of Maine,** Graduate School, College of Natural Sciences, Forestry, and Agriculture, Department of Molecular and Biomedical Sciences, Orono, ME 04469. Offers microbiology (PhD). *Faculty:* 10 full-time (5 women). *Students:* 24 full-time (14 women), 6 part-time (5 women); includes 3 minority (1 Black or African American, non-Hispanic/Latino; 1 Asian, non-Hispanic/Latino; 1 Two or more races, non-Hispanic/Latino), 7 international. Average age 29. 41 applicants, 46% accepted, 8 enrolled. In 2019, 2 master's, 3 doctorates awarded. *Degree requirements:* For master's, thesis (for some programs); for doctorate, comprehensive exam, thesis/dissertation. *Entrance requirements:* For master's and doctorate, GRE General Test. Additional exam

requirements/recommendations for international students: required—TOEFL (minimum score 580 paper-based; 92 iBT), IELTS (minimum score 7). *Application deadline:* For fall admission, 1/15 for domestic and international students; for spring admission, 9/15 for domestic and international students. Applications are processed on a rolling basis. Application fee: $65. Electronic applications accepted. *Expenses: Tuition, area resident:* Full-time $8100; part-time $450 per credit hour. Tuition, state resident: full-time $8100; part-time $450 per credit hour. Tuition, nonresident: full-time $26,388; part-time $1466 per credit hour. *International tuition:* $26,388 full-time. *Required fees:* $1257; $278 per semester. Tuition and fees vary according to course load. *Financial support:* In 2019–20, 60 students received support, including 1 fellowship with full tuition reimbursement available (averaging $34,000 per year), 49 research assistantships with full tuition reimbursements available (averaging $22,000 per year), 10 teaching assistantships with full tuition reimbursements available (averaging $15,850 per year); tuition waivers (full and partial) also available. Financial award application deadline: 3/1; financial award applicants required to submit FAFSA. *Unit head:* Dr. Robert Gundersen, Chair, 207-581-2802, Fax: 207-581-2801. *Application contact:* Scott G. Delcourt, Assistant Vice President for Graduate Studies and Senior Associate Dean, 207-581-3291, Fax: 207-581-3232, E-mail: graduate@maine.edu.
Website: http://umaine.edu/biomed/

**The University of Manchester,** School of Biological Sciences, Manchester, United Kingdom. Offers adaptive organismal biology (M Phil, PhD); animal biology (M Phil, PhD); biochemistry (M Phil, PhD); bioinformatics (M Phil, PhD); biomolecular sciences (M Phil, PhD); biotechnology (M Phil, PhD); cell biology (M Phil, PhD); cell matrix research (M Phil, PhD); channels and transporters (M Phil, PhD); developmental biology (M Phil, PhD); environmental biology (M Phil, PhD); evolutionary biology (M Phil, PhD); gene expression (M Phil, PhD); genetics (M Phil, PhD); history of science, technology and medicine (M Phil, PhD); immunology (M Phil, PhD); integrative neurobiology and behavior (M Phil, PhD); membrane trafficking (M Phil, PhD); microbiology (M Phil, PhD); molecular and cellular neuroscience (M Phil, PhD); molecular biology (M Phil, PhD); molecular cancer studies (M Phil, PhD); neuroscience (M Phil, PhD); ophthalmology (M Phil, PhD); optometry (M Phil, PhD); organelle function (M Phil, PhD); pharmacology (M Phil, PhD); physiology (M Phil, PhD); plant sciences (M Phil, PhD); stem cell research (M Phil, PhD); structural biology (M Phil, PhD); systems neuroscience (M Phil, PhD); toxicology (M Phil, PhD).

**University of Manitoba,** Faculty of Graduate Studies, Faculty of Science, Department of Microbiology, Winnipeg, MB R3T 2N2, Canada. Offers M Sc, PhD. *Degree requirements:* For master's, thesis; for doctorate, one foreign language, thesis/dissertation.

**University of Maryland, Baltimore,** Graduate School, Graduate Program in Life Sciences, Program in Molecular Microbiology and Immunology, Baltimore, MD 21201. Offers PhD, MD/PhD. *Degree requirements:* For doctorate, comprehensive exam, thesis/dissertation. *Entrance requirements:* For doctorate, GRE General Test, minimum GPA of 3.0, curriculum vitae, essay, 3 letters of recommendation. Additional exam requirements/recommendations for international students: required—TOEFL (minimum score 80 iBT); recommended—IELTS (minimum score 7). Electronic applications accepted.

**University of Massachusetts Amherst,** Graduate School, College of Natural Sciences, Department of Microbiology, Amherst, MA 01003. Offers MS, PhD. *Program availability:* Part-time. Terminal master's awarded for partial completion of doctoral program. *Degree requirements:* For master's, thesis or alternative; for doctorate, comprehensive exam, thesis/dissertation. *Entrance requirements:* For master's and doctorate, GRE General Test. Additional exam requirements/recommendations for international students: required—TOEFL (minimum score 550 paper-based; 80 iBT), IELTS (minimum score 6.5). Electronic applications accepted.

**University of Massachusetts Medical School,** Graduate School of Biomedical Sciences, Worcester, MA 01655. Offers biomedical sciences (PhD), including biochemistry and molecular pharmacology, bioinformatics and computational biology, cancer biology, immunology and microbiology, interdisciplinary, neuroscience, translational science; biomedical sciences (millennium program) (PhD); clinical and population health research (PhD); clinical investigation (MS). *Faculty:* 1,258 full-time (525 women), 372 part-time/adjunct (238 women). *Students:* 344 full-time (198 women), 1 (woman) part-time; includes 73 minority (12 Black or African American, non-Hispanic/Latino; 1 American Indian or Alaska Native, non-Hispanic/Latino; 45 Asian, non-Hispanic/Latino; 15 Hispanic/Latino), 120 international. Average age 29. 581 applicants, 23% accepted, 56 enrolled. In 2019, 6 master's, 49 doctorates awarded. Terminal master's awarded for partial completion of doctoral program. *Degree requirements:* For master's, comprehensive exam, thesis; for doctorate, comprehensive exam, thesis/dissertation. *Entrance requirements:* For master's, MD, PhD, DVM, or PharmD; for doctorate, bachelor's degree. Additional exam requirements/recommendations for international students: required—TOEFL, IELTS, TOEFL (minimum score 100 IBT) or IELTS (minimum score 7.0). *Application deadline:* For fall admission, 12/1 for domestic and international students. Applications are processed on a rolling basis. Application fee: $80. Electronic applications accepted. Application fee is waived when completed online. *Expenses:* Contact institution. *Financial support:* In 2019–20, 22 fellowships with full tuition reimbursements (averaging $33,061 per year), 322 research assistantships with full tuition reimbursements (averaging $32,850 per year) were awarded; institutionally sponsored loans and scholarships/grants also available. Financial award application deadline: 5/15. *Unit head:* Dr. Mary Ellen Lane, Dean, 508-856-4018, E-mail: maryellen.lane@umassmed.edu. *Application contact:* Dr. Kendall Knight, Assistant Vice Provost for Admissions, 508-856-5628, Fax: 508-856-3659, E-mail: kendall.knight@umassmed.edu.
Website: http://www.umassmed.edu/gsbs/

**University of Miami,** Graduate School, Miller School of Medicine, Graduate Programs in Medicine, Department of Microbiology and Immunology, Miami, FL 33124. Offers PhD, MD/PhD. *Faculty:* 22 full-time (6 women). *Students:* 24 full-time (19 women); includes 14 minority (4 Black or African American, non-Hispanic/Latino; 3 Asian, non-Hispanic/Latino; 6 Hispanic/Latino; 1 Two or more races, non-Hispanic/Latino). Average age 27. In 2019, 4 doctorates awarded. *Degree requirements:* For doctorate, thesis/dissertation, oral and written qualifying exams. *Entrance requirements:* For doctorate, GRE General Test. Additional exam requirements/recommendations for international students: required—TOEFL. *Application deadline:* For fall admission, 12/31 for domestic students. Applications are processed on a rolling basis. Application fee: $50. Electronic applications accepted. *Financial support:* In 2019–20, 22 students received support, including 22 fellowships with full tuition reimbursements available (averaging $30,000 per year), 22 research assistantships with full tuition reimbursements available (averaging $30,000 per year); institutionally sponsored loans also available. *Unit head:* Dr. Thomas Malek, Chairman, 305-243-5627, Fax: 305-243-5522, E-mail: tmalek@miami.edu. *Application contact:* Dr. Zhibin Chen, Director, Graduate Program, 305-243-8348, Fax: 305-243-5522, E-mail: zchen@med.miami.edu.
Website: http://micro.med.miami.edu/

**University of Michigan,** Rackham Graduate School, Program in Biomedical Sciences (PIBS), Department of Microbiology and Immunology, Ann Arbor, MI 48109-5620. Offers MS, PhD. *Program availability:* Part-time. Terminal master's awarded for partial

completion of doctoral program. *Degree requirements:* For master's, thesis optional; for doctorate, comprehensive exam, thesis/dissertation, oral defense of dissertation, preliminary exam. *Entrance requirements:* For master's and doctorate, GRE General Test. Additional exam requirements/recommendations for international students: required—TOEFL (minimum score 600 paper-based; 84 iBT), TWE. Electronic applications accepted.

**University of Minnesota, Twin Cities Campus,** Graduate School, PhD Program in Microbiology, Immunology and Cancer Biology, Minneapolis, MN 55455-0213. Offers PhD. *Degree requirements:* For doctorate, thesis/dissertation. *Entrance requirements:* For doctorate, GRE General Test. Additional exam requirements/recommendations for international students: required—TOEFL (minimum score 600 paper-based). Electronic applications accepted.

**University of Mississippi Medical Center,** School of Graduate Studies in Health Sciences, Department of Microbiology, Jackson, MS 39216-4505. Offers PhD, MD/PhD. *Degree requirements:* For doctorate, comprehensive exam, thesis/dissertation, first authored publication. *Entrance requirements:* For doctorate, GRE General Test (minimum score of 300), minimum GPA of 3.0. Additional exam requirements/recommendations for international students: recommended—TOEFL (minimum score 550 paper-based; 79 iBT), IELTS (minimum score 6.5), TSE (minimum score 53). Electronic applications accepted.

**University of Missouri,** School of Medicine and Office of Research and Graduate Studies, Graduate Programs in Medicine, Department of Molecular Microbiology and Immunology, Columbia, MO 65211. Offers PhD. Terminal master's awarded for partial completion of doctoral program. *Degree requirements:* For doctorate, thesis/dissertation. *Entrance requirements:* For doctorate, GRE General Test, minimum GPA of 3.0. Additional exam requirements/recommendations for international students: required—TOEFL.

**University of Montana,** Graduate School, College of Humanities and Sciences, Division of Biological Sciences, Program in Cellular, Molecular and Microbial Biology, Missoula, MT 59812. Offers cellular and developmental biology (PhD); microbial evolution and ecology (PhD); microbiology and immunology (PhD); molecular biology and biochemistry (PhD). Terminal master's awarded for partial completion of doctoral program. *Degree requirements:* For doctorate, variable foreign language requirement, thesis/dissertation. *Entrance requirements:* For doctorate, GRE General Test.

**University of New Hampshire,** Graduate School, College of Life Sciences and Agriculture, Department of Molecular, Cellular and Biomedical Sciences, Program in Microbiology, Durham, NH 03824. Offers MS, PhD. *Program availability:* Part-time. *Students:* 7 full-time (3 women), 6 part-time (all women); includes 1 minority (Two or more races, non-Hispanic/Latino). Average age 26. 20 applicants, 15% accepted, 2 enrolled. In 2019, 1 master's awarded. Terminal master's awarded for partial completion of doctoral program. *Entrance requirements:* For master's and doctorate, GRE General Test. Additional exam requirements/recommendations for international students: required—TOEFL (minimum score 550 paper-based; 80 iBT), IELTS, PTE. *Application deadline:* For fall admission, 1/15 for domestic students, 4/1 for international students. Application fee: $65. Electronic applications accepted. *Financial support:* In 2019–20, 11 students received support, including 2 research assistantships, 9 teaching assistantships; fellowships, career-related internships or fieldwork, Federal Work-Study, scholarships/grants, and tuition waivers (full and partial) also available. Support available to part-time students. Financial award application deadline: 2/15. *Unit head:* Louis Tisa, Chair, 603-862-2442. *Application contact:* Paul Boisselle, Administrative Assistant, 603-862-4814, E-mail: paul.boisselle@unh.edu.
Website: https://colsa.unh.edu/molecular-cellular-biomedical-sciences

**University of New Mexico,** Graduate Studies, Health Sciences Center, Program in Biomedical Sciences, Albuquerque, NM 87131-5196. Offers biochemistry and molecular biology (MS, PhD); cell biology and physiology (MS, PhD); molecular genetics and microbiology (MS, PhD); neuroscience (MS, PhD); pathology (MS, PhD); toxicology (MS, PhD). *Program availability:* Part-time. Terminal master's awarded for partial completion of doctoral program. *Degree requirements:* For master's, thesis; for doctorate, comprehensive exam, thesis/dissertation, qualifying exam at the end of year 1/core curriculum. *Entrance requirements:* For master's and doctorate, GRE General Test, minimum undergraduate GPA of 3.0. Additional exam requirements/recommendations for international students: required—TOEFL. Electronic applications accepted. *Expenses: Tuition,* state resident: full-time $7633; part-time $972 per year. Tuition, nonresident: full-time $22,586; part-time $3840 per year. *International tuition:* $23,292 full-time. *Required fees:* $8608. Tuition and fees vary according to course level, course load, degree level, program and student level.

**The University of North Carolina at Chapel Hill,** School of Medicine and Graduate School, Biological and Biomedical Sciences Program, Department of Microbiology and Immunology, Chapel Hill, NC 27599-7290. Offers immunology (MS, PhD); microbiology (MS, PhD). *Faculty:* 65 full-time (20 women). *Students:* 55 full-time (39 women); includes 4 minority (3 Asian, non-Hispanic/Latino; 1 Two or more races, non-Hispanic/Latino), 5 international. Average age 26. In 2019, 2 master's, 5 doctorates awarded. Terminal master's awarded for partial completion of doctoral program. *Degree requirements:* For doctorate, comprehensive exam, thesis/dissertation. *Entrance requirements:* Additional exam requirements/recommendations for international students: required—TOEFL. *Application deadline:* For fall admission, 12/3 priority date for domestic and international students. Applications are processed on a rolling basis. Electronic applications accepted. *Financial support:* In 2019–20, 3 fellowships with full tuition reimbursements (averaging $32,000 per year), 69 research assistantships with full tuition reimbursements (averaging $32,000 per year) were awarded; career-related internships or fieldwork, health care benefits, and tuition waivers (full) also available. *Unit head:* Dr. Bob Bourret, Director of Graduate Studies, E-mail: bourrett@med.unc.edu. *Application contact:* Jeffrey Steinbach, Assistant Director of Admissions, 919-843-7129, E-mail: jsteinba@email.unc.edu.
Website: http://www.med.unc.edu/microimm/

**University of North Texas Health Science Center at Fort Worth,** Graduate School of Biomedical Sciences, Fort Worth, TX 76107-2699. Offers biochemistry and cancer biology (MS, PhD); biotechnology (MS); cell biology, immunology and microbiology (MS, PhD); clinical research management (MS); forensic genetics (MS); genetics (MS, PhD); integrative physiology (MS, PhD); medical sciences (MS); pharmaceutical sciences and pharmacotherapy (MS, PhD); pharmacology and neuroscience (MS, PhD); structural anatomy and rehabilitation sciences (MS, PhD); DO/MS; DO/PhD. Terminal master's awarded for partial completion of doctoral program. *Degree requirements:* For master's, thesis; for doctorate, thesis/dissertation. *Entrance requirements:* For master's and doctorate, GRE General Test. Additional exam requirements/recommendations for international students: required—TOEFL. *Expenses:* Contact institution.

**University of Oklahoma,** College of Arts and Sciences, Department of Microbiology and Plant Biology, Norman, OK 73019-0390. Offers microbiology (MS, PhD); plant biology (MS, PhD), including ecology and evolutionary biology (PhD), plant biology. Terminal master's awarded for partial completion of doctoral program. *Degree requirements:* For master's, comprehensive exam, thesis; for doctorate, comprehensive exam, thesis/dissertation. *Entrance requirements:* For master's and doctorate, GRE, 3

recommendation letters, letter of intent, bachelor's degree. Additional exam requirements/recommendations for international students: required—TOEFL (minimum score 80 iBT) or IELTS (minimum score 6.5). Electronic applications accepted. *Expenses:* Tuition, state resident: full-time $6583.20; part-time $274.30 per credit hour. Tuition, nonresident: full-time $21,242; part-time $885.10 per credit hour. *International tuition:* $21,242.40 full-time. *Required fees:* $1994.20; $72.55 per credit hour. $126.50 per semester. Tuition and fees vary according to course load and degree level.

**University of Oklahoma Health Sciences Center,** College of Medicine and Graduate College, Graduate Programs in Medicine, Department of Microbiology and Immunology, Oklahoma City, OK 73190. Offers immunology (MS, PhD); microbiology (MS, PhD). *Program availability:* Part-time. Terminal master's awarded for partial completion of doctoral program. *Degree requirements:* For master's, thesis or alternative; for doctorate, one foreign language, thesis/dissertation. *Entrance requirements:* For doctorate, GRE General Test, 3 letters of recommendation. Additional exam requirements/recommendations for international students: required—TOEFL.

**University of Ottawa,** Faculty of Graduate and Postdoctoral Studies, Faculty of Medicine, Department of Biochemistry, Microbiology and Immunology, Ottawa, ON K1N 6N5, Canada. Offers biochemistry (M Sc, PhD); microbiology and immunology (M Sc, PhD). *Degree requirements:* For master's, thesis; for doctorate, comprehensive exam, thesis/dissertation, seminar. *Entrance requirements:* For master's, honors degree or equivalent, minimum B average; for doctorate, master's degree, minimum B+ average. Electronic applications accepted.

**University of Pennsylvania,** Perelman School of Medicine, Biomedical Graduate Studies, Graduate Group in Cell and Molecular Biology, Philadelphia, PA 19104. Offers cancer biology (PhD); cell biology, physiology, and metabolism (PhD); developmental stem cell regenerative biology (PhD); gene therapy and vaccines (PhD); genetics and gene regulation (PhD); microbiology, virology, and parasitology (PhD); MD/PhD; VMD/PhD. *Faculty:* 400 full-time (118 women). *Students:* 378 full-time (221 women); includes 134 minority (6 Black or African American, non-Hispanic/Latino; 56 Asian, non-Hispanic/Latino; 58 Hispanic/Latino; 2 Native Hawaiian or other Pacific Islander, non-Hispanic/Latino; 12 Two or more races, non-Hispanic/Latino), 52 international. 851 applicants, 14% accepted, 59 enrolled. In 2019, 43 doctorates awarded. *Unit head:* Dr. Daniel Kessler, Graduate Group Chair, 215-898-1478. *Application contact:* Meagan Schofer, Associate Director, 215-898-1478.
Website: http://www.med.upenn.edu/camb/

**University of Pittsburgh,** Graduate School of Public Health, Department of Infectious Diseases and Microbiology, Pittsburgh, PA 15261. Offers infectious diseases and microbiology (MS, PhD); management, intervention, and community practice (MPH); pathogenesis, eradication, and laboratory practice (MPH). *Program availability:* Part-time. *Faculty:* 17 full-time (7 women), 4 part-time/adjunct (0 women). *Students:* 56 full-time (44 women), 20 part-time (10 women); includes 19 minority (6 Black or African American, non-Hispanic/Latino; 5 Asian, non-Hispanic/Latino; 3 Hispanic/Latino; 5 Two or more races, non-Hispanic/Latino), 6 international. Average age 26. 146 applicants, 80% accepted, 38 enrolled. In 2019, 24 master's, 2 doctorates awarded. Terminal master's awarded for partial completion of doctoral program. *Degree requirements:* For master's, comprehensive exam (for some programs), thesis; for doctorate, comprehensive exam, thesis/dissertation, preliminary exam, dissertation defense. *Entrance requirements:* Additional exam requirements/recommendations for international students: required—TOEFL (minimum score 550 paper-based; 80 iBT), IELTS (minimum score 6.5), TOEFL or IELTS, WES evaluation for foreign education. *Application deadline:* For fall admission, 1/15 for domestic students, 3/15 priority date for international students. Applications are processed on a rolling basis. Application fee: $135. Electronic applications accepted. *Expenses:* $13,379 state resident per term full-time, $23,407 non-state resident per term full-time, $1122 state resident per credit part-time, $1916 non-state resident per credit part-time, $500 per term for full-time dissertation research, $475 per term full-time fees, $295 per term part-time fees. *Financial support:* In 2019–20, 38 students received support. Scholarships/grants, traineeships, health care benefits, and unspecified assistantships available. Financial award applicants required to submit FAFSA. *Unit head:* Robin Tierno, Department Administrator, 412-624-3105, Fax: 412-624-4953, E-mail: rtierno@pitt.edu. *Application contact:* Chelsea Yonash, Student Services Coordinator, 412-624-3331, E-mail: cry8@pitt.edu.
Website: http://www.publichealth.pitt.edu/idm

**University of Pittsburgh,** School of Medicine, Graduate Programs in Medicine, Microbiology and Immunology Program, Pittsburgh, PA 15260. Offers PhD. *Degree requirements:* For doctorate, comprehensive exam, thesis/dissertation, 34 course credits, 38 dissertation credits, published paper. *Entrance requirements:* For doctorate, GRE General Test. Additional exam requirements/recommendations for international students: required—TOEFL (minimum score 600 paper-based; 100 iBT), IELTS (minimum score 7). Electronic applications accepted. *Expenses:* Contact institution.

**University of Puerto Rico - Medical Sciences Campus,** School of Medicine, Biomedical Sciences Graduate Program, Department of Microbiology and Medical Zoology, San Juan, PR 00936-5067. Offers MS, PhD. *Degree requirements:* For master's, one foreign language, thesis; for doctorate, one foreign language, comprehensive exam, thesis/dissertation. *Entrance requirements:* For master's and doctorate, GRE General Test, GRE Subject Test, interview, minimum GPA of 3.0, 3 letters of recommendation.

**University of Rhode Island,** Graduate School, College of the Environment and Life Sciences, Department of Cell and Molecular Biology, Kingston, RI 02881. Offers biochemistry (MS, PhD); clinical laboratory sciences (MS), including biotechnology, clinical laboratory science, cytopathology; microbiology (MS, PhD); molecular genetics (MS, PhD). *Program availability:* Part-time. *Faculty:* 20 full-time (9 women). *Students:* 1 (woman) part-time. In 2019, 16 master's awarded. *Entrance requirements:* Additional exam requirements/recommendations for international students: required—TOEFL. *Application deadline:* For fall admission, 1/15 for domestic and international students. Application fee: $65. Electronic applications accepted. *Expenses: Tuition, area resident:* Full-time $13,734; part-time $763 per credit. Tuition, state resident: full-time $13,734; part-time $763 per credit. Tuition, nonresident: full-time $26,512; part-time $1473 per credit. *International tuition:* $26,512 full-time. *Required fees:* $1780; $52 per credit. $35 per term. One-time fee: $165. *Financial support:* In 2019–20, 11 teaching assistantships with tuition reimbursements (averaging $10,985 per year) were awarded; traineeships also available. Financial award application deadline: 1/15; financial award applicants required to submit FAFSA. *Unit head:* Dr. Joel Chandlee, Chair, E-mail: joelchandlee@uri.edu. *Application contact:* Dr. Steven Gregory, Graduate Program Director, 401-874-5947, E-mail: stgregory@uri.edu.
Website: https://web.uri.edu/cmb/

**University of Rochester,** School of Medicine and Dentistry, Graduate Programs in Medicine and Dentistry, Department of Microbiology and Immunology, Program in Medical Microbiology, Rochester, NY 14627. Offers MS, PhD.

**University of Rochester,** School of Medicine and Dentistry, Graduate Programs in Medicine and Dentistry, Department of Microbiology and Immunology, Program in Microbiology and Immunology, Rochester, NY 14627. Offers MS, PhD.

**University of Saskatchewan,** College of Medicine, Department of Biochemistry, Microbiology and Immunology, Saskatoon, SK S7N 5A2, Canada. Offers biochemistry (M Sc, PhD); microbiology and immunology (M Sc, PhD). *Degree requirements:* For master's, thesis; for doctorate, thesis/dissertation. *Entrance requirements:* Additional exam requirements/recommendations for international students: required—TOEFL.

**University of Saskatchewan,** Western College of Veterinary Medicine and College of Graduate and Postdoctoral Studies, Graduate Programs in Veterinary Medicine, Department of Veterinary Microbiology, Saskatoon, SK S7N 5A2, Canada. Offers M Sc, M Vet Sc, PhD. *Degree requirements:* For master's, thesis; for doctorate, comprehensive exam (for some programs), thesis/dissertation. *Entrance requirements:* Additional exam requirements/recommendations for international students: required—TOEFL (minimum score 80 iBT) or IELTS (minimum score 6.5). Electronic applications accepted.

**University of South Dakota,** Graduate School, Sanford School of Medicine and Graduate School, Biomedical Sciences Graduate Program, Molecular Microbiology and Immunology Group, Vermillion, SD 57069. Offers MS, PhD. Terminal master's awarded for partial completion of doctoral program. *Degree requirements:* For master's, thesis; for doctorate, comprehensive exam, thesis/dissertation. *Entrance requirements:* For master's and doctorate, GRE General Test, minimum GPA of 3.0. Additional exam requirements/recommendations for international students: required—TOEFL (minimum score 550 paper-based; 80 iBT), IELTS (minimum score 6). Electronic applications accepted. *Expenses:* Contact institution.

**University of Southern California,** Keck School of Medicine and Graduate School, Graduate Programs in Medicine, Department of Molecular Microbiology and Immunology, Los Angeles, CA 90089. Offers MS. *Program availability:* Part-time. *Faculty:* 19 full-time (4 women). *Students:* 41 full-time (24 women); includes 31 minority (1 Black or African American, non-Hispanic/Latino; 26 Asian, non-Hispanic/Latino; 4 Hispanic/Latino). Average age 26. 72 applicants, 76% accepted, 20 enrolled. In 2019, 15 master's awarded. Terminal master's awarded for partial completion of doctoral program. *Degree requirements:* For master's, comprehensive exam (for some programs), thesis optional. *Entrance requirements:* For master's, GRE General Test preferred (Verbal and Quantitative), MCAT (on a case-by-case basis). Additional exam requirements/recommendations for international students: required—TOEFL (minimum score 100 iBT), IELTS (minimum score 6.5). *Application deadline:* For fall admission, 6/1 for domestic students, 5/1 for international students; for spring admission, 11/1 for domestic students, 10/1 for international students. Applications are processed on a rolling basis. Application fee: $90. Electronic applications accepted. *Financial support:* Career-related internships or fieldwork, Federal Work-Study, institutionally sponsored loans, scholarships/grants, and health care benefits available. Financial award application deadline: 3/1; financial award applicants required to submit FAFSA. *Unit head:* Dr. Axel H. Schonthal, Associate Professor/Program Director, 323-442-1730, Fax: 323-442-1721, E-mail: schontha@usc.edu. *Application contact:* Monica C. Pan, Program Administrator, E-mail: monicap@med.usc.edu.
Website: http://keck.usc.edu/molecular-microbiology-and-immunology/

**University of South Florida,** College of Arts and Sciences, Department of Cell Biology, Microbiology, and Molecular Biology, Tampa, FL 33620-9951. Offers biology (MS), including cell biology, microbiology and molecular biology; cancer biology (PhD); cancer chemical biology (PhD); cancer immunology and immunotherapy (PhD); cell and molecular biology (PhD); microbiology (MS). *Faculty:* 21 full-time (8 women). *Students:* 85 full-time (50 women), 4 part-time (all women); includes 10 minority (1 Black or African American, non-Hispanic/Latino; 3 Asian, non-Hispanic/Latino; 4 Hispanic/Latino; 2 Two or more races, non-Hispanic/Latino), 35 international. Average age 27. 178 applicants, 15% accepted, 20 enrolled. In 2019, 12 master's, 12 doctorates awarded. *Degree requirements:* For master's, thesis or alternative; for doctorate, comprehensive exam, thesis/dissertation. *Entrance requirements:* For master's and doctorate, GRE General Test, minimum GPA of 3.0, extensive background in biology or chemistry. Additional exam requirements/recommendations for international students: required—TOEFL (minimum score 570 paper-based; 79 iBT) or IELTS (minimum score 6.5). *Application deadline:* For fall admission, 11/30 priority date for domestic and international students; for spring admission, 7/1 priority date for domestic students, 7/1 for international students. Application fee: $30. *Financial support:* In 2019–20, 9 students received support. Career-related internships or fieldwork, health care benefits, and unspecified assistantships available. Financial award application deadline: 4/1. *Unit head:* Dr. James Garey, Professor/Chair, 813-974-7103, Fax: 813-974-1614, E-mail: garey@usf.edu. *Application contact:* Dr. Kenneth Wright, Associate Professor of Cancer Biology, H. Lee Moffitt Cancer Center and Research Institute, 813-745-3918, Fax: 813-974-1614, E-mail: ken.wright@moffitt.org.
Website: http://biology.usf.edu/cmmb/

**University of South Florida,** College of Arts and Sciences, Department of Integrative Biology, Tampa, FL 33620-9951. Offers biology (MS), including ecology and evolution, environmental and ecological microbiology, physiology and morphology. *Program availability:* Part-time. *Faculty:* 12 full-time (4 women). *Students:* 27 full-time (15 women), 3 part-time (all women); includes 5 minority (1 Black or African American, non-Hispanic/Latino; 2 Asian, non-Hispanic/Latino; 2 Hispanic/Latino), 3 international. Average age 32. 37 applicants, 24% accepted, 6 enrolled. In 2019, 4 master's, 3 doctorates awarded. *Degree requirements:* For master's, comprehensive exam, thesis (for some programs); for doctorate, comprehensive exam, thesis/dissertation. *Entrance requirements:* For master's, GRE: Preferred scores of 155V (69th percentile), 150Q (38th percentile), 4.5AW, minimum GPA of 3.0; Acceptance by faculty member; 3 letters of recommendation (see student recommendation form on department website); statement of research and professional goals; TA application; It is expected that candidates will have completed courses equivalent to those required for the BS in Biology at USF; for doctorate, GRE: 155+ (70%)V, 150+ (70%)Q, 4.5 (70%) AW, Bachelor of Science required. It is expected that candidates for the Ph.D. degree will have completed courses equivalent to those required for the B.S. in Biology at U.S.F. Acceptance by a faculty member in the Department of Integrative Biology is mandatory. Additional exam requirements/recommendations for international students: required—TOEFL. *Application deadline:* For fall admission, 11/30 priority date for domestic and international students; for spring admission, 7/1 priority date for domestic and international students. Application fee: $30. Electronic applications accepted. *Financial support:* In 2019–20, 11 students received support. Research assistantships, teaching assistantships, and unspecified assistantships available. Financial award application deadline: 6/30; financial award applicants required to submit FAFSA. *Unit head:* Dr. Valerie Harwood, Professor and Chair, 813-974-1524, Fax: 813-974-3263, E-mail: vharwood@usf.edu. *Application contact:* Dr. Stephen Deban, Associate Professor and Graduate Program Director, 813-974-2242, E-mail: sdeban@usf.edu.
Website: http://biology.usf.edu/ib/grad/

**The University of Tennessee,** Graduate School, College of Arts and Sciences, Department of Microbiology, Knoxville, TN 37996. Offers MS, PhD. *Program availability:* Part-time. *Degree requirements:* For master's, thesis; for doctorate, thesis/dissertation. *Entrance requirements:* For master's and doctorate, GRE General Test, minimum GPA of 2.7. Additional exam requirements/recommendations for international students: required—TOEFL. Electronic applications accepted.

## *Microbiology*

**The University of Texas at Austin,** Graduate School, College of Natural Sciences, School of Biological Sciences, Program in Microbiology, Austin, TX 78712-1111. Offers PhD. *Entrance requirements:* For doctorate, GRE General Test. Electronic applications accepted.

**The University of Texas Health Science Center at Houston,** MD Anderson UTHealth Graduate School, Houston, TX 77225-0036. Offers biochemistry and cell biology (PhD); biomedical sciences (MS); cancer biology (PhD); genetic counseling (MS); genetics and epigenetics (PhD); immunology (PhD); medical physics (MS, PhD); microbiology and infectious diseases (PhD); neuroscience (PhD); quantitative sciences (PhD); therapeutics and pharmacology (PhD); MD/PhD. Terminal master's awarded for partial completion of doctoral program. *Degree requirements:* For master's, thesis; for doctorate, thesis/dissertation. *Entrance requirements:* For master's and doctorate, GRE General Test. Additional exam requirements/recommendations for international students: required—TOEFL. Electronic applications accepted.

**The University of Texas Health Science Center at San Antonio,** Graduate School of Biomedical Sciences, Department of Microbiology and Immunology, San Antonio, TX 78229-3900. Offers MS, PhD. *Degree requirements:* For master's, thesis; for doctorate, comprehensive exam, thesis/dissertation.

**The University of Texas Medical Branch,** Graduate School of Biomedical Sciences, Program in Microbiology and Immunology, Galveston, TX 77555. Offers MS, PhD. Terminal master's awarded for partial completion of doctoral program. *Degree requirements:* For master's, thesis or alternative; for doctorate, thesis/dissertation. *Entrance requirements:* For doctorate, GRE General Test, minimum GPA of 3.0. Additional exam requirements/recommendations for international students: required—TOEFL (minimum score 550 paper-based). Electronic applications accepted.

**The University of Texas Southwestern Medical Center,** Southwestern Graduate School of Biomedical Sciences, Division of Basic Science, Program in Molecular Microbiology, Dallas, TX 75390. Offers PhD. *Degree requirements:* For doctorate, thesis/dissertation, oral and written exams. *Entrance requirements:* For doctorate, GRE General Test, minimum GPA of 3.0. Additional exam requirements/recommendations for international students: required—TOEFL. Electronic applications accepted.

**University of Victoria,** Faculty of Graduate Studies, Faculty of Science, Department of Biochemistry and Microbiology, Victoria, BC V8W 2Y2, Canada. Offers biochemistry (M Sc, PhD); microbiology (M Sc, PhD). *Degree requirements:* For master's, thesis, seminar; for doctorate, thesis/dissertation, seminar, candidacy exam. *Entrance requirements:* For master's, GRE General Test, minimum B+ average; for doctorate, GRE General Test, minimum B+ average, M Sc. Additional exam requirements/recommendations for international students: required—TOEFL (minimum score 600 paper-based). Electronic applications accepted.

**University of Virginia,** School of Medicine, Department of Microbiology, Immunology, and Cancer Biology, Charlottesville, VA 22903. Offers PhD, MD/PhD. *Degree requirements:* For doctorate, thesis/dissertation. *Entrance requirements:* For doctorate, GRE General Test, 2 or more letters of recommendation. Additional exam requirements/recommendations for international students: required—TOEFL (minimum score 600 paper-based; 90 iBT). Electronic applications accepted.

**University of Washington,** Graduate School, School of Medicine, Graduate Programs in Medicine, Department of Microbiology, Seattle, WA 98195. Offers PhD. *Degree requirements:* For doctorate, thesis/dissertation. *Entrance requirements:* For doctorate, GRE General Test, GRE Subject Test (recommended). Electronic applications accepted.

**The University of Western Ontario,** Schulich School of Medicine and Dentistry, Department of Microbiology and Immunology, London, ON N6A 3K7, Canada. Offers M Sc, PhD. *Degree requirements:* For master's, thesis, oral and written exam; for doctorate, thesis/dissertation, oral and written exam. *Entrance requirements:* For master's, honors degree or equivalent in microbiology, immunology, or other biological science; minimum B average; for doctorate, M Sc in microbiology and immunology. Additional exam requirements/recommendations for international students: required—TOEFL.

**University of Wisconsin–La Crosse,** College of Science and Health, Department of Biology, La Crosse, WI 54601. Offers aquatic sciences (MS); biology (MS); cellular and molecular biology (MS); clinical microbiology (MS); microbiology (MS); nurse anesthesia (MS); physiology (MS). *Accreditation:* AANA/CANAEP. *Program availability:* Part-time. *Faculty:* 19 full-time (7 women). *Students:* 12 full-time (6 women), 39 part-time (15 women); includes 2 minority (1 Black or African American, non-Hispanic/Latino; 1 Asian, non-Hispanic/Latino). Average age 28. 37 applicants, 68% accepted, 19 enrolled. In 2019, 19 master's awarded. *Degree requirements:* For master's, comprehensive exam, thesis. *Entrance requirements:* For master's, GRE General Test, minimum GPA of 2.85. Additional exam requirements/recommendations for international students: required—TOEFL (minimum score 550 paper-based; 79 iBT). *Application deadline:* For fall admission, 2/1 priority date for domestic and international students; for spring admission, 1/4 priority date for domestic and international students. Applications are processed on a rolling basis. Electronic applications accepted. *Financial support:* Research assistantships with partial tuition reimbursements, Federal Work-Study, scholarships/grants, health care benefits, and tuition waivers (partial) available. Support available to part-time students. Financial award application deadline: 3/15; financial award applicants required to submit FAFSA. *Unit head:* Dr. Michael Abler, Department Chair, 608-785-6962, E-mail: mabler@uwlax.edu. *Application contact:* Jennifer Weber, Senior Student Services Coordinator Graduate Admissions, 608-785-8939, E-mail: admissions@uwlax.edu.
Website: http://uwlax.edu/biology/

**University of Wisconsin–La Crosse,** College of Science and Health, Department of Microbiology, La Crosse, WI 54601-3742. Offers clinical microbiology (MS); microbiology (MS). *Faculty:* 7 full-time (2 women). *Students:* 9 full-time (4 women), 12 part-time (6 women); includes 1 minority (Two or more races, non-Hispanic/Latino), 1 international. Average age 26. 9 applicants, 89% accepted, 6 enrolled. In 2019, 7 master's awarded. *Unit head:* Dr. Michael Hoffman, Chair/Program Director, 608-785-6984, E-mail: mhoffman@uwlax.edu. *Application contact:* Jennifer Weber, Senior Student Service Coordinator Graduate Admissions, 608-785-8939, E-mail: admissions@uwlax.edu.
Website: http://www.uwlax.edu/microbiology/

**University of Wisconsin–Madison,** Graduate School, College of Agricultural and Life Sciences, Microbiology Doctoral Training Program, Madison, WI 53706. Offers PhD.

**University of Wisconsin–Milwaukee,** Graduate School, College of Letters and Science, Department of Biological Sciences, Milwaukee, WI 53201-0413. Offers cellular and molecular biology (MS, PhD); microbiology (MS, PhD). *Degree requirements:* For master's, thesis; for doctorate, thesis/dissertation, 1 foreign language or data analysis proficiency. *Entrance requirements:* For master's and doctorate, GRE General Test. Additional exam requirements/recommendations for international students: required—TOEFL (minimum score 550 paper-based; 79 iBT), IELTS (minimum score 6.5). Electronic applications accepted.

**University of Wisconsin–Oshkosh,** Graduate Studies, College of Letters and Science, Department of Biology and Microbiology, Oshkosh, WI 54901. Offers biology (MS), including botany, microbiology, zoology. *Degree requirements:* For master's, comprehensive exam, thesis. *Entrance requirements:* For master's, GRE General Test, minimum GPA of 3.0, BS in biology. Additional exam requirements/recommendations for international students: required—TOEFL (minimum score 550 paper-based; 79 iBT). Electronic applications accepted.

**University of Wyoming,** Graduate Program in Molecular and Cellular Life Sciences, Laramie, WY 82071. Offers PhD. *Degree requirements:* For doctorate, thesis/dissertation, four eight-week laboratory rotations, comprehensive basic practical exam, two-part qualifying exam, seminars, symposium.

**Université Laval,** Faculty of Agricultural and Food Sciences, Program in Agricultural Microbiology, Québec, QC G1K 7P4, Canada. Offers agricultural microbiology (M Sc); agro-food microbiology (PhD). Terminal master's awarded for partial completion of doctoral program. *Degree requirements:* For master's, thesis; for doctorate, comprehensive exam, thesis/dissertation. *Entrance requirements:* For master's and doctorate, knowledge of French and English. Electronic applications accepted.

**Université Laval,** Faculty of Medicine, Graduate Programs in Medicine, Programs in Microbiology-Immunology, Québec, QC G1K 7P4, Canada. Offers M Sc, PhD. Terminal master's awarded for partial completion of doctoral program. *Degree requirements:* For master's, thesis; for doctorate, comprehensive exam, thesis/dissertation. *Entrance requirements:* For master's and doctorate, knowledge of French, comprehension of written English. Electronic applications accepted.

**Université Laval,** Faculty of Sciences and Engineering, Department of Biochemistry and Microbiology, Programs in Microbiology, Québec, QC G1K 7P4, Canada. Offers M Sc, PhD. Terminal master's awarded for partial completion of doctoral program. *Degree requirements:* For master's, thesis; for doctorate, comprehensive exam, thesis/dissertation. *Entrance requirements:* For master's and doctorate, knowledge of French, comprehension of written English. Electronic applications accepted.

**Vanderbilt University,** School of Medicine, Microbe Host Interactions, Nashville, TN 37240-1001. Offers MS, PhD, MD/PhD. *Faculty:* 35 full-time (13 women). *Students:* 51 full-time (30 women); includes 17 minority (3 Black or African American, non-Hispanic/Latino; 6 Asian, non-Hispanic/Latino; 4 Hispanic/Latino; 4 Two or more races, non-Hispanic/Latino), 1 international. Average age 26. In 2019, 2 master's, 12 doctorates awarded. Terminal master's awarded for partial completion of doctoral program. *Degree requirements:* For master's, thesis; for doctorate, thesis/dissertation, final and qualifying exams. *Entrance requirements:* For master's and doctorate, GRE General Test, GRE Subject Test (recommended). Additional exam requirements/recommendations for international students: required—TOEFL (minimum score 570 paper-based; 88 iBT). *Application deadline:* For fall admission, 1/15 for domestic and international students. Electronic applications accepted. *Expenses: Tuition:* Full-time $51,018; part-time $2087 per hour. *Required fees:* $542. Tuition and fees vary according to program. *Financial support:* Fellowships with full tuition reimbursements, research assistantships with full tuition reimbursements, Federal Work-Study, institutionally sponsored loans, scholarships/grants, traineeships, health care benefits, and tuition waivers (partial) available. Financial award application deadline: 1/15; financial award applicants required to submit CSS PROFILE or FAFSA. *Unit head:* Dr. Roger Cone, Acting Chair, 615-322-7000, Fax: 615-322-5551, E-mail: roger.cone@vanderbilt.edu. *Application contact:* Jay Jerome, Director of Graduate Studies, 615-322-2123, E-mail: jay.jerome@vanderbilt.edu.
Website: http://www.mc.vanderbilt.edu/root/vumc.php?site-vmcpathology

**Virginia Commonwealth University,** Medical College of Virginia-Professional Programs, School of Medicine, Graduate Programs in Medicine, Department of Microbiology and Immunology, Richmond, VA 23284-9005. Offers microbiology and immunology (MS, PhD); MD/PhD. *Degree requirements:* For master's, thesis; for doctorate, thesis/dissertation, comprehensive oral and written exams. *Entrance requirements:* For master's and doctorate, GRE General Test or MCAT. Additional exam requirements/recommendations for international students: required—TOEFL (minimum score 600 paper-based; 100 iBT). Electronic applications accepted.

**Wagner College,** Division of Graduate Studies, Program in Microbiology, Staten Island, NY 10301-4495. Offers MS. *Program availability:* Part-time, evening/weekend. *Degree requirements:* For master's, comprehensive exam or thesis. *Entrance requirements:* For master's, minimum GPA of 3.0, proficiency in statistics, undergraduate major in biological science or chemistry, undergraduate microbiology course, 16 credits of chemistry including organic chemistry with lab. Additional exam requirements/recommendations for international students: required—TOEFL (minimum score 550 paper-based; 79 iBT), IELTS (minimum score 6.5). Electronic applications accepted.

**Wake Forest University,** School of Medicine and Graduate School of Arts and Sciences, Graduate Programs in Medicine, Department of Microbiology and Immunology, Winston-Salem, NC 27109. Offers PhD, MD/PhD. *Degree requirements:* For doctorate, thesis/dissertation. *Entrance requirements:* For doctorate, GRE General Test. Additional exam requirements/recommendations for international students: required—TOEFL. Electronic applications accepted.

**Washington University in St. Louis,** The Graduate School, Division of Biology and Biomedical Sciences, Program in Molecular Microbiology and Microbial Pathogenesis, St. Louis, MO 63130-4899. Offers PhD. *Degree requirements:* For doctorate, thesis/dissertation. *Entrance requirements:* For doctorate, GRE General Test, GRE Subject Test. Additional exam requirements/recommendations for international students: required—TOEFL. Electronic applications accepted.

**Wright State University,** Graduate School, College of Science and Mathematics, Program in Microbiology and Immunology, Dayton, OH 45435. Offers MS. *Program availability:* Part-time. *Degree requirements:* For master's, thesis. *Entrance requirements:* Additional exam requirements/recommendations for international students: required—TOEFL.

**Yale University,** Yale School of Medicine and Graduate School of Arts and Sciences, Combined Program in Biological and Biomedical Sciences (BBS), Microbiology Track, New Haven, CT 06520. Offers PhD, MD/PhD. *Degree requirements:* For doctorate, thesis/dissertation. *Entrance requirements:* For doctorate, GRE General Test, GRE Subject Test. Additional exam requirements/recommendations for international students: required—TOEFL. Electronic applications accepted.

**Youngstown State University,** College of Graduate Studies, College of Science, Technology, Engineering and Mathematics, Department of Biological Sciences, Youngstown, OH 44555-0001. Offers environmental biology (MS); molecular biology, microbiology, and genetics (MS); physiology and anatomy (MS). *Program availability:* Part-time. *Degree requirements:* For master's, comprehensive exam, thesis, oral review. *Entrance requirements:* For master's, GRE General Test, minimum GPA of 2.7. Additional exam requirements/recommendations for international students: required—TOEFL.

# Virology

**Baylor College of Medicine,** Graduate School of Biomedical Sciences, Department of Molecular Virology and Microbiology, Houston, TX 77030-3498. Offers PhD, MD/PhD. *Degree requirements:* For doctorate, thesis/dissertation, public defense. *Entrance requirements:* For doctorate, GRE General Test, GRE Subject Test (strongly recommended), minimum GPA of 3.0. Additional exam requirements/recommendations for international students: required—TOEFL. Electronic applications accepted.

**Baylor College of Medicine,** Graduate School of Biomedical Sciences, Interdepartmental Program in Cell and Molecular Biology, Houston, TX 77030-3498. Offers biochemistry (PhD); cell and molecular biology (PhD); genetics (PhD); human genetics (PhD); immunology (PhD); microbiology (PhD); virology (PhD); MD/PhD. *Degree requirements:* For doctorate, thesis/dissertation, public defense. *Entrance requirements:* For doctorate, GRE General Test, GRE Subject Test (strongly recommended), minimum GPA of 3.0. Additional exam requirements/recommendations for international students: required—TOEFL. Electronic applications accepted.

**Case Western Reserve University,** School of Medicine and School of Graduate Studies, Graduate Programs in Medicine, Department of Molecular Biology and Microbiology, Program in Molecular Virology, Cleveland, OH 44106. Offers PhD. *Entrance requirements:* Additional exam requirements/recommendations for international students: required—TOEFL (minimum score 550 paper-based).

**Mayo Clinic Graduate School of Biomedical Sciences,** Program in Virology and Gene Therapy, Rochester, MN 55905. Offers PhD. *Degree requirements:* For doctorate, comprehensive exam, thesis/dissertation. *Entrance requirements:* Additional exam requirements/recommendations for international students: required—TOEFL. Electronic applications accepted.

**McMaster University,** Faculty of Health Sciences and School of Graduate Studies, Program in Medical Sciences, Hamilton, ON L8S 4M2, Canada. Offers blood and vascular (M Sc, PhD); genetics and cancer (M Sc, PhD); immunity and infection (M Sc, PhD); metabolism and nutrition (M Sc, PhD); neurosciences and behavioral sciences (M Sc, PhD); physiology/pharmacology (M Sc, PhD); MD/PhD. *Degree requirements:* For master's, thesis; for doctorate, comprehensive exam, thesis/dissertation. *Entrance requirements:* For master's, honors B Sc, B+ average in related field; for doctorate, M Sc, minimum B+ average. Additional exam requirements/recommendations for international students: required—TOEFL (minimum score 580 paper-based; 92 iBT).

**Oregon State University,** College of Science, Program in Microbiology, Corvallis, OR 97331. Offers environmental microbiology (MA, MS, PhD); food microbiology (MA, MS, PhD); genomics (MA, MS, PhD); immunology (MA, MS, PhD); microbial ecology (MA, MS, PhD); microbial evolution (MA, MS, PhD); parasitology (MA, MS, PhD); pathogenic microbiology (MA, MS, PhD); virology (MA). Terminal master's awarded for partial completion of doctoral program. *Entrance requirements:* For master's and doctorate, GRE. Additional exam requirements/recommendations for international students: required—TOEFL (minimum score 600 paper-based; 100 iBT).

**Oregon State University,** Interdisciplinary/Institutional Programs, Program in Molecular and Cellular Biology, Corvallis, OR 97331. Offers bioinformatics (PhD); biotechnology (PhD); genome biology (PhD); molecular virology (PhD); plant molecular biology (PhD). *Degree requirements:* For doctorate, thesis/dissertation, oral and written qualifying exams. *Entrance requirements:* For doctorate, GRE. Additional exam requirements/recommendations for international students: required—TOEFL (minimum score 80 iBT), IELTS (minimum score 6.5).

**Penn State Hershey Medical Center,** College of Medicine, Graduate School Programs in the Biomedical Sciences, Graduate Program in Biomedical Sciences, Hershey, PA 17033. Offers biochemistry and molecular genetics (MS, PhD); biomedical sciences (MS, PhD); cellular and integrative physiology (MS, PhD); translational therapeutics (MS, PhD); virology and immunology (MS, PhD); MD/PhD; PhD/MBA. Terminal master's awarded for partial completion of doctoral program. *Degree requirements:* For master's, thesis; for doctorate, comprehensive exam, thesis/dissertation, candidacy exam. *Entrance requirements:* For doctorate, GRE General Test. Additional exam requirements/recommendations for international students: required—TOEFL (minimum score 550 paper-based; 81 iBT). Electronic applications accepted.

**Purdue University,** Graduate School, PULSe - Purdue University Life Sciences Program, West Lafayette, IN 47907. Offers biomolecular structure and biophysics (PhD); biotechnology (PhD); chemical biology (PhD); chromatin and regulation of gene expression (PhD); integrative neuroscience (PhD); integrative plant sciences (PhD); membrane biology (PhD); microbiology (PhD); molecular evolutionary and cancer biology (PhD); molecular evolutionary genetics (PhD); molecular virology (PhD). *Students:* 37 full-time (23 women); includes 7 minority (1 Black or African American, non-Hispanic/Latino; 2 Asian, non-Hispanic/Latino; 4 Hispanic/Latino), 22 international. Average age 25. 162 applicants, 36% accepted, 19 enrolled. *Entrance requirements:* For doctorate, GRE, minimum undergraduate GPA of 3.0. Additional exam requirements/recommendations for international students: required—TOEFL (minimum score 550 paper-based; 77 iBT). *Application deadline:* For fall admission, 1/15 priority date for domestic and international students. Applications are processed on a rolling basis. Application fee: $60 ($75 for international students). Electronic applications accepted. *Financial support:* In 2019–20, research assistantships with tuition reimbursements (averaging $22,500 per year), teaching assistantships with tuition reimbursements (averaging $22,500 per year) were awarded. *Application contact:* Lindsey Springer, Graduate Contact for Admissions, 765-496-9667, E-mail: lbcampbe@purdue.edu.
Website: http://www.gradschool.purdue.edu/pulse

**Purdue University,** School of Veterinary Medicine and Graduate School, Graduate Programs in Veterinary Medicine, Department of Comparative Pathobiology, West Lafayette, IN 47907-2027. Offers comparative epidemiology and public health (MS); comparative epidemiology and public heath (PhD); comparative microbiology and immunology (MS, PhD); comparative pathobiology (MS, PhD); interdisciplinary studies (PhD), including microbial pathogenesis, molecular signaling and cancer biology, molecular virology; lab animal medicine (MS); veterinary anatomic pathology (MS); veterinary clinical pathology (MS). Terminal master's awarded for partial completion of doctoral program. *Degree requirements:* For master's, thesis (for some programs); for

doctorate, thesis/dissertation. *Entrance requirements:* For master's and doctorate, GRE General Test. Additional exam requirements/recommendations for international students: required—TOEFL (minimum score 575 paper-based), IELTS (minimum score 6.5), TWE (minimum score 4). Electronic applications accepted.

**Rush University,** Graduate College, Division of Immunology and Microbiology, Program in Immunology/Microbiology, Chicago, IL 60612-3832. Offers immunology (MS, PhD); virology (MS, PhD); MD/PhD. *Program availability:* Part-time. Terminal master's awarded for partial completion of doctoral program. *Degree requirements:* For master's, thesis; for doctorate, thesis/dissertation, comprehensive preliminary exam. *Entrance requirements:* For master's, GRE General Test; for doctorate, GRE General Test, interview, minimum GPA of 3.0. Additional exam requirements/recommendations for international students: required—TOEFL. Electronic applications accepted.

**Rutgers University - New Brunswick,** Graduate School-New Brunswick, Programs in the Molecular Biosciences, Piscataway, NJ 08854-8097. Offers biochemistry (PhD); cell and developmental biology (MS, PhD); microbiology and molecular genetics (MS, PhD), including applied microbiology, clinical microbiology, computational molecular biology (PhD), immunology, microbial biochemistry, molecular genetics, virology.

**Université de Montréal,** Faculty of Veterinary Medicine, Program in Virology and Immunology, Montréal, QC H3C 3J7, Canada. Offers PhD. *Degree requirements:* For doctorate, thesis/dissertation, general exam. *Entrance requirements:* For doctorate, proficiency in French, knowledge of English. Electronic applications accepted.

**Université du Québec, Institut National de la Recherche Scientifique,** Graduate Programs, Armand-Frappier Santé Biotechnologie, Laval, QC H7V 1B7, Canada. Offers applied microbiology (M Sc); biology (PhD); experimental health sciences (M Sc); virology and immunology (M Sc, PhD). *Program availability:* Part-time. *Faculty:* 46 full-time. *Students:* 157 full-time (94 women), 9 part-time (4 women), 100 international. Average age 30. 23 applicants, 96% accepted, 21 enrolled. In 2019, 19 master's, 20 doctorates awarded. *Degree requirements:* For master's, thesis; for doctorate, thesis/dissertation. *Entrance requirements:* For master's, appropriate bachelor's degree, proficiency in French; for doctorate, appropriate master's degree, proficiency in French. *Application deadline:* For fall admission, 3/30 for domestic and international students; for winter admission, 11/1 for domestic and international students; for spring admission, 3/1 for domestic and international students. Application fee: $45 Canadian dollars. Electronic applications accepted. *Financial support:* In 2019–20, fellowships (averaging $16,500 per year) were awarded; research assistantships also available. *Unit head:* Claude Guertin, Director, 450-687-5010, Fax: 450-686-5501, E-mail: claude.guertin@iaf.inrs.ca. *Application contact:* Sean Otto, Registrar, 418-654-2518, Fax: 418-654-3858, E-mail: sean.otto@inrs.ca.
Website: http://www.iaf.inrs.ca

**The University of Iowa,** Roy J. and Lucille A. Carver College of Medicine and Graduate College, Graduate Programs in Medicine, Department of Microbiology, Iowa City, IA 52242-1316. Offers general microbiology and microbial physiology (MS, PhD); immunology (MS, PhD); microbial genetics (MS, PhD); pathogenic bacteriology (MS, PhD); virology (MS, PhD). *Degree requirements:* For master's, thesis; for doctorate, comprehensive exam, thesis/dissertation. *Entrance requirements:* For master's and doctorate, GRE General Test. Additional exam requirements/recommendations for international students: required—TOEFL (minimum score 600 paper-based). Electronic applications accepted.

**University of Minnesota, Twin Cities Campus,** Graduate School, PhD Program in Microbiology, Immunology and Cancer Biology, Minneapolis, MN 55455-0213. Offers PhD. *Degree requirements:* For doctorate, thesis/dissertation. *Entrance requirements:* For doctorate, GRE General Test. Additional exam requirements/recommendations for international students: required—TOEFL (minimum score 600 paper-based). Electronic applications accepted.

**University of Pennsylvania,** Perelman School of Medicine, Biomedical Graduate Studies, Graduate Group in Cell and Molecular Biology, Philadelphia, PA 19104. Offers cancer biology (PhD); cell biology, physiology, and metabolism (PhD); developmental stem cell regenerative biology (PhD); gene therapy and vaccines (PhD); genetics and gene regulation (PhD); microbiology, virology, and parasitology (PhD); MD/PhD; VMD/PhD. *Faculty:* 400 full-time (118 women). *Students:* 378 full-time (221 women); includes 134 minority (6 Black or African American, non-Hispanic/Latino; 56 Asian, non-Hispanic/Latino; 58 Hispanic/Latino; 2 Native Hawaiian or other Pacific Islander, non-Hispanic/Latino; 12 Two or more races, non-Hispanic/Latino), 52 international. 851 applicants, 14% accepted, 59 enrolled. In 2019, 43 doctorates awarded. *Unit head:* Dr. Daniel Kessler, Graduate Group Chair, 215-898-1478. *Application contact:* Meagan Schofer, Associate Director, 215-898-1478.
Website: http://www.med.upenn.edu/camb/

**University of Prince Edward Island,** Atlantic Veterinary College, Graduate Program in Veterinary Medicine, Charlottetown, PE C1A 4P3, Canada. Offers anatomy (M Sc, PhD); bacteriology (M Sc, PhD); clinical pharmacology (M Sc, PhD); clinical sciences (M Sc, PhD); epidemiology (M Sc, PhD), including reproduction; fish health (M Sc, PhD); food animal nutrition (M Sc, PhD); immunology (M Sc, PhD); microanatomy (M Sc, PhD); parasitology (M Sc, PhD); pathology (M Sc, PhD); pharmacology (M Sc, PhD); physiology (M Sc, PhD); toxicology (M Sc, PhD); veterinary science (M Vet Sc); virology (M Sc, PhD). *Program availability:* Part-time. *Degree requirements:* For master's, thesis; for doctorate, thesis/dissertation. *Entrance requirements:* For master's, DVM, B Sc honors degree, or equivalent; for doctorate, M Sc. Additional exam requirements/recommendations for international students: required—TOEFL (minimum score 550 paper-based; 80 iBT). *Expenses:* Contact institution.

**Yale University,** Yale School of Medicine and Graduate School of Arts and Sciences, Combined Program in Biological and Biomedical Sciences (BBS), Microbiology Track, New Haven, CT 06520. Offers PhD, MD/PhD. *Degree requirements:* For doctorate, thesis/dissertation. *Entrance requirements:* For doctorate, GRE General Test, GRE Subject Test. Additional exam requirements/recommendations for international students: required—TOEFL. Electronic applications accepted.

Virology

# Section 13
# Neuroscience and Neurobiology

This section contains a directory of institutions offering graduate work in neuroscience and neurobiology, followed by in-depth entries submitted by institutions that chose to prepare detailed program descriptions. Additional information about programs listed in the directory but not augmented by an in-depth entry may be obtained by writing directly to the dean of a graduate school or chair of a department at the address given in the directory.

For programs offering related work, see also in this book *Anatomy; Biochemistry; Biological and Biomedical Sciences; Biophysics; Cell, Molecular, and Structural Biology; Genetics, Developmental Biology, and Reproductive Biology; Optometry and Vision Sciences; Pathology and Pathobiology; Pharmacology and Toxicology; Physiology;* and *Zoology.* In another guide in this series:

**Graduate Programs in the Humanities, Arts & Social Sciences**
See *Psychology and Counseling*

## CONTENTS
### Program Directories

# Biopsychology

**American University,** College of Arts and Sciences, Department of Psychology, Washington, DC 22016-8062. Offers addiction and addictive behavior (Certificate); behavior, cognition, and neuroscience (PhD); clinical psychology (PhD); psychobiology of healing (Certificate); psychology (MA). *Accreditation:* APA. *Program availability:* Part-time. *Degree requirements:* For master's, comprehensive exam, thesis or alternative; for doctorate, comprehensive exam, thesis/dissertation. *Entrance requirements:* For master's, GRE General Test, GRE Subject Test; Please website: https://www.american.edu/cas/psychology/, statement of purpose, transcripts, 2 letters of recommendation; for doctorate, GRE General Test, GRE Subject Test, 3 letters of recommendation, statement of purpose, transcripts, resume. Additional exam requirements/recommendations for international students: required—TOEFL (minimum score 600 paper-based; 100 iBT). *Expenses:* Contact institution.

**Argosy University, Atlanta,** Georgia School of Professional Psychology, Atlanta, GA 30328. Offers clinical psychology (MA, Psy D, Postdoctoral Respecialization Certificate), including child and family psychology (Psy D), general adult clinical (Psy D), health psychology (Psy D), neuropsychology/geropsychology (Psy D); community counseling (MA), including marriage and family therapy; counselor education and supervision (Ed D); forensic psychology (MA); industrial organizational psychology (MA); marriage and family therapy (Certificate); sport-exercise psychology (MA). *Accreditation:* APA.

**Argosy University, Twin Cities,** Minnesota School of Professional Psychology, Eagan, MN 55121. Offers clinical psychology (MA, Psy D), including child and family psychology (Psy D), forensic psychology (Psy D), health and neuropsychology (Psy D), trauma (Psy D); forensic counseling (Post-Graduate Certificate); forensic psychology (MA); industrial organizational psychology (MA); marriage and family therapy (MA, DMFT), including forensic counseling (MA). *Accreditation:* AAMFT; AAMFT/COAMFTE; APA.

**Binghamton University, State University of New York,** Graduate School, Harpur College of Arts and Sciences, Department of Psychology, Program in Psychology - Behavioral Neuroscience, Binghamton, NY 13902-6000. Offers PhD. *Program availability:* Part-time. Terminal master's awarded for partial completion of doctoral program. *Degree requirements:* For doctorate, thesis/dissertation. *Entrance requirements:* For doctorate, GRE General Test. Additional exam requirements/recommendations for international students: required—TOEFL (minimum score 550 paper-based; 80 iBT). Electronic applications accepted.

**Boston University,** School of Medicine, Graduate Medical Sciences, Program in Mental Health Counseling and Behavioral Medicine, Boston, MA 02215. Offers MA. *Unit head:* Dr. Stephen Brady, Director, 617-414-2320, Fax: 617-414-2323, E-mail: sbrady@bu.edu. *Application contact:* GMS Admissions Office, 617-358-9518, Fax: 617-358-2913, E-mail: gmsbusm@bu.edu.
Website: http://www.bumc.bu.edu/gms/mhcbm/

**Carnegie Mellon University,** Dietrich College of Humanities and Social Sciences, Department of Psychology, Area of Cognitive Neuroscience, Pittsburgh, PA 15213-3891. Offers PhD. *Degree requirements:* For doctorate, comprehensive exam, thesis/dissertation. *Entrance requirements:* For doctorate, GRE General Test. Additional exam requirements/recommendations for international students: required—TOEFL.

**Cornell University,** Graduate School, Graduate Fields of Arts and Sciences, Field of Psychology, Ithaca, NY 14853. Offers biopsychology (PhD); human experimental psychology (PhD); personality and social psychology (PhD). *Degree requirements:* For doctorate, comprehensive exam, thesis/dissertation, 2 semesters of teaching experience. *Entrance requirements:* For doctorate, GRE General Test, 3 letters of recommendation. Additional exam requirements/recommendations for international students: required—TOEFL (minimum score 550 paper-based; 77 iBT). Electronic applications accepted.

**Drexel University,** College of Arts and Sciences, Department of Psychology, Philadelphia, PA 19104-2875. Offers clinical psychology (PhD), including clinical psychology, forensic psychology, health psychology, neuropsychology; psychology (MS); JD/PhD. *Accreditation:* APA (one or more programs are accredited). *Degree requirements:* For doctorate, thesis/dissertation, internship. *Entrance requirements:* For doctorate, GRE General Test. Additional exam requirements/recommendations for international students: required—TOEFL. Electronic applications accepted. *Expenses:* Contact institution.

**Duke University,** Graduate School, Department of Psychology and Neuroscience, Durham, NC 27708. Offers biological psychology (PhD); clinical psychology (PhD); cognitive psychology (PhD); developmental psychology (PhD); experimental psychology (PhD); health psychology (PhD); human social development (PhD); JD/MA. *Accreditation:* APA (one or more programs are accredited). *Degree requirements:* For doctorate, thesis/dissertation. *Entrance requirements:* For doctorate, GRE General Test. Additional exam requirements/recommendations for international students: required—TOEFL (minimum score 577 paper-based; 90 iBT) or IELTS (minimum score 7). Electronic applications accepted.

**Florida State University,** The Graduate School, College of Arts and Sciences, Interdisciplinary Program in Neuroscience, Tallahassee, FL 32306. Offers neuroscience (PhD); psychobiology (MS). Terminal master's awarded for partial completion of doctoral program. *Degree requirements:* For master's, thesis; for doctorate, comprehensive exam, thesis/dissertation. *Entrance requirements:* For doctorate, GRE General Test (suggested minimum score above 60th percentile on both verbal and quantitative sections), minimum GPA of 3.0, research experience, letters of recommendation. Additional exam requirements/recommendations for international students: required—TOEFL (minimum score 80 iBT). Electronic applications accepted.

**The Graduate Center, City University of New York,** Graduate Studies, Program in Psychology, New York, NY 10016-4039. Offers basic applied neurocognition (PhD); biopsychology (PhD); clinical psychology (PhD); developmental psychology (PhD); environmental psychology (PhD); experimental psychology (PhD); industrial psychology (PhD); learning processes (PhD); neuropsychology (PhD); psychology (PhD); social personality (PhD). *Degree requirements:* For doctorate, one foreign language, thesis/dissertation. *Entrance requirements:* For doctorate, GRE General Test. Additional exam requirements/recommendations for international students: required—TOEFL. Electronic applications accepted.

**Harvard University,** Graduate School of Arts and Sciences, Department of Psychology, Cambridge, MA 02138. Offers psychology (PhD), including behavior and decision analysis, cognition, developmental psychology, experimental psychology, personality, psychobiology, psychopathology; social psychology (PhD). *Accreditation:* APA. *Degree requirements:* For doctorate, thesis/dissertation, general exams. *Entrance requirements:* For doctorate, GRE General Test. Additional exam requirements/recommendations for international students: required—TOEFL.

**Howard University,** Graduate School, Department of Psychology, Washington, DC 20059-0002. Offers clinical psychology (PhD); developmental psychology (PhD); experimental psychology (PhD); neuropsychology (PhD); personality psychology (PhD); psychology (MS); social psychology (PhD). *Accreditation:* APA (one or more programs are accredited). *Program availability:* Part-time. *Degree requirements:* For master's, thesis; for doctorate, comprehensive exam, thesis/dissertation, qualifying exam. *Entrance requirements:* For master's, GRE General Test, minimum GPA of 2.5, bachelor's degree in psychology or related field; for doctorate, GRE General Test, minimum GPA of 3.0.

**Liberty University,** School of Health Sciences, Lynchburg, VA 24515. Offers anatomy and cell biology (PhD); biomedical sciences (MS); epidemiology (MPH); exercise science (MS), including clinical, community physical activity, human performance, nutrition; global health (MPH); health promotion (MPH); medical sciences (MA), including biopsychology, business management, health informatics, molecular medicine, public health; nutrition (MPH). *Program availability:* Part-time, online learning. *Students:* 820 full-time (588 women), 889 part-time (612 women); includes 611 minority (402 Black or African American, non-Hispanic/Latino; 10 American Indian or Alaska Native, non-Hispanic/Latino; 43 Asian, non-Hispanic/Latino; 85 Hispanic/Latino; 1 Native Hawaiian or other Pacific Islander, non-Hispanic/Latino; 70 Two or more races, non-Hispanic/Latino), 67 international. Average age 32. 2,610 applicants, 33% accepted, 406 enrolled. In 2019, 445 master's awarded. *Degree requirements:* For master's, thesis (for some programs); for doctorate, thesis/dissertation. *Entrance requirements:* For doctorate, MAT or GRE, minimum GPA of 3.25 in master's program, 2-3 recommendations, writing samples (for some programs), letter of intent, professional vitae. Additional exam requirements/recommendations for international students: required—TOEFL (minimum score 600 paper-based; 100 iBT). Application fee: $50. *Expenses:* Tuition: Full-time $545; part-time $410 per credit hour. One-time fee: $50. *Financial support:* In 2019–20, 918 students received support. Federal Work-Study available. Financial award applicants required to submit FAFSA. *Unit head:* Dr. Ralph Linstra, Dean. *Application contact:* Jay Bridge, Director of Admissions, 800-424-9595, Fax: 800-628-7977, E-mail: gradadmissions@liberty.edu.
Website: https://www.liberty.edu/health-sciences/

**Louisiana State University and Agricultural & Mechanical College,** Graduate School, College of Humanities and Social Sciences, Department of Psychology, Baton Rouge, LA 70803. Offers biological psychology (MA, PhD); clinical psychology (MA, PhD); cognitive psychology (MA, PhD); developmental psychology (MA, PhD); school psychology (MA, PhD). *Accreditation:* APA (one or more programs are accredited).

**Memorial University of Newfoundland,** School of Graduate Studies, Interdisciplinary Program in Cognitive and Behavioral Ecology, St. John's, NL A1C 5S7, Canada. Offers M Sc, PhD. *Degree requirements:* For master's, thesis, public lecture; for doctorate, comprehensive exam, thesis/dissertation, oral defense of dissertation. *Entrance requirements:* For master's, honors degree (minimum 2nd class standing) in related field; for doctorate, master's degree. Electronic applications accepted.

**Northwestern University,** Feinberg School of Medicine and The Graduate School, Program in Clinical Psychology, Evanston, IL 60208. Offers clinical psychology (PhD), including clinical neuropsychology. *Accreditation:* APA. *Degree requirements:* For doctorate, thesis/dissertation, clinical internship. *Entrance requirements:* For doctorate, GRE General Test, GRE Subject Test, minimum GPA of 3.2, course work in psychology. Additional exam requirements/recommendations for international students: required—TOEFL.

**Northwestern University,** The Graduate School, Judd A. and Marjorie Weinberg College of Arts and Sciences, Department of Psychology, Evanston, IL 60208. Offers brain, behavior and cognition (PhD); clinical psychology (PhD); cognitive psychology (PhD); personality psychology (PhD); social psychology (PhD); JD/PhD. *Accreditation:* APA (one or more programs are accredited). *Program availability:* Part-time. *Degree requirements:* For doctorate, thesis/dissertation. *Entrance requirements:* For doctorate, GRE General Test, GRE Subject Test. Additional exam requirements/recommendations for international students: required—TOEFL. Electronic applications accepted.

**Oregon Health & Science University,** School of Medicine, Graduate Programs in Medicine, Department of Behavioral Neuroscience, Portland, OR 97239-3098. Offers PhD. Terminal master's awarded for partial completion of doctoral program. *Degree requirements:* For doctorate, comprehensive exam, thesis/dissertation, qualifying exam. *Entrance requirements:* For doctorate, GRE General Test (minimum scores: 153 Verbal/148 Quantitative/4.5 Analytical), undergraduate coursework in biopsychology and other basic science areas. Electronic applications accepted.

**Palo Alto University,** PGSP-Stanford Psy D Consortium Program, Palo Alto, CA 94304. Offers Psy D. *Accreditation:* APA. *Degree requirements:* For doctorate, comprehensive exam, thesis/dissertation, 2000-hour clinical internship. *Entrance requirements:* For doctorate, GRE General Test (minimum overall score 1200); GRE Subject Test in psychology (highly recommended), undergraduate degree in psychology or related area with minimum GPA of 3.3. Additional exam requirements/recommendations for international students: required—TOEFL, IELTS. Electronic applications accepted. *Expenses:* Contact institution.

**Penn State University Park,** Graduate School, College of Health and Human Development, Department of Biobehavioral Health, University Park, PA 16802. Offers MS, PhD.

**Philadelphia College of Osteopathic Medicine,** Graduate and Professional Programs, School of Professional and Applied Psychology, Philadelphia, PA 19131. Offers applied behavior analysis (Certificate); clinical health psychology (Post-Doctoral Certificate); clinical neuropsychology (Post-Doctoral Certificate); clinical psychology (Psy D); educational psychology (PhD); mental health counseling (MS); organizational development and leadership (MS); psychology (Certificate); public health management and administration (MS); school psychology (MS, Psy D, Ed S). *Accreditation:* APA. *Faculty:* 19 full-time (11 women), 122 part-time/adjunct (58 women). *Students:* 342 (285 women); includes 108 minority (65 Black or African American, non-Hispanic/Latino; 1 American Indian or Alaska Native, non-Hispanic/Latino; 10 Asian, non-Hispanic/Latino; 14 Hispanic/Latino; 18 Two or more races, non-Hispanic/Latino). Average age 25. 357 applicants, 51% accepted, 113 enrolled. In 2019, 79 master's, 38 doctorates, 16 other advanced degrees awarded. Terminal master's awarded for partial completion of doctoral program. *Degree requirements:* For master's, comprehensive exam (for some programs), thesis (for some programs); for doctorate, comprehensive exam, thesis/dissertation. *Entrance requirements:* For master's, GRE or MAT, minimum GPA of 3.0; bachelor's degree from regionally-accredited college or university; for doctorate, PRAXIS II (for Psy D in school psychology), minimum undergraduate GPA of 3.0; for other advanced degree, GRE (for Ed S). Additional exam requirements/

recommendations for international students: required—TOEFL (minimum score 79 iBT). *Application deadline:* Applications are processed on a rolling basis. Application fee: $50. Electronic applications accepted. *Financial support:* In 2019–20, 28 teaching assistantships were awarded; Federal Work-Study, institutionally sponsored loans, and scholarships/grants also available. Financial award application deadline: 3/15; financial award applicants required to submit FAFSA. *Unit head:* Dr. Robert DiTomasso, Chairman, 215-871-6442, Fax: 215-871-6458, E-mail: robertd@pcom.edu. *Application contact:* Johnathan Cox, Associate Director of Admissions, 215-871-6700, Fax: 215-871-6719, E-mail: johnathancox@pcom.edu.
Website: pcom.edu

**Rutgers University - Newark,** Graduate School, Program in Psychology, Newark, NJ 07102. Offers cognitive neuroscience (PhD); cognitive science (PhD); perception (PhD); psychobiology (PhD); social cognition (PhD). *Degree requirements:* For doctorate, comprehensive exam, thesis/dissertation. *Entrance requirements:* For doctorate, GRE General Test, GRE Subject Test, minimum undergraduate B average. Electronic applications accepted.

**Rutgers University - New Brunswick,** Graduate School-New Brunswick, Program in Psychology, Piscataway, NJ 08854-8097. Offers behavioral neuroscience (PhD); clinical psychology (PhD); cognitive psychology (PhD); interdisciplinary health psychology (PhD); social psychology (PhD). *Accreditation:* APA. *Degree requirements:* For doctorate, comprehensive exam, thesis/dissertation. *Entrance requirements:* For doctorate, GRE General Test, 3 letters of recommendation. Additional exam requirements/recommendations for international students: required—TOEFL (minimum score 577 paper-based). Electronic applications accepted.

**The University of British Columbia,** Faculty of Arts, Department of Psychology, Vancouver, BC V6T 1Z4, Canada. Offers behavioral neuroscience (MA, PhD); clinical psychology (MA, PhD); cognitive science (MA, PhD); developmental psychology (MA, PhD); health psychology (MA, PhD); quantitative methods (MA, PhD); social/personality psychology (MA, PhD). *Accreditation:* APA (one or more programs are accredited). Terminal master's awarded for partial completion of doctoral program. *Degree requirements:* For master's, thesis; for doctorate, comprehensive exam, thesis/dissertation. *Entrance requirements:* For master's and doctorate, GRE General Test. Additional exam requirements/recommendations for international students: required—TOEFL. Electronic applications accepted. *Expenses:* Contact institution.

**University of Connecticut,** Graduate School, College of Liberal Arts and Sciences, Department of Psychological Sciences, Storrs, CT 06269. Offers behavioral neuroscience (PhD); biopsychology (PhD); clinical psychology (MA, PhD); cognition and instruction (PhD); developmental psychology (MA, PhD); ecological psychology (PhD); experimental psychology (PhD); general psychology (MA, PhD); industrial/organizational psychology (PhD); language and cognition (PhD); neuroscience (PhD); social psychology (MA, PhD). *Accreditation:* APA. Terminal master's awarded for partial completion of doctoral program. *Degree requirements:* For master's, comprehensive exam; for doctorate, thesis/dissertation. *Entrance requirements:* For master's and doctorate, GRE General Test, GRE Subject Test. Additional exam requirements/recommendations for international students: required—TOEFL (minimum score 550 paper-based). Electronic applications accepted.

**University of Michigan,** Rackham Graduate School, College of Literature, Science, and the Arts, Department of Psychology, Ann Arbor, MI 48109. Offers biopsychology (PhD); clinical science (PhD); cognition and cognitive neuroscience (PhD); developmental psychology (PhD); personality and social contexts (PhD); social psychology (PhD). *Accreditation:* APA. Terminal master's awarded for partial completion of doctoral program. *Degree requirements:* For doctorate, comprehensive exam, thesis/dissertation, oral defense of dissertation, preliminary exam. *Entrance requirements:* For doctorate, GRE (Biopsychology, Cognition and Cognitive Neuroscience, Developmental, Social, and Clinical); GRE Subject Test also strongly recommended (Clinical); GRE not required (Personality and Social Contexts). Additional exam requirements/recommendations for international students: required—TOEFL. Electronic applications accepted.

**University of Minnesota, Twin Cities Campus,** Graduate School, College of Liberal Arts, Department of Psychology, Program in Cognitive and Biological Psychology, Minneapolis, MN 55455-0213. Offers PhD. *Degree requirements:* For doctorate, comprehensive exam, thesis/dissertation. *Entrance requirements:* For doctorate, GRE General Test, GRE Subject Test (recommended), 12 credits of upper-level psychology courses, including a course in statistics or psychological measurement. Additional exam requirements/recommendations for international students: required—TOEFL (minimum score 550 paper-based; 79 iBT).

**University of Nebraska–Lincoln,** Graduate College, College of Arts and Sciences, Department of Psychology, Lincoln, NE 68588. Offers biopsychology (PhD); clinical psychology (PhD); cognitive psychology (PhD); developmental psychology (PhD); psychology (MA); social/personality psychology (PhD); JD/MA; JD/PhD. *Accreditation:* APA (one or more programs are accredited). *Degree requirements:* For master's, thesis optional; for doctorate, comprehensive exam, thesis/dissertation. *Entrance requirements:* For master's and doctorate, GRE General Test. Additional exam requirements/recommendations for international students: required—TOEFL (minimum score 550 paper-based). Electronic applications accepted.

**The University of North Carolina at Chapel Hill,** Graduate School, College of Arts and Sciences, Department of Psychology, Chapel Hill, NC 27599-3270. Offers behavioral neuroscience psychology (PhD); clinical psychology (PhD); cognitive psychology (PhD); developmental psychology (PhD); quantitative psychology (PhD); social psychology (PhD). *Accreditation:* APA. *Degree requirements:* For doctorate, comprehensive exam, thesis/dissertation. *Entrance requirements:* For doctorate, GRE General Test, minimum GPA of 3.0. Additional exam requirements/recommendations for international students: required—TOEFL (minimum score 550 paper-based; 79 iBT), IELTS (minimum score 7). Electronic applications accepted.

**University of Oklahoma Health Sciences Center,** College of Medicine and Graduate College, Graduate Programs in Medicine, Department of Psychiatry and Behavioral Sciences, Oklahoma City, OK 73190. Offers biological psychology (MS, PhD). *Degree requirements:* For master's, thesis; for doctorate, thesis/dissertation. *Entrance requirements:* For doctorate, GRE General Test, 3 letters of recommendation. Additional exam requirements/recommendations for international students: required—TOEFL.

**University of Oregon,** Graduate School, College of Arts and Sciences, Department of Psychology, Eugene, OR 97403. Offers clinical psychology (PhD); cognitive psychology (MA, MS, PhD); developmental psychology (MA, MS, PhD); physiological psychology (MA, MS, PhD); psychology (MA, MS, PhD); social/personality psychology (MA, MS, PhD). *Accreditation:* APA (one or more programs are accredited). Terminal master's awarded for partial completion of doctoral program. *Degree requirements:* For doctorate, thesis/dissertation. *Entrance requirements:* For master's, GRE General Test, minimum GPA of 3.0; for doctorate, GRE General Test. Additional exam requirements/recommendations for international students: required—TOEFL.

**The University of Texas at Austin,** Graduate School, The Institute for Neuroscience, Austin, TX 78712-1111. Offers PhD, MD/PhD. Terminal master's awarded for partial completion of doctoral program. *Degree requirements:* For doctorate, thesis/dissertation. *Entrance requirements:* For doctorate, GRE. Electronic applications accepted.

**University of Windsor,** Faculty of Graduate Studies, Faculty of Arts and Social Sciences, Department of Psychology, Windsor, ON N9B 3P4, Canada. Offers adult clinical (MA, PhD); applied social psychology (MA, PhD); child clinical (MA, PhD); clinical neuropsychology (MA, PhD). *Degree requirements:* For master's, thesis; for doctorate, comprehensive exam, thesis/dissertation. *Entrance requirements:* For master's, GRE General Test, GRE Subject Test in psychology, minimum B average; for doctorate, GRE General Test, GRE Subject Test in psychology, master's degree. Additional exam requirements/recommendations for international students: required—TOEFL (minimum score 600 paper-based). Electronic applications accepted.

**University of Wisconsin–Madison,** Graduate School, College of Letters and Science, Department of Psychology, Program in Biology of Brain and Behavior, Madison, WI 53706-1380. Offers PhD. *Degree requirements:* For doctorate, comprehensive exam, thesis/dissertation. *Entrance requirements:* For doctorate, GRE General Test, minimum undergraduate GPA of 3.0. Additional exam requirements/recommendations for international students: required—TOEFL. Electronic applications accepted.

# Neurobiology

**Boston University,** School of Medicine, Graduate Medical Sciences, Department of Anatomy and Neurobiology, Boston, MA 02118. Offers MA, PhD, MD/PhD. *Program availability:* Part-time. Terminal master's awarded for partial completion of doctoral program. *Degree requirements:* For master's, thesis; for doctorate, thesis/dissertation. *Application deadline:* For fall admission, 1/15 for domestic students; for spring admission, 10/15 for domestic students. *Unit head:* Dr. Mark Moss, Chairman, 617-638-4200, Fax: 617-638-4216. *Application contact:* GMS Admissions Office, 617-358-9518, Fax: 617-358-2913, E-mail: gmsbusm@bu.edu.
Website: http://www.bumc.bu.edu/anatneuro/

**Brandeis University,** Graduate School of Arts and Sciences, Department of Biology, Waltham, MA 02454-9110. Offers genetics (PhD); microbiology (PhD); molecular and cell biology (MS, PhD); molecular biology (PhD); neurobiology (PhD); quantitative biology (PhD). *Program availability:* Part-time. *Faculty:* 28 full-time (14 women), 1 part-time/adjunct (0 women). *Students:* 44 full-time (26 women), 1 (woman) part-time; includes 15 minority (1 American Indian or Alaska Native, non-Hispanic/Latino; 7 Asian, non-Hispanic/Latino; 7 Hispanic/Latino), 10 international. Average age 27. 202 applicants, 22% accepted, 12 enrolled. In 2019, 9 master's, 6 doctorates awarded. Terminal master's awarded for partial completion of doctoral program. *Degree requirements:* For master's, thesis optional; for doctorate, comprehensive exam, thesis/dissertation. *Entrance requirements:* For master's, transcripts, letters of recommendation, resume, statement of purpose; for doctorate, transcripts, letters of recommendation, resume, program questions, statement of purpose. Additional exam requirements/recommendations for international students: required—TOEFL, IELTS, PTE. *Application deadline:* For fall admission, 12/1 priority date for domestic and international students; for spring admission, 10/15 for domestic students, 11/15 for international students. Applications are processed on a rolling basis. Application fee: $75. Electronic applications accepted. *Financial support:* In 2019–20, 50 fellowships with full tuition reimbursements (averaging $35,000 per year), 21 teaching assistantships (averaging $3,550 per year) were awarded; research assistantships, scholarships/grants, health care benefits, and tuition waivers also available. Support available to part-time students. *Unit head:* Dr. Michael Marr, Director of Graduate Studies, 781-736-2481, E-mail: mmarr@brandeis.edu. *Application contact:* Maryanna Aldrich, Administrator, 781-736-2352, E-mail: scigradoffice@brandeis.edu.
Website: http://www.brandeis.edu/gsas/programs/mcbio.html

**California Institute of Technology,** Division of Biology and Biological Engineering, Program in Neurobiology, Pasadena, CA 91125-0001. Offers PhD. *Degree requirements:* For doctorate, thesis/dissertation, qualifying exam. *Entrance requirements:* For doctorate, GRE General Test.

**Carnegie Mellon University,** Mellon College of Science, Department of Biological Sciences, Pittsburgh, PA 15213-3891. Offers biochemistry (PhD); biophysics (PhD); cell and developmental biology (PhD); computational biology (MS, PhD); genetics (PhD); molecular biology (PhD); neuroscience (PhD); structural biology (PhD). *Degree requirements:* For doctorate, comprehensive exam, thesis/dissertation. *Entrance requirements:* For doctorate, GRE General Test, GRE Subject Test, interview. Electronic applications accepted.

**Columbia University,** College of Physicians and Surgeons, Program in Neurobiology and Behavior, New York, NY 10032. Offers PhD. *Degree requirements:* For doctorate, thesis/dissertation. *Entrance requirements:* For doctorate, GRE General Test. Additional exam requirements/recommendations for international students: required—TOEFL. *Expenses:* Contact institution.

**Cornell University,** Graduate School, Graduate Fields of Agriculture and Life Sciences, Field of Neurobiology and Behavior, Ithaca, NY 14853. Offers behavioral biology (PhD), including behavioral ecology, chemical ecology, ethology, neuroethology, sociobiology; neurobiology (PhD), including cellular and molecular neurobiology, neuroanatomy, neurochemistry, neuropharmacology, neurophysiology, sensory physiology. *Degree requirements:* For doctorate, comprehensive exam, thesis/dissertation, 1 year of teaching experience, seminar presentation. *Entrance requirements:* For doctorate, GRE General Test, GRE Subject Test (biology), 3 letters of recommendation. Additional exam requirements/recommendations for international students: required—TOEFL (minimum score 550 paper-based; 77 iBT). Electronic applications accepted.

**Duke University,** Graduate School, Department of Evolutionary Anthropology, Durham, NC 27708. Offers cellular and molecular biology (PhD); gross anatomy and physical anthropology (PhD), including comparative morphology of human and non-human

primates, primate social behavior, vertebrate paleontology; neuroanatomy (PhD). *Degree requirements:* For doctorate, one foreign language, thesis/dissertation. *Entrance requirements:* For doctorate, GRE General Test. Additional exam requirements/recommendations for international students: required—TOEFL (minimum score 577 paper-based; 90 iBT) or IELTS (minimum score 7). Electronic applications accepted.

**Duke University,** Graduate School, Department of Neurobiology, Durham, NC 27710. Offers PhD. *Degree requirements:* For doctorate, variable foreign language requirement, thesis/dissertation. *Entrance requirements:* For doctorate, GRE General Test. Additional exam requirements/recommendations for international students: required—TOEFL (minimum score 577 paper-based; 90 iBT) or IELTS (minimum score 7). Electronic applications accepted.

**Georgia State University,** College of Arts and Sciences, Department of Biology, Program in Neurobiology and Behavior, Atlanta, GA 30302-3083. Offers bioinformatics (MS); neurobiology and behavior (MS, PhD). *Program availability:* Part-time. Terminal master's awarded for partial completion of doctoral program. *Entrance requirements:* For master's and doctorate, GRE. *Application deadline:* Applications are processed on a rolling basis. Application fee: $50. Electronic applications accepted. *Expenses: Tuition, area resident:* Full-time $7164; part-time $398 per credit hour. Tuition, state resident: full-time $7164; part-time $398 per credit hour. Tuition, nonresident: full-time $22,662; part-time $1259 per credit hour. *International tuition:* $22,662 full-time. *Required fees:* $2128; $312 per credit hour. Tuition and fees vary according to course load and program. *Financial support:* Fellowships and research assistantships available. Financial award application deadline: 12/3. *Unit head:* Dr. Geert de Vries, Chair, 404-413-5658, Fax: 404-413-3518, E-mail: devries@gsu.edu. *Application contact:* Dr. Geert de Vries, Chair, 404-413-5658, Fax: 404-413-3518, E-mail: devries@gsu.edu.
Website: http://biology.gsu.edu/

**Harvard University,** Graduate School of Arts and Sciences, Program in Neuroscience, Boston, MA 02115. Offers neurobiology (PhD). *Degree requirements:* For doctorate, thesis/dissertation, qualifying exam. *Entrance requirements:* For doctorate, GRE General Test, GRE Subject Test. Additional exam requirements/recommendations for international students: required—TOEFL.

**Illinois State University,** Graduate School, College of Arts and Sciences, School of Biological Sciences, Normal, IL 61790. Offers animal behavior (MS); bacteriology (MS); biochemistry (MS); biological sciences (MS); biology (PhD); biophysics (MS); biotechnology (MS); botany (MS, PhD); cell biology (MS); conservation biology (MS); developmental biology (MS); ecology (MS, PhD); entomology (MS); evolutionary biology (MS); genetics (MS, PhD); immunology (MS); microbiology (MS, PhD); molecular biology (MS); molecular genetics (MS); neurobiology (MS); neuroscience (MS); parasitology (MS); physiology (MS, PhD); plant biology (MS); plant molecular biology (MS); plant sciences (MS); structural biology (MS); zoology (MS, PhD). *Program availability:* Part-time. *Faculty:* 26 full-time (6 women), 7 part-time/adjunct (2 women). *Students:* 51 full-time (33 women), 15 part-time (8 women). Average age 27. 71 applicants, 28% accepted, 9 enrolled. In 2019, 14 master's, 3 doctorates awarded. *Degree requirements:* For master's, thesis or alternative; for doctorate, variable foreign language requirement, thesis/dissertation, 2 terms of residency. *Entrance requirements:* For master's, GRE General Test, minimum GPA of 2.6 in last 60 hours of course work; for doctorate, GRE General Test. *Application deadline:* Applications are processed on a rolling basis. Application fee: $50. *Expenses: Tuition, area resident:* Full-time $7956; part-time $9767 per year. Tuition, nonresident: full-time $9233; part-time $17,592 per year. *Required fees:* $1797. *Financial support:* In 2019–20, 20 research assistantships, 41 teaching assistantships were awarded; Federal Work-Study, tuition waivers (full), and unspecified assistantships also available. Financial award application deadline: 4/1. *Unit head:* Dr. Craig Gatto, School Director, 309-438-3087, E-mail: cgatto@IllinoisState.edu. *Application contact:* Dr. Ben Sadd, Assistant Chair for Graduate Studies, 309-438-2651, E-mail: bmsadd@IllinoisState.edu.
Website: http://www.bio.ilstu.edu/

**Indiana University-Purdue University Indianapolis,** Indiana University School of Medicine, Stark Neurosciences Research Institute, Indianapolis, IN 46202. Offers medical neuroscience (PhD). *Degree requirements:* For doctorate, thesis/dissertation. *Entrance requirements:* For doctorate, GRE General Test, previous course work in calculus, organic chemistry, and physics.

**Louisiana State University Health Sciences Center,** School of Graduate Studies in New Orleans, Department of Cell Biology and Anatomy, New Orleans, LA 70112-2223. Offers cell biology and anatomy (PhD), including clinical anatomy, development, cell, and neurobiology; MD/PhD. *Degree requirements:* For doctorate, comprehensive exam, thesis/dissertation. *Entrance requirements:* For doctorate, GRE General Test, minimum undergraduate GPA of 3.0. Additional exam requirements/recommendations for international students: recommended—TOEFL, IELTS.

**Massachusetts Institute of Technology,** School of Science, Department of Biology, Cambridge, MA 02139. Offers biochemistry (PhD); biological oceanography (PhD); biology (PhD); biophysical chemistry and molecular structure (PhD); cell biology (PhD); computational and systems biology (PhD); developmental biology (PhD); genetics (PhD); immunology (PhD); microbiology (PhD); molecular biology (PhD); neurobiology (PhD). *Degree requirements:* For doctorate, comprehensive exam, thesis/dissertation, teaching assistantship during two semesters. *Entrance requirements:* For doctorate, GRE General Test. Additional exam requirements/recommendations for international students: required—TOEFL, IELTS. Electronic applications accepted.

**New York University,** Graduate School of Arts and Science, Department of Biology, New York, NY 10012-1019. Offers biology (PhD); biomedical journalism (MS); cancer and molecular biology (PhD); computational biology (PhD); computers in biological research (MS); developmental genetics (PhD); general biology (MS); immunology and microbiology (PhD); molecular genetics (PhD); neurobiology (PhD); oral biology (MS); plant biology (PhD); recombinant DNA technology (MS); MS/MBA. *Program availability:* Part-time. Terminal master's awarded for partial completion of doctoral program. *Degree requirements:* For master's, thesis or alternative, qualifying paper; for doctorate, comprehensive exam, thesis/dissertation. *Entrance requirements:* For master's and doctorate, GRE General Test. Additional exam requirements/recommendations for international students: required—TOEFL, IELTS.

**Northwestern University,** The Graduate School, Interdisciplinary Biological Sciences Program (IBiS), Evanston, IL 60208. Offers biochemistry (PhD); bioengineering and biotechnology (PhD); biotechnology (PhD); cell and molecular biology (PhD); developmental and systems biology (PhD); nanotechnology (PhD); neurobiology (PhD); structural biology and biophysics (PhD). *Degree requirements:* For doctorate, thesis/dissertation, qualifying exam. *Entrance requirements:* For doctorate, GRE General Test. Additional exam requirements/recommendations for international students: required—TOEFL (minimum score 600 paper-based). Electronic applications accepted.

**Northwestern University,** The Graduate School, Judd A. and Marjorie Weinberg College of Arts and Sciences, Department of Neurobiology, Evanston, IL 60208. Offers neurobiology and physiology (MS). *Program availability:* Part-time. *Degree requirements:* For master's, thesis. *Entrance requirements:* For master's, GRE General Test and MCAT (strongly recommended). Additional exam requirements/recommendations for international students: required—TOEFL. Electronic applications accepted. *Expenses:* Contact institution.

**Penn State Hershey Medical Center,** College of Medicine, Graduate School Programs in the Biomedical Sciences, Huck Institutes of the Life Sciences, Intercollege Graduate Program in Molecular Cellular and Integrative Biosciences, Hershey, PA 17033. Offers cell and developmental biology (PhD); molecular medicine (PhD); molecular toxicology (PhD); neurobiology (PhD). *Degree requirements:* For doctorate, comprehensive exam, thesis/dissertation, oral exam. *Entrance requirements:* For doctorate, GRE, minimum GPA of 3.0. Additional exam requirements/recommendations for international students: required—TOEFL (minimum score 500 paper-based). Electronic applications accepted.

**Purdue University,** Graduate School, College of Science, Department of Biological Sciences, West Lafayette, IN 47907. Offers cell and developmental biology (PhD); genetics (MS); microbiology (MS, PhD); neurobiology (MS, PhD). *Faculty:* 43 full-time (14 women), 6 part-time/adjunct (1 woman). *Students:* 117 full-time (58 women), 10 part-time (6 women); includes 24 minority (5 Black or African American, non-Hispanic/Latino; 12 Asian, non-Hispanic/Latino; 4 Hispanic/Latino; 3 Two or more races, non-Hispanic/Latino), 56 international. Average age 27. 146 applicants, 32% accepted, 27 enrolled. In 2019, 7 master's, 18 doctorates awarded. Terminal master's awarded for partial completion of doctoral program. *Degree requirements:* For master's, thesis (for some programs); for doctorate, thesis/dissertation, seminars, teaching experience. *Entrance requirements:* For master's, GRE General Test (minimum analytical writing score of 3.5), minimum undergraduate GPA of 3.0; for doctorate, GRE General Test (minimum analytical writing score of 3.5), minimum undergraduate GPA of 3.5. Additional exam requirements/recommendations for international students: required—TOEFL minimum score 600 paper-based; 107 iBT (for MS), 80 iBT (for PhD). *Application deadline:* For fall admission, 12/7 for domestic and international students. Applications are processed on a rolling basis. Application fee: $60 ($75 for international students). Electronic applications accepted. *Financial support:* Fellowships, research assistantships, and teaching assistantships available. Support available to part-time students. Financial award application deadline: 2/15; financial award applicants required to submit FAFSA. *Unit head:* Janice P. Evans, Head, 765-494-4407, E-mail: janiceevans@purdue.edu. *Application contact:* Georgina E. Rupp, Graduate Coordinator, 765-494-8142, E-mail: ruppg@purdue.edu.
Website: http://www.bio.purdue.edu/

**University of Arkansas for Medical Sciences,** Graduate School, Little Rock, AR 72205. Offers biochemistry and molecular biology (MS, PhD); bioinformatics (MS, PhD); cellular physiology and molecular biophysics (MS, PhD); clinical nutrition (MS); interdisciplinary biomedical sciences (MS, PhD, Certificate); interdisciplinary toxicology (MS); microbiology and immunology (PhD); neurobiology and developmental sciences (PhD); pharmacology (PhD); MD/PhD. *Program availability:* Part-time. Terminal master's awarded for partial completion of doctoral program. *Degree requirements:* For master's, comprehensive exam (for some programs), thesis (for some programs); for doctorate, thesis/dissertation. *Entrance requirements:* For master's and doctorate, GRE. Additional exam requirements/recommendations for international students: required—TOEFL. Electronic applications accepted. *Expenses:* Contact institution.

**University of California, Irvine,** School of Biological Sciences, Department of Neurobiology and Behavior, Irvine, CA 92697. Offers biological sciences (MS, PhD); MD/PhD. *Students:* 45 full-time (26 women); includes 20 minority (2 Black or African American, non-Hispanic/Latino; 1 American Indian or Alaska Native, non-Hispanic/Latino; 8 Asian, non-Hispanic/Latino; 9 Hispanic/Latino), 3 international. Average age 28. In 2019, 7 master's, 2 doctorates awarded. *Entrance requirements:* For master's and doctorate, GRE General Test, GRE Subject Test, minimum GPA of 3.0. Additional exam requirements/recommendations for international students: required—TOEFL (minimum score 550 paper-based). *Application deadline:* For fall admission, 1/15 priority date for domestic students, 1/15 for international students. Applications are processed on a rolling basis. Application fee: $120 ($140 for international students). Electronic applications accepted. *Financial support:* Fellowships, research assistantships with full tuition reimbursements, teaching assistantships, institutionally sponsored loans, traineeships, health care benefits, and unspecified assistantships available. Financial award application deadline: 3/1; financial award applicants required to submit FAFSA. *Unit head:* Marcelo A. Wood, Chair, 949-824-6114, Fax: 949-824-2447, E-mail: mwood@uci.edu. *Application contact:* Sally Dabiri, Department Administrator, 949-824-4727, Fax: 949-824-2447, E-mail: sfdabiri@uci.edu.
Website: http://neurobiology.uci.edu/

**University of California, Irvine,** School of Medicine and School of Biological Sciences, Department of Anatomy and Neurobiology, Irvine, CA 92697. Offers biological sciences (MS, PhD); MD/PhD. *Students:* 15 full-time (9 women), 3 part-time (2 women); includes 8 minority (5 Asian, non-Hispanic/Latino; 3 Hispanic/Latino), 2 international. Average age 28. *Entrance requirements:* For master's and doctorate, GRE General Test, GRE Subject Test. Additional exam requirements/recommendations for international students: required—TOEFL (minimum score 550 paper-based). *Application deadline:* For fall admission, 1/15 priority date for domestic students, 1/15 for international students. Applications are processed on a rolling basis. Application fee: $120 ($140 for international students). Electronic applications accepted. *Financial support:* Fellowships, research assistantships with full tuition reimbursements, teaching assistantships, institutionally sponsored loans, traineeships, health care benefits, and unspecified assistantships available. Financial award application deadline: 3/1; financial award applicants required to submit FAFSA. *Unit head:* Prof. Christine Gall, Interim Chair, 949-824-8652, Fax: 949-824-1255, E-mail: cmgall@uci.edu. *Application contact:* David Lyon, Director of Graduate Studies, 949-824-0447, E-mail: dclyon@uci.edu.
Website: http://anatomy.uci.edu/

**University of California, Los Angeles,** David Geffen School of Medicine and Graduate Division, Graduate Programs in Medicine, Department of Neurobiology, Los Angeles, CA 90095. Offers MS, PhD. Terminal master's awarded for partial completion of doctoral program. *Degree requirements:* For master's, comprehensive exam; for doctorate, thesis/dissertation, oral and written qualifying exams; 2 quarters of teaching experience. *Entrance requirements:* For doctorate, GRE General Test; GRE Subject Test, bachelor's degree; minimum undergraduate GPA of 3.0 (or its equivalent if letter grade system not used). Additional exam requirements/recommendations for international students: required—TOEFL. Electronic applications accepted.

**University of California, Los Angeles,** Graduate Division, College of Letters and Science and David Geffen School of Medicine, UCLA ACCESS to Programs in the Molecular, Cellular and Integrative Life Sciences, Los Angeles, CA 90095. Offers biochemistry and molecular biology (PhD); biological chemistry (PhD); cellular and molecular pathology (PhD); human genetics (PhD); microbiology, immunology, and molecular genetics (PhD); molecular biology (PhD); molecular toxicology (PhD); molecular, cellular and integrative physiology (PhD); neurobiology (PhD); oral biology (PhD); physiology (PhD). *Degree requirements:* For doctorate, thesis/dissertation, oral and written qualifying exams. *Entrance requirements:* For doctorate, GRE General Test, bachelor's degree; minimum undergraduate GPA of 3.0 (or its equivalent if letter grade system not used). Additional exam requirements/recommendations for international students: required—TOEFL. Electronic applications accepted.

**University of Chicago,** Division of the Biological Sciences, Program in Neurobiology, Chicago, IL 60637. Offers PhD. *Degree requirements:* For doctorate, comprehensive exam, thesis/dissertation, ethics class, 2 teaching assistantships. *Entrance requirements:* For doctorate, GRE General Test, transcripts, statement of purpose, 3 letters of recommendation. Additional exam requirements/recommendations for international students: required—TOEFL (minimum score 600 paper-based; 104 iBT), IELTS (minimum score 7). Electronic applications accepted.

**University of Connecticut,** Graduate School, College of Liberal Arts and Sciences, Department of Physiology and Neurobiology, Storrs, CT 06269. Offers comparative physiology (MS, PhD). Terminal master's awarded for partial completion of doctoral program. *Degree requirements:* For master's, comprehensive exam; for doctorate, thesis/dissertation. *Entrance requirements:* For master's and doctorate, GRE General Test, GRE Subject Test. Additional exam requirements/recommendations for international students: required—TOEFL (minimum score 550 paper-based). Electronic applications accepted.

**The University of Iowa,** Graduate College, College of Liberal Arts and Sciences, Department of Biology, Iowa City, IA 52242-1324. Offers biology (MS, PhD); cell and developmental biology (MS, PhD); evolution (MS, PhD); genetics (MS, PhD); neurobiology (MS, PhD). Terminal master's awarded for partial completion of doctoral program. *Degree requirements:* For master's, thesis optional, exam; for doctorate, comprehensive exam, thesis/dissertation. *Entrance requirements:* For master's and doctorate, GRE General Test, minimum GPA of 3.0. Additional exam requirements/ recommendations for international students: required—TOEFL (minimum score 600 paper-based; 100 iBT). Electronic applications accepted.

**University of Kentucky,** Graduate School, Graduate School Programs from the College of Medicine, Program in Anatomy and Neurobiology, Lexington, KY 40506-0032. Offers PhD. *Degree requirements:* For doctorate, comprehensive exam, thesis/ dissertation. *Entrance requirements:* For doctorate, GRE General Test, minimum undergraduate GPA of 2.75. Additional exam requirements/recommendations for international students: required—TOEFL (minimum score 550 paper-based). Electronic applications accepted.

**University of Louisville,** School of Medicine, Department of Anatomical Sciences and Neurobiology, Louisville, KY 40292-0001. Offers MS, PhD, MD/PhD. *Faculty:* 16 full-time (5 women), 2 part-time/adjunct (0 women). *Students:* 24 full-time (7 women), 4 part-time (2 women); includes 2 minority (1 Asian, non-Hispanic/Latino; 1 Hispanic/Latino), 3 international. Average age 30. 29 applicants, 52% accepted, 10 enrolled. In 2019, 9 master's, 6 doctorates awarded. Terminal master's awarded for partial completion of doctoral program. *Degree requirements:* For master's, thesis (for some programs); for doctorate, comprehensive exam, thesis/dissertation. *Entrance requirements:* For master's and doctorate, GRE General Test (Verbal + Quantitative score of 300), Minimum GPA 3.0. Additional exam requirements/recommendations for international students: required—TOEFL (minimum score 550 paper-based; 79 iBT). *Application deadline:* For fall admission, 2/15 priority date for domestic and international students. Application fee: $65. Electronic applications accepted. *Expenses: Tuition, area resident:* Full-time $13,000; part-time $723 per credit hour. Tuition, state resident: full-time $13,000; part-time $723 per credit hour. Tuition, nonresident: full-time $27,114; part-time $1507 per credit hour. *International tuition:* $27,114 full-time. *Required fees:* $196. Tuition and fees vary according to program and reciprocity agreements. *Financial support:* In 2019–20, 25 students received support, including 6 fellowships with full tuition reimbursements available (averaging $25,000 per year); health care benefits and unspecified assistantships also available. Financial award application deadline: 2/15. *Unit head:* Dr. William Guido, Professor and Chair, 502-852-5165, Fax: 502-852-6228, E-mail: w0guid01@gwise.louisville.edu. *Application contact:* Dr. Patrick Moore, Admissions Director, 502-852-1311, E-mail: jpmoor03@louisville.edu. Website: http://louisville.edu/medicine/departments/anatomy

**The University of Manchester,** School of Biological Sciences, Manchester, United Kingdom. Offers adaptive organismal biology (M Phil, PhD); animal biology (M Phil, PhD); biochemistry (M Phil, PhD); bioinformatics (M Phil, PhD); biomolecular sciences (M Phil, PhD); biotechnology (M Phil, PhD); cell biology (M Phil, PhD); cell matrix research (M Phil, PhD); channels and transporters (M Phil, PhD); developmental biology (M Phil, PhD); environmental biology (M Phil, PhD); evolutionary biology (M Phil, PhD); gene expression (M Phil, PhD); genetics (M Phil, PhD); history of science, technology and medicine (M Phil, PhD); immunology (M Phil, PhD); integrative neurobiology and behavior (M Phil, PhD); membrane trafficking (M Phil, PhD); microbiology (M Phil, PhD); molecular and cellular neuroscience (M Phil, PhD); molecular biology (M Phil, PhD); molecular cancer studies (M Phil, PhD); neuroscience (M Phil, PhD); ophthalmology (M Phil, PhD); optometry (M Phil, PhD); organelle function (M Phil, PhD); pharmacology (M Phil, PhD); physiology (M Phil, PhD); plant sciences (M Phil, PhD); stem cell research (M Phil, PhD); structural biology (M Phil, PhD); systems neuroscience (M Phil, PhD); toxicology (M Phil, PhD).

**University of Maryland, Baltimore,** Graduate School, Graduate Program in Life Sciences, Program in Neuroscience, Baltimore, MD 21201. Offers PhD, MD/PhD. *Program availability:* Part-time. *Degree requirements:* For doctorate, comprehensive exam, thesis/dissertation. *Entrance requirements:* For doctorate, GRE General Test, minimum GPA of 3.0, curriculum vitae, essay, 3 letters of recommendation. Additional exam requirements/recommendations for international students: required—TOEFL (minimum score 80 iBT); recommended—IELTS (minimum score 7). Electronic applications accepted.

**University of Minnesota, Twin Cities Campus,** Graduate School, Graduate Program in Neuroscience, Minneapolis, MN 55455-0213. Offers MS, PhD. Terminal master's awarded for partial completion of doctoral program. *Degree requirements:* For master's, thesis; for doctorate, thesis/dissertation. *Entrance requirements:* For doctorate, GRE. Additional exam requirements/recommendations for international students: required—TOEFL. Electronic applications accepted.

**The University of North Carolina at Chapel Hill,** School of Medicine and Graduate School, Biological and Biomedical Sciences Program, Curriculum in Neuroscience, Chapel Hill, NC 27599. Offers PhD. *Faculty:* 68 full-time (21 women), 15 part-time/ adjunct (2 women). *Students:* 32 full-time (22 women); includes 11 minority (5 Black or African American, non-Hispanic/Latino; 4 Asian, non-Hispanic/Latino; 1 Hispanic/Latino; 1 Two or more races, non-Hispanic/Latino), 3 international. Average age 26. In 2019, 9 doctorates awarded. *Degree requirements:* For doctorate, comprehensive exam, thesis/ dissertation. *Entrance requirements:* Additional exam requirements/recommendations for international students: required—TOEFL. *Application deadline:* For fall admission, 12/3 priority date for domestic and international students. Applications are processed on a rolling basis. Application fee: $55. Electronic applications accepted. *Financial support:* In 2019–20, 11 fellowships with full tuition reimbursements (averaging $32,000 per year), 26 research assistantships with full tuition reimbursements (averaging $32,000 per year) were awarded; career-related internships or fieldwork, health care benefits, and tuition waivers (full) also available. *Unit head:* Dr. Jay Brenman, Director, 919-843-

3637, E-mail: jay_brenman@med.unc.edu. *Application contact:* Jeffrey Steinbach, Assistant Director of Admissions, 919-843-7129, E-mail: jsteinba@email.unc.edu. Website: https://www.med.unc.edu/neuroscience/curriculum/

**University of Oklahoma,** College of Arts and Sciences, Department of Biology, Norman, OK 73019. Offers biology (MS, PhD); cellular and behavioral neurobiology (PhD), including biology; ecology and evolutionary biology (PhD), including biology. *Degree requirements:* For master's, thesis, course in biostatistics; for doctorate, comprehensive exam, thesis/dissertation, course in biostatistics, 2 semesters as teaching assistant. *Entrance requirements:* For master's and doctorate, GRE General Test, transcripts, 3 letters of recommendation, personal statement, curriculum vitae. Additional exam requirements/recommendations for international students: required— TOEFL (minimum score 79 iBT) or IELTS (minimum score 6.5). Electronic applications accepted. *Expenses:* Tuition, state resident: full-time $6583.20; part-time $274.30 per credit hour. Tuition, nonresident: full-time $21,242; part-time $885.10 per credit hour. *International tuition:* $21,242.40 full-time. *Required fees:* $1994.20; $72.55 per credit hour. $126.50 per semester. Tuition and fees vary according to course load and degree level.

**University of Rochester,** School of Medicine and Dentistry, Graduate Programs in Medicine and Dentistry, Department of Neurobiology and Anatomy, Programs in Neurobiology and Anatomy, Rochester, NY 14627. Offers PhD, MD/MS. *Degree requirements:* For doctorate, thesis/dissertation, qualifying exam. *Entrance requirements:* For doctorate, GRE General Test.

**University of Southern California,** Graduate School, Dana and David Dornsife College of Letters, Arts and Sciences, Department of Biological Sciences, Program in Neurobiology, Los Angeles, CA 90089. Offers PhD. Terminal master's awarded for partial completion of doctoral program. *Degree requirements:* For doctorate, comprehensive exam, thesis/dissertation, qualifying examination, dissertation defense. *Entrance requirements:* For doctorate, GRE, 3 letters of recommendation, personal statement, resume, minimum GPA of 3.0. Additional exam requirements/ recommendations for international students: required—TOEFL (minimum score 600 paper-based; 100 iBT). Electronic applications accepted.

**The University of Texas at Austin,** Graduate School, The Institute for Neuroscience, Austin, TX 78712-1111. Offers PhD, MD/PhD. Terminal master's awarded for partial completion of doctoral program. *Degree requirements:* For doctorate, thesis/ dissertation. *Entrance requirements:* For doctorate, GRE. Electronic applications accepted.

**The University of Texas at San Antonio,** College of Sciences, Department of Biology, San Antonio, TX 78249-0617. Offers biology (MS); biotechnology (MS); cell and molecular biology (PhD); neurobiology (PhD). Terminal master's awarded for partial completion of doctoral program. *Degree requirements:* For master's, comprehensive exam, thesis or alternative; for doctorate, comprehensive exam, thesis/dissertation. *Entrance requirements:* For master's, GRE General Test, bachelor's degree with 18 credit hours in field of study or in another appropriate field of study; for doctorate, GRE General Test, 3 letters of recommendation, statement of purpose, resume. Additional exam requirements/recommendations for international students: required—TOEFL (minimum score 500 paper-based; 100 iBT), IELTS (minimum score 5). Electronic applications accepted.

**University of Utah,** School of Medicine and Graduate School, Graduate Programs in Medicine, Department of Neurobiology and Anatomy, Salt Lake City, UT 84112-1107. Offers PhD. *Program availability:* Part-time. Terminal master's awarded for partial completion of doctoral program. *Degree requirements:* For doctorate, comprehensive exam, thesis/dissertation. *Entrance requirements:* For doctorate, GRE General Test. Additional exam requirements/recommendations for international students: required— TOEFL. *Expenses:* Tuition, state resident: full-time $7085; part-time $272.51 per credit hour. Tuition, nonresident: full-time $24,937; part-time $959.12 per credit hour. *Required fees:* $880.52; $880.52 per semester. Tuition and fees vary according to degree level, program and student level.

**University of Washington,** Graduate School, School of Medicine, Graduate Programs in Medicine, Graduate Program in Neurobiology and Behavior, Seattle, WA 98195. Offers PhD. *Degree requirements:* For doctorate, thesis/dissertation. *Entrance requirements:* For doctorate, GRE. Additional exam requirements/recommendations for international students: required—TOEFL. Electronic applications accepted.

**Université Laval,** Faculty of Medicine, Graduate Programs in Medicine, Programs in Neurobiology, Québec, QC G1K 7P4, Canada. Offers M Sc, PhD. Terminal master's awarded for partial completion of doctoral program. *Degree requirements:* For master's, thesis; for doctorate, comprehensive exam, thesis/dissertation. *Entrance requirements:* For master's and doctorate, knowledge of French and English. Electronic applications accepted.

**Virginia Commonwealth University,** Medical College of Virginia-Professional Programs, School of Medicine, Graduate Programs in Medicine, Department of Anatomy and Neurobiology, Richmond, VA 23284-9005. Offers MS. *Degree requirements:* For master's, thesis. *Entrance requirements:* For master's, GRE, MCAT or DAT. Electronic applications accepted.

**Wake Forest University,** School of Medicine and Graduate School of Arts and Sciences, Graduate Programs in Medicine, Department of Neurobiology and Anatomy, Winston-Salem, NC 27109. Offers PhD, MD/PhD. *Degree requirements:* For doctorate, thesis/dissertation. *Entrance requirements:* For doctorate, GRE General Test. Additional exam requirements/recommendations for international students: required—TOEFL. Electronic applications accepted.

**Wesleyan University,** Graduate Studies, Department of Biology, Middletown, CT 06459. Offers cell and developmental biology (PhD); evolution and ecology (PhD); genetics and genomics (PhD), including bioinformatics; neurobiology and behavior (PhD). Terminal master's awarded for partial completion of doctoral program. *Degree requirements:* For doctorate, comprehensive exam, thesis/dissertation, public seminar. *Entrance requirements:* For doctorate, GRE, official transcripts, three recommendation letters, essay. Additional exam requirements/recommendations for international students: required—TOEFL. Electronic applications accepted.

**Yale University,** Graduate School of Arts and Sciences, Department of Molecular, Cellular, and Developmental Biology, Program in Neurobiology, New Haven, CT 06520. Offers PhD. *Degree requirements:* For doctorate, thesis/dissertation. *Entrance requirements:* For doctorate, GRE General Test, GRE Subject Test.

**Yale University,** Yale School of Medicine and Graduate School of Arts and Sciences, Combined Program in Biological and Biomedical Sciences (BBS), Department of Neurobiology, New Haven, CT 06520. Offers PhD. *Degree requirements:* For doctorate, thesis/dissertation. *Entrance requirements:* For doctorate, GRE General Test, GRE Subject Test.

# Neuroscience

**Albany Medical College,** Center for Neuropharmacology and Neuroscience, Albany, NY 12208-3479. Offers MS, PhD. Terminal master's awarded for partial completion of doctoral program. *Degree requirements:* For master's, thesis; for doctorate, comprehensive exam, thesis/dissertation. *Entrance requirements:* For master's, GRE General Test, all transcripts, letters of recommendation; for doctorate, GRE General Test, letters of recommendation. Additional exam requirements/recommendations for international students: required—TOEFL.

**Albert Einstein College of Medicine,** Graduate Programs in the Biomedical Sciences, Dominick P. Purpura Department of Neuroscience, Bronx, NY 10461. Offers PhD, MD/PhD. *Degree requirements:* For doctorate, thesis/dissertation, qualifying exam. *Entrance requirements:* For doctorate, GRE General Test. Additional exam requirements/recommendations for international students: required—TOEFL.

**Alliant International University - San Diego,** Shirley M. Hufstedler School of Education, Educational Psychology Programs, San Diego, CA 92131. Offers educational psychology (Psy D); pupil personnel services (Credential); school neuropsychology (Certificate); school psychology (MA); school-based mental health (Certificate). *Program availability:* Part-time. *Degree requirements:* For doctorate, comprehensive exam, thesis/dissertation, internship. *Entrance requirements:* For master's, minimum GPA of 2.5, letters of recommendation; for doctorate, minimum GPA of 3.0, letters of recommendation. Additional exam requirements/recommendations for international students: required—TOEFL (minimum score 550 paper-based; 80 iBT), TWE (minimum score 5). Electronic applications accepted.

**American University,** College of Arts and Sciences, Department of Psychology, Washington, DC 22016-8062. Offers addiction and addictive behavior (Certificate); behavior, cognition, and neuroscience (PhD); clinical psychology (PhD); psychobiology of healing (Certificate); psychology (MA). *Accreditation:* APA. *Program availability:* Part-time. *Degree requirements:* For master's, comprehensive exam, thesis or alternative; for doctorate, comprehensive exam, thesis/dissertation. *Entrance requirements:* For master's, GRE General Test, GRE Subject Test; Please website: https://www.american.edu/cas/psychology/, statement of purpose, transcripts, 2 letters of recommendation; for doctorate, GRE General Test, GRE Subject Test, 3 letters of recommendation, statement of purpose, transcripts, resume. Additional exam requirements/recommendations for international students: required—TOEFL (minimum score 600 paper-based; 100 iBT). *Expenses:* Contact institution.

**Argosy University, Chicago,** Illinois School of Professional Psychology, Doctoral Program in Clinical Psychology, Chicago, IL 60601. Offers child and adolescent psychology (Psy D); client-centered and experiential psychotherapies (Psy D); diversity and multicultural psychology (Psy D); family psychology (Psy D); forensic psychology (Psy D); health psychology (Psy D); neuropsychology (Psy D); organizational consulting (Psy D); psychoanalytic psychology (Psy D); psychology and spirituality (Psy D). *Accreditation:* APA.

**Argosy University, Phoenix,** Arizona School of Professional Psychology, Program in Clinical Psychology, Phoenix, AZ 85021. Offers clinical psychology (MA); neuropsychology (Psy D); sports-exercise psychology (Psy D).

**Argosy University, Phoenix,** Arizona School of Professional Psychology, Program in Neuropsychology, Phoenix, AZ 85021. Offers Psy D.

**Argosy University, Tampa,** Florida School of Professional Psychology, Program in Clinical Psychology, Tampa, FL 33607. Offers clinical psychology (MA, Psy D), including child and adolescent psychology (Psy D), geropsychology (Psy D), marriage/couples and family therapy (Psy D), neuropsychology (Psy D). *Accreditation:* APA.

**Arizona State University at Tempe,** College of Liberal Arts and Sciences, Department of Psychology, Tempe, AZ 85287-1104. Offers applied behavior analysis (MS); behavioral neuroscience (PhD); clinical psychology (PhD); cognitive science (PhD); developmental psychology (PhD); quantitative psychology (PhD); social psychology (PhD). *Accreditation:* APA. *Degree requirements:* For doctorate, comprehensive exam, thesis/dissertation, interactive Program of Study (iPOS) submitted before completing 50 percent of required credit hours. *Entrance requirements:* For doctorate, GRE General Test, GRE Subject Test, minimum GPA of 3.0 or equivalent in last 2 years of work leading to bachelor's degree. Additional exam requirements/recommendations for international students: required—TOEFL, IELTS, or PTE. Electronic applications accepted.

**Arizona State University at Tempe,** College of Liberal Arts and Sciences, School of Life Sciences, Tempe, AZ 85287-4601. Offers animal behavior (PhD); applied ethics (biomedical and health ethics) (MA); biology (MS, PhD), including biology, biology and society, complex adaptive systems science (PhD), plant biology and conservation (MS); environmental life sciences (PhD); evolutionary biology (PhD); history and philosophy of science (PhD); human and social dimensions of science and technology (PhD); microbiology (PhD); molecular and cellular biology (PhD); neuroscience (PhD). Terminal master's awarded for partial completion of doctoral program. *Degree requirements:* For master's, thesis (for some programs), interactive Program of Study (iPOS) submitted before completing 50 percent of required credit hours; for doctorate, variable foreign language requirement, comprehensive exam, thesis/dissertation, interactive Program of Study (iPOS) submitted before completing 50 percent of required credit hours. *Entrance requirements:* For master's and doctorate, GRE, minimum GPA of 3.0 or equivalent in last 2 years of work leading to bachelor's degree. Additional exam requirements/recommendations for international students: required—TOEFL (minimum score 600 paper-based; 100 iBT). Electronic applications accepted.

**Arizona State University at Tempe,** Graduate College, Interdisciplinary Graduate Program in Neuroscience, Tempe, AZ 85287-1003. Offers PhD. Terminal master's awarded for partial completion of doctoral program. *Degree requirements:* For doctorate, comprehensive exam, thesis/dissertation, all students must submit an interactive Program of Study (iPOS) before completing 50 percent of the credit hours required for their degree program. A student is not eligible to apply for the Foreign Language Examination (if appl), comprehensive exams, dissertation proposal/prospectus or dissertation defense (if appl) without an approved iPOS. *Entrance requirements:* For doctorate, GRE, GPA of 3.0 or better in the last 2 years of work leading to the bachelor's degree, 3 letters of recommendation, statement of research interests and goals, CV or resume, and the completed Interdisciplinary Neuroscience Academic Record form. Additional exam requirements/recommendations for international students: required—TOEFL (minimum score 550 paper-based; 80 iBT), IELTS (minimum score 6.5). Electronic applications accepted.

**Augusta University,** Program in Neuroscience, Augusta, GA 30912. Offers PhD. *Degree requirements:* For doctorate, comprehensive exam, thesis/dissertation. *Entrance requirements:* For doctorate, GRE General Test. Additional exam requirements/recommendations for international students: required—TOEFL (minimum score 550 paper-based; 79 iBT). Electronic applications accepted.

**Ball State University,** Graduate School, Teachers College, Department of Educational Psychology, Muncie, IN 47306. Offers educational psychology (MA, MS), including educational psychology (MA, MS, PhD); educational psychology (PhD), including educational psychology (MA, MS, PhD); gifted and talented education (Certificate); human development and learning (Certificate); instructional design and assessment (Certificate); neuropsychology (Certificate); quantitative psychology (MS); response to intervention (Certificate); school psychology (MA, PhD), including school psychology (MA, PhD, Ed S); school psychology (Ed S), including school psychology (MA, PhD, Ed S). *Program availability:* 100% online. *Degree requirements:* For doctorate, thesis/dissertation; for other advanced degree, thesis. *Entrance requirements:* For master's, GRE General Test, minimum baccalaureate GPA of 2.75 or 3.0 in latter half of baccalaureate, professional goals and self-assessment; for doctorate, GRE General Test, minimum graduate GPA of 3.2; for other advanced degree, GRE General Test. Additional exam requirements/recommendations for international students: required—TOEFL (minimum score 550 paper-based; 79 iBT), IELTS (minimum score 6.5). Electronic applications accepted. *Expenses: Tuition, area resident:* Full-time $7506; part-time $417 per credit hour. Tuition, nonresident: full-time $20,610; part-time $1145 per credit hour. *Required fees:* $2126. Tuition and fees vary according to course load, campus/location and program.

**Baylor College of Medicine,** Graduate School of Biomedical Sciences, Department of Neuroscience, Houston, TX 77030-3498. Offers PhD, MD/PhD. *Degree requirements:* For doctorate, thesis/dissertation, public defense. *Entrance requirements:* For doctorate, GRE General Test, GRE Subject Test (strongly recommended), minimum GPA of 3.0. Additional exam requirements/recommendations for international students: required—TOEFL. Electronic applications accepted.

**Boston University,** School of Medicine, Graduate Medical Sciences, Graduate Program for Neuroscience, Boston, MA 02215. Offers PhD. *Unit head:* Dr. Shelley Russek, Director, E-mail: srussek@bu.edu. *Application contact:* GMS Admissions Office, 617-358-9518, Fax: 617-358-2913, E-mail: gmsbusm@bu.edu.
Website: http://www.bu.edu/neuro/graduate/

**Boston University,** School of Medicine, Graduate Medical Sciences, Program in Behavioral Neuroscience, Boston, MA 02215. Offers PhD. *Program availability:* Part-time. *Application deadline:* For fall admission, 1/15 for domestic students; for spring admission, 10/15 for domestic students. *Financial support:* Federal Work-Study, scholarships/grants, and traineeships available. *Unit head:* Dr. Carole Palumbo, Director, E-mail: cpalumbo@bu.edu. *Application contact:* GMS Admissions Office, 617-358-9518, Fax: 617-358-2913, E-mail: gmsbusm@bu.edu.
Website: http://www.bumc.bu.edu/gms/behavioral-neuroscience/

**Brandeis University,** Graduate School of Arts and Sciences, Department of Neuroscience, Waltham, MA 02454-9110. Offers neuroscience (MS, PhD); quantitative biology (PhD). *Program availability:* Part-time. *Faculty:* 26 full-time (12 women). *Students:* 60 full-time (29 women), 2 part-time (0 women); includes 18 minority (2 Black or African American, non-Hispanic/Latino; 1 American Indian or Alaska Native, non-Hispanic/Latino; 3 Asian, non-Hispanic/Latino; 9 Hispanic/Latino; 3 Two or more races, non-Hispanic/Latino), 13 international. Average age 27. 169 applicants, 27% accepted, 13 enrolled. In 2019, 13 master's, 7 doctorates awarded. Terminal master's awarded for partial completion of doctoral program. *Degree requirements:* For master's, thesis optional; for doctorate, comprehensive exam, thesis/dissertation. *Entrance requirements:* For master's, transcripts, letters of recommendation, resume, statement of purpose; for doctorate, transcripts, letters of recommendation, resume, program questions, statement of purpose. Additional exam requirements/recommendations for international students: required—TOEFL, IELTS, PTE. *Application deadline:* For fall admission, 12/1 priority date for domestic and international students. Applications are processed on a rolling basis. Application fee: $75. Electronic applications accepted. *Financial support:* In 2019–20, 64 fellowships with full tuition reimbursements (averaging $35,000 per year), 10 teaching assistantships (averaging $3,550 per year) were awarded; scholarships/grants, health care benefits, and tuition waivers also available. Support available to part-time students. *Unit head:* Dr. Susan Birren, Director of Graduate Studies, 781-736-2680, E-mail: birren@brandeis.edu. *Application contact:* Maryanna Aldrich, Administrator, 781-736-2352, E-mail: scigradoffice@brandeis.edu.
Website: http://www.brandeis.edu/gsas/programs/neuroscience.html

**Brandeis University,** Graduate School of Arts and Sciences, Department of Psychology, Waltham, MA 02454-9110. Offers brain, body and behavior (PhD); cognitive neuroscience (PhD); general psychology (MA); social/developmental psychology (PhD). *Program availability:* Part-time. *Faculty:* 14 full-time (7 women), 3 part-time/adjunct (all women). *Students:* 31 full-time (21 women), 1 (woman) part-time; includes 6 minority (4 Asian, non-Hispanic/Latino; 2 Hispanic/Latino), 8 international. Average age 26. 157 applicants, 14% accepted, 12 enrolled. In 2019, 18 master's, 2 doctorates awarded. Terminal master's awarded for partial completion of doctoral program. *Degree requirements:* For master's, thesis (for some programs); for doctorate, thesis/dissertation. *Entrance requirements:* For master's and doctorate, GRE General (GRE Subject recommended), transcripts, letters of recommendation, resume, statement of purpose. Additional exam requirements/recommendations for international students: required—TOEFL, IELTS, PTE. *Application deadline:* For fall admission, 12/1 priority date for domestic and international students. Applications are processed on a rolling basis. Application fee: $75. Electronic applications accepted. *Financial support:* In 2019–20, 23 fellowships with full tuition reimbursements (averaging $25,000 per year), 16 teaching assistantships (averaging $3,550 per year) were awarded; research assistantships, scholarships/grants, traineeships, health care benefits, and tuition waivers also available. Support available to part-time students. *Unit head:* Dr. Angela Gutchess, Director of Graduate Studies, 781-736-3247, E-mail: gutchess@brandeis.edu. *Application contact:* Sarah Lupis, Administrator, 781-736-3303, E-mail: slupis@brandeis.edu.
Website: http://www.brandeis.edu/gsas/programs/psychology.html

**Brigham Young University,** Graduate Studies, College of Family, Home, and Social Sciences, Department of Psychology, Provo, UT 84602. Offers clinical psychology (PhD); cognitive and behavioral neuroscience (PhD). *Accreditation:* APA. *Faculty:* 24 full-time (9 women), 3 part-time/adjunct (0 women). *Students:* 62 full-time (39 women); includes 10 minority (3 Black or African American, non-Hispanic/Latino; 1 American Indian or Alaska Native, non-Hispanic/Latino; 5 Asian, non-Hispanic/Latino; 1 Hispanic/Latino), 4 international. Average age 29. 76 applicants, 22% accepted, 11 enrolled. In 2019, 8 doctorates awarded. *Degree requirements:* For doctorate, comprehensive exam, thesis/dissertation, publishable paper. *Entrance requirements:* For doctorate, GRE General Test, minimum GPA of 3.0. Additional exam requirements/

recommendations for international students: required—TOEFL (minimum score 580 paper-based; 85 iBT). *Application deadline:* For fall admission, 12/1 for domestic and international students. Application fee: $50. Electronic applications accepted. *Expenses:* $18,226/LDS $25,512/Non-LDS. *Financial support:* In 2019–20, 41 students received support, including 43 research assistantships with partial tuition reimbursements available (averaging $12,000 per year), 7 teaching assistantships with partial tuition reimbursements available (averaging $12,000 per year); scholarships/grants and unspecified assistantships also available. Financial award application deadline: 5/31. *Unit head:* Dr. Gary Burlingame, Chair, 801-422-7557, Fax: 801-422-0602, E-mail: gary_burlingame@byu.edu. *Application contact:* Rachelle Gunderson, Coordinator of Student Programs, 801-422-4560, Fax: 801-422-0602, E-mail: leesa_scott@byu.edu. Website: http://psychology.byu.edu/

**Brigham Young University,** Graduate Studies, College of Life Sciences, Department of Physiology and Developmental Biology, Provo, UT 84602. Offers neuroscience (MS, PhD); physiology and developmental biology (MS, PhD). *Program availability:* Part-time. *Faculty:* 22 full-time (1 woman). *Students:* 15 full-time (7 women); includes 5 minority (all Asian, non-Hispanic/Latino). Average age 31. 7 applicants, 29% accepted. In 2019, 5 master's, 1 doctorate awarded. Terminal master's awarded for partial completion of doctoral program. *Degree requirements:* For master's, thesis, Coursework Oral Exam; for doctorate, comprehensive exam, thesis/dissertation. *Entrance requirements:* For master's, GRE General Test, MCAT, or DAT, minimum GPA of 3.0 during previous 2 years; for doctorate, GRE General Test, minimum GPA of 3.0 overall. Additional exam requirements/recommendations for international students: required—TOEFL (minimum score 580 paper-based; 85 iBT), E3PT; recommended—IELTS. *Application deadline:* For fall admission, 1/15 priority date for domestic and international students. Application fee: $50. Electronic applications accepted. *Financial support:* In 2019–20, 16 students received support, including 1 fellowship with full tuition reimbursement available (averaging $7,200 per year), 12 research assistantships with full tuition reimbursements available (averaging $6,400 per year), 2 teaching assistantships with partial tuition reimbursements available (averaging $6,000 per year); career-related internships or fieldwork, institutionally sponsored loans, scholarships/grants, tuition waivers (full and partial), unspecified assistantships, and tuition awards also available. Financial award application deadline: 2/1; financial award applicants required to submit FAFSA. *Unit head:* Dr. Michael R. Stark, Chair, 801-422-9498, Fax: 801-422-0004, E-mail: michael_stark@byu.edu. *Application contact:* Connie L. Provost, Graduate Program Manager, 801-422-3706, Fax: 801-422-0004, E-mail: connie_provost@byu.edu. Website: http://pdbio.byu.edu

**Brock University,** Faculty of Graduate Studies, Faculty of Social Sciences, Program in Psychology, St. Catharines, ON L2S 3A1, Canada. Offers behavioral neuroscience (MA, PhD); life span development (MA, PhD); social personality (MA, PhD). *Program availability:* Part-time. *Degree requirements:* For master's, thesis; for doctorate, thesis/dissertation. *Entrance requirements:* For master's, GRE, honors degree; for doctorate, GRE, master's degree. Additional exam requirements/recommendations for international students: required—TOEFL (minimum score 550 paper-based; 80 iBT), IELTS (minimum score 6.5), TWE (minimum score 4). Electronic applications accepted.

**Brown University,** Graduate School, Division of Biology and Medicine, Department of Neuroscience, Providence, RI 02912. Offers PhD. *Degree requirements:* For doctorate, thesis/dissertation, preliminary exam. *Entrance requirements:* For doctorate, GRE General Test, GRE Subject Test. Additional exam requirements/recommendations for international students: required—TOEFL. Electronic applications accepted.

**Brown University,** National Institutes of Health Sponsored Programs, Providence, RI 02912. Offers neuroscience (PhD).

**California Institute of Technology,** Division of Engineering and Applied Science, Option in Computation and Neural Systems, Pasadena, CA 91125-0001. Offers MS, PhD. Terminal master's awarded for partial completion of doctoral program. *Degree requirements:* For doctorate, thesis/dissertation, qualifying exam. *Entrance requirements:* For doctorate, GRE General Test.

**Carleton University,** Faculty of Graduate Studies, Faculty of Arts and Social Sciences, Department of Psychology, Ottawa, ON K1S 5B6, Canada. Offers neuroscience (M Sc); psychology (MA, PhD). *Program availability:* Part-time. *Degree requirements:* For master's, thesis; for doctorate, comprehensive exam, thesis/dissertation. *Entrance requirements:* For master's, honors degree; for doctorate, GRE, master's degree. Additional exam requirements/recommendations for international students: required—TOEFL.

**Carnegie Mellon University,** Center for the Neural Basis of Cognition, Pittsburgh, PA 15213-3891. Offers PhD.

**Case Western Reserve University,** School of Medicine and School of Graduate Studies, Graduate Programs in Medicine, Department of Neurosciences, Cleveland, OH 44106. Offers neuroscience (PhD); MD/PhD. Terminal master's awarded for partial completion of doctoral program. *Degree requirements:* For doctorate, thesis/dissertation. *Entrance requirements:* For doctorate, GRE General Test, 3 letters of recommendation. Additional exam requirements/recommendations for international students: required—TOEFL (minimum score 90 iBT). Electronic applications accepted.

**Central Michigan University,** College of Graduate Studies, College of Liberal Arts and Social Sciences, Department of Psychology, Program in Neuroscience, Mount Pleasant, MI 48859. Offers MS, PhD. *Degree requirements:* For master's, comprehensive exam, thesis or alternative; for doctorate, thesis/dissertation. *Entrance requirements:* For master's and doctorate, GRE. Electronic applications accepted. *Expenses: Tuition, area resident:* Full-time $12,267; part-time $8178 per year. Tuition, state resident: full-time $12,267; part-time $8178 per year. Tuition, nonresident: full-time $12,267; part-time $8178 per year. *International tuition:* $16,110 full-time. *Required fees:* $225 per semester. Tuition and fees vary according to degree level and program.

**College of Staten Island of the City University of New York,** Graduate Programs, Division of Science and Technology, Program in Neuroscience and Developmental Disabilities, Staten Island, NY 10314-6600. Offers MS. *Program availability:* Part-time, evening/weekend. *Faculty:* 8. *Students:* 25. 28 applicants, 46% accepted, 8 enrolled. In 2019, 7 master's awarded. *Degree requirements:* For master's, comprehensive exam, thesis, 37 credits (31 in courses, 6 in thesis research), oral preliminary exam, thesis defense. *Entrance requirements:* For master's, three letters of recommendation; minimum GPA of 3.0 in undergraduate biology, mathematics, psychology or other science; interview. Additional exam requirements/recommendations for international students: required—TOEFL (minimum score 550 paper-based; 79 iBT), IELTS (minimum score 6.5). *Application deadline:* For fall admission, 4/25 priority date for domestic students, 4/25 for international students; for spring admission, 11/25 priority date for domestic students, 11/25 for international students. Applications are processed on a rolling basis. Application fee: $125. Electronic applications accepted. *Expenses: Tuition, area resident:* Full-time $11,090; part-time $470 per credit. Tuition, state resident: full-time $11,090; part-time $470 per credit. Tuition, nonresident: full-time $20,520; part-time $855 per credit. *International tuition:* $20,520 full-time. *Required fees:* $559; $181 per semester. Tuition and fees vary according to program. *Unit head:* Prof. Greg Phillips, Graduate Program Coordinator, 718-982-3723, E-mail: greg.phillips@csi.cuny.edu. *Application contact:* Sasha Spence, Associate Director for Graduate

Admissions, 718-982-2019, Fax: 718-982-2500, E-mail: sasha.spence@csi.cuny.edu. Website: https://www.csi.cuny.edu/admissions/graduate-admissions/graduate-programs-and-requirements/neuroscience

**Dalhousie University,** Faculty of Graduate Studies, Department of Medical Neuroscience, Halifax, NS B3H 4H7, Canada. Offers anatomy and neuroscience (M Sc, PhD). *Degree requirements:* For doctorate, thesis/dissertation. *Entrance requirements:* For master's and doctorate, 4 year honors degree or equivalent, minimum A- average. Additional exam requirements/recommendations for international students: required—1 of 5 approved tests: TOEFL, IELTS, CANTEST, CAEL, Michigan English Language Assessment Battery. Electronic applications accepted.

**Dalhousie University,** Faculty of Science, Department of Psychology and Neuroscience, Halifax, NS B3H 4R2, Canada. Offers clinical psychology (PhD); psychology (M Sc, PhD); psychology/neuroscience (M Sc, PhD). *Degree requirements:* For master's, thesis; for doctorate, thesis/dissertation. *Entrance requirements:* For doctorate, GRE General Test. Additional exam requirements/recommendations for international students: required—TOEFL, IELTS, CANTEST, CAEL, or Michigan English Language Assessment Battery. Electronic applications accepted.

**Dartmouth College,** Guarini School of Graduate and Advanced Studies, Department of Psychological and Brain Sciences, Hanover, NH 03755. Offers cognitive neuroscience (PhD); psychology (PhD). *Entrance requirements:* For doctorate, GRE General Test, GRE Subject Test. Additional exam requirements/recommendations for international students: required—TOEFL. Electronic applications accepted.

**Delaware State University,** Graduate Programs, Department of Biological Sciences, Dover, DE 19901-2277. Offers biological sciences (MA, MS); biology education (MS); molecular and cellular neuroscience (MS); neuroscience (PhD). *Program availability:* Part-time, evening/weekend. *Degree requirements:* For master's, thesis (for some programs). *Entrance requirements:* For master's, GRE, minimum GPA of 3.0 in major, 2.75 overall. Additional exam requirements/recommendations for international students: required—TOEFL (minimum score 550 paper-based). Electronic applications accepted.

**Drexel University,** College of Arts and Sciences, Department of Psychology, Clinical Psychology Program, Philadelphia, PA 19104-2875. Offers clinical psychology (PhD); forensic psychology (PhD); health psychology (PhD); neuropsychology (PhD). *Accreditation:* APA. Terminal master's awarded for partial completion of doctoral program. *Degree requirements:* For doctorate, thesis/dissertation, qualifying exam. *Entrance requirements:* For doctorate, GRE General Test, GRE Subject Test, minimum GPA of 3.0. Electronic applications accepted. *Expenses:* Contact institution.

**Drexel University,** College of Medicine, Biomedical Graduate Programs, Program in Neuroscience, Philadelphia, PA 19104-2875. Offers MS, PhD, MD/PhD. *Degree requirements:* For doctorate, thesis/dissertation, qualifying exam. *Entrance requirements:* For doctorate, GRE General Test or MCAT, minimum GPA of 2.75. Additional exam requirements/recommendations for international students: required—TOEFL. Electronic applications accepted.

**Duke University,** Graduate School, Cognitive Neuroscience Admitting Program, Durham, NC 27708. Offers PhD, Certificate. *Degree requirements:* For doctorate, thesis/dissertation. *Entrance requirements:* For doctorate, GRE General Test. Additional exam requirements/recommendations for international students: required—TOEFL (minimum score 577 paper-based; 90 iBT) or IELTS (minimum score 7). Electronic applications accepted.

**Emory University,** Laney Graduate School, Department of Psychology, Atlanta, GA 30322-1100. Offers clinical psychology (PhD); cognition and development (PhD); neuroscience and animal behavior (PhD). *Accreditation:* APA. *Degree requirements:* For doctorate, comprehensive exam, thesis/dissertation. *Entrance requirements:* For doctorate, GRE General Test, minimum GPA of 3.25. Additional exam requirements/recommendations for international students: required—TOEFL. Electronic applications accepted.

**Emory University,** Laney Graduate School, Division of Biological and Biomedical Sciences, Program in Neuroscience, Atlanta, GA 30322-1100. Offers PhD. *Degree requirements:* For doctorate, comprehensive exam, thesis/dissertation. *Entrance requirements:* For doctorate, GRE General Test, minimum GPA of 3.0 in science course work (recommended). Additional exam requirements/recommendations for international students: required—TOEFL. Electronic applications accepted.

**Fielding Graduate University,** Graduate Programs, School of Psychology, Post Doctoral Certificate Program in Neuropsychology, Santa Barbara, CA 93105-3814. Offers Post-Doctoral Certificate. *Program availability:* Part-time-only, evening/weekend. *Entrance requirements:* For degree, PhD, Psy D, or Ed D in psychology; minimum GPA of 3.0; curriculum vitae; psychologist license or certificate; official transcript. Electronic applications accepted. *Expenses:* Contact institution.

**Florida Atlantic University,** Charles E. Schmidt College of Science, Center for Complex Systems and Brain Sciences, Boca Raton, FL 33431-0991. Offers PhD. *Faculty:* 1 full-time (0 women). *Students:* 6 full-time (4 women), 7 part-time (0 women); includes 3 minority (1 Black or African American, non-Hispanic/Latino; 2 Two or more races, non-Hispanic/Latino), 2 international. Average age 31. 8 applicants, 13% accepted, 1 enrolled. In 2019, 3 doctorates awarded. *Entrance requirements:* For doctorate, GRE General Test, minimum GPA of 3.0 in last 60 hours of undergraduate course work. Additional exam requirements/recommendations for international students: required—TOEFL (minimum score 500 paper-based; 61 iBT), IELTS (minimum score 6). *Application deadline:* For fall admission, 1/15 priority date for domestic and international students. Application fee: $30. *Expenses: Tuition:* Full-time $20,536; part-time $371.82 per credit hour. Tuition and fees vary according to program. *Financial support:* Fellowships with full tuition reimbursements, research assistantships with partial tuition reimbursements, teaching assistantships with partial tuition reimbursements, Federal Work-Study, and traineeships available. *Unit head:* Keyla Thamsten, Assistant Director, Academic Support Services, 561-297-2231, E-mail: thamsten@fau.edu. *Application contact:* Keyla Thamsten, Assistant Director, Academic Support Services, 561-297-2231, E-mail: thamsten@fau.edu. Website: http://www.ccs.fau.edu/

**Florida International University,** College of Arts, Sciences, and Education, Department of Psychology, Miami, FL 33199. Offers behavioral analysis (MS); clinical science (PhD); cognitive neuroscience (PhD); counseling psychology (MS); developmental science (MS, PhD); legal psychology (MS, PhD); organizational psychology (MS, PhD). *Accreditation:* APA. *Program availability:* Part-time, evening/weekend. *Faculty:* 52 full-time (33 women), 50 part-time/adjunct (37 women). *Students:* 203 full-time (159 women), 2 part-time (both women); includes 117 minority (15 Black or African American, non-Hispanic/Latino; 8 Asian, non-Hispanic/Latino; 86 Hispanic/Latino; 8 Two or more races, non-Hispanic/Latino), 15 international. Average age 26. 410 applicants, 19% accepted, 60 enrolled. In 2019, 57 master's, 7 doctorates awarded. Terminal master's awarded for partial completion of doctoral program. *Degree requirements:* For master's, thesis; for doctorate, comprehensive exam, thesis/dissertation. *Entrance requirements:* For master's, GRE General Test, minimum GPA of 3.0, resume, 3 letters of recommendation; for doctorate, GRE General Test, 3 letters of recommendation, resume, letter of intent, two writing samples, minimum GPA of 3.0.

Additional exam requirements/recommendations for international students: required—TOEFL (minimum score 550 paper-based; 80 iBT). *Application deadline:* For fall admission, 12/15 for domestic and international students. Application fee: $30. Electronic applications accepted. *Expenses: Tuition, area resident:* Full-time $8912; part-time $446 per credit hour. Tuition, state resident: full-time $8912; part-time $446 per credit hour. Tuition, nonresident: full-time $21,393; part-time $992 per credit hour. *Required fees:* $2194. *Financial support:* Institutionally sponsored loans and scholarships/grants available. Financial award application deadline: 3/1. *Unit head:* Dr. Jeremy Pettit, Interim Chair, 305-348-1671, Fax: 305-348-2880, E-mail: jeremy.pettit@fiu.edu. *Application contact:* Nanett Rojas, Manager, Admissions Operations, 305-348-7464, Fax: 305-348-7441, E-mail: gradadm@fiu.edu.

**Florida State University,** College of Medicine, Division of Research and Graduate Programs, Tallahassee, FL 32306-4300. Offers biomedical sciences (PhD); neuroscience (PhD). *Faculty:* 31 full-time (8 women). *Students:* 48 full-time (30 women), 1 (woman) part-time; includes 7 minority (2 Black or African American, non-Hispanic/Latino; 1 Asian, non-Hispanic/Latino; 4 Two or more races, non-Hispanic/Latino), 12 international. Average age 27. 42 applicants, 33% accepted, 8 enrolled. In 2019, 4 doctorates awarded. *Degree requirements:* For doctorate, comprehensive exam, thesis/dissertation, seminar; published peer-reviewed manuscript. *Entrance requirements:* For doctorate, GRE. Additional exam requirements/recommendations for international students: required—TOEFL (minimum score 550 paper-based; 80 iBT). *Application deadline:* For fall admission, 12/1 for domestic and international students. Application fee: $30. Electronic applications accepted. *Expenses:* $13,011.64 per year for five years, nine credit hours per semester for three semesters (in-state rate). *Financial support:* In 2019–20, 34 students received support, including 34 research assistantships with full tuition reimbursements available (averaging $30,485 per year); tuition waivers (full) also available. Financial award application deadline: 12/1. *Unit head:* Dr. Jeffrey N. Joyce, Senior Associate Dean for Research and Graduate Programs, 850-644-2190, Fax: 850-644-9399, E-mail: jeffrey.joyce@med.fsu.edu. *Application contact:* Robin Ryan, Academic Program Specialist, 850-645-6420, Fax: 850-644-5781, E-mail: robin.ryan@med.fsu.edu.

**Florida State University,** The Graduate School, College of Arts and Sciences, Interdisciplinary Program in Neuroscience, Tallahassee, FL 32306. Offers neuroscience (PhD); psychobiology (MS). Terminal master's awarded for partial completion of doctoral program. *Degree requirements:* For master's, thesis; for doctorate, comprehensive exam, thesis/dissertation. *Entrance requirements:* For doctorate, GRE General Test (suggested minimum score above 60th percentile on both verbal and quantitative sections), minimum GPA of 3.0, research experience, letters of recommendation. Additional exam requirements/recommendations for international students: required—TOEFL (minimum score 80 iBT). Electronic applications accepted.

**Gallaudet University,** The Graduate School, Washington, DC 20002. Offers American Sign Language/English bilingual early childhood deaf education: birth to 5 (Certificate); audiology (Au D); clinical psychology (PhD); deaf and hard of hearing infants, toddlers, and their families (Certificate); deaf education (MA, Ed S); deaf history (Certificate); deaf studies (Certificate); educating deaf students with disabilities (Certificate); education: teacher preparation (MA), including deaf education, early childhood education and deaf education, elementary education and deaf education, secondary education and deaf education; educational neuroscience (PhD); hearing, speech and language sciences (MS, PhD); international development (MA); interpretation (MA, PhD), including combined interpreting practice and research (MA); interpreting research (MA); linguistics (MA, PhD); mental health counseling (MA); peer mentoring (Certificate); public administration (MPA); school counseling (MA); school psychology (Psy S); sign language teaching (MA); social work (MSW); speech-language pathology (MS). *Program availability:* Part-time. *Faculty:* 101 full-time (70 women). *Students:* 267 full-time (208 women), 139 part-time (95 women); includes 120 minority (38 Black or African American, non-Hispanic/Latino; 20 Asian, non-Hispanic/Latino; 44 Hispanic/Latino; 18 Two or more races, non-Hispanic/Latino), 19 international. Average age 30. 484 applicants, 50% accepted, 162 enrolled. In 2019, 138 master's, 25 doctorates, 14 other advanced degrees awarded. Terminal master's awarded for partial completion of doctoral program. *Degree requirements:* For master's, comprehensive exam (for some programs), thesis optional; for doctorate, comprehensive exam, thesis/dissertation. *Entrance requirements:* For master's and doctorate, GRE General Test or MAT, letters of recommendation, interviews, goals statement, American Sign Language proficiency interview, written English competency. Additional exam requirements/recommendations for international students: required—TOEFL. *Application deadline:* For fall admission, 2/15 for domestic students. Applications are processed on a rolling basis. Application fee: $75. Electronic applications accepted. *Expenses: Tuition:* Full-time $18,180; part-time $688 per credit. *Required fees:* $526; $526. Tuition and fees vary according to course load. *Financial support:* In 2019–20, 50 students received support. Fellowships, research assistantships, teaching assistantships, career-related internships or fieldwork, Federal Work-Study, scholarships/grants, tuition waivers (partial), and unspecified assistantships available. Support available to part-time students. Financial award application deadline: 7/1; financial award applicants required to submit FAFSA. *Unit head:* Dr. Gaurav Mathur, Dean, Graduate School and Continuing Studies, 202-250-2380, Fax: 202-651-5027, E-mail: gaurav.mathur@gallaudet.edu. *Application contact:* Heidi Zornes-Foster, Senior Graduate Admissions Counselor, 202-650-5436, Fax: 202-651-5295, E-mail: graduate.school@gallaudet.edu.
Website: www.gallaudet.edu

**George Mason University,** College of Humanities and Social Sciences, Department of Psychology, Fairfax, VA 22030. Offers applied developmental psychology (MA, PhD); clinical psychology (PhD); cognitive and behavioral neuroscience (MA, PhD); cognitive neuroscience (Certificate); human factors/applied cognition (MA, PhD, Certificate), including transportation human factors (Certificate), usability (Certificate); industrial/organizational psychology (MA, PhD). *Accreditation:* APA. *Degree requirements:* For master's, comprehensive exam, thesis or practicum research; for doctorate, comprehensive exam, thesis/dissertation, 2nd-year project. *Entrance requirements:* For master's, GRE, 2 official transcripts; goals statement; 15 undergraduate credits in concentration for which the applicant is applying; for doctorate, GRE, 3 letters of recommendation; resume; goals statement; minimum GPA of 3.0 overall for last 60 undergraduate credits, 3.25 in psychology courses; 15 undergraduate credits in concentration for which the applicant is applying; 2 official transcripts; for Certificate, GRE, 2 official transcripts; expanded goals statement; 3 letters of recommendation. Additional exam requirements/recommendations for international students: required—TOEFL (minimum score 575 paper-based; 88 iBT), IELTS (minimum score 6.5), PTE (minimum score 59). Electronic applications accepted.

**George Mason University,** College of Science, Program in Neuroscience, Fairfax, VA 22030. Offers PhD. *Degree requirements:* For doctorate, comprehensive exam, thesis/dissertation, at least one publication in a refereed journal (print or press). *Entrance requirements:* For doctorate, GRE, bachelor's degree in related field with minimum GPA of 3.25; expanded goals statement; 2 copies of official transcripts; 3 letters of recommendation. Additional exam requirements/recommendations for international students: required—TOEFL (minimum score 575 paper-based; 88 iBT), IELTS (minimum score 6.5), PTE (minimum score 59). Electronic applications accepted.

**Georgetown University,** Graduate School of Arts and Sciences, Department of Psychology, Washington, DC 20005. Offers human development and public policy (PhD); lifespan cognitive neuroscience (PhD); PhD/MPP. *Faculty:* 14 full-time (9 women). *Students:* 16 full-time (9 women); includes 3 minority (1 Asian, non-Hispanic/Latino; 2 Hispanic/Latino). Average age 25. 101 applicants, 5 enrolled. In 2019, 4 doctorates awarded. *Degree requirements:* For doctorate, thesis/dissertation, area paper. *Entrance requirements:* For doctorate, GRE General Test, GRE Subject Test. Additional exam requirements/recommendations for international students: required—TOEFL. *Application deadline:* For fall admission, 12/1 for domestic and international students. Application fee: $51 ($50 for international students). Electronic applications accepted. *Financial support:* In 2019–20, 16 students received support, including 16 teaching assistantships with full tuition reimbursements available (averaging $28,000 per year); research assistantships also available. Financial award application deadline: 2/1; financial award applicants required to submit FAFSA. *Unit head:* Dr. Jennifer Woolard, Interim Chair, 202-687-9258, Fax: 202-687-6050, E-mail: jlw47@georgetown.edu. *Application contact:* Graduate School Admissions Office, 202-687-5568, E-mail: gradmail@georgetown.edu.
Website: https://psychology.georgetown.edu

**Georgetown University,** Graduate School of Arts and Sciences, Interdisciplinary Program in Neuroscience, Washington, DC 20057. Offers PhD, MD/PhD. *Degree requirements:* For doctorate, thesis/dissertation. *Entrance requirements:* For doctorate, GRE General Test. Additional exam requirements/recommendations for international students: required—TOEFL.

**Georgia State University,** College of Arts and Sciences, Department of Psychology, Atlanta, GA 30302-3083. Offers clinical psychology (PhD); cognitive sciences (PhD); community psychology (PhD); developmental psychology (PhD); neuropsychology and behavioral neuroscience (PhD). *Accreditation:* APA. *Faculty:* 29 full-time (17 women). *Students:* 107 full-time (85 women), 2 part-time (both women); includes 23 minority (9 Black or African American, non-Hispanic/Latino; 6 Asian, non-Hispanic/Latino; 7 Hispanic/Latino; 1 Two or more races, non-Hispanic/Latino), 13 international. Average age 28. 498 applicants, 5% accepted, 17 enrolled. In 2019, 18 doctorates awarded. *Entrance requirements:* For doctorate, GRE. Additional exam requirements/recommendations for international students: required—TOEFL (minimum score 550 paper-based; 80 iBT). *Application deadline:* For fall admission, 12/1 for domestic and international students. Application fee: $50. Electronic applications accepted. *Expenses: Tuition, area resident:* Full-time $7164; part-time $398 per credit hour. Tuition, state resident: full-time $7164; part-time $398 per credit hour. Tuition, nonresident: full-time $22,662; part-time $1259 per credit hour. *International tuition:* $22,662 full-time. *Required fees:* $2128; $312 per credit hour. Tuition and fees vary according to course load and program. *Financial support:* In 2019–20, fellowships with full tuition reimbursements (averaging $19,282 per year), research assistantships with full tuition reimbursements (averaging $5,173 per year), teaching assistantships with full tuition reimbursements (averaging $6,389 per year) were awarded; scholarships/grants, traineeships, health care benefits, and unspecified assistantships also available. Financial award applicants required to submit FAFSA. *Unit head:* Dr. Lisa Armistead, Professor, Associate Provost for Graduate Programs, 404-413-2091, Fax: 404-413-6207, E-mail: lparmistead@gsu.edu. *Application contact:* Dr. Lindsey Cohen, Director of Graduate Studies, 404-413-6263, Fax: 404-413-6207, E-mail: llcohen@gsu.edu.
Website: https://psychology.gsu.edu/

**Georgia State University,** College of Arts and Sciences, Neuroscience Institute, Atlanta, GA 30302-3083. Offers PhD. *Faculty:* 19 full-time (8 women). *Students:* 61 full-time (37 women), 2 part-time (1 woman); includes 19 minority (4 Black or African American, non-Hispanic/Latino; 6 Asian, non-Hispanic/Latino; 8 Hispanic/Latino; 1 Two or more races, non-Hispanic/Latino), 10 international. Average age 29. 64 applicants, 44% accepted, 20 enrolled. In 2019, 6 doctorates awarded. Terminal master's awarded for partial completion of doctoral program. *Entrance requirements:* For doctorate, GRE. Additional exam requirements/recommendations for international students: required—TOEFL. *Application deadline:* For fall admission, 12/10 for domestic and international students. Application fee: $50. Electronic applications accepted. *Expenses: Tuition, area resident:* Full-time $7164; part-time $398 per credit hour. Tuition, state resident: full-time $7164; part-time $398 per credit hour. Tuition, nonresident: full-time $22,662; part-time $1259 per credit hour. *International tuition:* $22,662 full-time. *Required fees:* $2128; $312 per credit hour. Tuition and fees vary according to course load and program. *Financial support:* In 2019–20, fellowships (averaging $22,000 per year), research assistantships (averaging $22,000 per year) were awarded. Financial award applicants required to submit FAFSA. *Application contact:* Dr. Laura L. Carruth, Director of Graduate Studies, 404-413-5340, E-mail: lcarruth@gsu.edu.
Website: http://www.neuroscience.gsu.edu/

**The Graduate Center, City University of New York,** Graduate Studies, Program in Cognitive Neuroscience, New York, NY 10016-4039. Offers MS.

**The Graduate Center, City University of New York,** Graduate Studies, Program in Psychology, New York, NY 10016-4039. Offers basic applied neurocognition (PhD); biopsychology (PhD); clinical psychology (PhD); developmental psychology (PhD); environmental psychology (PhD); experimental psychology (PhD); industrial psychology (PhD); learning processes (PhD); neuropsychology (PhD); psychology (PhD); social personality (PhD). *Degree requirements:* For doctorate, one foreign language, thesis/dissertation. *Entrance requirements:* For doctorate, GRE General Test. Additional exam requirements/recommendations for international students: required—TOEFL. Electronic applications accepted.

**Harvard University,** Graduate School of Arts and Sciences, Program in Neuroscience, Boston, MA 02115. Offers neurobiology (PhD). *Degree requirements:* For doctorate, thesis/dissertation, qualifying exam. *Entrance requirements:* For doctorate, GRE General Test, GRE Subject Test. Additional exam requirements/recommendations for international students: required—TOEFL.

**Icahn School of Medicine at Mount Sinai,** Graduate School of Biomedical Sciences, New York, NY 10029-6504. Offers biomedical sciences (MS, PhD); clinical research education (MS, PhD); community medicine (MPH); genetic counseling (MS); neurosciences (PhD); MD/PhD. Terminal master's awarded for partial completion of doctoral program. *Degree requirements:* For master's, thesis; for doctorate, comprehensive exam, thesis/dissertation. *Entrance requirements:* For master's, GRE General Test; for doctorate, GRE General Test, GRE Subject Test, 3 years of college pre-med course work. Additional exam requirements/recommendations for international students: required—TOEFL. Electronic applications accepted.

**Illinois State University,** Graduate School, College of Arts and Sciences, School of Biological Sciences, Normal, IL 61790. Offers animal behavior (MS); bacteriology (MS); biochemistry (MS); biological sciences (MS); biology (PhD); biophysics (MS); biotechnology (MS); botany (MS, PhD); cell biology (MS); conservation biology (MS); developmental biology (MS); ecology (MS, PhD); entomology (MS); evolutionary biology (MS); genetics (MS, PhD); immunology (MS); microbiology (MS, PhD); molecular biology (MS); molecular genetics (MS); neurobiology (MS); neuroscience (MS); parasitology (MS); physiology (MS, PhD); plant biology (MS); plant molecular biology (MS); plant sciences (MS); structural biology (MS); zoology (MS, PhD). *Program*

*availability:* Part-time. *Faculty:* 26 full-time (6 women), 7 part-time/adjunct (2 women). *Students:* 51 full-time (33 women), 15 part-time (8 women). Average age 27. 71 applicants, 28% accepted, 9 enrolled. In 2019, 14 master's, 3 doctorates awarded. *Degree requirements:* For master's, thesis or alternative; for doctorate, variable foreign language requirement, thesis/dissertation, 2 terms of residency. *Entrance requirements:* For master's, GRE General Test, minimum GPA of 2.6 in last 60 hours of course work; for doctorate, GRE General Test. *Application deadline:* Applications are processed on a rolling basis. Application fee: $50. *Expenses: Tuition, area resident:* Full-time $7956; part-time $9767 per year. Tuition, nonresident: full-time $9233; part-time $17,592 per year. *Required fees:* $1797. *Financial support:* In 2019–20, 20 research assistantships, 41 teaching assistantships were awarded; Federal Work-Study, tuition waivers (full), and unspecified assistantships also available. Financial award application deadline: 4/1. *Unit head:* Dr. Craig Gatto, School Director, 309-438-3087, E-mail: cgatto@IllinoisState.edu. *Application contact:* Dr. Ben Sadd, Assistant Chair for Graduate Studies, 309-438-2651, E-mail: bmsadd@IllinoisState.edu.
Website: http://www.bio.ilstu.edu/

**Immaculata University,** College of Graduate Studies, Department of Psychology, Immaculata, PA 19345. Offers clinical mental health counseling (MA); clinical psychology (Psy D); forensic psychology (Graduate Certificate); integrative psychotherapy (Graduate Certificate); neuropsychology (Graduate Certificate); psychodynamic psychotherapy (Graduate Certificate); psychological testing (Graduate Certificate); school counseling (MA, Graduate Certificate); school psychology (MA). *Accreditation:* APA. *Program availability:* Part-time, evening/weekend. Terminal master's awarded for partial completion of doctoral program. *Degree requirements:* For master's, comprehensive exam, thesis optional; for doctorate, comprehensive exam, thesis/dissertation. *Entrance requirements:* For master's, GRE General Test or MAT, minimum GPA of 3.0; for doctorate, GRE General Test or MAT, minimum GPA of 3.5. Additional exam requirements/recommendations for international students: required—TOEFL, IELTS. Electronic applications accepted.

**Indiana University Bloomington,** University Graduate School, College of Arts and Sciences, Department of Psychological and Brain Sciences, Bloomington, IN 47405. Offers clinical science (PhD); cognitive neuroscience (PhD); cognitive psychology (PhD); developmental psychology (PhD); methods of behavior (PhD); molecular systems neuroscience (PhD); social psychology (PhD). *Accreditation:* APA. *Degree requirements:* For doctorate, comprehensive exam, 90 credit hours, 2 advanced statistics/methods courses, 2 written research projects, the teaching of psychology course, teaching 1 semester of undergraduate methods course, qualifying examination, minor or a second major, first-year research seminar course, dissertation defense, written dissertation. *Entrance requirements:* For doctorate, GRE. Additional exam requirements/recommendations for international students: required—TOEFL (minimum score 550 paper-based; 79 iBT). Electronic applications accepted.

**Indiana University Bloomington,** University Graduate School, College of Arts and Sciences, Program in Neuroscience, Bloomington, IN 47405. Offers PhD. *Degree requirements:* For doctorate, comprehensive exam, thesis/dissertation, qualifying exam. *Entrance requirements:* For doctorate, GRE, bachelor's degree. Additional exam requirements/recommendations for international students: required—TOEFL. Electronic applications accepted.

**Iowa State University of Science and Technology,** Program in Neuroscience, Ames, IA 50011. Offers MS, PhD. *Degree requirements:* For master's, thesis; for doctorate, thesis/dissertation. *Entrance requirements:* For master's and doctorate, GRE General Test, resume. Additional exam requirements/recommendations for international students: required—TOEFL (minimum score 580 paper-based; 85 iBT), IELTS (minimum score 7). Electronic applications accepted.

**Irell & Manella Graduate School of Biological Sciences,** Graduate Program, Duarte, CA 91010. Offers brain metastatic cancer (PhD); cancer and stem cell metabolism (PhD); cancer biology (PhD); cancer biology and developmental therapeutics (PhD); cell biology (PhD); chemical biology (PhD); chromosomal break repair (PhD); diabetes and pancreatic progenitor cell biology (PhD); DNA repair and cancer biology (PhD); germline epigenetic remodeling and endocrine disruptors (PhD); hematology and hematopoietic cell transplantation (PhD); hematology and immunology (PhD); inflammation and cancer (PhD); micrornas and gene regulation in cardiovascular disease (PhD); mixed chimerism for reversal of autoimmunity (PhD); molecular and cellular biology (PhD); molecular biology and genetics (PhD); nanoparticle mediated twist1 silencing in metastatic cancer (PhD); neuro-oncology and stem cell biology (PhD); neuroscience (PhD); RNA directed therapies for HIV-1 (PhD); small RNA-induced transcriptional gene activation (PhD); stem cell regulation by the microenvironment (PhD); translational oncology and pharmaceutical sciences (PhD); tumor biology (PhD). *Degree requirements:* For doctorate, comprehensive exam, thesis/dissertation, qualifying exams, two advanced courses. *Entrance requirements:* For doctorate, GRE General Test; GRE Subject Test (recommended), 2 years of course work in chemistry (general and organic); 1 year of course work each in biochemistry, general biology, and general physics; 2 semesters of course work in mathematics; significant research laboratory experience. Additional exam requirements/recommendations for international students: required—TOEFL. Electronic applications accepted.

**Johns Hopkins University,** School of Medicine, Graduate Programs in Medicine, Neuroscience Training Program, Baltimore, MD 21218. Offers PhD. *Degree requirements:* For doctorate, comprehensive exam, thesis/dissertation, thesis defense. *Entrance requirements:* For doctorate, GRE General Test, bachelor's degree in science or mathematics. Additional exam requirements/recommendations for international students: required—TOEFL. Electronic applications accepted. *Expenses:* Contact institution.

**Kent State University,** College of Arts and Sciences, School of Biomedical Sciences, Kent, OH 44242-0001. Offers biological anthropology (PhD); biomedical mathematics (MS, PhD); cellular and molecular biology (MS, PhD), including cellular biology and structures, molecular biology and genetics; neurosciences (MS, PhD); pharmacology (MS, PhD); physiology (MS, PhD). *Faculty:* 17 full-time (8 women). *Students:* 73 full-time (48 women), 2 part-time (1 woman); includes 9 minority (2 Black or African American, non-Hispanic/Latino; 1 Asian, non-Hispanic/Latino; 3 Hispanic/Latino; 3 Two or more races, non-Hispanic/Latino), 53 international. Average age 29. 78 applicants, 17% accepted, 9 enrolled. In 2019, 2 master's, 5 doctorates awarded. *Degree requirements:* For master's, thesis; for doctorate, comprehensive exam, thesis/dissertation. *Entrance requirements:* For master's, GRE, bachelor's degree, transcripts, minimum GPA of 3.0 undergraduate GPA, goal statement, three letters of recommendation, academic preparation adequate to perform graduate work in the desired field (typically two years of chemistry, one year of mathematics, one year of physics and courses in anthropology, biology and psychology); for doctorate, GRE, master's degree, minimum GPA of 3.0, transcripts, goal statement, three letters of recommendation. Additional exam requirements/recommendations for international students: required—TOEFL (minimum score 100 iBT), IELTS (minimum score 7), PTE (minimum score 68), Michigan English Language Assessment Battery (minimum score 85). *Application deadline:* For fall admission, 1/1 for domestic students, 12/15 for international students. Applications are processed on a rolling basis. Application fee: $45 ($70 for international students). Electronic applications accepted. *Financial support:* Research assistantships with full tuition reimbursements, teaching assistantships, health care benefits, and unspecified assistantships available. Financial award application deadline: 1/1. *Unit head:* Dr. Ernest J. Freeman, Director, School of Biomedical Sciences, 330-672-2363, E-mail: efreema2@kent.edu. *Application contact:* School of Biomedical Sciences, 330-6722263, Fax: 330-6729391.
Website: http://www.kent.edu/biomedical/

**Louisiana State University Health Sciences Center,** School of Graduate Studies in New Orleans, Interdisciplinary Neuroscience Graduate Program, New Orleans, LA 70112-2223. Offers PhD, MD/PhD. *Degree requirements:* For doctorate, comprehensive exam, thesis/dissertation. *Entrance requirements:* For doctorate, GRE General Test, previous course work in chemistry, mathematics, physics, and computer science. Additional exam requirements/recommendations for international students: recommended—TOEFL, IELTS.

**Loyola University Chicago,** Graduate School, Integrated Program in Biomedical Sciences, Maywood, IL 60660. Offers biochemistry and molecular biology (MS, PhD); cell and molecular physiology (MS, PhD); infectious disease and immunology (MS); integrative cell biology (MS, PhD); microbiology and immunology (MS, PhD); molecular pharmacology and therapeutics (MS, PhD); neuroscience (MS, PhD). *Students:* Average age 25. 773 applicants, 34% accepted, 122 enrolled. In 2019, 46 master's, 12 doctorates awarded. *Degree requirements:* For master's, thesis; for doctorate, comprehensive exam, thesis/dissertation. *Entrance requirements:* For doctorate, GRE. Additional exam requirements/recommendations for international students: required—TOEFL (minimum score 94 iBT), IELTS (minimum score 7.5). *Application deadline:* For fall admission, 2/7 for domestic students. Applications are processed on a rolling basis. Electronic applications accepted. *Expenses:* Contact institution. *Financial support:* In 2019–20, 20 students received support. Schmitt Fellowships and yearly tuition scholarships (averaging $25,032) available. Financial award application deadline: 6/15; financial award applicants required to submit FAFSA. *Unit head:* Dr. Leanne L. Cribbs, Associate Dean, Graduate Education, 708-327-2817, Fax: 708-216-8216, E-mail: lcribbs@luc.edu. *Application contact:* Margarita Quesada, Graduate Program Secretary, 708-216-3532, Fax: 708-216-8216, E-mail: mquesad@luc.edu.
Website: http://ssom.luc.edu/graduate_school/degree-programs/ipbsphd/

**Marquette University,** Graduate School, College of Arts and Sciences, Department of Biological Sciences, Milwaukee, WI 53201-1881. Offers cell biology (MS, PhD); developmental biology (MS, PhD); ecology (MS, PhD); epithelial physiology (MS, PhD); genetics (MS, PhD); microbiology (MS, PhD); molecular biology (MS, PhD); muscle and exercise physiology (MS, PhD); neuroscience (PhD). Terminal master's awarded for partial completion of doctoral program. *Degree requirements:* For master's, comprehensive exam, thesis, 1 year of teaching experience or equivalent; for doctorate, thesis/dissertation, 1 year of teaching experience or equivalent, qualifying exam. *Entrance requirements:* For master's and doctorate, GRE General Test, GRE Subject Test, official transcripts from all current and previous colleges/universities except Marquette, statement of professional goals and aspirations, three letters of recommendation. Additional exam requirements/recommendations for international students: required—TOEFL (minimum score 530 paper-based). Electronic applications accepted.

**Massachusetts Institute of Technology,** School of Science, Department of Brain and Cognitive Sciences, Cambridge, MA 02139. Offers cognitive science (PhD); neuroscience (PhD). *Degree requirements:* For doctorate, comprehensive exam, thesis/dissertation. *Entrance requirements:* For doctorate, GRE General Test. Additional exam requirements/recommendations for international students: required—TOEFL, IELTS. Electronic applications accepted.

**Mayo Clinic Graduate School of Biomedical Sciences,** Program in Neuroscience, Rochester, MN 55905. Offers MS, PhD. *Degree requirements:* For doctorate, comprehensive exam, thesis/dissertation, oral defense of dissertation, qualifying oral and written exam. *Entrance requirements:* For doctorate, GRE, 1 year of chemistry, biology, calculus, and physics. Additional exam requirements/recommendations for international students: required—TOEFL. Electronic applications accepted.

**McGill University,** Faculty of Graduate and Postdoctoral Studies, Faculty of Medicine, Department of Neurology and Neurosurgery, Montréal, QC H3A 2T5, Canada. Offers M Sc, PhD.

**McMaster University,** Faculty of Health Sciences and School of Graduate Studies, Program in Medical Sciences, Neurosciences and Behavioral Sciences Area, Hamilton, ON L8S 4M2, Canada. Offers M Sc, PhD, MD/PhD. *Degree requirements:* For master's, thesis; for doctorate, comprehensive exam, thesis/dissertation. *Entrance requirements:* For master's, honors B Sc, B+ average in related field; for doctorate, M Sc, minimum B+ average, students with proven research experience and an A average may be admitted with a B Sc degree. Additional exam requirements/recommendations for international students: required—TOEFL (minimum score 580 paper-based).

**Medical College of Wisconsin,** Graduate School, Neuroscience Doctoral Program, Milwaukee, WI 53226. Offers PhD, MD/PhD. *Students:* 10 full-time (5 women); includes 2 minority (1 Asian, non-Hispanic/Latino; 1 Hispanic/Latino). Average age 25. 32 applicants, 28% accepted, 6 enrolled. *Degree requirements:* For doctorate, comprehensive exam, thesis/dissertation. *Entrance requirements:* For doctorate, GRE, official transcripts, three letters of recommendation. Additional exam requirements/recommendations for international students: required—TOEFL. *Application deadline:* For fall admission, 1/15 for domestic and international students. Applications are processed on a rolling basis. Application fee: $50. Electronic applications accepted. *Expenses:* $1,250 per credit PhD students; $155 per year full-time student fees. *Financial support:* In 2019–20, 10 students received support, including fellowships with full tuition reimbursements available (averaging $30,000 per year), research assistantships with full tuition reimbursements available (averaging $30,000 per year); institutionally sponsored loans, scholarships/grants, and annual stipends also available. Support available to part-time students. Financial award application deadline: 2/15. *Unit head:* Dr. Cheryl Stucky, Director, 414-955-8373, Fax: 414-955-6555, E-mail: cstucky@mcw.edu. *Application contact:* Recruitment Office, 414-955-4402, Fax: 414-955-6555, E-mail: gradschoolrecruit@mcw.edu.
Website: http://www.mcw.edu/Graduate-School/Programs/Neuroscience-PhD-Program.htm

**Medical University of South Carolina,** College of Graduate Studies, Department of Neurosciences, Charleston, SC 29425. Offers MS, PhD, DMD/PhD, MD/PhD. Terminal master's awarded for partial completion of doctoral program. *Degree requirements:* For master's, thesis; for doctorate, thesis/dissertation, oral and written exams. *Entrance requirements:* For master's, GRE General Test; for doctorate, GRE General Test, interview, minimum GPA of 3.0. Additional exam requirements/recommendations for international students: required—TOEFL (minimum score 600 paper-based; 100 iBT). Electronic applications accepted.

**Meharry Medical College,** School of Graduate Studies, Program in Biomedical Sciences, Neuroscience Emphasis, Nashville, TN 37208-9989. Offers PhD, MD/PhD. *Degree requirements:* For doctorate, comprehensive exam, thesis/dissertation. *Entrance requirements:* For doctorate, GRE. Additional exam requirements/recommendations for international students: required—TOEFL. *Application deadline:*

For fall admission, 6/1 for domestic students. Applications are processed on a rolling basis. Application fee: $65. *Financial support:* Fellowships and institutionally sponsored loans available. Financial award application deadline: 4/15; financial award applicants required to submit FAFSA. *Unit head:* Dr. Sukhbir S. Mokha, Professor, 615-327-6933, E-mail: smokha@mmc.edu. *Application contact:* Dr. Sukhbir S. Mokha, Professor, 615-327-6933, E-mail: smokha@mmc.edu.
Website: https://home.mmc.edu/school-of-graduate-studies-research/neuroscience/

**Memorial University of Newfoundland,** Faculty of Medicine and School of Graduate Studies, Graduate Programs in Medicine, Division of Biomedical Sciences, St. John's, NL A1C 5S7, Canada. Offers cancer (M Sc, PhD); cardiovascular (M Sc, PhD); immunology (M Sc, PhD); neuroscience (M Sc, PhD). *Program availability:* Part-time. *Degree requirements:* For master's, thesis; for doctorate, comprehensive exam, thesis/dissertation, oral defense of thesis. *Entrance requirements:* For master's, MD or B Sc; for doctorate, MD or M Sc. Additional exam requirements/recommendations for international students: required—TOEFL.

**Michigan State University,** The Graduate School, College of Natural Science, Program in Neuroscience, East Lansing, MI 48824. Offers MS, PhD. *Entrance requirements:* Additional exam requirements/recommendations for international students: required—TOEFL. Electronic applications accepted.

**Montana State University,** The Graduate School, College of Letters and Science, Department of Cell Biology and Neuroscience, Bozeman, MT 59717. Offers biological sciences (PhD); neuroscience (MS, PhD). *Program availability:* Part-time. *Degree requirements:* For master's, comprehensive exam; for doctorate, comprehensive exam, thesis/dissertation. *Entrance requirements:* For master's and doctorate, GRE General Test. Additional exam requirements/recommendations for international students: required—TOEFL (minimum score 550 paper-based). Electronic applications accepted.

**New York University,** Graduate School of Arts and Science, Center for Neural Science, New York, NY 10012-1019. Offers PhD. *Degree requirements:* For doctorate, one foreign language, thesis/dissertation. *Entrance requirements:* For doctorate, GRE, interview. Additional exam requirements/recommendations for international students: required—TOEFL, IELTS.

**Northwestern University,** Feinberg School of Medicine, Department of Physical Therapy and Human Movement Sciences, Chicago, IL 60611-2814. Offers neuroscience (PhD), including movement and rehabilitation science; physical therapy (DPT); DPT/MPH; DPT/PhD. *Accreditation:* APTA. *Degree requirements:* For doctorate, research project. *Entrance requirements:* For doctorate, GRE General Test (for DPT), baccalaureate degree with minimum GPA of 3.0 in required course work (DPT). Additional exam requirements/recommendations for international students: required—TOEFL (minimum score 100 iBT). Electronic applications accepted. *Expenses:* Contact institution.

**Northwestern University,** The Graduate School, Interdepartmental Neuroscience Program, Evanston, IL 60208. Offers PhD. *Degree requirements:* For doctorate, thesis/dissertation. *Entrance requirements:* For doctorate, GRE General Test. Additional exam requirements/recommendations for international students: required—TOEFL.

**The Ohio State University,** Graduate School, College of Arts and Sciences, Division of Natural and Mathematical Sciences, Neuroscience Graduate Program, Columbus, OH 43210. Offers PhD. *Degree requirements:* For doctorate, comprehensive exam, thesis/dissertation. *Entrance requirements:* For doctorate, GRE General Test, GRE Subject Test in biology, psychology, biochemistry, or cell and molecular biology (recommended). Additional exam requirements/recommendations for international students: required—TOEFL (minimum score 600 paper-based; 100 iBT); recommended—IELTS (minimum score 8). Electronic applications accepted.

**The Ohio State University,** Graduate School, College of Arts and Sciences, Division of Social and Behavioral Sciences, Department of Psychology, Columbus, OH 43210. Offers behavioral neuroscience (PhD); clinical psychology (PhD); cognitive psychology (PhD); developmental psychology (PhD); intellectual and developmental disabilities psychology (PhD); quantitative psychology (PhD); social psychology (PhD). *Accreditation:* APA. *Entrance requirements:* For doctorate, GRE General Test. Additional exam requirements/recommendations for international students: required—TOEFL (minimum score 600 paper-based; 100 iBT); recommended—IELTS (minimum score 8). Electronic applications accepted.

**Ohio University,** Graduate College, College of Arts and Sciences, Department of Biological Sciences, Athens, OH 45701-2979. Offers biological sciences (MS, PhD); cell biology and physiology (MS, PhD); ecology and evolutionary biology (MS, PhD); exercise physiology and muscle biology (MS, PhD); microbiology (MS, PhD); neuroscience (MS, PhD). Terminal master's awarded for partial completion of doctoral program. *Degree requirements:* For master's, comprehensive exam, thesis, 1 quarter of teaching experience; for doctorate, comprehensive exam, thesis/dissertation, 2 quarters of teaching experience. *Entrance requirements:* For master's, GRE General Test, names of three faculty members whose research interests most closely match the applicant's interest; for doctorate, GRE General Test, essay concerning prior training, research interest and career goals, plus names of three faculty members whose research interests most closely match the applicant's interest. Additional exam requirements/recommendations for international students: required—TOEFL (minimum score 620 paper-based; 105 iBT) or IELTS (minimum score 7.5). Electronic applications accepted.

**Oregon Health & Science University,** School of Medicine, Graduate Programs in Medicine, Department of Behavioral Neuroscience, Portland, OR 97239-3098. Offers PhD. Terminal master's awarded for partial completion of doctoral program. *Degree requirements:* For doctorate, comprehensive exam, thesis/dissertation, qualifying exam. *Entrance requirements:* For doctorate, GRE General Test (minimum scores: 153 Verbal/148 Quantitative/4.5 Analytical), undergraduate coursework in biopsychology and other basic science areas. Electronic applications accepted.

**Oregon Health & Science University,** School of Medicine, Graduate Programs in Medicine, Neuroscience Graduate Program, Portland, OR 97239-3098. Offers PhD. Terminal master's awarded for partial completion of doctoral program. *Degree requirements:* For doctorate, comprehensive exam, thesis/dissertation, qualifying exam. *Entrance requirements:* For doctorate, GRE General Test (minimum scores: 153 Verbal/148 Quantitative/4.5 Analytical) or MCAT (for some programs). Electronic applications accepted.

**Penn State Hershey Medical Center,** College of Medicine, Graduate School Programs in the Biomedical Sciences, Huck Institutes of the Life Sciences, Intercollege Graduate Program in Neuroscience, Hershey, PA 17033. Offers MS, PhD, MD/PhD. Terminal master's awarded for partial completion of doctoral program. *Degree requirements:* For master's, thesis or alternative; for doctorate, comprehensive exam, thesis/dissertation, oral exam. *Entrance requirements:* For master's, GRE General Test; for doctorate, GRE General Test, minimum GPA of 3.0. Additional exam requirements/recommendations for international students: required—TOEFL (minimum score 81 iBT). Electronic applications accepted.

**Princeton University,** Graduate School, Department of Psychology, Princeton, NJ 08544-1019. Offers neuroscience (PhD); psychology (PhD). *Degree requirements:* For doctorate, thesis/dissertation. *Entrance requirements:* For doctorate, GRE General Test, GRE Subject Test. Additional exam requirements/recommendations for international students: required—TOEFL (minimum score 550 paper-based). Electronic applications accepted.

**Princeton University,** Princeton Neuroscience Institute, Princeton, NJ 08544-1019. Offers PhD. Electronic applications accepted.

**Purdue University,** College of Pharmacy and Graduate School, Graduate Programs in Pharmacy and Pharmacal Sciences, Department of Medicinal Chemistry and Molecular Pharmacology, West Lafayette, IN 47907. Offers biophysical and computational chemistry (PhD); cancer research (PhD); immunology and infectious disease (PhD); medicinal biochemistry and molecular biology (PhD); medicinal chemistry and chemical biology (PhD); molecular pharmacology (PhD); neuropharmacology, neurodegeneration, and neurotoxicity (PhD); systems biology and functional genomics (PhD). *Faculty:* 20 full-time (5 women), 7 part-time/adjunct (2 women). *Students:* 80 full-time (40 women), 2 part-time (0 women); includes 9 minority (5 Asian, non-Hispanic/Latino; 2 Hispanic/Latino; 2 Two or more races, non-Hispanic/Latino), 44 international. Average age 26. 162 applicants, 20% accepted, 15 enrolled. In 2019, 11 doctorates awarded. *Degree requirements:* For doctorate, thesis/dissertation. *Entrance requirements:* For doctorate, GRE General Test; GRE Subject Test in biology, biochemistry, and chemistry (recommended), minimum undergraduate GPA of 3.0. Additional exam requirements/recommendations for international students: required—TOEFL (minimum score 550 paper-based; 77 iBT); recommended—TWE. *Application deadline:* For fall admission, 2/1 for domestic and international students. Applications are processed on a rolling basis. Application fee: $60 ($75 for international students). Electronic applications accepted. *Financial support:* Fellowships, research assistantships, teaching assistantships, and traineeships available. Support available to part-time students. Financial award applicants required to submit FAFSA. *Unit head:* Zhong-Yin Zhang, Head, 765-494-1403, E-mail: zhang-yn@purdue.edu. *Application contact:* Delayne Graham, Graduate Contact, 765-494-1362, E-mail: dkgraham@purdue.edu.

**Purdue University,** Graduate School, College of Health and Human Sciences, Department of Psychological Sciences, West Lafayette, IN 47907. Offers behavioral neuroscience (PhD); clinical psychology (PhD); cognitive psychology (PhD); industrial/organizational psychology (PhD); mathematical and computational cognitive science (PhD). *Accreditation:* APA. *Faculty:* 43 full-time (17 women), 2 part-time/adjunct (both women). *Students:* 69 full-time (55 women), 4 part-time (2 women); includes 18 minority (2 Black or African American, non-Hispanic/Latino; 2 Asian, non-Hispanic/Latino; 11 Hispanic/Latino; 3 Two or more races, non-Hispanic/Latino), 19 international. Average age 28. 314 applicants, 15% accepted, 28 enrolled. In 2019, 12 doctorates awarded. Terminal master's awarded for partial completion of doctoral program. *Degree requirements:* For doctorate, thesis/dissertation. *Entrance requirements:* For doctorate, GRE General Test, minimum undergraduate GPA of 3.0 or equivalent. Additional exam requirements/recommendations for international students: required—TOEFL (minimum score 550 paper-based; 77 iBT); recommended—TWE. *Application deadline:* For fall admission, 12/3 for domestic and international students. Applications are processed on a rolling basis. Application fee: $60 ($75 for international students). Electronic applications accepted. *Financial support:* Fellowships with partial tuition reimbursements, research assistantships with partial tuition reimbursements, teaching assistantships with partial tuition reimbursements, and career-related internships or fieldwork available. Support available to part-time students. Financial award applicants required to submit FAFSA. *Unit head:* Dr. Jefferey D. Karpicke, Head, 765-494-6061, E-mail: karpicke@purdue.edu. *Application contact:* Nancy A. O'Brien, Graduate Contact, 765-494-6067, E-mail: nobrien@psych.pardue.edu.
Website: http://www.psych.purdue.edu/

**Purdue University,** Graduate School, PULSe - Purdue University Life Sciences Program, West Lafayette, IN 47907. Offers biomolecular structure and biophysics (PhD); biotechnology (PhD); chemical biology (PhD); chromatin and regulation of gene expression (PhD); integrative neuroscience (PhD); integrative plant sciences (PhD); membrane biology (PhD); microbiology (PhD); molecular evolutionary and cancer biology (PhD); molecular evolutionary genetics (PhD); molecular virology (PhD). *Students:* 37 full-time (23 women); includes 7 minority (1 Black or African American, non-Hispanic/Latino; 2 Asian, non-Hispanic/Latino; 4 Hispanic/Latino), 22 international. Average age 25. 162 applicants, 36% accepted, 19 enrolled. *Entrance requirements:* For doctorate, GRE, minimum undergraduate GPA of 3.0. Additional exam requirements/recommendations for international students: required—TOEFL (minimum score 550 paper-based; 77 iBT). *Application deadline:* For fall admission, 1/15 priority date for domestic and international students. Applications are processed on a rolling basis. Application fee: $60 ($75 for international students). Electronic applications accepted. *Financial support:* In 2019–20, research assistantships with tuition reimbursements (averaging $22,500 per year), teaching assistantships with tuition reimbursements (averaging $22,500 per year) were awarded. *Application contact:* Lindsey Springer, Graduate Contact for Admissions, 765-496-9667, E-mail: lbcampbe@purdue.edu.
Website: http://www.gradschool.purdue.edu/pulse

**Queens College of the City University of New York,** Mathematics and Natural Sciences Division, Department of Psychology, Queens, NY 11367-1597. Offers applied behavior analysis (MA); behavioral neuroscience (MA); general psychology (MA). *Program availability:* Part-time. Terminal master's awarded for partial completion of doctoral program. *Degree requirements:* For master's, comprehensive exam (for some programs), thesis (for some programs). *Entrance requirements:* For master's, GRE for Behavioral Neuroscience MA, minimum GPA of 3.0. Additional exam requirements/recommendations for international students: required—TOEFL (minimum score 100 iBT), IELTS (minimum score 7). Electronic applications accepted.

**Rosalind Franklin University of Medicine and Science,** School of Graduate and Postdoctoral Studies - Interdisciplinary Graduate Program in Biomedical Sciences, Department of Neuroscience, North Chicago, IL 60064-3095. Offers PhD, MD/PhD. *Degree requirements:* For doctorate, comprehensive exam, thesis/dissertation, original research project. *Entrance requirements:* For doctorate, GRE General Test. Additional exam requirements/recommendations for international students: required—TOEFL, TWE.

**Rush University,** Graduate College, Division of Neuroscience, Chicago, IL 60612-3832. Offers MS, PhD. Terminal master's awarded for partial completion of doctoral program. *Degree requirements:* For master's, thesis; for doctorate, thesis/dissertation. *Entrance requirements:* For master's and doctorate, GRE General Test. Additional exam requirements/recommendations for international students: required—TOEFL. Electronic applications accepted.

**Rutgers University - Newark,** Graduate School of Biomedical Sciences, Program in Integrative Neuroscience, Newark, NJ 07107. Offers PhD. *Degree requirements:* For doctorate, thesis/dissertation, qualifying exam. *Entrance requirements:* For doctorate, GRE General Test, minimum GPA of 3.5. Additional exam requirements/recommendations for international students: required—TOEFL. Electronic applications accepted.

**Rutgers University - Newark,** Graduate School, Program in Psychology, Newark, NJ 07102. Offers cognitive neuroscience (PhD); cognitive science (PhD); perception (PhD); psychobiology (PhD); social cognition (PhD). *Degree requirements:* For doctorate, comprehensive exam, thesis/dissertation. *Entrance requirements:* For doctorate, GRE General Test, GRE Subject Test, minimum undergraduate B average. Electronic applications accepted.

**Rutgers University - New Brunswick,** Graduate School-New Brunswick, Program in Endocrinology and Animal Biosciences, Piscataway, NJ 08854-8097. Offers MS, PhD. Terminal master's awarded for partial completion of doctoral program. *Degree requirements:* For master's, thesis; for doctorate, comprehensive exam, thesis/ dissertation. *Entrance requirements:* For master's and doctorate, GRE General Test. Additional exam requirements/recommendations for international students: required— TOEFL. Electronic applications accepted.

**Rutgers University - New Brunswick,** Graduate School of Biomedical Sciences, Program in Neuroscience, Piscataway, NJ 08854-5635. Offers MS, PhD, MD/PhD. *Degree requirements:* For master's, thesis, qualifying exam; for doctorate, thesis/ dissertation, qualifying exam. *Entrance requirements:* Additional exam requirements/ recommendations for international students: required—TOEFL. Electronic applications accepted.

**Seton Hall University,** College of Arts and Sciences, Department of Biological Sciences, South Orange, NJ 07079-2697. Offers biology (MS); biology/business administration (MS); microbiology (MS); molecular bioscience (PhD); molecular bioscience/neuroscience (PhD). *Program availability:* Part-time, evening/weekend. *Degree requirements:* For master's, thesis optional; for doctorate, comprehensive exam, thesis/dissertation. *Entrance requirements:* For master's, GRE or undergraduate degree (BS in biological sciences) with minimum GPA of 3.0 from accredited U.S. institution; for doctorate, GRE. Additional exam requirements/recommendations for international students: required—TOEFL. Electronic applications accepted.

**State University of New York Downstate Medical Center,** School of Graduate Studies, Program in Neural and Behavioral Science, Brooklyn, NY 11203-2098. Offers PhD, MD/PhD. *Degree requirements:* For doctorate, comprehensive exam, thesis/ dissertation. *Entrance requirements:* For doctorate, GRE. Additional exam requirements/recommendations for international students: recommended—TOEFL.

**State University of New York Upstate Medical University,** College of Graduate Studies, Program in Neuroscience, Syracuse, NY 13210. Offers PhD. *Degree requirements:* For doctorate, comprehensive exam, thesis/dissertation. *Entrance requirements:* For doctorate, GRE General Test, telephone interview. Additional exam requirements/recommendations for international students: required—TOEFL. Electronic applications accepted.

**Stony Brook University, State University of New York,** Graduate School, College of Arts and Sciences, Department of Neurobiology and Behavior, Stony Brook, NY 11794. Offers neuroscience (MS, PhD). *Faculty:* 16 full-time (3 women), 2 part-time/adjunct (0 women). *Students:* 38 full-time (20 women), 1 (woman) part-time; includes 12 minority (2 Black or African American, non-Hispanic/Latino; 7 Asian, non-Hispanic/Latino; 3 Hispanic/Latino), 7 international. Average age 27. 61 applicants, 21% accepted, 4 enrolled. In 2019, 6 doctorates awarded. *Degree requirements:* For doctorate, comprehensive exam, thesis/dissertation, teaching experience. *Entrance requirements:* For doctorate, GRE General Test, GRE Subject Test, minimum GPA of 3.0. Additional exam requirements/recommendations for international students: required—TOEFL (minimum score 90 iBT). *Application deadline:* For fall admission, 1/15 for domestic students; for spring admission, 10/1 for domestic students. Application fee: $100. Electronic applications accepted. *Expenses:* Contact institution. *Financial support:* In 2019–20, 9 fellowships, 15 research assistantships, 6 teaching assistantships were awarded; Federal Work-Study also available. *Unit head:* Dr. Alfredo Fontanini, Chair, 631-632-4100, Fax: 631-632-6661, E-mail: Alfredo.Fontanini@stonybrook.edu. *Application contact:* Odalis Hernandez, Coordinator, 631-632-8078, Fax: 631-632-6661, E-mail: odalis.hernandez@stonybrook.edu.
Website: http://medicine.stonybrookmedicine.edu/neurobiology/

**Stony Brook University, State University of New York,** Graduate School, College of Arts and Sciences, Department of Psychology, Program in Integrative Neuroscience, Stony Brook, NY 11794. Offers PhD. *Students:* 9 full-time (7 women); includes 3 minority (1 Black or African American, non-Hispanic/Latino; 1 Asian, non-Hispanic/Latino; 1 Hispanic/Latino), 2 international. Average age 27. 16 applicants, 19% accepted. In 2019, 3 doctorates awarded. *Entrance requirements:* For doctorate, GRE General Test, GRE Subject Test. Additional exam requirements/recommendations for international students: required—TOEFL (minimum score 90 iBT). *Application deadline:* For fall admission, 1/15 for domestic students; for spring admission, 10/1 for domestic students. Application fee: $100. Electronic applications accepted. *Expenses:* Contact institution. *Financial support:* In 2019–20, 9 fellowships, 15 research assistantships, 13 teaching assistantships were awarded. *Unit head:* Dr. Sheri Levy, Chair, 631-632-4355, E-mail: sheri.levy@stonybrook.edu. *Application contact:* Marilynn Wollmuth, Coordinator, 631-632-7855, Fax: 631-632-7876, E-mail: marilyn.wollmuth@stonybrook.edu.
Website: http://www.stonybrook.edu/commcms/psychology/integrative_neuroscience/overview.html

**Syracuse University,** College of Arts and Sciences, Department of Biology, Syracuse, NY 13244. Offers biology (MS, PhD); neuroscience (PhD). Terminal master's awarded for partial completion of doctoral program. *Entrance requirements:* For master's and doctorate, GRE General Test, GRE Subject Test (recommended), BS or BA, at least a minimal background in both physical and biological sciences, three letters of recommendation, personal statement, transcripts. Additional exam requirements/ recommendations for international students: required—TOEFL (minimum score 100 iBT). Electronic applications accepted.

**Teachers College, Columbia University,** Department of Biobehavioral Sciences, New York, NY 10027-6696. Offers applied exercise physiology (Ed M, MA, Ed D); communication sciences and disorders (MS, Ed D, PhD); kinesiology (PhD); motor learning and control (Ed M, MA); motor learning/movement science (Ed D); neuroscience and education (MS); physical education (MA, Ed D). *Accreditation:* ASHA. *Faculty:* 9 full-time (8 women). *Students:* 153 full-time (134 women), 149 part-time (106 women); includes 122 minority (25 Black or African American, non-Hispanic/Latino; 32 Asian, non-Hispanic/Latino; 55 Hispanic/Latino; 10 Two or more races, non-Hispanic/ Latino), 37 international. 582 applicants, 51% accepted, 165 enrolled. *Unit head:* Dr. Carol Scheffner Hammer, E-mail: cjh2207@tc.columbia.edu. *Application contact:* Kelly Sutton Skinner, Director of Admission and New Student Enrollment, 212-678-3710, E-mail: kms2237@tc.columbia.edu.
Website: http://www.tc.columbia.edu/biobehavioral-sciences/

**Texas Christian University,** College of Science and Engineering, Department of Psychology, Fort Worth, TX 76129-0002. Offers developmental trauma (MS); experimental psychology (PhD), including cognition/developmental, learning, neuroscience, social. *Faculty:* 14 full-time (7 women), 1 part-time/adjunct (0 women). *Students:* 31 full-time (26 women); includes 2 minority (both Asian, non-Hispanic/ Latino), 2 international. Average age 25. 52 applicants, 35% accepted, 13 enrolled. In 2019, 10 master's, 4 doctorates awarded. Terminal master's awarded for partial

completion of doctoral program. *Entrance requirements:* For doctorate, GRE General Test. Additional exam requirements/recommendations for international students: required—TOEFL (minimum score 550 paper-based; 80 iBT). *Application deadline:* For fall admission, 1/1 for domestic and international students. Application fee: $60. Electronic applications accepted. Full-time tuition and fees vary according to program. *Financial support:* In 2019–20, 23 students received support, including 23 teaching assistantships with full tuition reimbursements available (averaging $19,750 per year); scholarships/grants also available. Financial award application deadline: 1/1; financial award applicants required to submit FAFSA. *Unit head:* Dr. Anna I. Petursdottir, Chair, 817-257-7410, Fax: 817-257-7681, E-mail: a.petursdottir@tcu.edu. *Application contact:* Cindy Hayes, Administrative Assistant, 817-257-7410, Fax: 817-257-7681, E-mail: c.hayes@tcu.edu.
Website: https://psychology.tcu.edu/

**Thomas Jefferson University,** Jefferson College of Life Sciences, PhD Program in Neuroscience, Philadelphia, PA 19107. Offers PhD. *Degree requirements:* For doctorate, comprehensive exam, thesis/dissertation. *Entrance requirements:* For doctorate, GRE General Test, strong background in the sciences, interview, previous research experience. Additional exam requirements/recommendations for international students: required—TOEFL, IELTS (minimum score 7). Electronic applications accepted.

**Tufts University,** Cummings School of Veterinary Medicine, North Grafton, MA 01536. Offers animals and public policy (MS); biomedical sciences (PhD), including digestive diseases, infectious diseases, neuroscience and reproductive biology, pathology; conservation medicine (MS); veterinary medicine (DVM); DVM/MPH; DVM/MS. *Accreditation:* AVMA (one or more programs are accredited). *Degree requirements:* For master's, thesis (for some programs); for doctorate, comprehensive exam, thesis/ dissertation (for some programs). *Entrance requirements:* For master's and doctorate, GRE General Test. Additional exam requirements/recommendations for international students: required—TOEFL or IELTS. Electronic applications accepted. *Expenses:* Contact institution.

**Tufts University,** Graduate School of Biomedical Sciences, Neuroscience Program, Medford, MA 02155. Offers PhD. *Faculty:* 47 full-time (13 women). *Students:* 26 full-time (19 women); includes 10 minority (5 Asian, non-Hispanic/Latino; 2 Hispanic/Latino; 3 Two or more races, non-Hispanic/Latino), 3 international. Average age 28. 95 applicants, 15% accepted, 5 enrolled. In 2019, 8 doctorates awarded. Terminal master's awarded for partial completion of doctoral program. *Degree requirements:* For doctorate, comprehensive exam, thesis/dissertation. *Entrance requirements:* For doctorate, 3 letters of reference, personal statement, resume. *Application deadline:* For fall admission, 12/1 priority date for domestic and international students. Application fee: $90. Electronic applications accepted. *Expenses: Tuition:* Part-time $1799 per credit hour. Full-time tuition and fees vary according to degree level, program and student level. Part-time tuition and fees vary according to course load. *Financial support:* Application deadline: 12/1. *Unit head:* Dr. Chris Dulla, Program Director, 617-636-3796, E-mail: chris.dulla@tufts.edu. *Application contact:* Jeff Miller, Admissions Coordinator, 617-636-6767, Fax: 617-636-0375, E-mail: GSBS-Admissions@tufts.edu.
Website: https://gsbs.tufts.edu/academics/neuroscience

**Tulane University,** School of Medicine, Graduate Programs in Biomedical Sciences, Program in Neuroscience, New Orleans, LA 70118-5669. Offers MS, PhD, MD/PhD. *Degree requirements:* For doctorate, thesis/dissertation, qualifying exam. *Entrance requirements:* For doctorate, GRE General Test. Additional exam requirements/ recommendations for international students: required—TOEFL. Electronic applications accepted. *Expenses: Tuition:* Full-time $57,004; part-time $3167 per credit hour. *Required fees:* $2086; $44.50 per credit hour. $80 per term. Tuition and fees vary according to course load, degree level and program.

**Tulane University,** School of Science and Engineering, Neuroscience Program, New Orleans, LA 70118-5669. Offers MS, PhD. *Expenses: Tuition:* Full-time $57,004; part-time $3167 per credit hour. *Required fees:* $2086; $44.50 per credit hour. $80 per term. Tuition and fees vary according to course load, degree level and program.

**Uniformed Services University of the Health Sciences,** F. Edward Hebert School of Medicine, Graduate Programs in the Biomedical Sciences and Public Health, Graduate Program in Neuroscience, Bethesda, MD 20814-4799. Offers PhD. *Degree requirements:* For doctorate, comprehensive exam, thesis/dissertation, qualifying exams. *Entrance requirements:* For doctorate, GRE General Test, minimum GPA of 3.0; course work in biology, general chemistry, organic chemistry. Electronic applications accepted.

**Universidad de Iberoamerica,** Graduate School, San Jose, Costa Rica. Offers clinical neuropsychology (PhD); clinical psychology (M Psych); educational psychology (M Psych); forensic psychology (M Psych); hospital management (MHA); intensive care nursing (MN); medicine (MD).

**Université de Montréal,** Faculty of Medicine, Department of Physiology, Program in Neurological Sciences, Montréal, QC H3C 3J7, Canada. Offers M Sc, PhD. Terminal master's awarded for partial completion of doctoral program. *Degree requirements:* For master's, thesis; for doctorate, thesis/dissertation, general exam. *Entrance requirements:* For master's and doctorate, proficiency in French, knowledge of English. Electronic applications accepted.

**University at Albany, State University of New York,** College of Arts and Sciences, Department of Psychology, Albany, NY 12222-0001. Offers behavioral neuroscience (PhD); clinical psychology (PhD); cognitive psychology (PhD); industrial/organizational psychology (MA, PhD); social-personality psychology (PhD). *Accreditation:* APA (one or more programs are accredited). *Program availability:* Blended/hybrid learning. *Faculty:* 31 full-time (14 women), 6 part-time/adjunct (4 women). *Students:* 68 full-time (44 women), 53 part-time (35 women); includes 30 minority (3 Black or African American, non-Hispanic/Latino; 10 Asian, non-Hispanic/Latino; 11 Hispanic/Latino; 6 Two or more races, non-Hispanic/Latino), 9 international. 253 applicants, 21% accepted, 28 enrolled. In 2019, 22 master's, 11 doctorates awarded. *Degree requirements:* For doctorate, thesis/dissertation. *Entrance requirements:* For master's, transcripts of all schools attended; statement of background and goals; departmental questionnaire; resume; names and contact information for 3 recommenders; for doctorate, GRE General Test, GRE Subject Test, transcripts of all schools attended; statement of background and goals; departmental questionnaire; resume; names and contact information for 3 recommenders. Additional exam requirements/recommendations for international students: required—TOEFL (minimum score 550 paper-based). *Application deadline:* For fall admission, 1/15 for domestic and international students; for spring admission, 11/15 for domestic students. Application fee: $75. Electronic applications accepted. *Expenses: Tuition,* area resident: Full-time $11,530; part-time $480 per credit hour. Tuition, nonresident: full-time $23,530; part-time $980 per credit hour. *International tuition:* $23,530 full-time. *Required fees:* $2185; $96 per credit hour. Part-time tuition and fees vary according to course load and program. *Financial support:* Fellowships, research assistantships, teaching assistantships, and career-related internships or fieldwork available. Financial award application deadline: 2/1. *Unit head:* Christine K. Wagner, Chair, 518-442-4820, Fax: 518-442-4867, E-mail: cwagner@albany.edu. *Application contact:* Michael DeRensis, Director, Graduate Admissions, 518-442-3980,

Fax: 518-442-3922, E-mail: graduate@albany.edu.
Website: https://www.albany.edu/psychology/

**University at Buffalo, the State University of New York,** Graduate School, Jacobs School of Medicine and Biomedical Sciences, Graduate Programs in Medicine and Biomedical Sciences, Neuroscience Program, Buffalo, NY 14260. Offers MS, PhD. *Faculty:* 88 full-time (24 women), 1 part-time/adjunct (0 women). *Students:* Average age 25. 46 applicants, 30% accepted, 10 enrolled. In 2019, 5 master's, 3 doctorates awarded. Terminal master's awarded for partial completion of doctoral program. *Degree requirements:* For master's, thesis or project; for doctorate, comprehensive exam, thesis/dissertation. *Entrance requirements:* For master's, GRE General Test, 3 letters of recommendation, transcripts; for doctorate, GRE General Test or MCAT. Additional exam requirements/recommendations for international students: required—TOEFL (minimum score 550 paper-based; 80 iBT). *Application deadline:* For fall admission, 4/30 priority date for domestic and international students. Applications are processed on a rolling basis. Application fee: $85. Electronic applications accepted. *Expenses:* Contact institution. *Financial support:* In 2019–20, 19 students received support, including 19 research assistantships with full tuition reimbursements available (averaging $27,000 per year); scholarships/grants and health care benefits also available. Financial award application deadline: 9/1; financial award applicants required to submit FAFSA. *Unit head:* Dr. Fraser Sim, Associate Professor, 716-829-2151, E-mail: fjsim@buffalo.edu. *Application contact:* Lisa M. Zander, Graduate Programs Coordinator, 716-881-7507, E-mail: lzander@buffalo.edu.
Website: http://medicine.buffalo.edu/education/neuroscience.html

**The University of Alabama at Birmingham,** College of Arts and Sciences, Program in Psychology, Birmingham, AL 35294. Offers behavioral neuroscience (PhD); lifespan developmental psychology (PhD); medical/clinical psychology (PhD); psychology (MA). *Accreditation:* APA (one or more programs are accredited). *Faculty:* 27 full-time (12 women), 1 (woman) part-time/adjunct. *Students:* 81 full-time (55 women), 3 part-time (all women); includes 22 minority (10 Black or African American, non-Hispanic/Latino; 4 Asian, non-Hispanic/Latino; 6 Hispanic/Latino; 2 Two or more races, non-Hispanic/Latino), 3 international. Average age 27. 199 applicants, 7% accepted, 12 enrolled. In 2019, 8 master's, 15 doctorates awarded. *Entrance requirements:* For master's and doctorate, GRE General Test, letters of recommendation. *Application deadline:* Applications are processed on a rolling basis. Electronic applications accepted. *Financial support:* Fellowships, research assistantships, and teaching assistantships available. *Unit head:* Dr. Karlene K. Ball, Chair, 205-934-2610, Fax: 205-975-2295, E-mail: psych-dept@uab.edu. *Application contact:* Susan Noblitt Banks, Director of Graduate School Operations, 205-934-8227, Fax: 205-934-8413, E-mail: gradschool@uab.edu.
Website: http://www.uab.edu/cas/psychology/graduate

**The University of Alabama at Birmingham,** Joint Health Sciences, Neuroscience Theme, Birmingham, AL 35294. Offers PhD. *Students:* Average age 26. 92 applicants, 11% accepted, 1 enrolled. In 2019, 2 doctorates awarded. *Degree requirements:* For doctorate, comprehensive exam, thesis/dissertation. *Entrance requirements:* For doctorate, personal statement, resume or curriculum vitae, letters of recommendation, research experience, interview. Additional exam requirements/recommendations for international students: required—TOEFL (minimum score 53 iBT), IELTS (minimum score 6.5). *Application deadline:* For fall admission, 12/31 for domestic and international students. Applications are processed on a rolling basis. Electronic applications accepted. *Financial support:* In 2019–20, fellowships with full tuition reimbursements (averaging $30,000 per year), research assistantships with full tuition reimbursements (averaging $31,000 per year) were awarded; health care benefits also available. *Unit head:* Dr. Karen Gamble, Theme Director, 205-934-4663, E-mail: klgamble@uab.edu. *Application contact:* Alyssa Zasada, Admissions Manager for Graduate Biomedical Sciences, 205-934-3857, E-mail: grad-gbs@uab.edu.
Website: http://www.uab.edu/gbs/home/themes/nesc

**University of Alaska Fairbanks,** College of Natural Science and Mathematics, Department of Chemistry and Biochemistry, Fairbanks, AK 99775-6160. Offers biochemistry and neuroscience (PhD); chemistry (MA, MS), including chemistry (MS); environmental chemistry (PhD). *Program availability:* Part-time. *Degree requirements:* For master's, comprehensive exam, thesis (for some programs), oral defense of project or thesis; for doctorate, comprehensive exam, thesis/dissertation, oral defense of dissertation. *Entrance requirements:* For master's, GRE General Test (for MS), bachelor's degree from accredited institution with minimum cumulative undergraduate and major GPA of 3.0; for doctorate, GRE General Test, minimum cumulative GPA of 3.0. Additional exam requirements/recommendations for international students: required—TOEFL (minimum score 550 paper-based; 79 iBT), TWE. Electronic applications accepted.

**University of Alberta,** Neuroscience and Mental Health Institute, Edmonton, AB T6G 2E1, Canada. Offers neuroscience (M Sc, PhD). Terminal master's awarded for partial completion of doctoral program. *Degree requirements:* For master's, thesis; for doctorate, thesis/dissertation. *Entrance requirements:* For master's and doctorate, minimum GPA of 3.3. Additional exam requirements/recommendations for international students: required—TOEFL (minimum score 600 paper-based). Electronic applications accepted.

**The University of Arizona,** Graduate Interdisciplinary Programs, Graduate Interdisciplinary Program in Neuroscience, Tucson, AZ 85719. Offers PhD. *Degree requirements:* For doctorate, thesis/dissertation. *Entrance requirements:* For doctorate, GRE (minimum score 1100), minimum GPA of 3.5, 3 letters of recommendation. Additional exam requirements/recommendations for international students: required—TOEFL (minimum score 550 paper-based; 79 iBT). Electronic applications accepted.

**The University of British Columbia,** Faculty of Arts, Department of Psychology, Vancouver, BC V6T 1Z4, Canada. Offers behavioral neuroscience (MA, PhD); clinical psychology (MA, PhD); cognitive science (MA, PhD); developmental psychology (MA, PhD); health psychology (MA, PhD); quantitative methods (MA, PhD); social/personality psychology (MA, PhD). *Accreditation:* APA (one or more programs are accredited). Terminal master's awarded for partial completion of doctoral program. *Degree requirements:* For master's, thesis; for doctorate, comprehensive exam, thesis/dissertation. *Entrance requirements:* For master's and doctorate, GRE General Test. Additional exam requirements/recommendations for international students: required—TOEFL. Electronic applications accepted. *Expenses:* Contact institution.

**The University of British Columbia,** Faculty of Medicine, Department of Cellular and Physiological Sciences, Vancouver, BC V6T 1Z3, Canada. Offers bioinformatics (M Sc, PhD); cell and developmental biology (M Sc, PhD); genome science and technology (M Sc, PhD); neuroscience (M Sc, PhD). *Degree requirements:* For master's, thesis, oral defense; for doctorate, comprehensive exam, thesis/dissertation, oral defense. *Entrance requirements:* For master's, minimum overall B+ average in third- and fourth-year courses; for doctorate, minimum overall B+ average in master's degree (or equivalent) from approved institution with clear evidence of research ability or potential. Additional exam requirements/recommendations for international students: required—TOEFL, IELTS. *Expenses:* Contact institution.

**University of Calgary,** Cumming School of Medicine and Faculty of Graduate Studies, Program in Neuroscience, Calgary, AB T2N 1N4, Canada. Offers M Sc, PhD. *Degree requirements:* For master's, thesis, oral thesis exam; for doctorate, thesis/dissertation, candidacy exam, oral thesis exam. *Entrance requirements:* For master's and doctorate, minimum GPA of 3.2 during previous 2 years. Additional exam requirements/recommendations for international students: required—TOEFL (minimum score 580 paper-based). Electronic applications accepted.

**University of California, Berkeley,** Graduate Division, Neuroscience Graduate Program, Berkeley, CA 94720-3200. Offers PhD. *Degree requirements:* For doctorate, qualifying exam, teaching requirement, research thesis/dissertation. *Entrance requirements:* For doctorate, GRE General Test, minimum GPA of 3.0, 3 letters of recommendation, at least one year of laboratory experience. Additional exam requirements/recommendations for international students: required—TOEFL or IELTS. Electronic applications accepted.

**University of California, Davis,** Graduate Studies, Graduate Group in Neuroscience, Davis, CA 95616. Offers PhD. *Degree requirements:* For doctorate, thesis/dissertation. *Entrance requirements:* For doctorate, GRE General Test, GRE Subject Test. Additional exam requirements/recommendations for international students: required—TOEFL (minimum score 550 paper-based). Electronic applications accepted.

**University of California, Irvine,** School of Biological Sciences, Interdepartmental Neuroscience Program, Irvine, CA 92697. Offers PhD. *Students:* 15 full-time (10 women); includes 8 minority (1 Black or African American, non-Hispanic/Latino; 3 Asian, non-Hispanic/Latino; 4 Hispanic/Latino), 1 international. Average age 25. 183 applicants, 20% accepted, 15 enrolled. *Application deadline:* For fall admission, 12/2 for domestic students. Application fee: $120 ($140 for international students). Electronic applications accepted. *Unit head:* Prof. Karina S. Cramer, Director, 949-824-4211, Fax: 949-824-2447, E-mail: cramerk@uci.edu. *Application contact:* Gary R. Roman, Program Administrator, 949-824-6226, Fax: 949-824-4150, E-mail: gary.roman@uci.edu.
Website: http://www.inp.uci.edu/

**University of California, Los Angeles,** David Geffen School of Medicine and Graduate Division, Graduate Programs in Medicine, Interdepartmental Program in Neuroscience, Los Angeles, CA 90095. Offers PhD. *Degree requirements:* For doctorate, thesis/dissertation, oral and written qualifying exams; 1 quarter of teaching experience. *Entrance requirements:* For doctorate, GRE General Test or MCAT, bachelor's degree; minimum undergraduate GPA of 3.0 (or its equivalent if letter grade system not used). Additional exam requirements/recommendations for international students: required—TOEFL. Electronic applications accepted.

**University of California, Riverside,** Graduate Division, Program in Neuroscience, Riverside, CA 92521. Offers PhD. *Degree requirements:* For doctorate, comprehensive exam, thesis/dissertation, 2 quarters of teaching experience, qualifying exams. *Entrance requirements:* For doctorate, GRE General Test, minimum GPA of 3.25. Additional exam requirements/recommendations for international students: required—TOEFL (minimum score 550 paper-based; 80 iBT); recommended—IELTS. Electronic applications accepted.

**University of California, San Diego,** Graduate Division, Department of Physics, La Jolla, CA 92093. Offers biophysics (PhD); computational neuroscience (PhD); computational science (PhD); multi-scale biology (PhD); physics (MS, PhD); quantitative biology (PhD). *Students:* 166 full-time (26 women), 2 part-time (1 woman). 566 applicants, 22% accepted, 22 enrolled. In 2019, 9 master's, 23 doctorates awarded. *Degree requirements:* For doctorate, comprehensive exam, thesis/dissertation, 1-quarter teaching assistantship. *Entrance requirements:* For doctorate, GRE General Test, GRE Subject Test, statement of purpose, three letters of reference. Additional exam requirements/recommendations for international students: required—TOEFL (minimum score 550 paper-based; 80 iBT), IELTS (minimum score 7). *Application deadline:* For fall admission, 12/18 for domestic students. Application fee: $105 ($125 for international students). Electronic applications accepted. *Financial support:* Fellowships, research assistantships, teaching assistantships, scholarships/grants, and unspecified assistantships available. Financial award applicants required to submit FAFSA. *Unit head:* Brian Maple, Chair, 858-534-6857, E-mail: chair@physics.ucsd.edu. *Application contact:* Saixious Dominguez-Kilday, Graduate Admissions Coordinator, 858-534-3293, E-mail: skilday@physics.ucsd.edu.
Website: http://physics.ucsd.edu/

**University of California, San Diego,** School of Medicine and Graduate Division, Program in Neurosciences, La Jolla, CA 92093. Offers PhD. *Students:* 91 full-time (51 women), 2 part-time (1 woman). 509 applicants, 10% accepted, 14 enrolled. In 2019, 27 doctorates awarded. *Degree requirements:* For doctorate, comprehensive exam, thesis/dissertation, 1-quarter teaching assistantship, 3 research rotations. *Entrance requirements:* For doctorate, GRE General Test, three letters of recommendation, statement of purpose. Additional exam requirements/recommendations for international students: required—TOEFL (minimum score 550 paper-based; 80 iBT), IELTS (minimum score 7). *Application deadline:* For fall admission, 11/26 for domestic students. Application fee: $105 ($125 for international students). Electronic applications accepted. *Financial support:* Fellowships, research assistantships, teaching assistantships, scholarships/grants, traineeships, unspecified assistantships, and readerships available. Financial award applicants required to submit FAFSA. *Unit head:* Timothy Gentner, Chair, 858-822-6763, E-mail: tgentner@ucsd.edu. *Application contact:* Erin Gilbert, Graduate Coordinator, 858-534-3377, E-mail: neurograd@ucsd.edu.
Website: http://neurograd.ucsd.edu

**University of California, San Francisco,** Graduate Division, Program in Neuroscience, San Francisco, CA 94143. Offers PhD. *Degree requirements:* For doctorate, thesis/dissertation. *Entrance requirements:* For doctorate, GRE General Test or MCAT, official transcripts, two letters of recommendation. Additional exam requirements/recommendations for international students: required—TOEFL. Electronic applications accepted.

**University of California, Santa Barbara,** Graduate Division, College of Letters and Sciences, Division of Mathematics, Life, and Physical Sciences, Interdepartmental Graduate Program in Dynamical Neuroscience, Santa Barbara, CA 93106-2014. Offers PhD. *Degree requirements:* For doctorate, comprehensive exam, thesis/dissertation. *Entrance requirements:* Additional exam requirements/recommendations for international students: required—TOEFL. Electronic applications accepted.

**University of Chicago,** Division of the Biological Sciences, Program in Computational Neuroscience, Chicago, IL 60637-1513. Offers PhD. *Degree requirements:* For doctorate, thesis/dissertation, ethics class, 2 teaching assistantships. *Entrance requirements:* For doctorate, GRE General Test, transcripts, statement of purpose, 3 letters of recommendation. Additional exam requirements/recommendations for international students: required—TOEFL (minimum score 600 paper-based; 104 iBT), IELTS (minimum score 7). Electronic applications accepted.

**University of Cincinnati,** Graduate School, Neuroscience Graduate Program, Cincinnati, OH 45267. Offers PhD. *Degree requirements:* For doctorate, thesis/dissertation, qualifying exam. *Entrance requirements:* For doctorate, GRE General Test.

Additional exam requirements/recommendations for international students: required—TOEFL (minimum score 100 iBT), IELTS (minimum score 6.5). Electronic applications accepted.

**University of Colorado Denver,** School of Medicine, Program in Neuroscience, Aurora, CO 80206. Offers PhD. *Degree requirements:* For doctorate, comprehensive exam, thesis/dissertation, structured class schedule each year paired with lab rotations. *Entrance requirements:* For doctorate, GRE, baccalaureate degree in a biological science, chemistry, physics or engineering (recommended); minimum GPA of 3.2. Additional exam requirements/recommendations for international students: required—TOEFL (minimum score 550 paper-based; 80 iBT). Electronic applications accepted. Tuition and fees vary according to course load, program and reciprocity agreements.

**University of Connecticut,** Graduate School, College of Liberal Arts and Sciences, Department of Psychological Sciences, Storrs, CT 06269. Offers behavioral neuroscience (PhD); biopsychology (PhD); clinical psychology (MA, PhD); cognition and instruction (PhD); developmental psychology (MA, PhD); ecological psychology (PhD); experimental psychology (PhD); general psychology (MA, PhD); industrial/organizational psychology (PhD); language and cognition (PhD); neuroscience (PhD); social psychology (MA, PhD). *Accreditation:* APA. Terminal master's awarded for partial completion of doctoral program. *Degree requirements:* For master's, comprehensive exam; for doctorate, thesis/dissertation. *Entrance requirements:* For master's and doctorate, GRE General Test, GRE Subject Test. Additional exam requirements/recommendations for international students: required—TOEFL (minimum score 550 paper-based). Electronic applications accepted.

**University of Connecticut Health Center,** Graduate School, Programs in Biomedical Sciences, Program in Neuroscience, Farmington, CT 06030. Offers PhD, DMD/PhD, MD/PhD. *Degree requirements:* For doctorate, comprehensive exam, thesis/dissertation. *Entrance requirements:* For doctorate, GRE General Test, interview (recommended). Additional exam requirements/recommendations for international students: required—TOEFL (minimum score 600 paper-based). Electronic applications accepted.

**University of Delaware,** College of Arts and Sciences, Department of Psychology, Newark, DE 19716. Offers behavioral neuroscience (PhD); clinical psychology (PhD); cognitive psychology (PhD); social psychology (PhD). *Accreditation:* APA. *Degree requirements:* For doctorate, thesis/dissertation. *Entrance requirements:* For doctorate, GRE General Test. Additional exam requirements/recommendations for international students: required—TOEFL (minimum score 600 paper-based). Electronic applications accepted.

**University of Florida,** College of Medicine and Graduate School, Interdisciplinary Program in Biomedical Sciences, Concentration in Neuroscience, Gainesville, FL 32611. Offers PhD. *Degree requirements:* For doctorate, thesis/dissertation. *Entrance requirements:* For doctorate, GRE General Test, minimum GPA of 3.0, biochemistry before enrollment. Additional exam requirements/recommendations for international students: required—TOEFL. Electronic applications accepted.

**University of Georgia,** Biomedical and Health Sciences Institute, Athens, GA 30602. Offers neuroscience (PhD). *Entrance requirements:* For doctorate, GRE, official transcripts, 3 letters of recommendation, statement of interest. Additional exam requirements/recommendations for international students: required—TOEFL.

**University of Guelph,** Ontario Veterinary College and Office of Graduate and Postdoctoral Studies, Graduate Programs in Veterinary Sciences, Department of Biomedical Sciences, Guelph, ON N1G 2W1, Canada. Offers morphology (M Sc, DV Sc, PhD); neuroscience (M Sc, DV Sc, PhD); pharmacology (M Sc, DV Sc, PhD); physiology (M Sc, DV Sc, PhD); toxicology (M Sc, DV Sc, PhD). *Program availability:* Part-time. *Degree requirements:* For master's, thesis; for doctorate, comprehensive exam, thesis/dissertation. *Entrance requirements:* For master's, honors B Sc, minimum 75% average in last 20 courses; for doctorate, M Sc with thesis from accredited institution. Additional exam requirements/recommendations for international students: required—TOEFL (minimum score 550 paper-based; 89 iBT). Electronic applications accepted.

**University of Guelph,** Ontario Veterinary College and Office of Graduate and Postdoctoral Studies, Graduate Programs in Veterinary Sciences, Department of Clinical Studies, Guelph, ON N1G 2W1, Canada. Offers anesthesiology (M Sc, DV Sc); cardiology (DV Sc, Diploma); clinical studies (Diploma); dermatology (M Sc); diagnostic imaging (M Sc, DV Sc); emergency/critical care (M Sc, DV Sc, Diploma); medicine (M Sc, DV Sc); neurology (M Sc, DV Sc); ophthalmology (M Sc, DV Sc); surgery (M Sc, DV Sc). *Degree requirements:* For master's, thesis; for doctorate, comprehensive exam, thesis/dissertation. *Entrance requirements:* Additional exam requirements/recommendations for international students: required—TOEFL (minimum score 550 paper-based), IELTS (minimum score 6.5). Electronic applications accepted.

**University of Hartford,** College of Arts and Sciences, Department of Biology, Program in Neuroscience, West Hartford, CT 06117-1599. Offers MS. *Program availability:* Part-time, evening/weekend. *Students:* 16 full-time (6 women), 14 part-time (4 women); includes 7 minority (5 Black or African American, non-Hispanic/Latino; 2 Hispanic/Latino), 3 international. Average age 25. *Degree requirements:* For master's, comprehensive exam, thesis optional, oral exams. *Entrance requirements:* For master's, GRE General Test, GRE Subject Test, MCAT. Additional exam requirements/recommendations for international students: required—TOEFL (minimum score 550 paper-based). *Application deadline:* Applications are processed on a rolling basis. Application fee: $40. Electronic applications accepted. *Expenses: Tuition:* Full-time $23,700; part-time $645 per credit. *Required fees:* $510; $510 per unit. Tuition and fees vary according to course load, degree level and program. *Financial support:* Research assistantships with partial tuition reimbursements and teaching assistantships with partial tuition reimbursements available. Financial award application deadline: 6/1. *Unit head:* Dr. Jacob Harney, Head, 860-768-5372, Fax: 860-768-5002, E-mail: harney@hartford.edu. *Application contact:* Renee Murphy, Assistant Director of Graduate Admissions, 860-768-4371, Fax: 860-768-5160, E-mail: gettoknow@hartford.edu.
Website: http://www.uhaweb.hartford.edu/biology/

**University of Illinois at Chicago,** Program in Neuroscience, Chicago, IL 60607. Offers cellular and systems neuroscience and cell biology (PhD); neuroscience (MS).

**University of Illinois at Urbana-Champaign,** Graduate College, College of Liberal Arts and Sciences, School of Molecular and Cellular Biology, Neuroscience Program, Champaign, IL 61820. Offers PhD.

**The University of Iowa,** Graduate College, Program in Neuroscience, Iowa City, IA 52242-1316. Offers PhD. *Degree requirements:* For doctorate, comprehensive exam, thesis/dissertation. *Entrance requirements:* For doctorate, GRE General Test, minimum GPA of 3.0. Additional exam requirements/recommendations for international students: required—TOEFL (minimum score 600 paper-based; 100 iBT). Electronic applications accepted.

**The University of Kansas,** Graduate Studies, School of Pharmacy, Program in Neurosciences, Lawrence, KS 66045. Offers MS, PhD. *Program availability:* Part-time. *Students:* 6 full-time (1 woman), 3 part-time (2 women); includes 1 minority (Hispanic/Latino), 1 international. Average age 32. 12 applicants, 8% accepted, 1 enrolled. In 2019, 2 doctorates awarded. *Entrance requirements:* For master's and doctorate, GRE, BA or BS in neuroscience or a related study, three letters of recommendation, personal statement, minimum GPA of 3.0. Additional exam requirements/recommendations for international students: required—TOEFL, IELTS. *Application deadline:* For fall admission, 1/15 priority date for domestic and international students. Application fee: $65 ($85 for international students). Electronic applications accepted. *Expenses:* Tuition, state resident: full-time $9989. Tuition, nonresident: full-time $23,950. *International tuition:* $23,950 full-time. *Required fees:* $984; $81.99 per credit hour. Tuition and fees vary according to course load, campus/location and program. *Financial support:* Fellowships, research assistantships, teaching assistantships, and scholarships/grants available. Financial award application deadline: 1/15. *Unit head:* Rick Dobrowsky, Chair, 785-864-3531, E-mail: dobrowsky@ku.edu. *Application contact:* Patti Steffan, Graduate Admission Contact, 785-864-3893, E-mail: psteffan@ku.edu.
Website: http://www.neuroscience.ku.edu/

**The University of Kansas,** University of Kansas Medical Center, School of Medicine, Neuroscience Graduate Program, Kansas City, KS 66045-7582. Offers PhD, MD/PhD. *Students:* 8 full-time (2 women), 1 international. Average age 29. In 2019, 2 doctorates awarded. Terminal master's awarded for partial completion of doctoral program. *Degree requirements:* For doctorate, comprehensive exam, thesis/dissertation. *Entrance requirements:* For doctorate, GRE. Additional exam requirements/recommendations for international students: required—TOEFL. Application fee: $60. Application fee is waived when completed online. *Expenses:* Tuition, state resident: full-time $9989. Tuition, nonresident: full-time $23,950. *International tuition:* $23,950 full-time. *Required fees:* $984; $81.99 per credit hour. Tuition and fees vary according to course load, campus/location and program. *Financial support:* Fellowships with partial tuition reimbursements, research assistantships with full tuition reimbursements, and teaching assistantships with full tuition reimbursements available. Financial award application deadline: 3/1; financial award applicants required to submit FAFSA. *Unit head:* Dr. Doug Wright, Professor, Director of KUMC Neuroscience Graduate Program, 913-588-2713, Fax: 913-588-2710, E-mail: dwright@kumc.edu. *Application contact:* Marcia Jones, Director of Graduate Studies, 913-588-1238, Fax: 913-588-5242, E-mail: mjones@kumc.edu.
Website: http://www.kumc.edu/school-of-medicine/neuroscience.html

**University of Lethbridge,** School of Graduate Studies, Lethbridge, AB T1K 3M4, Canada. Offers addictions counseling (M Sc); agricultural biotechnology (M Sc); agricultural studies (M Sc, MA); anthropology (MA); archaeology (M Sc, MA); art (MA, MFA); biochemistry (M Sc); biological sciences (M Sc); biomolecular science (PhD); biosystems and biodiversity (PhD); Canadian studies (MA); chemistry (M Sc); computer science (M Sc); computer science and geographical information science (M Sc); counseling (MC); counseling psychology (M Ed); dramatic arts (MA); earth, space, and physical science (PhD); economics (MA); education (MA, PhD); educational leadership (M Ed); English (MA); environmental science (M Sc); evolution and behavior (PhD); exercise science (M Sc); French (MA); French/German (MA); French/Spanish (MA); general education (M Ed); geography (M Sc, MA); German (MA); health sciences (M Sc); individualized multidisciplinary (M Sc, MA); kinesiology (M Sc, MA); management (M Sc), including accounting, finance, human resource management and labor relations, information systems, international management, marketing, policy and strategy; mathematics (M Sc); music (M Mus, MA); Native American studies (MA); neuroscience (M Sc, PhD); new media (MA, MFA); nursing (M Sc, MN); philosophy (MA); physics (M Sc); political science (MA); psychology (M Sc, MA); religious studies (MA); sociology (MA); theatre and dramatic arts (MFA); theoretical and computational science (PhD); urban and regional studies (MA); women and gender studies (MA). *Program availability:* Part-time, evening/weekend. *Degree requirements:* For master's, thesis (for some programs); for doctorate, comprehensive exam, thesis/dissertation. *Entrance requirements:* For master's, GMAT (for M Sc in management), bachelor's degree in related field, minimum GPA of 3.0 during previous 20 graded semester courses, 2 years' teaching or related experience (M Ed); for doctorate, master's degree, minimum graduate GPA of 3.5. Additional exam requirements/recommendations for international students: required—TOEFL (minimum score 580 paper-based; 93 iBT). Electronic applications accepted.

**The University of Manchester,** School of Biological Sciences, Manchester, United Kingdom. Offers adaptive organismal biology (M Phil, PhD); animal biology (M Phil, PhD); biochemistry (M Phil, PhD); bioinformatics (M Phil, PhD); biomolecular sciences (M Phil, PhD); biotechnology (M Phil, PhD); cell biology (M Phil, PhD); cell matrix research (M Phil, PhD); channels and transporters (M Phil, PhD); developmental biology (M Phil, PhD); environmental biology (M Phil, PhD); evolutionary biology (M Phil, PhD); gene expression (M Phil, PhD); genetics (M Phil, PhD); history of science, technology and medicine (M Phil, PhD); immunology (M Phil, PhD); integrative neurobiology and behavior (M Phil, PhD); membrane trafficking (M Phil, PhD); microbiology (M Phil, PhD); molecular and cellular neuroscience (M Phil, PhD); molecular biology (M Phil, PhD); molecular cancer studies (M Phil, PhD); neuroscience (M Phil, PhD); ophthalmology (M Phil, PhD); optometry (M Phil, PhD); organelle function (M Phil, PhD); pharmacology (M Phil, PhD); physiology (M Phil, PhD); plant sciences (M Phil, PhD); stem cell research (M Phil, PhD); structural biology (M Phil, PhD); systems neuroscience (M Phil, PhD); toxicology (M Phil, PhD).

**University of Maryland, Baltimore,** Graduate School, Graduate Program in Life Sciences, Program in Neuroscience, Baltimore, MD 21201. Offers PhD, MD/PhD. *Program availability:* Part-time. *Degree requirements:* For doctorate, comprehensive exam, thesis/dissertation. *Entrance requirements:* For doctorate, GRE General Test, minimum GPA of 3.0, curriculum vitae, essay, 3 letters of recommendation. Additional exam requirements/recommendations for international students: required—TOEFL (minimum score 80 iBT); recommended—IELTS (minimum score 7). Electronic applications accepted.

**University of Maryland, Baltimore County,** The Graduate School, College of Natural and Mathematical Sciences, Department of Biological Sciences, Program in Neuroscience and Cognitive Sciences, Baltimore, MD 21250. Offers PhD. *Faculty:* 6 full-time (3 women). *Students:* 6 full-time (4 women); includes 3 minority (1 Black or African American, non-Hispanic/Latino; 2 Asian, non-Hispanic/Latino). Average age 25. 7 applicants. *Degree requirements:* For doctorate, thesis/dissertation. *Entrance requirements:* For doctorate, GRE General Test, minimum GPA of 3.0. Additional exam requirements/recommendations for international students: required—TOEFL (minimum score 80 iBT), IELTS (minimum score 6.5). *Application deadline:* For fall admission, 4/15 priority date for domestic and international students. Application fee: $50. Electronic applications accepted. *Expenses: Tuition, area resident:* Full-time $659. Tuition, state resident: full-time $659. Tuition, nonresident: full-time $1132. *International tuition:* $1132 full-time. *Required fees:* $140; $140 per credit hour. *Financial support:* In 2019–20, 5 students received support, including 1 research assistantship with full tuition reimbursement available (averaging $24,600 per year), 4 teaching assistantships with full tuition reimbursements available (averaging $23,518 per year); health care benefits and unspecified assistantships also available. *Unit head:* Dr. Michelle Starz-Gaiano, Director, 410-455-2217, Fax: 410-455-3875, E-mail: biograd@umbc.edu. *Application contact:* Brandy Darcey, Graduate Program Coordinator, 410-455-3669, E-mail:

bdarcey@umbc.edu.
Website: http://biology.umbc.edu

**University of Maryland, College Park,** Academic Affairs, College of Behavioral and Social Sciences, Department of Hearing and Speech Sciences, College Park, MD 20742. Offers audiology (MA, PhD); hearing and speech sciences (Au D); language pathology (MA, PhD); neuroscience (PhD); speech (MA, PhD). *Accreditation:* ASHA (one or more programs are accredited). *Degree requirements:* For master's, thesis optional; for doctorate, thesis/dissertation, written and oral exams. *Entrance requirements:* For master's, GRE General Test, minimum GPA of 3.5, 3 letters of recommendation; for doctorate, GRE General Test, minimum GPA of 3.5. Additional exam requirements/recommendations for international students: required—TOEFL. Electronic applications accepted.

**University of Maryland, College Park,** Academic Affairs, College of Behavioral and Social Sciences, Program in Neurosciences and Cognitive Sciences, College Park, MD 20742. Offers PhD. *Degree requirements:* For doctorate, comprehensive exam, thesis/dissertation. *Entrance requirements:* For doctorate, GRE General Test, 3 letters of recommendation. Additional exam requirements/recommendations for international students: required—TOEFL. Electronic applications accepted.

**University of Massachusetts Amherst,** Graduate School, Interdisciplinary Programs, Program in Neuroscience and Behavior, Amherst, MA 01003. Offers animal behavior and learning (PhD); molecular and cellular neuroscience (PhD); neural and behavioral development (PhD); neuroendocrinology (PhD); neuroscience and behavior (MS); sensorimotor, cognitive, and computational neuroscience (PhD). Terminal master's awarded for partial completion of doctoral program. *Degree requirements:* For master's, thesis or alternative; for doctorate, comprehensive exam, thesis/dissertation. *Entrance requirements:* For master's, GRE General Test; for doctorate, GRE General Test; GRE Subject Test in psychology, biology, or mathematics (recommended). Additional exam requirements/recommendations for international students: required—TOEFL (minimum score 550 paper-based; 80 iBT), IELTS (minimum score 6.5). Electronic applications accepted.

**University of Massachusetts Medical School,** Graduate School of Biomedical Sciences, Worcester, MA 01655. Offers biomedical sciences (PhD), including biochemistry and molecular pharmacology, bioinformatics and computational biology, cancer biology, immunology and microbiology, interdisciplinary, neuroscience, translational science; biomedical sciences (millennium program) (PhD); clinical and population health research (PhD); clinical investigation (MS). *Faculty:* 1,258 full-time (525 women), 372 part-time/adjunct (238 women). *Students:* 344 full-time (198 women), 1 (woman) part-time; includes 73 minority (12 Black or African American, non-Hispanic/Latino; 1 American Indian or Alaska Native, non-Hispanic/Latino; 45 Asian, non-Hispanic/Latino; 15 Hispanic/Latino), 120 international. Average age 29. 581 applicants, 23% accepted, 56 enrolled. In 2019, 6 master's, 49 doctorates awarded. Terminal master's awarded for partial completion of doctoral program. *Degree requirements:* For master's, comprehensive exam, thesis; for doctorate, comprehensive exam, thesis/dissertation. *Entrance requirements:* For master's, MD, PhD, DVM, or PharmD; for doctorate, bachelor's degree. Additional exam requirements/recommendations for international students: required—TOEFL, IELTS, TOEFL (minimum score 100 IBT) or IELTS (minimum score 7.0). *Application deadline:* For fall admission, 12/1 for domestic and international students. Applications are processed on a rolling basis. Application fee: $80. Electronic applications accepted. Application fee is waived when completed online. *Expenses:* Contact institution. *Financial support:* In 2019–20, 22 fellowships with full tuition reimbursements (averaging $33,061 per year), 322 research assistantships with full tuition reimbursements (averaging $32,850 per year) were awarded; institutionally sponsored loans and scholarships/grants also available. Financial award application deadline: 5/15. *Unit head:* Dr. Mary Ellen Lane, Dean, 508-856-4018, E-mail: maryellen.lane@umassmed.edu. *Application contact:* Dr. Kendall Knight, Assistant Vice Provost for Admissions, 508-856-5628, Fax: 508-856-3659, E-mail: kendall.knight@umassmed.edu.
Website: http://www.umassmed.edu/gsbs/

**University of Miami,** Graduate School, College of Arts and Sciences, Department of Psychology, Coral Gables, FL 33124. Offers adult clinical (PhD); behavioral neuroscience (PhD); child clinical (PhD); developmental psychology (PhD); health clinical (PhD); psychology (MS). *Accreditation:* APA (one or more programs are accredited). *Degree requirements:* For doctorate, comprehensive exam, thesis/dissertation. *Entrance requirements:* For doctorate, GRE General Test, minimum GPA of 3.5. Additional exam requirements/recommendations for international students: required—TOEFL. Electronic applications accepted.

**University of Miami,** Graduate School, Miller School of Medicine, Graduate Programs in Medicine, Neuroscience Program, Miami, FL 33124. Offers neuroscience (PhD); MD/PhD. *Faculty:* 31 full-time (14 women), 1 part-time/adjunct (0 women). *Students:* 30 full-time (15 women); includes 5 minority (4 Hispanic/Latino; 1 Two or more races, non-Hispanic/Latino), 5 international. Average age 28. 25 applicants. In 2019, 5 doctorates awarded. *Degree requirements:* For doctorate, thesis/dissertation, 1st-author publication; Qualifying examination. *Entrance requirements:* For doctorate, GRE General Test. Additional exam requirements/recommendations for international students: required—TOEFL (minimum score 80 paper-based), IELTS (minimum score 6.5). *Application deadline:* For fall admission, 12/1 priority date for domestic and international students. Applications are processed on a rolling basis. Application fee: $100. Electronic applications accepted. *Financial support:* In 2019–20, 30 students received support, including 30 fellowships with full tuition reimbursements available (averaging $30,000 per year), 30 research assistantships with full tuition reimbursements available (averaging $30,000 per year); institutionally sponsored loans and health care benefits also available. Financial award applicants required to submit FAFSA. *Unit head:* Dr. Coleen M. Atkins, Director, Neuroscience Graduate Program, 305-243-4698, Fax: 305-243-3914, E-mail: catkins@miami.edu. *Application contact:* Maya Kono, Graduate Coordinator, 305-243-3368, Fax: 305-243-2970, E-mail: neuroscience@miami.edu.
Website: Administrative Organization (parent) hhttp://biomed.miami.edu/graduate-programs/neuroscience

**University of Michigan,** Rackham Graduate School, College of Literature, Science, and the Arts, Department of Psychology, Ann Arbor, MI 48109. Offers biopsychology (PhD); clinical science (PhD); cognition and cognitive neuroscience (PhD); developmental psychology (PhD); personality and social contexts (PhD); social psychology (PhD). *Accreditation:* APA. Terminal master's awarded for partial completion of doctoral program. *Degree requirements:* For doctorate, comprehensive exam, thesis/dissertation, oral defense of dissertation, preliminary exam. *Entrance requirements:* For doctorate, GRE (Biopsychology, Cognition and Cognitive Neuroscience, Developmental, Social, and Clinical); GRE Subject Test also strongly recommended (Clinical); GRE not required (Personality and Social Contexts). Additional exam requirements/recommendations for international students: required—TOEFL. Electronic applications accepted.

**University of Michigan,** Rackham Graduate School, Program in Biomedical Sciences (PIBS), Neuroscience Graduate Program, Ann Arbor, MI 48072-2215. Offers PhD. *Degree requirements:* For doctorate, thesis/dissertation, oral defense of dissertation, preliminary exam. *Entrance requirements:* For doctorate, 3 letters of recommendation, research experience. Additional exam requirements/recommendations for international students: required—TOEFL (minimum score 84 iBT). Electronic applications accepted.

**University of Michigan–Flint,** College of Health Sciences, Program in Physical Therapy, Flint, MI 48502-1950. Offers adult neurology (PhD); neurology (Certificate); orthopedics (PhD, Certificate); pediatrics (PhD, Certificate); physical therapy (DPT). *Accreditation:* APTA. *Program availability:* Part-time, evening/weekend, 100% online. *Faculty:* 16 full-time (12 women), 14 part-time/adjunct (7 women). *Students:* 184 full-time (123 women), 37 part-time (23 women); includes 24 minority (3 Black or African American, non-Hispanic/Latino; 1 American Indian or Alaska Native, non-Hispanic/Latino; 10 Asian, non-Hispanic/Latino; 3 Hispanic/Latino; 7 Two or more races, non-Hispanic/Latino), 14 international. Average age 28. 294 applicants, 44% accepted, 62 enrolled. In 2019, 68 doctorates awarded. *Degree requirements:* For doctorate, thesis/dissertation or alternative. *Entrance requirements:* For degree, DPT from accredited institution; current physical therapy license in the United States or Canada; minimum overall GPA of 3.0 in the physical therapy degree; current CPR certification. Additional exam requirements/recommendations for international students: required—TOEFL (minimum score 84 iBT), IELTS (minimum score 6.5). *Application deadline:* For fall admission, 5/1 for domestic students, 2/1 for international students; for winter admission, 7/31 for domestic students, 4/1 for international students; for spring admission, 3/1 for domestic students, 12/1 for international students. Application fee: $55. Electronic applications accepted. *Expenses:* Contact institution. *Financial support:* Federal Work-Study, scholarships/grants, and unspecified assistantships available. Support available to part-time students. Financial award application deadline: 3/1; financial award applicants required to submit FAFSA. *Unit head:* Dr. Amy Yorke, Department Admissions Chair, 810-762-3373, E-mail: amyorke@umflint.edu. *Application contact:* Frank Fanzone, Senior Administrative Assistant, 810-762-3373, Fax: 810-766-6668, E-mail: ffanzone@umflint.edu.
Website: https://www.umflint.edu/pt

**University of Minnesota, Twin Cities Campus,** Graduate School, Graduate Program in Neuroscience, Minneapolis, MN 55455-0213. Offers MS, PhD. Terminal master's awarded for partial completion of doctoral program. *Degree requirements:* For master's, thesis; for doctorate, thesis/dissertation. *Entrance requirements:* For doctorate, GRE. Additional exam requirements/recommendations for international students: required—TOEFL. Electronic applications accepted.

**University of Mississippi Medical Center,** School of Graduate Studies in Health Sciences, Program in Neuroscience, Jackson, MS 39216-4505. Offers PhD. *Degree requirements:* For doctorate, comprehensive exam, thesis/dissertation, 1st authored publication. *Entrance requirements:* For doctorate, GRE, BA, BS. Additional exam requirements/recommendations for international students: required—TOEFL (minimum score 550 paper-based, 79 iBT), IELTS (minimum score 6.5), or PTE (minimum score 53). Electronic applications accepted.

**University of Missouri,** Office of Research and Graduate Studies, Interdisciplinary Neuroscience Program, Columbia, MO 65211. Offers MS, PhD, Graduate Certificate. *Entrance requirements:* For master's and doctorate, GRE (minimum score: Verbal and Quantitative 1200), bachelor's degree or its equivalent. Additional exam requirements/recommendations for international students: required—TOEFL (minimum score 600 paper-based; 100 iBT), IELTS (minimum score 6.5). Electronic applications accepted.

**University of Missouri–St. Louis,** College of Arts and Sciences, Department of Psychological Sciences, St. Louis, MO 63121. Offers behavioral neuroscience (MA, PhD); clinical psychology (PhD); trauma studies (Certificate). *Accreditation:* APA (one or more programs are accredited). *Program availability:* Evening/weekend. Terminal master's awarded for partial completion of doctoral program. *Degree requirements:* For master's, thesis; for doctorate, thesis/dissertation. *Entrance requirements:* For master's, GRE General Test, 3 letters of recommendation; for doctorate, GRE General Test, GRE Subject Test, 3 letters of recommendation. Additional exam requirements/recommendations for international students: required—TOEFL (minimum score 550 paper-based; 79 iBT), IELTS (minimum score 6.5). Electronic applications accepted. *Expenses: Tuition, area resident:* Full-time $9005.40; part-time $6003.60 per credit hour. Tuition, state resident: full-time $9005.40; part-time $6003.60 per credit hour. Tuition, nonresident: full-time $22,108; part-time $14,738.40 per credit hour. *International tuition:* $22,108 full-time. Tuition and fees vary according to course load.

**University of Montana,** Graduate School, College of Health Professions and Biomedical Sciences, Skaggs School of Pharmacy, Department of Biomedical and Pharmaceutical Sciences, Missoula, MT 59812. Offers biomedical sciences (PhD); medicinal chemistry (MS, PhD); molecular and cellular toxicology (MS, PhD); neuroscience (PhD); pharmaceutical sciences (MS). *Accreditation:* ACPE. *Degree requirements:* For master's, oral defense of thesis; for doctorate, research dissertation defense. *Entrance requirements:* For master's and doctorate, GRE General Test. Additional exam requirements/recommendations for international students: required—TOEFL (minimum score 540 paper-based). Electronic applications accepted.

**University of Nebraska Medical Center,** Interdisciplinary Graduate Program in Biomedical Sciences, Department of Pharmacology and Experimental Neuroscience, Omaha, NE 68198. Offers PhD. Terminal master's awarded for partial completion of doctoral program. *Degree requirements:* For doctorate, comprehensive exam, thesis/dissertation. *Entrance requirements:* For doctorate, GRE General Test. Additional exam requirements/recommendations for international students: required—TOEFL (minimum score 90 iBT). Electronic applications accepted.

**University of New Mexico,** Graduate Studies, College of Arts and Sciences, Program in Psychology, Albuquerque, NM 87131-2039. Offers behavioral neuroscience (PhD); clinical psychology (PhD); cognitive neuroimaging (PhD); developmental psychology (PhD); evolution (PhD); health psychology (PhD); quantitative methodology (PhD). *Accreditation:* APA. *Degree requirements:* For doctorate, comprehensive exam, thesis/dissertation. *Entrance requirements:* For doctorate, GRE General Test, GRE Subject Test (psychology), minimum GPA of 3.0. Additional exam requirements/recommendations for international students: required—TOEFL (minimum score 550 paper-based; 79 iBT), IELTS (minimum score 6.5). Electronic applications accepted. *Expenses:* Tuition, state resident: full-time $7633; part-time $972 per year. Tuition, nonresident: full-time $22,586; part-time $3840 per year. *International tuition:* $23,292 full-time. *Required fees:* $8608. Tuition and fees vary according to course level, course load, degree level, program and student level.

**University of New Mexico,** Graduate Studies, Health Sciences Center, Program in Biomedical Sciences, Albuquerque, NM 87131-5196. Offers biochemistry and molecular biology (MS, PhD); cell biology and physiology (MS, PhD); molecular genetics and microbiology (MS, PhD); neuroscience (MS, PhD); pathology (MS, PhD); toxicology (MS, PhD). *Program availability:* Part-time. Terminal master's awarded for partial completion of doctoral program. *Degree requirements:* For master's, thesis; for doctorate, comprehensive exam, thesis/dissertation, qualifying exam at the end of year 1/core curriculum. *Entrance requirements:* For master's and doctorate, GRE General Test, minimum undergraduate GPA of 3.0. Additional exam requirements/recommendations for international students: required—TOEFL. Electronic applications

accepted. *Expenses:* Tuition, state resident: full-time $7633; part-time $972 per year. Tuition, nonresident: full-time $22,586; part-time $3840 per year. *International tuition:* $23,292 full-time. *Required fees:* $8608. Tuition and fees vary according to course level, course load, degree level, program and student level.

**The University of North Carolina at Chapel Hill,** Graduate School, College of Arts and Sciences, Department of Psychology, Chapel Hill, NC 27599-3270. Offers behavioral neuroscience psychology (PhD); clinical psychology (PhD); cognitive psychology (PhD); developmental psychology (PhD); quantitative psychology (PhD); social psychology (PhD). *Accreditation:* APA. *Degree requirements:* For doctorate, comprehensive exam, thesis/dissertation. *Entrance requirements:* For doctorate, GRE General Test, minimum GPA of 3.0. Additional exam requirements/recommendations for international students: required—TOEFL (minimum score 550 paper-based; 79 iBT), IELTS (minimum score 7). Electronic applications accepted.

**University of North Texas Health Science Center at Fort Worth,** Graduate School of Biomedical Sciences, Fort Worth, TX 76107-2699. Offers biochemistry and cancer biology (MS, PhD); biotechnology (MS); cell biology, immunology and microbiology (MS, PhD); clinical research management (MS); forensic genetics (MS); genetics (MS, PhD); integrative physiology (MS, PhD); medical sciences (MS); pharmaceutical sciences and pharmacotherapy (MS, PhD); pharmacology and neuroscience (MS, PhD); structural anatomy and rehabilitation sciences (MS, PhD); DO/MS; DO/PhD. Terminal master's awarded for partial completion of doctoral program. *Degree requirements:* For master's, thesis; for doctorate, thesis/dissertation. *Entrance requirements:* For master's and doctorate, GRE General Test. Additional exam requirements/recommendations for international students: required—TOEFL. *Expenses:* Contact institution.

**University of Oklahoma Health Sciences Center,** College of Medicine and Graduate College, Graduate Programs in Medicine, Department of Neuroscience, Oklahoma City, OK 73190. Offers MS, PhD. *Degree requirements:* For doctorate, thesis/dissertation. *Entrance requirements:* For master's and doctorate, GRE General Test, 3 letters of recommendation. Additional exam requirements/recommendations for international students: required—TOEFL.

**University of Oregon,** Graduate School, College of Arts and Sciences, Department of Biology, Eugene, OR 97403. Offers ecology and evolution (MA, MS, PhD); marine biology (MA, MS, PhD); molecular, cellular and genetic biology (PhD); neuroscience and development (PhD). Terminal master's awarded for partial completion of doctoral program. *Degree requirements:* For master's, thesis (for some programs); for doctorate, thesis/dissertation. *Entrance requirements:* For master's and doctorate, GRE General Test, minimum GPA of 3.2. Additional exam requirements/recommendations for international students: required—TOEFL.

**University of Pennsylvania,** Perelman School of Medicine, Biomedical Graduate Studies, Graduate Group in Neuroscience, Philadelphia, PA 19104. Offers PhD, MD/PhD, VMD/PhD. *Faculty:* 187 full-time (63 women). *Students:* 133 full-time (84 women); includes 50 minority (5 Black or African American, non-Hispanic/Latino; 1 American Indian or Alaska Native, non-Hispanic/Latino; 14 Asian, non-Hispanic/Latino; 25 Hispanic/Latino; 5 Two or more races, non-Hispanic/Latino), 3 international. 497 applicants, 9% accepted, 19 enrolled. In 2019, 11 doctorates awarded. *Unit head:* Dr. Joshua Gold, Chair, 215-746-0028. *Application contact:* Mary Taylor, Graduate Coordinator, 215-573-4394.
Website: http://www.med.upenn.edu/ngg

**University of Pittsburgh,** Kenneth P. Dietrich School of Arts and Sciences, Center for Neuroscience, Pittsburgh, PA 15260. Offers PhD. *Degree requirements:* For doctorate, comprehensive exam, thesis/dissertation. *Entrance requirements:* For doctorate, GRE, interview. Additional exam requirements/recommendations for international students: required—TOEFL (minimum score 100 iBT), IELTS (minimum score 7). Electronic applications accepted. *Expenses:* Contact institution.

**University of Puerto Rico at Rio Piedras,** College of Natural Sciences, Department of Biology, San Juan, PR 00931-3300. Offers ecology/systematics (MS, PhD); evolution/genetics (MS, PhD); molecular/cellular biology (MS, PhD); neuroscience (MS, PhD). *Program availability:* Part-time. *Degree requirements:* For master's, one foreign language, comprehensive exam, thesis; for doctorate, one foreign language, comprehensive exam, thesis/dissertation. *Entrance requirements:* For master's, GRE Subject Test, interview, minimum GPA of 3.0, letter of recommendation; for doctorate, GRE Subject Test, interview, master's degree, minimum GPA of 3.0, letter of recommendation.

**University of Rochester,** School of Medicine and Dentistry, Graduate Programs in Medicine and Dentistry, Department of Neurobiology and Anatomy, Interdepartmental Programs in Neuroscience, Rochester, NY 14627. Offers PhD. Terminal master's awarded for partial completion of doctoral program. *Degree requirements:* For doctorate, one foreign language, thesis/dissertation, qualifying exam. *Entrance requirements:* For doctorate, GRE General Test.

**University of South Dakota,** Graduate School, Sanford School of Medicine and Graduate School, Biomedical Sciences Graduate Program, Program in Neuroscience, Vermillion, SD 57069. Offers MS, PhD. Terminal master's awarded for partial completion of doctoral program. *Degree requirements:* For master's, thesis; for doctorate, comprehensive exam, thesis/dissertation. *Entrance requirements:* For master's and doctorate, GRE General Test, minimum GPA of 3.0. Additional exam requirements/recommendations for international students: required—TOEFL (minimum score 550 paper-based; 80 iBT), IELTS (minimum score 6). Electronic applications accepted. *Expenses:* Contact institution.

**University of Southern California,** Program in Neuroscience, Los Angeles, CA 90089. Offers MS, PhD. Terminal master's awarded for partial completion of doctoral program. *Degree requirements:* For master's, research paper; for doctorate, comprehensive exam, thesis/dissertation, qualifying examination, dissertation defense. *Entrance requirements:* For doctorate, GRE, 3 letters of recommendation, personal statement, resume. Additional exam requirements/recommendations for international students: required—TOEFL (minimum score 600 paper-based; 100 iBT). Electronic applications accepted.

**University of South Florida,** College of Arts and Sciences, Department of Psychology, Tampa, FL 33620-9951. Offers psychology (PhD), including clinical psychology, cognition, neuroscience and social psychology, industrial-organizational psychology. *Accreditation:* APA. *Faculty:* 30 full-time (11 women). *Students:* 79 full-time (55 women), 12 part-time (8 women); includes 16 minority (2 Black or African American, non-Hispanic/Latino; 6 Asian, non-Hispanic/Latino; 6 Hispanic/Latino; 2 Two or more races, non-Hispanic/Latino), 8 international. Average age 28. 355 applicants, 5% accepted, 19 enrolled. In 2019, 17 doctorates awarded. *Degree requirements:* For doctorate, comprehensive exam, thesis/dissertation, internship. *Entrance requirements:* For doctorate, a GRE Score Report with a strong preference for GRE V and Q scores each at the 50th percentile or better, statement of purpose; Research Interests and Faculty Matches Form (http://psychology.usf.edu/forms/ResearchInterest.aspx); 3 letters of recommendation; GPA worksheet (http://www.grad.usf.edu/inc/linked-files/gpa.pdf). Additional exam requirements/recommendations for international students: required—TOEFL, TOEFL (minimum score 550 paper-based; 79 iBT) or IELTS (minimum score 6.5). *Application deadline:* For fall admission, 12/1 priority date for domestic and international students. Application fee: $30. Electronic applications accepted. *Expenses:* Contact institution. *Financial support:* In 2019–20, 44 students received support, including 18 research assistantships with tuition reimbursements available (averaging $14,727 per year), 57 teaching assistantships with tuition reimbursements available (averaging $14,543 per year); tuition waivers (partial) and unspecified assistantships also available. Financial award applicants required to submit FAFSA. *Unit head:* Dr. Toru Shimizu, Chairperson, 813-974-0352, Fax: 813-974-4617, E-mail: shimizu@usf.edu. *Application contact:* Dr. Sandra Schneider, Professor and Graduate Program Director, 813-974-0928, E-mail: sandra@usf.edu.
Website: http://psychology.usf.edu/

**University of South Florida,** Innovative Education, Tampa, FL 33620-9951. Offers adult, career and higher education (Graduate Certificate), including college teaching, leadership in developing human resources, leadership in higher education; Africana studies (Graduate Certificate), including diasporas and health disparities, genocide and human rights; aging studies (Graduate Certificate), including gerontology; art research (Graduate Certificate), including museum studies; business foundations (Graduate Certificate); chemical and biomedical engineering (Graduate Certificate), including materials science and engineering, water, health and sustainability; child and family studies (Graduate Certificate), including positive behavior support; civil and industrial engineering (Graduate Certificate), including transportation systems analysis; community and family health (Graduate Certificate), including maternal and child health, social marketing and public health, violence and injury: prevention and intervention, women's health; criminology (Graduate Certificate), including criminal justice administration; data science for public administration (Graduate Certificate); digital humanities (Graduate Certificate); educational measurement and research (Graduate Certificate), including evaluation; English (Graduate Certificate), including comparative literary studies, creative writing, professional and technical communication; entrepreneurship (Graduate Certificate); environmental health (Graduate Certificate), including safety management; epidemiology and biostatistics (Graduate Certificate), including applied biostatistics, biostatistics, concepts and tools of epidemiology, epidemiology, epidemiology of infectious diseases; geography, environment and planning (Graduate Certificate), including community development, environmental policy and management, geographical information systems; geology (Graduate Certificate), including hydrogeology; global health (Graduate Certificate), including disaster management, global health and Latin American and Caribbean studies, global health practice, humanitarian assistance, infection control; government and international affairs (Graduate Certificate), including Cuban studies, globalization studies; health policy and management (Graduate Certificate), including health management and leadership, public health policy and programs; hearing specialist: early intervention (Graduate Certificate); industrial and management systems engineering (Graduate Certificate), including systems engineering, technology management; information studies (Graduate Certificate), including school library media specialist; information systems/decision sciences (Graduate Certificate), including analytics and business intelligence; instructional technology (Graduate Certificate), including distance education, Florida digital/virtual educator, instructional design, multimedia design, Web design; internal medicine, bioethics and medical humanities (Graduate Certificate), including biomedical ethics; Latin American and Caribbean studies (Graduate Certificate); leadership for coastal resiliency planning (Graduate Certificate); mass communications (Graduate Certificate), including multimedia journalism; mathematics and statistics (Graduate Certificate), including mathematics; medicine (Graduate Certificate), including aging and neuroscience, bioinformatics, biotechnology, brain fitness and memory management, clinical investigation, hand and upper limb rehabilitation, health informatics, health sciences, integrative weight management, intellectual property, medicine and gender, metabolic and nutritional medicine, metabolic cardiology, pharmacy sciences; national and competitive intelligence (Graduate Certificate); nursing (Graduate Certificate), including simulation based academic fellowship in advanced pain management; psychological and social foundations (Graduate Certificate), including career counseling, college teaching, diversity in education, mental health counseling, school counseling; public affairs (Graduate Certificate), including nonprofit management, public management, research administration; public health (Graduate Certificate), including assessing chemical toxicity and public health risks, health equity, pharmacoepidemiology, public health generalist, toxicology, translational research in adolescent behavioral health; public health practices (Graduate Certificate), including planning for healthy communities; rehabilitation and mental health counseling (Graduate Certificate), including integrative mental health care, marriage and family therapy, rehabilitation technology; secondary education (Graduate Certificate), including ESOL, foreign language education: culture and content, foreign language education: professional; social work (Graduate Certificate), including geriatric social work/clinical gerontology; special education (Graduate Certificate), including autism spectrum disorder, disabilities education: severe/profound; world languages (Graduate Certificate), including teaching English as a second language (TESL) or foreign language. *Unit head:* Dr. Cynthia DeLuca, Associate Vice President and Assistant Vice Provost, 813-974-3077, Fax: 813-974-7061, E-mail: deluca@usf.edu. *Application contact:* Owen Hooper, Director, Summer and Alternative Calendar Programs, 813-974-6917, E-mail: hooper@usf.edu.
Website: http://www.usf.edu/innovative-education/

**The University of Texas at Austin,** Graduate School, College of Liberal Arts, Department of Psychology, Austin, TX 78712-1111. Offers behavioral neuroscience (PhD); clinical psychology (PhD); cognitive systems (PhD); developmental psychology (PhD); individual differences and evolutionary psychology (PhD); perceptual systems (PhD); social psychology (PhD). *Accreditation:* APA. *Degree requirements:* For doctorate, thesis/dissertation. *Entrance requirements:* For doctorate, GRE General Test. Electronic applications accepted.

**The University of Texas at Austin,** Graduate School, The Institute for Neuroscience, Austin, TX 78712-1111. Offers PhD, MD/PhD. Terminal master's awarded for partial completion of doctoral program. *Degree requirements:* For doctorate, thesis/dissertation. *Entrance requirements:* For doctorate, GRE. Electronic applications accepted.

**The University of Texas at Dallas,** School of Behavioral and Brain Sciences, Program in Cognition and Neuroscience, Richardson, TX 75080. Offers applied cognition and neuroscience (MS); cognition and neuroscience (PhD). *Program availability:* Part-time, evening/weekend. *Faculty:* 24 full-time (4 women), 7 part-time/adjunct (4 women). *Students:* 189 full-time (113 women), 43 part-time (25 women); includes 65 minority (6 Black or African American, non-Hispanic/Latino; 1 American Indian or Alaska Native, non-Hispanic/Latino; 31 Asian, non-Hispanic/Latino; 18 Hispanic/Latino; 9 Two or more races, non-Hispanic/Latino), 54 international. Average age 28. 182 applicants, 47% accepted, 69 enrolled. In 2019, 63 master's, 5 doctorates awarded. *Degree requirements:* For master's, internship; for doctorate, thesis/dissertation. *Entrance requirements:* For master's and doctorate, GRE General Test, minimum GPA of 3.0 in upper-level coursework in field. Additional exam requirements/recommendations for international students: required—TOEFL (minimum score 550 paper-based). *Application deadline:* For fall admission, 7/15 for domestic students, 5/1 priority date for international students; for spring admission, 11/15 for domestic students, 9/1 priority date for

international students. Applications are processed on a rolling basis. Application fee: $50 ($100 for international students). Electronic applications accepted. *Expenses: Tuition, area resident:* Full-time $16,504. Tuition, state resident: full-time $16,504. Tuition, nonresident: full-time $34,266. Tuition and fees vary according to course load. *Financial support:* In 2019–20, 75 students received support, including 2 fellowships (averaging $3,000 per year), 32 research assistantships with partial tuition reimbursements available (averaging $28,597 per year), 43 teaching assistantships with partial tuition reimbursements available (averaging $19,530 per year); career-related internships or fieldwork, Federal Work-Study, institutionally sponsored loans, scholarships/grants, and unspecified assistantships also available. Support available to part-time students. Financial award application deadline: 4/30; financial award applicants required to submit FAFSA. *Unit head:* Dr. Kristen Kennedy, Area Head, 972-883-3739, Fax: 972-883-3491, E-mail: kmk082000@utdallas.edu. *Application contact:* Dr. Theodore Price, Area Head, 972-883-4311, Fax: 972-883-3491, E-mail: theodore.price@utdallas.edu.
Website: https://bbs.utdallas.edu/degrees/cn-degrees/

**The University of Texas Health Science Center at Houston,** MD Anderson UTHealth Graduate School, Houston, TX 77225-0036. Offers biochemistry and cell biology (PhD); biomedical sciences (MS); cancer biology (PhD); genetic counseling (MS); genetics and epigenetics (PhD); immunology (PhD); medical physics (MS, PhD); microbiology and infectious diseases (PhD); neuroscience (PhD); quantitative sciences (PhD); therapeutics and pharmacology (PhD); MD/PhD. Terminal master's awarded for partial completion of doctoral program. *Degree requirements:* For master's, thesis; for doctorate, thesis/dissertation. *Entrance requirements:* For master's and doctorate, GRE General Test. Additional exam requirements/recommendations for international students: required—TOEFL. Electronic applications accepted.

**The University of Texas Health Science Center at San Antonio,** Graduate School of Biomedical Sciences, Department of Pharmacology, San Antonio, TX 78229-3900. Offers neuroscience (PhD). *Degree requirements:* For doctorate, comprehensive exam, thesis/dissertation.

**The University of Texas Medical Branch,** Graduate School of Biomedical Sciences, Program in Neuroscience, Galveston, TX 77555. Offers PhD. *Degree requirements:* For doctorate, thesis/dissertation. *Entrance requirements:* For doctorate, GRE General Test. Additional exam requirements/recommendations for international students: required—TOEFL (minimum score 550 paper-based). Electronic applications accepted.

**The University of Texas Southwestern Medical Center,** Southwestern Graduate School of Biomedical Sciences, Division of Basic Science, Program in Neuroscience, Dallas, TX 75390. Offers PhD. *Degree requirements:* For doctorate, thesis/dissertation, qualifying exam. *Entrance requirements:* For doctorate, GRE General Test, minimum GPA of 3.0. Additional exam requirements/recommendations for international students: required—TOEFL. Electronic applications accepted.

**The University of Toledo,** College of Graduate Studies, College of Medicine and Life Sciences, Department of Neurosciences, Toledo, OH 43606-3390. Offers MSBS, PhD, MD/MSBS, MD/PhD. Terminal master's awarded for partial completion of doctoral program. *Degree requirements:* For master's, thesis, qualifying exam; for doctorate, thesis/dissertation, qualifying exam. *Entrance requirements:* For master's and doctorate, GRE, minimum undergraduate GPA of 3.0, three letters of recommendation, statement of purpose, transcripts from all prior institutions attended, resume. Additional exam requirements/recommendations for international students: required—TOEFL (minimum score 550 paper-based; 80 iBT). Electronic applications accepted.

**University of Utah,** Graduate School, College of Social and Behavioral Science, Department of Psychology, Salt Lake City, UT 84112. Offers clinical psychology (PhD); psychology (PhD), including cognitive neuroscience, developmental psychology, social psychology. *Accreditation:* APA. *Faculty:* 27 full-time (14 women), 1 (woman) part-time/adjunct. *Students:* 53 full-time (40 women); includes 8 minority (1 Black or African American, non-Hispanic/Latino; 4 Hispanic/Latino; 3 Two or more races, non-Hispanic/Latino), 6 international. Average age 28. 295 applicants, 8% accepted, 13 enrolled. In 2019, 11 doctorates awarded. *Degree requirements:* For doctorate, thesis/dissertation. *Entrance requirements:* For doctorate, GRE General Test. Additional exam requirements/recommendations for international students: required—TOEFL (minimum score 500 paper-based). *Application deadline:* For fall admission, 12/1 for domestic and international students. Application fee: $55 ($65 for international students). Electronic applications accepted. *Expenses:* Tuition, state resident: full-time $7085; part-time $272.51 per credit hour. Tuition, nonresident: full-time $24,937; part-time $959.12 per credit hour. *Required fees:* $880.52; $880.52 per semester. Tuition and fees vary according to degree level, program and student level. *Financial support:* In 2019–20, 5 fellowships (averaging $13,400 per year), 22 research assistantships (averaging $15,000 per year), 33 teaching assistantships (averaging $14,909 per year) were awarded; unspecified assistantships also available. Financial award applicants required to submit FAFSA. *Unit head:* Dr. Bert N. Uchino, Chair, 801-581-8925, Fax: 801-581-5841, E-mail: bert.uchino@psych.utah.edu. *Application contact:* Nancy Seegmiller, Program Manager, 801-581-8925, Fax: 801-581-5841, E-mail: nancy.seegmiller@psych.utah.edu.
Website: http://www.psych.utah.edu/

**University of Utah,** School of Medicine and Graduate School, Graduate Programs in Medicine, Program in Neuroscience, Salt Lake City, UT 84112-1107. Offers PhD. *Degree requirements:* For doctorate, thesis/dissertation. *Entrance requirements:* For doctorate, GRE General Test, minimum GPA of 3.0. Additional exam requirements/recommendations for international students: required—TOEFL (minimum score 500 paper-based); recommended—TWE (minimum score 6). Electronic applications accepted. *Expenses:* Tuition, state resident: full-time $7085; part-time $272.51 per credit hour. Tuition, nonresident: full-time $24,937; part-time $959.12 per credit hour. *Required fees:* $880.52; $880.52 per semester. Tuition and fees vary according to degree level, program and student level.

**University of Vermont,** Graduate College, Cross-College Interdisciplinary Program, Graduate Program in Neuroscience, Burlington, VT 05405. Offers PhD. *Degree requirements:* For doctorate, thesis/dissertation. *Entrance requirements:* For doctorate, GRE General Test. Additional exam requirements/recommendations for international students: required—TOEFL (minimum score 550 paper-based, 100 iBT) or IELTS (7). Electronic applications accepted.

**University of Virginia,** School of Medicine, Department of Neuroscience, Charlottesville, VA 22903. Offers PhD, MD/PhD. *Degree requirements:* For doctorate, thesis/dissertation. *Entrance requirements:* For doctorate, GRE General Test, 2 letters of recommendation. Additional exam requirements/recommendations for international students: required—TOEFL. Electronic applications accepted.

**University of Washington,** Graduate School, College of Arts and Sciences, Department of Psychology, Seattle, WA 98195. Offers animal behavior (PhD); applied child and adolescent psychology: prevention and treatment (MA); behavioral neuroscience (PhD); clinical psychology (PhD); cognition and perception (PhD); developmental psychology (PhD); quantitative psychology (PhD); social psychology and personality (PhD). *Accreditation:* APA (one or more programs are accredited). *Degree requirements:* For doctorate, thesis/dissertation. *Entrance requirements:* For doctorate, GRE General Test, minimum GPA of 3.0. Electronic applications accepted.

**The University of Western Ontario,** Schulich School of Medicine and Dentistry, Department of Clinical Neurological Sciences, London, ON N6A 3K7, Canada. Offers M Sc, PhD. Terminal master's awarded for partial completion of doctoral program. *Degree requirements:* For master's, thesis; for doctorate, thesis/dissertation. *Entrance requirements:* For master's, honors degree or equivalent, minimum B+ average; for doctorate, master's degree, minimum B+ average.

**University of Wisconsin–Madison,** Graduate School, College of Letters and Science, Department of Psychology, Program in Cognitive Neurosciences, Madison, WI 53706-1380. Offers PhD. *Degree requirements:* For doctorate, comprehensive exam, thesis/dissertation. *Entrance requirements:* For doctorate, GRE General Test, minimum undergraduate GPA of 3.0. Additional exam requirements/recommendations for international students: required—TOEFL. Electronic applications accepted.

**University of Wisconsin–Madison,** School of Medicine and Public Health, Neuroscience Training Program, Madison, WI 53706. Offers PhD, MD/PhD, PhD/JD.

**Virginia Commonwealth University,** Medical College of Virginia-Professional Programs, School of Medicine, Graduate Program in Neuroscience, Richmond, VA 23284-9005. Offers PhD. *Entrance requirements:* For doctorate, GRE or MCAT. Additional exam requirements/recommendations for international students: required—TOEFL (minimum score 600 paper-based; 100 iBT). Electronic applications accepted.

**Virginia Commonwealth University,** Medical College of Virginia-Professional Programs, School of Medicine, Graduate Programs in Medicine, Department of Pharmacology and Toxicology, Richmond, VA 23284-9005. Offers neuroscience (PhD); pharmacology (Certificate); pharmacology and toxicology (MS, PhD); MD/PhD. Terminal master's awarded for partial completion of doctoral program. *Degree requirements:* For master's, thesis; for doctorate, thesis/dissertation, comprehensive oral and written exams. *Entrance requirements:* For master's and doctorate, GRE or MCAT. Additional exam requirements/recommendations for international students: required—TOEFL (minimum score 600 paper-based; 100 iBT). Electronic applications accepted.

**Wake Forest University,** School of Medicine and Graduate School of Arts and Sciences, Graduate Programs in Medicine, Interdisciplinary Program in Neuroscience, Winston-Salem, NC 27109. Offers PhD, MD/PhD. *Degree requirements:* For doctorate, thesis/dissertation. *Entrance requirements:* For doctorate, GRE General Test. Additional exam requirements/recommendations for international students: required—TOEFL. Electronic applications accepted.

**Washington State University,** College of Veterinary Medicine, Program in Neuroscience, Pullman, WA 99164-6520. Offers MS, PhD. *Program availability:* Part-time. *Faculty:* 52 full-time (16 women). *Students:* 29 full-time (15 women); includes 10 minority (1 Black or African American, non-Hispanic/Latino; 3 Asian, non-Hispanic/Latino; 6 Hispanic/Latino). Average age 28. 59 applicants, 19% accepted, 10 enrolled. In 2019, 1 master's, 2 doctorates awarded. Terminal master's awarded for partial completion of doctoral program. *Degree requirements:* For master's, thesis, written exam; for doctorate, thesis/dissertation, written exam, oral exam. *Entrance requirements:* For master's and doctorate, GRE General Test, minimum GPA of 3.0. Additional exam requirements/recommendations for international students: required—TOEFL (minimum score 550 paper-based; 100 iBT). *Application deadline:* For fall admission, 12/15 priority date for domestic and international students. Applications are processed on a rolling basis. Application fee: $75. Electronic applications accepted. *Financial support:* In 2019–20, 23 students received support, including 19 research assistantships with full tuition reimbursements available (averaging $27,018 per year), 6 teaching assistantships with full tuition reimbursements available (averaging $27,018 per year); fellowships, scholarships/grants, health care benefits, and unspecified assistantships also available. Financial award application deadline: 1/31. *Unit head:* Dr. Steve Simasko, Chair, 509-335-6624, Fax: 509-335-4650, E-mail: steve_simasko@wsu.edu. *Application contact:* Becky Morton, Department Manager, 509-335-6621, Fax: 509-335-4650, E-mail: grad.neuro@wsu.edu.
Website: http://ipn.vetmed.wsu.edu/neuroscience/graduate

**Washington University in St. Louis,** The Graduate School, Department of Philosophy, Program in Philosophy-Neuroscience-Psychology, St. Louis, MO 63130-4899. Offers PhD. *Degree requirements:* For doctorate, thesis/dissertation. *Entrance requirements:* For doctorate, GRE General Test, sample of written work. Additional exam requirements/recommendations for international students: required—TOEFL. Electronic applications accepted.

**Washington University in St. Louis,** The Graduate School, Division of Biology and Biomedical Sciences, Program in Neurosciences, St. Louis, MO 63130-4899. Offers PhD. *Degree requirements:* For doctorate, thesis/dissertation. *Entrance requirements:* For doctorate, GRE General Test, GRE Subject Test. Additional exam requirements/recommendations for international students: required—TOEFL. Electronic applications accepted.

**Wayne State University,** College of Liberal Arts and Sciences, Department of Psychology, Detroit, MI 48202. Offers behavioral and cognitive neuroscience (PhD); clinical psychology (PhD); developmental science (PhD); industrial/organizational psychology (MA, PhD); social personality (PhD). *Accreditation:* APA (one or more programs are accredited). *Faculty:* 40. *Students:* 92 full-time (66 women), 42 part-time (27 women); includes 23 minority (4 Black or African American, non-Hispanic/Latino; 2 Asian, non-Hispanic/Latino; 9 Hispanic/Latino; 8 Two or more races, non-Hispanic/Latino), 10 international. Average age 27. 433 applicants, 15% accepted, 36 enrolled. In 2019, 28 master's, 13 doctorates awarded. Terminal master's awarded for partial completion of doctoral program. *Degree requirements:* For master's, thesis (for some programs); for doctorate, comprehensive exam, thesis/dissertation, training assignments. *Entrance requirements:* For master's, GRE General Test, minimum undergraduate upper-division cumulative GPA of 3.0, courses in psychology and statistics; for doctorate, GRE General Test, bachelor's, master's, or other advanced degree; at least twelve credits in psychology with minimum GPA of 3.0; courses in laboratory psychology and statistical methods in psychology; at least three letters of recommendation; statement of purpose. Additional exam requirements/recommendations for international students: required—TOEFL (minimum score 550 paper-based; 79 iBT), TWE (minimum score 5.5), Michigan English Language Assessment Battery (minimum score 85); recommended—IELTS (minimum score 6.5). Application fee: $50. Electronic applications accepted. *Expenses: Tuition:* Full-time $34,567. *Financial support:* In 2019–20, 93 students received support, including 11 fellowships with tuition reimbursements available (averaging $21,181 per year), 8 research assistantships with tuition reimbursements available (averaging $20,965 per year), 48 teaching assistantships with tuition reimbursements available (averaging $19,952 per year); scholarships/grants, health care benefits, and unspecified assistantships also available. Financial award applicants required to submit FAFSA. *Unit head:* Scott Bowen, PhD, Chair/Professor, 313-577-2803, E-mail: ad4771@wayne.edu. *Application contact:* Alia Allen, Academic Services Officer III, 313-577-2823, E-mail: aallen@wayne.edu.
Website: http://clas.wayne.edu/psychology/

**Weill Cornell Medicine,** Weill Cornell Graduate School of Medical Sciences, Neuroscience Program, New York, NY 10065. Offers MS, PhD. Terminal master's awarded for partial completion of doctoral program. *Degree requirements:* For master's, comprehensive exam; for doctorate, thesis/dissertation, final exam. *Entrance requirements:* For doctorate, GRE General Test, undergraduate training in biology, organic chemistry, physics, and mathematics. Additional exam requirements/recommendations for international students: required—TOEFL. Electronic applications accepted.

**Wilfrid Laurier University,** Faculty of Graduate and Postdoctoral Studies, Faculty of Science, Department of Psychology, Waterloo, ON N2L 3C5, Canada. Offers behavioral neuroscience (M Sc, PhD); cognitive neuroscience (M Sc, PhD); community psychology (MA, PhD); social and developmental psychology (MA, PhD). *Program availability:* Part-time. *Degree requirements:* For master's, thesis; for doctorate, thesis/dissertation. *Entrance requirements:* For master's, GRE General Test, honors BA or the equivalent in psychology, minimum B average in undergraduate course work; for doctorate, GRE General Test, master's degree, minimum A- average. Additional exam requirements/recommendations for international students: required—TOEFL (minimum score 89 iBT). Electronic applications accepted.

**Wright State University,** Graduate School, College of Science and Mathematics, Department of Neuroscience, Cell Biology, and Physiology, Dayton, OH 45435. Offers anatomy (MS); physiology and neuroscience (MS). *Degree requirements:* For master's, thesis optional. *Entrance requirements:* Additional exam requirements/recommendations for international students: required—TOEFL.

**Yale University,** Graduate School of Arts and Sciences, Department of Psychology, New Haven, CT 06520. Offers behavioral neuroscience (PhD); clinical psychology (PhD); cognitive psychology (PhD); developmental psychology (PhD); social/personality psychology (PhD). *Accreditation:* APA. *Degree requirements:* For doctorate, thesis/dissertation. *Entrance requirements:* For doctorate, GRE General Test.

**Yale University,** Graduate School of Arts and Sciences, Interdepartmental Neuroscience Program, New Haven, CT 06520. Offers PhD. *Degree requirements:* For doctorate, thesis/dissertation. *Entrance requirements:* For doctorate, GRE General Test. *Expenses:* Contact institution.

**Yale University,** Yale School of Medicine and Graduate School of Arts and Sciences, Combined Program in Biological and Biomedical Sciences (BBS), Neuroscience Track, New Haven, CT 06520. Offers PhD, MD/PhD. *Degree requirements:* For doctorate, thesis/dissertation. *Entrance requirements:* For doctorate, GRE General Test. Additional exam requirements/recommendations for international students: required—TOEFL. Electronic applications accepted.

# Section 14
# Nutrition

This section contains a directory of institutions offering graduate work in nutrition, followed by an in-depth entry submitted by an institution that chose to prepare a detailed program description. Additional information about programs listed in the directory but not augmented by an in-depth entry may be obtained by writing directly to the dean of a graduate school or chair of a department at the address given in the directory.

For programs offering related work, see also in this book *Allied Health, Biochemistry, Biological and Biomedical Sciences, Botany and Plant Biology, Microbiological Sciences, Pathology and Pathobiology, Pharmacology and Toxicology, Physiology, Public Health,* and *Veterinary Medicine and Sciences*. In the other guides in this series:

**Graduate Programs in the Humanities, Arts & Social Sciences**

See *Economics (Agricultural Economics and Agribusiness)* and *Family and Consumer Sciences*

**Graduate Programs in the Physical Sciences, Mathematics, Agricultural Sciences, the Environment & Natural Resources**

See *Agricultural and Food Sciences* and *Chemistry*

**Graduate Programs in Engineering & Applied Sciences**

See *Agricultural Engineering and Bioengineering* and *Biomedical Engineering and Biotechnology*

## CONTENTS

### Program Directory

# Nutrition

**Abilene Christian University,** Office of Graduate Programs, College of Education and Human Services, Department of Kinesiology and Nutrition, Abilene, TX 79699. Offers dietetic internship (Certificate); nutrition (MS). *Faculty:* 2 full-time (1 woman), 3 part-time/adjunct (all women). *Students:* 30 full-time (24 women), 2 part-time (1 woman); includes 8 minority (5 Black or African American, non-Hispanic/Latino; 2 Hispanic/Latino; 1 Two or more races, non-Hispanic/Latino). 107 applicants, 22% accepted, 18 enrolled. In 2019, 2 master's, 11 other advanced degrees awarded. *Entrance requirements:* For master's, official transcripts, recommendations, Purpose Statement; for Certificate, official transcripts, Purpose Statement, Resume. Additional exam requirements/recommendations for international students: required—TOEFL (minimum score 80 iBT), IELTS (minimum score 6), PTE (minimum score 51). *Application deadline:* For fall admission, 3/1 priority date for domestic students. Application fee: $65. *Expenses:* $875 per hour for nutrition; $850 per hour for athletic training. *Financial support:* In 2019–20, 20 students received support. Scholarships/grants available. Financial award application deadline: 4/1; financial award applicants required to submit FAFSA. *Unit head:* Dr. Sheila Jones, Program Director, 325-674-2089, Fax: 325-674-6788, E-mail: joness@acu.edu. *Application contact:* Graduate Admissions, 325-674-6911, E-mail: gradinfo@acu.edu.
Website: http://www.acu.edu/on-campus/graduate/college-of-education-and-human-services/kinesiology-nutrition.html

**Adelphi University,** College of Nursing and Public Health, Garden City, NY 11530. Offers adult gerontology primary care nurse practitioner (Advanced Certificate); adult health nurse (MS); nurse practitioner in adult health nursing (Certificate); nursing (PhD); nursing administration (MS, Certificate); nursing education (MS, Certificate); nutrition (MS); public health (MPH). *Accreditation:* AACN. *Program availability:* Part-time, evening/weekend. *Entrance requirements:* For master's, BSN, clinical experience, course in basic statistics, minimum GPA of 3.0, 2 letters of recommendation, resume or curriculum vitae; for doctorate, GRE, licensure as RN in New York, professional writing sample (scholarly writing), 3 letters of recommendation, resume or curriculum vitae; for other advanced degree, MSN. Additional exam requirements/recommendations for international students: required—TOEFL (minimum score 550 paper-based; 80 iBT), IELTS (minimum score 6.5). Electronic applications accepted. *Expenses:* Contact institution.

**Alabama Agricultural and Mechanical University,** School of Graduate Studies, College of Agricultural, Life and Natural Sciences, Department of Family and Consumer Sciences, Huntsville, AL 35811. Offers apparel, merchandising and design (MS); family and consumer sciences (MS); human development and family studies (MS); nutrition and hospitality management (MS). *Program availability:* Part-time, evening/weekend. *Degree requirements:* For master's, comprehensive exam, thesis optional. *Entrance requirements:* For master's, GRE General Test. Additional exam requirements/recommendations for international students: required—TOEFL (minimum score 500 paper-based; 61 iBT). Electronic applications accepted.

**American College of Healthcare Sciences,** Graduate Programs, Portland, OR 97239-3719. Offers anatomy and physiology (Graduate Certificate); aromatherapy (MS, Graduate Certificate); botanical safety (Graduate Certificate); complementary alternative medicine (MS, Graduate Certificate); health and wellness (MS); herbal medicine (MS, Graduate Certificate); holistic nutrition (MS, Graduate Certificate); wellness coaching (Graduate Certificate). *Program availability:* Part-time, evening/weekend, online learning. *Degree requirements:* For master's, capstone project. *Entrance requirements:* For master's, interview, letters of recommendation, essay.

**American University,** College of Arts and Sciences, Department of Health Studies, Washington, DC 20016. Offers health promotion management (MS), including health promotion management; nutrition education (MS, Certificate). *Program availability:* 100% online, blended/hybrid learning. *Degree requirements:* For master's, comprehensive exam (for some programs), thesis or alternative. *Entrance requirements:* For master's, Please visit the website: https://www.american.edu/cas/health/, statement of purpose, transcripts, 2 letters of recommendation, resume. Additional exam requirements/recommendations for international students: required—TOEFL. Electronic applications accepted. *Expenses:* Contact institution.

**Andrews University,** College of Health and Human Services, School of Population Health, Nutrition & Wellness, Berrien Springs, MI 49104. Offers nutrition (MS); nutrition and dietetics (Certificate); public health (MPH). *Accreditation:* CEPH. *Program availability:* Part-time. *Faculty:* 1 (woman) full-time, 7 part-time/adjunct (2 women). *Students:* 20 full-time (19 women), 41 part-time (31 women); includes 24 minority (15 Black or African American, non-Hispanic/Latino; 2 Asian, non-Hispanic/Latino; 6 Hispanic/Latino; 1 Two or more races, non-Hispanic/Latino), 12 international. Average age 33. In 2019, 6 master's, 14 other advanced degrees awarded. *Entrance requirements:* For master's, GRE. Additional exam requirements/recommendations for international students: required—TOEFL (minimum score 550 paper-based). *Application deadline:* Applications are processed on a rolling basis. Application fee: $60. Electronic applications accepted. *Financial support:* Research assistantships, teaching assistantships, Federal Work-Study, institutionally sponsored loans, and scholarships/grants available. *Unit head:* Dr. Padma Tadiupala, Chairperson, 269-471-3370. *Application contact:* Jillian Panigot, Director, University Admissions, 800-253-2874, Fax: 269-471-6321, E-mail: graduate@andrews.edu.
Website: https://www.andrews.edu/shp/publichealth/

**Appalachian State University,** Cratis D. Williams School of Graduate Studies, Department of Nutrition and Health Care Management, Boone, NC 28608. Offers nutrition (MS). *Program availability:* Part-time. Electronic applications accepted.

**Arizona State University at Tempe,** College of Health Solutions, School of Nutrition and Health Promotion, Tempe, AZ 85287. Offers clinical exercise physiology (MS); exercise and wellness (MS); nutrition (MS), including dietetics, human nutrition; obesity prevention and management (MS); physical activity, nutrition and wellness (PhD).

**Auburn University,** Graduate School, College of Human Sciences, Department of Nutrition, Dietetics, and Hospitality Management, Auburn University, AL 36849. Offers MS, PhD, Graduate Certificate. *Program availability:* Part-time. *Faculty:* 18 full-time (7 women). *Students:* 30 full-time (26 women), 34 part-time (23 women); includes 10 minority (4 Black or African American, non-Hispanic/Latino; 1 American Indian or Alaska Native, non-Hispanic/Latino; 1 Asian, non-Hispanic/Latino; 3 Hispanic/Latino; 1 Two or more races, non-Hispanic/Latino), 15 international. Average age 30. 56 applicants, 66% accepted, 19 enrolled. In 2019, 12 master's, 3 doctorates, 16 other advanced degrees awarded. *Degree requirements:* For master's, thesis (for some programs); for doctorate, thesis/dissertation. *Entrance requirements:* For master's and doctorate, GRE General Test. Additional exam requirements/recommendations for international students: required—iTEP; recommended—TOEFL (minimum score 550 paper-based; 79 iBT), IELTS (minimum score 6.5). *Application deadline:* Applications are processed on a rolling basis. Application fee: $60 ($70 for international students). Electronic applications accepted. *Expenses: Tuition, area resident:* Full-time $9828; part-time $546 per credit hour. Tuition, state resident: full-time $9828; part-time $546 per credit hour. Tuition, nonresident: full-time $29,484; part-time $1638 per credit hour. *International tuition:* $29,744 full-time. Tuition and fees vary according to course load, program and reciprocity agreements. *Financial support:* In 2019–20, 35 fellowships with tuition reimbursements, 16 research assistantships with tuition reimbursements (averaging $14,239 per year), 8 teaching assistantships with tuition reimbursements (averaging $17,192 per year) were awarded; career-related internships or fieldwork and Federal Work-Study also available. Support available to part-time students. Financial award application deadline: 3/15; financial award applicants required to submit FAFSA. *Unit head:* Dr. Martin O'Neill, Head, 334-844-3266. *Application contact:* Dr. George Flowers, Dean of the Graduate School, 334-844-2125.
Website: http://www.humsci.auburn.edu/ndhm/grad.php

**Ball State University,** Graduate School, Teachers College, Department of Family, Consumer, and Technology Education, Muncie, IN 47306. Offers family and consumer science (MS), including apparel design (MA, MS), fashion merchandising (MA, MS), interior design (MA, MS), residential property management (MA, MS); family and consumer sciences (MA), including apparel design (MA, MS), fashion merchandising (MA, MS), interior design (MA, MS), residential property management (MA, MS); nutrition and dietetics (MA, MS). *Program availability:* Part-time, evening/weekend, 100% online. *Entrance requirements:* For master's, letter of intent, resume, two letters of recommendation, portfolio (for interior design option). Additional exam requirements/recommendations for international students: required—TOEFL (minimum score 550 paper-based; 79 iBT), IELTS (minimum score 6.5). Electronic applications accepted. *Expenses: Tuition, area resident:* Full-time $7506; part-time $417 per credit hour. Tuition, nonresident: full-time $20,610; part-time $1145 per credit hour. *Required fees:* $2126. Tuition and fees vary according to course load, campus/location and program.

**Bastyr University,** School of Natural Health Arts and Sciences, Kenmore, WA 98028-4966. Offers counseling psychology (MA); maternal-child health systems (MA); midwifery (MS); nutrition (Certificate); nutrition and clinical health psychology (MS); nutrition and wellness (MS). *Accreditation:* AND; MEAC. *Program availability:* Part-time. *Degree requirements:* For master's, thesis optional. *Entrance requirements:* For master's, 1-2 years' basic sciences course work (depending on program). Additional exam requirements/recommendations for international students: required—TOEFL (minimum score 550 paper-based; 79 iBT).

**Baylor University,** Graduate School, Robbins College of Health and Human Sciences, Department of Family and Consumer Sciences, Waco, TX 76798. Offers nutrition sciences (MS). *Program availability:* Part-time. *Faculty:* 6 full-time (all women), 2 part-time/adjunct (both women). *Students:* 17 full-time (14 women), 1 (woman) part-time; includes 2 minority (1 Hispanic/Latino; 1 Two or more races, non-Hispanic/Latino), 4 international. Average age 24. 28 applicants, 82% accepted, 9 enrolled. In 2019, 2 master's awarded. *Degree requirements:* For master's, comprehensive exam (for some programs), thesis (for some programs), 30-36 credit hours, 3.0 GPA. *Entrance requirements:* For master's, minimum GPA of 3.0 for acceptance (less than 3.0 is considered probationary acceptance), 3 letters of recommendation, undergraduate transcript showing baccalaureate degree completion. Additional exam requirements/recommendations for international students: required—TOEFL. *Application deadline:* For fall admission, 4/12 priority date for domestic and international students. Application fee: $500. Electronic applications accepted. *Financial support:* In 2019–20, 8 research assistantships with partial tuition reimbursements (averaging $6,000 per year), 5 teaching assistantships with partial tuition reimbursements (averaging $7,200 per year) were awarded; tuition waivers also available. Financial award application deadline: 4/15. *Unit head:* Sheri L. Dragoo, PhD, Department Chair, 254-710-3626, E-mail: Sheri_Dragoo@Baylor.edu. *Application contact:* Maria Boccia, PhD, Graduate Program Director, 254-710-6193, E-mail: Maria_Boccia@Baylor.edu.
Website: http://www.baylor.edu/fcs/

**Baylor University,** Graduate School, Robbins College of Health and Human Sciences, Department of Health, Human Performance and Recreation, Waco, TX 76798. Offers athletic training (MS); exercise physiology (MS); kinesiology, exercise nutrition, and health promotion (PhD); sport pedagogy (MS). *Accreditation:* NCATE. *Faculty:* 15 full-time (5 women). *Students:* 87 full-time (47 women), 14 part-time (7 women); includes 21 minority (5 Black or African American, non-Hispanic/Latino; 1 American Indian or Alaska Native, non-Hispanic/Latino; 1 Asian, non-Hispanic/Latino; 8 Hispanic/Latino; 6 Two or more races, non-Hispanic/Latino), 5 international. Average age 24. 115 applicants, 77% accepted, 56 enrolled. In 2019, 42 master's, 7 doctorates awarded. *Degree requirements:* For master's, comprehensive exam, thesis optional; for doctorate, comprehensive exam, thesis/dissertation. *Entrance requirements:* For master's, GRE for MS in Exercise Science, transcripts, resume, 3 letters of recommendation; for doctorate, GRE, transcripts, resume, 3 letters of recommendation, statement of purpose, clinical/research experience, writing samples. Additional exam requirements/recommendations for international students: required—TOEFL (minimum score 550 paper-based; 80 iBT), IELTS (minimum score 6.5). *Application deadline:* For fall admission, 4/1 for domestic and international students; for spring admission, 10/1 for domestic and international students; for summer admission, 11/1 priority date for domestic and international students. Applications are processed on a rolling basis. Application fee: $50. Electronic applications accepted. *Financial support:* In 2019–20, 70 students received support, including 4 research assistantships with full tuition reimbursements available (averaging $15,000 per year), 25 teaching assistantships with full and partial tuition reimbursements available (averaging $11,000 per year); health care benefits, tuition waivers (full and partial), and unspecified assistantships also available. Financial award application deadline: 2/15. *Unit head:* Dr. Dale Connally, Interim Chair and Professor, 254-710-4004, Fax: 254-710-3527, E-mail: Dale_Connally@baylor.edu. *Application contact:* Deepa George, Graduate Program Coordinator, 254-710-3526, Fax: 254-710-3527, E-mail: deepa_morris@baylor.edu.
Website: www.baylor.edu/hhpr

**Baylor University,** Graduate School, Robbins College of Health and Human Sciences, Department of Nutrition, Waco, TX 76798. Offers MS. *Program availability:* Part-time. *Faculty:* 3 full-time (all women). *Students:* 4 full-time (3 women); includes 3 minority (2 Asian, non-Hispanic/Latino; 1 Hispanic/Latino). In 2019, 8 master's awarded. *Degree requirements:* For master's, comprehensive exam, thesis or alternative. *Entrance requirements:* For master's, GRE. Additional exam requirements/recommendations for international students: required—TOEFL (minimum score 550 paper-based; 80 iBT), IELTS (minimum score 6.5). Application fee: $50. Electronic applications accepted. *Financial support:* Federal Work-Study available. Financial award application deadline: 2/15; financial award applicants required to submit FAFSA. *Unit head:* Denny Kramer, Associate Dean, 254-710-4178, E-mail: Denny_Kramer@baylor.edu. *Application*

*contact:* Denny Kramer, Associate Dean, 254-710-4178, E-mail: Denny_Kramer@baylor.edu.
Website: www.baylor.edu/chhs

**Benedictine University,** Graduate Programs, Program in Public Health, Lisle, IL 60532. Offers administration of health care institutions (MPH); dietetics (MPH); disaster management (MPH); health education (MPH); health information systems (MPH); management information systems (MPH/MS); MBA/MPH; MPH/MS. *Accreditation:* CEPH. *Program availability:* Part-time, evening/weekend, 100% online. *Entrance requirements:* For master's, GRE, MAT, GMAT, LSAT, DAT or other graduate professional exams, official transcript; 2 letters of recommendation from individuals familiar with the applicant's professional or academic work, excluding family or personal friends; essay describing the candidate's career path. Additional exam requirements/recommendations for international students: required—TOEFL (minimum score 600 paper-based; 79 iBT), IELTS (minimum score 6.5). Electronic applications accepted.

**Boston University,** College of Health and Rehabilitation Sciences: Sargent College, Program in Nutrition, Boston, MA 02215. Offers MS. *Faculty:* 5 full-time (all women), 5 part-time/adjunct (4 women). *Students:* 50 full-time (43 women), 3 part-time (all women); includes 10 minority (4 Asian, non-Hispanic/Latino; 6 Hispanic/Latino), 8 international. Average age 24. 122 applicants, 37% accepted, 22 enrolled. In 2019, 20 master's awarded. *Entrance requirements:* Additional exam requirements/recommendations for international students: required—TOEFL. Application fee: $95. Electronic applications accepted. *Financial support:* Teaching assistantships, career-related internships or fieldwork, Federal Work-Study, institutionally sponsored loans, scholarships/grants, and unspecified assistantships available. Financial award applicants required to submit FAFSA. *Unit head:* Dr. Paula Quatromoni, Chair, 617-353-5797, Fax: 617-353-7567, E-mail: paulaq@bu.edu. *Application contact:* Sharon Sankey, Assistant Dean, Student Services, 617-353-2713, Fax: 617-353-7500, E-mail: ssankey@bu.edu.

**Boston University,** School of Medicine, Graduate Medical Sciences, Program in Nutrition and Metabolism, Boston, MA 02215. Offers MS, PhD. *Application deadline:* For fall admission, 1/15 for domestic students; for spring admission, 10/15 for domestic students. *Unit head:* Dr. Lynn L. Moore, Director, 617-358-1325, E-mail: llmoore@bu.edu. *Application contact:* Cassandra Kocek, Program Administrator, 617-358-5677, Fax: 617-3585677, E-mail: ckocek@bu.edu.
Website: http://www.bumc.bu.edu/gms/nutrition-metabolism/

**Bradley University,** The Graduate School, College of Education and Health Sciences, Department of Family and Consumer Sciences, Peoria, IL 61625-0002. Offers dietetic internship (MS). *Faculty:* 8 full-time (7 women). *Students:* 17 full-time (all women), 3 part-time (2 women); includes 5 minority (2 Asian, non-Hispanic/Latino; 3 Hispanic/Latino). Average age 24. 15 applicants, 60% accepted, 9 enrolled. In 2019, 8 master's awarded. *Degree requirements:* For master's, comprehensive exam, thesis. *Entrance requirements:* For master's, minimum GPA of 2.5, essays, recommendation letters, transcripts. Additional exam requirements/recommendations for international students: required—TOEFL (minimum score 550 paper-based; 79 iBT), IELTS (minimum score 6.5), PTE (minimum score 58). *Application deadline:* For fall admission, 5/15 for domestic and international students; for spring admission, 10/15 for domestic and international students. *Expenses: Tuition:* Part-time $930 per credit hour. *Financial support:* Research assistantships available. *Unit head:* Teresa Drake, Department Chair & Professor, 309-677-3879, E-mail: tdrake@bradley.edu. *Application contact:* Rachel Webb, Director of On-Campus Graduate Admissions and International Student and Scholar Services, 309-677-2375, E-mail: rkwebb@bradley.edu.
Website: http://www.bradley.edu/academic/departments/fcs/

**Brigham Young University,** Graduate Studies, College of Life Sciences, Department of Nutrition, Dietetics and Food Science, Provo, UT 84602-1001. Offers food science (MS); nutrition (MS), including dietetics, nutritional science. *Faculty:* 17 full-time (6 women). *Students:* 30 full-time (25 women); includes 2 minority (both Hispanic/Latino), 3 international. Average age 25. 16 applicants, 50% accepted, 7 enrolled. In 2019, 10 master's awarded. *Degree requirements:* For master's, thesis, MS/DI program requires a project and internship instead of a thesis. *Entrance requirements:* For master's, GRE, MCAT, DAT, GMAT, LSAT. Additional exam requirements/recommendations for international students: required—TOEFL (minimum score 580 paper-based; 85 iBT); recommended—IELTS (minimum score 7). *Application deadline:* For fall admission, 3/1 priority date for domestic and international students; for winter admission, 6/30 priority date for domestic and international students; for spring admission, 3/1 priority date for domestic and international students; for summer admission, 3/1 priority date for domestic and international students. Application fee: $50. Electronic applications accepted. *Financial support:* In 2019–20, 39 students received support, including 32 research assistantships with partial tuition reimbursements available (averaging $14,400 per year); institutionally sponsored loans and scholarships/grants also available. Financial award application deadline: 4/1; financial award applicants required to submit FAFSA. *Unit head:* Dr. Merrill J. Christensen, Chair, 801-422-5255, Fax: 801-422-0258, E-mail: merrill_christensen@byu.edu. *Application contact:* Judy A. Stoudt, Graduate Program Manager, 801-422-4296, Fax: 801-422-0258, E-mail: judy.stoudt@byu.edu.
Website: http://ndfs.byu.edu/

**Brooklyn College of the City University of New York,** School of Natural and Behavioral Sciences, Department of Health and Nutrition Sciences, Program in Nutrition, Brooklyn, NY 11210-2889. Offers MS. *Program availability:* Part-time. *Degree requirements:* For master's, thesis or comprehensive exam. *Entrance requirements:* For master's, 18 credits in health-related areas, 2 letters of recommendation, essay. Additional exam requirements/recommendations for international students: required—TOEFL. Electronic applications accepted.

**Buffalo State College, State University of New York,** The Graduate School, Program in Multidisciplinary Studies, Buffalo, NY 14222-1095. Offers data science and analytics (MS); individualized studies (MA, MS); nutrition (MS). *Program availability:* Part-time, evening/weekend. *Degree requirements:* For master's, thesis or project. *Entrance requirements:* For master's, minimum GPA of 2.5. Additional exam requirements/recommendations for international students: required—TOEFL (minimum score 550 paper-based).

**California Polytechnic State University, San Luis Obispo,** College of Agriculture, Food and Environmental Sciences, Department of Food Science and Nutrition, San Luis Obispo, CA 93407. Offers food science (MS); nutrition (MS). *Students:* 9 full-time (all women), 6 part-time (4 women); includes 8 minority (3 Asian, non-Hispanic/Latino; 4 Hispanic/Latino; 1 Two or more races, non-Hispanic/Latino), 1 international. Average age 26. 33 applicants, 30% accepted, 7 enrolled. In 2019, 3 master's awarded. *Entrance requirements:* For master's, GRE. Additional exam requirements/recommendations for international students: required—TOEFL (minimum score 80 iBT). *Application deadline:* For fall admission, 4/1 for domestic students. Application fee: $55. *Expenses:* Tuition, state resident: full-time $7176; part-time $4164 per year. Tuition, nonresident: full-time $18,690; part-time $8916 per year. *Required fees:* $4206; $3185 per unit. $1061 per term. *Financial support:* Fellowships, research assistantships, teaching assistantships, scholarships/grants, health care benefits, tuition waivers, and unspecified assistantships available. Financial award application deadline: 3/2; financial award applicants required to submit FAFSA. *Unit head:* Dr. Johan Ubbink, Head, 805-756-2660, E-mail: jubbink@calpoly.edu. *Application contact:* Dr. Jim Prince, Associate Dean, Research and Graduate Programs, 805-756-5104, E-mail: jpprince@calpoly.edu.
Website: http://www.fsn.calpoly.edu

**California State University, Chico,** Office of Graduate Studies, College of Natural Sciences, Department of Nutrition and Food Science, Chico, CA 95929-0722. Offers general nutritional science (MS); nutrition education (MS). *Program availability:* Part-time. *Degree requirements:* For master's, thesis, professional paper, or oral defense. *Entrance requirements:* For master's, GRE General Test, two letters of recommendation, statement of purpose, department pre-requisite course clearance forms, resume, department letter of recommendation access waiver form. Additional exam requirements/recommendations for international students: required—TOEFL (minimum score 550 paper-based; 80 iBT), IELTS (minimum score 6.5), PTE (minimum score 59). Electronic applications accepted.

**California State University, Long Beach,** Graduate Studies, College of Health and Human Services, Department of Kinesiology, Long Beach, CA 90840. Offers adapted physical education (MA); coaching and student athlete development (MA); exercise physiology and nutrition (MS); exercise science (MS); individualized studies (MA); kinesiology (MA); pedagogical studies (MA); sport and exercise psychology (MS); sport management (MA); sports medicine and injury studies (MS). *Program availability:* Part-time. *Degree requirements:* For master's, oral and written comprehensive exams or thesis. *Entrance requirements:* For master's, GRE General Test, minimum GPA of 2.75 during previous 2 years of course work. Electronic applications accepted.

**California State University, Los Angeles,** Graduate Studies, College of Health and Human Services, Department of Kinesiology and Nutritional Sciences, Los Angeles, CA 90032-8530. Offers nutritional science (MS); physical education and kinesiology (MA). *Accreditation:* AND. *Program availability:* Part-time, evening/weekend. *Degree requirements:* For master's, comprehensive exam, project or thesis. *Entrance requirements:* For master's, minimum GPA of 2.75. Additional exam requirements/recommendations for international students: required—TOEFL (minimum score 500 paper-based). *Expenses: Tuition, area resident:* Full-time $7176; part-time $4164 per year. Tuition, state resident: full-time $7176; part-time $4164 per year. Tuition, nonresident: full-time $14,304; part-time $8916 per year. *International tuition:* $14,304 full-time. *Required fees:* $1037.76; $1037.76 per unit. Tuition and fees vary according to degree level and program.

**California University of Pennsylvania,** School of Graduate Studies and Research, College of Education and Human Services, Department of Exercise Science and Sport Studies, California, PA 15419-1394. Offers applied sport science (MS); exercise science (MS), including group fitness leadership, nutrition, performance enhancement and injury prevention, rehabilitation science; group fitness leadership (MS); nutrition (MS); wellness coaching (MS). *Program availability:* Part-time, evening/weekend, online learning. *Degree requirements:* For master's, comprehensive exam, thesis optional. *Entrance requirements:* For master's, minimum GPA of 3.0. Additional exam requirements/recommendations for international students: required—TOEFL (minimum score 550 paper-based; 80 iBT). Electronic applications accepted. *Expenses:* Contact institution.

**Canisius College,** Graduate Division, School of Education and Human Services, Office of Professional Studies, Buffalo, NY 14208-1098. Offers applied nutrition (MS, Certificate); community and school health (MS); health and human performance (MS); health information technology (MS); respiratory care (MS). *Program availability:* Part-time, evening/weekend, 100% online, blended/hybrid learning. *Faculty:* 1 full-time (0 women), 20 part-time/adjunct (11 women). *Students:* 12 full-time (8 women), 28 part-time (17 women); includes 9 minority (3 Black or African American, non-Hispanic/Latino; 1 Asian, non-Hispanic/Latino; 3 Hispanic/Latino; 2 Two or more races, non-Hispanic/Latino). Average age 33. 24 applicants, 88% accepted, 11 enrolled. In 2019, 27 master's awarded. *Degree requirements:* For master's, thesis (for some programs), Programs require Thesis/Project or Internship. *Entrance requirements:* For master's, GRE recommended, bachelor's degree transcript, two letters of recommendation, current licensure (for applied nutrition), minimum GPA of 2.7, current resume. Additional exam requirements/recommendations for international students: required—TOEFL (550+ PBT or 79+ IBT), IELTS (6.5+), or CAEL (70+). *Application deadline:* Applications are processed on a rolling basis. Electronic applications accepted. *Expenses: Tuition:* Part-time $900 per credit. *Required fees:* $25 per credit hour. $65 per term. Part-time tuition and fees vary according to course load and program. *Financial support:* Career-related internships or fieldwork, Federal Work-Study, scholarships/grants, tuition waivers (partial), and unspecified assistantships available. Support available to part-time students. Financial award application deadline: 4/30; financial award applicants required to submit FAFSA. *Unit head:* Dennis W. Koch, Director, Office of Professional Studies, 716-888-8292, E-mail: koch5@canisius.edu. *Application contact:* Dennis W. Koch, Director, Office of Professional Studies, 716-888-8292, E-mail: koch5@canisius.edu.
Website: http://www.canisius.edu/graduate/

**Case Western Reserve University,** School of Medicine and School of Graduate Studies, Graduate Programs in Medicine, Department of Nutrition, Cleveland, OH 44106. Offers dietetics (MS); molecular nutrition (MS); nutrition (MS, PhD), including molecular nutrition (PhD); nutritional biochemistry and metabolism (MS); public health nutrition (MS). *Program availability:* Part-time. Terminal master's awarded for partial completion of doctoral program. *Degree requirements:* For master's, thesis (for some programs); for doctorate, thesis/dissertation. *Entrance requirements:* For master's, GRE General Test; for doctorate, GRE General Test, GRE Subject Test. Additional exam requirements/recommendations for international students: required—TOEFL.

**Cedar Crest College,** Dietetic Internship Certificate Program, Allentown, PA 18104-6196. Offers Graduate Certificate. *Program availability:* Part-time, evening/weekend, blended/hybrid learning. *Entrance requirements:* For degree, two semesters of medical nutrition therapy coursework completed no more than four years prior to application; one biochemistry course completed no more than five years prior to application. Electronic applications accepted. *Expenses:* Contact institution.

**Central Michigan University,** Central Michigan University Global Campus, Program in Health Administration, Mount Pleasant, MI 48859. Offers health administration (DHA); international health (Certificate); nutrition and dietetics (MS). *Program availability:* Part-time, evening/weekend, online learning. Electronic applications accepted. *Expenses: Tuition, area resident:* Full-time $12,267; part-time $8178 per year. Tuition, state resident: full-time $12,267; part-time $8178 per year. Tuition, nonresident: full-time $12,267; part-time $8178 per year. *International tuition:* $16,110 full-time. *Required fees:* $225 per semester. Tuition and fees vary according to degree level and program.

**Central Michigan University,** College of Graduate Studies, College of Education and Human Services, Department of Human Environmental Studies, Mount Pleasant, MI 48859. Offers apparel product development and merchandising technology (MS); gerontology (Graduate Certificate); human development and family studies (MA); nutrition and dietetics (MS). *Program availability:* Part-time, evening/weekend. *Degree requirements:* For master's, thesis or alternative. Electronic applications accepted. *Expenses: Tuition, area resident:* Full-time $12,267; part-time $8178 per year. Tuition, state resident: full-time $12,267; part-time $8178 per year. Tuition, nonresident: full-time

$12,267; part-time $8178 per year. *International tuition:* $16,110 full-time. *Required fees:* $225 per semester. Tuition and fees vary according to degree level and program.

**Central Washington University,** School of Graduate Studies and Research, College of Education and Professional Studies, Department of Health Sciences, Ellensburg, WA 98926. Offers integrative human physiology (MS); nutrition (MS). *Program availability:* Part-time. *Entrance requirements:* For master's, GRE, minimum GPA of 3.0. Additional exam requirements/recommendations for international students: required—TOEFL (minimum score 550 paper-based; 79 iBT). Electronic applications accepted.

**Chapman University,** Schmid College of Science and Technology, Food Science Program, Orange, CA 92866. Offers MS, MS/MBA. *Program availability:* Part-time, evening/weekend. *Faculty:* 4 full-time (3 women), 7 part-time/adjunct (all women). *Students:* 4 full-time (1 woman), 24 part-time (17 women); includes 14 minority (1 Black or African American, non-Hispanic/Latino; 8 Asian, non-Hispanic/Latino; 4 Hispanic/Latino; 1 Two or more races, non-Hispanic/Latino), 7 international. Average age 27. 21 applicants, 71% accepted, 6 enrolled. In 2019, 24 master's awarded. *Degree requirements:* For master's, thesis or alternative. *Entrance requirements:* For master's, GRE or GMAT. Additional exam requirements/recommendations for international students: required—TOEFL (minimum score 80 iBT), IELTS (minimum score 6.5), PTE (minimum score 53). *Application deadline:* For fall admission, 2/1 priority date for domestic students. Applications are processed on a rolling basis. Application fee: $60. Electronic applications accepted. *Expenses:* $1,095 per unit. *Financial support:* Fellowships, research assistantships, teaching assistantships, Federal Work-Study, and scholarships/grants available. Financial award applicants required to submit FAFSA. *Unit head:* Dr. Anuradha Prakash, Program Director, 714-744-7895, E-mail: prakash@chapman.edu. *Application contact:* Sharnique Dow, Graduate Admission Counselor, 714-997-6770, E-mail: sdow@chapman.edu.
Website: https://www.chapman.edu/scst/graduate/index.aspx

**Clemson University,** Graduate School, College of Agriculture, Forestry and Life Sciences, Department of Food, Nutrition and Packaging Sciences, Clemson, SC 29634. Offers food technology (PhD); food, nutrition and culinary sciences (MS); packaging science (MS). *Program availability:* Part-time. *Students:* Average age 30. 79 applicants, 39% accepted, 24 enrolled. In 2019, 12 master's, 4 doctorates awarded. *Degree requirements:* For master's, thesis or alternative; for doctorate, comprehensive exam, thesis/dissertation. *Entrance requirements:* For master's and doctorate, GRE General Test, unofficial transcripts, letters of recommendation. Additional exam requirements/recommendations for international students: required—TOEFL (minimum score 80 paper-based; 80 iBT); recommended—IELTS (minimum score 6.5), TSE (minimum score 54). *Application deadline:* For fall admission, 4/15 for international students; for spring admission, 10/15 for international students. Applications are processed on a rolling basis. Application fee: $80 ($90 for international students). Electronic applications accepted. *Expenses:* Contact institution. *Financial support:* In 2019–20, 37 students received support, including 1 fellowship with full and partial tuition reimbursement available (averaging $5,000 per year), 15 research assistantships with full and partial tuition reimbursements available (averaging $13,366 per year), 15 teaching assistantships with full and partial tuition reimbursements available (averaging $11,008 per year); career-related internships or fieldwork and unspecified assistantships also available. *Unit head:* Dr. E. Jeffery Rhodehamel, Department Chair, 864-656-1211, E-mail: jrhode@clemson.edu. *Application contact:* Dr. Paul Dawson, Graduate Coordinator, 864-656-1138, E-mail: pdawson@clemson.edu.
Website: http://www.clemson.edu/cafls/departments/fnps/

**College of Saint Elizabeth,** Department of Foods and Nutrition, Morristown, NJ 07960-6989. Offers dietetics verification (Certificate); nutrition (MS), including community nutrition and wellness, entrepreneurial nutrition practice; nutrition/dietetic internship (MS). *Program availability:* Part-time, blended/hybrid learning. *Degree requirements:* For master's, thesis. *Entrance requirements:* Additional exam requirements/recommendations for international students: required—TOEFL (minimum score 550 paper-based; 79 iBT), IELTS (minimum score 6.5). Electronic applications accepted. Application fee is waived when completed online.

**Colorado State University,** College of Health and Human Sciences, Department of Food Science and Human Nutrition, Fort Collins, CO 80523-1571. Offers dietetics (MS); food science and human nutrition (PhD); food science and nutrition (MS); nutrition and exercise science (MS). *Accreditation:* AND. *Program availability:* Part-time, 100% online. *Faculty:* 11 full-time (7 women), 4 part-time/adjunct (2 women). *Students:* 30 full-time (27 women), 41 part-time (35 women); includes 10 minority (1 Black or African American, non-Hispanic/Latino; 2 Asian, non-Hispanic/Latino; 3 Hispanic/Latino; 4 Two or more races, non-Hispanic/Latino), 2 international. Average age 31. 90 applicants, 38% accepted, 18 enrolled. In 2019, 22 master's, 2 doctorates awarded. Terminal master's awarded for partial completion of doctoral program. *Degree requirements:* For master's, thesis; for doctorate, thesis/dissertation. *Entrance requirements:* For master's, 3.0 GPA, prerequisites, letters of recommendation, personal statement, resume; for doctorate, 3.0 GPA, advisor identified, prerequisites, letters of recommendation, personal statement, resume. Additional exam requirements/recommendations for international students: required—TOEFL (minimum score 550 paper-based; 80 iBT), IELTS (minimum score 6.5). *Application deadline:* For fall admission, 2/1 priority date for domestic and international students. Application fee: $60 ($70 for international students). Electronic applications accepted. *Expenses:* 2019-20 full-time (9 credits), in-state tuition & fees = $12,745.82 (includes $20.75/credit facility fee). *Financial support:* In 2019–20, 8 research assistantships (averaging $10,933 per year), 10 teaching assistantships (averaging $11,408 per year) were awarded; fellowships, scholarships/grants, and unspecified assistantships also available. Financial award application deadline: 2/1. *Unit head:* Dr. Michael Pagliassotti, Department Head, 970-491-1390, E-mail: michael.pagliassotti@colostate.edu. *Application contact:* Paula Coleman, Administrative Assistant, 970-491-3819, Fax: 970-491-3875, E-mail: paula.coleman@colostate.edu.
Website: http://www.fshn.chhs.colostate.edu/

**Colorado State University,** College of Health and Human Sciences, Department of Health and Exercise Science, Fort Collins, CO 80523-1582. Offers exercise science and nutrition (MS); human bioenergetics (PhD). *Program availability:* Part-time. *Faculty:* 8 full-time (4 women), 1 (woman) part-time/adjunct. *Students:* 30 full-time (20 women), 5 part-time (2 women); includes 2 minority (1 Hispanic/Latino; 1 Two or more races, non-Hispanic/Latino), 2 international. Average age 28. 37 applicants, 14% accepted, 5 enrolled. In 2019, 10 master's, 1 doctorate awarded. Terminal master's awarded for partial completion of doctoral program. *Degree requirements:* For master's, thesis; for doctorate, comprehensive exam, thesis/dissertation. *Entrance requirements:* For master's, minimum GPA of 3.0, personal statement, identification of faculty lab mentor, specific prerequisite undergrad courses; for doctorate, letter of application to the eepartment, statement of career goals and research interests, 3 letters of recommendation from former/current professors, graduate faculty adviser approval of application and financial support plan. Additional exam requirements/recommendations for international students: recommended—TOEFL. *Application deadline:* For fall admission, 12/31 for domestic students, 11/30 for international students; for spring admission, 8/31 for domestic and international students. Electronic applications accepted. *Expenses:* Tuition, state resident: full-time $10,520; part-time $5844 per credit hour. Tuition, nonresident: full-time $25,791; part-time $14,328 per credit hour. *International tuition:* $25,791 full-time. *Required fees:* $2512.80. Part-time tuition and fees vary according to course level, course load, degree level, program and student level. *Financial support:* In 2019–20, 28 students received support, including 1 fellowship with full tuition reimbursement available (averaging $20,933 per year), 11 research assistantships with full tuition reimbursements available (averaging $17,950 per year), 17 teaching assistantships with full tuition reimbursements available (averaging $15,358 per year); scholarships/grants, health care benefits, and unspecified assistantships also available. Financial award application deadline: 3/1; financial award applicants required to submit FAFSA. *Unit head:* Dr. Barry Braun, Professor and Department Head, 970-491-7875, Fax: 970-491-0445, E-mail: barry.braun@colostate.edu. *Application contact:* Dr. Matt Hickey, Professor, 970-491-5727, Fax: 970-491-0445, E-mail: matthew.hickey@colostate.edu.
Website: https://www.chhs.colostate.edu/hes

**Columbia University,** College of Physicians and Surgeons, Institute of Human Nutrition, MS Program in Nutrition, New York, NY 10032. Offers MS, MPH/MS. *Program availability:* Part-time. *Degree requirements:* For master's, thesis. *Entrance requirements:* For master's, GRE General Test, MCAT. Additional exam requirements/recommendations for international students: required—TOEFL; recommended—IELTS. Electronic applications accepted. *Expenses: Tuition:* Full-time $47,600; part-time $1880 per credit. One-time fee: $105.

**Columbia University,** College of Physicians and Surgeons, Institute of Human Nutrition, PhD Program in Nutrition, New York, NY 10032. Offers PhD. *Degree requirements:* For doctorate, thesis/dissertation. *Entrance requirements:* For doctorate, GRE General Test. Additional exam requirements/recommendations for international students: required—TOEFL. *Expenses: Tuition:* Full-time $47,600; part-time $1880 per credit. One-time fee: $105.

**Cornell University,** Graduate School, Graduate Fields of Agriculture and Life Sciences, Field of Global Development, Ithaca, NY 14853. Offers development policy (MPS); international agriculture and development (MPS); international development (MPS); international nutrition (MPS); international planning (MPS); international population (MPS); science and technology policy (MPS). *Degree requirements:* For master's, project paper. *Entrance requirements:* For master's, GRE General Test (recommended), 2 years of development experience, 2 letters of recommendation. Additional exam requirements/recommendations for international students: required—TOEFL (minimum score 550 paper-based; 77 iBT). Electronic applications accepted.

**Cornell University,** Graduate School, Graduate Fields of Agriculture and Life Sciences and Graduate Fields of Human Ecology, Field of Nutrition, Ithaca, NY 14853. Offers animal nutrition (MPS, PhD); community nutrition (MPS, PhD); human nutrition (MPS, PhD); international nutrition (MPS, PhD); molecular biochemistry (MPS, PhD). *Degree requirements:* For master's, thesis (MS), project papers (MPS); for doctorate, comprehensive exam, thesis/dissertation. *Entrance requirements:* For master's and doctorate, GRE General Test, previous course work in organic chemistry (with laboratory) and biochemistry; 2 letters of recommendation. Additional exam requirements/recommendations for international students: required—TOEFL (minimum score 550 paper-based; 77 iBT). Electronic applications accepted.

**D'Youville College,** Department of Dietetics, Buffalo, NY 14201-1084. Offers MS. *Degree requirements:* For master's, thesis. *Entrance requirements:* Additional exam requirements/recommendations for international students: required—TOEFL (minimum score 500 paper-based). Electronic applications accepted.

**East Carolina University,** Graduate School, College of Allied Health Sciences, Department of Nutrition Science, Greenville, NC 27858-4353. Offers MS. *Program availability:* Part-time, online learning. *Application deadline:* For fall admission, 3/1 for domestic students. *Expenses: Tuition, area resident:* Full-time $4749; part-time $185 per credit hour. Tuition, state resident: full-time $4749; part-time $185 per credit hour. Tuition, nonresident: full-time $17,898; part-time $864 per credit hour. *International tuition:* $17,898 full-time. *Required fees:* $2787. *Financial support:* Application deadline: 3/1. *Unit head:* Dr. Michael Wheeler, Chair, 252-744-1027, E-mail: wheelerm@ecu.edu. *Application contact:* Graduate School Admissions, 252-328-6012, Fax: 252-328-6071, E-mail: gradschool@ecu.edu.
Website: http://www.ecu.edu/nutr/

**Eastern Illinois University,** Graduate School, College of Health and Human Services, Program in Nutrition and Dietetics, Charleston, IL 61920. Offers MS. *Program availability:* Part-time, evening/weekend. *Degree requirements:* For master's, comprehensive exam (for some programs), thesis (for some programs). *Entrance requirements:* For master's, GMAT or GRE. Additional exam requirements/recommendations for international students: required—TOEFL (minimum score 500 paper-based; 61 iBT), IELTS (minimum score 6). Electronic applications accepted.

**Eastern Kentucky University,** The Graduate School, College of Health Sciences, Department of Family and Consumer Sciences, Richmond, KY 40475-3102. Offers M Ed. *Program availability:* Part-time. *Entrance requirements:* For master's, GRE General Test, minimum GPA of 2.5.

**Eastern Kentucky University,** The Graduate School, College of Health Sciences, Program in Public Health, Richmond, KY 40475-3102. Offers community health education (MPH); environmental health science (MPH); industrial hygiene (MPH); public health nutrition (MPH). *Accreditation:* CEPH. *Degree requirements:* For master's, comprehensive exam, thesis optional, practicum, capstone course. *Entrance requirements:* For master's, GRE.

**Eastern Michigan University,** Graduate School, College of Health and Human Services, School of Health Sciences, Programs in Dietetics and Human Nutrition, Ypsilanti, MI 48197. Offers dietetics (MS); human nutrition (MS). *Program availability:* Part-time, evening/weekend, online learning. *Students:* 27 full-time (25 women), 26 part-time (24 women); includes 11 minority (4 Black or African American, non-Hispanic/Latino; 3 Asian, non-Hispanic/Latino; 3 Hispanic/Latino; 1 Two or more races, non-Hispanic/Latino), 2 international. Average age 33. 36 applicants, 44% accepted, 12 enrolled. In 2019, 24 master's awarded. *Entrance requirements:* Additional exam requirements/recommendations for international students: required—TOEFL. *Application deadline:* Applications are processed on a rolling basis. Application fee: $45. *Financial support:* Fellowships, research assistantships with full tuition reimbursements, teaching assistantships with full tuition reimbursements, career-related internships or fieldwork, Federal Work-Study, institutionally sponsored loans, scholarships/grants, tuition waivers (partial), and unspecified assistantships available. Support available to part-time students. Financial award applicants required to submit FAFSA. *Application contact:* Dr. Alice Jo Rainville, Program Coordinator, 734-487-0430, Fax: 734-487-4095, E-mail: arainville@emich.edu.

**East Tennessee State University,** College of Graduate and Continuing Studies, College of Clinical and Rehabilitative Health Sciences, Department of Allied Health Sciences, Elizabethton, TN 37643. Offers allied health (MSAH); clinical nutrition (MS). *Program availability:* Part-time, online learning. *Degree requirements:* For master's, comprehensive exam, thesis or advanced practice seminar (for MSAH); internship (for MS). *Entrance requirements:* For master's, GRE General Test, professional license in

allied health discipline, minimum GPA of 2.75, and three professional letters of recommendation (for MSAH); bachelor's degree from an undergraduate didactic program in dietetics with minimum GPA of 3.0 in DPD coursework and three letters of recommendation (for MS). Additional exam requirements/recommendations for international students: required—TOEFL (minimum score 550 paper-based; 79 iBT). Electronic applications accepted.

**Emory University,** Laney Graduate School, Division of Biological and Biomedical Sciences, Program in Nutrition and Health Sciences, Atlanta, GA 30322-1100. Offers PhD. *Degree requirements:* For doctorate, comprehensive exam, thesis/dissertation. *Entrance requirements:* For doctorate, GRE General Test, minimum GPA of 3.0 in science course work (recommended). Additional exam requirements/recommendations for international students: required—TOEFL. Electronic applications accepted.

**Emory University,** Rollins School of Public Health, Hubert Department of Global Health, Atlanta, GA 30322-1100. Offers global health (MPH); public nutrition (MSPH). *Degree requirements:* For master's, thesis, practicum. *Entrance requirements:* For master's, GRE General Test. Additional exam requirements/recommendations for international students: required—TOEFL (minimum score 550 paper-based; 80 iBT). Electronic applications accepted.

**Florida International University,** Robert Stempel College of Public Health and Social Work, Department of Dietetics and Nutrition, Miami, FL 33199. Offers MS, PhD. *Program availability:* Part-time. *Faculty:* 12 full-time (11 women), 9 part-time/adjunct (all women). *Students:* 76 full-time (64 women), 48 part-time (43 women); includes 84 minority (11 Black or African American, non-Hispanic/Latino; 8 Asian, non-Hispanic/Latino; 62 Hispanic/Latino; 3 Two or more races, non-Hispanic/Latino), 15 international. Average age 29. 79 applicants, 59% accepted, 28 enrolled. In 2019, 45 master's, 4 doctorates awarded. *Degree requirements:* For master's, thesis; for doctorate, comprehensive exam, thesis/dissertation. *Entrance requirements:* For master's, minimum GPA of 3.0; for doctorate, GRE General Test, minimum GPA of 3.0, resume, letters of recommendation, faculty sponsor. Additional exam requirements/recommendations for international students: required—TOEFL (minimum score 550 paper-based; 80 iBT). *Application deadline:* For fall admission, 6/1 for domestic students, 4/1 for international students; for spring admission, 10/1 for domestic students, 9/1 for international students. Applications are processed on a rolling basis. Application fee: $30. Electronic applications accepted. *Expenses: Tuition, area resident:* Full-time $8912; part-time $446 per credit hour. Tuition, state resident: full-time $8912; part-time $446 per credit hour. Tuition, nonresident: full-time $21,393; part-time $992 per credit hour. *Required fees:* $2194. *Financial support:* Career-related internships or fieldwork, Federal Work-Study, institutionally sponsored loans, and scholarships/grants available. Financial award application deadline: 3/1; financial award applicants required to submit FAFSA. *Unit head:* Dr. Adriana Campa, Chair, 305-348-2871, Fax: 305-348-0383, E-mail: Adriana.Campa@fiu.edu. *Application contact:* Nanett Rojas, Manager, Admissions Operations, 305-348-7464, Fax: 305-348-7441, E-mail: gradadm@fiu.edu.

**Florida State University,** The Graduate School, College of Human Sciences, Department of Nutrition, Food and Exercise Sciences, Tallahassee, FL 32306-1493. Offers exercise physiology (MS, PhD); nutrition and food science (MS, PhD), including nutrition education and health promotion (MS); sports nutrition (MS); sports sciences (MS). *Program availability:* Part-time. *Faculty:* 25 full-time (11 women). *Students:* 79 full-time (49 women), 19 part-time (14 women); includes 16 minority (2 Black or African American, non-Hispanic/Latino; 4 Asian, non-Hispanic/Latino; 10 Two or more races, non-Hispanic/Latino), 13 international. 118 applicants, 62% accepted, 38 enrolled. In 2019, 20 master's, 6 doctorates awarded. *Degree requirements:* For master's, comprehensive exam (for some programs), thesis optional; for doctorate, thesis/dissertation, preliminary examination, minimum of 24 credit hours dissertation, dissertation defense. *Entrance requirements:* For master's, GRE General Test, minimum upper-division GPA of 3.0, prerequisites listed on website; for doctorate, GRE General Test, minimum upper-division GPA of 3.0 or awarded master's degree. Additional exam requirements/recommendations for international students: required—TOEFL (minimum score 550 paper-based; 80 iBT). *Application deadline:* For fall admission, 4/1 for domestic and international students; for spring admission, 10/1 for domestic and international students. Applications are processed on a rolling basis. Application fee: $30. Electronic applications accepted. *Financial support:* In 2019–20, 67 students received support, including 16 research assistantships with full tuition reimbursements available (averaging $25,462 per year), 34 teaching assistantships with full tuition reimbursements available (averaging $25,462 per year); career-related internships or fieldwork, Federal Work-Study, institutionally sponsored loans, scholarships/grants, and unspecified assistantships also available. Financial award application deadline: 2/1; financial award applicants required to submit FAFSA. *Unit head:* Dr. Chester Ray, Department Chair, 850-644-1850, E-mail: caray@fsu.edu. *Application contact:* Mary-Sue McLemore, Academic Support Assistant, 850-644-1117, E-mail: mmclemore@fsu.edu.
Website: https://humansciences.fsu.edu/nutrition-food-exercise-sciences/students/graduate-programs/

**Framingham State University,** Graduate Studies, Programs in Food and Nutrition, Coordinated Program in Dietetics, Framingham, MA 01701-9101. Offers MS.

**Framingham State University,** Graduate Studies, Programs in Food and Nutrition, Program in Nutrition Science and Informatics, Framingham, MA 01701-9101. Offers MS. *Program availability:* Part-time, evening/weekend. *Entrance requirements:* For master's, GRE General Test.

**Franciscan Missionaries of Our Lady University,** School of Health Professions, Baton Rouge, LA 70808. Offers health administration (MHA); nutritional sciences (MS); physical therapy (DPT); physician assistant studies (MMS).

**George Mason University,** College of Health and Human Services, Department of Nutrition and Food Studies, Fairfax, VA 22030. Offers food security (Certificate); nutrition (MS). *Program availability:* Part-time. *Degree requirements:* For master's, comprehensive exam, thesis optional. *Entrance requirements:* For master's, resume, 2 letters of recommendation, expanded goal statement, college transcripts; for Certificate, college transcripts, goals statement, 2 recommendation letters, resume. Additional exam requirements/recommendations for international students: required—TOEFL (minimum score 575 paper-based; 88 iBT), IELTS (minimum score 6.5), PTE (minimum score 59). Electronic applications accepted.

**Georgia Southern University,** Jack N. Averitt College of Graduate Studies, Waters College of Health Professions, Department of Health Sciences and Kinesiology, Dietetic Internship Program, Statesboro, GA 30458. Offers Certificate. *Students:* 6 part-time (all women); all minorities (5 Black or African American, non-Hispanic/Latino; 1 Hispanic/Latino). Average age 26. *Degree requirements:* For Certificate, 1,200 hours of supervised practice experiences. *Entrance requirements:* For degree, Verification of Completion of a Didactic Program in Dietetics, accredited by the Accreditation Council for Education of Nutrition & Dietetics. Additional exam requirements/recommendations for international students: required—TOEFL (minimum score 550 paper-based; 80 iBT). *Application deadline:* For fall admission, 1/16 for domestic students. Electronic applications accepted. *Expenses: Tuition, area resident:* Full-time $4986; part-time $277 per credit hour. Tuition, nonresident: full-time $19,890; part-time $1105 per credit hour.

*International tuition:* $19,890 full-time. *Required fees:* $2114; $1057 per semester. $1057 per semester. Tuition and fees vary according to course load, campus/location and program. *Financial support:* In 2019–20, 2 students received support. Applicants required to submit FAFSA. *Unit head:* Dr. Karen Spears, Dietetic Internship Coordinator, 912-478-2123, E-mail: kspears@georgiasouthern.edu. *Application contact:* Dr. Karen Spears, Dietetic Internship Coordinator, 912-478-2123, E-mail: kspears@georgiasouthern.edu. Website: https://chp.georgiasouthern.edu/hk/graduate/dietetic-internship/

**Georgia State University,** Byrdine F. Lewis School of Nursing, Division of Nutrition, Atlanta, GA 30302-3083. Offers MS. *Program availability:* Part-time. *Faculty:* 9 full-time (7 women), 1 (woman) part-time/adjunct. *Students:* 44 full-time (38 women); includes 17 minority (10 Black or African American, non-Hispanic/Latino; 2 Asian, non-Hispanic/Latino; 4 Hispanic/Latino; 1 Two or more races, non-Hispanic/Latino). Average age 29. 45 applicants, 58% accepted, 23 enrolled. In 2019, 23 master's awarded. *Entrance requirements:* For master's, GRE, prerequisite courses in inorganic chemistry (1 semester), organic chemistry (1 semester), and human anatomy and physiology (2 semesters); transcripts; resume; statement of goals; letters of recommendation. Additional exam requirements/recommendations for international students: required—TOEFL (minimum score 550 paper-based; 80 iBT). *Application deadline:* For fall admission, 5/15 for domestic and international students; for spring admission, 10/1 for domestic and international students. Application fee: $50. Electronic applications accepted. *Expenses: Tuition, area resident:* Full-time $7164; part-time $398 per credit hour. Tuition, state resident: full-time $7164; part-time $398 per credit hour. Tuition, nonresident: full-time $22,662; part-time $1259 per credit hour. *International tuition:* $22,662 full-time. *Required fees:* $2128; $312 per credit hour. Tuition and fees vary according to course load and program. *Financial support:* In 2019–20, research assistantships with tuition reimbursements (averaging $1,647 per year), teaching assistantships with full tuition reimbursements (averaging $2,666 per year) were awarded. Financial award application deadline: 4/1. *Unit head:* Dr. Anita Nucci, Associate Professor and Graduate Program Director, 404-413-1234, Fax: 404-413-1228, E-mail: anucci@gsu.edu. *Application contact:* Dr. Anita Nucci, Associate Professor and Graduate Program Director, 404-413-1234, Fax: 404-413-1228, E-mail: anucci@gsu.edu.
Website: http://nutrition.gsu.edu/

**Grand Valley State University,** College of Health Professions, Clinical Dietetics Program, Allendale, MI 49401-9403. Offers MS. *Program availability:* Part-time. *Students:* 46 full-time (43 women), 2 part-time (both women); includes 9 minority (2 Black or African American, non-Hispanic/Latino; 5 Asian, non-Hispanic/Latino; 2 Two or more races, non-Hispanic/Latino). Average age 24. 27 applicants, 96% accepted, 23 enrolled. In 2019, 25 master's awarded. *Degree requirements:* For master's, thesis optional, project or thesis. *Entrance requirements:* For master's, minimum cumulative undergraduate GPA of 3.0, 2.7 in clinical or advanced nutrition, pharmacology, pathophysiology, and biochemistry courses; resume; personal statement; two professional or academic recommendations. Additional exam requirements/recommendations for international students: required—TOEFL (minimum iBT score of 80), IELTS (6.5), or Michigan English Language Assessment Battery (77). *Application deadline:* For fall admission, 4/1 for domestic students. Applications are processed on a rolling basis. Application fee: $30. Electronic applications accepted. *Expenses:* $733 per credit hour, track A = 49-52 credit hours, track B = 39-42 credit hours. *Financial support:* In 2019–20, 3 students received support, including 3 fellowships; unspecified assistantships also available. *Unit head:* Dr. Jody Vogelzang, Director, 616-331-5059, Fax: 616-331-5550, E-mail: vogelzjo@gvsu.edu. *Application contact:* Darlene Zwart, Student Services Coordinator/Recruiting Contact, 616-331-3958, Fax: 616-331-5999, E-mail: zwartda@gvsu.edu.
Website: http://www.gvsu.edu/grad/clinicaldiet/

**Harvard University,** Harvard T.H. Chan School of Public Health, Department of Nutrition, Boston, MA 02115-6096. Offers population health sciences (PhD). *Accreditation:* CEPH. *Faculty:* 29 full-time (8 women), 16 part-time/adjunct (7 women). *Students:* 4 full-time (all women), 2 international. Average age 29. In 2019, 5 doctorates awarded. *Degree requirements:* For doctorate, thesis/dissertation, qualifying exam. *Entrance requirements:* For doctorate, GRE. Additional exam requirements/recommendations for international students: recommended—TOEFL (minimum score 600 paper-based; 100 iBT), IELTS (minimum score 7). *Application deadline:* For fall admission, 12/1 for domestic and international students. Application fee: $140. Electronic applications accepted. *Financial support:* Fellowships, research assistantships, teaching assistantships, Federal Work-Study, scholarships/grants, traineeships, and unspecified assistantships available. Support available to part-time students. Financial award application deadline: 2/15; financial award applicants required to submit FAFSA. *Unit head:* Dr. Frank Hu, Chair. *Application contact:* Vincent W. James, Director of Admissions, 617-432-1031, Fax: 617-432-7080, E-mail: admissions@hsph.harvard.edu.
Website: http://www.hsph.harvard.edu/nutrition/

**Harvard University,** Harvard T.H. Chan School of Public Health, PhD Program in Population Health Sciences, Boston, MA 02138. Offers environmental health (PhD); epidemiology (PhD); global health and population (PhD); nutrition (PhD); social and behavioral sciences (PhD). *Students:* 159 full-time (0 women). Average age 29. In 2019, 5 doctorates awarded. *Entrance requirements:* Additional exam requirements/recommendations for international students: recommended—TOEFL, IELTS. *Application deadline:* For fall admission, 12/1 for domestic and international students. Electronic applications accepted. *Financial support:* Application deadline: 2/15; applicants required to submit FAFSA. *Unit head:* Bruce Villineau, Assistant Director, 617-432-6076, E-mail: phdphs@hsph.harvard.edu. *Application contact:* Bruce Villineau, Assistant Director, 617-432-6076, E-mail: phdphs@hsph.harvard.edu.

**Howard University,** Graduate School, Department of Nutritional Sciences, Washington, DC 20059-0002. Offers nutrition (MS, PhD). *Program availability:* Part-time, evening/weekend. *Degree requirements:* For master's, comprehensive exam, thesis; for doctorate, comprehensive exam, thesis/dissertation. *Entrance requirements:* For master's and doctorate, minimum GPA of 3.0, general chemistry, organic chemistry, biochemistry, nutrition. Additional exam requirements/recommendations for international students: required—TOEFL. Electronic applications accepted.

**Hunter College of the City University of New York,** Graduate School, School of Urban Public Health, Program in Nutrition, New York, NY 10065-5085. Offers MS. *Accreditation:* AND. *Program availability:* Part-time, evening/weekend. *Degree requirements:* For master's, comprehensive exam, thesis optional, internship. *Entrance requirements:* For master's, GRE General Test, previous course work in calculus and statistics. Additional exam requirements/recommendations for international students: required—TOEFL.

**Huntington University of Health Sciences,** Program in Nutrition, Knoxville, TN 37918. Offers clinical nutrition (DHS); nutrition (MS); personalized option (DHS). *Program availability:* Part-time, evening/weekend, online learning. *Degree requirements:* For doctorate, comprehensive exam, thesis/dissertation. *Entrance requirements:* For master's, bachelor's degree, essay, resume/curriculum vitae; for doctorate, master's degree, essay, references, interview, resume/curriculum vitae. Additional exam

requirements/recommendations for international students: required—TOEFL (minimum score 550 paper-based; 80 iBT); recommended—IELTS. Electronic applications accepted.

**Immaculata University,** College of Graduate Studies, Program in Nutrition Education, Immaculata, PA 19345. Offers nutrition education for the registered dietitian (MA); nutrition education with dietetic internship (MA); nutrition education with wellness promotion (MA). *Program availability:* Part-time, evening/weekend. *Degree requirements:* For master's, comprehensive exam, thesis optional. *Entrance requirements:* For master's, GRE or MAT, minimum GPA of 3.0. Additional exam requirements/recommendations for international students: required—TOEFL. Electronic applications accepted.

**Indiana University Bloomington,** School of Public Health, Department of Applied Health Science, Bloomington, IN 47405. Offers behavioral, social, and community health (MPH); family health (MPH); health behavior (PhD); nutrition science (MS); professional health education (MPH); public health administration (MPH); safety management (MS); school and college health education (MS). *Degree requirements:* For master's, thesis optional; for doctorate, comprehensive exam, thesis/dissertation. *Entrance requirements:* For master's, GRE (for MS in nutrition science), 3 recommendations; for doctorate, GRE, 3 recommendations. Additional exam requirements/recommendations for international students: required—TOEFL (minimum score 550 paper-based; 80 iBT). Electronic applications accepted.

**Indiana University of Pennsylvania,** School of Graduate Studies and Research, College of Health and Human Services, Department of Food and Nutrition, Indiana, PA 15705. Offers MS. *Program availability:* Part-time, blended/hybrid learning. *Faculty:* 4 full-time (3 women). *Students:* 13 full-time (11 women), 50 part-time (46 women); includes 7 minority (4 Black or African American, non-Hispanic/Latino; 2 Asian, non-Hispanic/Latino; 1 Two or more races, non-Hispanic/Latino). Average age 28. 44 applicants, 95% accepted, 36 enrolled. In 2019, 30 master's awarded. *Degree requirements:* For master's, thesis optional. *Entrance requirements:* For master's, GRE General Test, 2 letters of recommendation, official transcripts, goal statement. Additional exam requirements/recommendations for international students: required—TOEFL (minimum score 540 paper-based; 76 iBT); recommended—IELTS (minimum score 6). *Application deadline:* Applications are processed on a rolling basis. Application fee: $50. Electronic applications accepted. *Expenses: Tuition, area resident:* Full-time $9288; part-time $516 per credit. Tuition, nonresident: full-time $13,932; part-time $774 per credit. *Required fees:* $4454. One-time fee: $115 full-time. Tuition and fees vary according to course load and program. *Financial support:* In 2019–20, 1 fellowship with tuition reimbursement (averaging $1,100 per year), 8 research assistantships with full and partial tuition reimbursements (averaging $5,770 per year) were awarded; Federal Work-Study also available. Support available to part-time students. Financial award application deadline: 4/15; financial award applicants required to submit FAFSA. *Unit head:* Dr. Stephanie Taylor-Davis, Chairperson, 724-357-7773, E-mail: stdavis@iup.edu. *Application contact:* Dr. Pao Ying Hsiao, Graduate Coordinator, 724-357-7917, E-mail: pyhsiao@iup.edu.

**Indiana University of Pennsylvania,** School of Graduate Studies and Research, College of Health and Human Services, Department of Food and Nutrition, MS Program in Food and Nutrition, Indiana, PA 15705. Offers MS. *Program availability:* Part-time. *Degree requirements:* For master's, thesis optional. *Entrance requirements:* For master's, GRE General Test, 2 letters of recommendation. Additional exam requirements/recommendations for international students: required—TOEFL (minimum score 540 paper-based). Electronic applications accepted. *Expenses: Tuition, area resident:* Full-time $9288; part-time $516 per credit. Tuition, nonresident: full-time $13,932; part-time $774 per credit. *Required fees:* $4454. One-time fee: $115 full-time. Tuition and fees vary according to course load and program.

**Indiana University-Purdue University Indianapolis,** School of Health and Rehabilitation Sciences, Indianapolis, IN 46202. Offers health and rehabilitation sciences (PhD); health sciences (MS); nutrition and dietetics (MS); occupational therapy (OTD); physical therapy (DPT); physician assistant (MPAS). *Accreditation:* AOTA. *Program availability:* Part-time, evening/weekend. *Degree requirements:* For master's, thesis (for some programs). *Entrance requirements:* For master's, GRE General Test, minimum GPA of 3.0 (for MS in health sciences, nutrition and dietetics), 3.2 (for MS in occupational therapy), 3.0 cumulative and prerequisite math/science (for MPAS); for doctorate, GRE, minimum cumulative and prerequisite math/science GPA of 3.2. Additional exam requirements/recommendations for international students: required—TOEFL (minimum score 550 paper-based; 79 iBT), IELTS (minimum score 6.5), PTE (minimum score 54). Electronic applications accepted. *Expenses:* Contact institution.

**Instituto Tecnologico de Santo Domingo,** Graduate School, Area of Health Sciences, Santo Domingo, Dominican Republic. Offers bioethics (M Bioethics); clinical bioethics (Certificate); clinical nutrition (Certificate); comprehensive adolescent health (MS); comprehensive health and the adolescent (Certificate); health and social security (M Mgmt).

**Iowa State University of Science and Technology,** Program in Diet and Exercise, Ames, IA 50011. Offers MS. *Entrance requirements:* For master's, GRE, minimum GPA of 3.5, 3 letters of recommendation. Additional exam requirements/recommendations for international students: required—TOEFL (minimum score 550 paper-based; 79 iBT), IELTS (minimum score 6.5). Electronic applications accepted.

**Iowa State University of Science and Technology,** Program in Nutritional Sciences, Ames, IA 50011. Offers MS, PhD. *Entrance requirements:* For master's and doctorate, GRE General Test. Additional exam requirements/recommendations for international students: required—TOEFL (minimum score 550 paper-based; 79 iBT), IELTS (minimum score 6.5). Electronic applications accepted.

**James Madison University,** The Graduate School, College of Health and Behavioral Studies, Program in Health Sciences, Harrisonburg, VA 22807. Offers nutrition and physical activity (MS). *Program availability:* Part-time. *Students:* 8 full-time (5 women), 2 part-time (1 woman); includes 1 minority (Black or African American, non-Hispanic/Latino), 1 international. Average age 30. Application fee: $60. Electronic applications accepted. *Financial support:* In 2019–20, 5 students received support. Federal Work-Study and assistantships (averaging $7911) available. Financial award application deadline: 3/1; financial award applicants required to submit FAFSA. *Unit head:* Dr. Allen Lewis, Department Head, 540-568-6510, E-mail: amatohk@jmu.edu. *Application contact:* Lynette D. Michael, Director of Graduate Admissions and Student Records, 540-568-6131 Ext. 6395, Fax: 540-568-7860, E-mail: michaeld@jmu.edu.
Website: http://www.healthsci.jmu.edu/index.html

**James Madison University,** The Graduate School, College of Health and Behavioral Studies, Program in Kinesiology, Harrisonburg, VA 22807. Offers clinical exercise physiology (MS); exercise physiology (MS); kinesiology (MAT, MS); nutrition and exercise (MS); physical and health education (MAT); sport and recreation leadership (MS). *Program availability:* Part-time, evening/weekend. *Students:* 35 full-time (19 women), 1 (woman) part-time; includes 5 minority (3 Black or African American, non-Hispanic/Latino; 2 Hispanic/Latino). Average age 30. In 2019, 16 master's awarded. Application fee: $60. Electronic applications accepted. *Financial support:* In 2019–20, 17 students received support, including 14 teaching assistantships with full tuition reimbursements available (averaging $8,837 per year); Federal Work-Study and assistantships (averaging $7911), athletic assistantships (averaging $9284) also available. Financial award application deadline: 3/1; financial award applicants required to submit FAFSA. *Unit head:* Dr. Christopher J. Womack, Department Head, 540-568-6145, E-mail: womackcx@jmu.edu. *Application contact:* Lynette D. Michael, Director of Graduate Admissions, 540-568-6131 Ext. 6395, Fax: 540-568-7860, E-mail: michaeld@jmu.edu.
Website: http://www.jmu.edu/kinesiology/

**Johns Hopkins University,** Bloomberg School of Public Health, Department of International Health, Baltimore, MD 21205. Offers global disease epidemiology and control (MSPH, PhD); global health economics (MHS); health systems (MSPH, PhD); human nutrition (MSPH, PhD); social and behavioral interventions (MSPH, PhD). *Degree requirements:* For master's, comprehensive exam, thesis (for some programs), 1-year full-time residency, 4-9 month internship; for doctorate, comprehensive exam, thesis/dissertation or alternative, 1.5 years' full-time residency, oral and written exams. *Entrance requirements:* For master's, GRE General Test or MCAT, 3 letters of recommendation, resume; for doctorate, GRE General Test or MCAT, 3 letters of recommendation, resume, transcripts. Additional exam requirements/recommendations for international students: required—TOEFL (minimum score 600 paper-based; 100 iBT); recommended—IELTS (minimum score 7). Electronic applications accepted.

**Kansas State University,** Graduate School, College of Human Ecology, Department of Food, Nutrition, Dietetics and Health, Manhattan, KS 66506. Offers dietetics (MS); human nutrition (PhD); nutrition, dietetics and sensory sciences (MS); nutritional sciences (PhD); public health nutrition (PhD); public health physical activity (PhD); sensory analysis and consumer behavior (PhD). *Program availability:* Part-time. *Degree requirements:* For master's, thesis or alternative, residency; for doctorate, thesis/dissertation, residency. *Entrance requirements:* For master's, GRE General Test, minimum undergraduate GPA of 3.0; for doctorate, GRE General Test, minimum graduate GPA of 3.0. Additional exam requirements/recommendations for international students: required—TOEFL (minimum score 550 paper-based; 79 iBT), IELTS (minimum score 6.5). Electronic applications accepted.

**Kent State University,** College of Education, Health and Human Services, School of Health Sciences, Program in Nutrition, Kent, OH 44242-0001. Offers MS. *Degree requirements:* For master's, thesis optional. *Entrance requirements:* For master's, 3 letters of reference, goals statement, minimum GPA of 3.0. Additional exam requirements/recommendations for international students: required—TOEFL (minimum score 550 paper-based; 80 iBT). Electronic applications accepted.

**Lehman College of the City University of New York,** School of Health Sciences, Human Services and Nursing, Department of Health Sciences, Program in Nutrition, Bronx, NY 10468-1589. Offers clinical nutrition (MS); community nutrition (MS); dietetic internship (MS). *Degree requirements:* For master's, thesis or alternative. *Expenses: Tuition, area resident:* Full-time $5545; part-time $470 per credit. Tuition, nonresident: part-time $855 per credit. *Required fees:* $240.

**Liberty University,** School of Health Sciences, Lynchburg, VA 24515. Offers anatomy and cell biology (PhD); biomedical sciences (MS); epidemiology (MPH); exercise science (MS), including clinical, community physical activity, human performance, nutrition; global health (MPH); health promotion (MPH); medical sciences (MA), including biopsychology, business management, health informatics, molecular medicine, public health; nutrition (MPH). *Program availability:* Part-time, online learning. *Students:* 820 full-time (588 women), 889 part-time (612 women); includes 611 minority (402 Black or African American, non-Hispanic/Latino; 10 American Indian or Alaska Native, non-Hispanic/Latino; 43 Asian, non-Hispanic/Latino; 85 Hispanic/Latino; 1 Native Hawaiian or other Pacific Islander, non-Hispanic/Latino; 70 Two or more races, non-Hispanic/Latino), 67 international. Average age 32. 2,610 applicants, 33% accepted, 406 enrolled. In 2019, 445 master's awarded. *Degree requirements:* For master's, thesis (for some programs); for doctorate, thesis/dissertation. *Entrance requirements:* For doctorate, MAT or GRE, minimum GPA of 3.25 in master's program, 2-3 recommendations, writing samples (for some programs), letter of intent, professional vitae. Additional exam requirements/recommendations for international students: required—TOEFL (minimum score 600 paper-based; 100 iBT). Application fee: $50. *Expenses: Tuition:* Full-time $545; part-time $410 per credit hour. One-time fee: $50. *Financial support:* In 2019–20, 918 students received support. Federal Work-Study available. Financial award applicants required to submit FAFSA. *Unit head:* Dr. Ralph Linstra, Dean. *Application contact:* Jay Bridge, Director of Admissions, 800-424-9595, Fax: 800-628-7977, E-mail: gradadmissions@liberty.edu.
Website: https://www.liberty.edu/health-sciences/

**Life University,** College of Graduate and Undergraduate Studies, Marietta, GA 30060-2903. Offers athletic training (MAT); chiropractic sport science (MS); nutrition and sport science (MS), including chiropractic sport science; positive psychology (MS), including life coaching psychology; sport coaching (MS), including exercise sport science; sport injury management (MS), including nutrition and sport science; sports health science (MS), including sports injury management. *Program availability:* Part-time, 100% online, blended/hybrid learning. *Degree requirements:* For master's, comprehensive exam (for some programs), thesis optional. *Entrance requirements:* For master's, GRE General Test, minimum GPA of 3.0, 3 letters of recommendation, curriculum vitae. Additional exam requirements/recommendations for international students: required—TOEFL (minimum score 500 paper-based). Electronic applications accepted. *Expenses:* Contact institution.

**Lipscomb University,** Program in Exercise and Nutrition Science, Nashville, TN 37204-3951. Offers MS. *Program availability:* Part-time, evening/weekend. *Degree requirements:* For master's, comprehensive exam (for some programs), thesis optional. *Entrance requirements:* For master's, GRE (minimum score of 800), minimum GPA of 2.75 on all undergraduate work; 2 letters of recommendation; resume. Additional exam requirements/recommendations for international students: required—TOEFL (minimum score 570 paper-based; 80 iBT). Electronic applications accepted. *Expenses:* Contact institution.

**Logan University,** College of Health Sciences, Chesterfield, MO 63017. Offers health informatics (MS); health professions education (DHPE); nutrition and human performance (MS); sports science and rehabilitation (MS). *Program availability:* Part-time, online only, 100% online. *Entrance requirements:* For master's, minimum GPA of 2.5; 6 hours of biology and physical science; bachelor's degree and 9 hours of business health administration (for health informatics). Additional exam requirements/recommendations for international students: required—TOEFL (minimum score 500 paper-based; 79 iBT); recommended—IELTS (minimum score 6.5). Electronic applications accepted. *Expenses:* Contact institution.

**Loma Linda University,** School of Public Health, Programs in Nutrition, Loma Linda, CA 92350. Offers public health nutrition (MPH, Dr PH). *Degree requirements:* For doctorate, thesis/dissertation. *Entrance requirements:* For doctorate, GRE General Test. Additional exam requirements/recommendations for international students: required—Michigan English Language Assessment Battery or TOEFL. *Expenses:* Contact institution.

**London Metropolitan University,** Graduate Programs, London, United Kingdom. Offers applied psychology (M Sc); architecture (MA); biomedical science (M Sc); blood science (M Sc); cancer pharmacology (M Sc); computer networking and cyber security (M Sc); computing and information systems (M Sc); conference interpreting (MA); counter-terrorism studies (M Sc); creative, digital and professional writing (MA); crime, violence and prevention (M Sc); criminology (M Sc); curating contemporary art (MA); data analytics (M Sc); digital media (MA); early childhood studies (MA); education (MA, Ed D); financial services law, regulation and compliance (LL M); food science (M Sc); forensic psychology (M Sc); health and social care management and policy (M Sc); human nutrition (M Sc); human resource management (MA); human rights and international conflict (MA); information technology (M Sc); intelligence and security studies (M Sc); international oil, gas and energy law (LL M); international relations (MA); interpreting (MA); learning and teaching in higher education (MA); legal practice (LL M); media and entertainment law (LL M); organizational and consumer psychology (M Sc); psychological therapy (M Sc); psychology of mental health (M Sc); public health (M Sc); public policy and management (MPA); security studies (M Sc); social work (M Sc); spatial planning and urban design (MA); sports therapy (M Sc); supporting older children and young people with dyslexia (MA); teaching languages (MA), including Arabic, English; translation (MA); woman and child abuse (MA).

**Long Island University - Post,** School of Health Professions and Nursing, Brookville, NY 11548-1300. Offers biomedical science (MS); cardiovascular perfusion (MS); clinical lab sciences (MS); clinical laboratory management (MS); dietetic internship (Advanced Certificate); family nurse practitioner (MS, Advanced Certificate); forensic social work (Advanced Certificate); gerontology (Advanced Certificate); health administration (MPA); non-profit management (Advanced Certificate); nursing education (MS); nutrition (MS); public administration (MPA); social work (MSW). *Program availability:* Part-time, blended/hybrid learning. *Degree requirements:* For master's, comprehensive exam (for some programs), thesis (for some programs). *Entrance requirements:* Additional exam requirements/recommendations for international students: required—TOEFL (minimum score 85 iBT) or IELTS (7.5). Electronic applications accepted.

**Louisiana State University and Agricultural & Mechanical College,** Graduate School, College of Agriculture, School of Nutrition and Food Sciences, Baton Rouge, LA 70803. Offers MS, PhD.

**Louisiana Tech University,** Graduate School, College of Applied and Natural Sciences, Ruston, LA 71272. Offers biology (MS); dietetics (Graduate Certificate); health informatics (MHI); molecular science and nanotechnology (MS, PhD). *Program availability:* Part-time. *Degree requirements:* For master's, comprehensive exam (for some programs), thesis (for some programs); for doctorate, comprehensive exam, thesis/dissertation. *Entrance requirements:* For master's and doctorate, GRE General Test, transcript with bachelor's degree awarded; for Graduate Certificate, transcript with bachelor's degree awarded. Additional exam requirements/recommendations for international students: required—TOEFL (minimum score 550 paper-based; 80 iBT), IELTS (minimum score 6.5). Electronic applications accepted. *Expenses: Tuition, area resident:* Full-time $6592; part-time $400 per credit. Tuition, state resident: full-time $6592; part-time $400 per credit. Tuition, nonresident: full-time $13,333; part-time $681 per credit. *International tuition:* $13,333 full-time. *Required fees:* $3011; $3011 per unit.

**Loyola University Chicago,** Graduate School, Marcella Niehoff School of Nursing, Maywood, IL 60153. Offers adult clinical nurse specialist (MSN, Certificate); adult nurse practitioner (Certificate); dietetics (MS); family nurse practitioner (Certificate); family, adult, and women's health nurse practitioner (MSN); health systems leadership (MSN); healthcare quality using education in safety and technology (DNP); infection prevention (MSN, DNP); nursing science (PhD); women's health clinical nurse specialist (Certificate). *Accreditation:* AACN. *Program availability:* Part-time, blended/hybrid learning. *Faculty:* 36 full-time (32 women), 18 part-time/adjunct (16 women). *Students:* 182 full-time (168 women), 198 part-time (175 women); includes 95 minority (26 Black or African American, non-Hispanic/Latino; 29 Asian, non-Hispanic/Latino; 37 Hispanic/Latino; 3 Two or more races, non-Hispanic/Latino), 7 international. Average age 35. 148 applicants, 59% accepted, 54 enrolled. In 2019, 84 master's, 16 doctorates, 27 other advanced degrees awarded. *Degree requirements:* For master's, comprehensive exam; for doctorate, thesis/dissertation, qualifying examination (for PhD); project (for DNP). *Entrance requirements:* For master's, BSN, minimum nursing GPA of 3.0, Illinois RN license, 3 letters of recommendation, 1000 hours of experience in area of specialty prior to starting clinical rotations, personal statement; for doctorate, BSN or MSN, minimum GPA of 3.0, professional nursing license, 3 letters of recommendation, personal statement. Additional exam requirements/recommendations for international students: required—TOEFL (minimum score 550 paper-based; 79 iBT), IELTS (minimum score 6), PTE (minimum score 53). *Application deadline:* For fall admission, 7/1 priority date for domestic and international students; for spring admission, 12/1 priority date for domestic and international students; for summer admission, 4/1 priority date for domestic and international students. Applications are processed on a rolling basis. Electronic applications accepted. Application fee is waived when completed online. *Expenses:* Contact institution. *Financial support:* In 2019–20, 53 students received support, including 3 research assistantships with full tuition reimbursements available (averaging $18,000 per year), 1 teaching assistantship with full tuition reimbursement available (averaging $18,000 per year); scholarships/grants, unspecified assistantships, and Nurse Faculty Loan Program also available. Financial award application deadline: 5/1; financial award applicants required to submit FAFSA. *Unit head:* Dr. Lorna Finnegan, Dean and Professor, 708-216-5448, Fax: 708-216-9555, E-mail: lornaf@luc.edu. *Application contact:* Glenda Runnels, Enrollment Advisor, 708-216-3751, Fax: 708-216-9555, E-mail: grunnels@luc.edu.
Website: http://www.luc.edu/nursing/

**Loyola University Chicago,** Parkinson School of Health Sciences and Public Health, Dietetics Program, Chicago, IL 60660. Offers MS, Certificate. *Students:* 19 full-time (18 women), 12 part-time (11 women); includes 5 minority (2 Asian, non-Hispanic/Latino; 3 Hispanic/Latino), 2 international. Average age 25. 23 applicants, 91% accepted, 20 enrolled. In 2019, 9 master's, 18 other advanced degrees awarded. *Entrance requirements:* For master's, BSN, minimum nursing GPA of 3.0, Illinois RN license, 3 letters of recommendation, 1000 hours of experience in area of specialty prior to starting clinical rotations. Additional exam requirements/recommendations for international students: required—TOEFL (minimum score 550 paper-based) or IELTS (minimum score 6.5). *Application deadline:* For fall admission, 8/1 priority date for domestic and international students; for spring admission, 12/15 priority date for domestic and international students. Applications are processed on a rolling basis. Application fee: $50. Electronic applications accepted. *Expenses:* Contact institution. *Financial support:* Nurse faculty loan program available. Financial award applicants required to submit FAFSA. *Unit head:* Dr. Vicky Keough, Dean, 708-216-5448, Fax: 708-216-9555, E-mail: vkeough@luc.edu. *Application contact:* Bri Lauka, Enrollment Advisor, School of Nursing, 708-216-3751, Fax: 708-216-9555, E-mail: blauka@luc.edu.
Website: http://www.luc.edu/nursing/

**Marshall University,** Academic Affairs Division, College of Health Professions, Department of Dietetics, Huntington, WV 25755. Offers MS, Certificate.

**Maryland University of Integrative Health,** Programs in Nutrition, Laurel, MD 20723. Offers clinical nutrition (DCN); nutrition and integrative health (MS, Post Master's Certificate).

**Marywood University,** Academic Affairs, College of Health and Human Services, Department of Nutrition and Dietetics, Program in Dietetic Internship, Scranton, PA 18509-1598. Offers Certificate. *Program availability:* Online learning. Electronic applications accepted.

**Marywood University,** Academic Affairs, College of Health and Human Services, Department of Nutrition and Dietetics, Program in Nutrition, Scranton, PA 18509-1598. Offers MS. *Program availability:* Part-time. Electronic applications accepted.

**Marywood University,** Academic Affairs, College of Health and Human Services, Department of Nutrition and Dietetics, Program in Sports Nutrition and Exercise Science, Scranton, PA 18509-1598. Offers MS. *Program availability:* Part-time. Electronic applications accepted.

**McGill University,** Faculty of Graduate and Postdoctoral Studies, Faculty of Agricultural and Environmental Sciences, School of Dietetics and Human Nutrition, Montréal, QC H3A 2T5, Canada. Offers dietetics (M Sc A, Graduate Diploma); human nutrition (M Sc, M Sc A, PhD).

**McMaster University,** Faculty of Health Sciences and School of Graduate Studies, Program in Medical Sciences, Metabolism and Nutrition Area, Hamilton, ON L8S 4M2, Canada. Offers M Sc, PhD, MD/PhD. *Degree requirements:* For master's, thesis; for doctorate, comprehensive exam, thesis/dissertation. *Entrance requirements:* For master's, honors B Sc, B+ average in related field; for doctorate, M Sc, minimum B+ average, students with proven research experience and an A average may be admitted with a B Sc degree. Additional exam requirements/recommendations for international students: required—TOEFL (minimum score 580 paper-based; 92 iBT).

**McNeese State University,** Doré School of Graduate Studies, Burton College of Education, Department of Health and Human Performance, Lake Charles, LA 70609. Offers exercise physiology (MS); health promotion (MS); nutrition and wellness (MS). *Accreditation:* NCATE. *Program availability:* Evening/weekend. *Entrance requirements:* For master's, GRE, undergraduate major or minor in health and human performance or related field of study.

**Meredith College,** School of Education, Health and Human Sciences, Nutrition, Health and Human Performance Department, Raleigh, NC 27607-5298. Offers dietetic internship (Postbaccalaureate Certificate); nutrition (MS). *Accreditation:* AND. *Degree requirements:* For master's, thesis optional. *Entrance requirements:* For master's, GRE, recommendations, interview. Additional exam requirements/recommendations for international students: required—TOEFL. Electronic applications accepted. *Expenses:* Contact institution.

**Michigan State University,** The Graduate School, College of Agriculture and Natural Resources, Department of Food Science and Human Nutrition, East Lansing, MI 48824. Offers food science (MS, PhD); food science - environmental toxicology (PhD); human nutrition (MS, PhD); human nutrition-environmental toxicology (PhD). *Entrance requirements:* Additional exam requirements/recommendations for international students: required—TOEFL (minimum score 550 paper-based), Michigan State University ELT ( minimum score 85), Michigan English Language Assessment Battery (minimum score 83). Electronic applications accepted.

**Mississippi State University,** College of Agriculture and Life Sciences, Department of Food Science, Nutrition and Health Promotion, Mississippi State, MS 39762. Offers food science and technology (MS, PhD); health promotion (MS); nutrition (MS, PhD). *Program availability:* Blended/hybrid learning. *Faculty:* 16 full-time (6 women). *Students:* 53 full-time (43 women), 36 part-time (27 women); includes 15 minority (10 Black or African American, non-Hispanic/Latino; 4 Hispanic/Latino; 1 Two or more races, non-Hispanic/Latino), 19 international. Average age 29. 44 applicants, 57% accepted, 18 enrolled. In 2019, 31 master's, 1 doctorate awarded. *Degree requirements:* For master's, comprehensive exam, thesis; for doctorate, comprehensive exam, thesis/dissertation. *Entrance requirements:* For master's, GRE General Test, minimum GPA of 2.75; for doctorate, GRE General Test, minimum GPA of 2.75 undergraduate, 3.0 graduate. Additional exam requirements/recommendations for international students: required—TOEFL (minimum score 550 paper-based; 79 iBT); recommended—IELTS (minimum score 6.5). *Application deadline:* For fall admission, 7/1 for domestic students, 5/1 for international students; for spring admission, 11/1 for domestic students, 9/1 for international students. Applications are processed on a rolling basis. Application fee: $60 ($80 for international students). Electronic applications accepted. *Expenses: Tuition, area resident:* Full-time $8880; part-time $456 per credit hour. Tuition, state resident: full-time $8880. Tuition, nonresident: full-time $23,840; part-time $1236 per credit hour. *Required fees:* $110; $11.12 per credit hour. Tuition and fees vary according to course load. *Financial support:* In 2019–20, 13 research assistantships (averaging $15,416 per year), 2 teaching assistantships (averaging $11,452 per year) were awarded; Federal Work-Study, institutionally sponsored loans, scholarships/grants, and unspecified assistantships also available. Financial award application deadline: 4/1; financial award applicants required to submit FAFSA. *Unit head:* Dr. Marion Will Evans, Professor and Head, 662-325-5508, Fax: 662-325-8728, E-mail: mwe59@msstate.edu. *Application contact:* Ryan King, Admissions and Enrollment Assistant, 662-325-8951, E-mail: rjk101@grad.msstate.edu.
Website: http://www.fsnhp.msstate.edu

**Missouri State University,** Graduate College, College of Health and Human Services, Department of Biomedical Sciences, Springfield, MO 65897. Offers cell and molecular biology (MS); dietetic internship (Certificate); nurse anesthesia (DNAP). *Accreditation:* AANA/CANAEP (one or more programs are accredited). *Program availability:* Part-time. *Degree requirements:* For master's, thesis or alternative, oral exam. *Entrance requirements:* For master's, GRE, minimum GPA of 3.0. Additional exam requirements/recommendations for international students: required—TOEFL (minimum score 550 paper-based; 79 iBT), IELTS (minimum score 6). Electronic applications accepted. *Expenses: Tuition, area resident:* Full-time $2600; part-time $1735 per credit hour. Tuition, nonresident: full-time $5240; part-time $3495 per credit hour. *International tuition:* $5240 full-time. *Required fees:* $530; $438 per credit hour. Tuition and fees vary according to class time, course level, course load, degree level, campus/location and program.

**Montclair State University,** The Graduate School, College of Education and Human Services, American Dietetics Certificate Program, Montclair, NJ 07043-1624. Offers Postbaccalaureate Certificate. *Program availability:* Part-time, evening/weekend. *Entrance requirements:* Additional exam requirements/recommendations for international students: required—TOEFL (minimum score 65 iBT), IELTS. Electronic applications accepted.

**Montclair State University,** The Graduate School, College of Education and Human Services, Nutrition and Exercise Science Certificate Program, Montclair, NJ 07043-1624. Offers Certificate. Electronic applications accepted.

**Montclair State University,** The Graduate School, College of Education and Human Services, Program in Nutrition and Food Science, Montclair, NJ 07043-1624. Offers MS. *Program availability:* Part-time, evening/weekend. *Degree requirements:* For master's,

comprehensive exam, thesis or alternative. *Entrance requirements:* For master's, GRE General Test, essay, 2 letters of recommendation. Additional exam requirements/recommendations for international students: required—TOEFL (minimum score 83 iBT), IELTS (minimum score 6.5). Electronic applications accepted.

**Mount Mary University,** Graduate Programs, Program in Dietetics, Milwaukee, WI 53222-4597. Offers dietetics (MS); dietetics internship (MS). *Program availability:* Part-time, evening/weekend. *Degree requirements:* For master's, thesis or alternative. *Entrance requirements:* For master's, minimum GPA of 2.75, completion of ADA and DPD requirements. Additional exam requirements/recommendations for international students: required—TOEFL (minimum score 550 paper-based; 80 iBT); recommended—IELTS (minimum score 6.5). Electronic applications accepted. *Expenses:* Contact institution.

**Mount Saint Vincent University,** Graduate Programs, Department of Applied Human Nutrition, Halifax, NS B3M 2J6, Canada. Offers M Sc AHN, MAHN. *Program availability:* Part-time, evening/weekend. *Degree requirements:* For master's, thesis (for some programs). *Entrance requirements:* For master's, bachelor's degree in related field, minimum GPA of 3.0, professional experience. Electronic applications accepted.

**Murray State University,** School of Nursing and Health Professions, Department of Applied Health Sciences, Murray, KY 42071. Offers nutrition (MS); registered dietitian (Certificate). *Program availability:* Part-time, evening/weekend, 100% online. *Entrance requirements:* For master's and Certificate, GRE or GMAT, minimum university GPA of 2.75. Additional exam requirements/recommendations for international students: required—TOEFL (minimum score 527 paper-based; 71 iBT). Electronic applications accepted.

**National University of Natural Medicine,** School of Undergraduate and Graduate Studies, Portland, OR 97201. Offers Ayurveda (MS); global health (MS); integrative medicine research (MS); integrative mental health (MS); nutrition (MS). *Program availability:* 100% online. *Students:* 92 full-time (83 women), 6 part-time (all women); includes 13 minority (1 Black or African American, non-Hispanic/Latino; 4 Asian, non-Hispanic/Latino; 3 Hispanic/Latino; 5 Two or more races, non-Hispanic/Latino). Average age 31. 114 applicants, 88% accepted, 60 enrolled. In 2019, 72 master's awarded. *Degree requirements:* For master's, thesis. *Entrance requirements:* For master's, Bachelor's degree from a regionally accredited institution and prerequisite courses. Additional exam requirements/recommendations for international students: required—TOEFL (minimum score 550 paper-based; 80 iBT), We accept IETS and PTE. *Application deadline:* For fall admission, 5/1 for domestic and international students. Applications are processed on a rolling basis. Application fee: $75. Electronic applications accepted. *Expenses: Tuition:* Part-time $464 per credit hour. *Financial support:* Federal Work-Study and scholarships/grants available. Financial award application deadline: 2/15; financial award applicants required to submit FAFSA. *Unit head:* Dr. Tim Irving, Program Director - School of Undergraduate and Graduate Studies, 503-552-1660, Fax: 503-499-0027, E-mail: admission@nunm.edu. *Application contact:* Ryan Hollister, Director of Admissions, 503-552-1665, Fax: 503-499-0027, E-mail: admissions@numn.edu.
Website: http://nunm.edu/academics/school-of-research-graduate-studies/

**New York Chiropractic College,** Program in Applied Clinical Nutrition, Seneca Falls, NY 13148-0800. Offers MS. *Program availability:* Part-time, evening/weekend. *Entrance requirements:* For master's, minimum GPA of 2.5, transcripts, writing sample. Additional exam requirements/recommendations for international students: recommended—TOEFL. Electronic applications accepted.

**New York Institute of Technology,** School of Health Professions, Department of Interdisciplinary Health Sciences, Old Westbury, NY 11568. Offers clinical nutrition (MS). *Program availability:* Part-time, evening/weekend, online only, 100% online. *Faculty:* 2 full-time (both women), 8 part-time/adjunct (7 women). *Students:* 2 full-time (both women), 17 part-time (15 women); includes 8 minority (2 Black or African American, non-Hispanic/Latino; 4 Asian, non-Hispanic/Latino; 2 Hispanic/Latino). Average age 31. 30 applicants, 47% accepted, 6 enrolled. In 2019, 8 master's awarded. *Degree requirements:* For master's, comprehensive exam, thesis. *Entrance requirements:* For master's, GRE scores may be required for students whose preparation is marginal. Additional exam requirements/recommendations for international students: required—TOEFL (minimum score 79 iBT), IELTS (minimum score 6), PTE (minimum score 53), Duolingo English Test. *Application deadline:* For fall admission, 6/1 for international students; for spring admission, 12/1 for international students. Applications are processed on a rolling basis. Application fee: $50. Electronic applications accepted. *Expenses:* $700 per credit plus $130 full-time graduate fee or $110 part-time graduate fee. *Financial support:* In 2019–20, 3 students received support. Scholarships/grants and unspecified assistantships available. Support available to part-time students. Financial award application deadline: 2/15; financial award applicants required to submit FAFSA. *Unit head:* Dr. Mindy Haar, Chair, 516-686-3818, Fax: 516-686-3795, E-mail: mhaar@nyit.edu. *Application contact:* Alice Dolitsky, Director, Graduate Admissions, 800-345-6948, Fax: 516-686-1116, E-mail: grad@nyit.edu.
Website: https://www.nyit.edu/health_professions/department_of_interdisciplinary_health_sciences

**New York University,** College of Global Public Health, New York, NY 10012. Offers biological basis of public health (PhD); community and international health (MPH); global health leadership (MPH); health systems and health services research (PhD); population and community health (PhD); public health nutrition (MPH); social and behavioral sciences (MPH); socio-behavioral health (PhD). *Accreditation:* CEPH. *Program availability:* Part-time, online learning. *Degree requirements:* For master's, thesis (for some programs); for doctorate, thesis/dissertation. *Entrance requirements:* For master's and doctorate, GRE. Additional exam requirements/recommendations for international students: required—TOEFL. Electronic applications accepted. *Expenses:* Contact institution.

**New York University,** Steinhardt School of Culture, Education, and Human Development, Department of Nutrition, Food Studies, and Public Health, Programs in Nutrition and Dietetics, New York, NY 10012. Offers clinical nutrition (MS); nutrition and dietetics (MS, PhD), including food and nutrition (MS); rehabilitation sciences (PhD). *Program availability:* Part-time. *Entrance requirements:* For doctorate, GRE General Test, interview. Additional exam requirements/recommendations for international students: required—TOEFL (minimum score 100 iBT). Electronic applications accepted.

**North Carolina Agricultural and Technical State University,** The Graduate College, College of Agriculture and Environmental Sciences, Department of Family and Consumer Sciences, Greensboro, NC 27411. Offers child development, early education and family studies (MAT); family and consumer sciences education (MAT); food and nutritional sciences (MS). *Program availability:* Part-time, evening/weekend. *Degree requirements:* For master's, comprehensive exam, thesis or alternative, qualifying exam. *Entrance requirements:* For master's, GRE General Test, minimum GPA of 2.6.

**North Carolina State University,** Graduate School, College of Agriculture and Life Sciences, Department of Food, Bioprocessing and Nutrition Sciences, Raleigh, NC 27695. Offers MFS, MS, PhD. *Degree requirements:* For master's, thesis (for some programs); for doctorate, thesis/dissertation. *Entrance requirements:* For master's and doctorate, GRE. Electronic applications accepted.

**North Dakota State University,** College of Graduate and Interdisciplinary Studies, College of Human Development and Education, Department of Health, Nutrition, and Exercise Sciences, Fargo, ND 58102. Offers advanced athletic training (MS); athletic training (MAT); dietetics (MS); exercise science and nutrition (PhD); health, nutrition and exercise science (MS). *Program availability:* Part-time, evening/weekend, online learning. *Entrance requirements:* For master's, minimum GPA of 3.0. Additional exam requirements/recommendations for international students: required—TOEFL (minimum score 525 paper-based; 71 iBT). Electronic applications accepted. Tuition and fees vary according to program and reciprocity agreements.

**Northeastern University,** College of Professional Studies, Boston, MA 02115-5096. Offers applied nutrition (MS); college athletics administration (MSL); commerce and economic development (MS); corporate and organizational communication (MS); criminal justice (MS); digital media (MPS); elearning and instructional design (M Ed); elementary education (MAT); geographic information technology (MPS); global studies and international relations (MS); higher education administration (M Ed); homeland security (MA); human services (MS); informatics (MPS); leadership (MS); learning analytics (M Ed); learning and instruction (M Ed); nonprofit management (MS); professional sports administration (MSL); project management (MS); regulatory affairs for drugs, biologics, and medical devices (MS); respiratory care leadership (MS); special education (M Ed); technical communication (MS). *Program availability:* Part-time, evening/weekend, 100% online, blended/hybrid learning. *Faculty:* 85 full-time (53 women), 892 part-time/adjunct (379 women). *Students:* 5,699 part-time (3,305 women). In 2019, 1,787 master's awarded. *Application deadline:* Applications are processed on a rolling basis. Electronic applications accepted. *Expenses:* Contact institution. *Financial support:* Applicants required to submit FAFSA. *Unit head:* Dr. Mary Loeffelholz, Dean of the College of Professional Studies, 617-373-6060. *Application contact:* Dr. Mary Loeffelholz, Dean of the College of Professional Studies, 617-373-6060.
Website: https://cps.northeastern.edu/

**Northern Illinois University,** Graduate School, College of Health and Human Sciences, Ph.D Health Sciences, De Kalb, IL 60115-2854. Offers nutrition and dietetics (MS); public health (MPH). *Accreditation:* CEPH. *Students:* 4 full-time (3 women), 42 part-time (28 women); includes 13 minority (5 Black or African American, non-Hispanic/Latino; 4 Asian, non-Hispanic/Latino; 2 Hispanic/Latino; 2 Two or more races, non-Hispanic/Latino), 2 international. Average age 40. 38 applicants, 37% accepted, 4 enrolled. In 2019, 4 master's awarded. *Entrance requirements:* Additional exam requirements/recommendations for international students: required—TOEFL (minimum score 550 paper-based). *Application deadline:* Applications are processed on a rolling basis. Electronic applications accepted. *Unit head:* Daniel Boutin, Chair, 815-753-1384. *Application contact:* Graduate School Office, 815-753-0395, E-mail: gradsch@niu.edu.
Website: http://chhs.niu.edu/health-studies/

**Northwestern Health Sciences University,** College of Health and Wellness, Bloomington, MN 55431-1599. Offers acupuncture (M Ac); applied clinical nutrition (MHS); Oriental medicine (MOM). *Accreditation:* ACAOM. *Entrance requirements:* For master's, 60 semester credits of course work with minimum GPA of 2.5. Additional exam requirements/recommendations for international students: required—TOEFL (minimum score 540 paper-based; 76 iBT). Electronic applications accepted.

**Nova Southeastern University,** Dr. Kiran C. Patel College of Osteopathic Medicine, Fort Lauderdale, FL 33314-7796. Offers biomedical informatics (MS, Graduate Certificate), including biomedical informatics (MS), clinical informatics (Graduate Certificate), public health informatics (Graduate Certificate); disaster and emergency management (MS); medical education (MS); nutrition (MS, Graduate Certificate), including functional nutrition and herbal therapy (Graduate Certificate); osteopathic medicine (DO); public health (MPH, Graduate Certificate), including health education (Graduate Certificate); social medicine (Graduate Certificate); DO/DMD. *Accreditation:* AOsA; CEPH. *Program availability:* Part-time, 100% online, blended/hybrid learning. *Faculty:* 73 full-time (43 women), 35 part-time/adjunct (14 women). *Students:* 1,410 full-time (740 women), 182 part-time (118 women); includes 895 minority (126 Black or African American, non-Hispanic/Latino; 1 American Indian or Alaska Native, non-Hispanic/Latino; 416 Asian, non-Hispanic/Latino; 309 Hispanic/Latino; 1 Native Hawaiian or other Pacific Islander, non-Hispanic/Latino; 42 Two or more races, non-Hispanic/Latino), 70 international. Average age 26. 5,078 applicants, 10% accepted, 495 enrolled. In 2019, 117 master's, 233 doctorates, 3 other advanced degrees awarded. *Degree requirements:* For master's, comprehensive exam (for MPH); field/special projects; for doctorate, comprehensive exam, COMLEX Board Exams; for Graduate Certificate, thesis or alternative. *Entrance requirements:* For master's, GRE; for doctorate, MCAT, coursework in biology, chemistry, organic chemistry, physics (all with labs), biochemistry, and English. *Application deadline:* For fall admission, 1/15 for domestic students. Applications are processed on a rolling basis. Application fee: $50. Electronic applications accepted. *Expenses:* Contact institution. *Financial support:* In 2019–20, 83 students received support, including 24 fellowships with tuition reimbursements available; Federal Work-Study and scholarships/grants also available. Financial award application deadline: 6/1; financial award applicants required to submit FAFSA. *Unit head:* Elaine M. Wallace, Dean, 954-262-1457, Fax: 954-262-2250, E-mail: ewallace@nova.edu. *Application contact:* HPD Admissions, 877-640-0218, E-mail: hpdinfo@nova.edu.
Website: https://www.osteopathic.nova.edu/

**The Ohio State University,** Graduate School, College of Education and Human Ecology, Department of Human Sciences, Columbus, OH 43210. Offers consumer sciences (MS, PhD); human development and family science (PhD); human nutrition (MS, PhD); kinesiology (MA, Ed D, PhD). *Program availability:* Part-time. *Degree requirements:* For master's, thesis optional; for doctorate, thesis/dissertation. *Entrance requirements:* For master's and doctorate, GRE. Additional exam requirements/recommendations for international students: required—TOEFL (minimum score 550 paper-based; 79 iBT), Michigan English Language Assessment Battery (minimum score 82); recommended—IELTS (minimum score 7). Electronic applications accepted.

**The Ohio State University,** Graduate School, College of Education and Human Ecology, Human Nutrition Program, Columbus, OH 43210. Offers PhD. *Degree requirements:* For doctorate, thesis/dissertation. *Entrance requirements:* For doctorate, GRE. Additional exam requirements/recommendations for international students: required—TOEFL (minimum score 600 paper-based; 100 iBT); recommended—IELTS (minimum score 8). Electronic applications accepted.

**Ohio University,** Graduate College, College of Health Sciences and Professions, School of Applied Health Sciences and Wellness, Program in Food and Nutrition, Athens, OH 45701-2979. Offers human and consumer sciences (MS).

**Oklahoma State University,** College of Human Sciences, Department of Nutritional Sciences, Stillwater, OK 74078. Offers MS, PhD. *Program availability:* Online learning. *Faculty:* 15 full-time (11 women). *Students:* 18 full-time (16 women), 26 part-time (18 women); includes 9 minority (2 Black or African American, non-Hispanic/Latino; 1 American Indian or Alaska Native, non-Hispanic/Latino; 3 Asian, non-Hispanic/Latino; 1 Hispanic/Latino; 2 Two or more races, non-Hispanic/Latino), 11 international. Average

age 27. 28 applicants, 68% accepted, 15 enrolled. In 2019, 10 master's, 1 doctorate awarded. *Entrance requirements:* For master's and doctorate, GRE or GMAT. Additional exam requirements/recommendations for international students: required—TOEFL (minimum score 550 paper-based; 79 iBT). *Application deadline:* For fall admission, 3/1 priority date for international students; for spring admission, 8/1 priority date for international students. Applications are processed on a rolling basis. Application fee: $50 ($75 for international students). Electronic applications accepted. *Expenses: Tuition, area resident:* Full-time $4148.10; part-time $2765.40 per credit hour. Tuition, state resident: full-time $4148.10; part-time $2765.40 per credit hour. Tuition, nonresident: full-time $15,775; part-time $10,516.80 per credit hour. *International tuition:* $15,775.20 full-time. *Required fees:* $2196.90; $122.05 per credit hour. Tuition and fees vary according to course load, campus/location and program. *Financial support:* In 2019–20, 8 research assistantships (averaging $1,200 per year), 18 teaching assistantships (averaging $1,054 per year) were awarded; career-related internships or fieldwork, Federal Work-Study, scholarships/grants, health care benefits, tuition waivers (partial), and unspecified assistantships also available. Support available to part-time students. Financial award application deadline: 3/1; financial award applicants required to submit FAFSA. *Unit head:* Dr. Stephen Clarke, Department Head, 405-744-5041, Fax: 405-744-1357, E-mail: stephen.clarke@okstate.edu. *Application contact:* Dr. Sheryl Tucker, Vice Prov/Dean/Prof, 405-744-6368, E-mail: gradi@okstate.edu.
Website: https://education.okstate.edu/departments-programs/nutritional-sciences/index.html

**Oregon Health & Science University,** School of Medicine, Graduate Programs in Medicine, Program in Clinical Nutrition, Portland, OR 97239-3098. Offers dietetics (Certificate); human nutrition (MS). *Program availability:* Part-time. *Degree requirements:* For master's, thesis optional. *Entrance requirements:* For master's, GRE General Test (minimum scores: 153 Verbal/148 Quantitative/4.5 Analytical), Registered Dietitian.

**Oregon State University,** College of Public Health and Human Sciences, Program in Nutrition, Corvallis, OR 97331. Offers MS, PhD. *Entrance requirements:* For master's and doctorate, GRE, minimum GPA of 3.0 in last 90 hours of course work. Additional exam requirements/recommendations for international students: required—TOEFL (minimum score 80 iBT), IELTS (minimum score 6.5). Electronic applications accepted.

**Penn State University Park,** Graduate School, College of Health and Human Development, Department of Nutritional Sciences, University Park, PA 16802. Offers MS, PhD.

**Purdue University,** Graduate School, College of Health and Human Sciences, Department of Nutrition Science, West Lafayette, IN 47907. Offers animal health (MS, PhD); biochemical and molecular nutrition (MS, PhD); growth and development (MS, PhD); human and clinical nutrition (MS, PhD); public health and education (MS, PhD). *Faculty:* 19 full-time (13 women), 1 part-time/adjunct (0 women). *Students:* 41 full-time (34 women), 2 part-time (both women); includes 2 minority (1 Black or African American, non-Hispanic/Latino; 1 Two or more races, non-Hispanic/Latino), 17 international. Average age 26. 43 applicants, 35% accepted, 10 enrolled. In 2019, 2 master's, 9 doctorates awarded. *Degree requirements:* For master's, thesis; for doctorate, thesis/dissertation. *Entrance requirements:* For master's and doctorate, GRE General Test (minimum scores in verbal and quantitative areas of 1000 or 300 on new scoring), minimum undergraduate GPA of 3.0 or equivalent. Additional exam requirements/recommendations for international students: required—TOEFL (minimum score 600 paper-based; 77 iBT). *Application deadline:* For fall admission, 1/10 for domestic and international students. Applications are processed on a rolling basis. Application fee: $60 ($75 for international students). Electronic applications accepted. *Financial support:* Fellowships, research assistantships, and teaching assistantships available. Support available to part-time students. Financial award applicants required to submit FAFSA. *Unit head:* Amanda Siedl, Interim Head, 765-496-3570, E-mail: asiedl@purdue.edu. *Application contact:* Kim Buhman, Graduate Contact for Admissions, 765-496-6872, E-mail: kbuhman@purdue.edu.
Website: http://www.cfs.purdue.edu/fn/

**Queens College of the City University of New York,** Mathematics and Natural Sciences Division, Department of Family, Nutrition and Exercise Sciences, Queens, NY 11367-1597. Offers exercise science specialist (MS); family and consumer science (K-12) (AC); family and consumer science/teaching curriculum (K-12) (MS Ed); nutrition and exercise science (MS); nutrition specialist (MS); physical education (K-12) (AC); physical education/teaching curriculum (pre K-12) (MS Ed). *Program availability:* Part-time, evening/weekend. *Degree requirements:* For master's, research project or comprehensive examination. *Entrance requirements:* For master's, minimum GPA of 3.0. Additional exam requirements/recommendations for international students: required—TOEFL (minimum paper-based score of 600) or IELTS=7 (for program in nutrition). Electronic applications accepted.

**Rosalind Franklin University of Medicine and Science,** College of Health Professions, Department of Nutrition, North Chicago, IL 60064-3095. Offers clinical nutrition (MS); health promotion and wellness (MS); nutrition education (MS). *Program availability:* Part-time, evening/weekend, online learning. *Degree requirements:* For master's, thesis optional, portfolio. *Entrance requirements:* For master's, minimum GPA of 2.75, registered dietitian (RD), professional certificate or license. Additional exam requirements/recommendations for international students: required—TOEFL. *Expenses:* Contact institution.

**Rush University,** College of Health Sciences, Department of Clinical Nutrition, Chicago, IL 60612. Offers MS. *Program availability:* Part-time. *Entrance requirements:* For master's, GRE General Test, minimum GPA of 3.0, course work in statistics, undergraduate didactic program approved by the American Dietetic Association, for CNDI. Additional exam requirements/recommendations for international students: required—TOEFL. Electronic applications accepted. *Financial support:* Career-related internships or fieldwork, Federal Work-Study, institutionally sponsored loans, and scholarships/grants available. Support available to part-time students. Financial award applicants required to submit FAFSA. *Unit head:* Dr. Sarah Peterson, Interim Program Director. *Application contact:* Dr. Sarah Peterson, Interim Program Director.
Website: http://www.rushu.rush.edu/nutrition/

**Rutgers University - Newark,** School of Health Related Professions, Department of Nutritional Sciences, Dietetic Internship Program, Newark, NJ 07102. Offers Certificate. *Program availability:* Online learning. *Entrance requirements:* For degree, bachelor's degree in dietetics, nutrition, or related field; interview; minimum GPA of 2.9. Additional exam requirements/recommendations for international students: required—TOEFL (minimum score 500 paper-based; 79 iBT). Electronic applications accepted.

**Rutgers University - Newark,** School of Health Related Professions, Department of Nutritional Sciences, Program in Clinical Nutrition, Newark, NJ 07102. Offers MS, DCN. *Program availability:* Part-time, evening/weekend, online learning. *Entrance requirements:* For master's, statement of career goals, minimum GPA of 3.2, proof of registered dietician status, interview, transcript of highest degree, bachelor's degree, 1 reference letter; for doctorate, minimum GPA of 3.4, transcript of highest degree, statement of career goals, interview, master's degree, 1 reference letter. Additional exam requirements/recommendations for international students: required—TOEFL (minimum score 500 paper-based; 79 iBT). Electronic applications accepted.

**Rutgers University - New Brunswick,** Graduate School-New Brunswick, Program in Nutritional Sciences, Piscataway, NJ 08854-8097. Offers MS, PhD. *Program availability:* Part-time. Terminal master's awarded for partial completion of doctoral program. *Degree requirements:* For master's, thesis; for doctorate, thesis/dissertation, written qualifying exam. *Entrance requirements:* For master's and doctorate, GRE General Test, 3 letters of recommendation. Additional exam requirements/recommendations for international students: required—TOEFL (minimum score 560 paper-based; 83 iBT). Electronic applications accepted.

**Sacred Heart University,** Graduate Programs, College of Health Professions, Department of Exercise Science, Fairfield, CT 06825. Offers exercise science and nutrition (MS). *Program availability:* Part-time, evening/weekend. *Degree requirements:* For master's, thesis. *Entrance requirements:* For master's, bachelor's degree in related major, minimum GPA of 3.0, anatomy and physiology (with labs), exercise physiology, nutrition, statistics or health/exercise-specific research methods course, kinesiology (preferred). Additional exam requirements/recommendations for international students: required—TOEFL (minimum score 570 paper-based, 80 iBT), TWE, or IELTS (6.5). Electronic applications accepted. *Expenses:* Contact institution.

**Sage Graduate School,** School of Health Sciences, Program in Nutrition, Troy, NY 12180-4115. Offers applied nutrition (MS); dietetic internship (Certificate); nutrition (Certificate). *Program availability:* Part-time, evening/weekend, 100% online. *Faculty:* 5 full-time (4 women), 4 part-time/adjunct (all women). *Students:* 53 full-time (50 women), 37 part-time (35 women); includes 9 minority (3 Black or African American, non-Hispanic/Latino; 1 American Indian or Alaska Native, non-Hispanic/Latino; 2 Asian, non-Hispanic/Latino; 1 Hispanic/Latino; 2 Two or more races, non-Hispanic/Latino), 5 international. Average age 29. 145 applicants, 46% accepted, 36 enrolled. In 2019, 31 master's, 40 other advanced degrees awarded. *Entrance requirements:* For master's, Applicants to the program must meet the general admission requirements for Sage Graduate schools. A GPA of 3.0 or higher is required for consideration into the program; 2 letters of recommendation; interview with Director. Additional exam requirements/recommendations for international students: required—TOEFL (minimum score 550 paper-based). *Application deadline:* Applications are processed on a rolling basis. Application fee: $30. Electronic applications accepted. *Expenses: Tuition:* Part-time $730 per credit hour. Tuition and fees vary according to course load, degree level and program. *Financial support:* Fellowships, research assistantships, and scholarships/grants available. Financial award applicants required to submit FAFSA. *Unit head:* Dr. Kathleen Kelly, Dean, School of Health Sciences, 518-244-2030, Fax: 518-244-4571, E-mail: kellyk5@sage.edu. *Application contact:* Samara Joy Nielsen, Program Director, Nutrition, 518-244-2396, E-mail: nielss2@sage.edu.

**Saint Louis University,** Graduate Programs, Doisy College of Health Sciences, Department of Nutrition and Dietetics, St. Louis, MO 63103. Offers medical dietetics (MS); nutrition and physical performance (MS). *Program availability:* Part-time. *Degree requirements:* For master's, comprehensive exam (for some programs). *Entrance requirements:* For master's, GRE General Test, letters of recommendation, resume, interview. Additional exam requirements/recommendations for international students: required—TOEFL (minimum score 525 paper-based). Electronic applications accepted.

**Samford University,** School of Public Health, Birmingham, AL 35229. Offers health informatics (MSHI); healthcare administration (MHA); nutrition (MS); public health (MPH); social work (MSW). *Accreditation:* CSWE. *Program availability:* Part-time, online only, 100% online. *Faculty:* 16 full-time (9 women), 5 part-time/adjunct (4 women). *Students:* 76 full-time (71 women), 16 part-time (14 women); includes 19 minority (14 Black or African American, non-Hispanic/Latino; 1 Asian, non-Hispanic/Latino; 1 Hispanic/Latino; 3 Two or more races, non-Hispanic/Latino). Average age 28. 74 applicants, 78% accepted, 39 enrolled. In 2019, 51 master's awarded. *Degree requirements:* For master's, capstone course. *Entrance requirements:* For master's, GRE, MAT, recommendations, resume, personal statement, transcripts, application. Additional exam requirements/recommendations for international students: required—TOEFL (minimum score 590 paper-based; 90 iBT), IELTS (minimum score 6.5). *Application deadline:* For fall admission, 10/1 for domestic students; for winter admission, 12/1 for domestic students; for spring admission, 5/1 for domestic students. Applications are processed on a rolling basis. Application fee: $75. Electronic applications accepted. *Expenses: Tuition:* Full-time $17,754; part-time $862 per credit hour. *Required fees:* $550; $550 per unit. Full-time tuition and fees vary according to course load, program and student level. *Financial support:* In 2019–20, 30 students received support. Scholarships/grants available. Financial award application deadline: 5/1; financial award applicants required to submit FAFSA. *Unit head:* Dr. Keith Elder, Ph.D., Dean, School of Public Health, 205-726-4655, E-mail: kelder@samford.edu. *Application contact:* Dr. Marian Carter, Ed.D, Assistant Dean of Enrollment Management, 205-726-2611, E-mail: mwcarter@samford.edu.
Website: http://www.samford.edu/publichealth

**Sam Houston State University,** College of Health Sciences, Department of Family and Consumer Sciences, Huntsville, TX 77341. Offers dietetics (MS); family and consumer sciences (MS). *Program availability:* Part-time, evening/weekend. *Degree requirements:* For master's, comprehensive exam, thesis optional, internship. *Entrance requirements:* For master's, GRE General Test, letters of recommendation, personal statement, writing sample. Additional exam requirements/recommendations for international students: required—TOEFL (minimum score 550 paper-based; 79 iBT), IELTS (minimum score 6.5). Electronic applications accepted.

**San Diego State University,** Graduate and Research Affairs, College of Health and Human Services, School of Exercise and Nutritional Sciences, Program in Nutritional Sciences, San Diego, CA 92182. Offers MS, MS/MS. *Degree requirements:* For master's, thesis. *Entrance requirements:* For master's, GRE General Test, 2 letters of reference. Additional exam requirements/recommendations for international students: required—TOEFL. Electronic applications accepted.

**San Jose State University,** Program in Nutrition, Food Science, and Packaging, San Jose, CA 95192-0058. Offers nutritional science (MS). *Faculty:* 6 full-time (4 women), 4 part-time/adjunct (3 women). *Students:* 25 full-time (20 women), 18 part-time (17 women); includes 19 minority (11 Asian, non-Hispanic/Latino; 8 Hispanic/Latino), 2 international. Average age 32. 51 applicants, 35% accepted, 9 enrolled. In 2019, 7 master's awarded. *Application deadline:* For fall admission, 2/1 for domestic and international students. Applications are processed on a rolling basis. Application fee: $70. Electronic applications accepted. *Expenses: Tuition, area resident:* Full-time $7176; part-time $4164 per credit hour. Tuition, state resident: full-time $7176; part-time $4164 per credit hour. Tuition, nonresident: full-time $7176; part-time $4165 per credit hour. *International tuition:* $7176 full-time. *Required fees:* $2110; $2110. *Financial support:* In 2019–20, 8 students received support. Scholarships/grants available. Financial award application deadline: 5/1; financial award applicants required to submit FAFSA. *Unit head:* Ashwini Wagle, Department Chair, 408-924-3100, E-mail: ashwini.wagle@sjsu.edu. *Application contact:* Adrianne Widaman, Assistant Professor, E-mail: adrianne.widaman@sjsu.edu.
Website: http://www.sjsu.edu/nufspkg/

*Nutrition*

**Saybrook University,** School of Mind-Body Medicine, San Francisco, CA 94612. Offers MS, PhD, Certificate. *Entrance requirements:* Additional exam requirements/recommendations for international students: required—TOEFL (minimum score 580 paper-based; 93 iBT). Electronic applications accepted.

**Simmons University,** Gwen Ifill College of Media, Arts, and Humanities, Boston, MA 02115. Offers behavior analysis (MS, PhD, Ed S); children's literature (MA); dietetics (Certificate); elementary education (MAT); English (MA); gender/cultural studies (MA); history (MA); nutrition and health promotion (MS); physical therapy (DPT); public health (MPH); public policy (MPP); special education: moderate and severe disabilities (MS Ed); sports nutrition (Certificate); writing for children (MFA). *Program availability:* Part-time. *Faculty:* 10 full-time (9 women), 7 part-time/adjunct (6 women). *Students:* 2 full-time (both women), 67 part-time (57 women); includes 13 minority (3 Black or African American, non-Hispanic/Latino; 4 Asian, non-Hispanic/Latino; 3 Hispanic/Latino; 3 Two or more races, non-Hispanic/Latino), 1 international. Average age 31. 42 applicants, 62% accepted, 23 enrolled. In 2019, 24 master's awarded. *Degree requirements:* For master's, thesis optional. *Entrance requirements:* For master's, GRE, bachelor's degree from accredited college or university; minimum B average (preferred). Additional exam requirements/recommendations for international students: required—TOEFL (minimum score 600 paper-based; 100 iBT). *Application deadline:* For fall admission, 8/1 for domestic and international students; for spring admission, 12/15 for domestic and international students; for summer admission, 5/1 for domestic and international students. Applications are processed on a rolling basis. Application fee: $35. Electronic applications accepted. *Expenses:* Contact institution. *Financial support:* In 2019–20, 14 students received support, including 1 fellowship (averaging $15,360 per year), 13 teaching assistantships (averaging $2,000 per year); scholarships/grants also available. Financial award applicants required to submit FAFSA. *Unit head:* Dr. Brian Norman, Dean, 617-521-2472, E-mail: brian.norman@simmons.edu. *Application contact:* Patricia Flaherty, Director, Graduate Studies Admission, 617-521-3902, Fax: 617-521-3058, E-mail: gsa@simmons.edu.
Website: https://www.simmons.edu/academics/colleges-schools-departments/ifill

**South Carolina State University,** College of Graduate and Professional Studies, Department of Family and Consumer Sciences, Orangeburg, SC 29117-0001. Offers individual and family development (MS); nutritional sciences (MS). *Program availability:* Part-time, evening/weekend. *Degree requirements:* For master's, comprehensive exam, thesis optional, departmental qualifying exam. *Entrance requirements:* For master's, GRE, MAT, or NTE, minimum GPA of 2.7. Electronic applications accepted.

**South Dakota State University,** Graduate School, College of Education and Human Sciences, Department of Health and Nutritional Sciences, Brookings, SD 57007. Offers athletic training (MS); dietetics (MS); nutrition and exercise sciences (MS, PhD); sport and recreation studies (MS). *Program availability:* Part-time. *Degree requirements:* For master's, comprehensive exam (for some programs), thesis (for some programs), oral exam. *Entrance requirements:* Additional exam requirements/recommendations for international students: required—TOEFL (minimum score 525 paper-based).

**Southern Illinois University Carbondale,** Graduate School, College of Agriculture, Department of Animal Science, Food and Nutrition, Program in Food and Nutrition, Carbondale, IL 62901-4701. Offers MS. *Degree requirements:* For master's, thesis or alternative. *Entrance requirements:* For master's, GRE, minimum GPA of 2.7. Additional exam requirements/recommendations for international students: required—TOEFL (minimum score 550 paper-based; 80 iBT). Electronic applications accepted.

**State University of New York College at Oneonta,** Graduate Programs, Department of Human Ecology, Oneonta, NY 13820-4015. Offers nutrition and dietetics (MS). *Program availability:* Online learning.

**Stony Brook University, State University of New York,** Stony Brook Medicine, Renaissance School of Medicine and Graduate School, Graduate Programs in Medicine, Department of Family, Population and Preventive Medicine, Stony Brook, NY 11794. Offers nutrition (MS, Advanced Certificate). *Program availability:* Online learning. *Faculty:* 14 full-time (7 women), 6 part-time/adjunct (5 women). *Students:* 3 full-time (all women), 74 part-time (69 women); includes 17 minority (2 American Indian or Alaska Native, non-Hispanic/Latino; 7 Asian, non-Hispanic/Latino; 6 Hispanic/Latino; 2 Two or more races, non-Hispanic/Latino). Average age 30. 8 applicants, 100% accepted, 6 enrolled. In 2019, 23 master's, 4 other advanced degrees awarded. *Entrance requirements:* For master's, baccalaureate degree with minimum preferred GPA of 3.0; physiology (laboratory not required) and statistics; for Advanced Certificate, physiology (laboratory not required). Additional exam requirements/recommendations for international students: required—TOEFL. *Application deadline:* For fall admission, 7/1 for domestic students; for spring admission, 12/1 for domestic students; for summer admission, 4/7 for domestic students. Application fee: $100. Electronic applications accepted. *Expenses:* Contact institution. *Unit head:* Dr. Iris A. Granek, Founding Chair, 631-444-3936, Fax: 631-444-1122, E-mail: emily.birgeles@stonybrookmedicine.edu. *Application contact:* Emily Birgeles, Assistant to the Chair, 631-638-3936, Fax: 631-444-1122, E-mail: emily.birgeles@stonybrookmedicine.edu.
Website: https://renaissance.stonybrookmedicine.edu/family_population_preventive_medicine

**Syracuse University,** David B. Falk College of Sport and Human Dynamics, Programs in Nutrition Science, Syracuse, NY 13244. Offers MA, MS, PhD. *Program availability:* Part-time. *Degree requirements:* For master's, comprehensive exam, thesis. *Entrance requirements:* For master's, GRE General Test, personal statement, resume, official transcripts, three letters of recommendation. Additional exam requirements/recommendations for international students: required—TOEFL (minimum score 100 iBT). Electronic applications accepted.

**Teachers College, Columbia University,** Department of Health and Behavior Studies, New York, NY 10027-6696. Offers applied behavior analysis (MA, PhD); applied educational psychology: school psychology (Ed M, PhD); behavioral nutrition (PhD), including nutrition (Ed D, PhD); community health education (MS); community nutrition education (Ed M), including community nutrition education; education of deaf and hard of hearing (MA, PhD); health education (MA, Ed D); hearing impairment (Ed D); intellectual disability/autism (MA, Ed D, PhD); nursing education (Ed D, Advanced Certificate); nutrition and education (MS); nutrition and exercise physiology (MS); nutrition and public health (MS); nutrition education (Ed D), including nutrition (Ed D, PhD); physical disabilities (Ed D); reading specialist (MA); severe or multiple disabilities (MA); special education (Ed M, MA, Ed D); teaching of sign language (MA). *Faculty:* 17 full-time (11 women). *Students:* 243 full-time (225 women), 246 part-time (211 women); includes 172 minority (33 Black or African American, non-Hispanic/Latino; 2 American Indian or Alaska Native, non-Hispanic/Latino; 63 Asian, non-Hispanic/Latino; 63 Hispanic/Latino; 11 Two or more races, non-Hispanic/Latino), 67 international. 515 applicants, 68% accepted, 170 enrolled. *Unit head:* Dr. Dolores Perin, Chair, 212-678-3091, E-mail: dp111@tc.columbia.edu. *Application contact:* Kelly Sutton-Skinner, Director of Admission and New Student Enrollment, E-mail: kms2237@tc.columbia.edu.
Website: http://www.tc.columbia.edu/health-and-behavior-studies/

**Texas A&M University,** College of Agriculture and Life Sciences, Department of Food Science and Technology, College Station, TX 77843. Offers food science and technology (M Agr, MS); nutrition (MS, PhD). *Faculty:* 14. *Students:* 58 full-time (36 women), 7 part-time (5 women); includes 13 minority (4 Black or African American, non-Hispanic/Latino; 8 Hispanic/Latino; 1 Two or more races, non-Hispanic/Latino), 30 international. Average age 30. 56 applicants, 34% accepted, 15 enrolled. In 2019, 5 master's, 4 doctorates awarded. *Degree requirements:* For master's, thesis (for some programs); for doctorate, thesis/dissertation. *Entrance requirements:* For master's and doctorate, GRE General Test. Additional exam requirements/recommendations for international students: required—TOEFL (minimum score 550 paper-based; 80 iBT), IELTS (minimum score 6), PTE (minimum score 53). *Application deadline:* For fall admission, 12/1 priority date for domestic and international students; for spring admission, 9/1 priority date for domestic and international students; for summer admission, 12/1 priority date for domestic and international students. Applications are processed on a rolling basis. Application fee: $65 ($90 for international students). Electronic applications accepted. *Expenses:* Contact institution. *Financial support:* In 2019–20, 59 students received support, including 3 fellowships with tuition reimbursements available (averaging $9,216 per year), 27 research assistantships with tuition reimbursements available (averaging $12,468 per year), 23 teaching assistantships with tuition reimbursements available (averaging $12,118 per year); career-related internships or fieldwork, institutionally sponsored loans, scholarships/grants, traineeships, health care benefits, tuition waivers (full and partial), and unspecified assistantships also available. Support available to part-time students. Financial award application deadline: 3/15; financial award applicants required to submit FAFSA. *Unit head:* Dr. Boon Chew, Department Head, 979-862-6655, E-mail: boon.chew@tamu.edu. *Application contact:* Graduate Program, 979-845-2142, E-mail: nfscadvisors@tamu.edu.
Website: http://nfs.tamu.edu

**Texas State University,** The Graduate College, College of Applied Arts, Program in Human Nutrition, San Marcos, TX 78666. Offers MS. *Program availability:* Part-time. *Degree requirements:* For master's, comprehensive exam, thesis (for some programs). *Entrance requirements:* For master's, baccalaureate degree from regionally-accredited institution with minimum GPA of 3.0 in last 60 hours of undergraduate work; 3 letters of reference; statement of goals and professional aspirations; curriculum vitae/resume; background course work in physiology, biochemistry, biology, nutrition, and chemistry. Additional exam requirements/recommendations for international students: required—TOEFL (minimum score 550 paper-based; 78 iBT), IELTS (minimum score 6.5). Electronic applications accepted.

**Texas Tech University,** Graduate School, College of Human Sciences, Department of Nutritional Sciences, Lubbock, TX 79409-1270. Offers nutrition and dietetics (MS); nutritional sciences (MS, PhD). *Program availability:* Part-time, 100% online. *Faculty:* 19 full-time (13 women), 5 part-time/adjunct (all women). *Students:* 67 full-time (57 women), 44 part-time (39 women); includes 23 minority (4 Black or African American, non-Hispanic/Latino; 5 Asian, non-Hispanic/Latino; 10 Hispanic/Latino; 4 Two or more races, non-Hispanic/Latino), 26 international. Average age 28. 55 applicants, 87% accepted, 39 enrolled. In 2019, 24 master's, 8 doctorates awarded. Terminal master's awarded for partial completion of doctoral program. *Degree requirements:* For master's, comprehensive exam (for some programs), thesis (for some programs); for doctorate, thesis/dissertation. *Entrance requirements:* For master's, GRE, minimum undergraduate cumulative GPA of 3.0; for doctorate, GRE, minimum undergraduate or graduate cumulative GPA of 3.0. Additional exam requirements/recommendations for international students: required—TOEFL (minimum score 550 paper-based; 80 iBT), IELTS (minimum score 6.5), TOEFL (minimum score 550 paper-based, 80 iBT) or IELTS (6.5). *Application deadline:* For fall admission, 6/1 priority date for domestic students, 1/15 priority date for international students; for spring admission, 9/1 priority date for domestic students, 6/15 priority date for international students. Applications are processed on a rolling basis. Application fee: $65. Electronic applications accepted. *Expenses:* Contact institution. *Financial support:* In 2019–20, 78 students received support, including 77 fellowships (averaging $4,130 per year), 16 research assistantships (averaging $16,328 per year), 17 teaching assistantships (averaging $13,067 per year); Federal Work-Study, scholarships/grants, and unspecified assistantships also available. Financial award application deadline: 1/15; financial award applicants required to submit FAFSA. *Unit head:* Dr. Nikhil V. Dhurandhar, Chairperson and Professor, 806-742-5270, Fax: 806-742-2926, E-mail: nikhil.dhurandhar@ttu.edu. *Application contact:* Taylor Reasoner, Coordinator, 806-834-6321, Fax: 806-742-2926, E-mail: taylor.r.reasoner@ttu.edu.
Website: www.ns.ttu.edu

**Texas Woman's University,** Graduate School, College of Health Sciences, Department of Nutrition and Food Sciences, Denton, TX 76204. Offers exercise and sports nutrition (MS); food science and flavor chemistry (MS); food systems administration (MS); nutrition (MS, PhD). *Program availability:* Part-time, evening/weekend, 100% online. *Faculty:* 17 full-time (11 women), 1 (woman) part-time/adjunct. *Students:* 70 full-time (61 women), 75 part-time (68 women); includes 52 minority (6 Black or African American, non-Hispanic/Latino; 17 Asian, non-Hispanic/Latino; 23 Hispanic/Latino; 6 Two or more races, non-Hispanic/Latino), 11 international. Average age 29. 98 applicants, 82% accepted, 45 enrolled. In 2019, 70 master's, 1 doctorate awarded. *Degree requirements:* For master's, thesis or alternative, thesis (for food and flavor chemistry); thesis or coursework (for exercise and sports nutrition, nutrition), capstone; for doctorate, comprehensive exam, thesis/dissertation, qualifying exam, 50% of all required hours must be earned at TWU. *Entrance requirements:* For master's, GRE General Test (143 verbal,141 quantitative), GMAT (330 total or verbal 21 quantitative 17), or MCAT (total 500-507, 125-126 critical analysis/reading and 125-126 biological and biochemical foundations of living systems), minimum GPA of 3.25 for last 60 undergraduate hours, resume, personal statement of interest (food science and flavor chemistry only); for doctorate, GRE General Test (143 verbal,141 quantitative), GMAT (330 total or verbal 21 quantitative 17), or MCAT (total 500-507, 125-126 critical analysis/reading and 125-126 biological and biochemical foundations of living systems), minimum GPA of 3.5 on last 60 undergraduate hours and graduate course work, 2 letters of reference, resume, statement of purpose. Additional exam requirements/recommendations for international students: required—TOEFL (minimum score 79 iBT); recommended—IELTS (minimum score 6.5), TSE (minimum score 53). *Application deadline:* For fall admission, 6/15 for domestic students, 3/1 priority date for international students; for spring admission, 10/1 for domestic students, 7/1 priority date for international students; for summer admission, 4/1 for domestic students, 2/1 priority date for international students. Application fee: $50 ($75 for international students). Electronic applications accepted. *Expenses: Tuition, area resident:* Full-time $4973.40; part-time $276.30 per semester hour. Tuition, state resident: full-time $4973.40; part-time $276.30 per semester hour. Tuition, nonresident: full-time $12,569; part-time $698.30 per semester hour. *International tuition:* $12,569.40 full-time. *Required fees:* $2524.30. Tuition and fees vary according to course level, course load, degree level and program. *Financial support:* In 2019–20, 67 students received support, including 6 research assistantships (averaging $4,352 per year), 18 teaching assistantships (averaging $6,539 per year); career-related internships or fieldwork, scholarships/grants, health care benefits, and unspecified assistantships also available. Support available to part-time students. Financial award application deadline: 3/1; financial award applicants required to submit FAFSA. *Unit head:* Dr. K. Shane Broughton, Chair, 940-898-2636, Fax: 940-898-2634, E-mail: nutrfdsci@twu.edu. *Application contact:* Korie Hawkins, Associate Director of Admissions, Graduate

Recruitment, 940-898-3188, Fax: 940-898-3081, E-mail: admissions@twu.edu.
Website: http://www.twu.edu/nutrition-food-sciences/

**Tufts University,** The Gerald J. and Dorothy R. Friedman School of Nutrition Science and Policy, Boston, MA 02111. Offers agriculture, food and environment (MS, PhD); biochemical and molecular nutrition (MS, PhD); dietetic internship (MS); food and nutrition policy (MS, PhD); humanitarian assistance (MAHA); nutrition (MS, PhD); nutrition data science (MS, PhD); nutrition interventions, communication, and behavior change (MS, PhD); sustainable water management (MS). *Program availability:* Part-time. *Degree requirements:* For doctorate, comprehensive exam, thesis/dissertation. *Entrance requirements:* For master's and doctorate, GRE General Test. Additional exam requirements/recommendations for international students: required—TOEFL. Electronic applications accepted. *Expenses:* Contact institution.

**Tufts University,** School of Medicine, Public Health and Professional Degree Programs, Boston, MA 02111. Offers biomedical sciences (MS); health communication (MS, Certificate); pain research, education and policy (MS, Certificate); physician assistant (MS); public health (MPH, Dr PH), including behavioral science (MPH), biostatistics (MPH), epidemiology (MPH), health communication (MPH), health services (MPH), management and policy (MPH), nutrition (MPH); DMD/MPH; DVM/MPH; JD/MPH; MD/MPH; MMS/MPH; MS/MBA; MS/MPH. *Accreditation:* CEPH (one or more programs are accredited). *Program availability:* Part-time, evening/weekend. *Students:* 450 full-time (291 women), 68 part-time (58 women); includes 201 minority (34 Black or African American, non-Hispanic/Latino; 1 American Indian or Alaska Native, non-Hispanic/Latino; 106 Asian, non-Hispanic/Latino; 41 Hispanic/Latino; 1 Native Hawaiian or other Pacific Islander, non-Hispanic/Latino; 18 Two or more races, non-Hispanic/Latino), 16 international. Average age 27. 1,076 applicants, 70% accepted, 213 enrolled. In 2019, 268 master's, 2 doctorates awarded. Terminal master's awarded for partial completion of doctoral program. *Degree requirements:* For master's, thesis (for some programs); for doctorate, thesis/dissertation. *Entrance requirements:* For master's, GRE General Test, MCAT, or GMAT; LSAT for applicants to the JD/MPH combined degree; for doctorate, GRE General Test or MCAT. Additional exam requirements/recommendations for international students: required—TOEFL (minimum score 100 iBT); recommended—IELTS (minimum score 7), TSE. *Application deadline:* For fall admission, 1/15 priority date for domestic and international students; for spring admission, 10/25 priority date for domestic and international students. Applications are processed on a rolling basis. Application fee: $70. Electronic applications accepted. *Expenses:* Contact institution. *Financial support:* In 2019–20, 13 students received support, including 1 fellowship (averaging $3,000 per year), 50 research assistantships (averaging $1,000 per year), 65 teaching assistantships (averaging $2,000 per year); Federal Work-Study and scholarships/grants also available. Financial award application deadline: 2/23; financial award applicants required to submit FAFSA. *Unit head:* Dr. Aviva Must, Dean, 617-636-0935, Fax: 617-636-0898, E-mail: aviva.must@tufts.edu. *Application contact:* Emily Keily, Director of Admissions, 617-636-0935, Fax: 617-636-0898, E-mail: med-phpd@tufts.edu.
Website: http://publichealth.tufts.edu

**Tuskegee University,** Graduate Programs, College of Agriculture, Environment and Nutrition Sciences, Department of Food and Nutritional Sciences, Tuskegee, AL 36088. Offers MS. *Degree requirements:* For master's, thesis. *Entrance requirements:* For master's, GRE General Test. Additional exam requirements/recommendations for international students: required—TOEFL (minimum score 500 paper-based).

**Université de Moncton,** School of Food Science, Nutrition and Family Studies, Moncton, NB E1A 3E9, Canada. Offers foods/nutrition (M Sc). *Program availability:* Part-time. *Degree requirements:* For master's, one foreign language, thesis. *Entrance requirements:* For master's, previous course work in statistics. Electronic applications accepted.

**Université de Montréal,** Faculty of Medicine, Department of Nutrition, Montréal, QC H3C 3J7, Canada. Offers M Sc, PhD, DESS. Terminal master's awarded for partial completion of doctoral program. *Degree requirements:* For master's, thesis; for doctorate, thesis/dissertation, general exam. *Entrance requirements:* For master's, MD, B Sc in nutrition or equivalent, proficiency in French; for doctorate, M Sc in nutrition or equivalent, proficiency in French. Electronic applications accepted.

**University at Buffalo, the State University of New York,** Graduate School, School of Public Health and Health Professions, Department of Exercise and Nutrition Sciences, Buffalo, NY 14260. Offers exercise science (MS, PhD); nutrition (MS, Advanced Certificate). *Program availability:* Part-time. *Entrance requirements:* For master's, doctorate, and Advanced Certificate, GRE General Test, minimum GPA of 3.0. Additional exam requirements/recommendations for international students: required—TOEFL (minimum score 550 paper-based; 79 iBT), IELTS (minimum score 6.5). Electronic applications accepted. *Expenses: Tuition, area resident:* Full-time $11,310; part-time $471 per credit hour. Tuition, state resident: full-time $11,310; part-time $471 per credit hour. Tuition, nonresident: full-time $23,100; part-time $963 per credit hour. *International tuition:* $23,100 full-time. *Required fees:* $2820.

**The University of Alabama,** Graduate School, College of Human Environmental Sciences, Department of Human Nutrition and Hospitality Management, Tuscaloosa, AL 35487. Offers MSHES. *Program availability:* Part-time, online only, 100% online. *Faculty:* 15 full-time (12 women). *Students:* 40 full-time (36 women), 183 part-time (177 women); includes 31 minority (10 Black or African American, non-Hispanic/Latino; 6 Asian, non-Hispanic/Latino; 11 Hispanic/Latino; 4 Two or more races, non-Hispanic/Latino), 5 international. Average age 30. 167 applicants, 69% accepted, 87 enrolled. In 2019, 54 master's awarded. *Degree requirements:* For master's, comprehensive exam, thesis optional. *Entrance requirements:* For master's, minimum GPA of 3.0. Additional exam requirements/recommendations for international students: required—TOEFL, IELTS. *Application deadline:* For fall admission, 6/1 for domestic students; for spring admission, 11/1 for domestic students; for summer admission, 4/1 for domestic students. Applications are processed on a rolling basis. Application fee: $50 ($60 for international students). Electronic applications accepted. *Expenses: Tuition, area resident:* Full-time $10,780; part-time $440 per credit hour. Tuition, nonresident: full-time $30,250; part-time $1550 per credit hour. *Financial support:* In 2019–20, 11 students received support. Research assistantships, teaching assistantships, and career-related internships or fieldwork available. Financial award application deadline: 3/15. *Unit head:* Dr. Kristi Crowe-White, Chair/Associate Professor, 205-348-6173, Fax: 205-348-2982, E-mail: kcrowe@ches.ua.edu. *Application contact:* Patrick D. Fuller, Admissions Officer, 205-348-5923, Fax: 205-348-0400, E-mail: patrick.d.fuller@ua.edu.
Website: http://www.nhm.ches.ua.edu/

**The University of Alabama at Birmingham,** School of Health Professions, Program in Nutrition Sciences, Birmingham, AL 35294. Offers MS, PhD. *Students:* 30 full-time (25 women), 8 part-time (6 women); includes 8 minority (6 Black or African American, non-Hispanic/Latino; 1 Asian, non-Hispanic/Latino; 1 Hispanic/Latino), 5 international. Average age 28. 65 applicants, 77% accepted, 45 enrolled. In 2019, 17 master's awarded. Terminal master's awarded for partial completion of doctoral program. *Degree requirements:* For master's, thesis optional; for doctorate, thesis/dissertation. *Entrance requirements:* For master's, GRE or MAT, letters of recommendation; for doctorate, GRE. Additional exam requirements/recommendations for international students: required—TOEFL. *Financial support:* Fellowships with tuition reimbursements, research assistantships with tuition reimbursements, career-related internships or fieldwork, and scholarships/grants available. *Unit head:* Dr. Timothy Garvey, MD, Chair, 205-934-6103, Fax: 205-975-4065, E-mail: garveyt@uab.edu. *Application contact:* Susan Noblitt Banks, Director of Graduate School Operations, 205-934-8227, Fax: 205-934-8413, E-mail: gradschool@uab.edu.
Website: http://www.uab.edu/shp/nutrition/

**The University of Arizona,** College of Agriculture and Life Sciences, Department of Nutritional Sciences, Tucson, AZ 85721. Offers MS, PhD. *Entrance requirements:* For master's, GRE, minimum GPA of 3.0, 2 letters of recommendation; for doctorate, GRE, minimum GPA of 3.0, 2 letters of recommendation, statement of purpose. Additional exam requirements/recommendations for international students: required—TOEFL (minimum score 550 paper-based; 79 iBT). Electronic applications accepted.

**University of Arkansas for Medical Sciences,** Graduate School, Little Rock, AR 72205. Offers biochemistry and molecular biology (MS, PhD); bioinformatics (MS, PhD); cellular physiology and molecular biophysics (MS, PhD); clinical nutrition (MS); interdisciplinary biomedical sciences (MS, PhD, Certificate); interdisciplinary toxicology (MS); microbiology and immunology (PhD); neurobiology and developmental sciences (PhD); pharmacology (PhD); MD/PhD. *Program availability:* Part-time. Terminal master's awarded for partial completion of doctoral program. *Degree requirements:* For master's, comprehensive exam (for some programs), thesis (for some programs); for doctorate, thesis/dissertation. *Entrance requirements:* For master's and doctorate, GRE. Additional exam requirements/recommendations for international students: required—TOEFL. Electronic applications accepted. *Expenses:* Contact institution.

**University of Bridgeport,** Nutrition Institute, Bridgeport, CT 06604. Offers human nutrition (MS). *Program availability:* Part-time, evening/weekend, online learning. *Degree requirements:* For master's, thesis, research project. *Entrance requirements:* For master's, previous course work in anatomy, biochemistry, organic chemistry, or physiology. Additional exam requirements/recommendations for international students: recommended—TOEFL (minimum score 550 paper-based; 80 iBT), IELTS (minimum score 6.5). Electronic applications accepted. *Expenses:* Contact institution.

**The University of British Columbia,** Faculty of Land and Food Systems, Human Nutrition Program, Vancouver, BC V6T 1Z4, Canada. Offers M Sc, PhD. *Program availability:* Part-time. Terminal master's awarded for partial completion of doctoral program. *Degree requirements:* For master's, thesis; for doctorate, comprehensive exam, thesis/dissertation. *Entrance requirements:* Additional exam requirements/recommendations for international students: required—TOEFL, IELTS. Electronic applications accepted. *Expenses:* Contact institution.

**University of California, Berkeley,** Graduate Division, College of Natural Resources, Program in Metabolic Biology, Berkeley, CA 94720. Offers MS, PhD. *Degree requirements:* For doctorate, thesis/dissertation, qualifying exam. *Entrance requirements:* For doctorate, GRE General Test, minimum GPA of 3.0, 3 letters of recommendation. Additional exam requirements/recommendations for international students: required—TOEFL. Electronic applications accepted.

**University of California, Davis,** Graduate Studies, Graduate Group in Nutritional Biology, Davis, CA 95616. Offers MS, PhD. *Degree requirements:* For master's, thesis; for doctorate, thesis/dissertation. *Entrance requirements:* For master's and doctorate, GRE General Test, minimum GPA of 3.0. Additional exam requirements/recommendations for international students: required—TOEFL (minimum score 550 paper-based). Electronic applications accepted.

**University of California, Davis,** Graduate Studies, Program in Maternal and Child Nutrition, Davis, CA 95616. Offers MAS. *Degree requirements:* For master's, comprehensive exam. *Entrance requirements:* Additional exam requirements/recommendations for international students: required—TOEFL (minimum score 550 paper-based).

**University of Central Arkansas,** Graduate School, College of Health and Behavioral Sciences, Department of Family and Consumer Sciences, Conway, AR 72035-0001. Offers family and consumer sciences (MS); nutrition (MS). *Program availability:* Part-time, evening/weekend, online learning. *Degree requirements:* For master's, comprehensive exam, thesis optional. *Entrance requirements:* For master's, GRE General Test, minimum GPA of 2.7. Additional exam requirements/recommendations for international students: required—TOEFL (minimum score 550 paper-based). Electronic applications accepted. *Expenses:* Contact institution.

**University of Central Oklahoma,** The Jackson College of Graduate Studies, College of Education and Professional Studies, Department of Human Environmental Sciences, Edmond, OK 73034-5209. Offers family and child studies (MS), including family life education, infant/child specialist, marriage and family therapy; nutrition-food science (MS). *Program availability:* Part-time. *Degree requirements:* For master's, comprehensive exam (for some programs), thesis (for some programs). *Entrance requirements:* For master's, GRE, essay, physical, CPR and First Aid training. Additional exam requirements/recommendations for international students: required—TOEFL (minimum score 550 paper-based; 79 iBT), IELTS (minimum score 6.5). Electronic applications accepted.

**University of Chicago,** Division of the Biological Sciences, Committee on Molecular Metabolism and Nutrition, Chicago, IL 60637. Offers PhD. *Degree requirements:* For doctorate, thesis/dissertation, ethics class, 2 teaching assistantships, mock grant proposal. *Entrance requirements:* For doctorate, GRE General Test, transcripts, statement of purpose, 3 letters of recommendation. Additional exam requirements/recommendations for international students: required—TOEFL (minimum score 600 paper-based; 104 iBT), IELTS (minimum score 7). Electronic applications accepted.

**University of Cincinnati,** Graduate School, College of Allied Health Sciences, Department of Rehabilitation, Exercise, and Nutrition Sciences, Cincinnati, OH 45267-0394. Offers nutritional sciences (MS). *Program availability:* Part-time. *Degree requirements:* For master's, thesis optional. *Entrance requirements:* For master's, GRE General Test. Additional exam requirements/recommendations for international students: required—TOEFL (minimum score 550 paper-based). Electronic applications accepted.

**University of Connecticut,** Graduate School, College of Agriculture, Health and Natural Resources, Department of Nutritional Sciences, Storrs, CT 06269. Offers MS, PhD. Terminal master's awarded for partial completion of doctoral program. *Degree requirements:* For master's, comprehensive exam, thesis; for doctorate, thesis/dissertation. *Entrance requirements:* For master's and doctorate, GRE General Test. Additional exam requirements/recommendations for international students: required—TOEFL (minimum score 550 paper-based). Electronic applications accepted.

**University of Delaware,** College of Health Sciences, Department of Behavioral Health and Nutrition, Newark, DE 19716. Offers health promotion (MS); human nutrition (MS). *Program availability:* Part-time. *Degree requirements:* For master's, thesis. *Entrance requirements:* For master's, GRE General Test, interview, minimum GPA of 3.0. Additional exam requirements/recommendations for international students: required—TOEFL (minimum score 550 paper-based). Electronic applications accepted.

## Nutrition

**University of Florida,** Graduate School, College of Agricultural and Life Sciences, Department of Food Science and Human Nutrition, Gainesville, FL 32611. Offers food science (PhD), including toxicology; food science and human nutrition (MS), including nutritional sciences; nutritional sciences (MS, PhD), including clinical and translational science (PhD). *Degree requirements:* For master's, thesis optional; for doctorate, thesis/dissertation. *Entrance requirements:* For master's and doctorate, GRE General Test, minimum GPA of 3.0. Additional exam requirements/recommendations for international students: required—TOEFL. Electronic applications accepted.

**University of Georgia,** College of Family and Consumer Sciences, Department of Foods and Nutrition, Athens, GA 30602. Offers MS, PhD. *Degree requirements:* For master's, thesis (MS); for doctorate, thesis/dissertation. *Entrance requirements:* For master's, GRE General Test, minimum GPA of 3.0, course work in biochemistry and physiology; for doctorate, GRE General Test, master's degree, minimum GPA of 3.0. Electronic applications accepted.

**University of Guelph,** Office of Graduate and Postdoctoral Studies, College of Biological Science, Department of Human Health and Nutritional Sciences, Guelph, ON N1G 2W1, Canada. Offers nutritional sciences (M Sc, PhD). *Program availability:* Part-time. *Degree requirements:* For master's, thesis (for some programs); for doctorate, comprehensive exam, thesis/dissertation. *Entrance requirements:* For master's, minimum B-average during previous 2 years of coursework; for doctorate, minimum A-average. Additional exam requirements/recommendations for international students: required—TOEFL (minimum score 550 paper-based). Electronic applications accepted.

**University of Guelph,** Office of Graduate and Postdoctoral Studies, College of Social and Applied Human Sciences, Department of Family Relations and Applied Nutrition, Guelph, ON N1G 2W1, Canada. Offers applied nutrition (MAN); family relations and human development (M Sc, PhD), including applied human nutrition, couple and family therapy (M Sc), family relations and human development. *Accreditation:* AAMFT/COAMFTE (one or more programs are accredited). *Program availability:* Part-time. *Degree requirements:* For master's, thesis (for some programs); for doctorate, comprehensive exam, thesis/dissertation. *Entrance requirements:* For master's, minimum B+ average; for doctorate, master's degree in family relations and human development or related field with a minimum B+ average or master's degree in applied human nutrition. Additional exam requirements/recommendations for international students: required—TOEFL (minimum score 600 paper-based). Electronic applications accepted.

**University of Hawaii at Manoa,** Office of Graduate Education, College of Tropical Agriculture and Human Resources, Department of Human Nutrition, Food and Animal Sciences, Program in Nutrition, Honolulu, HI 96822. Offers PhD. *Program availability:* Part-time. *Degree requirements:* For doctorate, comprehensive exam, thesis/dissertation. *Entrance requirements:* For doctorate, GRE General Test. Additional exam requirements/recommendations for international students: required—TOEFL (minimum score 580 paper-based; 92 iBT), IELTS (minimum score 5).

**University of Hawaii at Manoa,** Office of Graduate Education, College of Tropical Agriculture and Human Resources, Department of Human Nutrition, Food and Animal Sciences, Program in Nutritional Sciences, Honolulu, HI 96822. Offers MS, PhD. *Program availability:* Part-time. *Degree requirements:* For master's, thesis optional; for doctorate, comprehensive exam, thesis/dissertation. *Entrance requirements:* For master's and doctorate, GRE General Test. Additional exam requirements/recommendations for international students: required—TOEFL (minimum score 580 paper-based; 92 iBT), IELTS (minimum score 5).

**University of Houston,** College of Liberal Arts and Social Sciences, Department of Health and Human Performance, Houston, TX 77204. Offers exercise science (MS); human nutrition (MS); human space exploration sciences (MS); kinesiology (PhD); physical education (M Ed). *Accreditation:* NCATE (one or more programs are accredited). *Program availability:* Part-time, evening/weekend. *Degree requirements:* For master's, comprehensive exam (for some programs), thesis (for some programs); for doctorate, comprehensive exam, thesis/dissertation, qualifying exam, candidacy paper. *Entrance requirements:* For master's, GRE (minimum 35th percentile on each section), minimum cumulative GPA of 3.0; for doctorate, GRE (minimum 35th percentile on each section), minimum cumulative GPA of 3.3. Additional exam requirements/recommendations for international students: required—TOEFL (minimum score 550 paper-based; 79 iBT). Electronic applications accepted.

**University of Illinois at Chicago,** College of Applied Health Sciences, Program in Nutrition, Chicago, IL 60607-7128. Offers MS, PhD. *Degree requirements:* For master's, thesis; for doctorate, thesis/dissertation. *Entrance requirements:* For master's and doctorate, GRE General Test, minimum GPA of 2.75. Additional exam requirements/recommendations for international students: required—TOEFL. Electronic applications accepted. *Expenses:* Contact institution.

**University of Illinois at Urbana-Champaign,** Graduate College, College of Agricultural, Consumer and Environmental Sciences, Department of Food Science and Human Nutrition, Champaign, IL 61820. Offers food science (MS); food science and human nutrition (MS, PhD), including professional science (MS); human nutrition (MS). *Program availability:* Part-time, online learning.

**University of Illinois at Urbana-Champaign,** Graduate College, College of Agricultural, Consumer and Environmental Sciences, Division of Nutritional Sciences, Champaign, IL 61820. Offers MS, PhD, PhD/MPH.

**The University of Kansas,** University of Kansas Medical Center, School of Health Professions, Department of Dietetics and Nutrition, Kansas City, KS 66045. Offers dietetic internship (Graduate Certificate); dietetics and nutrition (MS); medical nutrition science (PhD). *Program availability:* Part-time, 100% online. *Faculty:* 28. *Students:* 44 full-time (39 women), 28 part-time (all women); includes 1 minority (Asian, non-Hispanic/Latino), 5 international. Average age 28. In 2019, 25 master's, 24 other advanced degrees awarded. *Degree requirements:* For master's, comprehensive exam, thesis optional; for doctorate, comprehensive exam, thesis/dissertation. *Entrance requirements:* For master's, GRE, prerequisite courses in nutrition, biochemistry, and physiology; minimum cumulative GPA of 3.0; for doctorate and Graduate Certificate, GRE, minimum cumulative GPA of 3.0. Additional exam requirements/recommendations for international students: required—TOEFL. *Application deadline:* For fall admission, 7/1 for domestic students; for spring admission, 12/1 for domestic students; for summer admission, 5/1 for domestic students. Applications are processed on a rolling basis. Application fee: $75. Electronic applications accepted. *Expenses:* Tuition, state resident: full-time $9989. Tuition, nonresident: full-time $23,950. *International tuition:* $23,950 full-time. *Required fees:* $984; $81.99 per credit hour. Tuition and fees vary according to course load, campus/location and program. *Financial support:* Research assistantships with full and partial tuition reimbursements, teaching assistantships with full tuition reimbursements, career-related internships or fieldwork, Federal Work-Study, institutionally sponsored loans, scholarships/grants, traineeships, and unspecified assistantships available. Support available to part-time students. Financial award application deadline: 3/1; financial award applicants required to submit FAFSA. *Unit head:* Dr. Debra Kay Sullivan, Department Chair, Midwest Dairy Council Professor in Clinical Nutrition, 913-588-5357, E-mail: dsulliva@kumc.edu. *Application contact:* Dr.

Heather Gibbs, Program Director, Master's in Dietetics and Nutrition, 913-945-9138. Website: http://www.kumc.edu/school-of-health-professions/dietetics-and-nutrition.html

**University of Kentucky,** Graduate School, College of Agriculture, Food and Environment, Program in Hospitality and Dietetics Administration, Lexington, KY 40506-0032. Offers MS. *Degree requirements:* For master's, comprehensive exam, thesis optional. *Entrance requirements:* For master's, GRE General Test, minimum undergraduate GPA of 2.75. Additional exam requirements/recommendations for international students: required—TOEFL (minimum score 550 paper-based). Electronic applications accepted.

**University of Kentucky,** Graduate School, College of Health Sciences, Program in Nutritional Sciences, Lexington, KY 40506-0032. Offers MSNS, PhD. *Degree requirements:* For doctorate, comprehensive exam, thesis/dissertation. *Entrance requirements:* For master's, GRE General Test, minimum undergraduate GPA of 2.75; for doctorate, GRE General Test, minimum graduate GPA of 3.0. Additional exam requirements/recommendations for international students: required—TOEFL (minimum score 550 paper-based). Electronic applications accepted.

**University of Manitoba,** Faculty of Graduate Studies, Faculty of Agricultural and Food Sciences, Department of Food and Human Nutritional Sciences, Winnipeg, MB R3T 2N2, Canada. Offers food science (M Sc, PhD); human nutritional sciences (M Sc, PhD). *Degree requirements:* For master's, thesis.

**University of Maryland, College Park,** Academic Affairs, College of Agriculture and Natural Resources, Department of Nutrition and Food Science, Program in Nutrition, College Park, MD 20742. Offers MS, PhD. *Degree requirements:* For master's, thesis; for doctorate, comprehensive exam, thesis/dissertation, candidacy exam. *Entrance requirements:* For master's, GRE General Test, minimum GPA of 3.0, 3 letters of recommendation; for doctorate, GRE General Test, minimum GPA of 3.0. Additional exam requirements/recommendations for international students: required—TOEFL. Electronic applications accepted.

**University of Massachusetts Amherst,** Graduate School, School of Public Health and Health Sciences, Department of Nutrition, Amherst, MA 01003. Offers community nutrition (MS); nutrition (MPH); nutrition science (MS). *Program availability:* Part-time, evening/weekend, online learning. Terminal master's awarded for partial completion of doctoral program. *Degree requirements:* For master's, thesis or alternative. *Entrance requirements:* For master's, GRE General Test. Additional exam requirements/recommendations for international students: required—TOEFL (minimum score 550 paper-based; 80 iBT), IELTS (minimum score 6.5). Electronic applications accepted.

**University of Massachusetts Amherst,** Graduate School, School of Public Health and Health Sciences, Department of Public Health, Amherst, MA 01003. Offers biostatistics (MPH, MS, PhD); community health education (MPH, MS, PhD); environmental health sciences (MPH, MS, PhD); epidemiology (MPH, MS, PhD); health policy and management (MPH, MS, PhD); nutrition (MPH, PhD); public health practice (MPH); MPH/MPPA. *Accreditation:* CEPH. *Program availability:* Part-time, evening/weekend, online learning. Terminal master's awarded for partial completion of doctoral program. *Degree requirements:* For master's, thesis (for some programs); for doctorate, comprehensive exam, thesis/dissertation. *Entrance requirements:* For master's and doctorate, GRE General Test. Additional exam requirements/recommendations for international students: required—TOEFL (minimum score 550 paper-based; 80 iBT), IELTS (minimum score 6.5). Electronic applications accepted.

**University of Memphis,** Graduate School, School of Health Studies, Memphis, TN 38152. Offers faith and health (Graduate Certificate); health studies (MS), including exercise, sport and movement sciences, health promotion, physical education teacher education; nutrition (MS), including clinical nutrition, environmental nutrition, nutrition science; sport nutrition and dietary supplementation (Graduate Certificate). *Program availability:* 100% online. *Faculty:* 19 full-time (11 women), 2 part-time/adjunct (1 woman). *Students:* 56 full-time (44 women), 42 part-time (33 women); includes 39 minority (24 Black or African American, non-Hispanic/Latino; 4 Asian, non-Hispanic/Latino; 4 Hispanic/Latino; 2 Native Hawaiian or other Pacific Islander, non-Hispanic/Latino; 5 Two or more races, non-Hispanic/Latino), 6 international. Average age 29. 63 applicants, 84% accepted, 37 enrolled. In 2019, 38 master's, 2 other advanced degrees awarded. *Degree requirements:* For master's, comprehensive exam, thesis or alternative, culminating experience; for Graduate Certificate, practicum. *Entrance requirements:* For master's, GRE or PRAXIS II, letters of recommendation, statement of goals, minimum undergraduate GPA of 2.5; for Graduate Certificate, minimum undergraduate GPA of 2.5. Additional exam requirements/recommendations for international students: required—TOEFL (minimum score 550 paper-based; 79 iBT). *Application deadline:* For fall admission, 4/15 priority date for domestic students; for spring admission, 10/15 priority date for domestic students; for summer admission, 4/15 priority date for domestic students. Application fee: $35 ($60 for international students). *Expenses: Tuition, area resident:* Full-time $9216; part-time $512 per credit hour. Tuition, state resident: full-time $9216; part-time $512 per credit hour. Tuition, nonresident: full-time $12,672; part-time $704 per credit hour. *International tuition:* $16,128 full-time. *Required fees:* $1530; $85 per credit hour. Tuition and fees vary according to program. *Financial support:* Research assistantships, teaching assistantships, career-related internships or fieldwork, Federal Work-Study, scholarships/grants, and unspecified assistantships available. Financial award application deadline: 2/1; financial award applicants required to submit FAFSA. *Unit head:* Dr. Richard Bloomer, Dean, 901-678-4316, Fax: 901-678-3591, E-mail: rbloomer@memphis.edu. *Application contact:* Dr. Richard Bloomer, Dean, 901-678-4316, Fax: 901-678-3591, E-mail: rbloomer@memphis.edu. Website: http://www.memphis.edu/shs/

**University of Miami,** Graduate School, School of Education and Human Development, Department of Kinesiology and Sport Sciences, Program in Nutrition for Health and Human Performance, Coral Gables, FL 33124. Offers MS Ed. *Program availability:* Part-time, evening/weekend. *Students:* 7 full-time (5 women), 1 (woman) part-time; includes 5 minority (2 Black or African American, non-Hispanic/Latino; 1 Asian, non-Hispanic/Latino; 2 Hispanic/Latino). Average age 23. 17 applicants, 65% accepted, 6 enrolled. In 2019, 11 master's awarded. *Degree requirements:* For master's, comprehensive exam. *Entrance requirements:* For master's, GRE General Test. Additional exam requirements/recommendations for international students: required—TOEFL (minimum score 550 paper-based; 80 iBT); recommended—IELTS (minimum score 6.5). *Application deadline:* For fall admission, 10/1 for international students. Applications are processed on a rolling basis. Application fee: $85. Electronic applications accepted. *Financial support:* Application deadline: 3/1; applicants required to submit FAFSA. *Unit head:* Dr. Brian Biagioli, Graduate Program Director, 305-284-6772, Fax: 305-284-5168, E-mail: b.biagioli@miami.edu. *Application contact:* Dr. Brian Biagioli, Graduate Program Director, 305-284-6772, Fax: 305-284-5168, E-mail: b.biagioli@miami.edu. Website: http://www.education.miami.edu

**University of Michigan,** School of Public Health, Department of Nutritional Sciences, Ann Arbor, MI 48109. Offers dietetics (MPH); nutritional sciences (MPH, MS, PhD). *Accreditation:* AND. *Entrance requirements:* For master's, GRE, MCAT; for doctorate, GRE. Additional exam requirements/recommendations for international students: required—TOEFL (minimum score 100 iBT). Electronic applications accepted.

**University of Minnesota, Twin Cities Campus,** Graduate School, College of Food, Agricultural and Natural Resource Sciences, Program in Nutrition, St. Paul, MN 55455-0213. Offers MS, PhD. *Program availability:* Part-time. Terminal master's awarded for partial completion of doctoral program. *Degree requirements:* For master's, comprehensive exam, thesis; for doctorate, comprehensive exam, thesis/dissertation. *Entrance requirements:* For master's, GRE General Test, previous course work in general chemistry, organic chemistry, physiology, biology, biochemistry, and statistics; minimum GPA of 3.0 (preferred); for doctorate, GRE General Test, previous course work in general chemistry, organic chemistry, biology, physiology, biochemistry, and statistics; minimum GPA of 3.0 (preferred). Additional exam requirements/recommendations for international students: required—TOEFL (minimum score 550 paper-based; 79 iBT), IELTS (minimum score 6.5). Electronic applications accepted. *Expenses:* Contact institution.

**University of Minnesota, Twin Cities Campus,** School of Public Health, Major in Public Health Nutrition, Minneapolis, MN 55455-0213. Offers MPH. *Program availability:* Part-time. *Degree requirements:* For master's, fieldwork, project. *Entrance requirements:* For master's, GRE General Test. Additional exam requirements/recommendations for international students: required—TOEFL. Electronic applications accepted. *Expenses:* Contact institution.

**University of Mississippi,** Graduate School, School of Applied Sciences, University, MS 38677. Offers communicative disorders (MS); criminal justice (MCJ); exercise science (MS); food and nutrition services (MS); health and kinesiology (PhD); health promotion (MS); nutrition and hospitality management (PhD); park and recreation management (MA); social welfare (PhD); social work (MSW). *Students:* 188 full-time (149 women), 37 part-time (18 women); includes 47 minority (35 Black or African American, non-Hispanic/Latino; 2 American Indian or Alaska Native, non-Hispanic/Latino; 1 Asian, non-Hispanic/Latino; 5 Hispanic/Latino; 1 Native Hawaiian or other Pacific Islander, non-Hispanic/Latino; 3 Two or more races, non-Hispanic/Latino), 23 international. Average age 26. *Expenses:* Tuition, state resident: full-time $8718; part-time $484.25 per credit hour. Tuition, nonresident: full-time $24,990; part-time $1388.25 per credit hour. *Required fees:* $100; $4.16 per credit hour. *Unit head:* Dr. Peter Grandjean, Dean of Applied Sciences, 662-915-7900, Fax: 662-915-7901, E-mail: applsci@olemiss.edu. *Application contact:* Temeka Smith, Graduate Activities Specialist for Admissions, 662-915-7474, Fax: 662-915-7577, E-mail: gschool@olemiss.edu.
Website: applsci@olemiss.edu

**University of Missouri,** Office of Research and Graduate Studies, College of Human Environmental Sciences, Department of Nutrition and Exercise Physiology, Columbia, MO 65211. Offers exercise physiology (MS, PhD); nutritional sciences (MS, PhD). *Entrance requirements:* For master's and doctorate, GRE General Test, minimum GPA of 3.0. Additional exam requirements/recommendations for international students: required—TOEFL.

**University of Nebraska–Lincoln,** Graduate College, College of Agricultural Sciences and Natural Resources, Interdepartmental Area of Nutrition, Lincoln, NE 68588. Offers MS, PhD. *Degree requirements:* For master's, thesis optional; for doctorate, comprehensive exam, thesis/dissertation. *Entrance requirements:* For master's and doctorate, GRE General Test. Additional exam requirements/recommendations for international students: required—TOEFL (minimum score 550 paper-based). Electronic applications accepted.

**University of Nebraska–Lincoln,** Graduate College, College of Education and Human Sciences, Department of Nutrition and Health Sciences, Lincoln, NE 68588. Offers community nutrition and health promotion (MS); nutrition (MS, PhD); nutrition and exercise (MS); nutrition and health sciences (MS, PhD). *Degree requirements:* For master's, thesis optional. *Entrance requirements:* For master's, GRE General Test. Additional exam requirements/recommendations for international students: required—TOEFL (minimum score 550 paper-based). Electronic applications accepted.

**University of Nebraska Medical Center,** College of Allied Health Professions, Program in Medical Nutrition, Omaha, NE 68198. Offers Certificate. *Entrance requirements:* Additional exam requirements/recommendations for international students: required—TOEFL.

**University of Nevada, Las Vegas,** Graduate College, School of Integrated Health Sciences, Department of Kinesiology and Nutrition Sciences, Las Vegas, NV 89154-3034. Offers exercise kinesiology (MS); kinesiology (PhD); nutrition sciences (MS). *Program availability:* Part-time. *Faculty:* 13 full-time (7 women), 1 part-time/adjunct (0 women). *Students:* 28 full-time (22 women), 10 part-time (4 women); includes 13 minority (2 Black or African American, non-Hispanic/Latino; 2 Asian, non-Hispanic/Latino; 7 Hispanic/Latino; 1 Native Hawaiian or other Pacific Islander, non-Hispanic/Latino; 1 Two or more races, non-Hispanic/Latino), 2 international. Average age 28. 44 applicants, 48% accepted, 16 enrolled. In 2019, 17 master's, 2 doctorates awarded. *Degree requirements:* For master's, thesis (for some programs), professional paper; for doctorate, comprehensive exam, thesis/dissertation. *Entrance requirements:* For master's, GRE General Test, bachelor's degree; statement of purpose; 2 letters of recommendation; for doctorate, GRE General Test (minimum 70th percentile on the Verbal section), master's degree/bachelor's degree with minimum GPA of 3.25; 3 letters of recommendation; statement of purpose; personal interview. Additional exam requirements/recommendations for international students: required—TOEFL (minimum score 550 paper-based; 80 iBT), IELTS (minimum score 7). Application fee: $60 ($95 for international students). Electronic applications accepted. *Expenses:* Contact institution. *Financial support:* In 2019–20, 24 students received support, including 9 research assistantships with full tuition reimbursements available (averaging $12,222 per year), 15 teaching assistantships with full tuition reimbursements available (averaging $12,267 per year); institutionally sponsored loans, scholarships/grants, health care benefits, and unspecified assistantships also available. Financial award application deadline: 3/15; financial award applicants required to submit FAFSA. *Unit head:* Dr. John Mercer, Professor/Acting Chair, 702-895-4672, Fax: 702-895-1356, E-mail: kns.chair@unlv.edu. *Application contact:* Dr. James Navalta, Graduate Coordinator, 702-895-2344, E-mail: kinesiology.gradcoord@unlv.edu.

**University of Nevada, Reno,** Graduate School, College of Agriculture, Biotechnology and Natural Resources, Program in Nutrition, Reno, NV 89557. Offers MS. *Degree requirements:* For master's, thesis optional. *Entrance requirements:* For master's, GRE, minimum GPA of 2.75. Additional exam requirements/recommendations for international students: required—TOEFL (minimum score 500 paper-based; 61 iBT), IELTS (minimum score 6). Electronic applications accepted.

**University of New England,** College of Graduate and Professional Studies, Portland, ME 04005-9526. Offers advanced educational leadership (CAGS); applied nutrition (MS); career and technical education (MS Ed); curriculum and instruction (MS Ed); education (CAGS, Post-Master's Certificate); educational leadership (MS Ed, Ed D); generalist (MS Ed); health informatics (MS, Graduate Certificate); inclusion education (MS Ed); literacy K-12 (MS Ed); medical education leadership (MMEL); public health (MPH, Graduate Certificate); reading specialist (MS Ed); social work (MSW). *Program availability:* Part-time, evening/weekend, online only, 100% online. *Faculty:* 2 full-time (1 woman), 63 part-time/adjunct (44 women). *Students:* 1,001 full-time (795 women), 470 part-time (378 women); includes 306 minority (211 Black or African American, non-Hispanic/Latino; 12 American Indian or Alaska Native, non-Hispanic/Latino; 61 Asian, non-Hispanic/Latino; 14 Hispanic/Latino; 4 Native Hawaiian or other Pacific Islander, non-Hispanic/Latino; 4 Two or more races, non-Hispanic/Latino). Average age 36. In 2019, 614 master's, 85 doctorates, 79 other advanced degrees awarded. *Application deadline:* Applications are processed on a rolling basis. Electronic applications accepted. *Financial support:* Application deadline: 5/1; applicants required to submit FAFSA. *Unit head:* Dr. Martha Wilson, Dean of the College of Graduate and Professional Studies, 207-221-4985, E-mail: mwilson13@une.edu. *Application contact:* Nicole Lindsay, Director of Online Admissions, 207-221-4966, E-mail: nlindsay1@une.edu.
Website: http://online.une.edu

**University of New Hampshire,** Graduate School, College of Life Sciences and Agriculture, Department of Molecular, Cellular and Biomedical Sciences, Program in Nutritional Science, Durham, NH 03824. Offers agricultural sciences (MS, PhD); nutritional sciences (MS, PhD). *Program availability:* Part-time. *Students:* Average age 28. 19 applicants, 42% accepted, 7 enrolled. In 2019, 1 master's, 3 doctorates awarded. *Entrance requirements:* For master's and doctorate, GRE. Additional exam requirements/recommendations for international students: required—TOEFL (minimum score 550 paper-based; 80 iBT). *Application deadline:* For fall admission, 3/15 for domestic and international students; for spring admission, 12/1 for domestic students. Application fee: $65. Electronic applications accepted. *Financial support:* In 2019–20, 13 students received support. Fellowships, research assistantships, teaching assistantships, scholarships/grants, traineeships, and unspecified assistantships available. Support available to part-time students. Financial award application deadline: 2/15. *Unit head:* Joanne Curran-Celentana, Chair, 603-862-2573. *Application contact:* Jen Surina, Administrative Assistant, 603-862-0822, E-mail: ansc.grad.program.info@unh.edu.

**University of New Mexico,** Graduate Studies, College of Education and Human Sciences, Program in Nutrition, Albuquerque, NM 87131-2039. Offers MS. *Program availability:* Part-time. *Entrance requirements:* For master's, GRE. Additional exam requirements/recommendations for international students: required—TOEFL. Electronic applications accepted. *Expenses:* Tuition, state resident: full-time $7633; part-time $972 per year. Tuition, nonresident: full-time $22,586; part-time $3840 per year. *International tuition:* $23,292 full-time. *Required fees:* $8608. Tuition and fees vary according to course level, course load, degree level, program and student level.

**The University of North Carolina at Chapel Hill,** Graduate School, Gillings School of Global Public Health, Department of Nutrition, Chapel Hill, NC 27599. Offers nutrition (MPH, PhD); nutrition/registered dietitian (MPH); nutritional biochemistry (MS). *Accreditation:* AND. *Program availability:* Part-time, evening/weekend, 100% online. *Faculty:* 42 full-time (28 women), 20 part-time/adjunct (18 women). *Students:* 96 full-time (82 women), 1 (woman) part-time; includes 24 minority (8 Black or African American, non-Hispanic/Latino; 4 Asian, non-Hispanic/Latino; 8 Hispanic/Latino; 4 Two or more races, non-Hispanic/Latino), 8 international. Average age 28. 51 applicants, 33% accepted, 13 enrolled. In 2019, 27 master's, 6 doctorates awarded. *Degree requirements:* For master's, comprehensive exam, thesis, major paper, 10 weeks of advanced nutrition field work; for doctorate, comprehensive exam, thesis/dissertation. *Entrance requirements:* For master's, GRE General Test, MCAT, or DAT, three letters of recommendation (academic and/or professional; academic preferred); coursework in biochemistry, anatomy and physiology, organic chemistry, microbiology with lab, psychology, sociology or anthropology, and human nutrition; for doctorate, GRE General Test, MCAT, or DAT, three letters of recommendation (academic and/or professional; academic preferred); coursework in biochemistry, anatomy and physiology, organic chemistry, and human nutrition. Additional exam requirements/recommendations for international students: required—TOEFL (minimum score 90 iBT), IELTS (minimum score 7). *Application deadline:* For fall admission, 1/8 for domestic and international students. Application fee: $90. Electronic applications accepted. *Financial support:* Fellowships with tuition reimbursements, research assistantships with tuition reimbursements, teaching assistantships with tuition reimbursements, career-related internships or fieldwork, Federal Work-Study, institutionally sponsored loans, scholarships/grants, traineeships, health care benefits, and unspecified assistantships available. Financial award application deadline: 12/10; financial award applicants required to submit FAFSA. *Unit head:* Dr. Elizabeth Mayer-Davis, Chair, 919-966-7218, Fax: 919-966-7215, E-mail: mayerdav@email.unc.edu. *Application contact:* Jonathan Earnest, Student Services Manager, 919-966-7212, E-mail: earnestj@email.unc.edu.
Website: https://sph.unc.edu/nutr/unc-nutrition/

**The University of North Carolina at Greensboro,** Graduate School, School of Health and Human Sciences, Department of Nutrition, Greensboro, NC 27412-5001. Offers MS, PhD. *Degree requirements:* For master's, thesis; for doctorate, thesis/dissertation. *Entrance requirements:* For master's and doctorate, GRE General Test. Additional exam requirements/recommendations for international students: required—TOEFL. Electronic applications accepted.

**University of North Florida,** Brooks College of Health, Department of Nutrition and Dietetics, Jacksonville, FL 32224. Offers MSH. *Program availability:* Part-time. *Entrance requirements:* For master's, GRE General Test, minimum GPA of 3.0 in last 60 hours. Additional exam requirements/recommendations for international students: required—TOEFL (minimum score 500 paper-based; 61 iBT). Electronic applications accepted.

**University of Oklahoma Health Sciences Center,** Graduate College, College of Allied Health, Department of Nutritional Sciences, Oklahoma City, OK 73190. Offers MS. *Degree requirements:* For master's, comprehensive exam, thesis optional. *Entrance requirements:* For master's, GRE General Test, interview, 3 letters of reference. Additional exam requirements/recommendations for international students: required—TOEFL (minimum score 550 paper-based).

**University of Pittsburgh,** School of Health and Rehabilitation Sciences, Department of Sports Medicine and Nutrition, Pittsburgh, PA 15260. Offers health and rehabilitation sciences (MS), including sports medicine, wellness and human performance; nutrition and dietetics (MS). *Faculty:* 15 full-time (8 women), 3 part-time/adjunct (all women). *Students:* 58 full-time (46 women), 1 part-time (0 women); includes 7 minority (1 Black or African American, non-Hispanic/Latino; 3 Asian, non-Hispanic/Latino; 2 Hispanic/Latino; 1 Two or more races, non-Hispanic/Latino), 1 international. Average age 24. 122 applicants, 70% accepted, 32 enrolled. In 2019, 28 master's awarded. *Degree requirements:* For master's, comprehensive exam (for some programs). *Entrance requirements:* For master's, Varies by program. Additional exam requirements/recommendations for international students: required—International applicants may provide Duolingo English Test, IELTS or TOEFL scores to verify English language proficiency. Application fee: $50. Electronic applications accepted. *Financial support:* In 2019–20, 13 students received support, including 7 research assistantships with full tuition reimbursements available (averaging $28,200 per year); traineeships also available. *Unit head:* Dr. Kevin Conley, Associate Dean for Undergraduate Studies, SHRS, Chair and Associate Professor, Department of Sports Medicine and Nutrition, 412-383-6737, Fax: 412-383-6636, E-mail: kconley@pitt.edu. *Application contact:* Jessica Maguire, Director of Admissions, 412-383-6557, Fax: 412-383-6535, E-mail: maguire@pitt.edu.
Website: http://www.shrs.pitt.edu/smn

**University of Puerto Rico at Rio Piedras,** College of Education, Program in Family Ecology and Nutrition, San Juan, PR 00931-3300. Offers M Ed. *Program availability:* Part-time. *Degree requirements:* For master's, thesis. *Entrance requirements:* For master's, PAEG or GRE, minimum GPA of 3.0, letter of recommendation.

**University of Puerto Rico - Medical Sciences Campus,** Graduate School of Public Health, Department of Human Development, Program in Nutrition, San Juan, PR 00936-5067. Offers MS. *Program availability:* Part-time. *Degree requirements:* For master's, thesis. *Entrance requirements:* For master's, GRE, previous course work in algebra, biochemistry, biology, chemistry, and social sciences.

**University of Puerto Rico - Medical Sciences Campus,** School of Health Professions, Program in Dietetics Internship, San Juan, PR 00936-5067. Offers Certificate. *Degree requirements:* For Certificate, one foreign language, clinical practice. *Entrance requirements:* For degree, minimum GPA of 2.5, interview, participation in the computer matching process by the American Dietetic Association.

**University of Puerto Rico - Medical Sciences Campus,** School of Medicine, Biomedical Sciences Graduate Program, Department of Biochemistry, San Juan, PR 00936-5067. Offers MS, PhD. *Degree requirements:* For master's, thesis; for doctorate, comprehensive exam, thesis/dissertation. *Entrance requirements:* For master's and doctorate, GRE General Test, GRE Subject Test, interview, minimum GPA of 3.0. Electronic applications accepted.

**University of Rhode Island,** Graduate School, College of Health Sciences, Department of Nutrition and Food Sciences, Kingston, RI 02881. Offers dietetic internship (MS); nutrition (MS); online dietetics (MS). *Program availability:* Part-time, 100% online. *Faculty:* 11 full-time (10 women), 1 (woman) part-time/adjunct. *Students:* 48 full-time (all women), 42 part-time (39 women); includes 7 minority (6 Asian, non-Hispanic/Latino; 1 Hispanic/Latino), 2 international. 20 applicants, 70% accepted, 7 enrolled. In 2019, 41 master's awarded. *Entrance requirements:* Additional exam requirements/recommendations for international students: required—TOEFL. *Application deadline:* For fall admission, 2/15 for domestic students, 2/1 for international students. Application fee: $65. Electronic applications accepted. *Expenses: Tuition, area resident:* Full-time $13,734; part-time $763 per credit. Tuition, state resident: full-time $13,734; part-time $763 per credit. Tuition, nonresident: full-time $26,512; part-time $1473 per credit. *International tuition:* $26,512 full-time. *Required fees:* $1780; $52 per credit. $35 per term. One-time fee: $165. *Financial support:* In 2019–20, 4 research assistantships with tuition reimbursements (averaging $7,953 per year), 7 teaching assistantships (averaging $16,859 per year) were awarded. Financial award application deadline: 2/1; financial award applicants required to submit FAFSA. *Unit head:* Dr. Cathy English, Chair, 401-874-5689, Fax: 401-874-5974, E-mail: cathy@uri.edu. *Application contact:* Dr. Ingrid Lofgren, Graduate Coordinator, 401-874-5706, E-mail: ingridlofgren@uri.edu.
Website: http://web.uri.edu/nfs/

**University of Saint Joseph,** Department of Nutrition and Public Health, West Hartford, CT 06117-2700. Offers nutrition (MS); public health (MPH). *Program availability:* Part-time, evening/weekend, online learning. *Entrance requirements:* For master's, 2 letters of recommendation, letter of intent. Electronic applications accepted. Application fee is waived when completed online.

**University of Saskatchewan,** College of Graduate and Postdoctoral Studies, College of Pharmacy and Nutrition, Saskatoon, SK S7N 5A2, Canada. Offers nutrition (M Sc, PhD); pharmacy (M Sc, PhD). *Degree requirements:* For master's, thesis; for doctorate, thesis/dissertation. *Entrance requirements:* Additional exam requirements/recommendations for international students: required—TOEFL.

**University of South Florida,** Innovative Education, Tampa, FL 33620-9951. Offers adult, career and higher education (Graduate Certificate), including college teaching, leadership in developing human resources, leadership in higher education; Africana studies (Graduate Certificate), including diasporas and health disparities, genocide and human rights; aging studies (Graduate Certificate), including gerontology; art research (Graduate Certificate), including museum studies; business foundations (Graduate Certificate); chemical and biomedical engineering (Graduate Certificate), including materials science and engineering, water, health and sustainability; child and family studies (Graduate Certificate), including positive behavior support; civil and industrial engineering (Graduate Certificate), including transportation systems analysis; community and family health (Graduate Certificate), including maternal and child health, social marketing and public health, violence and injury: prevention and intervention, women's health; criminology (Graduate Certificate), including criminal justice administration; data science for public administration (Graduate Certificate); digital humanities (Graduate Certificate); educational measurement and research (Graduate Certificate), including evaluation; English (Graduate Certificate), including comparative literary studies, creative writing, professional and technical communication; entrepreneurship (Graduate Certificate); environmental health (Graduate Certificate), including safety management; epidemiology and biostatistics (Graduate Certificate), including applied biostatistics, biostatistics, concepts and tools of epidemiology, epidemiology, epidemiology of infectious diseases; geography, environment and planning (Graduate Certificate), including community development, environmental policy and management, geographical information systems; geology (Graduate Certificate), including hydrogeology; global health (Graduate Certificate), including disaster management, global health and Latin American and Caribbean studies, global health practice, humanitarian assistance, infection control; government and international affairs (Graduate Certificate), including Cuban studies, globalization studies; health policy and management (Graduate Certificate), including health management and leadership, public health policy and programs; hearing specialist: early intervention (Graduate Certificate); industrial and management systems engineering (Graduate Certificate), including systems engineering, technology management; information studies (Graduate Certificate), including school library media specialist; information systems/decision sciences (Graduate Certificate), including analytics and business intelligence; instructional technology (Graduate Certificate), including distance education, Florida digital/virtual educator, instructional design, multimedia design, Web design; internal medicine, bioethics and medical humanities (Graduate Certificate), including biomedical ethics; Latin American and Caribbean studies (Graduate Certificate); leadership for coastal resiliency planning (Graduate Certificate); mass communications (Graduate Certificate), including multimedia journalism; mathematics and statistics (Graduate Certificate), including mathematics; medicine (Graduate Certificate), including aging and neuroscience, bioinformatics, biotechnology, brain fitness and memory management, clinical investigation, hand and upper limb rehabilitation, health informatics, health sciences, integrative weight management, intellectual property, medicine and gender, metabolic and nutritional medicine, metabolic cardiology, pharmacy sciences; national and competitive intelligence (Graduate Certificate); nursing (Graduate Certificate), including simulation based academic fellowship in advanced pain management; psychological and social foundations (Graduate Certificate), including career counseling, college teaching, diversity in education, mental health counseling, school counseling; public affairs (Graduate Certificate), including nonprofit management, public management, research administration; public health (Graduate Certificate), including assessing chemical toxicity and public health risks, health equity, pharmacoepidemiology, public health generalist, toxicology, translational research in adolescent behavioral health; public health practices (Graduate Certificate), including planning for healthy communities; rehabilitation and mental health counseling (Graduate Certificate), including integrative mental health care, marriage and family therapy, rehabilitation technology; secondary education (Graduate Certificate), including ESOL, foreign language education: culture and content, foreign language education: professional; social work (Graduate Certificate), including geriatric social work/clinical gerontology; special education (Graduate Certificate), including autism spectrum disorder, disabilities education: severe/profound; world languages (Graduate Certificate), including teaching English as a second language (TESL) or foreign language. *Unit head:* Dr. Cynthia DeLuca, Associate Vice President and Assistant Vice Provost, 813-974-3077, Fax: 813-974-7061, E-mail: deluca@usf.edu. *Application contact:* Owen Hooper, Director, Summer and Alternative Calendar Programs, 813-974-6917, E-mail: hooper@usf.edu.
Website: http://www.usf.edu/innovative-education/

**The University of Tampa,** Program in Exercise and Nutrition Science, Tampa, FL 33606-1490. Offers MS. *Program availability:* Part-time, evening/weekend. *Degree requirements:* For master's, comprehensive exam, practicum. *Entrance requirements:* For master's, GMAT or GRE, official transcripts from all colleges and/or universities previously attended, resume, personal statement, letters of recommendation, bachelor's degree in related field. Additional exam requirements/recommendations for international students: required—TOEFL (minimum score 577 paper-based; 90 iBT), IELTS (minimum score 7.5). Electronic applications accepted. *Expenses:* Contact institution.

**The University of Tennessee,** Graduate School, College of Education, Health and Human Sciences, Department of Nutrition, Knoxville, TN 37996. Offers nutrition (MS), including nutrition science, public health nutrition; MS/MPH. *Program availability:* Part-time. *Degree requirements:* For master's, thesis or alternative. *Entrance requirements:* For master's, GRE General Test, minimum GPA of 2.7. Additional exam requirements/recommendations for international students: required—TOEFL. Electronic applications accepted.

**The University of Tennessee at Martin,** Graduate Programs, College of Agriculture and Applied Sciences, Department of Family and Consumer Sciences, Martin, TN 38238. Offers dietetics (MSFCS); general family and consumer sciences (MSFCS). *Program availability:* Part-time, 100% online. *Faculty:* 7. *Students:* 1 full-time (0 women), 29 part-time (27 women); includes 3 minority (2 Black or African American, non-Hispanic/Latino; 1 Hispanic/Latino). Average age 29. 47 applicants, 70% accepted, 12 enrolled. In 2019, 12 master's awarded. *Degree requirements:* For master's, comprehensive exam, thesis optional. *Entrance requirements:* For master's, GRE General Test, minimum GPA of 2.5. Additional exam requirements/recommendations for international students: required—TOEFL (minimum score 525 paper-based; 71 iBT). *Application deadline:* For fall admission, 7/28 priority date for domestic and international students; for spring admission, 12/17 priority date for domestic and international students; for summer admission, 5/10 priority date for domestic and international students. Applications are processed on a rolling basis. Application fee: $30 ($130 for international students). Electronic applications accepted. *Expenses: Tuition, area resident:* Full-time $9096; part-time $505 per credit hour. Tuition, state resident: full-time $9096; part-time $505 per credit hour. Tuition, nonresident: full-time $15,136; part-time $841 per credit hour. *International tuition:* $23,040 full-time. *Required fees:* $1520; $85 per credit hour. Part-time tuition and fees vary according to course load. *Financial support:* In 2019–20, 10 students received support, including 2 teaching assistantships with full tuition reimbursements available (averaging $6,912 per year); research assistantships with full tuition reimbursements available, scholarships/grants, and tuition waivers (full and partial) also available. Financial award application deadline: 2/1; financial award applicants required to submit FAFSA. *Unit head:* Dr. Lisa LeBleu, Coordinator, 731-881-7116, Fax: 731-881-7106, E-mail: llebleu@utm.edu. *Application contact:* Jolene L. Cunningham, Student Services Specialist, 731-881-7012, Fax: 731-881-7499, E-mail: jcunningham@utm.edu.
Website: http://www.utm.edu/departments/caas/fcs/index.php

**The University of Texas at Austin,** Graduate School, College of Natural Sciences, School of Human Ecology, Program in Nutritional Sciences, Austin, TX 78712-1111. Offers nutrition (MA); nutritional sciences (MS, PhD). *Program availability:* Online learning. *Degree requirements:* For master's, thesis; for doctorate, thesis/dissertation. *Entrance requirements:* For master's and doctorate, GRE General Test. Additional exam requirements/recommendations for international students: required—TOEFL. Electronic applications accepted.

**The University of Texas Rio Grande Valley,** College of Health Affairs, Department of Health and Biomedical Sciences, Edinburg, TX 78539. Offers clinical laboratory sciences (MSHS); health care administration (MSHS); nutrition (MSHS). *Program availability:* Part-time, online only, 100% online. *Faculty:* 4 full-time (all women), 2 part-time/adjunct (both women). *Students:* 148 part-time (92 women); includes 120 minority (10 Black or African American, non-Hispanic/Latino; 5 American Indian or Alaska Native, non-Hispanic/Latino; 105 Hispanic/Latino), 3 international. Average age 34. 70 applicants, 77% accepted, 39 enrolled. In 2019, 110 master's awarded. *Entrance requirements:* For master's, Not required, 2 letters of recommendation and a letter of intent, UG degree in a health related profession. CLS - BS in CLS and ASCP MLS Certification; NUTR - 3 hrs. UG & A&P with a "C" or higher; Healthcare Informatics - UG degree in health field and experience with EMR highly recommended. Additional exam requirements/recommendations for international students: required—as required by grad. college; program does not require entrance exams. *Application deadline:* For fall admission, 7/23 for domestic and international students; for spring admission, 12/1 for domestic and international students. Applications are processed on a rolling basis. Application fee: $50 ($100 for international students). Electronic applications accepted. *Expenses:* 444.44 per semester credit hour. *Financial support:* Research assistantships and scholarships/grants available. Financial award application deadline: 7/23; financial award applicants required to submit FAFSA. *Unit head:* Dr. Saraswathy Nair, Associate Professor and Chair, 956-882-5108, Fax: 956-882-6835, E-mail: saraswathy.nair@utrgv.edu. *Application contact:* Kim Garcia, Lecturer III/Associate Chair, Health and Biomedical Sciences, 956-665-4781, E-mail: kim.garcia@utrgv.edu.
Website: http://www.utrgv.edu/hbs/

**The University of Texas Southwestern Medical Center,** Southwestern School of Health Professions, Clinical Nutrition Program, Dallas, TX 75390. Offers MCN.

**University of the District of Columbia,** College of Agriculture, Urban Sustainability and Environmental Sciences, Program in Nutrition and Dietetics, Washington, DC 20008-1175. Offers MS. *Degree requirements:* For master's, thesis. *Entrance requirements:* For master's, GRE, 3 letters of recommendation, personal interview.

**University of the Incarnate Word,** School of Mathematics, Science, and Engineering, San Antonio, TX 78209-6397. Offers applied statistics (MS); biology (MA, MS); mathematics (MA), including teaching; multidisciplinary sciences (MA); nutrition (MS). *Program availability:* Part-time, evening/weekend. *Faculty:* 2 full-time (1 woman), 1 part-time/adjunct (0 women). *Students:* 19 full-time (17 women), 5 part-time (3 women); includes 14 minority (1 Black or African American, non-Hispanic/Latino; 13 Hispanic/Latino), 3 international. 15 applicants, 87% accepted, 5 enrolled. In 2019, 18 master's awarded. *Degree requirements:* For master's, comprehensive exam (for some programs), thesis optional, capstone. *Entrance requirements:* For master's, GRE,

recommendation letter. Additional exam requirements/recommendations for international students: required—TOEFL (minimum score 560 paper-based; 83 iBT). *Application deadline:* Applications are processed on a rolling basis. Application fee: $20. Electronic applications accepted. *Expenses: Tuition:* Full-time $11,520; part-time $960 per credit hour. *Required fees:* $1128; $94 per credit hour. Tuition and fees vary according to degree level, campus/location, program and student level. *Financial support:* Research assistantships, Federal Work-Study, scholarships/grants, tuition waivers (partial), and unspecified assistantships available. Financial award applicants required to submit FAFSA. *Unit head:* Dr. Carlos A. Garcia, Dean, 210-829-2717, Fax: 210-829-3153, E-mail: cagarci9@uiwtx.edu. *Application contact:* Jessica Delarosa, Director of Admissions, 210-8296005, Fax: 210-829-3921, E-mail: admis@uiwtx.edu. Website: https://www.uiw.edu/smse/index.html

**The University of Toledo,** College of Graduate Studies, College of Medicine and Life Sciences, Department of Public Health and Preventative Medicine, Toledo, OH 43606-3390. Offers biostatistics and epidemiology (Certificate); contemporary gerontological practice (Certificate); environmental and occupational health and safety (MPH); epidemiology (Certificate); global public health (Certificate); health promotion and education (MPH); industrial hygiene (MSOH); medical and health science teaching and learning (Certificate); occupational health (Certificate); public health administration (MPH); public health and emergency response (Certificate); public health epidemiology (MPH); public health nutrition (MPH); MD/MPH. *Program availability:* Part-time, evening/weekend. *Degree requirements:* For master's, thesis or alternative. *Entrance requirements:* For master's, GRE, minimum undergraduate GPA of 3.0, three letters of recommendation, statement of purpose, transcripts from all prior institutions attended, resume; for Certificate, minimum undergraduate GPA of 3.0, three letters of recommendation, statement of purpose, transcripts from all prior institutions attended, resume. Additional exam requirements/recommendations for international students: required—TOEFL (minimum score 550 paper-based; 80 iBT), IELTS (minimum score 6.5). Electronic applications accepted.

**University of Toronto,** Faculty of Medicine, Department of Nutritional Sciences, Toronto, ON M5S 1A1, Canada. Offers M Sc, PhD. *Program availability:* Part-time. *Degree requirements:* For master's, thesis, oral thesis defense; for doctorate, comprehensive exam, thesis/dissertation, departmental examination, oral examination. *Entrance requirements:* For master's, minimum B average, background in nutrition or an area of biological or health sciences, 2 letters of reference; for doctorate, minimum B+ average in final 2 years, background in nutrition or an area of biological or health sciences, 2 letters of reference. Additional exam requirements/recommendations for international students: required—TOEFL (minimum score 580 paper-based), TWE (minimum score 5), IELTS (minimum score 7), Michigan English Language Assessment Battery (minimum score 85), or COPE (minimum score 4). Electronic applications accepted.

**University of Toronto,** School of Graduate Studies, Department of Public Health Sciences, Toronto, ON M5S 1A1, Canada. Offers biostatistics (M Sc, PhD); community health (M Sc); community nutrition (MPH), including nutrition and dietetics; epidemiology (MPH, PhD); family and community medicine (MPH); occupational and environmental health (MPH); social and behavioral health science (PhD); social and behavioral health sciences (MPH), including health promotion. *Accreditation:* CAHME (one or more programs are accredited). *Program availability:* Part-time. *Degree requirements:* For master's, thesis (for some programs), practicum; for doctorate, comprehensive exam, thesis/dissertation, oral thesis defense. *Entrance requirements:* For master's, 2 letters of reference, relevant professional/research experience, minimum B average in final year; for doctorate, 2 letters of reference, relevant professional/research experience, minimum B+ average. Additional exam requirements/recommendations for international students: required—TOEFL (minimum score 580 paper-based; 93 iBT), TWE (minimum score 5). Electronic applications accepted. *Expenses:* Contact institution.

**University of Utah,** Graduate School, College of Health, Department of Nutrition and Integrative Physiology, Salt Lake City, UT 84112. Offers nutrition and integrative physiology (MS, PhD), including integrative physiology, nutrition, nutrition and dietetics (MS). *Program availability:* Part-time, evening/weekend, 100% online. *Faculty:* 35 full-time (24 women), 33 part-time/adjunct (17 women). *Students:* 69 full-time (49 women), 5 part-time (all women); includes 7 minority (2 Asian, non-Hispanic/Latino; 2 Hispanic/Latino; 3 Two or more races, non-Hispanic/Latino), 7 international. 77 applicants, 35% accepted, 24 enrolled. In 2019, 22 master's awarded. Terminal master's awarded for partial completion of doctoral program. *Degree requirements:* For master's, comprehensive exam, thesis (for some programs); for doctorate, comprehensive exam, thesis/dissertation. *Entrance requirements:* Additional exam requirements/recommendations for international students: required—TOEFL (minimum score 80 paper-based; 550 iBT). *Application deadline:* For fall admission, 2/15 priority date for domestic students, 1/1 priority date for international students. Applications are processed on a rolling basis. Application fee: $50. Electronic applications accepted. *Expenses:* MS Dietetics: $9924 per semester resident (for 15 credits), $22,479 per semester non-resident (for 15 credits); all other MS and PhD: $5581 resident (for 15 credits), $18,146 non-resident and international (for 15 credits). *Financial support:* In 2019–20, 53 students received support, including 5 fellowships with full and partial tuition reimbursements available (averaging $25,310 per year), 19 research assistantships with full and partial tuition reimbursements available (averaging $24,750 per year), 21 teaching assistantships with full and partial tuition reimbursements available (averaging $9,871 per year); scholarships/grants and unspecified assistantships also available. Financial award application deadline: 2/15. *Unit head:* Dr. Scott Summers, Professor and Chair Department of Nutrition and Integrative Physiology, 801-581-8537, Fax: 801-585-3874, E-mail: scott.a.summers@health.utah.edu. *Application contact:* Dr. Thunder Jalili, Director of Undergraduate and Graduate Studies, 801-581-0399, Fax: 801-585-3874, E-mail: thunder.jalili@utah.edu. Website: http://www.health.utah.edu/fdnu/

**University of Vermont,** Graduate College, College of Agriculture and Life Sciences, Program in Dietetics, Burlington, VT 05405-0086. Offers dietetics (MS), including community health and nutrition. *Entrance requirements:* For master's, GRE General Test. Additional exam requirements/recommendations for international students: required—TOEFL (minimum score 550 paper-based, 90 iBT) or IELTS (6.5). Electronic applications accepted.

**University of Vermont,** Graduate College, College of Agriculture and Life Sciences, Program in Nutrition and Food Sciences, Burlington, VT 05405-0086. Offers nutrition and food sciences (MS). *Accreditation:* AND. *Degree requirements:* For master's, thesis. *Entrance requirements:* For master's, GRE General Test. Additional exam requirements/recommendations for international students: required—TOEFL (minimum score 550 paper-based, 90 iBT) or IELTS (6.5). Electronic applications accepted.

**University of Washington,** Graduate School, School of Public Health, Nutritional Sciences Program, Seattle, WA 98195. Offers nutritional sciences (PhD); nutritional sciences, dietetics practice (MS); public health nutrition, public health nutrition practice (MPH). *Program availability:* Part-time. *Students:* 34 full-time (32 women), 3 part-time (2 women); includes 8 minority (1 American Indian or Alaska Native, non-Hispanic/Latino; 4 Asian, non-Hispanic/Latino; 3 Hispanic/Latino), 3 international. Average age 29. 141

applicants, 25% accepted, 20 enrolled. In 2019, 11 master's awarded. Terminal master's awarded for partial completion of doctoral program. *Degree requirements:* For master's, thesis (for some programs); for doctorate, thesis/dissertation. *Entrance requirements:* For master's and doctorate, GRE. Additional exam requirements/recommendations for international students: required—TOEFL (minimum score 580 paper-based; 92 iBT). *Application deadline:* For fall admission, 12/1 for domestic and international students. Application fee: $85. Electronic applications accepted. *Financial support:* Fellowships, research assistantships, teaching assistantships, and scholarships/grants available. *Unit head:* Dr. Adam Drewnowski, Director. *Application contact:* Susan Inman, Manager of Student and Academic Services, 206-543-1730, E-mail: nutr@uw.edu. Website: http://nutr.uw.edu/

**University of Wisconsin–Madison,** Graduate School, College of Agricultural and Life Sciences, Department of Nutritional Sciences, Madison, WI 53706. Offers MS, PhD. Terminal master's awarded for partial completion of doctoral program. *Degree requirements:* For master's, thesis or research report; for doctorate, comprehensive exam, thesis/dissertation. *Entrance requirements:* For master's and doctorate, GRE General Test. Additional exam requirements/recommendations for international students: required—TOEFL (minimum score 550 paper-based; 80 iBT). Electronic applications accepted.

**University of Wisconsin–Milwaukee,** Graduate School, College of Health Sciences, Department of Kinesiology, Milwaukee, WI 53201-0413. Offers athletic training (MS); kinesiology (MS, PhD), including exercise and nutrition in health and disease (MS), integrative human performance (MS); neuromechanics (MS); physical therapy (DPT). *Program availability:* Part-time. *Degree requirements:* For master's, comprehensive exam, thesis optional. *Entrance requirements:* For master's, GRE General Test. Additional exam requirements/recommendations for international students: required—TOEFL (minimum score 550 paper-based; 79 iBT), IELTS (minimum score 6.5).

**University of Wisconsin–Stevens Point,** College of Professional Studies, School of Health Promotion and Human Development, Program in Sustainable and Resilient Food Systems, Stevens Point, WI 54481-3897. Offers MS. *Program availability:* Part-time. *Degree requirements:* For master's, thesis or alternative. *Entrance requirements:* For master's, minimum GPA of 2.75.

**University of Wisconsin–Stout,** Graduate School, College of Education, Health and Human Sciences, Program in Food and Nutritional Sciences, Menomonie, WI 54751. Offers MS. *Program availability:* Part-time. *Degree requirements:* For master's, thesis. *Entrance requirements:* For master's, minimum GPA of 3.0. Additional exam requirements/recommendations for international students: required—TOEFL (minimum score 500 paper-based; 61 iBT). Electronic applications accepted.

**University of Wyoming,** College of Agriculture and Natural Resources, Department of Animal Science, Program in Food Science and Human Nutrition, Laramie, WY 82071. Offers MS. *Degree requirements:* For master's, thesis. *Entrance requirements:* For master's, GRE General Test, minimum GPA of 3.0. Additional exam requirements/recommendations for international students: required—TOEFL (minimum score 525 paper-based). Electronic applications accepted.

**Université Laval,** Faculty of Agricultural and Food Sciences, Department of Food Sciences and Nutrition, Programs in Nutrition, Québec, QC G1K 7P4, Canada. Offers M Sc, PhD. Terminal master's awarded for partial completion of doctoral program. *Degree requirements:* For master's, thesis; for doctorate, comprehensive exam, thesis/dissertation. *Entrance requirements:* For master's and doctorate, knowledge of French and English. Electronic applications accepted.

**Utah State University,** School of Graduate Studies, College of Agriculture and Applied Sciences, Department of Nutrition, Dietetics, and Food Sciences, Logan, UT 84322. Offers dietetic administration (MDA); nutrition and food sciences (MS, PhD). *Program availability:* Online learning. *Degree requirements:* For master's, thesis; for doctorate, comprehensive exam, thesis/dissertation, teaching experience. *Entrance requirements:* For master's, GRE General Test, minimum GPA of 3.0, course work in chemistry, biochemistry, physics, math, bacteriology, physiology; for doctorate, GRE General Test, minimum GPA of 3.2, course work in chemistry, MS or manuscript in referred journal. Additional exam requirements/recommendations for international students: required—TOEFL (minimum score 550 paper-based). Electronic applications accepted.

**Virginia Polytechnic Institute and State University,** Graduate School, College of Agriculture and Life Sciences, Blacksburg, VA 24061. Offers agricultural and applied economics (MS, PhD); agricultural and life sciences (MS); agriculture, leadership, and community education (MS, PhD); animal and poultry science (MS, PhD); biochemistry (MS, PhD); crop and soil environmental sciences (MS, PhD); dairy science (MS, PhD); entomology (MS, PhD); food science and technology (MS, PhD); horticulture (PhD); human nutrition, foods and exercise (MS, PhD); plant pathology, physiology, and weed science (MS, PhD). *Faculty:* 246 full-time (83 women). *Students:* 364 full-time (213 women), 106 part-time (68 women); includes 79 minority (29 Black or African American, non-Hispanic/Latino; 1 American Indian or Alaska Native, non-Hispanic/Latino; 13 Asian, non-Hispanic/Latino; 16 Hispanic/Latino; 20 Two or more races, non-Hispanic/Latino), 106 international. Average age 28. 314 applicants, 57% accepted, 130 enrolled. In 2019, 92 master's, 59 doctorates awarded. *Degree requirements:* For master's, comprehensive exam (for some programs), thesis (for some programs); for doctorate, comprehensive exam (for some programs), thesis/dissertation (for some programs). *Entrance requirements:* For master's and doctorate, GRE/GMAT. Additional exam requirements/recommendations for international students: required—TOEFL (minimum score 90 iBT). *Application deadline:* For fall admission, 8/1 for domestic students, 4/1 for international students; for spring admission, 1/1 for domestic students, 9/1 for international students. Applications are processed on a rolling basis. Application fee: $75. Electronic applications accepted. *Expenses:* Tuition, state resident: full-time $13,700; part-time $761.25 per credit hour. Tuition, nonresident: full-time $27,614; part-time $1534 per credit hour. *Required fees:* $886.50 per term. Tuition and fees vary according to campus/location and program. *Financial support:* In 2019–20, 248 research assistantships with full tuition reimbursements (averaging $20,360 per year), 127 teaching assistantships with full tuition reimbursements (averaging $18,183 per year) were awarded; fellowships, scholarships/grants, and unspecified assistantships also available. Financial award application deadline: 3/1; financial award applicants required to submit FAFSA. *Unit head:* Dr. Alan L. Grant, Dean, 540-231-4152, Fax: 540-231-4163, E-mail: algrant@vt.edu. *Application contact:* Crystal Tawney, Administrative Assistant, 540-231-4152, Fax: 540-231-4163, E-mail: cdtawney@vt.edu. Website: http://www.cals.vt.edu/

**Virginia University of Integrative Medicine,** Graduate Programs, Fairfax, VA 22031. Offers acupuncture (MS, D Ac); acupuncture and Oriental medicine (DAOM); East Asian nutrition (Certificate); Oriental medicine (MSOM, DOM). *Expenses: Tuition:* Part-time $300 per credit.

**Washington State University,** College of Pharmacy and Pharmaceutical Sciences, Nutrition and Exercise Physiology Program, Pullman, WA 99164. Offers MS. *Degree requirements:* For master's, internship. *Entrance requirements:* For master's, BS in nutrition and exercise physiology, exercise science, human nutrition, or related degree; interview.

## Nutrition

**Wayne State University,** College of Liberal Arts and Sciences, Department of Nutrition and Food Science, Detroit, MI 48201. Offers dietetics (Postbaccalaureate Certificate); food science (PhD); nutrition (PhD); nutrition and food science (MA, MS); MA/MPH. *Faculty:* 8 full-time (4 women). *Students:* 27 full-time (23 women), 8 part-time (4 women); includes 3 minority (1 Asian, non-Hispanic/Latino; 1 Hispanic/Latino; 1 Two or more races, non-Hispanic/Latino, 14 international. Average age 31. 78 applicants, 14% accepted, 6 enrolled. In 2019, 7 master's, 3 doctorates awarded. *Degree requirements:* For master's, thesis (for some programs), essay (for MA); for doctorate, thesis/dissertation. *Entrance requirements:* For master's, GRE General Test (recommended), two letters of recommendation; minimum GPA of 3.0; undergraduate degree in science; for doctorate, GRE (recommended), MS in nutrition and/or food science or in a cognate science with minimum GPA of 3.5; three letters of recommendation; personal statement; interview (live or Web-based). Additional exam requirements/recommendations for international students: required—TOEFL (minimum score 550 paper-based; 79 iBT), TWE (minimum score 5.5), Michigan English Language Assessment Battery (minimum score 85); recommended—IELTS (minimum score 6.5). *Application deadline:* For fall admission, 3/1 priority date for domestic and international students. Applications are processed on a rolling basis. Application fee: $50. Electronic applications accepted. *Expenses: Tuition:* Full-time $34,567. *Financial support:* In 2019–20, 15 students received support, including 1 fellowship with tuition reimbursement available (averaging $20,000 per year), 1 research assistantship with tuition reimbursement available (averaging $20,000 per year), 8 teaching assistantships with tuition reimbursements available (averaging $20,792 per year); scholarships/grants, health care benefits, and unspecified assistantships also available. Financial award applicants required to submit FAFSA. *Unit head:* Dr. Ahmad R. Heydari, Professor and Chair, 313-577-2500, Fax: 313-577-8616, E-mail: ahmad.heydari@wayne.edu. *Application contact:* Dr. Diane Ryen Cress, Associate Professor and Graduate Officer, 313-577-5978, Fax: 313-577-8616, E-mail: gradprogramnfs@wayne.edu.
Website: http://clas.wayne.edu/nfs/

**West Virginia University,** Davis College of Agriculture, Forestry and Consumer Sciences, Morgantown, WV 26506. Offers agricultural and extension education (MS, PhD); agriculture and resource management (MS); agriculture, natural resources and design (M Agr); agronomy (MS); animal and food science (PhD); animal physiology (MS); applied and environmental microbiology (MS); design and merchandising (MS); entomology (MS); forest resource science (PhD); forestry (MSF); genetics and developmental biology (MS, PhD); horticulture (MS); human and community development (PhD); landscape architecture (MLA); natural resource economics (PhD); nutritional and food science (MS); plant and soil science (PhD); plant pathology (MS); recreation, parks and tourism resources (MS); reproductive physiology (MS, PhD); wildlife and fisheries resources (PhD). *Accreditation:* ASLA. *Program availability:* Part-time. *Degree requirements:* For master's, thesis. *Entrance requirements:* Additional exam requirements/recommendations for international students: required—TOEFL (minimum score 550 paper-based). Electronic applications accepted.

**Winthrop University,** College of Arts and Sciences, Department of Human Nutrition, Rock Hill, SC 29733. Offers dietetics (Certificate); human nutrition (MS). *Program availability:* Part-time. *Degree requirements:* For master's, thesis. *Entrance requirements:* For master's, GRE General Test, PRAXIS, or MAT, interview, minimum GPA of 3.0. Additional exam requirements/recommendations for international students: required—TOEFL (minimum score 550 paper-based; 79 iBT), IELTS (minimum score 6). Electronic applications accepted. *Expenses: Tuition, area resident:* Full-time $7659; part-time $641 per credit hour. Tuition, state resident: full-time $7659; part-time $641 per credit hour. Tuition, nonresident: full-time $14,753; part-time $1234 per credit hour.

# Section 15
# Parasitology

This section contains a directory of institutions offering graduate work in parasitology. Additional information about programs listed in the directory may be obtained by writing directly to the dean of a graduate school or chair of a department at the address given in the directory.

For programs offering related work, see also in this book *Allied Health, Biological and Biomedical Sciences, Microbiological Sciences,* and *Public Health.*

## CONTENTS

### Program Directory

# Parasitology

**Illinois State University,** Graduate School, College of Arts and Sciences, School of Biological Sciences, Normal, IL 61790. Offers animal behavior (MS); bacteriology (MS); biochemistry (MS); biological sciences (MS); biology (PhD); biophysics (MS); biotechnology (MS); botany (MS, PhD); cell biology (MS); conservation biology (MS); developmental biology (MS); ecology (MS, PhD); entomology (MS); evolutionary biology (MS); genetics (MS, PhD); immunology (MS); microbiology (MS, PhD); molecular biology (MS); molecular genetics (MS); neurobiology (MS); neuroscience (MS); parasitology (MS); physiology (MS, PhD); plant biology (MS); plant molecular biology (MS); plant sciences (MS); structural biology (MS); zoology (MS, PhD). *Program availability:* Part-time. *Faculty:* 26 full-time (6 women), 7 part-time/adjunct (2 women). *Students:* 51 full-time (33 women), 15 part-time (8 women). Average age 27. 71 applicants, 28% accepted, 9 enrolled. In 2019, 14 master's, 3 doctorates awarded. *Degree requirements:* For master's, thesis or alternative; for doctorate, variable foreign language requirement, thesis/dissertation, 2 terms of residency. *Entrance requirements:* For master's, GRE General Test, minimum GPA of 2.6 in last 60 hours of course work; for doctorate, GRE General Test. *Application deadline:* Applications are processed on a rolling basis. Application fee: $50. *Expenses: Tuition, area resident:* Full-time $7956; part-time $9767 per year. Tuition, nonresident: full-time $9233; part-time $17,592 per year. *Required fees:* $1797. *Financial support:* In 2019–20, 20 research assistantships, 41 teaching assistantships were awarded; Federal Work-Study, tuition waivers (full), and unspecified assistantships also available. Financial award application deadline: 4/1. *Unit head:* Dr. Craig Gatto, School Director, 309-438-3087, E-mail: cgatto@IllinoisState.edu. *Application contact:* Dr. Ben Sadd, Assistant Chair for Graduate Studies, 309-438-2651, E-mail: bmsadd@IllinoisState.edu.
Website: http://www.bio.ilstu.edu/

**Louisiana State University Health Sciences Center,** School of Graduate Studies in New Orleans, Department of Microbiology, Immunology, and Parasitology, New Orleans, LA 70112-1393. Offers microbiology and immunology (PhD); MD/PhD. *Degree requirements:* For doctorate, comprehensive exam, thesis/dissertation, preliminary exam, qualifying exam. *Entrance requirements:* For doctorate, GRE General Test. Additional exam requirements/recommendations for international students: recommended—TOEFL, IELTS.

**McGill University,** Faculty of Graduate and Postdoctoral Studies, Faculty of Agricultural and Environmental Sciences, Institute of Parasitology, Montréal, QC H3A 2T5, Canada. Offers biotechnology (M Sc A, Certificate); parasitology (M Sc, PhD).

**Oregon State University,** College of Science, Program in Microbiology, Corvallis, OR 97331. Offers environmental microbiology (MA, MS, PhD); food microbiology (MA, MS, PhD); genomics (MA, MS, PhD); immunology (MA, MS, PhD); microbial ecology (MA, MS, PhD); microbial evolution (MA, MS, PhD); parasitology (MA, MS, PhD); pathogenic microbiology (MA, MS, PhD); virology (MA). Terminal master's awarded for partial completion of doctoral program. *Entrance requirements:* For master's and doctorate, GRE. Additional exam requirements/recommendations for international students: required—TOEFL (minimum score 600 paper-based; 100 iBT).

**Tulane University,** School of Public Health and Tropical Medicine, Department of Tropical Medicine, New Orleans, LA 70118-5669. Offers Clinical Tropical Medicine and Traveler's Health (Diploma); parasitology (PhD); public health (MSPH); public health and tropical medicine (MPHTM); MD/MPHTM. *Degree requirements:* For master's, thesis; for doctorate, comprehensive exam, thesis/dissertation. *Entrance requirements:* For master's, GRE General Test, minimum B average in undergraduate course work; for doctorate, GRE General Test. Additional exam requirements/recommendations for international students: required—TOEFL. *Expenses: Tuition:* Full-time $57,004; part-time $3167 per credit hour. *Required fees:* $2086; $44.50 per credit hour. $80 per term. Tuition and fees vary according to course load, degree level and program.

**University of Notre Dame,** The Graduate School, College of Science, Department of Biological Sciences, Notre Dame, IN 46556. Offers aquatic ecology, evolution and environmental biology (MS, PhD); cellular and molecular biology (MS, PhD); genetics (MS, PhD); physiology (MS, PhD); vector biology and parasitology (MS, PhD). Terminal master's awarded for partial completion of doctoral program. *Degree requirements:* For master's, comprehensive exam, thesis; for doctorate, comprehensive exam, thesis/dissertation, candidacy exam. *Entrance requirements:* For master's and doctorate, GRE General Test. Additional exam requirements/recommendations for international students: required—TOEFL (minimum score 600 paper-based; 80 iBT). Electronic applications accepted.

**University of Prince Edward Island,** Atlantic Veterinary College, Graduate Program in Veterinary Medicine, Charlottetown, PE C1A 4P3, Canada. Offers anatomy (M Sc, PhD); bacteriology (M Sc, PhD); clinical pharmacology (M Sc, PhD); clinical sciences (M Sc, PhD); epidemiology (M Sc, PhD), including reproduction; fish health (M Sc, PhD); food animal nutrition (M Sc, PhD); immunology (M Sc, PhD); microanatomy (M Sc, PhD); parasitology (M Sc, PhD); pathology (M Sc, PhD); pharmacology (M Sc, PhD); physiology (M Sc, PhD); toxicology (M Sc, PhD); veterinary science (M Vet Sc); virology (M Sc, PhD). *Program availability:* Part-time. *Degree requirements:* For master's, thesis; for doctorate, thesis/dissertation. *Entrance requirements:* For master's, DVM, B Sc honors degree, or equivalent; for doctorate, M Sc. Additional exam requirements/recommendations for international students: required—TOEFL (minimum score 550 paper-based; 80 iBT). *Expenses:* Contact institution.

# Section 16
# Pathology and Pathobiology

This section contains a directory of institutions offering graduate work in pathology and pathobiology, followed by an in-depth entry submitted by an institution that chose to submit a detailed program description. Additional information about programs listed in the directory but not augmented by an in-depth entry may be obtained by writing directly to the dean of a graduate school or chair of a department at the address given in the directory.

For programs offering related work, see also in this book *Allied Health; Anatomy; Biochemistry; Biological and Biomedical Sciences; Cell, Molecular, and Structural Biology; Genetics, Developmental Biology, and Reproductive Biology; Microbiological Sciences; Pharmacology and Toxicology; Physiology, Public Health,* and *Veterinary Medicine and Sciences.*

## CONTENTS

### Program Directories

# Molecular Pathogenesis

**Dartmouth College,** Guarini School of Graduate and Advanced Studies, Graduate Programs in Biological Sciences, Graduate Program in Molecular and Cellular Biology, Department of Microbiology and Immunology, Hanover, NH 03755. Offers microbiology and molecular pathogenesis (PhD); MBA/PhD; MD/PhD. *Entrance requirements:* For doctorate, GRE General Test, letters of recommendation, minimum GPA of 3.0. Electronic applications accepted.

**Emory University,** Laney Graduate School, Division of Biological and Biomedical Sciences, Program in Immunology and Molecular Pathogenesis, Atlanta, GA 30322-1100. Offers PhD. *Degree requirements:* For doctorate, comprehensive exam, thesis/dissertation. *Entrance requirements:* For doctorate, GRE General Test, minimum GPA of 3.0 in science course work (recommended). Additional exam requirements/recommendations for international students: required—TOEFL. Electronic applications accepted.

**North Dakota State University,** College of Graduate and Interdisciplinary Studies, College of Agriculture, Food Systems, and Natural Resources, Department of Microbiological Sciences, Fargo, ND 58102. Offers microbiology (MS); molecular pathogenesis (PhD). *Program availability:* Part-time. *Degree requirements:* For master's, thesis; for doctorate, thesis/dissertation, oral and written preliminary exams. *Entrance requirements:* For master's and doctorate, GRE. Additional exam requirements/recommendations for international students: required—TOEFL (minimum score 525 paper-based; 71 iBT). Tuition and fees vary according to program and reciprocity agreements.

**Washington University in St. Louis,** The Graduate School, Division of Biology and Biomedical Sciences, Program in Molecular Microbiology and Microbial Pathogenesis, St. Louis, MO 63130-4899. Offers PhD. *Degree requirements:* For doctorate, thesis/dissertation. *Entrance requirements:* For doctorate, GRE General Test, GRE Subject Test. Additional exam requirements/recommendations for international students: required—TOEFL. Electronic applications accepted.

# Molecular Pathology

**Rutgers University - Newark,** Graduate School of Biomedical Sciences, Program in Molecular Pathology and Immunology, Newark, NJ 07107. Offers PhD. *Entrance requirements:* Additional exam requirements/recommendations for international students: required—TOEFL. Electronic applications accepted.

**Texas Tech University Health Sciences Center,** School of Health Professions, Program in Molecular Pathology, Lubbock, TX 79430. Offers MS. *Faculty:* 5 full-time (3 women), 2 part-time/adjunct (both women). *Students:* 28 full-time (15 women); includes 12 minority (2 Black or African American, non-Hispanic/Latino; 9 Hispanic/Latino; 1 Two or more races, non-Hispanic/Latino). Average age 23. 46 applicants, 65% accepted, 28 enrolled. In 2019, 27 master's awarded. *Entrance requirements:* Additional exam requirements/recommendations for international students: required—TOEFL (minimum score 550 paper-based; 79 iBT). *Application deadline:* For spring admission, 2/1 priority date for domestic students. Applications are processed on a rolling basis. Application fee: $75. Electronic applications accepted. *Financial support:* In 2019–20, 19 students received support. Institutionally sponsored loans and scholarships/grants available. Financial award application deadline: 9/1; financial award applicants required to submit FAFSA. *Unit head:* Dr. Ericka Hendrix, Program Director, 806-743-4473, Fax: 806-743-4470, E-mail: health.professions@ttuhsc.edu. *Application contact:* Lindsay Johnson, Associate Dean for Admissions and Student Affairs, 806-743-3220, Fax: 806-743-2994, E-mail: health.professions@ttuhsc.edu.
Website: http://www.ttuhsc.edu/health-professions/master-of-science-molecular-pathology/

**University of California, Los Angeles,** Graduate Division, College of Letters and Science and David Geffen School of Medicine, UCLA ACCESS to Programs in the Molecular, Cellular and Integrative Life Sciences, Los Angeles, CA 90095. Offers biochemistry and molecular biology (PhD); biological chemistry (PhD); cellular and molecular pathology (PhD); human genetics (PhD); microbiology, immunology, and molecular genetics (PhD); molecular biology (PhD); molecular toxicology (PhD); molecular, cellular and integrative physiology (PhD); neurobiology (PhD); oral biology (PhD); physiology (PhD). *Degree requirements:* For doctorate, thesis/dissertation, oral and written qualifying exams. *Entrance requirements:* For doctorate, GRE General Test, bachelor's degree; minimum undergraduate GPA of 3.0 (or its equivalent if letter grade system not used). Additional exam requirements/recommendations for international students: required—TOEFL. Electronic applications accepted.

**University of Michigan,** Rackham Graduate School, Program in Biomedical Sciences (PIBS), Program in Molecular and Cellular Pathology, Ann Arbor, MI 48109. Offers PhD. *Degree requirements:* For doctorate, comprehensive exam, thesis/dissertation, preliminary exam; oral defense of dissertation. *Entrance requirements:* For doctorate, 3 letters of recommendation, research experience, personal statement. Additional exam requirements/recommendations for international students: required—TOEFL (minimum score 84 iBT). Electronic applications accepted.

**University of Wisconsin–Madison,** School of Medicine and Public Health, Cellular and Molecular Pathology Graduate Program, Madison, WI 53706-1380. Offers PhD.

# Pathobiology

**Brown University,** Graduate School, Division of Biology and Medicine, Department of Pathology and Laboratory Medicine, Providence, RI 02912. Offers Sc M, PhD, MD/PhD. Terminal master's awarded for partial completion of doctoral program. *Degree requirements:* For doctorate, thesis/dissertation, preliminary exam. *Entrance requirements:* For master's and doctorate, GRE General Test, GRE Subject Test. Additional exam requirements/recommendations for international students: required—TOEFL. Electronic applications accepted.

**Columbia University,** College of Physicians and Surgeons, Department of Pathology, New York, NY 10032. Offers pathobiology (M Phil, MA, PhD); MD/PhD. Terminal master's awarded for partial completion of doctoral program. *Degree requirements:* For doctorate, thesis/dissertation. *Entrance requirements:* For master's and doctorate, GRE General Test. Additional exam requirements/recommendations for international students: required—TOEFL. *Expenses: Tuition:* Full-time $47,600; part-time $1880 per credit. One-time fee: $105.

**Drexel University,** College of Medicine, Biomedical Graduate Programs, Interdisciplinary Program in Molecular Pathobiology, Philadelphia, PA 19104-2875. Offers MS, PhD, MD/PhD. *Degree requirements:* For doctorate, comprehensive exam, thesis/dissertation, qualifying exams. *Entrance requirements:* For doctorate, GRE General Test, minimum GPA of 3.0. Additional exam requirements/recommendations for international students: required—TOEFL. Electronic applications accepted.

**Johns Hopkins University,** School of Medicine, Graduate Programs in Medicine, Graduate Program in Pathobiology, Baltimore, MD 21205. Offers pathobiology (PhD). *Degree requirements:* For doctorate, thesis/dissertation, qualifying oral exam. *Entrance requirements:* For doctorate, GRE General Test, previous course work with laboratory in organic and inorganic chemistry, general biology, calculus; interview. Additional exam requirements/recommendations for international students: required—TOEFL. Electronic applications accepted.

**Kansas State University,** Graduate School, College of Veterinary Medicine, Department of Diagnostic Medicine/Pathobiology, Manhattan, KS 66506. Offers biomedical science (MS); diagnostic medicine/pathobiology (PhD). Terminal master's awarded for partial completion of doctoral program. *Degree requirements:* For doctorate, thesis/dissertation. *Entrance requirements:* For master's and doctorate, interviews. Additional exam requirements/recommendations for international students: required—TOEFL (minimum score 550 paper-based). Electronic applications accepted.

**Medical University of South Carolina,** College of Graduate Studies, Program in Molecular and Cellular Biology and Pathobiology, Charleston, SC 29425. Offers cancer biology (PhD); cardiovascular biology (PhD); cardiovascular imaging (PhD); cell regulation (PhD); craniofacial biology (PhD); genetics and development (PhD); marine biomedicine (PhD); DMD/PhD; MD/PhD. *Degree requirements:* For doctorate, thesis/ dissertation, oral and written exams. *Entrance requirements:* For doctorate, GRE General Test, interview, minimum GPA of 3.0. Additional exam requirements/recommendations for international students: required—TOEFL (minimum score 600 paper-based; 100 iBT). Electronic applications accepted.

**Michigan State University,** College of Veterinary Medicine and The Graduate School, Graduate Programs in Veterinary Medicine, Department of Pathobiology and Diagnostic Investigation, East Lansing, MI 48824. Offers pathology (MS, PhD); pathology–environmental toxicology (PhD). *Entrance requirements:* Additional exam requirements/recommendations for international students: required—TOEFL. Electronic applications accepted.

**Penn State University Park,** Graduate School, College of Agricultural Sciences, Department of Veterinary and Biomedical Sciences, University Park, PA 16802. Offers pathobiology (MS, PhD).

**Purdue University,** School of Veterinary Medicine and Graduate School, Graduate Programs in Veterinary Medicine, Department of Comparative Pathobiology, West Lafayette, IN 47907-2027. Offers comparative epidemiology and public health (MS); comparative epidemiology and public heath (PhD); comparative microbiology and immunology (MS, PhD); comparative pathobiology (MS, PhD); interdisciplinary studies (PhD), including microbial pathogenesis, molecular signaling and cancer biology, molecular virology; lab animal medicine (MS); veterinary anatomic pathology (MS); veterinary clinical pathology (MS). Terminal master's awarded for partial completion of doctoral program. *Degree requirements:* For master's, thesis (for some programs); for doctorate, thesis/dissertation. *Entrance requirements:* For master's and doctorate, GRE General Test. Additional exam requirements/recommendations for international students: required—TOEFL (minimum score 575 paper-based), IELTS (minimum score 6.5), TWE (minimum score 4). Electronic applications accepted.

**The University of Alabama at Birmingham,** Joint Health Sciences, Pathobiology and Molecular Medicine Theme, Birmingham, AL 35294. Offers PhD. *Students:* Average age 28. 41 applicants, 15% accepted, 4 enrolled. In 2019, 9 doctorates awarded. *Degree requirements:* For doctorate, comprehensive exam, thesis/dissertation. *Entrance requirements:* For doctorate, personal statement, resume or curriculum vitae, letters of recommendation, research experience, interview. Additional exam requirements/recommendations for international students: required—TOEFL (minimum score 80 iBT), IELTS (minimum score 6.5). *Application deadline:* For fall admission, 12/31 for domestic and international students. Applications are processed on a rolling basis. Electronic applications accepted. *Financial support:* In 2019–20, fellowships with full tuition reimbursements (averaging $30,000 per year), research assistantships with full tuition reimbursements (averaging $31,000 per year) were awarded; health care benefits also available. *Unit head:* Dr. Yabing Chen, Theme Director, 205-996-6293, E-mail:

ybchen@uab.edu. *Application contact:* Alyssa Zasada, Admissions Manager for Graduate Biomedical Sciences, 205-934-3857, E-mail: grad-gbs@uab.edu. Website: http://www.uab.edu/gbs/home/themes/pbmm

**University of Cincinnati,** Graduate School, College of Medicine, Graduate Programs in Biomedical Sciences, Program in Pathobiology and Molecular Medicine, Cincinnati, OH 45267-0529. Offers pathology (PhD), including anatomic pathology, laboratory medicine, pathobiology and molecular medicine. *Degree requirements:* For doctorate, thesis/dissertation, qualifying exam. *Entrance requirements:* For doctorate, GRE General Test. Additional exam requirements/recommendations for international students: required—TOEFL. Electronic applications accepted.

**University of Connecticut,** Graduate School, College of Agriculture, Health and Natural Resources, Department of Pathobiology and Veterinary Science, Storrs, CT 06269. Offers pathobiology (MS, PhD). Terminal master's awarded for partial completion of doctoral program. *Degree requirements:* For master's, comprehensive exam; for doctorate, thesis/dissertation. *Entrance requirements:* For master's and doctorate, GRE General Test, GRE Subject Test. Additional exam requirements/recommendations for international students: required—TOEFL (minimum score 550 paper-based). Electronic applications accepted.

**University of Illinois at Urbana-Champaign,** College of Veterinary Medicine, Department of Pathobiology, Urbana, IL 61802. Offers MS, PhD, DVM/PhD. Terminal master's awarded for partial completion of doctoral program. *Degree requirements:* For doctorate, thesis/dissertation.

**University of Missouri,** College of Veterinary Medicine and Office of Research and Graduate Studies, Graduate Programs in Veterinary Medicine, Department of Veterinary Pathobiology, Columbia, MO 65211. Offers comparative medicine (MS); pathobiology (MS, PhD). *Entrance requirements:* For master's and doctorate, GRE General Test, minimum GPA of 3.0.

**University of Toronto,** Faculty of Medicine, Department of Laboratory Medicine and Pathobiology, Toronto, ON M5S 1A1, Canada. Offers M Sc, PhD. *Degree requirements:*

For master's, thesis; for doctorate, thesis/dissertation, oral defense of thesis. *Entrance requirements:* For master's, minimum B+ average in final 2 years, research experience, 2 letters of recommendation, resume, interview; for doctorate, minimum A- average, 2 letters of recommendation, research experience, resume, interview. Additional exam requirements/recommendations for international students: required—TOEFL (minimum score 600 paper-based), TWE (minimum score 5, or IELTS (minimum score 7). Electronic applications accepted.

**University of Washington,** Graduate School, School of Public Health, Department of Global Health, Interdisciplinary Doctoral Program in Pathobiology, Seattle, WA 98195. Offers PhD. *Faculty:* 57 full-time (20 women). *Students:* 30 full-time (23 women); includes 10 minority (6 Asian, non-Hispanic/Latino; 4 Hispanic/Latino), 4 international. Average age 28. 87 applicants, 14% accepted, 7 enrolled. In 2019, 5 doctorates awarded. Terminal master's awarded for partial completion of doctoral program. *Degree requirements:* For doctorate, comprehensive exam, thesis/dissertation. *Entrance requirements:* For doctorate, GRE. Additional exam requirements/recommendations for international students: required—TOEFL (minimum score 500 paper-based; 80 iBT). *Application deadline:* For fall admission, 12/1 for domestic and international students. Application fee: $85. Electronic applications accepted. *Financial support:* In 2019–20, 29 students received support, including 3 fellowships (averaging $4,000 per year), 29 research assistantships with tuition reimbursements available (averaging $34,200 per year); institutionally sponsored loans, scholarships/grants, traineeships, and health care benefits also available. *Application contact:* Ernest Lefler, 206-543-4338, E-mail: pabio@u.washington.edu. Website: https://globalhealth.washington.edu/education-training/phd-pathobiology

**University of Wyoming,** College of Agriculture and Natural Resources, Department of Veterinary Sciences, Laramie, WY 82071. Offers pathobiology (MS). *Degree requirements:* For master's, thesis. *Entrance requirements:* For master's, GRE General Test, minimum GPA of 3.0. Additional exam requirements/recommendations for international students: required—TOEFL.

# Pathology

**Albert Einstein College of Medicine,** Graduate Programs in the Biomedical Sciences, Department of Pathology, Bronx, NY 10461. Offers PhD, MD/PhD. *Degree requirements:* For doctorate, thesis/dissertation. *Entrance requirements:* For doctorate, GRE General Test. Additional exam requirements/recommendations for international students: required—TOEFL.

**Boston University,** School of Medicine, Graduate Medical Sciences, Department of Pathology and Laboratory Medicine, Boston, MA 02118. Offers MS, PhD, MD/PhD. *Program availability:* Part-time. *Entrance requirements:* Additional exam requirements/recommendations for international students: required—TOEFL. *Application deadline:* For fall admission, 1/15 for domestic students; for spring admission, 10/15 for domestic students. *Financial support:* Scholarships/grants and traineeships available. Financial award applicants required to submit FAFSA. *Unit head:* Dr. Daniel G. Remick, Chairman, 617-414-7043, E-mail: remickd@bu.edu. *Application contact:* GMS Admissions Office, 617-358-9518, Fax: 617-358-2913, E-mail: gmsbusm@bu.edu. Website: http://www.bumc.bu.edu/busm-pathology/

**Case Western Reserve University,** School of Medicine and School of Graduate Studies, Graduate Programs in Medicine, Programs in Molecular and Cellular Basis of Disease/Pathology, Cleveland, OH 44106. Offers molecular and cellular basis of disease (PhD); pathology (MS); MD/PhD. Terminal master's awarded for partial completion of doctoral program. *Degree requirements:* For master's, thesis; for doctorate, thesis/dissertation. *Entrance requirements:* For master's and doctorate, GRE General Test, GRE Subject Test. Additional exam requirements/recommendations for international students: required—TOEFL (minimum score 550 paper-based). Electronic applications accepted.

**Colorado State University,** College of Veterinary Medicine and Biomedical Sciences, Department of Microbiology, Immunology and Pathology, Fort Collins, CO 80523. Offers microbiology, immunology and pathology (MS, PhD); pathology (PhD). *Faculty:* 76 full-time (35 women), 12 part-time/adjunct (8 women). *Students:* 64 full-time (46 women), 39 part-time (30 women); includes 10 minority (1 Black or African American, non-Hispanic/Latino; 1 American Indian or Alaska Native, non-Hispanic/Latino; 4 Hispanic/Latino; 4 Two or more races, non-Hispanic/Latino), 3 international. Average age 28. 187 applicants, 30% accepted, 45 enrolled. In 2019, 28 master's, 9 doctorates awarded. Terminal master's awarded for partial completion of doctoral program. *Degree requirements:* For master's, thesis (for some programs); for doctorate, comprehensive exam, thesis/dissertation. *Entrance requirements:* Additional exam requirements/recommendations for international students: required—TOEFL (minimum score 550 paper-based; 80 iBT), IELTS (minimum score 6.5), PTE (minimum score 58). *Application deadline:* For fall admission, 12/15 for domestic and international students. Application fee: $60 ($70 for international students). *Expenses:* For non-thesis MS, addition fee of $120 per credit. *Financial support:* In 2019–20, 27 students received support, including 24 research assistantships with full and partial tuition reimbursements available (averaging $25,025 per year), 6 teaching assistantships with full and partial tuition reimbursements available (averaging $18,612 per year); health care benefits also available. Financial award application deadline: 12/15. *Unit head:* Dr. Gregg Dean, Department Head, 970-491-6144, E-mail: Gregg.Dean@colostate.edu. *Application contact:* Heidi Runge, Academic Support Coordinator for Graduate Studies, 970-491-1630, Fax: 970-491-1815, E-mail: heidi.runge@colostate.edu. Website: https://vetmedbiosci.colostate.edu/mip/

**Columbia University,** College of Physicians and Surgeons, Department of Pathology, New York, NY 10032. Offers pathobiology (M Phil, MA, PhD); MD/PhD. Terminal master's awarded for partial completion of doctoral program. *Degree requirements:* For doctorate, thesis/dissertation. *Entrance requirements:* For master's and doctorate, GRE General Test. Additional exam requirements/recommendations for international students: required—TOEFL. *Expenses:* Tuition: Full-time $47,600; part-time $1880 per credit. One-time fee: $105.

**Dalhousie University,** Faculty of Graduate Studies and Faculty of Medicine, Graduate Programs in Medicine, Department of Pathology, Halifax, NS B3H 4R2, Canada. Offers M Sc, PhD. *Degree requirements:* For master's, oral defense of thesis. *Entrance requirements:* Additional exam requirements/recommendations for international students: required—1 of 5 approved tests: TOEFL, IELTS, CANTEST, CAEL, Michigan English Language Assessment Battery. Electronic applications accepted.

**Duke University,** Graduate School, Department of Pathology, Durham, NC 27710. Offers PhD. *Accreditation:* NAACLS. *Degree requirements:* For doctorate, thesis/dissertation. *Entrance requirements:* For doctorate, GRE General Test, GRE Subject Test (recommended). Additional exam requirements/recommendations for international students: required—TOEFL (minimum score 577 paper-based; 90 iBT) or IELTS (minimum score 7). Electronic applications accepted.

**Duke University,** School of Medicine, Masters of Health Sciences - Pathologists' Assistant, Durham, NC 27708. Offers MHS. *Accreditation:* NAACLS. *Degree requirements:* For master's, comprehensive exam. *Entrance requirements:* For master's, GRE. Additional exam requirements/recommendations for international students: required—TOEFL, IELTS. Electronic applications accepted. Application fee is waived when completed online.

**Harvard University,** Graduate School of Arts and Sciences, Division of Medical Sciences, Boston, MA 02115. Offers biological chemistry and molecular pharmacology (PhD); cell biology (PhD); genetics (PhD); microbiology and molecular genetics (PhD); pathology (PhD), including experimental pathology. *Degree requirements:* For doctorate, thesis/dissertation. *Entrance requirements:* For doctorate, GRE General Test, GRE Subject Test. Additional exam requirements/recommendations for international students: required—TOEFL.

**Indiana University-Purdue University Indianapolis,** Indiana University School of Medicine, Department of Pathology and Laboratory Medicine, Indianapolis, IN 46202. Offers MS, PhD, MD/PhD. *Accreditation:* NAACLS. *Degree requirements:* For master's, thesis; for doctorate, thesis/dissertation. *Entrance requirements:* For master's and doctorate, GRE General Test. Additional exam requirements/recommendations for international students: required—TOEFL.

**Iowa State University of Science and Technology,** Department of Veterinary Pathology, Ames, IA 50011. Offers MS, PhD. *Entrance requirements:* For master's and doctorate, GRE General Test. Additional exam requirements/recommendations for international students: recommended—TOEFL (minimum score 550 paper-based; 79 iBT), IELTS (minimum score 6.5). Electronic applications accepted.

**Johns Hopkins University,** School of Medicine, Graduate Programs in Medicine, Graduate Program in Pathobiology, Baltimore, MD 21205. Offers pathobiology (PhD). *Degree requirements:* For doctorate, thesis/dissertation, qualifying oral exam. *Entrance requirements:* For doctorate, GRE General Test, previous course work with laboratory in organic and inorganic chemistry, general biology, calculus; interview. Additional exam requirements/recommendations for international students: required—TOEFL. Electronic applications accepted.

**Loma Linda University,** School of Medicine, Programs in Pathology and Human Anatomy, Loma Linda, CA 92350. Offers human anatomy (PhD); pathology (PhD). *Accreditation:* NAACLS. *Program availability:* Part-time. Terminal master's awarded for partial completion of doctoral program. *Degree requirements:* For doctorate, 2 foreign languages, thesis/dissertation. *Entrance requirements:* For doctorate, GRE General Test. Additional exam requirements/recommendations for international students: required—TOEFL (minimum score 550 paper-based).

**McGill University,** Faculty of Graduate and Postdoctoral Studies, Faculty of Medicine, Department of Pathology, Montréal, QC H3A 2T5, Canada. Offers M Sc, PhD.

**Medical University of South Carolina,** College of Graduate Studies, Department of Pathology and Laboratory Medicine, Charleston, SC 29425. Offers MS, PhD, DMD/PhD, MD/PhD. Terminal master's awarded for partial completion of doctoral program. *Degree requirements:* For master's, thesis; for doctorate, thesis/dissertation, oral and written exams. *Entrance requirements:* For master's, GRE General Test; for doctorate, GRE General Test, interview, minimum GPA of 3.0. Additional exam requirements/recommendations for international students: required—TOEFL (minimum score 600 paper-based; 100 iBT). Electronic applications accepted.

**Michigan State University,** College of Veterinary Medicine and The Graduate School, Graduate Programs in Veterinary Medicine, Department of Pathobiology and Diagnostic Investigation, East Lansing, MI 48824. Offers pathology (MS, PhD); pathology-environmental toxicology (PhD). *Entrance requirements:* Additional exam requirements/recommendations for international students: required—TOEFL. Electronic applications accepted.

## Pathology

**New York Medical College,** Graduate School of Basic Medical Sciences, Valhalla, NY 10595. Offers biochemistry and molecular biology (MS, PhD); cell biology (MS, PhD); microbiology and immunology (MS, PhD); pathology (MS, PhD); pharmacology (MS, PhD); physiology (MS, PhD); MD/PhD. *Program availability:* Part-time, evening/weekend. *Faculty:* 98 full-time (24 women). *Students:* 141 full-time (90 women), 17 part-time (3 women); includes 68 minority (16 Black or African American, non-Hispanic/Latino; 32 Asian, non-Hispanic/Latino; 15 Hispanic/Latino; 1 Native Hawaiian or other Pacific Islander, non-Hispanic/Latino; 4 Two or more races, non-Hispanic/Latino), 19 international. Average age 26. 351 applicants, 62% accepted, 86 enrolled. In 2019, 28 master's, 5 doctorates awarded. Terminal master's awarded for partial completion of doctoral program. *Degree requirements:* For master's, thesis; for doctorate, comprehensive exam, thesis/dissertation. *Entrance requirements:* For master's, GRE General Test, MCAT, or DAT, OAT. Additional exam requirements/recommendations for international students: required—TOEFL (minimum score 90 iBT), TOEFL or IELTS; one of the two exams are required. *Application deadline:* For fall admission, 6/1 priority date for domestic students, 5/1 priority date for international students. Applications are processed on a rolling basis. Application fee: $75 ($100 for international students). Electronic applications accepted. *Expenses:* $1200 credit and $620 fees. *Financial support:* In 2019–20, 400 students received support. Federal Work-Study, scholarships/grants, unspecified assistantships, and Student Federal Loans available. Financial award application deadline: 4/30; financial award applicants required to submit FAFSA. *Unit head:* Dr. Marina K Holz, Dean, 914-594-4110, Fax: 914-594-4944, E-mail: mholz@nymc.edu. *Application contact:* Valerie Romeo-Messana, Director of Admissions, 914-594-4110, Fax: 914-594-4944, E-mail: v_romeomessana@nymc.edu. Website: https://www.nymc.edu/graduate-school-of-basic-medical-sciences-gsbms/gsbms-academics/

**North Carolina State University,** College of Veterinary Medicine, Program in Comparative Biomedical Sciences, Raleigh, NC 27695. Offers cell biology (MS, PhD); infectious disease (MS, PhD); pathology (MS, PhD); pharmacology (MS, PhD); population medicine (MS, PhD). *Program availability:* Part-time. *Degree requirements:* For master's, thesis; for doctorate, thesis/dissertation. *Entrance requirements:* For master's and doctorate, GRE General Test. Additional exam requirements/recommendations for international students: required—TOEFL (minimum score 550 paper-based). Electronic applications accepted. *Expenses:* Contact institution.

**North Dakota State University,** College of Graduate and Interdisciplinary Studies, College of Agriculture, Food Systems, and Natural Resources, Department of Microbiological Sciences, Fargo, ND 58102. Offers microbiology (MS); molecular pathogenesis (PhD). *Program availability:* Part-time. *Degree requirements:* For master's, thesis; for doctorate, thesis/dissertation, oral and written preliminary exams. *Entrance requirements:* For master's and doctorate, GRE. Additional exam requirements/recommendations for international students: required—TOEFL (minimum score 525 paper-based; 71 iBT). Tuition and fees vary according to program and reciprocity agreements.

**Purdue University,** School of Veterinary Medicine and Graduate School, Graduate Programs in Veterinary Medicine, Department of Comparative Pathobiology, West Lafayette, IN 47907-2027. Offers comparative epidemiology and public health (MS); comparative epidemiology and public heath (PhD); comparative microbiology and immunology (MS, PhD); comparative pathobiology (MS, PhD); interdisciplinary studies (PhD), including microbial pathogenesis, molecular signaling and cancer biology, molecular virology; lab animal medicine (MS); veterinary anatomic pathology (MS); veterinary clinical pathology (MS). Terminal master's awarded for partial completion of doctoral program. *Degree requirements:* For master's, thesis (for some programs); for doctorate, thesis/dissertation. *Entrance requirements:* For master's and doctorate, GRE General Test. Additional exam requirements/recommendations for international students: required—TOEFL (minimum score 575 paper-based), IELTS (minimum score 6.5), TWE (minimum score 4). Electronic applications accepted.

**Queen's University at Kingston,** School of Graduate Studies, Faculty of Health Sciences, Department of Pathology and Molecular Medicine, Kingston, ON K7L 3N6, Canada. Offers M Sc, PhD. *Program availability:* Part-time. *Degree requirements:* For master's, thesis; for doctorate, comprehensive exam, thesis/dissertation. *Entrance requirements:* Additional exam requirements/recommendations for international students: required—TOEFL.

**Quinnipiac University,** School of Health Sciences, Program for Pathologists' Assistant, Hamden, CT 06518-1940. Offers MHS. *Accreditation:* NAACLS. *Degree requirements:* For master's, residency. *Entrance requirements:* For master's, interview, coursework in biological and health sciences, minimum GPA of 3.0. Electronic applications accepted. *Expenses: Tuition:* Part-time $1055 per credit. *Required fees:* $945 per semester. Tuition and fees vary according to course load and program.

**Rosalind Franklin University of Medicine and Science,** College of Health Professions, Pathologists' Assistant Department, North Chicago, IL 60064-3095. Offers MS. *Accreditation:* NAACLS. *Entrance requirements:* For master's, bachelor's degree from an accredited college or university, minimum cumulative GPA of 3.0. Additional exam requirements/recommendations for international students: required—TOEFL.

**Rutgers University - Newark,** Graduate School of Biomedical Sciences, Program in Molecular Pathology and Immunology, Newark, NJ 07107. Offers PhD. *Entrance requirements:* Additional exam requirements/recommendations for international students: required—TOEFL. Electronic applications accepted.

**Saint Louis University,** Graduate Programs, School of Medicine, Graduate Programs in Biomedical Sciences and Graduate Programs, Department of Pathology, St. Louis, MO 63103. Offers PhD. *Degree requirements:* For doctorate, comprehensive exam, thesis/dissertation, oral and written preliminary exams, oral defense of dissertation. *Entrance requirements:* For doctorate, GRE General Test (GRE Subject Test optional), letters of recommendation, resume, interview. Additional exam requirements/recommendations for international students: required—TOEFL (minimum score 525 paper-based). Electronic applications accepted.

**Stony Brook University, State University of New York,** Graduate School, College of Arts and Sciences, Department of Biochemistry and Cell Biology, Stony Brook, NY 11794. Offers biochemistry and structural biology (PhD); molecular and cellular biology (MA, PhD), including biochemistry and molecular biology (PhD), biological sciences (MA), cellular and developmental biology (PhD), immunology and pathology (PhD), molecular and cellular biology (PhD). *Faculty:* 18 full-time (5 women), 1 part-time/adjunct (0 women). *Students:* 104 full-time (61 women), 7 part-time (4 women); includes 28 minority (6 Black or African American, non-Hispanic/Latino; 15 Asian, non-Hispanic/Latino; 7 Hispanic/Latino), 48 international. Average age 26. 205 applicants, 37% accepted, 35 enrolled. In 2019, 11 master's, 17 doctorates awarded. *Degree requirements:* For doctorate, comprehensive exam, thesis/dissertation, teaching experience. *Entrance requirements:* For doctorate, GRE General Test, GRE Subject Test. Additional exam requirements/recommendations for international students: required—TOEFL (minimum score 90 iBT). *Application deadline:* For fall admission, 1/15 for domestic students; for spring admission, 10/15 for domestic students. Application fee: $100. *Expenses:* Contact institution. *Financial support:* In 2019–20, 6 fellowships, 41 research assistantships, 17 teaching assistantships were awarded; Federal Work-

Study also available. *Unit head:* Prof. Aaron Neiman, Chair, 631-632-1543, Fax: 631-632-8575, E-mail: aaron.neiman@stonybrook.edu. *Application contact:* Amy Saas, Coordinator, 631-632-8613, Fax: 631-632-9730, E-mail: Amy.Saas@stonybrook.edu. Website: http://www.sunysb.edu/biochem/

**Tufts University,** Cummings School of Veterinary Medicine, North Grafton, MA 01536. Offers animals and public policy (MS); biomedical sciences (PhD), including digestive diseases, infectious diseases, neuroscience and reproductive biology, pathology; conservation medicine (MS); veterinary medicine (DVM); DVM/MPH; DVM/MS. *Accreditation:* AVMA (one or more programs are accredited). *Degree requirements:* For master's, thesis (for some programs); for doctorate, comprehensive exam, thesis/dissertation (for some programs). *Entrance requirements:* For master's and doctorate, GRE General Test. Additional exam requirements/recommendations for international students: required—TOEFL or IELTS. Electronic applications accepted. *Expenses:* Contact institution.

**Université de Montréal,** Faculty of Medicine, Department of Pathology and Cellular Biology, Montréal, QC H3C 3J7, Canada. Offers M Sc, PhD. Terminal master's awarded for partial completion of doctoral program. *Degree requirements:* For master's, thesis; for doctorate, thesis/dissertation, general exam. *Entrance requirements:* For master's and doctorate, proficiency in French, knowledge of English. Electronic applications accepted.

**University at Buffalo, the State University of New York,** Graduate School, Jacobs School of Medicine and Biomedical Sciences, Graduate Programs in Medicine and Biomedical Sciences, Department of Pathology and Anatomical Sciences, Buffalo, NY 14203. Offers anatomical sciences (MA, PhD); computational cell biology, anatomy, and pathology (PhD); pathology (MA, PhD). *Faculty:* 14 full-time (2 women). *Students:* 16 full-time (6 women); includes 2 minority (1 American Indian or Alaska Native, non-Hispanic/Latino; 1 Asian, non-Hispanic/Latino), 1 international. Average age 29. 26 applicants, 27% accepted, 3 enrolled. In 2019, 2 master's, 2 doctorates awarded. *Degree requirements:* For master's, thesis; for doctorate, thesis/dissertation. *Entrance requirements:* For master's and doctorate, 3 letters of recommendation. Additional exam requirements/recommendations for international students: required—TOEFL (minimum score 600 paper-based; 100 iBT). *Application deadline:* For fall admission, 5/1 priority date for domestic students, 3/1 priority date for international students. Applications are processed on a rolling basis. Application fee: $85. Electronic applications accepted. *Expenses:* Contact institution. *Financial support:* In 2019–20, 7 students received support, including 1 research assistantship with full tuition reimbursement available (averaging $24,900 per year), 1 teaching assistantship with full tuition reimbursement available (averaging $24,900 per year); Federal Work-Study, scholarships/grants, health care benefits, and unspecified assistantships also available. Financial award application deadline: 2/1; financial award applicants required to submit FAFSA. *Unit head:* Dr. John E. Tomaszewski, Department Chair, 716-829-2846, Fax: 716-829-2911, E-mail: johntoma@buffalo.edu. *Application contact:* Lannette M. Garcia, Assistant for Academic Activity, 716-829-5204, E-mail: ubpathad@buffalo.edu. Website: http://medicine.buffalo.edu/departments/pathology.html

**University of Alberta,** Faculty of Medicine and Dentistry and Faculty of Graduate Studies and Research, Graduate Programs in Medicine, Department of Laboratory Medicine and Pathology, Edmonton, AB T6G 2E1, Canada. Offers medical sciences (M Sc, PhD). *Program availability:* Part-time. Terminal master's awarded for partial completion of doctoral program. *Degree requirements:* For master's, thesis; for doctorate, thesis/dissertation, candidacy exam. *Entrance requirements:* For master's and doctorate, 3 letters of recommendation, minimum GPA of 3.0. Additional exam requirements/recommendations for international students: required—TOEFL.

**The University of British Columbia,** Faculty of Medicine, Department of Pathology and Laboratory Medicine, Vancouver, BC V6T 2B5, Canada. Offers pathology (M Sc, PhD). *Degree requirements:* For master's, thesis; for doctorate, comprehensive exam, thesis/dissertation, internal oral defense. *Entrance requirements:* For master's, GRE, upper-level course work in biochemistry and physiology; for doctorate, GRE. Additional exam requirements/recommendations for international students: required—TOEFL, IELTS. Electronic applications accepted. *Expenses:* Contact institution.

**University of Calgary,** Cumming School of Medicine and Faculty of Graduate Studies, Program in Medical Science, Calgary, AB T2N 1N4, Canada. Offers cancer biology (M Sc, PhD); critical care medicine (M Sc, PhD); joint injury and arthritis (M Sc, PhD); molecular and medical genetics (M Sc, PhD); mountain medicine and high altitude physiology (M Sc, PhD); pathologists' assistant (M Sc, PhD). *Degree requirements:* For master's, thesis; for doctorate, thesis/dissertation, candidacy exam. *Entrance requirements:* For master's, minimum undergraduate GPA of 3.2; for doctorate, minimum graduate GPA of 3.2. Additional exam requirements/recommendations for international students: required—TOEFL (minimum score 600 paper-based). Electronic applications accepted.

**University of California, Davis,** Graduate Studies, Graduate Group in Comparative Pathology, Davis, CA 95616. Offers MS, PhD. *Accreditation:* NAACLS. Terminal master's awarded for partial completion of doctoral program. *Degree requirements:* For master's, comprehensive exam (for some programs), thesis (for some programs); for doctorate, thesis/dissertation. *Entrance requirements:* For master's and doctorate, GRE General Test. Additional exam requirements/recommendations for international students: required—TOEFL (minimum score 550 paper-based). Electronic applications accepted.

**University of California, Irvine,** School of Medicine, Department of Pathology and Laboratory Medicine, Irvine, CA 92697. Offers experimental pathology (PhD). *Accreditation:* NAACLS. *Students:* 3 full-time (0 women), 1 part-time (0 women). Average age 29. In 2019, 1 doctorate awarded. Application fee: $120 ($140 for international students). *Unit head:* Dr. Edwin S. Monuki, Chair, 949-824-9604, Fax: 949-824-2160, E-mail: emonuki@uci.edu. *Application contact:* Stefani Ching, Graduate Student Coordinator, 949-824-5367, E-mail: shching@uci.edu. Website: http://www.pathology.uci.edu/

**University of California, Los Angeles,** David Geffen School of Medicine and Graduate Division, Graduate Programs in Medicine, Program in Cellular and Molecular Pathology, Los Angeles, CA 90095. Offers MS, PhD. Terminal master's awarded for partial completion of doctoral program. *Degree requirements:* For master's, thesis; for doctorate, thesis/dissertation, written and oral qualifying examinations; 2 quarters of teaching experience. *Entrance requirements:* For doctorate, GRE General Test, bachelor's degree; minimum undergraduate GPA of 3.0 (or its equivalent if letter grade system not used). Additional exam requirements/recommendations for international students: required—TOEFL. Electronic applications accepted.

**University of California, Los Angeles,** David Geffen School of Medicine and Graduate Division, Graduate Programs in Medicine, Program in Experimental Pathology, Los Angeles, CA 90095. Offers MS, PhD. *Degree requirements:* For doctorate, thesis/dissertation, oral and written qualifying exams. *Entrance requirements:* For master's, GRE General Test; for doctorate, GRE General Test, previous course work in physical chemistry and physics.

**University of California, Los Angeles,** Graduate Division, College of Letters and Science and David Geffen School of Medicine, UCLA ACCESS to Programs in the Molecular, Cellular and Integrative Life Sciences, Los Angeles, CA 90095. Offers biochemistry and molecular biology (PhD); biological chemistry (PhD); cellular and molecular pathology (PhD); human genetics (PhD); microbiology, immunology, and molecular genetics (PhD); molecular biology (PhD); molecular toxicology (PhD); molecular, cellular and integrative physiology (PhD); neurobiology (PhD); oral biology (PhD); physiology (PhD). *Degree requirements:* For doctorate, thesis/dissertation, oral and written qualifying exams. *Entrance requirements:* For doctorate, GRE General Test, bachelor's degree; minimum undergraduate GPA of 3.0 (or its equivalent if letter grade system not used). Additional exam requirements/recommendations for international students: required—TOEFL. Electronic applications accepted.

**University of Cincinnati,** Graduate School, College of Medicine, Graduate Programs in Biomedical Sciences, Program in Pathobiology and Molecular Medicine, Cincinnati, OH 45267-0529. Offers pathology (PhD), including anatomic pathology, laboratory medicine, pathobiology and molecular medicine. *Degree requirements:* For doctorate, thesis/dissertation, qualifying exam. *Entrance requirements:* For doctorate, GRE General Test. Additional exam requirements/recommendations for international students: required—TOEFL. Electronic applications accepted.

**University of Georgia,** College of Veterinary Medicine, Department of Veterinary Pathology, Athens, GA 30602. Offers MS, PhD. *Degree requirements:* For master's, thesis; for doctorate, one foreign language, thesis/dissertation. *Entrance requirements:* For master's and doctorate, GRE General Test. Electronic applications accepted.

**University of Guelph,** Ontario Veterinary College and Office of Graduate and Postdoctoral Studies, Graduate Programs in Veterinary Sciences, Department of Pathobiology, Guelph, ON N1G 2W1, Canada. Offers anatomic pathology (DV Sc, Diploma); clinical pathology (Diploma); comparative pathology (M Sc, PhD); immunology (M Sc, PhD); laboratory animal science (DV Sc); pathology (M Sc, PhD, Diploma); veterinary infectious diseases (M Sc, PhD); zoo animal/wildlife medicine (DV Sc). *Degree requirements:* For master's, thesis; for doctorate, thesis/dissertation. *Entrance requirements:* For master's, DVM with B average or an honours degree in biological sciences; for doctorate, DVM or MSC degree, minimum B+ average. Additional exam requirements/recommendations for international students: required—TOEFL (minimum score 550 paper-based).

**The University of Iowa,** Roy J. and Lucille A. Carver College of Medicine and Graduate College, Graduate Programs in Medicine, Department of Pathology, Iowa City, IA 52242-1316. Offers MS. *Degree requirements:* For master's, thesis. *Entrance requirements:* For master's, GRE, minimum GPA of 3.0. Additional exam requirements/recommendations for international students: required—TOEFL. Electronic applications accepted.

**The University of Kansas,** University of Kansas Medical Center, School of Medicine, Department of Pathology and Laboratory Medicine, Kansas City, KS 66160. Offers MS, PhD, MD/PhD. *Accreditation:* NAACLS. *Faculty:* 19. *Students:* 9 full-time (6 women); includes 1 minority (Asian, non-Hispanic/Latino), 3 international. Average age 30. In 2019, 1 master's, 2 doctorates awarded. Terminal master's awarded for partial completion of doctoral program. *Degree requirements:* For master's, thesis; for doctorate, one foreign language, comprehensive exam, thesis/dissertation. *Entrance requirements:* For master's, GRE, curriculum vitae, official transcripts for all undergraduate coursework, 3 reference letters; for doctorate, GRE, curriculum vitae, statement of research and career interests, official transcripts for all undergraduate and graduate coursework, 3 reference letters. Additional exam requirements/recommendations for international students: required—TOEFL, TOEFL (preferred) or IELTS. *Application deadline:* For fall admission, 12/1 priority date for domestic and international students. Applications are processed on a rolling basis. Application fee: $60. Electronic applications accepted. *Expenses:* Tuition, state resident: full-time $9989. Tuition, nonresident: full-time $23,950. *International tuition:* $23,950 full-time. *Required fees:* $984; $81.99 per credit hour. Tuition and fees vary according to course load, campus/location and program. *Financial support:* Fellowships with full tuition reimbursements, research assistantships with full tuition reimbursements, teaching assistantships with full tuition reimbursements, Federal Work-Study, scholarships/grants, traineeships, and unspecified assistantships available. Financial award application deadline: 3/1; financial award applicants required to submit FAFSA. *Unit head:* Dr. Long Zheng, Professor and Russell J Eilers Endowed Chair, 913-588-7071, Fax: 913-588-7073, E-mail: xzheng2@kumc.edu. *Application contact:* Dr. Soumen Paul, Professor and Director of Graduate Studies, E-mail: spaul2@kumc.edu. Website: http://www.kumc.edu/school-of-medicine/pathology.html

**University of Manitoba,** Max Rady College of Medicine and Faculty of Graduate Studies, Graduate Programs in Medicine, Department of Pathology, Winnipeg, MB R3E 3P5, Canada. Offers M Sc. *Degree requirements:* For master's, thesis. *Entrance requirements:* For master's, B Sc honours degree. Additional exam requirements/recommendations for international students: required—TOEFL (minimum score 550 paper-based; 80 iBT), IELTS (minimum score 6.5).

**University of Maryland, Baltimore,** School of Medicine, Department of Pathology, Baltimore, MD 21201. Offers pathologists' assistant (MS). *Accreditation:* NAACLS. *Students:* 20 full-time (16 women); includes 5 minority (2 Black or African American, non-Hispanic/Latino; 2 Asian, non-Hispanic/Latino; 1 Hispanic/Latino), 2 international. Average age 25. 91 applicants, 64% accepted, 10 enrolled. In 2019, 10 master's awarded. *Entrance requirements:* For master's, GRE General Test. Additional exam requirements/recommendations for international students: required—TOEFL (minimum score 600 paper-based; 100 iBT); recommended—IELTS (minimum score 8). *Application deadline:* For fall admission, 2/1 for domestic and international students. Application fee: $75. Electronic applications accepted. *Expenses:* Contact institution. *Financial support:* Application deadline: 3/1; applicants required to submit FAFSA. *Unit head:* Dr. Rudy Castellani, Program Director, 410-328-5555, Fax: 410-706-8414, E-mail: rcastellani@som.umaryland.edu. *Application contact:* Carlen Miller, Associate Program Director, 410-328-5555, Fax: 410-706-8414, E-mail: cmiller@som.umaryland.edu. Website: http://medschool.umaryland.edu/pathology/pa/default.asp

**University of Michigan,** Rackham Graduate School, Program in Biomedical Sciences (PIBS), Program in Molecular and Cellular Pathology, Ann Arbor, MI 48109. Offers PhD. *Degree requirements:* For doctorate, comprehensive exam, thesis/dissertation, preliminary exam; oral defense of dissertation. *Entrance requirements:* For doctorate, 3 letters of recommendation, research experience, personal statement. Additional exam requirements/recommendations for international students: required—TOEFL (minimum score 84 iBT). Electronic applications accepted.

**University of Mississippi Medical Center,** School of Graduate Studies in Health Sciences, Department of Pathology, Jackson, MS 39216-4505. Offers PhD, MD/PhD. *Accreditation:* NAACLS. *Degree requirements:* For doctorate, thesis/dissertation, first authored publication in peer-reviewed journal. *Entrance requirements:* For doctorate, GRE General Test, GRE Subject Test, minimum GPA of 3.0. Additional exam requirements/recommendations for international students: required—TOEFL.

**University of Missouri,** School of Medicine and Office of Research and Graduate Studies, Graduate Programs in Medicine, Department of Pathology and Anatomical Sciences, Columbia, MO 65211. Offers MS, PhD. *Entrance requirements:* For master's, GRE (minimum Verbal and Analytical score of 1250), letters of recommendation, minimum GPA of 3.5. Additional exam requirements/recommendations for international students: required—TOEFL. Electronic applications accepted.

**University of Nebraska Medical Center,** Interdisciplinary Graduate Program in Biomedical Sciences, Immunology, Pathology and Infectious Disease Graduate Program, Omaha, NE 68198. Offers MS, PhD. *Program availability:* Part-time. Terminal master's awarded for partial completion of doctoral program. *Degree requirements:* For master's, comprehensive exam, thesis; for doctorate, comprehensive exam, thesis/dissertation. *Entrance requirements:* For master's and doctorate, previous course work in biology, chemistry, mathematics, and physics. Additional exam requirements/recommendations for international students: required—TOEFL (minimum score 550 paper-based; 90 iBT), IELTS (minimum score 6.5). Electronic applications accepted. Application fee is waived when completed online.

**University of New Mexico,** Graduate Studies, Health Sciences Center, Program in Biomedical Sciences, Albuquerque, NM 87131-5196. Offers biochemistry and molecular biology (MS, PhD); cell biology and physiology (MS, PhD); molecular genetics and microbiology (MS, PhD); neuroscience (MS, PhD); pathology (MS, PhD); toxicology (MS, PhD). *Program availability:* Part-time. Terminal master's awarded for partial completion of doctoral program. *Degree requirements:* For master's, thesis; for doctorate, comprehensive exam, thesis/dissertation, qualifying exam at the end of year 1/core curriculum. *Entrance requirements:* For master's and doctorate, GRE General Test, minimum undergraduate GPA of 3.0. Additional exam requirements/recommendations for international students: required—TOEFL. Electronic applications accepted. *Expenses:* Tuition, state resident: full-time $7633; part-time $972 per year. Tuition, nonresident: full-time $22,586; part-time $3840 per year. *International tuition:* $23,292 full-time. *Required fees:* $8608. Tuition and fees vary according to course level, course load, degree level, program and student level.

**The University of North Carolina at Chapel Hill,** School of Medicine and Graduate School, Biological and Biomedical Sciences Program, Pathobiology & Translational Science, Chapel Hill, NC 27599-7525. Offers experimental pathology (PhD). *Accreditation:* NAACLS. *Faculty:* 69 full-time (26 women), 5 part-time/adjunct (0 women). *Students:* 21 full-time (14 women); includes 3 minority (all Black or African American, non-Hispanic/Latino), 3 international. Average age 26. In 2019, 3 doctorates awarded. *Degree requirements:* For doctorate, comprehensive exam, thesis/dissertation. *Entrance requirements:* Additional exam requirements/recommendations for international students: required—TOEFL. *Application deadline:* For fall admission, 12/3 priority date for domestic and international students. Applications are processed on a rolling basis. Application fee: $77. Electronic applications accepted. *Financial support:* In 2019–20, 15 fellowships with full and partial tuition reimbursements (averaging $32,000 per year), 9 research assistantships with full and partial tuition reimbursements (averaging $32,000 per year) were awarded; career-related internships or fieldwork, health care benefits, and tuition waivers (full) also available. *Unit head:* Dr. Jon Homeister, Director of Graduate Studies, E-mail: homeiste@med.unc.edu. *Application contact:* Jeffrey Steinbach, Assistant Director for Admissions, 919-843-7129, E-mail: jsteinba@email.unc.edu. Website: https://www.med.unc.edu/pathology/mcp/pbts/

**University of Oklahoma Health Sciences Center,** College of Medicine and Graduate College, Graduate Programs in Medicine, Department of Pathology, Oklahoma City, OK 73190. Offers PhD. *Degree requirements:* For doctorate, thesis/dissertation. *Entrance requirements:* For doctorate, GRE General Test, 3 letters of recommendation. Additional exam requirements/recommendations for international students: required—TOEFL.

**University of Prince Edward Island,** Atlantic Veterinary College, Graduate Program in Veterinary Medicine, Charlottetown, PE C1A 4P3, Canada. Offers anatomy (M Sc, PhD); bacteriology (M Sc, PhD); clinical pharmacology (M Sc, PhD); clinical sciences (M Sc, PhD); epidemiology (M Sc, PhD), including reproduction; fish health (M Sc, PhD); food animal nutrition (M Sc, PhD); immunology (M Sc, PhD); microanatomy (M Sc, PhD); parasitology (M Sc, PhD); pathology (M Sc, PhD); pharmacology (M Sc, PhD); physiology (M Sc, PhD); toxicology (M Sc, PhD); veterinary science (M Vet Sc); virology (M Sc, PhD). *Program availability:* Part-time. *Degree requirements:* For master's, thesis; for doctorate, thesis/dissertation. *Entrance requirements:* For master's, DVM, B Sc honors degree, or equivalent; for doctorate, M Sc. Additional exam requirements/recommendations for international students: required—TOEFL (minimum score 550 paper-based; 80 iBT). *Expenses:* Contact institution.

**University of Rochester,** School of Medicine and Dentistry, Graduate Programs in Medicine and Dentistry, Department of Pathology and Laboratory Medicine, Rochester, NY 14627. Offers pathology (PhD). *Degree requirements:* For doctorate, variable foreign language requirement, thesis/dissertation, qualifying exam. *Entrance requirements:* For doctorate, GRE General Test, GRE Subject Test.

**University of Saskatchewan,** College of Medicine, Department of Pathology and Lab Medicine, Saskatoon, SK S7N 5A2, Canada. Offers M Sc, PhD. *Degree requirements:* For master's, thesis; for doctorate, thesis/dissertation. *Entrance requirements:* Additional exam requirements/recommendations for international students: required—TOEFL.

**University of Saskatchewan,** Western College of Veterinary Medicine and College of Graduate and Postdoctoral Studies, Graduate Programs in Veterinary Medicine, Department of Veterinary Pathology, Saskatoon, SK S7N 5A2, Canada. Offers M Sc, M Vet Sc, PhD. *Degree requirements:* For master's, thesis; for doctorate, comprehensive exam (for some programs), thesis/dissertation. *Entrance requirements:* Additional exam requirements/recommendations for international students: required—TOEFL or IELTS (minimum score 6.5). Electronic applications accepted.

**University of Southern California,** Keck School of Medicine and Graduate School, Graduate Programs in Medicine, Department of Pathology, Los Angeles, CA 90089. Offers experimental and molecular pathology (MS). *Degree requirements:* For master's, experiment-based thesis or theory-based scholarly review. *Entrance requirements:* For master's, GRE General Test, Minimum GPA of 3.0. Additional exam requirements/recommendations for international students: required—TOEFL (minimum score 600 paper-based; 100 iBT); recommended—IELTS (minimum score 6.5). Electronic applications accepted.

**The University of Tennessee Health Science Center,** College of Health Professions, Memphis, TN 38163-0002. Offers audiology (MS, Au D); clinical laboratory science (MSCLS); cytopathology practice (MCP); health informatics and information management (MHIIM); occupational therapy (MOT); physical therapy (DPT, ScDPT); physician assistant (MMS); speech-language pathology (MS). *Accreditation:* AOTA; APTA. *Program availability:* Part-time, evening/weekend, online learning. Terminal master's awarded for partial completion of doctoral program. *Degree requirements:* For master's, comprehensive exam, thesis; for doctorate, comprehensive exam, residency. *Entrance requirements:* For master's, GRE (MOT, MSCLS), minimum GPA of 3.0, 3 letters of reference, national accreditation (MSCLS), GRE if GPA is less than 3.0 (MCP); for doctorate, GRE. Additional exam requirements/recommendations for international students: required—TOEFL (minimum score 550 paper-based; 80 iBT). Electronic applications accepted. *Expenses:* Contact institution.

## Pathology

**The University of Texas Medical Branch,** Graduate School of Biomedical Sciences, Program in Experimental Pathology, Galveston, TX 77555. Offers PhD. *Degree requirements:* For doctorate, thesis/dissertation. *Entrance requirements:* For doctorate, GRE General Test. Additional exam requirements/recommendations for international students: required—TOEFL (minimum score 550 paper-based). Electronic applications accepted.

**The University of Toledo,** College of Graduate Studies, College of Medicine and Life Sciences, Department of Pathology, Toledo, OH 43606-3390. Offers pathology (Certificate); pathology assistant (MSBS). *Entrance requirements:* For degree, second-year medical student in good academic standing with recommendation by UT Medical School. Electronic applications accepted.

**University of Utah,** School of Medicine and Graduate School, Graduate Programs in Medicine, Department of Pathology, Salt Lake City, UT 84112-1107. Offers experimental pathology (PhD); laboratory medicine and biomedical science (MS). *Degree requirements:* For doctorate, comprehensive exam, thesis/dissertation. *Entrance requirements:* For doctorate, GRE, minimum GPA of 3.0. *Expenses:* Tuition, state resident: full-time $7085; part-time $272.51 per credit hour. Tuition, nonresident: full-time $24,937; part-time $959.12 per credit hour. *Required fees:* $880.52; $880.52 per semester. Tuition and fees vary according to degree level, program and student level.

**University of Vermont,** The Robert Larner, MD College of Medicine and Graduate College, Graduate Programs in Medicine, Department of Pathology and Laboratory Medicine, Burlington, VT 05405. Offers MS. Terminal master's awarded for partial completion of doctoral program. *Entrance requirements:* For master's, GRE General Test or MCAT. Additional exam requirements/recommendations for international students: required—TOEFL (minimum score 550 paper-based, 90 iBT) or IELTS (6.5). Electronic applications accepted.

**University of Virginia,** School of Medicine, Department of Pathology, Charlottesville, VA 22903. Offers PhD. *Degree requirements:* For doctorate, thesis/dissertation, oral defense of thesis. *Entrance requirements:* For doctorate, GRE General Test; GRE Subject Test (recommended), 2 letters of recommendation. Additional exam requirements/recommendations for international students: required—TOEFL.

**University of Washington,** Graduate School, School of Medicine, Graduate Programs in Medicine, Department of Pathology, Seattle, WA 98195. Offers molecular medicine and mechanisms of disease (PhD). *Degree requirements:* For doctorate, thesis/dissertation. *Entrance requirements:* For doctorate, GRE General Test.

**The University of Western Ontario,** Schulich School of Medicine and Dentistry, Department of Pathology, London, ON N6A 3K7, Canada. Offers M Sc, PhD. *Degree requirements:* For master's, thesis; for doctorate, comprehensive exam, thesis/dissertation. *Entrance requirements:* For master's and doctorate, minimum B+ average, honors degree. Additional exam requirements/recommendations for international students: required—TOEFL.

**University of Wisconsin–Madison,** School of Medicine and Public Health, Cellular and Molecular Pathology Graduate Program, Madison, WI 53706-1380. Offers PhD.

**Université Laval,** Faculty of Medicine, Post-Professional Programs in Medical Studies, Québec, QC G1K 7P4, Canada. Offers anatomy–pathology (DESS); anesthesiology (DESS); cardiology (DESS); care of older people (Diploma); clinical research (DESS); community health (DESS); dermatology (DESS); diagnostic radiology (DESS); emergency medicine (Diploma); family medicine (DESS); general surgery (DESS); geriatrics (DESS); hematology (DESS); internal medicine (DESS); maternal and fetal medicine (Diploma); medical biochemistry (DESS); medical microbiology and infectious diseases (DESS); medical oncology (DESS); nephrology (DESS); neurology (DESS); neurosurgery (DESS); obstetrics and gynecology (DESS); ophthalmology (DESS); orthopedic surgery (DESS); oto-rhino-laryngology (DESS); palliative medicine (Diploma); pediatrics (DESS); plastic surgery (DESS); psychiatry (DESS); pulmonary medicine (DESS); radiology–oncology (DESS); thoracic surgery (DESS); urology (DESS). *Degree requirements:* For other advanced degree, comprehensive exam. *Entrance requirements:* For degree, knowledge of French. Electronic applications accepted.

**Vanderbilt University,** School of Medicine, Department of Molecular Pathology and Immunology, Nashville, TN 37240-1001. Offers PhD, MD/PhD. *Faculty:* 35 full-time (13 women), 1 (woman) part-time/adjunct. *Students:* 26 full-time (16 women); includes 5 minority (1 Black or African American, non-Hispanic/Latino; 1 Asian, non-Hispanic/Latino; 3 Hispanic/Latino), 4 international. Average age 26. In 2019, 1 doctorate awarded. *Degree requirements:* For doctorate, thesis/dissertation, qualifying and final exams. *Entrance requirements:* For doctorate, GRE General Test. Additional exam requirements/recommendations for international students: required—TOEFL (minimum score 570 paper-based; 88 iBT). *Application deadline:* For fall admission, 1/15 for domestic and international students. Electronic applications accepted. *Expenses:* Tuition: Full-time $51,018; part-time $2087 per hour. *Required fees:* $542. Tuition and fees vary according to program. *Financial support:* Fellowships with full tuition reimbursements, research assistantships with full tuition reimbursements, Federal Work-Study, institutionally sponsored loans, traineeships, health care benefits, and tuition waivers (partial) available. Financial award application deadline: 1/15; financial award applicants required to submit CSS PROFILE or FAFSA. *Unit head:* Jay Jerome, Director of Graduate Studies, 615-322-2123, Fax: 615-322-0576, E-mail: jay.jerome@vanderbilt.edu. *Application contact:* Kristi Hargrove, Program Manager, 615-322-2294, E-mail: kristi.l.hargrove@vanderbilt.edu.
Website: https://medschool.vanderbilt.edu/igp/molecular-pathology-immunology

**West Virginia University,** School of Medicine, Morgantown, WV 26506. Offers biochemistry and molecular biology (PhD); biomedical science (MS); cancer cell biology (PhD); cellular and integrative physiology (PhD); exercise physiology (MS, PhD); health sciences (MS); immunology (PhD); medicine (MD); occupational therapy (MOT); pathologists assistant (MHS); physical therapy (DPT). *Accreditation:* AOTA; LCME/AMA. *Program availability:* Part-time, evening/weekend. *Entrance requirements:* Additional exam requirements/recommendations for international students: required—TOEFL. Electronic applications accepted. *Expenses:* Contact institution.

**Yale University,** Graduate School of Arts and Sciences, Department of Experimental Pathology, New Haven, CT 06520. Offers MS, PhD. *Degree requirements:* For doctorate, thesis/dissertation, qualifying exam. *Entrance requirements:* For doctorate, GRE General Test.

# Section 17
# Pharmacology and Toxicology

This section contains a directory of institutions offering graduate work in pharmacology and toxicology. Additional information about programs listed in the directory but not augmented by an in-depth entry may be obtained by writing directly to the dean of a graduate school or chair of a department at the address given in the directory.

For programs offering related work, see also in this book *Biochemistry; Biological and Biomedical Sciences; Cell, Molecular, and Structural Biology; Ecology, Environmental Biology, and Evolutionary Biology; Genetics, Developmental Biology, and Reproductive Biology; Neuroscience and Neurobiology; Nutrition; Pathology and Pathobiology; Pharmacy and Pharmaceutical Sciences; Physiology; Public Health;* and *Veterinary Medicine and Sciences.* In the other guides in this series:

**Graduate Programs in the Humanities, Arts & Social Sciences**
See *Psychology and Counseling*
**Graduate Programs in the Physical Sciences, Mathematics, Agricultural Sciences, the Environment & Natural Resources**
See *Chemistry* and *Environmental Sciences and Management*
**Graduate Programs in Engineering & Applied Sciences**
See *Chemical Engineering* and *Civil and Environmental Engineering*

## CONTENTS

### Program Directories

# Molecular Pharmacology

**Albert Einstein College of Medicine,** Graduate Programs in the Biomedical Sciences, Department of Molecular Pharmacology, Bronx, NY 10461. Offers PhD, MD/PhD. *Degree requirements:* For doctorate, thesis/dissertation. *Entrance requirements:* For doctorate, GRE General Test. Additional exam requirements/recommendations for international students: required—TOEFL.

**Brown University,** Graduate School, Division of Biology and Medicine, Department of Molecular Pharmacology, Physiology and Biotechnology, Providence, RI 02912. Offers biomedical engineering (Sc M, PhD); biotechnology (PhD); molecular pharmacology and physiology (PhD); MD/PhD. *Degree requirements:* For doctorate, thesis/dissertation, preliminary exam. *Entrance requirements:* For master's and doctorate, GRE General Test, GRE Subject Test. Additional exam requirements/recommendations for international students: required—TOEFL. Electronic applications accepted.

**Harvard University,** Graduate School of Arts and Sciences, Division of Medical Sciences, Boston, MA 02115. Offers biological chemistry and molecular pharmacology (PhD); cell biology (PhD); genetics (PhD); microbiology and molecular genetics (PhD); pathology (PhD), including experimental pathology. *Degree requirements:* For doctorate, thesis/dissertation. *Entrance requirements:* For doctorate, GRE General Test, GRE Subject Test. Additional exam requirements/recommendations for international students: required—TOEFL.

**Loyola University Chicago,** Graduate School, Integrated Program in Biomedical Sciences, Maywood, IL 60660. Offers biochemistry and molecular biology (MS, PhD); cell and molecular physiology (MS, PhD); infectious disease and immunology (MS); integrative cell biology (MS, PhD); microbiology and immunology (MS, PhD); molecular pharmacology and therapeutics (MS, PhD); neuroscience (MS, PhD). *Students:* Average age 25. 773 applicants, 34% accepted, 122 enrolled. In 2019, 46 master's, 12 doctorates awarded. *Degree requirements:* For master's, thesis; for doctorate, comprehensive exam, thesis/dissertation. *Entrance requirements:* For doctorate, GRE. Additional exam requirements/recommendations for international students: required—TOEFL (minimum score 94 iBT), IELTS (minimum score 7.5). *Application deadline:* For fall admission, 2/7 for domestic students. Applications are processed on a rolling basis. Electronic applications accepted. *Expenses:* Contact institution. *Financial support:* In 2019–20, 20 students received support. Schmitt Fellowships and yearly tuition scholarships (averaging $25,032) available. Financial award application deadline: 6/15; financial award applicants required to submit FAFSA. *Unit head:* Dr. Leanne L. Cribbs, Associate Dean, Graduate Education, 708-327-2817, Fax: 708-216-8216, E-mail: lcribbs@luc.edu. *Application contact:* Margarita Quesada, Graduate Program Secretary, 708-216-3532, Fax: 708-216-8216, E-mail: mquesad@luc.edu.
Website: http://ssom.luc.edu/graduate_school/degree-programs/ipbsphd/

**Mayo Clinic Graduate School of Biomedical Sciences,** Program in Molecular Pharmacology and Experimental Therapeutics, Rochester, MN 55905. Offers MS, PhD. Terminal master's awarded for partial completion of doctoral program. *Degree requirements:* For master's, thesis; for doctorate, comprehensive exam, thesis/dissertation, oral defense of dissertation, qualifying oral and written exam. *Entrance requirements:* For doctorate, GRE, 1 year of chemistry, biology, calculus, and physics. Additional exam requirements/recommendations for international students: required—TOEFL. Electronic applications accepted.

**Medical University of South Carolina,** College of Graduate Studies, Program in Cell and Molecular Pharmacology and Experimental Therapeutics, Charleston, SC 29425. Offers MS, PhD, DMD/PhD, MD/PhD. Terminal master's awarded for partial completion of doctoral program. *Degree requirements:* For master's, thesis; for doctorate, comprehensive exam, thesis/dissertation, oral and written exams. *Entrance requirements:* For master's, GRE General Test; for doctorate, GRE General Test, interview, minimum GPA of 3.0. Additional exam requirements/recommendations for international students: required—TOEFL (minimum score 600 paper-based; 100 iBT). Electronic applications accepted.

**Purdue University,** College of Pharmacy and Graduate School, Graduate Programs in Pharmacy and Pharmacal Sciences, Department of Medicinal Chemistry and Molecular Pharmacology, West Lafayette, IN 47907. Offers biophysical and computational chemistry (PhD); cancer research (PhD); immunology and infectious disease (PhD); medicinal biochemistry and molecular biology (PhD); medicinal chemistry and chemical biology (PhD); molecular pharmacology (PhD); neuropharmacology, neurodegeneration, and neurotoxicity (PhD); systems biology and functional genomics (PhD). *Faculty:* 20 full-time (5 women), 7 part-time/adjunct (2 women). *Students:* 80 full-time (40 women), 2 part-time (0 women); includes 9 minority (5 Asian, non-Hispanic/Latino; 2 Hispanic/Latino; 2 Two or more races, non-Hispanic/Latino), 44 international. Average age 26. 162 applicants, 20% accepted, 15 enrolled. In 2019, 11 doctorates awarded. *Degree requirements:* For doctorate, thesis/dissertation. *Entrance requirements:* For doctorate, GRE General Test; GRE Subject Test in biology, biochemistry, and chemistry (recommended), minimum undergraduate GPA of 3.0. Additional exam requirements/recommendations for international students: required—TOEFL (minimum score 550 paper-based; 77 iBT); recommended—TWE. *Application deadline:* For fall admission, 2/1 for domestic and international students. Applications are processed on a rolling basis. Application fee: $60 ($75 for international students). Electronic applications accepted. *Financial support:* Fellowships, research assistantships, teaching assistantships, and traineeships available. Support available to part-time students. Financial award applicants required to submit FAFSA. *Unit head:* Zhong-Yin Zhang, Head, 765-494-1403, E-mail: zhang-yn@purdue.edu. *Application contact:* Delayne Graham, Graduate Contact, 765-494-1362, E-mail: dkgraham@purdue.edu.

**Rosalind Franklin University of Medicine and Science,** School of Graduate and Postdoctoral Studies - Interdisciplinary Graduate Program in Biomedical Sciences, Department of Cellular and Molecular Pharmacology, North Chicago, IL 60064-3095. Offers MS, PhD, MD/PhD. Terminal master's awarded for partial completion of doctoral program. *Degree requirements:* For master's, comprehensive exam, thesis; for doctorate, comprehensive exam, thesis/dissertation. *Entrance requirements:* For master's and doctorate, GRE General Test. Additional exam requirements/recommendations for international students: required—TOEFL, TWE. Electronic applications accepted.

**Rutgers University - New Brunswick,** Graduate School of Biomedical Sciences, Program in Cellular and Molecular Pharmacology, Piscataway, NJ 08854-5635. Offers MS, PhD, MD/PhD. *Degree requirements:* For master's, thesis, qualifying exam; for doctorate, thesis/dissertation, qualifying exam. *Entrance requirements:* Additional exam requirements/recommendations for international students: required—TOEFL. Electronic applications accepted.

**Thomas Jefferson University,** Jefferson College of Life Sciences, PhD Program in Biochemistry and Molecular Pharmacology, Philadelphia, PA 19107. Offers PhD. *Degree requirements:* For doctorate, comprehensive exam, thesis/dissertation. *Entrance requirements:* For doctorate, GRE General Test or MCAT, minimum GPA of 3.2. Additional exam requirements/recommendations for international students: required—TOEFL, IELTS (minimum score 7). Electronic applications accepted.

**University at Buffalo, the State University of New York,** Graduate School, Graduate Programs in Cancer Research and Biomedical Sciences at Roswell Park Cancer Institute, Buffalo, NY 14260. Offers cancer pathology and prevention (PhD); cellular and molecular biology (PhD); immunology (PhD); interdisciplinary natural sciences (MS); molecular and cellular biophysics and biochemistry (PhD); molecular pharmacology and cancer therapeutics (PhD). Terminal master's awarded for partial completion of doctoral program. *Degree requirements:* For master's, thesis, oral defense of thesis; for doctorate, comprehensive exam, thesis/dissertation, oral defense of dissertation. *Entrance requirements:* For master's and doctorate, GRE General Test. Additional exam requirements/recommendations for international students: required—TOEFL (minimum score 79 iBT). Electronic applications accepted. *Expenses: Tuition, area resident:* Full-time $11,310; part-time $471 per credit hour. Tuition, state resident: full-time $11,310; part-time $471 per credit hour. Tuition, nonresident: full-time $23,100; part-time $963 per credit hour. *International tuition:* $23,100 full-time. *Required fees:* $2820.

**University of Maryland, Baltimore,** Graduate School, Graduate Program in Life Sciences, Program in Molecular Medicine, Baltimore, MD 21201. Offers applied pharmacology and toxicology (PhD); cancer biology (PhD); genome biology (PhD); molecular and cellular physiology (PhD); MD/PhD. *Degree requirements:* For doctorate, comprehensive exam, thesis/dissertation. *Entrance requirements:* For doctorate, GRE, minimum GPA of 3.0, curriculum vitae, essay, 3 letters of recommendation. Additional exam requirements/recommendations for international students: required—TOEFL (minimum score 80 iBT); recommended—IELTS (minimum score 7). Electronic applications accepted.

**University of Massachusetts Medical School,** Graduate School of Biomedical Sciences, Worcester, MA 01655. Offers biomedical sciences (PhD), including biochemistry and molecular pharmacology, bioinformatics and computational biology, cancer biology, immunology and microbiology, interdisciplinary, neuroscience, translational science; biomedical sciences (millennium program) (PhD); clinical and population health research (PhD); clinical investigation (MS). *Faculty:* 1,258 full-time (525 women), 372 part-time/adjunct (238 women). *Students:* 344 full-time (198 women), 1 (woman) part-time; includes 73 minority (12 Black or African American, non-Hispanic/Latino; 1 American Indian or Alaska Native, non-Hispanic/Latino; 45 Asian, non-Hispanic/Latino; 15 Hispanic/Latino), 120 international. Average age 29. 581 applicants, 23% accepted, 56 enrolled. In 2019, 6 master's, 49 doctorates awarded. Terminal master's awarded for partial completion of doctoral program. *Degree requirements:* For master's, comprehensive exam, thesis; for doctorate, comprehensive exam, thesis/dissertation. *Entrance requirements:* For master's, MD, PhD, DVM, or PharmD; for doctorate, bachelor's degree. Additional exam requirements/recommendations for international students: required—TOEFL, IELTS, TOEFL (minimum score 100 IBT) or IELTS (minimum score 7.0). *Application deadline:* For fall admission, 12/1 for domestic and international students. Applications are processed on a rolling basis. Application fee: $80. Electronic applications accepted. Application fee is waived when completed online. *Expenses:* Contact institution. *Financial support:* In 2019–20, 22 fellowships with full tuition reimbursements (averaging $33,061 per year), 322 research assistantships with full tuition reimbursements (averaging $32,850 per year) were awarded; institutionally sponsored loans and scholarships/grants also available. Financial award application deadline: 5/15. *Unit head:* Dr. Mary Ellen Lane, Dean, 508-856-4018, E-mail: maryellen.lane@umassmed.edu. *Application contact:* Dr. Kendall Knight, Assistant Vice Provost for Admissions, 508-856-5628, Fax: 508-856-3659, E-mail: kendall.knight@umassmed.edu.
Website: http://www.umassmed.edu/gsbs/

**University of Nevada, Reno,** Graduate School, Interdisciplinary Program in Cellular and Molecular Pharmacology and Physiology, Reno, NV 89557. Offers PhD. *Degree requirements:* For doctorate, one foreign language, thesis/dissertation. *Entrance requirements:* For doctorate, GRE General Test or MCAT, minimum GPA of 3.0. Additional exam requirements/recommendations for international students: required—TOEFL (minimum score 500 paper-based; 61 iBT), IELTS (minimum score 6). Electronic applications accepted.

**University of Southern California,** Graduate School, School of Pharmacy, Graduate Programs in Molecular Pharmacology and Toxicology, Los Angeles, CA 90033. Offers pharmacology and pharmaceutical sciences (MS, PhD). Terminal master's awarded for partial completion of doctoral program. *Degree requirements:* For master's, comprehensive exam, thesis, 24 units of formal course work, excluding research and seminar courses; for doctorate, comprehensive exam, thesis/dissertation, 24 units of formal course work, excluding research and seminar courses. *Entrance requirements:* For master's and doctorate, GRE. Additional exam requirements/recommendations for international students: required—TOEFL (minimum score 603 paper-based; 100 iBT). Electronic applications accepted. *Expenses:* Contact institution.

# Molecular Toxicology

**Massachusetts Institute of Technology,** School of Science, Department of Biology, Cambridge, MA 02139. Offers biochemistry (PhD); biological oceanography (PhD); biology (PhD); biophysical chemistry and molecular structure (PhD); cell biology (PhD); computational and systems biology (PhD); developmental biology (PhD); genetics

(PhD); immunology (PhD); microbiology (PhD); molecular biology (PhD); neurobiology (PhD). *Degree requirements:* For doctorate, comprehensive exam, thesis/dissertation, teaching assistantship during two semesters. *Entrance requirements:* For doctorate, GRE General Test. Additional exam requirements/recommendations for international students: required—TOEFL, IELTS. Electronic applications accepted.

**Oregon State University,** College of Agricultural Sciences, Program in Toxicology, Corvallis, OR 97331. Offers environmental chemistry and ecotoxicology (MS, PhD); mechanistic toxicology (MS, PhD); molecular and cellular toxicology (MS, PhD); neurotoxicology (MS, PhD). *Degree requirements:* For master's, thesis; for doctorate, thesis/dissertation. *Entrance requirements:* For master's and doctorate, GRE, bachelor's degree in chemistry or biological sciences, minimum GPA of 3.0 in last 90 hours of course work. Additional exam requirements/recommendations for international students: required—TOEFL (minimum score 80 iBT), IELTS (minimum score 6.5).

**Penn State Hershey Medical Center,** College of Medicine, Graduate School Programs in the Biomedical Sciences, Huck Institutes of the Life Sciences, Intercollege Graduate Program in Molecular Cellular and Integrative Biosciences, Hershey, PA 17033. Offers cell and developmental biology (PhD); molecular medicine (PhD); molecular toxicology (PhD); neurobiology (PhD). *Degree requirements:* For doctorate, comprehensive exam, thesis/dissertation, oral exam. *Entrance requirements:* For doctorate, GRE, minimum GPA of 3.0. Additional exam requirements/recommendations for international students: required—TOEFL (minimum score 500 paper-based). Electronic applications accepted.

**University of California, Berkeley,** Graduate Division, College of Natural Resources, Group in Molecular Toxicology, Berkeley, CA 94720. Offers PhD. *Entrance requirements:* For doctorate, GRE General Test, 3 letters of recommendation.

**University of California, Los Angeles,** Graduate Division, College of Letters and Science and David Geffen School of Medicine, UCLA ACCESS to Programs in the Molecular, Cellular and Integrative Life Sciences, Los Angeles, CA 90095. Offers biochemistry and molecular biology (PhD); biological chemistry (PhD); cellular and molecular pathology (PhD); human genetics (PhD); microbiology, immunology, and

molecular genetics (PhD); molecular biology (PhD); molecular toxicology (PhD); molecular, cellular and integrative physiology (PhD); neurobiology (PhD); oral biology (PhD); physiology (PhD). *Degree requirements:* For doctorate, thesis/dissertation, oral and written qualifying exams. *Entrance requirements:* For doctorate, GRE General Test, bachelor's degree; minimum undergraduate GPA of 3.0 (or its equivalent if letter grade system not used). Additional exam requirements/recommendations for international students: required—TOEFL. Electronic applications accepted.

**University of California, Los Angeles,** Graduate Division, Fielding School of Public Health, Department of Environmental Health Sciences, Interdepartmental Program in Molecular Toxicology, Los Angeles, CA 90095. Offers PhD. *Degree requirements:* For doctorate, thesis/dissertation, oral and written qualifying exams. *Entrance requirements:* For doctorate, GRE General Test. Electronic applications accepted.

**University of Cincinnati,** Graduate School, College of Medicine, Graduate Programs in Biomedical Sciences, Department of Environmental Health, Programs in Environmental Genetics and Molecular Toxicology, Cincinnati, OH 45221. Offers MS, PhD. *Degree requirements:* For doctorate, thesis/dissertation. *Entrance requirements:* For master's, GRE, minimum GPA of 3.0, 3 letters of recommendation. Additional exam requirements/recommendations for international students: required—TOEFL (minimum score 520 paper-based).

**University of Maryland, Baltimore,** Graduate School, Graduate Program in Life Sciences, Program in Molecular Medicine, Baltimore, MD 21201. Offers applied pharmacology and toxicology (PhD); cancer biology (PhD); genome biology (PhD); molecular and cellular physiology (PhD); MD/PhD. *Degree requirements:* For doctorate, comprehensive exam, thesis/dissertation. *Entrance requirements:* For doctorate, GRE, minimum GPA of 3.0, curriculum vitae, essay, 3 letters of recommendation. Additional exam requirements/recommendations for international students: required—TOEFL (minimum score 80 iBT); recommended—IELTS (minimum score 7). Electronic applications accepted.

# Pharmacology

**Albany College of Pharmacy and Health Sciences,** School of Pharmacy and Pharmaceutical Sciences, Albany, NY 12208. Offers health outcomes research (MS); pharmaceutical sciences (MS), including pharmaceutics, pharmacology; pharmacy (Pharm D). *Accreditation:* ACPE. *Degree requirements:* For master's, thesis; for doctorate, practice experience. *Entrance requirements:* For master's, GRE, minimum GPA of 3.0; for doctorate, PCAT, minimum GPA of 2.5. Additional exam requirements/ recommendations for international students: required—TOEFL (minimum score 84 iBT). Electronic applications accepted.

**Albany Medical College,** Center for Neuropharmacology and Neuroscience, Albany, NY 12208-3479. Offers MS, PhD. Terminal master's awarded for partial completion of doctoral program. *Degree requirements:* For master's, thesis; for doctorate, comprehensive exam, thesis/dissertation. *Entrance requirements:* For master's, GRE General Test, all transcripts, letters of recommendation; for doctorate, GRE General Test, letters of recommendation. Additional exam requirements/recommendations for international students: required—TOEFL.

**Alliant International University–San Francisco,** California School of Professional Psychology, Program in Psychopharmacology, San Francisco, CA 94133. Offers Post-Doctoral MS. *Program availability:* Part-time, online learning. *Entrance requirements:* For master's, doctorate in clinical psychology. Additional exam requirements/ recommendations for international students: required—TOEFL (minimum score 550 paper-based; 80 iBT), TWE (minimum score 5). Electronic applications accepted.

**Argosy University, Hawaii,** Hawai'i School of Professional Psychology, Program in Psychopharmacology, Honolulu, HI 96813. Offers MS, Certificate.

**Augusta University,** Program in Pharmacology, Augusta, GA 30912. Offers PhD. *Degree requirements:* For doctorate, comprehensive exam, thesis/dissertation. *Entrance requirements:* For doctorate, GRE General Test. Additional exam requirements/recommendations for international students: required—TOEFL (minimum score 550 paper-based; 79 iBT). Electronic applications accepted.

**Baylor College of Medicine,** Graduate School of Biomedical Sciences, Department of Pharmacology, Houston, TX 77030-3498. Offers PhD, MD/PhD. *Degree requirements:* For doctorate, thesis/dissertation, public defense. *Entrance requirements:* For doctorate, GRE General Test, GRE Subject Test (strongly recommended), minimum GPA of 3.0. Additional exam requirements/recommendations for international students: required—TOEFL. Electronic applications accepted.

**Boston University,** School of Medicine, Graduate Medical Sciences, Department of Pharmacology and Experimental Therapeutics, Boston, MA 02118. Offers PhD, MD/PhD. Terminal master's awarded for partial completion of doctoral program. *Application deadline:* For fall admission, 1/15 for domestic students; for spring admission, 10/15 for domestic students. *Unit head:* Dr. David H. Farb, Chairman, E-mail: dfarb@bu.edu. *Application contact:* GMS Admissions Office, 617-358-9518, Fax: 617-358-2913, E-mail: gmsbusm@bu.edu.
Website: http://www.bumc.bu.edu/busm-pm/

**Boston University,** School of Medicine, Graduate Medical Sciences, Program in Clinical Research, Boston, MA 02215. Offers MA. *Application deadline:* For spring admission, 10/15 for domestic students. *Unit head:* Dr. Janice Weinberg, Director, E-mail: janicew@bu.edu. *Application contact:* Stacey Hess Pino, Assistant Director, E-mail: sahess@bu.edu.
Website: http://www.bumc.bu.edu/gms/mscr/

**Case Western Reserve University,** School of Medicine and School of Graduate Studies, Graduate Programs in Medicine, Department of Pharmacology, Cleveland, OH 44106. Offers PhD, MD/PhD. Terminal master's awarded for partial completion of doctoral program. *Degree requirements:* For doctorate, comprehensive exam, thesis/dissertation. *Entrance requirements:* For doctorate, GRE General Test or MCAT. Additional exam requirements/recommendations for international students: required—TOEFL (minimum score 577 paper-based; 90 iBT). Electronic applications accepted.

**The Chicago School of Professional Psychology: Online,** Program in Clinical Psychopharmacology, Chicago, IL 60654. Offers MS. *Program availability:* Online learning.

**Columbia University,** College of Physicians and Surgeons, Department of Pharmacology, New York, NY 10032. Offers pharmacology (M Phil, MA, PhD); pharmacology-toxicology (M Phil, MA, PhD); MD/PhD. Terminal master's awarded for

partial completion of doctoral program. *Degree requirements:* For doctorate, thesis/dissertation. *Entrance requirements:* For master's and doctorate, GRE General Test. Additional exam requirements/recommendations for international students: required—TOEFL. *Expenses: Tuition:* Full-time $47,600; part-time $1880 per credit. One-time fee: $105.

**Creighton University,** School of Medicine and Graduate School, Graduate Programs in Medicine, Department of Pharmacology, Omaha, NE 68178-0001. Offers pharmaceutical sciences (MS); pharmacology (MS, PhD); Pharm D/MS. Terminal master's awarded for partial completion of doctoral program. *Degree requirements:* For master's, comprehensive exam, thesis; for doctorate, comprehensive exam, thesis/dissertation, oral and written preliminary exams. *Entrance requirements:* For master's and doctorate, GRE General Test, minimum GPA of 3.0, undergraduate degree in sciences. Additional exam requirements/recommendations for international students: required—TOEFL. Electronic applications accepted.

**Dalhousie University,** Faculty of Graduate Studies and Faculty of Medicine, Graduate Programs in Medicine, Department of Pharmacology, Halifax, NS B3H 4R2, Canada. Offers M Sc, PhD. *Degree requirements:* For master's, thesis; for doctorate, comprehensive exam, thesis/dissertation. *Entrance requirements:* Additional exam requirements/recommendations for international students: required—1 of 5 approved tests: TOEFL, IELTS, CANTEST, CAEL, Michigan English Language Assessment Battery. Electronic applications accepted.

**Drexel University,** College of Medicine, Biomedical Graduate Programs, Pharmacology and Physiology Program, Philadelphia, PA 19104-2875. Offers MS, PhD, MD/PhD. *Program availability:* Part-time. Terminal master's awarded for partial completion of doctoral program. *Degree requirements:* For master's, comprehensive exam; for doctorate, thesis/dissertation, qualifying exam. *Entrance requirements:* For master's, GRE General Test, minimum GPA of 2.75; for doctorate, GRE General Test, minimum GPA of 3.0. Additional exam requirements/recommendations for international students: required—TOEFL. Electronic applications accepted.

**Duke University,** Graduate School, Department of Pharmacology and Cancer Biology, Durham, NC 27710. Offers pharmacology (PhD). *Faculty:* 43 full-time. *Students:* 41 full-time (31 women); includes 25 minority (6 Black or African American, non-Hispanic/Latino; 14 Asian, non-Hispanic/Latino; 2 Hispanic/Latino; 1 Native Hawaiian or other Pacific Islander, non-Hispanic/Latino; 2 Two or more races, non-Hispanic/Latino), 10 international. Average age 23. 85 applicants, 19% accepted, 6 enrolled. In 2019, 13 doctorates awarded. *Degree requirements:* For doctorate, thesis/dissertation. *Entrance requirements:* For doctorate, GRE Optional, minimum GPA of 3.0. Additional exam requirements/recommendations for international students: required—TOEFL (minimum score 577 paper-based; 90 iBT), IELTS (minimum score 7), TOEFL or IELTS. *Application deadline:* For fall admission, 12/6 priority date for domestic and international students. Application fee: $95. Electronic applications accepted. *Financial support:* In 2019–20, 10 fellowships with tuition reimbursements (averaging $31,800 per year), 13 research assistantships with tuition reimbursements (averaging $31,800 per year) were awarded; scholarships/grants, traineeships, health care benefits, and unspecified assistantships also available. Financial award application deadline: 12/6. *Unit head:* Dr. David MacAlpine, Director of Graduate Studies, 919-681-6077, E-mail: david.macalpine@duke.edu. *Application contact:* Jamie Baize-Smith, Assistant Director of Graduate Studies, 919-613-8600, E-mail: baize@duke.edu.
Website: http://pharmacology.mc.duke.edu/

**Duquesne University,** School of Pharmacy, Graduate School of Pharmaceutical Sciences, Program in Pharmacology, Pittsburgh, PA 15282-0001. Offers MS, PhD. *Degree requirements:* For master's, thesis; for doctorate, comprehensive exam, thesis/dissertation. *Entrance requirements:* For master's and doctorate, GRE General Test. Additional exam requirements/recommendations for international students: required—TOEFL (minimum score 100 iBT). Electronic applications accepted. *Expenses:* Contact institution.

**East Carolina University,** Brody School of Medicine, Department of Pharmacology and Toxicology, Greenville, NC 27858-4353. Offers PhD. *Students:* 16 full-time (8 women); includes 1 minority (Hispanic/Latino), 2 international. Average age 29. *Entrance requirements:* For doctorate, GRE General Test, GRE Subject Test. *Expenses: Tuition,* area resident: Full-time $4749; part-time $185 per credit hour. Tuition, state resident: full-time $4749; part-time $185 per credit hour. Tuition, nonresident: full-time $17,898;

part-time $864 per credit hour. *International tuition:* $17,898 full-time. *Required fees:* $2787. *Financial support:* Fellowships with full tuition reimbursements available. Financial award application deadline: 6/1. *Unit head:* Dr. Rukiyah Van Dross, Chairman, 252-744-3301, E-mail: vandrossr@ecu.edu. *Application contact:* Contact Center, 252-744-1020.
Website: https://pharmacology-toxicology.ecu.edu/

**East Carolina University,** Brody School of Medicine, Office of Research and Graduate Studies, Greenville, NC 27858-4353. Offers anatomy and cell biology (PhD); biochemistry and molecular biology (PhD); biomedical science (MS); microbiology and immunology (PhD); pharmacology and toxicology (PhD); physiology (PhD). *Students:* 102 full-time (44 women), 1 part-time (0 women); includes 16 minority (4 Black or African American, non-Hispanic/Latino; 7 Asian, non-Hispanic/Latino; 4 Hispanic/Latino; 1 Two or more races, non-Hispanic/Latino), 13 international. Average age 28. 83 applicants, 40% accepted, 20 enrolled. In 2019, 3 master's, 10 doctorates awarded. *Degree requirements:* For doctorate, comprehensive exam, thesis/dissertation. *Entrance requirements:* For doctorate, GRE General Test. Additional exam requirements/recommendations for international students: required—some international applicants may be required to demonstrate English proficiency via the TOEFL, IELTS, or PTE exam.; recommended—TOEFL (minimum score 78 iBT), IELTS (minimum score 6.5), TSE (minimum score 65). *Application deadline:* For fall admission, 8/15 for domestic students; for spring admission, 12/20 for domestic students. Applications are processed on a rolling basis. Application fee: $75. Electronic applications accepted. *Expenses: Tuition, area resident:* Full-time $4749; part-time $185 per credit hour. Tuition, state resident: full-time $4749; part-time $185 per credit hour. Tuition, nonresident: full-time $17,898; part-time $864 per credit hour. *International tuition:* $17,898 full-time. *Required fees:* $2787. *Financial support:* Fellowships available. Financial award application deadline: 6/1. *Unit head:* Dr. Russ Price, Associate Dean, 252-744-9346, E-mail: pricest17@ecu.edu. *Application contact:* Dr. Russ Price, Associate Dean, 252-744-9346, E-mail: pricest17@ecu.edu.
Website: http://www.ecu.edu/cs-dhs/bsomresearchgradstudies/index.cfm

**East Tennessee State University,** Quillen College of Medicine, Department of Biomedical Sciences, Johnson City, TN 37614. Offers anatomy (PhD); biochemistry (PhD); microbiology (PhD); pharmaceutical sciences (PhD); pharmacology (PhD); physiology (PhD); quantitative biosciences (PhD). *Degree requirements:* For doctorate, comprehensive exam, thesis/dissertation, comprehensive qualifying exam; one-year residency. *Entrance requirements:* For doctorate, GRE General Test, GRE Subject Test, 3 letters of recommendation, minimum of 60 credit hours beyond the baccalaureate degree. Additional exam requirements/recommendations for international students: required—TOEFL (minimum score 550 paper-based; 79 iBT). Electronic applications accepted. *Expenses:* Contact institution.

**Emory University,** Laney Graduate School, Division of Biological and Biomedical Sciences, Program in Molecular and Systems Pharmacology, Atlanta, GA 30322-1100. Offers PhD. *Degree requirements:* For doctorate, comprehensive exam, thesis/dissertation. *Entrance requirements:* For doctorate, GRE General Test, minimum GPA of 3.0 in science course work (recommended). Additional exam requirements/recommendations for international students: required—TOEFL. Electronic applications accepted.

**Fairleigh Dickinson University, Florham Campus,** Silberman College of Business, Program in Pharmaceutical Studies, Madison, NJ 07940-1099. Offers MBA, Certificate.

**Florida Agricultural and Mechanical University,** Division of Graduate Studies, Research, and Continuing Education, College of Pharmacy and Pharmaceutical Sciences, Graduate Programs in Pharmaceutical Sciences, Tallahassee, FL 32307-3200. Offers environmental toxicology (PhD); health outcomes research and pharmacoeconomics (PhD); medicinal chemistry (MS, PhD); pharmaceutics (MS, PhD); pharmacology/toxicology (MS, PhD); pharmacy administration (MS). *Accreditation:* CEPH. *Degree requirements:* For master's, comprehensive exam, thesis, publishable paper; for doctorate, comprehensive exam, thesis/dissertation, publishable paper. *Entrance requirements:* For master's and doctorate, GRE General Test, minimum GPA of 3.0 in last 60 hours. Additional exam requirements/recommendations for international students: required—TOEFL.

**Georgetown University,** Graduate School of Arts and Sciences, Department of Pharmacology and Physiology, Washington, DC 20057. Offers pharmacology (MS, PhD, MD/PhD); physiology (MS); MD/PhD. *Program availability:* Part-time. *Degree requirements:* For doctorate, comprehensive exam, thesis/dissertation. *Entrance requirements:* For doctorate, GRE General Test, previous course work in biology and chemistry. Additional exam requirements/recommendations for international students: required—TOEFL (minimum score 550 paper-based; 80 iBT). Electronic applications accepted.

**Howard University,** College of Medicine, Department of Pharmacology, Washington, DC 20059-0002. Offers MS, PhD, MD/PhD. *Program availability:* Part-time. *Degree requirements:* For master's, comprehensive exam, thesis; for doctorate, one foreign language, comprehensive exam, thesis/dissertation, qualifying exam. *Entrance requirements:* For master's, GRE General Test, minimum GPA of 3.2, BS in chemistry, biology, pharmacy, psychology or related field; for doctorate, GRE General Test, minimum graduate GPA of 3.2. Additional exam requirements/recommendations for international students: recommended—TOEFL.

**Husson University,** School of Pharmacy, Bangor, ME 04401-2999. Offers pharmacology (MS); pharmacy (Pharm D). *Accreditation:* ACPE. *Entrance requirements:* For doctorate, PCAT, PharmCAS application. Additional exam requirements/recommendations for international students: required—TOEFL (minimum score 550 paper-based; 80 iBT), IELTS (minimum score 6.5). Electronic applications accepted. *Expenses:* Contact institution.

**Idaho State University,** Graduate School, College of Pharmacy, Department of Biomedical and Pharmaceutical Sciences, Pocatello, ID 83209-8334. Offers biopharmaceutical analysis (PhD); drug delivery (PhD); medicinal chemistry (PhD); pharmaceutical sciences (MS); pharmacology (PhD). *Program availability:* Part-time. *Degree requirements:* For master's, one foreign language, comprehensive exam, thesis, thesis research, classes in speech and technical writing; for doctorate, comprehensive exam, thesis/dissertation, written and oral exams, classes in speech and technical writing. *Entrance requirements:* For master's, GRE General Test, minimum GPA of 3.0, 3 letters of recommendation; for doctorate, GRE General Test, BS in pharmacy or related field, minimum GPA of 3.0, 3 letters of recommendation. Additional exam requirements/recommendations for international students: required—TOEFL (minimum score 550 paper-based; 80 iBT). Electronic applications accepted. *Expenses:* Contact institution.

**Indiana University-Purdue University Indianapolis,** Indiana University School of Medicine, Department of Pharmacology and Toxicology, Indianapolis, IN 46202. Offers pharmacology (MS, PhD); toxicology (MS, PhD); MD/PhD. *Degree requirements:* For master's, thesis; for doctorate, thesis/dissertation. *Entrance requirements:* For master's, GRE General Test, GRE Subject Test, minimum GPA of 3.2 in core science courses; for doctorate, GRE General Test, GRE Subject Test. Additional exam requirements/recommendations for international students: required—TOEFL, IELTS, GRE or MCAT. Electronic applications accepted. *Expenses:* Contact institution.

**Johns Hopkins University,** School of Medicine, Graduate Programs in Medicine, Department of Pharmacology and Molecular Sciences, Baltimore, MD 21205. Offers PhD. *Degree requirements:* For doctorate, comprehensive exam, thesis/dissertation, departmental seminar. *Entrance requirements:* Additional exam requirements/recommendations for international students: required—TOEFL. Electronic applications accepted.

**Kent State University,** College of Arts and Sciences, School of Biomedical Sciences, Kent, OH 44242-0001. Offers biological anthropology (PhD); biomedical mathematics (MS, PhD); cellular and molecular biology (MS, PhD), including cellular biology and structures, molecular biology and genetics; neurosciences (MS, PhD); pharmacology (MS, PhD); physiology (MS, PhD). *Faculty:* 17 full-time (8 women). *Students:* 73 full-time (48 women), 2 part-time (1 woman); includes 9 minority (2 Black or African American, non-Hispanic/Latino; 1 Asian, non-Hispanic/Latino; 3 Hispanic/Latino; 3 Two or more races, non-Hispanic/Latino), 53 international. Average age 29. 78 applicants, 17% accepted, 9 enrolled. In 2019, 2 master's, 5 doctorates awarded. *Degree requirements:* For master's, thesis; for doctorate, comprehensive exam, thesis/dissertation. *Entrance requirements:* For master's, GRE, bachelor's degree, transcripts, minimum GPA of 3.0 undergraduate GPA, goal statement, three letters of recommendation, academic preparation adequate to perform graduate work in the desired field (typically two years of chemistry, one year of mathematics, one year of physics and courses in anthropology, biology and psychology); for doctorate, GRE, master's degree, minimum GPA of 3.0, transcripts, goal statement, three letters of recommendation. Additional exam requirements/recommendations for international students: required—TOEFL (minimum score 100 iBT), IELTS (minimum score 7), PTE (minimum score 68), Michigan English Language Assessment Battery (minimum score 85). *Application deadline:* For fall admission, 1/1 for domestic students, 12/15 for international students. Applications are processed on a rolling basis. Application fee: $45 ($70 for international students). Electronic applications accepted. *Financial support:* Research assistantships with full tuition reimbursements, teaching assistantships, health care benefits, and unspecified assistantships available. Financial award application deadline: 1/1. *Unit head:* Dr. Ernest J. Freeman, Director, School of Biomedical Sciences, 330-672-2363, E-mail: efreema2@kent.edu. *Application contact:* School of Biomedical Sciences, 330-6722263, Fax: 330-6729391.
Website: http://www.kent.edu/biomedical/

**Loma Linda University,** School of Medicine, Programs in Physiology and Pharmacology, Loma Linda, CA 92350. Offers pharmacology (PhD); physiology (PhD). *Program availability:* Part-time. *Degree requirements:* For doctorate, 2 foreign languages, thesis/dissertation. *Entrance requirements:* For doctorate, GRE General Test.

**London Metropolitan University,** Graduate Programs, London, United Kingdom. Offers applied psychology (M Sc); architecture (MA); biomedical science (M Sc); blood science (M Sc); cancer pharmacology (M Sc); computer networking and cyber security (M Sc); computing and information systems (M Sc); conference interpreting (MA); counter-terrorism studies (M Sc); creative, digital and professional writing (MA); crime, violence and prevention (M Sc); criminology (M Sc); curating contemporary art (MA); data analytics (M Sc); digital media (MA); early childhood studies (MA); education (MA, Ed D); financial services law, regulation and compliance (LL M); food science (M Sc); forensic psychology (M Sc); health and social care management and policy (M Sc); human nutrition (M Sc); human resource management (MA); human rights and international conflict (MA); information technology (M Sc); intelligence and security studies (M Sc); international oil, gas and energy law (LL M); international relations (MA); interpreting (MA); learning and teaching in higher education (MA); legal practice (LL M); media and entertainment law (LL M); organizational and consumer psychology (M Sc); psychological therapy (M Sc); psychology of mental health (M Sc); public health (M Sc); public policy and management (MPA); security studies (M Sc); social work (M Sc); spatial planning and urban design (MA); sports therapy (M Sc); supporting older children and young people with dyslexia (MA); teaching languages (MA), including Arabic, English; translation (MA); woman and child abuse (MA).

**Long Island University - Brooklyn,** Arnold and Marie Schwartz College of Pharmacy and Health Sciences, Brooklyn, NY 11201-8423. Offers drug regulatory affairs (MS); pharmaceutics (MS, PhD), including cosmetic science (MS), industrial pharmacy (MS); pharmacology and toxicology (MS); pharmacy (Pharm D). *Accreditation:* ACPE. *Program availability:* Part-time. Terminal master's awarded for partial completion of doctoral program. *Degree requirements:* For master's, comprehensive exam, thesis; for doctorate, comprehensive exam, thesis/dissertation. *Entrance requirements:* For master's and doctorate, GRE. Additional exam requirements/recommendations for international students: required—TOEFL (minimum score 550 paper-based, 79 iBT) or IELTS. Electronic applications accepted. *Expenses:* Contact institution.

**Louisiana State University Health Sciences Center,** School of Graduate Studies in New Orleans, Department of Pharmacology and Experimental Therapeutics, New Orleans, LA 70112-2223. Offers PhD, MD/PhD. *Degree requirements:* For doctorate, comprehensive exam, thesis/dissertation. *Entrance requirements:* For doctorate, GRE General Test. Additional exam requirements/recommendations for international students: recommended—TOEFL, IELTS.

**Louisiana State University Health Sciences Center at Shreveport,** Department of Pharmacology, Toxicology and Neuroscience, Shreveport, LA 71130-3932. Offers pharmacology (PhD); MD/PhD. Terminal master's awarded for partial completion of doctoral program. *Degree requirements:* For master's, thesis; for doctorate, thesis/dissertation. *Entrance requirements:* For master's, GRE General Test; for doctorate, GRE General Test, minimum GPA of 3.0. Additional exam requirements/recommendations for international students: required—TOEFL (minimum score 550 paper-based).

**McGill University,** Faculty of Graduate and Postdoctoral Studies, Faculty of Medicine, Department of Pharmacology and Therapeutics, Montréal, QC H3A 2T5, Canada. Offers M Sc, PhD.

**McMaster University,** Faculty of Health Sciences and School of Graduate Studies, Program in Medical Sciences, Physiology/Pharmacology Area, Hamilton, ON L8S 4M2, Canada. Offers M Sc, PhD, MD/PhD. *Degree requirements:* For master's, thesis; for doctorate, comprehensive exam, thesis/dissertation. *Entrance requirements:* For master's, honors B Sc, B+ average in related field; for doctorate, M Sc, minimum B+ average, students with proven research experience and an A average may be admitted with a B Sc degree. Additional exam requirements/recommendations for international students: required—TOEFL (minimum score 580 paper-based; 92 iBT).

**MCPHS University,** Graduate Studies, Program in Pharmacology, Boston, MA 02115-5896. Offers MS, PhD. *Accreditation:* ACPE (one or more programs are accredited). Terminal master's awarded for partial completion of doctoral program. *Degree requirements:* For master's, oral defense of thesis; for doctorate, one foreign language, oral defense of dissertation, qualifying exam. *Entrance requirements:* For master's and doctorate, GRE General Test, minimum QPA of 3.0. Additional exam requirements/

recommendations for international students: required—TOEFL (minimum score 550 paper-based; 79 iBT).

**Medical College of Wisconsin,** Graduate School, Department of Pharmacology and Toxicology, Milwaukee, WI 53226. Offers PhD, MD/PhD. *Students:* 10 full-time (4 women), 3 international. Average age 29. 3 applicants, 33% accepted. In 2019, 1 doctorate awarded. *Degree requirements:* For doctorate, comprehensive exam, thesis/dissertation, oral and written qualifying exams. *Entrance requirements:* For doctorate, GRE, official transcripts, three letters of recommendation. Additional exam requirements/recommendations for international students: required—TOEFL. *Application deadline:* For fall admission, 12/15 priority date for domestic and international students. Applications are processed on a rolling basis. Application fee: $50. Electronic applications accepted. *Expenses:* $1,250 per credit PhD students; $155 per year full-time student fees. *Financial support:* In 2019–20, 8 students received support, including fellowships (averaging $30,000 per year), research assistantships (averaging $30,000 per year); career-related internships or fieldwork, institutionally sponsored loans, and scholarships/grants also available. Financial award application deadline: 2/15; financial award applicants required to submit FAFSA. *Unit head:* Dr. William D. Campbell, Chair, 414-955-8267, Fax: 414-955-6555, E-mail: gradschool@mcw.edu. *Application contact:* Recruitment Office, 414-955-4402, Fax: 414-955-6555, E-mail: gradschoolrecruit@mcw.edu.
Website: https://www.mcw.edu/Pharmacology.htm

**Meharry Medical College,** School of Graduate Studies, Program in Biomedical Sciences, Pharmacology Emphasis, Nashville, TN 37208-9989. Offers PhD, MD/PhD. *Degree requirements:* For doctorate, comprehensive exam, thesis/dissertation. *Entrance requirements:* For doctorate, GRE. Additional exam requirements/recommendations for international students: required—TOEFL. *Application deadline:* For fall admission, 6/1 for domestic students. Applications are processed on a rolling basis. Application fee: $65. *Financial support:* Fellowships, research assistantships, teaching assistantships, Federal Work-Study, institutionally sponsored loans, and tuition waivers (full) available. Support available to part-time students. Financial award application deadline: 4/15. *Unit head:* Dr. Aramandla Ramesh, Associate Professor, 615-327-6486, E-mail: aramesh@mmc.edu. *Application contact:* Dr. Aramandla Ramesh, Associate Professor, 615-327-6486, E-mail: aramesh@mmc.edu.
Website: https://home.mmc.edu/school-of-graduate-studies-research/pharmacology/

**Michigan State University,** College of Human Medicine and The Graduate School, Graduate Programs in Human Medicine, East Lansing, MI 48824. Offers biochemistry and molecular biology (MS, PhD); epidemiology (MS, PhD); microbiology (MS); microbiology and molecular genetics (PhD); pharmacology and toxicology (MS, PhD); physiology (MS, PhD); public health (MPH). *Entrance requirements:* Additional exam requirements/recommendations for international students: required—TOEFL.

**Michigan State University,** College of Osteopathic Medicine and The Graduate School, Graduate Studies in Osteopathic Medicine and College of Human Medicine and College of Veterinary Medicine, Department of Pharmacology and Toxicology, East Lansing, MI 48824. Offers integrative pharmacology (MS); pharmacology and toxicology (MS, PhD); pharmacology and toxicology-environmental toxicology (PhD). *Entrance requirements:* Additional exam requirements/recommendations for international students: required—TOEFL (minimum score 600 paper-based). Electronic applications accepted.

**Michigan State University,** College of Veterinary Medicine and The Graduate School, Graduate Programs in Veterinary Medicine, East Lansing, MI 48824. Offers comparative medicine and integrative biology (MS, PhD), including comparative medicine and integrative biology, comparative medicine and integrative biology–environmental toxicology (PhD); food safety and toxicology (MS), including food safety; integrative toxicology (PhD), including animal science–environmental toxicology, biochemistry and molecular biology–environmental toxicology, chemistry–environmental toxicology, crop and soil sciences–environmental toxicology, environmental engineering–environmental toxicology, environmental geosciences–environmental toxicology, fisheries and wildlife–environmental toxicology, food science–environmental toxicology, forestry–environmental toxicology, genetics–environmental toxicology, human nutrition–environmental toxicology, microbiology–environmental toxicology, pharmacology and toxicology–environmental toxicology, zoology–environmental toxicology; large animal clinical sciences (MS, PhD); microbiology and molecular genetics (MS, PhD), including industrial microbiology, microbiology, microbiology and molecular genetics, microbiology–environmental toxicology (PhD); pathobiology and diagnostic investigation (MS, PhD), including pathology, pathology–environmental toxicology (PhD); pharmacology and toxicology (MS, PhD); pharmacology and toxicology–environmental toxicology (PhD); physiology (MS, PhD); small animal clinical sciences (MS). Electronic applications accepted.

**Montclair State University,** The Graduate School, College of Science and Mathematics, Program in Pharmaceutical Biochemistry, Montclair, NJ 07043-1624. Offers MS. *Program availability:* Part-time, evening/weekend. *Entrance requirements:* For master's, GRE General Test, 24 undergraduate credits in chemistry, 2 letters of recommendation, essay. Electronic applications accepted.

**New Jersey Institute of Technology,** Newark College of Engineering, Newark, NJ 07102. Offers biomedical engineering (MS, PhD); biopharmaceutical engineering (MS); chemical engineering (MS, PhD); civil engineering (MS, PhD); computer engineering (MS); critical infrastructure systems (MS); electrical engineering (MS, PhD); engineering management (MS); engineering science (MS); environmental engineering (MS, PhD); healthcare systems management (MS); industrial engineering (MS, PhD); internet engineering (MS); manufacturing systems engineering (MS); materials science & engineering (PhD); materials science and engineering (MS); mechanical engineering (MS, PhD); occupational safety and health engineering (MS). *Program availability:* Part-time, evening/weekend. *Faculty:* 151 full-time (29 women), 135 part-time/adjunct (15 women). *Students:* 576 full-time (161 women), 528 part-time (111 women); includes 366 minority (61 Black or African American, non-Hispanic/Latino; 1 American Indian or Alaska Native, non-Hispanic/Latino; 166 Asian, non-Hispanic/Latino; 115 Hispanic/Latino; 23 Two or more races, non-Hispanic/Latino), 450 international. Average age 28. 2,053 applicants, 67% accepted, 338 enrolled. In 2019, 474 master's, 30 doctorates awarded. Terminal master's awarded for partial completion of doctoral program. *Degree requirements:* For master's, thesis (for some programs); for doctorate, thesis/dissertation. *Entrance requirements:* For master's, GRE General Test, minimum GPA 2.8, personal statement, 1 letter of recommendation, transcripts; for doctorate, GRE General Test, minimum GPA of 3.5, personal statement, 3 letters of recommendation, transcripts. Additional exam requirements/recommendations for international students: required—TOEFL (minimum score 550 paper-based; 79 iBT), IELTS (minimum score 6.5). *Application deadline:* For fall admission, 6/1 priority date for domestic students, 5/1 priority date for international students; for spring admission, 11/15 priority date for domestic and international students. Applications are processed on a rolling basis. Application fee: $75. Electronic applications accepted. *Expenses:* $23,828 per year (in-state), $33,744 per year (out-of-state). *Financial support:* In 2019–20, 352 students received support, including 33 fellowships with full tuition reimbursements available (averaging $24,000 per year), 89 research assistantships with full tuition reimbursements available (averaging $24,000 per year), 112 teaching assistantships with full tuition reimbursements available (averaging $24,000 per year); career-related internships or fieldwork, Federal Work-Study, scholarships/grants, and unspecified assistantships also available. Financial award application deadline: 1/15. *Unit head:* Dr. Moshe Kam, Dean, 973-596-5534, Fax: 973-596-2316, E-mail: moshe.kam@njit.edu. *Application contact:* Stephen Eck, Executive Director of University Admissions, 973-596-3300, Fax: 973-596-3461, E-mail: admissions@njit.edu.
Website: http://engineering.njit.edu/

**New York Medical College,** Graduate School of Basic Medical Sciences, Valhalla, NY 10595. Offers biochemistry and molecular biology (MS, PhD); cell biology (MS, PhD); microbiology and immunology (MS, PhD); pathology (MS, PhD); pharmacology (MS, PhD); physiology (MS, PhD); MD/PhD. *Program availability:* Part-time, evening/weekend. *Faculty:* 98 full-time (24 women). *Students:* 141 full-time (90 women), 17 part-time (3 women); includes 68 minority (16 Black or African American, non-Hispanic/Latino; 32 Asian, non-Hispanic/Latino; 15 Hispanic/Latino; 1 Native Hawaiian or other Pacific Islander, non-Hispanic/Latino; 4 Two or more races, non-Hispanic/Latino), 19 international. Average age 26. 351 applicants, 62% accepted, 86 enrolled. In 2019, 28 master's, 5 doctorates awarded. Terminal master's awarded for partial completion of doctoral program. *Degree requirements:* For master's, thesis; for doctorate, comprehensive exam, thesis/dissertation. *Entrance requirements:* For master's, GRE General Test, MCAT, or DAT, OAT. Additional exam requirements/recommendations for international students: required—TOEFL (minimum score 90 iBT), TOEFL or IELTS; one of the two exams are required. *Application deadline:* For fall admission, 6/1 priority date for domestic students, 5/1 priority date for international students. Applications are processed on a rolling basis. Application fee: $75 ($100 for international students). Electronic applications accepted. *Expenses:* $1200 credit and $620 fees. *Financial support:* In 2019–20, 400 students received support. Federal Work-Study, scholarships/grants, unspecified assistantships, and Student Federal Loans available. Financial award application deadline: 4/30; financial award applicants required to submit FAFSA. *Unit head:* Dr. Marina K Holz, Dean, 914-594-4110, Fax: 914-594-4944, E-mail: mholz@nymc.edu. *Application contact:* Valerie Romeo-Messana, Director of Admissions, 914-594-4110, Fax: 914-594-4944, E-mail: v_romeomessana@nymc.edu.
Website: https://www.nymc.edu/graduate-school-of-basic-medical-sciences-gsbms/gsbms-academics/

**North Carolina State University,** College of Veterinary Medicine, Program in Comparative Biomedical Sciences, Raleigh, NC 27695. Offers cell biology (MS, PhD); infectious disease (MS, PhD); pathology (MS, PhD); pharmacology (MS, PhD); population medicine (MS, PhD). *Program availability:* Part-time. *Degree requirements:* For master's, thesis; for doctorate, thesis/dissertation. *Entrance requirements:* For master's and doctorate, GRE General Test. Additional exam requirements/recommendations for international students: required—TOEFL (minimum score 550 paper-based). Electronic applications accepted. *Expenses:* Contact institution.

**Northeastern University,** Bouvé College of Health Sciences, Boston, MA 02115-5096. Offers applied behavior analysis (MS); audiology (Au D); counseling psychology (MS, PhD, CAGS); exercise science (MS); nursing (MS, PhD, CAGS), including administration (MS), adult-gerontology acute care nurse practitioner (MS, CAGS), adult-gerontology primary care nurse practitioner (MS, CAGS), anesthesia (MS), family nurse practitioner (MS, CAGS), neonatal nurse practitioner (MS, CAGS), pediatric nurse practitioner (MS, CAGS), psychiatric mental health nurse practitioner (MS, CAGS); nursing practice (DNP); pharmaceutical sciences (MS, PhD), including interdisciplinary concentration, pharmaceutics and drug delivery systems; pharmacology (MS); pharmacy (Pharm D); school psychology (PhD); speech-language pathology (MS); urban health (MPH); MS/MBA. *Accreditation:* AANA/CANAEP; ACPE (one or more programs are accredited); ASHA; CEPH. *Program availability:* Part-time, evening/weekend, online learning. *Degree requirements:* For doctorate, thesis/dissertation (for some programs); for CAGS, comprehensive exam. Electronic applications accepted. *Expenses:* Contact institution.

**The Ohio State University,** College of Pharmacy, Columbus, OH 43210. Offers MS, PhD, Pharm D, Pharm D/MBA, Pharm D/MPH, Pharm D/PhD. *Accreditation:* ACPE (one or more programs are accredited). Terminal master's awarded for partial completion of doctoral program. *Degree requirements:* For doctorate, comprehensive exam (for some programs), thesis/dissertation (for some programs). *Entrance requirements:* For master's, GRE General Test, minimum GPA of 3.0; for doctorate, GRE General Test; PCAT (for PharmD), minimum GPA of 3.0. Additional exam requirements/recommendations for international students: required—TOEFL minimum score 600 paper-based, 100 iBT (for MS and PhD); TOEFL minimum score 577 paper-based; 90 iBT, Michigan English Language Assessment Battery minimum score 84, IELTS minimum score 7.5 (for PharmD). Electronic applications accepted. *Expenses:* Contact institution.

**Oregon Health & Science University,** School of Medicine, Graduate Programs in Medicine, Program in Molecular and Cellular Biosciences, Department of Physiology and Pharmacology, Portland, OR 97239-3098. Offers PhD. *Degree requirements:* For doctorate, comprehensive exam, thesis/dissertation. *Entrance requirements:* For doctorate, GRE General Test (minimum scores: 153 Verbal/148 Quantitative/4.5 Analytical) or MCAT (for some programs). Electronic applications accepted.

**Purdue University,** College of Pharmacy and Graduate School, Graduate Programs in Pharmacy and Pharmacal Sciences, Department of Medicinal Chemistry and Molecular Pharmacology, West Lafayette, IN 47907. Offers biophysical and computational chemistry (PhD); cancer research (PhD); immunology and infectious disease (PhD); medicinal biochemistry and molecular biology (PhD); medicinal chemistry and chemical biology (PhD); molecular pharmacology (PhD); neuropharmacology, neurodegeneration, and neurotoxicity (PhD); systems biology and functional genomics (PhD). *Faculty:* 20 full-time (5 women), 7 part-time/adjunct (2 women). *Students:* 80 full-time (40 women), 2 part-time (0 women); includes 9 minority (5 Asian, non-Hispanic/Latino; 2 Hispanic/Latino; 2 Two or more races, non-Hispanic/Latino), 44 international. Average age 26. 162 applicants, 20% accepted, 15 enrolled. In 2019, 11 doctorates awarded. *Degree requirements:* For doctorate, thesis/dissertation. *Entrance requirements:* For doctorate, GRE General Test; GRE Subject Test in biology, biochemistry, and chemistry (recommended), minimum undergraduate GPA of 3.0. Additional exam requirements/recommendations for international students: required—TOEFL (minimum score 550 paper-based; 77 iBT); recommended—TWE. *Application deadline:* For fall admission, 2/1 for domestic and international students. Applications are processed on a rolling basis. Application fee: $60 ($75 for international students). Electronic applications accepted. *Financial support:* Fellowships, research assistantships, teaching assistantships, and traineeships available. Support available to part-time students. Financial award applicants required to submit FAFSA. *Unit head:* Zhong-Yin Zhang, Head, 765-494-1403, E-mail: zhang-yn@purdue.edu. *Application contact:* Delayne Graham, Graduate Contact, 765-494-1362, E-mail: dkgraham@purdue.edu.

**Purdue University,** School of Veterinary Medicine and Graduate School, Graduate Programs in Veterinary Medicine, Department of Basic Medical Sciences, West Lafayette, IN 47907. Offers anatomy (MS, PhD); pharmacology (MS, PhD); physiology (MS, PhD). *Program availability:* Part-time. Terminal master's awarded for partial completion of doctoral program. *Degree requirements:* For master's, thesis; for

doctorate, thesis/dissertation. *Entrance requirements:* For master's and doctorate, GRE General Test. Additional exam requirements/recommendations for international students: required—TOEFL. Electronic applications accepted.

**Rush University,** Graduate College, Division of Pharmacology, Chicago, IL 60612-3832. Offers clinical research (MS); pharmacology (MS, PhD); MD/PhD. Terminal master's awarded for partial completion of doctoral program. *Degree requirements:* For master's, thesis; for doctorate, thesis/dissertation. *Entrance requirements:* For master's and doctorate, GRE General Test, interview. Additional exam requirements/recommendations for international students: required—TOEFL (minimum score 550 paper-based).

**Rutgers University - Newark,** Graduate School of Biomedical Sciences, Department of Pharmacology and Physiology, Newark, NJ 07107. Offers PhD. *Degree requirements:* For doctorate, thesis/dissertation, qualifying exam. *Entrance requirements:* For doctorate, GRE General Test. Additional exam requirements/recommendations for international students: required—TOEFL. Electronic applications accepted.

**Saint Louis University,** Graduate Programs, School of Medicine, Graduate Programs in Biomedical Sciences and Graduate Programs, Department of Pharmacological and Physiological Science, St. Louis, MO 63103. Offers PhD. *Degree requirements:* For doctorate, comprehensive exam, thesis/dissertation, departmental qualifying exams. *Entrance requirements:* For doctorate, GRE General Test (GRE Subject Test optional), letters of recommendation, resume, interview. Additional exam requirements/recommendations for international students: required—TOEFL (minimum score 525 paper-based). Electronic applications accepted.

**Southern Illinois University Carbondale,** Graduate School, Graduate Programs in Medicine, Program in Pharmacology, Springfield, IL 62794-9629. Offers MS, PhD. *Degree requirements:* For master's, thesis; for doctorate, thesis/dissertation. *Entrance requirements:* For master's, GRE, minimum GPA of 3.0; for doctorate, GRE, minimum GPA of 3.25. Additional exam requirements/recommendations for international students: required—TOEFL.

**State University of New York Upstate Medical University,** College of Graduate Studies, Program in Pharmacology, Syracuse, NY 13210. Offers PhD, MD/PhD. Terminal master's awarded for partial completion of doctoral program. *Degree requirements:* For doctorate, comprehensive exam, thesis/dissertation. *Entrance requirements:* For doctorate, GRE General Test, telephone interview. Additional exam requirements/recommendations for international students: required—TOEFL. Electronic applications accepted.

**Stony Brook University, State University of New York,** Stony Brook Medicine, Renaissance School of Medicine and Graduate School, Graduate Programs in Medicine, Department of Pharmacological Sciences, Graduate Program in Molecular and Cellular Pharmacology, Stony Brook, NY 11794. Offers MS, PhD. *Faculty:* 20 full-time (6 women). *Students:* 55 full-time (29 women), 1 (woman) part-time; includes 25 minority (5 Black or African American, non-Hispanic/Latino; 12 Asian, non-Hispanic/Latino; 7 Hispanic/Latino; 1 Two or more races, non-Hispanic/Latino), 8 international. Average age 27. 26 applicants, 42% accepted, 5 enrolled. In 2019, 8 doctorates awarded. *Degree requirements:* For doctorate, thesis/dissertation, departmental qualifying exam. *Entrance requirements:* For doctorate, GRE General Test. Additional exam requirements/recommendations for international students: required—TOEFL. *Application deadline:* For fall admission, 1/15 priority date for domestic students; for spring admission, 10/1 for domestic students. Applications are processed on a rolling basis. Application fee: $100. Electronic applications accepted. *Expenses:* Contact institution. *Financial support:* In 2019–20, 23 fellowships, 17 research assistantships were awarded; teaching assistantships and Federal Work-Study also available. Financial award application deadline: 3/15; financial award applicants required to submit FAFSA. *Unit head:* Dr. Michael A. Frohman, Chair, 631-444-3050, Fax: 631-444-9749, E-mail: michael.frohman@stonybrook.edu. *Application contact:* Odalis Hernandez, Coordinator, 631-444-3057, Fax: 631-444-9749, E-mail: odalis.hernandez@stonybrook.edu.
Website: http://www.pharm.stonybrook.edu/about-graduate-program

**Thomas Jefferson University,** Jefferson College of Life Sciences, MS Program in Pharmacology, Philadelphia, PA 19107. Offers MS. *Program availability:* Part-time, evening/weekend. *Degree requirements:* For master's, thesis, clerkship. *Entrance requirements:* For master's, GRE General Test or MCAT, minimum GPA of 3.0. Additional exam requirements/recommendations for international students: required—TOEFL, IELTS (minimum score 7). Electronic applications accepted.

**Tulane University,** School of Medicine, Graduate Programs in Biomedical Sciences, Department of Pharmacology, New Orleans, LA 70118-5669. Offers MS. *Degree requirements:* For master's, one foreign language, thesis. *Entrance requirements:* For master's, GRE General Test, minimum B average in undergraduate course work. Additional exam requirements/recommendations for international students: required—TOEFL. Electronic applications accepted. *Expenses:* Tuition: Full-time $57,004; part-time $3167 per credit hour. *Required fees:* $2086; $44.50 per credit hour. $80 per term. Tuition and fees vary according to course load, degree level and program.

**Universidad Central del Caribe,** School of Medicine, Program in Biomedical Sciences, Bayamón, PR 00960-6032. Offers anatomy and cell biology (MA, MS); biochemistry (MS); biomedical sciences (MA); cellular and molecular biology (PhD); microbiology and immunology (MA, MS); pharmacology (MS); physiology (MS).

**Université de Montréal,** Faculty of Medicine, Department of Pharmacology, Montréal, QC H3C 3J7, Canada. Offers M Sc, PhD. Terminal master's awarded for partial completion of doctoral program. *Degree requirements:* For master's, thesis; for doctorate, thesis/dissertation, general exam. *Entrance requirements:* For master's, proficiency in French, knowledge of English; for doctorate, master's degree, proficiency in French. Electronic applications accepted.

**Université de Sherbrooke,** Faculty of Medicine and Health Sciences, Graduate Programs in Medicine, Department of Pharmacology, Sherbrooke, QC J1H 5N4, Canada. Offers M Sc, PhD. Terminal master's awarded for partial completion of doctoral program. *Degree requirements:* For master's, thesis; for doctorate, thesis/dissertation. Electronic applications accepted.

**University at Buffalo, the State University of New York,** Graduate School, Jacobs School of Medicine and Biomedical Sciences, Graduate Programs in Medicine and Biomedical Sciences, Department of Pharmacology and Toxicology, Buffalo, NY 14203. Offers pharmacology (MS, PhD); MD/PhD. *Faculty:* 22 full-time (4 women), 1 part-time/adjunct (0 women). *Students:* 29 full-time (20 women); includes 7 minority (2 Black or African American, non-Hispanic/Latino; 2 Asian, non-Hispanic/Latino; 3 Hispanic/Latino), 10 international. Average age 25. 44 applicants, 52% accepted, 9 enrolled. In 2019, 10 master's, 6 doctorates awarded. Terminal master's awarded for partial completion of doctoral program. *Degree requirements:* For master's, thesis; for doctorate, thesis/dissertation. *Entrance requirements:* For master's and doctorate, 3 letters of recommendation. Additional exam requirements/recommendations for international students: required—TOEFL (minimum score 79 iBT). *Application deadline:* For fall admission, 2/14 priority date for domestic and international students. Applications are processed on a rolling basis. Application fee: $85. Electronic applications accepted. *Expenses: Tuition, area resident:* Full-time $11,310; part-time $471 per credit hour. *Tuition, state resident:* full-time $11,310; part-time $471 per credit hour. *Tuition, nonresident:* full-time $23,100; part-time $963 per credit hour. *International tuition:* $23,100 full-time. *Required fees:* $2820. *Financial support:* In 2019–20, 2 students received support, including 2 fellowships with full tuition reimbursements available (averaging $27,000 per year), 7 research assistantships with full tuition reimbursements available (averaging $27,000 per year); teaching assistantships, Federal Work-Study, scholarships/grants, health care benefits, and unspecified assistantships also available. Financial award application deadline: 2/14; financial award applicants required to submit FAFSA. *Unit head:* Dr. David Dietz, Associate Professor/Chair, 716-829-2071, Fax: 716-829-2801, E-mail: ddietz@buffalo.edu. *Application contact:* Linda M. LeRoy, Admissions Assistant, 716-829-2800, Fax: 716-829-2801, E-mail: pmygrad@buffalo.edu.
Website: http://medicine.buffalo.edu/pharmtox

**The University of Alabama at Birmingham,** Joint Health Sciences, Program in Pharmacology and Toxicology, Birmingham, AL 35294. Offers PhD. *Degree requirements:* For doctorate, thesis/dissertation. *Entrance requirements:* For doctorate, GRE General Test; GRE Subject Test (recommended), interview. Additional exam requirements/recommendations for international students: required—TOEFL, TWE. Electronic applications accepted. *Expenses:* Contact institution.

**University of Alberta,** Faculty of Medicine and Dentistry, Department of Pharmacology, Edmonton, AB T6G 2E1, Canada. Offers M Sc, PhD. Terminal master's awarded for partial completion of doctoral program. *Degree requirements:* For master's, thesis; for doctorate, thesis/dissertation. *Entrance requirements:* For master's, B Sc, minimum GPA of 3.3; for doctorate, M Sc in pharmacology or closely related field, honors B Sc in pharmacology.

**The University of Arizona,** College of Pharmacy, Department of Pharmacology and Toxicology, Graduate Program in Medical Pharmacology, Tucson, AZ 85721. Offers medical pharmacology (PhD); perfusion science (MS). *Degree requirements:* For master's, thesis; for doctorate, comprehensive exam, thesis/dissertation. *Entrance requirements:* For master's, GRE General Test, 3 letters of recommendation; for doctorate, GRE General Test, personal statement, 3 letters of recommendation. Additional exam requirements/recommendations for international students: required—TOEFL (minimum score 550 paper-based; 79 iBT). Electronic applications accepted.

**University of Arkansas for Medical Sciences,** Graduate School, Little Rock, AR 72205. Offers biochemistry and molecular biology (MS, PhD); bioinformatics (MS, PhD); cellular physiology and molecular biophysics (MS, PhD); clinical nutrition (MS); interdisciplinary biomedical sciences (MS, PhD, Certificate); interdisciplinary toxicology (MS); microbiology and immunology (PhD); neurobiology and developmental sciences (PhD); pharmacology (PhD); MD/PhD. *Program availability:* Part-time. Terminal master's awarded for partial completion of doctoral program. *Degree requirements:* For master's, comprehensive exam (for some programs), thesis (for some programs); for doctorate, thesis/dissertation. *Entrance requirements:* For master's and doctorate, GRE. Additional exam requirements/recommendations for international students: required—TOEFL. Electronic applications accepted. *Expenses:* Contact institution.

**The University of British Columbia,** Faculty of Medicine, Department of Anesthesiology, Pharmacology and Therapeutics, Vancouver, BC V6T 1Z3, Canada. Offers pharmacology (M Sc, PhD). Terminal master's awarded for partial completion of doctoral program. *Degree requirements:* For master's, thesis; for doctorate, comprehensive exam, thesis/dissertation. *Entrance requirements:* For master's, MD or appropriate bachelor's degree; for doctorate, MD or M Sc. Additional exam requirements/recommendations for international students: required—TOEFL. Electronic applications accepted. *Expenses:* Contact institution.

**University of California, Davis,** Graduate Studies, Graduate Group in Pharmacology and Toxicology, Davis, CA 95616. Offers MS, PhD. Terminal master's awarded for partial completion of doctoral program. *Degree requirements:* For master's, comprehensive exam or thesis; for doctorate, thesis/dissertation, qualifying exam. *Entrance requirements:* For master's and doctorate, GRE General Test, minimum GPA of 3.0, course work in biochemistry and/or physiology. Additional exam requirements/recommendations for international students: required—TOEFL (minimum score 550 paper-based). Electronic applications accepted.

**University of California, Los Angeles,** David Geffen School of Medicine and Graduate Division, Graduate Programs in Medicine, Department of Molecular and Medical Pharmacology, Los Angeles, CA 90095. Offers MS, PhD. *Degree requirements:* For master's, thesis; for doctorate, thesis/dissertation, written and oral qualifying exams; 2 quarters of teaching experience. *Entrance requirements:* For doctorate, GRE General Test, bachelor's degree; minimum undergraduate GPA of 3.0 (or its equivalent if letter grade system not used). Additional exam requirements/recommendations for international students: required—TOEFL. Electronic applications accepted.

**University of California, San Francisco,** School of Pharmacy and Graduate Division, Pharmaceutical Sciences and Pharmacogenomics Program, San Francisco, CA 94158-0775. Offers PhD. *Degree requirements:* For doctorate, comprehensive exam, thesis/dissertation. *Entrance requirements:* For doctorate, GRE General Test, bachelor's degree, 3 letters of recommendation, personal statement. Additional exam requirements/recommendations for international students: required—TOEFL. Electronic applications accepted.

**University of Cincinnati,** Graduate School, College of Medicine, Graduate Programs in Biomedical Sciences, Department of Pharmacology and Cell Biophysics, Cincinnati, OH 45221. Offers cell biophysics (PhD); pharmacology (PhD). *Degree requirements:* For doctorate, thesis/dissertation, qualifying exam. *Entrance requirements:* For doctorate, GRE General Test. Additional exam requirements/recommendations for international students: required—TOEFL. Electronic applications accepted.

**University of Colorado Denver,** School of Medicine, Program in Pharmacology, Aurora, CO 80206. Offers bioinformatics (PhD); biomolecular structure (PhD). *Degree requirements:* For doctorate, comprehensive exam, thesis/dissertation, major seminar, 3 research rotations in the first year, 30 hours each of course work and thesis. *Entrance requirements:* For doctorate, GRE General Test, three letters of recommendation, personal statement. Additional exam requirements/recommendations for international students: required—TOEFL (minimum score 550 paper-based; 80 iBT). Electronic applications accepted. Tuition and fees vary according to course load, program and reciprocity agreements.

**University of Connecticut,** Graduate School, School of Pharmacy, Department of Pharmaceutical Sciences, Graduate Program in Pharmacology and Toxicology, Storrs, CT 06269. Offers pharmacology (MS, PhD); toxicology (MS, PhD). Terminal master's awarded for partial completion of doctoral program. *Degree requirements:* For master's, comprehensive exam, thesis; for doctorate, thesis/dissertation. *Entrance requirements:* For master's and doctorate, GRE General Test. Additional exam requirements/recommendations for international students: required—TOEFL (minimum score 550 paper-based). Electronic applications accepted.

**University of Florida,** College of Medicine and Graduate School, Interdisciplinary Program in Biomedical Sciences, Concentration in Physiology and Pharmacology,

Gainesville, FL 32611. Offers PhD. *Degree requirements:* For doctorate, thesis/dissertation. *Entrance requirements:* For doctorate, GRE General Test, minimum GPA of 3.0, biochemistry before enrollment. Electronic applications accepted.

**University of Florida,** Graduate School, College of Pharmacy, Graduate Programs in Pharmacy, Department of Pharmacodynamics, Gainesville, FL 32611. Offers MSP, PhD, Pharm D/PhD. *Degree requirements:* For doctorate, comprehensive exam, thesis/dissertation. *Entrance requirements:* For master's and doctorate, GRE General Test, minimum GPA of 3.0. Additional exam requirements/recommendations for international students: required—TOEFL (minimum score 550 paper-based; 80 iBT), IELTS (minimum score 6). Electronic applications accepted.

**University of Georgia,** College of Veterinary Medicine, Department of Physiology and Pharmacology, Athens, GA 30602. Offers pharmacology (MS, PhD). *Degree requirements:* For master's, thesis; for doctorate, one foreign language, thesis/dissertation. *Entrance requirements:* For master's and doctorate, GRE General Test. Electronic applications accepted.

**University of Guelph,** Ontario Veterinary College and Office of Graduate and Postdoctoral Studies, Graduate Programs in Veterinary Sciences, Department of Biomedical Sciences, Guelph, ON N1G 2W1, Canada. Offers morphology (M Sc, DV Sc, PhD); neuroscience (M Sc, DV Sc, PhD); pharmacology (M Sc, DV Sc, PhD); physiology (M Sc, DV Sc, PhD); toxicology (M Sc, DV Sc, PhD). *Program availability:* Part-time. *Degree requirements:* For master's, thesis; for doctorate, comprehensive exam, thesis/dissertation. *Entrance requirements:* For master's, honors B Sc, minimum 75% average in last 20 courses; for doctorate, M Sc with thesis from accredited institution. Additional exam requirements/recommendations for international students: required—TOEFL (minimum score 550 paper-based; 89 iBT). Electronic applications accepted.

**University of Hawaii at Hilo,** Program in Clinical Psychopharmacology, Hilo, HI 96720-4091. Offers MS. *Entrance requirements:* Additional exam requirements/recommendations for international students: required—TOEFL, IELTS. Electronic applications accepted.

**University of Houston,** College of Pharmacy, Houston, TX 77204. Offers pharmaceutics (MSPHR, PhD); pharmacology (MSPHR, PhD); pharmacy (Pharm D); pharmacy administration (MSPHR, PhD). *Accreditation:* ACPE. *Program availability:* Part-time. Terminal master's awarded for partial completion of doctoral program. *Entrance requirements:* For doctorate, PCAT (for Pharm D). Additional exam requirements/recommendations for international students: required—TOEFL. Electronic applications accepted.

**University of Illinois at Chicago,** College of Medicine, Graduate Programs in Medicine, Department of Pharmacology, Chicago, IL 60612. Offers PhD, MD/PhD. *Degree requirements:* For doctorate, thesis/dissertation. *Entrance requirements:* For doctorate, GRE General Test. Additional exam requirements/recommendations for international students: required—TOEFL.

**The University of Iowa,** Roy J. and Lucille A. Carver College of Medicine and Graduate College, Graduate Programs in Medicine, Department of Pharmacology, Iowa City, IA 52242-1316. Offers MS, PhD. Terminal master's awarded for partial completion of doctoral program. *Degree requirements:* For master's, thesis. *Entrance requirements:* For master's, GRE General Test. Additional exam requirements/recommendations for international students: required—TOEFL (minimum score 600 paper-based). Electronic applications accepted.

**The University of Kansas,** Graduate Studies, School of Pharmacy, Department of Pharmacology and Toxicology, Lawrence, KS 66045. Offers MS, PhD. *Students:* 15 full-time (10 women), 1 part-time (0 women); includes 1 minority (Hispanic/Latino), 9 international. Average age 27. 52 applicants, 17% accepted, 6 enrolled. In 2019, 3 master's, 2 doctorates awarded. Terminal master's awarded for partial completion of doctoral program. *Entrance requirements:* For master's and doctorate, GRE General Test, bachelor's degree in related field, 3 letters of recommendation, resume or curriculum vitae, official transcripts, 1-2 page personal statement. Additional exam requirements/recommendations for international students: required—TOEFL, IELTS. *Application deadline:* For fall admission, 4/15 for domestic and international students. Application fee: $65 ($85 for international students). Electronic applications accepted. *Expenses:* Tuition, state resident: full-time $9989. Tuition, nonresident: full-time $23,950. *International tuition:* $23,950 full-time. *Required fees:* $984; $81.99 per credit hour. Tuition and fees vary according to course load, campus/location and program. *Financial support:* Fellowships, research assistantships, and teaching assistantships available. Financial award application deadline: 2/1. *Unit head:* Nancy Muma, Chair, 785-864-4002, E-mail: nmuma@ku.edu. *Application contact:* Sarah Hoadley, Graduate Admissions Contact, 785-864-4002, E-mail: sarahhoadley@ku.edu. Website: http://pharmtox.ku.edu/

**The University of Kansas,** University of Kansas Medical Center, School of Medicine, Department of Pharmacology, Toxicology and Therapeutics, Kansas City, KS 66160. Offers pharmacology (PhD); toxicology (PhD); MD/PhD. *Faculty:* 14. *Students:* 16 full-time (9 women); includes 4 minority (3 Black or African American, non-Hispanic/Latino; 1 Asian, non-Hispanic/Latino), 8 international. Average age 28. In 2019, 4 doctorates awarded. Terminal master's awarded for partial completion of doctoral program. *Degree requirements:* For doctorate, one foreign language, comprehensive exam, thesis/dissertation. *Entrance requirements:* For doctorate, GRE. Additional exam requirements/recommendations for international students: required—TOEFL. *Application deadline:* For fall admission, 12/1 priority date for domestic and international students. Applications are processed on a rolling basis. Application fee: $60. Electronic applications accepted. Application fee is waived when completed online. *Expenses:* Tuition, state resident: full-time $9989. Tuition, nonresident: full-time $23,950. *International tuition:* $23,950 full-time. *Required fees:* $984; $81.99 per credit hour. Tuition and fees vary according to course load, campus/location and program. *Financial support:* Fellowships with full tuition reimbursements, research assistantships with full tuition reimbursements, teaching assistantships with full tuition reimbursements, Federal Work-Study, scholarships/grants, traineeships, and unspecified assistantships available. Support available to part-time students. Financial award application deadline: 3/1; financial award applicants required to submit FAFSA. *Unit head:* Dr. Hartmut Jaeschke, University Distinguished Professor and Chair, 913-588-7500, Fax: 913-588-7501, E-mail: hjaeschke@kumc.edu. *Application contact:* Dr. Bruno Hagenbuch, Professor and Graduate Director, 913-588-7500, Fax: 913-588-7501, E-mail: bhagenbuch@kumc.edu. Website: http://www.kumc.edu/school-of-medicine/pharmacology-toxicology-and-therapeutics.html

**University of Kentucky,** Graduate School, Graduate School Programs from the College of Medicine, Program in Molecular and Biomedical Pharmacology, Lexington, KY 40506-0032. Offers PhD, MD/PhD. *Degree requirements:* For doctorate, comprehensive exam, thesis/dissertation. *Entrance requirements:* For doctorate, GRE General Test, minimum undergraduate GPA of 2.75, graduate 3.0. Additional exam requirements/recommendations for international students: required—TOEFL (minimum score 550 paper-based). Electronic applications accepted.

**University of Louisville,** School of Medicine, Department of Pharmacology and Toxicology, Louisville, KY 40292-0001. Offers pharmacology and toxicology (MS; MD/PhD. *Program availability:* Part-time. *Faculty:* 17 full-time (3 women), 2 part-time/adjunct (0 women). *Students:* 38 full-time (19 women), 6 part-time (3 women); includes 11 minority (3 Black or African American, non-Hispanic/Latino; 4 Asian, non-Hispanic/Latino; 4 Two or more races, non-Hispanic/Latino), 12 international. Average age 30. 24 applicants, 54% accepted, 12 enrolled. In 2019, 7 master's, 10 doctorates awarded. Terminal master's awarded for partial completion of doctoral program. *Degree requirements:* For master's, thesis; for doctorate, comprehensive exam, thesis/dissertation. *Entrance requirements:* Additional exam requirements/recommendations for international students: required—TOEFL, Certified Translated official transcript; recommended—IELTS. *Application deadline:* For fall admission, 1/1 priority date for domestic and international students. Applications are processed on a rolling basis. Application fee: $65. Electronic applications accepted. *Expenses: Tuition, area resident:* Full-time $13,000; part-time $723 per credit hour. Tuition, state resident: full-time $13,000; part-time $723 per credit hour. Tuition, nonresident: full-time $27,114; part-time $1507 per credit hour. *International tuition:* $27,114 full-time. *Required fees:* $196. Tuition and fees vary according to program and reciprocity agreements. *Financial support:* In 2019–20, 39 students received support, including 11 fellowships with full tuition reimbursements available (averaging $26,000 per year), 26 research assistantships (averaging $26,000 per year); scholarships/grants, traineeships, health care benefits, tuition waivers, unspecified assistantships, and Tuition Waivers reducing out of state tuition to in state tuition rate for students on fellowships/assistantships (benefits unit, not student) also available. Financial award application deadline: 1/1. *Unit head:* Dr. David W. Hein, Peter K. Knoefel Endowed Chair, 502-852-6252, E-mail: david.hein@louisville.edu. *Application contact:* Sonya Cary, Unit Business Manager/Graduate Coordinator, 502-852-6254, E-mail: sonya.cary@louisville.edu. Website: http://louisville.edu/medicine/departments/pharmacology

**The University of Manchester,** School of Biological Sciences, Manchester, United Kingdom. Offers adaptive organismal biology (M Phil, PhD); animal biology (M Phil, PhD); biochemistry (M Phil, PhD); bioinformatics (M Phil, PhD); biomolecular sciences (M Phil, PhD); biotechnology (M Phil, PhD); cell biology (M Phil, PhD); cell matrix research (M Phil, PhD); channels and transporters (M Phil, PhD); developmental biology (M Phil, PhD); environmental biology (M Phil, PhD); evolutionary biology (M Phil, PhD); gene expression (M Phil, PhD); genetics (M Phil, PhD); history of science, technology and medicine (M Phil, PhD); immunology (M Phil, PhD); integrative neurobiology and behavior (M Phil, PhD); membrane trafficking (M Phil, PhD); microbiology (M Phil, PhD); molecular and cellular neuroscience (M Phil, PhD); molecular biology (M Phil, PhD); molecular cancer studies (M Phil, PhD); neuroscience (M Phil, PhD); ophthalmology (M Phil, PhD); optometry (M Phil, PhD); organelle function (M Phil, PhD); pharmacology (M Phil, PhD); physiology (M Phil, PhD); plant sciences (M Phil, PhD); stem cell research (M Phil, PhD); structural biology (M Phil, PhD); systems neuroscience (M Phil, PhD); toxicology (M Phil, PhD).

**University of Manitoba,** Max Rady College of Medicine and Faculty of Graduate Studies, Graduate Programs in Medicine, Department of Pharmacology and Therapeutics, Winnipeg, MB R3T 2N2, Canada. Offers M Sc, PhD. *Program availability:* Part-time. Terminal master's awarded for partial completion of doctoral program. *Degree requirements:* For master's, thesis; for doctorate, thesis/dissertation. *Entrance requirements:* For master's and doctorate, GRE. Additional exam requirements/recommendations for international students: required—TOEFL.

**University of Maryland, Baltimore,** Graduate School, Graduate Programs in Pharmacy, Program in Pharmacometrics, Baltimore, MD 21201. Offers MS.

**University of Miami,** Graduate School, Miller School of Medicine, Graduate Programs in Medicine, Department of Molecular and Cellular Pharmacology, Miami, FL 33124. Offers PhD, MD/PhD. *Faculty:* 14 full-time (7 women). *Students:* 23 full-time (8 women); includes 5 minority (1 Black or African American, non-Hispanic/Latino; 2 Asian, non-Hispanic/Latino; 1 Hispanic/Latino; 1 Two or more races, non-Hispanic/Latino). Average age 29. 5 applicants. In 2019, 3 doctorates awarded. *Degree requirements:* For doctorate, thesis/dissertation, Qualifying exam (QE). *Entrance requirements:* For doctorate, GRE General Test. Additional exam requirements/recommendations for international students: required—TOEFL (minimum score 550 paper-based). Application fee: $95. Electronic applications accepted. *Financial support:* In 2019–20, 25 students received support, including 25 fellowships (averaging $29,500 per year), research assistantships (averaging $29,500 per year); tuition waivers (full) also available. *Unit head:* Dr. Kerry Burnstein, Department Chair and Professor, 305-243-3299, Fax: 305-243-4555, E-mail: kburnstein@med.miami.edu. *Application contact:* Dr. Vladlen Z. Slepak, Director of Graduate Studies, 305-243-3419, Fax: 305-243-3420, E-mail: vslepak@med.miami.edu. Website: http://pharmacology.med.miami.edu

**University of Michigan,** Rackham Graduate School, Program in Biomedical Sciences (PIBS), Department of Pharmacology, Ann Arbor, MI 48109-5632. Offers MS, PhD. Terminal master's awarded for partial completion of doctoral program. *Degree requirements:* For master's, thesis, oral presentation; for doctorate, comprehensive exam, thesis/dissertation. *Entrance requirements:* For master's and doctorate, 3 letters of recommendation, research experience, all undergraduate transcripts. Additional exam requirements/recommendations for international students: required—TOEFL (minimum score 560 paper-based; 84 iBT). Electronic applications accepted. *Expenses:* Contact institution.

**University of Minnesota, Duluth,** Medical School, Program in Pharmacology, Duluth, MN 55812-2496. Offers MS, PhD. Terminal master's awarded for partial completion of doctoral program. *Degree requirements:* For master's, thesis, final oral exam; for doctorate, thesis/dissertation, final oral exam, oral and written preliminary exams. *Entrance requirements:* For master's and doctorate, GRE General Test. Additional exam requirements/recommendations for international students: required—TOEFL.

**University of Minnesota, Twin Cities Campus,** College of Pharmacy and Graduate School, Graduate Programs in Pharmacy, Graduate Program in Experimental and Clinical Pharmacology, Minneapolis, MN 55455-0213. Offers MS, PhD. *Degree requirements:* For doctorate, thesis/dissertation.

**University of Minnesota, Twin Cities Campus,** Medical School, Department of Pharmacology, Minneapolis, MN 55455. Offers MS, PhD. Terminal master's awarded for partial completion of doctoral program. *Degree requirements:* For master's, thesis (for some programs); for doctorate, thesis/dissertation. *Entrance requirements:* For master's and doctorate, GRE General Test. Additional exam requirements/recommendations for international students: required—TOEFL (minimum score 603 paper-based; 100 iBT). Electronic applications accepted.

**University of Mississippi,** Graduate School, School of Pharmacy, University, MS 38677. Offers environmental toxicology (MS, PhD); industrial pharmacy (MS); medicinal chemistry (MS, PhD); pharmaceutics (MS, PhD); pharmacognosy (MS, PhD); pharmacology (MS, PhD); pharmacy (Pharm D); pharmacy administration (MS, PhD). *Accreditation:* ACPE (one or more programs are accredited). *Program availability:* Part-time. *Faculty:* 68 full-time (33 women), 13 part-time/adjunct (5 women). *Students:* 223 full-time (137 women), 215 part-time (137 women); includes 71 minority (29 Black or

African American, non-Hispanic/Latino; 1 American Indian or Alaska Native, non-Hispanic/Latino; 31 Asian, non-Hispanic/Latino; 4 Hispanic/Latino; 6 Two or more races, non-Hispanic/Latino), 90 international. Average age 25. In 2019, 29 master's, 13 doctorates awarded. Terminal master's awarded for partial completion of doctoral program. *Degree requirements:* For master's, thesis; for doctorate, thesis/dissertation (for some programs). *Entrance requirements:* For master's, GRE General Test, minimum GPA of 3.0; for doctorate, GRE General Test (for PhD). Additional exam requirements/recommendations for international students: required—TOEFL. *Application deadline:* Applications are processed on a rolling basis. Application fee: $50. Electronic applications accepted. *Expenses:* Tuition, state resident: full-time $8718; part-time $484.25 per credit hour. Tuition, nonresident: full-time $24,990; part-time $1388.25 per credit hour. *Required fees:* $100; $4.16 per credit hour. *Financial support:* Fellowships, research assistantships, teaching assistantships, career-related internships or fieldwork, Federal Work-Study, institutionally sponsored loans, scholarships/grants, tuition waivers (full), and unspecified assistantships available. Financial award application deadline: 3/1; financial award applicants required to submit FAFSA. *Unit head:* Dr. David Allen, Dean, School of Pharmacy, 662-915-7265, Fax: 662-9155704, E-mail: sopdean@olemiss.edu. *Application contact:* Temeka Smith, Graduate Activities Specialist for Admissions, 662-915-7474, Fax: 662-915-7577, E-mail: gschool@olemiss.edu.
Website: http://www.pharmacy.olemiss.edu/

**University of Mississippi Medical Center,** School of Graduate Studies in Health Sciences, Department of Pharmacology and Toxicology, Jackson, MS 39216-4505. Offers PhD. *Degree requirements:* For doctorate, comprehensive exam, thesis/dissertation, first authored publication. *Entrance requirements:* For doctorate, GRE General Test, minimum GPA of 3.0. Additional exam requirements/recommendations for international students: required—TOEFL (minimum score 550 paper-based, 79 iBT), IELTS or PTE. Electronic applications accepted.

**University of Missouri,** School of Medicine and Office of Research and Graduate Studies, Graduate Programs in Medicine, Department of Medical Pharmacology and Physiology, Columbia, MO 65211. Offers MS, PhD. *Degree requirements:* For master's, thesis; for doctorate, thesis/dissertation. *Entrance requirements:* For master's and doctorate, GRE General Test, minimum GPA of 3.0. Additional exam requirements/recommendations for international students: required—TOEFL (minimum score 500 paper-based; 61 iBT).

**University of Nebraska Medical Center,** Interdisciplinary Graduate Program in Biomedical Sciences, Department of Pharmacology and Experimental Neuroscience, Omaha, NE 68198. Offers PhD. Terminal master's awarded for partial completion of doctoral program. *Degree requirements:* For doctorate, comprehensive exam, thesis/dissertation. *Entrance requirements:* For doctorate, GRE General Test. Additional exam requirements/recommendations for international students: required—TOEFL (minimum score 90 iBT). Electronic applications accepted.

**The University of North Carolina at Chapel Hill,** School of Medicine and Graduate School, Biological and Biomedical Sciences Program, Department of Pharmacology, Chapel Hill, NC 27599-7365. Offers PhD. *Faculty:* 45 full-time (11 women), 8 part-time/adjunct (0 women). *Students:* 36 full-time (20 women); includes 6 minority (3 Black or African American, non-Hispanic/Latino; 2 Asian, non-Hispanic/Latino; 1 Hispanic/Latino), 5 international. Average age 26. In 2019, 7 doctorates awarded. *Degree requirements:* For doctorate, comprehensive exam, thesis/dissertation. *Entrance requirements:* Additional exam requirements/recommendations for international students: required—TOEFL. *Application deadline:* For fall admission, 12/3 priority date for domestic and international students. Applications are processed on a rolling basis. Application fee: $77. Electronic applications accepted. *Financial support:* In 2019–20, 17 fellowships with full tuition reimbursements (averaging $32,000 per year), 22 research assistantships with full tuition reimbursements (averaging $32,000 per year) were awarded; career-related internships or fieldwork, health care benefits, and tuition waivers (full) also available. *Unit head:* Dr. Mauro Calabrese, Director of Graduate Studies, E-mail: jmcalabr@med.unc.edu. *Application contact:* Jeffrey Steinbach, Assistant Director of Admissions, 919-843-7129, E-mail: jsteinba@email.unc.edu.
Website: http://www.med.unc.edu/pharm/

**University of North Texas Health Science Center at Fort Worth,** Graduate School of Biomedical Sciences, Fort Worth, TX 76107-2699. Offers biochemistry and cancer biology (MS, PhD); biotechnology (MS); cell biology, immunology and microbiology (MS, PhD); clinical research management (MS); forensic genetics (MS); genetics (MS, PhD); integrative physiology (MS, PhD); medical sciences (MS); pharmaceutical sciences and pharmacotherapy (MS, PhD); pharmacology and neuroscience (MS, PhD); structural anatomy and rehabilitation sciences (MS, PhD); DO/MS; DO/PhD. Terminal master's awarded for partial completion of doctoral program. *Degree requirements:* For master's, thesis; for doctorate, thesis/dissertation. *Entrance requirements:* For master's and doctorate, GRE General Test. Additional exam requirements/recommendations for international students: required—TOEFL. *Expenses:* Contact institution.

**University of Pennsylvania,** Perelman School of Medicine, Biomedical Graduate Studies, Graduate Group in Pharmacology, Philadelphia, PA 19104. Offers PhD, MD/PhD, VMD/PhD. *Faculty:* 142 full-time (33 women). *Students:* 71 full-time (38 women); includes 25 minority (6 Black or African American, non-Hispanic/Latino; 9 Asian, non-Hispanic/Latino; 10 Hispanic/Latino), 7 international. 144 applicants, 13% accepted, 12 enrolled. In 2019, 9 doctorates awarded. *Unit head:* Dr. Julie Blendy, Chair, 215-898-0730. *Application contact:* Sarah Squire, Coordinator, 215-898-1790.
Website: http://www.med.upenn.edu/ggps

**University of Prince Edward Island,** Atlantic Veterinary College, Graduate Program in Veterinary Medicine, Charlottetown, PE C1A 4P3, Canada. Offers anatomy (M Sc, PhD); bacteriology (M Sc, PhD); clinical pharmacology (M Sc, PhD); clinical sciences (M Sc, PhD); epidemiology (M Sc, PhD), including reproduction; fish health (M Sc, PhD); food animal nutrition (M Sc, PhD); immunology (M Sc, PhD); microanatomy (M Sc, PhD); parasitology (M Sc, PhD); pathology (M Sc, PhD); pharmacology (M Sc, PhD); physiology (M Sc, PhD); toxicology (M Sc, PhD); veterinary science (M Vet Sc); virology (M Sc, PhD). *Program availability:* Part-time. *Degree requirements:* For master's, thesis; for doctorate, thesis/dissertation. *Entrance requirements:* For master's, DVM, B Sc honors degree, or equivalent; for doctorate, M Sc. Additional exam requirements/recommendations for international students: required—TOEFL (minimum score 550 paper-based; 80 iBT). *Expenses:* Contact institution.

**University of Puerto Rico - Medical Sciences Campus,** School of Medicine, Biomedical Sciences Graduate Program, Department of Pharmacology and Toxicology, San Juan, PR 00936-5067. Offers MS, PhD. *Degree requirements:* For master's, one foreign language, thesis; for doctorate, one foreign language, comprehensive exam, thesis/dissertation. *Entrance requirements:* For master's and doctorate, GRE General Test, GRE Subject Test, interview, minimum GPA of 3.0, 3 letters of recommendation. Electronic applications accepted.

**University of Rhode Island,** Graduate School, College of Pharmacy, Department of Biomedical and Pharmaceutical Sciences, Kingston, RI 02881. Offers health outcomes (MS, PhD); medicinal chemistry and pharmacognosy (MS, PhD); pharmaceutics and pharmacokinetics (MS, PhD); pharmacology and toxicology (MS, PhD). *Program availability:* Part-time. *Faculty:* 23 full-time (11 women). *Students:* 42 full-time (20 women), 11 part-time (6 women); includes 8 minority (1 American Indian or Alaska Native, non-Hispanic/Latino; 5 Asian, non-Hispanic/Latino; 2 Hispanic/Latino), 19 international. In 2019, 4 master's, 11 doctorates awarded. *Entrance requirements:* Additional exam requirements/recommendations for international students: required—TOEFL. *Application deadline:* For fall admission, 7/15 for domestic students, 2/1 for international students. Application fee: $65. Electronic applications accepted. *Expenses:* *Tuition, area resident:* Full-time $13,734; part-time $763 per credit. Tuition, state resident: full-time $13,734; part-time $763 per credit. Tuition, nonresident: full-time $26,512; part-time $1473 per credit. *International tuition:* $26,512 full-time. *Required fees:* $1780; $52 per credit. $35 per term. One-time fee: $165. *Financial support:* In 2019–20, 112 research assistantships with tuition reimbursements (averaging $8,040 per year), 17 teaching assistantships with tuition reimbursements (averaging $11,829 per year) were awarded. Financial award application deadline: 2/1; financial award applicants required to submit FAFSA. *Unit head:* Dr. Navindra Seeram, Chair, E-mail: nseeram@uri.edu. *Application contact:* Dr. Navindra Seeram, Chair, E-mail: nseeram@uri.edu.
Website: http://www.uri.edu/pharmacy/departments/bps/index.shtml

**University of Rochester,** School of Medicine and Dentistry, Graduate Programs in Medicine and Dentistry, Department of Pharmacology and Physiology, Programs in Pharmacology, Rochester, NY 14627. Offers MS, PhD. Terminal master's awarded for partial completion of doctoral program. *Degree requirements:* For master's, thesis; for doctorate, thesis/dissertation, qualifying exam. *Entrance requirements:* For master's and doctorate, GRE General Test.

**University of Saskatchewan,** College of Medicine, Department of Anatomy, Physiology and Pharmacology, Saskatoon, SK S7N 5A2, Canada. Offers anatomy and cell biology (M Sc, PhD); pharmacology (M Sc, PhD); physiology (M Sc, PhD). *Degree requirements:* For master's, thesis; for doctorate, thesis/dissertation. *Entrance requirements:* Additional exam requirements/recommendations for international students: required—TOEFL.

**University of South Dakota,** Graduate School, Sanford School of Medicine and Graduate School, Biomedical Sciences Graduate Program, Physiology and Pharmacology Group, Vermillion, SD 57069. Offers MS, PhD. Terminal master's awarded for partial completion of doctoral program. *Degree requirements:* For master's, thesis; for doctorate, comprehensive exam, thesis/dissertation. *Entrance requirements:* For master's and doctorate, GRE General Test, minimum GPA of 3.0. Additional exam requirements/recommendations for international students: required—TOEFL (minimum score 550 paper-based; 80 iBT), IELTS (minimum score 6). Electronic applications accepted. *Expenses:* Contact institution.

**The University of Tennessee Health Science Center,** College of Graduate Health Sciences, Memphis, TN 38163. Offers biomedical engineering (MS, PhD); biomedical sciences (PhD); dental sciences (MDS); epidemiology (MS); health outcomes and policy research (PhD); laboratory research and management (MS); nursing science (PhD); pharmaceutical sciences (PhD); pharmacology (MS); speech and hearing science (PhD); DDS/PhD; DNP/PhD; MD/PhD; Pharm D/PhD. Terminal master's awarded for partial completion of doctoral program. *Degree requirements:* For master's, comprehensive exam, thesis; for doctorate, thesis/dissertation, oral and written preliminary and comprehensive exams. *Entrance requirements:* For master's and doctorate, GRE General Test, minimum GPA of 3.0. Additional exam requirements/recommendations for international students: recommended—TOEFL (minimum score 79 iBT), IELTS (minimum score 6.5). Electronic applications accepted. *Expenses:* Contact institution.

**The University of Texas at Austin,** Graduate School, College of Pharmacy, Graduate Programs in Pharmacy, Austin, TX 78712-1111. Offers health outcomes and pharmacy practice (MS, PhD); medicinal chemistry (PhD); pharmaceutics (PhD); pharmacology and toxicology (PhD); pharmacotherapy (MS, PhD); translational science (PhD). *Degree requirements:* For master's, thesis; for doctorate, thesis/dissertation. *Entrance requirements:* For master's and doctorate, GRE General Test. Electronic applications accepted.

**The University of Texas Health Science Center at Houston,** MD Anderson UTHealth Graduate School, Houston, TX 77225-0036. Offers biochemistry and cell biology (PhD); biomedical sciences (MS); cancer biology (PhD); genetic counseling (MS); genetics and epigenetics (PhD); immunology (PhD); medical physics (MS, PhD); microbiology and infectious diseases (PhD); neuroscience (PhD); quantitative sciences (PhD); therapeutics and pharmacology (PhD); MD/PhD. Terminal master's awarded for partial completion of doctoral program. *Degree requirements:* For master's, thesis; for doctorate, thesis/dissertation. *Entrance requirements:* For master's and doctorate, GRE General Test. Additional exam requirements/recommendations for international students: required—TOEFL. Electronic applications accepted.

**The University of Texas Health Science Center at San Antonio,** Graduate School of Biomedical Sciences, Department of Pharmacology, San Antonio, TX 78229-3900. Offers neuroscience (PhD). *Degree requirements:* For doctorate, comprehensive exam, thesis/dissertation.

**The University of Texas Medical Branch,** Graduate School of Biomedical Sciences, Program in Pharmacology and Toxicology, Galveston, TX 77555. Offers pharmacology (MS); pharmacology and toxicology (PhD). *Degree requirements:* For master's, thesis or alternative; for doctorate, thesis/dissertation. *Entrance requirements:* For master's and doctorate, GRE General Test. Additional exam requirements/recommendations for international students: required—TOEFL (minimum score 550 paper-based).

**University of the Sciences,** Program in Chemistry, Biochemistry and Pharmacognosy, Philadelphia, PA 19104-4495. Offers biochemistry (MS, PhD); chemistry (MS, PhD); pharmacognosy (MS, PhD). *Program availability:* Part-time. *Degree requirements:* For master's, thesis, qualifying exams; for doctorate, comprehensive exam, thesis/dissertation, qualifying exams. *Entrance requirements:* For master's and doctorate, GRE General Test, GRE Subject Test. Additional exam requirements/recommendations for international students: required—TOEFL, TWE. *Expenses:* Contact institution.

**University of the Sciences,** Program in Pharmacology and Toxicology, Philadelphia, PA 19104-4495. Offers pharmacology (MS, PhD); toxicology (MS, PhD). Terminal master's awarded for partial completion of doctoral program. *Degree requirements:* For master's, thesis; for doctorate, comprehensive exam, thesis/dissertation. *Entrance requirements:* For master's and doctorate, GRE General Test. Additional exam requirements/recommendations for international students: required—TOEFL, TWE. *Expenses:* Contact institution.

**The University of Toledo,** College of Graduate Studies, College of Pharmacy and Pharmaceutical Sciences, Program in Experimental Therapeutics, Toledo, OH 43606-3390. Offers PhD. *Entrance requirements:* For doctorate, GRE, bachelor's degree in chemistry, biology, pharmaceutical sciences, pharmacy or a related discipline. Additional exam requirements/recommendations for international students: required—TOEFL.

**The University of Toledo,** College of Graduate Studies, College of Pharmacy and Pharmaceutical Sciences, Program in Pharmaceutical Sciences, Toledo, OH 43606-

3390. Offers administrative pharmacy (MSPS); industrial pharmacy (MSPS); pharmacology toxicology (MSPS). *Degree requirements:* For master's, thesis. *Entrance requirements:* For master's, GRE General Test. Additional exam requirements/recommendations for international students: required—TOEFL (minimum score 550 paper-based; 80 iBT). Electronic applications accepted.

**University of Toronto,** Faculty of Medicine, Department of Pharmacology and Toxicology, Toronto, ON M5S 1A1, Canada. Offers pharmacology (M Sc, PhD). *Program availability:* Part-time. *Degree requirements:* For master's, thesis; for doctorate, thesis/dissertation. *Entrance requirements:* For master's, B Sc or equivalent; background in pharmacology, biochemistry, and physiology; minimum B+ earned in at least 4 senior level classes; for doctorate, minimum B+ average. Additional exam requirements/recommendations for international students: required—TOEFL (minimum score 580 paper-based; 93 iBT), TWE (minimum score 5). Electronic applications accepted.

**University of Utah,** Graduate School, College of Pharmacy, Department of Pharmacology and Toxicology, Salt Lake City, UT 84112. Offers PhD. *Faculty:* 5 full-time (1 woman). *Students:* 4 full-time (all women), 1 (woman) part-time; includes 2 minority (1 Asian, non-Hispanic/Latino; 1 Hispanic/Latino). Average age 28. In 2019, 1 doctorate awarded. Terminal master's awarded for partial completion of doctoral program. *Degree requirements:* For doctorate, thesis/dissertation. *Application deadline:* For fall admission, 12/1 for domestic and international students. Application fee: $55. Electronic applications accepted. Application fee is waived when completed online. *Expenses:* Tuition, state resident: full-time $7085; part-time $272.51 per credit hour. Tuition, nonresident: full-time $24,937; part-time $959.12 per credit hour. *Required fees:* $880.52; $880.52 per semester. Tuition and fees vary according to degree level, program and student level. *Financial support:* In 2019–20, 3 students received support, including 3 research assistantships (averaging $17,000 per year); health care benefits also available. *Unit head:* Dr. Karen Wilcox, Chair Department Pharmacology and Toxicology, 801-581-5684, Fax: 801-585-5111, E-mail: karen.wilcox@hsc.utah.edu. *Application contact:* Linda Wright, Executive Secretary, 801-581-6287, Fax: 801-585-5111, E-mail: linda.wright@utah.edu.
Website: http://www.pharmacy.utah.edu/pharmtox/

**University of Vermont,** The Robert Larner, MD College of Medicine and Graduate College, Graduate Programs in Medicine, Department of Pharmacology, Burlington, VT 05405-0068. Offers MS, PhD. *Degree requirements:* For master's, thesis optional; for doctorate, thesis/dissertation. *Entrance requirements:* For doctorate, GRE General Test. Additional exam requirements/recommendations for international students: required—TOEFL (minimum score 550 paper-based, 90 iBT) or IELTS (6.5). Electronic applications accepted.

**University of Virginia,** School of Medicine, Department of Pharmacology, Charlottesville, VA 22903. Offers PhD, MD/PhD. *Degree requirements:* For doctorate, thesis/dissertation. *Entrance requirements:* For doctorate, GRE General Test, GRE Subject Test (recommended), 2 letters of recommendation. Additional exam requirements/recommendations for international students: required—TOEFL. Electronic applications accepted.

**University of Washington,** Graduate School, School of Medicine, Graduate Programs in Medicine, Department of Pharmacology, Seattle, WA 98195. Offers PhD. *Degree requirements:* For doctorate, thesis/dissertation. *Entrance requirements:* For doctorate, GRE General Test, minimum GPA of 3.0.

**University of Wisconsin–Madison,** School of Medicine and Public Health, Molecular and Cellular Pharmacology Graduate Training Program, Madison, WI 53705. Offers PhD. *Degree requirements:* For doctorate, comprehensive exam, thesis/dissertation. *Entrance requirements:* Additional exam requirements/recommendations for international students: required—TOEFL (minimum score 580 paper-based; 92 iBT). Electronic applications accepted.

**Vanderbilt University,** School of Medicine, Department of Pharmacology, Nashville, TN 37240-1001. Offers PhD, MD/PhD. *Faculty:* 26 full-time (12 women). *Students:* 44 full-time (22 women); includes 14 minority (2 Black or African American, non-Hispanic/Latino; 5 Asian, non-Hispanic/Latino; 4 Hispanic/Latino; 3 Two or more races, non-Hispanic/Latino), 3 international. Average age 27. In 2019, 9 doctorates awarded. *Degree requirements:* For doctorate, comprehensive exam, thesis/dissertation, preliminary, qualifying, and final exams. *Entrance requirements:* For doctorate, GRE General Test, GRE Subject Test (recommended). Additional exam requirements/

recommendations for international students: required—TOEFL (minimum score 570 paper-based; 88 iBT). *Application deadline:* For fall admission, 1/15 for domestic and international students. Electronic applications accepted. *Expenses:* Tuition: Full-time $51,018; part-time $2087 per hour. *Required fees:* $542. Tuition and fees vary according to program. *Financial support:* Fellowships with full tuition reimbursements, research assistantships with full tuition reimbursements, Federal Work-Study, institutionally sponsored loans, scholarships/grants, traineeships, health care benefits, and tuition waivers (partial) available. Financial award application deadline: 1/15; financial award applicants required to submit CSS PROFILE or FAFSA. *Unit head:* Dr. David Sweatt, Chair, 615-322-2207, Fax: 615-936-3910, E-mail: david.sweatt@vanderbilt.edu. *Application contact:* Christine Konradi, Director of Graduate Studies, 615-322-2207, E-mail: christine.konradi@vanderbilt.edu.
Website: http://medschool.vanderbilt.edu/pharmacology/

**Virginia Commonwealth University,** Medical College of Virginia-Professional Programs, School of Medicine, Graduate Programs in Medicine, Department of Pharmacology and Toxicology, Richmond, VA 23284-9005. Offers neuroscience (PhD); pharmacology (Certificate); pharmacology and toxicology (MS, PhD); MD/PhD. Terminal master's awarded for partial completion of doctoral program. *Degree requirements:* For master's, thesis; for doctorate, thesis/dissertation, comprehensive oral and written exams. *Entrance requirements:* For master's and doctorate, GRE or MCAT. Additional exam requirements/recommendations for international students: required—TOEFL (minimum score 600 paper-based; 100 iBT). Electronic applications accepted.

**Wake Forest University,** School of Medicine and Graduate School of Arts and Sciences, Graduate Programs in Medicine, Department of Physiology and Pharmacology, Winston-Salem, NC 27109. Offers pharmacology (PhD); physiology (PhD); MD/PhD. *Degree requirements:* For doctorate, thesis/dissertation. *Entrance requirements:* For doctorate, GRE General Test. Additional exam requirements/recommendations for international students: required—TOEFL. Electronic applications accepted.

**Wayne State University,** Eugene Applebaum College of Pharmacy and Health Sciences, Applied Health Sciences, Detroit, MI 48202. Offers medicinal chemistry (MS, PhD); pharmaceutics (MS, PhD), including medicinal chemistry (PhD); pharmacology and toxicology (MS, PhD). *Entrance requirements:* For master's, GRE General Test, bachelor's degree; adequate background in biology, physics, calculus, and chemistry; three letters of recommendation; personal statement; for doctorate, GRE General Test, bachelor's or master's degree in one of the behavioral, biological, pharmaceutical or physical sciences; three letters of recommendation. Additional exam requirements/recommendations for international students: required—TOEFL (minimum score 550 paper-based; 79 iBT), Michigan English Language Assessment Battery (minimum score 85); recommended—IELTS (minimum score 6.5), TWE (minimum score 5.5). Electronic applications accepted. *Expenses:* Contact institution.

**Weill Cornell Medicine,** Weill Cornell Graduate School of Medical Sciences, Pharmacology Program, New York, NY 10065. Offers MS, PhD. Terminal master's awarded for partial completion of doctoral program. *Degree requirements:* For master's, comprehensive exam; for doctorate, thesis/dissertation, final exam. *Entrance requirements:* For doctorate, GRE General Test, previous course work in natural and/or health sciences. Additional exam requirements/recommendations for international students: required—TOEFL.

**Wright State University,** Boonshoft School of Medicine, Program in Pharmacology and Toxicology, Dayton, OH 45435. Offers MS. *Degree requirements:* For master's, thesis optional.

**Yale University,** Yale School of Medicine and Graduate School of Arts and Sciences, Combined Program in Biological and Biomedical Sciences (BBS), Department of Pharmacology, New Haven, CT 06520. Offers PhD. *Degree requirements:* For doctorate, thesis/dissertation. *Entrance requirements:* For doctorate, GRE General Test. Additional exam requirements/recommendations for international students: required—TOEFL. *Expenses:* Contact institution.

**Yale University,** Yale School of Medicine and Graduate School of Arts and Sciences, Combined Program in Biological and Biomedical Sciences (BBS), Pharmacological Sciences and Molecular Medicine Track, New Haven, CT 06520. Offers PhD, MD/PhD. *Degree requirements:* For doctorate, thesis/dissertation. *Entrance requirements:* For doctorate, GRE General Test. Additional exam requirements/recommendations for international students: required—TOEFL. Electronic applications accepted.

# Toxicology

**Clemson University,** Graduate School, College of Science, Department of Biological Sciences, Clemson, SC 29634. Offers biological sciences (MS, PhD); biological sciences for science educators (MBS); environmental toxicology (MS, PhD); microbiology (MS, PhD). *Program availability:* Part-time, 100% online. *Faculty:* 48 full-time (22 women), 5 part-time/adjunct (0 women). *Students:* 72 full-time (40 women), 221 part-time (148 women); includes 39 minority (7 Black or African American, non-Hispanic/Latino; 2 American Indian or Alaska Native, non-Hispanic/Latino; 4 Asian, non-Hispanic/Latino; 14 Hispanic/Latino; 1 Native Hawaiian or other Pacific Islander, non-Hispanic/Latino; 11 Two or more races, non-Hispanic/Latino), 11 international. Average age 34. 206 applicants, 76% accepted, 122 enrolled. In 2019, 111 master's, 8 doctorates awarded. *Degree requirements:* For master's, comprehensive exam (for some programs), thesis (for some programs); for doctorate, comprehensive exam, thesis/dissertation. *Entrance requirements:* For master's and doctorate, GRE General Test, unofficial transcripts, letters of recommendation. Additional exam requirements/recommendations for international students: required—TOEFL (minimum score 102 paper-based; 102 iBT); recommended—IELTS (minimum score 7.5), TSE (minimum score 72). *Application deadline:* For fall admission, 12/10 priority date for domestic and international students. Applications are processed on a rolling basis. Application fee: $80 ($90 for international students). Electronic applications accepted. *Expenses:* Full-Time Student per Semester: Tuition: $4600 (in-state), $9525 (out-of-state), Fees: $598; Graduate Assistant Per Semester: $1144; Part-Time Student Per Credit Hour: $556 (in-state), $1106 (out-of-state), Fees: $617; other fees apply depending on program, credit hours, campus & residency. Doctoral Base Fee per Semester: $4938 (in-state), $10405 (out-of-state). *Financial support:* In 2019–20, 59 students received support, including 5 fellowships with full and partial tuition reimbursements available (averaging $3,622 per year), 11 research assistantships with full and partial tuition reimbursements available (averaging $23,227 per year), 43 teaching assistantships with full and partial tuition reimbursements available (averaging $22,326 per year); unspecified assistantships also available. Financial award application deadline: 12/10. *Unit head:* Dr. Saara Dewalt,

Department Chair, 864-656-1112, E-mail: saarad@clemson.edu. *Application contact:* Jay Lyn Martin, Graduate Student Services Coordinator, 864-656-3587, E-mail: jaylyn@clemson.edu.
Website: http://www.clemson.edu/science/departments/biosci/

**Columbia University,** College of Physicians and Surgeons, Department of Pharmacology, New York, NY 10032. Offers pharmacology (M Phil, MA, PhD); pharmacology-toxicology (M Phil, MA, PhD); MD/PhD. Terminal master's awarded for partial completion of doctoral program. *Degree requirements:* For doctorate, thesis/dissertation. *Entrance requirements:* For master's and doctorate, GRE General Test. Additional exam requirements/recommendations for international students: required—TOEFL. *Expenses: Tuition:* Full-time $47,600; part-time $1880 per credit. One-time fee: $105.

**Columbia University,** Columbia University Mailman School of Public Health, Department of Environmental Health Sciences, New York, NY 10032. Offers environmental health sciences (MPH, Dr PH, PhD); radiological sciences (MS); toxicology (MS). *Accreditation:* CEPH (one or more programs are accredited). *Program availability:* Part-time. *Students:* 45 full-time (37 women), 27 part-time (17 women); includes 27 minority (1 Black or African American, non-Hispanic/Latino; 1 American Indian or Alaska Native, non-Hispanic/Latino; 12 Asian, non-Hispanic/Latino; 7 Hispanic/Latino; 1 Native Hawaiian or other Pacific Islander, non-Hispanic/Latino; 5 Two or more races, non-Hispanic/Latino), 12 international. Average age 27. 161 applicants, 54% accepted, 33 enrolled. In 2019, 28 master's, 2 doctorates awarded. *Degree requirements:* For master's, thesis optional; for doctorate, thesis/dissertation. *Entrance requirements:* For master's, GRE General Test, 1 year of course work in biology, general chemistry, organic chemistry, and mathematics; for doctorate, GRE General Test, MPH or equivalent (for Dr PH). Additional exam requirements/recommendations for international students: required—TOEFL (minimum score 600 paper-based; 100 iBT). *Application deadline:* For fall admission, 12/1 priority date for domestic and international students. Applications are processed on a rolling basis. Application fee:

$120. Electronic applications accepted. *Expenses: Tuition:* Full-time $47,600; part-time $1880 per credit. One-time fee: $105. *Financial support:* Research assistantships, teaching assistantships, career-related internships or fieldwork, and Federal Work-Study available. Support available to part-time students. Financial award application deadline: 2/1; financial award applicants required to submit FAFSA. *Unit head:* Dr. Andrea Baccarelli, Chair, 212-305-3466, Fax: 212-305-4012. *Application contact:* Clare Norton, Associate Dean for Enrollment Management, 212-305-8698, Fax: 212-342-1861, E-mail: ph-admit@columbia.edu.
Website: https://www.mailman.columbia.edu/become-student/departments/environmental-health-sciences

**Cornell University,** Graduate School, Graduate Fields of Agriculture and Life Sciences, Field of Environmental Toxicology, Ithaca, NY 14853. Offers cellular and molecular toxicology (MS, PhD); ecotoxicology and environmental chemistry (MS, PhD); nutritional and food toxicology (MS, PhD); risk assessment, management and public policy (MS, PhD). *Degree requirements:* For master's, thesis; for doctorate, comprehensive exam, thesis/dissertation. *Entrance requirements:* For master's and doctorate, GRE General Test, GRE Subject Test (biology or chemistry recommended), 2 letters of recommendation. Additional exam requirements/recommendations for international students: required—TOEFL (minimum score 600 paper-based; 77 iBT). Electronic applications accepted.

**Duke University,** Graduate School, Integrated Toxicology and Environmental Health Program, Durham, NC 27708. Offers Certificate. *Entrance requirements:* Additional exam requirements/recommendations for international students: required—TOEFL (minimum score 577 paper-based; 90 iBT) or IELTS (minimum score 7). Electronic applications accepted.

**East Carolina University,** Brody School of Medicine, Office of Research and Graduate Studies, Greenville, NC 27858-4353. Offers anatomy and cell biology (PhD); biochemistry and molecular biology (PhD); biomedical science (MS); microbiology and immunology (PhD); pharmacology and toxicology (PhD); physiology (PhD). *Students:* 102 full-time (44 women), 1 part-time (0 women); includes 16 minority (4 Black or African American, non-Hispanic/Latino; 7 Asian, non-Hispanic/Latino; 4 Hispanic/Latino; 1 Two or more races, non-Hispanic/Latino), 13 international. Average age 28. 83 applicants, 40% accepted, 20 enrolled. In 2019, 3 master's, 10 doctorates awarded. *Degree requirements:* For doctorate, comprehensive exam, thesis/dissertation. *Entrance requirements:* For doctorate, GRE General Test. Additional exam requirements/recommendations for international students: required—some international applicants may be required to demonstrate English proficiency via the TOEFL, IELTS, or PTE exam.; recommended—TOEFL (minimum score 78 iBT), IELTS (minimum score 6.5), TSE (minimum score 65). *Application deadline:* For fall admission, 8/15 for domestic students; for spring admission, 12/20 for domestic students. Applications are processed on a rolling basis. Application fee: $75. Electronic applications accepted. *Expenses: Tuition, area resident:* Full-time $4749; part-time $185 per credit hour. Tuition, state resident: full-time $4749; part-time $185 per credit hour. Tuition, nonresident: full-time $17,898; part-time $864 per credit hour. *International tuition:* $17,898 full-time. *Required fees:* $2787. *Financial support:* Fellowships available. Financial award application deadline: 6/1. *Unit head:* Dr. Russ Price, Associate Dean, 252-744-9346, E-mail: pricest17@ecu.edu. *Application contact:* Dr. Russ Price, Associate Dean, 252-744-9346, E-mail: pricest17@ecu.edu.
Website: http://www.ecu.edu/cs-dhs/bsomresearchgradstudies/index.cfm

**Florida Agricultural and Mechanical University,** Division of Graduate Studies, Research, and Continuing Education, College of Pharmacy and Pharmaceutical Sciences, Graduate Programs in Pharmaceutical Sciences, Tallahassee, FL 32307-3200. Offers environmental toxicology (PhD); health outcomes research and pharmacoeconomics (PhD); medicinal chemistry (MS, PhD); pharmaceutics (MS, PhD); pharmacology/toxicology (MS, PhD); pharmacy administration (MS). *Accreditation:* CEPH. *Degree requirements:* For master's, comprehensive exam, thesis, publishable paper; for doctorate, comprehensive exam, thesis/dissertation, publishable paper. *Entrance requirements:* For master's and doctorate, GRE General Test, minimum GPA of 3.0 in last 60 hours. Additional exam requirements/recommendations for international students: required—TOEFL.

**The George Washington University,** Columbian College of Arts and Sciences, Department of Forensic Sciences, Washington, DC 20052. Offers crime scene investigation (MFS); forensic chemistry (MFS); forensic molecular biology (MFS); forensic toxicology (MFS); high-technology crime investigation (MS); security management (MFS). *Program availability:* Part-time, evening/weekend. *Entrance requirements:* For master's, GRE General Test, minimum GPA of 3.0. Additional exam requirements/recommendations for international students: required—TOEFL (minimum score 550 paper-based; 80 iBT). Electronic applications accepted.

**Indiana University Bloomington,** School of Public and Environmental Affairs, Environmental Science Programs, Bloomington, IN 47405. Offers applied ecology (MSES); energy (MSES); environmental chemistry, toxicology, and risk assessment (MSES); environmental science (PhD); hazardous materials management (Certificate); specialized environmental science (MSES); water resources (MSES); JD/MSES; MSES/MA; MSES/MPA; MSES/MS. *Program availability:* Part-time. Terminal master's awarded for partial completion of doctoral program. *Degree requirements:* For master's, capstone or thesis; internship; for doctorate, comprehensive exam, thesis/dissertation. *Entrance requirements:* For master's, GRE General Test or GMAT, official transcripts, 3 letters of recommendation, resume, personal statement; for doctorate, GRE General Test or LSAT, official transcripts, 3 letters of recommendation, resume or curriculum vitae, statement of purpose. Additional exam requirements/recommendations for international students: required—TOEFL (minimum score 600 paper-based; 96 iBT); recommended—IELTS (minimum score 7). Electronic applications accepted.

**Indiana University-Purdue University Indianapolis,** Indiana University School of Medicine, Department of Pharmacology and Toxicology, Indianapolis, IN 46202. Offers pharmacology (MS, PhD); toxicology (MS, PhD); MD/PhD. *Degree requirements:* For master's, thesis; for doctorate, thesis/dissertation. *Entrance requirements:* For master's, GRE General Test, GRE Subject Test, minimum GPA of 3.2 in core science courses; for doctorate, GRE General Test, GRE Subject Test. Additional exam requirements/recommendations for international students: required—TOEFL, IELTS, GRE or MCAT. Electronic applications accepted. *Expenses:* Contact institution.

**Iowa State University of Science and Technology,** Program in Toxicology, Ames, IA 50011. Offers MS, PhD. *Entrance requirements:* For master's and doctorate, GRE General Test. Additional exam requirements/recommendations for international students: required—TOEFL (minimum score 550 paper-based; 79 iBT), IELTS (minimum score 6.5). Electronic applications accepted.

**Long Island University - Brooklyn,** Arnold and Marie Schwartz College of Pharmacy and Health Sciences, Brooklyn, NY 11201-8423. Offers drug regulatory affairs (MS); pharmaceutics (MS, PhD), including cosmetic science (MS), industrial pharmacy (MS); pharmacology and toxicology (MS); pharmacy (Pharm D). *Accreditation:* ACPE. *Program availability:* Part-time. Terminal master's awarded for partial completion of doctoral program. *Degree requirements:* For master's, comprehensive exam, thesis; for doctorate, comprehensive exam, thesis/dissertation. *Entrance requirements:* For master's and doctorate, GRE. Additional exam requirements/recommendations for international students: required—TOEFL (minimum score 550 paper-based, 79 iBT) or IELTS. Electronic applications accepted. *Expenses:* Contact institution.

**Louisiana State University and Agricultural & Mechanical College,** Graduate School, School of the Coast and Environment, Department of Environmental Sciences, Baton Rouge, LA 70803. Offers environmental planning and management (MS); environmental science (PhD); environmental toxicology (MS).

**Massachusetts Institute of Technology,** School of Engineering, Department of Biological Engineering, Cambridge, MA 02139. Offers applied biosciences (PhD, Sc D); bioengineering (PhD, Sc D); biological engineering (PhD, Sc D); biomedical engineering (M Eng); toxicology (SM); SM/MBA. Terminal master's awarded for partial completion of doctoral program. *Degree requirements:* For master's, thesis; for doctorate, comprehensive exam, thesis/dissertation. *Entrance requirements:* For master's and doctorate, GRE General Test. Additional exam requirements/recommendations for international students: required—IELTS. Electronic applications accepted.

**Medical College of Wisconsin,** Graduate School, Department of Pharmacology and Toxicology, Milwaukee, WI 53226. Offers PhD, MD/PhD. *Students:* 10 full-time (4 women), 3 international. Average age 29. 3 applicants, 33% accepted. In 2019, 1 doctorate awarded. *Degree requirements:* For doctorate, comprehensive exam, thesis/dissertation, oral and written qualifying exams. *Entrance requirements:* For doctorate, GRE, official transcripts, three letters of recommendation. Additional exam requirements/recommendations for international students: required—TOEFL. *Application deadline:* For fall admission, 12/15 priority date for domestic and international students. Applications are processed on a rolling basis. Application fee: $50. Electronic applications accepted. *Expenses:* $1,250 per credit PhD students; $155 per year full-time student fees. *Financial support:* In 2019–20, 8 students received support, including fellowships (averaging $30,000 per year), research assistantships (averaging $30,000 per year); career-related internships or fieldwork, institutionally sponsored loans, and scholarships/grants also available. Financial award application deadline: 2/15; financial award applicants required to submit FAFSA. *Unit head:* Dr. William D. Campbell, Chair, 414-955-8267, Fax: 414-955-6555, E-mail: gradschool@mcw.edu. *Application contact:* Recruitment Office, 414-955-4402, Fax: 414-955-6555, E-mail: gradschoolrecruit@mcw.edu.
Website: https://www.mcw.edu/Pharmacology.htm

**Medical University of South Carolina,** College of Graduate Studies, Department of Pharmaceutical and Biomedical Sciences, Charleston, SC 29425. Offers cell injury and repair (PhD); drug discovery (PhD); medicinal chemistry (PhD); toxicology (PhD); DMD/PhD; MD/PhD; Pharm D/PhD. *Degree requirements:* For doctorate, thesis/dissertation, oral and written exams, teaching and research seminar. *Entrance requirements:* For doctorate, GRE General Test, interview, minimum GPA of 3.0. Additional exam requirements/recommendations for international students: required—TOEFL (minimum score 600 paper-based; 100 iBT). Electronic applications accepted.

**Michigan State University,** College of Human Medicine and The Graduate School, Graduate Programs in Human Medicine, East Lansing, MI 48824. Offers biochemistry and molecular biology (MS, PhD); epidemiology (MS, PhD); microbiology (MS); microbiology and molecular genetics (PhD); pharmacology and toxicology (MS, PhD); physiology (MS, PhD); public health (MPH). *Entrance requirements:* Additional exam requirements/recommendations for international students: required—TOEFL.

**Michigan State University,** College of Osteopathic Medicine and The Graduate School, Graduate Studies in Osteopathic Medicine and College of Human Medicine and College of Veterinary Medicine, Department of Pharmacology and Toxicology, East Lansing, MI 48824. Offers integrative pharmacology (MS); pharmacology and toxicology (MS, PhD); pharmacology and toxicology-environmental toxicology (PhD). *Entrance requirements:* Additional exam requirements/recommendations for international students: required—TOEFL (minimum score 600 paper-based). Electronic applications accepted.

**Michigan State University,** College of Veterinary Medicine and The Graduate School, Graduate Programs in Veterinary Medicine, Center for Integrative Toxicology, East Lansing, MI 48824. Offers animal science–environmental toxicology (PhD); biochemistry and molecular biology–environmental toxicology (PhD); chemistry–environmental toxicology (PhD); crop and soil sciences–environmental toxicology (PhD); environmental engineering–environmental toxicology (PhD); environmental geosciences–environmental toxicology (PhD); fisheries and wildlife–environmental toxicology (PhD); food science–environmental toxicology (PhD); forestry–environmental toxicology (PhD); genetics–environmental toxicology (PhD); human nutrition–environmental toxicology (PhD); microbiology–environmental toxicology (PhD); pharmacology and toxicology–environmental toxicology (PhD); zoology–environmental toxicology (PhD). *Entrance requirements:* Additional exam requirements/recommendations for international students: required—TOEFL (minimum score 550 paper-based), Michigan State University ELT ( minimum score 85), Michigan English Language Assessment Battery (minimum score 83). Electronic applications accepted.

**Michigan State University,** The Graduate School, College of Agriculture and Natural Resources, Department of Animal Science, East Lansing, MI 48824. Offers animal science (MS, PhD); animal science-environmental toxicology (PhD). *Entrance requirements:* Additional exam requirements/recommendations for international students: required—TOEFL (minimum score 550 paper-based), Michigan State University ELT ( minimum score 85), Michigan English Language Assessment Battery (minimum score 83). Electronic applications accepted.

**Michigan State University,** The Graduate School, College of Agriculture and Natural Resources, Department of Food Science and Human Nutrition, East Lansing, MI 48824. Offers food science (MS, PhD); food science - environmental toxicology (PhD); human nutrition (MS, PhD); human nutrition-environmental toxicology (PhD). *Entrance requirements:* Additional exam requirements/recommendations for international students: required—TOEFL (minimum score 550 paper-based), Michigan State University ELT ( minimum score 85), Michigan English Language Assessment Battery (minimum score 83). Electronic applications accepted.

**Michigan State University,** The Graduate School, College of Agriculture and Natural Resources, Department of Plant, Soil and Microbial Sciences, East Lansing, MI 48824. Offers crop and soil sciences (MS, PhD); crop and soil sciences-environmental toxicology (PhD); plant breeding and genetics-crop and soil sciences (MS); plant breeding, genetics and biotechnology-crop and soil sciences (PhD); plant pathology (MS, PhD). *Entrance requirements:* Additional exam requirements/recommendations for international students: required—TOEFL (minimum score 550 paper-based), Michigan State University ELT ( minimum score 85), Michigan Michigan English Language Assessment Battery (minimum score 83). Electronic applications accepted.

**Michigan State University,** The Graduate School, College of Engineering, Department of Civil and Environmental Engineering, East Lansing, MI 48824. Offers civil engineering (MS, PhD); environmental engineering (MS, PhD); environmental engineering-environmental toxicology (PhD). *Program availability:* Part-time. *Entrance requirements:* Additional exam requirements/recommendations for international students: required—TOEFL. Electronic applications accepted.

**Michigan State University,** The Graduate School, College of Natural Science, Department of Biochemistry and Molecular Biology, East Lansing, MI 48824. Offers biochemistry and molecular biology (MS, PhD); biochemistry and molecular biology/environmental toxicology (PhD). *Entrance requirements:* Additional exam requirements/recommendations for international students: required—TOEFL. Electronic applications accepted.

**Michigan State University,** The Graduate School, College of Natural Science, Department of Chemistry, East Lansing, MI 48824. Offers chemical physics (PhD); chemistry (MS, PhD); chemistry-environmental toxicology (PhD); computational chemistry (MS). *Entrance requirements:* Additional exam requirements/recommendations for international students: required—TOEFL. Electronic applications accepted.

**Michigan State University,** The Graduate School, College of Natural Science, Department of Earth and Environmental Sciences, East Lansing, MI 48824. Offers environmental geosciences (MS, PhD); environmental geosciences-environmental toxicology (PhD); geological sciences (MS, PhD). *Degree requirements:* For master's, thesis (for those without prior thesis work); for doctorate, thesis/dissertation. *Entrance requirements:* For master's, GRE General Test, minimum GPA of 3.0, course work in geoscience, 3 letters of recommendation; for doctorate, GRE General Test, 3 letters of recommendation. Additional exam requirements/recommendations for international students: required—TOEFL (minimum score 550 paper-based), Michigan State University ELT (minimum score 85), Michigan English Language Assessment Battery (minimum score 83). Electronic applications accepted.

**Michigan State University,** The Graduate School, College of Natural Science, Department of Microbiology and Molecular Genetics, East Lansing, MI 48824. Offers industrial microbiology (MS, PhD); microbiology (MS, PhD); microbiology and molecular genetics (MS, PhD); microbiology–environmental toxicology (PhD). *Entrance requirements:* For master's, GRE General Test. Additional exam requirements/recommendations for international students: required—TOEFL (minimum score 550 paper-based), Michigan State University ELT ( minimum score 85), Michigan English Language Assessment Battery (minimum score 83). Electronic applications accepted.

**Michigan State University,** The Graduate School, College of Natural Science, Program in Genetics, East Lansing, MI 48824. Offers genetics (MS, PhD); genetics–environmental toxicology (PhD). *Entrance requirements:* Additional exam requirements/recommendations for international students: required—TOEFL. Electronic applications accepted.

**Oklahoma State University Center for Health Sciences,** Graduate Program in Forensic Sciences, Tulsa, OK 74107-1898. Offers forensic sciences (MS), including arson and explosives investigation, forensic biology/DNA, forensic document examination, forensic pathology/death scene investigations, forensic psychology, forensic science administration, forensic toxicology/trace evidence. *Program availability:* Part-time, evening/weekend, 100% online, blended/hybrid learning. *Degree requirements:* For master's, comprehensive exam, thesis (for some programs), thesis or creative component. *Entrance requirements:* For master's, GRE (for thesis tracks); GRE or MAT (for options in arson and explosives investigation, forensic science administration, and forensic document examination), professional experience (for options in arson and explosives investigation, forensic science administration and forensic document examination). Additional exam requirements/recommendations for international students: required—TOEFL (minimum score 100 iBT) or IELTS (minimum score 7.0). Electronic applications accepted.

**Oregon State University,** College of Agricultural Sciences, Program in Fisheries Science, Corvallis, OR 97331. Offers aquaculture (MS); conservation biology (MS, PhD); fish genetics (MS, PhD); ichthyology (MS, PhD); limnology (MS, PhD); parasites and diseases (MS, PhD); physiology and ecology of marine and freshwater fishes (MS, PhD); stream ecology (MS, PhD); toxicology (MS, PhD); water pollution biology (MS, PhD). *Program availability:* Part-time. *Entrance requirements:* For master's and doctorate, GRE, minimum GPA of 3.0 in last 90 hours. Additional exam requirements/recommendations for international students: required—TOEFL (minimum score 80 iBT), IELTS (minimum score 6.5).

**Oregon State University,** College of Agricultural Sciences, Program in Toxicology, Corvallis, OR 97331. Offers environmental chemistry and ecotoxicology (MS, PhD); mechanistic toxicology (MS, PhD); molecular and cellular toxicology (MS, PhD); neurotoxicology (MS, PhD). *Degree requirements:* For master's, thesis; for doctorate, thesis/dissertation. *Entrance requirements:* For master's and doctorate, GRE, bachelor's degree in chemistry or biological sciences, minimum GPA of 3.0 in last 90 hours of course work. Additional exam requirements/recommendations for international students: required—TOEFL (minimum score 80 iBT), IELTS (minimum score 6.5).

**Purdue University,** Graduate School, College of Health and Human Sciences, School of Health Sciences, West Lafayette, IN 47907. Offers health physics (MS, PhD); medical physics (MS, PhD); occupational and environmental health science (MS, PhD), including aerosol deposition and lung disease, ergonomics, exposure and risk assessment, indoor air quality and bioaerosols (PhD), liver/lung toxicology, radiological health (PhD); toxicology (PhD); MS/PhD. *Program availability:* Part-time. *Faculty:* 15 full-time (6 women), 1 part-time/adjunct (0 women). *Students:* 39 full-time (22 women), 6 part-time (3 women); includes 12 minority (2 Black or African American, non-Hispanic/Latino; 1 American Indian or Alaska Native, non-Hispanic/Latino; 3 Asian, non-Hispanic/Latino; 1 Hispanic/Latino; 5 Two or more races, non-Hispanic/Latino), 15 international. Average age 28. 61 applicants, 43% accepted, 14 enrolled. In 2019, 15 master's, 6 doctorates awarded. *Degree requirements:* For master's, thesis optional; for doctorate, one foreign language, thesis/dissertation. *Entrance requirements:* For master's and doctorate, GRE General Test, minimum undergraduate GPA of 3.0 or equivalent. Additional exam requirements/recommendations for international students: required—TOEFL (minimum score 550 paper-based; 77 iBT); recommended—TWE. *Application deadline:* For fall admission, 5/15 for domestic and international students; for spring admission, 10/15 for domestic and international students. Applications are processed on a rolling basis. Application fee: $60 ($75 for international students). Electronic applications accepted. *Financial support:* In 2019–20, fellowships with tuition reimbursements (averaging $14,400 per year), research assistantships with tuition reimbursements (averaging $12,000 per year), teaching assistantships with tuition reimbursements (averaging $12,000 per year) were awarded; career-related internships or fieldwork and traineeships also available. Support available to part-time students. Financial award applicants required to submit FAFSA. *Unit head:* Aaron Bowman, Head of the Graduate Program, 765-494-2684, E-mail: bowma117@purdue.edu. *Application contact:* Karen E. Walker, Graduate Contact, 765-494-1419, E-mail: kwalker@purdue.edu. Website: https://www.purdue.edu/hhs/hsci/

**Rutgers University - New Brunswick,** Graduate School-New Brunswick, Department of Environmental Sciences, Piscataway, NJ 08854-8097. Offers air pollution and resources (MS, PhD); aquatic biology (MS, PhD); aquatic chemistry (MS, PhD); atmospheric science (MS, PhD); chemistry and physics of aerosol and hydrosol systems (MS, PhD); environmental chemistry (MS, PhD); environmental microbiology (MS, PhD); environmental toxicology (PhD); exposure assessment (PhD); fate and effects of pollutants (MS, PhD); pollution prevention and control (MS, PhD); water and wastewater treatment (MS, PhD); water resources (MS, PhD). Terminal master's awarded for partial completion of doctoral program. *Degree requirements:* For master's, comprehensive exam, thesis or alternative, oral final exam; for doctorate, comprehensive exam, thesis/dissertation, thesis defense, qualifying exam. *Entrance requirements:* For master's and doctorate, GRE General Test. Additional exam requirements/recommendations for international students: required—TOEFL. Electronic applications accepted.

**Rutgers University - New Brunswick,** Graduate School-New Brunswick, Joint Program in Toxicology, Piscataway, NJ 08854-8097. Offers environmental toxicology (MS, PhD); industrial-occupational toxicology (MS, PhD); nutritional toxicology (MS, PhD); pharmaceutical toxicology (MS, PhD). *Degree requirements:* For master's, thesis; for doctorate, comprehensive exam, thesis/dissertation, qualifying exams (written and oral). *Entrance requirements:* For master's and doctorate, GRE General Test. Additional exam requirements/recommendations for international students: required—TOEFL. Electronic applications accepted.

**Rutgers University - New Brunswick,** Graduate School of Biomedical Sciences, Piscataway, NJ 08854-5635. Offers biochemistry and molecular biology (MS, PhD); biomedical engineering (MS, PhD); biomedical science (MS); cellular and molecular pharmacology (MS, PhD); clinical and translational science (MS); environmental sciences/exposure assessment (PhD); molecular genetics, microbiology and immunology (MS, PhD); neuroscience (MS, PhD); physiology and integrative biology (MS, PhD); toxicology (PhD); MD/PhD. Terminal master's awarded for partial completion of doctoral program. *Degree requirements:* For master's, thesis (for some programs), ethics training; for doctorate, comprehensive exam, thesis/dissertation, ethics training. *Entrance requirements:* For master's, GRE General Test, MCAT, DAT; for doctorate, GRE General Test. Additional exam requirements/recommendations for international students: required—TOEFL. Electronic applications accepted.

**St. John's University,** College of Pharmacy and Health Sciences, Graduate Programs in Pharmaceutical Sciences, Program in Toxicology, Queens, NY 11439. Offers MS. *Program availability:* Part-time. Terminal master's awarded for partial completion of doctoral program. *Degree requirements:* For master's, comprehensive exam (for some programs), thesis (for some programs). *Entrance requirements:* For master's, GRE General Test, letters of recommendation, transcripts, resume, personal statement. Additional exam requirements/recommendations for international students: required—TOEFL (minimum score 100 iBT), IELTS (minimum score 7). Electronic applications accepted. *Expenses:* Contact institution.

**San Diego State University,** Graduate and Research Affairs, College of Health and Human Services, School of Public Health, San Diego, CA 92182. Offers environmental health (MPH); epidemiology (MPH, PhD), including biostatistics (MPH); global emergency preparedness and response (MS); global health (PhD); health behavior (PhD); health promotion (MPH); health services administration (MPH); toxicology (MS); MPH/MA; MSW/MPH. *Accreditation:* CAHME (one or more programs are accredited); CEPH. *Program availability:* Part-time. *Degree requirements:* For master's, comprehensive exam (for some programs), thesis (for some programs); for doctorate, thesis/dissertation. *Entrance requirements:* For master's, GMAT (MPH in health services administration), GRE General Test; for doctorate, GRE General Test. Additional exam requirements/recommendations for international students: required—TOEFL.

**Simon Fraser University,** Office of Graduate Studies and Postdoctoral Fellows, Faculty of Science, Department of Biological Sciences, Burnaby, BC V5A 1S6, Canada. Offers bioinformatics (Graduate Diploma); biological sciences (M Sc, PhD); environmental toxicology (MET); pest management (MPM). *Degree requirements:* For master's, thesis; for doctorate, thesis/dissertation, candidacy exam; for Graduate Diploma, practicum. *Entrance requirements:* For master's, minimum GPA of 3.0 (on scale of 4.33) or 3.33 based on last 60 credits of undergraduate courses; for doctorate, minimum GPA of 3.5 (on scale of 4.33); for Graduate Diploma, minimum GPA of 2.5 (on scale of 4.33) or 2.67 based on last 60 credits of undergraduate courses. Additional exam requirements/recommendations for international students: recommended—TOEFL (minimum score 580 paper-based; 93 iBT), IELTS (minimum score 7), TWE (minimum score 5). Electronic applications accepted.

**Texas Southern University,** School of Science and Technology, Program in Environmental Toxicology, Houston, TX 77004-4584. Offers MS, PhD. *Program availability:* Part-time. *Degree requirements:* For master's, thesis; for doctorate, thesis/dissertation. *Entrance requirements:* For master's, minimum GPA of 2.75; for doctorate, GRE, minimum GPA of 2.75. Electronic applications accepted. *Expenses:* Contact institution.

**Texas Tech University,** Graduate School, College of Arts and Sciences, Department of Environmental Toxicology, Lubbock, TX 79409-1163. Offers MS, PhD, JD/MS, MBA/MS. *Program availability:* Part-time. *Faculty:* 14 full-time (4 women). *Students:* 52 full-time (34 women), 3 part-time (2 women); includes 13 minority (5 Black or African American, non-Hispanic/Latino; 6 Hispanic/Latino; 2 Two or more races, non-Hispanic/Latino), 15 international. Average age 28. 32 applicants, 78% accepted, 19 enrolled. In 2019, 11 master's, 7 doctorates awarded. Terminal master's awarded for partial completion of doctoral program. *Degree requirements:* For master's, thesis; for doctorate, comprehensive exam, thesis/dissertation. *Entrance requirements:* For master's and doctorate, GRE. Additional exam requirements/recommendations for international students: required—TOEFL (minimum score 550 paper-based; 79 iBT); recommended—IELTS (minimum score 6.5), TSE (minimum score 60). *Application deadline:* For fall admission, 6/1 priority date for domestic students, 1/15 priority date for international students; for spring admission, 9/1 priority date for domestic students, 6/15 priority date for international students. Applications are processed on a rolling basis. Application fee: $65. Electronic applications accepted. *Expenses:* Contact institution. *Financial support:* In 2019–20, 51 students received support, including 42 fellowships (averaging $1,838 per year), 42 research assistantships (averaging $14,400 per year); teaching assistantships, Federal Work-Study, institutionally sponsored loans, scholarships/grants, health care benefits, and unspecified assistantships also available. Financial award application deadline: 5/15; financial award applicants required to submit FAFSA. *Unit head:* Dr. Steven M. Presley, Chair and Professor, 806-885-4567 Ext. 236, Fax: 806-885-2132, E-mail: steve.presley@ttu.edu. *Application contact:* Dr. Kamaleshwar Singh, Graduate Officer, 806-834-8407, Fax: 806-885-2132, E-mail: kamaleshwar.singh@ttu.edu. Website: www.tiehh.ttu.edu/

**Thomas Jefferson University,** Jefferson College of Life Sciences, MS Program in Forensic Toxicology, Philadelphia, PA 19107. Offers MS. *Program availability:* Part-time, evening/weekend. *Degree requirements:* For master's, thesis, clerkship. *Entrance requirements:* For master's, GRE General Test or MCAT, minimum GPA of 3.0. Additional exam requirements/recommendations for international students: required—TOEFL, IELTS (minimum score 7). Electronic applications accepted.

**Université de Montréal,** Faculty of Medicine, Program in Toxicology and Risk Analysis, Montréal, QC H3C 3J7, Canada. Offers DESS. Electronic applications accepted.

**University at Albany, State University of New York,** School of Public Health, Department of Environmental Health Sciences, Albany, NY 12222-0001. Offers environmental and occupational health (MS, PhD); environmental chemistry (MS, PhD); toxicology (MS, PhD). *Program availability:* Blended/hybrid learning. *Faculty:* 8 full-time

(6 women), 1 (woman) part-time/adjunct. *Students:* 15 full-time (8 women), 8 part-time (7 women); includes 7 minority (5 Black or African American, non-Hispanic/Latino; 2 Asian, non-Hispanic/Latino), 7 international. 19 applicants, 74% accepted, 7 enrolled. In 2019, 2 doctorates awarded. *Degree requirements:* For master's, thesis; for doctorate, comprehensive exam, thesis/dissertation. *Entrance requirements:* For master's and doctorate, transcripts of all schools attended; statement of background and goals; departmental questionnaire; resume; names and contact information for 3 recommenders. Additional exam requirements/recommendations for international students: required—TOEFL (minimum score 600 paper-based). *Application deadline:* For fall admission, 1/15 for domestic and international students; for winter admission, 4/1 for domestic and international students; for spring admission, 11/15 for domestic and international students. Applications are processed on a rolling basis. Application fee: $75. Electronic applications accepted. *Expenses: Tuition, area resident:* Full-time $11,530; part-time $480 per credit hour. Tuition, nonresident: full-time $23,530; part-time $980 per credit hour. *International tuition:* $23,530 full-time. *Required fees:* $2185; $96 per credit hour. Part-time tuition and fees vary according to course load and program. *Financial support:* Fellowships, research assistantships with full tuition reimbursements, teaching assistantships with full tuition reimbursements, scholarships/grants, health care benefits, tuition waivers (partial), and unspecified assistantships available. Financial award application deadline: 1/15. *Unit head:* Dr. David Lawrence, Chair, 518-474-7161, E-mail: dalawrence@albany.edu. *Application contact:* Dr. David Lawrence, Chair, 518-474-7161, E-mail: dalawrence@albany.edu.
Website: https://www.albany.edu/sph/programs/ms-environmental-health

**University at Buffalo, the State University of New York,** Graduate School, Jacobs School of Medicine and Biomedical Sciences, Graduate Programs in Medicine and Biomedical Sciences, Department of Pharmacology and Toxicology, Buffalo, NY 14203. Offers pharmacology (MS, PhD); MD/PhD. *Faculty:* 22 full-time (4 women), 1 part-time/adjunct (0 women). *Students:* 29 full-time (20 women); includes 7 minority (2 Black or African American, non-Hispanic/Latino; 2 Asian, non-Hispanic/Latino; 3 Hispanic/Latino), 10 international. Average age 25. 44 applicants, 52% accepted, 9 enrolled. In 2019, 10 master's, 6 doctorates awarded. Terminal master's awarded for partial completion of doctoral program. *Degree requirements:* For master's, thesis; for doctorate, thesis/dissertation. *Entrance requirements:* For master's and doctorate, 3 letters of recommendation. Additional exam requirements/recommendations for international students: required—TOEFL (minimum score 79 iBT). *Application deadline:* For fall admission, 2/14 priority date for domestic and international students. Applications are processed on a rolling basis. Application fee: $85. Electronic applications accepted. *Expenses: Tuition, area resident:* Full-time $11,310; part-time $471 per credit hour. Tuition, state resident: full-time $11,310; part-time $471 per credit hour. Tuition, nonresident: full-time $23,100; part-time $963 per credit hour. *International tuition:* $23,100 full-time. *Required fees:* $2820. *Financial support:* In 2019–20, 2 students received support, including 2 fellowships with full tuition reimbursements available (averaging $27,000 per year), 7 research assistantships with full tuition reimbursements available (averaging $27,000 per year); teaching assistantships, Federal Work-Study, scholarships/grants, health care benefits, and unspecified assistantships also available. Financial award application deadline: 2/14; financial award applicants required to submit FAFSA. *Unit head:* Dr. David Dietz, Associate Professor/Chair, 716-829-2071, Fax: 716-829-2801, E-mail: ddietz@buffalo.edu. *Application contact:* Linda M. LeRoy, Admissions Assistant, 716-829-2800, Fax: 716-829-2801, E-mail: pmygrad@buffalo.edu.
Website: http://medicine.buffalo.edu/pharmtox

**The University of Alabama at Birmingham,** Joint Health Sciences, Program in Pharmacology and Toxicology, Birmingham, AL 35294. Offers PhD. *Degree requirements:* For doctorate, thesis/dissertation. *Entrance requirements:* For doctorate, GRE General Test; GRE Subject Test (recommended), interview. Additional exam requirements/recommendations for international students: required—TOEFL, TWE. Electronic applications accepted. *Expenses:* Contact institution.

**The University of Alabama at Birmingham,** School of Public Health, Program in Health Care Organization and Policy, Birmingham, AL 35294. Offers applied epidemiology and pharmacoepidemiology (MSPH); biostatistics (MPH); clinical and translational science (MSPH); environmental health (MPH); environmental health and toxicology (MSPH); epidemiology (MPH); general theory and practice (MPH); health behavior (MPH); health care organization (MPH, Dr PH); health policy (MPH); industrial hygiene (MPH, MSPH); maternal and child health policy (Dr PH); maternal and child health policy and leadership (MPH); occupational health and safety (MPH); outcomes research (MSPH, Dr PH); public health (PhD); public health preparedness management (MPH). *Accreditation:* CEPH. *Program availability:* Part-time, 100% online, blended/hybrid learning. *Faculty:* 14 full-time (6 women). *Students:* 53 full-time (37 women), 61 part-time (45 women); includes 37 minority (12 Black or African American, non-Hispanic/Latino; 20 Asian, non-Hispanic/Latino; 1 Hispanic/Latino; 4 Two or more races, non-Hispanic/Latino), 17 international. Average age 31. 136 applicants, 59% accepted, 44 enrolled. In 2019, 36 master's, 4 doctorates awarded. *Degree requirements:* For master's, comprehensive exam (for some programs), thesis (for some programs); for doctorate, comprehensive exam, thesis/dissertation. *Entrance requirements:* For doctorate, GRE. Additional exam requirements/recommendations for international students: required—TOEFL (minimum score 80 iBT), IELTS (minimum score 6.5). *Application deadline:* For fall admission, 4/1 priority date for domestic students, 4/1 for international students; for spring admission, 11/1 for domestic students; for summer admission, 4/1 for domestic students. Application fee: $50 ($60 for international students). Electronic applications accepted. *Financial support:* Fellowships, research assistantships, teaching assistantships, scholarships/grants, traineeships, and unspecified assistantships available. Financial award application deadline: 3/1; financial award applicants required to submit FAFSA. *Unit head:* Dr. Martha Wingate, Program Director, 205-934-6783, Fax: 205-975-5484, E-mail: mslay@uab.edu. *Application contact:* Dustin Shaw, Coordinator, Student Admissions and Record, 205-934-3939, E-mail: bcampbel@uab.edu.
Website: http://www.soph.uab.edu

**University of Arkansas for Medical Sciences,** Graduate School, Little Rock, AR 72205. Offers biochemistry and molecular biology (MS, PhD); bioinformatics (MS, PhD); cellular physiology and molecular biophysics (MS, PhD); clinical nutrition (MS); interdisciplinary biomedical sciences (MS, PhD, Certificate); interdisciplinary toxicology (MS); microbiology and immunology (PhD); neurobiology and developmental sciences (PhD); pharmacology (PhD); MD/PhD. *Program availability:* Part-time. Terminal master's awarded for partial completion of doctoral program. *Degree requirements:* For master's, comprehensive exam (for some programs), thesis (for some programs); for doctorate, thesis/dissertation. *Entrance requirements:* For master's and doctorate, GRE. Additional exam requirements/recommendations for international students: required—TOEFL. Electronic applications accepted. *Expenses:* Contact institution.

**University of California, Davis,** Graduate Studies, Graduate Group in Pharmacology and Toxicology, Davis, CA 95616. Offers MS, PhD. Terminal master's awarded for partial completion of doctoral program. *Degree requirements:* For master's, comprehensive exam or thesis; for doctorate, thesis/dissertation, qualifying exam. *Entrance requirements:* For master's and doctorate, GRE General Test, minimum GPA of 3.0, course work in biochemistry and/or physiology. Additional exam requirements/recommendations for international students: required—TOEFL (minimum score 550 paper-based). Electronic applications accepted.

**University of California, Irvine,** School of Medicine, Program in Environmental Health Sciences, Irvine, CA 92697. Offers environmental health sciences (MS); environmental toxicology (PhD); exposure sciences and risk assessment (PhD). *Students:* 19 full-time (11 women); includes 6 minority (1 Black or African American, non-Hispanic/Latino; 2 Asian, non-Hispanic/Latino; 2 Hispanic/Latino; 1 Two or more races, non-Hispanic/Latino), 3 international. Average age 30. 17 applicants, 53% accepted, 4 enrolled. In 2019, 2 master's, 1 doctorate awarded. Terminal master's awarded for partial completion of doctoral program. *Degree requirements:* For master's, comprehensive exam; for doctorate, comprehensive exam, thesis/dissertation. *Entrance requirements:* For master's and doctorate, GRE General Test, GRE Subject Test, minimum GPA of 3.0. Additional exam requirements/recommendations for international students: required—TOEFL (minimum score 550 paper-based). *Application deadline:* For fall admission, 1/15 for domestic students. Applications are processed on a rolling basis. Application fee: $120 ($140 for international students). Electronic applications accepted. *Financial support:* Fellowships, research assistantships with full tuition reimbursements, teaching assistantships, institutionally sponsored loans, traineeships, health care benefits, and unspecified assistantships available. Financial award application deadline: 12/15; financial award applicants required to submit FAFSA. *Unit head:* Dr. Ulrike Luderer, Director, 949-824-8848, E-mail: uluderer@uci.edu. *Application contact:* Armando Villalpando, Student Affairs Officer, 949-824-8848, E-mail: afvillal@uci.edu.
Website: http://www.medicine.uci.edu/occupational/graduate.asp

**University of California, Riverside,** Graduate Division, Program in Environmental Toxicology, Riverside, CA 92521. Offers MS, PhD. Terminal master's awarded for partial completion of doctoral program. *Degree requirements:* For master's, thesis; for doctorate, comprehensive exam, thesis/dissertation, preliminary written exam, oral qualifying exam. *Entrance requirements:* For master's and doctorate, GRE General Test, minimum GPA of 3.25. Additional exam requirements/recommendations for international students: required—TOEFL (minimum score 550 paper-based, 80 iBT) or IELTS. Electronic applications accepted.

**University of California, Santa Cruz,** Division of Graduate Studies, Division of Physical and Biological Sciences, Department of Microbiology and Environmental Toxicology, Santa Cruz, CA 95064. Offers MS, PhD. Terminal master's awarded for partial completion of doctoral program. *Degree requirements:* For master's, comprehensive exam, thesis; for doctorate, thesis/dissertation, qualifying exams. *Entrance requirements:* For master's and doctorate, GRE. Additional exam requirements/recommendations for international students: required—TOEFL (minimum score 550 paper-based; 83 iBT); recommended—IELTS (minimum score 8). Electronic applications accepted.

**University of Colorado Denver,** Skaggs School of Pharmacy and Pharmaceutical Sciences, Program in Toxicology, Aurora, CO 80045. Offers PhD. *Entrance requirements:* For doctorate, GRE, minimum undergraduate GPA of 3.0; prior coursework in general chemistry, organic chemistry, calculus, biology, and physics. Additional exam requirements/recommendations for international students: required—TOEFL. Tuition and fees vary according to course load, program and reciprocity agreements.

**University of Connecticut,** Graduate School, School of Pharmacy, Department of Pharmaceutical Sciences, Graduate Program in Pharmacology and Toxicology, Storrs, CT 06269. Offers pharmacology (MS, PhD); toxicology (MS, PhD). Terminal master's awarded for partial completion of doctoral program. *Degree requirements:* For master's, comprehensive exam, thesis; for doctorate, thesis/dissertation. *Entrance requirements:* For master's and doctorate, GRE General Test. Additional exam requirements/recommendations for international students: required—TOEFL (minimum score 550 paper-based). Electronic applications accepted.

**University of Florida,** College of Veterinary Medicine, Graduate Program in Veterinary Medical Sciences, Gainesville, FL 32611. Offers forensic toxicology (Certificate); veterinary medical sciences (MS, PhD), including forensic toxicology (MS). *Program availability:* Online learning. Terminal master's awarded for partial completion of doctoral program. *Degree requirements:* For master's, thesis; for doctorate, thesis/dissertation. *Entrance requirements:* For master's and doctorate, GRE General Test, minimum GPA of 3.0. Additional exam requirements/recommendations for international students: required—TOEFL (minimum score 550 paper-based). Electronic applications accepted. *Expenses:* Contact institution.

**University of Florida,** Graduate School, College of Pharmacy, Programs in Forensic Science, Gainesville, FL 32611. Offers clinical toxicology (Certificate); drug chemistry (Certificate); environmental forensics (Certificate); forensic death investigation (Certificate); forensic DNA and serology (MSP, Certificate); forensic drug chemistry (MSP); forensic science (MSP); forensic toxicology (Certificate). *Program availability:* Part-time, evening/weekend, online learning. *Degree requirements:* For master's, comprehensive exam. *Entrance requirements:* For master's, GRE General Test, minimum GPA of 3.0. Additional exam requirements/recommendations for international students: required—TOEFL (minimum score 550 paper-based; 80 iBT), IELTS (minimum score 6).

**University of Guelph,** Office of Graduate and Postdoctoral Studies, Ontario Agricultural College, Department of Environmental Biology, Guelph, ON N1G 2W1, Canada. Offers entomology (M Sc, PhD); environmental microbiology and biotechnology (M Sc, PhD); environmental toxicology (M Sc, PhD); plant and forest systems (M Sc, PhD); plant pathology (M Sc, PhD). *Program availability:* Part-time. *Degree requirements:* For master's, thesis; for doctorate, comprehensive exam, thesis/dissertation. *Entrance requirements:* For master's, minimum 75% average during previous 2 years of course work; for doctorate, minimum 75% average. Additional exam requirements/recommendations for international students: required—TOEFL or IELTS. Electronic applications accepted.

**University of Guelph,** Ontario Veterinary College and Office of Graduate and Postdoctoral Studies, Graduate Programs in Veterinary Sciences, Department of Biomedical Sciences, Guelph, ON N1G 2W1, Canada. Offers morphology (M Sc, DV Sc, PhD); neuroscience (M Sc, DV Sc, PhD); pharmacology (M Sc, DV Sc, PhD); physiology (M Sc, DV Sc, PhD); toxicology (M Sc, DV Sc, PhD). *Program availability:* Part-time. *Degree requirements:* For master's, thesis; for doctorate, comprehensive exam, thesis/dissertation. *Entrance requirements:* For master's, honors B Sc, minimum 75% average in last 20 courses; for doctorate, M Sc with thesis from accredited institution. Additional exam requirements/recommendations for international students: required—TOEFL (minimum score 550 paper-based; 89 iBT). Electronic applications accepted.

**University of Guelph,** Ontario Veterinary College, Interdepartmental Program in Toxicology, Guelph, ON N1G 2W1, Canada. Offers M Sc, PhD. *Program availability:* Part-time. *Degree requirements:* For master's, thesis (for some programs); for doctorate, comprehensive exam, thesis/dissertation. *Entrance requirements:* For master's, B Sc; for doctorate, M Sc. Additional exam requirements/recommendations for international students: required—TOEFL (minimum score 550 paper-based; 89 iBT).

**University of Illinois at Chicago,** College of Pharmacy, Graduate Programs in Pharmacy, Chicago, IL 60607-7128. Offers comparative effectiveness research (MS); forensic science (MS); forensic toxicology (MS); medicinal chemistry (MS, PhD); pharmacognosy (MS, PhD); pharmacy (PhD). Terminal master's awarded for partial completion of doctoral program. *Degree requirements:* For master's, variable foreign language requirement, thesis; for doctorate, variable foreign language requirement, thesis/dissertation. *Entrance requirements:* For master's and doctorate, GRE General Test. Additional exam requirements/recommendations for international students: required—TOEFL. Electronic applications accepted.

**The University of Iowa,** Graduate College, Program in Human Toxicology, Iowa City, IA 52242-1316. Offers MS, PhD. *Degree requirements:* For master's, thesis; for doctorate, comprehensive exam, thesis/dissertation. *Entrance requirements:* For master's and doctorate, GRE General Test, minimum GPA of 3.0. Additional exam requirements/recommendations for international students: required—TOEFL (minimum score 600 paper-based; 100 iBT). Electronic applications accepted.

**The University of Kansas,** Graduate Studies, School of Pharmacy, Department of Pharmacology and Toxicology, Lawrence, KS 66045. Offers MS, PhD. *Students:* 15 full-time (10 women), 1 part-time (0 women); includes 1 minority (Hispanic/Latino), 9 international. Average age 27. 52 applicants, 17% accepted, 6 enrolled. In 2019, 3 master's, 2 doctorates awarded. Terminal master's awarded for partial completion of doctoral program. *Entrance requirements:* For master's and doctorate, GRE General Test, bachelor's degree in related field, 3 letters of recommendation, resume or curriculum vitae, official transcripts, 1-2 page personal statement. Additional exam requirements/recommendations for international students: required—TOEFL, IELTS. *Application deadline:* For fall admission, 4/15 for domestic and international students. Application fee: $65 ($85 for international students). Electronic applications accepted. *Expenses:* Tuition, state resident: full-time $9989. Tuition, nonresident: full-time $23,950. *International tuition:* $23,950 full-time. *Required fees:* $984; $81.99 per credit hour. Tuition and fees vary according to course load, campus/location and program. *Financial support:* Fellowships, research assistantships, and teaching assistantships available. Financial award application deadline: 2/1. *Unit head:* Nancy Muma, Chair, 785-864-4002, E-mail: nmuma@ku.edu. *Application contact:* Sarah Hoadley, Graduate Admissions Contact, 785-864-4002, E-mail: sarahhoadley@ku.edu.
Website: http://pharmtox.ku.edu/

**The University of Kansas,** University of Kansas Medical Center, School of Medicine, Department of Pharmacology, Toxicology and Therapeutics, Kansas City, KS 66160. Offers pharmacology (PhD); toxicology (PhD); MD/PhD. *Faculty:* 14. *Students:* 16 full-time (9 women); includes 4 minority (3 Black or African American, non-Hispanic/Latino; 1 Asian, non-Hispanic/Latino), 8 international. Average age 28. In 2019, 4 doctorates awarded. Terminal master's awarded for partial completion of doctoral program. *Degree requirements:* For doctorate, one foreign language, comprehensive exam, thesis/dissertation. *Entrance requirements:* For doctorate, GRE. Additional exam requirements/recommendations for international students: required—TOEFL. *Application deadline:* For fall admission, 12/1 priority date for domestic and international students. Applications are processed on a rolling basis. Application fee: $60. Electronic applications accepted. Application fee is waived when completed online. *Expenses:* Tuition, state resident: full-time $9989. Tuition, nonresident: full-time $23,950. *International tuition:* $23,950 full-time. *Required fees:* $984; $81.99 per credit hour. Tuition and fees vary according to course load, campus/location and program. *Financial support:* Fellowships with full tuition reimbursements, research assistantships with full tuition reimbursements, teaching assistantships with full tuition reimbursements, Federal Work-Study, scholarships/grants, traineeships, and unspecified assistantships available. Support available to part-time students. Financial award application deadline: 3/1; financial award applicants required to submit FAFSA. *Unit head:* Dr. Hartmut Jaeschke, University Distinguished Professor and Chair, 913-588-7500, Fax: 913-588-7501, E-mail: hjaeschke@kumc.edu. *Application contact:* Dr. Bruno Hagenbuch, Professor and Graduate Director, 913-588-7500, Fax: 913-588-7501, E-mail: bhagenbuch@kumc.edu.
Website: http://www.kumc.edu/school-of-medicine/pharmacology-toxicology-and-therapeutics.html

**University of Kentucky,** Graduate School, Graduate School Programs from the College of Medicine, Program in Toxicology, Lexington, KY 40506-0032. Offers MS, PhD. Terminal master's awarded for partial completion of doctoral program. *Degree requirements:* For master's, comprehensive exam, thesis optional; for doctorate, comprehensive exam, thesis/dissertation. *Entrance requirements:* For master's, GRE General Test, minimum undergraduate GPA of 2.75; for doctorate, GRE General Test, minimum graduate GPA of 3.0. Additional exam requirements/recommendations for international students: required—TOEFL (minimum score 550 paper-based). Electronic applications accepted.

**University of Louisiana at Monroe,** Graduate School, College of Pharmacy, Monroe, LA 71209-0001. Offers pharmacy (PhD); toxicology (PhD). *Accreditation:* ACPE. *Faculty:* 19 full-time (10 women). *Students:* 371 full-time (228 women), 1 part-time (0 women); includes 91 minority (42 Black or African American, non-Hispanic/Latino; 2 American Indian or Alaska Native, non-Hispanic/Latino; 32 Asian, non-Hispanic/Latino; 6 Hispanic/Latino; 9 Two or more races, non-Hispanic/Latino), 29 international. Average age 24. 147 applicants, 66% accepted, 86 enrolled. In 2019, 104 doctorates awarded. *Degree requirements:* For doctorate, comprehensive exam, thesis/dissertation (for some programs). *Entrance requirements:* For doctorate, GRE General Test, PCAT, minimum undergraduate GPA of 2.5. Additional exam requirements/recommendations for international students: required—TOEFL (minimum score 500 paper-based; 61 iBT); recommended—IELTS (minimum score 5.5). *Application deadline:* For fall admission, 3/1 for domestic and international students; for spring admission, 9/1 for domestic and international students. Applications are processed on a rolling basis. Electronic applications accepted. *Expenses:* Contact institution. *Financial support:* In 2019–20, 130 students received support. Research assistantships with full tuition reimbursements available, career-related internships or fieldwork, Federal Work-Study, scholarships/grants, and unspecified assistantships available. Financial award application deadline: 2/15; financial award applicants required to submit FAFSA. *Unit head:* Dr. Glenn Anderson, Dean, 318-342-1600, E-mail: ganderson@ulm.edu. *Application contact:* Dr. Kevin Baer, Director of Graduate Studies and Research, 318-342-1698, E-mail: baer@ulm.edu.
Website: http://www.ulm.edu/pharmacy/

**University of Louisville,** School of Medicine, Department of Pharmacology and Toxicology, Louisville, KY 40292-0001. Offers pharmacology and toxicology (MS); MD/PhD. *Program availability:* Part-time. *Faculty:* 17 full-time (3 women), 2 part-time/adjunct (0 women). *Students:* 38 full-time (19 women), 6 part-time (3 women); includes 11 minority (3 Black or African American, non-Hispanic/Latino; 4 Asian, non-Hispanic/Latino; 4 Two or more races, non-Hispanic/Latino), 12 international. Average age 30. 24 applicants, 54% accepted, 12 enrolled. In 2019, 7 master's, 10 doctorates awarded. Terminal master's awarded for partial completion of doctoral program. *Degree requirements:* For master's, thesis; for doctorate, comprehensive exam, thesis/dissertation. *Entrance requirements:* Additional exam requirements/recommendations for international students: required—TOEFL, Certified Translated official transcript;

recommended—IELTS. *Application deadline:* For fall admission, 1/1 priority date for domestic and international students. Applications are processed on a rolling basis. Application fee: $65. Electronic applications accepted. *Expenses: Tuition, area resident:* Full-time $13,000; part-time $723 per credit hour. *Tuition, state resident:* full-time $13,000; part-time $723 per credit hour. *Tuition, nonresident:* full-time $27,114; part-time $1507 per credit hour. *International tuition:* $27,114 full-time. *Required fees:* $196. Tuition and fees vary according to program and reciprocity agreements. *Financial support:* In 2019–20, 39 students received support, including 11 fellowships with full tuition reimbursements available (averaging $26,000 per year), 26 research assistantships (averaging $26,000 per year); scholarships/grants, traineeships, health care benefits, tuition waivers, unspecified assistantships, and Tuition Waivers reducing out of state tuition to in state tuition rate for students on fellowships/assistantships (benefits unit, not student) also available. Financial award application deadline: 1/1. *Unit head:* Dr. David W. Hein, Peter K. Knoefel Endowed Chair, 502-852-6252, E-mail: david.hein@louisville.edu. *Application contact:* Sonya Cary, Unit Business Manager/Graduate Coordinator, 502-852-6254, E-mail: sonya.cary@louisville.edu.
Website: http://louisville.edu/medicine/departments/pharmacology

**The University of Manchester,** School of Biological Sciences, Manchester, United Kingdom. Offers adaptive organismal biology (M Phil, PhD); animal biology (M Phil, PhD); biochemistry (M Phil, PhD); bioinformatics (M Phil, PhD); biomolecular sciences (M Phil, PhD); biotechnology (M Phil, PhD); cell biology (M Phil, PhD); cell matrix research (M Phil, PhD); channels and transporters (M Phil, PhD); developmental biology (M Phil, PhD); environmental biology (M Phil, PhD); evolutionary biology (M Phil, PhD); gene expression (M Phil, PhD); genetics (M Phil, PhD); history of science, technology and medicine (M Phil, PhD); immunology (M Phil, PhD); integrative neurobiology and behavior (M Phil, PhD); membrane trafficking (M Phil, PhD); microbiology (M Phil, PhD); molecular and cellular neuroscience (M Phil, PhD); molecular biology (M Phil, PhD); molecular cancer studies (M Phil, PhD); neuroscience (M Phil, PhD); ophthalmology (M Phil, PhD); optometry (M Phil, PhD); organelle function (M Phil, PhD); pharmacology (M Phil, PhD); physiology (M Phil, PhD); plant sciences (M Phil, PhD); stem cell research (M Phil, PhD); structural biology (M Phil, PhD); systems neuroscience (M Phil, PhD); toxicology (M Phil, PhD).

**University of Maryland, Baltimore,** Graduate School, Graduate Program in Life Sciences, Program in Toxicology, Baltimore, MD 21201. Offers MS, PhD, MD/MS, MD/PhD. *Program availability:* Part-time. *Degree requirements:* For master's, thesis (for some programs). *Entrance requirements:* For master's, GRE General Test, GRE Subject Test, minimum GPA of 3.0, curriculum vitae, essay, 3 letters of recommendation. Additional exam requirements/recommendations for international students: required—TOEFL (minimum score 80 iBT); recommended—IELTS (minimum score 7). Electronic applications accepted.

**University of Maryland, Baltimore,** School of Medicine, Department of Epidemiology and Public Health, Baltimore, MD 21201. Offers biostatistics (MS); clinical research (MS); epidemiology and preventive medicine (MPH, MS, PhD); gerontology (PhD); human genetics and genomic medicine (MS, PhD); molecular epidemiology (MS, PhD); toxicology (MS, PhD); JD/MS; MD/PhD; MS/PhD. *Accreditation:* CEPH. *Program availability:* Part-time. *Students:* 75 full-time (51 women), 32 part-time (28 women); includes 29 minority (11 Black or African American, non-Hispanic/Latino; 11 Asian, non-Hispanic/Latino; 5 Hispanic/Latino; 2 Two or more races, non-Hispanic/Latino), 24 international. Average age 31. In 2019, 27 master's, 9 doctorates awarded. *Degree requirements:* For doctorate, comprehensive exam, thesis/dissertation. *Entrance requirements:* For master's and doctorate, GRE General Test. Additional exam requirements/recommendations for international students: required—TOEFL (minimum score 550 paper-based; 80 iBT); recommended—IELTS (minimum score 7). *Application deadline:* For fall admission, 1/15 for domestic and international students. Application fee: $75. Electronic applications accepted. *Expenses:* Contact institution. *Financial support:* In 2019–20, research assistantships with partial tuition reimbursements (averaging $26,000 per year) were awarded; fellowships, Federal Work-Study, scholarships/grants, and unspecified assistantships also available. Financial award application deadline: 3/1; financial award applicants required to submit FAFSA. *Unit head:* Dr. Laura Hungerford, Program Director, 410-706-8492, Fax: 410-706-4225. *Application contact:* Jessica Kelley, Program Coordinator, 410-706-8492, Fax: 410-706-4225, E-mail: jkelley@som.umaryland.edu.
Website: http://lifesciences.umaryland.edu/epidemiology/

**University of Maryland Eastern Shore,** Graduate Programs, Department of Natural Sciences, Program in Toxicology, Princess Anne, MD 21853. Offers MS, PhD.

**University of Michigan,** School of Public Health, Department of Environmental Health Sciences, Ann Arbor, MI 48109. Offers environmental health policy and promotion (MPH); environmental health sciences (MS, PhD); environmental quality, sustainability and health (MPH); industrial hygiene (MPH, MS); occupational and environmental epidemiology (MPH); toxicology (MPH, MS, PhD). *Accreditation:* CEPH (one or more programs are accredited). Terminal master's awarded for partial completion of doctoral program. *Degree requirements:* For master's, thesis (for some programs); for doctorate, thesis/dissertation, preliminary exam, oral defense of dissertation. *Entrance requirements:* For master's and doctorate, GRE General Test and/or MCAT. Additional exam requirements/recommendations for international students: required—TOEFL (minimum score 100 iBT). Electronic applications accepted.

**University of Minnesota, Duluth,** Graduate School, Program in Toxicology, Duluth, MN 55812-2496. Offers MS, PhD. Terminal master's awarded for partial completion of doctoral program. *Degree requirements:* For master's, thesis; for doctorate, comprehensive exam, thesis/dissertation, written and oral preliminary and final exams. *Entrance requirements:* For master's and doctorate, GRE General Test, BS in basic science; full year each of biology, chemistry, and physics; mathematics coursework through calculus. Additional exam requirements/recommendations for international students: required—TOEFL (minimum score 550 paper-based; 79 iBT). Electronic applications accepted.

**University of Minnesota, Duluth,** Medical School, Department of Biochemistry, Molecular Biology and Biophysics, Duluth, MN 55812-2496. Offers biochemistry, molecular biology and biophysics (MS); biology and biophysics (PhD); social, administrative, and clinical pharmacy (MS, PhD); toxicology (MS, PhD). Terminal master's awarded for partial completion of doctoral program. *Degree requirements:* For master's, comprehensive exam, thesis; for doctorate, comprehensive exam, thesis/dissertation. *Entrance requirements:* For master's and doctorate, GRE General Test. Additional exam requirements/recommendations for international students: required—TOEFL. Electronic applications accepted.

**University of Minnesota, Twin Cities Campus,** School of Public Health, Division of Environmental Health Sciences, Area in Environmental Toxicology, Minneapolis, MN 55455-0213. Offers MPH, MS, PhD. *Degree requirements:* For doctorate, thesis/dissertation. *Entrance requirements:* For master's and doctorate, GRE General Test. Electronic applications accepted.

**University of Mississippi,** Graduate School, School of Pharmacy, University, MS 38677. Offers environmental toxicology (MS, PhD); industrial pharmacy (MS); medicinal chemistry (MS, PhD); pharmaceutics (MS, PhD); pharmacognosy (MS, PhD);

pharmacology (MS, PhD); pharmacy (Pharm D); pharmacy administration (MS, PhD). *Accreditation:* ACPE (one or more programs are accredited). *Program availability:* Part-time. *Faculty:* 68 full-time (33 women), 13 part-time/adjunct (5 women). *Students:* 223 full-time (137 women), 215 part-time (137 women); includes 71 minority (29 Black or African American, non-Hispanic/Latino; 1 American Indian or Alaska Native, non-Hispanic/Latino; 31 Asian, non-Hispanic/Latino; 4 Hispanic/Latino; 6 Two or more races, non-Hispanic/Latino), 90 international. Average age 25. In 2019, 29 master's, 13 doctorates awarded. Terminal master's awarded for partial completion of doctoral program. *Degree requirements:* For master's, thesis; for doctorate, thesis/dissertation (for some programs). *Entrance requirements:* For master's, GRE General Test, minimum GPA of 3.0; for doctorate, GRE General Test (for PhD). Additional exam requirements/recommendations for international students: required—TOEFL. *Application deadline:* Applications are processed on a rolling basis. Application fee: $50. Electronic applications accepted. *Expenses:* Tuition, state resident: full-time $8718; part-time $484.25 per credit hour. Tuition, nonresident: full-time $24,990; part-time $1388.25 per credit hour. *Required fees:* $100; $4.16 per credit hour. *Financial support:* Fellowships, research assistantships, teaching assistantships, career-related internships or fieldwork, Federal Work-Study, institutionally sponsored loans, scholarships/grants, tuition waivers (full), and unspecified assistantships available. Financial award application deadline: 3/1; financial award applicants required to submit FAFSA. *Unit head:* Dr. David Allen, Dean, School of Pharmacy, 662-915-7265, Fax: 662-9155704, E-mail: sopdean@olemiss.edu. *Application contact:* Temeka Smith, Graduate Activities Specialist for Admissions, 662-915-7474, Fax: 662-915-7577, E-mail: gschool@olemiss.edu.
Website: http://www.pharmacy.olemiss.edu/

**University of Mississippi Medical Center,** School of Graduate Studies in Health Sciences, Department of Pharmacology and Toxicology, Jackson, MS 39216-4505. Offers PhD. *Degree requirements:* For doctorate, comprehensive exam, thesis/dissertation, first authored publication. *Entrance requirements:* For doctorate, GRE General Test, minimum GPA of 3.0. Additional exam requirements/recommendations for international students: required—TOEFL (minimum score 550 paper-based, 79 iBT), IELTS or PTE. Electronic applications accepted.

**University of Montana,** Graduate School, College of Health Professions and Biomedical Sciences, Skaggs School of Pharmacy, Department of Biomedical and Pharmaceutical Sciences, Missoula, MT 59812. Offers biomedical sciences (PhD); medicinal chemistry (MS, PhD); molecular and cellular toxicology (MS, PhD); neuroscience (PhD); pharmaceutical sciences (MS). *Accreditation:* ACPE. *Degree requirements:* For master's, oral defense of thesis; for doctorate, research dissertation defense. *Entrance requirements:* For master's and doctorate, GRE General Test. Additional exam requirements/recommendations for international students: required—TOEFL (minimum score 540 paper-based). Electronic applications accepted.

**University of Nebraska–Lincoln,** Graduate College, Interdepartmental Area of Environmental Health, Occupational Health and Toxicology, Lincoln, NE 68588. Offers MS, PhD. *Entrance requirements:* Additional exam requirements/recommendations for international students: required—TOEFL (minimum score 550 paper-based). Electronic applications accepted.

**University of Nebraska Medical Center,** Environmental Health, Occupational Health and Toxicology Graduate Program, Omaha, NE 68198-4388. Offers PhD. *Degree requirements:* For doctorate, comprehensive exam, thesis/dissertation. *Entrance requirements:* For doctorate, GRE General Test, BS in chemistry, biology, biochemistry or related area. Additional exam requirements/recommendations for international students: required—TOEFL (minimum score 550 paper-based; 80 iBT). Electronic applications accepted.

**University of New Mexico,** Graduate Studies, Health Sciences Center, Program in Biomedical Sciences, Albuquerque, NM 87131-5196. Offers biochemistry and molecular biology (MS, PhD); cell biology and physiology (MS, PhD); molecular genetics and microbiology (MS, PhD); neuroscience (MS, PhD); pathology (MS, PhD); toxicology (MS, PhD). *Program availability:* Part-time. Terminal master's awarded for partial completion of doctoral program. *Degree requirements:* For master's, thesis; for doctorate, comprehensive exam, thesis/dissertation, qualifying exam at the end of year 1/core curriculum. *Entrance requirements:* For master's and doctorate, GRE General Test, minimum undergraduate GPA of 3.0. Additional exam requirements/recommendations for international students: required—TOEFL. Electronic applications accepted. *Expenses:* Tuition, state resident: full-time $7633; part-time $972 per year. Tuition, nonresident: full-time $22,586; part-time $3840 per year. *International tuition:* $23,292 full-time. *Required fees:* $8608. Tuition and fees vary according to course level, course load, degree level, program and student level.

**The University of North Carolina at Chapel Hill,** School of Medicine, Curriculum in Toxicology, Chapel Hill, NC 27599. Offers MS, PhD. Terminal master's awarded for partial completion of doctoral program. *Degree requirements:* For master's, comprehensive exam, thesis; for doctorate, comprehensive exam, thesis/dissertation. *Entrance requirements:* For doctorate, GRE General Test. Electronic applications accepted.

**University of Prince Edward Island,** Atlantic Veterinary College, Graduate Program in Veterinary Medicine, Charlottetown, PE C1A 4P3, Canada. Offers anatomy (M Sc, PhD); bacteriology (M Sc, PhD); clinical pharmacology (M Sc, PhD); clinical sciences (M Sc, PhD); epidemiology (M Sc, PhD), including reproduction; fish health (M Sc, PhD); food animal nutrition (M Sc, PhD); immunology (M Sc, PhD); microanatomy (M Sc, PhD); parasitology (M Sc, PhD); pathology (M Sc, PhD); pharmacology (M Sc, PhD); physiology (M Sc, PhD); toxicology (M Sc, PhD); veterinary science (M Vet Sc); virology (M Sc, PhD). *Program availability:* Part-time. *Degree requirements:* For master's, thesis; for doctorate, thesis/dissertation. *Entrance requirements:* For master's, DVM, B Sc honors degree, or equivalent; for doctorate, M Sc. Additional exam requirements/recommendations for international students: required—TOEFL (minimum score 550 paper-based; 80 iBT). *Expenses:* Contact institution.

**University of Puerto Rico - Medical Sciences Campus,** School of Medicine, Biomedical Sciences Graduate Program, Department of Pharmacology and Toxicology, San Juan, PR 00936-5067. Offers MS, PhD. *Degree requirements:* For master's, one foreign language, thesis; for doctorate, one foreign language, comprehensive exam, thesis/dissertation. *Entrance requirements:* For master's and doctorate, GRE General Test, GRE Subject Test, interview, minimum GPA of 3.0, 3 letters of recommendation. Electronic applications accepted.

**University of Rhode Island,** Graduate School, College of Pharmacy, Department of Biomedical and Pharmaceutical Sciences, Kingston, RI 02881. Offers health outcomes (MS, PhD); medicinal chemistry and pharmacognosy (MS, PhD); pharmaceutics and pharmacokinetics (MS, PhD); pharmacology and toxicology (MS, PhD). *Program availability:* Part-time. *Faculty:* 23 full-time (11 women). *Students:* 42 full-time (20 women), 11 part-time (6 women); includes 8 minority (1 American Indian or Alaska Native, non-Hispanic/Latino; 5 Asian, non-Hispanic/Latino; 2 Hispanic/Latino), 19 international. In 2019, 4 master's, 11 doctorates awarded. *Entrance requirements:* Additional exam requirements/recommendations for international students: required—TOEFL. *Application deadline:* For fall admission, 7/15 for domestic students, 2/1 for international students. Application fee: $65. Electronic applications accepted. *Expenses: Tuition, area resident:* Full-time $13,734; part-time $763 per credit. Tuition, state resident: full-time $13,734; part-time $763 per credit. Tuition, nonresident: full-time $26,512; part-time $1473 per credit. *International tuition:* $26,512 full-time. *Required fees:* $1780; $52 per credit. $35 per term. One-time fee: $165. *Financial support:* In 2019–20, 112 research assistantships with tuition reimbursements (averaging $8,040 per year), 17 teaching assistantships with tuition reimbursements (averaging $11,829 per year) were awarded. Financial award application deadline: 2/1; financial award applicants required to submit FAFSA. *Unit head:* Dr. Navindra Seeram, Chair, E-mail: nseeram@uri.edu. *Application contact:* Dr. Navindra Seeram, Chair, E-mail: nseeram@uri.edu.
Website: http://www.uri.edu/pharmacy/departments/bps/index.shtml

**University of Rochester,** School of Medicine and Dentistry, Graduate Programs in Medicine and Dentistry, Department of Environmental Medicine, Programs in Toxicology, Rochester, NY 14627. Offers PhD. *Degree requirements:* For doctorate, thesis/dissertation, qualifying exam. *Entrance requirements:* For doctorate, GRE General Test.

**University of Saskatchewan,** College of Graduate and Postdoctoral Studies, Toxicology Centre, Saskatoon, SK S7N 5A2, Canada. Offers M Sc, PhD, Diploma. *Degree requirements:* For master's, thesis; for doctorate, thesis/dissertation. *Entrance requirements:* Additional exam requirements/recommendations for international students: required—TOEFL.

**University of South Alabama,** Graduate School, Program in Environmental Toxicology, Mobile, AL 36688-0002. Offers basic medical sciences (MS); biology (MS); chemistry (MS); environmental toxicology (MS); exposure route and chemical transport (MS). *Faculty:* 4 full-time (0 women). *Students:* 7 full-time (5 women), 4 part-time (1 woman); includes 1 minority (Black or African American, non-Hispanic/Latino), 1 international. Average age 26. 2 applicants, 50% accepted, 1 enrolled. In 2019, 3 master's awarded. *Degree requirements:* For master's, comprehensive exam, thesis optional, research project or thesis. *Entrance requirements:* For master's, GRE. Additional exam requirements/recommendations for international students: required—TOEFL (minimum score 525 paper-based; 71 iBT). *Application deadline:* For fall admission, 7/1 for domestic students, 3/1 for international students; for spring admission, 12/1 for domestic students, 11/1 for international students. Application fee: $50. Electronic applications accepted. *Expenses: Tuition, area resident:* Part-time $442 per credit hour. Tuition, state resident: full-time $10,608; part-time $442 per credit hour. Tuition, nonresident: full-time $21,216; part-time $884 per credit hour. *Financial support:* Fellowships, research assistantships, teaching assistantships, career-related internships or fieldwork, Federal Work-Study, institutionally sponsored loans, scholarships/grants, and unspecified assistantships available. Support available to part-time students. Financial award application deadline: 3/31; financial award applicants required to submit FAFSA. *Unit head:* Dr. Sean Powers, Chair, Marine Sciences, 251-460-7136, E-mail: spowers@disl.org. *Application contact:* Dr. David Forbes, Graduate Coordinator/Director, Environmental Toxicology, 251-460-6181, E-mail: dforbes@southalabama.edu.
Website: https://www.southalabama.edu/colleges/graduateschool/etox/

**University of Southern California,** Graduate School, School of Pharmacy, Graduate Programs in Molecular Pharmacology and Toxicology, Los Angeles, CA 90033. Offers pharmacology and pharmaceutical sciences (MS, PhD). Terminal master's awarded for partial completion of doctoral program. *Degree requirements:* For master's, comprehensive exam, thesis, 24 units of formal course work, excluding research and seminar courses; for doctorate, comprehensive exam, thesis/dissertation, 24 units of formal course work, excluding research and seminar courses. *Entrance requirements:* For master's and doctorate, GRE. Additional exam requirements/recommendations for international students: required—TOEFL (minimum score 603 paper-based; 100 iBT). Electronic applications accepted. *Expenses:* Contact institution.

**University of South Florida,** Innovative Education, Tampa, FL 33620-9951. Offers adult, career and higher education (Graduate Certificate), including college teaching, leadership in developing human resources, leadership in higher education; Africana studies (Graduate Certificate), including diasporas and health disparities, genocide and human rights; aging studies (Graduate Certificate), including gerontology; art research (Graduate Certificate), including museum studies; business foundations (Graduate Certificate); chemical and biomedical engineering (Graduate Certificate), including materials science and engineering, water, health and sustainability; child and family studies (Graduate Certificate), including positive behavior support; civil and industrial engineering (Graduate Certificate), including transportation systems analysis; community and family health (Graduate Certificate), including maternal and child health, social marketing and public health, violence and injury: prevention and intervention, women's health; criminology (Graduate Certificate), including criminal justice administration; data science for public administration (Graduate Certificate); digital humanities (Graduate Certificate); educational measurement and research (Graduate Certificate), including evaluation; English (Graduate Certificate), including comparative literary studies, creative writing, professional and technical communication; entrepreneurship (Graduate Certificate); environmental health (Graduate Certificate), including safety management; epidemiology and biostatistics (Graduate Certificate), including applied biostatistics, biostatistics, concepts and tools of epidemiology, epidemiology, epidemiology of infectious diseases; geography, environment and planning (Graduate Certificate), including community development, environmental policy and management, geographical information systems; geology (Graduate Certificate), including hydrogeology; global health (Graduate Certificate), including disaster management, global health and Latin American and Caribbean studies, global health practice, humanitarian assistance, infection control; government and international affairs (Graduate Certificate), including Cuban studies, globalization studies; health policy and management (Graduate Certificate), including health management and leadership, public health policy and programs; hearing specialist: early intervention (Graduate Certificate); industrial and management systems engineering (Graduate Certificate), including systems engineering, technology management; information studies (Graduate Certificate), including school library media specialist; information systems/decision sciences (Graduate Certificate), including analytics and business intelligence; instructional technology (Graduate Certificate), including distance education, Florida digital/virtual educator, instructional design, multimedia design, Web design; internal medicine, bioethics and medical humanities (Graduate Certificate), including biomedical ethics; Latin American and Caribbean studies (Graduate Certificate); leadership for coastal resiliency planning (Graduate Certificate); mass communications (Graduate Certificate), including multimedia journalism; mathematics and statistics (Graduate Certificate), including mathematics; medicine (Graduate Certificate), including aging and neuroscience, bioinformatics, biotechnology, brain fitness and memory management, clinical investigation, hand and upper limb rehabilitation, health informatics, health sciences, integrative weight management, intellectual property, medicine and gender, metabolic and nutritional medicine, metabolic cardiology, pharmacy sciences; national and competitive intelligence (Graduate Certificate); nursing (Graduate Certificate), including simulation based academic fellowship in advanced pain management; psychological and social foundations (Graduate Certificate), including career

counseling, college teaching, diversity in education, mental health counseling, school counseling; public affairs (Graduate Certificate), including nonprofit management, public management, research administration; public health (Graduate Certificate), including assessing chemical toxicity and public health risks, health equity, pharmacoepidemiology, public health generalist, toxicology, translational research in adolescent behavioral health; public health practices (Graduate Certificate), including planning for healthy communities; rehabilitation and mental health counseling (Graduate Certificate), including integrative mental health care, marriage and family therapy, rehabilitation technology; secondary education (Graduate Certificate), including ESOL, foreign language education: culture and content, foreign language education: professional; social work (Graduate Certificate), including geriatric social work/clinical gerontology; special education (Graduate Certificate), including autism spectrum disorder, disabilities education: severe/profound; world languages (Graduate Certificate), including teaching English as a second language (TESL) or foreign language. *Unit head:* Dr. Cynthia DeLuca, Associate Vice President and Assistant Vice Provost, 813-974-3077, Fax: 813-974-7061, E-mail: deluca@usf.edu. *Application contact:* Owen Hooper, Director, Summer and Alternative Calendar Programs, 813-974-6917, E-mail: hooper@usf.edu.
Website: http://www.usf.edu/innovative-education/

**The University of Texas at Austin,** Graduate School, College of Pharmacy, Graduate Programs in Pharmacy, Austin, TX 78712-1111. Offers health outcomes and pharmacy practice (MS, PhD); medicinal chemistry (PhD); pharmaceutics (PhD); pharmacology and toxicology (PhD); pharmacotherapy (MS, PhD); translational science (PhD). *Degree requirements:* For master's, thesis; for doctorate, thesis/dissertation. *Entrance requirements:* For master's and doctorate, GRE General Test. Electronic applications accepted.

**The University of Texas Health Science Center at San Antonio,** Graduate School of Biomedical Sciences, Program in Toxicology, San Antonio, TX 78229-3900. Offers MS.

**The University of Texas Medical Branch,** Graduate School of Biomedical Sciences, Program in Pharmacology and Toxicology, Galveston, TX 77555. Offers pharmacology (MS); pharmacology and toxicology (PhD). *Degree requirements:* For master's, thesis or alternative; for doctorate, thesis/dissertation. *Entrance requirements:* For master's and doctorate, GRE General Test. Additional exam requirements/recommendations for international students: required—TOEFL (minimum score 550 paper-based).

**University of the Sciences,** Program in Pharmacology and Toxicology, Philadelphia, PA 19104-4495. Offers pharmacology (MS, PhD); toxicology (MS, PhD). Terminal master's awarded for partial completion of doctoral program. *Degree requirements:* For master's, thesis; for doctorate, comprehensive exam, thesis/dissertation. *Entrance requirements:* For master's and doctorate, GRE General Test. Additional exam requirements/recommendations for international students: required—TOEFL, TWE. *Expenses:* Contact institution.

**University of Utah,** Graduate School, College of Pharmacy, Department of Pharmacology and Toxicology, Salt Lake City, UT 84112. Offers PhD. *Faculty:* 5 full-time (1 woman). *Students:* 4 full-time (all women), 1 (woman) part-time; includes 2 minority (1 Asian, non-Hispanic/Latino; 1 Hispanic/Latino). Average age 28. In 2019, 1 doctorate awarded. Terminal master's awarded for partial completion of doctoral program. *Degree requirements:* For doctorate, thesis/dissertation. *Application deadline:* For fall admission, 12/1 for domestic and international students. Application fee: $55. Electronic applications accepted. Application fee is waived when completed online. *Expenses:* Tuition, state resident: full-time $7085; part-time $272.51 per credit hour. Tuition, nonresident: full-time $24,937; part-time $959.12 per credit hour. *Required fees:* $880.52; $880.52 per semester. Tuition and fees vary according to degree level, program and student level. *Financial support:* In 2019–20, 3 students received support, including 3 research assistantships (averaging $17,000 per year); health care benefits also available. *Unit head:* Dr. Karen Wilcox, Chair Department Pharmacology and Toxicology, 801-581-5684, Fax: 801-585-5111, E-mail: karen.wilcox@hsc.utah.edu. *Application contact:* Linda Wright, Executive Secretary, 801-581-6287, Fax: 801-585-5111, E-mail: linda.wright@utah.edu.
Website: http://www.pharmacy.utah.edu/pharmtox/

**University of Washington,** Graduate School, School of Public Health, Department of Environmental and Occupational Health Sciences, Seattle, WA 98195. Offers applied toxicology (MS); environmental and occupational health (MPH); environmental and occupational hygiene (PhD); environmental health (MS); environmental toxicology (MS, PhD); occupational and environmental exposure sciences (MS); occupational and environmental medicine (MPH). *Accreditation:* CEPH. *Program availability:* Part-time. *Faculty:* 35 full-time (16 women), 14 part-time/adjunct (5 women). *Students:* 61 full-time (39 women), 8 part-time (6 women); includes 24 minority (3 Black or African American, non-Hispanic/Latino; 13 Asian, non-Hispanic/Latino; 6 Hispanic/Latino; 2 Native Hawaiian or other Pacific Islander, non-Hispanic/Latino), 6 international. Average age 32. 106 applicants, 66% accepted, 40 enrolled. In 2019, 27 master's, 6 doctorates awarded. Terminal master's awarded for partial completion of doctoral program. *Entrance requirements:* For master's and doctorate, GRE General Test. Additional exam requirements/recommendations for international students: required—TOEFL. *Application deadline:* For fall admission, 12/1 for domestic and international students. Application fee: $85. Electronic applications accepted. *Expenses:* Contact institution. *Financial support:* Fellowships, research assistantships, teaching assistantships, career-related internships or fieldwork, institutionally sponsored loans, scholarships/grants, traineeships, health care benefits, and unspecified assistantships available. *Unit head:* Dr. Michael Yost, Chair, 206-543-3199, Fax: 206-543-9616. *Application contact:* Trina Sterry, Manager of Student and Academic Services, 206-543-3199, E-mail: ehgrad@uw.edu.
Website: http://deohs.washington.edu/

**University of Wisconsin–Madison,** School of Medicine and Public Health, Molecular and Environmental Toxicology Graduate Program, Madison, WI 53706. Offers MS, PhD.

**Utah State University,** School of Graduate Studies, College of Agriculture and Applied Sciences, Program in Toxicology, Logan, UT 84322. Offers MS, PhD. Terminal master's awarded for partial completion of doctoral program. *Degree requirements:* For master's, thesis; for doctorate, thesis/dissertation. *Entrance requirements:* For master's and doctorate, GRE General Test, minimum GPA of 3.0. Additional exam requirements/recommendations for international students: required—TOEFL.

**Virginia Commonwealth University,** Graduate School, College of Humanities and Sciences, Department of Forensic Science, Richmond, VA 23284-9005. Offers forensic biology (MS); forensic chemistry/drugs and toxicology (MS); forensic chemistry/trace evidence (MS); forensic physical analysis (MS). *Program availability:* Part-time. *Entrance requirements:* For master's, GRE General Test, bachelor's degree in a natural science discipline, including forensic science, or a degree with equivalent work. Additional exam requirements/recommendations for international students: required—TOEFL (minimum score 600 paper-based; 100 iBT) or IELTS (minimum score 6.5). Electronic applications accepted.

**Virginia Commonwealth University,** Medical College of Virginia-Professional Programs, School of Medicine, Graduate Programs in Medicine, Department of Pharmacology and Toxicology, Richmond, VA 23284-9005. Offers neuroscience (PhD); pharmacology (Certificate); pharmacology and toxicology (MS, PhD); MD/PhD. Terminal master's awarded for partial completion of doctoral program. *Degree requirements:* For master's, thesis; for doctorate, thesis/dissertation, comprehensive oral and written exams. *Entrance requirements:* For master's and doctorate, GRE or MCAT. Additional exam requirements/recommendations for international students: required—TOEFL (minimum score 600 paper-based; 100 iBT). Electronic applications accepted.

**Wayne State University,** Eugene Applebaum College of Pharmacy and Health Sciences, Applied Health Sciences, Detroit, MI 48202. Offers medicinal chemistry (MS, PhD); pharmaceutics (MS, PhD), including medicinal chemistry (PhD); pharmacology and toxicology (MS, PhD). *Entrance requirements:* For master's, GRE General Test, bachelor's degree; adequate background in biology, physics, calculus, and chemistry; three letters of recommendation; personal statement; for doctorate, GRE General Test, bachelor's or master's degree in one of the behavioral, biological, pharmaceutical or physical sciences; three letters of recommendation. Additional exam requirements/recommendations for international students: required—TOEFL (minimum score 550 paper-based; 79 iBT), Michigan English Language Assessment Battery (minimum score 85); recommended—IELTS (minimum score 6.5), TWE (minimum score 5.5). Electronic applications accepted. *Expenses:* Contact institution.

**Wright State University,** Boonshoft School of Medicine, Program in Pharmacology and Toxicology, Dayton, OH 45435. Offers MS. *Degree requirements:* For master's, thesis optional.

# Section 18
# Physiology

This section contains a directory of institutions offering graduate work in physiology, followed by an in-depth entry submitted by an institution that chose to prepare a detailed program description. Additional information about programs listed in the directory but not augmented by an in-depth entry may be obtained by writing directly to the dean of a graduate school or chair of a department at the address given in the directory.

For programs offering related work, see also all other sections in this book. In the other guides in this series:

**Graduate Programs in the Physical Sciences, Mathematics, Agricultural Sciences, the Environment & Natural Resources**

See *Agricultural and Food Sciences, Chemistry,* and *Marine Sciences and Oceanography*

**Graduate Programs in Engineering & Applied Sciences**

See *Agricultural Engineering and Bioengineering, Biomedical Engineering and Biotechnology, Electrical and Computer Engineering,* and *Mechanical Engineering and Mechanics*

## CONTENTS

### Program Directories

# Cardiovascular Sciences

**Albany Medical College,** Center for Cardiovascular Sciences, Albany, NY 12208-3479. Offers MS, PhD. *Program availability:* Part-time. Terminal master's awarded for partial completion of doctoral program. *Degree requirements:* For master's, thesis; for doctorate, comprehensive exam, thesis/dissertation, candidacy exam, written preliminary exam, 1 published paper-peer review. *Entrance requirements:* For master's, GRE General Test, letters of recommendation; for doctorate, GRE General Test, all transcripts, letters of recommendation. Additional exam requirements/recommendations for international students: required—TOEFL.

**Augusta University,** Program in Vascular Biology, Augusta, GA 30912. Offers PhD. *Degree requirements:* For doctorate, comprehensive exam, thesis/dissertation. *Entrance requirements:* For doctorate, GRE General Test. Additional exam requirements/recommendations for international students: required—TOEFL.

**Baylor College of Medicine,** Graduate School of Biomedical Sciences, Department of Molecular Physiology and Biophysics, Houston, TX 77030-3498. Offers cardiovascular sciences (PhD); molecular physiology and biophysics (PhD); MD/PhD. *Degree requirements:* For doctorate, thesis/dissertation, public defense. *Entrance requirements:* For doctorate, GRE General Test, GRE Subject Test (strongly recommended), minimum GPA of 3.0. Additional exam requirements/recommendations for international students: required—TOEFL. Electronic applications accepted.

**Johns Hopkins University,** Bloomberg School of Public Health, Department of Epidemiology, Baltimore, MD 21205. Offers cancer epidemiology (MHS, Sc M, PhD, Sc D); cardiovascular disease and clinical epidemiology (MHS, Sc M, PhD, Sc D); clinical trials (PhD, Sc D); clinical trials and evidence synthesis (MHS, Sc M, PhD, Sc D); environmental epidemiology (MHS, Sc M, PhD, Sc D); epidemiology of aging (MHS, Sc M, PhD, Sc D); general epidemiology and methodology (MHS, Sc M); genetic epidemiology (MHS, Sc M, PhD, Sc D); infectious disease epidemiology (MHS, Sc M, PhD, Sc D). *Degree requirements:* For master's, comprehensive exam, thesis, 1-year full-time residency; for doctorate, comprehensive exam, thesis/dissertation, 2 years' full-time residency, oral and written exams, student teaching. *Entrance requirements:* For master's, GRE General Test or MCAT, 3 letters of recommendation, curriculum vitae; for doctorate, GRE General Test, minimum 1 year of work experience, 3 letters of recommendation, curriculum vitae, academic records from all schools. Additional exam requirements/recommendations for international students: required—TOEFL (minimum score 100 iBT), IELTS (minimum score 7.5). Electronic applications accepted.

**Marquette University,** Graduate School, Program in Transfusion Medicine, Milwaukee, WI 53201-1881. Offers MSTM. *Program availability:* Part-time. *Entrance requirements:* For master's, official transcripts from all current and previous colleges, three letters of recommendation. Additional exam requirements/recommendations for international students: required—TOEFL.

**McMaster University,** Faculty of Health Sciences and School of Graduate Studies, Program in Medical Sciences, Blood and Vascular Area, Hamilton, ON L8S 4M2, Canada. Offers M Sc, PhD, MD/PhD. *Degree requirements:* For master's, thesis; for doctorate, comprehensive exam, thesis/dissertation. *Entrance requirements:* For master's, honors B Sc, B+ average in related field; for doctorate, M Sc, minimum B+ average, students with proven research experience and an A average may be admitted with a B Sc degree. Additional exam requirements/recommendations for international students: required—TOEFL (minimum score 580 paper-based; 92 iBT).

**Medical University of South Carolina,** College of Graduate Studies, Program in Molecular and Cellular Biology and Pathobiology, Charleston, SC 29425. Offers cancer biology (PhD); cardiovascular biology (PhD); cardiovascular imaging (PhD); cell regulation (PhD); craniofacial biology (PhD); genetics and development (PhD); marine biomedicine (PhD); DMD/PhD; MD/PhD. *Degree requirements:* For doctorate, thesis/dissertation, oral and written exams. *Entrance requirements:* For doctorate, GRE General Test, interview, minimum GPA of 3.0. Additional exam requirements/recommendations for international students: required—TOEFL (minimum score 600 paper-based; 100 iBT). Electronic applications accepted.

**Memorial University of Newfoundland,** Faculty of Medicine and School of Graduate Studies, Graduate Programs in Medicine, Division of Biomedical Sciences, St. John's, NL A1C 5S7, Canada. Offers cancer (M Sc, PhD); cardiovascular (M Sc, PhD); immunology (M Sc, PhD); neuroscience (M Sc, PhD). *Program availability:* Part-time. *Degree requirements:* For master's, thesis; for doctorate, comprehensive exam, thesis/dissertation, oral defense of thesis. *Entrance requirements:* For master's, MD or B Sc; for doctorate, MD or M Sc. Additional exam requirements/recommendations for international students: required—TOEFL.

**Midwestern University, Glendale Campus,** College of Health Sciences, Arizona Campus, Program in Cardiovascular Science, Glendale, AZ 85308. Offers MCVS. *Expenses:* Contact institution.

**Milwaukee School of Engineering,** MS Program in Perfusion, Milwaukee, WI 53202-3109. Offers MS. *Degree requirements:* For master's, comprehensive exam, thesis. *Entrance requirements:* For master's, GRE General Test (percentiles must average 50% or better), baccalaureate degree with minimum undergraduate GPA of 2.8; at least one undergraduate course in each of the following areas: physiology (or anatomy and physiology), chemistry, mathematics and physics; 3 letters of recommendation; personal interview; observation of 2 perfusion clinical cases. Additional exam requirements/recommendations for international students: required—TOEFL (minimum score 90 iBT), IELTS (minimum score 7). Electronic applications accepted.

**Quinnipiac University,** School of Health Sciences, Program in Cardiovascular Perfusion, Hamden, CT 06518-1940. Offers MHS. *Entrance requirements:* For master's, bachelor's degree in science or health-related discipline from an accredited American or Canadian college or university; 2 years of health care work experience; interview. Electronic applications accepted. *Expenses: Tuition:* Part-time $1055 per credit. *Required fees:* $945 per semester. Tuition and fees vary according to course load and program.

**University of Calgary,** Cumming School of Medicine and Faculty of Graduate Studies, Program in Cardiovascular and Respiratory Sciences, Calgary, AB T2N 1N4, Canada. Offers M Sc, PhD. *Degree requirements:* For master's, thesis; for doctorate, thesis/dissertation, candidacy exam. *Entrance requirements:* For master's and doctorate, minimum GPA of 3.2. Additional exam requirements/recommendations for international students: required—TOEFL (minimum score 600 paper-based). Electronic applications accepted.

**University of Guelph,** Ontario Veterinary College and Office of Graduate and Postdoctoral Studies, Graduate Programs in Veterinary Sciences, Department of Clinical Studies, Guelph, ON N1G 2W1, Canada. Offers anesthesiology (M Sc, DV Sc); cardiology (DV Sc, Diploma); clinical studies (Diploma); dermatology (M Sc); diagnostic imaging (M Sc, DV Sc); emergency/critical care (M Sc, DV Sc, Diploma); medicine (M Sc, DV Sc); neurology (M Sc, DV Sc); ophthalmology (M Sc, DV Sc); surgery (M Sc, DV Sc). *Degree requirements:* For master's, thesis; for doctorate, comprehensive exam, thesis/dissertation. *Entrance requirements:* Additional exam requirements/recommendations for international students: required—TOEFL (minimum score 550 paper-based), IELTS (minimum score 6.5). Electronic applications accepted.

**University of Mary,** School of Health Sciences, Program in Respiratory Therapy, Bismarck, ND 58504-9652. Offers MS. *Entrance requirements:* For master's, minimum GPA of 3.0, 3 letters of reference, interview. Additional exam requirements/recommendations for international students: required—TOEFL (minimum score 500 paper-based; 71 iBT). Electronic applications accepted.

**University of South Dakota,** Graduate School, Sanford School of Medicine and Graduate School, Biomedical Sciences Graduate Program, Cardiovascular Research Program, Vermillion, SD 57069. Offers MS, PhD. Terminal master's awarded for partial completion of doctoral program. *Degree requirements:* For master's, thesis; for doctorate, comprehensive exam, thesis/dissertation. *Entrance requirements:* For master's and doctorate, GRE General Test, minimum GPA of 3.0. Additional exam requirements/recommendations for international students: required—TOEFL (minimum score 550 paper-based; 80 iBT), IELTS (minimum score 6). Electronic applications accepted. *Expenses:* Contact institution.

**University of South Florida,** Innovative Education, Tampa, FL 33620-9951. Offers adult, career and higher education (Graduate Certificate), including college teaching, leadership in developing human resources, leadership in higher education; Africana studies (Graduate Certificate), including diasporas and health disparities, genocide and human rights; aging studies (Graduate Certificate), including gerontology; art research (Graduate Certificate), including museum studies; business foundations (Graduate Certificate); chemical and biomedical engineering (Graduate Certificate), including materials science and engineering, water, health and sustainability; child and family studies (Graduate Certificate), including positive behavior support; civil and industrial engineering (Graduate Certificate), including transportation systems analysis; community and family health (Graduate Certificate), including maternal and child health, social marketing and public health, violence and injury: prevention and intervention, women's health; criminology (Graduate Certificate), including criminal justice administration; data science for public administration (Graduate Certificate); digital humanities (Graduate Certificate); educational measurement and research (Graduate Certificate), including evaluation; English (Graduate Certificate), including comparative literary studies, creative writing, professional and technical communication; entrepreneurship (Graduate Certificate); environmental health (Graduate Certificate), including safety management; epidemiology and biostatistics (Graduate Certificate), including applied biostatistics, biostatistics, concepts and tools of epidemiology, epidemiology, epidemiology of infectious diseases; geography, environment and planning (Graduate Certificate), including community development, environmental policy and management, geographical information systems; geology (Graduate Certificate), including hydrogeology; global health (Graduate Certificate), including disaster management, global health and Latin American and Caribbean studies, global health practice, humanitarian assistance, infection control; government and international affairs (Graduate Certificate), including Cuban studies, globalization studies; health policy and management (Graduate Certificate), including health management and leadership, public health policy and programs; hearing specialist: early intervention (Graduate Certificate); industrial and management systems engineering (Graduate Certificate), including systems engineering, technology management; information studies (Graduate Certificate), including school library media specialist; information systems/decision sciences (Graduate Certificate), including analytics and business intelligence; instructional technology (Graduate Certificate), including distance education, Florida digital/virtual educator, instructional design, multimedia design, Web design; internal medicine, bioethics and medical humanities (Graduate Certificate), including biomedical ethics; Latin American and Caribbean studies (Graduate Certificate); leadership for coastal resiliency planning (Graduate Certificate); mass communications (Graduate Certificate), including multimedia journalism; mathematics and statistics (Graduate Certificate), including mathematics; medicine (Graduate Certificate), including aging and neuroscience, bioinformatics, biotechnology, brain fitness and memory management, clinical investigation, hand and upper limb rehabilitation, health informatics, health sciences, integrative weight management, intellectual property, medicine and gender, metabolic and nutritional medicine, metabolic cardiology, pharmacy sciences; national and competitive intelligence (Graduate Certificate); nursing (Graduate Certificate), including simulation based academic fellowship in advanced pain management; psychological and social foundations (Graduate Certificate), including career counseling, college teaching, diversity in education, mental health counseling, school counseling; public affairs (Graduate Certificate), including nonprofit management, public management, research administration; public health (Graduate Certificate), including assessing chemical toxicity and public health risks, health equity, pharmacoepidemiology, public health generalist, toxicology, translational research in adolescent behavioral health; public health practices (Graduate Certificate), including planning for healthy communities; rehabilitation and mental health counseling (Graduate Certificate), including integrative mental health care, marriage and family therapy, rehabilitation technology; secondary education (Graduate Certificate), including ESOL, foreign language education: culture and content, foreign language education: professional; social work (Graduate Certificate), including geriatric social work/clinical gerontology; special education (Graduate Certificate), including autism spectrum disorder, disabilities education: severe/profound; world languages (Graduate Certificate), including teaching English as a second language (TESL) or foreign language. *Unit head:* Dr. Cynthia DeLuca, Associate Vice President and Assistant Vice Provost, 813-974-3077, Fax: 813-974-7061, E-mail: deluca@usf.edu. *Application contact:* Owen Hooper, Director, Summer and Alternative Calendar Programs, 813-974-6917, E-mail: hooper@usf.edu.
Website: http://www.usf.edu/innovative-education/

**The University of Toledo,** College of Graduate Studies, College of Medicine and Life Sciences, Department of Physiology and Pharmacology, Toledo, OH 43606-3390. Offers cardiovascular and metabolic diseases (MSBS, PhD); MD/MSBS; MD/PhD. Terminal master's awarded for partial completion of doctoral program. *Degree requirements:* For master's, thesis, qualifying exam; for doctorate, thesis/dissertation, qualifying exam. *Entrance requirements:* For master's and doctorate, GRE, minimum undergraduate GPA of 3.0, three letters of recommendation, statement of purpose, transcripts from all prior institutions attended, resume. Additional exam requirements/recommendations for international students: required—TOEFL (minimum score 550 paper-based; 80 iBT). Electronic applications accepted.

**Université Laval,** Faculty of Medicine, Post-Professional Programs in Medical Studies, Québec, QC G1K 7P4, Canada. Offers anatomy–pathology (DESS); anesthesiology (DESS); cardiology (DESS); care of older people (Diploma); clinical research (DESS); community health (DESS); dermatology (DESS); diagnostic radiology (DESS); emergency medicine (Diploma); family medicine (DESS); general surgery (DESS); geriatrics (DESS); hematology (DESS); internal medicine (DESS); maternal and fetal medicine (Diploma); medical biochemistry (DESS); medical microbiology and infectious diseases (DESS); medical oncology (DESS); nephrology (DESS); neurology (DESS);

neurosurgery (DESS); obstetrics and gynecology (DESS); ophthalmology (DESS); orthopedic surgery (DESS); oto-rhino-laryngology (DESS); palliative medicine (Diploma); pediatrics (DESS); plastic surgery (DESS); psychiatry (DESS); pulmonary medicine (DESS); radiology–oncology (DESS); thoracic surgery (DESS); urology (DESS). *Degree requirements:* For other advanced degree, comprehensive exam. *Entrance requirements:* For degree, knowledge of French. Electronic applications accepted.

# Molecular Physiology

**Baylor College of Medicine,** Graduate School of Biomedical Sciences, Department of Molecular Physiology and Biophysics, Houston, TX 77030-3498. Offers cardiovascular sciences (PhD); molecular physiology and biophysics (PhD); MD/PhD. *Degree requirements:* For doctorate, thesis/dissertation, public defense. *Entrance requirements:* For doctorate, GRE General Test, GRE Subject Test (strongly recommended), minimum GPA of 3.0. Additional exam requirements/recommendations for international students: required—TOEFL. Electronic applications accepted.

**Loyola University Chicago,** Graduate School, Integrated Program in Biomedical Sciences, Maywood, IL 60660. Offers biochemistry and molecular biology (MS, PhD); cell and molecular physiology (MS, PhD); infectious disease and immunology (MS); integrative cell biology (MS, PhD); microbiology and immunology (MS, PhD); molecular pharmacology and therapeutics (MS, PhD); neuroscience (MS, PhD). *Students:* Average age 25. 773 applicants, 34% accepted, 122 enrolled. In 2019, 46 master's, 12 doctorates awarded. *Degree requirements:* For master's, thesis; for doctorate, comprehensive exam, thesis/dissertation. *Entrance requirements:* For doctorate, GRE. Additional exam requirements/recommendations for international students: required—TOEFL (minimum score 94 iBT), IELTS (minimum score 7.5). *Application deadline:* For fall admission, 2/7 for domestic students. Applications are processed on a rolling basis. Electronic applications accepted. *Expenses:* Contact institution. *Financial support:* In 2019–20, 20 students received support. Schmitt Fellowships and yearly tuition scholarships (averaging $25,032) available. Financial award application deadline: 6/15; financial award applicants required to submit FAFSA. *Unit head:* Dr. Leanne L. Cribbs, Associate Dean, Graduate Education, 708-327-2817, Fax: 708-216-8216, E-mail: lcribbs@luc.edu. *Application contact:* Margarita Quesada, Graduate Program Secretary, 708-216-3532, Fax: 708-216-8216, E-mail: mquesad@luc.edu. Website: http://ssom.luc.edu/graduate_school/degree-programs/ipbsphd/

**Rutgers University - New Brunswick,** Graduate School-New Brunswick, Program in Endocrinology and Animal Biosciences, Piscataway, NJ 08854-8097. Offers MS, PhD. Terminal master's awarded for partial completion of doctoral program. *Degree requirements:* For master's, thesis; for doctorate, comprehensive exam, thesis/dissertation. *Entrance requirements:* For master's and doctorate, GRE General Test. Additional exam requirements/recommendations for international students: required—TOEFL. Electronic applications accepted.

**Stony Brook University, State University of New York,** Stony Brook Medicine, Renaissance School of Medicine and Graduate School, Graduate Programs in Medicine, Department of Physiology and Biophysics, Stony Brook, NY 11794. Offers PhD. *Faculty:* 11 full-time (4 women), 2 part-time/adjunct (1 woman). *Students:* 22 full-time (14 women), 4 part-time (all women); includes 17 minority (7 Black or African American, non-Hispanic/Latino; 4 Asian, non-Hispanic/Latino; 6 Hispanic/Latino). Average age 23. 4 applicants, 25% accepted, 1 enrolled. *Degree requirements:* For doctorate, comprehensive exam, thesis/dissertation. *Entrance requirements:* For doctorate, GRE General Test, GRE Subject Test, BS in related field, minimum GPA of 3.0, recommendation. Additional exam requirements/recommendations for international students: required—TOEFL (minimum score 550 paper-based). *Application deadline:* For fall admission, 1/15 for domestic students; for spring admission, 10/1 for domestic students. Application fee: $100. *Expenses:* Contact institution. *Financial support:* In 2019–20, 3 research assistantships were awarded; fellowships, teaching assistantships, and Federal Work-Study also available. Financial award application deadline: 3/15. *Unit head:* Dr. Todd Miller, Chair, 631-444-3533, Fax: 631-444-3432, E-mail: todd.miller@stonybrook.edu. *Application contact:* Odalis Hernandez, Coordinator, 631-444-3057, Fax: 631-444-9749, E-mail: odalis.hernandez@stonybrook.edu. Website: https://renaissance.stonybrookmedicine.edu/pnb

**University of California, Los Angeles,** Graduate Division, College of Letters and Science, Program in Molecular, Cellular and Integrative Physiology, Los Angeles, CA 90095. Offers PhD. *Degree requirements:* For doctorate, thesis/dissertation, oral and written qualifying exams. *Entrance requirements:* For doctorate, GRE General Test; GRE Subject Test (biology or applicant's undergraduate major), bachelor's degree;

minimum undergraduate GPA of 3.0 (or its equivalent if letter grade system not used); interview. Additional exam requirements/recommendations for international students: required—TOEFL. Electronic applications accepted.

**University of Illinois at Urbana-Champaign,** Graduate College, College of Liberal Arts and Sciences, School of Molecular and Cellular Biology, Department of Molecular and Integrative Physiology, Champaign, IL 61820. Offers MS, PhD.

**The University of North Carolina at Chapel Hill,** School of Medicine and Graduate School, Biological and Biomedical Sciences Program, Cell Biology & Physiology, Chapel Hill, NC 27599. Offers PhD. *Faculty:* 27 full-time (9 women), 14 part-time/adjunct (4 women). *Students:* 30 full-time (18 women); includes 5 minority (1 Black or African American, non-Hispanic/Latino; 1 Asian, non-Hispanic/Latino; 3 Two or more races, non-Hispanic/Latino), 4 international. Average age 26. In 2019, 3 doctorates awarded. Terminal master's awarded for partial completion of doctoral program. *Degree requirements:* For doctorate, comprehensive exam, thesis/dissertation, ethics training. *Entrance requirements:* Additional exam requirements/recommendations for international students: required—TOEFL. *Application deadline:* For fall admission, 12/3 priority date for domestic and international students. Applications are processed on a rolling basis. Application fee: $77. Electronic applications accepted. *Financial support:* In 2019–20, 2 fellowships with full tuition reimbursements (averaging $32,000 per year), 16 research assistantships with full tuition reimbursements (averaging $32,000 per year) were awarded; career-related internships or fieldwork, health care benefits, and tuition waivers (full) also available. *Unit head:* Dr. Jay Brenman, Director of Graduate Studies, E-mail: brenman@med.unc.edu. *Application contact:* Jeffrey Steinbach, Assistant Director of Admissions, 919-843-7129, E-mail: jsteinba@email.unc.edu. Website: https://www.med.unc.edu/cellbiophysio/education-training/cell-biology-and-physiology-curriculum/

**University of Virginia,** School of Medicine, Department of Molecular Physiology and Biological Physics, Charlottesville, VA 22903. Offers biological and physical sciences (MS); physiology (PhD); MD/PhD. *Entrance requirements:* For doctorate, GRE General Test, GRE Subject Test. Additional exam requirements/recommendations for international students: required—TOEFL. Electronic applications accepted.

**Vanderbilt University,** School of Medicine, Department of Molecular Physiology and Biophysics, Nashville, TN 37240-1001. Offers MS, PhD, MD/PhD. *Faculty:* 23 full-time (2 women). *Students:* 26 full-time (16 women); includes 9 minority (4 Black or African American, non-Hispanic/Latino; 1 Asian, non-Hispanic/Latino; 3 Hispanic/Latino; 1 Two or more races, non-Hispanic/Latino), 5 international. Average age 26. In 2019, 12 doctorates awarded. *Degree requirements:* For doctorate, comprehensive exam, thesis/dissertation, preliminary, qualifying, and final exams. *Entrance requirements:* For doctorate, GRE General Test, GRE Subject Test (recommended). Additional exam requirements/recommendations for international students: required—TOEFL (minimum score 570 paper-based; 88 iBT). *Application deadline:* For fall admission, 1/15 for domestic and international students. Electronic applications accepted. *Expenses:* Tuition: Full-time $51,018; part-time $2087 per hour. *Required fees:* $542. Tuition and fees vary according to program. *Financial support:* Fellowships with full tuition reimbursements, research assistantships with full tuition reimbursements, Federal Work-Study, institutionally sponsored loans, scholarships/grants, traineeships, health care benefits, and tuition waivers (partial) available. Financial award application deadline: 1/15; financial award applicants required to submit CSS PROFILE or FAFSA. *Unit head:* Dr. Roger Cone, Acting Chair, 615-322-7000, Fax: 615-343-0490, E-mail: roger.cone@vanderbilt.edu. *Application contact:* Richard O'Brien, Director of Graduate Studies, 615-322-7000, E-mail: richard.obrien@vanderbilt.edu. Website: http://www.mc.vanderbilt.edu/root/vumc.php?site-MPB

**Yale University,** Graduate School of Arts and Sciences, Department of Cellular and Molecular Physiology, New Haven, CT 06520. Offers PhD. *Degree requirements:* For doctorate, thesis/dissertation. *Entrance requirements:* For doctorate, GRE General Test, GRE Subject Test.

# Physiology

**Albert Einstein College of Medicine,** Graduate Programs in the Biomedical Sciences, Department of Physiology and Biophysics, Bronx, NY 10461. Offers PhD, MD/PhD. *Degree requirements:* For doctorate, thesis/dissertation. *Entrance requirements:* For doctorate, GRE General Test. Additional exam requirements/recommendations for international students: required—TOEFL.

**American College of Healthcare Sciences,** Graduate Programs, Portland, OR 97239-3719. Offers anatomy and physiology (Graduate Certificate); aromatherapy (MS, Graduate Certificate); botanical safety (Graduate Certificate); complementary alternative medicine (MS, Graduate Certificate); health and wellness (MS); herbal medicine (MS, Graduate Certificate); holistic nutrition (MS, Graduate Certificate); wellness coaching (Graduate Certificate). *Program availability:* Part-time, evening/weekend, online learning. *Degree requirements:* For master's, capstone project. *Entrance requirements:* For master's, interview, letters of recommendation, essay.

**Augusta University,** Program in Physiology, Augusta, GA 30912. Offers PhD. *Degree requirements:* For doctorate, comprehensive exam, thesis/dissertation. *Entrance requirements:* For doctorate, GRE General Test. Additional exam requirements/

recommendations for international students: required—TOEFL. Electronic applications accepted.

**Ball State University,** Graduate School, College of Sciences and Humanities, Department of Biology, Program in Physiology, Muncie, IN 47306. Offers MA, MS. *Program availability:* Part-time. *Entrance requirements:* For master's, minimum baccalaureate GPA of 2.75 or 3.0 in latter half of baccalaureate, three letters of recommendation, resume or curriculum vitae. Additional exam requirements/ recommendations for international students: required—TOEFL (minimum score 550 paper-based; 79 iBT), IELTS (minimum score 6.5). Electronic applications accepted. *Expenses: Tuition, area resident:* Full-time $7506; part-time $417 per credit hour. Tuition, nonresident: full-time $20,610; part-time $1145 per credit hour. *Required fees:* $2126. Tuition and fees vary according to course load, campus/location and program.

**Baylor University,** Graduate School, Robbins College of Health and Human Sciences, Department of Health, Human Performance and Recreation, Waco, TX 76798. Offers athletic training (MS); exercise physiology (MS); kinesiology, exercise nutrition, and health promotion (PhD); sport pedagogy (MS). *Accreditation:* NCATE. *Faculty:* 15 full-time (5 women). *Students:* 87 full-time (47 women), 14 part-time (7 women); includes 21

minority (5 Black or African American, non-Hispanic/Latino; 1 American Indian or Alaska Native, non-Hispanic/Latino; 1 Asian, non-Hispanic/Latino; 8 Hispanic/Latino; 6 Two or more races, non-Hispanic/Latino), 5 international. Average age 24. 115 applicants, 77% accepted, 56 enrolled. In 2019, 42 master's, 7 doctorates awarded. *Degree requirements:* For master's, comprehensive exam, thesis optional; for doctorate, comprehensive exam, thesis/dissertation. *Entrance requirements:* For master's, GRE for MS in Exercise Science, transcripts, resume, 3 letters of recommendation; for doctorate, GRE, transcripts, resume, 3 letters of recommendation, statement of purpose, clinical/research experience, writing samples. Additional exam requirements/recommendations for international students: required—TOEFL (minimum score 550 paper-based; 80 iBT), IELTS (minimum score 6.5). *Application deadline:* For fall admission, 4/1 for domestic and international students; for spring admission, 10/1 for domestic and international students; for summer admission, 11/1 priority date for domestic and international students. Applications are processed on a rolling basis. Application fee: $50. Electronic applications accepted. *Financial support:* In 2019–20, 70 students received support, including 4 research assistantships with full tuition reimbursements available (averaging $15,000 per year), 25 teaching assistantships with full and partial tuition reimbursements available (averaging $11,000 per year); health care benefits, tuition waivers (full and partial), and unspecified assistantships also available. Financial award application deadline: 2/15. *Unit head:* Dr. Dale Connally, Interim Chair and Professor, 254-710-4004, Fax: 254-710-3527, E-mail: Dale_Connally@baylor.edu. *Application contact:* Deepa George, Graduate Program Coordinator, 254-710-3526, Fax: 254-710-3527, E-mail: deepa_morris@baylor.edu.
Website: www.baylor.edu/hhpr

**Boston University,** College of Health and Rehabilitation Sciences: Sargent College, Programs in Human Physiology, Boston, MA 02215. Offers MS, PhD. *Faculty:* 9 full-time (6 women), 7 part-time/adjunct (3 women). *Students:* 7 full-time (5 women), 4 part-time (3 women); includes 1 minority (Asian, non-Hispanic/Latino), 3 international. Average age 23. 40 applicants, 48% accepted, 7 enrolled. In 2019, 11 master's awarded. Terminal master's awarded for partial completion of doctoral program. *Entrance requirements:* Additional exam requirements/recommendations for international students: required—TOEFL. Application fee: $95. Electronic applications accepted. *Financial support:* Research assistantships, career-related internships or fieldwork, Federal Work-Study, institutionally sponsored loans, scholarships/grants, and unspecified assistantships available. Support available to part-time students. Financial award applicants required to submit FAFSA. *Unit head:* Dr. Paula Quatromoni, Chair, 617-353-5797, Fax: 617-353-7567, E-mail: paulaq@bu.edu. *Application contact:* Sharon Sankey, Assistant Dean, Student Services, 617-353-2713, Fax: 617-353-7500, E-mail: ssankey@bu.edu.

**Boston University,** School of Medicine, Graduate Medical Sciences, Department of Physiology and Biophysics, Boston, MA 02118. Offers MA, PhD, MD/PhD. *Program availability:* Part-time. Terminal master's awarded for partial completion of doctoral program. *Application deadline:* For fall admission, 1/15 for domestic students; for spring admission, 10/15 for domestic students. *Unit head:* Dr. David Atkinson, Chairman, E-mail: atkinson@bu.edu. *Application contact:* GMS Admissions Office, 617-358-9518, Fax: 617-358-2913, E-mail: gmsbusm@bu.edu.
Website: http://www.bumc.bu.edu/phys-biophys/

**Brigham Young University,** Graduate Studies, College of Life Sciences, Department of Physiology and Developmental Biology, Provo, UT 84602. Offers neuroscience (MS, PhD); physiology and developmental biology (MS, PhD). *Program availability:* Part-time. *Faculty:* 22 full-time (1 woman). *Students:* 15 full-time (7 women); includes 5 minority (all Asian, non-Hispanic/Latino). Average age 31. 7 applicants, 29% accepted. In 2019, 5 master's, 1 doctorate awarded. Terminal master's awarded for partial completion of doctoral program. *Degree requirements:* For master's, thesis, Coursework Oral Exam; for doctorate, comprehensive exam, thesis/dissertation. *Entrance requirements:* For master's, GRE General Test, MCAT, or DAT, minimum GPA of 3.0 during previous 2 years; for doctorate, GRE General Test, minimum GPA of 3.0 overall. Additional exam requirements/recommendations for international students: required—TOEFL (minimum score 580 paper-based; 85 iBT), E3PT; recommended—IELTS. *Application deadline:* For fall admission, 1/15 priority date for domestic and international students. Application fee: $50. Electronic applications accepted. *Financial support:* In 2019–20, 16 students received support, including 1 fellowship with full tuition reimbursement available (averaging $7,200 per year), 12 research assistantships with full tuition reimbursements available (averaging $6,400 per year), 2 teaching assistantships with partial tuition reimbursements available (averaging $6,000 per year); career-related internships or fieldwork, institutionally sponsored loans, scholarships/grants, tuition waivers (full and partial), unspecified assistantships, and tuition awards also available. Financial award application deadline: 2/1; financial award applicants required to submit FAFSA. *Unit head:* Dr. Michael R. Stark, Chair, 801-422-9498, Fax: 801-422-0004, E-mail: michael_stark@byu.edu. *Application contact:* Connie L. Provost, Graduate Program Manager, 801-422-3706, Fax: 801-422-0004, E-mail: connie_provost@byu.edu.
Website: http://pdbio.byu.edu

**Brown University,** Graduate School, Division of Biology and Medicine, Department of Molecular Pharmacology, Physiology and Biotechnology, Providence, RI 02912. Offers biomedical engineering (Sc M, PhD); biotechnology (PhD); molecular pharmacology and physiology (PhD); MD/PhD. *Degree requirements:* For doctorate, thesis/dissertation, preliminary exam. *Entrance requirements:* For master's and doctorate, GRE General Test, GRE Subject Test. Additional exam requirements/recommendations for international students: required—TOEFL. Electronic applications accepted.

**Case Western Reserve University,** School of Medicine and School of Graduate Studies, Graduate Programs in Medicine, Department of Physiology and Biophysics, Cleveland, OH 44106. Offers medical physiology (MS); physiology and biophysics (PhD); MD/PhD. Terminal master's awarded for partial completion of doctoral program. *Degree requirements:* For master's, thesis; for doctorate, thesis/dissertation. *Entrance requirements:* For master's, GRE General Test, minimum GPA of 3.28; for doctorate, GRE General Test, minimum GPA of 3.6. Additional exam requirements/recommendations for international students: required—TOEFL. Electronic applications accepted.

**Central Washington University,** School of Graduate Studies and Research, College of Education and Professional Studies, Department of Health Sciences, Ellensburg, WA 98926. Offers integrative human physiology (MS); nutrition (MS). *Program availability:* Part-time. *Entrance requirements:* For master's, GRE, minimum GPA of 3.0. Additional exam requirements/recommendations for international students: required—TOEFL (minimum score 550 paper-based; 79 iBT). Electronic applications accepted.

**Columbia University,** College of Physicians and Surgeons, Department of Physiology and Cellular Biophysics, New York, NY 10032. Offers M Phil, MA, PhD, MD/PhD. Terminal master's awarded for partial completion of doctoral program. *Degree requirements:* For doctorate, thesis/dissertation. *Entrance requirements:* For master's and doctorate, GRE General Test. Additional exam requirements/recommendations for international students: required—TOEFL. *Expenses: Tuition:* Full-time $47,600; part-time $1880 per credit. One-time fee: $105.

**Cornell University,** Graduate School, Graduate Fields of Agriculture and Life Sciences, Field of Horticulture, Ithaca, NY 14853. Offers breeding of horticultural crops (MPS); horticultural crop management systems (MPS); human-plant interactions (MPS, PhD); physiology and ecology of horticultural crops (MPS, MS, PhD). *Degree requirements:* For master's, thesis (MS); for doctorate, comprehensive exam, thesis/dissertation. *Entrance requirements:* For master's and doctorate, GRE General Test, 3 letters of recommendation. Additional exam requirements/recommendations for international students: required—TOEFL (minimum score 550 paper-based; 77 iBT). Electronic applications accepted.

**Dalhousie University,** Faculty of Agriculture, Halifax, NS B3H 4R2, Canada. Offers agriculture (M Sc), including air quality, animal behavior, animal molecular genetics, animal nutrition, animal technology, aquaculture, botany, crop management, crop physiology, ecology, environmental microbiology, food science, horticulture, nutrient management, pest management, physiology, plant biotechnology, plant pathology, soil chemistry, soil fertility, waste management and composting, water quality. *Program availability:* Part-time. *Degree requirements:* For master's, thesis, ATC Exam Teaching Assistantship. *Entrance requirements:* For master's, honors B Sc, minimum GPA of 3.0. Additional exam requirements/recommendations for international students: required—TOEFL (minimum score 580 paper-based; 92 iBT), IELTS, Michigan English Language Assessment Battery, CanTEST, CAEL.

**Dalhousie University,** Faculty of Medicine, Department of Physiology and Biophysics, Halifax, NS B3H 1X5, Canada. Offers M Sc, PhD, M Sc/PhD. *Degree requirements:* For master's, thesis; for doctorate, thesis/dissertation. *Entrance requirements:* For master's and doctorate, GRE Subject Test (for international students). Additional exam requirements/recommendations for international students: required—1 of 5 approved tests: TOEFL, IELTS, CANTEST, CAEL, Michigan English Language Assessment Battery. Electronic applications accepted.

**East Carolina University,** Brody School of Medicine, Office of Research and Graduate Studies, Greenville, NC 27858-4353. Offers anatomy and cell biology (PhD); biochemistry and molecular biology (PhD); biomedical science (MS); microbiology and immunology (PhD); pharmacology and toxicology (PhD); physiology (PhD). *Students:* 102 full-time (44 women), 1 part-time (0 women); includes 16 minority (4 Black or African American, non-Hispanic/Latino; 7 Asian, non-Hispanic/Latino; 4 Hispanic/Latino; 1 Two or more races, non-Hispanic/Latino), 13 international. Average age 28. 83 applicants, 40% accepted, 20 enrolled. In 2019, 3 master's, 10 doctorates awarded. *Degree requirements:* For doctorate, comprehensive exam, thesis/dissertation. *Entrance requirements:* For doctorate, GRE General Test. Additional exam requirements/recommendations for international students: required—some international applicants may be required to demonstrate English proficiency via the TOEFL, IELTS, or PTE exam.; recommended—TOEFL (minimum score 78 iBT), IELTS (minimum score 6.5), TSE (minimum score 65). *Application deadline:* For fall admission, 8/15 for domestic students; for spring admission, 12/20 for domestic students. Applications are processed on a rolling basis. Application fee: $75. Electronic applications accepted. *Expenses: Tuition, area resident:* Full-time $4749; part-time $185 per credit hour. Tuition, state resident: full-time $4749; part-time $185 per credit hour. Tuition, nonresident: full-time $17,898; part-time $864 per credit hour. *International tuition:* $17,898 full-time. *Required fees:* $2787. *Financial support:* Fellowships available. Financial award application deadline: 6/1. *Unit head:* Dr. Russ Price, Associate Dean, 252-744-9346, E-mail: pricest17@ecu.edu. *Application contact:* Dr. Russ Price, Associate Dean, 252-744-9346, E-mail: pricest17@ecu.edu.
Website: http://www.ecu.edu/cs-dhs/bsomresearchgradstudies/index.cfm

**Eastern Michigan University,** Graduate School, College of Health and Human Services, School of Health Promotion and Human Performance, Programs in Exercise Physiology, Ypsilanti, MI 48197. Offers exercise physiology (MS); sports medicine-biomechanics (MS); sports medicine-corporate adult fitness (MS); sports medicine-exercise physiology (MS). *Program availability:* Part-time, evening/weekend. *Students:* 16 full-time (4 women), 15 part-time (9 women); includes 4 minority (1 Asian, non-Hispanic/Latino; 3 Hispanic/Latino), 2 international. Average age 27. 44 applicants, 75% accepted, 13 enrolled. In 2019, 10 master's awarded. *Degree requirements:* For master's, comprehensive exam, thesis or 450-hour internship. *Entrance requirements:* Additional exam requirements/recommendations for international students: required—TOEFL. *Application deadline:* For fall admission, 8/1 for domestic students, 5/1 for international students; for winter admission, 12/1 for domestic students, 10/1 for international students; for spring admission, 3/15 for domestic students, 3/1 for international students. Application fee: $45. *Application contact:* Dr. Becca Moore, Program Coordinator, 734-487-2824, Fax: 734-487-2024, E-mail: rmoore41@emich.edu.

**East Tennessee State University,** Quillen College of Medicine, Department of Biomedical Sciences, Johnson City, TN 37614. Offers anatomy (PhD); biochemistry (PhD); microbiology (PhD); pharmaceutical sciences (PhD); pharmacology (PhD); physiology (PhD); quantitative biosciences (PhD). *Degree requirements:* For doctorate, comprehensive exam, thesis/dissertation, comprehensive qualifying exam; one-year residency. *Entrance requirements:* For doctorate, GRE General Test, GRE Subject Test, 3 letters of recommendation, minimum of 60 credit hours beyond the baccalaureate degree. Additional exam requirements/recommendations for international students: required—TOEFL (minimum score 550 paper-based; 79 iBT). Electronic applications accepted. *Expenses:* Contact institution.

**Georgetown University,** Graduate School of Arts and Sciences, Department of Pharmacology and Physiology, Washington, DC 20057. Offers pharmacology (MS, PhD, MD/PhD); physiology (MS); MD/PhD. *Program availability:* Part-time. *Degree requirements:* For doctorate, comprehensive exam, thesis/dissertation. *Entrance requirements:* For doctorate, GRE General Test, previous course work in biology and chemistry. Additional exam requirements/recommendations for international students: required—TOEFL (minimum score 550 paper-based; 80 iBT). Electronic applications accepted.

**Georgia Institute of Technology,** Graduate Studies, College of Sciences, School of Biological Sciences, Atlanta, GA 30332. Offers applied physiology (PhD); biology (MS, PhD); prosthetics and orthotics (MS). *Program availability:* Part-time. *Faculty:* 47 full-time (10 women), 1 part-time/adjunct (0 women). *Students:* 206 full-time (117 women), 15 part-time (3 women); includes 39 minority (7 Black or African American, non-Hispanic/Latino; 1 American Indian or Alaska Native, non-Hispanic/Latino; 20 Asian, non-Hispanic/Latino; 7 Hispanic/Latino; 4 Two or more races, non-Hispanic/Latino), 111 international. Average age 27. 287 applicants, 41% accepted, 59 enrolled. In 2019, 62 master's, 19 doctorates awarded. Terminal master's awarded for partial completion of doctoral program. *Degree requirements:* For master's, thesis; for doctorate, thesis/dissertation, qualifying exam. *Entrance requirements:* For master's and doctorate, GRE General Test. Additional exam requirements/recommendations for international students: required—TOEFL (minimum score 600 paper-based; 100 iBT), IELTS (minimum score 7.5). *Application deadline:* For fall admission, 12/1 priority date for domestic and international students. Applications are processed on a rolling basis. Application fee: $75 ($85 for international students). Electronic applications accepted. *Expenses: Tuition, area resident:* Full-time $14,064; part-time $586 per credit hour. Tuition, state resident: full-time $14,064; part-time $586 per credit hour. Tuition,

nonresident: full-time $29,140; part-time $1215 per credit hour. *International tuition:* $29,140 full-time. *Required fees:* $2024; $840 per semester. $2096. Tuition and fees vary according to course load. *Financial support:* In 2019–20, 7 fellowships, 94 research assistantships, 42 teaching assistantships were awarded; career-related internships or fieldwork, Federal Work-Study, institutionally sponsored loans, tuition waivers (full and partial), and unspecified assistantships also available. Support available to part-time students. Financial award application deadline: 7/1; financial award applicants required to submit FAFSA. *Unit head:* Todd Streelman, School Chair, 404-894-3700, Fax: 404-894-0519, E-mail: todd.streelman@biology.gatech.edu. *Application contact:* Marla Bruner, Director of Graduate Studies, 404-894-1610, Fax: 404-894-1609, E-mail: gradinfo@mail.gatech.edu.
Website: https://biosciences.gatech.edu

**Georgia State University,** College of Arts and Sciences, Department of Biology, Program in Cellular and Molecular Biology and Physiology, Atlanta, GA 30302-3083. Offers bioinformatics (MS); cellular and molecular biology and physiology (MS, PhD). *Program availability:* Part-time. Terminal master's awarded for partial completion of doctoral program. *Entrance requirements:* For master's and doctorate, GRE. *Application deadline:* Applications are processed on a rolling basis. Application fee: $50. Electronic applications accepted. *Expenses: Tuition, area resident:* Full-time $7164; part-time $398 per credit hour. Tuition, state resident: full-time $7164; part-time $398 per credit hour. Tuition, nonresident: full-time $22,662; part-time $1259 per credit hour. *International tuition:* $22,662 full-time. *Required fees:* $2128; $312 per credit hour. Tuition and fees vary according to course load and program. *Financial support:* Fellowships and research assistantships available. Financial award application deadline: 12/3. *Unit head:* Dr. Charles Derby, Director of Graduate Studies, 404-413-5393, Fax: 404-413-5446, E-mail: cderby@gsu.edu. *Application contact:* Dr. Charles Derby, Director of Graduate Studies, 404-413-5393, Fax: 404-413-5446, E-mail: cderby@gsu.edu.
Website: http://biology.gsu.edu/

**Gonzaga University,** School of Nursing and Human Physiology, Spokane, WA 99258. Offers MSN, DNP, DNP-A. *Accreditation:* AACN; AANA/CANAEP. *Program availability:* Part-time, evening/weekend, 100% online, immersion weekends. *Entrance requirements:* For master's, MAT or GRE within the last 5 years if GPA is lower than 3.0, official transcripts, two letters of recommendation, statement of purpose, current resume/curriculum vitae, current registered nurse license. Additional exam requirements/recommendations for international students: required—TOEFL (minimum score 88 iBT) or IELTS (minimum score 6.5). Electronic applications accepted. *Expenses:* Contact institution.

**Howard University,** Graduate School, Department of Physiology and Biophysics, Washington, DC 20059-0002. Offers biophysics (PhD); physiology (PhD). *Degree requirements:* For doctorate, comprehensive exam, thesis/dissertation. *Entrance requirements:* For doctorate, GRE General Test, minimum B average in field.

**Illinois State University,** Graduate School, College of Arts and Sciences, School of Biological Sciences, Normal, IL 61790. Offers animal behavior (MS); bacteriology (MS); biochemistry (MS); biological sciences (MS); biology (PhD); biophysics (MS); biotechnology (MS); botany (MS, PhD); cell biology (MS); conservation biology (MS); developmental biology (MS); ecology (MS, PhD); entomology (MS); evolutionary biology (MS); genetics (MS, PhD); immunology (MS); microbiology (MS, PhD); molecular biology (MS); molecular genetics (MS); neurobiology (MS); neuroscience (MS); parasitology (MS); physiology (MS, PhD); plant biology (MS); plant molecular biology (MS); plant sciences (MS); structural biology (MS); zoology (MS, PhD). *Program availability:* Part-time. *Faculty:* 26 full-time (6 women), 7 part-time/adjunct (2 women). *Students:* 51 full-time (33 women), 15 part-time (8 women). Average age 27. 71 applicants, 28% accepted, 9 enrolled. In 2019, 14 master's, 3 doctorates awarded. *Degree requirements:* For master's, thesis or alternative; for doctorate, variable foreign language requirement, thesis/dissertation, 2 terms of residency. *Entrance requirements:* For master's, GRE General Test, minimum GPA of 2.6 in last 60 hours of course work; for doctorate, GRE General Test. *Application deadline:* Applications are processed on a rolling basis. Application fee: $50. *Expenses: Tuition, area resident:* Full-time $7956; part-time $9767 per year. Tuition, nonresident: full-time $9233; part-time $17,592 per year. *Required fees:* $1797. *Financial support:* In 2019–20, 20 research assistantships, 41 teaching assistantships were awarded; Federal Work-Study, tuition waivers (full), and unspecified assistantships also available. Financial award application deadline: 4/1. *Unit head:* Dr. Craig Gatto, School Director, 309-438-3087, E-mail: cgatto@IllinoisState.edu. *Application contact:* Dr. Ben Sadd, Assistant Chair for Graduate Studies, 309-438-2651, E-mail: bmsadd@IllinoisState.edu.
Website: http://www.bio.ilstu.edu/

**Indiana State University,** College of Graduate and Professional Studies, College of Arts and Sciences, Department of Biology, Terre Haute, IN 47809. Offers cellular and molecular biology (PhD); ecology, systematics and evolution (PhD); life sciences (MS); physiology (PhD); science education (MS). *Degree requirements:* For master's, thesis optional; for doctorate, comprehensive exam, thesis/dissertation. *Entrance requirements:* For master's and doctorate, GRE General Test. Electronic applications accepted.

**James Madison University,** The Graduate School, College of Health and Behavioral Studies, Program in Kinesiology, Harrisonburg, VA 22807. Offers clinical exercise physiology (MS); exercise physiology (MS); kinesiology (MAT, MS); nutrition and exercise (MS); physical and health education (MAT); sport and recreation leadership (MS). *Program availability:* Part-time, evening/weekend. *Students:* 35 full-time (19 women), 1 (woman) part-time; includes 5 minority (3 Black or African American, non-Hispanic/Latino; 2 Hispanic/Latino). Average age 30. In 2019, 16 master's awarded. Application fee: $60. Electronic applications accepted. *Financial support:* In 2019–20, 17 students received support, including 14 teaching assistantships with full tuition reimbursements available (averaging $8,837 per year); Federal Work-Study and assistantships (averaging $7911), athletic assistantships (averaging $9284) also available. Financial award application deadline: 3/1; financial award applicants required to submit FAFSA. *Unit head:* Dr. Christopher J. Womack, Department Head, 540-568-6145, E-mail: womackcx@jmu.edu. *Application contact:* Lynette D. Michael, Director of Graduate Admissions, 540-568-6131 Ext. 6395, Fax: 540-568-7860, E-mail: michaeld@jmu.edu.
Website: http://www.jmu.edu/kinesiology/

**Johns Hopkins University,** School of Medicine, Graduate Programs in Medicine, Department of Physiology, Baltimore, MD 21205. Offers cellular and molecular physiology (PhD); physiology (PhD). *Degree requirements:* For doctorate, thesis/dissertation, oral and qualifying exams. *Entrance requirements:* For doctorate, previous course work in biology, calculus, chemistry, and physics. Additional exam requirements/recommendations for international students: required—TOEFL. Electronic applications accepted. *Expenses:* Contact institution.

**Kansas State University,** Graduate School, College of Agriculture, Department of Animal Sciences and Industry, Manhattan, KS 66506. Offers genetics (MS, PhD); meat science (MS, PhD); monogastric nutrition (MS, PhD); physiology (MS, PhD); ruminant nutrition (MS, PhD). *Degree requirements:* For master's, comprehensive exam, thesis, oral exam; for doctorate, comprehensive exam, thesis/dissertation, preliminary exams. *Entrance requirements:* Additional exam requirements/recommendations for international students: required—TOEFL (minimum score 550 paper-based; 79 iBT). Electronic applications accepted.

**Kansas State University,** Graduate School, College of Veterinary Medicine, Department of Anatomy and Physiology, Manhattan, KS 66506. Offers physiology (PhD). Terminal master's awarded for partial completion of doctoral program. *Entrance requirements:* For doctorate, GRE. Additional exam requirements/recommendations for international students: required—TOEFL. Electronic applications accepted.

**Kent State University,** College of Arts and Sciences, Department of Biological Sciences, Kent, OH 44242. Offers biological sciences (MA, MS, PhD), including botany (MS, PhD), cell biology (MS, PhD), ecology (MS, PhD), physiology (MS, PhD). *Program availability:* Part-time. *Faculty:* 19 full-time (5 women), 2 part-time/adjunct (1 woman). *Students:* 51 full-time (35 women), 9 part-time (4 women); includes 1 minority (Two or more races, non-Hispanic/Latino), 10 international. Average age 29. 53 applicants, 38% accepted, 14 enrolled. In 2019, 8 master's, 9 doctorates awarded. Terminal master's awarded for partial completion of doctoral program. *Degree requirements:* For master's, thesis (for some programs), departmental seminar presentation about research (for MS); for doctorate, thesis/dissertation, departmental seminar presentation about research, admitted to doctoral candidacy following written and oral candidacy. *Entrance requirements:* For master's, GRE, minimum GPA of 3.0, official transcripts, goal statement, three letters of recommendation, list of up to five potential faculty advisors, undergraduate coursework roughly equivalent to a biology minor, acceptance of student by a faculty advisor; for doctorate, GRE; After completing the required coursework, students complete the doctoral program by being admitted to candidacy, by proposing a research project to the faculty, and by completing and defending that research with a written dissertation before a faculty committee, official transcripts, goal statement, three letters of recommendation, list of up to five potential faculty advisors, baccalaureate degree with strong background in biology and related subjects such as chemistry and mathematics, acceptance of the student by a faculty advisor. Additional exam requirements/recommendations for international students: required—TOEFL (minimum score 94 iBT), IELTS (minimum score 7), PTE (minimum score 65), Michigan English Language Assessment Battery (minimum score 82). *Application deadline:* For fall admission, 12/15 for domestic students, 12/5 for international students. Applications are processed on a rolling basis. Application fee: $45 ($70 for international students). Electronic applications accepted. *Financial support:* Research assistantships with full tuition reimbursements, teaching assistantships with full tuition reimbursements, Federal Work-Study, scholarships/grants, health care benefits, and unspecified assistantships available. Financial award application deadline: 12/15. *Unit head:* Dr. James L. Blank, Dean, 330-672-2650, E-mail: jblank@kent.edu. *Application contact:* Dr. Heather K. Caldwell, Associate Professor and Graduate Coordinator, 330-672-3636, E-mail: hcaldwel@kent.edu.
Website: http://www.kent.edu/biology

**Kent State University,** College of Arts and Sciences, School of Biomedical Sciences, Kent, OH 44242-0001. Offers biological anthropology (PhD); biomedical mathematics (MS, PhD); cellular and molecular biology (MS, PhD), including cellular biology and structures, molecular biology and genetics; neurosciences (MS, PhD); pharmacology (MS, PhD); physiology (MS, PhD). *Faculty:* 17 full-time (8 women). *Students:* 73 full-time (48 women), 2 part-time (1 woman); includes 9 minority (2 Black or African American, non-Hispanic/Latino; 1 Asian, non-Hispanic/Latino; 3 Hispanic/Latino; 3 Two or more races, non-Hispanic/Latino), 53 international. Average age 29. 78 applicants, 17% accepted, 9 enrolled. In 2019, 2 master's, 5 doctorates awarded. *Degree requirements:* For master's, thesis; for doctorate, comprehensive exam, thesis/dissertation. *Entrance requirements:* For master's, GRE, bachelor's degree, transcripts, minimum GPA of 3.0 undergraduate GPA, goal statement, three letters of recommendation, academic preparation adequate to perform graduate work in the desired field (typically two years of chemistry, one year of mathematics, one year of physics and courses in anthropology, biology and psychology); for doctorate, GRE, master's degree, minimum GPA of 3.0, transcripts, goal statement, three letters of recommendation. Additional exam requirements/recommendations for international students: required—TOEFL (minimum score 100 iBT), IELTS (minimum score 7), PTE (minimum score 68), Michigan English Language Assessment Battery (minimum score 85). *Application deadline:* For fall admission, 1/1 for domestic students, 12/15 for international students. Applications are processed on a rolling basis. Application fee: $45 ($70 for international students). Electronic applications accepted. *Financial support:* Research assistantships with full tuition reimbursements, teaching assistantships, health care benefits, and unspecified assistantships available. Financial award application deadline: 1/1. *Unit head:* Dr. Ernest J. Freeman, Director, School of Biomedical Sciences, 330-672-2363, E-mail: efreema2@kent.edu. *Application contact:* School of Biomedical Sciences, 330-6722263, Fax: 330-6729391.
Website: http://www.kent.edu/biomedical/

**Loma Linda University,** School of Medicine, Programs in Physiology and Pharmacology, Loma Linda, CA 92350. Offers pharmacology (PhD); physiology (PhD). *Program availability:* Part-time. *Degree requirements:* For doctorate, 2 foreign languages, thesis/dissertation. *Entrance requirements:* For doctorate, GRE General Test.

**Louisiana State University Health Sciences Center,** School of Graduate Studies in New Orleans, Department of Physiology, New Orleans, LA 70112-2223. Offers PhD, MD/PhD. *Degree requirements:* For doctorate, comprehensive exam, thesis/dissertation. *Entrance requirements:* For doctorate, GRE General Test. Additional exam requirements/recommendations for international students: recommended—TOEFL, IELTS.

**Louisiana State University Health Sciences Center at Shreveport,** Department of Molecular and Cellular Physiology, Shreveport, LA 71130-3932. Offers physiology (MS, PhD); MD/PhD. *Degree requirements:* For master's, thesis; for doctorate, thesis/dissertation. *Entrance requirements:* For master's and doctorate, GRE General Test. Additional exam requirements/recommendations for international students: required—TOEFL (minimum score 550 paper-based). *Expenses:* Contact institution.

**Loyola University Chicago,** Graduate School, Integrated Program in Biomedical Sciences, Maywood, IL 60660. Offers biochemistry and molecular biology (MS, PhD); cell and molecular physiology (MS, PhD); infectious disease and immunology (MS); integrative cell biology (MS, PhD); microbiology and immunology (MS, PhD); molecular pharmacology and therapeutics (MS, PhD); neuroscience (MS, PhD). *Students:* Average age 25. 773 applicants, 34% accepted, 122 enrolled. In 2019, 46 master's, 12 doctorates awarded. *Degree requirements:* For master's, thesis; for doctorate, comprehensive exam, thesis/dissertation. *Entrance requirements:* For doctorate, GRE. Additional exam requirements/recommendations for international students: required—TOEFL (minimum score 94 iBT), IELTS (minimum score 7.5). *Application deadline:* For fall admission, 2/7 for domestic students. Applications are processed on a rolling basis. Electronic applications accepted. *Expenses:* Contact institution. *Financial support:* In 2019–20, 20 students received support. Schmitt Fellowships and yearly tuition scholarships (averaging $25,032) available. Financial award application deadline: 6/15; financial award applicants required to submit FAFSA. *Unit head:* Dr. Leanne L. Cribbs, Associate Dean, Graduate Education, 708-327-2817, Fax: 708-216-8216, E-mail:

lcribbs@luc.edu. *Application contact:* Margarita Quesada, Graduate Program Secretary, 708-216-3532, Fax: 708-216-8216, E-mail: mquesad@luc.edu.
Website: http://ssom.luc.edu/graduate_school/degree-programs/ipbsphd/

**Maharishi International University,** Graduate Studies, Program in Physiology, Fairfield, IA 52557. Offers PhD. *Degree requirements:* For doctorate, thesis/dissertation.

**Marquette University,** Graduate School, College of Arts and Sciences, Department of Biological Sciences, Milwaukee, WI 53201-1881. Offers cell biology (MS, PhD); developmental biology (MS, PhD); ecology (MS, PhD); epithelial physiology (MS, PhD); genetics (MS, PhD); microbiology (MS, PhD); molecular biology (MS, PhD); muscle and exercise physiology (MS, PhD); neuroscience (PhD). Terminal master's awarded for partial completion of doctoral program. *Degree requirements:* For master's, comprehensive exam, thesis, 1 year of teaching experience or equivalent; for doctorate, thesis/dissertation, 1 year of teaching experience or equivalent, qualifying exam. *Entrance requirements:* For master's and doctorate, GRE General Test, GRE Subject Test, official transcripts from all current and previous colleges/universities except Marquette, statement of professional goals and aspirations, three letters of recommendation. Additional exam requirements/recommendations for international students: required—TOEFL (minimum score 530 paper-based). Electronic applications accepted.

**Mayo Clinic Graduate School of Biomedical Sciences,** Program in Biomedical Engineering and Physiology, Rochester, MN 55905. Offers MS, PhD. Terminal master's awarded for partial completion of doctoral program. *Degree requirements:* For master's, thesis; for doctorate, comprehensive exam, thesis/dissertation, oral defense of dissertation, qualifying oral and written exam. *Entrance requirements:* For doctorate, GRE, 1 year of chemistry, biology, calculus, and physics; courses in quantitative science and engineering, e.g., signal processing, computer science, instrumentation (encouraged). Additional exam requirements/recommendations for international students: required—TOEFL. Electronic applications accepted.

**McGill University,** Faculty of Graduate and Postdoctoral Studies, Faculty of Medicine, Department of Physiology, Montréal, QC H3A 2T5, Canada. Offers M Sc, PhD.

**McMaster University,** Faculty of Health Sciences and School of Graduate Studies, Program in Medical Sciences, Physiology/Pharmacology Area, Hamilton, ON L8S 4M2, Canada. Offers M Sc, PhD, MD/PhD. *Degree requirements:* For master's, thesis; for doctorate, comprehensive exam, thesis/dissertation. *Entrance requirements:* For master's, honors B Sc, B+ average in related field; for doctorate, M Sc, minimum B+ average, students with proven research experience and an A average may be admitted with a B Sc degree. Additional exam requirements/recommendations for international students: required—TOEFL (minimum score 580 paper-based; 92 iBT).

**Medical College of Wisconsin,** Graduate School, Department of Physiology, Milwaukee, WI 53226. Offers PhD, MD/PhD. *Students:* 45 full-time (27 women); includes 11 minority (5 Black or African American, non-Hispanic/Latino; 3 Asian, non-Hispanic/Latino; 2 Hispanic/Latino; 1 Two or more races, non-Hispanic/Latino), 5 international. Average age 26. 55 applicants, 56% accepted, 23 enrolled. In 2019, 3 doctorates awarded. *Degree requirements:* For doctorate, comprehensive exam, thesis/dissertation. *Entrance requirements:* For doctorate, GRE, official transcripts, three letters of recommendation. Additional exam requirements/recommendations for international students: required—TOEFL. *Application deadline:* For fall admission, 1/15 for domestic and international students. Applications are processed on a rolling basis. Application fee: $50. Electronic applications accepted. *Expenses:* $1,250 per credit for PhD students; $42,000 per year flat fee for Master of Medical Physiology students; $155 per year full-time student fees. *Financial support:* In 2019–20, 28 students received support, including fellowships with full tuition reimbursements available (averaging $30,000 per year), research assistantships with full tuition reimbursements available (averaging $30,000 per year); institutionally sponsored loans and scholarships/grants also available. Support available to part-time students. Financial award application deadline: 2/15. *Unit head:* Dr. Allen W. Cowley, Jr., Chair, 414-955-8277, Fax: 414-955-6555, E-mail: cowley@mcw.edu. *Application contact:* Recruitment Office, 414-955-4402, Fax: 414-955-6555, E-mail: gradschoolrecruit@mcw.edu.
Website: https://www.mcw.edu/Physiology/Education.htm

**Michigan State University,** College of Human Medicine and The Graduate School, Graduate Programs in Human Medicine, East Lansing, MI 48824. Offers biochemistry and molecular biology (MS, PhD); epidemiology (MS, PhD); microbiology (MS); microbiology and molecular genetics (PhD); pharmacology and toxicology (MS, PhD); physiology (MS, PhD); public health (MPH). *Entrance requirements:* Additional exam requirements/recommendations for international students: required—TOEFL.

**Michigan State University,** College of Osteopathic Medicine and The Graduate School, Graduate Studies in Osteopathic Medicine, East Lansing, MI 48824. Offers biochemistry and molecular biology (MS, PhD); microbiology (MS); microbiology and molecular genetics (PhD); pharmacology and toxicology (MS, PhD), including integrative pharmacology (MS), pharmacology and toxicology, pharmacology and toxicology-environmental toxicology (PhD); physiology (MS, PhD).

**Michigan State University,** College of Veterinary Medicine and The Graduate School, Graduate Programs in Veterinary Medicine, East Lansing, MI 48824. Offers comparative medicine and integrative biology (MS, PhD), including comparative medicine and integrative biology, comparative medicine and integrative biology–environmental toxicology (PhD); food safety and toxicology (MS), including food safety; integrative toxicology (PhD), including animal science–environmental toxicology, biochemistry and molecular biology–environmental toxicology, chemistry–environmental toxicology, crop and soil sciences–environmental toxicology, environmental engineering–environmental toxicology, environmental geosciences–environmental toxicology, fisheries and wildlife–environmental toxicology, food science–environmental toxicology, forestry–environmental toxicology, genetics–environmental toxicology, human nutrition–environmental toxicology, microbiology–environmental toxicology, pharmacology and toxicology–environmental toxicology, zoology–environmental toxicology; large animal clinical sciences (MS, PhD); microbiology and molecular genetics (MS, PhD), including industrial microbiology, microbiology, microbiology and molecular genetics, microbiology–environmental toxicology (PhD); pathobiology and diagnostic investigation (MS, PhD), including pathology, pathology–environmental toxicology (PhD); pharmacology and toxicology (MS, PhD); pharmacology and toxicology–environmental toxicology (PhD); physiology (MS, PhD); small animal clinical sciences (MS). Electronic applications accepted.

**Michigan State University,** The Graduate School, College of Natural Science and College of Human Medicine and College of Osteopathic Medicine, Department of Physiology, East Lansing, MI 48824. Offers MS, PhD. *Entrance requirements:* Additional exam requirements/recommendations for international students: required—TOEFL (minimum score 600 paper-based). Electronic applications accepted.

**Montclair State University,** The Graduate School, College of Science and Mathematics, Program in Biology, Montclair, NJ 07043-1624. Offers biological science/education (MS); biology (MS); ecology and evolution (MS); physiology (MS).

**New York Medical College,** Graduate School of Basic Medical Sciences, Valhalla, NY 10595. Offers biochemistry and molecular biology (MS, PhD); cell biology (MS, PhD); microbiology and immunology (MS, PhD); pathology (MS, PhD); pharmacology (MS, PhD); physiology (MS, PhD); MD/PhD. *Program availability:* Part-time, evening/weekend. *Faculty:* 98 full-time (24 women). *Students:* 141 full-time (90 women), 17 part-time (3 women); includes 68 minority (16 Black or African American, non-Hispanic/Latino; 32 Asian, non-Hispanic/Latino; 15 Hispanic/Latino; 1 Native Hawaiian or other Pacific Islander, non-Hispanic/Latino; 4 Two or more races, non-Hispanic/Latino), 19 international. Average age 26. 351 applicants, 62% accepted, 86 enrolled. In 2019, 28 master's, 5 doctorates awarded. Terminal master's awarded for partial completion of doctoral program. *Degree requirements:* For master's, thesis; for doctorate, comprehensive exam, thesis/dissertation. *Entrance requirements:* For master's, GRE General Test, MCAT, or DAT, OAT. Additional exam requirements/recommendations for international students: required—TOEFL (minimum score 90 iBT), TOEFL or IELTS; one of the two exams are required. *Application deadline:* For fall admission, 6/1 priority date for domestic students, 5/1 priority date for international students. Applications are processed on a rolling basis. Application fee: $75 ($100 for international students). Electronic applications accepted. *Expenses:* $1200 credit and $620 fees. *Financial support:* In 2019–20, 400 students received support. Federal Work-Study, scholarships/grants, unspecified assistantships, and Student Federal Loans available. Financial award application deadline: 4/30; financial award applicants required to submit FAFSA. *Unit head:* Dr. Marina K Holz, Dean, 914-594-4110, Fax: 914-594-4944, E-mail: mholz@nymc.edu. *Application contact:* Valerie Romeo-Messana, Director of Admissions, 914-594-4110, Fax: 914-594-4944, E-mail: v_romeomessana@nymc.edu.
Website: https://www.nymc.edu/graduate-school-of-basic-medical-sciences-gsbms/gsbms-academics/

**Northwestern University,** The Graduate School, Judd A. and Marjorie Weinberg College of Arts and Sciences, Department of Neurobiology, Evanston, IL 60208. Offers neurobiology and physiology (MS). *Program availability:* Part-time. *Degree requirements:* For master's, thesis. *Entrance requirements:* For master's, GRE General Test and MCAT (strongly recommended). Additional exam requirements/recommendations for international students: required—TOEFL. Electronic applications accepted. *Expenses:* Contact institution.

**Ohio University,** Graduate College, College of Arts and Sciences, Department of Biological Sciences, Athens, OH 45701-2979. Offers biological sciences (MS, PhD); cell biology and physiology (MS, PhD); ecology and evolutionary biology (MS, PhD); exercise physiology and muscle biology (MS, PhD); microbiology (MS, PhD); neuroscience (MS, PhD). Terminal master's awarded for partial completion of doctoral program. *Degree requirements:* For master's, comprehensive exam, thesis, 1 quarter of teaching experience; for doctorate, comprehensive exam, thesis/dissertation, 2 quarters of teaching experience. *Entrance requirements:* For master's, GRE General Test, names of three faculty members whose research interests most closely match the applicant's interest; for doctorate, GRE General Test, essay concerning prior training, research interest and career goals, plus names of three faculty members whose research interests most closely match the applicant's interest. Additional exam requirements/recommendations for international students: required—TOEFL (minimum score 620 paper-based; 105 iBT) or IELTS (minimum score 7.5). Electronic applications accepted.

**Oregon Health & Science University,** School of Medicine, Graduate Programs in Medicine, Program in Molecular and Cellular Biosciences, Department of Physiology and Pharmacology, Portland, OR 97239-3098. Offers PhD. *Degree requirements:* For doctorate, comprehensive exam, thesis/dissertation. *Entrance requirements:* For doctorate, GRE General Test (minimum scores: 153 Verbal/148 Quantitative/4.5 Analytical) or MCAT (for some programs). Electronic applications accepted.

**Oregon State University,** College of Agricultural Sciences, Program in Fisheries Science, Corvallis, OR 97331. Offers aquaculture (MS); conservation biology (MS, PhD); fish genetics (MS, PhD); ichthyology (MS, PhD); limnology (MS, PhD); parasites and diseases (MS, PhD); physiology and ecology of marine and freshwater fishes (MS, PhD); stream ecology (MS, PhD); toxicology (MS, PhD); water pollution biology (MS, PhD). *Program availability:* Part-time. *Entrance requirements:* For master's and doctorate, GRE, minimum GPA of 3.0 in last 90 hours. Additional exam requirements/recommendations for international students: required—TOEFL (minimum score 80 iBT), IELTS (minimum score 6.5).

**Penn State University Park,** Graduate School, Intercollege Graduate Programs, Integrative and Biomedical Physiology Program, University Park, PA 16802. Offers MS, PhD.

**Purdue University,** School of Veterinary Medicine and Graduate School, Graduate Programs in Veterinary Medicine, Department of Basic Medical Sciences, West Lafayette, IN 47907. Offers anatomy (MS, PhD); pharmacology (MS, PhD); physiology (MS, PhD). *Program availability:* Part-time. Terminal master's awarded for partial completion of doctoral program. *Degree requirements:* For master's, thesis; for doctorate, thesis/dissertation. *Entrance requirements:* For master's and doctorate, GRE General Test. Additional exam requirements/recommendations for international students: required—TOEFL. Electronic applications accepted.

**Rocky Mountain University of Health Professions,** Doctor of Science Program in Clinical Electrophysiology, Provo, UT 84606. Offers D Sc. *Program availability:* Online learning. *Degree requirements:* For doctorate, thesis/dissertation. *Entrance requirements:* For doctorate, clinical entry-level master's or doctorate degree; professional licensure as a chiropractor, nurse practitioner, occupational therapist, physical therapist, physician or physician assistant; minimum of 100 hours experience in electroneuromyography.

**Rosalind Franklin University of Medicine and Science,** School of Graduate and Postdoctoral Studies - Interdisciplinary Graduate Program in Biomedical Sciences, Department of Physiology and Biophysics, North Chicago, IL 60064-3095. Offers MS, PhD, MD/PhD. Terminal master's awarded for partial completion of doctoral program. *Degree requirements:* For master's, comprehensive exam, thesis; for doctorate, comprehensive exam, thesis/dissertation. *Entrance requirements:* For master's and doctorate, GRE General Test. Additional exam requirements/recommendations for international students: required—TOEFL, TWE.

**Rush University,** Graduate College, Department of Molecular Biophysics and Physiology, Chicago, IL 60612-3832. Offers physiology (PhD); MD/PhD. *Degree requirements:* For doctorate, thesis/dissertation. *Entrance requirements:* For doctorate, GRE General Test. Additional exam requirements/recommendations for international students: required—TOEFL.

**Rutgers University - Newark,** Graduate School of Biomedical Sciences, Department of Pharmacology and Physiology, Newark, NJ 07107. Offers PhD. *Degree requirements:* For doctorate, thesis/dissertation, qualifying exam. *Entrance requirements:* For doctorate, GRE General Test. Additional exam requirements/recommendations for international students: required—TOEFL. Electronic applications accepted.

**Rutgers University - New Brunswick,** Graduate School-New Brunswick, Program in Endocrinology and Animal Biosciences, Piscataway, NJ 08854-8097. Offers MS, PhD. Terminal master's awarded for partial completion of doctoral program. *Degree requirements:* For master's, thesis; for doctorate, comprehensive exam, thesis/

dissertation. *Entrance requirements:* For master's and doctorate, GRE General Test. Additional exam requirements/recommendations for international students: required—TOEFL. Electronic applications accepted.

**Rutgers University - New Brunswick,** Graduate School of Biomedical Sciences, Program in Physiology and Integrative Biology, Piscataway, NJ 08854-5635. Offers MS, PhD, MD/PhD. *Entrance requirements:* Additional exam requirements/recommendations for international students: required—TOEFL. Electronic applications accepted.

**Saint Louis University,** Graduate Programs, School of Medicine, Graduate Programs in Biomedical Sciences and Graduate Programs, Department of Pharmacological and Physiological Science, St. Louis, MO 63103. Offers PhD. *Degree requirements:* For doctorate, comprehensive exam, thesis/dissertation, departmental qualifying exams. *Entrance requirements:* For doctorate, GRE General Test (GRE Subject Test optional), letters of recommendation, resume, interview. Additional exam requirements/recommendations for international students: required—TOEFL (minimum score 525 paper-based). Electronic applications accepted.

**Salisbury University,** Program in Applied Health Physiology, Salisbury, MD 21801-6837. Offers MS. *Faculty:* 8 full-time (0 women). *Students:* 23 full-time (8 women), 5 part-time (4 women); includes 9 minority (3 Black or African American, non-Hispanic/Latino; 1 Asian, non-Hispanic/Latino; 2 Hispanic/Latino; 3 Two or more races, non-Hispanic/Latino). Average age 25. 26 applicants, 73% accepted, 15 enrolled. In 2019, 16 master's awarded. *Degree requirements:* For master's, Internships; Credentialing exam (external). *Entrance requirements:* For master's, GRE, transcripts; personal statement; minimum GPA of 3.0; two letters of recommendation; pre-requisite undergraduate courses include human anatomy and physiology, exercise physiology, stress testing and exercise prescription, and kinesiology or biomechanics. Additional exam requirements/recommendations for international students: required—TOEFL (minimum score 550 paper-based; 79 iBT), IELTS (minimum score 6.5). *Application deadline:* For fall admission, 8/1 for domestic and international students; for spring admission, 12/1 for domestic and international students. Application fee: $65. Electronic applications accepted. *Expenses:* Contact institution. *Financial support:* In 2019–20, 10 students received support, including 1 research assistantship with full tuition reimbursement available (averaging $8,000 per year), 12 teaching assistantships with full tuition reimbursements available (averaging $8,083 per year); career-related internships or fieldwork and scholarships/grants also available. Support available to part-time students. Financial award application deadline: 3/1; financial award applicants required to submit FAFSA. *Unit head:* Dr. Scott Mazzetti, Graduate Program Chair, 410-677-0151, E-mail: szmazetti@salisbury.edu. *Application contact:* Dr. Scott Mazzetti, Graduate Program Chair, 410-677-0151, E-mail: szmazetti@salisbury.edu.
Website: https://www.salisbury.edu/explore-academics/programs/graduate-degree-programs/applied-health-physiology-master/

**San Francisco State University,** Division of Graduate Studies, College of Science and Engineering, Department of Biology, Program in Physiology and Behavioral Biology, San Francisco, CA 94132-1722. Offers MS. *Application deadline:* Applications are processed on a rolling basis. *Expenses: Tuition, area resident:* Full-time $7176; part-time $4164 per year. Tuition, state resident: full-time $7176; part-time $4164 per year. Tuition, nonresident: full-time $16,680; part-time $396 per unit. *International tuition:* $16,680 full-time. *Required fees:* $1524; $1524 per unit. $762 per semester. Tuition and fees vary according to degree level and program. *Unit head:* Dr. Andy Zink, Coordinator, 415-405-2761, Fax: 415-338-6136, E-mail: zink@sfsu.edu. *Application contact:* Dr. Andy Zink, Coordinator, 415-405-2761, Fax: 415-338-6136, E-mail: zink@sfsu.edu.
Website: http://biology.sfsu.edu/graduate/physiology_and_behavior

**San Jose State University,** Program in Biological Sciences, San Jose, CA 95192-0001. Offers biological sciences (MA, MS); molecular biology and microbiology (MS); organismal biology, conservation and ecology (MS); physiology (MS). *Program availability:* Part-time. *Entrance requirements:* For master's, GRE. Electronic applications accepted. *Expenses: Tuition, area resident:* Full-time $7176; part-time $4164 per credit hour. Tuition, state resident: full-time $7176; part-time $4164 per credit hour. Tuition, nonresident: full-time $7176; part-time $4165 per credit hour. *International tuition:* $7176 full-time. *Required fees:* $2110; $2110.

**Southern Illinois University Carbondale,** Graduate School, Graduate Programs in Medicine, Program in Molecular, Cellular and Systemic Physiology, Carbondale, IL 62901-4701. Offers MS, PhD. *Degree requirements:* For doctorate, thesis/dissertation. *Entrance requirements:* For master's and doctorate, GRE.

**Southern Methodist University,** Simmons School of Education and Human Development, Department of Allied Physiology and Wellness, Dallas, TX 75275. Offers applied physiology (PhD); health promotion management (MS); sport management (MS). *Entrance requirements:* For master's, GMAT, resume, essays, transcripts from all colleges and universities attended, two references. Additional exam requirements/recommendations for international students: required—TOEFL or PTE.

**Stanford University,** School of Medicine, Graduate Programs in Medicine, Department of Molecular and Cellular Physiology, Stanford, CA 94305-2004. Offers PhD. *Expenses: Tuition:* Full-time $52,479; part-time $34,110 per unit. *Required fees:* $672; $224 per quarter. Tuition and fees vary according to program and student level.

**State University of New York Upstate Medical University,** College of Graduate Studies, Program in Physiology, Syracuse, NY 13210. Offers MS, PhD, MD/PhD. Terminal master's awarded for partial completion of doctoral program. *Degree requirements:* For master's, thesis; for doctorate, comprehensive exam, thesis/dissertation. *Entrance requirements:* For master's, GRE General Test, interview; for doctorate, GRE General Test, telephone interview. Additional exam requirements/recommendations for international students: required—TOEFL. Electronic applications accepted.

**Stony Brook University, State University of New York,** Stony Brook Medicine, Renaissance School of Medicine and Graduate School, Graduate Programs in Medicine, Department of Physiology and Biophysics, Stony Brook, NY 11794. Offers PhD. *Faculty:* 11 full-time (4 women), 2 part-time/adjunct (1 woman). *Students:* 22 full-time (14 women), 4 part-time (all women); includes 17 minority (7 Black or African American, non-Hispanic/Latino; 4 Asian, non-Hispanic/Latino; 6 Hispanic/Latino). Average age 23. 4 applicants, 25% accepted, 1 enrolled. *Degree requirements:* For doctorate, comprehensive exam, thesis/dissertation. *Entrance requirements:* For doctorate, GRE General Test, GRE Subject Test, BS in related field, minimum GPA of 3.0, recommendation. Additional exam requirements/recommendations for international students: required—TOEFL (minimum score 550 paper-based). *Application deadline:* For fall admission, 1/15 for domestic students; for spring admission, 10/1 for domestic students. Application fee: $100. *Expenses:* Contact institution. *Financial support:* In 2019–20, 3 research assistantships were awarded; fellowships, teaching assistantships, and Federal Work-Study also available. Financial award application deadline: 3/15. *Unit head:* Dr. Todd Miller, Chair, 631-444-3533, Fax: 631-444-3432, E-mail: todd.miller@stonybrook.edu. *Application contact:* Odalis Hernandez, Coordinator, 631-444-3057, Fax: 631-444-9749, E-mail: odalis.hernandez@stonybrook.edu.
Website: https://renaissance.stonybrookmedicine.edu/pnb

**Teachers College, Columbia University,** Department of Biobehavioral Sciences, New York, NY 10027-6696. Offers applied exercise physiology (Ed M, MA, Ed D); communication sciences and disorders (MS, Ed D, PhD); kinesiology (PhD); motor learning and control (Ed M, MA); motor learning/movement science (Ed D); neuroscience and education (MS); physical education (MA, Ed D). *Accreditation:* ASHA. *Faculty:* 9 full-time (8 women). *Students:* 153 full-time (134 women), 149 part-time (106 women); includes 122 minority (25 Black or African American, non-Hispanic/Latino; 32 Asian, non-Hispanic/Latino; 55 Hispanic/Latino; 10 Two or more races, non-Hispanic/Latino), 37 international. 582 applicants, 51% accepted, 165 enrolled. *Unit head:* Dr. Carol Scheffner Hammer, E-mail: cjh2207@tc.columbia.edu. *Application contact:* Kelly Sutton Skinner, Director of Admission and New Student Enrollment, 212-678-3710, E-mail: kms2237@tc.columbia.edu.
Website: http://www.tc.columbia.edu/biobehavioral-sciences/

**Tulane University,** School of Medicine, Graduate Programs in Biomedical Sciences, Department of Physiology, New Orleans, LA 70118-5669. Offers MS. *Degree requirements:* For master's, one foreign language, thesis. *Entrance requirements:* For master's, GRE General Test, minimum B average in undergraduate course work. Additional exam requirements/recommendations for international students: required—TOEFL. Electronic applications accepted. *Expenses: Tuition:* Full-time $57,004; part-time $3167 per credit hour. *Required fees:* $2086; $44.50 per credit hour. $80 per term. Tuition and fees vary according to course load, degree level and program.

**Universidad Central del Caribe,** School of Medicine, Program in Biomedical Sciences, Bayamón, PR 00960-6032. Offers anatomy and cell biology (MA, MS); biochemistry (MS); biomedical sciences (MA); cellular and molecular biology (PhD); microbiology and immunology (MA, MS); pharmacology (MS); physiology (MS).

**Université de Montréal,** Faculty of Medicine, Department of Physiology, Montréal, QC H3C 3J7, Canada. Offers neurological sciences (M Sc, PhD); physiology (M Sc, PhD). Terminal master's awarded for partial completion of doctoral program. *Degree requirements:* For master's, thesis; for doctorate, thesis/dissertation, general exam. *Entrance requirements:* For master's and doctorate, proficiency in French, knowledge of English. Electronic applications accepted.

**Université de Sherbrooke,** Faculty of Medicine and Health Sciences, Graduate Programs in Medicine, Department of Physiology and Biophysics, Sherbrooke, QC J1H 5N4, Canada. Offers M Sc, PhD. Terminal master's awarded for partial completion of doctoral program. *Degree requirements:* For master's, thesis; for doctorate, thesis/dissertation. Electronic applications accepted.

**University at Buffalo, the State University of New York,** Graduate School, Jacobs School of Medicine and Biomedical Sciences, Graduate Programs in Medicine and Biomedical Sciences, Department of Physiology and Biophysics, Buffalo, NY 14260. Offers biophysics (MS, PhD); physiology (MA, PhD). *Faculty:* 17 full-time (4 women). *Students:* 5 full-time (1 woman); includes 3 minority (1 Black or African American, non-Hispanic/Latino; 2 Asian, non-Hispanic/Latino). Average age 27. 10 applicants, 10% accepted, 1 enrolled. In 2019, 2 master's awarded. Terminal master's awarded for partial completion of doctoral program. *Degree requirements:* For master's, comprehensive exam, thesis or alternative, oral exam, project; for doctorate, comprehensive exam, thesis/dissertation, oral and written qualifying exam or 2 research proposals. *Entrance requirements:* For master's, GRE General Test, unofficial transcripts, 3 letters of recommendation, personal statement, curriculum vitae; for doctorate, GRE General Test or MCAT, unofficial transcripts, 3 letters of recommendation, personal statement, curriculum vitae. Additional exam requirements/recommendations for international students: required—TOEFL (minimum score 550 paper-based; 79 iBT). *Application deadline:* Applications are processed on a rolling basis. Application fee: $85. Electronic applications accepted. *Expenses: Tuition, area resident:* Full-time $11,310; part-time $471 per credit hour. Tuition, state resident: full-time $11,310; part-time $471 per credit hour. Tuition, nonresident: full-time $23,100; part-time $963 per credit hour. *International tuition:* $23,100 full-time. *Required fees:* $2820. *Financial support:* In 2019–20, 2 students received support, including 2 research assistantships with full tuition reimbursements available (averaging $27,000 per year); health care benefits also available. Financial award applicants required to submit FAFSA. *Unit head:* Dr. Perry M. Hogan, Chair, 716-829-2738, Fax: 716-829-2344, E-mail: phogan@buffalo.edu. *Application contact:* Kara M. Rickicki, Assistant Director of Academic Administration, 716-829-2417, Fax: 716-829-2801, E-mail: rickicki@buffalo.edu.
Website: https://medicine.buffalo.edu/departments/physiology.html

**University of Alberta,** Faculty of Graduate Studies and Research, Department of Biological Sciences, Edmonton, AB T6G 2E1, Canada. Offers environmental biology and ecology (M Sc, PhD); microbiology and biotechnology (M Sc, PhD); molecular biology and genetics (M Sc, PhD); physiology and cell biology (M Sc, PhD); plant biology (M Sc, PhD); systematics and evolution (M Sc, PhD). Terminal master's awarded for partial completion of doctoral program. *Degree requirements:* For master's, thesis; for doctorate, thesis/dissertation. *Entrance requirements:* Additional exam requirements/recommendations for international students: required—TOEFL.

**University of Alberta,** Faculty of Medicine and Dentistry and Faculty of Graduate Studies and Research, Graduate Programs in Medicine, Department of Physiology, Edmonton, AB T6G 2E1, Canada. Offers M Sc, PhD. Terminal master's awarded for partial completion of doctoral program. *Degree requirements:* For master's, thesis; for doctorate, thesis/dissertation. *Entrance requirements:* For master's and doctorate, minimum GPA of 3.0. Additional exam requirements/recommendations for international students: required—TOEFL (minimum score 580 paper-based). Electronic applications accepted.

**The University of Arizona,** Graduate Interdisciplinary Programs, Graduate Interdisciplinary Program in Physiological Sciences, Tucson, AZ 85721. Offers MS, PhD. *Degree requirements:* For doctorate, thesis/dissertation. *Entrance requirements:* For master's, GRE General Test, 3 letters of recommendation, statement of purpose; for doctorate, GRE General Test, 3 letters of recommendation. Additional exam requirements/recommendations for international students: required—TOEFL (minimum score 600 paper-based). Electronic applications accepted.

**University of Arkansas for Medical Sciences,** Graduate School, Little Rock, AR 72205. Offers biochemistry and molecular biology (MS, PhD); bioinformatics (MS, PhD); cellular physiology and molecular biophysics (MS, PhD); clinical nutrition (MS); interdisciplinary biomedical sciences (MS, PhD, Certificate); interdisciplinary toxicology (MS); microbiology and immunology (PhD); neurobiology and developmental sciences (PhD); pharmacology (PhD); MD/PhD. *Program availability:* Part-time. Terminal master's awarded for partial completion of doctoral program. *Degree requirements:* For master's, comprehensive exam (for some programs), thesis (for some programs); for doctorate, thesis/dissertation. *Entrance requirements:* For master's and doctorate, GRE. Additional exam requirements/recommendations for international students: required—TOEFL. Electronic applications accepted. *Expenses:* Contact institution.

**University of Calgary,** Cumming School of Medicine and Faculty of Graduate Studies, Program in Gastrointestinal Sciences, Calgary, AB T2N 1N4, Canada. Offers M Sc, PhD. *Degree requirements:* For master's, thesis; for doctorate, thesis/dissertation, candidacy exam. *Entrance requirements:* For master's and doctorate, minimum GPA of

3.2 during previous 2 years. Additional exam requirements/recommendations for international students: required—TOEFL. Electronic applications accepted.

**University of Calgary,** Cumming School of Medicine and Faculty of Graduate Studies, Program in Medical Science, Calgary, AB T2N 1N4, Canada. Offers cancer biology (M Sc, PhD); critical care medicine (M Sc, PhD); joint injury and arthritis (M Sc, PhD); molecular and medical genetics (M Sc, PhD); mountain medicine and high altitude physiology (M Sc, PhD); pathologists' assistant (M Sc, PhD). *Degree requirements:* For master's, thesis; for doctorate, thesis/dissertation, candidacy exam. *Entrance requirements:* For master's, minimum undergraduate GPA of 3.2; for doctorate, minimum graduate GPA of 3.2. Additional exam requirements/recommendations for international students: required—TOEFL (minimum score 600 paper-based). Electronic applications accepted.

**University of California, Berkeley,** Graduate Division, College of Letters and Science, Group in Endocrinology, Berkeley, CA 94720. Offers MA, PhD. *Degree requirements:* For doctorate, thesis/dissertation, oral qualifying exam. *Entrance requirements:* For master's, GRE General Test or the equivalent (MCAT), minimum GPA of 3.0, 3 letters of recommendation; for doctorate, GRE General Test or the equivalent (MCAT), minimum GPA of 3.4, 3 letters of recommendation. Additional exam requirements/recommendations for international students: required—TOEFL. Electronic applications accepted.

**University of California, Davis,** Graduate Studies, Molecular, Cellular and Integrative Physiology Graduate Group, Davis, CA 95616. Offers MS, PhD. *Degree requirements:* For master's, comprehensive exam (for some programs), thesis (for some programs); for doctorate, thesis/dissertation. *Entrance requirements:* For master's and doctorate, GRE General Test. Additional exam requirements/recommendations for international students: required—TOEFL (minimum score 550 paper-based). Electronic applications accepted.

**University of California, Irvine,** School of Medicine and School of Biological Sciences, Department of Physiology and Biophysics, Irvine, CA 92697. Offers biological sciences (PhD); MD/PhD. *Students:* 20 full-time (8 women); includes 9 minority (1 American Indian or Alaska Native, non-Hispanic/Latino; 7 Asian, non-Hispanic/Latino; 1 Hispanic/Latino), 3 international. Average age 29. In 2019, 2 doctorates awarded. *Entrance requirements:* For doctorate, GRE General Test, GRE Subject Test, minimum GPA of 3.0. Additional exam requirements/recommendations for international students: required—TOEFL (minimum score 550 paper-based). *Application deadline:* For fall admission, 1/15 priority date for domestic students, 1/15 for international students. Application fee: $120 ($140 for international students). Electronic applications accepted. *Financial support:* Fellowships, research assistantships with full tuition reimbursements, teaching assistantships, institutionally sponsored loans, traineeships, health care benefits, and unspecified assistantships available. Financial award application deadline: 3/1; financial award applicants required to submit FAFSA. *Unit head:* Prof. Michael Cahalan, Chair, 949-824-7776, Fax: 949-824-3143, E-mail: mcahalan@uci.edu. *Application contact:* Janita Parpana, Chief Administrative Officer, 949-824-6833, Fax: 949-824-8540, E-mail: jparpana@uci.edu.
Website: http://www.physiology.uci.edu/

**University of California, Los Angeles,** David Geffen School of Medicine and Graduate Division, Graduate Programs in Medicine, Department of Physiology, Los Angeles, CA 90095. Offers PhD. *Degree requirements:* For doctorate, thesis/dissertation, oral and written qualifying exams. *Entrance requirements:* For doctorate, GRE General Test, GRE Subject Test.

**University of California, Los Angeles,** Graduate Division, College of Letters and Science, Department of Integrative Biology and Physiology, Los Angeles, CA 90095. Offers physiological science (MS). *Degree requirements:* For master's, thesis. *Entrance requirements:* For master's, GRE General Test or MCAT, bachelor's degree; minimum undergraduate GPA of 3.0 (or its equivalent if letter grade system not used). Additional exam requirements/recommendations for international students: required—TOEFL. Electronic applications accepted.

**University of California, Los Angeles,** Graduate Division, College of Letters and Science and David Geffen School of Medicine, UCLA ACCESS to Programs in the Molecular, Cellular and Integrative Life Sciences, Los Angeles, CA 90095. Offers biochemistry and molecular biology (PhD); biological chemistry (PhD); cellular and molecular pathology (PhD); human genetics (PhD); microbiology, immunology, and molecular genetics (PhD); molecular biology (PhD); molecular toxicology (PhD); molecular, cellular and integrative physiology (PhD); neurobiology (PhD); oral biology (PhD); physiology (PhD). *Degree requirements:* For doctorate, thesis/dissertation, oral and written qualifying exams. *Entrance requirements:* For doctorate, GRE General Test, bachelor's degree; minimum undergraduate GPA of 3.0 (or its equivalent if letter grade system not used). Additional exam requirements/recommendations for international students: required—TOEFL. Electronic applications accepted.

**University of Central Florida,** College of Community Innovation and Education, Department of Learning Science and Educational Research, Education Doctoral Programs, Orlando, FL 32816. Offers applied learning and instruction (MA); curriculum and instruction (M Ed); instructional design and technology (MA, Certificate), including e-learning (Certificate), educational technology (Certificate), instructional design (Certificate), instructional design and technology (MA), instructional design for simulations (Certificate); sport and exercise science (MS), including applied exercise physiology. *Program availability:* Part-time, evening/weekend. *Students:* 1 full-time (0 women), 2 part-time (1 woman); includes 1 minority (Black or African American, non-Hispanic/Latino). Average age 41. *Entrance requirements:* Additional exam requirements/recommendations for international students: required—TOEFL. Application fee: $30. Electronic applications accepted. *Financial support:* Scholarships/grants, health care benefits, and unspecified assistantships available. Financial award application deadline: 3/1; financial award applicants required to submit FAFSA. *Unit head:* Dr. Jeffrey Stout, Chair, 407-823-0211, E-mail: jeffrey.stout@ucf.edu. *Application contact:* Associate Director, Graduate Admissions, 407-823-2766, Fax: 407-823-6442, E-mail: gradadmissions@ucf.edu.
Website: https://ccie.ucf.edu/lser/

**University of Colorado Boulder,** Graduate School, College of Arts and Sciences, Department of Integrative Physiology, Boulder, CO 80309. Offers MS, PhD. Terminal master's awarded for partial completion of doctoral program. *Degree requirements:* For master's, comprehensive exam, thesis or alternative; for doctorate, thesis/dissertation. *Entrance requirements:* For master's, GRE General Test, minimum undergraduate GPA of 2.75. Electronic applications accepted. Application fee is waived when completed online.

**University of Connecticut,** Graduate School, College of Liberal Arts and Sciences, Department of Physiology and Neurobiology, Storrs, CT 06269. Offers comparative physiology (MS, PhD). Terminal master's awarded for partial completion of doctoral program. *Degree requirements:* For master's, comprehensive exam; for doctorate, thesis/dissertation. *Entrance requirements:* For master's and doctorate, GRE General Test, GRE Subject Test. Additional exam requirements/recommendations for international students: required—TOEFL (minimum score 550 paper-based). Electronic applications accepted.

**University of Delaware,** College of Arts and Sciences, Department of Biological Sciences, Newark, DE 19716. Offers biotechnology (MS); cancer biology (MS, PhD); cell and extracellular matrix biology (MS, PhD); cell and systems physiology (MS, PhD); developmental biology (MS, PhD); ecology and evolution (MS, PhD); microbiology (MS, PhD); molecular biology and genetics (MS, PhD). Terminal master's awarded for partial completion of doctoral program. *Degree requirements:* For master's, thesis, preliminary exam; for doctorate, comprehensive exam, thesis/dissertation, preliminary exam. *Entrance requirements:* For master's and doctorate, GRE General Test. Additional exam requirements/recommendations for international students: required—TOEFL (minimum score 600 paper-based); recommended—TWE. Electronic applications accepted.

**University of Delaware,** College of Health Sciences, Department of Kinesiology and Applied Physiology, Newark, DE 19716. Offers MS, PhD.

**University of Florida,** College of Medicine and Graduate School, Interdisciplinary Program in Biomedical Sciences, Concentration in Physiology and Pharmacology, Gainesville, FL 32611. Offers PhD. *Degree requirements:* For doctorate, thesis/dissertation. *Entrance requirements:* For doctorate, GRE General Test, minimum GPA of 3.0, biochemistry before enrollment. Electronic applications accepted.

**University of Florida,** Graduate School, College of Health and Human Performance, Department of Applied Physiology and Kinesiology, Gainesville, FL 32611. Offers applied physiology and kinesiology (MS); athletic training/sports medicine (MS); biobehavioral science (MS); clinical exercise physiology (MS); exercise physiology (MS); health and human performance (PhD), including applied physiology and kinesiology, biobehavioral science, exercise physiology; human performance (MS). *Degree requirements:* For master's, comprehensive exam, thesis (for some programs); for doctorate, comprehensive exam, thesis/dissertation. *Entrance requirements:* For master's and doctorate, GRE General Test, minimum GPA of 3.0. Additional exam requirements/recommendations for international students: required—TOEFL (minimum score 550 paper-based; 80 iBT), IELTS (minimum score 6). Electronic applications accepted.

**University of Georgia,** College of Veterinary Medicine, Department of Physiology and Pharmacology, Athens, GA 30602. Offers pharmacology (MS, PhD). *Degree requirements:* For master's, thesis; for doctorate, one foreign language, thesis/dissertation. *Entrance requirements:* For master's and doctorate, GRE General Test. Electronic applications accepted.

**University of Guelph,** Ontario Veterinary College and Office of Graduate and Postdoctoral Studies, Graduate Programs in Veterinary Sciences, Department of Biomedical Sciences, Guelph, ON N1G 2W1, Canada. Offers morphology (M Sc, DV Sc, PhD); neuroscience (M Sc, DV Sc, PhD); pharmacology (M Sc, DV Sc, PhD); physiology (M Sc, DV Sc, PhD); toxicology (M Sc, DV Sc, PhD). *Program availability:* Part-time. *Degree requirements:* For master's, thesis; for doctorate, comprehensive exam, thesis/dissertation. *Entrance requirements:* For master's, honors B Sc, minimum 75% average in last 20 courses; for doctorate, M Sc with thesis from accredited institution. Additional exam requirements/recommendations for international students: required—TOEFL (minimum score 550 paper-based; 89 iBT). Electronic applications accepted.

**University of Hawaii at Manoa,** John A. Burns School of Medicine, Program in Developmental and Reproductive Biology, Honolulu, HI 96813. Offers MS, PhD. *Program availability:* Part-time. *Degree requirements:* For doctorate, thesis/dissertation. *Entrance requirements:* For doctorate, GRE General Test, GRE Subject Test. Additional exam requirements/recommendations for international students: recommended—TOEFL (minimum score 560 paper-based), IELTS (minimum score 5).

**University of Illinois at Chicago,** College of Medicine, Graduate Programs in Medicine, Department of Physiology and Biophysics, Chicago, IL 60607-7128. Offers MS, PhD. Terminal master's awarded for partial completion of doctoral program. *Degree requirements:* For master's, thesis; for doctorate, thesis/dissertation. *Entrance requirements:* For master's and doctorate, GRE General Test. Additional exam requirements/recommendations for international students: required—TOEFL. Electronic applications accepted.

**University of Illinois at Urbana-Champaign,** Graduate College, College of Liberal Arts and Sciences, School of Molecular and Cellular Biology, Department of Molecular and Integrative Physiology, Champaign, IL 61820. Offers MS, PhD.

**The University of Iowa,** Roy J. and Lucille A. Carver College of Medicine and Graduate College, Graduate Programs in Medicine, Department of Molecular Physiology and Biophysics, Iowa City, IA 52242-1316. Offers MS, PhD. *Faculty:* 9 full-time (2 women). *Students:* 10 full-time (2 women); includes 3 minority (2 Asian, non-Hispanic/Latino; 1 Hispanic/Latino), 1 international. Average age 23. 5 applicants, 60% accepted, 3 enrolled. In 2019, 1 doctorate awarded. *Degree requirements:* For master's, comprehensive exam; for doctorate, comprehensive exam, thesis/dissertation. *Entrance requirements:* Additional exam requirements/recommendations for international students: required—TOEFL. *Application deadline:* For fall admission, 4/1 for domestic students, 3/1 for international students; for spring admission, 10/1 for domestic students, 9/1 for international students. Applications are processed on a rolling basis. Application fee: $60 ($80 for international students). Electronic applications accepted. *Financial support:* In 2019–20, 1 fellowship with full tuition reimbursement (averaging $26,000 per year), 14 research assistantships with full tuition reimbursements (averaging $26,000 per year) were awarded; traineeships also available. Financial award application deadline: 4/1. *Unit head:* Dr. Kevin P. Campbell, Chair and Department Executive Officer, 319-335-7800, Fax: 319-335-7330, E-mail: kevin-campbell@uiowa.edu. *Application contact:* Dr. Mark Stamnes, Director of Graduate Studies, 319-335-7858, Fax: 319-335-7330, E-mail: mark-stamnes@uiowa.edu.
Website: http://www.physiology.uiowa.edu/

**The University of Kansas,** University of Kansas Medical Center, School of Medicine, Department of Molecular and Integrative Physiology, Kansas City, KS 66160. Offers PhD, MD/PhD. *Faculty:* 29. *Students:* 19 full-time (15 women); includes 1 minority (Two or more races, non-Hispanic/Latino), 7 international. Average age 28. In 2019, 6 doctorates awarded. Terminal master's awarded for partial completion of doctoral program. *Degree requirements:* For doctorate, comprehensive exam, thesis/dissertation. *Entrance requirements:* For doctorate, GRE. Additional exam requirements/recommendations for international students: required—TOEFL. *Application deadline:* For fall admission, 12/1 priority date for domestic and international students. Applications are processed on a rolling basis. Application fee: $60. Electronic applications accepted. *Expenses:* Tuition, state resident: full-time $9989. Tuition, nonresident: full-time $23,950. *International tuition:* $23,950 full-time. *Required fees:* $984; $81.99 per credit hour. Tuition and fees vary according to course load, campus/location and program. *Financial support:* Fellowships with full tuition reimbursements, research assistantships with partial tuition reimbursements, teaching assistantships with full tuition reimbursements, scholarships/grants, and unspecified assistantships available. Financial award application deadline: 3/1; financial award applicants required to submit FAFSA. *Unit head:* Dr. Victor G. Blanco, Professor and Kathleen M. Osborn Chair, 913-588-7400, E-mail: gblanco@kumc.edu. *Application contact:* Dr. Michael W. Wolfe, Director of Graduate Studies, 913-588-7418, E-mail: mwolfe2@kumc.edu.

Website: http://www.kumc.edu/school-of-medicine/molecular-and-integrative-physiology.html

**University of Kentucky,** Graduate School, Graduate School Programs from the College of Medicine, Program in Physiology, Lexington, KY 40506-0032. Offers PhD. *Degree requirements:* For doctorate, comprehensive exam, thesis/dissertation. *Entrance requirements:* For doctorate, GRE General Test, minimum undergraduate GPA of 2.75, graduate 3.0. Additional exam requirements/recommendations for international students: required—TOEFL (minimum score 550 paper-based). Electronic applications accepted.

**University of Louisville,** School of Medicine, Department of Physiology, Louisville, KY 40292-0001. Offers physiology (MS); MD/PhD. *Faculty:* 14 full-time (2 women), 4 part-time/adjunct (0 women). *Students:* 44 full-time (26 women), 7 part-time (4 women); includes 21 minority (12 Black or African American, non-Hispanic/Latino; 5 Asian, non-Hispanic/Latino; 2 Hispanic/Latino; 2 Two or more races, non-Hispanic/Latino; 3 international. Average age 27. 64 applicants, 66% accepted, 31 enrolled. In 2019, 30 master's awarded. *Degree requirements:* For doctorate, comprehensive exam, thesis/dissertation. *Entrance requirements:* Additional exam requirements/recommendations for international students: required—TOEFL (minimum score 550 paper-based; 213 iBT); recommended—IELTS. *Application deadline:* For fall admission, 12/15 for domestic and international students; for winter admission, 2/15 for international students; for spring admission, 2/15 for domestic students; for summer admission, 7/15 for domestic students, 7/1 for international students. Applications are processed on a rolling basis. Application fee: $65. Electronic applications accepted. *Expenses: Tuition, area resident:* Full-time $13,000; part-time $723 per credit hour. Tuition, state resident: full-time $13,000; part-time $723 per credit hour. Tuition, nonresident: full-time $27,114; part-time $1507 per credit hour. *International tuition:* $27,114 full-time. *Required fees:* $196. Tuition and fees vary according to program and reciprocity agreements. *Financial support:* In 2019–20, 19 students received support, including 4 fellowships with full tuition reimbursements available (averaging $25,000 per year); health care benefits also available. Financial award application deadline: 4/15. *Unit head:* Dr. Irving G. Joshua, Professor and Chair, 502-852-5371, Fax: 502-852-6239, E-mail: igjosh01@louisville.edu. *Application contact:* Dr. Dale Schuschke, Professor and Vice Chairman, 502-852-7553, Fax: 502-852-6239, E-mail: dale.schuschke@louisville.edu. Website: http://louisville.edu/medicine/departments/physiology

**The University of Manchester,** School of Biological Sciences, Manchester, United Kingdom. Offers adaptive organismal biology (M Phil, PhD); animal biology (M Phil, PhD); biochemistry (M Phil, PhD); bioinformatics (M Phil, PhD); biomolecular sciences (M Phil, PhD); biotechnology (M Phil, PhD); cell biology (M Phil, PhD); cell matrix research (M Phil, PhD); channels and transporters (M Phil, PhD); developmental biology (M Phil, PhD); environmental biology (M Phil, PhD); evolutionary biology (M Phil, PhD); gene expression (M Phil, PhD); genetics (M Phil, PhD); history of science, technology and medicine (M Phil, PhD); immunology (M Phil, PhD); integrative neurobiology and behavior (M Phil, PhD); membrane trafficking (M Phil, PhD); microbiology (M Phil, PhD); molecular and cellular neuroscience (M Phil, PhD); molecular biology (M Phil, PhD); molecular cancer studies (M Phil, PhD); neuroscience (M Phil, PhD); ophthalmology (M Phil, PhD); optometry (M Phil, PhD); organelle function (M Phil, PhD); pharmacology (M Phil, PhD); physiology (M Phil, PhD); plant sciences (M Phil, PhD); stem cell research (M Phil, PhD); structural biology (M Phil, PhD); systems neuroscience (M Phil, PhD); toxicology (M Phil, PhD).

**University of Manitoba,** Max Rady College of Medicine and Faculty of Graduate Studies, Graduate Programs in Medicine, Department of Physiology and Pathophysiology, Winnipeg, MB R3T 2N2, Canada. Offers M Sc, PhD, MD/PhD. Terminal master's awarded for partial completion of doctoral program. *Degree requirements:* For master's, one foreign language, thesis; for doctorate, one foreign language, thesis/dissertation. *Entrance requirements:* For master's, minimum GPA of 3.5; for doctorate, minimum GPA of 3.5, M Sc.

**University of Massachusetts Amherst,** Graduate School, Interdisciplinary Programs, Program in Plant Biology, Amherst, MA 01003. Offers biochemistry and metabolism (MS, PhD); cell biology and physiology (MS, PhD); environmental, ecological and integrative biology (MS, PhD); genetics and evolution (MS, PhD). *Degree requirements:* For master's, thesis; for doctorate, 2 foreign languages, comprehensive exam, thesis/dissertation. *Entrance requirements:* For master's and doctorate, GRE General Test. Additional exam requirements/recommendations for international students: required—TOEFL (minimum score 550 paper-based; 80 iBT), IELTS (minimum score 6.5). Electronic applications accepted.

**University of Miami,** Graduate School, Miller School of Medicine, Graduate Programs in Medicine, Department of Physiology and Biophysics, Miami, FL 33124. Offers cellular physiology and molecular biophysics (MD/PhD); MD/PhD. *Faculty:* 12 full-time (3 women), 1 part-time/adjunct (0 women). *Students:* 7 full-time (5 women); includes 1 minority (Black or African American, non-Hispanic/Latino), 2 international. Average age 27. *Degree requirements:* For doctorate, thesis/dissertation, qualifying exam. *Entrance requirements:* For doctorate, GRE General Test, minimum GPA of 3.0 in sciences. Additional exam requirements/recommendations for international students: required—TOEFL (minimum score 80 paper-based), IELTS (minimum score 6.5). *Application deadline:* For fall admission, 12/1 priority date for domestic students, 12/1 for international students. Applications are processed on a rolling basis. Application fee: $100. Electronic applications accepted. *Financial support:* In 2019–20, 7 students received support, including 7 fellowships with full tuition reimbursements available (averaging $30,000 per year), 7 research assistantships with full tuition reimbursements available (averaging $30,000 per year); health care benefits and tuition waivers (full) also available. Financial award applicants required to submit FAFSA. *Unit head:* Dr. Karl Magleby, Chairman, 305-243-6236, Fax: 305-243-6898, E-mail: kmagleby@miami.edu. *Application contact:* Dr. Hans Peter Larsson, Graduate Program Director, 305-243-1021, E-mail: plarsson@miami.edu. Website: http://physiology-biophysics.med.miami.edu/

**University of Michigan,** Rackham Graduate School, Program in Biomedical Sciences (PIBS), Department of Molecular and Integrative Physiology, Ann Arbor, MI 48109-5622. Offers MS, PhD. *Degree requirements:* For master's, thesis (for some programs), capstone project (for some programs); for doctorate, thesis/dissertation, oral defense of dissertation, preliminary exam. *Entrance requirements:* For master's, GRE, MCAT, DAT or PCAT, minimum science and overall GPA of 3.0; for doctorate, GRE General Test, 3 letters of recommendation, research experience. Additional exam requirements/recommendations for international students: required—TOEFL (minimum score 84 iBT) or Michigan English Language Assessment Battery. Electronic applications accepted.

**University of Minnesota, Duluth,** Medical School, Graduate Program in Physiology, Duluth, MN 55812-2496. Offers MS, PhD. Terminal master's awarded for partial completion of doctoral program. *Degree requirements:* For master's, thesis; for doctorate, thesis/dissertation. *Entrance requirements:* For master's, GRE or MCAT; for doctorate, GRE or MCAT, 1 year of course work in each calculus, physics, and biology; 2 years of course work in chemistry; minimum GPA of 3.0 in science. Additional exam requirements/recommendations for international students: required—TOEFL.

**University of Minnesota, Twin Cities Campus,** Graduate School, Department of Integrative Biology and Physiology, Minneapolis, MN 55455-0213. Offers PhD. *Program availability:* Part-time. *Degree requirements:* For doctorate, comprehensive exam, thesis/dissertation. *Entrance requirements:* For doctorate, GRE General Test. Electronic applications accepted.

**University of Mississippi Medical Center,** School of Graduate Studies in Health Sciences, Department of Physiology and Biophysics, Jackson, MS 39216-4505. Offers PhD, MD/PhD. *Degree requirements:* For doctorate, thesis/dissertation, first authored publication. *Entrance requirements:* For doctorate, GRE General Test, minimum GPA of 3.0.

**University of Missouri,** School of Medicine and Office of Research and Graduate Studies, Graduate Programs in Medicine, Department of Medical Pharmacology and Physiology, Columbia, MO 65211. Offers MS, PhD. *Degree requirements:* For master's, thesis; for doctorate, thesis/dissertation. *Entrance requirements:* For master's and doctorate, GRE General Test, minimum GPA of 3.0. Additional exam requirements/recommendations for international students: required—TOEFL (minimum score 500 paper-based; 61 iBT).

**University of Nebraska Medical Center,** Interdisciplinary Graduate Program in Biomedical Sciences, Integrative Physiology and Molecular Medicine Doctoral Program, Omaha, NE 68198. Offers PhD. *Program availability:* Part-time. *Degree requirements:* For doctorate, comprehensive exam, thesis/dissertation, at least one first-author research publication. *Entrance requirements:* For doctorate, GRE General Test or MCAT, course work in biology, chemistry, mathematics, and physics; minimum GPA of 3.25. Additional exam requirements/recommendations for international students: required—TOEFL (minimum score 600 paper-based; 95 iBT), IELTS (minimum score 7). Electronic applications accepted.

**University of Nevada, Reno,** Graduate School, Interdisciplinary Program in Cellular and Molecular Pharmacology and Physiology, Reno, NV 89557. Offers PhD. *Degree requirements:* For doctorate, one foreign language, thesis/dissertation. *Entrance requirements:* For doctorate, GRE General Test or MCAT, minimum GPA of 3.0. Additional exam requirements/recommendations for international students: required—TOEFL (minimum score 500 paper-based; 61 iBT), IELTS (minimum score 6). Electronic applications accepted.

**University of New Mexico,** Graduate Studies, Health Sciences Center, Program in Biomedical Sciences, Albuquerque, NM 87131-5196. Offers biochemistry and molecular biology (MS, PhD); cell biology and physiology (MS, PhD); molecular genetics and microbiology (MS, PhD); neuroscience (MS, PhD); pathology (MS, PhD); toxicology (MS, PhD). *Program availability:* Part-time. Terminal master's awarded for partial completion of doctoral program. *Degree requirements:* For master's, thesis; for doctorate, comprehensive exam, thesis/dissertation, qualifying exam at the end of year 1/core curriculum. *Entrance requirements:* For master's and doctorate, GRE General Test, minimum undergraduate GPA of 3.0. Additional exam requirements/recommendations for international students: required—TOEFL. Electronic applications accepted. *Expenses:* Tuition, state resident: full-time $7633; part-time $972 per year. Tuition, nonresident: full-time $22,586; part-time $3840 per year. *International tuition:* $23,292 full-time. *Required fees:* $8608. Tuition and fees vary according to course level, course load, degree level, program and student level.

**University of North Texas Health Science Center at Fort Worth,** Graduate School of Biomedical Sciences, Fort Worth, TX 76107-2699. Offers biochemistry and cancer biology (MS, PhD); biotechnology (MS); cell biology, immunology and microbiology (MS, PhD); clinical research management (MS); forensic genetics (MS); genetics (MS, PhD); integrative physiology (MS, PhD); medical sciences (MS); pharmaceutical sciences and pharmacotherapy (MS, PhD); pharmacology and neuroscience (MS, PhD); structural anatomy and rehabilitation sciences (MS, PhD); DO/MS; DO/PhD. Terminal master's awarded for partial completion of doctoral program. *Degree requirements:* For master's, thesis; for doctorate, thesis/dissertation. *Entrance requirements:* For master's and doctorate, GRE General Test. Additional exam requirements/recommendations for international students: required—TOEFL. *Expenses:* Contact institution.

**University of Notre Dame,** The Graduate School, College of Science, Department of Biological Sciences, Notre Dame, IN 46556. Offers aquatic ecology, evolution and environmental biology (MS, PhD); cellular and molecular biology (MS, PhD); genetics (MS, PhD); physiology (MS, PhD); vector biology and parasitology (MS, PhD). Terminal master's awarded for partial completion of doctoral program. *Degree requirements:* For master's, comprehensive exam, thesis; for doctorate, comprehensive exam, thesis/dissertation, candidacy exam. *Entrance requirements:* For master's and doctorate, GRE General Test. Additional exam requirements/recommendations for international students: required—TOEFL (minimum score 600 paper-based; 80 iBT). Electronic applications accepted.

**University of Oklahoma Health Sciences Center,** College of Medicine and Graduate College, Graduate Programs in Medicine, Department of Physiology, Oklahoma City, OK 73190. Offers MS, PhD. *Program availability:* Part-time. Terminal master's awarded for partial completion of doctoral program. *Degree requirements:* For master's, thesis (for some programs); for doctorate, thesis/dissertation. *Entrance requirements:* For master's, GRE General Test, statement of career goals, 3 letters of recommendation; for doctorate, GRE General Test, 3 letters of recommendation. Additional exam requirements/recommendations for international students: required—TOEFL.

**University of Oregon,** Graduate School, College of Arts and Sciences, Department of Human Physiology, Eugene, OR 97403. Offers MS, PhD. *Degree requirements:* For master's, thesis optional; for doctorate, one foreign language, thesis/dissertation. *Entrance requirements:* For master's, GRE General Test, minimum GPA of 2.75 in undergraduate course work; for doctorate, GRE General Test.

**University of Pennsylvania,** Perelman School of Medicine, Biomedical Graduate Studies, Graduate Group in Cell and Molecular Biology, Philadelphia, PA 19104. Offers cancer biology (PhD); cell biology, physiology, and metabolism (PhD); developmental stem cell regenerative biology (PhD); gene therapy and vaccines (PhD); genetics and gene regulation (PhD); microbiology, virology, and parasitology (PhD); MD/PhD; VMD/PhD. *Faculty:* 400 full-time (118 women). *Students:* 378 full-time (221 women); includes 134 minority (6 Black or African American, non-Hispanic/Latino; 56 Asian, non-Hispanic/Latino; 58 Hispanic/Latino; 2 Native Hawaiian or other Pacific Islander, non-Hispanic/Latino; 12 Two or more races, non-Hispanic/Latino), 52 international. 851 applicants, 14% accepted, 59 enrolled. In 2019, 43 doctorates awarded. *Unit head:* Dr. Daniel Kessler, Graduate Group Chair, 215-898-1478. *Application contact:* Meagan Schofer, Associate Director, 215-898-1478. Website: http://www.med.upenn.edu/camb/

**University of Prince Edward Island,** Atlantic Veterinary College, Graduate Program in Veterinary Medicine, Charlottetown, PE C1A 4P3, Canada. Offers anatomy (M Sc, PhD); bacteriology (M Sc, PhD); clinical pharmacology (M Sc, PhD); clinical sciences (M Sc, PhD); epidemiology (M Sc, PhD), including reproduction; fish health (M Sc, PhD); food animal nutrition (M Sc, PhD); immunology (M Sc, PhD); microanatomy (M Sc, PhD); parasitology (M Sc, PhD); pathology (M Sc, PhD); pharmacology (M Sc, PhD); physiology (M Sc, PhD); toxicology (M Sc, PhD); veterinary science (M Vet Sc); virology

(M Sc, PhD). *Program availability:* Part-time. *Degree requirements:* For master's, thesis; for doctorate, thesis/dissertation. *Entrance requirements:* For master's, DVM, B Sc honors degree, or equivalent; for doctorate, M Sc. Additional exam requirements/recommendations for international students: required—TOEFL (minimum score 550 paper-based; 80 iBT). *Expenses:* Contact institution.

**University of Puerto Rico - Medical Sciences Campus,** School of Medicine, Biomedical Sciences Graduate Program, Department of Physiology, San Juan, PR 00936-5067. Offers MS, PhD. Terminal master's awarded for partial completion of doctoral program. *Degree requirements:* For master's, one foreign language, thesis; for doctorate, one foreign language, comprehensive exam, thesis/dissertation. *Entrance requirements:* For master's and doctorate, GRE General Test, GRE Subject Test, interview; course work in biology, chemistry and physics; minimum GPA of 3.0; 3 letters of recommendation. Electronic applications accepted.

**University of Rochester,** School of Medicine and Dentistry, Graduate Programs in Medicine and Dentistry, Department of Pharmacology and Physiology, Programs in Physiology, Rochester, NY 14627. Offers MS, PhD. Terminal master's awarded for partial completion of doctoral program. *Degree requirements:* For master's, thesis; for doctorate, thesis/dissertation, qualifying exam. *Entrance requirements:* For master's and doctorate, GRE General Test.

**University of Saskatchewan,** College of Medicine, Department of Anatomy, Physiology and Pharmacology, Saskatoon, SK S7N 5A2, Canada. Offers anatomy and cell biology (M Sc, PhD); pharmacology (M Sc, PhD); physiology (M Sc, PhD). *Degree requirements:* For master's, thesis; for doctorate, thesis/dissertation. *Entrance requirements:* Additional exam requirements/recommendations for international students: required—TOEFL.

**University of Saskatchewan,** Western College of Veterinary Medicine and College of Graduate and Postdoctoral Studies, Graduate Programs in Veterinary Medicine, Department of Veterinary Biomedical Sciences, Saskatoon, SK S7N 5A2, Canada. Offers veterinary anatomy (M Sc); veterinary biomedical sciences (M Vet Sc); veterinary physiological sciences (M Sc, PhD). *Degree requirements:* For master's, thesis; for doctorate, comprehensive exam (for some programs), thesis/dissertation. *Entrance requirements:* Additional exam requirements/recommendations for international students: required—TOEFL (minimum score 80 iBT); recommended—IELTS (minimum score 6.5). Electronic applications accepted.

**University of South Dakota,** Graduate School, Sanford School of Medicine and Graduate School, Biomedical Sciences Graduate Program, Physiology and Pharmacology Group, Vermillion, SD 57069. Offers MS, PhD. Terminal master's awarded for partial completion of doctoral program. *Degree requirements:* For master's, thesis; for doctorate, comprehensive exam, thesis/dissertation. *Entrance requirements:* For master's and doctorate, GRE General Test, minimum GPA of 3.0. Additional exam requirements/recommendations for international students: required—TOEFL (minimum score 550 paper-based; 80 iBT), IELTS (minimum score 6). Electronic applications accepted. *Expenses:* Contact institution.

**University of Southern California,** Keck School of Medicine and Graduate School, Graduate Programs in Medicine, Department of Physiology and Neuroscience, Los Angeles, CA 90089. Offers medical biophysics (MS); medical physiology (MS). *Program availability:* Part-time. *Faculty:* 13 full-time (2 women). *Students:* 2 full-time (both women); both minorities (both Asian, non-Hispanic/Latino). Average age 23. 10 applicants, 30% accepted, 2 enrolled. In 2019, 2 master's awarded. *Degree requirements:* For master's, thesis. *Entrance requirements:* For master's, GRE General Test, minimum GPA of 3.0. Additional exam requirements/recommendations for international students: required—TOEFL (minimum score 600 paper-based; 100 iBT). *Application deadline:* For fall admission, 4/15 priority date for domestic and international students. Applications are processed on a rolling basis. Application fee: $90. Electronic applications accepted. *Expenses:* Contact institution. *Financial support:* Application deadline: 4/15; applicants required to submit FAFSA. *Unit head:* Dr. Berislav Zlokavic, Chair, 323-442-2566, Fax: 323-442-2230, E-mail: zlokovic@usc.edu. *Application contact:* Monica Pan, Student Services Advisor, 323-442-0230, Fax: 323-442-1610, E-mail: monicap@med.usc.edu.
Website: https://keck.usc.edu/physiology-and-neuroscience/

**University of South Florida,** College of Arts and Sciences, Department of Integrative Biology, Tampa, FL 33620-9951. Offers biology (MS), including ecology and evolution, environmental and ecological microbiology, physiology and morphology. *Program availability:* Part-time. *Faculty:* 12 full-time (4 women). *Students:* 27 full-time (15 women), 3 part-time (all women); includes 5 minority (1 Black or African American, non-Hispanic/Latino; 2 Asian, non-Hispanic/Latino; 2 Hispanic/Latino), 3 international. Average age 32. 37 applicants, 24% accepted, 6 enrolled. In 2019, 4 master's, 3 doctorates awarded. *Degree requirements:* For master's, comprehensive exam, thesis (for some programs); for doctorate, comprehensive exam, thesis/dissertation. *Entrance requirements:* For master's, GRE: Preferred scores of 155V (69th percentile), 150Q (38th percentile), 4.5AW, minimum GPA of 3.0; Acceptance by faculty member; 3 letters of recommendation (see student recommendation form on department website); statement of research and professional goals; TA application; It is expected that candidates will have completed courses equivalent to those required for the BS in Biology at USF; for doctorate, GRE: 155+ (70%)V, 150+ (70%)Q, 4.5 (70%) AW, Bachelor of Science required. It is expected that candidates for the Ph.D. degree will have completed courses equivalent to those required for the B.S. in Biology at U.S.F. Acceptance by a faculty member in the Department of Integrative Biology is mandatory. Additional exam requirements/recommendations for international students: required—TOEFL. *Application deadline:* For fall admission, 11/30 priority date for domestic and international students; for spring admission, 7/1 priority date for domestic and international students. Application fee: $30. Electronic applications accepted. *Financial support:* In 2019–20, 11 students received support. Research assistantships, teaching assistantships, and unspecified assistantships available. Financial award application deadline: 6/30; financial award applicants required to submit FAFSA. *Unit head:* Dr. Valerie Harwood, Professor and Chair, 813-974-1524, Fax: 813-974-3263, E-mail: vharwood@usf.edu. *Application contact:* Dr. Stephen Deban, Associate Professor and Graduate Program Director, 813-974-2242, E-mail: sdeban@usf.edu.
Website: http://biology.usf.edu/ib/grad/

**The University of Tennessee,** Graduate School, College of Agricultural Sciences and Natural Resources, Department of Animal Science, Knoxville, TN 37996. Offers animal anatomy (PhD); breeding (MS, PhD); management (MS, PhD); nutrition (MS, PhD); physiology (MS, PhD). *Program availability:* Part-time. *Degree requirements:* For master's, thesis; for doctorate, thesis/dissertation. *Entrance requirements:* For master's and doctorate, GRE General Test, minimum GPA of 2.7. Additional exam requirements/recommendations for international students: required—TOEFL. Electronic applications accepted.

**The University of Texas Medical Branch,** Graduate School of Biomedical Sciences, Program in Human Pathophysiology and Translational Medicine, Galveston, TX 77555. Offers MS, PhD. *Degree requirements:* For master's, thesis or alternative; for doctorate, thesis/dissertation. *Entrance requirements:* For master's and doctorate, GRE General Test. Additional exam requirements/recommendations for international students: required—TOEFL (minimum score 550 paper-based). Electronic applications accepted.

**University of Toronto,** Faculty of Medicine, Department of Physiology, Toronto, ON M5S 1A1, Canada. Offers M Sc, PhD, MD/PhD. *Degree requirements:* For master's, thesis; for doctorate, thesis/dissertation. *Entrance requirements:* For master's and doctorate, minimum B+ average in final year, 2 letters of reference. Additional exam requirements/recommendations for international students: required—TOEFL (minimum score 600 paper-based), Michigan English Language Assessment Battery (minimum score 95), IELTS (minimum score 8), or COPE (minimum score 5). Electronic applications accepted.

**University of Utah,** Graduate School, College of Health, Department of Nutrition and Integrative Physiology, Salt Lake City, UT 84112. Offers nutrition and integrative physiology (MS, PhD), including integrative physiology, nutrition, nutrition and dietetics (MS). *Program availability:* Part-time, evening/weekend, 100% online. *Faculty:* 35 full-time (24 women), 33 part-time/adjunct (17 women). *Students:* 69 full-time (49 women), 5 part-time (all women); includes 7 minority (2 Asian, non-Hispanic/Latino; 2 Hispanic/Latino; 3 Two or more races, non-Hispanic/Latino), 7 international. 77 applicants, 35% accepted, 24 enrolled. In 2019, 22 master's awarded. Terminal master's awarded for partial completion of doctoral program. *Degree requirements:* For master's, comprehensive exam, thesis (for some programs); for doctorate, comprehensive exam, thesis/dissertation. *Entrance requirements:* Additional exam requirements/recommendations for international students: required—TOEFL (minimum score 80 paper-based; 550 iBT). *Application deadline:* For fall admission, 2/15 priority date for domestic students, 1/1 priority date for international students. Applications are processed on a rolling basis. Application fee: $50. Electronic applications accepted. *Expenses:* MS Dietetics: $9924 per semester resident (for 15 credits), $22,479 per semester non-resident (for 15 credits); all other MS and PhD: $5581 resident (for 15 credits), $18,146 non-resident and international (for 15 credits). *Financial support:* In 2019–20, 53 students received support, including 5 fellowships with full and partial tuition reimbursements available (averaging $25,310 per year), 19 research assistantships with full and partial tuition reimbursements available (averaging $24,750 per year), 21 teaching assistantships with full and partial tuition reimbursements available (averaging $9,871 per year); scholarships/grants and unspecified assistantships also available. Financial award application deadline: 2/15. *Unit head:* Dr. Scott Summers, Professor and Chair Department of Nutrition and Integrative Physiology, 801-581-8537, Fax: 801-585-3874, E-mail: scott.a.summers@health.utah.edu. *Application contact:* Dr. Thunder Jalili, Director of Undergraduate and Graduate Studies, 801-581-0399, Fax: 801-585-3874, E-mail: thunder.jalili@utah.edu.
Website: http://www.health.utah.edu/fdnu/

**University of Utah,** School of Medicine and Graduate School, Graduate Programs in Medicine, Department of Physiology, Salt Lake City, UT 84112-1107. Offers PhD. *Degree requirements:* For doctorate, thesis/dissertation, comprehensive qualifying exam, preliminary exam. *Entrance requirements:* For doctorate, GRE General Test, GRE Subject Test, minimum GPA of 3.0. Additional exam requirements/recommendations for international students: required—TOEFL (minimum score 650 paper-based; 100 iBT); recommended—TWE (minimum score 6). Electronic applications accepted. *Expenses:* Tuition, state resident: full-time $7085; part-time $272.51 per credit hour. Tuition, nonresident: full-time $24,937; part-time $959.12 per credit hour. *Required fees:* $880.52; $880.52 per semester. Tuition and fees vary according to degree level, program and student level.

**University of Virginia,** School of Medicine, Department of Molecular Physiology and Biological Physics, Program in Physiology, Charlottesville, VA 22903. Offers PhD, MD/PhD. *Entrance requirements:* For doctorate, GRE General Test, 2 letters of recommendation. Additional exam requirements/recommendations for international students: required—TOEFL. Electronic applications accepted.

**University of Washington,** Graduate School, School of Medicine, Graduate Programs in Medicine, Department of Physiology and Biophysics, Seattle, WA 98195. Offers PhD. *Degree requirements:* For doctorate, thesis/dissertation. *Entrance requirements:* For doctorate, GRE General Test. Additional exam requirements/recommendations for international students: required—TOEFL (minimum score 580 paper-based; 70 iBT).

**The University of Western Ontario,** Schulich School of Medicine and Dentistry, Department of Physiology and Pharmacology, London, ON N6A 3K7, Canada. Offers M Sc, PhD. *Degree requirements:* For master's, thesis, seminar course; for doctorate, comprehensive exam, thesis/dissertation. *Entrance requirements:* For master's, minimum B average, honors degree; for doctorate, minimum B average, honors degree, M Sc.

**University of Wisconsin–La Crosse,** College of Science and Health, Department of Biology, La Crosse, WI 54601. Offers aquatic sciences (MS); biology (MS); cellular and molecular biology (MS); clinical microbiology (MS); microbiology (MS); nurse anesthesia (MS); physiology (MS). *Accreditation:* AANA/CANAEP. *Program availability:* Part-time. *Faculty:* 19 full-time (7 women). *Students:* 12 full-time (6 women), 39 part-time (15 women); includes 2 minority (1 Black or African American, non-Hispanic/Latino; 1 Asian, non-Hispanic/Latino). Average age 28. 37 applicants, 68% accepted, 19 enrolled. In 2019, 19 master's awarded. *Degree requirements:* For master's, comprehensive exam, thesis. *Entrance requirements:* For master's, GRE General Test, minimum GPA of 2.85. Additional exam requirements/recommendations for international students: required—TOEFL (minimum score 550 paper-based; 79 iBT). *Application deadline:* For fall admission, 2/1 priority date for domestic and international students; for spring admission, 1/4 priority date for domestic and international students. Applications are processed on a rolling basis. Electronic applications accepted. *Financial support:* Research assistantships with partial tuition reimbursements, Federal Work-Study, scholarships/grants, health care benefits, and tuition waivers (partial) available. Support available to part-time students. Financial award application deadline: 3/15; financial award applicants required to submit FAFSA. *Unit head:* Dr. Michael Abler, Department Chair, 608-785-6962, E-mail: mabler@uwlax.edu. *Application contact:* Jennifer Weber, Senior Student Services Coordinator Graduate Admissions, 608-785-8939, E-mail: admissions@uwlax.edu.
Website: http://uwlax.edu/biology/

**University of Wisconsin–Madison,** School of Medicine and Public Health, Endocrinology-Reproductive Physiology Graduate Program, Madison, WI 53706-1380. Offers MS, PhD.

**University of Wyoming,** College of Arts and Sciences, Department of Zoology and Physiology, Laramie, WY 82071. Offers MS, PhD. *Program availability:* Part-time. *Degree requirements:* For master's, comprehensive exam (for some programs), thesis; for doctorate, comprehensive exam (for some programs), thesis/dissertation. *Entrance requirements:* For master's and doctorate, GRE General Test, minimum GPA of 3.0. Additional exam requirements/recommendations for international students: required—TOEFL. Electronic applications accepted.

**Université Laval,** Faculty of Medicine, Graduate Programs in Medicine, Programs in Physiology-Endocrinology, Québec, QC G1K 7P4, Canada. Offers M Sc, PhD. Terminal master's awarded for partial completion of doctoral program. *Degree requirements:* For

master's, thesis; for doctorate, comprehensive exam, thesis/dissertation. Electronic applications accepted.

**Virginia Commonwealth University,** Medical College of Virginia-Professional Programs, School of Medicine, Graduate Programs in Medicine, Department of Physiology and Biophysics, Richmond, VA 23284-9005. Offers molecular biology and genetics (MS); physical therapy (PhD); physiology (MS, PhD); MD/PhD. Terminal master's awarded for partial completion of doctoral program. *Degree requirements:* For master's, thesis; for doctorate, thesis/dissertation, comprehensive oral and written exams. *Entrance requirements:* For master's, GRE General Test, MCAT, or DAT; for doctorate, GRE, MCAT or DAT. Additional exam requirements/recommendations for international students: required—TOEFL (minimum score 600 paper-based; 100 iBT). Electronic applications accepted.

**Wake Forest University,** School of Medicine and Graduate School of Arts and Sciences, Graduate Programs in Medicine, Department of Physiology and Pharmacology, Winston-Salem, NC 27109. Offers pharmacology (PhD); physiology (PhD); MD/PhD. *Degree requirements:* For doctorate, thesis/dissertation. *Entrance requirements:* For doctorate, GRE General Test. Additional exam requirements/ recommendations for international students: required—TOEFL. Electronic applications accepted.

**Weill Cornell Medicine,** Weill Cornell Graduate School of Medical Sciences, Physiology, Biophysics and Systems Biology Program, New York, NY 10065. Offers MS, PhD. Terminal master's awarded for partial completion of doctoral program. *Degree requirements:* For master's, comprehensive exam; for doctorate, thesis/dissertation, final exam. *Entrance requirements:* For doctorate, GRE General Test, introductory courses in biology, inorganic and organic chemistry, physics, and mathematics.

Additional exam requirements/recommendations for international students: required— TOEFL.

**Western Michigan University,** Graduate College, College of Education and Human Development, Department of Health, Physical Education and Recreation, Kalamazoo, MI 49008. Offers athletic training (MS), including exercise physiology; sport management (MA), including pedagogy, special physical education.

**Wright State University,** Graduate School, College of Science and Mathematics, Department of Neuroscience, Cell Biology, and Physiology, Dayton, OH 45435. Offers anatomy (MS); physiology and neuroscience (MS). *Degree requirements:* For master's, thesis optional. *Entrance requirements:* Additional exam requirements/ recommendations for international students: required—TOEFL.

**Yale University,** Yale School of Medicine and Graduate School of Arts and Sciences, Combined Program in Biological and Biomedical Sciences (BBS), Physiology and Integrative Medical Biology Track, New Haven, CT 06520. Offers PhD, MD/PhD. *Entrance requirements:* Additional exam requirements/recommendations for international students: required—TOEFL.

**Youngstown State University,** College of Graduate Studies, College of Science, Technology, Engineering and Mathematics, Department of Biological Sciences, Youngstown, OH 44555-0001. Offers environmental biology (MS); molecular biology, microbiology, and genetics (MS); physiology and anatomy (MS). *Program availability:* Part-time. *Degree requirements:* For master's, comprehensive exam, thesis, oral review. *Entrance requirements:* For master's, GRE General Test, minimum GPA of 2.7. Additional exam requirements/recommendations for international students: required— TOEFL.

# Section 19
# Zoology

This section contains a directory of institutions offering graduate work in zoology. Additional information about programs listed in the directory may be obtained by writing directly to the dean of a graduate school or chair of a department at the address given in the directory.

For programs offering related work, see also in this book *Anatomy; Biochemistry; Biological and Biomedical Sciences; Cell, Molecular, and Structural Biology; Ecology, Environmental Biology, and Evolutionary Biology; Entomology; Genetics, Developmental Biology, and Reproductive Biology; Microbiological Sciences; Neuroscience and Neurobiology; Neurobiology; Physiology;* and *Veterinary Medicine and Sciences.* In the other guides in this series:

**Graduate Programs in the Physical Sciences, Mathematics, Agricultural Sciences, the Environment & Natural Resources**
See *Agricultural and Food Sciences, Environmental Sciences and Management,* and *Marine Sciences and Oceanography*
**Graduate Programs in Engineering & Applied Sciences**
See *Agricultural Engineering and Bioengineering* and *Ocean Engineering*

## CONTENTS

### Program Directories

# Animal Behavior

**Arizona State University at Tempe,** College of Liberal Arts and Sciences, School of Life Sciences, Tempe, AZ 85287-4601. Offers animal behavior (PhD); applied ethics (biomedical and health ethics) (MA); biology (MS, PhD), including biology, biology and society, complex adaptive systems science (PhD), plant biology and conservation (MS); environmental life sciences (PhD); evolutionary biology (PhD); history and philosophy of science (PhD); human and social dimensions of science and technology (PhD); microbiology (PhD); molecular and cellular biology (PhD); neuroscience (PhD). Terminal master's awarded for partial completion of doctoral program. *Degree requirements:* For master's, thesis (for some programs), interactive Program of Study (iPOS) submitted before completing 50 percent of required credit hours; for doctorate, variable foreign language requirement, comprehensive exam, thesis/dissertation, interactive Program of Study (iPOS) submitted before completing 50 percent of required credit hours. *Entrance requirements:* For master's and doctorate, GRE, minimum GPA of 3.0 or equivalent in last 2 years of work leading to bachelor's degree. Additional exam requirements/recommendations for international students: required—TOEFL (minimum score 600 paper-based; 100 iBT). Electronic applications accepted.

**Bucknell University,** Graduate Studies, College of Arts and Sciences, Department of Animal Behavior, Lewisburg, PA 17837. Offers MS. *Degree requirements:* For master's, thesis. *Entrance requirements:* For master's, GRE General Test, GRE Subject Test, minimum GPA of 3.0. Additional exam requirements/recommendations for international students: required—TOEFL (minimum score 600 paper-based).

**Cornell University,** Graduate School, Graduate Fields of Agriculture and Life Sciences, Field of Neurobiology and Behavior, Ithaca, NY 14853. Offers behavioral biology (PhD), including behavioral ecology, chemical ecology, ethology, neuroethology, sociobiology; neurobiology (PhD), including cellular and molecular neurobiology, neuroanatomy, neurochemistry, neuropharmacology, neurophysiology, sensory physiology. *Degree requirements:* For doctorate, comprehensive exam, thesis/dissertation, 1 year of teaching experience, seminar presentation. *Entrance requirements:* For doctorate, GRE General Test, GRE Subject Test (biology), 3 letters of recommendation. Additional exam requirements/recommendations for international students: required—TOEFL (minimum score 550 paper-based; 77 iBT). Electronic applications accepted.

**Emory University,** Laney Graduate School, Department of Psychology, Atlanta, GA 30322-1100. Offers clinical psychology (PhD); cognition and development (PhD); neuroscience and animal behavior (PhD). *Accreditation:* APA. *Degree requirements:* For doctorate, comprehensive exam, thesis/dissertation. *Entrance requirements:* For doctorate, GRE General Test, minimum GPA of 3.25. Additional exam requirements/recommendations for international students: required—TOEFL. Electronic applications accepted.

**Hunter College of the City University of New York,** Graduate School, School of Arts and Sciences, Department of Psychology, New York, NY 10065-5085. Offers animal behavior and conservation (MA, Certificate); general psychology (MA). *Program availability:* Part-time, evening/weekend. *Degree requirements:* For master's, comprehensive exam, thesis. *Entrance requirements:* For master's, GRE General Test, minimum 12 credits of course work in psychology, including statistics and experimental psychology; 2 letters of recommendation. Additional exam requirements/recommendations for international students: required—TOEFL.

**Illinois State University,** Graduate School, College of Arts and Sciences, School of Biological Sciences, Normal, IL 61790. Offers animal behavior (MS); bacteriology (MS); biochemistry (MS); biological sciences (MS); biology (PhD); biophysics (MS); biotechnology (MS); botany (MS, PhD); cell biology (MS); conservation biology (MS); developmental biology (MS); ecology (MS, PhD); entomology (MS); evolutionary biology (MS); genetics (MS, PhD); immunology (MS); microbiology (MS, PhD); molecular biology (MS); molecular genetics (MS); neurobiology (MS); neuroscience (MS); parasitology (MS); physiology (MS, PhD); plant biology (MS); plant molecular biology (MS); plant sciences (MS); structural biology (MS); zoology (MS, PhD). *Program availability:* Part-time. *Faculty:* 26 full-time (6 women), 7 part-time/adjunct (2 women). *Students:* 51 full-time (33 women), 15 part-time (8 women). Average age 27. 71 applicants, 28% accepted, 9 enrolled. In 2019, 14 master's, 3 doctorates awarded. *Degree requirements:* For master's, thesis or alternative; for doctorate, variable foreign language requirement, thesis/dissertation, 2 terms of residency. *Entrance requirements:* For master's, GRE General Test, minimum GPA of 2.6 in last 60 hours of course work; for doctorate, GRE General Test. *Application deadline:* Applications are processed on a rolling basis. Application fee: $50. *Expenses: Tuition, area resident:* Full-time $7956; part-time $9767 per year. Tuition, nonresident: full-time $9233; part-time $17,592 per

year. *Required fees:* $1797. *Financial support:* In 2019–20, 20 research assistantships, 41 teaching assistantships were awarded; Federal Work-Study, tuition waivers (full), and unspecified assistantships also available. Financial award application deadline: 4/1. *Unit head:* Dr. Craig Gatto, School Director, 309-438-3087, E-mail: cgatto@IllinoisState.edu. *Application contact:* Dr. Ben Sadd, Assistant Chair for Graduate Studies, 309-438-2651, E-mail: bmsadd@IllinoisState.edu.
Website: http://www.bio.ilstu.edu/

**University of California, Davis,** Graduate Studies, Graduate Group in Animal Behavior, Davis, CA 95616. Offers PhD. *Degree requirements:* For doctorate, thesis/dissertation. *Entrance requirements:* For doctorate, GRE General Test. Additional exam requirements/recommendations for international students: required—TOEFL (minimum score 550 paper-based), IELTS (minimum score 7). Electronic applications accepted.

**University of Massachusetts Amherst,** Graduate School, Interdisciplinary Programs, Program in Neuroscience and Behavior, Amherst, MA 01003. Offers animal behavior and learning (PhD); molecular and cellular neuroscience (PhD); neural and behavioral development (PhD); neuroendocrinology (PhD); neuroscience and behavior (MS); sensorimotor, cognitive, and computational neuroscience (PhD). Terminal master's awarded for partial completion of doctoral program. *Degree requirements:* For master's, thesis or alternative; for doctorate, comprehensive exam, thesis/dissertation. *Entrance requirements:* For master's, GRE General Test; for doctorate, GRE General Test; GRE Subject Test in psychology, biology, or mathematics (recommended). Additional exam requirements/recommendations for international students: required—TOEFL (minimum score 550 paper-based; 80 iBT), IELTS (minimum score 6.5). Electronic applications accepted.

**University of Minnesota, Twin Cities Campus,** Graduate School, College of Biological Sciences, Department of Ecology, Evolution, and Behavior, St. Paul, MN 55418. Offers MS, PhD. Terminal master's awarded for partial completion of doctoral program. *Degree requirements:* For master's, comprehensive exam, thesis or projects; for doctorate, comprehensive exam, thesis/dissertation. *Entrance requirements:* For master's and doctorate, GRE General Test, minimum GPA of 3.0. Additional exam requirements/recommendations for international students: required—TOEFL (minimum score 550 paper-based; 79 iBT), Michigan English Language Assessment Battery. Electronic applications accepted.

**University of Montana,** Graduate School, College of Humanities and Sciences, Department of Psychology, Missoula, MT 59812. Offers clinical psychology (PhD); experimental psychology (PhD), including animal behavior psychology, developmental psychology; school psychology (MA, PhD, Ed S). *Accreditation:* APA (one or more programs are accredited). Terminal master's awarded for partial completion of doctoral program. *Degree requirements:* For master's, thesis; for doctorate, thesis/dissertation. *Entrance requirements:* For master's, doctorate, and Ed S, GRE General Test. Additional exam requirements/recommendations for international students: required—TOEFL.

**The University of Tennessee,** Graduate School, College of Arts and Sciences, Department of Ecology and Evolutionary Biology, Knoxville, TN 37996. Offers behavior (MS, PhD); ecology (MS, PhD); evolutionary biology (MS, PhD). *Program availability:* Part-time. *Degree requirements:* For master's, thesis; for doctorate, thesis/dissertation. *Entrance requirements:* For master's and doctorate, GRE General Test, minimum GPA of 2.7. Additional exam requirements/recommendations for international students: required—TOEFL. Electronic applications accepted.

**The University of Texas at Austin,** Graduate School, College of Natural Sciences, School of Biological Sciences, Program in Ecology, Evolution and Behavior, Austin, TX 78712-1111. Offers PhD. *Entrance requirements:* For doctorate, GRE General Test. Additional exam requirements/recommendations for international students: required—TOEFL. Electronic applications accepted.

**University of Washington,** Graduate School, College of Arts and Sciences, Department of Psychology, Seattle, WA 98195. Offers animal behavior (PhD); applied child and adolescent psychology: prevention and treatment (MA); behavioral neuroscience (PhD); clinical psychology (PhD); cognition and perception (PhD); developmental psychology (PhD); quantitative psychology (PhD); social psychology and personality (PhD). *Accreditation:* APA (one or more programs are accredited). *Degree requirements:* For doctorate, thesis/dissertation. *Entrance requirements:* For doctorate, GRE General Test, minimum GPA of 3.0. Electronic applications accepted.

# Zoology

**Auburn University,** Graduate School, College of Sciences and Mathematics, Department of Biological Sciences, Auburn, AL 36849. Offers botany (MS); zoology (MS). *Program availability:* Part-time. *Faculty:* 44 full-time (22 women), 2 part-time/adjunct (1 woman). *Students:* 56 full-time (35 women), 70 part-time (39 women); includes 27 minority (10 Black or African American, non-Hispanic/Latino; 4 Asian, non-Hispanic/Latino; 5 Hispanic/Latino; 8 Two or more races, non-Hispanic/Latino), 23 international. Average age 28. 102 applicants, 48% accepted, 44 enrolled. In 2019, 26 master's, 6 doctorates awarded. *Degree requirements:* For master's, thesis (for some programs); for doctorate, thesis/dissertation. *Entrance requirements:* For master's and doctorate, GRE General Test. Additional exam requirements/recommendations for international students: required—iTEP; recommended—TOEFL (minimum score 550 paper-based; 79 iBT), IELTS (minimum score 6.5). *Application deadline:* Applications are processed on a rolling basis. Application fee: $60 ($70 for international students). Electronic applications accepted. *Expenses: Tuition, area resident:* Full-time $9828; part-time $546 per credit hour. Tuition, state resident: full-time $9828; part-time $546 per credit hour. Tuition, nonresident: full-time $29,484; part-time $1638 per credit hour. International tuition: $29,744 full-time. Tuition and fees vary according to course load, program and reciprocity agreements. *Financial support:* In 2019–20, 61 fellowships with tuition reimbursements, 28 research assistantships with tuition reimbursements (averaging $22,237 per year), 81 teaching assistantships with tuition reimbursements (averaging $27,166 per year) were awarded. Financial award application deadline: 3/15; financial award applicants required to submit FAFSA. *Unit head:* Dr. Scott R. Santos,

Chair, 334-844-7410, Fax: 334-844-1645, E-mail: santos@auburn.edu. *Application contact:* Dr. George Flowers, Dean of the Graduate School, 334-844-2125. Website: http://www.auburn.edu/cosam/departments/biology/

**Colorado State University,** College of Natural Sciences, Programs in Natural Sciences Education, Fort Collins, CO 80523. Offers material science and engineering (PhD); natural science education (MNSE); zoo, aquarium, and animal shelter management (MS). *Program availability:* 100% online. *Degree requirements:* For master's, comprehensive exam (for some programs), thesis (for some programs); for doctorate, comprehensive exam (for some programs), thesis/dissertation. *Entrance requirements:* Additional exam requirements/recommendations for international students: required—TOEFL (minimum score 550 paper-based). Electronic applications accepted. *Expenses:* Contact institution.

**Emporia State University,** Department of Biological Sciences, Emporia, KS 66801-5415. Offers botany (MS); environmental biology (MS); forensic science (MS); general biology (MS); microbial and cellular biology (MS); zoology (MS). *Program availability:* Part-time. *Degree requirements:* For master's, comprehensive exam or thesis. *Entrance requirements:* For master's, GRE, appropriate undergraduate degree, interview, letters of reference. Additional exam requirements/recommendations for international students: required—TOEFL (minimum score 520 paper-based; 68 iBT). Electronic applications accepted. *Expenses: Tuition, area resident:* Full-time $6394; part-time $266.41 per credit hour. Tuition, state resident: full-time $6394; part-time $266.41 per credit hour. Tuition, nonresident: full-time $20,128; part-time $828.66 per credit hour. *International*

tuition: $20,128 full-time. *Required fees:* $2183; $90.95 per credit hour. Tuition and fees vary according to campus/location and program.

**Illinois State University,** Graduate School, College of Arts and Sciences, School of Biological Sciences, Normal, IL 61790. Offers animal behavior (MS); bacteriology (MS); biochemistry (MS); biological sciences (MS); biology (PhD); biophysics (MS); biotechnology (MS); botany (MS, PhD); cell biology (MS); conservation biology (MS); developmental biology (MS); ecology (MS, PhD); entomology (MS); evolutionary biology (MS); genetics (MS, PhD); immunology (MS); microbiology (MS, PhD); molecular biology (MS); molecular genetics (MS); neurobiology (MS); neuroscience (MS); parasitology (MS); physiology (MS, PhD); plant biology (MS); plant molecular biology (MS); plant sciences (MS); structural biology (MS); zoology (MS, PhD). *Program availability:* Part-time. *Faculty:* 26 full-time (6 women), 7 part-time/adjunct (2 women). *Students:* 51 full-time (33 women), 15 part-time (8 women). Average age 27. 71 applicants, 28% accepted, 9 enrolled. In 2019, 14 master's, 3 doctorates awarded. *Degree requirements:* For master's, thesis or alternative; for doctorate, variable foreign language requirement, thesis/dissertation, 2 terms of residency. *Entrance requirements:* For master's, GRE General Test, minimum GPA of 2.6 in last 60 hours of course work; for doctorate, GRE General Test. *Application deadline:* Applications are processed on a rolling basis. Application fee: $50. *Expenses: Tuition, area resident:* Full-time $7956; part-time $9767 per year. Tuition, nonresident: full-time $9233; part-time $17,592 per year. *Required fees:* $1797. *Financial support:* In 2019–20, 20 research assistantships, 41 teaching assistantships were awarded; Federal Work-Study, tuition waivers (full), and unspecified assistantships also available. Financial award application deadline: 4/1. *Unit head:* Dr. Craig Gatto, School Director, 309-438-3087, E-mail: cgatto@IllinoisState.edu. *Application contact:* Dr. Ben Sadd, Assistant Chair for Graduate Studies, 309-438-2651, E-mail: bmsadd@IllinoisState.edu.
Website: http://www.bio.ilstu.edu/

**Indiana University Bloomington,** University Graduate School, College of Arts and Sciences, Department of Biology, Bloomington, IN 47405. Offers biology teaching (MAT); biotechnology (MA); evolution, ecology, and behavior (MA, PhD); genetics (PhD); microbiology (MA, PhD); molecular, cellular, and developmental biology (PhD); plant sciences (MA, PhD); zoology (MA, PhD). Terminal master's awarded for partial completion of doctoral program. *Degree requirements:* For master's, thesis, oral defense; for doctorate, thesis/dissertation, oral defense. *Entrance requirements:* For master's and doctorate, GRE General Test. Additional exam requirements/recommendations for international students: required—TOEFL (minimum score 100 iBT). Electronic applications accepted.

**Michigan State University,** The Graduate School, College of Natural Science, Department of Integrative Biology, East Lansing, MI 48824. Offers MS, PhD. *Entrance requirements:* Additional exam requirements/recommendations for international students: required—TOEFL. Electronic applications accepted.

**North Dakota State University,** College of Graduate and Interdisciplinary Studies, College of Science and Mathematics, Department of Biological Sciences, Fargo, ND 58102. Offers biology (MS); botany (MS, PhD); zoology (MS, PhD). *Entrance requirements:* For master's and doctorate, GRE General Test. Additional exam requirements/recommendations for international students: required—TOEFL. Electronic applications accepted. Tuition and fees vary according to program and reciprocity agreements.

**Southern Illinois University Carbondale,** Graduate School, College of Science, Department of Zoology, Carbondale, IL 62901-4701. Offers MS, PhD. *Degree requirements:* For master's, thesis; for doctorate, thesis/dissertation. *Entrance requirements:* For master's, GRE, minimum GPA of 2.7; for doctorate, GRE, minimum GPA of 3.25. Additional exam requirements/recommendations for international students: required—TOEFL.

**Texas Tech University,** Graduate School, College of Arts and Sciences, Department of Biological Sciences, Lubbock, TX 79409-3131. Offers biology (MS, PhD); environmental sustainability and natural resource management (PSM); microbiology (MS); zoology (MS, PhD). *Program availability:* Part-time, blended/hybrid learning. *Faculty:* 45 full-time (16 women). *Students:* 131 full-time (71 women), 21 part-time (12 women); includes 22 minority (4 Black or African American, non-Hispanic/Latino; 1 Asian, non-Hispanic/Latino; 11 Hispanic/Latino; 6 Two or more races, non-Hispanic/Latino), 66 international. Average age 29. 80 applicants, 48% accepted, 34 enrolled. In 2019, 13 master's, 6 doctorates awarded. *Degree requirements:* For master's, comprehensive exam, thesis or alternative; for doctorate, comprehensive exam, thesis/dissertation. *Entrance requirements:* For master's and doctorate, GRE General Test. Additional exam requirements/recommendations for international students: required—TOEFL (minimum score 550 paper-based; 79 iBT). *Application deadline:* For fall admission, 6/1 priority date for domestic students, 1/15 priority date for international students; for spring admission, 9/1 priority date for domestic students, 6/15 priority date for international students. Applications are processed on a rolling basis. Application fee: $65. Electronic applications accepted. *Expenses:* Contact institution. *Financial support:* In 2019–20, 140 students received support, including 114 fellowships (averaging $1,560 per year), 22 research assistantships (averaging $19,738 per year), 114 teaching assistantships (averaging $17,489 per year); Federal Work-Study and health care benefits also available. Financial award application deadline: 2/15; financial award applicants required to submit FAFSA. *Unit head:* Dr. John Zak, Professor, Chair and Associate Dean, 806-834-2682, Fax: 806-742-2963, E-mail: john.zak@ttu.edu. *Application contact:* Dr. Lou Densmore, Graduate Adviser, 806-834-6479, Fax: 806-742-2963, E-mail: lou.densmore@ttu.edu.
Website: www.depts.ttu.edu/biology/

**Uniformed Services University of the Health Sciences,** F. Edward Hebert School of Medicine, Graduate Programs in the Biomedical Sciences and Public Health, Bethesda, MD 20814. Offers emerging infectious diseases (PhD); medical and clinical psychology (PhD), including clinical psychology, medical psychology; medicine (MS, PhD), including health professions education; molecular and cell biology (MS, PhD); neuroscience (PhD); preventive medicine and biometrics (MPH, MS, MSPH, MTMH, PhD), including environmental health sciences (PhD), healthcare administration and policy (MS), medical zoology (PhD), public health (MPH, MSPH), tropical medicine and hygiene (MTMH). Terminal master's awarded for partial completion of doctoral program. *Degree requirements:* For master's, comprehensive exam, thesis or alternative; for doctorate, comprehensive exam, thesis/dissertation, qualifying exam. *Entrance requirements:* For master's, GRE General Test; for doctorate, GRE General Test, minimum GPA of 3.0. Electronic applications accepted. *Expenses:* Contact institution.

**Uniformed Services University of the Health Sciences,** F. Edward Hebert School of Medicine, Graduate Programs in the Biomedical Sciences and Public Health, Department of Preventive Medicine and Biostatistics, Program in Medical Zoology, Bethesda, MD 20814-4799. Offers PhD. *Degree requirements:* For doctorate, comprehensive exam, thesis/dissertation, qualifying exam. *Entrance requirements:* For doctorate, GRE General Test, GRE Subject Test, minimum GPA of 3.0, U.S. citizenship. Additional exam requirements/recommendations for international students: required—TOEFL.

**The University of British Columbia,** Faculty of Science, Department of Zoology, Vancouver, BC V6T 1Z4, Canada. Offers M Sc, PhD. *Degree requirements:* For master's, thesis, final defense; for doctorate, comprehensive exam, thesis/dissertation, final defense. *Entrance requirements:* For master's and doctorate, faculty support. Additional exam requirements/recommendations for international students: required—TOEFL. Electronic applications accepted. *Expenses:* Contact institution.

**University of California, Davis,** Graduate Studies, Graduate Group in Avian Sciences, Davis, CA 95616. Offers MS. *Degree requirements:* For master's, comprehensive exam (for some programs), thesis (for some programs). *Entrance requirements:* For master's, GRE General Test, minimum GPA of 3.0. Additional exam requirements/recommendations for international students: required—TOEFL (minimum score 550 paper-based). Electronic applications accepted.

**University of Florida,** Graduate School, College of Liberal Arts and Sciences, Department of Biology, Gainesville, FL 32611. Offers botany (MS, MST, PhD), including botany, tropical conservation and development, wetland sciences; zoology (MS, MST, PhD), including animal molecular and cellular biology (PhD), tropical conservation and development, wetland sciences, zoology. *Degree requirements:* For master's, comprehensive exam (for some programs), thesis; for doctorate, comprehensive exam, thesis/dissertation. *Entrance requirements:* For master's and doctorate, GRE General Test, minimum GPA of 3.0. Additional exam requirements/recommendations for international students: required—TOEFL (minimum score 550 paper-based; 80 iBT), IELTS (minimum score 6). Electronic applications accepted.

**University of Guelph,** Office of Graduate and Postdoctoral Studies, College of Biological Science, Department of Integrative Biology, Botany and Zoology, Guelph, ON N1G 2W1, Canada. Offers botany (M Sc, PhD); zoology (M Sc, PhD). *Program availability:* Part-time. *Degree requirements:* For master's, thesis, research proposal; for doctorate, thesis/dissertation, research proposal, qualifying exam. *Entrance requirements:* For master's, minimum B average during previous 2 years of course work. Additional exam requirements/recommendations for international students: required—TOEFL (minimum score 550 paper-based), IELTS (minimum score 6.5). Electronic applications accepted.

**University of Hawaii at Manoa,** Office of Graduate Education, College of Natural Sciences, Department of Biology, Honolulu, HI 96822. Offers zoology (MS, PhD). *Program availability:* Part-time. *Degree requirements:* For master's, one foreign language, thesis optional; for doctorate, one foreign language, comprehensive exam, thesis/dissertation, seminar. *Entrance requirements:* For master's and doctorate, GRE General Test, GRE Subject Test. Additional exam requirements/recommendations for international students: required—TOEFL (minimum score 600 paper-based; 100 iBT), IELTS (minimum score 7).

**University of Illinois at Urbana-Champaign,** Graduate College, College of Liberal Arts and Sciences, School of Integrative Biology, Department of Animal Biology, Champaign, IL 61820. Offers animal biology (ecology, ethology and evolution) (MS, PhD).

**University of Maine,** Graduate School, College of Natural Sciences, Forestry, and Agriculture, School of Biology and Ecology, Orono, ME 04469. Offers biological sciences (PhD); botany and plant pathology (MS); entomology (MS); zoology (MS, PhD). *Program availability:* Part-time. *Faculty:* 30 full-time (16 women), 2 part-time/adjunct (1 woman). *Students:* 84 full-time (54 women), 12 part-time (6 women); includes 9 minority (1 Black or African American, non-Hispanic/Latino; 1 American Indian or Alaska Native, non-Hispanic/Latino; 1 Asian, non-Hispanic/Latino; 5 Hispanic/Latino; 1 Two or more races, non-Hispanic/Latino), 21 international. Average age 30. 62 applicants, 40% accepted, 22 enrolled. In 2019, 12 master's, 12 doctorates awarded. Terminal master's awarded for partial completion of doctoral program. *Degree requirements:* For master's, thesis (for some programs); for doctorate, comprehensive exam, thesis/dissertation. *Entrance requirements:* For master's and doctorate, GRE General Test. Additional exam requirements/recommendations for international students: required—TOEFL (minimum score 80 iBT), IELTS (minimum score 6.5). *Application deadline:* For fall admission, 2/1 priority date for domestic students. Applications are processed on a rolling basis. Application fee: $65. Electronic applications accepted. *Expenses: Tuition, area resident:* Full-time $8100; part-time $450 per credit hour. Tuition, state resident: full-time $8100; part-time $450 per credit hour. Tuition, nonresident: full-time $26,388; part-time $1466 per credit hour. *International tuition:* $26,388 full-time. *Required fees:* $1257; $278 per semester. Tuition and fees vary according to course load. *Financial support:* In 2019–20, 108 students received support, including 1 fellowship with full tuition reimbursement available (averaging $25,000 per year), 79 research assistantships with full tuition reimbursements available (averaging $15,825 per year), 23 teaching assistantships with full tuition reimbursements available (averaging $15,825 per year); career-related internships or fieldwork, Federal Work-Study, institutionally sponsored loans, tuition waivers (full and partial), and unspecified assistantships also available. Financial award application deadline: 3/1; financial award applicants required to submit FAFSA. *Unit head:* Dr. Andrei Aloykhin, Director, 207-581-2977, Fax: 207-581-2537. *Application contact:* Scott G. Delcourt, Assistant Vice President for Graduate Studies and Senior Associate Dean, 207-581-3291, Fax: 207-581-3232, E-mail: graduate@maine.edu.
Website: http://sbe.umaine.edu/

**University of Manitoba,** Faculty of Graduate Studies, Faculty of Science, Department of Biological Sciences, Winnipeg, MB R3T 2N2, Canada. Offers botany (M Sc, PhD); ecology (M Sc, PhD); zoology (M Sc, PhD).

**University of Montana,** Graduate School, College of Humanities and Sciences, Division of Biological Sciences, Program in Organismal Biology and Ecology, Missoula, MT 59812. Offers MS, PhD. Terminal master's awarded for partial completion of doctoral program. *Degree requirements:* For master's, one foreign language, thesis; for doctorate, 2 foreign languages, thesis/dissertation. *Entrance requirements:* For master's and doctorate, GRE General Test.

**University of North Dakota,** Graduate School, College of Arts and Sciences, Department of Biology, Grand Forks, ND 58202. Offers biology (MS); fisheries/wildlife (PhD); genetics (PhD); zoology (PhD). Terminal master's awarded for partial completion of doctoral program. *Degree requirements:* For master's, thesis, final exam; for doctorate, comprehensive exam, thesis/dissertation, final exam. *Entrance requirements:* For master's, GRE General Test, GRE Subject Test, minimum GPA of 3.0; for doctorate, GRE General Test, GRE Subject Test, minimum GPA of 3.5. Additional exam requirements/recommendations for international students: required—TOEFL (minimum score 550 paper-based; 79 iBT), IELTS (minimum score 6.5). Electronic applications accepted.

**University of Wisconsin–Madison,** Graduate School, College of Letters and Science, Department of Zoology, Madison, WI 53706-1380. Offers MA, MS, PhD. *Program availability:* Part-time. *Degree requirements:* For master's, thesis; for doctorate, one foreign language, thesis/dissertation. *Entrance requirements:* For master's and doctorate, GRE General Test. Additional exam requirements/recommendations for international students: required—TOEFL. Electronic applications accepted.

**University of Wisconsin–Oshkosh,** Graduate Studies, College of Letters and Science, Department of Biology and Microbiology, Oshkosh, WI 54901. Offers biology (MS),

## Zoology

including botany, microbiology, zoology. *Degree requirements:* For master's, comprehensive exam, thesis. *Entrance requirements:* For master's, GRE General Test, minimum GPA of 3.0, BS in biology. Additional exam requirements/recommendations for international students: required—TOEFL (minimum score 550 paper-based; 79 iBT). Electronic applications accepted.

**University of Wyoming,** College of Arts and Sciences, Department of Zoology and Physiology, Laramie, WY 82071. Offers MS, PhD. *Program availability:* Part-time. *Degree requirements:* For master's, comprehensive exam (for some programs), thesis; for doctorate, comprehensive exam (for some programs), thesis/dissertation. *Entrance requirements:* For master's and doctorate, GRE General Test, minimum GPA of 3.0. Additional exam requirements/recommendations for international students: required—TOEFL. Electronic applications accepted.

**Western Illinois University,** School of Graduate Studies, College of Arts and Sciences, Department of Biological Sciences, Macomb, IL 61455-1390. Offers biology (MS); environmental GIS (Certificate); zoo and aquarium studies (Certificate). *Program availability:* Part-time. *Entrance requirements:* Additional exam requirements/ recommendations for international students: required—TOEFL (minimum score 550 paper-based; 80 iBT); recommended—IELTS. Electronic applications accepted.

**West Liberty University,** College of Sciences, West Liberty, WV 26074. Offers biology (MA, MS); biomedical science (MA); physician assistant studies (MS); zoo science (MA, MS).

# ACADEMIC AND PROFESSIONAL PROGRAMS IN HEALTH-RELATED PROFESSIONS

# Section 20
# Allied Health

This section contains a directory of institutions offering graduate work in allied health, followed by an in-depth entry submitted by an institution that chose to prepare a detailed program description. Additional information about programs listed in the directory but not augmented by an in-depth entry may be obtained by writing directly to the dean of a graduate school or chair of a department at the address given in the directory.

For programs offering related work, see also in this book *Anatomy, Biophysics, Dentistry and Dental Sciences, Health Services, Microbiological Sciences, Pathology and Pathobiology, Physiology,* and *Public Health.* In the other guides in this series:

**Graduate Programs in the Humanities, Arts & Social Sciences**

See *Art and Art History (Art Therapy), Family and Consumer Sciences (Gerontology), Performing Arts (Therapies),* and *Psychology and Counseling'*

**Graduate Programs in the Physical Sciences, Mathematics, Agricultural Sciences, the Environment & Natural Resources**

See *Physics (Acoustics)*

**Graduate Programs in Engineering & Applied Sciences**

See *Agricultural Engineering and Bioengineering (Bioengineering), Biomedical Engineering and Biotechnology,* and *Energy and Power Engineering (Nuclear Engineering)*

**Graduate Programs in Business, Education, Information Studies, Law & Social Work**

See *Administration, Instruction, and Theory (Educational Psychology); Special Focus (Education of the Multiply Handicapped); Social Work;* and *Subject Areas (Counselor Education)*

## CONTENTS

### Program Directories

# Allied Health—General

**Alabama State University,** College of Health Sciences, Montgomery, AL 36101-0271. Offers MRC, MS, DPT. *Program availability:* Part-time. *Faculty:* 19 full-time (16 women), 19 part-time/adjunct (10 women). *Students:* 183 full-time (128 women), 1 part-time (0 women); includes 76 minority (64 Black or African American, non-Hispanic/Latino; 1 American Indian or Alaska Native, non-Hispanic/Latino; 6 Hispanic/Latino; 5 Two or more races, non-Hispanic/Latino). Average age 25. 146 applicants, 50% accepted, 71 enrolled. In 2019, 33 master's, 23 doctorates awarded. Terminal master's awarded for partial completion of doctoral program. *Degree requirements:* For master's, comprehensive exam; for doctorate, thesis/dissertation or alternative. *Entrance requirements:* For doctorate, GRE (recommended minimum scores: Verbal 145, Quantitative 140), baccalaureate degree from accredited educational institution with minimum cumulative GPA of 3.0. Additional exam requirements/recommendations for international students: required—TOEFL (minimum score 500 paper-based). *Application deadline:* For fall admission, 4/15 for domestic and international students; for spring admission, 11/15 for domestic and international students; for summer admission, 3/15 for domestic and international students. Applications are processed on a rolling basis. Application fee: $25. Electronic applications accepted. *Financial support:* In 2019–20, 3 students received support. Research assistantships, Federal Work-Study, scholarships/grants, tuition waivers (partial), and unspecified assistantships available. Financial award application deadline: 6/30; financial award applicants required to submit FAFSA. *Unit head:* Dr. Charlene Portee, Dean, College of Health Sciences, 334-229-5053, E-mail: cportee@alasu.edu. *Application contact:* Dr. Ed Brown, Dean of Graduate Studies, 334-229-4274, Fax: 334-229-4928, E-mail: ebrown@alasu.edu.
Website: http://www.alasu.edu/academics/colleges—departments/health-sciences/index.aspx

**American College of Healthcare Sciences,** Graduate Programs, Portland, OR 97239-3719. Offers anatomy and physiology (Graduate Certificate); aromatherapy (MS, Graduate Certificate); botanical safety (Graduate Certificate); complementary alternative medicine (MS, Graduate Certificate); health and wellness (MS); herbal medicine (MS, Graduate Certificate); holistic nutrition (MS, Graduate Certificate); wellness coaching (Graduate Certificate). *Program availability:* Part-time, evening/weekend, online learning. *Degree requirements:* For master's, capstone project. *Entrance requirements:* For master's, interview, letters of recommendation, essay.

**Andrews University,** College of Health and Human Services, Department of Medical Laboratory Sciences, Berrien Springs, MI 49104. Offers MSMLS. *Accreditation:* APTA. *Faculty:* 2 full-time (1 woman). *Students:* 4 full-time (2 women); includes 2 minority (1 Asian, non-Hispanic/Latino; 1 Hispanic/Latino), 2 international. Average age 33. In 2019, 1 master's awarded. *Entrance requirements:* For master's, GRE. Additional exam requirements/recommendations for international students: required—TOEFL (minimum score 550 paper-based). *Application deadline:* Applications are processed on a rolling basis. Application fee: $60. Electronic applications accepted. *Financial support:* Research assistantships, teaching assistantships, Federal Work-Study, institutionally sponsored loans, and scholarships/grants available. *Unit head:* Karen Reiner, Chair, 269-471-3336. *Application contact:* Jillian Panigot, Director, University Admissions, 800-253-2874, Fax: 269-471-6321, E-mail: graduate@andrews.edu.
Website: http://www.andrews.edu/shp/mls/

**Athabasca University,** Faculty of Health Disciplines, Athabasca, AB T9S 3A3, Canada. Offers advanced nursing practice (MN, Advanced Diploma); generalist (MN); health studies (MHS). *Program availability:* Part-time, online learning. *Degree requirements:* For master's, comprehensive exam (for some programs). *Entrance requirements:* For master's, bachelor's degree in health-related field and 2 years of professional health service experience (MHS); bachelor's degree in nursing and 2 years' nursing experience (MN); minimum GPA of 3.0 in final 30 credits; for Advanced Diploma, RN license, 2 years of health care experience. Electronic applications accepted. *Expenses:* Contact institution.

**A.T. Still University,** Arizona School of Health Sciences, Mesa, AZ 85206. Offers advanced occupational therapy (MS); advanced physician assistant studies (MS); athletic training (MS, DAT); audiology (Au D); clinical decision making in athletic training (Graduate Certificate); occupational therapy (MS, OTD); orthopedic rehabilitation (Graduate Certificate); physical therapy (DPT); physician assistant studies (MS); post-professional audiology (Au D); post-professional physical therapy (DPT). *Accreditation:* AOTA (one or more programs are accredited); ASHA. *Program availability:* Part-time, evening/weekend, online only, 100% online, blended/hybrid learning. *Faculty:* 94 full-time (74 women), 203 part-time/adjunct (145 women). *Students:* 736 full-time (528 women), 289 part-time (195 women); includes 315 minority (53 Black or African American, non-Hispanic/Latino; 7 American Indian or Alaska Native, non-Hispanic/Latino; 94 Asian, non-Hispanic/Latino; 134 Hispanic/Latino; 2 Native Hawaiian or other Pacific Islander, non-Hispanic/Latino; 25 Two or more races, non-Hispanic/Latino), 79 international. Average age 32. 4,387 applicants, 20% accepted, 514 enrolled. In 2019, 153 master's, 344 doctorates, 2 other advanced degrees awarded. *Degree requirements:* For master's, thesis (for some programs); for doctorate, thesis/dissertation (for some programs). *Entrance requirements:* For master's, GRE General Test; for doctorate, GRE, Physical Therapist Evaluation Tool (for DPT), current state licensure. Additional exam requirements/recommendations for international students: required—TOEFL (minimum score 80 iBT). *Application deadline:* For fall admission, 7/7 for domestic and international students; for winter admission, 10/3 for domestic and international students; for spring admission, 1/16 for domestic and international students; for summer admission, 4/17 for domestic and international students. Applications are processed on a rolling basis. Application fee: $70. *Financial support:* In 2019–20, 170 students received support. Federal Work-Study and scholarships/grants available. Financial award application deadline: 6/1; financial award applicants required to submit FAFSA. *Unit head:* Dr. Ann Lee Burch, Dean, 480-219-6061, E-mail: aburch@atsu.edu. *Application contact:* Donna Sparks, Director, Admissions Processing, 660-626-2117, Fax: 660-626-2969, E-mail: admissions@atsu.edu.
Website: http://www.atsu.edu/ashs

**Augusta University,** College of Allied Health Sciences, Program in Applied Health Sciences, Augusta, GA 30912. Offers diagnostic sciences (PhD); health care outcomes (PhD); rehabilitation science (PhD). *Program availability:* Part-time, online learning. *Entrance requirements:* For doctorate, GRE General Test, bachelor's degree, official transcripts, minimum undergraduate GPA of 3.0, three letters of recommendation. Additional exam requirements/recommendations for international students: required—TOEFL (minimum score 550 paper-based; 79 iBT). Electronic applications accepted.

**Belmont University,** College of Health Sciences, Nashville, TN 37212. Offers nursing (MSN, DNP); occupational therapy (MSOT, OTD); physical therapy (DPT). *Program availability:* Part-time, blended/hybrid learning. *Faculty:* 26 full-time (20 women), 30 part-time/adjunct (21 women). *Students:* 416 full-time (362 women), 8 part-time (7 women); includes 36 minority (7 Black or African American, non-Hispanic/Latino; 12 Asian, non-Hispanic/Latino; 9 Hispanic/Latino; 8 Two or more races, non-Hispanic/Latino). Average age 26. *Degree requirements:* For master's, comprehensive exam, thesis; for doctorate, comprehensive exam. *Entrance requirements:* For master's, GRE, BSN, minimum GPA of 3.0. Additional exam requirements/recommendations for international students: required—TOEFL (minimum score 550 paper-based). *Application deadline:* Applications are processed on a rolling basis. Application fee: $50. Electronic applications accepted. *Expenses:* Contact institution. *Financial support:* Teaching assistantships with full tuition reimbursements, career-related internships or fieldwork, scholarships/grants, and traineeships available. Financial award application deadline: 3/1; financial award applicants required to submit FAFSA. *Unit head:* Dr. Cathy Taylor, Dean, 615-460-6916, Fax: 615-460-6750. *Application contact:* Bill Nichols, Director of Enrollment Services, 615-460-6107, E-mail: bill.nichols@belmont.edu.
Website: http://www.belmont.edu/healthsciences/

**Bennington College,** Graduate Programs, Post Baccalaureate Premedical Program, Bennington, VT 05201. Offers allied and health sciences (Certificate). Electronic applications accepted. *Expenses:* Contact institution.

**Boston University,** College of Health and Rehabilitation Sciences: Sargent College, Boston, MA 02215. Offers MS, DPT, OTD, PhD. *Accreditation:* APTA (one or more programs are accredited). *Program availability:* Blended/hybrid learning. *Faculty:* 58 full-time (44 women), 27 part-time/adjunct (18 women). *Students:* 443 full-time (350 women), 90 part-time (82 women); includes 128 minority (12 Black or African American, non-Hispanic/Latino; 64 Asian, non-Hispanic/Latino; 35 Hispanic/Latino; 1 Native Hawaiian or other Pacific Islander, non-Hispanic/Latino; 16 Two or more races, non-Hispanic/Latino), 43 international. Average age 26. 1,536 applicants, 31% accepted, 168 enrolled. In 2019, 73 master's, 96 doctorates awarded. Terminal master's awarded for partial completion of doctoral program. *Entrance requirements:* Additional exam requirements/recommendations for international students: required—TOEFL. Application fee: $95. Electronic applications accepted. *Financial support:* Research assistantships, teaching assistantships, career-related internships or fieldwork, Federal Work-Study, institutionally sponsored loans, scholarships/grants, and health care benefits available. Support available to part-time students. Financial award applicants required to submit FAFSA. *Unit head:* Dr. Christopher Moore, Dean, 617-353-2705, Fax: 617-353-7500, E-mail: mooreca@bu.edu. *Application contact:* Sharon Sankey, Assistant Dean, Student Services, 617-353-2713, Fax: 617-353-7500, E-mail: ssankey@bu.edu.
Website: http://www.bu.edu/sargent/

**Brock University,** Faculty of Graduate Studies, Faculty of Applied Health Sciences, St. Catharines, ON L2S 3A1, Canada. Offers M Sc, MA, PhD. *Degree requirements:* For master's, thesis. *Entrance requirements:* For master's, honors degree, BA and/or B Sc. Additional exam requirements/recommendations for international students: required—TOEFL (minimum score 550 paper-based; 80 iBT), IELTS (minimum score 6.5), TWE (minimum score 4). Electronic applications accepted.

**Canisius College,** Graduate Division, School of Education and Human Services, Office of Professional Studies, Buffalo, NY 14208-1098. Offers applied nutrition (MS, Certificate); community and school health (MS); health and human performance (MS); health information technology (MS); respiratory care (MS). *Program availability:* Part-time, evening/weekend, 100% online, blended/hybrid learning. *Faculty:* 1 full-time (0 women), 20 part-time/adjunct (11 women). *Students:* 12 full-time (8 women), 28 part-time (17 women); includes 9 minority (3 Black or African American, non-Hispanic/Latino; 1 Asian, non-Hispanic/Latino; 3 Hispanic/Latino; 2 Two or more races, non-Hispanic/Latino). Average age 33. 24 applicants, 88% accepted, 11 enrolled. In 2019, 27 master's awarded. *Degree requirements:* For master's, thesis (for some programs), Programs require Thesis/Project or Internship. *Entrance requirements:* For master's, GRE recommended, bachelor's degree transcript, two letters of recommendation, current licensure (for applied nutrition), minimum GPA of 2.7, current resume. Additional exam requirements/recommendations for international students: required—TOEFL (550+ PBT or 79+ IBT), IELTS (6.5+), or CAEL (70+). *Application deadline:* Applications are processed on a rolling basis. Electronic applications accepted. *Expenses: Tuition:* Part-time $900 per credit. *Required fees:* $25 per credit hour. $65 per term. Part-time tuition and fees vary according to course load and program. *Financial support:* Career-related internships or fieldwork, Federal Work-Study, scholarships/grants, tuition waivers (partial), and unspecified assistantships available. Support available to part-time students. Financial award application deadline: 4/30; financial award applicants required to submit FAFSA. *Unit head:* Dennis W. Koch, Director, Office of Professional Studies, 716-888-8292, E-mail: koch5@canisius.edu. *Application contact:* Dennis W. Koch, Director, Office of Professional Studies, 716-888-8292, E-mail: koch5@canisius.edu.
Website: http://www.canisius.edu/graduate/

**Cleveland State University,** College of Graduate Studies, College of Sciences and Health Professions, School of Health Sciences, Program in Health Sciences, Cleveland, OH 44115. Offers health sciences (MS); physician assistant science (MS). *Program availability:* Part-time, evening/weekend, online learning. *Entrance requirements:* For master's, GRE (minimum scores of 50th percentile in all areas; analytical writing 3.5), bachelor's degree from accredited institution, minimum prerequisite course GPA of 3.0, all courses completed with minimum grade of C. Additional exam requirements/recommendations for international students: required—TOEFL (minimum score 550 paper-based; 78 iBT). Electronic applications accepted. *Expenses:* Tuition, state resident: full-time $10,215; part-time $6810 per credit hour. Tuition, nonresident: full-time $17,496; part-time $11,664 per credit hour. *International tuition:* $19,316 full-time. Tuition and fees vary according to degree level and program.

**Concordia University, St. Paul,** College of Health and Science, St. Paul, MN 55104-5494. Offers exercise science (MS); orthotics and prosthetics (MS); physical therapy (DPT); sports management (MA). *Program availability:* Part-time, evening/weekend, 100% online, blended/hybrid learning. *Degree requirements:* For master's, comprehensive exam (for some programs), thesis (for some programs); for doctorate, at least one 8-12 week clinical rotation outside the St. Paul area. *Entrance requirements:* For master's, official transcripts from regionally-accredited institution stating the conferral of a bachelor's degree with minimum cumulative GPA of 3.0; personal statement; resume; for doctorate, GRE, official transcript from regionally-accredited institution showing bachelor's degree and minimum coursework GPA of 3.0; 100 physical therapy observation hours; two letters of professional recommendation. Additional exam requirements/recommendations for international students: recommended—TOEFL (minimum score 547 paper-based; 78 iBT), IELTS (minimum score 6), TSE (minimum score 52). Electronic applications accepted. *Expenses:* Contact institution.

**Creighton University,** School of Pharmacy and Health Professions, Omaha, NE 68178-0001. Offers MS, DPT, OTD, Pharm D, Pharm D/MS. *Accreditation:* ACPE (one or more programs are accredited). *Program availability:* Online learning. *Entrance requirements:* For doctorate, PCAT (for Pharm D); GRE (for DPT). Electronic applications accepted. *Expenses:* Contact institution.

**Dominican College,** Division of Allied Health, Orangeburg, NY 10962-1210. Offers MS, DPT. *Program availability:* Part-time, evening/weekend, online learning. *Degree requirements:* For master's, Official transcripts, personal statement, interview, resume (MBA) and 3 letters of recommendation are required; for doctorate, Official transcripts showing 3.0 GPA in undergraduate coursework and 3.5 GPA in graduate coursework, personal statement, interview, resume, Current Licensure as a Registered Nurse and Advanced Practice Nursing and 3 letters of recommendation are required. *Entrance requirements:* Additional exam requirements/recommendations for international students: required—TOEFL (minimum score 550 paper-based; 90 iBT). Electronic applications accepted. *Expenses:* Contact institution.

**Drexel University,** College of Nursing and Health Professions, Philadelphia, PA 19104-2875. Offers MA, MFT, MHS, MS, MSN, DPT, Dr NP, PPDPT, PhD, Certificate, PMC. *Accreditation:* ACEN. *Program availability:* Part-time, evening/weekend. Terminal master's awarded for partial completion of doctoral program. *Degree requirements:* For master's, comprehensive exam, thesis (for some programs); for doctorate, thesis/dissertation, qualifying exam. *Entrance requirements:* For doctorate, GRE General Test. Electronic applications accepted.

**Duquesne University,** John G. Rangos, Sr. School of Health Sciences, Pittsburgh, PA 15282-0001. Offers health management systems (MHMS); occupational therapy (MS, OTD); physical therapy (DPT); physician assistant studies (MPAS); rehabilitation science (MS, PhD); speech-language pathology (MS). *Accreditation:* AOTA (one or more programs are accredited); APTA (one or more programs are accredited); ASHA. *Program availability:* Part-time, minimal on-campus study. *Degree requirements:* For doctorate, comprehensive exam (for some programs), thesis/dissertation (for some programs). *Entrance requirements:* For master's, GRE General Test (speech-language pathology), 3 letters of recommendation; minimum GPA of 2.75 (health management systems), 3.0 (speech-language pathology); for doctorate, GRE General Test (for physical therapy and rehabilitation science), 3 letters of recommendation, minimum GPA of 3.0, personal interview. Additional exam requirements/recommendations for international students: required—TOEFL (minimum score 550 paper-based; 90 iBT); recommended—IELTS. Electronic applications accepted. *Expenses:* Contact institution.

**Duquesne University,** Post-Baccalaureate Pre-Medical and Health Professions Program, Pittsburgh, PA 15282-0001. Offers Postbaccalaureate Certificate. *Entrance requirements:* For degree, undergraduate degree from accredited college or university; minimum cumulative undergraduate GPA of 3.0, 2.75 for all relevant math/science courses taken; official transcripts with no final grades of D or F. Electronic applications accepted.

**East Carolina University,** Graduate School, College of Allied Health Sciences, Greenville, NC 27858-4353. Offers MS, MSOT, Au D, DPT, PhD, Certificate. *Program availability:* Part-time, evening/weekend, online learning. *Application deadline:* For fall admission, 2/1 for domestic and international students; for spring admission, 9/1 for domestic students, 10/1 for international students. *Expenses: Tuition, area resident:* Full-time $4749; part-time $185 per credit hour. Tuition, state resident: full-time $4749; part-time $185 per credit hour. Tuition, nonresident: full-time $17,898; part-time $864 per credit hour. *International tuition:* $17,898 full-time. *Required fees:* $2787. *Financial support:* Application deadline: 3/1. *Unit head:* Dr. Robert F Orlikoff, Dean, 252-744-6010. *Application contact:* Graduate School Admissions, 252-328-6012, Fax: 252-328-6071, E-mail: gradschool@ecu.edu.
Website: http://www.ecu.edu/cs-dhs/ah/

**Eastern Kentucky University,** The Graduate School, College of Health Sciences, Richmond, KY 40475-3102. Offers MPH, MS, MSN. *Program availability:* Part-time. *Entrance requirements:* For master's, GRE General Test, minimum GPA of 2.75.

**East Tennessee State University,** College of Graduate and Continuing Studies, College of Clinical and Rehabilitative Health Sciences, Department of Allied Health Sciences, Elizabethton, TN 37643. Offers allied health (MSAH); clinical nutrition (MS). *Program availability:* Part-time, online learning. *Degree requirements:* For master's, comprehensive exam, thesis or advanced practice seminar (for MSAH); internship (for MS). *Entrance requirements:* For master's, GRE General Test, professional license in allied health discipline, minimum GPA of 2.75, and three professional letters of recommendation (for MSAH); bachelor's degree from an undergraduate didactic program in dietetics with minimum GPA of 3.0 in DPD coursework and three letters of recommendation (for MS). Additional exam requirements/recommendations for international students: required—TOEFL (minimum score 550 paper-based; 79 iBT). Electronic applications accepted.

**Emory University,** School of Medicine, Programs in Allied Health Professions, Atlanta, GA 30322-1100. Offers anesthesiology assistant (MM Sc); genetic counseling (MM Sc), including human genetics and genetic counseling; physical therapy (DPT); physician assistant (MM Sc). *Entrance requirements:* For master's, GRE or MCAT; for doctorate, GRE. Electronic applications accepted. *Expenses:* Contact institution.

**Ferris State University,** College of Health Professions, Big Rapids, MI 49307. Offers MHA, MPH, MSN. *Program availability:* Part-time, evening/weekend, 100% online. *Faculty:* 16 full-time (13 women), 1 (woman) part-time/adjunct. *Students:* 37 full-time (31 women), 133 part-time (123 women); includes 34 minority (10 Black or African American, non-Hispanic/Latino; 8 American Indian or Alaska Native, non-Hispanic/Latino; 7 Asian, non-Hispanic/Latino; 4 Hispanic/Latino; 5 Two or more races, non-Hispanic/Latino). Average age 34. 56 applicants, 95% accepted, 43 enrolled. In 2019, 36 master's awarded. *Degree requirements:* For master's, comprehensive exam, thesis, practicum, practicum project, capstone program portfolio with thesis. *Entrance requirements:* For master's, GRE (if GPA is below a 3.5 or does not have a health related certification), Minimum GPA of 3.0. Additional exam requirements/recommendations for international students: required—TOEFL (minimum score 550 paper-based; 61 iBT), TOEFL 500 (for health administration), TOEFL 550 (for public health), TOEFL 550 (for nursing). *Application deadline:* For fall admission, 4/15 priority date for domestic students; for spring admission, 10/15 for domestic students; for summer admission, 4/1 for domestic and international students. Applications are processed on a rolling basis. Application fee: $0 ($30 for international students). Electronic applications accepted. Tuition and fees vary according to degree level, program and student level. *Financial support:* In 2019–20, 14 students received support. Career-related internships or fieldwork and scholarships/grants available. Financial award application deadline: 4/15; financial award applicants required to submit FAFSA. *Unit head:* Dr. Lincoln Gibbs, Dean, 231-591-2273, E-mail: LincolnGibbs@ferris.edu. *Application contact:* Dr. Kristen Salomonson, Dean of Enrollment Services and Director of Admissions and Records, 231-591-3963, Fax: 231-591-3179, E-mail: kristensalomonson@ferris.edu.
Website: http://www.ferris.edu/htmls/colleges/alliedhe/

**Florida Agricultural and Mechanical University,** Division of Graduate Studies, Research, and Continuing Education, School of Allied Health Sciences, Tallahassee, FL 32307-3200. Offers health administration (MS); occupational therapy (MOT); physical therapy (DPT). *Degree requirements:* For master's, thesis (for some programs). *Entrance requirements:* For master's, GRE General Test or GMAT, minimum GPA of 3.0. Additional exam requirements/recommendations for international students: required—TOEFL (minimum score 550 paper-based).

**Florida Gulf Coast University,** Elaine Nicpon Marieb College of Health and Human Services, Fort Myers, FL 33965-6565. Offers MA, MPAS, MS, MSN, MSW, DNP, DPT. *Accreditation:* AOTA. *Program availability:* Part-time, evening/weekend, online learning. *Degree requirements:* For master's, thesis or alternative. *Entrance requirements:* For master's, GRE General Test or MAT, minimum GPA of 3.0. Additional exam requirements/recommendations for international students: required—TOEFL (minimum score 550 paper-based). Electronic applications accepted. *Expenses: Tuition, area resident:* Full-time $6974; part-time $4350 per credit hour. Tuition, state resident: full-time $6974; part-time $4350 per credit hour. Tuition, nonresident: full-time $28,169; part-time $17,595 per credit hour. *International tuition:* $28,169 full-time. *Required fees:* $2027; $1267 per credit hour. $507 per semester. Tuition and fees vary according to course load.

**Georgia Southern University,** Jack N. Averitt College of Graduate Studies, Waters College of Health Professions, Statesboro, GA 30460. Offers MHA, MS, MSN, MSSM, DNP, DPT, Certificate. *Program availability:* Part-time, evening/weekend, 100% online, blended/hybrid learning. *Faculty:* 99 full-time (63 women), 8 part-time/adjunct (7 women). *Students:* 274 full-time (193 women), 262 part-time (178 women); includes 163 minority (110 Black or African American, non-Hispanic/Latino; 12 Asian, non-Hispanic/Latino; 26 Hispanic/Latino; 15 Two or more races, non-Hispanic/Latino), 9 international. Average age 29. 380 applicants, 56% accepted, 153 enrolled. In 2019, 173 master's, 39 doctorates, 19 other advanced degrees awarded. *Degree requirements:* For master's, comprehensive exam (for some programs), thesis (for some programs), exams; for doctorate, comprehensive exam, practicum. *Entrance requirements:* For master's, GRE General Test, MAT or GMAT; for doctorate, GRE or MAT. Additional exam requirements/recommendations for international students: required—TOEFL (minimum score 550 paper-based; 80 iBT), IELTS (minimum score 6). *Application deadline:* For fall admission, 3/1 priority date for domestic students, 3/1 for international students; for spring admission, 10/1 priority date for domestic students, 10/1 for international students. Applications are processed on a rolling basis. Application fee: $50. Electronic applications accepted. *Expenses: Tuition, area resident:* Full-time $4986; part-time $277 per credit hour. Tuition, nonresident: full-time $19,890; part-time $1105 per credit hour. *International tuition:* $19,890 full-time. *Required fees:* $2114; $1057 per semester. $1057 per semester. Tuition and fees vary according to course load, campus/location and program. *Financial support:* In 2019–20, 223 students received support, including 24 fellowships with full tuition reimbursements available (averaging $7,750 per year), 9 research assistantships with full tuition reimbursements available (averaging $7,750 per year), 33 teaching assistantships with full tuition reimbursements available (averaging $7,750 per year); career-related internships or fieldwork, Federal Work-Study, scholarships/grants, traineeships, and unspecified assistantships also available. Support available to part-time students. Financial award application deadline: 4/15; financial award applicants required to submit FAFSA. *Unit head:* Dr. Barry Joyner, Dean, 912-478-5322, Fax: 912-478-5349, E-mail: joyner@georgiasouthern.edu.
Website: https://chp.georgiasouthern.edu/

**Georgia State University,** Byrdine F. Lewis School of Nursing, Division of Respiratory Therapy, Atlanta, GA 30302-3083. Offers MS. *Faculty:* 8 full-time (3 women). *Students:* 62 full-time (22 women), 7 part-time (5 women); includes 17 minority (7 Black or African American, non-Hispanic/Latino; 7 Asian, non-Hispanic/Latino; 2 Hispanic/Latino; 1 Two or more races, non-Hispanic/Latino), 44 international. Average age 32. 81 applicants, 64% accepted, 29 enrolled. In 2019, 20 master's awarded. *Degree requirements:* For master's, thesis. *Entrance requirements:* For master's, GRE, transcripts, resume, statement of goals, letters of recommendation. Additional exam requirements/recommendations for international students: required—TOEFL (minimum score 550 paper-based; 80 iBT). *Application deadline:* For fall admission, 5/1 for domestic and international students; for spring admission, 9/15 for domestic and international students. Application fee: $50. Electronic applications accepted. *Expenses: Tuition, area resident:* Full-time $7164; part-time $398 per credit hour. Tuition, state resident: full-time $7164; part-time $398 per credit hour. Tuition, nonresident: full-time $22,662; part-time $1259 per credit hour. *International tuition:* $22,662 full-time. *Required fees:* $2128; $312 per credit hour. Tuition and fees vary according to course load and program. *Financial support:* In 2019–20, research assistantships with full tuition reimbursements (averaging $2,000 per year), teaching assistantships with full tuition reimbursements (averaging $2,000 per year) were awarded; scholarships/grants and unspecified assistantships also available. Financial award application deadline: 6/1; financial award applicants required to submit FAFSA. *Unit head:* Dr. Douglas Gardenhire, Department Head, 404-413-1270, Fax: 404-413-1230, E-mail: dgardenhire@gsu.edu. *Application contact:* Dr. Douglas Gardenhire, Department Head, 404-413-1270, Fax: 404-413-1230, E-mail: dgardenhire@gsu.edu.
Website: http://respiratorytherapy.gsu.edu/

**Grand Valley State University,** College of Health Professions, Allendale, MI 49401-9403. Offers MPAS, MPH, MS, DPT. *Faculty:* 61 full-time (49 women), 17 part-time/adjunct (14 women). *Students:* 672 full-time (554 women), 40 part-time (37 women); includes 75 minority (18 Black or African American, non-Hispanic/Latino; 1 American Indian or Alaska Native, non-Hispanic/Latino; 17 Asian, non-Hispanic/Latino; 22 Hispanic/Latino; 17 Two or more races, non-Hispanic/Latino), 9 international. Average age 25. 1,196 applicants, 34% accepted, 292 enrolled. In 2019, 221 master's, 60 doctorates awarded. *Entrance requirements:* For master's, volunteer work, interview, minimum GPA of 3.0, writing sample; for doctorate, GRE, 50 hours of volunteer work, interview, minimum GPA of 3.0 in last 60 hours and in prerequisites, writing sample. Additional exam requirements/recommendations for international students: required—TOEFL (minimum score 610 paper-based). *Application deadline:* For winter admission, 1/15 priority date for domestic and international students. Applications are processed on a rolling basis. Electronic applications accepted. *Expenses:* Tuition, state resident: full-time $12,654; part-time $3515 per credit hour. Tuition, nonresident: full-time $12,654; part-time $3515 per credit hour. *International tuition:* $12,654 full-time. Tuition and fees vary according to degree level and program. *Financial support:* In 2019–20, 122 students received support, including 84 fellowships, 46 research assistantships with full and partial tuition reimbursements available (averaging $8,000 per year); career-related internships or fieldwork, Federal Work-Study, institutionally sponsored loans, and scholarships/grants also available. Financial award application deadline: 2/15. *Unit head:* Dr. Roy Olsson, Dean, 616-331-3356, Fax: 616-331-3350, E-mail: olssonr@gvsu.edu. *Application contact:* Darlene Zwart, Student Services Coordinator, 616-331-3958, E-mail: zwartda@gvsu.edu.
Website: http://www.gvsu.edu/shp/

**Hampton University,** School of Science, Program in Medical Science, Hampton, VA 23668. Offers MS. *Students:* 43 full-time (29 women), 2 part-time (1 woman); all minorities (44 Black or African American, non-Hispanic/Latino; 1 Hispanic/Latino). Average age 25. 72 applicants, 38% accepted, 17 enrolled. In 2019, 23 master's awarded. *Degree requirements:* For master's, comprehensive exam. *Entrance*

*requirements:* For master's, MCAT or DAT. Additional exam requirements/recommendations for international students: required—TOEFL (minimum score 525 paper-based) or IELTS (6.5). *Application deadline:* For fall admission, 6/1 priority date for domestic students, 4/1 priority date for international students; for summer admission, 6/1 for domestic students. Applications are processed on a rolling basis. Application fee: $35. Electronic applications accepted. *Financial support:* In 2019–20, 4 students received support. Unspecified assistantships available. Financial award application deadline: 6/30; financial award applicants required to submit FAFSA. *Unit head:* Michael Darnell Druitt, Medical Science Coordinator, 757-727-5795, E-mail: michael.druitt@hamptonu.edu. *Application contact:* Michael Darnell Druitt, Medical Science Coordinator, 757-727-5795, E-mail: michael.druitt@hamptonu.edu.
Website: http://science.hamptonu.edu/prehealth/mprograms.cfm

**Harding University,** College of Allied Health, Searcy, AR 72149-0001. Offers MS, DPT. *Faculty:* 14 full-time (4 women). *Students:* 254 full-time (179 women), 2 part-time (both women); includes 39 minority (10 Black or African American, non-Hispanic/Latino; 2 American Indian or Alaska Native, non-Hispanic/Latino; 14 Asian, non-Hispanic/Latino; 10 Hispanic/Latino; 3 Two or more races, non-Hispanic/Latino). Average age 26. 1,055 applicants, 12% accepted, 85 enrolled. In 2019, 54 master's, 31 doctorates awarded. *Entrance requirements:* Additional exam requirements/recommendations for international students: required—TOEFL. *Financial support:* In 2019–20, 6 students received support. *Application contact:* Dr. Julie Hixson-Wallace, Vice Provost, 501-279-5205, Fax: 501-279-5192, E-mail: jahixson@harding.edu.
Website: http://www.harding.edu/academics/colleges-departments/allied-health

**Howard University,** College of Nursing and Allied Health Sciences, Division of Allied Health Sciences, Washington, DC 20059-0002. Offers occupational therapy (MSOT); physical therapy (DPT); physician assistant (MPA). *Accreditation:* AOTA.

**Idaho State University,** Graduate School, College of Health Professions, Pocatello, ID 83209-8090. Offers M Coun, MHE, MPH, MS, PhD, Ed S. *Accreditation:* APTA (one or more programs are accredited). *Program availability:* Part-time. *Degree requirements:* For master's, comprehensive exam, thesis (for some programs), 8-week externship; for doctorate, comprehensive exam, thesis/dissertation, clinical rotation (for some programs); for Ed S, comprehensive exam, thesis, case study, oral exam. *Entrance requirements:* For master's, GRE General Test or MAT, minimum GPA of 3.0, 3 letters of recommendation; for doctorate, GRE General Test or MAT, minimum GPA of 3.0, counseling license, professional research, interview, work experience, 3 letters of recommendation; for Ed S, GRE General Test or MAT, master's degree in similar field of study, 3 letters of recommendation, 2 years of work experience. Additional exam requirements/recommendations for international students: required—TOEFL (minimum score 600 paper-based; 80 iBT). Electronic applications accepted. *Expenses:* Contact institution.

**Ithaca College,** School of Health Sciences and Human Performance, Ithaca, NY 14850. Offers MS, DPT. *Program availability:* Part-time. *Faculty:* 56 full-time (37 women), 1 (woman) part-time/adjunct. *Students:* 284 full-time (230 women), 22 part-time (16 women); includes 40 minority (4 Black or African American, non-Hispanic/Latino; 14 Asian, non-Hispanic/Latino; 13 Hispanic/Latino; 9 Two or more races, non-Hispanic/Latino), 4 international. Average age 23. 280 applicants, 64% accepted, 173 enrolled. In 2019, 95 master's, 82 doctorates awarded. *Entrance requirements:* Additional exam requirements/recommendations for international students: required—TOEFL (minimum score 550 paper-based; 80 iBT). *Application deadline:* Applications are processed on a rolling basis. Application fee: $40. Electronic applications accepted. *Expenses:* Contact institution. *Financial support:* In 2019–20, 205 students received support, including 62 research assistantships (averaging $12,603 per year); Federal Work-Study and scholarships/grants also available. Support available to part-time students. Financial award application deadline: 3/1; financial award applicants required to submit FAFSA. *Unit head:* Dr. Linda Petrosino, Dean, School of Health Sciences and Human Performance, 607-274-3237, Fax: 607-274-1263, E-mail: lpetrosino@ithaca.edu. *Application contact:* Nicole Eversley Bradwell, Director, Office of Admission, 607-800-429-4274, Fax: 607-274-1263, E-mail: admission@ithaca.edu.
Website: https://www.ithaca.edu/academics/school-health-sciences-and-human-performance/graduate-programs

**Jacksonville University,** Brooks Rehabilitation College of Healthcare Sciences, School of Applied Health Sciences, Jacksonville, FL 32211. Offers clinical mental health counseling (MS), including clinical mental health counseling; health informatics (MS); kinesiological sciences (MS); occupational therapy (OTD); speech-language pathology (MS); sport management (MS). *Program availability:* Part-time, 100% online, blended/hybrid learning. *Students:* 187 full-time (160 women), 38 part-time (21 women); includes 73 minority (37 Black or African American, non-Hispanic/Latino; 2 American Indian or Alaska Native, non-Hispanic/Latino; 10 Asian, non-Hispanic/Latino; 19 Hispanic/Latino; 5 Two or more races, non-Hispanic/Latino), 8 international. Average age 29. 428 applicants, 43% accepted, 86 enrolled. In 2019, 114 master's awarded. *Degree requirements:* For doctorate, observation of occupational therapy practice; minimum of 40 hours total among three different settings (hospital, school system, home health, clinic, etc.). *Entrance requirements:* For master's, GRE (for speech language pathology and kinesiological sciences), baccalaureate degree from accredited college or university with minimum GPA of 3.0; official transcripts; essay on professional goals (minimum 1000 words); resume (education, work experience); 3 letters of recommendation; interview; for doctorate, GRE, baccalaureate degree from accredited college or university with minimum GPA of 3.0; official transcripts; observation of occupational therapy practice with minimum of 40 hours total among three settings (hospital, school system, home health, clinic, etc.); interview. Additional exam requirements/recommendations for international students: required—TOEFL (minimum score 650 paper-based; 114 iBT), IELTS (minimum score 8). *Application deadline:* Applications are processed on a rolling basis. Application fee: $50. Electronic applications accepted. *Expenses:* Contact institution. *Financial support:* Federal Work-Study, institutionally sponsored loans, scholarships/grants, and health care benefits available. Support available to part-time students. Financial award application deadline: 3/15; financial award applicants required to submit FAFSA. *Unit head:* Dr. Mark Tillman, Dean, Brooks Rehabilitation College of Healthcare Sciences, 904-256-7977, E-mail: mtillma3@ju.edu. *Application contact:* Pam Adrian, Assistant Director of Enrollment and Advising, 904-256-7245, E-mail: padrian@ju.edu.
Website: https://www.ju.edu/appliedhealth/index.php

**Loma Linda University,** School of Allied Health Professions, Loma Linda, CA 92350. Offers MOT, MPA, MS, DPT, OTD, PhD, SLPD. *Accreditation:* AOTA; APTA. *Entrance requirements:* For master's, minimum GPA of 2.0; for doctorate, minimum GPA of 2.0, associate degree in physical therapy. Additional exam requirements/recommendations for international students: required—TOEFL (minimum score 550 paper-based). Electronic applications accepted.

**Long Island University - Post,** School of Health Professions and Nursing, Brookville, NY 11548-1300. Offers biomedical science (MS); cardiovascular perfusion (MS); clinical lab sciences (MS); clinical laboratory management (MS); dietetic internship (Advanced Certificate); family nurse practitioner (MS, Advanced Certificate); forensic social work (Advanced Certificate); gerontology (Advanced Certificate); health administration (MPA); non-profit management (Advanced Certificate); nursing education (MS); nutrition (MS); public administration (MPA); social work (MSW). *Program availability:* Part-time, blended/hybrid learning. *Degree requirements:* For master's, comprehensive exam (for some programs), thesis (for some programs). *Entrance requirements:* Additional exam requirements/recommendations for international students: required—TOEFL (minimum score 85 iBT) or IELTS (7.5). Electronic applications accepted.

**Marymount University,** Malek School of Health Professions, Arlington, VA 22207-4299. Offers MS, MSN, DNP, DPT, Certificate. *Program availability:* Part-time, evening/weekend. *Faculty:* 15 full-time (14 women), 19 part-time/adjunct (13 women). *Students:* 175 full-time (119 women), 50 part-time (42 women); includes 54 minority (16 Black or African American, non-Hispanic/Latino; 14 Asian, non-Hispanic/Latino; 14 Hispanic/Latino; 10 Two or more races, non-Hispanic/Latino), 37 international. Average age 29. 473 applicants, 55% accepted, 81 enrolled. In 2019, 27 master's, 45 doctorates, 1 other advanced degree awarded. *Degree requirements:* For master's, comprehensive exam (for some programs), thesis (for some programs), internship/clinical practicum; for doctorate, comprehensive exam (for some programs), thesis/dissertation, research presentation/residency; for Certificate, comprehensive exam (for some programs), clinical practicum. *Entrance requirements:* For master's, GRE, MAT, or qualify for test waiver, 2 letters of recommendation, interview, resume, personal statement; for doctorate, GRE, 2 letters of recommendation, interview, resume, personal statement, other program-specific items. Additional exam requirements/recommendations for international students: required—TOEFL (minimum score 600 paper-based; 96 iBT), IELTS (minimum score 6.5), PTE (minimum score 58). *Application deadline:* For fall admission, 3/1 priority date for domestic and international students; for spring admission, 11/1 priority date for domestic and international students. Applications are processed on a rolling basis. Application fee: $40. Electronic applications accepted. *Expenses: Tuition:* Part-time $1050 per credit. *Required fees:* $22 per credit. One-time fee: $270 part-time. Tuition and fees vary according to program. *Financial support:* In 2019–20, 28 students received support. Research assistantships, teaching assistantships, career-related internships or fieldwork, scholarships/grants, and unspecified assistantships available. Support available to part-time students. Financial award application deadline: 3/1; financial award applicants required to submit FAFSA. *Unit head:* Dr. Michelle Walter-Edwards, Interim Dean, 703-284-1580, Fax: 703-284-3819, E-mail: michelle.walters-edwards@marymount.edu. *Application contact:* Fiona McDonnell, Administrative Assistant, 703-284-5901, E-mail: gadmissi@marymount.edu.
Website: http://www.marymount.edu/Academics/Malek-School-of-Health-Professions

**Maryville University of Saint Louis,** Myrtle E. and Earl E. Walker College of Health Professions, St. Louis, MO 63141-7299. Offers MARC, MMT, MOT, MS, MSN, DNP, DPT, Post-MSN Certificate. *Accreditation:* CORE. *Program availability:* Part-time, 100% online, blended/hybrid learning. *Faculty:* 56 full-time (48 women), 229 part-time/adjunct (197 women). *Students:* 323 full-time (284 women), 3,726 part-time (3,242 women); includes 1,113 minority (565 Black or African American, non-Hispanic/Latino; 41 American Indian or Alaska Native, non-Hispanic/Latino; 177 Asian, non-Hispanic/Latino; 235 Hispanic/Latino; 95 Two or more races, non-Hispanic/Latino), 9 international. Average age 36. In 2019, 1,109 master's, 91 doctorates awarded. *Entrance requirements:* Additional exam requirements/recommendations for international students: required—TOEFL (minimum score 550 paper-based). *Application deadline:* Applications are processed on a rolling basis. Electronic applications accepted. *Expenses: Tuition:* Full-time $26,070; part-time $714 per credit hour. *Required fees:* $450 per semester. *Financial support:* Career-related internships or fieldwork, Federal Work-Study, and campus employment available. Financial award application deadline: 4/1; financial award applicants required to submit FAFSA. *Unit head:* Michelle Jenkins-Unterberg, Dean, 314-529-9590, Fax: 314-529-9495, E-mail: munterberg@maryville.edu. *Application contact:* Jeannie DeLuca, Director of Admissions and Advising, 314-529-9355, Fax: 314-529-9927, E-mail: jdeluca@maryville.edu.
Website: http://www.maryville.edu/hp/

**Medical University of South Carolina,** College of Health Professions, Charleston, SC 29425. Offers MHA, MS, MSNA, MSOT, DHA, DPT, PhD. *Accreditation:* CAHME (one or more programs are accredited). *Program availability:* Part-time. *Degree requirements:* For doctorate, comprehensive exam, thesis/dissertation. *Entrance requirements:* For master's, GRE. Additional exam requirements/recommendations for international students: required—TOEFL (minimum score 600 paper-based). Electronic applications accepted. *Expenses:* Contact institution.

**Mercy College,** School of Health and Natural Sciences, Dobbs Ferry, NY 10522-1189. Offers communication disorders (MS); nursing (MS), including nursing administration, nursing education; occupational therapy (MS); physical therapy (DPT); physician assistant studies (MS). *Program availability:* Part-time, evening/weekend, 100% online, blended/hybrid learning. *Students:* 353 full-time (273 women), 295 part-time (256 women); includes 334 minority (123 Black or African American, non-Hispanic/Latino; 78 Asian, non-Hispanic/Latino; 105 Hispanic/Latino; 3 Native Hawaiian or other Pacific Islander, non-Hispanic/Latino; 25 Two or more races, non-Hispanic/Latino), 5 international. Average age 32. 1,012 applicants, 35% accepted, 241 enrolled. In 2019, 194 master's, 31 doctorates awarded. *Degree requirements:* For master's and doctorate, comprehensive exam (for some programs), Capstone project and clinical practice required for most programs. *Entrance requirements:* For master's, Some programs may require completion of the GRE, individual program application along with general graduate application; transcript(s); letters of recommendation; some programs may additionally require the following: interview, essay, and/or resume; for doctorate, GRE, program application along with general graduate application; transcript(s); two letters of recommendation; interview; demonstrated volunteer or work-related experience in physical therapy. Additional exam requirements/recommendations for international students: required—TOEFL (minimum score 80 iBT), IELTS (minimum score 6.5). *Application deadline:* Applications are processed on a rolling basis. Application fee: $40. Electronic applications accepted. *Expenses:* Contact institution. *Financial support:* Career-related internships or fieldwork, Federal Work-Study, scholarships/grants, and unspecified assistantships available. Support available to part-time students. Financial award applicants required to submit FAFSA. *Unit head:* Dr. Joan Toglia, Dean, School of Health and Natural Sciences, 914-674-7746, E-mail: jtoglia@mercy.edu. *Application contact:* Allison Gurdineer, Executive Director of Admissions, 877-637-2946, Fax: 914-674-7382, E-mail: admissions@mercy.edu.
Website: https://www.mercy.edu/health-and-natural-sciences/graduate

**Midwestern University, Glendale Campus,** College of Health Sciences, Arizona Campus, Glendale, AZ 85308. Offers MA, MBS, MCVS, MMS, MOT, MS, DPM, DPT, Psy D. *Program availability:* Part-time. *Expenses:* Contact institution.

**Minnesota State University Mankato,** College of Graduate Studies and Research, College of Allied Health and Nursing, Mankato, MN 56001. Offers MA, MS, MSN, DNP, Postbaccalaureate Certificate. *Program availability:* Part-time. *Degree requirements:* For master's, comprehensive exam; for Postbaccalaureate Certificate, thesis. *Entrance requirements:* For master's, GRE (for some programs), minimum GPA of 3.0 during previous 2 years; for Postbaccalaureate Certificate, GRE General Test, minimum GPA of 3.0. Electronic applications accepted.

**Misericordia University,** College of Health Sciences and Education, Dallas, PA 18612-1098. Offers MS, MSN, MSOT, MSSLP, DNP, DPT, OTD. *Program availability:* Part-time, evening/weekend. *Entrance requirements:* For doctorate, interview, references.

Additional exam requirements/recommendations for international students: required—TOEFL. Electronic applications accepted.

**New Jersey City University,** College of Professional Studies, Department of Health Sciences, Jersey City, NJ 07305-1597. Offers community health education (MS); health administration (MS); school health education (MS). *Program availability:* Part-time, evening/weekend. *Degree requirements:* For master's, thesis or alternative, internship. *Entrance requirements:* Additional exam requirements/recommendations for international students: required—TOEFL (minimum score 79 iBT).

**Northeastern University,** Bouvé College of Health Sciences, Boston, MA 02115-5096. Offers applied behavior analysis (MS); audiology (Au D); counseling psychology (MS, PhD, CAGS); exercise science (MS); nursing (MS, PhD, CAGS), including administration (MS), adult-gerontology acute care nurse practitioner (MS, CAGS), adult-gerontology primary care nurse practitioner (MS, CAGS), anesthesia (MS), family nurse practitioner (MS, CAGS), neonatal nurse practitioner (MS, CAGS), pediatric nurse practitioner (MS, CAGS), psychiatric mental health nurse practitioner (MS, CAGS); nursing practice (DNP); pharmaceutical sciences (MS, PhD), including interdisciplinary concentration, pharmaceutics and drug delivery systems; pharmacology (MS); pharmacy (Pharm D); school psychology (PhD); speech-language pathology (MS); urban health (MPH); MS/MBA. *Accreditation:* AANA/CANAEP; ACPE (one or more programs are accredited); ASHA; CEPH. *Program availability:* Part-time, evening/weekend, online learning. *Degree requirements:* For doctorate, thesis/dissertation (for some programs); for CAGS, comprehensive exam. Electronic applications accepted. *Expenses:* Contact institution.

**Northern Arizona University,** College of Health and Human Services, Flagstaff, AZ 86011. Offers MPAS, MS, DNP, DPT, OTD, Certificate. *Accreditation:* APTA (one or more programs are accredited). *Program availability:* Part-time, 100% online, blended/hybrid learning. *Degree requirements:* For master's, variable foreign language requirement, comprehensive exam (for some programs), thesis (for some programs); for doctorate, variable foreign language requirement, comprehensive exam (for some programs), thesis/dissertation (for some programs); for Certificate, comprehensive exam (for some programs). *Entrance requirements:* Additional exam requirements/recommendations for international students: required—TOEFL (minimum score 80 iBT), IELTS (minimum score 6.5). Electronic applications accepted.

**Northern Kentucky University,** Office of Graduate Programs, School of Nursing and Health Professions, Program in Health Science, Highland Heights, KY 41099. Offers MS. *Program availability:* Online learning. *Degree requirements:* For master's, capstone, internship. *Entrance requirements:* For master's, official transcripts, minimum GPA of 3.0 on last 40 hours of undergraduate work, letter of intent, resume, undergraduate course in statistical methods with minimum C grade, interview. Additional exam requirements/recommendations for international students: required—TOEFL (minimum score 79 iBT); recommended—IELTS (minimum score 6.5).

**Nova Southeastern University,** Dr. Pallavi Patel College of Health Care Sciences, Fort Lauderdale, FL 33314-7796. Offers anesthesiologist assistant (MSA); audiology (Au D); health science (MH Sc, DHSc, PhD); occupational therapy (MOT, Dr OT, PhD); physical therapy (DPT, TDPT); physician assistant (MMS); speech-language pathology (MS). *Accreditation:* AOTA; ASHA. *Program availability:* Part-time, 100% online, blended/hybrid learning. *Faculty:* 127 full-time (85 women), 107 part-time/adjunct (79 women). *Students:* 1,336 full-time (992 women), 950 part-time (824 women); includes 839 minority (195 Black or African American, non-Hispanic/Latino; 4 American Indian or Alaska Native, non-Hispanic/Latino; 165 Asian, non-Hispanic/Latino; 397 Hispanic/Latino; 3 Native Hawaiian or other Pacific Islander, non-Hispanic/Latino; 75 Two or more races, non-Hispanic/Latino), 26 international. Average age 30. 634 applicants, 28% accepted, 159 enrolled. In 2019, 613 master's, 261 doctorates awarded. Terminal master's awarded for partial completion of doctoral program. *Degree requirements:* For doctorate, comprehensive exam, thesis/dissertation (for some programs), 12-month full-time clinical externship experience. *Entrance requirements:* For master's, GRE General Test; for doctorate, personal interview, essay in application,additional letters may be requested by the program after initial review of application if so warranted. *Application deadline:* Applications are processed on a rolling basis. Application fee: $50. Electronic applications accepted. *Expenses:* Contact institution. *Financial support:* Federal Work-Study, institutionally sponsored loans, and scholarships/grants available. Financial award application deadline: 4/15; financial award applicants required to submit FAFSA. *Unit head:* Dr. Stanley Wilson, Dean, 954-262-1203, E-mail: swilson@nova.edu. *Application contact:* Joycelyn Vogt, Director of Admissions and Outreach, 954-262-1200, Fax: 954-262-1181, E-mail: joycelyn.vogt@nova.edu.
Website: http://healthsciences.nova.edu/

**Oakland University,** Graduate Study and Lifelong Learning, School of Health Sciences, Rochester, MI 48309-4401. Offers MS, DPT, Dr Sc PT, TDPT, Graduate Certificate. *Accreditation:* APTA (one or more programs are accredited). *Entrance requirements:* Additional exam requirements/recommendations for international students: required—TOEFL (minimum score 550 paper-based; 79 iBT), IELTS (minimum score 6.5). Electronic applications accepted. *Expenses:* Contact institution.

**The Ohio State University,** College of Medicine, School of Health and Rehabilitation Sciences, Program in Allied Health, Columbus, OH 43210. Offers MS. *Entrance requirements:* For master's, GRE. Additional exam requirements/recommendations for international students: required—TOEFL (minimum score 550 paper-based; 79 iBT), Michigan English Language Assessment Battery (minimum score 82); recommended—IELTS (minimum score 7). Electronic applications accepted.

**Old Dominion University,** College of Health Sciences, Norfolk, VA 23529. Offers MS, MSAT, MSN, DNP, DPT, PhD. *Program availability:* Part-time, evening/weekend, 100% online, blended/hybrid learning. *Degree requirements:* For master's, comprehensive exam; for doctorate, comprehensive exam, thesis/dissertation. *Entrance requirements:* For master's and doctorate, GRE or MAT. Additional exam requirements/recommendations for international students: required—TOEFL (minimum score 550 paper-based; 79 iBT). Electronic applications accepted.

**Oregon State University,** Interdisciplinary/Institutional Programs, Program in Comparative Health Sciences, Corvallis, OR 97331. Offers biomedical sciences (MS, PhD). *Entrance requirements:* For master's and doctorate, GRE. Additional exam requirements/recommendations for international students: required—TOEFL (minimum score 80 iBT), IELTS (minimum score 6.5).

**Purdue University,** Graduate School, College of Health and Human Sciences, School of Health Sciences, West Lafayette, IN 47907. Offers health physics (MS, PhD); medical physics (MS, PhD); occupational and environmental health science (MS, PhD), including aerosol deposition and lung disease, ergonomics, exposure and risk assessment, indoor air quality and bioaerosols (PhD), liver/lung toxicology; radiological health (PhD); toxicology (PhD); MS/PhD. *Program availability:* Part-time. *Faculty:* 15 full-time (6 women), 1 part-time/adjunct (0 women). *Students:* 39 full-time (22 women), 6 part-time (3 women); includes 12 minority (2 Black or African American, non-Hispanic/Latino; 1 American Indian or Alaska Native, non-Hispanic/Latino; 3 Asian, non-Hispanic/Latino; 1 Hispanic/Latino; 5 Two or more races, non-Hispanic/Latino), 15 international. Average age 28. 61 applicants, 43% accepted, 14 enrolled. In 2019, 15 master's, 6 doctorates awarded. *Degree requirements:* For master's, thesis optional; for doctorate, one foreign language, thesis/dissertation. *Entrance requirements:* For master's and doctorate, GRE General Test, minimum undergraduate GPA of 3.0 or equivalent. Additional exam requirements/recommendations for international students: required—TOEFL (minimum score 550 paper-based; 77 iBT); recommended—TWE. *Application deadline:* For fall admission, 5/15 for domestic and international students; for spring admission, 10/15 for domestic and international students. Applications are processed on a rolling basis. Application fee: $60 ($75 for international students). Electronic applications accepted. *Financial support:* In 2019–20, fellowships with tuition reimbursements (averaging $14,400 per year), research assistantships with tuition reimbursements (averaging $12,000 per year), teaching assistantships with tuition reimbursements (averaging $12,000 per year) were awarded; career-related internships or fieldwork and traineeships also available. Support available to part-time students. Financial award applicants required to submit FAFSA. *Unit head:* Aaron Bowman, Head of the Graduate Program, 765-494-2684, E-mail: bowma117@purdue.edu. *Application contact:* Karen E. Walker, Graduate Contact, 765-494-1419, E-mail: kwalker@purdue.edu.
Website: https://www.purdue.edu/hhs/hsci/

**Quinnipiac University,** School of Health Sciences, Hamden, CT 06518-1940. Offers MHS, MSW. *Accreditation:* AOTA. *Entrance requirements:* Additional exam requirements/recommendations for international students: required—TOEFL (minimum score 575 paper-based; 90 iBT), IELTS (minimum score 6.5). Electronic applications accepted. *Expenses: Tuition:* Part-time $1055 per credit. *Required fees:* $945 per semester. Tuition and fees vary according to course load and program.

**Regis University,** Rueckert-Hartman College for Health Professions, Denver, CO 80221-1099. Offers advanced practice nurse (DNP); counseling (MA); counseling children and adolescents (Post-Graduate Certificate); counseling military families (Post-Graduate Certificate); depth psychotherapy (Post-Graduate Certificate); fellowship in orthopedic manual physical therapy (Certificate); health care business management (Certificate); health care quality and patient safety (Certificate); health industry leadership (MBA); health services administration (MS); marriage and family therapy (MA, Post-Graduate Certificate); neonatal nurse practitioner (MSN); nursing education (MSN); nursing leadership (MSN); occupational therapy (OTD); pharmacy (Pharm D); physical therapy (DPT). *Accreditation:* ACPE. *Program availability:* Part-time, evening/weekend, 100% online, blended/hybrid learning. *Degree requirements:* For master's, thesis (for some programs), internship. *Entrance requirements:* For master's, official transcript reflecting baccalaureate degree awarded from regionally-accredited college or university. Additional exam requirements/recommendations for international students: required—TOEFL (minimum score 550 paper-based; 82 iBT). Electronic applications accepted. *Expenses:* Contact institution.

**Rosalind Franklin University of Medicine and Science,** College of Health Professions, North Chicago, IL 60064-3095. Offers MS, D Sc, DNAP, DPT, PhD, TDPT, Certificate. *Program availability:* Part-time, online learning. Terminal master's awarded for partial completion of doctoral program.

**Rutgers University - Newark,** School of Health Related Professions, Newark, NJ 07102. Offers MS, DCN, DPT, PhD, Certificate, DMD/MS, MD/MS. *Accreditation:* APTA (one or more programs are accredited); NAACLS. *Program availability:* Part-time. *Degree requirements:* For master's, thesis (for some programs). *Entrance requirements:* Additional exam requirements/recommendations for international students: required—TOEFL. Electronic applications accepted. *Expenses:* Contact institution.

**Saint Louis University,** Graduate Programs, Doisy College of Health Sciences, St. Louis, MO 63103. Offers MAT, MMS, MOT, MS, DPT, PhD, Certificate. *Program availability:* Part-time. *Degree requirements:* For master's, comprehensive exam. *Entrance requirements:* Additional exam requirements/recommendations for international students: required—TOEFL (minimum score 525 paper-based).

**Sam Houston State University,** College of Health Sciences, Department of Health Services and Promotion, Huntsville, TX 77341. Offers health (MA). *Accreditation:* NCATE. *Program availability:* Part-time. *Degree requirements:* For master's, comprehensive exam, thesis optional, internship. *Entrance requirements:* For master's, GRE General Test, MAT, letters of recommendation, statement of interest/intent. Additional exam requirements/recommendations for international students: required—TOEFL (minimum score 550 paper-based; 79 iBT), IELTS (minimum score 6.5). Electronic applications accepted.

**Seton Hall University,** School of Health and Medical Sciences, Program in Health Sciences, South Orange, NJ 07079-2697. Offers PhD. *Program availability:* Part-time, evening/weekend. *Degree requirements:* For doctorate, comprehensive exam (for some programs), thesis/dissertation, candidacy exam, practicum, research projects. *Entrance requirements:* For doctorate, GRE (preferred), interview, minimum GPA of 3.0, letters of recommendation. Additional exam requirements/recommendations for international students: required—TOEFL. Electronic applications accepted.

**Shenandoah University,** School of Health Professions, Winchester, VA 22601. Offers athletic training (MSAT); occupational therapy (MS); performing arts medicine (Certificate); physical therapy (DPT); physician assistant studies (MS); public health (MPH, Certificate). *Program availability:* Part-time, 100% online. *Faculty:* 1 (woman) full-time, 2 part-time/adjunct (both women). *Students:* 3 full-time (2 women), 25 part-time (20 women); includes 8 minority (4 Black or African American, non-Hispanic/Latino; 2 Asian, non-Hispanic/Latino; 2 Hispanic/Latino). Average age 34. 35 applicants, 97% accepted, 6 enrolled. In 2019, 1 other advanced degree awarded. *Degree requirements:* For master's, Practicum experience. *Entrance requirements:* For master's, Minimum GPA: 3.0 cumulative; Prerequisites: Bachelor's Degree or higher. Additional exam requirements/recommendations for international students: required—TOEFL (minimum score 83 iBT). *Application deadline:* For fall admission, 8/1 for domestic students; for spring admission, 12/1 for domestic students. Applications are processed on a rolling basis. Application fee: $30. Electronic applications accepted. *Expenses:* $700 per credit hour; 32 credit hours for program completion. *Financial support:* In 2019–20, 17 students received support, including 1 fellowship (averaging $210 per year); scholarships/grants and Faculty staff grant Public Health Discount (graduate) Valley Health SU Discretionary Award Anatomy and physiology graduate also available. Financial award application deadline: 8/1; financial award applicants required to submit FAFSA. *Unit head:* Michelle Gamber, DrPH, MA, Director, 540-665-5560, Fax: 540-665-5519, E-mail: mgamber@su.edu. *Application contact:* Katie Olivo, Associate Director of Admission, 540-665-5441, Fax: 540-665-4627, E-mail: kolivo@su.edu.
Website: su.edu/public-health/

**South Carolina State University,** College of Graduate and Professional Studies, Department of Health Sciences, Orangeburg, SC 29117-0001. Offers speech pathology and audiology (MA). *Accreditation:* ASHA. *Program availability:* Part-time, evening/weekend. *Degree requirements:* For master's, thesis optional, departmental qualifying exam. *Entrance requirements:* For master's, GRE or NTE, minimum GPA of 3.0. Electronic applications accepted.

**Temple University,** College of Public Health, Philadelphia, PA 19122-6096. Offers MA, MOT, MPH, MS, MSAT, MSW, DAT, DNP, DOT, DPT, PhD, TDPT. *Accreditation:* APTA (one or more programs are accredited). *Program availability:* Part-time, evening/weekend, online learning. *Faculty:* 130 full-time (93 women), 48 part-time/adjunct (32 women). *Students:* 698 full-time (541 women), 369 part-time (304 women); includes 340

minority (168 Black or African American, non-Hispanic/Latino; 3 American Indian or Alaska Native, non-Hispanic/Latino; 61 Asian, non-Hispanic/Latino; 74 Hispanic/Latino; 34 Two or more races, non-Hispanic/Latino), 44 international. 1,237 applicants, 50% accepted, 267 enrolled. In 2019, 295 master's, 89 doctorates awarded. *Entrance requirements:* Additional exam requirements/recommendations for international students: required—TOEFL, IELTS, PTE, one of three is required. Application fee: $60. *Expenses:* Contact institution. *Financial support:* Fellowships, research assistantships, teaching assistantships, Federal Work-Study, scholarships/grants, health care benefits, and unspecified assistantships available. Support available to part-time students. Financial award applicants required to submit FAFSA. *Unit head:* Laura Siminoff, Dean, 215-707-8624, E-mail: laura.siminoff@temple.edu. *Application contact:* Michael Usino, Assistant Dean of Admissions, 215-204-5717, E-mail: michael.usino@temple.edu. Website: http://cph.temple.edu/

**Tennessee State University,** The School of Graduate Studies and Research, College of Health Sciences, Nashville, TN 37209-1561. Offers MA Ed, MOT, MPH, MS, MSN, DPT, Certificate. *Accreditation:* ASHA (one or more programs are accredited). *Program availability:* Part-time, evening/weekend. *Entrance requirements:* For master's, GRE General Test, MAT, minimum GPA of 3.5. Electronic applications accepted.

**Texas Christian University,** Harris College of Nursing and Health Sciences, Fort Worth, TX 76129-0002. Offers MS, MSN, MSW, DNP, DNP-A, Certificate. *Program availability:* Part-time, 100% online, blended/hybrid learning. *Faculty:* 66 full-time (53 women), 5 part-time/adjunct (2 women). *Students:* 345 full-time (259 women), 25 part-time (19 women); includes 96 minority (18 Black or African American, non-Hispanic/Latino; 2 American Indian or Alaska Native, non-Hispanic/Latino; 25 Asian, non-Hispanic/Latino; 40 Hispanic/Latino; 11 Two or more races, non-Hispanic/Latino), 6 international. Average age 31. 628 applicants, 33% accepted, 163 enrolled. In 2019, 63 master's, 77 doctorates, 12 other advanced degrees awarded. *Degree requirements:* For master's and Certificate, comprehensive exam (for some programs), thesis (for some programs); for doctorate, comprehensive exam (for some programs), thesis/dissertation (for some programs). *Entrance requirements:* For master's, GRE (for some programs), resume, two transcripts from each institution attended, bachelor's degree in related field, recommendation letters; certification or license (for some programs); for doctorate, GRE (for some programs), resume, two transcripts from each institution attended, bachelor's degree in related field, recommendation letters; certification or license (for some programs); master's degree (for some programs); for Certificate, resume, two transcripts from each institution attended, bachelor's degree in related field, recommendation letters; certification or license (for some programs); master's degree (for some programs). Additional exam requirements/recommendations for international students: required—TOEFL (minimum score 550 paper-based, 80 iBT) or IELTS (6.5). Application fee: $60. Electronic applications accepted. *Expenses:* Contact institution. *Financial support:* Application deadline: 5/1; applicants required to submit FAFSA. *Unit head:* Dr. Suzy Lockwood, Interim Dean, 817-257-6749, E-mail: s.lockwood@tcu.edu. *Application contact:* Debbie Rhea, Associate Dean, 817-257-5263, E-mail: d.rhea@tcu.edu.
Website: http://www.harriscollege.tcu.edu/

**Texas State University,** The Graduate College, College of Health Professions, San Marcos, TX 78666. Offers MA, MHA, MHIIM, MSCD, MSN, DPT. *Program availability:* Part-time. *Faculty:* 67 full-time (44 women), 21 part-time/adjunct (13 women). *Students:* 307 full-time (244 women), 110 part-time (84 women); includes 171 minority (45 Black or African American, non-Hispanic/Latino; 22 Asian, non-Hispanic/Latino; 93 Hispanic/Latino; 11 Two or more races, non-Hispanic/Latino), 6 international. Average age 29. 1,226 applicants, 24% accepted, 203 enrolled. In 2019, 109 master's awarded. *Degree requirements:* For master's and doctorate, comprehensive exam. *Entrance requirements:* For master's, GRE General Test (for some programs) with competitive scores, baccalaureate degree from regionally-accredited institution; for doctorate, baccalaureate degree from regionally-accredited institution in physical therapy with minimum GPA of 3.0 on last 60 hours of undergraduate work. Additional exam requirements/recommendations for international students: required—TOEFL (minimum score 550 paper-based; 78 iBT), IELTS (minimum score 6.5). *Application deadline:* For fall admission, 1/15 priority date for domestic and international students; for spring admission, 10/1 for domestic and international students; for summer admission, 10/1 for domestic students, 10/1 priority date for international students. Applications are processed on a rolling basis. Application fee: $55 ($90 for international students). Electronic applications accepted. *Financial support:* In 2019–20, 175 students received support, including 2 fellowships with partial tuition reimbursements available (averaging $144 per year), 6 research assistantships (averaging $9,883 per year), 35 teaching assistantships (averaging $10,777 per year); career-related internships or fieldwork, Federal Work-Study, institutionally sponsored loans, scholarships/grants, unspecified assistantships, and stipends also available. Support available to part-time students. Financial award application deadline: 1/15; financial award applicants required to submit FAFSA. *Unit head:* Dr. Ruth Welborn, Dean, 512-245-3300, Fax: 512-245-3791, E-mail: rw01@txstate.edu. *Application contact:* Dr. Andrea Golato, Dean of Graduate School, 512-245-2581, Fax: 512-245-8365, E-mail: gradcollege@txstate.edu.
Website: http://www.health.txstate.edu/

**Texas Woman's University,** Graduate School, College of Health Sciences, Denton, TX 76204. Offers MA, MOT, MS, DPT, OTD, PhD. *Program availability:* Part-time, evening/weekend, 100% online, blended/hybrid learning. *Faculty:* 99 full-time (75 women), 19 part-time/adjunct (17 women). *Students:* 1,004 full-time (885 women), 373 part-time (314 women); includes 534 minority (105 Black or African American, non-Hispanic/Latino; 1 American Indian or Alaska Native, non-Hispanic/Latino; 129 Asian, non-Hispanic/Latino; 254 Hispanic/Latino; 45 Two or more races, non-Hispanic/Latino), 33 international. Average age 29. 1,572 applicants, 28% accepted, 365 enrolled. In 2019, 434 master's, 128 doctorates awarded. *Degree requirements:* For master's, comprehensive exam (for some programs), thesis (for some programs); for doctorate, comprehensive exam, thesis/dissertation, qualifying exam. *Entrance requirements:* For master's and doctorate, minimum GPA of 3.0. Additional exam requirements/recommendations for international students: required—TOEFL (minimum score 79 iBT); recommended—IELTS (minimum score 6.5), TSE (minimum score 53). *Application deadline:* For fall admission, 3/1 priority date for domestic and international students; for spring admission, 11/1 priority date for domestic students, 7/1 priority date for international students; for summer admission, 5/1 priority date for domestic students, 2/1 priority date for international students. Applications are processed on a rolling basis. Application fee: $50 ($75 for international students). Electronic applications accepted. *Expenses:* Based on course taken. *Financial support:* In 2019–20, 746 students received support, including 16 research assistantships (averaging $5,198 per year), 53 teaching assistantships (averaging $6,886 per year); career-related internships or fieldwork, scholarships/grants, health care benefits, and unspecified assistantships also available. Support available to part-time students. Financial award application deadline: 3/1; financial award applicants required to submit FAFSA. *Unit head:* Dr. Christopher T. Ray, Dean, 940-898-2852, Fax: 940-898-2853. *Application contact:* Korie Hawkins, Associate Director of Admissions, Graduate Recruitment, 940-898-3188, Fax: 940-898-3081, E-mail: admissions@twu.edu.
Website: http://www.twu.edu/college-health-sciences/

**Towson University,** College of Health Professions, Program in Health Science, Towson, MD 21252-0001. Offers MS. *Program availability:* Part-time, evening/weekend. *Students:* 32 full-time (28 women), 50 part-time (41 women); includes 51 minority (42 Black or African American, non-Hispanic/Latino; 4 Asian, non-Hispanic/Latino; 4 Hispanic/Latino; 1 Two or more races, non-Hispanic/Latino), 2 international. *Entrance requirements:* For master's, undergraduate degree in a health science field or substantial upper-division course work in those fields, or experience in those same areas; minimum B grade in previous statistics course; minimum GPA of 3.0. *Application deadline:* For fall admission, 1/17 for domestic students, 5/15 for international students; for spring admission, 10/15 for domestic students, 12/1 for international students. Applications are processed on a rolling basis. Application fee: $45. Electronic applications accepted. *Expenses:* Tuition, area resident: Full-time $7920; part-time $439 per credit. Tuition, nonresident: full-time $16,344; part-time $908 per credit. *International tuition:* $16,344 full-time. *Required fees:* $2628; $146 per credit. $876 per term. *Financial support:* Application deadline: 4/1. *Unit head:* Dr. Niya Werts, Program Director, 410-704-4049, E-mail: nwerts@towson.edu. *Application contact:* Coverley Beidleman, Assistant Director of Graduate Admissions, 410-704-5630, Fax: 410-704-3030, E-mail: grads@towson.edu.
Website: https://www.towson.edu/chp/departments/health-sciences/grad/health-science/

**University at Buffalo, the State University of New York,** Graduate School, School of Public Health and Health Professions, Buffalo, NY 14260. Offers MA, MPH, MS, DPT, PhD, Advanced Certificate, Certificate. *Program availability:* Part-time. Terminal master's awarded for partial completion of doctoral program. *Degree requirements:* For master's, comprehensive exam (for some programs), thesis (for some programs); for doctorate, comprehensive exam, thesis/dissertation. *Entrance requirements:* For master's and doctorate, GRE General Test. Additional exam requirements/recommendations for international students: required—TOEFL (minimum score 79 iBT). Electronic applications accepted. *Expenses:* Tuition, area resident: Full-time $11,310; part-time $471 per credit hour. Tuition, state resident: full-time $11,310; part-time $471 per credit hour. Tuition, nonresident: full-time $23,100; part-time $963 per credit hour. *International tuition:* $23,100 full-time. *Required fees:* $2820.

**The University of Alabama at Birmingham,** School of Health Professions, Birmingham, AL 35294. Offers MS, MSHA, MSHI, MSPAS, D Sc, DPT, PhD, Certificate. *Accreditation:* AANA/CANAEP (one or more programs are accredited); APTA (one or more programs are accredited); CAHME (one or more programs are accredited). *Program availability:* Part-time, online learning. *Faculty:* 113 full-time (65 women), 8 part-time/adjunct (2 women). *Students:* 740 full-time (539 women), 182 part-time (123 women); includes 159 minority (87 Black or African American, non-Hispanic/Latino; 3 American Indian or Alaska Native, non-Hispanic/Latino; 36 Asian, non-Hispanic/Latino; 17 Hispanic/Latino; 1 Native Hawaiian or other Pacific Islander, non-Hispanic/Latino; 15 Two or more races, non-Hispanic/Latino), 28 international. Average age 30. 1,015 applicants, 56% accepted, 417 enrolled. In 2019, 252 master's, 41 doctorates awarded. *Degree requirements:* For doctorate, thesis/dissertation. Application fee: $0 ($60 for international students). Electronic applications accepted. *Expenses:* Contact institution. *Financial support:* Fellowships, research assistantships, teaching assistantships, career-related internships or fieldwork, Federal Work-Study, institutionally sponsored loans, scholarships/grants, traineeships, and unspecified assistantships available. Support available to part-time students. *Unit head:* Dr. Harold P. Jones, Dean, 205-934-5149, Fax: 205-934-2412, E-mail: jonesh@uab.edu. *Application contact:* Susan Noblitt Banks, Director of Graduate School Operations, 205-934-8227, Fax: 205-934-8413, E-mail: gradschool@uab.edu.
Website: http://www.uab.edu/shp/

**University of Detroit Mercy,** College of Health Professions, Detroit, MI 48221. Offers clinical nurse leader (MSN); family nurse practitioner (MSN); health services administration (MHSA); health systems management (MSN); nurse anesthesia (MS); nursing (DNP); nursing education (MSN, Certificate); nursing leadership and financial management (Certificate); outcomes performance management (Certificate); physician assistant (MS). *Accreditation:* AANA/CANAEP. *Entrance requirements:* For master's, GRE General Test, minimum GPA of 3.0.

**University of Florida,** Graduate School, College of Public Health and Health Professions, Gainesville, FL 32611. Offers MA, MHA, MHS, MHS, MOT, MPH, MS, Au D, DPT, PhD, Certificate, DPT/MPH, DVM/MPH, JD/MPH, MBA/MHA, MD/MPH, PhD/MPH, Pharm D/MPH. *Accreditation:* CAHME (one or more programs are accredited). *Program availability:* Part-time. Terminal master's awarded for partial completion of doctoral program. *Degree requirements:* For master's, thesis (for some programs); for doctorate, comprehensive exam, thesis/dissertation. *Entrance requirements:* For master's and doctorate, GRE General Test, minimum GPA of 3.0. Additional exam requirements/recommendations for international students: required—TOEFL (minimum score 550 paper-based; 80 iBT), IELTS (minimum score 6). Electronic applications accepted.

**University of Illinois at Chicago,** College of Applied Health Sciences, Chicago, IL 60607-7128. Offers MS, DPT, OTD, PhD, CAS, Certificate. *Accreditation:* AOTA. *Program availability:* Part-time. *Degree requirements:* For doctorate, thesis/dissertation. *Entrance requirements:* For master's, GRE General Test, minimum GPA of 2.75. Additional exam requirements/recommendations for international students: required—TOEFL. Electronic applications accepted. *Expenses:* Contact institution.

**The University of Kansas,** University of Kansas Medical Center, School of Health Professions, Kansas City, KS 66045. Offers MOT, MS, Au D, DNAP, DPT, OTD, PhD, SLPD, Graduate Certificate. *Faculty:* 118. *Students:* 477 full-time (350 women), 65 part-time (60 women); includes 71 minority (9 Black or African American, non-Hispanic/Latino; 2 American Indian or Alaska Native, non-Hispanic/Latino; 17 Asian, non-Hispanic/Latino; 28 Hispanic/Latino; 1 Native Hawaiian or other Pacific Islander, non-Hispanic/Latino; 14 Two or more races, non-Hispanic/Latino), 17 international. Average age 27. In 2019, 68 master's, 103 doctorates, 24 other advanced degrees awarded. *Expenses:* Tuition, state resident: full-time $9989. Tuition, nonresident: full-time $23,950. *International tuition:* $23,950 full-time. *Required fees:* $984; $81.99 per credit hour. Tuition and fees vary according to course load, campus/location and program. *Unit head:* Dr. Abiodun Akinwuntan, Dean, 913-588-5235, Fax: 913-588-5254, E-mail: aakinwuntan@kumc.edu. *Application contact:* Dr. Abiodun Akinwuntan, Dean, 913-588-5235, Fax: 913-588-5254, E-mail: aakinwuntan@kumc.edu.
Website: http://www.kumc.edu/school-of-health-professions.html

**University of Kentucky,** Graduate School, College of Health Sciences, Lexington, KY 40506-0032. Offers MHA, MS, MSCD, MSHP, MSNS, MSPAS, MSPT, MSRMP, DS, PhD. *Program availability:* Part-time. *Degree requirements:* For master's, comprehensive exam, thesis (for some programs). *Entrance requirements:* For master's, GRE General Test, minimum undergraduate GPA of 2.75; for doctorate, GRE General Test, minimum undergraduate GPA of 3.0. Additional exam requirements/recommendations for international students: required—TOEFL (minimum score 550 paper-based). Electronic applications accepted.

**University of Maryland, Baltimore,** Graduate School, Program in Health Science, Baltimore, MD 21201. Offers MS. *Degree requirements:* For master's, comprehensive

exam, thesis optional. *Entrance requirements:* For master's, GRE, minimum GPA of 3.0, curriculum vitae, essay, three letters of recommendation. Additional exam requirements/recommendations for international students: required—TOEFL (minimum score 80 iBT); recommended—IELTS (minimum score 7). Electronic applications accepted.

**University of Massachusetts Lowell,** College of Health Sciences, Lowell, MA 01854. Offers MS, DNP, DPT, PhD. *Accreditation:* APTA (one or more programs are accredited). *Program availability:* Part-time. *Degree requirements:* For master's, thesis optional; for doctorate, thesis/dissertation. *Entrance requirements:* For master's and doctorate, GRE General Test.

**University of Memphis,** Graduate School, School of Health Studies, Memphis, TN 38152. Offers faith and health (Graduate Certificate); health studies (MS), including exercise, sport and movement sciences, health promotion, physical education teacher education; nutrition (MS), including clinical nutrition, environmental nutrition, nutrition science; sport nutrition and dietary supplementation (Graduate Certificate). *Program availability:* 100% online. *Faculty:* 19 full-time (11 women), 2 part-time/adjunct (1 woman). *Students:* 56 full-time (44 women), 42 part-time (33 women); includes 39 minority (24 Black or African American, non-Hispanic/Latino; 4 Asian, non-Hispanic/Latino; 4 Hispanic/Latino; 2 Native Hawaiian or other Pacific Islander, non-Hispanic/Latino; 5 Two or more races, non-Hispanic/Latino), 6 international. Average age 29. 63 applicants, 84% accepted, 37 enrolled. In 2019, 38 master's, 2 other advanced degrees awarded. *Degree requirements:* For master's, comprehensive exam, thesis or alternative, culminating experience; for Graduate Certificate, practicum. *Entrance requirements:* For master's, GRE or PRAXIS II, letters of recommendation, statement of goals, minimum undergraduate GPA of 2.5; for Graduate Certificate, minimum undergraduate GPA of 2.5. Additional exam requirements/recommendations for international students: required—TOEFL (minimum score 550 paper-based; 79 iBT). *Application deadline:* For fall admission, 4/15 priority date for domestic students; for spring admission, 10/15 priority date for domestic students; for summer admission, 4/15 priority date for domestic students. Application fee: $35 ($60 for international students). *Expenses: Tuition, area resident:* Full-time $9216; part-time $512 per credit hour. Tuition, state resident: full-time $9216; part-time $512 per credit hour. Tuition, nonresident: full-time $12,672; part-time $704 per credit hour. *International tuition:* $16,128 full-time. *Required fees:* $1530; $85 per credit hour. Tuition and fees vary according to program. *Financial support:* Research assistantships, teaching assistantships, career-related internships or fieldwork, Federal Work-Study, scholarships/grants, and unspecified assistantships available. Financial award application deadline: 2/1; financial award applicants required to submit FAFSA. *Unit head:* Dr. Richard Bloomer, Dean, 901-678-4316, Fax: 901-678-3591, E-mail: rbloomer@memphis.edu. *Application contact:* Dr. Richard Bloomer, Dean, 901-678-4316, Fax: 901-678-3591, E-mail: rbloomer@memphis.edu.
Website: http://www.memphis.edu/shs/

**University of Mississippi Medical Center,** School of Health Related Professions, Jackson, MS 39216-4505. Offers MOT, MPT. *Accreditation:* AOTA; NAACLS. *Program availability:* Part-time.

**University of Nebraska Medical Center,** College of Allied Health Professions, Omaha, NE 68198-4000. Offers MPAS, MPS, DPT, Certificate. *Accreditation:* APTA (one or more programs are accredited). *Entrance requirements:* For master's and doctorate, GRE. Additional exam requirements/recommendations for international students: required—TOEFL.

**University of Nevada, Las Vegas,** Graduate College, School of Integrated Health Sciences, Las Vegas, NV 89154-3018. Offers MS, DMP, DPT, PhD, Advanced Certificate. *Program availability:* Part-time. *Faculty:* 22 full-time (10 women), 12 part-time/adjunct (7 women). *Students:* 197 full-time (99 women), 22 part-time (8 women); includes 86 minority (6 Black or African American, non-Hispanic/Latino; 1 American Indian or Alaska Native, non-Hispanic/Latino; 34 Asian, non-Hispanic/Latino; 30 Hispanic/Latino; 1 Native Hawaiian or other Pacific Islander, non-Hispanic/Latino; 14 Two or more races, non-Hispanic/Latino), 11 international. Average age 28. 88 applicants, 43% accepted, 26 enrolled. In 2019, 20 master's, 39 doctorates awarded. *Degree requirements:* For master's, thesis (for some programs); for doctorate, comprehensive exam (for some programs), thesis/dissertation. *Entrance requirements:* For master's and doctorate, GRE General Test, letter of recommendation; statement of purpose. Additional exam requirements/recommendations for international students: required—TOEFL (minimum score 550 paper-based; 80 iBT), IELTS (minimum score 7). Application fee: $60 ($95 for international students). Electronic applications accepted. *Expenses:* Contact institution. *Financial support:* In 2019–20, 56 students received support, including 24 research assistantships with full tuition reimbursements available (averaging $16,521 per year), 32 teaching assistantships with full tuition reimbursements available (averaging $15,257 per year); institutionally sponsored loans, scholarships/grants, health care benefits, and unspecified assistantships also available. Financial award application deadline: 3/15; financial award applicants required to submit FAFSA. *Unit head:* Dr. Ronald T. Brown, Dean, 702-895-3693, Fax: 702-895-1356, E-mail: ihs.dean@unlv.edu. *Application contact:* Dr. Ronald T. Brown, Dean, 702-895-3693, Fax: 702-895-1356, E-mail: ihs.dean@unlv.edu.
Website: https://www.unlv.edu/ahs

**University of New Mexico,** Graduate Studies, Health Sciences Center, Albuquerque, NM 87131-2039. Offers MOT, MPH, MPT, MS, MSN, DNP, DPT, MD, PhD, Pharm D, Certificate, MSN/MA. *Expenses:* Tuition, state resident: full-time $7633; part-time $972 per year. Tuition, nonresident: full-time $22,586; part-time $3840 per year. *International tuition:* $23,292 full-time. *Required fees:* $8608. Tuition and fees vary according to course level, course load, degree level, program and student level.

**University of Northern Iowa,** Graduate College, College of Education, Ed D Program in Education, Cedar Falls, IA 50614. Offers allied health, recreation, and community services (Ed D); curriculum and instruction (Ed D); educational leadership (Ed D). *Program availability:* Part-time, evening/weekend. *Degree requirements:* For doctorate, thesis/dissertation. *Entrance requirements:* For doctorate, GRE, minimum GPA of 3.0, master's degree. Additional exam requirements/recommendations for international students: required—TOEFL (minimum score 500 paper-based; 61 iBT).

**University of Northern Iowa,** Graduate College, College of Education, School of Kinesiology, Allied Health and Human Services, Cedar Falls, IA 50614. Offers athletic training (MS); health education (MA), including community health education, health promotion/fitness management, school health education; leisure, youth and human services (MA); physical education (MA), including kinesiology, teaching/coaching. *Program availability:* Part-time, evening/weekend. *Degree requirements:* For master's, comprehensive exam, thesis or alternative. *Entrance requirements:* For master's, minimum GPA of 3.0. Additional exam requirements/recommendations for international students: required—TOEFL (minimum score 500 paper-based; 61 iBT).

**University of North Florida,** Brooks College of Health, Jacksonville, FL 32224. Offers MHA, MPH, MS, MSH, MSN, DNP, DPT, Certificate. *Program availability:* Part-time, evening/weekend. *Entrance requirements:* For master's, GRE General Test, minimum GPA of 3.0 in last 60 hours. Additional exam requirements/recommendations for international students: required—TOEFL (minimum score 500 paper-based; 61 iBT). Electronic applications accepted. *Expenses:* Contact institution.

**University of Oklahoma Health Sciences Center,** Graduate College, College of Allied Health, Oklahoma City, OK 73190. Offers MOT, MPT, MS, Au D, PhD, Certificate. *Accreditation:* AOTA; APTA. *Program availability:* Part-time. Terminal master's awarded for partial completion of doctoral program. *Degree requirements:* For master's, comprehensive exam, thesis optional; for doctorate, one foreign language, comprehensive exam, thesis/dissertation. *Entrance requirements:* For master's and doctorate, GRE General Test, 3 letters of recommendation. Additional exam requirements/recommendations for international students: required—TOEFL.

**University of Phoenix - Las Vegas Campus,** College of Human Services, Las Vegas, NV 89135. Offers marriage, family, and child therapy (MSC); mental health counseling (MSC); school counseling (MSC). *Program availability:* Online learning. *Entrance requirements:* For master's, minimum undergraduate GPA of 2.5, 3 years of work experience. Additional exam requirements/recommendations for international students: required—TOEFL (minimum score 550 paper-based; 79 iBT). Electronic applications accepted.

**University of Puerto Rico - Medical Sciences Campus,** School of Health Professions, San Juan, PR 00936-5067. Offers MS, Au D, Certificate. *Degree requirements:* For master's, one foreign language, thesis (for some programs). *Entrance requirements:* For master's, GRE or EXADEP, interview; for doctorate, EXADEP; for Certificate, Allied Health Professions Admissions Test, minimum GPA of 2.5, interview. Electronic applications accepted.

**University of South Alabama,** Pat Capps Covey College of Allied Health Professions, Mobile, AL 36688-0002. Offers MHS, MS, Au D, DPT, PhD. *Faculty:* 36 full-time (30 women), 7 part-time/adjunct (6 women). *Students:* 418 full-time (336 women), 1 (woman) part-time; includes 27 minority (5 Black or African American, non-Hispanic/Latino; 5 American Indian or Alaska Native, non-Hispanic/Latino; 7 Asian, non-Hispanic/Latino; 5 Hispanic/Latino; 1 Native Hawaiian or other Pacific Islander, non-Hispanic/Latino; 4 Two or more races, non-Hispanic/Latino), 26 international. Average age 24. 796 applicants, 44% accepted, 139 enrolled. In 2019, 92 master's, 54 doctorates awarded. *Entrance requirements:* Additional exam requirements/recommendations for international students: required—TOEFL (minimum score 600 paper-based; 100 iBT). *Application deadline:* Applications are processed on a rolling basis. Application fee: $75. Electronic applications accepted. *Expenses:* Contact institution. *Financial support:* Fellowships, research assistantships, teaching assistantships, career-related internships or fieldwork, Federal Work-Study, institutionally sponsored loans, scholarships/grants, and unspecified assistantships available. Support available to part-time students. Financial award application deadline: 3/31; financial award applicants required to submit FAFSA. *Unit head:* Dr. Susan Gordon-Hickey, Interim Dean, College of Allied Health, 251-445-9250, Fax: 251-445-9259, E-mail: gordonhickey@southalabama.edu. *Application contact:* Dr. Susan Gordon-Hickey, Interim Dean, College of Allied Health, 251-445-9250, Fax: 251-445-9259, E-mail: gordonhickey@southalabama.edu.
Website: https://www.southalabama.edu/colleges/alliedhealth/

**University of South Dakota,** Graduate School, School of Health Sciences, Vermillion, SD 57069. Offers MA, MPH, MS, MSW, DPT, OTD, PhD, Graduate Certificate. *Program availability:* Part-time. *Entrance requirements:* For master's, GRE General Test, GRE Subject Test.

**The University of Tennessee Health Science Center,** College of Graduate Health Sciences, Memphis, TN 38163. Offers biomedical engineering (MS, PhD); biomedical sciences (PhD); dental sciences (MDS); epidemiology (MS); health outcomes and policy research (PhD); laboratory research and management (MS); nursing science (PhD); pharmaceutical sciences (PhD); pharmacology (MS); speech and hearing science (PhD); DDS/PhD; DNP/PhD; MD/PhD; Pharm D/PhD. Terminal master's awarded for partial completion of doctoral program. *Degree requirements:* For master's, comprehensive exam, thesis; for doctorate, thesis/dissertation, oral and written preliminary and comprehensive exams. *Entrance requirements:* For master's and doctorate, GRE General Test, minimum GPA of 3.0. Additional exam requirements/recommendations for international students: recommended—TOEFL (minimum score 79 iBT), IELTS (minimum score 6.5). Electronic applications accepted. *Expenses:* Contact institution.

**The University of Tennessee Health Science Center,** College of Health Professions, Memphis, TN 38163-0002. Offers audiology (MS, Au D); clinical laboratory science (MSCLS); cytopathology practice (MCP); health informatics and information management (MHIIM); occupational therapy (MOT); physical therapy (DPT, ScDPT); physician assistant (MMS); speech-language pathology (MS). *Accreditation:* AOTA; APTA. *Program availability:* Part-time, evening/weekend, online learning. Terminal master's awarded for partial completion of doctoral program. *Degree requirements:* For master's, comprehensive exam, thesis; for doctorate, comprehensive exam, residency. *Entrance requirements:* For master's, GRE (MOT, MSCLS), minimum GPA of 3.0, 3 letters of reference, national accreditation (MSCLS), GRE if GPA is less than 3.0 (MCP); for doctorate, GRE. Additional exam requirements/recommendations for international students: required—TOEFL (minimum score 550 paper-based; 80 iBT). Electronic applications accepted. *Expenses:* Contact institution.

**The University of Texas at El Paso,** Graduate School, College of Health Sciences, Program in Interdisciplinary Health Sciences, El Paso, TX 79968-0001. Offers PhD. *Degree requirements:* For doctorate, thesis/dissertation. *Entrance requirements:* For doctorate, GRE, three letters of reference, relevant personal/professional experience, evidence of a master's degree (MS or MA) or other terminal degree, official transcripts. Additional exam requirements/recommendations for international students: required—TOEFL (minimum score 550 paper-based); recommended—IELTS. Electronic applications accepted.

**The University of Texas Medical Branch,** School of Health Professions, Galveston, TX 77555. Offers MOT, MPAS, MPT, DPT. *Degree requirements:* For master's, thesis or alternative; for doctorate, thesis/dissertation or alternative. *Entrance requirements:* For master's, GRE, experience in field, minimum GPA of 3.0; for doctorate, GRE, documentation of 40 hours experience. Additional exam requirements/recommendations for international students: required—TOEFL (minimum score 550 paper-based). Electronic applications accepted.

**University of Vermont,** Graduate College, College of Nursing and Health Sciences, Burlington, VT 05405-0068. Offers MS, DNP, DPT, PhD, Post-Graduate Certificate. *Degree requirements:* For master's, thesis. *Entrance requirements:* For master's and doctorate, GRE General Test. Additional exam requirements/recommendations for international students: required—TOEFL (minimum score 550 paper-based, 90 iBT) or IELTS (6.5). Electronic applications accepted.

**University of Wisconsin–Milwaukee,** Graduate School, College of Health Sciences, Milwaukee, WI 53211. Offers MHA, MS, DPT, PhD, Graduate Certificate. *Program availability:* Part-time. *Degree requirements:* For master's, thesis; for doctorate, comprehensive exam, thesis/dissertation. *Entrance requirements:* For doctorate, GRE General Test, master's degree. Additional exam requirements/recommendations for international students: required—TOEFL (minimum score 600 paper-based), IELTS (minimum score 6.5). *Expenses:* Contact institution.

*Allied Health—General*

**Virginia Commonwealth University,** Graduate School, School of Allied Health Professions, Doctoral Program in Health Related Sciences, Richmond, VA 23284-9005. Offers clinical laboratory sciences (PhD); gerontology (PhD); health administration (PhD); nurse anesthesia (PhD); occupational therapy (PhD); physical therapy (PhD); radiation sciences (PhD); rehabilitation leadership (PhD). *Entrance requirements:* For doctorate, GRE General Test or MAT, minimum GPA of 3.3 in master's degree. Additional exam requirements/recommendations for international students: required—TOEFL (minimum score 600 paper-based; 100 iBT); recommended—IELTS (minimum score 6.5). Electronic applications accepted.

**Western University of Health Sciences,** College of Health Sciences, Pomona, CA 91766-1854. Offers health sciences (MS). *Accreditation:* APTA (one or more programs are accredited). *Program availability:* Blended/hybrid learning. *Faculty:* 25 full-time (17 women), 17 part-time/adjunct (10 women). *Students:* 354 full-time (243 women), 23 part-time (18 women); includes 230 minority (14 Black or African American, non-Hispanic/Latino; 3 American Indian or Alaska Native, non-Hispanic/Latino; 82 Asian, non-Hispanic/Latino; 91 Hispanic/Latino; 2 Native Hawaiian or other Pacific Islander, non-Hispanic/Latino; 38 Two or more races, non-Hispanic/Latino). Average age 28. 2,873 applicants, 10% accepted, 158 enrolled. In 2019, 102 master's, 56 doctorates awarded. *Degree requirements:* For master's, thesis; for doctorate, comprehensive exam (for some programs), thesis/dissertation (for some programs). *Entrance requirements:* For master's, GRE (minimum score of 3.5 on analytical writing), minimum overall, science and prerequisite GPA of 3.0; letters of recommendation; interview; demonstrated history of ongoing community service and involvement; health screenings and immunizations; background check; statement of purpose; current curriculum vitae; for doctorate, GRE, letters of recommendation, bachelor's degree, minimum GPA of 3.0, volunteer or paid work experience, access to a computer meeting minimum technical standards, health screening and immunization, background check. Additional exam requirements/recommendations for international students: required—TOEFL (minimum score 540 paper-based; 79 iBT). *Application deadline:* Applications are processed on a rolling basis. Electronic applications accepted. *Expenses:* Tuition and fees vary among programs. *Financial support:* In 2019–20, 76 students received support. Career-related internships or fieldwork, scholarships/grants, and traineeships available. Financial award application deadline: 3/2; financial award applicants required to submit FAFSA. *Unit head:* Dr. Dee Schilling, Interim Dean, 909-469-5300, Fax: 909-469-5438, E-mail: dschilling@westernu.edu. *Application contact:* Office of Admissions, 909-469-5650, Fax: 909-469-5570, E-mail: admissions@westernu.edu.
Website: https://www.westernu.edu/health-sciences/

**Wichita State University,** Graduate School, College of Health Professions, Wichita, KS 67260. Offers MA, MPA, MSN, Au D, DNP, DPT, PhD. *Accreditation:* APTA (one or more programs are accredited). *Program availability:* Part-time.

# Anesthesiologist Assistant Studies

**Case Western Reserve University,** School of Medicine and School of Graduate Studies, Graduate Programs in Medicine, Anesthesiologist Assistant Program, Cleveland, OH 44106. Offers MS. *Degree requirements:* For master's, thesis. *Entrance requirements:* For master's, MCAT. Additional exam requirements/recommendations for international students: required—TOEFL. Electronic applications accepted. *Expenses:* Contact institution.

**Emory University,** School of Medicine, Programs in Allied Health Professions, Anesthesiology Assistant Program, Atlanta, GA 30322. Offers MM Sc. *Entrance requirements:* For master's, GRE General Test, MCAT. Additional exam requirements/recommendations for international students: required—TOEFL (minimum score 600 paper-based; 94 iBT). Electronic applications accepted. *Expenses:* Contact institution.

**Medical College of Wisconsin,** Medical School, Program in Anesthesiology, Milwaukee, WI 53226. Offers MSA. *Students:* 45 full-time (27 women); includes 7 minority (1 Black or African American, non-Hispanic/Latino; 6 Asian, non-Hispanic/Latino), 1 international. Average age 26. 227 applicants, 9% accepted, 16 enrolled. In 2019, 12 master's awarded. *Application deadline:* For fall admission, 2/1 for domestic students. Applications are processed on a rolling basis. Application fee: $160. Electronic applications accepted. *Expenses:* $46,540 tuition per year for years one and two; $23,270 tuition for year three; $832.50 fees for year one; $766 fees for year two; $388 fees for year three; $3,636.93 per year for single health insurance. *Financial support:* Application deadline: 2/1; applicants required to submit FAFSA. *Unit head:* Dr. Michael Stout, Program Director, E-mail: mistout@mcw.edu. *Application contact:* Registrar, 414-456-8733.
Website: https://www.mcw.edu/departments/anesthesiology/education/master-of-science-in-anesthesia-program

**Nova Southeastern University,** Dr. Pallavi Patel College of Health Care Sciences, Fort Lauderdale, FL 33314-7796. Offers anesthesiologist assistant (MSA); audiology (Au D); health science (MH Sc, DHSc, PhD); occupational therapy (MOT, Dr OT, PhD); physical therapy (DPT, TDPT); physician assistant (MMS); speech-language pathology (MS). *Accreditation:* AOTA; ASHA. *Program availability:* Part-time, 100% online, blended/hybrid learning. *Faculty:* 127 full-time (85 women), 107 part-time/adjunct (79 women). *Students:* 1,336 full-time (992 women), 950 part-time (824 women); includes 839 minority (195 Black or African American, non-Hispanic/Latino; 4 American Indian or Alaska Native, non-Hispanic/Latino; 165 Asian, non-Hispanic/Latino; 397 Hispanic/Latino; 3 Native Hawaiian or other Pacific Islander, non-Hispanic/Latino; 75 Two or more races, non-Hispanic/Latino), 26 international. Average age 30. 634 applicants, 28% accepted, 159 enrolled. In 2019, 613 master's, 261 doctorates awarded. Terminal master's awarded for partial completion of doctoral program. *Degree requirements:* For doctorate, comprehensive exam, thesis/dissertation (for some programs), 12-month full-time clinical externship experience. *Entrance requirements:* For master's, GRE General Test; for doctorate, personal interview, essay in application,additional letters may be requested by the program after initial review of application if so warranted. *Application deadline:* Applications are processed on a rolling basis. Application fee: $50. Electronic applications accepted. *Expenses:* Contact institution. *Financial support:* Federal Work-Study, institutionally sponsored loans, and scholarships/grants available. Financial award application deadline: 4/15; financial award applicants required to submit FAFSA. *Unit head:* Dr. Stanley Wilson, Dean, 954-262-1203, E-mail: swilson@nova.edu. *Application contact:* Joycelyn Vogt, Director of Admissions and Outreach, 954-262-1200, Fax: 954-262-1181, E-mail: joycelyn.vogt@nova.edu.
Website: http://healthsciences.nova.edu/

**Quinnipiac University,** Frank H. Netter MD School of Medicine, Program for Anesthesiologist Assistant, Hamden, CT 06518-1940. Offers MMS. *Degree requirements:* For master's, comprehensive exam. *Entrance requirements:* For master's, GRE or MCAT, bachelor's degree; official transcripts of all undergraduate and graduate course work; three letters of recommendation; essay; interview; criminal background check. Additional exam requirements/recommendations for international students: required—TOEFL. Electronic applications accepted. *Expenses:* Contact institution.

**South University - Savannah,** Graduate Programs, College of Health Professions, Program in Anesthesiologist Assistant, Savannah, GA 31406. Offers MM Sc.

**University of Colorado Denver,** School of Medicine, Program in Anesthesiology, Aurora, CO 80045. Offers MS. *Entrance requirements:* For master's, GRE or MCAT, three letters of recommendation; curriculum vitae or resume; statement of purpose. Additional exam requirements/recommendations for international students: required—TOEFL. Tuition and fees vary according to course load, program and reciprocity agreements.

**University of Guelph,** Ontario Veterinary College and Office of Graduate and Postdoctoral Studies, Graduate Programs in Veterinary Sciences, Department of Clinical Studies, Guelph, ON N1G 2W1, Canada. Offers anesthesiology (M Sc, DV Sc); cardiology (DV Sc, Diploma); clinical studies (Diploma); dermatology (M Sc); diagnostic imaging (M Sc, DV Sc); emergency/critical care (M Sc, DV Sc, Diploma); medicine (M Sc, DV Sc); neurology (M Sc, DV Sc); ophthalmology (M Sc, DV Sc); surgery (M Sc, DV Sc). *Degree requirements:* For master's, thesis; for doctorate, comprehensive exam, thesis/dissertation. *Entrance requirements:* Additional exam requirements/recommendations for international students: required—TOEFL (minimum score 550 paper-based), IELTS (minimum score 6.5). Electronic applications accepted.

**Université Laval,** Faculty of Medicine, Post-Professional Programs in Medical Studies, Québec, QC G1K 7P4, Canada. Offers anatomy–pathology (DESS); anesthesiology (DESS); cardiology (DESS); care of older people (Diploma); clinical research (DESS); community health (DESS); dermatology (DESS); diagnostic radiology (DESS); emergency medicine (Diploma); family medicine (DESS); general surgery (DESS); geriatrics (DESS); hematology (DESS); internal medicine (DESS); maternal and fetal medicine (Diploma); medical biochemistry (DESS); medical microbiology and infectious diseases (DESS); medical oncology (DESS); nephrology (DESS); neurology (DESS); neurosurgery (DESS); obstetrics and gynecology (DESS); ophthalmology (DESS); orthopedic surgery (DESS); oto-rhino-laryngology (DESS); palliative medicine (Diploma); pediatrics (DESS); plastic surgery (DESS); psychiatry (DESS); pulmonary medicine (DESS); radiology–oncology (DESS); thoracic surgery (DESS); urology (DESS). *Degree requirements:* For other advanced degree, comprehensive exam. *Entrance requirements:* For degree, knowledge of French. Electronic applications accepted.

# Clinical Laboratory Sciences/Medical Technology

**Albany College of Pharmacy and Health Sciences,** School of Arts and Sciences, Albany, NY 12208. Offers clinical laboratory sciences (MS); cytotechnology and molecular cytology (MS); health outcomes research (MS); molecular biosciences (MS). *Degree requirements:* For master's, thesis. *Entrance requirements:* For master's, GRE, minimum GPA of 3.0. Additional exam requirements/recommendations for international students: required—TOEFL (minimum score 84 iBT). Electronic applications accepted.

**Austin Peay State University,** College of Graduate Studies, College of Science, Technology, Engineering and Mathematics, Department of Biology, Clarksville, TN 37044. Offers clinical laboratory science (MS). *Program availability:* Part-time. *Faculty:* 12 full-time (5 women). *Students:* 10 full-time (4 women), 22 part-time (13 women); includes 7 minority (2 Black or African American, non-Hispanic/Latino; 2 Hispanic/Latino; 3 Two or more races, non-Hispanic/Latino), 3 international. Average age 27. 21 applicants, 100% accepted, 6 enrolled. In 2019, 4 master's awarded. *Degree requirements:* For master's, comprehensive exam, thesis optional. *Entrance requirements:* For master's, GRE General Test, 3 letters of recommendation, minimum undergraduate GPA of 2.75. Additional exam requirements/recommendations for international students: required—TOEFL (minimum score 500 paper-based). *Application deadline:* For fall admission, 8/5 priority date for domestic students. Applications are processed on a rolling basis. Application fee: $45 ($55 for international students). Electronic applications accepted. *Financial support:* Research assistantships with full tuition reimbursements, career-related internships or fieldwork, Federal Work-Study, institutionally sponsored loans, scholarships/grants, and unspecified assistantships available. Support available to part-time students. Financial award application deadline: 7/1; financial award applicants required to submit FAFSA. *Unit head:* Dr. Don Dailey, Chair, 931-221-7781, Fax: 931-221-6323, E-mail: daileyd@apsu.edu. *Application contact:* Megan Mitchell, Coordinator of Graduate Admissions, 800-859-4723, Fax: 931-221-7641, E-mail: gradadmissions@apsu.edu.
Website: http://www.apsu.edu/biology/

**Baylor College of Medicine,** Graduate School of Biomedical Sciences, Program in Clinical Scientist Training, Houston, TX 77030-3498. Offers MS, PhD. Terminal master's awarded for partial completion of doctoral program. *Degree requirements:* For master's, thesis; for doctorate, thesis/dissertation, public defense. Electronic applications accepted.

**The Catholic University of America,** School of Arts and Sciences, Department of Biology, Washington, DC 20064. Offers biotechnology (MS); cell and microbial biology (MS, PhD), including cell biology; clinical laboratory science (MS, PhD); MSLS/MS. *Program availability:* Part-time. *Faculty:* 10 full-time (4 women), 3 part-time/adjunct (1 woman). *Students:* 16 full-time (13 women), 36 part-time (19 women); includes 11 minority (4 Black or African American, non-Hispanic/Latino; 3 Asian, non-Hispanic/Latino; 4 Two or more races, non-Hispanic/Latino), 33 international. Average age 31. 46 applicants, 65% accepted, 12 enrolled. In 2019, 15 master's, 8 doctorates awarded. Terminal master's awarded for partial completion of doctoral program. *Degree requirements:* For master's and doctorate, comprehensive exam. *Entrance requirements:* For master's and doctorate, GRE General Test, GRE Subject Test, statement of purpose, official copies of academic transcripts, three letters of recommendation. Additional exam requirements/recommendations for international students: required—TOEFL (minimum score 550 paper-based; 80 iBT). *Application deadline:* For fall admission, 7/15 priority date for domestic students, 7/1 for international students; for spring admission, 11/15 priority date for domestic students, 11/1 for international students. Applications are processed on a rolling basis. Application fee: $55. Electronic applications accepted. *Expenses:* Contact institution. *Financial support:* Fellowships, research assistantships, teaching assistantships, Federal Work-Study, scholarships/grants, tuition waivers (full and partial), and unspecified assistantships available. Financial award application deadline: 2/1; financial award applicants required to submit FAFSA. *Unit head:* Dr. Venigalla Rao, Chair, 202-319-5271, Fax: 202-319-5721, E-mail: rao@cua.edu. *Application contact:* Dr. Steven Brown, Director of Graduate Admissions, 202-319-5057, Fax: 202-319-6533, E-mail: cua-admissions@cua.edu.
Website: http://biology.cua.edu/

**Dominican University of California,** School of Health and Natural Sciences, Program in Clinical Laboratory Sciences, San Rafael, CA 94901-2298. Offers MS. *Program availability:* Part-time, evening/weekend. *Degree requirements:* For master's, thesis. *Entrance requirements:* For master's, GRE, minimum GPA of 3.0. Additional exam requirements/recommendations for international students: required—TOEFL (minimum score 550 paper-based; 80 iBT), IELTS (minimum score 6.5). Electronic applications accepted. *Expenses:* Contact institution.

**Fairleigh Dickinson University, Metropolitan Campus,** University College: Arts, Sciences, and Professional Studies, Henry P. Becton School of Nursing and Allied Health, Program in Medical Technology, Teaneck, NJ 07666-1914. Offers MS.

**Inter American University of Puerto Rico, Metropolitan Campus,** Graduate Programs, Program in Medical Technology, San Juan, PR 00919-1293. Offers administration of clinical laboratories (MS); molecular microbiology (MS). *Accreditation:* NAACLS. *Program availability:* Part-time. *Degree requirements:* For master's, comprehensive exam. *Entrance requirements:* For master's, BS in medical technology, minimum GPA of 2.5. Electronic applications accepted.

**Lipscomb University,** Program in Biomolecular Science, Nashville, TN 37204-3951. Offers human disease (MS); laboratory research (MS). *Program availability:* Part-time, evening/weekend. *Degree requirements:* For master's, capstone project. *Entrance requirements:* For master's, GRE (minimum score of 300/1000 on prior scoring system), MCAT (minimum score of 24), DAT (minimum score of 17), BS in related field, transcripts, minimum undergraduate GPA of 3.0, 2 letters of recommendation, resume. Additional exam requirements/recommendations for international students: required—TOEFL (minimum score 570 paper-based). Electronic applications accepted. *Expenses:* Contact institution.

**Mayo Clinic Graduate School of Biomedical Sciences,** Program in Clinical and Translational Science, Rochester, MN 55905. Offers clinical and translational science (MS); laboratory-based translational science (PhD); patient-based translational science (PhD); population-based translational science (PhD). Terminal master's awarded for partial completion of doctoral program. *Degree requirements:* For master's, thesis; for doctorate, comprehensive exam, thesis/dissertation. Electronic applications accepted.

**Medical College of Wisconsin,** Graduate School, Program in Clinical and Translational Science, Milwaukee, WI 53226. Offers MS. *Program availability:* Part-time, evening/weekend. *Students:* 23 part-time (13 women); includes 7 minority (2 Black or African American, non-Hispanic/Latino; 3 Asian, non-Hispanic/Latino; 1 Hispanic/Latino; 1 Two or more races, non-Hispanic/Latino), 9 international. Average age 34. 37 applicants, 62% accepted, 19 enrolled. In 2019, 13 master's awarded. *Entrance requirements:* For master's, GRE, official transcripts, three letters of recommendation. Additional exam requirements/recommendations for international students: required—TOEFL (minimum score 600 paper-based; 100 iBT). *Application deadline:* For fall admission, 7/1 for domestic and international students; for spring admission, 11/1 for domestic and international students; for summer admission, 4/1 for domestic and international students. Application fee: $50. Electronic applications accepted. *Expenses:* $1,056 per credit for masters and certificate students; $155 per year fees for full time students. *Financial support:* Applicants required to submit FAFSA. *Unit head:* Leonard Egede, MD, Director, 414-955-8218, Fax: 414-955-6555, E-mail: legede@mcw.edu. *Application contact:* Recruitment Office, 414-955-4402, Fax: 414-955-6555, E-mail: gradschoolrecruit@mcw.edu.
Website: http://ctsi.mcw.edu/

**Michigan State University,** The Graduate School, College of Natural Science, Biomedical Laboratory Diagnostics Program, East Lansing, MI 48824. Offers biomedical laboratory operations (MS); clinical laboratory sciences (MS). *Entrance requirements:* Additional exam requirements/recommendations for international students: required—TOEFL. Electronic applications accepted.

**Milwaukee School of Engineering,** MS Program in Perfusion, Milwaukee, WI 53202-3109. Offers MS. *Degree requirements:* For master's, comprehensive exam, thesis. *Entrance requirements:* For master's, GRE General Test (percentiles must average 50% or better), baccalaureate degree with minimum undergraduate GPA of 2.8; at least one undergraduate course in each of the following areas: physiology (or anatomy and physiology), chemistry, mathematics and physics; 3 letters of recommendation; personal interview; observation of 2 perfusion clinical cases. Additional exam requirements/recommendations for international students: required—TOEFL (minimum score 90 iBT), IELTS (minimum score 7). Electronic applications accepted.

**Northern Michigan University,** Office of Graduate Education and Research, College of Health Sciences and Professional Studies, School of Clinical Sciences, Marquette, MI 49855-5301. Offers clinical molecular genetics (MS). *Accreditation:* NAACLS. *Program availability:* Part-time. *Degree requirements:* For master's, thesis or project to be presented as a seminar at the conclusion of the program. *Entrance requirements:* For master's, minimum undergraduate GPA of 3.0; bachelor's degree in clinical laboratory science or biology; laboratory experience; statement of intent that includes lab skills and experiences along with reason for pursuing this degree; 3 letters of recommendation (instructors or professional references). Additional exam requirements/recommendations for international students: required—TOEFL (minimum score 500 paper-based; 61 iBT), IELTS (minimum score 6). *Application deadline:* For fall admission, 7/1 for domestic students; for winter admission, 12/1 for domestic students; for summer admission, 4/1 for domestic students. Applications are processed on a rolling basis. Application fee: $50. Electronic applications accepted. *Financial support:* Application deadline: 3/1; applicants required to submit FAFSA. *Unit head:* Dr. Paul Mann, Associate Dean/Director, 906-227-2338, E-mail: pmann@nmu.edu. *Application contact:* Dr. Matthew Jennings, Assistant Professor, 906-227-1661, E-mail: majennin@nmu.edu.
Website: http://www.nmu.edu/clinicalsciences/

**Northwestern University,** School of Professional Studies, Program in Regulatory Compliance, Evanston, IL 60208. Offers clinical research (MS); healthcare compliance (MS); quality systems (MS). *Program availability:* Part-time, evening/weekend.

**Pontifical Catholic University of Puerto Rico,** College of Sciences, School of Medical Technology, Ponce, PR 00717-0777. Offers Certificate. *Accreditation:* NAACLS. *Entrance requirements:* For degree, letters of recommendation, interview, minimum GPA of 2.75.

**Rush University,** College of Health Sciences, Department of Medical Laboratory Science, Chicago, IL 60612-3832. Offers clinical laboratory management (MS); medical laboratory science (MS). *Accreditation:* NAACLS. *Degree requirements:* For master's, comprehensive exam, project. *Entrance requirements:* For master's, 16 semester hours of chemistry, 12 semester hours of biology, 3 semester hours of mathematics, interview. Additional exam requirements/recommendations for international students: required—TOEFL. *Application deadline:* For fall admission, 8/1 for domestic students. Electronic applications accepted. *Financial support:* Federal Work-Study, institutionally sponsored loans, and scholarships/grants available. Support available to part-time students. Financial award application deadline: 4/15; financial award applicants required to submit FAFSA. *Unit head:* Dr. Maribeth Flaws, Acting Chair, 312-942-2115, E-mail: maribeth_l_flaws@rush.edu. *Application contact:* Dr. Maribeth Flaws, Acting Chair, 312-942-2115, E-mail: maribeth_l_flaws@rush.edu.
Website: http://www.rushu.rush.edu/mls

**Rutgers University - Newark,** School of Health Related Professions, Department of Clinical Laboratory Sciences, Newark, NJ 07102. Offers MS. *Accreditation:* NAACLS. *Program availability:* Part-time, online learning. *Degree requirements:* For master's, project. *Entrance requirements:* For master's, two recommendations, personal statement, current resume or curriculum vita, minimum GPA of 2.75. Additional exam requirements/recommendations for international students: required—TOEFL.

**Rutgers University - New Brunswick,** Graduate School of Biomedical Sciences, Program in Clinical and Translational Science, Piscataway, NJ 08854-8097. Offers MS. *Program availability:* Part-time. *Degree requirements:* For master's, thesis.

**State University of New York Upstate Medical University,** Program in Medical Technology, Syracuse, NY 13210. Offers MS. *Accreditation:* NAACLS. *Degree requirements:* For master's, thesis. *Entrance requirements:* For master's, GRE General Test, GRE Subject Test, 2 years of medical technology experience.

**Tarleton State University,** College of Graduate Studies, College of Health Sciences and Human Services, Department of Medical Laboratory Sciences and Public Health, Fort Worth, TX 76402. Offers medical laboratory sciences (MS). *Accreditation:* NAACLS. *Program availability:* Part-time. *Faculty:* 6 full-time (5 women), 1 (woman) part-time/adjunct. *Students:* 10 full-time (8 women), 13 part-time (9 women); includes 12 minority (3 Black or African American, non-Hispanic/Latino; 1 American Indian or Alaska Native, non-Hispanic/Latino; 4 Asian, non-Hispanic/Latino; 4 Hispanic/Latino), 2 international. Average age 30. 24 applicants, 71% accepted, 13 enrolled. In 2019, 1 master's awarded. *Degree requirements:* For master's, comprehensive exam, thesis optional. *Entrance requirements:* For master's, GRE, minimum GPA of 2.5. Additional exam requirements/recommendations for international students: required—TOEFL (minimum score 520 paper-based; 69 iBT); recommended—IELTS (minimum score 6), TSE (minimum score 50). *Application deadline:* For fall admission, 8/15 for domestic students; for spring admission, 1/7 for domestic students. Applications are processed on a rolling basis. Application fee: $50 ($130 for international students). Electronic applications accepted. *Expenses:* Tuition, state resident: part-time $221.73 per credit hour. Tuition, nonresident: part-time $636.73 per credit hour. *Required fees:* $198 per credit hour. $100 per semester. Tuition and fees vary according to degree level. *Financial support:* Career-related internships or fieldwork, Federal Work-Study, and scholarships/grants available. Support available to part-time students. Financial award application deadline: 5/1; financial award applicants required to submit FAFSA. *Unit head:* Sally Lewis, Head, 817-926-1101, E-mail: slewis@tarleton.edu. *Application contact:* Wendy Weiss, Graduate Admissions Coordinator, 254-968-9104, Fax: 254-968-9670, E-mail: weiss@tarleton.edu.
Website: http://www.tarleton.edu/degrees/masters/ms-medical-laboratory-science/

**Thomas Jefferson University,** Jefferson College of Health Professions, Department of Medical Laboratory Sciences and Biotechnology, Philadelphia, PA 19107. Offers biotechnology (MS); cytotechnology (MS); medical laboratory science (MS). *Accreditation:* NAACLS. *Program availability:* Part-time. *Degree requirements:* For master's, comprehensive exam. *Entrance requirements:* Additional exam requirements/recommendations for international students: required—TOEFL (minimum score 87 iBT), IELTS (minimum score 6.5). Electronic applications accepted. *Expenses:* Contact institution.

**Tufts University,** Graduate School of Biomedical Sciences, Clinical and Translational Science Program, Medford, MA 02155. Offers MS, PhD, Certificate. *Faculty:* 33 full-time (11 women), 4 part-time/adjunct (0 women). *Students:* 21 full-time (13 women); includes 8 minority (1 Black or African American, non-Hispanic/Latino; 5 Asian, non-Hispanic/Latino; 1 Hispanic/Latino; 1 Two or more races, non-Hispanic/Latino), 4 international. Average age 38. 18 applicants, 39% accepted, 6 enrolled. In 2019, 3 master's awarded. *Degree requirements:* For master's, thesis; for doctorate, comprehensive exam, thesis/dissertation. *Entrance requirements:* For master's and doctorate, strong clinical research background; resume; personal statement; 3 letters of recommendation. *Application deadline:* For fall admission, 5/1 for domestic and international students. Applications are processed on a rolling basis. Application fee: $90. Electronic applications accepted. *Expenses:* Contact institution. *Unit head:* Dr. David Kent, Program Director, 617-636-3234, Fax: 617-636-8023, E-mail: dkent@tuftsmedicalcenter.edu. *Application contact:* Dr. Elizabeth Wiltrout, Program Manager, 617-636-2563, E-mail: ewiltrout@tuftsmedicalcenter.org.
Website: https://gsbs.tufts.edu/academics/CTS

**Universidad de las Américas Puebla,** Division of Graduate Studies, School of Sciences, Program in Clinical Analysis (Biomedicine), Puebla, Mexico. Offers MS. *Program availability:* Part-time, evening/weekend. *Degree requirements:* For master's, one foreign language, thesis.

**Université de Sherbrooke,** Faculty of Medicine and Health Sciences, Graduate Programs in Medicine, Program in Clinical Sciences, Sherbrooke, QC J1H 5N4, Canada. Offers M Sc, PhD. *Program availability:* Part-time. Terminal master's awarded for partial completion of doctoral program. *Degree requirements:* For master's, thesis; for doctorate, thesis/dissertation. Electronic applications accepted.

**University at Buffalo, the State University of New York,** Graduate School, Jacobs School of Medicine and Biomedical Sciences, Graduate Programs in Medicine and Biomedical Sciences, Department of Biotechnical and Clinical Laboratory Sciences,

Buffalo, NY 14214. Offers biotechnology (MS). *Accreditation:* NAACLS. *Program availability:* Part-time. *Faculty:* 6 full-time (2 women). *Students:* 6 full-time (3 women); includes 3 minority (all Asian, non-Hispanic/Latino), 2 international. Average age 27. 57 applicants, 21% accepted, 6 enrolled. In 2019, 6 master's awarded. *Degree requirements:* For master's, thesis. *Entrance requirements:* For master's, minimum GPA of 3.0 or equivalent. Additional exam requirements/recommendations for international students: required—TOEFL (minimum score 79 iBT), IELTS (minimum score 6.5). *Application deadline:* For fall admission, 3/1 priority date for domestic students, 2/1 priority date for international students. Applications are processed on a rolling basis. Application fee: $85. Electronic applications accepted. *Expenses: Tuition, area resident:* Full-time $11,310; part-time $471 per credit hour. Tuition, state resident: full-time $11,310; part-time $471 per credit hour. Tuition, nonresident: full-time $23,100; part-time $963 per credit hour. *International tuition:* $23,100 full-time. *Required fees:* $2820. *Financial support:* In 2019–20, 6 students received support, including 1 research assistantship with tuition reimbursement available (averaging $15,000 per year), 5 teaching assistantships with full tuition reimbursements available (averaging $10,000 per year). Financial award application deadline: 3/1. *Unit head:* Dr. Paul J. Kostyniak, Chair, 716-829-5188, Fax: 716-829-3601, E-mail: pjkost@buffalo.edu. *Application contact:* Dr. Stephen T. Koury, Director of Graduate Studies, 716-829-5188, Fax: 716-829-3601, E-mail: stvkoury@buffalo.edu.
Website: http://www.smbs.buffalo.edu/cls/biotech-ms.html

**The University of Alabama at Birmingham,** School of Health Professions, Program in Clinical Laboratory Science, Birmingham, AL 35294. Offers MS. *Accreditation:* NAACLS. *Students:* 34 full-time (22 women), 2 part-time (1 woman); includes 11 minority (9 Black or African American, non-Hispanic/Latino; 2 Asian, non-Hispanic/Latino). Average age 27. 49 applicants, 55% accepted, 16 enrolled. In 2019, 17 master's awarded. *Degree requirements:* For master's, thesis optional. *Entrance requirements:* For master's, GRE General Test, interview, related undergraduate major, minimum undergraduate GPA of 3.0 computed from all undergraduate credits or from the last 60 semester hours of undergraduate course credit. Additional exam requirements/recommendations for international students: required—TOEFL (minimum score 550 paper-based; 80 iBT), TWE. *Application deadline:* For fall admission, 2/1 priority date for domestic students. Application fee: $0 ($60 for international students). Electronic applications accepted. *Financial support:* Application deadline: 4/15. *Unit head:* Dr. Janelle Chiasera, Graduate Program Director, 205-934-5994, E-mail: chiasera@uab.edu. *Application contact:* Susan Noblitt Banks, Director of Graduate School Operations, 205-934-8227, Fax: 205-934-8413, E-mail: gradschool@uab.edu.
Website: http://www.uab.edu/shp/cds/clinical-laboratory-sciences

**The University of Alabama at Birmingham,** School of Public Health, Program in Health Care Organization and Policy, Birmingham, AL 35294. Offers applied epidemiology and pharmacoepidemiology (MSPH); biostatistics (MPH); clinical and translational science (MSPH); environmental health (MPH); environmental health and toxicology (MSPH); epidemiology (MPH); general theory and practice (MPH); health behavior (MPH); health care organization (MPH, Dr PH); health policy (MPH); industrial hygiene (MPH, MSPH); maternal and child health policy (Dr PH); maternal and child health policy and leadership (MPH); occupational health and safety (MPH); outcomes research (MSPH, Dr PH); public health (PhD); public health preparedness management (MPH). *Accreditation:* CEPH. *Program availability:* Part-time, 100% online, blended/hybrid learning. *Faculty:* 14 full-time (6 women). *Students:* 53 full-time (37 women), 61 part-time (45 women); includes 37 minority (12 Black or African American, non-Hispanic/Latino; 20 Asian, non-Hispanic/Latino; 1 Hispanic/Latino; 4 Two or more races, non-Hispanic/Latino), 17 international. Average age 31. 136 applicants, 59% accepted, 44 enrolled. In 2019, 36 master's, 4 doctorates awarded. *Degree requirements:* For master's, comprehensive exam (for some programs), thesis (for some programs); for doctorate, comprehensive exam, thesis/dissertation. *Entrance requirements:* For doctorate, GRE. Additional exam requirements/recommendations for international students: required—TOEFL (minimum score 80 iBT), IELTS (minimum score 6.5). *Application deadline:* For fall admission, 4/1 priority date for domestic students, 4/1 for international students; for spring admission, 11/1 for domestic students; for summer admission, 4/1 for domestic students. Application fee: $50 ($60 for international students). Electronic applications accepted. *Financial support:* Fellowships, research assistantships, teaching assistantships, scholarships/grants, traineeships, and unspecified assistantships available. Financial award application deadline: 3/1; financial award applicants required to submit FAFSA. *Unit head:* Dr. Martha Wingate, Program Director, 205-934-6783, Fax: 205-975-5484, E-mail: mslay@uab.edu. *Application contact:* Dustin Shaw, Coordinator, Student Admissions and Record, 205-934-3939, E-mail: bcampbel@uab.edu.
Website: http://www.soph.uab.edu

**University of Alberta,** Faculty of Medicine and Dentistry and Faculty of Graduate Studies and Research, Graduate Programs in Medicine, Department of Laboratory Medicine and Pathology, Edmonton, AB T6G 2E1, Canada. Offers medical sciences (M Sc, PhD). *Program availability:* Part-time. Terminal master's awarded for partial completion of doctoral program. *Degree requirements:* For master's, thesis; for doctorate, thesis/dissertation, candidacy exam. *Entrance requirements:* For master's and doctorate, 3 letters of recommendation, minimum GPA of 3.0. Additional exam requirements/recommendations for international students: required—TOEFL.

**University of California, San Diego,** Graduate Division, Department of Electrical and Computer Engineering, La Jolla, CA 92093. Offers applied ocean science (MS, PhD); applied physics (MS, PhD); communication theory and systems (MS, PhD); computer engineering (MS, PhD); electronic circuits and systems (MS, PhD); intelligent systems, robotics and control (MS, PhD); medical devices and systems (MS, PhD); nanoscale devices and systems (MS, PhD); photonics (MS, PhD); signal and image processing (MS, PhD). *Students:* 983 full-time (216 women), 80 part-time (15 women). 3,675 applicants, 33% accepted, 430 enrolled. In 2019, 287 master's, 50 doctorates awarded. Terminal master's awarded for partial completion of doctoral program. *Degree requirements:* For master's, comprehensive exam (for some programs), thesis (for some programs); for doctorate, comprehensive exam, thesis/dissertation. *Entrance requirements:* For master's and doctorate, GRE General Test, minimum GPA of 3.0, resume or curriculum vitae (recommended). Additional exam requirements/recommendations for international students: required—TOEFL (minimum score 550 paper-based; 80 iBT), IELTS (minimum score 7), PTE (minimum score 65). *Application deadline:* For fall admission, 12/18 for domestic students. Application fee: $105 ($125 for international students). Electronic applications accepted. *Financial support:* Fellowships, research assistantships, teaching assistantships, scholarships/grants, traineeships, and unspecified assistantships available. Financial award applicants required to submit FAFSA. *Unit head:* Bill Lin, Chair, 858-822-1383, E-mail: billin@ucsd.edu. *Application contact:* Sean Jones, Graduate Admissions Coordinator, 858-534-3213, E-mail: ecegradapps@ece.ucsd.edu.
Website: http://ece.ucsd.edu/

**University of Colorado Denver,** School of Medicine, Clinical Science Graduate Program, Aurora, CO 80045. Offers clinical investigation (PhD); clinical sciences (MS); health information technology (PhD); health services research (PhD). *Degree requirements:* For master's, thesis, minimum of 30 credit hours, defense/final exam of thesis or publishable paper; for doctorate, comprehensive exam, thesis/dissertation, at least 30 credit hours of thesis work. *Entrance requirements:* For master's, GRE General Test or MCAT (waived if candidate has earned MS/MA or PhD from accredited U.S. school), minimum undergraduate GPA of 3.0, 3-4 letters of recommendation; for doctorate, GRE General Test or MCAT (waived if candidate has earned MS/MA or PhD from accredited U.S. school), health care graduate, professional degree, or graduate degree related to health sciences; minimum GPA of 3.0; 3-4 letters of recommendation. Additional exam requirements/recommendations for international students: required—TOEFL (minimum score 550 paper-based; 80 iBT). Electronic applications accepted. Tuition and fees vary according to course load, program and reciprocity agreements.

**University of Florida,** Graduate School, College of Nursing, Gainesville, FL 32611. Offers clinical and translational science (PhD); clinical nursing (DNP); nursing (MSN); nursing sciences (PhD). *Accreditation:* AACN; ACNM/ACME (one or more programs are accredited). *Program availability:* Part-time. *Degree requirements:* For master's, thesis optional; for doctorate, thesis/dissertation. *Entrance requirements:* For master's and doctorate, GRE General Test, minimum GPA of 3.0. Additional exam requirements/recommendations for international students: required—TOEFL (minimum score 550 paper-based; 80 iBT), IELTS (minimum score 6). Electronic applications accepted.

**University of Florida,** Graduate School, College of Pharmacy, Graduate Programs in Pharmacy, Department of Pharmaceutics, Gainesville, FL 32611. Offers clinical and translational sciences (PhD); pharmaceutical sciences (MSP, PhD); pharmacy (MSP, PhD). *Degree requirements:* For doctorate, comprehensive exam, thesis/dissertation. *Entrance requirements:* For master's and doctorate, GRE General Test, minimum GPA of 3.0. Additional exam requirements/recommendations for international students: required—TOEFL (minimum score 550 paper-based; 80 iBT), IELTS (minimum score 6). Electronic applications accepted.

**University of Florida,** Graduate School, College of Public Health and Health Professions, Department of Clinical and Health Psychology, Gainesville, FL 32611. Offers clinical and translational science (PhD); psychology (MS). *Accreditation:* APA (one or more programs are accredited). *Degree requirements:* For doctorate, comprehensive exam, thesis/dissertation, pre-doctoral internship. *Entrance requirements:* For master's and doctorate, GRE General Test, minimum GPA of 3.0. Additional exam requirements/recommendations for international students: required—TOEFL (minimum score 550 paper-based; 80 iBT), IELTS (minimum score 6). Electronic applications accepted.

**University of Florida,** Graduate School, College of Public Health and Health Professions, Department of Epidemiology, Gainesville, FL 32611. Offers clinical and translational science (PhD); epidemiology (MS, PhD). *Degree requirements:* For master's, thesis; for doctorate, thesis/dissertation. *Entrance requirements:* For master's and doctorate, GRE (minimum score verbal/quantitative combined 300), minimum GPA of 3.0. Additional exam requirements/recommendations for international students: required—TOEFL (minimum score 550 paper-based; 80 iBT), IELTS (minimum score 6).

**University of Florida,** Graduate School, Herbert Wertheim College of Engineering, Department of Materials Science and Engineering, Gainesville, FL 32611. Offers material science and engineering (MS), including clinical and translational science; materials science and engineering (ME, PhD); nuclear engineering (ME, PhD), including imaging science and technology (PhD), nuclear engineering sciences (ME, MS, PhD); nuclear engineering (MS), including nuclear engineering sciences (ME, MS, PhD); JD/MS. *Program availability:* Part-time, online learning. Terminal master's awarded for partial completion of doctoral program. *Degree requirements:* For master's, comprehensive exam, thesis; for doctorate, comprehensive exam, thesis/dissertation. *Entrance requirements:* For master's and doctorate, minimum GPA of 3.0. Additional exam requirements/recommendations for international students: required—TOEFL (minimum score 550 paper-based; 80 iBT), IELTS (minimum score 6). Electronic applications accepted.

**University of Maryland, Baltimore,** Graduate School, Department of Medical and Research Technology, Baltimore, MD 21201. Offers MS. *Accreditation:* NAACLS. *Program availability:* Part-time. *Degree requirements:* For master's, thesis or management project. *Entrance requirements:* For master's, GRE General Test, minimum GPA of 3.0, curriculum vitae, essay, 3 letters of recommendation. Additional exam requirements/recommendations for international students: required—TOEFL (minimum score 80 iBT) or IELTS (minimum score 7). Electronic applications accepted.

**University of Massachusetts Lowell,** College of Health Sciences, Department of Clinical Laboratory and Nutritional Sciences, Lowell, MA 01854. Offers clinical laboratory sciences (MS). *Accreditation:* NAACLS. *Program availability:* Part-time, online learning. *Degree requirements:* For master's, thesis optional. *Entrance requirements:* For master's, GRE General Test, minimum GPA of 3.0, letters of recommendation.

**University of Minnesota, Twin Cities Campus,** College of Science and Engineering, Technological Leadership Institute, Program in Medical Device Innovation, Minneapolis, MN 55455-0213. Offers MS. *Entrance requirements:* Additional exam requirements/recommendations for international students: required—TOEFL. Electronic applications accepted.

**University of Nebraska Medical Center,** College of Allied Health Professions, Program in Clinical Perfusion Education, Omaha, NE 68198-4144. Offers MPS. *Accreditation:* NAACLS. *Program availability:* Online learning. *Degree requirements:* For master's, comprehensive exam, thesis. *Entrance requirements:* For master's, GRE. Electronic applications accepted.

**University of Nebraska Medical Center,** College of Allied Health Professions, Program in Cytotechnology, Omaha, NE 68198. Offers Certificate. *Accreditation:* NAACLS. *Program availability:* Online learning. Electronic applications accepted.

**University of New Mexico,** Graduate Studies, Health Sciences Center, Master's in Clinical Laboratory Science Program, Albuquerque, NM 87131-2039. Offers education (MS); laboratory management (MS); research and development (MS). *Program availability:* Part-time. *Entrance requirements:* For master's, ASCP Board of Certification Exam. Additional exam requirements/recommendations for international students: required—TOEFL. Electronic applications accepted. *Expenses:* Tuition, state resident: full-time $7633; part-time $972 per year. Tuition, nonresident: full-time $22,586; part-time $3840 per year. *International tuition:* $23,292 full-time. *Required fees:* $8608. Tuition and fees vary according to course level, course load, degree level, program and student level.

**University of New Mexico,** Graduate Studies, Health Sciences Center, Program in Clinical and Translational Science, Albuquerque, NM 87131-2039. Offers Certificate. *Expenses:* Tuition, state resident: full-time $7633; part-time $972 per year. Tuition, nonresident: full-time $22,586; part-time $3840 per year. *International tuition:* $23,292 full-time. *Required fees:* $8608. Tuition and fees vary according to course level, course load, degree level, program and student level.

**University of North Dakota,** Graduate School, Graduate Programs in Medicine, Department of Clinical Translation Science, Grand Forks, ND 58202. Offers MS, PhD. *Accreditation:* NAACLS. *Program availability:* Online learning. *Degree requirements:* For master's, comprehensive exam, thesis or alternative. *Entrance requirements:* For

master's, minimum GPA of 3.0. Additional exam requirements/recommendations for international students: required—TOEFL (minimum score 550 paper-based; 79 iBT), IELTS (minimum score 5.5). Electronic applications accepted.

**University of Pennsylvania,** Perelman School of Medicine, Master of Regulatory Affairs Program, Philadelphia, PA 19104. Offers MRA. *Unit head:* Dr. Andrew Fesnak, Director, E-mail: fesnak@pennmedicine.upenn.edu. *Application contact:* Dr. Bethany Germany, Associate Director, 662-4619.
Website: http://www.itmat.upenn.edu/mra.html

**University of Pennsylvania,** Perelman School of Medicine, Master of Science in Translational Research Program, Philadelphia, PA 19104-4283. Offers MTR. *Program availability:* Part-time, online learning. *Entrance requirements:* Additional exam requirements/recommendations for international students: required—TOEFL. *Financial support:* Fellowships, research assistantships, teaching assistantships, and tuition waivers available. *Unit head:* Dr. Emma Meagher, Director. *Application contact:* Megan Maxwell, Associate Director, 215-662-4581.
Website: www.itmat.upenn.edu/mstr

**University of Pittsburgh,** School of Medicine, Graduate Programs in Medicine, Clinical and Translational Science Graduate Program, Pittsburgh, PA 15260. Offers PhD. *Program availability:* Part-time, blended/hybrid learning. *Degree requirements:* For doctorate, comprehensive exam, thesis/dissertation, 8 hours of responsible conduct in research training. *Entrance requirements:* For doctorate, MCAT or GRE, transcripts, curriculum vitae, 2 letters of recommendation. Additional exam requirements/recommendations for international students: required—TOEFL (minimum score 600 paper-based; 100 iBT), IELTS (minimum score 7). Electronic applications accepted. *Expenses:* Contact institution.

**University of Puerto Rico - Medical Sciences Campus,** School of Health Professions, Program in Clinical Laboratory Science, San Juan, PR 00936-5067. Offers MS. *Accreditation:* NAACLS. *Program availability:* Part-time, evening/weekend. *Degree requirements:* For master's, one foreign language, thesis or alternative. *Entrance requirements:* For master's, EXADEP or GRE General Test, minimum GPA of 2.75, bachelor's degree in medical technology, 1 year lab experience, interview.

**University of Puerto Rico - Medical Sciences Campus,** School of Health Professions, Program in Cytotechnology, San Juan, PR 00936-5067. Offers Certificate. *Degree requirements:* For Certificate, one foreign language, research project. *Entrance requirements:* For degree, minimum GPA of 2.5, interview.

**University of Puerto Rico - Medical Sciences Campus,** School of Health Professions, Program in Medical Technology, San Juan, PR 00936-5067. Offers Certificate. *Program availability:* Part-time. *Degree requirements:* For Certificate, one foreign language, clinical practice. *Entrance requirements:* For degree, bachelor's degree in science, minimum GPA of 2.5.

**University of Rhode Island,** Graduate School, College of the Environment and Life Sciences, Department of Cell and Molecular Biology, Kingston, RI 02881. Offers biochemistry (MS, PhD); clinical laboratory sciences (MS), including biotechnology, clinical laboratory science, cytopathology; microbiology (MS, PhD); molecular genetics (MS, PhD). *Program availability:* Part-time. *Faculty:* 20 full-time (9 women). *Students:* 1 (woman) part-time. In 2019, 16 master's awarded. *Entrance requirements:* Additional exam requirements/recommendations for international students: required—TOEFL. *Application deadline:* For fall admission, 1/15 for domestic and international students. Application fee: $65. Electronic applications accepted. *Expenses: Tuition, area resident:* Full-time $13,734; part-time $763 per credit. Tuition, state resident: full-time $13,734; part-time $763 per credit. Tuition, nonresident: full-time $26,512; part-time $1473 per credit. *International tuition:* $26,512 full-time. *Required fees:* $1780; $52 per credit. $35 per term. One-time fee: $165. *Financial support:* In 2019–20, 11 teaching assistantships with tuition reimbursements (averaging $10,985 per year) were awarded; traineeships also available. Financial award application deadline: 1/15; financial award applicants required to submit FAFSA. *Unit head:* Dr. Joel Chandlee, Chair, E-mail: joelchandlee@uri.edu. *Application contact:* Dr. Steven Gregory, Graduate Program Director, 401-874-5947, E-mail: stgregory@uri.edu.
Website: https://web.uri.edu/cmb/

**The University of Tennessee Health Science Center,** College of Graduate Health Sciences, Memphis, TN 38163. Offers biomedical engineering (MS, PhD); biomedical sciences (PhD); dental sciences (MDS); epidemiology (MS); health outcomes and policy research (PhD); laboratory research and management (MS); nursing science (PhD); pharmaceutical sciences (PhD); pharmacology (MS); speech and hearing science (PhD); DDS/PhD; DNP/PhD; MD/PhD; Pharm D/PhD. Terminal master's awarded for partial completion of doctoral program. *Degree requirements:* For master's, comprehensive exam, thesis; for doctorate, thesis/dissertation, oral and written preliminary and comprehensive exams. *Entrance requirements:* For master's and doctorate, GRE General Test, minimum GPA of 3.0. Additional exam requirements/recommendations for international students: recommended—TOEFL (minimum score 79 iBT), IELTS (minimum score 6.5). Electronic applications accepted. *Expenses:* Contact institution.

**The University of Tennessee Health Science Center,** College of Health Professions, Memphis, TN 38163-0002. Offers audiology (MS, Au D); clinical laboratory science (MSCLS); cytopathology practice (MCP); health informatics and information management (MHIIM); occupational therapy (MOT); physical therapy (DPT, ScDPT); physician assistant (MMS); speech-language pathology (MS). *Accreditation:* AOTA; APTA. *Program availability:* Part-time, evening/weekend, online learning. Terminal master's awarded for partial completion of doctoral program. *Degree requirements:* For master's, comprehensive exam, thesis; for doctorate, comprehensive exam, residency. *Entrance requirements:* For master's, GRE (MOT, MSCLS), minimum GPA of 3.0, 3 letters of reference, national accreditation (MSCLS), GRE if GPA is less than 3.0 (MCP); for doctorate, GRE. Additional exam requirements/recommendations for international students: required—TOEFL (minimum score 550 paper-based; 80 iBT). Electronic applications accepted. *Expenses:* Contact institution.

**The University of Texas at Austin,** Graduate School, College of Pharmacy, Graduate Programs in Pharmacy, Austin, TX 78712-1111. Offers health outcomes and pharmacy practice (MS, PhD); medicinal chemistry (PhD); pharmaceutics (PhD); pharmacology and toxicology (PhD); pharmacotherapy (MS, PhD); translational science (PhD). *Degree requirements:* For master's, thesis; for doctorate, thesis/dissertation. *Entrance requirements:* For master's and doctorate, GRE General Test. Electronic applications accepted.

**The University of Texas Health Science Center at San Antonio,** Graduate School of Biomedical Sciences, Translational Science Program, San Antonio, TX 78229-3900. Offers PhD. *Program availability:* Part-time. *Degree requirements:* For doctorate, comprehensive exam, thesis/dissertation.

**The University of Texas Medical Branch,** Graduate School of Biomedical Sciences, Program in Clinical Science, Galveston, TX 77555. Offers MS, PhD. *Accreditation:* NAACLS.

**The University of Texas Rio Grande Valley,** College of Health Affairs, Department of Health and Biomedical Sciences, Edinburg, TX 78539. Offers clinical laboratory sciences (MSHS); health care administration (MSHS); nutrition (MSHS). *Program availability:* Part-time, online only, 100% online. *Faculty:* 4 full-time (all women), 2 part-time/adjunct (both women). *Students:* 148 part-time (92 women); includes 120 minority (10 Black or African American, non-Hispanic/Latino; 5 American Indian or Alaska Native, non-Hispanic/Latino; 105 Hispanic/Latino), 3 international. Average age 34. 70 applicants, 77% accepted, 39 enrolled. In 2019, 110 master's awarded. *Entrance requirements:* For master's, Not required, 2 letters of recommendation and a letter of intent, UG degree in a health related profession. CLS - BS in CLS and ASCP MLS Certification; NUTR - 3 hrs. UG & A&P with a "C" or higher; Healthcare Informatics - UG degree in health field and experience with EMR highly recommended. Additional exam requirements/recommendations for international students: required—as required by grad. college; program does not require entrance exams. *Application deadline:* For fall admission, 7/23 for domestic and international students; for spring admission, 12/1 for domestic and international students. Applications are processed on a rolling basis. Application fee: $50 ($100 for international students). Electronic applications accepted. *Expenses:* 444.44 per semester credit hour. *Financial support:* Research assistantships and scholarships/grants available. Financial award application deadline: 7/23; financial award applicants required to submit FAFSA. *Unit head:* Dr. Saraswathy Nair, Associate Professor and Chair, 956-882-5108, Fax: 956-882-6835, E-mail: saraswathy.nair@utrgv.edu. *Application contact:* Kim Garcia, Lecturer III/Associate Chair, Health and Biomedical Sciences, 956-665-4781, E-mail: kim.garcia@utrgv.edu.
Website: http://www.utrgv.edu/hbs/

**University of Utah,** School of Medicine and Graduate School, Graduate Programs in Medicine, Department of Pathology, Program in Laboratory Medicine and Biomedical Science, Salt Lake City, UT 84112-1107. Offers MS. *Program availability:* Part-time. *Degree requirements:* For master's, comprehensive exam, thesis, thesis research. *Entrance requirements:* For master's, minimum GPA of 3.0 during last 2 years of undergraduate course work, BS in medical laboratory science or related field. Additional exam requirements/recommendations for international students: required—TOEFL (minimum score 550 paper-based). *Expenses:* Tuition, state resident: full-time $7085; part-time $272.51 per credit hour. Tuition, nonresident: full-time $24,937; part-time $959.12 per credit hour. *Required fees:* $880.52; $880.52 per semester. Tuition and fees vary according to degree level, program and student level.

**University of Vermont,** Graduate College, College of Nursing and Health Sciences, Program in Medical Laboratory Science, Burlington, VT 05405. Offers MS. *Accreditation:* NAACLS. *Entrance requirements:* For master's, GRE General Test. Additional exam requirements/recommendations for international students: required—TOEFL (minimum iBT score of 90) or IELTS (6.5). Electronic applications accepted.

**University of Vermont,** The Robert Larner, MD College of Medicine and Graduate College, Graduate Programs in Medicine, Program in Clinical and Translational Science, Burlington, VT 05405. Offers MS, PhD, Certificate. Terminal master's awarded for partial completion of doctoral program. *Degree requirements:* For master's, thesis; for doctorate, thesis/dissertation. *Entrance requirements:* For master's and doctorate, GRE (recommended). Additional exam requirements/recommendations for international students: required—TOEFL (minimum score 550 paper-based; 90 iBT), IELTS (minimum score 6.5). Electronic applications accepted.

**University of Washington,** Graduate School, School of Medicine, Graduate Programs in Medicine, Department of Laboratory Medicine, Seattle, WA 98195. Offers MS. *Accreditation:* NAACLS. *Program availability:* Part-time. *Degree requirements:* For master's, thesis. *Entrance requirements:* For master's, GRE General Test, medical technology certification or specialist in an area of laboratory medicine.

**Virginia Commonwealth University,** Graduate School, School of Allied Health Professions, Department of Clinical Laboratory Sciences, Richmond, VA 23284-9005. Offers MS. *Accreditation:* NAACLS. *Degree requirements:* For master's, one foreign language, thesis. *Entrance requirements:* For master's, GRE General Test, major in clinical laboratory sciences, biology, or chemistry; minimum GPA of 2.7. Additional exam requirements/recommendations for international students: required—TOEFL (minimum score 600 paper-based; 100 iBT); recommended—IELTS (minimum score 6.5). Electronic applications accepted.

**Virginia Commonwealth University,** Graduate School, School of Allied Health Professions, Doctoral Program in Health Related Sciences, Richmond, VA 23284-9005. Offers clinical laboratory sciences (PhD); gerontology (PhD); health administration (PhD); nurse anesthesia (PhD); occupational therapy (PhD); physical therapy (PhD); radiation sciences (PhD); rehabilitation leadership (PhD). *Entrance requirements:* For doctorate, GRE General Test or MAT, minimum GPA of 3.3 in master's degree. Additional exam requirements/recommendations for international students: required—TOEFL (minimum score 600 paper-based; 100 iBT); recommended—IELTS (minimum score 6.5). Electronic applications accepted.

**Wake Forest University,** School of Medicine and Graduate School of Arts and Sciences, Graduate Programs in Medicine, Department of Comparative Medicine, Winston-Salem, NC 27109. Offers MS. *Degree requirements:* For master's, thesis. *Entrance requirements:* For master's, GRE General Test. Additional exam requirements/recommendations for international students: required—TOEFL. Electronic applications accepted.

# Clinical Research

---

**Albert Einstein College of Medicine,** Graduate Programs in the Biomedical Sciences, Clinical Investigation Program, Bronx, NY 10461. Offers PhD.

**American University of Health Sciences,** School of Clinical Research, Signal Hill, CA 90755. Offers MSCR.

## Clinical Research

**Augusta University,** College of Allied Health Sciences, Program in Clinical Laboratory Sciences, Augusta, GA 30912. Offers MHS.

**Boston University,** School of Medicine, Graduate Medical Sciences, Program in Clinical Research, Boston, MA 02215. Offers MA. *Application deadline:* For spring admission, 10/15 for domestic students. *Unit head:* Dr. Janice Weinberg, Director, E-mail: janicew@bu.edu. *Application contact:* Stacey Hess Pino, Assistant Director, E-mail: sahess@bu.edu.
Website: http://www.bumc.bu.edu/gms/mscr/

**Case Western Reserve University,** School of Medicine, Clinical Research Scholars Program, Cleveland, OH 44106. Offers MS, PhD.

**Clemson University,** Graduate School, College of Behavioral, Social and Health Sciences, Department of Public Health Sciences, Clemson, SC 29634. Offers applied health research and evaluation (MS, PhD); biomedical data science and informatics (PhD); clinical and translational research (Certificate). *Faculty:* 23 full-time (13 women). *Students:* 20 full-time (13 women), 41 part-time (31 women); includes 11 minority (2 Black or African American, non-Hispanic/Latino; 6 Asian, non-Hispanic/Latino; 2 Hispanic/Latino; 1 Two or more races, non-Hispanic/Latino), 3 international. Average age 32. 50 applicants, 84% accepted, 36 enrolled. In 2019, 11 master's, 3 other advanced degrees awarded. *Expenses:* Full-Time Student per Semester: Tuition: $6225 (in-state), $13425 (out-of-state), Fees: $598; Graduate Assistant Per Semester: $1144; Part-Time Student Per Credit Hour: $833 (in-state), $1731 (out-of-state), Fees: $617; other fees apply depending on program, credit hours, campus & residency. Doctoral Base Fee per Semester: $4938 (in-state), $10405 (out-of-state). *Financial support:* In 2019–20, 24 students received support, including 2 fellowships with full and partial tuition reimbursements available (averaging $5,000 per year), 9 research assistantships with full and partial tuition reimbursements available (averaging $18,428 per year), 7 teaching assistantships with full and partial tuition reimbursements available (averaging $17,325 per year); career-related internships or fieldwork and unspecified assistantships also available. *Application contact:* Dr. Sarah Griffin, Graduate Program Director, 864-656-1622, E-mail: sgriffi@clemson.edu.
Website: http://www.clemson.edu/cbshs/departments/public-health/index.html

**Clemson University,** Graduate School, College of Behavioral, Social and Health Sciences, School of Nursing, Clemson, SC 29634. Offers clinical and translational research (PhD); global health (Certificate), including low resource countries; healthcare genetics (PhD); nursing (MS, DNP), including adult/gerontology nurse practitioner (MS), family nurse practitioner (MS). *Accreditation:* AACN. *Program availability:* Part-time, 100% online, blended/hybrid learning. *Faculty:* 47 full-time (45 women), 1 (woman) part-time/adjunct. *Students:* 67 full-time (59 women), 66 part-time (49 women); includes 18 minority (10 Black or African American, non-Hispanic/Latino; 4 Asian, non-Hispanic/Latino; 4 Two or more races, non-Hispanic/Latino), 7 international. Average age 35. 109 applicants, 62% accepted, 49 enrolled. In 2019, 56 master's, 8 doctorates awarded. *Degree requirements:* For master's, comprehensive exam, thesis or alternative; for doctorate, comprehensive exam, thesis/dissertation. *Entrance requirements:* For master's, GRE General Test, South Carolina RN license, unofficial transcripts, resume, letters of recommendation; for doctorate, GRE General Test, unofficial transcripts, MS/MA thesis or publications, curriculum vitae, statement of career goals, letters of recommendation. Additional exam requirements/recommendations for international students: required—TOEFL (minimum score 80 paper-based; 80 iBT); recommended—IELTS (minimum score 6.5), TSE (minimum score 54). *Application deadline:* For fall admission, 4/15 priority date for international students; for spring admission, 10/15 priority date for international students. Applications are processed on a rolling basis. Application fee: $80 ($90 for international students). Electronic applications accepted. *Expenses:* MS Nursing Full-Time Student per Semester: Tuition: $9075 (in-state), $16051 (out-of-state), Fees: $598; Graduate Assistant Per Semester: $1144; Part-Time Student Per Credit Hour: $1009 (in-state), $1784 (out-of-state), Fees: $46; other fees apply depending on program, credit hours, campus & residency. Doctoral Base Fee per Semester: $4938 (in-state), $10405 (out-of-state). *Financial support:* In 2019–20, 47 students received support, including 46 teaching assistantships with full and partial tuition reimbursements available (averaging $6,766 per year); career-related internships or fieldwork and unspecified assistantships also available. *Unit head:* Dr. Kathleen Valentine, Chief Academic Nursing Officer & Director, 864-656-4758, E-mail: klvalen@clemson.edu. *Application contact:* Dr. Stephanie Davis, Director of Graduate Programs, 864-656-2588, E-mail: stephad@clemson.edu.
Website: http://www.clemson.edu/cbshs/departments/nursing/

**Duke University,** School of Medicine, Clinical Research Program, Durham, NC 27708. Offers MHS. *Program availability:* Part-time. *Degree requirements:* For master's, research project. *Entrance requirements:* For master's, GRE, An advanced degree in a clinical health science or two years of medical school from an accredited institution. Additional exam requirements/recommendations for international students: recommended—TOEFL, IELTS.

**Eastern Michigan University,** Graduate School, College of Health and Human Services, School of Health Sciences, Programs in Clinical Research Administration, Ypsilanti, MI 48197. Offers MS, Graduate Certificate. *Program availability:* Part-time, evening/weekend, online learning. *Students:* 8 full-time (7 women), 21 part-time (19 women); includes 8 minority (2 Black or African American, non-Hispanic/Latino; 4 Asian, non-Hispanic/Latino; 2 Two or more races, non-Hispanic/Latino), 8 international. Average age 33. 34 applicants, 76% accepted, 14 enrolled. In 2019, 13 master's awarded. *Entrance requirements:* Additional exam requirements/recommendations for international students: required—TOEFL. *Application deadline:* Applications are processed on a rolling basis. Application fee: $45. *Financial support:* Fellowships, research assistantships with full tuition reimbursements, teaching assistantships with full tuition reimbursements, career-related internships or fieldwork, Federal Work-Study, institutionally sponsored loans, scholarships/grants, tuition waivers (partial), and unspecified assistantships available. Support available to part-time students. Financial award applicants required to submit FAFSA. *Application contact:* Dr. Jean Rowan, Program Director, 734-487-1238, Fax: 734-487-4095, E-mail: jrowan3@emich.edu.

**Emory University,** Laney Graduate School, Program in Clinical Research, Atlanta, GA 30322-1100. Offers MS. *Degree requirements:* For master's, thesis. *Entrance requirements:* Additional exam requirements/recommendations for international students: recommended—TOEFL. Electronic applications accepted.

**Fordham University,** Graduate School of Arts and Sciences, Department of Psychology, Program in Clinical Research Methods, New York, NY 10458. Offers MS. *Program availability:* Part-time. *Students:* 55 applicants, 40% accepted, 6 enrolled. In 2019, 11 master's awarded. *Degree requirements:* For master's, thesis, practicum. *Entrance requirements:* Additional exam requirements/recommendations for international students: required—TOEFL. Application fee: $70. *Unit head:* Dr. Barry Rosenfeld, Chair, 718-817-3794, Fax: 718-817-3699, E-mail: rosenfeld@fordham.edu. *Application contact:* Garrett Marino, Director of Graduate Admissions, 718-817-4419, Fax: 718-817-3566, E-mail: gmarino10@fordham.edu.

**Icahn School of Medicine at Mount Sinai,** Graduate School of Biomedical Sciences, New York, NY 10029-6504. Offers biomedical sciences (MS, PhD); clinical research education (MS, PhD); community medicine (MPH); genetic counseling (MS); neurosciences (PhD); MD/PhD. Terminal master's awarded for partial completion of doctoral program. *Degree requirements:* For master's, thesis; for doctorate, comprehensive exam, thesis/dissertation. *Entrance requirements:* For master's, GRE General Test; for doctorate, GRE General Test, GRE Subject Test, 3 years of college pre-med course work. Additional exam requirements/recommendations for international students: required—TOEFL. Electronic applications accepted.

**Johns Hopkins University,** Bloomberg School of Public Health, Graduate Training Program in Clinical Investigation, Baltimore, MD 21205. Offers MHS, PhD. *Degree requirements:* For master's, comprehensive exam, thesis; for doctorate, comprehensive exam, thesis/dissertation. *Entrance requirements:* For master's, GRE or MCAT; United States Medical Licensing Exam, 2 letters of recommendation, curriculum vitae, transcripts, statement of purpose; for doctorate, GRE or MCAT; United States Medical Licensing Exam, 2 letters of recommendation, curriculum vitae. Additional exam requirements/recommendations for international students: required—TOEFL (minimum score 600 paper-based), IELTS. Electronic applications accepted.

**Loyola University Chicago,** Graduate School, Program in Clinical Research Methods, Chicago, IL 60660. Offers MS. *Program availability:* Part-time-only. *Faculty:* 5 full-time (2 women). *Students:* 5 part-time (3 women); includes 2 minority (both Asian, non-Hispanic/Latino). Average age 36. 8 applicants, 38% accepted, 3 enrolled. In 2019, 4 master's awarded. *Entrance requirements:* For master's, MCAT; GRE. Additional exam requirements/recommendations for international students: recommended—TOEFL (minimum score 550 paper-based; 79 iBT). *Application deadline:* For fall admission, 5/15 for domestic students, 5/1 for international students; for spring admission, 11/15 for domestic students, 11/1 for international students. Applications are processed on a rolling basis. Electronic applications accepted. *Expenses:* Contact institution. *Financial support:* Applicants required to submit FAFSA. *Unit head:* Dr. David Shoham, MPH Program Director, 708-327-9006, Fax: 708-327-9009, E-mail: dshoham@luc.edu. *Application contact:* Ilze Berzina-Galbreath, Administrative Coordinator, 708-327-9224, E-mail: iberzin@luc.edu.

**Medical College of Wisconsin,** Graduate School, Medical Scientist Training Program, Milwaukee, WI 53226. Offers MD/PhD. *Students:* 53 full-time (25 women); includes 12 minority (1 Black or African American, non-Hispanic/Latino; 7 Asian, non-Hispanic/Latino; 1 Hispanic/Latino; 3 Two or more races, non-Hispanic/Latino), 6 international. Average age 27. 6 applicants, 100% accepted, 6 enrolled. *Entrance requirements:* Additional exam requirements/recommendations for international students: required—TOEFL. *Application deadline:* For fall admission, 12/1 for domestic and international students. Application fee: $50. *Expenses: Tuition:* Full-time $55,130; part-time $1056 per credit. *Required fees:* $555.50. One-time fee: $72 full-time; $50 part-time. Tuition and fees vary according to degree level and program. *Financial support:* Applicants required to submit FAFSA. *Unit head:* Dr. Joseph T. Barbieri, Director, 414-456-8412, E-mail: jtb01@mcw.edu. *Application contact:* Dr. Joseph T. Barbieri, Director, 414-456-8412, E-mail: jtb01@mcw.edu.
Website: https://www.mcw.edu/Medical-Scientist-Training-Program-MSTP.htm

**Medical University of South Carolina,** College of Graduate Studies, South Carolina Clinical and Translational Research Institute, Charleston, SC 29425-5010. Offers MS. *Program availability:* Online learning. *Degree requirements:* For master's, thesis, oral dissertation of grant proposal. *Entrance requirements:* For master's, essay, letter of support. Additional exam requirements/recommendations for international students: required—TOEFL (minimum score 600 paper-based; 100 iBT). Electronic applications accepted.

**Memorial University of Newfoundland,** Faculty of Medicine and School of Graduate Studies, Graduate Programs in Medicine, Division of Applied Health Services Research, St. John's, NL A1C 5S7, Canada. Offers M Sc.

**Morehouse School of Medicine,** Master of Science in Clinical Research Program, Atlanta, GA 30310-1495. Offers MS. *Program availability:* Part-time. *Degree requirements:* For master's, thesis. Electronic applications accepted.

**National University of Natural Medicine,** School of Undergraduate and Graduate Studies, Portland, OR 97201. Offers Ayurveda (MS); global health (MS); integrative medicine research (MS); integrative mental health (MS); nutrition (MS). *Program availability:* 100% online. *Students:* 92 full-time (83 women), 6 part-time (all women); includes 13 minority (1 Black or African American, non-Hispanic/Latino; 4 Asian, non-Hispanic/Latino; 3 Hispanic/Latino; 5 Two or more races, non-Hispanic/Latino). Average age 31. 114 applicants, 88% accepted, 60 enrolled. In 2019, 72 master's awarded. *Degree requirements:* For master's, thesis. *Entrance requirements:* For master's, Bachelor's degree from a regionally accredited institution and prerequisite courses. Additional exam requirements/recommendations for international students: required—TOEFL (minimum score 550 paper-based; 80 iBT), We accept IETS and PTE. *Application deadline:* For fall admission, 5/1 for domestic and international students. Applications are processed on a rolling basis. Application fee: $75. Electronic applications accepted. *Expenses: Tuition:* Part-time $464 per credit hour. *Financial support:* Federal Work-Study and scholarships/grants available. Financial award application deadline: 2/15; financial award applicants required to submit FAFSA. *Unit head:* Dr. Tim Irving, Program Director - School of Undergraduate and Graduate Studies, 503-552-1660, Fax: 503-499-0027, E-mail: admission@nunm.edu. *Application contact:* Ryan Hollister, Director of Admissions, 503-552-1665, Fax: 503-499-0027, E-mail: admissions@numn.edu.
Website: http://nunm.edu/academics/school-of-research-graduate-studies/

**New York University,** College of Dentistry, Program in Clinical Research, New York, NY 10010. Offers MS. *Program availability:* Part-time. *Entrance requirements:* For master's, GRE or GRE or another standardized test (such as DAT, CDAT, National Dental Board Part I and National Dental Board Part II), academic transcripts, personal statement, resume or curriculum vitae, three letters of recommendation. Additional exam requirements/recommendations for international students: required—TOEFL (minimum score 600 paper-based; 100 iBT). Electronic applications accepted. *Expenses:* Contact institution.

**Northwestern University,** Feinberg School of Medicine, Program in Clinical Investigation, Evanston, IL 60208. Offers MSCI. *Program availability:* Part-time, evening/weekend. *Entrance requirements:* For master's, GRE or MCAT, doctoral degree in healthcare-related field. Additional exam requirements/recommendations for international students: required—TOEFL. Electronic applications accepted.

**Northwestern University,** The Graduate School, Program in Clinical Investigation, Evanston, IL 60208. Offers MSCI, Certificate. *Program availability:* Part-time, evening/weekend.

**Northwestern University,** School of Professional Studies, Program in Regulatory Compliance, Evanston, IL 60208. Offers clinical research (MS); healthcare compliance (MS); quality systems (MS). *Program availability:* Part-time, evening/weekend.

**Oregon Health & Science University,** School of Medicine, Graduate Programs in Medicine, Human Investigations Program, Portland, OR 97239-3098. Offers MCR, Certificate. *Program availability:* Part-time-only. *Entrance requirements:* For master's and Certificate, MD, MD/PhD, DO, DDS, DMD, DC, Pharm D, OD, ND or PhD with clinical responsibilities or patient-oriented research; faculty or staff member, clinical or

post-doctoral fellows and graduate students at OHSU, Kaiser Permanente, Portland VA Medical Center or other health care facilities in Oregon or the Northwest. Electronic applications accepted.

**Palmer College of Chiropractic,** Division of Graduate Studies, Davenport, IA 52803-5287. Offers clinical research (MS). *Program availability:* Part-time. *Degree requirements:* For master's, 2 mentored practicum projects. *Entrance requirements:* For master's, GRE General Test, minimum GPA of 2.5, bachelor's and doctoral-level health professions degrees. Additional exam requirements/recommendations for international students: required—TOEFL. Electronic applications accepted. *Expenses:* Contact institution.

**Stanford University,** School of Medicine, Graduate Programs in Medicine, Department of Health Research and Policy, Program in Epidemiology and Clinical Research, Stanford, CA 94305-2004. Offers MS, PhD. *Expenses: Tuition:* Full-time $52,479; part-time $34,110 per unit. *Required fees:* $672; $224 per quarter. Tuition and fees vary according to program and student level.
Website: http://med.stanford.edu/epidemiology/

**Thomas Jefferson University,** Jefferson College of Life Sciences, Certificate Program in Clinical Research and Trials: Implementation, Philadelphia, PA 19107. Offers Certificate. *Program availability:* Part-time. *Entrance requirements:* For degree, GRE General Test (recommended), scientific/medical background. Additional exam requirements/recommendations for international students: required—TOEFL, IELTS (minimum score 7).

**Thomas Jefferson University,** Jefferson College of Life Sciences, Certificate Program in Clinical Research: Operations, Philadelphia, PA 19107. Offers Certificate. *Entrance requirements:* For degree, BA. Additional exam requirements/recommendations for international students: required—TOEFL, IELTS (minimum score 7).

**Thomas Jefferson University,** Jefferson College of Life Sciences, Certificate Program in Human Clinical Investigation: Theory, Philadelphia, PA 19107. Offers Certificate. *Program availability:* Part-time. *Entrance requirements:* For degree, GRE General Test (recommended), scientific/medical background. Additional exam requirements/recommendations for international students: required—TOEFL, IELTS (minimum score 7).

**Thomas Jefferson University,** Jefferson College of Life Sciences, MS Program in Clinical Research, Philadelphia, PA 19107. Offers MS. *Program availability:* Part-time, evening/weekend. *Degree requirements:* For master's, thesis, clerkship. *Entrance requirements:* For master's, GRE General Test or MCAT, minimum GPA of 3.0. Additional exam requirements/recommendations for international students: required—TOEFL, IELTS (minimum score 7). Electronic applications accepted.

**Trident University International,** College of Health Sciences, Program in Health Sciences, Cypress, CA 90630. Offers clinical research administration (MS, Certificate); emergency and disaster management (MS, Certificate); environmental health science (Certificate); health care administration (PhD); health care management (MS), including health informatics; health education (MS, Certificate); health informatics (Certificate); health sciences (PhD); international health (MS); international health: educator or researcher option (PhD); international health: practitioner option (PhD); law and expert witness studies (MS, Certificate); public health (MS); quality assurance (Certificate). *Program availability:* Part-time, evening/weekend, online learning. *Degree requirements:* For doctorate, comprehensive exam, thesis/dissertation, defense of dissertation. *Entrance requirements:* For master's, minimum GPA of 2.5 (students with GPA 3.0 or greater may transfer up to 30% of graduate level credits); for doctorate, minimum GPA of 3.4, curriculum vitae, course work in research methods or statistics. Additional exam requirements/recommendations for international students: required—TOEFL. Electronic applications accepted.

**University of California, Berkeley,** UC Berkeley Extension, Certificate Programs in Sciences, Biotechnology and Mathematics, Berkeley, CA 94720. Offers clinical research conduct and management (Certificate). *Program availability:* Online learning.

**University of California, Davis,** Graduate Studies, Graduate Group in Clinical Research, Davis, CA 95616. Offers MAS. *Degree requirements:* For master's, comprehensive exam. *Entrance requirements:* Additional exam requirements/recommendations for international students: required—TOEFL (minimum score 550 paper-based).

**University of California, Los Angeles,** David Geffen School of Medicine and Graduate Division, Graduate Programs in Medicine, Department of Biomathematics, Program in Clinical Research, Los Angeles, CA 90095. Offers MS. *Degree requirements:* For master's, thesis. *Entrance requirements:* For master's, GRE General Test, bachelor's degree; minimum undergraduate GPA of 3.0 (or its equivalent if letter grade system not used). Additional exam requirements/recommendations for international students: required—TOEFL. Electronic applications accepted.

**University of California, San Diego,** School of Medicine, Program in Clinical Research, La Jolla, CA 92093. Offers MAS. *Program availability:* Part-time, evening/weekend. *Students:* 20 full-time (13 women), 24 part-time (17 women). 66 applicants, 76% accepted, 27 enrolled. In 2019, 10 master's awarded. *Degree requirements:* For master's, independent study project. *Entrance requirements:* For master's, minimum GPA of 3.0, advanced degree (recommended); professional work experience in clinical research, medical practice, or related field (recommended); resume or curriculum vitae, statement of purpose, three letters of recommendation. Additional exam requirements/recommendations for international students: required—TOEFL (minimum score 550 paper-based; 80 iBT), IELTS (minimum score 7). *Application deadline:* For fall admission, 7/4 for domestic students. Application fee: $105 ($125 for international students). Electronic applications accepted. *Expenses:* Contact institution. *Financial support:* Scholarships/grants available. Financial award applicants required to submit FAFSA. *Unit head:* Ravindra Mehta, Chair, 619-543-7310, E-mail: rmehta@ucsd.edu. *Application contact:* Ravindra Mehta, Chair, 619-543-7310, E-mail: rmehta@ucsd.edu. Website: http://clre.ucsd.edu/

**University of Colorado Denver,** School of Medicine, Clinical Science Graduate Program, Aurora, CO 80045. Offers clinical investigation (PhD); clinical sciences (MS); health information technology (PhD); health services research (PhD). *Degree requirements:* For master's, thesis, minimum of 30 credit hours, defense/final exam of thesis or publishable paper; for doctorate, comprehensive exam, thesis/dissertation, at least 30 credit hours of thesis work. *Entrance requirements:* For master's, GRE General Test or MCAT (waived if candidate has earned MS/MA or PhD from accredited U.S. school), minimum undergraduate GPA of 3.0, 3-4 letters of recommendation; for doctorate, GRE General Test or MCAT (waived if candidate has earned MS/MA or PhD from accredited U.S. school), health care graduate, professional degree, or graduate degree related to health sciences; minimum GPA of 3.0; 3-4 letters of recommendation. Additional exam requirements/recommendations for international students: required—TOEFL (minimum score 550 paper-based; 80 iBT). Electronic applications accepted. Tuition and fees vary according to course load, program and reciprocity agreements.

**University of Connecticut Health Center,** Graduate School, Program in Clinical and Translational Research, Farmington, CT 06030. Offers MS. *Program availability:* Part-time. *Entrance requirements:* For master's, GRE. Additional exam requirements/

recommendations for international students: required—TOEFL (minimum score 600 paper-based).

**University of Florida,** College of Medicine, Program in Clinical Investigation, Gainesville, FL 32611. Offers clinical investigation (MS); epidemiology (MS); public health (MPH). *Program availability:* Part-time. *Entrance requirements:* For master's, GRE, MD, PhD, DMD/DDS or Pharm D.

**University of Florida,** Graduate School, Herbert Wertheim College of Engineering, J. Crayton Pruitt Family Department of Biomedical Engineering, Gainesville, FL 32611. Offers biomedical engineering (ME, MS, PhD, Certificate); clinical and translational science (PhD); medical physics (MS, PhD); MD/PhD. Terminal master's awarded for partial completion of doctoral program. *Degree requirements:* For master's, comprehensive exam (for some programs), thesis (for some programs); for doctorate, comprehensive exam (for some programs), thesis/dissertation (for some programs). *Entrance requirements:* Additional exam requirements/recommendations for international students: required—TOEFL (minimum score 550 paper-based; 80 iBT), IELTS (minimum score 6). Electronic applications accepted.

**The University of Iowa,** Graduate College, College of Public Health, Department of Epidemiology, Iowa City, IA 52242-1316. Offers clinical investigation (MS); epidemiology (MPH, MS, PhD). *Degree requirements:* For master's, thesis optional, exam; for doctorate, comprehensive exam, thesis/dissertation. *Entrance requirements:* For master's and doctorate, GRE General Test, minimum GPA of 3.0. Additional exam requirements/recommendations for international students: required—TOEFL (minimum score 600 paper-based; 100 iBT). Electronic applications accepted.

**The University of Kansas,** University of Kansas Medical Center, School of Medicine, Department of Population Health, Kansas City, KS 66160. Offers clinical research (MS); epidemiology (MPH); public health management (MPH); social and behavioral health (MPH); MD/MPH; PhD/MPH. *Accreditation:* CEPH. *Program availability:* Part-time. *Faculty:* 100. *Students:* 73 full-time (54 women), 49 part-time (35 women); includes 37 minority (9 Black or African American, non-Hispanic/Latino; 3 American Indian or Alaska Native, non-Hispanic/Latino; 9 Asian, non-Hispanic/Latino; 11 Hispanic/Latino; 5 Two or more races, non-Hispanic/Latino), 5 international. Average age 30. In 2019, 52 master's awarded. *Degree requirements:* For master's, thesis, capstone practicum defense. *Entrance requirements:* For master's, GRE for MHSA Program; GRE for MPH Program; GRE, MCAT, LSAT, GMAT or other equivalent graduate professional exam for MS Clinical Research Program. Additional exam requirements/recommendations for international students: required—TOEFL. *Application deadline:* For fall admission, 3/1 for domestic and international students; for spring admission, 11/1 for domestic and international students. Applications are processed on a rolling basis. Application fee: $60. Electronic applications accepted. *Expenses:* Tuition, state resident: full-time $9989. Tuition, nonresident: full-time $23,950. *International tuition:* $23,950 full-time. *Required fees:* $984; $81.99 per credit hour. Tuition and fees vary according to course load, campus/location and program. *Financial support:* Research assistantships, career-related internships or fieldwork, Federal Work-Study, scholarships/grants, and unspecified assistantships available. Support available to part-time students. Financial award application deadline: 3/1; financial award applicants required to submit FAFSA. *Unit head:* Dr. Edward F. Ellerbeck, Professor and Chair, 913-588-2775, Fax: 913-588-2780, E-mail: eellerbe@kumc.edu. *Application contact:* Dr. Edward F. Ellerbeck, Professor and Chair, 913-588-2775, Fax: 913-588-2780, E-mail: eellerbe@kumc.edu. Website: http://www.kumc.edu/school-of-medicine/population-health.html

**University of Kentucky,** Graduate School, College of Public Health, Program in Clinical Research Design, Lexington, KY 40506-0032. Offers MS.

**University of Maryland, Baltimore,** Graduate School, Clinical Research Certificate Program, Baltimore, MD 21201. Offers Postbaccalaureate Certificate. *Entrance requirements:* For degree, GRE General Test, minimum GPA of 3.0, curriculum vitae, essay. Additional exam requirements/recommendations for international students: required—TOEFL (minimum score 80 iBT); recommended—IELTS (minimum score 7). Electronic applications accepted.

**University of Maryland, Baltimore,** Graduate School, Graduate Program in Life Sciences, Baltimore, MD 21201. Offers biochemistry and molecular biology (MS, PhD), including biochemistry; cellular and molecular biomedical science (MS); clinical research (Postbaccalaureate Certificate); epidemiology (PhD); gerontology (PhD); molecular medicine (PhD), including applied pharmacology and toxicology, cancer biology, genome biology, molecular and cellular physiology; molecular microbiology and immunology (PhD); neuroscience (PhD); physical rehabilitation science (PhD); toxicology (MS, PhD); MD/MS; MD/PhD. *Degree requirements:* For master's, comprehensive exam (for some programs), thesis (for some programs); for doctorate, comprehensive exam, thesis/dissertation. *Entrance requirements:* For master's and doctorate, GRE. Additional exam requirements/recommendations for international students: required—TOEFL (minimum score 80 iBT); recommended—IELTS (minimum score 7). Electronic applications accepted.

**University of Maryland, Baltimore,** School of Medicine, Department of Epidemiology and Public Health, Baltimore, MD 21201. Offers biostatistics (MS); clinical research (MS); epidemiology and preventive medicine (MPH, MS, PhD); gerontology (PhD); human genetics and genomic medicine (MS, PhD); molecular epidemiology (MS, PhD); toxicology (MS, PhD); JD/MS; MD/PhD; MS/PhD. *Accreditation:* CEPH. *Program availability:* Part-time. *Students:* 75 full-time (51 women), 32 part-time (28 women); includes 29 minority (11 Black or African American, non-Hispanic/Latino; 11 Asian, non-Hispanic/Latino; 5 Hispanic/Latino; 2 Two or more races, non-Hispanic/Latino), 24 international. Average age 31. In 2019, 27 master's, 9 doctorates awarded. *Degree requirements:* For doctorate, comprehensive exam, thesis/dissertation. *Entrance requirements:* For master's and doctorate, GRE General Test. Additional exam requirements/recommendations for international students: required—TOEFL (minimum score 550 paper-based; 80 iBT); recommended—IELTS (minimum score 7). *Application deadline:* For fall admission, 1/15 for domestic and international students. Application fee: $75. Electronic applications accepted. *Expenses:* Contact institution. *Financial support:* In 2019–20, research assistantships with partial tuition reimbursements (averaging $26,000 per year) were awarded; fellowships, Federal Work-Study, scholarships/grants, and unspecified assistantships also available. Financial award application deadline: 3/1; financial award applicants required to submit FAFSA. *Unit head:* Dr. Laura Hungerford, Program Director, 410-706-8492, Fax: 410-706-4225. *Application contact:* Jessica Kelley, Program Coordinator, 410-706-8492, Fax: 410-706-4225, E-mail: jkelley@som.umaryland.edu. Website: http://lifesciences.umaryland.edu/epidemiology/

**University of Massachusetts Medical School,** Graduate School of Biomedical Sciences, Worcester, MA 01655. Offers biomedical sciences (PhD), including biochemistry and molecular pharmacology, bioinformatics and computational biology, cancer biology, immunology and microbiology, interdisciplinary, neuroscience, translational science; biomedical sciences (millennium program) (PhD); clinical and population health research (PhD); clinical investigation (MS). *Faculty:* 1,258 full-time (525 women), 372 part-time/adjunct (238 women). *Students:* 344 full-time (198 women), 1 (woman) part-time; includes 73 minority (12 Black or African American, non-Hispanic/Latino; 1 American Indian or Alaska Native, non-Hispanic/Latino; 45 Asian, non-

Hispanic/Latino; 15 Hispanic/Latino), 120 international. Average age 29. 581 applicants, 23% accepted, 56 enrolled. In 2019, 6 master's, 49 doctorates awarded. Terminal master's awarded for partial completion of doctoral program. *Degree requirements:* For master's, comprehensive exam, thesis; for doctorate, comprehensive exam, thesis/dissertation. *Entrance requirements:* For master's, MD, PhD, DVM, or PharmD; for doctorate, bachelor's degree. Additional exam requirements/recommendations for international students: required—TOEFL, IELTS, TOEFL (minimum score 100 IBT) or IELTS (minimum score 7.0). *Application deadline:* For fall admission, 12/1 for domestic and international students. Applications are processed on a rolling basis. Application fee: $80. Electronic applications accepted. Application fee is waived when completed online. *Expenses:* Contact institution. *Financial support:* In 2019–20, 22 fellowships with full tuition reimbursements (averaging $33,061 per year), 322 research assistantships with full tuition reimbursements (averaging $32,850 per year) were awarded; institutionally sponsored loans and scholarships/grants also available. Financial award application deadline: 5/15. *Unit head:* Dr. Mary Ellen Lane, Dean, 508-856-4018, E-mail: maryellen.lane@umassmed.edu. *Application contact:* Dr. Kendall Knight, Assistant Vice Provost for Admissions, 508-856-5628, Fax: 508-856-3659, E-mail: kendall.knight@umassmed.edu.
Website: http://www.umassmed.edu/gsbs/

**University of Michigan,** School of Public Health, Program in Clinical Research Design and Statistical Analysis, Ann Arbor, MI 48109. Offers MS. *Program availability:* Evening/weekend. *Degree requirements:* For master's, comprehensive exam. *Entrance requirements:* For master's, GRE General Test or MCAT. Additional exam requirements/recommendations for international students: recommended—TOEFL (minimum score 560 paper-based; 100 iBT). Electronic applications accepted. *Expenses:* Contact institution.

**University of Minnesota, Twin Cities Campus,** School of Public Health, Major in Clinical Research, Minneapolis, MN 55455-0213. Offers MS. *Program availability:* Part-time. *Degree requirements:* For master's, thesis. *Entrance requirements:* For master's, advanced health professional degree. Additional exam requirements/recommendations for international students: required—TOEFL. Electronic applications accepted.

**The University of North Carolina at Chapel Hill,** Graduate School, Gillings School of Global Public Health, Department of Epidemiology, Chapel Hill, NC 27599. Offers clinical research (MSCR); epidemiology (MPH, PhD); veterinary epidemiology (MPH); Pharm D/MPH. *Faculty:* 54 full-time (34 women), 81 part-time/adjunct (42 women). *Students:* 160 full-time (121 women), 20 part-time (9 women); includes 61 minority (17 Black or African American, non-Hispanic/Latino; 26 Asian, non-Hispanic/Latino; 9 Hispanic/Latino; 9 Two or more races, non-Hispanic/Latino), 23 international. Average age 30. 232 applicants, 28% accepted, 34 enrolled. In 2019, 21 master's, 31 doctorates awarded. Terminal master's awarded for partial completion of doctoral program. *Degree requirements:* For master's, comprehensive exam, major paper; for doctorate, comprehensive exam, thesis/dissertation. *Entrance requirements:* For master's, GRE General Test or MCAT, doctoral degree (completed or in-progress); for doctorate, GRE General Test, strong quantitative and biological preparation, 3 letters of recommendation (academic and/or professional). Additional exam requirements/recommendations for international students: required—TOEFL (minimum score 90 iBT), IELTS (minimum score 7). *Application deadline:* For fall admission, 12/11 for domestic and international students. Application fee: $90. Electronic applications accepted. *Financial support:* Fellowships with tuition reimbursements, research assistantships with tuition reimbursements, teaching assistantships with tuition reimbursements, career-related internships or fieldwork, Federal Work-Study, institutionally sponsored loans, scholarships/grants, traineeships, health care benefits, and unspecified assistantships available. Support available to part-time students. Financial award application deadline: 12/10; financial award applicants required to submit FAFSA. *Unit head:* Dr. Til Sturmer, Chair, 919-966-7433, Fax: 919-966-2089, E-mail: sturmer@unc.edu. *Application contact:* Valerie Hudock, Academic Coordinator, 919-966-7459, E-mail: vhudock@email.unc.edu.
Website: https://sph.unc.edu/epid/epidemiology-landing/

**The University of North Carolina Wilmington,** School of Nursing, Wilmington, NC 28403-3297. Offers clinical research and product development (MS); family nurse practitioner (Post-Master's Certificate); nurse educator (Post-Master's Certificate); nursing (MSN); nursing practice (DNP). *Accreditation:* AACN; ACEN. *Program availability:* Part-time, 100% online, blended/hybrid learning. *Faculty:* 51 full-time (46 women). *Students:* 171 full-time (156 women), 423 part-time (387 women); includes 117 minority (73 Black or African American, non-Hispanic/Latino; 6 American Indian or Alaska Native, non-Hispanic/Latino; 12 Asian, non-Hispanic/Latino; 16 Hispanic/Latino; 1 Native Hawaiian or other Pacific Islander, non-Hispanic/Latino; 9 Two or more races, non-Hispanic/Latino). Average age 38. 527 applicants, 57% accepted, 199 enrolled. In 2019, 149 master's, 9 doctorates awarded. *Degree requirements:* For master's, thesis or alternative, research/capstone project, presentation; for doctorate, comprehensive exam, clinical scholarly project, 1000 clinical hours. *Entrance requirements:* For master's, GRE General Test if overall Bachelor degree GPA under 3.0 (MSN degree); No tests for MCRD degree, 3 recommendations; statement of interest; resume; bachelor's degree, preferably in a life science, health care discipline, or mathematics/statistics; experience working in the biopharmaceutical or related field (MCRD degree); RN license in NC & must have 2.69 or higher Bachelor's GPA (for MSN); for doctorate, GRE General Test or MAT if Bachelor's GPA below 3.0 (FNP & Psychiatric Mental Health Nurse concentration), Varies based on concentration (Family Nurse Practitioner, Nurse Executive Leadership, Post APRN, and Psychiatric Mental Health Nurse); All require 3 professional references and an RN license. Additional exam requirements/recommendations for international students: required—TOEFL (minimum score 79 iBT), IELTS (minimum score 6.5). *Application deadline:* For fall admission, 4/15 for domestic students. Applications are processed on a rolling basis. Application fee: $75. Electronic applications accepted. *Expenses:* $324.70 per credit hour in-state (for DNP Program), $1,002.59 per credit hour out-of-state (for DNP Program), $259.01 per credit hour in-state (for the remaining online programs), $936.91 per credit hour out-of-state (for the remaining online programs), $3,728.47 entire year in-state (for main campus programs), $10,642.97 entire year out-of-state (for main campus programs). *Financial support:* Scholarships/grants available. Financial award application deadline: 1/1; financial award applicants required to submit FAFSA. *Unit head:* Dr. Linda Haddad, Director, 910-962-7410, Fax: 910-962-3723, E-mail: haddadl@uncw.edu. *Application contact:* Dr. Sarah Hubbell, MSN Graduate Coordinator, 910-962-0561, E-mail: hubbells@uncw.edu.
Website: https://uncw.edu/chhs/son/

**University of Pittsburgh,** School of Medicine, Graduate Programs in Medicine, Clinical Research Graduate Programs, Pittsburgh, PA 15260. Offers MS, Certificate. *Program availability:* Part-time, blended/hybrid learning. *Degree requirements:* For master's, thesis, 8 hours of responsible conduct in research training. *Entrance requirements:* For master's, MCAT or GRE, official transcripts, 2 letters of recommendation, curriculum vitae. Additional exam requirements/recommendations for international students: required—TOEFL (minimum score 600 paper-based; 100 iBT), IELTS (minimum score 7). Electronic applications accepted. *Expenses:* Contact institution.

**University of Puerto Rico - Medical Sciences Campus,** School of Health Professions, Program in Clinical Research, San Juan, PR 00936-5067. Offers MS, Graduate Certificate.

**University of Rochester,** School of Medicine and Dentistry, Graduate Programs in Medicine and Dentistry, Department of Community and Preventive Medicine, Programs in Public Health and Clinical Investigation, Rochester, NY 14627. Offers clinical investigation (MS); public health (MPH); MBA/MPH; MD/MPH; MPH/MS; MPH/PhD. *Accreditation:* CEPH. *Entrance requirements:* For master's, GRE General Test.

**University of Rochester,** School of Medicine and Dentistry, Graduate Programs in Medicine and Dentistry, Interdepartmental Program in Clinical Translational Research, Rochester, NY 14627. Offers MS.

**University of Southern California,** Graduate School, School of Pharmacy, Regulatory Science Programs, Los Angeles, CA 90089. Offers clinical research design and management (Graduate Certificate); food safety (Graduate Certificate); patient and product safety (Graduate Certificate); preclinical drug development (Graduate Certificate); regulatory and clinical affairs (Graduate Certificate); regulatory science (MS, DRSc). *Program availability:* Part-time, evening/weekend, online learning. Terminal master's awarded for partial completion of doctoral program. *Degree requirements:* For master's, thesis optional; for doctorate, comprehensive exam, thesis/dissertation. *Entrance requirements:* For master's, GRE. Additional exam requirements/recommendations for international students: required—TOEFL (minimum score 603 paper-based; 100 iBT). Electronic applications accepted.

**University of South Florida,** Innovative Education, Tampa, FL 33620-9951. Offers adult, career and higher education (Graduate Certificate), including college teaching, leadership in developing human resources, leadership in higher education; Africana studies (Graduate Certificate), including diasporas and health disparities, genocide and human rights; aging studies (Graduate Certificate), including gerontology; art research (Graduate Certificate), including museum studies; business foundations (Graduate Certificate); chemical and biomedical engineering (Graduate Certificate), including materials science and engineering, water, health and sustainability; child and family studies (Graduate Certificate), including positive behavior support; civil and industrial engineering (Graduate Certificate), including transportation systems analysis; community and family health (Graduate Certificate), including maternal and child health, social marketing and public health, violence and injury: prevention and intervention, women's health; criminology (Graduate Certificate), including criminal justice administration; data science for public administration (Graduate Certificate); digital humanities (Graduate Certificate); educational measurement and research (Graduate Certificate), including evaluation; English (Graduate Certificate), including comparative literary studies, creative writing, professional and technical communication; entrepreneurship (Graduate Certificate); environmental health (Graduate Certificate), including safety management; epidemiology and biostatistics (Graduate Certificate), including applied biostatistics, biostatistics, concepts and tools of epidemiology, epidemiology, epidemiology of infectious diseases; geography, environment and planning (Graduate Certificate), including community development, environmental policy and management, geographical information systems; geology (Graduate Certificate), including hydrogeology; global health (Graduate Certificate), including disaster management, global health and Latin American and Caribbean studies, global health practice, humanitarian assistance, infection control; government and international affairs (Graduate Certificate), including Cuban studies, globalization studies; health policy and management (Graduate Certificate), including health management and leadership, public health policy and programs; hearing specialist: early intervention (Graduate Certificate); industrial and management systems engineering (Graduate Certificate), including systems engineering, technology management; information studies (Graduate Certificate), including school library media specialist; information systems/decision sciences (Graduate Certificate), including analytics and business intelligence; instructional technology (Graduate Certificate), including distance education, Florida digital/virtual educator, instructional design, multimedia design, Web design; internal medicine, bioethics and medical humanities (Graduate Certificate), including biomedical ethics; Latin American and Caribbean studies (Graduate Certificate); leadership for coastal resiliency planning (Graduate Certificate); mass communications (Graduate Certificate), including multimedia journalism; mathematics and statistics (Graduate Certificate), including mathematics; medicine (Graduate Certificate), including aging and neuroscience, bioinformatics, biotechnology, brain fitness and memory management, clinical investigation, hand and upper limb rehabilitation, health informatics, health sciences, integrative weight management, intellectual property, medicine and gender, metabolic and nutritional medicine, metabolic cardiology, pharmacy sciences; national and competitive intelligence (Graduate Certificate); nursing (Graduate Certificate), including simulation based academic fellowship in advanced pain management; psychological and social foundations (Graduate Certificate), including career counseling, college teaching, diversity in education, mental health counseling, school counseling; public affairs (Graduate Certificate), including nonprofit management, public management, research administration; public health (Graduate Certificate), including assessing chemical toxicity and public health risks, health equity, pharmacoepidemiology, public health generalist, toxicology, translational research in adolescent behavioral health; public health practices (Graduate Certificate), including planning for healthy communities; rehabilitation and mental health counseling (Graduate Certificate), including integrative mental health care, marriage and family therapy, rehabilitation technology; secondary education (Graduate Certificate), including ESOL, foreign language education: culture and content, foreign language education: professional; social work (Graduate Certificate), including geriatric social work/clinical gerontology; special education (Graduate Certificate), including autism spectrum disorder, disabilities education: severe/profound; world languages (Graduate Certificate), including teaching English as a second language (TESL) or foreign language. *Unit head:* Dr. Cynthia DeLuca, Associate Vice President and Assistant Vice Provost, 813-974-3077, Fax: 813-974-7061, E-mail: deluca@usf.edu. *Application contact:* Owen Hooper, Director, Summer and Alternative Calendar Programs, 813-974-6917, E-mail: hooper@usf.edu.
Website: http://www.usf.edu/innovative-education/

**The University of Texas Health Science Center at San Antonio,** Graduate School of Biomedical Sciences, Master of Science in Clinical Investigation Program, San Antonio, TX 78229-3900. Offers MS. *Program availability:* Part-time. *Degree requirements:* For master's, comprehensive exam.

**University of Virginia,** School of Medicine, Department of Public Health Sciences, Program in Clinical Research, Charlottesville, VA 22903. Offers clinical investigation and patient-oriented research (MS); informatics in medicine (MS). *Program availability:* Part-time. *Degree requirements:* For master's, thesis (for some programs). *Entrance requirements:* For master's, 2 letters of recommendation. Additional exam requirements/recommendations for international students: required—TOEFL (minimum score 600 paper-based; 90 iBT). Electronic applications accepted.

**University of Washington,** Graduate School, School of Public Health, Department of Epidemiology, Seattle, WA 98195. Offers clinical and translational research methods (MS); epidemiology (PhD); general epidemiology (MPH, MS); global health (MPH); maternal and child health (MPH); MPH/MPA. *Accreditation:* CEPH (one or more

programs are accredited). *Program availability:* Part-time. *Faculty:* 54 full-time (36 women), 60 part-time/adjunct (27 women). *Students:* 161 full-time (116 women), 43 part-time (33 women); includes 54 minority (8 Black or African American, non-Hispanic/Latino; 4 American Indian or Alaska Native, non-Hispanic/Latino; 34 Asian, non-Hispanic/Latino; 8 Hispanic/Latino), 30 international. Average age 32. 393 applicants, 56% accepted, 91 enrolled. In 2019, 37 master's, 21 doctorates awarded. *Degree requirements:* For master's, thesis; for doctorate, comprehensive exam, thesis/dissertation. *Entrance requirements:* For master's, GRE (except for MDs from US institutions), Earned Bachelor's degree; for doctorate, GRE, Earned Master's degree. Additional exam requirements/recommendations for international students: required—TOEFL (minimum score 80 iBT). *Application deadline:* For fall admission, 12/1 for domestic and international students. Application fee: $85. Electronic applications accepted. *Financial support:* In 2019–20, 135 students received support, including 55 fellowships with full and partial tuition reimbursements available (averaging $38,000 per year), 50 research assistantships with full and partial tuition reimbursements available (averaging $30,000 per year), 15 teaching assistantships with full and partial tuition reimbursements available (averaging $24,000 per year); career-related internships or fieldwork, Federal Work-Study, institutionally sponsored loans, scholarships/grants, traineeships, health care benefits, tuition waivers (full and partial), and unspecified assistantships also available. Support available to part-time students. Financial award application deadline: 12/1. *Unit head:* Dr. Stephen E. Hawes, Professor and Chair, 206-685-0146, E-mail: epiadmin@uw.edu. *Application contact:* John Paulson, Assistant Director of Student Academic Services, 206-685-1762, E-mail: epi@uw.edu. Website: https://epi.washington.edu/

**University of Wisconsin–Madison,** School of Medicine and Public Health, Clinical Investigation Graduate Program, Madison, WI 53705. Offers MS, PhD.

**Walden University,** Graduate Programs, School of Health Sciences, Minneapolis, MN 55401. Offers clinical research administration (MS, Graduate Certificate); health education and promotion (MS, PhD), including behavioral health (PhD), disease surveillance (PhD), emergency preparedness (MS), general (MHA, MS), global health (PhD), health policy (PhD), health policy and advocacy (MS), population health (PhD); health informatics (MS); health services (PhD), including community health, healthcare administration, leadership, public health policy, self-designed; healthcare administration (MHA, DHA), including general (MHA, MS); leadership and organizational development (MHA); public health (MPH, Dr PH, PhD, Graduate Certificate), including community health education (PhD), epidemiology (PhD); systems policy (MHA). *Program availability:* Part-time, evening/weekend, online only, 100% online. *Degree requirements:* For doctorate, thesis/dissertation, residency. *Entrance requirements:* For master's, bachelor's degree or higher; minimum GPA of 2.5; official transcripts; goal statement (for some programs); access to computer and Internet; for doctorate, master's degree or higher; three years of related professional or academic experience (preferred); minimum GPA of 3.0; goal statement and current resume (for select programs); official transcripts; access to computer and Internet; for Graduate Certificate, relevant work experience; access to computer and Internet. Additional exam requirements/recommendations for international students: required—TOEFL (minimum score 550 paper-based, 79 iBT), IELTS (minimum score 6.5), Michigan English Language Assessment Battery (minimum score 82), or PTE (minimum score 53). Electronic applications accepted.

**Washington University in St. Louis,** School of Medicine, Program in Clinical Investigation, St. Louis, MO 63130-4899. Offers clinical investigation (MS), including bioethics, entrepreneurship, genetics/genomics, translational medicine. *Program availability:* Part-time, evening/weekend. *Degree requirements:* For master's, thesis. *Entrance requirements:* For master's, doctoral-level degree or in process of obtaining doctoral-level degree. Electronic applications accepted.

# Communication Disorders

**Abilene Christian University,** Office of Graduate Programs, College of Education and Human Services, Department of Communication Sciences and Disorders, Abilene, TX 79699. Offers MS. *Accreditation:* ASHA. *Faculty:* 10 part-time/adjunct (9 women). *Students:* 104 full-time (all women), 1 (woman) part-time; includes 29 minority (6 Black or African American, non-Hispanic/Latino; 1 American Indian or Alaska Native, non-Hispanic/Latino; 2 Asian, non-Hispanic/Latino; 15 Hispanic/Latino; 5 Two or more races, non-Hispanic/Latino). 353 applicants, 38% accepted, 56 enrolled. In 2019, 50 master's awarded. *Degree requirements:* For master's, one foreign language, comprehensive exam. *Entrance requirements:* For master's, GRE General Test, official transcripts, recommendations, Purpose Statement, Resume, interview. Additional exam requirements/recommendations for international students: required—TOEFL (minimum score 80 iBT), IELTS (minimum score 6), PTE (minimum score 51). *Application deadline:* For fall admission, 1/15 priority date for domestic students. Applications are processed on a rolling basis. Application fee: $65. Electronic applications accepted. *Expenses:* $1105 per hour. *Financial support:* In 2019–20, 73 students received support, including 12 research assistantships with partial tuition reimbursements available; scholarships/grants also available. Financial award application deadline: 4/1; financial award applicants required to submit FAFSA. *Unit head:* Dr. Lynette Austin, Chair, 325-674-2090, Fax: 325-674-6272, E-mail: dla08a@acu.edu. *Application contact:* Graduate Admission, 325-674-6911, E-mail: gradinfo@acu.edu. Website: http://www.acu.edu/on-campus/graduate/college-of-education-and-human-services/communication-sciences-disorders.html

**Alabama Agricultural and Mechanical University,** School of Graduate Studies, College of Education, Humanities, and Behavioral Sciences, Department of Health Sciences, Human Performance, and Communicative Disorders, Huntsville, AL 35811. Offers kinesiology (MS); physical education (MS); speech-language pathology (MS). *Program availability:* Part-time, evening/weekend. *Degree requirements:* For master's, comprehensive exam. *Entrance requirements:* For master's, GRE General Test. Additional exam requirements/recommendations for international students: required—TOEFL (minimum score 500 paper-based; 61 iBT). Electronic applications accepted.

**Albizu University - Miami,** Graduate Programs, Doral, FL 33172. Offers clinical psychology (PhD, Psy D); entrepreneurship (MBA); exceptional student education (MS); human services (PhD); industrial/organizational psychology (MS); marriage and family therapy (MS); mental health counseling (MS); nonprofit management (MBA); organizational management (MBA); school counseling (MS); speech and language pathology (MS); teaching English for speakers of other languages (MS). *Accreditation:* APA. *Program availability:* Part-time, 100% online, blended/hybrid learning. *Faculty:* 28 full-time (21 women), 27 part-time/adjunct (15 women). *Students:* 410 full-time (351 women), 190 part-time (163 women); includes 519 minority (33 Black or African American, non-Hispanic/Latino; 3 Asian, non-Hispanic/Latino; 477 Hispanic/Latino; 6 Two or more races, non-Hispanic/Latino), 21 international. Average age 33. 286 applicants, 66% accepted, 127 enrolled. In 2019, 96 master's, 54 doctorates awarded. Terminal master's awarded for partial completion of doctoral program. *Degree requirements:* For master's, comprehensive exam (for some programs), integrative project (for MBA); research project (for exceptional student education, teaching English as a second language); comprehensive examination for Speech and Language Pathology; for doctorate, comprehensive exam, thesis/dissertation, comprehensive examinations, internship, project/dissertation. *Entrance requirements:* For master's, GRE/EXADEP, bachelor's degree from accredited institution, minimum GPA of 3.0, 3 letters of recommendation, interview, resume, statement of purpose, official transcripts; for doctorate, GRE (for Psy D), 3 letters of recommendation, resume, interview, statement of purpose, official transcripts; bachelor's degree and minimum GPA of 3.25 (for Psy D); master's degree and minimum GPA of 3.0 (for PhD). Additional exam requirements/recommendations for international students: required—Michigan Test of English Language Proficiency. *Application deadline:* For fall admission, 4/1 priority date for domestic students, 5/1 priority date for international students; for spring admission, 11/1 priority date for domestic students, 9/1 priority date for international students. Applications are processed on a rolling basis. Application fee: $50. Electronic applications accepted. Application fee is waived when completed online. *Expenses:* $600 per credit or $620 per credit or $650 per credit (for master's depending on field); $800 per credit or $1,050 per credit (for doctoral depending on program). *Financial support:* In 2019–20, 158 students received support. Federal Work-Study, scholarships/grants, unspecified assistantships, and tuition discounts available. Financial award application deadline: 6/1; financial award applicants required to submit FAFSA. *Unit head:* Dr. Tilokie Depoo, PhD, Chancellor, 305-593-1223 Ext. 3138, Fax: 305-477-8983, E-mail: tdepoo@albizu.edu. *Application contact:* Nancy Alvarez, Director of Enrollment Management, 305-593-1223 Ext. 3136, Fax: 305-593-1854, E-mail: nalvarez@albizu.edu. Website: www.albizu.edu

**Albizu University - San Juan,** Graduate Programs, San Juan, PR 00901. Offers clinical psychology (MS, PhD, Psy D); general psychology (PhD); industrial/organizational psychology (MS, PhD); speech and language pathology (MS). *Accreditation:* APA (one or more programs are accredited). *Program availability:* Part-time, evening/weekend. Terminal master's awarded for partial completion of doctoral program. *Degree requirements:* For master's, one foreign language, comprehensive exam, thesis; for doctorate, one foreign language, comprehensive exam, thesis/dissertation, written qualifying exams. *Entrance requirements:* For master's, GRE General Test or EXADEP, interview; minimum GPA of 2.8 (industrial/organizational psychology); for doctorate, GRE General Test or EXADEP, interview; minimum GPA of 3.0 (PhD in industrial/organizational psychology and clinical psychology), 3.25 (Psy D).

**Andrews University,** College of Health and Human Services, School of Communication Sciences and Disorders, Berrien Springs, MI 49104. Offers speech-language pathology (MS). *Faculty:* 5 full-time (all women). *Students:* 40 full-time (39 women); includes 17 minority (4 Black or African American, non-Hispanic/Latino; 7 Asian, non-Hispanic/Latino; 6 Hispanic/Latino), 2 international. Average age 25. In 2019, 16 master's awarded. *Application deadline:* Applications are processed on a rolling basis. Application fee: $60. Electronic applications accepted. *Financial support:* Research assistantships, teaching assistantships, Federal Work-Study, institutionally sponsored loans, and scholarships/grants available. *Unit head:* Heather Ferguson, Chair, 269-471-6369, E-mail: hferguson@andrews.edu. *Application contact:* Jillian Panigot, Director, University Admissions, 800-253-2874, Fax: 269-471-3228, E-mail: graduate@andrews.edu. Website: http://www.andrews.edu/shp/speech/

**Appalachian State University,** Cratis D. Williams School of Graduate Studies, Department of Communication Sciences and Disorders, Boone, NC 28608. Offers speech-language pathology (MS). *Accreditation:* ASHA. *Program availability:* Part-time. *Degree requirements:* For master's, comprehensive exam, thesis optional. *Entrance requirements:* For master's, GRE General Test, 3 letters of recommendation. Additional exam requirements/recommendations for international students: required—TOEFL (minimum score 570 paper-based), IELTS (minimum score 6.5). Electronic applications accepted.

**Arizona State University at Tempe,** College of Health Solutions, Department of Speech and Hearing Science, Tempe, AZ 85287-0102. Offers audiology (Au D); communication disorders (MS); speech and hearing science (PhD). *Accreditation:* ASHA (one or more programs are accredited). *Degree requirements:* For master's, comprehensive exam (for some programs), thesis optional, interactive Program of Study (iPOS) submitted before completing 50 percent of required credit hours; for doctorate, comprehensive exam, thesis/dissertation (for some programs), academic/practicum components (Au D); interactive Program of Study (iPOS) submitted before completing 50 percent of required credit hours. *Entrance requirements:* For master's and doctorate, GRE, minimum GPA of 3.0 or equivalent in last 2 years of work leading to bachelor's degree. Additional exam requirements/recommendations for international students: required—TOEFL, IELTS, or PTE. *Expenses:* Contact institution.

**Arkansas State University,** Graduate School, College of Nursing and Health Professions, Department of Communication Disorders, State University, AR 72467. Offers communication disorders (MCD); dyslexia therapy (Graduate Certificate). *Accreditation:* ASHA. *Program availability:* Part-time. *Degree requirements:* For master's, comprehensive exam, thesis or alternative. *Entrance requirements:* For master's, GRE General Test, appropriate bachelor's degree, letters of recommendation, official transcripts, immunization records. Additional exam requirements/recommendations for international students: required—TOEFL (minimum score 550 paper-based; 79 iBT), IELTS (minimum score 6), PTE (minimum score 56). Electronic applications accepted. *Expenses:* Contact institution.

**A.T. Still University,** Arizona School of Health Sciences, Mesa, AZ 85206. Offers advanced occupational therapy (MS); advanced physician assistant studies (MS); athletic training (MS, DAT); audiology (Au D); clinical decision making in athletic training (Graduate Certificate); occupational therapy (MS, OTD); orthopedic rehabilitation (Graduate Certificate); physical therapy (DPT); physician assistant studies (MS); post-professional audiology (Au D); post-professional physical therapy (DPT). *Accreditation:* AOTA (one or more programs are accredited); ASHA. *Program availability:* Part-time,

evening/weekend, online only, 100% online, blended/hybrid learning. *Faculty:* 94 full-time (74 women), 203 part-time/adjunct (145 women). *Students:* 736 full-time (528 women), 289 part-time (195 women); includes 315 minority (53 Black or African American, non-Hispanic/Latino; 7 American Indian or Alaska Native, non-Hispanic/Latino; 94 Asian, non-Hispanic/Latino; 134 Hispanic/Latino; 2 Native Hawaiian or other Pacific Islander, non-Hispanic/Latino; 25 Two or more races, non-Hispanic/Latino), 79 international. Average age 32. 4,387 applicants, 20% accepted, 514 enrolled. In 2019, 153 master's, 344 doctorates, 2 other advanced degrees awarded. *Degree requirements:* For master's, thesis (for some programs); for doctorate, thesis/dissertation (for some programs). *Entrance requirements:* For master's, GRE General Test; for doctorate, GRE, Physical Therapist Evaluation Tool (for DPT), current state licensure. Additional exam requirements/recommendations for international students: required—TOEFL (minimum score 80 iBT). *Application deadline:* For fall admission, 7/7 for domestic and international students; for winter admission, 10/3 for domestic and international students; for spring admission, 1/16 for domestic and international students; for summer admission, 4/17 for domestic and international students. Applications are processed on a rolling basis. Application fee: $70. *Financial support:* In 2019–20, 170 students received support. Federal Work-Study and scholarships/grants available. Financial award application deadline: 6/1; financial award applicants required to submit FAFSA. *Unit head:* Dr. Ann Lee Burch, Dean, 480-219-6061, E-mail: aburch@atsu.edu. *Application contact:* Donna Sparks, Director, Admissions Processing, 660-626-2117, Fax: 660-626-2969, E-mail: admissions@atsu.edu.
Website: http://www.atsu.edu/ashs

**Auburn University,** Graduate School, College of Liberal Arts, Department of Speech, Language, and Hearing Sciences, Auburn, AL 36849. Offers audiology (MCD, Au D). *Accreditation:* ASHA (one or more programs are accredited). *Program availability:* Part-time. *Faculty:* 19 full-time (15 women), 3 part-time/adjunct (2 women). *Students:* 78 full-time (71 women), 9 part-time (8 women); includes 10 minority (3 Black or African American, non-Hispanic/Latino; 1 American Indian or Alaska Native, non-Hispanic/Latino; 2 Asian, non-Hispanic/Latino; 4 Hispanic/Latino), 2 international. Average age 25. 262 applicants, 16% accepted, 34 enrolled. In 2019, 26 master's, 9 doctorates awarded. *Degree requirements:* For master's, thesis (for some programs), comprehensive exam (MCD), thesis (MS); for doctorate, thesis/dissertation. *Entrance requirements:* For master's and doctorate, GRE General Test. Additional exam requirements/recommendations for international students: recommended—TOEFL (minimum score 550 paper-based; 79 iBT). *Application deadline:* Applications are processed on a rolling basis. Application fee: $60 ($70 for international students). Electronic applications accepted. *Expenses: Tuition, area resident:* Full-time $9828; part-time $546 per credit hour. Tuition, state resident: full-time $9828; part-time $546 per credit hour. Tuition, nonresident: full-time $29,484; part-time $1638 per credit hour. *International tuition:* $29,744 full-time. Tuition and fees vary according to course load, program and reciprocity agreements. *Financial support:* In 2019–20, 10 fellowships with tuition reimbursements, 17 research assistantships with tuition reimbursements (averaging $10,611 per year) were awarded; teaching assistantships and Federal Work-Study also available. Support available to part-time students. Financial award application deadline: 3/15; financial award applicants required to submit FAFSA. *Unit head:* Dr. Laura W. Plexico, Chair, 334-844-9620, E-mail: lwp0002@auburn.edu. *Application contact:* Dr. George Flowers, Dean of the Graduate School, 334-844-2125.
Website: http://www.cla.auburn.edu/communicationdisorders/

**Baldwin Wallace University,** Graduate Programs, Speech-Language Pathology Program, Berea, OH 44017-2088. Offers MS. *Faculty:* 10 full-time (9 women), 7 part-time/adjunct (all women). *Students:* 48 full-time (46 women); includes 6 minority (2 Black or African American, non-Hispanic/Latino; 2 Asian, non-Hispanic/Latino; 1 Hispanic/Latino; 1 Two or more races, non-Hispanic/Latino). Average age 23. 155 applicants, 46% accepted, 28 enrolled. In 2019, 22 master's awarded. *Entrance requirements:* For master's, GRE, 3 letters of recommendation, bachelor's degree, 25 clinical observation hours in speech and/or language therapy or evaluation, CSDCAS online application. Additional exam requirements/recommendations for international students: required—TOEFL. *Application deadline:* For fall admission, 1/15 for domestic students. Applications are processed on a rolling basis. Electronic applications accepted. *Expenses:* Total cost - $70,000. *Financial support:* Unspecified assistantships available. Financial award applicants required to submit FAFSA. *Unit head:* Stephen D. Stahl, Provost, Academic Affairs, 440-826-2251, Fax: 440-826-2329, E-mail: sstahl@bw.edu. *Application contact:* Kate Glaser, Associate Director of Admission, Graduate and Professional Studies, 440-826-8016, Fax: 440-826-3830, E-mail: slp@bw.edu.
Website: http://www.bw.edu/slp

**Ball State University,** Graduate School, College of Health, Department of Speech Pathology and Audiology, Muncie, IN 47306. Offers audiology (Au D); speech-language pathology (MA). *Accreditation:* ASHA. *Degree requirements:* For doctorate, comprehensive exam. *Entrance requirements:* For master's, GRE General Test (minimum preferred combined score of 900 on verbal and quantitative sections), minimum baccalaureate GPA of 3.0, three letters of reference, transcripts of all previous course work; for doctorate, GRE General Test, statement of purpose, on-campus interview. Additional exam requirements/recommendations for international students: required—TOEFL (minimum score 550 paper-based; 79 iBT), IELTS (minimum score 6.5). Electronic applications accepted. *Expenses: Tuition, area resident:* Full-time $7506; part-time $417 per credit hour. Tuition, nonresident: full-time $20,610; part-time $1145 per credit hour. *Required fees:* $2126. Tuition and fees vary according to course load, campus/location and program.

**Barry University,** School of Education, Program in Education for Teachers of Students with Hearing Impairments, Miami Shores, FL 33161-6695. Offers MS.

**Baylor University,** Graduate School, Robbins College of Health and Human Sciences, Department of Communication Sciences and Disorders, Waco, TX 76798. Offers MS. *Accreditation:* ASHA. *Entrance requirements:* For master's, GRE General Test. Additional exam requirements/recommendations for international students: required—TOEFL. Electronic applications accepted. *Expenses:* Contact institution.

**Bloomsburg University of Pennsylvania,** School of Graduate Studies, College of Education, Department of Exceptionality Programs, Program in Education of the Deaf/Hard of Hearing, Bloomsburg, PA 17815-1301. Offers MS. *Degree requirements:* For master's, thesis, minimum QPA of 3.0, practicum. *Entrance requirements:* For master's, PRAXIS, GRE, minimum QPA of 3.0, letter of intent, 3 letters of recommendation, interview. Additional exam requirements/recommendations for international students: required—TOEFL (minimum score 550 paper-based), IELTS. Electronic applications accepted.

**Bloomsburg University of Pennsylvania,** School of Graduate Studies, College of Science and Technology, Department of Audiology and Speech Pathology, Program in Audiology, Bloomsburg, PA 17815-1301. Offers Au D. *Accreditation:* ASHA. *Degree requirements:* For doctorate, comprehensive exam, thesis/dissertation, minimum QPA of 3.0, practicum. *Entrance requirements:* For doctorate, GRE, 3 letters of recommendation, interview, personal statement, minimum QPA of 3.0. Additional exam requirements/recommendations for international students: required—TOEFL, IELTS. Electronic applications accepted. *Expenses:* Contact institution.

**Bloomsburg University of Pennsylvania,** School of Graduate Studies, College of Science and Technology, Department of Audiology and Speech Pathology, Program in Speech Pathology, Bloomsburg, PA 17815-1301. Offers speech-language pathology (MS). *Accreditation:* ASHA. *Degree requirements:* For master's, thesis optional, minimum QPA of 3.0, clinical experience. *Entrance requirements:* For master's, GRE, minimum QPA of 3.0, 3 letters of recommendation, personal statement. Additional exam requirements/recommendations for international students: required—TOEFL (minimum score 550 paper-based), IELTS. Electronic applications accepted. *Expenses:* Contact institution.

**Boston University,** College of Health and Rehabilitation Sciences: Sargent College, Department of Speech, Language and Hearing Sciences, Boston, MA 02215. Offers speech, language and hearing sciences (PhD); speech-language pathology (MS). *Accreditation:* ASHA. *Faculty:* 10 full-time (9 women), 8 part-time/adjunct (6 women). *Students:* 88 full-time (82 women); includes 11 minority (4 Asian, non-Hispanic/Latino; 4 Hispanic/Latino; 3 Two or more races, non-Hispanic/Latino), 8 international. Average age 24. 407 applicants, 53% accepted, 40 enrolled. In 2019, 32 master's, 4 doctorates awarded. Terminal master's awarded for partial completion of doctoral program. *Entrance requirements:* Additional exam requirements/recommendations for international students: required—TOEFL. Application fee: $133. Electronic applications accepted. *Financial support:* Research assistantships, teaching assistantships, career-related internships or fieldwork, Federal Work-Study, institutionally sponsored loans, scholarships/grants, and tuition waivers (full and partial) available. Financial award applicants required to submit FAFSA. *Unit head:* Dr. Michelle Mentis, Chair, 617-353-7840, E-mail: slhs@bu.edu. *Application contact:* Sharon Sankey, Assistant Dean, Student Services, 617-353-2713, Fax: 617-353-7500, E-mail: ssankey@bu.edu.
Website: http://www.bu.edu/sargent/

**Bowling Green State University,** Graduate College, College of Health and Human Services, Department of Communication Sciences and Disorders, Bowling Green, OH 43403. Offers communication disorders (PhD); speech-language pathology (MS). *Accreditation:* ASHA (one or more programs are accredited). *Degree requirements:* For master's, thesis or alternative; for doctorate, comprehensive exam, thesis/dissertation, foreign language or research tool. *Entrance requirements:* For master's, GRE General Test, minimum GPA of 3.0; for doctorate, GRE General Test, minimum GPA of 3.2. Additional exam requirements/recommendations for international students: required—TOEFL. Electronic applications accepted.

**Bridgewater State University,** College of Graduate Studies, College of Education and Allied Studies, Department of Communication Sciences and Disorders, Bridgewater, MA 02325. Offers speech/language pathology (MS).

**Brigham Young University,** Graduate Studies, David O. McKay School of Education, Department of Communication Disorders, Provo, UT 84602-1001. Offers speech language pathology (MS). *Accreditation:* ASHA. *Faculty:* 8 full-time (3 women). *Students:* 23 full-time (22 women), 21 part-time (all women); includes 2 minority (1 American Indian or Alaska Native, non-Hispanic/Latino; 1 Hispanic/Latino). Average age 26. 101 applicants, 25% accepted, 23 enrolled. In 2019, 20 master's awarded. *Degree requirements:* For master's, comprehensive exam, thesis, exit interview, PRAXIS. *Entrance requirements:* For master's, GRE General Test, 3 letters of recommendation; letter of intent; all transcripts. Additional exam requirements/recommendations for international students: required—TOEFL (minimum score 580 paper-based; 85 iBT). *Application deadline:* For fall admission, 2/1 for domestic and international students. Application fee: $50. Electronic applications accepted. *Expenses:* 4 semesters @. *Financial support:* In 2019–20, 42 students received support, including 20 research assistantships (averaging $1,701 per year), 18 teaching assistantships (averaging $2,700 per year); scholarships/grants also available. *Unit head:* Dr. Christoper D. Dromey, Department Chair, Professor, 801-422-6461, Fax: 801-422-0197, E-mail: dromey@byu.edu. *Application contact:* Dr. Douglas Bryan Petersen, Graduate Coordinator, Professor, 801-422-0453, Fax: 801-422-0197, E-mail: dpeter39@byu.edu.
Website: https://education.byu.edu/comd

**Brooklyn College of the City University of New York,** School of Humanities and Social Sciences, Department of Speech Communication Arts and Sciences, Brooklyn, NY 11210-2889. Offers audiology (Au D); speech (MA), including public communication; speech-language pathology (MS). *Accreditation:* ASHA (one or more programs are accredited). *Program availability:* Part-time. Terminal master's awarded for partial completion of doctoral program. *Degree requirements:* For master's, comprehensive exam, NTE. *Entrance requirements:* For master's, GRE, minimum GPA of 3.0, interview, essay. Additional exam requirements/recommendations for international students: required—TOEFL (minimum score 500 paper-based; 61 iBT). Electronic applications accepted.

**Buffalo State College, State University of New York,** The Graduate School, School of the Professions, Department of Speech-Language Pathology, Buffalo, NY 14222-1095. Offers MS Ed. *Accreditation:* ASHA. *Program availability:* Part-time, evening/weekend. *Degree requirements:* For master's, thesis or alternative, project. *Entrance requirements:* For master's, minimum GPA of 3.0 in last 60 hours, 22 hours in communication disorders. Additional exam requirements/recommendations for international students: required—TOEFL (minimum score 550 paper-based).

**California Baptist University,** Program in Speech Language Pathology, Riverside, CA 92504-3206. Offers MS. *Program availability:* Part-time. *Degree requirements:* For master's, comprehensive exam, capstone, PRAXIS, clinical practicum. *Entrance requirements:* For master's, minimum undergraduate GPA of 3.0, bachelor's transcripts, three letters of recommendation, essay, resume, interview. Additional exam requirements/recommendations for international students: required—TOEFL (minimum score 80 iBT). Electronic applications accepted. *Expenses:* Contact institution.

**California State University, Chico,** Office of Graduate Studies, College of Communication and Education, Department of Communication Arts and Sciences, Program in Communication Sciences and Disorders, Chico, CA 95929-0722. Offers MA. *Accreditation:* ASHA. *Degree requirements:* For master's, thesis or comprehensive exam. *Entrance requirements:* For master's, GRE, deadline is January 15th; fall admission only; 3 letters of recommendation, resume, personal essay, transcripts using http://www.capcsd.org/csdcas/; GPA of 3.0. Additional exam requirements/recommendations for international students: required—TOEFL (minimum score 550 paper-based; 80 iBT), IELTS (minimum score 6.5), PTE (minimum score 59). Electronic applications accepted.

**California State University, East Bay,** Office of Graduate Studies, College of Letters, Arts, and Social Sciences, Department of Speech, Language, and Hearing Sciences, Hayward, CA 94542-3000. Offers speech-language pathology (MS). *Accreditation:* ASHA. *Program availability:* Part-time. *Degree requirements:* For master's, comprehensive exam, internship or thesis. *Entrance requirements:* For master's, minimum GPA of 3.0 in last 2 years of course work; baccalaureate degree in speech pathology and audiology; minimum of 60 hours' supervised clinical practice. Additional exam requirements/recommendations for international students: required—TOEFL (minimum score 550 paper-based). Electronic applications accepted.

**California State University, Fresno,** Division of Research and Graduate Studies, College of Health and Human Services, Department of Communicative Sciences and

Deaf Studies, Fresno, CA 93740-8027. Offers communicative disorders (MA), including deaf education, speech/language pathology. *Accreditation:* ASHA. *Program availability:* Part-time. *Degree requirements:* For master's, thesis or alternative. *Entrance requirements:* For master's, GRE General Test, minimum GPA of 3.0. Additional exam requirements/recommendations for international students: required—TOEFL. Electronic applications accepted. *Expenses:* Tuition, state resident: full-time $4012; part-time $2506 per semester.

**California State University, Fullerton,** Graduate Studies, College of Communications, Department of Communication Sciences and Disorders, Fullerton, CA 92831-3599. Offers communicative disorders (MA). *Accreditation:* ASHA.

**California State University, Long Beach,** Graduate Studies, College of Health and Human Services, Department of Speech-Language Pathology, Long Beach, CA 90840. Offers MA. *Accreditation:* ASHA. *Program availability:* Part-time. *Degree requirements:* For master's, comprehensive exam or thesis. *Entrance requirements:* For master's, GRE, minimum GPA of 3.0 in last 60 units. Electronic applications accepted.

**California State University, Los Angeles,** Graduate Studies, College of Health and Human Services, Department of Communication Disorders, Los Angeles, CA 90032-8530. Offers speech and hearing (MA); speech-language pathology (MA). *Accreditation:* ASHA. *Program availability:* Part-time, evening/weekend. *Degree requirements:* For master's, comprehensive exam. *Entrance requirements:* For master's, undergraduate major in communication disorders or related area, minimum GPA of 2.75 in last 90 units. Additional exam requirements/recommendations for international students: required—TOEFL (minimum score 500 paper-based). *Expenses: Tuition, area resident:* Full-time $7176; part-time $4164 per year. Tuition, state resident: full-time $7176; part-time $4164 per year. Tuition, nonresident: full-time $14,304; part-time $8916 per year. *International tuition:* $14,304 full-time. *Required fees:* $1037.76; $1037.76 per unit. Tuition and fees vary according to degree level and program.

**California State University, Northridge,** Graduate Studies, College of Health and Human Development, Department of Communication Disorders and Sciences, Northridge, CA 91330. Offers audiology (MS); speech language pathology (MS). *Accreditation:* ASHA. *Degree requirements:* For master's, PRAXIS. *Entrance requirements:* For master's, GRE or minimum GPA of 3.5. Additional exam requirements/recommendations for international students: required—TOEFL.

**California State University, Sacramento,** College of Health and Human Services, Department of Communication Sciences and Disorders, Sacramento, CA 95819. Offers communication sciences and disorders (MS). *Accreditation:* ASHA. *Program availability:* Part-time. *Degree requirements:* For master's, thesis, project, or comprehensive exam; writing proficiency exam. *Entrance requirements:* For master's, GRE General Test; CBEST, appropriate bachelor's degree, minimum GPA of 3.0 in last 2 years of course work. Additional exam requirements/recommendations for international students: required—TOEFL (minimum score 550 paper-based; 80 iBT); recommended—IELTS, TSE. Electronic applications accepted. *Expenses:* Contact institution.

**California State University, San Marcos,** College of Education, Health and Human Services, Department of Speech-Language Pathology, San Marcos, CA 92096-0001. Offers MS. *Accreditation:* ASHA. *Expenses:* Contact institution.

**California University of Pennsylvania,** School of Graduate Studies and Research, College of Education and Human Services, Department of Communication Disorders, California, PA 15419-1394. Offers MS. *Accreditation:* ASHA. *Program availability:* Part-time, evening/weekend. *Degree requirements:* For master's, comprehensive exam, thesis optional. *Entrance requirements:* For master's, GRE General Test, minimum GPA of 3.0, references. Additional exam requirements/recommendations for international students: required—TOEFL (minimum score 550 paper-based; 80 iBT). Electronic applications accepted. *Expenses: Tuition, area resident:* Full-time $9288; part-time $516 per credit. Tuition, state resident: full-time $9288; part-time $516 per credit. Tuition, nonresident: full-time $13,932; part-time $774 per credit. *Required fees:* $3631; $291.13 per credit. Part-time tuition and fees vary according to course load.

**Calvin College,** Program in Speech Pathology, Grand Rapids, MI 49546-4388. Offers MA.

**Canisius College,** Graduate Division, School of Education and Human Services, Department of Graduate Education and Leadership, Buffalo, NY 14208-1098. Offers business and marketing education (MS Ed); college student personnel (MS Ed); deaf education (MS Ed); deaf/adolescent education, grades 7-12 (MS Ed); deaf/childhood education, grades 1-6 (MS Ed); differentiated instruction (MS Ed); education administration (MS); educational administration (MS Ed); educational technologies (Certificate); gifted education extension (Certificate); literacy (MS Ed); reading (Certificate); school building leadership (MS Ed, Certificate); school district leadership (Certificate); teacher leader (Certificate); TESOL (MS Ed). *Accreditation:* NCATE. *Program availability:* Part-time, evening/weekend, 100% online, blended/hybrid learning. *Faculty:* 3 full-time (2 women), 40 part-time/adjunct (29 women). *Students:* 63 full-time (51 women), 131 part-time (104 women); includes 43 minority (23 Black or African American, non-Hispanic/Latino; 3 Asian, non-Hispanic/Latino; 11 Hispanic/Latino; 6 Two or more races, non-Hispanic/Latino), 4 international. Average age 32. 154 applicants, 90% accepted, 88 enrolled. In 2019, 85 master's, 13 other advanced degrees awarded. *Entrance requirements:* For master's, GRE (if cumulative GPA less than 2.7), transcripts, two letters of recommendation. Additional exam requirements/ recommendations for international students: required—TOEFL (550+ PBT or 79+ IBT), IELTS (6.5+), or CAEL (70+). *Application deadline:* Applications are processed on a rolling basis. Electronic applications accepted. *Expenses: Tuition:* Part-time $900 per credit. *Required fees:* $25 per credit hour. $65 per term. Part-time tuition and fees vary according to course load and program. *Financial support:* Career-related internships or fieldwork, Federal Work-Study, scholarships/grants, tuition waivers (partial), and unspecified assistantships available. Support available to part-time students. Financial award application deadline: 4/30; financial award applicants required to submit FAFSA. *Unit head:* Dr. Nancy V Wallace, Interim Dean, School of Education and Health Services, 716-888-3205, Fax: 716-888-3164, E-mail: wallacen@canisius.edu. *Application contact:* Dr. Nancy V Wallace, Interim Dean, School of Education and Health Services, 716-888-3205, Fax: 716-888-3164, E-mail: wallacen@canisius.edu.

**Case Western Reserve University,** School of Graduate Studies, Psychological Sciences Department, Program in Communication Sciences, Cleveland, OH 44106. Offers speech-language pathology (MA, PhD). *Accreditation:* ASHA (one or more programs are accredited). *Program availability:* Part-time. *Students:* 20 full-time (19 women), 1 (woman) part-time; includes 4 minority (1 Black or African American, non-Hispanic/Latino; 1 Asian, non-Hispanic/Latino; 1 Hispanic/Latino; 1 Two or more races, non-Hispanic/Latino). Average age 27. 106 applicants, 18% accepted, 12 enrolled. In 2019, 10 master's awarded. Terminal master's awarded for partial completion of doctoral program. *Degree requirements:* For master's, comprehensive exam, thesis optional; for doctorate, thesis/dissertation. *Entrance requirements:* For master's and doctorate, GRE General Test, statement of objectives; curriculum vitae; 3 letters of recommendation; interview. Additional exam requirements/recommendations for international students: required—TOEFL (minimum score 577 paper-based; 90 iBT); recommended—IELTS (minimum score 7). *Application deadline:* For fall admission, 1/15 for domestic students. Application fee: $50. Electronic applications accepted.

*Financial support:* Research assistantships, health care benefits, tuition waivers (partial), and unspecified assistantships available. Financial award application deadline: 1/15; financial award applicants required to submit FAFSA. *Unit head:* Dr. Heath Demaree, Professor and Chair, 216-368-6468, E-mail: psychsciences@case.edu. *Application contact:* Kori Kosek, Department Administrator, 216-368-6469, Fax: 216-368-6078, E-mail: psychsciences@case.edu.
Website: http://psychsciences.case.edu/graduate/

**Central Michigan University,** College of Graduate Studies, The Herbert H. and Grace A. Dow College of Health Professions, Department of Communication Sciences and Disorders, Doctor of Audiology Program, Mount Pleasant, MI 48859. Offers Au D. *Accreditation:* ASHA. *Degree requirements:* For doctorate, comprehensive exam, thesis/ dissertation or alternative. *Entrance requirements:* For doctorate, GRE, interview. Electronic applications accepted. *Expenses: Tuition, area resident:* Full-time $12,267; part-time $8178 per year. Tuition, state resident: full-time $12,267; part-time $8178 per year. Tuition, nonresident: full-time $12,267; part-time $8178 per year. *International tuition:* $16,110 full-time. *Required fees:* $225 per semester. Tuition and fees vary according to degree level and program.

**Central Michigan University,** College of Graduate Studies, The Herbert H. and Grace A. Dow College of Health Professions, Department of Communication Sciences and Disorders, Program in Speech-Language Pathology, Mount Pleasant, MI 48859. Offers MA. *Accreditation:* ASHA. *Degree requirements:* For master's, thesis or alternative. Electronic applications accepted. *Expenses:* Contact institution.

**Chapman University,** Crean College of Health and Behavioral Sciences, Department of Communication Sciences and Disorders, Irvine, CA 92618. Offers MS. *Accreditation:* ASHA. *Program availability:* Evening/weekend. *Faculty:* 5 full-time (all women), 10 part-time/adjunct (all women). *Students:* 91 full-time (85 women); includes 48 minority (3 Black or African American, non-Hispanic/Latino; 20 Asian, non-Hispanic/Latino; 18 Hispanic/Latino; 7 Two or more races, non-Hispanic/Latino). Average age 26. In 2019, 42 master's awarded. *Degree requirements:* For master's, comprehensive exam, thesis, 400 hours of supervised practicum. *Entrance requirements:* For master's, GRE. Additional exam requirements/recommendations for international students: required— TOEFL (minimum score 80 iBT), IELTS (minimum score 6.5), PTE (minimum score 53). *Application deadline:* For fall admission, 1/15 for domestic students. Electronic applications accepted. *Expenses:* $11,786 per trimester. *Financial support:* Fellowships, scholarships/grants, and unspecified assistantships available. Financial award applicants required to submit FAFSA. *Unit head:* Dr. Mary Kennedy, Chair, 714-744-2132, E-mail: markenne@chapman.edu. *Application contact:* Catherine Dee, Admissions Specialist, 714-516-4535, E-mail: dee@chapman.edu.
Website: https://www.chapman.edu/crean/academic-programs/graduate-programs/ms-communication-sciences-and-disorders/index.aspx

**Clarion University of Pennsylvania,** College of Health Sciences & Human Services, MS Program in Speech Language Pathology, Clarion, PA 16214. Offers MS. *Accreditation:* ASHA. *Program availability:* Part-time. *Faculty:* 8 full-time (7 women), 5 part-time/adjunct (4 women). *Students:* 79 full-time (74 women), 18 part-time (all women); includes 5 minority (1 Black or African American, non-Hispanic/Latino; 1 Hispanic/Latino; 3 Two or more races, non-Hispanic/Latino). Average age 23. 149 applicants, 31% accepted, 45 enrolled. In 2019, 60 master's awarded. *Degree requirements:* For master's, comprehensive exam, thesis. *Entrance requirements:* For master's, GRE, minimum QPA of 3.0. Additional exam requirements/recommendations for international students: required—TOEFL (minimum score 573 paper-based; 89 iBT), TOEFL (minimum iBT scores: 21 listening, 18 reading, 26 speaking, 24 writing). *Application deadline:* For fall admission, 1/31 priority date for domestic students, 7/15 priority date for international students. Applications are processed on a rolling basis. Application fee: $40. Electronic applications accepted. *Expenses:* $770.50 per credit including fees. *Financial support:* Federal Work-Study and scholarships/grants available. Financial award application deadline: 3/1; financial award applicants required to submit FAFSA. *Unit head:* Dr. Janis Jarecki-Liu, Department Chair, 814-393-2581, Fax: 814-393-2206, E-mail: jjareckiliu@clarion.edu. *Application contact:* Susan Staub, Graduate Programs Counselor, 814-393-2337, Fax: 814-393-2722, E-mail: gradstudies@clarion.edu.

**Cleveland State University,** College of Graduate Studies, College of Sciences and Health Professions, School of Health Sciences, Program in Speech-Language Pathology, Cleveland, OH 44115. Offers MA. *Accreditation:* ASHA. *Faculty:* 7 full-time (6 women), 5 part-time/adjunct (all women). *Students:* 70 full-time (67 women); includes 11 minority (2 Black or African American, non-Hispanic/Latino; 2 Asian, non-Hispanic/Latino; 3 Hispanic/Latino; 4 Two or more races, non-Hispanic/Latino). Average age 23. In 2019, 38 master's awarded. *Entrance requirements:* For master's, GRE. Additional exam requirements/recommendations for international students: required—TOEFL (minimum score 550 paper-based; 78 iBT). Application fee: $40. Electronic applications accepted. *Expenses:* Tuition, state resident: full-time $10,215; part-time $6810 per credit hour. Tuition, nonresident: full-time $17,496; part-time $11,664 per credit hour. *International tuition:* $19,316 full-time. Tuition and fees vary according to degree level and program. *Financial support:* In 2019–20, 9 students received support, including 12 research assistantships (averaging $6,960 per year); teaching assistantships with partial tuition reimbursements available, career-related internships or fieldwork, Federal Work-Study, and unspecified assistantships also available. Financial award application deadline: 2/1; financial award applicants required to submit FAFSA. *Unit head:* Dr. Monica Gordon Pershey, Program Director, 216-687-4534, Fax: 216-687-6993, E-mail: m.pershey@csuohio.edu. *Application contact:* Donna Helwig, Administrative Coordinator to the Chairperson, 216-687-3807, Fax: 216-687-6993, E-mail: d.helwig@csuohio.edu.
Website: http://www.csuohio.edu/sciences/dept/healthsciences/graduate/SPH/index.html

**The College of Saint Rose,** Graduate Studies, Thelma P. Lally School of Education, Program in Communication Sciences and Disorders, Albany, NY 12203-1419. Offers MS Ed. *Accreditation:* ASHA. *Students:* 111 full-time (107 women), 6 part-time (all women); includes 23 minority (14 Black or African American, non-Hispanic/Latino; 4 Hispanic/Latino; 5 Two or more races, non-Hispanic/Latino), 1 international. Average age 24. 181 applicants, 55% accepted, 43 enrolled. In 2019, 56 master's awarded. *Degree requirements:* For master's, comprehensive exam (for some programs), thesis (for some programs), comprehensive exam or thesis. *Entrance requirements:* For master's, minimum undergraduate GPA of 3.0, on-campus interview, 32 undergraduate credits (if undergraduate degree is not in communication disorders). Additional exam requirements/recommendations for international students: required—TOEFL (minimum score 550 paper-based; 80 iBT), IELTS (minimum score 6), PTE (minimum score 56). *Application deadline:* For fall admission, 1/15 for domestic and international students; for spring admission, 9/15 for domestic and international students; for summer admission, 1/15 for domestic and international students. Application fee: $125. Electronic applications accepted. *Expenses: Tuition:* Full-time $14,382; part-time $799 per credit hour. *Required fees:* $954; $698. Tuition and fees vary according to course load. *Financial support:* Career-related internships or fieldwork, scholarships/grants, tuition waivers, and unspecified assistantships available. Support available to part-time students. Financial award application deadline: 4/15. *Unit head:* Dr. Jim Feeney, Chair,

518-454-5255, E-mail: feenyj@strose.edu. *Application contact:* Daniel Gallagher, Assistant Vice President for Graduate Recruitment and Enrollment, 518-485-3390, E-mail: grad@strose.edu.
Website: https://www.strose.edu/communication-sciences-disorders-ms/

**Dalhousie University,** Faculty of Health, School of Communication Sciences and Disorders, Halifax, NS B3H 1R2, Canada. Offers audiology (M Sc); speech-language pathology (M Sc). *Degree requirements:* For master's, thesis or alternative. *Entrance requirements:* Additional exam requirements/recommendations for international students: required—TOEFL, IELTS, CANTEST, CAEL, or Michigan English Language Assessment Battery. Electronic applications accepted. *Expenses:* Contact institution.

**Duquesne University,** John G. Rangos, Sr. School of Health Sciences, Pittsburgh, PA 15282-0001. Offers health management systems (MHMS); occupational therapy (MS, OTD); physical therapy (DPT); physician assistant studies (MPAS); rehabilitation science (MS, PhD); speech-language pathology (MS). *Accreditation:* AOTA (one or more programs are accredited); APTA (one or more programs are accredited); ASHA. *Program availability:* Part-time, minimal on-campus study. *Degree requirements:* For doctorate, comprehensive exam (for some programs), thesis/dissertation (for some programs). *Entrance requirements:* For master's, GRE General Test (speech-language pathology), 3 letters of recommendation; minimum GPA of 2.75 (health management systems), 3.0 (speech-language pathology); for doctorate, GRE General Test (for physical therapy and rehabilitation science), 3 letters of recommendation, minimum GPA of 3.0, personal interview. Additional exam requirements/recommendations for international students: required—TOEFL (minimum score 550 paper-based; 90 iBT); recommended—IELTS. Electronic applications accepted. *Expenses:* Contact institution.

**East Carolina University,** Graduate School, College of Allied Health Sciences, Department of Communication Sciences and Disorders, Greenville, NC 27858-4353. Offers MS, Au D, PhD. *Accreditation:* ASHA (one or more programs are accredited). *Program availability:* Online learning. *Degree requirements:* For master's, comprehensive exam, thesis or alternative, clinical clock hours; for doctorate, comprehensive exam, thesis/dissertation. *Entrance requirements:* Additional exam requirements/recommendations for international students: recommended—TOEFL, IELTS. *Application deadline:* For fall admission, 1/15 for domestic students. Applications are processed on a rolling basis. Electronic applications accepted. *Expenses: Tuition, area resident:* Full-time $4749; part-time $185 per credit hour. Tuition, state resident: full-time $4749; part-time $185 per credit hour. Tuition, nonresident: full-time $17,898; part-time $864 per credit hour. *International tuition:* $17,898 full-time. *Required fees:* $2787. *Financial support:* Research assistantships with partial tuition reimbursements, teaching assistantships with partial tuition reimbursements, and unspecified assistantships available. Financial award application deadline: 3/1; financial award applicants required to submit FAFSA. *Unit head:* Jamie Perry, Department Chair, 252-744-6100, E-mail: perryja@ecu.edu. *Application contact:* Graduate School Admissions, 252-328-6012, Fax: 252-328-6071, E-mail: gradschool@ecu.edu.
Website: http://www.ecu.edu/ah/

**Eastern Illinois University,** Graduate School, College of Health and Human Services, Department of Communication Disorders and Sciences, Charleston, IL 61920. Offers communication disorders and sciences (MS). *Accreditation:* ASHA. *Program availability:* Part-time, evening/weekend. *Degree requirements:* For master's, comprehensive exam (for some programs), thesis (for some programs). *Entrance requirements:* For master's, GMAT or GRE. Additional exam requirements/recommendations for international students: required—TOEFL (minimum score 500 paper-based; 61 iBT), IELTS (minimum score 6). Electronic applications accepted.

**Eastern Kentucky University,** The Graduate School, College of Education, Department of Special Education, Program in Communication Disorders, Richmond, KY 40475-3102. Offers MA Ed. *Accreditation:* ASHA. *Degree requirements:* For master's, comprehensive exam, thesis optional, 375 clinical clock hours. *Entrance requirements:* For master's, GRE General Test, minimum GPA of 3.0.

**Eastern Michigan University,** Graduate School, College of Education, Department of Special Education & Communication Sciences and Disorders, Program in Communication Sciences and Disorders, Ypsilanti, MI 48197. Offers MA. *Accreditation:* ASHA. *Program availability:* Part-time, evening/weekend, online learning. *Students:* 6 full-time (5 women), 1 (woman) part-time; includes 2 minority (1 Black or African American, non-Hispanic/Latino; 1 Asian, non-Hispanic/Latino). Average age 22. 143 applicants, 22% accepted, 26 enrolled. In 2019, 43 master's awarded. *Entrance requirements:* For master's, GRE General Test. Additional exam requirements/recommendations for international students: required—TOEFL. *Application deadline:* Applications are processed on a rolling basis. Application fee: $45. *Financial support:* Fellowships, research assistantships with full tuition reimbursements, teaching assistantships with full tuition reimbursements, career-related internships or fieldwork, Federal Work-Study, institutionally sponsored loans, scholarships/grants, tuition waivers (partial), and unspecified assistantships available. Support available to part-time students. Financial award applicants required to submit FAFSA. *Application contact:* Dr. Ana Claudia Harten, Program Director, 734-487-3300, Fax: 734-487-2473, E-mail: aharten@emich.edu.
Website: http://www.emich.edu/coe/slp/

**Eastern New Mexico University,** Graduate School, College of Liberal Arts and Sciences, Department of Health and Human Services, Portales, NM 88130. Offers communicative disorders (MS); nursing (MSN). *Accreditation:* ASHA. *Program availability:* Part-time, online learning. *Degree requirements:* For master's, thesis optional, oral and written comprehensive exam, oral presentation of professional portfolio. *Entrance requirements:* For master's, GRE, three letters of recommendation, resume, two essays. Additional exam requirements/recommendations for international students: required—TOEFL (minimum score 550 paper-based; 79 iBT), IELTS (minimum score 6). Electronic applications accepted. *Expenses: Tuition, area resident:* Full-time $5283; part-time $389.25 per credit hour. Tuition, state resident: full-time $5283; part-time $389.25 per credit hour. Tuition, nonresident: full-time $7007; part-time $389.25 per credit hour. *International tuition:* $7007 full-time. *Required fees:* $36; $35 per semester. One-time fee: $25.

**Eastern Washington University,** Graduate Studies, College of Health Science and Public Health, Department of Communication Sciences and Disorders, Cheney, WA 99004-2431. Offers MS. *Accreditation:* ASHA. *Faculty:* 12 full-time (all women). *Students:* 49 full-time (47 women), 4 part-time (0 women); includes 3 minority (2 Asian, non-Hispanic/Latino; 1 Hispanic/Latino), 1 international. Average age 27. 170 applicants, 15% accepted, 25 enrolled. In 2019, 24 master's awarded. *Degree requirements:* For master's, comprehensive exam, thesis or alternative. *Entrance requirements:* For master's, GRE General Test, minimum GPA of 3.0. Additional exam requirements/recommendations for international students: required—TOEFL (minimum score 580 paper-based; 92 iBT), IELTS (minimum score 7), PTE (minimum score 63). *Application deadline:* For fall admission, 3/1 for domestic students. Applications are processed on a rolling basis. Application fee: $75. Electronic applications accepted. *Financial support:* Teaching assistantships with partial tuition reimbursements, career-related internships or fieldwork, Federal Work-Study, institutionally sponsored loans, scholarships/grants, health care benefits, tuition waivers (partial), and unspecified assistantships available. Support available to part-time students. Financial award application deadline: 2/1; financial award applicants required to submit FAFSA. *Unit head:* Lesli Cleveland, PhD, 509.828.1328, E-mail: lcleveland@ewu.edu. *Application contact:* Lesli Cleveland, PhD, 509.828.1328, E-mail: lcleveland@ewu.edu.
Website: http://www.ewu.edu/CSHE/Programs/Communication-Disorders/ComD-Degrees/MSCD.xml

**East Stroudsburg University of Pennsylvania,** Graduate and Extended Studies, College of Health Sciences, Department of Communication Sciences and Disorders, East Stroudsburg, PA 18301-2999. Offers MS. *Accreditation:* ASHA. *Program availability:* Part-time, evening/weekend, online learning. *Degree requirements:* For master's, comprehensive exam, portfolio. *Entrance requirements:* For master's, GRE General Test, minimum undergraduate QPA of 3.0 overall and in major, 3 letters of recommendation. Additional exam requirements/recommendations for international students: recommended—TOEFL (minimum score 560 paper-based; 83 iBT), IELTS. Electronic applications accepted.

**East Tennessee State University,** College of Graduate and Continuing Studies, College of Clinical and Rehabilitative Health Sciences, Department of Audiology and Speech-Language Pathology, Johnson City, TN 37614-1710. Offers audiology (Au D); speech-language pathology (MS). *Accreditation:* ASHA (one or more programs are accredited). *Degree requirements:* For master's, comprehensive exam, case study or thesis; for doctorate, comprehensive exam, externship, research project. *Entrance requirements:* For master's, GRE General Test, minimum GPA of 3.0; 3 letters of recommendation; resume; 3 credits each in biological science, physical science, and statistics; 6 credits in the behavioral and/or social sciences; 15 credits in basic human communication processes; 25 clinical observation credits; for doctorate, GRE General Test, minimum GPA of 3.25, three letters of recommendation, 6 credit hours each in college-level mathematics (of which at least 3 must statistics) and in the behavioral and/or social sciences, interview. Additional exam requirements/recommendations for international students: required—TOEFL (minimum score 550 paper-based; 79 iBT). Electronic applications accepted.

**Edinboro University of Pennsylvania,** Department of Communication Sciences and Disorders, Edinboro, PA 16444. Offers speech language pathology (MA). *Accreditation:* ASHA. *Program availability:* Part-time, evening/weekend. *Faculty:* 5 full-time (3 women), 4 part-time/adjunct (all women). *Students:* 40 full-time (39 women); includes 5 minority (3 Asian, non-Hispanic/Latino; 1 Native Hawaiian or other Pacific Islander, non-Hispanic/Latino; 1 Two or more races, non-Hispanic/Latino). Average age 25. 161 applicants, 12% accepted, 15 enrolled. In 2019, 25 master's awarded. *Degree requirements:* For master's, thesis or alternative, complete the National Examination for Speech-Language Pathology (PRAXIS II: Speech- Language Pathology). *Entrance requirements:* For master's, GRE or MAT, minimum undergraduate GOA of 3.0/4.0. Additional exam requirements/recommendations for international students: required—TOEFL (minimum score 550 paper-based; 213 iBT), IELTS (minimum score 6.5). *Application deadline:* Applications are processed on a rolling basis. Application fee: $30. Electronic applications accepted. *Expenses:* Tuition & fees: 740.15/credit for PA resident; 1079.4/credit for non-PA resident; 1024.65/credit for International student. *Financial support:* In 2019–20, 28 students received support. Research assistantships with tuition reimbursements available, career-related internships or fieldwork, Federal Work-Study, scholarships/grants, and unspecified assistantships available. Support available to part-time students. Financial award application deadline: 2/15; financial award applicants required to submit FAFSA. *Unit head:* Craig Coleman, Chairperson, 814-732-1407, E-mail: ccoleman@edinboro.edu. *Application contact:* Craig Coleman, Chairperson, 814-732-1407, E-mail: ccoleman@edinboro.edu.
Website: https://www.edinboro.edu/academics/schools-and-departments/cshp/departments/speech/

**Elmhurst University,** Graduate Programs, Program in Communication Sciences and Disorders, Elmhurst, IL 60126-3296. Offers MS. *Accreditation:* ASHA. *Faculty:* 6 full-time (all women), 3 part-time/adjunct (all women). *Students:* 47 full-time (45 women); includes 6 minority (1 Asian, non-Hispanic/Latino; 5 Hispanic/Latino). Average age 23. 449 applicants, 33% accepted, 24 enrolled. In 2019, 23 master's awarded. *Degree requirements:* For master's, clinical practicum. *Entrance requirements:* For master's, GRE General Test, 3 recommendations, resume, statement of purpose. Additional exam requirements/recommendations for international students: required—TOEFL (minimum score 550 paper-based; 79 iBT), IELTS (minimum score 6.5). *Application deadline:* For fall admission, 1/15 for domestic students. Electronic applications accepted. *Expenses:* $32,000 per year. *Financial support:* In 2019–20, 43 students received support. Fellowships and scholarships/grants available. Financial award application deadline: 1/15; financial award applicants required to submit FAFSA. *Unit head:* Ruiying Ding, Director, 630-617-3107, E-mail: ruiying.ding@elmhurst.edu. *Application contact:* Timothy J. Panfil, Senior Director of Graduate Admission and Enrollment Management, 630-617-3300 Ext. 3256, Fax: 630-617-6471, E-mail: panfilt@elmhurst.edu.
Website: http://www.elmhurst.edu/masters_communication_sciences_disorders

**Florida Atlantic University,** College of Education, Department of Communication Sciences and Disorders, Boca Raton, FL 33431-0991. Offers speech-language pathology (MS). *Accreditation:* ASHA. *Faculty:* 4 full-time (2 women). *Students:* 50 full-time (47 women), 1 (woman) part-time; includes 17 minority (2 Asian, non-Hispanic/Latino; 15 Hispanic/Latino). Average age 24. 271 applicants, 11% accepted, 25 enrolled. In 2019, 21 master's awarded. *Entrance requirements:* For master's, GRE General Test, minimum undergraduate GPA of 3.0 in last 60 hours of course work or graduate 3.5. Additional exam requirements/recommendations for international students: required—TOEFL (minimum score 500 paper-based; 61 iBT), IELTS (minimum score 6). *Application deadline:* For fall admission, 2/1 for domestic and international students. Application fee: $30. *Expenses: Tuition:* Full-time $20,536; part-time $371.82 per credit hour. Tuition and fees vary according to program. *Financial support:* Career-related internships or fieldwork available. *Unit head:* Dr. Dale Williams, Chair, 561-297-3238, Fax: 561-297-2268, E-mail: dwilliam@fau.edu. *Application contact:* Dr. Deborah W. Shepherd, Associate Dean, 561-297-3570, E-mail: dshep@fau.edu.
Website: http://www.coe.fau.edu/academicdepartments/csd/

**Florida International University,** Nicole Wertheim College of Nursing and Health Sciences, Department of Communication Sciences and Disorders, Miami, FL 33199. Offers speech-language pathology (MS). *Accreditation:* ASHA. *Program availability:* Part-time, evening/weekend. *Faculty:* 5 full-time (4 women), 8 part-time/adjunct (6 women). *Students:* 88 full-time (82 women), 5 part-time (all women); includes 78 minority (2 Black or African American, non-Hispanic/Latino; 2 Asian, non-Hispanic/Latino; 72 Hispanic/Latino; 2 Two or more races, non-Hispanic/Latino). Average age 26. 200 applicants, 27% accepted, 46 enrolled. In 2019, 43 master's awarded. *Entrance requirements:* For master's, minimum undergraduate GPA of 3.0 in upper-level coursework; letter of intent; 2 letters of recommendation. Additional exam requirements/recommendations for international students: required—TOEFL (minimum score 550 paper-based; 80 iBT). *Application deadline:* For fall admission, 2/1 for domestic and international students. Application fee: $30. Electronic applications accepted. *Expenses: Tuition, area resident:* Full-time $8912; part-time $446 per credit hour. Tuition, state resident: full-time $8912; part-time $446 per credit hour. Tuition, nonresident: full-time $21,393; part-time $992 per credit hour. *Required fees:* $2194. *Financial support:*

Institutionally sponsored loans, scholarships/grants, and unspecified assistantships available. Financial award application deadline: 3/1; financial award applicants required to submit FAFSA. *Unit head:* Dr. Monica Hough, Chair, 305-348-2710, E-mail: monica.hough@fiu.edu. *Application contact:* Nanett Rojas, Manager, Admissions Operations, 305-348-7464, Fax: 305-348-7441, E-mail: gradadm@fiu.edu.

**Florida State University,** The Graduate School, College of Communication and Information, School of Communication Science and Disorders, Tallahassee, FL 32306-1200. Offers speech-language pathology (PhD). *Accreditation:* ASHA (one or more programs are accredited). *Program availability:* Part-time, blended/hybrid learning. *Faculty:* 20 full-time (17 women), 2 part-time/adjunct (1 woman). *Students:* 71 full-time (all women), 100 part-time (96 women); includes 60 minority (9 Black or African American, non-Hispanic/Latino; 4 Asian, non-Hispanic/Latino; 32 Hispanic/Latino; 15 Two or more races, non-Hispanic/Latino). Average age 22. 359 applicants, 36% accepted, 68 enrolled. In 2019, 62 master's, 6 doctorates awarded. *Degree requirements:* For master's, comprehensive exam, thesis optional; for doctorate, thesis/dissertation. *Entrance requirements:* For master's, GRE General Test, minimum GPA of 3.0; for doctorate, GRE General Test, minimum GPA of 3.0 (undergraduate), 3.5 (graduate). Additional exam requirements/recommendations for international students: required—TOEFL (minimum score 550 paper-based; 80 iBT). *Application deadline:* For fall admission, 1/15 for domestic and international students. Application fee: $30. Electronic applications accepted. *Financial support:* In 2019–20, 60 students received support, including 5 fellowships with full tuition reimbursements available (averaging $35,000 per year), 17 research assistantships with partial tuition reimbursements available (averaging $12,000 per year), 6 teaching assistantships with partial tuition reimbursements available (averaging $6,000 per year); career-related internships or fieldwork, Federal Work-Study, institutionally sponsored loans, scholarships/grants, tuition waivers (full and partial), and unspecified assistantships also available. Financial award application deadline: 1/1; financial award applicants required to submit FAFSA. *Unit head:* Dr. Hugh W. Catts, Director, 850-644-6566, Fax: 850-645-8994, E-mail: hugh.catts@cci.fsu.edu. *Application contact:* Jennifer Boss Kekelis, Assistant Director, Academic and Student Services, 850-644-2253, Fax: 850-644-8994, E-mail: jennifer.kekelis@cci.fsu.edu.
Website: http://commdisorders.cci.fsu.edu/Academic-Programs-Admissions/Doctoral-Program-Admissions/?_ga-1.91886682.1375024079.1443718977

**Fontbonne University,** Graduate Programs, St. Louis, MO 63105-3098. Offers accounting (MBA, MS); art (MA); art (K-12) (MAT); business (MBA); computer science (MS); deaf education (MA); early intervention in deaf education (MA); education (MA), including autism spectrum disorders, curriculum and instruction, diverse learners, early childhood education, reading, special education; elementary education (MAT); family and consumer sciences (MA), including multidisciplinary health communication studies; fine arts (MFA); instructional design and technology (MS); management and leadership (MM); middle school education (MAT); secondary education (MAT); special education (MAT); speech-language pathology (MS); supply chain management (MS); theatre (MA). *Accreditation:* ASHA. *Program availability:* Part-time, evening/weekend, online learning. *Degree requirements:* For master's, comprehensive exam (for some programs), thesis (for some programs). *Entrance requirements:* Additional exam requirements/recommendations for international students: required—TOEFL (minimum score 500 paper-based; 65 iBT). Electronic applications accepted. *Expenses: Tuition:* Full-time $6975; part-time $775 per credit hour. *Required fees:* $225; $25 per credit hour. Tuition and fees vary according to degree level and program.

**Fort Hays State University,** Graduate School, College of Health and Behavioral Sciences, Department of Communication Sciences and Disorders, Hays, KS 67601-4099. Offers speech-language pathology (MS). *Accreditation:* ASHA. *Program availability:* Part-time. *Degree requirements:* For master's, comprehensive exam, thesis optional. *Entrance requirements:* For master's, GRE General Test. Additional exam requirements/recommendations for international students: required—TOEFL (minimum score 550 paper-based). Electronic applications accepted.

**Francis Marion University,** Graduate Programs, Department of Speech-Language Pathology, Florence, SC 29502-0547. Offers MSLP. *Expenses: Tuition, area resident:* Full-time $10,612; part-time $530.60 per credit hour. Tuition, state resident: full-time $10,612; part-time $530.60 per credit hour. Tuition, nonresident: full-time $21,224; part-time $1061.20 per credit hour. *International tuition:* $21,224 full-time. *Required fees:* $312; $156 per credit hour. $332 per semester. Tuition and fees vary according to program.

**Gallaudet University,** The Graduate School, Washington, DC 20002. Offers American Sign Language/English bilingual early childhood deaf education: birth to 5 (Certificate); audiology (Au D); clinical psychology (PhD); deaf and hard of hearing infants, toddlers, and their families (Certificate); deaf education (MA, Ed S); deaf history (Certificate); deaf studies (Certificate); educating deaf students with disabilities (Certificate); education: teacher preparation (MA), including deaf education, early childhood education and deaf education, elementary education and deaf education, secondary education and deaf education; educational neuroscience (PhD); hearing, speech and language sciences (MS, PhD); international development (MA); interpretation (MA, PhD), including combined interpreting practice and research (MA), interpreting research (MA); linguistics (MA, PhD); mental health counseling (MA); peer mentoring (Certificate); public administration (MPA); school counseling (MA); school psychology (Psy S); sign language teaching (MA); social work (MSW); speech-language pathology (MS). *Program availability:* Part-time. *Faculty:* 101 full-time (70 women). *Students:* 267 full-time (208 women), 139 part-time (95 women); includes 120 minority (38 Black or African American, non-Hispanic/Latino; 20 Asian, non-Hispanic/Latino; 44 Hispanic/Latino; 18 Two or more races, non-Hispanic/Latino), 19 international. Average age 30. 484 applicants, 50% accepted, 162 enrolled. In 2019, 138 master's, 25 doctorates, 14 other advanced degrees awarded. Terminal master's awarded for partial completion of doctoral program. *Degree requirements:* For master's, comprehensive exam (for some programs), thesis optional; for doctorate, comprehensive exam, thesis/dissertation. *Entrance requirements:* For master's and doctorate, GRE General Test or MAT, letters of recommendation, interviews, goals statement, American Sign Language proficiency interview, written English competency. Additional exam requirements/recommendations for international students: required—TOEFL. *Application deadline:* For fall admission, 2/15 for domestic students. Applications are processed on a rolling basis. Application fee: $75. Electronic applications accepted. *Expenses: Tuition:* Full-time $18,180; part-time $688 per credit. *Required fees:* $526; $526. Tuition and fees vary according to course load. *Financial support:* In 2019–20, 50 students received support. Fellowships, research assistantships, teaching assistantships, career-related internships or fieldwork, Federal Work-Study, scholarships/grants, tuition waivers (partial), and unspecified assistantships available. Support available to part-time students. Financial award application deadline: 7/1; financial award applicants required to submit FAFSA. *Unit head:* Dr. Gaurav Mathur, Dean, Graduate School and Continuing Studies, 202-250-2380, Fax: 202-651-5027, E-mail: gaurav.mathur@gallaudet.edu. *Application contact:* Heidi Zornes-Foster, Senior Graduate Admissions Counselor, 202-650-5436, Fax: 202-651-5295, E-mail: graduate.school@gallaudet.edu.
Website: www.gallaudet.edu

**The George Washington University,** Columbian College of Arts and Sciences, Department of Speech, Language and Hearing Sciences, Washington, DC 20052. Offers speech-language pathology (MA). *Accreditation:* ASHA. *Degree requirements:* For master's, comprehensive exam, thesis or alternative. *Entrance requirements:* For master's, GRE General Test, interview, minimum GPA of 3.0. Additional exam requirements/recommendations for international students: required—TOEFL (minimum score 550 paper-based; 80 iBT). Electronic applications accepted.

**Georgia Southern University,** Jack N. Averitt College of Graduate Studies, Waters College of Health Professions, Program in Communication Sciences and Disorders, Statesboro, GA 30458. Offers MS. *Accreditation:* ASHA. *Students:* 40 full-time (all women); includes 10 minority (5 Black or African American, non-Hispanic/Latino; 1 Asian, non-Hispanic/Latino; 3 Hispanic/Latino; 1 Two or more races, non-Hispanic/Latino). Average age 24. 21 applicants, 100% accepted, 20 enrolled. In 2019, 20 master's awarded. *Degree requirements:* For master's, comprehensive exam, 400 client contact hours, PRAXIS II, minimum B average. *Entrance requirements:* For master's, GRE, minimum GPA of 3.0, recommendations, letter of interest. Additional exam requirements/recommendations for international students: required—TOEFL (minimum score 523 paper-based; 70 iBT). *Application deadline:* For fall admission, 1/15 for domestic and international students. Applications are processed on a rolling basis. Application fee: $30. Electronic applications accepted. *Expenses: Tuition, area resident:* Full-time $4986; part-time $277 per credit hour. Tuition, nonresident: full-time $19,890; part-time $1105 per credit hour. *International tuition:* $19,890 full-time. *Required fees:* $2114; $1057 per semester. $1057 per semester. Tuition and fees vary according to course load, campus/location and program. *Financial support:* In 2019–20, 12 students received support, including 1 research assistantship with full tuition reimbursement available (averaging $5,000 per year); teaching assistantships, Federal Work-Study, scholarships/grants, and unspecified assistantships also available. Support available to part-time students. Financial award application deadline: 3/15; financial award applicants required to submit FAFSA. *Unit head:* Dr. Walter Jenkins, Dept. Chair, 912-344-2969, Fax: 912-344-3439, E-mail: wjenkins@armstrong.edu. *Application contact:* McKenzie Peterman, Graduate Admissions Specialist, 912-478-5678, Fax: 912-478-0740, E-mail: mpeterman@georgiasouthern.edu.
Website: https://chp.georgiasouthern.edu/rehabilitation/graduate-programs/master-of-science-in-communication-sciences-and-disorders/

**Georgia State University,** College of Education and Human Development, Department of Learning Sciences, Program in Communication Disorders, Atlanta, GA 30302-3083. Offers M Ed. *Accreditation:* ASHA; NCATE. *Entrance requirements:* For master's, GRE, minimum undergraduate GPA of 3.0. Additional exam requirements/recommendations for international students: required—TOEFL (minimum score 550 paper-based; 79 iBT), IELTS (minimum score 6.5). Application fee: $50. Electronic applications accepted. *Expenses: Tuition, area resident:* Full-time $7164; part-time $398 per credit hour. Tuition, state resident: full-time $7164; part-time $398 per credit hour. Tuition, nonresident: full-time $22,662; part-time $1259 per credit hour. *International tuition:* $22,662 full-time. *Required fees:* $2128; $312 per credit hour. Tuition and fees vary according to course load and program. *Unit head:* Dr. Julie Washington, Chair, 404-413-8340, E-mail: jwashington@gsu.edu. *Application contact:* Sandy Vaughn, Senior Administrative Coordinator, 404-413-8318, Fax: 404-413-8043, E-mail: svaughn@gsu.edu.
Website: https://education.gsu.edu/csd/

**Georgia State University,** College of Education and Human Development, Department of Learning Sciences, Program in Education of Students with Exceptionalities, Atlanta, GA 30302-3083. Offers autism spectrum disorders (PhD); behavior disorders (PhD); communication disorders (PhD); early childhood special education (PhD); learning disabilities (PhD); mental retardation (PhD); orthopedic impairments (PhD); sensory impairments (PhD). *Accreditation:* NCATE. *Program availability:* Part-time, evening/weekend. Application fee: $50. Electronic applications accepted. *Expenses: Tuition, area resident:* Full-time $7164; part-time $398 per credit hour. Tuition, state resident: full-time $7164; part-time $398 per credit hour. Tuition, nonresident: full-time $22,662; part-time $1259 per credit hour. *International tuition:* $22,662 full-time. *Required fees:* $2128; $312 per credit hour. Tuition and fees vary according to course load and program. *Financial support:* Fellowships, research assistantships, scholarships/grants, health care benefits, and unspecified assistantships available. *Unit head:* Dr. Brendan Calandra, Chair, 404-413-8420, Fax: 404-413-8420, E-mail: bcalandra@gsu.edu. *Application contact:* Sandy Vaughn, Senior Administrative Coordinator, 404-413-8318, Fax: 404-413-8043, E-mail: svaughn@gsu.edu.
Website: https://education.gsu.edu/program/phd-education-students-exceptionalities/

**Governors State University,** College of Health and Human Services, Program in Communication Disorders, University Park, IL 60484. Offers MHS. *Accreditation:* ASHA. *Program availability:* Part-time. *Faculty:* 7 full-time (6 women), 15 part-time/adjunct (14 women). *Students:* 46 full-time (42 women), 48 part-time (46 women); includes 36 minority (13 Black or African American, non-Hispanic/Latino; 4 Asian, non-Hispanic/Latino; 18 Hispanic/Latino; 1 Two or more races, non-Hispanic/Latino). Average age 28. 208 applicants, 12% accepted, 25 enrolled. In 2019, 31 master's awarded. *Application deadline:* For fall admission, 4/1 for domestic students. Applications are processed on a rolling basis. Application fee: $50. Electronic applications accepted. *Expenses: Tuition, area resident:* Full-time $8472; part-time $353 per credit hour. Tuition, state resident: full-time $8472; part-time $353 per credit hour. Tuition, nonresident: full-time $16,944; part-time $706 per credit hour. *International tuition:* $16,944 full-time. *Required fees:* $2520; $105 per credit hour. $38 per term. Tuition and fees vary according to course load, degree level and program. *Financial support:* Application deadline: 5/1; applicants required to submit FAFSA. *Unit head:* Jessica Bonner, Chair, Department of Communication Disorders, 708-534-5000 Ext. 4591, E-mail: jbonner@govst.edu. *Application contact:* Jessica Bonner, Chair, Department of Communication Disorders, 708-534-5000 Ext. 4591, E-mail: jbonner@govst.edu.

**The Graduate Center, City University of New York,** Graduate Studies, Program in Audiology, New York, NY 10016-4039. Offers Au D. *Accreditation:* ASHA. *Entrance requirements:* For doctorate, GRE General Test. Additional exam requirements/recommendations for international students: required—TOEFL. Electronic applications accepted.

**The Graduate Center, City University of New York,** Graduate Studies, Program in Speech-Language-Hearing Sciences, New York, NY 10016-4039. Offers speech-language-hearing sciences (PhD). *Degree requirements:* For doctorate, comprehensive exam, thesis/dissertation. *Entrance requirements:* For doctorate, GRE General Test. Additional exam requirements/recommendations for international students: required—TOEFL, IELTS. Electronic applications accepted.

**Grand Valley State University,** College of Health Professions, Speech-Language Pathology Program, Allendale, MI 49401-9403. Offers MS. *Accreditation:* ASHA. *Program availability:* Part-time. *Faculty:* 11 full-time (10 women), 1 (woman) part-time/adjunct. *Students:* 89 full-time (87 women); includes 11 minority (2 Black or African American, non-Hispanic/Latino; 3 Asian, non-Hispanic/Latino; 5 Hispanic/Latino; 1 Two or more races, non-Hispanic/Latino), 1 international. Average age 24. 195 applicants, 27% accepted, 48 enrolled. In 2019, 31 master's awarded. *Degree requirements:* For master's, thesis optional, internship. *Entrance requirements:* For master's, GRE,

minimum GPA of 3.0, professional vita or resume, 3 letters of reference, interview. Additional exam requirements/recommendations for international students: required—TOEFL (minimum iBT score of 80), IELTS (6.5), or Michigan English Language Assessment Battery (77). *Application deadline:* For fall admission, 1/15 for domestic and international students. Applications are processed on a rolling basis. Application fee: $30. Electronic applications accepted. *Expenses:* $733 per credit hour, 60 credit hours. *Financial support:* In 2019–20, 10 students received support, including 2 fellowships, 1 research assistantship with full and partial tuition reimbursement available (averaging $8,000 per year); unspecified assistantships also available. *Unit head:* Dr. Dan Halling, Department Chair, 616-331-5604, Fax: 616-331-5556, E-mail: halling@gvsu.edu. *Application contact:* Dr. Courtney Karasinski, Graduate Program Director, 616-331-5670, Fax: 616-331-5544, E-mail: karasinc@gvsu.edu.

**Hampton University,** School of Science, Department of Communicative Sciences and Disorders, Hampton, VA 23668. Offers MA. *Accreditation:* ASHA. *Program availability:* Part-time, online learning. *Students:* 30 full-time (all women), 5 part-time (all women); includes 25 minority (17 Black or African American, non-Hispanic/Latino; 2 American Indian or Alaska Native, non-Hispanic/Latino; 4 Asian, non-Hispanic/Latino; 2 Hispanic/Latino). Average age 25. 62 applicants, 26% accepted, 11 enrolled. In 2019, 40 master's awarded. *Degree requirements:* For master's, comprehensive exam. *Entrance requirements:* For master's, GRE General Test. Additional exam requirements/recommendations for international students: required—TOEFL (minimum score 525 paper-based) or IELTS (6.5). *Application deadline:* For fall admission, 6/1 priority date for domestic students, 4/1 priority date for international students; for spring admission, 11/1 for domestic and international students. Applications are processed on a rolling basis. Application fee: $35. Electronic applications accepted. *Financial support:* Fellowships, research assistantships, teaching assistantships, career-related internships or fieldwork, Federal Work-Study, institutionally sponsored loans, and scholarships/grants available. Support available to part-time students. Financial award application deadline: 6/30; financial award applicants required to submit FAFSA. *Unit head:* Dr. Dorian Lee-Wilkerson, Chairperson, Department of Communicative Sciences and Disorders, 757-727-5435, Fax: 757-727-5765, E-mail: dorian.wilkerson@hamptonu.edu. *Application contact:* Dr. Jessica Sullivan, Graduate Coordinator, Department of Communicative Sciences and Disorders, 757-727-5763, Fax: 757-727-5765, E-mail: jessica.sullivan@hamptonu.edu.
Website: http://science.hamptonu.edu/csad/

**Harding University,** College of Allied Health, Program in Communication Sciences and Disorders, SEARCY, AR 72149-5615. Offers MS. *Accreditation:* ASHA. *Faculty:* 9 full-time (8 women). *Students:* 45 full-time (42 women), 1 (woman) part-time; includes 4 minority (1 Black or African American, non-Hispanic/Latino; 1 Asian, non-Hispanic/Latino; 1 Hispanic/Latino; 1 Two or more races, non-Hispanic/Latino), 1 international. Average age 24. 101 applicants, 23% accepted, 16 enrolled. In 2019, 18 master's awarded. *Application deadline:* For fall admission, 3/1 for domestic and international students. Application fee: $40. *Financial support:* In 2019–20, 6 students received support. Application deadline: 3/1; applicants required to submit FAFSA. *Unit head:* Dr. Dan Tullos, Professor and Chair, 501-279-4633, Fax: 501-279-4325, E-mail: tullos@harding.edu. *Application contact:* Martha Vendetti, Administrative Assistant, 501-279-4335, Fax: 501-279-5192, E-mail: mvendett@harding.edu.
Website: http://www.harding.edu/academics/colleges-departments/allied-health/communication-sciences-disorders/graduate-program

**Hofstra University,** School of Health Professions and Human Services, Programs in Health, Hempstead, NY 11549. Offers foundations of public health (Advanced Certificate); health administration (MHA); health informatics (MS); occupational therapy (MS); public health (MPH); security and privacy in health information systems (Advanced Certificate); sports science (MS); teacher of students with speech-language disabilities (Advanced Certificate). *Program availability:* Part-time, evening/weekend. *Students:* 291 full-time (220 women), 128 part-time (88 women); includes 192 minority (69 Black or African American, non-Hispanic/Latino; 3 American Indian or Alaska Native, non-Hispanic/Latino; 72 Asian, non-Hispanic/Latino; 37 Hispanic/Latino; 4 Native Hawaiian or other Pacific Islander, non-Hispanic/Latino; 7 Two or more races, non-Hispanic/Latino), 25 international. Average age 29. 676 applicants, 52% accepted, 132 enrolled. In 2019, 170 master's, 1 other advanced degree awarded. *Degree requirements:* For master's, internship, minimum GPA of 3.0. *Entrance requirements:* For master's, interview, 2 letters of recommendation, essay, resume. Additional exam requirements/recommendations for international students: required—TOEFL (minimum score 550 paper-based; 80 iBT); recommended—IELTS (minimum score 6.5). *Application deadline:* Applications are processed on a rolling basis. Application fee: $75. Electronic applications accepted. *Expenses: Tuition:* Full-time $25,164; part-time $1398 per credit. *Required fees:* $580; $165 per semester. Tuition and fees vary according to course load, degree level and program. *Financial support:* In 2019–20, 181 students received support, including 104 fellowships with full and partial tuition reimbursements available (averaging $3,465 per year), 5 research assistantships with full and partial tuition reimbursements available (averaging $7,172 per year); career-related internships or fieldwork, Federal Work-Study, institutionally sponsored loans, scholarships/grants, traineeships, tuition waivers (full and partial), unspecified assistantships, and scholarships and endowed scholarships also available. Support available to part-time students. Financial award applicants required to submit FAFSA. *Unit head:* Dr. Corinne Kyriacou, Chairperson, 516-463-4553, E-mail: corinne.m.kyriacou@hofstra.edu. *Application contact:* Sunil Samuel, Assistant Vice President of Admissions, 516-463-4723, Fax: 516-463-4664, E-mail: graduateadmission@hofstra.edu.
Website: http://www.hofstra.edu/academics/colleges/healthscienceshumanservices/

**Hofstra University,** School of Health Professions and Human Services, Programs in Speech Language Pathology and Audiology, Hempstead, NY 11549. Offers audiology (Au D); speech-language pathology (MA). *Accreditation:* ASHA (one or more programs are accredited). *Students:* 112 full-time (109 women), 2 part-time (both women); includes 16 minority (3 Black or African American, non-Hispanic/Latino; 4 Asian, non-Hispanic/Latino; 9 Hispanic/Latino), 2 international. Average age 23. 363 applicants, 58% accepted, 49 enrolled. In 2019, 47 master's, 7 doctorates awarded. *Degree requirements:* For master's, comprehensive exam, thesis optional; for doctorate, comprehensive exam, thesis/dissertation. *Entrance requirements:* For master's, GRE, 3 letters of recommendation, essay; for doctorate, GRE or master's degree, 3 letters of recommendation, essay. Additional exam requirements/recommendations for international students: required—TOEFL (minimum score 550 paper-based; 80 iBT); recommended—IELTS (minimum score 6.5). *Application deadline:* For fall admission, 1/15 for domestic and international students. Application fee: $75. Electronic applications accepted. *Expenses: Tuition:* Full-time $25,164; part-time $1398 per credit. *Required fees:* $580; $165 per semester. Tuition and fees vary according to course load, degree level and program. *Financial support:* In 2019–20, 31 students received support, including 31 fellowships with full and partial tuition reimbursements available (averaging $5,701 per year), 2 research assistantships with full and partial tuition reimbursements available (averaging $6,590 per year); career-related internships or fieldwork, Federal Work-Study, institutionally sponsored loans, scholarships/grants, traineeships, tuition waivers (full and partial), unspecified assistantships, and scholarships and endowed scholarships also available. Support available to part-time students. Financial award applicants required to submit FAFSA. *Unit head:* Dr. Jenny Roberts, Chairperson, 516-463-5514, E-mail: jennifer.a.roberts@hofstra.edu. *Application contact:* Sunil Samuel, Assistant Vice President of Admissions, 516-463-4723, Fax: 516-463-4664, E-mail: graduateadmission@hofstra.edu.
Website: http://www.hofstra.edu/academics/colleges/healthscienceshumanservices/

**Howard University,** Cathy Hughes School of Communications, Department of Communication Sciences and Disorders, Washington, DC 20059-0002. Offers communication sciences (PhD); speech pathology (MS). *Accreditation:* ASHA (one or more programs are accredited). *Program availability:* Part-time. *Degree requirements:* For master's, comprehensive exam, thesis or alternative; for doctorate, one foreign language, comprehensive exam, thesis/dissertation. *Entrance requirements:* For master's, GRE General Test, minimum GPA of 3.2; for doctorate, GRE General Test, minimum GPA of 3.5. Additional exam requirements/recommendations for international students: required—TOEFL. Electronic applications accepted.

**Hunter College of the City University of New York,** Graduate School, School of Health Professions, Department of Speech-Language Pathology and Audiology, New York, NY 10065-5085. Offers speech-language pathology (MS). *Accreditation:* ASHA. *Program availability:* Part-time. *Degree requirements:* For master's, comprehensive exam (for some programs), NTE, research project. *Entrance requirements:* For master's, GRE, letters of reference. Additional exam requirements/recommendations for international students: required—TOEFL.

**Idaho State University,** Graduate School, College of Rehabilitation and Communication Sciences, Department of Communication Sciences and Disorders, Pocatello, ID 83209-8116. Offers audiology (Au D); speech language pathology (MS). *Accreditation:* ASHA (one or more programs are accredited). *Program availability:* Part-time. *Degree requirements:* For master's, thesis optional, written and oral comprehensive exams; for doctorate, comprehensive exam, thesis/dissertation optional, externship, 1 year full time clinical practicum, 3rd year spent in Boise. *Entrance requirements:* For master's, GRE General Test, minimum GPA of 3.0, 3 letters of recommendation; for doctorate, GRE General Test (at least 2 scores minimum 40th percentile), minimum GPA of 3.0, 3 letters of recommendation, bachelor's degree. Additional exam requirements/recommendations for international students: required—TOEFL (minimum score 600 paper-based; 80 iBT). Electronic applications accepted.

**Illinois State University,** Graduate School, College of Arts and Sciences, Department of Communication Sciences and Disorders, Normal, IL 61790. Offers MA, MS. *Accreditation:* ASHA. *Faculty:* 11 full-time (8 women), 1 (woman) part-time/adjunct. *Students:* 105 full-time (all women). Average age 24. 87 applicants, 33% accepted, 10 enrolled. In 2019, 38 master's awarded. *Degree requirements:* For master's, thesis or alternative, 1 term of residency, 2 practica. *Entrance requirements:* For master's, GRE General Test, minimum GPA of 3.0 in last 60 hours. *Application deadline:* Applications are processed on a rolling basis. Application fee: $50. *Expenses: Tuition, area resident:* Full-time $7956; part-time $9767 per year. Tuition, nonresident: full-time $9233; part-time $17,592 per year. *Required fees:* $1797. *Financial support:* In 2019–20, 7 research assistantships, 5 teaching assistantships were awarded; tuition waivers (full) and unspecified assistantships also available. Financial award application deadline: 4/1. *Unit head:* Dr. Candice Osenga, Director of Clinical Education, 309-438-5794, E-mail: cjoseng@ilstu.edu. *Application contact:* Heidi Verticchio, Clinical Director, 309-438-3266, E-mail: hrfritz@IllinoisState.edu.
Website: http://www.speechpathaud.ilstu.edu/

**Indiana State University,** College of Graduate and Professional Studies, Bayh College of Education, Department of Communication Disorders and Counseling, School, and Educational Psychology, Terre Haute, IN 47809. Offers clinical mental health counseling (MS); communication disorders (MS); school counseling (M Ed); school psychology (PhD, Ed S); MA/MS. *Accreditation:* ACA; ASHA; NCATE. *Program availability:* Part-time, evening/weekend. *Degree requirements:* For master's, thesis optional; for doctorate, thesis/dissertation, research tools proficiency tests. *Entrance requirements:* For master's, GRE General Test or MAT, minimum undergraduate GPA of 2.75; for doctorate, GRE General Test, master's degree, minimum undergraduate GPA of 3.5. Electronic applications accepted.

**Indiana University Bloomington,** University Graduate School, College of Arts and Sciences, Department of Speech and Hearing Sciences, Clinical Program in Audiology, Bloomington, IN 47405-7000. Offers Au D. *Accreditation:* ASHA.

**Indiana University Bloomington,** University Graduate School, College of Arts and Sciences, Department of Speech and Hearing Sciences, Program in Speech and Hearing Sciences, Bloomington, IN 47405-7000. Offers auditory sciences (Au D, PhD); language sciences (PhD); speech and voice sciences (PhD); speech-language pathology (MA). *Accreditation:* ASHA.

**Indiana University of Pennsylvania,** School of Graduate Studies and Research, College of Education and Communications, Department of Communication Disorders, Special Education, and Disability Services, Program in Speech-Language Pathology, Indiana, PA 15705. Offers MS. *Accreditation:* ASHA. *Program availability:* Part-time. *Faculty:* 9 full-time (8 women), 2 part-time/adjunct (both women). *Students:* 42 full-time (40 women); includes 4 minority (1 Black or African American, non-Hispanic/Latino; 1 Asian, non-Hispanic/Latino; 1 Hispanic/Latino; 1 Two or more races, non-Hispanic/Latino), 1 international. Average age 23. 127 applicants, 18% accepted, 23 enrolled. In 2019, 24 master's awarded. *Degree requirements:* For master's, comprehensive exam, thesis optional. *Entrance requirements:* For master's, 2 letters of recommendation, minimum undergraduate GPA of 3.0 & an interview, official transcripts, goal statement. Additional exam requirements/recommendations for international students: required—TOEFL (minimum score 600 paper-based; 100 iBT), IELTS (minimum score 6.5), TOEFL or IELTS. *Application deadline:* For fall admission, 2/15 priority date for domestic students. Application fee: $50. Electronic applications accepted. *Expenses:* Contact institution. *Financial support:* In 2019–20, 3 fellowships with tuition reimbursements (averaging $733 per year), 14 research assistantships with full and partial tuition reimbursements (averaging $2,864 per year) were awarded; career-related internships or fieldwork, Federal Work-Study, scholarships/grants, and unspecified assistantships also available. Support available to part-time students. Financial award application deadline: 4/15; financial award applicants required to submit FAFSA. *Unit head:* Lisa Hammet Price, Professor/Program Director, 724-357-5687, E-mail: lisa.price@iup.edu. *Application contact:* Amber Dworek, Director of Graduate Admissions, 724-357-2222, E-mail: graduate-admissions@iup.edu.
Website: http://www.iup.edu/grad/speechlanguage/default.aspx

**Iona College,** School of Arts and Science, Department of Speech Communication Studies, New Rochelle, NY 10801-1890. Offers communication sciences and disorders (MA). *Faculty:* 4 full-time (all women), 10 part-time/adjunct (9 women). *Students:* 46 full-time (45 women); includes 12 minority (1 Black or African American, non-Hispanic/Latino; 1 Asian, non-Hispanic/Latino; 8 Hispanic/Latino; 2 Two or more races, non-Hispanic/Latino). Average age 23. 123 applicants, 100% accepted, 26 enrolled. In 2019, 22 master's awarded. *Entrance requirements:* For master's, GRE, 3 letters of recommendation, personal statement, interview. Additional exam requirements/recommendations for international students: required—TOEFL (minimum score 550 paper-based; 80 iBT). *Application deadline:* For fall admission, 2/1 priority date for domestic students, 2/1 for international students. Application fee: $50. *Expenses:*

Contact institution. *Financial support:* In 2019–20, 24 students received support. Scholarships/grants available. Support available to part-time students. Financial award application deadline: 4/15; financial award applicants required to submit FAFSA. *Unit head:* Jennifer Gerometta, PhD, CCC-SLP, Department Chair, Speech Communications Studies, 914-633-2036, Fax: 914-633-2023, E-mail: jgerometta@iona.edu. *Application contact:* RoseDeline Martinez, Director of Graduate Admissions, School of Arts and Science, 914-633-2427, Fax: 914-633-2277, E-mail: rmartinez@iona.edu.
Website: https://www.iona.edu/academics/school-of-arts-science/departments/speech-communication.aspx

**Ithaca College,** School of Health Sciences and Human Performance, Program in Speech-Language Pathology, Ithaca, NY 14850. Offers MS. *Accreditation:* ASHA. *Faculty:* 10 full-time (8 women). *Students:* 29 full-time (26 women); includes 3 minority (1 Black or African American, non-Hispanic/Latino; 1 Asian, non-Hispanic/Latino; 1 Hispanic/Latino). Average age 23. 116 applicants, 66% accepted, 16 enrolled. In 2019, 17 master's awarded. *Entrance requirements:* For master's, GRE General Test. Additional exam requirements/recommendations for international students: required—TOEFL (minimum score 550 paper-based; 80 iBT). *Application deadline:* For fall admission, 2/1 for domestic and international students. Applications are processed on a rolling basis. Application fee: $40. Electronic applications accepted. *Expenses:* Contact institution. *Financial support:* In 2019–20, 18 students received support, including 17 research assistantships (averaging $10,558 per year); Federal Work-Study and scholarships/grants also available. Support available to part-time students. Financial award application deadline: 3/1; financial award applicants required to submit FAFSA. *Unit head:* Jana Waller, Graduate Program Chair, Department of Speech-Language Pathology and Audiology, 607-274-3733, E-mail: slpgrad@ithaca.edu. *Application contact:* Nicole Eversley Bradwell, Director, Office of Admission, 800-429-4274, Fax: 607-274-1263, E-mail: admission@ithaca.edu.
Website: https://www.ithaca.edu/academics/school-health-sciences-and-human-performance/graduate-programs/speech-language-pathology-and-audiology

**Jackson State University,** Graduate School, School of Public Health, Department of Communicative Disorders, Jackson, MS 39217. Offers MS. *Accreditation:* ASHA. *Degree requirements:* For master's, comprehensive exam. *Entrance requirements:* For master's, GRE General Test. Additional exam requirements/recommendations for international students: required—TOEFL (minimum score 520 paper-based; 67 iBT).

**Jacksonville University,** Brooks Rehabilitation College of Healthcare Sciences, School of Applied Health Sciences, Program in Speech-Language Pathology, Jacksonville, FL 32211. Offers MS. *Accreditation:* ASHA. *Program availability:* Part-time. *Students:* 70 full-time (69 women); includes 16 minority (5 Black or African American, non-Hispanic/Latino; 1 American Indian or Alaska Native, non-Hispanic/Latino; 3 Asian, non-Hispanic/Latino; 6 Hispanic/Latino; 1 Two or more races, non-Hispanic/Latino), 2 international. Average age 25. 216 applicants, 32% accepted, 30 enrolled. In 2019, 33 master's awarded. *Entrance requirements:* For master's, GRE (quantitative, verbal and writing components), baccalaureate degree from accredited college or university with minimum GPA of 3.0; official transcripts; essay on personal professional goals (minimum 1000 words); resume (education, work experience); 3 letters of recommendation; interview. Additional exam requirements/recommendations for international students: required—TOEFL (minimum score 650 paper-based; 114 iBT), IELTS (minimum score 8). *Application deadline:* Applications are processed on a rolling basis. Application fee: $50. Electronic applications accepted. *Expenses:* Contact institution. *Financial support:* Federal Work-Study, institutionally sponsored loans, scholarships/grants, and health care benefits available. Support available to part-time students. Financial award application deadline: 3/15; financial award applicants required to submit FAFSA. *Unit head:* Dr. Judith M. Wingate, Department Chair and Associate Professor of Communication Sciences and Disorders, 904-256-8912, E-mail: jwingat2@ju.edu. *Application contact:* Antonio Starke, Assistant Director of Graduate Admissions, 904-256-7472, E-mail: astarke2@ju.edu.
Website: https://www.ju.edu/communicationsciences/programs/ms-speech-language-pathology.php

**James Madison University,** The Graduate School, College of Health and Behavioral Studies, Program in Audiology, Harrisonburg, VA 22807. Offers Au D. *Accreditation:* ASHA. *Program availability:* Part-time. *Students:* 25 full-time (23 women). Average age 30. In 2019, 5 doctorates awarded. Application fee: $60. Electronic applications accepted. *Financial support:* In 2019–20, 16 students received support, including 1 teaching assistantship (averaging $7,000 per year); fellowships, Federal Work-Study, and assistantships (averaging $7911), doctoral assistantships (stipend varies) also available. Financial award application deadline: 3/1; financial award applicants required to submit FAFSA. *Unit head:* Dr. Cynthia R. O'Donoghue, Department Head, 540-568-6440, E-mail: odonogcr@jmu.edu. *Application contact:* Lynette D. Michael, Director of Graduate Admissions, 540-568-6131 Ext. 6395, Fax: 540-568-7860, E-mail: michaeld@jmu.edu.
Website: http://www.csd.jmu.edu/aud/

**James Madison University,** The Graduate School, College of Health and Behavioral Studies, Program in Communication Sciences and Disorders, Harrisonburg, VA 22807. Offers PhD. *Accreditation:* ASHA. *Program availability:* Part-time. *Students:* 6 full-time (4 women), 1 (woman) part-time; includes 1 minority (Hispanic/Latino), 3 international. Average age 30. In 2019, 3 doctorates awarded. *Application deadline:* For fall admission, 7/1 priority date for domestic students. Applications are processed on a rolling basis. Application fee: $60. *Financial support:* In 2019–20, 5 students received support. Teaching assistantships, Federal Work-Study, unspecified assistantships, and doctoral assistantships (stipend varies) available. Financial award application deadline: 3/1; financial award applicants required to submit FAFSA. *Unit head:* Dr. Sharon E. Lovell, Dean, 540-568-2705, Fax: 540-568-2747, E-mail: lovellse@jmu.edu. *Application contact:* Lynette D. Michael, Director of Graduate Admissions, 540-568-6131 Ext. 6395, Fax: 540-568-7860, E-mail: michaeld@jmu.edu.

**James Madison University,** The Graduate School, College of Health and Behavioral Studies, Program in Speech-Language Pathology, Harrisonburg, VA 22807. Offers MS. *Accreditation:* ASHA. *Program availability:* Part-time. *Students:* 53 full-time (all women), 36 part-time (all women); includes 12 minority (3 Asian, non-Hispanic/Latino; 5 Hispanic/Latino; 4 Two or more races, non-Hispanic/Latino). Average age 30. In 2019, 36 master's awarded. Application fee: $60. Electronic applications accepted. *Financial support:* In 2019–20, 20 students received support. Fellowships, Federal Work-Study, and assistantships (averaging $7911) available. Financial award application deadline: 3/1; financial award applicants required to submit FAFSA. *Unit head:* Dr. Cynthia R. O'Donoghue, Department Head, 540-568-6440, E-mail: odonogcr@jmu.edu. *Application contact:* Lynette D. Michael, Director of Graduate Admissions, 540-568-6131 Ext. 6395, Fax: 540-568-7860, E-mail: michaeld@jmu.edu.
Website: http://www.csd.jmu.edu/MS-SLP/

**Kansas State University,** Graduate School, College of Human Ecology, School of Family Studies and Human Services, Manhattan, KS 66506-1403. Offers applied family sciences (MS); communication sciences and disorders (MS); conflict resolution (Graduate Certificate); couple and family therapy (MS); early childhood education (MS); family and community service (MS); life-span human development (MS); personal financial planning (MS, PhD, Graduate Certificate); youth development (MS, Graduate Certificate). *Accreditation:* AAMFT/COAMFTE; ASHA. *Program availability:* Part-time, online learning. *Degree requirements:* For master's, comprehensive exam (for some programs), thesis optional. *Entrance requirements:* For master's, GRE, minimum GPA of 3.0 in last 2 years (60 semester hours) of undergraduate study; for doctorate, GRE. Additional exam requirements/recommendations for international students: required—TOEFL (minimum score 600 paper-based). Electronic applications accepted.

**Kean University,** Nathan Weiss Graduate College, Doctorate Program in Speech-Language Pathology, Union, NJ 07083. Offers SLPD. *Faculty:* 8 full-time (7 women). *Students:* 20 part-time (all women); includes 5 minority (2 Black or African American, non-Hispanic/Latino; 3 Hispanic/Latino). Average age 41. 18 applicants, 56% accepted, 10 enrolled. *Entrance requirements:* For doctorate, master's degree in speech-language pathology or its equivalent from accredited institution of higher education; minimum master's GPA of 3.2; curriculum vitae; three letters of recommendation; statement of goals and research career interests; personal interview. Additional exam requirements/recommendations for international students: required—TOEFL (minimum score 550 paper-based; 79 iBT), IELTS (minimum score 6.5). *Application deadline:* For fall admission, 4/15 for domestic students. Application fee: $75. Electronic applications accepted. *Expenses:* Contact institution. *Financial support:* Scholarships/grants and unspecified assistantships available. Financial award applicants required to submit FAFSA. *Unit head:* Dr. Mahchid Namazi, Coordinator, 908-737-5804, E-mail: mnamazi@kean.edu. *Application contact:* Helen Ramirez, Associate Director, Graduate Admissions, 908-737-7100, E-mail: gradadmissions@kean.edu.
Website: https://www.kean.edu/academics/programs/speech-language-pathology-doctorate-slpd

**Kean University,** Nathan Weiss Graduate College, Program in Speech-Language Pathology, Union, NJ 07083. Offers MA. *Accreditation:* ASHA. *Program availability:* Part-time. *Faculty:* 8 full-time (7 women). *Students:* 94 full-time (90 women), 2 part-time (both women); includes 29 minority (5 Black or African American, non-Hispanic/Latino; 3 Asian, non-Hispanic/Latino; 21 Hispanic/Latino), 1 international. Average age 25. 256 applicants, 32% accepted, 48 enrolled. In 2019, 46 master's awarded. *Degree requirements:* For master's, comprehensive exam, thesis, six credits of research, minimum of 400 supervised clinical hours, PRAXIS. *Entrance requirements:* For master's, GRE General Test, minimum cumulative GPA of 3.2, official transcripts from all institutions attended, personal statement, three letters of recommendation, professional resume/curriculum vitae. Additional exam requirements/recommendations for international students: required—TOEFL (minimum score 550 paper-based; 79 iBT), IELTS (minimum score 6.5). *Application deadline:* For fall admission, 2/15 for domestic and international students; for summer admission, 1/15 for domestic and international students. Application fee: $75. Electronic applications accepted. *Expenses:* Contact institution. *Financial support:* Scholarships/grants and unspecified assistantships available. Financial award applicants required to submit FAFSA. *Unit head:* Dr. JoAnne Cascia, Program Coordinator, 908-737-5822, E-mail: gradcoordinatorcdd@kean.edu. *Application contact:* Helen Ramirez, Associate Director, Graduate Admissions, 908-737-7137, E-mail: gradadmissions@kean.edu.
Website: http://grad.kean.edu/slp

**Kent State University,** College of Education, Health and Human Services, School of Health Sciences, Program in Audiology, Kent, OH 44242-0001. Offers Au D, PhD. *Entrance requirements:* For doctorate, GRE, 3 letters of reference, goals statement. Additional exam requirements/recommendations for international students: required—TOEFL (minimum score 550 paper-based; 80 iBT). Electronic applications accepted.

**Kent State University,** College of Education, Health and Human Services, School of Health Sciences, Program in Speech Language Pathology, Kent, OH 44242-0001. Offers MA, PhD. *Accreditation:* ASHA. *Degree requirements:* For doctorate, comprehensive exam, thesis/dissertation. *Entrance requirements:* For master's and doctorate, GRE, 3 letters of reference, goals statement. Additional exam requirements/recommendations for international students: required—TOEFL (minimum score 550 paper-based; 80 iBT). Electronic applications accepted.

**Kent State University,** College of Education, Health and Human Services, School of Lifespan Development and Educational Sciences, Program in Special Education, Kent, OH 44242-0001. Offers deaf education (M Ed); early childhood education (M Ed); educational interpreter K-12 (M Ed); general special education (M Ed); mild/moderate intervention (M Ed); special education (PhD, Ed S); transition to work (M Ed). *Accreditation:* NCATE. *Degree requirements:* For doctorate, comprehensive exam, thesis/dissertation. *Entrance requirements:* For master's, minimum undergraduate GPA of 2.75, moral character form, 2 letters of reference, goals statement; for doctorate and Ed S, GRE General Test, goals statement, 2 letters of reference, interview, resume. Additional exam requirements/recommendations for international students: required—TOEFL (minimum score 550 paper-based; 80 iBT). Electronic applications accepted.

**Lamar University,** College of Graduate Studies, College of Fine Arts and Communication, Department of Speech and Hearing Science, Beaumont, TX 77710. Offers audiology (Au D); speech language pathology (MS). *Accreditation:* ASHA. *Faculty:* 14 full-time (10 women), 3 part-time/adjunct (all women). *Students:* 94 full-time (91 women), 21 part-time (19 women); includes 38 minority (9 Black or African American, non-Hispanic/Latino; 6 Asian, non-Hispanic/Latino; 22 Hispanic/Latino; 1 Two or more races, non-Hispanic/Latino), 4 international. Average age 25. 229 applicants, 27% accepted, 33 enrolled. In 2019, 29 master's, 8 doctorates awarded. *Degree requirements:* For master's, thesis optional; for doctorate, thesis/dissertation. *Entrance requirements:* For master's, GRE General Test, performance IQ score of 115 (for deaf students), minimum GPA of 2.5; for doctorate, GRE General Test, performance IQ score of 115 (for deaf students). Additional exam requirements/recommendations for international students: required—TOEFL (minimum score 550 paper-based; 79 iBT), IELTS (minimum score 6.5). *Application deadline:* Applications are processed on a rolling basis. Application fee: $25 ($50 for international students). Electronic applications accepted. *Expenses: Tuition, area resident:* Full-time $6324; part-time $351 per credit. Tuition, state resident: full-time $6324; part-time $351 per credit. Tuition, nonresident: full-time $13,920; part-time $773 per credit. *International tuition:* $13,920 full-time. *Required fees:* $2462; $327 per credit. Tuition and fees vary according to course load, campus/location and reciprocity agreements. *Financial support:* In 2019–20, 103 students received support. Fellowships with tuition reimbursements available, teaching assistantships, and institutionally sponsored loans available. Support available to part-time students. Financial award applicants required to submit FAFSA. *Unit head:* Dr. Monica Harn, Chair, 409-880-8338. *Application contact:* Celeste Contreas, Director, Admissions and Academic Services, 409-880-8888, Fax: 409-880-7419, E-mail: gradmissions@lamar.edu.
Website: http://fineartscomm.lamar.edu/speech-and-hearing-sciences

**La Salle University,** School of Nursing and Health Sciences, Program in Speech-Language Pathology, Philadelphia, PA 19141-1199. Offers MS. *Accreditation:* ASHA. *Degree requirements:* For master's, comprehensive exam, capstone project, which includes a written manuscript suitable for publication in a scholarly journal. *Entrance requirements:* For master's, GRE, personal essay; 3 letters of recommendation; CSDCAS centralized application. Additional exam requirements/recommendations for international students: required—TOEFL. *Expenses:* Contact institution.

## Communication Disorders

**Lebanon Valley College,** Program in Speech-Language Pathology, Annville, PA 17003-1400. Offers MSLP. *Expenses:* Contact institution.

**Lehman College of the City University of New York,** School of Health Sciences, Human Services and Nursing, Department of Speech–Language–Hearing Sciences, Bronx, NY 10468-1589. Offers speech-language pathology (MA). *Accreditation:* ASHA. *Program availability:* Part-time, evening/weekend. *Degree requirements:* For master's, thesis or alternative. *Expenses: Tuition, area resident:* Full-time $5545; part-time $470 per credit. Tuition, nonresident: part-time $855 per credit. *Required fees:* $240.

**Lewis & Clark College,** Graduate School of Education and Counseling, Department of Teacher Education, Program in Special Education, Portland, OR 97219-7899. Offers M Ed. *Accreditation:* NCATE. *Program availability:* Part-time, evening/weekend. *Entrance requirements:* For master's, minimum GPA of 2.75. Additional exam requirements/recommendations for international students: required—TOEFL (minimum score 575 paper-based). Electronic applications accepted.

**Lindenwood University,** Graduate Programs, School of Education, St. Charles, MO 63301-1695. Offers behavioral analysis (MA); education (MA), including autism spectrum disorders, character education, early intervention in autism and sensory impairment, gifted, technology; educational administration (MA, Ed D, Ed S); English to speakers of other languages (MA); instructional leadership (Ed D, Ed S); library media (MA); professional counseling (MA); school administration (MA, Ed S); school counseling (MA); teaching (MA). *Program availability:* Part-time, evening/weekend, 100% online, blended/hybrid learning. *Faculty:* 39 full-time (28 women), 133 part-time/adjunct (83 women). *Students:* 391 full-time (287 women), 1,149 part-time (889 women); includes 358 minority (284 Black or African American, non-Hispanic/Latino; 8 American Indian or Alaska Native, non-Hispanic/Latino; 6 Asian, non-Hispanic/Latino; 32 Hispanic/Latino; 28 Two or more races, non-Hispanic/Latino), 11 international. Average age 35. 465 applicants, 71% accepted, 229 enrolled. In 2019, 432 master's, 60 doctorates, 77 other advanced degrees awarded. *Degree requirements:* For master's, thesis (for some programs), minimum GPA of 3.0; for doctorate, thesis/dissertation, minimum GPA of 3.0; for Ed S, comprehensive exam, project, minimum GPA of 3.0. *Entrance requirements:* For master's, interview, minimum undergraduate cumulative GPA of 3.0, writing sample, letter of recommendation; for doctorate, minimum graduate GPA of 3.4, resume, interview, writing sample, 4 letters of recommendation; for Ed S, master's degree in education, relevant work experience. Additional exam requirements/recommendations for international students: required—TOEFL (minimum score 553 paper-based; 81 iBT); recommended—IELTS (minimum score 6.5). *Application deadline:* For fall admission, 8/9 priority date for domestic students, 6/1 priority date for international students; for spring admission, 12/20 priority date for domestic students, 11/1 priority date for international students; for summer admission, 5/15 priority date for domestic students, 3/27 priority date for international students. Applications are processed on a rolling basis. Application fee: $0 ($100 for international students). Electronic applications accepted. *Expenses: Tuition:* Full-time $8910; part-time $495 per credit. Tuition and fees vary according to course load, degree level and program. *Financial support:* In 2019–20, 198 students received support. Career-related internships or fieldwork, Federal Work-Study, institutionally sponsored loans, scholarships/grants, tuition waivers (partial), and unspecified assistantships available. Financial award application deadline: 6/30; financial award applicants required to submit FAFSA. *Unit head:* Dr. Anthony Scheffler, Dean, School of Education, 636-949-4618, Fax: 636-949-4197, E-mail: ascheffler@lindenwood.edu. *Application contact:* Kara Schilli, Assistant Vice President, University Admissions, 636-949-4349, Fax: 636-949-4109, E-mail: adultadmissions@lindenwood.edu.
Website: https://www.lindenwood.edu/academics/academic-schools/school-of-education/

**Loma Linda University,** School of Allied Health Professions, Department of Communication Sciences and Disorders, Loma Linda, CA 92350. Offers speech-language pathology (MS, SLPD). *Accreditation:* ASHA (one or more programs are accredited). *Program availability:* Part-time. *Degree requirements:* For master's, thesis or alternative. *Entrance requirements:* For master's, GRE General Test. Additional exam requirements/recommendations for international students: required—TOEFL (minimum score 550 paper-based). Electronic applications accepted.

**Long Island University - Brooklyn,** School of Health Professions, Brooklyn, NY 11201-8423. Offers athletic training and sport sciences (MS); community health (MS Ed); exercise science (MS); forensic social work (Advanced Certificate); occupational therapy (MS); physical therapy (DPT); physician assistant (MS); public health (MPH); social work (MSW); speech-language pathology (MS). *Accreditation:* AOTA; CEPH. *Degree requirements:* For master's, comprehensive exam (for some programs), thesis (for some programs); for doctorate, comprehensive exam (for some programs). *Entrance requirements:* For master's and doctorate, GRE. Additional exam requirements/recommendations for international students: required—TOEFL (minimum score 550 paper-based; 79 iBT). Electronic applications accepted.

**Long Island University - Post,** College of Education, Information and Technology, Brookville, NY 11548-1300. Offers adolescence education (MS); adolescence education 7-12 (MS); archives and records management (AC); art education (MS); childhood education (MS); childhood education/literacy B-6 (MS); childhood education/special education (MS); clinical mental health counseling (MS, AC); early childhood education (MS); early childhood education/childhood education (MS); educational leadership (AC); educational technology (MS); information studies (PhD); interdisciplinary educational studies (Ed D); middle childhood education (MS); music education (MS); public library administration (AC); school counselor (MS); special education (MS Ed); speech-language pathology (MA); students with disabilities, 7-12 generalist (AC); TESOL (MA). *Accreditation:* ASHA; TEAC. *Program availability:* Part-time, 100% online, blended/hybrid learning. Terminal master's awarded for partial completion of doctoral program. *Degree requirements:* For master's, variable foreign language requirement, comprehensive exam (for some programs), thesis optional; for doctorate, comprehensive exam, thesis/dissertation. *Entrance requirements:* For master's and AC, GRE (for some programs). Additional exam requirements/recommendations for international students: required—TOEFL (minimum score 550 paper-based, 75 iBT), IELTS, or PTE. Electronic applications accepted.

**Longwood University,** College of Graduate and Professional Studies, College of Education and Human Services, Department of Social Work and Communication Sciences and Disorders, Farmville, VA 23909. Offers communication sciences and disorders (MS). *Accreditation:* ASHA. *Degree requirements:* For master's, comprehensive exam, thesis optional. *Entrance requirements:* For master's, GRE, bachelor's degree from regionally-accredited institution, minimum GPA of 3.0, CSDCAS application. Additional exam requirements/recommendations for international students: required—TOEFL (minimum score 570 paper-based), IELTS (minimum score 6.5). Electronic applications accepted. *Expenses:* Contact institution.

**Louisiana State University and Agricultural & Mechanical College,** Graduate School, College of Humanities and Social Sciences, Department of Communication Sciences and Disorders, Baton Rouge, LA 70803. Offers MA, PhD. *Accreditation:* ASHA (one or more programs are accredited).

**Louisiana State University Health Sciences Center,** School of Allied Health Professions, Department of Communication Disorders, New Orleans, LA 70112-2223. Offers audiology (Au D); speech pathology (MCD). *Accreditation:* ASHA (one or more programs are accredited). *Faculty:* 9 full-time (6 women), 3 part-time/adjunct (all women). *Students:* 89 full-time (86 women); includes 7 minority (2 Black or African American, non-Hispanic/Latino; 1 Asian, non-Hispanic/Latino; 1 Hispanic/Latino; 3 Two or more races, non-Hispanic/Latino). Average age 24. 341 applicants, 9% accepted, 32 enrolled. In 2019, 19 master's, 12 doctorates awarded. *Degree requirements:* For master's, comprehensive exam or thesis. *Entrance requirements:* For master's, GRE General Test (minimum score of 296), 3 letters of recommendation, minimum GPA of 3.0; for doctorate, GRE General Test (minimum score of 294), 3 letters of recommendation, minimum GPA of 3.0. Additional exam requirements/recommendations for international students: required—TOEFL (minimum score 550 paper-based; 79 iBT). *Application deadline:* For fall admission, 2/15 for domestic students; for summer admission, 1/15 for domestic students. Application fee: $125. Electronic applications accepted. *Expenses:* Contact institution. *Financial support:* Application deadline: 4/15; applicants required to submit FAFSA. *Unit head:* Dr. Annette E. Hurley-Larmeu, Department Head, 504-568-4337, Fax: 504-568-4352, E-mail: ahurle@lsuhsc.edu. *Application contact:* Yudialys D. Cazanas, Student Affairs Director, 504-568-4253, Fax: 504-568-3185, E-mail: ydelga@lsuhsc.edu.
Website: http://alliedhealth.lsuhsc.edu/cd/default.aspx

**Louisiana Tech University,** Graduate School, College of Liberal Arts, Ruston, LA 71272. Offers architecture (M Arch); art (MFA), including graphic design, photography, studio; audiology (Au D); communication (MA), including speech communication, theatre; English (MA), including literature, technical writing; history (MA); speech pathology (MA); technical writing and communication (Graduate Certificate). *Accreditation:* ASHA. *Program availability:* Part-time. *Degree requirements:* For master's, thesis (for some programs); for doctorate, thesis/dissertation. *Entrance requirements:* For master's, GRE General Test; for doctorate, GRE General Test, bachelor's degree, minimum GPA of 3.0 or 3.2 on last 60 hours attempted. Additional exam requirements/recommendations for international students: required—TOEFL (minimum score 550 paper-based; 80 iBT), IELTS (minimum score 6.5). Electronic applications accepted. *Expenses: Tuition, area resident:* Full-time $6592; part-time $400 per credit. Tuition, state resident: full-time $6592; part-time $400 per credit. Tuition, nonresident: full-time $13,333; part-time $681 per credit. *International tuition:* $13,333 full-time. *Required fees:* $3011; $3011 per unit.

**Loyola University Maryland,** Graduate Programs, Loyola College of Arts and Sciences, Department of Speech-Language-Hearing Sciences, Baltimore, MD 21210-2699. Offers speech-language pathology (MS). *Accreditation:* ASHA. *Students:* 104 full-time (103 women), 1 (woman) part-time; includes 14 minority (4 Black or African American, non-Hispanic/Latino; 3 Asian, non-Hispanic/Latino; 6 Hispanic/Latino; 1 Two or more races, non-Hispanic/Latino), 1 international. Average age 25. 272 applicants, 75% accepted, 55 enrolled. In 2019, 48 master's awarded. *Degree requirements:* For master's, comprehensive exam, thesis optional, r-bachelors; appropriate prereq coursework if bachelor's is not Communication Science Disorders. *Entrance requirements:* For master's, essay, official transcripts, 3 letters of recomendation, course form if undergraduate degree was not completed at Loyola, supplemental form if international. Additional exam requirements/recommendations for international students: required—TOEFL (minimum score 550 paper-based; 80 iBT), IELTS (minimum score 7), TOEFL (minimum score 550 paper-based, 80iBT) or ILETS (minimum score 7). *Application deadline:* For fall admission, 2/15 for domestic and international students. Application fee: $60. Electronic applications accepted. *Expenses:* Contact institution. *Financial support:* Scholarships/grants, tuition waivers, and unspecified assistantships available. Financial award application deadline: 4/15; financial award applicants required to submit FAFSA. *Unit head:* Marie Kerins, Chair, 410-617-7246, E-mail: mkerins@loyola.edu. *Application contact:* Office of Graduate Admissions, 410-617-5020, E-mail: graduate@loyola.edu.
Website: https://www.loyola.edu/academics/speech/graduate

**Marquette University,** Graduate School, College of Health Sciences, Department of Speech Pathology and Audiology, Milwaukee, WI 53201-1881. Offers bilingual English/Spanish (Certificate); speech-language pathology (MS). *Accreditation:* ASHA (one or more programs are accredited). *Program availability:* Part-time. *Degree requirements:* For master's, comprehensive exam, thesis (for some programs). *Entrance requirements:* For master's, GRE General Test, official transcripts from all current and previous colleges/universities except Marquette, three letters of recommendation, personal statement. Additional exam requirements/recommendations for international students: required—TOEFL (minimum score 530 paper-based). Electronic applications accepted.

**Marshall University,** Academic Affairs Division, College of Health Professions, Department of Communication Disorders, Huntington, WV 25755. Offers MS. *Accreditation:* ASHA. *Entrance requirements:* For master's, GRE General Test.

**Maryville University of Saint Louis,** Myrtle E. and Earl E. Walker College of Health Professions, Program in Speech-Language Pathology, St. Louis, MO 63141-7299. Offers MS. *Faculty:* 7 full-time (all women), 1 (woman) part-time/adjunct. *Students:* 43 full-time (42 women); includes 7 minority (4 Black or African American, non-Hispanic/Latino; 2 Hispanic/Latino; 1 Two or more races, non-Hispanic/Latino). Average age 25. In 2019, 22 master's awarded. *Entrance requirements:* For master's, application; official transcripts; minimum cumulative GPA of 3.0; bachelors degree from a regionally accredited university; GRE scores, including Verbal, Analytical, and Writing components; 3 letters of recommendation; resume or vitae. Additional exam requirements/recommendations for international students: required—TOEFL (minimum score 603 paper-based; 100 iBT). *Application deadline:* For fall admission, 2/1 for domestic students. Applications are processed on a rolling basis. Electronic applications accepted. *Expenses:* Contact institution. *Financial support:* Application deadline: 4/1; applicants required to submit FAFSA. *Unit head:* Renee Schuster, Director Speech Pathology, 314-529-9548, Fax: 314-529-9495, E-mail: rschuster@maryville.edu. *Application contact:* Jeannie DeLuca, Director, Admissions and Advising, 314-529-9355, Fax: 314-529-9927, E-mail: jdeluca@maryville.edu.
Website: http://www.maryville.edu/hp/speech-language-pathology/

**Marywood University,** Academic Affairs, Reap College of Education and Human Development, Department of Communication Sciences and Disorders, Scranton, PA 18509-1598. Offers speech-language pathology (MS). *Accreditation:* ASHA. *Program availability:* Part-time. Electronic applications accepted.

**Massachusetts Institute of Technology,** School of Engineering, Harvard-MIT Health Sciences and Technology Program, Cambridge, MA 02139. Offers health sciences and technology (SM, PhD, Sc D), including bioastronautics (PhD, Sc D), bioinformatics and integrative genomics (PhD, Sc D), medical engineering and medical physics (PhD, Sc D), speech and hearing bioscience and technology (PhD, Sc D). Terminal master's awarded for partial completion of doctoral program. *Degree requirements:* For doctorate, comprehensive exam, thesis/dissertation. *Entrance requirements:* For doctorate, GRE General Test. Additional exam requirements/recommendations for international students: required—TOEFL, IELTS. Electronic applications accepted.

**McGill University,** Faculty of Graduate and Postdoctoral Studies, Faculty of Medicine, School of Communication Sciences and Disorders, Montréal, QC H3A 2T5, Canada. Offers communication science and disorders (M Sc); communication sciences and disorders (PhD); speech-language pathology (M Sc A). *Accreditation:* ASHA.

**Mercy College,** School of Health and Natural Sciences, Program in Communication Disorders, Dobbs Ferry, NY 10522-1189. Offers MS. *Accreditation:* ASHA. *Program availability:* Part-time, evening/weekend. *Students:* 83 full-time (81 women), 11 part-time (9 women); includes 34 minority (6 Black or African American, non-Hispanic/Latino; 6 Asian, non-Hispanic/Latino; 19 Hispanic/Latino; 3 Two or more races, non-Hispanic/Latino). Average age 24. 241 applicants, 38% accepted, 43 enrolled. In 2019, 40 master's awarded. *Degree requirements:* For master's, comprehensive exam, Clinical practicum. *Entrance requirements:* For master's, GRE, program application; transcript(s); two letters of recommendation; essay; resume; interview. Additional exam requirements/recommendations for international students: required—TOEFL (minimum score 80 iBT), IELTS (minimum score 6.5). *Application deadline:* For fall admission, 1/15 for domestic students. Application fee: $62. Electronic applications accepted. *Expenses:* Contact institution. *Financial support:* Career-related internships or fieldwork, Federal Work-Study, scholarships/grants, and unspecified assistantships available. Support available to part-time students. Financial award applicants required to submit FAFSA. *Unit head:* Dr. Joan Toglia, Dean, School of Health and Natural Sciences, 914-674-7746, E-mail: jtoglia@mercy.edu. *Application contact:* Allison Gurdineer, Executive Director of Admissions, 877-637-2946, Fax: 914-674-7382, E-mail: admissions@mercy.edu.
Website: https://www.mercy.edu/degrees-programs/ms-communication-disorders

**MGH Institute of Health Professions,** School of Health and Rehabilitation Sciences, Department of Communication Sciences and Disorders, Boston, MA 02129. Offers reading (Certificate); speech-language pathology (MS). *Accreditation:* ASHA (one or more programs are accredited). *Program availability:* Part-time. *Degree requirements:* For master's, thesis or alternative, research proposal. *Entrance requirements:* For master's, GRE General Test, bachelor's degree from regionally-accredited college or university. Additional exam requirements/recommendations for international students: required—TOEFL (minimum score 550 paper-based; 80 iBT). Electronic applications accepted.

**Miami University,** College of Arts and Science, Department of Speech Pathology and Audiology, Oxford, OH 45056. Offers MA, MS. *Accreditation:* ASHA.

**Michigan State University,** The Graduate School, College of Communication Arts and Sciences, Department of Communicative Sciences and Disorders, East Lansing, MI 48824. Offers MA, PhD. *Accreditation:* ASHA (one or more programs are accredited). *Entrance requirements:* Additional exam requirements/recommendations for international students: required—TOEFL. Electronic applications accepted.

**Midwestern University, Downers Grove Campus,** College of Health Sciences, Illinois Campus, Program in Speech-Language Pathology, Downers Grove, IL 60515-1235. Offers MS. *Accreditation:* ASHA. *Entrance requirements:* For master's, bachelor's degree, minimum cumulative GPA of 3.0.

**Midwestern University, Glendale Campus,** College of Health Sciences, Arizona Campus, Program in Speech-Language Pathology, Glendale, AZ 85308. Offers MS. *Entrance requirements:* For master's, bachelor's degree, minimum cumulative GPA of 3.0.

**Minnesota State University Mankato,** College of Graduate Studies and Research, College of Allied Health and Nursing, Program in Communication Disorders, Mankato, MN 56001. Offers MS. *Accreditation:* ASHA. *Program availability:* Part-time. *Degree requirements:* For master's, thesis or alternative, internship. *Entrance requirements:* For master's, GRE General Test, minimum GPA of 3.0 during previous 2 years, references, writing sample. Additional exam requirements/recommendations for international students: required—TOEFL.

**Minot State University,** Graduate School, Department of Communication Disorders, Minot, ND 58707-0002. Offers speech-language pathology (MS). *Accreditation:* ASHA. *Degree requirements:* For master's, comprehensive exam (for some programs), thesis (for some programs). *Entrance requirements:* For master's, GRE General Test, minimum GPA of 3.25. Additional exam requirements/recommendations for international students: required—TOEFL (minimum score 79 iBT), IELTS (minimum score 6).

**Minot State University,** Graduate School, Program in Special Education, Minot, ND 58707-0002. Offers deaf/hard of hearing education (MS); specific learning disabilities (MS). *Accreditation:* NCATE. *Degree requirements:* For master's, comprehensive exam (for some programs), thesis (for some programs). *Entrance requirements:* For master's, minimum GPA of 2.75, bachelor's degree in education or related field, teacher licensure (for some concentrations). Additional exam requirements/recommendations for international students: required—TOEFL (minimum score 79 iBT), IELTS (minimum score 6).

**Misericordia University,** College of Health Sciences and Education, Program in Speech-Language Pathology, Dallas, PA 18612-1098. Offers MSSLP. *Accreditation:* ASHA. *Entrance requirements:* For master's, GRE, minimum undergraduate GPA of 3.5. Additional exam requirements/recommendations for international students: required—TOEFL.

**Mississippi University for Women,** Graduate School, College of Nursing and Health Sciences, Columbus, MS 39701-9998. Offers nursing (MSN, DNP, PMC); public health education (MPH); speech-language pathology (MS). *Accreditation:* AACN; ASHA. *Program availability:* Part-time. *Degree requirements:* For master's, comprehensive exam, thesis. *Entrance requirements:* For master's, GRE General Test, bachelor's degree in nursing, previous course work in statistics, proficiency in English.

**Missouri State University,** Graduate College, College of Health and Human Services, Department of Communication Sciences and Disorders, Springfield, MO 65897. Offers communication sciences and disorders (Au D); speech language pathology (MS). *Accreditation:* ASHA (one or more programs are accredited). *Degree requirements:* For master's, comprehensive exam, thesis or alternative; for doctorate, comprehensive exam, thesis/dissertation or alternative, clinical externship. *Entrance requirements:* For master's and doctorate, GRE, minimum GPA of 3.0. Additional exam requirements/recommendations for international students: required—TOEFL (minimum score 550 paper-based; 79 iBT), IELTS (minimum score 6). Electronic applications accepted. *Expenses: Tuition, area resident:* Full-time $2600; part-time $1735 per credit hour. Tuition, nonresident: full-time $5240; part-time $3495 per credit hour. *International tuition:* $5240 full-time. *Required fees:* $530; $438 per credit hour. Tuition and fees vary according to class time, course level, course load, degree level, campus/location and program.

**Molloy College,** Graduate Speech-Language Pathology Program, Rockville Centre, NY 11571. Offers speech-language pathology (MS). *Accreditation:* ASHA. *Program availability:* Part-time, evening/weekend. *Faculty:* 7 full-time (all women), 5 part-time/adjunct (all women). *Students:* 85 full-time (83 women); includes 27 minority (7 Black or African American, non-Hispanic/Latino; 1 Asian, non-Hispanic/Latino; 16 Hispanic/Latino; 3 Two or more races, non-Hispanic/Latino). Average age 24. 193 applicants, 47% accepted, 42 enrolled. In 2019, 42 master's awarded. *Entrance requirements:* For master's, GRE, Three (3) letters of reference (professors preferred); Professional goals statement; Official transcripts from all institutions attended; A personal interview; Submit prerequisite coursework. Additional exam requirements/recommendations for international students: required—TOEFL (minimum score 550 paper-based; 79 iBT). *Application deadline:* Applications are processed on a rolling basis. Application fee: $60. Electronic applications accepted. *Expenses: Tuition:* Full-time $21,510; part-time $1195 per credit hour. *Required fees:* $1100. Tuition and fees vary according to course load, degree level and program. *Financial support:* Application deadline: 3/1; applicants required to submit FAFSA. *Unit head:* Dr. Susan Alimonti, Associate Dean, Communication Sciences and Disorders, 516-323-3517, E-mail: salimonti@molloy.edu. *Application contact:* Faye Hood, Assistant Director for Admissions, 516-323-4009, E-mail: fhood@molloy.edu.
Website: https://www.molloy.edu/academics/graduate-programs/graduate-speech-language-pathology

**Monmouth University,** Graduate Studies, School of Education, West Long Branch, NJ 07764-1898. Offers applied behavior analysis (Certificate); autism (Certificate); director of school counseling services (Post-Master's Certificate); early childhood (M Ed); educational leadership (Ed D); elementary education (MAT), including elementary level, secondary level; English as a second language (M Ed); learning disabilities teacher-consultant (Post-Master's Certificate); literacy (MS Ed); school counseling (MS Ed); special education (MS Ed), including autism, learning disabilities teacher-consultant, teacher of students with disabilities, teaching in inclusive settings; speech-language pathology (MS Ed); student affairs and college counseling (MS Ed); supervisor (Post-Master's Certificate); teaching English to speakers of other languages (Certificate). *Accreditation:* NCATE. *Program availability:* Part-time, evening/weekend, 100% online, blended/hybrid learning. *Faculty:* 28 full-time (19 women), 34 part-time/adjunct (25 women). *Students:* 168 full-time (144 women), 225 part-time (197 women); includes 66 minority (20 Black or African American, non-Hispanic/Latino; 6 Asian, non-Hispanic/Latino; 37 Hispanic/Latino; 3 Two or more races, non-Hispanic/Latino), 2 international. Average age 30. In 2019, 108 master's, 9 other advanced degrees awarded. *Degree requirements:* For master's, thesis (for some programs); for doctorate, thesis/dissertation, Project. *Entrance requirements:* For master's, GRE taken within last 5 years (for MS Ed in speech-language pathology); SAT (minimum combined score of 1660 in 3 sections), ACT (23), GRE (minimum score of 4.0 on analytical writing section and minimum combined score of 310 on quantitative and verbal sections), or passing scores on 3 parts of Core Academic Skills Educators, minimum GPA of 3.0 in major; 2 letters of recommendation (for some programs); resume, personal statement or essay (depending on program). Additional exam requirements/recommendations for international students: required—TOEFL (minimum score 550 paper-based; 79 iBT), IELTS (minimum score 6), Michigan English Language Assessment Battery (minimum score 77) or Certificate of Advanced English (minimum score 160). *Application deadline:* For fall admission, 7/15 priority date for domestic students, 7/1 for international students; for spring admission, 12/1 priority date for domestic students, 11/1 for international students; for summer admission, 5/1 for domestic students. Applications are processed on a rolling basis. Application fee: $50. Electronic applications accepted. *Expenses: Tuition:* Full-time $22,194; part-time $14,796 per credit. *Required fees:* $712; $178 per semester. $178 per semester. Tuition and fees vary according to course load. *Financial support:* In 2019–20, 337 students received support. Research assistantships, teaching assistantships, scholarships/grants, and unspecified assistantships available. Support available to part-time students. Financial award applicants required to submit FAFSA. *Unit head:* Dr. John E. Henning, Dean, 732-263-5513, Fax: 732-263-5277, E-mail: kodonnel@monmouth.edu. *Application contact:* Kirsten Sneeringer, Graduate Admission Counselor, 732-571-3452, Fax: 732-263-5123, E-mail: gradadm@monmouth.edu.
Website: http://www.monmouth.edu/academics/schools/education/default.asp

**Montclair State University,** The Graduate School, College of Humanities and Social Sciences, Doctoral Program in Audiology, Montclair, NJ 07043-1624. Offers Sc D. *Accreditation:* ASHA. *Program availability:* Part-time, evening/weekend. *Degree requirements:* For doctorate, comprehensive exam (for some programs), thesis/dissertation (for some programs). *Entrance requirements:* For doctorate, GRE General Test, essay, 2 letters of recommendation. Additional exam requirements/recommendations for international students: required—TOEFL (minimum score 83 iBT), IELTS (minimum score 6.5). Electronic applications accepted.

**Montclair State University,** The Graduate School, College of Humanities and Social Sciences, Program in Communication Sciences and Disorders, Montclair, NJ 07043-1624. Offers MA. *Accreditation:* ASHA. *Program availability:* Part-time, evening/weekend. *Degree requirements:* For master's, comprehensive exam, thesis (for some programs). *Entrance requirements:* For master's, GRE General Test, 2 letters of recommendation, essay. Additional exam requirements/recommendations for international students: required—TOEFL (minimum score 83 iBT), IELTS (minimum score 6.5). Electronic applications accepted.

**Moravian College,** Graduate and Continuing Studies, Rehabilitation Science Programs, Bethlehem, PA 18018-6650. Offers athletic training (MS, DAT); speech-language pathology (MS). *Program availability:* Part-time, 100% online. *Faculty:* 10 full-time (8 women), 3 part-time/adjunct (2 women). *Students:* 101 full-time (82 women), 4 part-time (2 women); includes 13 minority (3 Black or African American, non-Hispanic/Latino; 2 Asian, non-Hispanic/Latino; 6 Hispanic/Latino; 1 Native Hawaiian or other Pacific Islander, non-Hispanic/Latino; 1 Two or more races, non-Hispanic/Latino). Average age 27. 364 applicants, 48% accepted, 88 enrolled. In 2019, 13 master's awarded. *Degree requirements:* For master's, completion of clinical rotation. *Entrance requirements:* For master's, official transcripts, bachelor's degree from accredited institution, minimum undergraduate GPA of 3.0, documentation of clinical observation with supervision of certified/licensed athletic trainer, interview, essay; for doctorate, current ATC credentials in good standing, current AT State License if applicable, currently practicing, 5 years of full-time practice preferred. *Application deadline:* For summer admission, 5/1 priority date for domestic and international students. Applications are processed on a rolling basis. Electronic applications accepted. *Expenses:* Contact institution. *Financial support:* Applicants required to submit FAFSA. *Unit head:* Dr. James Scifers, Chair, 610-625-7210, E-mail: scifersj@moravian.edu. *Application contact:* Kristina Sullivan, Director of Student Recruitment Operations, 610-861-1400, Fax: 610-861-1466, E-mail: graduate@moravian.edu.
Website: https://www.moravian.edu/graduate/programs/rehabilitation-sciences#/

**Murray State University,** College of Education and Human Services, Center for Communication Disorders, Murray, KY 42071. Offers interdisciplinary brain injury studies (Certificate); speech-language pathology (MS). *Accreditation:* ASHA (one or more programs are accredited). *Program availability:* Part-time. *Entrance requirements:* For master's and Certificate, GRE or GMAT, minimum university GPA of 2.75. Additional exam requirements/recommendations for international students: required—TOEFL (minimum score 527 paper-based; 71 iBT). Electronic applications accepted.

**Nazareth College of Rochester,** Graduate Studies, Department of Speech-Language Pathology, Communication Sciences and Disorders Program, Rochester, NY 14618. Offers MS. *Accreditation:* ASHA. *Program availability:* Part-time. *Entrance requirements:*

For master's, GRE General Test, minimum GPA of 3.0. Additional exam requirements/ recommendations for international students: required—TOEFL or IELTS.

**New Mexico State University,** College of Education, Department of Special Education and Communication Disorders, Las Cruces, NM 88003-8001. Offers communication disorders (MA); curriculum and instruction (Ed S), including special education (MA, Ed S), special education/deaf-hard of hearing (MA, Ed S); education (MA), including autism spectrum disorders (MA, Ed D, PhD), special education (MA, Ed S), special education/deaf-hard of hearing (MA, Ed S), speech-language pathology; special education (Ed D, PhD), including autism spectrum disorders (MA, Ed D, PhD), bilingual/ multicultural special education. *Accreditation:* ASHA (one or more programs are accredited); NCATE. *Program availability:* Part-time, evening/weekend, online learning. *Faculty:* 10 full-time (9 women), 2 part-time/adjunct (1 woman). *Students:* 54 full-time (50 women), 36 part-time (31 women); includes 59 minority (3 Asian, non-Hispanic/ Latino; 52 Hispanic/Latino; 4 Two or more races, non-Hispanic/Latino), 2 international. Average age 31. 125 applicants, 35% accepted, 27 enrolled. In 2019, 25 master's, 3 doctorates, 4 other advanced degrees awarded. *Degree requirements:* For master's, comprehensive exam, thesis optional; for doctorate, comprehensive exam, thesis/ dissertation. *Entrance requirements:* For master's, GRE General Test or MAT. Additional exam requirements/recommendations for international students: required—TOEFL (minimum score 550 paper-based; 79 iBT), IELTS (minimum score 6.5). *Application deadline:* For fall admission, 2/1 priority date for domestic students. Applications are processed on a rolling basis. Application fee: $40 ($50 for international students). Electronic applications accepted. *Financial support:* In 2019–20, 46 students received support, including 1 fellowship (averaging $4,844 per year), 1 research assistantship (averaging $9,082 per year), 8 teaching assistantships (averaging $9,082 per year); career-related internships or fieldwork, Federal Work-Study, scholarships/ grants, traineeships, health care benefits, and unspecified assistantships also available. Support available to part-time students. Financial award application deadline: 3/1.
Website: spedcd.education.nmsu.edu

**New York Medical College,** School of Health Sciences and Practice, Valhalla, NY 10595. Offers behavioral sciences and health promotion (MPH); biostatistics (MS); children with special health care (Graduate Certificate); emergency preparedness (Graduate Certificate); environmental health science (MPH); epidemiology (MPH, MS); global health (Graduate Certificate); health education (Graduate Certificate); health policy and management (MPH, Dr PH); industrial hygiene (Graduate Certificate); pediatric dysphagia (Post-Graduate Certificate); physical therapy (DPT); public health (Graduate Certificate); speech-language pathology (MS). *Accreditation:* ASHA; CEPH. *Program availability:* Part-time, evening/weekend, 100% online, blended/hybrid learning. *Faculty:* 47 full-time (34 women), 203 part-time/adjunct (125 women). *Students:* 230 full-time (171 women), 292 part-time (207 women); includes 204 minority (73 Black or African American, non-Hispanic/Latino; 4 American Indian or Alaska Native, non-Hispanic/Latino; 59 Asian, non-Hispanic/Latino; 54 Hispanic/Latino; 1 Native Hawaiian or other Pacific Islander, non-Hispanic/Latino; 13 Two or more races, non-Hispanic/ Latino), 35 international. Average age 29. 790 applicants, 61% accepted, 162 enrolled. In 2019, 113 master's, 47 doctorates awarded. *Degree requirements:* For master's, comprehensive exam (for some programs), thesis (for some programs); for doctorate, thesis/dissertation. *Entrance requirements:* For master's, GRE (for MS in speech-language pathology); for doctorate, GRE (for Doctor of Physical Therapy and Doctor of Public Health). Additional exam requirements/recommendations for international students: required—TOEFL (minimum score 96 paper-based; 24 iBT), IELTS (minimum score 7). *Application deadline:* For fall admission, 8/1 for domestic students, 4/15 for international students; for spring admission, 12/1 for domestic students; for summer admission, 5/1 for domestic students, 4/15 for international students. Applications are processed on a rolling basis. Application fee: $128 ($120 for international students). Electronic applications accepted. *Expenses:* $1195 credit fee, academic support fee $200, Student activities fee $140 per year, technology fee $150. *Financial support:* In 2019–20, 18 students received support. Federal Work-Study, scholarships/grants, unspecified assistantships, and Federal student loans available. Financial award application deadline: 4/30; financial award applicants required to submit FAFSA. *Unit head:* Ben Johnson, PhD, Vice Dean, 914-594-4531, E-mail: bjohnson23@nymc.edu. *Application contact:* Irene Bundziak, Assistant to Director of Admissions, 914-594-4905, E-mail: irene_bundziak@nymc.edu.
Website: http://www.nymc.edu/school-of-health-sciences-and-practice-shsp/

**New York University,** Steinhardt School of Culture, Education, and Human Development, Department of Communication Sciences and Disorders, New York, NY 10003-6860. Offers MS, PhD. *Accreditation:* ASHA. *Program availability:* Part-time. *Entrance requirements:* For master's, GRE General Test; for doctorate, GRE General Test, interview. Additional exam requirements/recommendations for international students: required—TOEFL (minimum score 100 iBT). Electronic applications accepted.

**North Carolina Central University,** School of Education, Program in Communication Disorders, Durham, NC 27707-3129. Offers MS. *Accreditation:* ASHA. *Program availability:* Part-time, evening/weekend. *Degree requirements:* For master's, comprehensive exam, thesis or alternative. *Entrance requirements:* For master's, GRE, minimum GPA of 3.0 in major, 2.5 overall. Additional exam requirements/ recommendations for international students: required—TOEFL.

**Northeastern State University,** College of Science and Health Professions, Department of Health Professions, Program in Speech-Language Pathology, Tahlequah, OK 74464-2399. Offers MS. *Accreditation:* ASHA. *Program availability:* Part-time, evening/weekend. *Faculty:* 3 full-time (2 women), 1 (woman) part-time/adjunct. *Students:* 71 full-time (69 women), 1 (woman) part-time; includes 26 minority (1 Black or African American, non-Hispanic/Latino; 12 American Indian or Alaska Native, non-Hispanic/Latino; 2 Hispanic/Latino; 11 Two or more races, non-Hispanic/Latino). Average age 24. In 2019, 46 master's awarded. *Degree requirements:* For master's, thesis, capstone experience. *Entrance requirements:* For master's, GRE, minimum GPA of 2.75. Additional exam requirements/recommendations for international students: required—TOEFL. *Application deadline:* For fall admission, 6/1 priority date for domestic students. Applications are processed on a rolling basis. Application fee: $25. Electronic applications accepted. *Expenses: Tuition, area resident:* Full-time $250; part-time $250 per credit hour. Tuition, state resident: full-time $250; part-time $250 per credit hour. Tuition, nonresident: full-time $556; part-time $555.50 per credit hour. *Required fees:* $33.40 per credit hour. *Financial support:* Teaching assistantships, career-related internships or fieldwork, and Federal Work-Study available. Financial award application deadline: 3/1. *Unit head:* Brooke Klintworth, Program Chair, 918-444-3778, E-mail: klintwob@nsuok.edu. *Application contact:* Josh McCollum, Graduate Coordinator, 918-444-2093, E-mail: mccolluj@nsuok.edu.
Website: https://academics.nsuok.edu/healthprofessions/DegreePrograms/Speech-LangPath.aspx

**Northeastern University,** Bouvé College of Health Sciences, Boston, MA 02115-5096. Offers applied behavior analysis (MS); audiology (Au D); counseling psychology (MS, PhD, CAGS); exercise science (MS); nursing (MS, PhD, CAGS), including administration (MS), adult-gerontology acute care nurse practitioner (MS, CAGS), adult-gerontology primary care nurse practitioner (MS, CAGS), anesthesia (MS), family nurse practitioner (MS, CAGS), neonatal nurse practitioner (MS, CAGS), pediatric nurse practitioner (MS, CAGS), psychiatric mental health nurse practitioner (MS, CAGS); nursing practice (DNP); pharmaceutical sciences (MS, PhD), including interdisciplinary concentration, pharmaceutics and drug delivery systems; pharmacology (MS); pharmacy (Pharm D); school psychology (PhD); speech-language pathology (MS); urban health (MPH); MS/MBA. *Accreditation:* AANA/CANAEP; ACPE (one or more programs are accredited); ASHA; CEPH. *Program availability:* Part-time, evening/ weekend, online learning. *Degree requirements:* For doctorate, thesis/dissertation (for some programs); for CAGS, comprehensive exam. Electronic applications accepted. *Expenses:* Contact institution.

**Northern Arizona University,** College of Health and Human Services, Department of Communication Sciences and Disorders, Flagstaff, AZ 86011. Offers clinical speech-language pathology (MS). *Accreditation:* ASHA. *Program availability:* Part-time. *Degree requirements:* For master's, variable foreign language requirement, comprehensive exam (for some programs), thesis (for some programs). *Entrance requirements:* For master's, GRE General Test. Additional exam requirements/recommendations for international students: required—TOEFL (minimum score 100 iBT), IELTS (minimum score 6.5). Electronic applications accepted.

**Northern Illinois University,** Graduate School, College of Health and Human Sciences, School of Allied Health and Communicative Disorders, De Kalb, IL 60115-2854. Offers communicative disorders (MA, Au D), including audiology (Au D), speech-language pathology (MA); physical therapy (DPT). *Students:* 160 full-time (111 women), 2 part-time (1 woman); includes 41 minority (1 Black or African American, non-Hispanic/ Latino; 12 Asian, non-Hispanic/Latino; 22 Hispanic/Latino; 6 Two or more races, non-Hispanic/Latino), 1 international. Average age 25. 211 applicants, 41% accepted, 26 enrolled. In 2019, 25 master's, 38 doctorates awarded. Application fee: $40. *Financial support:* In 2019–20, 16 research assistantships, 3 teaching assistantships were awarded; staff assistantships also available. *Unit head:* Dr. Sherrill Morris, Chair, 815-753-1486, Fax: 815-753-6169, E-mail: ahcd@niu.edu. *Application contact:* Graduate School Office, 815-753-0395, E-mail: gradsch@niu.edu.
Website: http://www.chhs.niu.edu/ahcd

**Northwestern University,** The Graduate School, School of Communication, Roxelyn and Richard Pepper Department of Communication Sciences and Disorders, Evanston, IL 60208. Offers audiology (Au D); communication sciences and disorders (PhD); speech, language, and learning (MS). *Accreditation:* ASHA (one or more programs are accredited). Terminal master's awarded for partial completion of doctoral program. *Degree requirements:* For master's, seminar paper; for doctorate, thesis/dissertation, pre-dissertation research project, qualifying exam. *Entrance requirements:* For master's and doctorate, GRE General Test, letters of recommendation. Additional exam requirements/recommendations for international students: required—TOEFL.

**Nova Southeastern University,** Dr. Pallavi Patel College of Health Care Sciences, Fort Lauderdale, FL 33314-7796. Offers anesthesiologist assistant (MSA); audiology (Au D); health science (MH Sc, DHSc, PhD); occupational therapy (MOT, Dr OT, PhD); physical therapy (DPT, TDPT); physician assistant (MMS); speech-language pathology (MS). *Accreditation:* AOTA; ASHA. *Program availability:* Part-time, 100% online, blended/ hybrid learning. *Faculty:* 127 full-time (85 women), 107 part-time/adjunct (79 women). *Students:* 1,336 full-time (992 women), 950 part-time (824 women); includes 839 minority (195 Black or African American, non-Hispanic/Latino; 4 American Indian or Alaska Native, non-Hispanic/Latino; 165 Asian, non-Hispanic/Latino; 397 Hispanic/ Latino; 3 Native Hawaiian or other Pacific Islander, non-Hispanic/Latino; 75 Two or more races, non-Hispanic/Latino), 26 international. Average age 30. 634 applicants, 28% accepted, 159 enrolled. In 2019, 613 master's, 261 doctorates awarded. Terminal master's awarded for partial completion of doctoral program. *Degree requirements:* For doctorate, comprehensive exam, thesis/dissertation (for some programs), 12-month full-time clinical externship experience. *Entrance requirements:* For master's, GRE General Test; for doctorate, personal interview, essay in application,additional letters may be requested by the program after initial review of application if so warranted. *Application deadline:* Applications are processed on a rolling basis. Application fee: $50. Electronic applications accepted. *Expenses:* Contact institution. *Financial support:* Federal Work-Study, institutionally sponsored loans, and scholarships/grants available. Financial award application deadline: 4/15; financial award applicants required to submit FAFSA. *Unit head:* Dr. Stanley Wilson, Dean, 954-262-1203, E-mail: swilson@nova.edu. *Application contact:* Joycelyn Vogt, Director of Admissions and Outreach, 954-262-1200, Fax: 954-262-1181, E-mail: joycelyn.vogt@nova.edu.
Website: http://healthsciences.nova.edu/

**The Ohio State University,** Graduate School, College of Arts and Sciences, Division of Social and Behavioral Sciences, Department of Speech and Hearing Science, Columbus, OH 43210. Offers audiology (Au D); hearing science (PhD); speech-language pathology (MA); speech-language science (PhD). *Accreditation:* ASHA (one or more programs are accredited). *Entrance requirements:* For master's and doctorate, GRE General Test. Additional exam requirements/recommendations for international students: required—TOEFL (minimum score 600 paper-based; 100 iBT); recommended—IELTS (minimum score 9). Electronic applications accepted.

**Ohio University,** Graduate College, College of Health Sciences and Professions, School of Rehabilitation and Communication Sciences, Division of Communication Sciences and Disorders, Athens, OH 45701-2979. Offers clinical audiology (Au D); hearing science (PhD); speech language pathology (MA); speech language science (PhD). *Accreditation:* ASHA.

**Oklahoma State University,** College of Arts and Sciences, Department of Communication Sciences and Disorders, Stillwater, OK 74078. Offers MS. *Accreditation:* ASHA. *Faculty:* 8 full-time (4 women), 2 part-time/adjunct (both women). *Students:* 49 full-time (48 women), 4 part-time (all women); includes 11 minority (2 Black or African American, non-Hispanic/Latino; 3 American Indian or Alaska Native, non-Hispanic/Latino; 1 Asian, non-Hispanic/Latino; 4 Hispanic/Latino; 1 Two or more races, non-Hispanic/Latino). Average age 23. 95 applicants, 23% accepted, 20 enrolled. In 2019, 22 master's awarded. *Entrance requirements:* For master's, GRE, minimum GPA of 3.0 in undergraduate major. Additional exam requirements/recommendations for international students: required—TOEFL (minimum score 550 paper-based; 79 iBT). *Application deadline:* For fall admission, 3/1 priority date for international students; for spring admission, 8/1 priority date for international students. Applications are processed on a rolling basis. Application fee: $50 ($75 for international students). Electronic applications accepted. *Expenses: Tuition, area resident:* Full-time $4148.10; part-time $2765.40 per credit hour. Tuition, state resident: full-time $4148.10; part-time $2765.40 per credit hour. Tuition, nonresident: full-time $15,775; part-time $10,516.80 per credit hour. *International tuition:* $15,775.20 full-time. *Required fees:* $2196.90; $122.05 per credit hour. Tuition and fees vary according to course load, campus/location and program. *Financial support:* In 2019–20, 1 research assistantship (averaging $751 per year), 14 teaching assistantships (averaging $751 per year) were awarded; career-related internships or fieldwork, Federal Work-Study, scholarships/grants, health care benefits, tuition waivers (partial), and unspecified assistantships also available. Support available to part-time students. Financial award application deadline: 3/1; financial award applicants required to submit FAFSA. *Unit head:* Dr. Ramesh Kaipa, Department Head, 405-744-8938, E-mail: ramesh.kaipa@okstate.edu. *Application contact:* Dr.

Sheryl Tucker, Vice Prov/Dean/Prof, 405-744-6368, E-mail: gradi@okstate.edu. Website: http://cdis.okstate.edu/

**Old Dominion University,** Darden College of Education, Program in Speech-Language Pathology, Norfolk, VA 23529. Offers MS. *Accreditation:* ASHA. *Degree requirements:* For master's, comprehensive exam, written exams, case studies paper, practica. *Entrance requirements:* For master's, GRE General Test, minimum GPA of 3.0 in major, 2.8 overall. Additional exam requirements/recommendations for international students: required—TOEFL, IELTS. Electronic applications accepted. *Expenses:* Contact institution.

**Our Lady of the Lake University,** College of Professional Studies, Program in Communication and Learning Disorders, San Antonio, TX 78207-4689. Offers MA. *Accreditation:* ASHA. *Program availability:* Part-time. *Degree requirements:* For master's, comprehensive exam, comprehensive clinical practicum. *Entrance requirements:* For master's, GRE General Test, official transcripts. Additional exam requirements/recommendations for international students: required—TOEFL. Electronic applications accepted. Application fee is waived when completed online.

**Pace University,** College of Health Professions, Department of Communication Sciences and Disorders, New York, NY 10038. Offers MS. *Entrance requirements:* Additional exam requirements/recommendations for international students: required—TOEFL.

**Pacific University,** College of Education, Forest Grove, OR 97116-1797. Offers early childhood education (MAT); education (MAE); elementary education (MAT); ESOL (MAT); high school education (MAT); middle school education (MAT); special education (MAT); speech-language pathology (MS); STEM education (MAT); talented and gifted (M Ed); visual function in learning (M Ed). *Accreditation:* ASHA; NCATE. *Program availability:* Part-time, evening/weekend. *Degree requirements:* For master's, research project. *Entrance requirements:* For master's, California Basic Educational Skills Test, PRAXIS II, minimum undergraduate GPA of 2.75, 3.0 graduate. Additional exam requirements/recommendations for international students: required—TOEFL. Electronic applications accepted. *Expenses:* Contact institution.

**Pacific University,** School of Audiology, Forest Grove, OR 97116-1797. Offers Au D. *Accreditation:* ASHA.

**Penn State University Park,** Graduate School, College of Health and Human Development, Department of Communication Sciences and Disorders, University Park, PA 16802. Offers MS, PhD, Certificate. *Accreditation:* ASHA (one or more programs are accredited).

**Portland State University,** Graduate Studies, College of Liberal Arts and Sciences, Department of Speech and Hearing Sciences, Portland, OR 97207-0751. Offers speech-language pathology (MA, MS). *Accreditation:* ASHA (one or more programs are accredited). *Faculty:* 17 full-time (13 women), 5 part-time/adjunct (all women). *Students:* 71 full-time (68 women), 8 part-time (6 women); includes 25 minority (1 American Indian or Alaska Native, non-Hispanic/Latino; 6 Asian, non-Hispanic/Latino; 13 Hispanic/Latino; 5 Two or more races, non-Hispanic/Latino), 5 international. Average age 29. In 2019, 42 master's awarded. *Degree requirements:* For master's, variable foreign language requirement, thesis or alternative, oral exam, clinic. *Entrance requirements:* For master's, GRE General Test, minimum GPA of 3.0 overall, BA/BS in speech and hearing sciences. Additional exam requirements/recommendations for international students: required—TOEFL (minimum score 550 paper-based; 80 iBT), IELTS (minimum score 6.5). *Application deadline:* For fall admission, 12/15 for domestic and international students. Application fee: $65. Electronic applications accepted. *Expenses:* $456 per credit hour resident, $686 per credit hour non-resident. *Financial support:* In 2019–20, 3 teaching assistantships with full and partial tuition reimbursements (averaging $10,540 per year) were awarded; research assistantships, career-related internships or fieldwork, Federal Work-Study, and institutionally sponsored loans also available. Support available to part-time students. Financial award application deadline: 3/1; financial award applicants required to submit FAFSA. *Unit head:* Christina Gildersleeve-Neumann, PhD, Chair, 503-725-3230, Fax: 503-725-5385, E-mail: cegn@pdx.edu. *Application contact:* Dr. Sarah Key-DeLyria, Graduate Program Coordinator, 503-725-3698, E-mail: keydel@pdx.edu. Website: http://www.pdx.edu/sphr/

**Purdue University,** Graduate School, College of Health and Human Sciences, Department of Speech, Language, and Hearing Sciences, West Lafayette, IN 47907. Offers audiology clinic (MS, Au D, PhD); linguistics (MS, PhD); speech and hearing science (MS, PhD); speech-language pathology (MS, PhD). *Accreditation:* ASHA. *Faculty:* 20 full-time (14 women), 9 part-time/adjunct (5 women). *Students:* 96 full-time (91 women), 12 part-time (10 women); includes 13 minority (3 Black or African American, non-Hispanic/Latino; 5 Asian, non-Hispanic/Latino; 3 Hispanic/Latino; 2 Two or more races, non-Hispanic/Latino), 4 international. Average age 24. 270 applicants, 34% accepted, 38 enrolled. In 2019, 32 master's, 10 doctorates awarded. *Degree requirements:* For master's, comprehensive exam (for some programs), thesis optional; for doctorate, comprehensive exam, thesis/dissertation. *Entrance requirements:* For master's and doctorate, GRE General Test, minimum undergraduate GPA of 3.0 or equivalent. Additional exam requirements/recommendations for international students: required—TOEFL (minimum score 77 iBT). *Application deadline:* For fall admission, 1/1 priority date for domestic and international students; for spring admission, 8/1 priority date for domestic and international students. Applications are processed on a rolling basis. Application fee: $60 ($75 for international students). Electronic applications accepted. *Financial support:* Fellowships with full tuition reimbursements, research assistantships with full tuition reimbursements, teaching assistantships with full tuition reimbursements, career-related internships or fieldwork, and scholarships/grants available. Support available to part-time students. Financial award application deadline: 2/1; financial award applicants required to submit FAFSA. *Unit head:* Preeti Sivasankar, Head, 765-494-3788, E-mail: preeti@purdue.edu. *Application contact:* Vickie L. Parker-Black, Graduate Contact, 765-494-3786, E-mail: vpblack@purdue.edu. Website: http://www.purdue.edu/hhs/slhs/

**Queens College of the City University of New York,** Arts and Humanities Division, Department of Linguistics and Communication Disorders, Queens, NY 11367-1597. Offers applied linguistics (MA); speech-language pathology (MA); TESOL (MS Ed, Post-Master's Certificate); TESOL and bilingual education (Post-Master's Certificate). *Accreditation:* ASHA. *Program availability:* Part-time. *Entrance requirements:* For master's, minimum GPA of 3.0. Additional exam requirements/recommendations for international students: required—TOEFL, IELTS. Electronic applications accepted. *Expenses:* Contact institution.

**Radford University,** College of Graduate Studies and Research, Communication Sciences and Disorders, MS, Radford, VA 24142. Offers MA, MS. *Accreditation:* ASHA (one or more programs are accredited). *Program availability:* Part-time. *Degree requirements:* For master's, comprehensive exam, thesis (for some programs). *Entrance requirements:* For master's, GRE, minimum GPA of 3.0; completed CSDCAS application with 3 letters of reference; personal essay; resume. Additional exam requirements/recommendations for international students: required—TOEFL (minimum score 550 paper-based; 79 iBT), IELTS (minimum score 6.5). Electronic applications accepted.

**Rockhurst University,** College of Health and Human Services, Program in Communication Sciences and Disorders, Kansas City, MO 64110-2561. Offers MS. *Accreditation:* ASHA. *Program availability:* Part-time. *Entrance requirements:* For master's, GRE General Test, interview, minimum GPA of 3.0, letters of recommendation. Additional exam requirements/recommendations for international students: required—TOEFL (minimum score 550 paper-based; 79 iBT). Electronic applications accepted. *Expenses:* Contact institution.

**Rocky Mountain University of Health Professions,** Program in Speech-Language Pathology, Provo, UT 84606. Offers Clin Sc D.

**Rush University,** College of Health Sciences, Department of Communication Disorders and Sciences, Chicago, IL 60612-3832. Offers audiology (Au D); speech-language pathology (MS). *Accreditation:* ASHA (one or more programs are accredited). *Degree requirements:* For master's, comprehensive exam, thesis optional; for doctorate, comprehensive exam, investigative project. *Entrance requirements:* For master's and doctorate, GRE General Test, minimum GPA of 3.0. Additional exam requirements/recommendations for international students: required—TOEFL. *Application deadline:* For fall admission, 1/1 for domestic students. Electronic applications accepted. *Financial support:* Research assistantships with partial tuition reimbursements, career-related internships or fieldwork, Federal Work-Study, institutionally sponsored loans, scholarships/grants, traineeships, and tuition waivers (partial) available. Support available to part-time students. Financial award application deadline: 4/1; financial award applicants required to submit FAFSA. *Unit head:* Dr. Emily Wang, Chairperson. *Application contact:* Dr. Emily Wang, Chairperson.

**Sacred Heart University,** Graduate Programs, College of Health Professions, Department of Speech-Language Pathology, Fairfield, CT 06825. Offers MS. *Degree requirements:* For master's, capstone. *Entrance requirements:* For master's, GRE, bachelor's degree with minimum GPA of 3.0. Additional exam requirements/recommendations for international students: required—TOEFL (minimum score 570 paper-based, 80 iBT), TWE, or IELTS (6.5). Electronic applications accepted. *Expenses:* Contact institution.

**St. Ambrose University,** College of Health and Human Services, Program in Speech-Language Pathology, Davenport, IA 52803-2898. Offers MSLP. *Accreditation:* ASHA. *Program availability:* Part-time, evening/weekend. *Entrance requirements:* Additional exam requirements/recommendations for international students: required—TOEFL. Electronic applications accepted.

**St. Cloud State University,** School of Graduate Studies, School of Health and Human Services, Department of Communication Sciences and Disorders, St. Cloud, MN 56301-4498. Offers MS. *Accreditation:* ASHA. *Degree requirements:* For master's, comprehensive exam (for some programs), thesis or alternative. *Entrance requirements:* For master's, GRE General Test, minimum GPA of 2.75. Additional exam requirements/recommendations for international students: required—Michigan English Language Assessment Battery; recommended—TOEFL (minimum score 550 paper-based), IELTS (minimum score 6.5). Electronic applications accepted.

**St. John's University,** St. John's College of Liberal Arts and Sciences, Department of Communication Sciences and Disorders, Queens, NY 11439. Offers audiology (Au D); speech language pathology (MA). *Accreditation:* ASHA. *Program availability:* Evening/weekend. *Degree requirements:* For master's, comprehensive exam, thesis, practicum, residency; for doctorate, practicum. *Entrance requirements:* For master's, GRE, letters of recommendation, transcripts, resume, personal statement, 21 prerequisite credits in speech language pathology; for doctorate, GRE, letters of recommendation, transcripts, resume, personal statement. Additional exam requirements/recommendations for international students: required—TOEFL (minimum score 80 iBT), IELTS (minimum score 6.5). Electronic applications accepted. *Expenses:* Contact institution.

**Saint Joseph's University,** School of Health Studies and Education, Graduate Programs in Education, Philadelphia, PA 19131-1395. Offers curriculum supervisor (Certificate); educational leadership (MS, Ed D); elementary education (MS, Certificate); elementary/middle school education (Certificate); organizational development and leadership (MS); principal (Certificate); professional education (MS); reading specialist (MS, Certificate); reading supervisor (Certificate); secondary education (MS, Certificate); special education (MS); special education 7-12 (Certificate); special education PK-8 (Certificate); superintendent's letter of eligibility (Certificate); supervisor of special education (Certificate); teacher of the deaf and hard of hearing (Certificate). *Program availability:* Part-time, evening/weekend, blended/hybrid learning. *Degree requirements:* For master's, thesis or alternative; for doctorate, comprehensive exam, thesis/dissertation. *Entrance requirements:* For master's, 2 letters of recommendation, minimum GPA of 3.0, official transcripts, personal statement; for doctorate, GRE, master's degree from accredited institution, minimum graduate GPA of 3.5, computer competence, interview with program director. Additional exam requirements/recommendations for international students: required—TOEFL (minimum score 550 paper-based; 80 iBT), IELTS (minimum score 6.5), PTE (minimum score 60). Electronic applications accepted. *Expenses:* Contact institution.

**Saint Louis University,** Graduate Programs, Doisy College of Health Sciences, Department of Communication Sciences and Disorders, St. Louis, MO 63103. Offers MA. *Accreditation:* ASHA. *Degree requirements:* For master's, thesis optional, comprehensive oral and written exams. *Entrance requirements:* For master's, GRE General Test, letters of recommendation, resume. Additional exam requirements/recommendations for international students: required—TOEFL (minimum score 525 paper-based). Electronic applications accepted.

**Saint Mary's College,** Graduate Studies, Master of Science Program in Speech Language Pathology, Notre Dame, IN 46556. Offers speech language pathology (MS). *Faculty:* 8 full-time (7 women). *Students:* 60 full-time (all women); includes 10 minority (2 Black or African American, non-Hispanic/Latino; 1 Asian, non-Hispanic/Latino; 6 Hispanic/Latino; 1 Two or more races, non-Hispanic/Latino). Average age 28. 188 applicants, 60% accepted, 30 enrolled. In 2019, 32 master's awarded. *Degree requirements:* For master's, comprehensive exam (for some programs), thesis optional, 400 hours of a supervised clinical practicum. *Entrance requirements:* For master's, GRE, bachelor's degree in communication sciences and disorders or related field, official transcripts, current resume or curriculum vitae, 3 letters of recommendation, personal statement, video interview. Additional exam requirements/recommendations for international students: recommended—TOEFL (minimum score 80 iBT), IELTS (minimum score 6.5). *Application deadline:* For fall admission, 2/1 for domestic and international students. Electronic applications accepted. *Expenses:* $11,678 per semester. *Financial support:* In 2019–20, 7 students received support. Scholarships/grants available. Financial award application deadline: 3/1; financial award applicants required to submit FAFSA. *Unit head:* Susan Latham, Program Director, Master of Science in Speech Language Pathology, 574-284-4686, E-mail: slatham@saintmarys.edu. *Application contact:* Melissa Fruscione, Director, Graduate Studies, 574-284-5098, E-mail: graduateadmission@saintmarys.edu. Website: http://grad.saintmarys.edu/academic-programs/ms-speech-pathology

**Saint Xavier University,** Graduate Studies, College of Arts and Sciences, Department of Communication Sciences and Disorders, Chicago, IL 60655-3105. Offers speech-language pathology (MS). *Accreditation:* ASHA. *Entrance requirements:* For master's,

GRE General Test, minimum GPA of 3.0, undergraduate course work in speech. *Expenses:* Contact institution.

**Salus University,** College of Education and Rehabilitation, Elkins Park, PA 19027-1598. Offers education of children and youth with visual and multiple impairments (M Ed, Certificate); low vision rehabilitation (MS, Certificate); occupational therapy (MS); orientation and mobility therapy (MS, Certificate); speech-language pathology (MS); vision rehabilitation therapy (MS, Certificate); OD/MS. *Accreditation:* AOTA. *Program availability:* Part-time, online learning. *Entrance requirements:* For master's, GRE or MAT, 3 letters of reference, 2 interviews. Additional exam requirements/recommendations for international students: required—TOEFL, TWE. *Expenses:* Contact institution.

**Salus University,** Osborne College of Audiology, Elkins Park, PA 19027-1598. Offers Au D. *Accreditation:* ASHA. *Entrance requirements:* Additional exam requirements/recommendations for international students: required—TOEFL. Electronic applications accepted.

**Samford University,** School of Health Professions, Birmingham, AL 35229. Offers athletic training (MAT); physical therapy (DPT); physician assistant (MS); speech language pathology (MS). *Faculty:* 24 full-time (9 women), 2 part-time/adjunct (both women). *Students:* 193 full-time (152 women), 3 part-time (all women); includes 23 minority (7 Black or African American, non-Hispanic/Latino; 1 American Indian or Alaska Native, non-Hispanic/Latino; 3 Asian, non-Hispanic/Latino; 4 Hispanic/Latino; 8 Two or more races, non-Hispanic/Latino). Average age 24. 897 applicants, 25% accepted, 42 enrolled. In 2019, 52 master's awarded. *Degree requirements:* For master's and doctorate, capstone course. *Entrance requirements:* For master's, GRE, PA-CAT, MCAT, recommendations, resume, on-campus interview, personal statement, shadowing hours, transcripts; for doctorate, GRE, recommendations, resume, on-campus interview, personal statement, shadowing hours, transcripts. Additional exam requirements/recommendations for international students: required—TOEFL (minimum score 575 paper-based; 90 iBT), IELTS (minimum score 6.5). *Application deadline:* For fall admission, 8/1 for domestic students; for winter admission, 10/1 for domestic students; for spring admission, 1/1 for domestic students. Application fee: $120. Electronic applications accepted. *Expenses: Tuition:* Full-time $17,754; part-time $862 per credit hour. *Required fees:* $550; $550 per unit. Full-time tuition and fees vary according to course load, program and student level. *Financial support:* In 2019–20, 32 students received support. Scholarships/grants available. Financial award application deadline: 5/1; financial award applicants required to submit FAFSA. *Unit head:* Dr. Alan Jung, Ph.D., Dean of the School of Health Professions, 205-726-2716, E-mail: apjung@samford.edu. *Application contact:* Dr. Marian Carter, Ed.D., Assistant Dean of Enrollment Management and Student Services, 205-726-2611, E-mail: mwcarter@samford.edu.
Website: http://www.samford.edu/healthprofessions

**San Diego State University,** Graduate and Research Affairs, College of Health and Human Services, School of Speech, Language, and Hearing Sciences, San Diego, CA 92182. Offers audiology (Au D); communicative disorders (MA); language and communicative disorders (PhD). *Accreditation:* ASHA. *Program availability:* Part-time. *Degree requirements:* For master's, comprehensive exam (for some programs), thesis (for some programs); for doctorate, thesis/dissertation. *Entrance requirements:* For master's and doctorate, GRE General Test. Additional exam requirements/recommendations for international students: required—TOEFL. Electronic applications accepted.

**San Francisco State University,** Division of Graduate Studies, College of Education, Department of Speech, Language and Hearing Sciences, San Francisco, CA 94132-1722. Offers communicative disorders (MS). *Accreditation:* ASHA. *Expenses: Tuition, area resident:* Full-time $7176; part-time $4164 per year. Tuition, state resident: full-time $7176; part-time $4164 per year. Tuition, nonresident: full-time $16,680; part-time $396 per unit. *International tuition:* $16,680 full-time. *Required fees:* $1524; $1524 per unit. $762 per semester. Tuition and fees vary according to degree level and program. *Unit head:* Dr. Laura Epstein, Chair, 415-405-2170, Fax: 415-338-0916, E-mail: lepstein@sfsu.edu. *Application contact:* Mallorie Desimone, Administrative Office Coordinator, 415-338.1001, Fax: 415-338-0916, E-mail: mallorie@sfsu.edu.
Website: http://slhs.sfsu.edu/

**San Jose State University,** Program in Communicative Disorders and Sciences, San Jose, CA 95192-0112. Offers speech-language pathology (MA). *Accreditation:* ASHA. *Faculty:* 8 full-time (7 women), 7 part-time/adjunct (all women). *Students:* 109 full-time (100 women), 1 (woman) part-time; includes 63 minority (3 Black or African American, non-Hispanic/Latino; 37 Asian, non-Hispanic/Latino; 15 Hispanic/Latino; 8 Native Hawaiian or other Pacific Islander, non-Hispanic/Latino), 2 international. Average age 28. 264 applicants, 13% accepted, 35 enrolled. In 2019, 42 master's awarded. *Degree requirements:* For master's, comprehensive exam, thesis optional, current accreditation standards mandate completion of a minimum 400-hour clinical practicum requirement. *Entrance requirements:* For master's, GRE not required for Fall 2021 admissions. Additional exam requirements/recommendations for international students: required—TOEFL, GRE. *Application deadline:* For fall admission, 2/1 for domestic and international students. Applications are processed on a rolling basis. Application fee: $70. Electronic applications accepted. *Expenses: Tuition, area resident:* Full-time $7176; part-time $4164 per credit hour. Tuition, state resident: full-time $7176; part-time $4164 per credit hour. Tuition, nonresident: full-time $7176; part-time $4165 per credit hour. *International tuition:* $7176 full-time. *Required fees:* $2110; $2110. *Financial support:* In 2019–20, 57 students received support, including 1 fellowship (averaging $5,250 per year); research assistantships, scholarships/grants, traineeships, and Tutor jobs, student assistants also available. Financial award application deadline: 5/1; financial award applicants required to submit FAFSA. *Unit head:* Nidhi Mahendra, Department Chair, 408-924-8161, E-mail: nidhi.mahendra@sjsu.edu. *Application contact:* Cindy Aubrey, Administrative Support Coordinator, 408-924-3659, E-mail: communicative-disorders-sciences@sjsu.edu.
Website: http://www.sjsu.edu/cds/

**Seton Hall University,** School of Health and Medical Sciences, Program in Speech-Language Pathology, South Orange, NJ 07079-2697. Offers MS. *Accreditation:* ASHA. *Entrance requirements:* For master's, GRE, bachelor's degree, clinical experience; minimum GPA of 3.0, undergraduate preprofessional coursework in communication sciences and disorders. Additional exam requirements/recommendations for international students: recommended—TOEFL. Electronic applications accepted.

**South Carolina State University,** College of Graduate and Professional Studies, Department of Health Sciences, Orangeburg, SC 29117-0001. Offers speech pathology and audiology (MA). *Accreditation:* ASHA. *Program availability:* Part-time, evening/weekend. *Degree requirements:* For master's, thesis optional, departmental qualifying exam. *Entrance requirements:* For master's, GRE or NTE, minimum GPA of 3.0. Electronic applications accepted.

**Southeastern Louisiana University,** College of Nursing and Health Sciences, Department of Health and Human Sciences, Hammond, LA 70402. Offers communication sciences and disorders (MS); counseling (MS). *Accreditation:* ACA; ASHA; NCATE. *Program availability:* Part-time, 100% online. *Faculty:* 17 full-time (16 women), 1 (woman) part-time/adjunct. *Students:* 116 full-time (109 women), 47 part-time (39 women); includes 35 minority (14 Black or African American, non-Hispanic/Latino; 1 American Indian or Alaska Native, non-Hispanic/Latino; 16 Hispanic/Latino; 4 Two or more races, non-Hispanic/Latino), 1 international. Average age 26. 166 applicants, 70% accepted, 46 enrolled. In 2019, 59 master's awarded. *Degree requirements:* For master's, comprehensive exam, thesis optional. *Entrance requirements:* For master's, Counseling: GRE minimum 279; Communication Sciences and Disorders: GRE verbal 138, quantitative 138, writing 3.0, Counseling: minimum GPA of 2.8, three references, resume, letter of interest, autobiographical narrative; Child Life: minimum GPA of 3.25, personal statement, resume, 2 letters of recommendation, volunteer or paid work experience; Communication Sciences and Disorders: minimum 2.75 GPA, three reference letters, writing sample, resume. Additional exam requirements/recommendations for international students: required—TOEFL (minimum score 500 paper-based; 61 iBT). *Application deadline:* For fall admission, 7/15 priority date for domestic students, 6/1 priority date for international students; for spring admission, 12/1 priority date for domestic students, 10/1 priority date for international students. Applications are processed on a rolling basis. Application fee: $20 ($30 for international students). Electronic applications accepted. *Expenses: Tuition, area resident:* Full-time $6684; part-time $489 per credit hour. Tuition, state resident: full-time $6684; part-time $489 per credit hour. Tuition, nonresident: full-time $19,162; part-time $1183 per credit hour. *International tuition:* $19,162 full-time. *Required fees:* $2124. *Financial support:* In 2019–20, 90 students received support, including 1 fellowship with tuition reimbursement available (averaging $1,250 per year); career-related internships or fieldwork, institutionally sponsored loans, and unspecified assistantships also available. Financial award application deadline: 5/1; financial award applicants required to submit FAFSA. *Unit head:* Dr. Jacqueline Guendouzi, Department Head, 985-549-2309, Fax: 985-549-3758, E-mail: jguendouzi@southeastern.edu. *Application contact:* Office of Admissions, 985-549-5637, Fax: 985-549-5632, E-mail: admissions@southeastern.edu.
Website: http://www.southeastern.edu/acad_research/depts/hhs/index.html

**Southeast Missouri State University,** School of Graduate Studies, Department of Communication Disorders, Cape Girardeau, MO 63701-4799. Offers MA. *Accreditation:* ASHA. *Faculty:* 8 full-time (all women). *Students:* 30 full-time (29 women), 7 part-time (all women). Average age 23. 92 applicants, 20% accepted, 18 enrolled. In 2019, 16 master's awarded. *Degree requirements:* For master's, comprehensive exam, thesis optional, National Praxis Exam or Graduate Comprehensive Exam. *Entrance requirements:* For master's, GRE, TOEFL (for international students), Application to SEMO, Applications through CSDCAS. Additional exam requirements/recommendations for international students: recommended—TOEFL. *Application deadline:* For fall admission, 1/15 for domestic and international students. Applications are processed on a rolling basis. Application fee: $30 ($40 for international students). Electronic applications accepted. *Expenses:* Additional $35 per credit hour program fee. *Financial support:* In 2019–20, 9 students received support. Teaching assistantships with full tuition reimbursements available, career-related internships or fieldwork, Federal Work-Study, scholarships/grants, traineeships, tuition waivers (full), and unspecified assistantships available. Financial award application deadline: 2/1; financial award applicants required to submit FAFSA. *Unit head:* Dr. Jayanti Ray, Chairperson and Professor, 573-986-6404, E-mail: jray@semo.edu. *Application contact:* Dr. Jayanti Ray, Chairperson and Professor, 573-986-6404, E-mail: jray@semo.edu.
Website: https://semo.edu/commdisorders/index.html

**Southern Connecticut State University,** School of Graduate Studies, School of Health and Human Services, Department of Communication Disorders, New Haven, CT 06515-1355. Offers speech pathology (MS). *Accreditation:* ASHA. *Program availability:* Part-time. *Degree requirements:* For master's, thesis or alternative, clinical experience. *Entrance requirements:* For master's, GRE, interview, minimum QPA of 3.0. Electronic applications accepted.

**Southern Illinois University Carbondale,** Graduate School, College of Education and Human Services, Department of Communication Disorders and Sciences, Carbondale, IL 62901-4701. Offers MS. *Accreditation:* ASHA. *Degree requirements:* For master's, thesis. *Entrance requirements:* For master's, GRE, minimum GPA of 3.0. Additional exam requirements/recommendations for international students: required—TOEFL (minimum score 550 paper-based; 80 iBT). Electronic applications accepted.

**Southern Illinois University Edwardsville,** Graduate School, School of Education, Health, and Human Behavior, Department of Special Education and Communication Disorders, Program in Speech-Language Pathology, Edwardsville, IL 62026. Offers MS. *Accreditation:* ASHA. *Program availability:* Part-time, evening/weekend. *Degree requirements:* For master's, thesis (for some programs), final exam. *Entrance requirements:* For master's, GRE, minimum GPA of 3.0. Additional exam requirements/recommendations for international students: required—TOEFL (minimum score 550 paper-based; 79 iBT), IELTS (minimum score 6.5). Electronic applications accepted.

**Southern University and Agricultural and Mechanical College,** College of Nursing and Allied Health, Department of Speech-Language Pathology and Audiology, Baton Rouge, LA 70813. Offers MS. *Accreditation:* ASHA.

**State University of New York at Fredonia,** College of Liberal Arts and Sciences, Fredonia, NY 14063-1136. Offers biology (MS); English (MA); English education 7-12 (MA); interdisciplinary studies (MA, MS); math education (MS Ed); professional writing (CAS); speech pathology (MS); MA/MS. *Program availability:* Part-time, evening/weekend. *Degree requirements:* For master's, comprehensive exam (for some programs), thesis (for some programs). *Entrance requirements:* For master's, GRE. Additional exam requirements/recommendations for international students: required—TOEFL (minimum score 79 iBT), IELTS (minimum score 6.5). Electronic applications accepted.

**State University of New York at New Paltz,** Graduate and Extended Learning School, School of Liberal Arts and Sciences, Department of Communication Disorders, New Paltz, NY 12561. Offers communication disorders (MS), including speech-language disabilities, speech-language pathology. *Accreditation:* ASHA. *Program availability:* Part-time, evening/weekend. *Faculty:* 10 full-time (all women), 6 part-time/adjunct (all women). *Students:* 64 full-time (62 women), 2 part-time (1 woman); includes 14 minority (2 Black or African American, non-Hispanic/Latino; 2 Asian, non-Hispanic/Latino; 7 Hispanic/Latino; 3 Two or more races, non-Hispanic/Latino). 42 applicants, 67% accepted. In 2019, 25 master's awarded. *Degree requirements:* For master's, comprehensive exam, thesis. *Entrance requirements:* For master's, GRE General Test or MAT, minimum GPA of 3.0. Additional exam requirements/recommendations for international students: required—TOEFL (minimum score 550 paper-based; 80 iBT), IELTS (minimum score 6.5). *Application deadline:* For fall admission, 3/1 for domestic and international students. Application fee: $50. Electronic applications accepted. *Expenses: Tuition, area resident:* Full-time $11,310; part-time $471 per credit. Tuition, state resident: full-time $11,310; part-time $471 per credit. Tuition, nonresident: full-time $23,100; part-time $963 per credit. *International tuition:* $23,100 full-time. *Required fees:* $1432; $41.83 per credit. *Financial support:* In 2019–20, 4 teaching assistantships with partial tuition reimbursements (averaging $5,000 per year) were awarded. Financial award application deadline: 8/1. *Unit head:* Dr. Wendy Bower, Program Coordinator, 845-257-3452, E-mail: commdisgrad@newpaltz.edu. *Application contact:* Vika Shock,

Director of Graduate Admissions, 845-257-3286, E-mail: gradstudies@newpaltz.edu.
Website: http://www.newpaltz.edu/commdis/

**State University of New York at Plattsburgh,** School of Education, Health, and Human Services, Department of Communication Sciences and Disorders, Plattsburgh, NY 12901-2681. Offers speech-language pathology (MA). *Accreditation:* ASHA. *Program availability:* Part-time. *Entrance requirements:* For master's, GRE General Test, minimum GPA of 3.0. Additional exam requirements/recommendations for international students: required—TOEFL.

**State University of New York College at Cortland,** Graduate Studies, School of Professional Studies, Department of Communication Disorders and Sciences, Cortland, NY 13045. Offers communication sciences and disorders (MS). *Accreditation:* ASHA.

**Stephen F. Austin State University,** Graduate School, James I. Perkins College of Education, Department of Human Services, Nacogdoches, TX 75962. Offers counseling (MA); school psychology (MA); special education (M Ed); speech-language pathology (MS). *Accreditation:* ACA (one or more programs are accredited); ASHA (one or more programs are accredited); CORE; NCATE. *Degree requirements:* For master's, comprehensive exam, thesis (for some programs). *Entrance requirements:* For master's, GRE General Test, minimum GPA of 2.8. Additional exam requirements/ recommendations for international students: required—TOEFL.

**Stockton University,** Office of Graduate Studies, Program in Communication Disorders, Galloway, NJ 08205-9441. Offers MS. *Accreditation:* ASHA. *Faculty:* 5 full-time (4 women), 7 part-time/adjunct (all women). *Students:* 43 full-time (40 women), 20 part-time (all women); includes 11 minority (1 Black or African American, non-Hispanic/ Latino; 2 Asian, non-Hispanic/Latino; 6 Hispanic/Latino; 2 Two or more races, non-Hispanic/Latino). Average age 23. 235 applicants, 42% accepted, 32 enrolled. In 2019, 31 master's awarded. *Degree requirements:* For master's, comprehensive exam (for some programs), thesis optional. *Entrance requirements:* For master's, GRE, 3 letters of recommendation, official transcripts from all colleges/universities attended, minimum undergraduate cumulative GPA of 3.2. *Application deadline:* For fall admission, 2/1 for domestic students. Application fee: $50. Electronic applications accepted. *Expenses: Tuition, area resident:* Full-time $750.92; part-time $78.58 per credit hour. Tuition, state resident: full-time $750.92; part-time $78.58 per credit hour. Tuition, nonresident: full-time $846; part-time $78.58 per credit hour. *International tuition:* $1195.96 full-time. *Required fees:* $1464; $78.58 per credit hour. One-time fee: $50 full-time. *Financial support:* Fellowships, research assistantships with partial tuition reimbursements, career-related internships or fieldwork, Federal Work-Study, scholarships/grants, and unspecified assistantships available. Support available to part-time students. Financial award application deadline: 3/1. *Unit head:* Dr. Stacy Cassel, Program Director, 609-626-3640, E-mail: graduatestudies@stockton.edu. *Application contact:* Tara Williams, Assistant Director of Enrollment Management, 609-626-3640, Fax: 609-626-6050, E-mail: gradschool@stockton.edu.

**Syracuse University,** College of Arts and Sciences, MS Program in Speech-Language Pathology, Syracuse, NY 13244. Offers MS. *Accreditation:* ASHA. *Degree requirements:* For master's, comprehensive exam, thesis or alternative. *Entrance requirements:* For master's, GRE, three letters of recommendation, personal statement, resume, transcripts. Additional exam requirements/recommendations for international students: required—TOEFL (minimum score 100 iBT). Electronic applications accepted.

**Syracuse University,** College of Arts and Sciences, Programs in Audiology, Syracuse, NY 13244. Offers Au D, PhD. *Accreditation:* ASHA. *Program availability:* Part-time. *Degree requirements:* For doctorate, thesis/dissertation, internship. *Entrance requirements:* For doctorate, GRE General Test, undergraduate and graduate transcripts, three letters of recommendation, resume, personal statement. Additional exam requirements/recommendations for international students: required—TOEFL (minimum score 620 paper-based; 105 iBT). Electronic applications accepted.

**Teachers College, Columbia University,** Department of Biobehavioral Sciences, New York, NY 10027-6696. Offers applied exercise physiology (Ed M, MA, Ed D); communication sciences and disorders (MS, Ed D, PhD); kinesiology (PhD); motor learning and control (Ed M, MA); motor learning/movement science (Ed D); neuroscience and education (MS); physical education (MA, Ed D). *Accreditation:* ASHA. *Faculty:* 9 full-time (8 women). *Students:* 153 full-time (134 women), 149 part-time (106 women); includes 122 minority (25 Black or African American, non-Hispanic/Latino; 32 Asian, non-Hispanic/Latino; 55 Hispanic/Latino; 10 Two or more races, non-Hispanic/ Latino), 37 international. 582 applicants, 51% accepted, 165 enrolled. *Unit head:* Dr. Carol Scheffner Hammer, E-mail: cjh2207@tc.columbia.edu. *Application contact:* Kelly Sutton Skinner, Director of Admission and New Student Enrollment, 212-678-3710, E-mail: kms2237@tc.columbia.edu.
Website: http://www.tc.columbia.edu/biobehavioral-sciences/

**Teachers College, Columbia University,** Department of Health and Behavior Studies, New York, NY 10027-6696. Offers applied behavior analysis (MA, PhD); applied educational psychology: school psychology (Ed M, PhD); behavioral nutrition (PhD), including nutrition (Ed D, PhD); community health education (MS); community nutrition education (Ed M), including community nutrition education; education of deaf and hard of hearing (MA, PhD); health education (MA, Ed D); hearing impairment (Ed D); intellectual disability/autism (MA, Ed D, PhD); nursing education (Ed D, Advanced Certificate); nutrition and education (MS); nutrition and exercise physiology (MS); nutrition and public health (MS); nutrition education (Ed D), including nutrition (Ed D, PhD); physical disabilities (Ed D); reading specialist (MA); severe or multiple disabilities (MA); special education (Ed M, MA, Ed D); teaching of sign language (MA). *Faculty:* 17 full-time (11 women). *Students:* 243 full-time (225 women), 246 part-time (211 women); includes 172 minority (33 Black or African American, non-Hispanic/Latino; 2 American Indian or Alaska Native, non-Hispanic/Latino; 63 Asian, non-Hispanic/Latino; 63 Hispanic/Latino; 11 Two or more races, non-Hispanic/Latino), 67 international. 515 applicants, 68% accepted, 170 enrolled. *Unit head:* Dr. Dolores Perin, Chair, 212-678-3091, E-mail: dp111@tc.columbia.edu. *Application contact:* Kelly Sutton-Skinner, Director of Admission and New Student Enrollment, E-mail: kms2237@tc.columbia.edu.
Website: http://www.tc.columbia.edu/health-and-behavior-studies/

**Temple University,** College of Public Health, Department of Communication Sciences and Disorders, Philadelphia, PA 19122-6096. Offers communication sciences and disorders (PhD); speech-language-hearing (MA). *Accreditation:* ASHA. *Faculty:* 19 full-time (14 women), 3 part-time/adjunct (all women). *Students:* 69 full-time (64 women); includes 12 minority (4 Black or African American, non-Hispanic/Latino; 3 Asian, non-Hispanic/Latino; 3 Hispanic/Latino; 2 Two or more races, non-Hispanic/Latino), 2 international. 41 applicants, 83% accepted, 11 enrolled. In 2019, 27 master's awarded. *Degree requirements:* For master's, comprehensive exam, thesis optional; for doctorate, thesis/dissertation. *Entrance requirements:* For master's, GRE, minimum GPA of 3.0, 3 letters of reference, statement of goals; for doctorate, GRE, 3 letters of reference, statement of goals, writing sample, resume. Additional exam requirements/ recommendations for international students: required—TOEFL (minimum score 79 iBT), IELTS, PTE, one of three is required. Application fee: $60. Electronic applications accepted. *Expenses:* Contact institution. *Financial support:* Research assistantships, teaching assistantships, Federal Work-Study, health care benefits, and unspecified assistantships available. Financial award applicants required to submit FAFSA. *Unit head:* Lisa Bedore, Chairperson, 215-204-7543, E-mail: lisa.bedore@temple.edu. *Application contact:* Annemarie Szambelak, Assistant Director of Admissions, 215-204-4526, E-mail: aszambelak@temple.edu.
Website: https://cph.temple.edu/commsci/home

**Tennessee State University,** The School of Graduate Studies and Research, College of Health Sciences, Department of Speech Pathology and Audiology, Nashville, TN 37209-1561. Offers speech and hearing science (MS). *Accreditation:* ASHA. *Program availability:* Part-time, online learning. *Degree requirements:* For master's, comprehensive exam, thesis optional. *Entrance requirements:* For master's, GRE General Test or MAT, minimum GPA of 3.5. Additional exam requirements/ recommendations for international students: required—TOEFL.

**Texas A&M University–Kingsville,** College of Graduate Studies, College of Arts and Sciences, Program in Communication Sciences and Disorders, Kingsville, TX 78363. Offers MS. *Accreditation:* ASHA. *Entrance requirements:* Additional exam requirements/recommendations for international students: required—TOEFL (minimum score 550 paper-based; 79 iBT); recommended—IELTS. Electronic applications accepted.

**Texas Christian University,** Harris College of Nursing and Health Sciences, Davies School of Communication Sciences and Disorders, Fort Worth, TX 76129-0002. Offers speech-language pathology (MS). *Accreditation:* ASHA. *Faculty:* 9 full-time (8 women), 1 part-time/adjunct. *Students:* 42 full-time (40 women); includes 11 minority (2 Asian, non-Hispanic/Latino; 8 Hispanic/Latino; 1 Two or more races, non-Hispanic/Latino), 2 international. Average age 24. 212 applicants, 10% accepted, 20 enrolled. In 2019, 19 master's awarded. *Degree requirements:* For master's, comprehensive exam, thesis optional. *Entrance requirements:* For master's, GRE General Test. Additional exam requirements/recommendations for international students: required—TOEFL. *Application deadline:* For fall admission, 1/15 for domestic and international students. Application fee: $60. Electronic applications accepted. Full-time tuition and fees vary according to program. *Financial support:* In 2019–20, 40 students received support, including 40 research assistantships (averaging $35,000 per year); tuition waivers (partial) and unspecified assistantships also available. Financial award application deadline: 1/15; financial award applicants required to submit FAFSA. *Unit head:* Dr. Christopher Watts, Director, 817-257-7620, E-mail: c.watts@tcu.edu. *Application contact:* Janet Schwartz, Administrative Assistant, 817-257-7620, E-mail: janet.schwartz@tcu.edu.
Website: http://csd.tcu.edu

**Texas State University,** The Graduate College, College of Health Professions, Program in Communication Disorders, San Marcos, TX 78666. Offers MA, MSCD. *Accreditation:* ASHA (one or more programs are accredited). *Degree requirements:* For master's, comprehensive exam, thesis (for some programs), clinical practicum. *Entrance requirements:* For master's, baccalaureate degree in communication disorders from regionally-accredited institution with minimum GPA of 3.0 in communication disorders courses and in last 60 hours of course work; 3 forms of recommendation; resume; statement of purpose and interests. Additional exam requirements/recommendations for international students: required—TOEFL (minimum score 550 paper-based; 78 iBT), IELTS (minimum score 6.5). Electronic applications accepted.

**Texas Tech University Health Sciences Center,** School of Health Professions, Program in Audiology, Lubbock, TX 79430. Offers Au D. *Accreditation:* ASHA. *Faculty:* 9 full-time (8 women). *Students:* 35 full-time (33 women), 4 part-time (all women); includes 15 minority (1 Asian, non-Hispanic/Latino; 12 Hispanic/Latino; 2 Two or more races, non-Hispanic/Latino). Average age 24. 77 applicants, 16% accepted, 12 enrolled. In 2019, 11 doctorates awarded. *Degree requirements:* For doctorate, comprehensive exam. *Entrance requirements:* For doctorate, GRE, official transcripts, bachelor's degree, minimum cumulative GPA of 3.0. Additional exam requirements/ recommendations for international students: required—TOEFL (minimum score 550 paper-based; 79 iBT). *Application deadline:* For fall admission, 11/1 for domestic students; for spring admission, 2/1 for domestic students. Applications are processed on a rolling basis. Application fee: $75. Electronic applications accepted. *Financial support:* In 2019–20, 33 students received support. Career-related internships or fieldwork, scholarships/grants, and unspecified assistantships available. Support available to part-time students. Financial award application deadline: 9/1; financial award applicants required to submit FAFSA. *Unit head:* Dr. Candace Hicks, Program Director, 806-743-5660, Fax: 806-743-5670, E-mail: health.professions@ttuhsc.edu. *Application contact:* Lindsay Johnson, Associate Dean for Admissions and Student Affairs, 806-743-3220, Fax: 806-743-2994, E-mail: health.professions@ttuhsc.edu.
Website: http://www.ttuhsc.edu/health-professions/doctor-of-audiology/

**Texas Tech University Health Sciences Center,** School of Health Professions, Program in Speech-Language Pathology, Lubbock, TX 79430. Offers MS. *Accreditation:* ASHA. *Faculty:* 14 full-time (12 women). *Students:* 85 full-time (80 women), 1 (woman) part-time; includes 23 minority (3 Black or African American, non-Hispanic/Latino; 1 American Indian or Alaska Native, non-Hispanic/Latino; 3 Asian, non-Hispanic/Latino; 13 Hispanic/Latino; 3 Two or more races, non-Hispanic/Latino). Average age 23. 171 applicants, 25% accepted, 43 enrolled. In 2019, 41 master's awarded. *Degree requirements:* For master's, comprehensive exam, thesis optional. *Entrance requirements:* For master's, GRE. Additional exam requirements/recommendations for international students: required—TOEFL (minimum score 550 paper-based; 79 iBT). *Application deadline:* For winter admission, 2/1 for domestic students. Applications are processed on a rolling basis. Application fee: $75. Electronic applications accepted. *Financial support:* In 2019–20, 40 students received support. Institutionally sponsored loans, scholarships/grants, and unspecified assistantships available. Financial award application deadline: 9/1; financial award applicants required to submit FAFSA. *Unit head:* Sherry Sancibrian, Program Director, 806-743-5660, Fax: 806-743-5670, E-mail: health.professions@ttuhsc.edu. *Application contact:* Lindsay Johnson, Associate Dean for Admissions and Student Affairs, 806-743-3220, Fax: 806-742-2994, E-mail: health.professions@ttuhsc.edu.
Website: http://www.ttuhsc.edu/health-professions/master-of-science-speech-language-pathology/

**Texas Woman's University,** Graduate School, College of Health Sciences, Communication Sciences and Oral Health, Denton, TX 76204. Offers education of the deaf (MS); speech-language pathology (MS). *Accreditation:* ASHA. *Program availability:* Part-time, 100% online, blended/hybrid learning. *Faculty:* 16 full-time (14 women), 3 part-time/adjunct (all women). *Students:* 166 full-time (162 women), 34 part-time (33 women); includes 94 minority (9 Black or African American, non-Hispanic/Latino; 1 American Indian or Alaska Native, non-Hispanic/Latino; 9 Asian, non-Hispanic/Latino; 68 Hispanic/Latino; 7 Two or more races, non-Hispanic/Latino). Average age 31. 194 applicants, 11% accepted, 18 enrolled. In 2019, 145 master's awarded. *Degree requirements:* For master's, comprehensive exam, thesis or alternative, internship, practicum. *Entrance requirements:* For master's, GRE for SLP, 2 letters of reference (3 for speech/language pathology), personal essay, minimum GPA of 3.0 in last 60 hours of undergraduate work and all graduate course work, letter of intent, sign proficiency (Educ. of the Deaf). Additional exam requirements/recommendations for international students: required—TOEFL (minimum score 79 iBT); recommended—IELTS (minimum score 6.5), TSE (minimum score 53). *Application deadline:* For fall admission, 3/1

priority date for domestic and international students; for spring admission, 11/1 priority date for domestic students, 7/1 priority date for international students; for summer admission, 5/1 priority date for domestic students, 2/1 priority date for international students. Application fee: $50 ($75 for international students). Electronic applications accepted. *Expenses:* All are estimates. Tuition for 10 hours = $2,763; Fees for 10 hours = $1,342. Communication science courses require additional $20/SCH. *Financial support:* In 2019–20, 78 students received support, including 10 teaching assistantships (averaging $4,988 per year); career-related internships or fieldwork, scholarships/grants, health care benefits, and unspecified assistantships also available. Support available to part-time students. Financial award application deadline: 3/1; financial award applicants required to submit FAFSA. *Unit head:* Dr. Erika Armstrong, Chair, 940-898-2025, Fax: 940-898-2070, E-mail: coms@twu.edu. *Application contact:* Korie Hawkins, Associate Director of Admissions, Graduate Recruitment, 940-898-3188, Fax: 940-898-3081, E-mail: admissions@twu.edu.
Website: http://www.twu.edu/communication-sciences/

**Towson University,** College of Health Professions, Program in Audiology, Towson, MD 21252-0001. Offers Au D. *Accreditation:* ASHA. *Students:* 58 full-time (57 women); includes 11 minority (4 Black or African American, non-Hispanic/Latino; 2 Asian, non-Hispanic/Latino; 3 Hispanic/Latino; 2 Two or more races, non-Hispanic/Latino). *Entrance requirements:* For doctorate, GRE, 3 letters of recommendation, minimum GPA of 3.0, interview, essay. Additional exam requirements/recommendations for international students: required—TOEFL (minimum score 600 paper-based). *Application deadline:* For fall admission, 1/17 for domestic students, 5/15 for international students; for spring admission, 10/15 for domestic students, 12/1 for international students. Applications are processed on a rolling basis. Application fee: $45. Electronic applications accepted. *Expenses: Tuition, area resident:* Full-time $7920; part-time $439 per credit. Tuition, nonresident: full-time $16,344; part-time $908 per credit. *International tuition:* $16,344 full-time. *Required fees:* $2628; $146 per credit. $876 per term. *Financial support:* Application deadline: 4/1. *Unit head:* Dr. Jennifer Smart, Program Director, 410-704-3105, E-mail: audiology@towson.edu. *Application contact:* Coverley Beidleman, Assistant Director of Graduate Admissions, 410-704-5630, Fax: 410-704-3030, E-mail: grads@towson.edu.
Website: https://www.towson.edu/chp/departments/asld/grad/audiology/

**Towson University,** College of Health Professions, Program in Speech-Language Pathology, Towson, MD 21252-0001. Offers MS. *Accreditation:* ASHA. *Students:* 86 full-time (82 women); includes 8 minority (2 Black or African American, non-Hispanic/Latino; 2 Asian, non-Hispanic/Latino; 2 Hispanic/Latino; 2 Two or more races, non-Hispanic/Latino), 1 international. *Entrance requirements:* For master's, GRE, bachelor's degree in speech-language pathology and audiology; CLEP or advanced placement (AP) examination credits in biological sciences, physical sciences, social/behavioral sciences and statistics; minimum GPA of 3.0 in major; 3 letters of recommendation; essay. Additional exam requirements/recommendations for international students: required—TOEFL (minimum score 600 paper-based). *Application deadline:* For fall admission, 1/17 for domestic students, 5/15 for international students; for spring admission, 10/15 for domestic students, 12/1 for international students. Applications are processed on a rolling basis. Application fee: $45. Electronic applications accepted. *Expenses: Tuition, area resident:* Full-time $7920; part-time $439 per credit. Tuition, nonresident: full-time $16,344; part-time $908 per credit. *International tuition:* $16,344 full-time. *Required fees:* $2628; $146 per credit. $876 per term. *Financial support:* Application deadline: 4/1. *Unit head:* Dr. Karen Fallon, Program Director, 410-704-2437, E-mail: slpgradprogram@towson.edu. *Application contact:* Coverley Beidleman, Assistant Director of Graduate Admissions, 410-704-5630, Fax: 410-704-3030, E-mail: grads@towson.edu.
Website: https://www.towson.edu/chp/departments/asld/grad/speech/

**Truman State University,** Office of Graduate Studies, School of Health Sciences and Education, Program in Communication Disorders, Kirksville, MO 63501-4221. Offers MA. *Accreditation:* ASHA. *Degree requirements:* For master's, comprehensive exam, thesis optional. *Entrance requirements:* For master's, GRE General Test, minimum GPA of 3.0. Additional exam requirements/recommendations for international students: required—TOEFL (minimum score 550 paper-based). Electronic applications accepted. *Expenses:* Tuition, state resident: full-time $4630; part-time $385.50 per credit hour. Tuition, nonresident: full-time $8018; part-time $668 per credit hour. *International tuition:* $8018 full-time. *Required fees:* $324. Full-time tuition and fees vary according to course level, course load, program and reciprocity agreements.

**Universidad del Turabo,** Graduate Programs, School of Health Sciences, Program in Speech and Language Pathology, Gurabo, PR 00778-3030. Offers MS. *Accreditation:* ASHA. *Entrance requirements:* For master's, EXADEP, GRE OR GMAT, interview, essay, official transcript, recommendation letters. Electronic applications accepted.

**Université de Montréal,** Faculty of Medicine, School of Speech Therapy and Audiology, Montréal, QC H3C 3J7, Canada. Offers audiology (PMS); speech therapy (PMS, DESS). *Degree requirements:* For master's, thesis. *Entrance requirements:* For master's, B Sc in speech-language pathology and audiology, proficiency in French. Electronic applications accepted.

**University at Buffalo, the State University of New York,** Graduate School, College of Arts and Sciences, Department of Communicative Disorders and Sciences, Buffalo, NY 14260. Offers audiology (Au D); communicative disorders and sciences (MA, PhD). *Accreditation:* ASHA (one or more programs are accredited). *Degree requirements:* For master's, thesis or alternative, exam; for doctorate, thesis/dissertation, exams. *Entrance requirements:* For master's and doctorate, GRE General Test, minimum GPA of 3.0. Additional exam requirements/recommendations for international students: required—TOEFL (minimum score 550 paper-based; 79 iBT). Electronic applications accepted. *Expenses:* Contact institution.

**The University of Akron,** Graduate School, College of Health Professions, School of Speech-Language Pathology and Audiology, Program in Audiology, Akron, OH 44325. Offers Au D. *Degree requirements:* For doctorate, 2,000 clock hours of clinical experience, academic and clinical competency-based exams. *Entrance requirements:* For doctorate, GRE, minimum GPA of 3.0, letters of recommendation, statement of purpose, interview. Additional exam requirements/recommendations for international students: required—TOEFL (minimum score 79 iBT), IELTS (minimum score 6.5). Electronic applications accepted.

**The University of Akron,** Graduate School, College of Health Professions, School of Speech-Language Pathology and Audiology, Program in Speech-Language Pathology, Akron, OH 44325. Offers MA. *Accreditation:* ASHA. *Entrance requirements:* For master's, GRE, baccalaureate degree in speech-language pathology, minimum GPA of 3.0, three letters of recommendation, statement of purpose, resume, interview. Additional exam requirements/recommendations for international students: required—TOEFL (minimum score 79 iBT), IELTS (minimum score 6.5). Electronic applications accepted.

**The University of Alabama,** Graduate School, College of Arts and Sciences, Department of Communicative Disorders, Tuscaloosa, AL 35487. Offers speech language pathology (MS). *Accreditation:* ASHA. *Faculty:* 9 full-time (8 women). *Students:* 61 full-time (60 women); includes 7 minority (2 Black or African American, non-Hispanic/Latino; 1 Asian, non-Hispanic/Latino; 3 Hispanic/Latino; 1 Two or more races, non-Hispanic/Latino). Average age 24. 211 applicants, 30% accepted, 36 enrolled. In 2019, 25 master's awarded. *Degree requirements:* For master's, comprehensive exam, thesis optional. *Entrance requirements:* For master's, GRE or MAT, minimum GPA of 3.0. Additional exam requirements/recommendations for international students: required—TOEFL. *Application deadline:* For fall and spring admission, 1/15 for domestic and international students. Application fee: $50 ($60 for international students). Electronic applications accepted. *Expenses: Tuition, area resident:* Full-time $10,780; part-time $440 per credit hour. Tuition, nonresident: full-time $30,250; part-time $1550 per credit hour. *Financial support:* In 2019–20, 12 students received support. Fellowships with tuition reimbursements available, teaching assistantships with partial tuition reimbursements available, career-related internships or fieldwork, Federal Work-Study, scholarships/grants, traineeships, health care benefits, and unspecified assistantships available. Financial award application deadline: 1/15. *Unit head:* Dr. Angela B. Barber, Associate Professor and Chair, 205-348-2010, Fax: 205-348-1845, E-mail: abarber@ua.edu. *Application contact:* Lacey Watts, Office Associate, 205-348-7131, Fax: 205-348-1845, E-mail: lwatts@ua.edu.
Website: http://cd.ua.edu/

**University of Alberta,** Faculty of Graduate Studies and Research, Faculty of Rehabilitation Medicine, Department of Communication Sciences and Disorders, Edmonton, AB T6G 2E1, Canada. Offers speech-language pathology (M Sc). *Degree requirements:* For master's, thesis (for some programs), clinical practicum (MSLP). *Entrance requirements:* For master's, GRE, minimum GPA of 6.5 on a 9.0 scale. Additional exam requirements/recommendations for international students: required—TOEFL.

**The University of Arizona,** College of Science, Department of Speech, Language, and Hearing Sciences, Tucson, AZ 85721. Offers MS, PhD, Certificate. *Accreditation:* ASHA (one or more programs are accredited). *Degree requirements:* For master's, thesis optional; for doctorate, thesis/dissertation. *Entrance requirements:* For master's, GRE General Test, 3 letters of recommendation; for doctorate, GRE General Test, 3 letters of recommendation, personal statement, writing sample. Additional exam requirements/recommendations for international students: required—TOEFL (minimum score 550 paper-based; 79 iBT). Electronic applications accepted.

**University of Arkansas,** Graduate School, College of Education and Health Professions, Department of Rehabilitation, Human Resources and Communication Disorders, Program in Communication Disorders, Fayetteville, AR 72701. Offers MS. *Accreditation:* ASHA. *Program availability:* Part-time. *Students:* 32 full-time (31 women), 20 part-time (all women); includes 7 minority (5 Hispanic/Latino; 2 Two or more races, non-Hispanic/Latino), 2 international. 113 applicants, 27% accepted. In 2019, 23 master's awarded. *Degree requirements:* For master's, thesis optional, 8-week externship. *Entrance requirements:* For master's, GRE General Test. *Application deadline:* For fall admission, 8/1 for domestic students, 4/1 for international students; for spring admission, 12/1 for domestic students, 10/1 for international students; for summer admission, 4/15 for domestic students, 3/1 for international students. Applications are processed on a rolling basis. Application fee: $60. Electronic applications accepted. *Financial support:* In 2019–20, 5 research assistantships were awarded; fellowships, teaching assistantships, career-related internships or fieldwork, and Federal Work-Study also available. Support available to part-time students. Financial award application deadline: 4/1; financial award applicants required to submit FAFSA. *Unit head:* Dr. Michael Hevel, Program Coordinator, 479-575-4916, E-mail: hevel@uark.edu. *Application contact:* Dr. Rachel Glade, Graduate Coordinator, 479-575-3575, E-mail: rglade@uark.edu.
Website: http://cdis.uark.edu

**University of Arkansas for Medical Sciences,** College of Health Professions, Little Rock, AR 72205-7199. Offers audiology (Au D); communication sciences and disorders (MS, PhD); genetic counseling (MS); nuclear medicine advanced associate (MIS); physician assistant studies (MPAS); radiologist assistant (MIS). *Accreditation:* ASHA. *Program availability:* Part-time, online learning. *Degree requirements:* For master's, thesis (for some programs); for doctorate, comprehensive exam (for some programs), thesis/dissertation (for some programs). *Entrance requirements:* For master's, GRE. Additional exam requirements/recommendations for international students: required—TOEFL (minimum score 550 paper-based; 79 iBT). Electronic applications accepted. *Expenses:* Contact institution.

**The University of British Columbia,** Faculty of Medicine, School of Audiology and Speech Sciences, Vancouver, BC V6T 1Z3, Canada. Offers M Sc, PhD. *Accreditation:* ASHA. *Degree requirements:* For master's, thesis or alternative, externship; for doctorate, comprehensive exam, thesis/dissertation. *Entrance requirements:* For master's, 4-year undergraduate degree; for doctorate, master's degree, research proposal. Additional exam requirements/recommendations for international students: required—TOEFL, IELTS. Electronic applications accepted. *Expenses:* Contact institution.

**University of California, San Diego,** Graduate Division, Interdisciplinary Program in Language and Communicative Disorders, La Jolla, CA 92093. Offers PhD. *Students:* 1 (woman) full-time, 17 part-time (12 women). In 2019, 2 doctorates awarded. *Degree requirements:* For doctorate, one foreign language, comprehensive exam, thesis/dissertation, teaching assistantship. *Entrance requirements:* For doctorate, GRE General Test, minimum GPA of 3.25. Additional exam requirements/recommendations for international students: required—TOEFL (minimum score 550 paper-based; 80 iBT), IELTS (minimum score 7). *Application deadline:* For fall admission, 6/2 for domestic students. Electronic applications accepted. *Financial support:* Teaching assistantships available. Financial award applicants required to submit FAFSA. *Unit head:* Seana Coulson, Program Director, 858-534-7486, E-mail: scoulson@ucsd.edu. *Application contact:* Ethel Lu, Graduate Coordinator, 858-534-7141, E-mail: erlu@ucsd.edu.
Website: http://slhs.sdsu.edu/programs/phd/

**University of California, San Diego,** School of Medicine, Program in Audiology, La Jolla, CA 92093. Offers Au D. *Students:* 10 full-time (9 women), 3 part-time (all women). In 2019, 9 doctorates awarded. *Degree requirements:* For doctorate, comprehensive exam, thesis/dissertation, 2,950 clinic hours; externship. *Entrance requirements:* For doctorate, GRE General Test, minimum GPA of 3.0; at least one course in each of the following areas: statistics, biological science, physical science, and American Sign Language; additional courses in behavioral/social sciences and biological or physical sciences. Additional exam requirements/recommendations for international students: required—TOEFL (minimum score 550 paper-based; 80 iBT), IELTS (minimum score 7). Electronic applications accepted. *Expenses:* Contact institution. *Financial support:* Fellowships, research assistantships, scholarships/grants, and unspecified assistantships available. Financial award applicants required to submit FAFSA. *Unit head:* Erika Zettner, Chair, 858-657-8057, E-mail: ezettner@ucsd.edu. *Application contact:* Erika Zettner, Chair, 858-657-8057, E-mail: ezettner@ucsd.edu.
Website: http://slhs.sdsu.edu/programs/aud/

**University of Central Arkansas,** Graduate School, College of Health and Behavioral Sciences, Department of Communication Sciences and Disorders, Conway, AR 72035-0001. Offers communication sciences and disorders (PhD); speech-language pathology (MS). *Accreditation:* ASHA (one or more programs are accredited). *Degree*

*requirements:* For master's, comprehensive exam, thesis optional, portfolio, internship. *Entrance requirements:* For master's, GRE General Test, NTE, minimum GPA of 2.7. Additional exam requirements/recommendations for international students: required—TOEFL (minimum score 550 paper-based). Electronic applications accepted. *Expenses:* Contact institution.

**University of Central Florida,** College of Health Professions and Sciences, School of Communication Sciences and Disorders, Orlando, FL 32816. Offers MA, Certificate. *Accreditation:* ASHA (one or more programs are accredited). *Program availability:* Part-time, evening/weekend. *Students:* 189 full-time (183 women), 6 part-time (5 women); includes 63 minority (10 Black or African American, non-Hispanic/Latino; 7 Asian, non-Hispanic/Latino; 43 Hispanic/Latino; 3 Two or more races, non-Hispanic/Latino), 2 international. Average age 25. 297 applicants, 46% accepted, 27 enrolled. In 2019, 87 master's awarded. *Degree requirements:* For master's, comprehensive exam, thesis or alternative. *Entrance requirements:* For master's, GRE General Test, minimum GPA of 3.0 in last 60 hours, letters of recommendation, resume, personal statement. Additional exam requirements/recommendations for international students: required—TOEFL. *Application deadline:* For fall admission, 2/1 for domestic students; for spring admission, 10/1 for domestic students. Application fee: $30. Electronic applications accepted. *Financial support:* In 2019–20, 14 students received support, including 3 fellowships with partial tuition reimbursements available (averaging $5,200 per year), 6 research assistantships with partial tuition reimbursements available (averaging $5,084 per year), 6 teaching assistantships with partial tuition reimbursements available (averaging $5,668 per year); career-related internships or fieldwork, Federal Work-Study, institutionally sponsored loans, and unspecified assistantships also available. Financial award application deadline: 3/1; financial award applicants required to submit FAFSA. *Unit head:* Dr. Linda Rosa-Lugo, Program Coordinator, 407-823-4798, E-mail: csdgraduate@ucf.edu. *Application contact:* Associate Director, Graduate Admissions, 407-823-2766, Fax: 407-823-6442, E-mail: gradadmissions@ucf.edu.
Website: https://healthprofessions.ucf.edu/csd/

**University of Central Missouri,** The Graduate School, Warrensburg, MO 64093. Offers accountancy (MA); accounting (MBA); applied mathematics (MS); aviation safety (MA); biology (MS); business administration (MBA); career and technology education (MS); college student personnel administration (MS); communication (MA); computer information systems and information technology (MS); computer science (MS); counseling (MS); criminal justice and criminology (MS); educational leadership (Ed S); educational leadership and policy analysis (Ed D); educational technology (MS, Ed S); elementary and early childhood education (MSE); English (MA); english language learners - teaching english as a second language (MA); environmental studies (MA); finance (MBA); history (MA); industrial hygiene (MS); industrial management (MS); information systems (MBA); kinesiology (MS); library science and information services (MS); literacy education (MSE); marketing (MBA); mathematics (MS); music (MA); occupational safety management (MS); professional leadership - adult, career, and technical education (Ed S); professional leadership - counseling (Ed S); psychology (MS); rural family nursing (MS); school administration (MSE); social gerontology (MS); sociology (MA); special education (MSE); speech language pathology (MS); teaching (MAT); technology (MS); technology management (PhD); theatre (MA). *Accreditation:* ASHA. *Program availability:* Part-time, 100% online, blended/hybrid learning. *Faculty:* 236 full-time (113 women), 97 part-time/adjunct (61 women). *Students:* 787 full-time (448 women), 1,459 part-time (997 women); includes 213 minority (72 Black or African American, non-Hispanic/Latino; 5 American Indian or Alaska Native, non-Hispanic/Latino; 27 Asian, non-Hispanic/Latino; 59 Hispanic/Latino; 50 Two or more races, non-Hispanic/Latino), 574 international. Average age 30. 1,477 applicants, 68% accepted, 664 enrolled. In 2019, 831 master's, 93 other advanced degrees awarded. *Degree requirements:* For master's and Ed S, comprehensive exam (for some programs), thesis (for some programs). *Entrance requirements:* For master's, A GRE or GMAT test score may be required by some of the programs, A minimum GPA, letters of recommendation, a statement of purpose may be required by some of the programs; for Ed S, A master's degree is required for the application of an Education Specialist's degree program. Additional exam requirements/recommendations for international students: required—TOEFL (minimum score 550 paper-based; 79 iBT). *Application deadline:* For fall admission, 6/1 priority date for domestic and international students; for spring admission, 10/15 priority date for domestic and international students; for summer admission, 4/1 priority date for domestic and international students. Applications are processed on a rolling basis. Application fee: $30 ($75 for international students). Electronic applications accepted. *Expenses: Tuition, area resident:* Full-time $7524; part-time $313.50 per credit hour. Tuition, state resident: full-time $7524; part-time $313.50 per credit hour. Tuition, nonresident: full-time $15,048; part-time $627 per credit hour. *International tuition:* $15,048 full-time. *Required fees:* $915; $30.50 per credit hour. *Financial support:* In 2019–20, 89 students received support. Research assistantships, teaching assistantships, career-related internships or fieldwork, Federal Work-Study, scholarships/grants, unspecified assistantships, and administrative and laboratory assistantships available. Support available to part-time students. Financial award application deadline: 4/1; financial award applicants required to submit FAFSA. *Unit head:* Shellie Hewitt, Director of Graduate and International Student Services, 660-543-4621, Fax: 660-543-4778, E-mail: hewitt@ucmo.edu. *Application contact:* Shellie Hewitt, Director of Graduate and International Student Services, 660-543-4621, Fax: 660-543-4778, E-mail: hewitt@ucmo.edu.
Website: http://www.ucmo.edu/graduate/

**University of Central Oklahoma,** The Jackson College of Graduate Studies, College of Education and Professional Studies, Donna Nigh Department of Advanced Professional and Special Services, Edmond, OK 73034-5209. Offers educational leadership (M Ed); library media education (M Ed); reading (M Ed); school counseling (M Ed); special education (M Ed), including mild/moderate disabilities, severe-profound/multiple disabilities; speech-language pathology (MS). *Accreditation:* ASHA. *Program availability:* Part-time. *Degree requirements:* For master's, comprehensive exam (for some programs), thesis (for some programs). *Entrance requirements:* Additional exam requirements/recommendations for international students: required—TOEFL (minimum score 550 paper-based; 79 iBT), IELTS (minimum score 6.5). Electronic applications accepted.

**University of Cincinnati,** Graduate School, College of Allied Health Sciences, Department of Communication Sciences and Disorders, Cincinnati, OH 45221. Offers MA, Au D, PhD. *Accreditation:* ASHA (one or more programs are accredited). *Degree requirements:* For master's, thesis optional; for doctorate, comprehensive exam, thesis/dissertation. *Entrance requirements:* For master's and doctorate, GRE General Test, minimum GPA of 3.0. Additional exam requirements/recommendations for international students: required—TOEFL (minimum score 600 paper-based). Electronic applications accepted.

**University of Colorado Boulder,** Graduate School, College of Arts and Sciences, Department of Speech, Language and Hearing Sciences, Boulder, CO 80309. Offers MA, Au D, PhD. *Accreditation:* ASHA (one or more programs are accredited). Terminal master's awarded for partial completion of doctoral program. *Degree requirements:* For master's, comprehensive exam, thesis or alternative; for doctorate, one foreign language, thesis/dissertation. *Entrance requirements:* For master's, GRE General Test, minimum undergraduate GPA of 3.25; for doctorate, GRE General Test. Electronic applications accepted. Application fee is waived when completed online.

**University of Connecticut,** Graduate School, College of Liberal Arts and Sciences, Department of Speech, Language and Hearing Sciences, Storrs, CT 06269. Offers MA, Au D, PhD. *Accreditation:* ASHA. Terminal master's awarded for partial completion of doctoral program. *Degree requirements:* For master's, comprehensive exam, thesis optional; for doctorate, thesis/dissertation. *Entrance requirements:* For master's and doctorate, GRE General Test. Additional exam requirements/recommendations for international students: required—TOEFL (minimum score 550 paper-based). Electronic applications accepted.

**University of Delaware,** College of Health Sciences, Department of Communication Sciences and Disorders, Newark, DE 19716. Offers speech-language pathology (MA). *Entrance requirements:* For master's, GRE General Test, letters of recommendation, personal essay.

**University of Florida,** Graduate School, College of Public Health and Health Professions, Department of Speech, Language and Hearing Sciences, Gainesville, FL 32611. Offers audiology (Au D); communication sciences and disorders (MA, PhD). *Accreditation:* ASHA (one or more programs are accredited). *Degree requirements:* For master's, thesis optional; for doctorate, comprehensive exam, thesis/dissertation. *Entrance requirements:* For master's and doctorate, GRE General Test, minimum GPA of 3.0. Additional exam requirements/recommendations for international students: required—TOEFL (minimum score 550 paper-based; 80 iBT), IELTS (minimum score 6). Electronic applications accepted.

**University of Georgia,** College of Education, Department of Communication Sciences and Special Education, Athens, GA 30602. Offers communication science and disorders (M Ed, MA, PhD, Ed S); special education (Ed D). *Accreditation:* ASHA (one or more programs are accredited). Terminal master's awarded for partial completion of doctoral program. *Degree requirements:* For master's, comprehensive exam (for some programs), thesis (for some programs); for doctorate, thesis/dissertation. *Entrance requirements:* For master's, doctorate, and Ed S, GRE General Test. Additional exam requirements/recommendations for international students: required—TOEFL. Electronic applications accepted.

**University of Hawaii at Manoa,** John A. Burns School of Medicine, Department of Communication Sciences and Disorders, Honolulu, HI 96822. Offers MS. *Accreditation:* ASHA. *Program availability:* Part-time. *Degree requirements:* For master's, thesis optional. *Entrance requirements:* For master's, GRE General Test, minimum GPA of 3.0. Additional exam requirements/recommendations for international students: required—TOEFL (minimum score 580 paper-based; 92 iBT), IELTS (minimum score 5).

**University of Houston,** College of Liberal Arts and Social Sciences, Department of Communication Sciences and Disorders, Houston, TX 77204. Offers MA. *Accreditation:* ASHA. *Program availability:* Part-time. *Degree requirements:* For master's, comprehensive exam, thesis optional. *Entrance requirements:* For master's, GRE General Test, minimum GPA of 3.0 in last 60 hours. Additional exam requirements/recommendations for international students: required—TOEFL (minimum score 550 paper-based; 79 iBT).

**University of Illinois at Urbana-Champaign,** Graduate College, College of Applied Health Sciences, Department of Speech and Hearing Science, Champaign, IL 61820. Offers audiology (Au D); speech and hearing science (MA, PhD). *Accreditation:* ASHA (one or more programs are accredited).

**The University of Iowa,** Graduate College, College of Liberal Arts and Sciences, Department of Communication Sciences and Disorders, Iowa City, IA 52242-1316. Offers MA, Au D, PhD, Au D/PhD. *Accreditation:* ASHA. *Degree requirements:* For master's, thesis optional, exam; for doctorate, comprehensive exam (for some programs), thesis/dissertation (for some programs). *Entrance requirements:* For master's and doctorate, GRE General Test, minimum GPA of 3.0. Additional exam requirements/recommendations for international students: required—TOEFL (minimum score 550 paper-based; 81 iBT). Electronic applications accepted.

**The University of Kansas,** Graduate Studies, College of Liberal Arts and Sciences, Intercampus Program in Communicative Disorders: Speech-Language Pathology, Lawrence, KS 66045. Offers audiology (PhD); speech-language pathology (MA, PhD). *Accreditation:* ASHA. *Program availability:* Part-time. *Students:* 84 full-time (80 women), 4 part-time (all women); includes 14 minority (1 Black or African American, non-Hispanic/Latino; 2 American Indian or Alaska Native, non-Hispanic/Latino; 4 Asian, non-Hispanic/Latino; 4 Hispanic/Latino; 3 Two or more races, non-Hispanic/Latino), 5 international. Average age 26. 151 applicants, 58% accepted, 37 enrolled. In 2019, 29 master's, 4 doctorates awarded. Terminal master's awarded for partial completion of doctoral program. *Entrance requirements:* For master's, GRE General Test, minimum GPA of 3.0, bachelor's degree, one- to two-page resume, three letters of recommendation, official transcript, 500-word essay on one of three topics provided; for doctorate, GRE General Test, minimum GPA of 3.0, bachelor's degree, one- to two-page resume, three letters of recommendation, official transcript. Additional exam requirements/recommendations for international students: required—TOEFL, IELTS. *Application deadline:* For fall admission, 12/10 priority date for domestic and international students; for summer admission, 1/15 for domestic and international students. Application fee: $65 ($85 for international students). Electronic applications accepted. *Expenses:* Tuition, state resident: full-time $9989. Tuition, nonresident: full-time $23,950. *International tuition:* $23,950 full-time. *Required fees:* $984; $81.99 per credit hour. Tuition and fees vary according to course load, campus/location and program. *Financial support:* Research assistantships, teaching assistantships, career-related internships or fieldwork, Federal Work-Study, institutionally sponsored loans, scholarships/grants, traineeships, and unspecified assistantships available. Support available to part-time students. Financial award application deadline: 12/10; financial award applicants required to submit FAFSA. *Unit head:* Nancy C. Brady, Chair, 785-864-0762, E-mail: nbrady@ku.edu. *Application contact:* Angela Carrasco, Graduate Admissions Contact, 913-588-5935, E-mail: acarrasco@kumc.edu.
Website: http://splh.ku.edu/ipcd/

**The University of Kansas,** University of Kansas Medical Center, School of Health Professions, Intercampus Program in Communicative Disorders: Audiology and Speech-Language Pathology, Lawrence, KS 66045. Offers audiology (Au D); speech-language pathology (SLPD). *Accreditation:* ASHA. *Faculty:* 27. *Students:* 76 full-time (72 women), 3 part-time (all women); includes 9 minority (1 Black or African American, non-Hispanic/Latino; 1 Asian, non-Hispanic/Latino; 3 Hispanic/Latino; 4 Two or more races, non-Hispanic/Latino), 1 international. Average age 27. In 2019, 9 doctorates awarded. *Degree requirements:* For doctorate, comprehensive exam, oral comprehensive exam (for AuD); capstone oral exam (for SLPD). *Entrance requirements:* For doctorate, GRE (for AuD), bachelor's degree and/or prerequisites in communication sciences and disorders (for AuD); master's degree in speech-language pathology and ASHA certificate of clinical competence (for SLPD). Additional exam requirements/recommendations for international students: required—TOEFL or IELTS. *Application deadline:* For fall admission, 1/15 for domestic and international students. Application fee: $60. Electronic applications accepted. *Expenses:* Tuition, state resident: full-time $9989. Tuition, nonresident: full-time $23,950. *International tuition:* $23,950 full-time.

*Required fees:* $984; $81.99 per credit hour. Tuition and fees vary according to course load, campus/location and program. *Financial support:* Research assistantships with partial tuition reimbursements, teaching assistantships with partial tuition reimbursements, institutionally sponsored loans, scholarships/grants, traineeships, health care benefits, and unspecified assistantships available. Financial award application deadline: 3/1; financial award applicants required to submit FAFSA. *Unit head:* Dr. Tiffany A. Johnson, Associate Professor and Doughty-Kemp Endowed Chair, Department of Hearing and Speech, 913-588-5937, Fax: 913-588-5923, E-mail: tjohnson7@kumc.edu. *Application contact:* Angela Carrasco, Admissions Coordinator, 913-588-5935, Fax: 913-588-5923, E-mail: ipcd@ku.edu.
Website: http://ipcd.ku.edu

**University of Kentucky,** Graduate School, College of Health Sciences, Program in Communication Disorders, Lexington, KY 40506-0032. Offers MS. *Accreditation:* ASHA. *Degree requirements:* For master's, comprehensive exam. *Entrance requirements:* For master's, GRE General Test, minimum undergraduate GPA of 2.75. Additional exam requirements/recommendations for international students: required—TOEFL (minimum score 550 paper-based). Electronic applications accepted.

**University of Louisiana at Lafayette,** College of Liberal Arts, Department of Communicative Disorders, Lafayette, LA 70504. Offers applied language and speech sciences (PhD); speech pathology and audiology (MS). *Accreditation:* ASHA (one or more programs are accredited). *Entrance requirements:* For master's, GRE General Test, minimum GPA of 2.75. Additional exam requirements/recommendations for international students: required—TOEFL (minimum score 550 paper-based). *Expenses: Tuition, area resident:* Full-time $5511; part-time $1630 per credit hour. Tuition, state resident: full-time $5511; part-time $1630 per credit hour. Tuition, nonresident: full-time $19,239; part-time $2409 per credit hour. *Required fees:* $46,637.

**University of Louisiana at Monroe,** Graduate School, College of Health Sciences, Department of Speech-Language Pathology, Monroe, LA 71209-0001. Offers MS. *Accreditation:* ASHA. *Faculty:* 8 full-time (7 women). *Students:* 70 full-time (62 women), 33 part-time (31 women); includes 22 minority (17 Black or African American, non-Hispanic/Latino; 2 Asian, non-Hispanic/Latino; 1 Hispanic/Latino; 1 Native Hawaiian or other Pacific Islander, non-Hispanic/Latino; 1 Two or more races, non-Hispanic/Latino). Average age 36. 83 applicants, 25% accepted, 21 enrolled. In 2019, 18 master's awarded. *Degree requirements:* For master's, thesis optional, internships. *Entrance requirements:* For master's, GRE General Test (combined score of 286), minimum GPA of 2.5; 30 undergraduate credit hours in speech-language pathology. Additional exam requirements/recommendations for international students: required—TOEFL (minimum score 500 paper-based; 61 iBT); recommended—IELTS (minimum score 5.5). *Application deadline:* For fall admission, 2/1 for domestic and international students; for spring admission, 9/1 for domestic and international students. Applications are processed on a rolling basis. Application fee: $55. Electronic applications accepted. *Expenses: Tuition, area resident:* Full-time $6489. Tuition, state resident: full-time $6489. Tuition, nonresident: full-time $18,989. *Required fees:* $2748. Tuition and fees vary according to course load and program. *Financial support:* In 2019–20, 47 students received support. Research assistantships with full tuition reimbursements available, career-related internships or fieldwork, Federal Work-Study, scholarships/grants, and unspecified assistantships available. Financial award application deadline: 2/15; financial award applicants required to submit FAFSA. *Unit head:* Dr. David Irwin, Program Director, 318-342-1392, E-mail: irwin@ulm.edu. *Application contact:* Dr. David Irwin, Program Director, 318-342-1392, E-mail: irwin@ulm.edu.
Website: http://www.ulm.edu/slp/

**University of Louisville,** School of Medicine, Department of Speech-Language Pathology, Louisville, KY 40292-0001. Offers audiology (Au D); speech-language pathology (MS). *Accreditation:* ASHA. *Faculty:* 5 full-time (4 women), 2 part-time/adjunct (both women). *Students:* 63 full-time (61 women), 1 (woman) part-time; includes 1 minority (Two or more races, non-Hispanic/Latino). Average age 25. 154 applicants, 19% accepted, 26 enrolled. In 2019, 24 master's awarded. *Degree requirements:* For master's, comprehensive exam, thesis optional. *Entrance requirements:* For master's, GRE. Additional exam requirements/recommendations for international students: required—TOEFL (minimum score 79 iBT); recommended—IELTS. *Application deadline:* For fall admission, 2/1 priority date for domestic and international students. Application fee: $65. Electronic applications accepted. *Expenses: Tuition, area resident:* Full-time $13,000; part-time $723 per credit hour. Tuition, state resident: full-time $13,000; part-time $723 per credit hour. Tuition, nonresident: full-time $27,114; part-time $1507 per credit hour. *International tuition:* $27,114 full-time. *Required fees:* $196. Tuition and fees vary according to program and reciprocity agreements. *Financial support:* In 2019–20, 5 students received support. Stipends available. Financial award application deadline: 3/1; financial award applicants required to submit FAFSA. *Unit head:* Dr. Jeffrey M. Bumpous, Professor and Department Chair, 502-561-7268, Fax: 502-561-7280, E-mail: jmbump01@louisville.edu. *Application contact:* Dr. Alan F. Smith, Associate Professor and Program Director, 502-852-5274, Fax: 502-852-0865, E-mail: afsmit01@louisville.edu.
Website: https://louisville.edu/medicine/degrees/speechpathology

**University of Maine,** Graduate School, College of Natural Sciences, Forestry, and Agriculture, Department of Communication Sciences and Disorders, Orono, ME 04469. Offers MA. *Accreditation:* ASHA. *Faculty:* 9 full-time (8 women), 2 part-time/adjunct (1 woman). *Students:* 35 full-time (33 women); includes 1 minority (Hispanic/Latino), 6 international. Average age 25. 81 applicants, 62% accepted, 19 enrolled. In 2019, 14 master's awarded. *Degree requirements:* For master's, comprehensive exam. *Entrance requirements:* For master's, GRE General Test. Additional exam requirements/recommendations for international students: required—TOEFL (minimum score 80 paper-based), IELTS (minimum score 6.5), PTE (minimum score 60). *Application deadline:* For fall admission, 1/15 priority date for domestic students, 1/15 for international students. Applications are processed on a rolling basis. Application fee: $65. Electronic applications accepted. *Expenses: Tuition, area resident:* Full-time $8100; part-time $450 per credit hour. Tuition, state resident: full-time $8100; part-time $450 per credit hour. Tuition, nonresident: full-time $26,388; part-time $1466 per credit hour. *International tuition:* $26,388 full-time. *Required fees:* $1257; $278 per semester. Tuition and fees vary according to course load. *Financial support:* In 2019–20, 10 students received support, including 5 research assistantships with full tuition reimbursements available (averaging $7,800 per year); teaching assistantships, career-related internships or fieldwork, Federal Work-Study, institutionally sponsored loans, scholarships/grants, tuition waivers (full and partial), and unspecified assistantships also available. Support available to part-time students. Financial award application deadline: 3/1; financial award applicants required to submit FAFSA. *Unit head:* Dr. Nancy Hall, Chair, 207-581-2006, Fax: 207-581-1953. *Application contact:* Scott G. Delcourt, Assistant Vice President for Graduate Studies and Senior Associate Dean, 207-581-3291, Fax: 207-581-3232, E-mail: graduate@maine.edu.
Website: http://umaine.edu/comscidis/

**The University of Manchester,** School of Psychological Sciences, Manchester, United Kingdom. Offers audiology (M Phil, PhD); clinical psychology (M Phil, PhD, Psy D); psychology (M Phil, PhD).

**University of Mary,** School of Health Sciences, Program in Speech-Language Pathology, Bismarck, ND 58504-9652. Offers MS.

**University of Maryland, College Park,** Academic Affairs, College of Behavioral and Social Sciences, Department of Hearing and Speech Sciences, College Park, MD 20742. Offers audiology (MA, PhD); hearing and speech sciences (Au D); language pathology (MA, PhD); neuroscience (PhD); speech (MA, PhD). *Accreditation:* ASHA (one or more programs are accredited). *Degree requirements:* For master's, thesis optional; for doctorate, thesis/dissertation, written and oral exams. *Entrance requirements:* For master's, GRE General Test, minimum GPA of 3.5, 3 letters of recommendation; for doctorate, GRE General Test, minimum GPA of 3.5. Additional exam requirements/recommendations for international students: required—TOEFL. Electronic applications accepted.

**University of Massachusetts Amherst,** Graduate School, School of Public Health and Health Sciences, Department of Communication Disorders, Amherst, MA 01003. Offers audiology (Au D, PhD); clinical audiology (PhD); speech-language pathology (MA, PhD). *Accreditation:* ASHA (one or more programs are accredited). *Program availability:* Part-time. Terminal master's awarded for partial completion of doctoral program. *Degree requirements:* For master's, thesis optional; for doctorate, comprehensive exam, thesis/dissertation. *Entrance requirements:* For master's and doctorate, GRE General Test. Additional exam requirements/recommendations for international students: required—TOEFL (minimum score 550 paper-based; 80 iBT), IELTS (minimum score 6.5). Electronic applications accepted.

**University of Memphis,** Graduate School, School of Communication Sciences and Disorders, Memphis, TN 38152. Offers audiology (Au D); communication sciences and disorders (PhD), including hearing sciences and disorders; speech-language pathology (MA). *Accreditation:* ASHA. *Program availability:* Part-time. *Faculty:* 17 full-time (15 women), 3 part-time/adjunct (2 women). *Students:* 127 full-time (117 women), 20 part-time (17 women); includes 19 minority (10 Black or African American, non-Hispanic/Latino; 5 Asian, non-Hispanic/Latino; 3 Hispanic/Latino; 1 Two or more races, non-Hispanic/Latino), 4 international. Average age 25. 88 applicants, 95% accepted, 35 enrolled. In 2019, 21 master's, 17 doctorates awarded. Terminal master's awarded for partial completion of doctoral program. *Degree requirements:* For master's, comprehensive exam, thesis or alternative, clinical practicum; for doctorate, comprehensive exam, thesis/dissertation (for some programs), qualifying exam, research project, externship. *Entrance requirements:* For master's, GRE General Test, minimum GPA of 3.0, three letters of recommendation, personal statement, ASHA certification; for doctorate, GRE General Test, minimum GPA of 3.0, three letters of recommendation, personal statement, curriculum vitae, interview. Additional exam requirements/recommendations for international students: required—TOEFL (minimum score 550 paper-based; 79 iBT). *Application deadline:* For fall admission, 2/1 priority date for domestic students. Applications are processed on a rolling basis. Application fee: $35 ($60 for international students). Electronic applications accepted. *Expenses: Tuition, area resident:* Full-time $9216; part-time $512 per credit hour. Tuition, state resident: full-time $9216; part-time $512 per credit hour. Tuition, nonresident: full-time $12,672; part-time $704 per credit hour. *International tuition:* $16,128 full-time. *Required fees:* $1530; $85 per credit hour. Tuition and fees vary according to program. *Financial support:* Research assistantships with full tuition reimbursements, Federal Work-Study, scholarships/grants, and unspecified assistantships available. Financial award application deadline: 2/1; financial award applicants required to submit FAFSA. *Unit head:* Dr. Linda Jarmulowicz, Dean, 901-678-5800, Fax: 901-525-1282, E-mail: ljrmlwcz@memphis.edu. *Application contact:* Dr. Lisa Mendel, Interim Associate Dean of Graduate Studies, 901-678-5800, E-mail: lmendel@memphis.edu.
Website: http://www.memphis.edu/csd

**University of Minnesota, Duluth,** Graduate School, College of Education and Human Service Professions, Department of Communication Sciences and Disorders, Duluth, MN 55812-2496. Offers MA. *Accreditation:* ASHA. *Program availability:* Part-time. *Degree requirements:* For master's, research project, oral exam. *Entrance requirements:* For master's, minimum GPA of 3.0, undergraduate degree in communication sciences and disorders. Additional exam requirements/recommendations for international students: required—TOEFL (minimum score 550 paper-based).

**University of Minnesota, Twin Cities Campus,** Graduate School, College of Liberal Arts, Department of Speech-Language-Hearing Sciences, Minneapolis, MN 55455. Offers audiology (Au D); speech-language pathology (MA); speech-language-hearing sciences (PhD). *Accreditation:* ASHA. Terminal master's awarded for partial completion of doctoral program. *Degree requirements:* For master's, thesis, 375 client contact hours; for doctorate, comprehensive exam, thesis/dissertation. *Entrance requirements:* For master's and doctorate, GRE General Test, minimum GPA of 3.0. Additional exam requirements/recommendations for international students: required—TOEFL. Electronic applications accepted.

**University of Mississippi,** Graduate School, School of Applied Sciences, University, MS 38677. Offers communicative disorders (MS); criminal justice (MCJ); exercise science (MS); food and nutrition services (MS); health and kinesiology (PhD); health promotion (MS); nutrition and hospitality management (PhD); park and recreation management (MA); social welfare (PhD); social work (MSW). *Students:* 188 full-time (149 women), 37 part-time (18 women); includes 47 minority (35 Black or African American, non-Hispanic/Latino; 2 American Indian or Alaska Native, non-Hispanic/Latino; 1 Asian, non-Hispanic/Latino; 5 Hispanic/Latino; 1 Native Hawaiian or other Pacific Islander, non-Hispanic/Latino; 3 Two or more races, non-Hispanic/Latino), 23 international. Average age 26. *Expenses:* Tuition, state resident: full-time $8718; part-time $484.25 per credit hour. Tuition, nonresident: full-time $24,990; part-time $1388.25 per credit hour. *Required fees:* $100; $4.16 per credit hour. *Unit head:* Dr. Peter Grandjean, Dean of Applied Sciences, 662-915-7900, Fax: 662-915-7901, E-mail: applsci@olemiss.edu. *Application contact:* Temeka Smith, Graduate Activities Specialist for Admissions, 662-915-7474, Fax: 662-915-7577, E-mail: gschool@olemiss.edu.
Website: applsci@olemiss.edu

**University of Missouri,** School of Health Professions, Program in Communication Science and Disorders, Columbia, MO 65211. Offers MHS, PhD, MHS/PhD. *Accreditation:* ASHA (one or more programs are accredited). *Entrance requirements:* For master's, GRE General Test, minimum GPA of 3.0. Additional exam requirements/recommendations for international students: required—TOEFL. Electronic applications accepted.

**University of Montana,** Graduate School, Phyllis J. Washington College of Education and Human Sciences, Department of Communicative Sciences and Disorders, Missoula, MT 59812. Offers speech-language pathology (MS, Postbaccalaureate Certificate). *Accreditation:* ASHA.

**University of Montevallo,** College of Arts and Sciences, Department of Communication Science and Disorders, Montevallo, AL 35115. Offers MS. *Accreditation:* ASHA. *Students:* 54 full-time (52 women), 1 (woman) part-time; includes 4 minority (2 Black or African American, non-Hispanic/Latino; 1 Native Hawaiian or other Pacific Islander, non-Hispanic/Latino; 1 Two or more races, non-Hispanic/Latino). In 2019, 23 master's awarded. *Degree requirements:* For master's, comprehensive exam. *Entrance*

*requirements:* For master's, GRE General Test, MAT. Additional exam requirements/recommendations for international students: required—TOEFL (minimum score 550 paper-based). *Application deadline:* For fall admission, 7/15 for domestic students; for spring admission, 11/15 for domestic students. Application fee: $30. *Expenses: Tuition, area resident:* Full-time $10,512; part-time $438 per contact hour. Tuition, state resident: full-time $10,512; part-time $438 per credit hour. Tuition, nonresident: full-time $22,464; part-time $936 per credit hour. *International tuition:* $22,464 full-time. *Financial support:* Federal Work-Study, scholarships/grants, and unspecified assistantships available. *Unit head:* Dr. Claire Edwards, Chair, 205-665-6724, E-mail: edwardsc@montevallo.edu. *Application contact:* Christine Soria, Graduate Admissions Assistant, 205-665-6510, E-mail: csoria@montevallo.edu.
Website: http://www.montevallo.edu/csd/

**University of Nebraska at Kearney,** College of Education, Department of Communication Disorders, Kearney, NE 68849. Offers speech/language pathology (MS Ed). *Accreditation:* ASHA. *Faculty:* 5 full-time (4 women). *Students:* 36 full-time (35 women); includes 2 minority (1 Asian, non-Hispanic/Latino; 1 Two or more races, non-Hispanic/Latino), 1 international. Average age 25. 92 applicants, 45% accepted, 17 enrolled. In 2019, 18 master's awarded. *Degree requirements:* For master's, comprehensive exam, thesis optional. *Entrance requirements:* For master's, GRE General Test, personal statement, letters of recommendation, video response. Additional exam requirements/recommendations for international students: required—TOEFL (minimum score 550 paper-based; 79 iBT), IELTS (minimum score 6.5). *Application deadline:* For fall admission, 1/15 for domestic and international students. Application fee: $45. Electronic applications accepted. *Expenses: Tuition, area resident:* Full-time $4662; part-time $259 per credit hour. Tuition, nonresident: full-time $10,242; part-time $569 per credit hour. *International tuition:* $10,242 full-time. *Required fees:* $1222; $381.50 per term. Full-time tuition and fees vary according to course load, campus/location and program. *Financial support:* In 2019–20, 1 student received support, including 2 research assistantships with full tuition reimbursements available (averaging $10,980 per year), 1 teaching assistantship with full tuition reimbursement available (averaging $10,980 per year); career-related internships or fieldwork and unspecified assistantships also available. Support available to part-time students. Financial award application deadline: 2/28; financial award applicants required to submit FAFSA. *Unit head:* Dr. Whitney Schneider-Cline, Graduate Program Chair, 308-856-8612, Fax: 308-865-8397, E-mail: schneiderwm@unk.edu. *Application contact:* Linda Johnson, Director, Graduate Admissions and Programs, 800-717-7881, Fax: 308-865-8837, E-mail: gradstudies@unk.edu.
Website: http://www.unk.edu/academics/cdis/index.php

**University of Nebraska at Omaha,** Graduate Studies, College of Education, Department of Special Education and Communication Disorders, Omaha, NE 68182. Offers special education (MS); speech-language pathology (MS). *Accreditation:* ASHA; NCATE. *Program availability:* Part-time, evening/weekend. *Degree requirements:* For master's, comprehensive exam, thesis (for some programs). *Entrance requirements:* For master's, minimum GPA of 3.0, statement of purpose, 2 letters of recommendation, copy of teaching certificate. Additional exam requirements/recommendations for international students: required—TOEFL, IELTS, PTE. Electronic applications accepted.

**University of Nebraska–Lincoln,** Graduate College, College of Education and Human Sciences, Department of Special Education and Communication Disorders, Program in Speech-Language Pathology and Audiology, Lincoln, NE 68588. Offers audiology and hearing science (Au D); speech-language pathology and audiology (MS). *Accreditation:* ASHA. *Degree requirements:* For master's, thesis optional. *Entrance requirements:* For master's, GRE. Additional exam requirements/recommendations for international students: required—TOEFL (minimum score 500 paper-based). Electronic applications accepted.

**University of Nevada, Reno,** Graduate School, Department of Speech Pathology and Audiology, Reno, NV 89557. Offers speech pathology (PhD); speech pathology and audiology (MS). *Accreditation:* ASHA (one or more programs are accredited). Terminal master's awarded for partial completion of doctoral program. *Degree requirements:* For master's, thesis optional; for doctorate, thesis/dissertation. *Entrance requirements:* For master's, GRE General Test, minimum GPA of 2.75; for doctorate, GRE General Test, minimum GPA of 3.0. Additional exam requirements/recommendations for international students: required—TOEFL (minimum score 500 paper-based; 61 iBT), IELTS (minimum score 6). Electronic applications accepted.

**University of New Hampshire,** Graduate School, College of Health and Human Services, Department of Communication Sciences and Disorders, Durham, NH 03824. Offers adult neurogenic communication (MS); communication sciences and disorders (MS); early childhood intervention (MS); language and literacy disorders (MS). *Accreditation:* ASHA. *Program availability:* Part-time. *Students:* 53 full-time (51 women); includes 2 minority (both Two or more races, non-Hispanic/Latino). Average age 24. 107 applicants, 37% accepted. In 2019, 42 master's awarded. *Entrance requirements:* For master's, GRE General Test. Additional exam requirements/recommendations for international students: required—TOEFL (minimum score 550 paper-based; 80 iBT), IELTS, PTE. *Application deadline:* For summer admission, 1/15 for domestic students. Application fee: $65. Electronic applications accepted. *Financial support:* In 2019–20, 13 students received support, including 10 teaching assistantships; fellowships, research assistantships, career-related internships or fieldwork, Federal Work-Study, scholarships/grants, and tuition waivers (full and partial) also available. Support available to part-time students. Financial award application deadline: 2/15. *Unit head:* Don Robin, Chair, 603-862-3836. *Application contact:* Jane Dodge, Administrative Assistant III, 603-862-0965, E-mail: jane.dodge@unh.edu.
Website: http://chhs.unh.edu/csd

**University of New Mexico,** Graduate Studies, College of Arts and Sciences, Program in Speech-Language Pathology, Albuquerque, NM 87131-2039. Offers MS. *Accreditation:* ASHA. *Degree requirements:* For master's, comprehensive exam, thesis optional. *Entrance requirements:* For master's, GRE General Test, minimum GPA of 3.4 in speech and hearing sciences coursework. Additional exam requirements/recommendations for international students: required—TOEFL (minimum score 550 paper-based; 80 iBT). Electronic applications accepted. *Expenses:* Tuition, state resident: full-time $7633; part-time $972 per year. Tuition, nonresident: full-time $22,586; part-time $3840 per year. *International tuition:* $23,292 full-time. *Required fees:* $8608. Tuition and fees vary according to course level, course load, degree level, program and student level.

**The University of North Carolina at Greensboro,** Graduate School, School of Health and Human Sciences, Department of Communication Sciences and Disorders, Greensboro, NC 27412-5001. Offers speech language pathology (PhD); speech pathology and audiology (MA). *Accreditation:* ASHA. *Degree requirements:* For master's, thesis or alternative. *Entrance requirements:* For master's, GRE General Test. Additional exam requirements/recommendations for international students: required—TOEFL. Electronic applications accepted.

**University of North Dakota,** Graduate School, College of Arts and Sciences, Department of Communication Sciences and Disorders, Grand Forks, ND 58202. Offers speech-language pathology (MS). *Accreditation:* ASHA. *Program availability:* Part-time.

*Degree requirements:* For master's, comprehensive exam, thesis or alternative. *Entrance requirements:* For master's, GRE General Test, minimum GPA of 3.0. Additional exam requirements/recommendations for international students: required—TOEFL (minimum score 550 paper-based; 79 iBT), IELTS (minimum score 6.5). Electronic applications accepted.

**University of Northern Colorado,** Graduate School, College of Natural and Health Sciences, School of Human Sciences, Program in Audiology and Speech-Language Sciences, Greeley, CO 80639. Offers audiology (Au D); speech-language pathology (MA). *Accreditation:* ASHA (one or more programs are accredited). *Program availability:* Part-time, evening/weekend, online learning. *Degree requirements:* For master's, comprehensive exam, thesis or alternative; for doctorate, comprehensive exam, thesis/dissertation. *Entrance requirements:* For master's and doctorate, GRE General Test. Electronic applications accepted.

**University of Northern Iowa,** Graduate College, College of Humanities, Arts and Sciences, Department of Communication Sciences and Disorders, Cedar Falls, IA 50614. Offers speech-language pathology (MA). *Accreditation:* ASHA. *Program availability:* Part-time, evening/weekend. *Degree requirements:* For master's, comprehensive exam, thesis or alternative. *Entrance requirements:* For master's, GRE, minimum GPA of 3.0. Additional exam requirements/recommendations for international students: required—TOEFL (minimum score 500 paper-based; 61 iBT).

**University of North Florida,** College of Education and Human Services, Department of Exceptional, Deaf, and Interpreter Education, Jacksonville, FL 32224. Offers American Sign Language (MS); American Sign Language/English interpreting (M Ed); applied behavior analysis (M Ed); autism (M Ed); deaf education (M Ed); disability services (M Ed); exceptional student education (M Ed). *Accreditation:* NCATE. *Program availability:* Part-time, evening/weekend. *Entrance requirements:* For master's, GRE General Test, minimum GPA of 3.0 in last 60 hours, interview, 3 letters of recommendation. Additional exam requirements/recommendations for international students: required—TOEFL (minimum score 500 paper-based). Electronic applications accepted.

**University of North Texas,** Toulouse Graduate School, Denton, TX 76203-5459. Offers accounting (MS); applied anthropology (MA, MS); applied behavior analysis (Certificate); applied geography (MA); applied technology and performance improvement (M Ed, MS); art education (MA); art history (MA); arts leadership (Certificate); audiology (Au D); behavior analysis (MS); behavioral science (PhD); biochemistry and molecular biology (MS); biology (MA, MS); biomedical engineering (MS); business analysis (MS); chemistry (MS); clinical health psychology (PhD); communication studies (MA, MS); computer engineering (MS); computer science (MS); counseling (M Ed, MS), including clinical mental health counseling (MS), college and university counseling, elementary school counseling, secondary school counseling; creative writing (MA); criminal justice (MS); curriculum and instruction (M Ed); decision sciences (MBA); design (MA, MFA), including fashion design (MFA), innovation studies, interior design (MFA); early childhood studies (MS); economics (MS); educational leadership (M Ed, Ed D); educational psychology (MS, PhD), including family studies (MS), gifted and talented (MS), human development (MS), learning and cognition (MS), research, measurement and evaluation (MS); electrical engineering (MS); emergency management (MPA); engineering technology (MS); English (MA); English as a second language (MA); environmental science (MS); finance (MBA, MS); financial management (MPA); French (MA); health services management (MBA); higher education (M Ed, Ed D); history (MA, MS); hospitality management (MS); human resources management (MPA); information science (MS); information systems (PhD); information technologies (MBA); interdisciplinary studies (MA, MS); international studies (MA); international sustainable tourism (MS); jazz studies (MM); journalism (MA, MJ, Graduate Certificate), including interactive and virtual digital communication (Graduate Certificate), narrative journalism (Graduate Certificate), public relations (Graduate Certificate); kinesiology (MS); linguistics (MA); local government management (MPA); logistics (PhD); logistics and supply chain management (MBA); long-term care, senior housing, and aging services (MA); management (PhD); marketing (MBA); mathematics (MA, MS); mechanical and energy engineering (MS, PhD); music (MA), including ethnomusicology, music theory, musicology, performance; music composition (PhD); music education (MM Ed, PhD); nonprofit management (MPA); operations and supply chain management (MBA); performance (MM, DMA); philosophy (MA); political science (MA); professional and technical communication (MA); radio, television and film (MA, MFA); rehabilitation counseling (Certificate); sociology (MA); Spanish (MA); special education (M Ed); speech-language pathology (MA); strategic management (MBA); studio art (MFA); teaching (M Ed); MBA/MS. *Program availability:* Part-time, evening/weekend, online learning. Terminal master's awarded for partial completion of doctoral program. *Degree requirements:* For master's, variable foreign language requirement, comprehensive exam (for some programs), thesis (for some programs); for doctorate, variable foreign language requirement, comprehensive exam (for some programs), thesis/dissertation; for other advanced degree, variable foreign language requirement, comprehensive exam (for some programs). *Entrance requirements:* For master's and doctorate, GRE, GMAT. Additional exam requirements/recommendations for international students: required—TOEFL (minimum score 550 paper-based; 79 iBT). Electronic applications accepted.

**University of Oklahoma Health Sciences Center,** Graduate College, College of Allied Health, Department of Communication Sciences and Disorders, Oklahoma City, OK 73190. Offers audiology (MS, Au D, PhD); communication sciences and disorders (Certificate), including reading, speech-language pathology; education of the deaf (MS); speech-language pathology (MS, PhD). *Accreditation:* ASHA (one or more programs are accredited). *Program availability:* Part-time. Terminal master's awarded for partial completion of doctoral program. *Degree requirements:* For master's, comprehensive exam, thesis optional; for doctorate, one foreign language, comprehensive exam, thesis/dissertation. *Entrance requirements:* For master's and doctorate, GRE General Test, 3 letters of recommendation. Additional exam requirements/recommendations for international students: required—TOEFL (minimum score 550 paper-based).

**University of Oregon,** Graduate School, College of Education, Eugene, OR 97403. Offers communication disorders and sciences (MA, MS, PhD); counseling psychology (PhD); couples and family therapy (MS); critical and sociocultural studies in education (PhD); curriculum and teacher education (MA, MS); educational leadership (MS, D Ed, PhD); prevention science (M Ed, MS, PhD); school psychology (MS, PhD); special education (M Ed, MA, MS, PhD). *Accreditation:* ASHA. *Program availability:* Part-time. Terminal master's awarded for partial completion of doctoral program. *Degree requirements:* For master's, exam, paper, or project; for doctorate, comprehensive exam, thesis/dissertation. *Entrance requirements:* Additional exam requirements/recommendations for international students: required—TOEFL.

**University of Ottawa,** Faculty of Graduate and Postdoctoral Studies, Faculty of Health Sciences, School of Rehabilitation Sciences, Ottawa, ON K1N 6N5, Canada. Offers audiology (M Sc); orthophony (M Sc). *Program availability:* Part-time, evening/weekend. *Entrance requirements:* For master's, honors degree or equivalent, minimum B average. Electronic applications accepted.

## Communication Disorders

**University of Pittsburgh,** School of Health and Rehabilitation Sciences, Department of Communication Science and Disorders, Pittsburgh, PA 15260. Offers audiology (MA, MS, Au D); communication science and disorders (PhD); medical speech language pathology (CScD); speech language pathology (MA, MS). *Accreditation:* ASHA (one or more programs are accredited). *Faculty:* 19 full-time (12 women), 7 part-time/adjunct (5 women). *Students:* 124 full-time (114 women), 16 part-time (14 women); includes 11 minority (1 Black or African American, non-Hispanic/Latino; 4 Asian, non-Hispanic/Latino; 6 Hispanic/Latino), 4 international. Average age 25. 409 applicants, 48% accepted, 65 enrolled. In 2019, 49 master's, 21 doctorates awarded. *Degree requirements:* For master's, comprehensive exam, thesis (for some programs); for doctorate, comprehensive exam, thesis/dissertation (for some programs). *Entrance requirements:* For master's and doctorate, GRE General Test. Additional exam requirements/recommendations for international students: required—IELTS, International applicants may provide Duolingo English Test, IELTS or TOEFL scores to verify English language proficiency. Electronic applications accepted. *Financial support:* In 2019–20, 12 students received support, including 10 research assistantships with full tuition reimbursements available (averaging $18,000 per year), 2 teaching assistantships with full tuition reimbursements available (averaging $18,000 per year). *Unit head:* Dr. Bernard Rousseau, Chair and Professor, Department of Communication Science and Disorders, E-mail: rousseau.csd@pitt.edu. *Application contact:* Jessica Maguire, Director of Admissions, 412-383-6557, Fax: 412-383-6535, E-mail: maguire@pitt.edu.
Website: http://www.shrs.pitt.edu/csd

**University of Puerto Rico - Medical Sciences Campus,** School of Health Professions, Program in Audiology, San Juan, PR 00936-5067. Offers Au D. *Accreditation:* ASHA.

**University of Puerto Rico - Medical Sciences Campus,** School of Health Professions, Program in Speech-Language Pathology, San Juan, PR 00936-5067. Offers MS. *Accreditation:* ASHA. *Degree requirements:* For master's, one foreign language, comprehensive exam, thesis or alternative. *Entrance requirements:* For master's, EXADEP, interview; previous course work in linguistics, statistics, human development, and basic concepts in speech-language pathology; minimum GPA of 2.5.

**University of Redlands,** College of Arts and Sciences, Department of Communication Sciences and Disorders, Redlands, CA 92373-0999. Offers MS. *Accreditation:* ASHA. *Degree requirements:* For master's, final exam. *Entrance requirements:* For master's, GMAT or GRE, minimum GPA of 3.0, 3 letters of recommendation. Additional exam requirements/recommendations for international students: required—TOEFL (minimum score 550 paper-based). Electronic applications accepted. *Expenses:* Contact institution.

**University of Rhode Island,** Graduate School, College of Health Sciences, Department of Communicative Disorders, Kingston, RI 02881. Offers speech-language pathology (MS). *Accreditation:* ASHA. *Program availability:* Part-time. *Faculty:* 11 full-time (10 women). *Students:* 47 full-time (44 women), 1 (woman) part-time; includes 3 minority (1 Asian, non-Hispanic/Latino; 2 Hispanic/Latino). 126 applicants, 45% accepted, 22 enrolled. In 2019, 16 master's awarded. *Entrance requirements:* Additional exam requirements/recommendations for international students: required—TOEFL. *Application deadline:* For fall admission, 2/15 for domestic and international students; for spring admission, 10/15 for domestic and international students. Application fee: $65. Electronic applications accepted. *Expenses: Tuition, area resident:* Full-time $13,734; part-time $763 per credit. Tuition, state resident: full-time $13,734; part-time $763 per credit. Tuition, nonresident: full-time $26,512; part-time $1473 per credit. *International tuition:* $26,512 full-time. *Required fees:* $1780; $52 per credit. $35 per term. One-time fee: $165. *Financial support:* In 2019–20, 4 teaching assistantships with tuition reimbursements (averaging $9,493 per year) were awarded. Financial award application deadline: 2/1; financial award applicants required to submit FAFSA. *Unit head:* Dr. Dana Kovarsky, Chair, 401-874-2735, E-mail: dana@uri.edu. *Application contact:* Dr. Mikyong Kim, Graduate Program Coordinator, 401-874-4728, E-mail: mikyong@uri.edu.
Website: http://www.uri.edu/hss/cmd/

**University of South Alabama,** Pat Capps Covey College of Allied Health Professions, Department of Speech Pathology and Audiology, Mobile, AL 36688-0002. Offers audiology (Au D); communication sciences and disorders (PhD); speech-language pathology (MS). *Accreditation:* ASHA. *Faculty:* 17 full-time (16 women), 1 (woman) part-time/adjunct. *Students:* 100 full-time (94 women); includes 7 minority (2 Black or African American, non-Hispanic/Latino; 2 American Indian or Alaska Native, non-Hispanic/Latino; 1 Asian, non-Hispanic/Latino; 2 Hispanic/Latino), 7 international. Average age 24. 240 applicants, 60% accepted, 44 enrolled. In 2019, 25 master's, 15 doctorates awarded. *Degree requirements:* For master's, comprehensive exam, thesis optional; for doctorate, thesis/dissertation. *Entrance requirements:* For master's and doctorate, GRE. Additional exam requirements/recommendations for international students: required—TOEFL (minimum score 600 paper-based; 100 iBT). *Application deadline:* For fall admission, 1/15 for domestic students, 2/1 for international students. Applications are processed on a rolling basis. Application fee: $75. Electronic applications accepted. *Expenses:* Contact institution. *Financial support:* Fellowships, research assistantships, teaching assistantships, career-related internships or fieldwork, Federal Work-Study, institutionally sponsored loans, scholarships/grants, and unspecified assistantships available. Support available to part-time students. Financial award application deadline: 3/31; financial award applicants required to submit FAFSA. *Unit head:* Dr. Elizabeth Adams, Chair, Associate Professor, Department of Speech Pathology & Audiology, 251-445-9596, Fax: 251-445-9376, E-mail: eadams@southalabama.edu. *Application contact:* Dr. Elizabeth Adams, Chair, Associate Professor, Department of Speech Pathology & Audiology, 251-445-9596, Fax: 251-445-9376, E-mail: eadams@southalabama.edu.
Website: http://www.southalabama.edu/colleges/alliedhealth/speechandhearing/

**University of South Carolina,** The Graduate School, Arnold School of Public Health, Department of Communication Sciences and Disorders, Columbia, SC 29208. Offers MCD, MSP, PhD. *Accreditation:* ASHA (one or more programs are accredited). *Program availability:* Online learning. *Degree requirements:* For master's, thesis optional; for doctorate, comprehensive exam, thesis/dissertation. *Entrance requirements:* For master's, GRE General Test, minimum GPA of 3.0; for doctorate, GRE General Test. Electronic applications accepted.

**University of South Dakota,** Graduate School, College of Arts and Sciences, Department of Communication Sciences and Disorders, Vermillion, SD 57069. Offers audiology (Au D); speech-language pathology (MA). *Accreditation:* ASHA (one or more programs are accredited). *Program availability:* Part-time. *Degree requirements:* For master's, comprehensive exam; for doctorate, comprehensive exam, thesis/dissertation. *Entrance requirements:* For master's, GRE General Test, minimum GPA of 3.0. Additional exam requirements/recommendations for international students: required—TOEFL (minimum score 550 paper-based; 79 iBT). Electronic applications accepted.

**University of Southern Mississippi,** College of Nursing and Health Professions, School of Speech and Hearing Sciences, Hattiesburg, MS 39406-0001. Offers MA, MS, Au D. *Accreditation:* ASHA (one or more programs are accredited). *Students:* 82 full-time (79 women); includes 13 minority (10 Black or African American, non-Hispanic/Latino; 1 Asian, non-Hispanic/Latino; 1 Hispanic/Latino; 1 Two or more races, non-Hispanic/Latino), 3 international. 183 applicants, 44% accepted, 35 enrolled. In 2019, 27 master's, 7 doctorates awarded. *Degree requirements:* For master's, comprehensive exam, thesis or alternative; for doctorate, comprehensive exam, thesis/dissertation. *Entrance requirements:* For master's, GRE General Test, minimum GPA of 3.0 in field of study, 2.75 in last 60 hours; for doctorate, GRE General Test, minimum GPA of 3.5. Additional exam requirements/recommendations for international students: required—TOEFL, IELTS. *Application deadline:* For fall admission, 3/1 for domestic and international students; for spring admission, 1/10 priority date for domestic and international students. Application fee: $60. Electronic applications accepted. *Expenses: Tuition, area resident:* Full-time $4393; part-time $488 per credit hour. Tuition, nonresident: full-time $5393; part-time $600 per credit hour. *Required fees:* $6 per semester. *Financial support:* Research assistantships with full and partial tuition reimbursements, teaching assistantships with full and partial tuition reimbursements, career-related internships or fieldwork, Federal Work-Study, institutionally sponsored loans, scholarships/grants, health care benefits, and unspecified assistantships available. Financial award application deadline: 3/15; financial award applicants required to submit FAFSA. *Unit head:* Dr. Edward Goshorn, Chair, 601-266-5217, E-mail: Edward.Goshorn@usm.edu. *Application contact:* Dr. Edward Goshorn, Chair, 601-266-5217, E-mail: Edward.Goshorn@usm.edu.
Website: https://www.usm.edu/speech-hearing-sciences

**University of South Florida,** College of Behavioral and Community Sciences, Department of Communication Sciences and Disorders, Tampa, FL 33620. Offers MS, Au D, PhD. *Accreditation:* ASHA (one or more programs are accredited). *Program availability:* Part-time, evening/weekend, online learning. *Faculty:* 30 full-time (26 women). *Students:* 169 full-time (158 women), 58 part-time (54 women); includes 35 minority (5 Black or African American, non-Hispanic/Latino; 7 Asian, non-Hispanic/Latino; 22 Hispanic/Latino; 1 Two or more races, non-Hispanic/Latino), 7 international. Average age 25. 593 applicants, 16% accepted, 82 enrolled. In 2019, 75 master's, 18 doctorates awarded. *Degree requirements:* For master's, comprehensive exam, thesis (for some programs); for doctorate, comprehensive exam, thesis/dissertation. *Entrance requirements:* For master's, GRE with preferred scores of: 52nd percentile (approx. 151) on the verbal portion OR the 52nd percentile (approx. 4) on the writing section AND the 32nd percentile (approx. 148) on the quantitative section, 3 letters of recommendation; letter of intent; resume; demonstrate the following Essential Functions in accordance with the Council of Academic Programs in CSD; for doctorate, GRE with preferred scores at or above the 33rd percentile on both Verbal and Quantitative sections. GRE writing with a preferred score of 4.00 or better. For CSD program: GRE with preferred scores at the 33rd percentile for Verbal and, Quantitative, and a 3.50 or better on the Writing subtest, 3.5 GPA (for CSD Program); 3 letters of recommendation; letter of intent; demonstration of competency in communication skills as determined by the chairperson or delegate. Additional exam requirements/recommendations for international students: required—TOEFL, TOEFL (minimum score 550 paper-based; 79 iBT) or IELTS (minimum score 6.5). *Application deadline:* For fall admission, 12/1 for domestic and international students; for spring admission, 10/15 for domestic students, 9/15 for international students. Application fee: $30. Electronic applications accepted. *Financial support:* In 2019–20, 82 students received support, including 1 research assistantship with tuition reimbursement available (averaging $10,920 per year), 15 teaching assistantships with tuition reimbursements available (averaging $10,881 per year); career-related internships or fieldwork, traineeships, health care benefits, and unspecified assistantships also available. Financial award application deadline: 2/1; financial award applicants required to submit FAFSA. *Unit head:* Dr. Steven Surrency, Chair/Professor, 813-974-6204, E-mail: surrency@usf.edu. *Application contact:* Dr. Michelle Bourgeois, Graduate Director, 813-974-9778, E-mail: msbourgeois@usf.edu.
Website: http://csd.cbcs.usf.edu/

**University of South Florida,** Innovative Education, Tampa, FL 33620-9951. Offers adult, career and higher education (Graduate Certificate), including college teaching, leadership in developing human resources, leadership in higher education; Africana studies (Graduate Certificate), including diasporas and health disparities, genocide and human rights; aging studies (Graduate Certificate), including gerontology; art research (Graduate Certificate), including museum studies; business foundations (Graduate Certificate); chemical and biomedical engineering (Graduate Certificate), including materials science and engineering, water, health and sustainability; child and family studies (Graduate Certificate), including positive behavior support; civil and industrial engineering (Graduate Certificate), including transportation systems analysis; community and family health (Graduate Certificate), including maternal and child health, social marketing and public health, violence and injury: prevention and intervention, women's health; criminology (Graduate Certificate), including criminal justice administration; data science for public administration (Graduate Certificate); digital humanities (Graduate Certificate); educational measurement and research (Graduate Certificate), including evaluation; English (Graduate Certificate), including comparative literary studies, creative writing, professional and technical communication; entrepreneurship (Graduate Certificate); environmental health (Graduate Certificate), including safety management; epidemiology and biostatistics (Graduate Certificate), including applied biostatistics, biostatistics, concepts and tools of epidemiology, epidemiology, epidemiology of infectious diseases; geography, environment and planning (Graduate Certificate), including community development, environmental policy and management, geographical information systems; geology (Graduate Certificate), including hydrogeology; global health (Graduate Certificate), including disaster management, global health and Latin American and Caribbean studies, global health practice, humanitarian assistance, infection control; government and international affairs (Graduate Certificate), including Cuban studies, globalization studies; health policy and management (Graduate Certificate), including health management and leadership, public health policy and programs; hearing specialist: early intervention (Graduate Certificate); industrial and management systems engineering (Graduate Certificate), including systems engineering, technology management; information studies (Graduate Certificate), including school library media specialist; information systems/decision sciences (Graduate Certificate), including analytics and business intelligence; instructional technology (Graduate Certificate), including distance education, Florida digital/virtual educator, instructional design, multimedia design, Web design; internal medicine, bioethics and medical humanities (Graduate Certificate), including biomedical ethics; Latin American and Caribbean studies (Graduate Certificate); leadership for coastal resiliency planning (Graduate Certificate); mass communications (Graduate Certificate), including multimedia journalism; mathematics and statistics (Graduate Certificate), including mathematics; medicine (Graduate Certificate), including aging and neuroscience, bioinformatics, biotechnology, brain fitness and memory management, clinical investigation, hand and upper limb rehabilitation, health informatics, health sciences, integrative weight management, intellectual property, medicine and gender, metabolic and nutritional medicine, metabolic cardiology, pharmacy sciences; national and competitive intelligence (Graduate Certificate); nursing (Graduate Certificate), including simulation based academic fellowship in advanced pain management; psychological and social foundations (Graduate Certificate), including career counseling, college teaching, diversity in education, mental health counseling, school counseling; public affairs (Graduate Certificate), including nonprofit management, public management, research administration; public health (Graduate Certificate), including

assessing chemical toxicity and public health risks, health equity, pharmacoepidemiology, public health generalist, toxicology, translational research in adolescent behavioral health; public health practices (Graduate Certificate), including planning for healthy communities; rehabilitation and mental health counseling (Graduate Certificate), including integrative mental health care, marriage and family therapy, rehabilitation technology; secondary education (Graduate Certificate), including ESOL, foreign language education: culture and content, foreign language education: professional; social work (Graduate Certificate), including geriatric social work/clinical gerontology; special education (Graduate Certificate), including autism spectrum disorder, disabilities education: severe/profound; world languages (Graduate Certificate), including teaching English as a second language (TESL) or foreign language. *Unit head:* Dr. Cynthia DeLuca, Associate Vice President and Assistant Vice Provost, 813-974-3077, Fax: 813-974-7061, E-mail: deluca@usf.edu. *Application contact:* Owen Hooper, Director, Summer and Alternative Calendar Programs, 813-974-6917, E-mail: hooper@usf.edu.
Website: http://www.usf.edu/innovative-education/

**The University of Tennessee,** Graduate School, College of Arts and Sciences, Department of Audiology and Speech Pathology, Program in Audiology, Knoxville, TN 37996. Offers MA. *Degree requirements:* For master's, thesis or alternative. *Entrance requirements:* For master's, GRE General Test, minimum GPA of 2.7. Additional exam requirements/recommendations for international students: required—TOEFL. Electronic applications accepted.

**The University of Tennessee,** Graduate School, College of Arts and Sciences, Department of Audiology and Speech Pathology, Program in Speech and Hearing Science, Knoxville, TN 37996. Offers audiology (PhD); hearing science (PhD); speech and language pathology (PhD); speech and language science (PhD). *Degree requirements:* For doctorate, thesis/dissertation. *Entrance requirements:* For doctorate, GRE General Test, minimum GPA of 2.7. Additional exam requirements/recommendations for international students: required—TOEFL. Electronic applications accepted.

**The University of Tennessee,** Graduate School, College of Arts and Sciences, Department of Audiology and Speech Pathology, Program in Speech Pathology, Knoxville, TN 37996. Offers MA. *Degree requirements:* For master's, thesis or alternative. *Entrance requirements:* For master's, GRE General Test, minimum GPA of 2.7. Additional exam requirements/recommendations for international students: required—TOEFL. Electronic applications accepted.

**The University of Tennessee,** Graduate School, College of Education, Health and Human Sciences, Program in Education, Knoxville, TN 37996. Offers art education (MS); counseling education (PhD); cultural studies in education (PhD); curriculum (MS, Ed S); curriculum, educational research and evaluation (Ed D, PhD); early childhood education (PhD); early childhood special education (MS); education of deaf and hard of hearing (MS); educational administration and policy studies (Ed D, PhD); educational administration and supervision (Ed S); educational psychology (Ed D, PhD); elementary education (MS, Ed S); elementary teaching (MS); English education (MS, Ed S); exercise science (PhD); foreign language/ESL education (MS, Ed S); instructional technology (MS, Ed D, PhD, Ed S); literacy, language and ESL education (PhD); literacy, language education, and ESL education (Ed D); mathematics education (MS, Ed S); modified and comprehensive special education (MS); reading education (MS, Ed S); school counseling (Ed S); school psychology (PhD, Ed S); science education (MS, Ed S); secondary teaching (MS); social foundations (MS); social science education (MS, Ed S); socio-cultural foundations of sports and education (PhD); special education (Ed S); teacher education (Ed D, PhD). *Accreditation:* NCATE. *Program availability:* Part-time, evening/weekend. *Degree requirements:* For master's and Ed S, thesis optional; for doctorate, variable foreign language requirement, thesis/dissertation. *Entrance requirements:* For master's, minimum GPA of 2.7; for doctorate and Ed S, GRE General Test, minimum GPA of 2.7. Additional exam requirements/recommendations for international students: required—TOEFL. Electronic applications accepted.

**The University of Tennessee Health Science Center,** College of Graduate Health Sciences, Memphis, TN 38163. Offers biomedical engineering (MS, PhD); biomedical sciences (PhD); dental sciences (MDS); epidemiology (MS); health outcomes and policy research (PhD); laboratory research and management (MS); nursing science (PhD); pharmaceutical sciences (PhD); pharmacology (MS); speech and hearing science (PhD); DDS/PhD; DNP/PhD; MD/PhD; Pharm D/PhD. Terminal master's awarded for partial completion of doctoral program. *Degree requirements:* For master's, comprehensive exam, thesis; for doctorate, thesis/dissertation, oral and written preliminary and comprehensive exams. *Entrance requirements:* For master's and doctorate, GRE General Test, minimum GPA of 3.0. Additional exam requirements/recommendations for international students: recommended—TOEFL (minimum score 79 iBT), IELTS (minimum score 6.5). Electronic applications accepted. *Expenses:* Contact institution.

**The University of Tennessee Health Science Center,** College of Health Professions, Memphis, TN 38163-0002. Offers audiology (MS, Au D); clinical laboratory science (MSCLS); cytopathology practice (MCP); health informatics and information management (MHIIM); occupational therapy (MOT); physical therapy (DPT, ScDPT); physician assistant (MMS); speech-language pathology (MS). *Accreditation:* AOTA; APTA. *Program availability:* Part-time, evening/weekend, online learning. Terminal master's awarded for partial completion of doctoral program. *Degree requirements:* For master's, comprehensive exam, thesis; for doctorate, comprehensive exam, residency. *Entrance requirements:* For master's, GRE (MOT, MSCLS), minimum GPA of 3.0, 3 letters of reference, national accreditation (MSCLS), GRE if GPA is less than 3.0 (MCP); for doctorate, GRE. Additional exam requirements/recommendations for international students: required—TOEFL (minimum score 550 paper-based; 80 iBT). Electronic applications accepted. *Expenses:* Contact institution.

**The University of Texas at Austin,** Graduate School, College of Communication, Department of Communication Sciences and Disorders, Austin, TX 78712-1111. Offers audiology (Au D); communication sciences and disorders (PhD); speech language pathology (MA). *Accreditation:* ASHA (one or more programs are accredited). *Entrance requirements:* For master's and doctorate, GRE General Test.

**The University of Texas at Dallas,** School of Behavioral and Brain Sciences, Program in Communication Sciences and Disorders, Richardson, TX 75080. Offers audiology (Au D); communication disorders (MS); communication sciences and disorders (PhD). *Program availability:* Part-time, evening/weekend. *Faculty:* 15 full-time (9 women), 19 part-time/adjunct (18 women). *Students:* 289 full-time (279 women), 19 part-time (18 women); includes 68 minority (8 Black or African American, non-Hispanic/Latino; 24 Asian, non-Hispanic/Latino; 24 Hispanic/Latino; 12 Two or more races, non-Hispanic/Latino), 10 international. Average age 25. 519 applicants, 18% accepted, 83 enrolled. In 2019, 117 master's, 18 doctorates awarded. *Degree requirements:* For doctorate, thesis/dissertation. *Entrance requirements:* For master's and doctorate, GRE General Test, minimum GPA of 3.0 in upper-level course work in field. Additional exam requirements/recommendations for international students: required—TOEFL (minimum score 550 paper-based). *Application deadline:* For fall admission, 7/15 for domestic students, 5/1 priority date for international students; for spring admission, 11/15 for domestic students, 9/1 priority date for international students. Applications are processed on a rolling basis. Application fee: $50 ($100 for international students). Electronic applications accepted. *Expenses: Tuition, area resident:* Full-time $16,504. Tuition, state resident: full-time $16,504. Tuition, nonresident: full-time $34,266. Tuition and fees vary according to course load. *Financial support:* In 2019–20, 26 students received support, including 8 research assistantships with partial tuition reimbursements available (averaging $26,122 per year), 18 teaching assistantships with partial tuition reimbursements available (averaging $18,900 per year); fellowships, Federal Work-Study, institutionally sponsored loans, scholarships/grants, and unspecified assistantships also available. Support available to part-time students. Financial award application deadline: 4/30; financial award applicants required to submit FAFSA. *Unit head:* Dr. Robert D. Stillman, Area Head, 214-905-3106, Fax: 972-883-3022, E-mail: stillman@utdallas.edu. *Application contact:* Dr. Robert D. Stillman, Area Head, 214-905-3106, Fax: 972-883-3022, E-mail: stillman@utdallas.edu.
Website: https://bbs.utdallas.edu/degrees/csd-degrees/

**The University of Texas at El Paso,** Graduate School, College of Health Sciences, Program in Speech-Language Pathology, El Paso, TX 79968-0001. Offers MS. *Accreditation:* ASHA. *Degree requirements:* For master's, comprehensive exam, thesis optional. *Entrance requirements:* For master's, GRE, minimum GPA of 3.0, resume, letters of recommendation, writing sample, interview. Additional exam requirements/recommendations for international students: required—TOEFL; recommended—IELTS. Electronic applications accepted.

**The University of Texas Health Science Center at San Antonio,** Joe R. and Teresa Lozano Long School of Medicine, San Antonio, TX 78229-3900. Offers deaf education and hearing (MS); medicine (MD); MPH/MD. *Accreditation:* LCME/AMA. *Degree requirements:* For master's, comprehensive exam, practicum assignments. *Entrance requirements:* For master's, minimum GPA of 3.0, interview, 3 professional letters of recommendation; for doctorate, MCAT. Electronic applications accepted. *Expenses:* Contact institution.

**The University of Texas Health Science Center at San Antonio,** School of Health Professions, San Antonio, TX 78229-3900. Offers occupational therapy (MOT); physical therapy (DPT); physician assistant studies (MS); speech language pathology (MS). *Accreditation:* AOTA; APTA; ARC-PA; ASHA. *Degree requirements:* For master's, comprehensive exam, thesis (for some programs); for doctorate, comprehensive exam.

**The University of Texas Rio Grande Valley,** College of Health Affairs, Department of Communication Sciences and Disorders, Edinburg, TX 78539. Offers communication sciences and disorders (MS). *Accreditation:* ASHA. *Faculty:* 8 full-time (6 women), 2 part-time/adjunct (1 woman). *Students:* 25 full-time (all women), 24 part-time (22 women); includes 45 minority (1 Asian, non-Hispanic/Latino; 44 Hispanic/Latino), 1 international. Average age 25. 75 applicants, 35% accepted, 25 enrolled. In 2019, 23 master's awarded. *Degree requirements:* For master's, comprehensive exam, thesis or alternative, Must take the PRAXIS exam in speech-language pathology. *Entrance requirements:* For master's, GRE General Test (taken within prior five years), minimum GPA of 3.0, three letters of recommendation or reference check lists, resume, 500-word personal statement on goals in pursuing graduate degree, official transcripts from each institution attended, baccalaureate degree in communication sciences and disorders from a regionally accredited institution. Additional exam requirements/recommendations for international students: recommended—TOEFL (minimum score 550 paper-based; 79 iBT), IELTS (minimum score 6.5). *Application deadline:* For fall admission, 2/1 for domestic and international students. Applications are processed on a rolling basis. Application fee: $50 ($100 for international students). Electronic applications accepted. *Expenses:* 17,313. *Financial support:* In 2019–20, 4 research assistantships (averaging $2,500 per year) were awarded. Financial award application deadline: 9/1; financial award applicants required to submit FAFSA. *Unit head:* Dr. Donald R. Fuller, Professor/Chair, 956-665-2387, Fax: 956-665-5238, E-mail: donald.fuller@utrgv.edu. *Application contact:* Donald R. Fuller, Professor/Chair, 956-665-2387, Fax: 956-665-5238, E-mail: donald.fuller@utrgv.edu.
Website: http://www.utrgv.edu/communication-disorders/

**University of the District of Columbia,** College of Arts and Sciences, Program in Speech-Language Pathology, Washington, DC 20008-1175. Offers MS. *Accreditation:* ASHA. *Program availability:* Part-time. *Degree requirements:* For master's, comprehensive exam, thesis optional. *Entrance requirements:* For master's, GRE General Test, writing proficiency exam.

**University of the Pacific,** Thomas J. Long School of Pharmacy and Health Sciences, Department of Audiology, San Francisco, CA 94103. Offers Au D.

**University of the Pacific,** Thomas J. Long School of Pharmacy and Health Sciences, Department of Speech-Language Pathology, Stockton, CA 95211-0197. Offers MS. *Accreditation:* ASHA. *Entrance requirements:* For master's, GRE General Test. Additional exam requirements/recommendations for international students: required—TOEFL.

**The University of Toledo,** College of Graduate Studies, College of Health and Human Services, School of Intervention and Wellness, Toledo, OH 43606-3390. Offers counselor education (MA, PhD); school psychology (Ed S); speech-language pathology (MA). *Accreditation:* ACA (one or more programs are accredited); NCATE. *Degree requirements:* For master's, seminar paper. *Entrance requirements:* For master's, GRE General Test, interview, minimum GPA of 3.0. Electronic applications accepted.

**University of Toronto,** Faculty of Medicine, Department of Speech-Language Pathology, Toronto, ON M5S 1A1, Canada. Offers M Sc, MH Sc, PhD. *Program availability:* Part-time. *Degree requirements:* For master's, thesis (for some programs), clinical internship (MH Sc), oral thesis defense (M Sc); for doctorate, comprehensive exam, thesis/dissertation, oral thesis defense. *Entrance requirements:* For master's, minimum B+ average in last 2 years (MH Sc), B average in final year (M Sc); volunteer/work experience in a clinical setting (MH Sc); for doctorate, previous research experience or thesis, resume, 3 writing samples, 3 letters of recommendation. Electronic applications accepted.

**The University of Tulsa,** Graduate School, Oxley College of Health Sciences, Department of Communication Sciences and Disorders, Tulsa, OK 74104-3189. Offers MS. *Accreditation:* ASHA. *Program availability:* Part-time. *Degree requirements:* For master's, thesis optional. *Entrance requirements:* For master's, GRE General Test. Additional exam requirements/recommendations for international students: required—TOEFL (minimum score 577 paper-based; 90 iBT), IELTS (minimum score 6.5). Electronic applications accepted. *Expenses: Tuition:* Full-time $22,896; part-time $1272 per credit hour. *Required fees:* $6 per credit hour. Tuition and fees vary according to course load and program.

**University of Utah,** Graduate School, College of Education, Department of Special Education, Salt Lake City, UT 84112. Offers board certified behavior analyst (M Ed, MS, PhD); deaf and hard of hearing (M Ed); deafblind (M Ed, MS); early childhood deaf and hard of hearing (MS); early childhood special education (M Ed, MS, PhD); early childhood visual impairments (M Ed); mild/moderate disabilities (M Ed, MS, PhD); severe disabilities (M Ed, MS, PhD); visual impairments (M Ed, MS). *Program*

*availability:* Part-time, blended/hybrid learning, Interactive Video Conferencing. *Faculty:* 16 full-time (13 women), 4 part-time/adjunct (3 women). *Students:* 70 full-time (64 women), 22 part-time (21 women); includes 14 minority (1 Black or African American, non-Hispanic/Latino; 2 Asian, non-Hispanic/Latino; 9 Hispanic/Latino; 1 Native Hawaiian or other Pacific Islander, non-Hispanic/Latino; 1 Two or more races, non-Hispanic/Latino). Average age 33. 30 applicants, 87% accepted, 22 enrolled. In 2019, 20 master's, 2 doctorates awarded. Terminal master's awarded for partial completion of doctoral program. *Degree requirements:* For master's, comprehensive exam, thesis optional; for doctorate, comprehensive exam, thesis/dissertation. *Entrance requirements:* For master's, minimum GPA of 3.0; for doctorate, GRE General Test, minimum GPA of 3.5, Master's Degree. Additional exam requirements/recommendations for international students: required—TOEFL (minimum score 600 paper-based; 250 iBT). *Application deadline:* For fall admission, 10/1 for domestic and international students; for spring admission, 3/1 for domestic and international students; for summer admission, 5/16 for domestic and international students. Application fee: $55 ($65 for international students). Electronic applications accepted. *Expenses:* Contact institution. *Financial support:* In 2019–20, 51 students received support, including 41 fellowships with full and partial tuition reimbursements available (averaging $4,634 per year), 2 research assistantships with full and partial tuition reimbursements available (averaging $12,500 per year), 1 teaching assistantship with full tuition reimbursement available (averaging $9,000 per year); career-related internships or fieldwork, scholarships/grants, health care benefits, and unspecified assistantships also available. Financial award application deadline: 3/15. *Unit head:* Matt Jameson, PhD, Department Chair, 801-581-8121, E-mail: matt.jameson@utah.edu. *Application contact:* Matt Jameson, PhD, Department Chair, 801-581-8121, E-mail: matt.jameson@utah.edu.
Website: http://special-ed.utah.edu/

**University of Utah,** Graduate School, College of Health, Department of Communication Sciences and Disorders, Salt Lake City, UT 84112. Offers audiology (Au D); audiology/speech-language pathology (PhD); speech-language pathology (MA, MS, PhD). *Accreditation:* ASHA (one or more programs are accredited). *Faculty:* 14 full-time (9 women), 4 part-time/adjunct (2 women). *Students:* 142 full-time (132 women), 3 part-time (all women); includes 21 minority (1 Black or African American, non-Hispanic/Latino; 5 Asian, non-Hispanic/Latino; 13 Hispanic/Latino; 2 Two or more races, non-Hispanic/Latino), 6 international. Average age 27. 258 applicants, 46% accepted, 53 enrolled. In 2019, 38 master's, 15 doctorates awarded. Terminal master's awarded for partial completion of doctoral program. *Degree requirements:* For master's, comprehensive exam, thesis optional; for doctorate, comprehensive exam, thesis/dissertation. *Entrance requirements:* For master's and doctorate, GRE General Test, minimum GPA of 3.0. Additional exam requirements/recommendations for international students: required—TOEFL (minimum score 600 paper-based; 100 iBT). *Application deadline:* For fall admission, 1/15 for domestic and international students. Application fee: $55 ($65 for international students). Electronic applications accepted. *Expenses:* Tuition, state resident: full-time $7085; part-time $272.51 per credit hour. Tuition, nonresident: full-time $24,937; part-time $959.12 per credit hour. *Required fees:* $880.52; $880.52 per semester. Tuition and fees vary according to degree level, program and student level. *Financial support:* Research assistantships and unspecified assistantships available. *Unit head:* Dr. Michael Blomgren, Department Chair, 801-581-6725, Fax: 801-581-7955, E-mail: michael.blomgren@hsc.utah.edu. *Application contact:* Dr. Kathy Chapman, Director of Graduate Studies, 801-581-6725, Fax: 801-581-7955, E-mail: kathy.chapman@hsc.utah.edu.
Website: http://www.health.utah.edu/csd

**University of Vermont,** Graduate College, College of Nursing and Health Sciences, Department of Communication Sciences and Disorders, Burlington, VT 05405. Offers MS. *Accreditation:* ASHA. *Entrance requirements:* For master's, GRE General Test. Additional exam requirements/recommendations for international students: required—TOEFL (minimum iBT score of 90) or IELTS (6.5). Electronic applications accepted.

**University of Virginia,** Curry School of Education, Department of Human Services, Program in Speech Communication Disorders, Charlottesville, VA 22903. Offers M Ed, PhD. *Accreditation:* ASHA (one or more programs are accredited). *Entrance requirements:* For master's, GRE General Test, 2 letters of recommendation. Additional exam requirements/recommendations for international students: required—TOEFL (minimum score 600 paper-based; 90 iBT), IELTS (minimum score 7). Electronic applications accepted.

**University of Washington,** Graduate School, College of Arts and Sciences, Department of Speech and Hearing Sciences, Seattle, WA 98195. Offers audiology (Au D); speech and hearing sciences (PhD); speech-language pathology (MS). *Accreditation:* ASHA (one or more programs are accredited). *Degree requirements:* For master's, comprehensive exam, thesis or alternative; for doctorate, thesis/dissertation. *Entrance requirements:* For master's and doctorate, GRE, minimum GPA of 3.0. Additional exam requirements/recommendations for international students: required—TOEFL. Electronic applications accepted.

**The University of Western Ontario,** School of Graduate and Postdoctoral Studies, Faculty of Health Sciences, School of Communication Sciences and Disorders, London, ON N6A 3K7, Canada. Offers audiology (M Cl Sc, M Sc); speech-language pathology (M Cl Sc, M Sc). *Degree requirements:* For master's, thesis (for some programs), supervised clinical practicum. *Entrance requirements:* For master's, 14 hours volunteer experience in field of study, minimum B average during last 2 years, previous course work in developmental psychology and statistics, 4 year honors degree. Additional exam requirements/recommendations for international students: required—TOEFL (minimum score 620 paper-based).

**University of Wisconsin–Eau Claire,** College of Education and Human Sciences, Program in Communication Sciences and Disorders, Eau Claire, WI 54702-4004. Offers MS. *Accreditation:* ASHA. *Program availability:* Part-time. *Degree requirements:* For master's, comprehensive exam, thesis optional, written or oral exam with thesis, externship. *Entrance requirements:* For master's, GRE, Wisconsin residency; minimum GPA of 3.0 in communication disorders, 2.75 overall. Additional exam requirements/recommendations for international students: required—TOEFL (minimum score 79 iBT).

**University of Wisconsin–Madison,** Graduate School, College of Letters and Science, Department of Communication Sciences and Disorders, Madison, WI 53706-1380. Offers audiology (Au D); normal aspects of speech, language and hearing (MS, PhD); speech-language pathology (MS, PhD); MS/PhD. *Accreditation:* ASHA (one or more programs are accredited). *Degree requirements:* For doctorate, thesis/dissertation. *Entrance requirements:* For master's and doctorate, GRE. Electronic applications accepted.

**University of Wisconsin–Milwaukee,** Graduate School, College of Health Sciences, Department of Communication Sciences and Disorders, Milwaukee, WI 53211. Offers MS. *Accreditation:* ASHA. *Program availability:* Part-time. *Degree requirements:* For master's, comprehensive exam, thesis optional. *Entrance requirements:* For master's, GRE General Test, minimum GPA of 3.0. Additional exam requirements/recommendations for international students: required—TOEFL (minimum score 550 paper-based; 79 iBT), IELTS (minimum score 6.5).

**University of Wisconsin–River Falls,** Outreach and Graduate Studies, College of Education and Professional Studies, Department of Communication Sciences and Disorders, River Falls, WI 54022. Offers communicative disorders (MS); secondary education-communicative disorders (MSE). *Accreditation:* ASHA (one or more programs are accredited). *Program availability:* Part-time. *Degree requirements:* For master's, comprehensive exam. *Entrance requirements:* For master's, minimum GPA of 2.75, 3 letters of reference. Additional exam requirements/recommendations for international students: required—TOEFL (minimum score 500 paper-based; 65 iBT), IELTS (minimum score 5.5).

**University of Wisconsin–Stevens Point,** College of Professional Studies, School of Communication Sciences and Disorders, Stevens Point, WI 54481-3897. Offers audiology (Au D); speech and language pathology (MS). *Accreditation:* ASHA (one or more programs are accredited). *Degree requirements:* For master's, thesis optional, clinical semester and capstone project; for doctorate, capstone project, full-time clinical externship. *Entrance requirements:* For master's, completion of specific course contents and practicum experiences at the undergraduate level.

**University of Wisconsin–Whitewater,** School of Graduate Studies, College of Education and Professional Studies, Program in Communication Sciences and Disorders, Whitewater, WI 53190-1790. Offers MS. *Accreditation:* ASHA. *Program availability:* Part-time, evening/weekend, online learning. *Degree requirements:* For master's, comprehensive exam. *Entrance requirements:* For master's, 2 letters of recommendation. Additional exam requirements/recommendations for international students: required—TOEFL (minimum score 550 paper-based; 80 iBT), IELTS (minimum score 6). Electronic applications accepted.

**University of Wyoming,** College of Health Sciences, Division of Communication Disorders, Laramie, WY 82071. Offers speech-language pathology (MS). *Accreditation:* ASHA. *Program availability:* Part-time, online learning. *Entrance requirements:* For master's, GRE General Test, minimum GPA of 3.0. Additional exam requirements/recommendations for international students: required—TOEFL. Electronic applications accepted.

**Université Laval,** Faculty of Medicine, Graduate Programs in Medicine, Program in Speech Therapy, Québec, QC G1K 7P4, Canada. Offers M Sc. *Entrance requirements:* For master's, knowledge of French, interview. Electronic applications accepted.

**Utah State University,** School of Graduate Studies, Emma Eccles Jones College of Education and Human Services, Department of Communicative Disorders and Deaf Education, Logan, UT 84322. Offers audiology (Au D, Ed S); communication disorders and deaf education (M Ed); communicative disorders and deaf education (MA, MS). *Accreditation:* ASHA (one or more programs are accredited). *Program availability:* Evening/weekend, online learning. *Degree requirements:* For master's, thesis optional; for Ed S, thesis or alternative. *Entrance requirements:* For master's, GRE General Test, minimum GPA of 3.0, 3 recommendations; for doctorate, GRE General Test, interview, minimum GPA of 3.25. Additional exam requirements/recommendations for international students: required—TOEFL. *Expenses:* Contact institution.

**Valdosta State University,** Department of Communication Sciences and Disorders, Valdosta, GA 31698. Offers communication disorders (M Ed); communication sciences and disorders (SLPD); special education (MAT, Ed S). *Accreditation:* ASHA. *Degree requirements:* For master's, comprehensive exam. *Entrance requirements:* For master's, GRE or MAT. Additional exam requirements/recommendations for international students: required—TOEFL. Electronic applications accepted.

**Vanderbilt University,** School of Medicine, Department of Hearing and Speech Sciences, Nashville, TN 37240-1001. Offers audiology (Au D). *Accreditation:* ASHA. *Faculty:* 22 full-time (9 women). *Students:* 25 full-time (17 women); includes 2 minority (1 Asian, non-Hispanic/Latino; 1 Hispanic/Latino), 4 international. Average age 29. 26 applicants, 19% accepted, 4 enrolled. In 2019, 1 master's, 6 doctorates awarded. *Degree requirements:* For master's, thesis optional; for doctorate, thesis/dissertation, final and qualifying exams. *Entrance requirements:* For master's and doctorate, GRE General Test. Additional exam requirements/recommendations for international students: required—TOEFL. *Application deadline:* For fall admission, 1/15 for domestic and international students. Electronic applications accepted. *Expenses: Tuition:* Full-time $51,018; part-time $2087 per hour. *Required fees:* $542. Tuition and fees vary according to program. *Financial support:* Fellowships with full tuition reimbursements, research assistantships with full tuition reimbursements, career-related internships or fieldwork, institutionally sponsored loans, traineeships, and tuition waivers (full and partial) available. Financial award application deadline: 1/15; financial award applicants required to submit FAFSA. *Unit head:* Dr. Anne Marie Tharpe, Chair, 615-936-5103, Fax: 615-936-5014, E-mail: anne.m.tharpe@vanderbilt.edu. *Application contact:* Todd Ricketts, Director of Graduate Studies, 615-936-5103, Fax: 615-936-6914, E-mail: todd.a.ricketts@vanderbilt.edu.
Website: https://ww2.mc.vanderbilt.edu/ghss/

**Washington State University,** Elson S. Floyd College of Medicine, Program in Speech and Hearing Sciences, Spokane, WA 99210. Offers MS. *Accreditation:* ASHA. *Degree requirements:* For master's, comprehensive exam, thesis (for some programs). *Entrance requirements:* For master's, GRE, minimum GPA of 3.0, 3 letters of recommendation. Additional exam requirements/recommendations for international students: required—TOEFL (minimum score 550 paper-based). Electronic applications accepted.

**Washington University in St. Louis,** School of Medicine, Program in Audiology and Communication Sciences, St. Louis, MO 63110. Offers audiology (Au D); deaf education (MS); speech and hearing sciences (PhD). *Accreditation:* ASHA (one or more programs are accredited). *Faculty:* 22 full-time (12 women), 18 part-time/adjunct (12 women). *Students:* 80 full-time (78 women). Average age 23. 117 applicants, 33% accepted, 27 enrolled. In 2019, 7 master's, 15 doctorates awarded. *Degree requirements:* For master's, comprehensive exam, thesis, independent study project, oral exam; for doctorate, comprehensive exam, thesis/dissertation, capstone project. *Entrance requirements:* For master's and doctorate, GRE General Test, minimum B average in previous college/university coursework (recommended). Additional exam requirements/recommendations for international students: required—TOEFL (minimum score 100 iBT). *Application deadline:* For fall admission, 2/15 for domestic and international students. Application fee: $25. Electronic applications accepted. *Expenses:* $40,300 per year. *Financial support:* In 2019–20, 80 students received support, including 80 fellowships with full and partial tuition reimbursements available (averaging $19,000 per year), 6 teaching assistantships with partial tuition reimbursements available (averaging $2,000 per year); Federal Work-Study, scholarships/grants, traineeships, health care benefits, tuition waivers (partial), and unspecified assistantships also available. Financial award application deadline: 2/15; financial award applicants required to submit FAFSA. *Unit head:* Dr. William W. Clark, Program Director, 314-747-0104, Fax: 314-747-0105, E-mail: pacs@wustl.edu. *Application contact:* Beth Elliott, Director, Finance and Student/Academic Affairs, 314-747-0104, Fax: 314-747-0105, E-mail: elliottb@wustl.edu.
Website: http://pacs.wustl.edu/

**Wayne State University,** College of Liberal Arts and Sciences, Department of Communication Sciences and Disorders, Detroit, MI 48202. Offers audiology (Au D); communication disorders and science (PhD); speech-language pathology (MA).

*Accreditation:* ASHA (one or more programs are accredited). *Faculty:* 6. *Students:* 115 full-time (110 women), 2 part-time (both women); includes 9 minority (2 Black or African American, non-Hispanic/Latino; 3 Asian, non-Hispanic/Latino; 4 Hispanic/Latino), 12 international. Average age 25. 272 applicants, 21% accepted, 49 enrolled. In 2019, 32 master's, 7 doctorates awarded. *Degree requirements:* For master's, comprehensive exam (for some programs), thesis (for some programs); for doctorate, thesis/dissertation (for some programs), written and oral comprehensive examinations. *Entrance requirements:* For master's, GRE, minimum GPA of 3.0, three letters of recommendation, written statement of intent, official transcripts, CSDCAS Centralized Application Service; for doctorate, GRE, minimum GPA of 3.0, three letters of recommendation, written statement of intent, official transcripts, CSDCAS Centralized Application Service (for Doctor of Audiology applicants). Additional exam requirements/recommendations for international students: required—TOEFL (minimum score 620 paper-based; 105 iBT), TWE (minimum score 5.5), Michigan English Language Assessment Battery (minimum score 85); recommended—IELTS. *Application deadline:* For fall admission, 1/15 for domestic and international students. Application fee: $50. Electronic applications accepted. *Expenses: Tuition:* Full-time $34,567. *Financial support:* In 2019–20, 33 students received support, including 1 fellowship with tuition reimbursement available (averaging $20,000 per year), 1 research assistantship with tuition reimbursement available (averaging $19,600 per year); scholarships/grants and unspecified assistantships also available. Financial award applicants required to submit FAFSA. *Unit head:* Dr. Jinsheng Zhang, Professor and Chair, 313-577-0066, E-mail: jinzhang@wayne.edu. *Application contact:* Denise Walker, Program Records Clerk, 313-577-8386, E-mail: denise.walker@wayne.edu.
Website: http://clas.wayne.edu/csd/

**Webster University,** School of Education, Department of Communication Arts, Reading and Early Childhood, St. Louis, MO 63119-3194. Offers communication arts (MAT); reading (MA). *Entrance requirements:* For master's, minimum GPA of 2.5. Additional exam requirements/recommendations for international students: required—TOEFL.

**Western Carolina University,** Graduate School, College of Health and Human Sciences, Department of Communication Sciences and Disorders, Cullowhee, NC 28723. Offers MS. *Accreditation:* ASHA. *Program availability:* Part-time. *Degree requirements:* For master's, comprehensive exam, thesis or alternative. *Entrance requirements:* For master's, GRE, appropriate undergraduate degree with minimum GPA of 3.0, 3 letters of recommendation. Additional exam requirements/recommendations for international students: required—TOEFL (minimum score 550 paper-based; 79 iBT). *Expenses: Tuition, area resident:* Full-time $2217.50; part-time $1664 per semester. Tuition, state resident: full-time $2217.50; part-time $1664 per semester. Tuition, nonresident: full-time $7421; part-time $5566 per semester. *International tuition:* $7421 full-time. *Required fees:* $5598; $1954 per semester. Tuition and fees vary according to course load, campus/location and program.

**Western Illinois University,** School of Graduate Studies, College of Fine Arts and Communication, Department of Speech Pathology and Audiology, Macomb, IL 61455-1390. Offers MS. *Accreditation:* ASHA. *Program availability:* Part-time. *Degree requirements:* For master's, comprehensive exam, thesis or alternative. *Entrance requirements:* For master's, GRE, minimum GPA of 3.0. Additional exam requirements/recommendations for international students: required—TOEFL (minimum score 550 paper-based; 80 iBT). Electronic applications accepted.

**Western Kentucky University,** Graduate School, College of Health and Human Services, Department of Communication Sciences and Disorders, Bowling Green, KY 42101. Offers MS. *Accreditation:* ASHA. *Program availability:* Part-time, evening/weekend, online learning. *Degree requirements:* For master's, comprehensive exam, written exam. *Entrance requirements:* For master's, GRE General Test, 3 letters of recommendation. Additional exam requirements/recommendations for international students: required—TOEFL (minimum score 555 paper-based; 79 iBT).

**Western Michigan University,** Graduate College, College of Health and Human Services, Department of Speech, Language and Hearing Sciences, Kalamazoo, MI 49008. Offers audiology (Au D); speech pathology and audiology (MA). *Accreditation:* ASHA. *Degree requirements:* For master's, thesis optional.

**Western Washington University,** Graduate School, College of Humanities and Social Sciences, Department of Communication Sciences and Disorders, Bellingham, WA 98225-5996. Offers MA. *Accreditation:* ASHA. *Program availability:* Part-time. *Degree requirements:* For master's, comprehensive exam, thesis optional. *Entrance requirements:* For master's, GRE General Test, minimum GPA of 3.0 in last 60 semester hours or last 90 quarter hours. Additional exam requirements/recommendations for international students: required—TOEFL (minimum score 567 paper-based). Electronic applications accepted.

**West Texas A&M University,** College of Nursing and Health Sciences, Department of Communication Disorders, Canyon, TX 79015. Offers MS. *Accreditation:* ASHA. *Program availability:* Part-time. *Degree requirements:* For master's, comprehensive exam, thesis optional. *Entrance requirements:* For master's, GRE General Test, minimum B average in all clinical courses, liability insurance, immunizations. Additional exam requirements/recommendations for international students: required—TOEFL. Electronic applications accepted.

**West Virginia University,** College of Education and Human Services, Morgantown, WV 26506. Offers audiology (Au D); autism spectrum disorder (MA); clinical rehabilitation and mental health counseling (MS); communication science and disorders (PhD); counseling (MA); counseling psychology (PhD); curriculum and instruction (Ed D); early childhood education (MA); early intervention/ early childhood special education (MA); education (PhD); educational leadership (MA); educational leadership/ public school administration (Ed D); educational leadership/public school administration (MA); educational psychology (MA, Ed D); elementary education (MA); gifted education (MA); higher education administration (MA, Ed D); higher education curriculum and teaching (MA); institutional design and technology (MA); instructional design and technology (Ed D); literacy education (MA); secondary education (MA); secondary education/English (MA); special education (Ed D); speech pathology (MS). *Accreditation:* ASHA; NCATE. *Program availability:* Part-time, evening/weekend, online learning. *Degree requirements:* For master's, content exams; for doctorate, comprehensive exam, thesis/dissertation. *Entrance requirements:* Additional exam requirements/recommendations for international students: required—TOEFL (minimum score 500 paper-based; 61 iBT). Electronic applications accepted.

**Wichita State University,** Graduate School, College of Health Professions, Department of Communication Sciences and Disorders, Wichita, KS 67260. Offers MA, Au D, PhD. *Accreditation:* ASHA (one or more programs are accredited).

**Worcester State University,** Graduate School, Program in Speech-Language Pathology, Worcester, MA 01602-2597. Offers MS. *Accreditation:* ASHA. *Program availability:* Part-time, evening/weekend. *Faculty:* 6 full-time (4 women), 3 part-time/adjunct (all women). *Students:* 57 full-time (56 women), 29 part-time (28 women); includes 4 minority (1 Black or African American, non-Hispanic/Latino; 2 Asian, non-Hispanic/Latino; 1 Two or more races, non-Hispanic/Latino). Average age 25. 31 applicants, 100% accepted, 30 enrolled. In 2019, 24 master's awarded. *Degree requirements:* For master's, comprehensive exam, thesis, practicum; national licensing exam; clinical observation and participation in diagnostic/therapeutic work. For a detail list in Degree Completion requirements please see the graduate catalog at catalog.worcester.edu. *Entrance requirements:* For master's, GRE General Test or MAT, For a detail list in Degree Completion requirements please see the graduate catalog at catalog.worcester.edu. Additional exam requirements/recommendations for international students: required—TOEFL (minimum score 550 paper-based; 79 iBT), IELTS (minimum score 6). *Application deadline:* For fall admission, 3/1 priority date for domestic and international students; for spring admission, 11/1 for domestic and international students; for summer admission, 3/1 for domestic and international students. Applications are processed on a rolling basis. Application fee: $50. Electronic applications accepted. *Expenses:* Contact institution. *Financial support:* Career-related internships or fieldwork, scholarships/grants, and unspecified assistantships available. Financial award application deadline: 3/1; financial award applicants required to submit FAFSA. *Unit head:* Kristina Curro, Program Coordinator, 508-929-8881, Fax: 508-929-8100, E-mail: kcurro@worcester.edu. *Application contact:* Sara Grady, Associate Dean, Graduate Studies and Professional Development, 508-929-8130, Fax: 508-929-8100, E-mail: sara.grady@worcester.edu.

**Yeshiva University,** The Katz School, Program in Speech-Language Pathology, New York, NY 10033-3201. Offers MS.

# Dental Hygiene

**Eastern Washington University,** Graduate Studies, College of Health Science and Public Health, Department of Dental Hygiene, Cheney, WA 99004-2431. Offers MS. *Faculty:* 11 full-time (7 women). *Students:* 6 full-time (5 women), 14 part-time (13 women). Average age 44. 6 applicants, 83% accepted, 4 enrolled. In 2019, 2 master's awarded. *Degree requirements:* For master's, comprehensive exam, thesis. *Entrance requirements:* For master's, Dental Hygiene National Board examination, current dental hygiene license in the U.S. or Canada. Additional exam requirements/recommendations for international students: required—TOEFL (minimum score 580 paper-based; 92 iBT), IELTS (minimum score 7), PTE (minimum score 63). *Application deadline:* For fall admission, 7/1 for domestic students; for spring admission, 12/1 for domestic students. Applications are processed on a rolling basis. Application fee: $75. Electronic applications accepted. *Financial support:* Teaching assistantships with partial tuition reimbursements available. Financial award application deadline: 2/1; financial award applicants required to submit FAFSA. *Unit head:* Kasey Clark, 509-828-1317, E-mail: kclark56@ewu.edu. *Application contact:* Kasey Clark, 509-828-1317, E-mail: kclark56@ewu.edu.
Website: http://www.ewu.edu/cshe/programs/dental-hygiene.xml

**Idaho State University,** Graduate School, College of Health Professions, Department of Dental Hygiene, Pocatello, ID 83209-8048. Offers MS. *Program availability:* Part-time. *Degree requirements:* For master's, comprehensive exam, thesis, thesis defense, practicum experience, oral exam. *Entrance requirements:* For master's, GRE, MAT, baccalaureate degree in dental hygiene, minimum GPA of 3.0 in upper-division and dental hygiene coursework, current dental hygiene licensure in good standing. Additional exam requirements/recommendations for international students: required—TOEFL (minimum score 600 paper-based; 80 iBT). Electronic applications accepted.

**Missouri Southern State University,** Program in Dental Hygiene, Joplin, MO 64801-1595. Offers MS. *Program availability:* Part-time. *Degree requirements:* For master's, project. *Entrance requirements:* For master's, copy of current dental hygiene license. Electronic applications accepted.

**The Ohio State University,** College of Dentistry, Columbus, OH 43210. Offers dental anesthesiology (MS); dental hygiene (MDH); dentistry (DDS); endodontics (MS); oral and maxillofacial pathology (MS); oral and maxillofacial surgery (MS); oral biology (PhD); orthodontics (MS); pediatric dentistry (MS); periodontology (MS); prosthodontics (MS); DDS/PhD. *Accreditation:* ADA (one or more programs are accredited). Terminal master's awarded for partial completion of doctoral program. *Degree requirements:* For master's, thesis; for doctorate, thesis/dissertation (for some programs). *Entrance requirements:* For master's, GRE General Test (for all applicants with cumulative GPA below 3.0); for doctorate, DAT (for DDS); GRE General Test, GRE Subject Test in biology recommended (for PhD). Additional exam requirements/recommendations for international students: required—TOEFL (minimum score 550 paper-based; 79 iBT), IELTS (minimum score 7), Michigan English Language Assessment Battery (minimum score 82). Electronic applications accepted. *Expenses:* Contact institution.

**Old Dominion University,** College of Health Sciences, School of Dental Hygiene, Norfolk, VA 23529. Offers dental hygiene (MS), including community/public health, education, generalist, global health, marketing, modeling and simulation, research. *Program availability:* Part-time, evening/weekend, blended/hybrid learning. *Degree requirements:* For master's, comprehensive exam, thesis optional, writing proficiency exam, responsible conduct of research training. *Entrance requirements:* For master's, Dental Hygiene National Board Examination or copy of license to practice dental hygiene, BS or certificate in dental hygiene or related area, minimum GPA of 2.8 (3.0 in major), 4 letters of recommendation. Additional exam requirements/recommendations for international students: required—TOEFL (minimum score 550 paper-based, 79 iBT) or IELTS (minimum score 6.5). Electronic applications accepted. *Expenses:* Contact institution.

**Texas Woman's University,** Graduate School, College of Health Sciences, School of Health Promotion and Kinesiology, Denton, TX 76204. Offers health studies (MS, PhD), including dental hygiene (MS). *Program availability:* Part-time, evening/weekend, 100% online. *Faculty:* 20 full-time (10 women), 4 part-time/adjunct (all women). *Students:* 55 full-time (46 women), 151 part-time (119 women); includes 96 minority (49 Black or African American, non-Hispanic/Latino; 9 Asian, non-Hispanic/Latino; 31 Hispanic/Latino; 7 Two or more races, non-Hispanic/Latino), 11 international. Average age 35. 102 applicants, 53% accepted, 33 enrolled. In 2019, 63 master's, 9 doctorates awarded.

*Dental Hygiene*

*Degree requirements:* For master's, comprehensive exam, thesis or alternative, thesis, non-thesis options, or work-site health (for dental hygiene); for doctorate, comprehensive exam, thesis/dissertation, qualifying exam. *Entrance requirements:* For master's, GRE scores (for Kinesiology students in Biomechanics), minimum undergraduate GPA of 3.0 in last 60 credit hours of bachelor's degree, resume/curriculum vitae, 2 letters of recommendation, personal statement letter; for doctorate, GRE (for some), minimum GPA of 3.5 on all master's course work, 2 letters of recommendation, curriculum vitae, essay, writing sample, master's degree. Additional exam requirements/recommendations for international students: required—TOEFL (minimum score 79 iBT); recommended—IELTS (minimum score 6.5), TSE (minimum score 53). *Application deadline:* For fall admission, 3/1 for domestic and international students; for spring admission, 7/1 for domestic and international students; for summer admission, 3/1 for domestic and international students. Application fee: $50 ($75 for international students). Electronic applications accepted. *Expenses:* All are estimates. Tuition for 10 hours = $2,763; Fees for 10 hours = $1,342. Health studies courses require additional $40/SCH. *Financial support:* In 2019–20, 63 students received support, including 1 research assistantship, 17 teaching assistantships (averaging $9,109 per year); career-related internships or fieldwork, scholarships/grants, health care benefits, and unspecified assistantships also available. Support available to part-time students. Financial award application deadline: 3/1; financial award applicants required to submit FAFSA. *Unit head:* Dr. George King, Chair, 940-898-2860, Fax: 940-898-2859, E-mail: healthstudiesinfo@twu.edu. *Application contact:* Korie Hawkins, Associate Director of Admissions, Graduate Recruitment, 940-898-3188, Fax: 940-898-3081, E-mail: admissions@twu.edu.
Website: http://www.twu.edu/health-studies/

**Université de Montréal,** Faculty of Dental Medicine, Program in Stomatology Residency, Montréal, QC H3C 3J7, Canada. Offers Certificate.

**University of Alberta,** Faculty of Medicine and Dentistry, School of Dentistry, Program in Dental Hygiene, Edmonton, AB T6G 2E1, Canada. Offers Diploma. Electronic applications accepted.

**University of Bridgeport,** Fones School of Dental Hygiene, Bridgeport, CT 06604. Offers MS. *Program availability:* Part-time, evening/weekend, online learning. *Degree requirements:* For master's, thesis. *Entrance requirements:* For master's, Dental Hygiene National Board Examination. Additional exam requirements/recommendations for international students: recommended—TOEFL (minimum score 550 paper-based; 80 iBT), IELTS (minimum score 6.5). *Expenses:* Contact institution.

**University of Michigan,** School of Dentistry and Rackham Graduate School, Graduate Programs in Dentistry, Dental Hygiene Program, Ann Arbor, MI 48109-1078. Offers MS. *Program availability:* Part-time. *Degree requirements:* For master's, thesis. *Entrance*

*requirements:* For master's, Bachelor's degree in dental hygiene. Additional exam requirements/recommendations for international students: required—TOEFL (minimum score 84 iBT). Electronic applications accepted. *Expenses:* Contact institution.

**University of Missouri–Kansas City,** School of Dentistry, Kansas City, MO 64110-2499. Offers advanced education in dentistry (Graduate Dental Certificate); dental hygiene education (MS); endodontics (Graduate Dental Certificate); oral and maxillofacial surgery (Graduate Dental Certificate); oral biology (MS, PhD); orthodontics and dentofacial orthopedics (Graduate Dental Certificate); periodontics (Graduate Dental Certificate). *Accreditation:* ADA (one or more programs are accredited). *Degree requirements:* For master's, thesis; for doctorate, thesis/dissertation (for some programs). *Entrance requirements:* For master's, DAT, letters of evaluation, personal interview; for doctorate, DAT (for DDS); for Graduate Dental Certificate, DDS. Additional exam requirements/recommendations for international students: required—TOEFL (minimum score 550 paper-based; 80 iBT). *Expenses:* Contact institution.

**University of New Mexico,** Graduate Studies, Health Sciences Center, Program in Dental Hygiene, Albuquerque, NM 87131-2039. Offers MS. *Program availability:* Part-time, evening/weekend, online learning. *Expenses:* Tuition, state resident: full-time $7633; part-time $972 per year. Tuition, nonresident: full-time $22,586; part-time $3840 per year. *International tuition:* $23,292 full-time. *Required fees:* $8608. Tuition and fees vary according to course level, course load, degree level, program and student level.

**The University of North Carolina at Chapel Hill,** School of Dentistry and Graduate School, Graduate Programs in Dentistry, Chapel Hill, NC 27599. Offers dental hygiene (MS); endodontics (MS); epidemiology (PhD); operative dentistry (MS); oral and maxillofacial pathology (MS); oral and maxillofacial radiology (MS); oral biology (PhD); orthodontics (MS); pediatric dentistry (MS); periodontology (MS); prosthodontics (MS). *Degree requirements:* For master's, thesis; for doctorate, thesis/dissertation. *Entrance requirements:* For master's, GRE General Test (for orthodontics and oral biology only); National Dental Board Part I (Part II if available), dental degree (for all except dental hygiene); for doctorate, GRE General Test. Additional exam requirements/recommendations for international students: required—TOEFL (minimum score 550 paper-based; 79 iBT). Electronic applications accepted. *Expenses:* Contact institution.

**West Virginia University,** School of Dentistry, Morgantown, WV 26506. Offers dental hygiene (MS); dentistry (DDS); endodontics (MS); orthodontics (MS); periodontics (MS); prosthodontics (MS). *Accreditation:* ADA (one or more programs are accredited). *Degree requirements:* For master's, thesis; for doctorate, comprehensive exam. *Entrance requirements:* For doctorate, DAT, letters of recommendation, interview, minimum of 50 semester credit hours. Additional exam requirements/recommendations for international students: required—TOEFL (minimum score 500 paper-based). Electronic applications accepted. *Expenses:* Contact institution.

# Emergency Medical Services

**Creighton University,** Graduate School, Program in Emergency Medical Services, Omaha, NE 68178-0001. Offers MS. *Program availability:* Part-time, online only, 100% online, blended/hybrid learning. *Entrance requirements:* Additional exam requirements/recommendations for international students: required—TOEFL (minimum score 90 iBT). Electronic applications accepted.

**Drexel University,** College of Nursing and Health Professions, Emergency and Public Safety Services Program, Philadelphia, PA 19104-2875. Offers MS. *Program availability:* Part-time, evening/weekend. *Degree requirements:* For master's, comprehensive exam. *Entrance requirements:* For master's, GRE General Test, minimum GPA of 2.75.

**San Diego State University,** Graduate and Research Affairs, College of Health and Human Services, School of Public Health, San Diego, CA 92182. Offers environmental health (MPH); epidemiology (MPH, PhD), including biostatistics (MPH); global emergency preparedness and response (MS); global health (PhD); health behavior (PhD); health promotion (MPH); health services administration (MPH); toxicology (MS); MPH/MA; MSW/MPH. *Accreditation:* CAHME (one or more programs are accredited); CEPH. *Program availability:* Part-time. *Degree requirements:* For master's, comprehensive exam (for some programs), thesis (for some programs); for doctorate, thesis/dissertation. *Entrance requirements:* For master's, GMAT (MPH in health services administration), GRE General Test; for doctorate, GRE General Test. Additional exam requirements/recommendations for international students: required—TOEFL.

**University of Guelph,** Ontario Veterinary College and Office of Graduate and Postdoctoral Studies, Graduate Programs in Veterinary Sciences, Department of

Clinical Studies, Guelph, ON N1G 2W1, Canada. Offers anesthesiology (M Sc, DV Sc); cardiology (DV Sc, Diploma); clinical studies (Diploma); dermatology (M Sc); diagnostic imaging (M Sc, DV Sc); emergency/critical care (M Sc, DV Sc, Diploma); medicine (M Sc, DV Sc); neurology (M Sc, DV Sc); ophthalmology (M Sc, DV Sc); surgery (M Sc, DV Sc). *Degree requirements:* For master's, thesis; for doctorate, comprehensive exam, thesis/dissertation. *Entrance requirements:* Additional exam requirements/recommendations for international students: required—TOEFL (minimum score 550 paper-based), IELTS (minimum score 6.5). Electronic applications accepted.

**Université Laval,** Faculty of Medicine, Post-Professional Programs in Medical Studies, Québec, QC G1K 7P4, Canada. Offers anatomy–pathology (DESS); anesthesiology (DESS); cardiology (DESS); care of older people (Diploma); clinical research (DESS); community health (DESS); dermatology (DESS); diagnostic radiology (DESS); emergency medicine (Diploma); family medicine (DESS); general surgery (DESS); geriatrics (DESS); hematology (DESS); internal medicine (DESS); maternal and fetal medicine (Diploma); medical biochemistry (DESS); medical microbiology and infectious diseases (DESS); medical oncology (DESS); nephrology (DESS); neurology (DESS); neurosurgery (DESS); obstetrics and gynecology (DESS); ophthalmology (DESS); orthopedic surgery (DESS); oto-rhino-laryngology (DESS); palliative medicine (Diploma); pediatrics (DESS); plastic surgery (DESS); psychiatry (DESS); pulmonary medicine (DESS); radiology–oncology (DESS); thoracic surgery (DESS); urology (DESS). *Degree requirements:* For other advanced degree, comprehensive exam. *Entrance requirements:* For degree, knowledge of French. Electronic applications accepted.

# Occupational Therapy

**Abilene Christian University,** Office of Graduate Programs, College of Education and Human Services, Department of Occupational Therapy, Abilene, TX 79699. Offers MS. *Accreditation:* AOTA. *Faculty:* 4 full-time (all women), 2 part-time/adjunct (both women). *Students:* 90 full-time (81 women), 1 (woman) part-time; includes 39 minority (5 Black or African American, non-Hispanic/Latino; 4 Asian, non-Hispanic/Latino; 23 Hispanic/Latino; 7 Two or more races, non-Hispanic/Latino), 1 international. 604 applicants, 22% accepted, 45 enrolled. In 2019, 25 master's awarded. *Entrance requirements:* For master's, official transcripts, recommendations, observation hours, purpose of statement. Additional exam requirements/recommendations for international students: required—TOEFL (minimum score 80 iBT), IELTS (minimum score 6), PTE (minimum score 51). *Application deadline:* For fall admission, 12/14 for domestic students. Application fee: $65. *Expenses:* $1010 per hour. *Financial support:* In 2019–20, 9 students received support. Institutionally sponsored loans, scholarships/grants, and unspecified assistantships available. Support available to part-time students. Financial award application deadline: 4/1; financial award applicants required to submit FAFSA. *Unit head:* Dr. Catherine Candler, Program Director, 325-674-2474, Fax: 325-674-6568, E-mail: cfc15a@acu.edu. *Application contact:* Graduate Admissions, 325-674-6911, E-mail: gradinfo@acu.edu.
Website: http://www.acu.edu/on-campus/graduate/college-of-education-and-human-services/occupational-therapy-department.html

**AdventHealth University,** Program in Occupational Therapy, Orlando, FL 32803. Offers MOT. *Accreditation:* AOTA.

**Alabama State University,** College of Health Sciences, Department of Occupational Therapy, Montgomery, AL 36101-0271. Offers MS. *Accreditation:* AOTA. *Faculty:* 8 full-time (all women). *Students:* 67 full-time (61 women), 1 part-time (0 women); includes 16 minority (15 Black or African American, non-Hispanic/Latino; 1 American Indian or Alaska Native, non-Hispanic/Latino). Average age 24. 41 applicants, 59% accepted, 24 enrolled. In 2019, 33 master's awarded. *Degree requirements:* For master's, comprehensive exam. *Entrance requirements:* For master's, interview. Additional exam requirements/recommendations for international students: required—TOEFL. *Application deadline:* For fall admission, 4/15 for domestic and international students; for spring admission, 11/15 for domestic and international students; for summer admission, 3/15 for domestic and international students. Applications are processed on a rolling basis. Application fee: $25. Electronic applications accepted. *Financial support:* Fellowships, research assistantships, Federal Work-Study, scholarships/grants, tuition waivers, and unspecified assistantships available. Financial award application deadline: 6/30; financial award applicants required to submit FAFSA. *Unit head:* Dr. Susan Denham, Chair, 334-229-5056, Fax: 334-229-5882, E-mail: sdenham@alasu.edu. *Application contact:* Dr. Ed Brown, Dean of Graduate Studies, 334-229-4274, Fax: 334-229-4928, E-mail: ebrown@alasu.edu.

Website: http://www.alasu.edu/academics/colleges—departments/health-sciences/occupational-therapy/index.aspx

**Allen College,** Graduate Programs, Waterloo, IA 50703. Offers adult-gerontology acute care nurse practitioner (MSN); community/public health nursing (MSN); education (MSN); family nurse practitioner (MSN); health sciences (Ed D); leadership in health care delivery (MSN); leadership in health care informatics (MSN); nursing (DNP); occupational therapy (MS); psychiatric mental health nurse practitioner (MSN). *Accreditation:* AACN; ACEN. *Faculty:* 27 full-time (23 women), 9 part-time/adjunct (8 women). *Students:* 193 full-time (175 women), 95 part-time (84 women); includes 22 minority (6 Black or African American, non-Hispanic/Latino; 1 American Indian or Alaska Native, non-Hispanic/Latino; 4 Asian, non-Hispanic/Latino; 5 Hispanic/Latino; 6 Two or more races, non-Hispanic/Latino). Average age 32. 376 applicants, 53% accepted, 122 enrolled. *Application deadline:* For fall admission, 2/1 priority date for domestic students; for spring admission, 9/1 priority date for domestic students. Applications are processed on a rolling basis. Application fee: $50. Electronic applications accepted. *Financial support:* In 2019–20, 78 students received support. Federal Work-Study, institutionally sponsored loans, and scholarships/grants available. Support available to part-time students. Financial award application deadline: 8/1; financial award applicants required to submit FAFSA. *Unit head:* Dr. Bob Loch, Provost, 319-226-2040, Fax: 319-226-2070, E-mail: bob.loch@allencollege.edu. *Application contact:* Molly Quinn, Director of Admissions, 319-226-2001, Fax: 319-226-2010, E-mail: molly.quinn@allencollege.edu. Website: http://www.allencollege.edu/

**Alvernia University,** School of Graduate Studies, Program in Occupational Therapy, Reading, PA 19607-1799. Offers MSOT. *Accreditation:* AOTA. *Program availability:* Part-time, evening/weekend. *Degree requirements:* For master's, thesis optional. Electronic applications accepted.

**American International College,** School of Health Sciences, Springfield, MA 01109-3189. Offers exercise science (MS); family nurse practitioner (MSN, Post-Master's Certificate); nursing administrator (MSN); nursing educator (MSN); occupational therapy (MSOT, OTD); physical therapy (DPT). *Accreditation:* AOTA. *Program availability:* Part-time, 100% online. *Degree requirements:* For master's, practicum; for doctorate, thesis/dissertation, practicum. *Entrance requirements:* For master's, 3 letters of recommendation, personal goal statement; minimum GPA of 3.2, interview, BS or BA, and 2 clinical PT observations (for DPT); minimum GPA of 3.0, MSOT, OT licensen, and 2 clinical OT observations (for OTD); for doctorate, personal goal statement, 2 letters of recommendation; minimum GPA of 3.0, BS or BA, 2 clinical OT observations (for MSOT); RN license and minimum GPA of 3.0 (for MSN). Additional exam requirements/recommendations for international students: required—TOEFL (minimum score 577 paper-based; 91 iBT). Electronic applications accepted. *Expenses:* Contact institution.

**Arkansas State University,** Graduate School, College of Nursing and Health Professions, Program in Occupational Therapy, State University, AR 72467. Offers DOT. *Accreditation:* AOTA. *Degree requirements:* For doctorate, comprehensive exam, thesis/dissertation. *Entrance requirements:* For doctorate, GRE or MAT, bachelor's degree; transcripts; minimum GPA of 3.0 on prerequisites, 2.5 overall; 3 letters of recommendation; CPR Certification; TB Test; immunizations; health insurance; professional liability insurance; resume; personal statement. Additional exam requirements/recommendations for international students: required—TOEFL (minimum score 550 paper-based; 79 iBT), IELTS (minimum score 6), PTE (minimum score 56). Electronic applications accepted. *Expenses:* Contact institution.

**A.T. Still University,** Arizona School of Health Sciences, Mesa, AZ 85206. Offers advanced occupational therapy (MS); advanced physician assistant studies (MS); athletic training (MS, DAT); audiology (Au D); clinical decision making in athletic training (Graduate Certificate); occupational therapy (MS, OTD); orthopedic rehabilitation (Graduate Certificate); physical therapy (DPT); physician assistant studies (MS); post-professional audiology (Au D); post-professional physical therapy (DPT). *Accreditation:* AOTA (one or more programs are accredited); ASHA. *Program availability:* Part-time, evening/weekend, online only, 100% online, blended/hybrid learning. *Faculty:* 94 full-time (74 women), 203 part-time/adjunct (145 women). *Students:* 736 full-time (528 women), 289 part-time (195 women); includes 315 minority (53 Black or African American, non-Hispanic/Latino; 7 American Indian or Alaska Native, non-Hispanic/Latino; 94 Asian, non-Hispanic/Latino; 134 Hispanic/Latino; 2 Native Hawaiian or other Pacific Islander, non-Hispanic/Latino; 25 Two or more races, non-Hispanic/Latino), 79 international. Average age 32. 4,387 applicants, 20% accepted, 514 enrolled. In 2019, 153 master's, 344 doctorates, 2 other advanced degrees awarded. *Degree requirements:* For master's, thesis (for some programs); for doctorate, thesis/dissertation (for some programs). *Entrance requirements:* For master's, GRE General Test; for doctorate, GRE, Physical Therapist Evaluation Tool (for DPT), current state licensure. Additional exam requirements/recommendations for international students: required—TOEFL (minimum score 80 iBT). *Application deadline:* For fall admission, 7/7 for domestic and international students; for winter admission, 10/3 for domestic and international students; for spring admission, 1/16 for domestic and international students; for summer admission, 4/17 for domestic and international students. Applications are processed on a rolling basis. Application fee: $70. *Financial support:* In 2019–20, 170 students received support. Federal Work-Study and scholarships/grants available. Financial award application deadline: 6/1; financial award applicants required to submit FAFSA. *Unit head:* Dr. Ann Lee Burch, Dean, 480-219-6061, E-mail: aburch@atsu.edu. *Application contact:* Donna Sparks, Director, Admissions Processing, 660-626-2117, Fax: 660-626-2969, E-mail: admissions@atsu.edu. Website: http://www.atsu.edu/ashs

**Augusta University,** College of Allied Health Sciences, Occupational Therapy Program, Augusta, GA 30912. Offers MHS. *Accreditation:* AOTA. *Program availability:* Part-time. *Degree requirements:* For master's, thesis. *Entrance requirements:* For master's, GRE General Test. Additional exam requirements/recommendations for international students: required—TOEFL (minimum score 550 paper-based; 79 iBT). Electronic applications accepted.

**Baker College Center for Graduate Studies–Online,** Graduate Programs, Flint, MI 48507. Offers accounting (MBA); business administration (DBA); finance (MBA); general business (MBA); health care management (MBA); human resources management (MBA); information management (MBA); leadership studies (MBA); management information systems (MSIS); marketing (MBA); occupational therapy (MOT). *Program availability:* Part-time, evening/weekend, online learning. *Degree requirements:* For master's, portfolio. *Entrance requirements:* For master's, 3 years of work experience, minimum undergraduate GPA of 2.5, writing sample, 3 letters of recommendation; for doctorate, MBA or acceptable related master's degree from accredited association, 5 years work experience, minimum graduate GPA of 3.25, writing sample, 3 professional references. Additional exam requirements/recommendations for international students: required—TOEFL (minimum score 550 paper-based). Electronic applications accepted.

**Barry University,** College of Health Sciences, Program in Occupational Therapy, Miami Shores, FL 33161-6695. Offers MS. *Accreditation:* AOTA. Electronic applications accepted.

**Bay Path University,** Program in Occupational Therapy, Longmeadow, MA 01106-2292. Offers MOT, OTD. *Accreditation:* AOTA. *Program availability:* Part-time. *Entrance*

*requirements:* For master's, completed MOT application; official undergraduate and graduate transcripts (a GPA of 3.0 or higher); current resume; 2 recommendations; signed Essential Functions form; admission essay: what does the term "professionalism" mean to you? What professional quality do you think is most important for a student and an OT to have?; for doctorate, application, official undergraduate and graduate transcripts, original essay of at least 250 words on the topic: "Why the Post-Professional Occupational Therapy Doctorate is important to my personal and professional goals", writing sample in APA format, 2 recommendations, resume/curriculum vitae, NBCOT certificate. Electronic applications accepted. Application fee is waived when completed online. *Expenses:* Contact institution.

**Belmont University,** College of Health Sciences, Nashville, TN 37212. Offers nursing (MSN, DNP); occupational therapy (MSOT, OTD); physical therapy (DPT). *Program availability:* Part-time, blended/hybrid learning. *Faculty:* 26 full-time (20 women), 30 part-time/adjunct (21 women). *Students:* 416 full-time (362 women), 8 part-time (7 women); includes 36 minority (7 Black or African American, non-Hispanic/Latino; 12 Asian, non-Hispanic/Latino; 9 Hispanic/Latino; 8 Two or more races, non-Hispanic/Latino). Average age 26. *Degree requirements:* For master's, comprehensive exam, thesis; for doctorate, comprehensive exam. *Entrance requirements:* For master's, GRE, BSN, minimum GPA of 3.0. Additional exam requirements/recommendations for international students: required—TOEFL (minimum score 550 paper-based). *Application deadline:* Applications are processed on a rolling basis. Application fee: $50. Electronic applications accepted. *Expenses:* Contact institution. *Financial support:* Teaching assistantships with full tuition reimbursements, career-related internships or fieldwork, scholarships/grants, and traineeships available. Financial award application deadline: 3/1; financial award applicants required to submit FAFSA. *Unit head:* Dr. Cathy Taylor, Dean, 615-460-6916, Fax: 615-460-6750. *Application contact:* Bill Nichols, Director of Enrollment Services, 615-460-6107, E-mail: bill.nichols@belmont.edu. Website: http://www.belmont.edu/healthsciences/

**Boston University,** College of Health and Rehabilitation Sciences: Sargent College, Department of Occupational Therapy, Boston, MA 02215. Offers occupational therapy (OTD); rehabilitation sciences (PhD). *Accreditation:* AOTA (one or more programs are accredited). *Program availability:* Blended/hybrid learning. *Faculty:* 13 full-time (10 women). *Students:* 101 full-time (92 women), 83 part-time (76 women); includes 50 minority (9 Black or African American, non-Hispanic/Latino; 22 Asian, non-Hispanic/Latino; 12 Hispanic/Latino; 7 Two or more races, non-Hispanic/Latino), 10 international. Average age 30. 333 applicants, 35% accepted, 57 enrolled. In 2019, 31 doctorates awarded. *Entrance requirements:* Additional exam requirements/recommendations for international students: required—TOEFL. Application fee: $150. Electronic applications accepted. *Financial support:* Teaching assistantships, career-related internships or fieldwork, Federal Work-Study, institutionally sponsored loans, scholarships/grants, and unspecified assistantships available. Financial award applicants required to submit FAFSA. *Unit head:* Dr. Wendy Coster, Chair, 617-353-7518, E-mail: wjcoster@bu.edu. *Application contact:* Sharon Sankey, Assistant Dean, Student Services, 617-353-2713, Fax: 617-353-7500, E-mail: ssankey@bu.edu. Website: http://www.bu.edu/sargent/

**Brenau University,** Sydney O. Smith Graduate School, Ivester College of Health Sciences, Gainesville, GA 30501. Offers family nurse practitioner (MSN); general psychology (MS); nurse educator (MSN); nursing manager (MSN); occupational therapy (MS). *Accreditation:* AOTA. *Program availability:* Part-time, evening/weekend, 100% online, blended/hybrid learning. *Faculty:* 34 full-time (26 women), 11 part-time/adjunct (10 women). *Students:* 321 full-time (242 women), 209 part-time (197 women); includes 177 minority (104 Black or African American, non-Hispanic/Latino; 2 American Indian or Alaska Native, non-Hispanic/Latino; 24 Asian, non-Hispanic/Latino; 36 Hispanic/Latino; 2 Native Hawaiian or other Pacific Islander, non-Hispanic/Latino; 9 Two or more races, non-Hispanic/Latino), 3 international. Average age 29. 517 applicants, 47% accepted, 110 enrolled. In 2019, 174 master's awarded. *Entrance requirements:* For master's, GMAT, GRE, or MAT, minimum GPA 2.5. Additional exam requirements/recommendations for international students: required—TOEFL (minimum score 497 paper-based; 71 iBT); recommended—IELTS (minimum score 5.5). *Application deadline:* Applications are processed on a rolling basis. Application fee: $35. Electronic applications accepted. *Expenses:* $11,763 full-time tuition (average), $4,678 part-time tuition (average). *Financial support:* In 2019–20, 11 students received support. Scholarships/grants available. Financial award applicants required to submit FAFSA. *Unit head:* Dr. Gale Starich, Dean, 777-718-5305, Fax: 770-297-5929, E-mail: gstarich@brenau.edu. *Application contact:* Nathan Goss, Assistant Vice President for Recruitment, 770-534-6162, E-mail: ngoss@brenau.edu. Website: http://www.brenau.edu/healthsciences/

**Cabarrus College of Health Sciences,** Program in Occupational Therapy, Concord, NC 28025. Offers MOT. *Accreditation:* AOTA.

**California State University, Dominguez Hills,** College of Health, Human Services and Nursing, Program in Occupational Therapy, Carson, CA 90747-0001. Offers MS. *Accreditation:* AOTA. *Degree requirements:* For master's, comprehensive exam. *Entrance requirements:* For master's, GRE. Additional exam requirements/recommendations for international students: required—TOEFL, TWE. Electronic applications accepted.

**Carroll University,** Program in Occupational Therapy, Waukesha, WI 53186-5593. Offers MOT. *Accreditation:* AOTA.

**Chatham University,** Program in Occupational Therapy, Pittsburgh, PA 15232-2826. Offers MOT, OTD. *Accreditation:* AOTA. *Entrance requirements:* For master's, recommendation letter, community service, volunteer service. Additional exam requirements/recommendations for international students: required—TOEFL (minimum score 600 paper-based; 100 iBT), IELTS (minimum score 7), TWE. Electronic applications accepted. Application fee is waived when completed online. *Expenses:* Contact institution.

**Chicago State University,** School of Graduate and Professional Studies, College of Health Sciences, Department of Occupational Therapy, Chicago, IL 60628. Offers MOT. *Accreditation:* AOTA. *Program availability:* Part-time. *Entrance requirements:* For master's, bachelor's degree from accredited college or university with minimum GPA of 3.0 in final 60 semester credit hours; two recommendations; human service experience; essay; interview.

**Clarkson University,** Lewis School of Health Sciences, Department of Occupational Therapy, Potsdam, NY 13699. Offers MS. *Accreditation:* AOTA. *Faculty:* 7 full-time (6 women), 1 (woman) part-time/adjunct. *Students:* 56 full-time (47 women); includes 8 minority (2 Black or African American, non-Hispanic/Latino; 1 American Indian or Alaska Native, non-Hispanic/Latino; 5 Asian, non-Hispanic/Latino). 134 applicants, 49% accepted, 22 enrolled. In 2019, 17 master's awarded. *Entrance requirements:* For master's, minimum undergraduate GPA of 3.0; OTCAS application. *Application deadline:* For spring admission, 4/18 for domestic and international students. Applications are processed on a rolling basis. Application fee: $190. Electronic applications accepted. *Expenses:* Contact institution. *Financial support:* Scholarships/grants available. *Unit head:* Dr. Alisha Ohl, Interim Chair of Occupational Therapy, 315-268-2210, E-mail: ltebo@clarkson.edu. *Application contact:* Jennifer Zoanetti, Graduate

## Occupational Therapy

Admissions Coordinator, 315-268-4476, E-mail: jzoanett@clarkson.edu. Website: https://www.clarkson.edu/academics/graduate

**Cleveland State University,** College of Graduate Studies, College of Sciences and Health Professions, School of Health Sciences, Program in Occupational Therapy, Cleveland, OH 44115. Offers MOT. *Accreditation:* AOTA. *Entrance requirements:* For master's, GRE (if overall GPA less than 3.0). Additional exam requirements/recommendations for international students: recommended—TOEFL (minimum score 550 paper-based; 78 iBT), IELTS (minimum score 6). Electronic applications accepted. *Expenses:* Tuition, state resident: full-time $10,215; part-time $6810 per credit hour. Tuition, nonresident: full-time $17,496; part-time $11,664 per credit hour. *International tuition:* $19,316 full-time. Tuition and fees vary according to degree level and program.

**College of Saint Mary,** Program in Occupational Therapy, Omaha, NE 68106. Offers MOT. *Accreditation:* AOTA.

**The College of St. Scholastica,** Graduate Studies, Department of Occupational Therapy, Duluth, MN 55811-4199. Offers MA. *Accreditation:* AOTA. *Program availability:* Part-time. *Degree requirements:* For master's, thesis. *Entrance requirements:* Additional exam requirements/recommendations for international students: required—TOEFL (minimum score 550 paper-based; 79 iBT). Electronic applications accepted.

**Colorado State University,** College of Health and Human Sciences, Department of Occupational Therapy, Fort Collins, CO 80523-1573. Offers MOT, MS, PhD. *Accreditation:* AOTA. *Faculty:* 11 full-time (8 women), 5 part-time/adjunct (all women). *Students:* 115 full-time (106 women), 7 part-time (5 women); includes 15 minority (2 Asian, non-Hispanic/Latino; 8 Hispanic/Latino; 5 Two or more races, non-Hispanic/Latino), 1 international. Average age 27. 552 applicants, 16% accepted, 54 enrolled. In 2019, 51 master's, 2 doctorates awarded. Terminal master's awarded for partial completion of doctoral program. *Degree requirements:* For master's, thesis (for some programs); for doctorate, comprehensive exam, thesis/dissertation. *Entrance requirements:* For master's and doctorate, GRE General Test, OTCAS; departmental application. Additional exam requirements/recommendations for international students: required—TOEFL. *Application deadline:* For fall admission, 1/5 priority date for domestic and international students. Application fee: $60 ($70 for international students). Electronic applications accepted. *Expenses:* Contact institution. *Financial support:* In 2019–20, 7 fellowships with full and partial tuition reimbursements (averaging $7,605 per year), 6 research assistantships with full and partial tuition reimbursements (averaging $26,206 per year), 1 teaching assistantship with full and partial tuition reimbursement (averaging $7,605 per year) were awarded; scholarships/grants and unspecified assistantships also available. *Unit head:* Dr. Anita Bundy, Department Head, 970-491-3105, Fax: 970-491-6290, E-mail: anita.bundy@colostate.edu. *Application contact:* Linda McDowell, Graduate Programs Coordinator, 970-491-6243, Fax: 970-491-6290, E-mail: linda.mcdowell@colostate.edu. Website: https://www.chhs.colostate.edu/ot

**Columbia University,** College of Physicians and Surgeons, Programs in Occupational Therapy, New York, NY 10032. Offers movement science (Ed D), including occupational therapy; occupational therapy (MS); occupational therapy and cognition (OTD); MPH/MS. *Accreditation:* AOTA. *Degree requirements:* For master's, project, 6 months of fieldwork, thesis (for post-professional students); for doctorate, comprehensive exam, thesis/dissertation. *Entrance requirements:* For master's, undergraduate course work in anatomy, physiology, statistics, psychology, social sciences, humanities, and English composition; for doctorate, master's degree in occupational therapy (for OTD). Additional exam requirements/recommendations for international students: required—TOEFL (minimum score 100 iBT) or IELTS (minimum score 8). Electronic applications accepted. *Expenses:* Contact institution.

**Concordia University Wisconsin,** Graduate Programs, School of Health Professions, Program in Occupational Therapy, Mequon, WI 53097-2402. Offers MOT. *Accreditation:* AOTA. *Degree requirements:* For master's, comprehensive exam, thesis or alternative. *Entrance requirements:* Additional exam requirements/recommendations for international students: required—TOEFL.

**Cox College,** Program in Occupational Therapy, Springfield, MO 65802. Offers MSOT.

**Creighton University,** School of Pharmacy and Health Professions, Program in Occupational Therapy, Omaha, NE 68178-0001. Offers OTD. *Accreditation:* AOTA. *Program availability:* Online learning. *Entrance requirements:* Additional exam requirements/recommendations for international students: required—TOEFL. Electronic applications accepted.

**Dalhousie University,** Faculty of Health, School of Occupational Therapy, Halifax, NS B3H3J5, Canada. Offers occupational therapy (entry to profession) (M Sc); occupational therapy (post-professional) (M Sc). *Program availability:* Part-time, evening/weekend, online learning. *Degree requirements:* For master's, thesis. *Entrance requirements:* Additional exam requirements/recommendations for international students: required—TOEFL, IELTS, CANTEST, CAEL, or Michigan English Language Assessment Battery. Electronic applications accepted.

**Davenport University,** Sneden Graduate School, Grand Rapids, MI 49512. Offers accounting (MBA); business administration (EMBA); finance (MBA); health care management (MBA); human resources (MBA); information assurance (MS); occupational therapy (MSOT); public health (MPH); strategic management (MBA). *Program availability:* Evening/weekend. *Entrance requirements:* For master's, GMAT, minimum undergraduate GPA of 2.75. Additional exam requirements/recommendations for international students: required—TOEFL. Electronic applications accepted.

**Dominican College,** Division of Allied Health, Master's Degree in Occupational Therapy, Orangeburg, NY 10962-1210. Offers MS. *Accreditation:* AOTA. *Program availability:* Part-time, evening/weekend. *Degree requirements:* For master's, 2- Level 1 Fieldwork experience; 2 - Level 2 Fieldwork experience. *Entrance requirements:* For master's, minimum GPA of 3.0, writing sample, 3 letters of recommendation. Additional exam requirements/recommendations for international students: required—TOEFL (minimum score 550 paper-based; 90 iBT). Electronic applications accepted. *Expenses:* Contact institution.

**Dominican University of California,** School of Health and Natural Sciences, Program in Occupational Therapy, San Rafael, CA 94901-2298. Offers MS. *Accreditation:* AOTA. *Degree requirements:* For master's, thesis. *Entrance requirements:* For master's, GRE, minimum GPA of 3.0, minimum of 60 hours of volunteer experience. Additional exam requirements/recommendations for international students: required—TOEFL (minimum score 550 paper-based; 80 iBT), IELTS (minimum score 6.5). Electronic applications accepted. *Expenses:* Contact institution.

**Duquesne University,** John G. Rangos, Sr. School of Health Sciences, Pittsburgh, PA 15282-0001. Offers health management systems (MHMS); occupational therapy (MS, OTD); physical therapy (DPT); physician assistant studies (MPAS); rehabilitation science (MS, PhD); speech-language pathology (MS). *Accreditation:* AOTA (one or more programs are accredited); APTA (one or more programs are accredited); ASHA. *Program availability:* Part-time, minimal on-campus study. *Degree requirements:* For doctorate, comprehensive exam (for some programs), thesis/dissertation (for some programs). *Entrance requirements:* For master's, GRE General Test (speech-language pathology), 3 letters of recommendation; minimum GPA of 2.75 (health management

systems), 3.0 (speech-language pathology); for doctorate, GRE General Test (for physical therapy and rehabilitation science), 3 letters of recommendation, minimum GPA of 3.0, personal interview. Additional exam requirements/recommendations for international students: required—TOEFL (minimum score 550 paper-based; 90 iBT); recommended—IELTS. Electronic applications accepted. *Expenses:* Contact institution.

**D'Youville College,** Occupational Therapy Department, Buffalo, NY 14201-1084. Offers MS. *Accreditation:* AOTA. *Degree requirements:* For master's, research project or thesis. *Entrance requirements:* For master's, minimum undergraduate GPA of 3.0. Additional exam requirements/recommendations for international students: required—TOEFL (minimum score 500 paper-based). Electronic applications accepted.

**East Carolina University,** Graduate School, College of Allied Health Sciences, Department of Addictions and Rehabilitation Studies, Greenville, NC 27858-4353. Offers clinical counseling (MS); military and trauma counseling (Certificate); rehabilitation and career counseling (MS); rehabilitation counseling (Certificate); rehabilitation counseling and administration (PhD); substance abuse counseling (Certificate); vocational evaluation (Certificate). *Accreditation:* CORE. *Program availability:* Part-time, evening/weekend. *Students:* Average age 33. 51 applicants, 73% accepted, 31 enrolled. In 2019, 19 master's, 5 doctorates, 34 other advanced degrees awarded. *Degree requirements:* For master's, comprehensive exam, thesis or alternative, internship; for doctorate, thesis/dissertation, internship. *Entrance requirements:* For master's and doctorate, GRE General Test or MAT. Additional exam requirements/recommendations for international students: recommended—TOEFL (minimum score 78 iBT), IELTS (minimum score 6.5). *Application deadline:* For fall admission, 3/1 priority date for domestic students; for spring admission, 10/1 priority date for domestic students. Applications are processed on a rolling basis. Application fee: $75. Electronic applications accepted. *Expenses: Tuition, area resident:* Full-time $4749; part-time $185 per credit hour. Tuition, state resident: full-time $4749; part-time $185 per credit hour. Tuition, nonresident: full-time $17,898; part-time $864 per credit hour. *International tuition:* $17,898 full-time. *Required fees:* $2787. *Financial support:* Research assistantships with partial tuition reimbursements, teaching assistantships with partial tuition reimbursements, Federal Work-Study, scholarships/grants, and unspecified assistantships available. Support available to part-time students. Financial award application deadline: 3/1; financial award applicants required to submit FAFSA. *Unit head:* Dr. Paul Toriello, Chair, 252-744-6292, E-mail: toriellop@ecu.edu. *Application contact:* Graduate School Admissions, 252-328-6013, Fax: 252-328-6071, E-mail: gradschool@ecu.edu. Website: http://www.ecu.edu/rehb/

**East Carolina University,** Graduate School, College of Allied Health Sciences, Department of Occupational Therapy, Greenville, NC 27858-4353. Offers MSOT. *Accreditation:* AOTA. *Application deadline:* For fall admission, 11/1 for domestic students. *Expenses: Tuition, area resident:* Full-time $4749; part-time $185 per credit hour. Tuition, state resident: full-time $4749; part-time $185 per credit hour. Tuition, nonresident: full-time $17,898; part-time $864 per credit hour. *International tuition:* $17,898 full-time. *Required fees:* $2787. *Financial support:* Application deadline: 3/1. *Unit head:* Dr. Lynnne Murphy, Chair, 252-744-6193, E-mail: wilsonj@ecu.edu. *Application contact:* Graduate School Admissions, 252-328-6012, Fax: 252-328-6071, E-mail: gradschool@ecu.edu. Website: http://www.ecu.edu/ot/

**Eastern Kentucky University,** The Graduate School, College of Health Sciences, Department of Occupational Therapy, Richmond, KY 40475-3102. Offers MS. *Accreditation:* AOTA. *Program availability:* Part-time. *Degree requirements:* For master's, thesis optional. *Entrance requirements:* For master's, GRE General Test, minimum GPA of 3.0.

**Eastern Michigan University,** Graduate School, College of Health and Human Services, School of Health Sciences, Programs in Occupational Therapy, Ypsilanti, MI 48197. Offers MOT, MS. *Accreditation:* AOTA. *Program availability:* Part-time, evening/weekend, online learning. *Students:* 61 full-time (49 women), 3 part-time (2 women); includes 7 minority (2 Asian, non-Hispanic/Latino; 1 Hispanic/Latino; 4 Two or more races, non-Hispanic/Latino). Average age 25. 10 applicants, 20% accepted, 1 enrolled. In 2019, 38 master's awarded. *Entrance requirements:* Additional exam requirements/recommendations for international students: required—TOEFL. *Application deadline:* Applications are processed on a rolling basis. Application fee: $45. *Financial support:* Fellowships, research assistantships with full tuition reimbursements, teaching assistantships with full tuition reimbursements, career-related internships or fieldwork, Federal Work-Study, institutionally sponsored loans, scholarships/grants, tuition waivers (partial), and unspecified assistantships available. Support available to part-time students. Financial award applicants required to submit FAFSA. *Application contact:* Sharon Holt, Advisor, 734-487-0430, Fax: 734-487-4095, E-mail: ot_intent_advising@emich.edu.

**Eastern Washington University,** Graduate Studies, College of Health Science and Public Health, Department of Occupational Therapy, Cheney, WA 99004-2431. Offers MOT. *Accreditation:* AOTA. *Faculty:* 7 full-time (6 women). *Students:* 91 full-time (76 women), 5 part-time (1 woman); includes 2 minority (both Hispanic/Latino). Average age 29. 180 applicants, 14% accepted, 5 enrolled. In 2019, 31 master's awarded. *Degree requirements:* For master's, comprehensive exam. *Entrance requirements:* For master's, GRE. Additional exam requirements/recommendations for international students: required—TOEFL (minimum score 580 paper-based; 92 iBT), IELTS (minimum score 7), PTE (minimum score 63). *Application deadline:* For summer admission, 12/15 for domestic students. Applications are processed on a rolling basis. Application fee: $75. Electronic applications accepted. *Financial support:* Career-related internships or fieldwork, Federal Work-Study, institutionally sponsored loans, scholarships/grants, tuition waivers (partial), and unspecified assistantships available. Support available to part-time students. Financial award application deadline: 2/1; financial award applicants required to submit FAFSA. *Application contact:* Lee Knous, Senior Secretary, 509-8281344, E-mail: ot@ewu.edu. Website: http://www.ewu.edu/cshe/programs/occupational-therapy.xml

**Elizabethtown College,** Department of Occupational Therapy, Elizabethtown, PA 17022-2298. Offers MS. *Accreditation:* AOTA.

**Elmhurst University,** Graduate Programs, Program in Occupational Therapy, Elmhurst, IL 60126-3296. Offers MOT. *Accreditation:* AOTA. *Faculty:* 4 full-time (3 women). *Students:* 48 full-time (45 women); includes 11 minority (5 Asian, non-Hispanic/Latino; 6 Hispanic/Latino). Average age 24. 597 applicants, 11% accepted, 24 enrolled. In 2019, 18 master's awarded. *Entrance requirements:* For master's, GRE, minimum cumulative GPA of 3.2, 3 recommendations, resume, statement of purpose. Additional exam requirements/recommendations for international students: required—TOEFL (minimum score 550 paper-based; 79 iBT), IELTS (minimum score 6.5). *Application deadline:* Applications are processed on a rolling basis. Electronic applications accepted. *Expenses:* $33,000 per year. *Financial support:* In 2019–20, 41 students received support. Scholarships/grants available. Financial award applicants required to submit FAFSA. *Unit head:* Dr. Elizabeth Wanka, Program Director, 630-617-5854, E-mail: elizabeth.wanka@elmhurst.edu. *Application contact:* Timothy J. Panfil, Senior Director of Graduate Admission and Enrollment Management, 630-617-3300 Ext. 3256,

Fax: 630-617-6471, E-mail: panfilt@elmhurst.edu. Website: http://www.elmhurst.edu/admission/graduate/master_of_occupational_therapy

**Emory & Henry College,** Graduate Programs, Emory, VA 24327. Offers American history (MA Ed); education professional studies (M Ed); occupational therapy (MOT); organizational leadership (MCOL); physical therapy (DPT); physician assistant studies (MPAS); reading specialist (MA Ed). *Program availability:* Part-time. *Degree requirements:* For master's, thesis optional; for doctorate, thesis/dissertation optional. *Entrance requirements:* For master's, GRE or PRAXIS I, official transcripts from all colleges previously attended, three professional recommendations, essay. Additional exam requirements/recommendations for international students: recommended—TOEFL, IELTS (minimum score 6). Electronic applications accepted. *Expenses:* Contact institution.

**Florida Agricultural and Mechanical University,** Division of Graduate Studies, Research, and Continuing Education, School of Allied Health Sciences, Division of Occupational Therapy, Tallahassee, FL 32307-3200. Offers MOT. *Accreditation:* AOTA.

**Florida Gulf Coast University,** Elaine Nicpon Marieb College of Health and Human Services, Program in Occupational Therapy, Fort Myers, FL 33965-6565. Offers MS. *Accreditation:* AOTA. *Entrance requirements:* For master's, GRE General Test, MAT, minimum GPA of 3.0. Additional exam requirements/recommendations for international students: required—TOEFL (minimum score 550 paper-based). Electronic applications accepted. *Expenses: Tuition, area resident:* Full-time $6974; part-time $4350 per credit hour. Tuition, state resident: full-time $6974; part-time $4350 per credit hour. Tuition, nonresident: full-time $28,169; part-time $17,595 per credit hour. *International tuition:* $28,169 full-time. *Required fees:* $2027; $1267 per credit hour. $507 per semester. Tuition and fees vary according to course load.

**Florida International University,** Nicole Wertheim College of Nursing and Health Sciences, Department of Occupational Therapy, Miami, FL 33199. Offers MSOT. *Accreditation:* AOTA. *Program availability:* Part-time. *Faculty:* 6 full-time (5 women), 6 part-time/adjunct (all women). *Students:* 139 full-time (126 women), 3 part-time (all women); includes 110 minority (9 Black or African American, non-Hispanic/Latino; 5 Asian, non-Hispanic/Latino; 93 Hispanic/Latino; 3 Two or more races, non-Hispanic/Latino), 1 international. Average age 25. 177 applicants, 31% accepted, 48 enrolled. In 2019, 55 master's awarded. *Entrance requirements:* For master's, minimum undergraduate GPA of 3.0 in upper-level course work, letter of intent, 3 letters of recommendation, resume. Additional exam requirements/recommendations for international students: required—TOEFL (minimum score 550 paper-based; 80 iBT). *Application deadline:* For fall admission, 2/15 for domestic and international students. Applications are processed on a rolling basis. Application fee: $30. Electronic applications accepted. *Expenses:* Contact institution. *Financial support:* Career-related internships or fieldwork, Federal Work-Study, institutionally sponsored loans, scholarships/grants, and unspecified assistantships available. Financial award application deadline: 3/1; financial award applicants required to submit FAFSA. *Unit head:* Dr. Lynne Richard, Interim Chair, 305-348-2922, E-mail: lyrichar@fiu.edu. *Application contact:* Nanett Rojas, Manager, Admissions Operations, 305-348-7464, Fax: 305-348-7441, E-mail: gradadm@fiu.edu.

**Gannon University,** School of Graduate Studies, Morosky College of Health Professions and Sciences, School of Health Professions, Program in Occupational Therapy, Erie, PA 16541-0001. Offers MS, OTD. *Accreditation:* AOTA. *Degree requirements:* For master's, thesis, field work; for doctorate, thesis/dissertation. *Entrance requirements:* For master's, bachelor's degree, Student Self-Report Transcript Evaluation, minimum GPA of 3.0, 40 hours of volunteer experience; for doctorate, bachelor's degree from accredited college or university with minimum GPA of 3.0, transcript, minimum of 40 hours of volunteer experience in an OT setting, Student Self-Report Transcript Evaluation. Additional exam requirements/recommendations for international students: required—TOEFL (minimum score 79 iBT). Electronic applications accepted. Application fee is waived when completed online. *Expenses:* Contact institution.

**Georgia State University,** Byrdine F. Lewis School of Nursing, Department of Occupational Therapy, Atlanta, GA 30302-3083. Offers MOT. *Faculty:* 7 full-time (6 women). *Students:* 76 full-time (71 women), 16 part-time (1 woman); includes 20 minority (7 Black or African American, non-Hispanic/Latino; 6 Asian, non-Hispanic/Latino; 5 Hispanic/Latino; 2 Two or more races, non-Hispanic/Latino). Average age 26. 230 applicants, 31% accepted, 38 enrolled. In 2019, 48 master's awarded. *Application deadline:* For fall admission, 10/1 for domestic and international students. *Expenses: Tuition, area resident:* Full-time $7164; part-time $398 per credit hour. Tuition, state resident: full-time $7164; part-time $398 per credit hour. Tuition, nonresident: full-time $22,662; part-time $1259 per credit hour. *International tuition:* $22,662 full-time. *Required fees:* $2128; $312 per credit hour. Tuition and fees vary according to course load and program. *Unit head:* Dr. Kinsuk Maitra, Chair, 404-413-1446, Fax: 404-413-1090, E-mail: kmaitra@gsu.edu. *Application contact:* Dr. Kinsuk Maitra, Chair, 404-413-1446, Fax: 404-413-1090, E-mail: kmaitra@gsu.edu. Website: https://occupationaltherapy.gsu.edu/

**Governors State University,** College of Health and Human Services, Program in Occupational Therapy, University Park, IL 60484. Offers MOT. *Accreditation:* AOTA. *Program availability:* Part-time. *Faculty:* 7 full-time (6 women), 13 part-time/adjunct (all women). *Students:* 85 full-time (70 women); includes 20 minority (4 Black or African American, non-Hispanic/Latino; 9 Asian, non-Hispanic/Latino; 6 Hispanic/Latino; 1 Two or more races, non-Hispanic/Latino). Average age 26. 7 applicants. In 2019, 27 master's awarded. *Application deadline:* For fall admission, 4/1 for domestic students. Applications are processed on a rolling basis. Application fee: $50. Electronic applications accepted. *Expenses:* $797/credit hour; $9,564 in tuition/term; $10,862 in tuition and fees/term; $21,724/year. *Financial support:* Application deadline: 5/1; applicants required to submit FAFSA. *Unit head:* Caren Schranz, Chair, Department of Occupational Therapy, 708-534-5000 Ext. 7344, E-mail: cschranz@govst.edu. *Application contact:* Caren Schranz, Chair, Department of Occupational Therapy, 708-534-5000 Ext. 7344, E-mail: cschranz@govst.edu.

**Grand Valley State University,** College of Health Professions, Occupational Therapy Program, Allendale, MI 49401-9403. Offers MS. *Accreditation:* AOTA. *Program availability:* Part-time, evening/weekend. *Faculty:* 10 full-time (9 women), 7 part-time/adjunct (all women). *Students:* 120 full-time (112 women), 23 part-time (22 women); includes 13 minority (6 Black or African American, non-Hispanic/Latino; 1 Asian, non-Hispanic/Latino; 4 Hispanic/Latino; 2 Two or more races, non-Hispanic/Latino), 1 international. Average age 26. 197 applicants, 35% accepted, 61 enrolled. In 2019, 59 master's awarded. *Degree requirements:* For master's, thesis or alternative, fieldwork, project. *Entrance requirements:* For master's, minimum GPA of 3.0 in prerequisite courses and last 60 hours of work, 2 letters of recommendation, interview, volunteer work (minimum of 50 hours), writing sample, completion of Achievement Summary Form. Additional exam requirements/recommendations for international students: required—TOEFL (minimum iBT score of 80), IELTS (6.5), or Michigan English Language Assessment Battery (77). *Application deadline:* For fall admission, 1/15 for domestic and international students. Applications are processed on a rolling basis. Application fee: $30. Electronic applications accepted. *Expenses:* $733 per credit hour,

81-82 credit hours. *Financial support:* In 2019–20, 23 students received support, including 18 fellowships, 5 research assistantships; unspecified assistantships also available. Financial award application deadline: 2/15. *Unit head:* Dr. Scott Truskowski, Department Chair, 616-331-3128, Fax: 616-331-5654, E-mail: truskows@gvsu.edu. *Application contact:* Darlene Zwart, Student Services Coordinator, 616-331-3958, Fax: 616-331-5643, E-mail: zwartda@gvsu.edu. Website: http://www.gvsu.edu/ot/

**Hofstra University,** School of Health Professions and Human Services, Programs in Health, Hempstead, NY 11549. Offers foundations of public health (Advanced Certificate); health administration (MHA); health informatics (MS); occupational therapy (MS); public health (MPH); security and privacy in health information systems (Advanced Certificate); sports science (MS); teacher of students with speech-language disabilities (Advanced Certificate). *Program availability:* Part-time, evening/weekend. *Students:* 291 full-time (220 women), 128 part-time (88 women); includes 192 minority (69 Black or African American, non-Hispanic/Latino; 3 American Indian or Alaska Native, non-Hispanic/Latino; 72 Asian, non-Hispanic/Latino; 37 Hispanic/Latino; 4 Native Hawaiian or other Pacific Islander, non-Hispanic/Latino; 7 Two or more races, non-Hispanic/Latino), 25 international. Average age 29. 676 applicants, 52% accepted, 132 enrolled. In 2019, 170 master's, 1 other advanced degree awarded. *Degree requirements:* For master's, internship, minimum GPA of 3.0. *Entrance requirements:* For master's, interview, 2 letters of recommendation, essay, resume. Additional exam requirements/recommendations for international students: required—TOEFL (minimum score 550 paper-based; 80 iBT); recommended—IELTS (minimum score 6.5). *Application deadline:* Applications are processed on a rolling basis. Application fee: $75. Electronic applications accepted. *Expenses: Tuition:* Full-time $25,164; part-time $1398 per credit. *Required fees:* $580; $165 per semester. Tuition and fees vary according to course load, degree level and program. *Financial support:* In 2019–20, 181 students received support, including 104 fellowships with full and partial tuition reimbursements available (averaging $3,465 per year), 5 research assistantships with full and partial tuition reimbursements available (averaging $7,172 per year); career-related internships or fieldwork, Federal Work-Study, institutionally sponsored loans, scholarships/grants, traineeships, tuition waivers (full and partial), unspecified assistantships, and scholarships and endowed scholarships also available. Support available to part-time students. Financial award applicants required to submit FAFSA. *Unit head:* Dr. Corinne Kyriacou, Chairperson, 516-463-4553, E-mail: corinne.m.kyriacou@hofstra.edu. *Application contact:* Sunil Samuel, Assistant Vice President of Admissions, 516-463-4723, Fax: 516-463-4664, E-mail: graduateadmission@hofstra.edu. Website: http://www.hofstra.edu/academics/colleges/healthscienceshumanservices/

**Howard University,** College of Nursing and Allied Health Sciences, Division of Allied Health Sciences, Washington, DC 20059-0002. Offers occupational therapy (MSOT); physical therapy (DPT); physician assistant (MPA). *Accreditation:* AOTA.

**Huntington University,** Graduate School, Huntington, IN 46750-1299. Offers adolescent and young adult education (M Ed); business administration (MBA); counseling (MA), including licensed mental health counselor; early adolescent education (M Ed); elementary education (M Ed); global youth ministry (MA); occupational therapy (OTD); organizational leadership (MA); pastoral leadership (MA); TESOL education (M Ed). *Accreditation:* AOTA. *Program availability:* Part-time, online learning. *Degree requirements:* For master's, comprehensive exam (for some programs), thesis (for some programs). *Entrance requirements:* For master's, GRE (for counseling and education students only); for doctorate, GRE (for occupational therapy students). Additional exam requirements/recommendations for international students: required—TOEFL (minimum score 85 iBT), IELTS (minimum score 6.5). Electronic applications accepted. *Expenses:* Contact institution.

**Idaho State University,** Graduate School, College of Rehabilitation and Communication Sciences, Department of Physical and Occupational Therapy, Program in Occupational Therapy, Pocatello, ID 83209-8045. Offers MOT. *Accreditation:* AOTA. *Degree requirements:* For master's, comprehensive exam, thesis, oral and written exam. *Entrance requirements:* For master's, GRE General Test, minimum GPA of 3.0, 80 hours in 2 practice settings of occupational therapy. Additional exam requirements/recommendations for international students: required—TOEFL (minimum score 600 paper-based). Electronic applications accepted. *Expenses:* Contact institution.

**Indiana State University,** College of Graduate and Professional Studies, College of Health and Human Services, Department of Applied Medicine and Rehabilitation, Terre Haute, IN 47809. Offers athletic training (MS, DAT); occupational therapy (MS); physical therapy (DPT); physician assistant (MS). *Accreditation:* AOTA. *Degree requirements:* For master's, thesis or alternative. *Entrance requirements:* For master's, GRE General Test. Electronic applications accepted.

**Indiana University-Purdue University Indianapolis,** School of Health and Rehabilitation Sciences, Indianapolis, IN 46202. Offers health and rehabilitation sciences (PhD); health sciences (MS); nutrition and dietetics (MS); occupational therapy (OTD); physical therapy (DPT); physician assistant (MPAS). *Accreditation:* AOTA. *Program availability:* Part-time, evening/weekend. *Degree requirements:* For master's, thesis (for some programs). *Entrance requirements:* For master's, GRE General Test, minimum GPA of 3.0 (for MS in health sciences, nutrition and dietetics), 3.2 (for MS in occupational therapy), 3.0 cumulative and prerequisite math/science (for MPAS); for doctorate, GRE, minimum cumulative and prerequisite math/science GPA of 3.2. Additional exam requirements/recommendations for international students: required—TOEFL (minimum score 550 paper-based; 79 iBT), IELTS (minimum score 6.5), PTE (minimum score 54). Electronic applications accepted. *Expenses:* Contact institution.

**Indiana Wesleyan University,** Graduate School, School of Health Sciences, Marion, IN 46953-4974. Offers athletic training (MS); occupational therapy (OTD); public health (MPH).

**Ithaca College,** School of Health Sciences and Human Performance, Program in Occupational Therapy, Ithaca, NY 14850. Offers MS. *Accreditation:* AOTA. *Faculty:* 14 full-time (13 women), 1 (woman) part-time/adjunct. *Students:* 67 full-time (64 women), 1 (woman) part-time; includes 10 minority (4 Asian, non-Hispanic/Latino; 3 Hispanic/Latino; 3 Two or more races, non-Hispanic/Latino). Average age 23. 63 applicants, 92% accepted, 23 enrolled. In 2019, 53 master's awarded. *Entrance requirements:* Additional exam requirements/recommendations for international students: required—TOEFL (minimum score 550 paper-based; 80 iBT). *Application deadline:* For fall admission, 3/1 for domestic and international students. Applications are processed on a rolling basis. Application fee: $40. Electronic applications accepted. *Expenses:* Contact institution. *Financial support:* In 2019–20, 47 students received support, including 17 teaching assistantships (averaging $11,346 per year); Federal Work-Study and scholarships/grants also available. Support available to part-time students. Financial award application deadline: 3/1; financial award applicants required to submit FAFSA. *Unit head:* Dr. Michelle Bradshaw, Chair, Graduate Program, 607-274-3160, Fax: 607-274-1263, E-mail: mbradshaw@ithaca.edu. *Application contact:* Nicole Eversley Bradwell, Director, Office of Admission, 800-429-4274, Fax: 607-274-1263, E-mail: admission@ithaca.edu. Website: https://www.ithaca.edu/academics/school-health-sciences-and-human-

performance/occupational-therapy/professional-entry-level-masters-program-occupation

**Jacksonville University,** Brooks Rehabilitation College of Healthcare Sciences, School of Applied Health Sciences, Program in Occupational Therapy, Jacksonville, FL 32211. Offers OTD. *Students:* 43 full-time (41 women); includes 14 minority (7 Black or African American, non-Hispanic/Latino; 2 Asian, non-Hispanic/Latino; 4 Hispanic/Latino; 1 Two or more races, non-Hispanic/Latino). Average age 26. 131 applicants, 49% accepted, 28 enrolled. *Degree requirements:* For doctorate, observation of occupational therapy practice; minimum of 40 hours total among three different settings (hospital, school system, home health, clinic, etc.). *Entrance requirements:* For doctorate, GRE, baccalaureate degree from accredited college or university with minimum GPA of 3.0; official transcripts; observation of occupational therapy practice with minimum of 40 hours total among three different settings (hospital, school system, home health, clinic, etc.); interview. Additional exam requirements/recommendations for international students: required—TOEFL (minimum score 650 paper-based; 114 iBT), IELTS (minimum score 8). *Application deadline:* For spring admission, 10/30 for domestic and international students. Applications are processed on a rolling basis. Application fee: $50. Electronic applications accepted. *Expenses:* Contact institution. *Financial support:* Application deadline: 3/15; applicants required to submit FAFSA. *Unit head:* Dr. Michael Justiss, Professor and Department Chair, Doctor of Occupational Therapy (OTD) Program, 904-256-8917, E-mail: mjustis1@ju.edu. *Application contact:* Antonio Starke, Assistant Director of Graduate Admissions, 904-256-7472, E-mail: astarke2@ju.edu.
Website: https://www.ju.edu/occupationaltherapy/

**James Madison University,** The Graduate School, College of Health and Behavioral Studies, Program in Occupational Therapy, Harrisonburg, VA 22807. Offers MOT. *Accreditation:* AOTA. *Program availability:* Part-time. *Students:* 71 full-time (64 women), 1 (woman) part-time; includes 12 minority (4 Black or African American, non-Hispanic/Latino; 2 Asian, non-Hispanic/Latino; 3 Hispanic/Latino; 3 Two or more races, non-Hispanic/Latino), 2 international. Average age 30. In 2019, 22 master's awarded. Application fee: $60. Electronic applications accepted. *Financial support:* In 2019–20, 5 students received support. Fellowships available. Financial award application deadline: 3/1; financial award applicants required to submit FAFSA. *Unit head:* Dr. Kirk Armstrong, Academic Unit Head, Department of Health Professions, 540-568-6510. *Application contact:* Dr. Rachelle Dorne, Program Director, 540-568-2399, Fax: 540-568-3336, E-mail: otprogram@jmu.edu.
Website: http://healthprof.jmu.edu/ot/

**Jefferson College of Health Sciences,** Program in Occupational Therapy, Roanoke, VA 24013. Offers MS. *Accreditation:* AOTA. *Program availability:* Part-time. *Entrance requirements:* For master's, GRE. Additional exam requirements/recommendations for international students: required—TOEFL (minimum score 550 paper-based; 80 iBT). Electronic applications accepted.

**Johnson & Wales University,** Graduate Studies, Occupational Therapy Doctorate Program, Providence, RI 02903-3703. Offers OTD. *Entrance requirements:* For doctorate, GRE, bachelor's degree with minimum cumulative GPA of 3.0, 3 letters of recommendation, background check.

**Kean University,** Nathan Weiss Graduate College, Program in Occupational Therapy, Union, NJ 07083. Offers MS. *Accreditation:* AOTA. *Program availability:* Part-time. *Faculty:* 6 full-time (5 women). *Students:* 65 full-time (56 women), 35 part-time (32 women); includes 32 minority (8 Black or African American, non-Hispanic/Latino; 4 Asian, non-Hispanic/Latino; 17 Hispanic/Latino; 3 Two or more races, non-Hispanic/Latino), 1 international. Average age 26. 220 applicants, 16% accepted, 30 enrolled. In 2019, 33 master's awarded. *Degree requirements:* For master's, 6 months of field work, final project. *Entrance requirements:* Additional exam requirements/recommendations for international students: required—TOEFL (minimum score 550 paper-based; 79 iBT), IELTS (minimum score 6.5). *Application deadline:* For fall admission, 2/2 for domestic and international students. Applications are processed on a rolling basis. Application fee: $75. Electronic applications accepted. *Expenses:* Contact institution. *Financial support:* Scholarships/grants and unspecified assistantships available. Financial award applicants required to submit FAFSA. *Unit head:* Dr. Mariann Moran, Program Coordinator, 908-737-5850, Fax: 908-737-5855, E-mail: ot@kean.edu. *Application contact:* Brittany Gerstenhaber, Admissions Counselor, 908-737-7100, E-mail: gradadmissions@kean.edu.
Website: http://grad.kean.edu/ot

**Keiser University,** MS in Occupational Therapy Program, Fort Lauderdale, FL 33309. Offers MS. *Accreditation:* AOTA.

**Kettering College,** Program in Occupational Therapy, Kettering, OH 45429-1299. Offers OTD.

**Keuka College,** Program in Occupational Therapy, Keuka Park, NY 14478. Offers MS. *Accreditation:* AOTA. *Faculty:* 4 full-time (3 women). *Students:* 34 full-time (32 women); includes 2 minority (1 Asian, non-Hispanic/Latino; 1 Hispanic/Latino). Average age 22. In 2019, 33 master's awarded. *Entrance requirements:* For master's, Successfully complete the Keuka College undergraduate Bachelors of Science in occupational science degree meeting grade requirements of a 3.0 GPA and satisfactory completion (C or better) of all required courses. Additional exam requirements/recommendations for international students: required—TOEFL (minimum score 550 paper-based). *Application deadline:* For fall admission, 8/15 priority date for domestic students; for winter admission, 12/15 priority date for domestic students; for spring admission, 4/15 priority date for domestic students. Applications are processed on a rolling basis. Application fee: $50. Electronic applications accepted. *Expenses:* Contact institution. *Financial support:* Research assistantships, scholarships/grants, and tuition waivers (full and partial) available. Financial award applicants required to submit FAFSA. *Unit head:* Dr. Christopher Alterio, Division Chair of Occupational Therapy, 315-279-5483, Fax: 315-279-5439, E-mail: calterio1@keuka.edu. *Application contact:* Keuka College Admissions Office, 315-279-5254, Fax: 315-279-5386, E-mail: admissions@keuka.edu.
Website: https://www.keuka.edu/academics/programs/occupational-therapy

**Le Moyne College,** Department of Occupational Therapy, Syracuse, NY 13214. Offers occupational therapy (MS). *Accreditation:* AOTA. *Faculty:* 4 full-time (all women), 2 part-time/adjunct (1 woman). *Students:* 58 full-time (57 women), 1 part-time; includes 13 minority (4 Black or African American, non-Hispanic/Latino; 6 Asian, non-Hispanic/Latino; 2 Hispanic/Latino; 1 Native Hawaiian or other Pacific Islander, non-Hispanic/Latino). Average age 24. 78 applicants, 65% accepted, 22 enrolled. In 2019, 39 master's awarded. *Degree requirements:* For master's, 80-credit hours, fieldwork and clinical internship, capstone masters project. *Entrance requirements:* For master's, Miller Analogies Test (MAT) or Graduate Record Exam (GRE) score, bachelor's degree with minimum GPA of 3.0; three references from academic advisors, licensed occupational therapists, and/or work managers; background check, personal statement, interview, undergraduate prerequisites, 30 observation hours. Additional exam requirements/recommendations for international students: required—TOEFL (minimum score 79 iBT); recommended—IELTS (minimum score 6.5). *Application deadline:* For fall admission, 4/1 for domestic and international students. Applications are processed on a rolling basis. Application fee: $150. Electronic applications accepted. *Expenses:* Contact institution. *Financial support:* Career-related internships or fieldwork, Federal Work-Study, scholarships/grants, and health care benefits available. Financial award applicants required to submit FAFSA. *Unit head:* Caitlin O. Esposito, Chair and Assistant Professor, 315-445-5432, E-mail: occupationaltherapy@lemoyne.edu. *Application contact:* Teresa M. Renn, Director of Graduate Admission, 315-445-5444, Fax: 315-445-6092, E-mail: GradEducation@lemoyne.edu.
Website: http://www.lemoyne.edu/apply/graduate-and-professional-admission/occupational-therapy

**Lenoir-Rhyne University,** Graduate Programs, School of Occupational Therapy, Hickory, NC 28601. Offers MS. *Accreditation:* AOTA. *Entrance requirements:* For master's, GRE, official transcripts, three letters of recommendation, essay, criminal background check. *Expenses:* Contact institution.

**Loma Linda University,** School of Allied Health Professions, Department of Occupational Therapy, Loma Linda, CA 92350. Offers MOT, OTD. *Accreditation:* AOTA.

**Long Island University - Brooklyn,** School of Health Professions, Brooklyn, NY 11201-8423. Offers athletic training and sport sciences (MS); community health (MS Ed); exercise science (MS); forensic social work (Advanced Certificate); occupational therapy (MS); physical therapy (DPT); physician assistant (MS); public health (MPH); social work (MSW); speech-language pathology (MS). *Accreditation:* AOTA; CEPH. *Degree requirements:* For master's, comprehensive exam (for some programs), thesis (for some programs); for doctorate, comprehensive exam (for some programs). *Entrance requirements:* For master's and doctorate, GRE. Additional exam requirements/recommendations for international students: required—TOEFL (minimum score 550 paper-based; 79 iBT). Electronic applications accepted.

**Louisiana State University Health Sciences Center,** School of Allied Health Professions, Department of Occupational Therapy, New Orleans, LA 70112-2223. Offers MOT. *Accreditation:* AOTA. *Faculty:* 4 full-time (3 women). *Students:* 70 full-time (62 women); includes 12 minority (5 Black or African American, non-Hispanic/Latino; 3 Asian, non-Hispanic/Latino; 4 Two or more races, non-Hispanic/Latino). Average age 25. 156 applicants, 22% accepted, 35 enrolled. In 2019, 33 master's awarded. *Entrance requirements:* For master's, GRE (minimum scores: 150 verbal, 141 quantitative, and 3.5 analytical), bachelor's degree; 40 hours of observation in occupational therapy; minimum cumulative GPA of 2.8, cumulative prerequisite 3.0. Additional exam requirements/recommendations for international students: required—TOEFL (minimum score 550 paper-based; 79 iBT). *Application deadline:* For spring admission, 6/16 priority date for domestic students. Application fee: $140. Electronic applications accepted. *Expenses:* Contact institution. *Financial support:* Application deadline: 4/15; applicants required to submit FAFSA. *Unit head:* Dr. Kelly L. Alig, Department Head, 504-568-4303, Fax: 504-568-4306, E-mail: kalig@lsuhsc.edu. *Application contact:* Yudialys D. Cazanas, Student Affairs Director, 504-568-4253, Fax: 504-568-3185, E-mail: ydelga@lsuhsc.edu.
Website: http://alliedhealth.lsuhsc.edu/ot/default.aspx

**Mary Baldwin University,** Graduate Studies, Program in Occupational Therapy, Staunton, VA 24401-3610. Offers OTD. *Accreditation:* AOTA.

**Maryville University of Saint Louis,** Myrtle E. and Earl E. Walker College of Health Professions, Occupational Therapy Program, St. Louis, MO 63141-7299. Offers MOT. *Accreditation:* AOTA. *Faculty:* 7 full-time (all women), 4 part-time/adjunct (3 women). *Students:* 72 full-time (69 women), 40 part-time (37 women); includes 9 minority (5 Asian, non-Hispanic/Latino; 4 Hispanic/Latino). Average age 24. In 2019, 66 master's awarded. *Entrance requirements:* For master's, minimum cumulative GPA of 3.0, Personal Essay, Responses to Admissions Questions, Student Experiences and Achievements, Recommendations. Additional exam requirements/recommendations for international students: required—TOEFL (minimum score 563 paper-based), Revised TOEFL must achieve a speaking sub-score of 23, writing sub-score of 20, and listening scores of 21 or higher, and a combined score of 85+. *Application deadline:* Applications are processed on a rolling basis. Electronic applications accepted. *Expenses:* Contact institution. *Financial support:* Career-related internships or fieldwork, Federal Work-Study, and campus employment available. Financial award application deadline: 4/1; financial award applicants required to submit FAFSA. *Unit head:* Robert Cunningham, Director Occupational Therapy, 314-529-9682, Fax: 314-529-9191, E-mail: rcunningham@maryville.edu. *Application contact:* Jeannie DeLuca, Director of Admissions and Advising, 314-529-9355, Fax: 314-529-9927, E-mail: jdeluca@maryville.edu.
Website: https://www.maryville.edu/hp/master-occupational-therapy/

**McMaster University,** Faculty of Health Sciences, Professional Program in Occupational Therapy, Hamilton, ON L8S 4M2, Canada. Offers M Sc. *Degree requirements:* For master's, fieldwork and independent research project. *Entrance requirements:* For master's, minimum B average over last 60 undergraduate units. Additional exam requirements/recommendations for international students: required—TOEFL (minimum score 600 paper-based).

**Medical University of South Carolina,** College of Health Professions, Program in Occupational Therapy, Charleston, SC 29425. Offers MSOT. *Accreditation:* AOTA. *Degree requirements:* For master's, thesis or alternative, research project. *Entrance requirements:* For master's, GRE General Test, interview, minimum GPA of 3.0, references. Additional exam requirements/recommendations for international students: required—TOEFL (minimum score 600 paper-based). Electronic applications accepted.

**Mercy College,** School of Health and Natural Sciences, Program in Occupational Therapy, Dobbs Ferry, NY 10522-1189. Offers MS. *Accreditation:* AOTA. *Program availability:* Evening/weekend. *Students:* 70 full-time (60 women), 33 part-time (29 women); includes 46 minority (10 Black or African American, non-Hispanic/Latino; 7 Asian, non-Hispanic/Latino; 25 Hispanic/Latino; 4 Two or more races, non-Hispanic/Latino), 2 international. Average age 31. 163 applicants, 23% accepted, 36 enrolled. In 2019, 31 master's awarded. *Degree requirements:* For master's, Capstone project; clinical fieldwork. *Entrance requirements:* For master's, transcript(s); two letters of recommendation; course prerequisite form; sample of completed college work; essay; resume; interview. Additional exam requirements/recommendations for international students: required—TOEFL (minimum score 80 iBT), IELTS (minimum score 6.5). *Application deadline:* For fall admission, 6/1 for domestic students. Application fee: $62. Electronic applications accepted. *Expenses:* Contact institution. *Financial support:* Career-related internships or fieldwork, Federal Work-Study, scholarships/grants, and unspecified assistantships available. Support available to part-time students. Financial award applicants required to submit FAFSA. *Unit head:* Dr. Joan Toglia, Dean, School of Health and Natural Sciences, 914-674-7746, E-mail: jtoglia@mercy.edu. *Application contact:* Allison Gurdineer, Executive Director of Admissions, 877-637-2946, Fax: 914-674-7382, E-mail: admissions@mercy.edu.
Website: https://www.mercy.edu/degrees-programs/ms-occupational-therapy

**MGH Institute of Health Professions,** School of Health and Rehabilitation Sciences, Department of Occupational Therapy, Boston, MA 02129. Offers OTD. *Accreditation:* AOTA. *Entrance requirements:* For doctorate, GRE, bachelor's degree from regionally-accredited U.S. college or university with minimum undergraduate GPA of 3.0; official transcripts; personal statement; recommendation letters. Additional exam requirements/recommendations for international students: required—TOEFL (minimum score 80 iBT). Electronic applications accepted.

**Midwestern University, Downers Grove Campus,** College of Health Sciences, Illinois Campus, Program in Occupational Therapy, Downers Grove, IL 60515-1235. Offers MOT. *Accreditation:* AOTA. *Entrance requirements:* For master's, GRE General Test. *Expenses:* Contact institution.

**Midwestern University, Glendale Campus,** College of Health Sciences, Arizona Campus, Program in Occupational Therapy, Glendale, AZ 85308. Offers MOT. *Accreditation:* AOTA. *Entrance requirements:* For master's, GRE. *Expenses:* Contact institution.

**Milligan University,** Program in Occupational Therapy, Milligan College, TN 37682. Offers MSOT. *Accreditation:* AOTA. *Faculty:* 5 full-time (4 women), 4 part-time/adjunct (3 women). *Students:* 63 full-time (56 women), 31 part-time (26 women); includes 5 minority (1 Black or African American, non-Hispanic/Latino; 3 Hispanic/Latino; 1 Two or more races, non-Hispanic/Latino). Average age 25. 163 applicants, 44% accepted, 32 enrolled. In 2019, 32 master's awarded. *Degree requirements:* For master's, thesis or alternative. *Entrance requirements:* For master's, GRE. Additional exam requirements/recommendations for international students: required—TOEFL (minimum score 550 paper-based; 80 iBT). *Application deadline:* For spring admission, 11/15 for domestic and international students. Application fee: $120. Electronic applications accepted. *Expenses:* 79 hr program: $780/hr; $75 one-time records fee; $325/semester (technology and activity fees). *Financial support:* Career-related internships or fieldwork and institutionally sponsored loans available. Financial award application deadline: 4/15; financial award applicants required to submit FAFSA. *Unit head:* Dr. Christy Isbell, Program Director and Area Chair of Occupational Therapy;, 423-461-1548, Fax: 423-975-8019, E-mail: cisbell@milligan.edu. *Application contact:* Kristia Brown, Office Manager and Admissions Representative, 423-975-8010, Fax: 423-975-8019, E-mail: lkbrown@milligan.edu.
Website: http://www.milligan.edu/msot/

**Misericordia University,** College of Health Sciences and Education, Program in Occupational Therapy, Dallas, PA 18612-1098. Offers MSOT, OTD. *Accreditation:* AOTA. *Students:* 44 full-time (43 women), 69 part-time (65 women); includes 14 minority (2 Black or African American, non-Hispanic/Latino; 2 Asian, non-Hispanic/Latino; 5 Hispanic/Latino; 5 Two or more races, non-Hispanic/Latino). Average age 27. In 2019, 57 master's, 13 doctorates awarded. *Entrance requirements:* For master's, minimum undergraduate GPA of 2.8, 2 letters of reference; for doctorate, minimum graduate GPA of 3.0, interview, 3 letters of reference. Additional exam requirements/recommendations for international students: required—TOEFL. *Application deadline:* Applications are processed on a rolling basis. Application fee: $35. Electronic applications accepted. *Financial support:* Career-related internships or fieldwork and scholarships/grants available. Support available to part-time students. Financial award application deadline: 6/30; financial award applicants required to submit FAFSA. *Unit head:* Dr. Lori Charney, Chair, 570-674-3330, E-mail: lcharney@misericordia.edu. *Application contact:* Maureen Sheridan, Assistant Director of Admissions, Part-Time Undergraduate and Graduate Programs, 570-674-6451, E-mail: msherida@misericordia.edu.
Website: http://www.misericordia.edu/page.cfm?p-634

**Missouri State University,** Graduate College, College of Health and Human Services, Department of Sports Medicine and Athletic Training, Springfield, MO 65897. Offers athletic training (MS); occupational therapy (MOT). *Program availability:* Part-time. *Degree requirements:* For master's, comprehensive exam, thesis or alternative. *Entrance requirements:* For master's, GRE, current Professional Rescuer and AED certification, BOC certification, licensure as an athletic trainer, minimum undergraduate GPA of 3.0 (for MS); OTCAS application (for MOT). Additional exam requirements/recommendations for international students: required—TOEFL (minimum score 550 paper-based; 79 iBT), IELTS (minimum score 6). Electronic applications accepted. *Expenses: Tuition, area resident:* Full-time $2600; part-time $1735 per credit hour. Tuition, nonresident: full-time $5240; part-time $3495 per credit hour. *International tuition:* $5240 full-time. *Required fees:* $530; $438 per credit hour. Tuition and fees vary according to class time, course level, course load, degree level, campus/location and program.

**Mount Mary University,** Graduate Programs, Program in Occupational Therapy, Milwaukee, WI 53222-4597. Offers MS, OTD. *Accreditation:* AOTA. *Program availability:* Part-time, evening/weekend, 100% online, blended/hybrid learning. *Degree requirements:* For master's, comprehensive exam, thesis or alternative, professional development portfolio. *Entrance requirements:* For master's, minimum GPA of 3.0, occupational therapy license, 1 year of work experience. Additional exam requirements/recommendations for international students: required—TOEFL (minimum score 550 paper-based; 80 iBT); recommended—IELTS (minimum score 6.5). Electronic applications accepted. *Expenses:* Contact institution.

**Nebraska Methodist College,** Program in Occupational Therapy, Omaha, NE 68114. Offers MOT.

**New England Institute of Technology,** Program in Occupational Therapy, East Greenwich, RI 02818. Offers MS, OTD. *Accreditation:* AOTA. *Program availability:* Part-time, evening/weekend, 100% online, blended/hybrid learning. *Students:* 89 full-time (75 women), 6 part-time (all women); includes 14 minority (2 Black or African American, non-Hispanic/Latino; 5 Asian, non-Hispanic/Latino; 2 Hispanic/Latino; 5 Two or more races, non-Hispanic/Latino). Average age 30. In 2019, 25 master's awarded. *Degree requirements:* For master's, Fieldwork. *Entrance requirements:* For master's, Minimum GPA 3.0 awarded Bachelor's degree in related field from an accredited institution plus a personal statement. Additional exam requirements/recommendations for international students: required—TOEFL. *Application deadline:* Applications are processed on a rolling basis. Application fee: $50. Electronic applications accepted. *Unit head:* Dr. Douglas H. Sherman, Senior Vice President and Provost, 401-739-5000 Ext. 3481, Fax: 401-886-0859, E-mail: dsherman@neit.edu. *Application contact:* Tim Reardon, Vice President for Enrollment Management and Marketing, 800-736-7744, Fax: 401-886-0859, E-mail: treardon@neit.edu.
Website: http://www.neit.edu/Programs/Masters-Degree-Programs/Occupational-Therapy

**New York Institute of Technology,** School of Health Professions, Department of Occupational Therapy, Old Westbury, NY 11568. Offers MS. *Accreditation:* AOTA. *Faculty:* 7 full-time (5 women), 6 part-time/adjunct (all women). *Students:* 75 full-time (68 women), 39 part-time (34 women); includes 14 minority (2 Black or African American, non-Hispanic/Latino; 8 Asian, non-Hispanic/Latino; 2 Hispanic/Latino; 2 Two or more races, non-Hispanic/Latino), 1 international. Average age 24. 167 applicants, 63% accepted, 38 enrolled. In 2019, 42 master's awarded. *Entrance requirements:* For master's, Bachelor's degree or equivalent with cumulative GPA of 3.0; academic record that includes a balance of coursework in the humanities, social sciences, math, and life sciences, as well as competence in written and spoken English and basic computer skills; satisfactory completion of prerequisites; proof of 100 hours of volunteer work. Additional exam requirements/recommendations for international students: required—TOEFL (minimum score 79 iBT), IELTS (minimum score 6), PTE (minimum score 53), Duolingo English Test. *Application deadline:* For summer admission, 10/1 priority date for domestic and international students. Applications are processed on a rolling basis. Application fee: $50. Electronic applications accepted. *Expenses: Tuition:* Full-time $23,760; part-time $1320 per credit. *Required fees:* $260; $220 per unit. Full-time tuition and fees vary according to degree level and program. Part-time tuition and fees vary according to course load and program. *Financial support:* Research assistantships, teaching assistantships, Federal Work-Study, scholarships/grants, and unspecified assistantships available. Support available to part-time students. Financial award application deadline: 2/15; financial award applicants required to submit FAFSA. *Unit head:* Dr. Alexander Lopez, Chair, 516-686-3843, E-mail: alopez@nyit.edu. *Application contact:* Alice Dolitsky, Director, Graduate Admissions, 800-345-6948, Fax: 516-686-1116, E-mail: grad@nyit.edu.
Website: https://www.nyit.edu/health_professions/department_of_occupational_therapy

**New York University,** Steinhardt School of Culture, Education, and Human Development, Department of Occupational Therapy, New York, NY 10012. Offers advanced occupational therapy (MA); occupational therapy (MS, DPS); research in occupational therapy (PhD). *Accreditation:* AOTA (one or more programs are accredited). *Program availability:* Part-time. *Degree requirements:* For master's, thesis (for some programs), terminal project; fieldwork; for doctorate, thesis/dissertation, terminal project. *Entrance requirements:* For doctorate, GRE General Test, interview. Additional exam requirements/recommendations for international students: required—TOEFL (minimum score 100 iBT). Electronic applications accepted.

**Northeastern State University,** College of Science and Health Professions, Department of Health Professions, Program in Occupational Therapy, Tahlequah, OK 74464-2399. Offers MS. *Accreditation:* AOTA. *Faculty:* 3 full-time (2 women). *Students:* 39 full-time (35 women); includes 11 minority (4 American Indian or Alaska Native, non-Hispanic/Latino; 2 Asian, non-Hispanic/Latino; 2 Hispanic/Latino; 3 Two or more races, non-Hispanic/Latino). Average age 25. In 2019, 19 master's awarded. *Application deadline:* For fall admission, 7/1 priority date for domestic and international students. Applications are processed on a rolling basis. Electronic applications accepted. *Expenses: Tuition, area resident:* Full-time $250; part-time $250 per credit hour. Tuition, state resident: full-time $250; part-time $250 per credit hour. Tuition, nonresident: full-time $556; part-time $555.50 per credit hour. *Required fees:* $33.40 per credit hour. *Unit head:* Dr. Sydney Dorrough, Program Director, 918-444-5219, E-mail: dorrougs@nsuok.edu. *Application contact:* Josh McCollum, Graduate Coordinator, 918-444-2093, E-mail: mccolluj@nsuok.edu.
Website: http://academics.nsuok.edu/healthprofessions/DegreePrograms/Graduate/OccupatTherapy.aspx

**Northern Arizona University,** College of Health and Human Services, Department of Occupational Therapy, Phoenix, AZ 85004. Offers OTD. *Accreditation:* AOTA. *Program availability:* Blended/hybrid learning. *Degree requirements:* For doctorate, variable foreign language requirement, comprehensive exam (for some programs), thesis/dissertation (for some programs). *Entrance requirements:* For doctorate, minimum of 80 volunteer and observation hours. Additional exam requirements/recommendations for international students: required—TOEFL (minimum score 80 iBT), IELTS (minimum score 6.5). Electronic applications accepted.

**Nova Southeastern University,** Dr. Pallavi Patel College of Health Care Sciences, Fort Lauderdale, FL 33314-7796. Offers anesthesiologist assistant (MSA); audiology (Au D); health science (MH Sc, DHSc, PhD); occupational therapy (MOT, Dr OT, PhD); physical therapy (DPT, TDPT); physician assistant (MMS); speech-language pathology (MS). *Accreditation:* AOTA; ASHA. *Program availability:* Part-time, 100% online, blended/hybrid learning. *Faculty:* 127 full-time (85 women), 107 part-time/adjunct (79 women). *Students:* 1,336 full-time (992 women), 950 part-time (824 women); includes 839 minority (195 Black or African American, non-Hispanic/Latino; 4 American Indian or Alaska Native, non-Hispanic/Latino; 165 Asian, non-Hispanic/Latino; 397 Hispanic/Latino; 3 Native Hawaiian or other Pacific Islander, non-Hispanic/Latino; 75 Two or more races, non-Hispanic/Latino), 26 international. Average age 30. 634 applicants, 28% accepted, 159 enrolled. In 2019, 613 master's, 261 doctorates awarded. Terminal master's awarded for partial completion of doctoral program. *Degree requirements:* For doctorate, comprehensive exam, thesis/dissertation (for some programs), 12-month full-time clinical externship experience. *Entrance requirements:* For master's, GRE General Test; for doctorate, personal interview, essay in application, additional letters may be requested by the program after initial review of application if so warranted. *Application deadline:* Applications are processed on a rolling basis. Application fee: $50. Electronic applications accepted. *Expenses:* Contact institution. *Financial support:* Federal Work-Study, institutionally sponsored loans, and scholarships/grants available. Financial award application deadline: 4/15; financial award applicants required to submit FAFSA. *Unit head:* Dr. Stanley Wilson, Dean, 954-262-1203, E-mail: swilson@nova.edu. *Application contact:* Joycelyn Vogt, Director of Admissions and Outreach, 954-262-1200, Fax: 954-262-1181, E-mail: joycelyn.vogt@nova.edu.
Website: http://healthsciences.nova.edu/

**The Ohio State University,** College of Medicine, School of Health and Rehabilitation Sciences, Program in Occupational Therapy, Columbus, OH 43210. Offers MOT, MOT/PhD. *Accreditation:* AOTA. *Degree requirements:* For master's, fieldwork. *Entrance requirements:* For master's, GRE General Test. Additional exam requirements/recommendations for international students: required—TOEFL (minimum score 550 paper-based; 79 iBT), Michigan English Language Assessment Battery (minimum score 82); recommended—IELTS (minimum score 7). Electronic applications accepted.

**Pacific University,** School of Occupational Therapy, Forest Grove, OR 97116-1797. Offers OTD. *Accreditation:* AOTA. Electronic applications accepted. *Expenses:* Contact institution.

**Queen's University at Kingston,** School of Graduate Studies, Faculty of Health Sciences, School of Rehabilitation Therapy, Kingston, ON K7L 3N6, Canada. Offers occupational therapy (M Sc OT); physical therapy (M Sc PT); rehabilitation science (M Sc, PhD). *Program availability:* Part-time. *Degree requirements:* For master's, thesis; for doctorate, comprehensive exam, thesis/dissertation. *Entrance requirements:* Additional exam requirements/recommendations for international students: required—TOEFL.

**Radford University,** College of Graduate Studies and Research, Occupational Therapy, MOT, Radford, VA 24142. Offers MOT. *Accreditation:* AOTA. *Program availability:* Part-time, evening/weekend. *Degree requirements:* For master's, comprehensive exam. *Entrance requirements:* For master's, GRE, minimum GPA of 3.25, minimum B grade in prerequisite courses, 2 letters of recommendation, professional resume, 40 hours of observation, official transcripts, completion of a college or community course to learn a new occupation. Additional exam requirements/recommendations for international students: required—TOEFL (minimum score 550 paper-based; 79 iBT), IELTS (minimum score 6.5). Electronic applications accepted. *Expenses:* Contact institution.

**Regis College,** Nursing and Health Sciences School, Weston, MA 02493. Offers applied behavior analysis (MS); counseling psychology (MA); health administration (MS); nurse practitioner (Certificate); nursing (MS, DNP); nursing education (Certificate); occupational therapy (MS). *Accreditation:* ACEN. *Program availability:* Part-time, evening/weekend, 100% online, blended/hybrid learning. *Degree requirements:* For doctorate, thesis/dissertation. *Entrance requirements:* For master's, minimum GPA of 3.0, official transcripts, recommendations, personal statement, resume/curriculum vitae,

interview; for doctorate, GRE if GPA from master's lower than 3.5. Additional exam requirements/recommendations for international students: required—TOEFL (minimum score 560 paper-based; 79 iBT); recommended—IELTS (minimum score 6.5). *Application deadline:* Applications are processed on a rolling basis. Application fee: $75. Electronic applications accepted. *Financial support:* Federal Work-Study, scholarships/grants, and unspecified assistantships available. Support available to part-time students. Financial award applicants required to submit FAFSA. *Application contact:* Thomas May, Graduate Admission Counselor, 781-768-7162, E-mail: thomas.may@regiscollege.edu.

**Regis University,** Rueckert-Hartman College for Health Professions, Denver, CO 80221-1099. Offers advanced practice nurse (DNP); counseling (MA); counseling children and adolescents (Post-Graduate Certificate); counseling military families (Post-Graduate Certificate); depth psychotherapy (Post-Graduate Certificate); fellowship in orthopedic manual physical therapy (Certificate); health care business management (Certificate); health care quality and patient safety (Certificate); health industry leadership (MBA); health services administration (MS); marriage and family therapy (MA, Post-Graduate Certificate); neonatal nurse practitioner (MSN); nursing education (MSN); nursing leadership (MSN); occupational therapy (OTD); pharmacy (Pharm D); physical therapy (DPT). *Accreditation:* ACPE. *Program availability:* Part-time, evening/weekend, 100% online, blended/hybrid learning. *Degree requirements:* For master's, thesis (for some programs), internship. *Entrance requirements:* For master's, official transcript reflecting baccalaureate degree awarded from regionally-accredited college or university. Additional exam requirements/recommendations for international students: required—TOEFL (minimum score 550 paper-based; 82 iBT). Electronic applications accepted. *Expenses:* Contact institution.

**Rockhurst University,** College of Health and Human Services, Program in Occupational Therapy, Kansas City, MO 64110-2561. Offers MOT. *Accreditation:* AOTA. *Program availability:* Part-time. *Entrance requirements:* For master's, minimum GPA of 3.0. Additional exam requirements/recommendations for international students: required—TOEFL (minimum score 550 paper-based; 79 iBT). Electronic applications accepted. *Expenses:* Contact institution.

**Rocky Mountain College,** Program in Occupational Therapy, Billings, MT 59102-1796. Offers OTD. *Faculty:* 5 full-time (all women). *Students:* 30 full-time (26 women); includes 7 minority (1 Asian, non-Hispanic/Latino; 3 Hispanic/Latino; 3 Two or more races, non-Hispanic/Latino). Average age 25. *Entrance requirements:* For doctorate, GRE taken within 5 years of application, Bachelor's degree with a minimum GPA of 3.0. Additional exam requirements/recommendations for international students: required—TOEFL (minimum score 570 paper-based; 88 iBT), IELTS (minimum score 6.5). *Application deadline:* Applications are processed on a rolling basis. Application fee: $145. Electronic applications accepted. *Expenses:* Contact institution. *Financial support:* In 2019–20, 7 students received support. Unspecified assistantships and campus work-study available. Financial award applicants required to submit FAFSA. *Unit head:* Dr. Twylla M. Kirchen, Director, 406-657-1165, E-mail: twylla.kirchen@rocky.edu. *Application contact:* Cody Halverson, Coordinator of Admissions for Health Professions, 406-657-1198, E-mail: halversonc@rocky.edu.
Website: https://www.rocky.edu/otd

**Rocky Mountain University of Health Professions,** Program in Occupational Therapy, Provo, UT 84606. Offers OTD. *Program availability:* Online learning. *Entrance requirements:* For doctorate, bachelor's or master's degree from accredited institution with minimum cumulative GPA of 3.0; current U.S. occupational therapy license; resume/curriculum vitae; two letters of recommendation; official transcripts. Electronic applications accepted.

**Rush University,** College of Health Sciences, Department of Occupational Therapy, Chicago, IL 60612-3832. Offers OTD. *Accreditation:* AOTA. *Program availability:* Part-time. *Entrance requirements:* Additional exam requirements/recommendations for international students: required—TOEFL. *Application deadline:* For fall admission, 12/1 for domestic students. Electronic applications accepted. *Financial support:* Career-related internships or fieldwork, Federal Work-Study, institutionally sponsored loans, and scholarships/grants available. Support available to part-time students. Financial award application deadline: 3/15; financial award applicants required to submit FAFSA. *Unit head:* Dr. Linda M. Olson, Chairperson, 312-942-8721, E-mail: linda_m_olson@rush.edu. *Application contact:* Dr. Linda M. Olson, Chairperson, 312-942-8721, E-mail: linda_m_olson@rush.edu.
Website: http://www.rushu.rush.edu/occuth/

**Sacred Heart University,** Graduate Programs, College of Health Professions, Department of Occupational Therapy, Fairfield, CT 06825. Offers MSOT. *Accreditation:* AOTA. *Degree requirements:* For master's, capstone. *Entrance requirements:* For master's, GRE, minimum overall and prerequisites GPA of 3.2 (science 3.0) with no prerequisite course below a C; statistics and human anatomy and physiology completed in the past 10 years. Additional exam requirements/recommendations for international students: required—TOEFL (minimum score 570 paper-based, 80 iBT), TWE, or IELTS (6.5). Electronic applications accepted. *Expenses:* Contact institution.

**Sage Graduate School,** School of Health Sciences, Program in Occupational Therapy, Troy, NY 12180-4115. Offers MS. *Accreditation:* AOTA. *Faculty:* 9 full-time (all women), 2 part-time/adjunct (both women). *Students:* 73 full-time (72 women), 44 part-time (43 women); includes 13 minority (1 Black or African American, non-Hispanic/Latino; 4 Asian, non-Hispanic/Latino; 5 Hispanic/Latino; 3 Two or more races, non-Hispanic/Latino). Average age 23. 105 applicants, 50% accepted, 25 enrolled. In 2019, 37 master's awarded. *Entrance requirements:* For master's, Completed application; baccalaureate degree; minimum GPA of 3.25 in undergraduate study, including OT program pre-requisite courses. Earn a Science GPA of 3.0 in OT program pre-requisite courses. Provide 2 letters of reference, current resume, a career goals statement, and documentation of at least 20 hours of clinical observation. Additional exam requirements/recommendations for international students: required—TOEFL (minimum score 550 paper-based). *Application deadline:* For fall admission, 2/1 for domestic students. Applications are processed on a rolling basis. Application fee: $40. Electronic applications accepted. *Expenses:* Contact institution. *Financial support:* Fellowships, research assistantships, scholarships/grants, and unspecified assistantships available. Financial award applicants required to submit FAFSA. *Unit head:* Dr. Kathleen Kelly, Dean of Health Sciences/Program Director, 518-244-2030, Fax: 518-244-4524, E-mail: kellyk5@sage.edu. *Application contact:* Michael Jones, SR Associate Director of Graduate Enrollment Management, 518-292-8615, Fax: 518-292-1912, E-mail: jonesm4@sage.edu.

**Saginaw Valley State University,** College of Health and Human Services, Program in Occupational Therapy, University Center, MI 48710. Offers MSOT. *Accreditation:* AOTA. *Program availability:* Part-time, evening/weekend. *Students:* 121 full-time (104 women), 57 part-time (53 women); includes 12 minority (1 Asian, non-Hispanic/Latino; 5 Hispanic/Latino; 6 Two or more races, non-Hispanic/Latino), 1 international. Average age 24. In 2019, 51 master's awarded. *Entrance requirements:* For master's, minimum GPA of 3.0. Additional exam requirements/recommendations for international students: required—TOEFL (minimum score 525 paper-based; 71 iBT). *Application deadline:* For spring admission, 1/23 for domestic and international students. Applications are processed on a rolling basis. Application fee: $30 ($90 for international students). Electronic applications accepted. *Expenses: Tuition, area resident:* Full-time $11,212; part-time $622.90 per credit hour. Tuition, state resident: full-time $11,212; part-time $622.90 per credit hour. Tuition, nonresident: full-time $11,212; part-time $1253 per credit hour. *Required fees:* $263; $14.60 per credit hour. Tuition and fees vary according to course load, degree level and program. *Financial support:* Federal Work-Study and scholarships/grants available. Support available to part-time students. *Unit head:* Don Earley, Professor of Occupational Therapy, 989-964-4689, E-mail: dwe@svsu.edu. *Application contact:* Jenna Briggs, Director, Graduate and International Admissions, 989-964-6096, Fax: 989-964-2788, E-mail: gradadm@svsu.edu.

**St. Ambrose University,** College of Health and Human Services, Program in Occupational Therapy, Davenport, IA 52803-2898. Offers OTD. *Accreditation:* AOTA. *Entrance requirements:* Additional exam requirements/recommendations for international students: required—TOEFL. Electronic applications accepted.

**St. Catherine University,** Graduate Programs, Program in Occupational Therapy, St. Paul, MN 55105. Offers MA, OTD. *Accreditation:* AOTA. *Program availability:* Part-time, evening/weekend. *Degree requirements:* For master's, thesis. *Entrance requirements:* For master's, GRE, minimum GPA of 3.0. Additional exam requirements/recommendations for international students: required—Michigan English Language Assessment Battery or TOEFL. *Expenses:* Contact institution.

**Saint Francis University,** Department of Occupational Therapy, Loretto, PA 15940-0600. Offers MOT. *Accreditation:* AOTA. *Faculty:* 6 full-time (5 women). *Students:* 41 full-time (37 women); includes 3 minority (2 Black or African American, non-Hispanic/Latino; 1 Asian, non-Hispanic/Latino). Average age 22. 6 applicants, 100% accepted, 3 enrolled. In 2019, 39 master's awarded. *Degree requirements:* For master's, thesis. Application fee: $30. Electronic applications accepted. *Expenses:* 1142 per credit. 600 technology fee. 660 program fee. *Unit head:* Dr. Edward Mihelcic, Department Chair, 814-472-2760, E-mail: emihelcic@francis.edu. *Application contact:* Amy Hudkins, Instructor, 814-472-2792, E-mail: ahudkins@francis.edu.
Website: http://www.francis.edu/ot

**Saint Louis University,** Graduate Programs, Doisy College of Health Sciences, Department of Occupational Science and Occupational Therapy, St. Louis, MO 63103. Offers MOT. *Accreditation:* AOTA. *Degree requirements:* For master's, project. *Entrance requirements:* For master's, minimum GPA of 2.8. Additional exam requirements/recommendations for international students: required—TOEFL (minimum score 525 paper-based; 55 iBT). Electronic applications accepted.

**Salem State University,** School of Graduate Studies, Program in Occupational Therapy, Salem, MA 01970-5353. Offers MS. *Accreditation:* AOTA. *Program availability:* Part-time, evening/weekend. *Entrance requirements:* For master's, GRE or MAT. Additional exam requirements/recommendations for international students: required—TOEFL (minimum score 550 paper-based; 80 iBT), IELTS (minimum score 5.5).

**Salus University,** College of Education and Rehabilitation, Elkins Park, PA 19027-1598. Offers education of children and youth with visual and multiple impairments (M Ed, Certificate); low vision rehabilitation (MS, Certificate); occupational therapy (MS); orientation and mobility therapy (MS, Certificate); speech-language pathology (MS); vision rehabilitation therapy (MS, Certificate); OD/MS. *Accreditation:* AOTA. *Program availability:* Part-time, online learning. *Entrance requirements:* For master's, GRE or MAT, 3 letters of reference, 2 interviews. Additional exam requirements/recommendations for international students: required—TOEFL, TWE. *Expenses:* Contact institution.

**Samuel Merritt University,** Department of Occupational Therapy, Oakland, CA 94609-3108. Offers OTD. *Accreditation:* AOTA. *Degree requirements:* For doctorate, project. *Entrance requirements:* For doctorate, minimum GPA of 3.0 in science and overall; 40-70 hours of volunteer or professional occupational therapy experience; interview. Additional exam requirements/recommendations for international students: required—TOEFL (minimum score 100 iBT). Electronic applications accepted. *Expenses:* Contact institution.

**San Jose State University,** Program in Occupational Therapy, San Jose, CA 95192-0059. Offers MS. *Accreditation:* AOTA. *Faculty:* 9 full-time (7 women), 13 part-time/adjunct (12 women). *Students:* 156 full-time (128 women), 79 part-time (68 women); includes 88 minority (59 Asian, non-Hispanic/Latino; 29 Hispanic/Latino), 1 international. Average age 30. 216 applicants, 40% accepted, 76 enrolled. In 2019, 74 master's awarded. *Degree requirements:* For master's, thesis or alternative, Completion of two full time fieldwork experiences. *Entrance requirements:* For master's, GPA in the 8 prerequisite courses of 3.0 on a 4 point scale. Completion of volunteer hours and evaluation of volunteer service by an occupational therapist. *Application deadline:* For fall admission, 2/1 for domestic and international students. Applications are processed on a rolling basis. Application fee: $70. Electronic applications accepted. *Expenses: Tuition, area resident:* Full-time $7176; part-time $4164 per credit hour. Tuition, state resident: full-time $7176; part-time $4164 per credit hour. Tuition, nonresident: full-time $7176; part-time $4165 per credit hour. *International tuition:* $7176 full-time. *Required fees:* $2110; $2110. *Financial support:* In 2019–20, 107 students received support, including 3 fellowships (averaging $3,833 per year), 5 research assistantships (averaging $3,800 per year); scholarships/grants also available. Financial award application deadline: 5/1; financial award applicants required to submit FAFSA. *Unit head:* 408-924-3072, Fax: 408-924-3088, E-mail: winifred.schultz-krohn@sjsu.edu. *Application contact:* Dr. Jerilyn "Gigi"? Smith, PhD, OTR/L, FAOTA, Graduate Admissions Coordinator, 408-924-3081, Fax: 408-924-3088, E-mail: gigi.smith@sjsu.edu.
Website: http://www.sjsu.edu/occupationaltherapy/

**Seton Hall University,** School of Health and Medical Sciences, Program in Occupational Therapy, South Orange, NJ 07079-2697. Offers MS. *Accreditation:* AOTA. *Entrance requirements:* For master's, health care experience, minimum GPA of 3.0, 50 hours of occupational therapy volunteer work, pre-requisite courses. Additional exam requirements/recommendations for international students: required—TOEFL. Electronic applications accepted.

**Shawnee State University,** Program in Occupational Therapy, Portsmouth, OH 45662. Offers MOT. *Accreditation:* AOTA.

**Shenandoah University,** School of Health Professions, School of Occupational Therapy, Winchester, VA 22601. Offers MS. *Accreditation:* AOTA. *Program availability:* 100% online, blended/hybrid learning. *Faculty:* 6 full-time (all women), 6 part-time/adjunct (all women). *Students:* 106 full-time (95 women), 54 part-time (46 women); includes 7 minority (2 Black or African American, non-Hispanic/Latino; 2 Asian, non-Hispanic/Latino; 3 Hispanic/Latino). Average age 26. 120 applicants, 76% accepted, 53 enrolled. In 2019, 51 master's awarded. *Degree requirements:* For master's, thesis. *Entrance requirements:* Additional exam requirements/recommendations for international students: required—TOEFL (minimum score 558 paper-based; 83 iBT). *Application deadline:* For fall admission, 10/15 for domestic and international students. Application fee: $150. Electronic applications accepted. *Expenses:* $890 per credit hour tuition (75 credit hours), $165 student services fee per term (6 semesters), $175 technology fee per term (6 semesters), $305 IM Learning fee per term (6 semesters),

$305 attached to OT 641, $190.85 clinical toolkit supplies, $40 splinting kit supplies, $2,893.53 books. *Financial support:* In 2019–20, 11 students received support. Scholarships/grants available. Financial award application deadline: 8/1; financial award applicants required to submit FAFSA. *Unit head:* Dr. Cathy F. Shanholtz, OTD, Division Director, Occupational Therapy, 540-665-5441, Fax: 540-665-5564, E-mail: cshanhol2@su.edu. *Application contact:* Dr. Alicia Lutman, Associate Professor, 540-665-5563, Fax: 540-665-5564, E-mail: alutman@su.edu.
Website: https://www.su.edu/occupational-therapy/

**Sonoma State University,** School of Science and Technology, Department of Kinesiology, Rohnert Park, CA 94928. Offers exercise science/pre-physical therapy (MA); interdisciplinary (MA); interdisciplinary pre-occupational therapy (MA); lifetime physical activity (MA), including coach education, fitness and wellness. *Program availability:* Part-time. *Degree requirements:* For master's, thesis, oral exam. *Entrance requirements:* For master's, minimum GPA of 2.8. Additional exam requirements/recommendations for international students: required—TOEFL (minimum score 500 paper-based).

**South University - West Palm Beach,** Program in Occupational Therapy, Royal Palm Beach, FL 33411. Offers OTD.

**Spalding University,** Graduate Studies, Kosair College of Health and Natural Sciences, Auerbach School of Occupational Therapy, Louisville, KY 40203-2188. Offers MS. *Accreditation:* AOTA. *Entrance requirements:* For master's, interview, letters of recommendation, transcripts, 20 observation hours, MSOT mission alignment policy. Additional exam requirements/recommendations for international students: required—TOEFL (minimum score 535 paper-based).

**Springfield College,** Graduate Programs, Program in Occupational Therapy, Springfield, MA 01109-3797. Offers MS. *Accreditation:* AOTA. *Program availability:* Part-time. *Degree requirements:* For master's, comprehensive exam, research project; 6 months of full-time fieldwork. *Entrance requirements:* For master's, prerequisite courses in anatomy and physiology, other physical science, introduction to psychology, introduction to sociology, abnormal psychology, developmental psychology, English composition, additional English course, and statistics; minimum undergraduate GPA of 3.0; prior experience in/exposure to occupational therapy services. Additional exam requirements/recommendations for international students: required—TOEFL (minimum score 90 iBT); recommended—IELTS (minimum score 7). Electronic applications accepted.

**Stanbridge University,** Program in Occupational Therapy, Irvine, CA 92612. Offers MS. *Accreditation:* AOTA.

**State University of New York Downstate Medical Center,** School of Graduate Studies, Program in Occupational Therapy, Brooklyn, NY 11203-2098. Offers MS. *Accreditation:* AOTA.

**Stockton University,** Office of Graduate Studies, Program in Occupational Therapy, Galloway, NJ 08205-9441. Offers MSOT. *Accreditation:* AOTA. *Faculty:* 7 full-time (all women), 1 (woman) part-time/adjunct. *Students:* 60 full-time (56 women), 30 part-time (25 women); includes 19 minority (3 Black or African American, non-Hispanic/Latino; 4 Asian, non-Hispanic/Latino; 8 Hispanic/Latino; 1 Native Hawaiian or other Pacific Islander, non-Hispanic/Latino; 3 Two or more races, non-Hispanic/Latino). Average age 25. 402 applicants, 14% accepted, 30 enrolled. In 2019, 30 master's awarded. *Entrance requirements:* For master's, minimum GPA of 3.0; 60 hours of work, volunteer or community service. Additional exam requirements/recommendations for international students: required—TOEFL. *Application deadline:* For fall admission, 11/17 for domestic and international students. Application fee: $50. Electronic applications accepted. *Expenses: Tuition, area resident:* Full-time $750.92; part-time $78.58 per credit hour. Tuition, state resident: full-time $750.92; part-time $78.58 per credit hour. Tuition, nonresident: full-time $846; part-time $78.58 per credit hour. *International tuition:* $1195.96 full-time. *Required fees:* $1464; $78.58 per credit hour. One-time fee: $50 full-time. *Financial support:* Fellowships, research assistantships, career-related internships or fieldwork, institutionally sponsored loans, scholarships/grants, and unspecified assistantships available. Support available to part-time students. Financial award application deadline: 3/1; financial award applicants required to submit FAFSA. *Unit head:* Dr. Kim Furphy, Program Director, 609-626-3640, E-mail: msot@stockton.edu. *Application contact:* Tara Williams, Assistant Director of Graduate Enrollment Management, 609-626-3640, Fax: 609-626-6050, E-mail: gradschool@stockton.edu.

**Stony Brook University, State University of New York,** Stony Brook Medicine, School of Health Technology and Management, Stony Brook, NY 11794. Offers applied health informatics (MS); disability studies (Certificate); health administration (MHA); health and rehabilitation sciences (PhD); health care management (Advanced Certificate); health care policy and management (MS); occupational therapy (MS); physical therapy (DPT); physician assistant (MS). *Accreditation:* AOTA; APTA. *Faculty:* 53 full-time (37 women), 54 part-time/adjunct (34 women). *Students:* 605 full-time (417 women), 65 part-time (43 women); includes 225 minority (28 Black or African American, non-Hispanic/Latino; 110 Asian, non-Hispanic/Latino; 73 Hispanic/Latino; 1 Native Hawaiian or other Pacific Islander, non-Hispanic/Latino; 13 Two or more races, non-Hispanic/Latino), 9 international. Average age 26. 1,816 applicants, 21% accepted, 293 enrolled. In 2019, 152 master's, 86 doctorates, 21 other advanced degrees awarded. *Entrance requirements:* For master's, GRE General Test, minimum GPA of 3.0, work experience in field, references; for doctorate, GRE, three references, essay. Additional exam requirements/recommendations for international students: required—TOEFL (minimum score 550 paper-based). *Application deadline:* For fall admission, 1/15 for domestic students; for spring admission, 10/1 for domestic students. Application fee: $100. *Expenses:* Contact institution. *Financial support:* Fellowships, research assistantships, teaching assistantships, career-related internships or fieldwork, Federal Work-Study, and institutionally sponsored loans available. Financial award application deadline: 3/15. *Unit head:* Dr. Stacy Jafee Gropack, Dean and Professor, 631-444-2252, Fax: 631-444-7621, E-mail: stacy.jaffeegropack@stonybrook.edu. *Application contact:* Jessica M Rotolo, Executive Assistant to the Dean, 631-444-2252, Fax: 631-444-7621, E-mail: jessica.rotolo@stonybrook.edu.
Website: http://healthtechnology.stonybrookmedicine.edu/

**Temple University,** College of Public Health, Department of Health and Rehabilitation Sciences, Philadelphia, PA 19122-6096. Offers occupational therapy (MOT, DOT); recreational therapy (MS), including recreation therapy. *Accreditation:* AOTA. *Program availability:* Part-time, evening/weekend, online learning. *Faculty:* 29 full-time (19 women), 9 part-time/adjunct (6 women). *Students:* 290 full-time (212 women), 18 part-time (16 women); includes 57 minority (13 Black or African American, non-Hispanic/Latino; 18 Asian, non-Hispanic/Latino; 11 Hispanic/Latino; 15 Two or more races, non-Hispanic/Latino), 3 international. 33 applicants, 94% accepted, 23 enrolled. In 2019, 53 master's, 55 doctorates awarded. *Degree requirements:* For doctorate, thesis/dissertation (for some programs), area paper, capstone project, clinical experiences, practice project. *Entrance requirements:* For master's, GRE General Test, letters of recommendation, statement of goals, clearances for clinical/field education; for doctorate, GRE General Test, statement of goals, letters of recommendation. Additional exam requirements/recommendations for international students: required—TOEFL (minimum score 79 iBT), IELTS, PTE, one of three is required. Application fee: $60. Electronic applications accepted. *Expenses:* Contact institution. *Financial support:* Research assistantships, teaching assistantships, career-related internships or fieldwork, Federal Work-Study, health care benefits, and unspecified assistantships available. Financial award applicants required to submit FAFSA.
Website: https://cph.temple.edu/healthrehabsci/home

**Tennessee State University,** The School of Graduate Studies and Research, College of Health Sciences, Department of Occupational Therapy, Nashville, TN 37209-1561. Offers MOT. *Accreditation:* AOTA. *Entrance requirements:* For master's, GRE taken within the last 5 years, undergraduate degree with minimum GPA of 3.0; 30 hours of observation, volunteer, or work with an occupational therapist; 3 professional and/or academic references.

**Texas Tech University Health Sciences Center,** School of Health Professions, Program in Occupational Therapy, Lubbock, TX 79430. Offers MOT. *Accreditation:* AOTA. *Faculty:* 7 full-time (6 women), 10 part-time/adjunct (8 women). *Students:* 148 full-time (136 women); includes 39 minority (7 Black or African American, non-Hispanic/Latino; 6 Asian, non-Hispanic/Latino; 22 Hispanic/Latino; 1 Native Hawaiian or other Pacific Islander, non-Hispanic/Latino; 3 Two or more races, non-Hispanic/Latino). Average age 24. 476 applicants, 11% accepted, 52 enrolled. In 2019, 48 master's awarded. *Entrance requirements:* Additional exam requirements/recommendations for international students: required—TOEFL (minimum score 550 paper-based; 79 iBT). *Application deadline:* For summer admission, 11/15 priority date for domestic students. Applications are processed on a rolling basis. Application fee: $75. Electronic applications accepted. *Financial support:* In 2019–20, 101 students received support. Institutionally sponsored loans and scholarships/grants available. Financial award application deadline: 9/1; financial award applicants required to submit FAFSA. *Unit head:* Dr. Sandra Whisner, Program Director, 806-743-3240, Fax: 806-743-2189, E-mail: health.professions@ttuhsc.edu. *Application contact:* Lindsay Johnson, Associate Dean for Admissions and Student Affairs, 806-743-3220, Fax: 806-743-2994, E-mail: health.professions@ttuhsc.edu.
Website: http://www.ttuhsc.edu/health-professions/master-occupational-therapy/

**Texas Woman's University,** Graduate School, College of Health Sciences, School of Occupational Therapy, Denton, TX 76204. Offers MOT, OTD, PhD. *Accreditation:* AOTA (one or more programs are accredited). *Program availability:* Part-time, evening/weekend, blended/hybrid learning. *Faculty:* 23 full-time (21 women), 4 part-time/adjunct (3 women). *Students:* 413 full-time (389 women), 43 part-time (41 women); includes 151 minority (24 Black or African American, non-Hispanic/Latino; 46 Asian, non-Hispanic/Latino; 67 Hispanic/Latino; 14 Two or more races, non-Hispanic/Latino), 2 international. Average age 27. 565 applicants, 29% accepted, 156 enrolled. In 2019, 146 master's, 16 doctorates awarded. *Degree requirements:* For master's, comprehensive exam, thesis or alternative, capstone course, internship; for doctorate, comprehensive exam (for some programs), thesis/dissertation or alternative, capstone; completion of program within 6 years of initial registration (for OTD), 10 years (for PhD); qualification exam. *Entrance requirements:* For master's, GRE General Test (within 5 years of completion date), minimum GPA of 3.0 on prerequisites, interview, 20 hours of observation with one supervising OTR, 2 faculty references, medical terminology competency; for doctorate, GRE General Test (within last 5 years), post professional OTD: essay, interview, 3 letters of reference, certification and master's degree in occupational therapy or related field, minimum GPA of 3.2 in previous graduate work, occupational therapy license (OTD only), initial certification as an OT by NBCOT (PhD only). Additional exam requirements/recommendations for international students: required—TOEFL (minimum score 89 iBT); recommended—IELTS (minimum score 6.5), TSE (minimum score 53). *Application deadline:* For fall admission, 10/1 for domestic and international students. Application fee: $50 ($75 for international students). Electronic applications accepted. *Expenses:* All are estimates. Tuition for 10 hours = $2,763; Fees for 10 hours = $1,342. OT courses require additional $30/SCH. *Financial support:* In 2019–20, 294 students received support, including 9 research assistantships (averaging $4,988 per year), 8 teaching assistantships (averaging $5,312 per year); career-related internships or fieldwork, scholarships/grants, health care benefits, and unspecified assistantships also available. Support available to part-time students. Financial award application deadline: 3/1; financial award applicants required to submit FAFSA. *Unit head:* Dr. Cynthia Evetts, Director, 940-898-2801, Fax: 940-898-2806, E-mail: ot@twu.edu. *Application contact:* Korie Hawkins, Associate Director of Admissions, Graduate Recruitment, 940-898-3188, Fax: 940-898-3081, E-mail: admissions@twu.edu.
Website: http://www.twu.edu/occupational-therapy/

**Thomas Jefferson University,** Jefferson College of Rehabilitation Sciences, Program in Occupational Therapy, Philadelphia, PA 19107. Offers MS. *Accreditation:* AOTA. *Program availability:* Evening/weekend. *Degree requirements:* For master's, portfolio. *Entrance requirements:* For master's, GRE or MAT. Additional exam requirements/recommendations for international students: required—TOEFL (minimum score 550 paper-based; 79 iBT). Electronic applications accepted.

**Towson University,** College of Health Professions, Program in Occupational Therapy, Towson, MD 21252-0001. Offers MS. *Accreditation:* AOTA. *Students:* 126 full-time (115 women), 14 part-time (13 women); includes 29 minority (15 Black or African American, non-Hispanic/Latino; 5 Asian, non-Hispanic/Latino; 4 Hispanic/Latino; 5 Two or more races, non-Hispanic/Latino), 2 international. *Entrance requirements:* For master's, bachelor's degree with minimum GPA of 3.25, master's degree, or doctorate; 3 letters of recommendation; human service/OT observation hours; personal statement. *Application deadline:* For fall admission, 1/17 for domestic students, 5/15 for international students; for spring admission, 10/15 for domestic students, 12/1 for international students. Applications are processed on a rolling basis. Application fee: $45. Electronic applications accepted. *Expenses: Tuition, area resident:* Full-time $7920; part-time $439 per credit. Tuition, nonresident: full-time $16,344; part-time $908 per credit. *International tuition:* $16,344 full-time. *Required fees:* $2628; $146 per credit. $876 per term. *Financial support:* Application deadline: 4/1. *Unit head:* Dr. Beth Merryman, Department Chair, 410-704-2762, E-mail: otadmissions@towson.edu. *Application contact:* Coverley Beidleman, Assistant Director of Graduate Admissions, 410-704-5630, Fax: 410-704-3030, E-mail: grads@towson.edu.
Website: https://www.towson.edu/chp/departments/occutherapy/programs/

**Trinity Washington University,** School of Nursing and Health Professions, Washington, DC 20017-1094. Offers nursing (MSN); occupational therapy (MOT).

**Tufts University,** Graduate School of Arts and Sciences, Department of Occupational Therapy, Medford, MA 02155. Offers MS, OTD. *Accreditation:* AOTA. *Degree requirements:* For master's, thesis optional; for doctorate, leadership project. *Entrance requirements:* For master's and doctorate, GRE General Test. Additional exam requirements/recommendations for international students: required—TOEFL (minimum score 550 paper-based; 80 iBT), IELTS (minimum score 6.5). Electronic applications accepted. *Expenses:* Contact institution.

**Tufts University,** Graduate School of Arts and Sciences, Graduate Certificate Programs, Advanced Professional Study in Occupational Therapy Program, Medford, MA 02155. Offers Certificate. *Program availability:* Part-time, evening/weekend. Electronic applications accepted. *Expenses:* Contact institution.

*Occupational Therapy*

**Tuskegee University,** Graduate Programs, College of Veterinary Medicine, Nursing and Allied Health, School of Nursing and Allied Health, Tuskegee, AL 36088. Offers occupational therapy (MS). *Accreditation:* AOTA.

**Université de Montréal,** Faculty of Medicine, Programs in Ergonomics, Montréal, QC H3C 3J7, Canada. Offers occupational therapy (DESS).

**University at Buffalo, the State University of New York,** Graduate School, School of Public Health and Health Professions, Department of Rehabilitation Science, Program in Occupational Therapy, Buffalo, NY 14260. Offers MS. *Accreditation:* AOTA. *Entrance requirements:* Additional exam requirements/recommendations for international students: required—TOEFL (minimum score 79 iBT). Electronic applications accepted. *Expenses: Tuition, area resident:* Full-time $11,310; part-time $471 per credit hour. Tuition, state resident: full-time $11,310; part-time $471 per credit hour. Tuition, nonresident: full-time $23,100; part-time $963 per credit hour. *International tuition:* $23,100 full-time. *Required fees:* $2820.

**The University of Alabama at Birmingham,** School of Health Professions, Program in Occupational Therapy, Birmingham, AL 35294. Offers low vision rehabilitation (Certificate); occupational therapy (MS). *Accreditation:* AOTA. *Program availability:* Part-time, online learning. *Faculty:* 11 full-time (6 women). *Students:* 133 full-time (122 women), 11 part-time (10 women); includes 24 minority (14 Black or African American, non-Hispanic/Latino; 1 American Indian or Alaska Native, non-Hispanic/Latino; 4 Asian, non-Hispanic/Latino; 3 Hispanic/Latino; 2 Two or more races, non-Hispanic/Latino). Average age 27. 102 applicants, 82% accepted, 70 enrolled. In 2019, 54 master's awarded. *Entrance requirements:* Additional exam requirements/recommendations for international students: recommended—TOEFL, IELTS. *Unit head:* Dr. Brian J. Dudgeon, Director of Entry-Level Program, 205-975-6101, Fax: 205-934-0402. *Application contact:* Susan Noblitt Banks, Director of Graduate School Operations, 205-934-8227, Fax: 205-934-8413, E-mail: gradschool@uab.edu.

**University of Alberta,** Faculty of Graduate Studies and Research, Faculty of Rehabilitation Medicine, Department of Occupational Therapy, Edmonton, AB T6G 2E1, Canada. Offers M Sc, PhD. *Program availability:* Part-time. *Degree requirements:* For master's, thesis. *Entrance requirements:* For master's, bachelor's degree in occupational therapy, minimum GPA of 6.9 on a 9.0 scale. Additional exam requirements/recommendations for international students: required—TOEFL. Electronic applications accepted.

**The University of British Columbia,** Faculty of Medicine, Department of Occupational Science and Occupational Therapy, Vancouver, BC V6T 2B5, Canada. Offers occupational therapy (MOT). *Entrance requirements:* Additional exam requirements/recommendations for international students: required—TOEFL, IELTS. Electronic applications accepted. *Expenses:* Contact institution.

**University of Central Arkansas,** Graduate School, College of Health and Behavioral Sciences, Department of Occupational Therapy, Conway, AR 72035-0001. Offers MS. *Accreditation:* AOTA. *Degree requirements:* For master's, thesis optional, internship. *Entrance requirements:* For master's, GRE General Test, minimum GPA of 2.7. Additional exam requirements/recommendations for international students: required—TOEFL (minimum score 550 paper-based; 80 iBT). Electronic applications accepted. *Expenses:* Contact institution.

**The University of Findlay,** Office of Graduate Admissions, Findlay, OH 45840. Offers applied security and analytics (MSAS); athletic training (MAT); business (MBA), including certified management accountant, certified public accountant, health care management, hospitality management; education (MA Ed, Ed D), including children's literature (MA Ed), curriculum and teaching (MA Ed), education (MA Ed), educational administration (MA Ed), human resource development (MA Ed), mathematics (MA Ed), reading (MA Ed), science education (MA Ed), superintendent (Ed D), teaching (Ed D), technology (MA Ed); environmental, safety, and health management (MSEM); health informatics (MS); occupational therapy (MOT); pharmacy (Pharm D); physical therapy (DPT); physician assistant (MPA); rhetoric and writing (MA); teaching English to speakers of other languages (TESOL) and applied linguistics (MA). *Program availability:* Part-time, evening/weekend, 100% online, blended/hybrid learning. *Students:* 688 full-time (430 women), 553 part-time (308 women), 170 international. Average age 28. 865 applicants, 31% accepted, 235 enrolled. In 2019, 363 master's, 141 doctorates awarded. *Degree requirements:* For master's, comprehensive exam (for some programs), thesis (for some programs), cumulative project, capstone project; for doctorate, thesis/dissertation (for some programs). *Entrance requirements:* For master's, GRE/GMAT, bachelor's degree from accredited institution, minimum undergraduate GPA of 2.5 in last 64 hours of course work; for doctorate, GRE, MAT, minimum cumulative GPA of 3.0. Additional exam requirements/recommendations for international students: required—TOEFL (minimum score 79 iBT), IELTS (minimum score 7), PTE (minimum score 61). *Application deadline:* Applications are processed on a rolling basis. Electronic applications accepted. *Financial support:* In 2019–20, 10 research assistantships with partial tuition reimbursements (averaging $7,200 per year), 35 teaching assistantships with partial tuition reimbursements (averaging $7,200 per year) were awarded; Federal Work-Study, institutionally sponsored loans, and unspecified assistantships also available. Financial award applicants required to submit FAFSA. *Unit head:* Dave M. Emsweller, Director of Admissions, Interim, 419-434-4578, E-mail: emsweller@findlay.edu. *Application contact:* Amber Feehan, Graduate Admissions Counselor, 419-434-6933, Fax: 419-434-4898, E-mail: feehan@findlay.edu.
Website: http://www.findlay.edu/admissions/graduate/Pages/default.aspx

**University of Florida,** Graduate School, College of Public Health and Health Professions, Department of Occupational Therapy, Gainesville, FL 32611. Offers MHS, MOT. *Accreditation:* AOTA. *Degree requirements:* For master's, clinical rotations. *Entrance requirements:* For master's, GRE General Test, minimum GPA of 3.0. Additional exam requirements/recommendations for international students: required—TOEFL (minimum score 550 paper-based; 80 iBT), IELTS (minimum score 6). Electronic applications accepted.

**University of Illinois at Chicago,** College of Applied Health Sciences, Department of Occupational Therapy, Chicago, IL 60607-7128. Offers MS, OTD. *Accreditation:* AOTA. *Program availability:* Part-time. *Degree requirements:* For master's, thesis. *Entrance requirements:* For master's, GRE General Test, minimum GPA of 2.75, previous course work in statistics. Additional exam requirements/recommendations for international students: required—TOEFL. Electronic applications accepted. *Expenses:* Contact institution.

**University of Indianapolis,** Graduate Programs, College of Health Sciences, School of Occupational Therapy, Indianapolis, IN 46227-3697. Offers MOT, DHS, OTD. *Accreditation:* AOTA. *Program availability:* Part-time, evening/weekend. *Degree requirements:* For master's, thesis. *Entrance requirements:* For master's, minimum GPA of 3.0, interview; for doctorate, minimum GPA of 3.3, BA/BS or MA/MS from occupational therapy program, current state license, currently in practice as occupational therapist or have 1000 hours of practice in last 5 years. Additional exam requirements/recommendations for international students: required—TOEFL (minimum score 550 paper-based; 92 iBT), TWE (minimum score 5). *Expenses:* Contact institution.

**The University of Kansas,** University of Kansas Medical Center, School of Health Professions, Department of Occupational Therapy Education, Kansas City, KS 66160. Offers occupational therapy (MOT, OTD); therapeutic science (PhD). *Accreditation:* AOTA. *Program availability:* Part-time. *Faculty:* 14. *Students:* 128 full-time (112 women), 15 part-time (14 women); includes 21 minority (1 Black or African American, non-Hispanic/Latino; 4 Asian, non-Hispanic/Latino; 10 Hispanic/Latino; 6 Two or more races, non-Hispanic/Latino), 1 international. Average age 26. In 2019, 41 master's, 10 doctorates awarded. *Degree requirements:* For doctorate, comprehensive exam, thesis/dissertation, capstone and oral defense. *Entrance requirements:* For doctorate, GRE, For the Therapeutic Science PhD program, a minimum of 24 research-related course credits at the graduate level. Additional exam requirements/recommendations for international students: required—TOEFL; recommended—IELTS. *Application deadline:* For fall admission, 12/1 for domestic and international students. Application fee: $60. Electronic applications accepted. *Expenses:* Tuition, state resident: full-time $9989. Tuition, nonresident: full-time $23,950. *International tuition:* $23,950 full-time. *Required fees:* $984; $81.99 per credit hour. Tuition and fees vary according to course load, campus/location and program. *Financial support:* Research assistantships, teaching assistantships with full and partial tuition reimbursements, Federal Work-Study, scholarships/grants, traineeships, and unspecified assistantships available. Financial award application deadline: 3/1; financial award applicants required to submit FAFSA. *Unit head:* Dr. Dory Sabata, Interim Department Chair and Clinical Associate Professor, 913-588-7338, Fax: 913-588-4568, E-mail: dsabata@kumc.edu. *Application contact:* Bobbi Stidham, Program Manager, 913-588-7195, Fax: 913-588-4568, E-mail: bstidham@kumc.edu.
Website: http://www.kumc.edu/school-of-health-professions/occupational-therapy-education.html

**University of Louisiana at Monroe,** Graduate School, College of Health Sciences, Department of Occupational Therapy, Monroe, LA 71209-0001. Offers MOT. *Accreditation:* AOTA. *Program availability:* Part-time, evening/weekend, blended/hybrid learning. *Faculty:* 6 full-time (all women), 1 part-time/adjunct (0 women). *Students:* 59 full-time (55 women), 29 part-time (20 women); includes 13 minority (6 Black or African American, non-Hispanic/Latino; 1 American Indian or Alaska Native, non-Hispanic/Latino; 5 Hispanic/Latino; 1 Two or more races, non-Hispanic/Latino). Average age 31. 69 applicants, 43% accepted, 30 enrolled. In 2019, 27 master's awarded. *Degree requirements:* For master's, comprehensive exam (for some programs). *Entrance requirements:* For master's, certification as an OTA; Bachelor's degree; prerequisite courses; 2.5 minimum GPA, with 3.0 GPA for last 30 hours. Additional exam requirements/recommendations for international students: required—TOEFL (minimum score 500 paper-based; 61 iBT); recommended—IELTS (minimum score 5.5). *Application deadline:* For fall admission, 3/1 for domestic and international students. Applications are processed on a rolling basis. Application fee: $55. Electronic applications accepted. *Expenses: Tuition, area resident:* Full-time $6489. Tuition, state resident: full-time $6489. Tuition, nonresident: full-time $18,989. *Required fees:* $2748. Tuition and fees vary according to course load and program. *Financial support:* In 2019–20, 45 students received support. Career-related internships or fieldwork, Federal Work-Study, scholarships/grants, and unspecified assistantships available. Financial award application deadline: 2/15; financial award applicants required to submit FAFSA. *Unit head:* Dr. Patti Calk, Program Director, 318-342-5581, E-mail: calk@ulm.edu. *Application contact:* Dr. Patti Calk, Program Director, 318-342-5581, E-mail: calk@ulm.edu.
Website: http://www.ulm.edu/ot/

**University of Manitoba,** Faculty of Graduate Studies, College of Rehabilitation Sciences, Winnipeg, MB R3T 2N2, Canada. Offers applied health sciences (PhD); occupational therapy (MOT); physical therapy (MPT); rehabilitation sciences (M Sc).

**University of Mary,** School of Health Sciences, Program in Occupational Therapy, Bismarck, ND 58504-9652. Offers MSOT. *Accreditation:* AOTA. *Program availability:* Part-time, online learning. *Degree requirements:* For master's, thesis or alternative, seminar. *Entrance requirements:* For master's, minimum cumulative GPA of 3.0, 48 hours of volunteer experience, 3 letters of reference. Additional exam requirements/recommendations for international students: required—TOEFL (minimum score 550 paper-based). Electronic applications accepted. *Expenses:* Contact institution.

**University of Minnesota Rochester,** Graduate Programs, Rochester, MN 55904. Offers bioinformatics and computational biology (MS, PhD); business administration (MBA); occupational therapy (MOT). *Accreditation:* AOTA.

**University of Minnesota, Twin Cities Campus,** Graduate School, Program in Occupational Therapy, Minneapolis, MN 55455-0213. Offers MOT.

**University of Mississippi Medical Center,** School of Health Related Professions, Department of Occupational Therapy, Jackson, MS 39216-4505. Offers MOT. *Accreditation:* AOTA.

**University of New England,** Westbrook College of Health Professions, Biddeford, ME 04005-9526. Offers nurse anesthesia (MSNA); occupational therapy (MS); physical therapy (DPT); physician assistant (MS); social work (MSW). *Accreditation:* AANA/CANAEP; AOTA. *Program availability:* Part-time. *Faculty:* 42 full-time (32 women), 23 part-time/adjunct (16 women). *Students:* 493 full-time (361 women), 8 part-time (7 women); includes 59 minority (3 Black or African American, non-Hispanic/Latino; 2 American Indian or Alaska Native, non-Hispanic/Latino; 36 Asian, non-Hispanic/Latino; 10 Hispanic/Latino; 2 Native Hawaiian or other Pacific Islander, non-Hispanic/Latino; 6 Two or more races, non-Hispanic/Latino), 2 international. Average age 27. In 2019, 154 master's, 58 doctorates awarded. *Application deadline:* Applications are processed on a rolling basis. Electronic applications accepted. *Financial support:* Application deadline: 5/1; applicants required to submit FAFSA. *Unit head:* Dr. Karen T. Pardue, Dean, Westbrook College of Health Professions, 207-221-4361, E-mail: kpardue@une.edu. *Application contact:* Scott Steinberg, Vice President of University Admissions, 207-221-4225, Fax: 207-523-1925, E-mail: ssteinberg@une.edu.
Website: http://www.une.edu/wchp/index.cfm

**University of New Hampshire,** Graduate School, College of Health and Human Services, Department of Occupational Therapy, Durham, NH 03824. Offers assistive technology (Postbaccalaureate Certificate); occupational therapy (MS). *Accreditation:* AOTA. *Program availability:* Part-time. *Students:* 148 full-time (139 women), 10 part-time (9 women); includes 9 minority (4 Black or African American, non-Hispanic/Latino; 2 Asian, non-Hispanic/Latino; 2 Hispanic/Latino; 1 Two or more races, non-Hispanic/Latino). Average age 24. 101 applicants, 81% accepted, 69 enrolled. In 2019, 61 master's, 7 other advanced degrees awarded. *Entrance requirements:* Additional exam requirements/recommendations for international students: required—TOEFL (minimum score 550 paper-based; 80 iBT), IELTS, PTE. *Application deadline:* For fall admission, 1/15 for domestic and international students. Application fee: $65. Electronic applications accepted. *Financial support:* In 2019–20, 3 students received support. Fellowships, research assistantships, teaching assistantships, career-related internships or fieldwork, Federal Work-Study, and scholarships/grants available. Support available to part-time students. Financial award application deadline: 2/15. *Unit head:* Lou Ann Griswold, Chair, 603-862-3416. *Application contact:* Deb Smith,

Administrative Assistant, 603-862-3221, E-mail: deb.smith@unh.edu. Website: http://www.chhs.unh.edu/ot

**University of New Mexico,** Graduate Studies, Health Sciences Center, Program in Occupational Therapy, Albuquerque, NM 87131-5196. Offers MOT. *Accreditation:* AOTA. *Program availability:* Part-time. *Degree requirements:* For master's, thesis, clinical fieldwork. *Entrance requirements:* For master's, interview, writing sample, volunteer experience. Electronic applications accepted. *Expenses:* Tuition, state resident: full-time $7633; part-time $972 per year. Tuition, nonresident: full-time $22,586; part-time $3840 per year. *International tuition:* $23,292 full-time. *Required fees:* $8608. Tuition and fees vary according to course level, course load, degree level, program and student level.

**University of North Dakota,** Graduate School, Graduate Programs in Medicine, Department of Occupational Therapy, Grand Forks, ND 58202. Offers MOT. *Accreditation:* AOTA. *Program availability:* Part-time. *Entrance requirements:* For master's, letter of reference; volunteer or work experience, preferably from health-related field; interview; minimum GPA of 2.7. Additional exam requirements/recommendations for international students: required—TOEFL (minimum score 550 paper-based; 79 iBT), IELTS (minimum score 6.5). Electronic applications accepted.

**University of Oklahoma Health Sciences Center,** Graduate College, College of Allied Health, Department of Occupational Therapy, Oklahoma City, OK 73190. Offers MOT. *Accreditation:* AOTA.

**University of Pittsburgh,** School of Health and Rehabilitation Sciences, Department of Occupational Therapy, Pittsburgh, PA 15260. Offers MS, CScD, OTD. *Accreditation:* AOTA. *Program availability:* 100% online. *Faculty:* 17 full-time (16 women). *Students:* 162 full-time (153 women), 3 part-time (all women); includes 19 minority (2 Black or African American, non-Hispanic/Latino; 8 Asian, non-Hispanic/Latino; 5 Hispanic/Latino; 4 Two or more races, non-Hispanic/Latino), 7 international. Average age 24. 198 applicants, 56% accepted, 65 enrolled. In 2019, 11 master's, 4 doctorates awarded. *Degree requirements:* For master's and doctorate, comprehensive exam (for some programs). *Entrance requirements:* For doctorate, GRE General Test. Additional exam requirements/recommendations for international students: required—International applicants may provide Duolingo English Test, IELTS or TOEFL scores to verify English language proficiency. Application fee: $140. Electronic applications accepted. *Financial support:* In 2019–20, 6 students received support, including 6 research assistantships with full tuition reimbursements available (averaging $23,160 per year). *Unit head:* Dr. Elizabeth Skidmore, Associate Dean of Research, SHRS, Professor and Chair, Department of Occupational Therapy, 412-383-6617, Fax: 412-383-6613, E-mail: skidmore@pitt.edu. *Application contact:* Jessica Maguire, Director of Admissions, 412-383-6557, Fax: 412-383-6535, E-mail: maguire@pitt.edu. Website: http://www.shrs.pitt.edu/ot

**University of Puerto Rico - Medical Sciences Campus,** School of Health Professions, Program in Occupational Therapy, San Juan, PR 00936-5067. Offers MS. *Accreditation:* AOTA.

**University of Puget Sound,** School of Occupational Therapy, Tacoma, WA 98416. Offers MSOT, Dr OT. *Accreditation:* AOTA. *Degree requirements:* For master's, thesis, publishable paper or program development project. *Entrance requirements:* For master's, GRE General Test, minimum baccalaureate GPA of 3.0, three letters of recommendation. Additional exam requirements/recommendations for international students: required—TOEFL (minimum score 550 paper-based; 90 iBT). Electronic applications accepted. *Expenses:* Contact institution.

**University of St. Augustine for Health Sciences,** Graduate Programs, Doctor of Occupational Therapy Program, San Marcos, CA 92069. Offers OTD.

**University of St. Augustine for Health Sciences,** Graduate Programs, Master of Occupational Therapy Program, San Marcos, CA 92069. Offers MOT. *Accreditation:* AOTA. *Entrance requirements:* For master's, GRE General Test. Application fee is waived when completed online.

**University of St. Augustine for Health Sciences,** Graduate Programs, Post Professional Programs, San Marcos, CA 92069. Offers health science (DH Sc); health sciences education (Ed D); occupational therapy (TOTD); physical therapy (TDPT). *Program availability:* Part-time, online learning. *Entrance requirements:* For doctorate, GRE General Test, master's degree in related field. Additional exam requirements/recommendations for international students: required—TOEFL.

**The University of Scranton,** Panuska College of Professional Studies, Program in Occupational Therapy, Scranton, PA 18510. Offers MS. *Accreditation:* AOTA. *Degree requirements:* For master's, comprehensive exam (for some programs), thesis (for some programs), capstone experience. *Entrance requirements:* For master's, minimum GPA of 3.0, three letters of reference. Additional exam requirements/recommendations for international students: required—TOEFL (minimum score 500 paper-based; 80 iBT), IELTS (minimum score 6.5). Electronic applications accepted.

**University of South Alabama,** Pat Capps Covey College of Allied Health Professions, Department of Occupational Therapy, Mobile, AL 36688-0002. Offers MS. *Accreditation:* AOTA. *Faculty:* 7 full-time (all women), 2 part-time/adjunct (both women). *Students:* 106 full-time (97 women), 1 (woman) part-time; includes 9 minority (2 American Indian or Alaska Native, non-Hispanic/Latino; 3 Asian, non-Hispanic/Latino; 2 Hispanic/Latino; 1 Native Hawaiian or other Pacific Islander, non-Hispanic/Latino; 1 Two or more races, non-Hispanic/Latino), 5 international. Average age 24. 146 applicants, 70% accepted, 41 enrolled. In 2019, 28 master's awarded. *Degree requirements:* For master's, comprehensive exam. *Entrance requirements:* For master's, GRE. Additional exam requirements/recommendations for international students: required—TOEFL (minimum score 600 paper-based; 100 iBT). *Application deadline:* For fall admission, 12/1 for domestic students, 1/15 for international students. Application fee: $75. Electronic applications accepted. *Expenses:* Contact institution. *Financial support:* Fellowships, research assistantships, teaching assistantships, career-related internships or fieldwork, Federal Work-Study, institutionally sponsored loans, scholarships/grants, and unspecified assistantships available. Support available to part-time students. Financial award application deadline: 3/31; financial award applicants required to submit FAFSA. *Unit head:* Dr. Donna M. Wooster, Chair, Associate Professor, Department of Occupational Therapy, 251-445-9222, Fax: 251-445-9211, E-mail: otdept@southalabama.edu. *Application contact:* Dr. Donna M. Wooster, Chair, Associate Professor, Department of Occupational Therapy, 251-445-9222, Fax: 251-445-9211, E-mail: otdept@southalabama.edu. Website: http://www.southalabama.edu/colleges/alliedhealth/ot/

**University of South Dakota,** Graduate School, School of Health Sciences, Department of Occupational Therapy, Vermillion, SD 57069. Offers occupational therapy (OTD); post-professional clinical occupational therapy (OTD). *Accreditation:* AOTA. *Program availability:* Part-time. *Degree requirements:* For master's, thesis optional, 6 months of supervised fieldwork. *Entrance requirements:* For master's, courses in human anatomy, human physiology, general psychology, abnormal psychology, lifespan development, and statistics. Additional exam requirements/recommendations for international students: required—TOEFL (minimum score 550 paper-based). *Expenses:* Contact institution.

**University of Southern California,** Graduate School, Herman Ostrow School of Dentistry, Chan Division of Occupational Science and Occupational Therapy, Graduate Program in Occupational Science, Los Angeles, CA 90089. Offers PhD. *Accreditation:* AOTA. *Degree requirements:* For doctorate, thesis/dissertation, qualifying exam. *Entrance requirements:* For doctorate, GRE (minimum combined score of 1100), minimum GPA of 3.0. Additional exam requirements/recommendations for international students: required—TOEFL (minimum score 600 paper-based; 100 iBT). Electronic applications accepted.

**University of Southern California,** Graduate School, Herman Ostrow School of Dentistry, Chan Division of Occupational Science and Occupational Therapy, Graduate Programs in Occupational Therapy, Los Angeles, CA 90089. Offers MA, OTD. *Accreditation:* AOTA. *Program availability:* Part-time. *Degree requirements:* For master's, comprehensive exam (for some programs), thesis or alternative; for doctorate, residency, portfolio. *Entrance requirements:* For master's and doctorate, GRE (minimum score 1000), minimum cumulative GPA of 3.0. Additional exam requirements/recommendations for international students: required—TOEFL (minimum score 600 paper-based; 100 iBT). Electronic applications accepted.

**University of Southern Indiana,** Graduate Studies, College of Nursing and Health Professions, Program in Occupational Therapy, Evansville, IN 47712-3590. Offers MSOT. *Accreditation:* AOTA. *Program availability:* Part-time. *Entrance requirements:* For master's, minimum GPA of 3.0, two letters of recommendation (one professional letter from previous employer or practicing OT; one academic letter from professor or advisor from undergraduate degree). Additional exam requirements/recommendations for international students: required—TOEFL (minimum score 550 paper-based; 79 iBT), IELTS (minimum score 6). Electronic applications accepted. *Expenses:* Contact institution.

**University of Southern Maine,** Lewiston-Auburn College, Program in Occupational Therapy, Lewiston, ME 04240. Offers MOT. *Accreditation:* AOTA. *Degree requirements:* For master's, fieldwork, original research. *Entrance requirements:* For master's, minimum GPA of 3.0, writing sample, interview, reference letters, job shadow observation. Electronic applications accepted. *Expenses: Tuition, area resident:* Full-time $864; part-time $432 per credit hour. Tuition, state resident: full-time $864; part-time $432 per credit hour. Tuition, nonresident: full-time $2372; part-time $1186 per credit hour. *Required fees:* $141; $108 per credit hour. Tuition and fees vary according to course load.

**The University of Tennessee at Chattanooga,** Department of Occupational Therapy, Chattanooga, TN 37403. Offers OTD. *Accreditation:* AOTA. *Faculty:* 6 full-time (all women), 1 (woman) part-time/adjunct. *Students:* 70 full-time (65 women), 1 (woman) part-time; includes 4 minority (2 Asian, non-Hispanic/Latino; 2 Two or more races, non-Hispanic/Latino). Average age 24. 29 applicants, 83% accepted, 24 enrolled. In 2019, 24 doctorates awarded. *Degree requirements:* For doctorate, thesis/dissertation, internship. *Entrance requirements:* For doctorate, GRE General Test, OTCAS application, CPR certification. Additional exam requirements/recommendations for international students: required—TOEFL (minimum score 550 paper-based; 79 iBT), IELTS (minimum score 6). *Application deadline:* For fall admission, 6/15 priority date for domestic students, 7/1 for international students; for spring admission, 11/1 priority date for domestic students, 11/1 for international students. Applications are processed on a rolling basis. Application fee: $35 ($40 for international students). Electronic applications accepted. *Financial support:* Fellowships, research assistantships, career-related internships or fieldwork, scholarships/grants, and unspecified assistantships available. Support available to part-time students. Financial award application deadline: 7/1; financial award applicants required to submit FAFSA. *Unit head:* Susan McDonald, Department Head, 423-425-5759, E-mail: susan-mcdonald@utc.edu. *Application contact:* Dr. Joanne Romagni, Dean of the Graduate School, 423-425-4478, Fax: 423-425-5223, E-mail: joanne-romagni@utc.edu. Website: http://www.utc.edu/occupational-therapy/

**The University of Tennessee Health Science Center,** College of Health Professions, Memphis, TN 38163-0002. Offers audiology (MS, Au D); clinical laboratory science (MSCLS); cytopathology practice (MCP); health informatics and information management (MHIIM); occupational therapy (MOT); physical therapy (DPT, ScDPT); physician assistant (MMS); speech-language pathology (MS). *Accreditation:* AOTA; APTA. *Program availability:* Part-time, evening/weekend, online learning. Terminal master's awarded for partial completion of doctoral program. *Degree requirements:* For master's, comprehensive exam, thesis; for doctorate, comprehensive exam, residency. *Entrance requirements:* For master's, GRE (MOT, MSCLS), minimum GPA of 3.0, 3 letters of reference, national accreditation (MSCLS), GRE if GPA is less than 3.0 (MCP); for doctorate, GRE. Additional exam requirements/recommendations for international students: required—TOEFL (minimum score 550 paper-based; 80 iBT). Electronic applications accepted. *Expenses:* Contact institution.

**The University of Texas at El Paso,** Graduate School, College of Health Sciences, Master of Occupational Therapy Program, El Paso, TX 79968-0001. Offers MOT. *Accreditation:* AOTA. *Degree requirements:* For master's, thesis optional. *Entrance requirements:* For master's, GRE, minimum cumulative and prerequisite GPA of 3.0, bachelor's degree, 40 clock hours of supervised observations with an OT. Additional exam requirements/recommendations for international students: required—TOEFL; recommended—IELTS.

**The University of Texas Health Science Center at San Antonio,** School of Health Professions, San Antonio, TX 78229-3900. Offers occupational therapy (MOT); physical therapy (DPT); physician assistant studies (MS); speech language pathology (MS). *Accreditation:* AOTA; APTA; ARC-PA; ASHA. *Degree requirements:* For master's, comprehensive exam, thesis (for some programs); for doctorate, comprehensive exam.

**The University of Texas Medical Branch,** School of Health Professions, Department of Occupational Therapy, Galveston, TX 77555. Offers MOT. *Accreditation:* AOTA. *Entrance requirements:* For master's, MAT, 20 volunteer hours, telephone interview, 2 references.

**The University of Texas Rio Grande Valley,** College of Health Affairs, Department of Occupational Therapy, Edinburg, TX 78539. Offers MS. *Accreditation:* AOTA. *Faculty:* 6 full-time (2 women), 4 part-time/adjunct (all women). *Students:* 56 full-time (51 women), 31 part-time (23 women); includes 77 minority (1 Black or African American, non-Hispanic/Latino; 6 Asian, non-Hispanic/Latino; 70 Hispanic/Latino). Average age 26. 55 applicants, 58% accepted, 32 enrolled. In 2019, 15 master's awarded. *Degree requirements:* For master's, National Board of Certified Occupational Therapist (NBCOT). *Entrance requirements:* For master's, GRE. Additional exam requirements/recommendations for international students: required—TOEFL, IELTS. *Application deadline:* For spring admission, 2/1 for domestic students. Application fee: $35. Application fee is waived when completed online. *Expenses: Tuition, area resident:* Full-time $5959; part-time $440 per credit hour. Tuition, state resident: full-time $5959. Tuition, nonresident: full-time $5959. *International tuition:* $13,321 full-time. *Required fees:* $1169; $185 per credit hour. *Financial support:* In 2019–20, 3 research assistantships were awarded; Federal Work-Study, institutionally sponsored loans, scholarships/grants, and unspecified assistantships also available. Financial award applicants required to submit FAFSA. *Unit head:* Dr. Shirley A. Wells, Chair, 956-665-

2475, E-mail: shirley.wells@utrgv.edu. *Application contact:* Graduate Student Recruiter, 956-665-3558, E-mail: ucentrail@utrgv.edu.
Website: http://www.utrgv.edu/ot/

**University of the Sciences,** Program in Occupational Therapy, Philadelphia, PA 19104-4495. Offers MOT, Dr OT. *Accreditation:* AOTA. *Program availability:* Online learning. *Degree requirements:* For doctorate, capstone project. *Entrance requirements:* For doctorate, master's degree, two years of occupational therapy practice experience, 500-word essay. Electronic applications accepted.

**The University of Toledo,** College of Graduate Studies, College of Health and Human Services, School of Exercise and Rehabilitation Sciences, Toledo, OH 43606-3390. Offers athletic training (MSES); exercise physiology (MSES); exercise science (PhD); occupational therapy (OTD); physical therapy (DPT); recreation and leisure studies (MA), including recreation administration, recreation therapy. *Degree requirements:* For master's, comprehensive exam, thesis; for doctorate, thesis/dissertation or alternative. *Entrance requirements:* For master's, GRE, minimum cumulative GPA of 2.7 for all previous academic work, letters of recommendation; for doctorate, GRE, minimum cumulative GPA of 3.0 for all previous academic work, letters of recommendation; OTCAS or PTCAS application and UT supplemental application (for OTD and DPT). Additional exam requirements/recommendations for international students: required—TOEFL (minimum score 550 paper-based; 80 iBT). Electronic applications accepted.

**University of Toronto,** Faculty of Medicine, Department of Occupational Science and Occupational Therapy, Toronto, ON M5S 1A1, Canada. Offers occupational therapy (M Sc OT). *Entrance requirements:* For master's, bachelor's degree with high academic standing from recognized university with minimum B average in final year, personal statement. Additional exam requirements/recommendations for international students: required—TOEFL (minimum score 600 paper-based; 100 iBT), TWE (minimum score 5). Electronic applications accepted.

**University of Utah,** Graduate School, College of Health, Department of Occupational and Recreational Therapies, Salt Lake City, UT 84108. Offers MOT, OTD. *Accreditation:* AOTA. *Program availability:* Part-time, evening/weekend, 100% online. *Faculty:* 11 full-time (all women). *Students:* 104 full-time (83 women), 27 part-time (23 women); includes 24 minority (3 Black or African American, non-Hispanic/Latino; 9 Asian, non-Hispanic/Latino; 11 Hispanic/Latino; 1 Two or more races, non-Hispanic/Latino). Average age 32. In 2019, 32 master's, 6 doctorates awarded. *Expenses:* Tuition, state resident: full-time $7085; part-time $272.51 per credit hour. Tuition, nonresident: full-time $24,937; part-time $959.12 per credit hour. *Required fees:* $880.52; $880.52 per semester. Tuition and fees vary according to degree level, program and student level. *Financial support:* Teaching assistantships, Federal Work-Study, scholarships/grants, and unspecified assistantships available. *Unit head:* Dr. Lorie Richards, Chairperson, 801-585-1069, Fax: 801-585-1001, E-mail: lorie.richards@hsc.utah.edu. *Application contact:* Kelly C. Brown, Academic Advisor, 801-585-0555, Fax: 801-585-1001, E-mail: kelly.brown@hsc.utah.edu.
Website: http://health.utah.edu/occupational-recreational-therapies/

**University of Washington,** Graduate School, School of Medicine, Graduate Programs in Medicine, Department of Rehabilitation Medicine, Seattle, WA 98195-6490. Offers occupational therapy (MOT); physical therapy (DPT); prosthetics and orthotics (MPO); rehabilitation science (PhD). *Accreditation:* AOTA. *Degree requirements:* For doctorate, comprehensive exam (for some programs), thesis/dissertation (for some programs). *Entrance requirements:* For master's and doctorate, GRE. Additional exam requirements/recommendations for international students: required—TOEFL.

**The University of Western Ontario,** School of Graduate and Postdoctoral Studies, Faculty of Health Sciences, School of Occupational Therapy, London, ON N6A 3K7, Canada. Offers M Sc. *Program availability:* Part-time. *Degree requirements:* For master's, thesis. *Entrance requirements:* For master's, Canadian BA in occupational therapy or equivalent, minimum B+ average in last 2 years of 4 year degree. Additional exam requirements/recommendations for international students: required—TOEFL (minimum score 570 paper-based).

**University of Wisconsin–La Crosse,** College of Science and Health, Department of Health Professions, Program in Occupational Therapy, La Crosse, WI 54601-3742. Offers MS. *Accreditation:* AOTA. *Faculty:* 2 full-time (both women), 3 part-time/adjunct (all women). *Students:* 50 full-time (45 women), 22 part-time (21 women); includes 4 minority (3 Asian, non-Hispanic/Latino; 1 Two or more races, non-Hispanic/Latino). Average age 24. 207 applicants, 26% accepted, 25 enrolled. In 2019, 26 master's awarded. *Degree requirements:* For master's, 6-month clinical internship. *Entrance requirements:* For master's, minimum GPA of 3.0, 20 job shadowing hours. Additional exam requirements/recommendations for international students: required—TOEFL (minimum score 550 paper-based; 79 iBT). *Application deadline:* For fall admission, 1/4 for domestic students. Application fee: $50. Electronic applications accepted. *Expenses:* Contact institution. *Financial support:* Federal Work-Study, scholarships/grants, and health care benefits available. Support available to part-time students. Financial award application deadline: 3/15; financial award applicants required to submit FAFSA. *Unit head:* Dr. Laura Schaffer, Interim Program Director, 608-785-8462, E-mail: lschaffer@uwlax.edu. *Application contact:* Peter Amann, Senior Graduate Student Status Examiner, 608-785-6622, E-mail: pamann@uwlax.edu.
Website: http://www.uwlax.edu/ot/

**University of Wisconsin–Madison,** Graduate School, School of Education, Department of Kinesiology, Occupational Therapy Program, Madison, WI 53706-1380. Offers MS, PhD. *Accreditation:* AOTA. *Degree requirements:* For doctorate, thesis/dissertation.

**University of Wisconsin–Milwaukee,** Graduate School, College of Health Sciences, Department of Occupational Science and Technology, Milwaukee, WI 53201-0413. Offers assistive technology and design (MS); disability and occupation (MS); ergonomics (MS); therapeutic recreation (MS). *Accreditation:* AOTA. *Entrance requirements:* Additional exam requirements/recommendations for international students: required—TOEFL (minimum score 550 paper-based; 79 iBT), IELTS (minimum score 6.5).

**Utica College,** Program in Occupational Therapy, Utica, NY 13502. Offers MS. *Accreditation:* AOTA. *Program availability:* Part-time, evening/weekend. *Faculty:* 7 full-time (all women). *Students:* 88 full-time (80 women), 1 part-time (0 women); includes 10 minority (2 Black or African American, non-Hispanic/Latino; 2 Asian, non-Hispanic/Latino; 5 Hispanic/Latino; 1 Two or more races, non-Hispanic/Latino), 1 international. Average age 25. 65 applicants, 98% accepted, 57 enrolled. In 2019, 59 master's awarded. *Degree requirements:* For master's, thesis. *Entrance requirements:* For master's, physical health exam, CPR certification, 60 hours of volunteer experience, minimum GPA of 3.0. Additional exam requirements/recommendations for international students: required—TOEFL (minimum score 525 paper-based). *Application deadline:* Applications are processed on a rolling basis. Application fee: $50. Electronic applications accepted. *Expenses:* Contact institution. *Financial support:* Career-related internships or fieldwork, scholarships/grants, tuition waivers (partial), and unspecified assistantships available. Support available to part-time students. Financial award application deadline: 3/15; financial award applicants required to submit FAFSA. *Unit head:* Cora Bruns, Director, 315-792-3125, E-mail: cbruns@utica.edu. *Application contact:* John D. Rowe, Director of Graduate Admissions, 315-792-3824, Fax: 315-792-3003, E-mail: jrowe@utica.edu.
Website: https://www.utica.edu/academics/programs/occupational-therapy-graduate

**Virginia Commonwealth University,** Graduate School, School of Allied Health Professions, Department of Occupational Therapy, Richmond, VA 23284-9005. Offers MSOT, OTD. *Accreditation:* AOTA (one or more programs are accredited). *Degree requirements:* For master's, fieldwork. *Entrance requirements:* For master's, GRE General Test. Additional exam requirements/recommendations for international students: required—TOEFL (minimum score 600 paper-based; 100 iBT); recommended—IELTS (minimum score 6.5). Electronic applications accepted.

**Virginia Commonwealth University,** Graduate School, School of Allied Health Professions, Doctoral Program in Health Related Sciences, Richmond, VA 23284-9005. Offers clinical laboratory sciences (PhD); gerontology (PhD); health administration (PhD); nurse anesthesia (PhD); occupational therapy (PhD); physical therapy (PhD); radiation sciences (PhD); rehabilitation leadership (PhD). *Entrance requirements:* For doctorate, GRE General Test or MAT, minimum GPA of 3.3 in master's degree. Additional exam requirements/recommendations for international students: required—TOEFL (minimum score 600 paper-based; 100 iBT); recommended—IELTS (minimum score 6.5). Electronic applications accepted.

**Washington University in St. Louis,** School of Medicine, Program in Occupational Therapy, Saint Louis, MO 63108. Offers MSOT, OTD. *Accreditation:* AOTA. Terminal master's awarded for partial completion of doctoral program. *Degree requirements:* For master's, fieldwork experiences; for doctorate, fieldwork and apprenticeship experiences. *Entrance requirements:* For master's and doctorate, GRE General Test, bachelor's degree in another field or enrollment in an affiliated institution. Additional exam requirements/recommendations for international students: required—TOEFL, TWE (minimum score 5). Electronic applications accepted.

**Wayne State University,** Eugene Applebaum College of Pharmacy and Health Sciences, Department of Health Care Sciences, Detroit, MI 48201. Offers nurse anesthesia (MS, DNP-A, Certificate), including anesthesia (MS), nurse anesthesia practice (DNP-A), pediatric anesthesia (Certificate); occupational therapy (MOT); physical therapy (DPT); physician assistant studies (MS). *Faculty:* 5. *Students:* 310 full-time (209 women), 4 part-time (all women); includes 33 minority (7 Black or African American, non-Hispanic/Latino; 14 Asian, non-Hispanic/Latino; 8 Hispanic/Latino; 4 Two or more races, non-Hispanic/Latino), 4 international. Average age 26. 344 applicants, 20% accepted, 55 enrolled. In 2019, 97 master's, 36 doctorates awarded. *Entrance requirements:* Additional exam requirements/recommendations for international students: required—TOEFL (minimum score 550 paper-based; 79 iBT), Michigan English Language Assessment Battery (minimum score 85); recommended—IELTS (minimum score 6.5), TWE (minimum score 5.5). Application fee: $50. Electronic applications accepted. *Expenses:* Contact institution. *Financial support:* In 2019–20, 102 students received support. Fellowships and scholarships/grants available. Financial award applicants required to submit FAFSA. *Unit head:* Dr. Sara F Maher, Chair Department of Health Care Sciences, 313-577-5630, E-mail: sara.maher@wayne.edu. *Application contact:* Office of Student and Alumni Affairs, 313-577-1716, E-mail: cphsinfo@wayne.edu.
Website: http://cphs.wayne.edu/hcs/

**Wesley College,** Occupational Therapy Program, Dover, DE 19901-3875. Offers MOT.

**West Coast University,** Graduate Programs, North Hollywood, CA 91606. Offers advanced generalist (MSN); family nurse practitioner (MSN); health administration (MHA); occupational therapy (MS); pharmacy (Pharm D); physical therapy (DPT).

**Western Michigan University,** Graduate College, College of Health and Human Services, Department of Occupational Therapy, Kalamazoo, MI 49008. Offers MS. *Accreditation:* AOTA.

**Western New England University,** College of Pharmacy and Health Sciences, Doctor of Occupational Therapy Program, Springfield, MA 01119. Offers OTD. *Degree requirements:* For doctorate, thesis/dissertation. *Entrance requirements:* For doctorate, baccalaureate degree from accredited institution, documented volunteer/observation hours, two recommendations, personal statement. Additional exam requirements/recommendations for international students: required—TOEFL (minimum score 80 iBT). Electronic applications accepted. *Expenses:* Contact institution.

**Western New Mexico University,** Graduate Division, Program in Occupational Therapy, Silver City, NM 88062-0680. Offers MOT. *Program availability:* Part-time.

**West Virginia University,** School of Medicine, Morgantown, WV 26506. Offers biochemistry and molecular biology (PhD); biomedical science (MS); cancer cell biology (PhD); cellular and integrative physiology (PhD); exercise physiology (MS, PhD); health sciences (MS); immunology (PhD); medicine (MD); occupational therapy (MOT); pathologists assistant' (MHS); physical therapy (DPT). *Accreditation:* AOTA; LCME/AMA. *Program availability:* Part-time, evening/weekend. *Entrance requirements:* Additional exam requirements/recommendations for international students: required—TOEFL. Electronic applications accepted. *Expenses:* Contact institution.

**Winston-Salem State University,** Department of Occupational Therapy, Winston-Salem, NC 27110-0003. Offers MS. *Accreditation:* AOTA. *Entrance requirements:* For master's, GRE, 3 letters of recommendation (one from a licensed occupational therapist where volunteer or work experiences were performed; the other two from former professors or persons acquainted with academic potential); writing sample. Additional exam requirements/recommendations for international students: required—TOEFL. Electronic applications accepted.

**Worcester State University,** Graduate School, Program in Occupational Therapy, Worcester, MA 01602-2597. Offers MOT. *Accreditation:* AOTA. *Faculty:* 4 full-time (all women), 1 (woman) part-time/adjunct. *Students:* 58 full-time (52 women), 15 part-time (all women); includes 4 minority (1 Black or African American, non-Hispanic/Latino; 1 Asian, non-Hispanic/Latino; 2 Hispanic/Latino), 1 international. Average age 24. 37 applicants, 100% accepted, 36 enrolled. In 2019, 17 master's awarded. *Degree requirements:* For master's, comprehensive exam (for some programs), thesis, fieldwork. For a detail list in Degree Completion requirements please see the graduate catalog at catalog.worcester.edu. *Entrance requirements:* For master's, GRE General Test or MAT, For a detail list of entrance requirements please see the graduate catalog at catalog.worcester.edu. Additional exam requirements/recommendations for international students: required—TOEFL (minimum score 550 paper-based; 79 iBT), IELTS (minimum score 6). *Application deadline:* For fall admission, 3/1 priority date for domestic and international students; for spring admission, 11/1 for domestic and international students; for summer admission, 3/1 for domestic and international students. Applications are processed on a rolling basis. Application fee: $50. Electronic applications accepted. *Expenses:* Contact institution. *Financial support:* Career-related internships or fieldwork, scholarships/grants, and unspecified assistantships available. Financial award application deadline: 3/1; financial award applicants required to submit FAFSA. *Unit head:* Dr. Cheryl Lucas, Program Coordinator, 508-929-8795, Fax: 508-929-8178, E-mail: clucas2@worcester.edu. *Application contact:* Sara Grady, Associate Dean, Graduate Studies and Professional Development, 508-929-8130, Fax: 508-929-8100, E-mail: sara.grady@worcester.edu.

**Xavier University,** College of Professional Sciences, Department of Occupational Therapy, Cincinnati, OH 45207. Offers MOT. *Accreditation:* AOTA. *Degree requirements:* For master's, one foreign language, group research project. *Entrance requirements:* For master's, GRE (minimum of 33% average across all GRE sections - verbal, quantitative, analytical writing), minimum GPA of 3.0, completion of 40 volunteer hours, completion of all prerequisite courses with no more than 2 grades of C or lower; official transcript; personal statement; interview. Additional exam requirements/ recommendations for international students: required—TOEFL (minimum score 550 paper-based; 70 iBT) or IELTS. Electronic applications accepted. Application fee is waived when completed online. *Expenses:* Contact institution.

# Perfusion

**Long Island University - Post,** School of Health Professions and Nursing, Brookville, NY 11548-1300. Offers biomedical science (MS); cardiovascular perfusion (MS); clinical lab sciences (MS); clinical laboratory management (MS); dietetic internship (Advanced Certificate); family nurse practitioner (MS, Advanced Certificate); forensic social work (Advanced Certificate); gerontology (Advanced Certificate); health administration (MPA); non-profit management (Advanced Certificate); nursing education (MS); nutrition (MS); public administration (MPA); social work (MSW). *Program availability:* Part-time, blended/hybrid learning. *Degree requirements:* For master's, comprehensive exam (for some programs), thesis (for some programs). *Entrance requirements:* Additional exam requirements/recommendations for international students: required—TOEFL (minimum score 85 iBT) or IELTS (7.5). Electronic applications accepted.

**Milwaukee School of Engineering,** MS Program in Perfusion, Milwaukee, WI 53202-3109. Offers MS. *Degree requirements:* For master's, comprehensive exam, thesis. *Entrance requirements:* For master's, GRE General Test (percentiles must average 50% or better), baccalaureate degree with minimum undergraduate GPA of 2.8; at least one undergraduate course in each of the following areas: physiology (or anatomy and physiology), chemistry, mathematics and physics; 3 letters of recommendation; personal interview; observation of 2 perfusion clinical cases. Additional exam requirements/ recommendations for international students: required—TOEFL (minimum score 90 iBT), IELTS (minimum score 7). Electronic applications accepted.

**Quinnipiac University,** School of Health Sciences, Program in Cardiovascular Perfusion, Hamden, CT 06518-1940. Offers MHS. *Entrance requirements:* For master's, bachelor's degree in science or health-related discipline from an accredited American or Canadian college or university; 2 years of health care work experience; interview. Electronic applications accepted. *Expenses: Tuition:* Part-time $1055 per credit. *Required fees:* $945 per semester. Tuition and fees vary according to course load and program.

**Rush University,** College of Health Sciences, Cardiovascular Perfusion, Chicago, IL 60612-3832. Offers MS. *Entrance requirements:* Additional exam requirements/ recommendations for international students: required—TOEFL. *Financial support:* Scholarships/grants available. *Unit head:* Julie Collins, Program Director. *Application contact:* Julie Collins, Program Director.

**The University of Arizona,** College of Pharmacy, Department of Pharmacology and Toxicology, Graduate Program in Medical Pharmacology, Tucson, AZ 85721. Offers medical pharmacology (PhD); perfusion science (MS). *Degree requirements:* For master's, thesis; for doctorate, comprehensive exam, thesis/dissertation. *Entrance requirements:* For master's, GRE General Test, 3 letters of recommendation; for doctorate, GRE General Test, personal statement, 3 letters of recommendation. Additional exam requirements/recommendations for international students: required— TOEFL (minimum score 550 paper-based; 79 iBT). Electronic applications accepted.

**University of Nebraska Medical Center,** College of Allied Health Professions, Program in Clinical Perfusion Education, Omaha, NE 68198-4144. Offers MPS. *Accreditation:* NAACLS. *Program availability:* Online learning. *Degree requirements:* For master's, comprehensive exam, thesis. *Entrance requirements:* For master's, GRE. Electronic applications accepted.

# Physical Therapy

**AdventHealth University,** Program in Physical Therapy, Orlando, FL 32803. Offers DPT. *Entrance requirements:* For doctorate, minimum GPA of 3.0.

**Alabama State University,** College of Health Sciences, Department of Physical Therapy, Montgomery, AL 36101-0271. Offers physical therapy (DPT). *Accreditation:* APTA. *Faculty:* 5 full-time (3 women), 3 part-time/adjunct (0 women). *Students:* 69 full-time (39 women); includes 24 minority (18 Black or African American, non-Hispanic/Latino; 4 Hispanic/Latino; 2 Two or more races, non-Hispanic/Latino). Average age 25. 55 applicants, 42% accepted, 22 enrolled. In 2019, 23 doctorates awarded. Terminal master's awarded for partial completion of doctoral program. *Degree requirements:* For doctorate, comprehensive exam, thesis/dissertation or alternative. *Entrance requirements:* For doctorate, Scores are required with minimum scores of Verbal 150 or Analytic of 3.5, or Recommended MAT Score 385 GRE. Additional exam requirements/ recommendations for international students: required—TOEFL (minimum score 500 paper-based). *Application deadline:* For fall admission, 4/15 for domestic and international students; for spring admission, 11/15 for domestic and international students; for summer admission, 3/15 for domestic and international students. Applications are processed on a rolling basis. Application fee: $25. Electronic applications accepted. *Financial support:* Fellowships, research assistantships, teaching assistantships, scholarships/grants, tuition waivers (partial), and unspecified assistantships available. Financial award application deadline: 6/30; financial award applicants required to submit FAFSA. *Unit head:* Dr. Susan Denham, Interim Chair, 334-229-5611, Fax: 334-229-4945, E-mail: asupt@alasu.edu. *Application contact:* Dr. Ed Brown, Dean of Graduate Studies, 334-229-4274, Fax: 334-229-4928, E-mail: ebrown@ alasu.edu.
Website: http://www.alasu.edu/academics/colleges—departments/health-sciences/ physical-therapy/index.aspx

**American International College,** School of Health Sciences, Springfield, MA 01109-3189. Offers exercise science (MS); family nurse practitioner (MSN, Post-Master's Certificate); nursing administrator (MSN); nursing educator (MSN); occupational therapy (MSOT, OTD); physical therapy (DPT). *Accreditation:* AOTA. *Program availability:* Part-time, 100% online. *Degree requirements:* For master's, practicum; for doctorate, thesis/ dissertation, practicum. *Entrance requirements:* For master's, 3 letters of recommendation, personal goal statement; minimum GPA of 3.2, interview, BS or BA, and 2 clinical PT observations (for DPT); minimum GPA of 3.0, MSOT, OT licensen, and 2 clinical OT observations (for OTD); for doctorate, personal goal statement, 2 letters of recommendation; minimum GPA of 3.0, BS or BA, 2 clinical OT observations (for MSOT); RN license and minimum GPA of 3.0 (for MSN). Additional exam requirements/ recommendations for international students: required—TOEFL (minimum score 577 paper-based; 91 iBT). Electronic applications accepted. *Expenses:* Contact institution.

**Andrews University,** College of Health and Human Services, School of Rehabilitation Services, Postprofessional Physical Therapy Program, Berrien Springs, MI 49104. Offers orthopedic manual therapy (Dr Sc PT); physical therapy (TDPT). *Accreditation:* APTA. *Students:* 38 full-time (20 women), 50 part-time (20 women); includes 18 minority (3 Black or African American, non-Hispanic/Latino; 10 Asian, non-Hispanic/Latino; 5 Hispanic/Latino), 32 international. Average age 39. In 2019, 8 doctorates awarded. *Application deadline:* For fall admission, 12/1 priority date for domestic students. Applications are processed on a rolling basis. Application fee: $60. Electronic applications accepted. *Expenses:* Contact institution. *Financial support:* Federal Work-Study, institutionally sponsored loans, and scholarships/grants available. Financial award application deadline: 9/1; financial award applicants required to submit FAFSA. *Unit head:* Val Coolman, Director of Professional Programs, 269-471-6076, Fax: 269-471-2866, E-mail: berglund@andrews.edu. *Application contact:* Jillian Panigot, Director, Unverstiy Admissions, 800-827-2878, Fax: 269-471-2867, E-mail: pt-info@ andrews.edu.
Website: http://www.andrews.edu/PHTH/

**Angelo State University,** College of Graduate Studies and Research, Archer College of Health and Human Services, Department of Physical Therapy, San Angelo, TX 76909. Offers DPT. *Accreditation:* APTA. *Entrance requirements:* For doctorate, GRE General Test, interview, minimum undergraduate GPA of 3.0 in all prerequisite courses, essay, letters of recommendation, self-report transcript, volunteer hours. Additional exam requirements/recommendations for international students: required—TOEFL or IELTS. Electronic applications accepted.

**Arcadia University,** College of Health Sciences, Department of Physical Therapy, Glenside, PA 19038-3295. Offers DPT, DPT/MPH. *Accreditation:* APTA. *Program availability:* 100% online. *Students:* 119 full-time (89 women), 402 part-time (285 women); includes 81 minority (3 Black or African American, non-Hispanic/Latino; 1 American Indian or Alaska Native, non-Hispanic/Latino; 70 Asian, non-Hispanic/Latino; 4 Hispanic/Latino; 3 Two or more races, non-Hispanic/Latino), 123 international. In 2019, 313 doctorates awarded. *Degree requirements:* For doctorate, satisfactory completion of 6 semesters of classroom work; satisfactory completion of full-time clinical study; an overall minimum GPA of 2.70 maintained throughout the program; a grade below 'C' is not acceptable toward the degree; continuous enrollment; approval is required if extenuating circumstances make additional time necessary. *Entrance requirements:* For doctorate, GRE (taken within the last five years) scores for Individual Verbal (minimum 151), Quantitative (minimum 150), Combined Verbal and Quantitative Reasoning (minimum 303), Analytical Writing (minimum 4). Additional exam requirements/recommendations for international students: required—official results from the TOEFL or IELTS for all students for whom English is a second language. *Application deadline:* For fall admission, 11/1 for domestic students. *Expenses:* Contact institution. *Financial support:* Career-related internships or fieldwork, tuition waivers (partial), and unspecified assistantships available. *Unit head:* Dr. Phil McClure, Chair, 215-572-2863. *Application contact:* 215-572-2910, Fax: 215-572-4049, E-mail: admiss@arcadia.edu.

**Arkansas State University,** Graduate School, College of Nursing and Health Professions, Department of Physical Therapy, State University, AR 72467. Offers DPT. *Accreditation:* APTA. *Program availability:* Part-time. *Degree requirements:* For doctorate, comprehensive exam, thesis/dissertation. *Entrance requirements:* For doctorate, GRE, Allied Health Professions Admissions Test, appropriate bachelor's or master's degree, letters of reference, resume, official transcript, volunteer experience, criminal background check, immunization records, writing sample, PTCAS Application. Additional exam requirements/recommendations for international students: required— TOEFL (minimum score 550 paper-based; 79 iBT), IELTS (minimum score 6), PTE (minimum score 56). Electronic applications accepted. *Expenses:* Contact institution.

**A.T. Still University,** Arizona School of Health Sciences, Mesa, AZ 85206. Offers advanced occupational therapy (MS); advanced physician assistant studies (MS); athletic training (MS, DAT); audiology (Au D); clinical decision making in athletic training (Graduate Certificate); occupational therapy (MS, OTD); orthopedic rehabilitation (Graduate Certificate); physical therapy (DPT); physician assistant studies (MS); post-professional audiology (Au D); post-professional physical therapy (DPT). *Accreditation:* AOTA (one or more programs are accredited); ASHA. *Program availability:* Part-time, evening/weekend, online only, 100% online, blended/hybrid learning. *Faculty:* 94 full-time (74 women), 203 part-time/adjunct (145 women). *Students:* 736 full-time (528 women), 289 part-time (195 women); includes 315 minority (53 Black or African American, non-Hispanic/Latino; 7 American Indian or Alaska Native, non-Hispanic/ Latino; 94 Asian, non-Hispanic/Latino; 134 Hispanic/Latino; 2 Native Hawaiian or other Pacific Islander, non-Hispanic/Latino; 25 Two or more races, non-Hispanic/Latino), 79 international. Average age 32. 4,387 applicants, 20% accepted, 514 enrolled. In 2019, 153 master's, 344 doctorates, 2 other advanced degrees awarded. *Degree requirements:* For master's, thesis (for some programs); for doctorate, thesis/ dissertation (for some programs). *Entrance requirements:* For master's, GRE General Test; for doctorate, GRE, Physical Therapist Evaluation Tool (for DPT), current state

licensure. Additional exam requirements/recommendations for international students: required—TOEFL (minimum score 80 iBT). *Application deadline:* For fall admission, 7/7 for domestic and international students; for winter admission, 10/3 for domestic and international students; for spring admission, 1/16 for domestic and international students; for summer admission, 4/17 for domestic and international students. Applications are processed on a rolling basis. Application fee: $70. *Financial support:* In 2019–20, 170 students received support. Federal Work-Study and scholarships/grants available. Financial award application deadline: 6/1; financial award applicants required to submit FAFSA. *Unit head:* Dr. Ann Lee Burch, Dean, 480-219-6061, E-mail: aburch@atsu.edu. *Application contact:* Donna Sparks, Director, Admissions Processing, 660-626-2117, Fax: 660-626-2969, E-mail: admissions@atsu.edu.
Website: http://www.atsu.edu/ashs

**Augusta University,** College of Allied Health Sciences, Physical Therapy Program, Augusta, GA 30912. Offers DPT. *Accreditation:* APTA. *Program availability:* Part-time, online learning. *Degree requirements:* For doctorate, acute experience, rehabilitation experience. *Entrance requirements:* For doctorate, GRE, at least 100 hours of observational, volunteer or other work experiences in physical therapy settings. Additional exam requirements/recommendations for international students: required—TOEFL (minimum score 550 paper-based; 79 iBT). Electronic applications accepted.

**Azusa Pacific University,** School of Behavioral and Applied Sciences, Department of Physical Therapy, Azusa, CA 91702-7000. Offers DPT. *Accreditation:* APTA. *Degree requirements:* For doctorate, thesis/dissertation. *Entrance requirements:* For doctorate, GRE General Test. Additional exam requirements/recommendations for international students: required—TOEFL (minimum score 600 paper-based). Electronic applications accepted. *Expenses:* Contact institution.

**Bellarmine University,** College of Health Professions, School of Movement and Rehabilitation Sciences, Louisville, KY 40205. Offers athletic training (MSAT); physical therapy (DPT). *Program availability:* Part-time. *Faculty:* 28 full-time (20 women), 30 part-time/adjunct (21 women). *Students:* 220 full-time (134 women), 1 (woman) part-time; includes 29 minority (8 Black or African American, non-Hispanic/Latino; 6 Asian, non-Hispanic/Latino; 6 Hispanic/Latino; 9 Two or more races, non-Hispanic/Latino), 1 international. Average age 24. 522 applicants, 29% accepted, 75 enrolled. In 2019, 4 master's, 67 doctorates awarded. *Degree requirements:* For master's and doctorate, comprehensive exam. *Entrance requirements:* For master's, minimum undergraduate GPA of 2.75 or GRE, 3.0 in prerequisite courses; grade of C or better in all prerequisites; for doctorate, GRE, minimum undergraduate GPA of 2.75, 3.0 in prerequisite courses; grade of C or better in all prerequisites; documented work/volunteer hours in PT setting; physical ability to perform tasks required of a physical therapist. Additional exam requirements/recommendations for international students: required—TOEFL (minimum iBT score of 83, 26 on speaking test), IELTS (minimum score 7, speaking band score of 8). *Application deadline:* Applications are processed on a rolling basis. Application fee: $40. Electronic applications accepted. Tuition and fees vary according to degree level and program. *Financial support:* Applicants required to submit FAFSA. *Unit head:* Dr. Tony Brosky, Dean, 502-272-8375, E-mail: jbrosky@bellarmine.edu. *Application contact:* Dr. Sara Pettingill, Dean of Graduate Admission, 502-272-8401, Fax: 502-272-8002, E-mail: spettingill@bellarmine.edu.
Website: https://www.bellarmine.edu/movement/

**Belmont University,** College of Health Sciences, Nashville, TN 37212. Offers nursing (MSN, DNP); occupational therapy (MSOT, OTD); physical therapy (DPT). *Program availability:* Part-time, blended/hybrid learning. *Faculty:* 26 full-time (20 women), 30 part-time/adjunct (21 women). *Students:* 416 full-time (362 women), 8 part-time (7 women); includes 36 minority (7 Black or African American, non-Hispanic/Latino; 12 Asian, non-Hispanic/Latino; 9 Hispanic/Latino; 8 Two or more races, non-Hispanic/Latino). Average age 26. *Degree requirements:* For master's, comprehensive exam, thesis; for doctorate, comprehensive exam. *Entrance requirements:* For master's, GRE, BSN, minimum GPA of 3.0. Additional exam requirements/recommendations for international students: required—TOEFL (minimum score 550 paper-based). *Application deadline:* Applications are processed on a rolling basis. Application fee: $50. Electronic applications accepted. *Expenses:* Contact institution. *Financial support:* Teaching assistantships with full tuition reimbursements, career-related internships or fieldwork, scholarships/grants, and traineeships available. Financial award application deadline: 3/1; financial award applicants required to submit FAFSA. *Unit head:* Dr. Cathy Taylor, Dean, 615-460-6916, Fax: 615-460-6750. *Application contact:* Bill Nichols, Director of Enrollment Services, 615-460-6107, E-mail: bill.nichols@belmont.edu.
Website: http://www.belmont.edu/healthsciences/

**Boston University,** College of Health and Rehabilitation Sciences: Sargent College, Department of Physical Therapy and Athletic Training, Boston, MA 02215. Offers athletic training (MS); physical therapy (DPT); rehabilitation sciences (PhD). *Accreditation:* APTA (one or more programs are accredited). *Faculty:* 21 full-time (17 women), 1 (woman) part-time/adjunct. *Students:* 197 full-time (128 women); includes 56 minority (3 Black or African American, non-Hispanic/Latino; 33 Asian, non-Hispanic/Latino; 13 Hispanic/Latino; 1 Native Hawaiian or other Pacific Islander, non-Hispanic/Latino; 6 Two or more races, non-Hispanic/Latino), 14 international. Average age 25. 634 applicants, 13% accepted, 42 enrolled. In 2019, 10 master's, 61 doctorates awarded. *Entrance requirements:* Additional exam requirements/recommendations for international students: required—TOEFL. Application fee: $155. Electronic applications accepted. *Financial support:* Fellowships, research assistantships, teaching assistantships, career-related internships or fieldwork, Federal Work-Study, institutionally sponsored loans, scholarships/grants, tuition waivers (full and partial), and unspecified assistantships available. Financial award applicants required to submit FAFSA. *Unit head:* Dr. Theresa Ellis, Department Chair, 617-353-7571, E-mail: pt@bu.edu. *Application contact:* Sharon Sankey, Assistant Dean, Student Services, 617-353-2713, Fax: 617-353-7500, E-mail: ssankey@bu.edu.

**Bradley University,** The Graduate School, College of Education and Health Sciences, Department of Physical Therapy and Health Science, Peoria, IL 61625-0002. Offers physical therapy (DPT). *Accreditation:* APTA. *Faculty:* 10 full-time (6 women). *Students:* 75 full-time (40 women); includes 9 minority (1 Black or African American, non-Hispanic/Latino; 3 Asian, non-Hispanic/Latino; 2 Hispanic/Latino; 3 Two or more races, non-Hispanic/Latino), 1 international. Average age 25. In 2019, 24 doctorates awarded. *Degree requirements:* For doctorate, comprehensive exam. *Entrance requirements:* For doctorate, GRE, 2 letters of recommendation. Additional exam requirements/recommendations for international students: required—TOEFL (minimum score 600 paper-based; 100 iBT), IELTS (minimum score 6.5), PTE (minimum score 58). *Application deadline:* For summer admission, 8/15 priority date for domestic students. Applications are processed on a rolling basis. Application fee: $40 ($50 for international students). Electronic applications accepted. *Expenses:* Contact institution. *Financial support:* In 2019–20, 6 teaching assistantships with full and partial tuition reimbursements (averaging $16,380 per year) were awarded; research assistantships, scholarships/grants, and tuition waivers (full and partial) also available. Financial award application deadline: 4/1. *Unit head:* Steve Tippett, Chair, 309-677-2855, E-mail: srt@bradley.edu. *Application contact:* Rachel Webb, Director of On-Campus Graduate Admissions and International Student and Scholar Services, 309-677-2375, E-mail: rkwebb@bradley.edu.
Website: http://www.bradley.edu/academic/departments/pths/

**California State University, Fresno,** Division of Research and Graduate Studies, College of Health and Human Services, Department of Physical Therapy, Fresno, CA 93740-8027. Offers DPT. *Accreditation:* APTA. *Entrance requirements:* Additional exam requirements/recommendations for international students: required—TOEFL. Electronic applications accepted. *Expenses:* Tuition, state resident: full-time $4012; part-time $2506 per semester.

**California State University, Long Beach,** Graduate Studies, College of Health and Human Services, Department of Physical Therapy, Long Beach, CA 90840. Offers DPT. *Accreditation:* APTA. *Degree requirements:* For doctorate, Doctoral Project-required. *Entrance requirements:* Additional exam requirements/recommendations for international students: required—TOEFL (minimum score 550 paper-based; 80 iBT), GRE. Electronic applications accepted.

**California State University, Northridge,** Graduate Studies, College of Health and Human Development, Department of Physical Therapy, Northridge, CA 91330. Offers MPT. *Accreditation:* APTA. *Entrance requirements:* For master's, GRE General Test or minimum GPA of 3.0. Additional exam requirements/recommendations for international students: required—TOEFL.

**California State University, Sacramento,** College of Health and Human Services, Department of Physical Therapy, Sacramento, CA 95819. Offers DPT. *Degree requirements:* For doctorate, project. *Entrance requirements:* For doctorate, GRE. Additional exam requirements/recommendations for international students: required—TOEFL (minimum score 550 paper-based; 80 iBT); recommended—IELTS, TSE. Electronic applications accepted. *Expenses:* Contact institution.

**Campbell University,** Graduate and Professional Programs, College of Pharmacy and Health Sciences, Buies Creek, NC 27506. Offers athletic training (MAT); clinical research (MS); pharmaceutical sciences (MS); pharmacy (Pharm D); physical therapy (DPT); physician assistant (MPAP); public health (MS). *Accreditation:* ACPE; CEPH. *Program availability:* Part-time, evening/weekend. *Entrance requirements:* For master's, MCAT, PCAT, GRE, bachelor's degree in health sciences or related field; for doctorate, PCAT. Additional exam requirements/recommendations for international students: required—TOEFL (minimum score 550 paper-based; 79 iBT). Electronic applications accepted. *Expenses:* Contact institution.

**Carroll University,** Program in Physical Therapy, Waukesha, WI 53186-5593. Offers DPT. *Accreditation:* APTA. *Entrance requirements:* Additional exam requirements/recommendations for international students: required—TOEFL. *Expenses:* Contact institution.

**Central Michigan University,** College of Graduate Studies, The Herbert H. and Grace A. Dow College of Health Professions, School of Rehabilitation and Medical Sciences, Mount Pleasant, MI 48859. Offers physical therapy (DPT); physician assistant (MS). *Accreditation:* APTA; ARC-PA. *Degree requirements:* For master's, thesis or alternative; for doctorate, thesis/dissertation or alternative. *Entrance requirements:* For master's and doctorate, GRE. Electronic applications accepted. *Expenses: Tuition, area resident:* Full-time $12,267; part-time $8178 per year. Tuition, state resident: full-time $12,267; part-time $8178 per year. Tuition, nonresident: full-time $12,267; part-time $8178 per year. *International tuition:* $16,110 full-time. *Required fees:* $225 per semester. Tuition and fees vary according to degree level and program.

**Chapman University,** Crean College of Health and Behavioral Sciences, Department of Physical Therapy, Irvine, CA 92618. Offers DPT, TDPT. *Accreditation:* APTA. *Faculty:* 17 full-time (13 women), 24 part-time/adjunct (16 women). *Students:* 159 full-time (73 women), 96 part-time (45 women); includes 158 minority (1 Black or African American, non-Hispanic/Latino; 111 Asian, non-Hispanic/Latino; 24 Hispanic/Latino; 1 Native Hawaiian or other Pacific Islander, non-Hispanic/Latino; 21 Two or more races, non-Hispanic/Latino), 3 international. Average age 28. In 2019, 89 doctorates awarded. *Degree requirements:* For doctorate, 1440 hours of clinical experience, research/scholarly project. *Entrance requirements:* For doctorate, GRE. Additional exam requirements/recommendations for international students: required—TOEFL (minimum score 80 iBT), IELTS (minimum score 6.5), PTE (minimum score 53). *Application deadline:* For fall admission, 9/16 for domestic students; for summer admission, 9/16 for domestic students. Electronic applications accepted. *Expenses:* $16,284 per trimester. *Financial support:* Fellowships, Federal Work-Study, and scholarships/grants available. Financial award applicants required to submit FAFSA. *Unit head:* Dr. Emmanuel John, Chair, 714-744-7906, E-mail: john@chapman.edu. *Application contact:* Anu Nanjappa, Graduate Admissions Specialist, 714-744-7620, E-mail: cudptadmissions@chapman.edu.
Website: https://www.chapman.edu/crean/academic-programs/graduate-programs/physical-therapy/index.aspx

**Chatham University,** Program in Physical Therapy, Pittsburgh, PA 15232-2826. Offers DPT, TDPT. *Accreditation:* APTA. *Faculty:* 8 full-time (5 women). *Students:* 113 full-time (73 women), 5 part-time (2 women); includes 8 minority (1 Black or African American, non-Hispanic/Latino; 4 Asian, non-Hispanic/Latino; 2 Hispanic/Latino; 1 Two or more races, non-Hispanic/Latino). Average age 24. 368 applicants, 25% accepted, 40 enrolled. In 2019, 37 doctorates awarded. *Entrance requirements:* For doctorate, GRE, community service, interview, minimum GPA of 3.0, writing sample, volunteer/work experience, 3 references. Additional exam requirements/recommendations for international students: required—TOEFL (minimum score 600 paper-based; 100 iBT), IELTS (minimum score 7), TWE. *Application deadline:* For fall admission, 12/1 priority date for domestic and international students. Application fee: $45. Electronic applications accepted. Application fee is waived when completed online. *Expenses:* $12,687 tuition per semester, $265 campus fee per semester, $220 lab and insurance fee per semester. *Financial support:* Career-related internships or fieldwork available. Financial award applicants required to submit FAFSA. *Unit head:* Dr. Joseph Schreiber, Chair and Program Director, 412-365-1358, Fax: 412-365-1505, E-mail: jschreiber@chatham.edu. *Application contact:* Melanie Jo Elmer, Assistant Director of Graduate Admission, 412-365-1394, Fax: 412-365-1609, E-mail: gradadmissions@chatham.edu.
Website: http://www.chatham.edu/departments/healthmgmt/graduate/pt

**Clarke University,** Physical Therapy Program, Dubuque, IA 52001-3198. Offers DPT. *Accreditation:* APTA. *Entrance requirements:* For doctorate, GRE, minimum GPA of 3.0; total of 30 hours observing in three of the following areas: pediatrics, geriatrics, in-patient, acute/subacute care, neurological rehabilitation, orthopedics, or sports medicine; essay; three recommendations. Additional exam requirements/recommendations for international students: required—TOEFL (minimum score 550 paper-based; 80 iBT), IELTS (minimum score 6.5). Electronic applications accepted. *Expenses:* Contact institution.

**Clarkson University,** Lewis School of Health Sciences, Department of Physical Therapy, Potsdam, NY 13699. Offers DPT. *Accreditation:* APTA. *Faculty:* 9 full-time (6 women), 8 part-time/adjunct (5 women). *Students:* 67 full-time (45 women); includes 13 minority (5 Black or African American, non-Hispanic/Latino; 3 Asian, non-Hispanic/Latino; 3 Hispanic/Latino; 2 Two or more races, non-Hispanic/Latino), 2 international. 154 applicants, 45% accepted, 22 enrolled. In 2019, 20 doctorates awarded. *Entrance*

*requirements:* For doctorate, minimum undergraduate GPA of 3.2; PTCAS application. *Application deadline:* For fall admission, 3/1 for domestic and international students. Applications are processed on a rolling basis. Application fee: $140. Electronic applications accepted. *Expenses:* Contact institution. *Financial support:* Scholarships/ grants available. *Unit head:* Dr. Vicki LaFay, Clinical Associate Professor / Chair of Physical Therapy, 315-268-7622, E-mail: vlafay@clarkson.edu. *Application contact:* Daniel Capogna, Director of Graduate Admissions & Recruitment, 518-631-9910, E-mail: dcapogna@clarkson.edu.
Website: https://www.clarkson.edu/academics/graduate

**Cleveland State University,** College of Graduate Studies, College of Sciences and Health Professions, School of Health Sciences, Program in Physical Therapy, Cleveland, OH 44115. Offers DPT. *Accreditation:* APTA. *Entrance requirements:* For doctorate, GRE (minimum scores: 450 verbal; 550 quantitative; 4.0 analytical writing), minimum overall GPA of 3.0. Additional exam requirements/recommendations for international students: required—TOEFL (minimum score 550 paper-based; 78 iBT). Electronic applications accepted. Application fee is waived when completed online. *Expenses:* Contact institution.

**The College of St. Scholastica,** Graduate Studies, Department of Physical Therapy, Duluth, MN 55811-4199. Offers DPT. *Accreditation:* APTA. *Entrance requirements:* For doctorate, GRE. Additional exam requirements/recommendations for international students: required—TOEFL (minimum score 550 paper-based; 79 iBT). Electronic applications accepted.

**College of Staten Island of the City University of New York,** Graduate Programs, School of Health Sciences, Program in Physical Therapy, Staten Island, NY 10314-6600. Offers DPT. *Accreditation:* APTA. *Faculty:* 20. *Students:* 58. 153 applicants, 22% accepted, 19 enrolled. In 2019, 18 doctorates awarded. *Degree requirements:* For doctorate, comprehensive exam, 105 credits, first examination, second examination, 34 weeks of full-time clinical internships, and a publishable research paper. *Entrance requirements:* Additional exam requirements/recommendations for international students: required—TOEFL (minimum score 550 paper-based; 79 iBT), IELTS (minimum score 6.5). *Application deadline:* For fall admission, 11/1 for domestic and international students. Application fee: $75. Electronic applications accepted. *Expenses:* $11,970 per year (Full-time NY State Resident Level 1 enrolled prior to 2017-2018) $13,190 per year (Full-Time NY State Resident Level 1 entering 2017-2018) $8,260 per year (Full-time NY State Resident Level 2). *Unit head:* Zaghloul Ahmed, 718-982-3153, E-mail: zaghloul.ahmed@csi.cuny.edu. *Application contact:* Sasha Spence, Associate Director for Graduate Admissions, 718-982-2019, Fax: 718-982-2500, E-mail: sasha.spence@csi.cuny.edu.
Website: https://www.csi.cuny.edu/admissions/graduate-admissions/graduate-programs-and-requirements/physical-therapy

**Columbia University,** College of Physicians and Surgeons, Program in Physical Therapy, New York, NY 10032. Offers DPT. *Accreditation:* APTA. *Degree requirements:* For doctorate, fieldwork, capstone project. *Entrance requirements:* For doctorate, GRE General Test, undergraduate course work in biology, chemistry, physics, psychology, statistics and humanities. Additional exam requirements/recommendations for international students: required—TOEFL. Electronic applications accepted. *Expenses:* Contact institution.

**Concordia University, St. Paul,** College of Health and Science, St. Paul, MN 55104-5494. Offers exercise science (MS); orthotics and prosthetics (MS); physical therapy (DPT); sports management (MA). *Program availability:* Part-time, evening/weekend, 100% online, blended/hybrid learning. *Degree requirements:* For master's, comprehensive exam (for some programs), thesis (for some programs); for doctorate, at least one 8-12 week clinical rotation outside the St. Paul area. *Entrance requirements:* For master's, official transcripts from regionally-accredited institution stating the conferral of a bachelor's degree with minimum cumulative GPA of 3.0; personal statement; resume; for doctorate, GRE, official transcript from regionally-accredited institution showing bachelor's degree and minimum coursework GPA of 3.0; 100 physical therapy observation hours; two letters of professional recommendation. Additional exam requirements/recommendations for international students: recommended—TOEFL (minimum score 547 paper-based; 78 iBT), IELTS (minimum score 6), TSE (minimum score 52). Electronic applications accepted. *Expenses:* Contact institution.

**Concordia University Wisconsin,** Graduate Programs, School of Health Professions, Program in Physical Therapy, Mequon, WI 53097-2402. Offers DPT. *Accreditation:* APTA. *Entrance requirements:* Additional exam requirements/recommendations for international students: required—TOEFL. *Expenses:* Contact institution.

**Creighton University,** School of Pharmacy and Health Professions, Program in Physical Therapy, Omaha, NE 68178-0001. Offers DPT. *Accreditation:* APTA. *Entrance requirements:* For doctorate, GRE. Additional exam requirements/recommendations for international students: required—TOEFL. Electronic applications accepted.

**Daemen College,** Physical Therapy Programs, Amherst, NY 14226-3592. Offers orthopedic manual physical therapy (Advanced Certificate); physical therapy-direct entry (DPT); transitional (DPT). *Accreditation:* APTA. *Degree requirements:* For doctorate and Advanced Certificate, Satisfactory completion of all requirements as per the terms set forth by the Physical Therapy Department. *Entrance requirements:* For doctorate, baccalaureate degree with minimum GPA of 2.8 in science coursework; letter of intent; resume; 2 letters of reference; 120 hours of PT exposure; transcripts. Additional exam requirements/recommendations for international students: required—TOEFL (minimum score 77 paper-based), IELTS (minimum score 6.5). Electronic applications accepted. Application fee is waived when completed online.

**Dalhousie University,** Faculty of Health, School of Physiotherapy, Halifax, NS B3H 3J5, Canada. Offers physiotherapy (entry to profession) (M Sc); physiotherapy (rehabilitation research) (M Sc). *Entrance requirements:* Additional exam requirements/ recommendations for international students: required—TOEFL, IELTS, CANTEST, CAEL, or Michigan English Language Assessment Battery. Electronic applications accepted.

**Des Moines University,** College of Health Sciences, Program in Physical Therapy, Des Moines, IA 50312-4104. Offers DPT. *Accreditation:* APTA. *Entrance requirements:* For doctorate, GRE. Additional exam requirements/recommendations for international students: required—TOEFL. Electronic applications accepted. *Expenses:* Contact institution.

**Dominican College,** Division of Allied Health, Department of Physical Therapy, Orangeburg, NY 10962-1210. Offers MS, DPT. *Accreditation:* APTA. *Program availability:* Part-time, evening/weekend. *Faculty:* 22 full-time (12 women), 10 part-time/ adjunct (5 women). *Students:* 83 full-time (49 women), 107 part-time (64 women); includes 54 minority (2 Black or African American, non-Hispanic/Latino; 48 Asian, non-Hispanic/Latino; 3 Hispanic/Latino; 1 Two or more races, non-Hispanic/Latino), 25 international. Average age 32. In 2019, 109 doctorates awarded. *Degree requirements:* For doctorate, 3 clinical affiliations, 100 hours of voluntary or work experience in setting where licensed physical therapist is employed. *Entrance requirements:* For doctorate, Minimum GPA of 3.0 for undergraduate courses, 3.5 GPA for graduate courses. 3 letters

of recommendation, a personal statement, interview and resume are required. 60 hours of voluntary or work experience in settings where a licensed physical therapist is employed. These hours must be completed in diverse healthcare settings. Additional exam requirements/recommendations for international students: required—TOEFL (minimum score 550 paper-based; 90 iBT). *Application deadline:* For fall admission, 8/1 for domestic students, 6/1 for international students; for spring admission, 12/1 for domestic students; for summer admission, 3/2 for domestic students. Applications are processed on a rolling basis. Application fee: $50. Electronic applications accepted. *Expenses:* Doctoral (DPT) $1,026 per credit tuition, Master's (OT) $965 per credit tuition, $430 per term full-time registration fee, $200 per term part-time registration fee, $200 graduation fee. *Financial support:* Scholarships/grants available. Financial award application deadline: 1/1; financial award applicants required to submit FAFSA. *Unit head:* Dr. Emil Euaparadorn, Program Director, 845-848-6048, Fax: 845-398-4893, E-mail: emil.euaparadorn@dc.edu. *Application contact:* Ashley Scales, Assistant Director of Graduate Admissions, 845-848-7908, Fax: 845-365-3150, E-mail: ashley.scales@dc.edu.

**Drexel University,** College of Nursing and Health Professions, Department of Physical Therapy and Rehabilitation Sciences, Philadelphia, PA 19102. Offers clinical biomechanics and orthopedics (PhD); hand and upper quarter rehabilitation (Certificate); hand therapy (MHS, PPDPT); orthopedics (MHS, PPDPT); pediatric rehabilitation (Certificate); pediatrics (MHS, PPDPT, PhD); physical therapy (DPT). *Accreditation:* APTA. *Program availability:* Part-time. Terminal master's awarded for partial completion of doctoral program. *Degree requirements:* For master's, comprehensive exam; for doctorate, thesis/dissertation, qualifying exam. *Entrance requirements:* For master's and doctorate, GRE General Test. Additional exam requirements/recommendations for international students: required—TOEFL. Electronic applications accepted.

**Duke University,** School of Medicine, Doctor of Physical Therapy, Durham, NC 27708. Offers DPT. *Accreditation:* APTA. *Degree requirements:* For doctorate, comprehensive exam, scholarly project. *Entrance requirements:* For doctorate, GRE, previous course work in anatomy, physiology, biological sciences, chemistry, physics, psychology, and statistics. Electronic applications accepted.

**Duquesne University,** John G. Rangos, Sr. School of Health Sciences, Pittsburgh, PA 15282-0001. Offers health management systems (MHMS); occupational therapy (MS, OTD); physical therapy (DPT); physician assistant studies (MPAS); rehabilitation science (MS, PhD); speech-language pathology (MS). *Accreditation:* AOTA (one or more programs are accredited); APTA (one or more programs are accredited); ASHA. *Program availability:* Part-time, minimal on-campus study. *Degree requirements:* For doctorate, comprehensive exam (for some programs), thesis/dissertation (for some programs). *Entrance requirements:* For master's, GRE General Test (speech-language pathology), 3 letters of recommendation; minimum GPA of 2.75 (health management systems), 3.0 (speech-language pathology); for doctorate, GRE General Test (for physical therapy and rehabilitation science), 3 letters of recommendation, minimum GPA of 3.0, personal interview. Additional exam requirements/recommendations for international students: required—TOEFL (minimum score 550 paper-based; 90 iBT); recommended—IELTS. Electronic applications accepted. *Expenses:* Contact institution.

**D'Youville College,** Department of Physical Therapy, Buffalo, NY 14201-1084. Offers advanced orthopedic physical therapy (Certificate); manual physical therapy (Certificate); physical therapy (DPT). *Accreditation:* APTA. *Program availability:* Part-time, online learning. *Degree requirements:* For doctorate, comprehensive exam, project or thesis. *Entrance requirements:* For doctorate, bachelor's degree, minimum GPA of 3.0. Additional exam requirements/recommendations for international students: required—TOEFL (minimum score 500 paper-based). Electronic applications accepted.

**East Carolina University,** Graduate School, College of Allied Health Sciences, Department of Physical Therapy, Greenville, NC 27858-4353. Offers DPT. *Accreditation:* APTA. *Application deadline:* For fall admission, 10/2 for domestic students. *Expenses:* Tuition, area resident: Full-time $4749; part-time $185 per credit hour. Tuition, state resident: full-time $4749; part-time $185 per credit hour. Tuition, nonresident: full-time $17,898; part-time $864 per credit hour. *International tuition:* $17,898 full-time. *Required fees:* $2787. *Financial support:* Application deadline: 3/1. *Unit head:* Dr. John Wilson, Chair, 252-744-6241, E-mail: wilsonj@ecu.edu. *Application contact:* Graduate School Admissions, 252-328-6012, Fax: 252-328-6071, E-mail: gradschool@ecu.edu.
Website: http://www.ecu.edu/pt/

**Eastern Washington University,** Graduate Studies, College of Health Science and Public Health, Department of Physical Therapy, Cheney, WA 99004-2431. Offers DPT. *Accreditation:* APTA. *Faculty:* 9 full-time (6 women). *Students:* 111 full-time (68 women), 1 part-time (0 women). Average age 26. 380 applicants, 11% accepted, 38 enrolled. In 2019, 37 doctorates awarded. *Degree requirements:* For doctorate, comprehensive exam, thesis/dissertation or final project. *Entrance requirements:* For doctorate, GRE General Test (minimum score of 4.0 on writing section), minimum GPA of 3.0, 75 hours of experience, 3 letters of recommendation. Additional exam requirements/ recommendations for international students: required—TOEFL (minimum score 580 paper-based; 92 iBT), IELTS (minimum score 7), TWE, PTE (minimum score 63). *Application deadline:* For fall admission, 7/1 for domestic students. Application fee: $75. Electronic applications accepted. *Financial support:* In 2019–20, 1 teaching assistantship was awarded; career-related internships or fieldwork, Federal Work-Study, institutionally sponsored loans, scholarships/grants, health care benefits, tuition waivers (partial), and unspecified assistantships also available. Support available to part-time students. Financial award application deadline: 2/1; financial award applicants required to submit FAFSA. *Unit head:* Cindy Arlt, Program Specialist, 509-828-1374. *Application contact:* Cindy Arlt, Program Specialist, 509-828-1374.

**East Tennessee State University,** College of Graduate and Continuing Studies, College of Clinical and Rehabilitative Health Sciences, Department of Physical Therapy, Johnson City, TN 37614. Offers DPT. *Accreditation:* APTA. *Degree requirements:* For doctorate, comprehensive exam, internship. *Entrance requirements:* For doctorate, GRE General Test, minimum prerequisite GPA of 3.0, three letters of recommendation with at least one from a licensed PT, interview with the physical therapy Admissions Committee. Additional exam requirements/recommendations for international students: required—TOEFL (minimum score 550 paper-based; 79 iBT). Electronic applications accepted.

**Elon University,** Program in Physical Therapy, Elon, NC 27244-2010. Offers DPT. *Accreditation:* APTA. *Faculty:* 13 full-time (8 women), 14 part-time/adjunct (9 women). *Students:* 139 full-time (98 women); includes 20 minority (7 Black or African American, non-Hispanic/Latino; 3 Asian, non-Hispanic/Latino; 4 Hispanic/Latino; 6 Two or more races, non-Hispanic/Latino), 2 international. Average age 25. 814 applicants, 12% accepted, 46 enrolled. In 2019, 46 doctorates awarded. *Entrance requirements:* For doctorate, GRE General Test. Additional exam requirements/recommendations for international students: required—TOEFL (minimum score 550 paper-based; 79 iBT). *Application deadline:* For fall admission, 11/1 for domestic students; for winter admission, 1/10 priority date for domestic students. Applications are processed on a rolling basis. Electronic applications accepted. *Financial support:* Applicants required to submit FAFSA. *Unit head:* Dr. Becky Neiduski, Dean of the School of Health Sciences,

336-278-6350, E-mail: bneiduski@elon.edu. *Application contact:* Art Fadde, Director of Graduate Admissions, 800-334-8448 Ext. 3, Fax: 336-278-7699, E-mail: afadde@elon.edu.
Website: http://www.elon.edu/dpt/

**Emory & Henry College,** Graduate Programs, Emory, VA 24327. Offers American history (MA Ed); education professional studies (M Ed); occupational therapy (MOT); organizational leadership (MCOL); physical therapy (DPT); physician assistant studies (MPAS); reading specialist (MA Ed). *Program availability:* Part-time. *Degree requirements:* For master's, thesis optional; for doctorate, thesis/dissertation optional. *Entrance requirements:* For master's, GRE or PRAXIS I, official transcripts from all colleges previously attended, three professional recommendations, essay. Additional exam requirements/recommendations for international students: recommended—TOEFL, IELTS (minimum score 6). Electronic applications accepted. *Expenses:* Contact institution.

**Emory University,** School of Medicine, Programs in Allied Health Professions, Doctor of Physical Therapy Program, Atlanta, GA 30322. Offers DPT. *Accreditation:* APTA. *Entrance requirements:* For doctorate, GRE General Test. Additional exam requirements/recommendations for international students: recommended—TOEFL. Electronic applications accepted. *Expenses:* Contact institution.

**Florida Agricultural and Mechanical University,** Division of Graduate Studies, Research, and Continuing Education, School of Allied Health Sciences, Division of Physical Therapy, Tallahassee, FL 32307-3200. Offers DPT. *Accreditation:* APTA. *Entrance requirements:* Additional exam requirements/recommendations for international students: required—TOEFL.

**Florida Gulf Coast University,** Elaine Nicpon Marieb College of Health and Human Services, Program in Physical Therapy, Fort Myers, FL 33965-6565. Offers DPT. *Accreditation:* APTA. *Program availability:* Part-time, online learning. *Entrance requirements:* Additional exam requirements/recommendations for international students: required—TOEFL (minimum score 550 paper-based). Electronic applications accepted. *Expenses: Tuition, area resident:* Full-time $6974; part-time $4350 per credit hour. Tuition, state resident: full-time $6974; part-time $4350 per credit hour. Tuition, nonresident: full-time $28,169; part-time $17,595 per credit hour. *International tuition:* $28,169 full-time. *Required fees:* $2027; $1267 per credit hour. $507 per semester. Tuition and fees vary according to course load.

**Florida International University,** Nicole Wertheim College of Nursing and Health Sciences, Department of Physical Therapy, Miami, FL 33199. Offers DPT. *Accreditation:* APTA. *Program availability:* Part-time. *Faculty:* 10 full-time (6 women), 9 part-time/adjunct (4 women). *Students:* 186 full-time (122 women); includes 113 minority (16 Black or African American, non-Hispanic/Latino; 16 Asian, non-Hispanic/Latino; 73 Hispanic/Latino; 2 Native Hawaiian or other Pacific Islander, non-Hispanic/Latino; 6 Two or more races, non-Hispanic/Latino), 2 international. Average age 25. 633 applicants, 12% accepted, 62 enrolled. In 2019, 54 doctorates awarded. *Entrance requirements:* For doctorate, minimum undergraduate GPA of 3.0 in upper-level coursework; letter of intent; resume; at least 40 hours of observation within physical therapy clinic or facility. Additional exam requirements/recommendations for international students: required—TOEFL (minimum score 550 paper-based; 80 iBT). *Application deadline:* For fall admission, 1/15 for domestic and international students. Application fee: $30. Electronic applications accepted. *Expenses: Tuition, area resident:* Full-time $8912; part-time $446 per credit hour. Tuition, state resident: full-time $8912; part-time $446 per credit hour. Tuition, nonresident: full-time $21,393; part-time $992 per credit hour. *Required fees:* $2194. *Financial support:* Institutionally sponsored loans, scholarships/grants, and unspecified assistantships available. Financial award application deadline: 3/1; financial award applicants required to submit FAFSA. *Unit head:* Dr. Mark Rossi, Chair, 305-348-3478, Fax: 305-348-1979, E-mail: mark.rossi@fiu.edu. *Application contact:* Nanett Rojas, Manager, Admissions Operations, 305-348-7464, Fax: 305-348-7441, E-mail: gradadm@fiu.edu.

**Franciscan Missionaries of Our Lady University,** School of Health Professions, Baton Rouge, LA 70808. Offers health administration (MHA); nutritional sciences (MS); physical therapy (DPT); physician assistant studies (MMS).

**Franklin Pierce University,** Graduate and Professional Studies, Rindge, NH 03461-0060. Offers curriculum and instruction (M Ed); elementary education (MS Ed); emerging network technologies (Graduate Certificate); energy and sustainability studies (MBA, Graduate Certificate); health administration (MBA, Graduate Certificate); human resource management (MBA, Graduate Certificate); information technology (MBA); leadership (MBA); nursing education (MS); nursing leadership (MS); physical therapy (DPT); physician assistant studies (MPAS); special education (M Ed); sports management (MBA). *Accreditation:* APTA. *Program availability:* Part-time, 100% online, blended/hybrid learning. *Degree requirements:* For master's, concentrated original research projects; student teaching; fieldwork and/or internship; leadership project; PRAXIS I and II (for M Ed); for doctorate, concentrated original research projects, clinical fieldwork and/or internship, leadership project. *Entrance requirements:* For master's, minimum GPA of 2.5, 3 letters of recommendation; competencies in accounting, economics, statistics, and computer skills through life experience or undergraduate coursework (for MBA); certification/e-portfolio, minimum C grade in all education courses (for M Ed); license to practice as RN (for MS); for doctorate, GRE, 80 hours of observation/work in PT settings; completion of anatomy, chemistry, physics, and statistics; minimum GPA of 3.0. Additional exam requirements/recommendations for international students: required—TOEFL (minimum score 550 paper-based; 61 iBT). Electronic applications accepted.

**Gannon University,** School of Graduate Studies, Morosky College of Health Professions and Sciences, School of Health Professions, Program in Physical Therapy, Erie, PA 16541-0001. Offers DPT. *Accreditation:* APTA. *Degree requirements:* For doctorate, thesis/dissertation or alternative, research project, practicum. *Entrance requirements:* For doctorate, baccalaureate degree from accredited college or university with minimum GPA of 3.0, interview. Additional exam requirements/recommendations for international students: required—TOEFL (minimum score 79 iBT). Electronic applications accepted. *Expenses:* Contact institution.

**George Fox University,** Program in Physical Therapy, Newberg, OR 97132-2697. Offers DPT. *Accreditation:* APTA. *Entrance requirements:* For doctorate, bachelor's degree from regionally-accredited university or college, minimum GPA of 3.0. Additional exam requirements/recommendations for international students: required—TOEFL, IELTS. Electronic applications accepted.

**The George Washington University,** School of Medicine and Health Sciences, Health Sciences Programs, Program in Physical Therapy, Washington, DC 20052. Offers DPT. *Accreditation:* APTA. *Entrance requirements:* Additional exam requirements/recommendations for international students: required—TOEFL (minimum score 550 paper-based).

**Georgia Campus–Philadelphia College of Osteopathic Medicine,** Doctor of Physical Therapy Program, Suwanee, GA 30024. Offers DPT.

**Georgia Southern University,** Jack N. Averitt College of Graduate Studies, Waters College of Health Professions, Doctoral Program in Physical Therapy, savannah, GA 30458. Offers DPT. *Accreditation:* APTA. *Faculty:* 6 full-time (2 women). *Students:* 104 full-time (71 women); includes 13 minority (6 Black or African American, non-Hispanic/Latino; 1 Asian, non-Hispanic/Latino; 3 Hispanic/Latino; 3 Two or more races, non-Hispanic/Latino). Average age 24. 1 applicant. In 2019, 35 doctorates awarded. *Degree requirements:* For doctorate, thesis/dissertation, licensure exam. *Entrance requirements:* For doctorate, GRE General Test, CASPer, course work in general biology, chemistry, physical anatomy, physiology, and statistics; letters of recommendation; bachelor's degree; minimum GPA of 3.0; observation hours; PTCAS application. Additional exam requirements/recommendations for international students: required—TOEFL (minimum score 600 paper-based; 70 iBT). *Application deadline:* For fall admission, 10/15 priority date for domestic students; for summer admission, 8/15 priority date for domestic students. Applications are processed on a rolling basis. Application fee: $30. Electronic applications accepted. *Expenses: Tuition, area resident:* Full-time $4986; part-time $277 per credit hour. Tuition, nonresident: full-time $19,890; part-time $1105 per credit hour. *International tuition:* $19,890 full-time. *Required fees:* $2114; $1057 per semester. $1057 per semester. Tuition and fees vary according to course load, campus/location and program. *Financial support:* In 2019–20, 30 students received support. Scholarships/grants and unspecified assistantships available. Financial award application deadline: 3/5; financial award applicants required to submit FAFSA. *Unit head:* Dr. Walter Jenkins, Dept Chair, 912-344-2969, Fax: 912-344-3439, E-mail: wjenkins@georgiasouthern.edu. *Application contact:* Elizabeth Varner, Clinical Education Assistant, 912-344-3220, Fax: 912-344-3439, E-mail: evarner@georgiasouthern.edu.
Website: https://chp.georgiasouthern.edu/rehabilitation/graduate-programs/doctor-of-physical-therapy/

**Georgia State University,** Byrdine F. Lewis School of Nursing, Division of Physical Therapy, Atlanta, GA 30302-3083. Offers DPT. *Accreditation:* APTA. *Faculty:* 11 full-time (5 women), 1 (woman) part-time/adjunct. *Students:* 124 full-time (82 women), 1 (woman) part-time; includes 37 minority (12 Black or African American, non-Hispanic/Latino; 15 Asian, non-Hispanic/Latino; 5 Hispanic/Latino; 5 Two or more races, non-Hispanic/Latino). Average age 26. In 2019, 39 doctorates awarded. *Degree requirements:* For doctorate, comprehensive exam, thesis/dissertation or alternative, clinical education. *Entrance requirements:* For doctorate, GRE, transcripts, documentation of Physical Therapy Experience Form, statement of goals. Additional exam requirements/recommendations for international students: required—TOEFL (minimum score 550 paper-based; 80 iBT). *Application deadline:* For fall admission, 11/15 for domestic and international students. Application fee: $50. Electronic applications accepted. *Expenses:* Contact institution. *Financial support:* In 2019–20, research assistantships with full tuition reimbursements (averaging $2,000 per year), teaching assistantships with full tuition reimbursements (averaging $2,000 per year) were awarded; scholarships/grants, tuition waivers (partial), and unspecified assistantships also available. Financial award application deadline: 4/1; financial award applicants required to submit FAFSA. *Unit head:* Dr. Sujay Galen, Chair, 404-413-1243, Fax: 404-413-1230, E-mail: sgalen@gsu.edu. *Application contact:* Dr. Sujay Galen, Chair, 404-413-1243, Fax: 404-413-1230, E-mail: sgalen@gsu.edu.
Website: http://physicaltherapy.gsu.edu/

**Governors State University,** College of Health and Human Services, Program in Physical Therapy, University Park, IL 60484. Offers DPT. *Accreditation:* APTA. *Program availability:* Part-time. *Faculty:* 6 full-time (4 women), 13 part-time/adjunct (9 women). *Students:* 96 full-time (55 women), 1 (woman) part-time; includes 37 minority (8 Black or African American, non-Hispanic/Latino; 11 Asian, non-Hispanic/Latino; 15 Hispanic/Latino; 3 Two or more races, non-Hispanic/Latino), 1 international. Average age 25. 1 applicant, 100% accepted, 1 enrolled. In 2019, 38 doctorates awarded. *Application deadline:* For fall admission, 4/1 for domestic students. Applications are processed on a rolling basis. Application fee: $75. Electronic applications accepted. *Expenses:* $613/credit hour; $7,356 in tuition/term; $8,654 in tuition and fees/term; $17,308/year. *Financial support:* Application deadline: 5/1; applicants required to submit FAFSA. *Unit head:* Rebecca Wojcik, Chair, Department of Physical Therapy, 708-534-5000 Ext. 2231, E-mail: rwojcik@govst.edu. *Application contact:* Rebecca Wojcik, Chair, Department of Physical Therapy, 708-534-5000 Ext. 2231, E-mail: rwojcik@govst.edu.

**Grand Valley State University,** College of Health Professions, Physical Therapy Program, Allendale, MI 49401-9403. Offers DPT. *Accreditation:* APTA. *Faculty:* 15 full-time (10 women), 4 part-time/adjunct (3 women). *Students:* 176 full-time (132 women), 1 (woman) part-time; includes 12 minority (2 Asian, non-Hispanic/Latino; 4 Hispanic/Latino; 6 Two or more races, non-Hispanic/Latino). Average age 23. 290 applicants, 40% accepted, 58 enrolled. In 2019, 60 doctorates awarded. *Entrance requirements:* For doctorate, GRE, PTCAS Application, minimum GPA of 3.0 in most recent 60 hours and in prerequisites, official transcripts from all colleges/universities attended, 50 hours of volunteer work, writing sample, 2 recommendations. Additional exam requirements/recommendations for international students: required—TOEFL (minimum iBT score of 80), IELTS (6.5), or Michigan English Language Assessment Battery (77). *Application deadline:* For fall admission, 10/15 priority date for domestic and international students. Applications are processed on a rolling basis. Application fee: $30. Electronic applications accepted. *Expenses:* $847 per credit hour, 119 credit hours. *Financial support:* In 2019–20, 43 students received support, including 29 fellowships, 20 research assistantships with partial tuition reimbursements available (averaging $2,000 per year); career-related internships or fieldwork, Federal Work-Study, institutionally sponsored loans, and unspecified assistantships also available. Financial award application deadline: 2/15. *Unit head:* Dr. Daniel Vaughn, Director, 616-331-2678, Fax: 616-331-3350, E-mail: vaughnd@gvsu.edu. *Application contact:* Darlene Zwart, Student Services Coordinator, 616-331-3958, Fax: 616-331-5643, E-mail: zwartda@gvsu.edu.
Website: http://www.gvsu.edu/pt/

**Hampton University,** School of Science, Department of Physical Therapy, Hampton, VA 23668. Offers DPT. *Accreditation:* APTA. *Students:* 71 full-time (52 women), 2 part-time (1 woman); includes 54 minority (45 Black or African American, non-Hispanic/Latino; 4 Asian, non-Hispanic/Latino; 2 Hispanic/Latino; 3 Native Hawaiian or other Pacific Islander, non-Hispanic/Latino). Average age 25. 408 applicants, 7% accepted, 29 enrolled. In 2019, 23 doctorates awarded. *Degree requirements:* For doctorate, thesis/dissertation. *Entrance requirements:* For doctorate, GRE General Test, bachelor's degree, minimum cumulative and prerequisite GPA of 3.0. *Application deadline:* For fall admission, 1/15 priority date for domestic and international students; for winter admission, 1/15 for domestic students; for spring admission, 11/1 for domestic students. Application fee: $35. Electronic applications accepted. *Expenses:* Contact institution. *Financial support:* In 2019–20, 50 students received support. Scholarships/grants available. Financial award application deadline: 2/15; financial award applicants required to submit FAFSA. *Unit head:* Dr. Senobia D. Crawford, Chair, 757-727-5260, E-mail: senobia.crawford@hamptonu.edu. *Application contact:* Dr. Stephen Chris Owens, Admissions Coordinator, 757-727-5847, E-mail: stephen.owens@hamptonu.edu.
Website: http://science.hamptonu.edu/pt/

**Harding University,** College of Allied Health, Program in Physical Therapy, SEARCY, AR 72149-5615. Offers DPT. *Accreditation:* APTA. *Faculty:* 9 full-time (3 women). *Students:* 104 full-time (55 women), 1 (woman) part-time; includes 17 minority (5 Black

or African American, non-Hispanic/Latino; 5 Asian, non-Hispanic/Latino; 5 Hispanic/Latino; 2 Two or more races, non-Hispanic/Latino). Average age 26. 136 applicants, 46% accepted, 37 enrolled. In 2019, 31 doctorates awarded. *Entrance requirements:* For doctorate, GRE. Additional exam requirements/recommendations for international students: required—TOEFL (minimum score 550 paper-based). Application fee: $50. *Expenses:* Contact institution. *Unit head:* Dr. Michael McGalliard, Chair and Associate Professor, 501-279-5990, E-mail: mmcgalliard@harding.edu. *Application contact:* Dr. Michael McGalliard, Chair and Associate Professor, 501-279-5990, E-mail: mmcgalliard@harding.edu.
Website: http://www.harding.edu/pt/

**Hardin-Simmons University,** Graduate School, Holland School of Sciences and Mathematics, Department of Physical Therapy, Abilene, TX 79698. Offers DPT. *Accreditation:* APTA. *Faculty:* 9 full-time (4 women), 2 part-time/adjunct (0 women). *Students:* 95 full-time (59 women); includes 19 minority (3 Black or African American, non-Hispanic/Latino; 5 Asian, non-Hispanic/Latino; 11 Hispanic/Latino). Average age 23. 933 applicants, 5% accepted, 40 enrolled. In 2019, 28 doctorates awarded. *Degree requirements:* For doctorate, comprehensive exam, thesis/dissertation or alternative. *Entrance requirements:* For doctorate, GRE, letters of recommendation, interview, transcripts from all colleges attended. Additional exam requirements/recommendations for international students: required—TOEFL (minimum score 550 paper-based; 75 iBT). *Application deadline:* For spring admission, 3/1 priority date for domestic students. Applications are processed on a rolling basis. Application fee: $50. Electronic applications accepted. *Expenses:* 65,520 tuition 6,125 fees. *Financial support:* In 2019–20, 5 students received support. Scholarships/grants available. Financial award application deadline: 6/1; financial award applicants required to submit FAFSA. *Unit head:* Dr. Jacob Brewer, Associate Department Head/Professor, 325-671-2146, Fax: 325-670-5868, E-mail: jbrewer@hsutx.edu. *Application contact:* Dr. Jacob Brewer, Associate Department Head/Professor, 325-671-2146, Fax: 325-670-5868, E-mail: jbrewer@hsutx.edu.
Website: http://www.hsutx.edu/academics/holland/graduate/physicaltherapy

**High Point University,** Norcross Graduate School, High Point, NC 27268. Offers athletic training (MSAT); business administration (MBA); educational leadership (M Ed, Ed D); elementary education (M Ed, MAT); pharmacy (Pharm D); physical therapy (DPT); physician assistant studies (MPAS); secondary mathematics (M Ed, MAT); special education (M Ed); strategic communication (MA). *Accreditation:* NCATE. *Program availability:* Part-time, evening/weekend. *Degree requirements:* For master's, comprehensive exam (for some programs), thesis (for some programs). *Entrance requirements:* For master's, GMAT (MBA), GRE, MAT, minimum GPA of 3.0. Additional exam requirements/recommendations for international students: required—TOEFL (minimum score 550 paper-based). Electronic applications accepted.

**Howard University,** College of Nursing and Allied Health Sciences, Division of Allied Health Sciences, Washington, DC 20059-0002. Offers occupational therapy (MSOT); physical therapy (DPT); physician assistant (MPA). *Accreditation:* AOTA.

**Hunter College of the City University of New York,** Graduate School, School of Health Professions, Program in Physical Therapy, New York, NY 10065-5085. Offers DPT. *Accreditation:* APTA. *Entrance requirements:* For doctorate, 2 semesters of course work in biology, physics, chemistry, and psychology; 1 semester of mathematics, statistics, and English composition; CPR certification; minimum GPA of 3.0; documented clinical experience of at least 75 hours under the supervision of a licensed physical therapist, with a minimum of 50 hours in a hospital-based setting. Additional exam requirements/recommendations for international students: required—TOEFL (minimum score 550 paper-based). Electronic applications accepted.

**Husson University,** Doctorate in Physical Therapy Program, Bangor, ME 04401-2999. Offers DPT. *Accreditation:* APTA. *Degree requirements:* For doctorate, group research project. *Entrance requirements:* For doctorate, GRE, essay, minimum GPA of 3.0. Additional exam requirements/recommendations for international students: required—TOEFL (minimum score 550 paper-based; 75 iBT). Electronic applications accepted. *Expenses:* Contact institution.

**Idaho State University,** Graduate School, College of Rehabilitation and Communication Sciences, Department of Physical and Occupational Therapy, Program in Physical Therapy, Pocatello, ID 83209-8045. Offers DPT. *Accreditation:* APTA. *Degree requirements:* For doctorate, comprehensive exam, thesis/dissertation, oral and written exam. *Entrance requirements:* For doctorate, GRE General Test, minimum GPA of 3.0, 80 hours in 2 practice settings of physical therapy. Additional exam requirements/recommendations for international students: required—TOEFL (minimum score 600 paper-based). Electronic applications accepted. *Expenses:* Contact institution.

**Indiana State University,** College of Graduate and Professional Studies, College of Health and Human Services, Department of Applied Medicine and Rehabilitation, Terre Haute, IN 47809. Offers athletic training (MS, DAT); occupational therapy (MS); physical therapy (DPT); physician assistant (MS). *Accreditation:* AOTA. *Degree requirements:* For master's, thesis or alternative. *Entrance requirements:* For master's, GRE General Test. Electronic applications accepted.

**Indiana University-Purdue University Indianapolis,** School of Health and Rehabilitation Sciences, Indianapolis, IN 46202. Offers health and rehabilitation sciences (PhD); health sciences (MS); nutrition and dietetics (MS); occupational therapy (OTD); physical therapy (DPT); physician assistant (MPAS). *Accreditation:* AOTA. *Program availability:* Part-time, evening/weekend. *Degree requirements:* For master's, thesis (for some programs). *Entrance requirements:* For master's, GRE General Test, minimum GPA of 3.0 (for MS in health sciences, nutrition and dietetics), 3.2 (for MS in occupational therapy), 3.0 cumulative and prerequisite math/science (for MPAS); for doctorate, GRE, minimum cumulative and prerequisite math/science GPA of 3.2. Additional exam requirements/recommendations for international students: required—TOEFL (minimum score 550 paper-based; 79 iBT), IELTS (minimum score 6.5), PTE (minimum score 54). Electronic applications accepted. *Expenses:* Contact institution.

**Ithaca College,** School of Health Sciences and Human Performance, Program in Physical Therapy, Ithaca, NY 14850. Offers DPT. *Accreditation:* APTA. *Faculty:* 19 full-time (12 women). *Students:* 165 full-time (126 women), 3 part-time (all women); includes 22 minority (2 Black or African American, non-Hispanic/Latino; 9 Asian, non-Hispanic/Latino; 7 Hispanic/Latino; 4 Two or more races, non-Hispanic/Latino), 2 international. Average age 22. In 2019, 82 doctorates awarded. *Expenses:* Contact institution. *Financial support:* In 2019–20, 112 students received support. Federal Work-Study and scholarships/grants available. Support available to part-time students. Financial award application deadline: 3/1; financial award applicants required to submit FAFSA. *Unit head:* Dr. Laura Gras, Graduate Chair, Department of Physical Therapy, 607-274-7125, E-mail: lgras@ithaca.edu. *Application contact:* Nicole Eversley Bradwell, Director, Office of Admission, 800-429-4274, Fax: 607-274-1263, E-mail: admission@ithaca.edu.
Website: https://www.ithaca.edu/academics/majors-minors/clinical-health-studiesphysical-therapy-bsdpt

**Kean University,** Nathan Weiss Graduate College, Doctorate Program in Physical Therapy, Union, NJ 07083. Offers DPT. *Faculty:* 5 full-time (3 women). *Students:* 68 full-time (48 women); includes 9 minority (2 Black or African American, non-Hispanic/Latino; 3 Asian, non-Hispanic/Latino; 3 Hispanic/Latino; 1 Two or more races, non-Hispanic/Latino). Average age 25. 293 applicants, 11% accepted, 24 enrolled. In 2019, 22 doctorates awarded. *Entrance requirements:* For doctorate, GRE, minimum cumulative GPA of 3.0, satisfactory completion of all course prerequisites with minimum C grade, letters of recommendation, PT Experience form. Additional exam requirements/recommendations for international students: required—TOEFL (minimum score 550 paper-based; 79 iBT), IELTS (minimum score 6.5). *Application deadline:* For summer admission, 10/1 priority date for domestic and international students. Application fee: $75. Electronic applications accepted. *Expenses:* Contact institution. *Financial support:* Scholarships/grants and unspecified assistantships available. Financial award applicants required to submit FAFSA. *Unit head:* Dr. Timothy Clifford, Interim Executive Director, 908-737-6177, E-mail: marshati@kean.edu. *Application contact:* Pedro Lopes, Admissions Counselor, 908-737-7100, E-mail: gradadmissions@kean.edu.
Website: http://grad.kean.edu/dpt

**Langston University,** School of Physical Therapy, Langston, OK 73050. Offers DPT. *Accreditation:* APTA.

**Lebanon Valley College,** Program in Physical Therapy, Annville, PA 17003-1400. Offers DPT. *Accreditation:* APTA. *Degree requirements:* For doctorate, minimum GPA of 3.0. *Entrance requirements:* For doctorate, GRE, documented clinical hours; minimum overall undergraduate GPA of 3.0, 2.8 science. Additional exam requirements/recommendations for international students: required—TOEFL (minimum score 80 iBT). Electronic applications accepted. *Expenses:* Contact institution.

**Loma Linda University,** School of Allied Health Professions, Department of Physical Therapy, Loma Linda, CA 92350. Offers physical therapy (DPT, PhD); rehabilitation (MS). *Accreditation:* APTA. *Entrance requirements:* Additional exam requirements/recommendations for international students: required—TOEFL (minimum score 550 paper-based). Electronic applications accepted.

**Long Island University - Brooklyn,** School of Health Professions, Brooklyn, NY 11201-8423. Offers athletic training and sport sciences (MS); community health (MS Ed); exercise science (MS); forensic social work (Advanced Certificate); occupational therapy (MS); physical therapy (DPT); physician assistant (MS); public health (MPH); social work (MSW); speech-language pathology (MS). *Accreditation:* AOTA; CEPH. *Degree requirements:* For master's, comprehensive exam (for some programs), thesis (for some programs); for doctorate, comprehensive exam (for some programs). *Entrance requirements:* For master's and doctorate, GRE. Additional exam requirements/recommendations for international students: required—TOEFL (minimum score 550 paper-based; 79 iBT). Electronic applications accepted.

**Louisiana State University Health Sciences Center,** School of Allied Health Professions, Department of Physical Therapy, New Orleans, LA 70112-2223. Offers DPT. *Accreditation:* APTA. *Faculty:* 7 full-time (6 women). *Students:* 100 full-time (67 women); includes 8 minority (3 Black or African American, non-Hispanic/Latino; 3 Asian, non-Hispanic/Latino; 2 Two or more races, non-Hispanic/Latino). Average age 26. 216 applicants, 16% accepted, 35 enrolled. In 2019, 36 doctorates awarded. *Degree requirements:* For doctorate, thesis/dissertation optional. *Entrance requirements:* For doctorate, GRE General Test (minimum combined score: 296), 60 hours of experience in physical therapy, minimum GPA of 3.0 in math and science, bachelor's degree. *Application deadline:* For summer admission, 10/1 for domestic students. Application fee: $140. Electronic applications accepted. *Financial support:* Application deadline: 4/15; applicants required to submit FAFSA. *Unit head:* Dr. Jane M. Eason, Head, 504-568-4288, Fax: 504-568-6552, E-mail: jeason@lsuhsc.edu. *Application contact:* Yudialys D. Cazanas, Student Affairs Director, 504-568-4253, Fax: 504-568-3185, E-mail: ydelga@lsuhsc.edu.
Website: http://alliedhealth.lsuhsc.edu/pt/

**Marist College,** Graduate Programs, School of Science, Poughkeepsie, NY 12601-1387. Offers physical therapy (DPT).

**Marquette University,** Graduate School, College of Health Sciences, Department of Physical Therapy, Milwaukee, WI 53201-1881. Offers DPT. *Accreditation:* APTA. *Degree requirements:* For doctorate, clinical rotations. *Entrance requirements:* For doctorate, GRE General Test. Additional exam requirements/recommendations for international students: required—TOEFL. Electronic applications accepted. *Expenses:* Contact institution.

**Marshall University,** Academic Affairs Division, College of Health Professions, School of Physical Therapy, Huntington, WV 25755. Offers DPT. *Accreditation:* APTA.

**Mary Baldwin University,** Graduate Studies, Program in Physical Therapy, Staunton, VA 24401-3610. Offers DPT.

**Marymount University,** Malek School of Health Professions, Program in Physical Therapy, Arlington, VA 22207-4299. Offers physical therapy (DPT). *Accreditation:* APTA. *Faculty:* 8 full-time (7 women), 16 part-time/adjunct (11 women). *Students:* 118 full-time (73 women); includes 34 minority (9 Black or African American, non-Hispanic/Latino; 8 Asian, non-Hispanic/Latino; 9 Hispanic/Latino; 8 Two or more races, non-Hispanic/Latino). Average age 26. 389 applicants, 47% accepted, 38 enrolled. In 2019, 40 doctorates awarded. *Degree requirements:* For doctorate, comprehensive exam, thesis/dissertation, research presentation and full case report. *Entrance requirements:* For doctorate, GRE, 2 letters of recommendation, interview, resume, 40 hours of clinical work experience whether volunteer or observation, essay, minimum GPA of 3.0 from previous university coursework including many standard prerequisites. Additional exam requirements/recommendations for international students: required—TOEFL (minimum score 600 paper-based; 96 iBT), IELTS (minimum score 6.5), PTE (minimum score 58). *Application deadline:* For fall admission, 10/15 priority date for domestic and international students. Application fee: $180. Electronic applications accepted. *Expenses:* $39,600 per year. *Financial support:* In 2019–20, 11 students received support. Research assistantships, teaching assistantships, career-related internships or fieldwork, scholarships/grants, and unspecified assistantships available. Financial award application deadline: 3/1; financial award applicants required to submit FAFSA. *Unit head:* Dr. Jennifer Donovan, Chair, Physical Therapy, 703-284-5978, E-mail: jennifer.donovan@marymount.edu. *Application contact:* Fiona McDonnell, Administrative Assistant, 703-284-5901, E-mail: gadmissi@marymount.edu.
Website: https://www.marymount.edu/Academics/Malek-School-of-Health-Professions/Graduate-Programs/Physical-Therapy-(D-P-T-)

**Maryville University of Saint Louis,** Myrtle E. and Earl E. Walker College of Health Professions, Physical Therapy Program, St. Louis, MO 63141-7299. Offers DPT. *Accreditation:* APTA. *Faculty:* 14 full-time (10 women), 3 part-time/adjunct (2 women). *Students:* 83 full-time (62 women), 40 part-time (26 women); includes 4 minority (2 Asian, non-Hispanic/Latino; 2 Hispanic/Latino). Average age 23. In 2019, 37 doctorates awarded. *Degree requirements:* For doctorate, clinical rotations. *Entrance requirements:* For doctorate, minimum cumulative GPA of 3.25 from High School (3.0 Math & Science GPA) or ACT composite of 24, 2 letters of recommendation, interview, documentation of observation hours. Additional exam requirements/recommendations for international students: required—TOEFL (minimum score 573 paper-based). *Application deadline:* Applications are processed on a rolling basis. Electronic applications accepted. *Expenses:* Contact institution. *Financial support:* Career-related internships or fieldwork, Federal Work-Study, and campus employment available. Financial award

application deadline: 4/1; financial award applicants required to submit FAFSA. *Unit head:* Jill Heitzman, Director of Physical Therapy Program, 314-529-9563, Fax: 314-529-9946, E-mail: jheitzman@maryville.edu. *Application contact:* Jeannie DeLuca, Director of Admissions and Advising, 314-529-9355, Fax: 314-529-9927, E-mail: jdeluca@maryville.edu.
Website: http://www.maryville.edu/hp/physical-therapy/

**Mayo Clinic School of Health Sciences,** Program in Physical Therapy, Rochester, MN 55905. Offers DPT. *Accreditation:* APTA. *Degree requirements:* For doctorate, comprehensive exam. *Entrance requirements:* For doctorate, GRE, official transcripts, three letters of recommendation. Additional exam requirements/recommendations for international students: required—TOEFL. Electronic applications accepted. *Expenses:* Contact institution.

**McMaster University,** Faculty of Health Sciences, Professional Program in Physiotherapy, Hamilton, ON L8S 4M2, Canada. Offers M Sc. *Degree requirements:* For master's, clinical placements, independent research project. *Entrance requirements:* For master's, minimum B average over last 60 undergraduate units. Additional exam requirements/recommendations for international students: required—TOEFL (minimum score 600 paper-based).

**MCPHS University,** School of Physical Therapy, Boston, MA 02115-5896. Offers DPT.

**Medical University of South Carolina,** College of Health Professions, Program in Physical Therapy, Charleston, SC 29425. Offers DPT. *Accreditation:* APTA. *Program availability:* Online learning. *Entrance requirements:* For doctorate, GRE, references, minimum GPA of 3.0, volunteer hours. Additional exam requirements/recommendations for international students: required—TOEFL (minimum score 600 paper-based). Electronic applications accepted.

**Mercer University,** Graduate Studies, Cecil B. Day Campus, College of Health Professions, Atlanta, GA 31207. Offers athletic training (MAT); clinical medical psychology (Psy D); physical therapy (DPT); physician assistant studies (MM Sc); public health (MPH); DPT/MBA; DPT/MPH; MM Sc/MPH; Pharm D/MPH. *Accreditation:* CEPH. *Faculty:* 17 full-time (13 women), 17 part-time/adjunct (10 women). *Students:* 360 full-time (292 women), 74 part-time (58 women); includes 171 minority (100 Black or African American, non-Hispanic/Latino; 36 Asian, non-Hispanic/Latino; 31 Hispanic/Latino; 4 Two or more races, non-Hispanic/Latino), 10 international. Average age 26. In 2019, 141 master's, 51 doctorates awarded. *Expenses:* Contact institution. *Financial support:* Federal Work-Study, traineeships, and unspecified assistantships available. *Unit head:* Dr. Lisa Lundquist, Dean/Clinical Professor, 678-547-6308, E-mail: lundquist_lm@mercer.edu. *Application contact:* Laura Ellison, Director of Admissions and Student Affairs, 678-547-6391, E-mail: ellison_la@mercer.edu.
Website: http://chp.mercer.edu/

**Mercy College,** School of Health and Natural Sciences, Program in Physical Therapy, Dobbs Ferry, NY 10522-1189. Offers DPT. *Accreditation:* APTA. *Program availability:* Evening/weekend. *Students:* 85 full-time (39 women), 34 part-time (16 women); includes 52 minority (9 Black or African American, non-Hispanic/Latino; 18 Asian, non-Hispanic/Latino; 18 Hispanic/Latino; 7 Two or more races, non-Hispanic/Latino). Average age 28. 366 applicants, 14% accepted, 30 enrolled. In 2019, 31 doctorates awarded. *Degree requirements:* For doctorate, Capstone project; completion of research and clinical education requirements. *Entrance requirements:* For doctorate, GRE, program application; transcript(s); two letters of recommendation; interview; demonstrated volunteer or work-related experience in physical therapy. Additional exam requirements/recommendations for international students: required—TOEFL (minimum score 80 iBT), IELTS (minimum score 6.5). *Application deadline:* For fall admission, 1/15 for domestic students. Application fee: $40. Electronic applications accepted. *Expenses:* Contact institution. *Financial support:* Career-related internships or fieldwork, Federal Work-Study, scholarships/grants, and unspecified assistantships available. Support available to part-time students. Financial award applicants required to submit FAFSA. *Unit head:* Dr. Joan Toglia, Dean, School of Health and Natural Sciences, 914-674-7746, E-mail: jtoglia@mercy.edu. *Application contact:* Allison Gurdineer, Executive Director of Admissions, 877-637-2946, Fax: 914-674-7382, E-mail: admissions@mercy.edu.
Website: https://www.mercy.edu/degrees-programs/doctorate-physical-therapy

**MGH Institute of Health Professions,** School of Health and Rehabilitation Sciences, Doctor of Physical Therapy Program, Boston, MA 02129. Offers DPT. *Accreditation:* APTA. *Degree requirements:* For doctorate, thesis/dissertation or alternative, research project. *Entrance requirements:* For doctorate, GRE General Test, interview, minimum of 10 physical therapy observation hours, bachelor's degree from regionally-accredited college or university. Additional exam requirements/recommendations for international students: required—TOEFL (minimum score 550 paper-based; 80 iBT). Electronic applications accepted.

**MGH Institute of Health Professions,** School of Health and Rehabilitation Sciences, MS Program in Physical Therapy, Boston, MA 02129. Offers MS, Certificate. *Program availability:* Part-time, evening/weekend. *Degree requirements:* For master's, thesis, clinical preceptorship. *Entrance requirements:* For master's, GRE General Test, graduation from an approved program in physical therapy. Additional exam requirements/recommendations for international students: required—TOEFL (minimum score 550 paper-based; 80 iBT). Electronic applications accepted.

**Midwestern University, Downers Grove Campus,** College of Health Sciences, Illinois Campus, Program in Physical Therapy, Downers Grove, IL 60515-1235. Offers DPT. *Accreditation:* APTA. *Entrance requirements:* For doctorate, GRE General Test. *Expenses:* Contact institution.

**Midwestern University, Glendale Campus,** College of Health Sciences, Arizona Campus, Program in Physical Therapy, Glendale, AZ 85308. Offers DPT. *Accreditation:* APTA. *Entrance requirements:* For doctorate, GRE General Test, bachelor's degree, minimum cumulative GPA of 2.75.

**Misericordia University,** College of Health Sciences and Education, Program in Physical Therapy, Dallas, PA 18612-1098. Offers DPT. *Accreditation:* APTA. *Students:* 134 full-time (78 women), 4 part-time (3 women); includes 6 minority (1 Asian, non-Hispanic/Latino; 4 Hispanic/Latino; 1 Two or more races, non-Hispanic/Latino). Average age 23. In 2019, 47 doctorates awarded. *Entrance requirements:* For doctorate, GRE General Test, minimum undergraduate GPA of 3.0, volunteer experience. Additional exam requirements/recommendations for international students: required—TOEFL. *Application deadline:* For fall admission, 12/15 priority date for domestic students. Applications are processed on a rolling basis. Application fee: $35. Electronic applications accepted. *Financial support:* Career-related internships or fieldwork and scholarships/grants available. Support available to part-time students. Financial award application deadline: 6/30; financial award applicants required to submit FAFSA. *Unit head:* Dr. Susan Barker, Chair, 570-674-6422, E-mail: sbarker@misericordia.edu. *Application contact:* Dr. Susan Barker, Chair, 570-674-6422, E-mail: sbarker@misericordia.edu.
Website: http://www.misericordia.edu/page.cfm?p-654

**Missouri State University,** Graduate College, College of Health and Human Services, Department of Physical Therapy, Springfield, MO 65897. Offers DPT. *Accreditation:* APTA. *Degree requirements:* For doctorate, comprehensive exam, thesis/dissertation or alternative. *Entrance requirements:* For doctorate, GRE, minimum GPA of 3.0, PTCAS. Additional exam requirements/recommendations for international students: required—TOEFL (minimum score 550 paper-based; 79 iBT), IELTS (minimum score 6). Electronic applications accepted. *Expenses: Tuition, area resident:* Full-time $2600; part-time $1735 per credit hour. Tuition, nonresident: full-time $5240; part-time $3495 per credit hour. *International tuition:* $5240 full-time. *Required fees:* $530; $438 per credit hour. Tuition and fees vary according to class time, course level, course load, degree level, campus/location and program.

**Mount St. Joseph University,** Physical Therapy Program, Cincinnati, OH 45233-1670. Offers DPT. *Accreditation:* APTA. *Degree requirements:* For doctorate, clinical internship; integrative project. *Entrance requirements:* For doctorate, GRE, minimum GPA of 3.0; prerequisite coursework in sciences, humanities, social sciences, and statistics; 80 observation hours; at least 80 hours of clinical observation in 2 different physical therapy settings; PTCAS application. Additional exam requirements/recommendations for international students: required—TOEFL (minimum score 560 paper-based; 83 iBT). Electronic applications accepted. *Expenses:* Contact institution.

**Mount Saint Mary's University,** Graduate Division, Los Angeles, CA 90049. Offers business administration (MBA); counseling psychology (MS); creative writing (MFA); education (MS, Certificate); film and television (MFA); health policy and management (MS); humanities (MA); nursing (MSN, Certificate); physical therapy (DPT); religious studies (MA). *Program availability:* Part-time, evening/weekend. *Entrance requirements:* Additional exam requirements/recommendations for international students: required—TOEFL. Electronic applications accepted. *Expenses: Tuition:* Full-time $18,648; part-time $9324 per year. *Required fees:* $540; $540 per unit.

**Nazareth College of Rochester,** Graduate Studies, Department of Physical Therapy, Rochester, NY 14618. Offers DPT. *Entrance requirements:* For doctorate, minimum GPA of 3.0 in prerequisite coursework and overall. Additional exam requirements/recommendations for international students: required—TOEFL (minimum score 550 paper-based, 79 iBT) or IELTS (6.5). *Expenses:* Contact institution.

**Neumann University,** Program in Physical Therapy, Aston, PA 19014-1298. Offers DPT. *Accreditation:* APTA. *Program availability:* Evening/weekend. *Degree requirements:* For doctorate, comprehensive exam. *Entrance requirements:* For doctorate, GRE, official transcripts from all institutions attended, resume, letter of intent, documentation of at least 200 observation hours, 3 letters of recommendation. Additional exam requirements/recommendations for international students: required—TOEFL (minimum score 89 iBT). Electronic applications accepted. *Expenses:* Contact institution.

**New York Institute of Technology,** School of Health Professions, Department of Physical Therapy, Old Westbury, NY 11568. Offers DPT. *Accreditation:* APTA. *Faculty:* 10 full-time (5 women), 17 part-time/adjunct (8 women). *Students:* 114 full-time (56 women); includes 24 minority (2 Black or African American, non-Hispanic/Latino; 10 Asian, non-Hispanic/Latino; 8 Hispanic/Latino; 4 Two or more races, non-Hispanic/Latino), 1 international. Average age 25. 482 applicants, 12% accepted, 38 enrolled. In 2019, 41 doctorates awarded. *Entrance requirements:* Additional exam requirements/recommendations for international students: required—TOEFL (minimum score 79 iBT), IELTS (minimum score 6), PTE (minimum score 53), Duolingo English Test. *Application deadline:* For summer admission, 10/15 for domestic and international students. Application fee: $50. Electronic applications accepted. *Expenses: Tuition:* Full-time $23,760; part-time $1320 per credit. *Required fees:* $260; $220 per unit. Full-time tuition and fees vary according to degree level and program. Part-time tuition and fees vary according to course load and program. *Financial support:* Research assistantships, teaching assistantships, Federal Work-Study, scholarships/grants, and unspecified assistantships available. Financial award application deadline: 2/15; financial award applicants required to submit FAFSA. *Unit head:* Dr. Cheryl Hall, Interim Chair, 516-686-7670, Fax: 516-686-7699, E-mail: chall@nyit.edu. *Application contact:* Alice Dolitsky, Director, Graduate Admissions, 800-345-6948, Fax: 516-686-1116, E-mail: grad@nyit.edu.
Website: https://www.nyit.edu/health_professions/department_of_physical_therapy

**New York Medical College,** School of Health Sciences and Practice, Valhalla, NY 10595. Offers behavioral sciences and health promotion (MPH); biostatistics (MS); children with special health care (Graduate Certificate); emergency preparedness (Graduate Certificate); environmental health science (MPH); epidemiology (MPH, MS); global health (Graduate Certificate); health education (Graduate Certificate); health policy and management (MPH, Dr PH); industrial hygiene (Graduate Certificate); pediatric dysphagia (Post-Graduate Certificate); physical therapy (DPT); public health (Graduate Certificate); speech-language pathology (MS). *Accreditation:* ASHA; CEPH. *Program availability:* Part-time, evening/weekend, 100% online, blended/hybrid learning. *Faculty:* 47 full-time (34 women), 203 part-time/adjunct (125 women). *Students:* 230 full-time (171 women), 292 part-time (207 women); includes 204 minority (73 Black or African American, non-Hispanic/Latino; 4 American Indian or Alaska Native, non-Hispanic/Latino; 59 Asian, non-Hispanic/Latino; 54 Hispanic/Latino; 1 Native Hawaiian or other Pacific Islander, non-Hispanic/Latino; 13 Two or more races, non-Hispanic/Latino), 35 international. Average age 29. 790 applicants, 61% accepted, 162 enrolled. In 2019, 113 master's, 47 doctorates awarded. *Degree requirements:* For master's, comprehensive exam (for some programs), thesis (for some programs); for doctorate, thesis/dissertation. *Entrance requirements:* For master's, GRE (for MS in speech-language pathology); for doctorate, GRE (for Doctor of Physical Therapy and Doctor of Public Health). Additional exam requirements/recommendations for international students: required—TOEFL (minimum score 96 paper-based; 24 iBT), IELTS (minimum score 7). *Application deadline:* For fall admission, 8/1 for domestic students, 4/15 for international students; for spring admission, 12/1 for domestic students; for summer admission, 5/1 for domestic students, 4/15 for international students. Applications are processed on a rolling basis. Application fee: $128 ($120 for international students). Electronic applications accepted. *Expenses:* $1195 credit fee, academic support fee $200, Student activities fee $140 per year, technology fee $150. *Financial support:* In 2019–20, 18 students received support. Federal Work-Study, scholarships/grants, unspecified assistantships, and Federal student loans available. Financial award application deadline: 4/30; financial award applicants required to submit FAFSA. *Unit head:* Ben Johnson, PhD, Vice Dean, 914-594-4531, E-mail: bjohnson23@nymc.edu. *Application contact:* Irene Bundziak, Assistant to Director of Admissions, 914-594-4905, E-mail: irene_bundziak@nymc.edu.
Website: http://www.nymc.edu/school-of-health-sciences-and-practice-shsp/

**New York University,** Steinhardt School of Culture, Education, and Human Development, Department of Physical Therapy, New York, NY 10010-5615. Offers orthopedic physical therapy (Advanced Certificate); physical therapy (MA, DPT, PhD), including pathokinesiology (MA). *Accreditation:* APTA (one or more programs are accredited). *Program availability:* Part-time. *Entrance requirements:* For master's, physical therapy certificate; for doctorate, GRE General Test, interview, physical therapy certificate. Additional exam requirements/recommendations for international students: required—TOEFL (minimum score 100 iBT). Electronic applications accepted.

**Northern Arizona University,** College of Health and Human Services, Department of Physical Therapy, Flagstaff, AZ 86011. Offers DPT. *Accreditation:* APTA. *Program*

*availability:* Blended/hybrid learning. *Degree requirements:* For doctorate, variable foreign language requirement, comprehensive exam (for some programs), thesis/dissertation (for some programs), fieldwork experience/internship, individualized research. *Entrance requirements:* For doctorate, GRE General Test. Additional exam requirements/recommendations for international students: required—TOEFL (minimum score 100 iBT), IELTS (minimum score 6.5). Electronic applications accepted. *Expenses:* Contact institution.

**Northern Illinois University,** Graduate School, College of Health and Human Sciences, School of Allied Health and Communicative Disorders, De Kalb, IL 60115-2854. Offers communicative disorders (MA, Au D), including audiology (Au D), speech-language pathology (MA); physical therapy (DPT). *Students:* 160 full-time (111 women), 2 part-time (1 woman); includes 41 minority (1 Black or African American, non-Hispanic/Latino; 12 Asian, non-Hispanic/Latino; 22 Hispanic/Latino; 6 Two or more races, non-Hispanic/Latino), 1 international. Average age 25. 211 applicants, 41% accepted, 26 enrolled. In 2019, 25 master's, 38 doctorates awarded. Application fee: $40. *Financial support:* In 2019–20, 16 research assistantships, 3 teaching assistantships were awarded; staff assistantships also available. *Unit head:* Dr. Sherrill Morris, Chair, 815-753-1486, Fax: 815-753-6169, E-mail: ahcd@niu.edu. *Application contact:* Graduate School Office, 815-753-0395, E-mail: gradsch@niu.edu. Website: http://www.chhs.niu.edu/ahcd

**Northwestern University,** Feinberg School of Medicine, Department of Physical Therapy and Human Movement Sciences, Chicago, IL 60611-2814. Offers neuroscience (PhD), including movement and rehabilitation science; physical therapy (DPT); DPT/MPH; DPT/PhD. *Accreditation:* APTA. *Degree requirements:* For doctorate, research project. *Entrance requirements:* For doctorate, GRE General Test (for DPT), baccalaureate degree with minimum GPA of 3.0 in required course work (DPT). Additional exam requirements/recommendations for international students: required—TOEFL (minimum score 100 iBT). Electronic applications accepted. *Expenses:* Contact institution.

**Nova Southeastern University,** Dr. Pallavi Patel College of Health Care Sciences, Fort Lauderdale, FL 33314-7796. Offers anesthesiologist assistant (MSA); audiology (Au D); health science (MH Sc, DHSc, PhD); occupational therapy (MOT, Dr OT, PhD); physical therapy (DPT, TDPT); physician assistant (MMS); speech-language pathology (MS). *Accreditation:* AOTA; ASHA. *Program availability:* Part-time, 100% online, blended/hybrid learning. *Faculty:* 127 full-time (85 women), 107 part-time/adjunct (79 women). *Students:* 1,336 full-time (992 women), 950 part-time (824 women); includes 839 minority (195 Black or African American, non-Hispanic/Latino; 4 American Indian or Alaska Native, non-Hispanic/Latino; 165 Asian, non-Hispanic/Latino; 397 Hispanic/Latino; 3 Native Hawaiian or other Pacific Islander, non-Hispanic/Latino; 75 Two or more races, non-Hispanic/Latino), 26 international. Average age 30. 634 applicants, 28% accepted, 159 enrolled. In 2019, 613 master's, 261 doctorates awarded. Terminal master's awarded for partial completion of doctoral program. *Degree requirements:* For doctorate, comprehensive exam, thesis/dissertation (for some programs), 12-month full-time clinical externship experience. *Entrance requirements:* For master's, GRE General Test; for doctorate, personal interview, essay in application, additional letters may be requested by the program after initial review of application if so warranted. *Application deadline:* Applications are processed on a rolling basis. Application fee: $50. Electronic applications accepted. *Expenses:* Contact institution. *Financial support:* Federal Work-Study, institutionally sponsored loans, and scholarships/grants available. Financial award application deadline: 4/15; financial award applicants required to submit FAFSA. *Unit head:* Dr. Stanley Wilson, Dean, 954-262-1203, E-mail: swilson@nova.edu. *Application contact:* Joycelyn Vogt, Director of Admissions and Outreach, 954-262-1200, Fax: 954-262-1181, E-mail: joycelyn.vogt@nova.edu. Website: http://healthsciences.nova.edu/

**The Ohio State University,** College of Medicine, School of Health and Rehabilitation Sciences, Program in Physical Therapy, Columbus, OH 43210. Offers DPT. *Accreditation:* APTA. *Degree requirements:* For doctorate, thesis/dissertation. *Entrance requirements:* For doctorate, GRE General Test. Additional exam requirements/recommendations for international students: required—TOEFL (minimum score 550 paper-based; 79 iBT), Michigan English Language Assessment Battery (minimum score 82); recommended—IELTS (minimum score 7). Electronic applications accepted.

**Ohio University,** Graduate College, College of Health Sciences and Professions, School of Rehabilitation and Communication Sciences, Division of Physical Therapy, Athens, OH 45701-2979. Offers DPT. *Accreditation:* APTA. *Entrance requirements:* For doctorate, GRE. Additional exam requirements/recommendations for international students: required—TOEFL (minimum score 550 paper-based; 80 iBT) or IELTS (minimum score 6.5). Electronic applications accepted.

**Old Dominion University,** College of Health Sciences, School of Physical Therapy and Athletic Training, Doctor of Physical Therapy Program, Norfolk, VA 23529. Offers DPT. *Degree requirements:* For doctorate, 5 full-time two-month long supervised clinical experiences; oral and written comprehensive exams. *Entrance requirements:* For doctorate, GRE, bachelor's degree; completion of prerequisite courses in biology, anatomy and physiology, chemistry, physics, and psychology; 3 letters of recommendation (1 from a physical therapist); 80 hours of volunteer experience in two separate physical therapy settings (hospital, private practice, rehab center, home health agency). Additional exam requirements/recommendations for international students: required—TOEFL (minimum score 550 paper-based). Electronic applications accepted. *Expenses:* Contact institution.

**Pacific University,** School of Physical Therapy, Forest Grove, OR 97116-1797. Offers athletic training (MSAT); physical therapy (DPT). *Accreditation:* APTA. *Degree requirements:* For doctorate, evidence-based capstone project thesis. *Entrance requirements:* For doctorate, 100 hours of volunteer/observational hours, minimum cumulative GPA of 3.0, prerequisite courses with a C grade or better, minimum GPA of 2.5 in science/statistics. Additional exam requirements/recommendations for international students: required—TOEFL (minimum score 600 paper-based). Electronic applications accepted. *Expenses:* Contact institution.

**Queen's University at Kingston,** School of Graduate Studies, Faculty of Health Sciences, School of Rehabilitation Therapy, Kingston, ON K7L 3N6, Canada. Offers occupational therapy (M Sc OT); physical therapy (M Sc PT); rehabilitation science (M Sc, PhD). *Program availability:* Part-time. *Degree requirements:* For master's, thesis; for doctorate, comprehensive exam, thesis/dissertation. *Entrance requirements:* Additional exam requirements/recommendations for international students: required—TOEFL.

**Radford University,** College of Graduate Studies and Research, Physical Therapy, DPT, Roanoke, VA 24142. Offers DPT. *Accreditation:* APTA. *Degree requirements:* For doctorate, comprehensive exam, capstone research project suitable for publication. *Entrance requirements:* For doctorate, GRE, PTCAS application with 3 letters of reference, personal essay, resume; 40 hours of clinical experience, minimum overall GPA of 3.25, 3.0 in math and science prerequisites. Additional exam requirements/recommendations for international students: required—TOEFL (minimum score 575 paper-based; 88 iBT). Electronic applications accepted. *Expenses:* Contact institution.

**Regis University,** Rueckert-Hartman College for Health Professions, Denver, CO 80221-1099. Offers advanced practice nurse (DNP); counseling (MA); counseling children and adolescents (Post-Graduate Certificate); counseling military families (Post-Graduate Certificate); depth psychotherapy (Post-Graduate Certificate); fellowship in orthopedic manual physical therapy (Certificate); health care business management (Certificate); health care quality and patient safety (Certificate); health industry leadership (MBA); health services administration (MS); marriage and family therapy (MA, Post-Graduate Certificate); neonatal nurse practitioner (MSN); nursing education (MSN); nursing leadership (MSN); occupational therapy (OTD); pharmacy (Pharm D); physical therapy (DPT). *Accreditation:* ACPE. *Program availability:* Part-time, evening/weekend, 100% online, blended/hybrid learning. *Degree requirements:* For master's, thesis (for some programs), internship. *Entrance requirements:* For master's, official transcript reflecting baccalaureate degree awarded from regionally-accredited college or university. Additional exam requirements/recommendations for international students: required—TOEFL (minimum score 550 paper-based; 82 iBT). Electronic applications accepted. *Expenses:* Contact institution.

**Rockhurst University,** College of Health and Human Services, Program in Physical Therapy, Kansas City, MO 64110-2561. Offers DPT. *Accreditation:* APTA. *Entrance requirements:* For doctorate, 3 letters of recommendation, interview, minimum GPA of 3.0, physical therapy experience. Additional exam requirements/recommendations for international students: required—TOEFL (minimum score 550 paper-based; 79 iBT). Electronic applications accepted. *Expenses:* Contact institution.

**Rocky Mountain University of Health Professions,** Programs in Physical Therapy, Provo, UT 84606. Offers DPT, TDPT. *Accreditation:* APTA. *Entrance requirements:* For doctorate, GRE, bachelor's degree; two courses each of general chemistry and general physics with lab (for science majors); one course each in biology, human anatomy (with lab), and physiology (with lab); three semester hours of statistics; six semester hours in the behavioral sciences (life span development preferred); minimum cumulative GPA of 3.0.

**Rosalind Franklin University of Medicine and Science,** College of Health Professions, Department of Physical Therapy, North Chicago, IL 60064-3095. Offers MS, DPT, TDPT. *Accreditation:* APTA. *Program availability:* Online learning. *Degree requirements:* For master's, thesis. *Entrance requirements:* For master's, physical therapy license. Additional exam requirements/recommendations for international students: required—TOEFL.

**Rush University,** College of Health Sciences, Respiratory Care program, Chicago, IL 60612-3832. Offers MS. *Entrance requirements:* Additional exam requirements/recommendations for international students: required—TOEFL. Electronic applications accepted. *Financial support:* Scholarships/grants available. Financial award applicants required to submit FAFSA. *Unit head:* David L. Vines, Chairperson. *Application contact:* David L. Vines, Chairperson.

**Rutgers University - Camden,** Graduate School of Arts and Sciences, Program in Physical Therapy, Stratford, NJ 08084. Offers DPT. *Accreditation:* APTA. *Entrance requirements:* For doctorate, GRE, physical therapy experience, 3 letters of recommendation, statement of personal, professional and academic goals, resume. Additional exam requirements/recommendations for international students: required—TOEFL, IELTS. Electronic applications accepted.

**Rutgers University - Newark,** School of Health Related Professions, Department of Rehabilitation and Movement Sciences, Program in Physical Therapy–Newark, Newark, NJ 07102. Offers DPT. *Entrance requirements:* For doctorate, GRE, chemistry, physics, calculus, psychology, statistics, interview, 3 reference letters. Additional exam requirements/recommendations for international students: required—TOEFL (minimum score 500 paper-based; 79 iBT). Electronic applications accepted.

**Rutgers University - Newark,** School of Health Related Professions, Department of Rehabilitation and Movement Sciences, Program in Physical Therapy–Stratford, Newark, NJ 07102. Offers DPT. *Entrance requirements:* For doctorate, GRE, BS, 3 reference letters, interview. Additional exam requirements/recommendations for international students: required—TOEFL (minimum score 500 paper-based; 79 iBT). Electronic applications accepted.

**Sacred Heart University,** Graduate Programs, College of Health Professions, Department of Physical Therapy, Fairfield, CT 06825. Offers DPT. *Accreditation:* APTA. *Degree requirements:* For doctorate, capstone. *Entrance requirements:* For doctorate, GRE (recommended), minimum overall and prerequisites GPA of 3.2. Additional exam requirements/recommendations for international students: required—TOEFL (minimum score 570 paper-based, 80 iBT), TWE, or IELTS (6.5). *Expenses:* Contact institution.

**Sage Graduate School,** School of Health Sciences, Program in Physical Therapy, Troy, NY 12180-4115. Offers DPT. *Accreditation:* APTA. *Faculty:* 10 full-time (7 women), 3 part-time/adjunct (all women). *Students:* 91 full-time (56 women), 3 part-time (1 woman); includes 9 minority (2 Black or African American, non-Hispanic/Latino; 3 Asian, non-Hispanic/Latino; 2 Hispanic/Latino; 2 Two or more races, non-Hispanic/Latino). Average age 25. 128 applicants, 36% accepted, 23 enrolled. In 2019, 29 doctorates awarded. *Entrance requirements:* For doctorate, application; baccalaureate degree; current resume; 2 letters of recommendation; minimum GPA of 3.25 and in science pre-requisites; completion of all pre-requisite courses for the professional DPT program with a grade of "C" or better in each required course; completion of 40 hours of PT observation. Additional exam requirements/recommendations for international students: required—TOEFL (minimum score 550 paper-based). *Application deadline:* Applications are processed on a rolling basis. Application fee: $40. Electronic applications accepted. *Expenses:* Contact institution. *Financial support:* Scholarships/grants and unspecified assistantships available. Financial award application deadline: 3/1; financial award applicants required to submit FAFSA. *Unit head:* Dr. Kathleen Kelly, Dean, School of Health Sciences, 518-244-2030, Fax: 518-244-4571, E-mail: kellyk5@sage.edu. *Application contact:* Dr. James Brennan, Chair and Assistant Professor, 518-244-2058, Fax: 518-244-4524, E-mail: brennj@sage.edu.

**St. Ambrose University,** College of Health and Human Services, Program in Physical Therapy, Davenport, IA 52803-2898. Offers DPT. *Accreditation:* APTA. *Degree requirements:* For doctorate, board exams. *Entrance requirements:* For doctorate, GRE, interview. Additional exam requirements/recommendations for international students: required—TOEFL.

**St. Catherine University,** Graduate Programs, Program in Physical Therapy, St. Paul, MN 55105. Offers DPT. *Accreditation:* APTA. *Degree requirements:* For doctorate, research project. *Entrance requirements:* For doctorate, GRE, minimum GPA of 3.0; coursework in biology/zoology, anatomy, physiology, chemistry, physics, psychology, statistics, mathematics and medical terminology. Additional exam requirements/recommendations for international students: required—Michigan English Language Assessment Battery or TOEFL (minimum score 600 paper-based; 100 iBT). *Expenses:* Contact institution.

**Saint Francis University,** Department of Physical Therapy, Loretto, PA 15940-0600. Offers DPT. *Accreditation:* APTA. *Faculty:* 9 full-time (5 women), 2 part-time/adjunct (0 women). *Students:* 69 full-time (41 women), 1 part-time (0 women); includes 3 minority (2 Asian, non-Hispanic/Latino; 1 Hispanic/Latino). Average age 23. 264 applicants, 16%

accepted, 10 enrolled. In 2019, 29 doctorates awarded. *Entrance requirements:* Additional exam requirements/recommendations for international students: required—TOEFL. *Application deadline:* For winter admission, 1/15 for domestic and international students. Application fee: $30. Electronic applications accepted. *Expenses:* 1117 per credit, 600 technology fee, 660 program fee 4-6 years. *Financial support:* Teaching assistantships with partial tuition reimbursements and unspecified assistantships available. Financial award applicants required to submit FAFSA. *Unit head:* Dr. Ivan J. Mulligan, Chair/Associate Professor, 814-472-3123, Fax: 814-472-3140, E-mail: imulligan@francis.edu. *Application contact:* Dr. Ivan J. Mulligan, Chair/Associate Professor, 814-472-3123, Fax: 814-472-3140, E-mail: imulligan@francis.edu.

**Saint Louis University,** Graduate Programs, Doisy College of Health Sciences, Department of Physical Therapy, St. Louis, MO 63103. Offers athletic training (MAT); physical therapy (DPT). *Accreditation:* APTA. *Program availability:* Part-time. *Entrance requirements:* Additional exam requirements/recommendations for international students: required—TOEFL (minimum score 525 paper-based; 55 iBT). Electronic applications accepted.

**Samford University,** School of Health Professions, Birmingham, AL 35229. Offers athletic training (MAT); physical therapy (DPT); physician assistant (MS); speech language pathology (MS). *Faculty:* 24 full-time (9 women), 2 part-time/adjunct (both women). *Students:* 193 full-time (152 women), 3 part-time (all women); includes 23 minority (7 Black or African American, non-Hispanic/Latino; 1 American Indian or Alaska Native, non-Hispanic/Latino; 3 Asian, non-Hispanic/Latino; 4 Hispanic/Latino; 8 Two or more races, non-Hispanic/Latino). Average age 24. 897 applicants, 25% accepted, 42 enrolled. In 2019, 52 master's awarded. *Degree requirements:* For master's and doctorate, capstone course. *Entrance requirements:* For master's, GRE, PA-CAT, MCAT, recommendations, resume, on-campus interview, personal statement, shadowing hours, transcripts; for doctorate, GRE, recommendations, resume, on-campus interview, personal statement, shadowing hours, transcripts. Additional exam requirements/recommendations for international students: required—TOEFL (minimum score 575 paper-based; 90 iBT), IELTS (minimum score 6.5). *Application deadline:* For fall admission, 8/1 for domestic students; for winter admission, 10/1 for domestic students; for spring admission, 1/1 for domestic students. Application fee: $120. Electronic applications accepted. *Expenses: Tuition:* Full-time $17,754; part-time $862 per credit hour. *Required fees:* $550; $550 per unit. Full-time tuition and fees vary according to course load, program and student level. *Financial support:* In 2019–20, 32 students received support. Scholarships/grants available. Financial award application deadline: 5/1; financial award applicants required to submit FAFSA. *Unit head:* Dr. Alan Jung, Ph.D., Dean of the School of Health Professions, 205-726-2716, E-mail: apjung@samford.edu. *Application contact:* Dr. Marian Carter, Ed.D., Assistant Dean of Enrollment Management and Student Services, 205-726-2611, E-mail: mwcarter@samford.edu.
Website: http://www.samford.edu/healthprofessions

**Samuel Merritt University,** Department of Physical Therapy, Oakland, CA 94609-3108. Offers DPT. *Accreditation:* APTA. *Entrance requirements:* For doctorate, GRE General Test, minimum GPA of 3.0 in science and overall; related work experience; interview. Additional exam requirements/recommendations for international students: required—TOEFL (minimum score 100 iBT). Electronic applications accepted. *Expenses:* Contact institution.

**San Diego State University,** Graduate and Research Affairs, College of Health and Human Services, School of Exercise and Nutritional Sciences, Program in Physical Therapy, San Diego, CA 92182. Offers DPT. *Accreditation:* APTA.

**San Francisco State University,** Division of Graduate Studies, College of Health and Social Sciences, Department of Physical Therapy, San Francisco, CA 94132-1722. Offers DPT. *Accreditation:* APTA. *Expenses: Tuition, area resident:* Full-time $7176; part-time $4164 per year. Tuition, state resident: full-time $7176; part-time $4164 per year. Tuition, nonresident: full-time $16,680; part-time $396 per unit. *International tuition:* $16,680 full-time. *Required fees:* $1524; $1524 per unit. $762 per semester. Tuition and fees vary according to degree level and program. *Financial support:* Career-related internships or fieldwork and institutionally sponsored loans available. *Unit head:* Dr. Linda Wanek, Director, 415-338-2001, Fax: 415-338-0907, E-mail: lwanek@sfsu.edu. *Application contact:* Jill Lienau, Academic Office Coordinator, 415-338-2001, Fax: 415-338-0907, E-mail: jlienau@sfsu.edu.
Website: http://www.pt.sfsu.edu/

**Seton Hall University,** School of Health and Medical Sciences, Program in Physical Therapy, South Orange, NJ 07079-2697. Offers professional physical therapy (DPT). *Accreditation:* APTA. *Degree requirements:* For doctorate, research project. *Entrance requirements:* Additional exam requirements/recommendations for international students: required—TOEFL. Electronic applications accepted.

**Shenandoah University,** School of Health Professions, Division of Physical Therapy - Non-Traditional Physical Therapy, Winchester, VA 22601. Offers DPT. *Accreditation:* APTA. *Program availability:* Minimal on-campus study. *Degree requirements:* For doctorate, comprehensive exam, evidence-based practice research project. *Entrance requirements:* For doctorate, GRE General Test, minimum GPA of 2.8 in completed coursework; minimum grade of C in all prerequisites coursework; 2 letters of recommendation, one from a licensed practicing PT and one from a college professor; 40 documented hours of exposure to PT practice. Additional exam requirements/recommendations for international students: required—TOEFL (minimum score 558 paper-based; 83 iBT). Electronic applications accepted. *Expenses:* Contact institution.

**Simmons University,** Gwen Ifill College of Media, Arts, and Humanities, Boston, MA 02115. Offers behavior analysis (MS, PhD, Ed S); children's literature (MA); dietetics (Certificate); elementary education (MAT); English (MA); gender/cultural studies (MA); history (MA); nutrition and health promotion (MS); physical therapy (DPT); public health (MPH); public policy (MPP); special education: moderate and severe disabilities (MS Ed); sports nutrition (Certificate); writing for children (MFA). *Program availability:* Part-time. *Faculty:* 10 full-time (9 women), 7 part-time/adjunct (6 women). *Students:* 2 full-time (both women), 67 part-time (57 women); includes 13 minority (3 Black or African American, non-Hispanic/Latino; 4 Asian, non-Hispanic/Latino; 3 Hispanic/Latino; 3 Two or more races, non-Hispanic/Latino), 1 international. Average age 31. 42 applicants, 62% accepted, 23 enrolled. In 2019, 24 master's awarded. *Degree requirements:* For master's, thesis optional. *Entrance requirements:* For master's, GRE, bachelor's degree from accredited college or university; minimum B average (preferred). Additional exam requirements/recommendations for international students: required—TOEFL (minimum score 600 paper-based; 100 iBT). *Application deadline:* For fall admission, 8/1 for domestic and international students; for spring admission, 12/15 for domestic and international students; for summer admission, 5/1 for domestic and international students. Applications are processed on a rolling basis. Application fee: $35. Electronic applications accepted. *Expenses:* Contact institution. *Financial support:* In 2019–20, 14 students received support, including 1 fellowship (averaging $15,360 per year), 13 teaching assistantships (averaging $2,000 per year); scholarships/grants also available. Financial award applicants required to submit FAFSA. *Unit head:* Dr. Brian Norman, Dean, 617-521-2472, E-mail: brian.norman@simmons.edu. *Application contact:* Patricia Flaherty, Director, Graduate Studies Admission, 617-521-3902, Fax: 617-521-3058, E-mail: gsa@simmons.edu.
Website: https://www.simmons.edu/academics/colleges-schools-departments/ifill

**Slippery Rock University of Pennsylvania,** Graduate Studies (Recruitment), College of Health, Engineering, and Science, School of Physical Therapy, Slippery Rock, PA 16057-1383. Offers DPT. *Accreditation:* APTA. *Faculty:* 9 full-time (6 women), 1 (woman) part-time/adjunct. *Students:* 134 full-time (75 women); includes 10 minority (2 Black or African American, non-Hispanic/Latino; 5 Asian, non-Hispanic/Latino; 1 Hispanic/Latino; 2 Two or more races, non-Hispanic/Latino), 1 international. Average age 23. 242 applicants, 39% accepted, 35 enrolled. In 2019, 54 doctorates awarded. *Entrance requirements:* For doctorate, GRE General Test, minimum GPA of 3.0, three letters of recommendation, essay, 100 hours of PT experience with licensed physical therapist, CPR certification. Additional exam requirements/recommendations for international students: required—TOEFL (minimum score 550 paper-based; 80 iBT). *Application deadline:* For fall admission, 11/1 priority date for domestic and international students. Applications are processed on a rolling basis. Application fee: $35. Electronic applications accepted. *Expenses:* $516 per credit in-state tuition, $173.61 per credit in-state fees; $774 per credit out-of-state tuition, $224.31 per credit out-of-state fees; $516 per credit in-state tuition, $105.40 per credit in-state fees (for distance education); $526 per credit out-of-state tuition, $118.90 per credit out-of-state fees (for distance education). *Financial support:* In 2019–20, 48 students received support. Career-related internships or fieldwork, Federal Work-Study, institutionally sponsored loans, scholarships/grants, tuition waivers (partial), and unspecified assistantships available. Financial award application deadline: 5/1; financial award applicants required to submit FAFSA. *Unit head:* Dr. Kelly Lindenberg, Graduate Coordinator, 724-738-4368, Fax: 724-738-2113, E-mail: kelly.lindenberg@sru.edu. *Application contact:* Brandi Weber-Mortimer, Director of Graduate Admissions, 724-738-2051, Fax: 724-738-2146, E-mail: graduate.admissions@sru.edu.
Website: http://www.sru.edu/academics/graduate-programs/physical-therapy-doctor-of-physical-therapy

**Sonoma State University,** School of Science and Technology, Department of Kinesiology, Rohnert Park, CA 94928. Offers exercise science/pre-physical therapy (MA); interdisciplinary (MA); interdisciplinary pre-occupational therapy (MA); lifetime physical activity (MA), including coach education, fitness and wellness. *Program availability:* Part-time. *Degree requirements:* For master's, thesis, oral exam. *Entrance requirements:* For master's, minimum GPA of 2.8. Additional exam requirements/recommendations for international students: required—TOEFL (minimum score 500 paper-based).

**Southwest Baptist University,** Program in Physical Therapy, Bolivar, MO 65613-2597. Offers DPT. *Accreditation:* APTA. *Degree requirements:* For doctorate, comprehensive exam, 3-4 clinical education experiences. *Entrance requirements:* Additional exam requirements/recommendations for international students: required—TOEFL (minimum score 550 paper-based). *Expenses:* Contact institution.

**Springfield College,** Graduate Programs, Program in Physical Therapy, Springfield, MA 01109-3797. Offers DPT. *Accreditation:* APTA. *Program availability:* Part-time. *Degree requirements:* For doctorate, comprehensive exam, thesis/dissertation, research project. *Entrance requirements:* For doctorate, GRE General Test. Additional exam requirements/recommendations for international students: required—TOEFL (minimum score 550 paper-based); recommended—IELTS (minimum score 7). Electronic applications accepted.

**State University of New York Upstate Medical University,** Department of Physical Therapy, Syracuse, NY 13210. Offers DPT. *Accreditation:* APTA. *Program availability:* Part-time, evening/weekend, online learning. Electronic applications accepted.

**Stockton University,** Office of Graduate Studies, Program in Physical Therapy, Galloway, NJ 08205-9441. Offers DPT. *Accreditation:* APTA. *Faculty:* 10 full-time (7 women), 2 part-time/adjunct (1 woman). *Students:* 88 full-time (52 women), 1 part-time (0 women); includes 27 minority (3 Black or African American, non-Hispanic/Latino; 15 Asian, non-Hispanic/Latino; 5 Hispanic/Latino; 4 Two or more races, non-Hispanic/Latino), 1 international. Average age 24. 317 applicants, 29% accepted, 30 enrolled. In 2019, 30 doctorates awarded. *Entrance requirements:* For doctorate, GRE. Additional exam requirements/recommendations for international students: required—TOEFL. *Application deadline:* For fall admission, 10/15 priority date for domestic students, 10/15 for international students. Application fee: $50. Electronic applications accepted. *Expenses: Tuition, area resident:* Full-time $750.92; part-time $78.58 per credit hour. Tuition, state resident: full-time $750.92; part-time $78.58 per credit hour. Tuition, nonresident: full-time $846; part-time $78.58 per credit hour. *International tuition:* $1195.96 full-time. *Required fees:* $1464; $78.58 per credit hour. One-time fee: $50 full-time. *Financial support:* Fellowships, research assistantships, career-related internships or fieldwork, Federal Work-Study, scholarships/grants, and unspecified assistantships available. Support available to part-time students. Financial award application deadline: 3/1; financial award applicants required to submit FAFSA. *Unit head:* Dr. Bess Kathrins, Program Director, 609-626-3640, E-mail: gradschool@stockton.edu. *Application contact:* Tara Williams, Assistant Director of Graduate Enrollment Management, 609-626-3640, Fax: 609-626-6050, E-mail: gradschool@stockton.edu.

**Stony Brook University, State University of New York,** Stony Brook Medicine, School of Health Technology and Management, Stony Brook, NY 11794. Offers applied health informatics (MS); disability studies (Certificate); health administration (MHA); health and rehabilitation sciences (PhD); health care management (Advanced Certificate); health care policy and management (MS); occupational therapy (MS); physical therapy (DPT); physician assistant (MS). *Accreditation:* AOTA; APTA. *Faculty:* 53 full-time (37 women), 54 part-time/adjunct (34 women). *Students:* 605 full-time (417 women), 65 part-time (43 women); includes 225 minority (28 Black or African American, non-Hispanic/Latino; 110 Asian, non-Hispanic/Latino; 73 Hispanic/Latino; 1 Native Hawaiian or other Pacific Islander, non-Hispanic/Latino; 13 Two or more races, non-Hispanic/Latino), 9 international. Average age 26. 1,816 applicants, 21% accepted, 293 enrolled. In 2019, 152 master's, 86 doctorates, 21 other advanced degrees awarded. *Entrance requirements:* For master's, GRE General Test, minimum GPA of 3.0, work experience in field, references; for doctorate, GRE, three references, essay. Additional exam requirements/recommendations for international students: required—TOEFL (minimum score 550 paper-based). *Application deadline:* For fall admission, 1/15 for domestic students; for spring admission, 10/1 for domestic students. Application fee: $100. *Expenses:* Contact institution. *Financial support:* Fellowships, research assistantships, teaching assistantships, career-related internships or fieldwork, Federal Work-Study, and institutionally sponsored loans available. Financial award application deadline: 3/15. *Unit head:* Dr. Stacy Jafee Gropack, Dean and Professor, 631-444-2252, Fax: 631-444-7621, E-mail: stacy.jaffeegropack@stonybrook.edu. *Application contact:* Jessica M Rotolo, Executive Assistant to the Dean, 631-444-2252, Fax: 631-444-7621, E-mail: jessica.rotolo@stonybrook.edu.
Website: http://healthtechnology.stonybrookmedicine.edu/

**Tennessee State University,** The School of Graduate Studies and Research, College of Health Sciences, Department of Physical Therapy, Nashville, TN 37209-1561. Offers DPT. *Accreditation:* APTA. *Program availability:* Part-time, online learning. *Entrance*

*requirements:* For doctorate, GRE, baccalaureate degree, 2 letters of recommendation, interview, essay. Electronic applications accepted.

**Texas State University,** The Graduate College, College of Health Professions, Doctor of Physical Therapy Program, San Marcos, TX 78666. Offers DPT. *Accreditation:* APTA. *Degree requirements:* For doctorate, comprehensive exam. *Entrance requirements:* Additional exam requirements/recommendations for international students: required—TOEFL (minimum score 550 paper-based; 78 iBT). Electronic applications accepted.

**Texas Tech University Health Sciences Center,** School of Health Professions, Program in Physical Therapy, Lubbock, TX 79430. Offers DPT, Sc D, TDPT. *Accreditation:* APTA. *Program availability:* Blended/hybrid learning. *Faculty:* 11 full-time (6 women), 25 part-time/adjunct (15 women). *Students:* 207 full-time (132 women), 1 (woman) part-time; includes 72 minority (8 Black or African American, non-Hispanic/Latino; 25 Asian, non-Hispanic/Latino; 39 Hispanic/Latino), 1 international. Average age 24. 7,670 applicants, 1% accepted, 72 enrolled. In 2019, 103 doctorates awarded. *Entrance requirements:* For doctorate, GRE. Additional exam requirements/recommendations for international students: required—TOEFL (minimum score 550 paper-based; 79 iBT), IELTS. *Application deadline:* For summer admission, 10/1 priority date for domestic students. Applications are processed on a rolling basis. Application fee: $75. Electronic applications accepted. *Financial support:* In 2019–20, 164 students received support. Career-related internships or fieldwork, institutionally sponsored loans, and scholarships/grants available. Financial award application deadline: 9/1; financial award applicants required to submit FAFSA. *Unit head:* Dr. Kerry Gilbert, Program Director, 806-743-3226, Fax: 806-743-2189, E-mail: health.professions@ttuhsc.edu. *Application contact:* Lindsay Johnson, Associate Dean for Admissions and Student Affairs, 806-743-3220, Fax: 806-743-2994, E-mail: health.professions@ttuhsc.edu.
Website: http://www.ttuhsc.edu/health-professions/doctor-of-physical-therapy/

**Texas Woman's University,** Graduate School, College of Health Sciences, School of Physical Therapy, Houston, TX 76204. Offers DPT, PhD. *Accreditation:* APTA (one or more programs are accredited). *Program availability:* Part-time. *Faculty:* 23 full-time (19 women), 7 part-time/adjunct (6 women). *Students:* 300 full-time (227 women), 70 part-time (53 women); includes 141 minority (17 Black or African American, non-Hispanic/Latino; 48 Asian, non-Hispanic/Latino; 65 Hispanic/Latino; 11 Two or more races, non-Hispanic/Latino), 9 international. Average age 27. 604 applicants, 19% accepted, 109 enrolled. In 2019, 102 doctorates awarded. *Degree requirements:* For doctorate, comprehensive exam, thesis/dissertation or alternative, professional project, internship, residency (for PhD), qualification exam. *Entrance requirements:* For doctorate, GRE General Test (DPT only), interview, resume, essay; license to practice physical therapy (preferred) or eligibility for licensure and 3 letters of recommendation (PhD); 3 letters of recommendation on department form (DPT); minimum GPA of 3.0, CPR and AED certificates, 80 observation hours. Additional exam requirements/recommendations for international students: required—TOEFL (minimum score 79 iBT); recommended—IELTS (minimum score 6.5), TSE (minimum score 53). *Application deadline:* For fall admission, 10/15 for domestic and international students. Application fee: $50 ($75 for international students). Electronic applications accepted. *Expenses: Tuition, area resident:* Full-time $4973.40; part-time $276.30 per semester hour. Tuition, state resident: full-time $4973.40; part-time $276.30 per semester hour. Tuition, nonresident: full-time $12,569; part-time $698.30 per semester hour. *International tuition:* $12,569.40 full-time. *Required fees:* $2524.30. Tuition and fees vary according to course level, course load, degree level and program. *Financial support:* In 2019–20, 244 students received support. Career-related internships or fieldwork, scholarships/grants, health care benefits, and unspecified assistantships available. Support available to part-time students. Financial award application deadline: 3/1; financial award applicants required to submit FAFSA. *Unit head:* Dr. Ann Medley, Director, 713-794-2070, Fax: 713-794-2071, E-mail: pt@twu.edu. *Application contact:* Korie Hawkins, Associate Director of Admissions, Graduate Recruitment, 940-898-3188, Fax: 940-898-3081, E-mail: admissions@twu.edu.
Website: http://www.twu.edu/physical-therapy/

**Thomas Jefferson University,** Jefferson College of Rehabilitation Sciences, Department of Physical Therapy, Philadelphia, PA 19107. Offers DPT. *Accreditation:* APTA. *Degree requirements:* For doctorate, capstone project. *Entrance requirements:* Additional exam requirements/recommendations for international students: required—TOEFL (minimum score 87 iBT). Electronic applications accepted. *Expenses:* Contact institution.

**Trine University,** Program in Physical Therapy, Angola, IN 46703-1764. Offers DPT. *Accreditation:* APTA. *Degree requirements:* For doctorate, internship.

**University at Buffalo, the State University of New York,** Graduate School, School of Public Health and Health Professions, Department of Rehabilitation Science, Program in Physical Therapy, Buffalo, NY 14260. Offers DPT. *Accreditation:* APTA. *Entrance requirements:* For doctorate, GRE. Additional exam requirements/recommendations for international students: required—TOEFL (minimum score 79 iBT). Electronic applications accepted. *Expenses: Tuition, area resident:* Full-time $11,310; part-time $471 per credit hour. Tuition, state resident: full-time $11,310; part-time $471 per credit hour. Tuition, nonresident: full-time $23,100; part-time $963 per credit hour. *International tuition:* $23,100 full-time. *Required fees:* $2820.

**The University of Alabama at Birmingham,** School of Health Professions, Program in Physical Therapy, Birmingham, AL 35294. Offers DPT. *Accreditation:* APTA. *Faculty:* 17 full-time (8 women), 1 (woman) part-time/adjunct. *Students:* 146 full-time (101 women); includes 14 minority (8 Black or African American, non-Hispanic/Latino; 2 Asian, non-Hispanic/Latino; 1 Hispanic/Latino; 3 Two or more races, non-Hispanic/Latino), 1 international. Average age 25. In 2019, 45 doctorates awarded. *Entrance requirements:* For doctorate, GRE, interview; letters of recommendation; minimum GPA of 3.0 overall, in prerequisite courses, and last 60 hours; 40 hours of PT observation. *Application deadline:* For spring admission, 12/3 for domestic students. Electronic applications accepted. *Financial support:* Fellowships with tuition reimbursements, research assistantships, career-related internships or fieldwork, Federal Work-Study, and institutionally sponsored loans available. Financial award application deadline: 11/15. *Unit head:* Dr. Diane Clark, Program Director, 205-934-0419, Fax: 205-934-3566, E-mail: clark@uab.edu. *Application contact:* Susan Noblitt Banks, Director of Graduate School Operations, 205-934-8227, Fax: 205-934-8413, E-mail: gradschool@uab.edu.
Website: http://www.uab.edu/shp/pt/dpt

**University of Alberta,** Faculty of Graduate Studies and Research, Faculty of Rehabilitation Medicine, Department of Physical Therapy, Edmonton, AB T6G 2E1, Canada. Offers M Sc, PhD. *Program availability:* Part-time. *Degree requirements:* For master's, thesis. *Entrance requirements:* For master's, bachelor's degree in physical therapy, minimum GPA of 6.5 on a 9.0 scale. Additional exam requirements/recommendations for international students: required—TOEFL. Electronic applications accepted.

**The University of British Columbia,** Faculty of Medicine, Department of Physical Therapy, Vancouver, BC V6T 1Z1, Canada. Offers MPT.

**University of California, San Francisco,** Graduate Division, Program in Physical Therapy, San Francisco, CA 94143. Offers DPT, DPTSc. *Accreditation:* APTA. *Entrance requirements:* For doctorate, GRE General Test, letters of recommendation.

**University of Central Arkansas,** Graduate School, College of Health and Behavioral Sciences, Department of Physical Therapy, Conway, AR 72035-0001. Offers DPT, PhD. *Accreditation:* APTA. *Degree requirements:* For doctorate, comprehensive exam, thesis/dissertation. *Entrance requirements:* Additional exam requirements/recommendations for international students: required—TOEFL (minimum score 550 paper-based; 80 iBT). Electronic applications accepted. *Expenses:* Contact institution.

**University of Central Florida,** College of Health Professions and Sciences, School of Kinesiology and Physical Therapy, Program in Physical Therapy, Orlando, FL 32816. Offers physical therapy (DPT). *Accreditation:* APTA. *Students:* 109 full-time (67 women), 1 (woman) part-time; includes 39 minority (3 Black or African American, non-Hispanic/Latino; 6 Asian, non-Hispanic/Latino; 26 Hispanic/Latino; 4 Two or more races, non-Hispanic/Latino), 1 international. Average age 25. In 2019, 37 doctorates awarded. *Application deadline:* For summer admission, 11/1 for domestic students. Application fee: $30. Electronic applications accepted. *Expenses:* Contact institution. *Financial support:* In 2019–20, 7 students received support, including 7 fellowships with partial tuition reimbursements available (averaging $3,371 per year); career-related internships or fieldwork, institutionally sponsored loans, scholarships/grants, tuition waivers (partial), and unspecified assistantships also available. Financial award application deadline: 3/1; financial award applicants required to submit FAFSA. *Unit head:* Dr. Patrick Pabian, Program Director, 407-823-3457, E-mail: patrick.pabian@ucf.edu. *Application contact:* Associate Director, Graduate Admissions, 407-823-2766, Fax: 407-823-6442, E-mail: gradadmissions@ucf.edu.
Website: https://www.cohpa.ucf.edu/hp/physical-therapy-program/

**University of Cincinnati,** Graduate School, College of Allied Health Sciences, Department of Rehabilitation Sciences, Cincinnati, OH 45221. Offers physical therapy (DPT). *Accreditation:* APTA. *Entrance requirements:* For doctorate, GRE General Test, bachelor's degree with minimum GPA of 3.0, 50 hours volunteer/work in physical therapy setting. Additional exam requirements/recommendations for international students: required—TOEFL. Electronic applications accepted.

**University of Colorado Denver,** School of Medicine, Program in Physical Therapy, Aurora, CO 80045. Offers DPT. *Accreditation:* APTA. *Program availability:* Part-time. *Degree requirements:* For doctorate, thesis/dissertation or alternative, 116 credit hours, 44 weeks of clinical experiences, capstone project at end of year 3. *Entrance requirements:* For doctorate, GRE, minimum GPA of 3.0; prerequisite coursework in anatomy, physiology, chemistry, physics, psychology, English composition or writing, college-level math, statistics, and upper-level science; 45 hours of observation. Additional exam requirements/recommendations for international students: required—TOEFL (minimum score 550 paper-based). Electronic applications accepted. Tuition and fees vary according to course load, program and reciprocity agreements.

**University of Connecticut,** Graduate School, College of Agriculture, Health and Natural Resources, Department of Kinesiology, Program in Physical Therapy, Storrs, CT 06269. Offers DPT. *Accreditation:* APTA. *Entrance requirements:* Additional exam requirements/recommendations for international students: required—TOEFL (minimum score 550 paper-based). Electronic applications accepted.

**University of Dayton,** Department of Physical Therapy, Dayton, OH 45469. Offers DPT. *Accreditation:* APTA. *Degree requirements:* For doctorate, comprehensive exam, 4 clinical rotations; research project presented at a professional conference. *Entrance requirements:* For doctorate, GRE, bachelor's degree from accredited college or university; minimum cumulative GPA of 3.0 across all schools attended; minimum of 64 semester credits and four or more prerequisite science courses with labs; minimum grade of C+ in all prerequisite courses. Additional exam requirements/recommendations for international students: required—TOEFL (minimum score 550 paper-based; 89 iBT). Electronic applications accepted. *Expenses:* Contact institution.

**University of Delaware,** College of Health Sciences, Department of Physical Therapy, Newark, DE 19716. Offers DPT. *Accreditation:* APTA. *Entrance requirements:* For doctorate, GRE, 100 hours clinical experience, 3 letters of recommendation. Additional exam requirements/recommendations for international students: required—TOEFL (minimum score 550 paper-based). Electronic applications accepted.

**University of Evansville,** College of Education and Health Sciences, Department of Physical Therapy, Evansville, IN 47722. Offers DPT. *Accreditation:* APTA. *Entrance requirements:* Additional exam requirements/recommendations for international students: required—TOEFL (minimum score 88 iBT), IELTS (minimum score 6.5).

**The University of Findlay,** Office of Graduate Admissions, Findlay, OH 45840. Offers applied security and analytics (MSAS); athletic training (MAT); business (MBA), including certified management accountant, certified public accountant, health care management, hospitality management; education (MA Ed, Ed D), including children's literature (MA Ed), curriculum and teaching (MA Ed), education (MA Ed), educational administration (MA Ed), human resource development (MA Ed), mathematics (MA Ed), reading (MA Ed), science education (MA Ed), superintendent (Ed D), teaching (Ed D), technology (MA Ed); environmental, safety, and health management (MSEM); health informatics (MS); occupational therapy (MOT); pharmacy (Pharm D); physical therapy (DPT); physician assistant (MPA); rhetoric and writing (MA); teaching English to speakers of other languages (TESOL) and applied linguistics (MA). *Program availability:* Part-time, evening/weekend, 100% online, blended/hybrid learning. *Students:* 688 full-time (430 women), 553 part-time (308 women), 170 international. Average age 28. 865 applicants, 31% accepted, 235 enrolled. In 2019, 363 master's, 141 doctorates awarded. *Degree requirements:* For master's, comprehensive exam (for some programs), thesis (for some programs), cumulative project, capstone project; for doctorate, thesis/dissertation (for some programs). *Entrance requirements:* For master's, GRE/GMAT, bachelor's degree from accredited institution, minimum undergraduate GPA of 2.5 in last 64 hours of course work; for doctorate, GRE, MAT, minimum cumulative GPA of 3.0. Additional exam requirements/recommendations for international students: required—TOEFL (minimum score 79 iBT), IELTS (minimum score 7), PTE (minimum score 61). *Application deadline:* Applications are processed on a rolling basis. Electronic applications accepted. *Financial support:* In 2019–20, 10 research assistantships with partial tuition reimbursements (averaging $7,200 per year), 35 teaching assistantships with partial tuition reimbursements (averaging $7,200 per year) were awarded; Federal Work-Study, institutionally sponsored loans, and unspecified assistantships also available. Financial award applicants required to submit FAFSA. *Unit head:* Dave M. Emsweller, Director of Admissions, Interim, 419-434-4578, E-mail: emsweller@findlay.edu. *Application contact:* Amber Feehan, Graduate Admissions Counselor, 419-434-6933, Fax: 419-434-4898, E-mail: feehan@findlay.edu.
Website: http://www.findlay.edu/admissions/graduate/Pages/default.aspx

**University of Florida,** Graduate School, College of Public Health and Health Professions, Department of Physical Therapy, Gainesville, FL 32611. Offers DPT, DPT/MPH. *Accreditation:* APTA (one or more programs are accredited). *Entrance requirements:* For doctorate, GRE General Test, minimum GPA of 3.0. Additional exam requirements/recommendations for international students: required—TOEFL (minimum

score 515 paper-based; 80 iBT), IELTS (minimum score 6). Electronic applications accepted.

**University of Hartford,** College of Education, Nursing, and Health Professions, Program in Physical Therapy, West Hartford, CT 06117-1599. Offers MSPT, DPT. *Accreditation:* APTA. *Faculty:* 5 full-time (4 women), 5 part-time/adjunct (3 women). *Students:* 112 full-time (64 women), 1 (woman) part-time; includes 30 minority (8 Black or African American, non-Hispanic/Latino; 6 Asian, non-Hispanic/Latino; 15 Hispanic/Latino; 1 Two or more races, non-Hispanic/Latino). Average age 24. 4 applicants, 25% accepted. In 2019, 18 master's awarded. *Entrance requirements:* For master's, GRE, 3 letters of recommendation. Additional exam requirements/recommendations for international students: required—TOEFL (minimum score 550 paper-based). *Application deadline:* For fall admission, 2/1 for domestic students. Application fee: $45. *Expenses: Tuition:* Full-time $23,700; part-time $645 per credit. *Required fees:* $510; $510 per unit. Tuition and fees vary according to course load, degree level and program. *Financial support:* In 2019–20, 1 research assistantship (averaging $9,000 per year) was awarded; teaching assistantships also available. Financial award application deadline: 6/1; financial award applicants required to submit FAFSA. *Unit head:* Dr. Catherine Certo, Director, 860-768-5367, E-mail: certo@mail.hartford.edu. *Application contact:* Renee Murphy, Assistant Director of Graduate Admissions, 860-768-4371, Fax: 860-768-5160, E-mail: gettoknow@hartford.edu.
Website: http://www.hartford.edu/enhp/

**University of Illinois at Chicago,** College of Applied Health Sciences, Department of Physical Therapy, Chicago, IL 60607-7128. Offers MS, DPT. *Accreditation:* APTA. *Degree requirements:* For master's, thesis. *Entrance requirements:* For master's, GRE General Test, minimum GPA of 2.75. Additional exam requirements/recommendations for international students: required—TOEFL. Electronic applications accepted.

**University of Indianapolis,** Graduate Programs, College of Health Sciences, Krannert School of Physical Therapy, Indianapolis, IN 46227-3697. Offers MHS, DHS, DPT. *Accreditation:* APTA (one or more programs are accredited). *Program availability:* Part-time, evening/weekend. *Entrance requirements:* For doctorate, GRE General Test (for DPT), minimum GPA of 3.0 (for DPT), 3 letters of recommendation. Additional exam requirements/recommendations for international students: required—TOEFL (minimum score 100 iBT), TWE (minimum score 5). Electronic applications accepted. *Expenses:* Contact institution.

**The University of Iowa,** Roy J. and Lucille A. Carver College of Medicine and Graduate College, Graduate Programs in Medicine, Department of Physical Therapy and Rehabilitation Science, Iowa City, IA 52242. Offers physical rehabilitation science (MA, PhD); physical therapy (DPT). *Accreditation:* APTA (one or more programs are accredited). Terminal master's awarded for partial completion of doctoral program. *Degree requirements:* For master's, thesis (for some programs); for doctorate, comprehensive exam (for some programs), thesis/dissertation (for some programs). *Entrance requirements:* For master's and doctorate, GRE. Additional exam requirements/recommendations for international students: required—TOEFL. Electronic applications accepted. *Expenses:* Contact institution.

**University of Jamestown,** Program in Physical Therapy, Jamestown, ND 58405. Offers DPT. *Accreditation:* APTA. *Entrance requirements:* For doctorate, bachelor's degree.

**The University of Kansas,** University of Kansas Medical Center, School of Health Professions, Department of Physical Therapy and Rehabilitation Science, Kansas City, KS 66160. Offers physical therapy (DPT); rehabilitation science (PhD). *Accreditation:* APTA. *Faculty:* 27. *Students:* 186 full-time (120 women), 3 part-time (2 women); includes 22 minority (3 Black or African American, non-Hispanic/Latino; 6 Asian, non-Hispanic/Latino; 10 Hispanic/Latino; 1 Native Hawaiian or other Pacific Islander, non-Hispanic/Latino; 2 Two or more races, non-Hispanic/Latino), 9 international. Average age 25. In 2019, 60 doctorates awarded. *Degree requirements:* For doctorate, comprehensive exam, dissertation for PhD. *Entrance requirements:* For doctorate, GRE General Test, minimum GPA of 3.0. Additional exam requirements/recommendations for international students: required—TOEFL. *Application deadline:* For fall admission, 11/1 for domestic students. Application fee: $75. Electronic applications accepted. *Expenses:* Contact institution. *Financial support:* Research assistantships with tuition reimbursements, teaching assistantships with tuition reimbursements, career-related internships or fieldwork, Federal Work-Study, institutionally sponsored loans, scholarships/grants, traineeships, and unspecified assistantships available. Financial award application deadline: 3/1; financial award applicants required to submit FAFSA. *Unit head:* Dr. Patricia Kluding, Professor and Department Chair, 913-588-6799, Fax: 913-588-6910, E-mail: pkluding@kumc.edu. *Application contact:* Robert Bagley, Program Manager, 913-588-6799, Fax: 913-588-6910, E-mail: rbagley@kumc.edu.
Website: http://www.kumc.edu/school-of-health-professions/physical-therapy-and-rehabilitation-science.html

**University of Kentucky,** Graduate School, College of Health Sciences, Program in Physical Therapy, Lexington, KY 40506-0032. Offers DPT. *Accreditation:* APTA. *Degree requirements:* For doctorate, comprehensive exam, thesis/dissertation optional. *Entrance requirements:* For doctorate, GRE General Test, minimum undergraduate GPA of 2.75, U.S. physical therapist license. Additional exam requirements/recommendations for international students: required—TOEFL (minimum score 550 paper-based). Electronic applications accepted.

**University of Lynchburg,** Graduate Studies, Doctor of Physical Therapy Program, Lynchburg, VA 24501-3199. Offers physical therapy (DPT). *Accreditation:* APTA. *Degree requirements:* For doctorate, comprehensive exam, clinical internships; comprehensive review. *Entrance requirements:* For doctorate, GRE, baccalaureate degree from institution accredited by a CHEA-recognized regional accrediting organization; official transcripts; minimum GPA of 3.0 overall and for prerequisite science coursework; personal essay as described on PTCAS; 80 hours' experience under supervision of licensed physical therapist; 2 letters of recommendation. Additional exam requirements/recommendations for international students: required—TOEFL. Electronic applications accepted. *Expenses:* Contact institution.

**University of Manitoba,** Faculty of Graduate Studies, College of Rehabilitation Sciences, Winnipeg, MB R3T 2N2, Canada. Offers applied health sciences (PhD); occupational therapy (MOT); physical therapy (MPT); rehabilitation sciences (M Sc).

**University of Mary,** School of Health Sciences, Program in Physical Therapy, Bismarck, ND 58504-9652. Offers DPT. *Accreditation:* APTA. *Degree requirements:* For doctorate, comprehensive exam, professional paper. *Entrance requirements:* For doctorate, GRE, minimum GPA of 2.75, 3.0 in core requirements; 40 hours of paid/volunteer experience; 2 letters of recommendation. Additional exam requirements/recommendations for international students: required—TOEFL (minimum score 500 paper-based; 71 iBT). Electronic applications accepted. *Expenses:* Contact institution.

**University of Mary Hardin-Baylor,** Graduate Studies in Physical Therapy, Belton, TX 76513. Offers physical therapy (DPT). *Faculty:* 8 full-time (7 women), 10 part-time/adjunct (5 women). *Students:* 113 full-time (70 women); includes 28 minority (4 Black or African American, non-Hispanic/Latino; 7 Asian, non-Hispanic/Latino; 17 Hispanic/Latino). Average age 25. 337 applicants, 27% accepted, 40 enrolled. In 2019, 34 doctorates awarded. *Degree requirements:* For doctorate, comprehensive exam, professional portfolio. *Entrance requirements:* For doctorate, minimum GPA of 3.2 in last 60 hours of bachelor's or relevant master's degree, 3.0 in prerequisites; therapy and other healthcare-related experience; resume; letters of recommendation. Additional exam requirements/recommendations for international students: required—TOEFL (minimum score 60 iBT), IELTS (minimum score 4.5). *Application deadline:* For fall admission, 6/1 for domestic students, 4/30 priority date for international students; for spring admission, 11/1 for domestic students, 9/30 priority date for international students. Applications are processed on a rolling basis. Application fee: $35 ($135 for international students). Electronic applications accepted. *Expenses:* Contact institution. *Financial support:* In 2019–20, 113 students received support. Federal Work-Study, unspecified assistantships, and scholarships for some active duty military personnel available. Financial award applicants required to submit FAFSA. *Unit head:* Dr. Barbara Gresham, Director, Doctor of Physical Therapy Program/Associate Professor, 254-295-4921, E-mail: bgresham@umhb.edu. *Application contact:* Katherine Moore, Assistant Director, Graduate Admissions, 254-295-4924, E-mail: kmoore@umhb.edu.
Website: https://go.umhb.edu/graduate/physical-therapy/home

**University of Maryland, Baltimore,** School of Medicine, Department of Physical Therapy and Rehabilitation Science, Baltimore, MD 21201. Offers physical rehabilitation science (PhD); physical therapy and rehabilitation science (DPT). *Accreditation:* APTA. *Students:* 191 full-time (134 women), 1 (woman) part-time; includes 42 minority (10 Black or African American, non-Hispanic/Latino; 15 Asian, non-Hispanic/Latino; 6 Hispanic/Latino; 11 Two or more races, non-Hispanic/Latino), 1 international. Average age 25. 214 applicants, 93% accepted, 65 enrolled. In 2019, 61 doctorates awarded. *Entrance requirements:* For doctorate, GRE General Test, BS, science coursework. Additional exam requirements/recommendations for international students: required—TOEFL (minimum score 80 iBT). Electronic applications accepted. *Expenses:* Contact institution. *Financial support:* Career-related internships or fieldwork, Federal Work-Study, scholarships/grants, traineeships, health care benefits, and unspecified assistantships available. Financial award application deadline: 3/1; financial award applicants required to submit FAFSA. *Unit head:* Dr. Mark W. Rogers, Chair, 410-706-0841, Fax: 410-706-4903, E-mail: mrogers@som.umaryland.edu. *Application contact:* Aynsley Hamel, Program Coordinator, 410-706-0566, Fax: 410-706-6387, E-mail: ptadmissions@som.umaryland.edu.
Website: http://pt.umaryland.edu/pros.asp

**University of Maryland Eastern Shore,** Graduate Programs, Department of Physical Therapy, Princess Anne, MD 21853. Offers DPT. *Accreditation:* APTA. *Degree requirements:* For doctorate, thesis/dissertation, clinical practicum, research project. *Entrance requirements:* For doctorate, minimum GPA of 3.0, course work in science and mathematics, interview, knowledge of the physical therapy field. Additional exam requirements/recommendations for international students: required—TOEFL (minimum score 80 iBT). Electronic applications accepted.

**University of Massachusetts Lowell,** College of Health Sciences, Department of Physical Therapy, Lowell, MA 01854. Offers DPT. *Accreditation:* APTA. *Entrance requirements:* For doctorate, GRE General Test, minimum GPA of 3.0, 3 letters of recommendation. Additional exam requirements/recommendations for international students: required—TOEFL (minimum score 560 paper-based).

**University of Miami,** Graduate School, Miller School of Medicine, Graduate Programs in Medicine, Department of Physical Therapy, Coral Gables, FL 33124. Offers DPT, PhD. *Accreditation:* APTA (one or more programs are accredited). *Faculty:* 3 full-time (1 woman), 8 part-time/adjunct (5 women). *Students:* 192 full-time (110 women); includes 73 minority (8 Black or African American, non-Hispanic/Latino; 13 Asian, non-Hispanic/Latino; 48 Hispanic/Latino; 4 Two or more races, non-Hispanic/Latino), 5 international. Average age 26. In 2019, 61 doctorates awarded. *Degree requirements:* For doctorate, comprehensive exam, thesis/dissertation. *Entrance requirements:* For doctorate, GRE General Test. Additional exam requirements/recommendations for international students: required—TOEFL (minimum score 550 paper-based; 80 iBT). *Application deadline:* For fall admission, 10/15 for domestic and international students. Applications are processed on a rolling basis. Application fee: $40. Electronic applications accepted. *Expenses:* Contact institution. *Financial support:* In 2019–20, 10 students received support, including 8 research assistantships with full tuition reimbursements available (averaging $29,625 per year), 20 teaching assistantships with partial tuition reimbursements available (averaging $1,000 per year); Federal Work-Study, institutionally sponsored loans, scholarships/grants, health care benefits, tuition waivers (full and partial), unspecified assistantships, and stipends also available. Financial award application deadline: 5/15; financial award applicants required to submit FAFSA. *Unit head:* Dr. Neva Jillaine Kiek-Sanchez, Assoc. Professor and Chair, 305-284-4690, E-mail: nkirksanchez@miami.edu. *Application contact:* Jhelane Fuentes, Assoc. Director of Admissions and Student Services, 305-284-4535, Fax: 305-284-6128, E-mail: physicialtherapy@miami.edu.
Website: http://www.pt.med.miami.edu

**University of Michigan–Flint,** College of Health Sciences, Program in Physical Therapy, Flint, MI 48502-1950. Offers adult neurology (PhD); neurology (Certificate); orthopedics (PhD, Certificate); pediatrics (PhD, Certificate); physical therapy (DPT). *Accreditation:* APTA. *Program availability:* Part-time, evening/weekend, 100% online. *Faculty:* 16 full-time (12 women), 14 part-time/adjunct (7 women). *Students:* 184 full-time (123 women), 37 part-time (23 women); includes 24 minority (3 Black or African American, non-Hispanic/Latino; 1 American Indian or Alaska Native, non-Hispanic/Latino; 10 Asian, non-Hispanic/Latino; 3 Hispanic/Latino; 7 Two or more races, non-Hispanic/Latino), 14 international. Average age 28. 294 applicants, 44% accepted, 62 enrolled. In 2019, 68 doctorates awarded. *Degree requirements:* For doctorate, thesis/dissertation or alternative. *Entrance requirements:* For degree, DPT from accredited institution; current physical therapy license in the United States or Canada; minimum overall GPA of 3.0 in the physical therapy degree; current CPR certification. Additional exam requirements/recommendations for international students: required—TOEFL (minimum score 84 iBT), IELTS (minimum score 6.5). *Application deadline:* For fall admission, 5/1 for domestic students, 2/1 for international students; for winter admission, 7/31 for domestic students, 4/1 for international students; for spring admission, 3/1 for domestic students, 12/1 for international students. Application fee: $55. Electronic applications accepted. *Expenses:* Contact institution. *Financial support:* Federal Work-Study, scholarships/grants, and unspecified assistantships available. Support available to part-time students. Financial award application deadline: 3/1; financial award applicants required to submit FAFSA. *Unit head:* Dr. Amy Yorke, Department Admissions Chair, 810-762-3373, E-mail: amyorke@umflint.edu. *Application contact:* Frank Fanzone, Senior Administrative Assistant, 810-762-3373, Fax: 810-766-6668, E-mail: ffanzone@umflint.edu.
Website: https://www.umflint.edu/pt

**University of Minnesota, Twin Cities Campus,** Medical School, Minneapolis, MN 55455-0213. Offers MA, MS, DPT, MD, PhD, JD/MD, MD/MBA, MD/MHI, MD/MPH, MD/MS, MD/PhD. *Accreditation:* LCME/AMA. *Program availability:* Part-time, evening/weekend. *Expenses:* Contact institution.

**University of Mississippi Medical Center,** School of Health Related Professions, Department of Physical Therapy, Jackson, MS 39216-4505. Offers MPT. *Accreditation:* APTA.

**University of Montana,** Graduate School, College of Health Professions and Biomedical Sciences, School of Physical Therapy and Rehabilitation Science, Missoula, MT 59812. Offers physical therapy (DPT). *Accreditation:* APTA. *Degree requirements:* For doctorate, professional paper. *Entrance requirements:* For doctorate, GRE General Test. Additional exam requirements/recommendations for international students: required—TOEFL. Electronic applications accepted. *Expenses:* Contact institution.

**University of Mount Union,** Program in Physical Therapy, Alliance, OH 44601-3993. Offers DPT. *Entrance requirements:* Additional exam requirements/recommendations for international students: required—TOEFL (minimum score 89 iBT). Electronic applications accepted. *Expenses:* Contact institution.

**University of Nebraska Medical Center,** College of Allied Health Professions, Division of Physical Therapy Education, Omaha, NE 68198. Offers DPT. *Accreditation:* APTA.

**University of Nevada, Las Vegas,** Graduate College, School of Integrated Health Sciences, Department of Physical Therapy, Las Vegas, NV 89154-3029. Offers DPT. *Accreditation:* APTA. *Faculty:* 6 full-time (3 women), 8 part-time/adjunct (5 women). *Students:* 136 full-time (67 women); includes 56 minority (1 Black or African American, non-Hispanic/Latino; 25 Asian, non-Hispanic/Latino; 20 Hispanic/Latino; 10 Two or more races, non-Hispanic/Latino), 3 international. Average age 26. In 2019, 34 doctorates awarded. *Degree requirements:* For doctorate, comprehensive exam (for some programs), thesis/dissertation, final research report/professional paper/case report. *Entrance requirements:* For doctorate, GRE General Test, PTCAS application; hours of observation; 3 letters of recommendation; statement of purpose; personal interview; bachelor's degree. Additional exam requirements/recommendations for international students: required—TOEFL (minimum score 550 paper-based; 80 iBT), IELTS (minimum score 7). *Application deadline:* For summer admission, 10/1 for domestic and international students. Application fee: $60 ($95 for international students). Electronic applications accepted. *Expenses:* Contact institution. *Financial support:* In 2019–20, 5 students received support, including 5 research assistantships with full tuition reimbursements available (averaging $20,000 per year); institutionally sponsored loans, scholarships/grants, health care benefits, and unspecified assistantships also available. Financial award application deadline: 3/15; financial award applicants required to submit FAFSA. *Unit head:* Dr. Merrill Landers, Chair/Associate Professor, 702-895-1377, Fax: 702-895-4883, E-mail: pt.chair@unlv.edu. *Application contact:* Dr. Daniel Young, Graduate Coordinator, 702-895-2704, Fax: 702-895-4883, E-mail: dpt.gradcoord@unlv.edu.
Website: http://pt.unlv.edu/

**University of New England,** Westbrook College of Health Professions, Biddeford, ME 04005-9526. Offers nurse anesthesia (MSNA); occupational therapy (MS); physical therapy (DPT); physician assistant (MS); social work (MSW). *Accreditation:* AANA/CANAEP; AOTA. *Program availability:* Part-time. *Faculty:* 42 full-time (32 women), 23 part-time/adjunct (16 women). *Students:* 493 full-time (361 women), 8 part-time (7 women); includes 59 minority (3 Black or African American, non-Hispanic/Latino; 2 American Indian or Alaska Native, non-Hispanic/Latino; 36 Asian, non-Hispanic/Latino; 10 Hispanic/Latino; 2 Native Hawaiian or other Pacific Islander, non-Hispanic/Latino; 6 Two or more races, non-Hispanic/Latino), 2 international. Average age 27. In 2019, 154 master's, 58 doctorates awarded. *Application deadline:* Applications are processed on a rolling basis. Electronic applications accepted. *Financial support:* Application deadline: 5/1; applicants required to submit FAFSA. *Unit head:* Dr. Karen T. Pardue, Dean, Westbrook College of Health Professions, 207-221-4361, E-mail: kpardue@une.edu. *Application contact:* Scott Steinberg, Vice President of University Admissions, 207-221-4225, Fax: 207-523-1925, E-mail: ssteinberg@une.edu.
Website: http://www.une.edu/wchp/index.cfm

**University of New Mexico,** Graduate Studies, Health Sciences Center, Division of Physical Therapy, Albuquerque, NM 87131-2039. Offers DPT. *Accreditation:* APTA. *Degree requirements:* For doctorate, comprehensive exam, thesis/dissertation or alternative. *Entrance requirements:* For doctorate, GRE General Test, GRE Writing Assessment Test, interview, minimum GPA of 3.0. *Expenses:* Tuition, state resident: full-time $7633; part-time $972 per year. Tuition, nonresident: full-time $22,586; part-time $3840 per year. *International tuition:* $23,292 full-time. *Required fees:* $8608. Tuition and fees vary according to course level, course load, degree level, program and student level.

**University of North Dakota,** Graduate School, Graduate Programs in Medicine, Department of Physical Therapy, Grand Forks, ND 58202. Offers DPT. *Accreditation:* APTA. *Entrance requirements:* For doctorate, minimum GPA of 3.0, pre-physical therapy program. Additional exam requirements/recommendations for international students: required—TOEFL (minimum score 550 paper-based; 79 iBT), IELTS (minimum score 6.5).

**University of North Florida,** Brooks College of Health, Department of Clinical and Applied Movement Sciences, Jacksonville, FL 32224. Offers MSH, DPT. *Accreditation:* APTA. *Program availability:* Part-time, evening/weekend. *Entrance requirements:* For master's, GRE General Test, minimum GPA of 3.0 in last 60 hours, volunteer/observation experience. Additional exam requirements/recommendations for international students: required—TOEFL (minimum score 500 paper-based). Electronic applications accepted. *Expenses:* Contact institution.

**University of North Georgia,** Department of Physical Therapy, Dahlonega, GA 30597. Offers DPT. *Accreditation:* APTA. *Faculty:* 8 full-time (4 women). *Students:* 95 full-time (72 women), 4 part-time (3 women); includes 9 minority (1 Asian, non-Hispanic/Latino; 6 Hispanic/Latino; 2 Two or more races, non-Hispanic/Latino), 6 international. Average age 26. *Application deadline:* For summer admission, 10/1 for domestic students. Applications are processed on a rolling basis. Application fee: $50. Electronic applications accepted. *Unit head:* Dr. Susan Klappa, Department Head, E-mail: susan.klappa@ung.edu. *Application contact:* Cory Thornton, Director of Graduate Admissions, 706-867-2077, E-mail: cory.thornton@ung.edu.
Website: http://ung.edu/physical-therapy/

**University of North Texas Health Science Center at Fort Worth,** School of Health Professions, Fort Worth, TX 76107-2699. Offers physical therapy (DPT); physician assistant studies (MPAS). *Accreditation:* ARC-PA. *Degree requirements:* For master's, thesis or alternative, research paper. *Entrance requirements:* For master's, minimum GPA of 2.85.

**University of Oklahoma Health Sciences Center,** Graduate College, College of Allied Health, Department of Physical Therapy, Oklahoma City, OK 73190. Offers MPT. *Accreditation:* APTA.

**University of Pittsburgh,** School of Health and Rehabilitation Sciences, Department of Physical Therapy, Pittsburgh, PA 15260. Offers MS, DPT, DPT/PhD. *Accreditation:* APTA. *Faculty:* 31 full-time (13 women), 4 part-time/adjunct (2 women). *Students:* 211 full-time (141 women); includes 27 minority (4 Black or African American, non-Hispanic/Latino; 1 American Indian or Alaska Native, non-Hispanic/Latino; 12 Asian, non-Hispanic/Latino; 4 Hispanic/Latino; 6 Two or more races, non-Hispanic/Latino), 16 international. Average age 24. 553 applicants, 33% accepted, 85 enrolled. In 2019, 20 master's, 58 doctorates awarded. *Degree requirements:* For doctorate, comprehensive exam. *Entrance requirements:* For doctorate, GRE General Test. Additional exam requirements/recommendations for international students: required—International applicants may provide Duolingo English Test, IELTS or TOEFL scores to verify English language proficiency. Electronic applications accepted. *Financial support:* In 2019–20, 4 students received support, including 4 research assistantships with full tuition reimbursements available (averaging $28,400 per year). *Unit head:* Dr. James Irrgang, Chair/Professor, 412-383-9865, Fax: 412-648-5970, E-mail: jirrgang@pitt.edu. *Application contact:* Jessica Maguire, Director of Admissions, 412-383-6557, Fax: 412-383-6535, E-mail: maguire@pitt.edu.
Website: http://www.shrs.pitt.edu/pt

**University of Puerto Rico - Medical Sciences Campus,** School of Health Professions, Program in Physical Therapy, San Juan, PR 00936-5067. Offers MS. *Accreditation:* APTA. *Program availability:* Part-time, evening/weekend. *Degree requirements:* For master's, one foreign language, thesis. *Entrance requirements:* For master's, EXADEP, minimum GPA of 2.8, interview, first aid training and CPR certification.

**University of Puget Sound,** School of Physical Therapy, Tacoma, WA 98416. Offers DPT. *Accreditation:* APTA. *Degree requirements:* For doctorate, comprehensive exam, thesis/dissertation or alternative, successful completion of 36 weeks of full-time internships and a research project. *Entrance requirements:* For doctorate, GRE General Test, minimum baccalaureate GPA of 3.0, observation hours (at least 100 recommended), four letters of recommendation. Additional exam requirements/recommendations for international students: required—TOEFL. Electronic applications accepted. *Expenses:* Contact institution.

**University of Rhode Island,** Graduate School, College of Health Sciences, Physical Therapy Department, Kingston, RI 02881. Offers DPT. *Accreditation:* APTA. *Program availability:* Part-time. *Faculty:* 8 full-time (5 women). *Students:* 77 full-time (51 women), 28 part-time (18 women); includes 5 minority (1 Black or African American, non-Hispanic/Latino; 3 Asian, non-Hispanic/Latino; 1 Hispanic/Latino). 302 applicants, 20% accepted. In 2019, 30 doctorates awarded. *Entrance requirements:* Additional exam requirements/recommendations for international students: required—TOEFL. *Application deadline:* For fall admission, 10/15 for domestic and international students. Application fee: $65. Electronic applications accepted. *Expenses: Tuition, area resident:* Full-time $13,734; part-time $763 per credit. Tuition, state resident: full-time $13,734; part-time $763 per credit. Tuition, nonresident: full-time $26,512; part-time $1473 per credit. *International tuition:* $26,512 full-time. *Required fees:* $1780; $52 per credit. $35 per term. One-time fee: $165. *Financial support:* In 2019–20, 4 teaching assistantships with tuition reimbursements (averaging $5,086 per year) were awarded. Financial award application deadline: 10/15; financial award applicants required to submit FAFSA. *Unit head:* Dr. Peter Plenpied, Interim Chair, E-mail: blanpied@uri.edu. *Application contact:* Dr. Peter Plenpied, Interim Chair, E-mail: blanpied@uri.edu.
Website: http://www.uri.edu/hss/pt/

**University of St. Augustine for Health Sciences,** Graduate Programs, Doctor of Physical Therapy Program, San Marcos, CA 92069. Offers DPT. *Accreditation:* APTA. *Entrance requirements:* Additional exam requirements/recommendations for international students: required—TOEFL. Application fee is waived when completed online.

**University of St. Augustine for Health Sciences,** Graduate Programs, Post Professional Programs, San Marcos, CA 92069. Offers health science (DH Sc); health sciences education (Ed D); occupational therapy (TOTD); physical therapy (TDPT). *Program availability:* Part-time, online learning. *Entrance requirements:* For doctorate, GRE General Test, master's degree in related field. Additional exam requirements/recommendations for international students: required—TOEFL.

**University of Saint Mary,** Graduate Programs, Program in Physical Therapy, Leavenworth, KS 66048-5082. Offers DPT. *Accreditation:* APTA. *Students:* 122 full-time (72 women); includes 13 minority (1 Black or African American, non-Hispanic/Latino; 4 Asian, non-Hispanic/Latino; 7 Hispanic/Latino; 1 Two or more races, non-Hispanic/Latino). Average age 24. In 2019, 41 doctorates awarded. *Entrance requirements:* For doctorate, Pre-requisite courses, PTCAS application, minimum GPA of 3.0. *Application deadline:* Applications are processed on a rolling basis. Application fee: $35. Electronic applications accepted. *Expenses:* $840 per credit hour. *Financial support:* Applicants required to submit FAFSA. *Unit head:* Dr. Jamie Dehan, DPT Chair, 913-758-6106, E-mail: jamie.dehan@stmary.edu. *Application contact:* Dr. Jamie Dehan, DPT Chair, 913-758-6106, E-mail: jamie.dehan@stmary.edu.
Website: http://www.stmary.edu/DPT

**The University of Scranton,** Panuska College of Professional Studies, Department of Physical Therapy, Scranton, PA 18510. Offers DPT. *Accreditation:* APTA. *Program availability:* Part-time. *Degree requirements:* For doctorate, capstone experience. *Entrance requirements:* For doctorate, minimum undergraduate GPA of 3.0, minimum 60 hours of observation. Additional exam requirements/recommendations for international students: required—TOEFL (minimum score 500 paper-based; 80 iBT), IELTS (minimum score 6.5). Electronic applications accepted.

**University of South Alabama,** Pat Capps Covey College of Allied Health Professions, Department of Physical Therapy, Mobile, AL 36688-0002. Offers DPT. *Accreditation:* APTA. *Faculty:* 7 full-time (3 women), 2 part-time/adjunct (both women). *Students:* 133 full-time (86 women); includes 5 minority (2 Black or African American, non-Hispanic/Latino; 1 American Indian or Alaska Native, non-Hispanic/Latino; 1 Hispanic/Latino; 1 Two or more races, non-Hispanic/Latino), 14 international. Average age 24. 410 applicants, 25% accepted, 54 enrolled. In 2019, 39 doctorates awarded. *Degree requirements:* For doctorate, comprehensive exam. *Entrance requirements:* For doctorate, GRE. Additional exam requirements/recommendations for international students: required—TOEFL (minimum score 600 paper-based; 100 iBT), TWE (minimum score 4.5), TSE. *Application deadline:* For fall admission, 12/1 for domestic students, 10/15 for international students. Application fee: $75. Electronic applications accepted. *Expenses:* Contact institution. *Financial support:* Fellowships, research assistantships, teaching assistantships, career-related internships or fieldwork, Federal Work-Study, institutionally sponsored loans, scholarships/grants, and unspecified assistantships available. Support available to part-time students. Financial award application deadline: 3/31; financial award applicants required to submit FAFSA. *Unit head:* Dr. Barry Dale, Chair, Professor, Department of Physical Therapy, 251-445-9330, Fax: 251-445-9238, E-mail: ptdept@southalabama.edu. *Application contact:* Dr. Barry Dale, Chair, Professor, Department of Physical Therapy, 251-445-9330, Fax: 251-445-9238, E-mail: ptdept@southalabama.edu.
Website: http://www.southalabama.edu/alliedhealth/pt/

**University of South Dakota,** Graduate School, School of Health Sciences, Department of Physical Therapy, Vermillion, SD 57069. Offers DPT. *Accreditation:* APTA. *Entrance requirements:* For doctorate, GRE General Test. Additional exam requirements/recommendations for international students: required—TOEFL (minimum score 550 paper-based; 79 iBT), IELTS (minimum score 6). *Expenses:* Contact institution.

**University of Southern California,** Graduate School, Herman Ostrow School of Dentistry, Division of Biokinesiology and Physical Therapy, Los Angeles, CA 90089.

Offers biokinesiology (MS, PhD); physical therapy (DPT). *Accreditation:* APTA (one or more programs are accredited). *Degree requirements:* For master's, comprehensive exam; for doctorate, thesis/dissertation. *Entrance requirements:* For master's and doctorate, GRE (minimum combined score 1200, verbal 600, quantitative 600). Additional exam requirements/recommendations for international students: required—TOEFL. Electronic applications accepted. *Expenses:* Contact institution.

**University of South Florida,** Morsani College of Medicine, School of Physical Therapy, Tampa, FL 33620-9951. Offers physical therapy (DPT); rehabilitation sciences (PhD), including chronic disease, neuromusculoskeletal disability, veteran's health/reintegration. *Accreditation:* APTA. *Faculty:* 12 full-time (7 women). *Students:* 137 full-time (86 women); includes 29 minority (6 Black or African American, non-Hispanic/Latino; 9 Asian, non-Hispanic/Latino; 13 Hispanic/Latino; 1 Two or more races, non-Hispanic/Latino). Average age 24. 1,190 applicants, 4% accepted, 46 enrolled. In 2019, 44 doctorates awarded. *Degree requirements:* For doctorate, comprehensive exam, thesis/dissertation. *Entrance requirements:* For doctorate, GRE General Test, bachelor's degree from regionally-accredited university with minimum GPA of 3.0 in all upper-division coursework; interview; at least 20 hours of documented volunteer or work experience in hospital outpatient/inpatient physical therapy settings; written personal statement of values and purpose for attending. Additional exam requirements/recommendations for international students: required—TOEFL (minimum score 600 paper-based; 79 iBT). *Application deadline:* For fall admission, 6/1 for domestic students, 1/1 for international students; for spring admission, 10/15 for domestic students, 9/15 for international students. Application fee: $30. Electronic applications accepted. *Financial support:* In 2019–20, 64 students received support. Teaching assistantships available. *Unit head:* Dr. William S. Quillen, Director, 813-974-9863, Fax: 813-974-8915, E-mail: wquillen@health.usf.edu. *Application contact:* Dr. Gina Maria Musolino, Associate Professor and Coordinator for Clinical Education, 813-974-2254, Fax: 813-974-8915, E-mail: gmusolin@health.usf.edu.
Website: http://health.usf.edu/medicine/dpt/index.htm

**The University of Tennessee at Chattanooga,** Program in Physical Therapy, Chattanooga, TN 37403. Offers DPT. *Accreditation:* APTA. *Faculty:* 12 full-time (6 women). *Students:* 105 full-time (75 women); includes 7 minority (1 Black or African American, non-Hispanic/Latino; 2 Asian, non-Hispanic/Latino; 2 Hispanic/Latino; 2 Two or more races, non-Hispanic/Latino). Average age 24. 37 applicants, 97% accepted, 36 enrolled. In 2019, 34 doctorates awarded. *Degree requirements:* For doctorate, qualifying exams, internship. *Entrance requirements:* For doctorate, GRE, minimum GPA of 3.2 in science and overall, criminal background check, two letters of reference (one of which must be from a licensed physical therapist). Additional exam requirements/recommendations for international students: required—TOEFL (minimum score 550 paper-based; 79 iBT); recommended—IELTS (minimum score 6). *Application deadline:* For fall admission, 6/15 priority date for domestic students, 7/1 for international students; for spring admission, 11/1 priority date for domestic students, 11/1 for international students. Applications are processed on a rolling basis. Application fee: $35 ($40 for international students). Electronic applications accepted. *Financial support:* Research assistantships, teaching assistantships, career-related internships or fieldwork, scholarships/grants, and unspecified assistantships available. Support available to part-time students. Financial award application deadline: 7/1; financial award applicants required to submit FAFSA. *Unit head:* Dr. Nancy Fell, Department Head, 423-425-2240, Fax: 423-425-2380, E-mail: Nancy-Fell@utc.edu. *Application contact:* Dr. Joanne Romagni, Dean of the Graduate School, 423-425-4478, Fax: 423-425-5223, E-mail: joanne-romagni@utc.edu.
Website: http://www.utc.edu/physical-therapy/

**The University of Tennessee Health Science Center,** College of Health Professions, Memphis, TN 38163-0002. Offers audiology (MS, Au D); clinical laboratory science (MSCLS); cytopathology practice (MCP); health informatics and information management (MHIIM); occupational therapy (MOT); physical therapy (DPT, ScDPT); physician assistant (MMS); speech-language pathology (MS). *Accreditation:* AOTA; APTA. *Program availability:* Part-time, evening/weekend, online learning. Terminal master's awarded for partial completion of doctoral program. *Degree requirements:* For master's, comprehensive exam, thesis; for doctorate, comprehensive exam, residency. *Entrance requirements:* For master's, GRE (MOT, MSCLS), minimum GPA of 3.0, 3 letters of reference, national accreditation (MSCLS), GRE if GPA is less than 3.0 (MCP); for doctorate, GRE. Additional exam requirements/recommendations for international students: required—TOEFL (minimum score 550 paper-based; 80 iBT). Electronic applications accepted. *Expenses:* Contact institution.

**The University of Texas at El Paso,** Graduate School, College of Health Sciences, Program in Physical Therapy, El Paso, TX 79968-0001. Offers DPT. *Accreditation:* APTA. *Entrance requirements:* For doctorate, GRE General Test. Additional exam requirements/recommendations for international students: required—TOEFL. Electronic applications accepted.

**The University of Texas Health Science Center at San Antonio,** School of Health Professions, San Antonio, TX 78229-3900. Offers occupational therapy (MOT); physical therapy (DPT); physician assistant studies (MS); speech language pathology (MS). *Accreditation:* AOTA; APTA; ARC-PA; ASHA. *Degree requirements:* For master's, comprehensive exam, thesis (for some programs); for doctorate, comprehensive exam.

**The University of Texas Medical Branch,** School of Health Professions, Department of Physical Therapy, Galveston, TX 77555. Offers MPT, DPT. *Accreditation:* APTA. *Degree requirements:* For master's, thesis or alternative. *Entrance requirements:* For master's and doctorate, GRE, documentation of 40 hours' experience. Electronic applications accepted.

**The University of Texas Southwestern Medical Center,** Southwestern School of Health Professions, Physical Therapy Program, Dallas, TX 75390. Offers DPT. *Accreditation:* APTA. *Entrance requirements:* For doctorate, GRE, minimum GPA of 3.0. Additional exam requirements/recommendations for international students: required—TOEFL (minimum score 600 paper-based). Electronic applications accepted.

**University of the Incarnate Word,** School of Physical Therapy, San Antonio, TX 78209-6397. Offers DPT. *Accreditation:* APTA. *Faculty:* 16 full-time (9 women), 10 part-time/adjunct (8 women). *Students:* 103 full-time (57 women), 57 part-time (38 women); includes 91 minority (12 Black or African American, non-Hispanic/Latino; 17 Asian, non-Hispanic/Latino; 62 Hispanic/Latino). 68 applicants, 100% accepted, 55 enrolled. In 2019, 75 doctorates awarded. *Degree requirements:* For doctorate, comprehensive exam. *Entrance requirements:* For doctorate, GRE, minimum of 100 verified observation hours in at least two different physical therapy settings which focus on different physical therapy specialties; three letters of reference (at least one letter from licensed Physical Therapist). Additional exam requirements/recommendations for international students: required—TOEFL (minimum score 560 paper-based). *Application deadline:* For fall admission, 10/1 priority date for domestic students. Application fee: $50. *Expenses:* $950 per credit hour, $1,395 annual fees. *Financial support:* Scholarships/grants and unspecified assistantships available. Financial award applicants required to submit FAFSA. *Unit head:* Dr. Caroline Goulet, Dean, 210-283-6924, E-mail: goulet@uiwtx.edu. *Application contact:* Christina Immel, Director of Enrollment, 210-283-6918, E-mail: cimmel@uiwtx.edu.
Website: https://physical-therapy.uiw.edu/index.html

**University of the Pacific,** Thomas J. Long School of Pharmacy and Health Sciences, Department of Physical Therapy, Stockton, CA 95211-0197. Offers MS, DPT. *Accreditation:* APTA. *Entrance requirements:* For master's, GRE General Test, minimum GPA of 3.0. Additional exam requirements/recommendations for international students: required—TOEFL.

**University of the Sciences,** Doctor of Physical Therapy Program, Philadelphia, PA 19104-4495. Offers DPT. *Accreditation:* APTA. *Program availability:* Part-time, evening/weekend, online learning. *Entrance requirements:* For doctorate, interview. *Expenses:* Contact institution.

**The University of Toledo,** College of Graduate Studies, College of Health and Human Services, School of Exercise and Rehabilitation Sciences, Toledo, OH 43606-3390. Offers athletic training (MSES); exercise physiology (MSES); exercise science (PhD); occupational therapy (OTD); physical therapy (DPT); recreation and leisure studies (MA), including recreation administration, recreation therapy. *Degree requirements:* For master's, comprehensive exam, thesis; for doctorate, thesis/dissertation or alternative. *Entrance requirements:* For master's, GRE, minimum cumulative GPA of 2.7 for all previous academic work, letters of recommendation; for doctorate, GRE, minimum cumulative GPA of 3.0 for all previous academic work, letters of recommendation; OTCAS or PTCAS application and UT supplemental application (for OTD and DPT). Additional exam requirements/recommendations for international students: required—TOEFL (minimum score 550 paper-based; 80 iBT). Electronic applications accepted.

**The University of Toledo,** College of Graduate Studies, College of Medicine and Life Sciences, Department of Orthopedic Surgery, Toledo, OH 43606-3390. Offers MSBS. *Accreditation:* APTA. *Degree requirements:* For master's, thesis or alternative. *Entrance requirements:* For master's, GRE, minimum undergraduate GPA of 3.0, three letters of recommendation, statement of purpose, transcripts from all prior institutions attended, resume. Additional exam requirements/recommendations for international students: required—TOEFL (minimum score 550 paper-based; 80 iBT). Electronic applications accepted.

**University of Toronto,** Faculty of Medicine, Department of Physical Therapy, Toronto, ON M5S 1A1, Canada. Offers M Sc PT. *Accreditation:* APTA. *Entrance requirements:* For master's, minimum B average in final year, 2 references. Additional exam requirements/recommendations for international students: required—TOEFL (minimum score 600 paper-based; 100 iBT), TWE (minimum score 5). Electronic applications accepted.

**University of Utah,** Graduate School, College of Health, Department of Physical Therapy and Athletic Training, Salt Lake City, UT 84112-1290. Offers physical therapy (DPT); rehabilitation science (PhD). *Accreditation:* APTA. *Entrance requirements:* For doctorate, GRE, minimum GPA of 3.0, volunteer work, bachelor's degree. Additional exam requirements/recommendations for international students: required—TOEFL (minimum score 90 iBT); recommended—IELTS (minimum score 7). Electronic applications accepted. *Expenses:* Contact institution.

**University of Vermont,** Graduate College, College of Nursing and Health Sciences, Program in Physical Therapy, Burlington, VT 05405. Offers DPT. *Accreditation:* APTA. *Entrance requirements:* For doctorate, GRE General Test. Additional exam requirements/recommendations for international students: required—TOEFL (minimum score 550 paper-based; 90 iBT). Electronic applications accepted. *Expenses:* Contact institution.

**University of Washington,** Graduate School, School of Medicine, Graduate Programs in Medicine, Department of Rehabilitation Medicine, Seattle, WA 98195-6490. Offers occupational therapy (MOT); physical therapy (DPT); prosthetics and orthotics (MPO); rehabilitation science (PhD). *Accreditation:* AOTA. *Degree requirements:* For doctorate, comprehensive exam (for some programs), thesis/dissertation (for some programs). *Entrance requirements:* For master's and doctorate, GRE. Additional exam requirements/recommendations for international students: required—TOEFL.

**The University of Western Ontario,** School of Graduate and Postdoctoral Studies, Faculty of Health Sciences, School of Physical Therapy, London, ON N6A 3K7, Canada. Offers manipulative therapy (CAS); physical therapy (MPT); wound healing (CAS). *Program availability:* Part-time. *Degree requirements:* For master's, thesis. *Entrance requirements:* For master's, B Sc in physical therapy. Additional exam requirements/recommendations for international students: required—TOEFL.

**University of Wisconsin–La Crosse,** College of Science and Health, Department of Health Professions, Program in Physical Therapy, La Crosse, WI 54601-3742. Offers DPT. *Accreditation:* APTA. *Faculty:* 6 full-time (0 women), 6 part-time/adjunct (4 women). *Students:* 90 full-time (57 women), 43 part-time (23 women); includes 7 minority (2 Asian, non-Hispanic/Latino; 1 Hispanic/Latino; 4 Two or more races, non-Hispanic/Latino). Average age 24. 391 applicants, 14% accepted, 45 enrolled. In 2019, 41 doctorates awarded. *Entrance requirements:* Additional exam requirements/recommendations for international students: required—TOEFL (minimum score 550 paper-based; 79 iBT). Application fee: $50. Electronic applications accepted. *Expenses:* Contact institution. *Financial support:* Federal Work-Study, scholarships/grants, and health care benefits available. Support available to part-time students. Financial award application deadline: 11/1; financial award applicants required to submit FAFSA. *Unit head:* Dr. Patrick Grabowski, Program Director, 608-785-6623, E-mail: pgrabowski@uwlax.edu. *Application contact:* Peter Amann, Senior Graduate Student Status Examiner, 608-785-6622, E-mail: pamann@uwlax.edu.
Website: http://www.uwlax.edu/pt/

**University of Wisconsin–Madison,** School of Medicine and Public Health, Doctor of Physical Therapy Program, Madison, WI 53706. Offers DPT. *Accreditation:* APTA. *Entrance requirements:* For doctorate, GRE. Additional exam requirements/recommendations for international students: required—TOEFL (minimum score 580 paper-based; 92 iBT). Electronic applications accepted. *Expenses:* Contact institution.

**University of Wisconsin–Milwaukee,** Graduate School, College of Health Sciences, Department of Kinesiology, Milwaukee, WI 53201-0413. Offers athletic training (MS); kinesiology (MS, PhD), including exercise and nutrition in health and disease (MS), integrative human performance (MS), neuromechanics (MS); physical therapy (DPT). *Program availability:* Part-time. *Degree requirements:* For master's, comprehensive exam, thesis optional. *Entrance requirements:* For master's, GRE General Test. Additional exam requirements/recommendations for international students: required—TOEFL (minimum score 550 paper-based; 79 iBT), IELTS (minimum score 6.5).

**Utica College,** Department of Physical Therapy, Utica, NY 13502-4892. Offers DPT, TDPT. *Accreditation:* APTA. *Program availability:* Part-time, evening/weekend, online learning. *Faculty:* 10 full-time (4 women). *Students:* 86 full-time (46 women), 386 part-time (253 women); includes 246 minority (17 Black or African American, non-Hispanic/Latino; 220 Asian, non-Hispanic/Latino; 8 Hispanic/Latino; 1 Native Hawaiian or other Pacific Islander, non-Hispanic/Latino), 4 international. Average age 34. 240 applicants, 98% accepted, 232 enrolled. In 2019, 299 doctorates awarded. *Degree requirements:* For doctorate, comprehensive exam, thesis/dissertation (for some programs). *Entrance requirements:* For doctorate, GRE, MCAT, DAT or OPT, BS, minimum GPA of 3.0.

Additional exam requirements/recommendations for international students: required—TOEFL (minimum score 525 paper-based). *Application deadline:* Applications are processed on a rolling basis. Application fee: $50. Electronic applications accepted. *Expenses:* Contact institution. *Financial support:* Career-related internships or fieldwork, scholarships/grants, tuition waivers (partial), and unspecified assistantships available. Support available to part-time students. Financial award application deadline: 3/15; financial award applicants required to submit FAFSA. *Unit head:* Dr. Ashraf Elazzazi, Director, 315-792-3313, E-mail: aelazza@utica.edu. *Application contact:* John D. Rowe, Director of Graduate Admissions, 315-792-3824, Fax: 315-792-3003, E-mail: jrowe@utica.edu.

**Virginia Commonwealth University,** Graduate School, School of Allied Health Professions, Department of Physical Therapy, Richmond, VA 23284-9005. Offers DPT. *Accreditation:* APTA. *Degree requirements:* For doctorate, thesis/dissertation. *Entrance requirements:* For doctorate, GRE General Test, Physical Therapist Centralized Application Service (PTCAS). Additional exam requirements/recommendations for international students: required—TOEFL (minimum score 600 paper-based; 100 iBT). Electronic applications accepted.

**Virginia Commonwealth University,** Medical College of Virginia-Professional Programs, School of Medicine, Graduate Programs in Medicine, Department of Physiology and Biophysics, Richmond, VA 23284-9005. Offers molecular biology and genetics (MS); physical therapy (PhD); physiology (MS, PhD); MD/PhD. Terminal master's awarded for partial completion of doctoral program. *Degree requirements:* For master's, thesis; for doctorate, thesis/dissertation, comprehensive oral and written exams. *Entrance requirements:* For master's, GRE General Test, MCAT, or DAT; for doctorate, GRE, MCAT or DAT. Additional exam requirements/recommendations for international students: required—TOEFL (minimum score 600 paper-based; 100 iBT). Electronic applications accepted.

**Walsh University,** Doctor of Physical Therapy, North Canton, OH 44720. Offers DPT. *Accreditation:* APTA. *Faculty:* 7 full-time (5 women), 1 (woman) part-time/adjunct. *Students:* 95 full-time (66 women); includes 3 minority (1 Black or African American, non-Hispanic/Latino; 2 Two or more races, non-Hispanic/Latino). Average age 25. 201 applicants, 25% accepted, 30 enrolled. In 2019, 31 doctorates awarded. *Degree requirements:* For doctorate, comprehensive exam, research project, 3 clinical placements. *Entrance requirements:* For doctorate, GRE General Test (minimum scores: verbal 150, quantitative 150, or combined score of 291), previous coursework in anatomy, human physiology, exercise physiology, chemistry, statistics, psychology, biology, and physics; minimum GPA of 3.0. Additional exam requirements/recommendations for international students: required—TOEFL (minimum score 500 paper-based; 61 iBT). *Application deadline:* For fall admission, 10/1 priority date for domestic students. Electronic applications accepted. Application fee is waived when completed online. *Expenses:* $10,275 per semester, $50 technology fee. *Financial support:* In 2019–20, 3 students received support. Unspecified assistantships available. Financial award application deadline: 12/31; financial award applicants required to submit FAFSA. *Unit head:* Dr. Leigh Murray, Program Director, 330-490-7259, E-mail: lmurray@walsh.edu. *Application contact:* Mona McAuliffe, Associate Director of Graduate Admissions, 330-490-7406, Fax: 330-490-7406, E-mail: mmcauliffe@walsh.edu.
Website: www.walsh.edu

**Washington University in St. Louis,** School of Medicine, Program in Physical Therapy, Saint Louis, MO 63108. Offers DPT. *Accreditation:* APTA. *Degree requirements:* For doctorate, thesis/dissertation (for some programs). *Entrance requirements:* For doctorate, GRE. Additional exam requirements/recommendations for international students: required—TOEFL (minimum score 600 paper-based; 100 iBT), TWE (minimum score 5). Electronic applications accepted. *Expenses:* Contact institution.

**Wayne State University,** Eugene Applebaum College of Pharmacy and Health Sciences, Department of Health Care Sciences, Detroit, MI 48201. Offers nurse anesthesia (MS, DNP-A, Certificate), including anesthesia (MS), nurse anesthesia practice (DNP-A), pediatric anesthesia (Certificate); occupational therapy (MOT); physical therapy (DPT); physician assistant studies (MS). *Faculty:* 5. *Students:* 310 full-time (209 women), 4 part-time (all women); includes 33 minority (7 Black or African American, non-Hispanic/Latino; 14 Asian, non-Hispanic/Latino; 8 Hispanic/Latino; 4 Two or more races, non-Hispanic/Latino), 4 international. Average age 26. 344 applicants, 20% accepted, 55 enrolled. In 2019, 97 master's, 36 doctorates awarded. *Entrance requirements:* Additional exam requirements/recommendations for international students: required—TOEFL (minimum score 550 paper-based; 79 iBT), Michigan English Language Assessment Battery (minimum score 85); recommended—IELTS (minimum score 6.5), TWE (minimum score 5.5). Application fee: $50. Electronic applications accepted. *Expenses:* Contact institution. *Financial support:* In 2019–20, 102 students received support. Fellowships and scholarships/grants available. Financial award applicants required to submit FAFSA. *Unit head:* Dr. Sara F Maher, Chair

Department of Health Care Sciences, 313-577-5630, E-mail: sara.maher@wayne.edu. *Application contact:* Office of Student and Alumni Affairs, 313-577-1716, E-mail: cphsinfo@wayne.edu.
Website: http://cphs.wayne.edu/hcs/

**West Coast University,** Graduate Programs, North Hollywood, CA 91606. Offers advanced generalist (MSN); family nurse practitioner (MSN); health administration (MHA); occupational therapy (MS); pharmacy (Pharm D); physical therapy (DPT).

**Western Carolina University,** Graduate School, College of Health and Human Sciences, Department of Physical Therapy, Cullowhee, NC 28723. Offers DPT. *Accreditation:* APTA. *Entrance requirements:* Additional exam requirements/recommendations for international students: required—TOEFL (minimum score 550 paper-based; 79 iBT). *Expenses: Tuition, area resident:* Full-time $2217.50; part-time $1664 per semester. Tuition, state resident: full-time $2217.50; part-time $1664 per semester. Tuition, nonresident: full-time $7421; part-time $5566 per semester. *International tuition:* $7421 full-time. *Required fees:* $5598; $1954 per semester. Tuition and fees vary according to course load, campus/location and program.

**Western Kentucky University,** Graduate School, College of Health and Human Services, Department of Allied Health, Bowling Green, KY 42101. Offers physical therapy (DPT).

**Western University of Health Sciences,** College of Health Sciences, Program in Physical Therapy, Pomona, CA 91766-1854. Offers DPT. *Accreditation:* APTA. *Faculty:* 12 full-time (7 women), 11 part-time/adjunct (7 women). *Students:* 156 full-time (107 women), 7 part-time (6 women); includes 100 minority (5 Black or African American, non-Hispanic/Latino; 1 American Indian or Alaska Native, non-Hispanic/Latino; 36 Asian, non-Hispanic/Latino; 40 Hispanic/Latino; 1 Native Hawaiian or other Pacific Islander, non-Hispanic/Latino; 17 Two or more races, non-Hispanic/Latino). Average age 27. 818 applicants, 16% accepted, 55 enrolled. In 2019, 56 doctorates awarded. *Degree requirements:* For doctorate, comprehensive exam (for some programs). *Entrance requirements:* For doctorate, CASPer Assessment. Additional exam requirements/recommendations for international students: required—TOEFL, Or had taken English composition courses in the States. *Application deadline:* For fall admission, 11/1 for domestic and international students. Application fee: $60. Electronic applications accepted. *Expenses:* Tuition is about $42,630 per year. Student body fee and exam soft fee are $100. *Financial support:* In 2019–20, 6 students received support. Scholarships/grants available. Financial award application deadline: 3/2; financial award applicants required to submit FAFSA. *Unit head:* Dr. Robert Nithman, Chair, 909-469-5322, Fax: 909-469-5692, E-mail: rnithman@westernu.edu. *Application contact:* Christopher Calzada, Admissions Counselor, 909-706-3873, Fax: 909-469-5570, E-mail: ccalzada@westernu.edu.
Website: http://www.westernu.edu/allied-health/allied-health-dpt/

**West Virginia University,** School of Medicine, Morgantown, WV 26506. Offers biochemistry and molecular biology (PhD); biomedical science (MS); cancer cell biology (PhD); cellular and integrative physiology (PhD); exercise physiology (MS, PhD); health sciences (MS); immunology (PhD); medicine (MD); occupational therapy (MOT); pathologists assistant' (MHS); physical therapy (DPT). *Accreditation:* AOTA; LCME/AMA. *Program availability:* Part-time, evening/weekend. *Entrance requirements:* Additional exam requirements/recommendations for international students: required—TOEFL. Electronic applications accepted. *Expenses:* Contact institution.

**Wheeling Jesuit University,** Department of Physical Therapy, Wheeling, WV 26003-6295. Offers DPT. *Accreditation:* APTA. *Degree requirements:* For doctorate, comprehensive exam, thesis/dissertation. *Entrance requirements:* For doctorate, GRE, minimum GPA of 3.0. Additional exam requirements/recommendations for international students: required—TOEFL (minimum score 650 paper-based). Electronic applications accepted. Application fee is waived when completed online. *Expenses:* Contact institution.

**Wichita State University,** Graduate School, College of Health Professions, Department of Physical Therapy, Wichita, KS 67260. Offers DPT. *Accreditation:* APTA.

**Widener University,** School of Human Service Professions, Institute for Physical Therapy Education, Chester, PA 19013-5792. Offers MS, DPT. *Accreditation:* APTA. *Degree requirements:* For master's, thesis. *Entrance requirements:* For master's, GRE. *Expenses:* Contact institution.

**Wingate University,** Department of Physical Therapy, Wingate, NC 28174. Offers DPT.

**Winston-Salem State University,** Department of Physical Therapy, Winston-Salem, NC 27110-0003. Offers DPT. *Accreditation:* APTA. Electronic applications accepted.

**Youngstown State University,** College of Graduate Studies, Bitonte College of Health and Human Services, Department of Physical Therapy, Youngstown, OH 44555-0001. Offers DPT. *Accreditation:* APTA. *Entrance requirements:* Additional exam requirements/recommendations for international students: required—TOEFL.

# Physician Assistant Studies

**AdventHealth University,** Program in Physician Assistant Studies, Orlando, FL 32803. Offers MS. *Entrance requirements:* For master's, minimum GPA of 3.0.

**Albany Medical College,** Center for Physician Assistant Studies, Albany, NY 12208-3479. Offers MS. *Accreditation:* ARC-PA. *Degree requirements:* For master's, comprehensive exam, clinical portfolio. *Entrance requirements:* For master's, GRE. Additional exam requirements/recommendations for international students: required—TOEFL. Electronic applications accepted. *Expenses:* Contact institution.

**Alderson Broaddus University,** Program in Physician Assistant Studies, Philippi, WV 26416. Offers MPAS. *Degree requirements:* For master's, comprehensive exam, thesis. *Entrance requirements:* For master's, minimum 60 semester hours plus specific science. Electronic applications accepted.

**Arcadia University,** College of Health Sciences, Department of Medical Science, Glenside, PA 19038-3295. Offers dual physician assistant and public health (MMS/MPH); physician assistant (MMS); MMS/MPH. *Faculty:* 15 full-time (12 women). *Students:* 199 full-time (154 women); includes 40 minority (1 Black or African American, non-Hispanic/Latino; 29 Asian, non-Hispanic/Latino; 6 Hispanic/Latino; 1 Native Hawaiian or other Pacific Islander, non-Hispanic/Latino; 3 Two or more races, non-Hispanic/Latino), 1 international. In 2019, 99 master's awarded. *Degree requirements:* For master's, comprehensive exam. *Entrance requirements:* For master's, prerequisites that must be completed include biological sciences (5 courses to include anatomy, physiology, microbiology, biochemistry is recommended); chemistry (3 courses to

include minimum 1 semester of organic chemistry); psychology (1 course); statistics (1 course). Additional exam requirements/recommendations for international students: required—TOEFL. *Application deadline:* Applications are processed on a rolling basis. *Expenses:* Contact institution. *Financial support:* Tuition waivers (partial) available. *Unit head:* Renee Langstaff, Chair, 302-356-9447. *Application contact:* 215-572-2910, Fax: 215-572-4041, E-mail: admiss@arcadia.edu.

**A.T. Still University,** Arizona School of Health Sciences, Mesa, AZ 85206. Offers advanced occupational therapy (MS); advanced physician assistant studies (MS); athletic training (MS, DAT); audiology (Au D); clinical decision making in athletic training (Graduate Certificate); occupational therapy (MS, OTD); orthopedic rehabilitation (Graduate Certificate); physical therapy (DPT); physician assistant studies (MS); post-professional audiology (Au D); post-professional physical therapy (DPT). *Accreditation:* AOTA (one or more programs are accredited); ASHA. *Program availability:* Part-time, evening/weekend, online only, 100% online, blended/hybrid learning. *Faculty:* 94 full-time (74 women), 203 part-time/adjunct (145 women). *Students:* 736 full-time (528 women), 289 part-time (195 women); includes 315 minority (53 Black or African American, non-Hispanic/Latino; 7 American Indian or Alaska Native, non-Hispanic/Latino; 94 Asian, non-Hispanic/Latino; 134 Hispanic/Latino; 2 Native Hawaiian or other Pacific Islander, non-Hispanic/Latino; 25 Two or more races, non-Hispanic/Latino), 79 international. Average age 32. 4,387 applicants, 20% accepted, 514 enrolled. In 2019, 153 master's, 344 doctorates, 2 other advanced degrees awarded. *Degree requirements:* For master's, thesis (for some programs); for doctorate, thesis/

dissertation (for some programs). *Entrance requirements:* For master's, GRE General Test; for doctorate, GRE, Physical Therapist Evaluation Tool (for DPT), current state licensure. Additional exam requirements/recommendations for international students: required—TOEFL (minimum score 80 iBT). *Application deadline:* For fall admission, 7/7 for domestic and international students; for winter admission, 10/3 for domestic and international students; for spring admission, 1/16 for domestic and international students; for summer admission, 4/17 for domestic and international students. Applications are processed on a rolling basis. Application fee: $70. *Financial support:* In 2019–20, 170 students received support. Federal Work-Study and scholarships/grants available. Financial award application deadline: 6/1; financial award applicants required to submit FAFSA. *Unit head:* Dr. Ann Lee Burch, Dean, 480-219-6061, E-mail: aburch@atsu.edu. *Application contact:* Donna Sparks, Director, Admissions Processing, 660-626-2117, Fax: 660-626-2969, E-mail: admissions@atsu.edu.
Website: http://www.atsu.edu/ashs

**Augsburg University,** Program in Physician Assistant Studies, Minneapolis, MN 55454-1351. Offers MS. *Accreditation:* ARC-PA.

**Augusta University,** College of Allied Health Sciences, Physician Assistant Program, Augusta, GA 30912. Offers MPA. *Accreditation:* ARC-PA. *Program availability:* Part-time. *Degree requirements:* For master's, thesis or alternative. *Entrance requirements:* For master's, GRE General Test, minimum of 100 hours of hands-on health care experience. Additional exam requirements/recommendations for international students: required—TOEFL (minimum score 600 paper-based; 100 iBT), TWE. Electronic applications accepted.

**Baldwin Wallace University,** Graduate Programs, Physician Assistant Program, Berea, OH 44017-2088. Offers MMS. *Faculty:* 5 full-time (3 women), 2 part-time/adjunct (0 women). *Students:* 62 full-time (52 women), 1 (woman) part-time; includes 5 minority (1 Black or African American, non-Hispanic/Latino; 3 Asian, non-Hispanic/Latino; 1 Hispanic/Latino), 1 international. Average age 25. 600 applicants, 8% accepted, 32 enrolled. In 2019, 29 master's awarded. *Degree requirements:* For master's, comprehensive exam, thesis or alternative, capstone project. *Entrance requirements:* For master's, GRE, 3 letters of recommendation, personal statement, 40 hours of shadowing. Additional exam requirements/recommendations for international students: required—TOEFL (minimum score 550 paper-based; 100 iBT). *Application deadline:* For fall admission, 11/1 for domestic and international students. Applications are processed on a rolling basis. Electronic applications accepted. *Expenses:* Total cost is $80,000. *Financial support:* Applicants required to submit FAFSA. *Unit head:* Dr. Jared R. Pennington, Director/Chair, 440-826-2221, E-mail: jpenning@bw.edu. *Application contact:* Dr. Jared R. Pennington, Director/Chair, 440-826-2221, E-mail: jpenning@bw.edu.
Website: http://www.bw.edu/graduate/physician-assistant/

**Barry University,** Physician Assistant Program, Miami Shores, FL 33161-6695. Offers MCMS. *Accreditation:* ARC-PA. *Entrance requirements:* For master's, GRE General Test. Electronic applications accepted.

**Baylor College of Medicine,** School of Health Professions, Physician Assistant Program, Houston, TX 77030-3498. Offers MS. *Accreditation:* ARC-PA. *Degree requirements:* For master's, comprehensive exam, thesis. *Entrance requirements:* For master's, GRE General Test, bachelor's degree; minimum GPA of 3.0; prerequisite courses in general chemistry, organic chemistry, microbiology, general psychology, human anatomy, human physiology, statistics, and expository writing. Additional exam requirements/recommendations for international students: required—TOEFL. Electronic applications accepted. *Expenses:* Contact institution.

**Bay Path University,** Program in Physician Assistant Studies, Longmeadow, MA 01106-2292. Offers MS. *Entrance requirements:* For master's, minimum of 500 hours of patient contact hours; minimum of 24 hours of documented PA shadowing; all prerequisite courses completed with minimum C grade and cumulative GPA of 3.0. Electronic applications accepted. Application fee is waived when completed online. *Expenses:* Contact institution.

**Bethel University,** Graduate Programs, McKenzie, TN 38201. Offers administration and supervision (MA Ed); business administration (MBA); conflict resolution (MA); physician assistant studies (MS). *Program availability:* Part-time, evening/weekend. *Degree requirements:* For master's, thesis (for some programs). *Entrance requirements:* For master's, GRE General Test or MAT, minimum undergraduate GPA of 2.5.

**Bethel University,** Graduate School, St. Paul, MN 55112-6999. Offers business administration (MBA); classroom management (Certificate); counseling (MA); K-12 education (MA); leadership (Ed D); leadership foundations (Certificate); nurse educator (MS, Certificate); nurse-midwifery (MS); physician assistant (MS); special education (MA); strategic leadership (MA); teaching (MA); teaching and learning (Certificate). *Program availability:* Part-time, evening/weekend, 100% online, blended/hybrid learning. *Faculty:* 36 full-time (24 women), 112 part-time/adjunct (73 women). *Students:* 428 full-time (318 women), 825 part-time (482 women); includes 245 minority (95 Black or African American, non-Hispanic/Latino; 13 American Indian or Alaska Native, non-Hispanic/Latino; 52 Asian, non-Hispanic/Latino; 50 Hispanic/Latino; 2 Native Hawaiian or other Pacific Islander, non-Hispanic/Latino; 33 Two or more races, non-Hispanic/Latino), 28 international. Average age 38. 810 applicants, 45% accepted, 256 enrolled. In 2019, 320 master's, 34 doctorates, 112 other advanced degrees awarded. *Degree requirements:* For master's, comprehensive exam (for some programs), thesis (for some programs); for doctorate, comprehensive exam, thesis/dissertation. *Entrance requirements:* Additional exam requirements/recommendations for international students: required—TOEFL (minimum score 550 paper-based; 80 iBT), TOEFL (minimum score 550 paper-based, 80 iBT) or IELTS. *Application deadline:* Applications are processed on a rolling basis. Electronic applications accepted. *Expenses:* $420-$850/credit dependent on the program. *Financial support:* Teaching assistantships, career-related internships or fieldwork, and scholarships/grants available. Support available to part-time students. Financial award applicants required to submit FAFSA. *Unit head:* Dr. Randy Bergen, Associate Provost, 651-635-8000, Fax: 651-635-8004, E-mail: r-bergen@bethel.edu. *Application contact:* Director of Admissions, 651-635-8000, Fax: 651-635-8004, E-mail: gs@bethel.edu.
Website: https://www.bethel.edu/graduate/

**Boston University,** School of Medicine, Graduate Medical Sciences, Physician Assistant Program, Boston, MA 02215. Offers MS. *Entrance requirements:* For master's, GRE, three letters of recommendation. Additional exam requirements/recommendations for international students: required—TOEFL (minimum score 550 paper-based; 80 iBT). *Application deadline:* For spring admission, 10/1 for domestic students. Electronic applications accepted. *Financial support:* Applicants required to submit FAFSA. *Unit head:* Susan White, Director, E-mail: paoffice@bu.edu. *Application contact:* GMS Admissions Office, E-mail: paoffice@bu.edu.
Website: http://www.bu.edu/paprogram/

**Bryant University,** School of Health Sciences, Smithfield, RI 02917. Offers physician assistant studies (MPAS). *Degree requirements:* For master's, comprehensive exam. *Entrance requirements:* For master's, GRE (taken within past five years), baccalaureate degree, minimum overall undergraduate/pre-requiste GPA of 3.0, three professional references, 2000 hours of direct patient care experience. Additional exam requirements/recommendations for international students: required—TOEFL (minimum score 100 iBT). Electronic applications accepted. *Expenses:* Contact institution.

**Butler University,** College of Pharmacy and Health Sciences, Indianapolis, IN 46208-3485. Offers pharmaceutical science (MS); pharmacy (Pharm D), including medical Spanish, research; physician assistant studies (MS). *Accreditation:* ACPE (one or more programs are accredited). *Program availability:* Part-time, evening/weekend, 100% online. *Faculty:* 14 full-time (8 women). *Students:* 358 full-time (245 women), 2 part-time (0 women); includes 42 minority (1 Black or African American, non-Hispanic/Latino; 23 Asian, non-Hispanic/Latino; 12 Hispanic/Latino; 6 Two or more races, non-Hispanic/Latino), 4 international. Average age 24. 441 applicants, 17% accepted, 76 enrolled. In 2019, 77 master's, 106 doctorates awarded. *Degree requirements:* For master's, comprehensive exam (for some programs), thesis (for some programs), research paper or thesis; for doctorate, thesis/dissertation (for some programs). *Entrance requirements:* For master's, GRE General Test, CASPA application, official transcripts, baccalaureate degree from accredited institution (for physician assistant studies). Additional exam requirements/recommendations for international students: required—TOEFL (minimum score 550 paper-based; 79 iBT), IELTS (minimum score 6). *Application deadline:* For fall admission, 4/1 for domestic and international students. Electronic applications accepted. *Expenses:* Pharmacy: Pharmacy year 1 &2 (pre-Pharmacy) $20,685 per semester Pharmacy year 3-5 (P1-P3) $22,000 per semester; Pharm D (6th year only) (P4) $47,00 per year, billed summer ($4,780), fall* ($21,510), spring* ($21,510) Note: Rate is NOT based on number of hours enrolled. *Each hour above 20 hours is $1,830 for P1-P3. Master's of Science in Pharmaceutical Science: $760 per credit hour; Doctor of Medical Science: $800 per credit hour; PA Master's Program: $44,820 per year, billed summer ($4,482), fall* ($20,169), spring* ($20,169) Note: Rate is NOT based on number of hours enrolled. *each hour above 20 hours is $1,830 per credit hour. *Financial support:* In 2019–20, 4 students received support. Scholarships/grants, tuition waivers (full and partial), and unspecified assistantships available. Financial award applicants required to submit FAFSA. *Unit head:* Dr. Robert Soltis, Dean, 317-940-9322, E-mail: rsoltis@butler.edu. *Application contact:* Katie Clarizio, Academic Program Coordinator, 317-940-9297, E-mail: kclarizio@butler.edu.
Website: https://www.butler.edu/pharmacy-pa/about

**California Baptist University,** Program in Physician Assistant Studies, Riverside, CA 92504-3206. Offers MS. *Program availability:* Part-time. *Entrance requirements:* For master's, minimum undergraduate GPA of 3.0, bachelor's transcripts, three letters of recommendation, essay, interview. Additional exam requirements/recommendations for international students: required—TOEFL (minimum score 80 iBT). Electronic applications accepted. *Expenses:* Contact institution.

**Campbell University,** Graduate and Professional Programs, College of Pharmacy and Health Sciences, Buies Creek, NC 27506. Offers athletic training (MAT); clinical research (MS); pharmaceutical sciences (MS); pharmacy (Pharm D); physical therapy (DPT); physician assistant (MPAP); public health (MS). *Accreditation:* ACPE; CEPH. *Program availability:* Part-time, evening/weekend. *Entrance requirements:* For master's, MCAT, PCAT, GRE, bachelor's degree in health sciences or related field; for doctorate, PCAT. Additional exam requirements/recommendations for international students: required—TOEFL (minimum score 550 paper-based; 79 iBT). Electronic applications accepted. *Expenses:* Contact institution.

**Carroll University,** Program in Physician Assistant Studies, Waukesha, WI 53186-5593. Offers MS. *Entrance requirements:* For master's, GRE, three letters of reference, personal essay, patient care experience, transcripts. Additional exam requirements/recommendations for international students: required—TOEFL.

**Case Western Reserve University,** School of Medicine, Physician Assistant Program, Cleveland, OH 44106. Offers MS. *Degree requirements:* For master's, thesis. *Entrance requirements:* For master's, GRE, statement of objectives, letters of recommendation (minimum of 3). Additional exam requirements/recommendations for international students: required—TOEFL (minimum score 577 paper-based; 90 iBT); recommended—IELTS (minimum score 7). Electronic applications accepted.

**Central Michigan University,** College of Graduate Studies, The Herbert H. and Grace A. Dow College of Health Professions, School of Rehabilitation and Medical Sciences, Mount Pleasant, MI 48859. Offers physical therapy (DPT); physician assistant (MS). *Accreditation:* APTA; ARC-PA. *Degree requirements:* For master's, thesis or alternative; for doctorate, thesis/dissertation or alternative. *Entrance requirements:* For master's and doctorate, GRE. Electronic applications accepted. *Expenses: Tuition, area resident:* Full-time $12,267; part-time $8178 per year. Tuition, state resident: full-time $12,267; part-time $8178 per year. Tuition, nonresident: full-time $12,267; part-time $8178 per year. *International tuition:* $16,110 full-time. *Required fees:* $225 per semester. Tuition and fees vary according to degree level and program.

**Chapman University,** Crean College of Health and Behavioral Sciences, Physician Assistant Studies Program, Irvine, CA 92618. Offers MMS. *Faculty:* 8 full-time (5 women), 2 part-time/adjunct (0 women). *Students:* 85 full-time (71 women); includes 39 minority (3 Black or African American, non-Hispanic/Latino; 21 Asian, non-Hispanic/Latino; 11 Hispanic/Latino; 4 Two or more races, non-Hispanic/Latino). Average age 26. In 2019, 24 master's awarded. *Degree requirements:* For master's, clinical experience, capstone project. *Entrance requirements:* For master's, GRE. Additional exam requirements/recommendations for international students: required—TOEFL (minimum score 80 iBT), IELTS (minimum score 6.5), PTE (minimum score 53). *Application deadline:* For spring admission, 8/15 for domestic students. Electronic applications accepted. *Expenses:* $20,045 per trimester. *Financial support:* Applicants required to submit FAFSA. *Unit head:* Dr. Michael Burney, Chair, 714-744-5420, E-mail: paprogram@chapman.edu. *Application contact:* Howard Ying, Graduate Admissions Specialist, 714-744-2190, E-mail: paadmit@chapman.edu.
Website: https://www.chapman.edu/crean/academic-programs/graduate-programs/physician-assistant/index.aspx

**Chatham University,** Program in Physician Assistant Studies, Pittsburgh, PA 15232-2826. Offers MPAS. *Accreditation:* ARC-PA. *Degree requirements:* For master's, thesis, clinical experience, research project. *Entrance requirements:* For master's, community service, minimum GPA of 3.0, health science work or shadowing, volunteer work experience, PA shadowing form, 3 references. Additional exam requirements/recommendations for international students: required—TOEFL (minimum score 600 paper-based; 100 iBT), IELTS (minimum score 7), TWE. Electronic applications accepted. Application fee is waived when completed online. *Expenses:* Contact institution.

**Christian Brothers University,** School of Sciences, Memphis, TN 38104-5581. Offers physician assistant studies (MS).

**Clarkson University,** Lewis School of Health Sciences, Department of Physician Assistant Studies, Potsdam, NY 13699. Offers MS. *Faculty:* 6 full-time (4 women), 7 part-time/adjunct (4 women). *Students:* 58 full-time (45 women); includes 12 minority (1 Black or African American, non-Hispanic/Latino; 7 Asian, non-Hispanic/Latino; 2 Hispanic/Latino; 2 Two or more races, non-Hispanic/Latino), 2 international. 913 applicants, 14% accepted, 28 enrolled. In 2019, 28 master's awarded. *Entrance requirements:* For master's, minimum undergraduate GPA of 3.0; CASPA application. *Application deadline:* For fall admission, 3/1 for domestic and international students.

Applications are processed on a rolling basis. Application fee: $227. Electronic applications accepted. *Expenses:* Contact institution. *Financial support:* Scholarships/grants available. *Unit head:* Joan Caruso, Clinical Assistant Professor / Chair of Physician Assistant Studies / Director of Didactic Education, 315-268-7942, E-mail: jcaruso@clarkson.edu. *Application contact:* Amy Thompson, Graduate Admissions Coordinator, 315-268-2161, E-mail: athompso@clarkson.edu. Website: https://www.clarkson.edu/academics/graduate

**Cleveland State University,** College of Graduate Studies, College of Sciences and Health Professions, School of Health Sciences, Program in Health Sciences, Cleveland, OH 44115. Offers health sciences (MS); physician assistant science (MS). *Program availability:* Part-time, evening/weekend, online learning. *Entrance requirements:* For master's, GRE (minimum scores of 50th percentile in all areas; analytical writing 3.5), bachelor's degree from accredited institution, minimum prerequisite course GPA of 3.0, all courses completed with minimum grade of C. Additional exam requirements/recommendations for international students: required—TOEFL (minimum score 550 paper-based; 78 iBT). Electronic applications accepted. *Expenses:* Tuition, state resident: full-time $10,215; part-time $6810 per credit hour. Tuition, nonresident: full-time $17,496; part-time $11,664 per credit hour. *International tuition:* $19,316 full-time. Tuition and fees vary according to degree level and program.

**Daemen College,** Physician Assistant Programs, Amherst, NY 14226-3592. Offers MS. *Accreditation:* ARC-PA. *Degree requirements:* For master's, Satisfactory completion of all requirements as per the terms set forth by the Physician Assistant Department. *Entrance requirements:* For master's, baccalaureate degree, overall GPA of 3.0 or better, no more than two grades below C in any college level course, required science courses, 120 hours of direct patient contact experience. Additional exam requirements/recommendations for international students: required—TOEFL (minimum score 77 paper-based), IELTS (minimum score 6.5). Electronic applications accepted. Application fee is waived when completed online.

**Des Moines University,** College of Health Sciences, Physician Assistant Program, Des Moines, IA 50312-4104. Offers MS. *Accreditation:* ARC-PA. *Degree requirements:* For master's, research project. *Entrance requirements:* For master's, GRE, interview, minimum GPA of 2.8, related work experience. Additional exam requirements/recommendations for international students: recommended—TOEFL. Electronic applications accepted. *Expenses:* Contact institution.

**Drexel University,** College of Nursing and Health Professions, Physician Assistant Department, Philadelphia, PA 19104-2875. Offers MHS. *Accreditation:* ARC-PA. Electronic applications accepted.

**Duke University,** School of Medicine, Physician Assistant Program, Durham, NC 27701. Offers MHS. *Accreditation:* ARC-PA. *Entrance requirements:* For master's, GRE, bachelor's degree from regionally-accredited college; 8 core courses: anatomy, physiology, microbiology, biology (choice of 2), chemistry including labs (choice of 2), and statistics. Additional exam requirements/recommendations for international students: recommended—TOEFL. Electronic applications accepted.

**Duquesne University,** John G. Rangos, Sr. School of Health Sciences, Pittsburgh, PA 15282-0001. Offers health management systems (MHMS); occupational therapy (MS, OTD); physical therapy (DPT); physician assistant studies (MPAS); rehabilitation science (MS, PhD); speech-language pathology (MS). *Accreditation:* AOTA (one or more programs are accredited); APTA (one or more programs are accredited); ASHA. *Program availability:* Part-time, minimal on-campus study. *Degree requirements:* For doctorate, comprehensive exam (for some programs), thesis/dissertation (for some programs). *Entrance requirements:* For master's, GRE General Test (speech-language pathology), 3 letters of recommendation; minimum GPA of 2.75 (health management systems), 3.0 (speech-language pathology); for doctorate, GRE General Test (for physical therapy and rehabilitation science), 3 letters of recommendation, minimum GPA of 3.0, personal interview. Additional exam requirements/recommendations for international students: required—TOEFL (minimum score 550 paper-based; 90 iBT); recommended—IELTS. Electronic applications accepted. *Expenses:* Contact institution.

**D'Youville College,** Physician Assistant Department, Buffalo, NY 14201-1084. Offers MS. *Accreditation:* ARC-PA. *Entrance requirements:* For master's, BS, patient contact, 3 letters of recommendation. Additional exam requirements/recommendations for international students: required—TOEFL (minimum score 500 paper-based). Electronic applications accepted.

**East Carolina University,** Graduate School, College of Allied Health Sciences, Department of Physician Assistant Studies, Greenville, NC 27858-4353. Offers MS. *Accreditation:* ARC-PA. *Application deadline:* For fall admission, 9/1 for domestic students. *Expenses: Tuition, area resident:* Full-time $4749; part-time $185 per credit hour. Tuition, state resident: full-time $4749; part-time $185 per credit hour. Tuition, nonresident: full-time $17,898; part-time $864 per credit hour. *International tuition:* $17,898 full-time. *Required fees:* $2787. *Unit head:* Dr. Alan Gindoff, Chair, 252-744-6271, E-mail: gindoffa@ecu.edu. *Application contact:* Graduate School Admissions, 252-328-6012, Fax: 252-328-6071, E-mail: gradschool@ecu.edu. Website: http://www.ecu.edu/pa/

**Eastern Michigan University,** Graduate School, College of Health and Human Services, School of Health Promotion and Human Performance, Program in Physician Assistant Studies, Ypsilanti, MI 48197. Offers MS. *Program availability:* Part-time, evening/weekend. *Students:* 59 full-time (44 women); includes 12 minority (1 American Indian or Alaska Native, non-Hispanic/Latino; 6 Asian, non-Hispanic/Latino; 5 Hispanic/Latino). Average age 27. 29 applicants. In 2019, 30 master's awarded. *Entrance requirements:* Additional exam requirements/recommendations for international students: required—TOEFL. Application fee: $45. *Financial support:* Research assistantships with full tuition reimbursements, teaching assistantships with full tuition reimbursements, career-related internships or fieldwork, Federal Work-Study, institutionally sponsored loans, scholarships/grants, tuition waivers (full and partial), and unspecified assistantships available. Support available to part-time students. *Application contact:* Maria Keelon, Program Director, 734-487-0077, Fax: 734-483-1834, E-mail: mkeelon@emich.edu.

**Eastern Virginia Medical School,** Master of Physician Assistant Program, Norfolk, VA 23501-1980. Offers MPA. *Accreditation:* ARC-PA. *Entrance requirements:* Additional exam requirements/recommendations for international students: required—TOEFL. Electronic applications accepted. *Expenses:* Contact institution.

**Elon University,** Program in Physician Assistant Studies, Elon, NC 27244-2010. Offers physician assistant studies (MS). *Faculty:* 7 full-time (6 women), 2 part-time/adjunct (both women). *Students:* 75 full-time (60 women); includes 15 minority (2 Black or African American, non-Hispanic/Latino; 1 American Indian or Alaska Native, non-Hispanic/Latino; 3 Asian, non-Hispanic/Latino; 8 Hispanic/Latino; 1 Two or more races, non-Hispanic/Latino). Average age 27. 1,739 applicants, 4% accepted, 38 enrolled. In 2019, 38 master's awarded. *Entrance requirements:* For master's, GRE. Additional exam requirements/recommendations for international students: required—TOEFL (minimum score 550 paper-based; 79 iBT). *Application deadline:* For spring admission, 11/1 for domestic students. Applications are processed on a rolling basis. Electronic applications accepted. *Financial support:* Applicants required to submit FAFSA. *Unit*

*head:* Dr. Becky Neiduski, Dean of the School of Health Sciences, 336-278-6350, E-mail: bneiduski@elon.edu. *Application contact:* Art Fadde, Director of Graduate Admissions, 800-334-8448 Ext. 3, Fax: 336-278-7699, E-mail: afadde@elon.edu. Website: https://www.elon.edu/pa/

**Emory & Henry College,** Graduate Programs, Emory, VA 24327. Offers American history (MA Ed); education professional studies (M Ed); occupational therapy (MOT); organizational leadership (MCOL); physical therapy (DPT); physician assistant studies (MPAS); reading specialist (MA Ed). *Program availability:* Part-time. *Degree requirements:* For master's, thesis optional; for doctorate, thesis/dissertation optional. *Entrance requirements:* For master's, GRE or PRAXIS I, official transcripts from all colleges previously attended, three professional recommendations, essay. Additional exam requirements/recommendations for international students: recommended—TOEFL, IELTS (minimum score 6). Electronic applications accepted. *Expenses:* Contact institution.

**Emory University,** School of Medicine, Programs in Allied Health Professions, Physician Assistant Program, Atlanta, GA 30322. Offers MM Sc. *Accreditation:* ARC-PA. *Entrance requirements:* For master's, GRE General Test. Additional exam requirements/recommendations for international students: required—TOEFL (minimum score 69 iBT). Electronic applications accepted. *Expenses:* Contact institution.

**Florida Gulf Coast University,** Elaine Nicpon Marieb College of Health and Human Services, Program in Physician Assistant Studies, Fort Myers, FL 33965-6565. Offers MPAS. *Entrance requirements:* Additional exam requirements/recommendations for international students: required—TOEFL (minimum score 550 paper-based). Electronic applications accepted. *Expenses: Tuition, area resident:* Full-time $6974; part-time $4350 per credit hour. Tuition, state resident: full-time $6974; part-time $4350 per credit hour. Tuition, nonresident: full-time $28,169; part-time $17,595 per credit hour. *International tuition:* $28,169 full-time. *Required fees:* $2027; $1267 per credit hour. $507 per semester. Tuition and fees vary according to course load.

**Florida International University,** Herbert Wertheim College of Medicine, Miami, FL 33199. Offers biomedical sciences (PhD); medicine (MD); physician assistant studies (MPAS). *Accreditation:* LCME/AMA. *Faculty:* 75 full-time (36 women), 76 part-time/adjunct (23 women). *Students:* 632 full-time (366 women), 1 (woman) part-time; includes 416 minority (41 Black or African American, non-Hispanic/Latino; 112 Asian, non-Hispanic/Latino; 235 Hispanic/Latino; 28 Two or more races, non-Hispanic/Latino), 7 international. Average age 26. 5,124 applicants, 4% accepted, 171 enrolled. In 2019, 44 master's, 124 doctorates awarded. *Entrance requirements:* For doctorate, MCAT (minimum score of 25), minimum overall GPA of 3.0; 3 letters of recommendation, 2 from basic science faculty (biology, chemistry, physics, math) and 1 from any other faculty member. *Application deadline:* For fall admission, 12/15 for domestic students. Application fee: $160. Electronic applications accepted. *Expenses:* Contact institution. *Financial support:* Institutionally sponsored loans and scholarships/grants available. Financial award application deadline: 3/1; financial award applicants required to submit FAFSA. *Unit head:* Dr. Robert Sackstein, Dean, E-mail: med.admissions@fiu.edu. *Application contact:* Cristina M. Arabatzis, Assistant Director of Admissions, 305-348-0639, Fax: 305-348-0650, E-mail: carabatz@fiu.edu. Website: http://medicine.fiu.edu/

**Franciscan Missionaries of Our Lady University,** School of Health Professions, Baton Rouge, LA 70808. Offers health administration (MHA); nutritional sciences (MS); physical therapy (DPT); physician assistant studies (MMS).

**Francis Marion University,** Graduate Programs, Physician Assistant Program, Florence, SC 29502-0547. Offers MPAS. *Entrance requirements:* For master's, GRE, bachelor's degree with minimum GPA of 3.0, official transcripts, 3 letters of recommendation, 250 hours of clinical work, criminal background check, personal statement, proof of immunizations. Electronic applications accepted. *Expenses: Tuition, area resident:* Full-time $10,612; part-time $530.60 per credit hour. Tuition, state resident: full-time $10,612; part-time $530.60 per credit hour. Tuition, nonresident: full-time $21,224; part-time $1061.20 per credit hour. *International tuition:* $21,224 full-time. *Required fees:* $312; $156 per credit hour. $332 per semester. Tuition and fees vary according to program.

**Franklin Pierce University,** Graduate and Professional Studies, Rindge, NH 03461-0060. Offers curriculum and instruction (M Ed); elementary education (MS Ed); emerging network technologies (Graduate Certificate); energy and sustainability studies (MBA, Graduate Certificate); health administration (MBA, Graduate Certificate); human resource management (MBA, Graduate Certificate); information technology (MBA); leadership (MBA); nursing education (MS); nursing leadership (MS); physical therapy (DPT); physician assistant studies (MPAS); special education (M Ed); sports management (MBA). *Accreditation:* APTA. *Program availability:* Part-time, 100% online, blended/hybrid learning. *Degree requirements:* For master's, concentrated original research projects; student teaching; fieldwork and/or internship; leadership project; PRAXIS I and II (for M Ed); for doctorate, concentrated original research projects, clinical fieldwork and/or internship, leadership project. *Entrance requirements:* For master's, minimum GPA of 2.5, 3 letters of recommendation; competencies in accounting, economics, statistics, and computer skills through life experience or undergraduate coursework (for MBA); certification/e-portfolio, minimum C grade in all education courses (for M Ed); license to practice as RN (for MS); for doctorate, GRE, 80 hours of observation/work in PT settings; completion of anatomy, chemistry, physics, and statistics; minimum GPA of 3.0. Additional exam requirements/recommendations for international students: required—TOEFL (minimum score 550 paper-based; 61 iBT). Electronic applications accepted.

**Gannon University,** School of Graduate Studies, Morosky College of Health Professions and Sciences, School of Health Professions, Program in Physician Assistant Science, Erie, PA 16541-0001. Offers MPAS. *Accreditation:* ARC-PA. *Degree requirements:* For master's, thesis or alternative, research project, practicum. *Entrance requirements:* For master's, baccalaureate degree with minimum GPA of 3.0, 3 letters of recommendation, interview, transcript, 30 hours of documented volunteer/paid medical experience or shadowing a physician assistant. Additional exam requirements/recommendations for international students: required—TOEFL (minimum score 600 paper-based). Electronic applications accepted. Application fee is waived when completed online. *Expenses:* Contact institution.

**Gardner-Webb University,** Graduate School, Program in Physician Assistant Studies, Boiling Springs, NC 28017. Offers MPAS. *Expenses:* Contact institution.

**The George Washington University,** School of Medicine and Health Sciences, Health Sciences Programs, Physician Assistant Program, Washington, DC 20052. Offers MSHS. *Accreditation:* ARC-PA. *Entrance requirements:* For master's, GRE General Test, BA/BS with clinical experience. Electronic applications accepted.

**Grand Valley State University,** College of Health Professions, Physician Assistant Studies Program, Allendale, MI 49401-9403. Offers MPAS. *Accreditation:* ARC-PA. *Faculty:* 11 full-time (7 women), 2 part-time/adjunct (1 woman). *Students:* 140 full-time (101 women); includes 8 minority (1 American Indian or Alaska Native, non-Hispanic/Latino; 2 Asian, non-Hispanic/Latino; 2 Hispanic/Latino; 3 Two or more races, non-Hispanic/Latino). Average age 25. 382 applicants, 14% accepted, 48 enrolled. In 2019,

48 master's awarded. *Degree requirements:* For master's, thesis optional, clinical rotations, project. *Entrance requirements:* For master's, United States Medical Licensing Exam, minimum GPA of 3.0 overall, in last 60 hours, and on prerequisite courses; 2 recommendations; interview; minimum of 500 hours in volunteer, work, or observational experience in health care environment. Additional exam requirements/recommendations for international students: required—TOEFL (minimum iBT score of 80), IELTS (6.5), or Michigan English Language Assessment Battery (77). *Application deadline:* For fall admission, 9/15 priority date for domestic and international students. Application fee: $30. Electronic applications accepted. *Expenses:* $733 per credit hour, 103 credit hours. *Financial support:* In 2019–20, 17 students received support, including 17 fellowships, 2 research assistantships with full and partial tuition reimbursements available (averaging $8,000 per year); institutionally sponsored loans also available. Financial award application deadline: 2/15. *Unit head:* Dr. Andrew Booth, Director, 616-331-5991, Fax: 616-331-5654, E-mail: bootha@gvsu.edu. *Application contact:* Darlene Zwart, Student Services Coordinator, 616-331-3958, Fax: 616-331-5643, E-mail: zwartda@gvsu.edu.
Website: http://www.gvsu.edu/pas/

**Harding University,** College of Allied Health, Program in Physician Assistant, Searcy, AR 72149-0001. Offers MS. *Faculty:* 7 full-time (4 women), 1 part-time/adjunct. *Students:* 107 full-time (84 women); includes 19 minority (4 Black or African American, non-Hispanic/Latino; 2 American Indian or Alaska Native, non-Hispanic/Latino; 8 Asian, non-Hispanic/Latino; 4 Hispanic/Latino; 1 Two or more races, non-Hispanic/Latino). Average age 27. 881 applicants, 5% accepted, 36 enrolled. In 2019, 34 master's awarded. *Entrance requirements:* For master's, GRE. Additional exam requirements/recommendations for international students: required—TOEFL. *Application deadline:* For fall admission, 11/1 for domestic and international students. Application fee: $25. *Expenses:* Contact institution. *Unit head:* Dr. Mary Madill, Program Director, 501-279-5642, E-mail: mmadill@harding.edu. *Application contact:* Marcia Murphy, Admissions Director, 501-279-5642, Fax: 501-279-4811, E-mail: paprogram@harding.edu.
Website: http://www.harding.edu/paprogram/

**Hardin-Simmons University,** Graduate School, Holland School of Sciences and Mathematics, Abilene, TX 79698-0001. Offers physical therapy (DPT); physician assistant studies (MPAS). *Program availability:* Part-time. *Degree requirements:* For master's, comprehensive exam, thesis or alternative, internship; for doctorate, comprehensive exam, thesis/dissertation or alternative. *Entrance requirements:* For master's, minimum undergraduate GPA of 3.0 in major, 2.7 overall; 2 semesters of course work each in biology, chemistry and geology; interview; writing sample; occupational experience; for doctorate, letters of recommendation, interview, writing sample. Additional exam requirements/recommendations for international students: required—TOEFL (minimum score 550 paper-based; 79 iBT). Electronic applications accepted.

**High Point University,** Norcross Graduate School, High Point, NC 27268. Offers athletic training (MSAT); business administration (MBA); educational leadership (M Ed, Ed D); elementary education (M Ed, MAT); pharmacy (Pharm D); physical therapy (DPT); physician assistant studies (MPAS); secondary mathematics (M Ed, MAT); special education (M Ed); strategic communication (MA). *Accreditation:* NCATE. *Program availability:* Part-time, evening/weekend. *Degree requirements:* For master's, comprehensive exam (for some programs), thesis (for some programs). *Entrance requirements:* For master's, GMAT (MBA), GRE, MAT, minimum GPA of 3.0. Additional exam requirements/recommendations for international students: required—TOEFL (minimum score 550 paper-based). Electronic applications accepted.

**Hofstra University,** Hofstra Northwell School of Nursing and Physician Assistant Studies, Program in Physician Assistant, Hempstead, NY 11549. Offers physician assistant studies (MS). *Students:* 143 full-time (108 women); includes 24 minority (12 Asian, non-Hispanic/Latino; 10 Hispanic/Latino; 2 Native Hawaiian or other Pacific Islander, non-Hispanic/Latino), 1 international. Average age 24. 1,950 applicants, 4% accepted, 55 enrolled. In 2019, 47 master's awarded. *Degree requirements:* For master's, comprehensive exam, minimum GPA of 3.0. *Entrance requirements:* For master's, bachelor's degree in biology or equivalent, 2 letters of recommendation, essay, minimum GPA of 3.0. Additional exam requirements/recommendations for international students: required—TOEFL (minimum score 550 paper-based; 80 iBT); recommended—IELTS (minimum score 6.5). *Application deadline:* For fall admission, 10/1 for domestic students. Application fee: $75. Electronic applications accepted. *Expenses: Tuition:* Full-time $25,164; part-time $1398 per credit. *Required fees:* $580; $165 per semester. Tuition and fees vary according to course load, degree level and program. *Financial support:* In 2019–20, 11 students received support, including 11 fellowships with full and partial tuition reimbursements available (averaging $6,745 per year); research assistantships with full and partial tuition reimbursements available, career-related internships or fieldwork, Federal Work-Study, institutionally sponsored loans, scholarships/grants, traineeships, tuition waivers (full and partial), unspecified assistantships, and scholarships and endowed scholarships also available. Support available to part-time students. Financial award applicants required to submit FAFSA. *Unit head:* Carina Loscalzo, Chairperson, 516-463-4412, Fax: 516-463-5177, E-mail: carina.loscalzo@hofstra.edu. *Application contact:* Sunil Samuel, Assistant Vice President of Admissions, 516-463-4723, Fax: 516-463-4664, E-mail: graduateadmission@hofstra.edu.
Website: http://www.hofstra.edu/academics/colleges/healthscienceshumanservices/

**Howard University,** College of Nursing and Allied Health Sciences, Division of Allied Health Sciences, Washington, DC 20059-0002. Offers occupational therapy (MSOT); physical therapy (DPT); physician assistant (MPA). *Accreditation:* AOTA.

**Idaho State University,** Graduate School, College of Health Professions, Department of Physician Assistant Studies, Pocatello, ID 83209-8253. Offers MPAS. *Accreditation:* ARC-PA. *Degree requirements:* For master's, comprehensive exam, thesis (for some programs), portfolio, clinical year, oral case presentation. *Entrance requirements:* For master's, GRE General Test, minimum GPA of 3.0, letters of reference. Additional exam requirements/recommendations for international students: required—TOEFL (minimum score 500 paper-based). Electronic applications accepted. *Expenses:* Contact institution.

**Indiana State University,** College of Graduate and Professional Studies, College of Health and Human Services, Department of Applied Medicine and Rehabilitation, Terre Haute, IN 47809. Offers athletic training (MS, DAT); occupational therapy (MS); physical therapy (DPT); physician assistant (MS). *Accreditation:* AOTA. *Degree requirements:* For master's, thesis or alternative. *Entrance requirements:* For master's, GRE General Test. Electronic applications accepted.

**James Madison University,** The Graduate School, College of Health and Behavioral Studies, Program in Physician Assistant Studies, Harrisonburg, VA 22807. Offers MPAS. *Accreditation:* ARC-PA. *Program availability:* Part-time. *Students:* 91 full-time (69 women); includes 14 minority (2 Black or African American, non-Hispanic/Latino; 6 Asian, non-Hispanic/Latino; 3 Hispanic/Latino; 3 Two or more races, non-Hispanic/Latino). Average age 30. In 2019, 30 master's awarded. Application fee: $60. Electronic applications accepted. *Financial support:* Fellowships available. Financial award application deadline: 3/1; financial award applicants required to submit FAFSA. *Unit head:* Dr. Allen Lewis, Department Head, 540-568-6510, E-mail: lewis6an@jmu.edu. *Application contact:* Lynette D. Michael, Director of Graduate Admissions and Student Records, 540-568-6131 Ext. 6395, Fax: 540-568-7860, E-mail: michaeld@jmu.edu.
Website: http://www.healthsci.jmu.edu/PA/index.html

**Jefferson College of Health Sciences,** Program in Physician Assistant, Roanoke, VA 24013. Offers MS. *Accreditation:* ARC-PA. *Degree requirements:* For master's, rotations. *Entrance requirements:* For master's, GRE. Additional exam requirements/recommendations for international students: required—TOEFL (minimum score 550 paper-based; 80 iBT). Electronic applications accepted.

**Johnson & Wales University,** Graduate Studies, Master of Science Program in Physician Assistant Studies, Providence, RI 02903-3703. Offers MS.

**Keiser University,** MS in Physician Assistant Program, Fort Lauderdale, FL 33309. Offers MS.

**Kettering College,** Program in Physician Assistant Studies, Kettering, OH 45429-1299. Offers MPAS.

**King's College,** Program in Physician Assistant Studies, Wilkes-Barre, PA 18711-0801. Offers MSPAS. *Accreditation:* ARC-PA. *Degree requirements:* For master's, thesis. *Entrance requirements:* For master's, bachelor's degree; minimum cumulative GPA of 3.2 overall and in science; 500 clinical hours of health care experience; 2 letters of reference; personal statement. Additional exam requirements/recommendations for international students: required—TOEFL (minimum score 610 paper-based; 108 iBT). Electronic applications accepted. *Expenses:* Contact institution.

**Le Moyne College,** Department of Physician Assistant Studies, Syracuse, NY 13214. Offers physician assistant (MS). *Accreditation:* ARC-PA. *Faculty:* 4 full-time (2 women), 3 part-time/adjunct (all women). *Students:* 133 full-time (103 women), 1 (woman) part-time; includes 15 minority (3 Black or African American, non-Hispanic/Latino; 8 Asian, non-Hispanic/Latino; 4 Hispanic/Latino). Average age 25. 1,127 applicants, 7% accepted, 75 enrolled. In 2019, 67 master's awarded. *Degree requirements:* For master's, masters project, 12-month clinical curriculum comprised of eight rotations; NCCPA certification exam. *Entrance requirements:* For master's, bachelor's degree with minimum GPA of 3.2, 750 hours of documented patient contact, prerequisite courses, interview, 3 letters of recommendation. Additional exam requirements/recommendations for international students: required—TOEFL (minimum score 79 iBT); recommended—IELTS (minimum score 6.5). *Application deadline:* For fall admission, 10/1 for domestic and international students. Application fee: $179. Electronic applications accepted. *Expenses:* Contact institution. *Financial support:* In 2019–20, 17 students received support. Career-related internships or fieldwork, Federal Work-Study, scholarships/grants, and health care benefits available. Financial award applicants required to submit FAFSA. *Unit head:* Elizabeth W. Mercer, Program Director, Department of Physician Assistant Studies, 315-445-4745, Fax: 315-445-4602, E-mail: physassist@lemoyne.edu. *Application contact:* Teresa M. Renn, Director of Graduate Admission, 315-445-5444, Fax: 315-445-6092, E-mail: GradEducation@lemoyne.edu.
Website: http://www.lemoyne.edu/pa

**Lenoir-Rhyne University,** Graduate Programs, School of Physician Assistant Studies, Hickory, NC 28601. Offers MS. *Expenses:* Contact institution.

**Lock Haven University of Pennsylvania,** College of Natural, Behavioral and Health Sciences, Lock Haven, PA 17745-2390. Offers actuarial science (PSM); athletic training (MS); health promotion/education (MHS); healthcare management (MHS); physician assistant (MHS). *Accreditation:* ARC-PA. *Entrance requirements:* For master's, minimum undergraduate GPA of 3.0. Additional exam requirements/recommendations for international students: required—TOEFL. Electronic applications accepted.

**Loma Linda University,** School of Allied Health Professions, Department of Physician Assistant Sciences, Loma Linda, CA 92350. Offers MPA. *Accreditation:* ARC-PA. *Entrance requirements:* For master's, minimum GPA of 3.0. Additional exam requirements/recommendations for international students: required—TOEFL (minimum score 550 paper-based).

**Long Island University - Brooklyn,** School of Health Professions, Brooklyn, NY 11201-8423. Offers athletic training and sport sciences (MS); community health (MS Ed); exercise science (MS); forensic social work (Advanced Certificate); occupational therapy (MS); physical therapy (DPT); physician assistant (MS); public health (MPH); social work (MSW); speech-language pathology (MS). *Accreditation:* AOTA; CEPH. *Degree requirements:* For master's, comprehensive exam (for some programs), thesis (for some programs); for doctorate, comprehensive exam (for some programs). *Entrance requirements:* For master's and doctorate, GRE. Additional exam requirements/recommendations for international students: required—TOEFL (minimum score 550 paper-based; 79 iBT). Electronic applications accepted.

**Louisiana State University Health Sciences Center,** School of Allied Health Professions, Program in Physician Assistant Studies, New Orleans, LA 70112-2223. Offers MPAS. *Faculty:* 5 full-time (4 women). *Students:* 58 full-time (46 women); includes 16 minority (6 Black or African American, non-Hispanic/Latino; 4 Asian, non-Hispanic/Latino; 2 Hispanic/Latino; 4 Two or more races, non-Hispanic/Latino). Average age 25. 348 applicants, 9% accepted, 30 enrolled. In 2019, 30 master's awarded. *Entrance requirements:* For master's, GRE (minimum score 153 verbal, 144 quantitative, and 3.5 analytical), minimum cumulative and overall science GPA of 3.0, 80 hours of documented healthcare experience. Additional exam requirements/recommendations for international students: required—TOEFL (minimum score 550 paper-based; 79 iBT). *Application deadline:* For fall admission, 8/1 for domestic students. Application fee: $175. Electronic applications accepted. *Expenses:* Contact institution. *Financial support:* Application deadline: 4/15; applicants required to submit FAFSA. *Unit head:* Rachel Chappell, Program Director, 504-556-3424, Fax: 504-556-3421, E-mail: Rchap2@lsuhsc.edu. *Application contact:* Yudialys D. Cazanas, Student Affairs Director, 504-568-4253, Fax: 504-568-3185, E-mail: ydelga@lsuhsc.edu.
Website: http://alliedhealth.lsuhsc.edu/pa/

**Marietta College,** Program in Physician Assistant Studies, Marietta, OH 45750-4000. Offers MS. *Accreditation:* ARC-PA. *Faculty:* 7 full-time (2 women). *Students:* 70 full-time (58 women); includes 5 minority (2 Black or African American, non-Hispanic/Latino; 2 Asian, non-Hispanic/Latino; 1 Hispanic/Latino). Average age 25. 1,085 applicants, 6% accepted, 36 enrolled. In 2019, 35 master's awarded. *Entrance requirements:* For master's, MCAT and/or GRE, official transcripts. Additional exam requirements/recommendations for international students: recommended—TOEFL (minimum score 100 iBT). *Application deadline:* For fall admission, 11/1 for domestic students. Electronic applications accepted. *Expenses:* Contact institution. *Financial support:* Scholarships/grants available. *Unit head:* Miranda Collins, Director, 740-376-4953, E-mail: miranda.collins@marietta.edu. *Application contact:* Lori Hart, Administrative Coordinator, 740-376-4458, E-mail: lori.hart@marietta.edu.
Website: https://www.marietta.edu/pa-program

**Marquette University,** Graduate School, College of Health Sciences, Department of Physician Assistant Studies, Milwaukee, WI 53201-1881. Offers MPAS. *Accreditation:* ARC-PA. *Degree requirements:* For master's, clinical clerkship experience, capstone project. *Entrance requirements:* For master's, GRE General Test, three letters of recommendation, minimum GPA of 3.0, official transcripts from all current and previous institutions except Marquette. Additional exam requirements/recommendations for

international students: required—TOEFL (minimum score 530 paper-based). Electronic applications accepted. *Expenses:* Contact institution.

**Mary Baldwin University,** Graduate Studies, Program in Physician Assistant, Staunton, VA 24401-3610. Offers MSPA.

**Marywood University,** Academic Affairs, College of Health and Human Services, Department of Physician Assistant Studies, Scranton, PA 18509-1598. Offers MS. *Accreditation:* ARC-PA. Electronic applications accepted. *Expenses:* Contact institution.

**MCPHS University,** Graduate Studies, Programs in Physician Assistant Studies, Accelerated Program in Physician Assistant Studies (Manchester/Worcester), Boston, MA 02115-5896. Offers MPAS. *Accreditation:* ARC-PA. *Entrance requirements:* Additional exam requirements/recommendations for international students: required—TOEFL (minimum score 550 paper-based; 79 iBT). Electronic applications accepted.

**MCPHS University,** Graduate Studies, Programs in Physician Assistant Studies, Program in Physician Assistant Studies (Boston), Boston, MA 02115-5896. Offers MPAS. *Entrance requirements:* Additional exam requirements/recommendations for international students: required—TOEFL (minimum score 550 paper-based; 79 iBT).

**Medical University of South Carolina,** College of Health Professions, Physician Assistant Studies Program, Charleston, SC 29425. Offers MS. *Accreditation:* ARC-PA. *Degree requirements:* For master's, clinical clerkship, research project. *Entrance requirements:* For master's, GRE General Test, interview, minimum GPA of 3.0, 3 references. Additional exam requirements/recommendations for international students: required—TOEFL (minimum score 600 paper-based). Electronic applications accepted.

**Mercer University,** Graduate Studies, Cecil B. Day Campus, College of Health Professions, Atlanta, GA 31207. Offers athletic training (MAT); clinical medical psychology (Psy D); physical therapy (DPT); physician assistant studies (MM Sc); public health (MPH); DPT/MBA; DPT/MPH; MM Sc/MPH; Pharm D/MPH. *Accreditation:* CEPH. *Faculty:* 17 full-time (13 women), 17 part-time/adjunct (10 women). *Students:* 360 full-time (292 women), 74 part-time (58 women); includes 171 minority (100 Black or African American, non-Hispanic/Latino; 36 Asian, non-Hispanic/Latino; 31 Hispanic/Latino; 4 Two or more races, non-Hispanic/Latino), 10 international. Average age 26. In 2019, 141 master's, 51 doctorates awarded. *Expenses:* Contact institution. *Financial support:* Federal Work-Study, traineeships, and unspecified assistantships available. *Unit head:* Dr. Lisa Lundquist, Dean/Clinical Professor, 678-547-6308, E-mail: lundquist_lm@mercer.edu. *Application contact:* Laura Ellison, Director of Admissions and Student Affairs, 678-547-6391, E-mail: ellison_la@mercer.edu.
Website: http://chp.mercer.edu/

**Mercy College,** School of Health and Natural Sciences, Program in Physician Assistant Studies, Dobbs Ferry, NY 10522-1189. Offers MS. *Accreditation:* ARC-PA. *Students:* 106 full-time (85 women), 9 part-time (6 women); includes 51 minority (9 Black or African American, non-Hispanic/Latino; 26 Asian, non-Hispanic/Latino; 11 Hispanic/Latino; 5 Two or more races, non-Hispanic/Latino), 1 international. Average age 27. 295 applicants, 26% accepted, 54 enrolled. In 2019, 56 master's awarded. *Degree requirements:* For master's, Capstone project; clinical practicum. *Entrance requirements:* For master's, program application; transcript(s); three letters of recommendation; interview; personal statement; demonstrated experience working in a healthcare setting; completion of all prerequisite courses. Additional exam requirements/recommendations for international students: required—TOEFL (minimum score 80 iBT), IELTS (minimum score 6.5). *Application deadline:* For fall admission, 11/1 for domestic students. Application fee: $62. Electronic applications accepted. *Expenses:* Contact institution. *Financial support:* Career-related internships or fieldwork, Federal Work-Study, scholarships/grants, and unspecified assistantships available. Support available to part-time students. Financial award applicants required to submit FAFSA. *Unit head:* Dr. Joan Toglia, Dean, School of Health and Natural Sciences, 914-674-7746, E-mail: jtoglia@mercy.edu. *Application contact:* Allison Gurdineer, Executive Director of Admissions, 877-637-2946, Fax: 914-674-7382, E-mail: admissions@mercy.edu.
Website: https://www.mercy.edu/degrees-programs/ms-physician-assistant

**Mercyhurst University,** Graduate Studies, Program in Physician Assistant Studies, Erie, PA 16546. Offers MS.

**Methodist University,** School of Graduate Studies, Program in Physician Assistant Studies, Fayetteville, NC 28311-1498. Offers MMS. *Accreditation:* ARC-PA. *Degree requirements:* For master's, comprehensive exam. *Entrance requirements:* For master's, GRE, bachelor's degree from four-year, regionally-accredited college or university; minimum of 500 hours' clinical experience with direct patient contact; minimum GPA of 3.0 on all college level work attempted, 3.2 on medical core prerequisites (recommended). Additional exam requirements/recommendations for international students: required—TOEFL (minimum score 500 paper-based; 60 iBT).

**MGH Institute of Health Professions,** School of Health and Rehabilitation Sciences, Program in Physician Assistant Studies, Boston, MA 02129. Offers MPAS.

**Midwestern University, Downers Grove Campus,** College of Health Sciences, Illinois Campus, Program in Physician Assistant Studies, Downers Grove, IL 60515-1235. Offers MMS. *Accreditation:* ARC-PA. *Entrance requirements:* For master's, GRE General Test. *Expenses:* Contact institution.

**Midwestern University, Glendale Campus,** College of Health Sciences, Arizona Campus, Program in Physician Assistant Studies, Glendale, AZ 85308. Offers MMS. *Accreditation:* ARC-PA. *Entrance requirements:* For master's, GRE. *Expenses:* Contact institution.

**Milligan University,** Area of Physician Assistant Studies, Milligan College, TN 37682. Offers MSPAS. *Faculty:* 6 full-time (3 women), 4 part-time/adjunct (3 women). *Students:* 49 full-time (32 women); includes 3 minority (1 Black or African American, non-Hispanic/Latino; 1 Asian, non-Hispanic/Latino; 1 Two or more races, non-Hispanic/Latino). Average age 28. 226 applicants, 21% accepted, 26 enrolled. *Degree requirements:* For master's, thesis or alternative. *Entrance requirements:* For master's, GRE, CASPA application, baccalaureate degree with minimum cumulative GPA of 3.0 overall and for prerequisite science courses, health care experience with minimum of 300 documented hours of direct patient care or observation experience, three references, background check, CPR certification. Additional exam requirements/recommendations for international students: required—TOEFL (minimum score 550 paper-based, 79 iBT) or IELTS (6.5). *Application deadline:* For spring admission, 9/1 for domestic students. Application fee: $120. Electronic applications accepted. *Expenses:* 108 hr program: $770/hr; $75 one-time records fee; $325/semester (technology and activity fees). *Financial support:* Scholarships/grants available. Financial award application deadline: 12/1; financial award applicants required to submit FAFSA. *Unit head:* Andrew Hull, Area Chair and Director, 423-461-1558, Fax: 423-461-1518, E-mail: awhull@milligan.edu. *Application contact:* Rebekah Bess, Program Secretary, 423-461-1557, Fax: 423-461-1518, E-mail: rbess@milligan.edu.
Website: http://www.milligan.edu/pa/

**Missouri State University,** Graduate College, College of Health and Human Services, Department of Physician Assistant Studies, Springfield, MO 65897. Offers MS. *Accreditation:* ARC-PA. *Degree requirements:* For master's, comprehensive exam, thesis or alternative. *Entrance requirements:* For master's, GRE General Test, minimum GPA of 3.0; CASPA. Additional exam requirements/recommendations for international students: required—TOEFL (minimum score 550 paper-based; 79 iBT), IELTS (minimum score 6). Electronic applications accepted. *Expenses: Tuition, area resident:* Full-time $2600; part-time $1735 per credit hour. Tuition, nonresident: full-time $5240; part-time $3495 per credit hour. *International tuition:* $5240 full-time. *Required fees:* $530; $438 per credit hour. Tuition and fees vary according to class time, course level, course load, degree level, campus/location and program.

**New York Institute of Technology,** School of Health Professions, Department of Physician Assistant Studies, Old Westbury, NY 11568. Offers MS. *Accreditation:* ARC-PA. *Faculty:* 9 full-time (7 women), 16 part-time/adjunct (10 women). *Students:* 158 full-time (121 women), 2 part-time (both women); includes 28 minority (2 Black or African American, non-Hispanic/Latino; 16 Asian, non-Hispanic/Latino; 8 Hispanic/Latino; 2 Two or more races, non-Hispanic/Latino), 1 international. Average age 26. 1,547 applicants, 8% accepted, 56 enrolled. In 2019, 43 master's awarded. *Entrance requirements:* For master's, Bachelor's degree, preferably in a science or health-related; minimum GPA of 3.0, minimum GPA of 3.4 in science courses; minimum grade of B in all prerequisite courses; minimum of 250 hours of verifiable patient care experience in the U.S. healthcare system; 3 professional letters of recommendation. Additional exam requirements/recommendations for international students: required—TOEFL (minimum score 79 iBT), IELTS (minimum score 6), PTE (minimum score 53), Duolingo English Test. *Application deadline:* For fall admission, 10/1 for domestic and international students. Application fee: $50. Electronic applications accepted. *Expenses: Tuition:* Full-time $23,760; part-time $1320 per credit. *Required fees:* $260; $220 per unit. Full-time tuition and fees vary according to degree level and program. Part-time tuition and fees vary according to course load and program. *Financial support:* In 2019–20, 152 students received support. Research assistantships, teaching assistantships, Federal Work-Study, scholarships/grants, and unspecified assistantships available. Financial award application deadline: 2/15; financial award applicants required to submit FAFSA. *Unit head:* Dr. Anoma Zehra Ahmed, Department Chair, 516-686-3871, E-mail: zehra.ahmed@nyit.edu. *Application contact:* Alice Dolitsky, Director, Graduate Admissions, 800-345-6948, Fax: 516-686-1116, E-mail: grad@nyit.edu.
Website: https://www.nyit.edu/health_professions/department_of_physician_assistant_studies

**Northern Arizona University,** College of Health and Human Services, Department of Physician Assistant Studies, Phoenix, AZ 85004. Offers MPAS. *Degree requirements:* For master's, variable foreign language requirement, comprehensive exam (for some programs), thesis (for some programs), fieldwork experience/internship. *Entrance requirements:* For master's, GRE General Test, minimum overall and science course GPA of 3.0; minimum of 40 credits of science courses; minimum of 500 hours of direct patient care experience, paid or volunteer; in-person interview. Additional exam requirements/recommendations for international students: required—TOEFL (minimum score 80 iBT), IELTS (minimum score 6.5). Electronic applications accepted.

**Nova Southeastern University,** Dr. Pallavi Patel College of Health Care Sciences, Fort Lauderdale, FL 33314-7796. Offers anesthesiologist assistant (MSA); audiology (Au D); health science (MH Sc, DHSc, PhD); occupational therapy (MOT, Dr OT, PhD); physical therapy (DPT, TDPT); physician assistant (MMS); speech-language pathology (MS). *Accreditation:* AOTA; ASHA. *Program availability:* Part-time, 100% online, blended/hybrid learning. *Faculty:* 127 full-time (85 women), 107 part-time/adjunct (79 women). *Students:* 1,336 full-time (992 women), 950 part-time (824 women); includes 839 minority (195 Black or African American, non-Hispanic/Latino; 4 American Indian or Alaska Native, non-Hispanic/Latino; 165 Asian, non-Hispanic/Latino; 397 Hispanic/Latino; 3 Native Hawaiian or other Pacific Islander, non-Hispanic/Latino; 75 Two or more races, non-Hispanic/Latino), 26 international. Average age 30. 634 applicants, 28% accepted, 159 enrolled. In 2019, 613 master's, 261 doctorates awarded. Terminal master's awarded for partial completion of doctoral program. *Degree requirements:* For doctorate, comprehensive exam, thesis/dissertation (for some programs), 12-month full-time clinical externship experience. *Entrance requirements:* For master's, GRE General Test; for doctorate, personal interview, essay in application,additional letters may be requested by the program after initial review of application if so warranted. *Application deadline:* Applications are processed on a rolling basis. Application fee: $50. Electronic applications accepted. *Expenses:* Contact institution. *Financial support:* Federal Work-Study, institutionally sponsored loans, and scholarships/grants available. Financial award application deadline: 4/15; financial award applicants required to submit FAFSA. *Unit head:* Dr. Stanley Wilson, Dean, 954-262-1203, E-mail: swilson@nova.edu. *Application contact:* Joycelyn Vogt, Director of Admissions and Outreach, 954-262-1200, Fax: 954-262-1181, E-mail: joycelyn.vogt@nova.edu.
Website: http://healthsciences.nova.edu/

**Ohio Dominican University,** Division of Physician Assistant Studies, Columbus, OH 43219-2099. Offers physician assistant studies (MS). *Faculty:* 7 full-time (4 women), 2 part-time/adjunct (0 women). *Students:* 97 full-time (68 women), 50 part-time (39 women); includes 7 minority (1 Asian, non-Hispanic/Latino; 2 Hispanic/Latino; 4 Two or more races, non-Hispanic/Latino), 1 international. Average age 25. 651 applicants, 11% accepted, 50 enrolled. In 2019, 51 master's awarded. *Entrance requirements:* For master's, GRE and/or MCAT, bachelor's degree from accredited college or university with minimum GPA of 3.0 overall and in science; minimum of 250 hours of documented patient-care experience. Additional exam requirements/recommendations for international students: required—TOEFL (minimum score 550 paper-based), IELTS (minimum score 6.5). *Application deadline:* For fall admission, 10/1 for domestic and international students. Applications are processed on a rolling basis. Electronic applications accepted. *Expenses:* $823 per credit hour tuition. *Financial support:* Applicants required to submit FAFSA. *Unit head:* Prof. Shonna Riedlinger, Program Director, 614-251-8988, E-mail: riedlins@ohiodominican.edu. *Application contact:* John W. Naughton, Vice President for Enrollment and Student Success, 614-251-4721, Fax: 614-251-6654, E-mail: grad@ohiodominican.edu.
Website: http://www.ohiodominican.edu/academics/graduate/mspas

**Oregon Health & Science University,** School of Medicine, Graduate Programs in Medicine, Division of Physician Assistant Education, Portland, OR 97239-3098. Offers physician assistant studies (MPAS). *Accreditation:* ARC-PA. *Entrance requirements:* For master's, GRE, bachelor's degree, 2000 hours of health care experience. Electronic applications accepted. *Expenses:* Contact institution.

**Pace University,** College of Health Professions, Department of Physician Assistant Studies, New York, NY 10038. Offers MS. *Accreditation:* ARC-PA. *Degree requirements:* For master's, comprehensive exam, summative evaluations including 2 objective structured clinical evaluations and comprehensive written clinical exam; final paper; final project including clinical review article suitable for publication in JAAPA. *Entrance requirements:* For master's, baccalaureate degree from accredited institution, minimum science and cumulative GPA of 3.0, minimum 200 hours of direct patient care, 3 references from professionals (1 must be a health care professional), completion of all prerequisite courses at time of CASPA e-submission, no more than 1 grade that is less than a B- in a prerequisite course. Additional exam requirements/recommendations for international students: required—TOEFL, IELTS, PTE, TOEFL (minimum score 100 iBT), IELTS (minimum score 7.5) or PTE (minimum score 61). Electronic applications accepted.

**Pace University,** College of Health Professions, Physician Assistant Program - Pleasantville, New York, NY 10038. Offers MS. *Degree requirements:* For master's, comprehensive exam, https://www.pace.edu/college-health-professions/pa-pleasantville-standards-progression. *Entrance requirements:* For master's, https://www.pace.edu/college-health-professions/pa-pleasantville-academic-prerequisites. Additional exam requirements/recommendations for international students: required—TOEFL (minimum score 88 iBT); recommended—IELTS (minimum score 7), TSE (minimum score 60).

**Pacific University,** School of Physician Assistant Studies, Forest Grove, OR 97116-1797. Offers MS. *Accreditation:* ARC-PA. *Degree requirements:* For master's, comprehensive exam, thesis, clinical project. *Entrance requirements:* For master's, minimum of 1000 hours of direct clinical patient care, prerequisite coursework in science with minimum C average. Additional exam requirements/recommendations for international students: required—TOEFL (minimum score 600 paper-based). *Expenses:* Contact institution.

**Philadelphia College of Osteopathic Medicine,** Graduate and Professional Programs, Physician Assistant Studies Program, Philadelphia, PA 19131. Offers health sciences (MS). *Accreditation:* ARC-PA. *Faculty:* 9 full-time (6 women), 34 part-time/adjunct (11 women). *Students:* 111 full-time (93 women); includes 34 minority (5 Black or African American, non-Hispanic/Latino; 7 Asian, non-Hispanic/Latino; 5 Hispanic/Latino; 17 Two or more races, non-Hispanic/Latino), 1 international. Average age 25. 2,004 applicants, 4% accepted, 59 enrolled. In 2019, 55 master's awarded. *Degree requirements:* For master's, thesis. *Entrance requirements:* For master's, minimum GPA of 3.0; 200 hours of patient contact. Additional exam requirements/recommendations for international students: required—TOEFL (minimum score 79 iBT). *Application deadline:* For fall admission, 12/1 for domestic students. Applications are processed on a rolling basis. Application fee: $75. Electronic applications accepted. *Expenses:* Contact institution. *Financial support:* In 2019–20, 80 students received support. Federal Work-Study, institutionally sponsored loans, and scholarships/grants available. Financial award application deadline: 3/15; financial award applicants required to submit FAFSA. *Unit head:* Laura Levy, Program Director, 215-871-6772, E-mail: lauramo@pcom.edu. *Application contact:* Kevin A. Zajac, Assistant Director of Admissions, 215-871-6700, E-mail: kevinzaj@pcom.edu.
Website: http://www.pcom.edu

**Quinnipiac University,** School of Health Sciences, Program for Physician Assistant, Hamden, CT 06518-1940. Offers MHS. *Accreditation:* ARC-PA. *Degree requirements:* For master's, comprehensive exam. *Entrance requirements:* For master's, minimum GPA of 3.2; course work in biological, physical, and behavioral sciences; interviews; 2500 hours of direct patient care experience. Electronic applications accepted. *Expenses: Tuition:* Part-time $1055 per credit. *Required fees:* $945 per semester. Tuition and fees vary according to course load and program.

**Rocky Mountain College,** Program in Physician Assistant Studies, Billings, MT 59102-1796. Offers MPAS. *Accreditation:* ARC-PA. *Faculty:* 6 full-time (3 women), 2 part-time/adjunct (1 woman). *Students:* 72 full-time (50 women); includes 7 minority (3 Asian, non-Hispanic/Latino; 3 Hispanic/Latino; 1 Two or more races, non-Hispanic/Latino). Average age 27. In 2019, 36 master's awarded. *Entrance requirements:* For master's, GRE (minimum combined verbal and quantitative score of 291), 1500 hours of direct, hands-on patient care. Additional exam requirements/recommendations for international students: required—TOEFL (minimum score 570 paper-based; 88 iBT), IELTS (minimum score 6.5). *Application deadline:* Applications are processed on a rolling basis. Application fee: $80. Electronic applications accepted. *Expenses:* Contact institution. *Financial support:* Applicants required to submit FAFSA. *Unit head:* Adam Mattingly, Program Director, 406-657-1192, E-mail: adam.mattingly@rocky.edu. *Application contact:* Cody Halverson, Coordinator of Admissions for Health Professions, 406-657-1198, E-mail: halversonc@rocky.edu.
Website: https://www.rocky.edu/pa

**Rocky Mountain University of Health Professions,** Program in Physician Assistant Studies, Provo, UT 84606. Offers MPAS.

**Rocky Vista University,** Program in Physician Assistant Studies, Parker, CO 80134. Offers MPAS.

**Rosalind Franklin University of Medicine and Science,** College of Health Professions, Physician Assistant Department, North Chicago, IL 60064-3095. Offers MS. *Accreditation:* ARC-PA. *Degree requirements:* For master's, thesis. *Entrance requirements:* For master's, GRE, writing sample. Additional exam requirements/recommendations for international students: required—TOEFL. Electronic applications accepted.

**Rush University,** College of Health Sciences, Physician Assistant Studies Program, Chicago, IL 60612-3832. Offers MS. *Entrance requirements:* Additional exam requirements/recommendations for international students: required—TOEFL. *Application deadline:* For summer admission, 12/1 for domestic students. Electronic applications accepted. *Financial support:* Scholarships/grants available. Financial award applicants required to submit FAFSA. *Unit head:* Regina Chen, Director, 312-563-3234, E-mail: pa_admissions@rush.edu. *Application contact:* Regina Chen, Director, 312-563-3234, E-mail: pa_admissions@rush.edu.

**Rutgers University - Newark,** School of Health Related Professions, Department of Primary Care, Physician Assistant Program, Newark, NJ 07102. Offers MS. *Accreditation:* ARC-PA. *Degree requirements:* For master's, internship. *Entrance requirements:* For master's, GRE, interview, minimum GPA of 3.0, BS, 3 reference letters. Additional exam requirements/recommendations for international students: required—TOEFL. Electronic applications accepted.

**Sacred Heart University,** Graduate Programs, College of Health Professions, Department of Physician Assistant Studies, Fairfield, CT 06825. Offers MPAS. *Expenses:* Contact institution.

**St. Ambrose University,** College of Health and Human Services, Program in Physician Assistant Studies, Davenport, IA 52803-2898. Offers MPAS.

**St. Catherine University,** Graduate Programs, Program in Physician Assistant Studies, St. Paul, MN 55105. Offers MPAS. *Entrance requirements:* For master's, GRE, personal essay. *Expenses:* Contact institution.

**Saint Francis University,** Department of Physician Assistant Sciences, Loretto, PA 15940-0600. Offers MPAS. *Accreditation:* ARC-PA. *Faculty:* 9 full-time (7 women), 3 part-time/adjunct (2 women). *Students:* 59 full-time (46 women); includes 5 minority (all Asian, non-Hispanic/Latino). Average age 24. 64 applicants, 22% accepted, 9 enrolled. In 2019, 49 master's awarded. *Degree requirements:* For master's, comprehensive exam, capstone, summative evaluation. *Entrance requirements:* For master's, interview. Additional exam requirements/recommendations for international students: required—TOEFL (minimum score 550 paper-based; 70 iBT). *Application deadline:* For fall admission, 10/1 for domestic and international students. Applications are processed on a rolling basis. Application fee: $175. Electronic applications accepted. *Expenses:* 1142 per credit, 600 technology fee, 660 program fee in 4th and 5th year. *Financial support:* Unspecified assistantships available. Financial award applicants required to submit FAFSA. *Unit head:* Dr. Carrie Beebout, MPAS Program Director, 814-472-3128, E-mail: cbeebout@francis.edu. *Application contact:* Dr. Carrie Beebout, MPAS Program Director, 814-472-3128, E-mail: cbeebout@francis.edu.
Website: http://francis.edu/physician-assistant-science/

**Saint Louis University,** Graduate Programs, Doisy College of Health Sciences, Department of Physician Assistant Education, St. Louis, MO 63103. Offers MMS. *Accreditation:* ARC-PA. *Entrance requirements:* Additional exam requirements/recommendations for international students: required—TOEFL (minimum score 86 iBT). Electronic applications accepted.

**Salus University,** College of Health Sciences, Elkins Park, PA 19027-1598. Offers physician assistant (MMS); public health (MPH). *Accreditation:* ARC-PA. *Entrance requirements:* For master's, GRE (recommended). Additional exam requirements/recommendations for international students: required—TOEFL. Electronic applications accepted.

**Samuel Merritt University,** Department of Physician Assistant Studies, Oakland, CA 94609-3108. Offers MPA. *Accreditation:* ARC-PA. *Entrance requirements:* For master's, health care experience, minimum GPA of 3.0, previous course work in statistics. Additional exam requirements/recommendations for international students: required—TOEFL (minimum score 100 iBT). Electronic applications accepted. *Expenses:* Contact institution.

**Seton Hall University,** School of Health and Medical Sciences, Physician Assistant Program, South Orange, NJ 07079-2697. Offers MS. *Accreditation:* ARC-PA. *Entrance requirements:* For master's, GRE, health care experience, interview, minimum GPA of 3.0. Additional exam requirements/recommendations for international students: required—TOEFL. Electronic applications accepted.

**Seton Hill University,** Master of Science Program in Physician Assistant, Greensburg, PA 15601. Offers MS. *Accreditation:* ARC-PA. *Students:* 56. *Entrance requirements:* For master's, minimum GPA of 3.2, transcripts, 3 letters of recommendation, personal statement. Additional exam requirements/recommendations for international students: required—TOEFL (minimum score 650 paper-based; 114 iBT), IELTS (minimum score 7). *Application deadline:* Applications are processed on a rolling basis. Electronic applications accepted. *Expenses:* Contact institution. *Financial support:* Application deadline: 8/15; applicants required to submit FAFSA. *Application contact:* Lis Glessner, Enrollment Operations Director, 724-838-4208, E-mail: lglessner@setonhill.edu.
Website: http://www.setonhill.edu/academics/gradaute_programs/physician_assistant

**Shenandoah University,** School of Health Professions, Winchester, VA 22601. Offers athletic training (MSAT); occupational therapy (MS); performing arts medicine (Certificate); physical therapy (DPT); physician assistant studies (MS); public health (MPH, Certificate). *Program availability:* Part-time, 100% online. *Faculty:* 1 (woman) full-time, 2 part-time/adjunct (both women). *Students:* 3 full-time (2 women), 25 part-time (20 women); includes 8 minority (4 Black or African American, non-Hispanic/Latino; 2 Asian, non-Hispanic/Latino; 2 Hispanic/Latino). Average age 34. 35 applicants, 97% accepted, 6 enrolled. In 2019, 1 other advanced degree awarded. *Degree requirements:* For master's, Practicum experience. *Entrance requirements:* For master's, Minimum GPA: 3.0 cumulative; Prerequisites: Bachelor's Degree or higher. Additional exam requirements/recommendations for international students: required—TOEFL (minimum score 83 iBT). *Application deadline:* For fall admission, 8/1 for domestic students; for spring admission, 12/1 for domestic students. Applications are processed on a rolling basis. Application fee: $30. Electronic applications accepted. *Expenses:* $700 per credit hour; 32 credit hours for program completion. *Financial support:* In 2019–20, 17 students received support, including 1 fellowship (averaging $210 per year); scholarships/grants and Faculty staff grant Public Health Discount (graduate) Valley Health SU Discretionary Award Anatomy and physiology graduate also available. Financial award application deadline: 8/1; financial award applicants required to submit FAFSA. *Unit head:* Michelle Gamber, DrPH, MA, Director, 540-665-5560, Fax: 540-665-5519, E-mail: mgamber@su.edu. *Application contact:* Katie Olivo, Associate Director of Admission, 540-665-5441, Fax: 540-665-4627, E-mail: kolivo@su.edu.
Website: su.edu/public-health/

**Shenandoah University,** School of Health Professions, Division of Physician Assistant Studies, Winchester, VA 22601. Offers physician assistant (MS). *Accreditation:* ARC-PA. *Faculty:* 9 full-time (7 women), 5 part-time/adjunct (3 women). *Students:* 169 full-time (141 women), 1 (woman) part-time; includes 9 minority (1 Black or African American, non-Hispanic/Latino; 3 Asian, non-Hispanic/Latino; 3 Hispanic/Latino; 2 Two or more races, non-Hispanic/Latino), 4 international. Average age 27. 152 applicants, 59% accepted, 61 enrolled. In 2019, 52 master's awarded. *Degree requirements:* For master's, comprehensive exam. *Entrance requirements:* For master's, GRE, bachelor's degree, 3.0 GPA overall and in science, certain coursework, health care experience preferred but not required. Additional exam requirements/recommendations for international students: required—TOEFL (minimum score 83 paper-based); recommended—TSE (minimum score 53). *Application deadline:* For fall admission, 10/1 priority date for domestic students, 9/1 priority date for international students. Applications are processed on a rolling basis. Application fee: $179. Electronic applications accepted. *Expenses: Tuition:* Full-time $16,065; part-time $4075 per year. *Required fees:* $1240. Tuition and fees vary according to course load and program. *Financial support:* In 2019–20, 16 students received support. Institutionally sponsored loans and VTAG for Virginia residents, student loans, private sources available. Financial award application deadline: 8/1; financial award applicants required to submit FAFSA. *Unit head:* Anthony A. Miller, Distinguished Professor and Director, 540-545-7257, Fax: 540-542-6554, E-mail: amiller@su.edu. *Application contact:* Karen Marie O'Neil, Admissions Coordinator, 540-545-7381, Fax: 540-542-6554, E-mail: pa@su.edu.
Website: www.su.edu/pa

**Slippery Rock University of Pennsylvania,** Graduate Studies (Recruitment), College of Health, Engineering, and Science, Department of Physician Assistant Studies, Slippery Rock, PA 16057-1383. Offers MS. *Faculty:* 15 full-time (13 women), 4 part-time/adjunct (all women). *Students:* 91 full-time (71 women); includes 11 minority (1 Black or African American, non-Hispanic/Latino; 5 Asian, non-Hispanic/Latino; 3 Hispanic/Latino; 2 Two or more races, non-Hispanic/Latino). Average age 24. 439 applicants, 27% accepted, 44 enrolled. In 2019, 36 master's awarded. *Degree requirements:* For master's, clinical rotations. *Entrance requirements:* Additional exam requirements/recommendations for international students: required—TOEFL (minimum score 550 paper-based; 80 iBT). *Application deadline:* For summer admission, 5/1 priority date for domestic and international students. Applications are processed on a rolling basis. Application fee: $25 ($30 for international students). Electronic applications accepted. *Expenses:* $516 per credit in-state tuition, $173.61 per credit in-state fees; $774 per credit out-of-state tuition, $224.31 per credit out-of-state fees; $516 per credit in-state tuition, $105.40 per credit in-state fees (for distance education); $526 per credit out-of-state tuition, $118.90 per credit out-of-state fees (for distance education). *Financial support:* Career-related internships or fieldwork, Federal Work-Study, institutionally sponsored loans, scholarships/grants, tuition waivers (partial), and unspecified assistantships available. Support available to part-time students. Financial award application deadline: 5/1; financial award applicants required to submit FAFSA. *Unit head:* Megan Borger, Graduate Coordinator, 724-738-2425, Fax: 724-738-4669, E-mail: megan.borger@sru.edu. *Application contact:* Brandi Weber-Mortimer, Director of

Graduate Admissions, 724-738-2051, Fax: 724-738-2146, E-mail: graduate.admissions@sru.edu.
Website: http://www.sru.edu/academics/colleges-and-departments/ches/departments/physician-assistant-studies

**South College,** Program in Physician Assistant Studies, Knoxville, TN 37917. Offers MHS. *Accreditation:* ARC-PA.

**Southern Illinois University Carbondale,** Graduate School, Graduate Programs in Medicine, Program in Physician Assistant Studies, Carbondale, IL 62901-4701. Offers MSPA. *Accreditation:* ARC-PA. *Entrance requirements:* For master's, GRE, MAT, or MCAT. Additional exam requirements/recommendations for international students: required—TOEFL.

**South University - Savannah,** Graduate Programs, College of Health Professions, Program in Physician Assistant Studies, Savannah, GA 31406. Offers MS. *Accreditation:* ARC-PA.

**South University - Tampa,** Program in Physician Assistant Studies, Tampa, FL 33614. Offers MS.

**Springfield College,** Graduate Programs, Program in Physician Assistant, Springfield, MA 01109-3797. Offers MS. *Accreditation:* ARC-PA. *Program availability:* Part-time. *Degree requirements:* For master's, comprehensive exam. *Entrance requirements:* Additional exam requirements/recommendations for international students: required—TOEFL (minimum score 550 paper-based); recommended—IELTS (minimum score 7). Electronic applications accepted.

**Stephens College,** Division of Graduate and Continuing Studies, Columbia, MO 65215-0002. Offers counseling (M Ed), including addictions counseling, clinical mental health counseling, school counseling; health information administration (Postbaccalaureate Certificate); physician assistant studies (MPAS); TV and screenwriting (MFA). *Program availability:* Part-time, evening/weekend, online learning. *Entrance requirements:* For master's, minimum GPA of 3.0 in last 60 hours. Additional exam requirements/recommendations for international students: required—TOEFL (minimum score 79 iBT). Electronic applications accepted.

**Stony Brook University, State University of New York,** Stony Brook Medicine, School of Health Technology and Management, Stony Brook, NY 11794. Offers applied health informatics (MS); disability studies (Certificate); health administration (MHA); health and rehabilitation sciences (PhD); health care management (Advanced Certificate); health care policy and management (MS); occupational therapy (MS); physical therapy (DPT); physician assistant (MS). *Accreditation:* AOTA; APTA. *Faculty:* 53 full-time (37 women), 54 part-time/adjunct (34 women). *Students:* 605 full-time (417 women), 65 part-time (43 women); includes 225 minority (28 Black or African American, non-Hispanic/Latino; 110 Asian, non-Hispanic/Latino; 73 Hispanic/Latino; 1 Native Hawaiian or other Pacific Islander, non-Hispanic/Latino; 13 Two or more races, non-Hispanic/Latino), 9 international. Average age 26. 1,816 applicants, 21% accepted, 293 enrolled. In 2019, 152 master's, 86 doctorates, 21 other advanced degrees awarded. *Entrance requirements:* For master's, GRE General Test, minimum GPA of 3.0, work experience in field, references; for doctorate, GRE, three references, essay. Additional exam requirements/recommendations for international students: required—TOEFL (minimum score 550 paper-based). *Application deadline:* For fall admission, 1/15 for domestic students; for spring admission, 10/1 for domestic students. Application fee: $100. *Expenses:* Contact institution. *Financial support:* Fellowships, research assistantships, teaching assistantships, career-related internships or fieldwork, Federal Work-Study, and institutionally sponsored loans available. Financial award application deadline: 3/15. *Unit head:* Dr. Stacy Jafee Gropack, Dean and Professor, 631-444-2252, Fax: 631-444-7621, E-mail: stacy.jaffeegropack@stonybrook.edu. *Application contact:* Jessica M Rotolo, Executive Assistant to the Dean, 631-444-2252, Fax: 631-444-7621, E-mail: jessica.rotolo@stonybrook.edu.
Website: http://healthtechnology.stonybrookmedicine.edu/

**Texas Tech University Health Sciences Center,** School of Health Professions, Program in Physician Assistant Studies, Midland, TX 79430. Offers MPAS. *Accreditation:* ARC-PA. *Faculty:* 8 full-time (6 women), 9 part-time/adjunct (5 women). *Students:* 111 full-time (93 women); includes 51 minority (5 Black or African American, non-Hispanic/Latino; 14 Asian, non-Hispanic/Latino; 27 Hispanic/Latino; 5 Two or more races, non-Hispanic/Latino). Average age 26. 1,736 applicants, 3% accepted, 57 enrolled. In 2019, 54 master's awarded. *Entrance requirements:* For master's, GRE. Additional exam requirements/recommendations for international students: required—TOEFL. *Application deadline:* For summer admission, 10/1 priority date for domestic students. Applications are processed on a rolling basis. Application fee: $75. Electronic applications accepted. *Financial support:* In 2019–20, 114 students received support. Institutionally sponsored loans and scholarships/grants available. Financial award application deadline: 9/1; financial award applicants required to submit FAFSA. *Unit head:* Christina Robohm, Program Director, 432-620-1120, Fax: 432-620-8605, E-mail: health.professions@ttuhsc.edu. *Application contact:* Lindsay Johnson, Associate Dean for Admissions and Student Affairs, 806-743-3220, Fax: 806-743-2994, E-mail: health.professions@ttuhsc.edu.
Website: http://www.ttuhsc.edu/health-professions/master-physician-assistant-studies/

**Thomas Jefferson University,** Jefferson College of Health Professions, Department of Physician Assistant Studies, Philadelphia, PA 19107. Offers MS. *Degree requirements:* For master's, comprehensive exam, thesis. *Entrance requirements:* Additional exam requirements/recommendations for international students: required—TOEFL (minimum score 87 iBT). Electronic applications accepted.

**Towson University,** College of Health Professions, Program in Physician Assistant Studies, Towson, MD 21252-0001. Offers MS. *Accreditation:* ARC-PA. *Students:* 66 full-time (41 women); includes 19 minority (3 Black or African American, non-Hispanic/Latino; 9 Asian, non-Hispanic/Latino; 2 Hispanic/Latino; 5 Two or more races, non-Hispanic/Latino), 1 international. *Entrance requirements:* For master's, bachelor's degree with minimum GPA of 3.0, completion of prerequisite math and science courses, minimum of 800 hours of patient contact experience or medical/health-related experience. Additional exam requirements/recommendations for international students: required—TOEFL (minimum score 550 paper-based; 80 iBT). *Application deadline:* For fall admission, 1/17 for domestic students, 5/15 for international students; for spring admission, 10/15 for domestic students, 12/1 for international students. Applications are processed on a rolling basis. Application fee: $45. Electronic applications accepted. *Expenses:* Contact institution. *Financial support:* Application deadline: 4/1. *Unit head:* Dr. Marsha Davenport, Program Director, 410-704-4049, E-mail: paprogram@towson.edu. *Application contact:* Coverley Beidleman, Assistant Director of Graduate Admissions, 410-704-5630, Fax: 410-704-3030, E-mail: grads@towson.edu.
Website: https://www.towson.edu/chp/departments/health-sciences/grad/physician-assistant/

**Trevecca Nazarene University,** Graduate Physician Assistant Program, Nashville, TN 37210-2877. Offers MS. *Accreditation:* ARC-PA. *Degree requirements:* For master's, comprehensive exam, 9 clinical skills rotations, professional assessment, OSCE exam. *Entrance requirements:* Additional exam requirements/recommendations for

international students: required—TOEFL (minimum score 550 paper-based; 80 iBT). *Expenses:* Contact institution.

**Trine University,** Program in Physician Assistant Studies, Angola, IN 46703-1764. Offers MPAS. *Expenses:* Contact institution.

**Tufts University,** School of Medicine, Public Health and Professional Degree Programs, Boston, MA 02111. Offers biomedical sciences (MS); health communication (MS, Certificate); pain research, education and policy (MS, Certificate); physician assistant (MS); public health (MPH, Dr PH), including behavioral science (MPH), biostatistics (MPH), epidemiology (MPH), health communication (MPH), health services (MPH), management and policy (MPH), nutrition (MPH); DMD/MPH; DVM/MPH; JD/MPH; MD/MPH; MMS/MPH; MS/MBA; MS/MPH. *Accreditation:* CEPH (one or more programs are accredited). *Program availability:* Part-time, evening/weekend. *Students:* 450 full-time (291 women), 68 part-time (58 women); includes 201 minority (34 Black or African American, non-Hispanic/Latino; 1 American Indian or Alaska Native, non-Hispanic/Latino; 106 Asian, non-Hispanic/Latino; 41 Hispanic/Latino; 1 Native Hawaiian or other Pacific Islander, non-Hispanic/Latino; 18 Two or more races, non-Hispanic/Latino), 16 international. Average age 27. 1,076 applicants, 70% accepted, 213 enrolled. In 2019, 268 master's, 2 doctorates awarded. Terminal master's awarded for partial completion of doctoral program. *Degree requirements:* For master's, thesis (for some programs); for doctorate, thesis/dissertation. *Entrance requirements:* For master's, GRE General Test, MCAT, or GMAT; LSAT for applicants to the JD/MPH combined degree; for doctorate, GRE General Test or MCAT. Additional exam requirements/recommendations for international students: required—TOEFL (minimum score 100 iBT); recommended—IELTS (minimum score 7), TSE. *Application deadline:* For fall admission, 1/15 priority date for domestic and international students; for spring admission, 10/25 priority date for domestic and international students. Applications are processed on a rolling basis. Application fee: $70. Electronic applications accepted. *Expenses:* Contact institution. *Financial support:* In 2019–20, 13 students received support, including 1 fellowship (averaging $3,000 per year), 50 research assistantships (averaging $1,000 per year), 65 teaching assistantships (averaging $2,000 per year); Federal Work-Study and scholarships/grants also available. Financial award application deadline: 2/23; financial award applicants required to submit FAFSA. *Unit head:* Dr. Aviva Must, Dean, 617-636-0935, Fax: 617-636-0898, E-mail: aviva.must@tufts.edu. *Application contact:* Emily Keily, Director of Admissions, 617-636-0935, Fax: 617-636-0898, E-mail: med-phpd@tufts.edu.
Website: http://publichealth.tufts.edu

**Union College,** Physician Assistant Program, Lincoln, NE 68506-4300. Offers MPAS. *Accreditation:* ARC-PA. *Entrance requirements:* Additional exam requirements/recommendations for international students: required—TOEFL (minimum score 600 paper-based; 100 iBT). Electronic applications accepted. *Expenses:* Contact institution.

**The University of Alabama at Birmingham,** School of Health Professions, Program in Physician Assistant Studies, Birmingham, AL 35294. Offers MSPAS. *Accreditation:* ARC-PA. *Faculty:* 10 full-time (2 women), 13 part-time/adjunct (6 women). *Students:* 183 full-time (143 women); includes 17 minority (8 Black or African American, non-Hispanic/Latino; 5 Asian, non-Hispanic/Latino; 4 Hispanic/Latino). Average age 26. 85 applicants, 91% accepted, 75 enrolled. In 2019, 57 master's awarded. *Entrance requirements:* For master's, GRE or MCAT, minimum GPA of 3.0. Additional exam requirements/recommendations for international students: required—TOEFL. *Application deadline:* For fall admission, 8/1 for domestic students. Application fee: $75. Electronic applications accepted. *Financial support:* Scholarships/grants available. *Unit head:* Dr. James R. Kilgore, Program Director, 205-934-9142, E-mail: jrkilgo@uab.edu. *Application contact:* Dr. James R. Kilgore, Program Director, 205-934-9142, E-mail: jrkilgo@uab.edu.
Website: http://www.uab.edu/shp/cds/physician-assistant

**University of Alaska Anchorage,** College of Health, Department of Health Sciences, Anchorage, AK 99508. Offers physician assistant (MS); public health practice (MPH); MSW/MPH. *Accreditation:* CEPH. *Program availability:* Part-time. *Degree requirements:* For master's, comprehensive exam, thesis. *Entrance requirements:* For master's, writing sample. Additional exam requirements/recommendations for international students: required—TOEFL (minimum score 550 paper-based).

**University of Arkansas for Medical Sciences,** College of Health Professions, Little Rock, AR 72205-7199. Offers audiology (Au D); communication sciences and disorders (MS, PhD); genetic counseling (MS); nuclear medicine advanced associate (MIS); physician assistant studies (MPAS); radiologist assistant (MIS). *Accreditation:* ASHA. *Program availability:* Part-time, online learning. *Degree requirements:* For master's, thesis (for some programs); for doctorate, comprehensive exam (for some programs), thesis/dissertation (for some programs). *Entrance requirements:* For master's, GRE. Additional exam requirements/recommendations for international students: required—TOEFL (minimum score 550 paper-based; 79 iBT). Electronic applications accepted. *Expenses:* Contact institution.

**University of Bridgeport,** Physician Assistant Institute, Bridgeport, CT 06604. Offers MS. *Degree requirements:* For master's, thesis. *Entrance requirements:* Additional exam requirements/recommendations for international students: recommended—TOEFL (minimum score 550 paper-based; 80 iBT), IELTS (minimum score 6.5).

**University of Charleston,** Physician Assistant Program, Charleston, WV 25304-1099. Offers MPAS. Electronic applications accepted.

**University of Colorado Denver,** School of Medicine, Physician Assistant Program, Aurora, CO 80045. Offers child health associate (MPAS), including global health, leadership, education, advocacy, development, and scholarship, pediatric critical and acute care, rural health, urban/underserved populations. *Accreditation:* ARC-PA. *Degree requirements:* For master's, comprehensive exam. *Entrance requirements:* For master's, GRE General Test, minimum GPA of 2.8; 3 letters of recommendation; prerequisite courses in chemistry, biology, general genetics, psychology and statistics; interview. Additional exam requirements/recommendations for international students: required—TOEFL (minimum score 550 paper-based; 80 iBT). Electronic applications accepted. Tuition and fees vary according to course load, program and reciprocity agreements.

**University of Dayton,** Department of Physician Assistant Education, Dayton, OH 45469. Offers physician assistant practice (MPAP). *Degree requirements:* For master's, comprehensive exam. *Entrance requirements:* For master's, minimum GPA of 3.0, 250 hours' health care experience, interview, written and oral communication skills, 20 hours' community service, 20 hours' prior shadowing experience. Additional exam requirements/recommendations for international students: required—TOEFL (minimum score 550 paper-based; 85 iBT). Electronic applications accepted. *Expenses:* Contact institution.

**University of Detroit Mercy,** College of Health Professions, Detroit, MI 48221. Offers clinical nurse leader (MSN); family nurse practitioner (MSN); health services administration (MHSA); health systems management (MSN); nurse anesthesia (MS); nursing (DNP); nursing education (MSN, Certificate); nursing leadership and financial management (Certificate); outcomes performance management (Certificate); physician

assistant (MS). *Accreditation:* AANA/CANAEP. *Entrance requirements:* For master's, GRE General Test, minimum GPA of 3.0.

**The University of Findlay,** Office of Graduate Admissions, Findlay, OH 45840. Offers applied security and analytics (MSAS); athletic training (MAT); business (MBA), including certified management accountant, certified public accountant, health care management, hospitality management; education (MA Ed, Ed D), including children's literature (MA Ed), curriculum and teaching (MA Ed), education (MA Ed), educational administration (MA Ed), human resource development (MA Ed), mathematics (MA Ed), reading (MA Ed), science education (MA Ed), superintendent (Ed D), teaching (Ed D), technology (MA Ed); environmental, safety, and health management (MSEM); health informatics (MS); occupational therapy (MOT); pharmacy (Pharm D); physical therapy (DPT); physician assistant (MPA); rhetoric and writing (MA); teaching English to speakers of other languages (TESOL) and applied linguistics (MA). *Program availability:* Part-time, evening/weekend, 100% online, blended/hybrid learning. *Students:* 688 full-time (430 women), 553 part-time (308 women), 170 international. Average age 28. 865 applicants, 31% accepted, 235 enrolled. In 2019, 363 master's, 141 doctorates awarded. *Degree requirements:* For master's, comprehensive exam (for some programs), thesis (for some programs), cumulative project, capstone project; for doctorate, thesis/dissertation (for some programs). *Entrance requirements:* For master's, GRE/GMAT, bachelor's degree from accredited institution, minimum undergraduate GPA of 2.5 in last 64 hours of course work; for doctorate, GRE, MAT, minimum cumulative GPA of 3.0. Additional exam requirements/recommendations for international students: required—TOEFL (minimum score 79 iBT), IELTS (minimum score 7), PTE (minimum score 61). *Application deadline:* Applications are processed on a rolling basis. Electronic applications accepted. *Financial support:* In 2019–20, 10 research assistantships with partial tuition reimbursements (averaging $7,200 per year), 35 teaching assistantships with partial tuition reimbursements (averaging $7,200 per year) were awarded; Federal Work-Study, institutionally sponsored loans, and unspecified assistantships also available. Financial award applicants required to submit FAFSA. *Unit head:* Dave M. Emsweller, Director of Admissions, Interim, 419-434-4578, E-mail: emsweller@findlay.edu. *Application contact:* Amber Feehan, Graduate Admissions Counselor, 419-434-6933, Fax: 419-434-4898, E-mail: feehan@findlay.edu.
Website: http://www.findlay.edu/admissions/graduate/Pages/default.aspx

**University of Florida,** College of Medicine, Program in Physician Assistant, Gainesville, FL 32611. Offers MPAS. *Accreditation:* ARC-PA. *Entrance requirements:* For master's, GRE General Test, interview. Electronic applications accepted.

**The University of Iowa,** Roy J. and Lucille A. Carver College of Medicine and Graduate College, Graduate Programs in Medicine, Department of Physician Assistant Studies and Services, Iowa City, IA 52246. Offers MPAS. *Accreditation:* ARC-PA. *Faculty:* 3 full-time (2 women), 6 part-time/adjunct (4 women). *Students:* 75 full-time (41 women); includes 12 minority (2 Black or African American, non-Hispanic/Latino; 4 Asian, non-Hispanic/Latino; 4 Hispanic/Latino; 2 Two or more races, non-Hispanic/Latino). Average age 27. 693 applicants, 4% accepted, 25 enrolled. In 2019, 25 master's awarded. *Degree requirements:* For master's, comprehensive exam, comprehensive clinical exam, clinical presentation. *Entrance requirements:* For master's, GRE General Test or MCAT, minimum of 1,000 hours of health care and/or research experience. Additional exam requirements/recommendations for international students: required—TOEFL (minimum score 93 iBT). *Application deadline:* For fall admission, 10/1 for domestic students. Applications are processed on a rolling basis. Application fee: $60. Electronic applications accepted. *Expenses:* Contact institution. *Financial support:* In 2019–20, 68 students received support. Institutionally sponsored loans and scholarships/grants available. Financial award application deadline: 3/1; financial award applicants required to submit FAFSA. *Unit head:* Dr. David P. Asprey, Associate Dean and Chair/ Department Executive Officer, 319-335-8922, Fax: 319-335-8923, E-mail: david-asprey@uiowa.edu. *Application contact:* Dr. Thomas M. O'Shea, Director of Administrative and Student Services, 319-353-5956, Fax: 319-335-8923, E-mail: thomas-oshea@uiowa.edu.
Website: http://www.medicine.uiowa.edu/pa/

**University of Kentucky,** Graduate School, College of Health Sciences, Program in Physician Assistant Studies, Lexington, KY 40506-0032. Offers MSPAS. *Accreditation:* ARC-PA. *Degree requirements:* For master's, comprehensive exam. *Entrance requirements:* For master's, GRE General Test, minimum undergraduate GPA of 2.75. Additional exam requirements/recommendations for international students: required—TOEFL (minimum score 550 paper-based). Electronic applications accepted.

**University of Lynchburg,** Graduate Studies, MA Program in Physician Assistant Medicine, Lynchburg, VA 24501-3199. Offers MA. *Entrance requirements:* Additional exam requirements/recommendations for international students: required—TOEFL (minimum score 550 paper-based; 80 iBT). Electronic applications accepted. Application fee is waived when completed online. *Expenses:* Contact institution.

**University of Mount Union,** Program in Physician Assistant Studies, Alliance, OH 44601-3993. Offers MS. *Entrance requirements:* For master's, GRE, 40 hours of PA shadowing, interview, 3 letters of recommendation. Additional exam requirements/ recommendations for international students: required—TOEFL (minimum score 590 paper-based; 100 iBT). Electronic applications accepted. *Expenses:* Contact institution.

**University of Nebraska Medical Center,** College of Allied Health Professions, Division of Physician Assistant Education, Omaha, NE 68198-4300. Offers MPAS. *Accreditation:* ARC-PA. *Degree requirements:* For master's, comprehensive exam, research paper. *Entrance requirements:* For master's, GRE General Test, 16 undergraduate hours of course work in both biology and chemistry, 3 in math, 6 in English, 9 in psychology; minimum GPA of 3.0. Additional exam requirements/recommendations for international students: required—TOEFL (minimum score 600 paper-based; 100 iBT). Electronic applications accepted.

**University of New England,** Westbrook College of Health Professions, Biddeford, ME 04005-9526. Offers nurse anesthesia (MSNA); occupational therapy (MS); physical therapy (DPT); physician assistant (MS); social work (MSW). *Accreditation:* AANA/ CANAEP; AOTA. *Program availability:* Part-time. *Faculty:* 42 full-time (32 women), 23 part-time/adjunct (16 women). *Students:* 493 full-time (361 women), 8 part-time (7 women); includes 59 minority (3 Black or African American, non-Hispanic/Latino; 2 American Indian or Alaska Native, non-Hispanic/Latino; 36 Asian, non-Hispanic/Latino; 10 Hispanic/Latino; 2 Native Hawaiian or other Pacific Islander, non-Hispanic/Latino; 6 Two or more races, non-Hispanic/Latino), 2 international. Average age 27. In 2019, 154 master's, 58 doctorates awarded. *Application deadline:* Applications are processed on a rolling basis. Electronic applications accepted. *Financial support:* Application deadline: 5/1; applicants required to submit FAFSA. *Unit head:* Dr. Karen T. Pardue, Dean, Westbrook College of Health Professions, 207-221-4361, E-mail: kpardue@une.edu. *Application contact:* Scott Steinberg, Vice President of University Admissions, 207-221-4225, Fax: 207-523-1925, E-mail: ssteinberg@une.edu.
Website: http://www.une.edu/wchp/index.cfm

**University of New Mexico,** Graduate Studies, Health Sciences Center, Program in Physician Assistant Studies, Albuquerque, NM 87131-2039. Offers MS. *Accreditation:* ARC-PA. *Entrance requirements:* For master's, GRE. Additional exam requirements/ recommendations for international students: recommended—TOEFL. Electronic applications accepted. *Expenses:* Tuition, state resident: full-time $7633; part-time $972 per year. Tuition, nonresident: full-time $22,586; part-time $3840 per year. *International tuition:* $23,292 full-time. *Required fees:* $8608. Tuition and fees vary according to course level, course load, degree level, program and student level.

**University of North Dakota,** Graduate School, Graduate Programs in Medicine, Physician Assistant Program, Grand Forks, ND 58202. Offers MPAS. *Accreditation:* ARC-PA. *Entrance requirements:* For master's, current RN licensure, minimum of 4 years of clinical experience, current ACLS certification, interview, letters of recommendation. Additional exam requirements/recommendations for international students: required—TOEFL (minimum score 550 paper-based; 79 iBT), IELTS (minimum score 6.5).

**University of North Texas Health Science Center at Fort Worth,** School of Health Professions, Fort Worth, TX 76107-2699. Offers physical therapy (DPT); physician assistant studies (MPAS). *Accreditation:* ARC-PA. *Degree requirements:* For master's, thesis or alternative, research paper. *Entrance requirements:* For master's, minimum GPA of 2.85.

**University of Oklahoma Health Sciences Center,** College of Medicine, Program in Physician Associate, Oklahoma City, OK 73190. Offers MHS.

**University of Pittsburgh,** School of Health and Rehabilitation Sciences, Department of Rehabilitation Science and Technology, Pittsburgh, PA 15260. Offers clinical rehabilitation and mental health counseling (MS); physician assistant studies (MS); prosthetics and orthotics (DPT); rehabilitation technology (MS). *Program availability:* Part-time, blended/hybrid learning. *Faculty:* 26 full-time (15 women), 6 part-time/adjunct (3 women). *Students:* 97 full-time (57 women), 16 part-time (13 women); includes 19 minority (3 Black or African American, non-Hispanic/Latino; 5 Asian, non-Hispanic/ Latino; 3 Hispanic/Latino; 8 Two or more races, non-Hispanic/Latino), 9 international. Average age 26. 187 applicants, 58% accepted, 49 enrolled. In 2019, 50 master's awarded. *Degree requirements:* For master's, comprehensive exam (for some programs), thesis (for some programs). *Entrance requirements:* For master's, Varies by program, Varies by program. Additional exam requirements/recommendations for international students: required—International applicants may provide Duolingo English Test, IELTS or TOEFL scores to verify English language proficiency. Electronic applications accepted. *Financial support:* In 2019–20, 14 students received support, including 1 fellowship with full tuition reimbursement available (averaging $30,000 per year), 9 research assistantships with full tuition reimbursements available (averaging $30,000 per year); scholarships/grants also available. *Unit head:* Dr. Jonathan Pearlman, Chair and Associate Professor, Department of Rehabilitation Science and Technology, 412-383-3955, E-mail: jpearlman@pitt.edu. *Application contact:* Jessica Maguire, Director of Admissions, 412-383-6557, Fax: 412-383-6535, E-mail: maguire@ pitt.edu.
Website: http://www.shrs.pitt.edu/rst

**University of St. Francis,** College of Arts and Sciences, Joliet, IL 60435-6169. Offers forensic social work (Post-Master's Certificate); physician assistant practice (MS); social work (MSW). *Program availability:* Part-time. *Entrance requirements:* For master's, GRE (for MS). Additional exam requirements/recommendations for international students: required—TOEFL (minimum score 550 paper-based; 79 iBT), IELTS (minimum score 6). Electronic applications accepted. Application fee is waived when completed online. *Expenses:* Contact institution.

**University of Saint Francis,** Graduate School, Division of Allied Healthcare, Fort Wayne, IN 46808-3994. Offers MS. *Accreditation:* ARC-PA. *Faculty:* 6 full-time (3 women). *Students:* 49 full-time (41 women); includes 9 minority (2 Black or African American, non-Hispanic/Latino; 3 Asian, non-Hispanic/Latino; 3 Hispanic/Latino; 1 Two or more races, non-Hispanic/Latino). Average age 26. In 2019, 23 master's awarded. *Entrance requirements:* Additional exam requirements/recommendations for international students: required—TOEFL (minimum score 550 paper-based), IELTS (minimum score 6.5). *Application deadline:* For summer admission, 12/1 for domestic students. *Expenses:* $15,390 per semester. *Financial support:* Applicants required to submit FAFSA. *Unit head:* Joshua Fairbanks, Physician Assistant Program Director, 260-399-7700 Ext. 8511, E-mail: jfairbanks@sf.edu. *Application contact:* Kyle Richardson, Associate Director of Enrollment Management, 260-399-7700 Ext. 6310, E-mail: krichardson@sf.edu.
Website: https://majors.sf.edu/physician-assistant-studies/

**University of South Alabama,** Pat Capps Covey College of Allied Health Professions, Department of Physician Assistant Studies, Mobile, AL 36688-0002. Offers MHS. *Accreditation:* ARC-PA. *Faculty:* 5 full-time (4 women), 2 part-time/adjunct (1 woman). *Students:* 79 full-time (59 women); includes 6 minority (1 Black or African American, non-Hispanic/Latino; 3 Asian, non-Hispanic/Latino; 2 Two or more races, non-Hispanic/ Latino). Average age 26. 317 applicants, 21% accepted, 39 enrolled. In 2019, 39 master's awarded. *Degree requirements:* For master's, comprehensive exam. *Entrance requirements:* For master's, GRE. Additional exam requirements/recommendations for international students: required—TOEFL (minimum score 600 paper-based; 100 iBT). *Application deadline:* For fall admission, 9/1 for domestic students, 11/1 for international students. Application fee: $110. Electronic applications accepted. *Expenses:* Contact institution. *Financial support:* Fellowships, research assistantships, teaching assistantships, career-related internships or fieldwork, Federal Work-Study, institutionally sponsored loans, scholarships/grants, and unspecified assistantships available. Support available to part-time students. Financial award application deadline: 3/31; financial award applicants required to submit FAFSA. *Unit head:* Stephanie McGilvray, Chair, Program Director, Department of Physician Assistant Studies, 251-445-9334, Fax: 251-445-9336, E-mail: pastudies@southalabama.edu. *Application contact:* Stephanie McGilvray, Chair, Program Director, Department of Physician Assistant Studies, 251-445-9334, Fax: 251-445-9336, E-mail: pastudies@ southalabama.edu.
Website: http://www.southalabama.edu/colleges/alliedhealth/pa/

**University of South Dakota,** Graduate School, School of Health Sciences, Department of Physician Assistant Studies, Vermillion, SD 57069. Offers MS. *Accreditation:* ARC-PA. *Entrance requirements:* Additional exam requirements/recommendations for international students: required—TOEFL (minimum score 550 paper-based). Electronic applications accepted. *Expenses:* Contact institution.

**University of Southern California,** Keck School of Medicine and Graduate School, Graduate Programs in Medicine, Primary Care Physician Assistant Program, Alhambra, CA 90089. Offers MPAP. *Accreditation:* ARC-PA. *Faculty:* 13 full-time (9 women), 3 part-time/adjunct (2 women). *Students:* 172 full-time (139 women); includes 112 minority (7 Black or African American, non-Hispanic/Latino; 52 Asian, non-Hispanic/Latino; 49 Hispanic/Latino; 4 Two or more races, non-Hispanic/Latino). Average age 28. 886 applicants, 7% accepted, 60 enrolled. In 2019, 58 master's awarded. *Degree requirements:* For master's, one foreign language, comprehensive exam, clinical training. *Entrance requirements:* For master's, GRE or MCAT, bachelor's degree; minimum cumulative GPA of 3.0, cumulative science 2.75. Additional exam requirements/recommendations for international students: required—TOEFL (minimum score 90 iBT). *Application deadline:* For fall admission, 11/1 for domestic and international students. Applications are processed on a rolling basis. Application fee:

$50. Electronic applications accepted. *Expenses:* Contact institution. *Financial support:* In 2019–20, 26 students received support. Institutionally sponsored loans and scholarships/grants available. Financial award application deadline: 5/4; financial award applicants required to submit FAFSA. *Unit head:* Dr. Kevin C. Lohenry, Program Director and Vice-Chair for Education, 626-457-4262, Fax: 626-457-4245, E-mail: lohenry@med.usc.edu. *Application contact:* Sara Diosdado-Ortiz, Director of Admissions, 626-457-4264, Fax: 626-457-4245, E-mail: uscpa@usc.edu.
Website: https://keck.usc.edu/physician-assistant-program/

**The University of Tennessee Health Science Center,** College of Health Professions, Memphis, TN 38163-0002. Offers audiology (MS, Au D); clinical laboratory science (MSCLS); cytopathology practice (MCP); health informatics and information management (MHIIM); occupational therapy (MOT); physical therapy (DPT, ScDPT); physician assistant (MMS); speech-language pathology (MS). *Accreditation:* AOTA; APTA. *Program availability:* Part-time, evening/weekend, online learning. Terminal master's awarded for partial completion of doctoral program. *Degree requirements:* For master's, comprehensive exam, thesis; for doctorate, comprehensive exam, residency. *Entrance requirements:* For master's, GRE (MOT, MSCLS), minimum GPA of 3.0, 3 letters of reference, national accreditation (MSCLS), GRE if GPA is less than 3.0 (MCP); for doctorate, GRE. Additional exam requirements/recommendations for international students: required—TOEFL (minimum score 550 paper-based; 80 iBT). Electronic applications accepted. *Expenses:* Contact institution.

**The University of Texas Health Science Center at San Antonio,** School of Health Professions, San Antonio, TX 78229-3900. Offers occupational therapy (MOT); physical therapy (DPT); physician assistant studies (MS); speech language pathology (MS). *Accreditation:* AOTA; APTA; ARC-PA; ASHA. *Degree requirements:* For master's, comprehensive exam, thesis (for some programs); for doctorate, comprehensive exam.

**The University of Texas Medical Branch,** School of Health Professions, Department of Physician Assistant Studies, Galveston, TX 77555. Offers MPAS. *Accreditation:* ARC-PA. *Entrance requirements:* For master's, GRE, interview. Electronic applications accepted.

**The University of Texas Rio Grande Valley,** College of Health Affairs, Department of Physician Assistant Studies, Edinburg, TX 78539. Offers primary care (MPAS). *Program availability:* Blended/hybrid learning. *Faculty:* 17 full-time (11 women). *Students:* 254 full-time (180 women), 6 part-time (4 women); includes 193 minority (3 Black or African American, non-Hispanic/Latino; 1 American Indian or Alaska Native, non-Hispanic/Latino; 33 Asian, non-Hispanic/Latino; 155 Hispanic/Latino; 1 Native Hawaiian or other Pacific Islander, non-Hispanic/Latino), 4 international. Average age 28. 1,900 applicants, 5% accepted, 100 enrolled. In 2019, 92 master's awarded. *Entrance requirements:* For master's, GRE. Additional exam requirements/recommendations for international students: required—TOEFL (minimum score 550 paper-based; 79 iBT), IELTS (minimum score 6.5). *Application deadline:* Applications are processed on a rolling basis. Application fee: $50 ($100 for international students). Electronic applications accepted. *Expenses: Tuition, area resident:* Full-time $5959; part-time $440 per credit hour. Tuition, state resident: full-time $5959. Tuition, nonresident: full-time $5959. *International tuition:* $13,321 full-time. *Required fees:* $1169; $185 per credit hour. *Financial support:* In 2019–20, 90 students received support, including 15 research assistantships; scholarships/grants also available. Financial award applicants required to submit FAFSA. *Unit head:* Frank Ambriz, Chair, 956-665-7049, Fax: 956-665-2438, E-mail: pad@utrgv.edu. *Application contact:* Dr. Keith Joseph, Admissions Coordinator, 956-665-7049, Fax: 956-665-2438, E-mail: pad@utrgv.edu.
Website: http://www.utrgv.edu/pa/

**The University of Texas Southwestern Medical Center,** Southwestern School of Health Professions, Physician Assistant Studies Program, Dallas, TX 75390. Offers MPAS. *Accreditation:* ARC-PA. *Entrance requirements:* For master's, GRE, minimum GPA of 3.0. Electronic applications accepted.

**University of the Cumberlands,** Program in Physician Assistant Studies, Williamsburg, KY 40769-1372. Offers MPAS. *Accreditation:* ARC-PA. *Entrance requirements:* Additional exam requirements/recommendations for international students: required—TOEFL. Electronic applications accepted.

**The University of Toledo,** College of Graduate Studies, College of Medicine and Life Sciences, Department of Physician Assistant Studies, Toledo, OH 43606-3390. Offers MSBS. *Accreditation:* ARC-PA. *Degree requirements:* For master's, thesis or alternative, scholarly project. *Entrance requirements:* For master's, GRE, interview, minimum undergraduate GPA of 3.0, writing sample, transcripts. Additional exam requirements/recommendations for international students: required—TOEFL (minimum score 550 paper-based; 80 iBT). Electronic applications accepted. *Expenses:* Contact institution.

**University of Utah,** School of Medicine and Graduate School, Graduate Programs in Medicine, Department of Family and Preventive Medicine, Utah Physician Assistant Program, Salt Lake City, UT 84112-1107. Offers MPAS. *Accreditation:* ARC-PA. *Degree requirements:* For master's, comprehensive exam, thesis or alternative. *Entrance requirements:* Additional exam requirements/recommendations for international students: required—TOEFL (minimum score 550 paper-based). Electronic applications accepted. *Expenses:* Contact institution.

**University of Wisconsin–La Crosse,** College of Science and Health, Department of Health Professions, Program in Physician Assistant Studies, La Crosse, WI 54601-3742. Offers MS. *Accreditation:* ARC-PA. *Faculty:* 5 part-time/adjunct (all women). *Students:* 52 full-time (40 women); includes 2 minority (1 Hispanic/Latino; 1 Two or more races, non-Hispanic/Latino). Average age 24. 416 applicants, 10% accepted, 28 enrolled. In 2019, 18 master's awarded. *Degree requirements:* For master's, comprehensive exam. *Entrance requirements:* For master's, GRE. Additional exam requirements/recommendations for international students: required—TOEFL (minimum score 104 iBT). *Application deadline:* For fall admission, 8/1 for domestic and international students. Application fee: $50. Electronic applications accepted. *Expenses:* Contact institution. *Financial support:* Federal Work-Study and scholarships/grants available. Support available to part-time students. *Unit head:* Patricia Campbell, Program Director, 608-785-5067, E-mail: pcampbell@uwlax.edu. *Application contact:* Peter Amann, Senior Graduate Student Status Examiner, 608-785-6622, E-mail: pamann@uwlax.edu.
Website: https://www.uwlax.edu/grad/physician-assistant-studies/

**University of Wisconsin–Madison,** School of Medicine and Public Health, Physician Assistant Program, Madison, WI 53706-1380. Offers MPA.

**Valparaiso University,** Graduate School and Continuing Education, College of Nursing and Health Professions, Valparaiso, IN 46383. Offers nursing (DNP); nursing education (MSN, Certificate); physician assistant (MSPA); public health (MPH); MSN/MHA. *Accreditation:* AACN. *Program availability:* Part-time, evening/weekend, online learning. *Entrance requirements:* For master's, minimum GPA of 3.0, undergraduate major in nursing, Indiana registered nursing license, undergraduate courses in research and statistics. Additional exam requirements/recommendations for international students: required—TOEFL (minimum score 550 paper-based; 80 iBT), IELTS (minimum score 6). Electronic applications accepted. *Expenses:* Contact institution.

**Wayne State University,** Eugene Applebaum College of Pharmacy and Health Sciences, Department of Health Care Sciences, Detroit, MI 48201. Offers nurse anesthesia (MS, DNP-A, Certificate), including anesthesia (MS), nurse anesthesia practice (DNP-A), pediatric anesthesia (Certificate); occupational therapy (MOT); physical therapy (DPT); physician assistant studies (MS). *Faculty:* 5. *Students:* 310 full-time (209 women), 4 part-time (all women); includes 33 minority (7 Black or African American, non-Hispanic/Latino; 14 Asian, non-Hispanic/Latino; 8 Hispanic/Latino; 4 Two or more races, non-Hispanic/Latino), 4 international. Average age 26. 344 applicants, 20% accepted, 55 enrolled. In 2019, 97 master's, 36 doctorates awarded. *Entrance requirements:* Additional exam requirements/recommendations for international students: required—TOEFL (minimum score 550 paper-based; 79 iBT), Michigan English Language Assessment Battery (minimum score 85); recommended—IELTS (minimum score 6.5), TWE (minimum score 5.5). Application fee: $50. Electronic applications accepted. *Expenses:* Contact institution. *Financial support:* In 2019–20, 102 students received support. Fellowships and scholarships/grants available. Financial award applicants required to submit FAFSA. *Unit head:* Dr. Sara F Maher, Chair Department of Health Care Sciences, 313-577-5630, E-mail: sara.maher@wayne.edu. *Application contact:* Office of Student and Alumni Affairs, 313-577-1716, E-mail: cphsinfo@wayne.edu.
Website: http://cphs.wayne.edu/hcs/

**Weill Cornell Medicine,** Weill Cornell Graduate School of Medical Sciences, Physician Assistant Program, New York, NY 10022. Offers health sciences (MS), including surgery. *Accreditation:* ARC-PA. *Degree requirements:* For master's, thesis. *Entrance requirements:* For master's, GRE. Additional exam requirements/recommendations for international students: required—TOEFL. Electronic applications accepted.

**Western Michigan University,** Graduate College, College of Health and Human Services, Department of Physician Assistant, Kalamazoo, MI 49008. Offers MSM. *Accreditation:* ARC-PA. *Program availability:* Part-time.

**Western University of Health Sciences,** College of Health Sciences, Program in Physician Assistant Studies, Pomona, CA 91766-1854. Offers MS. *Accreditation:* ARC-PA. *Faculty:* 10 full-time (7 women), 3 part-time/adjunct (0 women). *Students:* 193 full-time (132 women); includes 116 minority (6 Black or African American, non-Hispanic/Latino; 2 American Indian or Alaska Native, non-Hispanic/Latino; 42 Asian, non-Hispanic/Latino; 46 Hispanic/Latino; 1 Native Hawaiian or other Pacific Islander, non-Hispanic/Latino; 19 Two or more races, non-Hispanic/Latino). Average age 27. 2,040 applicants, 7% accepted, 97 enrolled. In 2019, 93 master's awarded. *Degree requirements:* For master's, comprehensive exam, thesis. *Entrance requirements:* For master's, A bachelor's degree in any subject is acceptable and required, minimum overall, science and prerequisite GPAs of 3.0, letters of recommendation, interview, demonstrated history of ongoing community service and involvement, health screenings and immunizations, background check. *Application deadline:* For fall admission, 11/1 for domestic and international students. Application fee: $50. Electronic applications accepted. *Expenses:* The tuition is about $44,065 and the medical equipment fee is about $1000. *Financial support:* In 2019–20, 65 students received support. Scholarships/grants available. Financial award application deadline: 3/2; financial award applicants required to submit FAFSA. *Unit head:* Roy Guizado, Chair, 909-469-5445, Fax: 909-469-5407, E-mail: roygpac@westernu.edu. *Application contact:* Michael Haverkamp, Admissions Coordinator, 909-469-5571, Fax: 909-469-5570, E-mail: mhaverkamp@westernu.edu.
Website: http://www.westernu.edu/allied-health/allied-health-mspas/

**Westfield State University,** College of Graduate and Continuing Education, Department of Health Sciences, Westfield, MA 01086. Offers physician assistant studies (MS). *Degree requirements:* For master's, comprehensive exam, thesis. *Entrance requirements:* For master's, CASPA application, minimum of 500 hours of patient contact, completion of prerequisite courses within previous ten years. Additional exam requirements/recommendations for international students: required—TOEFL (minimum score 550 paper-based; 90 iBT). *Expenses:* Contact institution.

**West Liberty University,** College of Sciences, West Liberty, WV 26074. Offers biology (MA, MS); biomedical science (MA); physician assistant studies (MS); zoo science (MA, MS).

**Wichita State University,** Graduate School, College of Health Professions, Department of Physician Assistant, Wichita, KS 67260. Offers MPA. *Accreditation:* ARC-PA.

**Wingate University,** Harris Department of Physician Assistant Studies, Wingate, NC 28174. Offers MPAS.

**Yale University,** Yale School of Medicine, Physician Associate Program, New Haven, CT 06510. Offers MM Sc, MM Sc/MPH. *Accreditation:* ARC-PA. *Program availability:* Online learning. *Degree requirements:* For master's, thesis. *Entrance requirements:* For master's, GRE General Test, course work in science. Additional exam requirements/recommendations for international students: required—TOEFL. Electronic applications accepted. *Expenses:* Contact institution.

**York College of the City University of New York,** School of Health Sciences and Professional Programs, Jamaica, NY 11451. Offers physician assistant (MSPAS). *Entrance requirements:* For master's, GRE, bachelor's degree with minimum cumulative GPA of 3.0; 1 year each of general biology, general chemistry, human anatomy and physiology, and behavioral sciences; 1 semester each of biochemistry, microbiology (preferably clinical microbiology), and statistics; 500 hours of documented healthcare experience (volunteer or paid); personal interview.

# Rehabilitation Sciences

**Alabama State University,** College of Health Sciences, Department of Prosthetics and Orthotics, Montgomery, AL 36101-0271. Offers MS. *Faculty:* 4 full-time (0 women). *Students:* 20 full-time (6 women); includes 9 minority (4 Black or African American, non-Hispanic/Latino; 2 Hispanic/Latino; 3 Two or more races, non-Hispanic/Latino). Average age 26. 21 applicants, 48% accepted, 10 enrolled. *Degree requirements:* For master's, comprehensive exam. *Entrance requirements:* For master's, OPCAS application,

interviews. Additional exam requirements/recommendations for international students: required—TOEFL (minimum score 500 paper-based). *Application deadline:* For fall admission, 4/15 for domestic and international students; for spring admission, 11/15 for domestic and international students; for summer admission, 3/15 for domestic and international students. Applications are processed on a rolling basis. Application fee: $25. Electronic applications accepted. *Expenses:* Contact institution. *Financial support:* Fellowships, research assistantships, teaching assistantships, scholarships/grants, tuition waivers, and unspecified assistantships available. Financial award application deadline: 6/30; financial award applicants required to submit FAFSA. *Unit head:* Kimberly K. Hill, Interim Program Director, 334-229-5888, E-mail: asupando@alasu.edu. *Application contact:* Dr. William Person, Dean of Graduate Studies, 334-229-4274, Fax: 334-229-4928, E-mail: wperson@alasu.edu.
Website: http://www.alasu.edu/academics/colleges—departments/health-sciences/prosthetics-orthotics/index.aspx

**Augusta University,** College of Allied Health Sciences, Program in Applied Health Sciences, Augusta, GA 30912. Offers diagnostic sciences (PhD); health care outcomes (PhD); rehabilitation science (PhD). *Program availability:* Part-time, online learning. *Entrance requirements:* For doctorate, GRE General Test, bachelor's degree, official transcripts, minimum undergraduate GPA of 3.0, three letters of recommendation. Additional exam requirements/recommendations for international students: required—TOEFL (minimum score 550 paper-based; 79 iBT). Electronic applications accepted.

**Boston University,** College of Health and Rehabilitation Sciences: Sargent College, Department of Occupational Therapy, Boston, MA 02215. Offers occupational therapy (OTD); rehabilitation sciences (PhD). *Accreditation:* AOTA (one or more programs are accredited). *Program availability:* Blended/hybrid learning. *Faculty:* 13 full-time (10 women). *Students:* 101 full-time (92 women), 83 part-time (76 women); includes 50 minority (9 Black or African American, non-Hispanic/Latino; 22 Asian, non-Hispanic/Latino; 12 Hispanic/Latino; 7 Two or more races, non-Hispanic/Latino), 10 international. Average age 30. 333 applicants, 35% accepted, 57 enrolled. In 2019, 31 doctorates awarded. *Entrance requirements:* Additional exam requirements/recommendations for international students: required—TOEFL. Application fee: $150. Electronic applications accepted. *Financial support:* Teaching assistantships, career-related internships or fieldwork, Federal Work-Study, institutionally sponsored loans, scholarships/grants, and unspecified assistantships available. Financial award applicants required to submit FAFSA. *Unit head:* Dr. Wendy Coster, Chair, 617-353-7518, E-mail: wjcoster@bu.edu. *Application contact:* Sharon Sankey, Assistant Dean, Student Services, 617-353-2713, Fax: 617-353-7500, E-mail: ssankey@bu.edu.
Website: http://www.bu.edu/sargent/

**Boston University,** College of Health and Rehabilitation Sciences: Sargent College, Department of Physical Therapy and Athletic Training, Boston, MA 02215. Offers athletic training (MS); physical therapy (DPT); rehabilitation sciences (PhD). *Accreditation:* APTA (one or more programs are accredited). *Faculty:* 21 full-time (17 women), 1 (woman) part-time/adjunct. *Students:* 197 full-time (128 women); includes 56 minority (3 Black or African American, non-Hispanic/Latino; 33 Asian, non-Hispanic/Latino; 13 Hispanic/Latino; 1 Native Hawaiian or other Pacific Islander, non-Hispanic/Latino; 6 Two or more races, non-Hispanic/Latino), 14 international. Average age 25. 634 applicants, 13% accepted, 42 enrolled. In 2019, 10 master's, 61 doctorates awarded. *Entrance requirements:* Additional exam requirements/recommendations for international students: required—TOEFL. Application fee: $155. Electronic applications accepted. *Financial support:* Fellowships, research assistantships, teaching assistantships, career-related internships or fieldwork, Federal Work-Study, institutionally sponsored loans, scholarships/grants, tuition waivers (full and partial), and unspecified assistantships available. Financial award applicants required to submit FAFSA. *Unit head:* Dr. Theresa Ellis, Department Chair, 617-353-7571, E-mail: pt@bu.edu. *Application contact:* Sharon Sankey, Assistant Dean, Student Services, 617-353-2713, Fax: 617-353-7500, E-mail: ssankey@bu.edu.

**Central Michigan University,** College of Graduate Studies, The Herbert H. and Grace A. Dow College of Health Professions, School of Rehabilitation and Medical Sciences, Mount Pleasant, MI 48859. Offers physical therapy (DPT); physician assistant (MS). *Accreditation:* APTA; ARC-PA. *Degree requirements:* For master's, thesis or alternative; for doctorate, thesis/dissertation or alternative. *Entrance requirements:* For master's and doctorate, GRE. Electronic applications accepted. *Expenses: Tuition, area resident:* Full-time $12,267; part-time $8178 per year. Tuition, state resident: full-time $12,267; part-time $8178 per year. Tuition, nonresident: full-time $12,267; part-time $8178 per year. *International tuition:* $16,110 full-time. *Required fees:* $225 per semester. Tuition and fees vary according to degree level and program.

**Concordia University Wisconsin,** Graduate Programs, School of Health Professions, Program in Rehabilitation Science, Mequon, WI 53097-2402. Offers MSRS.

**Duquesne University,** John G. Rangos, Sr. School of Health Sciences, Pittsburgh, PA 15282-0001. Offers health management systems (MHMS); occupational therapy (MS, OTD); physical therapy (DPT); physician assistant studies (MPAS); rehabilitation science (MS, PhD); speech-language pathology (MS). *Accreditation:* AOTA (one or more programs are accredited); APTA (one or more programs are accredited); ASHA. *Program availability:* Part-time, minimal on-campus study. *Degree requirements:* For doctorate, comprehensive exam (for some programs), thesis/dissertation (for some programs). *Entrance requirements:* For master's, GRE General Test (speech-language pathology), 3 letters of recommendation; minimum GPA of 2.75 (health management systems), 3.0 (speech-language pathology); for doctorate, GRE General Test (for physical therapy and rehabilitation science), 3 letters of recommendation, minimum GPA of 3.0, personal interview. Additional exam requirements/recommendations for international students: required—TOEFL (minimum score 550 paper-based; 90 iBT); recommended—IELTS. Electronic applications accepted. *Expenses:* Contact institution.

**East Carolina University,** Graduate School, College of Allied Health Sciences, Department of Addictions and Rehabilitation Studies, Greenville, NC 27858-4353. Offers clinical counseling (MS); military and trauma counseling (Certificate); rehabilitation and career counseling (MS); rehabilitation counseling (Certificate); rehabilitation counseling and administration (PhD); substance abuse counseling (Certificate); vocational evaluation (Certificate). *Accreditation:* CORE. *Program availability:* Part-time, evening/weekend. *Students:* Average age 33. 51 applicants, 73% accepted, 31 enrolled. In 2019, 19 master's, 5 doctorates, 34 other advanced degrees awarded. *Degree requirements:* For master's, comprehensive exam, thesis or alternative, internship; for doctorate, thesis/dissertation, internship. *Entrance requirements:* For master's and doctorate, GRE General Test or MAT. Additional exam requirements/recommendations for international students: recommended—TOEFL (minimum score 78 iBT), IELTS (minimum score 6.5). *Application deadline:* For fall admission, 3/1 priority date for domestic students; for spring admission, 10/1 priority date for domestic students. Applications are processed on a rolling basis. Application fee: $75. Electronic applications accepted. *Expenses: Tuition, area resident:* Full-time $4749; part-time $185 per credit hour. Tuition, state resident: full-time $4749; part-time $185 per credit hour. Tuition, nonresident: full-time $17,898; part-time $864 per credit hour. *International tuition:* $17,898 full-time. *Required fees:* $2787. *Financial support:* Research assistantships with partial tuition reimbursements, teaching assistantships with partial tuition reimbursements, Federal Work-Study, scholarships/grants, and unspecified assistantships available. Support available to part-time students. Financial award application deadline: 3/1; financial award applicants required to submit FAFSA. *Unit head:* Dr. Paul Toriello, Chair, 252-744-6292, E-mail: toriellop@ecu.edu. *Application contact:* Graduate School Admissions, 252-328-6013, Fax: 252-328-6071, E-mail: gradschool@ecu.edu.
Website: http://www.ecu.edu/rehb/

**East Stroudsburg University of Pennsylvania,** Graduate and Extended Studies, College of Education, Department of Special Education and Rehabilitation, East Stroudsburg, PA 18301-2999. Offers special education (M Ed). *Program availability:* Part-time, evening/weekend, online learning. *Degree requirements:* For master's, comprehensive exam. *Entrance requirements:* For master's, PRAXIS/teacher certification, letter of recommendation, Pennsylvania Department of Education requirements. Additional exam requirements/recommendations for international students: recommended—TOEFL (minimum score 560 paper-based; 83 iBT), IELTS. Electronic applications accepted.

**George Mason University,** College of Health and Human Services, Department of Rehabilitation Science, Fairfax, VA 22030. Offers PhD, Certificate. *Program availability:* Part-time. *Degree requirements:* For doctorate, comprehensive exam, thesis/dissertation; for Certificate, 15 credits, minimum GPA of 3.0. *Entrance requirements:* For doctorate, GRE, college transcripts, expanded goals statement, 2 letters of recommendation, resume, professional and volunteer experience in related fields; for Certificate, college transcripts, expanded goals statement. 2 letters of recommendation, resume, bachelor's degree in a discipline related to health sciences from regionally-accredited institution, minimum GPA of 3.0, professional and volunteer experience in related fields. Additional exam requirements/recommendations for international students: required—TOEFL (minimum score 570 paper-based; 88 iBT), IELTS (minimum score 6.5), PTE (minimum score 59). Electronic applications accepted. *Expenses:* Contact institution.

**Indiana University-Purdue University Indianapolis,** School of Health and Rehabilitation Sciences, Indianapolis, IN 46202. Offers health and rehabilitation sciences (PhD); health sciences (MS); nutrition and dietetics (MS); occupational therapy (OTD); physical therapy (DPT); physician assistant (MPAS). *Accreditation:* AOTA. *Program availability:* Part-time, evening/weekend. *Degree requirements:* For master's, thesis (for some programs). *Entrance requirements:* For master's, GRE General Test, minimum GPA of 3.0 (for MS in health sciences, nutrition and dietetics), 3.2 (for MS in occupational therapy), 3.0 cumulative and prerequisite math/science (for MPAS); for doctorate, GRE, minimum cumulative and prerequisite math/science GPA of 3.2. Additional exam requirements/recommendations for international students: required—TOEFL (minimum score 550 paper-based; 79 iBT), IELTS (minimum score 6.5), PTE (minimum score 54). Electronic applications accepted. *Expenses:* Contact institution.

**Jackson State University,** Graduate School, College of Education and Human Development, Department of Counseling, Rehabilitation and Psychometric Services, Jackson, MS 39217. Offers clinical mental health (MS); rehabilitation counseling (MS); school counseling (MS Ed). *Accreditation:* ACA; CORE (one or more programs are accredited); NCATE. *Program availability:* Part-time, evening/weekend, 100% online, blended/hybrid learning. *Degree requirements:* For master's, comprehensive exam, thesis. *Entrance requirements:* For master's, GRE General Test. Additional exam requirements/recommendations for international students: required—TOEFL (minimum score 520 paper-based; 67 iBT). Electronic applications accepted. *Expenses:* Contact institution.

**Lasell College,** Graduate and Professional Studies in Rehabilitation Science, Newton, MA 02466-2709. Offers rehabilitation science (MS). *Program availability:* Part-time, evening/weekend, online only, 100% online. *Faculty:* 3 full-time (1 woman), 3 part-time/adjunct (2 women). *Students:* 15 full-time (10 women), 12 part-time (10 women); includes 5 minority (3 Black or African American, non-Hispanic/Latino; 2 Hispanic/Latino), 1 international. Average age 28. 22 applicants, 41% accepted, 5 enrolled. In 2019, 6 master's awarded. *Degree requirements:* For master's, minimum GPA of 3.0. *Entrance requirements:* For master's, one-page personal statement, 2 letters of recommendation, resume, bachelor's degree transcript, BA/BS in health-related field from accredited institution, minimum GPA of 2.75, 8 credits in anatomy and physiology, 3-4 credits in kinesiology, 3 credits in statistics. Additional exam requirements/recommendations for international students: required—TOEFL (minimum score 550 paper-based, 79 iBT) or IELTS (minimum score 6). *Application deadline:* For fall admission, 8/31 priority date for domestic students, 6/30 priority date for international students; for spring admission, 12/31 priority date for domestic students, 10/31 priority date for international students. Applications are processed on a rolling basis. Electronic applications accepted. *Expenses: Tuition:* Part-time $600 per credit. *Required fees:* $40 per semester. *Financial support:* Federal Work-Study, scholarships/grants, and tuition discounts available. Support available to part-time students. Financial award application deadline: 8/31; financial award applicants required to submit FAFSA. *Unit head:* Chrystal Porter, Vice President of Graduate and Professional Studies, 617-243-2083, Fax: 617-243-2450, E-mail: gradinfo@lasell.edu. *Application contact:* Adrienne Franciosi, Assistant Vice President of Graduate and Professional Studies, 617-243-2214, Fax: 617-243-2450, E-mail: gradinfo@lasell.edu.
Website: http://www.lasell.edu/academics/graduate-and-professional-studies/programs-of-study/master-of-science-in-rehabilitation-science.html

**Logan University,** College of Health Sciences, Chesterfield, MO 63017. Offers health informatics (MS); health professions education (DHPE); nutrition and human performance (MS); sports science and rehabilitation (MS). *Program availability:* Part-time, online only, 100% online. *Entrance requirements:* For master's, minimum GPA of 2.5; 6 hours of biology and physical science; bachelor's degree and 9 hours of business health administration (for health informatics). Additional exam requirements/recommendations for international students: required—TOEFL (minimum score 500 paper-based; 79 iBT); recommended—IELTS (minimum score 6.5). Electronic applications accepted. *Expenses:* Contact institution.

**Loma Linda University,** School of Allied Health Professions, Department of Physical Therapy, Loma Linda, CA 92350. Offers physical therapy (DPT, PhD); rehabilitation (MS). *Accreditation:* APTA. *Entrance requirements:* Additional exam requirements/recommendations for international students: required—TOEFL (minimum score 550 paper-based). Electronic applications accepted.

**Marquette University,** Graduate School, College of Health Sciences, Clinical and Translational Rehabilitation Science Program, Milwaukee, WI 53201-1881. Offers MS, PhD. *Entrance requirements:* For master's and doctorate, GRE, official transcripts, curriculum vitae, personal statement, three letters of recommendation, interview. Additional exam requirements/recommendations for international students: required—TOEFL (minimum score 90 iBT).

**McGill University,** Faculty of Graduate and Postdoctoral Studies, Faculty of Medicine, School of Physical and Occupational Therapy, Montréal, QC H3A 2T5, Canada. Offers assessing driving capability (PGC); rehabilitation science (M Sc, PhD).

**McMaster University,** Faculty of Health Sciences and School of Graduate Studies, Program in Rehabilitation Science (course-based), Hamilton, ON L8S 4M2, Canada. Offers M Sc. *Program availability:* Part-time. *Degree requirements:* For master's, online courses and scholarly paper. *Entrance requirements:* For master's, minimum B+

average in final year of a 4-year undergraduate health professional program or other relevant program. Additional exam requirements/recommendations for international students: required—TOEFL (minimum score 600 paper-based).

**McMaster University,** Faculty of Health Sciences and School of Graduate Studies, Program in Rehabilitation Science (Thesis Option), Hamilton, ON L8S 4M2, Canada. Offers M Sc, PhD. *Program availability:* Part-time. *Degree requirements:* For master's, thesis. *Entrance requirements:* For master's, minimum B+ average in final year of a 4-year undergraduate health professional program or other relevant program. Additional exam requirements/recommendations for international students: required—TOEFL (minimum score 600 paper-based).

**Medical University of South Carolina,** College of Health Professions, PhD Program in Health and Rehabilitation Science, Charleston, SC 29425. Offers PhD. *Degree requirements:* For doctorate, comprehensive exam, thesis/dissertation. *Entrance requirements:* Additional exam requirements/recommendations for international students: required—TOEFL (minimum score 600 paper-based). Electronic applications accepted.

**New York University,** Steinhardt School of Culture, Education, and Human Development, Department of Nutrition, Food Studies, and Public Health, Programs in Nutrition and Dietetics, New York, NY 10012. Offers clinical nutrition (MS); nutrition and dietetics (MS, PhD), including food and nutrition (MS); rehabilitation sciences (PhD). *Program availability:* Part-time. *Entrance requirements:* For doctorate, GRE General Test, interview. Additional exam requirements/recommendations for international students: required—TOEFL (minimum score 100 iBT). Electronic applications accepted.

**Northwestern University,** Feinberg School of Medicine, Department of Physical Therapy and Human Movement Sciences, Chicago, IL 60611-2814. Offers neuroscience (PhD), including movement and rehabilitation science; physical therapy (DPT); DPT/MPH; DPT/PhD. *Accreditation:* APTA. *Degree requirements:* For doctorate, research project. *Entrance requirements:* For doctorate, GRE General Test (for DPT), baccalaureate degree with minimum GPA of 3.0 in required course work (DPT). Additional exam requirements/recommendations for international students: required—TOEFL (minimum score 100 iBT). Electronic applications accepted. *Expenses:* Contact institution.

**The Ohio State University,** College of Medicine, School of Health and Rehabilitation Sciences, Program in Health and Rehabilitation Sciences, Columbus, OH 43210. Offers PhD. *Degree requirements:* For doctorate, thesis/dissertation. *Entrance requirements:* For doctorate, GRE. Additional exam requirements/recommendations for international students: required—TOEFL (minimum score 550 paper-based; 79 iBT), Michigan English Language Assessment Battery (minimum score 82); recommended—IELTS (minimum score 7). Electronic applications accepted.

**Old Dominion University,** College of Health Sciences, School of Physical Therapy and Athletic Training, Doctor of Kinesiology and Rehabilitation Program, Norfolk, VA 23529. Offers PhD. *Degree requirements:* For doctorate, comprehensive exam, thesis/dissertation. *Entrance requirements:* For doctorate, master's degree or higher in an associated area of basic science, such as kinesiology, exercise science, or biomechanics, or in a health profession such as athletic training, nursing, occupational therapy, physical therapy, or speech/language pathology. Additional exam requirements/recommendations for international students: recommended—TOEFL (minimum score 550 paper-based; 79 iBT), IELTS (minimum score 6.5). Electronic applications accepted. *Expenses:* Contact institution.

**Queen's University at Kingston,** School of Graduate Studies, Faculty of Health Sciences, School of Rehabilitation Therapy, Kingston, ON K7L 3N6, Canada. Offers occupational therapy (M Sc OT); physical therapy (M Sc PT); rehabilitation science (M Sc, PhD). *Program availability:* Part-time. *Degree requirements:* For master's, thesis; for doctorate, comprehensive exam, thesis/dissertation. *Entrance requirements:* Additional exam requirements/recommendations for international students: required—TOEFL.

**Salus University,** College of Education and Rehabilitation, Elkins Park, PA 19027-1598. Offers education of children and youth with visual and multiple impairments (M Ed, Certificate); low vision rehabilitation (MS, Certificate); occupational therapy (MS); orientation and mobility therapy (MS, Certificate); speech-language pathology (MS); vision rehabilitation therapy (MS, Certificate); OD/MS. *Accreditation:* AOTA. *Program availability:* Part-time, online learning. *Entrance requirements:* For master's, GRE or MAT, 3 letters of reference, 2 interviews. Additional exam requirements/recommendations for international students: required—TOEFL, TWE. *Expenses:* Contact institution.

**Stony Brook University, State University of New York,** Stony Brook Medicine, School of Health Technology and Management, Stony Brook, NY 11794. Offers applied health informatics (MS); disability studies (Certificate); health administration (MHA); health and rehabilitation sciences (PhD); health care management (Advanced Certificate); health care policy and management (MS); occupational therapy (MS); physical therapy (DPT); physician assistant (MS). *Accreditation:* AOTA; APTA. *Faculty:* 53 full-time (37 women), 54 part-time/adjunct (34 women). *Students:* 605 full-time (417 women), 65 part-time (43 women); includes 225 minority (28 Black or African American, non-Hispanic/Latino; 110 Asian, non-Hispanic/Latino; 73 Hispanic/Latino; 1 Native Hawaiian or other Pacific Islander, non-Hispanic/Latino; 13 Two or more races, non-Hispanic/Latino), 9 international. Average age 26. 1,816 applicants, 21% accepted, 293 enrolled. In 2019, 152 master's, 86 doctorates, 21 other advanced degrees awarded. *Entrance requirements:* For master's, GRE General Test, minimum GPA of 3.0, work experience in field, references; for doctorate, GRE, three references, essay. Additional exam requirements/recommendations for international students: required—TOEFL (minimum score 550 paper-based). *Application deadline:* For fall admission, 1/15 for domestic students; for spring admission, 10/1 for domestic students. Application fee: $100. *Expenses:* Contact institution. *Financial support:* Fellowships, research assistantships, teaching assistantships, career-related internships or fieldwork, Federal Work-Study, and institutionally sponsored loans available. Financial award application deadline: 3/15. *Unit head:* Dr. Stacy Jafee Gropack, Dean and Professor, 631-444-2252, Fax: 631-444-7621, E-mail: stacy.jaffeegropack@stonybrook.edu. *Application contact:* Jessica M Rotolo, Executive Assistant to the Dean, 631-444-2252, Fax: 631-444-7621, E-mail: jessica.rotolo@stonybrook.edu.
Website: http://healthtechnology.stonybrookmedicine.edu/

**Temple University,** College of Public Health, Department of Health and Rehabilitation Sciences, Philadelphia, PA 19122-6096. Offers occupational therapy (MOT, DOT); recreational therapy (MS), including recreation therapy. *Accreditation:* AOTA. *Program availability:* Part-time, evening/weekend, online learning. *Faculty:* 29 full-time (19 women), 9 part-time/adjunct (6 women). *Students:* 290 full-time (212 women), 18 part-time (16 women); includes 57 minority (13 Black or African American, non-Hispanic/Latino; 18 Asian, non-Hispanic/Latino; 11 Hispanic/Latino; 15 Two or more races, non-Hispanic/Latino), 3 international. 33 applicants, 94% accepted, 23 enrolled. In 2019, 53 master's, 55 doctorates awarded. *Degree requirements:* For doctorate, thesis/dissertation (for some programs), area paper, capstone project, clinical experiences, practice project. *Entrance requirements:* For master's, GRE General Test, letters of recommendation, statement of goals, clearances for clinical/field education; for

doctorate, GRE General Test, statement of goals, letters of recommendation. Additional exam requirements/recommendations for international students: required—TOEFL (minimum score 79 iBT), IELTS, PTE, one of three is required. Application fee: $60. Electronic applications accepted. *Expenses:* Contact institution. *Financial support:* Research assistantships, teaching assistantships, career-related internships or fieldwork, Federal Work-Study, health care benefits, and unspecified assistantships available. Financial award applicants required to submit FAFSA.
Website: https://cph.temple.edu/healthrehabsci/home

**Texas Tech University Health Sciences Center,** School of Health Professions, Program in Rehabilitation Science, Lubbock, TX 79430. Offers PhD. *Program availability:* Part-time. *Faculty:* 18 full-time (6 women). *Students:* 8 full-time (4 women), 11 part-time (7 women); includes 3 minority (2 Black or African American, non-Hispanic/Latino; 1 Hispanic/Latino), 5 international. Average age 34. 2 applicants, 50% accepted. In 2019, 1 doctorate awarded. *Degree requirements:* For doctorate, comprehensive exam, thesis/dissertation. *Entrance requirements:* For doctorate, GRE. Additional exam requirements/recommendations for international students: required—TOEFL (minimum score 550 paper-based; 79 iBT). *Application deadline:* For fall admission, 3/15 for domestic students; for spring admission, 10/15 for domestic students; for summer admission, 2/1 for domestic students. Applications are processed on a rolling basis. Application fee: $75. Electronic applications accepted. *Financial support:* In 2019–20, 6 students received support, including 1 teaching assistantship with tuition reimbursement available (averaging $18,000 per year); scholarships/grants and unspecified assistantships also available. Financial award application deadline: 9/1; financial award applicants required to submit FAFSA. *Unit head:* Dr. Roger James, Program Director, 806-743-3226, Fax: 806-743-2189, E-mail: health.professions@ttuhsc.edu. *Application contact:* Lindsay Johnson, Associate Dean for Admissions and Student Affairs, 806-743-3220, Fax: 806-743-2994, E-mail: health.professions@ttuhsc.edu.
Website: http://www.ttuhsc.edu/health-professions/phd-rehabilitation-science/default.aspx

**Université de Montréal,** Faculty of Medicine, Program in Mobility and Posture, Montréal, QC H3C 3J7, Canada. Offers DESS.

**University at Buffalo, the State University of New York,** Graduate School, School of Public Health and Health Professions, Department of Rehabilitation Science, Program in Assistive and Rehabilitation Technology, Buffalo, NY 14260. Offers Certificate. *Program availability:* Part-time. *Entrance requirements:* For degree, bachelor's degree. Additional exam requirements/recommendations for international students: required—TOEFL (minimum score 550 paper-based; 79 iBT). Electronic applications accepted. *Expenses:* Tuition, area resident: Full-time $11,310; part-time $471 per credit hour. Tuition, state resident: full-time $11,310; part-time $471 per credit hour. Tuition, nonresident: full-time $23,100; part-time $963 per credit hour. *International tuition:* $23,100 full-time. *Required fees:* $2820.

**The University of Alabama at Birmingham,** School of Health Professions, Program in Rehabilitation Science, Birmingham, AL 35294. Offers PhD. *Program availability:* Part-time. *Faculty:* 20 full-time (8 women). *Students:* 23 full-time (16 women), 1 part-time (0 women); includes 4 minority (2 Asian, non-Hispanic/Latino; 1 Hispanic/Latino; 1 Two or more races, non-Hispanic/Latino), 11 international. Average age 29. 28 applicants, 36% accepted, 9 enrolled. In 2019, 2 doctorates awarded. *Degree requirements:* For doctorate, comprehensive exam, thesis/dissertation. *Entrance requirements:* For doctorate, GRE, references, minimum GPA of 3.0, interview. Additional exam requirements/recommendations for international students: required—TOEFL (minimum score 500 paper-based; 80 iBT); recommended—IELTS (minimum score 5). *Application deadline:* For fall admission, 1/31 priority date for domestic and international students. Applications are processed on a rolling basis. Application fee: $50 ($60 for international students). Electronic applications accepted. *Financial support:* In 2019–20, 15 students received support, including 3 fellowships with full tuition reimbursements available (averaging $29,000 per year), 12 research assistantships with full tuition reimbursements available (averaging $29,000 per year); scholarships/grants, traineeships, and health care benefits also available. Financial award application deadline: 2/1. *Unit head:* Dr. David A. Brown, Graduate Program Director/Professor, 205-975-2788, E-mail: dbrownpt@uab.edu. *Application contact:* Holly Hebard, Director of Graduate School Operations, 205-934-8227, Fax: 205-934-8413, E-mail: gradschool@uab.edu.
Website: http://www.uab.edu/shp/pt/rsphd

**University of Alberta,** Faculty of Graduate Studies and Research, Faculty of Rehabilitation Medicine, Edmonton, AB T6G 2E1, Canada. Offers M Sc, PhD. *Degree requirements:* For doctorate, thesis/dissertation. *Entrance requirements:* For doctorate, GRE, minimum GPA of 7.0 on a 9.0 scale. Additional exam requirements/recommendations for international students: required—TOEFL. Electronic applications accepted.

**The University of British Columbia,** Faculty of Medicine, School of Rehabilitation Sciences, Vancouver, BC V6T 1Z3, Canada. Offers M Sc, MRSc, PhD. *Degree requirements:* For master's, thesis; for doctorate, comprehensive exam, thesis/dissertation. *Entrance requirements:* For master's, minimum B+ average; for doctorate, minimum B+ average, master's degree. Additional exam requirements/recommendations for international students: required—TOEFL. Electronic applications accepted. *Expenses:* Contact institution.

**University of Colorado Denver,** School of Medicine, Program in Rehabilitation Science, Aurora, CO 80045. Offers PhD. *Degree requirements:* For doctorate, comprehensive exam, 60 credit hours (30 of core coursework and 30 of thesis). *Entrance requirements:* For doctorate, GRE, bachelor's degree with minimum GPA of 3.0, research experience (preferred), three letters of recommendation, interview. Tuition and fees vary according to course load, program and reciprocity agreements.

**University of Florida,** Graduate School, College of Public Health and Health Professions, Program in Rehabilitation Science, Gainesville, FL 32611. Offers PhD, PhD/MPH. *Degree requirements:* For doctorate, comprehensive exam, thesis/dissertation. *Entrance requirements:* For doctorate, GRE (minimum scores: 150 Verbal, 145 Quantitative), minimum GPA of 3.0. Additional exam requirements/recommendations for international students: required—TOEFL (minimum score 550 paper-based; 80 iBT), IELTS (minimum score 6). Electronic applications accepted.

**University of Illinois at Urbana-Champaign,** Graduate College, College of Applied Health Sciences, Department of Kinesiology and Community Health, Champaign, IL 61820. Offers community health (MS, MSPH, PhD); kinesiology (MS, PhD); public health (MPH); rehabilitation (MS); PhD/MPH.

**The University of Iowa,** Roy J. and Lucille A. Carver College of Medicine and Graduate College, Graduate Programs in Medicine, Department of Physical Therapy and Rehabilitation Science, Iowa City, IA 52242. Offers physical rehabilitation science (MA, PhD); physical therapy (DPT). *Accreditation:* APTA (one or more programs are accredited). Terminal master's awarded for partial completion of doctoral program. *Degree requirements:* For master's, thesis (for some programs); for doctorate, comprehensive exam (for some programs), thesis/dissertation (for some programs). *Entrance requirements:* For master's and doctorate, GRE. Additional exam

requirements/recommendations for international students: required—TOEFL. Electronic applications accepted. *Expenses:* Contact institution.

**The University of Kansas,** University of Kansas Medical Center, School of Health Professions, Department of Occupational Therapy Education, Kansas City, KS 66160. Offers occupational therapy (MOT, OTD); therapeutic science (PhD). *Accreditation:* AOTA. *Program availability:* Part-time. *Faculty:* 14. *Students:* 128 full-time (112 women), 15 part-time (14 women); includes 21 minority (1 Black or African American, non-Hispanic/Latino; 4 Asian, non-Hispanic/Latino; 10 Hispanic/Latino; 6 Two or more races, non-Hispanic/Latino), 1 international. Average age 26. In 2019, 41 master's, 10 doctorates awarded. *Degree requirements:* For doctorate, comprehensive exam, thesis/dissertation, capstone and oral defense. *Entrance requirements:* For doctorate, GRE, For the Therapeutic Science PhD program, a minimum of 24 research-related course credits at the graduate level. Additional exam requirements/recommendations for international students: required—TOEFL; recommended—IELTS. *Application deadline:* For fall admission, 12/1 for domestic and international students. Application fee: $60. Electronic applications accepted. *Expenses:* Tuition, state resident: full-time $9989. Tuition, nonresident: full-time $23,950. *International tuition:* $23,950 full-time. *Required fees:* $984; $81.99 per credit hour. Tuition and fees vary according to course load, campus/location and program. *Financial support:* Research assistantships, teaching assistantships with full and partial tuition reimbursements, Federal Work-Study, scholarships/grants, traineeships, and unspecified assistantships available. Financial award application deadline: 3/1; financial award applicants required to submit FAFSA. *Unit head:* Dr. Dory Sabata, Interim Department Chair and Clinical Associate Professor, 913-588-7338, Fax: 913-588-4568, E-mail: dsabata@kumc.edu. *Application contact:* Bobbi Stidham, Program Manager, 913-588-7195, Fax: 913-588-4568, E-mail: bstidham@kumc.edu.
Website: http://www.kumc.edu/school-of-health-professions/occupational-therapy-education.html

**The University of Kansas,** University of Kansas Medical Center, School of Health Professions, Department of Physical Therapy and Rehabilitation Science, Kansas City, KS 66160. Offers physical therapy (DPT); rehabilitation science (PhD). *Accreditation:* APTA. *Faculty:* 27. *Students:* 186 full-time (120 women), 3 part-time (2 women); includes 22 minority (3 Black or African American, non-Hispanic/Latino; 6 Asian, non-Hispanic/Latino; 10 Hispanic/Latino; 1 Native Hawaiian or other Pacific Islander, non-Hispanic/Latino; 2 Two or more races, non-Hispanic/Latino), 9 international. Average age 25. In 2019, 60 doctorates awarded. *Degree requirements:* For doctorate, comprehensive exam, dissertation for PhD. *Entrance requirements:* For doctorate, GRE General Test, minimum GPA of 3.0. Additional exam requirements/recommendations for international students: required—TOEFL. *Application deadline:* For fall admission, 11/1 for domestic students. Application fee: $75. Electronic applications accepted. *Expenses:* Contact institution. *Financial support:* Research assistantships with tuition reimbursements, teaching assistantships with tuition reimbursements, career-related internships or fieldwork, Federal Work-Study, institutionally sponsored loans, scholarships/grants, traineeships, and unspecified assistantships available. Financial award application deadline: 3/1; financial award applicants required to submit FAFSA. *Unit head:* Dr. Patricia Kluding, Professor and Department Chair, 913-588-6799, Fax: 913-588-6910, E-mail: pkluding@kumc.edu. *Application contact:* Robert Bagley, Program Manager, 913-588-6799, Fax: 913-588-6910, E-mail: rbagley@kumc.edu.
Website: http://www.kumc.edu/school-of-health-professions/physical-therapy-and-rehabilitation-science.html

**University of Kentucky,** Graduate School, College of Health Sciences, Program in Rehabilitation Sciences, Lexington, KY 40506-0032. Offers PhD. *Degree requirements:* For doctorate, comprehensive exam, thesis/dissertation. *Entrance requirements:* For doctorate, GRE General Test, minimum undergraduate GPA of 2.75. Additional exam requirements/recommendations for international students: required—TOEFL (minimum score 550 paper-based). Electronic applications accepted.

**University of Manitoba,** Faculty of Graduate Studies, College of Rehabilitation Sciences, Winnipeg, MB R3T 2N2, Canada. Offers applied health sciences (PhD); occupational therapy (MOT); physical therapy (MPT); rehabilitation sciences (M Sc).

**University of Maryland, Baltimore,** Graduate School, Graduate Program in Life Sciences, Program in Physical Rehabilitation Science, Baltimore, MD 21201. Offers PhD, MD/PhD. *Degree requirements:* For doctorate, comprehensive exam, thesis/dissertation. *Entrance requirements:* For doctorate, GRE, minimum GPA of 3.0, curriculum vitae, essay, 3 letters of recommendation. Additional exam requirements/recommendations for international students: required—TOEFL (minimum score 80 iBT); recommended—IELTS (minimum score 7). Electronic applications accepted.

**University of Maryland, Baltimore,** School of Medicine, Department of Physical Therapy and Rehabilitation Science, Baltimore, MD 21201. Offers physical rehabilitation science (PhD); physical therapy and rehabilitation science (DPT). *Accreditation:* APTA. *Students:* 191 full-time (134 women), 1 (woman) part-time; includes 42 minority (10 Black or African American, non-Hispanic/Latino; 15 Asian, non-Hispanic/Latino; 6 Hispanic/Latino; 11 Two or more races, non-Hispanic/Latino), 1 international. Average age 25. 214 applicants, 93% accepted, 65 enrolled. In 2019, 61 doctorates awarded. *Entrance requirements:* For doctorate, GRE General Test, BS, science coursework. Additional exam requirements/recommendations for international students: required—TOEFL (minimum score 80 iBT). Electronic applications accepted. *Expenses:* Contact institution. *Financial support:* Career-related internships or fieldwork, Federal Work-Study, scholarships/grants, traineeships, health care benefits, and unspecified assistantships available. Financial award application deadline: 3/1; financial award applicants required to submit FAFSA. *Unit head:* Dr. Mark W. Rogers, Chair, 410-706-0841, Fax: 410-706-4903, E-mail: mrogers@som.umaryland.edu. *Application contact:* Aynsley Hamel, Program Coordinator, 410-706-0566, Fax: 410-706-6387, E-mail: ptadmissions@som.umaryland.edu.
Website: http://pt.umaryland.edu/pros.asp

**University of Maryland Eastern Shore,** Graduate Programs, Department of Rehabilitation Services, Princess Anne, MD 21853. Offers rehabilitation counseling (MS). *Accreditation:* CORE. *Program availability:* Part-time, evening/weekend. *Degree requirements:* For master's, internship. *Entrance requirements:* For master's, interview. Additional exam requirements/recommendations for international students: required—TOEFL (minimum score 80 iBT). Electronic applications accepted.

**University of Northern Colorado,** Graduate School, College of Natural and Health Sciences, School of Human Sciences, Program in Rehabilitation Counseling and Sciences, Greeley, CO 80639. Offers rehabilitation counseling (MA); rehabilitation sciences (PhD). *Accreditation:* CORE (one or more programs are accredited). *Program availability:* Part-time. *Degree requirements:* For master's, comprehensive exam, thesis or alternative; for doctorate, comprehensive exam, thesis/dissertation. *Entrance requirements:* For master's, GRE General Test or MAT, 2 letters of recommendation; for doctorate, GRE General Test, 2 letters of recommendation. Electronic applications accepted.

**University of North Texas Health Science Center at Fort Worth,** Graduate School of Biomedical Sciences, Fort Worth, TX 76107-2699. Offers biochemistry and cancer biology (MS, PhD); biotechnology (MS); cell biology, immunology and microbiology (MS, PhD); clinical research management (MS); forensic genetics (MS); genetics (MS, PhD); integrative physiology (MS, PhD); medical sciences (MS); pharmaceutical sciences and pharmacotherapy (MS, PhD); pharmacology and neuroscience (MS, PhD); structural anatomy and rehabilitation sciences (MS, PhD); DO/MS; DO/PhD. Terminal master's awarded for partial completion of doctoral program. *Degree requirements:* For master's, thesis; for doctorate, thesis/dissertation. *Entrance requirements:* For master's and doctorate, GRE General Test. Additional exam requirements/recommendations for international students: required—TOEFL. *Expenses:* Contact institution.

**University of Oklahoma Health Sciences Center,** Graduate College, College of Allied Health, Department of Rehabilitation Sciences, Oklahoma City, OK 73190. Offers MS. *Degree requirements:* For master's, comprehensive exam, thesis optional. *Entrance requirements:* For master's, GRE General Test, 2 years of clinical experience, 3 letters of reference. Additional exam requirements/recommendations for international students: required—TOEFL (minimum score 550 paper-based).

**University of Ottawa,** Faculty of Graduate and Postdoctoral Studies, Faculty of Health Sciences, School of Rehabilitation Sciences, Ottawa, ON K1N 6N5, Canada. Offers audiology (M Sc); orthophony (M Sc). *Program availability:* Part-time, evening/weekend. *Entrance requirements:* For master's, honors degree or equivalent, minimum B average. Electronic applications accepted.

**University of Pittsburgh,** School of Health and Rehabilitation Sciences, Department of Rehabilitation Science and Technology, Pittsburgh, PA 15260. Offers clinical rehabilitation and mental health counseling (MS); physician assistant studies (MS); prosthetics and orthotics (DPT); rehabilitation technology (MS). *Program availability:* Part-time, blended/hybrid learning. *Faculty:* 26 full-time (15 women), 6 part-time/adjunct (3 women). *Students:* 97 full-time (57 women), 16 part-time (13 women); includes 19 minority (3 Black or African American, non-Hispanic/Latino; 5 Asian, non-Hispanic/Latino; 3 Hispanic/Latino; 8 Two or more races, non-Hispanic/Latino), 9 international. Average age 26. 187 applicants, 58% accepted, 49 enrolled. In 2019, 50 master's awarded. *Degree requirements:* For master's, comprehensive exam (for some programs), thesis (for some programs). *Entrance requirements:* For master's, Varies by program, Varies by program. Additional exam requirements/recommendations for international students: required—International applicants may provide Duolingo English Test, IELTS or TOEFL scores to verify English language proficiency. Electronic applications accepted. *Financial support:* In 2019–20, 14 students received support, including 1 fellowship with full tuition reimbursement available (averaging $30,000 per year), 9 research assistantships with full tuition reimbursements available (averaging $30,000 per year); scholarships/grants also available. *Unit head:* Dr. Jonathan Pearlman, Chair and Associate Professor, Department of Rehabilitation Science and Technology, 412-383-3955, E-mail: jpearlman@pitt.edu. *Application contact:* Jessica Maguire, Director of Admissions, 412-383-6557, Fax: 412-383-6535, E-mail: maguire@pitt.edu.
Website: http://www.shrs.pitt.edu/rst

**University of Pittsburgh,** School of Health and Rehabilitation Sciences, Department of Sports Medicine and Nutrition, Pittsburgh, PA 15260. Offers health and rehabilitation sciences (MS), including sports medicine, wellness and human performance; nutrition and dietetics (MS). *Faculty:* 15 full-time (8 women), 3 part-time/adjunct (all women). *Students:* 58 full-time (46 women), 1 part-time (0 women); includes 7 minority (1 Black or African American, non-Hispanic/Latino; 3 Asian, non-Hispanic/Latino; 2 Hispanic/Latino; 1 Two or more races, non-Hispanic/Latino), 1 international. Average age 24. 122 applicants, 70% accepted, 32 enrolled. In 2019, 28 master's awarded. *Degree requirements:* For master's, comprehensive exam (for some programs). *Entrance requirements:* For master's, Varies by program. Additional exam requirements/recommendations for international students: required—International applicants may provide Duolingo English Test, IELTS or TOEFL scores to verify English language proficiency. Application fee: $50. Electronic applications accepted. *Financial support:* In 2019–20, 13 students received support, including 7 research assistantships with full tuition reimbursements available (averaging $28,200 per year); traineeships also available. *Unit head:* Dr. Kevin Conley, Associate Dean for Undergraduate Studies, SHRS, Chair and Associate Professor, Department of Sports Medicine and Nutrition, 412-383-6737, Fax: 412-383-6636, E-mail: kconley@pitt.edu. *Application contact:* Jessica Maguire, Director of Admissions, 412-383-6557, Fax: 412-383-6535, E-mail: maguire@pitt.edu.
Website: http://www.shrs.pitt.edu/smn

**University of Pittsburgh,** School of Health and Rehabilitation Sciences, PhD Program in Rehabilitation Science, Pittsburgh, PA 15260. Offers PhD. *Students:* 38 full-time (20 women), 1 (woman) part-time; includes 3 minority (1 Black or African American, non-Hispanic/Latino; 2 Two or more races, non-Hispanic/Latino), 10 international. Average age 32. 21 applicants, 62% accepted, 11 enrolled. In 2019, 6 doctorates awarded. *Degree requirements:* For doctorate, comprehensive exam, thesis/dissertation. *Entrance requirements:* For doctorate, GRE General Test. Additional exam requirements/recommendations for international students: required—International applicants may provide Duolingo English Test, IELTS or TOEFL scores to verify English language proficiency. *Application deadline:* Applications are processed on a rolling basis. Application fee: $50. Electronic applications accepted. *Unit head:* Dr. G. Kelley Fitzgerald, Associate Dean of Graduate Studies/Professor, 412-383-6643, Fax: 412-383-6535, E-mail: kfitzger@pitt.edu. *Application contact:* Jessica Maguire, Director of Admissions, 412-383-6557, Fax: 412-383-6535, E-mail: maguire@pitt.edu.
Website: http://www.shrs.pitt.edu/phdrs/

**University of South Carolina,** School of Medicine and The Graduate School, Graduate Programs in Medicine, Program in Rehabilitation Counseling, Columbia, SC 29208. Offers psychiatric rehabilitation (Certificate); rehabilitation counseling (MRC). *Accreditation:* CORE. *Program availability:* Part-time, evening/weekend. *Degree requirements:* For master's, comprehensive exam, internship, practicum. *Entrance requirements:* For master's and Certificate, GRE General Test or GMAT. Electronic applications accepted. *Expenses:* Contact institution.

**University of South Florida,** Morsani College of Medicine, School of Physical Therapy, Tampa, FL 33620-9951. Offers physical therapy (DPT); rehabilitation sciences (PhD), including chronic disease, neuromusculoskeletal disability, veteran's health/reintegration. *Accreditation:* APTA. *Faculty:* 12 full-time (7 women). *Students:* 137 full-time (86 women); includes 29 minority (6 Black or African American, non-Hispanic/Latino; 9 Asian, non-Hispanic/Latino; 13 Hispanic/Latino; 1 Two or more races, non-Hispanic/Latino). Average age 24. 1,190 applicants, 4% accepted, 46 enrolled. In 2019, 44 doctorates awarded. *Degree requirements:* For doctorate, comprehensive exam, thesis/dissertation. *Entrance requirements:* For doctorate, GRE General Test, bachelor's degree from regionally-accredited university with minimum GPA of 3.0 in all upper-division coursework; interview; at least 20 hours of documented volunteer or work experience in hospital outpatient/inpatient physical therapy settings; written personal statement of values and purpose for attending. Additional exam requirements/recommendations for international students: required—TOEFL (minimum score 600 paper-based; 79 iBT). *Application deadline:* For fall admission, 6/1 for domestic students, 1/1 for international students; for spring admission, 10/15 for domestic students, 9/15 for international students. Application fee: $30. Electronic applications accepted. *Financial support:* In 2019–20, 64 students received support. Teaching

assistantships available. *Unit head:* Dr. William S. Quillen, Director, 813-974-9863, Fax: 813-974-8915, E-mail: wquillen@health.usf.edu. *Application contact:* Dr. Gina Maria Musolino, Associate Professor and Coordinator for Clinical Education, 813-974-2254, Fax: 813-974-8915, E-mail: gmusolin@health.usf.edu. Website: http://health.usf.edu/medicine/dpt/index.htm

**The University of Texas Medical Branch,** Graduate School of Biomedical Sciences, Program in Rehabilitation Sciences, Galveston, TX 77555. Offers PhD. *Accreditation:* CEPH. *Degree requirements:* For doctorate, thesis/dissertation. *Entrance requirements:* For doctorate, GRE General Test. Additional exam requirements/recommendations for international students: required—TOEFL (minimum score 550 paper-based). Electronic applications accepted.

**University of Toronto,** Faculty of Medicine, Department of Rehabilitation Science, Toronto, ON M5S 1A1, Canada. Offers M Sc, PhD. *Degree requirements:* For master's, thesis. *Entrance requirements:* For master's, B Sc or equivalent; specialization in occupational therapy, physical therapy, or a related field; minimum B+ average in final 2 years. Additional exam requirements/recommendations for international students: required—TOEFL (minimum score 580 paper-based; 93 iBT), TWE (minimum score 5). Electronic applications accepted.

**The University of Tulsa,** Graduate School, Oxley College of Health Sciences, Department of Kinesiology and Rehabilitative Sciences, Tulsa, OK 74104-3189. Offers MAT. *Entrance requirements:* For master's, GRE General Test. Additional exam requirements/recommendations for international students: required—TOEFL (minimum score 577 paper-based; 90 iBT), IELTS (minimum score 6.5). *Expenses:* Contact institution.

**University of Utah,** Graduate School, College of Health, Department of Physical Therapy and Athletic Training, Salt Lake City, UT 84112-1290. Offers physical therapy (DPT); rehabilitation science (PhD). *Accreditation:* APTA. *Entrance requirements:* For doctorate, GRE, minimum GPA of 3.0, volunteer work, bachelor's degree. Additional exam requirements/recommendations for international students: required—TOEFL (minimum score 90 iBT); recommended—IELTS (minimum score 7). Electronic applications accepted. *Expenses:* Contact institution.

**University of Vermont,** Graduate College, College of Nursing and Health Sciences, Program in Human Functioning and Rehabilitation Science, Burlington, VT 05405. Offers PhD. *Entrance requirements:* For doctorate, GRE General Test. Additional exam requirements/recommendations for international students: required—TOEFL (minimum iBT score of 90) or IELTS (6.5). Electronic applications accepted.

**University of Washington,** Graduate School, School of Medicine, Graduate Programs in Medicine, Department of Rehabilitation Medicine, Seattle, WA 98195-6490. Offers occupational therapy (MOT); physical therapy (DPT); prosthetics and orthotics (MPO); rehabilitation science (PhD). *Accreditation:* AOTA. *Degree requirements:* For doctorate,

comprehensive exam (for some programs), thesis/dissertation (for some programs). *Entrance requirements:* For master's and doctorate, GRE. Additional exam requirements/recommendations for international students: required—TOEFL.

**University of Wisconsin–La Crosse,** College of Science and Health, Department of Exercise and Sport Science, Program in Clinical Exercise Physiology, La Crosse, WI 54601-3742. Offers MS. *Students:* 14 full-time (5 women); includes 2 minority (1 Asian, non-Hispanic/Latino; 1 Hispanic/Latino). Average age 24. 14 applicants, 100% accepted, 14 enrolled. In 2019, 14 master's awarded. *Degree requirements:* For master's, thesis optional. *Entrance requirements:* Additional exam requirements/recommendations for international students: required—TOEFL (minimum score 550 paper-based; 79 iBT). *Application deadline:* For fall admission, 2/1 priority date for domestic and international students. Electronic applications accepted. *Financial support:* Federal Work-Study, scholarships/grants, health care benefits, and tuition waivers (partial) available. Support available to part-time students. Financial award application deadline: 3/15; financial award applicants required to submit FAFSA. *Unit head:* Dr. John Porcari, Director, 608-785-8684, Fax: 608-785-8686, E-mail: porcari.john@uwlax.edu. *Application contact:* Jennifer Weber, Senior Student Service Coordinator Graduate Admissions, 608-785-8939, E-mail: admissions@uwlax.edu. Website: https://www.uwlax.edu/grad/clinical-exercise-physiology/

**University of Wisconsin–Milwaukee,** Graduate School, College of Health Sciences, Program in Health Sciences, Milwaukee, WI 53201-0413. Offers health sciences (PhD), including diagnostic and biomedical sciences, disability and rehabilitation, health administration and policy, human movement sciences, population health. *Degree requirements:* For doctorate, comprehensive exam, thesis/dissertation. *Entrance requirements:* For doctorate, GRE. Additional exam requirements/recommendations for international students: required—TOEFL (minimum score 600 paper-based), IELTS (minimum score 6.5).

**Virginia Commonwealth University,** Graduate School, College of Humanities and Sciences, Department of Kinesiology and Health Sciences, Program in Rehabilitation and Movement Science, Richmond, VA 23284-9005. Offers PhD. *Entrance requirements:* Additional exam requirements/recommendations for international students: required—TOEFL (minimum score 600 paper-based; 100 iBT). Electronic applications accepted.

**Washington University in St. Louis,** School of Medicine, Program in Rehabilitation and Participation Science, St. Louis, MO 63130-4899. Offers PhD.

**Western Michigan University,** Graduate College, College of Health and Human Services, Department of Blindness and Low Vision Studies, Kalamazoo, MI 49008. Offers orientation and mobility (MA); orientation and mobility of children (MA); vision rehabilitation therapy (MA). *Accreditation:* CORE.

# Section 21
# Health Sciences

This section contains a directory of institutions offering graduate work in health sciences. Additional information about programs listed in the directory may be obtained by writing directly to the dean of a graduate school or chair of a department at the address given in the directory.

For programs offering related work, see also in this book *Biological and Biomedical Sciences, Biophysics (Radiation Biology), Dentistry and Dental Sciences, Health Services, Medicine, Nursing,* and *Public Health.* In the other guides in this series:

**Graduate Programs in the Physical Sciences, Mathematics, Agricultural Sciences, the Environment & Natural Resources**

See *Physics*

**Graduate Programs in Engineering & Applied Sciences**

See *Agricultural Engineering and Bioengineering (Bioengineering), Biomedical Engineering and Biotechnology,* and *Energy and Power Engineering (Nuclear Engineering)*

## CONTENTS

## Program Directories

# Health Physics/Radiological Health

**East Carolina University,** Graduate School, Thomas Harriot College of Arts and Sciences, Department of Physics, Greenville, NC 27858-4353. Offers applied physics (MS); biomedical physics (PhD); health physics (MS); medical physics (MS). *Program availability:* Part-time. *Application deadline:* For fall admission, 3/1 priority date for domestic and international students. *Expenses: Tuition, area resident:* Full-time $4749; part-time $185 per credit hour. Tuition, state resident: full-time $4749; part-time $185 per credit hour. Tuition, nonresident: full-time $17,898; part-time $864 per credit hour. *International tuition:* $17,898 full-time. *Required fees:* $2787. *Financial support:* Application deadline: 3/1. *Unit head:* Dr. Jefferson Shinpaugh, Chair, 252-328-6739, E-mail: shinpaughj@ecu.edu. *Application contact:* Graduate School Admissions, 252-328-6012, Fax: 252-328-6071, E-mail: gradschool@ecu.edu.
Website: https://physics.ecu.edu/

**Georgetown University,** Graduate School of Arts and Sciences, Department of Health Physics and Radiation Protection, Washington, DC 20057. Offers health physics (MS); nuclear nonproliferation (MS). *Degree requirements:* For master's, thesis. *Entrance requirements:* Additional exam requirements/recommendations for international students: required—TOEFL.

**Georgia Institute of Technology,** Graduate Studies, College of Engineering, George W. Woodruff School of Mechanical Engineering, Atlanta, GA 30332-0405. Offers mechanical engineering (MS, MSME, PhD); nuclear and radiological engineering and medical physics (MS, MSMP, MSNE, PhD), including medical physics (MS, MSMP), nuclear and radiological engineering (PhD), nuclear engineering (MSNE). *Program availability:* Part-time, 100% online. *Faculty:* 100 full-time (13 women), 5 part-time/adjunct (1 woman). *Students:* 608 full-time (110 women), 200 part-time (43 women); includes 205 minority (19 Black or African American, non-Hispanic/Latino; 1 American Indian or Alaska Native, non-Hispanic/Latino; 107 Asian, non-Hispanic/Latino; 47 Hispanic/Latino; 31 Two or more races, non-Hispanic/Latino), 231 international. Average age 26. 1,352 applicants, 32% accepted, 200 enrolled. In 2019, 229 master's, 56 doctorates awarded. Terminal master's awarded for partial completion of doctoral program. *Degree requirements:* For master's, thesis; for doctorate, comprehensive exam, thesis/dissertation. *Entrance requirements:* For master's, GRE General Test, minimum 3.0 for the MSNRE and MSMP; for doctorate, GRE General Test, minimum GPA of 3.3. Additional exam requirements/recommendations for international students: required—TOEFL (minimum score 94 iBT), IELTS (minimum score 7), TOEFL is the preferred method with the requirements shown on the programs. *Application deadline:* For fall admission, 2/1 for domestic and international students; for spring admission, 11/1 for domestic students, 10/1 for international students. Applications are processed on a rolling basis. Application fee: $75 ($85 for international students). Electronic applications accepted. *Expenses: Tuition, area resident:* Full-time $14,064; part-time $586 per credit hour. Tuition, state resident: full-time $14,064; part-time $586 per credit hour. Tuition, nonresident: full-time $29,140; part-time $1215 per credit hour. *International tuition:* $29,140 full-time. *Required fees:* $2024; $840 per semester. $2096. Tuition and fees vary according to course load. *Financial support:* In 2019–20, 41 fellowships, 395 research assistantships, 8 teaching assistantships were awarded; career-related internships or fieldwork, Federal Work-Study, institutionally sponsored loans, tuition waivers (full and partial), and unspecified assistantships also available. Support available to part-time students. Financial award application deadline: 7/1; financial award applicants required to submit FAFSA. *Unit head:* Samuel Graham, School Chair, 404-894-3200, Fax: 404-894-1658, E-mail: sgraham@gatech.edu. *Application contact:* Marla Bruner, Director of Graduate Studies, 404-894-1610, Fax: 404-894-1609, E-mail: gradinfo@mail.gatech.edu.
Website: http://www.me.gatech.edu

**Idaho State University,** Graduate School, College of Science and Engineering, Department of Physics, Pocatello, ID 83209-8106. Offers applied physics (PhD); health physics (MS); physics (MNS). *Program availability:* Part-time. *Degree requirements:* For master's, comprehensive exam, thesis (for some programs), oral exam (for some programs); for doctorate, comprehensive exam, thesis/dissertation (for some programs), oral exam, written qualifying exam in physics or health physics after 1st year. *Entrance requirements:* For master's, GRE General Test, 3 letters of recommendation, BS or BA in physics, teaching certificate (MNS); for doctorate, GRE General Test (minimum 50th percentile), 3 letters of recommendation, statement of career goals. Additional exam requirements/recommendations for international students: required—TOEFL (minimum score 550 paper-based; 80 iBT). Electronic applications accepted.

**Illinois Institute of Technology,** Graduate College, College of Science, Department of Physics, Chicago, IL 60616. Offers applied physics (MS); health physics (MAS); physics (MS, PhD). *Program availability:* Part-time, evening/weekend, online learning. Terminal master's awarded for partial completion of doctoral program. *Degree requirements:* For master's, comprehensive exam (for some programs), thesis (for some programs); for doctorate, comprehensive exam, thesis/dissertation. *Entrance requirements:* For master's, GRE General Test (minimum score 295 Quantitative and Verbal, 2.5 Analytical Writing), minimum undergraduate GPA of 3.0; for doctorate, GRE General Test (minimum score 310 Quantitative and Verbal, 3.0 Analytical Writing); GRE Subject Test in physics (strongly recommended), minimum undergraduate GPA of 3.0. Additional exam requirements/recommendations for international students: required—TOEFL (minimum score 550 paper-based; 80 iBT). Electronic applications accepted.

**John Patrick University of Health and Applied Sciences,** Graduate Programs, South Bend, IN 46601. Offers medical dosimetry (MS); medical health physics (MS); medical physics (MS).

**McMaster University,** School of Graduate Studies, Faculty of Science, Department of Medical Physics and Applied Radiation Sciences, Hamilton, ON L8S 4M2, Canada. Offers health and radiation physics (M Sc); medical physics (M Sc, PhD). *Program availability:* Part-time. *Degree requirements:* For master's, thesis or alternative. *Entrance requirements:* For master's, minimum B+ average. Additional exam requirements/recommendations for international students: required—TOEFL (minimum score 550 paper-based).

**Midwestern State University,** Billie Doris McAda Graduate School, Robert D. and Carol Gunn College of Health Sciences and Human Services, Program in Radiologic Sciences, Wichita Falls, TX 76308. Offers MS. *Program availability:* Part-time, evening/weekend, online learning. *Degree requirements:* For master's, comprehensive exam, thesis optional. *Entrance requirements:* For master's, GRE General Test, MAT or GMAT, credentials in one of the medical imaging modalities or radiation therapy; 1 year of experience; 3 letters of recommendation from past and/or present educators and employers. Additional exam requirements/recommendations for international students: required—TOEFL (minimum score 550 paper-based). Electronic applications accepted.

**Northwestern State University of Louisiana,** Graduate Studies and Research, College of Nursing and School of Allied Health, Department of Radiologic Sciences, Natchitoches, LA 71497. Offers MS. *Degree requirements:* For master's, comprehensive exam, thesis (for some programs). *Entrance requirements:* Additional exam requirements/recommendations for international students: required—TOEFL. Electronic applications accepted.

**Oregon State University,** College of Engineering, Program in Radiation Health Physics, Corvallis, OR 97331. Offers application of nuclear techniques (MHP, MS, PhD). *Program availability:* Part-time, blended/hybrid learning. *Entrance requirements:* For master's and doctorate, GRE. Additional exam requirements/recommendations for international students: required—TOEFL (minimum score 80 iBT), IELTS (minimum score 6.5). *Expenses:* Contact institution.

**Purdue University,** Graduate School, College of Health and Human Sciences, School of Health Sciences, West Lafayette, IN 47907. Offers health physics (MS, PhD); medical physics (MS, PhD); occupational and environmental health science (MS, PhD), including aerosol deposition and lung disease, ergonomics, exposure and risk assessment, indoor air quality and bioaerosols (PhD), liver/lung toxicology; radiological health (PhD); toxicology (PhD); MS/PhD. *Program availability:* Part-time. *Faculty:* 15 full-time (6 women), 1 part-time/adjunct (0 women). *Students:* 39 full-time (22 women), 6 part-time (3 women); includes 12 minority (2 Black or African American, non-Hispanic/Latino; 1 American Indian or Alaska Native, non-Hispanic/Latino; 3 Asian, non-Hispanic/Latino; 1 Hispanic/Latino; 5 Two or more races, non-Hispanic/Latino), 15 international. Average age 28. 61 applicants, 43% accepted, 14 enrolled. In 2019, 15 master's, 6 doctorates awarded. *Degree requirements:* For master's, thesis optional; for doctorate, one foreign language, thesis/dissertation. *Entrance requirements:* For master's and doctorate, GRE General Test, minimum undergraduate GPA of 3.0 or equivalent. Additional exam requirements/recommendations for international students: required—TOEFL (minimum score 550 paper-based; 77 iBT); recommended—TWE. *Application deadline:* For fall admission, 5/15 for domestic and international students; for spring admission, 10/15 for domestic and international students. Applications are processed on a rolling basis. Application fee: $60 ($75 for international students). Electronic applications accepted. *Financial support:* In 2019–20, fellowships with tuition reimbursements (averaging $14,400 per year), research assistantships with tuition reimbursements (averaging $12,000 per year), teaching assistantships with tuition reimbursements (averaging $12,000 per year) were awarded; career-related internships or fieldwork and traineeships also available. Support available to part-time students. Financial award applicants required to submit FAFSA. *Unit head:* Aaron Bowman, Head of the Graduate Program, 765-494-2684, E-mail: bowma117@purdue.edu. *Application contact:* Karen E. Walker, Graduate Contact, 765-494-1419, E-mail: kwalker@purdue.edu.
Website: https://www.purdue.edu/hhs/hsci/

**Quinnipiac University,** School of Health Sciences, Program for Radiologist Assistant, Hamden, CT 06518-1940. Offers MHS. *Entrance requirements:* For master's, proof of certification from American Registry of Radiologic Technologists; 2000 hours of direct patient care; CPR certification. Additional exam requirements/recommendations for international students: required—TOEFL (minimum score 575 paper-based; 90 iBT), IELTS (minimum score 6.5). Electronic applications accepted. *Expenses: Tuition:* Part-time $1055 per credit. *Required fees:* $945 per semester. Tuition and fees vary according to course load and program.

**Rutgers University - Newark,** School of Health Related Professions, Department of Medical Imaging Sciences, Newark, NJ 07102. Offers radiologist assistant (MS). *Program availability:* Part-time, evening/weekend. *Entrance requirements:* For master's, BS with minimum GPA of 3.0, RT license, coursework in intro to pathopsychology, interview, all transcripts, personal statement, BCLS certification. Additional exam requirements/recommendations for international students: required—TOEFL (minimum score 500 paper-based; 79 iBT). Electronic applications accepted.

**San Diego State University,** Graduate and Research Affairs, College of Sciences, Department of Physics, Program in Radiological Physics, San Diego, CA 92182. Offers MS. *Program availability:* Part-time. *Degree requirements:* For master's, thesis optional, oral or written exam. *Entrance requirements:* For master's, GRE General Test, GRE Subject Test (physics), 2 letters of recommendation. Additional exam requirements/recommendations for international students: required—TOEFL. Electronic applications accepted.

**Thomas Jefferson University,** Jefferson College of Health Professions, Department of Medical Imaging and Radiation Sciences, Philadelphia, PA 19107. Offers medical physics (MS); radiologic and imaging sciences (MS). *Program availability:* Part-time. *Degree requirements:* For master's, capstone project. *Entrance requirements:* For master's, bachelor's degree. Additional exam requirements/recommendations for international students: required—TOEFL (minimum score 87 iBT), IELTS (minimum score 6.5). Electronic applications accepted.

**University of Alberta,** Faculty of Medicine and Dentistry and Faculty of Graduate Studies and Research, Graduate Programs in Medicine, Department of Radiology and Diagnostic Imaging, Edmonton, AB T6G 2E1, Canada. Offers medical sciences (PhD); radiology and diagnostic imaging (M Sc). Terminal master's awarded for partial completion of doctoral program. *Degree requirements:* For master's, thesis; for doctorate, thesis/dissertation. *Entrance requirements:* For master's, minimum GPA of 6.5 on a 9.0 scale; for doctorate, M Sc.

**University of Arkansas for Medical Sciences,** College of Health Professions, Little Rock, AR 72205-7199. Offers audiology (Au D); communication sciences and disorders (MS, PhD); genetic counseling (MS); nuclear medicine advanced associate (MIS); physician assistant studies (MPAS); radiologist assistant (MIS). *Accreditation:* ASHA. *Program availability:* Part-time, online learning. *Degree requirements:* For master's, thesis (for some programs); for doctorate, comprehensive exam (for some programs), thesis/dissertation (for some programs). *Entrance requirements:* For master's, GRE. Additional exam requirements/recommendations for international students: required—TOEFL (minimum score 550 paper-based; 79 iBT). Electronic applications accepted. *Expenses:* Contact institution.

**University of Cincinnati,** Graduate School, College of Medicine, Graduate Programs in Biomedical Sciences, Department of Radiology, Cincinnati, OH 45267. Offers medical physics (MS). *Program availability:* Part-time. *Degree requirements:* For master's, comprehensive exam, project. *Entrance requirements:* For master's, GRE General Test. Additional exam requirements/recommendations for international students: required—TOEFL (minimum score 575 paper-based). Electronic applications accepted.

**University of Kentucky,** Graduate School, Graduate School Programs from the College of Medicine, Program in Radiation Sciences, Lexington, KY 40506-0032. Offers MSRMP. *Program availability:* Part-time. *Degree requirements:* For master's, comprehensive exam, thesis. *Entrance requirements:* For master's, GRE General Test, minimum undergraduate GPA of 2.75. Additional exam requirements/recommendations

for international students: required—TOEFL (minimum score 550 paper-based). Electronic applications accepted.

**University of Massachusetts Lowell,** College of Sciences, Department of Physics, Program in Radiological Sciences and Protection, Lowell, MA 01854. Offers MS, PSM. *Degree requirements:* For master's, one foreign language, thesis. *Entrance requirements:* For master's, GRE General Test, 3 letters of reference. Additional exam requirements/recommendations for international students: required—TOEFL. Electronic applications accepted.

**University of Michigan,** College of Engineering, Department of Nuclear Engineering and Radiological Sciences, Ann Arbor, MI 48109. Offers nuclear engineering (Nuc E); nuclear engineering and radiological sciences (MSE, PhD); nuclear science (MS, PhD). Terminal master's awarded for partial completion of doctoral program. *Degree requirements:* For master's, thesis optional; for doctorate, thesis/dissertation, oral defense of dissertation, preliminary exams. *Entrance requirements:* For master's and doctorate, GRE General Test. Additional exam requirements/recommendations for international students: required—TOEFL. Electronic applications accepted.

**University of Missouri,** School of Health Professions, Department of Clinical and Diagnostic Sciences, Columbia, MO 65211. Offers diagnostic medical ultrasound (MHS). *Entrance requirements:* Additional exam requirements/recommendations for international students: required—TOEFL. Electronic applications accepted.

**University of Nevada, Las Vegas,** Graduate College, School of Integrated Health Sciences, Department of Health Physics and Diagnostic Sciences, Las Vegas, NV 89154-3037. Offers health physics (MS); interdisciplinary health sciences (PhD); medical physics (DMP, Advanced Certificate). *Accreditation:* ABET. *Program availability:* Part-time. *Faculty:* 3 full-time (0 women), 1 part-time/adjunct (0 women). *Students:* 33 full-time (10 women), 10 part-time (2 women); includes 16 minority (3 Black or African American, non-Hispanic/Latino; 1 American Indian or Alaska Native, non-Hispanic/Latino; 7 Asian, non-Hispanic/Latino; 3 Hispanic/Latino; 2 Two or more races, non-Hispanic/Latino), 6 international. Average age 32. 44 applicants, 39% accepted, 10 enrolled. In 2019, 3 master's, 3 doctorates awarded. *Degree requirements:* For master's, thesis, professional paper, oral exam; for doctorate, comprehensive exam (for some programs), thesis/dissertation. *Entrance requirements:* For master's and doctorate, GRE General Test, bachelor's degree with minimum GPA 3.0; 3 letters of recommendation; statement of purpose; for Advanced Certificate, GRE General Test, minimum overall GPA of 3.0 in graduate work. Additional exam requirements/recommendations for international students: required—TOEFL (minimum score 550 paper-based; 80 iBT), IELTS (minimum score 7). *Application deadline:* For fall admission, 6/15 for domestic students, 5/1 for international students; for spring admission, 11/15 for domestic students, 10/1 for international students. Application fee: $60 ($95 for international students). Electronic applications accepted. *Expenses:* Contact institution. *Financial support:* In 2019–20, 27 students received support, including 10 research assistantships with full tuition reimbursements available (averaging $18,650 per year), 17 teaching assistantships with full tuition reimbursements available (averaging $17,897 per year); institutionally sponsored loans, scholarships/grants, health care benefits, and unspecified assistantships also available. Financial award application deadline: 3/15; financial award applicants required to submit FAFSA. *Unit head:* Dr. Steen Madsen, Chair/Associate Professor, 702-895-1805, Fax: 702-895-4819, E-mail: hpds.chair@unlv.edu. *Application contact:* Dr. Steen Madsen, Chair/Associate Professor, 702-895-1805, Fax: 702-895-4819, E-mail: hpds.chair@unlv.edu. Website: http://healthphysics.unlv.edu/

**University of Oklahoma Health Sciences Center,** College of Medicine and Graduate College, Graduate Programs in Medicine, Department of Radiological Sciences, Oklahoma City, OK 73190. Offers medical radiation physics (MS, PhD), including diagnostic radiology, nuclear medicine, radiation therapy, ultrasound. *Program availability:* Part-time. Terminal master's awarded for partial completion of doctoral program. *Degree requirements:* For master's, thesis; for doctorate, thesis/dissertation. *Entrance requirements:* For master's, GRE General Test; for doctorate, GRE General Test, 3 letters of recommendation. Additional exam requirements/recommendations for international students: required—TOEFL.

**University of Toronto,** Faculty of Medicine, Institute of Medical Science, Toronto, ON M5S 1A1, Canada. Offers bioethics (MH Sc); biomedical communications (M Sc BMC); medical radiation science (MH Sc); medical science (PhD). *Degree requirements:* For master's, thesis; for doctorate, thesis/dissertation, thesis defense. *Entrance requirements:* For master's, minimum GPA of 3.7 in 3 of 4 years (M Sc), interview; for doctorate, M Sc or equivalent, defended thesis, minimum A- average, interview. Additional exam requirements/recommendations for international students: required—TOEFL (minimum score 600 paper-based; 93 iBT), TWE (minimum score 5). Electronic applications accepted.

**Université Laval,** Faculty of Medicine, Post-Professional Programs in Medical Studies, Québec, QC G1K 7P4, Canada. Offers anatomy–pathology (DESS); anesthesiology (DESS); cardiology (DESS); care of older people (Diploma); clinical research (DESS); community health (DESS); dermatology (DESS); diagnostic radiology (DESS); emergency medicine (Diploma); family medicine (DESS); general surgery (DESS); geriatrics (DESS); hematology (DESS); internal medicine (DESS); maternal and fetal medicine (Diploma); medical biochemistry (DESS); medical microbiology and infectious diseases (DESS); medical oncology (DESS); nephrology (DESS); neurology (DESS); neurosurgery (DESS); obstetrics and gynecology (DESS); ophthalmology (DESS); orthopedic surgery (DESS); oto-rhino-laryngology (DESS); palliative medicine (Diploma); pediatrics (DESS); plastic surgery (DESS); psychiatry (DESS); pulmonary medicine (DESS); radiology–oncology (DESS); thoracic surgery (DESS); urology (DESS). *Degree requirements:* For other advanced degree, comprehensive exam. *Entrance requirements:* For degree, knowledge of French. Electronic applications accepted.

**Virginia Commonwealth University,** Graduate School, School of Allied Health Professions, Doctoral Program in Health Related Sciences, Richmond, VA 23284-9005. Offers clinical laboratory sciences (PhD); gerontology (PhD); health administration (PhD); nurse anesthesia (PhD); occupational therapy (PhD); physical therapy (PhD); radiation sciences (PhD); rehabilitation leadership (PhD). *Entrance requirements:* For doctorate, GRE General Test or MAT, minimum GPA of 3.3 in master's degree. Additional exam requirements/recommendations for international students: required—TOEFL (minimum score 600 paper-based; 100 iBT); recommended—IELTS (minimum score 6.5). Electronic applications accepted.

**Weber State University,** Dumke College of Health Professions, Department of Radiologic Sciences, Ogden, UT 84408-1001. Offers MSRS. *Faculty:* 5 full-time (2 women), 1 (woman) part-time/adjunct. *Students:* 23 full-time (16 women), 2 part-time (0 women); includes 1 minority (Two or more races, non-Hispanic/Latino). Average age 36. In 2019, 12 master's awarded. *Degree requirements:* For master's, thesis. *Entrance requirements:* Additional exam requirements/recommendations for international students: required—TOEFL (minimum score 550 paper-based). *Application deadline:* For fall admission, 5/1 priority date for domestic and international students. Application fee: $60 ($90 for international students). Electronic applications accepted. *Expenses:* Contact institution. *Financial support:* In 2019–20, 14 students received support. Scholarships/grants available. Financial award application deadline: 4/1; financial award applicants required to submit FAFSA. *Unit head:* Dr. Robert Walker, Chair, School of Radiologic Sciences, 801-626-7156, Fax: 801-626-7683, E-mail: rwalker2@weber.edu. *Application contact:* Cathy Wells, Graduate Enrollment Director, 801-626-8538, Fax: 801-626-7966, E-mail: cathywells@weber.edu. Website: http://www.weber.edu/msrs

# Medical Imaging

**Boston University,** School of Medicine, Graduate Medical Sciences, Program in Bioimaging, Boston, MA 02118. Offers MS. *Financial support:* Applicants required to submit FAFSA. *Unit head:* Dr. Jennifer Luebke, Chair, 617-358-2200, E-mail: jluebke@bu.edu. *Application contact:* GMS Admissions Office, 617-358-9518, Fax: 617-358-2913, E-mail: gmsbusm@bu.edu. Website: http://www.bumc.bu.edu/gms/bioimaging/

**Cedars-Sinai Medical Center,** Graduate Programs, Los Angeles, CA 90048. Offers biomedical and translational sciences (PhD); magnetic resonance in medicine (MS). *Degree requirements:* For doctorate, comprehensive exam, thesis/dissertation. *Entrance requirements:* For doctorate, GRE, 3 letters of recommendation. Additional exam requirements/recommendations for international students: required—TOEFL (minimum score 550 paper-based; 80 iBT), IELTS (minimum score 6.5). Electronic applications accepted.

**Illinois Institute of Technology,** Graduate College, Armour College of Engineering, Department of Electrical and Computer Engineering, Chicago, IL 60616. Offers biomedical imaging and signals (MAS); computer engineering (MS, PhD); electrical engineering (MS, PhD); electricity markets (MAS); network engineering (MAS); power engineering (MAS); telecommunications and software engineering (MAS); VLSI and microelectronics (MAS); MS/MS. *Program availability:* Part-time, evening/weekend, online learning. Terminal master's awarded for partial completion of doctoral program. *Degree requirements:* For master's, comprehensive exam (for some programs), thesis (for some programs); for doctorate, comprehensive exam, thesis/dissertation. *Entrance requirements:* For master's and doctorate, GRE General Test (minimum score 1100 Quantitative and Verbal, 3.5 Analytical Writing), minimum undergraduate GPA of 3.0. Additional exam requirements/recommendations for international students: required—TOEFL (minimum score 550 paper-based; 80 iBT); recommended—IELTS (minimum score 5.5). Electronic applications accepted.

**Medical University of South Carolina,** College of Graduate Studies, Program in Molecular and Cellular Biology and Pathobiology, Charleston, SC 29425. Offers cancer biology (PhD); cardiovascular biology (PhD); cardiovascular imaging (PhD); cell regulation (PhD); craniofacial biology (PhD); genetics and development (PhD); marine biomedicine (PhD); DMD/PhD; MD/PhD. *Degree requirements:* For doctorate, thesis/dissertation, oral and written exams. *Entrance requirements:* For doctorate, GRE General Test, interview, minimum GPA of 3.0. Additional exam requirements/recommendations for international students: required—TOEFL (minimum score 600 paper-based; 100 iBT). Electronic applications accepted.

**National University of Health Sciences,** Graduate Programs, Lombard, IL 60148-4583. Offers acupuncture (MSAC); chiropractic (DC); diagnostic imaging (MS); naturopathic medicine (ND); Oriental medicine (MSOM). *Accreditation:* ACAOM; CCE; CNME.

**Oregon State University,** College of Engineering, Program in Bioengineering, Corvallis, OR 97331. Offers biomaterials (M Eng, MS, PhD); biomedical devices and instrumentation (M Eng, MS, PhD); human performance engineering (M Eng, MS, PhD); medical imaging (M Eng, MS, PhD); systems and computational biology (M Eng, MS, PhD). Electronic applications accepted. *Expenses:* Contact institution.

**Rutgers University - Newark,** School of Health Related Professions, Department of Medical Imaging Sciences, Newark, NJ 07102. Offers radiologist assistant (MS). *Program availability:* Part-time, evening/weekend. *Entrance requirements:* For master's, BS with minimum GPA of 3.0, RT license, coursework in intro to pathopsychology, interview, all transcripts, personal statement, BCLS certification. Additional exam requirements/recommendations for international students: required—TOEFL (minimum score 500 paper-based; 79 iBT). Electronic applications accepted.

**Thomas Jefferson University,** Jefferson College of Health Professions, Department of Medical Imaging and Radiation Sciences, Philadelphia, PA 19107. Offers medical physics (MS); radiologic and imaging sciences (MS). *Program availability:* Part-time. *Degree requirements:* For master's, capstone project. *Entrance requirements:* For master's, bachelor's degree. Additional exam requirements/recommendations for international students: required—TOEFL (minimum score 87 iBT), IELTS (minimum score 6.5). Electronic applications accepted.

**University of California, San Francisco,** Graduate Division, Biomedical Imaging Program, San Francisco, CA 94143. Offers MS. *Program availability:* Part-time. *Degree requirements:* For master's, comprehensive exam or thesis. *Entrance requirements:* For master's, MCAT or GRE General Test. Additional exam requirements/recommendations for international students: required—TOEFL (minimum score 550 paper-based, 80 iBT) or IELTS (minimum score 7.0). Electronic applications accepted. *Expenses:* Contact institution.

**University of Cincinnati,** Graduate School, College of Engineering and Applied Science, Department of Biomedical, Chemical and Environmental Engineering, Cincinnati, OH 45221. Offers biomechanics (PhD); chemical engineering (MS, PhD); environmental engineering (MS, PhD); environmental sciences (MS, PhD); medical imaging (PhD); tissue engineering (PhD). *Program availability:* Part-time. *Degree requirements:* For master's, thesis or alternative; for doctorate, one foreign language, thesis/dissertation. *Entrance requirements:* For master's and doctorate, GRE General Test. Additional exam requirements/recommendations for international students: required—TOEFL (minimum score 600 paper-based).

*Medical Imaging*

**University of Guelph,** Ontario Veterinary College and Office of Graduate and Postdoctoral Studies, Graduate Programs in Veterinary Sciences, Department of Clinical Studies, Guelph, ON N1G 2W1, Canada. Offers anesthesiology (M Sc, DV Sc); cardiology (DV Sc, Diploma); clinical studies (Diploma); dermatology (M Sc); diagnostic imaging (M Sc, DV Sc); emergency/critical care (M Sc, DV Sc, Diploma); medicine (M Sc, DV Sc); neurology (M Sc, DV Sc); ophthalmology (M Sc, DV Sc); surgery (M Sc, DV Sc). *Degree requirements:* For master's, thesis; for doctorate, comprehensive exam, thesis/dissertation. *Entrance requirements:* Additional exam requirements/ recommendations for international students: required—TOEFL (minimum score 550 paper-based), IELTS (minimum score 6.5). Electronic applications accepted.

**University of Southern California,** Graduate School, Viterbi School of Engineering, Department of Biomedical Engineering, Los Angeles, CA 90089. Offers biomedical engineering (PhD); medical device and diagnostic engineering (MS); medical imaging and imaging informatics (MS). *Program availability:* Online learning. Terminal master's awarded for partial completion of doctoral program. *Degree requirements:* For master's, thesis optional; for doctorate, thesis/dissertation. *Entrance requirements:* For master's and doctorate, GRE General Test. Additional exam requirements/recommendations for international students: recommended—TOEFL. Electronic applications accepted.

**University of Wisconsin–Milwaukee,** Graduate School, College of Engineering and Applied Science, Biomedical and Health Informatics Program, Milwaukee, WI 53201-0413. Offers health information systems (PhD); health services management and policy (PhD); knowledge based systems (PhD); medical imaging and instrumentation (PhD); public health informatics (PhD). *Degree requirements:* For doctorate, comprehensive exam, thesis/dissertation. *Entrance requirements:* For doctorate, GRE, GMAT or MCAT. Additional exam requirements/recommendations for international students: required—TOEFL (minimum score 600 paper-based; 79 iBT), IELTS (minimum score 6.5). Electronic applications accepted.

**Wayne State University,** College of Engineering, Department of Biomedical Engineering, Detroit, MI 48202. Offers biomedical engineering (MS, PhD), including biomedical imaging (PhD); injury biomechanics (Graduate Certificate). *Faculty:* 17. *Students:* 58 full-time (32 women), 37 part-time (17 women); includes 17 minority (6 Black or African American, non-Hispanic/Latino; 9 Asian, non-Hispanic/Latino; 2 Hispanic/Latino), 31 international. Average age 28. 88 applicants, 33% accepted, 18 enrolled. In 2019, 38 master's, 3 doctorates awarded. Terminal master's awarded for partial completion of doctoral program. *Degree requirements:* For master's, thesis optional; for doctorate, comprehensive exam, thesis/dissertation. *Entrance requirements:* For master's, GRE (recommended), bachelor's degree, minimum undergraduate GPA of 3.0, one-page statement of purpose, completion of prerequisite coursework in calculus and engineering physics; for doctorate, GRE, bachelor's degree in biomedical engineering with minimum undergraduate GPA of 3.5, or master's degree in biomedical engineering with minimum GPA of 3.3; personal statement; three letters of recommendation; for Graduate Certificate, minimum undergraduate GPA of 3.0, bachelor's degree in engineering or in a mathematics-based science program. Additional exam requirements/recommendations for international students: required—TOEFL (minimum score 550 paper-based; 79 iBT), TWE; recommended—IELTS (minimum score 6.5). *Application deadline:* For fall admission, 6/1 priority date for domestic students, 5/1 priority date for international students; for winter admission, 10/1 priority date for domestic students, 9/1 priority date for international students; for spring admission, 2/1 priority date for domestic students, 1/1 priority date for international students. Applications are processed on a rolling basis. Application fee: $50. Electronic applications accepted. *Expenses:* In-state: $790/credit hour Out-of-state: $1579/credit hour. Courses are 1-4 credits, majority 3 credits. Total 32-34 credits for MS program; 90 credits for PhD program. *Financial support:* In 2019–20, 38 students received support, including 4 fellowships with tuition reimbursements available (averaging $21,875 per year), 2 research assistantships with tuition reimbursements available (averaging $24,950 per year), 8 teaching assistantships with tuition reimbursements available (averaging $20,792 per year); Federal Work-Study, scholarships/grants, health care benefits, and unspecified assistantships also available. Support available to part-time students. Financial award applicants required to submit FAFSA. *Unit head:* Dr. Cynthia Bir, Department Chair, 313-577-7821, E-mail: cbir@wayne.edu. *Application contact:* Rob Carlson, Graduate Program Coordinator, 313-577-0409, Fax: 313-577-9615, E-mail: rcarlson@wayne.edu.
Website: http://engineering.wayne.edu/bme/

# Medical Physics

**Columbia University,** Fu Foundation School of Engineering and Applied Science, Department of Applied Physics and Applied Mathematics, New York, NY 10027. Offers applied mathematics (MS, Eng Sc D, PhD); applied physics (MS, Eng Sc D, PhD); materials science and engineering (MS, Eng Sc D, PhD); medical physics (MS). *Program availability:* Part-time, online learning. Terminal master's awarded for partial completion of doctoral program. *Degree requirements:* For master's, comprehensive exam; for doctorate, thesis/dissertation, qualifying exam. *Entrance requirements:* For master's, GRE General Test, GRE Subject Test (strongly recommended); for doctorate, GRE General Test, GRE Subject Test (applied physics). Additional exam requirements/recommendations for international students: required—TOEFL, IELTS, PTE. Electronic applications accepted. *Expenses: Tuition:* Full-time $47,600; part-time $1880 per credit. One-time fee: $105.

**Duke University,** Graduate School, Medical Physics Graduate Program, Durham, NC 27705. Offers MS, PhD. *Entrance requirements:* For master's and doctorate, GRE General Test. Additional exam requirements/recommendations for international students: required—TOEFL (minimum score 577 paper-based; 90 iBT) or IELTS (minimum score 7). Electronic applications accepted.

**East Carolina University,** Graduate School, Thomas Harriot College of Arts and Sciences, Department of Physics, Greenville, NC 27858-4353. Offers applied physics (MS); biomedical physics (PhD); health physics (MS); medical physics (MS). *Program availability:* Part-time. *Application deadline:* For fall admission, 3/1 priority date for domestic and international students. *Expenses: Tuition, area resident:* Full-time $4749; part-time $185 per credit hour. Tuition, state resident: full-time $4749; part-time $185 per credit hour. Tuition, nonresident: full-time $17,898; part-time $864 per credit hour. International tuition: $17,898 full-time. *Required fees:* $2787. *Financial support:* Application deadline: 3/1. *Unit head:* Dr. Jefferson Shinpaugh, Chair, 252-328-6739, E-mail: shinpaughj@ecu.edu. *Application contact:* Graduate School Admissions, 252-328-6012, Fax: 252-328-6071, E-mail: gradschool@ecu.edu.
Website: https://physics.ecu.edu/

**Hampton University,** School of Science, Department of Physics, Hampton, VA 23668. Offers medical physics (PhD); nuclear physics (MS, PhD); optical physics (MS, PhD). *Students:* 13 full-time (3 women), 2 part-time (1 woman); includes 3 minority (2 Black or African American, non-Hispanic/Latino; 1 Asian, non-Hispanic/Latino), 11 international. Average age 32. 8 applicants, 25% accepted, 1 enrolled. In 2019, 2 master's, 1 doctorate awarded. *Degree requirements:* For master's, thesis optional; for doctorate, thesis/dissertation, oral defense, qualifying exam. *Entrance requirements:* For master's, GRE General Test; for doctorate, GRE General Test, minimum GPA of 3.0 or master's degree in physics or related field. Additional exam requirements/recommendations for international students: required—TOEFL (minimum score 525 paper-based) or IELTS (6.5). *Application deadline:* For fall admission, 6/1 priority date for domestic students, 4/1 priority date for international students; for spring admission, 11/1 priority date for domestic students, 9/1 priority date for international students; for summer admission, 4/1 priority date for domestic students, 2/1 priority date for international students. Applications are processed on a rolling basis. Application fee: $35. Electronic applications accepted. *Financial support:* In 2019–20, 17 research assistantships were awarded; fellowships, teaching assistantships, career-related internships or fieldwork, Federal Work-Study, institutionally sponsored loans, and scholarships/grants also available. Support available to part-time students. Financial award application deadline: 6/30; financial award applicants required to submit FAFSA. *Unit head:* Dr. Paul Gueye, Chairperson, 757-727-5277. *Application contact:* Dr. Paul Gueye, Chairperson, 757-727-5277.
Website: http://science.hamptonu.edu/physics/

**Harvard University,** Graduate School of Arts and Sciences, Department of Physics, Cambridge, MA 02138. Offers experimental physics (PhD); medical engineering/medical physics (PhD), including applied physics, engineering sciences, physics; theoretical physics (PhD). *Degree requirements:* For doctorate, thesis/dissertation, final exams, laboratory experience. *Entrance requirements:* For doctorate, GRE General Test, GRE Subject Test. Additional exam requirements/recommendations for international students: required—TOEFL.

**Hofstra University,** College of Liberal Arts and Sciences, Program in Medical Physics, Hempstead, NY 11549. Offers medical physics (MS). *Program availability:* Part-time, evening/weekend. *Students:* 15 full-time (7 women); includes 5 minority (2 Asian, non-Hispanic/Latino; 2 Hispanic/Latino; 1 Two or more races, non-Hispanic/Latino), 3 international. Average age 27. 63 applicants, 40% accepted, 9 enrolled. In 2019, 2 master's awarded. *Degree requirements:* For master's, comprehensive exam, minimum GPA of 3.0. *Entrance requirements:* For master's, bachelor's degree in science, minimum GPA of 3.0, 2 letters of recommendation. Additional exam requirements/recommendations for international students: required—TOEFL (minimum score 550 paper-based; 80 iBT); recommended—IELTS (minimum score 6.5). *Application deadline:* Applications are processed on a rolling basis. Application fee: $75. Electronic applications accepted. *Expenses: Tuition:* Full-time $25,164; part-time $1398 per credit. *Required fees:* $580; $165 per semester. Tuition and fees vary according to course load, degree level and program. *Financial support:* In 2019–20, 12 students received support, including 8 fellowships with full and partial tuition reimbursements available (averaging $5,345 per year); research assistantships with full and partial tuition reimbursements available, career-related internships or fieldwork, Federal Work-Study, institutionally sponsored loans, scholarships/grants, traineeships, tuition waivers (full and partial), unspecified assistantships, and scholarships and endowed scholarships also available. Support available to part-time students. Financial award applicants required to submit FAFSA. *Unit head:* Dr. Gregory Levine, Chairperson, 516-463-5583, E-mail: gregory.c.levine@hofstra.edu. *Application contact:* Sunil Samuel, Assistant Vice President of Admissions, 516-463-4723, Fax: 516-463-4664, E-mail: graduateadmission@hofstra.edu.
Website: http://www.hofstra.edu/hclas

**Indiana University Bloomington,** University Graduate School, College of Arts and Sciences, Department of Physics, Bloomington, IN 47405. Offers medical physics (MS); physics (MAT, MS, PhD). *Program availability:* Part-time, online learning. Terminal master's awarded for partial completion of doctoral program. *Degree requirements:* For master's, comprehensive exam (for some programs), thesis (for some programs), qualifying exam; for doctorate, comprehensive exam, thesis/dissertation, qualifying exam. *Entrance requirements:* For master's and doctorate, GRE General Test, GRE Subject Test (physics), minimum GPA of 3.0. Additional exam requirements/recommendations for international students: required—TOEFL (minimum score 550 paper-based; 80 iBT) or IELTS (minimum score 6.5). Electronic applications accepted. *Expenses:* Contact institution.

**John Patrick University of Health and Applied Sciences,** Graduate Programs, South Bend, IN 46601. Offers medical dosimetry (MS); medical health physics (MS); medical physics (MS).

**Louisiana State University and Agricultural & Mechanical College,** Graduate School, College of Science, Department of Physics and Astronomy, Baton Rouge, LA 70803. Offers astronomy (PhD); astrophysics (PhD); medical physics (MS); physics (MS, PhD).

**Massachusetts Institute of Technology,** School of Engineering, Harvard-MIT Health Sciences and Technology Program, Cambridge, MA 02139. Offers health sciences and technology (SM, PhD, Sc D), including bioastronautics (PhD, Sc D), bioinformatics and integrative genomics (PhD, Sc D), medical engineering and medical physics (PhD, Sc D), speech and hearing bioscience and technology (PhD, Sc D). Terminal master's awarded for partial completion of doctoral program. *Degree requirements:* For doctorate, comprehensive exam, thesis/dissertation. *Entrance requirements:* For doctorate, GRE General Test. Additional exam requirements/recommendations for international students: required—TOEFL, IELTS. Electronic applications accepted.

**McGill University,** Faculty of Graduate and Postdoctoral Studies, Faculty of Medicine, Medical Physics Unit, Montréal, QC H3A 2T5, Canada. Offers M Sc, PhD. *Entrance requirements:* Additional exam requirements/recommendations for international students: required—TOEFL.

**McMaster University,** School of Graduate Studies, Faculty of Science, Department of Medical Physics and Applied Radiation Sciences, Hamilton, ON L8S 4M2, Canada. Offers health and radiation physics (M Sc); medical physics (M Sc, PhD). *Program availability:* Part-time. *Degree requirements:* For master's, thesis or alternative. *Entrance*

*requirements:* For master's, minimum B+ average. Additional exam requirements/recommendations for international students: required—TOEFL (minimum score 550 paper-based).

**Oakland University,** Graduate Study and Lifelong Learning, College of Arts and Sciences, Department of Physics, Rochester, MI 48309-4401. Offers medical physics (PhD); physics (MS). *Degree requirements:* For doctorate, thesis/dissertation. *Entrance requirements:* Additional exam requirements/recommendations for international students: required—TOEFL (minimum score 550 paper-based; 79 iBT), IELTS (minimum score 6.5). Electronic applications accepted. *Expenses: Tuition, area resident:* Full-time $12,328; part-time $770.50 per credit hour. Tuition, state resident: full-time $12,328; part-time $770.50 per credit hour. Tuition, nonresident: full-time $16,432; part-time $1027 per credit hour. *International tuition:* $16,432 full-time. Tuition and fees vary according to degree level and program.

**Oregon State University,** College of Engineering, Program in Medical Physics, Corvallis, OR 97331. Offers medical health physics (MMP, MS); therapeutic radiologic physics (PhD). *Entrance requirements:* For master's and doctorate, GRE. Additional exam requirements/recommendations for international students: required—TOEFL (minimum score 80 iBT), IELTS (minimum score 6.5). *Expenses:* Contact institution.

**Purdue University,** Graduate School, College of Health and Human Sciences, School of Health Sciences, West Lafayette, IN 47907. Offers health physics (MS, PhD); medical physics (MS, PhD); occupational and environmental health science (MS, PhD), including aerosol deposition and lung disease, ergonomics, exposure and risk assessment, indoor air quality and bioaerosols (PhD), liver/lung toxicology; radiological health (PhD); toxicology (PhD); MS/PhD. *Program availability:* Part-time. *Faculty:* 15 full-time (6 women), 1 part-time/adjunct (0 women). *Students:* 39 full-time (22 women), 6 part-time (3 women); includes 12 minority (2 Black or African American, non-Hispanic/Latino; 1 American Indian or Alaska Native, non-Hispanic/Latino; 3 Asian, non-Hispanic/Latino; 1 Hispanic/Latino; 5 Two or more races, non-Hispanic/Latino), 15 international. Average age 28. 61 applicants, 43% accepted, 14 enrolled. In 2019, 15 master's, 6 doctorates awarded. *Degree requirements:* For master's, thesis optional; for doctorate, one foreign language, thesis/dissertation. *Entrance requirements:* For master's and doctorate, GRE General Test, minimum undergraduate GPA of 3.0 or equivalent. Additional exam requirements/recommendations for international students: required—TOEFL (minimum score 550 paper-based; 77 iBT); recommended—TWE. *Application deadline:* For fall admission, 5/15 for domestic and international students; for spring admission, 10/15 for domestic and international students. Applications are processed on a rolling basis. Application fee: $60 ($75 for international students). Electronic applications accepted. *Financial support:* In 2019–20, fellowships with tuition reimbursements (averaging $14,400 per year), research assistantships with tuition reimbursements (averaging $12,000 per year), teaching assistantships with tuition reimbursements (averaging $12,000 per year) were awarded; career-related internships or fieldwork and traineeships also available. Support available to part-time students. Financial award applicants required to submit FAFSA. *Unit head:* Aaron Bowman, Head of the Graduate Program, 765-494-2684, E-mail: bowma117@purdue.edu. *Application contact:* Karen E. Walker, Graduate Contact, 765-494-1419, E-mail: kwalker@purdue.edu.
Website: https://www.purdue.edu/hhs/hsci/

**Rush University,** Graduate College, Division of Medical Physics, Chicago, IL 60612-3832. Offers MS, PhD. Terminal master's awarded for partial completion of doctoral program. *Degree requirements:* For master's, thesis, qualifying exam; for doctorate, thesis/dissertation, preliminary and qualifying exams. *Entrance requirements:* For master's, GRE General Test, BS in physics or physical science; for doctorate, GRE General Test, GRE Subject Test. Additional exam requirements/recommendations for international students: required—TOEFL. Electronic applications accepted.

**Southern Illinois University Carbondale,** Graduate School, College of Applied Science, Program in Medical Dosimetry, Carbondale, IL 62901-4701. Offers MS. *Entrance requirements:* Additional exam requirements/recommendations for international students: required—TOEFL. Electronic applications accepted.

**Stony Brook University, State University of New York,** Graduate School, College of Engineering and Applied Sciences, Department of Biomedical Engineering, Program in Medical Physics, Stony Brook, NY 11794. Offers MS, PhD. *Entrance requirements:* For doctorate, GRE. Additional exam requirements/recommendations for international students: required—TOEFL (minimum score 90 iBT). *Application deadline:* For fall admission, 1/1 for domestic students. Application fee: $100. *Expenses: Tuition, area resident:* Full-time $11,310; part-time $471 per credit. Tuition, state resident: full-time $11,310; part-time $471 per credit. Tuition, nonresident: full-time $23,100; part-time $963 per credit. *International tuition:* $23,100 full-time. *Required fees:* $2247.50. *Financial support:* Fellowships available. *Unit head:* Dr. Terry Button, Director, 631-444-3841, Fax: 631-444-7538, E-mail: terry.button@stonybrook.edu. *Application contact:* Erica Valdez, Graduate Program Coordinator, 631-632-8375, Fax: 631-632-8577, E-mail: Erica.Valdez@stonybrook.edu.
Website: https://www.stonybrook.edu/commcms/bme/graduate/medicalphys.php

**Thomas Jefferson University,** Jefferson College of Health Professions, Department of Medical Imaging and Radiation Sciences, Philadelphia, PA 19107. Offers medical physics (MS); radiologic and imaging sciences (MS). *Program availability:* Part-time. *Degree requirements:* For master's, capstone project. *Entrance requirements:* For master's, bachelor's degree. Additional exam requirements/recommendations for international students: required—TOEFL (minimum score 87 iBT), IELTS (minimum score 6.5). Electronic applications accepted.

**University at Buffalo, the State University of New York,** Graduate School, Jacobs School of Medicine and Biomedical Sciences, Graduate Programs in Medicine and Biomedical Sciences, Program in Medical Physics, Buffalo, NY 14260. Offers MS, PhD. *Faculty:* 15 full-time (2 women). *Students:* 27 full-time (8 women); includes 12 minority (all Asian, non-Hispanic/Latino). Average age 29. 39 applicants, 21% accepted, 3 enrolled. In 2019, 1 master's, 8 doctorates awarded. *Degree requirements:* For master's, thesis or project; for doctorate, thesis/dissertation. *Entrance requirements:* For master's and doctorate, GRE. Additional exam requirements/recommendations for international students: required—TOEFL (minimum score 550 paper-based; 79 iBT). *Application deadline:* For fall admission, 3/15 priority date for domestic and international students. Applications are processed on a rolling basis. Application fee: $85. Electronic applications accepted. *Expenses: Tuition, area resident:* Full-time $11,310; part-time $471 per credit hour. Tuition, state resident: full-time $11,310; part-time $471 per credit hour. Tuition, nonresident: full-time $23,100; part-time $963 per credit hour. *International tuition:* $23,100 full-time. *Required fees:* $2820. *Financial support:* Research assistantships and traineeships available. *Unit head:* Dr. Stephen Rudin, Director, 716-829-5408, E-mail: srudin@buffalo.edu. *Application contact:* Chris P. Root, Graduate Programs Coordinator, 716-829-6942, E-mail: cproot@buffalo.edu.
Website: http://medicine.buffalo.edu/education/medical-physics.html

**University of Alberta,** Faculty of Graduate Studies and Research, Department of Physics, Edmonton, AB T6G 2E1, Canada. Offers astrophysics (M Sc, PhD); condensed matter (M Sc, PhD); geophysics (M Sc, PhD); medical physics (M Sc, PhD); subatomic physics (M Sc, PhD). *Degree requirements:* For master's, thesis; for doctorate, thesis/dissertation. *Entrance requirements:* For master's and doctorate, minimum GPA of 7.0 on a 9.0 scale. Additional exam requirements/recommendations for international students: required—TOEFL.

**The University of Arizona,** College of Science, Department of Physics, Medical Physics Program, Tucson, AZ 85721. Offers PSM. *Program availability:* Part-time. *Degree requirements:* For master's, thesis or alternative, internship, colloquium, business courses. *Entrance requirements:* Additional exam requirements/recommendations for international students: required—TOEFL (minimum score 550 paper-based; 79 iBT). Electronic applications accepted.

**University of California, Los Angeles,** David Geffen School of Medicine and Graduate Division, Graduate Programs in Medicine, Program in Biomedical Physics, Los Angeles, CA 90095. Offers MS, PhD. Terminal master's awarded for partial completion of doctoral program. *Degree requirements:* For master's, comprehensive exam or thesis; for doctorate, thesis/dissertation, oral and written qualifying exams. *Entrance requirements:* For master's and doctorate, GRE General Test. Additional exam requirements/recommendations for international students: required—TOEFL. Electronic applications accepted.

**University of Chicago,** Division of the Biological Sciences, Committee on Medical Physics, Chicago, IL 60637-1513. Offers PhD. *Degree requirements:* For doctorate, comprehensive exam, thesis/dissertation, ethics class, 2 teaching assistantships. *Entrance requirements:* For doctorate, GRE General Test, transcripts, statement of purpose, 3 letters of recommendation. Additional exam requirements/recommendations for international students: required—TOEFL (minimum score 600 paper-based; 104 iBT), IELTS (minimum score 7). Electronic applications accepted.

**University of Cincinnati,** Graduate School, College of Medicine, Graduate Programs in Biomedical Sciences, Department of Radiology, Cincinnati, OH 45267. Offers medical physics (MS). *Program availability:* Part-time. *Degree requirements:* For master's, comprehensive exam, project. *Entrance requirements:* For master's, GRE General Test. Additional exam requirements/recommendations for international students: required—TOEFL (minimum score 575 paper-based). Electronic applications accepted.

**University of Florida,** Graduate School, Herbert Wertheim College of Engineering, J. Crayton Pruitt Family Department of Biomedical Engineering, Gainesville, FL 32611. Offers biomedical engineering (ME, MS, PhD, Certificate); clinical and translational science (PhD); medical physics (MS, PhD); MD/PhD. Terminal master's awarded for partial completion of doctoral program. *Degree requirements:* For master's, comprehensive exam (for some programs), thesis (for some programs); for doctorate, comprehensive exam (for some programs), thesis/dissertation (for some programs). *Entrance requirements:* Additional exam requirements/recommendations for international students: required—TOEFL (minimum score 550 paper-based; 80 iBT), IELTS (minimum score 6). Electronic applications accepted.

**University of Kentucky,** Graduate School, Graduate School Programs from the College of Medicine, Program in Radiation Sciences, Lexington, KY 40506-0032. Offers MSRMP. *Program availability:* Part-time. *Degree requirements:* For master's, comprehensive exam, thesis. *Entrance requirements:* For master's, GRE General Test, minimum undergraduate GPA of 2.75. Additional exam requirements/recommendations for international students: required—TOEFL (minimum score 550 paper-based). Electronic applications accepted.

**University of Minnesota, Twin Cities Campus,** Graduate School, Program in Biophysical Sciences and Medical Physics, Minneapolis, MN 55455-0213. Offers MS, PhD. *Program availability:* Part-time. *Degree requirements:* For master's, thesis optional, research paper, oral exam; for doctorate, thesis/dissertation, oral/written preliminary exam, oral final exam.

**University of Oklahoma Health Sciences Center,** College of Medicine and Graduate College, Graduate Programs in Medicine, Department of Radiological Sciences, Oklahoma City, OK 73190. Offers medical radiation physics (MS, PhD), including diagnostic radiology, nuclear medicine, radiation therapy, ultrasound. *Program availability:* Part-time. Terminal master's awarded for partial completion of doctoral program. *Degree requirements:* For master's, thesis; for doctorate, thesis/dissertation. *Entrance requirements:* For master's, GRE General Test; for doctorate, GRE General Test, 3 letters of recommendation. Additional exam requirements/recommendations for international students: required—TOEFL.

**University of Pennsylvania,** School of Arts and Sciences, College of Liberal and Professional Studies, Philadelphia, PA 19104. Offers applied geosciences (MSAG); applied positive psychology (MAP); chemical sciences (MCS); environmental studies (MES); individualized study (MLA); liberal arts (M Phil); medical physics (MMP); organization dynamics (M Phil). *Students:* 240 full-time (161 women), 290 part-time (180 women); includes 91 minority (31 Black or African American, non-Hispanic/Latino; 31 Asian, non-Hispanic/Latino; 14 Hispanic/Latino; 15 Two or more races, non-Hispanic/Latino), 136 international. Average age 33. 955 applicants, 44% accepted, 272 enrolled. In 2019, 203 master's awarded. *Unit head:* Nora Lewis, Vice Dean, Professional and Liberal Education, 215-898-7326, E-mail: nlewis@sas.upenn.edu. *Application contact:* Nora Lewis, Vice Dean, Professional and Liberal Education, 215-898-7326, E-mail: nlewis@sas.upenn.edu.
Website: http://www.sas.upenn.edu/lps/graduate

**University of Pennsylvania,** School of Arts and Sciences, Graduate Group in Physics and Astronomy, Philadelphia, PA 19104. Offers medical physics (MS); physics (PhD). *Program availability:* Part-time. *Faculty:* 45 full-time (8 women), 12 part-time/adjunct (0 women). *Students:* 95 full-time (27 women), 2 part-time (1 woman); includes 21 minority (2 Black or African American, non-Hispanic/Latino; 8 Asian, non-Hispanic/Latino; 8 Hispanic/Latino; 3 Two or more races, non-Hispanic/Latino), 33 international. Average age 26. 465 applicants, 9% accepted, 15 enrolled. In 2019, 11 master's, 21 doctorates awarded. Application fee: $90. *Financial support:* Application deadline: 12/1.
Website: http://www.physics.upenn.edu/graduate/

**University of Rhode Island,** Graduate School, College of Arts and Sciences, Department of Physics, Kingston, RI 02881. Offers medical physics (MS); physics (MS, PhD). *Program availability:* Part-time, evening/weekend. *Faculty:* 15 full-time (1 woman). *Students:* 20 full-time (5 women); includes 2 minority (1 Black or African American, non-Hispanic/Latino; 1 Asian, non-Hispanic/Latino), 5 international. 27 applicants, 41% accepted, 4 enrolled. In 2019, 5 master's awarded. *Entrance requirements:* For master's and doctorate, GRE General Test; GRE Subject Test in physics (recommended), 2 letters of recommendation. Additional exam requirements/recommendations for international students: required—TOEFL. *Application deadline:* For fall admission, 3/1 for domestic students, 2/1 for international students; for spring admission, 7/15 for international students. Application fee: $65. Electronic applications accepted. *Expenses: Tuition, area resident:* Full-time $13,734; part-time $763 per credit. Tuition, state resident: full-time $13,734; part-time $763 per credit. Tuition, nonresident: full-time $26,512; part-time $1473 per credit. *International tuition:* $26,512 full-time. *Required fees:* $1780; $52 per credit. $35 per term. One-time fee: $165. *Financial support:* In 2019–20, 18 teaching assistantships with tuition reimbursements (averaging $18,352 per year) were awarded. Financial award application deadline: 3/1; financial award applicants required to submit FAFSA. *Unit head:* Dr. Leonard Kahn, Chair, E-mail: lenkahn@uri.edu. *Application contact:* Dr. Alexander Meyerovich, Director of Graduate

## Medical Physics

Studies, 401-8742047, E-mail: sfo101@uri.edu. Website: https://web.uri.edu/physics/

**The University of Texas Health Science Center at Houston,** MD Anderson UTHealth Graduate School, Houston, TX 77225-0036. Offers biochemistry and cell biology (PhD); biomedical sciences (MS); cancer biology (PhD); genetic counseling (MS); genetics and epigenetics (PhD); immunology (PhD); medical physics (MS, PhD); microbiology and infectious diseases (PhD); neuroscience (PhD); quantitative sciences (PhD); therapeutics and pharmacology (PhD); MD/PhD. Terminal master's awarded for partial completion of doctoral program. *Degree requirements:* For master's, thesis; for doctorate, thesis/dissertation. *Entrance requirements:* For master's and doctorate, GRE General Test. Additional exam requirements/recommendations for international students: required—TOEFL. Electronic applications accepted.

**The University of Texas Health Science Center at San Antonio,** Graduate School of Biomedical Sciences, Radiological Sciences Graduate Program, San Antonio, TX 78229-3900. Offers PhD. *Degree requirements:* For doctorate, comprehensive exam, thesis/dissertation.

**The University of Toledo,** College of Graduate Studies, College of Medicine and Life Sciences, Program in Medical Physics, Toledo, OH 43606-3390. Offers MSBS. *Degree requirements:* For master's, thesis. *Entrance requirements:* For master's, GRE, minimum undergraduate GPA of 3.0, three letters of recommendation, statement of purpose, transcripts from all prior institutions attended, resume. Additional exam requirements/recommendations for international students: required—TOEFL (minimum score 550 paper-based; 80 iBT). Electronic applications accepted.

**The University of Toledo,** College of Graduate Studies, College of Natural Sciences and Mathematics, Department of Physics and Astronomy, Toledo, OH 43606-3390. Offers photovoltaics (PSM); physics (MS, PhD), including astrophysics (PhD), materials science, medical physics (PhD); MS/PhD. *Degree requirements:* For master's, thesis; for doctorate, thesis/dissertation, departmental qualifying exam. *Entrance requirements:* For master's and doctorate, GRE General Test, GRE Subject Test, minimum cumulative point-hour ratio of 2.7 for all previous academic work, three letters of recommendation, statement of purpose, transcripts from all prior institutions attended. Additional exam requirements/recommendations for international students: required—TOEFL (minimum score 550 paper-based; 80 iBT). Electronic applications accepted.

**University of Utah,** Graduate School, College of Science, Department of Physics and Astronomy, Salt Lake City, UT 84112. Offers chemical physics (PhD); medical physics (MS, PhD); physics (MA, MS, PhD); physics teaching (PhD). *Program availability:* Part-time. *Faculty:* 24 full-time (3 women). *Students:* 48 full-time (14 women), 19 part-time (6 women); includes 3 minority (all Hispanic/Latino), 32 international. Average age 29. In 2019, 35 master's, 17 doctorates awarded. Terminal master's awarded for partial completion of doctoral program. *Degree requirements:* For master's, comprehensive exam; for doctorate, comprehensive exam, thesis/dissertation. Application fee: $55 ($65 for international students). *Expenses:* Tuition, state resident: full-time $7085; part-time $272.51 per credit hour. Tuition, nonresident: full-time $24,937; part-time $959.12 per credit hour. *Required fees:* $880.52; $880.52 per semester. Tuition and fees vary according to degree level, program and student level. *Financial support:* In 2019–20, 23 research assistantships (averaging $8,000 per year), 31 teaching assistantships (averaging $16,548 per year) were awarded; scholarships/grants and unspecified assistantships also available. Financial award applicants required to submit FAFSA. *Unit head:* Dr. Christoph Bhoehme, Chair, 801-581-6806, Fax: 801-581-4801, E-mail: bhoeme@physics.utah.edu. *Application contact:* Bryce Nelson, Graduate Coordinator, 801-581-6861, Fax: 801-581-4801, E-mail: bryce@physics.utah.edu. Website: http://www.physics.utah.edu/

**University of Victoria,** Faculty of Graduate Studies, Faculty of Science, Department of Physics and Astronomy, Victoria, BC V8W 2Y2, Canada. Offers astronomy and astrophysics (M Sc, PhD); condensed matter physics (M Sc, PhD); experimental particle physics (M Sc, PhD); medical physics (M Sc, PhD); ocean physics (M Sc, PhD); theoretical physics (M Sc, PhD). *Degree requirements:* For master's, thesis; for doctorate, comprehensive exam, thesis/dissertation, candidacy exam. *Entrance requirements:* For master's and doctorate, GRE. Additional exam requirements/recommendations for international students: required—TOEFL (minimum score 575 paper-based), IELTS (minimum score 7). Electronic applications accepted.

**University of Wisconsin–Madison,** School of Medicine and Public Health, Medical Physics Graduate Program, Madison, WI 53705-2275. Offers medical physics (MS, PhD). *Program availability:* Part-time. Terminal master's awarded for partial completion of doctoral program. *Degree requirements:* For master's, comprehensive exam; for doctorate, comprehensive exam, thesis/dissertation. *Entrance requirements:* For master's and doctorate, GRE General Test, minimum GPA of 3.0. Additional exam requirements/recommendations for international students: required—TOEFL (minimum score 550 paper-based; 80 iBT), IELTS (minimum score 6.5). Electronic applications accepted.

**Virginia Commonwealth University,** Graduate School, College of Humanities and Sciences, Department of Physics, Programs in Medical Physics, Richmond, VA 23284-9005. Offers MS, PhD. *Entrance requirements:* For master's and doctorate, GRE General Test. Additional exam requirements/recommendations for international students: required—TOEFL (minimum score 600 paper-based; 100 iBT); recommended—IELTS (minimum score 6.5). Electronic applications accepted.

# Section 22
# Health Services

This section contains a directory of institutions offering graduate work in health services. Additional information about programs listed in the directory may be obtained by writing directly to the dean of a graduate school or chair of a department at the address given in the directory.

For programs offering related work, see also in this book *Allied Health, Nursing,* and *Public Health.* In another book in this series:

**Graduate Programs in Business, Education, Information Studies, Law & Social Work**

See *Business Administration and Management*

## CONTENTS

### Program Directories

### Featured School: Display and Close-Up

# Health Services Management and Hospital Administration

**Abilene Christian University,** College of Graduate and Professional Studies, School of Professional Studies, Addison, TX 75001. Offers business analytics (MBA); general management (MBA); healthcare administration (MBA); international business (MBA); management: business analytics (MS); management: healthcare administration (MS); management: international business (MS); management: marketing (MS); management: operations and supply chain management (MS); marketing (MBA); nonprofit leadership (MBA). *Program availability:* Part-time, online only, 100% online. *Faculty:* 7 full-time (1 woman), 13 part-time/adjunct (5 women). *Students:* 203 full-time (117 women), 108 part-time (69 women); includes 166 minority (85 Black or African American, non-Hispanic/Latino; 2 American Indian or Alaska Native, non-Hispanic/Latino; 4 Asian, non-Hispanic/Latino; 58 Hispanic/Latino; 1 Native Hawaiian or other Pacific Islander, non-Hispanic/Latino; 16 Two or more races, non-Hispanic/Latino), 5 international. 71 applicants, 99% accepted, 55 enrolled. In 2019, 141 master's awarded. *Entrance requirements:* Additional exam requirements/recommendations for international students: required—TOEFL (minimum score 80 iBT), IELTS (minimum score 6). *Application deadline:* For fall admission, 10/7 for domestic students; for winter admission, 12/20 for domestic students; for spring admission, 2/24 for domestic students; for summer admission, 4/20 for domestic students. Applications are processed on a rolling basis. Application fee: $50. Electronic applications accepted. *Expenses:* $732 per hour. *Financial support:* In 2019–20, 46 students received support. Scholarships/grants available. Financial award application deadline: 7/1; financial award applicants required to submit FAFSA. *Unit head:* Dr. Phil Vardiman, Program Director, 325-674-2153, E-mail: pxv02b@acu.edu. *Application contact:* Graduate Advisor, 855-219-7300, E-mail: onlineadmissions@acu.edu.
Website: https://www.acu.edu/online/graduate/school-of-professional-studies.html

**Adelphi University,** Robert B. Willumstad School of Business, MBA Program, Garden City, NY 11530-0701. Offers accounting (MBA); finance (MBA); health services administration (MBA); human resource management (MBA); management (MBA); management information systems (MBA); marketing (MBA); sport management (MBA). *Accreditation:* AACSB. *Program availability:* Part-time, evening/weekend. *Entrance requirements:* For master's, GMAT, official transcripts, bachelor's degree, 500 word essay, 2 letters of recommendation, resume. Additional exam requirements/recommendations for international students: required—TOEFL (minimum score 550 paper-based; 80 iBT), IELTS (minimum score 6.5). Electronic applications accepted.

**AdventHealth University,** Program in Healthcare Administration, Orlando, FL 32803. Offers MHA. *Entrance requirements:* For master's, minimum GPA of 3.0.

**Alaska Pacific University,** Graduate Programs, Business Administration Department, Program in Business Administration, Anchorage, AK 99508-4672. Offers business administration (MBA); health services administration (MBA). *Program availability:* Part-time, evening/weekend. *Degree requirements:* For master's, capstone course. *Entrance requirements:* For master's, GMAT or GRE General Test, minimum GPA of 3.0.

**Albany State University,** College of Arts and Humanities, Albany, GA 31705-2717. Offers criminal justice (MS); English education (M Ed); public administration (MPA), including community and economic development, criminal justice administration, health administration and policy, human resources management, public management, public policy, water resources management and policy; social work (MSW). *Accreditation:* NASPAA. *Program availability:* Part-time. *Degree requirements:* For master's, comprehensive exam, professional portfolio (for MPA), internship, capstone report. *Entrance requirements:* For master's, GRE, MAT, minimum GPA of 3.0, official transcript, pre-medical record/certificate of immunization, letters of reference. Electronic applications accepted.

**Albany State University,** College of Business, Albany, GA 31705-2717. Offers accounting (MBA); general business administration (MBA); healthcare (MBA); public administration (MBA); supply chain and logistics (MBA). *Accreditation:* ACBSP. *Program availability:* Part-time, evening/weekend. *Degree requirements:* For master's, comprehensive exam, internship, 3 hours of physical education. *Entrance requirements:* For master's, GMAT (minimum score of 450)/GRE (minimum score of 800) for those without earned master's degree or higher, minimum undergraduate GPA of 2.5, 2 letters of reference, official transcript, pre-entrance medical record and certificate of immunization. Electronic applications accepted.

**Albertus Magnus College,** Master of Business Administration Program, New Haven, CT 06511-1189. Offers accounting (MBA); general management (MBA); health care management (MBA); human resource management (MBA); leadership (MBA); project management (MBA). *Program availability:* Part-time, evening/weekend, 100% online, blended/hybrid learning. *Faculty:* 8 full-time (1 woman), 5 part-time/adjunct (2 women). *Students:* 57 full-time (40 women), 15 part-time (8 women); includes 32 minority (23 Black or African American, non-Hispanic/Latino; 1 Asian, non-Hispanic/Latino; 6 Hispanic/Latino; 2 Two or more races, non-Hispanic/Latino), 4 international. Average age 34. 30 applicants, 90% accepted, 23 enrolled. In 2019, 50 master's awarded. *Degree requirements:* For master's, comprehensive exam, thesis optional, Satisfactorily complete the business plan, min. cumulative GPA of 3.0, complete within 7 years, pay all tuition and fees. *Entrance requirements:* For master's, A bachelor's degree, min. cumulative GPA of 2.8, two letters of recommendations from former professors or professional associates, written 500-600 word essay. Additional exam requirements/recommendations for international students: required—One of the following: SAT or ACT, TOEFL, IELTS, DUO Lingo English Proficiency Test, 3+ years at a university/college with English as primary language. *Application deadline:* For fall admission, 7/15 for international students; for spring admission, 11/15 for international students. Applications are processed on a rolling basis. Application fee: $50. Electronic applications accepted. *Financial support:* In 2019–20, 5 students received support. Unspecified assistantships available. Financial award applicants required to submit FAFSA. *Unit head:* Dr. Wayne Gineo, Director of Master of Business Administration Programs, 203-672-6670, E-mail: wgineo@albertus.edu. *Application contact:* Annette Bosley-Boyce, Dean of the Division of Professional and Graduate Studies, 203-672-6688, E-mail: abosleyboyce@albertus.edu.
Website: https://www.albertus.edu/business-administration/ms/

**American InterContinental University Online,** Program in Business Administration, Schaumburg, IL 60173. Offers accounting and finance (MBA); finance (MBA); healthcare management (MBA); human resource management (MBA); international business (MBA); management (MBA); marketing (MBA); operations management (MBA); organizational psychology and development (MBA); project management (MBA). *Accreditation:* ACBSP. *Program availability:* Evening/weekend, online learning.

*Entrance requirements:* Additional exam requirements/recommendations for international students: required—TOEFL (minimum score 550 paper-based). Electronic applications accepted.

**American Sentinel University,** Graduate Programs, Aurora, CO 80014. Offers business administration (MBA); business intelligence (MS); computer science (MSCS); health information management (MS); healthcare (MBA); information systems (MSIS); nursing (MSN). *Program availability:* Part-time, evening/weekend, online learning. *Entrance requirements:* Additional exam requirements/recommendations for international students: required—TOEFL (minimum score 600 paper-based). Electronic applications accepted.

**American University,** School of Professional and Extended Studies, Washington, DC 20016. Offers agile project management (MS); healthcare management (MS, Graduate Certificate); human resource analytics and management (MS, Graduate Certificate); instructional design and learning analytics (MS); measurement and evaluation (MS); project monitoring and evaluation (Graduate Certificate); sports analytics and management (MS, Graduate Certificate). *Program availability:* Part-time, evening/weekend, 100% online, blended/hybrid learning. *Entrance requirements:* For master's, official transcript(s), resume. Additional exam requirements/recommendations for international students: required—TOEFL. Electronic applications accepted. *Expenses:* Contact institution.

**Anderson University,** College of Business, Anderson, SC 29621. Offers business administration (MBA); healthcare leadership (MBA); human resources (MBA); marketing (MBA); organizational leadership (MOL); supply chain management (MBA). *Accreditation:* ACBSP. *Application deadline:* Applications are processed on a rolling basis. Electronic applications accepted. *Financial support:* Scholarships/grants and tuition waivers available. Financial award application deadline: 3/1; financial award applicants required to submit FAFSA. *Unit head:* Steve Nail, Dean, 864-MBA-6000. *Application contact:* Sharon Vargo, Graduate Admission Counselor, 864-231-2000, E-mail: svargo@andersonuniversity.edu.
Website: http://www.andersonuniversity.edu/business

**Antioch University Midwest,** MBA Program in Healthcare Leadership, Yellow Springs, OH 45387-1609. Offers MBA. *Program availability:* Part-time, evening/weekend, online learning. *Degree requirements:* For master's, capstone (thesis or practicum). *Entrance requirements:* For master's, resume, interview, essay. Electronic applications accepted. *Expenses:* Contact institution.

**Aquinas Institute of Theology,** Graduate and Professional Programs, St. Louis, MO 63108. Offers biblical studies (Certificate); church music (MM); health care mission (MAHCM); ministry (M Div); pastoral care (Certificate); pastoral ministry (MAPM); pastoral studies (MAPS); preaching (D Min); spiritual direction (Certificate); theology (M Div, MA); Thomistic studies (Certificate); M Div/MA; MA/PhD; MAPS/MSW. *Accreditation:* ATS (one or more programs are accredited). *Program availability:* Part-time, evening/weekend, online learning. *Degree requirements:* For master's, variable foreign language requirement, comprehensive exam (for some programs), thesis (for some programs); for doctorate, thesis/dissertation. *Entrance requirements:* For master's and Certificate, MAT; for doctorate, 3 years of ministerial experience, 6 hours of graduate course work in homiletics, M Div or the equivalent, minimum GPA of 3.0. Additional exam requirements/recommendations for international students: required—TOEFL. *Expenses:* Contact institution.

**Argosy University, Atlanta,** College of Business, Atlanta, GA 30328. Offers accounting (DBA); corporate compliance (MBA); customized professional concentration (MBA, DBA); finance (MBA); healthcare administration (MBA); information systems (DBA); information systems management (MBA); international business (MBA, DBA); management (MBA, MSM, DBA); marketing (MBA, DBA). *Accreditation:* ACBSP.

**Argosy University, Chicago,** College of Business, Chicago, IL 60601. Offers accounting (DBA); customized professional concentration (MBA, DBA); finance (MBA); fraud examination (MBA); global business sustainability (DBA); healthcare administration (MBA); information systems (DBA); information systems management (MBA); international business (MBA, DBA); management (MBA, MSM, DBA); marketing (MBA, DBA); organizational leadership (Ed D); public administration (MBA); sustainable management (MBA). *Accreditation:* ACBSP. *Program availability:* Online learning.

**Argosy University, Hawaii,** College of Business, Honolulu, HI 96813. Offers accounting (DBA); corporate compliance (MBA); customized professional concentration (MBA, DBA); finance (MBA, Certificate); fraud examination (MBA); global business sustainability (DBA); healthcare administration (MBA, Certificate); information systems (DBA); information systems management (MBA, Certificate); international business (MBA, DBA, Certificate); management (MBA, MSM, DBA); marketing (MBA, DBA, Certificate); organizational leadership (Ed D); public administration (MBA); sustainable management (MBA).

**Argosy University, Los Angeles,** College of Business, Los Angeles, CA 90045. Offers accounting (DBA); corporate compliance (MBA); customized professional concentration (MBA, DBA); finance (MBA); fraud examination (MBA); global business sustainability (DBA); healthcare administration (MBA); information systems (DBA); information systems management (MBA); international business (MBA, DBA); management (MBA, MSM, DBA); marketing (MBA, DBA); organizational leadership (Ed D); public administration (MBA); sustainable management (MBA).

**Argosy University, Northern Virginia,** College of Business, Arlington, VA 22209. Offers accounting (DBA); customized professional concentration (MBA, DBA); finance (MBA); fraud examination (MBA); global business sustainability (DBA); healthcare administration (MBA); information systems (DBA); information systems management (MBA); international business (MBA, DBA, Certificate); management (MBA, MSM, DBA); marketing (MBA, DBA, Certificate); organizational leadership (Ed D); public administration (MBA); sustainable management (MBA).

**Argosy University, Orange County,** College of Business, Orange, CA 92868. Offers accounting (DBA, Adv C); corporate compliance (MBA); customized professional concentration (MBA, DBA); finance (MBA, Certificate); fraud examination (MBA); global business sustainability (DBA); healthcare administration (MBA, Certificate); information systems (DBA, Adv C, Certificate); information systems management (MBA); international business (MBA, DBA, Adv C, Certificate); management (MBA, MSM, DBA, Adv C); marketing (MBA, DBA, Adv C, Certificate); organizational leadership (Ed D); public administration (MBA, Certificate); sustainable management (MBA).

**Argosy University, Phoenix,** College of Business, Phoenix, AZ 85021. Offers accounting (DBA); corporate compliance (MBA); customized professional concentration (MBA, DBA); finance (MBA); fraud examination (MBA); global business sustainability (DBA); healthcare administration (MBA); information systems (DBA); information systems management (MBA); international business (MBA, DBA); management (MBA, DBA); marketing (MBA, DBA); public administration (MBA); sustainable management (MBA).

**Argosy University, Seattle,** College of Business, Seattle, WA 98121. Offers accounting (DBA); corporate compliance (MBA); customized professional concentration (MBA, DBA); finance (MBA); fraud examination (MBA); global business sustainability (DBA); healthcare administration (MBA); information systems (DBA); information systems management (MBA); international business (MBA, DBA); management (MBA, MSM, DBA); marketing (MBA, DBA); organizational leadership (Ed D); public administration (MBA); sustainable management (MBA).

**Argosy University, Tampa,** College of Business, Tampa, FL 33607. Offers accounting (DBA); corporate compliance (MBA); customized professional concentration (MBA, DBA); finance (MBA); fraud examination (MBA); global business sustainability (DBA); healthcare administration (MBA); information systems (DBA); information systems management (MBA); international business (MBA, DBA); management (MBA, MSM, DBA); marketing (MBA, DBA); organizational leadership (Ed D); public administration (MBA); sustainable management (MBA).

**Argosy University, Twin Cities,** College of Business, Eagan, MN 55121. Offers accounting (DBA); customized professional concentration (MBA, DBA); finance (MBA); fraud examination (MBA); global business sustainability (DBA); healthcare administration (MBA); information systems (DBA); information systems management (MBA); international business (MBA, DBA); management (MBA, MSM, DBA); marketing (MBA, DBA); organizational leadership (Ed D); public administration (MBA); sustainable management (MBA).

**Argosy University, Twin Cities,** College of Health Sciences, Eagan, MN 55121. Offers health services management (MS); public health (MPH).

**Arizona State University at Tempe,** W. P. Carey School of Business, Program in Business Administration, Tempe, AZ 85287-4906. Offers entrepreneurship (MBA); finance (MBA); health sector management (MBA); international business (MBA); leadership (MBA); marketing (MBA); organizational behavior (PhD); strategic management (PhD); supply chain management (MBA, PhD); JD/MBA; MBA/M Acc; MBA/M Arch. *Accreditation:* AACSB. *Program availability:* Part-time, evening/weekend, online learning. Terminal master's awarded for partial completion of doctoral program. *Degree requirements:* For master's, thesis or alternative, internship, interactive Program of Study (iPOS) submitted before completing 50 percent of required credit hours; for doctorate, comprehensive exam, thesis/dissertation, interactive Program of Study (iPOS) submitted before completing 50 percent of required credit hours. *Entrance requirements:* For master's, GMAT, minimum GPA of 3.0 in last 2 years of work leading to bachelor's degree, 2 letters of recommendation, professional resume, official transcripts, 3 essays; for doctorate, GMAT or GRE, minimum GPA of 3.0 in last 2 years of work leading to bachelor's degree, 3 letters of recommendation, resume, personal statement/essay. Additional exam requirements/recommendations for international students: required—TOEFL (minimum score 550 paper-based; 80 iBT), IELTS (minimum score 6.5). Electronic applications accepted. *Expenses:* Contact institution.

**Arkansas State University,** Graduate School, College of Nursing and Health Professions, School of Nursing, State University, AR 72467. Offers aging studies (Graduate Certificate); health care management (Graduate Certificate); health sciences (MS); health sciences education (Graduate Certificate); nurse anesthesia (MSN); nursing (MSN); nursing practice (DNP). *Accreditation:* AANA/CANAEP (one or more programs are accredited); ACEN. *Program availability:* Part-time. *Degree requirements:* For master's and Graduate Certificate, comprehensive exam, thesis or alternative; for doctorate, comprehensive exam, thesis/dissertation. *Entrance requirements:* For master's, GRE General Test or MAT, appropriate bachelor's degree, current Arkansas nursing license, CPR certification, physical examination, professional liability insurance, critical care experience, ACLS Certification, PALS Certification, interview, immunization records, personal goal statement, health assessment; for doctorate, GRE or MAT, NCLEX-RN Exam, appropriate master's degree, current Arkansas nursing license, CPR certification, physical examination, professional liability insurance, critical care experience, ACLS Certification, PALS Certification, interview, immunization records, personal goal statement, health assessment, TB skin test, background check; for Graduate Certificate, GRE or MAT, appropriate bachelor's degree, official transcripts, immunization records, proof of employment in healthcare, TB Skin Test, TB Mask Fit Test, CPR Certification. Additional exam requirements/recommendations for international students: required—TOEFL (minimum score 550 paper-based; 79 iBT), IELTS (minimum score 6), PTE (minimum score 56). Electronic applications accepted. *Expenses:* Contact institution.

**Ashland University,** Dauch College of Business and Economics, Ashland, OH 44805-3702. Offers accounting (MBA); business analytics (MBA); entrepreneurship (MBA); financial management (MBA); global management (MBA); health care management and leadership (MBA); human resource management (MBA); human resources (MBA); management information systems (MBA); project management (MBA); sport management (MBA); supply chain management (MBA). *Accreditation:* ACBSP. *Program availability:* Part-time, evening/weekend, 100% online, blended/hybrid learning. Terminal master's awarded for partial completion of doctoral program. *Degree requirements:* For master's, thesis optional, capstone course. *Entrance requirements:* For master's, 2 years of full-time work experience. Additional exam requirements/recommendations for international students: required—TOEFL (minimum score 550 paper-based; 78 iBT). Electronic applications accepted. *Expenses:* Contact institution.

**Ashworth College,** Graduate Programs, Norcross, GA 30092. Offers business administration (MBA); criminal justice (MS); health care administration (MBA, MS); human resource management (MBA, MS); international business (MBA); management (MS); marketing (MBA, MS).

**Assumption University,** Health Advocacy Program, Worcester, MA 01609-1296. Offers MA, Professional Certificate. *Program availability:* Part-time, evening/weekend, online only, 100% online. *Degree requirements:* For master's, research course, practicum, capstone. *Entrance requirements:* For master's and Professional Certificate, bachelor's degree, three letters of recommendation, official transcripts, personal statement, current resume. Additional exam requirements/recommendations for international students: required—TOEFL (minimum score 540 paper-based; 76 iBT), IELTS (minimum score 6). Electronic applications accepted. *Expenses: Tuition:* Full-time $12,690; part-time $705 per credit. *Required fees:* $70 per term.

**Assumption University,** Healthcare Management Program, Worcester, MA 01609-1296. Offers MBA, CAGS, CGS. *Program availability:* Part-time, evening/weekend, online only, 100% online, blended/hybrid learning. *Degree requirements:* For master's, capstone. *Entrance requirements:* For master's, bachelor's degree, three letters of recommendation, official transcripts, personal statement, current resume; for other advanced degree, three letters of recommendation, official transcripts, personal statement, current resume; bachelor's degree in closely-related field (for CGS); MBA or equivalent degree in closely-related field (for CAGS). Additional exam requirements/recommendations for international students: required—TOEFL (minimum score 540 paper-based; 76 iBT), IELTS (minimum score 6). Electronic applications accepted. *Expenses: Tuition:* Full-time $12,690; part-time $705 per credit. *Required fees:* $70 per term.

**Atlantis University,** School of Health Care, Miami, FL 33132. Offers healthcare management (MS).

**A.T. Still University,** College of Graduate Health Studies, Kirksville, MO 63501. Offers dental public health (MPH); exercise and sport psychology (Certificate); fundamentals of education (Certificate); geriatric exercise science (Certificate); global health (Certificate); health administration (MHA, DHA); health professions (Ed D); health sciences (DH Sc); kinesiology (MS); leadership and organizational behavior (Certificate); public health (MPH); sports conditioning (Certificate). *Accreditation:* CEPH. *Program availability:* Part-time, evening/weekend, online only, 100% online, blended/hybrid learning. *Faculty:* 49 full-time (36 women), 109 part-time/adjunct (66 women). *Students:* 601 full-time (406 women), 532 part-time (331 women); includes 457 minority (197 Black or African American, non-Hispanic/Latino; 15 American Indian or Alaska Native, non-Hispanic/Latino; 114 Asian, non-Hispanic/Latino; 105 Hispanic/Latino; 3 Native Hawaiian or other Pacific Islander, non-Hispanic/Latino; 23 Two or more races, non-Hispanic/Latino), 30 international. Average age 36. 339 applicants, 73% accepted, 217 enrolled. In 2019, 175 master's, 100 doctorates, 118 other advanced degrees awarded. *Degree requirements:* For master's, thesis, integrated terminal project, practicum; for doctorate, thesis/dissertation. *Entrance requirements:* For master's, minimum GPA of 2.5, bachelor's degree or equivalent, essay, resume, English proficiency; for doctorate, minimum GPA of 2.5, master's or terminal degree, essay, past experience in relevant field, resume, English proficiency. Additional exam requirements/recommendations for international students: required—TOEFL (minimum score 550 paper-based; 80 iBT). *Application deadline:* For fall admission, 6/24 for domestic and international students; for winter admission, 9/9 for domestic and international students; for spring admission, 12/9 for domestic and international students; for summer admission, 3/2 for domestic and international students. Applications are processed on a rolling basis. Application fee: $70. Electronic applications accepted. *Financial support:* In 2019–20, 13 students received support. Scholarships/grants available. Financial award applicants required to submit FAFSA. *Unit head:* Dr. Donald Altman, Dean, 480-219-6008, Fax: 660-626-2826, E-mail: daltman@atsu.edu. *Application contact:* Amie Waldemer, Associate Director, Online Admissions, 480-219-6146, E-mail: awaldemer@atsu.edu.
Website: http://www.atsu.edu/college-of-graduate-health-studies

**Baker College Center for Graduate Studies–Online,** Graduate Programs, Flint, MI 48507. Offers accounting (MBA); business administration (DBA); finance (MBA); general business (MBA); health care management (MBA); human resources management (MBA); information management (MBA); leadership studies (MBA); management information systems (MSIS); marketing (MBA); occupational therapy (MOT). *Program availability:* Part-time, evening/weekend, online learning. *Degree requirements:* For master's, portfolio. *Entrance requirements:* For master's, 3 years of work experience, minimum undergraduate GPA of 2.5, writing sample, 3 letters of recommendation; for doctorate, MBA or acceptable related master's degree from accredited association, 5 years work experience, minimum graduate GPA of 3.25, writing sample, 3 professional references. Additional exam requirements/recommendations for international students: required—TOEFL (minimum score 550 paper-based). Electronic applications accepted.

**Baldwin Wallace University,** Graduate Programs, School of Business, Program in Health Care, Berea, OH 44017-2088. Offers MBA. *Program availability:* Part-time, evening/weekend, Multi-modal - student can choose to take some or all classes online. *Students:* 33 full-time (19 women), 6 part-time (2 women); includes 9 minority (3 Black or African American, non-Hispanic/Latino; 2 Asian, non-Hispanic/Latino; 4 Hispanic/Latino), 3 international. Average age 42. 12 applicants, 75% accepted, 8 enrolled. In 2019, 24 master's awarded. *Degree requirements:* For master's, minimum overall GPA of 3.0. *Entrance requirements:* For master's, GMAT or minimum GPA or 3.0, interview, work experience, bachelor's degree in any field. Additional exam requirements/recommendations for international students: required—TOEFL (minimum score 550 paper-based; 79 iBT), IELTS can be accepted in place of TOEFL. *Application deadline:* For fall admission, 7/25 priority date for domestic students, 4/30 priority date for international students; for spring admission, 12/10 priority date for domestic students, 9/30 priority date for international students. Applications are processed on a rolling basis. Electronic applications accepted. *Expenses:* $948 per credit hour. *Financial support:* Scholarships/grants and tuition discounts available. Financial award applicants required to submit FAFSA. *Unit head:* Dr. Susan Kuznik, Associate Dean, Graduate Business Programs, 440-826-2053, Fax: 440-826-3868, E-mail: skuznik@bw.edu. *Application contact:* Laura Spencer, Graduate Business Admission Specialist, 440-826-2191, Fax: 440-826-3868, E-mail: lspencer@bw.edu.
Website: https://www.bw.edu/schools/business/graduate-professional/master-business-administration-mba/health-care/

**Barry University,** Andreas School of Business, Graduate Certificate Programs, Miami Shores, FL 33161-6695. Offers finance (Certificate); health services administration (Certificate); international business (Certificate); management (Certificate); management information systems (Certificate); marketing (Certificate).

**Barry University,** College of Health Sciences, Graduate Certificate Programs, Miami Shores, FL 33161-6695. Offers health care leadership (Certificate); health care planning and informatics (Certificate); histotechnology (Certificate); long term care management (Certificate); medical group practice management (Certificate); quality improvement and outcomes management (Certificate).

**Barry University,** College of Health Sciences, Program in Health Services Administration, Miami Shores, FL 33161-6695. Offers MS. *Program availability:* Part-time, evening/weekend. *Degree requirements:* For master's, comprehensive exam. *Entrance requirements:* For master's, GMAT or GRE General Test, 2 years of experience in the health field, minimum GPA of 3.0, 1 semester of course work in computer applications or the equivalent (business). Electronic applications accepted.

**Baruch College of the City University of New York,** Austin W. Marxe School of Public and International Affairs, Program in Public Administration, New York, NY 10010-5585. Offers general public administration (MPA); health care policy (MPA); nonprofit administration (MPA); policy analysis and evaluation (MPA); public management (MPA); urban development and sustainability (MPA); MS/MPA. *Accreditation:* NASPAA. *Program availability:* Part-time, evening/weekend. *Degree requirements:* For master's, thesis, capstone. *Entrance requirements:* For master's, GRE General Test. Additional exam requirements/recommendations for international students: required—TOEFL. Electronic applications accepted. *Expenses:* Contact institution.

**Baruch College of the City University of New York,** Zicklin School of Business, Zicklin Executive Programs, Baruch/Mt. Sinai Program in Health Care Administration, New York, NY 10010-5585. Offers MBA. *Accreditation:* CAHME. *Program availability:* Part-time, evening/weekend. *Entrance requirements:* For master's, GMAT, personal interview, work experience in health care. Additional exam requirements/recommendations for international students: required—TOEFL. Electronic applications accepted. *Expenses:* Contact institution.

## Health Services Management and Hospital Administration

**Baylor University,** Graduate School, Hankamer School of Business, Department of Health Care Administration, Waco, TX 76798. Offers MHA, MHA/MBA. *Accreditation:* CAHME. *Faculty:* 18 full-time (6 women), 5 part-time/adjunct (1 woman). *Students:* 86 full-time (32 women); includes 14 minority (2 Black or African American, non-Hispanic/Latino; 5 Asian, non-Hispanic/Latino; 4 Hispanic/Latino; 3 Two or more races, non-Hispanic/Latino). 40 applicants, 50% accepted, 13 enrolled. In 2019, 38 master's awarded. Terminal master's awarded for partial completion of doctoral program. *Degree requirements:* For master's, comprehensive exam, Administrative Residency; Capstone. *Entrance requirements:* For master's, GMAT or GRE. Additional exam requirements/recommendations for international students: recommended—TOEFL, IELTS. *Application deadline:* For fall admission, 5/15 for domestic students, 3/15 for international students. Applications are processed on a rolling basis. Application fee: $50. Electronic applications accepted. *Financial support:* Unspecified assistantships available. Financial award application deadline: 4/15. *Unit head:* Scott H. Garner, Colonel, 210-710-3072, E-mail: Scott_H_Garner@baylor.edu. *Application contact:* Dr. Forest Kim, Dr., 254-710-3729, Fax: 210-221-6010, E-mail: Forest_Kim@baylor.edu. Website: https://www.baylor.edu/business/healthpolicy/

**Bay Path University,** Program in Healthcare Management, Longmeadow, MA 01106-2292. Offers health informatics (MS); organizational excellence (MS). *Program availability:* Part-time, online only, 100% online. *Entrance requirements:* For master's, completed application; official undergraduate and graduate transcripts (a GPA of 3.0 or higher is preferred); original essay of at least 250 words on the topic: "Why the MS in Healthcare Management is important to my personal and professional goals"; current resume; 2 recommendations. Electronic applications accepted. Application fee is waived when completed online.

**Belhaven University,** School of Business, Jackson, MS 39202-1789. Offers business administration (MBA); health administration (MBA); human resources (MBA, MSL); leadership (MBA); sports administration (MBA, MSA). *Program availability:* Part-time, evening/weekend, 100% online. *Students:* Average age 35. 574 applicants, 75% accepted, 306 enrolled. In 2019, 326 master's awarded. *Degree requirements:* For master's, comprehensive exam (for some programs), thesis or alternative. *Entrance requirements:* For master's, minimum GPA of 2.8 (for MBA and MHA), 2.5 (for MSL, MPA and MSA). *Application deadline:* Applications are processed on a rolling basis. Application fee: $25. Electronic applications accepted. *Expenses:* Contact institution. *Financial support:* Applicants required to submit FAFSA. *Unit head:* Dr. Ralph Mason, Dean, 601-968-8949, Fax: 601-968-8951, E-mail: cmason@belhaven.edu. *Application contact:* Dr. Audrey Kelleher, Vice President of Adult and Graduate Marketing and Development, 407-804-1424, Fax: 407-620-5210, E-mail: akelleher@belhaven.edu. Website: http://www.belhaven.edu/campuses/index.htm

**Bellevue University,** Graduate School, College of Arts and Sciences, Bellevue, NE 68005-3098. Offers clinical counseling (MS); healthcare administration (MHA); human services (MA); international security and intelligence studies (MS); managerial communication (MA). *Program availability:* Online learning.

**Belmont University,** Jack C. Massey Graduate School of Business, Nashville, TN 37212. Offers accounting (M Acc); business (AMBA, PMBA); healthcare (MBA). *Accreditation:* AACSB. *Program availability:* Part-time, evening/weekend. *Faculty:* 29 full-time (9 women), 7 part-time/adjunct (3 women). *Students:* 175 full-time (77 women), 30 part-time (16 women); includes 24 minority (8 Black or African American, non-Hispanic/Latino; 7 Asian, non-Hispanic/Latino; 7 Hispanic/Latino; 2 Two or more races, non-Hispanic/Latino), 6 international. Average age 30. In 2019, 110 master's awarded. *Entrance requirements:* For master's, GMAT, 2 years of work experience (MBA). Additional exam requirements/recommendations for international students: required—TOEFL (minimum score 550 paper-based). *Application deadline:* For fall admission, 7/1 for domestic and international students; for spring admission, 11/1 for domestic and international students. Applications are processed on a rolling basis. Application fee: $50. Electronic applications accepted. *Expenses:* Contact institution. *Financial support:* In 2019–20, 86 students received support. Scholarships/grants, tuition waivers (partial), and unspecified assistantships available. Financial award application deadline: 7/1; financial award applicants required to submit FAFSA. *Unit head:* Dr. Sarah Gardial, Dean, 615-460-6480, Fax: 615-460-6455, E-mail: Sarah.Gardial@belmont.edu. *Application contact:* Dr. Sarah Gardial, Dean, 615-460-6480, Fax: 615-460-6455, E-mail: Sarah.Gardial@belmont.edu.

**Benedictine University,** Graduate Programs, Program in Business Administration, Lisle, IL 60532. Offers accounting (MBA); entrepreneurship and managing innovation (MBA); financial management (MBA); health administration (MBA); human resource management (MBA); information systems security (MBA); international business (MBA); management consulting (MBA); management information systems (MBA); marketing management (MBA); operations management and logistics (MBA); organizational leadership (MBA). *Program availability:* Part-time, evening/weekend, 100% online, blended/hybrid learning. *Entrance requirements:* For master's, GMAT or GRE test scores or completed test waiver form, official transcripts; 2 letters of reference from individuals familiar with the applicant's professional or academic work, excluding family or personal friends; a 1-2 page essay addressing educational and career goals; current résumé listing chronological work history; personal interview may be required prior to an admission decision. Additional exam requirements/recommendations for international students: required—TOEFL (minimum score 550 paper-based; 79 iBT), IELTS (minimum score 6.5). Electronic applications accepted.

**Benedictine University,** Graduate Programs, Program in Public Health, Lisle, IL 60532. Offers administration of health care institutions (MPH); dietetics (MPH); disaster management (MPH); health education (MPH); health information systems (MPH); management information systems (MPH/MS); MBA/MPH; MPH/MS. *Accreditation:* CEPH. *Program availability:* Part-time, evening/weekend, 100% online. *Entrance requirements:* For master's, GRE, MAT, GMAT, LSAT, DAT or other graduate professional exams, official transcript; 2 letters of recommendation from individuals familiar with the applicant's professional or academic work, excluding family or personal friends; essay describing the candidate's career path. Additional exam requirements/recommendations for international students: required—TOEFL (minimum score 600 paper-based; 79 iBT), IELTS (minimum score 6.5). Electronic applications accepted.

**Binghamton University, State University of New York,** Graduate School, School of Management, Program in Business Administration, Binghamton, NY 13902-6000. Offers business administration (MBA); corporate executive (MBA); executive business administration (MBA); health care professional executive (MBA); professional business administration (MBA). *Accreditation:* AACSB. *Program availability:* Part-time. *Entrance requirements:* For master's, GMAT. Additional exam requirements/recommendations for international students: required—TOEFL (minimum score 96 iBT). Electronic applications accepted. *Expenses:* Contact institution.

**Binghamton University, State University of New York,** Graduate School, Thomas J. Watson School of Engineering and Applied Science, Department of Systems Science and Industrial Engineering, Binghamton, NY 13902-6000. Offers executive health systems (MS); industrial and systems engineering (M Eng); systems science and industrial engineering (MS, PhD). *Program availability:* Part-time, evening/weekend, online learning. *Degree requirements:* For master's, thesis; for doctorate, thesis/

dissertation. *Entrance requirements:* For master's and doctorate, GRE General Test. Additional exam requirements/recommendations for international students: required—TOEFL (minimum score 550 paper-based; 80 iBT). Electronic applications accepted. *Expenses:* Contact institution.

**Bluffton University,** Graduate Programs in Business, Bluffton, OH 45817. Offers accounting and financial management (MBA); health care management (MBA); leadership (MAOM, MBA); production and operations management (MBA); sustainability management (MBA). *Program availability:* Evening/weekend, blended/hybrid learning, videoconference. *Degree requirements:* For master's, integrated research project (for some programs). *Entrance requirements:* For master's, current resume, official transcript, bachelor's degree, minimum GPA of 3.0, personal essay. Additional exam requirements/recommendations for international students: recommended—TOEFL (minimum score 550 paper-based). Electronic applications accepted. *Expenses:* Contact institution.

**Boston University,** School of Medicine, Graduate Medical Sciences, Program in Healthcare Emergency Management, Boston, MA 02215. Offers MS. *Financial support:* Applicants required to submit FAFSA. *Unit head:* Dr. Kevin Thomas, Director, 617-414-2316, Fax: 617-414-2332, E-mail: kipthoma@bu.edu. *Application contact:* Patricia Jones, E-mail: psterlin@bu.edu. Website: http://www.bumc.bu.edu/gms/hem/

**Boston University,** School of Medicine, Graduate Medical Sciences, Program in Medical Sciences, Boston, MA 02215. Offers MS, MS/MPH. *Program availability:* Part-time. *Entrance requirements:* For master's, MCAT or GRE. *Application deadline:* Applications are processed on a rolling basis. Application fee: $75. Electronic applications accepted. *Financial support:* Federal Work-Study available. Financial award applicants required to submit FAFSA. *Unit head:* Dr. Gwynneth D. Offner, Director, E-mail: goffner@bu.edu. *Application contact:* Devin Weaver, MAMS Admissions Counselor, 617-358-9518, Fax: 617-358-2913, E-mail: mams@bu.edu. Website: http://www.bumc.bu.edu/gms/mams/

**Bradley University,** The Graduate School, College of Education and Health Sciences, Department of Nursing, Peoria, IL 61625-0002. Offers family nurse practitioner (MSN, DNP, Certificate); leadership (DNP); nursing administration (MSN); nursing education (MSN, Certificate). *Accreditation:* AACN; ACEN. *Program availability:* Part-time, evening/weekend, 100% online. *Faculty:* 12 full-time (all women), 32 part-time/adjunct (28 women). *Students:* 91 full-time (79 women), 637 part-time (551 women); includes 253 minority (143 Black or African American, non-Hispanic/Latino; 13 American Indian or Alaska Native, non-Hispanic/Latino; 40 Asian, non-Hispanic/Latino; 45 Hispanic/Latino; 2 Native Hawaiian or other Pacific Islander, non-Hispanic/Latino; 10 Two or more races, non-Hispanic/Latino), 19 international. Average age 38. 229 applicants, 79% accepted, 114 enrolled. In 2019, 60 master's, 20 doctorates awarded. *Degree requirements:* For master's, comprehensive exam, thesis optional; for doctorate, comprehensive exam. *Entrance requirements:* For master's, GRE General Test or MAT, interview, Illinois RN license, advanced cardiac life support certification, pediatric advanced life support certification, 3 letters of recommendation. Additional exam requirements/recommendations for international students: required—TOEFL (minimum score 550 paper-based; 79 iBT), IELTS (minimum score 6.5), PTE (minimum score 58). *Application deadline:* For fall admission, 5/15 priority date for domestic and international students; for spring admission, 10/15 priority date for domestic and international students. Applications are processed on a rolling basis. Application fee: $40 ($50 for international students). Electronic applications accepted. *Expenses:* Tuition: Part-time $930 per credit hour. *Financial support:* Research assistantships, scholarships/grants, tuition waivers (partial), and unspecified assistantships available. Financial award application deadline: 4/1. *Unit head:* Jessica Clark, Associate Dean and Director of the Department of Nursing, 309-677-2547, E-mail: jclark@bradley.edu. *Application contact:* Rachel Webb, Director of On-Campus Graduate Admissions and International Student and Scholar Services, 309-677-2375, Fax: 309-677-3343, E-mail: rkwebb@bradley.edu. Website: http://www.bradley.edu/academic/departments/nur/

**Brandeis University,** The Heller School for Social Policy and Management, Program in Nonprofit Management, Waltham, MA 02454-9110. Offers child, youth, and family management (MBA); health care management (MBA); social impact management (MBA); social policy and management (MBA); sustainable development (MBA); MBA/MA; MBA/MD. *Accreditation:* AACSB. *Program availability:* Part-time. *Degree requirements:* For master's, team consulting project. *Entrance requirements:* For master's, GMAT (preferred) or GRE, 2 letters of recommendation, problem statement analysis, 3-5 years of professional experience. Additional exam requirements/recommendations for international students: required—TOEFL (minimum score 600 paper-based; 100 iBT). Electronic applications accepted. *Expenses:* Contact institution.

**Brandman University,** School of Business and Professional Studies, Irvine, CA 92618. Offers accounting (MBA); business administration (MBA); business intelligence and data analytics (MBA); e-business strategic management (MBA); entrepreneurship (MBA); finance (MBA); health administration (MBA); human resources (MBA, MS); international business (MBA); marketing (MBA); organizational leadership (MA, MBA, MPA); public administration (MPA).

**Brenau University,** Sydney O. Smith Graduate School, College of Business & Communication, Gainesville, GA 30501. Offers accounting (MBA); business administration (MBA); healthcare management (MBA); organizational leadership (MS); project management (MBA). *Accreditation:* ACBSP. *Program availability:* Part-time, evening/weekend, 100% online. *Faculty:* 17 full-time (7 women), 31 part-time/adjunct (15 women). *Students:* 53 full-time (38 women), 361 part-time (274 women); includes 240 minority (209 Black or African American, non-Hispanic/Latino; 2 American Indian or Alaska Native, non-Hispanic/Latino; 6 Asian, non-Hispanic/Latino; 21 Hispanic/Latino; 2 Two or more races, non-Hispanic/Latino), 7 international. Average age 36. 211 applicants, 64% accepted, 90 enrolled. In 2019, 158 master's awarded. *Entrance requirements:* For master's, GMAT, GRE, or MAT, resume, minimum undergraduate GPA of 2.5. Additional exam requirements/recommendations for international students: required—TOEFL (minimum score 497 paper-based; 71 iBT); recommended—IELTS (minimum score 5.5). *Application deadline:* Applications are processed on a rolling basis. Application fee: $35. Electronic applications accepted. *Expenses:* Tuition: Full-time $7339.65; part-time $3685.36 per year. *Required fees:* $740 per semester. Tuition and fees vary according to course load, degree level and program. *Financial support:* In 2019–20, 7 students received support. Scholarships/grants available. Financial award applicants required to submit FAFSA. *Unit head:* Dr. Suzanne Erickson, Dean, 770-531-3174, Fax: 770-537-4701, E-mail: serickson@brenau.edu. *Application contact:* Nathan Goss, Assistant Vice President for Recruitment, 770-534-6162, E-mail: ngoss@brenau.edu. Website: https://www.brenau.edu/businesscomm/

**Brigham Young University,** Graduate Studies, BYU Marriott School of Business, Master of Public Administration Program, Provo, UT 84602. Offers healthcare (MPA); local government (MPA); nonprofit management (MPA); state and federal government (MPA); JD/MPA. *Accreditation:* NASPAA. *Faculty:* 10 full-time (2 women), 10 part-time/adjunct (2 women). *Students:* 95 full-time (52 women); includes 10 minority (4 Black or African American, non-Hispanic/Latino; 1 American Indian or Alaska Native, non-

Hispanic/Latino; 1 Asian, non-Hispanic/Latino; 2 Hispanic/Latino; 2 Native Hawaiian or other Pacific Islander, non-Hispanic/Latino). Average age 26. 81 applicants, 85% accepted, 57 enrolled. In 2019, 45 master's awarded. *Entrance requirements:* For master's, GMAT or GRE, Statement of Intent, Resume, Bachelor's degree, 3 letters or recommendation, ecclesiastical endorsement. Additional exam requirements/ recommendations for international students: required—TOEFL (minimum score 580 paper-based; 85 iBT). *Application deadline:* For fall admission, 1/15 for domestic and international students. Application fee: $50. Electronic applications accepted. *Expenses:* Full-time LDS tuition $6,725 a semester in 2019, books, health insurance. *Financial support:* In 2019–20, 93 students received support. Scholarships/grants available. Financial award application deadline: 4/15; financial award applicants required to submit FAFSA. *Unit head:* Dr. Lori Wadsworth, Director, 801-422-5956, E-mail: lori_wadsworth@byu.edu. *Application contact:* Catherine Cooper, Associate Director, 801-422-9173, E-mail: clc@byu.edu.
Website: https://marriottschool.byu.edu/mpa/

**Broadview University–West Jordan,** Graduate Programs, West Jordan, UT 84088. Offers business administration (MBA); health care management (MSM); information technology (MSM); managerial leadership (MSM).

**Brooklyn College of the City University of New York,** School of Natural and Behavioral Sciences, Department of Health and Nutrition Sciences, Program in Public Health, Brooklyn, NY 11210-2889. Offers general public health (MPH); health care policy and administration (MPH). *Degree requirements:* For master's, thesis or alternative, 46 credits. *Entrance requirements:* For master's, GRE, 2 letters of recommendation, essay, interview. Electronic applications accepted.

**Bryan College,** MBA Program, Dayton, TN 37321. Offers business administration (MBA); healthcare administration (MBA); human resources (MBA); marketing (MBA); ministry (MBA); sports management (MBA). *Program availability:* Part-time, evening/ weekend, online only, 100% online. *Faculty:* 1 full-time (0 women), 13 part-time/adjunct (5 women). *Students:* 137 full-time (72 women), 26 part-time (11 women). 70 applicants, 100% accepted, 70 enrolled. In 2019, 28 master's awarded. *Degree requirements:* For master's, minimum gpa of 3.0. *Entrance requirements:* For master's, transcripts showing degree conferral; undergrad gpa of 2.75. Additional exam requirements/ recommendations for international students: required—TOEFL (minimum score 70 iBT). *Application deadline:* For fall admission, 9/1 for domestic and international students; for winter admission, 11/15 for domestic and international students; for spring admission, 2/ 1 for domestic and international students; for summer admission, 6/1 for domestic and international students. Applications are processed on a rolling basis. Electronic applications accepted. *Expenses:* 595 per credit hour, 36 credit hours required, 250 graduation fee, 65 tech fee per term. *Financial support:* Scholarships/grants available. Financial award applicants required to submit FAFSA. *Unit head:* Dr. Adina Scruggs, Dean of Adult and Graduate Studies, 423-775-7121, E-mail: adina.scruggs@bryan.edu. *Application contact:* Mandi K Sullivan, Director of Academic Programs, 423-664-9880, E-mail: mandi.sullivan@bryan.edu.
Website: http://www.bryan.edu/academics/adult-education/graduate/online-mba/

**California Baptist University,** Program in Business Administration, Riverside, CA 92504-3206. Offers accounting (MBA); construction management (MBA); healthcare management (MBA); management (MBA). *Accreditation:* ACBSP. *Program availability:* Part-time, evening/weekend, 100% online, blended/hybrid learning. *Degree requirements:* For master's, thesis, Interdisciplinary Capstone Project. *Entrance requirements:* For master's, GMAT, minimum GPA of 2.5; two recommendations; comprehensive essay; resume; interview. Additional exam requirements/ recommendations for international students: required—TOEFL (minimum score 80 iBT). Electronic applications accepted. *Expenses:* Contact institution.

**California Baptist University,** Program in Public Health, Riverside, CA 92504-3206. Offers health education and promotion (MPH); health policy and administration (MPH). *Accreditation:* CEPH. *Program availability:* Part-time, evening/weekend, 100% online, blended/hybrid learning. *Degree requirements:* For master's, capstone project; practicum. *Entrance requirements:* For master's, minimum undergraduate GPA of 2.75, two recommendations, 500-word essay, resume. Additional exam requirements/ recommendations for international students: required—TOEFL (minimum score 80 iBT). Electronic applications accepted. *Expenses:* Contact institution.

**California Coast University,** School of Administration and Management, Santa Ana, CA 92701. Offers business marketing (MBA); health care management (MBA); human resource management (MBA); management (MBA, MS). *Program availability:* Online learning. Electronic applications accepted.

**California Intercontinental University,** School of Healthcare, Irvine, CA 92614. Offers healthcare management and leadership (MBA, DBA).

**California State University, Chico,** Office of Graduate Studies, College of Behavioral and Social Sciences, Department of Political Science and Criminal Justice, Program in Public Administration, Chico, CA 95929-0722. Offers health administration (MPA); local government management (MPA). *Accreditation:* NASPAA. *Program availability:* Part-time. *Degree requirements:* For master's, thesis or culminating practicum. *Entrance requirements:* For master's, 2 letters of recommendation and statement of purpose. Additional exam requirements/recommendations for international students: required—TOEFL (minimum score 550 paper-based; 80 iBT), IELTS (minimum score 6.5), PTE. Electronic applications accepted.

**California State University, East Bay,** Office of Graduate Studies, College of Letters, Arts, and Social Sciences, Department of Public Affairs and Administration, Program in Health Care Administration, Hayward, CA 94542-3000. Offers management and change in health care (MS). *Program availability:* Part-time, evening/weekend, online learning. *Degree requirements:* For master's, thesis or alternative, final project. *Entrance requirements:* For master's, minimum undergraduate cumulative GPA of 2.5, statement of purpose, two letters of academic and/or professional recommendation, professional resume/curriculum vitae, all undergraduate/graduate transcripts. Additional exam requirements/recommendations for international students: required—TOEFL (minimum score 550 paper-based). Electronic applications accepted.

**California State University, East Bay,** Office of Graduate Studies, College of Letters, Arts, and Social Sciences, Department of Public Affairs and Administration, Program in Public Administration, Hayward, CA 94542-3000. Offers health care administration (MPA); public management and policy analysis (MPA). *Program availability:* Part-time, evening/weekend. *Degree requirements:* For master's, comprehensive exam (for some programs), comprehensive exam or thesis. *Entrance requirements:* For master's, minimum GPA of 2.5; statement of purpose; 2 letters of recommendation; professional resume/curriculum vitae. Additional exam requirements/recommendations for international students: required—TOEFL (minimum score 550 paper-based; 79 iBT). Electronic applications accepted.

**California State University, Fresno,** Division of Research and Graduate Studies, College of Health and Human Services, Department of Public Health, Fresno, CA 93740-8027. Offers health policy and management (MPH); health promotion (MPH). *Accreditation:* CEPH. *Program availability:* Part-time, evening/weekend. *Degree requirements:* For master's, thesis or alternative. *Entrance requirements:* For master's, GRE General Test, minimum GPA of 2.5. Additional exam requirements/ recommendations for international students: required—TOEFL. Electronic applications accepted. *Expenses:* Tuition, state resident: full-time $4012; part-time $2506 per semester.

**California State University, Long Beach,** Graduate Studies, College of Health and Human Services, Program in Health Care Administration, Long Beach, CA 90840. Offers MS. *Accreditation:* CAHME. *Program availability:* Part-time. *Degree requirements:* For master's, comprehensive exam or thesis. *Entrance requirements:* For master's, minimum GPA of 3.0. Electronic applications accepted.

**California State University, Los Angeles,** Graduate Studies, College of Business and Economics, Department of Management, Los Angeles, CA 90032-8530. Offers health care management (MS); management (MBA). *Accreditation:* AACSB. *Program availability:* Part-time, evening/weekend. *Entrance requirements:* For master's, GMAT, minimum GPA of 2.5 during previous 2 years of course work. Additional exam requirements/recommendations for international students: required—TOEFL (minimum score 550 paper-based). Electronic applications accepted. *Expenses: Tuition, area resident:* Full-time $7176; part-time $4164 per year. Tuition, state resident: full-time $7176; part-time $4164 per year. Tuition, nonresident: full-time $14,304; part-time $8916 per year. *International tuition:* $14,304 full-time. *Required fees:* $1037.76; $1037.76 per unit. Tuition and fees vary according to degree level and program.

**California State University, Northridge,** Graduate Studies, College of Health and Human Development, Department of Health Sciences, Northridge, CA 91330. Offers health administration (MS); public health (MPH), including applied epidemiology, community health education. *Accreditation:* CAHME; CEPH. *Entrance requirements:* For master's, GRE General Test or minimum GPA of 3.0. Additional exam requirements/ recommendations for international students: required—TOEFL.

**California State University, Northridge,** Graduate Studies, Tseng College, Program in Health Administration, Northridge, CA 91330. Offers MPA. *Program availability:* Online learning. *Degree requirements:* For master's, comprehensive exam. *Entrance requirements:* For master's, bachelor's degree from accredited college or university, minimum cumulative GPA of 2.5, at least two years of work experience. Additional exam requirements/recommendations for international students: required—TOEFL (minimum score of 563 paper-based, 85 iBT) or IELTS (minimum score of 7). Electronic applications accepted.

**California State University, San Bernardino,** Graduate Studies, College of Natural Sciences, Program in Health Services Administration, San Bernardino, CA 92407. Offers MS. *Faculty:* 4 full-time (3 women), 4 part-time/adjunct (2 women). *Students:* 12 full-time (5 women), 20 part-time (17 women); includes 22 minority (6 Black or African American, non-Hispanic/Latino; 2 Asian, non-Hispanic/Latino; 14 Hispanic/Latino), 3 international. Average age 28. 38 applicants, 58% accepted, 11 enrolled. In 2019, 15 master's awarded. *Degree requirements:* For master's, thesis or alternative. *Entrance requirements:* Additional exam requirements/recommendations for international students: required—TOEFL. *Application deadline:* For fall admission, 5/5 for domestic students. Application fee: $55. *Unit head:* Dr. Paulchris Okpala, Program Director, 909-537-5341, E-mail: pokpala@csusb.edu. *Application contact:* Dr. Dorota Huizinga, Dean of Graduate Studies, 909-537-3064, E-mail: dorota.huizinga@csusb.edu.

**California University of Pennsylvania,** School of Graduate Studies and Research, Eberly College of Science and Technology, Program in Business Administration, California, PA 15419-1394. Offers business analytics (MBA); entrepreneurship (MBA); healthcare management (MBA). *Program availability:* Part-time, evening/weekend. *Degree requirements:* For master's, comprehensive exam. *Entrance requirements:* For master's, minimum GPA of 3.0, official transcripts. Additional exam requirements/ recommendations for international students: required—TOEFL (minimum score 550 paper-based). Electronic applications accepted. *Expenses: Tuition, area resident:* Full-time $9288; part-time $516 per credit. Tuition, state resident: full-time $9288; part-time $516 per credit. Tuition, nonresident: full-time $13,932; part-time $774 per credit. *Required fees:* $3631; $291.13 per credit. Part-time tuition and fees vary according to course load.

**Cambridge College,** School of Management, Boston, MA 02129. Offers business administration (MBA); business negotiation and conflict resolution (M Mgt); general business (M Mgt); health care (MBA); health care management (M Mgt); small business development (M Mgt); technology management (M Mgt). *Program availability:* Part-time, evening/weekend, 100% online, blended/hybrid learning. *Degree requirements:* For master's, thesis, seminars. *Entrance requirements:* For master's, resume, 2 professional references. Additional exam requirements/recommendations for international students: required—TOEFL (minimum score 550 paper-based; 79 iBT), Michigan English Language Assessment Battery (minimum score 85); recommended—IELTS (minimum score 6). Electronic applications accepted. *Expenses:* Contact institution.

**Capella University,** School of Business and Technology, Master's Programs in Business, Minneapolis, MN 55402. Offers accounting (MBA); business analysis (MS); business intelligence (MBA); entrepreneurship (MBA); finance (MBA); general business administration (MBA); general human resource management (MS); general leadership (MS); health care management (MBA); human resource management (MBA); marketing (MBA); project management (MBA, MS). *Accreditation:* ACBSP.

**Capella University,** School of Public Service Leadership, Doctoral Programs in Healthcare, Minneapolis, MN 55402. Offers criminal justice (PhD); emergency management (PhD); epidemiology (Dr PH); general health administration (DHA); general public administration (DPA); health advocacy and leadership (Dr PH); health care administration (PhD); health care leadership (DHA); health policy advocacy (DHA); multidisciplinary human services (PhD); nonprofit management and leadership (PhD); public safety leadership (PhD); social and community services (PhD).

**Capella University,** School of Public Service Leadership, Master's Programs in Healthcare, Minneapolis, MN 55402. Offers criminal justice (MS); emergency management (MS); general public health (MPH); gerontology (MS); health administration (MHA); health care operations (MHA); health management policy (MPH); health policy (MHA); homeland security (MS); multidisciplinary human services (MS); public administration (MPA); public safety leadership (MS); social and community services (MS); social behavioral sciences (MPH); MS/MPA.

**Cardinal Stritch University,** College of Business and Management, Milwaukee, WI 53217-3985. Offers cyber security (MBA); healthcare management (MBA); justice administration (MBA); marketing (MBA). *Accreditation:* ACBSP. *Program availability:* Part-time, evening/weekend, 100% online, blended/hybrid learning. *Degree requirements:* For master's, thesis. *Entrance requirements:* For master's, 3 years of management or related experience, minimum GPA of 2.5. Additional exam requirements/recommendations for international students: required—TOEFL (minimum score 79 iBT), IELTS (minimum score 6.5). Electronic applications accepted. *Expenses:* Contact institution.

**Carlow University,** College of Leadership and Social Change, MBA Program, Pittsburgh, PA 15213-3165. Offers fraud and forensics (MBA); healthcare management (MBA); human resource management (MBA); leadership and management (MBA); project management (MBA). *Program availability:* Part-time, evening/weekend, 100%

online, blended/hybrid learning. *Students:* 52 full-time (39 women), 24 part-time (20 women); includes 28 minority (23 Black or African American, non-Hispanic/Latino; 3 Asian, non-Hispanic/Latino; 2 Two or more races, non-Hispanic/Latino). Average age 36. 33 applicants, 100% accepted, 24 enrolled. In 2019, 39 master's awarded. *Entrance requirements:* For master's, minimum undergraduate GPA of 3.0 (preferred); personal essay; resume; official transcripts; two professional recommendations. Additional exam requirements/recommendations for international students: required—TOEFL (minimum score 550 paper-based). *Application deadline:* Applications are processed on a rolling basis. Electronic applications accepted. *Financial support:* Application deadline: 4/1; applicants required to submit FAFSA. *Unit head:* Dr. Howard Stern, Program Director, MBA Program, 412-578-8828, E-mail: hastern@carlow.edu. *Application contact:* Dr. Howard Stern, Program Director, MBA Program, 412-578-8828, E-mail: hastern@carlow.edu.
Website: http://www.carlow.edu/Business_Administration.aspx

**Carnegie Mellon University,** Heinz College, School of Public Policy and Management, Master of Science Program in Health Care Policy and Management, Pittsburgh, PA 15213-3891. Offers MSHCPM. *Program availability:* Part-time, evening/weekend. *Degree requirements:* For master's, internship. *Entrance requirements:* For master's, GRE or GMAT, college-level course in advanced algebra/pre-calculus; college-level courses in economics and statistics (recommended). Additional exam requirements/recommendations for international students: required—TOEFL or IELTS. Electronic applications accepted.

**Carnegie Mellon University,** Heinz College, School of Public Policy and Management, Programs in Medical Management, Pittsburgh, PA 15213-3891. Offers MMM.

**Case Western Reserve University,** Weatherhead School of Management, Program in Healthcare, Cleveland, OH 44106. Offers MSM. *Program availability:* Evening/weekend. *Entrance requirements:* For master's, GMAT/GRE, master's degree or higher in a medical to management-related field, or bachelor's degree plus 5 years of experience working in the healthcare industry, essay, current resume, letters of recommendation. Electronic applications accepted.

**The Catholic University of America,** Metropolitan School of Professional Studies, Washington, DC 20064. Offers emergency service administration (MS); health administration (MHA); social service administration (MS). *Program availability:* Part-time, evening/weekend, 100% online. *Faculty:* 22 part-time/adjunct (13 women). *Students:* 32 full-time (17 women), 73 part-time (43 women); includes 57 minority (39 Black or African American, non-Hispanic/Latino; 4 Asian, non-Hispanic/Latino; 10 Hispanic/Latino; 4 Two or more races, non-Hispanic/Latino), 18 international. Average age 35. 78 applicants, 79% accepted, 34 enrolled. In 2019, 32 master's awarded. *Degree requirements:* For master's, minimum GPA of 3.0, capstone course. *Entrance requirements:* For master's, statement of purpose, official copies of academic transcripts, three letters of recommendation, resume. Additional exam requirements/recommendations for international students: required—TOEFL (minimum score 550 paper-based; 80 iBT). *Application deadline:* For fall admission, 7/15 priority date for domestic students, 7/1 for international students; for spring admission, 11/15 priority date for domestic students, 11/1 for international students. Applications are processed on a rolling basis. Application fee: $55. Electronic applications accepted. *Financial support:* Scholarships/grants available. Financial award application deadline: 3/15; financial award applicants required to submit FAFSA. *Unit head:* Dr. Vince Kiernan, Dean, 202-319-5256, Fax: 202-319-6260, E-mail: kiernan@cua.edu. *Application contact:* Dr. Steven Brown, Director of Graduate Admissions, 202-319-5057, Fax: 202-319-6533, E-mail: cua-admissions@cua.edu.
Website: https://metro.catholic.edu/

**Cedarville University,** Graduate Programs, Cedarville, OH 45314. Offers business administration (MBA); family nurse practitioner (MSN); global ministry (M Div); global public health nursing (MSN); healthcare administration (MBA); ministry (M Min); nurse educator (MSN); operations management (MBA); pharmacy (Pharm D). *Program availability:* Part-time, evening/weekend, 100% online, blended/hybrid learning. *Faculty:* 52 full-time (19 women), 21 part-time/adjunct (13 women). *Students:* 378 full-time (221 women), 45 part-time (23 women); includes 76 minority (46 Black or African American, non-Hispanic/Latino; 2 American Indian or Alaska Native, non-Hispanic/Latino; 22 Asian, non-Hispanic/Latino; 1 Hispanic/Latino; 5 Two or more races, non-Hispanic/Latino), 2 international. Average age 26. 398 applicants, 70% accepted, 172 enrolled. In 2019, 74 master's, 34 doctorates awarded. *Degree requirements:* For master's, portfolio; for doctorate, comprehensive exam. *Entrance requirements:* For master's, GRE may be required, 2 professional recommendations; for doctorate, PCAT, professional recommendation from a practicing pharmacist or current employer/supervisor, resume, essay, interview. Additional exam requirements/recommendations for international students: required—TOEFL (minimum score 550 paper-based; 80 iBT). *Application deadline:* For fall admission, 5/1 priority date for domestic and international students; for spring admission, 11/1 priority date for domestic and international students. Applications are processed on a rolling basis. Electronic applications accepted. *Expenses: Tuition:* Full-time $12,594; part-time $566 per credit hour. One-time fee: $100. Tuition and fees vary according to course load and program. *Financial support:* Scholarships/grants and unspecified assistantships available. Support available to part-time students. Financial award application deadline: 1/30; financial award applicants required to submit FAFSA. *Unit head:* Dr. Janice Supplee, Dean of Graduate Studies, 937-766-8000, E-mail: suppleej@cedarville.edu. *Application contact:* Alexis McKay, Graduate Admissions Counselor, 937-766-8000, E-mail: amckay@cedarville.edu.
Website: https://www.cedarville.edu/offices/graduate-school

**Central Michigan University,** Central Michigan University Global Campus, Program in Administration, Mount Pleasant, MI 48859. Offers acquisitions administration (MSA, Certificate); engineering management administration (MSA, Certificate); general administration (MSA, Certificate); health services administration (MSA, Certificate); human resources administration (MSA, Certificate); information resource management (MSA); information resource management administration (Certificate); international administration (MSA, Certificate); leadership (MSA, Certificate); philanthropy and fundraising administration (MSA, Certificate); public administration (MSA, Certificate); recreation and park administration (MSA); research administration (MSA, Certificate). *Program availability:* Part-time, evening/weekend, online learning. *Entrance requirements:* For master's, minimum GPA of 2.7 in major. Electronic applications accepted. *Expenses: Tuition, area resident:* Full-time $12,267; part-time $8178 per year. Tuition, state resident: full-time $12,267; part-time $8178 per year. Tuition, nonresident: full-time $12,267; part-time $8178 per year. *International tuition:* $16,110 full-time. *Required fees:* $225 per semester. Tuition and fees vary according to degree level and program.

**Central Michigan University,** Central Michigan University Global Campus, Program in Health Administration, Mount Pleasant, MI 48859. Offers health administration (DHA); international health (Certificate); nutrition and dietetics (MS). *Program availability:* Part-time, evening/weekend, online learning. Electronic applications accepted. *Expenses: Tuition, area resident:* Full-time $12,267; part-time $8178 per year. Tuition, state resident: full-time $12,267; part-time $8178 per year. Tuition, nonresident: full-time $12,267; part-time $8178 per year. *International tuition:* $16,110 full-time. *Required fees:* $225 per semester. Tuition and fees vary according to degree level and program.

**Central Michigan University,** College of Graduate Studies, The Herbert H. and Grace A. Dow College of Health Professions, School of Health Sciences, Mount Pleasant, MI 48859. Offers exercise science (MA); health administration (DHA). *Program availability:* Part-time, evening/weekend, online learning. *Degree requirements:* For doctorate, comprehensive exam, thesis/dissertation. *Entrance requirements:* For doctorate, accredited master's or doctoral degree, 5 years of related work experience. Electronic applications accepted. *Expenses: Tuition, area resident:* Full-time $12,267; part-time $8178 per year. Tuition, state resident: full-time $12,267; part-time $8178 per year. Tuition, nonresident: full-time $12,267; part-time $8178 per year. *International tuition:* $16,110 full-time. *Required fees:* $225 per semester. Tuition and fees vary according to degree level and program.

**Central Michigan University,** College of Graduate Studies, Interdisciplinary Administration Programs, Mount Pleasant, MI 48859. Offers acquisitions administration (MSA, Graduate Certificate); general administration (MSA, Graduate Certificate); health services administration (MSA, Graduate Certificate); human resource administration (Graduate Certificate); human resources administration (MSA); information resource management (MSA, Graduate Certificate); international administration (MSA, Graduate Certificate); leadership (MSA, Graduate Certificate); public administration (MSA, Graduate Certificate); research administration (Graduate Certificate); sport administration (MSA). *Accreditation:* AACSB. *Program availability:* Part-time, evening/weekend, online learning. *Degree requirements:* For master's, thesis or alternative. *Entrance requirements:* For master's, bachelor's degree with minimum GPA of 2.7. Electronic applications accepted. *Expenses: Tuition, area resident:* Full-time $12,267; part-time $8178 per year. Tuition, state resident: full-time $12,267; part-time $8178 per year. Tuition, nonresident: full-time $12,267; part-time $8178 per year. *International tuition:* $16,110 full-time. *Required fees:* $225 per semester. Tuition and fees vary according to degree level and program.

**Champlain College,** Graduate Studies, Burlington, VT 05402-0670. Offers business (MBA); digital forensic science (MS); early childhood education (M Ed); emergent media (MFA, MS); executive leadership (MS); health care administration (MS); information security operations (MS); law (MS); mediation and applied conflict studies (MS). *Program availability:* Part-time, online learning. *Degree requirements:* For master's, capstone project. *Entrance requirements:* Additional exam requirements/recommendations for international students: required—TOEFL (minimum score 550 paper-based; 80 iBT). Electronic applications accepted.

**The Chicago School of Professional Psychology: Online,** Program in Health Services Administration, Chicago, IL 60654. Offers MHSA. *Program availability:* Online learning.

**Clarion University of Pennsylvania,** College of Business Administration and Information Sciences, Master of Business Administration Program, Clarion, PA 16214. Offers accounting (MBA); finance (MBA); health care administration (MBA); innovation and entrepreneurship (MBA); non-profit business (MBA). *Accreditation:* AACSB. *Program availability:* Part-time, evening/weekend, online only, 100% online. *Faculty:* 13 full-time (2 women). *Students:* 18 full-time (10 women), 79 part-time (32 women); includes 13 minority (5 Black or African American, non-Hispanic/Latino; 6 Hispanic/Latino; 1 Native Hawaiian or other Pacific Islander, non-Hispanic/Latino; 1 Two or more races, non-Hispanic/Latino), 1 international. Average age 31. 81 applicants, 36% accepted, 26 enrolled. In 2019, 25 master's awarded. *Entrance requirements:* For master's, If GPA is below 3.0 submit the GMAT, minimum QPA of 2.75. Additional exam requirements/recommendations for international students: required—TOEFL (minimum score 550 paper-based; 80 iBT). *Application deadline:* For fall admission, 8/1 priority date for domestic students, 7/15 priority date for international students; for winter admission, 11/1 priority date for domestic students; for spring admission, 12/1 priority date for domestic students, 11/15 priority date for international students; for summer admission, 4/1 priority date for domestic students. Applications are processed on a rolling basis. Application fee: $40. Electronic applications accepted. *Expenses: Tuition, area resident:* Part-time $516 per credit hour. Tuition, state resident: part-time $516 per credit hour. Tuition, nonresident: part-time $557 per credit hour. *Required fees:* $161 per credit hour. One-time fee: $50 part-time. Tuition and fees vary according to degree level, campus/location and program. *Financial support:* Career-related internships or fieldwork, Federal Work-Study, institutionally sponsored loans, and scholarships/grants available. Support available to part-time students. Financial award application deadline: 3/1; financial award applicants required to submit FAFSA. *Unit head:* Juanice Vega, Interim Assistant Dean, 814-393-1892, Fax: 814-393-1910, E-mail: mba@clarion.edu. *Application contact:* Susan Staub, Graduate Admissions Counselor, 814-393-2337, Fax: 814-393-2722, E-mail: gradstudies@clarion.edu.
Website: http://www.clarion.edu/admissions/graduate/index.html

**Clarkson University,** David D. Reh School of Business, Master's Programs in Healthcare Management and Leadership, Schenectady, NY 13699. Offers clinical leadership in healthcare management (MS); healthcare data analytics (MS); healthcare management (MBA, Advanced Certificate). *Program availability:* Part-time, evening/weekend, blended/hybrid learning. *Faculty:* 20 full-time (7 women), 6 part-time/adjunct (1 woman). *Students:* 36 full-time (22 women), 36 part-time (18 women); includes 12 minority (6 Black or African American, non-Hispanic/Latino; 4 Asian, non-Hispanic/Latino; 2 Hispanic/Latino), 7 international. 46 applicants, 70% accepted, 24 enrolled. In 2019, 28 master's awarded. *Entrance requirements:* For master's, GRE or GMAT. Additional exam requirements/recommendations for international students: required—TOEFL (minimum score 550 paper-based, 80 iBT) or IELTS (6.5). *Application deadline:* Applications are processed on a rolling basis. Application fee: $50. Electronic applications accepted. *Expenses: Tuition:* Full-time $24,984; part-time $1388 per credit hour. *Required fees:* $225. Tuition and fees vary according to campus/location and program. *Financial support:* Scholarships/grants available. *Unit head:* Dr. John Huppertz, Associate Professor / Director of Healthcare Management, 518-631-9892, E-mail: jhuppert@clarkson.edu. *Application contact:* Daniel Capogna, Director of Graduate Admissions & Recruitment, 518-631-9910, E-mail: graduate@clarkson.edu.

**Cleary University,** Online Program in Business Administration, Howell, MI 48843. Offers analytics, technology, and innovation (MBA, Graduate Certificate); financial planning (Graduate Certificate); global leadership (MBA, Graduate Certificate); health care leadership (MBA, Graduate Certificate). *Program availability:* Part-time, evening/weekend, online learning. *Degree requirements:* For master's, thesis. *Entrance requirements:* For master's, bachelor's degree; minimum GPA of 2.5; professional resume indicating minimum of 2 years of management or related experience; undergraduate degree from accredited college or university with at least 18 quarter hours (or 12 semester hours) of accounting study (for MBA in accounting). Additional exam requirements/recommendations for international students: required—TOEFL (minimum score 550 paper-based; 79 iBT), Michigan English Language Assessment Battery (minimum score 75). Electronic applications accepted.

**Cleveland State University,** College of Graduate Studies, Monte Ahuja College of Business, Department of Management, Cleveland, OH 44115. Offers health care administration (MBA); labor relations and human resources (MLRHR). *Program availability:* Part-time, evening/weekend. *Faculty:* 6 full-time (3 women), 8 part-time/adjunct (1 woman). *Students:* 9 full-time (7 women), 15 part-time (14 women); includes 6 minority (3 Black or African American, non-Hispanic/Latino; 1 Asian, non-Hispanic/

Latino; 1 Hispanic/Latino; 1 Two or more races, non-Hispanic/Latino), 1 international. Average age 28. In 2019, 14 master's awarded. *Entrance requirements:* For master's, GMAT or GRE, minimum GPA of 3.0. Additional exam requirements/recommendations for international students: required—TOEFL (minimum score 550 paper-based; 78 iBT). *Application deadline:* For fall admission, 7/15 for domestic students; for spring admission, 12/15 for domestic students. Applications are processed on a rolling basis. Application fee: $40. Electronic applications accepted. *Expenses:* Tuition, state resident: full-time $10,215; part-time $6810 per credit hour. Tuition, nonresident: full-time $17,496; part-time $11,664 per credit hour. *International tuition:* $19,316 full-time. Tuition and fees vary according to degree level and program. *Financial support:* In 2019–20, 3 students received support. Career-related internships or fieldwork, scholarships/grants, and unspecified assistantships available. Financial award application deadline: 5/1; financial award applicants required to submit FAFSA. *Unit head:* Dr. Kenneth J. Dunegan, Chairperson, 216-687-4747, Fax: 216-687-4708, E-mail: t.degroot@csuohio.edu. *Application contact:* Lisa Marie Sample, Administrative Assistant, 216-687-4726, Fax: 216-687-6888, E-mail: l.m.sample@csuohio.edu. Website: https://www.csuohio.edu/business/management/management

**College of Saint Elizabeth,** Health Administration Program, Morristown, NJ 07960-6989. Offers MS. *Program availability:* Part-time. *Degree requirements:* For master's, thesis. *Entrance requirements:* For master's, minimum cumulative undergraduate GPA of 3.0, personal statement, resume, two letters of professional recommendation. Additional exam requirements/recommendations for international students: required—TOEFL (minimum score 550 paper-based; 79 iBT), IELTS (minimum score 6.5). Electronic applications accepted. Application fee is waived when completed online.

**College of Staten Island of the City University of New York,** Graduate Programs, Lucille and Jay Chazanoff School of Business, Program in Healthcare Management, Staten Island, NY 10314-6600. Offers MS. *Program availability:* Evening/weekend. *Faculty:* 5. *Students:* 20. 29 applicants, 48% accepted, 9 enrolled. *Degree requirements:* For master's, comprehensive exam, 33 credit hours. *Entrance requirements:* For master's, baccalaureate degree with overall GPA of 3.0 or higher; 1-2 page letter explaining your interest in pursuing a graduate program in Healthcare Management; brief 1-2 page resume; 2 letters of recommendation; 1 letter, whenever possible, should come from a current or former employer; transcripts. Additional exam requirements/recommendations for international students: required—TOEFL (minimum score 79 iBT), IELTS (minimum score 6.5). *Application deadline:* For fall admission, 6/30 priority date for domestic students, 6/30 for international students; for spring admission, 11/25 priority date for domestic students, 11/25 for international students. Applications are processed on a rolling basis. Application fee: $75. Electronic applications accepted. *Expenses: Tuition, area resident:* Full-time $11,090; part-time $470 per credit. *Tuition, state resident:* full-time $11,090; part-time $470 per credit. *Tuition, nonresident:* full-time $20,520; part-time $855 per credit. *International tuition:* $20,520 full-time. *Required fees:* $559; $181 per semester. Tuition and fees vary according to program. *Unit head:* Prof. Chandan Acharya, Department Chair, 718-982-2953, E-mail: chandan.acharya@csi.cuny.edu. *Application contact:* Sasha Spence, Associate Director for Graduate Admissions, 718-982-2019, Fax: 718-982-2500, E-mail: sasha.spence@csi.cuny.edu. Website: https://www.csi.cuny.edu/admissions/graduate-admissions/graduate-programs-and-requirements/healthcare-management

**Colorado State University–Global Campus,** Graduate Programs, Greenwood Village, CO 80111. Offers criminal justice and law enforcement administration (MS); education leadership (MS); finance (MS); healthcare administration and management (MS); human resource management (MHRM); information technology management (MITM); international management (MS); management (MS); organizational leadership (MS); professional accounting (MPA); project management (MS); teaching and learning (MS). *Accreditation:* ACBSP. *Program availability:* Online learning.

**Columbia Southern University,** MBA Program, Orange Beach, AL 36561. Offers finance (MBA); health care management (MBA); human resource management (MBA); marketing (MBA); project management (MBA); public administration (MBA). *Program availability:* Part-time, evening/weekend, online learning. *Entrance requirements:* For master's, bachelor's degree from accredited/approved institution. Additional exam requirements/recommendations for international students: required—TOEFL. Electronic applications accepted.

**Columbia University,** Columbia University Mailman School of Public Health, Department of Health Policy and Management, New York, NY 10032. Offers Exec MHA, Exec MPH, MHA, MPH. *Accreditation:* CAHME. *Program availability:* Part-time, evening/weekend. *Students:* 246 full-time (196 women), 156 part-time (110 women); includes 190 minority (30 Black or African American, non-Hispanic/Latino; 107 Asian, non-Hispanic/Latino; 41 Hispanic/Latino; 12 Two or more races, non-Hispanic/Latino), 51 international. Average age 29. 652 applicants, 71% accepted, 187 enrolled. In 2019, 163 master's awarded. *Degree requirements:* For master's, thesis optional. *Entrance requirements:* For master's, GRE General Test. Additional exam requirements/recommendations for international students: required—TOEFL (minimum score 600 paper-based; 100 iBT). *Application deadline:* For fall admission, 12/1 priority date for domestic and international students. Application fee: $120. Electronic applications accepted. *Expenses: Tuition:* Full-time $47,600; part-time $1880 per credit. One-time fee: $105. *Financial support:* Research assistantships, teaching assistantships, career-related internships or fieldwork, and Federal Work-Study available. Support available to part-time students. Financial award application deadline: 2/1; financial award applicants required to submit FAFSA. *Unit head:* Dr. Michael Sparer, Chairperson, 212-305-3924. *Application contact:* Clare Norton, Associate Dean for Enrollment Management, 212-305-8698, Fax: 212-342-1861, E-mail: ph-admit@columbia.edu. Website: https://www.mailman.columbia.edu/become-student/departments/health-policy-and-management

**Columbus State University,** Graduate Studies, College of Letters and Sciences, Department of Political Science and Public Administration, Columbus, GA 31907-5645. Offers public administration (MPA), including criminal justice, environmental policy, government administration, health services administration, political campaigning, urban policy. *Program availability:* Part-time, evening/weekend, 100% online, blended/hybrid learning. *Degree requirements:* For master's, comprehensive exam. *Entrance requirements:* For master's, GRE General Test, minimum GPA of 2.75, three letters of recommendation. Additional exam requirements/recommendations for international students: required—TOEFL (minimum score 550 paper-based; 79 iBT). Electronic applications accepted. *Expenses: Tuition, area resident:* Full-time $210; part-time $210 per credit hour. *Tuition, state resident:* full-time $210; part-time $210 per credit hour. *Tuition, nonresident:* full-time $817; part-time $817 per credit hour. *International tuition:* $817 full-time. *Required fees:* $802.50. Tuition and fees vary according to course load, degree level and program.

**Concordia University Irvine,** School of Professional Studies, Irvine, CA 92612-3299. Offers healthcare administration (MHA); international studies (MAIS), including Africa, China; nursing (MSN).

**Concordia University, St. Paul,** College of Business and Technology, St. Paul, MN 55104-5494. Offers business administration (MBA), including cyber-security leadership; health care management (MBA); human resource management (MA); information technology (MBA); leadership and management (MA); strategic communication management (MA). *Accreditation:* ACBSP. *Program availability:* Part-time, evening/weekend, 100% online, blended/hybrid learning. *Degree requirements:* For master's, thesis (for some programs). *Entrance requirements:* For master's, official transcripts from regionally-accredited institution stating the conferral of a bachelor's degree with minimum cumulative GPA of 3.0; personal statement; professional resume. Additional exam requirements/recommendations for international students: recommended—TOEFL (minimum score 547 paper-based; 78 iBT), IELTS (minimum score 6). Electronic applications accepted. *Expenses:* Contact institution.

**Concordia University Wisconsin,** Graduate Programs, Batterman School of Business, MBA Program, Mequon, WI 53097-2402. Offers finance (MBA); health care administration (MBA); human resource management (MBA); international business (MBA); international business-bilingual English/Chinese (MBA); management (MBA); management information systems (MBA); managerial communications (MBA); marketing (MBA); public administration (MBA); risk management (MBA). *Program availability:* Online learning. *Degree requirements:* For master's, comprehensive exam, thesis or alternative. *Entrance requirements:* Additional exam requirements/recommendations for international students: required—TOEFL. *Expenses:* Contact institution.

**Copenhagen Business School,** Graduate Programs, Copenhagen, Denmark. Offers business administration (Exec MBA, MBA, PhD); business administration and information systems (M Sc); business, language and culture (M Sc); economics and business administration (M Sc); health management (MHM); international business and politics (M Sc); public administration (MPA); shipping and logistics (Exec MBA); technology, market and organization (MBA).

**Cornell University,** Graduate School, Graduate Fields of Human Ecology, Field of Policy Analysis and Management, Ithaca, NY 14853. Offers consumer policy (PhD); family and social welfare policy (PhD); health administration (MHA); health management and policy (PhD); public policy (PhD). *Degree requirements:* For master's, thesis; for doctorate, thesis/dissertation. *Entrance requirements:* For master's, GRE General Test or GMAT, 2 letters of recommendation; for doctorate, GRE General Test, 2 letters of recommendation. Additional exam requirements/recommendations for international students: required—TOEFL (minimum score 550 paper-based; 77 iBT). Electronic applications accepted.

**Creighton University,** Graduate School, Department of Interdisciplinary Studies, Omaha, NE 68178-0001. Offers health and wellness coaching (MS); health care ethics (MS); healthcare management (MHM); leadership (Ed D); negotiation and conflict resolution (MS); organizational leadership (MS); public health (MPH). *Program availability:* Part-time, online only, blended/hybrid learning. *Degree requirements:* For master's, capstone project or practicum; for doctorate, thesis/dissertation. *Entrance requirements:* Additional exam requirements/recommendations for international students: required—TOEFL (minimum score 90 iBT). Electronic applications accepted. *Expenses:* Contact institution.

**Daemen College,** Leadership and Innovation Programs, Amherst, NY 14226-3592. Offers business (MS); health professions (MS); not-for-profit organizations (MS). *Program availability:* Part-time-only, evening/weekend. *Degree requirements:* For master's, thesis, minimum cumulative GPA of 3.00; student is allowed a maximum of 2 repeats before being dismissed. *Entrance requirements:* For master's, bachelor's degree, official transcripts, personal statement, resume, 2 letters of recommendation, interview with program director. Additional exam requirements/recommendations for international students: required—TOEFL (minimum score 77 paper-based), IELTS (minimum score 6.5). Electronic applications accepted. Application fee is waived when completed online.

**Dalhousie University,** Faculty of Health, School of Health Administration, Halifax, NS B3H 1R2, Canada. Offers MAHSR, MHA, MPH, PhD, LL B/MHA, MBA/MHA, MHA/MN. *Accreditation:* CAHME. *Program availability:* Part-time, online learning. *Entrance requirements:* For master's, GMAT. Additional exam requirements/recommendations for international students: required—TOEFL, IELTS, CANTEST, CAEL, or Michigan English Language Assessment Battery. Electronic applications accepted. *Expenses:* Contact institution.

**Dallas Baptist University,** College of Business, Management Program, Dallas, TX 75211-9299. Offers conflict resolution management (MA); general management (MA, MS); health care management (MA); human resource management (MA); professional sales and management optimization (MA). *Program availability:* Part-time, evening/weekend, online learning. *Application deadline:* Applications are processed on a rolling basis. Application fee: $25. Electronic applications accepted. Application fee is waived when completed online. *Expenses: Tuition:* Full-time $18,072; part-time $1004 per credit hour. *Required fees:* $1100; $550 per semester. Tuition and fees vary according to course level and degree level. *Unit head:* Dr. Sandra Reid, Chair, Graduate School of Business, 214-333-6860, E-mail: sandra@dbu.edu. *Application contact:* Dr. Justin Gandy, Program Director, 214-333-6840, E-mail: justing@dbu.edu. Website: https://www.dbu.edu/graduate/degree-programs/ma-management

**Dallas Baptist University,** College of Business, Master of Business Administration Program, Dallas, TX 75211-9299. Offers health care management (MBA); international business (MBA); management information systems (MBA). *Accreditation:* ACBSP. *Program availability:* Part-time, evening/weekend, online learning. *Application deadline:* Applications are processed on a rolling basis. Application fee: $25. Electronic applications accepted. Application fee is waived when completed online. *Expenses: Tuition:* Full-time $18,072; part-time $1004 per credit hour. *Required fees:* $1100; $550 per semester. Tuition and fees vary according to course level and degree level. *Unit head:* Dr. Sandra Reid, Chair of Graduate Business Programs, Program Director, 214-333-6860, E-mail: sandra@dbu.edu. *Application contact:* Dr. Sandra Reid, Chair of Graduate Business Programs, Program Director, 214-333-6860, E-mail: sandra@dbu.edu. Website: https://www.dbu.edu/graduate/degree-programs/mba

**Dartmouth College,** The Dartmouth Institute, Program in Health Policy and Clinical Practice, Hanover, NH 03755. Offers evaluative clinical sciences (MS, PhD). *Program availability:* Part-time. *Degree requirements:* For master's, research project or practicum; for doctorate, thesis/dissertation. *Entrance requirements:* For master's and doctorate, GRE or MCAT, 3 letters of recommendation. Additional exam requirements/recommendations for international students: required—TOEFL.

**Davenport University,** Sneden Graduate School, Grand Rapids, MI 49512. Offers accounting (MBA); business administration (EMBA); finance (MBA); health care management (MBA); human resources (MBA); information assurance (MS); occupational therapy (MSOT); public health (MPH); strategic management (MBA). *Program availability:* Evening/weekend. *Entrance requirements:* For master's, GMAT, minimum undergraduate GPA of 2.75. Additional exam requirements/recommendations for international students: required—TOEFL. Electronic applications accepted.

**Delta State University,** Graduate Programs, Robert E. Smith School of Nursing, Cleveland, MS 38733. Offers family nurse practitioner (MSN); nurse administrator (MSN); nurse educator (MSN). *Accreditation:* AACN. *Program availability:* Part-time.

*Degree requirements:* For master's, thesis optional. *Entrance requirements:* For master's, GRE General Test. Electronic applications accepted. *Expenses: Tuition, area resident:* Full-time $7501; part-time $417 per credit hour. Tuition, state resident: full-time $7501; part-time $417 per credit hour. Tuition, nonresident: full-time $7501; part-time $417 per credit hour. *International tuition:* $7501 full-time. *Required fees:* $170; $9.45 per credit hour. $9.45 per semester.

**DeSales University,** Division of Business, Center Valley, PA 18034-9568. Offers accounting (MBA); computer information systems (MBA); finance (MBA); health care systems management (MBA); human resources management (MBA); management (MBA); marketing (MBA); project management (MBA); self-design (MBA); supply chain management (MBA); DNP/MBA; MSN/MBA. *Accreditation:* ACBSP. *Program availability:* Part-time, evening/weekend, 100% online, blended/hybrid learning. *Faculty:* 16 full-time (9 women), 21 part-time/adjunct (6 women). *Students:* 66 full-time (37 women), 278 part-time (149 women); includes 70 minority (18 Black or African American, non-Hispanic/Latino; 1 American Indian or Alaska Native, non-Hispanic/Latino; 14 Asian, non-Hispanic/Latino; 29 Hispanic/Latino; 8 Two or more races, non-Hispanic/Latino), 2 international. Average age 35. 242 applicants, 60% accepted, 143 enrolled. In 2019, 108 master's awarded. *Entrance requirements:* For master's, GMAT (waived if undergraduate GPA is 3.0 or better), minimum GPA of 3.0 in undergraduate work, literacy in basic software, background or interest in the field of study, personal statement, 2 years of work experience. Additional exam requirements/recommendations for international students: required—TOEFL. *Application deadline:* Applications are processed on a rolling basis. Application fee: $50. Electronic applications accepted. *Expenses: Tuition:* Full-time $855; part-time $855 per credit hour. Tuition and fees vary according to program. *Financial support:* Applicants required to submit FAFSA. *Unit head:* Dr. Christopher R. Cocozza, Division Head, Division of Business, 610-282-1100 Ext. 1446, E-mail: Christopher.Cocozza@desales.edu. *Application contact:* Julia Ferraro, Director of Graduate Admissions, 610-282-1100 Ext. 1768, E-mail: gradadmissions@desales.edu.

**Des Moines University,** College of Health Sciences, Program in Healthcare Administration, Des Moines, IA 50312-4104. Offers MHA. *Accreditation:* CAHME. *Program availability:* Part-time, evening/weekend. *Entrance requirements:* For master's, minimum GPA of 3.0. Additional exam requirements/recommendations for international students: required—TOEFL (minimum score 600 paper-based). Electronic applications accepted. *Expenses:* Contact institution.

**Dominican College,** MBA Program, Orangeburg, NY 10962-1210. Offers accounting (MBA); healthcare management (MBA); management (MBA). *Program availability:* Part-time, evening/weekend. *Faculty:* 3 full-time (1 woman), 4 part-time/adjunct (2 women). *Students:* 1 (woman) full-time, 15 part-time (11 women); includes 8 minority (3 Black or African American, non-Hispanic/Latino; 4 Hispanic/Latino; 1 Native Hawaiian or other Pacific Islander, non-Hispanic/Latino), 1 international. Average age 35. 28 applicants, 16 enrolled. In 2019, 10 master's awarded. *Entrance requirements:* For master's, Application; official transcripts from all accredited institutions; GPA of at least 3.0; 2 letters of recommendation; Interview with the program director; Updated resume and a TOEFL score of at least 90 (IBT) if English is not first language. Additional exam requirements/recommendations for international students: required—TOEFL (minimum score 550 paper-based; 90 iBT). *Application deadline:* Applications are processed on a rolling basis. Application fee: $50. Electronic applications accepted. *Expenses:* $947/credit, Registration fee: Full-time- $430/term, Part-time - $200/term, Graduation fee - $200. *Financial support:* Scholarships/grants available. Financial award application deadline: 1/1; financial award applicants required to submit FAFSA. *Unit head:* Ken Mias, MBA Director, 845-848-4102, E-mail: ken.mias@dc.edu. *Application contact:* Christina Lifshey, Assistant Director of Graduate Admissions, 845-848-7908, Fax: 845-365-3150, E-mail: admissions@dc.edu.

**Drew University,** Caspersen School of Graduate Studies, Madison, NJ 07940-1493. Offers conflict resolution and leadership (Certificate), including community leadership, moderation, peace building; education (M Ed); finance (MA); history and culture (MA, PhD), including American history, book history, British history, European history, intellectual history, Irish history, print culture, public history; K-12 education (MAT), including art, biology, chemistry, elementary education, English, French, Italian, math, secondary education, special education, teacher of students with disabilities; liberal studies (M Litt, D Litt), including history, Irish/Irish-American studies, literature (M Litt, MMH, D Litt, DMH, CMH), religion, spirituality, teaching in the two-year college, writing; medical humanities (MMH, DMH, CMH), including arts, health, healthcare, literature (M Litt, MMH, D Litt, DMH, CMH), scientific research; poetry (MFA). *Program availability:* Part-time, evening/weekend. Terminal master's awarded for partial completion of doctoral program. *Degree requirements:* For master's and other advanced degree, thesis (for some programs); for doctorate, one foreign language, comprehensive exam (for some programs), thesis/dissertation. *Entrance requirements:* For master's, PRAXIS Core and Subject Area tests (for MAT), GRE/GMAT (for MFin MS in Data Analytics), resume, transcripts, writing sample, personal statement, letters of recommendation; for doctorate, GRE (PhD in history and culture), resume, transcripts, writing sample, personal statement, letters of recommendation; for other advanced degree, resume, transcripts, personal statement. Additional exam requirements/recommendations for international students: required—TOEFL (minimum score 587 paper-based; 80 iBT), IELTS (minimum score 6), TWE (minimum score 4). Electronic applications accepted.

**Duquesne University,** John G. Rangos, Sr. School of Health Sciences, Pittsburgh, PA 15282-0001. Offers health management systems (MHMS); occupational therapy (MS, OTD); physical therapy (DPT); physician assistant studies (MPAS); rehabilitation science (MS, PhD); speech-language pathology (MS). *Accreditation:* AOTA (one or more programs are accredited); APTA (one or more programs are accredited); ASHA. *Program availability:* Part-time, minimal on-campus study. *Degree requirements:* For doctorate, comprehensive exam (for some programs), thesis/dissertation (for some programs). *Entrance requirements:* For master's, GRE General Test (speech-language pathology), 3 letters of recommendation; minimum GPA of 2.75 (health management systems), 3.0 (speech-language pathology); for doctorate, GRE General Test (for physical therapy and rehabilitation science), 3 letters of recommendation, minimum GPA of 3.0, personal interview. Additional exam requirements/recommendations for international students: required—TOEFL (minimum score 550 paper-based; 90 iBT); recommended—IELTS. Electronic applications accepted. *Expenses:* Contact institution.

**D'Youville College,** Department of Health Services Administration, Buffalo, NY 14201-1084. Offers clinical research associate (Certificate); health administration (Ed D); health services administration (MS, Certificate); long term care administration (Certificate). *Program availability:* Part-time, evening/weekend. *Degree requirements:* For master's, project or thesis. *Entrance requirements:* For master's, minimum GPA of 3.0 in major. Additional exam requirements/recommendations for international students: required—TOEFL (minimum score 500 paper-based). Electronic applications accepted.

**East Carolina University,** Graduate School, College of Allied Health Sciences, Department of Health Services and Information Management, Greenville, NC 27858-4353. Offers health care administration (Certificate); health care management (Certificate); health informatics (Certificate); health informatics and information management (MS); health information management (Certificate). *Program availability:* Part-time, evening/weekend, online learning. *Degree requirements:* For master's, comprehensive exam, thesis optional. *Entrance requirements:* For master's, GRE General Test or GMAT. Additional exam requirements/recommendations for international students: recommended—TOEFL, IELTS. *Application deadline:* For fall admission, 5/1 priority date for domestic students; for spring admission, 10/15 priority date for domestic students. Applications are processed on a rolling basis. Electronic applications accepted. *Expenses: Tuition, area resident:* Full-time $4749; part-time $185 per credit hour. Tuition, state resident: full-time $4749; part-time $185 per credit hour. Tuition, nonresident: full-time $17,898; part-time $864 per credit hour. *International tuition:* $17,898 full-time. *Required fees:* $2787. *Unit head:* Dr. Leigh W Cellucci, Chair. *Application contact:* Graduate School Admissions, 252-328-6012, Fax: 252-328-6071, E-mail: gradschool@ecu.edu.
Website: http://www.ecu.edu/cs-dhs/hsim/index.cfm

**Eastern Kentucky University,** The Graduate School, College of Arts and Sciences, Department of Government, Program in General Public Administration, Richmond, KY 40475-3102. Offers community development (MPA); community health administration (MPA); general public administration (MPA). *Accreditation:* NASPAA. *Program availability:* Part-time, evening/weekend. *Entrance requirements:* For master's, GRE General Test, minimum GPA of 2.5.

**Eastern Mennonite University,** Program in Business Administration, Harrisonburg, VA 22802-2462. Offers general management (MBA); health services administration (MBA); non-profit leadership (MBA). *Program availability:* Part-time, evening/weekend. *Degree requirements:* For master's, final capstone course. *Entrance requirements:* For master's, GMAT, minimum GPA of 2.5, 2 years of work experience, 2 letters of reference. Additional exam requirements/recommendations for international students: required—TOEFL (minimum score 500 paper-based). Electronic applications accepted. *Expenses:* Contact institution.

**Eastern Michigan University,** Graduate School, College of Arts and Sciences, Department of Political Science, Programs in Public Administration, Ypsilanti, MI 48197. Offers general public management (Graduate Certificate); local government management (Graduate Certificate); management of public healthcare services (Graduate Certificate); nonprofit management (Graduate Certificate); public administration (MPA); public budget management (Graduate Certificate); public land planning and development management (Graduate Certificate); public personnel management (Graduate Certificate); public policy analysis (Graduate Certificate). *Accreditation:* NASPAA. *Students:* 12 full-time (7 women), 31 part-time (14 women); includes 13 minority (11 Black or African American, non-Hispanic/Latino; 1 Hispanic/Latino; 1 Two or more races, non-Hispanic/Latino), 2 international. Average age 35. 38 applicants, 82% accepted, 13 enrolled. In 2019, 16 master's, 9 other advanced degrees awarded. Application fee: $45. *Application contact:* Dr. Rose Jindal, MPA Coordinator, 734-487-3113, Fax: 734-487-3340, E-mail: rsoliven@emich.edu.
Website: http://www.emich.edu/polisci/

**Eastern Michigan University,** Graduate School, College of Health and Human Services, Interdisciplinary Program in Health & Human Services (Community Building), Ypsilanti, MI 48197. Offers Graduate Certificate. *Program availability:* Part-time, evening/weekend. *Students:* 1 (woman) part-time; minority (Black or African American, non-Hispanic/Latino). Average age 59. 3 applicants, 33% accepted, 1 enrolled. In 2019, 1 Graduate Certificate awarded. *Entrance requirements:* Additional exam requirements/recommendations for international students: required—TOEFL. Application fee: $45. *Unit head:* Dr. Marcia Bombyk, Program Coordinator, 734-487-0393, Fax: 734-487-8536, E-mail: mbombyk@emich.edu. *Application contact:* Graduate Admissions, 734-487-2400, Fax: 734-487-6559, E-mail: graduate.admissions@emich.edu.

**Eastern Michigan University,** Graduate School, College of Health and Human Services, School of Health Sciences, Programs in Health Administration, Ypsilanti, MI 48197. Offers MHA, MS, Graduate Certificate. *Students:* 9 full-time (8 women), 29 part-time (19 women); includes 19 minority (6 Black or African American, non-Hispanic/Latino; 8 Asian, non-Hispanic/Latino; 4 Hispanic/Latino; 1 Two or more races, non-Hispanic/Latino). Average age 32. 23 applicants, 70% accepted, 9 enrolled. In 2019, 7 master's, 4 other advanced degrees awarded. Application fee: $45. *Application contact:* Dr. Rodney K. McCurdy, Program Advisor, 734-487-6630, Fax: 734-487-4095, E-mail: mccurd3@emich.edu.

**Eastern University,** Graduate Programs in Business and Leadership, St. Davids, PA 19087-3696. Offers health administration (MBA); health services management (MS); management (MBA); organizational leadership (MA); social impact (MBA). *Program availability:* Part-time, evening/weekend, online learning. *Students:* 104 full-time (75 women), 182 part-time (109 women); includes 108 minority (73 Black or African American, non-Hispanic/Latino; 1 American Indian or Alaska Native, non-Hispanic/Latino; 10 Asian, non-Hispanic/Latino; 16 Hispanic/Latino; 8 Two or more races, non-Hispanic/Latino), 28 international. Average age 38. In 2019, 95 master's awarded. *Application deadline:* Applications are processed on a rolling basis. Application fee: $35. Electronic applications accepted. Application fee is waived when completed online. *Expenses:* Contact institution. *Financial support:* Applicants required to submit FAFSA. *Unit head:* Michael Dziedziak, Executive Director of Enrollment, 800-452-0996, E-mail: gpsadmissions@eastern.edu. *Application contact:* Michael Dziedziak, Executive Director of Enrollment, 800-452-0996, E-mail: gpsadmissions@eastern.edu.
Website: https://www.eastern.edu/academics/programs/graduate-business

**East Tennessee State University,** College of Graduate and Continuing Studies, College of Business and Technology, Department of Management and Marketing, Johnson City, TN 37614. Offers business administration (MBA, Postbaccalaureate Certificate); digital marketing (MS); entrepreneurial leadership (Postbaccalaureate Certificate); health care management (Postbaccalaureate Certificate). *Program availability:* Part-time, evening/weekend. *Degree requirements:* For master's, comprehensive exam, capstone. *Entrance requirements:* For master's, GMAT, minimum GPA of 2.5 (for MBA), 3.0 (for MS); current resume; three letters of recommendation; for Postbaccalaureate Certificate, minimum GPA of 2.5, undergraduate degree. Additional exam requirements/recommendations for international students: required—TOEFL (minimum score 550 paper-based; 79 iBT). Electronic applications accepted.

**East Tennessee State University,** College of Graduate and Continuing Studies, College of Public Health, Program in Public Health, Johnson City, TN 37614. Offers biostatistics (MPH, Postbaccalaureate Certificate); community health (MPH, DPH); environmental health (MPH); epidemiology (MPH, DPH, Postbaccalaureate Certificate); gerontology (Postbaccalaureate Certificate); global health (Postbaccalaureate Certificate); health care management (Postbaccalaureate Certificate); health management and policy (DPH); public health (Postbaccalaureate Certificate); public health services administration (MPH); rural health (Postbaccalaureate Certificate). *Accreditation:* CEPH. *Program availability:* Part-time, online learning. *Degree requirements:* For master's, comprehensive exam, field experience; for doctorate, thesis/dissertation, practicum. *Entrance requirements:* For master's, GRE General Test, minimum GPA of 2.75, SOPHAS application, three letters of recommendation; for doctorate, GRE General Test, SOPHAS application, three letters of recommendation; for Postbaccalaureate Certificate, minimum GPA of 2.5, three letters of recommendation, resume. Additional exam requirements/recommendations for

international students: required—TOEFL (minimum score 550 paper-based; 79 iBT), IELTS (minimum score 6.5). Electronic applications accepted.

**Elmhurst University,** Graduate Programs, Program in Health Care Management and Administration, Elmhurst, IL 60126-3296. Offers MHCA. *Program availability:* Part-time, evening/weekend, online learning. *Students:* Average age 26. *Entrance requirements:* For master's, undergraduate degree, undergraduate or graduate statistics course, at least two years of professional or military experience. Additional exam requirements/recommendations for international students: required—TOEFL (minimum score 550 paper-based; 79 iBT). *Application deadline:* Applications are processed on a rolling basis. Electronic applications accepted. *Expenses:* Contact institution. *Financial support:* In 2019–20, 2 students received support. Scholarships/grants available. Support available to part-time students. Financial award application deadline: 3/1; financial award applicants required to submit FAFSA. *Unit head:* Richard Pabst, Director, E-mail: richard.pabst@elmhurst.edu. *Application contact:* Timothy J. Panfil, Director of Enrollment Management, 630-617-3300 Ext. 3256, Fax: 630-617-6471, E-mail: panfilt@elmhurst.edu.

**Elms College,** Division of Business, Chicopee, MA 01013-2839. Offers accounting (MBA); accounting and finance (MS); financial planning (MBA, Certificate); healthcare leadership (MBA); lean entrepreneurship (MBA); management (MBA). *Program availability:* Part-time, evening/weekend. *Faculty:* 3 full-time (all women), 7 part-time/adjunct (4 women). *Students:* 38 part-time (22 women); includes 5 minority (3 Black or African American, non-Hispanic/Latino; 1 Asian, non-Hispanic/Latino; 1 Hispanic/Latino), 4 international. Average age 34. 11 applicants, 64% accepted, 7 enrolled. In 2019, 25 master's awarded. *Entrance requirements:* For master's, minimum GPA of 3.0. Additional exam requirements/recommendations for international students: required—TOEFL (minimum score 80 iBT). *Application deadline:* Applications are processed on a rolling basis. Electronic applications accepted. *Financial support:* Applicants required to submit FAFSA. *Unit head:* Kim Kenney-Rockwal, MBA Program Director, 413-265-2572, E-mail: kenneyrockwalk@elms.edu. *Application contact:* Nancy Davis, Director, Office of Graduate and Continuing Education Admissions, 413-265-2456, E-mail: grad@elms.edu.

**Emory University,** Rollins School of Public Health, Department of Health Policy and Management, Atlanta, GA 30322-1100. Offers health policy (MPH); health policy research (MSPH); health services management (MPH); health services research and health policy (PhD). *Program availability:* Part-time. *Degree requirements:* For master's, thesis (for some programs), practicum, capstone course. *Entrance requirements:* For master's, GRE General Test. Additional exam requirements/recommendations for international students: required—TOEFL (minimum score 550 paper-based; 80 iBT). Electronic applications accepted.

**Fairleigh Dickinson University, Florham Campus,** Silberman College of Business, Executive MBA Programs, Executive MBA Program for Health Care and Life Sciences Professionals, Madison, NJ 07940-1099. Offers EMBA.

**Fairleigh Dickinson University, Metropolitan Campus,** Silberman College of Business, Program in Healthcare and Life Sciences, Teaneck, NJ 07666-1914. Offers EMBA.

**Felician University,** Program in Health Care Administration, Lodi, NJ 07644-2117. Offers MSHA. *Program availability:* Part-time, evening/weekend. Terminal master's awarded for partial completion of doctoral program. *Degree requirements:* For master's, thesis, scholarly project. *Entrance requirements:* For master's, GRE, resume, personal statement, graduation from accredited baccalaureate program. Additional exam requirements/recommendations for international students: required—TOEFL (minimum score 550 paper-based; 79 iBT), IELTS (minimum score 6.5), PTE (minimum score 56). Electronic applications accepted. Application fee is waived when completed online. *Expenses:* Contact institution.

**Ferris State University,** College of Health Professions, Master of Healthcare Administration Program, Big Rapids, MI 49307. Offers MHA. *Program availability:* Part-time, evening/weekend, online only, 100% online course work, the 160-hour internship is onground. *Faculty:* 5 full-time (4 women). *Students:* 30 full-time (27 women), 10 part-time (all women); includes 13 minority (3 Black or African American, non-Hispanic/Latino; 2 American Indian or Alaska Native, non-Hispanic/Latino; 6 Asian, non-Hispanic/Latino; 2 Two or more races, non-Hispanic/Latino). Average age 32. 18 applicants, 89% accepted, 13 enrolled. In 2019, 8 master's awarded. *Degree requirements:* For master's, thesis, 160-hour capstone with thesis and a program competency portfolio. *Entrance requirements:* For master's, bachelor's degree from a regionally accredited university with an overall GPA of 3.0 or higher. International applicants only: a minimum TOEFL score of 550. Completion of courses in the areas of mathematics, biology, chemistry, social sciences & statistics with minimal grades of C. Personal statement of interest. Additional exam requirements/recommendations for international students: required—TOEFL (minimum score 550 paper-based). *Application deadline:* For fall admission, 7/18 for domestic students; for spring admission, 12/8 for domestic students. Application fee: $175. Electronic applications accepted. Tuition and fees vary according to degree level, program and student level. *Financial support:* In 2019–20, 3 students received support. Scholarships/grants and None available. Financial award applicants required to submit FAFSA. *Unit head:* Dr. Gail L Bullard, Program Director, 231-591-2279, E-mail: gailbullard@ferris.edu. *Application contact:* Dr. Gail L Bullard, Program Director, 231-359-2279, E-mail: GailBullard@ferris.edu.
Website: https://ferris.edu/HTMLS/colleges/alliedhe/csrchca/MHA/homepage.htm

**Florida Atlantic University,** College of Business, Department of Management, Boca Raton, FL 33431-0991. Offers business administration (MBA); entrepreneurship (MBA); health administration (MBA); international business (MBA); sport management (MBA). *Faculty:* 6 full-time (1 woman). *Students:* 70 full-time (49 women), 114 part-time (82 women); includes 115 minority (63 Black or African American, non-Hispanic/Latino; 7 Asian, non-Hispanic/Latino; 38 Hispanic/Latino; 7 Two or more races, non-Hispanic/Latino), 3 international. Average age 35. 108 applicants, 86% accepted, 74 enrolled. In 2019, 118 master's awarded. *Entrance requirements:* For master's, GMAT or GRE General Test, minimum GPA of 3.0 in last 60 hours of course work. Additional exam requirements/recommendations for international students: required—TOEFL (minimum score 600 paper-based; 61 iBT), IELTS (minimum score 6). *Application deadline:* For fall admission, 7/25 for domestic students, 2/15 for international students; for spring admission, 12/10 for domestic students, 7/15 for international students. Applications are processed on a rolling basis. Application fee: $30. Electronic applications accepted. *Expenses: Tuition:* Full-time $20,536; part-time $371.82 per credit hour. Tuition and fees vary according to program. *Financial support:* Research assistantships with full tuition reimbursements, career-related internships or fieldwork, tuition waivers (partial), and unspecified assistantships available. *Unit head:* Dr. Roland Kidwell, Chair, 561-297-4507, E-mail: kidwellr@fau.edu. *Application contact:* Dr. Roland Kidwell, Chair, 561-297-4507, E-mail: kidwellr@fau.edu.
Website: http://business.fau.edu/departments/management

**Florida Institute of Technology,** Aberdeen Education Center (Maryland), Program in Management, Melbourne, FL 32901-6975. Offers acquisition and contract management (MS, PMBA); business administration (MS, PMBA); contracts management (PMBA); financial management (MPA); global management (PMBA); health management (MS); human resources management (MS, PMBA); information systems (PMBA); logistics management (MS); management (MS), including information systems, operations research; materials acquisition management (MS); operations research (MS); public administration (MPA); research (PMBA); space systems (MS); space systems management (MS).

**Florida International University,** Nicole Wertheim College of Nursing and Health Sciences, Department of Health Services Administration, Miami, FL 33199. Offers MHSA. *Program availability:* Part-time. *Faculty:* 5 full-time (4 women), 27 part-time/adjunct (17 women). *Students:* 121 full-time (92 women), 39 part-time (28 women); includes 138 minority (43 Black or African American, non-Hispanic/Latino; 8 Asian, non-Hispanic/Latino; 82 Hispanic/Latino; 5 Two or more races, non-Hispanic/Latino), 6 international. Average age 28. 87 applicants, 66% accepted, 42 enrolled. In 2019, 40 master's awarded. *Entrance requirements:* For master's, GRE General Test, minimum GPA of 3.0. Additional exam requirements/recommendations for international students: required—TOEFL. *Application deadline:* For fall admission, 4/1 priority date for domestic students; for spring admission, 10/1 for domestic students. Applications are processed on a rolling basis. Application fee: $30. *Expenses: Tuition, area resident:* Full-time $8912; part-time $446 per credit hour. Tuition, state resident: full-time $8912; part-time $446 per credit hour. Tuition, nonresident: full-time $21,393; part-time $992 per credit hour. *Required fees:* $2194. *Financial support:* Fellowships, research assistantships, teaching assistantships, career-related internships or fieldwork, Federal Work-Study, and institutionally sponsored loans available. *Unit head:* Prof. Chanadra Young Whiting, Interim Chair, 305-919-4477, E-mail: chanadra.young@fiu.edu. *Application contact:* Nanett Rojas, Manager, Admissions Operations, 305-348-7464, Fax: 305-348-7441, E-mail: gradadm@fiu.edu.
Website: http://cnhs.fiu.edu/hsa/

**Florida International University,** Robert Stempel College of Public Health and Social Work, Programs in Public Health, Miami, FL 33199. Offers biostatistics (MPH); environmental and occupational health (MPH, PhD); epidemiology (MPH, PhD); health policy and management (MPH); health promotion and disease prevention (MPH, PhD). *Accreditation:* CEPH. *Program availability:* Part-time, evening/weekend, online learning. *Faculty:* 31 full-time (15 women), 8 part-time/adjunct (6 women). *Students:* 176 full-time (117 women), 58 part-time (42 women); includes 170 minority (57 Black or African American, non-Hispanic/Latino; 1 American Indian or Alaska Native, non-Hispanic/Latino; 14 Asian, non-Hispanic/Latino; 95 Hispanic/Latino; 3 Two or more races, non-Hispanic/Latino), 32 international. Average age 29. 260 applicants, 68% accepted, 68 enrolled. In 2019, 70 master's, 16 doctorates awarded. *Degree requirements:* For master's, thesis optional; for doctorate, comprehensive exam, thesis/dissertation. *Entrance requirements:* For master's, minimum GPA of 3.0, letters of recommendation; for doctorate, GRE, resume, minimum GPA of 3.0, letters of recommendation, letter of intent. Additional exam requirements/recommendations for international students: required—TOEFL (minimum score 550 paper-based; 80 iBT). *Application deadline:* For fall admission, 6/1 for domestic students, 4/1 for international students; for spring admission, 10/1 for domestic students, 9/1 for international students. Applications are processed on a rolling basis. Application fee: $30. Electronic applications accepted. *Expenses:* Contact institution. *Financial support:* Institutionally sponsored loans, scholarships/grants, and tuition waivers (full) available. Financial award application deadline: 3/1; financial award applicants required to submit FAFSA. *Unit head:* Dr. Kim Tieu, Chair, 305-348-0371, E-mail: kim.tieu@fiu.edu. *Application contact:* Nanett Rojas, Manager, Admissions Operations, 305-348-7464, Fax: 305-348-7441, E-mail: gradadm@fiu.edu.

**Florida National University,** Program in Business Administration, Hialeah, FL 33139. Offers accounting (MBA); finance (MBA); general management (MBA); health services administration (MBA); marketing (MBA); public management and leadership (MBA). *Program availability:* Part-time, online only, blended/hybrid learning. *Faculty:* 3 full-time (1 woman), 5 part-time/adjunct (2 women). *Students:* 23 full-time (15 women), 18 part-time (7 women); includes 37 minority (4 Black or African American, non-Hispanic/Latino; 1 American Indian or Alaska Native, non-Hispanic/Latino; 32 Hispanic/Latino), 1 international. Average age 35. 14 applicants, 100% accepted, 14 enrolled. In 2019, 13 master's awarded. *Degree requirements:* For master's, capstone. *Entrance requirements:* For master's, writing assessment, bachelor's degree from accredited institution; official undergraduate transcripts; minimum undergraduate GPA of 2.5, GMAT (minimum score of 400), or GRE (minimum score of 900); two letters of recommendation; resume. Additional exam requirements/recommendations for international students: required—TOEFL (minimum score 500 paper-based; 62 iBT), IELTS (minimum score 5.5). *Application deadline:* Applications are processed on a rolling basis. Electronic applications accepted. *Expenses:* Contact institution. *Financial support:* Federal Work-Study, institutionally sponsored loans, scholarships/grants, and tuition waivers (full and partial) available. Financial award applicants required to submit FAFSA. *Unit head:* Dr. James Bullen, Business and Economics Division Head, 305-821-3333 Ext. 1163, Fax: 305-362-0595, E-mail: jbullen@fnu.edu. *Application contact:* Dr. Ernesto Gonzalez, Business and Economics Department Head, 305-821- 3333 Ext. 1170, Fax: 305-362-0595, E-mail: egonzalez@fnu.edu.
Website: https://www.fnu.edu/prospective-students/our-programs/select-a-program/master-of-business-administration/business-administration-mba-masters/

**Florida National University,** Program in Health Services Administration, Hialeah, FL 333139. Offers MHSA. *Program availability:* Part-time, evening/weekend, 100% online, blended/hybrid learning. *Faculty:* 3 full-time (1 woman), 1 (woman) part-time/adjunct. *Students:* 9 full-time (4 women), 5 part-time (4 women); includes 12 minority (1 Black or African American, non-Hispanic/Latino; 11 Hispanic/Latino). Average age 35. 4 applicants, 100% accepted, 4 enrolled. In 2019, 12 master's awarded. *Degree requirements:* For master's, capstone project. *Entrance requirements:* For master's, writing assessment, bachelor's degree from an accredited institution; official undergraduate transcripts; minimum undergraduate GPA of 2.5, GMAT (minimum score of 400), or GRE (minimum score of 900). Additional exam requirements/recommendations for international students: required—TOEFL, IELTS. *Application deadline:* Applications are processed on a rolling basis. Electronic applications accepted. *Expenses:* Contact institution. *Financial support:* Scholarships/grants available. Financial award applicants required to submit FAFSA. *Unit head:* Dr. Loreto Almonte, Allied Health Division Head, 305-821-3333 Ext. 1074, Fax: 305-362-0595, E-mail: lalmonte@fnu.edu. *Application contact:* Dr. Loreto Almonte, Allied Health Division Head, 305-821-3333 Ext. 1074, Fax: 305-362-0595, E-mail: lalmonte@fnu.edu.
Website: https://www.fnu.edu/health-services-administration-hsa-master/

**Fordham University,** Gabelli School of Business, New York, NY 10023. Offers accounting (MBA, MS); applied statistics and decision-making (MS); business economics (DPS); capital markets (DPS); communications and media management (MBA); electronic business (MBA); entrepreneurship (MBA); finance (MBA, PhD); global finance (MS); global sustainability (MBA); health administration (MS); healthcare management (MBA); information systems (MBA, MS); investor relations (MS); management (EMBA, MBA, MS, PhD); marketing (MBA); marketing intelligence (MS); media management (MS); nonprofit leadership (MS); quantitative finance (MS); strategy and decision-making (DPS); taxation (MS); JD/MBA; MS/MBA. *Accreditation:* AACSB. *Program availability:* Part-time, evening/weekend, 100% online, blended/hybrid learning.

*Faculty:* 130 full-time (49 women), 73 part-time/adjunct (12 women). *Students:* 1,038 full-time, 503 part-time; includes 227 minority (57 Black or African American, non-Hispanic/Latino; 1 American Indian or Alaska Native, non-Hispanic/Latino; 65 Asian, non-Hispanic/Latino; 91 Hispanic/Latino; 1 Native Hawaiian or other Pacific Islander, non-Hispanic/Latino; 12 Two or more races, non-Hispanic/Latino), 985 international. Average age 27. 4,250 applicants, 62% accepted, 764 enrolled. In 2019, 899 master's awarded. Terminal master's awarded for partial completion of doctoral program. *Degree requirements:* For master's, internships (for some degrees); for doctorate, comprehensive exam (for some programs), thesis/dissertation. *Entrance requirements:* For master's, GMAT/GRE, 2 letters of recommendation, resume, 2 essays, transcripts, interview. Additional exam requirements/recommendations for international students: required—TOEFL (minimum score 100 iBT), IELTS (minimum score 7). *Application deadline:* For fall admission, 11/15 for domestic and international students; for winter admission, 1/10 for domestic students, 1/1 for international students; for spring admission, 5/15 for domestic students, 3/1 for international students; for summer admission, 7/10 for domestic students, 6/5 for international students. Application fee: $130. Electronic applications accepted. *Expenses:* Contact institution. *Financial support:* Career-related internships or fieldwork, institutionally sponsored loans, scholarships/grants, and unspecified assistantships available. Support available to part-time students. Financial award application deadline: 6/5; financial award applicants required to submit FAFSA. *Unit head:* Dr. Donna Rapaccioli, Dean, 212-636-6165, Fax: 212-307-1779, E-mail: rapaccioli@fordham.edu. *Application contact:* Lawrence Mur'ray, Senior Assistant Dean of Graduate Admissions and Advising, 212-636-6200, Fax: 212-636-7076, E-mail: admissionsgb@fordham.edu.
Website: http://www.fordham.edu/gabelli

**Framingham State University,** Graduate Studies, Program in Healthcare Administration, Framingham, MA 01701-9101. Offers MHA. *Program availability:* Part-time, evening/weekend.

**Franciscan Missionaries of Our Lady University,** School of Health Professions, Baton Rouge, LA 70808. Offers health administration (MHA); nutritional sciences (MS); physical therapy (DPT); physician assistant studies (MMS).

**Francis Marion University,** Graduate Programs, School of Business, Florence, SC 29502-0547. Offers business (MBA); health executive management (MBA). *Accreditation:* AACSB. *Program availability:* Part-time, evening/weekend. *Degree requirements:* For master's, comprehensive exam. *Entrance requirements:* For master's, GMAT or GRE, official transcripts, two letters of recommendation. Additional exam requirements/recommendations for international students: required—TOEFL (minimum score 550 paper-based; 79 iBT). *Expenses: Tuition, area resident:* Full-time $10,612; part-time $530.60 per credit hour. Tuition, state resident: full-time $10,612; part-time $530.60 per credit hour. Tuition, nonresident: full-time $21,224; part-time $1061.20 per credit hour. *International tuition:* $21,224 full-time. *Required fees:* $312; $156 per credit hour. $332 per semester. Tuition and fees vary according to program.

**Franklin Pierce University,** Graduate and Professional Studies, Rindge, NH 03461-0060. Offers curriculum and instruction (M Ed); elementary education (MS Ed); emerging network technologies (Graduate Certificate); energy and sustainability studies (MBA, Graduate Certificate); health administration (MBA, Graduate Certificate); human resource management (MBA, Graduate Certificate); information technology (MBA); leadership (MBA); nursing education (MS); nursing leadership (MS); physical therapy (DPT); physician assistant studies (MPAS); special education (M Ed); sports management (MBA). *Accreditation:* APTA. *Program availability:* Part-time, 100% online, blended/hybrid learning. *Degree requirements:* For master's, concentrated original research projects; student teaching; fieldwork and/or internship; leadership project; PRAXIS I and II (for M Ed); for doctorate, concentrated original research projects, clinical fieldwork and/or internship, leadership project. *Entrance requirements:* For master's, minimum GPA of 2.5, 3 letters of recommendation; competencies in accounting, economics, statistics, and computer skills through life experience or undergraduate coursework (for MBA); certification/e-portfolio, minimum C grade in all education courses (for M Ed); license to practice as RN (for MS); for doctorate, GRE, 80 hours of observation/work in PT settings; completion of anatomy, chemistry, physics, and statistics; minimum GPA of 3.0. Additional exam requirements/recommendations for international students: required—TOEFL (minimum score 550 paper-based; 61 iBT). Electronic applications accepted.

**Friends University,** Graduate School, Wichita, KS 67213. Offers family therapy (MSFT); global business administration (MBA), including accounting, business law, change management, health care leadership, management information systems, supply chain management and logistics; health care leadership (MHCL); management information systems (MMIS); professional business administration (MBA), including accounting, business law, change management, health care leadership, management information systems, supply chain management and logistics. *Program availability:* Part-time, evening/weekend, online learning. *Degree requirements:* For master's, research project. *Entrance requirements:* For master's, bachelor's degree from accredited institution, official transcripts, interview with program director, letter(s) of recommendation. Additional exam requirements/recommendations for international students: required—TOEFL (minimum score 560 paper-based). Electronic applications accepted.

**George Mason University,** College of Health and Human Services, Department of Health Administration and Policy, Fairfax, VA 22030. Offers health and medical policy (MS); health informatics (MS); health informatics and data analytics (Certificate); health services research (PhD); health systems management (MHA); quality improvement and outcomes management in health care systems (Certificate). *Accreditation:* CAHME. *Program availability:* Part-time, evening/weekend, 100% online. *Degree requirements:* For master's, comprehensive exam, internship; for doctorate, thesis/dissertation. *Entrance requirements:* For master's, GRE recommended if undergraduate GPA is below 3.0 (for MS in health and medical policy), 2 official transcripts; expanded goals statement; 3 letters of recommendation; resume; 1 year of work experience (for MHA in health systems management); minimum GPA of 3.25 preferred (for MS in health informatics); for doctorate, GRE, professional and volunteer experience, evidence of ability to write and conduct research at the doctoral level, master's degree or equivalent; for Certificate, 2 official transcripts; expanded goals statement; 3 letters of recommendation; resume. Additional exam requirements/recommendations for international students: required—TOEFL (minimum score 575 paper-based; 88 iBT), IELTS (minimum score 6.5), PTE (minimum score 59). Electronic applications accepted. *Expenses:* Contact institution.

**Georgetown University,** Graduate School of Arts and Sciences, School of Nursing and Health Studies, Washington, DC 20057. Offers acute care nurse practitioner (MS); clinical nurse specialist (MS); family nurse practitioner (MS); health systems administration (MS); nurse anesthesia (MS); nurse-midwifery (MS); nursing (DNP); nursing education (MS). *Accreditation:* AACN; AANA/CANAEP (one or more programs are accredited); ACNM/ACME (one or more programs are accredited). *Degree requirements:* For master's, thesis optional. *Entrance requirements:* For master's, GRE General Test or MAT, bachelor's degree in nursing from ACEN-accredited school, minimum undergraduate GPA of 3.0. Additional exam requirements/recommendations for international students: required—TOEFL.

**The George Washington University,** College of Professional Studies, Program in Healthcare Corporate Compliance, Washington, DC 20052. Offers Graduate Certificate. *Program availability:* Online learning.

**The George Washington University,** Milken Institute School of Public Health, Department of Health Policy and Management, Washington, DC 20052. Offers EMHA, MHA, MPH, MS, Graduate Certificate. *Accreditation:* CAHME. *Entrance requirements:* For master's, GMAT, GRE General Test, or MCAT. Additional exam requirements/recommendations for international students: required—TOEFL.

**The George Washington University,** School of Medicine and Health Sciences, Health Sciences Programs, Washington, DC 20052. Offers clinical practice management (MSHS); clinical research administration (MSHS); emergency services management (MSHS); end-of-life care (MSHS); immunohematology (MSHS); immunohematology and biotechnology (MSHS); physical therapy (DPT); physician assistant (MSHS). *Program availability:* Online learning. *Entrance requirements:* Additional exam requirements/recommendations for international students: required—TOEFL (minimum score 550 paper-based). *Expenses:* Contact institution.

**Georgia Institute of Technology,** Graduate Studies, College of Engineering, H. Milton Stewart School of Industrial and Systems Engineering, Atlanta, GA 30332. Offers health systems (MS); industrial and systems engineering (MS, PhD), including industrial engineering; international logistics (MS); operations research (MS, PhD). *Program availability:* Part-time, 100% online. *Faculty:* 54 full-time (11 women), 3 part-time/adjunct. *Students:* 416 full-time (140 women), 86 part-time (32 women); includes 63 minority (5 Black or African American, non-Hispanic/Latino; 36 Asian, non-Hispanic/Latino; 15 Hispanic/Latino; 7 Two or more races, non-Hispanic/Latino), 359 international. Average age 25. 1,533 applicants, 29% accepted, 206 enrolled. In 2019, 203 master's, 21 doctorates awarded. Terminal master's awarded for partial completion of doctoral program. *Degree requirements:* For doctorate, comprehensive exam, thesis/dissertation. *Entrance requirements:* For master's, GRE General Test, Must have an undergraduate Bachelor of Science degree or the equivalent. MS Analytics applicants may substitute Graduate Management Admission Test (GMAT) scores as a substitute, although the GRE is preferred. Should describe any relevant work experience in the personal statement; for doctorate, GRE General Test, transcripts of prior academic work, evidence of an earned bachelor's degree, statement of purpose, resume, 3 credible letters of reference. Additional exam requirements/recommendations for international students: required—TOEFL (minimum score 577 paper-based; 90 iBT), IELTS (minimum score 7), TOEFL is the preferred method with the requirements shown on the programs. *Application deadline:* For fall admission, 1/1 for domestic students, 12/15 for international students; for spring admission, 2/1 for domestic and international students. Applications are processed on a rolling basis. Application fee: $75 ($85 for international students). Electronic applications accepted. *Expenses: Tuition, area resident:* Full-time $14,064; part-time $586 per credit hour. Tuition, state resident: full-time $14,064; part-time $586 per credit hour. Tuition, nonresident: full-time $29,140; part-time $1215 per credit hour. *International tuition:* $29,140 full-time. *Required fees:* $2024; $840 per semester. $2096. Tuition and fees vary according to course load. *Financial support:* In 2019–20, 10 fellowships, 140 research assistantships, 50 teaching assistantships were awarded; career-related internships or fieldwork, Federal Work-Study, institutionally sponsored loans, tuition waivers (full and partial), and unspecified assistantships also available. Support available to part-time students. Financial award application deadline: 7/1; financial award applicants required to submit FAFSA. *Unit head:* Edwin Romeijn, School Chair, 404-894-2300, Fax: 404-894-2301, E-mail: edwin.romeijn@isye.gatech.edu. *Application contact:* Marla Bruner, Director of Graduate Studies, 404-894-1610, Fax: 404-894-1609, E-mail: gradinfo@mail.gatech.edu.
Website: http://www.isye.gatech.edu

**Georgia Southern University,** Jack N. Averitt College of Graduate Studies, Jiann-Ping Hsu College of Public Health, Program in Public Health, Statesboro, GA 30460. Offers biostatistics (MPH, Dr PH); community health behavior and education (Dr PH); community health education (MPH); environmental health sciences (MPH); epidemiology (MPH); health policy and management (MPH, Dr PH). *Program availability:* Part-time. *Faculty:* 42 full-time (22 women), 1 (woman) part-time/adjunct. *Students:* 142 full-time (105 women), 88 part-time (62 women); includes 132 minority (100 Black or African American, non-Hispanic/Latino; 10 Asian, non-Hispanic/Latino; 8 Hispanic/Latino; 14 Two or more races, non-Hispanic/Latino), 46 international. Average age 32. 195 applicants, 85% accepted, 59 enrolled. In 2019, 90 master's, 14 doctorates awarded. *Degree requirements:* For master's, thesis optional, practicum; for doctorate, comprehensive exam, thesis/dissertation, preceptorship. *Entrance requirements:* For master's, GRE General Test, minimum GPA of 2.75, 3 letters of recommendation, statement of purpose, resume or curriculum vitae; for doctorate, GRE, GMAT, MCAT, LSAT, minimum GPA of 3.0, 3 letters of recommendation, statement of purpose, resume or curriculum vitae. Additional exam requirements/recommendations for international students: required—TOEFL (minimum score 537 paper-based; 75 iBT), IELTS (minimum score 6). *Application deadline:* For fall admission, 6/1 for domestic students, 5/1 for international students. Applications are processed on a rolling basis. Application fee: $135. Electronic applications accepted. *Expenses:* Contact institution. *Financial support:* In 2019–20, 94 students received support, including 1 research assistantship with full tuition reimbursement available (averaging $12,350 per year), 6 teaching assistantships with full tuition reimbursements available (averaging $12,350 per year); scholarships/grants, tuition waivers (full), and unspecified assistantships also available. Financial award application deadline: 4/15; financial award applicants required to submit FAFSA. *Unit head:* Dr. Robert Greg Evans, Dean, 912-478-2674, E-mail: rgevans@georgiasouthern.edu. *Application contact:* Shamia Garrett, Coordinator, Office of Student Services, 912-478-2674, Fax: 912-478-5811, E-mail: jphcoph-gradadvisor@georgiasouthern.edu.
Website: http://jphcoph.georgiasouthern.edu/

**Georgia Southern University,** Jack N. Averitt College of Graduate Studies, Waters College of Health Professions, Department of Health Sciences and Kinesiology, Program in Health Administration, Statesboro, GA 30460. Offers MHA. *Students:* 30 full-time (17 women), 1 part-time (0 women); includes 15 minority (7 Black or African American, non-Hispanic/Latino; 3 Asian, non-Hispanic/Latino; 3 Hispanic/Latino; 2 Two or more races, non-Hispanic/Latino), 5 international. Average age 28. 10 applicants, 90% accepted, 6 enrolled. *Degree requirements:* For master's, comprehensive exam, 400 hour internship. *Entrance requirements:* For master's, GRE, GMAT, personal statement, three letters of recommendation, professional resume. Additional exam requirements/recommendations for international students: required—TOEFL (minimum score 537 paper-based; 75 iBT), IELTS (minimum score 6). *Application deadline:* For fall admission, 7/1 for domestic students, 5/1 for international students. Applications are processed on a rolling basis. Application fee: $135. Electronic applications accepted. *Expenses: Tuition, area resident:* Full-time $4986; part-time $277 per credit hour. Tuition, nonresident: full-time $19,890; part-time $1105 per credit hour. *International tuition:* $19,890 full-time. *Required fees:* $2114; $1057 per semester. $1057 per semester. Tuition and fees vary according to course load, campus/location and program. *Financial support:* In 2019–20, 34 students received support, including 1 research assistantship with full tuition reimbursement available (averaging $12,350 per year);

career-related internships or fieldwork, Federal Work-Study, scholarships/grants, tuition waivers (full), and unspecified assistantships also available. Financial award application deadline: 4/15; financial award applicants required to submit FAFSA. *Unit head:* Dr. John Dobson, Interim Chair, 912-478-0200, E-mail: jdobson@georgiasouthern.edu. *Application contact:* Dr. Joseph Crosby, Master of Health Administration Program Coordinator, 912-344-2657, E-mail: jfcrosby@georgiasouthern.edu.

**Georgia State University,** Andrew Young School of Policy Studies, Department of Public Management and Policy, Atlanta, GA 30303. Offers criminal justice (MPA); disaster management (Certificate); disaster policy (MPA); environmental policy (PhD); health policy (PhD); management and finance (MPA); nonprofit management (MPA, Certificate); nonprofit policy (MPA); planning and economic development (MPP, Certificate); policy analysis and evaluation (MPA), including planning and economic development; public and nonprofit management (PhD); public finance and budgeting (PhD), including science and technology policy, urban and regional economic development; public finance policy (MPA), including social policy; public health (MPA). *Accreditation:* NASPAA (one or more programs are accredited). *Program availability:* Part-time. *Faculty:* 13 full-time (7 women), 3 part-time/adjunct (1 woman). *Students:* 125 full-time (81 women), 91 part-time (66 women); includes 103 minority (78 Black or African American, non-Hispanic/Latino; 3 Asian, non-Hispanic/Latino; 14 Hispanic/Latino; 8 Two or more races, non-Hispanic/Latino), 31 international. Average age 32. 298 applicants, 60% accepted, 82 enrolled. In 2019, 70 master's, 8 other advanced degrees awarded. Terminal master's awarded for partial completion of doctoral program. *Degree requirements:* For master's, thesis optional; for doctorate, comprehensive exam, thesis/dissertation. *Entrance requirements:* For master's and doctorate, GRE. Additional exam requirements/recommendations for international students: required—TOEFL (minimum score 603 paper-based; 100 iBT) or IELTS (minimum score 7). *Application deadline:* For fall admission, 1/15 for domestic and international students. Application fee: $50. Electronic applications accepted. *Expenses: Tuition, area resident:* Full-time $7164; part-time $398 per credit hour. Tuition, state resident: full-time $7164; part-time $398 per credit hour. Tuition, nonresident: full-time $22,662; part-time $1259 per credit hour. *International tuition:* $22,662 full-time. *Required fees:* $2128; $312 per credit hour. Tuition and fees vary according to course load and program. *Financial support:* In 2019–20, fellowships (averaging $8,194 per year), research assistantships (averaging $8,068 per year), teaching assistantships (averaging $3,600 per year) were awarded; institutionally sponsored loans, scholarships/grants, health care benefits, and unspecified assistantships also available. Financial award application deadline: 2/1. *Unit head:* Dr. Cathy Yang Liu, Chair and Professor, 404-413-0102, Fax: 404-413-0104, E-mail: cyliu@gsu.edu. *Application contact:* Dr. Cathy Yang Liu, Chair and Professor, 404-413-0102, Fax: 404-413-0104, E-mail: cyliu@gsu.edu.
Website: https://aysps.gsu.edu/public-management-policy/

**Georgia State University,** J. Mack Robinson College of Business, Institute of Health Administration, Atlanta, GA 30302-3083. Offers health administration (MBA, MSHA); health informatics (MBA, MSCIS); MBA/MHA; PMBA/MHA. *Accreditation:* CAHME. *Program availability:* Part-time, evening/weekend. *Faculty:* 4 full-time (1 woman). *Students:* 37 full-time (18 women), 38 part-time (25 women); includes 37 minority (18 Black or African American, non-Hispanic/Latino; 11 Asian, non-Hispanic/Latino; 4 Hispanic/Latino; 4 Two or more races, non-Hispanic/Latino), 11 international. Average age 31. 57 applicants, 47% accepted, 19 enrolled. In 2019, 26 master's awarded. *Entrance requirements:* For master's, GRE or GMAT, transcripts from all institutions attended, resume, essays. Additional exam requirements/recommendations for international students: required—TOEFL (minimum score 610 paper-based; 101 iBT), IELTS (minimum score 7). *Application deadline:* For fall admission, 5/1 priority date for domestic students, 2/1 priority date for international students; for spring admission, 9/15 priority date for domestic students, 4/1 priority date for international students. Applications are processed on a rolling basis. Application fee: $50. Electronic applications accepted. *Expenses: Tuition, area resident:* Full-time $7164; part-time $398 per credit hour. Tuition, state resident: full-time $7164; part-time $398 per credit hour. Tuition, nonresident: full-time $22,662; part-time $1259 per credit hour. *International tuition:* $22,662 full-time. *Required fees:* $2128; $312 per credit hour. Tuition and fees vary according to course load and program. *Financial support:* Research assistantships, teaching assistantships, scholarships/grants, tuition waivers, and unspecified assistantships available. *Unit head:* Dr. Andrew T. Sumner, Chair in Health Administration/Director of the Institute of Health, 404-413-7630, Fax: 404-413-7631. *Application contact:* Toby McChesney, Assistant Dean for Graduate Recruiting and Student Services, 404-413-7167, Fax: 404-413-7162, E-mail: rcbgradadmissions@gsu.edu.
Website: https://robinson.gsu.edu/academic-departments/health-administration/

**Goldey-Beacom College,** Graduate Program, Wilmington, DE 19808-1999. Offers business administration (MBA); finance (MS); financial management (MBA); health care management (MBA); human resource management (MBA); information technology (MBA); international business management (MBA); major finance (MBA); major taxation (MBA); management (MM); marketing management (MBA); taxation (MBA, MS). *Accreditation:* ACBSP. *Program availability:* Part-time, evening/weekend. *Entrance requirements:* For master's, GMAT, MAT, GRE, minimum GPA of 3.0. Additional exam requirements/recommendations for international students: required—TOEFL (minimum score 65 iBT); recommended—IELTS (minimum score 6). Electronic applications accepted.

**Governors State University,** College of Health and Human Services, Program in Health Administration, University Park, IL 60484. Offers MHA. *Accreditation:* CAHME. *Program availability:* Part-time. *Faculty:* 7 full-time (4 women), 11 part-time/adjunct (8 women). *Students:* 24 full-time (21 women), 18 part-time (12 women); includes 28 minority (20 Black or African American, non-Hispanic/Latino; 6 Asian, non-Hispanic/Latino; 2 Hispanic/Latino), 5 international. Average age 32. 29 applicants, 62% accepted, 12 enrolled. In 2019, 14 master's awarded. *Application deadline:* For fall admission, 4/1 for domestic students. Applications are processed on a rolling basis. Application fee: $50. Electronic applications accepted. *Expenses: Tuition, area resident:* Full-time $8472; part-time $353 per credit hour. Tuition, state resident: full-time $8472; part-time $353 per credit hour. Tuition, nonresident: full-time $16,944; part-time $706 per credit hour. *International tuition:* $16,944 full-time. *Required fees:* $2520; $105 per credit hour. $38 per term. Tuition and fees vary according to course load, degree level and program. *Financial support:* Application deadline: 5/1; applicants required to submit FAFSA. *Unit head:* Ning Lu, Chair, Department of Health Administration, 708-534-5000 Ext. 4916, E-mail: nlu@govst.edu. *Application contact:* Ning Lu, Chair, Department of Health Administration, 708-534-5000 Ext. 4916, E-mail: nlu@govst.edu.

**Grambling State University,** School of Graduate Studies and Research, College of Arts and Sciences, Department of Political Science and Public Administration, Grambling, LA 71270. Offers health services administration (MPA); human resource management (MPA); public management (MPA); state and local government (MPA). *Accreditation:* NASPAA. *Program availability:* Part-time. *Degree requirements:* For master's, comprehensive exam (for some programs), thesis optional. *Entrance requirements:* For master's, GRE, minimum GPA of 2.75 on last degree. Additional exam requirements/recommendations for international students: required—TOEFL (minimum score 500 paper-based; 62 iBT). Electronic applications accepted.

**Grand Canyon University,** Colangelo College of Business, Phoenix, AZ 85017-1097. Offers accounting (MBA, MS); business analytics (MS); disaster preparedness and executive fire service leadership (MS); finance (MBA); general management (MBA); health systems management (MBA); information technology management (MS); leadership (MBA, MS); marketing (MBA); organizational leadership and entrepreneurship (MS); project management (MBA); sports business (MBA); strategic human resource management (MBA). *Accreditation:* ACBSP. *Program availability:* Part-time, evening/weekend, online learning. *Entrance requirements:* For master's, equivalent of two years' full-time professional work experience. Additional exam requirements/recommendations for international students: required—TOEFL (minimum score 575 paper-based; 90 iBT), IELTS (minimum score 7). Electronic applications accepted.

**Grand Canyon University,** College of Doctoral Studies, Phoenix, AZ 85017-1097. Offers data analytics (DBA); general psychology (PhD), including cognition and instruction, industrial and organizational psychology, integrating technology, learning, and psychology, performance psychology; management (DBA); marketing (DBA); organizational leadership (Ed D), including behavioral health, Christian ministry, health care administration, organizational development. *Degree requirements:* For doctorate, comprehensive exam, thesis/dissertation. *Entrance requirements:* For doctorate, minimum GPA of 3.4 on earned advanced degree from regionally-accredited institution; transcripts; goals statement.

**Grand Canyon University,** College of Nursing and Health Care Professions, Phoenix, AZ 85017-1097. Offers acute care nurse practitioner (MSN, PMC); family nurse practitioner (MSN, PMC); health care administration (MS); health care informatics (MS, MSN); leadership in health care systems (MSN); nursing (DNP); nursing education (MSN, PMC); public health (MPH, MSN); MBA/MSN. *Accreditation:* AACN. *Program availability:* Part-time, evening/weekend, online learning. *Degree requirements:* For master's and PMC, comprehensive exam (for some programs). *Entrance requirements:* For master's, minimum cumulative and science course undergraduate GPA of 3.0. Additional exam requirements/recommendations for international students: required—TOEFL (minimum score 575 paper-based; 90 iBT), IELTS (minimum score 7).

**Grand Valley State University,** College of Community and Public Service, School of Public, Nonprofit and Health Administration, Program in Health Administration, Allendale, MI 49401-9403. Offers MHA. *Program availability:* Part-time, evening/weekend. *Students:* 36 full-time (28 women), 34 part-time (22 women); includes 13 minority (4 Black or African American, non-Hispanic/Latino; 3 Asian, non-Hispanic/Latino; 3 Hispanic/Latino; 3 Two or more races, non-Hispanic/Latino), 8 international. Average age 27. 39 applicants, 97% accepted, 15 enrolled. In 2019, 18 master's awarded. *Degree requirements:* For master's, internship (for pre- and early-career students), capstone (for mid-career). *Entrance requirements:* For master's, minimum undergraduate GPA of 3.0, three letters of reference, 250-750 word essay on career and educational objectives, current resume. Additional exam requirements/recommendations for international students: required—TOEFL (minimum iBT score of 80), IELTS (6.5), or Michigan English Language Assessment Battery (77). *Application deadline:* For fall admission, 5/1 priority date for domestic students; for winter admission, 11/1 priority date for domestic students. Applications are processed on a rolling basis. Application fee: $30. Electronic applications accepted. *Expenses:* $671 per credit hour, 33 credit hours. *Financial support:* In 2019–20, 6 students received support, including 2 fellowships, 5 research assistantships with full and partial tuition reimbursements available (averaging $4,000 per year). Financial award application deadline: 5/1. *Unit head:* Dr. Richard Jelier, Director, 616-331-6575, Fax: 616-331-7120, E-mail: jelierr@gvsu.edu. *Application contact:* Dr. Ray Higbea, Graduate Program Director, 616-331-6869, Fax: 616-331-7120, E-mail: higbeara@gvsu.edu.
Website: http://www.gvsu.edu/spna

**Grantham University,** College of Nursing and Allied Health, Lenexa, KS 66219. Offers case management (MSN); health systems management (MS); healthcare administration (MHA); nursing education (MSN); nursing informatics (MSN); nursing management and organizational leadership (MSN). *Program availability:* Part-time, evening/weekend, online only, 100% online. *Students:* 180 full-time (135 women), 61 part-time (47 women); includes 124 minority (71 Black or African American, non-Hispanic/Latino; 1 American Indian or Alaska Native, non-Hispanic/Latino; 17 Asian, non-Hispanic/Latino; 17 Hispanic/Latino; 1 Native Hawaiian or other Pacific Islander, non-Hispanic/Latino; 17 Two or more races, non-Hispanic/Latino). Average age 40. 53 applicants, 89% accepted, 37 enrolled. In 2019, 100 master's awarded. *Entrance requirements:* For master's, Graduate: A minimum score of 530 on the paper-based TOEFL, or 71 on the internet-based TOEFL, 6.5 on the IELTS, or 50 on the PTE Academic Score Report. Additional exam requirements/recommendations for international students: required—TOEFL (minimum score 530 paper-based; 71 iBT), IELTS (minimum score 6.5), PTE (minimum score 50). *Application deadline:* Applications are processed on a rolling basis. Electronic applications accepted. *Expenses:* Contact institution. *Financial support:* Scholarships/grants available. Financial award applicants required to submit FAFSA. *Unit head:* Dr. Cheryl Rules, Dean of the College of Nursing and the School of Allied Health changing to College of Health Professions, 913-309-4783, Fax: 844-897-6490, E-mail: crules@grantham.edu. *Application contact:* Adam Wright, Associate VP, Enrollment Services, 800-955-2527 Ext. 803, Fax: 877-304-4467, E-mail: admissions@grantham.edu.
Website: http://www.grantham.edu/nursing-and-allied-health/

**Harvard University,** Graduate School of Arts and Sciences, Committee on Higher Degrees in Health Policy, Cambridge, MA 02138. Offers PhD. *Degree requirements:* For doctorate, thesis/dissertation. *Entrance requirements:* For doctorate, GMAT, GRE General Test, or MCAT. Additional exam requirements/recommendations for international students: required—TOEFL.

**Harvard University,** Harvard Business School, Doctoral Programs in Management, Boston, MA 02163. Offers accounting and management (DBA); business economics (PhD); health policy management (PhD); management (DBA); marketing (DBA); organizational behavior (PhD); science, technology and management (PhD); strategy (DBA); technology and operations management (DBA). *Degree requirements:* For doctorate, comprehensive exam (for some programs), thesis/dissertation. *Entrance requirements:* For doctorate, GRE General Test or GMAT. Additional exam requirements/recommendations for international students: required—TOEFL.

**Harvard University,** Harvard T.H. Chan School of Public Health, Department of Health Policy and Management, Boston, MA 02115-6096. Offers MHCM, SM, PhD. *Program availability:* Part-time. *Faculty:* 49 full-time (17 women), 21 part-time/adjunct (11 women). *Students:* 35 full-time (25 women), 55 part-time (20 women); includes 22 minority (5 Black or African American, non-Hispanic/Latino; 12 Asian, non-Hispanic/Latino; 2 Hispanic/Latino; 3 Two or more races, non-Hispanic/Latino), 13 international. Average age 29. 57 applicants, 77% accepted, 38 enrolled. In 2019, 28 master's, 10 doctorates awarded. *Degree requirements:* For doctorate, thesis/dissertation, qualifying exam. *Entrance requirements:* For master's, GRE, GMAT, MCAT; for doctorate, GRE. Additional exam requirements/recommendations for international students:

recommended—TOEFL (minimum score 600 paper-based; 100 iBT), IELTS (minimum score 7). *Application deadline:* For fall admission, 12/1 for domestic and international students. Application fee: $140. Electronic applications accepted. *Financial support:* Fellowships, research assistantships, teaching assistantships, Federal Work-Study, scholarships/grants, traineeships, and unspecified assistantships available. Support available to part-time students. Financial award application deadline: 2/15; financial award applicants required to submit FAFSA. *Unit head:* Dr. Arnold Epstein, Chair, 617-432-3415, Fax: 617-432-4494. *Application contact:* Vincent W. James, Director of Admissions, 617-432-1031, Fax: 617-432-7080, E-mail: admissions@hsph.harvard.edu.
Website: http://www.hsph.harvard.edu/departments/health-policy-and-management/

**Herzing University Online,** Program in Business Administration, Menomonee Falls, WI 53051. Offers accounting (MBA); business administration (MBA); business management (MBA); healthcare management (MBA); human resources (MBA); marketing (MBA); project management (MBA); technology management (MBA). *Program availability:* Online learning.

**Hilbert College,** Program in Public Administration, Hamburg, NY 14075-1597. Offers health administration (MPA); public administration (MPA). *Program availability:* Evening/weekend. *Degree requirements:* For master's, final capstone project. *Entrance requirements:* For master's, essay, official transcripts from all prior colleges, two letters of recommendation, current resume, relevant work experience, baccalaureate degree from accredited college or university with minimum cumulative GPA of 3.0, personal interview. Additional exam requirements/recommendations for international students: recommended—TOEFL. Electronic applications accepted. Application fee is waived when completed online. *Expenses:* Contact institution.

**Hodges University,** Graduate Programs, Naples, FL 34119. Offers accounting (M Acc); business administration (MBA); clinical mental health counseling (MS); health services administration (MS); information systems management (MIS); legal studies (MS); management (MSM). *Program availability:* Part-time, evening/weekend, 100% online, blended/hybrid learning. *Degree requirements:* For master's, comprehensive exam (for some programs), thesis (for some programs). *Entrance requirements:* For master's, essay. Additional exam requirements/recommendations for international students: recommended—TOEFL. Electronic applications accepted.

**Hofstra University,** Frank G. Zarb School of Business, Programs in Management and General Business, Hempstead, NY 11549. Offers business administration (MBA), including health services management, management, sports and entertainment management, strategic business management, strategic healthcare management; general management (Advanced Certificate); human resource management (MS, Advanced Certificate). *Program availability:* Part-time, evening/weekend, blended/hybrid learning. *Students:* 120 full-time (54 women), 126 part-time (61 women); includes 109 minority (29 Black or African American, non-Hispanic/Latino; 38 Asian, non-Hispanic/Latino; 39 Hispanic/Latino; 3 Two or more races, non-Hispanic/Latino), 14 international. Average age 34. 301 applicants, 73% accepted, 87 enrolled. In 2019, 95 master's awarded. *Degree requirements:* For master's, thesis optional, capstone course (for MBA), thesis (for MS), minimum GPA of 3.0. *Entrance requirements:* For master's, GMAT/GRE, 2 letters of recommendation, resume, essay. Additional exam requirements/recommendations for international students: required—TOEFL (minimum score 550 paper-based; 80 iBT); recommended—IELTS (minimum score 6.5). *Application deadline:* Applications are processed on a rolling basis. Application fee: $75. Electronic applications accepted. *Expenses:* $1,430 per credit plus fees. *Financial support:* In 2019–20, 86 students received support, including 71 fellowships with full and partial tuition reimbursements available (averaging $5,399 per year), 1 research assistantship with full and partial tuition reimbursement available (averaging $9,900 per year); career-related internships or fieldwork, Federal Work-Study, institutionally sponsored loans, scholarships/grants, tuition waivers (full and partial), unspecified assistantships, and scholarships and endowed scholarships also available. Support available to part-time students. Financial award applicants required to submit FAFSA. *Unit head:* Dr. Kaushik Sengupta, Chairperson, 516-463-7825, Fax: 516-463-4834, E-mail: kaushik.sengupta@hofstra.edu. *Application contact:* Sunil Samuel, Assistant Vice President of Admissions, 516-463-4723, Fax: 516-463-4664, E-mail: graduateadmission@hofstra.edu.
Website: http://www.hofstra.edu/business/

**Hofstra University,** School of Health Professions and Human Services, Programs in Health, Hempstead, NY 11549. Offers foundations of public health (Advanced Certificate); health administration (MHA); health informatics (MS); occupational therapy (MS); public health (MPH); security and privacy in health information systems (Advanced Certificate); sports science (MS); teacher of students with speech-language disabilities (Advanced Certificate). *Program availability:* Part-time, evening/weekend. *Students:* 291 full-time (220 women), 128 part-time (88 women); includes 192 minority (69 Black or African American, non-Hispanic/Latino; 3 American Indian or Alaska Native, non-Hispanic/Latino; 72 Asian, non-Hispanic/Latino; 37 Hispanic/Latino; 4 Native Hawaiian or other Pacific Islander, non-Hispanic/Latino; 7 Two or more races, non-Hispanic/Latino), 25 international. Average age 29. 676 applicants, 52% accepted, 132 enrolled. In 2019, 170 master's, 1 other advanced degree awarded. *Degree requirements:* For master's, internship, minimum GPA of 3.0. *Entrance requirements:* For master's, interview, 2 letters of recommendation, essay, resume. Additional exam requirements/recommendations for international students: required—TOEFL (minimum score 550 paper-based; 80 iBT); recommended—IELTS (minimum score 6.5). *Application deadline:* Applications are processed on a rolling basis. Application fee: $75. Electronic applications accepted. *Expenses: Tuition:* Full-time $25,164; part-time $1398 per credit. *Required fees:* $580; $165 per semester. Tuition and fees vary according to course load, degree level and program. *Financial support:* In 2019–20, 181 students received support, including 104 fellowships with full and partial tuition reimbursements available (averaging $3,465 per year), 5 research assistantships with full and partial tuition reimbursements available (averaging $7,172 per year); career-related internships or fieldwork, Federal Work-Study, institutionally sponsored loans, scholarships/grants, traineeships, tuition waivers (full and partial), unspecified assistantships, and scholarships and endowed scholarships also available. Support available to part-time students. Financial award applicants required to submit FAFSA. *Unit head:* Dr. Corinne Kyriacou, Chairperson, 516-463-4553, E-mail: corinne.m.kyriacou@hofstra.edu. *Application contact:* Sunil Samuel, Assistant Vice President of Admissions, 516-463-4723, Fax: 516-463-4664, E-mail: graduateadmission@hofstra.edu.
Website: http://www.hofstra.edu/academics/colleges/healthscienceshumanservices/

**Holy Family University,** Graduate and Professional Programs, School of Business Administration, Philadelphia, PA 19114. Offers accountancy (MS); finance (MBA); health care administration (MBA); human resource management (MBA); information systems management (MBA). *Accreditation:* ACBSP. *Program availability:* Part-time, evening/weekend. *Degree requirements:* For master's, comprehensive exam, thesis optional. *Entrance requirements:* For master's, minimum GPA of 3.0, interview, essay/personal statement, current resume, official transcript of all college or university work. Additional exam requirements/recommendations for international students: required—TOEFL (minimum score 550 paper-based; 79 iBT), IELTS (minimum score 6), PTE (minimum score 54). Electronic applications accepted.

**Husson University,** Master of Business Administration Program, Bangor, ME 04401-2999. Offers athletic administration (MBA); biotechnology and innovation (MBA); general business administration (MBA); healthcare management (MBA); hospitality and tourism management (MBA); organizational management (MBA); risk management (MBA). *Program availability:* Part-time, evening/weekend, 100% online, blended/hybrid learning. *Degree requirements:* For master's, comprehensive exam (for some programs), thesis optional. *Entrance requirements:* For master's, minimum GPA of 3.0, letter of recommendation. Additional exam requirements/recommendations for international students: required—TOEFL (minimum score 550 paper-based; 80 iBT), IELTS (minimum score 6.5). Electronic applications accepted. *Expenses:* Contact institution.

**IGlobal University,** Graduate Programs, Vienna, VA 22182. Offers accounting (MBA); data management and analytics (MSIT); entrepreneurship (MBA); finance (MBA); global business management (MBA); health care management (MBA); hospitality and tourism management (MBA); human resources management (MBA); information technology (MBA); information technology systems and management (MSIT); leadership and management (MBA); project management (MBA); public service and administration (MBA); software design and management (MSIT).

**Independence University,** Program in Business Administration in Health Care, Salt Lake City, UT 84107. Offers health care administration (MBA). *Program availability:* Part-time, evening/weekend, online learning. *Degree requirements:* For master's, fieldwork/internship.

**Independence University,** Program in Health Care Administration, Salt Lake City, UT 84107. Offers MSHCA. *Program availability:* Part-time, evening/weekend, online learning. *Degree requirements:* For master's, fieldwork, internship. *Entrance requirements:* For master's, previous course work in psychology.

**Independence University,** Program in Health Services, Salt Lake City, UT 84107. Offers community health (MSHS); wellness promotion (MSHS). *Program availability:* Part-time, evening/weekend, online learning. *Degree requirements:* For master's, fieldwork, internship, final project (wellness promotion). *Entrance requirements:* For master's, previous course work in psychology.

**Indiana Tech,** Program in Business Administration, Fort Wayne, IN 46803-1297. Offers accounting (MBA); health care management (MBA); human resources (MBA); management (MBA); marketing (MBA). *Program availability:* Part-time, evening/weekend, online learning. *Entrance requirements:* For master's, GMAT, bachelor's degree from regionally-accredited university; minimum undergraduate GPA of 2.5; 2 years of significant work experience; 3 letters of recommendation. Electronic applications accepted.

**Indiana University Bloomington,** School of Public Health, Department of Applied Health Science, Bloomington, IN 47405. Offers behavioral, social, and community health (MPH); family health (MPH); health behavior (PhD); nutrition science (MS); professional health education (MPH); public health administration (MPH); safety management (MS); school and college health education (MS). *Degree requirements:* For master's, thesis optional; for doctorate, comprehensive exam, thesis/dissertation. *Entrance requirements:* For master's, GRE (for MS in nutrition science), 3 recommendations; for doctorate, GRE, 3 recommendations. Additional exam requirements/recommendations for international students: required—TOEFL (minimum score 550 paper-based; 80 iBT). Electronic applications accepted.

**Indiana University Kokomo,** Department of Public Administration and Health Management, Kokomo, IN 46904. Offers health management (MPM, Graduate Certificate); public management (Graduate Certificate); public management and policy (MPM). *Program availability:* Part-time, evening/weekend. *Entrance requirements:* For master's, GRE/GMAT for GPAs lower than 3.0, letters of recommendation. Additional exam requirements/recommendations for international students: required—TOEFL (minimum score 550 paper-based; 73 iBT). Electronic applications accepted. *Expenses:* Contact institution.

**Indiana University Northwest,** School of Public and Environmental Affairs, Gary, IN 46408. Offers criminal justice (MPA); environmental affairs (Graduate Certificate); health services (MPA); nonprofit management (Certificate); public management (MPA, Graduate Certificate). *Accreditation:* NASPAA (one or more programs are accredited). *Program availability:* Part-time. *Entrance requirements:* For master's, GRE General Test (minimum combined verbal and quantitative score of 280), GMAT, or LSAT, letters of recommendation. Electronic applications accepted.

**Indiana University of Pennsylvania,** School of Graduate Studies and Research, College of Health and Human Services, Department of Employment and Labor Relations, Program in Health Services Administration, Indiana, PA 15705. Offers MS. *Program availability:* Part-time, evening/weekend, 100% online, blended/hybrid learning. *Faculty:* 4 full-time (0 women). *Students:* 18 full-time (13 women), 19 part-time (12 women); includes 8 minority (6 Black or African American, non-Hispanic/Latino; 2 Two or more races, non-Hispanic/Latino), 6 international. Average age 30. 29 applicants, 100% accepted, 15 enrolled. In 2019, 19 master's awarded. *Degree requirements:* For master's, thesis optional. *Entrance requirements:* For master's, letters of recommendation, goal statement, official transcripts. Additional exam requirements/recommendations for international students: required—TOEFL (minimum score 540 paper-based; 76 iBT); recommended—IELTS (minimum score 6). *Application deadline:* Applications are processed on a rolling basis. Application fee: $50. Electronic applications accepted. *Expenses: Tuition, area resident:* Full-time $9288; part-time $516 per credit. Tuition, nonresident: full-time $13,932; part-time $774 per credit. *Required fees:* $4454. One-time fee: $115 full-time. Tuition and fees vary according to course load and program. *Financial support:* In 2019–20, 1 fellowship (averaging $800 per year), 6 research assistantships with full and partial tuition reimbursements (averaging $2,667 per year) were awarded; career-related internships or fieldwork, Federal Work-Study, scholarships/grants, and unspecified assistantships also available. Financial award application deadline: 4/15; financial award applicants required to submit FAFSA. *Unit head:* Dr. Scott Decker, Graduate Coordinator, 724-357-4423, E-mail: s.e.decker@iup.edu. *Application contact:* Dr. Scott Decker, Graduate Coordinator, 724-357-4423, E-mail: s.e.decker@iup.edu.
Website: http://www.iup.edu/elr/grad/health-services-administration-ms/default.aspx

**Indiana University-Purdue University Indianapolis,** Kelley School of Business, Business of Medicine MBA Program, Indianapolis, IN 46202-5151. Offers MBA. *Program availability:* Part-time, evening/weekend, blended/hybrid learning. *Entrance requirements:* For master's, GMAT, previous course work in accounting and statistics; MD or DO with three years' experience post-residency. Electronic applications accepted.

**Indiana University-Purdue University Indianapolis,** Richard M. Fairbanks School of Public Health, Indianapolis, IN 46202. Offers biostatistics (MS, PhD); environmental health (MPH); epidemiology (MPH, PhD); global health leadership (Dr PH); health administration (MHA); health policy (Graduate Certificate); health policy and management (MPH, PhD); health systems management (Graduate Certificate); product stewardship (MS); public health (Graduate Certificate); social and behavioral sciences (MPH). *Accreditation:* CAHME; CEPH. *Expenses:* Contact institution.

**Indiana University-Purdue University Indianapolis,** School of Nursing, PhD Program in Nursing Science, Indianapolis, IN 46202. Offers clinical nursing science (PhD); health systems (PhD). *Program availability:* Part-time, blended/hybrid learning. *Degree requirements:* For doctorate, comprehensive exam, thesis/dissertation. *Entrance requirements:* For doctorate, GRE General Test, BSN or MSN from ACEN- or CCNE-accredited program; minimum baccalaureate cumulative GPA of 3.0 or master's degree 3.5. Additional exam requirements/recommendations for international students: required—TOEFL (minimum score 550 paper-based; 79 iBT). Electronic applications accepted. *Expenses:* Contact institution.

**Indiana University South Bend,** College of Liberal Arts and Sciences, South Bend, IN 46615. Offers advanced computer programming (Graduate Certificate); applied informatics (Graduate Certificate); applied mathematics and computer science (MS); behavior modification (Graduate Certificate); computer applications (Graduate Certificate); computer programming (Graduate Certificate); correctional management and supervision (Graduate Certificate); English (MA); health systems management (Graduate Certificate); international studies (Graduate Certificate); liberal studies (MLS); nonprofit management (Graduate Certificate); paralegal studies (Graduate Certificate); professional writing (Graduate Certificate); public affairs (MPA); public management (Graduate Certificate); social and cultural diversity (Graduate Certificate); strategic sustainability leadership (Graduate Certificate); technology for administration (Graduate Certificate). *Program availability:* Part-time, evening/weekend. *Degree requirements:* For master's, variable foreign language requirement, thesis (for some programs). *Entrance requirements:* For master's, minimum GPA of 3.0. Additional exam requirements/recommendations for international students: required—TOEFL (minimum score 550 paper-based; 80 iBT). *Expenses:* Contact institution.

**Indiana Wesleyan University,** College of Adult and Professional Studies, Graduate Studies in Business, Marion, IN 46953. Offers accounting (MBA, Graduate Certificate); applied management (MBA); business administration (MBA); health care (MBA, Graduate Certificate); human resources (MBA, Graduate Certificate); management (MS); organizational leadership (MA). *Program availability:* Part-time, evening/weekend, online learning. *Degree requirements:* For master's, applied business or management project. *Entrance requirements:* For master's, minimum GPA of 2.5, 2 years of related work experience. Additional exam requirements/recommendations for international students: required—TOEFL (minimum score 550 paper-based). Electronic applications accepted.

**Institute of Public Administration,** Programs in Public Administration, Dublin, Ireland. Offers healthcare management (MA); local government management (MA); public management (MA, Diploma).

**Iona College,** School of Business, Department of Management, Business Administration and Health Care Management, New Rochelle, NY 10801-1890. Offers health care analytics (AC); human resource management (PMC); management (MBA, PMC). *Program availability:* Part-time, evening/weekend. *Faculty:* 24 full-time (10 women), 6 part-time/adjunct (5 women). *Students:* 36 full-time (20 women), 84 part-time (48 women); includes 34 minority (15 Black or African American, non-Hispanic/Latino; 1 American Indian or Alaska Native, non-Hispanic/Latino; 3 Asian, non-Hispanic/Latino; 14 Hispanic/Latino; 1 Two or more races, non-Hispanic/Latino), 2 international. Average age 27. 80 applicants, 98% accepted, 40 enrolled. In 2019, 75 master's, 23 other advanced degrees awarded. *Entrance requirements:* For master's, GMAT, 2 letters of recommendation, minimum GPA of 3.0; for other advanced degree, GMAT, minimum GPA of 3.0. Additional exam requirements/recommendations for international students: required—TOEFL (minimum score 550 paper-based; 80 iBT), IELTS (minimum score 6.5). *Application deadline:* For fall admission, 8/15 priority date for domestic students, 8/1 priority date for international students; for winter admission, 11/15 priority date for domestic students, 11/1 priority date for international students; for spring admission, 2/15 priority date for domestic students, 2/1 priority date for international students; for summer admission, 5/15 priority date for domestic students, 5/1 priority date for international students. Applications are processed on a rolling basis. Application fee: $50. Electronic applications accepted. *Expenses:* Contact institution. *Financial support:* In 2019–20, 57 students received support. Scholarships/grants, tuition waivers (partial), and unspecified assistantships available. Support available to part-time students. Financial award application deadline: 4/15; financial award applicants required to submit FAFSA. *Unit head:* George DeFeis, Chair, 914-633-2631, E-mail: gdefeis@iona.edu. *Application contact:* Kimberly Kelly, Director of Graduate Business Admissions, 914-633-2271, Fax: 914-633-2012, E-mail: kkelly@iona.edu.
Website: http://www.iona.edu/Academics/Hagan-School-of-Business/Departments/Management-Business-Administration-Health-Car/Graduate-Programs.aspx

**John F. Kennedy University,** College of Business and Professional Studies, Program in Business Administration, Pleasant Hill, CA 94523-4817. Offers business administration (MBA); finance (MBA); health care (MBA); human resources (MBA); information technology (MBA); management (MBA); sales management (MBA); strategic management (MBA). *Program availability:* Part-time, evening/weekend, online learning. *Degree requirements:* For master's, thesis or alternative. *Entrance requirements:* For master's, interview. Additional exam requirements/recommendations for international students: required—TOEFL.

**Johns Hopkins University,** Bloomberg School of Public Health, Department of Health Policy and Management, Baltimore, MD 21205-1996. Offers bioethics and policy (PhD); health administration (MHA); health and public policy (PhD); health economics (MHS); health economics and policy (PhD); health finance and management (MHS); health policy (MSPH); health policy and management (Dr PH); health services research and policy (PhD); public policy (MPP). *Accreditation:* CAHME (one or more programs are accredited). *Program availability:* Part-time. *Degree requirements:* For master's, thesis (for some programs), internship (for some programs); for doctorate, comprehensive exam, thesis/dissertation, 1-year full-time residency (for some programs), oral and written exams. *Entrance requirements:* For master's, GRE General Test or GMAT, 3 letters of recommendation, curriculum vitae/resume; for doctorate, GRE General Test or GMAT, 3 letters of recommendation, curriculum vitae, transcripts. Additional exam requirements/recommendations for international students: required—TOEFL (minimum score 100 iBT), IELTS (minimum score 7). Electronic applications accepted.

**Johns Hopkins University,** Bloomberg School of Public Health, Department of International Health, Baltimore, MD 21205. Offers global disease epidemiology and control (MSPH, PhD); global health economics (MHS); health systems (MSPH, PhD); human nutrition (MSPH, PhD); social and behavioral interventions (MSPH, PhD). *Degree requirements:* For master's, comprehensive exam, thesis (for some programs), 1-year full-time residency, 4-9 month internship; for doctorate, comprehensive exam, thesis/dissertation or alternative, 1.5 years' full-time residency, oral and written exams. *Entrance requirements:* For master's, GRE General Test or MCAT, 3 letters of recommendation, resume; for doctorate, GRE General Test or MCAT, 3 letters of recommendation, resume, transcripts. Additional exam requirements/recommendations for international students: required—TOEFL (minimum score 600 paper-based; 100 iBT); recommended—IELTS (minimum score 7). Electronic applications accepted.

**Johns Hopkins University,** Carey Business School, MS in Health Care Management Program, Baltimore, MD 21218. Offers health care management (MS). *Program availability:* Part-time, evening/weekend, blended/hybrid learning, on-site residency requirement. *Entrance requirements:* For master's, GMAT or GRE. Additional exam requirements/recommendations for international students: required—TOEFL, IELTS. Electronic applications accepted. *Expenses:* Contact institution.

**Kean University,** College of Business and Public Management, Program in Public Administration, Union, NJ 07083. Offers health services administration (MPA); non-profit management (MPA); public administration (MPA). *Accreditation:* NASPAA. *Program availability:* Part-time. *Faculty:* 15 full-time (5 women). *Students:* 44 full-time (32 women), 56 part-time (33 women); includes 77 minority (45 Black or African American, non-Hispanic/Latino; 6 Asian, non-Hispanic/Latino; 25 Hispanic/Latino; 1 Two or more races, non-Hispanic/Latino), 2 international. Average age 31. 45 applicants, 93% accepted, 28 enrolled. In 2019, 31 master's awarded. *Degree requirements:* For master's, thesis, internship, research seminar. *Entrance requirements:* For master's, minimum cumulative GPA of 3.0, official transcripts from all institutions attended, two letters of recommendation, personal statement, writing sample, professional resume/curriculum vitae. Additional exam requirements/recommendations for international students: required—TOEFL (minimum score 550 paper-based; 79 iBT), IELTS (minimum score 6.5). *Application deadline:* For fall admission, 6/30 for domestic and international students; for spring admission, 12/1 for domestic and international students. Applications are processed on a rolling basis. Application fee: $75. Electronic applications accepted. *Expenses:* Tuition, state resident: full-time $15,326; part-time $748 per credit. Tuition, nonresident: full-time $20,288; part-time $902 per credit. *Required fees:* $2149.50; $91.25 per credit. Tuition and fees vary according to course level, course load, degree level and program. *Financial support:* Scholarships/grants and unspecified assistantships available. Financial award applicants required to submit FAFSA. *Unit head:* Dr. Deborah Mohammed-Spigner, Program Coordinator, 908-737-4037, E-mail: demohamm@kean.edu. *Application contact:* Pedro Lopes, Admissions Counselor, 908-737-7100, E-mail: gradadmissions@kean.edu.
Website: http://grad.kean.edu/masters-programs/public-administration

**Keiser University,** Master of Business Administration Program, Fort Lauderdale, FL 33309. Offers accounting (MBA); health services administration (MBA); international business (MBA); management (MBA); marketing (MBA); technology management (MBA). *Program availability:* Part-time, online learning.

**Kennesaw State University,** Coles College of Business, Program in Health Management and Informatics, Kennesaw, GA 30144. Offers MS. *Program availability:* Part-time-only, evening/weekend, online only, blended/hybrid learning. *Students:* 7 full-time (5 women), 73 part-time (55 women); includes 51 minority (33 Black or African American, non-Hispanic/Latino; 1 American Indian or Alaska Native, non-Hispanic/Latino; 9 Asian, non-Hispanic/Latino; 5 Hispanic/Latino; 3 Two or more races, non-Hispanic/Latino), 9 international. Average age 35. 39 applicants, 87% accepted, 34 enrolled. In 2019, 3 master's awarded. *Entrance requirements:* Additional exam requirements/recommendations for international students: required—TOEFL (minimum score 80 iBT), IELTS (minimum score 6.5). *Application deadline:* For fall admission, 7/1 for domestic and international students. Applications are processed on a rolling basis. Application fee: $60. Electronic applications accepted. *Expenses:* Contact institution. *Unit head:* Dr. Sweta Sneha, Director, 470-578-2436, E-mail: ssneha@kennesaw.edu. *Application contact:* Admissions Counselor, 470-578-4377, Fax: 470-578-9172, E-mail: ksugrad@kennesaw.edu.
Website: http://coles.kennesaw.edu/mshmi/

**Kent State University,** College of Public Health, Kent, OH 44242-0001. Offers public health (MPH, PhD), including biostatistics (MPH), environmental health sciences (MPH), epidemiology, health policy and management, prevention science (PhD), social and behavioral sciences (MPH). *Accreditation:* CEPH. *Program availability:* Part-time, 100% online. *Faculty:* 23 full-time (12 women), 4 part-time/adjunct (1 woman). *Students:* 136 full-time (98 women), 158 part-time (129 women); includes 71 minority (45 Black or African American, non-Hispanic/Latino; 12 Asian, non-Hispanic/Latino; 8 Hispanic/Latino; 6 Two or more races, non-Hispanic/Latino), 40 international. Average age 31. 187 applicants, 79% accepted, 85 enrolled. In 2019, 93 master's, 7 doctorates awarded. *Degree requirements:* For master's, comprehensive exam, between 150 - 300 hours' placement at public health agency, final portfolio and presentation; for doctorate, comprehensive exam, thesis/dissertation. *Entrance requirements:* For master's, GRE or other standardized graduate admission exam (GMAT, MCAT, LSAT or PCAT), minimum GPA of 3.0, transcripts, goal statement, 3 letters of recommendation; for doctorate, GRE or other standardized graduate admission exam with a quantitative component, Master's degree in related discipline, minimum GPA of 3.0, personal statement, resume, interview with faculty, 3 letters of recommendation, transcript(s). Additional exam requirements/recommendations for international students: required—TOEFL (minimum score 94 iBT), IELTS (minimum score 7), PTE (minimum score 65), For MPH: TOEFL iBT 79, Michigan English Language Assessment Battery (minimum score of 77), IELTS 6.5, PTE 58; For Ph.D.: see below and min MELAB 82. *Application deadline:* For fall admission, 6/15 for domestic and international students; for spring admission, 10/15 for domestic and international students; for summer admission, 3/15 for domestic and international students. Applications are processed on a rolling basis. Application fee: $45 ($70 for international students). Electronic applications accepted. *Financial support:* Career-related internships or fieldwork, Federal Work-Study, scholarships/grants, and unspecified assistantships available. *Unit head:* Dr. Sonia Alemagno, Dean and Professor of Health Policy and Management, 330-672-6500, E-mail: salemagn@kent.edu. *Application contact:* Dr. Jeffrey S. Hallam, Professor/Associate Dean for Research and Graduate Studies, 330-672-0679, E-mail: jhallam1@kent.edu.
Website: http://www.kent.edu/publichealth/

**King's College,** William G. McGowan School of Business, Wilkes-Barre, PA 18711-0801. Offers health care administration (MS). *Accreditation:* AACSB. *Program availability:* Part-time. *Entrance requirements:* Additional exam requirements/recommendations for international students: required—TOEFL (minimum score 600 paper-based).

**King University,** School of Business, Economics, and Technology, Bristol, TN 37620-2699. Offers accounting (MBA); finance (MBA); healthcare management (MBA); human resources management (MBA); leadership (MBA); management (MBA); marketing (MBA); project management (MBA). *Program availability:* Part-time, evening/weekend, 100% online, blended/hybrid learning. *Faculty:* 12 full-time (3 women), 8 part-time/adjunct (4 women). *Students:* 154 full-time (89 women), 14 part-time (11 women); includes 24 minority (17 Black or African American, non-Hispanic/Latino; 3 Asian, non-Hispanic/Latino; 4 Hispanic/Latino), 6 international. Average age 33. 127 applicants, 96% accepted, 60 enrolled. In 2019, 103 master's awarded. *Degree requirements:* For master's, comprehensive exam, thesis optional. *Entrance requirements:* For master's, resume which demonstrates a minimum of 2 years of full-time work experience, minimum cumulative GPA of 3.0 on a 4.0 scale. Students who do not meet this requirement may be conditionally accepted. Additional exam requirements/recommendations for international students: required—TOEFL (minimum score 84 paper-based; 84 iBT). *Application deadline:* Applications are processed on a rolling basis. Application fee: $50. Electronic applications accepted. *Expenses: Tuition:* Full-time $10,890; part-time $605 per semester hour. *Required fees:* $100 per course. *Financial support:* Unspecified assistantships available. Financial award applicants

required to submit FAFSA. *Unit head:* Dr. Mark Pate, Dean, School of Business, Economics and Technology, 423-652-4814, E-mail: mjpate@king.edu. *Application contact:* Nancy Beverly, Territory Manager/Enrollment Counselor, 423-341-9495, Fax: 423-652-4727, E-mail: nmbeverly@king.edu.

**Lake Erie College,** School of Business, Painesville, OH 44077-3389. Offers general management (MBA); health care administration (MBA); information technology management (MBA). *Program availability:* Part-time, evening/weekend. *Entrance requirements:* For master's, GMAT or minimum GPA of 3.0, resume, personal statement. Additional exam requirements/recommendations for international students: required—TOEFL (minimum score 550 paper-based; 79 iBT), IELTS (minimum score 6), STEP Eiken 1st and pre-1st grade level (for Japanese students). Electronic applications accepted. Application fee is waived when completed online. *Expenses:* Contact institution.

**Lake Forest Graduate School of Management,** The Leadership MBA Program, Lake Forest, IL 60045. Offers finance (MBA); global business (MBA); healthcare management (MBA); management (MBA); marketing (MBA); organizational behavior (MBA). *Program availability:* Part-time, evening/weekend. *Entrance requirements:* For master's, 4 years of work experience in field, interview, 2 letters of recommendation. Electronic applications accepted.

**Lasell College,** Graduate and Professional Studies in Management, Newton, MA 02466-2709. Offers business administration (MBA); elder care management (MSM); hospitality and event management (MSM); human resources management (MSM, Graduate Certificate); management (MSM, Graduate Certificate); marketing (MS, Graduate Certificate); project management (MSM, Graduate Certificate). *Accreditation:* ACBSP. *Program availability:* Part-time, evening/weekend, 100% online, blended/hybrid learning. *Faculty:* 3 full-time (1 woman), 14 part-time/adjunct (7 women). *Students:* 58 full-time (33 women), 84 part-time (54 women); includes 29 minority (15 Black or African American, non-Hispanic/Latino; 2 Asian, non-Hispanic/Latino; 9 Hispanic/Latino; 3 Two or more races, non-Hispanic/Latino), 21 international. Average age 30. 141 applicants, 40% accepted, 34 enrolled. In 2019, 73 master's, 1 other advanced degree awarded. *Degree requirements:* For master's, minimum GPA of 3.0; internship or research paper (for MSM). *Entrance requirements:* For master's, one-page personal statement, 2 letters of recommendation, resume, bachelor's degree transcript; proof of microeconomics and statistics (for MBA); for Graduate Certificate, bachelor's degree transcript, 2 letters of recommendation, 1-page personal statement, resume. Additional exam requirements/recommendations for international students: required—TOEFL (minimum score 550 paper-based, 79 iBT) or IELTS (minimum score 6). *Application deadline:* For fall admission, 8/31 priority date for domestic students, 6/30 priority date for international students; for spring admission, 12/31 priority date for domestic students, 10/31 priority date for international students. Applications are processed on a rolling basis. Electronic applications accepted. *Expenses: Tuition:* Part-time $600 per credit. *Required fees:* $40 per semester. *Financial support:* Federal Work-Study, scholarships/grants, and tuition discounts available. Support available to part-time students. Financial award application deadline: 8/31; financial award applicants required to submit FAFSA. *Unit head:* Chrystal Porter, Vice President of Graduate and Professional Studies, 617-243-2083, Fax: 617-243-2450, E-mail: gradinfo@lasell.edu. *Application contact:* Adrienne Franciosi, Assistant Vice President of Graduate and Professional Studies, 617-243-2214, Fax: 617-243-2450, E-mail: gradinfo@lasell.edu.
Website: http://www.lasell.edu/academics/graduate-and-professional-studies/programs-of-study/master-of-science-in-management.html

**Lawrence Technological University,** College of Management, Southfield, MI 48075-1058. Offers business administration (MBA, DBA), including business analytics (MBA, MS), cybersecurity (MBA, MS), finance (MBA), information systems (MBA), information technology (MBA), marketing (MBA), project management (MBA, MS); cybersecurity (Graduate Certificate); health IT management (Graduate Certificate); information assurance management (Graduate Certificate); information systems (MS), including enterprise resource planning, enterprise security management, project management (MBA, MS); information technology (MS, DM), including business analytics (MBA, MS), cybersecurity (MBA, MS), information assurance (MS), project management (MBA, MS); management (PhD); nonprofit management and leadership (Graduate Certificate); operations management (MS), including manufacturing operations, service operations; project management (Graduate Certificate). *Accreditation:* ACBSP. *Program availability:* Part-time, evening/weekend, 100% online. *Faculty:* 9 full-time (3 women), 12 part-time/adjunct (3 women). *Students:* 5 full-time (1 woman), 226 part-time (92 women); includes 51 minority (28 Black or African American, non-Hispanic/Latino; 1 American Indian or Alaska Native, non-Hispanic/Latino; 11 Asian, non-Hispanic/Latino; 6 Hispanic/Latino; 1 Native Hawaiian or other Pacific Islander, non-Hispanic/Latino; 4 Two or more races, non-Hispanic/Latino), 45 international. Average age 33. 123 applicants, 58% accepted, 49 enrolled. In 2019, 96 master's, 3 doctorates, 9 other advanced degrees awarded. Terminal master's awarded for partial completion of doctoral program. *Degree requirements:* For master's, thesis (for some programs); for doctorate, comprehensive exam, thesis/dissertation. *Entrance requirements:* Additional exam requirements/recommendations for international students: required—TOEFL (minimum score 550 paper-based; 79 iBT), IELTS (minimum score 6.5). *Application deadline:* For fall admission, 5/24 for international students; for spring admission, 10/13 for international students; for summer admission, 2/18 for international students. Applications are processed on a rolling basis. Application fee: $50. Electronic applications accepted. *Expenses: Tuition:* Full-time $16,618; part-time $8309 per year. *Required fees:* $600; $600. *Financial support:* In 2019–20, 25 students received support, including 8 research assistantships with partial tuition reimbursements available (averaging $3,360 per year); career-related internships or fieldwork, unspecified assistantships, and corporate tuition incentives also available. Financial award application deadline: 4/1; financial award applicants required to submit FAFSA. *Unit head:* Dr. Bahman Mirshab, Dean, 248-204-3050, E-mail: mgtdean@ltu.edu. *Application contact:* Jane Rohrback, Director of Admissions, 248-204-3160, Fax: 248-204-2228, E-mail: admissions@ltu.edu.
Website: http://www.ltu.edu/management/index.asp

**Lebanon Valley College,** Program in Business Administration, Annville, PA 17003-1400. Offers business administration (MBA); healthcare management (MBA); human resources (MBA); leadership and ethics (MBA); project management (MBA). *Program availability:* Part-time, evening/weekend. *Degree requirements:* For master's, capstone course. *Entrance requirements:* For master's, GMAT, 3 years of work experience, resume, professional statement (application form, resume, personal statement, transcripts). Additional exam requirements/recommendations for international students: required—TOEFL (minimum score 80 iBT), IELTS (minimum score 6.5) or STEP Eiken (grade 1). Electronic applications accepted. *Expenses:* Contact institution.

**Lehigh University,** P.C. Rossin College of Engineering and Applied Science, Department of Industrial and Systems Engineering, Program in Healthcare Systems Engineering, Bethlehem, PA 18015. Offers M Eng, Certificate. *Program availability:* Part-time, blended/hybrid learning. *Faculty:* 1 (woman) full-time, 2 part-time/adjunct (0 women). *Students:* 18 full-time (9 women), 14 part-time (10 women); includes 7 minority (3 Asian, non-Hispanic/Latino; 3 Hispanic/Latino; 1 Two or more races, non-Hispanic/Latino), 6 international. Average age 26. 20 applicants, 95% accepted, 17 enrolled. In 2019, 12 master's awarded. *Degree requirements:* For master's, comprehensive exam, thesis or alternative, 30 credits. *Entrance requirements:* For master's, GRE waived due to COVID-19. Additional exam requirements/recommendations for international students: required—TOEFL (minimum score 79 iBT). *Application deadline:* For fall admission, 8/12 for domestic students, 6/12 for international students; for spring admission, 12/15 for domestic students, 10/15 for international students; for summer admission, 4/30 for domestic students. Applications are processed on a rolling basis. Application fee: $75. Electronic applications accepted. *Financial support:* Unspecified assistantships available. Financial award application deadline: 1/15. *Unit head:* Prof. Ana Iulia Alexandrescu, Professor of Practice, 610-758-3865, Fax: 610-758-6766, E-mail: aia210@lehigh.edu. *Application contact:* Linda Wismer, Coordinator, 610-758-5867, Fax: 610-758-6766, E-mail: liw511@lehigh.edu.
Website: http://hse.lehigh.edu/

**Lenoir-Rhyne University,** Graduate Programs, Charles M. Snipes School of Business, Hickory, NC 28601. Offers accounting (MBA); business analytics and information technology (MBA); entrepreneurship (MBA); global business (MBA); healthcare administration (MBA); innovation and change management (MBA); leadership development (MBA). *Accreditation:* ACBSP. *Program availability:* Part-time, evening/weekend, online learning. *Degree requirements:* For master's, capstone course. *Entrance requirements:* For master's, GMAT, GRE, MAT, minimum undergraduate GPA of 2.7, graduate 3.0. Additional exam requirements/recommendations for international students: required—TOEFL (minimum score 600 paper-based). Electronic applications accepted. *Expenses:* Contact institution.

**LeTourneau University,** Graduate Programs, Longview, TX 75607-7001. Offers business administration (MBA); counseling (MA); curriculum and instruction (M Ed); educational administration (M Ed); engineering (ME, MS); engineering management (MEM); health care administration (MS); marriage and family therapy (MA); psychology (MA); strategic leadership (MSL); teacher leadership (M Ed); teaching and learning (M Ed). *Program availability:* Part-time, 100% online, blended/hybrid learning. *Students:* 45 full-time (34 women), 243 part-time (186 women); includes 142 minority (89 Black or African American, non-Hispanic/Latino; 1 Asian, non-Hispanic/Latino; 26 Hispanic/Latino; 26 Two or more races, non-Hispanic/Latino), 2 international. Average age 37. In 2019, 143 master's awarded. *Entrance requirements:* Additional exam requirements/recommendations for international students: required—TOEFL (minimum score 525 paper-based; 80 iBT) or IELTS (minimum score 6). *Application deadline:* Applications are processed on a rolling basis. Electronic applications accepted. *Financial support:* Unspecified assistantships and employee tuition waivers and institutionally sponsored loans available. Financial award applicants required to submit FAFSA.
Website: http://www.letu.edu

**Lewis University,** College of Business, Program in Business Administration, Romeoville, IL 60446. Offers accounting (MBA); custom elective option (MBA); e-business (MBA); finance (MBA); healthcare management (MBA); human resources management (MBA); international business (MBA); management information systems (MBA); marketing (MBA); project management (MBA); technology and operations management (MBA). *Program availability:* Part-time, evening/weekend. *Students:* 96 full-time (65 women), 153 part-time (96 women); includes 100 minority (33 Black or African American, non-Hispanic/Latino; 14 Asian, non-Hispanic/Latino; 49 Hispanic/Latino; 4 Two or more races, non-Hispanic/Latino), 20 international. Average age 31. In 2019, 99 master's awarded. *Entrance requirements:* For master's, interview, bachelor's degree, resume, two recommendations. Additional exam requirements/recommendations for international students: required—TOEFL (minimum score 550 paper-based), IELTS. *Application deadline:* For fall admission, 5/1 priority date for international students; for spring admission, 11/15 priority date for international students. Applications are processed on a rolling basis. Application fee: $40. Electronic applications accepted. *Financial support:* Federal Work-Study and unspecified assistantships available. Financial award application deadline: 5/1; financial award applicants required to submit FAFSA. *Unit head:* Dr. Ryan Butt, Dean, 815-836-5348, E-mail: culleema@lewisu.edu. *Application contact:* Linda Campbell, Graduate Admission Counselor, 815-836-5610, E-mail: grad@lewisu.edu.

**Lindenwood University,** Graduate Programs, School of Accelerated Degree Programs, St. Charles, MO 63301-1695. Offers administration (MSA), including management, marketing, project management; business administration (MBA); communications (MA), including digital and multimedia, media management, promotions, training and development; criminal justice and administration (MS); healthcare administration (MS); human resource management (MS); information technology (Certificate); managing information security (MS); managing information technology (MS); managing virtualization and cloud computing (MS); writing (MFA). *Program availability:* Part-time, evening/weekend, 100% online. *Faculty:* 11 full-time (6 women), 66 part-time/adjunct (23 women). *Students:* 408 full-time (262 women), 60 part-time (40 women); includes 149 minority (111 Black or African American, non-Hispanic/Latino; 2 American Indian or Alaska Native, non-Hispanic/Latino; 2 Asian, non-Hispanic/Latino; 18 Hispanic/Latino; 1 Native Hawaiian or other Pacific Islander, non-Hispanic/Latino; 15 Two or more races, non-Hispanic/Latino), 33 international. Average age 39. 268 applicants, 46% accepted, 99 enrolled. In 2019, 347 master's awarded. *Degree requirements:* For master's, thesis (for some programs), minimum cumulative GPA of 3.0; for Certificate, minimum cumulative GPA of 3.0. *Entrance requirements:* For master's, resume, personal statement, official undergraduate transcript, minimum undergraduate cumulative GPA of 3.0. Additional exam requirements/recommendations for international students: required—TOEFL (minimum score 553 paper-based; 81 iBT); recommended—IELTS (minimum score 6.5). *Application deadline:* For fall admission, 9/30 priority date for domestic and international students; for winter admission, 1/6 priority date for domestic and international students; for spring admission, 4/6 priority date for domestic and international students; for summer admission, 7/8 priority date for domestic and international students. Applications are processed on a rolling basis. Application fee: $0 ($100 for international students). Electronic applications accepted. *Expenses:* Contact institution. *Financial support:* In 2019–20, 145 students received support. Career-related internships or fieldwork, institutionally sponsored loans, scholarships/grants, tuition waivers (partial), and unspecified assistantships available. Financial award application deadline: 6/30; financial award applicants required to submit FAFSA. *Unit head:* Dr. Gina Ganahl, Dean, Accelerated Degree Programs, 636-949-4501, Fax: 636-949-4505, E-mail: gganahl@lindenwood.edu. *Application contact:* Kara Schilli, Assistant Vice President, University Admissions, 636-949-4349, Fax: 636-949-4109, E-mail: adultadmissions@lindenwood.edu.
Website: https://www.lindenwood.edu/academics/academic-schools/school-of-accelerated-degree-programs/

**Lindenwood University–Belleville,** Graduate Programs, Belleville, IL 62226. Offers business administration (MBA); communications (MA), including digital and multimedia, media management, promotions, training and development; counseling (MA); criminal justice administration (MS); education (MA); healthcare administration (MS); human resource management (MS); school administration (MA); teaching (MAT).

**Lipscomb University,** College of Business, Nashville, TN 37204-3951. Offers accounting and finance (MBA); audit/accounting (M Acc); business (Certificate); business administration (MM); healthcare management (MBA); leadership (MBA); tax (M Acc); MBA/MS; Pharm D/MM. *Accreditation:* ACBSP. *Program availability:* Part-time,

evening/weekend. *Entrance requirements:* For master's, GMAT, transcripts, interview, 2 references, resume. Additional exam requirements/recommendations for international students: required—TOEFL (minimum score 570 paper-based). Electronic applications accepted. *Expenses:* Contact institution.

**Lock Haven University of Pennsylvania,** College of Natural, Behavioral and Health Sciences, Lock Haven, PA 17745-2390. Offers actuarial science (PSM); athletic training (MS); health promotion/education (MHS); healthcare management (MHS); physician assistant (MHS). *Accreditation:* ARC-PA. *Entrance requirements:* For master's, minimum undergraduate GPA of 3.0. Additional exam requirements/recommendations for international students: required—TOEFL. Electronic applications accepted.

**Loma Linda University,** School of Public Health, Program in Healthcare Administration, Loma Linda, CA 92350. Offers MBA. *Entrance requirements:* Additional exam requirements/recommendations for international students: required—Michigan Test of English Language Proficiency or TOEFL.

**London Metropolitan University,** Graduate Programs, London, United Kingdom. Offers applied psychology (M Sc); architecture (MA); biomedical science (M Sc); blood science (M Sc); cancer pharmacology (M Sc); computer networking and cyber security (M Sc); computing and information systems (M Sc); conference interpreting (MA); counter-terrorism studies (M Sc); creative, digital and professional writing (MA); crime, violence and prevention (M Sc); criminology (M Sc); curating contemporary art (MA); data analytics (M Sc); digital media (MA); early childhood studies (MA); education (MA, Ed D); financial services law, regulation and compliance (LL M); food science (M Sc); forensic psychology (M Sc); health and social care management and policy (M Sc); human nutrition (M Sc); human resource management (MA); human rights and international conflict (MA); information technology (M Sc); intelligence and security studies (M Sc); international oil, gas and energy law (LL M); international relations (MA); interpreting (MA); learning and teaching in higher education (MA); legal practice (LL M); media and entertainment law (LL M); organizational and consumer psychology (M Sc); psychological therapy (M Sc); psychology of mental health (M Sc); public health (M Sc); public policy and management (MPA); security studies (M Sc); social work (M Sc); spatial planning and urban design (MA); sports therapy (M Sc); supporting older children and young people with dyslexia (MA); teaching languages (MA), including Arabic, English; translation (MA); woman and child abuse (MA).

**Long Island University - Brentwood Campus,** Graduate Programs, Brentwood, NY 11717. Offers childhood education (MS), including grades 1-6; childhood education/literacy B-6 (MS); childhood education/special education (grades 1-6) (MS); clinical mental health counseling (MS, Advanced Certificate); criminal justice (MS); early childhood education (MS); educational leadership (MS Ed); family nurse practitioner (MS, Advanced Certificate); health administration (MPA); library and information science (MS); literacy (B-6) (MS Ed); school counselor (MS, Advanced Certificate); social work (MSW); special education (MS Ed); students with disabilities generalist (grades 7-12) (Advanced Certificate). *Program availability:* Part-time. *Entrance requirements:* For master's and Advanced Certificate, GRE. Additional exam requirements/recommendations for international students: required—TOEFL or IELTS. Electronic applications accepted.

**Long Island University - Brooklyn,** School of Business, Public Administration and Information Sciences, Brooklyn, NY 11201-8423. Offers accounting (MBA); accounting (MS); business administration (MBA); computer science (MS); gerontology (Advanced Certificate); health administration (MPA); human resources management (MS); not-for-profit management (Advanced Certificate); public administration (MPA); taxation (MS). *Program availability:* Part-time, evening/weekend. *Entrance requirements:* Additional exam requirements/recommendations for international students: required—TOEFL (minimum score 550 paper-based; 75 iBT). Electronic applications accepted.

**Long Island University - Hudson,** Graduate School, Purchase, NY 10577. Offers autism (Advanced Certificate); bilingual education (Advanced Certificate); childhood education (MS Ed); crisis management (Advanced Certificate); early childhood education (MS Ed); educational leadership (MS Ed); health administration (MPA); literacy (MS Ed); marriage and family therapy (MS); mental health counseling (MS, Advanced Certificate), including credentialed alcoholism and substance abuse counselor (MS); middle childhood and adolescence education (MS Ed); pharmaceutics (MS), including cosmetic science, industrial pharmacy; public administration (MPA); school counseling (MS Ed, Advanced Certificate); school psychology (MS Ed); special education (MS Ed); TESOL (MS Ed); TESOL (all grades) (Advanced Certificate). *Program availability:* Part-time, evening/weekend. *Entrance requirements:* Additional exam requirements/recommendations for international students: required—TOEFL. Electronic applications accepted. *Expenses:* Contact institution.

**Long Island University - Post,** School of Health Professions and Nursing, Brookville, NY 11548-1300. Offers biomedical science (MS); cardiovascular perfusion (MS); clinical lab sciences (MS); clinical laboratory management (MS); dietetic internship (Advanced Certificate); family nurse practitioner (MS, Advanced Certificate); forensic social work (Advanced Certificate); gerontology (Advanced Certificate); health administration (MPA); non-profit management (Advanced Certificate); nursing education (MS); nutrition (MS); public administration (MPA); social work (MSW). *Program availability:* Part-time, blended/hybrid learning. *Degree requirements:* For master's, comprehensive exam (for some programs), thesis (for some programs). *Entrance requirements:* Additional exam requirements/recommendations for international students: required—TOEFL (minimum score 85 iBT) or IELTS (7.5). Electronic applications accepted.

**Louisiana State University Health Sciences Center,** School of Public Health, New Orleans, LA 70112. Offers behavioral and community health sciences (MPH); biostatistics (MPH, MS, PhD); community health sciences (PhD); environmental and occupational health sciences (MPH); epidemiology (MPH, PhD); health policy and systems management (MPH). *Accreditation:* CEPH. *Program availability:* Part-time. *Degree requirements:* For doctorate, thesis/dissertation. *Entrance requirements:* For master's, GRE General Test. Additional exam requirements/recommendations for international students: recommended—TOEFL (minimum score 550 paper-based; 79 iBT), IELTS. Electronic applications accepted.

**Louisiana State University in Shreveport,** College of Business, Education, and Human Development, Program in Health Administration, Shreveport, LA 71115-2399. Offers MHA. *Program availability:* Part-time, evening/weekend, online learning. *Entrance requirements:* For master's, GRE or GMAT, minimum GPA of 3.0, recommendations. Additional exam requirements/recommendations for international students: required—TOEFL (minimum score 550 paper-based; 61 iBT). Electronic applications accepted.

**Loyola University Chicago,** Quinlan School of Business, MBA Programs, Chicago, IL 60611. Offers accounting (MBA); business ethics (MBA); derivative markets (MBA); economics (MBA); entrepreneurship (MBA); finance (MBA); healthcare management (MBA); human resources management (MBA); information systems management (MBA); international business (MBA); management (MBA); marketing (MBA); risk management (MBA); supply chain management (MBA). *Program availability:* Part-time, evening/weekend. *Entrance requirements:* For master's, GMAT or GRE, official transcripts, two letters of recommendation, statement of purpose, resume. Additional

exam requirements/recommendations for international students: required—TOEFL (minimum score 90 iBT) or IELTS (minimum score 6.5). Electronic applications accepted. Application fee is waived when completed online. *Expenses:* Contact institution.

**Madonna University,** Program in Health Services, Livonia, MI 48150-1173. Offers MSHS. *Program availability:* Part-time. *Degree requirements:* For master's, thesis or alternative. *Entrance requirements:* For master's, GRE General Test or minimum GPA of 3.25. Additional exam requirements/recommendations for international students: required—TOEFL, TWE. Electronic applications accepted. *Expenses: Tuition:* Full-time $15,930; part-time $885 per credit hour. Tuition and fees vary according to degree level and program.

**Marshall University,** Academic Affairs Division, College of Business, Program in Health Care Administration, Huntington, WV 25755. Offers MS. *Program availability:* Part-time, evening/weekend. *Entrance requirements:* For master's, GMAT or GRE General Test.

**Marymount University,** School of Business and Technology, Program in Health Care Management, Arlington, VA 22207-4299. Offers health care management (MS); health care management with business administration (MS/MBA); health care management with information technology (MS/MS); MS/MBA; MS/MS. *Accreditation:* CAHME. *Program availability:* Part-time, evening/weekend. *Faculty:* 1 (woman) full-time, 3 part-time/adjunct (1 woman). *Students:* 22 full-time (17 women), 21 part-time (13 women); includes 27 minority (15 Black or African American, non-Hispanic/Latino; 3 Asian, non-Hispanic/Latino; 8 Hispanic/Latino; 1 Two or more races, non-Hispanic/Latino), 6 international. Average age 30. 38 applicants, 92% accepted, 17 enrolled. In 2019, 7 master's awarded. *Degree requirements:* For master's, capstone project. *Entrance requirements:* For master's, resume, interview. Additional exam requirements/recommendations for international students: required—TOEFL (minimum score 600 paper-based; 96 iBT), IELTS (minimum score 6.5), PTE (minimum score 58). *Application deadline:* For fall admission, 7/16 priority date for domestic and international students; for spring admission, 11/16 priority date for domestic and international students; for summer admission, 4/16 priority date for domestic and international students. Applications are processed on a rolling basis. Application fee: $40. Electronic applications accepted. *Expenses:* $1,060 per credit. *Financial support:* In 2019–20, 7 students received support. Research assistantships, teaching assistantships, career-related internships or fieldwork, scholarships/grants, and unspecified assistantships available. Support available to part-time students. Financial award application deadline: 3/1; financial award applicants required to submit FAFSA. *Unit head:* Dr. Uma Kelekar, Director, Healthcare Management, 703-284-4994, E-mail: uma.kelekar@marymount.edu. *Application contact:* Fiona McDonnell, Administrative Assistant, 703-284-5901, E-mail: gadmissi@marymount.edu.
Website: https://www.marymount.edu/Academics/School-of-Business-and-Technology/Graduate-Programs/Health-Care-Management-(M-S-)

**Maryville University of Saint Louis,** The John E. Simon School of Business, St. Louis, MO 63141-7299. Offers accounting (MBA, MS, Certificate); business studies (Certificate); cybersecurity (MBA, MS, Certificate); financial services (MBA, Certificate); health administration (MBA); healthcare administration (Certificate); human resource management (MBA); human resources management (Certificate); information technology (MBA); information technology management (Certificate); management (MBA, Certificate); management and leadership (MA); marketing (MBA, Certificate); project management (MBA, Certificate); sport business management (MBA); supply chain management (Certificate); supply chain management/logistics (MBA). *Accreditation:* ACBSP. *Program availability:* Part-time, 100% online, blended/hybrid learning. *Faculty:* 3 full-time (0 women), 107 part-time/adjunct (28 women). *Students:* 315 full-time (155 women), 738 part-time (344 women); includes 329 minority (186 Black or African American, non-Hispanic/Latino; 5 American Indian or Alaska Native, non-Hispanic/Latino; 48 Asian, non-Hispanic/Latino; 60 Hispanic/Latino; 30 Two or more races, non-Hispanic/Latino), 38 international. Average age 34. In 2019, 388 master's awarded. *Degree requirements:* For master's, capstone course (for MBA). *Entrance requirements:* Additional exam requirements/recommendations for international students: required—TOEFL (minimum score 563 paper-based; 85 iBT). *Application deadline:* Applications are processed on a rolling basis. Electronic applications accepted. *Expenses:* Contact institution. *Financial support:* Career-related internships or fieldwork, Federal Work-Study, tuition waivers (partial), and campus employment available. Financial award application deadline: 4/1; financial award applicants required to submit FAFSA. *Unit head:* Tammy Gocial, Associate Academic Vice President/Interim Dean, 314-529-9401, Fax: 314-529-9975, E-mail: tgocial@maryville.edu. *Application contact:* Chris Gourdine, Assistant Dean Business Administration, 314-529-6861, Fax: 314-529-9975, E-mail: cgourdine@maryville.edu.
Website: http://www.maryville.edu/bu/business-administration-masters/

**Marywood University,** Academic Affairs, College of Health and Human Services, School of Social Work, Program in Health Services Administration, Scranton, PA 18509-1598. Offers MHSA. *Program availability:* Part-time. Electronic applications accepted.

**MCPHS University,** Graduate Studies, Program in Drug Regulatory Affairs and Health Policy, Boston, MA 02115-5896. Offers MS. *Program availability:* Part-time, evening/weekend. *Degree requirements:* For master's, thesis, oral defense of thesis. *Entrance requirements:* For master's, GRE General Test, minimum GPA of 3.0. Additional exam requirements/recommendations for international students: required—TOEFL (minimum score 550 paper-based; 79 iBT). Electronic applications accepted.

**Medical University of South Carolina,** College of Health Professions, Doctoral Program in Health Administration, Charleston, SC 29425. Offers DHA. *Degree requirements:* For doctorate, comprehensive exam, thesis/dissertation. *Entrance requirements:* For doctorate, experience in health care, interview, master's degree in relevant field, resume, 3 references. Additional exam requirements/recommendations for international students: required—TOEFL (minimum score 600 paper-based).

**Medical University of South Carolina,** College of Health Professions, Program in Health Administration-Executive, Charleston, SC 29425. Offers MHA. *Accreditation:* CAHME. *Program availability:* Part-time, online learning. *Degree requirements:* For master's, 20 hours of community service. *Entrance requirements:* For master's, GRE General Test or GMAT, minimum GPA of 3.0. Additional exam requirements/recommendations for international students: required—TOEFL (minimum score 600 paper-based). Electronic applications accepted.

**Medical University of South Carolina,** College of Health Professions, Program in Health Administration-Global, Charleston, SC 29425. Offers MHA. *Entrance requirements:* Additional exam requirements/recommendations for international students: required—TOEFL.

**Medical University of South Carolina,** College of Health Professions, Program in Health Administration-Residential, Charleston, SC 29425. Offers MHA. *Accreditation:* CAHME. *Program availability:* Part-time, online learning. *Degree requirements:* For master's, 20 hours of community service, internship or field project. *Entrance requirements:* For master's, GRE General Test, GMAT, minimum GPA of 3.0, 3 references, interview. Additional exam requirements/recommendations for international students: required—TOEFL (minimum score 550 paper-based).

## Health Services Management and Hospital Administration

**Meharry Medical College,** School of Graduate Studies, Division of Public Health Practice, Nashville, TN 37208-9989. Offers occupational medicine (MSPH); public health administration (MSPH). *Accreditation:* CEPH. *Program availability:* Part-time, evening/weekend. *Degree requirements:* For master's, thesis, externship. *Entrance requirements:* For master's, GRE General Test, GMAT. Additional exam requirements/recommendations for international students: required—TOEFL. *Application deadline:* For fall admission, 6/1 for domestic students. Applications are processed on a rolling basis. Application fee: $65. *Expenses:* Contact institution. *Financial support:* Career-related internships or fieldwork, Federal Work-Study, institutionally sponsored loans, and scholarships/grants available. Support available to part-time students. Financial award application deadline: 7/15; financial award applicants required to submit FAFSA. *Unit head:* Stephanie Bailey, MD, Senior Associate Dean, 615-327-6069, E-mail: sbailey@mmc.edu. *Application contact:* Kimberlee Wyche-Etheridge, MD,MPH, Interim Program Director, 615-327-6675, E-mail: ketheridge@mmc.edu. Website: https://home.mmc.edu/school-of-graduate-studies-research/the-m-s-p-h-program/

**Mercy College,** School of Social and Behavioral Sciences, Program in Health Services Management, Dobbs Ferry, NY 10522-1189. Offers MPA, MS. *Program availability:* Part-time, evening/weekend, 100% online, blended/hybrid learning. *Students:* 42 full-time (34 women), 18 part-time (17 women); includes 48 minority (25 Black or African American, non-Hispanic/Latino; 3 Asian, non-Hispanic/Latino; 19 Hispanic/Latino; 1 Two or more races, non-Hispanic/Latino). Average age 33. 131 applicants, 80% accepted, 36 enrolled. In 2019, 14 master's awarded. *Degree requirements:* For master's, Capstone project or internship. *Entrance requirements:* For master's, transcript(s); two letters of recommendation; resume; essay; interview; demonstrated work experience in health care. Additional exam requirements/recommendations for international students: required—TOEFL (minimum score 80 iBT), IELTS (minimum score 6.5). *Application deadline:* Applications are processed on a rolling basis. Application fee: $40. Electronic applications accepted. *Expenses:* Contact institution. *Financial support:* Career-related internships or fieldwork, Federal Work-Study, scholarships/grants, and unspecified assistantships available. Support available to part-time students. Financial award applicants required to submit FAFSA. *Unit head:* Dr. Diana Juettner, Interim Dean, School of Social and Behavioral Sciences, 914-674-7546, E-mail: djuettner@mercy.edu. *Application contact:* Allison Gurdineer, Executive Director of Admissions, 877-637-2946, Fax: 914-674-7382, E-mail: admissions@mercy.edu. Website: https://www.mercy.edu/social-and-behavioral-sciences/social-sciences

**Mercy College of Ohio,** Program in Health Administration, Toledo, OH 43604. Offers MHA. *Program availability:* Part-time-only, online only, 100% online, Practicum may be required based on student prior experience. *Faculty:* 1 full-time, 14 part-time/adjunct. *Students:* 45 part-time (39 women). 43 applicants, 44% accepted, 14 enrolled. *Entrance requirements:* For master's, Possess a bachelor's degree or higher from an accredited higher education institution; submit a current professional resume or Curriculum Vitae and a statement of purpose; and provide three professional references. *Application deadline:* Applications are processed on a rolling basis. Electronic applications accepted. *Expenses:* Tuition: Part-time $649 per credit hour. *Required fees:* $450 per term. One-time fee: $250 part-time. Tuition and fees vary according to program. *Financial support:* Tuition discounts for alumni and Bon Secours/Mercy Health Employees available. Financial award applicants required to submit FAFSA. *Unit head:* Dr. Kimberly Watson, Dean Health Sciences; Program Director: Master of Health Administration, 419-251-1852, E-mail: kim.watson@mercycollege.edu. *Application contact:* Amy Mergen, Director of Enrollment Management, 888-806-3729, E-mail: admissions@mercycollege.edu. Website: https://mercycollege.edu/academics/programs/graduate/health-administration

**Midwestern State University,** Billie Doris McAda Graduate School, Robert D. and Carol Gunn College of Health Sciences and Human Services, Department of Criminal Justice and Health Services Administration, Wichita Falls, TX 76308. Offers criminal justice (MA); health information management (MHA); health services administration (Graduate Certificate); medical practice management (MHA); public and community sector health care management (MHA); rural and urban hospital management (MHA). *Program availability:* Part-time, evening/weekend. *Degree requirements:* For master's, comprehensive exam, thesis. *Entrance requirements:* For master's, GRE. Additional exam requirements/recommendations for international students: required—TOEFL (minimum score 550 paper-based). Electronic applications accepted.

**Milligan University,** Area of Business Administration, Milligan College, TN 37682. Offers health sector management (MBA, Graduate Certificate); leadership (MBA, Graduate Certificate); operations management (MBA, Graduate Certificate). *Faculty:* 4 full-time (0 women), 3 part-time/adjunct (1 woman). *Students:* 48 full-time (21 women); includes 2 minority (1 Asian, non-Hispanic/Latino; 1 Two or more races, non-Hispanic/Latino), 2 international. Average age 33. 55 applicants, 98% accepted, 34 enrolled. In 2019, 33 master's awarded. *Degree requirements:* For master's, thesis or alternative. *Entrance requirements:* For master's, GMAT if undergraduate GPA less than 3.0, undergraduate degree and supporting transcripts, relevant full-time work experience, essay/personal statement, professional recommendations. Additional exam requirements/recommendations for international students: required—TOEFL (minimum score 550 paper-based, 79 iBT) or IELTS (6.5). *Application deadline:* For fall admission, 8/1 for domestic students, 6/1 for international students; for spring admission, 1/15 for domestic students, 12/1 for international students. Applications are processed on a rolling basis. Application fee: $30. Electronic applications accepted. *Expenses:* 32 hr program: $600/hr; $75 one-time records fee; no other fees throughout program. *Financial support:* Scholarships/grants available. Financial award application deadline: 12/1; financial award applicants required to submit FAFSA. *Unit head:* Dr. David Campbell, Area Chair of Business, 423-461-8674, Fax: 423-461-8677, E-mail: dacampbell@milligan.edu. *Application contact:* Rebecca Banton, Graduate Admissions Recruiter, Business Area, 423-461-8662, Fax: 423-461-8789, E-mail: rbbanton@milligan.edu. Website: http://www.milligan.edu/GPS

**Milwaukee School of Engineering,** MS Program in Nursing - Leadership and Management, Milwaukee, WI 53202-3109. Offers MSN. *Program availability:* Part-time, evening/weekend, 100% online, blended/hybrid learning. *Entrance requirements:* For master's, GRE General Test or GMAT if undergraduate GPA less than 3.0, 2 letters of recommendation; BSN from accredited institution; current unrestricted licensure as a Registered Nurse. Additional exam requirements/recommendations for international students: required—TOEFL (minimum score 90 iBT), IELTS (minimum score 7). Electronic applications accepted.

**Minnesota State University Moorhead,** Graduate and Extended Learning, College of Science, Health and the Environment, Moorhead, MN 56563. Offers healthcare administration (MHA); nursing (MS); school psychology (MS, Psy S). *Program availability:* Part-time, evening/weekend, 100% online, blended/hybrid learning. *Students:* 30 full-time (26 women), 120 part-time (91 women). Average age 33. 77 applicants, 57% accepted. In 2019, 40 master's, 11 other advanced degrees awarded. *Degree requirements:* For master's, comprehensive exam (for some programs), thesis, final oral defense. *Entrance requirements:* For master's, GRE (for school psychology program), minimum GPA of 3.0, essay, letters of reference, RN license (for nursing

program). Additional exam requirements/recommendations for international students: required—TOEFL (minimum score 550 paper-based; 80 iBT); recommended—IELTS (minimum score 6.5). *Application deadline:* Applications are processed on a rolling basis. Application fee: $35. Electronic applications accepted. *Financial support:* Federal Work-Study and unspecified assistantships available. Financial award application deadline: 10/1; financial award applicants required to submit FAFSA. *Unit head:* Dr. Elizabeth Nawrot, Interim Dean, 218-477-5892, E-mail: nawrot@mnstate.edu. *Application contact:* Karla Wenger, Office Manager, 218-477-2344, Fax: 218-477-2482, E-mail: wengerk@mnstate.edu. Website: http://www.mnstate.edu/cshe

**Misericordia University,** College of Business, Master of Business Administration Program, Dallas, PA 18612-1098. Offers accounting (MBA); healthcare management (MBA); human resource management (MBA); management (MBA); sport management (MBA). *Program availability:* Part-time, evening/weekend, online learning. *Entrance requirements:* For master's, GMAT, MAT, GRE (50th percentile or higher), or minimum undergraduate GPA of 3.0, interview. Additional exam requirements/recommendations for international students: required—TOEFL. Electronic applications accepted. Application fee is waived when completed online. *Expenses:* Contact institution.

**Misericordia University,** College of Business, Program in Organizational Management, Dallas, PA 18612-1098. Offers healthcare management (MS); human resource management (MS); management (MS). *Program availability:* Part-time, evening/weekend, 100% online, blended/hybrid learning. *Students:* 68 part-time (47 women); includes 8 minority (3 Black or African American, non-Hispanic/Latino; 2 Asian, non-Hispanic/Latino; 2 Hispanic/Latino; 1 Two or more races, non-Hispanic/Latino). Average age 32. In 2019, 25 master's awarded. *Entrance requirements:* For master's, Undergraduate GPA of 3.0. Additional exam requirements/recommendations for international students: required—TOEFL. *Application deadline:* Applications are processed on a rolling basis. Application fee: $35. Electronic applications accepted. Application fee is waived when completed online. *Expenses:* $790 per credit. *Financial support:* Scholarships/grants and unspecified assistantships available. Support available to part-time students. Financial award application deadline: 6/30; financial award applicants required to submit FAFSA. *Unit head:* Dr. Corina Slaff, Chair of Business Department, 570-674-8022, E-mail: cslaff@misericordia.edu. *Application contact:* Karen Cefalo, Assistant Director of Admissions, 570-674-8094, Fax: 570-674-6232, E-mail: kcefalo@misericordia.edu. Website: http://www.misericordia.edu/page.cfm?p-1855

**Mississippi College,** Graduate School, Program in Health Services Administration, Clinton, MS 39058. Offers MHSA. *Program availability:* Part-time. *Degree requirements:* For master's, comprehensive exam. *Entrance requirements:* For master's, GRE General Test, minimum GPA of 2.5. Additional exam requirements/recommendations for international students: recommended—TOEFL, IELTS. Electronic applications accepted.

**Molloy College,** Graduate Business Program, Rockville Centre, NY 11571. Offers accounting (MBA); finance (MBA, Post-Master's Certificate, Postbaccalaureate Certificate); healthcare administration (MBA, Post-Master's Certificate, Postbaccalaureate Certificate); management (MBA); marketing (MBA, Post-Master's Certificate, Postbaccalaureate Certificate); personal financial planning (MBA). *Program availability:* Part-time, evening/weekend, online only, 100% online, blended/hybrid learning. *Faculty:* 11 full-time (3 women), 7 part-time/adjunct (4 women). *Students:* 76 full-time (36 women), 175 part-time (101 women); includes 105 minority (36 Black or African American, non-Hispanic/Latino; 1 American Indian or Alaska Native, non-Hispanic/Latino; 22 Asian, non-Hispanic/Latino; 37 Hispanic/Latino; 1 Native Hawaiian or other Pacific Islander, non-Hispanic/Latino; 8 Two or more races, non-Hispanic/Latino), 1 international. Average age 31. 97 applicants, 72% accepted, 63 enrolled. In 2019, 103 master's awarded. *Degree requirements:* For master's, Capstone. *Entrance requirements:* Additional exam requirements/recommendations for international students: required—TOEFL (minimum score 550 paper-based; 79 iBT). *Application deadline:* Applications are processed on a rolling basis. Application fee: $60. Electronic applications accepted. *Expenses:* Tuition: Full-time $21,510; part-time $1195 per credit hour. *Required fees:* $1100. Tuition and fees vary according to course load, degree level and program. *Financial support:* Application deadline: 3/1; applicants required to submit FAFSA. *Unit head:* Dr. Barbara Schmidt, Assistant Vice President for Academic Affairs, 516-323-3015, E-mail: MBAdean@molloy.edu. *Application contact:* Faye Hood, Assistant Director for Admissions, 516-323-4009, E-mail: fhood@molloy.edu. Website: https://www.molloy.edu/mba

**Molloy College,** Graduate Nursing Program, Rockville Centre, NY 11571-5002. Offers adult-gerontology clinical nurse specialist (DNP); adult-gerontology nurse practitioner (MS, DNP); clinical nurse specialist: adult-gerontology (MS); family nurse practitioner (MS, DNP); family psychiatric/mental health nurse practitioner (MS, DNP); nursing (PhD, Advanced Certificate); nursing administration with informatics (MS); nursing education (MS); pediatric nurse practitioner (MS, DNP). *Accreditation:* AACN. *Program availability:* Part-time, evening/weekend. *Faculty:* 30 full-time (28 women), 10 part-time/adjunct (6 women). *Students:* 18 full-time (17 women), 573 part-time (520 women); includes 340 minority (181 Black or African American, non-Hispanic/Latino; 2 American Indian or Alaska Native, non-Hispanic/Latino; 100 Asian, non-Hispanic/Latino; 42 Hispanic/Latino; 5 Native Hawaiian or other Pacific Islander, non-Hispanic/Latino; 10 Two or more races, non-Hispanic/Latino), 3 international. Average age 38. 332 applicants, 60% accepted, 149 enrolled. In 2019, 136 master's, 12 doctorates, 22 other advanced degrees awarded. *Degree requirements:* For doctorate, clinical research residency and scholarly clinical project (for DNP); dissertation and comprehensive exam (for PhD). *Entrance requirements:* Additional exam requirements/recommendations for international students: required—TOEFL (minimum score 550 paper-based; 79 iBT). *Application deadline:* Applications are processed on a rolling basis. Application fee: $60. Electronic applications accepted. *Expenses:* Tuition: Full-time $21,510; part-time $1195 per credit hour. *Required fees:* $1100. Tuition and fees vary according to course load, degree level and program. *Financial support:* Application deadline: 3/1; applicants required to submit FAFSA. *Unit head:* Dr. Marcia R. Gardner, Dean, The Barbara H. Hagan School of Nursing, 516-323-3651, E-mail: mgardner@molloy.edu. *Application contact:* Faye Hood, Assistant Director for Admissions, 516-323-4009, E-mail: fhood@molloy.edu. Website: https://www.molloy.edu/academics/graduate-programs/graduate-nursing-x25989

**Monroe College,** King Graduate School, Bronx, NY 10468. Offers accounting (MS); business administration (MBA), including entrepreneurship, finance, general business administration, healthcare management, human resources, information technology, marketing; computer science (MS); criminal justice (MS); hospitality management (MS); public health (MPH), including biostatistics and epidemiology, community health, health administration and leadership. *Program availability:* Online learning.

**Montana State University Billings,** College of Allied Health Professions, Program in Health Administration, Billings, MT 59101. Offers MHA. *Program availability:* Part-time, evening/weekend, 100% online, blended/hybrid learning. *Degree requirements:* For master's, thesis or professional paper and/or field experience. *Entrance requirements:* For master's, GRE General Test or GMAT, minimum undergraduate GPA of 3.0, graduate 3.25; 3 years' clinical or administrative experience in health care delivery or 5

years' experience in business or industry management. Additional exam requirements/recommendations for international students: required—TOEFL (minimum score 79 iBT), IELTS (minimum score 6.5). Electronic applications accepted.

**Moravian College,** Graduate and Continuing Studies, Business and Management Programs, Bethlehem, PA 18018-6614. Offers accounting (MBA); business management (MBA); health administration (MHA); HR leadership (MSHRM); supply chain management (MBA). *Program availability:* Part-time, evening/weekend, 100% online, blended/hybrid learning. *Faculty:* 1 (woman) full-time, 8 part-time/adjunct (3 women). *Students:* 14 full-time (8 women), 108 part-time (55 women); includes 17 minority (3 Black or African American, non-Hispanic/Latino; 1 American Indian or Alaska Native, non-Hispanic/Latino; 13 Hispanic/Latino), 2 international. Average age 31. 92 applicants, 85% accepted, 58 enrolled. In 2019, 37 master's awarded. *Entrance requirements:* For master's, current resume, official transcripts, 2 letters of recommendation. Additional exam requirements/recommendations for international students: required—TOEFL (minimum score 577 paper-based), IELTS (minimum score 6.5). *Application deadline:* For fall admission, 8/1 priority date for domestic and international students; for spring admission, 1/1 priority date for domestic and international students; for summer admission, 5/1 priority date for domestic and international students. Applications are processed on a rolling basis. Electronic applications accepted. *Expenses: Tuition:* Full-time $16,848; part-time $2808 per course. *Required fees:* $90; $45 per semester. Tuition and fees vary according to program. *Financial support:* Research assistantships available. Financial award applicants required to submit FAFSA. *Unit head:* Dr. Katie P. Desiderio, Executive Director, Graduate Business Programs, 610-861-1400, Fax: 610-861-1466, E-mail: graduate@moravian.edu. *Application contact:* Kristy Sullivan, Director of Student Recruitment Operations, 610-861-1400, Fax: 610-861-1466, E-mail: graduate@moravian.edu.
Website: https://www.moravian.edu/graduate/programs/business#/

**Mount Aloysius College,** Program in Business Administration, Cresson, PA 16630. Offers accounting (MBA); health and human services administration (MBA); non-profit management (MBA); project management (MBA). *Program availability:* Part-time, evening/weekend. *Entrance requirements:* Additional exam requirements/recommendations for international students: required—IELTS (minimum score 5.5); recommended—TOEFL. *Application deadline:* For fall admission, 8/1 for domestic students; for spring admission, 12/1 for domestic students. Applications are processed on a rolling basis. Application fee: $30. Electronic applications accepted. Application fee is waived when completed online. *Financial support:* Unspecified assistantships available. Financial award applicants required to submit FAFSA. *Application contact:* Matthew P. Bodenschatz, Director of Graduate and Continuing Education Admissions, 814-886-6556, Fax: 814-886-6441, E-mail: mbodenschatz@mtaloy.edu.

**Mount St. Joseph University,** Doctor of Nursing Practice Program, Cincinnati, OH 45233-1670. Offers health systems leadership (DNP). *Accreditation:* AACN. *Program availability:* Part-time-only. *Degree requirements:* For doctorate, capstone, minimum cumulative GPA of 3.0, completion of program within 5 years of enrollment, minimum of 75% of credits earned at Mount St. Joseph University, 1000 practicum hours between prior master's degree and DNP programs, minimum of 400 practicum hours in the DNP program. *Entrance requirements:* For doctorate, essay; MSN from regionally-accredited university; minimum graduate GPA of 3.0; professional resume; two professional references; interview; 2 years of clinical nursing experience; active RN license; minimum C grade in an undergraduate statistics course; official documentation of practicum hours post-BSN. Additional exam requirements/recommendations for international students: required—TOEFL (minimum score 560 paper-based; 83 iBT). Electronic applications accepted. *Expenses:* Contact institution.

**Mount Saint Mary's University,** Graduate Division, Los Angeles, CA 90049. Offers business administration (MBA); counseling psychology (MS); creative writing (MFA); education (MS, Certificate); film and television (MFA); health policy and management (MS); humanities (MA); nursing (MSN, Certificate); physical therapy (DPT); religious studies (MA). *Program availability:* Part-time, evening/weekend. *Entrance requirements:* Additional exam requirements/recommendations for international students: required—TOEFL. Electronic applications accepted. *Expenses: Tuition:* Full-time $18,648; part-time $9324 per year. *Required fees:* $540; $540 per unit.

**Mount St. Mary's University,** Program in Health Administration, Emmitsburg, MD 21727-7799. Offers MHA. *Program availability:* Part-time, evening/weekend. *Students:* 2 full-time (1 woman), 22 part-time (16 women); includes 10 minority (7 Black or African American, non-Hispanic/Latino; 1 Asian, non-Hispanic/Latino; 1 Hispanic/Latino; 1 Two or more races, non-Hispanic/Latino), 1 international. In 2019, 18 master's awarded. *Degree requirements:* For master's, health care field practicum. *Entrance requirements:* For master's, undergraduate degree, minimum cumulative undergraduate GPA of 2.75. Additional exam requirements/recommendations for international students: required—TOEFL (minimum score 550 paper-based; 83 iBT). *Application deadline:* Applications are processed on a rolling basis. Electronic applications accepted. *Expenses:* Contact institution. *Financial support:* Unspecified assistantships available. Financial award applicants required to submit FAFSA.
Website: https://msmary.edu/academics/graduate-programs/master-health-administration.html

**National American University,** Roueche Graduate Center, Austin, TX 78731. Offers accounting (MBA); aviation management (MBA, MM); care coordination (MSN); community college leadership (Ed D); criminal justice (MM); e-marketing (MBA, MM); health care administration (MBA, MM); higher education (MM); human resources management (MBA, MM); information technology management (MBA, MM); international business (MBA); leadership (EMBA); management (MBA); nursing administration (MSN); nursing education (MSN); nursing informatics (MSN); operations and configuration management (MBA, MM); project and process management (MBA, MM). *Program availability:* Part-time, evening/weekend, online learning. *Entrance requirements:* For master's, minimum undergraduate GPA of 2.75. Additional exam requirements/recommendations for international students: required—TOEFL, TWE. Electronic applications accepted.

**National University,** School of Health and Human Services, La Jolla, CA 92037-1011. Offers clinical affairs (MS); clinical regulatory affairs (MS); complementary and integrative healthcare (MS); family nurse practitioner (MSN); health and life science analytics (MS); health informatics (MS, Certificate); healthcare administration (MHA); nurse anesthesia (MSNA); nursing administration (MSN); nursing informatics (MSN); psychiatric-mental health nurse practitioner (MSN); public health (MPH), including health promotion, healthcare administration, mental health. *Accreditation:* CEPH. *Program availability:* Part-time, evening/weekend, 100% online, blended/hybrid learning. *Degree requirements:* For master's, thesis (for some programs). *Entrance requirements:* For master's, interview, minimum GPA of 2.5. Additional exam requirements/recommendations for international students: required—TOEFL (minimum score 550 paper-based; 79 iBT), IELTS (minimum score 6). Electronic applications accepted. *Expenses: Tuition:* Full-time $442; part-time $442 per unit.

**Nebraska Methodist College,** Program in Healthcare Operations Management, Omaha, NE 68114. Offers MS. *Program availability:* Part-time, evening/weekend, online learning. *Degree requirements:* For master's, thesis or alternative, capstone. *Entrance requirements:* Additional exam requirements/recommendations for international students: required—TOEFL (minimum score 550 paper-based; 80 iBT).

**New Charter University,** College of Business, Salt Lake City, UT 84101. Offers finance (MBA); health care management (MBA); management (MBA). *Program availability:* Part-time, evening/weekend, online only, 100% online. *Entrance requirements:* For master's, course work in calculus, statistics, macroeconomics. Additional exam requirements/recommendations for international students: required—TOEFL (minimum score 550 paper-based). Electronic applications accepted.

**New England College,** Program in Management, Henniker, NH 03242-3293. Offers accounting (MSA); healthcare administration (MS); international relations (MA); marketing management (MS); nonprofit leadership (MS); project management (MS); strategic leadership (MS). *Program availability:* Part-time, evening/weekend. *Degree requirements:* For master's, independent research project. Electronic applications accepted.

**New Jersey City University,** College of Professional Studies, Department of Health Sciences, Jersey City, NJ 07305-1597. Offers community health education (MS); health administration (MS); school health education (MS). *Program availability:* Part-time, evening/weekend. *Degree requirements:* For master's, thesis or alternative, internship. *Entrance requirements:* Additional exam requirements/recommendations for international students: required—TOEFL (minimum score 79 iBT).

**New Jersey Institute of Technology,** Newark College of Engineering, Newark, NJ 07102. Offers biomedical engineering (MS, PhD); biopharmaceutical engineering (MS); chemical engineering (MS, PhD); civil engineering (MS, PhD); computer engineering (MS); critical infrastructure systems (MS); electrical engineering (MS, PhD); engineering management (MS); engineering science (MS); environmental engineering (MS, PhD); healthcare systems management (MS); industrial engineering (MS, PhD); internet engineering (MS); manufacturing systems engineering (MS); materials science & engineering (PhD); materials science and engineering (MS); mechanical engineering (MS, PhD); occupational safety and health engineering (MS). *Program availability:* Part-time, evening/weekend. *Faculty:* 151 full-time (29 women), 135 part-time/adjunct (15 women). *Students:* 576 full-time (161 women), 528 part-time (111 women); includes 366 minority (61 Black or African American, non-Hispanic/Latino; 1 American Indian or Alaska Native, non-Hispanic/Latino; 166 Asian, non-Hispanic/Latino; 115 Hispanic/Latino; 23 Two or more races, non-Hispanic/Latino), 450 international. Average age 28. 2,053 applicants, 67% accepted, 338 enrolled. In 2019, 474 master's, 30 doctorates awarded. Terminal master's awarded for partial completion of doctoral program. *Degree requirements:* For master's, thesis (for some programs); for doctorate, thesis/dissertation. *Entrance requirements:* For master's, GRE General Test, minimum GPA 2.8, personal statement, 1 letter of recommendation, transcripts; for doctorate, GRE General Test, minimum GPA of 3.5, personal statement, 3 letters of recommendation, transcripts. Additional exam requirements/recommendations for international students: required—TOEFL (minimum score 550 paper-based; 79 iBT), IELTS (minimum score 6.5). *Application deadline:* For fall admission, 6/1 priority date for domestic students, 5/1 priority date for international students; for spring admission, 11/15 priority date for domestic and international students. Applications are processed on a rolling basis. Application fee: $75. Electronic applications accepted. *Expenses:* $23,828 per year (in-state), $33,744 per year (out-of-state). *Financial support:* In 2019–20, 352 students received support, including 33 fellowships with full tuition reimbursements available (averaging $24,000 per year), 89 research assistantships with full tuition reimbursements available (averaging $24,000 per year), 112 teaching assistantships with full tuition reimbursements available (averaging $24,000 per year); career-related internships or fieldwork, Federal Work-Study, scholarships/grants, and unspecified assistantships also available. Financial award application deadline: 1/15. *Unit head:* Dr. Moshe Kam, Dean, 973-596-5534, Fax: 973-596-2316, E-mail: moshe.kam@njit.edu. *Application contact:* Stephen Eck, Executive Director of University Admissions, 973-596-3300, Fax: 973-596-3461, E-mail: admissions@njit.edu.
Website: http://engineering.njit.edu/

**New York Medical College,** School of Health Sciences and Practice, Valhalla, NY 10595. Offers behavioral sciences and health promotion (MPH); biostatistics (MS); children with special health care (Graduate Certificate); emergency preparedness (Graduate Certificate); environmental health science (MPH); epidemiology (MPH, MS); global health (Graduate Certificate); health education (Graduate Certificate); health policy and management (MPH, Dr PH); industrial hygiene (Graduate Certificate); pediatric dysphagia (Post-Graduate Certificate); physical therapy (DPT); public health (Graduate Certificate); speech-language pathology (MS). *Accreditation:* ASHA; CEPH. *Program availability:* Part-time, evening/weekend, 100% online, blended/hybrid learning. *Faculty:* 47 full-time (34 women), 203 part-time/adjunct (125 women). *Students:* 230 full-time (171 women), 292 part-time (207 women); includes 204 minority (73 Black or African American, non-Hispanic/Latino; 4 American Indian or Alaska Native, non-Hispanic/Latino; 59 Asian, non-Hispanic/Latino; 54 Hispanic/Latino; 1 Native Hawaiian or other Pacific Islander, non-Hispanic/Latino; 13 Two or more races, non-Hispanic/Latino), 35 international. Average age 29. 790 applicants, 61% accepted, 162 enrolled. In 2019, 113 master's, 47 doctorates awarded. *Degree requirements:* For master's, comprehensive exam (for some programs), thesis (for some programs); for doctorate, thesis/dissertation. *Entrance requirements:* For master's, GRE (for MS in speech-language pathology); for doctorate, GRE (for Doctor of Physical Therapy and Doctor of Public Health). Additional exam requirements/recommendations for international students: required—TOEFL (minimum score 96 paper-based; 24 iBT), IELTS (minimum score 7). *Application deadline:* For fall admission, 8/1 for domestic students, 4/15 for international students; for spring admission, 12/1 for domestic students; for summer admission, 5/1 for domestic students, 4/15 for international students. Applications are processed on a rolling basis. Application fee: $128 ($120 for international students). Electronic applications accepted. *Expenses:* $1195 credit fee, academic support fee $200, Student activities fee $140 per year, technology fee $150. *Financial support:* In 2019–20, 18 students received support. Federal Work-Study, scholarships/grants, unspecified assistantships, and Federal student loans available. Financial award application deadline: 4/30; financial award applicants required to submit FAFSA. *Unit head:* Ben Johnson, PhD, Vice Dean, 914-594-4531, E-mail: bjohnson23@nymc.edu. *Application contact:* Irene Bundziak, Assistant to Director of Admissions, 914-594-4905, E-mail: irene_bundziak@nymc.edu.
Website: http://www.nymc.edu/school-of-health-sciences-and-practice-shsp/

**New York University,** College of Global Public Health, New York, NY 10012. Offers biological basis of public health (PhD); community and international health (MPH); global health leadership (MPH); health systems and health services research (PhD); population and community health (PhD); public health nutrition (MPH); social and behavioral sciences (MPH); socio-behavioral health (PhD). *Accreditation:* CEPH. *Program availability:* Part-time, online learning. *Degree requirements:* For master's, thesis (for some programs); for doctorate, thesis/dissertation. *Entrance requirements:* For master's and doctorate, GRE. Additional exam requirements/recommendations for international students: required—TOEFL. Electronic applications accepted. *Expenses:* Contact institution.

## Health Services Management and Hospital Administration

**New York University,** Wagner Graduate School of Public Service, Program in Health Policy and Management, New York, NY 10012. Offers health finance (MPA); health policy analysis (MPA); health services management (MPA); international health (MPA); MBA/MPA; MD/MPA; MPA/MPH. *Accreditation:* CAHME (one or more programs are accredited). *Program availability:* Part-time. *Degree requirements:* For master's, thesis or alternative, capstone end event. *Entrance requirements:* Additional exam requirements/recommendations for international students: required—TOEFL (minimum score 100 iBT), IELTS (minimum score 7.5), TWE. Electronic applications accepted. *Expenses:* Contact institution.

**Niagara University,** Graduate Division of Business Administration, Niagara University, NY 14109. Offers accounting (MBA); business administration (MBA); finance (MBA, MS); financial planning (MBA); healthcare administration (MBA, MHA); human resources (MBA); international business (MBA); marketing (MBA); professional accountancy (MBA); strategic management (MBA); supply chain management (MBA). *Accreditation:* AACSB. *Program availability:* Part-time, evening/weekend, 100% online, blended/hybrid learning. *Entrance requirements:* For master's, GMAT. Additional exam requirements/recommendations for international students: required—TOEFL (minimum score 550 paper-based; 79 iBT), IELTS (minimum score 6). Electronic applications accepted. *Expenses:* Contact institution.

**Northeast Ohio Medical University,** College of Graduate Studies, Rootstown, OH 44272-0095. Offers health-system pharmacy administration (MS); integrated pharmaceutical medicine (MS, PhD); medical ethics and humanities (MS, Certificate); public health (MPH). *Program availability:* Part-time, evening/weekend, 100% online, blended/hybrid learning. *Faculty:* 126 part-time/adjunct (62 women). *Students:* 24 full-time (12 women), 28 part-time (15 women); includes 21 minority (2 Black or African American, non-Hispanic/Latino; 10 Asian, non-Hispanic/Latino; 5 Hispanic/Latino; 4 Two or more races, non-Hispanic/Latino). Average age 26. 31 applicants, 97% accepted, 21 enrolled. In 2019, 15 master's, 13 other advanced degrees awarded. *Degree requirements:* For master's, thesis (for some programs), thesis (for MS in medical ethics and humanities, integrated pharmaceutical medicine, MS in MAS); for doctorate, thesis/dissertation, For IPM Ph.D Program. *Entrance requirements:* Additional exam requirements/recommendations for international students: recommended—TOEFL (minimum score 550 paper-based). *Application deadline:* For fall admission, 7/17 for domestic students. Applications are processed on a rolling basis. Application fee: $95. Electronic applications accepted. *Expenses:* Student health and fitness, student activities. *Financial support:* In 2019–20, 6 students received support. Scholarships/grants and tuition waivers (full and partial) available. Financial award application deadline: 3/15; financial award applicants required to submit FAFSA. *Unit head:* Dr. Steven Schmidt, Dean, 330-325-6290. *Application contact:* Dr. Steven Schmidt, Dean, 330-325-6290.
Website: https://www.neomed.edu/graduatestudies/

**Northern Arizona University,** College of Social and Behavioral Sciences and College of Health and Human Services, Interdisciplinary Health PhD Program, Flagstaff, AZ 86011. Offers PhD. *Program availability:* Part-time. *Entrance requirements:* Additional exam requirements/recommendations for international students: required—TOEFL (minimum score 550 paper-based; 80 iBT), IELTS (minimum score 7). Electronic applications accepted.

**Northwestern University,** Feinberg School of Medicine, Driskill Graduate Program in Life Sciences, Chicago, IL 60611. Offers biostatistics (PhD); epidemiology (PhD); health and biomedical informatics (PhD); health services and outcomes research (PhD); healthcare quality and patient safety (PhD); translational outcomes in science (PhD). *Degree requirements:* For doctorate, comprehensive exam, thesis/dissertation, written and oral qualifying exams. *Entrance requirements:* For doctorate, GRE General Test. Additional exam requirements/recommendations for international students: required—TOEFL (minimum score 600 paper-based). Electronic applications accepted.

**Northwestern University,** School of Professional Studies, Program in Public Policy and Administration, Evanston, IL 60208. Offers global policy (MA); health services policy (MA); public administration (MA); public policy (MA). *Program availability:* Part-time, evening/weekend, online learning.

**Ohio Christian University,** Graduate Programs, Circleville, OH 43113. Offers accounting (MBA); business administration (MBA); digital marketing (MBA); finance (MBA); healthcare management (MBA); human resources (MBA); management (MM); organizational leadership (MBA); pastoral care and counseling (MAM); practical theology (MAM).

**Ohio Dominican University,** Division of Business, Program in Healthcare Administration, Columbus, OH 43219-2099. Offers MS. *Program availability:* Part-time, evening/weekend, 100% online. *Faculty:* 2 full-time (0 women). *Students:* 5 full-time (all women), 14 part-time (10 women); includes 7 minority (6 Black or African American, non-Hispanic/Latino; 1 Asian, non-Hispanic/Latino), 6 international. Average age 28. 22 applicants, 82% accepted, 15 enrolled. In 2019, 11 master's awarded. *Entrance requirements:* For master's, minimum GPA of 3.0 in undergraduate degree from regionally-accredited institution, or 2.7 in the last 60 semester hours of bachelor's degree and at least two years of professional experience. Additional exam requirements/recommendations for international students: required—TOEFL (minimum score 550 paper-based), IELTS (minimum score 6.5). *Application deadline:* For fall admission, 8/15 for domestic students, 6/10 for international students; for spring admission, 1/4 for domestic students, 11/2 for international students; for summer admission, 5/30 for domestic students. Applications are processed on a rolling basis. Application fee: $25. Electronic applications accepted. *Expenses:* Tuition: Full-time $10,800; part-time $600 per credit hour. *Required fees:* $225 per semester. Tuition and fees vary according to program. *Financial support:* Applicants required to submit FAFSA. *Unit head:* Dr. Thomas Eveland, Director of Graduate Programs in Business, 614-251-4569, E-mail: evelandt@ohiodominican.edu. *Application contact:* John W Naughton, Vice President for Enrollment and Student Success, 614-251-4721, Fax: 614-251-6654, E-mail: grad@ohiodominican.edu.
Website: http://www.ohiodominican.edu/academics/graduate/msha

**The Ohio State University,** College of Public Health, Columbus, OH 43210. Offers MHA, MPH, MS, PhD, DVM/MPH, JD/MHA, MHA/MBA, MHA/MD, MHA/MPA, MHA/MS, MPH/MBA, MPH/MD, MPH/MSW. *Accreditation:* CAHME; CEPH. *Program availability:* Part-time. Terminal master's awarded for partial completion of doctoral program. *Degree requirements:* For master's, thesis optional, practicum; for doctorate, thesis/dissertation. *Entrance requirements:* For master's and doctorate, GRE. Additional exam requirements/recommendations for international students: required—TOEFL (minimum score 550 paper-based; 79 iBT); recommended—IELTS (minimum score 7). Electronic applications accepted.

**Ohio University,** Graduate College, College of Health Sciences and Professions, Department of Social and Public Health, Athens, OH 45701-2979. Offers early child development and family life (MS); family studies (MS); health administration (MHA); public health (MPH); social work (MSW). *Program availability:* Part-time, evening/weekend, online learning. *Degree requirements:* For master's, capstone (MPH). *Entrance requirements:* For master's, GMAT, GRE General Test, previous course work in accounting, management, and statistics; previous public health background (MHA,

MPH). Additional exam requirements/recommendations for international students: required—TOEFL (minimum score 550 paper-based; 80 iBT) or IELTS (minimum score 6.5). Electronic applications accepted. *Expenses:* Contact institution.

**Oklahoma Christian University,** Graduate School of Business, Oklahoma City, OK 73136-1100. Offers accounting (M Acc, MBA); financial services (MBA); general business (MBA); health services management (MBA); human resources (MBA); international business (MBA); leadership and organizational development (MBA); marketing (MBA); nonprofit management (MBA); project management (MBA). *Accreditation:* ACBSP. *Program availability:* Part-time, 100% online. *Entrance requirements:* For master's, bachelor's degree. Additional exam requirements/recommendations for international students: required—TOEFL (minimum score 550 paper-based). Electronic applications accepted. *Expenses:* Contact institution.

**Oklahoma State University Center for Health Sciences,** Program in Health Care Administration, Tulsa, OK 74107-1898. Offers MS. *Program availability:* Part-time, evening/weekend, 100% online. *Degree requirements:* For master's, thesis or alternative. *Entrance requirements:* For master's, official transcripts with minimum GPA of 3.0. Additional exam requirements/recommendations for international students: required—TOEFL.

**Oregon Health & Science University,** School of Medicine, Graduate Programs in Medicine, Division of Management, Portland, OR 97239-3098. Offers healthcare management (MBA, MS, Certificate). *Program availability:* Part-time. *Degree requirements:* For master's, thesis optional. *Entrance requirements:* For master's, GRE General Test (minimum scores: 153 Verbal/148 Quantitative/4.5 Analytical) or GMAT. Electronic applications accepted.

**Oregon State University,** College of Public Health and Human Sciences, Program in Public Health, Corvallis, OR 97331. Offers biostatistics (MPH); environmental and occupational health (MPH, PhD); epidemiology (MPH, PhD); global health (MPH, PhD). *Accreditation:* CEPH. Terminal master's awarded for partial completion of doctoral program. *Entrance requirements:* For master's and doctorate, GRE, minimum GPA of 3.0 in last 90 hours. Additional exam requirements/recommendations for international students: required—TOEFL (minimum score 80 iBT), IELTS (minimum score 6.5). Electronic applications accepted. *Expenses:* Contact institution.

**Our Lady of the Lake University,** School of Business and Leadership, Program in Healthcare Management, San Antonio, TX 78207-4689. Offers MBA. *Program availability:* Part-time, evening/weekend, 100% online, blended/hybrid learning. *Entrance requirements:* For master's, official transcripts showing 6 hours of coursework in economics and 3 hours of coursework in each of the following ares: statistics, management, business law, and finance; resume including detailed work history describing managerial or professional work experience. Additional exam requirements/recommendations for international students: required—TOEFL. Electronic applications accepted. Application fee is waived when completed online.

**Pace University,** Dyson College of Arts and Sciences, Department of Public Administration, New York, NY 10038. Offers government management (MPA); health care administration (MPA); not-for-profit management (MPA); JD/MPA. *Program availability:* Part-time, evening/weekend. *Degree requirements:* For master's, comprehensive exam, thesis (for some programs), capstone project. *Entrance requirements:* For master's, 2 letters of recommendation, resume, personal statement, official transcripts, essay. Additional exam requirements/recommendations for international students: required—TOEFL (minimum score 88 iBT), IELTS (minimum score 7) or PTE (minimum score 60). Electronic applications accepted.

**Pacific University,** Healthcare Administration Program, Forest Grove, OR 97116-1797. Offers MHA.

**Park University,** School of Graduate and Professional Studies, Kansas City, MO 54105. Offers adult education (M Ed); business and government leadership (Graduate Certificate); business, government, and global society (MPA); communication and leadership (MA); creative and life writing (Graduate Certificate); disaster and emergency management (MPA, Graduate Certificate); educational leadership (M Ed); finance (MBA, Graduate Certificate); general business (MBA); global business (Graduate Certificate); healthcare administration (MHA); healthcare services management and leadership (Graduate Certificate); international business (MBA); language and literacy (M Ed), including English for speakers of other languages, special reading teacher/literacy coach; leadership of international healthcare organizations (Graduate Certificate); management information systems (MBA, Graduate Certificate); music performance (ADP, Graduate Certificate), including cello (MM, ADP), piano (MM, ADP), viola (MM, ADP), violin (MM, ADP); nonprofit and community services management (MPA); nonprofit leadership (Graduate Certificate); performance (MM), including cello (MM, ADP), piano (MM, ADP), viola (MM, ADP), violin (MM, ADP); public management (MPA); social work (MSW); teacher leadership (M Ed), including curriculum and assessment, instructional leader. *Program availability:* Part-time, evening/weekend, online learning. *Degree requirements:* For master's, comprehensive exam (for some programs), thesis (for some programs), internship (for some programs); exam (for some programs). *Entrance requirements:* For master's, GRE or GMAT (for some programs), teacher certification (for some M Ed programs), letters of recommendation, essay, resume (for some programs). Additional exam requirements/recommendations for international students: required—TOEFL (minimum score 550 paper-based; 79 iBT), IELTS (minimum score 6). Electronic applications accepted.

**Penn State Great Valley,** Graduate Studies, Management Division, Malvern, PA 19355-1488. Offers business administration (MBA); cyber security (Certificate); data analytics (MPS, MS, Certificate); distributed energy and grid modernization (Certificate); finance (M Fin); health sector management (Certificate); human resource management (Certificate); information science (MSIS); leadership development (MLD); new ventures and entrepreneurship (Certificate); sustainable management practices (Certificate). *Accreditation:* AACSB.

**Penn State Harrisburg,** Graduate School, School of Public Affairs, Middletown, PA 17057. Offers criminal justice (MA); health administration (MHA); health administration: long term care (Certificate); homeland security (MPS, Certificate); public administration (MPA, PhD); public administration: non-profit administration (Certificate); public budgeting and financial management (Certificate); public sector human resource management (Certificate). *Accreditation:* NASPAA.

**Penn State University Park,** Graduate School, College of Health and Human Development, Department of Health Policy and Administration, University Park, PA 16802. Offers MHA, MS, PhD. *Accreditation:* CAHME.

**Pennsylvania College of Health Sciences,** Graduate Programs, Lancaster, PA 17601. Offers administration (MSN); education (MSHS, MSN); healthcare administration (MHA). *Degree requirements:* For master's, internship (for MHA, MSN in administration); practicum (for MSHS, MSN in education).

**Pfeiffer University,** Program in Health Administration, Misenheimer, NC 28109-0960. Offers MHA, MBA/MHA.

**Philadelphia College of Osteopathic Medicine,** Graduate and Professional Programs, School of Professional and Applied Psychology, Philadelphia, PA 19131. Offers applied

behavior analysis (Certificate); clinical health psychology (Post-Doctoral Certificate); clinical neuropsychology (Post-Doctoral Certificate); clinical psychology (Psy D); educational psychology (PhD); mental health counseling (MS); organizational development and leadership (MS); psychology (Certificate); public health management and administration (MS); school psychology (MS, Psy D, Ed S). *Accreditation:* APA. *Faculty:* 19 full-time (11 women), 122 part-time/adjunct (58 women). *Students:* 342 (285 women); includes 108 minority (65 Black or African American, non-Hispanic/Latino; 1 American Indian or Alaska Native, non-Hispanic/Latino; 10 Asian, non-Hispanic/Latino; 14 Hispanic/Latino; 18 Two or more races, non-Hispanic/Latino). Average age 25. 357 applicants, 51% accepted, 113 enrolled. In 2019, 79 master's, 38 doctorates, 16 other advanced degrees awarded. Terminal master's awarded for partial completion of doctoral program. *Degree requirements:* For master's, comprehensive exam (for some programs), thesis (for some programs); for doctorate, comprehensive exam, thesis/dissertation. *Entrance requirements:* For master's, GRE or MAT, minimum GPA of 3.0; bachelor's degree from regionally-accredited college or university; for doctorate, PRAXIS II (for Psy D in school psychology), minimum undergraduate GPA of 3.0; for other advanced degree, GRE (for Ed S). Additional exam requirements/recommendations for international students: required—TOEFL (minimum score 79 iBT). *Application deadline:* Applications are processed on a rolling basis. Application fee: $50. Electronic applications accepted. *Financial support:* In 2019–20, 28 teaching assistantships were awarded; Federal Work-Study, institutionally sponsored loans, and scholarships/grants also available. Financial award application deadline: 3/15; financial award applicants required to submit FAFSA. *Unit head:* Dr. Robert DiTomasso, Chairman, 215-871-6442, Fax: 215-871-6458, E-mail: robertd@pcom.edu. *Application contact:* Johnathan Cox, Associate Director of Admissions, 215-871-6700, Fax: 215-871-6719, E-mail: johnathancox@pcom.edu.
Website: pcom.edu

**Point Loma Nazarene University,** Fermanian School of Business, San Diego, CA 92108. Offers general business (MBA); healthcare management (MBA); innovation and entrepreneurship (MBA); organizational leadership (MBA); project management (MBA). *Accreditation:* ACBSP. *Program availability:* Part-time, evening/weekend. *Faculty:* 9 full-time (3 women), 6 part-time/adjunct (2 women). *Students:* 20 full-time (10 women), 81 part-time (44 women); includes 49 minority (4 Black or African American, non-Hispanic/Latino; 1 American Indian or Alaska Native, non-Hispanic/Latino; 10 Asian, non-Hispanic/Latino; 26 Hispanic/Latino; 8 Two or more races, non-Hispanic/Latino), 11 international. Average age 30. 80 applicants, 89% accepted, 49 enrolled. In 2019, 73 master's awarded. *Entrance requirements:* For master's, GMAT, letters of recommendation, essay, interview. Additional exam requirements/recommendations for international students: required—TOEFL. *Application deadline:* For fall admission, 7/26 priority date for domestic students; for spring admission, 11/29 priority date for domestic students; for summer admission, 4/2 priority date for domestic students. Applications are processed on a rolling basis. Application fee: $50. Electronic applications accepted. *Expenses:* $890 per unit. *Financial support:* In 2019–20, 43 students received support. Applicants required to submit FAFSA. *Unit head:* Dr. Jamie McIlwaine, Associate Dean, Graduate Business, 619-849-2721, E-mail: JamieMcIlwaine@pointloma.edu. *Application contact:* Dana Barger, Director of Recruitment and Admissions, Graduate and Professional Students, 619-329-6799, E-mail: gradinfo@pointloma.edu.
Website: https://www.pointloma.edu/schools-departments-colleges/fermanian-school-business

**Point Park University,** Rowland School of Business, Program in Management, Pittsburgh, PA 15222-1984. Offers health care administration and management (MS); leadership (MA). *Program availability:* 100% online.

**Portland State University,** Graduate Studies, College of Urban and Public Affairs, Hatfield School of Government, Department of Public Administration, Portland, OR 97207-0751. Offers collaborative governance (Certificate); energy policy and management (Certificate); global management and leadership (MPA); health administration (MPA); human resource management (MPA); local government (MPA); natural resource policy and administration (MPA); nonprofit and public management (Certificate); nonprofit management (MPA); public administration (EMPA); public affairs and policy (PhD); sustainable food systems (Certificate). *Accreditation:* CAHME; NASPAA (one or more programs are accredited). *Program availability:* Part-time, evening/weekend. *Faculty:* 14 full-time (6 women), 9 part-time/adjunct (5 women). *Students:* 86 full-time (55 women), 119 part-time (73 women); includes 46 minority (3 Black or African American, non-Hispanic/Latino; 4 American Indian or Alaska Native, non-Hispanic/Latino; 8 Asian, non-Hispanic/Latino; 18 Hispanic/Latino; 2 Native Hawaiian or other Pacific Islander, non-Hispanic/Latino; 11 Two or more races, non-Hispanic/Latino), 17 international. Average age 35. 138 applicants, 82% accepted, 67 enrolled. In 2019, 64 master's, 2 doctorates awarded. *Degree requirements:* For master's, integrative field experience (MPA), practicum (MPH); for doctorate, comprehensive exam, thesis/dissertation. *Entrance requirements:* For master's, GRE (minimum scores: verbal 150, quantitative 149, and analytic writing 4.5), minimum GPA of 3.0, 3 recommendation letters, resume, 500-word statement of intent; for doctorate, GRE, 3 recommendation letters, resume, 500-word personal essay. Additional exam requirements/recommendations for international students: required—TOEFL (minimum score 550 paper-based; 80 iBT), IELTS (minimum score 7). *Application deadline:* For fall admission, 8/15 for domestic and international students; for winter admission, 10/31 for domestic and international students; for spring admission, 1/31 for domestic and international students. Applications are processed on a rolling basis. Application fee: $65. Electronic applications accepted. *Expenses: Tuition, area resident:* Full-time $13,020; part-time $6510 per year. Tuition, state resident: full-time $13,020; part-time $6510 per year. Tuition, nonresident: full-time $19,830; part-time $9915 per year. *International tuition:* $19,830 full-time. *Required fees:* $1226. One-time fee: $350. Tuition and fees vary according to course load, program and reciprocity agreements. *Financial support:* In 2019–20, 1 research assistantship with full and partial tuition reimbursement (averaging $8,500 per year), 3 teaching assistantships (averaging $7,840 per year) were awarded; career-related internships or fieldwork, Federal Work-Study, scholarships/grants, and unspecified assistantships also available. Support available to part-time students. Financial award application deadline: 3/1; financial award applicants required to submit FAFSA. *Unit head:* Dr. Masami Nishishiba, Chair, 503-725-5151, E-mail: nishism@pdx.edu. *Application contact:* Megan Heljeson, Office Coordinator, 503-725-3921, Fax: 503-725-8250, E-mail: publicad@pdx.edu.
Website: https://www.pdx.edu/hatfieldschool/public-administration

**Portland State University,** Graduate Studies, OHSU-PSU School of Public Health, Health Management and Policy Program, Portland, OR 97207-0751. Offers health management and policy (MPH); health systems and policy (PhD). *Accreditation:* CAHME. *Program availability:* Part-time, evening/weekend. *Students:* 1 (woman) full-time, 9 part-time (7 women); includes 1 minority (American Indian or Alaska Native, non-Hispanic/Latino). Average age 38. In 2019, 6 master's, 1 doctorate awarded. *Degree requirements:* For master's, comprehensive exam (for some programs), thesis (for some programs), internship (MPA), practicum (MPH); for doctorate, comprehensive exam, thesis/dissertation. *Entrance requirements:* For master's, GRE (for MPH program), minimum GPA of 3.0 in upper-division course work or 2.75 overall, resume, 3 recommendation letters; for doctorate, GRE, transcripts, personal statement, resume, writing sample, 3 recommendation letters. Additional exam requirements/recommendations for international students: required—TOEFL (minimum score 550 paper-based; 80 iBT). *Application deadline:* For fall admission, 2/1 for domestic and international students. Applications are processed on a rolling basis. Application fee: $65. *Expenses: Tuition, area resident:* Full-time $13,020; part-time $6510 per year. Tuition, state resident: full-time $13,020; part-time $6510 per year. Tuition, nonresident: full-time $19,830; part-time $9915 per year. *International tuition:* $19,830 full-time. *Required fees:* $1226. One-time fee: $350. Tuition and fees vary according to course load, program and reciprocity agreements. *Financial support:* Research assistantships with full and partial tuition reimbursements, teaching assistantships with full and partial tuition reimbursements, career-related internships or fieldwork, Federal Work-Study, institutionally sponsored loans, scholarships/grants, and unspecified assistantships available. Support available to part-time students. Financial award application deadline: 3/1; financial award applicants required to submit FAFSA. *Unit head:* Dr. David Bangsberg, Founding Dean, 503-282-7537, E-mail: bangsber@ohsu.edu. *Application contact:* Dr. Jill Rissi, Associate Dean for Academic Affairs, 502-725-8217, E-mail: jrissi@pdx.edu.
Website: https://ohsu-psu-sph.org/

**Post University,** Program in Business Administration, Waterbury, CT 06723-2540. Offers accounting (MSA); business administration (MBA); corporate finance (MBA); corporate innovation (MBA); healthcare systems leadership (MBA); leadership (MBA); marketing (MBA); project management (MBA, MS). *Accreditation:* ACBSP. *Program availability:* Online learning. *Entrance requirements:* For master's, resume.

**Purdue University Global,** School of Business, Davenport, IA 52807. Offers business administration (MBA); change leadership (MS); entrepreneurship (MBA); finance (MBA); health care management (MBA, MS); human resource (MBA); international business (MBA); management (MS); marketing (MBA); project management (MBA, MS); supply chain management and logistics (MBA, MS). *Accreditation:* ACBSP. *Program availability:* Part-time, evening/weekend, online learning. *Entrance requirements:* Additional exam requirements/recommendations for international students: required—TOEFL (minimum score 550 paper-based; 80 iBT). Electronic applications accepted.

**Purdue University Global,** School of Legal Studies, Davenport, IA 52807. Offers health care delivery (MS); pathway to paralegal (Postbaccalaureate Certificate); state and local government (MS). *Program availability:* Part-time, evening/weekend, online learning. *Entrance requirements:* Additional exam requirements/recommendations for international students: required—TOEFL (minimum score 550 paper-based; 80 iBT).

**Quinnipiac University,** School of Business, Program in Business Administration, Hamden, CT 06518-1940. Offers finance (MBA); health care management (MBA); supply chain management (MBA); JD/MBA. *Accreditation:* AACSB. *Program availability:* Part-time, evening/weekend, 100% online, blended/hybrid learning. *Entrance requirements:* For master's, GMAT or GRE, minimum GPA of 3.0. Additional exam requirements/recommendations for international students: required—TOEFL (minimum score 575 paper-based; 90 iBT), IELTS (minimum score 6.5). Electronic applications accepted. *Expenses:* Contact institution.

**Regent University,** Graduate School, School of Business and Leadership, Virginia Beach, VA 23464. Offers business administration (MBA), including accounting, economics, entrepreneurship, finance and investing, general management, healthcare management (MA, MBA), human resource management (MA, MBA), innovation management, leadership, marketing, not-for-profit management (MA, MBA); business analytics (MS); business and design management (MA); church leadership (MA); leadership (Certificate); organizational leadership (MA, PhD), including ecclesial leadership (DSL, PhD), entrepreneurial leadership (PhD), healthcare management (MA, MBA), human resource development (PhD), human resource management (MA, MBA), individualized studies (DSL, PhD), interdisciplinary studies (MA), leadership coaching and mentoring (MA), not-for-profit management (MA, MBA), organizational development consulting (MA), servant leadership (MA, DSL); strategic leadership (DSL), including ecclesial leadership (DSL, PhD), global consulting, healthcare leadership, individualized studies (DSL, PhD), leadership coaching, servant leadership (MA, DSL), strategic foresight. *Program availability:* Part-time, evening/weekend, 100% online, blended/hybrid learning. *Faculty:* 9 full-time (2 women), 39 part-time/adjunct (14 women). *Students:* 397 full-time (229 women), 828 part-time (474 women); includes 698 minority (531 Black or African American, non-Hispanic/Latino; 5 American Indian or Alaska Native, non-Hispanic/Latino; 35 Asian, non-Hispanic/Latino; 87 Hispanic/Latino; 5 Native Hawaiian or other Pacific Islander, non-Hispanic/Latino; 35 Two or more races, non-Hispanic/Latino), 45 international. Average age 41. 615 applicants, 76% accepted, 275 enrolled. In 2019, 218 master's, 91 doctorates, 1 other advanced degree awarded. *Degree requirements:* For master's, thesis or alternative, 3-credit hour culminating experience; for doctorate, thesis/dissertation. *Entrance requirements:* For master's, college transcripts, resume, essay; for doctorate, college transcripts, resume, essay, writing sample; for Certificate, writing sample, resume, transcripts. Additional exam requirements/recommendations for international students: required—TOEFL (minimum score 577 paper-based). *Application deadline:* For fall admission, 5/1 priority date for domestic students; for spring admission, 10/1 priority date for domestic students. Applications are processed on a rolling basis. Application fee: $50. Electronic applications accepted. *Expenses:* Contact institution. *Financial support:* In 2019–20, 959 students received support. Career-related internships or fieldwork, scholarships/grants, health care benefits, and unspecified assistantships available. Support available to part-time students. Financial award applicants required to submit FAFSA. *Unit head:* Dr. Doris Gomez, Dean, 757-352-4686, Fax: 757-352-4634, E-mail: dorigom@regent.edu. *Application contact:* Heidi Cece, Assistant Vice President for Enrollment Management, 800-373-5504, Fax: 757-352-4381, E-mail: admissions@regent.edu.
Website: https://www.regent.edu/school-of-business-and-leadership/

**Regis College,** Nursing and Health Sciences School, Weston, MA 02493. Offers applied behavior analysis (MS); counseling psychology (MA); health administration (MS); nurse practitioner (Certificate); nursing (MS, DNP); nursing education (Certificate); occupational therapy (MS). *Accreditation:* ACEN. *Program availability:* Part-time, evening/weekend, 100% online, blended/hybrid learning. *Degree requirements:* For doctorate, thesis/dissertation. *Entrance requirements:* For master's, minimum GPA of 3.0, official transcripts, recommendations, personal statement, resume/curriculum vitae, interview; for doctorate, GRE if GPA from master's lower than 3.5. Additional exam requirements/recommendations for international students: required—TOEFL (minimum score 560 paper-based; 79 iBT); recommended—IELTS (minimum score 6.5). *Application deadline:* Applications are processed on a rolling basis. Application fee: $75. Electronic applications accepted. *Financial support:* Federal Work-Study, scholarships/grants, and unspecified assistantships available. Support available to part-time students. Financial award applicants required to submit FAFSA. *Application contact:* Thomas May, Graduate Admission Counselor, 781-768-7162, E-mail: thomas.may@regiscollege.edu.

**Regis University,** College of Business and Economics, Denver, CO 80221-1099. Offers accounting (MS); executive leadership (Certificate); finance (MS); finance and accounting (MBA); health industry leadership (MBA); human resource management and leadership (MSOL); management (MBA); marketing (MBA); nonprofit leadership (Post-Graduate Certificate); nonprofit management (MNM); nonprofit organizational capacity building (Certificate); operations management (MBA); organizational leadership and

management (MSOL); project leadership and management (MS, MSOL); strategic business management (Certificate); strategic human resource integration (Certificate); strategic management (MBA). *Program availability:* Part-time, evening/weekend, 100% online, blended/hybrid learning. *Degree requirements:* For master's, thesis (for some programs), capstone or final research project. *Entrance requirements:* For master's, official transcript reflecting baccalaureate degree awarded from regionally-accredited college or university, interview, 2 years of full-time related work experience, resume, letters of recommendation. Additional exam requirements/recommendations for international students: required—TOEFL (minimum score 550 paper-based; 82 iBT). Electronic applications accepted. *Expenses:* Contact institution.

**Regis University,** Rueckert-Hartman College for Health Professions, Denver, CO 80221-1099. Offers advanced practice nurse (DNP); counseling (MA); counseling children and adolescents (Post-Graduate Certificate); counseling military families (Post-Graduate Certificate); depth psychotherapy (Post-Graduate Certificate); fellowship in orthopedic manual physical therapy (Certificate); health care business management (Certificate); health care quality and patient safety (Certificate); health industry leadership (MBA); health services administration (MS); marriage and family therapy (MA, Post-Graduate Certificate); neonatal nurse practitioner (MSN); nursing education (MSN); nursing leadership (MSN); occupational therapy (OTD); pharmacy (Pharm D); physical therapy (DPT). *Accreditation:* ACPE. *Program availability:* Part-time, evening/weekend, 100% online, blended/hybrid learning. *Degree requirements:* For master's, thesis (for some programs), internship. *Entrance requirements:* For master's, official transcript reflecting baccalaureate degree awarded from regionally-accredited college or university. Additional exam requirements/recommendations for international students: required—TOEFL (minimum score 550 paper-based; 82 iBT). Electronic applications accepted. *Expenses:* Contact institution.

**Rhode Island College,** School of Graduate Studies, School of Business, Marketing and Management Department, Providence, RI 02908-1991. Offers MS. *Program availability:* Part-time, evening/weekend. *Faculty:* 5 full-time (2 women), 4 part-time/adjunct (1 woman). *Students:* 2 full-time (1 woman), 33 part-time (17 women); includes 9 minority (2 Black or African American, non-Hispanic/Latino; 2 Asian, non-Hispanic/Latino; 5 Hispanic/Latino). Average age 37. In 2019, 6 master's awarded. *Entrance requirements:* For master's, GMAT or GRE, bachelor's degree from accredited college or university; official transcripts; Three professional or academic references. Additional exam requirements/recommendations for international students: required—TOEFL (minimum score 550 paper-based; 80 iBT). *Application deadline:* Applications are processed on a rolling basis. Application fee: $50. Electronic applications accepted. *Expenses: Tuition, area resident:* Part-time $462 per credit hour. Tuition, state resident: part-time $462 per credit hour. *Required fees:* $720. One-time fee: $140. *Financial support:* Research assistantships and teaching assistantships available. Financial award application deadline: 5/15; financial award applicants required to submit FAFSA. *Unit head:* Dr. Connie Milbourne, Chair, 401-456-8096, E-mail: cmilbourne@ric.edu. *Application contact:* Dr. Connie Milbourne, Chair, 401-456-8096, E-mail: cmilbourne@ric.edu.
Website: http://www.ric.edu/managementMarketing/Pages/default.aspx

**Rice University,** Graduate Programs, Wiess School–Professional Science Master's Programs, Professional Master's Program in Bioscience Research and Health Policy, Houston, TX 77251-1892. Offers MS.

**Robert Morris University Illinois,** Morris Graduate School of Management, Chicago, IL 60605. Offers accounting (MBA); accounting/finance (MBA); business analytics (MIS); health care administration (MM); higher education administration (MM); human performance (MS); human resource management (MBA); information security (MIS); information systems management (MIS); law enforcement administration (MM); management (MBA); management/finance (MBA); management/human resource management (MBA); sports administration (MM). *Program availability:* Part-time, evening/weekend. *Entrance requirements:* For master's, official transcripts and letters of recommendation (for some programs); written personal statement. Additional exam requirements/recommendations for international students: required—TOEFL (minimum score 550 paper-based). Electronic applications accepted.

**Roberts Wesleyan College,** Health Administration Programs, Rochester, NY 14624-1997. Offers health administration (MS); healthcare informatics administration (MS). *Program availability:* Evening/weekend, online learning. *Degree requirements:* For master's, thesis or alternative. *Entrance requirements:* For master's, minimum GPA of 3.0, verifiable work experience or recommendation.

**Rochester Institute of Technology,** Graduate Enrollment Services, College of Health Sciences and Technology, Health Sciences Department, Advanced Certificate Program in Health Care Finance, Rochester, NY 14623-5603. Offers Advanced Certificate. *Program availability:* Part-time, evening/weekend, online only, 100% online. *Entrance requirements:* For degree, minimum GPA of 3.0 (recommended). Additional exam requirements/recommendations for international students: required—TOEFL (minimum score 570 paper-based; 88 iBT), IELTS (minimum score 6.5), PTE (minimum score 61). Electronic applications accepted. *Expenses:* Contact institution.

**Rochester Institute of Technology,** Graduate Enrollment Services, College of Health Sciences and Technology, Health Sciences Department, MS Program in Health Systems Administration, Rochester, NY 14623-5603. Offers MS. *Program availability:* Part-time, evening/weekend, online only, 100% online. *Degree requirements:* For master's, thesis or alternative, capstone. *Entrance requirements:* For master's, minimum GPA of 3.0 (recommended); related professional work experience. Additional exam requirements/recommendations for international students: required—TOEFL (minimum score 570 paper-based; 88 iBT), IELTS (minimum score 6.5), PTE (minimum score 61). Electronic applications accepted. *Expenses:* Contact institution.

**Rockhurst University,** Helzberg School of Management, Kansas City, MO 64110-2561. Offers accounting (MBA); business intelligence (MBA, Certificate); business intelligence and analytics (MS); data science (MBA, Certificate); entrepreneurship (MBA); finance (MBA); fundraising leadership (MBA, Certificate); healthcare management (MBA, Certificate); human capital (Certificate); international business (Certificate); management (MA, MBA, Certificate); nonprofit administration (Certificate); organizational development (Certificate); science leadership (Certificate). *Accreditation:* AACSB. *Program availability:* Part-time, evening/weekend. *Entrance requirements:* For master's, GMAT or GRE. Additional exam requirements/recommendations for international students: required—TOEFL (minimum score 550 paper-based; 79 iBT). Electronic applications accepted.

**Roger Williams University,** School of Justice Studies, Bristol, RI 02809. Offers criminal justice (MS); cybersecurity (MS); leadership (MS), including health care administration (MPA, MS), public management (MPA, MS); public administration (MPA), including health care administration (MPA, MS), public management (MPA, MS); MS/JD. *Program availability:* Part-time, evening/weekend, 100% online, blended/hybrid learning. *Faculty:* 1 (woman) full-time, 5 part-time/adjunct (0 women). *Students:* 24 full-time (15 women), 109 part-time (59 women); includes 31 minority (9 Black or African American, non-Hispanic/Latino; 1 Asian, non-Hispanic/Latino; 17 Hispanic/Latino; 4 Two or more races, non-Hispanic/Latino), 2 international. Average age 34. 94 applicants, 83% accepted, 46 enrolled. In 2019, 46 master's awarded. *Degree requirements:* For master's, thesis. *Entrance requirements:* For master's, letter of intent, transcripts, two letters of recommendation, resume, background check (cybersecurity). Additional exam requirements/recommendations for international students: required—TOEFL (minimum score 85 paper-based), IELTS (minimum score 6.5). *Application deadline:* Applications are processed on a rolling basis. Application fee: $50. Electronic applications accepted. Application fee is waived when completed online. *Expenses: Tuition:* Full-time $15,768. *Required fees:* $900; $450. *Financial support:* In 2019–20, 8 students received support. Scholarships/grants and unspecified assistantships available. Financial award application deadline: 3/15; financial award applicants required to submit FAFSA. *Unit head:* Dr. Eric Bronson, Dean and Professor of Criminal Justice, 401-254-3336, E-mail: ebronson@rwu.edu. *Application contact:* Marcus Hanscom, Director of Graduate Admission, 401-254-3345, Fax: 401-254-3557, E-mail: gradadmit@rwu.edu.
Website: http://www.rwu.edu/academics/departments/criminaljustice.htm#graduate

**Rosalind Franklin University of Medicine and Science,** College of Health Professions, Department of Interprofessional Healthcare Studies, Healthcare Administration and Management Program, North Chicago, IL 60064-3095. Offers MS, Certificate. *Program availability:* Part-time, evening/weekend, online learning. *Degree requirements:* For master's, capstone portfolio. *Entrance requirements:* For master's, minimum GPA of 2.75, BS/BA from accredited college or university. Additional exam requirements/recommendations for international students: required—TOEFL.

**Rush University,** College of Health Sciences, Department of Health Systems Management, Chicago, IL 60612-3832. Offers MS, PhD. *Accreditation:* CAHME. *Program availability:* Part-time. *Degree requirements:* For master's, thesis. *Entrance requirements:* For master's, GMAT or GRE General Test, previous undergraduate course work in accounting and statistics. Additional exam requirements/recommendations for international students: required—TOEFL. *Application deadline:* For fall admission, 2/15 for domestic students. Electronic applications accepted. *Financial support:* Career-related internships or fieldwork, Federal Work-Study, institutionally sponsored loans, scholarships/grants, and traineeships available. Support available to part-time students. Financial award applicants required to submit FAFSA. *Application contact:* Dr. Andrew N. Garman, Director, 312-942-5402, Fax: 312-942-4957, E-mail: andy_n_garman@rush.edu.
Website: http://www.rushu.rush.edu/hsm

**Rutgers University - Camden,** School of Public Health, Stratford, NJ 08084. Offers general public health (Certificate); health systems and policy (MPH); DO/MPH. *Program availability:* Part-time, evening/weekend. *Degree requirements:* For master's, thesis, internship. *Entrance requirements:* For master's, GRE General Test. Additional exam requirements/recommendations for international students: required—TOEFL. Electronic applications accepted.

**Rutgers University - Newark,** Graduate School, Program in Public Administration, Newark, NJ 07102. Offers health care administration (MPA); human resources administration (MPA); public administration (PhD); public management (MPA); public policy analysis (MPA); urban systems and issues (MPA). *Accreditation:* NASPAA (one or more programs are accredited). *Program availability:* Part-time, evening/weekend. *Degree requirements:* For master's, comprehensive exam, thesis or alternative; for doctorate, thesis/dissertation. *Entrance requirements:* For master's, GRE, minimum undergraduate B average; for doctorate, GRE, MPA, minimum B average. Electronic applications accepted.

**Rutgers University - Newark,** Rutgers Business School–Newark and New Brunswick, Program in Healthcare Services Management, Newark, NJ 07102. Offers MHSM.

**Rutgers University - Newark,** School of Health Related Professions, Department of Interdisciplinary Studies, Program in Health Care Management, Newark, NJ 07102. Offers MS. *Program availability:* Part-time, evening/weekend, online learning. *Entrance requirements:* For master's, minimum GPA of 3.0, bachelor's degree, statement of career goals, curriculum vitae, transcript of highest degree. Additional exam requirements/recommendations for international students: required—TOEFL (minimum score 500 paper-based; 79 iBT). Electronic applications accepted.

**Rutgers University - Newark,** School of Public Health, Newark, NJ 07107-1709. Offers clinical epidemiology (Certificate); dental public health (MPH); general public health (Certificate); public policy and oral health services administration (Certificate); quantitative methods (MPH); urban health (MPH); DMD/MPH; MD/MPH; MS/MPH. *Program availability:* Part-time, evening/weekend. *Degree requirements:* For master's, thesis, internship. *Entrance requirements:* For master's, GRE General Test. Additional exam requirements/recommendations for international students: required—TOEFL. Electronic applications accepted.

**Rutgers University - New Brunswick,** School of Public Health, Piscataway, NJ 08854. Offers biostatistics (MPH, MS, Dr PH, PhD); clinical epidemiology (Certificate); environmental and occupational health (MPH, Dr PH, PhD, Certificate); epidemiology (MPH, Dr PH, PhD); general public health (Certificate); health education and behavioral science (MPH, Dr PH, PhD); health systems and policy (MPH, PhD); public health (MPH, Dr PH, PhD); public health preparedness (Certificate); DO/MPH; JD/MPH; MBA/MPH; MD/MPH; MPH/MBA; MPH/MSPA; MS/MPH; Psy D/MPH. *Accreditation:* CEPH. *Program availability:* Part-time, evening/weekend. *Degree requirements:* For master's, thesis, internship; for doctorate, comprehensive exam, thesis/dissertation. *Entrance requirements:* For master's, GRE General Test; for doctorate, GRE General Test, MPH (Dr PH); MA, MPH, or MS (PhD). Additional exam requirements/recommendations for international students: required—TOEFL. Electronic applications accepted.

**Sage Graduate School,** School of Management, Program in Health Services Administration, Troy, NY 12180-4115. Offers gerontology (MS). *Program availability:* Part-time, evening/weekend, 100% online, blended/hybrid learning. *Faculty:* 5 full-time (3 women), 4 part-time/adjunct (1 woman). *Students:* 5 full-time (all women), 10 part-time (7 women); includes 4 minority (1 Black or African American, non-Hispanic/Latino; 1 Asian, non-Hispanic/Latino; 1 Hispanic/Latino; 1 Two or more races, non-Hispanic/Latino). Average age 32. 33 applicants, 30% accepted, 7 enrolled. In 2019, 10 master's awarded. *Entrance requirements:* For master's, application, minimum GPA 2.75, current resume, 2 letters of recommendation, career goals essay, official transcripts from each previous college attended. Additional exam requirements/recommendations for international students: required—TOEFL (minimum score 550 paper-based). *Application deadline:* Applications are processed on a rolling basis. Application fee: $30. Electronic applications accepted. *Expenses: Tuition:* Part-time $730 per credit hour. Tuition and fees vary according to course load, degree level and program. *Financial support:* Fellowships, research assistantships, and unspecified assistantships available. Financial award application deadline: 3/1; financial award applicants required to submit FAFSA. *Unit head:* Dr. Kimberly Fredericks, Dean, School of Management, 518-292-1782, Fax: 518-292-1964, E-mail: fredek1@sage.edu. *Application contact:* Michael Jones, SR Associate Director of Graduate Enrollment Management, 518-292-8615, Fax: 518-292-1912, E-mail: jonesm4@sage.edu.

**Saginaw Valley State University,** College of Health and Human Services, Program in Health Leadership, University Center, MI 48710. Offers MS. *Program availability:* Part-time, evening/weekend. *Students:* 36 part-time (21 women); includes 5 minority (2 Black or African American, non-Hispanic/Latino; 1 Asian, non-Hispanic/Latino; 2 Hispanic/Latino), 9 international. Average age 38. 16 applicants, 100% accepted, 14 enrolled. In 2019, 23 master's awarded. *Entrance requirements:* For master's, minimum GPA of 3.0.

Additional exam requirements/recommendations for international students: required—TOEFL (minimum score 580 paper-based; 92 iBT). *Application deadline:* For fall admission, 7/15 for international students; for winter admission, 11/15 for international students; for spring admission, 4/15 for international students. Applications are processed on a rolling basis. Application fee: $30 ($90 for international students). Electronic applications accepted. *Expenses: Tuition, area resident:* Full-time $11,212; part-time $622.90 per credit hour. Tuition, state resident: full-time $11,212; part-time $622.90 per credit hour. Tuition, nonresident: full-time $11,212; part-time $1253 per credit hour. *Required fees:* $263; $14.60 per credit hour. Tuition and fees vary according to course load, degree level and program. *Financial support:* Federal Work-Study and scholarships/grants available. Support available to part-time students. *Unit head:* Dr. Marilyn Skrocki, Program Coordinator, 989-964-7394, E-mail: mskrocki@svsu.edu. *Application contact:* Jenna Briggs, Director, Graduate and International Admissions, 989-964-6096, Fax: 989-964-2788, E-mail: gradadm@svsu.edu.

**St. Ambrose University,** College of Business, Program in Business Administration, Davenport, IA 52803-2898. Offers business administration (DBA); health care (MBA); human resources (MBA). *Accreditation:* ACBSP. *Program availability:* Part-time, evening/weekend. *Degree requirements:* For master's, comprehensive exam (for some programs), thesis or alternative, capstone seminar; for doctorate, comprehensive exam, thesis/dissertation, oral and written exams. *Entrance requirements:* For master's, GMAT; for doctorate, GMAT, master's degree. Additional exam requirements/recommendations for international students: required—TOEFL. Electronic applications accepted. *Expenses:* Contact institution.

**St. Catherine University,** Graduate Programs, Program in Business Administration, St. Paul, MN 55105. Offers healthcare (MBA); integrated marketing communications (MBA); management (MBA). *Program availability:* Part-time, evening/weekend. *Entrance requirements:* For master's, GMAT (if undergraduate GPA is less than 3.0), 2+ years' work or volunteer experience in professional setting(s). Additional exam requirements/recommendations for international students: required—TOEFL. *Expenses:* Contact institution.

**St. Joseph's College, Long Island Campus,** Programs in Health Care Administration, Field in Health Care Management, Patchogue, NY 11772-2399. Offers MBA. *Program availability:* Part-time, evening/weekend, 100% online, blended/hybrid learning. *Faculty:* 10 full-time (4 women), 18 part-time/adjunct (7 women). *Students:* 2 part-time (both women); both minorities (1 Black or African American, non-Hispanic/Latino; 1 Hispanic/Latino). Average age 26. *Entrance requirements:* For master's, Application, official transcripts, 2 letters of recommendation, current resume, 250 word written statement. Additional exam requirements/recommendations for international students: required—TOEFL (minimum score 80 iBT). *Application deadline:* Applications are processed on a rolling basis. Application fee: $25. Electronic applications accepted. *Expenses: Tuition:* Full-time $19,350; part-time $1075 per credit. *Required fees:* $410. *Unit head:* John Sardelis, Associate Chair and Professor, 631-687-1493, E-mail: jsardelis@sjcny.edu. *Application contact:* John Sardelis, Associate Chair and Professor, 631-687-1493, E-mail: jsardelis@sjcny.edu.
Website: https://www.sjcny.edu/long-island/academics/graduate/degree/health-care-management

**St. Joseph's College, Long Island Campus,** Programs in Management, Field in Health Care Management, Patchogue, NY 11772-2399. Offers MS. *Program availability:* Part-time, evening/weekend, 100% online, blended/hybrid learning. *Faculty:* 10 full-time (4 women), 18 part-time/adjunct (7 women). *Students:* 14 full-time (13 women), 69 part-time (59 women); includes 30 minority (12 Black or African American, non-Hispanic/Latino; 6 Asian, non-Hispanic/Latino; 11 Hispanic/Latino; 1 Two or more races, non-Hispanic/Latino). Average age 34. 91 applicants, 42% accepted, 25 enrolled. In 2019, 20 master's awarded. *Entrance requirements:* For master's, Application, official transcripts, 2 letters of recommendation, current resume, 250 word written statement. Additional exam requirements/recommendations for international students: required—TOEFL (minimum score 80 iBT). *Application deadline:* Applications are processed on a rolling basis. Application fee: $25. Electronic applications accepted. *Expenses: Tuition:* Full-time $19,350; part-time $1075 per credit. *Required fees:* $410. *Financial support:* In 2019–20, 13 students received support. *Unit head:* Mary A. Chance, Assistant Professor, Director of Graduate Management Studies, 631-687-1297, E-mail: mchance@sjcny.edu. *Application contact:* Mary A. Chance, Assistant Professor, Director of Graduate Management Studies, 631-687-1297, E-mail: mchance@sjcny.edu.
Website: https://www.sjcny.edu/long-island/academics/graduate/degree/management-health-care-management-concentration

**St. Joseph's College, New York,** Programs in Health Care Administration, Field in Health Care Management, Brooklyn, NY 11205-3688. Offers MBA. *Program availability:* Part-time, evening/weekend, 100% online, blended/hybrid learning. *Faculty:* 6 full-time (3 women), 11 part-time/adjunct (7 women). *Students:* 3 part-time (2 women); includes 2 minority (1 Black or African American, non-Hispanic/Latino; 1 Hispanic/Latino). Average age 44. In 2019, 2 master's awarded. *Entrance requirements:* For master's, Application, 2 letters of recommendation, current resume, 250 word essay, official transcripts. Additional exam requirements/recommendations for international students: required—TOEFL (minimum score 80 iBT). *Application deadline:* Applications are processed on a rolling basis. Application fee: $25. Electronic applications accepted. *Expenses: Tuition:* Full-time $19,350; part-time $1075 per credit. *Required fees:* $400. *Financial support:* In 2019–20, 1 student received support. *Unit head:* Dr. Lauren Pete, Chair, 718-940-5890, E-mail: lpete@sjcny.edu. *Application contact:* Dr. Lauren Pete, Chair, 718-940-5890, E-mail: lpete@sjcny.edu.
Website: https://www.sjcny.edu/brooklyn/academics/graduate/graduate-degrees/health-care-management

**St. Joseph's College, New York,** Programs in Health Care Administration, Field in Health Care Management - Health Information Systems, Brooklyn, NY 11205-3688. Offers MBA. *Program availability:* Part-time, evening/weekend, 100% online, blended/hybrid learning. *Faculty:* 6 full-time (3 women), 11 part-time/adjunct (7 women). *Students:* 7 part-time (6 women); includes 5 minority (3 Black or African American, non-Hispanic/Latino; 1 Asian, non-Hispanic/Latino; 1 Hispanic/Latino). Average age 37. 2 applicants, 50% accepted. In 2019, 5 master's awarded. *Entrance requirements:* For master's, Application, 2 letters of recommendation, current resume, 250 word essay, official transcripts. Additional exam requirements/recommendations for international students: required—TOEFL (minimum score 80 iBT). *Application deadline:* Applications are processed on a rolling basis. Application fee: $25. Electronic applications accepted. *Expenses: Tuition:* Full-time $19,350; part-time $1075 per credit. *Required fees:* $400. *Financial support:* In 2019–20, 1 student received support. *Unit head:* Dr. Lauren Pete, Chair, 718-940-5890, E-mail: lpete@sjcny.edu. *Application contact:* Dr. Lauren Pete, Chair, 718-940-5890, E-mail: lpete@sjcny.edu.
Website: https://www.sjcny.edu/brooklyn/academics/graduate/graduate-degrees/health-care-management-health-info-sys-concentration

**St. Joseph's College, New York,** Programs in Management, Field in Health Care Management, Brooklyn, NY 11205-3688. Offers MBA. *Program availability:* Part-time, evening/weekend, 100% online, blended/hybrid learning. *Faculty:* 6 full-time (3 women), 11 part-time/adjunct (7 women). *Students:* 6 full-time (5 women), 20 part-time (14 women); includes 20 minority (11 Black or African American, non-Hispanic/Latino; 1 Asian, non-Hispanic/Latino; 8 Hispanic/Latino), 1 international. Average age 34. 19 applicants, 63% accepted, 7 enrolled. In 2019, 12 master's awarded. *Entrance requirements:* For master's, Application, 2 letters of recommendation, current resume, 250 word essay, official transcripts. Additional exam requirements/recommendations for international students: required—TOEFL (minimum score 80 iBT). *Application deadline:* Applications are processed on a rolling basis. Application fee: $25. Electronic applications accepted. *Expenses: Tuition:* Full-time $19,350; part-time $1075 per credit. *Required fees:* $400. *Financial support:* In 2019–20, 1 student received support. *Unit head:* Dr. Lauren Pete, Associate Professor/Chair, 718-940-5890, E-mail: lpete@sjcny.edu. *Application contact:* Dr. Lauren Pete, Associate Professor/Chair, 718-940-5890, E-mail: lpete@sjcny.edu.
Website: https://www.sjcny.edu/brooklyn/academics/graduate/graduate-degrees/management-health-care-management-concentration

**Saint Joseph's College of Maine,** Master of Health Administration Program, Standish, ME 04084. Offers MHA. *Program availability:* Part-time, online learning. *Entrance requirements:* For master's, two years of experience in health care. Electronic applications accepted.

**Saint Joseph's University,** Erivan K. Haub School of Business, MBA Program, Philadelphia, PA 19131-1395. Offers accounting (MBA); business intelligence analytics (MBA); finance (MBA); financial analysis reporting (Postbaccalaureate Certificate); general business (MBA); health and medical services administration (MBA); international business (MBA); international marketing (MBA); leading (MBA); marketing (MBA); DO/MBA. *Program availability:* Part-time-only, evening/weekend, 100% online. *Degree requirements:* For master's, minimum GPA of 3.0. *Entrance requirements:* For master's, GMAT or GRE, 2 letters of recommendation, resume, personal statement, official undergraduate and graduate transcripts. Additional exam requirements/recommendations for international students: required—PTE, TOEFL, IELTS, or PTE. Electronic applications accepted. *Expenses:* Contact institution.

**Saint Joseph's University,** School of Health Studies and Education, Department of Health Services, Philadelphia, PA 19131-1395. Offers health administration (MS); health informatics (MS); organizations development and leadership (MS). *Program availability:* Part-time, evening/weekend. *Entrance requirements:* For master's, GRE (if GPA less than 2.75), 2 letters of recommendation, resume, personal statement, official transcripts. Additional exam requirements/recommendations for international students: required—TOEFL (minimum score 550 paper-based; 80 iBT), IELTS (minimum score 6.5). Electronic applications accepted. *Expenses:* Contact institution.

**Saint Leo University,** Graduate Studies in Business, Saint Leo, FL 33574-6665. Offers accounting (M Acc); cybersecurity management (MBA); health care management (MBA); human resource management (MBA); marketing (MBA); marketing research and social media analytics (MBA); software engineering (MS). *Accreditation:* ACBSP. *Program availability:* Part-time, evening/weekend, 100% online, blended/hybrid learning. *Faculty:* 51 full-time (15 women), 45 part-time/adjunct (18 women). *Students:* 8 full-time (2 women), 1,963 part-time (1,176 women); includes 1,147 minority (580 Black or African American, non-Hispanic/Latino; 8 American Indian or Alaska Native, non-Hispanic/Latino; 43 Asian, non-Hispanic/Latino; 250 Hispanic/Latino; 4 Native Hawaiian or other Pacific Islander, non-Hispanic/Latino; 262 Two or more races, non-Hispanic/Latino), 96 international. Average age 37. 818 applicants, 78% accepted, 424 enrolled. In 2019, 766 master's, 14 doctorates awarded. *Degree requirements:* For doctorate, comprehensive exam, thesis/dissertation. *Entrance requirements:* For master's, GMAT with minimum score 500 (for M Acc), official transcripts, current resume, 2 professional recommendations, personal statement, bachelor's degree from regionally-accredited university; undergraduate degree in accounting and minimum undergraduate GPA of 3.0 (for M Acc); minimum undergraduate GPA of 3.0 in final 2 years of undergraduate study and 2 years' work experience (for MBA); for doctorate, GMAT (minimum score of 550) if master's GPA is under 3.25, official transcripts, current resume, 2 professional recommendations, personal statement, master's degree from regionally-accredited university with minimum GPA of 3.25, 3 years' work experience, interview. Additional exam requirements/recommendations for international students: required—TOEFL (minimum score 550 paper-based; 78 iBT). *Application deadline:* For fall admission, 7/1 priority date for domestic and international students; for spring admission, 11/12 priority date for domestic students, 11/1 for international students. Applications are processed on a rolling basis. Electronic applications accepted. *Expenses:* DBA $16,350 per FT yr., MS Cybersecurity $14,010 per FT yr. *Financial support:* In 2019–20, 1,510 students received support. Scholarships/grants, unspecified assistantships, and tuition remission for Saint Leo employees and their dependents available. Financial award application deadline: 3/1; financial award applicants required to submit FAFSA. *Unit head:* Dr. Robyn Parker, Dean, School of Business, 352-588-8599, Fax: 352-588-8912, E-mail: mbaslu@saintleo.edu. *Application contact:* Saint Leo University Office of Graduate Admissions, 800-707-8846, Fax: 352-588-7873, E-mail: grad.admissions@saintleo.edu.
Website: https://www.saintleo.edu/college-of-business

**Saint Louis University,** Graduate Programs, College for Public Health and Social Justice, Department of Health Management and Policy, St. Louis, MO 63103. Offers health administration (MHA); health policy (MPH); public health studies (PhD). *Accreditation:* CAHME. *Program availability:* Part-time. *Degree requirements:* For master's, comprehensive exam, internship. *Entrance requirements:* For master's, GMAT or GRE General Test, LSAT, MCAT, letters of recommendation, resume. Additional exam requirements/recommendations for international students: required—TOEFL (minimum score 525 paper-based).

**Saint Mary-of-the-Woods College,** Master of Healthcare Administration Program, Saint Mary of the Woods, IN 47876. Offers MHA. *Program availability:* Part-time. *Faculty:* 1 (woman) full-time, 4 part-time/adjunct (all women). *Students:* 8 full-time (5 women), 1 (woman) part-time; includes 3 minority (1 Black or African American, non-Hispanic/Latino; 2 Two or more races, non-Hispanic/Latino). Average age 33. 7 applicants, 100% accepted, 5 enrolled. In 2019, 9 master's awarded. *Entrance requirements:* Additional exam requirements/recommendations for international students: required—TOEFL (minimum score 500 paper-based; 62 iBT), Other English proficiency tests may be accepted and will be reviewed on a case-by-case basis. *Application deadline:* Applications are processed on a rolling basis. Tuition and fees vary according to course load and program. *Financial support:* In 2019–20, 6 students received support. Scholarships/grants available. Financial award applicants required to submit FAFSA. *Unit head:* Dr. Michelle Ruiz, Assistant Professor, Healthcare Administration Program Director, 812-535-5112, E-mail: Michelle.Ruiz@smwc.edu. *Application contact:* Office of Admissions, 800-926-7692, E-mail: admissions@smwc.edu.
Website: https://www.smwc.edu/academics/departments/graduate-studies/master-healthcare-administration/

**Saint Mary's University of Minnesota,** Schools of Graduate and Professional Programs, Graduate School of Health and Human Services, Health and Human Services Administration Program, Winona, MN 55987-1399. Offers MA. *Unit head:* Amy Heinz, Director, 612-238-4549, E-mail: sdoherty@smumn.edu. *Application contact:* Laurie Roy, Director of Admission of Schools of Graduate and Professional Programs, 507-457-8606, Fax: 612-728-5121, E-mail: lroy@smumn.edu.

## Health Services Management and Hospital Administration

Website: http://www.smumn.edu/graduate-home/areas-of-study/graduate-school-of-health-human-services/ma-in-health-human-services-administration

**St. Norbert College,** Master of Business Administration Program, De Pere, WI 54115-2099. Offers business (MBA); health care (MBA); supply chain and manufacturing (MBA). *Program availability:* Part-time-only, evening/weekend. *Faculty:* 11 full-time (2 women), 4 part-time/adjunct (0 women). *Students:* 52 (29 women); includes 4 minority (all American Indian or Alaska Native, non-Hispanic/Latino). Average age 33. 23 applicants, 39% accepted, 9 enrolled. In 2019, 18 master's awarded. *Entrance requirements:* For master's, official transcripts, letters of recommendation, professional resume, essay. *Application deadline:* For fall admission, 7/31 for domestic students; for winter admission, 12/1 for domestic students; for spring admission, 1/1 for domestic students; for summer admission, 4/15 for domestic students. Applications are processed on a rolling basis. Application fee: $50. Electronic applications accepted. Application fee is waived when completed online. *Expenses:* $750 per credit tuition; $37.50 per course technology fee; $337.50 per credit for audit-only course; $1,500 for textbooks for entire program (estimated cost); $100 graduation application fee. *Financial support:* Application deadline: 1/1; applicants required to submit FAFSA. *Unit head:* Dr. Daniel Heiser, Dean of the Schneider School of Business and Economics, 920-403-3440, E-mail: dan.heiser@snc.edu. *Application contact:* Brenda Busch, Associate Director of Graduate Recruitment, 920-403-3942, E-mail: brenda.busch@snc.edu.
Website: https://schneiderschool.snc.edu/academics/mba/index.html

**Saint Peter's University,** Graduate Business Programs, MBA Program, Jersey City, NJ 07306-5997. Offers finance (MBA); health care administration (MBA); human resource management (MBA); international business (MBA); management (MBA); management information systems (MBA); marketing (MBA); risk management (MBA); MBA/MS. *Program availability:* Part-time, evening/weekend. *Entrance requirements:* Additional exam requirements/recommendations for international students: required—TOEFL. Electronic applications accepted.

**St. Thomas University - Florida,** School of Business, Department of Management, Miami Gardens, FL 33054-6459. Offers accounting (MBA); general management (MSM, Certificate); health management (MBA, MSM, Certificate); human resource management (MBA, MSM, Certificate); international business (MBA, MIB, MSM, Certificate); justice administration (MSM, Certificate); management accounting (MSM, Certificate); public management (MSM, Certificate); sports administration (MS). *Program availability:* Part-time, evening/weekend. *Degree requirements:* For master's, comprehensive exam. *Entrance requirements:* For master's, interview, minimum GPA of 3.0 or GMAT. Additional exam requirements/recommendations for international students: required—TOEFL (minimum score 550 paper-based; 79 iBT). Electronic applications accepted.

**Saint Xavier University,** Graduate Studies, Graham School of Management, Chicago, IL 60655-3105. Offers employee health benefits (Certificate); finance (MBA); financial fraud examination and management (MBA, Certificate); financial planning (MBA, Certificate); generalist/individualized (MBA); health administration (MBA); managed care (Certificate); management (MBA); marketing (MBA); project management (MBA, Certificate); MBA/MS. *Accreditation:* AACSB. *Program availability:* Part-time, evening/weekend. *Entrance requirements:* For master's, GMAT, minimum GPA of 3.0, 2 years of work experience. Electronic applications accepted. *Expenses:* Contact institution.

**Salve Regina University,** Program in Business Administration, Newport, RI 02840-4192. Offers cybersecurity issues in business (MBA); entrepreneurial enterprise (MBA); health care administration and management (MBA); nonprofit management (MBA); social ventures (MBA). *Program availability:* Part-time, evening/weekend, online learning. *Entrance requirements:* For master's, GMAT, GRE General Test, or MAT, 6 undergraduate credits each in accounting, economics, quantitative analysis and calculus or statistics. Additional exam requirements/recommendations for international students: required—TOEFL (minimum score 600 paper-based; 100 iBT) or IELTS. Electronic applications accepted.

**Salve Regina University,** Program in Healthcare Administration and Management, Newport, RI 02840-4192. Offers MS, CGS. *Program availability:* Part-time, evening/weekend, online learning. *Degree requirements:* For master's, internship. *Entrance requirements:* For master's, GMAT, GRE General Test, or MAT, health care work experience or 250 internship hours. Additional exam requirements/recommendations for international students: required—TOEFL (minimum score 600 paper-based; 100 iBT) or IELTS. Electronic applications accepted.

**Samford University,** School of Public Health, Birmingham, AL 35229. Offers health informatics (MSHI); healthcare administration (MHA); nutrition (MS); public health (MPH); social work (MSW). *Accreditation:* CSWE. *Program availability:* Part-time, online only, 100% online. *Faculty:* 16 full-time (9 women), 5 part-time/adjunct (4 women). *Students:* 76 full-time (71 women), 16 part-time (14 women); includes 19 minority (14 Black or African American, non-Hispanic/Latino; 1 Asian, non-Hispanic/Latino; 1 Hispanic/Latino; 3 Two or more races, non-Hispanic/Latino). Average age 28. 74 applicants, 78% accepted, 39 enrolled. In 2019, 51 master's awarded. *Degree requirements:* For master's, capstone course. *Entrance requirements:* For master's, GRE, MAT, recommendations, resume, personal statement, transcripts, application. Additional exam requirements/recommendations for international students: required—TOEFL (minimum score 590 paper-based; 90 iBT), IELTS (minimum score 6.5). *Application deadline:* For fall admission, 10/1 for domestic students; for winter admission, 12/1 for domestic students; for spring admission, 5/1 for domestic students. Applications are processed on a rolling basis. Application fee: $75. Electronic applications accepted. *Expenses:* Tuition: Full-time $17,754; part-time $862 per credit hour. *Required fees:* $550; $550 per unit. Full-time tuition and fees vary according to course load, program and student level. *Financial support:* In 2019–20, 30 students received support. Scholarships/grants available. Financial award application deadline: 5/1; financial award applicants required to submit FAFSA. *Unit head:* Dr. Keith Elder, Ph.D., Dean, School of Public Health, 205-726-4655, E-mail: kelder@samford.edu. *Application contact:* Dr. Marian Carter, Ed.D, Assistant Dean of Enrollment Management, 205-726-2611, E-mail: mwcarter@samford.edu.
Website: http://www.samford.edu/publichealth

**San Diego State University,** Graduate and Research Affairs, College of Health and Human Services, School of Public Health, San Diego, CA 92182. Offers environmental health (MPH); epidemiology (MPH, PhD), including biostatistics (MPH); global emergency preparedness and response (MS); global health (PhD); health behavior (PhD); health promotion (MPH); health services administration (MPH); toxicology (MS); MPH/MA; MSW/MPH. *Accreditation:* CAHME (one or more programs are accredited); CEPH. *Program availability:* Part-time. *Degree requirements:* For master's, comprehensive exam (for some programs), thesis (for some programs); for doctorate, thesis/dissertation. *Entrance requirements:* For master's, GMAT (MPH in health services administration), GRE General Test; for doctorate, GRE General Test. Additional exam requirements/recommendations for international students: required—TOEFL.

**San Francisco State University,** Division of Graduate Studies, Lam Family College of Business, Program in Business Administration, San Francisco, CA 94132-1722. Offers decision sciences/operations research (MBA); ethics and compliance (MBA); finance (MBA); global business and innovation (MBA); healthcare administration (MBA);

hospitality and tourism management (MBA); information systems (MBA); leadership (MBA); marketing (MBA); nonprofit and social enterprise leadership (MBA); sustainable business (MBA). *Accreditation:* AACSB. *Program availability:* Part-time, evening/weekend. *Degree requirements:* For master's, thesis, essay test. *Entrance requirements:* For master's, GMAT, minimum GPA of 2.7 in last 60 units. Additional exam requirements/recommendations for international students: required—TOEFL (minimum score 550 paper-based). *Application deadline:* For fall admission, 5/1 priority date for domestic students, 4/1 for international students; for spring admission, 11/1 for domestic students, 10/15 for international students. Applications are processed on a rolling basis. Application fee: $55. *Expenses: Tuition, area resident:* Full-time $7176; part-time $4164 per year. Tuition, state resident: full-time $7176; part-time $4164 per year. Tuition, nonresident: full-time $16,680; part-time $396 per unit. *International tuition:* $16,680 full-time. *Required fees:* $1524; $1524 per unit. $762 per semester. Tuition and fees vary according to degree level and program. *Financial support:* Application deadline: 3/1. *Unit head:* Dr. Sanjit Sengupta, Faculty Director, 415-817-4366, Fax: 415-817-4340, E-mail: sengupta@sfsu.edu. *Application contact:* Christopher Kingston, Director of Student Advising, 415-817-4322, Fax: 415-817-4340, E-mail: cak@sfsu.edu.
Website: http://cob.sfsu.edu/graduate-programs/mba

**Seton Hall University,** College of Nursing, South Orange, NJ 07079-2697. Offers advanced practice in primary health care (MSN, DNP), including adult/gerontological nurse practitioner, pediatric nurse practitioner; entry into practice (MSN); health systems administration (MSN, DNP); nursing (PhD); nursing case management (MSN); nursing education (MA); school nurse (MSN); MSN/MA. *Accreditation:* AACN. *Program availability:* Part-time, online learning. *Degree requirements:* For master's, research project; for doctorate, dissertation or scholarly project. *Entrance requirements:* For doctorate, GRE (waived for students with GPA of 3.5 or higher). Additional exam requirements/recommendations for international students: required—TOEFL. Electronic applications accepted.

**Seton Hall University,** School of Health and Medical Sciences, Program in Healthcare Administration, South Orange, NJ 07079-2697. Offers MHA. *Program availability:* Part-time, evening/weekend, online learning. *Entrance requirements:* For master's, GMAT, GRE General Test, or LSAT.

**Seton Hill University,** MBA Program, Greensburg, PA 15601. Offers entrepreneurship (MBA); forensic accounting and fraud examination (MBA); healthcare administration (MBA); management (MBA). *Program availability:* Part-time, evening/weekend. *Students:* 103. *Entrance requirements:* For master's, resume, 3 letters of recommendation, personal statement, transcripts. Additional exam requirements/recommendations for international students: required—TOEFL (minimum score 600 paper-based; 100 iBT), IELTS (minimum score 6.5). *Application deadline:* For fall admission, 8/10 for domestic students; 8/1 for international students; for spring admission, 12/10 for domestic students, 12/1 for international students. Applications are processed on a rolling basis. Electronic applications accepted. Application fee is waived when completed online. *Expenses:* Tuition: Full-time $29,196; part-time $811 per credit. *Required fees:* $550; $100 per unit. $25 per semester. Tuition and fees vary according to class time, course level, course load, degree level, campus/location, program, reciprocity agreements, student level and student's religious affiliation. *Financial support:* Federal Work-Study, scholarships/grants, unspecified assistantships, and tuition discounts available. Financial award application deadline: 8/15; financial award applicants required to submit FAFSA. *Unit head:* Dr. Douglas Nelson, Associate Professor, Business/MBA Program Director, E-mail: dnelson@setonhill.edu. *Application contact:* Ellen Monnich, Assistant Director, Graduate & Adult Studies, 724-838-4208, E-mail: monnich@setonhill.edu.
Website: www.setonhill.edu/mba

**Shenandoah University,** Eleanor Wade Custer School of Nursing, Winchester, VA 22601. Offers adult gerontology primary care nurse practitioner (Graduate Certificate); adult-gerontology primary care nurse practitioner (MSN); family nurse practitioner (MSN, DNP, Graduate Certificate); general (MSN); health systems leadership (DNP); health systems management (MSN, Graduate Certificate); nurse midwifery (MSN); nurse-midwifery (Graduate Certificate); nursing education (Graduate Certificate); nursing practice (DNP); psychiatric mental health nurse practitioner (MSN, DNP, Graduate Certificate). *Accreditation:* AACN; ACNM/ACME. *Entrance requirements:* For master's, United States RN license; minimum GPA of 3.0; 2080 hours of clinical experience; curriculum vitae; 3 letters of recommendation from former dean, faculty member, or advisor familiar with the applicant, and a former or current supervisor; two-to-three-page essay on a specified topic; for doctorate, MSN, minimum GPA of 3.0, 3 letters of recommendation, interview, BSN, two-to-three page essay on a specific topic, 500-word statement of clinical practice research interest, resume, current U.S. RN license, 2080 clinical hours; for Graduate Certificate, MSN, minimum GPA of 3.0, 2 letters of recommendation, minimum of one year (2080 hours) of clinical nursing experience, interview, two-to-three page essay on a specific topic, resume, current United States RN license. Additional exam requirements/recommendations for international students: required—TOEFL (minimum score 558 paper-based; 83 iBT). Electronic applications accepted. *Expenses:* Contact institution.

**Shippensburg University of Pennsylvania,** School of Graduate Studies, John L. Grove College of Business, Shippensburg, PA 17257-2299. Offers advanced studies in business (Certificate); advanced supply chain and logistics management (Certificate); business administration (MBA, DBA), including business administration (MBA), business analytics (MBA), finance (MBA), healthcare management (MBA), management information systems (MBA), supply chain management (MBA); finance (Certificate); health care management (Certificate); management information systems (Certificate). *Accreditation:* AACSB. *Program availability:* Part-time, evening/weekend, 100% online, blended/hybrid learning. *Faculty:* 21 full-time (4 women). *Students:* 46 full-time (23 women), 156 part-time (59 women); includes 35 minority (12 Black or African American, non-Hispanic/Latino; 6 Asian, non-Hispanic/Latino; 12 Hispanic/Latino; 5 Two or more races, non-Hispanic/Latino), 8 international. Average age 32. 192 applicants, 58% accepted, 71 enrolled. In 2019, 89 master's awarded. *Degree requirements:* For master's, comprehensive exam (for some programs), thesis optional, practicum capstone course; for doctorate, comprehensive exam, thesis/dissertation, comprehensive exam dissertation. *Entrance requirements:* For master's, GMAT (minimum score 450 if less than 5 years of mid-level experience, including management experience), current resume; relevant work/classroom experience; 500-word statement of purpose; prerequisites of quantitative analysis, computer usage, and oral and written communications; laptop computer; for doctorate, GMAT (minimum score of 600 if less than 5 years of substantive professional or teaching experience), 2 letters of recommendation from professionals in academia or industry; 2-3 page personal and professional statement; interview; resume. Additional exam requirements/recommendations for international students: required—TOEFL (minimum score 550 paper-based; 68 iBT), IELTS (minimum score 6), TOEFL (minimum score 550 paper-based, 68 iBT) or IELTS (minimum score 6). *Application deadline:* For fall admission, 4/30 for international students; for spring admission, 9/30 for international students. Applications are processed on a rolling basis. Application fee: $45. Electronic applications accepted. *Expenses:* Tuition, state resident: part-time $516 per credit.

## Health Services Management and Hospital Administration

Tuition, nonresident: part-time $774 per credit. *Required fees:* $149 per credit. *Financial support:* In 2019–20, 22 students received support. Career-related internships or fieldwork, scholarships/grants, unspecified assistantships, and resident hall director and student payroll positions available. Support available to part-time students. Financial award application deadline: 3/1; financial award applicants required to submit FAFSA. *Unit head:* Dr. John G. Kooti, Dean of the College of Business, 717-477-1435, Fax: 717-477-4003, E-mail: jgkooti@ship.edu. *Application contact:* Maya T. Mapp, Director of Admissions, 717-477-1231, Fax: 717-477-4016, E-mail: mtmapp@ship.edu. Website: http://www.ship.edu/business

**Siena Heights University,** Graduate College, Adrian, MI 49221-1796. Offers clinical mental health counseling (MA); educational leadership (Specialist); leadership (MA), including health care leadership, organizational leadership; teacher education (MA), including early childhood education, early childhood education: Montessori, education leadership: principal, elementary education: reading K-12, leadership: higher education, secondary education: reading K-12, special education: cognitive impairment, special education: learning disabilities. *Program availability:* Part-time, evening/weekend. *Degree requirements:* For master's, thesis, Presentation. *Entrance requirements:* For master's, Minimum GPA of 3.0, current resume, essay, all post-secondary transcripts, 3 letters of reference, conviction disclosure form; copy of teaching certificate (for some education programs); for Specialist, Master's degree, minimum GPA of 3.0, current resume, essay, all post-secondary transcripts, 3 letters of reference, conviction disclosure form; copy of teaching certificate (for some education programs). Additional exam requirements/recommendations for international students: recommended—TOEFL, IELTS, TWE, TSE. Electronic applications accepted.

**Simmons University,** College of Organizational, Computational, and Information Sciences, Boston, MA 02115. Offers business administration (MBA); health care (MBA); MBA/MSW. *Accreditation:* AACSB. *Program availability:* Part-time. *Faculty:* 32 full-time (19 women), 18 part-time/adjunct (15 women). *Students:* 300 full-time (250 women), 530 part-time (452 women); includes 131 minority (19 Black or African American, non-Hispanic/Latino; 31 Asian, non-Hispanic/Latino; 55 Hispanic/Latino; 1 Native Hawaiian or other Pacific Islander, non-Hispanic/Latino; 25 Two or more races, non-Hispanic/Latino), 16 international. Average age 31. 475 applicants, 67% accepted, 274 enrolled. In 2019, 342 master's awarded. *Degree requirements:* For master's, thesis (for some programs). *Entrance requirements:* For master's, GMAT or GRE. Additional exam requirements/recommendations for international students: required—TOEFL. *Application deadline:* For fall admission, 7/18 priority date for domestic students; for summer admission, 4/24 priority date for domestic students. Applications are processed on a rolling basis. Application fee: $65. Electronic applications accepted. *Expenses:* Contact institution. *Financial support:* In 2019–20, 16 students received support, including 6 fellowships (averaging $30,000 per year), 10 teaching assistantships (averaging $20,000 per year); scholarships/grants also available. Financial award applicants required to submit FAFSA. *Unit head:* Dr. Marie desJardins, Dean, E-mail: marie.desjardins@simmons.edu. *Application contact:* Kate Benson, Director, Library Science Admission Office, 617-5212801, E-mail: kate.benson@simmons.edu. Website: https://www.simmons.edu/academics/colleges-schools-departments/cocis

**South Carolina State University,** College of Graduate and Professional Studies, Department of Business Administration, Orangeburg, SC 29117-0001. Offers agribusiness (MBA); entrepreneurship (MBA); general business administration (MBA); healthcare management (MBA). *Program availability:* Part-time, evening/weekend. *Degree requirements:* For master's, comprehensive exam, business plan. *Entrance requirements:* For master's, GMAT, minimum GPA of 2.8. Additional exam requirements/recommendations for international students: required—TOEFL. Electronic applications accepted.

**Southeastern University,** Jannetides College of Business & Entrepreneurial Leadership, Lakeland, FL 33801. Offers executive leadership (MBA); global business administration (MBA); healthcare administration (MBA); missional leadership (MBA); organizational leadership (PhD); sport management (MBA); strategic leadership (DSL). *Accreditation:* ACBSP. *Program availability:* Evening/weekend, online learning. *Faculty:* 16 full-time (3 women). *Students:* 127 full-time (61 women), 80 part-time (41 women); includes 78 minority (37 Black or African American, non-Hispanic/Latino; 5 Asian, non-Hispanic/Latino; 34 Hispanic/Latino; 1 Native Hawaiian or other Pacific Islander, non-Hispanic/Latino; 1 Two or more races, non-Hispanic/Latino), 4 international. Average age 33. In 2019, 63 master's awarded. *Entrance requirements:* For master's, GMAT, minimum cumulative GPA of 3.0, writing sample. Additional exam requirements/recommendations for international students: required—TOEFL (minimum score 76 iBT), IELTS (minimum score 6). Application fee: $50. Electronic applications accepted. *Unit head:* Dr. Lyle L. Bowlin, Dean, 863-667-5118, E-mail: llbowlin@seu.edu. *Application contact:* Dr. Lyle L. Bowlin, Dean, 863-667-5118, E-mail: llbowlin@seu.edu. Website: http://www.seu.edu/business/

**Southern Adventist University,** School of Business, Collegedale, TN 37315-0370. Offers accounting (MBA); computer information systems (MBA); finance (MBA); healthcare administration (MBA); management (MBA). *Program availability:* Part-time, evening/weekend, 100% online. *Entrance requirements:* For master's, GMAT, minimum cumulative undergraduate GPA of 3.0. Additional exam requirements/recommendations for international students: required—TOEFL (minimum score 100 iBT). Electronic applications accepted.

**Southern Illinois University Carbondale,** School of Law, Program in Legal Studies, Carbondale, IL 62901-4701. Offers general law (MLS); health law and policy (MLS).

**Southern Nazarene University,** College of Professional and Graduate Studies, School of Business, Bethany, OK 73008. Offers business administration (MBA); health care management (MBA); management (MS Mgt). *Accreditation:* ACBSP. *Program availability:* Part-time, evening/weekend, online learning. *Degree requirements:* For master's, thesis optional. *Entrance requirements:* For master's, resume. Additional exam requirements/recommendations for international students: required—TOEFL (minimum score 550 paper-based; 80 iBT), IELTS (minimum score 7). Electronic applications accepted.

**Southern New Hampshire University,** School of Business, Manchester, NH 03106-1045. Offers accounting (MBA, Graduate Certificate); accounting finance (MS); accounting/auditing (MS); accounting/forensic accounting (MS); accounting/management accounting (MS); accounting/taxation (MS); applied economics (MS); athletic administration (MBA, Graduate Certificate); business administration (IMBA, Certificate), including business information systems (Certificate), human resource management (Certificate); business analytics (MBA); business intelligence (MBA); communication (MA), including new media and marketing, public relations; community economic development (MBA); criminal justice (MBA); data analytics (MS); economics (MBA); engineering management (MBA); entrepreneurship (MBA); finance (MBA, MS, Graduate Certificate); finance/corporate finance (MS); finance/investments (MS); forensic accounting (MBA); forensic accounting and fraud examination (Graduate Certificate); healthcare informatics (MS); healthcare management (MBA); human resource management (MS); human resources (MBA); information technology (MS); information technology management (MBA); international business (PhD); Internet marketing (MBA); leadership (MBA); leadership of nonprofit organizations (Graduate

Certificate); management (MS); marketing (MBA, MS, Graduate Certificate); music business (MBA); operations and project management (MS); operations and supply chain management (MBA, Graduate Certificate); organizational leadership (MS); project management (MBA, Graduate Certificate); public administration (MBA, Graduate Certificate); quantitative analysis (MBA); Six Sigma (Graduate Certificate); Six Sigma quality (MBA); social media marketing (MBA, Graduate Certificate); sport management (MBA, MS, Graduate Certificate); sustainability and environmental compliance (MBA); MBA/Certificate. *Accreditation:* ACBSP. *Program availability:* Part-time, evening/weekend, online learning. Terminal master's awarded for partial completion of doctoral program. *Degree requirements:* For master's, one foreign language, comprehensive exam (for some programs), thesis or alternative; for doctorate, one foreign language, comprehensive exam, thesis/dissertation. *Entrance requirements:* For master's, minimum GPA of 2.5; for doctorate, GMAT. Additional exam requirements/recommendations for international students: required—TOEFL (minimum score 500 paper-based). Electronic applications accepted.

**South University - Columbia,** Program in Healthcare Administration, Columbia, SC 29203. Offers MBA.

**South University - Montgomery,** Program in Healthcare Administration, Montgomery, AL 36116-1120. Offers MBA.

**South University - Savannah,** Graduate Programs, College of Business, Program in Healthcare Administration, Savannah, GA 31406. Offers MBA.

**South University - Tampa,** Program in Healthcare Administration, Tampa, FL 33614. Offers MBA.

**South University - West Palm Beach,** Program in Business Administration, Royal Palm Beach, FL 33411. Offers business administration (MBA); healthcare administration (MBA).

**Southwest Baptist University,** Program in Business, Bolivar, MO 65613-2597. Offers business administration (MBA); health administration (MBA). *Accreditation:* ACBSP. *Program availability:* Part-time, online learning. *Degree requirements:* For master's, comprehensive exam. *Entrance requirements:* For master's, interviews, minimum GPA of 2.75. Additional exam requirements/recommendations for international students: required—TOEFL (minimum score 550 paper-based).

**Stevenson University,** Program in Healthcare Management, Stevenson, MD 21153. Offers project management (MS); quality management and patient safety (MS). *Program availability:* Part-time, online only, 100% online. *Faculty:* 1 (woman) full-time, 5 part-time/adjunct (4 women). *Students:* 33 part-time (25 women); includes 13 minority (11 Black or African American, non-Hispanic/Latino; 2 Asian, non-Hispanic/Latino). Average age 35. 19 applicants, 42% accepted, 6 enrolled. In 2019, 18 master's awarded. *Entrance requirements:* For master's, personal statement (3-5 paragraphs); official college transcript from degree-granting institution; bachelor's degree from a regionally accredited institution; minimum cumulative GPA of 3.0 on a 4.0 scale in past academic work; 1 letter of recommendation from a current or past supervisor; professional resume. *Application deadline:* For fall admission, 8/9 priority date for domestic students; for spring admission, 1/11 priority date for domestic students; for summer admission, 5/1 priority date for domestic students. Applications are processed on a rolling basis. Electronic applications accepted. *Expenses:* $670 per credit. *Financial support:* Unspecified assistantships available. Financial award applicants required to submit FAFSA. *Unit head:* Dr. Sharon Buchbinder, Program Coordinator, 443-394-9290, Fax: 443-394-0538, E-mail: sbuchbinder@stevenson.edu. *Application contact:* Amanda Millar, Director, Admissions, 443-352-4243, Fax: 443-394-0538, E-mail: amillar@stevenson.edu. Website: https://www.stevenson.edu/online/academics/online-graduate-programs/healthcare-management/index.html

**Stony Brook University, State University of New York,** Graduate School, College of Business, Program in Business Administration, Stony Brook, NY 11794. Offers accounting (MBA); business administration (MBA); finance (MBA, Certificate); health care management (MBA); human resources (MBA); innovation (MBA); management (MBA); marketing (MBA); operations management (MBA). *Faculty:* 37 full-time (14 women), 7 part-time/adjunct (3 women). *Students:* 183 full-time (89 women), 140 part-time (67 women); includes 107 minority (18 Black or African American, non-Hispanic/Latino; 46 Asian, non-Hispanic/Latino; 36 Hispanic/Latino; 7 Two or more races, non-Hispanic/Latino), 45 international. Average age 27. 124 applicants, 80% accepted, 72 enrolled. In 2019, 62 master's awarded. *Entrance requirements:* For master's, GMAT, 3 letters of recommendation from current or former employers or professors, transcripts, personal statement, resume. Additional exam requirements/recommendations for international students: required—TOEFL (minimum score 550 paper-based; 80 iBT), IELTS (minimum score 6.5). *Application deadline:* For fall admission, 5/15 for domestic students, 3/15 for international students; for spring admission, 12/1 for domestic students, 10/15 for international students. Application fee: $100. *Expenses:* Contact institution. *Financial support:* Teaching assistantships available. *Unit head:* Dr. Manuel London, Dean, 631-632-7159, E-mail: manuel.london@stonybrook.edu. *Application contact:* Dr. Dmytro Holod, Associate Dean for Academic Programs/Graduate Director, 631-632-7183, Fax: 631-632-8181, E-mail: dmytro.holod@stonybrook.edu. Website: https://www.stonybrook.edu/commcms/business/

**Stony Brook University, State University of New York,** Stony Brook Medicine, School of Health Technology and Management, Stony Brook, NY 11794. Offers applied health informatics (MS); disability studies (Certificate); health administration (MHA); health and rehabilitation sciences (PhD); health care management (Advanced Certificate); health care policy and management (MS); occupational therapy (MS); physical therapy (DPT); physician assistant (MS). *Accreditation:* AOTA; APTA. *Faculty:* 53 full-time (37 women), 54 part-time/adjunct (34 women). *Students:* 605 full-time (417 women), 65 part-time (43 women); includes 225 minority (28 Black or African American, non-Hispanic/Latino; 110 Asian, non-Hispanic/Latino; 73 Hispanic/Latino; 1 Native Hawaiian or other Pacific Islander, non-Hispanic/Latino; 13 Two or more races, non-Hispanic/Latino), 9 international. Average age 26. 1,816 applicants, 21% accepted, 293 enrolled. In 2019, 152 master's, 86 doctorates, 21 other advanced degrees awarded. *Entrance requirements:* For master's, GRE General Test, minimum GPA of 3.0, work experience in field, references; for doctorate, GRE, three references, essay. Additional exam requirements/recommendations for international students: required—TOEFL (minimum score 550 paper-based). *Application deadline:* For fall admission, 1/15 for domestic students; for spring admission, 10/1 for domestic students. Application fee: $100. *Expenses:* Contact institution. *Financial support:* Fellowships, research assistantships, teaching assistantships, career-related internships or fieldwork, Federal Work-Study, and institutionally sponsored loans available. Financial award application deadline: 3/15. *Unit head:* Dr. Stacy Jafee Gropack, Dean and Professor, 631-444-2252, Fax: 631-444-7621, E-mail: stacy.jaffeegropack@stonybrook.edu. *Application contact:* Jessica M Rotolo, Executive Assistant to the Dean, 631-444-2252, Fax: 631-444-7621, E-mail: jessica.rotolo@stonybrook.edu. Website: http://healthtechnology.stonybrookmedicine.edu/

**Stratford University,** School of Graduate Studies, Falls Church, VA 22043. Offers accounting (MS); business administration (MBA, DBA); cyber security (MS); cyber security leadership and policy (MS); digital forensics (MS); healthcare administration

(MS); information systems (MS); information technology (DIT); networking and telecommunications (MS); software engineering (MS). *Program availability:* Part-time, evening/weekend, 100% online, blended/hybrid learning. *Degree requirements:* For master's, comprehensive exam, capstone project. *Entrance requirements:* For master's, GRE or GMAT, baccalaureate degree. Additional exam requirements/recommendations for international students: required—TOEFL (minimum score 79 iBT), IELTS (minimum score 6.5), PTE (minimum score 5). Electronic applications accepted.

**Strayer University,** Graduate Studies, Washington, DC 20005-2603. Offers accounting (MS); acquisition (MBA); business administration (MBA); communications technology (MS); educational management (M Ed); finance (MBA); health services administration (MHSA); hospitality and tourism management (MBA); human resource management (MBA); information systems (MS), including computer security management, decision support system management, enterprise resource management, network management, software engineering management, systems development management; management (MBA); management information systems (MS); marketing (MBA); professional accounting (MS), including accounting information systems, controllership, taxation; public administration (MPA); supply chain management (MBA); technology in education (M Ed). *Accreditation:* ACBSP. *Program availability:* Part-time, evening/weekend, online learning. *Degree requirements:* For master's, thesis. *Entrance requirements:* For master's, GMAT, GRE General Test, bachelor's degree from an accredited college or university, minimum undergraduate GPA of 2.75. Electronic applications accepted.

**Suffolk University,** Sawyer Business School, Master of Business Administration Program, Boston, MA 02108-2770. Offers accounting (MBA); entrepreneurship (MBA); executive business administration (EMBA); finance (MBA); global business administration (GMBA); health administration (MBA); international business (MBA); marketing (MBA); nonprofit management (MBA); organizational behavior (MBA); strategic management (MBA); supply chain management (MBA); taxation (MBA); JD/MBA; MBA/MHA; MBA/MSA; MBA/MSF; MBA/MST. *Accreditation:* AACSB. *Program availability:* Part-time, evening/weekend, 100% online. *Faculty:* 11 full-time (5 women), 3 part-time/adjunct (0 women). *Students:* 130 full-time (67 women), 266 part-time (153 women); includes 107 minority (39 Black or African American, non-Hispanic/Latino; 26 Asian, non-Hispanic/Latino; 39 Hispanic/Latino; 3 Two or more races, non-Hispanic/Latino), 80 international. Average age 29. 449 applicants, 72% accepted, 138 enrolled. In 2019, 121 master's awarded. *Entrance requirements:* For master's, GMAT, minimum undergraduate GPA of 2.75 (MBA), 5 years of managerial experience (EMBA). Additional exam requirements/recommendations for international students: required—TOEFL (minimum score 550 paper-based; 80 iBT). *Application deadline:* For fall admission, 3/15 priority date for domestic students, 10/15 priority date for international students; for spring admission, 10/15 priority date for domestic and international students. Applications are processed on a rolling basis. Application fee: $50. Electronic applications accepted. *Expenses:* Contact institution. *Financial support:* In 2019–20, 213 students received support, including 12 fellowships (averaging $3,225 per year); career-related internships or fieldwork, Federal Work-Study, institutionally sponsored loans, and scholarships/grants also available. Support available to part-time students. Financial award application deadline: 4/1; financial award applicants required to submit FAFSA. *Unit head:* Jodi Detjen, Director of MBA Programs, 617-573-8306, E-mail: jdetjen@suffolk.edu. *Application contact:* Mara Marzocchi, Associate Director of Graduate Admissions, 617-573-8302, Fax: 617-305-1733, E-mail: grad.admission@suffolk.edu.
Website: http://www.suffolk.edu/mba

**Suffolk University,** Sawyer Business School, Program in Healthcare Administration, Boston, MA 02108-2770. Offers community health (MPA); health (MBAH); healthcare administration (MHA). *Accreditation:* CAHME. *Program availability:* Part-time, evening/weekend. *Faculty:* 4 full-time (1 woman), 3 part-time/adjunct (1 woman). *Students:* 22 full-time (17 women), 32 part-time (26 women); includes 19 minority (7 Black or African American, non-Hispanic/Latino; 7 Asian, non-Hispanic/Latino; 3 Hispanic/Latino; 2 Two or more races, non-Hispanic/Latino), 9 international. Average age 28. 56 applicants, 80% accepted, 23 enrolled. In 2019, 41 master's awarded. *Entrance requirements:* Additional exam requirements/recommendations for international students: required—TOEFL (minimum score 550 paper-based; 80 iBT). *Application deadline:* For fall admission, 3/15 priority date for domestic and international students; for spring admission, 10/15 priority date for domestic and international students. Applications are processed on a rolling basis. Application fee: $50. Electronic applications accepted. *Expenses:* Contact institution. *Financial support:* In 2019–20, 31 students received support. Fellowships, career-related internships or fieldwork, Federal Work-Study, institutionally sponsored loans, scholarships/grants, and health care benefits available. Support available to part-time students. Financial award application deadline: 4/1; financial award applicants required to submit FAFSA. *Unit head:* Richard Gregg, Director of Programs in Healthcare Administration/Chair of Healthcare Department, 617-994-4246, E-mail: rgregg@suffolk.edu. *Application contact:* Mara Marzocchi, Associate Director of Graduate Admissions, 617-573-8302, Fax: 617-305-1733, E-mail: grad.admission@suffolk.edu.
Website: http://www.suffolk.edu/business/graduate/62398.php

**SUNY Brockport,** School of Business and Management, Department of Public Administration, Brockport, NY 14420-2997. Offers arts administration (AGC); nonprofit management (AGC); public administration (MPA), including health care management, nonprofit management, poverty studies, public management, public safety. *Accreditation:* NASPAA. *Program availability:* Part-time, evening/weekend. *Faculty:* 5 full-time (3 women), 7 part-time/adjunct (0 women). *Students:* 35 full-time (23 women), 92 part-time (56 women); includes 15 minority (10 Black or African American, non-Hispanic/Latino; 1 Asian, non-Hispanic/Latino; 3 Hispanic/Latino; 1 Native Hawaiian or other Pacific Islander, non-Hispanic/Latino). 41 applicants, 78% accepted, 23 enrolled. In 2019, 104 master's, 6 other advanced degrees awarded. *Degree requirements:* For master's, thesis or alternative. *Entrance requirements:* For master's, GRE or minimum GPA of 3.0, letters of recommendation, statement of objectives, current resume. Additional exam requirements/recommendations for international students: required—TOEFL (minimum score 550 paper-based; 79 iBT), IELTS (minimum score 6.5). *Application deadline:* For fall admission, 8/15 priority date for domestic and international students; for spring admission, 1/15 priority date for domestic and international students; for summer admission, 4/15 priority date for domestic and international students. Application fee: $50. Electronic applications accepted. *Expenses: Tuition, area resident:* Part-time $471 per credit hour. Tuition, nonresident: part-time $963 per credit hour. *Financial support:* In 2019–20, 1 fellowship with full tuition reimbursement (averaging $7,500 per year), 1 teaching assistantship with full tuition reimbursement (averaging $6,000 per year) were awarded; Federal Work-Study, scholarships/grants, and unspecified assistantships also available. Support available to part-time students. Financial award application deadline: 3/15; financial award applicants required to submit FAFSA. *Unit head:* Dr. Wendy Wright, Graduate Director, 585-395-5570, Fax: 585-395-2172, E-mail: wwright@brockport.edu. *Application contact:* Danielle A. Welch, Graduate Admissions Counselor, 585-395-2525, Fax: 585-395-2515.
Website: https://www.brockport.edu/academics/public_administration/graduate/masters.html

**Syracuse University,** Maxwell School of Citizenship and Public Affairs, CAS Program in Health Services Management and Policy, Syracuse, NY 13244. Offers CAS. *Program availability:* Part-time. *Entrance requirements:* For degree, 7 years of mid-level professional experience, resume, personal statement, three letters of recommendation, official transcripts. Additional exam requirements/recommendations for international students: required—TOEFL (minimum score 100 iBT). Electronic applications accepted.

**Temple University,** Fox School of Business, MBA Programs, Philadelphia, PA 19122-6096. Offers accounting (MBA); business management (MBA); financial management (MBA); healthcare and life sciences innovation (MBA); human resource management (MBA); international business (IMBA); IT management (MBA); marketing management (MBA); pharmaceutical management (MBA); strategic management (EMBA, MBA). *Accreditation:* AACSB. *Program availability:* Part-time, evening/weekend, online learning. *Entrance requirements:* For master's, GMAT, minimum undergraduate GPA of 3.0. Additional exam requirements/recommendations for international students: required—TOEFL (minimum score 600 paper-based; 100 iBT), IELTS (minimum score 7.5).

**Texas A&M University,** School of Public Health, College Station, TX 77843. Offers biostatistics (MPH, MSPH); environmental health (MPH, MSPH); epidemiology (MPH, MSPH); health administration (MHA); health policy and management (MPH); health services research (PhD); occupational safety and health (MPH). *Accreditation:* CAHME; CEPH. *Program availability:* Part-time, blended/hybrid learning. *Entrance requirements:* For master's, GRE General Test, 3 letters of recommendation; statement of purpose; current curriculum vitae or resume; official transcripts; for doctorate, GRE General Test, 3 letters of recommendation; statement of purpose; current curriculum vitae or resume; official transcripts; interview (in some cases). Additional exam requirements/recommendations for international students: required—TOEFL (minimum score 597 paper-based, 95 iBT) or GRE (minimum verbal score 153). Electronic applications accepted. *Expenses:* Contact institution.

**Texas A&M University–Corpus Christi,** College of Graduate Studies, College of Business, Corpus Christi, TX 78412. Offers accounting (M Acc); business (MBA); finance (MBA); health care administration (MBA); international business (MBA). *Accreditation:* AACSB. *Program availability:* Part-time, evening/weekend, 100% online, blended/hybrid learning. *Degree requirements:* For master's, 30 to 42 hours (for MBA; varies by concentration area, delivery format, and necessity for foundational courses for students with nonbusiness degrees). *Entrance requirements:* For master's, GMAT, GRE. Additional exam requirements/recommendations for international students: required—TOEFL (minimum score 550 paper-based; 79 iBT), IELTS (minimum score 6.5). Electronic applications accepted.

**Texas A&M University–Corpus Christi,** College of Graduate Studies, College of Nursing and Health Sciences, Corpus Christi, TX 78412. Offers family nurse practitioner (MSN); leadership in nursing systems (MSN); nurse educator (MSN); nursing practice (DNP). *Accreditation:* AACN. *Program availability:* Part-time, evening/weekend, online only, 100% online. *Degree requirements:* For master's, clinical capstone; for doctorate, capstone/scholarly project. *Entrance requirements:* For master's, essay, resume, 3 letters of recommendation, minimum GPA of 3.0, current valid unencumbered Texas nursing license. Additional exam requirements/recommendations for international students: required—TOEFL (minimum score 550 paper-based; 79 iBT), IELTS (minimum score 6.5). Electronic applications accepted.

**Texas Health and Science University,** Graduate Programs, Austin, TX 78704. Offers acupuncture and Oriental medicine (MS, DAOM); business administration (MBA); healthcare management (MBA). *Accreditation:* ACAOM. *Entrance requirements:* For master's, 60 hours applicable to bachelor's degree. Additional exam requirements/recommendations for international students: required—TOEFL (minimum score 500 paper-based), TWE. Electronic applications accepted. *Expenses:* *Tuition:* Full-time $11,780; part-time $3440 per credit. *Required fees:* $292; $146 per credit. $220 per trimester. One-time fee: $72. Tuition and fees vary according to course load and program.

**Texas Southern University,** College of Pharmacy and Health Sciences, Department of Health Sciences, Houston, TX 77004-4584. Offers health care administration (MS). *Program availability:* Online learning. *Entrance requirements:* For master's, PCAT. Electronic applications accepted.

**Texas State University,** The Graduate College, College of Health Professions, Program in Healthcare Administration, San Marcos, TX 78666. Offers MHA. *Accreditation:* CAHME. *Program availability:* Part-time, evening/weekend. *Degree requirements:* For master's, comprehensive exam, thesis optional, committee review. *Entrance requirements:* For master's, GRE General Test with preferred minimum of 575 on your admissions index: (last 60 hours GPA x 100) + GRE verbal section scores + GRE quantitative section scores, baccalaureate degree from regionally-accredited institution; minimum GPA of 2.75 for last 60 hours of undergraduate course work; 3 letters of reference; written statement of purpose; resume; prerequisite courses in statistics, economics, and financial accounting. Additional exam requirements/recommendations for international students: required—TOEFL (minimum score 550 paper-based; 78 iBT), IELTS (minimum score 6.5). Electronic applications accepted.

**Texas Tech University,** Rawls College of Business Administration, Lubbock, TX 79409-2101. Offers accounting (MSA, PhD), including audit/financial reporting (MSA), taxation (MSA); data science (MS); finance (PhD); general business (MBA); healthcare management (MS); information systems and operations management (PhD); management (PhD); marketing (PhD); STEM (MBA); JD/MBA; JD/MSA; MBA/M Arch; MBA/MD; MBA/MS; MBA/Pharm D. *Accreditation:* AACSB. *Program availability:* Part-time, evening/weekend, 100% online, blended/hybrid learning. *Faculty:* 90 full-time (20 women). *Students:* 505 full-time (209 women), 251 part-time (87 women); includes 239 minority (50 Black or African American, non-Hispanic/Latino; 2 American Indian or Alaska Native, non-Hispanic/Latino; 39 Asian, non-Hispanic/Latino; 112 Hispanic/Latino; 36 Two or more races, non-Hispanic/Latino), 96 international. Average age 28. 534 applicants, 57% accepted, 229 enrolled. In 2019, 415 master's, 10 doctorates awarded. *Degree requirements:* For master's, thesis (for MS); capstone course; for doctorate, comprehensive exam, thesis/dissertation, qualifying exams. *Entrance requirements:* For master's, GMAT, GRE, MCAT, PCAT, LSAT, or DAT, holistic review of academic credentials, resume, essay, letters of recommendation; for doctorate, GMAT, GRE, holistic review of academic credentials, resume, statement of purpose, letters of recommendation. Additional exam requirements/recommendations for international students: required—TOEFL (minimum score 550 paper-based; 79 iBT), IELTS (minimum score 6.5), PTE (minimum score 60). *Application deadline:* For fall admission, 7/1 priority date for domestic students, 1/15 for international students; for spring admission, 12/1 priority date for domestic students, 6/15 for international students; for summer admission, 5/1 priority date for domestic students, 1/15 for international students. Applications are processed on a rolling basis. Application fee: $60. Electronic applications accepted. *Expenses:* Tuition, state resident: full-time $7944; part-time $331 per credit hour. Tuition, nonresident: full-time $17,904; part-time $746 per credit hour. *Required fees:* $2556; $55.50 per credit hour. $612 per semester. Tuition and fees vary according to program. *Financial support:* In 2019–20, 373 students received support, including 1 fellowship with full tuition reimbursement available (averaging $34,000 per

year), 2 research assistantships with full tuition reimbursements available (averaging $21,742 per year), 57 teaching assistantships with full tuition reimbursements available (averaging $22,750 per year); career-related internships or fieldwork, Federal Work-Study, scholarships/grants, traineeships, health care benefits, and unspecified assistantships also available. Financial award application deadline: 3/1; financial award applicants required to submit FAFSA. *Unit head:* Dr. Margaret Williams, Dean, 806-834-2839, Fax: 806-742-1092, E-mail: margaret.l.williams@ttu.edu. *Application contact:* Elisa Dunman, Lead Administrator, Graduate and Professional Programs, 806-834-7772, E-mail: rawlsgrad@ttu.edu.
Website: http://www.depts.ttu.edu/rawlsbusiness/graduate/

**Texas Tech University Health Sciences Center,** School of Health Professions, Program in Healthcare Administration, Lubbock, TX 79430. Offers MS. *Accreditation:* CORE. *Program availability:* Part-time, online only, 100% online. *Faculty:* 6 full-time (3 women), 17 part-time/adjunct (10 women). *Students:* 371 full-time (259 women), 75 part-time (49 women); includes 242 minority (78 Black or African American, non-Hispanic/Latino; 4 American Indian or Alaska Native, non-Hispanic/Latino; 35 Asian, non-Hispanic/Latino; 105 Hispanic/Latino; 1 Native Hawaiian or other Pacific Islander, non-Hispanic/Latino; 19 Two or more races, non-Hispanic/Latino), 2 international. Average age 32. 214 applicants, 73% accepted, 144 enrolled. In 2019, 127 master's awarded. *Entrance requirements:* Additional exam requirements/recommendations for international students: required—TOEFL (minimum score 550 paper-based; 79 iBT). *Application deadline:* For fall admission, 7/1 for domestic students; for spring admission, 12/1 for domestic students; for summer admission, 4/1 for domestic students. Applications are processed on a rolling basis. Application fee: $75. Electronic applications accepted. *Financial support:* In 2019–20, 62 students received support. Institutionally sponsored loans available. Support available to part-time students. Financial award application deadline: 9/1; financial award applicants required to submit FAFSA. *Unit head:* Debra Flores, Program Director, 806-743-3220, Fax: 806-743-3244, E-mail: health.professions@ttuhsc.edu. *Application contact:* Lindsay Johnson, Associate Dean for Admissions and Student Affairs, 806-743-3220, Fax: 806-743-2994, E-mail: health.professions@ttuhsc.edu.
Website: http://www.ttuhsc.edu/health-professions/master-of-science-healthcare-administration/

**Texas Woman's University,** Graduate School, College of Business, Program in Healthcare Administration, Houston, TX 76204. Offers healthcare administration (MHA), including business analytics. *Accreditation:* CAHME. *Program availability:* Part-time, evening/weekend, 100% online, blended/hybrid learning. *Faculty:* 7 full-time (4 women), 4 part-time/adjunct (3 women). *Students:* 79 full-time (71 women), 76 part-time (65 women); includes 122 minority (53 Black or African American, non-Hispanic/Latino; 33 Asian, non-Hispanic/Latino; 32 Hispanic/Latino; 4 Two or more races, non-Hispanic/Latino), 6 international. Average age 30. 82 applicants, 89% accepted, 47 enrolled. In 2019, 53 master's awarded. *Degree requirements:* For master's, thesis or alternative, portfolio. *Entrance requirements:* For master's, GMAT or GRE (optional depending on GPA), resume, minimum GPA of 3.0 in last 60 hours of undergraduate degree and in all graduate course work. Additional exam requirements/recommendations for international students: required—TOEFL (minimum score 79 iBT); recommended—IELTS (minimum score 6.5), TSE (minimum score 53). *Application deadline:* For fall admission, 3/1 priority date for domestic and international students; for spring admission, 11/1 priority date for domestic students, 7/1 priority date for international students; for summer admission, 5/1 priority date for domestic students, 2/1 priority date for international students. Applications are processed on a rolling basis. Application fee: $50 ($75 for international students). Electronic applications accepted. *Expenses:* All are estimates. Tuition for 10 hours = $2,763; Fees for 10 hours = $1,342. Business courses require additional $80/SCH. *Financial support:* In 2019–20, 43 students received support, including 2 teaching assistantships; career-related internships or fieldwork, scholarships/grants, health care benefits, and unspecified assistantships also available. Support available to part-time students. Financial award application deadline: 3/1; financial award applicants required to submit FAFSA. *Unit head:* Dr. Gerald Goodman, Director, 940-898-2458, Fax: 940-898-2120, E-mail: hcahouston@twu.edu. *Application contact:* Korie Hawkins, Associate Director of Admissions, Graduate Recruitment, 940-898-3188, Fax: 940-898-3081, E-mail: admissions@twu.edu.
Website: https://www.twu.edu/business/graduate-programs-college-of-business/master-of-healthcare-administration/

**Thomas Jefferson University,** Jefferson College of Population Health, Program in Healthcare Quality and Safety, Philadelphia, PA 19107. Offers MS, PhD, Certificate. *Program availability:* Part-time, evening/weekend, online learning. *Entrance requirements:* For master's, GRE or other graduate examination, 2 letters of recommendation, interview, curriculum vitae; for doctorate, GRE (within the last 5 years), 3 letters of recommendation, interview, curriculum vitae. Additional exam requirements/recommendations for international students: required—TOEFL.

**Thomas Jefferson University,** Jefferson College of Population Health, Program in Health Policy, Philadelphia, PA 19107. Offers MS, PhD, Certificate. *Program availability:* Part-time, evening/weekend, online learning. *Entrance requirements:* For master's, GRE or other graduate exam, two letters of recommendation, curriculum vitae/resume, interview; for doctorate, GRE (taken within the last 5 years), three letters of recommendation, curriculum vitae/resume, interview. Additional exam requirements/recommendations for international students: required—TOEFL. Electronic applications accepted.

**Tiffin University,** Program in Business Administration, Tiffin, OH 44883-2161. Offers finance (MBA); general management (MBA); healthcare administration (MBA); human resource management (MBA); international business (MBA); leadership (MBA); marketing (MBA); non-profit management (MBA); sports management (MBA). *Accreditation:* ACBSP. *Program availability:* Part-time, evening/weekend, online learning. *Entrance requirements:* For master's, minimum undergraduate GPA of 2.5, work experience. Additional exam requirements/recommendations for international students: required—TOEFL (minimum score 550 paper-based; 79 iBT), IELTS. Electronic applications accepted. Application fee is waived when completed online.

**Towson University,** College of Health Professions, Program in Clinician to Administrator Transition, Towson, MD 21252-0001. Offers MS, Postbaccalaureate Certificate. *Students:* 1 (woman) full-time, 3 part-time (2 women); includes 1 minority (Hispanic/Latino). *Entrance requirements:* For degree, minimum GPA of 3.0; bachelor's or master's degree in a clinical field; licensure, licensure eligibility, or certificate in a clinical field. *Application deadline:* For fall admission, 1/17 for domestic students, 5/15 for international students; for spring admission, 10/15 for domestic students, 12/1 for international students. Applications are processed on a rolling basis. Application fee: $45. Electronic applications accepted. *Expenses: Tuition, area resident:* Full-time $7920; part-time $439 per credit. *Tuition, nonresident:* full-time $16,344; part-time $908 per credit. *International tuition:* $16,344 full-time. *Required fees:* $2628; $146 per credit. $876 per term. *Financial support:* Application deadline: 4/1. *Unit head:* Dr. Allison Kabel, Program Director, 410-704-4049, E-mail: akabel@towson.edu. *Application contact:* Coverley Beidleman, Assistant Director of Graduate Admissions, 410-704-5630, Fax: 410-704-3030, E-mail: grads@towson.edu.

Website: https://www.towson.edu/chp/departments/health-sciences/grad/clinician-administrator-certificate/

**Trevecca Nazarene University,** Graduate Business Programs, Nashville, TN 37210-2877. Offers business administration (MBA); health care leadership and innovation (MS); management (MSM). *Program availability:* Evening/weekend, online learning. *Entrance requirements:* For master's, minimum GPA of 2.75, resume, official transcript from regionally accredited institution, minimum math grade of C, minimum English composition grade of C. Additional exam requirements/recommendations for international students: required—TOEFL (minimum score 550 paper-based; 80 iBT). Electronic applications accepted. *Expenses:* Contact institution.

**Trident University International,** College of Health Sciences, Program in Health Sciences, Cypress, CA 90630. Offers clinical research administration (MS, Certificate); emergency and disaster management (MS, Certificate); environmental health science (Certificate); health care administration (PhD); health care management (MS), including health informatics; health education (MS, Certificate); health informatics (Certificate); health sciences (PhD); international health (MS); international health: educator or researcher option (PhD); international health: practitioner option (PhD); law and expert witness studies (MS, Certificate); public health (MS); quality assurance (Certificate). *Program availability:* Part-time, evening/weekend, online learning. *Degree requirements:* For doctorate, comprehensive exam, thesis/dissertation, defense of dissertation. *Entrance requirements:* For master's, minimum GPA of 2.5 (students with GPA 3.0 or greater may transfer up to 30% of graduate level credits); for doctorate, minimum GPA of 3.4, curriculum vitae, course work in research methods or statistics. Additional exam requirements/recommendations for international students: required—TOEFL. Electronic applications accepted.

**Trinity University,** Department of Health Care Administration, San Antonio, TX 78212-7200. Offers health care administration (MS). *Accreditation:* CAHME. *Program availability:* Part-time, online learning. *Faculty:* 4 full-time (1 woman), 9 part-time/adjunct (3 women). *Students:* 46 full-time (25 women), 39 part-time (25 women); includes 26 minority (5 Black or African American, non-Hispanic/Latino; 7 Asian, non-Hispanic/Latino; 11 Hispanic/Latino; 3 Two or more races, non-Hispanic/Latino). Average age 27. In 2019, 34 master's awarded. *Entrance requirements:* For master's, GRE or GMAT, resume or autobiographical sketch; statement of purpose; letters of recommendation. *Application deadline:* For fall admission, 6/1 for domestic students. Applications are processed on a rolling basis. Application fee: $50. Electronic applications accepted. *Financial support:* Fellowships, institutionally sponsored loans, scholarships/grants, and unspecified assistantships available. Support available to part-time students. Financial award application deadline: 5/1; financial award applicants required to submit FAFSA. *Unit head:* Dr. Ed Schumacher, Professor/Chair, 210-999-8137, E-mail: hca@trinity.edu. *Application contact:* Dr. Ed Schumacher, Professor/Chair, 210-999-8137, E-mail: hca@trinity.edu.
Website: http://new.trinity.edu/academics/departments/health-care-administration

**Trinity Western University,** School of Graduate Studies, Master of Arts in Leadership, Langley, BC V2Y 1Y1, Canada. Offers business (MA, Certificate); Christian ministry (MA); education (MA, Certificate); healthcare (MA, Certificate); non-profit (MA, Certificate). *Program availability:* Part-time, 100% online, blended/hybrid learning. *Degree requirements:* For master's, major project. *Entrance requirements:* Additional exam requirements/recommendations for international students: required—TOEFL (minimum score 100 iBT), IELTS (minimum score 7), DuoLingo. *Application deadline:* Applications are processed on a rolling basis. Electronic applications accepted. *Expenses:* Contact institution. *Financial support:* Research assistantships, teaching assistantships, and scholarships/grants available. Financial award application deadline: 5/1. *Unit head:* Dr. Philip Laird, Director, E-mail: laird@twu.ca. *Application contact:* Phil Kay, Director of Graduate Admissions, 604-513-2121 Ext. 3444, E-mail: phil.kay@twu.ca.
Website: http://www.twu.ca/leadership/

**Troy University,** Graduate School, College of Business, Program in Business Administration, Troy, AL 36082. Offers accounting (EMBA, MBA); criminal justice (EMBA); finance (MBA); general management (EMBA, MBA); healthcare management (EMBA); information systems (EMBA, MBA); international economic development (MBA). *Accreditation:* ACBSP. *Program availability:* Part-time, evening/weekend, online learning. *Faculty:* 15 full-time (5 women), 2 part-time/adjunct (0 women). *Students:* 49 full-time (17 women), 77 part-time (27 women); includes 23 minority (19 Black or African American, non-Hispanic/Latino; 1 Asian, non-Hispanic/Latino; 3 Hispanic/Latino), 21 international. Average age 29. 93 applicants, 60% accepted, 42 enrolled. In 2019, 59 master's awarded. *Degree requirements:* For master's, minimum GPA of 3.0, capstone course, research course. *Entrance requirements:* For master's, GMAT (500 or above) or GRE (1050 or above in verbal and quantitative), or 294 or above on the revised GRE (verbal and quantitative), bachelor's degree; minimum undergraduate GPA of 2.5 or 3.0 on last 30 semester hours, letter of recommendation. Additional exam requirements/recommendations for international students: required—TOEFL (minimum score 523 paper-based; 70 iBT), IELTS (minimum score 6). *Application deadline:* Applications are processed on a rolling basis. Application fee: $50. Electronic applications accepted. *Expenses: Tuition, area resident:* full-time $7650; part-time $2550 per semester hour. Tuition, state resident: full-time $7650; part-time $2550 per semester hour. *Tuition, nonresident:* full-time $15,300; part-time $5100 per semester hour. *International tuition:* $15,300 full-time. *Required fees:* $856; $352 per semester hour. $176 per semester. *Financial support:* In 2019–20, 50 students received support. Fellowships, research assistantships, teaching assistantships, career-related internships or fieldwork, Federal Work-Study, scholarships/grants, traineeships, tuition waivers, and unspecified assistantships available. Support available to part-time students. Financial award application deadline: 3/1; financial award applicants required to submit FAFSA. *Unit head:* Dr. Robert Wheatley, Professor, Director of Graduate Business Programs, 334-670-3416, Fax: 334-670-3708, E-mail: rwheat@troy.edu. *Application contact:* Haley McKinnon, Director of Graduate Admissions, 334-670-3178, Fax: 334-670-3733, E-mail: hmckinnon@troy.edu.
Website: https://www.troy.edu/academics/academic-programs/sorrell-college-business-programs.php

**Tufts University,** School of Medicine, Public Health and Professional Degree Programs, Boston, MA 02111. Offers biomedical sciences (MS); health communication (MS, Certificate); pain research, education and policy (MS, Certificate); physician assistant (MS); public health (MPH, Dr PH), including behavioral science (MPH), biostatistics (MPH), epidemiology (MPH), health communication (MPH), health services (MPH), management and policy (MPH), nutrition (MPH); DMD/MPH; DVM/MPH; JD/MPH; MD/MPH; MMS/MPH; MS/MBA; MS/MPH. *Accreditation:* CEPH (one or more programs are accredited). *Program availability:* Part-time, evening/weekend. *Students:* 450 full-time (291 women), 68 part-time (58 women); includes 201 minority (34 Black or African American, non-Hispanic/Latino; 1 American Indian or Alaska Native, non-Hispanic/Latino; 106 Asian, non-Hispanic/Latino; 41 Hispanic/Latino; 1 Native Hawaiian or other Pacific Islander, non-Hispanic/Latino; 18 Two or more races, non-Hispanic/Latino), 16 international. Average age 27. 1,076 applicants, 70% accepted, 213 enrolled. In 2019, 268 master's, 2 doctorates awarded. Terminal master's awarded for partial completion of doctoral program. *Degree requirements:* For master's, thesis (for some

programs); for doctorate, thesis/dissertation. *Entrance requirements:* For master's, GRE General Test, MCAT, or GMAT; LSAT for applicants to the JD/MPH combined degree; for doctorate, GRE General Test or MCAT. Additional exam requirements/recommendations for international students: required—TOEFL (minimum score 100 iBT); recommended—IELTS (minimum score 7), TSE. *Application deadline:* For fall admission, 1/15 priority date for domestic and international students; for spring admission, 10/25 priority date for domestic and international students. Applications are processed on a rolling basis. Application fee: $70. Electronic applications accepted. *Expenses:* Contact institution. *Financial support:* In 2019–20, 13 students received support, including 1 fellowship (averaging $3,000 per year), 50 research assistantships (averaging $1,000 per year), 65 teaching assistantships (averaging $2,000 per year); Federal Work-Study and scholarships/grants also available. Financial award application deadline: 2/23; financial award applicants required to submit FAFSA. *Unit head:* Dr. Aviva Must, Dean, 617-636-0935, Fax: 617-636-0898, E-mail: aviva.must@tufts.edu. *Application contact:* Emily Keily, Director of Admissions, 617-636-0935, Fax: 617-636-0898, E-mail: med-phpd@tufts.edu.
Website: http://publichealth.tufts.edu

**Tulane University,** School of Public Health and Tropical Medicine, Department of Health Policy and Management, New Orleans, LA 70118-5669. Offers MHA, MPH, PhD, Sc D, JD/MHA, MBA/MHA, MD/MPH, MSW/MPH. *Accreditation:* CAHME (one or more programs are accredited). *Degree requirements:* For doctorate, comprehensive exam, thesis/dissertation. *Entrance requirements:* For master's, GMAT, GRE General Test; for doctorate, GRE General Test. Additional exam requirements/recommendations for international students: required—TOEFL. Electronic applications accepted. *Expenses: Tuition:* Full-time $57,004; part-time $3167 per credit hour. *Required fees:* $2086; $44.50 per credit hour. $80 per term. Tuition and fees vary according to course load, degree level and program.

**Uniformed Services University of the Health Sciences,** F. Edward Hebert School of Medicine, Graduate Programs in the Biomedical Sciences and Public Health, Bethesda, MD 20814. Offers emerging infectious diseases (PhD); medical and clinical psychology (PhD), including clinical psychology, medical psychology; medicine (MS, PhD), including health professions education; molecular and cell biology (MS, PhD); neuroscience (PhD); preventive medicine and biometrics (MPH, MS, MSPH, MTMH, PhD), including environmental health sciences (PhD), healthcare administration and policy (MS), medical zoology (PhD), public health (MPH, MSPH), tropical medicine and hygiene (MTMH). Terminal master's awarded for partial completion of doctoral program. *Degree requirements:* For master's, comprehensive exam, thesis or alternative; for doctorate, comprehensive exam, thesis/dissertation, qualifying exam. *Entrance requirements:* For master's, GRE General Test; for doctorate, GRE General Test, minimum GPA of 3.0. Electronic applications accepted. *Expenses:* Contact institution.

**Uniformed Services University of the Health Sciences,** F. Edward Hebert School of Medicine, Graduate Programs in the Biomedical Sciences and Public Health, Department of Preventive Medicine and Biostatistics, Program in Healthcare Administration and Policy, Bethesda, MD 20814-4799. Offers MS. *Accreditation:* CAHME.

**Union Institute & University,** Master of Science Program in Healthcare Leadership, Cincinnati, OH 45206-1925. Offers MS.

**Universidad de Ciencias Medicas,** Graduate Programs, San Jose, Costa Rica. Offers dermatology (SP); family health (MS); health service center administration (MHA); human anatomy (MS); medical and surgery (MD); occupational medicine (MS); pharmacy (Pharm D). *Program availability:* Part-time. *Degree requirements:* For master's, thesis; for doctorate and SP, comprehensive exam. *Entrance requirements:* For master's, MD or bachelor's degree; for doctorate, admissions test; for SP, admissions test, MD.

**Universidad de Iberoamerica,** Graduate School, San Jose, Costa Rica. Offers clinical neuropsychology (PhD); clinical psychology (M Psych); educational psychology (M Psych); forensic psychology (M Psych); hospital management (MHA); intensive care nursing (MN); medicine (MD).

**Université de Montréal,** Faculty of Medicine, Department of Health Administration, Montréal, QC H3C 3J7, Canada. Offers M Sc, DESS. *Accreditation:* CAHME. *Degree requirements:* For master's, thesis. *Entrance requirements:* For master's, proficiency in French. Electronic applications accepted.

**University at Albany, State University of New York,** Nelson A. Rockefeller College of Public Affairs and Policy, Department of Public Administration and Policy, Albany, NY 12222-0001. Offers financial management and public economics (MPA); financial market regulation (MPA); health policy (MPA); healthcare management (MPA); homeland security (MPA); human resources management (MPA); information strategy and management (MPA); local government management (MPA); nonprofit management (MPA); nonprofit management and leadership (Certificate); organizational behavior and theory (MPA, PhD); planning and policy analysis (CAS); policy analysis (MPA); politics and administration (PhD); public finance (PhD); public management (PhD); public policy (PhD); public sector management (Certificate); women and public policy (Certificate); JD/MPA. *Accreditation:* NASPAA (one or more programs are accredited). *Program availability:* Blended/hybrid learning. *Faculty:* 19 full-time (8 women), 12 part-time/adjunct (4 women). *Students:* 119 full-time (71 women), 41 part-time (4 women); includes 45 minority (18 Black or African American, non-Hispanic/Latino; 7 Asian, non-Hispanic/Latino; 14 Hispanic/Latino; 6 Two or more races, non-Hispanic/Latino), 28 international. Average age 29. 172 applicants, 81% accepted, 85 enrolled. In 2019, 57 master's, 6 doctorates, 11 other advanced degrees awarded. *Degree requirements:* For doctorate, one foreign language, thesis/dissertation. *Entrance requirements:* For doctorate, GRE General Test. Additional exam requirements/recommendations for international students: required—TOEFL (minimum score 550 paper-based). *Application deadline:* For fall admission, 1/15 priority date for domestic students, 5/1 for international students; for spring admission, 11/15 for domestic students. Applications are processed on a rolling basis. Application fee: $75. Electronic applications accepted. *Expenses: Tuition, area resident:* Full-time $11,530; part-time $480 per credit hour. Tuition, nonresident: full-time $23,530; part-time $980 per credit hour. *International tuition:* $23,530 full-time. *Required fees:* $2185; $96 per credit hour. Part-time tuition and fees vary according to course load and program. *Financial support:* Research assistantships, teaching assistantships, and Federal Work-Study available. Financial award application deadline: 2/1. *Unit head:* Edmund Stazyk, Chair, 518-591-8723, E-mail: estazyk@albany.edu. *Application contact:* Luis Felipe Luna-Reyes, 518-442-5297, E-mail: llunareyes@albany.edu.
Website: http://www.albany.edu/rockefeller/pad.shtml

**University at Buffalo, the State University of New York,** Graduate School, School of Management, Buffalo, NY 14260. Offers accounting (MS); analytics (MBA); business administration (PMBA); consulting (MBA); finance (MBA, MS), including financial risk management (MS), quantitative finance (MS); healthcare (MBA); information assurance (MBA); information systems (MBA); international management (MBA); management (EMBA, PhD); management information systems (MS); marketing (MBA); supply chain and operations (MBA); supply chains and operations management (MS); Au D/MBA; DDS/MBA; JD/MBA; M Arch/MBA; MD/MBA; MPH/MBA; MSW/MBA; Pharm D/MBA. *Accreditation:* AACSB. *Program availability:* Part-time, evening/weekend. *Degree requirements:* For master's, capstone courses or projects; for doctorate, comprehensive exam, thesis/dissertation. *Entrance requirements:* For master's, GMAT (for MS in accounting, finance); GRE or GMAT (for MBA, MS in management information systems, supply chains and operations management), essays, letters of recommendation; for doctorate, GMAT or GRE, essays, writing sample, letters of recommendation. Additional exam requirements/recommendations for international students: required—TOEFL (minimum score 95 iBT) or IELTS (minimum score 6.5); recommended—TSE (minimum score 73). Electronic applications accepted. *Expenses:* Contact institution.

**The University of Alabama at Birmingham,** Collat School of Business, Program in Business Administration, Birmingham, AL 35294. Offers business administration (MBA), including finance, health care management, information technology management, marketing; MD/MBA. *Program availability:* Part-time, evening/weekend, 100% online, blended/hybrid learning. *Faculty:* 44 full-time (8 women), 11 part-time/adjunct (4 women). *Students:* 108 full-time (49 women), 369 part-time (154 women); includes 121 minority (78 Black or African American, non-Hispanic/Latino; 24 Asian, non-Hispanic/Latino; 8 Hispanic/Latino; 11 Two or more races, non-Hispanic/Latino), 59 international. Average age 33. 213 applicants, 62% accepted, 93 enrolled. In 2019, 114 master's awarded. *Entrance requirements:* For master's, GMAT. Additional exam requirements/recommendations for international students: required—TOEFL (minimum score 80 iBT), IELTS (minimum score 6.5). *Application deadline:* For fall admission, 7/1 for domestic and international students; for spring admission, 11/1 for domestic and international students; for summer admission, 4/1 for domestic and international students. Applications are processed on a rolling basis. Application fee: $60 ($75 for international students). Electronic applications accepted. *Unit head:* Dr. Ken Miller, Executive Director, MBA Programs, 205-934-8855, E-mail: klmiller@uab.edu. *Application contact:* Christy Manning, Coordinator of Graduate Programs in Business, 205-934-8817, E-mail: cmanning@uab.edu.
Website: http://www.uab.edu/business/home/mba

**The University of Alabama at Birmingham,** School of Education, Community Health and Human Services Program, Birmingham, AL 35294. Offers MA Ed. *Accreditation:* NCATE. *Faculty:* 4 full-time (2 women). *Students:* 12 full-time (11 women), 12 part-time (9 women); includes 14 minority (13 Black or African American, non-Hispanic/Latino; 1 Hispanic/Latino), 1 international. Average age 33. 19 applicants, 84% accepted, 9 enrolled. In 2019, 14 master's awarded. *Degree requirements:* For master's, comprehensive exam (for some programs), thesis optional. *Entrance requirements:* For master's, GRE General Test or MAT, minimum GPA of 3.0, references. *Application deadline:* Applications are processed on a rolling basis. Application fee: $35 ($60 for international students). Electronic applications accepted. *Unit head:* Dr. Kristi Menear, Chair, 205-975-7409, Fax: 205-975-8040, E-mail: kmenear@uab.edu. *Application contact:* Dr. Retta R. Evans, Program Coordinator, 205-996-2701, Fax: 205-975-8040, E-mail: rrevans@uab.edu.

**The University of Alabama at Birmingham,** School of Health Professions, Program in Administration/Health Services, Birmingham, AL 35294. Offers D Sc, PhD. *Faculty:* 32 full-time (19 women), 2 part-time/adjunct. *Students:* 29 full-time (12 women), 38 part-time (18 women); includes 19 minority (12 Black or African American, non-Hispanic/Latino; 3 Asian, non-Hispanic/Latino; 1 Hispanic/Latino; 1 Native Hawaiian or other Pacific Islander, non-Hispanic/Latino; 2 Two or more races, non-Hispanic/Latino), 8 international. Average age 43. 29 applicants, 52% accepted, 2 enrolled. In 2019, 10 doctorates awarded. *Degree requirements:* For doctorate, thesis/dissertation. *Entrance requirements:* For doctorate, GRE General Test. Additional exam requirements/recommendations for international students: required—TOEFL. *Application deadline:* For fall admission, 1/15 priority date for domestic students. *Financial support:* Fellowships, research assistantships, teaching assistantships, career-related internships or fieldwork, institutionally sponsored loans, and unspecified assistantships available. Financial award application deadline: 4/15. *Unit head:* Dr. S. Robert Hernandez, Director, Doctoral Programs, 205-924-1665, E-mail: hernande@uab.edu. *Application contact:* Susan Noblitt Banks, Director of Graduate School Operations, 205-934-8227, Fax: 205-934-8413, E-mail: gradschool@uab.edu.
Website: http://www.uab.edu/shp/hsa/phddsc

**The University of Alabama at Birmingham,** School of Health Professions, Program in Health Administration, Birmingham, AL 35294. Offers MSHA. *Accreditation:* CAHME. *Faculty:* 21 full-time (12 women), 15 part-time/adjunct (8 women). *Students:* 149 full-time (73 women); includes 37 minority (21 Black or African American, non-Hispanic/Latino; 1 American Indian or Alaska Native, non-Hispanic/Latino; 10 Asian, non-Hispanic/Latino; 5 Hispanic/Latino), 1 international. Average age 29. 141 applicants, 48% accepted, 56 enrolled. In 2019, 59 master's awarded. *Degree requirements:* For master's, administrative residency. *Entrance requirements:* For master's, GMAT or GRE General Test, minimum GPA of 3.0 in final 60 hours of undergraduate course work; 5 years of experience in health care organizations, either as manager or as clinical professional (for executive program). Additional exam requirements/recommendations for international students: required—TOEFL (minimum score 550 paper-based), TWE. *Application deadline:* For fall admission, 12/1 priority date for domestic students. Applications are processed on a rolling basis. Application fee: $70 ($85 for international students). Electronic applications accepted. *Financial support:* Career-related internships or fieldwork, Federal Work-Study, scholarships/grants, and traineeships available. Financial award application deadline: 5/1; financial award applicants required to submit FAFSA. *Unit head:* Amy Y. Landry, PhD, Director, 205-996-7767, E-mail: akyarb@uab.edu. *Application contact:* Pamela L. Armstrong, Admissions Coordinator, 205-934-1583, E-mail: parmstrong@uab.edu.
Website: http://www.uab.edu/shp/hsa/msha

**The University of Alabama at Birmingham,** School of Public Health, Program in Health Care Organization and Policy, Birmingham, AL 35294. Offers applied epidemiology and pharmacoepidemiology (MSPH); biostatistics (MPH); clinical and translational science (MSPH); environmental health (MPH); environmental health and toxicology (MSPH); epidemiology (MPH); general theory and practice (MPH); health behavior (MPH); health care organization (MPH, Dr PH); health policy (MPH); industrial hygiene (MPH, MSPH); maternal and child health policy (Dr PH); maternal and child health policy and leadership (MPH); occupational health and safety (MPH); outcomes research (MSPH, Dr PH); public health (PhD); public health preparedness management (MPH). *Accreditation:* CEPH. *Program availability:* Part-time, 100% online, blended/hybrid learning. *Faculty:* 14 full-time (6 women). *Students:* 53 full-time (37 women), 61 part-time (45 women); includes 37 minority (12 Black or African American, non-Hispanic/Latino; 20 Asian, non-Hispanic/Latino; 1 Hispanic/Latino; 4 Two or more races, non-Hispanic/Latino), 17 international. Average age 31. 136 applicants, 59% accepted, 44 enrolled. In 2019, 36 master's, 4 doctorates awarded. *Degree requirements:* For master's, comprehensive exam (for some programs), thesis (for some programs); for doctorate, comprehensive exam, thesis/dissertation. *Entrance requirements:* For doctorate, GRE. Additional exam requirements/recommendations for international students: required—TOEFL (minimum score 80 iBT), IELTS (minimum score 6.5). *Application deadline:* For fall admission, 4/1 priority date for domestic students, 4/1 for international students; for spring admission, 11/1 for domestic students; for summer admission, 4/1 for domestic students. Application fee: $50 ($60 for international

students). Electronic applications accepted. *Financial support:* Fellowships, research assistantships, teaching assistantships, scholarships/grants, traineeships, and unspecified assistantships available. Financial award application deadline: 3/1; financial award applicants required to submit FAFSA. *Unit head:* Dr. Martha Wingate, Program Director, 205-934-6783, Fax: 205-975-5484, E-mail: mslay@uab.edu. *Application contact:* Dustin Shaw, Coordinator, Student Admissions and Record, 205-934-3939, E-mail: bcampbel@uab.edu.
Website: http://www.soph.uab.edu

**The University of Alabama in Huntsville,** School of Graduate Studies, College of Nursing, Huntsville, AL 35899. Offers family nurse practitioner (Certificate); nursing (MSN, DNP), including adult-gerontology acute care nurse practitioner (MSN), adult-gerontology clinical nurse specialist (MSN), family nurse practitioner (MSN), leadership in health care systems (MSN); nursing education (Certificate). *Accreditation:* AACN. *Program availability:* Part-time. *Degree requirements:* For master's, comprehensive exam, thesis or alternative, oral and written exams. *Entrance requirements:* For master's, MAT or GRE, Alabama RN license, BSN, minimum GPA of 3.0; for doctorate, master's degree in nursing in an advanced practice area; for Certificate, MAT or GRE, minimum GPA of 3.0. Additional exam requirements/recommendations for international students: required—TOEFL (minimum score 500 paper-based; 80 iBT), IELTS (minimum score 6.5). Electronic applications accepted.

**University of Alberta,** School of Public Health, Department of Public Health Sciences, Edmonton, AB T6G 2E1, Canada. Offers clinical epidemiology (M Sc, MPH); environmental and occupational health (MPH); environmental health sciences (M Sc); epidemiology (M Sc); global health (M Sc, MPH); health policy and management (MPH); health policy research (M Sc); health technology assessment (MPH); occupational health (M Sc); population health (M Sc); public health leadership (MPH); public health sciences (PhD); quantitative methods (MPH). *Accreditation:* CEPH. Terminal master's awarded for partial completion of doctoral program. *Degree requirements:* For master's, thesis (for some programs); for doctorate, thesis/dissertation. *Entrance requirements:* For master's, GMAT or GRE General Test. Additional exam requirements/recommendations for international students: required—TOEFL (minimum score 550 paper-based) or IELTS (minimum score 6). Electronic applications accepted.

**University of Arkansas for Medical Sciences,** Fay W. Boozman College of Public Health, Little Rock, AR 72205-7199. Offers biostatistics (MPH); environmental and occupational health (MPH, Certificate); epidemiology (MPH, PhD); health behavior and health education (MPH); health policy and management (MPH); health promotion and prevention research (PhD); health services administration (MHSA); health systems research (PhD); public health (Certificate); public health leadership (Dr PH). *Accreditation:* CAHME; CEPH. *Program availability:* Part-time. *Degree requirements:* For master's, preceptorship, culminating experience, internship; for doctorate, comprehensive exam, capstone. *Entrance requirements:* For master's, GRE, GMAT, LSAT, PCAT, MCAT, DAT; for doctorate, GRE. Additional exam requirements/recommendations for international students: required—TOEFL (minimum score 80 iBT), IELTS. Electronic applications accepted. *Expenses:* Contact institution.

**University of Arkansas-Fort Smith,** Program in Healthcare Administration, Fort Smith, AR 72913-3649. Offers MS. *Program availability:* Online learning. *Degree requirements:* For master's, project. *Entrance requirements:* For master's, bachelor's degree with minimum GPA of 3.0.

**University of Baltimore,** Graduate School, College of Public Affairs, Program in Health Systems Management, Baltimore, MD 21201-5779. Offers MS. *Program availability:* Part-time, evening/weekend. *Entrance requirements:* For master's, minimum undergraduate GPA of 3.0. Additional exam requirements/recommendations for international students: required—TOEFL (minimum score 550 paper-based).

**The University of British Columbia,** Faculty of Medicine, School of Population and Public Health, Vancouver, BC V6T 1Z3, Canada. Offers health administration (MHA); health sciences (MH Sc); occupational and environmental hygiene (M Sc); population and public health (M Sc, MPH, PhD); MPH/MSN. *Program availability:* Online learning. *Degree requirements:* For master's, thesis (for some programs), major paper (MH Sc), research project (MHA); for doctorate, thesis/dissertation. *Entrance requirements:* For master's, GRE General Test or GMAT, PCAT, MCAT (for MHA), MD or equivalent (for MH Sc); 4-year undergraduate degree from accredited university with minimum B+ overall academic average and in math or statistics course at undergraduate level (for MPH); 4-year undergraduate degree from accredited university with minimum B+ overall academic average plus work experience (for MHA); for doctorate, master's degree from accredited university with minimum B+ overall academic average and in math or statistics course at undergraduate level. Additional exam requirements/recommendations for international students: required—TOEFL. Electronic applications accepted. *Expenses:* Contact institution.

**University of California, Berkeley,** Graduate Division, School of Public Health, Group in Health Policy, Berkeley, CA 94720. Offers PhD. *Degree requirements:* For doctorate, thesis/dissertation, qualifying exam. *Entrance requirements:* For doctorate, GRE General Test, minimum GPA of 3.0, 3 letters of recommendation. Electronic applications accepted.

**University of California, Irvine,** The Paul Merage School of Business, Health Care Executive MBA Program, Irvine, CA 92697. Offers MBA.

**University of California, Los Angeles,** Graduate Division, Fielding School of Public Health, Department of Health Services, Los Angeles, CA 90095. Offers MPH, MS, Dr PH, PhD, JD/MPH, MBA/MPH, MD/MPH. *Degree requirements:* For master's, comprehensive exam or thesis; for doctorate, thesis/dissertation, oral and written qualifying exams. *Entrance requirements:* For master's, GRE General Test, minimum GPA of 3.0; for doctorate, GRE General Test, minimum undergraduate GPA of 3.0. Electronic applications accepted.

**University of California, San Diego,** School of Medicine, Program in the Leadership of Healthcare Organizations, La Jolla, CA 92093. Offers MAS. *Program availability:* Part-time, evening/weekend. *Students:* 5 full-time (all women), 21 part-time (14 women). 19 applicants, 53% accepted, 6 enrolled. In 2019, 25 master's awarded. *Degree requirements:* For master's, independent study project. *Entrance requirements:* For master's, minimum GPA of 3.0, minimum 5 years of professional work/internship in health care or related field, resume or curriculum vitae, 3 letters of recommendation. Additional exam requirements/recommendations for international students: required—TOEFL (minimum score 550 paper-based; 80 iBT), IELTS (minimum score 7). *Application deadline:* Applications are processed on a rolling basis. Application fee: $105 ($125 for international students). Electronic applications accepted. *Expenses:* Contact institution. *Financial support:* Scholarships/grants available. Financial award applicants required to submit FAFSA. *Unit head:* Todd Gilmer, Chair, 858-534-7596, E-mail: tgilmer@ucsd.edu. *Application contact:* Katherine Lukens, Graduate Coordinator, E-mail: lhco@ucsd.edu.
Website: http://lhco.ucsd.edu/

**University of Central Florida,** College of Community Innovation and Education, Department of Health Management and Informatics, Orlando, FL 32816. Offers health administration (MHA); health care informatics (MS); health information administration (Certificate). *Accreditation:* CAHME. *Program availability:* Part-time, evening/weekend. *Students:* 169 full-time (106 women), 233 part-time (159 women); includes 247 minority (87 Black or African American, non-Hispanic/Latino; 61 Asian, non-Hispanic/Latino; 82 Hispanic/Latino; 17 Two or more races, non-Hispanic/Latino), 4 international. Average age 30. 316 applicants, 80% accepted, 165 enrolled. In 2019, 135 master's awarded. *Degree requirements:* For master's, comprehensive exam, thesis or alternative, research report. *Entrance requirements:* For master's, letters of recommendation, resume, goal statement. Additional exam requirements/recommendations for international students: required—TOEFL. *Application deadline:* For fall admission, 7/15 for domestic students; for spring admission, 12/1 for domestic students. Application fee: $30. Electronic applications accepted. *Financial support:* In 2019–20, 3 students received support, including 1 fellowship (averaging $10,000 per year), 1 research assistantship with partial tuition reimbursement available (averaging $4,704 per year), 1 teaching assistantship (averaging $9,074 per year); career-related internships or fieldwork, Federal Work-Study, institutionally sponsored loans, and unspecified assistantships also available. Financial award application deadline: 3/1; financial award applicants required to submit FAFSA. *Unit head:* Dr. Reid Oetjen, Interim Chair, 407-823-5668, E-mail: reid.oetjen@ucf.edu. *Application contact:* Associate Director, Graduate Admissions, 407-823-2766, Fax: 407-823-6442, E-mail: gradadmissions@ucf.edu.
Website: https://www.cohpa.ucf.edu/hmi/

**University of Chicago,** Booth School of Business, Full-Time MBA Program, Chicago, IL 60637. Offers accounting (MBA); analytic finance (MBA); analytic management (MBA); econometrics and statistics (MBA); economics (MBA); entrepreneurship (MBA); finance (MBA); general management (MBA); health administration and policy (Certificate); international business (MBA); managerial and organizational behavior (MBA); marketing analytics (MBA); marketing management (MBA); operations management (MBA); strategic management (MBA); MBA/AM; MBA/JD; MBA/MA; MBA/MD; MBA/MPP. *Accreditation:* AACSB. *Entrance requirements:* For master's, GMAT or GRE, transcripts, resume, 2 letters of recommendation, essays, interview. Additional exam requirements/recommendations for international students: required—TOEFL, IELTS, or PTE. Electronic applications accepted. *Expenses:* Contact institution.

**University of Colorado Denver,** Business School, Master of Business Administration Program, Denver, CO 80217. Offers business administration (MBA); health administration (MBA). *Accreditation:* AACSB. *Program availability:* Part-time, evening/weekend, 100% online, blended/hybrid learning. *Degree requirements:* For master's, 48 semester hours, including 30 of core courses, 3 in international business, and 15 in electives from over 50 other business courses. *Entrance requirements:* For master's, GMAT, resume, official transcripts, essay, two letters of recommendation, financial statements (for international applicants). Additional exam requirements/recommendations for international students: required—TOEFL (minimum score 560 paper-based; 83 iBT); recommended—IELTS (minimum score 6.5). Electronic applications accepted. *Expenses:* Contact institution.

**University of Colorado Denver,** Business School, Program in Health Administration, Denver, CO 80217. Offers MS. *Accreditation:* CAHME. *Program availability:* Part-time, evening/weekend. *Degree requirements:* For master's, 30 credit hours. *Entrance requirements:* For master's, GMAT, resume, essay, two letters of reference, financial statements (for international applicants). Additional exam requirements/recommendations for international students: required—TOEFL (minimum score 525 paper-based; 71 iBT); recommended—IELTS (minimum score 6.5). Electronic applications accepted. *Expenses:* Contact institution.

**University of Connecticut,** Graduate School, School of Business, Storrs, CT 06269. Offers accounting (MS, PhD); business (PhD); business administration (MBA); business analytics and project management (MS); finance (PhD); financial risk management (MS); health care management and insurance studies (MBA); human resource management (MS); management (PhD); management consulting (MBA); marketing (PhD); marketing intelligence (MBA); operations and information management (PhD). *Accreditation:* AACSB. *Degree requirements:* For master's, comprehensive exam; for doctorate, thesis/dissertation. *Entrance requirements:* For master's and doctorate, GMAT. Additional exam requirements/recommendations for international students: required—TOEFL (minimum score 550 paper-based). Electronic applications accepted.

**University of Dallas,** Satish and Yasmin Gupta College of Business, Irving, TX 75062. Offers accounting (MBA, MS); business administration (DBA); business analytics (MS); business management (MBA); corporate finance (MBA); cybersecurity (MS); finance (MS); financial services (MBA); global business (MBA, MS); health services management (MBA); human resource management (MBA); information and technology management (MS); information assurance (MBA); information technology (MBA); information technology service management (MBA); marketing management (MBA); organization development (MBA); project management (MBA); sports and entertainment management (MBA); strategic leadership (MBA); supply chain management (MBA). *Accreditation:* AACSB. *Program availability:* Part-time, evening/weekend, 100% online, blended/hybrid learning. *Students:* 120 full-time (53 women), 531 part-time (203 women); includes 353 minority (173 Black or African American, non-Hispanic/Latino; 1 American Indian or Alaska Native, non-Hispanic/Latino; 78 Asian, non-Hispanic/Latino; 92 Hispanic/Latino; 2 Native Hawaiian or other Pacific Islander, non-Hispanic/Latino; 7 Two or more races, non-Hispanic/Latino), 96 international. Average age 33. 291 applicants, 96% accepted, 141 enrolled. In 2019, 302 master's, 4 doctorates awarded. *Degree requirements:* For doctorate, thesis/dissertation. *Entrance requirements:* For master's and doctorate, U.S. bachelor's degree with a minimum cumulative GPA of 2.0 from a regionally accredited college or university (or comparable foreign degree); minimum 3.0 GPA in any graduate-level coursework completed; good academic standing with all colleges attended. Additional exam requirements/recommendations for international students: required—TOEFL (minimum score 80 iBT), IELTS (minimum score 6.5), PTE (minimum score 67). *Application deadline:* Applications are processed on a rolling basis. Application fee: $50. Electronic applications accepted. *Expenses:* $1,250 per credit hour, $160 matriculation fee, $100 graduation fee. *Financial support:* Research assistantships, teaching assistantships, scholarships/grants, and unspecified assistantships available. Support available to part-time students. Financial award application deadline: 2/15; financial award applicants required to submit FAFSA. *Unit head:* Brett J.L. Landry, Dean, 972-721-5356, E-mail: blandry@udallas.edu. *Application contact:* Breonna Collins, Director, Graduate Admissions, 972-7215304, E-mail: bcollins@udallas.edu.
Website: http://www.udallas.edu/cob/

**University of Denver,** University College, Denver, CO 80208. Offers arts and culture (MA, Certificate); communication management (MS, Certificate), including translation studies (Certificate), world history and culture (Certificate); environmental policy and management (MS); geographic information systems (MS); global affairs (MA, Certificate), including human capital in organizations (Certificate), philanthropic leadership (Certificate), project management (Certificate), strategic innovation and change (Certificate); healthcare leadership (MS); information communications and technology (MS); leadership and organizations (MS); professional creative writing (MA, Certificate), including emergency planning and response (Certificate), organizational security (Certificate); security management (MS, Certificate); strategic human resources

(Certificate). *Program availability:* Part-time, evening/weekend, 100% online, blended/hybrid learning. *Faculty:* 104 part-time/adjunct (52 women). *Students:* 59 full-time (33 women), 1,893 part-time (1,210 women); includes 545 minority (133 Black or African American, non-Hispanic/Latino; 16 American Indian or Alaska Native, non-Hispanic/Latino; 64 Asian, non-Hispanic/Latino; 252 Hispanic/Latino; 4 Native Hawaiian or other Pacific Islander, non-Hispanic/Latino; 76 Two or more races, non-Hispanic/Latino), 78 international. Average age 32. 1,290 applicants, 91% accepted, 752 enrolled. In 2019, 457 master's, 181 other advanced degrees awarded. *Degree requirements:* For master's, capstone project. *Entrance requirements:* For master's, baccalaureate degree, transcripts, two letters of recommendation, personal statement, resume, writing sample (Master of Arts in Professional Creative Writing). Additional exam requirements/recommendations for international students: required—TOEFL (minimum score 550 paper-based; 80 iBT). *Application deadline:* For fall admission, 6/19 priority date for domestic students, 6/14 priority date for international students; for winter admission, 10/25 priority date for domestic students, 9/27 priority date for international students; for spring admission, 2/7 priority date for domestic students, 1/10 priority date for international students; for summer admission, 4/24 priority date for domestic students, 3/27 priority date for international students. Applications are processed on a rolling basis. Application fee: $75. Electronic applications accepted. *Expenses:* Contact institution. *Financial support:* In 2019–20, 56 students received support. Teaching assistantships available. Financial award applicants required to submit FAFSA. *Unit head:* Dr. Michael McGuire, Dean, 303-871-3518, E-mail: michael.mcguire@du.edu. *Application contact:* Admission Team, 303-871-2291, E-mail: ucoladm@du.edu.
Website: http://universitycollege.du.edu/

**University of Detroit Mercy,** College of Health Professions, Detroit, MI 48221. Offers clinical nurse leader (MSN); family nurse practitioner (MSN); health services administration (MHSA); health systems management (MSN); nurse anesthesia (MS); nursing (DNP); nursing education (MSN, Certificate); nursing leadership and financial management (Certificate); outcomes performance management (Certificate); physician assistant (MS). *Accreditation:* AANA/CANAEP. *Entrance requirements:* For master's, GRE General Test, minimum GPA of 3.0.

**University of Evansville,** College of Education and Health Sciences, School of Health Sciences, Evansville, IN 47722. Offers athletic training (MSAT); health policy (MPH); health services administration (MS). *Program availability:* Part-time, evening/weekend. *Entrance requirements:* Additional exam requirements/recommendations for international students: required—TOEFL, IELTS (minimum score 6.5). *Expenses:* Contact institution.

**The University of Findlay,** Office of Graduate Admissions, Findlay, OH 45840. Offers applied security and analytics (MSAS); athletic training (MAT); business (MBA), including certified management accountant, certified public accountant, health care management, hospitality management; education (MA Ed, Ed D), including children's literature (MA Ed), curriculum and teaching (MA Ed), education (MA Ed), educational administration (MA Ed), human resource development (MA Ed), mathematics (MA Ed), reading (MA Ed), science education (MA Ed), superintendent (Ed D), teaching (Ed D), technology (MA Ed); environmental, safety, and health management (MSEM); health informatics (MS); occupational therapy (MOT); pharmacy (Pharm D); physical therapy (DPT); physician assistant (MPA); rhetoric and writing (MA); teaching English to speakers of other languages (TESOL) and applied linguistics (MA). *Program availability:* Part-time, evening/weekend, 100% online, blended/hybrid learning. *Students:* 688 full-time (430 women), 553 part-time (308 women), 170 international. Average age 28. 865 applicants, 31% accepted, 235 enrolled. In 2019, 363 master's, 141 doctorates awarded. *Degree requirements:* For master's, comprehensive exam (for some programs), thesis (for some programs), cumulative project, capstone project; for doctorate, thesis/dissertation (for some programs). *Entrance requirements:* For master's, GRE/GMAT, bachelor's degree from accredited institution, minimum undergraduate GPA of 2.5 in last 64 hours of course work; for doctorate, GRE, MAT, minimum cumulative GPA of 3.0. Additional exam requirements/recommendations for international students: required—TOEFL (minimum score 79 iBT), IELTS (minimum score 7), PTE (minimum score 61). *Application deadline:* Applications are processed on a rolling basis. Electronic applications accepted. *Financial support:* In 2019–20, 10 research assistantships with partial tuition reimbursements (averaging $7,200 per year), 35 teaching assistantships with partial tuition reimbursements (averaging $7,200 per year) were awarded; Federal Work-Study, institutionally sponsored loans, and unspecified assistantships also available. Financial award applicants required to submit FAFSA. *Unit head:* Dave M. Emsweller, Director of Admissions, Interim, 419-434-4578, E-mail: emsweller@findlay.edu. *Application contact:* Amber Feehan, Graduate Admissions Counselor, 419-434-6933, Fax: 419-434-4898, E-mail: feehan@findlay.edu.
Website: http://www.findlay.edu/admissions/graduate/Pages/default.aspx

**University of Florida,** Graduate School, College of Pharmacy, Graduate Programs in Pharmacy, Department of Pharmaceutical Outcomes and Policy, Gainesville, FL 32611. Offers MSP, PhD. *Program availability:* Part-time, online learning. *Degree requirements:* For doctorate, thesis/dissertation. *Entrance requirements:* For master's and doctorate, GRE General Test, minimum GPA of 3.0. Additional exam requirements/recommendations for international students: required—TOEFL (minimum score 550 paper-based; 80 iBT), IELTS (minimum score 6). Electronic applications accepted.

**University of Florida,** Graduate School, College of Public Health and Health Professions, Department of Health Services Research, Management and Policy, Gainesville, FL 32611. Offers health administration (MHA); health services research (PhD). *Accreditation:* CAHME. *Program availability:* Part-time. *Degree requirements:* For master's, internship. *Entrance requirements:* For master's, GRE General Test (minimum score 300) or GMAT (minimum score 500), minimum GPA of 3.0; for doctorate, GRE General Test, minimum GPA of 3.0. Additional exam requirements/recommendations for international students: required—TOEFL (minimum score 550 paper-based; 80 iBT), IELTS (minimum score 6). Electronic applications accepted.

**University of Florida,** Graduate School, Warrington College of Business Administration, Hough Graduate School of Business, Department of Management, Gainesville, FL 32611. Offers health care risk management (MS); international business (MA); management (MS, PhD). *Accreditation:* AACSB. *Program availability:* Online learning. *Degree requirements:* For master's, comprehensive exam, thesis. *Entrance requirements:* For master's, GMAT (minimum score of 465) or GRE General Test, minimum GPA of 3.0. Additional exam requirements/recommendations for international students: required—TOEFL (minimum score 550 paper-based; 80 iBT), IELTS (minimum score 6). Electronic applications accepted.

**University of Holy Cross,** Graduate Programs, New Orleans, LA 70131-7399. Offers biomedical sciences (MS); Catholic theology (MA); counseling (MA, PhD), including community counseling (MA), marriage and family counseling (MA), school counseling (MA); educational leadership (M Ed); executive leadership (Ed D); management (MS), including healthcare management, operations management; teaching and learning (M Ed). *Accreditation:* ACA; NCATE. *Program availability:* Part-time, evening/weekend, online learning. *Degree requirements:* For master's, thesis. *Entrance requirements:* For master's, GRE General Test, minimum GPA of 2.7.

**University of Houston–Clear Lake,** School of Business, Program in Healthcare Administration, Houston, TX 77058-1002. Offers MHA, MHA/MBA. *Degree requirements:* For master's, thesis optional. *Entrance requirements:* For master's, GMAT. Additional exam requirements/recommendations for international students: required—TOEFL (minimum score 550 paper-based).

**University of Illinois at Chicago,** School of Public Health, Division of Health Policy and Administration, Chicago, IL 60607-7128. Offers clinical and translational science (MS); health policy (PhD); health services research (PhD); healthcare administration (MHA); public health policy management (MPH). *Accreditation:* CAHME. *Program availability:* Part-time. Terminal master's awarded for partial completion of doctoral program. *Degree requirements:* For master's, thesis, field practicum; for doctorate, thesis/dissertation, independent research, internship. *Entrance requirements:* For master's and doctorate, GRE General Test, minimum GPA of 2.75. Additional exam requirements/recommendations for international students: required—TOEFL. Electronic applications accepted. *Expenses:* Contact institution.

**University of Illinois at Urbana-Champaign,** Graduate College, School of Social Work, Champaign, IL 61820. Offers advocacy, leadership, and social change (MSW); children, youth and family services (MSW); health care (MSW); mental health (MSW); school social work (MSW); social work (PhD). *Accreditation:* CSWE (one or more programs are accredited). *Entrance requirements:* For master's and doctorate, minimum GPA of 3.0.

**The University of Iowa,** Graduate College, College of Public Health, Department of Health Management and Policy, Iowa City, IA 52242-1316. Offers MHA, PhD, JD/MHA, MBA/MHA, MHA/MA, MHA/MS. *Accreditation:* CAHME (one or more programs are accredited). *Degree requirements:* For doctorate, comprehensive exam, thesis/dissertation. *Entrance requirements:* For master's, GRE General Test or equivalent, minimum GPA of 3.0; for doctorate, GRE General Test, minimum GPA of 3.0. Additional exam requirements/recommendations for international students: required—TOEFL (minimum score 550 paper-based; 81 iBT). Electronic applications accepted. *Expenses:* Contact institution.

**University of Kentucky,** Graduate School, College of Health Sciences, Program in Health Administration, Lexington, KY 40506-0032. Offers MHA. *Accreditation:* CAHME. *Degree requirements:* For master's, comprehensive exam. *Entrance requirements:* For master's, GRE General Test, minimum undergraduate GPA of 2.75. Additional exam requirements/recommendations for international students: required—TOEFL (minimum score 550 paper-based). Electronic applications accepted.

**University of La Verne,** College of Business and Public Management, Graduate Programs in Business Administration, La Verne, CA 91750-4443. Offers accounting (MBA, MBA-EP); finance (MBA, MBA-EP); health services management (MBA); information technology (MBA, MBA-EP); international business (MBA, MBA-EP); management and leadership (MBA, MBA-EP); marketing (MBA, MBA-EP); supply chain management (MBA, MBA-EP). *Program availability:* Part-time, evening/weekend. *Entrance requirements:* For master's, GMAT, MAT, or GRE, minimum undergraduate GPA of 3.0, 2 letters of recommendation, resume, statement of purpose. Additional exam requirements/recommendations for international students: required—TOEFL (minimum score 550 paper-based; 85 iBT).

**University of La Verne,** College of Business and Public Management, Program in Health Administration, La Verne, CA 91750-4443. Offers financial management (MHA); management and leadership (MHA); marketing and business development (MHA). *Program availability:* Part-time. *Entrance requirements:* For master's, bachelor's degree, experience in health services industry (preferred). Additional exam requirements/recommendations for international students: required—TOEFL (minimum score 550 paper-based). *Expenses:* Contact institution.

**University of La Verne,** Regional and Online Campuses, Graduate Programs, Bakersfield Campus, Bakersfield, CA 93311. Offers business administration for experienced professionals (MBA-EP); education (special emphasis) (M Ed); educational counseling (MS); educational leadership (M Ed); health administration (MHA); leadership and management (MS); mild/moderate education specialist (Credential); multiple subject (elementary) (Credential); organizational leadership (Ed D); preliminary administrative services (Credential); single subject (secondary) (Credential); special education studies (MS). *Program availability:* Part-time, evening/weekend. *Expenses:* Contact institution.

**University of La Verne,** Regional and Online Campuses, Graduate Programs, Inland Empire Campus, Ontario, CA 91730. Offers business administration (MBA, MBA-EP), including accounting (MBA), finance (MBA), health services management (MBA-EP), information technology (MBA-EP), international business (MBA), managed care (MBA), management and leadership (MBA-EP), marketing (MBA-EP), supply chain management (MBA); leadership and management (MS), including human resource management, nonprofit management, organizational development. *Program availability:* Part-time, evening/weekend. *Expenses:* Contact institution.

**University of La Verne,** Regional and Online Campuses, Graduate Programs, Orange County Campus, Irvine, CA 92840. Offers business administration for experienced professionals (MBA); educational counseling (MS); educational leadership (M Ed); health administration (MHA); leadership and management (MS); preliminary administrative services (Credential); pupil personnel services (Credential). *Program availability:* Part-time. *Expenses:* Contact institution.

**University of La Verne,** Regional and Online Campuses, Graduate Programs, Vandenberg Air Force Base Campuses, La Verne, CA 91750-4443. Offers business administration for experienced professionals (MBA), including health services management, information technology; leadership and management (MS). *Program availability:* Part-time. *Expenses:* Contact institution.

**University of Louisville,** Graduate School, College of Business, MBA Programs, Louisville, KY 40292-0001. Offers entrepreneurship (MBA); global business (MBA); health sector management (MBA). *Accreditation:* AACSB. *Program availability:* Part-time, evening/weekend, 100% online. *Faculty:* 26 full-time (9 women), 13 part-time/adjunct (2 women). *Students:* 246 full-time (87 women), 12 part-time (2 women); includes 74 minority (37 Black or African American, non-Hispanic/Latino; 1 American Indian or Alaska Native, non-Hispanic/Latino; 16 Asian, non-Hispanic/Latino; 17 Hispanic/Latino; 3 Two or more races, non-Hispanic/Latino), 13 international. Average age 32. 292 applicants, 74% accepted, 179 enrolled. In 2019, 165 master's awarded. *Degree requirements:* For master's, Completion of 45 credit hours. *Entrance requirements:* For master's, GMAT, Personal Statement, Resume, Letter of Recommendation and all official college transcripts. Additional exam requirements/recommendations for international students: required—TOEFL (minimum score 550 paper-based; 79 iBT), IELTS. *Application deadline:* For fall admission, 6/1 priority date for domestic students, 5/1 priority date for international students; for spring admission, 4/1 for domestic students. Applications are processed on a rolling basis. Application fee: $50. Electronic applications accepted. *Expenses: Tuition, area resident:* Full-time $13,000; part-time $723 per credit hour. Tuition, state resident: full-time $13,000; part-time $723 per credit hour. Tuition, nonresident: full-time $27,114; part-time $1507 per credit hour. *International tuition:* $27,114 full-time. *Required fees:* $196. Tuition and fees

vary according to program and reciprocity agreements. *Financial support:* In 2019–20, 84 students received support. Scholarships/grants, unspecified assistantships, and We offer 11-paid internships (competitive, not guaranteed) available. Financial award application deadline: 8/1; financial award applicants required to submit FAFSA. *Unit head:* Dr. Richard Germain, Associate Dean, 502-852-4680, E-mail: richard.germain@louisville.edu. *Application contact:* Dr. Richard Germain, Associate Dean, 502-852-4680, E-mail: richard.germain@louisville.edu.
Website: http://business.louisville.edu/mba

**University of Management and Technology,** Program in Health Administration, Arlington, VA 22209-1609. Offers MHA. *Expenses: Tuition:* Full-time $7020; part-time $390 per credit hour. *Required fees:* $90; $30 per semester.

**University of Mary,** Gary Tharaldson School of Business, Bismarck, ND 58504-9652. Offers business administration (MBA); energy management (MBA, MS); executive (MBA, MS); health care (MBA, MS); human resource management (MBA); project management (MBA, MPM); virtuous leadership (MBA, MPM, MS). *Program availability:* Part-time, evening/weekend. *Entrance requirements:* For master's, minimum GPA of 2.5. Additional exam requirements/recommendations for international students: required—TOEFL (minimum score 550 paper-based; 80 iBT). Electronic applications accepted.

**University of Maryland, Baltimore County,** The Graduate School, College of Arts, Humanities and Social Sciences, Department of Emergency Health Services, Baltimore, MD 21250. Offers emergency health services (MS), including administration, planning, and policy, preventive medicine and epidemiology; emergency management (Postbaccalaureate Certificate); public policy (PhD), including emergency health, emergency management. *Program availability:* Part-time, evening/weekend, 100% online, blended/hybrid learning. *Faculty:* 4 full-time (2 women), 8 part-time/adjunct (3 women). *Students:* 5 full-time (4 women), 9 part-time (5 women); includes 5 minority (2 Black or African American, non-Hispanic/Latino; 1 Asian, non-Hispanic/Latino; 2 Hispanic/Latino), 2 international. Average age 37. 19 applicants, 68% accepted, 3 enrolled. In 2019, 5 master's, 2 other advanced degrees awarded. Terminal master's awarded for partial completion of doctoral program. *Degree requirements:* For master's, comprehensive exam (for some programs), capstone project or thesis. *Entrance requirements:* For master's, GRE General Test if GPA is below 3.2, minimum GPA of 3.2. Additional exam requirements/recommendations for international students: required—TOEFL (minimum score 80 iBT), IELTS, or PTE. *Application deadline:* For fall admission, 6/15 for domestic students, 3/1 for international students; for spring admission, 12/1 for domestic students, 10/1 for international students. Applications are processed on a rolling basis. Application fee: $50. Electronic applications accepted. *Expenses:* $14,382 per year. *Financial support:* In 2019–20, 1 student received support, including 1 research assistantship with full tuition reimbursement available (averaging $16,875 per year); career-related internships or fieldwork, Federal Work-Study, health care benefits, and unspecified assistantships also available. Financial award application deadline: 5/30; financial award applicants required to submit FAFSA. *Unit head:* Dr. J. Lee Jenkins, Department Chair, 410-455-3216, Fax: 410-455-3045, E-mail: jleejenkins@umbc.edu. *Application contact:* Dr. Rick Bissell, Program Director, 410-455-3776, Fax: 410-455-3045, E-mail: bissell@umbc.edu.
Website: http://ehs.umbc.edu/

**University of Maryland, Baltimore County,** The Graduate School, College of Arts, Humanities and Social Sciences, School of Public Policy, Baltimore, MD 21250. Offers public policy (MPP, PhD), including economics (PhD), educational policy, emergency services (PhD), environmental policy (MPP), evaluation and analytical methods, health policy, policy history (PhD), public management, urban policy. *Program availability:* Part-time, evening/weekend. *Faculty:* 10 full-time (5 women). *Students:* 49 full-time (29 women), 63 part-time (31 women); includes 39 minority (18 Black or African American, non-Hispanic/Latino; 1 American Indian or Alaska Native, non-Hispanic/Latino; 9 Asian, non-Hispanic/Latino; 9 Hispanic/Latino; 2 Two or more races, non-Hispanic/Latino), 10 international. Average age 36. 73 applicants, 74% accepted, 31 enrolled. In 2019, 17 master's, 8 doctorates awarded. Terminal master's awarded for partial completion of doctoral program. *Degree requirements:* For master's, thesis, policy analysis paper, internship for pre-service; for doctorate, comprehensive exam, thesis/dissertation, comprehensive and field qualifying exams. *Entrance requirements:* For master's, GRE General Test, 3 academic letters of reference, resume, official transcripts; for doctorate, GRE General Test, 3 academic letters of reference, resume, research paper, official transcripts. Additional exam requirements/recommendations for international students: required—TOEFL (minimum score 550 paper-based; 80 iBT), IELTS (minimum score 6.5). *Application deadline:* For fall admission, 1/15 priority date for domestic students, 1/1 priority date for international students; for spring admission, 11/1 priority date for domestic students, 5/1 priority date for international students. Applications are processed on a rolling basis. Application fee: $50. Electronic applications accepted. *Expenses:* $14,382 per year. *Financial support:* In 2019–20, 26 students received support, including 23 research assistantships with full tuition reimbursements available (averaging $20,000 per year), 3 teaching assistantships; Federal Work-Study, scholarships/grants, health care benefits, and unspecified assistantships also available. Financial award application deadline: 1/1; financial award applicants required to submit FAFSA. *Unit head:* Dr. Susan Sterett, Director, 410-455-2140, Fax: 410-455-1172, E-mail: ssterett@umbc.edu. *Application contact:* Shelley Morris, Administrator of Academic Affairs, 410-455-3202, Fax: 410-455-1172, E-mail: shelleym@umbc.edu.
Website: http://publicpolicy.umbc.edu/

**University of Maryland, Baltimore County,** The Graduate School, Erickson School of Aging Studies, Baltimore, MD 21228. Offers management of aging services (MA). *Program availability:* Part-time. *Faculty:* 4 full-time (1 woman), 7 part-time/adjunct (1 woman). *Students:* 5 full-time (4 women), 7 part-time (all women); includes 5 minority (4 Black or African American, non-Hispanic/Latino; 1 Asian, non-Hispanic/Latino). Average age 32. 7 applicants, 57% accepted, 1 enrolled. In 2019, 13 master's awarded. *Entrance requirements:* For master's, essays. *Application deadline:* For fall admission, 6/1 for domestic students; for spring admission, 12/1 for domestic students. Applications are processed on a rolling basis. Application fee: $50. Electronic applications accepted. *Expenses:* $14,382 per year. *Financial support:* In 2019–20, 1 student received support, including 1 teaching assistantship with full tuition reimbursement available (averaging $21,600 per year). Financial award applicants required to submit FAFSA. *Unit head:* Bill Holman, Graduate Program Director, 443-543-5603, E-mail: holman1@umbc.edu. *Application contact:* Michelle Howell, Administrative Assistant, 443-543-5607, E-mail: mhowell@umbc.edu.
Website: http://www.umbc.edu/erickson/

**University of Maryland, College Park,** Academic Affairs, School of Public Health, Department of Health Services Administration, College Park, MD 20742. Offers MHA, PhD.

**University of Maryland Global Campus,** University of Maryland Global Campus, Health Care Administration, Adelphi, MD 20783. Offers MS. *Program availability:* Part-time, evening/weekend, online learning. *Students:* 14 full-time (9 women), 620 part-time (508 women); includes 400 minority (293 Black or African American, non-Hispanic/Latino; 2 American Indian or Alaska Native, non-Hispanic/Latino; 48 Asian, non-Hispanic/Latino; 42 Hispanic/Latino; 2 Native Hawaiian or other Pacific Islander, non-Hispanic/Latino; 13 Two or more races, non-Hispanic/Latino), 8 international. Average age 35. 334 applicants, 100% accepted, 119 enrolled. In 2019, 212 master's awarded. *Application deadline:* Applications are processed on a rolling basis. Application fee: $50. Electronic applications accepted. *Financial support:* Scholarships/grants available. Support available to part-time students. Financial award application deadline: 6/1; financial award applicants required to submit FAFSA. *Unit head:* Liliya Roberts, Program Director, 240-684-2400, E-mail: liliya.roberts@umgc.edu. *Application contact:* Admissions, 800-888-8682, E-mail: studentsfirst@umgc.edu.
Website: https://www.umgc.edu/academic-programs/masters-degrees/health-care-administration.cfm

**University of Massachusetts Amherst,** Graduate School, Isenberg School of Management, Program in Management, Amherst, MA 01003. Offers accounting (PhD); business administration (MBA); entrepreneurship (MBA); finance (MBA, PhD); healthcare administration (MBA); hospitality and tourism management (PhD); management science (PhD); marketing (MBA, PhD); organization studies (PhD); sport management (PhD); strategic management (PhD); MBA/MS. *Accreditation:* AACSB. *Program availability:* Part-time, evening/weekend, online learning. Terminal master's awarded for partial completion of doctoral program. *Degree requirements:* For doctorate, comprehensive exam, thesis/dissertation. *Entrance requirements:* For master's and doctorate, GMAT or GRE General Test. Additional exam requirements/recommendations for international students: required—TOEFL (minimum score 550 paper-based; 80 iBT), IELTS (minimum score 6.5). Electronic applications accepted.

**University of Massachusetts Amherst,** Graduate School, School of Public Health and Health Sciences, Department of Public Health, Amherst, MA 01003. Offers biostatistics (MPH, MS, PhD); community health education (MPH, MS, PhD); environmental health sciences (MPH, MS, PhD); epidemiology (MPH, MS, PhD); health policy and management (MPH, MS, PhD); nutrition (MPH, PhD); public health practice (MPH); MPH/MPPA. *Accreditation:* CEPH. *Program availability:* Part-time, evening/weekend, online learning. Terminal master's awarded for partial completion of doctoral program. *Degree requirements:* For master's, thesis (for some programs); for doctorate, comprehensive exam, thesis/dissertation. *Entrance requirements:* For master's and doctorate, GRE General Test. Additional exam requirements/recommendations for international students: required—TOEFL (minimum score 550 paper-based; 80 iBT), IELTS (minimum score 6.5). Electronic applications accepted.

**University of Massachusetts Dartmouth,** Graduate School, Charlton College of Business, Department of Decision and Information Sciences, North Dartmouth, MA 02747-2300. Offers healthcare management (MS); technology management (MS). *Program availability:* Part-time, 100% online, blended/hybrid learning. *Faculty:* 12 full-time (3 women), 5 part-time/adjunct (2 women). *Students:* 11 full-time (5 women), 54 part-time (34 women); includes 14 minority (4 Black or African American, non-Hispanic/Latino; 1 American Indian or Alaska Native, non-Hispanic/Latino; 6 Asian, non-Hispanic/Latino; 2 Hispanic/Latino; 1 Two or more races, non-Hispanic/Latino), 15 international. Average age 36. 48 applicants, 92% accepted, 17 enrolled. In 2019, 22 master's awarded. *Degree requirements:* For master's, thesis or alternative, thesis or project. *Entrance requirements:* For master's, GMAT or waiver, statement of purpose (minimum 300 words), resume, official transcripts, 1 letter of recommendation. Additional exam requirements/recommendations for international students: required—TOEFL (minimum score 80 iBT). *Application deadline:* Applications are processed on a rolling basis. Application fee: $60. Electronic applications accepted. *Expenses: Tuition, area resident:* Full-time $16,390; part-time $682.92 per credit. Tuition, state resident: full-time $16,390; part-time $682.92 per credit. Tuition, nonresident: full-time $29,578; part-time $1232.42 per credit. *Required fees:* $575. *Financial support:* Tuition waivers available. Financial award application deadline: 3/1; financial award applicants required to submit FAFSA. *Unit head:* Melissa Pacheco, Assistant Dean of Graduate Programs, 508-999-8543, Fax: 508-999-8646, E-mail: mpacheco@umassd.edu. *Application contact:* Scott Webster, Director of Graduate Studies and Admissions, 508-999-8604, Fax: 508-999-8183, E-mail: graduate@umassd.edu.
Website: http://www.umassd.edu/charlton/programs

**University of Memphis,** Graduate School, School of Public Health, Memphis, TN 38152. Offers biostatistics (MPH); environmental health (MPH); epidemiology (MPH, PhD); health systems and policy (PhD); health systems management (MPH); public health (MHA); social and behavioral sciences (MPH, PhD). *Accreditation:* CAHME; CEPH. *Program availability:* Part-time, evening/weekend, online learning. *Faculty:* 20 full-time (7 women), 10 part-time/adjunct (4 women). *Students:* 126 full-time (80 women), 77 part-time (60 women); includes 70 minority (40 Black or African American, non-Hispanic/Latino; 17 Asian, non-Hispanic/Latino; 9 Hispanic/Latino; 4 Two or more races, non-Hispanic/Latino), 29 international. Average age 30. 105 applicants, 97% accepted, 67 enrolled. In 2019, 47 master's, 9 doctorates awarded. *Degree requirements:* For master's, comprehensive exam, thesis (for some programs), practicum/field experience; for doctorate, comprehensive exam, thesis/dissertation, residency. *Entrance requirements:* For master's, GRE or GMAT, letters of recommendation; letter of intent; for doctorate, GRE, letters of recommendation; personal statement. Additional exam requirements/recommendations for international students: required—TOEFL (minimum score 550 paper-based; 79 iBT). *Application deadline:* For fall admission, 4/1 for domestic students; for spring admission, 11/1 for domestic students. Application fee: $35 ($60 for international students). Electronic applications accepted. *Expenses: Tuition, area resident:* Full-time $9216; part-time $512 per credit hour. Tuition, state resident: full-time $9216; part-time $512 per credit hour. Tuition, nonresident: full-time $12,672; part-time $704 per credit hour. *International tuition:* $16,128 full-time. *Required fees:* $1530; $85 per credit hour. Tuition and fees vary according to program. *Financial support:* Research assistantships with full tuition reimbursements, Federal Work-Study, scholarships/grants, and unspecified assistantships available. Financial award application deadline: 2/1; financial award applicants required to submit FAFSA. *Unit head:* Dr. James Gurney, Dean, 901-678-1673, E-mail: jggurney@memphis.edu. *Application contact:* Dr. Marian Levy, Associate Dean, 901-678-4514, E-mail: mlevy@memphis.edu.
Website: http://www.memphis.edu/sph/

**University of Miami,** Miami Business School, Coral Gables, FL 33146. Offers accounting (M Acc); business (PhD); business administration (MBA); business analytics (MSBA); economics (PhD); finance (MSF); health administration (MHA); international business (MIBS); real estate (MBA); taxation (MS Tax); JD/MBA; MD/MBA. *Accreditation:* AACSB; CAHME (one or more programs are accredited). *Program availability:* Part-time, evening/weekend, 100% online, blended/hybrid learning. Terminal master's awarded for partial completion of doctoral program. *Degree requirements:* For master's, comprehensive exam; for doctorate, comprehensive exam, thesis/dissertation. *Entrance requirements:* For master's, GMAT or GRE; for doctorate, GRE General Test. Additional exam requirements/recommendations for international students: required—TOEFL (minimum score 94 iBT), IELTS (minimum score 7), TOEFL (minimum score 587 paper-based, 94 iBT) or IELTS (7). Electronic applications accepted. *Expenses:* Contact institution.

**University of Michigan,** School of Public Health, Department of Health Management and Policy, Ann Arbor, MI 48109. Offers health management and policy (MHSA, MPH); health services organization and policy (PhD); JD/MHSA; MD/MPH; MHSA/MBA;

MHSA/MPP; MHSA/MSIOE; MPH/JD; MPH/MBA; MPH/MPP. *Accreditation:* CAHME (one or more programs are accredited). *Program availability:* Evening/weekend. *Degree requirements:* For doctorate, thesis/dissertation, oral defense of dissertation, preliminary exam. *Entrance requirements:* For master's, GMAT, GRE General Test; for doctorate, GRE General Test. Additional exam requirements/recommendations for international students: required—TOEFL (minimum score 600 paper-based; 100 iBT). Electronic applications accepted.

**University of Michigan–Flint,** College of Health Sciences, Program in Public Health, Flint, MI 48502-1950. Offers health administration (MPH); health education (MPH). *Program availability:* Part-time. *Faculty:* 15 full-time (11 women), 29 part-time/adjunct (15 women). *Students:* 19 full-time (16 women), 23 part-time (20 women); includes 15 minority (9 Black or African American, non-Hispanic/Latino; 2 Asian, non-Hispanic/Latino; 4 Hispanic/Latino), 5 international. Average age 32. 43 applicants, 65% accepted, 9 enrolled. In 2019, 22 master's awarded. *Entrance requirements:* For master's, bachelor's degree from accredited institution with sufficient preparation in algebra to succeed in epidemiology and biostatistics; minimum overall undergraduate GPA of 3.0; completion of BIO 104 or an equivalent course in anatomy and physiology. Additional exam requirements/recommendations for international students: required—TOEFL (minimum score 84 iBT), IELTS (minimum score 6.5). *Application deadline:* For fall admission, 8/1 for domestic students, 5/1 for international students; for winter admission, 11/15 for domestic students, 10/1 for international students; for spring admission, 3/15 for domestic students, 1/1 for international students. Applications are processed on a rolling basis. Application fee: $55. Electronic applications accepted. *Expenses:* Contact institution. *Financial support:* Federal Work-Study, scholarships/grants, and unspecified assistantships available. Support available to part-time students. Financial award application deadline: 3/1; financial award applicants required to submit FAFSA. *Unit head:* Dr. Shan Parker, Director, 810-762-3172, E-mail: shanpark@umflint.edu. *Application contact:* Matt Bohlen, Director of Graduate Admissions, 810-762-3171, Fax: 810-766-6789, E-mail: mbohlen@umflint.edu.
Website: http://www.umflint.edu/graduateprograms/public-health-mph

**University of Michigan–Flint,** Graduate Programs, Program in Public Administration, Flint, MI 48502-1950. Offers administration of non-profit agencies (MPA); criminal justice administration (MPA); educational administration (MPA); general public administration (MPA); healthcare administration (MPA). *Program availability:* Part-time. *Faculty:* 2 part-time/adjunct (1 woman). *Students:* 7 full-time (4 women), 79 part-time (54 women); includes 31 minority (27 Black or African American, non-Hispanic/Latino; 1 American Indian or Alaska Native, non-Hispanic/Latino; 2 Hispanic/Latino; 1 Two or more races, non-Hispanic/Latino), 2 international. Average age 38. 54 applicants, 72% accepted, 19 enrolled. In 2019, 40 master's awarded. *Degree requirements:* For master's, thesis or alternative, internship. *Entrance requirements:* For master's, bachelor's degree from regionally-accredited institution, minimum overall undergraduate GPA of 3.0 on 4.0 scale. Additional exam requirements/recommendations for international students: required—TOEFL (minimum score 84 iBT), IELTS (minimum score 6.5). *Application deadline:* For fall admission, 8/1 for domestic students, 5/1 for international students; for winter admission, 11/15 for domestic students, 10/1 for international students; for spring admission, 3/15 for domestic students, 1/1 for international students; for summer admission, 5/15 for domestic students. Applications are processed on a rolling basis. Application fee: $55. Electronic applications accepted. *Expenses:* Contact institution. *Financial support:* Career-related internships or fieldwork, Federal Work-Study, and scholarships/grants available. Support available to part-time students. Financial award application deadline: 3/1; financial award applicants required to submit FAFSA. *Unit head:* Dr. Kim Sacks McManaway, Director, 810-766-6628, E-mail: kimsaks@umflint.edu. *Application contact:* Matt Bohlen, Associate Director of Graduate Admissions, 810-762-3171, Fax: 810-766-6789, E-mail: mbohlen@umflint.edu.
Website: http://www.umflint.edu/graduateprograms/public-administration-mpa

**University of Michigan–Flint,** School of Management, Program in Business Administration, Flint, MI 48502-1950. Offers accounting (MBA); computer information systems (MBA); finance (MBA, Post-Master's Certificate); general business (Graduate Certificate); general business administration (MBA); health care management (MBA); international business (MBA, Post-Master's Certificate); lean manufacturing (MBA); marketing (Post-Master's Certificate); marketing and innovation management (MBA); organizational leadership (MBA). *Program availability:* Part-time, evening/weekend, mixed mode format. *Faculty:* 25 full-time (4 women), 11 part-time/adjunct (3 women). *Students:* 25 full-time (13 women), 161 part-time (81 women); includes 51 minority (22 Black or African American, non-Hispanic/Latino; 2 American Indian or Alaska Native, non-Hispanic/Latino; 9 Asian, non-Hispanic/Latino; 11 Hispanic/Latino; 7 Two or more races, non-Hispanic/Latino), 16 international. Average age 36. 121 applicants, 73% accepted, 43 enrolled. In 2019, 50 master's, 1 other advanced degree awarded. *Entrance requirements:* For master's, bachelor's degree in arts, sciences, engineering, or business administration from regionally-accredited college or university; for other advanced degree, bachelor's degree in arts, sciences, engineering, or business administration from regionally-accredited college or university. college-level math, statistics, or quantitative course (for Graduate Certificate); MBA or equivalent degree from regionally-accredited college or university (for Post Master's Certificate). Additional exam requirements/recommendations for international students: required—TOEFL (minimum score 84 iBT), IELTS (minimum score 6.5). *Application deadline:* For fall admission, 8/1 for domestic students, 5/1 for international students; for winter admission, 11/15 for domestic students, 10/1 for international students; for spring admission, 3/15 for domestic students, 1/1 for international students; for summer admission, 5/15 for domestic students. Applications are processed on a rolling basis. Application fee: $55. Electronic applications accepted. *Expenses:* Contact institution. *Financial support:* Federal Work-Study, scholarships/grants, and unspecified assistantships available. Support available to part-time students. Financial award application deadline: 3/1; financial award applicants required to submit FAFSA. *Unit head:* Dr. Scott Johnson, Dean, School of Management, 810-762-3164, Fax: 810-237-6685, E-mail: scotjohn@umflint.edu. *Application contact:* Matt Bohlen, Associate Director of Graduate Admissions, 810-762-3171, E-mail: mbohlen@umflint.edu.
Website: http://www.umflint.edu/graduateprograms/business-administration-mba

**University of Minnesota, Twin Cities Campus,** Carlson School of Management, Carlson Full-Time MBA Program, Minneapolis, MN 55455. Offers finance (MBA); information technology (MBA); management (MBA); marketing (MBA); medical industry orientation (MBA); supply chain and operations (MBA); JD/MBA; MBA/MPP; MBA/MSBA; MD/MBA; MHA/MBA; Pharm D/MBA. *Accreditation:* AACSB. *Entrance requirements:* For master's, GMAT or GRE, 2 recommendations, personal statement, resume. Additional exam requirements/recommendations for international students: required—TOEFL (minimum score 580 paper-based; 84 iBT), IELTS (minimum score 7), PTE. Electronic applications accepted. *Expenses:* Contact institution.

**University of Minnesota, Twin Cities Campus,** Carlson School of Management, Carlson Part-Time MBA Program, Minneapolis, MN 55455. Offers finance (MBA); information technology (MBA); management (MBA); marketing (MBA); medical industry orientation (MBA); supply chain and operations (MBA). *Program availability:* Part-time-only, evening/weekend, 100% online, blended/hybrid learning. *Entrance requirements:* For master's, GMAT or GRE, 2 recommendations, personal statement, current resume. Additional exam requirements/recommendations for international students: required—TOEFL (minimum score 580 paper-based; 84 iBT), IELTS (minimum score 7), PTE. Electronic applications accepted. *Expenses:* Contact institution.

**University of Minnesota, Twin Cities Campus,** School of Public Health, Major in Health Services Research, Policy, and Administration, Minneapolis, MN 55455-0213. Offers MS, PhD, JD/MS, JD/PhD, MD/PhD, MPP/MS. *Program availability:* Part-time. Terminal master's awarded for partial completion of doctoral program. *Degree requirements:* For master's, thesis, internship, final oral exam; for doctorate, thesis/dissertation, teaching experience, written preliminary exam, final oral exam, dissertation. *Entrance requirements:* For master's, GRE General Test, course work in mathematics; for doctorate, GRE General Test, prerequisite courses in calculus and statistics. Additional exam requirements/recommendations for international students: required—TOEFL (minimum score 600 paper-based; 100 iBT).

**University of Minnesota, Twin Cities Campus,** School of Public Health, Major in Public Health Administration and Policy, Minneapolis, MN 55455-0213. Offers MPH, MPH/JD, MPH/MSN. *Program availability:* Part-time. *Degree requirements:* For master's, thesis, field experience. *Entrance requirements:* For master's, GRE General Test. Additional exam requirements/recommendations for international students: required—TOEFL. Electronic applications accepted.

**University of Minnesota, Twin Cities Campus,** School of Public Health, Program in Healthcare Administration, Minneapolis, MN 55455-0213. Offers MHA. *Accreditation:* AACSB; CAHME. *Program availability:* Part-time, evening/weekend, online learning. *Degree requirements:* For master's, thesis, project. *Entrance requirements:* For master's, GMAT or GRE General Test, minimum GPA of 3.0. Additional exam requirements/recommendations for international students: required—TOEFL (minimum score 600 paper-based; 100 iBT). Electronic applications accepted. *Expenses:* Contact institution.

**University of Missouri,** School of Health Professions, Master of Public Health Program, Columbia, MO 65211. Offers global public health (Graduate Certificate); health promotion and policy (MPH); public health (Graduate Certificate); veterinary public health (MPH); DVM/MPH; MPH/MA; MPH/MPA. *Accreditation:* CEPH. *Entrance requirements:* Additional exam requirements/recommendations for international students: required—TOEFL (minimum score 550 paper-based; 80 iBT), IELTS (minimum score 6.5). Electronic applications accepted.

**University of Missouri,** School of Medicine and Office of Research and Graduate Studies, Graduate Programs in Medicine, Department of Health Management and Informatics, Columbia, MO 65211. Offers health administration (MHA); health informatics (MS, Certificate). *Accreditation:* CAHME. *Program availability:* Part-time. *Entrance requirements:* For master's, GRE General Test or GMAT, minimum GPA of 3.0. Additional exam requirements/recommendations for international students: required—TOEFL (minimum score 550 paper-based; 80 iBT), IELTS (minimum score 6.5). Electronic applications accepted.

**University of Nebraska Medical Center,** Department of Health Services Research and Administration, Omaha, NE 68198. Offers health administration (MHA); health services research, administration, and policy (PhD); public health administration and policy (MPH). *Program availability:* Part-time, 100% online, blended/hybrid learning. *Degree requirements:* For doctorate, comprehensive exam, thesis/dissertation. *Entrance requirements:* For doctorate, GRE, official transcripts, resume or curriculum vitae, three letters of recommendation, statement of intent. Additional exam requirements/recommendations for international students: required—TOEFL (minimum score 550 paper-based; 80 iBT), IELTS (minimum score 6.5). Electronic applications accepted. *Expenses:* Contact institution.

**University of Nevada, Las Vegas,** Graduate College, School of Public Health, Department of Health Care Administration and Policy, Las Vegas, NV 89154-3023. Offers health care administration (Exec MHA, MHA). *Accreditation:* CAHME. *Program availability:* Part-time, 100% online, blended/hybrid learning. *Faculty:* 6 full-time (2 women), 6 part-time/adjunct (4 women). *Students:* 46 full-time (24 women), 11 part-time (4 women); includes 31 minority (8 Black or African American, non-Hispanic/Latino; 1 American Indian or Alaska Native, non-Hispanic/Latino; 8 Asian, non-Hispanic/Latino; 8 Hispanic/Latino; 6 Two or more races, non-Hispanic/Latino), 2 international. Average age 31. 28 applicants, 82% accepted, 15 enrolled. In 2019, 23 master's awarded. *Degree requirements:* For master's, thesis (for some programs), capstone course. *Entrance requirements:* For master's, GRE General Test or GMAT, bachelor's degree with minimum GPA 3.0; personal essay; 3 letters of recommendation. Additional exam requirements/recommendations for international students: required—TOEFL (minimum score 550 paper-based; 80 iBT), IELTS (minimum score 7). *Application deadline:* For fall admission, 4/1 for domestic and international students; for spring admission, 12/1 for domestic students, 10/1 for international students. Application fee: $60 ($95 for international students). Electronic applications accepted. *Expenses:* Contact institution. *Financial support:* In 2019–20, 4 students received support, including 2 research assistantships with full tuition reimbursements available (averaging $11,250 per year), 2 teaching assistantships with full tuition reimbursements available (averaging $11,375 per year); institutionally sponsored loans, scholarships/grants, health care benefits, and unspecified assistantships also available. Financial award application deadline: 3/15; financial award applicants required to submit FAFSA. *Unit head:* Dr. Chris Cochran, Chair, 702-895-1400, Fax: 702-895-5573, E-mail: hca.chair@unlv.edu. *Application contact:* Dr. Michelle Sotero, Graduate Coordinator, 702-895-3091, E-mail: healthcareadmin.gradcoord@unlv.edu.
Website: http://hca.unlv.edu

**University of New England,** College of Graduate and Professional Studies, Portland, ME 04005-9526. Offers advanced educational leadership (CAGS); applied nutrition (MS); career and technical education (MS Ed); curriculum and instruction (MS Ed); education (CAGS, Post-Master's Certificate); educational leadership (MS Ed, Ed D); generalist (MS Ed); health informatics (MS, Graduate Certificate); inclusion education (MS Ed); literacy K-12 (MS Ed); medical education leadership (MMEL); public health (MPH, Graduate Certificate); reading specialist (MS Ed); social work (MSW). *Program availability:* Part-time, evening/weekend, online only, 100% online. *Faculty:* 2 full-time (1 woman), 63 part-time/adjunct (44 women). *Students:* 1,001 full-time (795 women), 470 part-time (378 women); includes 306 minority (211 Black or African American, non-Hispanic/Latino; 12 American Indian or Alaska Native, non-Hispanic/Latino; 61 Asian, non-Hispanic/Latino; 14 Hispanic/Latino; 4 Native Hawaiian or other Pacific Islander, non-Hispanic/Latino; 4 Two or more races, non-Hispanic/Latino). Average age 36. In 2019, 614 master's, 85 doctorates, 79 other advanced degrees awarded. *Application deadline:* Applications are processed on a rolling basis. Electronic applications accepted. *Financial support:* Application deadline: 5/1; applicants required to submit FAFSA. *Unit head:* Dr. Martha Wilson, Dean of the College of Graduate and Professional Studies, 207-221-4985, E-mail: mwilson13@une.edu. *Application contact:* Nicole Lindsay, Director of Online Admissions, 207-221-4966, E-mail: nlindsay1@une.edu.
Website: http://online.une.edu

**University of New Mexico,** Graduate Studies, Health Sciences Center, Program in Public Health, Albuquerque, NM 87131-5196. Offers community health (MPH);

## Health Services Management and Hospital Administration

epidemiology (MPH); health systems, services and policy (MPH). *Accreditation:* CEPH. *Program availability:* Part-time, online learning. *Entrance requirements:* For master's, GRE, MCAT, 2 years of experience in health field. Additional exam requirements/recommendations for international students: required—TOEFL. *Expenses:* Tuition, state resident: full-time $7633; part-time $972 per year. Tuition, nonresident: full-time $22,586; part-time $3840 per year. *International tuition:* $23,292 full-time. *Required fees:* $8608. Tuition and fees vary according to course level, course load, degree level, program and student level.

**University of New Mexico,** Graduate Studies, School of Public Administration, Program in Health Administration, Albuquerque, NM 87131-2039. Offers MHA. *Entrance requirements:* For master's, baccalaureate degree from accredited college or university with minimum undergraduate GPA of 3.0 for last 60 hours or overall major; letter of intent; three letters of recommendation; resume; official transcripts. Electronic applications accepted. *Expenses:* Tuition, state resident: full-time $7633; part-time $972 per year. Tuition, nonresident: full-time $22,586; part-time $3840 per year. *International tuition:* $23,292 full-time. *Required fees:* $8608. Tuition and fees vary according to course level, course load, degree level, program and student level.

**University of New Orleans,** Graduate School, College of Business Administration, Program in Health Care Management, New Orleans, LA 70148. Offers MS. *Degree requirements:* For master's, thesis optional. *Entrance requirements:* For master's, GRE or GMAT. Additional exam requirements/recommendations for international students: required—TOEFL (minimum score 550 paper-based; 79 iBT). Electronic applications accepted.

**University of North Alabama,** College of Business, Florence, AL 35632-0001. Offers business administration (MBA), including accounting, enterprise resource planning systems, executive, finance, health care management, information systems, international business, project management. *Accreditation:* AACSB; ACBSP. *Program availability:* Part-time, 100% online, blended/hybrid learning. *Entrance requirements:* For master's, GMAT, GRE, minimum GPA of 2.75 in last 60 hours, 2.5 overall (on a 3.0 scale); 27 hours of course work in business and economics. Additional exam requirements/recommendations for international students: required—TOEFL (minimum score 79 iBT), IELTS (minimum score 6), PTE (minimum score 54). Electronic applications accepted.

**The University of North Carolina at Chapel Hill,** Graduate School, Gillings School of Global Public Health, Department of Health Policy and Management, Chapel Hill, NC 27599. Offers MHA, MPH, MSPH, Dr PH, PhD, JD/MPH, MBA/MSPH, MHA/MBA, MHA/MCRP, MHA/MSIS, MHA/MSLS, MSPH/MCRP, MSPH/MSIS, MSPH/MSLS. *Accreditation:* CAHME (one or more programs are accredited). *Program availability:* Part-time, 100% online, blended/hybrid learning. *Faculty:* 31 full-time (19 women), 105 part-time/adjunct (40 women). *Students:* 229 full-time (147 women), 36 part-time (25 women); includes 87 minority (29 Black or African American, non-Hispanic/Latino; 31 Asian, non-Hispanic/Latino; 11 Hispanic/Latino; 16 Two or more races, non-Hispanic/Latino), 18 international. Average age 32. 320 applicants, 41% accepted, 83 enrolled. In 2019, 50 master's, 13 doctorates awarded. *Degree requirements:* For master's, comprehensive exam, thesis optional, capstone course or paper; for doctorate, comprehensive exam, thesis/dissertation. *Entrance requirements:* For master's, GRE General Test or GMAT, 3 letters of recommendation (academic and/or professional), interview; for doctorate, GRE General Test, prior graduate-level degree; UNC MPH Core if not awarded master's degree from accredited school of public health; 3 letters of recommendation (academic and/or professional); interview. Additional exam requirements/recommendations for international students: required—TOEFL, IELTS. *Application deadline:* For fall admission, 12/11 for domestic and international students. Application fee: $90. Electronic applications accepted. *Expenses:* Contact institution. *Financial support:* Fellowships with tuition reimbursements, research assistantships with tuition reimbursements, teaching assistantships with tuition reimbursements, career-related internships or fieldwork, Federal Work-Study, institutionally sponsored loans, scholarships/grants, traineeships, health care benefits, and unspecified assistantships available. Financial award application deadline: 12/10; financial award applicants required to submit FAFSA. *Unit head:* Dr. Morris Weinberger, Chair, 919-966-7385, Fax: 919-966-3671, E-mail: mweinber@email.unc.edu. *Application contact:* Lynnette Jones, Academic Coordinator, 919-966-7391, Fax: 919-843-4980, E-mail: lynnette_jones@unc.edu.
Website: https://sph.unc.edu/hpm/health-policy-and-management-home/

**The University of North Carolina at Charlotte,** College of Health and Human Services, Department of Public Health Sciences, Charlotte, NC 28223-0001. Offers community health (Certificate); health administration (MHA); public health (MPH), including community health practice, epidemiology, and population health analytics; public health core concepts (Graduate Certificate); public health sciences (PhD). *Accreditation:* CAHME; CEPH. *Program availability:* Part-time. *Faculty:* 30 full-time (18 women), 4 part-time/adjunct (2 women). *Students:* 103 full-time (85 women), 13 part-time (9 women); includes 43 minority (28 Black or African American, non-Hispanic/Latino; 8 Asian, non-Hispanic/Latino; 3 Hispanic/Latino; 1 Native Hawaiian or other Pacific Islander, non-Hispanic/Latino; 3 Two or more races, non-Hispanic/Latino), 10 international. Average age 26. 154 applicants, 77% accepted, 47 enrolled. In 2019, 49 master's, 3 doctorates, 1 other advanced degree awarded. *Degree requirements:* For master's, capstone; for doctorate, thesis/dissertation. *Entrance requirements:* For master's, GRE or MCAT (for MSPH); GRE or GMAT (for MHA), career goal statement, current resume, letters of recommendation, undergraduate major or coursework that prepares students for graduate work; for doctorate, GRE, master's degree in public health or a related field with minimum GPA of 3.5 in all graduate work; statement of purpose detailing why applicant wants to pursue a PhD in public health sciences in the specified concentration at UNC Charlotte; three letters of recommendation (including at least two letters from former professors); for other advanced degree, bachelor's degree from regionally-accredited university; minimum GPA of 2.75 on all post-secondary work attempted; transcripts; personal statement outlining why the applicant seeks admission to the program. Additional exam requirements/recommendations for international students: required—TOEFL (minimum score 557 paper-based; 83 iBT), IELTS (minimum score 6.5), TOEFL (minimum score 557 paper-based,83 iBT) or IELTS (6.5). *Application deadline:* Applications are processed on a rolling basis. Application fee: $75. Electronic applications accepted. *Expenses:* Contact institution. *Financial support:* In 2019–20, 27 students received support, including 4 research assistantships (averaging $14,323 per year), 15 teaching assistantships (averaging $7,966 per year); fellowships, career-related internships or fieldwork, Federal Work-Study, institutionally sponsored loans, scholarships/grants, and unspecified assistantships also available. Support available to part-time students. Financial award application deadline: 3/1; financial award applicants required to submit FAFSA. *Unit head:* Dr. Jan Warren-Findlow, Professor and Interim Chair, 704-687-7908, E-mail: jwarren1@uncc.edu. *Application contact:* Kathy B. Giddings, Director of Graduate Admissions, 704-687-5503, Fax: 704-687-1668, E-mail: gradadm@uncc.edu.
Website: http://publichealth.uncc.edu/

**The University of North Carolina at Pembroke,** The Graduate School, Department of Political Science and Public Administration, Pembroke, NC 28372-1510. Offers criminal justice (MPA); emergency management (MPA); health administration (MPA); public

management (MPA). *Program availability:* Part-time, evening/weekend, online learning. *Degree requirements:* For master's, comprehensive exam, thesis optional. *Entrance requirements:* For master's, GRE General Test or MAT, minimum GPA of 3.0 in major, 2.5 overall; interview. Additional exam requirements/recommendations for international students: required—TOEFL.

**University of Northern Colorado,** Graduate School, Monfort College of Business, Greeley, CO 80639. Offers accounting (MA); general business management (MBA); healthcare administration (MBA); human resources management (MBA). *Accreditation:* AACSB.

**University of North Florida,** Brooks College of Health, Department of Health Administration, Jacksonville, FL 32224. Offers MHA. *Program availability:* Part-time, evening/weekend.

**University of North Texas,** Toulouse Graduate School, Denton, TX 76203-5459. Offers accounting (MS); applied anthropology (MA, MS); applied behavior analysis (Certificate); applied geography (MA); applied technology and performance improvement (M Ed, MS); art education (MA); art history (MA); arts leadership (Certificate); audiology (Au D); behavior analysis (MS); behavioral science (PhD); biochemistry and molecular biology (MS); biology (MA, MS); biomedical engineering (MS); business analysis (MS); chemistry (MS); clinical health psychology (PhD); communication studies (MA, MS); computer engineering (MS); computer science (MS); counseling (M Ed, MS), including clinical mental health counseling (MS), college and university counseling, elementary school counseling, secondary school counseling; creative writing (MA); criminal justice (MS); curriculum and instruction (M Ed); decision sciences (MBA); design (MA, MFA), including fashion design (MFA), innovation studies, interior design (MFA); early childhood studies (MS); economics (MS); educational leadership (M Ed, Ed D); educational psychology (MS, PhD), including family studies (MS), gifted and talented (MS), human development (MS), learning and cognition (MS), research, measurement and evaluation (MS); electrical engineering (MS); emergency management (MPA); engineering technology (MS); English (MA); English as a second language (MA); environmental science (MS); finance (MBA, MS); financial management (MPA); French (MA); health services management (MBA); higher education (M Ed, Ed D); history (MA, MS); hospitality management (MS); human resources management (MPA); information science (MS); information systems (PhD); information technologies (MBA); interdisciplinary studies (MA, MS); international studies (MA); international sustainable tourism (MS); jazz studies (MM); journalism (MA, MJ, Graduate Certificate), including interactive and virtual digital communication (Graduate Certificate), narrative journalism (Graduate Certificate), public relations (Graduate Certificate); kinesiology (MS); linguistics (MA); local government management (MPA); logistics (PhD); logistics and supply chain management (MBA); long-term care, senior housing, and aging services (MA); management (PhD); marketing (MBA); mathematics (MA, MS); mechanical and energy engineering (MS, PhD); music (MA), including ethnomusicology, music theory, musicology, performance; music composition (PhD); music education (MM Ed, PhD); nonprofit management (MPA); operations and supply chain management (MBA); performance (MM, DMA); philosophy (MA); political science (MA); professional and technical communication (MA); radio, television and film (MA, MFA); rehabilitation counseling (Certificate); sociology (MA); Spanish (MA); special education (M Ed); speech-language pathology (MA); strategic management (MBA); studio art (MFA); teaching (M Ed); MBA/MS. *Program availability:* Part-time, evening/weekend, online learning. Terminal master's awarded for partial completion of doctoral program. *Degree requirements:* For master's, variable foreign language requirement, comprehensive exam (for some programs), thesis (for some programs); for doctorate, variable foreign language requirement, comprehensive exam (for some programs), thesis/dissertation; for other advanced degree, variable foreign language requirement, comprehensive exam (for some programs). *Entrance requirements:* For master's and doctorate, GRE, GMAT. Additional exam requirements/recommendations for international students: required—TOEFL (minimum score 550 paper-based; 79 iBT). Electronic applications accepted.

**University of North Texas Health Science Center at Fort Worth,** School of Public Health, Fort Worth, TX 76107-2699. Offers biostatistics (MS); epidemiology (MPH, MS, PhD); food security and public health (Graduate Certificate); GIS in public health (Graduate Certificate); global health (Graduate Certificate); global health for medical professionals (Graduate Certificate); health administration (MHA); health behavior research (MS, PhD); maternal and child health (MPH); public health (Graduate Certificate); public health practice (MPH); DO/MPH; MS/MPH. *Accreditation:* CAHME; CEPH. *Program availability:* Part-time, evening/weekend, 100% online. *Degree requirements:* For master's, thesis or alternative, supervised internship; for doctorate, thesis/dissertation, supervised internship. *Entrance requirements:* For master's, GRE General Test. Additional exam requirements/recommendations for international students: required—TOEFL. Electronic applications accepted. *Expenses:* Contact institution.

**University of Oklahoma,** College of Professional and Continuing Studies, Norman, OK 73019. Offers administrative leadership (MA, Graduate Certificate), including government and military leadership (MA), organizational leadership (MA), volunteer and non-profit leadership (MA); corrections management (Graduate Certificate); criminal justice (MS); integrated studies (MA), including human and health services administration, integrated studies; museum studies (MA); prevention science (MPS); restorative justice administration (Graduate Certificate). *Program availability:* Part-time, 100% online, blended/hybrid learning. *Degree requirements:* For master's, comprehensive exam, thesis optional, 33 credit hours; project/internship (for museum studies program only); for Graduate Certificate, 12 graduate credit hours (for Graduate Certificate). *Entrance requirements:* For master's and Graduate Certificate, minimum GPA of 3.0 in last 60 undergraduate hours; statement of goals; resume. Additional exam requirements/recommendations for international students: required—TOEFL (minimum score 79 iBT) or IELTS (minimum score 6.5). Electronic applications accepted. *Expenses:* Tuition, state resident: full-time $6583.20; part-time $274.30 per credit hour. Tuition, nonresident: full-time $21,242; part-time $885.10 per credit hour. *International tuition:* $21,242.40 full-time. *Required fees:* $1994.20; $72.55 per credit hour. $126.50 per semester. Tuition and fees vary according to course load and degree level.

**University of Oklahoma Health Sciences Center,** Graduate College, Hudson College of Public Health, Department of Health Administration and Policy, Oklahoma City, OK 73190. Offers MHA, MPH, MS, Dr PH, PhD, JD/MPH, MBA/MPH. *Accreditation:* CAHME. *Program availability:* Part-time. *Degree requirements:* For master's, comprehensive exam, thesis (for some programs); for doctorate, 2 foreign languages, comprehensive exam, thesis/dissertation. *Entrance requirements:* For master's, 3 letters of recommendation, resume; for doctorate, GRE General Test, letters of recommendation. Additional exam requirements/recommendations for international students: required—TOEFL (minimum score 570 paper-based).

**University of Ottawa,** Faculty of Graduate and Postdoctoral Studies, Telfer School of Management, Health Administration Program, Ottawa, ON K1N 6N5, Canada. Offers MHA. *Program availability:* Part-time. *Degree requirements:* For master's, thesis optional, residency. *Entrance requirements:* For master's, GMAT, bachelor's degree or equivalent, minimum B average. Additional exam requirements/recommendations for international students: recommended—TOEFL. Electronic applications accepted.

## Health Services Management and Hospital Administration

**University of Pennsylvania,** Wharton School, Health Care Management Department, Philadelphia, PA 19104. Offers MBA, PhD. *Degree requirements:* For doctorate, comprehensive exam, thesis/dissertation. *Entrance requirements:* For master's, GMAT; for doctorate, GMAT or GRE. Electronic applications accepted.

**University of Phoenix - Bay Area Campus,** School of Business, San Jose, CA 95134-1805. Offers accountancy (MS); accounting (MBA); business administration (MBA, DBA); energy management (MBA); global management (MBA); health care management (MBA); human resource management (MBA); human resources management (MM); management (MM); marketing (MBA); organizational leadership (DM); project management (MBA); public administration (MPA); technology management (MBA). *Accreditation:* ACBSP. *Program availability:* Evening/weekend, online learning. *Degree requirements:* For master's, thesis (for some programs). *Entrance requirements:* For master's, minimum undergraduate GPA of 3.0, 3 years of work experience. Additional exam requirements/recommendations for international students: required—TOEFL (minimum score 550 paper-based; 79 iBT). Electronic applications accepted.

**University of Phoenix - Central Valley Campus,** College of Nursing, Fresno, CA 93720-1552. Offers education (MHA); gerontology (MHA); health administration (MHA); nursing (MSN); MSN/MBA.

**University of Phoenix - Hawaii Campus,** College of Nursing, Honolulu, HI 96813-3800. Offers education (MHA); family nurse practitioner (MSN); gerontology (MHA); health administration (MHA); nursing (MSN); nursing/health care education (MSN); MSN/MBA. *Program availability:* Evening/weekend. *Degree requirements:* For master's, thesis (for some programs). *Entrance requirements:* For master's, minimum undergraduate GPA of 2.5, 3 years of work experience, RN license. Additional exam requirements/recommendations for international students: required—TOEFL (minimum score 550 paper-based; 79 iBT). Electronic applications accepted.

**University of Phoenix - Houston Campus,** College of Nursing, Houston, TX 77079-2004. Offers health administration (MHA). *Program availability:* Online learning. *Degree requirements:* For master's, thesis (for some programs). *Entrance requirements:* For master's, minimum undergraduate GPA of 2.5, 3 years of work experience. Additional exam requirements/recommendations for international students: required—TOEFL (minimum score 550 paper-based; 79 iBT). Electronic applications accepted.

**University of Phoenix–Online Campus,** School of Advanced Studies, Phoenix, AZ 85034-7209. Offers business administration (DBA); education (Ed S); educational leadership (Ed D), including curriculum and instruction, education technology, educational leadership; health administration (DHA); higher education administration (PhD); industrial/organizational psychology (PhD); nursing (PhD); organizational leadership (DM), including information systems and technology, organizational leadership. *Program availability:* Evening/weekend, online learning. *Degree requirements:* For doctorate, thesis/dissertation. *Entrance requirements:* Additional exam requirements/recommendations for international students: required—TOEFL, TOEIC (Test of English as an International Communication), Berlitz Online English Proficiency Exam, PTE, or IELTS. Electronic applications accepted. *Expenses:* Contact institution.

**University of Phoenix–Online Campus,** School of Business, Phoenix, AZ 85034-7209. Offers accountancy (MS); accounting (MBA, Certificate); business administration (MBA); energy management (MBA); global management (MBA); health care management (MBA); human resource management (MBA, Certificate); human resources management (MM); management (MM); marketing (MBA, Certificate); project management (MBA, Certificate); public administration (MBA, MM); technology management (MBA). *Program availability:* Evening/weekend, online learning. *Entrance requirements:* Additional exam requirements/recommendations for international students: required—TOEFL, TOEIC (Test of English as an International Communication), Berlitz Online English Proficiency Exam, PTE, or IELTS. Electronic applications accepted. *Expenses:* Contact institution.

**University of Phoenix - Phoenix Campus,** School of Business, Tempe, AZ 85282-2371. Offers accounting (MBA, MS, Certificate); business administration (MBA); energy management (MBA); global management (MBA); health care management (MBA); human resource management (MBA, Certificate); management (MM); marketing (MBA); project management (MBA); technology management (MBA). *Program availability:* Evening/weekend, online learning. *Entrance requirements:* Additional exam requirements/recommendations for international students: required—TOEFL, TOEIC (Test of English as an International Communication), Berlitz Online English Proficiency Exam, PTE, or IELTS. Electronic applications accepted. *Expenses:* Contact institution.

**University of Phoenix - Sacramento Valley Campus,** College of Nursing, Sacramento, CA 95833-4334. Offers family nurse practitioner (MSN); health administration (MHA); health care education (MSN); nursing (MSN); MSN/MBA. *Program availability:* Evening/weekend. *Degree requirements:* For master's, thesis (for some programs). *Entrance requirements:* For master's, RN license, minimum undergraduate GPA of 2.5, 3 years work experience. Additional exam requirements/recommendations for international students: required—TOEFL (minimum score 550 paper-based; 79 iBT). Electronic applications accepted.

**University of Phoenix - San Antonio Campus,** College of Nursing, San Antonio, TX 78230. Offers health administration (MHA).

**University of Pikeville,** Coleman College of Business, Pikeville, KY 41501. Offers business (MBA); entrepreneurship (MBA); healthcare (MBA). *Program availability:* Part-time, evening/weekend, online only, 100% online. *Faculty:* 5 part-time/adjunct (2 women). *Students:* 51 full-time (23 women), 7 part-time (2 women); includes 12 minority (6 Black or African American, non-Hispanic/Latino; 6 Asian, non-Hispanic/Latino). Average age 31. In 2019, 27 master's awarded. *Degree requirements:* For master's, comprehensive exam (for some programs). *Entrance requirements:* For master's, official transcripts, two professional letters of recommendation, three years of work experience. *Application deadline:* For fall admission, 8/15 for domestic students, 7/1 for international students. Applications are processed on a rolling basis. Application fee: $50. *Expenses:* $450 per credit hour (for 30 credit hours program). *Financial support:* In 2019–20, 19 students received support, including 15 teaching assistantships with full tuition reimbursements available; university employee grants also available. Financial award application deadline: 2/15; financial award applicants required to submit FAFSA. *Unit head:* Dr. Howard V. Roberts, Dean, 606-218-5019, Fax: 606-218-5031, E-mail: howardroberts@upike.edu. *Application contact:* Cathy Maynard, Secretary, Business and Economics, 606-218-5020, Fax: 606-218-5031, E-mail: cathymaynard@upike.edu.
Website: https://www.upike.edu/graduate-studies/master-of-business-administration-mba/

**University of Pittsburgh,** Graduate School of Public Health, Department of Behavioral and Community Health Sciences, Pittsburgh, PA 15261. Offers applied research and leadership in behavioral and community health sciences (Dr PH); applied social and behavioral concepts in public health (MPH); community-based participatory research (Certificate); evaluation of public health programs (Certificate); global health (Certificate); health equity (Certificate); LGBT health and wellness (Certificate); maternal and child health (MPH); MID/MPH; MPH/MPA; MPH/MSW; MPH/PhD. *Accreditation:* CEPH. *Program availability:* Part-time. *Faculty:* 7 full-time (5 women), 8 part-time/adjunct (4 women). *Students:* 98 full-time (85 women), 8 part-time (5 women); includes 18 minority (7 Black or African American, non-Hispanic/Latino; 5 Asian, non-Hispanic/Latino; 6 Hispanic/Latino), 4 international. Average age 28. 153 applicants, 48% accepted, 21 enrolled. In 2019, 42 master's, 10 doctorates awarded. *Degree requirements:* For master's, thesis or alternative, Master's students can either complete an Essay or a Thesis; for doctorate, comprehensive exam, thesis/dissertation. *Entrance requirements:* For master's, GRE, applicants must have completed and earned a C or better in a three-credit math or statistics class taken in a math or statistics department. They must also have completed six credits of social sciences (anthropology, economics, geography, political science, psychology, social psychology); for doctorate, GRE, PhD applicants must hold a post-baccalaureate degree e.g. a Master of Science degree in a discipline relevant to public health such as social work or anthropology or an MD or JD. Additional exam requirements/recommendations for international students: required—TOEFL (minimum score 100 iBT), TOEFL or IELTS, WES evaluation for foreign education. *Application deadline:* For fall admission, 7/15 for domestic students, 4/15 for international students; for spring admission, 10/15 for domestic students, 8/1 for international students. Applications are processed on a rolling basis. Application fee: $135. *Expenses:* $13,379 per term full-time resident, $23,407 per term full-time non-resident, $1122 per credit part-time resident, $1916 per credit part-time non-resident, $500 per term for full-time dissertation research, $475 per term full-time fees, $295 per term part-time fees. *Financial support:* In 2019–20, 1 fellowship with full tuition reimbursement (averaging $24,816 per year), 11 research assistantships with full tuition reimbursements (averaging $16,386 per year) were awarded; traineeships also available. Financial award application deadline: 10/1; financial award applicants required to submit FAFSA. *Unit head:* Susan Cotter, Department Administrator, 412-624-9594, Fax: 412-624-5510, E-mail: suecot@pitt.edu. *Application contact:* Paul J. Markgraf, Recruitment and Academic Affairs Administrator, 412-624-3107, Fax: 412-624-5510, E-mail: pjm111@pitt.edu.
Website: http://www.bchs.pitt.edu/

**University of Pittsburgh,** Graduate School of Public Health, Department of Health Policy and Management, Pittsburgh, PA 15261. Offers decision sciences (MS); health policy and economics (MS); health policy and management (MHA, MPH, PhD); JD/MPH. *Accreditation:* CAHME. *Program availability:* Part-time. *Faculty:* 18 full-time (8 women), 7 part-time/adjunct (3 women). *Students:* 71 full-time (46 women), 14 part-time (9 women); includes 22 minority (6 Black or African American, non-Hispanic/Latino; 11 Asian, non-Hispanic/Latino; 5 Hispanic/Latino), 3 international. Average age 27. 165 applicants, 61% accepted, 37 enrolled. In 2019, 32 master's, 2 doctorates awarded. Terminal master's awarded for partial completion of doctoral program. *Degree requirements:* For master's, comprehensive exam (for some programs), thesis (for some programs), Essay required for MPH and MHA degrees as well as a fellowship/residency experience; Thesis required for MS degree.; for doctorate, comprehensive exam, thesis/dissertation, Preliminary exam and dissertation overview are also required. *Entrance requirements:* For master's, GRE or GMAT, 3 Letters of recommendation; for doctorate, GRE, 3 letters of recommendation, writing sample. Additional exam requirements/recommendations for international students: required—TOEFL (minimum score 90 iBT), IELTS (minimum score 6.5), TOEFL or IELTS, WES evaluation for foreign education. *Application deadline:* For fall admission, 1/15 priority date for domestic and international students. Applications are processed on a rolling basis. Application fee: $135. Electronic applications accepted. *Financial support:* In 2019–20, 39 students received support, including 10 research assistantships with full tuition reimbursements available (averaging $24,096 per year), 1 teaching assistantship with full tuition reimbursement available (averaging $24,096 per year); scholarships/grants, health care benefits, and unspecified assistantships also available. Financial award application deadline: 1/15; financial award applicants required to submit FAFSA. *Unit head:* Tina Micale, Department Administrator, 412-624-2128, Fax: 412-624-3146, E-mail: tina.micale@pitt.edu. *Application contact:* Jessica Dornin, Recruitment and Academic Affairs Administrator, 412-624-3625, Fax: 412-624-3146, E-mail: jld115@pitt.edu.
Website: http://www.publichealth.pitt.edu/hpm

**University of Pittsburgh,** Katz Graduate School of Business, MBA/Master of Health Administration in Health Policy and Management Program, Pittsburgh, PA 15260. Offers MBA/MHA. *Program availability:* Part-time, evening/weekend. *Faculty:* 95 full-time (30 women), 30 part-time/adjunct (10 women). *Students:* 17 full-time (10 women), 1 part-time (0 women); includes 6 minority (4 Black or African American, non-Hispanic/Latino; 1 Asian, non-Hispanic/Latino; 1 Hispanic/Latino). Average age 27. 14 applicants, 57% accepted, 6 enrolled. *Entrance requirements:* Additional exam requirements/recommendations for international students: required—TOEFL (minimum score 100 iBT). *Application deadline:* For fall admission, 4/1 priority date for domestic students, 2/1 priority date for international students. Application fee: $50. Electronic applications accepted. *Financial support:* Research assistantships, teaching assistantships, Federal Work-Study, scholarships/grants, health care benefits, and unspecified assistantships available. Financial award application deadline: 6/1; financial award applicants required to submit FAFSA. *Unit head:* Dr. Arjang A. Assad, Dean, 412-648-1552, Fax: 412-648-1552, E-mail: aassad@katz.pitt.edu. *Application contact:* Thomas Keller, Director of Admissions, 412-648-1700, Fax: 412-648-1659, E-mail: admissions@katz.pitt.edu.
Website: http://www.katz.business.pitt.edu/mba/joint-and-dual/health-administration

**University of Pittsburgh,** School of Health and Rehabilitation Sciences, Department of Health Information Management, Pittsburgh, PA 15260. Offers health and rehabilitation sciences (MS), including health information systems, healthcare supervision and management. *Accreditation:* APTA. *Program availability:* Part-time, 100% online. *Faculty:* 7 full-time (4 women), 1 (woman) part-time/adjunct. *Students:* 17 full-time (9 women), 14 part-time (10 women); includes 7 minority (4 Black or African American, non-Hispanic/Latino; 1 Asian, non-Hispanic/Latino; 2 Hispanic/Latino), 8 international. Average age 29. 59 applicants, 78% accepted, 17 enrolled. In 2019, 17 master's awarded. *Entrance requirements:* Additional exam requirements/recommendations for international students: required—International applicants may provide Duolingo English Test, IELTS or TOEFL scores to verify English language proficiency. *Application deadline:* Applications are processed on a rolling basis. Application fee: $50. Electronic applications accepted. *Financial support:* In 2019–20, 3 students received support, including 3 research assistantships with full tuition reimbursements available (averaging $30,000 per year). *Unit head:* Dr. Bambang Parmanto, Professor and Chair, Department of Health Information Management, 412-383-6649, E-mail: parmanto@pitt.edu. *Application contact:* Jessica Maguire, Director of Admissions, 412-383-6557, Fax: 412-383-6535, E-mail: maguire@pitt.edu.
Website: http://www.shrs.pitt.edu/him

**University of Portland,** Dr. Robert B. Pamplin, Jr. School of Business, Portland, OR 97203-5798. Offers entrepreneurship (MBA); finance (MBA, MS); health care management (MBA); marketing (MBA); nonprofit management (EMBA); operations and technology management (MBA, MS); sustainability (MBA). *Accreditation:* AACSB. *Program availability:* Part-time, evening/weekend. *Entrance requirements:* For master's, GMAT or GRE, minimum GPA of 3.0, resume, statement of goals, 2 letters of recommendation. Additional exam requirements/recommendations for international students: required—TOEFL (minimum score 88 iBT), IELTS (minimum score 7). Electronic applications accepted. *Expenses:* Contact institution.

**University of Puerto Rico - Medical Sciences Campus,** Graduate School of Public Health, Department of Health Services Administration, Program in Health Services Administration, San Juan, PR 00936-5067. Offers MHSA. *Accreditation:* CAHME. *Program availability:* Part-time. *Degree requirements:* For master's, thesis. *Entrance requirements:* For master's, GRE, previous course work in accounting, statistics, economics, algebra, and managerial finance.

**University of Regina,** Faculty of Graduate Studies and Research, Johnson-Shoyama Graduate School of Public Policy, Regina, SK S4S 0A2, Canada. Offers economic analysis for public policy (Master's Certificate); health administration (MHA); health systems management (Master's Certificate); public management (MPA, Master's Certificate); public policy (MPA, MPP, PhD); public policy analysis (Master's Certificate). *Program availability:* Part-time. *Faculty:* 9 full-time (4 women), 19 part-time/adjunct (8 women). *Students:* 116 full-time (71 women), 202 part-time (155 women). Average age 30. 328 applicants, 50% accepted. In 2019, 67 master's, 12 other advanced degrees awarded. Terminal master's awarded for partial completion of doctoral program. *Degree requirements:* For master's, thesis (for some programs), course work, in person residencies; for doctorate, comprehensive exam, thesis/dissertation, seminar. *Entrance requirements:* For master's, 4 year undergraduate degree in any area, transcript, 2 letters of recommendation, authorization of release. Students without a background in economics may be required to complete introductory courses in micro and macro economics; for doctorate, master's degree, intended research program in an area of public policy, proposal. Additional exam requirements/recommendations for international students: required—TOEFL (minimum score 585 paper-based; 86 iBT), IELTS (minimum score 6.5), PTE (minimum score 63), Could be one of the listed above. Other options are MELAB, CANTEST, CAEI, and UR ESL. *Application deadline:* For fall admission, 5/1 for domestic and international students; for winter admission, 10/1 for domestic and international students. Application fee: $100. Electronic applications accepted. *Expenses:* Tuition fee is different for each program. See tuition and fees details on each program. *Financial support:* In 2019–20, 78 students received support, including 33 fellowships, 15 teaching assistantships (averaging $2,552 per year); research assistantships, career-related internships or fieldwork, Federal Work-Study, scholarships/grants, unspecified assistantships, and travel award and Graduate Scholarship Base funds also available. Support available to part-time students. Financial award application deadline: 9/30. *Unit head:* Dr. Doug Moen, Executive Director, 306-585-4921, Fax: 306-585-5461, E-mail: doeg.moen@uregina.ca. *Application contact:* John Bird, Academic Advisor, 306-585-5469, Fax: 306-585-5461, E-mail: john.bird@uregina.ca.
Website: http://www.schoolofpublicpolicy.sk.ca/

**University of Rhode Island,** Graduate School, College of Business, Kingston, RI 02881. Offers accounting (MS); business administration (MBA, PhD), including finance (MBA), general business (MBA), management (MBA), marketing, operations and supply chain management (PhD), supply chain management (MBA); finance (MBA, MS, PhD); general business (MBA); health care management (MBA); labor research (MS, Graduate Certificate), including labor relations and human resources; management (MBA); marketing (MBA); strategic innovation (MBA); supply chain management (MBA); textiles, fashion merchandising and design (MS, Certificate), including fashion merchandising (Certificate), master seamstress (Certificate), textiles, fashion merchandising and design (MS); MS/JD; Pharm D/MBA. *Accreditation:* AACSB. *Program availability:* Part-time, evening/weekend. *Faculty:* 62 full-time (30 women), 1 (woman) part-time/adjunct. *Students:* 84 full-time (40 women), 212 part-time (101 women); includes 42 minority (14 Black or African American, non-Hispanic/Latino; 1 American Indian or Alaska Native, non-Hispanic/Latino; 13 Asian, non-Hispanic/Latino; 10 Hispanic/Latino; 1 Native Hawaiian or other Pacific Islander, non-Hispanic/Latino; 3 Two or more races, non-Hispanic/Latino), 23 international. 218 applicants, 71% accepted, 93 enrolled. In 2019, 102 master's, 3 doctorates, 14 other advanced degrees awarded. *Entrance requirements:* Additional exam requirements/recommendations for international students: required—TOEFL. Application fee: $65. Electronic applications accepted. *Expenses: Tuition, area resident:* Full-time $13,734; part-time $763 per credit. Tuition, state resident: full-time $13,734; part-time $763 per credit. Tuition, nonresident: full-time $26,512; part-time $1473 per credit. *International tuition:* $26,512 full-time. *Required fees:* $1780; $52 per credit. $35 per term. One-time fee: $165. *Financial support:* In 2019–20, 20 teaching assistantships with tuition reimbursements (averaging $13,599 per year) were awarded. Financial award applicants required to submit FAFSA. *Unit head:* Dr. Maling Ebrahimpour, Dean, 401-874-4348, Fax: 401-874-4312, E-mail: mebrahimpour@uri.edu. *Application contact:* Lisa Lancellotta, Coordinator, MBA Programs, 401-874-4241, Fax: 401-874-4312, E-mail: mba@uri.edu.
Website: https://web.uri.edu/business/

**University of Rochester,** School of Nursing, Rochester, NY 14642. Offers adult gerontological acute care nurse practitioner (MS); adult gerontological primary care nurse practitioner (MS); clinical nurse leader (MS); family nurse practitioner (MS); family psychiatric mental health nurse practitioner (MS); health care organization management and leadership (MS); nursing (DNP); nursing and health science (PhD); nursing education (MS); pediatric nurse practitioner (MS); pediatric nurse practitioner/neonatal nurse practitioner (MS). *Accreditation:* AACN. *Program availability:* Part-time, 100% online, blended/hybrid learning. Terminal master's awarded for partial completion of doctoral program. *Degree requirements:* For master's, comprehensive exam; for doctorate, thesis/dissertation. *Entrance requirements:* For master's, BS in nursing, RN license; for doctorate, GRE General Test (for PhD), B.S. degree, RN license most programs. Additional exam requirements/recommendations for international students: required—TOEFL (minimum score 560 paper-based; 88 iBT), TOEFL (minimum score 560 paper-based; 88 iBT) or IELTS (minimum score 6.5) recommended. Electronic applications accepted. *Expenses:* Contact institution.

**University of Rochester,** Simon Business School, Full-Time Master's Program in Business Administration, Rochester, NY 14627. Offers business systems consulting (MBA); competitive and organizational strategy (MBA); computers and information systems (MBA); corporate accounting (MBA); entrepreneurship (MBA); finance (MBA); health sciences management (MBA); marketing (MBA); operations management (MBA); public accounting (MBA); strategy and organizations (MBA). *Accreditation:* AACSB. *Entrance requirements:* For master's, GMAT or GRE.

**University of Rochester,** Simon Business School, Part-Time MBA Program, Rochester, NY 14627. Offers business systems consulting (MBA); competitive and organizational strategy (MBA); computers and information systems (MBA); corporate accounting (MBA); entrepreneurship (MBA); finance (MBA); health sciences management (MBA); marketing (MBA), including brand management, marketing strategy, pricing; operations management (MBA); public accounting (MBA). *Program availability:* Part-time-only, evening/weekend. *Entrance requirements:* For master's, GRE or GMAT. Electronic applications accepted. *Expenses:* Contact institution.

**University of St. Augustine for Health Sciences,** Graduate Programs, Master of Health Administration Program, San Marcos, CA 92069. Offers MHA. *Program availability:* Online learning.

**University of St. Augustine for Health Sciences,** Graduate Programs, Master of Health Science Program, San Marcos, CA 92069. Offers athletic training (MHS); executive leadership (MHS); informatics (MHS); teaching and learning (MHS). *Program availability:* Online learning. *Degree requirements:* For master's, comprehensive project.

**University of St. Francis,** College of Business and Health Administration, Joliet, IL 60435-6169. Offers accounting (MBA, Certificate); business analytics (MBA, Certificate); e-learning (Certificate); finance (MBA, Certificate); health administration (MBA, MS); human resource management (MBA, Certificate); logistics (Certificate); management (MBA, MSM); management of training and development (Certificate); supply chain management (MBA); training and development (MBA); training specialist (Certificate). *Program availability:* Part-time, evening/weekend, 100% online, blended/hybrid learning. *Degree requirements:* For master's, comprehensive exam (for some programs). *Entrance requirements:* Additional exam requirements/recommendations for international students: required—TOEFL (minimum score 550 paper-based; 79 iBT), IELTS (minimum score 6). Electronic applications accepted. Application fee is waived when completed online. *Expenses:* Contact institution.

**University of Saint Francis,** Graduate School, Keith Busse School of Business and Entrepreneurial Leadership, Fort Wayne, IN 46808-3994. Offers business administration (MBA), including sustainability; environmental health (MEH); healthcare administration (MHA); organizational leadership (MOL). *Accreditation:* ACBSP. *Program availability:* Part-time, evening/weekend, online only, 100% online. *Faculty:* 1 full-time (0 women), 19 part-time/adjunct (6 women). *Students:* 59 full-time (40 women), 105 part-time (63 women); includes 43 minority (24 Black or African American, non-Hispanic/Latino; 2 American Indian or Alaska Native, non-Hispanic/Latino; 4 Asian, non-Hispanic/Latino; 7 Hispanic/Latino; 6 Two or more races, non-Hispanic/Latino), 1 international. Average age 36. 90 applicants, 100% accepted, 56 enrolled. In 2019, 98 master's awarded. *Entrance requirements:* Additional exam requirements/recommendations for international students: required—TOEFL (minimum score 550 paper-based), IELTS (minimum score 6.5). *Application deadline:* Applications are processed on a rolling basis. Electronic applications accepted. *Expenses: Tuition:* Full-time $9450; part-time $525 per semester hour. *Required fees:* $330 per semester. Tuition and fees vary according to course load, degree level, campus/location and program. *Financial support:* Applicants required to submit FAFSA. *Unit head:* Eye-Lynn Clarke, KBSOBEL Division Director, 260-399-7700 Ext. 8315, E-mail: eclarke@sf.edu. *Application contact:* Kyle Richardson, Associate Director of Enrollment Management, 260-399-7700 Ext. 6310, Fax: 260-399-8152, E-mail: krichardson@sf.edu.
Website: https://admissions.sf.edu/graduate/

**University of Saint Mary,** Graduate Programs, Program in Business Administration, Leavenworth, KS 66048-5082. Offers enterprise risk management (MBA); finance (MBA); general management (MBA); health care management (MBA); human resources management (MBA); marketing and advertising management (MBA). *Program availability:* Part-time, evening/weekend, 100% online, blended/hybrid learning. *Students:* 157 full-time (87 women), 38 part-time (22 women); includes 52 minority (19 Black or African American, non-Hispanic/Latino; 1 American Indian or Alaska Native, non-Hispanic/Latino; 7 Asian, non-Hispanic/Latino; 19 Hispanic/Latino; 1 Native Hawaiian or other Pacific Islander, non-Hispanic/Latino; 5 Two or more races, non-Hispanic/Latino), 7 international. Average age 34. 139 applicants, 90% accepted, 55 enrolled. In 2019, 99 master's awarded. *Degree requirements:* For master's, thesis. *Entrance requirements:* For master's, Minimum undergraduate GPA of 2.75, official transcripts. *Application deadline:* Applications are processed on a rolling basis. Application fee: $25. Electronic applications accepted. *Expenses:* $595 per credit hour. *Financial support:* Unspecified assistantships available. Financial award applicants required to submit FAFSA. *Unit head:* Mark Harvey, Director of Graduate Business Programs, 913-319-3011, E-mail: mark.harvey@stmary.edu. *Application contact:* Mark Harvey, Director of Graduate Business Programs, 913-319-3011, E-mail: mark.harvey@stmary.edu.
Website: https://www.stmary.edu/mba

**University of St. Thomas,** Opus College of Business, Health Care MBA Program, Minneapolis, MN 55403. Offers MBA. *Accreditation:* CAHME. *Program availability:* Blended/hybrid learning. *Entrance requirements:* For master's, minimum 5 years of work experience in related field, letters of recommendation, essays, interview. Electronic applications accepted. *Expenses:* Contact institution.

**University of San Francisco,** School of Management, Master of Public Administration Program, San Francisco, CA 94117. Offers health services administration (MPA); public administration (MPA). *Program availability:* Part-time, evening/weekend, online learning. *Faculty:* 6 full-time (2 women), 2 part-time/adjunct (0 women). *Students:* 99 full-time (72 women), 4 part-time (3 women); includes 68 minority (8 Black or African American, non-Hispanic/Latino; 1 American Indian or Alaska Native, non-Hispanic/Latino; 25 Asian, non-Hispanic/Latino; 30 Hispanic/Latino; 4 Two or more races, non-Hispanic/Latino). Average age 33. 95 applicants, 80% accepted, 37 enrolled. In 2019, 65 master's awarded. *Entrance requirements:* For master's, resume demonstrating minimum of two years of professional work experience, transcripts from each college or university attended, two letters of recommendation, personal statement. Additional exam requirements/recommendations for international students: required—TOEFL (minimum score 600 paper-based, 100 iBT), IELTS (minimum score 7) or PTE (minimum score 68). *Application deadline:* For fall admission, 6/15 for domestic students, 5/15 for international students. Application fee: $55. Electronic applications accepted. *Expenses:* Contact institution. *Financial support:* Scholarships/grants available. Financial award application deadline: 3/2; financial award applicants required to submit FAFSA. *Unit head:* Dr. Catherine Horiuchi, Director, 415-422-2221, E-mail: management@usfca.edu. *Application contact:* Office of Graduate Recruiting and Admissions, 415-422-2221, E-mail: management@usfca.edu.
Website: http://www.usfca.edu/mpa

**The University of Scranton,** Kania School of Management, Program in Business Administration, Scranton, PA 18510. Offers accounting (MBA); finance (MBA); general business administration (MBA); health care management (MBA); international business (MBA); management information systems (MBA); marketing (MBA); operations management (MBA). *Accreditation:* AACSB. *Program availability:* Part-time, evening/weekend, 100% online. *Entrance requirements:* For master's, GMAT (for MBA).

**The University of Scranton,** Panuska College of Professional Studies, Department of Health Administration and Human Resources, Program in Health Administration, Scranton, PA 18510. Offers MHA. *Accreditation:* CAHME. *Program availability:* Part-time, evening/weekend, online only, 100% online.

**University of Sioux Falls,** Vucurevich School of Business, Sioux Falls, SD 57105-1699. Offers entrepreneurial leadership (MBA); general management (MBA); health care management (MBA); marketing (MBA). *Program availability:* Part-time, evening/weekend. *Degree requirements:* For master's, project. *Entrance requirements:* For master's, minimum GPA of 3.0. Additional exam requirements/recommendations for international students: required—TOEFL. *Expenses:* Contact institution.

**University of South Africa,** College of Human Sciences, Pretoria, South Africa. Offers adult education (M Ed); African languages (MA, PhD); African politics (MA, PhD); Afrikaans (MA, PhD); ancient history (MA, PhD); ancient Near Eastern studies (MA, PhD); anthropology (MA, PhD); applied linguistics (MA); Arabic (MA, PhD); archaeology (MA); art history (MA); Biblical archaeology (MA); Biblical studies (M Th, D Th, PhD);

Christian spirituality (M Th, D Th); church history (M Th, D Th); classical studies (MA, PhD); clinical psychology (MA); communication (MA, PhD); comparative education (M Ed, Ed D); consulting psychology (D Admin, D Com, PhD); curriculum studies (M Ed, Ed D); development studies (M Admin, MA, D Admin, PhD); didactics (M Ed, Ed D); education (M Tech); education management (M Ed, Ed D); educational psychology (M Ed); English (MA); environmental education (M Ed); French (MA, PhD); German (MA, PhD); Greek (MA); guidance and counseling (M Ed); health studies (MA, PhD), including health sciences education (MA), health services management (MA), medical and surgical nursing science (critical care general) (MA), midwifery and neonatal nursing science (MA), trauma and emergency care (MA); history (MA, PhD); history of education (Ed D); inclusive education (M Ed, Ed D); information and communications technology policy and regulation (MA); information science (MA, MIS, PhD); international politics (MA, PhD); Islamic studies (MA, PhD); Italian (MA, PhD); Judaica (MA, PhD); linguistics (MA, PhD); mathematical education (M Ed); mathematics education (MA); missiology (M Th, D Th); modern Hebrew (MA, PhD); musicology (MA, MMus, D Mus, PhD); natural science education (M Ed); New Testament (M Th, D Th); Old Testament (D Th); pastoral therapy (M Th, D Th); philosophy (MA); philosophy of education (M Ed, Ed D); politics (MA, PhD); Portuguese (MA, PhD); practical theology (M Th, D Th); psychology (MA, MS, PhD); psychology of education (M Ed, Ed D); public health (MA); religious studies (MA, D Th, PhD); Romance languages (MA, PhD); Russian (MA, PhD); Semitic languages (MA, PhD); social behavior studies in HIV/AIDS (MA); social science (mental health) (MA); social science in development studies (MA); social science in psychology (MA); social science in social work (MA); social science in sociology (MA); social work (MSW, DSW, PhD); socio-education (M Ed, Ed D); sociolinguistics (MA); sociology (MA, PhD); Spanish (MA, PhD); systematic theology (M Th, D Th); TESOL (teaching English to speakers of other languages) (MA); theological ethics (M Th, D Th); theory of literature (MA, PhD); urban ministries (D Th); urban ministry (M Th).

**University of South Carolina,** The Graduate School, Arnold School of Public Health, Department of Health Services Policy and Management, Columbia, SC 29208. Offers MHA, MPH, Dr PH, PhD, JD/MHA, MPH/MSN, MSW/MPH. *Accreditation:* CAHME (one or more programs are accredited). *Program availability:* Part-time, evening/weekend. *Degree requirements:* For master's, comprehensive exam, thesis or alternative, internship (MHA); for doctorate, comprehensive exam, thesis/dissertation. *Entrance requirements:* For master's, GMAT (MHA), GRE General Test (MPH); for doctorate, GRE General Test. Additional exam requirements/recommendations for international students: required—TOEFL (minimum score 570 paper-based). Electronic applications accepted.

**University of South Dakota,** Graduate School, Beacom School of Business, Department of Business Administration, Vermillion, SD 57069. Offers business administration (MBA); business analytics (MBA, Graduate Certificate); health services administration (MBA); long term care management (Graduate Certificate); marketing (MBA, Graduate Certificate); operations and supply chain management (MBA, Graduate Certificate); JD/MBA. *Accreditation:* AACSB. *Program availability:* Part-time, blended/hybrid learning. *Degree requirements:* For master's, thesis or alternative. *Entrance requirements:* For master's, GMAT, minimum GPA of 2.7, resume. Additional exam requirements/recommendations for international students: required—TOEFL (minimum score 550 paper-based; 79 iBT), IELTS (minimum score 6). Electronic applications accepted. *Expenses:* Contact institution.

**University of South Dakota,** Graduate School, College of Arts and Sciences, Program in Administrative Studies, Vermillion, SD 57069. Offers addiction studies (MSA); criminal justice studies (MSA); health services administration (MSA); human resources (MSA); interdisciplinary studies (MSA); long term care administration (MSA); organizational leadership (MSA). *Program availability:* Part-time, evening/weekend, 100% online. *Degree requirements:* For master's, thesis or alternative. *Entrance requirements:* For master's, 3 years of work or experience, minimum GPA of 2.7, resume. Additional exam requirements/recommendations for international students: required—TOEFL (minimum score 550 paper-based; 79 iBT). Electronic applications accepted.

**University of Southern California,** Graduate School, Sol Price School of Public Policy, Executive Master of Health Administration Program, Los Angeles, CA 90089. Offers EMHA. *Program availability:* Part-time, evening/weekend, online learning. *Entrance requirements:* Additional exam requirements/recommendations for international students: required—TOEFL (minimum score 600 paper-based; 100 iBT). Electronic applications accepted. *Expenses:* Contact institution.

**University of Southern California,** Graduate School, Sol Price School of Public Policy, Master of Health Administration Program, Los Angeles, CA 90089. Offers ambulatory care (Graduate Certificate); health administration (MHA); long-term care (Graduate Certificate); MHA/MS. *Accreditation:* CAHME. *Program availability:* Part-time. *Degree requirements:* For master's, residency placement. *Entrance requirements:* For master's, GRE, GMAT. Additional exam requirements/recommendations for international students: required—TOEFL (minimum score 600 paper-based; 100 iBT). Electronic applications accepted.

**University of Southern Indiana,** Graduate Studies, College of Nursing and Health Professions, Program in Health Administration, Evansville, IN 47712-3590. Offers MHA. *Program availability:* Part-time, 3 required intensives in August (2.5 days), January (2.5 days) and May (2 days). *Entrance requirements:* For master's, GRE, minimum GPA of 3.0, curriculum vitae, letter of intent, three professional references, focused essay(s). Additional exam requirements/recommendations for international students: required—TOEFL (minimum score 550 paper-based; 79 iBT), IELTS (minimum score 6). Electronic applications accepted.

**University of Southern Indiana,** Graduate Studies, Romain College of Business, Program in Business Administration, Evansville, IN 47712-3590. Offers accounting (MBA); data analytics (MBA); engineering management (MBA); general business administration (MBA); healthcare administration (MBA); human resource management (MBA). *Accreditation:* AACSB. *Program availability:* Part-time, evening/weekend, 100% online, blended/hybrid learning. *Entrance requirements:* For master's, GMAT or GRE, minimum GPA of 2.5, resume, 3 professional references. Additional exam requirements/recommendations for international students: required—TOEFL (minimum score 550 paper-based; 79 iBT), IELTS (minimum score 6). Electronic applications accepted.

**University of Southern Maine,** College of Management and Human Service, School of Business, Portland, ME 04104-9300. Offers accounting (MBA); business administration (MBA); finance (MBA); health management and policy (MBA); sustainability (MBA); JD/MBA; MBA/MSA; MBA/MSN; MS/MBA. *Accreditation:* AACSB. *Program availability:* Part-time, evening/weekend. *Entrance requirements:* For master's, GMAT or GRE, minimum AACSB index of 1100. Additional exam requirements/recommendations for international students: required—TOEFL (minimum score 550 paper-based; 79 iBT). Electronic applications accepted. *Expenses: Tuition, area resident:* Full-time $864; part-time $432 per credit hour. Tuition, state resident: full-time $864; part-time $432 per credit hour. Tuition, nonresident: full-time $2372; part-time $1186 per credit hour. *Required fees:* $141; $108 per credit hour. Tuition and fees vary according to course load.

**University of Southern Mississippi,** College of Nursing and Health Professions, School of Health Professions, Hattiesburg, MS 39406-0001. Offers epidemiology and biostatistics (MPH); health policy and administration (MPH). *Accreditation:* CEPH. *Program availability:* Part-time, evening/weekend. *Students:* 58 full-time (41 women), 8 part-time (3 women); includes 25 minority (18 Black or African American, non-Hispanic/Latino; 2 Asian, non-Hispanic/Latino; 2 Hispanic/Latino; 3 Two or more races, non-Hispanic/Latino), 22 international. 125 applicants, 32% accepted, 23 enrolled. In 2019, 19 master's awarded. *Degree requirements:* For master's, comprehensive exam, thesis (for some programs). *Entrance requirements:* For master's, GRE General Test, minimum GPA of 2.75 in last 60 hours. Additional exam requirements/recommendations for international students: required—TOEFL, IELTS. *Application deadline:* For fall admission, 3/1 priority date for domestic and international students; for spring admission, 1/10 priority date for domestic and international students. Applications are processed on a rolling basis. Application fee: $60. Electronic applications accepted. *Expenses: Tuition, area resident:* Full-time $4393; part-time $488 per credit hour. Tuition, nonresident: full-time $5393; part-time $600 per credit hour. *Required fees:* $6 per semester. *Financial support:* Research assistantships with full tuition reimbursements, teaching assistantships with full tuition reimbursements, career-related internships or fieldwork, Federal Work-Study, institutionally sponsored loans, scholarships/grants, health care benefits, and unspecified assistantships available. Financial award application deadline: 3/15; financial award applicants required to submit FAFSA. *Unit head:* Hwanseok Choi, Director, 601-266-5435, Fax: 601-266-5043, E-mail: hwanseok.choi@usm.edu. *Application contact:* Hwanseok Choi, Director, 601-266-5435, Fax: 601-266-5043, E-mail: hwanseok.choi@usm.edu.
Website: http://www.usm.edu/community-public-health-sciences

**University of South Florida,** Innovative Education, Tampa, FL 33620-9951. Offers adult, career and higher education (Graduate Certificate), including college teaching, leadership in developing human resources, leadership in higher education; Africana studies (Graduate Certificate), including diasporas and health disparities, genocide and human rights; aging studies (Graduate Certificate), including gerontology; art research (Graduate Certificate), including museum studies; business foundations (Graduate Certificate); chemical and biomedical engineering (Graduate Certificate), including materials science and engineering, water, health and sustainability; child and family studies (Graduate Certificate), including positive behavior support; civil and industrial engineering (Graduate Certificate), including transportation systems analysis; community and family health (Graduate Certificate), including maternal and child health, social marketing and public health, violence and injury: prevention and intervention, women's health; criminology (Graduate Certificate), including criminal justice administration; data science for public administration (Graduate Certificate); digital humanities (Graduate Certificate); educational measurement and research (Graduate Certificate), including evaluation; English (Graduate Certificate), including comparative literary studies, creative writing, professional and technical communication; entrepreneurship (Graduate Certificate); environmental health (Graduate Certificate), including safety management; epidemiology and biostatistics (Graduate Certificate), including applied biostatistics, biostatistics, concepts and tools of epidemiology, epidemiology, epidemiology of infectious diseases; geography, environment and planning (Graduate Certificate), including community development, environmental policy and management, geographical information systems; geology (Graduate Certificate), including hydrogeology; global health (Graduate Certificate), including disaster management, global health and Latin American and Caribbean studies, global health practice, humanitarian assistance, infection control; government and international affairs (Graduate Certificate), including Cuban studies, globalization studies; health policy and management (Graduate Certificate), including health management and leadership, public health policy and programs; hearing specialist: early intervention (Graduate Certificate); industrial and management systems engineering (Graduate Certificate), including systems engineering, technology management; information studies (Graduate Certificate), including school library media specialist; information systems/decision sciences (Graduate Certificate), including analytics and business intelligence; instructional technology (Graduate Certificate), including distance education, Florida digital/virtual educator, instructional design, multimedia design, Web design; internal medicine, bioethics and medical humanities (Graduate Certificate), including biomedical ethics; Latin American and Caribbean studies (Graduate Certificate); leadership for coastal resiliency planning (Graduate Certificate); mass communications (Graduate Certificate), including multimedia journalism; mathematics and statistics (Graduate Certificate), including mathematics; medicine (Graduate Certificate), including aging and neuroscience, bioinformatics, biotechnology, brain fitness and memory management, clinical investigation, hand and upper limb rehabilitation, health informatics, health sciences, integrative weight management, intellectual property, medicine and gender, metabolic and nutritional medicine, metabolic cardiology, pharmacy sciences; national and competitive intelligence (Graduate Certificate); nursing (Graduate Certificate), including simulation based academic fellowship in advanced pain management; psychological and social foundations (Graduate Certificate), including career counseling, college teaching, diversity in education, mental health counseling, school counseling; public affairs (Graduate Certificate), including nonprofit management, public management, research administration; public health (Graduate Certificate), including assessing chemical toxicity and public health risks, health equity, pharmacoepidemiology, public health generalist, toxicology, translational research in adolescent behavioral health; public health practices (Graduate Certificate), including planning for healthy communities; rehabilitation and mental health counseling (Graduate Certificate), including integrative mental health care, marriage and family therapy, rehabilitation technology; secondary education (Graduate Certificate), including ESOL, foreign language education: culture and content, foreign language education: professional; social work (Graduate Certificate), including geriatric social work/clinical gerontology; special education (Graduate Certificate), including autism spectrum disorder, disabilities education: severe/profound; world languages (Graduate Certificate), including teaching English as a second language (TESL) or foreign language. *Unit head:* Dr. Cynthia DeLuca, Associate Vice President and Assistant Vice Provost, 813-974-3077, Fax: 813-974-7061, E-mail: deluca@usf.edu. *Application contact:* Owen Hooper, Director, Summer and Alternative Calendar Programs, 813-974-6917, E-mail: hooper@usf.edu.
Website: http://www.usf.edu/innovative-education/

**The University of Tennessee,** Graduate School, College of Education, Health and Human Sciences, Program in Public Health, Knoxville, TN 37996. Offers community health education (MPH); gerontology (MPH); health planning/administration (MPH); MS/MPH. *Accreditation:* CEPH. *Degree requirements:* For master's, thesis optional. *Entrance requirements:* For master's, minimum GPA of 2.7. Additional exam requirements/recommendations for international students: required—TOEFL. Electronic applications accepted.

**The University of Texas at Arlington,** Graduate School, College of Business, Program in Health Care Administration, Arlington, TX 76019. Offers MS. *Program availability:* Part-time, evening/weekend. *Degree requirements:* For master's, one foreign language, thesis optional. *Entrance requirements:* For master's, GRE General Test or GMAT, minimum GPA of 3.0, official undergraduate and graduate transcripts, current professional resume, personal statement, three letters of recommendation. Additional exam requirements/recommendations for international students: required—TOEFL (minimum score 550 paper-based; 79 iBT).

**The University of Texas at Dallas,** Naveen Jindal School of Management, Program in Organizations, Strategy and International Management, Richardson, TX 75080. Offers business administration (MBA); executive business administration (EMBA); global leadership (EMBA); healthcare leadership and management (MS); healthcare management (EMBA); innovation and entrepreneurship (MS); international management studies (MS, PhD); management science (MS, PhD); project management (EMBA); systems engineering and management (MS); MS/MBA. *Program availability:* Part-time, evening/weekend. *Faculty:* 18 full-time (5 women), 30 part-time/adjunct (5 women). *Students:* 611 full-time (245 women), 768 part-time (372 women); includes 423 minority (86 Black or African American, non-Hispanic/Latino; 2 American Indian or Alaska Native, non-Hispanic/Latino; 210 Asian, non-Hispanic/Latino; 88 Hispanic/Latino; 37 Two or more races, non-Hispanic/Latino), 335 international. Average age 35. 1,456 applicants, 41% accepted, 403 enrolled. In 2019, 570 master's, 19 doctorates awarded. *Degree requirements:* For doctorate, thesis/dissertation. *Entrance requirements:* For master's and doctorate, GMAT. Additional exam requirements/recommendations for international students: required—TOEFL (minimum score 550 paper-based). *Application deadline:* For fall admission, 7/15 for domestic students, 5/1 priority date for international students; for spring admission, 11/15 for domestic students, 9/1 priority date for international students. Applications are processed on a rolling basis. Application fee: $50 ($100 for international students). Electronic applications accepted. *Expenses: Tuition, area resident:* Full-time $16,504. Tuition, state resident: full-time $16,504. Tuition, nonresident: full-time $34,266. Tuition and fees vary according to course load. *Financial support:* In 2019–20, 122 students received support, including 28 research assistantships with partial tuition reimbursements available (averaging $36,900 per year), 82 teaching assistantships with partial tuition reimbursements available (averaging $24,763 per year); Federal Work-Study, institutionally sponsored loans, scholarships/grants, and unspecified assistantships also available. Support available to part-time students. Financial award application deadline: 4/30; financial award applicants required to submit FAFSA. *Unit head:* Dr. Seung-Hyun Lee, Area Coordinator, 972-883-6267, Fax: 972-883-5977, E-mail: sxl029100@utdallas.edu. *Application contact:* Dr. Seung-Hyun Lee, Area Coordinator, 972-883-6267, Fax: 972-883-5977, E-mail: sxl029100@utdallas.edu.
Website: http://jindal.utdallas.edu/osim/

**The University of Texas at El Paso,** Graduate School, School of Nursing, El Paso, TX 79968-0001. Offers family nurse practitioner (MSN); health care leadership and management (Certificate); interdisciplinary health sciences (PhD); nursing (DNP); nursing education (MSN, Certificate); nursing systems management (MSN). *Accreditation:* AACN. *Program availability:* Online learning. *Degree requirements:* For master's, thesis optional; for doctorate, thesis/dissertation. *Entrance requirements:* For master's, minimum GPA of 3.0, resume; for doctorate, GRE, letters of reference, relevant personal/professional experience; master's degree in nursing (for DNP); for Certificate, bachelor's degree in nursing. Additional exam requirements/recommendations for international students: required—TOEFL; recommended—IELTS. Electronic applications accepted.

**The University of Texas at Tyler,** Soules College of Business, Department of Management and Marketing, Tyler, TX 75799-0001. Offers cyber security (MBA); engineering management (MBA); general management (MBA); healthcare management (MBA); internal assurance and consulting (MBA); marketing (MBA); oil, gas and energy (MBA); organizational development (MBA); quality management (MBA). *Accreditation:* AACSB. *Program availability:* Part-time, online learning. *Faculty:* 13 full-time (5 women). *Students:* Average age 29. *Entrance requirements:* Additional exam requirements/recommendations for international students: required—TOEFL (minimum score 550 paper-based). *Application deadline:* For fall admission, 8/17 priority date for domestic students, 7/1 priority date for international students; for spring admission, 12/21 priority date for domestic students, 11/1 priority date for international students. Application fee: $25 ($50 for international students). *Unit head:* Dr. Krist Swimberghe, Chair, 903-565-5803, E-mail: kswimberghe@uttyler.edu. *Application contact:* Dr. Krist Swimberghe, Chair, 903-565-5803, E-mail: kswimberghe@uttyler.edu.
Website: https://www.uttyler.edu/cbt/manamark/

**The University of Texas Health Science Center at Houston,** School of Public Health, Houston, TX 77030. Offers behavioral science (PhD); biostatistics (MPH, MS, PhD); environmental health (MPH); epidemiology (MPH, MS, PhD); general public health (Certificate); genomics and bioinformatics (Certificate); health disparities (Certificate); health promotion/health education (MPH, Dr PH); healthcare management (Certificate); management, policy and community health (MPH, Dr PH, PhD); maternal and child health (Certificate); public health informatics (Certificate); DDS/MPH; JD/MPH; MBA/MPH; MD/MPH; MGPS/MPH; MP Aff/MPH; MS/MPH; MSN/MPH; MSW/MPH; PhD/MPH. *Accreditation:* CAHME; CEPH. *Program availability:* Part-time. *Degree requirements:* For master's (thesis for some programs); for doctorate, comprehensive exam, thesis/dissertation. *Entrance requirements:* For master's and doctorate, GRE General Test. Additional exam requirements/recommendations for international students: required—TOEFL (minimum score 600 paper-based, 100 iBT) or IELTS (7.5). Electronic applications accepted. *Expenses:* Contact institution.

**The University of Texas Health Science Center at Tyler,** School of Community and Rural Health, Tyler, TX 75708. Offers health administration (MHA); public health (MPH).

**The University of Texas Rio Grande Valley,** College of Health Affairs, Department of Health and Biomedical Sciences, Edinburg, TX 78539. Offers clinical laboratory sciences (MSHS); health care administration (MSHS); nutrition (MSHS). *Program availability:* Part-time, online only, 100% online. *Faculty:* 4 full-time (all women), 2 part-time/adjunct (both women). *Students:* 148 part-time (92 women); includes 120 minority (10 Black or African American, non-Hispanic/Latino; 5 American Indian or Alaska Native, non-Hispanic/Latino; 105 Hispanic/Latino), 3 international. Average age 34. 70 applicants, 77% accepted, 39 enrolled. In 2019, 110 master's awarded. *Entrance requirements:* For master's, Not required, 2 letters of recommendation and a letter of intent, UG degree in a health related profession. CLS - BS in CLS and ASCP MLS Certification; NUTR - 3 hrs. UG & A&P with a "C" or higher; Healthcare Informatics - UG degree in health field and experience with EMR highly recommended. Additional exam requirements/recommendations for international students: required—as required by grad. college; program does not require entrance exams. *Application deadline:* For fall admission, 7/23 for domestic and international students; for spring admission, 12/1 for domestic and international students. Applications are processed on a rolling basis. Application fee: $50 ($100 for international students). Electronic applications accepted. *Expenses:* 444.44 per semester credit hour. *Financial support:* Research assistantships and scholarships/grants available. Financial award application deadline: 7/23; financial award applicants required to submit FAFSA. *Unit head:* Dr. Saraswathy Nair, Associate Professor and Chair, 956-882-5108, Fax: 956-882-6835, E-mail: saraswathy.nair@utrgv.edu. *Application contact:* Kim Garcia, Lecturer III/Associate Chair, Health and Biomedical Sciences, 956-665-4781, E-mail: kim.garcia@utrgv.edu.
Website: http://www.utrgv.edu/hbs

**University of the Incarnate Word,** H-E-B School of Business and Administration, San Antonio, TX 78209-6397. Offers accounting (MS); business administration (MBA); health administration (MHA). *Program availability:* Part-time, evening/weekend. *Faculty:* 20 full-time (10 women), 9 part-time/adjunct (3 women). *Students:* 203 full-time (105 women),

27 part-time (11 women); includes 148 minority (22 Black or African American, non-Hispanic/Latino; 2 American Indian or Alaska Native, non-Hispanic/Latino; 6 Asian, non-Hispanic/Latino; 113 Hispanic/Latino; 1 Native Hawaiian or other Pacific Islander, non-Hispanic/Latino; 4 Two or more races, non-Hispanic/Latino), 27 international. 137 applicants, 95% accepted, 83 enrolled. In 2019, 136 master's awarded. *Degree requirements:* For master's, capstone. *Entrance requirements:* For master's, GMAT, GRE, writing sample, interview. Additional exam requirements/recommendations for international students: required—TOEFL (minimum score 560 paper-based; 83 iBT). *Application deadline:* Applications are processed on a rolling basis. Application fee: $20. Electronic applications accepted. *Expenses: Tuition:* Full-time $11,520; part-time $960 per credit hour. *Required fees:* $1128; $94 per credit hour. Tuition and fees vary according to degree level, campus/location, program and student level. *Financial support:* Research assistantships, Federal Work-Study, scholarships/grants, tuition waivers (partial), and unspecified assistantships available. Financial award applicants required to submit FAFSA. *Unit head:* Dr. Forrest Aven, Dean, 210-805-5884, Fax: 210-805-3564, E-mail: aven@uiwtx.edu. *Application contact:* Jessica Delarosa, Director of Admissions, 210-8296005, Fax: 210-829-3921, E-mail: admis@uiwtx.edu.
Website: https://www.uiw.edu/hebsba/index.html

**University of the Incarnate Word,** School of Professional Studies, San Antonio, TX 78209-6397. Offers communication arts (MAA), including applied administration, communication arts, healthcare administration, industrial and organizational psychology, organizational development; organizational development and leadership (MS); professional studies (DBA). *Program availability:* Part-time, evening/weekend, 100% online, blended/hybrid learning. *Faculty:* 16 full-time (12 women), 41 part-time/adjunct (18 women). *Students:* 503 full-time (236 women), 385 part-time (175 women); includes 571 minority (124 Black or African American, non-Hispanic/Latino; 5 American Indian or Alaska Native, non-Hispanic/Latino; 35 Asian, non-Hispanic/Latino; 382 Hispanic/Latino; 3 Native Hawaiian or other Pacific Islander, non-Hispanic/Latino; 22 Two or more races, non-Hispanic/Latino), 1 international. 670 applicants, 99% accepted, 296 enrolled. In 2019, 429 master's, 5 doctorates awarded. *Degree requirements:* For master's, comprehensive exam (for some programs), thesis or alternative. *Entrance requirements:* For master's, GMAT, GRE, official transcripts from all other colleges attended. Additional exam requirements/recommendations for international students: required—TOEFL (minimum score 560 paper-based; 83 iBT). *Application deadline:* Applications are processed on a rolling basis. Electronic applications accepted. *Expenses: Tuition:* Full-time $11,520; part-time $960 per credit hour. *Required fees:* $1128; $94 per credit hour. Tuition and fees vary according to degree level, campus/location, program and student level. *Financial support:* Scholarships/grants and unspecified assistantships available. Financial award applicants required to submit FAFSA. *Unit head:* Vincent Porter, Dean, 210-8292770, E-mail: porterv@uiwtx.edu. *Application contact:* Julie Weber, Director of Marketing and Recruitment, 210-318-1876, Fax: 210-829-2756, E-mail: eapadmission@uiwtx.edu.
Website: https://sps.uiw.edu/

**University of the Sciences,** Program in Health Policy, Philadelphia, PA 19104-4495. Offers MS, PhD. *Program availability:* Part-time, evening/weekend, online learning. *Degree requirements:* For doctorate, comprehensive exam, thesis/dissertation. *Entrance requirements:* For master's and doctorate, GRE General Test. Additional exam requirements/recommendations for international students: required—TOEFL, TWE. *Expenses:* Contact institution.

**The University of Toledo,** College of Graduate Studies, College of Languages, Literature and Social Sciences, Department of Political Science and Public Administration, Toledo, OH 43606-3390. Offers health care policy and administration (Certificate); management of non-profit organizations (Certificate); municipal administration (Certificate); political science (MA); public administration (MPA); JD/MPA. *Program availability:* Part-time. *Degree requirements:* For master's, comprehensive exam (for some programs), thesis. *Entrance requirements:* For master's, GRE General Test, minimum cumulative point-hour ratio of 2.7 (3.0 for MPA) for all previous academic work, three letters of recommendation, statement of purpose, transcripts from all prior institutions attended; for Certificate, minimum cumulative point-hour ratio of 2.7 for all previous academic work, three letters of recommendation, statement of purpose, transcripts from all prior institutions attended. Additional exam requirements/recommendations for international students: required—TOEFL (minimum score 550 paper-based; 80 iBT). Electronic applications accepted.

**The University of Toledo,** College of Graduate Studies, College of Medicine and Life Sciences, Department of Public Health and Preventative Medicine, Toledo, OH 43606-3390. Offers biostatistics and epidemiology (Certificate); contemporary gerontological practice (Certificate); environmental and occupational health and safety (MPH); epidemiology (Certificate); global public health (Certificate); health promotion and education (MPH); industrial hygiene (MSOH); medical and health science teaching and learning (Certificate); occupational health (Certificate); public health administration (MPH); public health and emergency response (Certificate); public health epidemiology (MPH); public health nutrition (MPH); MD/MPH. *Program availability:* Part-time, evening/weekend. *Degree requirements:* For master's, thesis or alternative. *Entrance requirements:* For master's, GRE, minimum undergraduate GPA of 3.0, three letters of recommendation, statement of purpose, transcripts from all prior institutions attended, resume; for Certificate, minimum undergraduate GPA of 3.0, three letters of recommendation, statement of purpose, transcripts from all prior institutions attended, resume. Additional exam requirements/recommendations for international students: required—TOEFL (minimum score 550 paper-based; 80 iBT), IELTS (minimum score 6.5). Electronic applications accepted.

**University of Toronto,** Faculty of Medicine, Institute of Health Policy, Management and Evaluation, Program in Health Administration, Toronto, ON M5S 1A1, Canada. Offers MH Sc. *Accreditation:* CAHME. *Entrance requirements:* For master's, minimum B+ average on each of the last two years of a four-year undergraduate program, minimum of three years relevant clinical or management experience. Additional exam requirements/recommendations for international students: required—TOEFL (minimum score 580 paper-based; 93 iBT), TWE (minimum score 5). Electronic applications accepted.

**University of Utah,** Graduate School, College of Pharmacy, Department of Pharmacotherapy, Salt Lake City, UT 84112. Offers health system pharmacy administration (MS); outcomes research and health policy (PhD). *Faculty:* 19 full-time (12 women). *Students:* 6 full-time (3 women), 7 part-time (1 woman); includes 1 minority (Asian, non-Hispanic/Latino), 4 international. Average age 33. 14 applicants, 43% accepted, 6 enrolled. In 2019, 1 master's, 1 doctorate awarded. Terminal master's awarded for partial completion of doctoral program. *Degree requirements:* For master's, comprehensive exam, thesis or alternative, project; for doctorate, comprehensive exam, thesis/dissertation. *Entrance requirements:* Additional exam requirements/recommendations for international students: required—TOEFL (minimum score 550 paper-based; 80 iBT), GRE. *Application deadline:* For fall admission, 1/10 for domestic students, 12/15 for international students. Application fee: $55 ($65 for international students). *Expenses:* Tuition, state resident: full-time $7085; part-time $272.51 per credit hour. Tuition, nonresident: full-time $24,937; part-time $959.12 per credit hour. *Required fees:* $880.52; $880.52 per semester. Tuition and fees vary according to

degree level, program and student level. *Financial support:* In 2019–20, 1 research assistantship (averaging $4,000 per year) was awarded. Financial award applicants required to submit CSS PROFILE or FAFSA. *Unit head:* Daniel Malone, Professor, 801-581-8054, Fax: 801-587-7923, E-mail: dan.malone@utah.edu. *Application contact:* Linda O'Connor, Education Coordinator, 801-585-1065, E-mail: linda.oconner@pharm.utah.edu.
Website: http://www.pharmacy.utah.edu/pharmacotherapy/

**University of Utah,** Graduate School, David Eccles School of Business, Master in Healthcare Administration Program, Salt Lake City, UT 4112. Offers MHA, MBA/MHA, MHA/MPA, MPH/MHA, PMBA/MHA. *Accreditation:* CAHME. *Program availability:* Part-time, evening/weekend. *Students:* 100 full-time (36 women), 8 part-time (3 women); includes 14 minority (1 Black or African American, non-Hispanic/Latino; 1 Asian, non-Hispanic/Latino; 11 Hispanic/Latino; 1 Native Hawaiian or other Pacific Islander, non-Hispanic/Latino), 2 international. Average age 30. In 2019, 31 master's awarded. *Entrance requirements:* For master's, GMAT, GRE, statistics course with minimum B grade; minimum undergraduate GPA of 3.0. Application fee: $55 ($65 for international students). *Expenses:* Tuition, state resident: full-time $7085; part-time $272.51 per credit hour. Tuition, nonresident: full-time $24,937; part-time $959.12 per credit hour. *Required fees:* $880.52; $880.52 per semester. Tuition and fees vary according to degree level, program and student level. *Financial support:* In 2019–20, 31 students received support. *Unit head:* Dr. Stephen Walston, MHA Program Director, 405-833-7774, E-mail: Steve.Walston@Eccles.Utah.edu. *Application contact:* Kayla Smartz, Admissions and Recruiting, 801-581-5790, Fax: 801-581-7785, E-mail: Kayla.Smartz@Eccles.Utah.edu.
Website: https://eccles.utah.edu/programs/master-of-healthcare-administration/

**University of Vermont,** The Robert Larner, MD College of Medicine and Graduate College, Graduate Programs in Medicine, Program in Public Health, Burlington, VT 05405. Offers epidemiology (Graduate Certificate); global and environmental health (Graduate Certificate); healthcare management and policy (Graduate Certificate); public health (MPH). *Program availability:* Online only, 100% online. *Entrance requirements:* For master's and Graduate Certificate, resume/curriculum vitae. Additional exam requirements/recommendations for international students: required—TOEFL (minimum iBT score of 90) or IELTS (6.5). Electronic applications accepted. *Expenses:* Contact institution.

**University of Virginia,** School of Medicine, Department of Public Health Sciences, Charlottesville, VA 22903. Offers clinical research (MS), including clinical investigation and patient-oriented research, informatics in medicine; public health (MPH); MPP/MPH. *Program availability:* Part-time. *Entrance requirements:* For master's, GRE General Test or MCAT. Additional exam requirements/recommendations for international students: required—TOEFL. Electronic applications accepted.

**University of Washington,** Graduate School, School of Public Health, Programs in Health Administration, Seattle, WA 98195. Offers EMHA, MHA, JD/MHA, MHA/MBA, MHA/MD, MHA/MPA. *Accreditation:* CAHME. *Students:* 117 full-time (78 women); includes 59 minority (6 Black or African American, non-Hispanic/Latino; 3 American Indian or Alaska Native, non-Hispanic/Latino; 40 Asian, non-Hispanic/Latino; 9 Hispanic/Latino; 1 Native Hawaiian or other Pacific Islander, non-Hispanic/Latino), 5 international. Average age 32. 114 applicants, 69% accepted, 55 enrolled. In 2019, 52 master's awarded. *Entrance requirements:* Additional exam requirements/recommendations for international students: required—See http://grad.uw.edu/policies-procedures/graduate-school-memoranda/memo-8-graduate-school-english-language-proficiency-requirements/. Electronic applications accepted. *Expenses:* Contact institution. *Financial support:* Scholarships/grants and unspecified assistantships available. Financial award applicants required to submit FAFSA. *Unit head:* Sarah H. Cave, Director, 206-543-8778, Fax: 206-543-3964, E-mail: scave@uw.edu. *Application contact:* Christine Fleming, Marketing and Recruitment Specialist, 206-543-4705, E-mail: mhap@uw.edu.
Website: https://www.mha.uw.edu/

**The University of Western Ontario,** Ivey Business School, London, ON N6A 3K7, Canada. Offers business (EMBA, PhD); corporate strategy and leadership elective (MBA); entrepreneurship elective (MBA); finance elective (MBA); health sector stream (MBA); international management elective (MBA); marketing elective (MBA); JD/MBA. *Degree requirements:* For master's, thesis (for some programs); for doctorate, thesis/dissertation. *Entrance requirements:* For master's, GMAT, 2 years of full-time work experience, interview. Additional exam requirements/recommendations for international students: required—TOEFL (minimum score 100 iBT) or IELTS (minimium score 6). Electronic applications accepted.

**University of West Florida,** Usha Kundu, MD College of Health, Department of Health Sciences and Administration, Pensacola, FL 32514-5750. Offers healthcare administration (MHA). *Program availability:* Part-time, evening/weekend, online learning. *Entrance requirements:* For master's, GRE General Test, letter of intent, names of references. Additional exam requirements/recommendations for international students: required—TOEFL (minimum score 550 paper-based).

**University of Wisconsin–Milwaukee,** Graduate School, College of Engineering and Applied Science, Biomedical and Health Informatics Program, Milwaukee, WI 53201-0413. Offers health information systems (PhD); health services management and policy (PhD); knowledge based systems (PhD); medical imaging and instrumentation (PhD); public health informatics (PhD). *Degree requirements:* For doctorate, comprehensive exam, thesis/dissertation. *Entrance requirements:* For doctorate, GRE, GMAT or MCAT. Additional exam requirements/recommendations for international students: required—TOEFL (minimum score 600 paper-based; 79 iBT), IELTS (minimum score 6.5). Electronic applications accepted.

**University of Wisconsin–Milwaukee,** Graduate School, College of Health Sciences, Department of Health Informatics and Administration, Milwaukee, WI 53201-0413. Offers health care informatics (MS); healthcare administration (MHA). *Degree requirements:* For master's, comprehensive exam, thesis optional. *Entrance requirements:* For master's, GRE General Test. Additional exam requirements/recommendations for international students: required—TOEFL (minimum score 550 paper-based; 79 iBT), IELTS (minimum score 6.5).

**University of Wisconsin–Milwaukee,** Graduate School, College of Health Sciences, Program in Health Sciences, Milwaukee, WI 53201-0413. Offers health sciences (PhD), including diagnostic and biomedical sciences, disability and rehabilitation, health administration and policy, human movement sciences, population health. *Degree requirements:* For doctorate, comprehensive exam, thesis/dissertation. *Entrance requirements:* For doctorate, GRE. Additional exam requirements/recommendations for international students: required—TOEFL (minimum score 600 paper-based), IELTS (minimum score 6.5).

**University of Wisconsin–Oshkosh,** Graduate Studies, College of Letters and Science, Department of Public Administration, Oshkosh, WI 54901. Offers general agency (MPA); health care (MPA). *Program availability:* Part-time, evening/weekend. *Degree requirements:* For master's, thesis or alternative. *Entrance requirements:* For master's, public service-related experience, resume, sample of written work. Additional exam requirements/recommendations for international students: required—TOEFL (minimum score 550 paper-based; 79 iBT). Electronic applications accepted.

**University of Wyoming,** College of Health Sciences, School of Pharmacy, Laramie, WY 82071. Offers health services administration (MS); pharmacy (Pharm D). *Accreditation:* ACPE (one or more programs are accredited). *Program availability:* Online learning. *Entrance requirements:* For doctorate, PCAT. Additional exam requirements/recommendations for international students: required—TOEFL.

**Utica College,** Program in Health Care Administration, Utica, NY 13502-4892. Offers MS. *Program availability:* Part-time, evening/weekend, online learning. *Degree requirements:* For master's, capstone (internship or research/program development project). *Entrance requirements:* For master's, BS, minimum GPA of 3.0, 2 recommendation letters, personal essay. Additional exam requirements/recommendations for international students: required—TOEFL (minimum score 525 paper-based). Electronic applications accepted. *Expenses:* Contact institution.

**Valdosta State University,** Langdale College of Business, Valdosta, GA 31698. Offers accountancy (M Acc); business administration (MBA); healthcare administration (MBA). *Accreditation:* AACSB. *Program availability:* Part-time, evening/weekend, 100% online, blended/hybrid learning. *Degree requirements:* For master's, comprehensive written and/or oral exams. *Entrance requirements:* For master's, GMAT or GRE, minimum GPA of 2.75. Additional exam requirements/recommendations for international students: required—TOEFL (minimum score 523 paper-based); recommended—IELTS. Electronic applications accepted. *Expenses:* Contact institution.

**Valparaiso University,** Graduate School and Continuing Education, Program in Health Administration, Valparaiso, IN 46383. Offers health administration (MHA); health care administration (MS). *Program availability:* Part-time, evening/weekend. *Degree requirements:* For master's, practicum, internship. *Entrance requirements:* For master's, minimum overall GPA of 3.0 or 5 years of work experience in the field; basic course in statistics; official transcripts; two letters of recommendation; essay. Additional exam requirements/recommendations for international students: required—TOEFL (minimum score 550 paper-based; 80 iBT), IELTS (minimum score 6). Electronic applications accepted.

**Vanderbilt University,** Vanderbilt University Owen Graduate School of Management, Master of Management in Health Care Program, Nashville, TN 37203. Offers MM. *Entrance requirements:* For master's, GMAT or GRE (recommended), undergraduate transcript, five years of relevant work experience, interview. Electronic applications accepted. *Expenses:* Contact institution.

**Vanderbilt University,** Vanderbilt University Owen Graduate School of Management, Vanderbilt MBA Program, Nashville, TN 37203. Offers accounting (MBA); finance (MBA); general management (MBA); health care (MBA); human and organizational performance (MBA); marketing (MBA); operations (MBA); strategy (MBA); MBA/JD; MBA/M Div; MBA/MD; MBA/MSN; MBA/MTS; MBA/PhD. *Accreditation:* AACSB. *Degree requirements:* For master's, 62 credit hours of coursework; completion of ethics course; minimum GPA of 3.0. *Entrance requirements:* For master's, GMAT (preferred) or GRE, 2 years of work experience (recommended). Additional exam requirements/recommendations for international students: required—TOEFL (minimum score 100 iBT). Electronic applications accepted. *Expenses:* Contact institution.

**Villanova University,** Villanova School of Business, MBA - The Fast Track Program, Villanova, PA 19085. Offers finance (MBA); healthcare (MBA); international business (MBA); strategic management (MBA). *Accreditation:* AACSB. *Program availability:* Part-time, evening/weekend. *Faculty:* 100 full-time (37 women), 34 part-time/adjunct (5 women). *Students:* 97 part-time (38 women); includes 21 minority (5 Black or African American, non-Hispanic/Latino; 6 Asian, non-Hispanic/Latino; 8 Hispanic/Latino; 2 Two or more races, non-Hispanic/Latino), 2 international. Average age 29. 80 applicants, 99% accepted, 69 enrolled. In 2019, 67 master's awarded. *Degree requirements:* For master's, minimum GPA of 3.0. *Entrance requirements:* For master's, GMAT or GRE, Application, official transcripts, 2 letters of recommendation, resume, 2 essays. Additional exam requirements/recommendations for international students: required—TOEFL (minimum score 550 paper-based; 100 iBT). *Application deadline:* For fall admission, 7/15 for domestic and international students. Applications are processed on a rolling basis. Application fee: $65. Electronic applications accepted. *Expenses:* Contact institution. *Financial support:* Scholarships/grants available. Financial award application deadline: 6/30; financial award applicants required to submit FAFSA. *Unit head:* Dr. Joyce E. A. Russell, Dean of Villanova School of Business, 610-519-6082, E-mail: joyce.russell@villanova.edu. *Application contact:* Kimberly Kane, Manager, Admissions, 610-519-3701, E-mail: kimberly.kane@villanova.edu.
Website: http://www1.villanova.edu/villanova/business/graduate/mba.html

**Villanova University,** Villanova School of Business, MBA - The Flex Track Program, Villanova, PA 19085. Offers healthcare (MBA); international business (MBA); marketing (MBA); real estate (MBA); strategic management (MBA); JD/MBA. *Accreditation:* AACSB. *Program availability:* Part-time, evening/weekend. *Faculty:* 100 full-time (37 women), 34 part-time/adjunct (5 women). *Students:* 10 full-time (5 women), 412 part-time (156 women); includes 69 minority (10 Black or African American, non-Hispanic/Latino; 32 Asian, non-Hispanic/Latino; 18 Hispanic/Latino; 9 Two or more races, non-Hispanic/Latino), 10 international. Average age 32. 80 applicants, 99% accepted, 69 enrolled. In 2019, 133 master's awarded. *Degree requirements:* For master's, minimum GPA of 3.0. *Entrance requirements:* For master's, GMAT or GRE, Application, official transcripts, 2 letters of recommendation, resume, 2 essays. Additional exam requirements/recommendations for international students: required—TOEFL (minimum score 550 paper-based; 100 iBT). *Application deadline:* For fall admission, 7/15 for domestic and international students; for spring admission, 11/30 for domestic and international students; for summer admission, 4/15 for domestic and international students. Applications are processed on a rolling basis. Application fee: $65. Electronic applications accepted. *Expenses:* Contact institution. *Financial support:* Research assistantships and scholarships/grants available. Financial award application deadline: 6/30; financial award applicants required to submit FAFSA. *Unit head:* Dr. Joyce E. A. Russell, Dean of Villanova School of Business, 610-519-6082, E-mail: joyce.russell@villanova.edu. *Application contact:* Nicholas Pontarelli, Coordinator, Admissions, 610-519-4336, E-mail: nicholas.pontarelli@villanova.edu.
Website: http://www1.villanova.edu/villanova/business/graduate/mba.html

**Virginia Commonwealth University,** Graduate School, School of Allied Health Professions, Department of Health Administration, Doctoral Program in Health Services Organization and Research, Richmond, VA 23284-9005. Offers PhD. *Degree requirements:* For doctorate, thesis/dissertation, residency. *Entrance requirements:* For doctorate, GMAT or GRE General Test, minimum graduate GPA of 3.0. Additional exam requirements/recommendations for international students: required—TOEFL (minimum score 600 paper-based; 100 iBT). Electronic applications accepted.

**Virginia Commonwealth University,** Graduate School, School of Allied Health Professions, Department of Health Administration, Master's Program in Health Administration, Richmond, VA 23284-9005. Offers MHA, JD/MHA, MHA/MD, MHA/MSIS. *Accreditation:* CAHME. *Degree requirements:* For master's, residency. *Entrance requirements:* For master's, GMAT or GRE General Test (preferred minimum score of 5.0 on analytical writing), course work in accounting, economics, and statistics; minimum GPA of 3.0. Additional exam requirements/recommendations for international students:

required—TOEFL (minimum score 600 paper-based; 100 iBT). Electronic applications accepted.

**Virginia Commonwealth University,** Graduate School, School of Allied Health Professions, Department of Health Administration, Professional Online Master of Science in Health Administration Program, Richmond, VA 23284-9005. Offers MSHA. *Accreditation:* CAHME. *Program availability:* Online learning. *Degree requirements:* For master's, residency. *Entrance requirements:* For master's, GMAT or GRE General Test. Additional exam requirements/recommendations for international students: required—TOEFL (minimum score 600 paper-based; 100 iBT). Electronic applications accepted.

**Virginia Commonwealth University,** Graduate School, School of Allied Health Professions, Doctoral Program in Health Related Sciences, Richmond, VA 23284-9005. Offers clinical laboratory sciences (PhD); gerontology (PhD); health administration (PhD); nurse anesthesia (PhD); occupational therapy (PhD); physical therapy (PhD); radiation sciences (PhD); rehabilitation leadership (PhD). *Entrance requirements:* For doctorate, GRE General Test or MAT, minimum GPA of 3.3 in master's degree. Additional exam requirements/recommendations for international students: required—TOEFL (minimum score 600 paper-based; 100 iBT); recommended—IELTS (minimum score 6.5). Electronic applications accepted.

**Virginia Commonwealth University,** Medical College of Virginia-Professional Programs, School of Medicine, Graduate Programs in Medicine, Department of Health Behavior and Policy, Richmond, VA 23284-9005. Offers healthcare policy and research (PhD); social and behavioral sciences (PhD). *Entrance requirements:* For doctorate, GRE General Test. Additional exam requirements/recommendations for international students: required—TOEFL (minimum score 600 paper-based; 100 iBT). Electronic applications accepted.

**Virginia International University,** School of Business, Fairfax, VA 22030. Offers accounting (MBA, MS); entrepreneurship (MBA); executive management (Graduate Certificate); global logistics (MBA); health care management (MBA); hospitality and tourism management (MBA); human resources management (MBA); international business management (MBA); international finance (MBA); marketing management (MBA); mass media and public relations (MBA); project management (MBA, MS). *Program availability:* Part-time, online learning. *Entrance requirements:* For master's and Graduate Certificate, bachelor's degree. Additional exam requirements/recommendations for international students: required—TOEFL (minimum score 550 paper-based; 80 iBT), IELTS (minimum score 6). Electronic applications accepted.

**Viterbo University,** Master of Business Administration Program, La Crosse, WI 54601-4797. Offers general business administration (MBA); health care management (MBA); international business (MBA); leadership (MBA); project management (MBA). *Accreditation:* ACBSP. *Program availability:* Part-time, evening/weekend. *Degree requirements:* For master's, 34 semester credits. *Entrance requirements:* For master's, bachelor's degree, transcripts, minimum undergraduate cumulative GPA of 3.0, 2 letters of reference, 3-5 page essay. Additional exam requirements/recommendations for international students: recommended—TOEFL (minimum score 550 paper-based). Electronic applications accepted. *Expenses:* Contact institution.

**Walden University,** Graduate Programs, School of Health Sciences, Minneapolis, MN 55401. Offers clinical research administration (MS, Graduate Certificate); health education and promotion (MS, PhD), including behavioral health (PhD), disease surveillance (PhD), emergency preparedness (MS), general (MHA, MS), global health (PhD), health policy (PhD), health policy and advocacy (MS), population health (PhD); health informatics (MS); health services (PhD), including community health, healthcare administration, leadership, public health policy, self-designed; healthcare administration (MHA, DHA), including general (MHA, MS); leadership and organizational development (MHA); public health (MPH, Dr PH, PhD, Graduate Certificate), including community health education (PhD), epidemiology (PhD); systems policy (MHA). *Program availability:* Part-time, evening/weekend, online only, 100% online. *Degree requirements:* For doctorate, thesis/dissertation, residency. *Entrance requirements:* For master's, bachelor's degree or higher; minimum GPA of 2.5; official transcripts; goal statement (for some programs); access to computer and Internet; for doctorate, master's degree or higher; three years of related professional or academic experience (preferred); minimum GPA of 3.0; goal statement and current resume (for select programs); official transcripts; access to computer and Internet; for Graduate Certificate, relevant work experience; access to computer and Internet. Additional exam requirements/recommendations for international students: required—TOEFL (minimum score 550 paper-based, 79 iBT), IELTS (minimum score 6.5), Michigan English Language Assessment Battery (minimum score 82), or PTE (minimum score 53). Electronic applications accepted.

**Walden University,** Graduate Programs, School of Management, Minneapolis, MN 55401. Offers accounting (MBA, MS, DBA), including accounting for the professional (MS), accounting with CPA emphasis (MS), self-designed (MS); advanced project management (Graduate Certificate); applied project management (Graduate Certificate); auditing (Graduate Certificate); bridge to business administration (Post-Doctoral Certificate); bridge to management (Post-Doctoral Certificate); business management (Graduate Certificate); communication (MBA); corporate finance (MBA); digital marketing (Graduate Certificate); entrepreneurship (DBA); entrepreneurship and small business (MBA); finance (MS, DBA), including finance for the professional (MS), finance with CFA/investment (MS), finance with CPA emphasis (MS); global supply chain management (DBA); healthcare management (MBA, DBA); human resource management (MBA, MS, Graduate Certificate), including functional human resource management (MS), general program (MS), integrating functional and strategic human resource management (MS), organizational strategy (MS); human resources management (DBA); information systems management (DBA); international business (MBA, DBA); leadership (MBA, MS, DBA, Graduate Certificate), including general program (MS), human resource leadership (MS), leader development (MS), self-designed (MS); management (MS, PhD), including communications (MS), finance (PhD), general program (MS), healthcare management (MS), human resource management (MS), human resources management (PhD), information systems management (PhD), international business (MS), leadership (MS), leadership and organizational change (PhD), marketing (MS), project management (MS), strategy and operations (MS); managerial accounting (Graduate Certificate); marketing (MBA, MS, DBA); project management (MBA, MS, DBA); self-designed (MBA, DBA); social impact management (DBA); technology entrepreneurship (DBA). *Accreditation:* ACBSP. *Program availability:* Part-time, evening/weekend, online only, 100% online. *Degree requirements:* For master's, thesis (for some programs), residency (for EMBA); for doctorate, thesis/dissertation (for some programs), residency. *Entrance requirements:* For master's, bachelor's degree or higher; minimum GPA of 2.5; official transcripts; goal statement (for some programs); access to computer and Internet; for doctorate, master's degree or higher; three years of related professional or academic experience (preferred); minimum GPA of 3.0; goal statement and current resume (for select programs); official transcripts; access to computer and Internet; for other advanced degree, relevant work experience; access to computer and Internet. Additional exam requirements/recommendations for international students: required—TOEFL (minimum score 550 paper-based, 79 iBT), IELTS (minimum score 6.5), Michigan English Language Assessment Battery (minimum score 82), or PTE (minimum score 53). Electronic applications accepted.

**Walden University,** Graduate Programs, School of Nursing, Minneapolis, MN 55401. Offers adult-gerontology acute care nurse practitioner (MSN); adult-gerontology nurse practitioner (MSN); education (MSN); family nurse practitioner (MSN); informatics (MSN); leadership and management (MSN); nursing (PhD, Post-Master's Certificate), including education (PhD), healthcare administration (PhD), interdisciplinary health (PhD), leadership (PhD), nursing education (Post-Master's Certificate), nursing informatics (Post-Master's Certificate), nursing leadership and management (Post-Master's Certificate), public health policy (PhD); nursing practice (DNP); psychiatric mental health (MSN). *Accreditation:* AACN. *Program availability:* Part-time, evening/weekend, online only, 100% online. *Degree requirements:* For doctorate, thesis/dissertation (for some programs), residency (for some programs), field experience (for some programs). *Entrance requirements:* For master's, bachelor's degree or equivalent in related field or RN; minimum GPA of 2.5; official transcripts; goal statement (for some programs); access to computer and Internet; for doctorate, master's degree or higher; RN; three years of related professional or academic experience; goal statement; access to computer and Internet; for Post-Master's Certificate, relevant work experience; access to computer and Internet. Additional exam requirements/recommendations for international students: required—TOEFL (minimum score 550 paper-based, 79 iBT), IELTS (minimum score 6.5), Michigan English Language Assessment Battery (minimum score 82), or PTE (minimum score 53). Electronic applications accepted.

**Walden University,** Graduate Programs, School of Public Policy and Administration, Minneapolis, MN 55401. Offers criminal justice (MPA, MPP, MS, Graduate Certificate), including emergency management (MS, PhD), general program (MS), global leadership (MS, PhD), homeland security and policy coordination (MS, PhD), law and public policy (MS, PhD), policy analysis (MS, PhD), public management and leadership (MS, PhD), self-designed (MS), terrorism, mediation, and peace (MS, PhD); criminal justice and executive management (MS), including global leadership (MS, PhD); criminal justice leadership and executive management (MS), including emergency management (MS, PhD), general program, homeland security and policy coordination (MS, PhD), law and public policy (MS, PhD), policy analysis (MS, PhD), public management and leadership (MS, PhD), self-designed, terrorism, mediation, and peace (MS, PhD); emergency management (MPA, MPP, MS), including criminal justice (MS, PhD), general program (MS), homeland security (MS), public management and leadership (MS, PhD), terrorism and emergency management (MS); general program (MPA, MPP); global leadership (MPA, MPP); government management (Graduate Certificate); health policy (MPA, MPP); homeland security (Graduate Certificate); homeland security and policy coordination (MPA, MPP); international nongovernmental organizations (MPA, MPP); law and public policy (MPA, MPP); local government management for sustainable communities (MPA, MPP); nonprofit management (Graduate Certificate); nonprofit management and leadership (MPA, MPP, MS), including global leadership (MS, PhD), international nongovernmental organization (MS), local government for sustainable communities (MS), self-designed (MS); online teaching in higher education (Post-Master's Certificate); policy analysis (MPA); public management and leadership (MPA, MPP, Graduate Certificate); public policy (Graduate Certificate); public policy and administration (PhD), including criminal justice (MS, PhD), emergency management (MS, PhD), global leadership (MS, PhD), health policy, homeland security and policy coordination (MS, PhD), international nongovernmental organizations, law and public policy (MS, PhD), local government management for sustainable communities, nonprofit management and leadership, policy analysis (MS, PhD), public management and leadership (MS, PhD), terrorism, mediation, and peace (MS, PhD); strategic planning and public policy (Graduate Certificate); terrorism, mediation, and peace (MPA, MPP). *Program availability:* Part-time, evening/weekend, online only, 100% online. *Degree requirements:* For doctorate, thesis/dissertation, residency. *Entrance requirements:* For master's, bachelor's degree or higher; minimum GPA of 2.5; official transcripts; goal statement (for some programs); access to computer and Internet; for doctorate, master's degree or higher; three years of related professional or academic experience (preferred); minimum GPA of 3.0; goal statement and current resume (for select programs); official transcripts; access to computer and Internet; for other advanced degree, relevant work experience; access to computer and Internet. Additional exam requirements/recommendations for international students: required—TOEFL (minimum score 550 paper-based, 79 iBT), IELTS (minimum score 6.5), Michigan English Language Assessment Battery (minimum score 82), or PTE (minimum score 53). Electronic applications accepted.

**Walsh University,** Master of Business Administration, North Canton, OH 44720. Offers healthcare management (MBA); management (MBA); marketing (MBA). *Program availability:* Part-time, evening/weekend, online only, 100% online. *Faculty:* 11 full-time (6 women), 9 part-time/adjunct (4 women). *Students:* 60 full-time (32 women), 128 part-time (67 women); includes 23 minority (12 Black or African American, non-Hispanic/Latino; 1 American Indian or Alaska Native, non-Hispanic/Latino; 1 Asian, non-Hispanic/Latino; 9 Two or more races, non-Hispanic/Latino), 4 international. Average age 39. 158 applicants, 50% accepted, 51 enrolled. In 2019, 52 master's awarded. *Degree requirements:* For master's, capstone course in strategic management. *Entrance requirements:* For master's, minimum GPA of 3.0, application, resume, transcripts. Additional exam requirements/recommendations for international students: required—TOEFL (minimum score 500 paper-based; 61 iBT), IELTS (minimum score 5.5). *Application deadline:* For fall admission, 7/15 priority date for domestic students. Applications are processed on a rolling basis. Electronic applications accepted. *Expenses:* $745 per credit hour, $50 technology fee. *Financial support:* In 2019–20, 4 students received support. Unspecified assistantships available. Financial award application deadline: 12/31; financial award applicants required to submit FAFSA. *Unit head:* Dr. Rajshekhar Javalgi, Dean, DeVille School of Business, 330-4907048, E-mail: rjavalgi@walsh.edu. *Application contact:* Dr. Rajshekhar Javalgi, Dean, DeVille School of Business, 330-4907048, E-mail: rjavalgi@walsh.edu.
Website: http://www.walsh.edu/

**Washington Adventist University,** Program in Health Care Administration, Takoma Park, MD 20912. Offers MA. *Program availability:* Part-time. *Entrance requirements:* Additional exam requirements/recommendations for international students: required—TOEFL (minimum score 550 paper-based; 80 iBT), IELTS (minimum score 6.5). Electronic applications accepted.

**Washington State University,** College of Pharmacy and Pharmaceutical Sciences, Department of Health Policy and Administration, Spokane, WA 99210. Offers MHPA. *Accreditation:* CAHME. *Program availability:* Part-time, evening/weekend. *Degree requirements:* For master's, comprehensive exam (for some programs), thesis (for some programs), oral exam. *Entrance requirements:* For master's, GRE General Test or GMAT, minimum GPA of 3.0, 3 letters of recommendation. Additional exam requirements/recommendations for international students: required—TOEFL (minimum score 550 paper-based) or IELTS (minimum score 7).

**Wayland Baptist University,** Graduate Programs, Programs in Business Administration/Management, Plainview, TX 79072-6998. Offers accounting (MBA); general business (MBA); health care administration (MAM, MBA); human resource management (MAM, MBA); international management (MBA); management (MBA,

D Mgt); management information systems (MBA); organization management (MAM); project management (MBA). *Program availability:* Part-time, evening/weekend, online learning. *Degree requirements:* For master's, capstone course. *Entrance requirements:* For master's, GMAT, GRE or MAT. Additional exam requirements/recommendations for international students: required—TOEFL (minimum score 500 paper-based; 61 iBT). Electronic applications accepted. *Expenses: Tuition:* Full-time $728; part-time $728 per semester. *Required fees:* $1218. Tuition and fees vary according to degree level, campus/location and program.

**Waynesburg University,** Graduate and Professional Studies, Canonsburg, PA 15370. Offers business (MBA), including energy management, finance, health systems, human resources, leadership, market development; counseling (MA), including addictions counseling, clinical mental health; counselor education and supervision (PhD); criminal investigation (MA); education (M Ed), including autism, curriculum and instruction, educational leadership, online teaching; nursing (MSN), including administration, education, informatics; nursing practice (DNP); special education (M Ed); technology (M Ed); MSN/MBA. *Accreditation:* AACN. *Program availability:* Part-time, evening/weekend. *Degree requirements:* For doctorate, thesis/dissertation. *Entrance requirements:* Additional exam requirements/recommendations for international students: required—TOEFL. Electronic applications accepted.

**Wayne State University,** College of Liberal Arts and Sciences, Department of Political Science, Detroit, MI 48202. Offers political science (MA, PhD); public administration (MPA), including economic development policy and management, health and human services policy and management, human and fiscal resource management, nonprofit policy and management, organizational behavior and management, urban and metropolitan policy and management; JD/MA. *Accreditation:* NASPAA. *Program availability:* Part-time, evening/weekend. *Faculty:* 22 full-time (9 women). *Students:* 50 full-time (22 women), 64 part-time (32 women); includes 28 minority (20 Black or African American, non-Hispanic/Latino; 2 Asian, non-Hispanic/Latino; 1 Hispanic/Latino; 5 Two or more races, non-Hispanic/Latino), 10 international. Average age 34. 105 applicants, 40% accepted, 24 enrolled. In 2019, 21 master's, 7 doctorates awarded. Terminal master's awarded for partial completion of doctoral program. *Degree requirements:* For master's, comprehensive exam (for some programs), thesis (for some programs); for doctorate, thesis/dissertation. *Entrance requirements:* For master's, GRE General Test, substantial undergraduate preparation in the social sciences, minimum upper-division undergraduate GPA of 3.0, two letters of recommendation, personal statement; for doctorate, GRE General Test, 3 letters of recommendation; personal statement; interview. Additional exam requirements/recommendations for international students: required—TOEFL (minimum score 550 paper-based; 79 iBT), TWE (minimum score 5.5), Michigan English Language Assessment Battery (minimum score 85); recommended—IELTS (minimum score 6.5). *Application deadline:* For fall admission, 5/15 for domestic students, 5/1 priority date for international students; for winter admission, 10/15 for domestic students, 9/1 priority date for international students. Applications are processed on a rolling basis. Application fee: $50. Electronic applications accepted. *Expenses:* $678.55 per credit in-state tuition, $1,469.75 per credit out-of-state tuition, $54.56 per credit hour student service fee, $315.70 registration fee. *Financial support:* In 2019–20, 48 students received support, including 4 fellowships with partial tuition reimbursements available (averaging $57,000 per year), 1 research assistantship with partial tuition reimbursement available (averaging $45,000 per year), 13 teaching assistantships with partial tuition reimbursements available (averaging $58,000 per year); scholarships/grants, health care benefits, and unspecified assistantships also available. Financial award applicants required to submit FAFSA. *Unit head:* Dr. Daniel Geller, Professor and Chair, 313-577-6328, E-mail: dgeller@wayne.edu. *Application contact:* Dr. Jeffrey Grynaviski, Graduate Director, 313-577-2620, E-mail: gradpolisci@wayne.edu.
Website: http://clas.wayne.edu/politicalscience/

**Weber State University,** Dumke College of Health Professions, Master of Health Administration Program, Ogden, UT 84408-1001. Offers MHA. *Accreditation:* CAHME. *Program availability:* Part-time, evening/weekend, 100% online. *Faculty:* 5 full-time (2 women), 4 part-time/adjunct (1 woman). *Students:* 80 full-time (36 women), 11 part-time (3 women); includes 5 minority (2 Black or African American, non-Hispanic/Latino; 3 Hispanic/Latino). Average age 33. In 2019, 38 master's awarded. *Entrance requirements:* For master's, GMAT or GRE. Additional exam requirements/recommendations for international students: required—TOEFL (minimum score 550 paper-based). *Application deadline:* For fall admission, 3/15 for domestic students, 2/20 for international students. Application fee: $60 ($95 for international students). Electronic applications accepted. *Expenses: Tuition, area resident:* Full-time $7197; part-time $4981 per credit. Tuition, state resident: full-time $7197; part-time $4981 per credit. Tuition, nonresident: full-time $16,560; part-time $11,589 per credit. *Required fees:* $643 per semester. One-time fee: $60. Tuition and fees vary according to course load and program. *Financial support:* In 2019–20, 12 students received support. Scholarships/grants available. Financial award application deadline: 4/1; financial award applicants required to submit FAFSA. *Unit head:* Darcy Carter, Program Director, 801-626-7549, Fax: 801-626-6475, E-mail: darcycarter@weber.edu. *Application contact:* Cory Moss, Assistant Professor, 801-626-7237, Fax: 801-626-6475, E-mail: cmoss@weber.edu.
Website: http://www.weber.edu/MHA/

**Webster University,** George Herbert Walker School of Business and Technology, Department of Management, St. Louis, MO 63119-3194. Offers business and organizational security management (MA); digital marketing management (Graduate Certificate); government contracting (Graduate Certificate); health administration (MHA); health care management (MA); health services management (MA); human resources development (MA); human resources management (MA); information technology management (MA, MS); management (D Mgt); management and leadership (MA); marketing (MA); nonprofit leadership (MA); nonprofit revenue development (Graduate Certificate); organizational development (Graduate Certificate); procurement and acquisitions management (MA); public administration (MPA); space systems operations management (MS). *Program availability:* Part-time, evening/weekend, online learning. *Degree requirements:* For master's, thesis (for some programs); for doctorate, thesis/dissertation, written exam. *Entrance requirements:* For doctorate, GMAT, 3 years of work experience, MBA. Additional exam requirements/recommendations for international students: required—TOEFL.

**Weill Cornell Medicine,** Weill Cornell Graduate School of Medical Sciences, Program in Healthcare Policy and Research, New York, NY 10065. Offers biostatistics and data science (MS); health informatics (MS); health policy and economics (MS). *Program availability:* Part-time. *Degree requirements:* For master's, thesis. *Entrance requirements:* For master's, GRE, MCAT, or GMAT (recommended), official transcripts, resume, personal statement, 3 letters of reference. Additional exam requirements/recommendations for international students: required—TOEFL. *Expenses:* Contact institution.

**West Coast University,** Graduate Programs, North Hollywood, CA 91606. Offers advanced generalist (MSN); family nurse practitioner (MSN); health administration (MHA); occupational therapy (MS); pharmacy (Pharm D); physical therapy (DPT).

**Western Carolina University,** Graduate School, College of Health and Human Sciences, School of Health Sciences, Cullowhee, NC 28723. Offers MHS. *Program availability:* Part-time, evening/weekend. *Degree requirements:* For master's, thesis or alternative. *Entrance requirements:* For master's, GRE General Test, appropriate undergraduate degree with minimum GPA of 3.0, 3 letters of recommendation. Additional exam requirements/recommendations for international students: required—TOEFL (minimum score 550 paper-based; 79 iBT). *Expenses: Tuition, area resident:* Full-time $2217.50; part-time $1664 per semester. Tuition, state resident: full-time $2217.50; part-time $1664 per semester. Tuition, nonresident: full-time $7421; part-time $5566 per semester. *International tuition:* $7421 full-time. *Required fees:* $5598; $1954 per semester. Tuition and fees vary according to course load, campus/location and program.

**Western Connecticut State University,** Division of Graduate Studies, Ancell School of Business, Program in Health Administration, Danbury, CT 06810-6885. Offers MHA. *Program availability:* Part-time. *Degree requirements:* For master's, comprehensive exam, completion of program within 6 years. *Entrance requirements:* For master's, GMAT, GRE, or MAT, minimum GPA of 2.5. Additional exam requirements/recommendations for international students: recommended—TOEFL (minimum score 550 paper-based; 79 iBT), IELTS (minimum score 6).

**Western Governors University,** College of Health Professions, Salt Lake City, UT 84107. Offers healthcare management (MBA); leadership and management (MSN); nursing education (MSN); nursing informatics (MSN). *Program availability:* Evening/weekend, online learning. *Degree requirements:* For master's, capstone project. *Entrance requirements:* For master's, transcripts. Additional exam requirements/recommendations for international students: required—TOEFL (minimum score 450 paper-based; 80 iBT). Electronic applications accepted. Application fee is waived when completed online.

**Western Kentucky University,** Graduate School, College of Health and Human Services, Department of Public Health, Bowling Green, KY 42101. Offers healthcare administration (MHA); public health (MPH). *Accreditation:* CEPH. *Program availability:* Part-time, evening/weekend. *Degree requirements:* For master's, comprehensive exam, thesis or alternative. *Entrance requirements:* For master's, GRE General Test, minimum GPA of 2.75. Additional exam requirements/recommendations for international students: required—TOEFL (minimum score 555 paper-based; 79 iBT).

**Western Michigan University,** Graduate College, College of Arts and Sciences, School of Public Affairs and Administration, Kalamazoo, MI 49008. Offers health care administration (MPA, Graduate Certificate); nonprofit leadership and administration (Graduate Certificate); public administration (PhD). *Accreditation:* NASPAA (one or more programs are accredited). *Degree requirements:* For doctorate, thesis/dissertation.

**Widener University,** School of Business Administration, Program in Health and Medical Services Administration, Chester, PA 19013-5792. Offers MBA, MHA, MD/MBA, MD/MHA, Psy D/MBA, Psy D/MHA. *Accreditation:* CAHME (one or more programs are accredited). *Program availability:* Part-time, evening/weekend, 100% online, blended/hybrid learning. *Degree requirements:* For master's, clerkship, residency. *Entrance requirements:* For master's, GMAT, interview, minimum GPA of 2.5. Electronic applications accepted. *Expenses: Tuition:* Full-time $48,750; part-time $917 per credit hour. Tuition and fees vary according to class time, degree level, campus/location and program.

**Widener University,** School of Human Service Professions, Institute for Graduate Clinical Psychology, Program in Clinical Psychology and Health and Medical Services Administration, Chester, PA 19013-5792. Offers Psy D/MBA, Psy D/MHA. *Accreditation:* APA (one or more programs are accredited). Electronic applications accepted. *Expenses: Tuition:* Full-time $48,750; part-time $917 per credit hour. Tuition and fees vary according to class time, degree level, campus/location and program.

**William Woods University,** Graduate and Adult Studies, Fulton, MO 65251-1098. Offers administration (M Ed, Ed S); athletic/activities administration (M Ed); curriculum and instruction (M Ed, Ed S); educational leadership (Ed D); equestrian education (M Ed); health management (MBA); human resources (MBA); leadership (MBA); marketing, advertising, and public relations (MBA); teaching and technology (M Ed). *Program availability:* Part-time, evening/weekend. *Degree requirements:* For master's, capstone course (MBA), action research (M Ed); for Ed S, field experience. *Entrance requirements:* Additional exam requirements/recommendations for international students: required—TOEFL (minimum score 550 paper-based). Electronic applications accepted. *Expenses:* Contact institution.

**Wilmington University,** College of Business, New Castle, DE 19720-6491. Offers accounting (MBA, MS); business administration (MBA, DBA); environmental stewardship (MBA); finance (MBA); health care administration (MBA, MSM); homeland security (MBA, MSM); human resource management (MSM); management information systems (MBA, MSN); marketing (MSM); marketing management (MBA); military leadership (MSM); organizational leadership (MBA, MSM); public administration (MSM). *Program availability:* Part-time, evening/weekend. *Entrance requirements:* Additional exam requirements/recommendations for international students: required—TOEFL (minimum score 500 paper-based). Electronic applications accepted.

**Wilson College,** Graduate Programs, Chambersburg, PA 17201-1285. Offers accounting (M Acc); choreography and visual art (MFA); education (M Ed); educational technology (MET); healthcare administration (MHA); humanities (MA), including art and culture, critical/cultural theory, English language and literature, women's studies; management (MSM); nursing (MSN), including nursing education, nursing leadership and management; special education (MSE). *Program availability:* Evening/weekend. *Degree requirements:* For master's, project. *Entrance requirements:* For master's, PRAXIS, minimum undergraduate cumulative GPA of 3.0, 2 letters of recommendation, current certification for eligibility to teach in grades K-12, resume, personal interview. Electronic applications accepted.

**Wingate University,** Porter B. Byrum School of Business, Wingate, NC 28174. Offers accounting (MAC); corporate innovation (MBA); finance (MBA); general management (MBA); healthcare management (MBA); marketing (MBA); project management (MBA). *Accreditation:* ACBSP. *Program availability:* Part-time, evening/weekend. *Entrance requirements:* For master's, GMAT, work experience, 2 letters of recommendation. Electronic applications accepted. *Expenses:* Contact institution.

**Winston-Salem State University,** Program in Health Administration, Winston-Salem, NC 27110-0003. Offers MHA. *Entrance requirements:* For master's, baccalaureate degree, minimum cumulative undergraduate GPA of 3.0, personal statement, three letters of recommendation, interview.

**Worcester State University,** Graduate School, Program in Health Care Administration, Worcester, MA 01602-2597. Offers MS. *Program availability:* Part-time, evening/weekend. *Faculty:* 1 full-time, 4 part-time/adjunct (2 women). *Students:* 13 part-time (7 women); includes 4 minority (2 Black or African American, non-Hispanic/Latino; 2 Asian, non-Hispanic/Latino), 5 international. Average age 36. 3 applicants, 100% accepted, 1 enrolled. In 2019, 1 master's awarded. *Degree requirements:* For master's, comprehensive exam (for some programs), thesis, capstone. For a detail list in Degree Completion requirements please see the graduate catalog at catalog.worcester.edu.

*Health Services Management and Hospital Administration*

*Entrance requirements:* For master's, GMAT (preferred), GRE, For a detail list of entrance requirements please see the graduate catalog at catalog.worcester.edu. Additional exam requirements/recommendations for international students: required—TOEFL (minimum score 550 paper-based; 79 iBT), IELTS (minimum score 6). *Application deadline:* For fall admission, 3/1 for domestic and international students; for spring admission, 11/1 for domestic and international students; for summer admission, 3/1 for domestic and international students. Applications are processed on a rolling basis. Application fee: $50. Electronic applications accepted. *Expenses: Tuition, area resident:* Full-time $3042; part-time $169 per credit hour. Tuition, state resident: full-time $3042; part-time $169 per credit hour. Tuition, nonresident: full-time $3042; part-time $169 per credit hour. *International tuition:* $3042 full-time. *Required fees:* $2754; $153 per credit hour. *Financial support:* Career-related internships or fieldwork, scholarships/grants, and unspecified assistantships available. Financial award application deadline: 3/1; financial award applicants required to submit FAFSA. *Unit head:* Dr. Robert Holmes, Program Coordinator, 508-929-8343, Fax: 508-929-8176, E-mail: rholmes3@worcester.edu. *Application contact:* Sara Grady, Associate Dean, Graduate Studies and Professional Development, 508-929-8130, Fax: 508-929-8100, E-mail: sara.grady@worcester.edu.

**Xavier University,** College of Professional Sciences, Department of Health Services Administration, Cincinnati, OH 45207. Offers MHSA, MHSA/MBA. *Accreditation:* CAHME. *Program availability:* Part-time. *Degree requirements:* For master's, thesis, residency, project. *Entrance requirements:* For master's, GMAT or GRE, resume, two letters of recommendation, statement of intent, official transcripts, interview, minimum accounting and statistics grade of C. Additional exam requirements/recommendations for international students: required—TOEFL (minimum score 550 paper-based; 80 iBT). Electronic applications accepted. Application fee is waived when completed online. *Expenses:* Contact institution.

**See Display below and Close-Up on page 429.**

**Xavier University,** Williams College of Business, Master of Business Administration Program, Cincinnati, OH 45207. Offers business administration (Exec MBA, MBA); business intelligence (MBA); finance (MBA); health industry (MBA); international business (MBA); marketing (MBA); values-based leadership (MBA); MBA/MHSA; MSN/MBA. *Accreditation:* AACSB. *Program availability:* Part-time, evening/weekend. *Degree requirements:* For master's, capstone course. *Entrance requirements:* For master's, GMAT or GRE, official transcript; resume. Additional exam requirements/recommendations for international students: required—TOEFL (minimum score 550 paper-based; 79 iBT). Electronic applications accepted. Application fee is waived when completed online. *Expenses:* Contact institution.

**Yale University,** Yale School of Medicine, Yale School of Public Health, New Haven, CT 06520. Offers applied biostatistics and epidemiology (APMPH); biostatistics (MPH, MS, PhD), including global health (MPH); chronic disease epidemiology (MPH, PhD), including global health (MPH); environmental health sciences (MPH, PhD), including global health (MPH); epidemiology of microbial diseases (MPH, PhD), including global health (MPH); global health (APMPH); health management (MPH), including global health; health policy (MPH), including global health; health policy and administration (APMPH, PhD); occupational and environmental medicine (APMPH); preventive medicine (APMPH); social and behavioral sciences (APMPH, MPH), including global health (MPH); JD/MPH; M Div/MPH; MBA/MPH; MD/MPH; MEM/MPH; MFS/MPH; MM Sc/MPH; MPH/MA; MSN/MPH. *Accreditation:* CEPH. *Faculty:* 161 full-time (71 women), 121 part-time/adjunct (57 women). *Students:* 534 full-time (386 women); includes 156 minority (24 Black or African American, non-Hispanic/Latino; 83 Asian, non-Hispanic/Latino; 30 Hispanic/Latino; 19 Two or more races, non-Hispanic/Latino), 220 international. Average age 25. 1,300 applicants, 220 enrolled. In 2019, 250 master's, 12 doctorates awarded. *Degree requirements:* For master's, thesis; for doctorate, comprehensive exam, thesis/dissertation. *Entrance requirements:* For master's, GMAT, GRE, or MCAT; for doctorate, GRE General Test. Additional exam requirements/recommendations for international students: required—TOEFL (minimum score 100 iBT). *Application deadline:* For fall admission, 12/15 for domestic and international students; for summer admission, 12/15 for domestic and international students. Applications are processed on a rolling basis. Application fee: $135. Electronic applications accepted. *Expenses:* Contact institution. *Financial support:* Fellowships with full tuition reimbursements, research assistantships with full tuition reimbursements, teaching assistantships with full tuition reimbursements, career-related internships or fieldwork, institutionally sponsored loans, scholarships/grants, and tuition waivers available. Support available to part-time students. Financial award application deadline: 3/1; financial award applicants required to submit FAFSA. *Unit head:* Dr. Sten Vermund, Dean and Anna M.R. Lauder Professor of Public Health, E-mail: sten.vermund@yale.edu. *Application contact:* Mary Keefe, Director of Admissions, 203-785-2844, E-mail: ysph.admissions@yale.edu.
Website: http://publichealth.yale.edu/

**York College of Pennsylvania,** Graham School of Business, York, PA 17403-3651. Offers financial management (MBA); health care management (MBA); self-designed (MBA). *Accreditation:* ACBSP. *Program availability:* Part-time, evening/weekend. *Faculty:* 15 full-time (7 women), 4 part-time/adjunct (3 women). *Students:* 10 full-time (3 women), 73 part-time (27 women); includes 11 minority (6 Black or African American, non-Hispanic/Latino; 1 Asian, non-Hispanic/Latino; 3 Hispanic/Latino; 1 Two or more races, non-Hispanic/Latino), 2 international. Average age 32. In 2019, 25 master's awarded. *Degree requirements:* For master's, directed study. *Application deadline:* For fall admission, 7/15 priority date for domestic students, 5/1 for international students; for spring admission, 11/15 priority date for domestic students, 9/1 for international students; for summer admission, 4/15 priority date for domestic students. Applications are processed on a rolling basis. Electronic applications accepted. *Expenses:* Contact institution. *Financial support:* In 2019–20, 3 students received support. Scholarships/grants available. Financial award applicants required to submit FAFSA. *Unit head:* Nicole Cornell Sadowski, MBA Director, 717-815-1491, Fax: 717-600-3999, E-mail: ncornell@ycp.edu. *Application contact:* MBA Office, 717-815-1491, Fax: 717-600-3999, E-mail: mba@ycp.edu.
Website: http://www.ycp.edu/mba

**Youngstown State University,** College of Graduate Studies, Bitonte College of Health and Human Services, Department of Health Professions, Youngstown, OH 44555-0001. Offers health and human services (MHHS); public health (MPH). *Accreditation:* NAACLS. *Program availability:* Part-time, evening/weekend. *Degree requirements:* For master's, thesis optional. *Entrance requirements:* For master's, GRE General Test, minimum GPA of 3.0. Additional exam requirements/recommendations for international students: required—TOEFL.

# Health Services Research

**Albany College of Pharmacy and Health Sciences,** School of Arts and Sciences, Albany, NY 12208. Offers clinical laboratory sciences (MS); cytotechnology and molecular cytology (MS); health outcomes research (MS); molecular biosciences (MS). *Degree requirements:* For master's, thesis. *Entrance requirements:* For master's, GRE, minimum GPA of 3.0. Additional exam requirements/recommendations for international students: required—TOEFL (minimum score 84 iBT). Electronic applications accepted.

**Albany College of Pharmacy and Health Sciences,** School of Pharmacy and Pharmaceutical Sciences, Albany, NY 12208. Offers health outcomes research (MS); pharmaceutical sciences (MS), including pharmaceutics, pharmacology; pharmacy (Pharm D). *Accreditation:* ACPE. *Degree requirements:* For master's, thesis; for doctorate, practice experience. *Entrance requirements:* For master's, GRE, minimum GPA of 3.0; for doctorate, PCAT, minimum GPA of 2.5. Additional exam requirements/ recommendations for international students: required—TOEFL (minimum score 84 iBT). Electronic applications accepted.

**Brown University,** Graduate School, Division of Biology and Medicine, School of Public Health, Department of Health Services, Policy and Practice, Providence, RI 02912. Offers PhD.

**Clarkson University,** School of Arts and Sciences, Program in Basic Science, Potsdam, NY 13699. Offers basic science (MS), including biology. *Students:* 2 full-time (0 women), 1 (woman) part-time; includes 2 minority (1 Black or African American, non-Hispanic/Latino; 1 Asian, non-Hispanic/Latino). 3 applicants, 100% accepted, 2 enrolled. In 2019, 5 master's awarded. *Entrance requirements:* For master's, GRE. Additional exam requirements/recommendations for international students: required—TOEFL (minimum score 550 paper-based, 80 iBT) or IELTS (6.5). *Application deadline:* Applications are processed on a rolling basis. Application fee: $50. Electronic applications accepted. *Expenses: Tuition:* Full-time $24,984; part-time $1388 per credit hour. *Required fees:* $225. Tuition and fees vary according to campus/location and program. *Financial support:* Scholarships/grants and unspecified assistantships available. *Unit head:* Dr. Charles Thorpe, Dean of the School of Arts and Sciences, 315-268-6544, E-mail: cthorpe@clarkson.edu. *Application contact:* Daniel Capogna, Director of Graduate Admissions & Recruitment, 518-631-9910, E-mail: graduate@clarkson.edu. Website: https://www.clarkson.edu/academics/graduate

**Dartmouth College,** The Dartmouth Institute, Hanover, NH 03755. Offers MPH, MS, PhD. *Program availability:* Part-time. *Degree requirements:* For master's, research project or practicum; for doctorate, thesis/dissertation. *Entrance requirements:* For master's, GRE, GMAT or MCAT, 2 letters of recommendation, current resume or curriculum vitae; for doctorate, GRE, 3 letters of recommendation, current resume or curriculum vitae.

**Emory University,** Rollins School of Public Health, Department of Health Policy and Management, Atlanta, GA 30322-1100. Offers health policy (MPH); health policy research (MSPH); health services management (MPH); health services research and health policy (PhD). *Program availability:* Part-time. *Degree requirements:* For master's, thesis (for some programs), practicum, capstone course. *Entrance requirements:* For master's, GRE General Test. Additional exam requirements/recommendations for international students: required—TOEFL (minimum score 550 paper-based; 80 iBT). Electronic applications accepted.

**Florida Agricultural and Mechanical University,** Division of Graduate Studies, Research, and Continuing Education, College of Pharmacy and Pharmaceutical Sciences, Graduate Programs in Pharmaceutical Sciences, Tallahassee, FL 32307-3200. Offers environmental toxicology (PhD); health outcomes research and pharmacoeconomics (PhD); medicinal chemistry (MS, PhD); pharmaceutics (MS, PhD); pharmacology/toxicology (MS, PhD); pharmacy administration (MS). *Accreditation:* CEPH. *Degree requirements:* For master's, comprehensive exam, thesis, publishable paper; for doctorate, comprehensive exam, thesis/dissertation, publishable paper. *Entrance requirements:* For master's and doctorate, GRE General Test, minimum GPA of 3.0 in last 60 hours. Additional exam requirements/recommendations for international students: required—TOEFL.

**George Mason University,** College of Health and Human Services, Department of Health Administration and Policy, Fairfax, VA 22030. Offers health and medical policy (MS); health informatics (MS); health informatics and data analytics (Certificate); health services research (PhD); health systems management (MHA); quality improvement and outcomes management in health care systems (Certificate). *Accreditation:* CAHME. *Program availability:* Part-time, evening/weekend, 100% online. *Degree requirements:* For master's, comprehensive exam, internship; for doctorate, thesis/dissertation. *Entrance requirements:* For master's, GRE recommended if undergraduate GPA is below 3.0 (for MS in health and medical policy), 2 official transcripts; expanded goals statement; 3 letters of recommendation; resume; 1 year of work experience (for MHA in health systems management); minimum GPA of 3.25 preferred (for MS in health informatics); for doctorate, GRE, professional and volunteer experience, evidence of ability to write and conduct research at the doctoral level, master's degree or equivalent; for Certificate, 2 official transcripts; expanded goals statement; 3 letters of recommendation; resume. Additional exam requirements/recommendations for international students: required—TOEFL (minimum score 575 paper-based; 88 iBT), IELTS (minimum score 6.5), PTE (minimum score 59). Electronic applications accepted. *Expenses:* Contact institution.

**The George Washington University,** School of Medicine and Health Sciences, Health Sciences Programs, Washington, DC 20052. Offers clinical practice management (MSHS); clinical research administration (MSHS); emergency services management (MSHS); end-of-life care (MSHS); immunohematology (MSHS); immunohematology and biotechnology (MSHS); physical therapy (DPT); physician assistant (MSHS). *Program availability:* Online learning. *Entrance requirements:* Additional exam requirements/recommendations for international students: required—TOEFL (minimum score 550 paper-based). *Expenses:* Contact institution.

**Lakehead University,** Graduate Studies, Faculty of Social Sciences and Humanities, Department of Sociology, Thunder Bay, ON P7B 5E1, Canada. Offers gerontology (MA); health services and policy research (MA); sociology (MA); women's studies (MA). *Program availability:* Part-time, evening/weekend. *Degree requirements:* For master's, research project or thesis. *Entrance requirements:* For master's, minimum B average. Additional exam requirements/recommendations for international students: required—TOEFL.

**McMaster University,** Faculty of Health Sciences and School of Graduate Studies, Program in Health Research Methodology, Hamilton, ON L8S 4M2, Canada. Offers M Sc, PhD. *Program availability:* Part-time. *Degree requirements:* For doctorate, comprehensive exam. *Entrance requirements:* For master's, honors degree, minimum B+ average in last year of undergraduate course work; for doctorate, M Sc, minimum B+

average. Additional exam requirements/recommendations for international students: required—TOEFL (minimum score 580 paper-based; 92 iBT).

**Northwestern University,** Feinberg School of Medicine, Driskill Graduate Program in Life Sciences, Chicago, IL 60611. Offers biostatistics (PhD); epidemiology (PhD); health and biomedical informatics (PhD); health services and outcomes research (PhD); healthcare quality and patient safety (PhD); translational outcomes in science (PhD). *Degree requirements:* For doctorate, comprehensive exam, thesis/dissertation, written and oral qualifying exams. *Entrance requirements:* For doctorate, GRE General Test. Additional exam requirements/recommendations for international students: required—TOEFL (minimum score 600 paper-based). Electronic applications accepted.

**Old Dominion University,** College of Health Sciences, Program in Health Services Research, Norfolk, VA 23529. Offers PhD. *Degree requirements:* For doctorate, comprehensive exam, thesis/dissertation, oral presentation of dissertation. *Entrance requirements:* For doctorate, GRE, minimum GPA of 3.25, master's degree, degree in health profession or health services, interview. Additional exam requirements/ recommendations for international students: required—TOEFL (minimum score 550 paper-based; 79 iBT). Electronic applications accepted. *Expenses:* Contact institution.

**Penn State Hershey Medical Center,** College of Medicine, Graduate School Programs in the Biomedical Sciences, Graduate Program in Public Health Sciences, Hershey, PA 17033. Offers MS. *Accreditation:* CEPH. *Program availability:* Part-time. *Entrance requirements:* For master's, GRE General Test. Additional exam requirements/ recommendations for international students: required—TOEFL (minimum score 81 iBT). Electronic applications accepted.

**Stanford University,** School of Medicine, Graduate Programs in Medicine, Department of Health Research and Policy, Stanford, CA 94305-2004. Offers biostatistics (PhD); epidemiology and clinical research (MS, PhD); health policy (MS, PhD). *Expenses: Tuition:* Full-time $52,479; part-time $34,110 per unit. *Required fees:* $672; $224 per quarter. Tuition and fees vary according to program and student level. Website: http://med.stanford.edu/hsr/

**Texas A&M University,** School of Public Health, College Station, TX 77843. Offers biostatistics (MPH, MSPH); environmental health (MPH, MSPH); epidemiology (MPH, MSPH); health administration (MHA); health policy and management (MPH); health services research (PhD); occupational safety and health (MPH). *Accreditation:* CAHME; CEPH. *Program availability:* Part-time, blended/hybrid learning. *Entrance requirements:* For master's, GRE General Test, 3 letters of recommendation; statement of purpose; current curriculum vitae or resume; official transcripts; for doctorate, GRE General Test, 3 letters of recommendation; statement of purpose; current curriculum vitae or resume; official transcripts; interview (in some cases). Additional exam requirements/ recommendations for international students: required—TOEFL (minimum score 597 paper-based, 95 iBT) or GRE (minimum verbal score 153). Electronic applications accepted. *Expenses:* Contact institution.

**Thomas Jefferson University,** Jefferson College of Life Sciences, Certificate Program in Patient-Centered Research, Philadelphia, PA 19107. Offers Certificate. *Program availability:* Part-time. *Entrance requirements:* For degree, GRE General Test (recommended). Additional exam requirements/recommendations for international students: required—TOEFL, IELTS (minimum score 7).

**Thomas Jefferson University,** Jefferson College of Population Health, Philadelphia, PA 19107. Offers applied health economics and outcomes research (MS, PhD, Certificate); behavioral health science (PhD); health policy (MS, Certificate); healthcare quality and safety (MS, PhD); population health (Certificate); public health (MPH, Certificate). *Program availability:* Part-time, evening/weekend, online learning. Terminal master's awarded for partial completion of doctoral program. *Degree requirements:* For master's, thesis; for doctorate, comprehensive exam, thesis/dissertation. *Entrance requirements:* For master's, GRE or other graduate entrance exam (MCAT, LSAT, DAT, etc.), two letters of recommendation, curriculum vitae, transcripts from all undergraduate and graduate institutions; for doctorate, GRE (taken within the last 5 years), three letters of recommendation, curriculum vitae, transcripts from all undergraduate and graduate institutions. Additional exam requirements/recommendations for international students: required—TOEFL. Electronic applications accepted.

**UNB Fredericton,** School of Graduate Studies, Applied Health Services Research Program, Fredericton, NB E3B 5A3, Canada. Offers MAHSR. *Program availability:* Part-time, online learning. *Faculty:* 3 full-time (1 woman). *Students:* 15 full-time (12 women), 5 part-time (all women), 3 international. Average age 31. In 2019, 1 master's awarded. *Degree requirements:* For master's, thesis. *Entrance requirements:* For master's, honors BA, minimum GPA of 3.0. Additional exam requirements/recommendations for international students: required—TWE (minimum score 4), TOEFL (minimum score 600 paper-based; 100 iBT) or IELTS (minimum score 7). *Application deadline:* For winter admission, 3/31 for domestic and international students. Applications are processed on a rolling basis. Application fee: $50 Canadian dollars. Electronic applications accepted. *Expenses: Tuition, area resident:* Full-time $6975 Canadian dollars; part-time $3423 Canadian dollars per year. Tuition, state resident: full-time $6975 Canadian dollars; part-time $3423 Canadian dollars per year. Tuition, Canadian resident: full-time $6975 Canadian dollars; part-time $3423 Canadian dollars per year. *International tuition:* $12,435 Canadian dollars full-time. *Required fees:* $92.25 Canadian dollars per term. Full-time tuition and fees vary according to degree level, campus/location, program, reciprocity agreements and student level. *Financial support:* Application deadline: 1/15. *Unit head:* Dr. Mary McKenna, Assistant Dean of Graduate Studies, 506-451 6872, Fax: 506-453-4817, E-mail: mmckenna@unb.ca. *Application contact:* Andrea Guevara, Graduate Programs Officer, 506-458-7558, Fax: 506-453-4817, E-mail: andrea.guevara@unb.ca. Website: http://www.artc-hsr.ca

**The University of Alabama at Birmingham,** School of Public Health, Program in Health Care Organization and Policy, Birmingham, AL 35294. Offers applied epidemiology and pharmacoepidemiology (MSPH); biostatistics (MPH); clinical and translational science (MSPH); environmental health (MPH); environmental health and toxicology (MSPH); epidemiology (MPH); general theory and practice (MPH); health behavior (MPH); health care organization (MPH, Dr PH); health policy (MPH); industrial hygiene (MPH, MSPH); maternal and child health policy (Dr PH); maternal and child health policy and leadership (MPH); occupational health and safety (MPH); outcomes research (MSPH, Dr PH); public health (PhD); public health preparedness management (MPH). *Accreditation:* CEPH. *Program availability:* Part-time, 100% online, blended/ hybrid learning. *Faculty:* 14 full-time (6 women). *Students:* 53 full-time (37 women), 61 part-time (45 women); includes 37 minority (12 Black or African American, non-Hispanic/ Latino; 20 Asian, non-Hispanic/Latino; 1 Hispanic/Latino; 4 Two or more races, non-Hispanic/Latino), 17 international. Average age 31. 136 applicants, 59% accepted, 44

enrolled. In 2019, 36 master's, 4 doctorates awarded. *Degree requirements:* For master's, comprehensive exam (for some programs), thesis (for some programs); for doctorate, comprehensive exam, thesis/dissertation. *Entrance requirements:* For doctorate, GRE. Additional exam requirements/recommendations for international students: required—TOEFL (minimum score 80 iBT), IELTS (minimum score 6.5). *Application deadline:* For fall admission, 4/1 priority date for domestic students, 4/1 for international students; for spring admission, 11/1 for domestic students; for summer admission, 4/1 for domestic students. Application fee: $50 ($60 for international students). Electronic applications accepted. *Financial support:* Fellowships, research assistantships, teaching assistantships, scholarships/grants, traineeships, and unspecified assistantships available. Financial award application deadline: 3/1; financial award applicants required to submit FAFSA. *Unit head:* Dr. Martha Wingate, Program Director, 205-934-6783, Fax: 205-975-5484, E-mail: mslay@uab.edu. *Application contact:* Dustin Shaw, Coordinator, Student Admissions and Record, 205-934-3939, E-mail: bcampbel@uab.edu.
Website: http://www.soph.uab.edu

**University of Alberta,** School of Public Health, Department of Public Health Sciences, Edmonton, AB T6G 2E1, Canada. Offers clinical epidemiology (M Sc, MPH); environmental and occupational health (MPH); environmental health sciences (M Sc); epidemiology (M Sc); global health (M Sc, MPH); health policy and management (MPH); health policy research (M Sc); health technology assessment (MPH); occupational health (M Sc); population health (M Sc); public health leadership (MPH); public health sciences (PhD); quantitative methods (MPH). *Accreditation:* CEPH. Terminal master's awarded for partial completion of doctoral program. *Degree requirements:* For master's, thesis (for some programs); for doctorate, thesis/dissertation. *Entrance requirements:* For master's, GMAT or GRE General Test. Additional exam requirements/recommendations for international students: required—TOEFL (minimum score 550 paper-based) or IELTS (minimum score 6). Electronic applications accepted.

**University of Arkansas for Medical Sciences,** Fay W. Boozman College of Public Health, Little Rock, AR 72205-7199. Offers biostatistics (MPH); environmental and occupational health (MPH, Certificate); epidemiology (MPH, PhD); health behavior and health education (MPH); health policy and management (MPH); health promotion and prevention research (PhD); health services administration (MHSA); health systems research (PhD); public health (Certificate); public health leadership (Dr PH). *Accreditation:* CAHME; CEPH. *Program availability:* Part-time. *Degree requirements:* For master's, preceptorship, culminating experience, internship; for doctorate, comprehensive exam, capstone. *Entrance requirements:* For master's, GRE, GMAT, LSAT, PCAT, MCAT, DAT; for doctorate, GRE. Additional exam requirements/recommendations for international students: required—TOEFL (minimum score 80 iBT), IELTS. Electronic applications accepted. *Expenses:* Contact institution.

**University of Cincinnati,** Graduate School, College of Medicine, Graduate Programs in Biomedical Sciences, Program in Biomedical Research, Cincinnati, OH 45221. Offers MS.

**University of Colorado Denver,** Colorado School of Public Health, Health Services Research Program, Aurora, CO 80045. Offers MS, PhD. *Program availability:* Part-time. *Entrance requirements:* For doctorate, GRE, MCAT, or MA, MS or PhD from an accredited school, minimum undergraduate GPA of 3.0. Tuition and fees vary according to course load, program and reciprocity agreements.

**University of Colorado Denver,** School of Medicine, Clinical Science Graduate Program, Aurora, CO 80045. Offers clinical investigation (PhD); clinical sciences (MS); health information technology (PhD); health services research (PhD). *Degree requirements:* For master's, thesis, minimum of 30 credit hours, defense/final exam of thesis or publishable paper; for doctorate, comprehensive exam, thesis/dissertation, at least 30 credit hours of thesis work. *Entrance requirements:* For master's, GRE General Test or MCAT (waived if candidate has earned MS/MA or PhD from accredited U.S. school), minimum undergraduate GPA of 3.0, 3-4 letters of recommendation; for doctorate, GRE General Test or MCAT (waived if candidate has earned MS/MA or PhD from accredited U.S. school), health care graduate, professional degree, or graduate degree related to health sciences; minimum GPA of 3.0; 3-4 letters of recommendation. Additional exam requirements/recommendations for international students: required—TOEFL (minimum score 550 paper-based; 80 iBT). Electronic applications accepted. Tuition and fees vary according to course load, program and reciprocity agreements.

**University of Florida,** Graduate School, College of Public Health and Health Professions, Department of Health Services Research, Management and Policy, Gainesville, FL 32611. Offers health administration (MHA); health services research (PhD). *Accreditation:* CAHME. *Program availability:* Part-time. *Degree requirements:* For master's, internship. *Entrance requirements:* For master's, GRE General Test (minimum score 300) or GMAT (minimum score 500), minimum GPA of 3.0; for doctorate, GRE General Test, minimum GPA of 3.0. Additional exam requirements/recommendations for international students: required—TOEFL (minimum score 550 paper-based; 80 iBT), IELTS (minimum score 6). Electronic applications accepted.

**University of Illinois at Chicago,** School of Public Health, Division of Health Policy and Administration, Chicago, IL 60607-7128. Offers clinical and translational science (MS); health policy (PhD); health services research (PhD); healthcare administration (MHA); public health policy management (MPH). *Accreditation:* CAHME. *Program availability:* Part-time. Terminal master's awarded for partial completion of doctoral program. *Degree requirements:* For master's, thesis, field practicum; for doctorate, thesis/dissertation, independent research, internship. *Entrance requirements:* For master's and doctorate, GRE General Test, minimum GPA of 2.75. Additional exam requirements/recommendations for international students: required—TOEFL. Electronic applications accepted. *Expenses:* Contact institution.

**University of La Verne,** College of Business and Public Management, Program in Health Administration, La Verne, CA 91750-4443. Offers financial management (MHA); management and leadership (MHA); marketing and business development (MHA). *Program availability:* Part-time. *Entrance requirements:* For master's, bachelor's degree, experience in health services industry (preferred). Additional exam requirements/recommendations for international students: required—TOEFL (minimum score 550 paper-based). *Expenses:* Contact institution.

**University of Maryland, Baltimore,** Graduate School, Graduate Programs in Pharmacy, Department of Pharmaceutical Health Service Research, Baltimore, MD 21201. Offers epidemiology (MS); pharmacy administration (PhD); Pharm D/PhD. *Degree requirements:* For doctorate, comprehensive exam, thesis/dissertation. *Entrance requirements:* For doctorate, GRE General Test. Additional exam requirements/recommendations for international students: required—TOEFL, IELTS. Electronic applications accepted.

**University of Massachusetts Medical School,** Graduate School of Biomedical Sciences, Worcester, MA 01655. Offers biomedical sciences (PhD), including biochemistry and molecular pharmacology, bioinformatics and computational biology, cancer biology, immunology and microbiology, interdisciplinary, neuroscience, translational science; biomedical sciences (millennium program) (PhD); clinical and population health research (PhD); clinical investigation (MS). *Faculty:* 1,258 full-time (525 women), 372 part-time/adjunct (238 women). *Students:* 344 full-time (198 women),

1 (woman) part-time; includes 73 minority (12 Black or African American, non-Hispanic/Latino; 1 American Indian or Alaska Native, non-Hispanic/Latino; 45 Asian, non-Hispanic/Latino; 15 Hispanic/Latino), 120 international. Average age 29. 581 applicants, 23% accepted, 56 enrolled. In 2019, 6 master's, 49 doctorates awarded. Terminal master's awarded for partial completion of doctoral program. *Degree requirements:* For master's, comprehensive exam, thesis; for doctorate, comprehensive exam, thesis/dissertation. *Entrance requirements:* For master's, MD, PhD, DVM, or PharmD; for doctorate, bachelor's degree. Additional exam requirements/recommendations for international students: required—TOEFL, IELTS, TOEFL (minimum score 100 IBT) or IELTS (minimum score 7.0). *Application deadline:* For fall admission, 12/1 for domestic and international students. Applications are processed on a rolling basis. Application fee: $80. Electronic applications accepted. Application fee is waived when completed online. *Expenses:* Contact institution. *Financial support:* In 2019–20, 22 fellowships with full tuition reimbursements (averaging $33,061 per year), 322 research assistantships with full tuition reimbursements (averaging $32,850 per year) were awarded; institutionally sponsored loans and scholarships/grants also available. Financial award application deadline: 5/15. *Unit head:* Dr. Mary Ellen Lane, Dean, 508-856-4018, E-mail: maryellen.lane@umassmed.edu. *Application contact:* Dr. Kendall Knight, Assistant Vice Provost for Admissions, 508-856-5628, Fax: 508-856-3659, E-mail: kendall.knight@umassmed.edu.
Website: http://www.umassmed.edu/gsbs/

**University of Minnesota, Twin Cities Campus,** School of Public Health, Major in Health Services Research, Policy, and Administration, Minneapolis, MN 55455-0213. Offers MS, PhD, JD/MS, JD/PhD, MD/PhD, MPP/MS. *Program availability:* Part-time. Terminal master's awarded for partial completion of doctoral program. *Degree requirements:* For master's, thesis, internship, final oral exam; for doctorate, thesis/dissertation, teaching experience, written preliminary exam, final oral exam, dissertation. *Entrance requirements:* For master's, GRE General Test, course work in mathematics; for doctorate, GRE General Test, prerequisite courses in calculus and statistics. Additional exam requirements/recommendations for international students: required—TOEFL (minimum score 600 paper-based; 100 iBT).

**University of Nebraska Medical Center,** Department of Health Services Research and Administration, Omaha, NE 68198. Offers health administration (MHA); health services research, administration, and policy (PhD); public health administration and policy (MPH). *Program availability:* Part-time, 100% online, blended/hybrid learning. *Degree requirements:* For doctorate, comprehensive exam, thesis/dissertation. *Entrance requirements:* For doctorate, GRE, official transcripts, resume or curriculum vitae, three letters of recommendation, statement of intent. Additional exam requirements/recommendations for international students: required—TOEFL (minimum score 550 paper-based; 80 iBT), IELTS (minimum score 6.5). Electronic applications accepted. *Expenses:* Contact institution.

**The University of North Carolina at Charlotte,** College of Health and Human Services, Program in Health Services Research, Charlotte, NC 28223-0001. Offers health services research (PhD). *Program availability:* Part-time. *Students:* 10 full-time (7 women), 10 part-time (5 women); includes 5 minority (3 Black or African American, non-Hispanic/Latino; 1 Asian, non-Hispanic/Latino; 1 Hispanic/Latino), 3 international. Average age 38. 8 applicants, 63% accepted, 2 enrolled. In 2019, 4 doctorates awarded. *Degree requirements:* For doctorate, thesis/dissertation. *Entrance requirements:* For doctorate, Master's or doctoral degree from regionally-accredited university in a health-related field; minimum graduate GPA of 3.5, essay, curriculum vitae, interviews, 3 reference letter. Additional exam requirements/recommendations for international students: required—TOEFL (minimum score 557 paper-based; 83 iBT), IELTS (minimum score 6.5), TOEFL (minimum score 557 paper-based, 83 iBT) or IELTS (6.5). *Application deadline:* For fall admission, 2/1 priority date for domestic students. Applications are processed on a rolling basis. Application fee: $75. Electronic applications accepted. *Expenses:* Tuition, state resident: full-time $4337. Tuition, nonresident: full-time $17,771. Required fees: $3093. Tuition and fees vary according to course load, degree level and program. *Financial support:* Career-related internships or fieldwork, institutionally sponsored loans, scholarships/grants, and unspecified assistantships available. Support available to part-time students. Financial award application deadline: 2/1; financial award applicants required to submit FAFSA. *Unit head:* Dr. Catrine Tudor-Locke, Dean, 704-687-7917, E-mail: tudor-locke@uncc.edu. *Application contact:* Kathy B. Giddings, Director of Graduate Admissions, 704-687-5503, Fax: 704-687-1668, E-mail: gradadm@uncc.edu.
Website: https://health.uncc.edu/academic-programs/hsr-phd-overview

**University of North Texas Health Science Center at Fort Worth,** School of Public Health, Fort Worth, TX 76107-2699. Offers biostatistics (MS); epidemiology (MPH, MS, PhD); food security and public health (Graduate Certificate); GIS in public health (Graduate Certificate); global health (Graduate Certificate); global health for medical professionals (Graduate Certificate); health administration (MHA); health behavior research (MS, PhD); maternal and child health (MPH); public health (Graduate Certificate); public health practice (MPH); DO/MPH; MS/MPH. *Accreditation:* CAHME; CEPH. *Program availability:* Part-time, evening/weekend, 100% online. *Degree requirements:* For master's, thesis or alternative, supervised internship; for doctorate, thesis/dissertation, supervised internship. *Entrance requirements:* For master's, GRE General Test. Additional exam requirements/recommendations for international students: required—TOEFL. Electronic applications accepted. *Expenses:* Contact institution.

**University of Ottawa,** Faculty of Graduate and Postdoctoral Studies, Interdisciplinary Programs, Ottawa, ON K1N 6N5, Canada. Offers e-business (Certificate); e-commerce (Certificate); finance (Certificate); health services and policies research (Diploma); population health (PhD); population health risk assessment and management (Certificate); public management and governance (Certificate); systems science (Certificate).

**University of Pennsylvania,** Perelman School of Medicine, Master of Science in Health Policy Research, Philadelphia, PA 19104. Offers MSHP, MD/MSHP. *Program availability:* Part-time. *Faculty:* 28 full-time (17 women). *Students:* 67 part-time (46 women); includes 24 minority (4 Black or African American, non-Hispanic/Latino; 14 Asian, non-Hispanic/Latino; 1 Hispanic/Latino; 5 Two or more races, non-Hispanic/Latino). Average age 33. 34 applicants, 82% accepted, 24 enrolled. *Degree requirements:* For master's, thesis optional. *Entrance requirements:* For master's, MCAT or waiver GRE. *Application deadline:* For fall admission, 11/1 for domestic and international students. Electronic applications accepted. *Financial support:* Fellowships, research assistantships, teaching assistantships, scholarships/grants, and tuition waivers (full and partial) available. Financial award application deadline: 4/1. *Unit head:* Dr. Judy Shea, Co-Director, 215-573-5111, E-mail: sheaja@pennmedicine.upenn.edu. *Application contact:* Kathlyn York, Graduate group Coordinator, 215-573-2740, E-mail: mshp@pennmedicine.upenn.edu.
Website: http://www.mshp.med.upenn.edu

**University of Pittsburgh,** School of Law, Master of Studies in Law Program, Pittsburgh, PA 15260. Offers biomedical and health services research (MSL); business law (MSL), including commercial law, corporate law, general business law, international business, tax law; Constitutional law (MSL); criminal law and justice (MSL); disability law (MSL);

elder and estate planning law (MSL); employment and labor law (MSL); energy law (MSL); environmental and real estate law (MSL); family law (MSL); health law (MSL); intellectual property and technology law (MSL); international and human rights law (MSL); jurisprudence (MSL); regulatory law (MSL); self-designed (MSL). *Program availability:* Part-time. *Entrance requirements:* Additional exam requirements/recommendations for international students: required—TOEFL (minimum score 600 paper-based; 100 iBT), IELTS (minimum score 7).

**University of Puerto Rico - Medical Sciences Campus,** Graduate School of Public Health, Department of Health Services Administration, Program in Evaluative Research of Health Systems, San Juan, PR 00936-5067. Offers MS. *Program availability:* Part-time. *Degree requirements:* For master's, thesis. *Entrance requirements:* For master's, GRE, previous course work in algebra and statistics. *Expenses:* Contact institution.

**University of Rochester,** School of Medicine and Dentistry, Graduate Programs in Medicine and Dentistry, Department of Community and Preventive Medicine, Program in Health Services Research and Policy, Rochester, NY 14627. Offers PhD, MPH/PhD. *Degree requirements:* For doctorate, thesis/dissertation, qualifying exam. *Entrance requirements:* For doctorate, GRE General Test.

**University of Southern California,** Keck School of Medicine and Graduate School, Graduate Programs in Medicine, Department of Preventive Medicine, Program in Health Behavior Research, Los Angeles, CA 90032. Offers PhD. *Faculty:* 21 full-time (12 women), 1 (woman) part-time/adjunct. *Students:* 34 full-time (29 women); includes 13 minority (1 American Indian or Alaska Native, non-Hispanic/Latino; 3 Asian, non-Hispanic/Latino; 5 Hispanic/Latino; 4 Two or more races, non-Hispanic/Latino), 5 international. Average age 30. 41 applicants, 32% accepted, 8 enrolled. In 2019, 4 doctorates awarded. *Degree requirements:* For doctorate, comprehensive exam, thesis/dissertation. *Entrance requirements:* For doctorate, GRE General Test (minimum preferred score for combined Verbal and Quantitative of 311), minimum GPA of 3.0 (3.5 preferred). Additional exam requirements/recommendations for international students: required—TOEFL (minimum score 600 paper-based; 100 iBT). *Application deadline:* For fall admission, 12/1 priority date for domestic and international students. Application fee: $95. Electronic applications accepted. *Financial support:* In 2019–20, 34 students received support, including 4 fellowships with full tuition reimbursements available (averaging $36,000 per year), 22 research assistantships with full tuition reimbursements available (averaging $36,000 per year), 1 teaching assistantship with full tuition reimbursement available (averaging $36,000 per year); institutionally sponsored loans, scholarships/grants, traineeships, health care benefits, and unspecified assistantships also available. Financial award application deadline: 6/30; financial award applicants required to submit CSS PROFILE or FAFSA. *Unit head:* Dr. Jennifer Unger, Director, 323-442-8234, E-mail: unger@usc.edu. *Application contact:* Sherri Fagan, Graduate Advisor, 323-442-8299, E-mail: sfagan@usc.edu.
Website: http://phdhbr.usc.edu

**The University of Tennessee Health Science Center,** College of Graduate Health Sciences, Memphis, TN 38163. Offers biomedical engineering (MS, PhD); biomedical sciences (PhD); dental sciences (MDS); epidemiology (MS); health outcomes and policy research (PhD); laboratory research and management (MS); nursing science (PhD); pharmaceutical sciences (PhD); pharmacology (MS); speech and hearing science (PhD); DDS/PhD; DNP/PhD; MD/PhD; Pharm D/PhD. Terminal master's awarded for partial completion of doctoral program. *Degree requirements:* For master's, comprehensive exam, thesis; for doctorate, thesis/dissertation, oral and written preliminary and comprehensive exams. *Entrance requirements:* For master's and doctorate, GRE General Test, minimum GPA of 3.0. Additional exam requirements/recommendations for international students: recommended—TOEFL (minimum score 79 iBT), IELTS (minimum score 6.5). Electronic applications accepted. *Expenses:* Contact institution.

**University of Utah,** Graduate School, College of Pharmacy, Department of Pharmacotherapy, Salt Lake City, UT 84112. Offers health system pharmacy administration (MS); outcomes research and health policy (PhD). *Faculty:* 19 full-time (12 women). *Students:* 6 full-time (3 women), 7 part-time (1 woman); includes 1 minority (Asian, non-Hispanic/Latino), 4 international. Average age 33. 14 applicants, 43% accepted, 6 enrolled. In 2019, 1 master's, 1 doctorate awarded. Terminal master's awarded for partial completion of doctoral program. *Degree requirements:* For master's, comprehensive exam, thesis or alternative, project; for doctorate, comprehensive exam, thesis/dissertation. *Entrance requirements:* Additional exam requirements/recommendations for international students: required—TOEFL (minimum score 550 paper-based; 80 iBT), GRE. *Application deadline:* For fall admission, 1/10 for domestic students, 12/15 for international students. Application fee: $55 ($65 for international students). *Expenses:* Tuition, state resident: full-time $7085; part-time $272.51 per credit hour. Tuition, nonresident: full-time $24,937; part-time $959.12 per credit hour. *Required fees:* $880.52; $880.52 per semester. Tuition and fees vary according to degree level, program and student level. *Financial support:* In 2019–20, 1 research assistantship (averaging $4,000 per year) was awarded. Financial award applicants required to submit CSS PROFILE or FAFSA. *Unit head:* Daniel Malone, Professor, 801-581-8054, Fax: 801-587-7923, E-mail: dan.malone@utah.edu. *Application contact:* Linda O'Connor, Education Coordinator, 801-585-1065, E-mail: linda.oconner@pharm.utah.edu.
Website: http://www.pharmacy.utah.edu/pharmacotherapy/

**University of Virginia,** School of Medicine, Department of Public Health Sciences, Charlottesville, VA 22903. Offers clinical research (MS), including clinical investigation and patient-oriented research, informatics in medicine; public health (MPH); MPP/MPH. *Program availability:* Part-time. *Entrance requirements:* For master's, GRE General Test or MCAT. Additional exam requirements/recommendations for international students: required—TOEFL. Electronic applications accepted.

**University of Washington,** Graduate School, School of Public Health, Department of Health Services, Seattle, WA 98195. Offers community-oriented public health practice (MPH); health services (MPH, MS, PhD); health systems and policy (MPH); maternal and child health (MPH); social and behavioral sciences (MPH); MPH/JD; MPH/MD; MPH/MN; MPH/MPA; MPH/MS; MPH/MSD; MPH/MSW; MPH/PhD. *Program availability:* Blended/hybrid learning. *Faculty:* 50 full-time (26 women), 71 part-time/adjunct (36 women). *Students:* 136 full-time (109 women), 16 part-time (all women); includes 62 minority (12 Black or African American, non-Hispanic/Latino; 6 American Indian or Alaska Native, non-Hispanic/Latino; 28 Asian, non-Hispanic/Latino; 14 Hispanic/Latino; 2 Native Hawaiian or other Pacific Islander, non-Hispanic/Latino), 9 international. Average age 31. 236 applicants, 62% accepted, 56 enrolled. In 2019, 63 master's, 10 doctorates awarded. Terminal master's awarded for partial completion of doctoral program. *Degree requirements:* For doctorate, comprehensive exam, thesis/dissertation. *Entrance requirements:* Additional exam requirements/recommendations for international students: required—TOEFL (minimum score 80 iBT). Application fee: $85. Electronic applications accepted. *Expenses:* MPH resident $22,476, MPH non-resident $38,316, resident MS & PhD $19,389, non-resident MS & PhD $32,775. *Financial support:* Fellowships, research assistantships, teaching assistantships, Federal Work-Study, institutionally sponsored loans, scholarships/grants, traineeships, health care benefits, and unspecified assistantships available. Financial award applicants required to submit FAFSA. *Unit head:* Dr. Jeffrey Harris, Chair, 206-616-2930, E-mail: hschair@uw.edu. *Application contact:* Marketing & Recruitment Specialist, 206-616-1397, E-mail: hservask@uw.edu.
Website: http://depts.washington.edu/hserv/

**Virginia Commonwealth University,** Graduate School, School of Allied Health Professions, Department of Health Administration, Doctoral Program in Health Services Organization and Research, Richmond, VA 23284-9005. Offers PhD. *Degree requirements:* For doctorate, thesis/dissertation, residency. *Entrance requirements:* For doctorate, GMAT or GRE General Test, minimum graduate GPA of 3.0. Additional exam requirements/recommendations for international students: required—TOEFL (minimum score 600 paper-based; 100 iBT). Electronic applications accepted.

**Virginia Commonwealth University,** Medical College of Virginia-Professional Programs, School of Medicine, Graduate Programs in Medicine, Department of Health Behavior and Policy, Richmond, VA 23284-9005. Offers healthcare policy and research (PhD); social and behavioral sciences (PhD). *Entrance requirements:* For doctorate, GRE General Test. Additional exam requirements/recommendations for international students: required—TOEFL (minimum score 600 paper-based; 100 iBT). Electronic applications accepted.

**Washington University in St. Louis,** School of Medicine, Program in Applied Health Behavior Research, St. Louis, MO 63110. Offers applied health behavior research (MS); health behavior planning and evaluation (Graduate Certificate). *Program availability:* Part-time, evening/weekend. *Entrance requirements:* For master's and Graduate Certificate, baccalaureate degree in psychology, biology, social work, public health, anthropology, allied health, sciences, or other related fields. Electronic applications accepted.

**Wayne State University,** College of Liberal Arts and Sciences, Department of Economics, Detroit, MI 48202. Offers applied macroeconomics (MA, PhD); health economics (MA, PhD); industrial organization (MA, PhD); international economics (MA, PhD); labor and human resources (MA, PhD); JD/MA. *Faculty:* 10. *Students:* 47 full-time (13 women), 6 part-time (2 women); includes 8 minority (4 Black or African American, non-Hispanic/Latino; 2 Asian, non-Hispanic/Latino; 2 Hispanic/Latino), 18 international. Average age 31. 67 applicants, 37% accepted, 8 enrolled. In 2019, 4 master's, 2 doctorates awarded. *Degree requirements:* For master's, comprehensive exam; for doctorate, comprehensive exam, thesis/dissertation, oral examination on research, completion of course work in quantitative methods, final lecture. *Entrance requirements:* For master's, minimum upper-division GPA of 3.0; prior coursework in intermediate microeconomic and macroeconomic theory, statistics, and elementary calculus; for doctorate, GRE, minimum upper-division GPA of 3.0, prior coursework in intermediate microeconomic and macroeconomic theory, statistics, two courses in calculus, three letters of recommendation from officials or teaching staff at institution(s) most recently attended, statement of purpose. Additional exam requirements/recommendations for international students: required—TOEFL (minimum score 550 paper-based; 79 iBT), TWE (minimum score 5.5), Michigan English Language Assessment Battery (minimum score 85); recommended—IELTS (minimum score 6.5). *Application deadline:* For fall admission, 5/1 for domestic and international students; for winter admission, 10/1 priority date for domestic students, 9/1 priority date for international students; for spring admission, 1/1 priority date for domestic and international students. Applications are processed on a rolling basis. Application fee: $50. Electronic applications accepted. *Expenses: Tuition:* Full-time $34,567. *Financial support:* In 2019–20, 30 students received support, including 2 fellowships with tuition reimbursements available (averaging $20,000 per year), 17 teaching assistantships with tuition reimbursements available (averaging $19,883 per year); research assistantships, scholarships/grants, health care benefits, and unspecified assistantships also available. Support available to part-time students. Financial award applicants required to submit FAFSA. *Unit head:* Dr. Kevin Cotter, Department Chair, 313-577-3345, E-mail: kevin.cotter@wayne.edu. *Application contact:* Dr. Allen Charles Goodman, Professor and Director of Graduate Studies, 313-577-3235, E-mail: aa1313@wayne.edu.
Website: http://clas.wayne.edu/economics/

**Weill Cornell Medicine,** Weill Cornell Graduate School of Medical Sciences, Program in Clinical Epidemiology and Health Services Research, New York, NY 10021. Offers MS. *Degree requirements:* For master's, thesis. *Entrance requirements:* For master's, 3 years of work experience, MD or RN certificate.

# XAVIER UNIVERSITY
*Graduate Program in Health Services Administration*

## Programs of Study

The Xavier University graduate program in Health Services Administration, the only program in the country to have received inaugural CAHME awards two years in a row, offers a rigorous curriculum that integrates both theory and practical experience. This combination fully equips its students to hold management, executive, and other leadership positions in a wide range of fields in the health services industry, including hospitals, health systems, group practice, insurance, consulting, government, and the military. Xavier's Master of Health Services Administration (M.H.S.A.) program is accredited by the Commission on the Accreditation of Healthcare Management Education (CAHME) and is one of only a handful of M.H.S.A. programs still requiring the eight- to twelve-month paid residency for full-time students. As one of the nation's oldest accredited health administration programs, the M.H.S.A. degree from Xavier has a tradition of excellence recognized throughout the healthcare industry since 1958.

The M.H.S.A. program offers both full-time and Executive M.H.S.A. degree options. The program also offers a concurrent degree with M.B.A.

The full-time day program prepares students for administrative and executive positions in healthcare organizations. This option consists of four semesters of on-campus coursework over a two-year period. After completing this coursework, students begin the required eight to twelve month paid residency (the average stipend in 2020 is $46,000) at a healthcare organization. With more than 150 approved residency sites across the country, the residency provides students with the opportunity to apply the knowledge and skills from their coursework to a real-world setting under the guidance of a senior manager.

The Executive M.H.S.A. (E.M.H.S.A.) program enables individuals with one or more years of professional health care experience to learn the administrative skills needed to progress in their careers and increase their value to their employers. The Executive M.H.S.A. track is offered 100% online and can be completed in as few as two years, with flexible scheduling options available.

The concurrent degree option provides an opportunity for students to pursue a business (M.B.A.) degree in addition to an M.H.S.A. degree. Students in this track must apply and be accepted into both programs. An M.B.A. may be earned over a two-year period by pursuing additional hours of M.B.A. graduate-level course work in the Williams College of Business at Xavier. The concurrent degree is designed to be completed within three years.

## Research Facilities

The McDonald Library at Xavier University contains most of the library's collections, including archives and special collections. Connected to this building is the Conaton Learning Commons (CLC), which hosts the "Connection Center," an integrated service point, blending library and help desk services. The library and CLC both provide study, lounge, conference, and instruction space along with access to photocopiers, computer workstations, and printers. The library emphasizes individual study while the CLC focuses on collaboration, housing thirteen group study rooms; nine of these rooms have plasma screen projection with Internet access. A food kiosk, vending machines, and kitchenette are available for students. Other student support services in the CLC include the Learning Assistance Center, Writing Center, Language Resource Center, and Digital Media Lab.

## Financial Aid

Internal scholarships are available from M.H.S.A. endowed funds. These awards are granted to students based on academic merit or a scholarship application. When available, graduate assistantships are offered which may include tuition remission and an hourly rate for work as determined by the University. Students who file a FAFSA and enroll at least half time may qualify for a Direct Loan, which is a long-term, low-interest loan. These students may also apply for a Graduate PLUS loan, which is credit-based. Various alternative loans are available for students who need additional assistance. Further information is available from the Financial Aid Office (phone: 513-745-3142) or by e-mailing hellkampal@xavier.edu.

## Cost of Study

Tuition for 2020–21 is $685 per credit hour. There is a $175 admissions fee for all full-time M.H.S.A. students. Textbooks are an additional cost.

## Living and Housing Costs

Xavier University does not provide graduate-specific housing on campus, as most graduate students live in neighboring areas of Cincinnati at affordable prices. Information regarding apartments located on campus is available at http://liveatustation.com.

## Student Group

There are between 20 and 30 students in each of the three full-time cohorts, while the Executive program consists of 6 to 10 new students per semester. The average age is 24 for full-time students and 32 for EMHSA students.

## Location

Xavier is located just north of downtown Cincinnati, Ohio which was named one of America's most livable cities (according to *Places Rated Almanac*). Cincinnati is known for great restaurants, shops, a major amusement park, and culture with Broadway theater, museums, a zoo, and aquarium. The city is home to major sports teams: the Cincinnati Reds, the Cincinnati Bengals, and FC Cincinnati.

## The University

Founded in 1831, Xavier is a private, coed university. As one of 28 Jesuit colleges/universities in the U.S., Xavier provides an education in the Jesuit Catholic tradition of preparing the whole person, developing knowledge, values, spiritual growth, and responsibility for others. The University's focus on ethics and values helps students ready themselves for moral decisions

*Xavier University*

they must make in their lives and careers. Xavier has 5,047 undergraduate students and 1,094 graduate students.

### The Faculty

#### M.H.S.A. Full-Time Faculty

- Rick Browne, Department Chair and Program Director, Associate Professor, Assistant Professor; Ph.D., Indiana University, 2002.
- Dwight Ellingwood, Professor; M.S., University of Utah, 1980.
- Lin Guo, Associate Professor; Ph.D., University of Cincinnati, 1995.
- Edmond Hooker, Professor; M.D., Eastern Virginia Medical School, 1985.
- Peter Mallow, Assistant Professor, Ph.D., University of Cincinnati, 2013.
- Thomas Ruthemeyer, Teaching Professor; M.B.A., Xavier University, 1984.
- France Weaver, Assistant Professor; Ph.D., University of North Carolina, 2005.

#### M.H.S.A. Adjunct Faculty

- Charlie Baverman, Adjunct Faculty, M.B.A., Xavier University
- Chris Boue, Adjunct Faculty; M.B.A., Florida Metropolitan University, 1993.
- Spencer Hale, Adjunct Faculty; M.B.A., Xavier University, 2012; M.H.S.A., Xavier University, 2016.
- Gayle Heintzelman, Adjunct Faculty; M.Ed., Xavier University, 2008.
- Lisa Taylor, Adjunct Faculty; J.D., Salmon P. Chase College of Law, 2000.
- RaNae Wright, Adjunct Faculty, M.H.S.A., Xavier University, 2010
- Karen Tepe, Adjunct Faculty; M.H.S.A., Xavier University, 1999; M.B.A., Xavier University, 2004.

### Applying

Full-time M.H.S.A. students matriculate in the fall each year. Deadlines to apply are January 1 for international students and June 1 for domestic students of the year in which they plan to enroll. Online Executive M.H.S.A. student matriculate in the fall and spring each year. The deadlines for E.M.H.S.A. student to apply are August 1 for fall and December 1 for spring. Application requirements include a completed online application form, two recommendation letters, a statement of intent, resume, and official transcripts from all previous college work. An interview is required for admission. Additional documents are required for international students.

### Correspondence and Information

Amy Hellkamp
Recruitment and Marketing Coordinator
Xavier University
Department of Health Services Administration
3800 Victory Parkway
Cincinnati, Ohio 45207-5141

Phone: 513-745-3687
E-mail: hellkampal@xavier.edu
Website: http://www.xavier.edu/mhsa/

Hinkle Hall, Xavier University.

Gallagher Student Center, Xavier University Green Space.

# Section 23
# Nursing

This section contains a directory of institutions offering graduate work in nursing, followed by in-depth entries submitted by institutions that chose to prepare detailed program descriptions. Additional information about programs listed in the directory but not augmented by an in-depth entry may be obtained by writing directly to the dean of a graduate school or chair of a department at the address given in the directory.

For programs offering related work, see also in this book *Health Services* and *Public Health*. In another guide in this series:

**Graduate Programs in the Humanities, Arts & Social Sciences**
See *Family and Consumer Sciences (Gerontology)*

## CONTENTS

### Program Directories

### Featured Schools: Displays and Close-Ups

# Nursing—General

**Abilene Christian University,** College of Graduate and Professional Studies, Program in Nursing Practice, Addison, TX 75001. Offers advanced practice nurse (DNP); executive nursing leadership (DNP); nursing education (DNP). *Program availability:* Part-time, online only, blended/hybrid learning. *Faculty:* 4 full-time (3 women), 1 (woman) part-time/adjunct. *Students:* 48 full-time (44 women), 64 part-time (55 women); includes 63 minority (35 Black or African American, non-Hispanic/Latino; 3 Asian, non-Hispanic/Latino; 24 Hispanic/Latino; 1 Two or more races, non-Hispanic/Latino), 2 international. 49 applicants, 100% accepted, 34 enrolled. In 2019, 10 doctorates awarded. *Entrance requirements:* For doctorate, master's degree in nursing, official transcripts, minimum graduate nursing cumulative GPA of 3.0, two recommendation letters, 500-word statement of purpose, professional curriculum vitae or resume. Additional exam requirements/recommendations for international students: required—TOEFL (minimum score 80 iBT), IELTS (minimum score 6). *Application deadline:* For fall admission, 10/7 for domestic students; for winter admission, 12/20 for domestic students; for spring admission, 2/24 for domestic students; for summer admission, 4/20 for domestic students. Applications are processed on a rolling basis. Application fee: $50. Electronic applications accepted. *Expenses:* $1000 per hour. *Financial support:* In 2019–20, 21 students received support. Scholarships/grants available. Financial award application deadline: 7/1; financial award applicants required to submit FAFSA. *Unit head:* Dr. Linda Gibson, Program Director, 214-305-9500, E-mail: lcg17a@acu.edu. *Application contact:* Graduate Advisor, 855-219-7300, E-mail: onlineadmissions@acu.edu.
Website: http://www.acu.edu/online/academics/doctor-of-nursing-practice.html

**Adelphi University,** College of Nursing and Public Health, PhD in Nursing Program, Garden City, NY 11530-0701. Offers PhD. *Entrance requirements:* Additional exam requirements/recommendations for international students: required—TOEFL (minimum score 550 paper-based; 80 iBT), IELTS (minimum score 6.5). *Expenses:* Contact institution.

**Albany State University,** Darton College of Health Professions, Albany, GA 31705-2717. Offers nursing (MSN), including family nurse practitioner, nurse educator. *Accreditation:* ACEN. *Program availability:* Part-time, evening/weekend, online learning. *Degree requirements:* For master's, comprehensive exam, thesis. *Entrance requirements:* For master's, GRE or MAT, official transcript, letters of recommendation, pre-medical/certificate of immunizations. Electronic applications accepted.

**Alcorn State University,** School of Graduate Studies, School of Nursing, Natchez, MS 39122-8399. Offers rural nursing (MSN). *Accreditation:* ACEN.

**Allen College,** Graduate Programs, Waterloo, IA 50703. Offers adult-gerontology acute care nurse practitioner (MSN); community/public health nursing (MSN); education (MSN); family nurse practitioner (MSN); health sciences (Ed D); leadership in health care delivery (MSN); leadership in health care informatics (MSN); nursing (DNP); occupational therapy (MS); psychiatric mental health nurse practitioner (MSN). *Accreditation:* AACN; ACEN. *Faculty:* 27 full-time (23 women), 9 part-time/adjunct (8 women). *Students:* 193 full-time (175 women), 95 part-time (84 women); includes 22 minority (6 Black or African American, non-Hispanic/Latino; 1 American Indian or Alaska Native, non-Hispanic/Latino; 4 Asian, non-Hispanic/Latino; 5 Hispanic/Latino; 6 Two or more races, non-Hispanic/Latino). Average age 32. 376 applicants, 53% accepted, 122 enrolled. *Application deadline:* For fall admission, 2/1 priority date for domestic students; for spring admission, 9/1 priority date for domestic students. Applications are processed on a rolling basis. Application fee: $50. Electronic applications accepted. *Financial support:* In 2019–20, 78 students received support. Federal Work-Study, institutionally sponsored loans, and scholarships/grants available. Support available to part-time students. Financial award application deadline: 8/1; financial award applicants required to submit FAFSA. *Unit head:* Dr. Bob Loch, Provost, 319-226-2040, Fax: 319-226-2070, E-mail: bob.loch@allencollege.edu. *Application contact:* Molly Quinn, Director of Admissions, 319-226-2001, Fax: 319-226-2010, E-mail: molly.quinn@allencollege.edu.
Website: http://www.allencollege.edu/

**Alvernia University,** School of Graduate Studies, Department of Nursing, Reading, PA 19607-1799. Offers adult gerontology nurse practitioner (DNP); family nurse practitioner (DNP); nursing education (MSN); nursing leadership (Graduate Certificate); nursing leadership and healthcare administration (MSN).

**Alverno College,** JoAnn McGrath School of Nursing and Health Professions, Milwaukee, WI 53234-3922. Offers clinical nurse specialist (MSN); family nurse practitioner (MSN); nursing practice (DNP); psychiatric mental health nurse practitioner (MSN). *Accreditation:* AACN. *Program availability:* Part-time, evening/weekend, 100% online, blended/hybrid learning. *Faculty:* 7 full-time (all women), 10 part-time/adjunct (8 women). *Students:* 117 full-time (110 women), 139 part-time (129 women); includes 68 minority (32 Black or African American, non-Hispanic/Latino; 8 Asian, non-Hispanic/Latino; 24 Hispanic/Latino; 4 Two or more races, non-Hispanic/Latino), 1 international. Average age 36. 94 applicants, 95% accepted, 60 enrolled. In 2019, 51 master's, 3 doctorates awarded. *Degree requirements:* For master's, 500 clinical hours, capstone; for doctorate, 1,000 post-BSN clinical hours. *Entrance requirements:* For master's, BSN, current license; for doctorate, MSN, nursing license. Additional exam requirements/recommendations for international students: required—TOEFL. *Application deadline:* For fall admission, 7/15 priority date for domestic and international students; for spring admission, 12/15 priority date for domestic and international students. Applications are processed on a rolling basis. Electronic applications accepted. *Expenses:* $1098 per credit hour. *Financial support:* In 2019–20, 4 students received support. Federal Work-Study and scholarships/grants available. Support available to part-time students. Financial award applicants required to submit FAFSA. *Unit head:* Patti Varga, Dean, 414-382-6303, Fax: 414-382-6354, E-mail: patti.varga@alverno.edu. *Application contact:* Janet Stikel, Director of Admissions, 414-382-6112, Fax: 414-382-6354, E-mail: janet.stikel@alverno.edu.
Website: http://www.alverno.edu/academics/academicdepartments/joannmcgrathschoolofnursing/

**American Public University System,** AMU/APU Graduate Programs, Charles Town, WV 25414. Offers accounting (MS); applied business analytics (MS); business administration (MBA); criminal justice (MA); cybersecurity studies (MS); educational leadership (M Ed); environmental policy and management (MS); global security (DGS); health information management (MS); history (MA), including American military history, American Revolution, civil war, war since 1945, World War II; information technology (MS); international relations and conflict resolution (MA), including American politics and government, comparative government and development, general, international relations, public policy; national security studies (MA); nursing (MSN); political science (MA); public policy (MPP); reverse logistics management (MA), including comparative and security issues, conflict resolution, international and transnational security issues, peacekeeping; space studies (MS); sports management (MS); strategic intelligence (DSI); teaching (M Ed), including secondary social studies; transportation and logistics management (MA). *Program availability:* Part-time, evening/weekend, online only, 100% online. *Students:* 461 full-time (193 women), 7,322 part-time (3,127 women); includes 3,089 minority (1,404 Black or African American, non-Hispanic/Latino; 30 American Indian or Alaska Native, non-Hispanic/Latino; 210 Asian, non-Hispanic/Latino; 753 Hispanic/Latino; 445 Native Hawaiian or other Pacific Islander, non-Hispanic/Latino; 247 Two or more races, non-Hispanic/Latino), 117 international. Average age 37. In 2019, 2,681 master's awarded. *Degree requirements:* For master's, comprehensive exam or practicum; for doctorate, practicum. *Entrance requirements:* For master's, official transcript showing earned bachelor's degree from institution accredited by recognized accrediting body. Additional exam requirements/recommendations for international students: required—TOEFL (minimum score 550 paper-based), IELTS (minimum score 6.5). *Application deadline:* Applications are processed on a rolling basis. Electronic applications accepted. *Financial support:* Scholarships/grants available. Financial award applicants required to submit FAFSA. *Unit head:* Dr. Wallace Boston, President, 877-468-6268, Fax: 304-728-2348, E-mail: president@apus.edu. *Application contact:* Yoci Deal, Associate Vice President, Graduate and International Admissions, 877-468-6268, Fax: 304-724-3764, E-mail: info@apus.edu.
Website: http://www.apus.edu

**American Sentinel University,** Graduate Programs, Aurora, CO 80014. Offers business administration (MBA); business intelligence (MS); computer science (MSCS); health information management (MS); healthcare (MBA); information systems (MSIS); nursing (MSN). *Program availability:* Part-time, evening/weekend, online learning. *Entrance requirements:* Additional exam requirements/recommendations for international students: required—TOEFL (minimum score 600 paper-based). Electronic applications accepted.

**Anderson University,** College of Health Professions, Anderson, SC 29621. Offers advanced practice (DNP); executive leadership (MSN, DNP); family nurse practitioner (MSN, DNP); nurse educator (MSN); psychiatric mental health nurse practitioner (MSN, DNP). *Program availability:* Online learning. *Application deadline:* Applications are processed on a rolling basis. Electronic applications accepted. *Expenses:* Contact institution. *Financial support:* Scholarships/grants available. *Unit head:* Dr. Donald M. Peace, Dean, 864-231-5513, E-mail: dpeace@andersonuniversity.edu. *Application contact:* Dr. Donald M. Peace, Dean, 864-231-5513, E-mail: dpeace@andersonuniversity.edu.
Website: http://www.andersonuniversity.edu/health-professions

**Andrews University,** College of Health and Human Services, School of Nursing, Berrien Springs, MI 49104. Offers MS, DNP. *Accreditation:* ACEN. *Program availability:* Part-time, evening/weekend. *Faculty:* 3 full-time (all women), 1 (woman) part-time/adjunct. *Students:* 19 full-time (all women), 12 part-time (8 women); includes 24 minority (17 Black or African American, non-Hispanic/Latino; 1 American Indian or Alaska Native, non-Hispanic/Latino; 2 Asian, non-Hispanic/Latino; 4 Hispanic/Latino). Average age 42. In 2019, 6 master's awarded. *Degree requirements:* For master's, thesis. *Entrance requirements:* For master's, GRE, minimum GPA of 2.5, 1 year of nursing experience, RN license. Additional exam requirements/recommendations for international students: required—TOEFL (minimum score 550 paper-based). *Application deadline:* Applications are processed on a rolling basis. Application fee: $60. Electronic applications accepted. *Financial support:* Research assistantships, Federal Work-Study, institutionally sponsored loans, and scholarships/grants available. *Unit head:* Dr. Jochebed Ade-Oshifogun, Chairperson, 269-471-3364. *Application contact:* Jillian Panigot, Director, University Admissions, 800-253-2874, Fax: 269-471-6321, E-mail: graduate@andrews.edu.
Website: http://www.andrews.edu/shp/nursing/

**Angelo State University,** College of Graduate Studies and Research, Archer College of Health and Human Services, Department of Nursing, San Angelo, TX 76909. Offers family nurse practitioner (MSN); nurse educator (MSN). *Accreditation:* AACN; ACEN. *Program availability:* Part-time, evening/weekend, online learning. *Entrance requirements:* For master's, essay, three letters of recommendation. Additional exam requirements/recommendations for international students: required—TOEFL or IELTS. Electronic applications accepted.

**Arizona State University at Tempe,** College of Nursing and Health Innovation, Phoenix, AZ 85004. Offers advanced nursing practice (DNP); clinical research management (MS); community and public health practice (Graduate Certificate); family mental health nurse practitioner (Graduate Certificate); family nurse practitioner (Graduate Certificate); geriatric nursing (Graduate Certificate); healthcare innovation (MHI); nurse education in academic and practice settings (Graduate Certificate); nurse educator (MS); nursing and healthcare innovation (PhD). *Accreditation:* AACN. *Program availability:* Online learning. *Degree requirements:* For master's, comprehensive exam (for some programs), thesis (for some programs), interactive Program of Study (iPOS) submitted before completing 50 percent of required credit hours; for doctorate, comprehensive exam, thesis/dissertation, interactive Program of Study (iPOS) submitted before completing 50 percent of required credit hours. *Entrance requirements:* For master's and doctorate, GRE, minimum GPA of 3.0 or equivalent in last 2 years of work leading to bachelor's degree. Additional exam requirements/recommendations for international students: required—TOEFL, IELTS, or PTE. Electronic applications accepted. *Expenses:* Contact institution.

**Arkansas State University,** Graduate School, College of Nursing and Health Professions, School of Nursing, State University, AR 72467. Offers aging studies (Graduate Certificate); health care management (Graduate Certificate); health sciences (MS); health sciences education (Graduate Certificate); nurse anesthesia (MSN); nursing (MSN); nursing practice (DNP). *Accreditation:* AANA/CANAEP (one or more programs are accredited); ACEN. *Program availability:* Part-time. *Degree requirements:* For master's and Graduate Certificate, comprehensive exam, thesis or alternative; for doctorate, comprehensive exam, thesis/dissertation. *Entrance requirements:* For master's, GRE General Test or MAT, appropriate bachelor's degree, current Arkansas nursing license, CPR certification, physical examination, professional liability insurance, critical care experience, ACLS Certification, PALS Certification, interview, immunization records, personal goal statement, health assessment; for doctorate, GRE or MAT, NCLEX-RN Exam, appropriate master's degree, current Arkansas nursing license, CPR certification, physical examination, professional liability insurance, critical care experience, ACLS Certification, PALS Certification, interview, immunization records, personal goal statement, health assessment, TB skin test, background check; for Graduate Certificate, GRE or MAT, appropriate bachelor's degree, official transcripts, immunization records, proof of employment in healthcare, TB Skin Test, TB Mask Fit Test, CPR Certification. Additional exam requirements/recommendations for international students: required—TOEFL (minimum score 550 paper-based; 79 iBT),

IELTS (minimum score 6), PTE (minimum score 56). Electronic applications accepted. *Expenses:* Contact institution.

**Arkansas Tech University,** College of Natural and Health Sciences, Russellville, AR 72801. Offers fisheries and wildlife biology (MS); health informatics (MS); nursing (MSN). *Program availability:* Part-time, evening/weekend, 100% online, blended/hybrid learning. *Students:* 6 full-time (2 women), 53 part-time (37 women); includes 7 minority (5 Black or African American, non-Hispanic/Latino; 1 Asian, non-Hispanic/Latino; 1 Hispanic/Latino). Average age 35. In 2019, 15 master's awarded. *Degree requirements:* For master's, thesis (for some programs), project. *Entrance requirements:* Additional exam requirements/recommendations for international students: required—TOEFL (minimum score 550 paper-based; 79 iBT), IELTS (minimum score 6.5), PTE (minimum score 58). *Application deadline:* For fall admission, 3/1 priority date for domestic students, 5/1 priority date for international students; for spring admission, 10/1 priority date for domestic and international students. Applications are processed on a rolling basis. Application fee: $40 ($90 for international students). Electronic applications accepted. *Expenses: Tuition, area resident:* Full-time $7008; part-time $292 per credit hour. Tuition, state resident: full-time $7008; part-time $292 per credit hour. Tuition, nonresident: full-time $14,016; part-time $584 per credit hour. *International tuition:* $14,016 full-time. *Required fees:* $343 per term. *Financial support:* In 2019–20, research assistantships with full and partial tuition reimbursements (averaging $4,800 per year), teaching assistantships with full and partial tuition reimbursements (averaging $4,800 per year) were awarded; career-related internships or fieldwork, Federal Work-Study, scholarships/grants, health care benefits, and unspecified assistantships also available. Support available to part-time students. Financial award application deadline: 4/15; financial award applicants required to submit FAFSA. *Unit head:* Dr. Jeff Robertson, Dean, 479-968-0498, E-mail: jrobertson@atu.edu. *Application contact:* Dr. Richard Schoephoerster, Dean of Graduate College and Research, 479-968-0398, Fax: 479-964-0542, E-mail: gradcollege@atu.edu.
Website: http://www.atu.edu/nhs/

**Ashland University,** Dwight Schar College of Nursing and Health Sciences, Department of Nursing, Ashland, OH 44805-3702. Offers family nurse practitioner (DNP). *Entrance requirements:* For doctorate, minimum GPA of 3.0, one year of clinical practice experience, 2-3 page paper, undergraduate- or graduate-level statistics course, interview. Additional exam requirements/recommendations for international students: recommended—TOEFL, IELTS, TSE. Electronic applications accepted. *Expenses: Tuition:* Full-time $10,800; part-time $5400 per credit hour. *Required fees:* $720; $360 per credit hour.

**Aspen University,** Program in Nursing, Denver, CO 80246-1930. Offers forensic nursing (MSN); informatics (MSN); nursing (MSN); nursing administration and management (MSN); nursing education (MSN); public health (MSN). *Program availability:* Part-time, evening/weekend, online only, 100% online. *Degree requirements:* For master's, comprehensive exam. *Entrance requirements:* For master's, www.aspen.edu, www.aspen.edu. Electronic applications accepted.

**Athabasca University,** Faculty of Health Disciplines, Athabasca, AB T9S 3A3, Canada. Offers advanced nursing practice (MN, Advanced Diploma); generalist (MN); health studies (MHS). *Program availability:* Part-time, online learning. *Degree requirements:* For master's, comprehensive exam (for some programs). *Entrance requirements:* For master's, bachelor's degree in health-related field and 2 years of professional health service experience (MHS); bachelor's degree in nursing and 2 years' nursing experience (MN); minimum GPA of 3.0 in final 30 credits; for Advanced Diploma, RN license, 2 years of health care experience. Electronic applications accepted. *Expenses:* Contact institution.

**Auburn University,** Graduate School, School of Nursing, Auburn, AL 36849. Offers nursing educator (MSN); primary care practitioner (MSN). *Accreditation:* AACN. *Program availability:* Part-time. *Faculty:* 30 full-time (27 women), 1 (woman) part-time/adjunct. *Students:* 13 full-time (all women), 132 part-time (117 women); includes 13 minority (7 Black or African American, non-Hispanic/Latino; 1 American Indian or Alaska Native, non-Hispanic/Latino; 2 Asian, non-Hispanic/Latino; 1 Hispanic/Latino; 2 Two or more races, non-Hispanic/Latino), 1 international. Average age 34. 88 applicants, 85% accepted, 58 enrolled. In 2019, 78 master's awarded. *Degree requirements:* For master's, Primary Care Practicum. *Entrance requirements:* For master's, BS in Nursing, license as a registered nurse in the US, C or better in undergraduate statistics course, BSN Nursing GPA of 3.0, Three professional references, Professional Goal Statement, resume or curriculum vitae. Additional exam requirements/recommendations for international students: required—TOEFL (minimum score 550 paper-based; 79 iBT). *Application deadline:* For fall admission, 6/1 priority date for domestic and international students; for spring admission, 10/1 priority date for domestic and international students; for summer admission, 3/1 priority date for domestic and international students. Application fee: $60 ($70 for international students). Electronic applications accepted. *Expenses:* $546 per credit hour state resident tuition, $1638 per credit hour nonresident tuition, $680 student services fee for GRA/GTA, $450 continuous enrollment fee, $450 clearing for graduation fee, $200 per clinical credit hour. *Financial support:* In 2019–20, 28 fellowships (averaging $28,714 per year), 2 teaching assistantships (averaging $9,696 per year) were awarded; scholarships/grants also available. Financial award application deadline: 3/15; financial award applicants required to submit FAFSA. *Unit head:* Dr. Gregg E. Newschwander, Dean, 334-844-3658, E-mail: gen0002@auburn.edu. *Application contact:* Dr. George Flowers, Dean of the Graduate School, 334-844-4700, E-mail: gradadm@auburn.edu.
Website: https://cws.auburn.edu/nursing/

**Auburn University at Montgomery,** College of Nursing and Health Sciences, Montgomery, AL 36124. Offers family nurse practitioner (MSN); nurse educator for interprofessional practice (MSN). *Accreditation:* AACN. *Program availability:* Part-time, evening/weekend, 100% online, blended/hybrid learning. *Faculty:* 3 full-time (all women), 4 part-time/adjunct (all women). *Students:* 37 part-time (32 women); includes 13 minority (all Black or African American, non-Hispanic/Latino). Average age 36. 56 applicants, 46% accepted, 22 enrolled. *Entrance requirements:* Additional exam requirements/recommendations for international students: recommended—TOEFL (minimum score 500 paper-based; 61 iBT), IELTS (minimum score 5.5), TSE (minimum score 44). *Application deadline:* For fall admission, 7/1 for domestic students; for spring admission, 10/1 for domestic students; for summer admission, 3/1 for domestic students. Applications are processed on a rolling basis. Application fee: $25. Electronic applications accepted. *Expenses: Tuition, area resident:* Full-time $7578; part-time $421 per credit hour. Tuition, state resident: full-time $7578; part-time $421 per credit hour. Tuition, nonresident: full-time $17,046; part-time $947 per credit hour. *International tuition:* $17,046 full-time. *Required fees:* $868. *Financial support:* Application deadline: 3/1. *Unit head:* Dr. Jean Leuner, Dean, 334-244-3658, E-mail: jleuner@aum.edu. *Application contact:* Christy Dearden, Senior Administrative Associate, 334-244-3658, E-mail: cdearden@aum.edu.
Website: http://conhs.aum.edu/academic-programs/graduate-programs/msn

**Augsburg University,** Programs in Nursing, Minneapolis, MN 55454-1351. Offers MA, DNP. *Accreditation:* AACN. *Degree requirements:* For master's, thesis or alternative.

**Augusta University,** College of Nursing, Doctor of Nursing Practice Program, Augusta, GA 30912. Offers adult gerontology acute care nurse practitioner (DNP); family nurse practitioner (DNP); nurse executive (DNP); nursing (DNP); nursing anesthesia (DNP); pediatric nurse practitioner (DNP); psychiatric mental health nurse practitioner (DNP). *Accreditation:* AACN; AANA/CANAEP. *Degree requirements:* For doctorate, thesis/dissertation or alternative. *Entrance requirements:* For doctorate, GRE General Test or MAT, master's degree in nursing or related field, current professional nurse licensure. Additional exam requirements/recommendations for international students: required—TOEFL (minimum score 600 paper-based; 100 iBT). Electronic applications accepted.

**Augusta University,** College of Nursing, Nursing PhD Program, Augusta, GA 30912. Offers PhD. *Degree requirements:* For doctorate, thesis/dissertation. *Entrance requirements:* For doctorate, GRE General Test, current GA nurse licensure. Additional exam requirements/recommendations for international students: required—TOEFL (minimum score 550 paper-based; 79 iBT). Electronic applications accepted.

**Austin Peay State University,** College of Graduate Studies, College of Behavioral and Health Sciences, School of Nursing, Clarksville, TN 37044. Offers family nurse practitioner (MSN); nursing administration (MSN); nursing education (MSN); nursing informatics (MSN). *Program availability:* Part-time, online learning. *Faculty:* 5 full-time (all women), 1 (woman) part-time/adjunct. *Students:* 12 full-time (11 women), 120 part-time (114 women); includes 25 minority (14 Black or African American, non-Hispanic/Latino; 3 Asian, non-Hispanic/Latino; 4 Hispanic/Latino; 4 Two or more races, non-Hispanic/Latino). Average age 34. 19 applicants, 84% accepted, 2 enrolled. In 2019, 51 master's awarded. *Degree requirements:* For master's, comprehensive exam. *Entrance requirements:* For master's, minimum GPA of 3.0, RN license eligibility, 3 letters of recommendation. Additional exam requirements/recommendations for international students: required—TOEFL (minimum score 500 paper-based). *Application deadline:* For fall admission, 8/5 priority date for domestic students. Applications are processed on a rolling basis. Application fee: $45 ($55 for international students). Electronic applications accepted. *Financial support:* Research assistantships with full tuition reimbursements, career-related internships or fieldwork, Federal Work-Study, institutionally sponsored loans, scholarships/grants, and unspecified assistantships available. Support available to part-time students. Financial award application deadline: 7/1; financial award applicants required to submit FAFSA. *Unit head:* Dr. Mary Rice, Interim Director of Nursing, 931-221-7483, Fax: 931-221-7595, E-mail: ricem@apsu.edu. *Application contact:* Megan Mitchell, Coordinator of Graduate Admissions, 931-221-6189, Fax: 931-221-7641, E-mail: mitchellm@apsu.edu.
Website: http://www.apsu.edu/nursing

**Azusa Pacific University,** School of Nursing, Azusa, CA 91702-7000. Offers adult clinical nurse specialist (MSN); adult-gerontology nurse practitioner (MSN); family nurse practitioner (MSN); healthcare administration and leadership (MSN); nursing (MSN, DNP, PhD); nursing education (MSN); parent-child clinical nurse specialist (MSN); psychiatric mental health nurse practitioner (MSN). *Accreditation:* AACN. *Program availability:* Part-time, evening/weekend. *Degree requirements:* For master's, thesis optional. *Entrance requirements:* For master's, BSN.

**Ball State University,** Graduate School, College of Health, School of Nursing, Muncie, IN 47304. Offers adult/gerontology nurse practitioner (Post Master's Certificate); evidence-based clinical practice (Postbaccalaureate Certificate); family nurse practitioner (Post Master's Certificate); nurse educator (Post Master's Certificate); nursing (MS), including family nurse practitioner, nurse administrator, nurse educator; nursing education (Postbaccalaureate Certificate); nursing practice (DNP). *Accreditation:* AACN. *Program availability:* Part-time-only, online only, 100% online. *Entrance requirements:* For master's, bachelor's degree in nursing, minimum GPA of 3.0, minimum C grade in at least 2 quarter or semester hours in an undergraduate research course, unencumbered license as a registered nurse in state of practice; for doctorate, advanced practice nurse (nurse practitioner, clinical nurse specialist, nurse midwife); master's degree in nursing from accredited program with minimum GPA of 3.2; graduate-level statistics, nursing research, and health assessment courses; unencumbered license as registered nurse in state of practice. Additional exam requirements/recommendations for international students: required—TOEFL (minimum score 550 paper-based; 79 iBT), IELTS (minimum score 6.5). Electronic applications accepted. *Expenses:* Contact institution.

**Barry University,** School of Adult and Continuing Education, Division of Nursing, Miami Shores, FL 33161-6695. Offers MSN, PhD, Certificate, MSN/MBA. *Program availability:* Part-time, evening/weekend. *Degree requirements:* For master's, research project or thesis; for doctorate, thesis/dissertation. *Entrance requirements:* For master's, GRE General Test or MAT, BSN, minimum GPA of 3.0, course work in statistics and research, Florida RN license; for doctorate, GRE General Test or MAT, minimum GPA of 3.3, MSN. Electronic applications accepted.

**Baylor University,** Graduate School, Louise Herrington School of Nursing, Dallas, TX 75246. Offers nursing practice (MSN), including executive nursing leadership. *Accreditation:* AACN; AANA/CANAEP; ACNM/ACME. *Program availability:* Part-time, online only, Online with on campus immersions. *Degree requirements:* For master's, oral presentation; for doctorate, DNP Project. *Entrance requirements:* Additional exam requirements/recommendations for international students: required—TOEFL (minimum score 550 paper-based; 80 iBT). Electronic applications accepted. *Expenses:* Contact institution.

**Bellarmine University,** College of Health Professions, Donna and Allan Lansing School of Nursing and Clinical Sciences, Louisville, KY 40205. Offers family nurse practitioner (MSN); health science (MHS); nursing administration (MSN); nursing education (MSN); nursing practice (DNP). *Accreditation:* AACN; APTA. *Program availability:* Part-time, evening/weekend. *Faculty:* 19 full-time (15 women), 7 part-time/adjunct (all women). *Students:* 142 full-time (104 women), 128 part-time (105 women); includes 55 minority (24 Black or African American, non-Hispanic/Latino; 1 American Indian or Alaska Native, non-Hispanic/Latino; 15 Asian, non-Hispanic/Latino; 10 Hispanic/Latino; 5 Two or more races, non-Hispanic/Latino), 10 international. Average age 30. 348 applicants, 82% accepted, 172 enrolled. In 2019, 29 master's, 4 doctorates awarded. *Degree requirements:* For master's, comprehensive exam, thesis (for some programs); for doctorate, comprehensive exam, thesis/dissertation. *Entrance requirements:* For master's, GRE General Test, minimum GPA of 3.0, interview, resume; BSN from CCNE- or ACEN-accredited program, professional references, goal statement, and RN license (for MSN); bachelor's degree with exposure to health issues and grade of C or better in math/science courses (for MHS); for doctorate, GRE General Test, MSN from CCNE- or ACEN-accredited program; minimum GPA of 3.5 in graduate coursework; professional references; goal statement; current curriculum vitae or resume; RN license; verification of post-baccalaureate clinical and practice hours. Additional exam requirements/recommendations for international students: required—TOEFL (minimum iBT score of 83, 26 on speaking test), IELTS (minimum score 7, speaking band score of 8), or language training at an approved center; recommended—TOEFL (minimum score 83 iBT), IELTS. *Application deadline:* Applications are processed on a rolling basis. Application fee: $40. Electronic applications accepted. *Expenses:* Accelerated BSN, May 2020 cohort: $905 per credit hour; Accelerated BSN, 2-yr. program, Summer 2020: $950 per credit hour; MHS: $770 per credit hour; MHS, Medical Lab Science: $665 per credit hour; MHS, Respiratory Therapy: $665 per credit hour; MSN, Education and

Administration: $770 per credit hour; MSN, Family Nurse Practitioner: $770 per credit hour ($85 per credit hour fee for FNP specialty courses); Doctor of Nursing Practice: $855 per credit hour; Radiation Therapy Second Degree: $665 per credit hour. *Financial support:* Career-related internships or fieldwork and scholarships/grants available. Financial award applicants required to submit FAFSA. *Unit head:* Dr. Nancy York, Dean, 502-272-8639, E-mail: nyork@bellarmine.edu. *Application contact:* Julie Armstrong-Binnix, Health Science Recruiter, 800-274-4723 Ext. 8364, E-mail: julieab@bellarmine.edu.
Website: http://www.bellarmine.edu/lansing

**Bellin College,** School of Nursing, Green Bay, WI 54305. Offers family nurse practitioner (MSN); nurse educator (MSN). *Accreditation:* AACN.

**Belmont University,** College of Health Sciences, Nashville, TN 37212. Offers nursing (MSN, DNP); occupational therapy (MSOT, OTD); physical therapy (DPT). *Program availability:* Part-time, blended/hybrid learning. *Faculty:* 26 full-time (20 women), 30 part-time/adjunct (21 women). *Students:* 416 full-time (362 women), 8 part-time (7 women); includes 36 minority (7 Black or African American, non-Hispanic/Latino; 12 Asian, non-Hispanic/Latino; 9 Hispanic/Latino; 8 Two or more races, non-Hispanic/Latino). Average age 26. *Degree requirements:* For master's, comprehensive exam, thesis; for doctorate, comprehensive exam. *Entrance requirements:* For master's, GRE, BSN, minimum GPA of 3.0. Additional exam requirements/recommendations for international students: required—TOEFL (minimum score 550 paper-based). *Application deadline:* Applications are processed on a rolling basis. Application fee: $50. Electronic applications accepted. *Expenses:* Contact institution. *Financial support:* Teaching assistantships with full tuition reimbursements, career-related internships or fieldwork, scholarships/grants, and traineeships available. Financial award application deadline: 3/1; financial award applicants required to submit FAFSA. *Unit head:* Dr. Cathy Taylor, Dean, 615-460-6916, Fax: 615-460-6750. *Application contact:* Bill Nichols, Director of Enrollment Services, 615-460-6107, E-mail: bill.nichols@belmont.edu.
Website: http://www.belmont.edu/healthsciences/

**Benedictine University,** Graduate Programs, Program in Nursing, Lisle, IL 60532. Offers MSN. *Accreditation:* AACN. *Program availability:* Part-time, evening/weekend, online only, 100% online. *Entrance requirements:* For master's, Proof of license as registered nurse; official transcripts; a statement of goals; one letter of professional recommendation from an individual familiar with the applicant's competence in the practice of nursing and potential for successful graduate education. Additional exam requirements/recommendations for international students: required—TOEFL (minimum score 550 paper-based; 79 iBT), IELTS (minimum score 6.5). Electronic applications accepted.

**Bethel University,** Adult and Graduate Programs, Program in Nursing, Mishawaka, IN 46545-5591. Offers MSN. *Accreditation:* ACEN. *Program availability:* Part-time, evening/weekend, 100% online, blended/hybrid learning. *Degree requirements:* For master's, thesis. *Entrance requirements:* Additional exam requirements/recommendations for international students: required—TOEFL (minimum score 540 paper-based). Electronic applications accepted.

**Binghamton University, State University of New York,** Graduate School, Decker School of Nursing, Binghamton, NY 13902-6000. Offers adult-gerontological nursing (MS, DNP, Certificate); community health nursing (MS, DNP, Certificate); family health nursing (MS, DNP, Certificate); family psychiatric mental health nursing (MS, DNP, Certificate); nursing (PhD). *Accreditation:* AACN. *Program availability:* Part-time, evening/weekend. Terminal master's awarded for partial completion of doctoral program. *Degree requirements:* For master's, comprehensive exam, thesis; for doctorate, comprehensive exam (for some programs), thesis/dissertation. *Entrance requirements:* For master's and doctorate, GRE General Test, nursing licensure. Additional exam requirements/recommendations for international students: required—TOEFL (minimum score 90 iBT). Electronic applications accepted. *Expenses:* Contact institution.

**Blessing-Rieman College of Nursing & Health Sciences,** Master of Science in Nursing Program, Quincy, IL 62305-7005. Offers nursing education (MSN); nursing leadership (MSN). *Program availability:* Part-time-only, evening/weekend, online only, 100% online. *Degree requirements:* For master's, thesis or project. *Entrance requirements:* Additional exam requirements/recommendations for international students: required—TOEFL (minimum score 500 paper-based; 80 iBT). Electronic applications accepted.

**Bloomsburg University of Pennsylvania,** School of Graduate Studies, College of Science and Technology, Department of Nursing, Bloomsburg, PA 17815-1301. Offers adult and family nurse practitioner (MSN); community health (MSN); nurse anesthesia (MSN); nursing (MSN, DNP); nursing administration (MSN). *Accreditation:* AACN. *Degree requirements:* For master's, thesis (for some programs), clinical experience. *Entrance requirements:* For master's, minimum QPA of 3.0, personal statement, 2 letters of recommendation, nursing license. Additional exam requirements/recommendations for international students: required—TOEFL, IELTS. Electronic applications accepted. *Expenses:* Contact institution.

**Boise State University,** College of Health Sciences, School of Nursing, Boise, ID 83725-0399. Offers acute care adult gerontology (Graduate Certificate); adult gerontology acute care (MSN); adult gerontology primary care (MSN); healthcare simulation (Graduate Certificate); nursing practice (DNP); primary care adult gerontology (Graduate Certificate). *Accreditation:* AACN. *Students:* 1 (woman) full-time, 91 part-time (73 women); includes 8 minority (4 Black or African American, non-Hispanic/Latino; 3 Asian, non-Hispanic/Latino; 1 Native Hawaiian or other Pacific Islander, non-Hispanic/Latino). *Entrance requirements:* Additional exam requirements/recommendations for international students: required—TOEFL, IELTS. Electronic applications accepted. *Expenses: Tuition, area resident:* Full-time $7110; part-time $470 per credit hour. Tuition, state resident: full-time $7110; part-time $470 per credit hour. Tuition, nonresident: full-time $24,030; part-time $827 per credit hour. *International tuition:* $24,030 full-time. *Required fees:* $2536. Tuition and fees vary according to course load and program. *Financial support:* Applicants required to submit FAFSA. *Unit head:* Dr. Ann Hubbert, Director, 208-426-3404, E-mail: annhubbert@boisestate.edu. *Application contact:* Dr. Nancy Loftus, Program Coordinator, 208-426-3819, E-mail: nancyloftus@boisestate.edu.
Website: https://www.boisestate.edu/nursing/

**Boston College,** William F. Connell School of Nursing, Chestnut Hill, MA 02467. Offers adult-gerontology primary care nurse practitioner (MS); family health nursing (MS); nurse anesthesia (MS); nursing (PhD); pediatric primary care nurse practitioner (MS), including pediatric and women's health; psychiatric-mental health nursing (MS); women's health nursing (MS); MBA/MS; MS/MA; MS/PhD. *Accreditation:* AACN; AANA/CANAEP (one or more programs are accredited). *Program availability:* Part-time. *Faculty:* 56 full-time (50 women). *Students:* 228 full-time (200 women), 82 part-time (71 women); includes 54 minority (10 Black or African American, non-Hispanic/Latino; 18 Asian, non-Hispanic/Latino; 20 Hispanic/Latino; 6 Two or more races, non-Hispanic/Latino), 7 international. Average age 28. 360 applicants, 56% accepted, 93 enrolled. In 2019, 107 master's, 7 doctorates awarded. *Degree requirements:* For master's, comprehensive exam; for doctorate, comprehensive exam, thesis/dissertation, computer

literacy exam or foreign language. *Entrance requirements:* For master's, bachelor's degree; for doctorate, GRE General Test, bachelor's in Nursing and master's degree in nursing or related field. Additional exam requirements/recommendations for international students: required—TOEFL (minimum score 600 paper-based; 100 iBT), IELTS (minimum score 7.5). *Application deadline:* For fall admission, 3/15 for domestic and international students; for spring admission, 9/30 for domestic and international students. Application fee: $40. Electronic applications accepted. *Expenses:* Contact institution. *Financial support:* In 2019–20, 135 students received support, including 12 fellowships with full tuition reimbursements available (averaging $24,504 per year), 29 teaching assistantships (averaging $4,380 per year); scholarships/grants, health care benefits, tuition waivers (partial), and unspecified assistantships also available. Support available to part-time students. Financial award application deadline: 4/18; financial award applicants required to submit FAFSA. *Unit head:* Dr. Susan Gennaro, Dean, 617-552-4251, Fax: 617-552-0931, E-mail: susan.gennaro@bc.edu. *Application contact:* Sean Sendall, Assistant Dean, Graduate Enrollment and Data Analytics, 617-552-4745, Fax: 617-552-2121, E-mail: sean.sendall@bc.edu.
Website: http://www.bc.edu/cson

**Bowie State University,** Graduate Programs, Department of Nursing, Bowie, MD 20715-9465. Offers administration of nursing services (MS); family nurse practitioner (MS); nursing education (MS). *Accreditation:* ACEN. *Program availability:* Part-time. *Degree requirements:* For master's, comprehensive exam, thesis, research paper. *Entrance requirements:* For master's, minimum GPA of 2.5. Electronic applications accepted. *Expenses: Tuition, area resident:* Full-time $11,942; part-time $423 per credit hour. Tuition, state resident: full-time $11,942; part-time $423 per credit hour. Tuition, nonresident: full-time $18,806; part-time $709 per credit hour. *International tuition:* $18,806 full-time. *Required fees:* $1106; $1106 per semester. $553 per semester.

**Bradley University,** The Graduate School, College of Education and Health Sciences, Department of Nursing, Peoria, IL 61625-0002. Offers family nurse practitioner (MSN, DNP, Certificate); leadership (DNP); nursing administration (MSN); nursing education (MSN, Certificate). *Accreditation:* AACN; ACEN. *Program availability:* Part-time, evening/weekend, 100% online. *Faculty:* 12 full-time (all women), 32 part-time/adjunct (28 women). *Students:* 91 full-time (79 women), 637 part-time (551 women); includes 253 minority (143 Black or African American, non-Hispanic/Latino; 13 American Indian or Alaska Native, non-Hispanic/Latino; 40 Asian, non-Hispanic/Latino; 45 Hispanic/Latino; 2 Native Hawaiian or other Pacific Islander, non-Hispanic/Latino; 10 Two or more races, non-Hispanic/Latino), 19 international. Average age 38. 229 applicants, 79% accepted, 114 enrolled. In 2019, 60 master's, 20 doctorates awarded. *Degree requirements:* For master's, comprehensive exam, thesis optional; for doctorate, comprehensive exam. *Entrance requirements:* For master's, GRE General Test or MAT, interview, Illinois RN license, advanced cardiac life support certification, pediatric advanced life support certification, 3 letters of recommendation. Additional exam requirements/recommendations for international students: required—TOEFL (minimum score 550 paper-based; 79 iBT), IELTS (minimum score 6.5), PTE (minimum score 58). *Application deadline:* For fall admission, 5/15 priority date for domestic and international students; for spring admission, 10/15 priority date for domestic and international students. Applications are processed on a rolling basis. Application fee: $40 ($50 for international students). Electronic applications accepted. *Expenses: Tuition:* Part-time $930 per credit hour. *Financial support:* Research assistantships, scholarships/grants, tuition waivers (partial), and unspecified assistantships available. Financial award application deadline: 4/1. *Unit head:* Jessica Clark, Associate Dean and Director of the Department of Nursing, 309-677-2547, E-mail: jclark@bradley.edu. *Application contact:* Rachel Webb, Director of On-Campus Graduate Admissions and International Student and Scholar Services, 309-677-2375, Fax: 309-677-3343, E-mail: rkwebb@bradley.edu.
Website: http://www.bradley.edu/academic/departments/nur/

**Brandman University,** Marybelle and S. Paul Musco School of Nursing and Health Professions, Irvine, CA 92618. Offers nursing (DNP). *Accreditation:* AACN.

**Briar Cliff University,** Graduate Nursing Programs, Sioux City, IA 51104-0100. Offers MSN, DNP, Post-Master's Certificate. *Accreditation:* AACN. *Program availability:* Part-time, online only, 100% online, blended/hybrid learning. *Degree requirements:* For master's, thesis optional. *Entrance requirements:* For master's, minimum undergraduate GPA of 3.0 for last 60 credits from accredited institution, current RN license, current CPR certification, 2000 hours of nursing experience, 2 letters of recommendation, personal development statement, official transcripts from all undergraduate institutions attended; for doctorate, minimum undergraduate GPA of 3.0 for last 60 credits from accredited institution, current RN license, current CPR certification, 2000 hours of nursing experience, 2 letters of recommendation, personal development statement, official transcripts from all undergraduate institutions attended, clinical hours completed from earned MSN. Additional exam requirements/recommendations for international students: recommended—TOEFL. Electronic applications accepted. *Expenses:* Contact institution.

**Brigham Young University,** Graduate Studies, College of Nursing, Provo, UT 84602. Offers family nurse practitioner (MS). *Accreditation:* AACN. *Faculty:* 16 full-time (9 women). *Students:* 30 full-time (26 women); includes 5 minority (1 Black or African American, non-Hispanic/Latino; 1 American Indian or Alaska Native, non-Hispanic/Latino; 2 Asian, non-Hispanic/Latino; 1 Hispanic/Latino), 1 international. Average age 33. 30 applicants, 50% accepted, 15 enrolled. In 2019, 15 master's awarded. *Degree requirements:* For master's, thesis or alternative. *Entrance requirements:* For master's, GRE, minimum cumulative undergraduate GPA of 3.0, baccalaureate degree in nursing from school with national nursing accreditation, interview, current RN license in Utah, pathophysiology and statistics classes, 3 letters of recommendation. Additional exam requirements/recommendations for international students: required—TOEFL (minimum score 580 paper-based; 85 iBT), IELTS (minimum score 7). *Application deadline:* For spring admission, 12/1 for domestic and international students. Application fee: $50. Electronic applications accepted. *Expenses:* $3,535 per semester. $8,838 per year. *Financial support:* In 2019–20, 30 students received support, including 1 research assistantship (averaging $6,000 per year); teaching assistantships, career-related internships or fieldwork, and scholarships/grants also available. Financial award application deadline: 8/13; financial award applicants required to submit FAFSA. *Unit head:* Dr. Beth Luthy, Dean, 801-422-6683, Fax: 801-422-0536, E-mail: beth-luthy@byu.edu. *Application contact:* Cherie Top, Graduate Secretary, 801-422-4142, Fax: 801-422-0538, E-mail: cherie-top@byu.edu.
Website: http://nursing.byu.edu/

**Brookline College - Phoenix Campus,** Nursing Programs, Phoenix, AZ 85021. Offers health systems administration (MSN); nursing (MSN). *Program availability:* Part-time, online learning.

**California Baptist University,** Doctor of Nursing Practice Program, Riverside, CA 92504-3206. Offers DNP. *Program availability:* Part-time. *Degree requirements:* For doctorate, thesis/dissertation, Translational Research Final Project. *Entrance requirements:* For doctorate, Completion of a master's degree in nursing from a regionally accredited institution or evaluated equivalency, minimum cumulative GPA of 3.3 for unconditional admission and a minimum 3.0 GPA for conditional admission, active California RN license, prerequisites of statistics and research (all prerequisites must be completed). Additional exam requirements/recommendations for international

students: required—TOEFL (minimum score 80 iBT). Electronic applications accepted. *Expenses:* Contact institution.

**California Baptist University,** Program in Nursing, Riverside, CA 92504-3206. Offers clinical nurse specialist (MSN); family nurse practitioner (MSN); healthcare systems management (MSN); teaching-learning (MSN). *Accreditation:* AACN. *Program availability:* Part-time. *Degree requirements:* For master's, comprehensive exam or directed project thesis; capstone practicum. *Entrance requirements:* For master's, GRE or California Critical Thinking Skills Test; Test of Essential Academic Skills (TEAS), minimum undergraduate GPA of 3.0; completion of prerequisite courses with minimum grade of C; CPR certification; background check clearance; health clearance; drug testing; proof of health insurance; proof of motor vehicle insurance; three letters of recommendation; 1000-word essay; interview. Additional exam requirements/recommendations for international students: required—TOEFL (minimum score 80 iBT). Electronic applications accepted. *Expenses:* Contact institution.

**California State University, Chico,** Office of Graduate Studies, College of Natural Sciences, School of Nursing, Chico, CA 95929-0722. Offers MSN. *Accreditation:* AACN. *Program availability:* Part-time, online learning. *Degree requirements:* For master's, project or thesis and oral exam. *Entrance requirements:* For master's, GRE, fall admission for even years only 2020, 2022, 2024; statement of purpose, course work in inferential statistics in the last seven years, BSN degree, California nursing license. Additional exam requirements/recommendations for international students: required—TOEFL (minimum score 550 paper-based; 80 iBT), IELTS (minimum score 6.5), PTE (minimum score 59). Electronic applications accepted.

**California State University, Dominguez Hills,** College of Health, Human Services and Nursing, Program in Nursing, Carson, CA 90747-0001. Offers MSN. *Accreditation:* AACN. *Program availability:* Part-time, online learning. *Degree requirements:* For master's, comprehensive exam. *Entrance requirements:* For master's, minimum GPA of 2.5, 3.0 in prior coursework in statistics, research, pathophysiology and assessment. Additional exam requirements/recommendations for international students: required—TOEFL. Electronic applications accepted.

**California State University, Fresno,** Division of Research and Graduate Studies, College of Health and Human Services, School of Nursing, Fresno, CA 93740-8027. Offers nursing (MS, DNP), including clinical nurse specialist (MS). *Accreditation:* AACN. *Program availability:* Part-time, evening/weekend. *Degree requirements:* For master's, thesis or alternative. *Entrance requirements:* For master's, GRE General Test, 1 year of clinical practice, previous course work in statistics, BSN, minimum GPA of 3.0 in nursing. Additional exam requirements/recommendations for international students: required—TOEFL. Electronic applications accepted. *Expenses:* Tuition, state resident: full-time $4012; part-time $2506 per semester.

**California State University, Fullerton,** Graduate Studies, College of Health and Human Development, School of Nursing, Fullerton, CA 92831-3599. Offers leadership (MS); nurse anesthesia (MS); nurse educator (MS); nursing (DNP); school nursing (MS); women's health care (MS). *Accreditation:* AACN. *Program availability:* Part-time.

**California State University, Long Beach,** Graduate Studies, College of Health and Human Services, School of Nursing, Long Beach, CA 90840. Offers MSN, DNP, Graduate Certificate. *Accreditation:* AACN. *Program availability:* Part-time. *Degree requirements:* For master's, thesis optional. *Entrance requirements:* For master's, minimum GPA of 3.0. Electronic applications accepted.

**California State University, Los Angeles,** Graduate Studies, College of Health and Human Services, School of Nursing, Los Angeles, CA 90032-8530. Offers MS, Post Master's Certificate. *Accreditation:* AACN. *Program availability:* Part-time, evening/weekend. *Degree requirements:* For master's, comprehensive exam, project or thesis. *Entrance requirements:* For master's, minimum GPA of 3.0 in nursing, course work in nursing and statistics. Additional exam requirements/recommendations for international students: required—TOEFL (minimum score 500 paper-based). *Expenses:* Tuition, area resident: Full-time $7176; part-time $4164 per year. Tuition, state resident: full-time $7176; part-time $4164 per year. Tuition, nonresident: full-time $14,304; part-time $8916 per year. *International tuition:* $14,304 full-time. *Required fees:* $1037.76; $1037.76 per unit. Tuition and fees vary according to degree level and program.

**California State University, Sacramento,** College of Health and Human Services, School of Nursing, Sacramento, CA 95819-6096. Offers MS. *Accreditation:* AACN. *Program availability:* Part-time. *Students:* 72 full-time (64 women), 100 part-time (95 women); includes 64 minority (8 Black or African American, non-Hispanic/Latino; 1 American Indian or Alaska Native, non-Hispanic/Latino; 24 Asian, non-Hispanic/Latino; 29 Hispanic/Latino; 2 Native Hawaiian or other Pacific Islander, non-Hispanic/Latino). Average age 38. 40 applicants, 85% accepted, 16 enrolled. In 2019, 56 master's awarded. *Degree requirements:* For master's, comprehensive exam, thesis optional, thesis or project, writing proficiency exam. *Entrance requirements:* For master's, bachelor's degree in nursing, minimum GPA of 3.0. Additional exam requirements/recommendations for international students: required—TOEFL (minimum score 550 paper-based; 80 iBT); recommended—IELTS (minimum score 7). *Application deadline:* For fall admission, 3/1 for domestic and international students; for spring admission, 12/1 for domestic students, 11/1 for international students. Applications are processed on a rolling basis. Application fee: $70. Electronic applications accepted. *Expenses:* Contact institution. *Financial support:* Teaching assistantships, career-related internships or fieldwork, Federal Work-Study, and scholarships/grants available. Support available to part-time students. Financial award application deadline: 3/1; financial award applicants required to submit FAFSA. *Unit head:* Dr. Tanya Altmann, Chair, 916-278-1504, E-mail: altmannt@csus.edu. *Application contact:* Jose Martinez, Graduate Admissions Supervisor, 916-278-6470, E-mail: martinj@skymail.csus.edu. Website: http://www.csus.edu/hhs/nrs/

**California State University, San Bernardino,** Graduate Studies, College of Natural Sciences, Program in Nursing, San Bernardino, CA 92407. Offers MSN. *Accreditation:* AACN. *Faculty:* 2 full-time (both women), 2 part-time/adjunct (1 woman). *Students:* 7 full-time (all women), 16 part-time (0 women); includes 17 minority (5 Black or African American, non-Hispanic/Latino; 12 Hispanic/Latino). Average age 36. 10 applicants, 50% accepted, 3 enrolled. In 2019, 10 master's awarded. *Degree requirements:* For master's, thesis optional. *Entrance requirements:* Additional exam requirements/recommendations for international students: required—TOEFL. *Application deadline:* For fall admission, 7/16 for domestic students; for winter admission, 10/16 for domestic students; for spring admission, 1/22 for domestic students. Application fee: $55. *Unit head:* Cheryl Brandt, MSN Coordinator, 909-537-7238, E-mail: cheryl.brandt@csusb.edu. *Application contact:* Dr. Dorota Huizinga, Dean of Graduate Studies, 909-537-3064, E-mail: dorota.huizinga@csusb.edu.

**California State University, San Marcos,** College of Education, Health and Human Services, School of Nursing, San Marcos, CA 92096-0001. Offers advanced practice nursing (MSN), including clinical nurse specialist, family nurse practitioner, psychiatric mental health nurse practitioner; clinical nurse leader (MSN); nursing education (MSN). *Expenses:* Tuition, area resident: Full-time $7176. Tuition, state resident: full-time $7176. Tuition, nonresident: full-time $18,640. *International tuition:* $18,640 full-time. *Required fees:* $1960.

**California State University, Stanislaus,** College of Science, Master's in Nursing Program, Turlock, CA 95382. Offers gerontological nursing (MS); nursing education (MS). *Accreditation:* AACN. *Program availability:* Part-time. *Degree requirements:* For master's, comprehensive exam, thesis or alternative. *Entrance requirements:* For master's, GRE or MAT, minimum GPA of 3.0, 3 letters of reference, RN. Additional exam requirements/recommendations for international students: required—TOEFL (minimum score 550 paper-based). Electronic applications accepted.

**California University of Pennsylvania,** School of Graduate Studies and Research, Eberly College of Science and Technology, Department of Nursing, California, PA 15419-1394. Offers nursing administration and leadership (MSN); nursing education (MSN). *Expenses: Tuition, area resident:* Full-time $9288; part-time $516 per credit. Tuition, state resident: full-time $9288; part-time $516 per credit. Tuition, nonresident: full-time $13,932; part-time $774 per credit. *Required fees:* $3631; $291.13 per credit. Part-time tuition and fees vary according to course load.

**Capella University,** School of Public Service Leadership, Doctoral Programs in Nursing, Minneapolis, MN 55402. Offers nursing education (PhD); nursing practice (DNP).

**Capella University,** School of Public Service Leadership, Master's Programs in Nursing, Minneapolis, MN 55402. Offers diabetes nursing (MSN); general nursing (MSN); gerontology nursing (MSN); health information management (MS); nurse educator (MSN); nursing leadership and administration (MSN). *Accreditation:* AACN.

**Capital University,** School of Nursing, Columbus, OH 43209-2394. Offers administration (MSN); legal studies (MSN); theological studies (MSN); JD/MSN; MBA/MSN; MSN/MTS. *Accreditation:* AACN. *Program availability:* Part-time, evening/weekend. *Degree requirements:* For master's, thesis or alternative. *Entrance requirements:* For master's, BSN, current RN license, minimum GPA of 3.0, undergraduate courses in statistics and research. Additional exam requirements/recommendations for international students: required—TOEFL (minimum score 550 paper-based). *Expenses:* Contact institution.

**Cardinal Stritch University,** Ruth S. Coleman College of Nursing and Health Sciences, Milwaukee, WI 53217-3985. Offers MSN. *Accreditation:* ACEN. *Program availability:* Part-time, evening/weekend. *Degree requirements:* For master's, thesis. *Entrance requirements:* For master's, interview; minimum GPA of 3.0; RN license; 3 letters of recommendation; undergraduate coursework in statistics and nursing research; computer literacy; curriculum vitae. Additional exam requirements/recommendations for international students: required—TOEFL (minimum score 79 iBT), IELTS (minimum score 6.5). Electronic applications accepted. Tuition and fees vary according to course load, degree level and program.

**Carlow University,** College of Health and Wellness, Doctor of Nursing Practice Program, Pittsburgh, PA 15213-3165. Offers DNP. *Accreditation:* AACN. *Program availability:* Part-time, evening/weekend, low-residency. *Students:* 8 full-time (6 women), 24 part-time (23 women); includes 2 minority (both Black or African American, non-Hispanic/Latino). Average age 43. 14 applicants, 100% accepted, 8 enrolled. In 2019, 16 doctorates awarded. *Degree requirements:* For doctorate, 3-semester scholarly inquiry. *Entrance requirements:* For doctorate, master's degree with minimum GPA of 3.0; BSN; current RN license; official transcripts from all undergraduate and graduate institutions; copy of RN license; current curriculum vitae; two letters of academic and/or professional recommendation; reflective essay describing career goals and expectations for education. Additional exam requirements/recommendations for international students: required—TOEFL (minimum score 550 paper-based). *Application deadline:* For fall admission, 4/1 priority date for domestic students. Applications are processed on a rolling basis. Electronic applications accepted. *Expenses:* Contact institution. *Financial support:* Application deadline: 4/1; applicants required to submit FAFSA. *Unit head:* Dr. Renee Ingel, Director, DNP Program, 412-578-6103, Fax: 412-578-6114, E-mail: rmingel@carlow.edu. *Application contact:* Dr. Renee Ingel, Director, DNP Program, 412-578-6103, Fax: 412-578-6114, E-mail: rmingel@carlow.edu. Website: http://www.carlow.edu/Nursing_Doctoral_Offering.aspx

**Case Western Reserve University,** Frances Payne Bolton School of Nursing, Doctor of Nursing Practice Program, Cleveland, OH 44106. Offers educational leadership (DNP); practice leadership (DNP). *Accreditation:* AACN. *Program availability:* Part-time. *Faculty:* 41 full-time (33 women), 1 (woman) part-time/adjunct. *Students:* 74 full-time (64 women), 44 part-time (39 women); includes 34 minority (17 Black or African American, non-Hispanic/Latino; 10 Asian, non-Hispanic/Latino; 7 Hispanic/Latino), 7 international. Average age 45. 15 applicants, 80% accepted, 8 enrolled. In 2019, 47 doctorates awarded. *Degree requirements:* For doctorate, thesis/dissertation, log of 1000 practicum hours. *Entrance requirements:* Additional exam requirements/recommendations for international students: required—TOEFL (minimum score 577 paper-based; 90 iBT), IELTS (minimum score 7). *Application deadline:* For fall admission, 6/1 for domestic and international students; for spring admission, 10/1 for domestic and international students; for summer admission, 3/1 for domestic and international students. Applications are processed on a rolling basis. Application fee: $75. Electronic applications accepted. *Expenses:* Activity fee $15; Graduate council fee $15; Tuition rate $2,133 per credit hour, Medical plan fee $1,165 per semester; One to One fitness fall $126 + tax; One to One fitness spring $157 + tax. *Financial support:* In 2019–20, 82 students received support, including 4 teaching assistantships with partial tuition reimbursements available (averaging $19,197 per year); scholarships/grants and nurse faculty loan program also available. Financial award application deadline: 5/15; financial award applicants required to submit FAFSA. *Unit head:* Dr. Latina Brooks, Director, 216-368-1196, Fax: 216-368-3542, E-mail: lmb3@case.edu. *Application contact:* Jackie Tepale, Admissions Coordinator, 216-368-5253, Fax: 216-368-3542, E-mail: yyd@case.edu. Website: https://case.edu/nursing/programs/dnp

**Case Western Reserve University,** Frances Payne Bolton School of Nursing, Master's Programs in Nursing, Cleveland, OH 44106. Offers nurse anesthesia (MSN); nurse education (MSN); nurse midwifery (MSN); nurse practitioner (MSN), including acute care/cardiovascular nursing, adult gerontology nurse practitioner, palliative care; nursing (MN). *Accreditation:* ACEN. *Program availability:* Part-time. *Faculty:* 40 full-time (36 women), 8 part-time/adjunct (7 women). *Students:* 160 full-time (131 women), 141 part-time (108 women); includes 72 minority (26 Black or African American, non-Hispanic/Latino; 22 Asian, non-Hispanic/Latino; 16 Hispanic/Latino; 8 Two or more races, non-Hispanic/Latino), 13 international. Average age 29. 273 applicants, 64% accepted, 100 enrolled. In 2019, 122 master's awarded. *Degree requirements:* For master's, thesis optional, minimum GPA of 3.0, Typhon log of clinical hours corresponding to requirements to sit for certification exam. *Entrance requirements:* For master's, GRE/MAT (scores not required for application, but may be requested for an admission decision), CCRN certification and 2 years ICU experience (for nurse anesthesia). Additional exam requirements/recommendations for international students: required—TOEFL (minimum score 577 paper-based; 90 iBT), IELTS (minimum score 7). *Application deadline:* For fall admission, 3/1 for domestic and international students; for spring admission, 10/1 for domestic and international students; for summer admission, 3/1 for domestic and international students. Applications are processed on a rolling basis. Application fee: $75. Electronic applications accepted. *Expenses:* MSN $2,133

per credit hour; MN $25,596 per semester; Lab fee $215; NCLEX $300; ACEMAPP $50; Clinical placement $75; Activity fee $15; Graduate Council fee $15. *Financial support:* In 2019–20, 126 students received support, including 49 teaching assistantships with partial tuition reimbursements available (averaging $19,197 per year); scholarships/grants and traineeships also available. Financial award application deadline: 5/15; financial award applicants required to submit FAFSA. *Unit head:* Dr. Latina Brooks, Director, 216-368-1196, Fax: 216-368-3542, E-mail: lmb3@case.edu. *Application contact:* Jackie Tepale, Admissions Coordinator, 216-368-5253, Fax: 216-368-3542, E-mail: yyd@case.edu.
Website: https://case.edu/nursing/programs/msn

**Case Western Reserve University,** Frances Payne Bolton School of Nursing, PhD in Nursing Program, Cleveland, OH 44106. Offers PhD. *Program availability:* Part-time. *Faculty:* 28 full-time (20 women). *Students:* 44 full-time (40 women), 1 (woman) part-time; includes 8 minority (6 Black or African American, non-Hispanic/Latino; 1 American Indian or Alaska Native, non-Hispanic/Latino; 1 Two or more races, non-Hispanic/Latino), 13 international. Average age 37. 14 applicants, 43% accepted, 6 enrolled. In 2019, 10 doctorates awarded. *Degree requirements:* For doctorate, comprehensive exam, thesis/dissertation, 240-hour research practicum. *Entrance requirements:* Additional exam requirements/recommendations for international students: required—TOEFL (minimum score 577 paper-based; 90 iBT), IELTS (minimum score 7). *Application deadline:* For fall admission, 2/1 for domestic and international students; for spring admission, 10/1 for domestic and international students. Applications are processed on a rolling basis. Application fee: $50. Electronic applications accepted. *Expenses:* $1,939 per credit hour tuition, $15 per semester graduate council fee, $15 per semester activity fee, $1,165 per semester medical plan, $126 + tax one-to-one fitness (fall), $157 + tax one-to-one fitness (spring). *Financial support:* In 2019–20, 21 students received support, including 3 fellowships with full tuition reimbursements available (averaging $39,428 per year), 3 research assistantships with partial tuition reimbursements available (averaging $17,064 per year), 1 teaching assistantship with partial tuition reimbursement available (averaging $17,064 per year); scholarships/grants and nurse faculty loan program also available. Financial award application deadline: 5/15; financial award applicants required to submit FAFSA. *Unit head:* Dr. Joachim Voss, Director, 216-368-5979, Fax: 216-368-3542, E-mail: jgv20@case.edu. *Application contact:* Jackie Tepale, Admissions Coordinator, Graduate Programs, 216-368-5253, Fax: 216-368-3542, E-mail: yyd@case.edu.
Website: https://case.edu/nursing/programs/phd

**The Catholic University of America,** School of Nursing, Washington, DC 20064. Offers MSN, DNP, PhD, Certificate. *Accreditation:* AACN. *Program availability:* Part-time, 100% online. *Faculty:* 22 full-time (21 women), 32 part-time/adjunct (31 women). *Students:* 20 full-time (18 women), 125 part-time (115 women); includes 41 minority (28 Black or African American, non-Hispanic/Latino; 4 Asian, non-Hispanic/Latino; 4 Hispanic/Latino; 5 Two or more races, non-Hispanic/Latino), 7 international. Average age 42. 79 applicants, 78% accepted, 26 enrolled. In 2019, 15 master's, 1 doctorate, 2 other advanced degrees awarded. *Degree requirements:* For master's, comprehensive exam, thesis optional; for doctorate, comprehensive exam, thesis/dissertation, minimum GPA of 3.0, oral proposal defense. *Entrance requirements:* For master's, GRE General Test, 3 letters of recommendation, BA in nursing, RN registration, official copies of academic transcripts, some post-baccalaureate nursing experience; for doctorate, GRE General Test, BA in nursing, professional portfolio (including statements, resume, copy of RN license, 3 letters of recommendation, narrative description of clinical practice), copy of research/scholarly paper related to clinical nursing; for Certificate, GRE General Test. Additional exam requirements/recommendations for international students: required—TOEFL (minimum score 550 paper-based; 80 iBT). *Application deadline:* For fall admission, 7/15 priority date for domestic students, 7/1 for international students; for spring admission, 11/15 priority date for domestic students, 11/1 for international students. Applications are processed on a rolling basis. Application fee: $55. Electronic applications accepted. *Expenses:* Contact institution. *Financial support:* Fellowships, research assistantships, teaching assistantships, Federal Work-Study, scholarships/grants, tuition waivers (full and partial), and unspecified assistantships available. Financial award application deadline: 2/1; financial award applicants required to submit FAFSA. *Unit head:* Dr. Patricia McMullen, Dean, 202-319-5403, Fax: 202-319-6485, E-mail: mcmullep@cua.edu. *Application contact:* Dr. Steven Brown, Director of Graduate Admissions, 202-319-5057, Fax: 202-319-6533, E-mail: cua-admissions@cua.edu.
Website: https://nursing.catholic.edu/

**Cedar Crest College,** School of Nursing, Allentown, PA 18104-6196. Offers nursing administration (MS); nursing education (MS). *Program availability:* Part-time. Electronic applications accepted. *Expenses:* Contact institution.

**Central Connecticut State University,** School of Graduate Studies, School of Education and Professional Studies, Department of Nursing, New Britain, CT 06050-4010. Offers hospice and palliative care (MSN). *Program availability:* Part-time, evening/weekend. *Degree requirements:* For master's, thesis, nursing capstone. *Entrance requirements:* For master's, minimum undergraduate GPA of 2.7, essay, letter of reference, minimum grade of C+ in an undergraduate statistics course. Additional exam requirements/recommendations for international students: required—TOEFL (minimum score 550 paper-based; 79 iBT); recommended—IELTS (minimum score 6.5). Electronic applications accepted.

**Central Methodist University,** College of Graduate and Extended Studies, Fayette, MO 65248-1198. Offers clinical counseling (MS); clinical nurse leader (MSN); education (M Ed); music education (MME); nurse educator (MSN). *Program availability:* Part-time, evening/weekend, online learning. *Degree requirements:* For master's, thesis. *Entrance requirements:* For master's, GRE General Test, minimum GPA of 2.75. Electronic applications accepted.

**Chatham University,** Nursing Programs, Pittsburgh, PA 15232-2826. Offers education/leadership (MSN); nursing (DNP). *Accreditation:* AACN. *Program availability:* Online learning. *Entrance requirements:* For master's, RN license, BSN, minimum GPA of 3.0; for doctorate, RN license, MSN. Additional exam requirements/recommendations for international students: required—TOEFL (minimum score 600 paper-based; 100 iBT), IELTS (minimum score 6.5), TWE. Electronic applications accepted. Application fee is waived when completed online. *Expenses:* Contact institution.

**Chicago State University,** School of Graduate and Professional Studies, College of Health Sciences, Department of Nursing, Chicago, IL 60628. Offers MSN.

**Clarion University of Pennsylvania,** College of Health Sciences & Human Services, Master of Science in Nursing Program, Clarion, PA 16214. Offers family nurse practitioner (MSN). *Accreditation:* ACEN. *Program availability:* Part-time, online only, 100% online, blended/hybrid learning. *Faculty:* 5 full-time (all women), 3 part-time/adjunct (2 women). *Students:* 98 part-time (79 women); includes 8 minority (2 Black or African American, non-Hispanic/Latino; 2 Asian, non-Hispanic/Latino; 3 Hispanic/Latino; 1 Two or more races, non-Hispanic/Latino). Average age 34. 112 applicants, 41% accepted, 45 enrolled. In 2019, 39 master's awarded. *Degree requirements:* For master's, comprehensive exam, thesis, portfolio. *Entrance requirements:* For master's, Bachelor degree in nursing. 2.75 or above. 2000 hours of clinical practice. Additional exam requirements/recommendations for international students: required—TOEFL (minimum score 550 paper-based; 80 iBT). *Application deadline:* For fall admission, 8/1 for domestic students, 7/1 priority date for international students. Applications are processed on a rolling basis. Application fee: $40. Electronic applications accepted. *Expenses:* $736.40 per credit including fees. *Financial support:* Federal Work-Study and scholarships/grants available. Financial award application deadline: 3/1; financial award applicants required to submit FAFSA. *Unit head:* Dr. Deborah J. Kelly, Chair and Nurse Administrator, 814-393-1258, E-mail: dkelly@clarion.edu. *Application contact:* Susan Staub, Graduate Programs Counselor, 814-393-2337, Fax: 814-393-2722, E-mail: gradstudies@clarion.edu.
Website: http://www.clarion.edu/admissions/graduate/index.html

**Clarke University,** Department of Nursing and Health, Dubuque, IA 52001-3198. Offers family nurse practitioner (DNP); health leadership and practice (DNP); psychiatric mental health nurse practitioner (DNP). *Accreditation:* AACN. *Program availability:* Part-time. *Degree requirements:* For doctorate, comprehensive exam, thesis/dissertation. *Entrance requirements:* For doctorate, GRE (if GPA under 3.0), bachelor's degree from accredited nursing program and accredited college or university; minimum GPA of 3.0; minimum C grade on undergraduate prerequisite courses; three recommendation forms; curriculum vitae; statement of goals; transcripts; copy of nursing license; proof of health insurance; interview. Additional exam requirements/recommendations for international students: required—TOEFL (minimum score 550 paper-based; 80 iBT), IELTS (minimum score 6.5). Electronic applications accepted. *Expenses:* Contact institution.

**Clarkson College,** Master of Science in Nursing Program, Omaha, NE 68131. Offers adult nurse practitioner (MSN, Post-Master's Certificate); family nurse practitioner (MSN, Post-Master's Certificate); nursing education (MSN, Post-Master's Certificate); nursing health care leadership (MSN, Post-Master's Certificate). *Accreditation:* AANA/CANAEP; ACEN. *Program availability:* Part-time, evening/weekend, online learning. *Degree requirements:* For master's, on-campus skills assessment (family nurse practitioner, adult nurse practitioner), comprehensive exam or thesis. *Entrance requirements:* For master's, minimum GPA of 3.0, 2 references, resume. Additional exam requirements/recommendations for international students: required—TOEFL (minimum score 600 paper-based; 100 iBT). Electronic applications accepted.

**Clayton State University,** School of Graduate Studies, College of Health, Program in Nursing, Morrow, GA 30260-0285. Offers family nurse practitioner (MSN). *Accreditation:* AACN. *Degree requirements:* For master's, thesis. *Entrance requirements:* For master's, GRE, official transcript, 3 letters of recommendation, statement of purpose, on-campus interview, 1-2 years of clinical nursing experience (preferred). Additional exam requirements/recommendations for international students: required—TOEFL (minimum score 550 paper-based; 80 iBT). Electronic applications accepted. *Expenses:* Contact institution.

**Clemson University,** Graduate School, College of Behavioral, Social and Health Sciences, School of Nursing, Clemson, SC 29634. Offers clinical and translational research (PhD); global health (Certificate), including low resource countries; healthcare genetics (PhD); nursing (MS, DNP), including adult/gerontology nurse practitioner (MS), family nurse practitioner (MS). *Accreditation:* AACN. *Program availability:* Part-time, 100% online, blended/hybrid learning. *Faculty:* 47 full-time (45 women), 1 (woman) part-time/adjunct. *Students:* 67 full-time (59 women), 66 part-time (49 women); includes 18 minority (10 Black or African American, non-Hispanic/Latino; 4 Asian, non-Hispanic/Latino; 4 Two or more races, non-Hispanic/Latino), 7 international. Average age 35. 109 applicants, 62% accepted, 49 enrolled. In 2019, 56 master's, 8 doctorates awarded. *Degree requirements:* For master's, comprehensive exam, thesis or alternative; for doctorate, comprehensive exam, thesis/dissertation. *Entrance requirements:* For master's, GRE General Test, South Carolina RN license, unofficial transcripts, resume, letters of recommendation; for doctorate, GRE General Test, unofficial transcripts, MS/MA thesis or publications, curriculum vitae, statement of career goals, letters of recommendation. Additional exam requirements/recommendations for international students: required—TOEFL (minimum score 80 paper-based; 80 iBT); recommended—IELTS (minimum score 6.5), TSE (minimum score 54). *Application deadline:* For fall admission, 4/15 priority date for international students; for spring admission, 10/15 priority date for international students. Applications are processed on a rolling basis. Application fee: $80 ($90 for international students). Electronic applications accepted. *Expenses:* MS Nursing Full-Time Student per Semester: Tuition: $9075 (in-state), $16051 (out-of-state), Fees: $598; Graduate Assistant Per Semester: $1144; Part-Time Student Per Credit Hour: $1009 (in-state), $1784 (out-of-state), Fees: $46; other fees apply depending on program, credit hours, campus & residency. Doctoral Base Fee per Semester: $4938 (in-state), $10405 (out-of-state). *Financial support:* In 2019–20, 47 students received support, including 46 teaching assistantships with full and partial tuition reimbursements available (averaging $6,766 per year); career-related internships or fieldwork and unspecified assistantships also available. *Unit head:* Dr. Kathleen Valentine, Chief Academic Nursing Officer & Director, 864-656-4758, E-mail: klvalen@clemson.edu. *Application contact:* Dr. Stephanie Davis, Director of Graduate Programs, 864-656-2588, E-mail: stephad@clemson.edu.
Website: http://www.clemson.edu/cbshs/departments/nursing/

**Cleveland State University,** College of Graduate Studies, School of Nursing, Cleveland, OH 44115. Offers MSN, PhD, MSN/MBA. *Accreditation:* AACN. *Program availability:* Part-time, 100% online. *Degree requirements:* For master's, thesis optional, portfolio, capstone practicum project; for doctorate, comprehensive exam, thesis/dissertation. *Entrance requirements:* For master's, RN license in the U.S., BSN with minimum cumulative GPA of 3.0, recent (within last 5 years) course work in statistics; for doctorate, GRE, MSN with minimum cumulative GPA of 3.25. Additional exam requirements/recommendations for international students: required—TOEFL (minimum score 550 paper-based; 78 iBT), IELTS (minimum score 6). Electronic applications accepted. *Expenses:* Tuition, state resident: full-time $10,215; part-time $6810 per credit hour. Tuition, nonresident: full-time $17,496; part-time $11,664 per credit hour. *International tuition:* $19,316 full-time. Tuition and fees vary according to degree level and program.

**College of Mount Saint Vincent,** School of Professional and Graduate Studies, Department of Nursing, Riverdale, NY 10471-1093. Offers family nurse practitioner (MSN, PMC); nurse educator (PMC); nursing administration (MSN); nursing education (MSN). *Accreditation:* AACN. *Program availability:* Part-time. *Entrance requirements:* For master's, BSN, interview, RN license, minimum GPA of 3.0, letters of reference. Additional exam requirements/recommendations for international students: required—TOEFL. *Expenses:* Contact institution.

**The College of New Jersey,** Office of Graduate and Advancing Education, School of Nursing, Health, and Exercise Science, Program in Nursing, Ewing, NJ 08628. Offers MSN, Certificate. *Accreditation:* AACN. *Program availability:* Part-time. *Degree requirements:* For master's, comprehensive exam. *Entrance requirements:* For master's, GRE, minimum GPA of 3.0 in field or 2.75 overall. Additional exam requirements/recommendations for international students: required—TOEFL. Electronic applications accepted.

**The College of New Rochelle,** Graduate School, Program in Nursing, New Rochelle, NY 10805-2308. Offers acute care nurse practitioner (MS, Certificate); clinical specialist

in holistic nursing (MS, Certificate); family nurse practitioner (MS, Certificate); nursing and health care management (MS); nursing education (Certificate). *Accreditation:* AACN. *Program availability:* Part-time. *Entrance requirements:* For master's, GRE General Test or MAT, BSN, malpractice insurance, minimum GPA of 3.0, RN license. Electronic applications accepted.

**College of Saint Elizabeth,** Department of Nursing, Morristown, NJ 07960-6989. Offers MSN. *Accreditation:* ACEN. *Program availability:* Part-time. *Degree requirements:* For master's, thesis. *Entrance requirements:* Additional exam requirements/recommendations for international students: required—TOEFL (minimum score 550 paper-based; 79 iBT), IELTS (minimum score 6.5). Electronic applications accepted. Application fee is waived when completed online.

**College of Saint Mary,** Program in Nursing, Omaha, NE 68106. Offers MSN. *Accreditation:* ACEN. *Program availability:* Part-time. *Entrance requirements:* For master's, bachelor's degree in nursing, Nebraska RN license, essay or scholarly writing, minimum cumulative GPA of 3.0, 2 references. Additional exam requirements/recommendations for international students: required—TOEFL.

**The College of St. Scholastica,** Graduate Studies, Department of Nursing, Duluth, MN 55811-4199. Offers MA, PMC. *Accreditation:* AACN. *Program availability:* Part-time, online learning. *Degree requirements:* For master's, thesis. *Entrance requirements:* For master's, GRE General Test. Additional exam requirements/recommendations for international students: required—TOEFL (minimum score 550 paper-based; 79 iBT). Electronic applications accepted.

**Colorado Mesa University,** Department of Health Sciences, Grand Junction, CO 81501-3122. Offers advanced nursing practice (MSN); family nurse practitioner (DNP); health information technology systems (Graduate Certificate); nursing education (MSN). *Accreditation:* AACN. *Program availability:* Part-time, evening/weekend, 100% online, blended/hybrid learning. *Degree requirements:* For master's and doctorate, capstone. *Entrance requirements:* For master's and doctorate, minimum GPA of 3.0 in BSN program. Additional exam requirements/recommendations for international students: required—TOEFL (minimum score 550 paper-based). Electronic applications accepted.

**Colorado State University-Pueblo,** College of Education, Engineering and Professional Studies, Nursing Department, Pueblo, CO 81001-4901. Offers MS. *Accreditation:* ACEN. *Degree requirements:* For master's, comprehensive exam or thesis. *Entrance requirements:* Additional exam requirements/recommendations for international students: required—TOEFL.

**Columbia College of Nursing,** Graduate Program, Glendale, WI 53212. Offers MSN. *Entrance requirements:* For master's, bachelor's degree, minimum cumulative GPA of 3.0, undergraduate or graduate statistics course, unencumbered Wisconsin RN license.

**Columbia University,** School of Nursing, New York, NY 10032. Offers MS, DNP, PhD, Adv C, MBA/MS, MPH/MS. *Accreditation:* AACN. *Degree requirements:* For master's, comprehensive exam; for doctorate, thesis/dissertation. *Entrance requirements:* For master's, GRE General Test, bachelor's degree, 1 year of clinical experience (preferred for most, required for some); for doctorate, GRE General Test. Additional exam requirements/recommendations for international students: required—TOEFL (minimum score 100 iBT). Electronic applications accepted. *Expenses:* Contact institution.

**Columbus State University,** Graduate Studies, College of Education and Health Professions, School of Nursing, Columbus, GA 31907-5645. Offers family nurse practitioner (MSN); nursing (MSN), including nurse educator, nurse informatics, nurse leader. *Program availability:* Part-time, online only, 100% online. *Entrance requirements:* For master's, GRE, BSN, minimum undergraduate GPA of 3.0. Additional exam requirements/recommendations for international students: required—TOEFL (minimum score 550 paper-based; 79 iBT). Electronic applications accepted. *Expenses:* Contact institution.

**Concordia University Irvine,** School of Professional Studies, Irvine, CA 92612-3299. Offers healthcare administration (MHA); international studies (MAIS), including Africa, China; nursing (MSN).

**Concordia University Wisconsin,** Graduate Programs, School of Nursing, Mequon, WI 53097-2402. Offers family nurse practitioner (MSN). *Accreditation:* AACN. *Program availability:* Online learning. *Degree requirements:* For master's, comprehensive exam, thesis or alternative. *Entrance requirements:* Additional exam requirements/recommendations for international students: required—TOEFL. *Expenses:* Contact institution.

**Coppin State University,** School of Graduate Studies, Helene Fuld School of Nursing, Baltimore, MD 21216-3698. Offers family nurse practitioner (PMC); nursing (MSN). *Accreditation:* AACN; ACEN. *Program availability:* Part-time, evening/weekend. *Degree requirements:* For master's, comprehensive exam, thesis, clinical internship. *Entrance requirements:* For master's, GRE, bachelor's degree in nursing, interview, minimum GPA of 3.0, RN license. Additional exam requirements/recommendations for international students: required—TOEFL (minimum score 550 paper-based).

**Cox College,** Programs in Nursing, Springfield, MO 65802. Offers clinical nurse leader (MSN); family nurse practitioner (MSN); nurse educator (MSN). *Accreditation:* AACN. *Entrance requirements:* For master's, RN license, essay, 2 letters of recommendation, official transcripts. Electronic applications accepted.

**Creighton University,** College of Nursing, Omaha, NE 68178-0001. Offers adult gerontology acute care nurse practitioner (DNP, Post-Master's Certificate); adult gerontology nurse practitioner (DNP); clinical nurse leader (MSN, Post-Graduate Certificate); clinical systems administration (MSN, DNP); family nurse practitioner (DNP, Post-Master's Certificate); neonatal nurse practitioner (DNP, Post-Master's Certificate); nursing (Post-Graduate Certificate); pediatric acute care nurse practitioner (DNP, Post-Master's Certificate); psychiatric mental health nurse practitioner (DNP). *Accreditation:* AACN. *Program availability:* Part-time, blended/hybrid learning. *Degree requirements:* For master's, capstone project; for doctorate, scholarly project. *Entrance requirements:* For master's and doctorate, BSN from ACEN- or CCNE-accredited nursing school, minimum cumulative GPA of 3.0, personal statement, active unencumbered RN license with NE eligibility, undergraduate statistics course, physical assessment course or equivalent, three recommendation letters; for other advanced degree, MSN or MS in nursing from ACEN- or CCNE-accredited nursing school, minimum cumulative GPA of 3.0, active unencumbered RN license with NE eligibility. Additional exam requirements/recommendations for international students: required—TOEFL (minimum score 600 paper-based, 100 iBT) or IELTS. Electronic applications accepted. *Expenses:* Contact institution.

**Curry College,** Graduate Studies, Program in Nursing, Milton, MA 02186-9984. Offers MSN. *Accreditation:* AACN.

**Daemen College,** Nursing Programs, Amherst, NY 14226-3592. Offers adult nurse practitioner (MS, Post Master's Certificate); nurse executive leadership (Post Master's Certificate); nursing education (MS, Post Master's Certificate); nursing executive leadership (MS); nursing practice (DNP); palliative care nursing (Post Master's Certificate). *Accreditation:* ACEN. *Program availability:* Part-time. *Degree requirements:* For master's, thesis, degree completed in 4 years; minimum GPA of 3.0 and a minimum grade of B in all courses; for doctorate, thesis/dissertation, degree completed in 5 years;

minimum GPA of 3.0 and a minimum grade of B in all courses. *Entrance requirements:* For master's, bachelor's degree in nursing from a NLNAC or CCNE accredited program, 1 year medical-surgical clinical experience, resume, official transcripts, undergraduate or graduate statistics course (grade of C or better), GPA 3.25 or above (below may be accepted on provisional basis), NYS Nursing license, interview with nursing faculty. Additional exam requirements/recommendations for international students: required—TOEFL (minimum score 77 paper-based), IELTS (minimum score 6.5). Electronic applications accepted. Application fee is waived when completed online.

**Dalhousie University,** Faculty of Health, School of Nursing, Halifax, NS B3H 3J5, Canada. Offers MN, PhD, MN/MHSA. *Program availability:* Part-time, online learning. *Degree requirements:* For master's, thesis optional. *Entrance requirements:* For master's, minimum GPA of 3.0; for doctorate, written support of faculty member who has agreed to be thesis supervisor. Additional exam requirements/recommendations for international students: required—TOEFL, IELTS, CANTEST, CAEL, or Michigan English Language Assessment Battery. Electronic applications accepted.

**Delaware State University,** Graduate Programs, College of Education, Health and Public Policy, Department of Nursing, Dover, DE 19901-2277. Offers MS. *Entrance requirements:* Additional exam requirements/recommendations for international students: required—TOEFL (minimum score 550 paper-based). Electronic applications accepted.

**Delta State University,** Graduate Programs, Robert E. Smith School of Nursing, Cleveland, MS 38733. Offers family nurse practitioner (MSN); nurse administrator (MSN); nurse educator (MSN). *Accreditation:* AACN. *Program availability:* Part-time. *Degree requirements:* For master's, thesis optional. *Entrance requirements:* For master's, GRE General Test. Electronic applications accepted. *Expenses: Tuition, area resident:* Full-time $7501; part-time $417 per credit hour. Tuition, state resident: full-time $7501; part-time $417 per credit hour. Tuition, nonresident: full-time $7501; part-time $417 per credit hour. *International tuition:* $7501 full-time. *Required fees:* $170; $9.45 per credit hour. $9.45 per semester.

**DePaul University,** College of Science and Health, Chicago, IL 60604-2287. Offers applied mathematics (MS); applied statistics (MS); biological sciences (MA, MS); chemistry (MS); environmental science (MS); mathematics education (MA); mathematics for teaching (MS); nursing (MS); nursing practice (DNP); physics (MS); polymer and coatings science (MS); psychology (MS); pure mathematics (MS); science education (MS); MA/PhD. *Accreditation:* AACN. Electronic applications accepted.

**DeSales University,** Division of Healthcare, Center Valley, PA 18034-9568. Offers adult-gerontology acute care (Post Master's Certificate); adult-gerontology acute care nurse practitioner (MSN); adult-gerontology acute certified nurse practitioner (Post Master's Certificate); adult-gerontology clinical nurse specialist (MSN, Post Master's Certificate); clinical leadership (DNP); family nurse practitioner (MSN, Post Master's Certificate); general nursing practice (DNP); nurse anesthetist (MSN); nurse educator (Post Master's Certificate, Postbaccalaureate Certificate); nurse midwife (MSN); nurse practitioner (MSN); psychiatric-mental health nurse practitioner (MSN, Post Master's Certificate); DNP/MBA. *Accreditation:* ACEN. *Program availability:* Part-time. *Faculty:* 31 full-time (23 women), 12 part-time/adjunct (9 women). *Students:* 294 full-time (219 women), 128 part-time (109 women); includes 71 minority (20 Black or African American, non-Hispanic/Latino; 1 American Indian or Alaska Native, non-Hispanic/Latino; 15 Asian, non-Hispanic/Latino; 30 Hispanic/Latino; 5 Two or more races, non-Hispanic/Latino). Average age 28. 2,666 applicants, 6% accepted, 142 enrolled. In 2019, 115 master's, 30 doctorates awarded. *Degree requirements:* For master's, minimum GPA of 3.0, portfolio; for doctorate, minimum GPA of 3.0, scholarly capstone project. *Entrance requirements:* For master's, GRE or MAT (waived if applicant has an undergraduate GPA of 3.0 or higher), BSN from ACEN- or CCNE-accredited program, minimum undergraduate GPA of 3.0, active RN license or eligibility, two letters of recommendation, essay, health care experience, personal interview; for doctorate, BSN or MSN from ACEN- or CCNE-accredited institution, minimum GPA of 3.3 in graduate program, current licensure as an RN. Additional exam requirements/recommendations for international students: required—TOEFL (minimum score 104 iBT). *Application deadline:* Applications are processed on a rolling basis. Application fee: $50. Electronic applications accepted. *Expenses:* Contact institution. *Financial support:* Applicants required to submit FAFSA. *Unit head:* Ronald Nordone, Dean of Graduate Education, 610-282-1100 Ext. 1289, E-mail: ronald.nordone@desales.edu. *Application contact:* Julia Ferraro, Director of Graduate Admissions, 610-282-1100 Ext. 1768, E-mail: gradadmissions@desales.edu.

**Drexel University,** College of Nursing and Health Professions, Division of Graduate Nursing, Philadelphia, PA 19104-2875. Offers adult acute care (MSN); adult psychiatric/mental health (MSN); advanced practice nursing (MSN); clinical trials research (MSN); family nurse practitioner (MSN); leadership in health systems management (MSN); nursing education (MSN); pediatric primary care (MSN); women's health (MSN). *Accreditation:* AACN. Electronic applications accepted.

**Drexel University,** College of Nursing and Health Professions, Doctor of Nursing Practice Program, Philadelphia, PA 19104-2875. Offers Dr NP. *Accreditation:* AACN.

**Duke University,** School of Nursing, PhD Program in Nursing, Durham, NC 27708. Offers PhD. *Degree requirements:* For doctorate, comprehensive exam, thesis/dissertation. *Entrance requirements:* For doctorate, GRE General Test, resume, personal statement, minimum cumulative undergraduate GPA of 3.2, recommendations, previous work in nursing, research course, graduate-level statistics course. Additional exam requirements/recommendations for international students: required—TOEFL (minimum score 577 paper-based; 90 iBT), IELTS (minimum score 7). Electronic applications accepted. *Expenses:* Contact institution.

**Duquesne University,** School of Nursing, Doctor of Nursing Practice Program, Pittsburgh, PA 15282-0001. Offers DNP. *Program availability:* Part-time, evening/weekend, 100% online. *Entrance requirements:* For doctorate, current RN license; BSN; master's degree with minimum GPA of 3.5; current certifications; phone interview. Additional exam requirements/recommendations for international students: required—TOEFL (minimum score 600 paper-based; 100 iBT). Electronic applications accepted. *Expenses:* Contact institution.

**Duquesne University,** School of Nursing, Doctor of Philosophy in Nursing Program, Pittsburgh, PA 15282-0001. Offers nursing (PhD); nursing ethics (PhD). *Program availability:* Part-time, evening/weekend, minimal on-campus study. *Degree requirements:* For doctorate, thesis/dissertation, preliminary exam. *Entrance requirements:* For doctorate, current RN license; BSN; master's degree with minimum GPA of 3.5. Additional exam requirements/recommendations for international students: required—TOEFL (minimum score 600 paper-based; 100 iBT). Electronic applications accepted. *Expenses:* Contact institution.

**Duquesne University,** School of Nursing, Master of Science in Nursing Program, Pittsburgh, PA 15282-0001. Offers family (individual across the life span) nurse practitioner (MSN); forensic nursing (MSN); nursing education and faculty role (MSN). *Accreditation:* AACN. *Program availability:* Part-time, evening/weekend, minimal on-campus study. *Entrance requirements:* For master's, current RN license; BSN with minimum GPA of 3.0; minimum of 1 year of full-time work experience as RN prior to

registration in clinical or specialty course. Additional exam requirements/recommendations for international students: required—TOEFL (minimum score 600 paper-based; 100 iBT). Electronic applications accepted. *Expenses:* Contact institution.

**Duquesne University,** School of Nursing, Post Master's Certificate Program, Pittsburgh, PA 15282-0001. Offers family (individual across the life span) nurse practitioner (Post-Master's Certificate); forensic nursing (Post-Master's Certificate); nursing education and faculty role (Post-Master's Certificate). *Program availability:* Part-time, evening/weekend, minimal on-campus study. *Entrance requirements:* For degree, current RN license, BSN, MSN. Additional exam requirements/recommendations for international students: required—TOEFL (minimum score 600 paper-based; 100 iBT). Electronic applications accepted. *Expenses:* Contact institution.

**D'Youville College,** School of Nursing, Buffalo, NY 14201-1084. Offers advanced practice nursing (DNP); family nurse practitioner (MSN, Certificate); nursing and health-related professions education (Certificate). *Accreditation:* AACN. *Program availability:* Part-time. *Degree requirements:* For master's, thesis or alternative. *Entrance requirements:* For master's, BS in nursing, minimum GPA of 3.0, course work in statistics and computers; for doctorate, BS in nursing, MS in advanced practice nursing specialty, minimum GPA of 3.25. Additional exam requirements/recommendations for international students: required—TOEFL (minimum score 500 paper-based). Electronic applications accepted.

**East Carolina University,** Graduate School, College of Nursing, Greenville, NC 27858-4353. Offers MSN, DNP, PhD. *Accreditation:* AACN; AANA/CANAEP (one or more programs are accredited); ACNM/ACME (one or more programs are accredited). *Program availability:* Part-time. *Application deadline:* For fall admission, 3/15 priority date for domestic students; for spring admission, 10/15 priority date for domestic students. *Expenses: Tuition, area resident:* Full-time $4749; part-time $185 per credit hour. Tuition, state resident: full-time $4749; part-time $185 per credit hour. Tuition, nonresident: full-time $17,898; part-time $864 per credit hour. *International tuition:* $17,898 full-time. *Required fees:* $2787. *Financial support:* Application deadline: 6/1. *Unit head:* Dr. Sylvia T Brown, Dean, 252-744-6372, E-mail: brownsy@ecu.edu. *Application contact:* Graduate School Admissions, 252-328-6012, Fax: 252-328-6071, E-mail: gradschool@ecu.edu.
Website: https://nursing.ecu.edu/

**Eastern Kentucky University,** The Graduate School, College of Health Sciences, Department of Nursing, Richmond, KY 40475-3102. Offers rural community health care (MSN); rural health family nurse practitioner (MSN). *Accreditation:* AACN. *Entrance requirements:* For master's, GRE General Test, minimum GPA of 2.75.

**Eastern Mennonite University,** Program in Nursing, Harrisonburg, VA 22802-2462. Offers leadership and management (MSN); leadership and school nursing (MSN); nursing management (DNP). *Accreditation:* AACN. *Program availability:* Part-time, online learning. *Degree requirements:* For master's, leadership project. *Entrance requirements:* For master's, RN license, one year of full-time work experience as RN, minimum GPA of 3.0. Additional exam requirements/recommendations for international students: required—TOEFL. Application fee is waived when completed online.

**Eastern New Mexico University,** Graduate School, College of Liberal Arts and Sciences, Department of Health and Human Services, Portales, NM 88130. Offers communicative disorders (MS); nursing (MSN). *Accreditation:* ASHA. *Program availability:* Part-time, online learning. *Degree requirements:* For master's, thesis optional, oral and written comprehensive exam, oral presentation of professional portfolio. *Entrance requirements:* For master's, GRE, three letters of recommendation, resume, two essays. Additional exam requirements/recommendations for international students: required—TOEFL (minimum score 550 paper-based; 79 iBT), IELTS (minimum score 6). Electronic applications accepted. *Expenses: Tuition, area resident:* Full-time $5283; part-time $389.25 per credit hour. Tuition, state resident: full-time $5283; part-time $389.25 per credit hour. Tuition, nonresident: full-time $7007; part-time $389.25 per credit hour. *International tuition:* $7007 full-time. *Required fees:* $36; $35 per semester. One-time fee: $25.

**East Tennessee State University,** College of Graduate and Continuing Studies, College of Nursing, Johnson City, TN 37614. Offers acute care nurse practitioner (DNP); adult-gerontology primary care nurse practitioner (DNP); adult/gerontological nurse practitioner (Postbaccalaureate Certificate); executive leadership in nursing (DNP, Postbaccalaureate Certificate); family nurse practitioner (MSN, DNP, Post-Master's Certificate, Postbaccalaureate Certificate); nursing (PhD); nursing administration (MSN); nursing education (MSN); pediatric primary care nurse practitioner (DNP); psychiatric mental health nurse practitioner (Postbaccalaureate Certificate); psychiatric/mental health nurse practitioner (MSN, DNP, Post-Master's Certificate); women's health care nurse practitioner (DNP). *Accreditation:* AACN. *Program availability:* Part-time, evening/weekend, online learning. *Degree requirements:* For master's and other advanced degree, comprehensive exam, practicum; for doctorate, comprehensive exam, thesis/dissertation (for some programs), practicum, internship, evidence of professional malpractice insurance, CPR certification. *Entrance requirements:* For master's, bachelor's degree, minimum GPA of 3.0, current RN license and eligibility to practice, resume, three letters of recommendation; for doctorate, GRE General Test, MSN (for PhD), BSN or MSN (for DNP), current RN license and eligibility to practice, 2 years of full-time registered nurse work experience or equivalent, three letters of recommendation, resume or curriculum vitae, interview, writing sample; for other advanced degree, MSN, minimum GPA of 3.0, current RN license and eligibility to practice, three letters of recommendation, resume or curriculum vitae; DNP with designated concentration in advanced clinical practice or nursing administration (for select programs). Additional exam requirements/recommendations for international students: required—TOEFL (minimum score 600 paper-based; 79 iBT). Electronic applications accepted.

**Edgewood College,** Henry Predolin School of Nursing, Madison, WI 53711. Offers MSN, DNP. *Accreditation:* AACN. *Degree requirements:* For master's, practicum, research project; for doctorate, practicum, capstone project. *Entrance requirements:* For master's, minimum GPA of 3.0, 2 letters of reference, current RN license. Additional exam requirements/recommendations for international students: required—TOEFL. *Application deadline:* For fall admission, 8/15 priority date for domestic students, 5/1 for international students; for spring admission, 1/8 priority date for domestic students, 11/1 for international students. Applications are processed on a rolling basis. Application fee: $30. Electronic applications accepted. *Expenses: Tuition:* Part-time $997 per credit. *Unit head:* Dr. Margaret Noreuil, Dean, 608-663-2820, Fax: 608-663-3291, E-mail: mnoreuil@edgewood.edu. *Application contact:* Dr. Margaret Noreuil, Dean, 608-663-2820, Fax: 608-663-3291, E-mail: mnoreuil@edgewood.edu.
Website: https://www.edgewood.edu/academics/schools/henry-predolin-school-of-nursing

**Edinboro University of Pennsylvania,** Department of Nursing, Edinboro, PA 16444. Offers advanced practice nursing (DNP); family nurse practitioner (MSN); nurse educator (MSN). *Program availability:* Part-time, evening/weekend. *Faculty:* 6 full-time (5 women), 1 (woman) part-time/adjunct. *Students:* 105 part-time (85 women); includes 9 minority (4 Black or African American, non-Hispanic/Latino; 2 Asian, non-Hispanic/Latino; 3 Hispanic/Latino). Average age 37. 57 applicants, 100% accepted, 57 enrolled.

*Degree requirements:* For master's, thesis, competency exam. *Entrance requirements:* For master's, GRE or MAT, minimum GPA 2.75; one year of recent full-time clinical practice or two years of part-time clinical practice; licensure as a registered nurse in the state where they plan to complete clinical practicum; for doctorate, minimum GPA 3.25; current unencumbered licenses as a Registered nurse. Additional exam requirements/recommendations for international students: required—TOEFL (minimum score 550 paper-based; 213 iBT), IELTS (minimum score 6.5). Application fee: $40. Electronic applications accepted. *Expenses:* Tuition & Fees: 889.8/credit for PA resident; 1025.24/credit for non-PA resident. *Financial support:* Application deadline: 2/15; applicants required to submit FAFSA. *Unit head:* Dr. Victoria Hedderick, Chair, 814-732-1655, E-mail: vhedderick@edinboro.edu. *Application contact:* Dr. Victoria Hedderick, Chair, 814-732-1655, E-mail: vhedderick@edinboro.edu.
Website: https://www.edinboro.edu/academics/schools-and-departments/cshp/departments/nursing/

**EDP University of Puerto Rico–San Sebastian,** Graduate School, San Sebastian, PR 00685. Offers nursing science (MS).

**Elmhurst University,** Graduate Programs, Nursing Master's Entry Program, Elmhurst, IL 60126-3296. Offers MS. *Faculty:* 11 full-time (all women), 6 part-time/adjunct (all women). *Students:* 34 full-time (27 women); includes 6 minority (1 Black or African American, non-Hispanic/Latino; 1 Asian, non-Hispanic/Latino; 4 Hispanic/Latino). Average age 27. 370 applicants, 16% accepted, 13 enrolled. In 2019, 19 master's awarded. *Entrance requirements:* For master's, baccalaureate degree in any field from regionally-accredited institution with minimum cumulative GPA of 3.2. Additional exam requirements/recommendations for international students: required—TOEFL (minimum score 550 paper-based; 79 iBT), IELTS (minimum score 6.5). *Application deadline:* For fall admission, 1/15 for domestic students. Electronic applications accepted. *Expenses:* $30,000 per year. *Financial support:* In 2019–20, 27 students received support. Scholarships/grants available. Financial award applicants required to submit FAFSA. *Unit head:* Dr. Elizabeth Davis, Director, 630-617-3549, E-mail: elizabeth.davis@elmhurst.edu. *Application contact:* Timothy J. Panfil, Senior Director of Graduate Admission and Enrollment Management, 630-617-3300 Ext. 3256, Fax: 630-617-6471, E-mail: panfilt@elmhurst.edu.
Website: http://www.elmhurst.edu/nursing_masters_entry

**Elmhurst University,** Graduate Programs, Program in Nursing, Elmhurst, IL 60126-3296. Offers MSN. *Accreditation:* AACN. *Program availability:* Part-time, evening/weekend. *Faculty:* 11 full-time (all women), 6 part-time/adjunct (all women). *Students:* 48 part-time (47 women); includes 4 minority (2 Asian, non-Hispanic/Latino; 2 Hispanic/Latino). Average age 33. 68 applicants, 34% accepted, 23 enrolled. In 2019, 37 master's awarded. *Entrance requirements:* For master's, 3 recommendations, resume, statement of purpose, current RN licensure in Illinois, interview. Additional exam requirements/recommendations for international students: required—TOEFL (minimum score 550 paper-based; 79 iBT), IELTS (minimum score 6.5). *Application deadline:* For fall admission, 6/1 for domestic students. Applications are processed on a rolling basis. Electronic applications accepted. *Expenses:* $750 per semester hour. *Financial support:* In 2019–20, 7 students received support. Scholarships/grants available. Support available to part-time students. Financial award applicants required to submit FAFSA. *Unit head:* Dr. Becky Hulett, Director, 630-617-3506, E-mail: becky.hulett@elmhurst.edu. *Application contact:* Timothy J. Panfil, Senior Director of Graduate Admission and Enrollment Management, 630-617-3300 Ext. 3256, Fax: 630-617-6471, E-mail: panfilt@elmhurst.edu.
Website: http://www.elmhurst.edu/nrs

**Elms College,** School of Nursing, Chicopee, MA 01013-2839. Offers adult-gerontology acute care nurse practitioner (DNP); family nurse practitioner (DNP); health systems innovation and leadership (DNP); nursing and health services management (MSN); nursing education (MSN). *Accreditation:* AACN. *Program availability:* Part-time, evening/weekend. *Faculty:* 3 full-time (2 women), 2 part-time/adjunct (both women). *Students:* 13 full-time (11 women), 97 part-time (91 women); includes 8 minority (4 Black or African American, non-Hispanic/Latino; 2 Hispanic/Latino; 2 Two or more races, non-Hispanic/Latino). Average age 38. 39 applicants, 87% accepted, 27 enrolled. In 2019, 4 master's, 20 doctorates awarded. *Entrance requirements:* Additional exam requirements/recommendations for international students: required—TOEFL (minimum score 80 iBT). *Application deadline:* For fall admission, 7/1 priority date for domestic students; for spring admission, 11/1 priority date for domestic students. Applications are processed on a rolling basis. Electronic applications accepted. *Financial support:* Applicants required to submit FAFSA. *Unit head:* Dr. Kathleen Scoble, Dean, School of Nursing, 413-265-2204, E-mail: scoblek@elms.edu. *Application contact:* Nancy Davis, Director, Office of Graduate and Continuing Education Admissions, 413-265-2456, E-mail: grad@elms.edu.

**Emmanuel College,** Graduate and Professional Programs, Graduate Program in Nursing, Boston, MA 02115. Offers education (MSN, Graduate Certificate); management (MSN, Graduate Certificate). *Accreditation:* AACN. *Program availability:* Part-time, evening/weekend. *Faculty:* 2 full-time (both women), 3 part-time/adjunct (all women). *Students:* 27 part-time (all women); includes 7 minority (3 Black or African American, non-Hispanic/Latino; 1 Asian, non-Hispanic/Latino; 3 Hispanic/Latino). Average age 43. In 2019, 14 master's awarded. *Degree requirements:* For master's, 30 credits (eight 3 credit courses and 1 6 credit course); for Graduate Certificate, 12 credits (two 3 credit courses and 1 6 credit course). *Entrance requirements:* For degree, completed application, transcripts from all regionally-accredited institutions attended (showing proof of bachelor's degree completion), proof of current RN license, 2 letters of recommendation, admissions essay, current resume. Additional exam requirements/recommendations for international students: required—TOEFL. *Application deadline:* Applications are processed on a rolling basis. Electronic applications accepted. *Expenses:* $2,581 per course. *Financial support:* Application deadline: 2/15; applicants required to submit FAFSA. *Unit head:* Diane Shea, Associate Dean for Nursing/Professor of Nursing Practice, 617-732-1604, E-mail: shead@emmanuel.edu. *Application contact:* Helen Muterperl, Director of Graduate and Professional Programs, 617-735-9700, Fax: 617-507-0434, E-mail: gpp@emmanuel.edu.
Website: http://www.emmanuel.edu/graduate-professional-programs/academics/nursing.html

**Emory University,** Laney Graduate School, Program in Nursing, Atlanta, GA 30322-1100. Offers PhD. *Accreditation:* AACN. *Degree requirements:* For doctorate, comprehensive exam, thesis/dissertation. *Entrance requirements:* For doctorate, GRE General Test. Additional exam requirements/recommendations for international students: required—TOEFL. Electronic applications accepted.

**Emory University,** Nell Hodgson Woodruff School of Nursing, Atlanta, GA 30322-1100. Offers adult nurse practitioner (MSN); emergency nurse practitioner (MSN); family nurse practitioner (MSN); family nurse-midwife (MSN); health systems leadership (MSN); nurse-midwifery (MSN); pediatric nurse practitioner acute and primary care (MSN); women's health care (Title X) (MSN); women's health nurse practitioner (MSN); MSN/MPH. *Accreditation:* AACN; ACNM/ACME (one or more programs are accredited). *Program availability:* Part-time. *Entrance requirements:* For master's, GRE General Test or MAT, minimum GPA of 3.0, BS in nursing from an accredited institution, RN license and additional course work, 3 letters of recommendation. Additional exam requirements/

recommendations for international students: required—TOEFL (minimum score 600 paper-based; 100 iBT). Electronic applications accepted. *Expenses:* Contact institution.

**Endicott College,** School of Nursing, Program in Nursing, Beverly, MA 01915. Offers family nurse practitioner (MSN, Post-Master's Certificate); global health (MSN); nursing administration (MSN); nursing administrator (Post-Master's Certificate); nursing educator (MSN, Post-Master's Certificate). *Program availability:* Part-time, evening/weekend, blended/hybrid learning. *Faculty:* 4 full-time (all women), 18 part-time/adjunct (13 women). *Students:* 20 full-time (19 women), 71 part-time (70 women); includes 11 minority (5 Black or African American, non-Hispanic/Latino; 3 Asian, non-Hispanic/Latino; 2 Hispanic/Latino; 1 Two or more races, non-Hispanic/Latino). Average age 37. 32 applicants, 41% accepted, 12 enrolled. In 2019, 34 master's, 6 other advanced degrees awarded. *Degree requirements:* For master's, thesis, Internship and Capstone portfolio (S); Minimum 600 faculty supervised clinical hours (S). *Entrance requirements:* Additional exam requirements/recommendations for international students: required—TOEFL. *Application deadline:* Applications are processed on a rolling basis. Application fee: $50. Electronic applications accepted. *Expenses:* Tuition varies by program. *Financial support:* Applicants required to submit FAFSA. *Unit head:* Nancy Meedzan, DNP, RN, CNE, Dean, School of Nursing, 978-232-2328, E-mail: nmeedzan@endicott.edu. *Application contact:* Ian Menchini, Director, Graduate Enrollment and Advising, 978-232-5292, Fax: 978-232-3000, E-mail: imenchin@endicott.edu. Website: https://www.endicott.edu/academics/schools/nursing/graduate-programs

**Fairfield University,** Marion Peckham Egan School of Nursing and Health Studies, Fairfield, CT 06824. Offers advanced practice (DNP); family nurse practitioner (MSN, DNP); nurse anesthesia (DNP); nursing leadership (MSN); psychiatric nurse practitioner (MSN, DNP). *Accreditation:* AACN; AANA/CANAEP. *Program availability:* Part-time, evening/weekend. *Faculty:* 13 full-time (all women), 12 part-time/adjunct (9 women). *Students:* 56 full-time (49 women), 165 part-time (149 women); includes 62 minority (24 Black or African American, non-Hispanic/Latino; 12 Asian, non-Hispanic/Latino; 25 Hispanic/Latino; 1 Two or more races, non-Hispanic/Latino). Average age 33. 129 applicants, 56% accepted, 62 enrolled. In 2019, 26 master's, 36 doctorates awarded. *Degree requirements:* For master's, capstone project. *Entrance requirements:* For master's, minimum QPA of 3.0, RN license, resume, 2 recommendations; for doctorate, MSN (minimum QPA of 3.2) or BSN (minimum QPA of 3.0); critical care nursing experience (for nurse anesthesia DNP candidates). Additional exam requirements/recommendations for international students: required—TOEFL (minimum score 550 paper-based; 80 iBT), IELTS (minimum score 6.5), TOEFL (minimum score 550 paper-based; 80 iBT) or IELTS (minimum score 6.5). *Application deadline:* For fall admission, 5/15 for international students; for spring admission, 10/15 for international students. Applications are processed on a rolling basis. Application fee: $60. Electronic applications accepted. *Expenses:* $875 per credit hour tuition (for MS), $1,010 per credit hour tuition (for Master of Healthcare Administration), $1,025 per credit hour tuition (for Doctorate in Clinical Nutrition), $1,050 per credit hour tuition (for DNP Nurse Anesthesia), $1,000 per credit hour tuition (for all other DNP programs), $150 per semester clinical placement fee (applicable programs, fall and spring semesters), $50 per semester registration fee, $65 per semester graduate student activity fee (fall and spring). *Financial support:* In 2019–20, 45 students received support. Scholarships/grants and unspecified assistantships available. Financial award applicants required to submit FAFSA. *Unit head:* Dr. Meredith Wallace Kazer, Dean, 203-254-4000 Ext. 2701, Fax: 203-254-4126, E-mail: mkazer@fairfield.edu. *Application contact:* Melanie Rogers, Director of Graduate Admission, 203-254-4184, Fax: 203-254-4073, E-mail: gradadmis@fairfield.edu.
Website: http://fairfield.edu/son

**Fairleigh Dickinson University, Florham Campus,** University College: Arts, Sciences, and Professional Studies, The Henry P. Becton School of Nursing and Allied Health, Madison, NJ 07940-1099. Offers adult gerontology primary care nurse practitioner (MSN); family psychiatric/mental health nurse practitioner (MSN). *Program availability:* Part-time, evening/weekend. *Entrance requirements:* For master's, BSN, minimum undergraduate GPA of 3.0, courses in statistics and nursing research at the undergraduate level, NJ Registered Nurse licensure, minimum of 1 year of clinical nursing experience, two letters of recommendation.

**Fairleigh Dickinson University, Metropolitan Campus,** University College: Arts, Sciences, and Professional Studies, Henry P. Becton School of Nursing and Allied Health, Program in Nursing, Teaneck, NJ 07666-1914. Offers MSN, Certificate. *Accreditation:* AACN.

**Fairleigh Dickinson University, Metropolitan Campus,** University College: Arts, Sciences, and Professional Studies, Henry P. Becton School of Nursing and Allied Health, Program in Nursing Practice, Teaneck, NJ 07666-1914. Offers DNP. *Accreditation:* AACN.

**Felician University,** Doctor of Nursing Practice Program, Lodi, NJ 07644-2117. Offers advanced practice (DNP); executive leadership (DNP). *Accreditation:* AACN. *Program availability:* Evening/weekend, online only, 100% online, blended/hybrid learning. *Degree requirements:* For doctorate, thesis/dissertation, scholarly project. *Entrance requirements:* For doctorate, 2 letters of recommendation; national certification as nurse executive/administrator (preferred); interview; minimum GPA of 3.0. Additional exam requirements/recommendations for international students: required—TOEFL (minimum score 550 paper-based; 79 iBT), IELTS (minimum score 6.5), PTE (minimum score 56). Electronic applications accepted. Application fee is waived when completed online. *Expenses:* Contact institution.

**Felician University,** Master of Science in Nursing Program, Lodi, NJ 07644-2117. Offers adult-gerontology nurse practitioner (MSN, PMC); executive leadership (MSN, PMC); family nurse practitioner (MSN, PMC); nursing education (MSN, PMC). *Accreditation:* AACN. *Program availability:* Evening/weekend, online only, 100% online, blended/hybrid learning. *Degree requirements:* For master's, thesis, clinical presentation; for PMC, thesis, education project. *Entrance requirements:* For master's, BSN; minimum GPA of 3.0; 2 letters of recommendation; NJ RN license; personal statement; for PMC, RN license, minimum GPA of 3.0. Additional exam requirements/recommendations for international students: required—TOEFL (minimum score 550 paper-based; 79 iBT), IELTS (minimum score 6.5), PTE (minimum score 56). Electronic applications accepted. Application fee is waived when completed online. *Expenses:* Contact institution.

**Ferris State University,** College of Health Professions, School of Nursing, Big Rapids, MI 49307. Offers nursing (MSN); nursing administration (MSN); nursing education (MSN); nursing informatics (MSN). *Accreditation:* ACEN. *Program availability:* Part-time, evening/weekend, online only, 100% online. *Faculty:* 7 full-time (all women), 1 (woman) part-time/adjunct. *Students:* 103 part-time (95 women); includes 14 minority (2 Black or African American, non-Hispanic/Latino; 6 American Indian or Alaska Native, non-Hispanic/Latino; 4 Hispanic/Latino; 2 Two or more races, non-Hispanic/Latino). Average age 38. 31 applicants, 97% accepted, 24 enrolled. In 2019, 24 master's awarded. *Degree requirements:* For master's, practicum, practicum project. *Entrance requirements:* For master's, BS in nursing (for nursing education track); BS in nursing or related field (for nursing administration and nursing informatics tracks); registered nurse license, writing sample, letters of reference, 2 years' clinical experience (recommended).

Additional exam requirements/recommendations for international students: required—TOEFL (minimum score 550 paper-based; 79 iBT). *Application deadline:* For fall admission, 4/15 priority date for domestic and international students; for spring admission, 10/15 for domestic and international students. Electronic applications accepted. Tuition and fees vary according to degree level, program and student level. *Financial support:* In 2019–20, 7 students received support. Career-related internships or fieldwork and scholarships/grants available. Financial award application deadline: 4/15; financial award applicants required to submit FAFSA. *Unit head:* Dr. Wendy Lenon, Chair, School of Nursing, 231-591-2267, Fax: 231-591-2325, E-mail: WendyLenon@ferris.edu. *Application contact:* Dr. Sharon Colley, MSN Program Coordinator, 231-591-2288, Fax: 231-591-2325, E-mail: colleys@ferris.edu.
Website: http://www.ferris.edu/htmls/colleges/alliedhe/Nursing/homepage.htm

**Florida Agricultural and Mechanical University,** Division of Graduate Studies, Research, and Continuing Education, School of Nursing, Tallahassee, FL 32307-3200. Offers MSN, PhD. *Accreditation:* ACEN. *Entrance requirements:* Additional exam requirements/recommendations for international students: required—TOEFL.

**Florida Atlantic University,** Christine E. Lynn College of Nursing, Boca Raton, FL 33431. Offers administrative and financial leadership in nursing and health care (Post Master's Certificate); nursing (MSN, PhD); nursing practice (DNP). *Accreditation:* AACN. *Program availability:* Part-time. *Faculty:* 37 full-time (35 women), 16 part-time/adjunct (15 women). *Students:* 75 full-time (66 women), 396 part-time (366 women); includes 272 minority (151 Black or African American, non-Hispanic/Latino; 24 Asian, non-Hispanic/Latino; 81 Hispanic/Latino; 16 Two or more races, non-Hispanic/Latino), 14 international. Average age 36. 515 applicants, 31% accepted, 131 enrolled. In 2019, 155 master's, 33 doctorates awarded. *Degree requirements:* For master's, thesis or alternative; for doctorate, comprehensive exam, thesis/dissertation. *Entrance requirements:* For master's, GRE General Test or MAT, bachelor's degree in nursing, Florida RN license, minimum GPA of 3.0, resume/curriculum vitae, letter of recommendation; for doctorate, GRE General Test or MAT, curriculum vitae, Florida RN license, minimum GPA of 3.5, master's degree in nursing, three letters of recommendation. *Application deadline:* For fall admission, 6/1 for domestic students, 2/15 for international students; for spring admission, 10/1 for domestic students, 7/15 for international students. Applications are processed on a rolling basis. Application fee: $30. *Expenses: Tuition:* Full-time $20,536; part-time $371.82 per credit hour. Tuition and fees vary according to program. *Financial support:* Research assistantships with partial tuition reimbursements, teaching assistantships with partial tuition reimbursements, career-related internships or fieldwork, Federal Work-Study, institutionally sponsored loans, scholarships/grants, and traineeships available. Support available to part-time students. *Unit head:* Safiya A George Damida, Dean, 561-297-3206, E-mail: sgeorge@health.fau.edu. *Application contact:* Safiya A George Damida, Dean, 561-297-3206, E-mail: sgeorge@health.fau.edu.
Website: http://nursing.fau.edu/

**Florida International University,** Nicole Wertheim College of Nursing and Health Sciences, Nursing Program, Miami, FL 33199. Offers adult health nursing (MSN); family health (MSN); nurse anesthetist (MSN); nursing practice (DNP); nursing science research (PhD); pediatric nurse (MSN); psychiatric and mental health nursing (MSN); registered nurse (MSN). *Accreditation:* AACN; AANA/CANAEP. *Program availability:* Part-time, evening/weekend. *Faculty:* 14 full-time (12 women), 19 part-time/adjunct (14 women). *Students:* 279 full-time (188 women), 109 part-time (87 women); includes 309 minority (110 Black or African American, non-Hispanic/Latino; 1 American Indian or Alaska Native, non-Hispanic/Latino; 29 Asian, non-Hispanic/Latino; 166 Hispanic/Latino; 2 Native Hawaiian or other Pacific Islander, non-Hispanic/Latino; 1 Two or more races, non-Hispanic/Latino), 6 international. Average age 35. 154 applicants, 61% accepted, 88 enrolled. In 2019, 167 master's, 46 doctorates awarded. *Degree requirements:* For master's, thesis or alternative; for doctorate, comprehensive exam, thesis/dissertation. *Entrance requirements:* For master's, bachelor's degree in nursing, minimum undergraduate GPA of 3.0 in upper-level coursework, letters of recommendation; for doctorate, GRE, letters of recommendation, minimum undergraduate GPA of 3.0 in upper-level coursework, interview. Additional exam requirements/recommendations for international students: required—TOEFL (minimum score 550 paper-based; 80 iBT). *Application deadline:* For fall admission, 6/1 for domestic students, 4/1 for international students; for spring admission, 10/1 for domestic students, 9/1 for international students. Applications are processed on a rolling basis. Application fee: $30. Electronic applications accepted. *Expenses: Tuition, area resident:* Full-time $8912; part-time $446 per credit hour. Tuition, state resident: full-time $8912; part-time $446 per credit hour. Tuition, nonresident: full-time $21,393; part-time $992 per credit hour. *Required fees:* $2194. *Financial support:* Institutionally sponsored loans and scholarships/grants available. Financial award application deadline: 3/1; financial award applicants required to submit FAFSA. *Unit head:* Dr. Yhovana Gordon, Chair, 305-348-7733, Fax: 305-348-7051, E-mail: gordony@fiu.edu. *Application contact:* Nanett Rojas, Manager, Admissions Operations, 305-348-7464, Fax: 305-348-7441, E-mail: gradadm@fiu.edu.
Website: http://cnhs.fiu.edu/

**Florida National University,** Program in Nursing, Hialeah, FL 33139. Offers family nurse practitioner (MSN); nurse educator (MSN); nurse leadership and management (MSN). *Program availability:* 100% online, blended/hybrid learning. *Faculty:* 6 full-time (4 women), 9 part-time/adjunct (7 women). *Students:* 14 full-time (10 women), 204 part-time (151 women); includes 213 minority (21 Black or African American, non-Hispanic/Latino; 1 Asian, non-Hispanic/Latino; 191 Hispanic/Latino). Average age 40. 54 applicants, 100% accepted, 54 enrolled. In 2019, 53 master's awarded. *Degree requirements:* For master's, practicum. *Entrance requirements:* For master's, active registered nurse license, BSN from accredited institution. Additional exam requirements/recommendations for international students: recommended—TOEFL. *Expenses:* Contact institution. *Financial support:* Scholarships/grants available. *Unit head:* Dr. Lydie Janvier, Master of Science in Nursing Program Director, 305-821-3333 Ext. 1056, Fax: 305-362-0595, E-mail: ljanvier@fnu.edu. *Application contact:* Dr. Lydie Janvier, Master of Science in Nursing Program Director, 305-821-3333 Ext. 1056, Fax: 305-362-0595, E-mail: ljanvier@fnu.edu.
Website: https://www.fnu.edu/prospective-students/our-programs/select-a-program/master-of-business-administration/nursing-msn-master/

**Florida Southern College,** School of Nursing and Health Sciences, Lakeland, FL 33801. Offers adult gerontology clinical nurse specialist (MSN); adult gerontology primary care nurse practitioner (MSN); family nurse practitioner (MSN); nurse educator (MSN); nursing administration (MSN). *Accreditation:* AACN. *Program availability:* Part-time, The Nurse Educator MSN degree concentration and NE postmasters certificate are fully online. The Nursing Administrative Leadership MSN degree concentration is delivered in blended/hybrid format. *Faculty:* 6 full-time (all women), 1 (woman) part-time/adjunct. *Students:* 145 full-time (131 women), 1 (woman) part-time; includes 70 minority (30 Black or African American, non-Hispanic/Latino; 11 Asian, non-Hispanic/Latino; 25 Hispanic/Latino; 4 Two or more races, non-Hispanic/Latino), 1 international. Average age 39. 81 applicants, 89% accepted, 50 enrolled. In 2019, 53 master's awarded. *Degree requirements:* For master's, comprehensive exam, 660 clinical hours (for Family Nurse Practitioner); 540 clinical hours (for Adult-Gerontology Primary Care Nurse Practitioner). *Entrance requirements:* For master's, Florida RN license, 3 letters of

*Nursing—General*

recommendation, professional statement, minimum GPA of 3.0 in the last 60 credit hours of BSN, BSN earned from a regionally accredited institution and a CCNE, CNEA, or ACEN accredited nursing program, resume, admission interview. Additional exam requirements/recommendations for international students: required—TOEFL (minimum score 550 paper-based; 79 iBT), IELTS (minimum score 6.5), International students from countries where English is not the standard for daily communication must submit either the TOEFL or IELTS. *Application deadline:* For fall admission, 6/1 for domestic and international students; for spring admission, 10/1 for domestic and international students. Applications are processed on a rolling basis. Electronic applications accepted. *Expenses:* DNP: $725 per credit hour tuition, $50 per semester technology fee (for 5-8 hours), $100 per semester technology fee (for 9-12 hours); MSN: $600 per credit hour tuition, $50 per semester technology fee (for 5-8 hours), $100 per semester technology fee (for 9-12 hours), $35 per semester insurance and lab supplies fees. *Financial support:* In 2019–20, 1 student received support. Employee tuition grants, athletic scholarships for students still eligible available. Financial award application deadline: 8/20; financial award applicants required to submit FAFSA. *Unit head:* Dr. Linda Comer, Dean, 863-680-3951, Fax: 863-680-3860, E-mail: lcomer@flsouthern.edu. *Application contact:* Kimberly Smith, Admission Counselor and Advisor for Nursing, 863-680-3090, Fax: 863-680-3872, E-mail: ksmith@flsouthern.edu. Website: www.flsouthern.edu/sage

**Florida State University,** The Graduate School, College of Nursing, Tallahassee, FL 32306-4310. Offers family nurse practitioner (DNP); psychiatric mental health (Certificate). *Accreditation:* AACN; AANA/CANAEP. *Program availability:* Part-time, online only, 100% online. *Faculty:* 31 full-time (27 women), 10 part-time/adjunct (9 women). *Students:* 66 full-time (59 women), 72 part-time (63 women); includes 61 minority (32 Black or African American, non-Hispanic/Latino; 1 American Indian or Alaska Native, non-Hispanic/Latino; 5 Asian, non-Hispanic/Latino; 20 Hispanic/Latino; 3 Two or more races, non-Hispanic/Latino). Average age 40. 156 applicants, 39% accepted, 54 enrolled. In 2019, 24 doctorates awarded. *Degree requirements:* For doctorate, thesis/dissertation, evidence-based project. *Entrance requirements:* For doctorate, GRE General Test, MAT, minimum GPA of 3.0, BSN or MSN, Florida RN license. Additional exam requirements/recommendations for international students: required—TOEFL (minimum score 550 paper-based). *Application deadline:* For fall admission, 3/1 for domestic and international students. Application fee: $30. Electronic applications accepted. *Expenses:* Contact institution. *Financial support:* In 2019–20, 27 students received support, including fellowships with partial tuition reimbursements available (averaging $6,300 per year), research assistantships with partial tuition reimbursements available (averaging $3,000 per year), 3 teaching assistantships with partial tuition reimbursements available (averaging $3,000 per year); career-related internships or fieldwork, Federal Work-Study, institutionally sponsored loans, scholarships/grants, traineeships, and tuition waivers (partial) also available. Financial award application deadline: 4/1; financial award applicants required to submit FAFSA. *Unit head:* Dr. Laurie Grubbs, Interim Dean, 850-644-6846, Fax: 850-644-7660, E-mail: lgrubbs@fsu.edu. *Application contact:* Carlos Urrutia, Assistant Director for Student Services, 850-644-5638, Fax: 850-645-7249, E-mail: currutia@fsu.edu. Website: http://nursing.fsu.edu/

**Fort Hays State University,** Graduate School, College of Health and Behavioral Sciences, Department of Nursing, Hays, KS 67601-4099. Offers MSN. *Accreditation:* AACN. *Degree requirements:* For master's, comprehensive exam, thesis optional. *Entrance requirements:* For master's, GRE General Test or MAT. Additional exam requirements/recommendations for international students: required—TOEFL (minimum score 550 paper-based). Electronic applications accepted.

**Framingham State University,** Graduate Studies, Program in Nursing, Framingham, MA 01701-9101. Offers nursing education (MSN); nursing leadership (MSN).

*Accreditation:* AACN. *Entrance requirements:* For master's, BSN; minimum cumulative undergraduate GPA of 3.0, 3.25 in nursing courses; coursework in statistics; 2 letters of recommendation; interview. Electronic applications accepted.

**Franciscan Missionaries of Our Lady University,** School of Nursing, Baton Rouge, LA 70808. Offers MSN, DNP. *Accreditation:* ACEN.

**Franciscan University of Steubenville,** Graduate Programs, Department of Nursing, Steubenville, OH 43952-1763. Offers MSN. *Accreditation:* ACEN. *Program availability:* Part-time, evening/weekend. *Degree requirements:* For master's, thesis. *Entrance requirements:* For master's, GRE General Test, MAT. Additional exam requirements/recommendations for international students: required—TOEFL. Electronic applications accepted. Application fee is waived when completed online.

**Francis Marion University,** Graduate Programs, Department of Nursing, Florence, SC 29502-0547. Offers family nurse practitioner (MSN); family nurse practitioner with nurse educator certificate (MSN); nurse educator (MSN). *Program availability:* Part-time. *Entrance requirements:* For master's, GRE, official transcripts, two letters of recommendation from professional associates or former professors, written statement of applicant's career goals, current nursing license. Additional exam requirements/recommendations for international students: required—TOEFL (minimum score 550 paper-based; 79 iBT). Electronic applications accepted. *Expenses:* Contact institution.

**Fresno Pacific University,** Graduate Programs, Program in Nursing, Fresno, CA 93702-4709. Offers family nurse practitioner (MSN). *Entrance requirements:* For master's, official transcripts verifying BSN from accredited nursing program; minimum cumulative GPA of 3.0; three reference forms; statement of intent; resume or curriculum vitae; personal interview; active California RN license; completion of statistics, chemistry and upper-division writing. *Expenses:* Contact institution.

**Frontier Nursing University,** Graduate Programs, Hyden, KY 41749. Offers family nurse practitioner (MSN, DNP, Post Master's Certificate); nurse-midwife (MSN, DNP, Post Master's Certificate); psychiatric-mental health nurse practitioner (MSN, DNP, Post Master's Certificate); women's health care nurse practitioner (MSN, DNP, Post Master's Certificate). *Accreditation:* ACEN. *Degree requirements:* For doctorate, capstone project, practicum.

**See Display below and Close-Up on page 593.**

**Frostburg State University,** College of Liberal Arts and Sciences, Department of Nursing, Frostburg, MD 21532-1099. Offers nursing administration (MSN); nursing education (MSN). *Program availability:* Part-time, online learning. *Entrance requirements:* For master's, current unrestricted RN license; BSN from a nursing program accredited by CCNE or ACEN. Additional exam requirements/recommendations for international students: required—TOEFL.

**Gannon University,** School of Graduate Studies, Morosky College of Health Professions and Sciences, Villa Maria School of Nursing, Program in Nursing Practice, Erie, PA 16541-0001. Offers DNP. *Program availability:* Part-time, evening/weekend, online only, 100% online. *Entrance requirements:* For doctorate, MSN; nurse practitioner, nurse midwife, or nurse anesthetist certification; transcripts; 3 letters of recommendation; portfolio; minimum GPA of 3.5. Additional exam requirements/recommendations for international students: required—TOEFL (minimum score 79 iBT). Electronic applications accepted. Application fee is waived when completed online. *Expenses:* Contact institution.

**Gardner-Webb University,** Graduate School, School of Nursing, Boiling Springs, NC 28017. Offers family nurse practitioner (MSN, DNP). *Accreditation:* ACEN. *Program availability:* Part-time, online learning. *Entrance requirements:* For master's, GRE or MAT, minimum undergraduate GPA of 2.7; unrestricted licensure to practice as an RN. *Expenses:* Contact institution.

**George Mason University,** College of Health and Human Services, School of Nursing, Fairfax, VA 22030. Offers adult gerontology (DNP); adult/gerontological nurse practitioner (MSN); family nurse practitioner (MSN, DNP); nurse educator (MSN); nursing (PhD); nursing administration (MSN, DNP); nursing education (Certificate); psychiatric mental health (DNP). *Accreditation:* AACN. *Program availability:* Part-time, evening/weekend, blended/hybrid learning. *Degree requirements:* For master's, comprehensive exam (for some programs), thesis in clinical classes; for doctorate, comprehensive exam (for some programs), thesis/dissertation (for some programs). *Entrance requirements:* For master's, 2 official transcripts; expanded goals statement; resume; BSN from accredited institution; minimum GPA of 3.0 in last 60 credits of undergraduate work; 2 letters of recommendation; completion of undergraduate statistics and graduate-level bivariate statistics; certification in professional CPR; for doctorate, GRE, 2 official transcripts; expanded goals statement; resume; 2 recommendation letters; nursing license; at least 1 year of work experience as an RN; interview; writing sample; evidence of graduate-level course in applied statistics; master's degree in nursing with minimum GPA of 3.5; for Certificate, 2 official transcripts; expanded goals statement; resume; master's degree from accredited institution or currently enrolled with minimum GPA of 3.0. Additional exam requirements/recommendations for international students: required—TOEFL (minimum score 570 paper-based; 88 iBT), IELTS (minimum score 6.5), PTE (minimum score 59). Electronic applications accepted. *Expenses:* Contact institution.

**Georgetown University,** Graduate School of Arts and Sciences, School of Nursing and Health Studies, Washington, DC 20057. Offers acute care nurse practitioner (MS); clinical nurse specialist (MS); family nurse practitioner (MS); health systems administration (MS); nurse anesthesia (MS); nurse-midwifery (MS); nursing (DNP); nursing education (MS). *Accreditation:* AACN; AANA/CANAEP (one or more programs are accredited); ACNM/ACME (one or more programs are accredited). *Degree requirements:* For master's, thesis optional. *Entrance requirements:* For master's, GRE General Test or MAT, bachelor's degree in nursing from ACEN-accredited school, minimum undergraduate GPA of 3.0. Additional exam requirements/recommendations for international students: required—TOEFL.

**The George Washington University,** School of Nursing, Washington, DC 20052. Offers adult nurse practitioner (MSN, DNP, Post-Master's Certificate); clinical research administration (MSN); family nurse practitioner (MSN, Post-Master's Certificate); health care quality (MSN, Post-Master's Certificate); nursing leadership and management (MSN); nursing practice (DNP); palliative care nurse practitioner (Post-Master's Certificate). *Accreditation:* AACN.

**Georgia College & State University,** The Graduate School, College of Health Sciences, Graduate Nursing Program, Milledgeville, GA 31061. Offers nursing (MSN, Post-MSN Certificate); nursing practice (DNP). *Accreditation:* AACN; ACEN. *Program availability:* Part-time, evening/weekend, online only, blended/hybrid learning. *Students:* 12 full-time (all women), 159 part-time (143 women); includes 57 minority (44 Black or African American, non-Hispanic/Latino; 3 Asian, non-Hispanic/Latino; 6 Hispanic/Latino; 4 Two or more races, non-Hispanic/Latino). Average age 39. 31 applicants, 100% accepted, 29 enrolled. In 2019, 34 master's, 8 doctorates, 10 other advanced degrees awarded. *Degree requirements:* For master's, comprehensive exam, minimum GPA of 3.0, electronic portfolio, completion of requirements within a period of 7 years; for doctorate, capstone project, complete all required courses within a period of 7 years; for Post-MSN Certificate, practicum. *Entrance requirements:* For master's, GRE (taken within last 5 years), bachelor's degree in nursing, RN license, 1 year of clinical experience, minimum GPA of 2.75 on last 60 undergraduate hours required in nursing major, statistics course, interview, 3 letters of reference, transcript, resume; for doctorate, master's degree in nursing or anesthesia, minimum graduate GPA of 3.2 in MSN program, unencumbered RN licensure, 500 faculty-supervised clinical hours in master's program, interview, computer access, resume; for Post-MSN Certificate, RN licensure, MSN with minimum GPA of 3.2, transcript, 2 letters of reference, resume, statement of professional goals. *Application deadline:* For fall admission, 1/1 priority date for domestic students. Applications are processed on a rolling basis. Application fee: $40. Electronic applications accepted. *Expenses:* $373 per credit hour. $343 per semester for fees. *Financial support:* In 2019–20, 7 students received support. Unspecified assistantships available. Financial award application deadline: 7/1; financial award applicants required to submit FAFSA. *Unit head:* Dr. Deborah MacMillan, School of Nursing Programs Director, 478-445-5122, E-mail: debby.macmillan@gcsu.edu. *Application contact:* Dr. Deborah MacMillan, School of Nursing Programs Director, 478-445-5122, E-mail: debby.macmillan@gcsu.edu.

**Georgia Southern University,** Jack N. Averitt College of Graduate Studies, Waters College of Health Professions, School of Nursing, Program in Nursing Science, Statesboro, GA 30460. Offers DNP. *Program availability:* Part-time, online learning. *Students:* 136 part-time (117 women); includes 55 minority (41 Black or African American, non-Hispanic/Latino; 4 Asian, non-Hispanic/Latino; 7 Hispanic/Latino; 3 Two or more races, non-Hispanic/Latino), 1 international. Average age 36. 146 applicants, 53% accepted, 37 enrolled. *Degree requirements:* For doctorate, comprehensive exam (for some programs), thesis/dissertation (for some programs). *Entrance requirements:* Additional exam requirements/recommendations for international students: required—TOEFL (minimum score 550 paper-based; 80 iBT), IELTS (minimum score 6). *Application deadline:* For fall admission, 6/1 priority date for domestic and international students; for spring admission, 10/1 priority date for domestic students, 10/1 for international students. Applications are processed on a rolling basis. Application fee: $50. Electronic applications accepted. *Expenses: Tuition, area resident:* Full-time $4986; part-time $277 per credit hour. Tuition, nonresident: full-time $19,890; part-time $1105 per credit hour. *International tuition:* $19,890 full-time. *Required fees:* $2114; $1057 per semester. $1057 per semester. Tuition and fees vary according to course load, campus/location and program. *Financial support:* In 2019–20, 54 students received support. Career-related internships or fieldwork, Federal Work-Study, scholarships/grants, traineeships, and tuition waivers available. Support available to part-time students. Financial award application deadline: 4/15; financial award applicants required to submit FAFSA. *Unit head:* Dr. Deborah Allen, Chair, 912-478-5770, Fax: 912-478-0536, E-mail: debbieallen@georgiasouthern.edu. *Application contact:* Dr. Deborah Allen, Chair, 912-478-5770, Fax: 912-478-0536, E-mail: debbieallen@georgiasouthern.edu.

**Georgia Southwestern State University,** College of Nursing and Health Sciences, Americus, GA 31709-4693. Offers family nurse practitioner (MSN); health informatics (Postbaccalaureate Certificate); nurse educator (Post Master's Certificate); nursing educator (MSN); nursing informatics (MSN); nursing leadership (MSN). *Program availability:* Part-time, online only, all theory courses are offered online. *Faculty:* 9 full-time (all women), 5 part-time/adjunct (all women). *Students:* 18 full-time (14 women), 104 part-time (91 women); includes 45 minority (31 Black or African American, non-Hispanic/Latino; 1 American Indian or Alaska Native, non-Hispanic/Latino; 4 Asian, non-Hispanic/Latino; 3 Hispanic/Latino; 6 Two or more races, non-Hispanic/Latino). Average age 36. 96 applicants, 45% accepted, 24 enrolled. In 2019, 53 master's awarded. *Degree requirements:* For master's, thesis (for some programs), minimum cumulative GPA of 3.0; maximum of 6 credit hours with C grade and no D grades; degree completed within 7 calendar years from initial enrollment date in graduate courses; for other advanced degree, minimum cumulative GPA of 3.0; maximum of 6 credit hours with C grade and no D grades; degree completed within 7 calendar years from initial enrollment date in graduate courses. *Entrance requirements:* For master's, baccalaureate degree in nursing from regionally-accredited institution and nationally-accredited nursing program with minimum GPA of 3.0; three completed recommendation forms from professional peer or clinical supervisor; current unencumbered RN license in state where clinical course requirements will be met; proof of immunizations; for other advanced degree, Baccalaureate or masters degree (depending upon certificate) in nursing; Minimum GPA of 3.0; 3 completed recommendation forms; current unencumbered RN license in state where clinical course requirements will be met. Application fee: $25. Electronic applications accepted. *Expenses:* $385.00 per credit hour tuition, plus fees, which vary according to enrolled credit hours. *Financial support:* Application deadline: 6/1; applicants required to submit FAFSA. *Unit head:* Dr. Sandra Daniel, Dean, 229-931-2275. *Application contact:* Office of Graduate Admissions, 800-338-0082, Fax: 229-931-2983, E-mail: graduateadmissions@gsw.edu.
Website: https://www.gsw.edu/academics/schools-and-departments/college-of-nursing-and-health-sciences/school-of-nursing/nursing-programs/graduate

**Georgia State University,** Byrdine F. Lewis School of Nursing, Atlanta, GA 30303. Offers adult health clinical nurse specialist/nurse practitioner (MS, Certificate); child health clinical nurse specialist/pediatric nurse practitioner (MS, Certificate); family nurse practitioner (MS, Certificate); family psychiatric mental health nurse practitioner (MS, Certificate); nursing (PhD); nursing leadership in healthcare innovations (MS), including nursing administration, nursing informatics; nutrition (MS); occupational therapy (MOT); perinatal clinical nurse specialist/women's health nurse practitioner (MS, Certificate); physical therapy (DPT); respiratory therapy (MS). *Accreditation:* AACN. *Program availability:* Part-time, blended/hybrid learning. *Faculty:* 57 full-time (40 women), 5 part-time/adjunct (4 women). *Students:* 388 full-time (290 women), 155 part-time (135 women); includes 217 minority (130 Black or African American, non-Hispanic/Latino; 47 Asian, non-Hispanic/Latino; 26 Hispanic/Latino; 14 Two or more races, non-Hispanic/Latino), 45 international. Average age 32. 480 applicants, 50% accepted, 164 enrolled. In 2019, 158 master's, 64 doctorates, 20 other advanced degrees awarded. *Degree requirements:* For doctorate, comprehensive exam, thesis/dissertation. *Entrance requirements:* For doctorate, GRE. Additional exam requirements/recommendations for international students: required—TOEFL. *Application deadline:* For fall admission, 2/1 priority date for domestic and international students; for spring admission, 9/15 for domestic and international students. Applications are processed on a rolling basis. Application fee: $50. Electronic applications accepted. *Expenses:* Contact institution. *Financial support:* In 2019–20, research assistantships with tuition reimbursements (averaging $1,666 per year), teaching assistantships with tuition reimbursements (averaging $1,920 per year) were awarded; scholarships/grants, tuition waivers (full and partial), and unspecified assistantships also available. Support available to part-time students. Financial award application deadline: 8/1; financial award applicants required to submit FAFSA. *Unit head:* Huanbiao Mo, Dean of Nursing. *Application contact:* Huanbiao Mo, Dean of Nursing.
Website: http://nursing.gsu.edu/

**Goldfarb School of Nursing at Barnes-Jewish College,** Graduate Programs, St. Louis, MO 63110. Offers adult-gerontology (MSN), including primary care nurse practitioner; adult-gerontology (MSN), including acute care nurse practitioner; health systems and population health leadership (MSN); nurse anesthesia (MSN). *Accreditation:* AACN; AANA/CANAEP. *Program availability:* Part-time, online learning. *Degree requirements:* For master's, thesis or alternative. *Entrance requirements:* For master's, 2 references, personal statement, curriculum vitae or resume. Additional exam requirements/recommendations for international students: required—TOEFL (minimum score 575 paper-based; 85 iBT).

**Gonzaga University,** School of Nursing and Human Physiology, Spokane, WA 99258. Offers MSN, DNP, DNP-A. *Accreditation:* AACN; AANA/CANAEP. *Program availability:* Part-time, evening/weekend, 100% online, immersion weekends. *Entrance requirements:* For master's, MAT or GRE within the last 5 years if GPA is lower than 3.0, official transcripts, two letters of recommendation, statement of purpose, current resume/curriculum vitae, current registered nurse license. Additional exam requirements/recommendations for international students: required—TOEFL (minimum score 88 iBT) or IELTS (minimum score 6.5). Electronic applications accepted. *Expenses:* Contact institution.

**Goshen College,** Graduate Program in Nursing, Goshen, IN 46526. Offers family nurse practitioner (MSN). *Accreditation:* AACN. *Program availability:* Part-time, evening/weekend. *Faculty:* 7 full-time (5 women). *Students:* 56 full-time (51 women), 5 part-time (all women); includes 11 minority (3 Black or African American, non-Hispanic/Latino; 2 Asian, non-Hispanic/Latino; 5 Hispanic/Latino; 1 Two or more races, non-Hispanic/Latino). Average age 35. 22 applicants, 100% accepted, 22 enrolled. In 2019, 21 master's awarded. *Degree requirements:* For master's, comprehensive exam (for some programs). *Entrance requirements:* For master's, minimum GPA of 3.0, curriculum vitae, bachelor's degree in nursing, active RN license in Indiana or Michigan, three professional references, essay, one year of clinical experience, statistics course, interview with program director. Additional exam requirements/recommendations for international students: required—TOEFL (minimum score 600 paper-based; 100 iBT), IELTS (minimum score 6.5). *Application deadline:* For fall admission, 3/15 priority date for domestic students. Applications are processed on a rolling basis. Application fee: $25. Electronic applications accepted. *Expenses:* $650 per credit hour (master's); $780 per credit hour (doctorate). *Financial support:* In 2019–20, 7 students received support. Scholarships/grants available. *Unit head:* Ruth Stoltzfus, Director, 574-535-7973, E-mail: ruthas@goshen.edu. *Application contact:* Ruth Stoltzfus, Director, 574-535-7973, E-mail: ruthas@goshen.edu.
Website: http://www.goshen.edu/graduate/nursing/

**Governors State University,** College of Health and Human Services, Program in Nursing, University Park, IL 60484. Offers MSN. *Accreditation:* ACEN. *Program availability:* Part-time. *Faculty:* 10 full-time (all women), 12 part-time/adjunct (11 women). *Students:* 3 full-time (all women), 108 part-time (92 women); includes 72 minority (50 Black or African American, non-Hispanic/Latino; 8 Asian, non-Hispanic/Latino; 10 Hispanic/Latino; 4 Two or more races, non-Hispanic/Latino), 1 international. Average age 41. 77 applicants, 49% accepted, 24 enrolled. In 2019, 36 master's awarded. *Application deadline:* For fall admission, 4/1 for domestic students. Applications are processed on a rolling basis. Application fee: $50. Electronic applications accepted. *Expenses:* $797/credit hour; $9,564 in tuition/term; $10,862 in tuition and fees/term; $21,724/year. *Financial support:* Application deadline: 5/1; applicants required to submit FAFSA. *Unit head:* Nancy MacMullen, Chair, Department of Nursing, 708-534-5000 Ext. 4043, E-mail: nmacmullen@govst.edu. *Application contact:* Nancy MacMullen, Chair, Department of Nursing, 708-534-5000 Ext. 4043, E-mail: nmacmullen@govst.edu.

**Graceland University,** School of Nursing, Independence, MO 64050-3434. Offers adult and gerontology acute care (MSN, PMC); family nurse practitioner (MSN, PMC); nurse educator (MSN, PMC); organizational leadership (DNP). *Accreditation:* AACN. *Program availability:* Part-time, online only, 100% online. *Degree requirements:* For master's,

comprehensive exam (for some programs), thesis optional, scholarly project; for doctorate, capstone project. *Entrance requirements:* For master's, BSN from nationally-accredited program, RN license, minimum GPA of 3.0, satisfactory criminal background check, three professional reference letters, professional goals statement of 150 words or less; for doctorate, MSN from nationally-accredited program, RN license, minimum GPA of 3.0, criminal background check. Additional exam requirements/recommendations for international students: required—TOEFL (minimum score 550 paper-based; 80 iBT). Electronic applications accepted. *Expenses:* Contact institution.

**The Graduate Center, City University of New York,** Graduate Studies, Program in Nursing, New York, NY 10016-4039. Offers PhD. *Degree requirements:* For doctorate, thesis/dissertation, exams. *Entrance requirements:* For doctorate, GRE, 2 letters of recommendation, personal statement. Additional exam requirements/recommendations for international students: required—TOEFL. Electronic applications accepted.

**Grambling State University,** School of Graduate Studies and Research, College of Professional Studies, School of Nursing, Grambling, LA 71245. Offers family nurse practitioner (PMC); nursing (MSN). *Accreditation:* ACEN. *Program availability:* Part-time. *Degree requirements:* For master's, comprehensive exam (for some programs), thesis (for some programs). *Entrance requirements:* For master's, GRE, minimum GPA of 3.0 on last degree, interview, 2 years of experience as RN. Additional exam requirements/recommendations for international students: required—TOEFL (minimum score 500 paper-based; 62 iBT). Electronic applications accepted.

**Grand Canyon University,** College of Nursing and Health Care Professions, Phoenix, AZ 85017-1097. Offers acute care nurse practitioner (MSN, PMC); family nurse practitioner (MSN, PMC); health care administration (MS); health care informatics (MS, MSN); leadership in health care systems (MSN); nursing (DNP); nursing education (MSN, PMC); public health (MPH, MSN); MBA/MSN. *Accreditation:* AACN. *Program availability:* Part-time, evening/weekend, online learning. *Degree requirements:* For master's and PMC, comprehensive exam (for some programs). *Entrance requirements:* For master's, minimum cumulative and science course undergraduate GPA of 3.0. Additional exam requirements/recommendations for international students: required—TOEFL (minimum score 575 paper-based; 90 iBT), IELTS (minimum score 7).

**Grand Valley State University,** Kirkhof College of Nursing, Grand Rapids, MI 49503-3314. Offers case management (MSN); nursing practice (DNP); MSN/MBA. *Accreditation:* AACN. *Program availability:* Part-time. *Faculty:* 14 full-time (all women), 4 part-time/adjunct (3 women). *Students:* 55 full-time (47 women), 21 part-time (19 women); includes 12 minority (5 Black or African American, non-Hispanic/Latino; 4 Asian, non-Hispanic/Latino; 2 Hispanic/Latino; 1 Two or more races, non-Hispanic/Latino), 1 international. Average age 32. 33 applicants, 94% accepted, 21 enrolled. In 2019, 7 master's, 49 doctorates awarded. *Degree requirements:* For master's, thesis optional, thesis or project; for doctorate, thesis/dissertation optional, thesis or project. *Entrance requirements:* For master's, GRE, minimum upper-division GPA of 3.0, course work in statistics, Michigan RN license, writing sample, interview, criminal background check and drug screen, health records; for doctorate, minimum GPA of 3.0 in master's-level coursework, writing sample, interview, RN in Michigan, criminal background check and drug screen, health records. Additional exam requirements/recommendations for international students: required—TOEFL (minimum iBT score of 80), IELTS (6.5), or Michigan English Language Assessment Battery (77). *Application deadline:* For fall admission, 3/15 priority date for domestic students. Applications are processed on a rolling basis. Application fee: $30. Electronic applications accepted. *Expenses:* $823 per credit hour, 75-77 credit hours. *Financial support:* In 2019–20, 39 students received support, including 14 fellowships, 20 research assistantships with partial tuition reimbursements available (averaging $4,000 per year); career-related internships or fieldwork, Federal Work-Study, institutionally sponsored loans, and traineeships also available. Financial award application deadline: 2/15. *Unit head:* Dr. Cynthia McCurren, Dean, 616-331-3558, Fax: 616-331-2510, E-mail: mccurrec@gvsu.edu. *Application contact:* Dr. Katherine Moran, Graduate Program Director, 616-331-5458, Fax: 616-331-2510, E-mail: morakath@gvsu.edu.
Website: http://www.gvsu.edu/kcon/

**Grantham University,** College of Nursing and Allied Health, Lenexa, KS 66219. Offers case management (MSN); health systems management (MS); healthcare administration (MHA); nursing education (MSN); nursing informatics (MSN); nursing management and organizational leadership (MSN). *Program availability:* Part-time, evening/weekend, online only, 100% online. *Students:* 180 full-time (135 women), 61 part-time (47 women); includes 124 minority (71 Black or African American, non-Hispanic/Latino; 1 American Indian or Alaska Native, non-Hispanic/Latino; 17 Asian, non-Hispanic/Latino; 17 Hispanic/Latino; 1 Native Hawaiian or other Pacific Islander, non-Hispanic/Latino; 17 Two or more races, non-Hispanic/Latino). Average age 40. 53 applicants, 89% accepted, 37 enrolled. In 2019, 100 master's awarded. *Entrance requirements:* For master's, Graduate: A minimum score of 530 on the paper-based TOEFL, or 71 on the internet-based TOEFL, 6.5 on the IELTS, or 50 on the PTE Academic Score Report. Additional exam requirements/recommendations for international students: required—TOEFL (minimum score 530 paper-based; 71 iBT), IELTS (minimum score 6.5), PTE (minimum score 50). *Application deadline:* Applications are processed on a rolling basis. Electronic applications accepted. *Expenses:* Contact institution. *Financial support:* Scholarships/grants available. Financial award applicants required to submit FAFSA. *Unit head:* Dr. Cheryl Rules, Dean of the College of Nursing and the School of Allied Health changing to College of Health Professions, 913-309-4783, Fax: 844-897-6490, E-mail: crules@grantham.edu. *Application contact:* Adam Wright, Associate VP, Enrollment Services, 800-955-2527 Ext. 803, Fax: 877-304-4467, E-mail: admissions@grantham.edu.
Website: http://www.grantham.edu/nursing-and-allied-health/

**Gwynedd Mercy University,** Frances M. Maguire School of Nursing and Health Professions, Gwynedd Valley, PA 19437-0901. Offers clinical nurse specialist (MSN), including gerontology, oncology, pediatrics; nurse educator (MSN); nurse practitioner (MSN), including adult health, pediatric health; nursing (DNP). *Accreditation:* ACEN. *Program availability:* Part-time, blended/hybrid learning. *Faculty:* 4 full-time (all women), 1 (woman) part-time/adjunct. *Students:* 52 full-time (47 women), 58 part-time (52 women); includes 28 minority (17 Black or African American, non-Hispanic/Latino; 9 Asian, non-Hispanic/Latino; 2 Hispanic/Latino). Average age 33. 35 applicants, 43% accepted, 14 enrolled. In 2019, 26 master's awarded. *Degree requirements:* For master's, thesis optional; for doctorate, evidence-based scholarly project. *Entrance requirements:* For master's, current nursing experience, physical assessment, course work in statistics, BSN from ACEN-accredited program, 2 letters of recommendation, personal interview. *Application deadline:* For fall admission, 4/15 for domestic and international students. Applications are processed on a rolling basis. Electronic applications accepted. *Expenses:* Contact institution. *Financial support:* Scholarships/grants, traineeships, and unspecified assistantships available. Financial award application deadline: 4/15. *Unit head:* Dr. Ann Phalen, Dean, 215-646-7300 Ext. 539, Fax: 215-641-5517, E-mail: phalen.a@gmercyu.edu. *Application contact:* Mary Hermann, Associate Dean, 215-646-7300, E-mail: herman.m@gmercyu.edu.
Website: http://www.gmercyu.edu/academics/graduate-programs/nursing

**Hampton University,** School of Nursing, Hampton, VA 23668. Offers community health nursing (MS); family nurse practitioner (MS); family research (PhD); nursing administration (MS); nursing education (MS). *Accreditation:* AACN. *Program availability:* Part-time, online learning. *Students:* 3 full-time (all women), 13 part-time (12 women); includes 15 minority (all Black or African American, non-Hispanic/Latino). Average age 49. 4 applicants, 25% accepted. In 2019, 3 master's, 5 doctorates awarded. *Degree requirements:* For master's, comprehensive exam, thesis optional; for doctorate, comprehensive exam, thesis/dissertation. *Entrance requirements:* For master's, GRE General Test. *Application deadline:* For fall admission, 6/1 priority date for domestic students, 4/1 priority date for international students; for spring admission, 11/1 priority date for domestic students, 9/1 priority date for international students; for summer admission, 4/1 priority date for domestic students, 2/1 priority date for international students. Applications are processed on a rolling basis. Application fee: $35. Electronic applications accepted. *Financial support:* In 2019–20, 2 students received support. Fellowships, research assistantships, teaching assistantships, career-related internships or fieldwork, Federal Work-Study, institutionally sponsored loans, and scholarships/grants available. Support available to part-time students. Financial award application deadline: 6/30; financial award applicants required to submit FAFSA. *Unit head:* Dr. Shevellanie Lott, Dean, 757-727-5654, E-mail: shevellanie.lott@hamptonu.edu. *Application contact:* Dr. Shevellanie Lott, Dean, 757-727-5654, E-mail: shevellanie.lott@hamptonu.edu.
Website: http://nursing.hamptonu.edu

**Hardin-Simmons University,** Graduate School, Patty Hanks Shelton School of Nursing, Abilene, TX 79698-0001. Offers education (MSN); family nurse practitioner (MSN). *Accreditation:* AACN. *Program availability:* Part-time. *Degree requirements:* For master's, comprehensive exam, thesis or alternative. *Entrance requirements:* For master's, GRE, minimum undergraduate GPA of 3.0; interview; upper-level course work in statistics; CPR certification; letters of recommendation. Additional exam requirements/recommendations for international students: required—TOEFL (minimum score 550 paper-based; 79 iBT). Electronic applications accepted. *Expenses:* Contact institution.

**Hawaii Pacific University,** College of Health and Society, Program in Nursing, Honolulu, HI 96813. Offers MSN, DNP. *Accreditation:* AACN. *Program availability:* Part-time, evening/weekend, 100% online, blended/hybrid learning. *Entrance requirements:* For master's, BN with minimum GPA of 3.0, proof of valid Hawai'i RN license; for doctorate, minimum graduate GPA of 3.0, U.S. State RN license, prerequisite or transfer equivalent coursework in statistics, curriculum vitae or resume, personal interview (phone/video conference) with DNP Program Coordinator and Graduate Program Chair, MSN with national certification in field of study, 2 letters of recommendation. Additional exam requirements/recommendations for international students: recommended—TOEFL (minimum score 550 paper-based; 80 iBT), IELTS (minimum score 6), TWE (minimum score 5). Electronic applications accepted. *Expenses:* Contact institution.

**Herzing University Online,** Program in Nursing, Menomonee Falls, WI 53051. Offers nursing (MSN); nursing education (MSN); nursing management (MSN). *Accreditation:* AACN. *Program availability:* Online learning.

**Hofstra University,** Hofstra Northwell School of Nursing and Physician Assistant Studies, Programs in Nursing, Hempstead, NY 11549. Offers adult-gerontology acute care nurse practitioner (MS); family nurse practitioner (MS); psychiatric-mental health np (MS). *Students:* 68 full-time (48 women), 159 part-time (138 women); includes 103 minority (24 Black or African American, non-Hispanic/Latino; 2 American Indian or Alaska Native, non-Hispanic/Latino; 41 Asian, non-Hispanic/Latino; 35 Hispanic/Latino; 1 Two or more races, non-Hispanic/Latino). Average age 33. 389 applicants, 32% accepted, 89 enrolled. In 2019, 44 master's awarded. *Degree requirements:* For master's, comprehensive exam, minimum GPA of 3.0. *Entrance requirements:* For master's, bachelor's degree in nursing, 3 letters of recommendation, essay, resume. Additional exam requirements/recommendations for international students: required—TOEFL (minimum score 550 paper-based; 80 iBT); recommended—IELTS (minimum score 6.5). Application fee: $75. Electronic applications accepted. *Expenses: Tuition:* Full-time $25,164; part-time $1398 per credit. *Required fees:* $580; $165 per semester. Tuition and fees vary according to course load, degree level and program. *Financial support:* In 2019–20, 56 students received support, including 5 fellowships with full and partial tuition reimbursements available (averaging $10,870 per year); research assistantships with full and partial tuition reimbursements available, career-related internships or fieldwork, Federal Work-Study, institutionally sponsored loans, scholarships/grants, traineeships, tuition waivers (full and partial), unspecified assistantships, and scholarships and endowed scholarships also available. Support available to part-time students. Financial award applicants required to submit FAFSA. *Unit head:* Dr. Kathleen Gallo, Dean, 516-463-7475, Fax: 516-463-7495, E-mail: kathleen.gallo@hofstra.edu. *Application contact:* Sunil Samuel, Assistant Vice President of Admissions, 516-463-4723, Fax: 516-463-4664, E-mail: graduateadmission@hofstra.edu.

**Holy Family University,** Graduate and Professional Programs, School of Nursing and Allied Health Professions, Philadelphia, PA 19114. Offers nursing administration (MSN); nursing education (MSN). *Accreditation:* AACN. *Program availability:* Part-time, evening/weekend. *Degree requirements:* For master's, thesis or alternative, comprehensive portfolio, clinical practicum. *Entrance requirements:* For master's, BSN or RN from appropriately-accredited program, minimum GPA of 3.0, professional references, official transcripts of all college or university work, essay/personal statement, current resume, completion of one undergraduate statistics course with minimum grade of C. Additional exam requirements/recommendations for international students: required—TOEFL (minimum score 550 paper-based; 79 iBT), IELTS (minimum score 6), or PTE (minimum score 54). Electronic applications accepted.

**Holy Names University,** Graduate Division, Department of Nursing, Oakland, CA 94619-1699. Offers administration/management (MSN, PMC); care transition management (MSN); family nurse practitioner (MSN, PMC); informatics (MSN); nurse educator (PMC); MSN/MBA. *Accreditation:* AACN. *Program availability:* Part-time, evening/weekend. *Entrance requirements:* For master's, bachelor's degree in nursing or related field; California RN license or eligibility; minimum cumulative GPA of 2.8, 3.0 in nursing courses from baccalaureate program; courses in pathophysiology, statistics, and research at the undergraduate level. Additional exam requirements/recommendations for international students: required—TOEFL (minimum score 550 paper-based; 79 iBT). Electronic applications accepted. Application fee is waived when completed online.

**Houston Baptist University,** School of Nursing and Allied Health, Program in Nursing, Houston, TX 77074-3298. Offers family nurse practitioner (MSN); pediatric nurse practitioner in primary care (MSN). *Program availability:* Part-time, evening/weekend, online only, 100% online. *Degree requirements:* For master's, comprehensive exam. *Entrance requirements:* For master's, GRE General Test, BSN from NLN or CCLE program, minimum GPA of 2.5, RN license in Texas; resume. Electronic applications accepted. Application fee is waived when completed online. *Expenses:* Contact institution.

**Howard University,** College of Nursing and Allied Health Sciences, Division of Nursing, Washington, DC 20059-0002. Offers family nurse practitioner (MSN); nurse educator (MSN). *Accreditation:* AACN. *Program availability:* Part-time. *Degree requirements:* For

master's, comprehensive exam, thesis optional. *Entrance requirements:* For master's, RN license, minimum GPA of 3.0, BS in nursing.

**Hunter College of the City University of New York,** Graduate School, Hunter-Bellevue School of Nursing, New York, NY 10010. Offers MS, DNP, AC. *Accreditation:* AACN. *Program availability:* Part-time. *Degree requirements:* For master's, practicum, portfolio. *Entrance requirements:* For master's, BSN, minimum GPA of 3.0, New York RN license, course work in basic statistics, resume; for AC, MSN, minimum GPA of 3.0. Additional exam requirements/recommendations for international students: required—TOEFL.

**Husson University,** Graduate Nursing Program, Bangor, ME 04401-2999. Offers educational leadership (MSN); family and community nurse practitioner (MSN, PMC); psychiatric mental health nurse practitioner (MSN, PMC). *Accreditation:* AACN. *Program availability:* Part-time, evening/weekend. *Degree requirements:* For master's, comprehensive exam (for some programs), research project. *Entrance requirements:* For master's, proof of RN licensure. Additional exam requirements/recommendations for international students: required—TOEFL (minimum score 550 paper-based; 80 iBT), IELTS (minimum score 6.5). Electronic applications accepted. *Expenses:* Contact institution.

**Idaho State University,** Graduate School, College of Nursing, Pocatello, ID 83209-8101. Offers MS, DNP, PhD. *Accreditation:* AACN. *Program availability:* Part-time. *Degree requirements:* For master's, comprehensive exam, thesis optional, practicum and/or clinical hours. *Entrance requirements:* For master's, GRE General Test, interview, 3 letters of reference, active RN license. Additional exam requirements/recommendations for international students: required—TOEFL (minimum score 600 paper-based). Electronic applications accepted.

**Illinois State University,** Graduate School, Mennonite College of Nursing, Normal, IL 61790. Offers family nurse practitioner (PMC); nursing (MSN, PhD). *Accreditation:* AACN. *Faculty:* 41 full-time (39 women), 47 part-time/adjunct (40 women). *Students:* 12 full-time (9 women), 118 part-time (102 women). Average age 37. 46 applicants, 83% accepted, 16 enrolled. In 2019, 32 master's, 11 doctorates awarded. *Degree requirements:* For master's, variable foreign language requirement, comprehensive exam; for doctorate, residency. *Entrance requirements:* For master's and doctorate, GRE. Application fee: $50. *Expenses:* Contact institution. *Financial support:* In 2019–20, 5 teaching assistantships were awarded. *Unit head:* Dr. Judy Neubrander, Dean of Mennonite College of Nursing, 309-438-2174, E-mail: jlneubr@IllinoisState.edu. *Application contact:* Dr. Noelle Selkow, Interim Director of Graduate Studies, 309-438-2583, Fax: 309-438-7912, E-mail: gradinfor@ilstu.edu.
Website: http://www.mcn.ilstu.edu/

**Immaculata University,** College of Graduate Studies, Division of Nursing, Immaculata, PA 19345. Offers nursing administration (MSN); nursing education (MSN). *Accreditation:* AACN. *Program availability:* Part-time, evening/weekend. *Entrance requirements:* For master's, MAT or GRE, BSN, minimum undergraduate GPA of 3.0. Additional exam requirements/recommendations for international students: required—TOEFL.

**Independence University,** Program in Nursing, Salt Lake City, UT 84107. Offers community health (MSN); gerontology (MSN); nursing administration (MSN); wellness promotion (MSN).

**Indiana State University,** College of Graduate and Professional Studies, College of Health and Human Services, Department of Advanced Practice Nursing, Terre Haute, IN 47809. Offers advanced practice nursing (DNP); family nurse practitioner (MS); nursing administration (MS); nursing education (MS). *Accreditation:* ACEN. *Program availability:* Part-time. *Degree requirements:* For master's, thesis or alternative. *Entrance requirements:* For master's, BSN, RN license, minimum undergraduate GPA of 3.0. Electronic applications accepted.

**Indiana University East,** School of Nursing, Richmond, IN 47374-1289. Offers MSN.

**Indiana University Kokomo,** School of Nursing, Kokomo, IN 46904. Offers family nurse practitioner (MSN); nurse administrator (MSN); nurse educator (MSN). Electronic applications accepted. *Expenses:* Contact institution.

**Indiana University of Pennsylvania,** School of Graduate Studies and Research, College of Health and Human Services, Department of Nursing and Allied Health Professions, Nursing DNP to PhD Pathway Program, Indiana, PA 15705. Offers PhD. *Program availability:* Part-time, evening/weekend. *Faculty:* 7 full-time (6 women). *Students:* 25 part-time (22 women); includes 8 minority (7 Black or African American, non-Hispanic/Latino; 1 Asian, non-Hispanic/Latino). Average age 48. 14 applicants, 93% accepted, 9 enrolled. *Degree requirements:* For doctorate, comprehensive exam, thesis/dissertation. *Entrance requirements:* For doctorate, Current nursing license; Current curriculum vitae; Personal interview. *Application deadline:* Applications are processed on a rolling basis. Application fee: $50. Electronic applications accepted. *Expenses:* Contact institution. *Financial support:* In 2019–20, 2 fellowships with tuition reimbursements (averaging $733 per year), 2 research assistantships with tuition reimbursements (averaging $3,750 per year) were awarded; career-related internships or fieldwork, Federal Work-Study, scholarships/grants, and unspecified assistantships also available. Financial award application deadline: 4/15; financial award applicants required to submit FAFSA. *Unit head:* Dr. Teresa Shellenbarger, Doctoral Coordinator, 724-357-2559, E-mail: TShell@iup.edu. *Application contact:* Dr. Teresa Shellenbarger, Doctoral Coordinator, 724-357-2559, E-mail: TShell@iup.edu.

**Indiana University of Pennsylvania,** School of Graduate Studies and Research, College of Health and Human Services, Department of Nursing and Allied Health Professions, PhD in Nursing Program, Indiana, PA 15705. Offers PhD. *Program availability:* Part-time. *Faculty:* 7 full-time (6 women). *Students:* 35 part-time (33 women); includes 3 minority (1 Black or African American, non-Hispanic/Latino; 1 Asian, non-Hispanic/Latino; 1 Hispanic/Latino). Average age 45. 2 applicants, 100% accepted, 2 enrolled. In 2019, 6 doctorates awarded. *Degree requirements:* For doctorate, comprehensive exam, thesis/dissertation. *Entrance requirements:* For doctorate, Current nursing license; Current curriculum vitae; Personal interview; goal statement; official transripts. Additional exam requirements/recommendations for international students: required—TOEFL (minimum score 540 paper-based; 76 iBT), IELTS (minimum score 6). *Application deadline:* Applications are processed on a rolling basis. Application fee: $50. Electronic applications accepted. *Expenses:* Contact institution. *Financial support:* In 2019–20, 1 fellowship with tuition reimbursement (averaging $734 per year), 5 research assistantships with tuition reimbursements (averaging $5,400 per year) were awarded; teaching assistantships with partial tuition reimbursements, career-related internships or fieldwork, Federal Work-Study, scholarships/grants, and unspecified assistantships also available. Financial award application deadline: 4/15; financial award applicants required to submit FAFSA. *Unit head:* Dr. Teresa Shellenbarger, Doctoral Coordinator, 724-357-2559, E-mail: TShell@iup.edu. *Application contact:* Dr. Teresa Shellenbarger, Doctoral Coordinator, 724-357-2559, E-mail: TShell@iup.edu.
Website: http://www.iup.edu/grad/nursingphd/default.aspx

**Indiana University-Purdue University Indianapolis,** School of Nursing, Doctor of Nursing Practice Program, Indianapolis, IN 46202. Offers executive leadership (DNP). *Accreditation:* AACN. *Program availability:* Blended/hybrid learning. *Entrance requirements:* For doctorate, MSN from ACEN- or CCNE-accredited program with minimum cumulative GPA of 3.3, documentation of supervised practice hours from accredited MSN program, unencumbered RN license, graduate-level course in statistics, three references indicating ability to succeed in DNP program. Additional exam requirements/recommendations for international students: required—TOEFL (minimum score 550 paper-based; 79 iBT). Electronic applications accepted. *Expenses:* Contact institution.

**Indiana University-Purdue University Indianapolis,** School of Nursing, MSN Program in Nursing, Indianapolis, IN 46202. Offers adult/gerontology acute care nurse practitioner (MSN); adult/gerontology clinical nurse specialist (MSN); adult/gerontology primary care nurse practitioner (MSN); family nurse practitioner (MSN); nursing education (MSN); nursing leadership in health systems (MSN); pediatric clinical nurse specialist (MSN); pediatric nurse practitioner (MSN). *Accreditation:* AACN. *Program availability:* Part-time, blended/hybrid learning. *Degree requirements:* For master's, thesis. *Entrance requirements:* For master's, BSN from ACEN- or CCNE-accredited program, minimum undergraduate GPA of 3.0 (preferred), professional resume or curriculum vitae, essay stating career goals and objectives, current unencumbered RN license, three references from individuals with knowledge of ability to succeed in graduate program. Additional exam requirements/recommendations for international students: required—TOEFL (minimum score 550 paper-based; 79 iBT). Electronic applications accepted. *Expenses:* Contact institution.

**Indiana University-Purdue University Indianapolis,** School of Nursing, PhD Program in Nursing Science, Indianapolis, IN 46202. Offers clinical nursing science (PhD); health systems (PhD). *Program availability:* Part-time, blended/hybrid learning. *Degree requirements:* For doctorate, comprehensive exam, thesis/dissertation. *Entrance requirements:* For doctorate, GRE General Test, BSN or MSN from ACEN- or CCNE-accredited program; minimum baccalaureate cumulative GPA of 3.0 or master's degree 3.5. Additional exam requirements/recommendations for international students: required—TOEFL (minimum score 550 paper-based; 79 iBT). Electronic applications accepted. *Expenses:* Contact institution.

**Indiana University South Bend,** Vera Z. Dwyer College of Health Sciences, School of Nursing, South Bend, IN 46615. Offers family nurse practitioner (MSN). *Accreditation:* AACN. *Program availability:* Part-time, evening/weekend. *Entrance requirements:* For master's, GRE General Test, minimum GPA of 3.0. *Expenses:* Contact institution.

**Indiana Wesleyan University,** Graduate School, School of Nursing, Marion, IN 46953-4974. Offers nursing administration (MS); nursing education (MS); primary care nursing (MS); MSN/MBA. *Accreditation:* AACN. *Program availability:* Part-time, online learning. *Degree requirements:* For master's, capstone project or thesis. *Entrance requirements:* For master's, writing sample, RN license, 1 year of related experience, graduate statistics course. Additional exam requirements/recommendations for international students: required—TOEFL. *Expenses:* Contact institution.

**Inter American University of Puerto Rico, Arecibo Campus,** Program in Nursing, Arecibo, PR 00614-4050. Offers critical care nursing (MSN); surgical nursing (MSN). *Entrance requirements:* For master's, EXADEP or GRE General Test or MAT, 2 letters of recommendation, bachelor's degree in nursing, minimum GPA of 2.5 in last 60 credits, minimum 1 year nursing experience, nursing license.

**Inter American University of Puerto Rico, Barranquitas Campus,** Program in Nursing, Barranquitas, PR 00794. Offers critical care nursing (MSN); medical surgical nursing (MSN). *Program availability:* Part-time, evening/weekend. *Degree requirements:* For master's, 2 foreign languages, comprehensive exam (for some programs), thesis optional, minimum grade of B on all courses, integration seminar. *Entrance requirements:* For master's, bachelor's degree in nursing from accredited institution, minimum GPA of 2.5, provisional or permanent nursing license for practicing nursing in Puerto Rico, official academic transcript from institution that conferred bachelor's degree, two recommendations letters. Electronic applications accepted. *Expenses:* Contact institution.

**Jacksonville State University,** Graduate Studies, Department of Nursing, Jacksonville, AL 36265-1602. Offers MSN. *Accreditation:* AACN. *Program availability:* Part-time, evening/weekend. *Degree requirements:* For master's, comprehensive exam, thesis (for some programs). *Entrance requirements:* For master's, GRE General Test or MAT. Additional exam requirements/recommendations for international students: required—TOEFL (minimum score 500 paper-based; 61 iBT). Electronic applications accepted.

**Jacksonville University,** Brooks Rehabilitation College of Healthcare Sciences, Keigwin School of Nursing, Doctor of Nursing Practice Program, Jacksonville, FL 32211. Offers DNP. *Program availability:* Part-time, blended/hybrid learning. *Students:* 22 full-time (18 women), 110 part-time (99 women); includes 45 minority (30 Black or African American, non-Hispanic/Latino; 6 Asian, non-Hispanic/Latino; 5 Hispanic/Latino; 4 Two or more races, non-Hispanic/Latino). Average age 40. 22 applicants, 59% accepted, 9 enrolled. In 2019, 15 doctorates awarded. *Degree requirements:* For doctorate, thesis/dissertation. *Entrance requirements:* For doctorate, official transcripts from all colleges/universities attended; MSN from ACEN- or CCNE-accredited program; licensure as RN or ARNP; 3 letters of reference (2 clinical, 1 professional/academic); curriculum vitae; graded essay. Additional exam requirements/recommendations for international students: required—TOEFL (minimum score 650 paper-based; 114 iBT), IELTS (minimum score 8). *Application deadline:* Applications are processed on a rolling basis. Application fee: $50. Electronic applications accepted. *Expenses:* Contact institution. *Financial support:* Federal Work-Study, institutionally sponsored loans, scholarships/grants, and health care benefits available. Support available to part-time students. Financial award application deadline: 3/15; financial award applicants required to submit FAFSA. *Unit head:* Dr. Hilary Morgan, Director, Graduate Nursing Programs/Associate Professor, 904-256-7601, E-mail: hmorgan@ju.edu. *Application contact:* Kristen Kirkendall, Associate Director of Graduate Admissions and Communications, 904-256-7169, E-mail: kgreene8@ju.edu.
Website: https://www.ju.edu/nursing/graduate/doctor-nursing-practice/

**Jacksonville University,** Brooks Rehabilitation College of Healthcare Sciences, Keigwin School of Nursing, Master of Science in Nursing Program, Jacksonville, FL 32211. Offers clinical nurse educator (MSN); family nurse practitioner (MSN); family nurse practitioner/emergency nurse practitioner (MSN); leadership in the healthcare system (MSN); nursing informatics (MSN); psychiatric nurse practitioner (MSN); MSN/MBA. *Program availability:* Part-time, 100% online, blended/hybrid learning. In 2019, 215 master's awarded. *Degree requirements:* For master's, thesis. *Entrance requirements:* For master's, GRE General Test or undergraduate GPA above 3.0, BSN from ACEN- or CCNE-accredited program; course work in statistics and physical assessment within last 5 years; Florida nursing license; CPR/BLS certification; 3 recommendations, 2 of which are professional references; statement of intent; resume. Additional exam requirements/recommendations for international students: required—TOEFL (minimum score 650 paper-based; 114 iBT), IELTS (minimum score 8). *Application deadline:* Applications are processed on a rolling basis. Application fee: $50. Electronic applications accepted. *Expenses:* Contact institution. *Financial support:* Federal Work-Study, institutionally sponsored loans, scholarships/grants, and health care benefits available. Support available to part-time students. Financial award

application deadline: 3/15; financial award applicants required to submit FAFSA. *Unit head:* Dr. Hilary Morgan, Director, Graduate Nursing Programs/Associate Professor, 904-256-7601, E-mail: hmorgan@ju.edu. *Application contact:* Kristen Kirkendall, Associate Director of Graduate Admissions and Communications, 904-256-7169, E-mail: kgreene8@ju.edu.
Website: https://www.ju.edu/nursing/graduate/master-science-nursing/index.php

**James Madison University,** The Graduate School, College of Health and Behavioral Studies, Program in Nursing, Harrisonburg, VA 22807. Offers adult/gerontology primary care nurse practitioner (MSN); clinical nurse leader (MSN); family nurse practitioner (MSN); nurse administrator (MSN); nurse midwifery (MSN); nursing (MSN, DNP); psychiatric mental health nurse practitioner (MSN). *Accreditation:* AACN. *Program availability:* Part-time, 100% online, blended/hybrid learning. *Students:* 15 full-time (14 women), 71 part-time (66 women); includes 10 minority (3 Black or African American, non-Hispanic/Latino; 6 Asian, non-Hispanic/Latino; 1 Hispanic/Latino). Average age 30. In 2019, 28 master's awarded. Application fee: $60. Electronic applications accepted. *Financial support:* In 2019–20, 2 students received support. Federal Work-Study and assistantships (averaging $7911) available. Financial award application deadline: 3/1; financial award applicants required to submit FAFSA. *Unit head:* Dr. Julie T. Sanford, Department Head, 540-568-6314, E-mail: sanforjt@jmu.edu. *Application contact:* Lynette D. Michael, Director of Graduate Admissions, 540-568-6131 Ext. 6395, Fax: 540-568-7860, E-mail: michaeld@jmu.edu.
Website: http://www.nursing.jmu.edu

**Jefferson College of Health Sciences,** Program in Nursing, Roanoke, VA 24013. Offers nursing education (MSN); nursing management (MSN). *Accreditation:* AACN. *Program availability:* Part-time. *Degree requirements:* For master's, project. *Entrance requirements:* For master's, MAT. Additional exam requirements/recommendations for international students: required—TOEFL (minimum score 550 paper-based; 80 iBT). Electronic applications accepted.

**Johns Hopkins University,** School of Nursing, Doctoral Program in Nursing, Baltimore, MD 21218. Offers adult/gerontological primary care nurse practitioner (PhD); nursing (PhD); nursing practice (DNP); DNP/PhD. *Faculty:* 39 full-time (35 women), 6 part-time/adjunct (5 women). *Students:* 9 full-time (all women), 1 (woman) part-time; includes 4 minority (2 Black or African American, non-Hispanic/Latino; 2 Asian, non-Hispanic/Latino). 7 applicants, 71% accepted, 3 enrolled. *Degree requirements:* For doctorate, comprehensive exam, thesis/dissertation, Preliminary and final oral exam. *Entrance requirements:* For doctorate, minimum GPA of 3.0, goal statement/essay, resume, letters of recommendation, official transcripts from all post-secondary institutions attended; BSN and RN license (for DNP); writing sample (for PhD), work experience for some tracks. Additional exam requirements/recommendations for international students: required—TOEFL (minimum score 600 paper-based; 100 iBT), IELTS (minimum score 7). *Application deadline:* For summer admission, 12/1 priority date for domestic and international students. Application fee: $75. Electronic applications accepted. *Expenses:* $2,053 per credit. *Financial support:* In 2019–20, 10 students received support. Federal Work-Study, scholarships/grants, and tuition waivers (partial) available. Support available to part-time students. Financial award application deadline: 3/1; financial award applicants required to submit FAFSA. *Unit head:* Dr. Jason Farley, 410-502-7563, E-mail: jfarley1@jhu.edu. *Application contact:* Cathy Wilson, Director of Admissions, 410-955-7548, Fax: 410-614-7086, E-mail: jhuson@jhu.edu.
Website: http://nursing.jhu.edu/

**Johns Hopkins University,** School of Nursing, MSN Entry into Nursing Program, Baltimore, MD 21218. Offers MSN. *Faculty:* 26 full-time (23 women). *Students:* 430 full-time (374 women), 1 part-time (0 women); includes 165 minority (45 Black or African American, non-Hispanic/Latino; 1 American Indian or Alaska Native, non-Hispanic/Latino; 58 Asian, non-Hispanic/Latino; 45 Hispanic/Latino; 16 Two or more races, non-Hispanic/Latino), 3 international. 652 applicants, 53% accepted, 168 enrolled. In 2019, 241 master's awarded. *Entrance requirements:* For master's, Bachelor's degree (in a discipline other than nursing), minimum GPA of 3.0, goal statement/essay, resume, letters of recommendation, official transcripts from all post-secondary institutions attended, prerequisite coursework. Additional exam requirements/recommendations for international students: required—TOEFL (minimum score 600 paper-based; 100 iBT), IELTS (minimum score 7). *Application deadline:* For fall admission, 11/1 priority date for domestic and international students; for spring admission, 7/1 priority date for domestic and international students. Application fee: $75. Electronic applications accepted. *Expenses:* $1,688 per credit. *Financial support:* In 2019–20, 519 students received support. Federal Work-Study, institutionally sponsored loans, and scholarships/grants available. Financial award application deadline: 3/1; financial award applicants required to submit FAFSA. *Unit head:* Dr. Joanne Flagg, 410-614-4082, E-mail: jsilber1@jhu.edu. *Application contact:* Cathy Wilson, Director of Admissions, 410-955-7548, Fax: 410-614-7086, E-mail: jhuson@jhu.edu.
Website: http://nursing.jhu.edu/academics/programs/pre-licensure/masters-entry/

**Johns Hopkins University,** School of Nursing, PhD Program in Nursing, Baltimore, MD 21218. Offers PhD. *Faculty:* 9 full-time (7 women), 1 part-time/adjunct (0 women). *Students:* 42 full-time (32 women); includes 11 minority (3 Black or African American, non-Hispanic/Latino; 2 Asian, non-Hispanic/Latino; 2 Hispanic/Latino; 4 Two or more races, non-Hispanic/Latino), 8 international. 43 applicants, 40% accepted, 11 enrolled. In 2019, 6 doctorates awarded. *Degree requirements:* For doctorate, comprehensive exam, thesis/dissertation, Preliminary and final oral exam. *Entrance requirements:* For doctorate, minimum GPA of 3.0, goal statement/essay, resume, letters of recommendation, official transcripts from all post-secondary institutions attended; BSN and RN license; writing sample. Additional exam requirements/recommendations for international students: required—TOEFL (minimum score 600 paper-based; 100 iBT), IELTS (minimum score 7). *Application deadline:* For fall admission, 12/1 priority date for domestic and international students. Application fee: $75. Electronic applications accepted. *Expenses:* $2,334 per credit. *Financial support:* In 2019–20, 34 students received support, including 42 fellowships with full and partial tuition reimbursements available (averaging $5,000 per year), 21 research assistantships with full tuition reimbursements available (averaging $8,000 per year), 14 teaching assistantships (averaging $3,000 per year); Federal Work-Study, scholarships/grants, traineeships, health care benefits, and tuition waivers (full and partial) also available. Support available to part-time students. Financial award application deadline: 3/1; financial award applicants required to submit FAFSA. *Unit head:* Dr. Jason Farley, 410-502-7563, E-mail: jfarley1@jhu.edu. *Application contact:* Cathy Wilson, Director of Admissions, 410-955-7548, E-mail: cathy.wilson@jhu.edu.
Website: http://nursing.jhu.edu/academics/programs/doctoral/phd/

**Johns Hopkins University,** School of Nursing, Post Master's Certificate Program in Nursing, Baltimore, MD 21218. Offers nursing education (Certificate); pediatric acute care nurse practitioner (Certificate); psychiatric mental health nurse practitioner (Certificate). *Program availability:* Part-time-only, online only, 100% online. *Faculty:* 4 full-time (all women), 2 part-time/adjunct (both women). *Students:* 47 part-time (44 women); includes 9 minority (3 Black or African American, non-Hispanic/Latino; 2 Asian, non-Hispanic/Latino; 3 Hispanic/Latino; 1 Two or more races, non-Hispanic/Latino). 127 applicants, 44% accepted, 47 enrolled. In 2019, 46 Certificates awarded. *Entrance requirements:* For degree, Minimum GPA of 3.0, goal statement/essay, resume, letters of recommendation, official transcripts from all post-secondary institutions attended, MSN and RN licensure, NP license for some tracks, work experience and prerequisite coursework for some tracks. Additional exam requirements/recommendations for international students: required—TOEFL (minimum score 600 paper-based; 100 iBT), IELTS (minimum score 7). *Application deadline:* For fall admission, 1/1 priority date for domestic students. Application fee: $75. Electronic applications accepted. *Expenses:* $1,688 per credit. *Financial support:* In 2019–20, 1 student received support. Federal Work-Study available. Financial award application deadline: 3/1; financial award applicants required to submit FAFSA. *Unit head:* Dr. Susan Renda, 410-955-7139, E-mail: srenda1@jhu.edu. *Application contact:* Cathy Wilson, Director of Admissions, 410-955-7548, Fax: 410-614-7086, E-mail: jhuson@jhu.edu.
Website: http://nursing.jhu.edu/

**Kean University,** Nathan Weiss Graduate College, Program in Nursing, Union, NJ 07083. Offers clinical management (MSN); community health nursing (MSN). *Accreditation:* ACEN. *Program availability:* Part-time. *Faculty:* 5 full-time (all women). *Students:* 2 full-time (both women), 28 part-time (26 women); includes 15 minority (10 Black or African American, non-Hispanic/Latino; 2 Asian, non-Hispanic/Latino; 1 Hispanic/Latino; 2 Two or more races, non-Hispanic/Latino). Average age 45. 5 applicants, 100% accepted, 2 enrolled. In 2019, 10 master's awarded. *Degree requirements:* For master's, thesis or alternative, clinical field experience. *Entrance requirements:* For master's, minimum GPA of 3.0; BS in nursing; RN license; 2 letters of recommendation; interview; official transcripts from all institutions attended. Additional exam requirements/recommendations for international students: required—TOEFL (minimum score 550 paper-based; 79 iBT), IELTS (minimum score 6.5). *Application deadline:* For fall admission, 6/30 for domestic and international students; for spring admission, 12/1 for domestic and international students. Applications are processed on a rolling basis. Application fee: $75. Electronic applications accepted. *Expenses:* Tuition, state resident: full-time $15,326; part-time $748 per credit. Tuition, nonresident: full-time $20,288; part-time $902 per credit. *Required fees:* $2149.50; $91.25 per credit. Tuition and fees vary according to course level, course load, degree level and program. *Financial support:* Scholarships/grants and unspecified assistantships available. Financial award applicants required to submit FAFSA. *Unit head:* Dr. Joan Valas, Program Coordinator, 908-737-6210, E-mail: nursing@kean.edu. *Application contact:* Pedro Lopes, Admissions Counselor, 908-737-7100, E-mail: gradadmissions@kean.edu.
Website: http://grad.kean.edu/masters-programs/nursing-clinical-management

**Keiser University,** Master of Science in Nursing Program, Fort Lauderdale, FL 33309. Offers family nurse practitioner (MSN); nursing (MSN). *Accreditation:* AANA/CANAEP.

**Kennesaw State University,** WellStar College of Health and Human Services, Program in Primary Care Nurse Practitioner, Kennesaw, GA 30144. Offers MSN. *Accreditation:* AACN. *Program availability:* Part-time, evening/weekend. *Students:* 33 full-time (31 women), 43 part-time (39 women); includes 26 minority (17 Black or African American, non-Hispanic/Latino; 5 Asian, non-Hispanic/Latino; 1 Hispanic/Latino; 1 Native Hawaiian or other Pacific Islander, non-Hispanic/Latino; 2 Two or more races, non-Hispanic/Latino). Average age 35. 123 applicants, 49% accepted, 42 enrolled. In 2019, 22 master's awarded. *Entrance requirements:* For master's, minimum GPA of 2.75, RN license. Additional exam requirements/recommendations for international students: required—TOEFL (minimum score 80 iBT), IELTS (minimum score 6.5). *Application deadline:* For fall admission, 3/1 for domestic and international students. Application fee: $60. Electronic applications accepted. *Expenses: Tuition, area resident:* Full-time $7104; part-time $296 per credit hour. Tuition, state resident: full-time $7104; part-time $296 per credit hour. Tuition, nonresident: full-time $25,584; part-time $1066 per credit hour. *International tuition:* $25,584 full-time. *Required fees:* $2006; $1706 per unit. $853 per semester. *Financial support:* Applicants required to submit FAFSA. *Application contact:* Admissions Counselor, 470-578-4377, Fax: 470-578-9172, E-mail: ksugrad@kennesaw.edu.
Website: http://wellstarcollege.kennesaw.edu/nursing/master-science-nursing/primary-nurse-practitioner.php

**Kent State University,** College of Nursing, Kent, OH 44242. Offers advanced nursing practice (DNP), including adult/gerontology acute care nurse practitioner (MSN, DNP); nursing (MSN, PhD), including adult/gerontology acute care nurse practitioner (MSN, DNP), adult/gerontology clinical nurse specialist (MSN), adult/gerontology primary care nurse practitioner (MSN), family nurse practitioner (MSN), nurse educator (MSN), nursing and healthcare management (MSN), pediatric primary care nurse practitioner (MSN), psychiatric/mental health nurse practitioner (MSN); MBA/MSN. *Accreditation:* AACN. *Program availability:* Part-time, online learning. *Faculty:* 28 full-time (26 women), 15 part-time/adjunct (13 women). *Students:* 138 full-time (123 women), 522 part-time (464 women); includes 80 minority (41 Black or African American, non-Hispanic/Latino; 16 Asian, non-Hispanic/Latino; 9 Hispanic/Latino; 1 Native Hawaiian or other Pacific Islander, non-Hispanic/Latino; 13 Two or more races, non-Hispanic/Latino), 7 international. Average age 35. 303 applicants, 68% accepted, 154 enrolled. In 2019, 156 master's, 8 doctorates awarded. *Degree requirements:* For master's, practicum for master's degrees; for doctorate, comprehensive exam, thesis/dissertation. *Entrance requirements:* For master's, GRE or GMAT, minimum GPA of 3.0, active RN license, statement of purpose, 3 letters of reference, undergraduate level statistics class (minimum C grade), baccalaureate or graduate-level nursing degree, curriculum vitae/resume; for doctorate, GRE, minimum GPA of 3.0, transcripts, 3 letters of reference, interview, active unrestricted Ohio RN license, statement of purpose, writing sample, curriculum vitae/resume, baccalaureate and master's degrees in nursing or DNP, undergraduate or graduate level statistics course with a minimum C grade. Additional exam requirements/recommendations for international students: required—TOEFL (minimum score 83 iBT), IELTS (minimum score 6.5), PTE (minimum score 55), Michigan English Language Assessment Battery (minimum score 78). *Application deadline:* For fall admission, 3/1 for domestic and international students; for spring admission, 10/1 for domestic and international students. Applications are processed on a rolling basis. Application fee: $45 ($70 for international students). Electronic applications accepted. *Financial support:* Federal Work-Study and scholarships/grants available. Financial award application deadline: 2/1. *Unit head:* Dr. Barbara Broome, Ph.D., Dean, 330-672-3777, E-mail: bbroome1@kent.edu. *Application contact:* Dr. Wendy A. Umberger, Ph.D., Associate Dean for Graduate Programs/Professor, 330-672-8813, E-mail: wlewando@kent.edu.
Website: http://www.kent.edu/nursing/

**Keuka College,** Program in Nursing, Keuka Park, NY 14478. Offers adult gerontology (MS); nursing education (MS). *Accreditation:* AACN. *Degree requirements:* For master's, exam or thesis. *Entrance requirements:* For master's, bachelor's degree from accredited institution, minimum GPA of 3.0, unencumbered NY State license, and current registration as RN (for nursing); currently full-time or part-time working RN and 2 clinical letters of recommendation (for adult gerontology nurse practitioner). Additional exam requirements/recommendations for international students: required—TOEFL (minimum score 550 paper-based). Electronic applications accepted. *Expenses:* Contact institution.

**King University,** School of Nursing, Bristol, TN 37620-2699. Offers family nurse practitioner (MSN, Post-Master's Certificate); nurse educator (MSN, Post-Master's

Certificate); nursing (DNP); nursing administration (MSN); pediatric nurse practitioner (MSN). *Program availability:* Part-time, evening/weekend, 100% online, blended/hybrid learning. *Faculty:* 13 full-time (12 women), 4 part-time/adjunct (2 women). *Students:* 115 full-time (103 women), 35 part-time (28 women); includes 12 minority (9 Black or African American, non-Hispanic/Latino; 1 Asian, non-Hispanic/Latino; 1 Hispanic/Latino; 1 Native Hawaiian or other Pacific Islander, non-Hispanic/Latino). Average age 37. 141 applicants, 96% accepted, 63 enrolled. In 2019, 89 master's, 1 doctorate, 6 other advanced degrees awarded. *Degree requirements:* For master's and post-master's certificate, comprehensive exam (for some programs), thesis optional; for doctorate, comprehensive exam (for some programs), thesis/dissertation. *Entrance requirements:* For master's, Submit evidence of graduation from an accredited baccalaureate nursing program with a minimum cumulative undergraduate GPA of 3.0 on a 4.0 scale prior to enrolling; for doctorate, bachelor's and master's degree in nursing with a GPA of 3.25 or higher from a master's degree program accredited by the Accreditation Commission for Nursing Education (ACNE) or the Commission on Collegiate Nursing Education (CCNE); for Post-Master's Certificate, FNP and PNP applicants must complete an interview with the MSN Admissions Committee. Additional exam requirements/ recommendations for international students: required—TOEFL (minimum score 84 paper-based; 84 iBT). *Application deadline:* Applications are processed on a rolling basis. Application fee: $50. Electronic applications accepted. *Expenses: Tuition:* Full-time $10,890; part-time $605 per semester hour. *Required fees:* $100 per course. *Financial support:* Unspecified assistantships available. Financial award applicants required to submit FAFSA. *Unit head:* Dr. Tracy Slemp, Dean, School of Nursing, 423-652-6335, E-mail: tjslemp@king.edu. *Application contact:* Natalie Blankenship, Territory Manager/Enrollment Counselor, 652-652-4159, Fax: 652-652-4727, E-mail: nblankenship@king.edu.

**Lamar University,** College of Graduate Studies, College of Arts and Sciences, JoAnne Gay Dishman Department of Nursing, Beaumont, TX 77710. Offers nursing administration (MSN); nursing education (MSN); MSN/MBA. *Accreditation:* ACEN. *Program availability:* Part-time, evening/weekend, online learning. *Faculty:* 33 full-time (30 women), 7 part-time/adjunct (6 women). *Students:* 1 (woman) full-time, 95 part-time (88 women); includes 42 minority (27 Black or African American, non-Hispanic/Latino; 2 American Indian or Alaska Native, non-Hispanic/Latino; 5 Asian, non-Hispanic/Latino; 8 Hispanic/Latino). Average age 40. 63 applicants, 79% accepted, 16 enrolled. In 2019, 29 master's awarded. *Degree requirements:* For master's, comprehensive exam, practicum project presentation, evidence-based project. *Entrance requirements:* For master's, GRE General Test, MAT, criminal background check, RN license, ACEN-accredited BSN, college course work in statistics in past 5 years, letters of recommendation, minimum undergraduate GPA of 3.0. Additional exam requirements/ recommendations for international students: required—TOEFL (minimum score 550 paper-based; 79 iBT), IELTS (minimum score 6.5). *Application deadline:* Applications are processed on a rolling basis. Application fee: $25 ($50 for international students). Electronic applications accepted. *Expenses:* $13,098 total program cost. *Financial support:* In 2019–20, 3 students received support, including 2 teaching assistantships (averaging $24,000 per year); scholarships/grants and traineeships also available. Financial award applicants required to submit FAFSA. *Unit head:* Dr. Cynthia Stinson, School of Nursing Chair, 409-880-8817, Fax: 409-880-8698. *Application contact:* Celeste Contreas, Director, Admissions and Academic Services, 409-880-8888, Fax: 409-880-7419, E-mail: gradmissions@lamar.edu.
Website: http://artssciences.lamar.edu/nursing

**Lander University,** Graduate Studies, Greenwood, SC 29649-2099. Offers clinical nurse leader (MSN); emergency management (MS); Montessori education (M Ed); teaching and learning (M Ed). *Accreditation:* NCATE. *Program availability:* Part-time, online learning. *Degree requirements:* For master's, comprehensive exam, thesis or alternative. *Entrance requirements:* For master's, GRE General Test. Additional exam requirements/recommendations for international students: required—TOEFL (minimum score 550 paper-based). Electronic applications accepted.

**La Roche University,** School of Graduate Studies and Adult Education, Program in Nursing, Pittsburgh, PA 15237-5898. Offers clinical nurse leader (MSN); nursing education (MSN); nursing management (MSN). *Accreditation:* ACEN. *Program availability:* Part-time, evening/weekend, online only, 100% online. *Faculty:* 3 full-time (all women), 3 part-time/adjunct (all women). *Students:* 10 full-time (all women), 27 part-time (22 women); includes 4 minority (1 Black or African American, non-Hispanic/Latino; 2 Hispanic/Latino; 1 Native Hawaiian or other Pacific Islander, non-Hispanic/Latino). Average age 36. 9 applicants, 100% accepted, 7 enrolled. In 2019, 10 master's awarded. *Degree requirements:* For master's, thesis optional, internship, practicum. *Entrance requirements:* For master's, GRE General Test, BSN, nursing license, work experience. Additional exam requirements/recommendations for international students: recommended—TOEFL (minimum score 550 paper-based). *Application deadline:* For fall admission, 8/15 priority date for domestic students, 8/15 for international students; for spring admission, 12/15 priority date for domestic students, 12/15 for international students. Applications are processed on a rolling basis. Application fee: $50. Electronic applications accepted. *Expenses:* Contact institution. *Financial support:* Application deadline: 3/31; applicants required to submit FAFSA. *Unit head:* Dr. Terri Liberto, Professor, Master of Science in Nursing Department Chair, 412-847-1813, Fax: 412-536-1175, E-mail: terri.liberto@laroche.edu. *Application contact:* Erin Pottgen, Assistant Director, Graduate Admissions, 412-847-2509, Fax: 412-536-1283, E-mail: erin.pottgen@laroche.edu.

**La Salle University,** School of Nursing and Health Sciences, Program in Nursing, Philadelphia, PA 19141-1199. Offers adult gerontology primary care nurse practitioner (MSN, Certificate); adult health and illness clinical nurse specialist (MSN); adult-gerontology clinical nurse specialist (MSN, Certificate); clinical nurse leader (MSN); family primary care nurse practitioner (MSN, Certificate); gerontology (Certificate); nurse anesthetist (MSN, Certificate); nursing (MSN, Certificate); nursing administration (MSN, Certificate); nursing education (Certificate); nursing practice (DNP); nursing service administration (MSN); public health nursing (MSN, Certificate); school nursing (Certificate); MSN/MBA; MSN/MPH. *Accreditation:* AACN. *Program availability:* Part-time, evening/weekend, 100% online. *Degree requirements:* For doctorate, minimum of 1,000 hours of post baccalaureate clinical practice supervised by preceptors. *Entrance requirements:* For master's, GRE, MAT, or GMAT (for students with BSN GPA of less than 3.2), baccalaureate degree in nursing from ACEN- or CCNE-accredited program or an MSN Bridge program; Pennsylvania RN license; 2 letters of reference; resume; statement of philosophy articulating professional values and future educational goal; 1 year of work experience as a registered nurse; for doctorate, GRE (waived for applicants with MSN cumulative GPA of 3.7 or above), MSN, master's degree, MBA or MHA from nationally-accredited program; resume or curriculum vitae; 2 letters of reference; interview; for Certificate, GRE, MAT, or GMAT (for students with BSN GPA of less than 3.2, baccalaureate degree in nursing from ACEN- or CCNE-accredited program or an MSN Bridge program), Pennsylvania RN license; 2 letters of reference; resume; statement of philosophy articulating professional values and future educational goal; 1 year of work experience as a registered nurse. Additional exam requirements/ recommendations for international students: required—TOEFL. Electronic applications accepted. Application fee is waived when completed online. *Expenses:* Contact institution.

**Laurentian University,** School of Graduate Studies and Research, Programme in Nursing, Sudbury, ON P3E 2C6, Canada. Offers M Sc N.

**Lehman College of the City University of New York,** School of Health Sciences, Human Services and Nursing, Department of Nursing, Bronx, NY 10468-1589. Offers adult health nursing (MS); nursing of older adults (MS); parent-child nursing (MS); pediatric nurse practitioner (MS). *Accreditation:* AACN. *Program availability:* Part-time, evening/weekend. *Entrance requirements:* For master's, bachelor's degree in nursing, New York RN license. *Expenses: Tuition, area resident:* Full-time $5545; part-time $470 per credit. Tuition, nonresident: part-time $855 per credit. *Required fees:* $240.

**Le Moyne College,** Department of Nursing, Syracuse, NY 13214. Offers family nurse practitioner (MS, CAS); informatics (MS, CAS); nursing administration (MS, CAS); nursing education (MS, CAS). *Accreditation:* AACN. *Program availability:* Part-time, evening/weekend. *Faculty:* 4 full-time (all women), 6 part-time/adjunct (4 women). *Students:* 18 full-time (17 women), 57 part-time (52 women); includes 7 minority (1 Black or African American, non-Hispanic/Latino; 1 Asian, non-Hispanic/Latino; 4 Hispanic/Latino; 1 Two or more races, non-Hispanic/Latino). Average age 31. 43 applicants, 84% accepted, 32 enrolled. In 2019, 33 master's, 3 other advanced degrees awarded. *Degree requirements:* For master's, 39-45 credit hours, varies by program, practicum, scholarly project; for CAS, Varies by experience or incoming degree. *Entrance requirements:* For master's, earned bachelor's degree transcripts, New York RN license, 2-3 letters of recommendation, personal statement, interview. Additional exam requirements/recommendations for international students: required—TOEFL (minimum score 79 iBT); recommended—IELTS (minimum score 6.5). *Application deadline:* For fall admission, 4/1 priority date for domestic students, 4/1 for international students; for spring admission, 11/1 priority date for domestic students, 11/1 for international students; for summer admission, 5/1 priority date for domestic students, 5/1 for international students. Applications are processed on a rolling basis. Electronic applications accepted. *Expenses:* $764-$951 per credit hour depending upon program, $75 fee per semester. *Financial support:* In 2019–20, 1 student received support. Career-related internships or fieldwork, Federal Work-Study, scholarships/grants, health care benefits, and unspecified assistantships available. Support available to part-time students. Financial award applicants required to submit FAFSA. *Unit head:* Catherine A. Brownell, Professor - Chair of Nursing, 315-445-5426, Fax: 315-445-6024, E-mail: nursing@lemoyne.edu. *Application contact:* Teresa M. Renn, Director of Graduate Admission, 315-445-5444, Fax: 315-445-6092, E-mail: GradAdmission@lemoyne.edu. Website: http://www.lemoyne.edu/nursing

**Lenoir-Rhyne University,** Graduate Programs, School of Nursing, Program in Nursing, Hickory, NC 28601. Offers nursing administration (MSN); nursing education (MSN). *Accreditation:* AACN. *Program availability:* Online learning. *Degree requirements:* For master's, comprehensive exam, thesis optional. *Entrance requirements:* For master's, official transcripts, two recommendations, essay, resume, unrestricted RN license, criminal background check. Additional exam requirements/recommendations for international students: required—TOEFL (minimum score 600 paper-based). Electronic applications accepted. *Expenses:* Contact institution.

**Lewis University,** College of Nursing and Health Sciences, Program in Nursing, Romeoville, IL 60446. Offers adult gerontology clinical nurse specialist (MSN); adult gerontology primary care nurse practitioner (MSN); family nurse practitioner (MSN); healthcare systems leadership (MSN); nursing education (MSN); school nurse (MSN). *Accreditation:* AACN. *Program availability:* Part-time, evening/weekend, 100% online, blended/hybrid learning. *Students:* 7 full-time (all women), 411 part-time (372 women); includes 113 minority (15 Black or African American, non-Hispanic/Latino; 43 Asian, non-Hispanic/Latino; 47 Hispanic/Latino; 8 Two or more races, non-Hispanic/Latino; 2 international. Average age 35. *Degree requirements:* For master's, clinical practicum. *Entrance requirements:* For master's, minimum undergraduate GPA of 3.0, degree in nursing, RN license, letter of recommendation, interview, resume or curriculum vitae. Additional exam requirements/recommendations for international students: required— TOEFL (minimum score 550 paper-based; 80 iBT), IELTS. *Application deadline:* For fall admission, 5/1 priority date for international students; for spring admission, 11/15 priority date for international students. Applications are processed on a rolling basis. Application fee: $40. Electronic applications accepted. *Financial support:* Federal Work-Study, scholarships/grants, tuition waivers (full and partial), and unspecified assistantships available. Financial award application deadline: 5/1; financial award applicants required to submit FAFSA. *Unit head:* Dr. Mary Desmond, Program Director. *Application contact:* Nancy Wiksten, Graduate Admission Counselor, 815-836-5610, E-mail: grad@lewisu.edu.

**Lewis University,** College of Nursing and Health Sciences and College of Business, Program in Nursing/Business, Romeoville, IL 60446. Offers MSN/MBA. *Program availability:* Part-time, evening/weekend. *Students:* 27 part-time (23 women); includes 7 minority (2 Black or African American, non-Hispanic/Latino; 2 Asian, non-Hispanic/Latino; 2 Hispanic/Latino; 1 Two or more races, non-Hispanic/Latino). Average age 36. *Entrance requirements:* Additional exam requirements/recommendations for international students: required—TOEFL (minimum score 550 paper-based; 80 iBT), IELTS. *Application deadline:* For fall admission, 4/2 priority date for domestic students, 5/1 priority date for international students; for spring admission, 11/15 priority date for international students. Applications are processed on a rolling basis. Electronic applications accepted. *Financial support:* Federal Work-Study and unspecified assistantships available. Financial award application deadline: 5/1; financial award applicants required to submit FAFSA. *Unit head:* Dr. Mary Desmond, Program Director. *Application contact:* Nancy Wiksten, Graduate Admission Counselor, 815-838-5610, E-mail: grad@lewisu.edu.

**Liberty University,** School of Nursing, Lynchburg, VA 24515. Offers family nurse practitioner (DNP); nurse educator (MSN); nursing administration (MSN); nursing informatics (MSN). *Accreditation:* AACN. *Program availability:* Part-time, online learning. *Students:* 279 full-time (257 women), 505 part-time (449 women); includes 170 minority (118 Black or African American, non-Hispanic/Latino; 2 American Indian or Alaska Native, non-Hispanic/Latino; 19 Asian, non-Hispanic/Latino; 25 Hispanic/Latino; 6 Two or more races, non-Hispanic/Latino), 11 international. Average age 39. 1,154 applicants, 27% accepted, 171 enrolled. In 2019, 138 master's, 26 doctorates awarded. *Entrance requirements:* For master's, minimum cumulative undergraduate GPA of 3.0; for doctorate, minimum GPA of 3.25 in most current nursing program completed. Additional exam requirements/recommendations for international students: recommended— TOEFL. *Application deadline:* Applications are processed on a rolling basis. Application fee: $50. Electronic applications accepted. *Expenses: Tuition:* Full-time $545; part-time $410 per credit hour. One-time fee: $50. *Financial support:* In 2019–20, 128 students received support. Federal Work-Study available. Financial award applicants required to submit FAFSA. *Unit head:* Dr. Shanna Akers, Dean, 434-592-3618, E-mail: lusondean@liberty.edu. *Application contact:* Jay Bridge, Director of Admissions, 800-424-9595, Fax: 800-628-7977, E-mail: gradadmissions@liberty.edu. Website: https://www.liberty.edu/nursing/

**Lincoln Memorial University,** Caylor School of Nursing, Harrogate, TN 37752-1901. Offers family nurse practitioner (MSN); nurse anesthesia (MSN); psychiatric mental health nurse practitioner (MSN). *Accreditation:* AANA/CANAEP; ACEN. *Program availability:* Part-time. *Entrance requirements:* For master's, GRE.

## Nursing—General

**Lindenwood University,** Graduate Programs, School of Health Sciences, St. Charles, MO 63301-1695. Offers human performance (MS); nursing (MS). *Program availability:* Part-time, blended/hybrid learning. *Faculty:* 8 full-time (3 women), 8 part-time/adjunct (5 women). *Students:* 22 full-time (11 women), 25 part-time (18 women); includes 5 minority (3 Black or African American, non-Hispanic/Latino; 1 Hispanic/Latino; 1 Native Hawaiian or other Pacific Islander, non-Hispanic/Latino), 6 international. Average age 30. 43 applicants, 37% accepted, 12 enrolled. In 2019, 31 master's awarded. *Degree requirements:* For master's, minimum cumulative GPA of 3.0. *Entrance requirements:* For master's, minimum cumulative GPA of 3.0. Additional exam requirements/recommendations for international students: required—TOEFL (minimum score 553 paper-based; 81 iBT); recommended—IELTS (minimum score 6.5). *Application deadline:* For fall admission, 8/9 priority date for domestic students, 6/1 priority date for international students; for spring admission, 12/20 priority date for domestic students, 11/1 priority date for international students; for summer admission, 5/15 priority date for domestic students, 3/27 priority date for international students. Applications are processed on a rolling basis. Application fee: $0 ($100 for international students). Electronic applications accepted. *Expenses: Tuition:* Full-time $8910; part-time $495 per credit. Tuition and fees vary according to course load, degree level and program. *Financial support:* In 2019–20, 25 students received support. Career-related internships or fieldwork, Federal Work-Study, institutionally sponsored loans, scholarships/grants, tuition waivers (partial), and unspecified assistantships available. Financial award application deadline: 6/30; financial award applicants required to submit FAFSA. *Unit head:* Dr. Cynthia Schroeder, Dean, School of Health Sciences, 636-949-4318, E-mail: cschroeder@lindenwood.edu. *Application contact:* Kara Schilli, Assistant Vice President, University Admissions, 636-949-4349, Fax: 636-949-4109, E-mail: adultadmissions@lindenwood.edu.
Website: https://www.lindenwood.edu/academics/academic-schools/school-of-health-sciences/

**Loma Linda University,** School of Nursing, Program in Nursing, Loma Linda, CA 92350. Offers DNP, PhD. *Accreditation:* AACN. *Program availability:* Part-time. *Entrance requirements:* Additional exam requirements/recommendations for international students: required—TOEFL. Electronic applications accepted.

**Long Island University - Brooklyn,** Harriet Rothkopf Heilbrunn School of Nursing, Brooklyn, NY 11201-8423. Offers adult nurse practitioner (MS, Advanced Certificate); family nurse practitioner (MS, Advanced Certificate); nurse educator (MS). *Accreditation:* AACN. *Program availability:* Part-time, evening/weekend, blended/hybrid learning. *Entrance requirements:* Additional exam requirements/recommendations for international students: required—TOEFL or IELTS. Electronic applications accepted.

**Louisiana College,** Graduate Programs, Pineville, LA 71359-0001. Offers clinical nurse leadership (MSN); educational leadership (M Ed); social work (MSW); teaching (MAT).

**Louisiana State University Health Sciences Center,** School of Nursing, New Orleans, LA 70112. Offers adult gerontology acute care nurse practitioner (DNP, Post-Master's Certificate); adult gerontology clinical nurse specialist (DNP, Post-Master's Certificate); adult gerontology primary care nurse practitioner (DNP, Post-Master's Certificate); clinical nurse leader (MSN); executive nurse leader (DNP, Post-Master's Certificate); neonatal nurse practitioner (DNP, Post-Master's Certificate); nurse anesthesia (DNP, Post-Master's Certificate); nurse educator (MSN); nursing (DNS); primary care family nurse practitioner (DNP, Post-Master's Certificate); public/community health nursing (DNP, Post-Master's Certificate). *Accreditation:* AACN; AANA/CANAEP (one or more programs are accredited). *Program availability:* Part-time. *Faculty:* 25 full-time (21 women), 25 part-time/adjunct (13 women). *Students:* 182 full-time (127 women), 70 part-time (59 women); includes 82 minority (52 Black or African American, non-Hispanic/Latino; 2 American Indian or Alaska Native, non-Hispanic/Latino; 14 Asian, non-Hispanic/Latino; 14 Hispanic/Latino), 1 international. Average age 34. 34 applicants, 62% accepted, 21 enrolled. In 2019, 72 doctorates awarded. *Degree requirements:* For master's, thesis optional; for doctorate, thesis/dissertation. *Entrance requirements:* For master's, GRE, minimum GPA of 3.0; for doctorate, GRE, minimum GPA of 3.0 (for DNP), 3.5 (for DNS). Additional exam requirements/recommendations for international students: required—TOEFL (minimum score 550 paper-based; 79 iBT). *Application deadline:* For fall admission, 6/1 priority date for domestic and international students; for spring admission, 10/1 priority date for domestic and international students; for summer admission, 3/1 priority date for domestic and international students. Applications are processed on a rolling basis. Application fee: $100. Electronic applications accepted. *Expenses:* MSN and DNS: $13,354.50, $24,982.25 non-resident, $586 per hour (fall and spring), $467 per hour (summer), $1,102 per hour non-resident (fall and spring), $858 per hour non-resident (summer); DNP (Except Nurse Anethesia): $21,907.50, $38,262.23 non-resident, $973 per hour (fall and spring), $733 per hour (summer), $1,700 per hour non-resident (fall and spring), $1,278 per hour non-resident (summer); Nurse Anesthesia DNP: $26,407.50, $42,762.23 non-resident, $1,173 per hour (fall and spring), $883 per hour (summer), $1,900 per hour non-resident (fall and spring), $1,428 per hour non-resident (summer). *Financial support:* In 2019–20, 20 students received support. Institutionally sponsored loans, scholarships/grants, unspecified assistantships, and DNS Scholars Program available. Financial award application deadline: 4/15; financial award applicants required to submit FAFSA. *Unit head:* Dr. Demetrius James Porche, Dean, 504-568-4106, Fax: 504-599-0573, E-mail: dporch@lsuhsc.edu. *Application contact:* Tracie Gravolet, Director, Office of Student Affairs, 504-568-4114, Fax: 504-568-5711, E-mail: tgravo@lsuhsc.edu.
Website: http://nursing.lsuhsc.edu/

**Loyola University Chicago,** Graduate School, Marcella Niehoff School of Nursing, Maywood, IL 60153. Offers adult clinical nurse specialist (MSN, Certificate); adult nurse practitioner (Certificate); dietetics (MS); family nurse practitioner (Certificate); family, adult, and women's health nurse practitioner (MSN); health systems leadership (MSN); healthcare quality using education in safety and technology (DNP); infection prevention (MSN, DNP); nursing science (PhD); women's health clinical nurse specialist (Certificate). *Accreditation:* AACN. *Program availability:* Part-time, blended/hybrid learning. *Faculty:* 36 full-time (32 women), 18 part-time/adjunct (16 women). *Students:* 182 full-time (168 women), 198 part-time (175 women); includes 95 minority (26 Black or African American, non-Hispanic/Latino; 29 Asian, non-Hispanic/Latino; 37 Hispanic/Latino; 3 Two or more races, non-Hispanic/Latino), 7 international. Average age 35. 148 applicants, 59% accepted, 54 enrolled. In 2019, 84 master's, 16 doctorates, 27 other advanced degrees awarded. *Degree requirements:* For master's, comprehensive exam; for doctorate, thesis/dissertation, qualifying examination (for PhD); project (for DNP). *Entrance requirements:* For master's, BSN, minimum nursing GPA of 3.0, Illinois RN license, 3 letters of recommendation, 1000 hours of experience in area of specialty prior to starting clinical rotations, personal statement; for doctorate, BSN or MSN, minimum GPA of 3.0, professional nursing license, 3 letters of recommendation, personal statement. Additional exam requirements/recommendations for international students: required—TOEFL (minimum score 550 paper-based; 79 iBT), IELTS (minimum score 6), PTE (minimum score 53). *Application deadline:* For fall admission, 7/1 priority date for domestic and international students; for spring admission, 12/1 priority date for domestic and international students; for summer admission, 4/1 priority date for domestic and international students. Applications are processed on a rolling basis. Electronic applications accepted. Application fee is waived when completed online. *Expenses:* Contact institution. *Financial support:* In 2019–20, 53 students received support, including 3 research assistantships with full tuition reimbursements available (averaging $18,000 per year), 1 teaching assistantship with full tuition reimbursement available (averaging $18,000 per year); scholarships/grants, unspecified assistantships, and Nurse Faculty Loan Program also available. Financial award application deadline: 5/1; financial award applicants required to submit FAFSA. *Unit head:* Dr. Lorna Finnegan, Dean and Professor, 708-216-5448, Fax: 708-216-9555, E-mail: lornaf@luc.edu. *Application contact:* Glenda Runnels, Enrollment Advisor, 708-216-3751, Fax: 708-216-9555, E-mail: grunnels@luc.edu.
Website: http://www.luc.edu/nursing/

**Loyola University New Orleans,** College of Nursing and Health, School of Nursing, New Orleans, LA 70118. Offers family nurse practitioner (DNP); nursing (MSN). *Accreditation:* AACN; ACEN. *Program availability:* Part-time, online only, 100% online. *Faculty:* 15 full-time (13 women), 5 part-time/adjunct (4 women). *Students:* 78 full-time (74 women), 222 part-time (198 women); includes 86 minority (62 Black or African American, non-Hispanic/Latino; 3 American Indian or Alaska Native, non-Hispanic/Latino; 4 Asian, non-Hispanic/Latino; 15 Hispanic/Latino; 2 Native Hawaiian or other Pacific Islander, non-Hispanic/Latino). Average age 39. 209 applicants, 70% accepted, 60 enrolled. In 2019, 89 master's, 19 doctorates awarded. *Degree requirements:* For master's, Practicum 180-720 hours depending on track; for doctorate, DNP Scholarly Project with 1000+ graduate practicum hours. *Entrance requirements:* Additional exam requirements/recommendations for international students: recommended—TOEFL (minimum score 550 paper-based; 79 iBT). *Application deadline:* For fall admission, 7/15 priority date for domestic students; for spring admission, 11/15 priority date for domestic students; for summer admission, 4/15 priority date for domestic students. Applications are processed on a rolling basis. Electronic applications accepted. *Expenses:* MSN FNP (Most students) - $818/cr hr tution * 48 cr hrs + 4 * $850 practicum fee + $275/sem technology fee * 6 semesters (minimum) + $300 graduation fee = $44,614. MSN HSAL (36 cr & 1 practicum $500) $31,598. MSN NE (39 and 1 practicum $500) $34,052. BSN to DNP (78 credits, 7 practicum, 4 - $850, 3 - $500) $71,179. MSN to DNP (39 credits & 3 practicum $500) $35,052. *Financial support:* Traineeships and Incumbent Workers Training Program grants available. Financial award application deadline: 5/1; financial award applicants required to submit FAFSA. *Unit head:* Dr. Laurie Anne Ferguson, Dean and Director, 504-865-2880, Fax: 504-865-3254, E-mail: nursing@loyno.edu. *Application contact:* Jennifer Brackett, SON Office Manager & Admissions Coordinator, 504-865-2823, Fax: 504-865-3254, E-mail: edwadswo@loyno.edu.
Website: http://gps.loyno.edu/nursing

**Madonna University,** Program in Nursing, Livonia, MI 48150-1173. Offers adult health: chronic health conditions (MSN); adult nurse practitioner (MSN); nursing administration (MSN); MSN/MSBA. *Accreditation:* AACN. *Program availability:* Part-time. *Degree requirements:* For master's, thesis or alternative. *Entrance requirements:* For master's, GRE General Test, Michigan nursing license. Electronic applications accepted. *Expenses: Tuition:* Full-time $15,930; part-time $885 per credit hour. Tuition and fees vary according to degree level and program.

**Malone University,** Graduate Program in Nursing, Canton, OH 44709. Offers family nurse practitioner (MSN). *Accreditation:* AACN. *Program availability:* Part-time, evening/weekend. *Faculty:* 10 full-time (all women), 14 part-time/adjunct (13 women). *Students:* 30 part-time (24 women). Average age 30. In 2019, 26 master's awarded. *Degree requirements:* For master's, thesis. *Entrance requirements:* For master's, minimum GPA of 3.0 from BSN program, interview, Ohio RN license. Additional exam requirements/recommendations for international students: required—This program is not open to international students, because of course offerings and visa course requirements. *Application deadline:* Applications are processed on a rolling basis. *Financial support:* Unspecified assistantships available. *Unit head:* Dr. Sheri Hartman, Director, 330-471-8330, Fax: 330-471-8607, E-mail: shartman@malone.edu. *Application contact:* Dr. Sheri Hartman, Director, 330-471-8330, Fax: 330-471-8607, E-mail: shartman@malone.edu.
Website: http://www.malone.edu/admissions/graduate/nursing/

**Mansfield University of Pennsylvania,** Graduate Studies, Program in Nursing, Mansfield, PA 16933. Offers MSN. *Accreditation:* ACEN. *Program availability:* Part-time, evening/weekend, online learning. *Degree requirements:* For master's, comprehensive exam, thesis optional. *Entrance requirements:* For master's, minimum GPA of 3.0. Additional exam requirements/recommendations for international students: required—TOEFL (minimum score 550 paper-based). Electronic applications accepted.

**Marian University,** Leighton School of Nursing, Indianapolis, IN 46222-1997. Offers family nurse practitioner (DNP); nurse anesthesia (DNP); nursing education (MSN). *Accreditation:* AANA/CANAEP. *Program availability:* Part-time. *Degree requirements:* For master's, 38 credits, designed to be completed in 2 years; 225-hour practicum including a culminating project; for doctorate, 70 credit hours (for family nurse practitioner track); 85 credits (for nurse anesthesia track); minimum of 1000 hours of supervised practice. *Entrance requirements:* For master's, degree in nursing from NLNAC- or CCNE-accredited program; current, valid RN license in State of Indiana; minimum undergraduate GPA of 3.0; 3 recommendations; interview with admissions committee; current resume; 500-word essay describing career goals; for doctorate, BSN from NSNAC- or CCNE-accredited program; minimum undergraduate GPA of 3.0; cureent, valid RN license; current resume or curriculum vitae; 500-word essay addressing career goals; 3 letters of recommendation; interview with Admissions Committee. Additional exam requirements/recommendations for international students: required—TOEFL (minimum score 550 paper-based; 79 iBT). Electronic applications accepted. Application fee is waived when completed online. *Expenses:* Contact institution.

**Marian University,** School of Nursing and Health Professions, Fond du Lac, WI 54935-4699. Offers adult nurse practitioner (MSN); nurse educator (MSN); thanatology (MS). *Accreditation:* AACN. *Program availability:* Part-time, evening/weekend. *Degree requirements:* For master's, thesis, 675 clinical practicum hours. *Entrance requirements:* For master's, 3 letters of professional recommendation; undergraduate work in nursing research, statistics, health assessment. Additional exam requirements/recommendations for international students: required—TOEFL (minimum score 525 paper-based; 70 iBT). Electronic applications accepted. *Expenses:* Contact institution.

**Marquette University,** Graduate School, College of Nursing, Milwaukee, WI 53201-1881. Offers acute care nurse practitioner (Certificate); adult clinical nurse specialist (Certificate); adult nurse practitioner (Certificate); advanced practice nursing (MSN, DNP), including adult-older adult acute care (DNP), adults (MSN), adults-older adults (DNP), clinical nurse leader (MSN), health care systems leadership (DNP), nurse-midwifery (MSN), older adults (MSN), pediatrics-acute care, pediatrics-primary care, primary care (DNP), systems leadership and healthcare quality (MSN); family nurse practitioner (Certificate); nurse-midwifery (Certificate); nursing (PhD); pediatric acute care (Certificate); pediatric primary care (Certificate); systems leadership and healthcare quality (Certificate). *Accreditation:* AACN; AANA/CANAEP; ACNM/ACME. Terminal master's awarded for partial completion of doctoral program. *Degree requirements:* For master's, comprehensive exam, thesis or alternative. *Entrance requirements:* For master's, GRE General Test, BSN, Wisconsin RN license, official transcripts from all current and previous colleges/universities except Marquette, three completed recommendation forms, resume, written statement of professional goals; for doctorate,

GRE General Test, official transcripts from all current and previous colleges/universities except Marquette, three letters of recommendation, resume, written statement of professional goals, sample of scholarly writing. Additional exam requirements/recommendations for international students: required—TOEFL (minimum score 530 paper-based). Electronic applications accepted.

**Marshall University,** Academic Affairs Division, College of Health Professions, Department of Nursing, Huntington, WV 25755. Offers MSN, Certificate. *Entrance requirements:* For master's, GRE General Test.

**Mary Baldwin University,** Graduate Studies, Program in Nursing, Staunton, VA 24401-3610. Offers patient safety and healthcare quality (MSN); MSN/MBA; MSN/MHA.

**Marymount University,** Malek School of Health Professions, Program in Nursing, Arlington, VA 22207-4299. Offers family nurse practitioner (MSN, DNP, Certificate). *Accreditation:* AACN. *Program availability:* Part-time, evening/weekend. *Faculty:* 3 full-time (all women), 2 part-time/adjunct (1 woman). *Students:* 14 full-time (13 women), 38 part-time (35 women); includes 15 minority (6 Black or African American, non-Hispanic/Latino; 5 Asian, non-Hispanic/Latino; 3 Hispanic/Latino; 1 Two or more races, non-Hispanic/Latino), 2 international. Average age 36. 30 applicants, 83% accepted, 16 enrolled. In 2019, 21 master's, 5 doctorates, 1 other advanced degree awarded. *Degree requirements:* For master's and Certificate, comprehensive exam, clinical practicum; for doctorate, thesis/dissertation, research presentation/residency. *Entrance requirements:* For master's, 2 letters of recommendation, interview, resume, current RN license, personal statement, minimum 3.0 GPA; for doctorate, 2 letters of recommendation, interview, resume, RN license, personal statement, APN licensure if applicable; for Certificate, interview, master's degree in nursing with a minimum of 3.3 GPA, current RN licensure, 2 letters of recommendation, personal statement, APN licnesure if applicable. Additional exam requirements/recommendations for international students: required—TOEFL (minimum score 600 paper-based; 96 iBT), IELTS (minimum score 6.5), PTE (minimum score 58). *Application deadline:* For fall admission, 3/1 priority date for domestic and international students; for spring admission, 11/1 priority date for domestic and international students. Application fee: $40. Electronic applications accepted. *Expenses: Tuition:* Part-time $1050 per credit. *Required fees:* $22 per credit. One-time fee: $270 part-time. Tuition and fees vary according to program. *Financial support:* In 2019–20, 11 students received support. Research assistantships, teaching assistantships, career-related internships or fieldwork, scholarships/grants, and unspecified assistantships available. Support available to part-time students. Financial award application deadline: 3/1; financial award applicants required to submit FAFSA. *Unit head:* Dr. Maureen Moriarty, Program Director, 703-284-1590, E-mail: maureen.moriarty@marymount.edu. *Application contact:* Fiona McDonnell, Administrative Assistant, 703-284-5901, E-mail: gadmissi@marymount.edu.
Website: https://www.marymount.edu/Academics/Malek-School-of-Health-Professions/Graduate-Programs

**Maryville University of Saint Louis,** Myrtle E. and Earl E. Walker College of Health Professions, The Catherine McAuley School of Nursing, St. Louis, MO 63141-7299. Offers acute care nurse practitioner (MSN); adult gerontology nurse practitioner (MSN); advanced practice nursing (DNP); family nurse practitioner (MSN); pediatric nurse practitioner (MSN). *Accreditation:* AACN. *Program availability:* 100% online, blended/hybrid learning. *Faculty:* 14 full-time (all women), 131 part-time/adjunct (114 women). *Students:* 103 full-time (91 women), 3,493 part-time (3,050 women); includes 1,039 minority (530 Black or African American, non-Hispanic/Latino; 41 American Indian or Alaska Native, non-Hispanic/Latino; 157 Asian, non-Hispanic/Latino; 221 Hispanic/Latino; 90 Two or more races, non-Hispanic/Latino), 9 international. Average age 37. In 2019, 1,012 master's, 54 doctorates awarded. *Degree requirements:* For master's, practicum. *Entrance requirements:* For master's, BSN, current licensure, minimum GPA of 3.0, 3 letters of recommendation, curriculum vitae. Additional exam requirements/recommendations for international students: required—TOEFL (minimum score 550 paper-based). *Application deadline:* Applications are processed on a rolling basis. Electronic applications accepted. *Expenses:* Contact institution. *Financial support:* Federal Work-Study and campus employment available. Support available to part-time students. Financial award application deadline: 4/1; financial award applicants required to submit FAFSA. *Unit head:* Karla Larson, Assistant Dean Nursing, 314-529-6856, Fax: 314-529-9139, E-mail: klarson@maryville.edu. *Application contact:* Jeannie DeLuca, Director of Admissions and Advising, 314-929-9355, Fax: 314-529-9927, E-mail: jdeluca@maryville.edu.
Website: http://www.maryville.edu/hp/nursing/

**McGill University,** Faculty of Graduate and Postdoctoral Studies, Faculty of Medicine, Ingram School of Nursing, Montréal, QC H3A 2T5, Canada. Offers nurse practitioner (Graduate Diploma); nursing (M Sc A, PhD).

**McKendree University,** Graduate Programs, Master of Science in Nursing Program, Lebanon, IL 62254-1299. Offers nursing education (MSN); nursing management/administration (MSN). *Accreditation:* AACN. *Program availability:* Part-time, evening/weekend, online learning. *Degree requirements:* For master's, research project or thesis. *Entrance requirements:* For master's, resume, references, valid Professional Registered Nurse license. Additional exam requirements/recommendations for international students: required—TOEFL. Electronic applications accepted.

**McMaster University,** Faculty of Health Sciences and School of Graduate Studies, Program in Nursing (course-based), Hamilton, ON L8S 4M2, Canada. Offers M Sc. *Degree requirements:* For master's, scholarly paper. *Entrance requirements:* For master's, 4 year honors BSCN, minimum B+ average in last 60 units. Additional exam requirements/recommendations for international students: required—TOEFL (minimum score 580 paper-based; 92 iBT).

**McMaster University,** Faculty of Health Sciences and School of Graduate Studies, Program in Nursing (thesis), Hamilton, ON L8S 4M2, Canada. Offers M Sc, PhD. *Degree requirements:* For master's, thesis; for doctorate, comprehensive exam, thesis/dissertation. *Entrance requirements:* For master's, honors B Sc N, B+ average in last 60 units; for doctorate, M Sc, minimum B+ average. Additional exam requirements/recommendations for international students: required—TOEFL (minimum score 580 paper-based; 92 iBT).

**McMurry University,** Graduate Studies, Abilene, TX 79697. Offers education (MSN); family nurse practitioner (MSN).

**McNeese State University,** Doré School of Graduate Studies, College of Nursing and Health Professions, Lake Charles, LA 70609. Offers MSN, PMC. *Accreditation:* AACN. *Entrance requirements:* For master's, GRE, eligibility for unencumbered licensure as RN in Louisiana.

**MCPHS University,** Graduate Studies, Program in Nursing, Boston, MA 02115-5896. Offers MS. *Accreditation:* AACN. *Program availability:* Part-time, online learning. *Entrance requirements:* For master's, BSN. Additional exam requirements/recommendations for international students: required—TOEFL (minimum score 550 paper-based; 79 iBT). Electronic applications accepted.

**Medical University of South Carolina,** College of Nursing, PhD in Nursing Program, Charleston, SC 29425. Offers PhD. *Accreditation:* AACN. *Program availability:* Part-time, online learning. *Degree requirements:* For doctorate, comprehensive exam, thesis/dissertation, mentored teaching and research seminar. *Entrance requirements:* For doctorate, BSN or MSN from accredited ACEN or CCNE program, minimum GPA of 3.5, documentation of RN license from state of residence, curriculum vitae, personal statement, 3 references, interview, evidence of computer literacy. Additional exam requirements/recommendations for international students: required—TOEFL (minimum score 550 paper-based; 80 iBT). Electronic applications accepted.

**Medical University of South Carolina,** College of Nursing, Post-MSN Doctor of Nursing Practice Program, Charleston, SC 29425. Offers advanced practice nursing (DNP). *Accreditation:* AACN. *Program availability:* Part-time, online learning. *Degree requirements:* For doctorate, final project. *Entrance requirements:* For doctorate, BSN and MSN from nationally-accredited program, minimum cumulative GPA of 3.0 for undergraduate and graduate coursework, active APRN License and specialty certification, 3 confidential references, current curriculum vitae or resume, statement of goals. Additional exam requirements/recommendations for international students: required—TOEFL (minimum score 550 paper-based; 80 iBT). Electronic applications accepted.

**Memorial University of Newfoundland,** School of Graduate Studies, School of Nursing, St. John's, NL A1C 5S7, Canada. Offers MN, PhD. *Program availability:* Part-time. *Degree requirements:* For master's, thesis optional. *Entrance requirements:* For master's, bachelor's degree in nursing, 1 year of experience in nursing practice, practicing license. Electronic applications accepted.

**Mercer University,** Graduate Studies, Cecil B. Day Campus, Georgia Baptist College of Nursing, Atlanta, GA 30341. Offers adult gerontology acute care nurse practitioner (MSN, Certificate); family nurse practitioner (MSN, Certificate); nursing (PhD); nursing practice (DNP). *Accreditation:* AACN. *Program availability:* Part-time, blended/hybrid learning. *Faculty:* 26 full-time (23 women), 13 part-time/adjunct (11 women). *Students:* 69 full-time (64 women), 45 part-time (41 women); includes 61 minority (42 Black or African American, non-Hispanic/Latino; 12 Asian, non-Hispanic/Latino; 4 Hispanic/Latino; 1 Native Hawaiian or other Pacific Islander, non-Hispanic/Latino; 2 Two or more races, non-Hispanic/Latino), 1 international. Average age 35. 92 applicants, 75% accepted, 57 enrolled. In 2019, 14 master's, 10 doctorates awarded. *Degree requirements:* For master's, thesis or alternative, capstone project; for doctorate, comprehensive exam (for some programs), scholarly project (for DNP); dissertation (for PhD). *Entrance requirements:* For master's, bachelor's degree from accredited nursing program, minimum GPA 3.0, unencumbered license to practice as a Registered Nurse in Georgia, essay, three professional references; for doctorate, master's degree from accredited nursing program depending on program, unencumbered license to practice as a Registered Nurse, graduate statistics course, essay, three professional references; for Certificate, APRN license for post-master's certificate programs. Additional exam requirements/recommendations for international students: required—TOEFL (minimum score 100 iBT). *Application deadline:* For fall admission, 7/1 for domestic students; for spring admission, 12/1 for domestic students; for summer admission, 4/15 for domestic students. Applications are processed on a rolling basis. Application fee: $50. Electronic applications accepted. *Expenses:* Contact institution. *Financial support:* In 2019–20, 23 students received support, including 1 research assistantship with partial tuition reimbursement available (averaging $10,500 per year); scholarships/grants also available. Financial award application deadline: 6/30; financial award applicants required to submit FAFSA. *Unit head:* Dr. Linda Streit, Dean/Professor, 678-547-6793, Fax: 678-547-6796, E-mail: streit_la@mercer.edu. *Application contact:* Janda Anderson, Director of Admissions, 678-547-6700, Fax: 678-547-6794, E-mail: anderson_j@mercer.edu.
Website: http://www.nursing.mercer.edu

**Mercy College,** School of Health and Natural Sciences, Programs in Nursing, Dobbs Ferry, NY 10522-1189. Offers nursing administration (MS); nursing education (MS). *Accreditation:* AACN. *Program availability:* Part-time, evening/weekend, 100% online, blended/hybrid learning. *Students:* 9 full-time (8 women), 208 part-time (196 women); includes 151 minority (89 Black or African American, non-Hispanic/Latino; 21 Asian, non-Hispanic/Latino; 32 Hispanic/Latino; 3 Native Hawaiian or other Pacific Islander, non-Hispanic/Latino; 6 Two or more races, non-Hispanic/Latino). Average age 40. 242 applicants, 73% accepted, 132 enrolled. In 2019, 67 master's awarded. *Degree requirements:* For master's, Capstone project and/or clinical practicum required for some programs. *Entrance requirements:* For master's, program application; transcript(s); RN registered in the U.S. Additional exam requirements/recommendations for international students: required—TOEFL (minimum score 80 iBT), IELTS (minimum score 6.5). *Application deadline:* Applications are processed on a rolling basis. Application fee: $40. Electronic applications accepted. *Expenses: Tuition:* Full-time $16,146; part-time $897 per credit. *Required fees:* $332; $166 per semester. Tuition and fees vary according to course load and program. *Financial support:* Career-related internships or fieldwork, Federal Work-Study, scholarships/grants, and unspecified assistantships available. Support available to part-time students. Financial award applicants required to submit FAFSA. *Unit head:* Dr. Joan Toglia, Dean, School of Health and Natural Sciences, 914-674-7746, E-mail: jtoglia@mercy.edu. *Application contact:* Allison Gurdineer, Executive Director of Admissions, 877-637-2946, Fax: 914-674-7382, E-mail: admissions@mercy.edu.
Website: https://www.mercy.edu/health-and-natural-sciences/graduate

**Mercy College of Ohio,** Program in Nursing, Toledo, OH 43604. Offers MSN, Post Master's Certificate. *Program availability:* Part-time-only, online only, 100% online, Practicum Experiences: 140 hours total. *Faculty:* 1 (woman) full-time, 8 part-time/adjunct (7 women). *Students:* 15 part-time (13 women). 22 applicants, 50% accepted, 5 enrolled. In 2019, 10 master's awarded. *Degree requirements:* For master's, R MSN: Evidence-based practice project. *Entrance requirements:* For master's, A degree in nursing at bachelor's level or higher from an accredited institution and professionally-accredited (ACEN or CCNE) program; minimum overall GPA of 3.0 on undergraduate and graduate course work; proof of active unencumbered RN license; and submit items as specified in the College catalog; for Post Master's Certificate, Possess a degree in nursing at the master's level or higher from an accredited institution and a professionally accredited program; have proof of an active unencumbered RN license; and submit items as specified in the College catalog. *Application deadline:* Applications are processed on a rolling basis. Electronic applications accepted. *Expenses:* $649 per credit and college fees (for MSN); $4,200 per program (for post-master's certificates). *Financial support:* Scholarships/grants and Tuition discounts for alumni and Bon Secours/Mercy Health Employees available. Financial award applicants required to submit FAFSA. *Unit head:* Dr. Deborah Karns, MSN Program Director, 419-251-1718, E-mail: deborah.karns@mercycollege.edu. *Application contact:* Amy Mergen, Director of Enrollment Management, 888-806-3729, E-mail: admissions@mercycollege.edu.
Website: https://mercycollege.edu/academics/programs/graduate

**Metropolitan State University,** College of Nursing and Health Sciences, St. Paul, MN 55106-5000. Offers advanced dental therapy (MS); leadership and management (MSN); nurse educator (MSN); nursing (DNP). *Accreditation:* AACN. *Program availability:* Part-time. *Degree requirements:* For master's, thesis or alternative; for doctorate, thesis/dissertation or alternative. *Entrance requirements:* For master's, GRE General Test, minimum GPA of 3.0, RN license, BS/BA; for doctorate, minimum GPA of 3.0, RN license, MSN. Additional exam requirements/recommendations for international students: required—TOEFL (minimum score 550 paper-based).

*Nursing—General*

**MGH Institute of Health Professions,** School of Nursing, Boston, MA 02129. Offers advanced practice nursing (MSN); gerontological nursing (MSN); nursing (DNP); pediatric nursing (MSN); psychiatric nursing (MSN); teaching and learning for health care education (Certificate); women's health nursing (MSN). *Accreditation:* AACN. *Degree requirements:* For master's, thesis or alternative. *Entrance requirements:* For master's, GRE General Test, bachelor's degree from regionally-accredited college or university. Additional exam requirements/recommendations for international students: required—TOEFL (minimum score 550 paper-based; 80 iBT). Electronic applications accepted.

**Miami Regional University,** School of Nursing and Health Sciences, Miami Springs, FL 33166. Offers nursing (MSN); nursing education (MSN); nursing leadership (MSN).

**Michigan State University,** The Graduate School, College of Nursing, East Lansing, MI 48824. Offers MSN, PhD. *Accreditation:* AACN; AANA/CANAEP. *Program availability:* Part-time, online learning. *Entrance requirements:* Additional exam requirements/recommendations for international students: required—TOEFL (minimum score 580 paper-based), Michigan State University ELT ( minimum score 85), Michigan English Language Assessment Battery (minimum score 83). Electronic applications accepted.

**MidAmerica Nazarene University,** School of Nursing and Health Science, Olathe, KS 66062. Offers healthcare administration (MSN); healthcare quality management (MSN); nursing education (MSN); public health (MSN); MSN/MBA. *Accreditation:* AACN. *Program availability:* Part-time, evening/weekend, 100% online. *Faculty:* 5 full-time (all women), 9 part-time/adjunct (7 women). *Students:* 14 full-time (12 women), 79 part-time (74 women); includes 12 minority (10 Black or African American, non-Hispanic/Latino; 1 American Indian or Alaska Native, non-Hispanic/Latino; 1 Hispanic/Latino), 2 international. Average age 38. 87 applicants, 39% accepted, 14 enrolled. In 2019, 39 master's awarded. *Entrance requirements:* For master's, BSN, minimum GPA of 3.0, active unencumbered RN license, undergraduate statistics course. Additional exam requirements/recommendations for international students: required—TOEFL (minimum score 81 iBT). *Application deadline:* Applications are processed on a rolling basis. Electronic applications accepted. *Expenses:* Tuition $499 per credit hour, technology fee $34.00 per credit hour, graduation fee $100, carrying fee $13 per course, other fee $215. *Financial support:* Unspecified assistantships available. Financial award applicants required to submit FAFSA. *Unit head:* Dr. Karen Wiegman, Dean, 913-971-3839, E-mail: kdwiegman@mnu.edu. *Application contact:* JoVonda Merrell, Compliance Coordinator, 913-971-3844, E-mail: jkmerrell@mnu.edu.
Website: http://www.mnu.edu/nursing.html

**Middle Tennessee State University,** College of Graduate Studies, College of Behavioral and Health Sciences, School of Nursing, Murfreesboro, TN 37132. Offers MSN, Graduate Certificate. *Program availability:* Part-time, evening/weekend, online learning. *Entrance requirements:* Additional exam requirements/recommendations for international students: required—TOEFL (minimum score 525 paper-based; 71 iBT) or IELTS (minimum score 6). Electronic applications accepted.

**Midwestern State University,** Billie Doris McAda Graduate School, Robert D. and Carol Gunn College of Health Sciences and Human Services, Wilson School of Nursing, Wichita Falls, TX 76308. Offers family nurse practitioner (MSN); family psychiatric mental health nurse practitioner (MSN); nurse educator (MSN). *Accreditation:* AACN. *Program availability:* Part-time, evening/weekend. *Degree requirements:* For master's, comprehensive exam, thesis optional. *Entrance requirements:* For master's, GRE General Test or MAT. Additional exam requirements/recommendations for international students: required—TOEFL (minimum score 550 paper-based). Electronic applications accepted.

**Millersville University of Pennsylvania,** College of Graduate Studies and Adult Learning, College of Science and Technology, Department of Nursing, Millersville, PA 17551-0302. Offers family nurse practitioner (MSN, Post-Master's Certificate); nursing education (MSN, Post-Master's Certificate); nursing practice (DNP). *Accreditation:* ACEN. *Program availability:* Part-time. *Faculty:* 6 full-time (all women), 9 part-time/adjunct (8 women). *Students:* 122 part-time (100 women); includes 22 minority (8 Black or African American, non-Hispanic/Latino; 6 Asian, non-Hispanic/Latino; 7 Hispanic/Latino; 1 Two or more races, non-Hispanic/Latino). Average age 39. 44 applicants, 68% accepted, 26 enrolled. In 2019, 30 master's, 27 other advanced degrees awarded. *Entrance requirements:* For master's, resume, including minimum of 2 years of pertinent clinical experience (3-5 years preferred); copy of RN license; 3.0 GPA required; interview; minimum of one year of current clinical experience in nursing; for doctorate, goal statement, 3-5 page (APA 6th Ed.) Writing Sample Defining a Specific Issue or Problem in Nursing Practices, current resume/CV, verification of MSN Clinical Hours, completed MSN or MPH, with a minimum 3.5 GPA. Additional exam requirements/recommendations for international students: required—TOEFL, IELTS (minimum score 6), PTE (minimum score 60). Application fee: $40. Electronic applications accepted. *Expenses:* Tuition, area resident: Part-time $516 per credit. Tuition, state resident: part-time $516 per credit. Tuition, nonresident: part-time $774 per credit. *Required fees:* $118.75 per credit. Tuition and fees vary according to course load, degree level and program. *Financial support:* In 2019–20, 16 students received support. Scholarships/grants and unspecified assistantships available. Financial award application deadline: 3/15; financial award applicants required to submit FAFSA. *Unit head:* Dr. Kelly A. Kuhns, Chairperson, 717-871-5276, Fax: 717-871-4877, E-mail: kelly.kuhns@millersville.edu. *Application contact:* Dr. James A. Delle, Acting Dean of College of Graduate Studies and Adult Learning/Associate Provost, Academic Administration, 717-871-7462, E-mail: James.Delle@millersville.edu.
Website: https://www.millersville.edu/nursing/index.php

**Millersville University of Pennsylvania,** College of Graduate Studies and Adult Learning, College of Science and Technology, Department of Nursing, Doctor of Nursing Practice, Millersville, PA 17551-0302. Offers nursing practice (DNP). *Program availability:* Part-time. *Students:* 15 part-time (14 women); includes 2 minority (1 Black or African American, non-Hispanic/Latino; 1 Hispanic/Latino). Average age 46. 5 applicants, 100% accepted, 4 enrolled. *Entrance requirements:* For doctorate, Goal Statement; 3-5 Page (APA 6th Ed.) Writing Sample Defining a Specific Issue or Problem in Nursing Practices; Current Resume/CV; Verification of MSN Clinical Hours; Completed MSN or MPH, With a Minimum 3.5 GPA. Additional exam requirements/recommendations for international students: required—TOEFL, IELTS (minimum score 6), PTE (minimum score 60). *Application deadline:* For summer admission, 3/1 priority date for domestic students. Application fee: $40. Electronic applications accepted. *Expenses:* Doctor of Nursing Practice: $568 per credit resident tuition, $851 per credit non-resident tuition, $115 per credit doctoral fee (resident and non-resident), $28 per credit resident technology fee, $40 per credit non-resident technology fee. *Financial support:* In 2019–20, 1 student received support. Scholarships/grants and unspecified assistantships available. Financial award application deadline: 3/15; financial award applicants required to submit FAFSA. *Unit head:* Dr. Kelly A. Kuhns, Chairperson and DNP Coordinator, 717-871-5276, Fax: 717-871-4877, E-mail: kelly.kuhns@millersville.edu. *Application contact:* Dr. James A. Delle, Acting Dean of College of Graduate Studies and Adult Learning/Associate Provost, Academic Administration, 717-871-7462, E-mail: James.Delle@millersville.edu.
Website: https://www.millersville.edu/nursing/dnp.php

**Millikin University,** School of Nursing, Decatur, IL 62522-2084. Offers completion program (DNP); entry into nursing practice (MSN). *Accreditation:* AACN. *Program availability:* Part-time. *Faculty:* 18 full-time (15 women), 8 part-time/adjunct (7 women). *Students:* 45 full-time (31 women), 17 part-time (12 women); includes 19 minority (11 Black or African American, non-Hispanic/Latino; 4 Asian, non-Hispanic/Latino; 4 Hispanic/Latino), 1 international. Average age 31. 129 applicants, 35% accepted, 19 enrolled. In 2019, 5 master's, 14 doctorates awarded. *Degree requirements:* For master's, thesis or alternative, scholarly project; for doctorate, thesis/dissertation or alternative, scholarly project. *Entrance requirements:* For master's and doctorate, GRE (if undergraduate cumulative GPA is below 3.0), official academic transcript(s), written statement, resume/vitae, 3 letters of recommendation, RN license. Additional exam requirements/recommendations for international students: required—TOEFL (minimum score 550 paper-based; 79 iBT), IELTS (minimum score 6.5). *Application deadline:* For winter admission, 1/15 priority date for domestic and international students; for summer admission, 1/15 priority date for domestic and international students. Applications are processed on a rolling basis. Electronic applications accepted. *Expenses:* The MSN program is $861 per credit hour; Clinical Nurse Leader and Nurse Educator are 36 credit hours; the Master's Entry into Nursing Practice is 83 credit hours. The DNP program is $983 per credit hour. *Financial support:* Traineeships and unspecified assistantships available. Financial award applicants required to submit FAFSA. *Unit head:* Dr. Elizabeth Gephart, Interim Director, 217-424-6397, E-mail: egephart@millikin.edu. *Application contact:* Marianne Taylor, Director, Graduate Admission, 217-420-6771, Fax: 217-425-4669, E-mail: mgtaylor@millikin.edu.
Website: https://millikin.edu/grad-nursing

**Minnesota State University Mankato,** College of Graduate Studies and Research, College of Allied Health and Nursing, School of Nursing, Mankato, MN 56001. Offers family nurse practitioner (MSN), including family nurse practitioner; nurse educator (MSN); nursing (DNP). *Accreditation:* AACN. *Degree requirements:* For master's, comprehensive exam, internships, research project or thesis; for doctorate, capstone project. *Entrance requirements:* For master's, GRE General Test or on-campus essay, minimum GPA of 3.0 during previous 2 years, BSN or equivalent references; for doctorate, master's degree in nursing. Additional exam requirements/recommendations for international students: required—TOEFL. Electronic applications accepted.

**Minnesota State University Moorhead,** Graduate and Extended Learning, College of Science, Health and the Environment, Moorhead, MN 56563. Offers healthcare administration (MHA); nursing (MS); school psychology (MS, Psy S). *Program availability:* Part-time, evening/weekend, 100% online, blended/hybrid learning. *Students:* 30 full-time (26 women), 120 part-time (91 women). Average age 33. 77 applicants, 57% accepted. In 2019, 40 master's, 11 other advanced degrees awarded. *Degree requirements:* For master's, comprehensive exam (for some programs), thesis, final oral defense. *Entrance requirements:* For master's, GRE (for school psychology program), minimum GPA of 3.0, essay, letters of reference, RN license (for nursing program). Additional exam requirements/recommendations for international students: required—TOEFL (minimum score 550 paper-based; 80 iBT); recommended—IELTS (minimum score 6.5). *Application deadline:* Applications are processed on a rolling basis. Application fee: $35. Electronic applications accepted. *Financial support:* Federal Work-Study and unspecified assistantships available. Financial award application deadline: 10/1; financial award applicants required to submit FAFSA. *Unit head:* Dr. Elizabeth Nawrot, Interim Dean, 218-477-5892, E-mail: nawrot@mnstate.edu. *Application contact:* Karla Wenger, Office Manager, 218-477-2344, Fax: 218-477-2482, E-mail: wengerk@mnstate.edu.
Website: http://www.mnstate.edu/cshe/

**Misericordia University,** College of Health Sciences and Education, Department of Nursing, Dallas, PA 18612. Offers MSN, DNP. *Accreditation:* AACN. *Program availability:* Part-time, evening/weekend, 100% online, blended/hybrid learning. *Students:* 55 part-time (47 women); includes 4 minority (1 Black or African American, non-Hispanic/Latino; 1 Asian, non-Hispanic/Latino; 2 Hispanic/Latino). Average age 31. In 2019, 10 master's, 7 doctorates awarded. *Degree requirements:* For master's, thesis optional, practicum. *Entrance requirements:* For master's, interview, minimum GPA of 3.0; for doctorate, official transcripts of all previous college work, MSN from CCNE- or ACEN-accredited institution, copy of unencumbered RN license, license to practice as an advanced practice nurse, minimum graduate GPA of 3.0, two letters of reference, 500-word statement/writing sample of personal and professional goals, telephone interview. Additional exam requirements/recommendations for international students: required—TOEFL. *Application deadline:* For fall admission, 8/7 priority date for domestic students; for spring admission, 1/3 for domestic students. Applications are processed on a rolling basis. Application fee: $35. Electronic applications accepted. *Expenses:* $775 per credit. *Financial support:* Career-related internships or fieldwork and scholarships/grants available. Support available to part-time students. Financial award application deadline: 6/30; financial award applicants required to submit FAFSA. *Unit head:* Dr. Pamela Dwyer, Graduate Nursing Program Chair, 570-674-6177, E-mail: pdwyer@misericordia.edu. *Application contact:* Maureen Sheridan, Assistant Director of Admissions, Part-Time Undergraduate and Graduate Programs, 570-674-6451, Fax: 570-674-6232, E-mail: msherida@misericordia.edu.
Website: http://www.misericordia.edu/page.cfm?p-632

**Mississippi University for Women,** Graduate School, College of Nursing and Health Sciences, Columbus, MS 39701-9998. Offers nursing (MSN, DNP, PMC); public health education (MPH); speech-language pathology (MS). *Accreditation:* AACN; ASHA. *Program availability:* Part-time. *Degree requirements:* For master's, comprehensive exam, thesis. *Entrance requirements:* For master's, GRE General Test, bachelor's degree in nursing, previous course work in statistics, proficiency in English.

**Missouri Southern State University,** Program in Nursing, Joplin, MO 64801-1595. Offers MSN. *Accreditation:* AACN. *Program availability:* Part-time. *Entrance requirements:* For master's, minimum cumulative GPA of 3.2 for the last 60 hours of the BSN program, resume, RN licensure, CPR certification, course work in statistics and health assessment. Electronic applications accepted.

**Missouri State University,** Graduate College, College of Health and Human Services, School of Nursing, Springfield, MO 65897. Offers nursing (MSN), including family nurse practitioner, nurse educator; nursing practice (DNP). *Accreditation:* AACN. *Program availability:* 100% online, blended/hybrid learning. *Degree requirements:* For master's, comprehensive exam, thesis or alternative. *Entrance requirements:* For master's, GRE General Test, minimum GPA of 3.0, RN license (for MSN), 1 year of work experience (for MPH). Additional exam requirements/recommendations for international students: required—TOEFL (minimum score 550 paper-based; 79 iBT), IELTS (minimum score 6). Electronic applications accepted. *Expenses:* Tuition, area resident: Full-time $2600; part-time $1735 per credit hour. Tuition, nonresident: full-time $5240; part-time $3495 per credit hour. *International tuition:* $5240 full-time. *Required fees:* $530; $438 per credit hour. Tuition and fees vary according to class time, course level, course load, degree level, campus/location and program.

**Missouri Western State University,** Program in Nursing, St. Joseph, MO 64507-2294. Offers health care leadership (MSN); nurse educator (MSN, Graduate Certificate). *Program availability:* Part-time. *Students:* 2 full-time (both women), 29 part-time (all women); includes 3 minority (1 Black or African American, non-Hispanic/Latino; 1 Asian,

non-Hispanic/Latino; 1 Hispanic/Latino), 1 international. Average age 37. 13 applicants, 100% accepted, 12 enrolled. In 2019, 12 master's, 1 other advanced degree awarded. *Entrance requirements:* For master's, Minimum undergraduate GPA of 2.75 and nursing GPA 3.0 or higher. B.S.N. from a CCNE or NLNAC accredited college or university. Evidence of current, unencumbered RN license. Completion of undergraduate statistics and research methods courses with a minimum of "B" in each. Curriculum vitae/resume. A supporting statement of interest. Additional exam requirements/recommendations for international students: recommended—TOEFL (minimum score 79 iBT), IELTS (minimum score 6). *Application deadline:* For fall admission, 7/15 for domestic and international students; for spring admission, 11/1 for domestic and international students; for summer admission, 4/29 for domestic and international students. Applications are processed on a rolling basis. Application fee: $45 ($50 for international students). Electronic applications accepted. *Expenses:* Tuition, state resident: full-time $6469.02; part-time $359.39 per credit hour. Tuition, nonresident: full-time $11,581; part-time $643.39 per credit hour. *Required fees:* $345.20; $99.10 per credit hour. Tuition and fees vary according to course load, campus/location and program. *Financial support:* Scholarships/grants and unspecified assistantships available. Support available to part-time students. *Unit head:* Dr. Jacklyn Gentry, MSN Program Director and Assistant Professor, 816-271-4415, E-mail: jgentry8@missouriwestern.edu. *Application contact:* Dr. Jacklyn Gentry, MSN Program Director and Assistant Professor, 816-271-4415, E-mail: jgentry8@missouriwestern.edu.
Website: https://www.missouriwestern.edu/nursing/msn/

**Molloy College,** Graduate Nursing Program, Rockville Centre, NY 11571-5002. Offers adult-gerontology clinical nurse specialist (DNP); adult-gerontology nurse practitioner (MS, DNP); clinical nurse specialist: adult-gerontology (MS); family nurse practitioner (MS, DNP); family psychiatric/mental health nurse practitioner (MS, DNP); nursing (PhD, Advanced Certificate); nursing administration with informatics (MS); nursing education (MS); pediatric nurse practitioner (MS, DNP). *Accreditation:* AACN. *Program availability:* Part-time, evening/weekend. *Faculty:* 30 full-time (28 women), 10 part-time/adjunct (6 women). *Students:* 18 full-time (17 women), 573 part-time (520 women); includes 340 minority (181 Black or African American, non-Hispanic/Latino; 2 American Indian or Alaska Native, non-Hispanic/Latino; 100 Asian, non-Hispanic/Latino; 42 Hispanic/Latino; 5 Native Hawaiian or other Pacific Islander, non-Hispanic/Latino; 10 Two or more races, non-Hispanic/Latino), 3 international. Average age 38. 332 applicants, 60% accepted, 149 enrolled. In 2019, 136 master's, 12 doctorates, 22 other advanced degrees awarded. *Degree requirements:* For doctorate, clinical research residency and scholarly clinical project (for DNP); dissertation and comprehensive exam (for PhD). *Entrance requirements:* Additional exam requirements/recommendations for international students: required—TOEFL (minimum score 550 paper-based; 79 iBT). *Application deadline:* Applications are processed on a rolling basis. Application fee: $60. Electronic applications accepted. *Expenses:* Tuition: Full-time $21,510; part-time $1195 per credit hour. *Required fees:* $1100. Tuition and fees vary according to course load, degree level and program. *Financial support:* Application deadline: 3/1; applicants required to submit FAFSA. *Unit head:* Dr. Marcia R. Gardner, Dean, The Barbara H. Hagan School of Nursing, 516-323-3651, E-mail: mgardner@molloy.edu. *Application contact:* Faye Hood, Assistant Director for Admissions, 516-323-4009, E-mail: fhood@molloy.edu.
Website: https://www.molloy.edu/academics/graduate-programs/graduate-nursing-x25989

**Monmouth University,** Graduate Studies, Marjorie K. Unterberg School of Nursing and Health Studies, West Long Branch, NJ 07764-1898. Offers adult-gerontological primary care nurse practitioner (Post-Master's Certificate); forensic nursing (MSN). *Accreditation:* AACN. *Program availability:* Part-time, evening/weekend, 100% online, blended/hybrid learning. *Faculty:* 13 full-time (all women), 9 part-time/adjunct (8 women). *Students:* 1 (woman) full-time, 284 part-time (261 women); includes 108 minority (37 Black or African American, non-Hispanic/Latino; 38 Asian, non-Hispanic/Latino; 32 Hispanic/Latino; 1 Two or more races, non-Hispanic/Latino). Average age 39. In 2019, 100 master's, 14 doctorates, 10 other advanced degrees awarded. *Degree requirements:* For master's, practicum (for some tracks); for doctorate, practicum, capstone course. *Entrance requirements:* For master's, GRE General Test (waived for MSN applicants with minimum B grade in each of the first four courses and for MS applicants with master's degree), BSN with minimum GPA of 2.75, current RN license, proof of liability and malpractice policy, personal statement, two letters of recommendation, college course work in health assessment, resume; CASPA application (for MS); for doctorate, accredited master's nursing program degree with minimum GPA of 3.2, active RN license, national certification as nurse practitioner or nurse administrator, working knowledge of statistics, statement of goals and vision for change, 2 letters of recommendation (professional or academic), resume, interview. Additional exam requirements/recommendations for international students: required—TOEFL (minimum score 550 paper-based; 79 iBT), IELTS (minimum score 6) or Michigan English Language Assessment Battery (minimum score 77). *Application deadline:* For fall admission, 7/15 priority date for domestic students, 6/1 for international students; for spring admission, 12/1 priority date for domestic students, 11/1 for international students; for summer admission, 5/1 for domestic students. Applications are processed on a rolling basis. Application fee: $50. Electronic applications accepted. *Expenses:* $1,233 per credit. *Financial support:* In 2019–20, 251 students received support. Research assistantships, teaching assistantships, scholarships/grants, and unspecified assistantships available. Support available to part-time students. Financial award applicants required to submit FAFSA. *Unit head:* Dr. Ann Marie Mauro, Dean, 732-571-3443, Fax: 732-263-5131, E-mail: amauro@monmouth.edu. *Application contact:* Laurie Kuhn, Associate Director of Graduate Admission, 732-571-3452, Fax: 732-263-5123, E-mail: gradadm@monmouth.edu.
Website: https://www.monmouth.edu/graduate/nursing-programs-of-study/

**Montana State University,** The Graduate School, College of Nursing, Bozeman, MT 59717. Offers clinical nurse leader (MN); family and individual nurse practitioner (DNP); family nurse practitioner (MN, Post-Master's Certificate); nursing education (Certificate, Post-Master's Certificate); psychiatric mental health nurse practitioner (MN); psychiatric/mental health nurse practitioner (DNP). *Accreditation:* AACN. *Program availability:* Part-time, online learning. *Degree requirements:* For master's, comprehensive exam, thesis (for some programs); for doctorate, thesis/dissertation, 1,125 hours in clinical settings. *Entrance requirements:* For master's, GRE General Test, minimum GPA of 3.0 for undergraduate and post-baccalaureate work. Additional exam requirements/recommendations for international students: required—TOEFL (minimum score 580 paper-based). Electronic applications accepted.

**Moravian College,** Graduate and Continuing Studies, Helen S. Breidegam School of Nursing, Bethlehem, PA 18018-6614. Offers clinical nurse leader (MS); nurse administrator - (MS); nurse educator (MS); nurse practitioner - acute care (MS); nurse practitioner - primary care (MS). *Accreditation:* AACN. *Program availability:* Part-time, evening/weekend. *Faculty:* 2 full-time (both women), 3 part-time/adjunct (2 women). *Students:* 5 full-time (4 women), 103 part-time (95 women); includes 19 minority (4 Black or African American, non-Hispanic/Latino; 8 Asian, non-Hispanic/Latino; 7 Hispanic/Latino), 1 international. Average age 37. 131 applicants, 69% accepted, 85 enrolled. In 2019, 25 master's awarded. *Degree requirements:* For master's, comprehensive exam (for some programs), evidence-based practice project. *Entrance requirements:* For master's, BSN with minimum GPA of 3.0, active RN license, statistics course with

minimum C grade, 2 professional references, written statement of goals, professional resume, interview, official transcripts. *Application deadline:* For fall admission, 8/1 priority date for domestic and international students; for spring admission, 1/1 priority date for domestic and international students; for summer admission, 5/1 priority date for domestic and international students. Applications are processed on a rolling basis. Electronic applications accepted. *Expenses:* Contact institution. *Financial support:* Applicants required to submit FAFSA. *Unit head:* Dr. Dawn Goodolf, 610-861-1412, Fax: 610-861-1466, E-mail: nursing@moravian.edu. *Application contact:* Caroline Bechtel, Student Experience Mentor, 610-861-1400, Fax: 610-861-1466, E-mail: graduate@moravian.edu.
Website: https://www.moravian.edu/graduate/programs/nursing#/

**Morgan State University,** School of Graduate Studies, School of Community Health and Policy, Program in Nursing, Baltimore, MD 21251. Offers MS, PhD. *Accreditation:* AACN. *Program availability:* Part-time, evening/weekend. *Faculty:* 5 full-time (all women), 16 part-time/adjunct (13 women). *Students:* 4 full-time (3 women), 4 part-time (all women); all minorities (all Black or African American, non-Hispanic/Latino). Average age 53. 4 applicants, 100% accepted, 1 enrolled. In 2019, 5 master's awarded. *Degree requirements:* For master's, comprehensive exam. *Entrance requirements:* For master's, Minimum 3.0, GRE. Additional exam requirements/recommendations for international students: required—TOEFL (minimum score 570 paper-based; 70 iBT). *Application deadline:* For fall admission, 5/1 for domestic students, 4/1 for international students; for spring admission, 11/15 for domestic students, 10/1 for international students. Applications are processed on a rolling basis. Application fee: $50 ($70 for international students). Electronic applications accepted. *Expenses:* Tuition, state resident: full-time $455; part-time $455 per credit hour. Tuition, nonresident: full-time $894; part-time $894 per credit hour. *Required fees:* $82; $82 per credit hour. *Financial support:* In 2019–20, 12 students received support. Fellowships with full and partial tuition reimbursements available, research assistantships with full and partial tuition reimbursements available, teaching assistantships with full and partial tuition reimbursements available, career-related internships or fieldwork, Federal Work-Study, scholarships/grants, tuition waivers (full and partial), and unspecified assistantships available. Support available to part-time students. Financial award application deadline: 2/1. *Unit head:* Dr. Maija Anderson, Program Director, 443-885-4144, E-mail: maija.anderson@morgan.edu. *Application contact:* Dr. Jahmaine Smith, Director of Admissions, 443-885-3185, Fax: 443-885-8226, E-mail: gradapply@morgan.edu.
Website: https://morgan.edu/nursing

**Morningside College,** Graduate Programs, Nylen School of Nursing, Sioux City, IA 51106. Offers adult gerontology primary care nurse practitioner (MSN); clinical nurse leader (MSN); family primary care nurse practitioner (MSN). *Program availability:* Part-time, online only, 100% online. Electronic applications accepted. *Expenses:* Contact institution.

**Mount Carmel College of Nursing,** Nursing Program, Columbus, OH 43222. Offers adult gerontology acute care nurse practitioner (MS); adult health clinical nurse specialist (MS); family nurse practitioner (MS); nursing (DNP); nursing administration (MS); nursing education (MS). *Accreditation:* AACN. *Program availability:* Part-time. *Faculty:* 6 full-time (all women), 10 part-time/adjunct (9 women). *Students:* 101 full-time (82 women), 109 part-time (95 women); includes 43 minority (27 Black or African American, non-Hispanic/Latino; 4 Asian, non-Hispanic/Latino; 5 Hispanic/Latino; 7 Two or more races, non-Hispanic/Latino). Average age 32. 133 applicants, 84% accepted, 95 enrolled. In 2019, 66 master's, 2 doctorates awarded. *Degree requirements:* For master's, professional manuscript; for doctorate, practicum. *Entrance requirements:* For master's, letters of recommendation, statement of purpose, current resume, baccalaureate degree in nursing, current Ohio RN license, minimum cumulative GPA of 3.0; for doctorate, master's degree in nursing from program accredited by either ACEN or CCNE. Additional exam requirements/recommendations for international students: required—TOEFL (minimum score 550 paper-based; 80 iBT). *Application deadline:* For fall admission, 2/1 priority date for domestic students; for spring admission, 11/1 priority date for domestic students. Applications are processed on a rolling basis. Application fee: $30. Electronic applications accepted. *Expenses:* Tuition: Full-time $27,936; part-time $27,936 per year. *Required fees:* $360. *Financial support:* In 2019–20, 13 students received support. Institutionally sponsored loans and scholarships/grants available. Financial award application deadline: 3/1; financial award applicants required to submit FAFSA. *Unit head:* Dr. Jami Nininger, Interim Associate Dean Graduate Studies, 614-234-1777, Fax: 614-234-2875, E-mail: jnininger@mccn.edu. *Application contact:* Dr. Kim Campbell, Director of Recruitment and Admissions, 614-234-5144, Fax: 614-234-5427, E-mail: kcampbell@mccn.edu.
Website: www.mccn.edu

**Mount Marty University,** Graduate Studies Division, Yankton, SD 57078-3724. Offers business administration (MBA); nurse anesthesia (MS); nursing (MSN); pastoral ministries (MPM). *Accreditation:* AANA/CANAEP (one or more programs are accredited). *Degree requirements:* For master's, thesis or alternative. *Entrance requirements:* For master's, GRE General Test, minimum GPA of 3.0. Electronic applications accepted.

**Mount Mercy University,** Program in Nursing, Cedar Rapids, IA 52402-4797. Offers health advocacy (MSN); nurse administration (MSN); nurse education (MSN). *Accreditation:* AACN. *Program availability:* Evening/weekend. *Degree requirements:* For master's, project/practicum.

**Mount St. Joseph University,** Doctor of Nursing Practice Program, Cincinnati, OH 45233-1670. Offers health systems leadership (DNP). *Accreditation:* AACN. *Program availability:* Part-time-only. *Degree requirements:* For doctorate, capstone, minimum cumulative GPA of 3.0, completion of program within 5 years of enrollment, minimum of 75% of credits earned at Mount St. Joseph University, 1000 practicum hours between prior master's degree and DNP programs, minimum of 400 practicum hours in the DNP program. *Entrance requirements:* For doctorate, essay; MSN from regionally-accredited university; minimum graduate GPA of 3.0; professional resume; two professional references; interview; 2 years of clinical nursing experience; active RN license; minimum C grade in an undergraduate statistics course; official documentation of practicum hours post-BSN. Additional exam requirements/recommendations for international students: required—TOEFL (minimum score 560 paper-based; 83 iBT). Electronic applications accepted. *Expenses:* Contact institution.

**Mount St. Joseph University,** Master of Science in Nursing Program, Cincinnati, OH 45233-1670. Offers administration (MSN); clinical nurse leader (MSN); education (MSN). *Accreditation:* AACN. *Program availability:* Part-time. *Entrance requirements:* For master's, essay; BSN from regionally-accredited university; minimum undergraduate GPA of 3.25 or GRE; professional resume; three professional references; interview; 2 years of clinical nursing experience; active RN license; criminal background check. Additional exam requirements/recommendations for international students: required—TOEFL (minimum score 560 paper-based; 83 iBT). Electronic applications accepted. *Expenses:* Contact institution.

**Mount St. Joseph University,** Master's Graduate Entry-Level into Nursing (MAGELIN) Program, Cincinnati, OH 45233-1670. Offers MSN. *Accreditation:* AACN. *Degree requirements:* For master's, evidence-based project, preceptorship. *Entrance*

*requirements:* For master's, GRE or minimum GPA of 3.0, interview; course work in chemistry, anatomy, physiology, microbiology, psychology, sociology, statistics, life span development, and nutrition; non-nursing bachelor's degree; statement of goals; transcripts; criminal background check. Additional exam requirements/recommendations for international students: required—TOEFL (minimum score 560 paper-based; 83 iBT). Electronic applications accepted. *Expenses:* Contact institution.

**Mount Saint Mary College,** School of Nursing, Newburgh, NY 12550. Offers adult nurse practitioner (MS, Advanced Certificate), including nursing education (MS), nursing management (MS); nursing education (Advanced Certificate). *Accreditation:* AACN. *Program availability:* Part-time, evening/weekend, blended/hybrid learning. *Faculty:* 6 full-time (all women), 11 part-time/adjunct (10 women). *Students:* 1 (woman) full-time, 186 part-time (171 women); includes 36 minority (16 Black or African American, non-Hispanic/Latino; 1 American Indian or Alaska Native, non-Hispanic/Latino; 5 Asian, non-Hispanic/Latino; 11 Hispanic/Latino; 1 Native Hawaiian or other Pacific Islander, non-Hispanic/Latino; 2 Two or more races, non-Hispanic/Latino), 1 international. Average age 37. 37 applicants, 84% accepted, 22 enrolled. In 2019, 33 master's, 4 other advanced degrees awarded. *Degree requirements:* For master's, research utilization project. *Entrance requirements:* For master's, BSN, minimum GPA of 3.0, RN license. Additional exam requirements/recommendations for international students: required—TOEFL (minimum score 80 iBT). *Application deadline:* For fall admission, 6/3 priority date for domestic students; for spring admission, 10/31 priority date for domestic students. Applications are processed on a rolling basis. Application fee: $45. Electronic applications accepted. Application fee is waived when completed online. *Expenses: Tuition:* Full-time $15,192; part-time $844 per credit. *Required fees:* $180; $90 per semester. *Financial support:* In 2019–20, 10 students received support. Scholarships/grants and unspecified assistantships available. Financial award application deadline: 4/15; financial award applicants required to submit FAFSA. *Unit head:* Christine Berte, Graduate Coordinator, 845-569-3141, Fax: 845-562-6762, E-mail: christine.berte@msmc.edu. *Application contact:* Eileen Bardney, Director of Admissions, 845-569-3254, Fax: 845-569-3438, E-mail: GraduateAdmissions@msmc.edu.
Website: http://www.msmc.edu/Academics/Graduate_Programs/Master_of_Science_in_Nursing

**Mount Saint Mary's University,** Graduate Division, Los Angeles, CA 90049. Offers business administration (MBA); counseling psychology (MS); creative writing (MFA); education (MS, Certificate); film and television (MFA); health policy and management (MS); humanities (MA); nursing (MSN, Certificate); physical therapy (DPT); religious studies (MA). *Program availability:* Part-time, evening/weekend. *Entrance requirements:* Additional exam requirements/recommendations for international students: required—TOEFL. Electronic applications accepted. *Expenses: Tuition:* Full-time $18,648; part-time $9324 per year. *Required fees:* $540; $540 per unit.

**Murray State University,** School of Nursing and Health Professions, Department of Nursing, Murray, KY 42071. Offers family nurse practitioner (DNP); nurse anesthetist (DNP). *Accreditation:* AACN; AANA/CANAEP. *Program availability:* Evening/weekend, 100% online, blended/hybrid learning. *Entrance requirements:* For doctorate, GRE, minimum university GPA of 2.75. Additional exam requirements/recommendations for international students: required—TOEFL (minimum score 527 paper-based; 71 iBT). Electronic applications accepted.

**Nebraska Methodist College,** Program in Nursing, Omaha, NE 68114. Offers nurse educator (MSN); nurse executive (MSN). *Accreditation:* AACN. *Program availability:* Evening/weekend, online learning. *Degree requirements:* For master's, thesis or alternative, Evidence Based Practice (EBP) project. *Entrance requirements:* For master's, interview. Additional exam requirements/recommendations for international students: required—TOEFL (minimum score 550 paper-based; 80 iBT).

**Nebraska Wesleyan University,** Program in Nursing, Lincoln, NE 68504. Offers MSN. *Accreditation:* AACN; ACEN. *Program availability:* Part-time. *Faculty:* 6 full-time (all women), 9 part-time/adjunct (4 women). *Students:* 1 (woman) full-time, 50 part-time (48 women); includes 3 minority (1 Hispanic/Latino; 2 Two or more races, non-Hispanic/Latino), 1 international. Average age 42. 12 applicants, 75% accepted, 9 enrolled. In 2019, 21 master's awarded. *Application deadline:* Applications are processed on a rolling basis. Electronic applications accepted. *Expenses:* Contact institution. *Unit head:* Charlotte Liggett, Nursing Department Chair, 402-465-7521, E-mail: cliggett@nebrwesleyan.edu. *Application contact:* Graduate, Adult and Transfer Admissions, 402-465-2329, Fax: 402-465-2179, E-mail: adultadmissions@nebrwesleyan.edu.
Website: https://www.nebrwesleyan.edu/academics/graduate-programs/master-science-nursing/master-science-nursing

**Neumann University,** Graduate Program in Nursing, Aston, PA 19014-1298. Offers adult-gerontology nurse practitioner (MS, Certificate). *Accreditation:* ACEN. *Program availability:* Part-time, evening/weekend. *Entrance requirements:* For master's, official transcripts from all institutions attended, resume, letter of intent, current registered nursing license, two letters of reference; for Certificate, BSN, MSN, official transcripts from all institutions attended, resume, letter of intent, current registered nursing license, two official letters of reference. Additional exam requirements/recommendations for international students: required—TOEFL (minimum score 84 iBT). Electronic applications accepted.

**New Mexico State University,** College of Health and Social Services, School of Nursing, Las Cruces, NM 88003. Offers family nurse practitioner (Graduate Certificate); nursing (MSN); nursing practice (DNP); nursing science (PhD); psychiatric/mental health nurse practitioner (Graduate Certificate). *Accreditation:* AACN. *Program availability:* Part-time, blended/hybrid learning. *Faculty:* 12 full-time (all women). *Students:* 29. 57 applicants, 98% accepted. In 2019, 4 master's, 20 doctorates, 5 other advanced degrees awarded. *Degree requirements:* For master's, comprehensive exam, thesis optional, clinical practicum; for doctorate, comprehensive exam, thesis/dissertation. *Entrance requirements:* For master's, NCLEX exam, BSN, minimum GPA of 3.0, course work in statistics, 3 letters of reference, writing sample, RN license, CPR certification, proof of liability, immunizations, criminal background check; for doctorate, NCLEX exam, MSN, minimum GPA of 3.0, 3 letters of reference, writing sample, RN license, CPR certification, proof of liability, immunizations, criminal background check, statistics course. Additional exam requirements/recommendations for international students: required—TOEFL (minimum score 550 paper-based; 79 iBT), IELTS (minimum score 6.5). *Application deadline:* For fall admission, 2/1 priority date for domestic students, 2/1 for international students. Application fee: $40 ($50 for international students). Electronic applications accepted. *Financial support:* In 2019–20, 7 teaching assistantships (averaging $10,499 per year) were awarded; career-related internships or fieldwork, Federal Work-Study, scholarships/grants, traineeships, health care benefits, and unspecified assistantships also available. Support available to part-time students. Financial award application deadline: 3/1. *Unit head:* Dr. Alexa Doig, Director, 575-646-3812, Fax: 575-646-2167, E-mail: adoig@nmsu.edu. *Application contact:* Alyce Kolenovsky, Academic Advisor, 575-646-3812, Fax: 575-646-2167, E-mail: nursing@nmsu.edu.
Website: http://schoolofnursing.nmsu.edu

**New York University,** Rory Meyers College of Nursing, Doctor of Nursing Practice Program, New York, NY 10012-1019. Offers nursing (DNP), including adult-gerontology acute care nurse practitioner, adult-gerontology primary care nurse practitioner, family nurse practitioner, nurse-midwifery, pediatrics nurse practitioner, psychiatric-mental health nurse practitioner. *Accreditation:* AACN. *Program availability:* Part-time, evening/weekend. *Degree requirements:* For doctorate, thesis/dissertation, project. *Entrance requirements:* For doctorate, MS, RN license, interview, Nurse Practitioner Certification, writing sample. Additional exam requirements/recommendations for international students: required—TOEFL (minimum score 100 iBT), IELTS (minimum score 7). Electronic applications accepted. *Expenses:* Contact institution.

**New York University,** Rory Meyers College of Nursing, Doctor of Philosophy in Nursing Program, New York, NY 10012-1019. Offers nursing research and theory development (PhD). *Program availability:* Part-time. *Degree requirements:* For doctorate, thesis/dissertation, candidacy exam. *Entrance requirements:* For doctorate, GRE General Test, interview. Additional exam requirements/recommendations for international students: required—TOEFL (minimum score 100 iBT), IELTS (minimum score 7). Electronic applications accepted. *Expenses:* Contact institution.

**New York University,** Rory Meyers College of Nursing, Programs in Advanced Practice Nursing, New York, NY 10012-1019. Offers adult-gerontology acute care nurse practitioner (MS, Advanced Certificate); adult-gerontology primary care nurse practitioner (MS, Advanced Certificate); family nurse practitioner (MS, Advanced Certificate); gerontology nurse practitioner (Advanced Certificate); nurse-midwifery (MS, Advanced Certificate); nursing administration (MS, Advanced Certificate); nursing education (MS, Advanced Certificate); nursing informatics (MS, Advanced Certificate); pediatrics nurse practitioner (MS, Advanced Certificate); psychiatric-mental health nurse practitioner (MS, Advanced Certificate); MS/MPH. *Accreditation:* AACN; ACNM/ACME. *Program availability:* Part-time, evening/weekend. *Degree requirements:* For master's, thesis (for some programs), capstone. *Entrance requirements:* For master's, BS in nursing, AS in nursing with another BS/BA, interview, RN license, 1 year of clinical experience (3 for the MS in nursing education program); for Advanced Certificate, master's degree in nursing. Additional exam requirements/recommendations for international students: required—TOEFL (minimum score 100 iBT), IELTS (minimum score 7). Electronic applications accepted. *Expenses:* Contact institution.

**Nicholls State University,** Graduate Studies, College of Nursing and Allied Health, Thibodaux, LA 70310. Offers family nurse practitioner (MSN); nurse executive (MSN); nursing education (MSN); psychiatric/mental health nurse practitioner (MSN).

**North Dakota State University,** College of Graduate and Interdisciplinary Studies, College of Health Professions, School of Nursing, Fargo, ND 58102. Offers DNP. *Accreditation:* AACN. *Program availability:* Part-time, online learning. *Degree requirements:* For doctorate, thesis/dissertation or alternative, oral defense. *Entrance requirements:* For doctorate, bachelor's or master's degree with a nursing major, minimum GPA of 3.0 in nursing courses, RN license. Additional exam requirements/recommendations for international students: required—TOEFL, IELTS. Electronic applications accepted. *Expenses:* Contact institution.

**Northeastern University,** Bouvé College of Health Sciences, Boston, MA 02115-5096. Offers applied behavior analysis (MS); audiology (Au D); counseling psychology (MS, PhD, CAGS); exercise science (MS); nursing (MS, PhD, CAGS), including administration (MS), adult-gerontology acute care nurse practitioner (MS, CAGS), adult-gerontology primary care nurse practitioner (MS, CAGS), anesthesia (MS), family nurse practitioner (MS, CAGS), neonatal nurse practitioner (MS, CAGS), pediatric nurse practitioner (MS, CAGS), psychiatric mental health nurse practitioner (MS, CAGS); nursing practice (DNP); pharmaceutical sciences (MS, PhD), including interdisciplinary concentration, pharmaceutics and drug delivery systems; pharmacology (MS); pharmacy (Pharm D); school psychology (PhD); speech-language pathology (MS); urban health (MPH); MS/MBA. *Accreditation:* AANA/CANAEP; ACPE (one or more programs are accredited); ASHA; CEPH. *Program availability:* Part-time, evening/weekend, online learning. *Degree requirements:* For doctorate, thesis/dissertation (for some programs); for CAGS, comprehensive exam. Electronic applications accepted. *Expenses:* Contact institution.

**Northern Arizona University,** College of Health and Human Services, School of Nursing, Flagstaff, AZ 86011. Offers family nurse practitioner (Certificate); nursing (MS), including family nurse practitioner, generalist; nursing practice (DNP). *Accreditation:* AACN. *Program availability:* Part-time, 100% online, blended/hybrid learning. *Degree requirements:* For master's, variable foreign language requirement, comprehensive exam (for some programs), thesis (for some programs); for doctorate, variable foreign language requirement, comprehensive exam (for some programs), thesis/dissertation (for some programs), oral defense, individualized research. *Entrance requirements:* For master's, bachelor's degree in nursing from accredited program or associate's degree in nursing from accredited program with bachelor's degree in another field; minimum GPA of 3.0 in all nursing coursework; current RN license in good standing; for doctorate, master's degree in nursing from regionally-accredited university and nationally-accredited nursing program; minimum cumulative GPA of 3.0 in all nursing coursework of master's degree program; current RN license in good standing to practice. Additional exam requirements/recommendations for international students: required—TOEFL (minimum score 80 iBT), IELTS (minimum score 6.5). Electronic applications accepted.

**Northern Illinois University,** Graduate School, College of Health and Human Sciences, School of Nursing, De Kalb, IL 60115-2854. Offers MS, DNP. *Accreditation:* AACN. *Program availability:* Part-time. *Faculty:* 12 full-time (11 women), 1 (woman) part-time/adjunct. *Students:* 4 full-time (all women), 161 part-time (144 women); includes 47 minority (12 Black or African American, non-Hispanic/Latino; 2 American Indian or Alaska Native, non-Hispanic/Latino; 8 Asian, non-Hispanic/Latino; 23 Hispanic/Latino; 2 Two or more races, non-Hispanic/Latino), 3 international. Average age 36. 56 applicants, 61% accepted, 21 enrolled. In 2019, 23 master's awarded. *Degree requirements:* For master's, thesis optional, internship. *Entrance requirements:* For master's, minimum GPA of 3.0 in last 60 hours, BA in nursing, nursing license. Additional exam requirements/recommendations for international students: required—TOEFL (minimum score 550 paper-based). *Application deadline:* For fall admission, 6/1 for domestic students, 5/1 for international students; for spring admission, 11/1 for domestic students, 10/1 for international students. Applications are processed on a rolling basis. Application fee: $40. Electronic applications accepted. *Financial support:* In 2019–20, 1 research assistantship with full tuition reimbursement, 16 teaching assistantships with full tuition reimbursements were awarded; fellowships with full tuition reimbursements, career-related internships or fieldwork, Federal Work-Study, scholarships/grants, tuition waivers (full), and unspecified assistantships also available. Support available to part-time students. Financial award applicants required to submit FAFSA. *Unit head:* Dr. Susan Caplan, Chair, 815-753-6550, Fax: 815-753-0814. *Application contact:* Graduate School Office, 815-753-0395, E-mail: gradsch@niu.edu.
Website: http://www.chhs.niu.edu/nursing/

**Northern Kentucky University,** Office of Graduate Programs, School of Nursing and Health Professions, Online Doctor of Nursing Practice Program, Highland Heights, KY 41099. Offers DNP. *Accreditation:* AANA/CANAEP. *Program availability:* Part-time, online learning. *Degree requirements:* For doctorate, thesis/dissertation. *Entrance requirements:* For doctorate, RN license, master's degree in nursing, minimum GPA of 3.25, course in upper-division statistics, course in informatics, 3 professional

recommendations (2 from nurses), resume or curriculum vitae, all official transcripts, graduate paper of intent, interview. Additional exam requirements/recommendations for international students: required—TOEFL (minimum score 79 iBT); recommended—IELTS (minimum score 6.5). *Expenses:* Contact institution.

**Northern Kentucky University,** Office of Graduate Programs, School of Nursing and Health Professions, Program in Nursing, Highland Heights, KY 41099. Offers MSHS, MSN, Certificate, Post-Master's Certificate. *Accreditation:* ACEN. *Program availability:* Part-time, evening/weekend, online learning. *Degree requirements:* For master's, comprehensive exam, thesis optional. *Entrance requirements:* For master's, BS in nursing, letter from employer on letterhead indicating a minimum of 1,000 clinical hours of RN practice, updated resume, letter of purpose, official transcripts, proof of current licensure, minimum GPA of 3.0, two electronic letters of reference, successful completion of elementary statistics. Additional exam requirements/recommendations for international students: required—TOEFL (minimum score 550 paper-based; 79 iBT); recommended—IELTS (minimum score 6.5). Electronic applications accepted.

**Northern Michigan University,** Office of Graduate Education and Research, College of Health Sciences and Professional Studies, School of Nursing, Marquette, MI 49855-5301. Offers DNP. *Accreditation:* AACN. *Program availability:* Part-time, online learning. *Entrance requirements:* For doctorate, Michigan RN license; minimum undergraduate GPA of 3.0; 3 letters of recommendation; written personal goal statement. Additional exam requirements/recommendations for international students: required—TOEFL (minimum score 550 paper-based; 79 iBT), IELTS (minimum score 6.5). Electronic applications accepted.

**North Park University,** School of Nursing and Health Sciences, Chicago, IL 60625-4895. Offers advanced practice nursing (MS); leadership and management (MS); MBA/MS; MM/MSN; MS/MHR; MS/MNA. *Accreditation:* AACN. *Program availability:* Part-time, evening/weekend. *Degree requirements:* For master's, thesis. *Entrance requirements:* For master's, GMAT, MAT.

**Northwestern State University of Louisiana,** Graduate Studies and Research, College of Nursing and School of Allied Health, Shreveport, LA 71101-4653. Offers MS, MSN. *Accreditation:* AACN. *Program availability:* Part-time. *Degree requirements:* For master's, comprehensive exam, thesis or alternative. *Entrance requirements:* For master's, GRE General Test, 6 months of clinical nursing experience, BS in nursing, minimum GPA of 3.0. Additional exam requirements/recommendations for international students: required—TOEFL. Electronic applications accepted.

**Norwich University,** College of Graduate and Continuing Studies, Master of Science in Nursing Program, Northfield, VT 05663. Offers nursing administration (MSN); nursing education (MSN). *Accreditation:* AACN. *Program availability:* Evening/weekend, online only, mostly all online with a week-long residency requirement. *Entrance requirements:* For master's, minimum undergraduate GPA of 3.0. Additional exam requirements/ recommendations for international students: required—TOEFL (minimum score 550 paper-based; 80 iBT), IELTS (minimum score 6.5). Electronic applications accepted. *Expenses:* Contact institution.

**Nova Southeastern University,** Ron and Kathy Assaf College of Nursing, Fort Lauderdale, FL 33314-7796. Offers advanced practice registered nurse (MSN), including adult-gerontology acute care nurse practitioner, family nurse practitioner, psychiatric mental health nurse practitioner; executive nurse leadership (MSN); nursing (PhD), including nursing education; nursing education (MSN); nursing informatics (MSN); nursing practice (DNP). *Accreditation:* AACN. *Program availability:* Part-time, evening/weekend, 100% online, blended/hybrid learning, annual one-week summer institute delivered face-to-face on main campus. *Faculty:* 32 full-time (29 women), 34 part-time/adjunct (31 women). *Students:* 4 full-time (3 women), 658 part-time (585 women); includes 427 minority (182 Black or African American, non-Hispanic/Latino; 35 Asian, non-Hispanic/Latino; 197 Hispanic/Latino; 13 Two or more races, non-Hispanic/Latino), 3 international. Average age 38. 157 applicants, 93% accepted, 146 enrolled. In 2019, 184 master's, 12 doctorates awarded. *Degree requirements:* For doctorate, comprehensive exam, thesis/dissertation. *Entrance requirements:* For master's, minimum GPA of 3.0, RN, BSN, BS or BA; for doctorate, minimum GPA of 3.5, MSN, RN. Additional exam requirements/recommendations for international students: recommended—TOEFL. *Application deadline:* For fall admission, 8/1 for domestic students, 3/1 for international students; for winter admission, 12/9 for domestic students, 11/1 for international students. Applications are processed on a rolling basis. Application fee: $50. Electronic applications accepted. *Expenses:* Contact institution. *Financial support:* Application deadline: 4/15; applicants required to submit FAFSA. *Unit head:* Dr. Marcella M. Rutherford, Dean, 954-262-1963, E-mail: rmarcell@nova.edu. *Application contact:* Dianna Murphey, Director of Operations, 954-262-1975, E-mail: dgardner1@nova.edu.
Website: http://www.nova.edu/nursing/

**Oakland University,** Graduate Study and Lifelong Learning, School of Nursing, Rochester, MI 48309-4401. Offers MSN, DNP, PMC. *Accreditation:* AACN. *Program availability:* Part-time, evening/weekend. *Entrance requirements:* Additional exam requirements/recommendations for international students: required—TOEFL (minimum score 550 paper-based; 79 iBT), IELTS (minimum score 6.5). Electronic applications accepted. *Expenses: Tuition, area resident:* Full-time $12,328; part-time $770.50 per credit hour. Tuition, state resident: full-time $12,328; part-time $770.50 per credit hour. Tuition, nonresident: full-time $16,432; part-time $1027 per credit hour. *International tuition:* $16,432 full-time. Tuition and fees vary according to degree level and program.

**The Ohio State University,** Graduate School, College of Nursing, Columbus, OH 43210. Offers MHI, MS, DNP, PhD. *Accreditation:* AACN; ACNM/ACME. *Program availability:* Part-time. *Degree requirements:* For master's, thesis optional; for doctorate, thesis/dissertation. *Entrance requirements:* For doctorate, GRE (for PhD). Additional exam requirements/recommendations for international students: required—TOEFL (minimum score 600 paper-based; 100 iBT); recommended—IELTS (minimum score 8). Electronic applications accepted.

**Ohio University,** Graduate College, College of Health Sciences and Professions, School of Nursing, Athens, OH 45701-2979. Offers advanced clinical practice (DNP); executive practice (DNP); family nurse practitioner (MSN); nurse educator (MSN). *Accreditation:* AACN. *Degree requirements:* For master's, capstone project. *Entrance requirements:* For master's, GRE, bachelor's degree in nursing from accredited college or university, minimum overall undergraduate GPA of 3.0, official transcripts, statement of goals and objectives, resume, 3 letters of recommendation. Additional exam requirements/recommendations for international students: required—TOEFL (minimum score 550 paper-based; 80 iBT) or IELTS (minimum score 6.5). Electronic applications accepted.

**Oklahoma Baptist University,** Program in Nursing, Shawnee, OK 74804. Offers global nursing (MSN); nursing education (MSN). *Accreditation:* AACN.

**Oklahoma City University,** Kramer School of Nursing, Oklahoma City, OK 73106-1402. Offers clinical nurse leader (MSN); nursing (DNP, PhD); nursing education (MSN). *Accreditation:* ACEN. *Program availability:* Part-time, evening/weekend, online learning. *Degree requirements:* For master's, thesis, minimum GPA of 3.0; for doctorate, comprehensive exam, thesis/dissertation, minimum GPA of 3.0. *Entrance requirements:*

For master's, registered nurse licensure, minimum undergraduate GPA of 3.0, BSN from nationally-accredited nursing program, completion of courses in health assessment and statistics; for doctorate, GRE, current RN licensure; bachelor's and master's degrees from accredited programs (at least one of which must be in nursing); minimum graduate GPA of 3.5; personal essay; approved scholarly paper or published article/paper in a refereed journal. Additional exam requirements/recommendations for international students: required—TOEFL (minimum score 550 paper-based; 80 iBT), IELTS (minimum score 6). Electronic applications accepted. *Expenses:* Contact institution.

**Old Dominion University,** College of Health Sciences, School of Nursing, Doctor of Nursing Practice Program, Norfolk, VA 23529. Offers advanced practice (DNP); nurse executive (DNP). *Accreditation:* AACN. *Program availability:* Part-time, blended/hybrid learning. Terminal master's awarded for partial completion of doctoral program. *Degree requirements:* For doctorate, thesis/dissertation, capstone project. *Entrance requirements:* For doctorate, 3 letters of recommendation, essay, resume, transcripts. Additional exam requirements/recommendations for international students: required—TOEFL. Electronic applications accepted. *Expenses:* Contact institution.

**Olivet Nazarene University,** Graduate School, Department of Nursing, Bourbonnais, IL 60914. Offers family nurse practitioner (MSN); nursing (MSN).

**Oregon Health & Science University,** School of Nursing, Portland, OR 97239-2941. Offers MN, DNP, PhD, Post Master's Certificate. *Accreditation:* AACN; ACNM/ACME (one or more programs are accredited). *Program availability:* Part-time, 100% online, blended/hybrid learning. *Degree requirements:* For master's, thesis optional; for doctorate, thesis/dissertation (for some programs). *Entrance requirements:* For master's, GRE General Test, bachelor's degree in nursing, minimum undergraduate GPA of 3.0, previous course work in statistics; for doctorate, GRE General Test, master's degree in nursing; minimum undergraduate GPA of 3.0, 3.5 graduate; for Post Master's Certificate, master's degree in nursing. Additional exam requirements/recommendations for international students: required—TOEFL (minimum score 83 iBT). Electronic applications accepted. *Expenses:* Contact institution.

**Otterbein University,** Department of Nursing, Westerville, OH 43081. Offers advanced practice nurse educator (Certificate); clinical nurse leader (MSN); family nurse practitioner (MSN, Certificate); nurse anesthesia (MSN, Certificate); nursing (DNP); nursing service administration (MSN). *Accreditation:* AACN; AANA/CANAEP; ACEN. *Program availability:* Part-time, evening/weekend, online learning. *Degree requirements:* For master's, comprehensive exam (for some programs), thesis (for some programs). *Entrance requirements:* For master's, 2 reference forms, resume; for Certificate, official transcripts, 2 reference forms, essay, resumé. Additional exam requirements/recommendations for international students: required—TOEFL (minimum score 550 paper-based; 79 iBT).

**Pace University,** College of Health Professions, Lienhard School of Nursing, New York, NY 10038. Offers adult acute care nurse practitioner (MS, CAGS); family nurse practitioner (MS, CAGS); nursing (DNP, PhD); professional nursing leadership (MS, CAGS). *Accreditation:* AACN. *Program availability:* Part-time. Terminal master's awarded for partial completion of doctoral program. *Entrance requirements:* For master's, RN license, resume, personal statement, 2 letters of recommendation, official transcripts, minimum GPA of 3.0, undergraduate statistics; for doctorate, RN license, resume, personal statement, 2 letters of recommendation, official transcripts, accredited master's degree in nursing, minimum GPA of 3.3, state certification and board eligibility as FNP or ANP; for CAGS, RN license, resume, personal statement, 2 letters of recommendation, official transcripts, minimum GPA of 3.0, undergraduate statistics, completion of 2nd degree in nursing. Additional exam requirements/recommendations for international students: required—TOEFL (minimum score 100 iBT), IELTS or PTE. Electronic applications accepted. *Expenses:* Contact institution.

**Pacific Lutheran University,** School of Nursing, Tacoma, WA 98447. Offers MSN, DNP. *Accreditation:* AACN. *Degree requirements:* For master's, thesis or alternative. *Entrance requirements:* For master's, GRE General Test, minimum undergraduate GPA of 3.0. Additional exam requirements/recommendations for international students: required—TOEFL (minimum score 550 paper-based; 86 iBT). Electronic applications accepted. *Expenses:* Contact institution.

**Palm Beach Atlantic University,** School of Nursing, West Palm Beach, FL 33416-4708. Offers family nurse practitioner (DNP); health systems leadership (MSN). *Accreditation:* AACN. *Program availability:* Part-time. *Degree requirements:* For master's, capstone course. *Entrance requirements:* For master's, minimum GPA of 3.0; active RN license; personal interview; for doctorate, minimum GPA of 3.0; one year of experience as an RN; personal interview. Additional exam requirements/recommendations for international students: required—TOEFL (minimum score 550 paper-based; 79 iBT). Electronic applications accepted. *Expenses:* Contact institution.

**Penn State University Park,** Graduate School, College of Nursing, University Park, PA 16802. Offers nursing (MSN). *Accreditation:* AACN; ACEN. *Program availability:* Part-time, evening/weekend. *Entrance requirements:* Additional exam requirements/recommendations for international students: required—TOEFL (minimum score 550 paper-based; 80 iBT), IELTS. Electronic applications accepted. *Expenses:* Contact institution.

**Pensacola Christian College,** Graduate Studies, Pensacola, FL 32503-2267. Offers business administration (MBA); curriculum and instruction (MS, Ed D, Ed S); dramatics (MFA); educational leadership (MS, Ed D, Ed S); graphic design (MA, MFA); music (MA); nursing (MSN); performance studies (MA); studio art (MA, MFA).

**Pittsburg State University,** Graduate School, College of Arts and Sciences, Irene Ransom Bailey School of Nursing, Pittsburg, KS 66762. Offers nursing (DNP); nursing education (MSN). *Accreditation:* AACN. *Program availability:* Part-time. *Degree requirements:* For master's, thesis optional; for doctorate, thesis/dissertation optional. *Entrance requirements:* For master's, GRE General Test. Additional exam requirements/recommendations for international students: required—TOEFL (minimum score 550 paper-based; 79 iBT), IELTS (minimum score 6.5), PTE (minimum score 53). Electronic applications accepted. *Expenses:* Contact institution.

**Point Loma Nazarene University,** School of Nursing, Doctorate of Nursing Practice Program, San Diego, CA 92106. Offers DNP. *Program availability:* Online learning. *Students:* 20 part-time (18 women); includes 13 minority (2 Black or African American, non-Hispanic/Latino; 5 Asian, non-Hispanic/Latino; 3 Hispanic/Latino; 1 Native Hawaiian or other Pacific Islander, non-Hispanic/Latino; 2 Two or more races, non-Hispanic/Latino). Average age 49. 10 applicants, 70% accepted, 6 enrolled. Application fee: $50. Electronic applications accepted. *Expenses:* $1,160 per unit (2020-21 academic year). *Financial support:* In 2019–20, 6 students received support. *Unit head:* Dr. Larry Rankin, Associate Dean, 619-849-7813, E-mail: LarryRankin@pointloma.edu. *Application contact:* Dana Barger, Director of Recruitment and Admissions, Graduate and Professional Students, 619-329-6799, E-mail: gradinfo@pointloma.edu.
Website: https://www.pointloma.edu/graduate-studies/programs/doctorate-nursing-practice

**Point Loma Nazarene University,** School of Nursing, MS in Nursing Program, San Diego, CA 92106. Offers adult/gerontology (MSN); family/individual health (MSN); pediatrics (MSN). *Program availability:* Part-time. *Students:* 4 full-time (3 women), 49

part-time (41 women); includes 29 minority (5 Black or African American, non-Hispanic/Latino; 8 Asian, non-Hispanic/Latino; 14 Hispanic/Latino; 2 Two or more races, non-Hispanic/Latino). Average age 37. 30 applicants, 83% accepted, 14 enrolled. In 2019, 25 master's awarded. *Entrance requirements:* For master's, NCLEX exam, ADN or BSN in nursing, interview, RN license, essay, letters of recommendation, interview. *Application deadline:* For fall admission, 7/5 priority date for domestic students; for spring admission, 11/1 priority date for domestic students; for summer admission, 3/22 priority date for domestic students. Applications are processed on a rolling basis. Application fee: $50. Electronic applications accepted. *Expenses:* $820 per unit. *Financial support:* In 2019–20, 9 students received support. Scholarships/grants available. Financial award applicants required to submit FAFSA. *Unit head:* Dr. Larry Rankin, Associate Dean, 619-849-7813, E-mail: LarryRankin@pointloma.edu. *Application contact:* Dana Barger, Director of Recruitment and Admissions, Graduate and Professional Students, 619-329-6799, E-mail: gradinfo@pointloma.edu.
Website: https://www.pointloma.edu/graduate-studies/programs/nursing-ms

**Point Loma Nazarene University,** School of Nursing, Post-MSN Clinical Nurse Specialist Certificate Program, San Diego, CA 92106. Offers Post-MSN Certificate. *Program availability:* Online learning. *Students:* 2 part-time (1 woman); includes 1 minority (Asian, non-Hispanic/Latino). Average age 43. 2 applicants, 100% accepted, 1 enrolled. In 2019, 3 Post-MSN Certificates awarded. Application fee: $50. Electronic applications accepted. *Expenses:* $820 per unit. *Unit head:* Dr. Larry Rankin, Associate Dean, 619-849-7813, E-mail: LarryRankin@pointloma.edu. *Application contact:* Dana Barger, Director of Recruitment and Admissions, Graduate and Professional Students, 619-329-6799, E-mail: gradinfo@pointloma.edu.
Website: https://www.pointloma.edu/graduate-studies/programs/post-msn-cns-certificate

**Pontifical Catholic University of Puerto Rico,** College of Sciences, Department of Nursing, Ponce, PR 00717-0777. Offers medical-surgical nursing (MSN); mental health and psychiatric nursing (MSN). *Accreditation:* ACEN. *Program availability:* Part-time, evening/weekend. *Degree requirements:* For master's, comprehensive exam (for some programs), thesis, clinical research paper. *Entrance requirements:* For master's, GRE General Test, 2 letters of recommendation, interview, minimum GPA of 2.5. Electronic applications accepted.

**Prairie View A&M University,** College of Nursing, Houston, TX 77030. Offers MSN, DNP. *Accreditation:* AACN; ACEN. *Program availability:* Part-time, evening/weekend. *Faculty:* 8 full-time (7 women), 3 part-time/adjunct (2 women). *Students:* 39 full-time (30 women), 49 part-time (45 women); includes 82 minority (63 Black or African American, non-Hispanic/Latino; 13 Asian, non-Hispanic/Latino; 6 Hispanic/Latino). Average age 37. 23 applicants, 91% accepted, 18 enrolled. In 2019, 41 master's, 4 doctorates awarded. *Degree requirements:* For master's, comprehensive exam, thesis. *Entrance requirements:* For master's, MAT or GRE, BS in nursing; minimum 1 year of experience as registered nurse; minimum GPA of 2.75; 3 letters of recommendation from professional nurses; for doctorate, GRE, minimum GPA of 3.0 undergraduate, 3.3 graduate; 3 letters of recommendation from professional nurses. Additional exam requirements/recommendations for international students: required—TOEFL (minimum score 550 paper-based; 79 iBT). *Application deadline:* For fall admission, 5/1 priority date for domestic and international students; for spring admission, 10/1 priority date for domestic students, 9/1 priority date for international students; for summer admission, 3/1 priority date for domestic students, 2/1 priority date for international students. Applications are processed on a rolling basis. Application fee: $50. Electronic applications accepted. *Expenses: Tuition, area resident:* Full-time $5479.68. Tuition, state resident: full-time $5479.68. Tuition, nonresident: full-time $15,439. *International tuition:* $15,439 full-time. *Required fees:* $2149.32. *Financial support:* Career-related internships or fieldwork, Federal Work-Study, institutionally sponsored loans, scholarships/grants, and traineeships available. Support available to part-time students. Financial award application deadline: 4/1; financial award applicants required to submit FAFSA. *Unit head:* Dr. Betty N. Adams, Dean, 713-797-7009, Fax: 713-797-7013, E-mail: bnadams@pvamu.edu. *Application contact:* Dr. Forest Smith, Director of Student Services and Admissions, 713-797-7031, Fax: 713-797-7012, E-mail: fdsmith@pvamu.edu.
Website: http://www.pvamu.edu/nursing/

**Purdue University,** Graduate School, College of Health and Human Sciences, School of Nursing, West Lafayette, IN 47907. Offers adult gerontology primary care nurse practitioner (MS, Post Master's Certificate); nursing (DNP, PhD); primary care family nurse practitioner (MS, Post Master's Certificate); primary care pediatric nurse practitioner (MS, Post Master's Certificate). *Faculty:* 41 full-time (40 women), 9 part-time/adjunct (8 women). *Students:* 84 full-time (72 women), 46 part-time (43 women); includes 19 minority (7 Black or African American, non-Hispanic/Latino; 6 Asian, non-Hispanic/Latino; 4 Hispanic/Latino; 2 Two or more races, non-Hispanic/Latino), 1 international. Average age 33. 85 applicants, 80% accepted, 55 enrolled. In 2019, 29 master's, 7 doctorates, 2 other advanced degrees awarded. *Unit head:* Nancy E. Edwards, Head of the Graduate Program, 765-494-4015, E-mail: edwardsn@purdue.edu. *Application contact:* Reanne Hall, Graduate Contact, 765-494-9248, E-mail: gradnursing@purdue.edu.
Website: http://www.purdue.edu/hhs/nur/

**Purdue University Fort Wayne,** College of Health and Human Services, Department of Nursing, Fort Wayne, IN 46805-1499. Offers adult-gerontology primary care nurse practitioner (MS); family nurse practitioner (MS); nurse executive (MS); nursing administration (Certificate); nursing education (MS). *Accreditation:* ACEN. *Program availability:* Part-time. *Entrance requirements:* For master's, GRE Writing Test (if GPA below 3.0), BS in nursing, eligibility for Indiana RN license, minimum GPA of 3.0, essay, copy of resume, three references, undergraduate course work in research and statistics within last 5 years. Additional exam requirements/recommendations for international students: required—TOEFL (minimum score 550 paper-based; 79 iBT); recommended—TWE. Electronic applications accepted.

**Purdue University Global,** School of Nursing, Davenport, IA 52807. Offers nurse administrator (MS); nurse educator (MS). *Program availability:* Part-time, evening/weekend, online learning. *Entrance requirements:* For master's, RN. Additional exam requirements/recommendations for international students: required—TOEFL (minimum score 550 paper-based).

**Purdue University Northwest,** Graduate Studies Office, School of Nursing, Hammond, IN 46323-2094. Offers adult health clinical nurse specialist (MS); critical care clinical nurse specialist (MS); family nurse practitioner (MS); nurse executive (MS). *Accreditation:* ACEN. *Program availability:* Part-time, online learning. *Entrance requirements:* For master's, BSN. Additional exam requirements/recommendations for international students: required—TOEFL. Electronic applications accepted.

**Queen's University at Kingston,** School of Graduate Studies, Faculty of Health Sciences, School of Nursing, Kingston, ON K7L 3N6, Canada. Offers health and chronic illness (M Sc); nurse scientist (PhD); primary health care nurse practitioner (Certificate); women's and children's health (M Sc). *Degree requirements:* For master's, thesis. *Entrance requirements:* For master's, RN license. Additional exam requirements/recommendations for international students: required—TOEFL.

**Queens University of Charlotte,** Presbyterian School of Nursing, Charlotte, NC 28274-0002. Offers clinical nurse leader (MSN); nurse educator (MSN); nursing administrator (MSN). *Accreditation:* AACN. *Degree requirements:* For master's, research project. *Entrance requirements:* For master's, minimum GPA of 3.0. Additional exam requirements/recommendations for international students: required—TOEFL. Electronic applications accepted. *Expenses:* Contact institution.

**Quinnipiac University,** School of Nursing, Hamden, CT 06518-1940. Offers DNP. *Accreditation:* AACN. *Entrance requirements:* Additional exam requirements/recommendations for international students: required—TOEFL (minimum score 575 paper-based; 90 iBT), IELTS (minimum score 6.5). Electronic applications accepted. *Expenses: Tuition:* Part-time $1055 per credit. *Required fees:* $945 per semester. Tuition and fees vary according to course load and program.

**Radford University,** College of Graduate Studies and Research, Nursing Practice, DNP, Radford, VA 24142. Offers DNP. *Accreditation:* AACN. *Program availability:* Part-time, evening/weekend, online learning. *Degree requirements:* For doctorate, thesis/dissertation. *Entrance requirements:* For doctorate, GRE, current license to practice as RN; minimum undergraduate GPA of 3.0, graduate 3.5; 3-5 page essay; professional writing sample; three letters of reference; personal interview; resume or curriculum vitae; official transcripts; 2,000 hours of RN clinical experience; certification in BLS or ACLS; BSN. Additional exam requirements/recommendations for international students: required—TOEFL (minimum score 550 paper-based; 79 iBT), IELTS (minimum score 6.5). Electronic applications accepted. *Expenses:* Contact institution.

**Ramapo College of New Jersey,** Master of Science in Nursing Program, Mahwah, NJ 07430. Offers family nurse practitioner (MSN); nursing administrator (MSN); nursing education (MSN). *Accreditation:* ACEN. *Program availability:* Part-time. *Degree requirements:* For master's, thesis or alternative. *Entrance requirements:* For master's, official transcript; personal statement; 2 letters of recommendation; resume; current licensure as a Registered Nurse, or eligibility for licensure; evidence of one year of recent experience as RN prior to entry into clinical practicum courses; evidence of undergraduate statistics course; criminal background check. Additional exam requirements/recommendations for international students: required—TOEFL (minimum score 550 paper-based; 90 iBT); recommended—IELTS (minimum score 6). Electronic applications accepted. *Expenses:* Contact institution.

**Regis College,** Nursing and Health Sciences School, Weston, MA 02493. Offers applied behavior analysis (MS); counseling psychology (MA); health administration (MS); nurse practitioner (Certificate); nursing (MS, DNP); nursing education (Certificate); occupational therapy (MS). *Accreditation:* ACEN. *Program availability:* Part-time, evening/weekend, 100% online, blended/hybrid learning. *Degree requirements:* For doctorate, thesis/dissertation. *Entrance requirements:* For master's, minimum GPA of 3.0, official transcripts, recommendations, personal statement, resume/curriculum vitae, interview; for doctorate, GRE if GPA from master's lower than 3.5. Additional exam requirements/recommendations for international students: required—TOEFL (minimum score 560 paper-based; 79 iBT); recommended—IELTS (minimum score 6.5). *Application deadline:* Applications are processed on a rolling basis. Application fee: $75. Electronic applications accepted. *Financial support:* Federal Work-Study, scholarships/grants, and unspecified assistantships available. Support available to part-time students. Financial award applicants required to submit FAFSA. *Application contact:* Thomas May, Graduate Admission Counselor, 781-768-7162, E-mail: thomas.may@regiscollege.edu.

**Resurrection University,** Nursing Program, Chicago, IL 60622. Offers MSN. *Accreditation:* AACN. *Entrance requirements:* For master's, letter of recommendation.

**Rhode Island College,** School of Graduate Studies, School of Nursing, Providence, RI 02908-1991. Offers MSN, DNP. *Accreditation:* AACN; AANA/CANAEP. *Program availability:* Part-time. *Faculty:* 14 full-time (13 women), 16 part-time/adjunct (15 women). *Students:* 22 full-time (16 women), 83 part-time (70 women); includes 21 minority (5 Black or African American, non-Hispanic/Latino; 3 Asian, non-Hispanic/Latino; 9 Hispanic/Latino; 1 Native Hawaiian or other Pacific Islander, non-Hispanic/Latino; 3 Two or more races, non-Hispanic/Latino). Average age 36. In 2019, 30 master's, 4 doctorates awarded. *Entrance requirements:* For master's, GRE or Miller Analogies test, undergraduate transcripts, minimum undergraduate GPA of 3.0; 3 professional letters of recommendation at least one clinical; evidence of current unrestricted Rhode Island RN licensure; professional resume; letter of intent. Additional exam requirements/recommendations for international students: required—TOEFL (minimum score 550 paper-based; 80 iBT). *Application deadline:* For fall admission, 2/15 for domestic students. Applications are processed on a rolling basis. Application fee: $50. Electronic applications accepted. *Expenses: Tuition, area resident:* Part-time $462 per credit hour. Tuition, state resident: part-time $462 per credit hour. *Required fees:* $720. One-time fee: $140. *Financial support:* Teaching assistantships, Federal Work-Study, scholarships/grants, health care benefits, and unspecified assistantships available. Support available to part-time students. Financial award application deadline: 5/15; financial award applicants required to submit FAFSA. *Unit head:* Carolynn Masters, Dean, 401-456-8014, E-mail: cmasters@ric.edu. *Application contact:* Carolynn Masters, Dean, 401-456-8014, E-mail: cmasters@ric.edu.
Website: http://www.ric.edu/nursing/Pages/default.aspx

**Rivier University,** School of Graduate Studies, Division of Nursing and Health Professions, Nashua, NH 03060. Offers family nurse practitioner (MS); leadership in health systems management (MS); nursing education (MS); nursing practice (DNP); psychiatric/mental health nurse practitioner (MS); public health (MPH). *Accreditation:* ACEN. *Program availability:* Part-time, evening/weekend. *Entrance requirements:* For master's, GRE, MAT. Electronic applications accepted.

**Robert Morris University,** School of Nursing, Education and Human Studies, Moon Township, PA 15108. Offers MSN, DNP. *Accreditation:* AACN. *Program availability:* Part-time-only, evening/weekend, 100% online. *Faculty:* 16 full-time (13 women), 5 part-time/adjunct (4 women). *Students:* 351 part-time (266 women); includes 45 minority (31 Black or African American, non-Hispanic/Latino; 5 Asian, non-Hispanic/Latino; 3 Hispanic/Latino; 1 Native Hawaiian or other Pacific Islander, non-Hispanic/Latino; 5 Two or more races, non-Hispanic/Latino), 5 international. Average age 35. In 2019, 52 master's, 69 doctorates awarded. *Degree requirements:* For master's, Completion of 30 credits; for doctorate, Credits required varies by program. *Entrance requirements:* For master's, letters of recommendation. Additional exam requirements/recommendations for international students: required—TOEFL (minimum score 550 paper-based; 79 iBT). *Application deadline:* For fall admission, 7/1 priority date for domestic and international students; for spring admission, 11/1 priority date for domestic and international students. Applications are processed on a rolling basis. Application fee: $35. Electronic applications accepted. *Expenses:* Contact institution. *Financial support:* Federal Work-Study, institutionally sponsored loans, and unspecified assistantships available. Financial award application deadline: 5/1; financial award applicants required to submit FAFSA. *Application contact:* Kellie Laurenzi, Associate Vice President, Enrollment Management, 412-397-5200, E-mail: graduateadmissions@rmu.edu.
Website: https://www.rmu.edu/academics/schools/snehs

**Roberts Wesleyan College,** Department of Nursing, Rochester, NY 14624-1997. Offers nursing education (MSN); nursing informatics (MSN); nursing leadership and

administration (MSN). *Accreditation:* AACN. *Program availability:* Evening/weekend, online learning. *Degree requirements:* For master's, thesis. *Entrance requirements:* For master's, minimum GPA of 3.0; BS in nursing; interview; RN license; resume; course work in statistics. Additional exam requirements/recommendations for international students: required—TOEFL (minimum score 90 iBT), IELTS (minimum score 6.5). Electronic applications accepted.

**Rowan University,** Graduate School, College of Science and Mathematics, Department of Nursing, Glassboro, NJ 08028-1701. Offers MS. *Accreditation:* AACN. Electronic applications accepted. *Expenses: Tuition, area resident:* Part-time $715.50 per semester hour. Tuition, state resident: part-time $715.50 per semester hour. Tuition, nonresident: part-time $715.50 per semester hour. *Required fees:* $161.55 per semester hour.

**Rutgers University - Camden,** School of Nursing–Camden, Camden, NJ 08102-1401. Offers adult gerontology primary care nurse practitioner (DNP); family nurse practitioner (DNP). *Degree requirements:* For doctorate, minimum of 1,000 clinical residency hours, evidence-based clinical project.

**Rutgers University - Newark,** Rutgers School of Nursing, Newark, NJ 07107-3001. Offers adult health (MSN); adult occupational health (MSN); advanced practice nursing (MSN, Post Master's Certificate); family nurse practitioner (MSN); nurse anesthesia (MSN); nursing (MSN); nursing informatics (MSN); urban health (PhD); women's health practitioner (MSN). *Accreditation:* AANA/CANAEP. *Program availability:* Part-time. *Entrance requirements:* For master's, GRE, RN license; basic life support, statistics, and health assessment experience. Additional exam requirements/recommendations for international students: required—TOEFL. Electronic applications accepted. *Expenses:* Contact institution.

**Sacred Heart University,** Graduate Programs, College of Nursing, Fairfield, CT 06825. Offers clinical (DNP); clinical nurse leader (MSN); family nurse practitioner (MSN, Post-Master's Certificate); leadership (DNP); nursing education (MSN); nursing management and executive leadership (MSN). *Accreditation:* AACN. *Program availability:* Part-time, evening/weekend, 100% online, blended/hybrid learning. *Degree requirements:* For master's, thesis, 500 clinical hours; for doctorate, capstone. *Entrance requirements:* For master's, minimum GPA of 3.0, BSN or RN plus BS (for MSN); for doctorate, minimum GPA of 3.0, MSN or BSN plus MS in related field (for DNP). Additional exam requirements/recommendations for international students: required—TOEFL (minimum score 570 paper-based, 80 iBT), TWE, or IELTS (6.5). Electronic applications accepted. *Expenses:* Contact institution.

**Sage Graduate School,** School of Health Sciences, Department of Nursing, Troy, NY 12180-4115. Offers MS, DNS, Certificate, Post Master's Certificate. *Accreditation:* AACN. *Program availability:* Part-time, evening/weekend. *Faculty:* 8 full-time (all women), 13 part-time/adjunct (12 women). *Students:* 51 full-time (46 women), 172 part-time (156 women); includes 47 minority (15 Black or African American, non-Hispanic/Latino; 2 American Indian or Alaska Native, non-Hispanic/Latino; 18 Asian, non-Hispanic/Latino; 8 Hispanic/Latino; 4 Two or more races, non-Hispanic/Latino), 2 international. Average age 36. 186 applicants, 35% accepted, 38 enrolled. In 2019, 41 master's, 4 doctorates, 14 other advanced degrees awarded. *Degree requirements:* For master's, thesis or alternative. *Entrance requirements:* For master's, applicants must be currently licensed as a registered professional nurse in the state where they practice; bachelor's degree in nursing from a nationally accredited program; a GPA of 3.0 or higher; official transcripts of all previous UG/GR study; 2 letters of reference; 1-2 page statement of professional goals; current resume. Additional exam requirements/recommendations for international students: required—TOEFL (minimum score 550 paper-based). *Application deadline:* Applications are processed on a rolling basis. Application fee: $40. Electronic applications accepted. *Expenses: Tuition:* Part-time $730 per credit hour. Tuition and fees vary according to course load, degree level and program. *Financial support:* Fellowships, research assistantships, scholarships/grants, and unspecified assistantships available. Financial award application deadline: 3/1; financial award applicants required to submit FAFSA. *Unit head:* Dr. Kathleen Kelly, Dean, School of Health Sciences, 518-244-2030, Fax: 518-244-2009, E-mail: kellyk5@sage.edu. *Application contact:* Erin Menzer, Associate Director of Transfer and Nursing Enrollment Management, 518-244-4565, Fax: 518-244-6880, E-mail: menzee@sage.edu.

**Saginaw Valley State University,** College of Health and Human Services, Program in Clinical Nurse Specialist, University Center, MI 48710. Offers MSN. *Accreditation:* AACN. *Program availability:* Part-time, evening/weekend. *Degree requirements:* For master's, thesis optional. *Entrance requirements:* Additional exam requirements/recommendations for international students: required—TOEFL (minimum score 580 paper-based; 92 iBT). *Application deadline:* For fall admission, 7/15 for international students; for winter admission, 11/15 for international students; for spring admission, 4/15 for international students. Applications are processed on a rolling basis. Application fee: $30 ($90 for international students). Electronic applications accepted. *Expenses: Tuition, area resident:* Full-time $11,212; part-time $622.90 per credit hour. Tuition, state resident: full-time $11,212; part-time $622.90 per credit hour. Tuition, nonresident: full-time $11,212; part-time $1253 per credit hour. *Required fees:* $263; $14.60 per credit hour. Tuition and fees vary according to course load, degree level and program. *Financial support:* Federal Work-Study and scholarships/grants available. Support available to part-time students. Financial award application deadline: 4/1; financial award applicants required to submit FAFSA. *Unit head:* Dr. Karen Brown-Fackler, Associate Professor of Nursing, 989-964-2185, Fax: 989-964-4925, E-mail: kmbrown4@svsu.edu. *Application contact:* Jenna Briggs, Director, Graduate and International Admissions, 989-964-6096, Fax: 989-964-2788, E-mail: gradadm@svsu.edu.

**Saginaw Valley State University,** College of Health and Human Services, Program in Nursing, University Center, MI 48710. Offers MSN. *Accreditation:* AACN. *Program availability:* Part-time, evening/weekend. *Students:* 9 part-time (all women); includes 1 minority (Black or African American, non-Hispanic/Latino). Average age 38. 1 applicant. In 2019, 2 master's awarded. *Entrance requirements:* For master's, GRE, minimum GPA of 3.0. Additional exam requirements/recommendations for international students: required—TOEFL (minimum score 580 paper-based; 92 iBT). *Application deadline:* For fall admission, 7/15 for international students; for winter admission, 11/15 for international students; for spring admission, 4/15 for international students. Applications are processed on a rolling basis. Application fee: $30 ($90 for international students). Electronic applications accepted. *Expenses: Tuition, area resident:* Full-time $11,212; part-time $622.90 per credit hour. Tuition, state resident: full-time $11,212; part-time $622.90 per credit hour. Tuition, nonresident: full-time $11,212; part-time $1253 per credit hour. *Required fees:* $263; $14.60 per credit hour. Tuition and fees vary according to course load, degree level and program. *Financial support:* Federal Work-Study and scholarships/grants available. Support available to part-time students. *Unit head:* Dr. Karen Brown-Fackler, Coordinator, 989-964-2185, Fax: 989-964-4925, E-mail: kmbrown4@svsu.edu. *Application contact:* Jenna Briggs, Director, Graduate and International Admissions, 989-964-6096, Fax: 989-964-2788, E-mail: gradadm@svsu.edu.

**Saint Anthony College of Nursing,** Graduate Program, Rockford, IL 61114. Offers adult-gerontology acute care nurse practitioner (MSN). *Accreditation:* AACN. *Program availability:* Part-time, evening/weekend. *Faculty:* 6 full-time (5 women), 13 part-time/adjunct (11 women). *Students:* 3 full-time (all women), 75 part-time (69 women); includes 13 minority (5 Black or African American, non-Hispanic/Latino; 4 Asian, non-Hispanic/Latino; 4 Hispanic/Latino). Average age 37. In 2019, 12 master's awarded. *Application deadline:* For fall admission, 7/1 for domestic students; for spring admission, 12/1 for domestic students; for summer admission, 4/1 for domestic students. Applications are processed on a rolling basis. Application fee: $75. Electronic applications accepted. *Expenses: Tuition:* Full-time $17,712; part-time $984 per credit. *Required fees:* $605; $605 per unit. Tuition and fees vary according to course load. *Financial support:* Scholarships/grants available. Financial award applicants required to submit FAFSA. *Unit head:* Dr. Shannon Lizer, Dean, Graduate Affairs & Research, 815-282-7900, Fax: 815-282-7901, E-mail: shannonlizer@sacn.edu. *Application contact:* Jean Odom, Student Affairs Specialist - Graduate Program, 815-282-7900, Fax: 815-282-7901, E-mail: GradAdmissions@sacn.edu.
Website: https://www.osfhealthcare.org/sacn/admissions/graduate/dnp/

**St. Catherine University,** Graduate Programs, Program in Nursing, St. Paul, MN 55105. Offers adult-gerontological nurse practitioner (MS); nurse educator (MS); nursing (DNP); nursing: entry-level (MS); pediatric nurse practitioner (MS). *Accreditation:* ACEN. *Program availability:* Part-time, evening/weekend. *Degree requirements:* For master's, thesis; for doctorate, portfolio, systems change project. *Entrance requirements:* For master's, GRE General Test, bachelor's degree in nursing, current nursing license, 2 years of recent clinical practice; for doctorate, master's degree in nursing, RN license, advanced nursing position. Additional exam requirements/recommendations for international students: required—TOEFL (minimum score 600 paper-based; 100 iBT). *Expenses:* Contact institution.

**Saint Francis Medical Center College of Nursing,** SFMC College of Nursing Graduate Programs, Peoria, IL 61603-3783. Offers adult gerontology (MSN); clinical nurse leader (MSN); family nurse practitioner (MSN, Post-Graduate Certificate); family psychiatric mental health nurse practitioner (MSN); neonatal nurse practitioner (MSN); nurse clinician (Post-Graduate Certificate); nurse educator (MSN, Post-Graduate Certificate); nursing (DNP), including leadership/ clinician; nursing management leadership (MSN). *Accreditation:* ACEN. *Program availability:* Part-time, online only, 100% online, blended/hybrid learning. *Faculty:* 12 full-time (all women), 10 part-time/adjunct (all women). *Students:* 1 (woman) full-time, 188 part-time (157 women); includes 20 minority (10 Black or African American, non-Hispanic/Latino; 3 Asian, non-Hispanic/Latino; 3 Hispanic/Latino; 4 Two or more races, non-Hispanic/Latino). Average age 40. 54 applicants, 91% accepted, 18 enrolled. In 2019, 51 master's, 11 doctorates awarded. *Degree requirements:* For master's, research experience, portfolio, practicum; for doctorate, practicum. *Entrance requirements:* For master's, Nursing research, health assessment, RN license; for doctorate, Master's degree in nursing, professional portfolio, graduate statistics, transcripts, RN license. Additional exam requirements/recommendations for international students: required—TOEFL (minimum score 550 paper-based; 79 iBT). *Application deadline:* For fall admission, 6/1 priority date for domestic and international students; for spring admission, 11/15 priority date for domestic and international students. Applications are processed on a rolling basis. Application fee: $50. *Expenses: Tuition:* Part-time $705 per credit hour. *Required fees:* $270 per unit. *Financial support:* In 2019–20, 13 students received support. Scholarships/grants available. Support available to part-time students. Financial award application deadline: 6/15; financial award applicants required to submit FAFSA. *Unit head:* Dr. Sandie S Soldwisch, President of OSF Colleges of Health Sciences, 815-282-7909, Fax: 309-624-8973, E-mail: Sandie.S.Soldwisch@osfhealthcare.org. *Application contact:* Dr. Kim A. Mitchell, Dean, Graduate Program, 309-655-2201, Fax: 309-624-8973, E-mail: kim.a.mitchell@osfhealthcare.org.
Website: http://www.sfmccon.edu/graduate-programs/

**Saint Francis University,** Nursing Program, Loretto, PA 15940-0600. Offers leadership/education (MSN). *Program availability:* Part-time, online only, blended/hybrid learning. *Faculty:* 2 full-time (both women), 4 part-time/adjunct (all women). *Students:* 7 part-time (all women). Average age 44. 9 applicants, 78% accepted, 4 enrolled. In 2019, 10 master's awarded. *Entrance requirements:* Additional exam requirements/recommendations for international students: required—TOEFL. Application fee: $30. Electronic applications accepted. *Expenses:* 625 per credit, 48 credits. *Financial support:* Applicants required to submit FAFSA. *Unit head:* Dr. Camille Wendekier, RN, Coordinator, 814-472-2843, E-mail: cwendekier@francis.edu. *Application contact:* Dr. Peter Raymond Skoner.
Website: https://www.francis.edu/Nursing-Masters/

**St. John Fisher College,** Wegmans School of Nursing, Advanced Practice Nursing Program, Rochester, NY 14618-3597. Offers MS, Certificate. *Accreditation:* AACN. *Program availability:* Part-time, evening/weekend. *Faculty:* 13 full-time (12 women), 1 part-time/adjunct (0 women). *Students:* 2 full-time (both women), 261 part-time (229 women); includes 19 minority (1 Black or African American, non-Hispanic/Latino; 1 American Indian or Alaska Native, non-Hispanic/Latino; 7 Asian, non-Hispanic/Latino; 5 Hispanic/Latino; 5 Two or more races, non-Hispanic/Latino). Average age 31. 146 applicants, 55% accepted, 54 enrolled. In 2019, 52 master's awarded. *Degree requirements:* For master's, clinical practice, project; for Certificate, clinical practice. *Entrance requirements:* For master's, BSN; undergraduate course work in statistics, health assessment, and nursing research; current New York State RN license; 2 letters of recommendation; current resume. Additional exam requirements/recommendations for international students: required—TOEFL (minimum score 575 paper-based; 80 iBT). *Application deadline:* Applications are processed on a rolling basis. Application fee: $30. Electronic applications accepted. *Expenses:* Contact institution. *Financial support:* Scholarships/grants and traineeships available. Financial award applicants required to submit FAFSA. *Unit head:* Dr. Colleen Donegan, Graduate Director, 585-899-3788, Fax: 585-385-8466, E-mail: cdonegan@sjfc.edu. *Application contact:* Michelle Gosier, Director of Transfer and Graduate Admissions, 585-385-8064, E-mail: mgosier@sjfc.edu.
Website: https://www.sjfc.edu/graduate-programs/ms-in-nursing-programs/

**St. John Fisher College,** Wegmans School of Nursing, Doctor of Nursing Practice Program, Rochester, NY 14618-3597. Offers DNP. *Accreditation:* AACN. *Program availability:* Part-time, evening/weekend. *Faculty:* 6 full-time (5 women), 1 part-time/adjunct (0 women). *Students:* 12 part-time (9 women); includes 2 minority (1 Black or African American, non-Hispanic/Latino; 1 Asian, non-Hispanic/Latino). Average age 38. 12 applicants, 50% accepted, 4 enrolled. In 2019, 2 doctorates awarded. *Degree requirements:* For doctorate, 1,000 hours of clinical practice, clinical scholarship project. *Entrance requirements:* For doctorate, New York State RN license; New York State Certificate as advanced practice nurse (APN) or eligibility and National Professional Certification in APN specialty; currently practicing as APN; 2 letters of recommendation; writing sample. *Application deadline:* For fall admission, 8/1 for domestic students; for spring admission, 12/1 for domestic students. Applications are processed on a rolling basis. Electronic applications accepted. *Expenses:* Contact institution. *Financial support:* Scholarships/grants available. Financial award applicants required to submit FAFSA. *Unit head:* Dr. John Kirchgessner, Program Director, 585-899-3739, E-mail:

jKirchgessner@sjfc.edu. *Application contact:* Michelle Gosier, Director of Transfer and Graduate Admissions, 585-385-8064, E-mail: mgosier@sjfc.edu. Website: https://www.sjfc.edu/graduate-programs/doctor-of-nursing-practice-dnp/

**St. Joseph's College, Long Island Campus,** Program in Nursing, Patchogue, NY 11772-2399. Offers adult-gerontology clinical nurse specialist (MS); adult-gerontology primary care nurse practitioner (MS); nursing education (MS). *Program availability:* Part-time, evening/weekend. *Faculty:* 7 full-time (6 women), 1 (woman) part-time/adjunct. *Students:* 54 part-time (48 women); includes 18 minority (7 Black or African American, non-Hispanic/Latino; 2 Asian, non-Hispanic/Latino; 8 Hispanic/Latino; 1 Two or more races, non-Hispanic/Latino). Average age 38. 57 applicants, 51% accepted, 22 enrolled. In 2019, 14 master's awarded. *Entrance requirements:* For master's, Application, proof of New York State R.N. license, curriculum vitae, personal statement, 2 letters of reference, official transcripts, verification of employment form, proof of malpractice insurance. Additional exam requirements/recommendations for international students: required—TOEFL (minimum score 80 iBT). *Application deadline:* Applications are processed on a rolling basis. Application fee: $25. Electronic applications accepted. *Expenses: Tuition:* Full-time $19,350; part-time $1075 per credit. *Required fees:* $410. *Financial support:* In 2019–20, 33 students received support. *Unit head:* Dr. Maria Fletcher, RN, Director, Associate Professor, 631-687-5180, E-mail: mfletcher@sjcny.edu. *Application contact:* Dr. Maria Fletcher, RN, Director, Associate Professor, 631-687-5180, E-mail: mfletcher@sjcny.edu. Website: https://www.sjcny.edu/nursingli

**St. Joseph's College, New York,** Program in Nursing, Brooklyn, NY 11205-3688. Offers adult-gerontology clinical nurse specialist (MS); adult-gerontology primary care nurse practitioner (MS); nursing education (MS). *Accreditation:* ACEN. *Program availability:* Part-time, evening/weekend. *Faculty:* 3 full-time (all women), 2 part-time/adjunct (both women). *Students:* 52 part-time (47 women); includes 43 minority (40 Black or African American, non-Hispanic/Latino; 2 Asian, non-Hispanic/Latino; 1 Two or more races, non-Hispanic/Latino). Average age 43. 49 applicants, 67% accepted, 21 enrolled. In 2019, 19 master's awarded. *Entrance requirements:* Additional exam requirements/recommendations for international students: required—TOEFL (minimum score 80 iBT). *Application deadline:* Applications are processed on a rolling basis. Application fee: $25. Electronic applications accepted. *Expenses: Tuition:* Full-time $19,350; part-time $1075 per credit. *Required fees:* $400. *Financial support:* In 2019–20, 9 students received support. *Unit head:* Maria Fletcher, Director, Associate Professor, 718-940-5891, E-mail: mfletcher@sjcny.edu. *Application contact:* Maria Fletcher, Director, Associate Professor, 718-940-5891, E-mail: mfletcher@sjcny.edu. Website: https://www.sjcny.edu/brooklyn/academics/graduate/graduate-degrees/nursing-clinical-nurse-specialist/m.s.-in-nursing-major

**Saint Joseph's College of Maine,** Master of Science in Nursing Program, Standish, ME 04084. Offers administration (MSN); education (MSN); family nurse practitioner (MSN); nursing administration and leadership (Certificate); nursing and health care education (Certificate). *Accreditation:* AACN. *Program availability:* Part-time, online learning. *Entrance requirements:* For master's, MAT. Electronic applications accepted.

**Saint Louis University,** Graduate Programs, School of Nursing, St. Louis, MO 63104-1099. Offers MSN, DNP, PhD, Certificate. *Accreditation:* AACN. *Program availability:* Part-time, online learning. *Degree requirements:* For master's, comprehensive exam, thesis optional; for doctorate, comprehensive exam, thesis/dissertation, preliminary exams. *Entrance requirements:* For master's, 3 letters of recommendation, resumé, transcripts; for doctorate, GRE General Test, 3 letters of recommendation, curriculum vitae; for Certificate, 3 letters of recommendation, resumé, transcripts, copy of RN license, personal statement. Additional exam requirements/recommendations for international students: required—TOEFL (minimum score 525 paper-based). Electronic applications accepted.

**Saint Mary-of-the-Woods College,** Master of Science in Nursing Program, Saint Mary of the Woods, IN 47876. Offers MSN. *Faculty:* 2 full-time (both women). *Students:* 16 full-time (14 women), 1 (woman) part-time; includes 9 minority (all Two or more races, non-Hispanic/Latino). Average age 38. 12 applicants, 100% accepted, 11 enrolled. *Entrance requirements:* For master's, Baccalaureate degree in nursing from an accredited college or university. Cumulative GPA of 3.0 / 4.0 or higher on any undergraduate work. Cumulative GPA of 3.0 / 4.0 or higher on any graduate work. Must have current unencumbered license as a registered nurse. Additional exam requirements/recommendations for international students: required—TOEFL (minimum score 500 paper-based; 62 iBT), Other English proficiency tests may be accepted and will be reviewed on a case-by-case basis. Tuition and fees vary according to course load and program. *Financial support:* Scholarships/grants available. Financial award applicants required to submit FAFSA. *Unit head:* Marcia Miller, Chair, 812-535-5119, E-mail: mmiller5@smwc.edu. *Application contact:* Marcia Miller, Chair, 812-535-5119, E-mail: mmiller5@smwc.edu. Website: https://www.smwc.edu/academics/departments/graduate-studies/master-science-nursing/

**Saint Mary's College,** Graduate Studies, Doctor of Nursing Practice Program, Notre Dame, IN 46556. Offers adult - gerontology acute care nurse practitioner (DNP); adult - gerontology primary care nurse practitioner (DNP); family nurse practitioner (DNP). *Program availability:* Part-time-only, evening/weekend, online only, 100% online. *Faculty:* 11. *Students:* 58 part-time (53 women); includes 15 minority (8 Black or African American, non-Hispanic/Latino; 3 Asian, non-Hispanic/Latino; 4 Hispanic/Latino). Average age 30. 24 applicants, 75% accepted, 15 enrolled. In 2019, 1 doctorate awarded. *Degree requirements:* For doctorate, comprehensive exam, thesis/dissertation. *Entrance requirements:* For doctorate, BSN or MSN, unencumbered RN license or eligibility for RN licensure, official transcripts from previously-attended institutions, 3 letters of recommendation, personal statement, resume or curriculum vitae. Additional exam requirements/recommendations for international students: recommended—TOEFL (minimum score 80 iBT), IELTS (minimum score 6.5). *Application deadline:* For fall admission, 3/31 priority date for domestic and international students. Applications are processed on a rolling basis. Application fee: $70. Electronic applications accepted. *Expenses:* $5765 per semester. *Financial support:* In 2019–20, 3 students received support. Scholarships/grants available. Financial award application deadline: 3/1; financial award applicants required to submit FAFSA. *Unit head:* Sue Anderson, Program Director, Doctor of Nursing Practice, 574-284-4682, E-mail: sanderson@saintmarys.edu. *Application contact:* Melissa Fruscione, Director, Graduate Studies, 574-284-5098, E-mail: graduateadmission@saintmarys.edu. Website: https://grad.saintmarys.edu/academic-programs/doctor-nursing-practice

**Saint Peter's University,** School of Nursing, Nursing Program, Jersey City, NJ 07306-5997. Offers adult nurse practitioner (MSN, Certificate); advanced practice (DNP); case management (MSN, DNP). *Accreditation:* AACN. *Program availability:* Part-time, evening/weekend. *Entrance requirements:* Additional exam requirements/recommendations for international students: required—TOEFL. Electronic applications accepted.

**Saint Xavier University,** Graduate Studies, School of Nursing, Chicago, IL 60655-3105. Offers MSN, Certificate, MBA/MS. *Accreditation:* AACN. *Program availability:*

Part-time, evening/weekend. *Entrance requirements:* For master's, GRE General Test or MAT, minimum GPA of 3.0, RN license.

**Salem State University,** School of Graduate Studies, Program in Nursing, Salem, MA 01970-5353. Offers adult-gerontology primary care nursing (MSN); nursing administration (MSN); nursing education (MSN); MBA/MSN. *Accreditation:* AACN. *Program availability:* Part-time, evening/weekend. *Entrance requirements:* For master's, GRE or MAT. Additional exam requirements/recommendations for international students: required—TOEFL (minimum score 550 paper-based; 80 iBT) or IELTS (minimum score 5.5).

**Salisbury University,** DNP Program, Salisbury, MD 21801. Offers family nurse practitioner (DNP); nursing leadership (DNP). *Accreditation:* AACN. *Program availability:* Part-time, evening/weekend, 100% online, blended/hybrid learning. *Faculty:* 14 full-time (13 women), 4 part-time/adjunct (all women). *Students:* 25 full-time (22 women), 8 part-time (all women); includes 8 minority (5 Black or African American, non-Hispanic/Latino; 1 Hispanic/Latino; 2 Two or more races, non-Hispanic/Latino). Average age 34. 17 applicants, 71% accepted, 8 enrolled. In 2019, 7 doctorates awarded. *Degree requirements:* For doctorate, Evidence based project. *Entrance requirements:* For doctorate, transcripts; resume or CV; personal statement; proof of certification or licensure; minimum GPA of 3.0; three letters of recommendation; undergraduate degree in nursing. *Application deadline:* For fall admission, 3/1 priority date for domestic and international students. Applications are processed on a rolling basis. Application fee: $65. Electronic applications accepted. *Expenses:* Contact institution. *Financial support:* Career-related internships or fieldwork and scholarships/grants available. Support available to part-time students. Financial award application deadline: 3/1; financial award applicants required to submit FAFSA. *Unit head:* Dr. Annette Barnes, Graduate Program Chair, 410-546-4380, E-mail: ahbarnes@salisbury.edu. *Application contact:* Kristi Jenkins, Administrative Assistant II, 410-548-2242, E-mail: kljenkins@salisbury.edu. Website: https://www.salisbury.edu/explore-academics/programs/graduate-degree-programs/nursing-practice-doctor/

**Salisbury University,** MS in Nursing Program, Salisbury, MD 21801-6837. Offers nursing (MS), including clinical nurse educator, health care leadership. *Accreditation:* AACN. *Program availability:* Part-time, evening/weekend, 100% online, blended/hybrid learning. *Faculty:* 14 full-time (13 women), 4 part-time/adjunct (all women). *Students:* 1 (woman) full-time, 4 part-time (all women); includes 2 minority (1 Asian, non-Hispanic/Latino; 1 Hispanic/Latino). Average age 27. 3 applicants, 100% accepted, 3 enrolled. *Degree requirements:* For master's, internship, capstone or thesis. *Entrance requirements:* For master's, transcripts; resume or CV; personal statement; proof of certification or licensure; minimum GPA of 3.0; two letters of recommendation; undergraduate degree in nursing; undergraduate statistics. *Application deadline:* For fall admission, 3/1 priority date for domestic and international students. Application fee: $65. Electronic applications accepted. *Expenses:* Contact institution. *Financial support:* In 2019–20, 1 student received support, including 1 research assistantship with full tuition reimbursement available (averaging $8,000 per year), 1 teaching assistantship with full tuition reimbursement available (averaging $9,000 per year); career-related internships or fieldwork and scholarships/grants also available. Support available to part-time students. Financial award application deadline: 3/1; financial award applicants required to submit FAFSA. *Unit head:* Dr. Annette Barnes, Graduate Program Chair, 410-546-4380, E-mail: ahbarnes@salisbury.edu. *Application contact:* Kristi Jenkins, Administrative Assistant II, 410-548-2242, E-mail: kljenkins@salisbury.edu. Website: https://www.salisbury.edu/explore-academics/programs/graduate-degree-programs/nursing-master/

**Salve Regina University,** Program in Nursing, Newport, RI 02840-4192. Offers DNP. *Program availability:* Part-time, evening/weekend, online only, 100% online. *Degree requirements:* For doctorate, thesis/dissertation. *Entrance requirements:* For doctorate, copy of active, unencumbered RN license issued in the U.S., copy of unencumbered APRN license and certification (if applicable), evidence of completion of 3 credits in statistics, evidence of completion of 3 credits in master's-level advanced research course. Additional exam requirements/recommendations for international students: required—TOEFL (minimum score 100 iBT), IELTS (minimum score 7). *Application deadline:* For fall admission, 7/1 for domestic students, 3/15 priority date for international students; for spring admission, 11/1 for domestic students, 9/15 priority date for international students. Applications are processed on a rolling basis. Electronic applications accepted. Application fee is waived when completed online. *Expenses:* Contact institution. *Financial support:* Application deadline: 3/1; applicants required to submit FAFSA. *Unit head:* Dr. Sharon Stager, Director, 401-341-3297, E-mail: sharon.stager@salve.edu. *Application contact:* Laurie Reilly, Graduate Admissions Manager, 401-341-2153, Fax: 401-341-2973, E-mail: laurie.reilly@salve.edu. Website: http://www.salve.edu/graduate-studies/nursing

**Samford University,** Ida Moffett School of Nursing, Birmingham, AL 35229. Offers advanced practice (DNP), including emergency nurse practitioner, family nurse practitioner, transformation of care; family nurse practitioner (MSN, DNP), including emergency nurse practitioner specialty (MSN); nurse anesthesia (DNP); nursing administration (DNP); psychiatric mental health nurse practitioner (DNP). *Accreditation:* AACN; AANA/CANAEP. *Program availability:* Part-time, evening/weekend, blended/hybrid learning. *Faculty:* 16 full-time (all women), 3 part-time/adjunct (0 women). *Students:* 281 full-time (239 women), 39 part-time (38 women); includes 68 minority (39 Black or African American, non-Hispanic/Latino; 2 American Indian or Alaska Native, non-Hispanic/Latino; 10 Asian, non-Hispanic/Latino; 10 Hispanic/Latino; 1 Native Hawaiian or other Pacific Islander, non-Hispanic/Latino; 6 Two or more races, non-Hispanic/Latino). Average age 35. 59 applicants, 97% accepted, 29 enrolled. In 2019, 47 master's, 68 doctorates awarded. *Degree requirements:* For doctorate, DNP project with poster presentation. *Entrance requirements:* For doctorate, GRE is required for the Nurse Anesthesia Program. Additional exam requirements/recommendations for international students: required—TOEFL (minimum score 575 paper-based; 90 iBT), IELTS (minimum score 6.5). *Application deadline:* For fall admission, 4/1 for domestic and international students; for spring admission, 8/1 for domestic and international students; for summer admission, 1/1 for domestic and international students. Application fee: $50. Electronic applications accepted. *Expenses: Tuition:* Full-time $17,754; part-time $862 per credit hour. *Required fees:* $550; $550 per unit. Full-time tuition and fees vary according to course load, program and student level. *Financial support:* In 2019–20, 30 students received support. Application deadline: 2/15; applicants required to submit FAFSA. *Unit head:* Dr. Jane S. Martin, Interim Dean and Professor, Ida Moffett School of Nursing, 205-726-2760, E-mail: jsmartin@samford.edu. *Application contact:* Allyson Maddox, Director of Graduate Student Services, 205-726-2047, E-mail: amaddox@samford.edu. Website: http://samford.edu/nursing

**Samuel Merritt University,** School of Nursing, Oakland, CA 94609-3108. Offers case management (MSN); family nurse practitioner (MSN, DNP, Certificate); nurse anesthetist (MSN, Certificate); nursing (DNP). *Accreditation:* AACN; AANA/CANAEP (one or more programs are accredited). *Program availability:* Part-time, evening/weekend, 100% online, blended/hybrid learning. *Degree requirements:* For master's, thesis or alternative; for doctorate, project. *Entrance requirements:* For master's, GRE

General Test (for nurse anesthetist program), minimum GPA of 2.5 in science, 3.0 overall; previous course work in statistics; current RN license; for doctorate and Certificate, minimum GPA of 2.5 in science, 3.0 overall; previous course work in statistics; current RN license. Additional exam requirements/recommendations for international students: required—TOEFL (minimum score 100 iBT). Electronic applications accepted. *Expenses:* Contact institution.

**San Diego State University,** Graduate and Research Affairs, College of Health and Human Services, School of Nursing, San Diego, CA 92182. Offers MS. *Accreditation:* AACN; ACNM/ACME. *Program availability:* Part-time, evening/weekend. *Entrance requirements:* For master's, GRE General Test, previous course work in statistics and physical assessment, 3 letters of recommendation, California RN license. Additional exam requirements/recommendations for international students: required—TOEFL. Electronic applications accepted.

**San Francisco State University,** Division of Graduate Studies, College of Health and Social Sciences, School of Nursing, San Francisco, CA 94132-1722. Offers adult acute care (MS); clinical nurse specialist (MS); community/public health nursing (MS); family nurse practitioner (Certificate); nursing administration (MS); pediatrics (MS); women's health (MS). *Accreditation:* AACN. *Program availability:* Part-time. *Application deadline:* Applications are processed on a rolling basis. *Expenses: Tuition, area resident:* Full-time $7176; part-time $4164 per year. Tuition, state resident: full-time $7176; part-time $4164 per year. Tuition, nonresident: full-time $16,680; part-time $396 per unit. *International tuition:* $16,680 full-time. *Required fees:* $1524; $1524 per unit. $762 per semester. Tuition and fees vary according to degree level and program. *Financial support:* Career-related internships or fieldwork available. *Unit head:* Dr. Mary-Ann van Dam, 415-338-1802, Fax: 415-338-0555, E-mail: vandam@sfsu.edu. *Application contact:* Prof. Fang-yu Chou, Assistant Director of Graduate Programs, 415-338-6853, Fax: 415-338-0555, E-mail: fchou@sfsu.edu.
Website: http://nursing.sfsu.edu

**San Jose State University,** Program in Nursing, San Jose, CA 95192-0057. Offers gerontology nurse practitioner (MS); nursing (Certificate); nursing administration (MS); nursing education (MS). *Accreditation:* AACN. *Faculty:* 5 full-time (all women), 3 part-time/adjunct (all women). *Students:* 21 full-time (17 women), 52 part-time (49 women); includes 45 minority (4 Black or African American, non-Hispanic/Latino; 29 Asian, non-Hispanic/Latino; 12 Hispanic/Latino), 3 international. Average age 37. 30 applicants, 97% accepted, 23 enrolled. In 2019, 22 master's awarded. *Degree requirements:* For master's, comprehensive exam, thesis. *Entrance requirements:* For master's, BSN. *Application deadline:* For fall admission, 3/1 for domestic students. Applications are processed on a rolling basis. Application fee: $70. Electronic applications accepted. *Expenses:* Contact institution. *Financial support:* Application deadline: 5/1; applicants required to submit FAFSA. *Unit head:* Colleen O'Leary-Kelley, Department Chair, 408-924-1319, Fax: 408-924-3135, E-mail: colleen.oleary-kelley@sjsu.edu. *Application contact:* Karen Wilcox, FNP Program Analyst, 408-924-3153, Fax: 408-924-3135, E-mail: karen.wilcox@sjsu.edu.
Website: http://www.sjsu.edu/nursing/

**Seattle Pacific University,** MS in Nursing Program, Seattle, WA 98119-1997. Offers administration (MSN); adult/gerontology nurse practitioner (MSN); clinical nurse specialist (MSN); family nurse practitioner (MSN, Certificate); informatics (MSN); nurse educator (MSN). *Accreditation:* AACN. *Program availability:* Part-time. *Students:* 42 full-time (38 women), 18 part-time (16 women); includes 28 minority (5 Black or African American, non-Hispanic/Latino; 18 Asian, non-Hispanic/Latino; 5 Hispanic/Latino), 2 international. Average age 33. 59 applicants, 41% accepted. In 2019, 10 master's awarded. *Degree requirements:* For master's, thesis. *Entrance requirements:* For master's, personal statement, transcripts, undergraduate nursing degree, proof of undergraduate statistics course with minimum GPA of 2.0, 2 recommendations. *Application deadline:* For fall admission, 1/15 priority date for domestic students; for spring admission, 1/15 for domestic students. Applications are processed on a rolling basis. Application fee: $50. Electronic applications accepted. *Expenses:* Contact institution. *Financial support:* Fellowships and scholarships/grants available. Financial award applicants required to submit FAFSA. *Unit head:* Dr. Antwinett Lee, Associate Dean, 206-281-2607, E-mail: leea30@spu.edu. *Application contact:* Dr. Antwinett Lee, Associate Dean, 206-281-2607, E-mail: leea30@spu.edu.
Website: http://spu.edu/academics/school-of-health-sciences/undergraduate-programs/nursing

**Seattle University,** College of Nursing, Doctor of Nursing Practice Program, Seattle, WA 98122-1090. Offers DNP. *Accreditation:* AACN. *Program availability:* Evening/weekend. *Students:* Average age 40. In 2019, 9 doctorates awarded. *Entrance requirements:* For doctorate, letter of intent. *Application deadline:* For fall admission, 11/1 priority date for domestic students. *Financial support:* In 2019–20, 4 students received support. *Unit head:* Dr. Kristen Swanson, Dean, 206-296-5670, E-mail: swansonk@seattleu.edu. *Application contact:* Janet Shandley, Director of Graduate Admissions, 206-296-5900, Fax: 206-298-5656, E-mail: grad_admissions@seattleu.edu.
Website: https://www.seattleu.edu/nursing/dnp/

**Seton Hall University,** College of Nursing, South Orange, NJ 07079-2697. Offers advanced practice in primary health care (MSN, DNP), including adult/gerontological nurse practitioner, pediatric nurse practitioner; entry into practice (MSN); health systems administration (MSN, DNP); nursing (PhD); nursing case management (MSN); nursing education (MA); school nurse (MSN); MSN/MA. *Accreditation:* AACN. *Program availability:* Part-time, online learning. *Degree requirements:* For master's, research project; for doctorate, dissertation or scholarly project. *Entrance requirements:* For doctorate, GRE (waived for students with GPA of 3.5 or higher). Additional exam requirements/recommendations for international students: required—TOEFL. Electronic applications accepted.

**Shenandoah University,** Eleanor Wade Custer School of Nursing, Winchester, VA 22601. Offers adult gerontology primary care nurse practitioner (Graduate Certificate); adult-gerontology primary care nurse practitioner (MSN); family nurse practitioner (MSN, DNP, Graduate Certificate); general (MSN); health systems leadership (DNP); health systems management (MSN, Graduate Certificate); nurse midwifery (MSN); nurse-midwifery (Graduate Certificate); nursing education (Graduate Certificate); nursing practice (DNP); psychiatric mental health nurse practitioner (MSN, DNP, Graduate Certificate). *Accreditation:* AACN; ACNM/ACME. *Entrance requirements:* For master's, United States RN license; minimum GPA of 3.0; 2080 hours of clinical experience; curriculum vitae; 3 letters of recommendation from former dean, faculty member, or advisor familiar with the applicant, and a former or current supervisor; two-to-three-page essay on a specified topic; for doctorate, MSN, minimum GPA of 3.0, 3 letters of recommendation, interview, BSN, two-to-three page essay on a specific topic, 500-word statement of clinical practice research interest, resume, current U.S. RN license, 2080 clinical hours; for Graduate Certificate, MSN, minimum GPA of 3.0, 2 letters of recommendation, minimum of one year (2080 hours) of clinical nursing experience, interview, two-to-three page essay on a specific topic, resume, current United States RN license. Additional exam requirements/recommendations for international students: required—TOEFL (minimum score 558 paper-based; 83 iBT). Electronic applications accepted. *Expenses:* Contact institution.

**Simmons University,** College of Natural, Behavioral, and Health Sciences, Boston, MA 02115. Offers nursing (MS, MSN), including family nurse practitioner (MS); nursing practice (DNP). *Accreditation:* AACN. *Program availability:* Part-time. *Faculty:* 39 full-time (33 women), 194 part-time/adjunct (180 women). *Students:* 418 full-time (374 women), 1,868 part-time (1,682 women); includes 477 minority (161 Black or African American, non-Hispanic/Latino; 4 American Indian or Alaska Native, non-Hispanic/Latino; 138 Asian, non-Hispanic/Latino; 124 Hispanic/Latino; 1 Native Hawaiian or other Pacific Islander, non-Hispanic/Latino; 49 Two or more races, non-Hispanic/Latino), 22 international. Average age 32. 1,442 applicants, 62% accepted, 501 enrolled. In 2019, 630 master's, 39 doctorates awarded. *Degree requirements:* For master's, thesis optional; for doctorate, thesis/dissertation (for some programs). *Entrance requirements:* For doctorate, GRE. Additional exam requirements/recommendations for international students: required—TOEFL (minimum score 570 paper-based; 88 iBT). *Application deadline:* For fall admission, 6/1 for international students. Applications are processed on a rolling basis. Application fee: $50. Electronic applications accepted. *Expenses:* Contact institution. *Financial support:* In 2019–20, 25 students received support, including 25 fellowships (averaging $3,015 per year); teaching assistantships and scholarships/grants also available. Financial award applicants required to submit FAFSA. *Unit head:* Dr. Lepaine Sharp-McHenry, Dean. *Application contact:* Brett DiMarzo, Director of Graduate Admission, 617-521-2651, Fax: 617-521-3137, E-mail: brett.dimarzo@simmons.edu.
Website: https://www.simmons.edu/academics/colleges-schools-departments/cnbhs

**Sonoma State University,** School of Science and Technology, Family Nurse Practitioner Program, Rohnert Park, CA 94928. Offers MSN. *Accreditation:* ACEN. *Program availability:* Part-time. *Degree requirements:* For master's, comprehensive exam, thesis or alternative, oral exams. *Entrance requirements:* For master's, GRE General Test, BSN, minimum GPA of 3.0, course work in statistics, physical assessment, RN license. Additional exam requirements/recommendations for international students: required—TOEFL (minimum score 500 paper-based).

**South Dakota State University,** Graduate School, College of Nursing, Brookings, SD 57007. Offers MS, PhD. *Accreditation:* AACN. *Program availability:* Part-time, evening/weekend, online learning. *Degree requirements:* For master's, comprehensive exam, thesis (for some programs), oral exam. *Entrance requirements:* For master's, nurse registration; for doctorate, nurse registration, MS. Additional exam requirements/recommendations for international students: required—TOEFL (minimum score 525 paper-based; 71 iBT). *Expenses:* Contact institution.

**Southeastern Louisiana University,** College of Nursing and Health Sciences, School of Nursing, Hammond, LA 70402. Offers nurse practitioner (DNP); nursing (MSN). *Accreditation:* AACN. *Program availability:* Part-time, 100% online. *Faculty:* 16 full-time (15 women), 1 (woman) part-time/adjunct. *Students:* 24 full-time (19 women), 127 part-time (116 women); includes 37 minority (23 Black or African American, non-Hispanic/Latino; 1 American Indian or Alaska Native, non-Hispanic/Latino; 2 Asian, non-Hispanic/Latino; 4 Hispanic/Latino; 7 Two or more races, non-Hispanic/Latino). Average age 35. 63 applicants, 49% accepted, 19 enrolled. In 2019, 40 master's, 9 doctorates awarded. *Degree requirements:* For master's, comprehensive exam, thesis optional; for doctorate, comprehensive exam, thesis/dissertation optional. *Entrance requirements:* For master's, GRE; Please check with the Graduate Coordinator for additional information, evidence of valid, unencumbered Louisiana Registered Nurse license, curriculum vita, statement of intent/purpose, letters of recommendation, 2.7 GPA, completion of a course in introductory statistics with minimum grade of "C" for doctorate, GRE (BSN to DNP); Please check with the Graduate Coordinator for additional information, current unencumbered U.S. nursing license, resume or curriculum vita, statement of purpose, 3 recommendation statements, verification of clinical hours from MSN program (Post-MSN DNP program), 3.3 GPA on master's level coursework (Post-MSN DNP program). Additional exam requirements/recommendations for international students: required—TOEFL (minimum score 500 paper-based; 61 iBT). *Application deadline:* For fall admission, 4/1 for domestic and international students; for spring admission, 10/1 for domestic and international students. Applications are processed on a rolling basis. Application fee: $20 ($30 for international students). Electronic applications accepted. *Expenses: Tuition, area resident:* Full-time $6684; part-time $489 per credit hour. Tuition, state resident: full-time $6684; part-time $489 per credit hour. Tuition, nonresident: full-time $19,162; part-time $1183 per credit hour. *International tuition:* $19,162 full-time. *Required fees:* $2124. *Financial support:* Institutionally sponsored loans and unspecified assistantships available. Financial award application deadline: 5/1; financial award applicants required to submit FAFSA. *Unit head:* Dr. Ken Tillman, Department Head, School of Nursing, 985-549-2156, Fax: 985-549-2869, E-mail: nursing@southeastern.edu. *Application contact:* Office of Admissions, 985-549-5637, Fax: 985-549-5632, E-mail: admissions@southeastern.edu.
Website: http://www.southeastern.edu/acad_research/depts/nurs/index.html

**Southeast Missouri State University,** School of Graduate Studies, Department of Nursing, Cape Girardeau, MO 63701-4799. Offers MSN. *Accreditation:* AACN. *Faculty:* 6 full-time (all women). *Students:* 10 full-time (all women), 10 part-time (7 women). Average age 30. 25 applicants, 52% accepted, 12 enrolled. In 2019, 10 master's awarded. *Degree requirements:* For master's, comprehensive exam, scholarly portfolio. *Entrance requirements:* For master's, BSN from a CCNE or NLN accredited program, minimum GPA of 3.25, MO RN licensure or eligibility for that licensure, evidence of professional liability insurance. Additional exam requirements/recommendations for international students: required—TOEFL (minimum score 550 paper-based; 79 iBT), IELTS (minimum score 6), PTE (minimum score 53). *Application deadline:* For fall admission, 4/1 for domestic and international students. Applications are processed on a rolling basis. Application fee: $30 ($40 for international students). Electronic applications accepted. *Expenses:* Additional $50 per credit hour program fee. *Financial support:* In 2019–20, 9 students received support, including 8 teaching assistantships with full tuition reimbursements available; career-related internships or fieldwork, Federal Work-Study, scholarships/grants, traineeships, tuition waivers (full), and unspecified assistantships also available. Financial award application deadline: 2/1; financial award applicants required to submit FAFSA. *Unit head:* Dr. Gloria Green, Chairperson, 573-651-2585, Fax: 573-651-2142, E-mail: gjgreen@semo.edu. *Application contact:* Dr. Michele Tanz, Graduate Director, 573-651-2585, Fax: 573-651-2142, E-mail: mtanz@semo.edu.
Website: http://www.semo.edu/nursing/

**Southern Adventist University,** School of Nursing, Collegedale, TN 37315-0370. Offers acute care-adult/gerontology nurse practitioner (MSN, DNP); healthcare administration (MSN/MBA); lifestyle medicine (DNP); nurse educator (MSN, DNP); primary care-adult/gerontology nurse practitioner (MSN); primary care-family nurse practitioner (MSN, DNP); primary care-psychiatric mental health nurse practitioner (MSN, DNP); MSN/MBA. *Accreditation:* ACEN. *Program availability:* Part-time, 100% online. *Degree requirements:* For master's, thesis or project; for doctorate, scholarly project. *Entrance requirements:* For master's, RN license. Additional exam requirements/recommendations for international students: required—TOEFL (minimum score 100 iBT). Electronic applications accepted.

**Southern Connecticut State University,** School of Graduate Studies, School of Health and Human Services, Department of Nursing, New Haven, CT 06515-1355. Offers

family nurse practitioner (MSN); nursing (Ed D); nursing education (MSN). *Accreditation:* AACN. *Program availability:* Part-time, evening/weekend. *Degree requirements:* For master's, thesis. *Entrance requirements:* For master's, GRE, MAT, interview, minimum QPA of 2.8, RN license, minimum 1 year of professional nursing experience. Electronic applications accepted.

**Southern Illinois University Edwardsville,** Graduate School, School of Nursing, Edwardsville, IL 62026. Offers MS, DNP, Post-Master's Certificate. *Accreditation:* AACN; AANA/CANAEP. *Program availability:* Part-time, evening/weekend. *Degree requirements:* For master's, comprehensive exam (for some programs), thesis or alternative; for doctorate, thesis/dissertation or alternative, project. *Entrance requirements:* For master's, appropriate bachelor's degree, RN license; for Post-Master's Certificate, minimum graduate nursing GPA of 3.0, completion of graduate-level statistics and epidemiology courses with minimum B grade, current unencumbered RN licensure. Additional exam requirements/recommendations for international students: required—TOEFL (minimum score 550 paper-based; 79 iBT), IELTS (minimum score 6.5). Electronic applications accepted.

**Southern Nazarene University,** College of Professional and Graduate Studies, School of Nursing, Bethany, OK 73008. Offers nursing education (MS); nursing leadership (MS). *Accreditation:* AACN. *Program availability:* Part-time, evening/weekend. *Degree requirements:* For master's, thesis. *Entrance requirements:* For master's, minimum undergraduate cumulative GPA of 3.0; baccalaureate degree in nursing from nationally-accredited program; current unencumbered registered nurse licensure in Oklahoma or eligibility for same; documentation of basic computer skills; basic statistics course; statement of professional goals; three letters of recommendation. Additional exam requirements/recommendations for international students: required—TOEFL (minimum score 550 paper-based).

**Southern New Hampshire University,** Program in Nursing, Manchester, NH 03106-1045. Offers clinical nurse leader (MSN); nurse educator (MSN); nursing (MSN); patient safety and quality (MSN, Post Master's Certificate). *Program availability:* Online only, 100% online. *Entrance requirements:* For master's, undergraduate transcripts, active unencumbered license, bachelor's degree with minimum cumulative GPA of 3.0. Electronic applications accepted.

**Southern University and Agricultural and Mechanical College,** College of Nursing and Allied Health, School of Nursing, Baton Rouge, LA 70813. Offers educator/administrator (PhD); family health nursing (MSN); family nurse practitioner (Post Master's Certificate); geriatric nurse practitioner/gerontology (PhD); nursing (DNP). *Accreditation:* AACN. *Program availability:* Part-time. *Degree requirements:* For master's, comprehensive exam, thesis; for doctorate, comprehensive exam, thesis/dissertation. *Entrance requirements:* For master's, GRE General Test, BSN, minimum GPA of 2.7; for doctorate, GRE General Test; for Post Master's Certificate, MSN. Additional exam requirements/recommendations for international students: required—TOEFL (minimum score 525 paper-based).

**South University - Columbia,** Program in Nursing, Columbia, SC 29203. Offers MSN.

**South University - Montgomery,** Program in Nursing, Montgomery, AL 36116-1120. Offers MSN.

**South University - Richmond,** Program in Nursing, Glen Allen, VA 23060. Offers MSN.

**South University - Savannah,** Graduate Programs, College of Nursing, Savannah, GA 31406. Offers nurse educator (MS). *Accreditation:* AACN.

**South University - Tampa,** Program in Nursing, Tampa, FL 33614. Offers adult health nurse practitioner (MS); family nurse practitioner (MS); nurse educator (MS).

**South University - Virginia Beach,** Program in Nursing, Virginia Beach, VA 23452. Offers family nurse practitioner (MSN).

**South University - West Palm Beach,** Program in Nursing, Royal Palm Beach, FL 33411. Offers family nurse practitioner (MS).

**Spalding University,** Graduate Studies, Kosair College of Health and Natural Sciences, School of Nursing, Louisville, KY 40203-2188. Offers adult nurse practitioner (MSN); family nurse practitioner (MSN); leadership in nursing and healthcare (MSN); nurse educator (Post-Master's Certificate); nurse practitioner (Post-Master's Certificate); pediatric nurse practitioner (MSN). *Accreditation:* AACN. *Program availability:* Part-time, evening/weekend. *Degree requirements:* For master's, comprehensive exam (for some programs), thesis. *Entrance requirements:* For master's, GRE General Test, BSN or bachelor's degree in related field, RN licensure, autobiographical statement, transcripts, letters of recommendation. Additional exam requirements/recommendations for international students: required—TOEFL (minimum score 535 paper-based).

**Spring Arbor University,** School of Human Services, Spring Arbor, MI 49283-9799. Offers counseling (MAC); family studies (MAFS); nursing (MSN); social work (MSW). *Program availability:* Part-time, evening/weekend, online learning. *Entrance requirements:* For master's, bachelor's degree from regionally-accredited college or university, minimum GPA of 3.0 for at least the last two years of the bachelor's degree, at least two recommendations from professional/academic individuals. Additional exam requirements/recommendations for international students: required—TOEFL (minimum score 600 paper-based). Electronic applications accepted.

**Spring Hill College,** Graduate Programs, Program in Nursing, Mobile, AL 36608-1791. Offers MSN, Post-Master's Certificate. *Accreditation:* AACN. *Program availability:* Part-time, evening/weekend, online only, 100% online. *Degree requirements:* For master's, comprehensive exam, capstone courses, completion of program within 6 calendar years; for Post-Master's Certificate, 460 clinical integration hours. *Entrance requirements:* For master's, RN license in state where practicing nursing; 1 year of clinical nursing experience; work in clinical setting or access to health care facility for clinical integration/research; 3 written references; employer verification; resume; 500-word essay explaining how becoming a CNL will help applicant achieve personal and professional goals; for Post-Master's Certificate, RN license; master's degree in nursing. Additional exam requirements/recommendations for international students: required—TOEFL (minimum score 550 paper-based; 80 iBT), IELTS (minimum score 6.5), CPE or CAE (minimum score C), Michigan English Language Assessment Battery (minimum score 90). *Application deadline:* For fall admission, 8/1 priority date for domestic and international students; for spring admission, 12/1 priority date for domestic and international students. Applications are processed on a rolling basis. Application fee: $25 ($35 for international students). Electronic applications accepted. *Expenses:* Contact institution. *Financial support:* Fellowships, research assistantships, teaching assistantships, and tuition waivers available. Financial award applicants required to submit FAFSA. *Unit head:* Dr. Terran Mathers, Director, 251-380-4485, Fax: 251-460-4495, E-mail: tmathers@shc.edu. *Application contact:* Gary Bracken, Vice President of Enrollment Management, 251-380-3038, Fax: 251-460-2186, E-mail: gbracken@shc.edu.
Website: http://ug.shc.edu/graduate-degrees/master-science-nursing/

**Stanbridge University,** Program in Nursing, Irvine, CA 92612. Offers MSN. *Program availability:* Online learning.

**State University of New York College of Technology at Delhi,** Program in Nursing, Delhi, NY 13753. Offers nursing administration (MS); nursing education (MS). *Program availability:* Part-time, online only, 100% online. *Faculty:* 6 full-time (all women), 2 part-time/adjunct (both women). *Students:* 10 full-time (7 women), 77 part-time (70 women); includes 13 minority (7 Black or African American, non-Hispanic/Latino; 2 Asian, non-Hispanic/Latino; 4 Hispanic/Latino). Average age 38. 70 applicants, 71% accepted, 37 enrolled. In 2019, 15 master's awarded. *Application deadline:* For fall admission, 7/15 for domestic and international students; for spring admission, 11/15 for domestic and international students. Applications are processed on a rolling basis. Application fee: $75. Electronic applications accepted. *Expenses: Tuition, area resident:* Full-time $11,310; part-time $471 per credit hour. Tuition, state resident: full-time $11,310; part-time $471 per credit hour. Tuition, nonresident: full-time $13,570; part-time $565 per credit hour. *International tuition:* $13,570 full-time. *Required fees:* $420; $21.70 per credit hour. $21.70. *Financial support:* In 2019–20, 4 students received support. Scholarships/grants available. Financial award applicants required to submit FAFSA. *Unit head:* Susan Deane, Dean of the School of Nursing, 607-746-4550, Fax: 607-746-4104, E-mail: deanesg@delhi.edu. *Application contact:* Misty Fields, Associate Director of Admission, 607-746-4546, E-mail: fieldsmr@delhi.edu.

**State University of New York Downstate Medical Center,** College of Nursing, Graduate Programs in Nursing, Brooklyn, NY 11203-2098. Offers clinical nurse specialist (MS, Post Master's Certificate); nurse anesthesia (MS); nurse midwifery (MS, Post Master's Certificate); nurse practitioner (MS, Post Master's Certificate); nursing (MS). *Accreditation:* AACN. *Program availability:* Part-time. *Degree requirements:* For master's, thesis optional, clinical research project. *Entrance requirements:* For master's, GRE, BSN; minimum GPA of 3.0; previous undergraduate course work in statistics, health assessment, and nursing research; RN license; for Post Master's Certificate, BSN; minimum GPA of 3.0; RN license; previous undergraduate course work in statistics, health assessment, and nursing research.

**State University of New York Upstate Medical University,** College of Nursing, Syracuse, NY 13210. Offers nurse practitioner (Post Master's Certificate); nursing (MS). *Accreditation:* AACN. *Program availability:* Part-time, online learning. *Degree requirements:* For master's, thesis or alternative. *Entrance requirements:* For master's, 3 years of work experience. Electronic applications accepted.

**Stephen F. Austin State University,** Graduate School, College of Sciences and Mathematics, Richard and Lucille DeWitt School of Nursing, Nacogdoches, TX 75962. Offers family nurse practitioner (MSN).

**Stevenson University,** Program in Nursing, Stevenson, MD 21153. Offers nursing education (MS); nursing leadership/management (MS); population-based care coordination (MS). *Accreditation:* AACN. *Program availability:* Part-time, blended/hybrid learning. *Faculty:* 2 full-time (both women), 5 part-time/adjunct (all women). *Students:* 144 part-time (138 women); includes 33 minority (24 Black or African American, non-Hispanic/Latino; 3 Asian, non-Hispanic/Latino; 4 Hispanic/Latino; 2 Two or more races, non-Hispanic/Latino). Average age 37. 56 applicants, 73% accepted, 30 enrolled. In 2019, 50 master's awarded. *Degree requirements:* For master's, capstone course. *Entrance requirements:* For master's, Personal statement; Official college transcript; Bachelor's degree in nursing; Cumulative GPA of 3.0; current registered nurse's license in good standing; 1 letter of recommendation; Professional Resume. *Application deadline:* For fall admission, 8/9 priority date for domestic students; for spring admission, 1/11 priority date for domestic students; for summer admission, 5/1 priority date for domestic students. Applications are processed on a rolling basis. Electronic applications accepted. *Expenses:* $625 per credit. *Financial support:* Unspecified assistantships available. Financial award applicants required to submit FAFSA. *Unit head:* Dr. Judith Feustle, Associate Dean, 443-394-9818, Fax: 443-394-0538, E-mail: jfeustle@stevenson.edu. *Application contact:* Amanda Millar, Director, Admissions, 443-352-4243, Fax: 443-394-0538, E-mail: amillar@stevenson.edu.
Website: https://www.stevenson.edu/online/academics/online-graduate-programs/nursing/

**Stockton University,** Office of Graduate Studies, Program in Nursing, Galloway, NJ 08205-9441. Offers MSN. *Accreditation:* AACN. *Program availability:* Part-time. *Faculty:* 6 full-time (4 women), 2 part-time/adjunct (1 woman). *Students:* 45 part-time (36 women); includes 12 minority (3 Black or African American, non-Hispanic/Latino; 5 Asian, non-Hispanic/Latino; 2 Hispanic/Latino; 2 Two or more races, non-Hispanic/Latino). Average age 34. 23 applicants, 57% accepted, 11 enrolled. In 2019, 9 master's awarded. *Entrance requirements:* For master's, CPR certification, minimum GPA of 3.0, RN license. Additional exam requirements/recommendations for international students: required—TOEFL. *Application deadline:* For fall admission, 5/1 for domestic and international students; for spring admission, 12/1 for domestic students, 11/1 for international students. Applications are processed on a rolling basis. Application fee: $50. Electronic applications accepted. *Expenses: Tuition, area resident:* Full-time $750.92; part-time $78.58 per credit hour. Tuition, state resident: full-time $750.92; part-time $78.58 per credit hour. Tuition, nonresident: full-time $846; part-time $78.58 per credit hour. *International tuition:* $1195.96 full-time. *Required fees:* $1464; $78.58 per credit hour. One-time fee: $50 full-time. *Financial support:* Fellowships, research assistantships, career-related internships or fieldwork, Federal Work-Study, scholarships/grants, and unspecified assistantships available. Support available to part-time students. Financial award application deadline: 3/1; financial award applicants required to submit FAFSA. *Unit head:* Dr. Larider Ruffin, Interim Graduate Nursing Coordinator, 609-626-3640, E-mail: Larider.Ruffin@stockton.edu. *Application contact:* Tara Williams, Associate Director of Admissions, 609-626-3640, Fax: 609-626-6050, E-mail: gradschool@stockton.edu.

**Stony Brook University, State University of New York,** Stony Brook Medicine, School of Nursing, Stony Brook, NY 11794. Offers MS, DNP, PhD, Certificate. *Accreditation:* AACN; ACNM/ACME. *Program availability:* Blended/hybrid learning. *Faculty:* 34 full-time (31 women), 49 part-time/adjunct (45 women). *Students:* 16 full-time (15 women), 1,033 part-time (917 women); includes 364 minority (129 Black or African American, non-Hispanic/Latino; 1 American Indian or Alaska Native, non-Hispanic/Latino; 105 Asian, non-Hispanic/Latino; 106 Hispanic/Latino; 3 Native Hawaiian or other Pacific Islander, non-Hispanic/Latino; 20 Two or more races, non-Hispanic/Latino), 2 international. Average age 35. 965 applicants, 57% accepted, 488 enrolled. In 2019, 337 master's, 12 doctorates, 23 other advanced degrees awarded. *Degree requirements:* For master's, thesis; for doctorate, thesis/dissertation. *Entrance requirements:* For master's, BSN, minimum GPA of 3.0, course work in statistics; for doctorate, GRE General Test (for PhD). Additional exam requirements/recommendations for international students: required—TOEFL, TOEFL (minimum iBT score of 90, 22 on each section). *Application deadline:* For fall admission, 2/27 for domestic students. Application fee: $100. Electronic applications accepted. *Expenses:* Contact institution. *Financial support:* Fellowships, research assistantships, teaching assistantships, career-related internships or fieldwork, Federal Work-Study, institutionally sponsored loans, and traineeships available. Financial award application deadline: 3/15. *Unit head:* Dr. Annette B Wysocki, Dean, 631-444-3200, Fax: 631-444-3136, E-mail: annette.wysocki@stonybrook.edu. *Application contact:* Karen Allard, Admissions Coordinator, 631-444-6628, Fax: 631-444-3136, E-mail: karen.allard@stonybrook.edu.
Website: http://www.nursing.stonybrookmedicine.edu/

**Tarleton State University,** College of Graduate Studies, College of Health Sciences and Human Services, School of Nursing, Stephenville, TX 76402. Offers nursing

administration (MSN); nursing education (MSN). *Accreditation:* AACN. *Program availability:* Part-time, evening/weekend, 100% online, blended/hybrid learning. *Faculty:* 3 full-time (all women), 1 (woman) part-time/adjunct. *Students:* 5 part-time (4 women); includes 1 minority (Black or African American, non-Hispanic/Latino), 1 international. Average age 42. 7 applicants, 100% accepted, 1 enrolled. In 2019, 2 master's awarded. *Degree requirements:* For master's, comprehensive exam. *Entrance requirements:* For master's, GRE General Test, minimum GPA of 2.5. Additional exam requirements/recommendations for international students: required—TOEFL (minimum score 520 paper-based; 69 iBT); recommended—IELTS (minimum score 6), TSE (minimum score 50). *Application deadline:* For fall admission, 8/15 priority date for domestic students; for spring admission, 1/7 for domestic students. Applications are processed on a rolling basis. Application fee: $50 ($130 for international students). Electronic applications accepted. *Expenses:* Contact institution. *Financial support:* Career-related internships or fieldwork, Federal Work-Study, and institutionally sponsored loans available. Support available to part-time students. Financial award applicants required to submit FAFSA. *Unit head:* Dr. Jennifer Mundine, Department Head, 254-968-1827, E-mail: mundine@tarleton.edu. *Application contact:* Wendy Weiss, Graduate Admissions Coordinator, 254-968-9104, Fax: 254-968-9670, E-mail: weiss@tarleton.edu.
Website: https://www.tarleton.edu/nursing/index.html

**Temple University,** College of Public Health, Department of Nursing, Philadelphia, PA 19122-6096. Offers adult-gerontology primary care (DNP); family-individual across the lifespan (DNP); nursing (DNP). *Accreditation:* AACN. *Program availability:* Part-time. *Faculty:* 15 full-time (13 women), 6 part-time/adjunct (5 women). *Students:* 3 full-time (1 woman), 55 part-time (50 women); includes 27 minority (13 Black or African American, non-Hispanic/Latino; 11 Asian, non-Hispanic/Latino; 2 Hispanic/Latino; 1 Two or more races, non-Hispanic/Latino). 26 applicants, 54% accepted, 14 enrolled. In 2019, 11 doctorates awarded. *Degree requirements:* For doctorate, evidence-based practice project. *Entrance requirements:* For doctorate, GRE/MAT (waived for those who enter post-master's), 2 letters of reference, statement of goals, RN license, interview, statement of purpose, resume. Additional exam requirements/recommendations for international students: required—TOEFL (minimum score 79 iBT), IELTS (minimum score 6.5), PTE (minimum score 53), one of three is required. *Application deadline:* For fall admission, 3/1 for domestic students. Application fee: $60. Electronic applications accepted. *Expenses:* Contact institution. *Financial support:* Federal Work-Study and scholarships/grants available. Support available to part-time students. Financial award applicants required to submit FAFSA. *Unit head:* Martha Y Kubik, Chairperson, 215-707-4687, E-mail: martha.kubik@temple.edu. *Application contact:* Amy Costik, Assistant Director of Admissions, 215-204-5229, E-mail: amy.costik@temple.edu.
Website: https://cph.temple.edu/nursing/home

**Tennessee State University,** The School of Graduate Studies and Research, College of Health Sciences, School of Nursing, Nashville, TN 37209-1561. Offers family nurse practitioner (MSN, Certificate); holistic nurse practitioner (MSN); holistic nursing (Certificate); nursing education (MSN, Certificate). *Accreditation:* ACEN. *Entrance requirements:* For master's, GRE General Test or MAT, BSN, current RN license, minimum GPA of 3.0.

**Tennessee Technological University,** Whitson-Hester School of Nursing, Cookeville, TN 38505. Offers MSN, DNP. *Program availability:* Part-time, evening/weekend, online learning. *Students:* 22 full-time (19 women), 122 part-time (105 women); includes 10 minority (6 Black or African American, non-Hispanic/Latino; 1 Asian, non-Hispanic/Latino; 1 Hispanic/Latino; 2 Two or more races, non-Hispanic/Latino). 80 applicants, 69% accepted, 39 enrolled. In 2019, 29 master's awarded. *Degree requirements:* For master's, comprehensive exam, thesis or alternative. *Entrance requirements:* Additional exam requirements/recommendations for international students: required—TOEFL (minimum score 600 paper-based; 100 iBT), IELTS (minimum score 5.5), PTE, or TOEIC (Test of English as an International Communication). *Application deadline:* For fall admission, 7/1 for domestic students, 5/1 for international students; for spring admission, 11/1 for domestic students, 10/1 for international students; for summer admission, 5/1 for domestic students, 2/1 for international students. Applications are processed on a rolling basis. Application fee: $35 ($40 for international students). Electronic applications accepted. *Expenses: Tuition, area resident:* Part-time $597 per credit hour. Tuition, state resident: part-time $597 per credit hour. Tuition, nonresident: part-time $1323 per credit hour. *Financial support:* Teaching assistantships available. Financial award application deadline: 4/1. *Unit head:* Dr. Kim Hanna, Dean, 931-372-3547, Fax: 931-372-6244, E-mail: khanna@tntech.edu. *Application contact:* Shelia K. Kendrick, Coordinator of Graduate Studies, 931-372-3808, Fax: 931-372-3497, E-mail: skendrick@tntech.edu.

**Texas A&M International University,** Office of Graduate Studies and Research, College of Nursing and Health Sciences, Laredo, TX 78041. Offers family nurse practitioner (MSN). *Accreditation:* ACEN. *Entrance requirements:* Additional exam requirements/recommendations for international students: required—TOEFL (minimum score 550 paper-based; 79 iBT).

**Texas A&M University,** College of Nursing, Bryan, TX 77843. Offers family nurse practitioner (MSN); forensic nursing (MSN); nursing education (MSN). *Expenses:* Contact institution.

**Texas A&M University–Corpus Christi,** College of Graduate Studies, College of Nursing and Health Sciences, Corpus Christi, TX 78412. Offers family nurse practitioner (MSN); leadership in nursing systems (MSN); nurse educator (MSN); nursing practice (DNP). *Accreditation:* AACN. *Program availability:* Part-time, evening/weekend, online only, 100% online. *Degree requirements:* For master's, clinical capstone; for doctorate, capstone/scholarly project. *Entrance requirements:* For master's, essay, resume, 3 letters of recommendation, minimum GPA of 3.0, current valid unencumbered Texas nursing license. Additional exam requirements/recommendations for international students: required—TOEFL (minimum score 550 paper-based; 79 iBT), IELTS (minimum score 6.5). Electronic applications accepted.

**Texas Christian University,** Harris College of Nursing and Health Sciences, Doctor of Nursing Practice Program, Fort Worth, TX 76129-0002. Offers clinical nurse specialist - adult/gerontology nursing (DNP); clinical nurse specialist - pediatrics (DNP); family nurse practitioner (DNP); general (DNP); nursing administration (DNP). *Accreditation:* AACN. *Program availability:* Part-time, 100% online, blended/hybrid learning. *Faculty:* 29 full-time (26 women), 1 (woman) part-time/adjunct. *Students:* 49 full-time (45 women), 13 part-time (10 women); includes 18 minority (9 Black or African American, non-Hispanic/Latino; 1 American Indian or Alaska Native, non-Hispanic/Latino; 3 Asian, non-Hispanic/Latino; 4 Hispanic/Latino; 1 Two or more races, non-Hispanic/Latino), 2 international. Average age 37. 57 applicants, 70% accepted, 24 enrolled. In 2019, 27 doctorates awarded. *Degree requirements:* For doctorate, thesis/dissertation or alternative, practicum. *Entrance requirements:* For doctorate, three reference letters, essay, resume, two official transcripts from each institution attended, APRN recognition or MSN with experience or certification in nursing administration, as applicable per track, current RN license, successful completion of interview. Additional exam requirements/recommendations for international students: required—TOEFL (minimum score 550 paper-based; 80 iBT). *Application deadline:* For summer admission, 1/15 for domestic and international students. Application fee: $60. Electronic applications accepted. Full-time tuition and fees vary according to program. *Financial support:* In 2019–20, 20 students received support. Scholarships/grants available. Financial award application deadline: 2/15; financial award applicants required to submit FAFSA. *Unit head:* Dr. Kathy Ellis, Division Director, Graduate Nursing, 817-257-6726, Fax: 817-257-7944, E-mail: kathryn.ellis@tcu.edu. *Application contact:* Beth Janke, Academic Program Specialist, 817-257-6726, Fax: 817-257-7944, E-mail: graduatenursing@tcu.edu.
Website: http://dnp.tcu.edu/

**Texas Christian University,** Harris College of Nursing and Health Sciences, Master's Program in Nursing, Fort Worth, TX 76129-0002. Offers administration and leadership (MSN); clinical nurse leader (MSN, Certificate); clinical nurse specialist (MSN), including adult/gerontology nursing, pediatrics; nursing education (MSN). *Accreditation:* AACN. *Program availability:* Part-time, online only, 100% online. *Faculty:* 29 full-time (26 women), 1 (woman) part-time/adjunct. *Students:* 12 full-time (all women), 5 part-time (all women); includes 5 minority (1 Asian, non-Hispanic/Latino; 4 Hispanic/Latino). Average age 34. 41 applicants, 59% accepted, 8 enrolled. In 2019, 10 master's awarded. *Degree requirements:* For master's, thesis or alternative, practicum. *Entrance requirements:* For master's, 3 letters of reference, essay, resume, two official transcripts from every institution attended, current license to practice as a registered nurse. Additional exam requirements/recommendations for international students: required—TOEFL (minimum score 550 paper-based; 80 iBT). *Application deadline:* For spring admission, 8/15 for domestic and international students; for summer admission, 1/15 for domestic and international students. Application fee: $60. Electronic applications accepted. Full-time tuition and fees vary according to program. *Financial support:* In 2019–20, 15 students received support. Scholarships/grants available. Financial award application deadline: 2/15; financial award applicants required to submit FAFSA. *Unit head:* Dr. Kathy Ellis, Division Director, Graduate Nursing, 817-257-6726, Fax: 817-257-7944, E-mail: kathryn.ellis@tcu.edu. *Application contact:* Beth Janke, Academic Program Specialist, 817-257-6726, Fax: 817-257-7944, E-mail: graduatenursing@tcu.edu.
Website: http://www.nursing.tcu.edu/graduate.asp

**Texas Tech University Health Sciences Center,** School of Nursing, Lubbock, TX 79430. Offers acute care nurse practitioner (MSN, Certificate); administration (MSN); advanced practice (DNP); education (MSN); executive leadership (DNP); family nurse practitioner (MSN, Certificate); geriatric nurse practitioner (MSN, Certificate); pediatric nurse practitioner (MSN, Certificate). *Accreditation:* AACN. *Program availability:* Part-time, online learning. *Degree requirements:* For master's, thesis optional. *Entrance requirements:* For master's, minimum GPA of 3.0, 3 letters of reference, BSN, RN license; for Certificate, minimum GPA of 3.0, 3 letters of reference, RN license. Additional exam requirements/recommendations for international students: required—TOEFL (minimum score 550 paper-based).

**Texas Tech University Health Sciences Center El Paso,** Gayle Greve Hunt School of Nursing, El Paso, TX 79905. Offers MSN.

**Texas Woman's University,** Graduate School, College of Nursing, Denton, TX 76204. Offers adult health clinical nurse specialist (MS); adult health nurse practitioner (MS); adult/gerontology acute care nurse practitioner (MS); child health clinical nurse specialist (MS); clinical nurse leader (MS); family nurse practitioner (MS); health systems management (MS); nursing education (MS); nursing practice (DNP); nursing science (PhD); pediatric nurse practitioner (MS); women's health clinical nurse specialist (MS); women's health nurse practitioner (MS). *Accreditation:* AACN. *Program availability:* Part-time, 100% online, blended/hybrid learning. *Faculty:* 48 full-time (47 women), 31 part-time/adjunct (24 women). *Students:* 42 full-time (40 women), 811 part-time (756 women); includes 481 minority (168 Black or African American, non-Hispanic/Latino; 2 American Indian or Alaska Native, non-Hispanic/Latino; 165 Asian, non-Hispanic/Latino; 118 Hispanic/Latino; 1 Native Hawaiian or other Pacific Islander, non-Hispanic/Latino; 27 Two or more races, non-Hispanic/Latino), 26 international. Average age 36. 435 applicants, 71% accepted, 172 enrolled. In 2019, 203 master's, 37 doctorates awarded. *Degree requirements:* For master's, comprehensive exam, thesis or alternative, 6-year time limit for completion of degree, professional or clinical project; for doctorate, comprehensive exam, thesis/dissertation, 10-year time limit for completion of degree; dissertation (PhD), assessment practicum (DPT). *Entrance requirements:* For master's, minimum GPA of 3.0 on last 60 hours in undergraduate nursing degree and overall, RN license, BS in nursing, basic statistics course; for doctorate, MS in nursing, minimum preferred GPA of 3.5, RN or APRN license, statistics course, 2 letters of reference, curriculum vitae, graduate nursing-theory course, graduate research course, statement of professional goals and research interests, 1 yr APRN experience. Additional exam requirements/recommendations for international students: required—TOEFL (minimum score 79 iBT); recommended—IELTS (minimum score 6.5), TSE (minimum score 53). *Application deadline:* For fall admission, 5/1 for domestic students, 3/1 priority date for international students; for spring admission, 9/15 for domestic students, 7/1 priority date for international students. Application fee: $50 ($75 for international students). Electronic applications accepted. *Expenses:* All are estimates. Tuition for 10 hours = $2,763; Fees for 10 hours = $1,342. Master's Nursing courses require additional $75/SCH; Doctoral Nursing courses require additional $80/SCH. *Financial support:* In 2019–20, 212 students received support, including 1 research assistantship, 6 teaching assistantships (averaging $12,029 per year); career-related internships or fieldwork, scholarships/grants, health care benefits, and unspecified assistantships also available. Support available to part-time students. Financial award application deadline: 3/1; financial award applicants required to submit FAFSA. *Unit head:* Dr. Rosalie Mainous, Dean, 940-898-2401, Fax: 940-898-2437, E-mail: nursing@twu.edu. *Application contact:* Korie Hawkins, Associate Director of Admissions, Graduate Recruitment, 940-898-3188, Fax: 940-898-3081, E-mail: admissions@twu.edu.
Website: http://www.twu.edu/nursing/

**Thomas Edison State University,** W. Cary Edwards School of Nursing, Doctor of Nursing Practice Program, Trenton, NJ 08608. Offers systems-level leadership (DNP). *Accreditation:* AACN. *Program availability:* Part-time, 100% online. *Entrance requirements:* Additional exam requirements/recommendations for international students: required—TOEFL (minimum score 550 paper-based; 79 iBT). Electronic applications accepted.

**Thomas Edison State University,** W. Cary Edwards School of Nursing, Master of Science in Nursing Program, Trenton, NJ 08608. Offers nurse educator (MSN); nursing administration (MSN); nursing informatics (MSN). *Accreditation:* AACN; ACEN. *Program availability:* Part-time, online learning. *Degree requirements:* For master's, nursing education seminar, onground practicum, online practicum. *Entrance requirements:* For master's, BSN. Additional exam requirements/recommendations for international students: required—TOEFL (minimum score 550 paper-based; 79 iBT). Electronic applications accepted.

**Thomas Jefferson University,** Jefferson College of Nursing, Philadelphia, PA 19107. Offers MS, DNP. *Accreditation:* AACN; AANA/CANAEP. *Program availability:* Part-time, online only, 100% online, blended/hybrid learning. *Degree requirements:* For master's, thesis; for doctorate, thesis/dissertation. *Entrance requirements:* For doctorate, GRE (only for those under 3.2 GPA). Electronic applications accepted.

**Thomas University,** Department of Nursing, Thomasville, GA 31792-7499. Offers MSN. *Accreditation:* ACEN. *Program availability:* Part-time. *Entrance requirements:* For

master's, resume, 3 academic/professional references. Additional exam requirements/ recommendations for international students: required—TOEFL (minimum score 600 paper-based). Electronic applications accepted.

**Trinity Washington University,** School of Nursing and Health Professions, Washington, DC 20017-1094. Offers nursing (MSN); occupational therapy (MOT).

**Trinity Western University,** School of Graduate Studies, Master of Science in Nursing, Langley, BC V2Y 1Y1, Canada. Offers MSN. *Program availability:* Part-time, 100% online, blended/hybrid learning. *Students:* Average age 32. 43 applicants, 60% accepted, 12 enrolled. *Degree requirements:* For master's, thesis optional, capstone project: knowledge translation project or thesis. *Entrance requirements:* For master's, DuoLingo - 125 Approved nursing certification. Additional exam requirements/ recommendations for international students: required—TOEFL (minimum score 105 iBT), IELTS (minimum score 7.5), DuoLingo. *Application deadline:* For spring admission, 10/1 for domestic and international students; for summer admission, 2/1 for domestic and international students. Application fee: $150 Canadian dollars for international students. Electronic applications accepted. *Expenses:* $740 per semester hour program tuition (for 31 semester hours is $22,940), $28 per semester hour student fees (for 31 semester hours is $868). *Financial support:* Research assistantships, teaching assistantships, scholarships/grants, and unspecified assistantships available. Support available to part-time students. *Unit head:* Dr. Barb Astle, Program Director, E-mail: barbara.astle@twu.ca. *Application contact:* Tim Macfarlane, Senior Enrolment Advisor, 604-513-2121 Ext. 3046, E-mail: tim.macfarlane@twu.ca.
Website: http://www.twu.ca/msn

**Troy University,** Graduate School, College of Health and Human Services, Program in Nursing, Troy, AL 36082. Offers adult health (MSN); family nurse practitioner (DNP); maternal infant (MSN); nursing informatics specialist (MSN). *Accreditation:* ACEN. *Program availability:* Part-time, evening/weekend, online learning. *Faculty:* 14 full-time (all women). *Students:* 67 full-time (64 women), 160 part-time (139 women); includes 46 minority (37 Black or African American, non-Hispanic/Latino; 1 American Indian or Alaska Native, non-Hispanic/Latino; 1 Asian, non-Hispanic/Latino; 7 Hispanic/Latino). Average age 35. 64 applicants, 97% accepted, 59 enrolled. In 2019, 73 master's, 20 doctorates awarded. *Degree requirements:* For master's, comprehensive exam, minimum GPA of 3.0, candidacy; for doctorate, minimum GPA of 3.0, submission of approved comprehensive e-portfolio, completion of residency synthesis project, minimum of 1000 hours of clinical practice, qualifying exam. *Entrance requirements:* For master's, Score of 396 or higher on the Miller's Analogy Test (MAT) or score of 290 on Graduate Record Exam (850 on the old exam)(verbal plus quantitative); GRE or MAT required for every applicant, minimum GPA of 3.0, BSN, current RN licensure, 2 letters of reference, undergraduate health assessment course; for doctorate, GRE (minimum score of 850 on old exam or 294 on new exam), BSN or MSN, minimum GPA of 3.0, 2 letters of reference, current RN licensure, essay. Additional exam requirements/ recommendations for international students: required—TOEFL (minimum score 523 paper-based; 70 iBT), IELTS (minimum score 6). *Application deadline:* For fall admission, 5/1 for domestic students; for spring admission, 10/1 for domestic students; for summer admission, 3/1 for domestic students. Applications are processed on a rolling basis. Application fee: $50. Electronic applications accepted. *Expenses: Tuition, area resident:* Full-time $7650; part-time $2550 per semester hour. Tuition, state resident: full-time $7650; part-time $2550 per semester hour. Tuition, nonresident: full-time $15,300; part-time $5100 per semester hour. *International tuition:* $15,300 full-time. *Required fees:* $856; $352 per semester hour. $176 per semester. *Financial support:* In 2019–20, 20 students received support. Fellowships, research assistantships, teaching assistantships, career-related internships or fieldwork, Federal Work-Study, scholarships/grants, traineeships, tuition waivers, and unspecified assistantships available. Support available to part-time students. Financial award application deadline: 3/1; financial award applicants required to submit FAFSA. *Unit head:* Dr. Wade Forehand, Professor, Director, School of Nursing, 334-670-3745, Fax: 334-670-3743, E-mail: jforehand@troy.edu. *Application contact:* Crystal G. Bishop, Director of Graduate Admissions, School of Nursing, 334-241-8631, E-mail: cdgodwin@troy.edu.
Website: https://www.troy.edu/academics/academic-programs/college-health-human-services-programs.php

**Tusculum University,** Program in Nursing, Greeneville, TN 37743-9997. Offers family nurse practitioner (MSN). *Program availability:* Part-time. *Entrance requirements:* For master's, GRE. Additional exam requirements/recommendations for international students: required—TOEFL.

**UNB Fredericton,** School of Graduate Studies, Faculty of Nursing, Fredericton, NB E3B 5A3, Canada. Offers nurse educator (MN); nurse practitioner (MN); nursing (MN). *Program availability:* Part-time, online learning. *Faculty:* 41 full-time (37 women). *Students:* 14 full-time (13 women), 13 part-time (all women). Average age 36. In 2019, 10 master's awarded. *Degree requirements:* For master's, comprehensive exam (for some programs), thesis (for some programs). *Entrance requirements:* For master's, undergraduate coursework in statistics and nursing research, minimum GPA of 3.3, registration as a nurse (or eligibility) in New Brunswick. Additional exam requirements/ recommendations for international students: required—TOEFL (minimum score 600 paper-based). *Application deadline:* For winter admission, 1/2 priority date for domestic students. Application fee: $50 Canadian dollars. Electronic applications accepted. *Expenses: Tuition, area resident:* Full-time $6975 Canadian dollars; part-time $3423 Canadian dollars per year. Tuition, state resident: full-time $6975 Canadian dollars; part-time $3423 Canadian dollars per year. Tuition, Canadian resident: full-time $6975 Canadian dollars; part-time $3423 Canadian dollars per year. *International tuition:* $12,435 Canadian dollars full-time. *Required fees:* $92.25 Canadian dollars per term. Full-time tuition and fees vary according to degree level, campus/location, program, reciprocity agreements and student level. *Financial support:* Fellowships and research assistantships available. Financial award application deadline: 1/15. *Unit head:* Lorna Butler, Dean, 506-458 7625, Fax: 506-447 3057, E-mail: Lorna.butler@unb.ca. *Application contact:* Tricia Canning, Graduate Secretary, 506-458 7650, Fax: 506-447-3057, E-mail: canningt@unb.ca.
Website: http://www.unb.ca/fredericton/nursing/graduate/

**Uniformed Services University of the Health Sciences,** Daniel K. Inouye Graduate School of Nursing, Bethesda, MD 20814. Offers adult-gerontology clinical nurse specialist (MSN, DNP); family nurse practitioner (DNP); nurse anesthesia (DNP); nursing science (PhD); psychiatric mental health nurse practitioner (DNP); women's health nurse practitioner (DNP). *Accreditation:* AACN; AANA/CANAEP. *Program availability:* Part-time. *Faculty:* 50 full-time (32 women), 1 part-time/adjunct (0 women). *Students:* 170 full-time (98 women); includes 51 minority (21 Black or African American, non-Hispanic/Latino; 17 Asian, non-Hispanic/Latino; 11 Hispanic/Latino; 2 Native Hawaiian or other Pacific Islander, non-Hispanic/Latino). Average age 34. 88 applicants, 75% accepted, 66 enrolled. In 2019, 2 master's, 42 doctorates awarded. *Degree requirements:* For master's, thesis, scholarly project; for doctorate, dissertation (for PhD); project (for DNP). *Entrance requirements:* For master's, GRE, BSN, clinical experience, minimum GPA of 3.0, previous course work in science; for doctorate, GRE, BSN, minimum GPA of 3.0, undergraduate/graduate science course within past 5 years, writing example, interview (for some programs), and 3 letters of reference (for DNP); master's degree, minimum GPA of 3.0 in nursing or related field, personal statement, 3 references, and interview (for PhD). *Application deadline:* For winter admission, 2/15 for domestic students; for summer admission, 8/15 for domestic students. Electronic applications accepted. *Financial support:* Robert Wood Johnson and Jonas scholars available. *Unit head:* Dr. Diane C. Seibert, Associate Dean for Academic Affairs, 301-295-1080, Fax: 301-295-1707, E-mail: diane.seibert@usuhs.edu. *Application contact:* Maureen Jackson, Student Admissions Program Manager, 301-295-1055, E-mail: maureen.jackson.ctr@usuhs.edu.
Website: http://www.usuhs.edu/gsn/

**Union University,** School of Nursing, Jackson, TN 38305-3697. Offers executive leadership (DNP); nurse anesthesia (DNP); nurse practitioner (DNP); nursing education (MSN, PMC). *Accreditation:* AACN; AANA/CANAEP. *Degree requirements:* For master's, thesis or alternative. *Entrance requirements:* For master's, GRE, 3 letters of reference, bachelor's degree in nursing, minimum GPA of 3.0. Additional exam requirements/recommendations for international students: required—TOEFL (minimum score 560 paper-based). Electronic applications accepted.

**Universidad Metropolitana,** School of Health Sciences, Department of Nursing, San Juan, PR 00928-1150. Offers case management (Certificate); nursing (MSN); oncology nursing (Certificate). *Accreditation:* ACEN.

**Université de Montréal,** Faculty of Nursing, Montréal, QC H3C 3J7, Canada. Offers M Sc, PhD, Certificate, DESS. *Program availability:* Part-time. *Degree requirements:* For master's, one foreign language, thesis optional; for doctorate, thesis/dissertation, general exam; for other advanced degree, one foreign language. *Entrance requirements:* For master's, doctorate, and other advanced degree, proficiency in French. Electronic applications accepted.

**Université du Québec à Rimouski,** Graduate Programs, Program in Nursing Studies, Rimouski, QC G5L 3A1, Canada. Offers M Sc, Diploma.

**Université du Québec à Trois-Rivières,** Graduate Programs, Program in Nursing Sciences, Trois-Rivières, QC G9A 5H7, Canada. Offers M Sc, DESS. *Program availability:* Part-time.

**Université du Québec en Outaouais,** Graduate Programs, Program in Nursing, Gatineau, QC J8X 3X7, Canada. Offers M Sc, DESS, Diploma. *Program availability:* Part-time, evening/weekend. *Degree requirements:* For master's, thesis (for some programs). *Entrance requirements:* For master's, appropriate bachelor's degree, proficiency in French.

**University at Buffalo, the State University of New York,** Graduate School, School of Nursing, Buffalo, NY 14260. Offers adult gerontology nurse practitioner (DNP); family nurse practitioner (DNP); health care systems and leadership (MS); nurse anesthetist (DNP); nursing (PhD); nursing education (Certificate); psychiatric/mental health nurse practitioner (DNP). *Accreditation:* AACN; AANA/CANAEP (one or more programs are accredited). *Program availability:* Part-time, 100% online. *Degree requirements:* For master's, thesis optional; for doctorate, comprehensive exam (for some programs), capstone (for DNP), dissertation (for PhD). *Entrance requirements:* For master's, GRE or MAT; for doctorate, GRE or MAT, minimum GPA of 3.0 (for DNP), 3.25 (for PhD); RN license; BS or MS in nursing; 3 references; writing sample; resume; personal statement; for Certificate, interview, minimum GPA of 3.0 or GRE General Test, RN license, MS in nursing, professional certification. Additional exam requirements/recommendations for international students: required—TOEFL (minimum score 550 paper-based; 79 iBT), IELTS (minimum score 6.5). Electronic applications accepted. *Expenses:* Contact institution.

**The University of Akron,** Graduate School, College of Health Professions, School of Nursing, Akron, OH 44325-3701. Offers MSN, DNP. *Accreditation:* AACN; AANA/CANAEP (one or more programs are accredited). *Program availability:* Part-time. *Degree requirements:* For doctorate, one foreign language, thesis/dissertation, qualifying exam. *Entrance requirements:* For master's, current Ohio state license as registered nurse, three letters of reference, 300-word essay, interview with program coordinator; for doctorate, GRE, minimum GPA of 3.0, MSN, nursing license or eligibility for licensure, writing sample, letters of recommendation, interview, resume, personal statement of research interests and career goals. Additional exam requirements/ recommendations for international students: required—TOEFL (minimum score 79 iBT), IELTS (minimum score 6.5). Electronic applications accepted.

**The University of Alabama,** Graduate School, Capstone College of Nursing, Tuscaloosa, AL 35487. Offers MSN, DNP. *Accreditation:* AACN. *Program availability:* Part-time, online learning. *Faculty:* 32 full-time (30 women), 2 part-time/adjunct (1 woman). *Students:* 117 full-time (99 women), 190 part-time (164 women); includes 98 minority (69 Black or African American, non-Hispanic/Latino; 1 American Indian or Alaska Native, non-Hispanic/Latino; 10 Asian, non-Hispanic/Latino; 12 Hispanic/Latino; 6 Two or more races, non-Hispanic/Latino). Average age 40. 322 applicants, 42% accepted, 124 enrolled. In 2019, 84 master's, 53 doctorates awarded. *Degree requirements:* For master's, thesis optional; for doctorate, comprehensive exam, thesis/ dissertation, scholarly practice project. *Entrance requirements:* For master's, GRE or MAT (if GPA is below 3.0), minimum GPA of 3.0 overall and/or last 60 hours; BSN; current unencumbered RN licensure in the U.S.; drug and background screen deemed acceptable by university officials; statement of purpose; resume; 2 recommendation letters. Additional exam requirements/recommendations for international students: required—TOEFL (minimum score 550 paper-based; 79 iBT), IELTS (minimum score 6.5), PTE (minimum score 59). *Application deadline:* For fall admission, 3/1 priority date for domestic students. Applications are processed on a rolling basis. Application fee: $50 ($60 for international students). Electronic applications accepted. *Expenses: Tuition, area resident:* Full-time $10,780; part-time $440 per credit hour. Tuition, nonresident: full-time $30,250; part-time $1550 per credit hour. *Financial support:* Scholarships/grants available. Financial award application deadline: 6/15; financial award applicants required to submit FAFSA. *Unit head:* Dr. Suzanne Prevost, Dean, 205-348-1040, Fax: 205-348-5559, E-mail: sprevost@ua.edu. *Application contact:* Vickie L. Samuel, Graduate Recruitment and Retention Liaison, 205-348-8163, Fax: 205-348-6674, E-mail: vsamuel@ua.edu.
Website: http://nursing.ua.edu/

**The University of Alabama at Birmingham,** School of Nursing, Birmingham, AL 35294. Offers clinical nurse leader (MSN); nurse anesthesia (DNP); nurse practitioner (MSN, DNP), including adult-gerontology acute care (MSN), adult-gerontology primary care (MSN), family (MSN), pediatric (MSN), psychiatric/mental health (MSN), women's health (MSN); nursing (MSN, DNP, PhD); nursing health systems administration (MSN); nursing informatics (MSN). *Accreditation:* AACN; AANA/CANAEP. *Program availability:* Part-time, online only, blended/hybrid learning. *Faculty:* 86 full-time (79 women), 42 part-time/adjunct (35 women). *Students:* 228 full-time (165 women), 1,393 part-time (1,234 women); includes 398 minority (267 Black or African American, non-Hispanic/Latino; 4 American Indian or Alaska Native, non-Hispanic/Latino; 52 Asian, non-Hispanic/Latino; 41 Hispanic/Latino; 34 Two or more races, non-Hispanic/Latino), 3 international. Average age 33. 1,027 applicants, 55% accepted, 421 enrolled. In 2019, 557 master's, 19 doctorates awarded. Terminal master's awarded for partial completion of doctoral program. *Degree requirements:* For master's, comprehensive exam; for doctorate, comprehensive exam, thesis/dissertation, research mentorship experience (for PhD); scholarly project (for DNP). *Entrance requirements:* For master's, GRE, GMAT, or MAT,

minimum cumulative undergraduate GPA of 3.0 or on last 60 semesters hours; letters of recommendation; for doctorate, GRE General Test, computer literacy, course work in statistics, interview, minimum GPA of 3.0, MS in nursing, references, writing sample. Additional exam requirements/recommendations for international students: required—TOEFL (minimum score 500 paper-based, 80 iBT) or IELTS (5.5). *Application deadline:* For fall admission, 2/24 for domestic students; for summer admission, 10/15 for domestic students. Application fee: $50. Electronic applications accepted. *Expenses:* Contact institution. *Financial support:* In 2019–20, 23 fellowships (averaging $34,685 per year), 12 research assistantships (averaging $9,042 per year), 2 teaching assistantships (averaging $22,000 per year) were awarded; scholarships/grants, traineeships, health care benefits, and unspecified assistantships also available. Support available to part-time students. *Unit head:* Dr. Doreen C. Harper, Dean, 205-934-5360, Fax: 205-934-1894, E-mail: dcharper@uab.edu. *Application contact:* John Updegraff, Director of Student Affairs, 205-975-3370, Fax: 205-934-5490, E-mail: jupde22@uab.edu.
Website: http://www.uab.edu/nursing/home/

**The University of Alabama in Huntsville,** School of Graduate Studies, College of Nursing, Huntsville, AL 35899. Offers family nurse practitioner (Certificate); nursing (MSN, DNP), including adult-gerontology acute care nurse practitioner (MSN), adult-gerontology clinical nurse specialist (MSN), family nurse practitioner (MSN), leadership in health care systems (MSN); nursing education (Certificate). *Accreditation:* AACN. *Program availability:* Part-time. *Degree requirements:* For master's, comprehensive exam, thesis or alternative, oral and written exams. *Entrance requirements:* For master's, MAT or GRE, Alabama RN license, BSN, minimum GPA of 3.0; for doctorate, master's degree in nursing in an advanced practice area; for Certificate, MAT or GRE, minimum GPA of 3.0. Additional exam requirements/recommendations for international students: required—TOEFL (minimum score 500 paper-based; 80 iBT), IELTS (minimum score 6.5). Electronic applications accepted.

**University of Alaska Anchorage,** College of Health, School of Nursing, Anchorage, AK 99508. Offers MS, DNP, Graduate Certificate. *Accreditation:* ACEN. *Program availability:* Part-time, evening/weekend. *Degree requirements:* For master's, comprehensive exam, individual project. *Entrance requirements:* For master's, GRE or MAT, BS in nursing, interview, minimum GPA of 3.0, RN license, 1 year of part-time or 6 months of full-time clinical experience. Additional exam requirements/recommendations for international students: required—TOEFL (minimum score 550 paper-based).

**University of Alberta,** Faculty of Graduate Studies and Research, Faculty of Nursing, Edmonton, AB T6G 2E1, Canada. Offers MN, PhD. *Program availability:* Part-time. *Degree requirements:* For master's, thesis optional, clinical practice; for doctorate, thesis/dissertation. *Entrance requirements:* For master's, B Sc N, 1 year of clinical nursing experience in specialty area; for doctorate, MN. Additional exam requirements/recommendations for international students: required—TOEFL (minimum score 550 paper-based).

**The University of Arizona,** College of Nursing, Tucson, AZ 85721. Offers health care informatics (Certificate); nurse practitioner (MS); nursing (DNP, PhD). *Accreditation:* AACN; AANA/CANAEP. *Program availability:* Part-time, online learning. Terminal master's awarded for partial completion of doctoral program. *Degree requirements:* For master's, thesis optional; for doctorate, comprehensive exam, thesis/dissertation. *Entrance requirements:* For master's, BSN, eligibility for RN license; for doctorate, BSN; for Certificate, GRE General Test, Arizona RN license, BSN, minimum GPA of 3.0. Additional exam requirements/recommendations for international students: required—TOEFL (minimum score 550 paper-based; 79 iBT). Electronic applications accepted. *Expenses:* Contact institution.

**University of Arkansas,** Graduate School, College of Education and Health Professions, Eleanor Mann School of Nursing, Fayetteville, AR 72701. Offers MSN. *Accreditation:* AACN. *Program availability:* Online learning. *Students:* 30 full-time (27 women), 38 part-time (35 women); includes 12 minority (6 Black or African American, non-Hispanic/Latino; 1 Asian, non-Hispanic/Latino; 4 Hispanic/Latino; 1 Two or more races, non-Hispanic/Latino). In 2019, 3 master's awarded. *Application deadline:* For fall admission, 8/1 for domestic students, 4/1 for international students; for spring admission, 12/1 for domestic students, 10/1 for international students; for summer admission, 4/15 for domestic students, 3/1 for international students. Applications are processed on a rolling basis. Application fee: $60. Electronic applications accepted. *Financial support:* Fellowships, research assistantships, and teaching assistantships available. *Unit head:* Dr. Susan Kane Patton, Director, 479-575-3907, Fax: 479-575-3218, E-mail: skpatton@uark.edu. *Application contact:* Dr. Martha Butler, Graduate Admissions, 479-575-4280, Fax: 479-575-3218, E-mail: mrbutler@uark.edu.
Website: http://nurs.uark.edu/

**University of Arkansas for Medical Sciences,** College of Nursing, Little Rock, AR 72205-7199. Offers PhD. *Accreditation:* AACN. *Program availability:* Part-time. *Entrance requirements:* For doctorate, GRE. Additional exam requirements/recommendations for international students: required—TOEFL. *Expenses:* Contact institution.

**The University of British Columbia,** Faculty of Applied Science, School of Nursing, Vancouver, BC V6T 2B5, Canada. Offers nurse practitioner (MN); nursing (MSN, PhD). *Program availability:* Part-time. *Degree requirements:* For doctorate, comprehensive exam, thesis/dissertation. *Entrance requirements:* Additional exam requirements/recommendations for international students: required—TOEFL. Electronic applications accepted. *Expenses:* Contact institution.

**University of Calgary,** Faculty of Graduate Studies, Faculty of Nursing, Calgary, AB T2N 1N4, Canada. Offers MN, PhD, PMD. *Program availability:* Part-time. *Degree requirements:* For master's, comprehensive exam (for some programs), thesis (for some programs); for doctorate, thesis/dissertation; for PMD, comprehensive exam. *Entrance requirements:* For master's and PMD, nursing experience, nursing registration; for doctorate, nursing registration. Additional exam requirements/recommendations for international students: required—TOEFL (minimum score 600 paper-based), IELTS (minimum score 7), Michigan English Language Assessment Battery. Electronic applications accepted. *Expenses:* Contact institution.

**University of California, Irvine,** Programs in Health Sciences, Sue & Bill Gross School of Nursing, Irvine, CA 92697. Offers MSN. *Accreditation:* AACN. *Students:* 40 full-time (35 women), 38 part-time (32 women); includes 43 minority (5 Black or African American, non-Hispanic/Latino; 17 Asian, non-Hispanic/Latino; 19 Hispanic/Latino; 2 Two or more races, non-Hispanic/Latino), 3 international. Average age 32. 547 applicants, 14% accepted, 53 enrolled. In 2019, 19 master's awarded. Application fee: $120 ($140 for international students). *Unit head:* Adey Nyamathi, Dean, 949-824-1514, E-mail: anyamath@uci.edu. *Application contact:* Julie Aird, Director, Student Affairs and Support Services, 949-824-1514, E-mail: jaird@uci.edu.
Website: http://www.nursing.uci.edu/

**University of California, Los Angeles,** Graduate Division, School of Nursing, Los Angeles, CA 90095. Offers MSN, PhD, MBA/MSN. *Accreditation:* AACN. *Degree requirements:* For master's, comprehensive exam; for doctorate, thesis/dissertation, oral and written qualifying exams. *Entrance requirements:* For master's, bachelor's degree in nursing; minimum undergraduate GPA of 3.0 (or its equivalent if letter grade system not used); for doctorate, bachelor's degree in nursing; minimum undergraduate GPA of 3.5

(or its equivalent if letter grade system not used); writing sample. Additional exam requirements/recommendations for international students: required—TOEFL. Electronic applications accepted. *Expenses:* Contact institution.

**University of California, San Francisco,** Graduate Division, School of Nursing, Program in Nursing, San Francisco, CA 94143. Offers MS, PhD. *Accreditation:* AACN; ACNM/ACME (one or more programs are accredited). *Degree requirements:* For master's, comprehensive exam, thesis or alternative; for doctorate, thesis/dissertation. *Entrance requirements:* For master's and doctorate, GRE General Test. *Expenses:* Contact institution.

**University of Central Arkansas,** Graduate School, College of Health and Behavioral Sciences, Department of Nursing, Conway, AR 72035-0001. Offers adult nurse practitioner (PMC); clinical nurse leader (PMC); clinical nurse specialist (MSN); family nurse practitioner (PMC); nurse educator (PMC); nurse practitioner (MSN). *Accreditation:* AACN. *Program availability:* Part-time, evening/weekend, online learning. *Degree requirements:* For master's, comprehensive exam, thesis optional, clinicals. *Entrance requirements:* For master's, GRE General Test, minimum GPA of 2.7. Additional exam requirements/recommendations for international students: required—TOEFL (minimum score 550 paper-based; 80 iBT). Electronic applications accepted. *Expenses:* Contact institution.

**University of Central Florida,** College of Nursing, Orlando, FL 32816. Offers MSN, DNP, PhD, Certificate, Post-Master's Certificate. *Accreditation:* AACN. *Program availability:* Part-time, evening/weekend. *Faculty:* 60 full-time (50 women), 95 part-time/adjunct (85 women). *Students:* 88 full-time (82 women), 382 part-time (336 women); includes 153 minority (56 Black or African American, non-Hispanic/Latino; 2 American Indian or Alaska Native, non-Hispanic/Latino; 27 Asian, non-Hispanic/Latino; 60 Hispanic/Latino; 8 Two or more races, non-Hispanic/Latino). Average age 38. 319 applicants, 61% accepted, 139 enrolled. In 2019, 97 master's, 14 doctorates, 16 other advanced degrees awarded. *Degree requirements:* For master's, thesis or alternative; for doctorate, comprehensive exam, thesis/dissertation. *Entrance requirements:* For master's, essay, curriculum vitae; for doctorate, GRE General Test, letters of recommendation, resume, essay. Additional exam requirements/recommendations for international students: required—TOEFL. *Application deadline:* For fall admission, 3/15 for domestic students; for spring admission, 10/15 for domestic students. Application fee: $30. Electronic applications accepted. *Financial support:* In 2019–20, 30 students received support, including 25 fellowships with partial tuition reimbursements available (averaging $10,218 per year), 3 research assistantships with partial tuition reimbursements available (averaging $4,815 per year), 3 teaching assistantships (averaging $6,050 per year); career-related internships or fieldwork, Federal Work-Study, institutionally sponsored loans, traineeships, and unspecified assistantships also available. Financial award application deadline: 3/1; financial award applicants required to submit FAFSA. *Unit head:* Dr. Mary Lou Sole, Dean, 407-823-5496, Fax: 407-823-5675, E-mail: mary.sole@ucf.edu. *Application contact:* Associate Director, Graduate Admissions, 407-823-2766, Fax: 407-823-6442, E-mail: gradadmissions@ucf.edu.
Website: http://nursing.ucf.edu/

**University of Central Missouri,** The Graduate School, Warrensburg, MO 64093. Offers accountancy (MA); accounting (MBA); applied mathematics (MS); aviation safety (MA); biology (MS); business administration (MBA); career and technology education (MS); college student personnel administration (MS); communication (MA); computer information systems and information technology (MS); computer science (MS); counseling (MS); criminal justice and criminology (MS); educational leadership (Ed S); educational leadership and policy analysis (Ed D); educational technology (MS, Ed S); elementary and early childhood education (MSE); English (MA); english language learners - teaching english as a second language (MA); environmental studies (MA); finance (MBA); history (MA); industrial hygiene (MS); industrial management (MS); information systems (MBA); kinesiology (MS); library science and information services (MS); literacy education (MSE); marketing (MBA); mathematics (MS); music (MA); occupational safety management (MS); professional leadership - adult, career, and technical education (Ed S); professional leadership - counseling (Ed S); psychology (MS); rural family nursing (MS); school administration (MSE); social gerontology (MS); sociology (MA); special education (MSE); speech language pathology (MS); teaching (MAT); technology (MS); technology management (PhD); theatre (MA). *Accreditation:* ASHA. *Program availability:* Part-time, 100% online, blended/hybrid learning. *Faculty:* 236 full-time (113 women), 97 part-time/adjunct (61 women). *Students:* 787 full-time (448 women), 1,459 part-time (997 women); includes 213 minority (72 Black or African American, non-Hispanic/Latino; 5 American Indian or Alaska Native, non-Hispanic/Latino; 27 Asian, non-Hispanic/Latino; 59 Hispanic/Latino; 50 Two or more races, non-Hispanic/Latino), 574 international. Average age 30. 1,477 applicants, 68% accepted, 664 enrolled. In 2019, 831 master's, 93 other advanced degrees awarded. *Degree requirements:* For master's and Ed S, comprehensive exam (for some programs), thesis (for some programs). *Entrance requirements:* For master's, A GRE or GMAT test score may be required by some of the programs, A minimum GPA, letters of recommendation, a statement of purpose may be required by some of the programs; for Ed S, A master's degree is required for the application of an Education Specialist's degree program. Additional exam requirements/recommendations for international students: required—TOEFL (minimum score 550 paper-based; 79 iBT). *Application deadline:* For fall admission, 6/1 priority date for domestic and international students; for spring admission, 10/15 priority date for domestic and international students; for summer admission, 4/1 priority date for domestic and international students. Applications are processed on a rolling basis. Application fee: $30 ($75 for international students). Electronic applications accepted. *Expenses: Tuition, area resident:* Full-time $7524; part-time $313.50 per credit hour. *Tuition, state resident:* full-time $7524; part-time $313.50 per credit hour. *Tuition, nonresident:* full-time $15,048; part-time $627 per credit hour. *International tuition:* $15,048 full-time. *Required fees:* $915; $30.50 per credit hour. *Financial support:* In 2019–20, 89 students received support. Research assistantships, teaching assistantships, career-related internships or fieldwork, Federal Work-Study, scholarships/grants, unspecified assistantships, and administrative and laboratory assistantships available. Support available to part-time students. Financial award application deadline: 4/1; financial award applicants required to submit FAFSA. *Unit head:* Shellie Hewitt, Director of Graduate and International Student Services, 660-543-4621, Fax: 660-543-4778, E-mail: hewitt@ucmo.edu. *Application contact:* Shellie Hewitt, Director of Graduate and International Student Services, 660-543-4621, Fax: 660-543-4778, E-mail: hewitt@ucmo.edu.
Website: http://www.ucmo.edu/graduate/

**University of Central Oklahoma,** The Jackson College of Graduate Studies, College of Mathematics and Science, Department of Nursing, Edmond, OK 73034-5209. Offers MS. *Accreditation:* AACN. *Program availability:* Part-time. *Degree requirements:* For master's, thesis (for some programs). *Entrance requirements:* For master's, minimum undergraduate GPA of 3.0 in nursing; bachelor's degree in nursing; RN license (preferred). Additional exam requirements/recommendations for international students: required—TOEFL (minimum score 550 paper-based; 79 iBT), IELTS (minimum score 6.5). Electronic applications accepted. *Expenses:* Contact institution.

**University of Cincinnati,** Graduate School, College of Nursing, Cincinnati, OH 45221-0038. Offers nurse midwifery (MSN); nurse practitioner (MSN, DNP), including acute

care pediatrics (DNP), adult-gerontology acute care, adult-gerontology primary care, anesthesia (DNP), family (MSN), leadership (DNP), neonatal (MSN), women's health (MSN); nursing (MSN, PhD), including occupational health (MSN). *Accreditation:* AACN; AANA/CANAEP (one or more programs are accredited); ACNM/ACME. *Program availability:* Part-time, 100% online, blended/hybrid learning. *Faculty:* 62 full-time (55 women), 125 part-time/adjunct (114 women). *Students:* 429 full-time (355 women), 1,547 part-time (1,390 women); includes 453 minority (226 Black or African American, non-Hispanic/Latino; 5 American Indian or Alaska Native, non-Hispanic/Latino; 68 Asian, non-Hispanic/Latino; 103 Hispanic/Latino; 3 Native Hawaiian or other Pacific Islander, non-Hispanic/Latino; 48 Two or more races, non-Hispanic/Latino), 15 international. Average age 36. 779 applicants, 78% accepted, 464 enrolled. In 2019, 518 master's, 47 doctorates awarded. *Degree requirements:* For master's, thesis or alternative; for doctorate, comprehensive exam (for some programs), thesis/dissertation (for some programs). *Entrance requirements:* For master's, GRE required only for the Direct-Entry Accelerated Program. Additional exam requirements/recommendations for international students: required—TOEFL (minimum score 600 paper-based; 100 iBT); recommended—IELTS (minimum score 7). *Application deadline:* For fall admission, 4/1 priority date for domestic and international students; for spring admission, 9/1 priority date for domestic and international students; for summer admission, 2/1 priority date for domestic and international students. Applications are processed on a rolling basis. Application fee: $135 ($140 for international students). Electronic applications accepted. *Expenses:* Contact institution. *Financial support:* In 2019–20, 103 students received support, including 9 fellowships with full tuition reimbursements available (averaging $18,595 per year), 7 research assistantships with full tuition reimbursements available (averaging $12,991 per year), 8 teaching assistantships with full tuition reimbursements available (averaging $12,991 per year); institutionally sponsored loans, scholarships/grants, traineeships, health care benefits, tuition waivers (partial), and unspecified assistantships also available. Support available to part-time students. Financial award application deadline: 4/1; financial award applicants required to submit FAFSA. *Unit head:* Dr. Greer Glazer, Dean, 513-558-5330, Fax: 513-558-9030, E-mail: greer.glazer@uc.edu. *Application contact:* Office of Student Affairs, 513-558-8400, E-mail: nursingbearcats@uc.edu.
Website: https://nursing.uc.edu/

**University of Colorado Colorado Springs,** Helen and Arthur E. Johnson Beth-El College of Nursing and Health Sciences, Colorado Springs, CO 80918. Offers nursing practice (MSN, DNP). *Accreditation:* AACN. *Program availability:* Part-time, 100% online. *Faculty:* 62 full-time (47 women), 77 part-time/adjunct (68 women). *Students:* 20 full-time (18 women), 295 part-time (261 women); includes 74 minority (14 Black or African American, non-Hispanic/Latino; 2 American Indian or Alaska Native, non-Hispanic/Latino; 16 Asian, non-Hispanic/Latino; 26 Hispanic/Latino; 1 Native Hawaiian or other Pacific Islander, non-Hispanic/Latino; 15 Two or more races, non-Hispanic/Latino). Average age 36. 147 applicants, 44% accepted, 49 enrolled. In 2019, 63 master's, 4 doctorates awarded. *Degree requirements:* For master's, comprehensive exam, thesis optional; for doctorate, capstone project. *Entrance requirements:* For master's, completion of an accredited (programmatic) baccalaureate degree in nursing including undergraduate coursework in: Introduction to Statistics, nursing research, health assessment; curriculum vitae or resume; 3 letters of recommendation; minimum overall GPA of 2.75 for cumulative undergraduate course work and BSN GPA of 3.3 or higher; for doctorate, active RN license in state of practice; Master of Science Degree in Nursing from an accredited (CCNE/NLN) program; undergraduate cumulative GPA of 2.75 or higher and graduate cumulative GPA 3.3 or higher; National Certification* as NP or CNS; curriculum vitae; completion of application essay. Additional exam requirements/recommendations for international students: required—TOEFL (minimum score 80 iBT). *Application deadline:* For fall admission, 3/15 priority date for domestic students, 3/15 for international students; for spring admission, 8/15 for domestic and international students. Applications are processed on a rolling basis. Application fee: $60 ($100 for international students). Electronic applications accepted. *Expenses:* Contact institution. *Financial support:* In 2019–20, 14 students received support, including 1 research assistantship (averaging $20,800 per year), 9 teaching assistantships (averaging $3,000 per year); career-related internships or fieldwork, Federal Work-Study, and scholarships/grants also available. Support available to part-time students. Financial award application deadline: 3/1; financial award applicants required to submit FAFSA. *Unit head:* Dr. Deborah Pollard, Nursing Department Chair, 719-255-3577, Fax: 719-255-4416, E-mail: dpollard@uccs.edu. *Application contact:* Diane Busch, Program Assistant II, 719-255-4424, Fax: 719-255-4416, E-mail: dbusch@uccs.edu.
Website: https://www.uccs.edu/johnsonbethel/

**University of Colorado Denver,** College of Nursing, Aurora, CO 80045. Offers adult clinical nurse specialist (MS); adult nurse practitioner (MS); family nurse practitioner (MS); family psychiatric mental health nurse practitioner (MS); health care informatics (MS); nurse-midwifery (MS); nursing (DNP, PhD); nursing leadership and health care systems (MS); pediatric nurse practitioner (MS); women's health (MS); MS/PhD. *Accreditation:* ACNM/ACME (one or more programs are accredited). *Program availability:* Part-time, evening/weekend, online learning. Terminal master's awarded for partial completion of doctoral program. *Degree requirements:* For master's, thesis optional; for doctorate, comprehensive exam, thesis/dissertation, 42 credits of coursework. *Entrance requirements:* For master's, GRE if cumulative undergraduate GPA is less than 3.0, undergraduate nursing degree from ACEN- or CCNE-accredited school or university; completion of research and statistics courses with minimum grade of C; copy of current and unencumbered nursing license; for doctorate, GRE, bachelor's and/or master's degrees in nursing from ACEN- or CCNE-accredited institution; portfolio; minimum undergraduate GPA of 3.0, graduate 3.5; graduate-level intermediate statistics and master's-level nursing theory courses with minimum B grade; interview. Additional exam requirements/recommendations for international students: required—TOEFL (minimum score 560 paper-based; 83 iBT). Electronic applications accepted. *Expenses:* Contact institution.

**University of Connecticut,** Graduate School, School of Nursing, Doctorate of Nursing Practice Program, Storrs, CT 06269. Offers DNP. *Program availability:* Part-time, online learning. *Entrance requirements:* For doctorate, current licensure as registered professional nurse; minimum GPA of 3.0; three reference letters; personal statement; personal interview; master's degree from accredited college or university. Additional exam requirements/recommendations for international students: required—TOEFL (minimum score 550 paper-based). Electronic applications accepted.

**University of Connecticut,** Graduate School, School of Nursing, MS Program in Nursing, Storrs, CT 06269. Offers adult gerontological acute care nurse practitioner (MS); adult gerontological primary care nurse practitioner (MS); family nurse practitioner (MS); neonatal nurse practitioner (MS). *Accreditation:* AACN. *Program availability:* Part-time, online learning. *Degree requirements:* For master's, comprehensive exam. *Entrance requirements:* For master's, official transcripts, Connecticut RN license, three letters of reference, curriculum vitae or resume, personal statement. Additional exam requirements/recommendations for international students: required—TOEFL (minimum score 550 paper-based). Electronic applications accepted.

**University of Connecticut,** Graduate School, School of Nursing, PhD Program in Nursing, Storrs, CT 06269. Offers PhD.

**University of Connecticut,** Graduate School, School of Nursing, Post-Master's Certificate Programs, Storrs, CT 06269. Offers adult gerontology acute care nurse practitioner (Post-Master's Certificate); adult gerontology primary care nurse practitioner (Post-Master's Certificate); neonatal nurse practitioner (Post-Master's Certificate). *Entrance requirements:* For degree, minimum graduate GPA of 3.0, current Connecticut RN license, three letters of recommendation, current resume/curriculum vitae.

**University of Delaware,** College of Health Sciences, School of Nursing, Newark, DE 19716. Offers adult nurse practitioner (MSN, PMC); cardiopulmonary clinical nurse specialist (MSN, PMC); cardiopulmonary clinical nurse specialist/adult nurse practitioner (MSN, PMC); family nurse practitioner (MSN, PMC); gerontology clinical nurse specialist (MSN, PMC); gerontology clinical nurse specialist geriatric nurse practitioner (PMC); gerontology clinical nurse specialist/geriatric nurse practitioner (MSN); health services administration (MSN, PMC); nursing of children clinical nurse specialist (MSN, PMC); nursing of children clinical nurse specialist/pediatric nurse practitioner (MSN, PMC); oncology/immune deficiency clinical nurse specialist (MSN, PMC); oncology/immune deficiency clinical nurse specialist/adult nurse practitioner (MSN, PMC); perinatal/women's health clinical nurse specialist (MSN, PMC); perinatal/women's health clinical nurse specialist/women's health nurse practitioner (MSN, PMC); psychiatric nursing clinical nurse specialist (MSN, PMC). *Accreditation:* AACN. *Program availability:* Part-time, evening/weekend, online learning. *Degree requirements:* For master's, thesis optional. *Entrance requirements:* For master's, BSN, interview, RN license. Electronic applications accepted.

**University of Detroit Mercy,** College of Health Professions, Detroit, MI 48221. Offers clinical nurse leader (MSN); family nurse practitioner (MSN); health services administration (MHSA); health systems management (MSN); nurse anesthesia (MS); nursing (DNP); nursing education (MSN, Certificate); nursing leadership and financial management (Certificate); outcomes performance management (Certificate); physician assistant (MS). *Accreditation:* AANA/CANAEP. *Entrance requirements:* For master's, GRE General Test, minimum GPA of 3.0.

**University of Florida,** Graduate School, College of Nursing, Gainesville, FL 32611. Offers clinical and translational science (PhD); clinical nursing (DNP); nursing (MSN); nursing sciences (PhD). *Accreditation:* AACN; ACNM/ACME (one or more programs are accredited). *Program availability:* Part-time. *Degree requirements:* For master's, thesis optional; for doctorate, thesis/dissertation. *Entrance requirements:* For master's and doctorate, GRE General Test, minimum GPA of 3.0. Additional exam requirements/recommendations for international students: required—TOEFL (minimum score 550 paper-based; 80 iBT), IELTS (minimum score 6). Electronic applications accepted.

**University of Hartford,** College of Education, Nursing, and Health Professions, Program in Nursing, West Hartford, CT 06117-1599. Offers community/public health nursing (MSN); nursing education (MSN); nursing management (MSN). *Accreditation:* AACN. *Program availability:* Part-time, evening/weekend. *Faculty:* 9 full-time (8 women), 5 part-time/adjunct (all women). *Students:* 7 full-time (all women), 100 part-time (94 women); includes 22 minority (12 Black or African American, non-Hispanic/Latino; 2 Asian, non-Hispanic/Latino; 6 Hispanic/Latino; 2 Two or more races, non-Hispanic/Latino), 9 international. Average age 39. 50 applicants, 96% accepted, 45 enrolled. In 2019, 65 master's awarded. *Entrance requirements:* For master's, BSN, Connecticut RN license. Additional exam requirements/recommendations for international students: required—TOEFL (minimum score 550 paper-based). *Application deadline:* For fall admission, 4/15 priority date for domestic students; for spring admission, 12/1 for domestic students. Application fee: $45. Electronic applications accepted. *Expenses:* Contact institution. *Financial support:* Teaching assistantships and Federal Work-Study available. Support available to part-time students. Financial award application deadline: 6/1; financial award applicants required to submit FAFSA. *Unit head:* Jane Williams, Chair, 860-768-4217, Fax: 860-768-5346. *Application contact:* Marlene Hall, Assistant Dean, 860-768-5116, E-mail: mhall@hartford.edu.
Website: http://www.hartford.edu/enhp/

**University of Hawaii at Hilo,** Program in Nursing Practice, Hilo, HI 96720-4091. Offers DNP. *Accreditation:* AACN. *Entrance requirements:* Additional exam requirements/recommendations for international students: required—TOEFL, IELTS. Electronic applications accepted.

**University of Hawaii at Manoa,** Office of Graduate Education, School of Nursing and Dental Hygiene, Honolulu, HI 96822. Offers clinical nurse specialist (MS), including adult health, community mental health; nurse practitioner (MS), including adult health, community mental health, family nurse practitioner; nursing (PhD, Graduate Certificate); nursing administration (MS). *Accreditation:* AACN. *Program availability:* Part-time, online learning. *Degree requirements:* For master's, thesis optional; for doctorate, comprehensive exam, thesis/dissertation. *Entrance requirements:* For master's, Hawaii RN license. Additional exam requirements/recommendations for international students: required—TOEFL (minimum score 580 paper-based; 92 iBT), IELTS (minimum score 5). *Expenses:* Contact institution.

**University of Houston,** College of Nursing, Sugar Land, TX 77479. Offers family nurse practitioner (MSN); nursing administration (MSN); nursing education (MSN). *Accreditation:* AACN. *Faculty:* 8 full-time (7 women). *Students:* 18 full-time (12 women), 33 part-time (32 women); includes 30 minority (13 Black or African American, non-Hispanic/Latino; 4 Asian, non-Hispanic/Latino; 12 Hispanic/Latino; 1 Native Hawaiian or other Pacific Islander, non-Hispanic/Latino). Average age 36. 38 applicants, 74% accepted, 20 enrolled. In 2019, 12 master's awarded. *Entrance requirements:* For master's, minimum GPA of 3.0, unencumbered Texas RN license, 2 letters of recommendation, essay, resume, interview required. Additional exam requirements/recommendations for international students: required—TOEFL. *Application deadline:* For fall admission, 6/1 for domestic and international students; for spring admission, 11/1 for domestic and international students; for summer admission, 4/1 for domestic and international students. Application fee: $75. Electronic applications accepted. *Financial support:* In 2019–20, 19 students received support. Federal Work-Study, scholarships/grants, and unspecified assistantships available. Support available to part-time students. Financial award application deadline: 7/1; financial award applicants required to submit FAFSA. *Unit head:* Dr. Kathryn Tart, Dean, 832-842-8200, E-mail: kmtart@uh.edu. *Application contact:* Tammy N. Whatley, Student Affairs Director, 832-842-8220, E-mail: tnwhatley@uh.edu.
Website: http://www.uh.edu/nursing

**University of Illinois at Chicago,** College of Nursing, Chicago, IL 60607-7128. Offers MS, DNP, PhD, Certificate, MBA/MS, MPH/MS. *Accreditation:* AACN; ACNM/ACME. *Program availability:* Part-time. *Degree requirements:* For master's, thesis or alternative; for doctorate, thesis/dissertation. *Entrance requirements:* For master's and doctorate, GRE General Test, minimum GPA of 2.75. Additional exam requirements/recommendations for international students: required—TOEFL. Electronic applications accepted. *Expenses:* Contact institution.

**University of Indianapolis,** Graduate Programs, School of Nursing, Indianapolis, IN 46227-3697. Offers advanced practice nursing (DNP); family nurse practitioner (MSN); gerontological nurse practitioner (MSN); neonatal nurse practitioner (MSN); nurse-

midwifery (MSN); nursing (MSN); nursing and health systems leadership (MSN); nursing education (MSN); women's health nurse practitioner (MSN); MBA/MSN. *Accreditation:* AACN. *Entrance requirements:* For master's, minimum GPA of 3.0, interview, letters of recommendation, resume, IN nursing license, 1 year of professional practice; for doctorate, graduate of ACEN- or CCNE-accredited nursing program; MSN or MA with nursing major and minimum cumulative GPA of 3.25; unencumbered RN license with eligibility for licensure in Indiana; completion of graduate-level statistics course within last 5 years with minimum grade of B; resume; essay; official transcripts from all academic institutions. Additional exam requirements/recommendations for international students: required—TOEFL (minimum score 550 paper-based). Electronic applications accepted.

**The University of Iowa,** Graduate College, College of Nursing, Iowa City, IA 52242-1316. Offers MSN, DNP, PhD. *Accreditation:* AACN; AANA/CANAEP (one or more programs are accredited). *Degree requirements:* For master's, thesis optional, portfolio, project; for doctorate, comprehensive exam, thesis/dissertation. *Entrance requirements:* For master's, minimum GPA of 3.0; for doctorate, GRE General Test, minimum GPA of 3.0. Additional exam requirements/recommendations for international students: required—TOEFL (minimum score 550 paper-based; 81 iBT). Electronic applications accepted. *Expenses:* Contact institution.

**The University of Kansas,** University of Kansas Medical Center, School of Nursing, Kansas City, KS 66045. Offers adult/gerontological clinical nurse specialist (PMC); adult/gerontological nurse practitioner (PMC); health care informatics (PMC); health professions educator (PMC); nurse midwife (PMC); nursing (MS, DNP, PhD); organizational leadership (PMC); psychiatric/mental health nurse practitioner (PMC); public health nursing (PMC). *Accreditation:* AACN; ACNM/ACME. *Program availability:* Part-time, 100% online, blended/hybrid learning. *Faculty:* 65. *Students:* 57 full-time (53 women), 267 part-time (242 women); includes 65 minority (14 Black or African American, non-Hispanic/Latino; 2 American Indian or Alaska Native, non-Hispanic/Latino; 21 Asian, non-Hispanic/Latino; 9 Hispanic/Latino; 1 Native Hawaiian or other Pacific Islander, non-Hispanic/Latino; 18 Two or more races, non-Hispanic/Latino), 2 international. Average age 35. In 2019, 26 master's, 48 doctorates, 5 other advanced degrees awarded. Terminal master's awarded for partial completion of doctoral program. *Degree requirements:* For master's, comprehensive exam, thesis (for some programs), general oral exam; for doctorate, thesis/dissertation or alternative, comprehensive oral exam (for DNP); comprehensive written and oral exam, or three publications (for PhD). *Entrance requirements:* For master's, bachelor's degree in nursing, minimum GPA of 3.0, 1 year of clinical experience, RN license in KS and MO; for doctorate, GRE General Test (for PhD only), bachelor's degree in nursing, minimum GPA of 3.5, RN license in KS and MO. Additional exam requirements/recommendations for international students: required—TOEFL. *Application deadline:* For fall admission, 4/1 for domestic and international students; for spring admission, 9/1 for domestic and international students. Application fee: $75. Electronic applications accepted. *Expenses:* Contact institution. *Financial support:* Research assistantships with tuition reimbursements, teaching assistantships with tuition reimbursements, scholarships/grants, and traineeships available. Financial award application deadline: 3/1; financial award applicants required to submit FAFSA. *Unit head:* Dr. Sally Maliski, Professor and Dean, 913-588-1601, Fax: 913-588-1660, E-mail: smaliski@kumc.edu. *Application contact:* Dr. Pamela K. Barnes, Associate Dean, Student Affairs and Enrollment Management, 913-588-1619, Fax: 913-588-1615, E-mail: pbarnes2@kumc.edu.
Website: http://nursing.kumc.edu

**University of Kentucky,** Graduate School, College of Nursing, Lexington, KY 40506-0032. Offers DNP, PhD. *Accreditation:* AACN. *Degree requirements:* For doctorate, comprehensive exam, thesis/dissertation. *Entrance requirements:* For doctorate, GRE General Test, minimum undergraduate GPA of 3.0. Additional exam requirements/recommendations for international students: required—TOEFL (minimum score 550 paper-based). Electronic applications accepted.

**University of Lethbridge,** School of Graduate Studies, Lethbridge, AB T1K 3M4, Canada. Offers addictions counseling (M Sc); agricultural biotechnology (M Sc); agricultural studies (M Sc, MA); anthropology (MA); archaeology (M Sc, MA); art (MA, MFA); biochemistry (M Sc); biological sciences (M Sc); biomolecular science (PhD); biosystems and biodiversity (PhD); Canadian studies (MA); chemistry (M Sc); computer science (M Sc); computer science and geographical information science (M Sc); counseling (MC); counseling psychology (M Ed); dramatic arts (MA); earth, space, and physical science (PhD); economics (MA); education (MA, PhD); educational leadership (M Ed); English (MA); environmental science (M Sc); evolution and behavior (PhD); exercise science (M Sc); French (MA); French/German (MA); French/Spanish (MA); general education (M Ed); geography (M Sc, MA); German (MA); health sciences (M Sc); individualized multidisciplinary (M Sc, MA); kinesiology (M Sc, MA); management (M Sc), including accounting, finance, human resource management and labor relations, information systems, international management, marketing, policy and strategy; mathematics (M Sc); music (M Mus, MA); Native American studies (MA); neuroscience (M Sc, PhD); new media (MA, MFA); nursing (M Sc, MN); philosophy (MA); physics (M Sc); political science (MA); psychology (M Sc, MA); religious studies (MA); sociology (MA); theatre and dramatic arts (MFA); theoretical and computational science (PhD); urban and regional studies (MA); women and gender studies (MA). *Program availability:* Part-time, evening/weekend. *Degree requirements:* For master's, thesis (for some programs); for doctorate, comprehensive exam, thesis/dissertation. *Entrance requirements:* For master's, GMAT (for M Sc in management), bachelor's degree in related field, minimum GPA of 3.0 during previous 20 graded semester courses, 2 years' teaching or related experience (M Ed); for doctorate, master's degree, minimum graduate GPA of 3.5. Additional exam requirements/recommendations for international students: required—TOEFL (minimum score 580 paper-based; 93 iBT). Electronic applications accepted.

**University of Louisiana at Lafayette,** College of Nursing and Allied Health Professions, Lafayette, LA 70504. Offers family nurse practitioner (MSN); nursing (DNP); nursing education (MSN). *Accreditation:* AACN. *Entrance requirements:* For master's, GRE General Test, minimum GPA of 2.75. Additional exam requirements/recommendations for international students: required—TOEFL (minimum score 550 paper-based). Electronic applications accepted. *Expenses: Tuition, area resident:* Full-time $5511; part-time $1630 per credit hour. Tuition, state resident: full-time $5511; part-time $1630 per credit hour. Tuition, nonresident: full-time $19,239; part-time $2409 per credit hour. *Required fees:* $46,637.

**University of Louisville,** Graduate School, School of Nursing, Louisville, KY 40202. Offers adult gerontology nurse practitioner (MSN, DNP); education and administration (MSN); family nurse practitioner (MSN, DNP); neonatal nurse practitioner (MSN, DNP); nursing research (PhD); psychiatric/mental health nurse practitioner (MSN, DNP); women's health nurse practitioner (MSN). *Accreditation:* AACN. *Program availability:* Part-time, blended/hybrid learning. *Faculty:* 49 full-time (46 women), 91 part-time/adjunct (86 women). *Students:* 164 full-time (140 women), 47 part-time (39 women); includes 45 minority (21 Black or African American, non-Hispanic/Latino; 5 Asian, non-Hispanic/Latino; 9 Hispanic/Latino; 10 Two or more races, non-Hispanic/Latino), 4 international. Average age 33. 84 applicants, 63% accepted, 48 enrolled. In 2019, 25 master's, 5 doctorates awarded. *Degree requirements:* For master's, varies; for doctorate, comprehensive exam (for some programs), thesis/dissertation (for some programs), varies. *Entrance requirements:* For master's, Our only master's degree is an accelerated program meant for students who have a bachelor's degree in another discipline who are transitioning into nursing. Thus, the main requirement is a bachelor's degree from a nationally-accredited college, and the completion of 6 prerequisite courses. Must have a minimum undergraduate GPA of 3.0; for doctorate, PhD program: GRE requirement omitted, DNP & PhD doctoral programs: 3 letters of professional reference. BSN applicants must have a 3.0 GPA. MSN applicants must have 3.25 GPA. Written statement of career goals, areas of expertise, reasons for pursuing doctoral degree, resume, and RN license. Additional exam requirements/recommendations for international students: recommended—TOEFL (minimum score 560 paper-based), IELTS (minimum score 6.5). *Application deadline:* For fall admission, 1/15 priority date for domestic and international students; for summer admission, 10/15 priority date for domestic students. Application fee: $60. Electronic applications accepted. *Expenses:* 17871. *Financial support:* In 2019–20, 47 students received support, including 2 fellowships with full tuition reimbursements available (averaging $20,000 per year), 9 research assistantships with full tuition reimbursements available (averaging $20,000 per year), 3 teaching assistantships with full tuition reimbursements available (averaging $15,000 per year); scholarships/grants, health care benefits, unspecified assistantships, and Jonas Nurse Leader Fellowships also available. Financial award application deadline: 10/1; financial award applicants required to submit FAFSA. *Unit head:* 502-852-8300, Fax: 502-852-5044, E-mail: sonya.hardin@louisville.edu. *Application contact:* Trish Hart, MA, Assistant Dean for Student Affairs, 502-852-5825, Fax: 502-852-8783, E-mail: trish.hart@louisville.edu.
Website: http://www.louisville.edu/nursing/

**University of Maine,** Graduate School, College of Natural Sciences, Forestry, and Agriculture, School of Nursing, Orono, ME 04469. Offers individualized (MS); nursing education (CGS); rural health family nurse practitioner (MS, CAS). *Accreditation:* AACN. *Faculty:* 6 full-time (all women), 6 part-time/adjunct (4 women). *Students:* 24 full-time (21 women), 20 part-time (18 women); includes 4 minority (2 American Indian or Alaska Native, non-Hispanic/Latino; 2 Hispanic/Latino). Average age 34. 14 applicants, 100% accepted, 10 enrolled. In 2019, 11 master's, 4 other advanced degrees awarded. *Entrance requirements:* For master's, GRE General Test; for other advanced degree, master's degree. Additional exam requirements/recommendations for international students: required—TOEFL. *Application deadline:* For fall admission, 7/1 for domestic students; for spring admission, 12/15 for domestic students; for summer admission, 4/15 for domestic students. Applications are processed on a rolling basis. Application fee: $65. Electronic applications accepted. *Expenses: Tuition, area resident:* Full-time $8100; part-time $450 per credit hour. Tuition, state resident: full-time $8100; part-time $450 per credit hour. Tuition, nonresident: full-time $26,388; part-time $1466 per credit hour. *International tuition:* $26,388 full-time. *Required fees:* $1257; $278 per semester. Tuition and fees vary according to course load. *Financial support:* Career-related internships or fieldwork, Federal Work-Study, institutionally sponsored loans, tuition waivers (full and partial), and unspecified assistantships available. Support available to part-time students. Financial award application deadline: 3/1. *Unit head:* Dr. Nancy Fishwick, Director, 207-581-2505, Fax: 207-581-2585. *Application contact:* Scott G. Delcourt, Assistant Vice President for Graduate Studies and Senior Associate Dean, 207-581-3291, Fax: 207-581-3232, E-mail: graduate@maine.edu.
Website: http://umaine.edu/nursing/

**The University of Manchester,** School of Nursing, Midwifery and Social Work, Manchester, United Kingdom. Offers nursing (M Phil, PhD); social work (M Phil, PhD).

**University of Manitoba,** Faculty of Graduate Studies, College of Nursing, Winnipeg, MB R3T 2N2, Canada. Offers cancer nursing (MN); nursing (MN). *Degree requirements:* For master's, thesis.

**University of Mary,** School of Health Sciences, Division of Nursing, Bismarck, ND 58504-9652. Offers family nurse practitioner (DNP); nurse administrator (MSN); nursing educator (MSN); MSN/MBA. *Accreditation:* AACN. *Program availability:* Part-time, evening/weekend, online learning. *Degree requirements:* For master's, comprehensive exam (for some programs), thesis (for some programs), internship (family nurse practitioner), teaching practice. *Entrance requirements:* For master's, minimum GPA of 2.75 in nursing, interview, letters of recommendation, criminal background check, immunizations, statement of professional goals. Additional exam requirements/recommendations for international students: required—TOEFL (minimum score 500 paper-based; 71 iBT). Electronic applications accepted.

**University of Mary Hardin-Baylor,** Graduate Studies in Nursing, Belton, TX 76513. Offers family nurse practitioner (MSN, Post-Master's Certificate); nursing education (MSN); nursing practice (DNP). *Accreditation:* AACN. *Program availability:* Evening/weekend. *Faculty:* 8 full-time (all women), 5 part-time/adjunct (3 women). *Students:* 22 full-time (20 women), 9 part-time (8 women); includes 15 minority (4 Black or African American, non-Hispanic/Latino; 3 Asian, non-Hispanic/Latino; 7 Hispanic/Latino; 1 Two or more races, non-Hispanic/Latino), 1 international. Average age 36. 26 applicants, 62% accepted, 15 enrolled. In 2019, 17 master's, 2 other advanced degrees awarded. *Degree requirements:* For master's, comprehensive exam, practicum; for doctorate, scholarly project. *Entrance requirements:* For master's, baccalaureate degree in nursing, current licensure as Registered Nurse in the state of Texas, minimum GPA of 3.0 in last 60 hours of undergraduate program, two letters of recommendation, full-time RN for 1 year, personal interview with director of MSN program; for doctorate, master's degree as an advanced practice nurse, nurse leader or nurse educator; three letters of recommendation; current RN license and approval to practice as an advanced practice nurse; essay; curriculum vitae; interview. Additional exam requirements/recommendations for international students: required—TOEFL (minimum score 60 iBT), IELTS (minimum score 4.5). *Application deadline:* For fall admission, 6/1 for domestic students, 4/30 priority date for international students; for spring admission, 11/1 for domestic students, 9/30 priority date for international students. Applications are processed on a rolling basis. Application fee: $35 ($135 for international students). Electronic applications accepted. *Expenses:* Contact institution. *Financial support:* In 2019–20, 24 students received support. Federal Work-Study, unspecified assistantships, and scholarships for some active duty military personnel available. Support available to part-time students. Financial award applicants required to submit FAFSA. *Unit head:* Dr. Elizabeth Jimenez, Director, Master of Science in Nursing Program & Assistant Professor, 254-295-4769, E-mail: ejimenez@umhb.edu. *Application contact:* Katherine Moore, Assistant Director, Graduate Admissions, 254-295-4924, E-mail: kmoore@umhb.edu.
Website: https://go.umhb.edu/graduate/nursing/home

**University of Maryland, Baltimore,** University of Maryland School of Nursing, Baltimore, MD 21201. Offers adult-gerontology acute care nurse practitioner (DNP); adult-gerontology primary care nurse practitioner (DNP); clinical nurse leader (MS); community/public health nursing (MS); family nurse practitioner (DNP); global health (Postbaccalaureate Certificate); health services leadership and management (MS); neonatal nurse practitioner (DNP); nurse anesthesia (DNP); nursing (PhD); nursing informatics (MS, Postbaccalaureate Certificate); pediatric acute/primary care nurse practitioner (DNP); psychiatric mental health nurse practitioner (DNP); teaching in nursing and health professions (Postbaccalaureate Certificate); MS/MBA. *Accreditation:*

AANA/CANAEP. *Program availability:* Part-time. *Faculty:* 130 full-time (117 women), 125 part-time/adjunct (114 women). *Students:* 539 full-time (463 women), 586 part-time (506 women); includes 485 minority (259 Black or African American, non-Hispanic/Latino; 3 American Indian or Alaska Native, non-Hispanic/Latino; 124 Asian, non-Hispanic/Latino; 66 Hispanic/Latino; 1 Native Hawaiian or other Pacific Islander, non-Hispanic/Latino; 32 Two or more races, non-Hispanic/Latino), 18 international. Average age 33. 964 applicants, 54% accepted, 347 enrolled. In 2019, 197 master's, 114 doctorates, 12 other advanced degrees awarded. *Degree requirements:* For master's and Postbaccalaureate Certificate, thesis (for some programs); for doctorate, comprehensive exam, thesis/dissertation. *Entrance requirements:* Additional exam requirements/recommendations for international students: required—TOEFL (minimum score 550 paper-based; 79 iBT); recommended—IELTS (minimum score 7). *Application deadline:* For fall admission, 11/1 priority date for domestic and international students; for spring admission, 12/15 for domestic and international students; for summer admission, 9/1 for domestic and international students. Applications are processed on a rolling basis. Application fee: $75. Electronic applications accepted. *Financial support:* In 2019–20, 257 students received support, including 31 research assistantships with full and partial tuition reimbursements available (averaging $25,000 per year), 21 teaching assistantships with full and partial tuition reimbursements available (averaging $19,000 per year); scholarships/grants, traineeships, and unspecified assistantships also available. Support available to part-time students. Financial award application deadline: 3/1; financial award applicants required to submit FAFSA. *Unit head:* Dr. Jane Kirschling, Dean, 410-706-4359, E-mail: kirschling@umaryland.edu. *Application contact:* Larry Fillian, Associate Dean of Student and Academic Services, 410-706-6298, E-mail: lfillian@umaryland.edu.
Website: http://www.nursing.umaryland.edu/

**University of Massachusetts Amherst,** Graduate School, College of Nursing, Amherst, MA 01003. Offers adult gerontology primary care nurse practitioner (DNP); clinical nurse leader (MS); family nurse practitioner (DNP); nursing (PhD); public health nurse leader (DNP). *Accreditation:* AACN. *Program availability:* Part-time, online learning. Terminal master's awarded for partial completion of doctoral program. *Degree requirements:* For master's, thesis optional; for doctorate, comprehensive exam, thesis/dissertation. *Entrance requirements:* Additional exam requirements/recommendations for international students: required—TOEFL (minimum score 550 paper-based; 80 iBT), IELTS (minimum score 6.5). Electronic applications accepted.

**University of Massachusetts Boston,** College of Nursing and Health Sciences, Program in Nursing, Boston, MA 02125-3393. Offers MS, PhD. *Program availability:* Part-time, evening/weekend. *Entrance requirements:* For master's, GRE General Test, minimum GPA of 2.75, RN license; for doctorate, GRE General Test, master's degree, minimum GPA of 3.3, RN license or eligibility.

**University of Massachusetts Boston,** College of Nursing and Health Sciences, Program in Nursing Practice, Boston, MA 02125-3393. Offers DNP.

**University of Massachusetts Dartmouth,** Graduate School, College of Nursing and Health Sciences, North Dartmouth, MA 02747-2300. Offers MS, DNP, PhD. *Accreditation:* AACN. *Program availability:* Part-time, 100% online, blended/hybrid learning. *Faculty:* 26 full-time (all women), 45 part-time/adjunct (all women). *Students:* 2 full-time (both women), 122 part-time (111 women); includes 25 minority (10 Black or African American, non-Hispanic/Latino; 9 Asian, non-Hispanic/Latino; 4 Hispanic/Latino; 2 Two or more races, non-Hispanic/Latino), 1 international. Average age 38. 39 applicants, 95% accepted, 32 enrolled. In 2019, 1 master's, 12 doctorates awarded. *Degree requirements:* For master's, capstone project; for doctorate, comprehensive exam, thesis/dissertation, project (for DNP); dissertation (qualifying exam for PhD). *Entrance requirements:* For master's, statement of purpose (minimum of 300 words), resume, 2 letters of reference, official transcripts, BS Nursing, copy of RN license or license number; for doctorate, Personal statement, Current Mass registered Nurse license, 1 year professional Nursing experience, resume, official transcripts, scholarly writing samples (min 10 pages) and 3 letters of recommendation. Additional exam requirements/recommendations for international students: required—TOEFL. *Application deadline:* Applications are processed on a rolling basis. Application fee: $60. Electronic applications accepted. *Expenses: Tuition, area resident:* Full-time $16,390; part-time $682.92 per credit. Tuition, state resident: full-time $16,390; part-time $682.92 per credit. Tuition, nonresident: full-time $29,578; part-time $1232.42 per credit. *Required fees:* $575. *Financial support:* In 2019–20, 7 teaching assistantships (averaging $7,714 per year) were awarded; tuition waivers (partial) and doctoral support also available. Financial award application deadline: 3/1; financial award applicants required to submit FAFSA. *Unit head:* June Horowitz, Associate Dean for Graduate Programs and Research, 508-999-8251, E-mail: jhorowitz@umassd.edu. *Application contact:* Scott Webster, Director of Graduate Studies and Admissions, 508-999-8604, Fax: 508-999-8183, E-mail: graduate@umassd.edu.
Website: http://www.umassd.edu/nursing

**University of Massachusetts Lowell,** College of Health Sciences, School of Nursing, Lowell, MA 01854. Offers adult/gerontological nursing (MS); family health nursing (MS); nursing (DNP, PhD). *Accreditation:* AACN. *Degree requirements:* For master's, thesis optional; for doctorate, thesis/dissertation. *Entrance requirements:* For master's and doctorate, GRE General Test.

**University of Massachusetts Medical School,** Graduate School of Nursing, Worcester, MA 01655. Offers adult gerontological acute care nurse practitioner (DNP, Post Master's Certificate); adult gerontological primary care nurse practitioner (DNP, Post Master's Certificate); family nursing practitioner (DNP); nurse administrator (DNP); nurse educator (MS); nursing (PhD); psychiatric mental health (Post Master's Certificate). *Accreditation:* AACN. *Program availability:* Blended/hybrid learning. *Faculty:* 26 full-time (22 women), 51 part-time/adjunct (40 women). *Students:* 176 full-time (152 women), 33 part-time (27 women); includes 61 minority (21 Black or African American, non-Hispanic/Latino; 1 American Indian or Alaska Native, non-Hispanic/Latino; 18 Asian, non-Hispanic/Latino; 20 Hispanic/Latino; 1 Native Hawaiian or other Pacific Islander, non-Hispanic/Latino). Average age 32. 131 applicants, 66% accepted, 58 enrolled. In 2019, 28 master's, 34 doctorates, 1 other advanced degree awarded. *Degree requirements:* For doctorate, thesis/dissertation (for some programs), comprehensive exam and manuscript (for PhD); scholarly project (for DNP). *Entrance requirements:* For master's, GRE General Test, bachelor's degree in nursing, course work in statistics, unrestricted Massachusetts license as registered nurse; for doctorate, GRE General Test, bachelor's or master's degree; for Post Master's Certificate, GRE General Test, MS in nursing. Additional exam requirements/recommendations for international students: required—TOEFL (minimum score 400 paper-based; 81 iBT). *Application deadline:* For fall admission, 12/1 priority date for domestic students. Applications are processed on a rolling basis. Application fee: $100. Electronic applications accepted. *Expenses:* Contact institution. *Financial support:* In 2019–20, 103 students received support. Scholarships/grants available. Support available to part-time students. Financial award application deadline: 5/15; financial award applicants required to submit FAFSA. *Unit head:* Dr. Joan Vitello-Cicciu, Dean, 508-856-5081, Fax: 508-856-6552, E-mail: joan.vitello@umassmed.edu. *Application contact:* Diane Brescia, Admissions Coordinator, 508-856-3488, Fax: 508-856-5851, E-mail: diane.brescia@umassmed.edu.
Website: http://www.umassmed.edu/gsn/

**University of Memphis,** Loewenberg College of Nursing, Memphis, TN 38152. Offers advanced practice nursing (Graduate Certificate); executive leadership (MSN); family nurse practitioner (MSN); nursing administration (MSN, Graduate Certificate); nursing education (MSN, Graduate Certificate). *Accreditation:* AACN. *Program availability:* Part-time, evening/weekend, online learning. *Faculty:* 21 full-time (19 women), 11 part-time/adjunct (10 women). *Students:* 19 full-time (17 women), 281 part-time (254 women); includes 104 minority (87 Black or African American, non-Hispanic/Latino; 5 Asian, non-Hispanic/Latino; 7 Hispanic/Latino; 5 Two or more races, non-Hispanic/Latino), 2 international. Average age 34. 117 applicants, 79% accepted, 48 enrolled. In 2019, 71 master's, 3 other advanced degrees awarded. *Degree requirements:* For master's, comprehensive exam, thesis optional, scholarly project; clinical practicum hours. *Entrance requirements:* For master's, NCLEX exam, minimum undergraduate GPA of 2.8, letter of interest, letters of recommendation, interview, resume, nursing licensure; for Graduate Certificate, unrestricted license to practice as RN in TN, current CPR certification, evidence of vaccination, annual flu shot, evidence of current professional malpractice insurance, letters of recommendation, letter of intent, resume. Additional exam requirements/recommendations for international students: required—TOEFL (minimum score 550 paper-based; 79 iBT). *Application deadline:* For fall admission, 2/15 for domestic and international students; for spring admission, 10/1 for domestic and international students. Application fee: $35 ($60 for international students). *Expenses: Tuition, area resident:* Full-time $9216; part-time $512 per credit hour. Tuition, state resident: full-time $9216; part-time $512 per credit hour. Tuition, nonresident: full-time $12,672; part-time $704 per credit hour. *International tuition:* $16,128 full-time. *Required fees:* $1530; $85 per credit hour. Tuition and fees vary according to program. *Financial support:* Federal Work-Study and scholarships/grants available. Financial award application deadline: 2/1; financial award applicants required to submit FAFSA. *Unit head:* Dr. Lin Zhan, Dean, 901-678-2020, E-mail: lzhan@memphis.edu. *Application contact:* Dr. Lin Zhan, Dean, 901-678-2020, E-mail: lzhan@memphis.edu.
Website: http://www.memphis.edu/nursing

**University of Miami,** Graduate School, School of Nursing and Health Studies, Coral Gables, FL 33124. Offers acute care (MSN), including acute care nurse practitioner, nurse anesthesia; nursing (PhD); primary care (MSN), including adult nurse practitioner, family nurse practitioner, nurse midwifery, women's health practitioner. *Accreditation:* AACN; AANA/CANAEP; ACNM/ACME (one or more programs are accredited). *Program availability:* Part-time. *Degree requirements:* For master's, thesis optional; for doctorate, thesis/dissertation. *Entrance requirements:* For master's, GRE General Test, BSN, minimum GPA of 3.0, Florida RN license; for doctorate, GRE General Test, BSN or MSN, minimum GPA of 3.0. Additional exam requirements/recommendations for international students: required—TOEFL (minimum score 550 paper-based). Electronic applications accepted.

**University of Michigan,** Rackham Graduate School, School of Nursing, Ann Arbor, MI 48109. Offers acute care pediatric nurse practitioner (MS); nursing (DNP, PhD, Post Master's Certificate). *Accreditation:* AACN; ACNM/ACME (one or more programs are accredited). *Program availability:* Part-time, online learning. Terminal master's awarded for partial completion of doctoral program. *Degree requirements:* For doctorate, thesis/dissertation.

**University of Michigan–Flint,** School of Nursing, Flint, MI 48502-1950. Offers adult-gerontology acute care (DNP); adult-gerontology primary care (DNP); family nurse practitioner (DNP); nursing (MSN); psychiatric mental health (DNP); psychiatric mental health nurse practitioner (Certificate). *Accreditation:* AACN. *Program availability:* Part-time, evening/weekend, 100% online. *Faculty:* 32 full-time (31 women), 80 part-time/adjunct (71 women). *Students:* 198 full-time (174 women), 188 part-time (162 women); includes 55 minority (6 Black or African American, non-Hispanic/Latino; 3 American Indian or Alaska Native, non-Hispanic/Latino; 21 Asian, non-Hispanic/Latino; 18 Hispanic/Latino; 1 Native Hawaiian or other Pacific Islander, non-Hispanic/Latino; 6 Two or more races, non-Hispanic/Latino), 1 international. Average age 37. 140 applicants, 84% accepted, 75 enrolled. In 2019, 52 master's, 22 doctorates, 8 other advanced degrees awarded. *Entrance requirements:* For master's, BSN from regionally-accredited college; minimum GPA of 3.2; current unencumbered RN license in the United States; three or more credits in college-level chemistry or statistics with minimum C grade; for Certificate, completion of nurse practitioner program with MS from regionally-accredited college or university with minimum overall GPA of 3.2; current unencumbered RN license in the United States; current unencumbered license as nurse practitioner; current certification as nurse practitioner in specialty other than discipline of study. Additional exam requirements/recommendations for international students: required—TOEFL (minimum score 84 iBT), IELTS (minimum score 6.5). *Application deadline:* For fall admission, 7/1 for domestic students, 5/1 for international students; for winter admission, 11/15 for domestic students, 10/1 for international students; for spring admission, 3/15 for domestic students, 1/1 for international students; for summer admission, 5/15 for domestic students. Applications are processed on a rolling basis. Application fee: $55. Electronic applications accepted. *Expenses:* Contact institution. *Financial support:* Federal Work-Study, scholarships/grants, and unspecified assistantships available. Support available to part-time students. Financial award application deadline: 3/1; financial award applicants required to submit FAFSA. *Unit head:* Dr. Constance J. Creech, Director, 810-762-3420, Fax: 810-766-6851, E-mail: ccreech@umflint.edu. *Application contact:* Matt Bohlen, Director of Graduate Admissions, 810-762-3171, Fax: 810-766-6789, E-mail: mbohlen@umflint.edu.
Website: https://www.umflint.edu/nursing/graduate-nursing-programs

**University of Minnesota, Twin Cities Campus,** Graduate School, School of Nursing, Minneapolis, MN 55455-0213. Offers adult/gerontological clinical nurse specialist (DNP); adult/gerontological primary care nurse practitioner (DNP); family nurse practitioner (DNP); health innovation and leadership (DNP); integrative health and healing (DNP); nurse anesthesia (DNP); nurse midwifery (DNP); nursing (MN, PhD); nursing informatics (DNP); pediatric clinical nurse specialist (DNP); primary care certified pediatric nurse practitioner (DNP); psychiatric/mental health nurse practitioner (DNP); women's health nurse practitioner (DNP). *Accreditation:* AACN; AANA/CANAEP; ACNM/ACME (one or more programs are accredited). *Program availability:* Part-time, online learning. Terminal master's awarded for partial completion of doctoral program. *Degree requirements:* For master's, final oral exam, project or thesis; for doctorate, thesis/dissertation. *Entrance requirements:* For master's and doctorate, GRE General Test. Additional exam requirements/recommendations for international students: required—TOEFL (minimum score 586 paper-based). *Expenses:* Contact institution.

**University of Mississippi Medical Center,** School of Nursing, Jackson, MS 39216-4505. Offers MSN, DNP, PhD. *Accreditation:* AACN. *Program availability:* Part-time, evening/weekend, online learning. *Degree requirements:* For master's, thesis optional; for doctorate, comprehensive exam, thesis/dissertation, publishable paper. *Entrance requirements:* For master's, GRE, 1 year of clinical experience (acute care nurse practitioner only), RN license; for doctorate, GRE, RN license, professional nursing experience. Additional exam requirements/recommendations for international students: required—TOEFL (minimum score 550 paper-based; 79 iBT). Electronic applications accepted. *Expenses:* Contact institution.

**University of Missouri,** Office of Research and Graduate Studies, Sinclair School of Nursing, Columbia, MO 65211. Offers adult-gerontology clinical nurse specialist (DNP, Certificate); family nurse practitioner (DNP); family psychiatric and mental health nurse practitioner (DNP); nursing (MS, PhD); nursing leadership and innovations in health care (DNP); pediatric clinical nurse specialist (DNP, Certificate); pediatric nurse practitioner (DNP). *Accreditation:* AACN. *Program availability:* Part-time. *Degree requirements:* For master's, thesis optional, oral exam; for doctorate, thesis/dissertation. *Entrance requirements:* For master's, GRE General Test, BSN, minimum GPA of 3.0 during last 60 hours, nursing license. Additional exam requirements/recommendations for international students: required—TOEFL, IELTS. Electronic applications accepted.

**University of Missouri–Kansas City,** School of Nursing and Health Studies, Kansas City, MO 64110-2499. Offers adult clinical nurse specialist (MSN), including adult nurse practitioner, women's health nurse practitioner (MSN, DNP); adult clinical nursing practice (DNP), including adult gerontology nurse practitioner, women's health nurse practitioner (MSN, DNP); clinical nursing practice (DNP), including family nurse practitioner; neonatal nurse practitioner (MSN); nurse educator (MSN); nurse executive (MSN); nursing practice (DNP); pediatric clinical nursing practice (DNP), including pediatric nurse practitioner; pediatric nurse practitioner (MSN). *Accreditation:* AACN. *Program availability:* Part-time, online learning. *Degree requirements:* For master's, thesis or alternative. *Entrance requirements:* For master's, minimum undergraduate GPA of 3.2; for doctorate, GRE, 3 letters of reference. Additional exam requirements/recommendations for international students: required—TOEFL (minimum score 550 paper-based; 80 iBT).

**University of Missouri–St. Louis,** College of Nursing, St. Louis, MO 63121. Offers adult/geriatric nurse practitioner (Post Master's Certificate); family nurse practitioner (Post Master's Certificate); nursing (DNP, PhD); pediatric acute care nurse practitioner (Post Master's Certificate); pediatric nurse practitioner (Post Master's Certificate); psychiatric-mental health nurse practitioner (Post Master's Certificate); women's health nurse practitioner (Post Master's Certificate). *Accreditation:* AACN. *Program availability:* Part-time. *Degree requirements:* For doctorate, comprehensive exam, thesis/dissertation; for Post Master's Certificate, thesis. *Entrance requirements:* For doctorate, GRE, 2 letters of recommendation, MSN, minimum GPA of 3.2, course in differential/inferential statistics; for Post Master's Certificate, 2 recommendation letters; MSN; advanced practice certificate; minimum GPA of 3.0; essay. Additional exam requirements/recommendations for international students: recommended—TOEFL (minimum score 550 paper-based; 79 iBT), IELTS (minimum score 6.5). Electronic applications accepted. *Expenses: Tuition, area resident:* Full-time $9005.40; part-time $6003.60 per credit hour. Tuition, state resident: full-time $9005.40; part-time $6003.60 per credit hour. Tuition, nonresident: full-time $22,108; part-time $14,738.40 per credit hour. *International tuition:* $22,108 full-time. Tuition and fees vary according to course load.

**University of Mobile,** Graduate Studies, School of Nursing, Mobile, AL 36613. Offers education/administration (MSN); nurse practitioner (DNP). *Accreditation:* AACN. *Program availability:* Part-time, evening/weekend. *Degree requirements:* For master's, comprehensive exam, thesis or alternative; for doctorate, comprehensive exam. *Entrance requirements:* For master's, minimum cumulative GPA of 2.5, unencumbered license to practice as a registered nurse. See catalog for additional requirements. Additional exam requirements/recommendations for international students: required—TOEFL (minimum score 550 paper-based; 80 iBT). Electronic applications accepted.

**University of Mount Olive,** Graduate Programs, Mount Olive, NC 28365. Offers business (MBA); education (M Ed); nursing (MSN). *Program availability:* Online learning.

**University of Nebraska Medical Center,** PhD in Nursing Program, Omaha, NE 68198. Offers PhD. *Accreditation:* AACN. *Program availability:* Part-time, blended/hybrid learning. *Degree requirements:* For doctorate, comprehensive exam, thesis/dissertation. *Entrance requirements:* For doctorate, GRE General Test, NCLEX, minimum GPA of 3.2, BSN or MSN from accredited school, students without an MSN may be accepted into BSN-PhD program. Additional exam requirements/recommendations for international students: required—TOEFL (minimum score 550 paper-based; 80 iBT), IELTS (minimum score 6.5), Will accept TOEFL or IELTS. Electronic applications accepted. *Expenses:* Contact institution.

**University of Nevada, Las Vegas,** Graduate College, School of Nursing, Las Vegas, NV 89154-3018. Offers biobehavioral nursing (Advanced Certificate); family nurse practitioner (Advanced Certificate); nursing (MS, DNP, PhD); nursing education (Advanced Certificate). *Accreditation:* AACN. *Program availability:* Part-time, 100% online, blended/hybrid learning. *Faculty:* 15 full-time (13 women), 9 part-time/adjunct (8 women). *Students:* 44 full-time (41 women), 111 part-time (96 women); includes 48 minority (9 Black or African American, non-Hispanic/Latino; 16 Asian, non-Hispanic/Latino; 15 Hispanic/Latino; 1 Native Hawaiian or other Pacific Islander, non-Hispanic/Latino; 7 Two or more races, non-Hispanic/Latino), 1 international. Average age 38. 218 applicants, 33% accepted, 63 enrolled. In 2019, 19 master's, 14 doctorates, 2 other advanced degrees awarded. *Degree requirements:* For master's, comprehensive exam, thesis; for doctorate, comprehensive exam (for some programs), thesis/dissertation, project defense (for DNP). *Entrance requirements:* For master's, bachelor's degree with minimum GPA 3.0; 2 letters of recommendation; valid RN license; statement of purpose; for doctorate, GRE General Test, bachelor's degree; statement of purpose; 3 letters of recommendation; for Advanced Certificate, 2 letters of recommendation; statement of purpose; valid RN license. Additional exam requirements/recommendations for international students: recommended—TOEFL (minimum score 550 paper-based; 80 iBT), IELTS (minimum score 7). Application fee: $60 ($95 for international students). Electronic applications accepted. *Expenses:* Contact institution. *Financial support:* In 2019–20, 2 students received support, including 1 research assistantship with full tuition reimbursement available (averaging $20,250 per year), 1 teaching assistantship with full tuition reimbursement available (averaging $20,250 per year); institutionally sponsored loans, scholarships/grants, health care benefits, and unspecified assistantships also available. Financial award application deadline: 3/15; financial award applicants required to submit FAFSA. *Unit head:* Dr. Angela Amar, Dean/Professor, 702-895-3906, Fax: 702-895-4807, E-mail: nursing.dean@unlv.edu. *Application contact:* Dr. Angela Amar, Dean/Professor, 702-895-3906, Fax: 702-895-4807, E-mail: nursing.dean@unlv.edu. Website: http://nursing.unlv.edu/

**University of Nevada, Reno,** Graduate School, Division of Health Sciences, Orvis School of Nursing, Reno, NV 89557. Offers MSN, DNP, MPH/MSN. *Accreditation:* AACN. *Degree requirements:* For master's, thesis optional. *Entrance requirements:* For master's, minimum GPA of 3.0 in bachelor's degree from accredited school. Additional exam requirements/recommendations for international students: required—TOEFL (minimum score 500 paper-based; 61 iBT), IELTS (minimum score 6). Electronic applications accepted.

**University of New Hampshire,** Graduate School, College of Health and Human Services, Department of Nursing, Durham, NH 03824. Offers family nurse practitioner (Postbaccalaureate Certificate); nursing (MS, DNP); psychiatric mental health (Postbaccalaureate Certificate). *Accreditation:* AACN. *Program availability:* Part-time, online learning. *Students:* 46 full-time (27 women), 11 part-time (8 women); includes 6 minority (1 Black or African American, non-Hispanic/Latino; 1 Asian, non-Hispanic/

Latino; 2 Hispanic/Latino; 2 Two or more races, non-Hispanic/Latino), 3 international. Average age 34. 17 applicants, 71% accepted, 10 enrolled. In 2019, 7 doctorates awarded. *Entrance requirements:* Additional exam requirements/recommendations for international students: required—TOEFL (minimum score 550 paper-based; 80 iBT), IELTS, PTE. *Application deadline:* For fall admission, 7/1 for domestic students; for spring admission, 11/1 for domestic students. Application fee: $65. Electronic applications accepted. *Financial support:* In 2019–20, 36 students received support, including 4 fellowships, 15 research assistantships, 13 teaching assistantships; Federal Work-Study, scholarships/grants, and tuition waivers (full and partial) also available. Financial award application deadline: 2/15. *Unit head:* Dr. Gene Harkless, Chair, 603-862-2285. *Application contact:* Pan DiNapoli, Administrative Assistant, 603-862-3976, E-mail: pam.dinapoli@unh.edu.
Website: https://chhs.unh.edu/nursing/graduate-program-nursing

**University of New Mexico,** Graduate Studies, Health Sciences Center, Program in Nursing, Albuquerque, NM 87131-2039. Offers MSN, DNP, PhD. *Accreditation:* AACN; ACNM/ACME (one or more programs are accredited). *Program availability:* Part-time, online learning. *Degree requirements:* For master's, comprehensive exam, thesis optional; for doctorate, comprehensive exam, thesis/dissertation. *Entrance requirements:* For master's, minimum GPA of 3.0, course work in statistics (recommended), interview (for some concentrations), BSN or RN with BA; for doctorate, interview, minimum GPA of 3.0, writing sample, MSN or BSN with MA. Additional exam requirements/recommendations for international students: required—TOEFL. Electronic applications accepted. *Expenses:* Tuition, state resident: full-time $7633; part-time $972 per year. Tuition, nonresident: full-time $22,586; part-time $3840 per year. *International tuition:* $23,292 full-time. *Required fees:* $8608. Tuition and fees vary according to course level, course load, degree level, program and student level.

**University of North Alabama,** Anderson College of Nursing, Florence, AL 35632-0001. Offers MSN. *Accreditation:* AACN. *Program availability:* Part-time, online only, 100% online, blended/hybrid learning. *Entrance requirements:* For master's, one year of clinical practice as registered nurse. Additional exam requirements/recommendations for international students: required—TOEFL (minimum score 550 paper-based; 79 iBT), IELTS (minimum score 6), PTE (minimum score 54). Electronic applications accepted.

**The University of North Carolina at Chapel Hill,** School of Nursing, Chapel Hill, NC 27599-7460. Offers advanced practice registered nurse (DNP); nursing (MSN, PhD, PMC), including administration (MSN), adult gerontology primary care nurse practitioner (MSN), clinical nurse leader (MSN), education (MSN), health care systems (PMC), informatics (MSN, PMC), nursing leadership (PMC), outcomes management (MSN), primary care family nurse practitioner (MSN), primary care pediatric nurse practitioner (MSN), psychiatric/mental health nurse practitioner (MSN, PMC). *Accreditation:* AACN; ACEN (one or more programs are accredited). *Program availability:* Part-time. *Degree requirements:* For master's, comprehensive exam, thesis; for doctorate, thesis/dissertation, 3 exams; for PMC, thesis. *Entrance requirements:* Additional exam requirements/recommendations for international students: required—TOEFL (minimum score 575 paper-based; 89 iBT), IELTS (minimum score 8). Electronic applications accepted.

**The University of North Carolina at Charlotte,** College of Health and Human Services, School of Nursing, Charlotte, NC 28223-0001. Offers adult-gerontology acute care nurse practitioner (Post-Master's Certificate); advanced clinical nursing (MSN), including adult psychiatric mental health, adult-gerontology acute care nurse practitioner, family nurse practitioner across the lifespan; family nurse practitioner across the lifespan (Post-Master's Certificate); nurse anesthesia (MSN), including nurse anesthesia across the lifespan; nurse anesthesia across the lifespan (Post-Master's Certificate); nursing (DNP); nursing administrator (Graduate Certificate); nursing educator (Graduate Certificate); systems/population nursing (MSN), including community/public health nursing, nurse administrator, nurse educator. *Accreditation:* AACN; AANA/CANAEP. *Program availability:* Part-time, blended/hybrid learning. *Students:* 126 full-time (96 women), 142 part-time (127 women); includes 70 minority (48 Black or African American, non-Hispanic/Latino; 8 Asian, non-Hispanic/Latino; 9 Hispanic/Latino; 5 Two or more races, non-Hispanic/Latino), 1 international. Average age 35. 347 applicants, 37% accepted, 104 enrolled. In 2019, 102 master's, 10 doctorates, 10 other advanced degrees awarded. Terminal master's awarded for partial completion of doctoral program. *Entrance requirements:* For master's, GRE General Test, current unrestricted license as Registered Nurse in North Carolina; BSN from nationally-accredited program; one year of professional nursing practice in acute/critical care; minimum overall GPA of 3.0 in last degree; completion of undergraduate statistics course with minimum grade of C; statement of purpose; for doctorate, GRE or MAT, master's degree in nursing in an advanced nursing practice specialty from nationally-accredited program; minimum overall GPA of 3.5 in MSN program; current RN licensure in U.S. at time of application with eligibility for NC licensure; essay; resume/curriculum vitae; professional recommendations; clinical hours; for other advanced degree, GRE. Additional exam requirements/recommendations for international students: required—TOEFL (minimum score 557 paper-based; 83 iBT), IELTS (minimum score 6.5), TOEFL (minimum score 557 paper-based, 83 iBT) or IELTS (6.5). *Application deadline:* Applications are processed on a rolling basis. Application fee: $75. Electronic applications accepted. *Expenses:* Contact institution. *Financial support:* In 2019–20, 6 students received support, including 4 research assistantships (averaging $4,856 per year), 2 teaching assistantships (averaging $3,615 per year); career-related internships or fieldwork, institutionally sponsored loans, scholarships/grants, traineeships, and unspecified assistantships also available. Support available to part-time students. Financial award application deadline: 3/1; financial award applicants required to submit FAFSA. *Unit head:* Dr. Dena Evans, Director, 704-687-7974, E-mail: devans37@uncc.edu. *Application contact:* Kathy B. Giddings, Director of Graduate Admissions, 704-687-5503, Fax: 704-687-1668, E-mail: gradadm@uncc.edu.
Website: http://nursing.uncc.edu/

**The University of North Carolina at Greensboro,** Graduate School, School of Nursing, Greensboro, NC 27412-5001. Offers adult clinical nurse specialist (MSN, PMC); adult/gerontological nurse practitioner (MSN, PMC); nurse anesthesia (MSN, PMC); nursing (PhD); nursing administration (MSN); nursing education (MSN); MSN/MBA. *Accreditation:* ACEN. *Degree requirements:* For master's, thesis or alternative. *Entrance requirements:* For master's, GRE General Test or MAT, BSN, clinical experience, liability insurance, RN license; for PMC, liability insurance, MSN, RN license. Additional exam requirements/recommendations for international students: required—TOEFL. Electronic applications accepted.

**The University of North Carolina at Pembroke,** The Graduate School, Department of Nursing, Pembroke, NC 28372-1510. Offers clinical nurse leader (MSN); nurse educator (MSN); rural case manager (MSN). *Accreditation:* AACN. *Program availability:* Part-time.

**The University of North Carolina Wilmington,** School of Nursing, Wilmington, NC 28403-3297. Offers clinical research and product development (MS); family nurse practitioner (Post-Master's Certificate); nurse educator (Post-Master's Certificate); nursing (MSN); nursing practice (DNP). *Accreditation:* AACN; ACEN. *Program availability:* Part-time, 100% online, blended/hybrid learning. *Faculty:* 51 full-time (46 women). *Students:* 171 full-time (156 women), 423 part-time (387 women); includes 117 minority (73 Black or African American, non-Hispanic/Latino; 6 American Indian or

Alaska Native, non-Hispanic/Latino; 12 Asian, non-Hispanic/Latino; 16 Hispanic/Latino; 1 Native Hawaiian or other Pacific Islander, non-Hispanic/Latino; 9 Two or more races, non-Hispanic/Latino). Average age 38. 527 applicants, 57% accepted, 199 enrolled. In 2019, 149 master's, 9 doctorates awarded. *Degree requirements:* For master's, thesis or alternative, research/capstone project, presentation; for doctorate, comprehensive exam, clinical scholarly project, 1000 clinical hours. *Entrance requirements:* For master's, GRE General Test if overall Bachelor degree GPA under 3.0 (MSN degree); No tests for MCRD degree, 3 recommendations; statement of interest; resume; bachelor's degree, preferably in a life science, health care discipline, or mathematics/statistics; experience working in the biopharmaceutical or related field (MCRD degree); RN license in NC & must have 2.69 or higher Bachelor's GPA (for MSN); for doctorate, GRE General Test or MAT if Bachelor's GPA below 3.0 (FNP & Psychiatric Mental Health Nurse concentration), Varies based on concentration (Family Nurse Practitioner, Nurse Executive Leadership, Post APRN, and Psychiatric Mental Health Nurse); All require 3 professional references and an RN license. Additional exam requirements/recommendations for international students: required—TOEFL (minimum score 79 iBT), IELTS (minimum score 6.5). *Application deadline:* For fall admission, 4/15 for domestic students. Applications are processed on a rolling basis. Application fee: $75. Electronic applications accepted. *Expenses:* $324.70 per credit hour in-state (for DNP Program), $1,002.59 per credit hour out-of-state (for DNP Program), $259.01 per credit hour in-state (for the remaining online programs), $936.91 per credit hour out-of-state (for the remaining online programs), $3,728.47 entire year in-state (for main campus programs), $10,642.97 entire year out-of-state (for main campus programs). *Financial support:* Scholarships/grants available. Financial award application deadline: 1/1; financial award applicants required to submit FAFSA. *Unit head:* Dr. Linda Haddad, Director, 910-962-7410, Fax: 910-962-3723, E-mail: haddadl@uncw.edu. *Application contact:* Dr. Sarah Hubbell, MSN Graduate Coordinator, 910-962-0561, E-mail: hubbells@uncw.edu.
Website: https://uncw.edu/chhs/son/

**University of North Dakota,** Graduate School, College of Nursing and Professional Disciplines, Department of Nursing, Grand Forks, ND 58202. Offers adult-gerontological nurse practitioner (MS); advanced public health nurse (MS); family nurse practitioner (MS); nurse anesthesia (MS); nurse educator (MS); nursing (PhD, Post-Master's Certificate); nursing practice (DNP); psychiatric and mental health nurse practitioner (MS). *Accreditation:* AANA/CANAEP.

**University of Northern Colorado,** Graduate School, College of Natural and Health Sciences, School of Nursing, Greeley, CO 80639. Offers adult-gerontology acute care nurse practitioner (MSN, DNP); family nurse practitioner (MSN, DNP); nursing education (PhD); nursing practice (DNP). *Accreditation:* AACN. *Program availability:* Online learning. *Degree requirements:* For master's, comprehensive exam, thesis or alternative; for doctorate, comprehensive exam, thesis/dissertation. *Entrance requirements:* For master's and doctorate, GRE General Test, minimum GPA of 3.0 in last 60 hours, BS in nursing, 2 letters of recommendation. Electronic applications accepted.

**University of North Florida,** Brooks College of Health, School of Nursing, Jacksonville, FL 32224. Offers family nurse practitioner (Certificate); nurse anesthetist (MSN). *Accreditation:* AACN; AANA/CANAEP. *Program availability:* Part-time. *Degree requirements:* For master's, thesis optional. *Entrance requirements:* For master's, GRE General Test, minimum GPA of 3.0 in last 60 hours of course work, BSN, clinical experience, resume; for doctorate, GRE, master's degree in nursing specialty from nationally-accredited program; national certification in one of the following APRN roles: CNE, CNM, CNS, CRNA, CNP; minimum graduate GPA of 3.3; three letters of reference which address academic ability and clinical skills; active license as registered nurse or advanced practice registered nurse. Additional exam requirements/recommendations for international students: required—TOEFL (minimum score 500 paper-based; 61 iBT). Electronic applications accepted. *Expenses:* Contact institution.

**University of Oklahoma Health Sciences Center,** Graduate College, College of Nursing, Oklahoma City, OK 73190. Offers MS, MS/MBA. *Accreditation:* AACN; ACEN. *Program availability:* Part-time. *Degree requirements:* For master's, comprehensive exam, thesis optional. *Entrance requirements:* For master's, 3 letters of recommendation, Oklahoma RN license, statistics course, research methods, computer course or completion of a computer literacy test.

**University of Ottawa,** Faculty of Graduate and Postdoctoral Studies, Faculty of Health Sciences, School of Nursing, Ottawa, ON K1N 6N5, Canada. Offers nurse practitioner (Certificate); nursing (M Sc, PhD); nursing/primary health care (M Sc). *Program availability:* Part-time, evening/weekend. *Degree requirements:* For master's, thesis or alternative. *Entrance requirements:* For master's, honors degree or equivalent, minimum B average. Electronic applications accepted.

**University of Pennsylvania,** School of Nursing, Philadelphia, PA 19104. Offers MSN, PhD, Certificate, MBA/MSN, MBA/PhD, MSN/PhD. *Accreditation:* AACN; AANA/CANAEP. *Program availability:* Part-time, online learning. *Faculty:* 60 full-time (52 women), 33 part-time/adjunct (29 women). *Students:* 249 full-time (211 women), 471 part-time (418 women); includes 199 minority (57 Black or African American, non-Hispanic/Latino; 77 Asian, non-Hispanic/Latino; 45 Hispanic/Latino; 20 Two or more races, non-Hispanic/Latino), 14 international. Average age 32. 587 applicants, 60% accepted, 282 enrolled. In 2019, 321 master's, 15 doctorates awarded. Terminal master's awarded for partial completion of doctoral program. *Unit head:* Dr. Antonia M. Villarruel, Dean, 215-898-4271, Fax: 215-573-8439, E-mail: amvillar@nursing.upenn.edu. *Application contact:* Sylvia English, Admissions Officer, Enrollment Management, 215-898-8439, Fax: 215-573-8439, E-mail: sylviaj@nursing.upenn.edu.
Website: http://www.nursing.upenn.edu/

**University of Phoenix - Bay Area Campus,** College of Nursing, San Jose, CA 95134-1805. Offers education (MHA); gerontology (MHA); health administration (MHA, DHA); informatics (MHA, MSN); nursing (MSN, PhD); nursing/health care education (MSN); MSN/MBA. *Program availability:* Evening/weekend, online learning. *Degree requirements:* For master's, thesis (for some programs). *Entrance requirements:* For master's, minimum undergraduate GPA of 2.5, 3 years of work experience, RN license. Additional exam requirements/recommendations for international students: required—TOEFL (minimum score 550 paper-based; 79 iBT). Electronic applications accepted.

**University of Phoenix - Central Valley Campus,** College of Nursing, Fresno, CA 93720-1552. Offers education (MHA); gerontology (MHA); health administration (MHA); nursing (MSN); MSN/MBA.

**University of Phoenix - Hawaii Campus,** College of Nursing, Honolulu, HI 96813-3800. Offers education (MHA); family nurse practitioner (MSN); gerontology (MHA); health administration (MHA); nursing (MSN); nursing/health care education (MSN); MSN/MBA. *Program availability:* Evening/weekend. *Degree requirements:* For master's, thesis (for some programs). *Entrance requirements:* For master's, minimum undergraduate GPA of 2.5, 3 years of work experience, RN license. Additional exam requirements/recommendations for international students: required—TOEFL (minimum score 550 paper-based; 79 iBT). Electronic applications accepted.

**University of Phoenix - Houston Campus,** College of Nursing, Houston, TX 77079-2004. Offers health administration (MHA). *Program availability:* Online learning. *Degree requirements:* For master's, thesis (for some programs). *Entrance requirements:* For master's, minimum undergraduate GPA of 2.5, 3 years of work experience. Additional exam requirements/recommendations for international students: required—TOEFL (minimum score 550 paper-based; 79 iBT). Electronic applications accepted.

**University of Phoenix–Online Campus,** College of Health Sciences and Nursing, Phoenix, AZ 85034-7209. Offers family nurse practitioner (Certificate); health care (Certificate); health care education (Certificate); health care informatics (Certificate); informatics (MSN); nursing (MSN); nursing and health care education (MSN); MSN/MBA; MSN/MHA. *Accreditation:* AACN. *Program availability:* Evening/weekend, online learning. *Entrance requirements:* Additional exam requirements/recommendations for international students: required—TOEFL, TOEIC (Test of English as an International Communication), Berlitz Online English Proficiency Exam, PTE, or IELTS. Electronic applications accepted. *Expenses:* Contact institution.

**University of Phoenix–Online Campus,** School of Advanced Studies, Phoenix, AZ 85034-7209. Offers business administration (DBA); education (Ed S); educational leadership (Ed D), including curriculum and instruction, education technology, educational leadership; health administration (DHA); higher education administration (PhD); industrial/organizational psychology (PhD); nursing (PhD); organizational leadership (DM), including information systems and technology, organizational leadership. *Program availability:* Evening/weekend, online learning. *Degree requirements:* For doctorate, thesis/dissertation. *Entrance requirements:* Additional exam requirements/recommendations for international students: required—TOEFL, TOEIC (Test of English as an International Communication), Berlitz Online English Proficiency Exam, PTE, or IELTS. Electronic applications accepted. *Expenses:* Contact institution.

**University of Phoenix - Phoenix Campus,** College of Health Sciences and Nursing, Tempe, AZ 85282-2371. Offers family nurse practitioner (MSN, Certificate); gerontology health care (Certificate); health care education (MSN, Certificate); health care informatics (Certificate); informatics (MSN); nursing (MSN); MSN/MHA. *Program availability:* Evening/weekend, online learning. *Entrance requirements:* Additional exam requirements/recommendations for international students: required—TOEFL, TOEIC (Test of English as an International Communication), Berlitz Online English Proficiency Exam, PTE, or IELTS. Electronic applications accepted. *Expenses:* Contact institution.

**University of Phoenix - Sacramento Valley Campus,** College of Nursing, Sacramento, CA 95833-4334. Offers family nurse practitioner (MSN); health administration (MHA); health care education (MSN); nursing (MSN); MSN/MBA. *Program availability:* Evening/weekend. *Degree requirements:* For master's, thesis (for some programs). *Entrance requirements:* For master's, RN license, minimum undergraduate GPA of 2.5, 3 years work experience. Additional exam requirements/recommendations for international students: required—TOEFL (minimum score 550 paper-based; 79 iBT). Electronic applications accepted.

**University of Phoenix - San Antonio Campus,** College of Nursing, San Antonio, TX 78230. Offers health administration (MHA).

**University of Phoenix - San Diego Campus,** College of Nursing, San Diego, CA 92123. Offers health care education (MSN); nursing (MSN); MSN/MBA. *Program availability:* Evening/weekend. *Degree requirements:* For master's, thesis (for some programs). *Entrance requirements:* For master's, minimum undergraduate GPA of 2.5, 3 years work experience, RN license. Additional exam requirements/recommendations for international students: required—TOEFL (minimum score 550 paper-based; 79 iBT). Electronic applications accepted.

**University of Pittsburgh,** School of Nursing, Clinical Nurse Specialist Program, Pittsburgh, PA 15260. Offers clinical nurse specialist (DNP), including adult gerontology. *Accreditation:* AACN. *Program availability:* Part-time. *Faculty:* 1 full-time (0 women). *Students:* 3 full-time (all women), 4 part-time (all women). Average age 39. 4 applicants, 100% accepted, 1 enrolled. In 2019, 2 doctorates awarded. *Degree requirements:* For doctorate, comprehensive exam, thesis/dissertation or alternative, capstone project required. *Entrance requirements:* For doctorate, GRE, BSN, RN license, course work in statistics, resume/essay, 3 letters of recommendation. Additional exam requirements/recommendations for international students: required—TOEFL (minimum score 600 paper-based; 100 iBT), IELTS (minimum score 7), TOEFL (minimum score 600 paper-based; 100 IBT) or IELTS (minimum score 7.0). *Application deadline:* For fall admission, 6/1 priority date for domestic students, 2/15 priority date for international students. Application fee: $50. Electronic applications accepted. *Expenses:* $13,795 per term full-time resident tuition, $475 per term full-time resident fees, $1,122 per credit part-time resident tuition, $295 per term part-time resident fees, $16,474 per term full-time non-resident tuition, $475 per term full-time non-resident fees, $1,345 per credit part-time non-resident tuition, $295 per term part-time non-resident fees. *Financial support:* In 2019–20, 7 students received support, including 4 fellowships (averaging $15,188 per year); scholarships/grants and Matching Funds also available. Financial award application deadline: 6/1; financial award applicants required to submit FAFSA. *Unit head:* Dr. Sandra Engberg, Associate Dean for Clinical Education, 412-624-3835, Fax: 412-624-8521, E-mail: sje1@pitt.edu. *Application contact:* Laurie Lapsley, Graduate Administrator, 412-624-9670, Fax: 412-624-2409, E-mail: lapsleyl@pitt.edu.

**University of Pittsburgh,** School of Nursing, PhD Program in Nursing, Pittsburgh, PA 15261. Offers doctor of philosophy (PhD). *Program availability:* Part-time. *Faculty:* 27 full-time (22 women), 1 (woman) part-time/adjunct. *Students:* 29 full-time (28 women), 2 part-time (both women); includes 1 minority (Hispanic/Latino), 12 international. Average age 32. 15 applicants, 67% accepted, 8 enrolled. In 2019, 6 doctorates awarded. *Degree requirements:* For doctorate, comprehensive exam, thesis/dissertation. *Entrance requirements:* For doctorate, GRE, BSN/MSN, 3 letters of recommendation, resume/essay, course work in statistics. Additional exam requirements/recommendations for international students: required—TOEFL (minimum score 600 paper-based; 100 iBT), IELTS (minimum score 7), TOEFL (minimum score 600 paper-based; 100 IBT) or IELTS (minimum score 7.0). *Application deadline:* For fall admission, 6/1 for domestic students, 2/1 priority date for international students. Application fee: $50. Electronic applications accepted. *Expenses:* $13,795 per term full-time resident tuition, $475 per term full-time resident fees, $1,122 per credit part-time resident tuition, $295 per term part-time resident fees, $16,474 per term full-time non-resident tuition, $475 per term full-time non-resident fees, $1,345 per credit part-time non-resident tuition, $295 per term part-time non-resident fees. *Financial support:* In 2019–20, 28 students received support, including 4 fellowships (averaging $14,664 per year), 12 research assistantships (averaging $15,010 per year), 4 teaching assistantships (averaging $11,054 per year); scholarships/grants, unspecified assistantships, and Matching Funds also available. Financial award application deadline: 6/1; financial award applicants required to submit FAFSA. *Unit head:* Dr. Marilyn Hravnak, Director, PhD Program, 412-383-5148, Fax: 412-624-2401, E-mail: mhra@pitt.edu. *Application contact:* Laurie Lapsley, Graduate Administrator, 412-624-9670, Fax: 412-624-2409, E-mail: lapsleyl@pitt.edu.
Website: http://www.nursing.pitt.edu/

**University of Portland,** School of Nursing, Portland, OR 97203-5798. Offers clinical nurse leader (MS); family nurse practitioner (DNP); nurse educator (MS). *Accreditation:* AACN. *Program availability:* Part-time, evening/weekend. *Entrance requirements:* For doctorate, RN license, BSN or MSN, 3 letters of recommendation, resume, writing

sample, official transcripts. Additional exam requirements/recommendations for international students: required—TOEFL (minimum score 100 iBT), IELTS (minimum score 7.5). Electronic applications accepted. *Expenses:* Contact institution.

**University of Puerto Rico - Medical Sciences Campus,** School of Nursing, San Juan, PR 00936-5067. Offers adult and elderly nursing (MSN); child and adolescent nursing (MSN); critical care nursing (MSN); family and community nursing (MSN); family nurse practitioner (MSN); maternity nursing (MSN); mental health and psychiatric nursing (MSN). *Accreditation:* AACN; AANA/CANAEP. *Entrance requirements:* For master's, GRE or EXADEP, interview, Puerto Rico RN license or professional license for international students, general and specific point average, article analysis. Electronic applications accepted.

**University of Regina,** Faculty of Graduate Studies and Research, Faculty of Nursing, Regina, SK S4S 0A2, Canada. Offers nurse practitioner clinical nurse specialist (MN); nursing (M Sc, PhD). *Faculty:* 18 full-time (15 women), 11 part-time/adjunct (10 women). *Students:* 19 full-time (17 women), 36 part-time (29 women). Average age 30. 59 applicants, 54% accepted. In 2019, 14 master's awarded. *Degree requirements:* For master's, course work, internship/residency; for doctorate, thesis/dissertation, course work. *Entrance requirements:* For master's, proof of licensure or registration as an RN including registration number in a Canadian province or territory, 2 years of clinical practice within last 5 years, essay, minimum overall GPA of 75% in all 3rd- and 4th-year nursing courses taken at a Canadian-accredited or provincially-approved baccalaureate nursing education program. Additional exam requirements/recommendations for international students: required—TOEFL (minimum score 580 paper-based; 80 iBT), IELTS (minimum score 6.5), PTE (minimum score 59), Other options are MELAB, CAEL, CANTEST, and UR ESL. *Application deadline:* For fall admission, 3/15 for domestic and international students. Application fee: $100 Canadian dollars. Electronic applications accepted. *Expenses:* 11,036.50 - This amount is based on three semesters tuition, registered in 6 credit hours per semester. Plus student fees and books. There might be some other fees while in the work placement. *Financial support:* In 2019–20, 40 students received support, including 36 fellowships, 2 teaching assistantships (averaging $2,552 per year); career-related internships or fieldwork, Federal Work-Study, scholarships/grants, unspecified assistantships, and travel Award and Graduate Scholarship Base Funds also available. Support available to part-time students. Financial award application deadline: 9/30. *Unit head:* Dr. Joan Wagner, Associate Dean, Graduate Programs and Research, 306-585-4070, Fax: 306-337-8493, E-mail: joan.wagner@uregina.ca. *Application contact:* Gillian Borys, Graduate Program Assistant, 306-337-3355, Fax: 306-337-8493, E-mail: gillian.borys@uregina.ca. Website: http://www.uregina.ca/nursing

**University of Rhode Island,** Graduate School, College of Nursing, Kingston, RI 02881. Offers acute care nurse practitioner (adult-gerontology focus) (Post Master's Certificate); adult gerontology nurse practitioner/clinical nurse specialist (Post Master's Certificate); adult-gerontological acute care nurse practitioner (MS); adult-gerontological nurse practitioner/clinical nurse specialist (MS); family nurse practitioner (MS, Post Master's Certificate); nursing (DNP, PhD); nursing education (MS, Post Master's Certificate). *Accreditation:* AACN; ACNM/ACME (one or more programs are accredited). *Program availability:* Part-time, evening/weekend, 100% online, blended/hybrid learning. *Faculty:* 27 full-time (26 women). *Students:* 51 full-time (47 women), 72 part-time (65 women); includes 21 minority (9 Black or African American, non-Hispanic/Latino; 5 Asian, non-Hispanic/Latino; 4 Hispanic/Latino; 2 Native Hawaiian or other Pacific Islander, non-Hispanic/Latino; 1 Two or more races, non-Hispanic/Latino), 6 international. 32 applicants, 88% accepted, 21 enrolled. In 2019, 34 master's, 9 doctorates, 1 other advanced degree awarded. *Entrance requirements:* For master's, GRE or MAT, 2 letters of recommendation, scholarly papers; for doctorate, GRE, 3 letters of recommendation, scholarly papers. Additional exam requirements/recommendations for international students: required—TOEFL. *Application deadline:* For fall admission, 2/15 for domestic students, 2/1 for international students; for spring admission, 10/15 for domestic students, 7/15 for international students. Application fee: $65. Electronic applications accepted. *Expenses: Tuition, area resident:* Full-time $13,734; part-time $763 per credit. Tuition, state resident: full-time $13,734; part-time $763 per credit. Tuition, nonresident: full-time $26,512; part-time $1473 per credit. *International tuition:* $26,512 full-time. *Required fees:* $1780; $52 per credit. $35 per term. One-time fee: $165. *Financial support:* In 2019–20, 7 teaching assistantships with tuition reimbursements (averaging $13,376 per year) were awarded. Financial award application deadline: 2/1; financial award applicants required to submit FAFSA. *Unit head:* Dr. Barbara Wolfe, Dean, 401-874-5324, E-mail: bwolfe@uri.edu. *Application contact:* Dr. Denise Coppa, Associate Professor/Interim Associate Dean for Graduate Programs, 401-874-5036, E-mail: dcoppa@uri.edu.
Website: http://www.uri.edu/nursing/

**University of Rochester,** School of Nursing, Rochester, NY 14642. Offers adult gerontological acute care nurse practitioner (MS); adult gerontological primary care nurse practitioner (MS); clinical nurse leader (MS); family nurse practitioner (MS); family psychiatric mental health nurse practitioner (MS); health care organization management and leadership (MS); nursing (DNP); nursing and health science (PhD); nursing education (MS); pediatric nurse practitioner (MS); pediatric nurse practitioner/neonatal nurse practitioner (MS). *Accreditation:* AACN. *Program availability:* Part-time, 100% online, blended/hybrid learning. Terminal master's awarded for partial completion of doctoral program. *Degree requirements:* For master's, comprehensive exam; for doctorate, thesis/dissertation. *Entrance requirements:* For master's, BS in nursing, RN license; for doctorate, GRE General Test (for PhD), B.S. degree, RN license most programs. Additional exam requirements/recommendations for international students: required—TOEFL (minimum score 560 paper-based; 88 iBT), TOEFL (minimum score 560 paper-based; 88 iBT) or IELTS (minimum score 6.5) recommended. Electronic applications accepted. *Expenses:* Contact institution.

**University of St. Augustine for Health Sciences,** Graduate Programs, Doctor of Nursing Practice Program, San Marcos, CA 92069. Offers DNP.

**University of St. Augustine for Health Sciences,** Graduate Programs, Master of Science in Nursing Program, San Marcos, CA 92069. Offers nurse educator (MSN); nurse executive (MSN); nurse informatics (MSN). *Program availability:* Part-time, online learning.

**University of Saint Francis,** Graduate School, Division of Nursing, Fort Wayne, IN 46808. Offers family nurse practitioner (MSN, Post Master's Certificate); nurse anesthesia (DNP); nursing practice (DNP). *Accreditation:* AACN. *Program availability:* Part-time, blended/hybrid learning. *Faculty:* 12 full-time (10 women), 3 part-time/adjunct (2 women). *Students:* 67 full-time (45 women), 70 part-time (64 women); includes 22 minority (13 Black or African American, non-Hispanic/Latino; 1 Asian, non-Hispanic/Latino; 7 Hispanic/Latino; 1 Two or more races, non-Hispanic/Latino). Average age 32. 44 applicants, 98% accepted, 34 enrolled. In 2019, 37 master's, 1 other advanced degree awarded. *Entrance requirements:* Additional exam requirements/recommendations for international students: required—TOEFL (minimum score 550 paper-based), IELTS (minimum score 6.5). *Application deadline:* Applications are processed on a rolling basis. Electronic applications accepted. *Expenses:* MSN - $700 per semester hour; DNP - $1,055 per semester hour. *Financial support:* Applicants required to submit FAFSA. *Unit head:* Dr. Wendy Clark, Graduate Nursing Program

Director, 260-399-7700 Ext. 8534, E-mail: wclark@sf.edu. *Application contact:* Kyle Richardson, Associate Director of Enrollment Management, 260-399-7700 Ext. 6310, Fax: 260-399-8152, E-mail: krichardson@sf.edu.

**University of St. Francis,** Leach College of Nursing, Joliet, IL 60435-6169. Offers family nurse practitioner (MSN, Post-Master's Certificate); nursing administration (MSN); nursing education (MSN); nursing practice (DNP); psychology/mental health nurse practitioner (MSN, Post-Master's Certificate); teaching in nursing (Certificate). *Accreditation:* AACN. *Program availability:* Part-time, evening/weekend, 100% online. *Degree requirements:* For master's, comprehensive exam. *Entrance requirements:* Additional exam requirements/recommendations for international students: required—TOEFL (minimum score 550 paper-based; 79 iBT), IELTS (minimum score 6). Electronic applications accepted. Application fee is waived when completed online. *Expenses:* Contact institution.

**University of Saint Joseph,** Department of Nursing, West Hartford, CT 06117-2700. Offers family nurse practitioner (MS); nurse educator (MS); nursing practice (DNP); psychiatric/mental health nurse practitioner (MS). *Accreditation:* AACN. *Program availability:* Part-time, evening/weekend. *Degree requirements:* For master's, thesis. *Entrance requirements:* For master's, 2 letters of recommendation. Electronic applications accepted. Application fee is waived when completed online.

**University of Saint Mary,** Graduate Programs, Program in Nursing, Leavenworth, KS 66048-5082. Offers nurse administrator (MSN); nurse educator (MSN). *Accreditation:* AACN. *Program availability:* Part-time, online only, 100% online. *Students:* 10 full-time (all women), 12 part-time (10 women); includes 2 minority (1 Hispanic/Latino; 1 Native Hawaiian or other Pacific Islander, non-Hispanic/Latino). Average age 40. In 2019, 19 master's awarded. *Degree requirements:* For master's, practicum. *Entrance requirements:* For master's, BSN from CCNE- or ACEN-accredited baccalaureate nursing program at regionally-accredited institution. *Application deadline:* Applications are processed on a rolling basis. Application fee: $25. Electronic applications accepted. *Expenses:* $615 per credit hour. *Financial support:* Applicants required to submit FAFSA. *Unit head:* Michelle Birdashaw, Division Chair of Nursing, E-mail: michelle.birdashaw@stmary.edu. *Application contact:* Michelle Birdashaw, Division Chair of Nursing, E-mail: michelle.birdashaw@stmary.edu.
Website: http://online.stmary.edu/msn

**University of San Diego,** Hahn School of Nursing and Health Science, San Diego, CA 92110-2492. Offers adult-gerontology clinical nurse specialist (MSN); adult-gerontology nurse practitioner/family nurse practitioner (MSN); clinical nurse leader (MSN); executive nurse leader (MSN); family nurse practitioner (MSN); healthcare informatics (MS); master's entry program in clinical nursing (for non-rns) (MSN); nursing (PhD); nursing informatics (MSN); nursing practice (DNP); psychiatric-mental health nurse practitioner (MSN). *Accreditation:* AACN. *Program availability:* Part-time, evening/weekend. *Faculty:* 28 full-time (23 women), 43 part-time/adjunct (32 women). *Students:* 252 full-time (202 women), 288 part-time (227 women); includes 261 minority (53 Black or African American, non-Hispanic/Latino; 2 American Indian or Alaska Native, non-Hispanic/Latino; 106 Asian, non-Hispanic/Latino; 76 Hispanic/Latino; 24 Two or more races, non-Hispanic/Latino), 24 international. Average age 34. In 2019, 174 master's, 47 doctorates awarded. *Degree requirements:* For doctorate, thesis/dissertation (for some programs), residency (DNP). *Entrance requirements:* For master's, GRE General Test (for entry-level nursing), BSN, current California RN licensure (except for entry-level nursing), minimum GPA of 3.0; for doctorate, minimum GPA of 3.5, MSN, current California RN licensure. Additional exam requirements/recommendations for international students: required—TOEFL (minimum score 580 paper-based; 83 iBT), TWE. *Application deadline:* Applications are processed on a rolling basis. Application fee: $55. Electronic applications accepted. *Financial support:* In 2019–20, 284 students received support. Institutionally sponsored loans, scholarships/grants, and traineeships available. Support available to part-time students. Financial award application deadline: 4/1; financial award applicants required to submit FAFSA. *Unit head:* Dr. Jane Georges, Dean, Hahn School of Nursing and Health Science, 619-260-4550, Fax: 619-260-6814, E-mail: nursing@sandiego.edu. *Application contact:* Erika Garwood, Associate Director of Graduate Admissions, 619-260-4524, Fax: 619-260-4158, E-mail: grads@sandiego.edu.
Website: http://www.sandiego.edu/nursing/

**University of San Francisco,** School of Nursing and Health Professions, Doctor of Nursing Practice Program, San Francisco, CA 94117. Offers DNP. *Program availability:* Part-time, evening/weekend, online learning. *Students:* 115 full-time (97 women), 46 part-time (41 women); includes 97 minority (24 Black or African American, non-Hispanic/Latino; 42 Asian, non-Hispanic/Latino; 24 Hispanic/Latino; 1 Native Hawaiian or other Pacific Islander, non-Hispanic/Latino; 6 Two or more races, non-Hispanic/Latino), 2 international. Average age 40. 66 applicants, 77% accepted, 30 enrolled. In 2019, 25 doctorates awarded. *Entrance requirements:* Additional exam requirements/recommendations for international students: required—TOEFL (minimum score 600 paper-based; 100 iBT), IELTS. *Application deadline:* For fall admission, 12/15 for domestic students. Applications are processed on a rolling basis. Application fee: $55. Electronic applications accepted. *Financial support:* Scholarships/grants available. *Unit head:* Dr. Mary Donnelly, Department Chair, 415-422-3627, E-mail: nursing@usfca.edu. *Application contact:* Tamara White, Director, Graduate Enrollment Management, 415-422-3627, E-mail: twhite3@usfca.edu.
Website: https://www.usfca.edu/nursing/programs/doctoral/dnp

**University of Saskatchewan,** College of Graduate and Postdoctoral Studies, College of Nursing, Saskatoon, SK S7N 5E5, Canada. Offers MN, PhD. *Program availability:* Part-time. *Entrance requirements:* Additional exam requirements/recommendations for international students: required—TOEFL.

**The University of Scranton,** Panuska College of Professional Studies, Department of Nursing, Scranton, PA 18510-4595. Offers family nurse practitioner (MSN, PMC); nurse anesthesia (MSN, PMC); nursing leadership (DNP). *Accreditation:* AACN; AANA/CANAEP. *Program availability:* Part-time, evening/weekend. *Degree requirements:* For master's, comprehensive exam (for some programs), thesis (for some programs), capstone experience. *Entrance requirements:* For master's, minimum GPA of 3.0, three letters of reference; for doctorate, RN licensure and evidence of certification in advanced practice nursing specialty. Additional exam requirements/recommendations for international students: required—TOEFL (minimum score 500 paper-based; 80 iBT), IELTS (minimum score 6.5). Electronic applications accepted.

**University of South Alabama,** College of Nursing, Mobile, AL 36688-0002. Offers nursing (MSN, DNP); nursing administration (Certificate); nursing education (Certificate); nursing practice (Certificate). *Accreditation:* AACN. *Program availability:* Part-time, online learning. *Faculty:* 72 full-time (66 women), 116 part-time/adjunct (103 women). *Students:* 2,311 full-time (2,024 women), 716 part-time (636 women); includes 955 minority (613 Black or African American, non-Hispanic/Latino; 28 American Indian or Alaska Native, non-Hispanic/Latino; 121 Asian, non-Hispanic/Latino; 123 Hispanic/Latino; 4 Native Hawaiian or other Pacific Islander, non-Hispanic/Latino; 66 Two or more races, non-Hispanic/Latino). Average age 35. 884 applicants, 93% accepted, 624 enrolled. In 2019, 744 master's, 157 doctorates, 94 other advanced degrees awarded. *Degree requirements:* For master's, thesis optional. *Entrance requirements:* Additional

exam requirements/recommendations for international students: required—TOEFL (minimum score 600 paper-based; 100 iBT). *Application deadline:* For fall admission, 2/15 priority date for domestic students, 1/15 priority date for international students; for spring admission, 7/15 priority date for domestic students, 6/15 priority date for international students; for summer admission, 11/15 priority date for domestic students, 10/15 priority date for international students. Applications are processed on a rolling basis. Application fee: $100. Electronic applications accepted. *Expenses:* Contact institution. *Financial support:* Fellowships, research assistantships, teaching assistantships, career-related internships or fieldwork, Federal Work-Study, institutionally sponsored loans, scholarships/grants, and unspecified assistantships available. Support available to part-time students. Financial award application deadline: 3/31; financial award applicants required to submit FAFSA. *Unit head:* Dr. Heather Hall, Dean, College of Nursing, 251-445-9400, Fax: 251-445-9416, E-mail: heatherhall@southalabama.edu. *Application contact:* Jennifer Bouvier, Academic Advisor II, 251-445-9400, Fax: 251-445-9416, E-mail: jcamp@southalabama.edu.
Website: http://www.southalabama.edu/colleges/con/index.html

**University of South Carolina,** The Graduate School, College of Nursing, Program in Advanced Practice Clinical Nursing, Columbia, SC 29208. Offers acute care nurse practitioner (Certificate); advanced practice clinical nursing (MSN). *Accreditation:* AACN. *Program availability:* Part-time, online learning. *Entrance requirements:* For master's, master's degree in nursing, RN license; for Certificate, MSN. Additional exam requirements/recommendations for international students: required—TOEFL (minimum score 570 paper-based). Electronic applications accepted.

**University of South Carolina,** The Graduate School, College of Nursing, Program in Advanced Practice Nursing in Primary Care, Columbia, SC 29208. Offers MSN, Certificate. *Accreditation:* AACN. *Entrance requirements:* For master's, master's degree in nursing, RN license; for Certificate, MSN. Additional exam requirements/recommendations for international students: required—TOEFL (minimum score 570 paper-based). Electronic applications accepted.

**University of Southern Indiana,** Graduate Studies, College of Nursing and Health Professions, Program in Nursing, Evansville, IN 47712-3590. Offers adult-gerontology acute care nurse practitioner (MSN, PMC); adult-gerontology clinical nurse specialist (MSN, PMC); adult-gerontology primary care nurse practitioner (MSN, PMC); advanced nursing practice (DNP); family nurse practitioner (MSN, PMC); nursing education (MSN, PMC); nursing management and leadership (MSN, PMC); organizational and systems leadership (DNP); psychiatric mental health nurse practitioner (MSN, PMC). *Accreditation:* AACN. *Program availability:* Part-time, online learning. *Entrance requirements:* For master's, BSN from nationally-accredited school; minimum cumulative GPA of 3.0; satisfactory completion of a course in undergraduate statistics (minimum grade C); one year of full-time experience or 2,000 hours of clinical practice as an RN (recommended), unencumbered U.S. RN license; for doctorate, minimum GPA of 3.0, completion of graduate research course with minimum B grade, unencumbered RN license, resume/curriculum vitae, three professional references, 1-2 page narrative of practice experience and professional goals, Capstone Project Information form. Additional exam requirements/recommendations for international students: required—TOEFL (minimum score 550 paper-based; 79 iBT), IELTS (minimum score 6). Electronic applications accepted. *Expenses:* Contact institution.

**University of Southern Maine,** College of Science, Technology, and Health, School of Nursing, Portland, ME 04103. Offers adult-gerontology primary care nurse practitioner (MS, PMC); education (MS); family nurse practitioner (MS, PMC); family psychiatric/mental health nurse practitioner (MS); management (MS); nursing (CAS, CGS); psychiatric-mental health nurse practitioner (PMC). *Accreditation:* AACN. *Program availability:* Part-time. *Degree requirements:* For master's, thesis optional. *Entrance requirements:* For master's, GRE General Test or MAT, minimum GPA of 3.0; for doctorate, GRE. Additional exam requirements/recommendations for international students: required—TOEFL (minimum score 550 paper-based). Electronic applications accepted. *Expenses: Tuition, area resident:* Full-time $864; part-time $432 per credit hour. Tuition, state resident: full-time $864; part-time $432 per credit hour. Tuition, nonresident: full-time $2372; part-time $1186 per credit hour. *Required fees:* $141; $108 per credit hour. Tuition and fees vary according to course load.

**University of Southern Mississippi,** College of Nursing and Health Professions, School of Leadership and Advanced Practice Nursing, Hattiesburg, MS 39406-0001. Offers MSN, DNP, PhD, Graduate Certificate. *Accreditation:* AACN; AANA/CANAEP. *Program availability:* Part-time, evening/weekend. *Students:* 175 full-time (126 women), 22 part-time (17 women); includes 54 minority (43 Black or African American, non-Hispanic/Latino; 3 Asian, non-Hispanic/Latino; 2 Hispanic/Latino; 6 Two or more races, non-Hispanic/Latino), 3 international. 161 applicants, 24% accepted, 27 enrolled. In 2019, 60 master's, 33 doctorates, 2 other advanced degrees awarded. *Degree requirements:* For master's, comprehensive exam, thesis optional; for doctorate, comprehensive exam, thesis/dissertation. *Entrance requirements:* For master's, GRE General Test, minimum GPA of 2.75 during last 60 hours, nursing license, BS in nursing; for doctorate, GRE General Test, master's degree in nursing, minimum GPA of 3.5. Additional exam requirements/recommendations for international students: required—TOEFL, IELTS. *Application deadline:* For fall admission, 3/15 priority date for domestic students, 5/1 for international students; for spring admission, 1/10 priority date for domestic and international students. Applications are processed on a rolling basis. Application fee: $60. Electronic applications accepted. *Expenses: Tuition, area resident:* Full-time $4393; part-time $488 per credit hour. Tuition, nonresident: full-time $5393; part-time $600 per credit hour. *Required fees:* $6 per semester. *Financial support:* Research assistantships with full tuition reimbursements, teaching assistantships, Federal Work-Study, institutionally sponsored loans, scholarships/grants, traineeships, health care benefits, and unspecified assistantships available. Financial award application deadline: 3/15; financial award applicants required to submit FAFSA. *Unit head:* Dr. Lachel Story, Director, 601-266-6485, Fax: 601-266-5927, E-mail: lachel.story@usm.edu. *Application contact:* Dr. Lachel Story, Director, 601-266-6485, Fax: 601-266-5927, E-mail: lachel.story@usm.edu.
Website: https://www.usm.edu/nursing-health-professions

**University of South Florida,** College of Nursing, Tampa, FL 33612. Offers nurse anesthesia (DNP); nursing (MS, DNP), including adult-gerontology acute care nursing, adult-gerontology primary care nursing, family health nursing, nurse anesthesia (MS), nursing education (MS), occupational health nursing/adult-gerontology primary care nursing, oncology nursing/adult-gerontology primary care nursing (DNP), pediatric health nursing; nursing education (Post Master's Certificate); nursing science (PhD); simulation based academic fellowship in advanced pain management (Graduate Certificate). *Accreditation:* AACN; AANA/CANAEP. *Program availability:* Part-time. *Faculty:* 34 full-time (28 women), 2 part-time/adjunct (1 woman). *Students:* 265 full-time (207 women), 687 part-time (594 women); includes 343 minority (113 Black or African American, non-Hispanic/Latino; 1 American Indian or Alaska Native, non-Hispanic/Latino; 60 Asian, non-Hispanic/Latino; 141 Hispanic/Latino; 1 Native Hawaiian or other Pacific Islander, non-Hispanic/Latino; 27 Two or more races, non-Hispanic/Latino), 2 international. Average age 33. 955 applicants, 44% accepted, 343 enrolled. In 2019, 281 master's, 80 doctorates awarded. *Degree requirements:* For master's, comprehensive exam, thesis optional; for doctorate, comprehensive exam, thesis/dissertation (for some programs). *Entrance requirements:* For master's, GRE General Test, bachelor's in nursing or RN with Bachelor's in relevant field; current license as Registered Nurse; resume or CV; interview; pre-reqs may be required; for doctorate, GRE General Test (recommended), bachelor's degree in nursing from ACEN or CCNE regionally-accredited institution with minimum GPA of 3.0 in all coursework or in all upper-division coursework; current license as Registered Nurse in Florida; undergraduate statistics course with minimum B grade; 3 letters of recommendation; statement of goals; resume; interview. Additional exam requirements/recommendations for international students: required—TOEFL (minimum score 550 paper-based; 79 iBT). *Application deadline:* For fall admission, 12/15 for domestic and international students; for spring admission, 10/1 for domestic students, 9/15 for international students. Application fee: $30. Electronic applications accepted. *Financial support:* In 2019–20, 181 students received support, including 7 research assistantships with tuition reimbursements available (averaging $18,935 per year), 29 teaching assistantships with tuition reimbursements available (averaging $30,814 per year); tuition waivers (partial) and unspecified assistantships also available. Financial award application deadline: 2/1; financial award applicants required to submit FAFSA. *Unit head:* Dr. Victoria Rich, Dean, College of Nursing, 813-974-8939, Fax: 813-974-5418, E-mail: victoriarich@health.usf.edu. *Application contact:* Dr. Denise Maguire, Vice Dean, Graduate Programs, 813-396-9962, E-mail: dmaguire@health.usf.edu.
Website: http://health.usf.edu/nursing/index.htm

**The University of Tampa,** Program in Nursing, Tampa, FL 33606-1490. Offers adult nursing practitioner (MSN); family nursing practitioner (MSN); nursing (MS). *Accreditation:* ACEN. *Program availability:* Part-time, evening/weekend. *Degree requirements:* For master's, comprehensive exam, oral exam, practicum. *Entrance requirements:* For master's, GMAT or GRE, current licensure as registered nurse in state of Florida; minimum GPA of 3.0 in last 60 credit hours; minimum of one year of direct patient care experience within the past five years (recommended). Additional exam requirements/recommendations for international students: required—TOEFL (minimum score 577 paper-based; 90 iBT), IELTS (minimum score 7.5). Electronic applications accepted. *Expenses:* Contact institution.

**The University of Tennessee,** Graduate School, College of Nursing, Knoxville, TN 37996. Offers MSN, PhD. *Accreditation:* AACN; AANA/CANAEP. *Program availability:* Part-time. *Degree requirements:* For master's, thesis or alternative; for doctorate, thesis/dissertation. *Entrance requirements:* For master's and doctorate, GRE General Test, minimum GPA of 2.7. Additional exam requirements/recommendations for international students: required—TOEFL. Electronic applications accepted.

**The University of Tennessee at Chattanooga,** School of Nursing, Chattanooga, TN 37403. Offers certified nurse anesthetist (Post-Master's Certificate); family nurse practitioner (MSN, Post-Master's Certificate); gerontology acute care (MSN, Post-Master's Certificate); nurse anesthesia (MSN); nurse education (Post-Master's Certificate); nursing (DNP). *Accreditation:* AACN; AANA/CANAEP (one or more programs are accredited). *Program availability:* 100% online. *Faculty:* 32 full-time (29 women), 14 part-time/adjunct (10 women). *Students:* 78 full-time (49 women), 51 part-time (43 women); includes 24 minority (11 Black or African American, non-Hispanic/Latino; 2 American Indian or Alaska Native, non-Hispanic/Latino; 4 Asian, non-Hispanic/Latino; 5 Hispanic/Latino; 2 Two or more races, non-Hispanic/Latino). Average age 34. 50 applicants, 100% accepted, 46 enrolled. In 2019, 38 master's, 16 doctorates, 2 other advanced degrees awarded. *Degree requirements:* For master's, thesis optional, practicum; for doctorate, professional project; for Post-Master's Certificate, practicum. *Entrance requirements:* For master's, GRE General Test, MAT, BSN, minimum GPA of 3.0, eligibility for Tennessee RN license, 1 year of direct patient care experience; for doctorate, GRE General Test or MAT (if applicant does not have MSN), minimum GPA of 3.0 for highest degree earned; for Post-Master's Certificate, GRE General Test, MAT, MSN, minimum GPA of 3.0, eligibility for Tennessee RN license, one year of direct patient care experience. Additional exam requirements/recommendations for international students: required—TOEFL (minimum score 550 paper-based; 79 iBT), IELTS (minimum score 6). *Application deadline:* For fall admission, 6/15 priority date for domestic students, 7/1 for international students; for spring admission, 11/1 priority date for domestic students, 11/1 for international students. Applications are processed on a rolling basis. Application fee: $35 ($40 for international students). Electronic applications accepted. *Financial support:* Teaching assistantships, career-related internships or fieldwork, and scholarships/grants available. Support available to part-time students. Financial award application deadline: 7/1; financial award applicants required to submit FAFSA. *Unit head:* Dr. Chris Smith, Director, 423-425-4665, Fax: 423-425-4668, E-mail: chris-smith@utc.edu. *Application contact:* Dr. Joanne Romagni, Dean of the Graduate School, 423-425-4478, Fax: 423-425-5223, E-mail: joanne-romagni@utc.edu.
Website: http://www.utc.edu/nursing/

**The University of Tennessee Health Science Center,** College of Graduate Health Sciences, Memphis, TN 38163. Offers biomedical engineering (MS, PhD); biomedical sciences (PhD); dental sciences (MDS); epidemiology (MS); health outcomes and policy research (PhD); laboratory research and management (MS); nursing science (PhD); pharmaceutical sciences (PhD); pharmacology (MS); speech and hearing science (PhD); DDS/PhD; DNP/PhD; MD/PhD; Pharm D/PhD. Terminal master's awarded for partial completion of doctoral program. *Degree requirements:* For master's, comprehensive exam, thesis; for doctorate, thesis/dissertation, oral and written preliminary and comprehensive exams. *Entrance requirements:* For master's and doctorate, GRE General Test, minimum GPA of 3.0. Additional exam requirements/recommendations for international students: recommended—TOEFL (minimum score 79 iBT), IELTS (minimum score 6.5). Electronic applications accepted. *Expenses:* Contact institution.

**The University of Tennessee Health Science Center,** College of Nursing, Memphis, TN 38163. Offers adult-gerontology acute care nurse practitioner (Post Master's Certificate); advance practice nursing (DNP); family nurse practitioner (Post-Doctoral Certificate); pediatric acute care nurse practitioner (Post-Doctoral Certificate); pediatric primary care nurse practitioner (Post-Doctoral Certificate); psychiatric/mental health nurse practitioner (Post-Doctoral Certificate); registered nurse first assistant (Certificate). *Accreditation:* AACN; AANA/CANAEP. *Program availability:* Part-time, blended/hybrid learning. *Faculty:* 62 full-time (55 women), 7 part-time/adjunct (2 women). *Students:* 226 full-time (187 women), 28 part-time (26 women); includes 80 minority (63 Black or African American, non-Hispanic/Latino; 15 Asian, non-Hispanic/Latino; 2 Hispanic/Latino). Average age 33. 652 applicants, 20% accepted, 104 enrolled. In 2019, 86 doctorates, 2 Certificates awarded. *Degree requirements:* For doctorate, project. *Entrance requirements:* For doctorate, RN license, minimum GPA of 3.0; http://www.uthsc.edu/nursing/dnp-admission-requirements.php; for other advanced degree, MSN, APN license, minimum GPA of 3.0; http://www.uthsc.edu/nursing/dnp-admission-requirements.php. Additional exam requirements/recommendations for international students: required—TOEFL (minimum score 550 paper-based; 80 iBT). *Application deadline:* For fall admission, 1/15 for domestic students; for spring admission, 8/15 for domestic students. Application fee: $70. Electronic applications accepted. *Expenses:* $5400 tuition, $450 fees, $110 loan fees, $5790 room/board, $2137 books/supplies, $1260 transportation, $2339 miscellaneous, $450 out-of-state tuition surcharge. *Financial support:* In 2019–20, 112 students received support, including 16 research

assistantships (averaging $229,578 per year); Federal Work-Study, institutionally sponsored loans, scholarships/grants, and tuition waivers (partial) also available. Financial award application deadline: 3/15; financial award applicants required to submit FAFSA. *Unit head:* Dr. Wendy Likes, Dean, 901-448-6135, Fax: 901-448-4121, E-mail: wlikes@uthsc.edu. *Application contact:* Glynis Blackard, Assistant Dean for Student Affairs, 901-448-6139, Fax: 901-448-4121, E-mail: gblackar@uthsc.edu.
Website: http://uthsc.edu/nursing/

**The University of Texas at Arlington,** Graduate School, College of Nursing and Health Innovation, Arlington, TX 76019. Offers athletic training (MS); exercise science (MS); kinesiology (PhD); nurse practitioner (MSN); nursing (PhD); nursing administration (MSN); nursing education (MSN); nursing practice (DNP). *Accreditation:* AACN. *Program availability:* Part-time, evening/weekend, online learning. *Degree requirements:* For master's, practicum course; for doctorate, comprehensive exam (for some programs), thesis/dissertation (for some programs), proposal defense dissertation (for PhD); scholarship project (for DNP). *Entrance requirements:* For master's, GRE General Test if GPA less than 3.0, minimum GPA of 3.0, Texas nursing license, minimum C grade in undergraduate statistics course; for doctorate, GRE General Test (waived for MSN-to-PhD applicants), minimum undergraduate, graduate and statistics GPA of 3.0; Texas RN license; interview; written statement of goals. Additional exam requirements/recommendations for international students: required—TOEFL (minimum score 550 paper-based), IELTS (minimum score 7).

**The University of Texas at Austin,** Graduate School, School of Nursing, Austin, TX 78712-1111. Offers adult - gerontology clinical nurse specialist (MSN); child health (MSN), including administration, public health nursing, teaching; family nurse practitioner (MSN); family psychiatric/mental health nurse practitioner (MSN); holistic adult health (MSN), including administration, teaching; maternity (MSN), including administration, public health nursing, teaching; nursing (PhD); nursing administration and healthcare systems management (MSN); nursing practice (DNP); pediatric nurse practitioner (MSN); public health nursing (MSN). *Accreditation:* AACN. *Program availability:* Part-time. *Degree requirements:* For master's, thesis optional; for doctorate, thesis/dissertation. *Entrance requirements:* For master's and doctorate, GRE General Test. Additional exam requirements/recommendations for international students: required—TOEFL (minimum score 550 paper-based). Electronic applications accepted.

**The University of Texas at El Paso,** Graduate School, School of Nursing, El Paso, TX 79968-0001. Offers family nurse practitioner (MSN); health care leadership and management (Certificate); interdisciplinary health sciences (PhD); nursing (DNP); nursing education (MSN, Certificate); nursing systems management (MSN). *Accreditation:* AACN. *Program availability:* Online learning. *Degree requirements:* For master's, thesis optional; for doctorate, thesis/dissertation. *Entrance requirements:* For master's, minimum GPA of 3.0, resume; for doctorate, GRE, letters of reference, relevant personal/professional experience; master's degree in nursing (for DNP); for Certificate, bachelor's degree in nursing. Additional exam requirements/recommendations for international students: required—TOEFL; recommended—IELTS. Electronic applications accepted.

**The University of Texas at Tyler,** College of Nursing and Health Sciences, School of Nursing, Tyler, TX 75799. Offers nurse practitioner (MSN); nursing (PhD); nursing administration (MSN); nursing education (MSN); MSN/MBA. *Accreditation:* AACN. *Program availability:* Part-time, evening/weekend, online learning. *Faculty:* 27 full-time (all women), 4 part-time/adjunct (all women). *Students:* 101 full-time (83 women), 351 part-time (303 women); includes 149 minority (53 Black or African American, non-Hispanic/Latino; 1 American Indian or Alaska Native, non-Hispanic/Latino; 27 Asian, non-Hispanic/Latino; 51 Hispanic/Latino; 17 Two or more races, non-Hispanic/Latino), 5 international. Average age 37. 128 applicants, 67% accepted, 81 enrolled. In 2019, 86 master's, 21 doctorates awarded. *Degree requirements:* For master's, comprehensive exam (for some programs), thesis (for some programs); for doctorate, thesis/dissertation. *Entrance requirements:* For master's, GRE General Test or MAT, GMAT, minimum undergraduate GPA of 3.0, course work in statistics, RN license, BSN. Additional exam requirements/recommendations for international students: required—TOEFL. *Application deadline:* For fall admission, 8/17 priority date for domestic students, 7/1 priority date for international students; for spring admission, 12/21 priority date for domestic students, 11/1 priority date for international students. Applications are processed on a rolling basis. Application fee: $25 ($50 for international students). Electronic applications accepted. *Financial support:* In 2019–20, 15 students received support, including 1 fellowship (averaging $10,000 per year), 3 research assistantships (averaging $2,200 per year); institutionally sponsored loans and scholarships/grants also available. Financial award application deadline: 7/1; financial award applicants required to submit FAFSA. *Unit head:* Dr. Barbara Haas, Associate Dean, 903-566-7021, E-mail: bhaas@uttyler.edu. *Application contact:* Dr. Barbara Haas, Associate Dean, 903-566-7021, E-mail: bhaas@uttyler.edu.
Website: https://www.uttyler.edu/nursing/

**The University of Texas Health Science Center at Houston,** Cizik School of Nursing, Houston, TX 77030. Offers MSN, DNP, PhD, MSN/MPH. *Accreditation:* AACN; AANA/CANAEP. *Program availability:* Part-time. *Degree requirements:* For master's, thesis, research project, or clinical project; for doctorate, thesis/dissertation. *Entrance requirements:* For master's, GRE or MAT, BSN, Texas RN license, related work experience, interview, writing sample; for doctorate, GRE, interview, Texas RN license, portfolio, master's degree. Additional exam requirements/recommendations for international students: required—TOEFL (minimum score 550 paper-based; 86 iBT). Electronic applications accepted.

**The University of Texas Health Science Center at San Antonio,** Graduate School of Biomedical Sciences, Program in Nursing Science, San Antonio, TX 78229-3900. Offers PhD.

**The University of Texas Health Science Center at San Antonio,** School of Nursing, San Antonio, TX 78229-3900. Offers administrative management (MSN); adult-gerontology acute care nurse practitioner (PGC); advanced practice leadership (DNP); clinical nurse leader (MSN); executive administrative management (DNP); family nurse practitioner (MSN, PGC); nursing (MSN, PhD); nursing education (MSN, PGC); pediatric nurse practitioner primary care (PGC); psychiatric mental health nurse practitioner (PGC); public health nurse leader (DNP). *Accreditation:* AACN. *Program availability:* Part-time. Terminal master's awarded for partial completion of doctoral program. *Degree requirements:* For master's, thesis optional; for doctorate, comprehensive exam, thesis/dissertation.

**The University of Texas Medical Branch,** Graduate School of Biomedical Sciences, Doctoral Program in Nursing, Galveston, TX 77555. Offers PhD. *Degree requirements:* For doctorate, comprehensive exam, thesis/dissertation. *Entrance requirements:* For doctorate, GRE General Test, minimum GPA of 3.0, BSN and MSN or equivalent advanced degree, 2 writing samples, 3 letters of reference, curriculum vitae or resume. Additional exam requirements/recommendations for international students: required—TOEFL (minimum score 550 paper-based). Electronic applications accepted.

**The University of Texas Medical Branch,** School of Nursing, Master's Program in Nursing, Galveston, TX 77555. Offers MSN. *Accreditation:* AACN. *Program availability:* Part-time, online learning. *Entrance requirements:* For master's, GRE General Test or MAT, minimum BSN GPA of 3.0, 3 references, interview, 1 year nursing experience. Additional exam requirements/recommendations for international students: required—TOEFL (minimum score 550 paper-based).

**University of the Incarnate Word,** Ila Faye Miller School of Nursing and Health Professions, San Antonio, TX 78209-6397. Offers kinesiology (MS); nursing (MSN, DNP); sport management (MS). *Program availability:* Part-time, evening/weekend. *Faculty:* 13 full-time (9 women), 1 (woman) part-time/adjunct. *Students:* 104 full-time (71 women), 6 part-time (5 women); includes 68 minority (24 Black or African American, non-Hispanic/Latino; 1 American Indian or Alaska Native, non-Hispanic/Latino; 2 Asian, non-Hispanic/Latino; 40 Hispanic/Latino; 1 Two or more races, non-Hispanic/Latino), 2 international. 30 applicants, 100% accepted, 20 enrolled. In 2019, 19 master's, 20 doctorates awarded. *Degree requirements:* For master's, comprehensive exam (for some programs), thesis or alternative, capstone. *Entrance requirements:* For master's, GRE General Test, MAT, baccalaureate degree in ACEN- or CCNE-accredited nursing program with health assessment and statistics; minimum cumulative GPA of 2.5 (3.0 in upper-division courses); three professional references; Texas State license or multi-state compact. Additional exam requirements/recommendations for international students: required—TOEFL (minimum score 560 paper-based; 83 iBT). *Application deadline:* Applications are processed on a rolling basis. Application fee: $20. Electronic applications accepted. *Expenses:* $980 per credit hour for DNP program. *Financial support:* Research assistantships, Federal Work-Study, scholarships/grants, tuition waivers (partial), and unspecified assistantships available. Financial award applicants required to submit FAFSA. *Unit head:* Dr. Holly Cassells, Dean, 210-829-3982, Fax: 210-829-3174, E-mail: cassells@uiwtx.edu. *Application contact:* Jessica Delarosa, Director of Admissions, 210-8296005, Fax: 210-829-3921, E-mail: admis@uiwtx.edu.
Website: https://nursing-and-health-professions.uiw.edu/

**The University of Toledo,** College of Graduate Studies, College of Nursing, Toledo, OH 43614. Offers MSN, DNP, Certificate. *Accreditation:* AACN. *Program availability:* Part-time, online learning. *Degree requirements:* For master's, thesis or scholarly project; for doctorate, thesis/dissertation or alternative, evidence-based project. *Entrance requirements:* For master's, GRE, BS in nursing, minimum undergraduate GPA of 3.0, statement of purpose, two letters of recommendation, transcripts from all prior institutions attended, resume, Nursing CAS application, UT supplemental application; for doctorate, minimum undergraduate GPA of 3.0, statement of purpose, three letters of recommendation, transcripts from all prior institutions attended, resume, Nursing CAS application, UT supplemental application. Additional exam requirements/recommendations for international students: required—TOEFL (minimum score 550 paper-based; 80 iBT). Electronic applications accepted. *Expenses:* Contact institution.

**University of Toronto,** School of Graduate Studies, Department of Nursing Science, Toronto, ON M5S 1A1, Canada. Offers MN, PhD, MHSc/MN. *Program availability:* Part-time. *Degree requirements:* For doctorate, thesis/dissertation, departmental and final oral exam/thesis defense. *Entrance requirements:* For master's, B Sc N or equivalent, minimum B average in next-to-final year, resume, 3 letters of reference; for doctorate, minimum B+ average, master's degree in nursing or a related area, resume, 2 letters of recommendation. Additional exam requirements/recommendations for international students: required—TOEFL (minimum score 580 paper-based; 93 iBT), TWE (minimum score 5). Electronic applications accepted. *Expenses:* Contact institution.

**The University of Tulsa,** Graduate School, Oxley College of Health Sciences, School of Nursing, Tulsa, OK 74104-3189. Offers adult-gerontology acute care nurse practitioner (DNP); family nurse practitioner (DNP). *Degree requirements:* For doctorate, comprehensive exam, thesis/dissertation. *Entrance requirements:* Additional exam requirements/recommendations for international students: required—TOEFL (minimum score 550 paper-based; 91 iBT), IELTS (minimum score 6.5). Electronic applications accepted. *Expenses:* Contact institution.

**University of Utah,** Graduate School, College of Nursing, Department of Nursing, Salt Lake City, UT 84112. Offers MS, DNP, PhD. *Accreditation:* AACN. *Program availability:* Part-time, 100% online, blended/hybrid learning. *Faculty:* 49 full-time (47 women), 9 part-time/adjunct (7 women). *Students:* 325 full-time (259 women), 52 part-time (42 women); includes 62 minority (5 Black or African American, non-Hispanic/Latino; 15 Asian, non-Hispanic/Latino; 26 Hispanic/Latino; 3 Native Hawaiian or other Pacific Islander, non-Hispanic/Latino; 13 Two or more races, non-Hispanic/Latino), 7 international. Average age 35. 287 applicants, 54% accepted, 126 enrolled. In 2019, 16 master's, 100 doctorates awarded. *Degree requirements:* For doctorate, comprehensive exam (for some programs), thesis/dissertation (for some programs). *Entrance requirements:* For doctorate, GRE (PhD only). Additional exam requirements/recommendations for international students: required—TOEFL (minimum score 80 iBT), IELTS (minimum score 6.5). *Application deadline:* For fall admission, 12/1 for domestic and international students. Application fee: $55 ($65 for international students). Electronic applications accepted. *Expenses:* MS in Nursing Informatics: $33,000.71; MS in Nursing Education: $30,127.91; MS in Care Management: $25,578.86; MS in Nursing Informatics: $33,000.71; MS in Nursing Education: $30,127.91; MS in Care Management: $25,578.86. Graduate degrees vary widely by specific track. These are program of study cost projections for students beginning in Fall 2019 (resident tuition rates). Each projection is an estimate of the cost of the entire program through graduation, based on full time enrollment and an estimated 5% annual tuition increase. *Financial support:* In 2019–20, 71 students received support, including 147 fellowships with partial tuition reimbursements available (averaging $10,617 per year), 11 research assistantships with partial tuition reimbursements available (averaging $12,626 per year), 25 teaching assistantships with partial tuition reimbursements available (averaging $12,761 per year); Federal Work-Study, institutionally sponsored loans, scholarships/grants, traineeships, and unspecified assistantships also available. Support available to part-time students. Financial award application deadline: 1/20. *Unit head:* Dr. Barbara Wilson, PhD, Interim Dean, Associate Dean of Academic Programs, 801-581-8262, Fax: 801-581-4642, E-mail: barbara.wilson@nurs.utah.edu. *Application contact:* Carrie Radmall, Executive Associate Director, Student Services, 801-581-8798, Fax: 801-585-3414, E-mail: carrie.radmall@nurs.utah.edu.
Website: http://www.nursing.utah.edu/

**University of Vermont,** Graduate College, College of Nursing and Health Sciences, Department of Nursing, Burlington, VT 05405. Offers MS, DNP, Post-Graduate Certificate. *Accreditation:* AACN. *Entrance requirements:* For master's, GRE General Test; for doctorate, GRE. Additional exam requirements/recommendations for international students: required—TOEFL (minimum iBT score of 90) or IELTS (6.5). Electronic applications accepted. *Expenses:* Contact institution.

**University of Victoria,** Faculty of Graduate Studies, Faculty of Human and Social Development, School of Nursing, Victoria, BC V8W 2Y2, Canada. Offers advanced nursing practice (advanced practice leadership option) (MN); advanced nursing practice (nurse educator option) (MN); advanced nursing practice (nurse practitioner option) (MN); nursing (PhD). *Program availability:* Part-time, online learning. *Entrance requirements:* Additional exam requirements/recommendations for international students: required—TOEFL (minimum score 575 paper-based), IELTS (minimum score 7). Electronic applications accepted.

*Nursing—General*

**University of Virginia,** School of Nursing, Charlottesville, VA 22903. Offers acute and specialty care (MSN); acute care nurse practitioner (MSN); clinical nurse leadership (MSN); community-public health leadership (MSN); nursing (DNP, PhD); psychiatric mental health counseling (MSN); MSN/MBA. *Accreditation:* AACN. *Program availability:* Part-time. *Degree requirements:* For doctorate, comprehensive exam (for some programs), capstone project (DNP), dissertation (PhD). *Entrance requirements:* For master's, GRE General Test, MAT; for doctorate, GRE General Test. Additional exam requirements/recommendations for international students: required—TOEFL, IELTS. Electronic applications accepted.

**University of Washington,** Graduate School, School of Nursing, Seattle, WA 98195. Offers MN, MS, DNP, PhD, Graduate Certificate, MN/MPH. *Accreditation:* AACN; ACNM/ACME (one or more programs are accredited). *Program availability:* Part-time. *Degree requirements:* For master's, thesis (for some programs); for doctorate, thesis/dissertation. *Entrance requirements:* For master's, GRE, minimum GPA of 3.0, resume; for doctorate, GRE, minimum GPA of 3.0. Additional exam requirements/recommendations for international students: required—TOEFL.

**University of Washington, Bothell,** Program in Nursing, Bothell, WA 98011. Offers MN. *Program availability:* Part-time. *Degree requirements:* For master's, scholarly project. *Entrance requirements:* For master's, BSN (or other bachelor's degree with additional prerequisite work); current license as registered nurse in Washington state; minimum GPA of 3.0 in last 90 college credits, 2.0 in college statistics course. Additional exam requirements/recommendations for international students: required—TOEFL (minimum score 580 paper-based). Electronic applications accepted. *Expenses:* Contact institution.

**University of Washington, Tacoma,** Graduate Programs, Program in Nursing, Tacoma, WA 98402-3100. Offers communities, populations and health (MN); leadership in healthcare (MN); nurse educator (MN). *Program availability:* Part-time. *Degree requirements:* For master's, thesis (for some programs), advance fieldwork. *Entrance requirements:* For master's, Washington State NCLEX exam, minimum GPA of 3.0. Additional exam requirements/recommendations for international students: required—TOEFL (minimum score 580 paper-based; 70 iBT); recommended—IELTS (minimum score 7).

**The University of Western Ontario,** School of Graduate and Postdoctoral Studies, Faculty of Health Sciences, Arthur Labatt Family School of Nursing, London, ON N6A 3K7, Canada. Offers M Sc N, MN NP, PhD. *Program availability:* Part-time. *Degree requirements:* For master's, thesis; for doctorate, thesis/dissertation. *Entrance requirements:* Additional exam requirements/recommendations for international students: required—TOEFL.

**University of West Florida,** Usha Kundu, MD College of Health, School of Nursing, Pensacola, FL 32514-5750. Offers MSN. *Accreditation:* AACN. *Program availability:* Part-time, evening/weekend. *Entrance requirements:* For master's, GRE or MAT, letter of intent; current curriculum vitae/resume. Additional exam requirements/recommendations for international students: required—TOEFL (minimum score 550 paper-based).

**University of Windsor,** Faculty of Graduate Studies, Faculty of Nursing, Windsor, ON N9B 3P4, Canada. Offers M Sc, MN. *Degree requirements:* For master's, thesis or alternative. *Entrance requirements:* For master's, minimum B average, certificate of competence (nurse registration). Additional exam requirements/recommendations for international students: required—TOEFL (minimum score 560 paper-based). Electronic applications accepted.

**University of Wisconsin–Eau Claire,** College of Nursing and Health Sciences, Program in Nursing, Eau Claire, WI 54702-4004. Offers adult-gerontological administration (DNP); adult-gerontological clinical nurse specialist (DNP); adult-gerontological education (MSN); adult-gerontological primary care nurse practitioner (DNP); family health administration (DNP); family health in education (MSN); family health nurse practitioner (DNP); nursing (MSN); nursing practice (DNP). *Accreditation:* AACN. *Program availability:* Part-time. Terminal master's awarded for partial completion of doctoral program. *Degree requirements:* For master's, thesis optional, 500-600 hours clinical practicum, oral and written exams. *Entrance requirements:* For master's, Wisconsin RN license, minimum GPA of 3.0, undergraduate statistics, course work in health assessment. Additional exam requirements/recommendations for international students: required—TOEFL (minimum score 79 iBT). *Expenses:* Contact institution.

**University of Wisconsin–Madison,** School of Nursing, Madison, WI 53705. Offers adult/gerontology (DNP), including clinical nurse specialist; adult/gerontology acute care (DNP), including nurse practitioner; adult/gerontology primary care (DNP), including nurse practitioner; nursing (PhD); MS/MPH. *Accreditation:* AACN. *Program availability:* Part-time. *Degree requirements:* For doctorate, comprehensive exam, thesis/dissertation. *Entrance requirements:* For doctorate, GRE, bachelor's degree in nursing, undergraduate GPA of at least 3.0 on the last 60 credits, academic references, 2 original papers or other scholarly work, essay, RN license (for DNP), 1 year of professional nursing experience (for DNP). Additional exam requirements/recommendations for international students: required—TOEFL (minimum score 580 paper-based; 92 iBT), IELTS (minimum score 7). Electronic applications accepted. *Expenses:* Contact institution.

**University of Wisconsin–Milwaukee,** Graduate School, College of Nursing, Milwaukee, WI 53201. Offers clinical nurse specialist (Graduate Certificate); family nurse practitioner (Graduate Certificate); nursing (MN, DNP, PhD); sustainable peacebuilding (MSP). *Accreditation:* AACN. *Program availability:* Part-time. *Entrance requirements:* For master's, GRE General Test or MAT, autobiographical sketch; for doctorate, GRE, minimum GPA of 3.2. Additional exam requirements/recommendations for international students: required—TOEFL (minimum score 550 paper-based; 79 iBT), IELTS (minimum score 6.5). Electronic applications accepted.

**See Display below and Close-Up on page 595.**

**University of Wisconsin–Oshkosh,** Graduate Studies, College of Nursing, Oshkosh, WI 54901. Offers adult health and illness (MSN); family nurse practitioner (MSN). *Accreditation:* AACN; AANA/CANAEP. *Program availability:* Part-time. *Degree requirements:* For master's, thesis or alternative, clinical paper. *Entrance requirements:* For master's, RN license, BSN, previous course work in statistics and health assessment, minimum undergraduate GPA of 3.0, letters of recommendation. Additional exam requirements/recommendations for international students: required—TOEFL (minimum score 550 paper-based; 79 iBT). Electronic applications accepted.

**University of Wyoming,** College of Health Sciences, Fay W. Whitney School of Nursing, Laramie, WY 82071. Offers MS. *Accreditation:* AACN. *Program availability:* Part-time, online learning. *Degree requirements:* For master's, thesis. *Entrance requirements:* For master's, GRE General Test, BSN from CCNE or NCN-accredited school, minimum GPA of 3.0. Additional exam requirements/recommendations for international students: required—TOEFL.

**Université Laval,** Faculty of Nursing, Programs in Nursing, Québec, QC G1K 7P4, Canada. Offers M Sc, PhD, DESS, Diploma. *Degree requirements:* For master's, thesis (for some programs). *Entrance requirements:* For master's, French exam, knowledge of English; for other advanced degree, knowledge of French. Electronic applications accepted.

**Urbana University–A Branch Campus of Franklin University,** College of Nursing and Allied Health, Urbana, OH 43078-2091. Offers nursing (MSN). *Accreditation:* AACN.

*Entrance requirements:* For master's, baccalaureate degree in nursing with minimum cumulative undergraduate GPA of 3.0, official transcripts, Ohio RN license, background check, statement of goals and objectives, resume, 3 letters of recommendation, interview.

**Ursuline College,** School of Graduate and Professional Studies, Programs in Nursing, Pepper Pike, OH 44124-4398. Offers acute-care nurse practitioner (MSN); adult nurse practitioner (MSN); adult-gerontology acute care nurse practitioner (MSN); adult-gerontology clinical nurse specialist (MSN); adult-gerontology nurse practitioner (MSN); care management (MSN); clinical nurse specialist (MSN); family nurse practitioner (MSN); nursing (DNP); nursing education (MSN); palliative care (MSN). *Accreditation:* AACN. *Program availability:* Part-time, 100% online. *Faculty:* 6 full-time (all women), 25 part-time/adjunct (19 women). *Students:* 106 full-time (99 women), 117 part-time (105 women); includes 71 minority (46 Black or African American, non-Hispanic/Latino; 2 American Indian or Alaska Native, non-Hispanic/Latino; 12 Asian, non-Hispanic/Latino; 6 Hispanic/Latino; 5 Two or more races, non-Hispanic/Latino). Average age 38. 265 applicants, 98% accepted, 61 enrolled. In 2019, 68 master's, 2 doctorates awarded. *Degree requirements:* For master's, comprehensive exam; for doctorate, thesis/dissertation. *Entrance requirements:* For master's, minimum undergraduate GPA of 3.0, bachelor's degree in nursing, eligibility for or current Ohio RN license. Additional exam requirements/recommendations for international students: required—TOEFL (minimum score 500 paper-based). *Application deadline:* For fall admission, 8/1 priority date for domestic students. Applications are processed on a rolling basis. Application fee: $25. Electronic applications accepted. *Expenses: Tuition:* Full-time $18,784; part-time $1174 per credit hour. *Required fees:* $320; $240 per unit. One-time fee: $100. Tuition and fees vary according to course level and program. *Financial support:* In 2019–20, 10 students received support. Scholarships/grants, tuition waivers (partial), and College Free Credit available. Financial award application deadline: 3/1; financial award applicants required to submit FAFSA. *Unit head:* Dr. Janet Baker, Associate Dean of Graduate Nursing, 440-864-8172, Fax: 440-684-6053, E-mail: jbaker@ursuline.edu. *Application contact:* Melanie Steele, Director, Graduate Admission, 440-646-8119, Fax: 440-684-6138, E-mail: graduateadmissions@ursuline.edu.

**Utah Valley University,** Program in Nursing, Orem, UT 84058-5999. Offers MSN. *Accreditation:* ACEN. *Program availability:* Part-time, online learning. Terminal master's awarded for partial completion of doctoral program. *Degree requirements:* For master's, project or thesis. *Entrance requirements:* For master's, GRE, baccalaureate degree in nursing, nurse licensure, undergraduate course in statistics, minimum undergraduate GPA of 3.2 overall or in last 60 semester hours of coursework, 3 letters of recommendation. Additional exam requirements/recommendations for international students: required—TOEFL (minimum score 83 iBT). Electronic applications accepted. *Expenses:* Contact institution.

**Valdosta State University,** College of Nursing and Health Sciences, Valdosta, GA 31698. Offers adult gerontology nurse practitioner (MSN); exercise physiology (MS); family nurse practitioner (MSN); family psychiatric mental health nurse practitioner (MSN). *Accreditation:* AACN. *Program availability:* Part-time, online learning. *Degree requirements:* For master's, thesis (for some programs), comprehensive written and/or oral exams. *Entrance requirements:* For master's, minimum GPA of 2.8. Additional exam requirements/recommendations for international students: required—TOEFL (minimum score 523 paper-based). Electronic applications accepted.

**Valparaiso University,** Graduate School and Continuing Education, College of Nursing and Health Professions, Valparaiso, IN 46383. Offers nursing (DNP); nursing education (MSN, Certificate); physician assistant (MSPA); public health (MPH); MSN/MHA. *Accreditation:* AACN. *Program availability:* Part-time, evening/weekend, online learning. *Entrance requirements:* For master's, minimum GPA of 3.0, undergraduate major in nursing, Indiana registered nursing license, undergraduate courses in research and statistics. Additional exam requirements/recommendations for international students: required—TOEFL (minimum score 550 paper-based; 80 iBT), IELTS (minimum score 6). Electronic applications accepted. *Expenses:* Contact institution.

**Vanderbilt University,** Program in Nursing Science, Nashville, TN 37240-1001. Offers PhD. *Faculty:* 22 full-time (20 women), 3 part-time/adjunct (all women). *Students:* 28 full-time (26 women), 2 part-time (both women); includes 7 minority (1 Asian, non-Hispanic/Latino; 3 Hispanic/Latino; 3 Two or more races, non-Hispanic/Latino). Average age 37. 20 applicants, 40% accepted, 6 enrolled. In 2019, 5 doctorates awarded. *Degree requirements:* For doctorate, comprehensive exam, thesis/dissertation, final and qualifying exams. *Entrance requirements:* For doctorate, GRE General Test. Additional exam requirements/recommendations for international students: required—TOEFL (minimum score 570 paper-based; 88 iBT). *Application deadline:* For fall admission, 1/15 for domestic and international students. Electronic applications accepted. *Expenses: Tuition:* Full-time $51,018; part-time $2087 per hour. *Required fees:* $542. Tuition and fees vary according to program. *Financial support:* Fellowships with full tuition reimbursements, research assistantships with full tuition reimbursements, teaching assistantships with full tuition reimbursements, career-related internships or fieldwork, Federal Work-Study, institutionally sponsored loans, scholarships/grants, health care benefits, and tuition waivers (full and partial) available. Financial award application deadline: 1/15; financial award applicants required to submit CSS PROFILE or FAFSA. *Unit head:* Sheila Ridner, Director of Graduate Studies, 615-322-3800, Fax: 615-343-5898, E-mail: sheila.ridner@vanderbilt.edu. *Application contact:* Judy Vesterfelt, Program Manager, 615-322-7410, E-mail: judy.vesterfelt@vanderbilt.edu.
Website: http://www.nursing.vanderbilt.edu/

**Vanderbilt University,** Vanderbilt University School of Nursing, Nashville, TN 37240. Offers advanced clinical practice, advanced systems practice; executive leadership (DNP); agacnp; agpcnp; enp; fnp; enp/fnp; nhcl; ni; nnp; nm; nm;fnp; pmhnp; pnp-ac; pnp-pc; whnp; whnp/agpacnp (MSN), including agacnp - intensivist; agacnp - hospitalist; clinical research; health services research (PhD); MSN/M Div; MSN/MTS. *Accreditation:* AACN; ACEN (one or more programs are accredited); ACNM/ACME. *Program availability:* Part-time, blended/hybrid learning. *Faculty:* 134 full-time (120 women), 30 part-time/adjunct (26 women). *Students:* 600 full-time (527 women), 295 part-time (267 women); includes 203 minority (64 Black or African American, non-Hispanic/Latino; 5 American Indian or Alaska Native, non-Hispanic/Latino; 38 Asian, non-Hispanic/Latino; 59 Hispanic/Latino; 2 Native Hawaiian or other Pacific Islander, non-Hispanic/Latino; 35 Two or more races, non-Hispanic/Latino), 1 international. Average age 30. 1,548 applicants, 48% accepted, 521 enrolled. In 2019, 354 master's, 63 doctorates, 3 other advanced degrees awarded. *Degree requirements:* For doctorate, comprehensive exam, thesis/dissertation, PhD requires dissertation including other oral defense. *Entrance requirements:* For master's, GPA of 3.0 or greater, 3 letters of recommendation, statement of purpose, application essays, official transcripts; for doctorate, GPA and gt;- 3.5, 3 letters of recommendation, statement of purpose, application essays, official transcripts, writing samples, interview, 3 letters of recommendation from doctorally-prepared faculty, MSN, essay. Additional exam requirements/recommendations for international students: required—TOEFL (minimum score 600 paper-based; 100 iBT), IELTS (minimum score 6.5). *Application deadline:* For fall admission, 11/1 priority date for domestic and international students. Applications are processed on a rolling basis. Application fee: $50. Electronic applications accepted. *Expenses:* Contact institution. *Financial support:* In 2019–20, 645 students received support. Scholarships/grants available. Financial award application deadline: 3/15; financial award applicants required to submit FAFSA. *Unit head:* Dr. Linda Norman, Dean, 615-343-8876, Fax: 615-343-7711, E-mail: linda.norman@vanderbilt.edu. *Application contact:* Patricia Peerman, Assistant Dean for Enrollment Management, 615-322-3800, Fax: 615-343-0333, E-mail: vusn-admissions@vanderbilt.edu.
Website: https://nursing.vanderbilt.edu/

**Vanguard University of Southern California,** Graduate Program in Nursing, Costa Mesa, CA 92626. Offers MSN. *Accreditation:* AACN. *Program availability:* Part-time, evening/weekend, blended/hybrid learning. *Degree requirements:* For master's, thesis, two 55-hour practicums. *Entrance requirements:* For master's, free and clear RN license in California. *Expenses:* Contact institution.

**Villanova University,** M. Louise Fitzpatrick College of Nursing, Villanova, PA 19085. Offers adult-gerontology primary care nurse practitioner (MSN, Post Master's Certificate); family primary care nurse practitioner (MSN, Post Master's Certificate); nurse anesthesia (DNP); nursing (PhD); nursing education (MSN, Post Master's Certificate); nursing practice (DNP); pediatric primary care nurse practitioner (MSN, Post Master's Certificate). *Accreditation:* AACN; AANA/CANAEP. *Program availability:* Part-time, online learning. *Entrance requirements:* Additional exam requirements/recommendations for international students: required—TOEFL, IELTS. Electronic applications accepted.

**Virginia Commonwealth University,** Graduate School, School of Nursing, Richmond, VA 23284-9005. Offers adult health acute nursing (MS); adult health primary nursing (MS); biobehavioral clinical research (PhD); child health nursing (MS); clinical nurse leader (MS); family health nursing (MS); nurse educator (MS); nurse practitioner (MS); nursing (Certificate); nursing administration (MS), including clinical nurse manager; psychiatric-mental health nursing (MS); quality and safety in health care (DNP); women's health nursing (MS). *Accreditation:* AACN; ACEN (one or more programs are accredited). *Program availability:* Part-time, evening/weekend, online learning. *Degree requirements:* For master's, thesis optional; for doctorate, thesis/dissertation. *Entrance requirements:* For master's, GRE General Test, BSN, minimum GPA of 2.8; for doctorate, GRE General Test. Additional exam requirements/recommendations for international students: required—TOEFL (minimum score 600 paper-based; 100 iBT). Electronic applications accepted.

**Viterbo University,** Graduate Program in Nursing, La Crosse, WI 54601-4797. Offers DNP. *Accreditation:* AACN. *Program availability:* Part-time. *Degree requirements:* For doctorate, project. *Entrance requirements:* For doctorate, GRE General Test or MAT, bachelor's degree in nursing, minimum GPA of 3.0, RN license, one year of practice as an RN prior to beginning classes. Electronic applications accepted. *Expenses:* Contact institution.

**Wagner College,** Division of Graduate Studies, Evelyn L. Spiro School of Nursing, Staten Island, NY 10301-4495. Offers family nurse practitioner (MS, Certificate); nurse educator (MS); nursing (DNP). *Accreditation:* ACEN (one or more programs are accredited). *Program availability:* Part-time, evening/weekend. *Degree requirements:* For master's, thesis optional. *Entrance requirements:* For master's, BS in nursing, current clinical experience, minimum GPA of 3.3; for Certificate, master's degree in nursing from an NLN-accredited program, minimum GPA of 3.0. Additional exam requirements/recommendations for international students: required—TOEFL (minimum score 550 paper-based; 79 iBT), IELTS (minimum score 6.5). Electronic applications accepted.

**Walden University,** Graduate Programs, School of Nursing, Minneapolis, MN 55401. Offers adult-gerontology acute care nurse practitioner (MSN); adult-gerontology nurse practitioner (MSN); education (MSN); family nurse practitioner (MSN); informatics (MSN); leadership and management (MSN); nursing (PhD, Post-Master's Certificate), including education (PhD), healthcare administration (PhD), interdisciplinary health (PhD), leadership (PhD), nursing education (Post-Master's Certificate), nursing informatics (Post-Master's Certificate), nursing leadership and management (Post-Master's Certificate), public health policy (PhD); nursing practice (DNP); psychiatric mental health (MSN). *Accreditation:* AACN. *Program availability:* Part-time, evening/weekend, online only, 100% online. *Degree requirements:* For doctorate, thesis/dissertation (for some programs), residency (for some programs), field experience (for some programs). *Entrance requirements:* For master's, bachelor's degree or equivalent in related field or RN; minimum GPA of 2.5; official transcripts; goal statement (for some programs); access to computer and Internet; for doctorate, master's degree or higher; RN; three years of related professional or academic experience; goal statement; access to computer and Internet; for Post-Master's Certificate, relevant work experience; access to computer and Internet. Additional exam requirements/recommendations for international students: required—TOEFL (minimum score 550 paper-based, 79 iBT), IELTS (minimum score 6.5), Michigan English Language Assessment Battery (minimum score 82), or PTE (minimum score 53). Electronic applications accepted.

**Walsh University,** Master of Science in Nursing, North Canton, OH 44720-3396. Offers academic nurse educator (MSN); adult acute care nurse practitioner (MSN); clinical nurse leader (MSN); nursing practice (DNP). *Accreditation:* AACN. *Program availability:* Part-time, 100% online, blended/hybrid learning. *Faculty:* 5 full-time (4 women), 11 part-time/adjunct (10 women). *Students:* 80 full-time (68 women), 83 part-time (73 women); includes 12 minority (5 Black or African American, non-Hispanic/Latino; 1 Asian, non-Hispanic/Latino; 6 Two or more races, non-Hispanic/Latino). Average age 35. 76 applicants, 93% accepted, 55 enrolled. In 2019, 38 master's, 2 doctorates awarded. *Degree requirements:* For doctorate, scholarly project; residency practicum. *Entrance requirements:* For master's, Registered Nurse license(s), 1 year of experience as a Registered Nurse; Official transcripts documenting a baccalaureate degree in nursing from an accredited program, Minimum 3.0 cumulative GPA, completion of a statistics course, 2 letters of recommendation, resume or CV, personal statement. Additional exam requirements/recommendations for international students: required—TOEFL. *Application deadline:* Applications are processed on a rolling basis. Electronic applications accepted. *Expenses:* $725 per credit hour, $50 technology fee. *Financial support:* In 2019–20, 1 student received support. Research assistantships available. Financial award application deadline: 12/31; financial award applicants required to submit FAFSA. *Unit head:* Dr. Judy Kreye, Dean, Byers School of Nursing, 330-2444757, Fax: 330-4907206, E-mail: jkreye@walsh.edu. *Application contact:* Dr. Janet Finneran, Director of Graduate Nursing Programs, 330-2444759, Fax: 330-4907206, E-mail: jfinneran@walsh.edu.
Website: http://www.walsh.edu/master-of-science-in-nursing

**Washburn University,** School of Nursing, Topeka, KS 66621. Offers clinical nurse leader (MSN); nursing (DNP); psychiatric mental health nurse practitioner (Post-Graduate Certificate). *Accreditation:* AACN. *Program availability:* Part-time. *Entrance requirements:* Additional exam requirements/recommendations for international students: required—TOEFL (minimum score 550 paper-based).

**Washington Adventist University,** Program in Nursing - Business Leadership, Takoma Park, MD 20912. Offers MSN. *Program availability:* Part-time. *Entrance requirements:* Additional exam requirements/recommendations for international students: required—TOEFL (minimum score 550 paper-based), IELTS (minimum score 5).

## Nursing—General

**Washington State University,** College of Nursing, Spokane, WA 99210. Offers advanced population health (MN, DNP); family nurse practitioner (MN, DNP); nursing (PhD); psychiatric/mental health nurse practitioner (DNP); psychiatric/mental health practitioner (MN). *Accreditation:* AACN. *Degree requirements:* For master's, comprehensive exam (for some programs), thesis (for some programs), oral exam, research project. *Entrance requirements:* For master's, minimum GPA of 3.0, Washington state RN license, physical assessment skills, course work in statistics, recommendations, written interview (for nurse practitioner).

**Waynesburg University,** Graduate and Professional Studies, Canonsburg, PA 15370. Offers business (MBA), including energy management, finance, health systems, human resources, leadership, market development; counseling (MA), including addictions counseling, clinical mental health; counselor education and supervision (PhD); criminal investigation (MA); education (M Ed), including autism, curriculum and instruction, educational leadership, online teaching; nursing (MSN), including administration, education, informatics; nursing practice (DNP); special education (M Ed); technology (M Ed); MSN/MBA. *Accreditation:* AACN. *Program availability:* Part-time, evening/weekend. *Degree requirements:* For doctorate, thesis/dissertation. *Entrance requirements:* Additional exam requirements/recommendations for international students: required—TOEFL. Electronic applications accepted.

**Wayne State University,** College of Nursing, Detroit, MI 48202. Offers adult gerontology acute care nurse practitioner (MSN); adult gerontology primary care nurse practitioner (MSN); advanced public health nursing (MSN); infant and mental health (DNP, PhD); neonatal nurse practitioner (MSN); nurse-midwifery (MSN); pediatric acute care nurse practitioner (MSN); pediatric primary care nurse practitioner (MSN); psychiatric mental health nurse practitioner (MSN); women's health nurse practitioner (MSN). *Accreditation:* AACN; ACNM/ACME. *Program availability:* Part-time. *Faculty:* 27. *Students:* 134 full-time (118 women), 216 part-time (187 women); includes 98 minority (51 Black or African American, non-Hispanic/Latino; 24 Asian, non-Hispanic/Latino; 6 Hispanic/Latino; 17 Two or more races, non-Hispanic/Latino), 18 international. Average age 33. 425 applicants, 37% accepted, 95 enrolled. In 2019, 58 master's, 31 doctorates awarded. *Degree requirements:* For doctorate, thesis/dissertation. *Entrance requirements:* For master's, Completed a Bachelor of Science in Nursing with a 3.0 or higher GPA. Official transcripts. Professional competence as documented by three references. Current Michigan Registered Nurse (RN) licensure. A personal statement of goals for graduate study; for doctorate, DNP: Minimum GPA of 3.0 or higher in BSN is required. Resume or Curriculum Vita that includes education, work and/or research experience. Two references, one from a doctorally prepared individual. RN license. PhD: BSN transcript; Two to three references from doctorally prepared individuals; goals statement; Resume or CV; Interview. Additional exam requirements/recommendations for international students: required—TOEFL (minimum score 101 iBT), TWE (minimum score 6), Michigan English Language Assessment Battery (minimum score 85); recommended—IELTS (minimum score 7). *Application deadline:* For fall admission, 1/31 for domestic students; for winter admission, 11/1 for domestic students. Applications are processed on a rolling basis. Application fee: $50. Electronic applications accepted. *Expenses:* $925.72 per credit hour in-state, $1,716.93 per credit hour out-of-state, $54.56 student service credit hour fee, $315.70 registration fee. *Financial support:* In 2019–20, 104 students received support, including 39 fellowships with tuition reimbursements available (averaging $6,456 per year), 1 research assistantship (averaging $24,950 per year), 5 teaching assistantships with tuition reimbursements available (averaging $25,000 per year); scholarships/grants, health care benefits, and unspecified assistantships also available. Support available to part-time students. Financial award application deadline: 3/1; financial award applicants required to submit FAFSA. *Unit head:* Dr. Laurie M Lauzon Clabo, Dean, College of Nursing, 313-577-4082, E-mail: laurie.lauzon.clabo@wayne.edu. *Application contact:* Dr. Laurie M Lauzon Clabo, Dean, College of Nursing, 313-577-4082, E-mail: laurie.lauzon.clabo@wayne.edu.
Website: http://nursing.wayne.edu/

**Weber State University,** Dumke College of Health Professions, School of Nursing, Ogden, UT 84408-1001. Offers educator (MSN); executive (MSN); nurse practitioner (MSN). *Program availability:* Part-time, evening/weekend, online only, 100% online. *Faculty:* 14 full-time (13 women), 2 part-time/adjunct (both women). *Students:* 85 full-time (73 women), 18 part-time (16 women); includes 6 minority (1 Asian, non-Hispanic/Latino; 4 Hispanic/Latino; 1 Two or more races, non-Hispanic/Latino). Average age 38. In 2019, 52 master's awarded. *Entrance requirements:* For master's, bachelor's degree in nursing from ACEN- or CCNE-accredited program. *Application deadline:* For fall admission, 4/1 priority date for domestic students. Application fee: $60 ($90 for international students). Electronic applications accepted. *Expenses: Tuition, area resident:* Full-time $7197; part-time $4981 per credit. Tuition, state resident: full-time $7197; part-time $4981 per credit. Tuition, nonresident: full-time $16,560; part-time $11,589 per credit. *Required fees:* $643 per semester. One-time fee: $60. Tuition and fees vary according to course load and program. *Financial support:* In 2019–20, 16 students received support. Scholarships/grants available. Financial award application deadline: 4/1; financial award applicants required to submit FAFSA. *Unit head:* Dr. Deborah Juff, MSN & DNP Program Director, 801-626-7833, Fax: 801-626-6397, E-mail: djudd@weber.edu. *Application contact:* Robert Holt, Director of Enrollment, 801-626-7774, Fax: 801-626-6397, E-mail: rholt@weber.edu.
Website: http://www.weber.edu/nursing

**Webster University,** College of Arts and Sciences, Department of Nursing, St. Louis, MO 63119-3194. Offers nurse educator (MSN). *Accreditation:* ACEN. *Degree requirements:* For master's, comprehensive exam. *Entrance requirements:* For master's, 1 year of clinical experience, BSN, interview, minimum C+ average in statistics and physical assessment, minimum GPA of 3.0, RN license. Additional exam requirements/recommendations for international students: required—TOEFL.

**Wesley College,** Nursing Program, Dover, DE 19901-3875. Offers MSN. *Accreditation:* ACEN. *Program availability:* Part-time, evening/weekend. *Degree requirements:* For master's, thesis optional, portfolio. *Entrance requirements:* For master's, GRE or MAT. Electronic applications accepted.

**West Coast University,** Graduate Programs, North Hollywood, CA 91606. Offers advanced generalist (MSN); family nurse practitioner (MSN); health administration (MHA); occupational therapy (MS); pharmacy (Pharm D); physical therapy (DPT).

**Western Carolina University,** Graduate School, College of Health and Human Sciences, School of Nursing, Cullowhee, NC 28723. Offers MS, DNP, Post-Master's Certificate, Postbaccalaureate Certificate. *Accreditation:* AACN; AANA/CANAEP. *Program availability:* Part-time, evening/weekend. *Degree requirements:* For master's, comprehensive exam, thesis or alternative. *Entrance requirements:* For master's, GRE General Test, BSN with minimum GPA of 3.0, 3 references, 1 year of clinical experience. Additional exam requirements/recommendations for international students: required—TOEFL (minimum score 550 paper-based; 79 iBT). *Expenses: Tuition, area resident:* Full-time $2217.50; part-time $1664 per semester. Tuition, state resident: full-time $2217.50; part-time $1664 per semester. Tuition, nonresident: full-time $7421; part-time $5566 per semester. *International tuition:* $7421 full-time. *Required fees:* $5598; $1954 per semester. Tuition and fees vary according to course load, campus/location and program.

**Western Connecticut State University,** Division of Graduate Studies, School of Professional Studies, Nursing Department, Danbury, CT 06810-6885. Offers adult gerontology clinical nurse specialist (MSN); adult gerontology nurse practitioner (MSN); nursing education (Ed D). *Accreditation:* AACN. *Program availability:* Part-time. *Entrance requirements:* For master's, MAT (if GPA less than 3.0), bachelor's degree in nursing, minimum GPA of 3.0, previous course work in statistics and nursing research, RN license. Additional exam requirements/recommendations for international students: recommended—TOEFL (minimum score 550 paper-based; 79 iBT), IELTS (minimum score 6). *Expenses:* Contact institution.

**Western Kentucky University,** Graduate School, College of Health and Human Services, School of Nursing, Bowling Green, KY 42101. Offers MSN. *Accreditation:* AACN. *Program availability:* Part-time, evening/weekend. *Degree requirements:* For master's, comprehensive exam, thesis optional. *Entrance requirements:* For master's, GRE General Test, minimum GPA of 2.75. Additional exam requirements/recommendations for international students: required—TOEFL (minimum score 555 paper-based; 79 iBT).

**Western Michigan University,** Graduate College, College of Health and Human Services, Bronson School of Nursing, Kalamazoo, MI 49008. Offers MSN. *Accreditation:* AACN.

**Western University of Health Sciences,** College of Graduate Nursing, Doctor of Nursing Practice Program, Pomona, CA 91766-1854. Offers DNP. *Accreditation:* AACN. *Program availability:* Part-time-only, evening/weekend, blended/hybrid learning. *Faculty:* 2 full-time (1 woman), 4 part-time/adjunct (3 women). *Students:* 17 full-time (all women), 17 part-time (14 women); includes 12 minority (1 Black or African American, non-Hispanic/Latino; 1 American Indian or Alaska Native, non-Hispanic/Latino; 5 Asian, non-Hispanic/Latino; 5 Hispanic/Latino), 2 international. Average age 48. 6 applicants, 83% accepted, 4 enrolled. In 2019, 12 doctorates awarded. *Degree requirements:* For doctorate, comprehensive exam (for some programs), thesis/dissertation, dissertation project. *Entrance requirements:* For doctorate, Personal statement, curriculum vitae, 2 reference forms, official transcripts of all schools attended, example of scholarly writing, copy of RN license and Advanced Practice certifications, verification of post-baccalaureate clinical/Practice hours. Additional exam requirements/recommendations for international students: required—TOEFL (minimum score 80 iBT). *Application deadline:* For fall admission, 5/1 for domestic and international students. Application fee: $60. Electronic applications accepted. *Expenses:* Tuition is 1205 per unit; clinical fee is 2031 and student body fee is 40. *Financial support:* In 2019–20, 6 students received support. Scholarships/grants and NFLP program available. Financial award application deadline: 3/2; financial award applicants required to submit FAFSA. *Unit head:* Dr. Mary Lopez, Dean, 909-706-3860, Fax: 909-469-5521, E-mail: mlopez@westernu.edu. *Application contact:* Chris Calzada, Admissions Counselor, 909-706-3873, Fax: 909-469-5570, E-mail: ccalzada@westernu.edu.
Website: http://www.westernu.edu/nursing-dnp

**Western University of Health Sciences,** College of Graduate Nursing, Master of Science in Nursing Program, Pomona, CA 91766-1854. Offers administrative nurse leader (MSN); ambulatory care nurse (MSN); clinical nurse leader (MSN). *Accreditation:* AACN. *Faculty:* 19 full-time (16 women), 40 part-time/adjunct (31 women). *Students:* 231 full-time (182 women), 2 part-time (both women); includes 181 minority (8 Black or African American, non-Hispanic/Latino; 2 American Indian or Alaska Native, non-Hispanic/Latino; 82 Asian, non-Hispanic/Latino; 65 Hispanic/Latino; 1 Native Hawaiian or other Pacific Islander, non-Hispanic/Latino; 23 Two or more races, non-Hispanic/Latino), 3 international. Average age 29. 640 applicants, 23% accepted, 85 enrolled. In 2019, 77 master's awarded. *Degree requirements:* For master's, comprehensive exam (for some programs), project. *Entrance requirements:* For master's, Bachelor's degree, essay questions, Resume/Curriculum Vitae, 2 reference forms, Official transcripts of all schools attended, prerequisite worksheet, repeated courses work sheet. Additional exam requirements/recommendations for international students: required—TOEFL (minimum score 80 iBT). *Application deadline:* For fall admission, 11/2 for domestic and international students. Application fee: $60. Electronic applications accepted. *Expenses:* Contact institution. *Financial support:* In 2019–20, 17 students received support. Scholarships/grants available. Financial award application deadline: 3/2; financial award applicants required to submit FAFSA. *Unit head:* Dr. Mary Lopez, Dean, 909-706-3860, Fax: 909-469-5521, E-mail: mlopez@westernu.edu. *Application contact:* Daniell Mendoza, Assistant Director of Admissions, 909-469-5541, Fax: 909-469-5570, E-mail: dmendoza@westernu.edu.

**Westminster College,** School of Nursing and Health Sciences, Salt Lake City, UT 84105-3697. Offers family nurse practitioner (MSN); nurse anesthesia (MSNA); public health (MPH). *Accreditation:* AACN; AANA/CANAEP; CEPH. *Degree requirements:* For master's, clinical practicum, 504 clinical practice hours. *Entrance requirements:* For master's, GRE (can be waived in select cases), personal statement, resume, 3 professional recommendations, copy of unrestricted Utah license to practice professional nursing, background check, minimum cumulative GPA of 3.0, documentation of current immunizations, physical and mental health certificate signed by primary care provider. Additional exam requirements/recommendations for international students: required—TOEFL (minimum score 84 iBT), IELTS (minimum score 7). Electronic applications accepted. *Expenses:* Contact institution.

**West Texas A&M University,** College of Nursing and Health Sciences, Department of Nursing, Canyon, TX 79015. Offers family nurse practitioner (MSN); nursing (MSN). *Accreditation:* AACN. *Program availability:* Part-time, online learning. *Degree requirements:* For master's, comprehensive exam, thesis optional. *Entrance requirements:* For master's, GRE General Test, bachelor's degree in nursing, minimum GPA of 3.0 in last 60 hours. Additional exam requirements/recommendations for international students: required—TOEFL (minimum score 550 paper-based). Electronic applications accepted.

**West Virginia University,** School of Nursing, Morgantown, WV 26506. Offers nurse practitioner (Certificate); nursing (MSN, DNP, PhD). *Accreditation:* AACN. *Program availability:* Part-time, online learning. *Degree requirements:* For master's, thesis or alternative; for doctorate, comprehensive exam, thesis/dissertation. *Entrance requirements:* For master's, GRE General Test, minimum GPA of 3.0, current U.S. RN license, BSN, course work in statistics and physical assessment; for doctorate, GRE General Test (for PhD), minimum graduate GPA of 3.0, minimum grade of B in graduate statistics course work. Additional exam requirements/recommendations for international students: required—TOEFL (minimum score 550 paper-based). Electronic applications accepted. *Expenses:* Contact institution.

**West Virginia Wesleyan College,** School of Nursing, Buckhannon, WV 26201. Offers family nurse practitioner (MS, Post Master's Certificate); nurse-midwifery (MS); nursing (DNP); nursing leadership (MS); psychiatric mental health nurse practitioner (MS); MSN/MBA. *Accreditation:* ACEN.

**Wheeling Jesuit University,** Department of Nursing, Wheeling, WV 26003-6295. Offers MSN. *Accreditation:* AACN. *Program availability:* Part-time, evening/weekend, online learning. *Degree requirements:* For master's, comprehensive exam (for some programs), thesis (for some programs). *Entrance requirements:* For master's, GRE General Test or MAT, BSN, minimum GPA of 3.0, course work in research and

statistics, U.S. nursing license. Additional exam requirements/recommendations for international students: required—TOEFL (minimum score 600 paper-based; 100 iBT). Electronic applications accepted. Application fee is waived when completed online.

**Wichita State University,** Graduate School, College of Health Professions, School of Nursing, Wichita, KS 67260. Offers nursing (MSN); nursing practice (DNP). *Accreditation:* AACN. *Program availability:* Part-time, 100% online, blended/hybrid learning.

**Widener University,** School of Nursing, Chester, PA 19013-5792. Offers MSN, DN Sc, PhD, PMC. *Accreditation:* AACN. *Program availability:* Part-time, evening/weekend. *Degree requirements:* For doctorate, thesis/dissertation. *Entrance requirements:* For master's, GRE General Test, BSN, undergraduate course in statistics; for doctorate, GRE General Test, MSN, undergraduate course in statistics. Electronic applications accepted. *Expenses:* Contact institution.

**William Carey University,** School of Nursing, Hattiesburg, MS 39401. Offers MSN. *Accreditation:* AACN. *Program availability:* Part-time. *Degree requirements:* For master's, thesis or alternative. *Entrance requirements:* For master's, GRE, minimum GPA of 3.0, RN license. Additional exam requirements/recommendations for international students: required—TOEFL (minimum score 500 paper-based).

**Wilmington University,** College of Health Professions, New Castle, DE 19720-6491. Offers adult nurse practitioner (MSN); family nurse practitioner (MSN); gerontology nurse practitioner (MSN); nursing (MSN); nursing leadership (MSN); nursing practice (DNP). *Accreditation:* AACN. *Program availability:* Part-time. *Degree requirements:* For master's, thesis. *Entrance requirements:* For master's, BSN, RN license, interview, 3 letters of recommendation. Additional exam requirements/recommendations for international students: required—TOEFL (minimum score 500 paper-based). Electronic applications accepted.

**Wilson College,** Graduate Programs, Chambersburg, PA 17201-1285. Offers accounting (M Acc); choreography and visual art (MFA); education (M Ed); educational technology (MET); healthcare administration (MHA); humanities (MA), including art and culture, critical/cultural theory, English language and literature, women's studies; management (MSM); nursing (MSN), including nursing education, nursing leadership and management; special education (MSE). *Program availability:* Evening/weekend. *Degree requirements:* For master's, project. *Entrance requirements:* For master's, PRAXIS, minimum undergraduate cumulative GPA of 3.0, 2 letters of recommendation, current certification for eligibility to teach in grades K-12, resume, personal interview. Electronic applications accepted.

**Winona State University,** College of Nursing and Health Sciences, Winona, MN 55987. Offers adult-gerontology acute care nurse practitioner (MS, DNP, Post Master's Certificate); adult-gerontology clinical nurse specialist (MS, DNP, Post Master's Certificate); adult-gerontology primary care nurse practitioner (MS, DNP, Post Master's Certificate); family nurse practitioner (MS, DNP, Post Master's Certificate); nurse educator (MS); nursing and organizational leadership (MS, DNP, Post Master's Certificate); practice and leadership innovations (DNP, Post Master's Certificate). *Accreditation:* AACN. *Program availability:* Part-time, online learning. *Degree requirements:* For master's, thesis; for doctorate, capstone. *Entrance requirements:* For master's, GRE (if GPA less than 3.0). Additional exam requirements/recommendations for international students: required—TOEFL (minimum score 550 paper-based).

**Winston-Salem State University,** Program in Nursing, Winston-Salem, NC 27110-0003. Offers advanced nurse educator (MSN); family nurse practitioner (MSN); nursing (DNP). *Accreditation:* AACN. *Program availability:* Part-time, evening/weekend, online learning. *Entrance requirements:* For master's, GRE, MAT, resume, NC or state compact license, 3 letters of recommendation. Electronic applications accepted.

**Wright State University,** Graduate School, College of Nursing and Health, Program in Nursing, Dayton, OH 45435. Offers administration of nursing and health care systems (MS); adult gerontology clinical nurse specialist (MS); adult-gerontology acute care

nurse practitioner (MS); family nurse practitioner (MS); neonatal nurse practitioner (MS); pediatric nurse practitioner-acute care (MS); pediatric nurse practitioner-primary care (MS); psychiatric mental health nurse practitioner (MS); school nurse (MS). *Accreditation:* AACN. *Program availability:* Part-time, evening/weekend. *Degree requirements:* For master's, thesis or alternative. *Entrance requirements:* For master's, GRE General Test, BSN from ACEN-accredited college, Ohio RN license. Additional exam requirements/recommendations for international students: required—TOEFL.

**Xavier University,** College of Professional Sciences, School of Nursing, Cincinnati, OH 45207. Offers MSN, DNP, PMC, MSN/M Ed, MSN/MBA, MSN/MS. *Accreditation:* AACN. *Program availability:* Part-time, evening/weekend. *Degree requirements:* For master's, thesis, scholarly project; for doctorate, thesis/dissertation, scholarly project; for PMC, practicum. *Entrance requirements:* For master's, GRE, resume; statement of purpose and/or portfolio; RN licensure or bachelor's degree; official transcript; 3 references/recommendations; for PMC, RN licensure; master's degree in nursing; licensed in state where participating in clinical experiences; official transcript. Additional exam requirements/recommendations for international students: required—TOEFL (minimum score 550 paper-based; 79 iBT). Electronic applications accepted. Application fee is waived when completed online. *Expenses:* Contact institution.

**Yale University,** School of Nursing, West Haven, CT 06516. Offers MSN, DNP, PhD, Post Master's Certificate, MAR/MSN, MSN/M Div, MSN/MPH. *Accreditation:* AACN. *Program availability:* Part-time, online learning. Terminal master's awarded for partial completion of doctoral program. *Degree requirements:* For master's, thesis; for doctorate, comprehensive exam, thesis/dissertation. *Entrance requirements:* For master's, GRE General Test, bachelor's degree; for doctorate, GRE General Test, MSN; for Post Master's Certificate, MSN. Additional exam requirements/recommendations for international students: required—TOEFL or IELTS. Electronic applications accepted. *Expenses:* Contact institution.

**York College of Pennsylvania,** The Stabler Department of Nursing, York, PA 17403-3651. Offers adult gerontology clinical nurse specialist (MS); nurse anesthetist (MS). *Accreditation:* AACN; AANA/CANAEP. *Program availability:* Part-time. *Faculty:* 6 full-time (all women), 5 part-time/adjunct (4 women). *Students:* 30 full-time (15 women), 36 part-time (30 women); includes 9 minority (1 Black or African American, non-Hispanic/Latino; 6 Asian, non-Hispanic/Latino; 1 Hispanic/Latino; 1 Two or more races, non-Hispanic/Latino), 1 international. Average age 34. 61 applicants, 46% accepted, 23 enrolled. In 2019, 24 master's awarded. *Entrance requirements:* For master's, bachelor's degree in nursing, minimum GPA of 3.0. Additional exam requirements/recommendations for international students: required—TOEFL (minimum score 530 paper-based; 72 iBT), IELTS. Electronic applications accepted. *Expenses:* Master's Programs (other than Psych/Mental Health NP): $820 per credit tuition; Master's Program, Psych/Mental Health NP: $775 per credit tuition; DNP Programs: $960 per credit tuition, $880 general fee. *Financial support:* In 2019–20, 1 student received support. Scholarships/grants available. Financial award applicants required to submit FAFSA. *Unit head:* Colleen Marshall-Fantaski, Director, Graduate Programs in Nursing, 717-815-1791, Fax: 717-849-1651, E-mail: cfantaski@ycp.edu. *Application contact:* Allison Malachosky, Administrative Assistant, 717-815-2290, Fax: 717-849-1651, E-mail: amalacho@ycp.edu.
Website: http://www.ycp.edu/academics/academic-departments/nursing/

**York University,** Faculty of Graduate Studies, Faculty of Health, Program in Nursing, Toronto, ON M3J 1P3, Canada. Offers M Sc N.

**Youngstown State University,** College of Graduate Studies, Bitonte College of Health and Human Services, Department of Nursing, Youngstown, OH 44555-0001. Offers MSN. *Accreditation:* ACEN. *Program availability:* Part-time, evening/weekend. *Degree requirements:* For master's, thesis optional. *Entrance requirements:* For master's, GRE General Test, BSN, CPR certification. Additional exam requirements/recommendations for international students: required—TOEFL.

# Acute Care/Critical Care Nursing

**Augusta University,** College of Nursing, Doctor of Nursing Practice Program, Augusta, GA 30912. Offers adult gerontology acute care nurse practitioner (DNP); family nurse practitioner (DNP); nurse executive (DNP); nursing (DNP); nursing anesthesia (DNP); pediatric nurse practitioner (DNP); psychiatric mental health nurse practitioner (DNP). *Accreditation:* AACN; AANA/CANAEP. *Degree requirements:* For doctorate, thesis/dissertation or alternative. *Entrance requirements:* For doctorate, GRE General Test or MAT, master's degree in nursing or related field, current professional nurse licensure. Additional exam requirements/recommendations for international students: required—TOEFL (minimum score 600 paper-based; 100 iBT). Electronic applications accepted.

**Barry University,** School of Adult and Continuing Education, Division of Nursing, Program in Nurse Practitioner, Miami Shores, FL 33161-6695. Offers acute care nurse practitioner (MSN); family nurse practitioner (MSN); nurse practitioner (Certificate). *Accreditation:* AACN. *Program availability:* Part-time, evening/weekend. *Degree requirements:* For master's, research project or thesis. *Entrance requirements:* For master's, GRE General Test or MAT, BSN, minimum GPA of 3.0, course work in statistics. Electronic applications accepted.

**Case Western Reserve University,** Frances Payne Bolton School of Nursing, Master's Programs in Nursing, Nurse Practitioner Program, Cleveland, OH 44106. Offers acute care pediatric nurse practitioner (MSN); acute care/cardiovascular nursing (MSN); adult gerontology acute care nurse practitioner (MSN); adult gerontology primary care nurse practitioner (MSN); family nurse practitioner (MSN); family systems psychiatric mental health nursing (MSN); neonatal nurse practitioner (MSN); palliative care (MSN); pediatric nurse practitioner in acute care (MSN); pediatric primary care nurse practitioner (MSN); women's health nurse practitioner (MSN). *Accreditation:* ACEN. *Program availability:* Part-time. *Faculty:* 30 full-time (25 women), 6 part-time/adjunct (all women). *Students:* 47 full-time (36 women), 70 part-time (59 women); includes 34 minority (12 Black or African American, non-Hispanic/Latino; 11 Asian, non-Hispanic/Latino; 9 Hispanic/Latino; 2 Two or more races, non-Hispanic/Latino), 9 international. Average age 30. 45 applicants, 82% accepted, 22 enrolled. In 2019, 46 master's awarded. *Degree requirements:* For master's, thesis optional, minimum GPA of 3.0, clinical hours corresponding to requirements to sit for certification exam, portfolio. *Entrance requirements:* For master's, GRE/MAT (scores not required for application, but may be requested for an admission decision). Additional exam requirements/recommendations for international students: required—TOEFL (minimum score 577 paper-based; 90 iBT), IELTS (minimum score 7). *Application deadline:* For fall admission, 3/15 for domestic and international students; for spring admission, 10/1 for domestic and international

students; for summer admission, 3/15 for domestic and international students. Applications are processed on a rolling basis. Application fee: $75. Electronic applications accepted. *Expenses:* Clinical placement $75; Activity fee $15 per semester; Graduate council fee $15 per semester; Tuition rate $2,133 per credit hour. *Financial support:* In 2019–20, 100 students received support, including 34 teaching assistantships with partial tuition reimbursements available (averaging $19,197 per year); scholarships/grants and traineeships also available. Financial award application deadline: 5/15; financial award applicants required to submit FAFSA. *Unit head:* Dr. Latina Brooks, Director, 216-368-1196, Fax: 216-368-3542, E-mail: lmb3@case.edu. *Application contact:* Jackie Tepale, Admissions Coordinator, 216-368-5253, Fax: 216-368-3542, E-mail: yyd@case.edu.
Website: https://case.edu/nursing/programs/msn

**The College of New Rochelle,** Graduate School, Program in Nursing, New Rochelle, NY 10805-2308. Offers acute care nurse practitioner (MS, Certificate); clinical specialist in holistic nursing (MS, Certificate); family nurse practitioner (MS, Certificate); nursing and health care management (MS); nursing education (Certificate). *Accreditation:* AACN. *Program availability:* Part-time. *Entrance requirements:* For master's, GRE General Test or MAT, BSN, malpractice insurance, minimum GPA of 3.0, RN license. Electronic applications accepted.

**Columbia University,** School of Nursing, Program in Adult-Gerontology Acute Care Nurse Practitioner, New York, NY 10032. Offers MS, Adv C. *Accreditation:* AACN. *Program availability:* Part-time. *Entrance requirements:* For master's, GRE General Test, NCLEX, 1 year of clinical experience, BSN; for Adv C, MSN. Additional exam requirements/recommendations for international students: required—TOEFL (minimum score 100 iBT). Electronic applications accepted. *Expenses:* Tuition: Full-time $47,600; part-time $1880 per credit. One-time fee: $105.

**Drexel University,** College of Nursing and Health Professions, Division of Graduate Nursing, Philadelphia, PA 19104-2875. Offers adult acute care (MSN); adult psychiatric/mental health (MSN); advanced practice nursing (MSN); clinical trials research (MSN); family nurse practitioner (MSN); leadership in health systems management (MSN); nursing education (MSN); pediatric primary care (MSN); women's health (MSN). *Accreditation:* AACN. Electronic applications accepted.

**Duke University,** School of Nursing, Durham, NC 27708. Offers acute care pediatric nurse practitioner (MSN, Post-Graduate Certificate); adult-gerontology nurse practitioner (MSN, Post-Graduate Certificate), including acute care, primary care; family nurse practitioner (MSN, Post-Graduate Certificate); neonatal nurse practitioner (MSN, Post-

Graduate Certificate); nurse anesthesia (DNP); nurse practitioner (DNP); nursing (PhD); nursing and health care leadership (MSN, Post-Graduate Certificate); nursing education (MSN, Post-Graduate Certificate); nursing informatics (MSN, Post-Graduate Certificate); pediatric nurse practitioner (MSN, Post-Graduate Certificate), including primary care; psychiatric mental health nurse practitioner (MSN, Post-Graduate Certificate); women's health nurse practitioner (MSN, Post-Graduate Certificate). *Accreditation:* AACN; AANA/CANAEP. *Program availability:* Part-time, evening/weekend, online with on-campus intensives. *Faculty:* 48 full-time (40 women), 32 part-time/adjunct (28 women). *Students:* 666 full-time (601 women), 157 part-time (139 women); includes 193 minority (61 Black or African American, non-Hispanic/Latino; 4 American Indian or Alaska Native, non-Hispanic/Latino; 57 Asian, non-Hispanic/Latino; 49 Hispanic/Latino; 1 Native Hawaiian or other Pacific Islander, non-Hispanic/Latino; 21 Two or more races, non-Hispanic/Latino), 8 international. Average age 34. 761 applicants, 33% accepted, 149 enrolled. In 2019, 213 master's, 74 doctorates, 18 other advanced degrees awarded. Terminal master's awarded for partial completion of doctoral program. *Degree requirements:* For master's, thesis optional; for doctorate, capstone project. *Entrance requirements:* For master's, MSN applicants are no longer required to take the GRE, 1 year of nursing experience (recommended), BSN, minimum GPA of 3.0, previous course work in statistics; for doctorate, GRE is required for the DNP in Nurse Anesthesia, BSN or MSN, minimum GPA of 3.0, resume, personal statement, graduate statistics and research methods course, current licensure as a registered nurse, transcripts from all post-secondary institutions; for Post-Graduate Certificate, MSN, licensure or eligibility as a professional nurse, transcripts from all post-secondary institutions, previous course work in statistics. Additional exam requirements/recommendations for international students: required—TOEFL (minimum score 100 iBT), IELTS (minimum score 7). *Application deadline:* For fall admission, 12/1 for domestic and international students; for spring admission, 5/1 for domestic and international students. Application fee: $50. Electronic applications accepted. *Expenses:* Contact institution. *Financial support:* Institutionally sponsored loans, scholarships/grants, and traineeships available. Support available to part-time students. Financial award applicants required to submit FAFSA. *Unit head:* Dr. Marion E. Broome, Dean/Vice Chancellor for Nursing Affairs/Associate Vice President for Academic Affairs for Nursing, 919-684-9446, Fax: 919-684-9414, E-mail: marion.broome@duke.edu. *Application contact:* Dr. Ernie Rushing, Director of Admissions and Recruitment, 919-668-6274, Fax: 919-668-4693, E-mail: ernie.rushing@dm.duke.edu.
Website: http://www.nursing.duke.edu/

**Elms College,** School of Nursing, Chicopee, MA 01013-2839. Offers adult-gerontology acute care nurse practitioner (DNP); family nurse practitioner (DNP); health systems innovation and leadership (DNP); nursing and health services management (MSN); nursing education (MSN). *Accreditation:* AACN. *Program availability:* Part-time, evening/weekend. *Faculty:* 3 full-time (2 women), 2 part-time/adjunct (both women). *Students:* 13 full-time (11 women), 97 part-time (91 women); includes 8 minority (4 Black or African American, non-Hispanic/Latino; 2 Hispanic/Latino; 2 Two or more races, non-Hispanic/Latino). Average age 38. 39 applicants, 87% accepted, 27 enrolled. In 2019, 4 master's, 20 doctorates awarded. *Entrance requirements:* Additional exam requirements/recommendations for international students: required—TOEFL (minimum score 80 iBT). *Application deadline:* For fall admission, 7/1 priority date for domestic students; for spring admission, 11/1 priority date for domestic students. Applications are processed on a rolling basis. Electronic applications accepted. *Financial support:* Applicants required to submit FAFSA. *Unit head:* Dr. Kathleen Scoble, Dean, School of Nursing, 413-265-2204, E-mail: scoblek@elms.edu. *Application contact:* Nancy Davis, Director, Office of Graduate and Continuing Education Admissions, 413-265-2456, E-mail: grad@elms.edu.

**Georgetown University,** Graduate School of Arts and Sciences, School of Nursing and Health Studies, Washington, DC 20057. Offers acute care nurse practitioner (MS); clinical nurse specialist (MS); family nurse practitioner (MS); health systems administration (MS); nurse anesthesia (MS); nurse-midwifery (MS); nursing (DNP); nursing education (MS). *Accreditation:* AACN; AANA/CANAEP (one or more programs are accredited); ACNM/ACME (one or more programs are accredited). *Degree requirements:* For master's, thesis optional. *Entrance requirements:* For master's, GRE General Test or MAT, bachelor's degree in nursing from ACEN-accredited school, minimum undergraduate GPA of 3.0. Additional exam requirements/recommendations for international students: required—TOEFL.

**Goldfarb School of Nursing at Barnes-Jewish College,** Graduate Programs, St. Louis, MO 63110. Offers adult-gerontology (MSN), including primary care nurse practitioner; adult-gerontology (MSN), including acute care nurse practitioner; health systems and population health leadership (MSN); nurse anesthesia (MSN). *Accreditation:* AACN; AANA/CANAEP. *Program availability:* Part-time, online learning. *Degree requirements:* For master's, thesis or alternative. *Entrance requirements:* For master's, 2 references, personal statement, curriculum vitae or resume. Additional exam requirements/recommendations for international students: required—TOEFL (minimum score 575 paper-based; 85 iBT).

**Grand Canyon University,** College of Nursing and Health Care Professions, Phoenix, AZ 85017-1097. Offers acute care nurse practitioner (MSN, PMC); family nurse practitioner (MSN, PMC); health care administration (MS); health care informatics (MS, MSN); leadership in health care systems (MSN); nursing (DNP); nursing education (MSN, PMC); public health (MPH, MSN); MBA/MSN. *Accreditation:* AACN. *Program availability:* Part-time, evening/weekend, online learning. *Degree requirements:* For master's and PMC, comprehensive exam (for some programs). *Entrance requirements:* For master's, minimum cumulative and science course undergraduate GPA of 3.0. Additional exam requirements/recommendations for international students: required—TOEFL (minimum score 575 paper-based; 90 iBT), IELTS (minimum score 7).

**Indiana University-Purdue University Indianapolis,** School of Nursing, MSN Program in Nursing, Indianapolis, IN 46202. Offers adult/gerontology acute care nurse practitioner (MSN); adult/gerontology clinical nurse specialist (MSN); adult/gerontology primary care nurse practitioner (MSN); family nurse practitioner (MSN); nursing education (MSN); nursing leadership in health systems (MSN); pediatric clinical nurse specialist (MSN); pediatric nurse practitioner (MSN). *Accreditation:* AACN. *Program availability:* Part-time, blended/hybrid learning. *Degree requirements:* For master's, thesis. *Entrance requirements:* For master's, BSN from ACEN- or CCNE-accredited program, minimum undergraduate GPA of 3.0 (preferred), professional resume or curriculum vitae, essay stating career goals and objectives, current unencumbered RN license, three references from individuals with knowledge of ability to succeed in graduate program. Additional exam requirements/recommendations for international students: required—TOEFL (minimum score 550 paper-based; 79 iBT). Electronic applications accepted. *Expenses:* Contact institution.

**Inter American University of Puerto Rico, Arecibo Campus,** Program in Nursing, Arecibo, PR 00614-4050. Offers critical care nursing (MSN); surgical nursing (MSN). *Entrance requirements:* For master's, EXADEP or GRE General Test or MAT, 2 letters of recommendation, bachelor's degree in nursing, minimum GPA of 2.5 in last 60 credits, minimum 1 year nursing experience, nursing license.

**Inter American University of Puerto Rico, Barranquitas Campus,** Program in Nursing, Barranquitas, PR 00794. Offers critical care nursing (MSN); medical surgical nursing (MSN). *Program availability:* Part-time, evening/weekend. *Degree requirements:* For master's, 2 foreign languages, comprehensive exam (for some programs), thesis optional, minimum grade of B on all courses, integration seminar. *Entrance requirements:* For master's, bachelor's degree in nursing from accredited institution, minimum GPA of 2.5, provisional or permanent nursing license for practicing nursing in Puerto Rico, official academic transcript from institution that conferred bachelor's degree, two recommendations letters. Electronic applications accepted. *Expenses:* Contact institution.

**Marquette University,** Graduate School, College of Nursing, Milwaukee, WI 53201-1881. Offers acute care nurse practitioner (Certificate); adult clinical nurse specialist (Certificate); adult nurse practitioner (Certificate); advanced practice nursing (MSN, DNP), including adult-older adult acute care (DNP), adults (MSN), adults-older adults (DNP), clinical nurse leader (MSN), health care systems leadership (DNP), nurse-midwifery (MSN), older adults (MSN), pediatrics-acute care, pediatrics-primary care, primary care (DNP), systems leadership and healthcare quality (MSN); family nurse practitioner (Certificate); nurse-midwifery (Certificate); nursing (PhD); pediatric acute care (Certificate); pediatric primary care (Certificate); systems leadership and healthcare quality (Certificate). *Accreditation:* AACN; AANA/CANAEP; ACNM/ACME. Terminal master's awarded for partial completion of doctoral program. *Degree requirements:* For master's, comprehensive exam, thesis or alternative. *Entrance requirements:* For master's, GRE General Test, BSN, Wisconsin RN license, official transcripts from all current and previous colleges/universities except Marquette, three completed recommendation forms, resume, written statement of professional goals; for doctorate, GRE General Test, official transcripts from all current and previous colleges/universities except Marquette, three letters of recommendation, resume, written statement of professional goals, sample of scholarly writing. Additional exam requirements/recommendations for international students: required—TOEFL (minimum score 530 paper-based). Electronic applications accepted.

**Maryville University of Saint Louis,** Myrtle E. and Earl E. Walker College of Health Professions, The Catherine McAuley School of Nursing, St. Louis, MO 63141-7299. Offers acute care nurse practitioner (MSN); adult gerontology nurse practitioner (MSN); advanced practice nursing (DNP); family nurse practitioner (MSN); pediatric nurse practitioner (MSN). *Accreditation:* AACN. *Program availability:* 100% online, blended/hybrid learning. *Faculty:* 14 full-time (all women), 131 part-time/adjunct (114 women). *Students:* 103 full-time (91 women), 3,493 part-time (3,050 women); includes 1,039 minority (530 Black or African American, non-Hispanic/Latino; 41 American Indian or Alaska Native, non-Hispanic/Latino; 157 Asian, non-Hispanic/Latino; 221 Hispanic/Latino; 90 Two or more races, non-Hispanic/Latino), 9 international. Average age 37. In 2019, 1,012 master's, 54 doctorates awarded. *Degree requirements:* For master's, practicum. *Entrance requirements:* For master's, BSN, current licensure, minimum GPA of 3.0, 3 letters of recommendation, curriculum vitae. Additional exam requirements/recommendations for international students: required—TOEFL (minimum score 550 paper-based). *Application deadline:* Applications are processed on a rolling basis. Electronic applications accepted. *Expenses:* Contact institution. *Financial support:* Federal Work-Study and campus employment available. Support available to part-time students. Financial award application deadline: 4/1; financial award applicants required to submit FAFSA. *Unit head:* Karla Larson, Assistant Dean Nursing, 314-529-6856, Fax: 314-529-9139, E-mail: klarson@maryville.edu. *Application contact:* Jeannie DeLuca, Director of Admissions and Advising, 314-929-9355, Fax: 314-529-9927, E-mail: jdeluca@maryville.edu.
Website: http://www.maryville.edu/hp/nursing/

**Moravian College,** Graduate and Continuing Studies, Helen S. Breidegam School of Nursing, Bethlehem, PA 18018-6614. Offers clinical nurse leader (MS); nurse administrator (MS); nurse educator (MS); nurse practitioner - acute care (MS); nurse practitioner - primary care (MS). *Accreditation:* AACN. *Program availability:* Part-time, evening/weekend. *Faculty:* 2 full-time (both women), 3 part-time/adjunct (2 women). *Students:* 5 full-time (4 women), 103 part-time (95 women); includes 19 minority (4 Black or African American, non-Hispanic/Latino; 8 Asian, non-Hispanic/Latino; 7 Hispanic/Latino), 1 international. Average age 37. 131 applicants, 69% accepted, 85 enrolled. In 2019, 25 master's awarded. *Degree requirements:* For master's, comprehensive exam (for some programs), evidence-based practice project. *Entrance requirements:* For master's, BSN with minimum GPA of 3.0, active RN license, statistics course with minimum C grade, 2 professional references, written statement of goals, professional resume, interview, official transcripts. *Application deadline:* For fall admission, 8/1 priority date for domestic and international students; for spring admission, 1/1 priority date for domestic and international students; for summer admission, 5/1 priority date for domestic and international students. Applications are processed on a rolling basis. Electronic applications accepted. *Expenses:* Contact institution. *Financial support:* Applicants required to submit FAFSA. *Unit head:* Dr. Dawn Goodolf, 610-861-1412, Fax: 610-861-1466, E-mail: nursing@moravian.edu. *Application contact:* Caroline Bechtel, Student Experience Mentor, 610-861-1400, Fax: 610-861-1466, E-mail: graduate@moravian.edu.
Website: https://www.moravian.edu/graduate/programs/nursing#/

**Mount Carmel College of Nursing,** Nursing Program, Columbus, OH 43222. Offers adult gerontology acute care nurse practitioner (MS); adult health clinical nurse specialist (MS); family nurse practitioner (MS); nursing (DNP); nursing administration (MS); nursing education (MS). *Accreditation:* AACN. *Program availability:* Part-time. *Faculty:* 6 full-time (all women), 10 part-time/adjunct (9 women). *Students:* 101 full-time (82 women), 109 part-time (95 women); includes 43 minority (27 Black or African American, non-Hispanic/Latino; 4 Asian, non-Hispanic/Latino; 5 Hispanic/Latino; 7 Two or more races, non-Hispanic/Latino). Average age 32. 133 applicants, 84% accepted, 95 enrolled. In 2019, 66 master's, 2 doctorates awarded. *Degree requirements:* For master's, professional manuscript; for doctorate, practicum. *Entrance requirements:* For master's, letters of recommendation, statement of purpose, current resume, baccalaureate degree in nursing, current Ohio RN license, minimum cumulative GPA of 3.0; for doctorate, master's degree in nursing from program accredited by either ACEN or CCNE. Additional exam requirements/recommendations for international students: required—TOEFL (minimum score 550 paper-based; 80 iBT). *Application deadline:* For fall admission, 2/1 priority date for domestic students; for spring admission, 11/1 priority date for domestic students. Applications are processed on a rolling basis. Application fee: $30. Electronic applications accepted. *Expenses: Tuition:* Full-time $27,936; part-time $27,936 per year. *Required fees:* $360. *Financial support:* In 2019–20, 13 students received support. Institutionally sponsored loans and scholarships/grants available. Financial award application deadline: 3/1; financial award applicants required to submit FAFSA. *Unit head:* Dr. Jami Nininger, Interim Associate Dean Graduate Studies, 614-234-1777, Fax: 614-234-2875, E-mail: jnininger@mccn.edu. *Application contact:* Dr. Kim Campbell, Director of Recruitment and Admissions, 614-234-5144, Fax: 614-234-5427, E-mail: kcampbell@mccn.edu.
Website: www.mccn.edu

**New York University,** Rory Meyers College of Nursing, Doctor of Nursing Practice Program, New York, NY 10012-1019. Offers nursing (DNP), including adult-gerontology acute care nurse practitioner, adult-gerontology primary care nurse practitioner, family nurse practitioner, nurse-midwifery, pediatrics nurse practitioner, psychiatric-mental

health nurse practitioner. *Accreditation:* AACN. *Program availability:* Part-time, evening/weekend. *Degree requirements:* For doctorate, thesis/dissertation, project. *Entrance requirements:* For doctorate, MS, RN license, interview, Nurse Practitioner Certification, writing sample. Additional exam requirements/recommendations for international students: required—TOEFL (minimum score 100 iBT), IELTS (minimum score 7). Electronic applications accepted. *Expenses:* Contact institution.

**New York University,** Rory Meyers College of Nursing, Programs in Advanced Practice Nursing, New York, NY 10012-1019. Offers adult-gerontology acute care nurse practitioner (MS, Advanced Certificate); adult-gerontology primary care nurse practitioner (MS, Advanced Certificate); family nurse practitioner (MS, Advanced Certificate); gerontology nurse practitioner (Advanced Certificate); nurse-midwifery (MS, Advanced Certificate); nursing administration (MS, Advanced Certificate); nursing education (MS, Advanced Certificate); nursing informatics (MS, Advanced Certificate); pediatrics nurse practitioner (MS, Advanced Certificate); psychiatric-mental health nurse practitioner (MS, Advanced Certificate); MS/MPH. *Accreditation:* AACN; ACNM/ACME. *Program availability:* Part-time, evening/weekend. *Degree requirements:* For master's, thesis (for some programs), capstone. *Entrance requirements:* For master's, BS in nursing, AS in nursing with another BS/BA, interview, RN license, 1 year of clinical experience (3 for the MS in nursing education program); for Advanced Certificate, master's degree in nursing. Additional exam requirements/recommendations for international students: required—TOEFL (minimum score 100 iBT), IELTS (minimum score 7). Electronic applications accepted. *Expenses:* Contact institution.

**Northeastern University,** Bouvé College of Health Sciences, Boston, MA 02115-5096. Offers applied behavior analysis (MS); audiology (Au D); counseling psychology (MS, PhD, CAGS); exercise science (MS); nursing (MS, PhD, CAGS), including administration (MS), adult-gerontology acute care nurse practitioner (MS, CAGS), adult-gerontology primary care nurse practitioner (MS, CAGS), anesthesia (MS), family nurse practitioner (MS, CAGS), neonatal nurse practitioner (MS, CAGS), pediatric nurse practitioner (MS, CAGS), psychiatric mental health nurse practitioner (MS, CAGS); nursing practice (DNP); pharmaceutical sciences (MS, PhD), including interdisciplinary concentration, pharmaceutics and drug delivery systems; pharmacology (MS); pharmacy (Pharm D); school psychology (PhD); speech-language pathology (MS); urban health (MPH); MS/MBA. *Accreditation:* AANA/CANAEP; ACPE (one or more programs are accredited); ASHA; CEPH. *Program availability:* Part-time, evening/weekend, online learning. *Degree requirements:* For doctorate, thesis/dissertation (for some programs); for CAGS, comprehensive exam. Electronic applications accepted. *Expenses:* Contact institution.

**Point Loma Nazarene University,** School of Nursing, MS in Nursing Program, San Diego, CA 92106. Offers adult/gerontology (MSN); family/individual health (MSN); pediatrics (MSN). *Program availability:* Part-time. *Students:* 4 full-time (3 women), 49 part-time (41 women); includes 29 minority (5 Black or African American, non-Hispanic/Latino; 8 Asian, non-Hispanic/Latino; 14 Hispanic/Latino; 2 Two or more races, non-Hispanic/Latino). Average age 37. 30 applicants, 83% accepted, 14 enrolled. In 2019, 25 master's awarded. *Entrance requirements:* For master's, NCLEX exam, ADN or BSN in nursing, interview, RN license, essay, letters of recommendation, interview. *Application deadline:* For fall admission, 7/5 priority date for domestic students; for spring admission, 11/1 priority date for domestic students; for summer admission, 3/22 priority date for domestic students. Applications are processed on a rolling basis. Application fee: $50. Electronic applications accepted. *Expenses:* $820 per unit. *Financial support:* In 2019–20, 9 students received support. Scholarships/grants available. Financial award applicants required to submit FAFSA. *Unit head:* Dr. Larry Rankin, Associate Dean, 619-849-7813, E-mail: LarryRankin@pointloma.edu. *Application contact:* Dana Barger, Director of Recruitment and Admissions, Graduate and Professional Students, 619-329-6799, E-mail: gradinfo@pointloma.edu. Website: https://www.pointloma.edu/graduate-studies/programs/nursing-ms

**Purdue University Northwest,** Graduate Studies Office, School of Nursing, Hammond, IN 46323-2094. Offers adult health clinical nurse specialist (MS); critical care clinical nurse specialist (MS); family nurse practitioner (MS); nurse executive (MS). *Accreditation:* ACEN. *Program availability:* Part-time, online learning. *Entrance requirements:* For master's, BSN. Additional exam requirements/recommendations for international students: required—TOEFL. Electronic applications accepted.

**San Francisco State University,** Division of Graduate Studies, College of Health and Social Sciences, School of Nursing, San Francisco, CA 94132-1722. Offers adult acute care (MS); clinical nurse specialist (MS); community/public health nursing (MS); family nurse practitioner (Certificate); nursing administration (MS); pediatrics (MS); women's health (MS). *Accreditation:* AACN. *Program availability:* Part-time. *Application deadline:* Applications are processed on a rolling basis. *Expenses: Tuition, area resident:* Full-time $7176; part-time $4164 per year. Tuition, state resident: full-time $7176; part-time $4164 per year. Tuition, nonresident: full-time $16,680; part-time $396 per unit. International tuition: $16,680 full-time. *Required fees:* $1524; $1524 per unit. $762 per semester. Tuition and fees vary according to degree level and program. *Financial support:* Career-related internships or fieldwork available. *Unit head:* Dr. Mary-Ann van Dam, 415-338-1802, Fax: 415-338-0555, E-mail: vandam@sfsu.edu. *Application contact:* Prof. Fang-yu Chou, Assistant Director of Graduate Programs, 415-338-6853, Fax: 415-338-0555, E-mail: fchou@sfsu.edu. Website: http://nursing.sfsu.edu

**Southern Adventist University,** School of Nursing, Collegedale, TN 37315-0370. Offers acute care-adult/gerontology nurse practitioner (MSN, DNP); healthcare administration (MSN/MBA); lifestyle medicine (DNP); nurse educator (MSN, DNP); primary care-adult/gerontology nurse practitioner (MSN); primary care-family nurse practitioner (MSN, DNP); primary care-psychiatric mental health nurse practitioner (MSN, DNP); MSN/MBA. *Accreditation:* ACEN. *Program availability:* Part-time, 100% online. *Degree requirements:* For master's, thesis or project; for doctorate, scholarly project. *Entrance requirements:* For master's, RN license. Additional exam requirements/recommendations for international students: required—TOEFL (minimum score 100 iBT). Electronic applications accepted.

**Tennessee Technological University,** Whitson-Hester School of Nursing, DNP Program, Cookeville, TN 38505. Offers adult-gerontology acute care nurse practitioner (DNP); executive leadership in nursing (DNP); family nurse practitioner (DNP); pediatric nurse practitioner-primary care (DNP); psychiatric/mental health nurse practitioner (DNP); women's health care nurse practitioner (DNP). *Program availability:* Part-time. *Students:* 20 full-time (17 women), 12 part-time (all women); includes 3 minority (2 Black or African American, non-Hispanic/Latino; 1 Two or more races, non-Hispanic/Latino). 25 applicants, 60% accepted, 10 enrolled. *Application deadline:* For fall admission, 7/1 for domestic students, 5/1 for international students; for spring admission, 12/1 for domestic students, 10/1 for international students; for summer admission, 5/1 for domestic students, 2/1 for international students. Applications are processed on a rolling basis. Application fee: $35 ($40 for international students). Electronic applications accepted. *Expenses: Tuition, area resident:* Part-time $597 per credit hour. Tuition, state resident: part-time $597 per credit hour. Tuition, nonresident: part-time $1323 per credit hour. *Financial support:* Application deadline: 4/1; applicants required to submit FAFSA. *Unit head:* Dr. Kim Hanna, Dean, Fax: 931-372-6244, E-mail: khanna@tntech.edu. *Application contact:* Shelia K. Kendrick, Coordinator of Graduate Studies,

931-372-3808, Fax: 931-372-3497, E-mail: skendrick@tntech.edu. Website: https://www.tntech.edu/nursing/doctor-of-nursing-practice/

**Texas Tech University Health Sciences Center,** School of Nursing, Lubbock, TX 79430. Offers acute care nurse practitioner (MSN, Certificate); administration (MSN); advanced practice (DNP); education (MSN); executive leadership (DNP); family nurse practitioner (MSN, Certificate); geriatric nurse practitioner (MSN, Certificate); pediatric nurse practitioner (MSN, Certificate). *Accreditation:* AACN. *Program availability:* Part-time, online learning. *Degree requirements:* For master's, thesis optional. *Entrance requirements:* For master's, minimum GPA of 3.0, 3 letters of reference, BSN, RN license; for Certificate, minimum GPA of 3.0, 3 letters of reference, RN license. Additional exam requirements/recommendations for international students: required—TOEFL (minimum score 550 paper-based).

**Texas Woman's University,** Graduate School, College of Nursing, Denton, TX 76204. Offers adult health clinical nurse specialist (MS); adult health nurse practitioner (MS); adult/gerontology acute care nurse practitioner (MS); child health clinical nurse specialist (MS); clinical nurse leader (MS); family nurse practitioner (MS); health systems management (MS); nursing education (MS); nursing practice (DNP); nursing science (PhD); pediatric nurse practitioner (MS); women's health clinical nurse specialist (MS); women's health nurse practitioner (MS). *Accreditation:* AACN. *Program availability:* Part-time, 100% online, blended/hybrid learning. *Faculty:* 48 full-time (47 women), 31 part-time/adjunct (24 women). *Students:* 42 full-time (40 women), 811 part-time (756 women); includes 481 minority (168 Black or African American, non-Hispanic/Latino; 2 American Indian or Alaska Native, non-Hispanic/Latino; 165 Asian, non-Hispanic/Latino; 118 Hispanic/Latino; 1 Native Hawaiian or other Pacific Islander, non-Hispanic/Latino; 27 Two or more races, non-Hispanic/Latino), 26 international. Average age 36. 435 applicants, 71% accepted, 172 enrolled. In 2019, 203 master's, 37 doctorates awarded. *Degree requirements:* For master's, comprehensive exam, thesis or alternative, 6-year time limit for completion of degree, professional or clinical project; for doctorate, comprehensive exam, thesis/dissertation, 10-year time limit for completion of degree; dissertation (PhD), assessment practicum (DPT). *Entrance requirements:* For master's, minimum GPA of 3.0 on last 60 hours in undergraduate nursing degree and overall, RN license, BS in nursing, basic statistics course; for doctorate, MS in nursing, minimum preferred GPA of 3.5, RN or APRN license, statistics course, 2 letters of reference, curriculum vitae, graduate nursing-theory course, graduate research course, statement of professional goals and research interests, 1 yr APRN experience. Additional exam requirements/recommendations for international students: required—TOEFL (minimum score 79 iBT); recommended—IELTS (minimum score 6.5), TSE (minimum score 53). *Application deadline:* For fall admission, 5/1 for domestic students, 3/1 priority date for international students; for spring admission, 9/15 for domestic students, 7/1 priority date for international students. Application fee: $50 ($75 for international students). Electronic applications accepted. *Expenses:* All are estimates. Tuition for 10 hours = $2,763; Fees for 10 hours = $1,342. Master's Nursing courses require additional $75/SCH; Doctoral Nursing courses require additional $80/SCH. *Financial support:* In 2019–20, 212 students received support, including 1 research assistantship, 6 teaching assistantships (averaging $12,029 per year); career-related internships or fieldwork, scholarships/grants, health care benefits, and unspecified assistantships also available. Support available to part-time students. Financial award application deadline: 3/1; financial award applicants required to submit FAFSA. *Unit head:* Dr. Rosalie Mainous, Dean, 940-898-2401, Fax: 940-898-2437, E-mail: nursing@twu.edu. *Application contact:* Korie Hawkins, Associate Director of Admissions, Graduate Recruitment, 940-898-3188, Fax: 940-898-3081, E-mail: admissions@twu.edu. Website: http://www.twu.edu/nursing/

**Universidad de Iberoamerica,** Graduate School, San Jose, Costa Rica. Offers clinical neuropsychology (PhD); clinical psychology (M Psych); educational psychology (M Psych); forensic psychology (M Psych); hospital management (MHA); intensive care nursing (MN); medicine (MD).

**The University of Alabama in Huntsville,** School of Graduate Studies, College of Nursing, Huntsville, AL 35899. Offers family nurse practitioner (Certificate); nursing (MSN, DNP), including adult-gerontology acute care nurse practitioner (MSN), adult-gerontology clinical nurse specialist (MSN), family nurse practitioner (MSN), leadership in health care systems (MSN); nursing education (Certificate). *Accreditation:* AACN. *Program availability:* Part-time. *Degree requirements:* For master's, comprehensive exam, thesis or alternative, oral and written exams. *Entrance requirements:* For master's, MAT or GRE, Alabama RN license, BSN, minimum GPA of 3.0; for doctorate, master's degree in nursing in an advanced practice area; for Certificate, MAT or GRE, minimum GPA of 3.0. Additional exam requirements/recommendations for international students: required—TOEFL (minimum score 500 paper-based; 80 iBT), IELTS (minimum score 6.5). Electronic applications accepted.

**University of Cincinnati,** Graduate School, College of Nursing, Cincinnati, OH 45221-0038. Offers nurse midwifery (MSN); nurse practitioner (MSN, DNP), including acute care pediatrics (DNP), adult-gerontology acute care, adult-gerontology primary care, anesthesia (DNP), family (MSN), leadership (DNP), neonatal (MSN), women's health (MSN); nursing (MSN, PhD), including occupational health (MSN). *Accreditation:* AACN; AANA/CANAEP (one or more programs are accredited); ACNM/ACME. *Program availability:* Part-time, 100% online, blended/hybrid learning. *Faculty:* 62 full-time (55 women), 125 part-time/adjunct (114 women). *Students:* 429 full-time (355 women), 1,547 part-time (1,390 women); includes 453 minority (226 Black or African American, non-Hispanic/Latino; 5 American Indian or Alaska Native, non-Hispanic/Latino; 68 Asian, non-Hispanic/Latino; 103 Hispanic/Latino; 3 Native Hawaiian or other Pacific Islander, non-Hispanic/Latino; 48 Two or more races, non-Hispanic/Latino), 15 international. Average age 36. 779 applicants, 78% accepted, 464 enrolled. In 2019, 518 master's, 47 doctorates awarded. *Degree requirements:* For master's, thesis or alternative; for doctorate, comprehensive exam (for some programs), thesis/dissertation (for some programs). *Entrance requirements:* For master's, GRE required only for the Direct-Entry Accelerated Program. Additional exam requirements/recommendations for international students: required—TOEFL (minimum score 600 paper-based; 100 iBT); recommended—IELTS (minimum score 7). *Application deadline:* For fall admission, 4/1 priority date for domestic and international students; for spring admission, 9/1 priority date for domestic and international students; for summer admission, 2/1 priority date for domestic and international students. Applications are processed on a rolling basis. Application fee: $135 ($140 for international students). Electronic applications accepted. *Expenses:* Contact institution. *Financial support:* In 2019–20, 103 students received support, including 9 fellowships with full tuition reimbursements available (averaging $18,595 per year), 7 research assistantships with full tuition reimbursements available (averaging $12,991 per year), 8 teaching assistantships with full tuition reimbursements available (averaging $12,991 per year); institutionally sponsored loans, scholarships/grants, traineeships, health care benefits, tuition waivers (partial), and unspecified assistantships also available. Support available to part-time students. Financial award application deadline: 4/1; financial award applicants required to submit FAFSA. *Unit head:* Dr. Greer Glazer, Dean, 513-558-5330, Fax: 513-558-9030, E-mail: greer.glazer@uc.edu. *Application contact:* Office of Student Affairs, 513-558-8400,

E-mail: nursingbearcats@uc.edu.
Website: https://nursing.uc.edu/

**University of Guelph,** Ontario Veterinary College and Office of Graduate and Postdoctoral Studies, Graduate Programs in Veterinary Sciences, Department of Clinical Studies, Guelph, ON N1G 2W1, Canada. Offers anesthesiology (M Sc, DV Sc); cardiology (DV Sc, Diploma); clinical studies (Diploma); dermatology (M Sc); diagnostic imaging (M Sc, DV Sc); emergency/critical care (M Sc, DV Sc, Diploma); medicine (M Sc, DV Sc); neurology (M Sc, DV Sc); ophthalmology (M Sc, DV Sc); surgery (M Sc, DV Sc). *Degree requirements:* For master's, thesis; for doctorate, comprehensive exam, thesis/dissertation. *Entrance requirements:* Additional exam requirements/recommendations for international students: required—TOEFL (minimum score 550 paper-based), IELTS (minimum score 6.5). Electronic applications accepted.

**University of Illinois at Chicago,** College of Nursing, Program in Nursing, Chicago, IL 60607-7128. Offers acute care clinical nurse specialist (MS); administrative nursing leadership (Certificate); adult nurse practitioner (MS); adult/geriatric nurse practitioner (MS); advanced community health nurse specialist (MS); family nurse practitioner (MS); geriatric clinical nurse specialist (MS); geriatric nurse practitioner (MS); nurse midwifery (MS); occupational health/advanced community health nurse specialist (MS); occupational health/family nurse practitioner (MS); pediatric nurse practitioner (MS); perinatal clinical nurse specialist (MS); school/advanced community health nurse specialist (MS); school/family nurse practitioner (MS); women's health nurse practitioner (MS). *Accreditation:* AACN. *Program availability:* Part-time. *Degree requirements:* For master's, thesis or alternative. *Entrance requirements:* For master's, GRE General Test, minimum GPA of 2.75. Additional exam requirements/recommendations for international students: required—TOEFL. Electronic applications accepted.

**University of Miami,** Graduate School, School of Nursing and Health Studies, Coral Gables, FL 33124. Offers acute care (MSN), including acute care nurse practitioner, nurse anesthesia; nursing (PhD); primary care (MSN), including adult nurse practitioner, family nurse practitioner, nurse midwifery, women's health practitioner. *Accreditation:* AACN; AANA/CANAEP; ACNM/ACME (one or more programs are accredited). *Program availability:* Part-time. *Degree requirements:* For master's, thesis optional; for doctorate, thesis/dissertation. *Entrance requirements:* For master's, GRE General Test, BSN, minimum GPA of 3.0, Florida RN license; for doctorate, GRE General Test, BSN or MSN, minimum GPA of 3.0. Additional exam requirements/recommendations for international students: required—TOEFL (minimum score 550 paper-based). Electronic applications accepted.

**The University of North Carolina at Charlotte,** College of Health and Human Services, School of Nursing, Charlotte, NC 28223-0001. Offers adult-gerontology acute care nurse practitioner (Post-Master's Certificate); advanced clinical nursing (MSN), including adult psychiatric mental health, adult-gerontology acute care nurse practitioner, family nurse practitioner across the lifespan; family nurse practitioner across the lifespan (Post-Master's Certificate); nurse anesthesia (MSN), including nurse anesthesia across the lifespan; nurse anesthesia across the lifespan (Post-Master's Certificate); nursing (DNP); nursing administrator (Graduate Certificate); nursing educator (Graduate Certificate); systems/population nursing (MSN), including community/public health nursing, nurse administrator, nurse educator. *Accreditation:* AACN; AANA/CANAEP. *Program availability:* Part-time, blended/hybrid learning. *Students:* 126 full-time (96 women), 142 part-time (127 women); includes 70 minority (48 Black or African American, non-Hispanic/Latino; 8 Asian, non-Hispanic/Latino; 9 Hispanic/Latino; 5 Two or more races, non-Hispanic/Latino), 1 international. Average age 35. 347 applicants, 37% accepted, 104 enrolled. In 2019, 102 master's, 10 doctorates, 10 other advanced degrees awarded. Terminal master's awarded for partial completion of doctoral program. *Entrance requirements:* For master's, GRE General Test, current unrestricted license as Registered Nurse in North Carolina; BSN from nationally-accredited program; one year of professional nursing practice in acute/critical care; minimum overall GPA of 3.0 in last degree; completion of undergraduate statistics course with minimum grade of C; statement of purpose; for doctorate, GRE or MAT, master's degree in nursing in an advanced nursing practice specialty from nationally-accredited program; minimum overall GPA of 3.5 in MSN program; current RN licensure in U.S. at time of application with eligibility for NC licensure; essay; resume/curriculum vitae; professional recommendations; clinical hours; for other advanced degree, GRE. Additional exam requirements/recommendations for international students: required—TOEFL (minimum score 557 paper-based; 83 iBT), IELTS (minimum score 6.5), TOEFL (minimum score 557 paper-based, 83 iBT) or IELTS (6.5). *Application deadline:* Applications are processed on a rolling basis. Application fee: $75. Electronic applications accepted. *Expenses:* Contact institution. *Financial support:* In 2019–20, 6 students received support, including 4 research assistantships (averaging $4,856 per year), 2 teaching assistantships (averaging $3,615 per year); career-related internships or fieldwork, institutionally sponsored loans, scholarships/grants, traineeships, and unspecified assistantships also available. Support available to part-time students. Financial award application deadline: 3/1; financial award applicants required to submit FAFSA. *Unit head:* Dr. Dena Evans, Director, 704-687-7974, E-mail: devans37@uncc.edu. *Application contact:* Kathy B. Giddings, Director of Graduate Admissions, 704-687-5503, Fax: 704-687-1668, E-mail: gradadm@uncc.edu.
Website: http://nursing.uncc.edu/

**University of Northern Colorado,** Graduate School, College of Natural and Health Sciences, School of Nursing, Greeley, CO 80639. Offers adult-gerontology acute care nurse practitioner (MSN, DNP); family nurse practitioner (MSN, DNP); nursing education (PhD); nursing practice (DNP). *Accreditation:* AACN. *Program availability:* Online learning. *Degree requirements:* For master's, comprehensive exam, thesis or alternative; for doctorate, comprehensive exam, thesis/dissertation. *Entrance requirements:* For master's and doctorate, GRE General Test, minimum GPA of 3.0 in last 60 hours, BS in nursing, 2 letters of recommendation. Electronic applications accepted.

**University of Pennsylvania,** School of Nursing, Adult-Gerontology Acute Care Nurse Practitioner Program, Philadelphia, PA 19104. Offers MSN. *Accreditation:* AACN. *Program availability:* Part-time, online learning. *Students:* 26 full-time (25 women), 245 part-time (216 women); includes 69 minority (21 Black or African American, non-Hispanic/Latino; 29 Asian, non-Hispanic/Latino; 13 Hispanic/Latino; 6 Two or more races, non-Hispanic/Latino), 2 international. Average age 36. 193 applicants, 84% accepted, 143 enrolled. In 2019, 165 master's awarded. *Entrance requirements:* For master's, GRE General Test. Application fee: $80. *Financial support:* Application deadline: 4/1. *Unit head:* Assistant Dean of Admissions and Financial Aid, 866-867-6877, Fax: 215-573-8439, E-mail: admissions@nursing.upenn.edu. *Application contact:* Deborah Becker, Program Director, 215-898-0432, E-mail: debecker@nursing.upenn.edu.
Website: http://www.nursing.upenn.edu/

**University of Pennsylvania,** School of Nursing, Pediatric Acute Care Nurse Practitioner Program, Philadelphia, PA 19104. Offers MSN. *Accreditation:* AACN. *Program availability:* Part-time, online learning. *Students:* 8 full-time (all women), 51 part-time (48 women); includes 8 minority (2 Black or African American, non-Hispanic/Latino; 5 Asian, non-Hispanic/Latino; 1 Two or more races, non-Hispanic/Latino), 1 international. Average age 27. 46 applicants, 74% accepted, 30 enrolled. In 2019, 34 master's awarded. Application fee: $80.

**University of Puerto Rico - Medical Sciences Campus,** School of Nursing, San Juan, PR 00936-5067. Offers adult and elderly nursing (MSN); child and adolescent nursing (MSN); critical care nursing (MSN); family and community nursing (MSN); family nurse practitioner (MSN); maternity nursing (MSN); mental health and psychiatric nursing (MSN). *Accreditation:* AACN; AANA/CANAEP. *Entrance requirements:* For master's, GRE or EXADEP, interview, Puerto Rico RN license or professional license for international students, general and specific point average, article analysis. Electronic applications accepted.

**University of Rhode Island,** Graduate School, College of Nursing, Kingston, RI 02881. Offers acute care nurse practitioner (adult-gerontology focus) (Post Master's Certificate); adult gerontology nurse practitioner/clinical nurse specialist (Post Master's Certificate); adult-gerontological acute care nurse practitioner (MS); adult-gerontological nurse practitioner/clinical nurse specialist (MS); family nurse practitioner (MS, Post Master's Certificate); nursing (DNP, PhD); nursing education (MS, Post Master's Certificate). *Accreditation:* AACN; ACNM/ACME (one or more programs are accredited). *Program availability:* Part-time, evening/weekend, 100% online, blended/hybrid learning. *Faculty:* 27 full-time (26 women). *Students:* 51 full-time (47 women), 72 part-time (65 women); includes 21 minority (9 Black or African American, non-Hispanic/Latino; 5 Asian, non-Hispanic/Latino; 4 Hispanic/Latino; 2 Native Hawaiian or other Pacific Islander, non-Hispanic/Latino; 1 Two or more races, non-Hispanic/Latino), 6 international. 32 applicants, 88% accepted, 21 enrolled. In 2019, 34 master's, 9 doctorates, 1 other advanced degree awarded. *Entrance requirements:* For master's, GRE or MAT, 2 letters of recommendation, scholarly papers; for doctorate, GRE, 3 letters of recommendation, scholarly papers. Additional exam requirements/recommendations for international students: required—TOEFL. *Application deadline:* For fall admission, 2/15 for domestic students, 2/1 for international students; for spring admission, 10/15 for domestic students, 7/15 for international students. Application fee: $65. Electronic applications accepted. *Expenses: Tuition, area resident:* Full-time $13,734; part-time $763 per credit. Tuition, state resident: full-time $13,734; part-time $763 per credit. Tuition, nonresident: full-time $26,512; part-time $1473 per credit. *International tuition:* $26,512 full-time. *Required fees:* $1780; $52 per credit. $35 per term. One-time fee: $165. *Financial support:* In 2019–20, 7 teaching assistantships with tuition reimbursements (averaging $13,376 per year) were awarded. Financial award application deadline: 2/1; financial award applicants required to submit FAFSA. *Unit head:* Dr. Barbara Wolfe, Dean, 401-874-5324, E-mail: bwolfe@uri.edu. *Application contact:* Dr. Denise Coppa, Associate Professor/Interim Associate Dean for Graduate Programs, 401-874-5036, E-mail: dcoppa@uri.edu.
Website: http://www.uri.edu/nursing/

**University of Rochester,** School of Nursing, Rochester, NY 14642. Offers adult gerontological acute care nurse practitioner (MS); adult gerontological primary care nurse practitioner (MS); clinical nurse leader (MS); family nurse practitioner (MS); family psychiatric mental health nurse practitioner (MS); health care organization management and leadership (MS); nursing (DNP); nursing and health science (PhD); nursing education (MS); pediatric nurse practitioner (MS); pediatric nurse practitioner/neonatal nurse practitioner (MS). *Accreditation:* AACN. *Program availability:* Part-time, 100% online, blended/hybrid learning. Terminal master's awarded for partial completion of doctoral program. *Degree requirements:* For master's, comprehensive exam; for doctorate, thesis/dissertation. *Entrance requirements:* For master's, BS in nursing, RN license; for doctorate, GRE General Test (for PhD), B.S. degree, RN license most programs. Additional exam requirements/recommendations for international students: required—TOEFL (minimum score 560 paper-based; 88 iBT), TOEFL (minimum score 560 paper-based; 88 iBT) or IELTS (minimum score 6.5) recommended. Electronic applications accepted. *Expenses:* Contact institution.

**University of South Africa,** College of Human Sciences, Pretoria, South Africa. Offers adult education (M Ed); African languages (MA, PhD); African politics (MA, PhD); Afrikaans (MA, PhD); ancient history (MA, PhD); ancient Near Eastern studies (MA, PhD); anthropology (MA, PhD); applied linguistics (MA); Arabic (MA, PhD); archaeology (MA); art history (MA); Biblical archaeology (MA); Biblical studies (M Th, D Th, PhD); Christian spirituality (M Th, D Th); church history (M Th, D Th); classical studies (MA, PhD); clinical psychology (MA); communication (MA, PhD); comparative education (M Ed, Ed D); consulting psychology (D Admin, D Com, PhD); curriculum studies (M Ed, Ed D); development studies (M Admin, MA, D Admin, PhD); didactics (M Ed, Ed D); education (M Tech); education management (M Ed, Ed D); educational psychology (M Ed); English (MA); environmental education (M Ed); French (MA, PhD); German (MA, PhD); Greek (MA); guidance and counseling (M Ed); health studies (MA, PhD), including health sciences education (MA), health services management (MA), medical and surgical nursing science (critical care general) (MA), midwifery and neonatal nursing science (MA), trauma and emergency care (MA); history (MA, PhD); history of education (Ed D); inclusive education (M Ed, Ed D); information and communications technology policy and regulation (MA); information science (MA, MIS, PhD); international politics (MA, PhD); Islamic studies (MA, PhD); Italian (MA, PhD); Judaica (MA, PhD); linguistics (MA, PhD); mathematical education (M Ed); mathematics education (MA); missiology (M Th, D Th); modern Hebrew (MA, PhD); musicology (MA, MMus, D Mus, PhD); natural science education (M Ed); New Testament (M Th, D Th); Old Testament (D Th); pastoral therapy (M Th, D Th); philosophy (MA); philosophy of education (M Ed, Ed D); politics (MA, PhD); Portuguese (MA, PhD); practical theology (M Th, D Th); psychology (MA, MS, PhD); psychology of education (M Ed, Ed D); public health (MA); religious studies (MA, D Th, PhD); Romance languages (MA); Russian (MA, PhD); Semitic languages (MA, PhD); social behavior studies in HIV/AIDS (MA); social science (mental health) (MA); social science in development studies (MA); social science in psychology (MA); social science in social work (MA); social science in sociology (MA); social work (MSW, DSW, PhD); socio-education (M Ed, Ed D); sociolinguistics (MA); sociology (MA, PhD); Spanish (MA, PhD); systematic theology (M Th, D Th); TESOL (teaching English to speakers of other languages) (MA); theological ethics (M Th, D Th); theory of literature (MA, PhD); urban ministries (D Th); urban ministry (M Th).

**University of South Carolina,** The Graduate School, College of Nursing, Program in Advanced Practice Clinical Nursing, Columbia, SC 29208. Offers acute care nurse practitioner (Certificate); advanced practice clinical nursing (MSN). *Accreditation:* AACN. *Program availability:* Part-time, online learning. *Entrance requirements:* For master's, master's degree in nursing, RN license; for Certificate, MSN. Additional exam requirements/recommendations for international students: required—TOEFL (minimum score 570 paper-based). Electronic applications accepted.

**University of South Carolina,** The Graduate School, College of Nursing, Program in Clinical Nursing, Columbia, SC 29208. Offers acute care clinical specialist (MSN); acute care nurse practitioner (MSN); women's health nurse practitioner (MSN). *Accreditation:* AACN. *Program availability:* Part-time. *Degree requirements:* For master's, thesis or alternative. *Entrance requirements:* For master's, GRE General Test or MAT, BS in nursing, RN licensure. Additional exam requirements/recommendations for international students: required—TOEFL (minimum score 570 paper-based). Electronic applications accepted.

**University of South Florida,** College of Nursing, Tampa, FL 33612. Offers nurse anesthesia (DNP); nursing (MS, DNP), including adult-gerontology acute care nursing, adult-gerontology primary care nursing, family health nursing, nurse anesthesia (MS), nursing education (MS), occupational health nursing/adult-gerontology primary care nursing, oncology nursing/adult-gerontology primary care nursing (DNP), pediatric health nursing; nursing education (Post Master's Certificate); nursing science (PhD); simulation based academic fellowship in advanced pain management (Graduate Certificate). *Accreditation:* AACN; AANA/CANAEP. *Program availability:* Part-time. *Faculty:* 34 full-time (28 women), 2 part-time/adjunct (1 woman). *Students:* 265 full-time (207 women), 687 part-time (594 women); includes 343 minority (113 Black or African American, non-Hispanic/Latino; 1 American Indian or Alaska Native, non-Hispanic/Latino; 60 Asian, non-Hispanic/Latino; 141 Hispanic/Latino; 1 Native Hawaiian or other Pacific Islander, non-Hispanic/Latino; 27 Two or more races, non-Hispanic/Latino), 2 international. Average age 33. 955 applicants, 44% accepted, 343 enrolled. In 2019, 281 master's, 80 doctorates awarded. *Degree requirements:* For master's, comprehensive exam, thesis optional; for doctorate, comprehensive exam, thesis/dissertation (for some programs). *Entrance requirements:* For master's, GRE General Test, bachelor's in nursing or RN with Bachelor's in relevant field; current license as Registered Nurse; resume or CV; interview; pre-reqs may be required; for doctorate, GRE General Test (recommended), bachelor's degree in nursing from ACEN or CCNE regionally-accredited institution with minimum GPA of 3.0 in all coursework or in all upper-division coursework; current license as Registered Nurse in Florida; undergraduate statistics course with minimum B grade; 3 letters of recommendation; statement of goals; resume; interview. Additional exam requirements/recommendations for international students: required—TOEFL (minimum score 550 paper-based; 79 iBT). *Application deadline:* For fall admission, 12/15 for domestic and international students; for spring admission, 10/1 for domestic students, 9/15 for international students. Application fee: $30. Electronic applications accepted. *Financial support:* In 2019–20, 181 students received support, including 7 research assistantships with tuition reimbursements available (averaging $18,935 per year), 29 teaching assistantships with tuition reimbursements available (averaging $30,814 per year); tuition waivers (partial) and unspecified assistantships also available. Financial award application deadline: 2/1; financial award applicants required to submit FAFSA. *Unit head:* Dr. Victoria Rich, Dean, College of Nursing, 813-974-8939, Fax: 813-974-5418, E-mail: victoriarich@health.usf.edu. *Application contact:* Dr. Denise Maguire, Vice Dean, Graduate Programs, 813-396-9962, E-mail: dmaguire@health.usf.edu.
Website: http://health.usf.edu/nursing/index.htm

**The University of Texas Health Science Center at San Antonio,** School of Nursing, San Antonio, TX 78229-3900. Offers administrative management (MSN); adult-gerontology acute care nurse practitioner (PGC); advanced practice leadership (DNP); clinical nurse leader (MSN); executive administrative management (DNP); family nurse practitioner (MSN, PGC); nursing (MSN, PhD); nursing education (MSN, PGC); pediatric nurse practitioner primary care (PGC); psychiatric mental health nurse practitioner (PGC); public health nurse leader (DNP). *Accreditation:* AACN. *Program availability:* Part-time. Terminal master's awarded for partial completion of doctoral program. *Degree requirements:* For master's, thesis optional; for doctorate, comprehensive exam, thesis/dissertation.

**University of Virginia,** School of Nursing, Charlottesville, VA 22903. Offers acute and specialty care (MSN); acute care nurse practitioner (MSN); clinical nurse leadership (MSN); community-public health leadership (MSN); nursing (DNP, PhD); psychiatric mental health counseling (MSN); MSN/MBA. *Accreditation:* AACN. *Program availability:* Part-time. *Degree requirements:* For doctorate, comprehensive exam (for some programs), capstone project (DNP), dissertation (PhD). *Entrance requirements:* For master's, GRE General Test, MAT; for doctorate, GRE General Test. Additional exam requirements/recommendations for international students: required—TOEFL, IELTS. Electronic applications accepted.

**Wayne State University,** College of Nursing, Detroit, MI 48202. Offers adult gerontology acute care nurse practitioner (MSN); adult gerontology primary care nurse practitioner (MSN); advanced public health nursing (MSN); infant and mental health (DNP, PhD); neonatal nurse practitioner (MSN); nurse-midwifery (MSN); pediatric acute care nurse practitioner (MSN); pediatric primary care nurse practitioner (MSN); psychiatric mental health nurse practitioner (MSN); women's health nurse practitioner (MSN). *Accreditation:* AACN; ACNM/ACME. *Program availability:* Part-time. *Faculty:* 27. *Students:* 134 full-time (118 women), 216 part-time (187 women); includes 98 minority (51 Black or African American, non-Hispanic/Latino; 24 Asian, non-Hispanic/Latino; 6 Hispanic/Latino; 17 Two or more races, non-Hispanic/Latino), 18 international. Average age 33. 425 applicants, 37% accepted, 95 enrolled. In 2019, 58 master's, 31 doctorates awarded. *Degree requirements:* For doctorate, thesis/dissertation. *Entrance requirements:* For master's, Completed a Bachelor of Science in Nursing with a 3.0 or higher GPA. Official transcripts. Professional competence as documented by three references. Current Michigan Registered Nurse (RN) licensure. A personal statement of goals for graduate study; for doctorate, DNP: Minimum GPA of 3.0 or higher in BSN is required. Resume or Curriculum Vita that includes education, work and/or research experience. Two references, one from a doctorally prepared individual. RN license. PhD: BSN transcript; Two to three references from doctorally prepared individuals; goals statement; Resume or CV; Interview. Additional exam requirements/recommendations for international students: required—TOEFL (minimum score 101 iBT), TWE (minimum score 6), Michigan English Language Assessment Battery (minimum score 85); recommended—IELTS (minimum score 7). *Application deadline:* For fall admission, 1/31 for domestic students; for winter admission, 11/1 for domestic students. Applications are processed on a rolling basis. Application fee: $50. Electronic applications accepted. *Expenses:* $925.72 per credit hour in-state, $1,716.93 per credit hour out-of-state, $54.56 student service credit hour fee, $315.70 registration fee. *Financial support:* In 2019–20, 104 students received support, including 39 fellowships with tuition reimbursements available (averaging $6,456 per year), 1 research assistantship (averaging $24,950 per year), 5 teaching assistantships with tuition reimbursements available (averaging $25,000 per year); scholarships/grants, health care benefits, and unspecified assistantships also available. Support available to part-time students. Financial award application deadline: 3/1; financial award applicants required to submit FAFSA. *Unit head:* Dr. Laurie M Lauzon Clabo, Dean, College of Nursing, 313-577-4082, E-mail: laurie.lauzon.clabo@wayne.edu. *Application contact:* Dr. Laurie M Lauzon Clabo, Dean, College of Nursing, 313-577-4082, E-mail: laurie.lauzon.clabo@wayne.edu.
Website: http://nursing.wayne.edu/

**Winona State University,** College of Nursing and Health Sciences, Winona, MN 55987. Offers adult-gerontology acute care nurse practitioner (MS, DNP, Post Master's Certificate); adult-gerontology clinical nurse specialist (MS, DNP, Post Master's Certificate); adult-gerontology primary care nurse practitioner (MS, DNP, Post Master's Certificate); family nurse practitioner (MS, DNP, Post Master's Certificate); nurse educator (MS); nursing and organizational leadership (MS, DNP, Post Master's Certificate); practice and leadership innovations (DNP, Post Master's Certificate). *Accreditation:* AACN. *Program availability:* Part-time, online learning. *Degree requirements:* For master's, thesis; for doctorate, capstone. *Entrance requirements:* For master's, GRE (if GPA less than 3.0). Additional exam requirements/recommendations for international students: required—TOEFL (minimum score 550 paper-based).

**Wright State University,** Graduate School, College of Nursing and Health, Program in Nursing, Dayton, OH 45435. Offers administration of nursing and health care systems (MS); adult gerontology clinical nurse specialist (MS); adult-gerontology acute care nurse practitioner (MS); family nurse practitioner (MS); neonatal nurse practitioner (MS); pediatric nurse practitioner-acute care (MS); pediatric nurse practitioner-primary care (MS); psychiatric mental health nurse practitioner (MS); school nurse (MS). *Accreditation:* AACN. *Program availability:* Part-time, evening/weekend. *Degree requirements:* For master's, thesis or alternative. *Entrance requirements:* For master's, GRE General Test, BSN from ACEN-accredited college, Ohio RN license. Additional exam requirements/recommendations for international students: required—TOEFL.

# Adult Nursing

**Adelphi University,** College of Nursing and Public Health, Program in Adult Health Nurse, Garden City, NY 11530-0701. Offers MS. *Entrance requirements:* Additional exam requirements/recommendations for international students: required—TOEFL (minimum score 550 paper-based; 80 iBT), IELTS (minimum score 6.5). *Expenses:* Contact institution.

**Allen College,** Graduate Programs, Waterloo, IA 50703. Offers adult-gerontology acute care nurse practitioner (MSN); community/public health nursing (MSN); education (MSN); family nurse practitioner (MSN); health sciences (Ed D); leadership in health care delivery (MSN); leadership in health care informatics (MSN); nursing (DNP); occupational therapy (MS); psychiatric mental health nurse practitioner (MSN). *Accreditation:* AACN; ACEN. *Faculty:* 27 full-time (23 women), 9 part-time/adjunct (8 women). *Students:* 193 full-time (175 women), 95 part-time (84 women); includes 22 minority (6 Black or African American, non-Hispanic/Latino; 1 American Indian or Alaska Native, non-Hispanic/Latino; 4 Asian, non-Hispanic/Latino; 5 Hispanic/Latino; 6 Two or more races, non-Hispanic/Latino). Average age 32. 376 applicants, 53% accepted, 122 enrolled. *Application deadline:* For fall admission, 2/1 priority date for domestic students; for spring admission, 9/1 priority date for domestic students. Applications are processed on a rolling basis. Application fee: $50. Electronic applications accepted. *Financial support:* In 2019–20, 78 students received support. Federal Work-Study, institutionally sponsored loans, and scholarships/grants available. Support available to part-time students. Financial award application deadline: 8/1; financial award applicants required to submit FAFSA. *Unit head:* Dr. Bob Loch, Provost, 319-226-2040, Fax: 319-226-2070, E-mail: bob.loch@allencollege.edu. *Application contact:* Molly Quinn, Director of Admissions, 319-226-2001, Fax: 319-226-2010, E-mail: molly.quinn@allencollege.edu.
Website: http://www.allencollege.edu/

**Azusa Pacific University,** School of Nursing, Azusa, CA 91702-7000. Offers adult clinical nurse specialist (MSN); adult-gerontology nurse practitioner (MSN); family nurse practitioner (MSN); healthcare administration and leadership (MSN); nursing (MSN, DNP, PhD); nursing education (MSN); parent-child clinical nurse specialist (MSN); psychiatric mental health nurse practitioner (MSN). *Accreditation:* AACN. *Program availability:* Part-time, evening/weekend. *Degree requirements:* For master's, thesis optional. *Entrance requirements:* For master's, BSN.

**Bloomsburg University of Pennsylvania,** School of Graduate Studies, College of Science and Technology, Department of Nursing, Bloomsburg, PA 17815-1301. Offers adult and family nurse practitioner (MSN); community health (MSN); nurse anesthesia (MSN); nursing (MSN, DNP); nursing administration (MSN). *Accreditation:* AACN. *Degree requirements:* For master's, thesis (for some programs), clinical experience. *Entrance requirements:* For master's, minimum QPA of 3.0, personal statement, 2 letters of recommendation, nursing license. Additional exam requirements/recommendations for international students: required—TOEFL, IELTS. Electronic applications accepted. *Expenses:* Contact institution.

**Boston College,** William F. Connell School of Nursing, Chestnut Hill, MA 02467. Offers adult-gerontology primary care nurse practitioner (MS); family health nursing (MS); nurse anesthesia (MS); nursing (PhD); pediatric primary care nurse practitioner (MS), including pediatric and women's health; psychiatric-mental health nursing (MS); women's health nursing (MS); MBA/MS; MS/MA; MS/PhD. *Accreditation:* AACN; AANA/CANAEP (one or more programs are accredited). *Program availability:* Part-time. *Faculty:* 56 full-time (50 women). *Students:* 228 full-time (200 women), 82 part-time (71 women); includes 54 minority (10 Black or African American, non-Hispanic/Latino; 18 Asian, non-Hispanic/Latino; 20 Hispanic/Latino; 6 Two or more races, non-Hispanic/Latino), 7 international. Average age 28. 360 applicants, 56% accepted, 93 enrolled. In 2019, 107 master's, 7 doctorates awarded. *Degree requirements:* For master's, comprehensive exam; for doctorate, comprehensive exam, thesis/dissertation, computer literacy exam or foreign language. *Entrance requirements:* For master's, bachelor's degree; for doctorate, GRE General Test, bachelor's in Nursing and master's degree in nursing or related field. Additional exam requirements/recommendations for international students: required—TOEFL (minimum score 600 paper-based; 100 iBT), IELTS (minimum score 7.5). *Application deadline:* For fall admission, 3/15 for domestic and international students; for spring admission, 9/30 for domestic and international students. Application fee: $40. Electronic applications accepted. *Expenses:* Contact institution. *Financial support:* In 2019–20, 135 students received support, including 12 fellowships with full tuition reimbursements available (averaging $24,504 per year), 29 teaching assistantships (averaging $4,380 per year); scholarships/grants, health care benefits, tuition waivers (partial), and unspecified assistantships also available. Support available to part-time students. Financial award application deadline: 4/18; financial award applicants required to submit FAFSA. *Unit head:* Dr. Susan Gennaro, Dean, 617-552-4251, Fax: 617-552-0931, E-mail: susan.gennaro@bc.edu. *Application contact:* Sean Sendall, Assistant Dean, Graduate Enrollment and Data Analytics, 617-552-4745, Fax: 617-552-2121, E-mail: sean.sendall@bc.edu.
Website: http://www.bc.edu/cson

## Adult Nursing

**California Baptist University,** Program in Nursing, Riverside, CA 92504-3206. Offers clinical nurse specialist (MSN); family nurse practitioner (MSN); healthcare systems management (MSN); teaching-learning (MSN). *Accreditation:* AACN. *Program availability:* Part-time. *Degree requirements:* For master's, comprehensive exam or directed project thesis; capstone practicum. *Entrance requirements:* For master's, GRE or California Critical Thinking Skills Test; Test of Essential Academic Skills (TEAS), minimum undergraduate GPA of 3.0; completion of prerequisite courses with minimum grade of C; CPR certification; background check clearance; health clearance; drug testing; proof of health insurance; proof of motor vehicle insurance; three letters of recommendation; 1000-word essay; interview. Additional exam requirements/recommendations for international students: required—TOEFL (minimum score 80 iBT). Electronic applications accepted. *Expenses:* Contact institution.

**Clarkson College,** Master of Science in Nursing Program, Omaha, NE 68131. Offers adult nurse practitioner (MSN, Post-Master's Certificate); family nurse practitioner (MSN, Post-Master's Certificate); nursing education (MSN, Post-Master's Certificate); nursing health care leadership (MSN, Post-Master's Certificate). *Accreditation:* AANA/CANAEP; ACEN. *Program availability:* Part-time, evening/weekend, online learning. *Degree requirements:* For master's, on-campus skills assessment (family nurse practitioner, adult nurse practitioner), comprehensive exam or thesis. *Entrance requirements:* For master's, minimum GPA of 3.0, 2 references, resume. Additional exam requirements/recommendations for international students: required—TOEFL (minimum score 600 paper-based; 100 iBT). Electronic applications accepted.

**College of Staten Island of the City University of New York,** Graduate Programs, School of Health Sciences, Program in Adult-Gerontological Nursing, Staten Island, NY 10314-6600. Offers adult-gerontological nursing (MS, Post Master's Certificate), including clinical nurse specialist, nurse practitioner. *Program availability:* Part-time, evening/weekend. *Faculty:* 8. *Students:* 63. 43 applicants, 51% accepted, 13 enrolled. In 2019, 12 master's, 3 other advanced degrees awarded. *Degree requirements:* For master's, thesis optional, 42 credits with minimum of 500 supervised hours toward development of clinical competencies for primary care of the adult-gerontological population (15 core credits, advanced practice core of nine credits, specialty courses of 12 credits, and six credits of elective courses); for Post Master's Certificate, 12-21 credits with minimum of 500 supervised hours toward development of Clinical Nurse Specialist or Nurse Practitioner competencies. *Entrance requirements:* For master's, Bachelor's degree in nursing with minimum GPA of 3.0, 2 letters of recommendation, personal statement, current New York State RN license, minimum 1 year of full-time experience as registered nurse, 3 years of appropriate full-time clinical experience in nursing, completion of required nursing, science, and math courses; for Post Master's Certificate, master's degree in nursing; master's-level courses in pathophysiology, health assessment and pharmacology. Additional exam requirements/recommendations for international students: required—TOEFL (minimum score 550 paper-based; 79 iBT), IELTS (minimum score 6.5). *Application deadline:* For spring admission, 10/15 for domestic and international students. Applications are processed on a rolling basis. Application fee: $75. Electronic applications accepted. *Expenses:* For the Master's and Advanced Certificates, the tuition and fees are the same as for the majority of graduate programs. For the DNP $14,630 per year (Full Time NY State Resident); $620 per equated credit (part Time NY State Resident); $1,000 per equated credit Full/Part Time Non-State Resident). *Unit head:* Dr. Catherine Paradiso, 718-982-3838, E-mail: catherine.paradiso@csi.cuny.edu. *Application contact:* Sasha Spence, Associate Director for Graduate Admissions, 718-982-2019, Fax: 718-982-2500, E-mail: sasha.spence@csi.cuny.edu.
Website: http://www.csi.cuny.edu/nursing/graduate.html

**Columbia University,** School of Nursing, Program in Adult-Gerontology Primary Care Nurse Practitioner, New York, NY 10032. Offers MS, Adv C. *Accreditation:* AACN. *Program availability:* Part-time. *Entrance requirements:* For master's, GRE General Test, NCLEX, BSN, 1 year of clinical experience (preferred); for Adv C, MSN. Additional exam requirements/recommendations for international students: required—TOEFL (minimum score 100 iBT). Electronic applications accepted. *Expenses: Tuition:* Full-time $47,600; part-time $1880 per credit. One-time fee: $105.

**Creighton University,** College of Nursing, Omaha, NE 68178-0001. Offers adult gerontology acute care nurse practitioner (DNP, Post-Master's Certificate); adult gerontology nurse practitioner (DNP); clinical nurse leader (MSN, Post-Graduate Certificate); clinical systems administration (MSN, DNP); family nurse practitioner (DNP, Post-Master's Certificate); neonatal nurse practitioner (DNP, Post-Master's Certificate); nursing (Post-Graduate Certificate); pediatric acute care nurse practitioner (DNP, Post-Master's Certificate); psychiatric mental health nurse practitioner (DNP). *Accreditation:* AACN. *Program availability:* Part-time, blended/hybrid learning. *Degree requirements:* For master's, capstone project; for doctorate, scholarly project. *Entrance requirements:* For master's and doctorate, BSN from ACEN- or CCNE-accredited nursing school, minimum cumulative GPA of 3.0, personal statement, active unencumbered RN license with NE eligibility, undergraduate statistics course, physical assessment course or equivalent, three recommendation letters; for other advanced degree, MSN or MS in nursing from ACEN- or CCNE-accredited nursing school, minimum cumulative GPA of 3.0, active unencumbered RN license with NE eligibility. Additional exam requirements/recommendations for international students: required—TOEFL (minimum score 600 paper-based, 100 iBT) or IELTS. Electronic applications accepted. *Expenses:* Contact institution.

**Daemen College,** Nursing Programs, Amherst, NY 14226-3592. Offers adult nurse practitioner (MS, Post Master's Certificate); nurse executive leadership (Post Master's Certificate); nursing education (MS, Post Master's Certificate); nursing executive leadership (MS); nursing practice (DNP); palliative care nursing (Post Master's Certificate). *Accreditation:* ACEN. *Program availability:* Part-time. *Degree requirements:* For master's, thesis, degree completed in 4 years; minimum GPA of 3.0 and a minimum grade of B in all courses; for doctorate, thesis/dissertation, degree completed in 5 years; minimum GPA of 3.0 and a minimum grade of B in all courses. *Entrance requirements:* For master's, bachelor's degree in nursing from a NLNAC or CCNE accredited program, 1 year medical-surgical clinical experience, resume, official transcripts, undergraduate or graduate statistics course (grade of C or better), GPA 3.25 or above (below may be accepted on provisional basis), NYS Nursing license, interview with nursing faculty. Additional exam requirements/recommendations for international students: required—TOEFL (minimum score 77 paper-based), IELTS (minimum score 6.5). Electronic applications accepted. Application fee is waived when completed online.

**Duke University,** School of Nursing, Durham, NC 27708. Offers acute care pediatric nurse practitioner (MSN, Post-Graduate Certificate); adult-gerontology nurse practitioner (MSN, Post-Graduate Certificate), including acute care, primary care; family nurse practitioner (MSN, Post-Graduate Certificate); neonatal nurse practitioner (MSN, Post-Graduate Certificate); nurse anesthesia (DNP); nurse practitioner (DNP); nursing (PhD); nursing and health care leadership (MSN, Post-Graduate Certificate); nursing education (MSN, Post-Graduate Certificate); nursing informatics (MSN, Post-Graduate Certificate); pediatric nurse practitioner (MSN, Post-Graduate Certificate), including primary care; psychiatric mental health nurse practitioner (MSN, Post-Graduate Certificate); women's health nurse practitioner (MSN, Post-Graduate Certificate). *Accreditation:* AACN; AANA/CANAEP. *Program availability:* Part-time, evening/weekend, online with on-campus intensives. *Faculty:* 48 full-time (40 women), 32 part-time/adjunct (28 women). *Students:* 666 full-time (601 women), 157 part-time (139 women); includes 193 minority (61 Black or African American, non-Hispanic/Latino; 4 American Indian or Alaska Native, non-Hispanic/Latino; 57 Asian, non-Hispanic/Latino; 49 Hispanic/Latino; 1 Native Hawaiian or other Pacific Islander, non-Hispanic/Latino; 21 Two or more races, non-Hispanic/Latino), 8 international. Average age 34. 761 applicants, 33% accepted, 149 enrolled. In 2019, 213 master's, 74 doctorates, 18 other advanced degrees awarded. Terminal master's awarded for partial completion of doctoral program. *Degree requirements:* For master's, thesis optional; for doctorate, capstone project. *Entrance requirements:* For master's, MSN applicants are no longer required to take the GRE, 1 year of nursing experience (recommended), BSN, minimum GPA of 3.0, previous course work in statistics; for doctorate, GRE is required for the DNP in Nurse Anesthesia, BSN or MSN, minimum GPA of 3.0, resume, personal statement, graduate statistics and research methods course, current licensure as a registered nurse, transcripts from all post-secondary institutions; for Post-Graduate Certificate, MSN, licensure or eligibility as a professional nurse, transcripts from all post-secondary institutions, previous course work in statistics. Additional exam requirements/recommendations for international students: required—TOEFL (minimum score 100 iBT), IELTS (minimum score 7). *Application deadline:* For fall admission, 12/1 for domestic and international students; for spring admission, 5/1 for domestic and international students. Application fee: $50. Electronic applications accepted. *Expenses:* Contact institution. *Financial support:* Institutionally sponsored loans, scholarships/grants, and traineeships available. Support available to part-time students. Financial award applicants required to submit FAFSA. *Unit head:* Dr. Marion E. Broome, Dean/Vice Chancellor for Nursing Affairs/Associate Vice President for Academic Affairs for Nursing, 919-684-9446, Fax: 919-684-9414, E-mail: marion.broome@duke.edu. *Application contact:* Dr. Ernie Rushing, Director of Admissions and Recruitment, 919-668-6274, Fax: 919-668-4693, E-mail: ernie.rushing@dm.duke.edu.
Website: http://www.nursing.duke.edu/

**Eastern Michigan University,** Graduate School, College of Health and Human Services, School of Nursing, Ypsilanti, MI 48197. Offers nursing (MSN); teaching in health care systems (MSN, Graduate Certificate). *Accreditation:* AACN. *Program availability:* Part-time, evening/weekend, online learning. *Faculty:* 27 full-time (24 women). *Students:* 23 full-time (17 women), 36 part-time (29 women); includes 19 minority (6 Black or African American, non-Hispanic/Latino; 5 Asian, non-Hispanic/Latino; 7 Hispanic/Latino; 1 Two or more races, non-Hispanic/Latino), 1 international. Average age 37. 27 applicants, 7% accepted. In 2019, 14 master's, 3 other advanced degrees awarded. *Entrance requirements:* For master's, GRE General Test, Michigan RN license. Additional exam requirements/recommendations for international students: required—TOEFL. *Application deadline:* Applications are processed on a rolling basis. Application fee: $45. *Financial support:* Fellowships, research assistantships with full tuition reimbursements, teaching assistantships with full tuition reimbursements, career-related internships or fieldwork, Federal Work-Study, institutionally sponsored loans, scholarships/grants, tuition waivers (partial), and unspecified assistantships available. Support available to part-time students. Financial award applicants required to submit FAFSA. *Unit head:* Dr. Michael Williams, Director, 734-487-2310, Fax: 734-487-6946, E-mail: mwilliams@emich.edu. *Application contact:* Deanna Kowaleski, Coordinator, School of Nursing, 734-487-6599, Fax: 734-487-6946, E-mail: dkowales@emich.edu.
Website: http://www.emich.edu/nursing

**Emory University,** Nell Hodgson Woodruff School of Nursing, Atlanta, GA 30322-1100. Offers adult nurse practitioner (MSN); emergency nurse practitioner (MSN); family nurse practitioner (MSN); family nurse-midwife (MSN); health systems leadership (MSN); nurse-midwifery (MSN); pediatric nurse practitioner acute and primary care (MSN); women's health care (Title X) (MSN); women's health nurse practitioner (MSN); MSN/MPH. *Accreditation:* AACN; ACNM/ACME (one or more programs are accredited). *Program availability:* Part-time. *Entrance requirements:* For master's, GRE General Test or MAT, minimum GPA of 3.0, BS in nursing from an accredited institution, RN license and additional course work, 3 letters of recommendation. Additional exam requirements/recommendations for international students: required—TOEFL (minimum score 600 paper-based; 100 iBT). Electronic applications accepted. *Expenses:* Contact institution.

**Felician University,** Master of Science in Nursing Program, Lodi, NJ 07644-2117. Offers adult-gerontology nurse practitioner (MSN, PMC); executive leadership (MSN, PMC); family nurse practitioner (MSN, PMC); nursing education (MSN, PMC). *Accreditation:* AACN. *Program availability:* Evening/weekend, online only, 100% online, blended/hybrid learning. *Degree requirements:* For master's, thesis, clinical presentation; for PMC, thesis, education project. *Entrance requirements:* For master's, BSN; minimum GPA of 3.0; 2 letters of recommendation; NJ RN license; personal statement; for PMC, RN license, minimum GPA of 3.0. Additional exam requirements/recommendations for international students: required—TOEFL (minimum score 550 paper-based; 79 iBT), IELTS (minimum score 6.5), PTE (minimum score 56). Electronic applications accepted. Application fee is waived when completed online. *Expenses:* Contact institution.

**Florida International University,** Nicole Wertheim College of Nursing and Health Sciences, Nursing Program, Miami, FL 33199. Offers adult health nursing (MSN); family health (MSN); nurse anesthetist (MSN); nursing practice (DNP); nursing science research (PhD); pediatric nurse (MSN); psychiatric and mental health nursing (MSN); registered nurse (MSN). *Accreditation:* AACN; AANA/CANAEP. *Program availability:* Part-time, evening/weekend. *Faculty:* 14 full-time (12 women), 19 part-time/adjunct (14 women). *Students:* 279 full-time (188 women), 109 part-time (87 women); includes 309 minority (110 Black or African American, non-Hispanic/Latino; 1 American Indian or Alaska Native, non-Hispanic/Latino; 29 Asian, non-Hispanic/Latino; 166 Hispanic/Latino; 2 Native Hawaiian or other Pacific Islander, non-Hispanic/Latino; 1 Two or more races, non-Hispanic/Latino), 6 international. Average age 35. 154 applicants, 61% accepted, 88 enrolled. In 2019, 167 master's, 46 doctorates awarded. *Degree requirements:* For master's, thesis or alternative; for doctorate, comprehensive exam, thesis/dissertation. *Entrance requirements:* For master's, bachelor's degree in nursing, minimum undergraduate GPA of 3.0 in upper-level coursework, letters of recommendation; for doctorate, GRE, letters of recommendation, minimum undergraduate GPA of 3.0 in upper-level coursework, interview. Additional exam requirements/recommendations for international students: required—TOEFL (minimum score 550 paper-based; 80 iBT). *Application deadline:* For fall admission, 6/1 for domestic students, 4/1 for international students; for spring admission, 10/1 for domestic students, 9/1 for international students. Applications are processed on a rolling basis. Application fee: $30. Electronic applications accepted. *Expenses: Tuition, area resident:* Full-time $8912; part-time $446 per credit hour. Tuition, state resident: full-time $8912; part-time $446 per credit hour. Tuition, nonresident: full-time $21,393; part-time $992 per credit hour. *Required fees:* $2194. *Financial support:* Institutionally sponsored loans and scholarships/grants available. Financial award application deadline: 3/1; financial award applicants required to submit FAFSA. *Unit head:* Dr. Yhovana Gordon, Chair, 305-348-7733, Fax: 305-348-7051, E-mail: gordony@fiu.edu. *Application contact:* Nanett Rojas, Manager, Admissions Operations, 305-348-7464, Fax: 305-348-7441, E-mail: gradadm@fiu.edu.
Website: http://cnhs.fiu.edu/

**Florida Southern College,** School of Nursing and Health Sciences, Lakeland, FL 33801. Offers adult gerontology clinical nurse specialist (MSN); adult gerontology primary care nurse practitioner (MSN); family nurse practitioner (MSN); nurse educator (MSN); nursing administration (MSN). *Accreditation:* AACN. *Program availability:* Part-time, The Nurse Educator MSN degree concentration and NE postmasters certificate are fully online. The Nursing Administrative Leadership MSN degree concentration is delivered in blended/hybrid format. *Faculty:* 6 full-time (all women), 1 (woman) part-time/adjunct. *Students:* 145 full-time (131 women), 1 (woman) part-time; includes 70 minority (30 Black or African American, non-Hispanic/Latino; 11 Asian, non-Hispanic/Latino; 25 Hispanic/Latino; 4 Two or more races, non-Hispanic/Latino), 1 international. Average age 39. 81 applicants, 89% accepted, 50 enrolled. In 2019, 53 master's awarded. *Degree requirements:* For master's, comprehensive exam, 660 clinical hours (for Family Nurse Practitioner); 540 clinical hours (for Adult-Gerontology Primary Care Nurse Practitioner). *Entrance requirements:* For master's, Florida RN license, 3 letters of recommendation, professional statement, minimum GPA of 3.0 in the last 60 credit hours of BSN, BSN earned from a regionally accredited institution and a CCNE, CNEA, or ACEN accredited nursing program, resume, admission interview. Additional exam requirements/recommendations for international students: required—TOEFL (minimum score 550 paper-based; 79 iBT), IELTS (minimum score 6.5), International students from countries where English is not the standard for daily communication must submit either the TOEFL or IELTS. *Application deadline:* For fall admission, 6/1 for domestic and international students; for spring admission, 10/1 for domestic and international students. Applications are processed on a rolling basis. Electronic applications accepted. *Expenses:* DNP: $725 per credit hour tuition, $50 per semester technology fee (for 5-8 hours), $100 per semester technology fee (for 9-12 hours); MSN: $600 per credit hour tuition, $50 per semester technology fee (for 5-8 hours), $100 per semester technology fee (for 9-12 hours), $35 per semester insurance and lab supplies fees. *Financial support:* In 2019–20, 1 student received support. Employee tuition grants, athletic scholarships for students still eligible available. Financial award application deadline: 8/20; financial award applicants required to submit FAFSA. *Unit head:* Dr. Linda Comer, Dean, 863-680-3951, Fax: 863-680-3860, E-mail: lcomer@flsouthern.edu. *Application contact:* Kimberly Smith, Admission Counselor and Advisor for Nursing, 863-680-3090, Fax: 863-680-3872, E-mail: ksmith@flsouthern.edu.
Website: www.flsouthern.edu/sage

**George Mason University,** College of Health and Human Services, School of Nursing, Fairfax, VA 22030. Offers adult gerontology (DNP); adult/gerontological nurse practitioner (MSN); family nurse practitioner (MSN, DNP); nurse educator (MSN); nursing (PhD); nursing administration (MSN, DNP); nursing education (Certificate); psychiatric mental health (DNP). *Accreditation:* AACN. *Program availability:* Part-time, evening/weekend, blended/hybrid learning. *Degree requirements:* For master's, comprehensive exam (for some programs), thesis in clinical classes; for doctorate, comprehensive exam (for some programs), thesis/dissertation (for some programs). *Entrance requirements:* For master's, 2 official transcripts; expanded goals statement; resume; BSN from accredited institution; minimum GPA of 3.0 in last 60 credits of undergraduate work; 2 letters of recommendation; completion of undergraduate statistics and graduate-level bivariate statistics; certification in professional CPR; for doctorate, GRE, 2 official transcripts; expanded goals statement; resume; 2 recommendation letters; nursing license; at least 1 year of work experience as an RN; interview; writing sample; evidence of graduate-level course in applied statistics; master's degree in nursing with minimum GPA of 3.5; for Certificate, 2 official transcripts; expanded goals statement; resume; master's degree from accredited institution or currently enrolled with minimum GPA of 3.0. Additional exam requirements/recommendations for international students: required—TOEFL (minimum score 570 paper-based; 88 iBT), IELTS (minimum score 6.5), PTE (minimum score 59). Electronic applications accepted. *Expenses:* Contact institution.

**The George Washington University,** School of Nursing, Washington, DC 20052. Offers adult nurse practitioner (MSN, DNP, Post-Master's Certificate); clinical research administration (MSN); family nurse practitioner (MSN, Post-Master's Certificate); health care quality (MSN, Post-Master's Certificate); nursing leadership and management (MSN); nursing practice (DNP); palliative care nurse practitioner (Post-Master's Certificate). *Accreditation:* AACN.

**Georgia State University,** Byrdine F. Lewis School of Nursing, Atlanta, GA 30303. Offers adult health clinical nurse specialist/nurse practitioner (MS, Certificate); child health clinical nurse specialist/pediatric nurse practitioner (MS, Certificate); family nurse practitioner (MS, Certificate); family psychiatric mental health nurse practitioner (MS, Certificate); nursing (PhD); nursing leadership in healthcare innovations (MS), including nursing administration, nursing informatics; nutrition (MS); occupational therapy (MOT); perinatal clinical nurse specialist/women's health nurse practitioner (MS, Certificate); physical therapy (DPT); respiratory therapy (MS). *Accreditation:* AACN. *Program availability:* Part-time, blended/hybrid learning. *Faculty:* 57 full-time (40 women), 5 part-time/adjunct (4 women). *Students:* 388 full-time (290 women), 155 part-time (135 women); includes 217 minority (130 Black or African American, non-Hispanic/Latino; 47 Asian, non-Hispanic/Latino; 26 Hispanic/Latino; 14 Two or more races, non-Hispanic/Latino), 45 international. Average age 32. 480 applicants, 50% accepted, 164 enrolled. In 2019, 158 master's, 64 doctorates, 20 other advanced degrees awarded. *Degree requirements:* For doctorate, comprehensive exam, thesis/dissertation. *Entrance requirements:* For doctorate, GRE. Additional exam requirements/recommendations for international students: required—TOEFL. *Application deadline:* For fall admission, 2/1 priority date for domestic and international students; for spring admission, 9/15 for domestic and international students. Applications are processed on a rolling basis. Application fee: $50. Electronic applications accepted. *Expenses:* Contact institution. *Financial support:* In 2019–20, research assistantships with tuition reimbursements (averaging $1,666 per year), teaching assistantships with tuition reimbursements (averaging $1,920 per year) were awarded; scholarships/grants, tuition waivers (full and partial), and unspecified assistantships also available. Support available to part-time students. Financial award application deadline: 8/1; financial award applicants required to submit FAFSA. *Unit head:* Huanbiao Mo, Dean of Nursing. *Application contact:* Huanbiao Mo, Dean of Nursing.
Website: http://nursing.gsu.edu/

**Gwynedd Mercy University,** Frances M. Maguire School of Nursing and Health Professions, Gwynedd Valley, PA 19437-0901. Offers clinical nurse specialist (MSN), including gerontology, oncology, pediatrics; nurse educator (MSN); nurse practitioner (MSN), including adult health, pediatric health; nursing (DNP). *Accreditation:* ACEN. *Program availability:* Part-time, blended/hybrid learning. *Faculty:* 4 full-time (all women), 1 (woman) part-time/adjunct. *Students:* 52 full-time (47 women), 58 part-time (52 women); includes 28 minority (17 Black or African American, non-Hispanic/Latino; 9 Asian, non-Hispanic/Latino; 2 Hispanic/Latino). Average age 33. 35 applicants, 43% accepted, 14 enrolled. In 2019, 26 master's awarded. *Degree requirements:* For master's, thesis optional; for doctorate, evidence-based scholarly project. *Entrance requirements:* For master's, current nursing experience, physical assessment, course work in statistics, BSN from ACEN-accredited program, 2 letters of recommendation, personal interview. *Application deadline:* For fall admission, 4/15 for domestic and international students. Applications are processed on a rolling basis. Electronic applications accepted. *Expenses:* Contact institution. *Financial support:* Scholarships/grants, traineeships, and unspecified assistantships available. Financial award application deadline: 4/15. *Unit head:* Dr. Ann Phalen, Dean, 215-646-7300 Ext. 539, Fax: 215-641-5517, E-mail: phalen.a@gmercyu.edu. *Application contact:* Mary Hermann, Associate Dean, 215-646-7300, E-mail: herman.m@gmercyu.edu.
Website: http://www.gmercyu.edu/academics/graduate-programs/nursing

**Hunter College of the City University of New York,** Graduate School, Hunter-Bellevue School of Nursing, Gerontological/Adult Nurse Practitioner Program, New York, NY 10065-5085. Offers MS. *Accreditation:* AACN. *Program availability:* Part-time. *Degree requirements:* For master's, practicum. *Entrance requirements:* For master's, minimum GPA of 3.0, New York RN license, 2 years of professional practice experience, BSN. Additional exam requirements/recommendations for international students: required—TOEFL.

**Hunter College of the City University of New York,** Graduate School, Hunter-Bellevue School of Nursing, Program in Adult-Gerontology Clinical Nurse Specialist, New York, NY 10065-5085. Offers MS. *Accreditation:* AACN. *Degree requirements:* For master's, practicum. *Entrance requirements:* For master's, minimum GPA of 3.0, New York RN license, 2 years of professional practice experience, BSN. Additional exam requirements/recommendations for international students: required—TOEFL.

**Jacksonville University,** Brooks Rehabilitation College of Healthcare Sciences, Keigwin School of Nursing, Jacksonville, FL 32211. Offers adult gerontology acute care nurse practitioner (MSN), including clinical nurse educator, family nurse practitioner, family nurse practitioner/emergency nurse practitioner, leadership in the healthcare system, nursing informatics, psychiatric nurse practitioner; adult-gerontology acute care nurse practitioner (Certificate); clinical nurse educator (Certificate); emergency nurse practitioner (Certificate); family nurse practitioner (Certificate); family nurse practitioner/emergency nurse practitioner (Certificate); leadership in healthcare systems (Certificate); nursing informatics (MSN, Certificate); nursing practice (DNP); psychiatric mental health nurse practitioner (Certificate); MSN/MBA. *Accreditation:* AACN. *Program availability:* Part-time, 100% online, blended/hybrid learning. *Students:* 49 full-time (39 women), 463 part-time (406 women); includes 153 minority (85 Black or African American, non-Hispanic/Latino; 2 American Indian or Alaska Native, non-Hispanic/Latino; 22 Asian, non-Hispanic/Latino; 32 Hispanic/Latino; 1 Native Hawaiian or other Pacific Islander, non-Hispanic/Latino; 11 Two or more races, non-Hispanic/Latino), 1 international. Average age 39. 203 applicants, 39% accepted, 67 enrolled. In 2019, 215 master's, 15 doctorates awarded. *Degree requirements:* For master's, thesis; for doctorate, thesis/dissertation. *Entrance requirements:* For master's, GRE General Test or undergraduate GPA above 3.0, BSN from ACEN- or CCNE-accredited program; course work in statistics and physical assessment within last 5 years; Florida nursing license; CPR/BLS certification; 3 recommendations, 2 of which are professional references; statement of intent; resume; for doctorate, official transcripts from all colleges/universities attended; MSN from ACEN- or CCNE-accredited program; licensure as RN or ARNP; 3 letters of reference (2 clinical, 1 professional/academic); curriculum vitae; graded essay; for Certificate, GRE (minimum score of 290, waived if undergraduate nursing GPA is 3.0 or higher), official transcripts from MSN; minimum graduate nursing GPA of 3.0; graduation from CCNE- or ACEN-accredited MSN program; 3 recommendations, 2 of which are professional references; 2 years of work experience in critical care setting; statement of intent; resume. Additional exam requirements/recommendations for international students: required—TOEFL (minimum score 650 paper-based; 114 iBT), IELTS (minimum score 8). *Application deadline:* Applications are processed on a rolling basis. Application fee: $50. Electronic applications accepted. *Expenses:* Contact institution. *Financial support:* Federal Work-Study, institutionally sponsored loans, scholarships/grants, and health care benefits available. Support available to part-time students. Financial award application deadline: 3/15; financial award applicants required to submit FAFSA. *Unit head:* Dr. Hilary Morgan, Director, Graduate Nursing Programs/Associate Professor, 904-256-7601, E-mail: hmorgan@ju.edu. *Application contact:* Kristen Kirkendall, Associate Director of Graduate Admissions and Communications, 904-256-7169, E-mail: kgreene8@ju.edu.
Website: http://www.ju.edu/chs/nursing/

**Kent State University,** College of Nursing, Kent, OH 44242. Offers advanced nursing practice (DNP), including adult/gerontology acute care nurse practitioner (MSN, DNP); nursing (MSN, PhD), including adult/gerontology acute care nurse practitioner (MSN, DNP), adult/gerontology clinical nurse specialist (MSN), adult/gerontology primary care nurse practitioner (MSN), family nurse practitioner (MSN), nurse educator (MSN), nursing and healthcare management (MSN), pediatric primary care nurse practitioner (MSN), psychiatric/mental health nurse practitioner (MSN); MBA/MSN. *Accreditation:* AACN. *Program availability:* Part-time, online learning. *Faculty:* 28 full-time (26 women), 15 part-time/adjunct (13 women). *Students:* 138 full-time (123 women), 522 part-time (464 women); includes 80 minority (41 Black or African American, non-Hispanic/Latino; 16 Asian, non-Hispanic/Latino; 9 Hispanic/Latino; 1 Native Hawaiian or other Pacific Islander, non-Hispanic/Latino; 13 Two or more races, non-Hispanic/Latino), 7 international. Average age 35. 303 applicants, 68% accepted, 154 enrolled. In 2019, 156 master's, 8 doctorates awarded. *Degree requirements:* For master's, practicum for master's degrees; for doctorate, comprehensive exam, thesis/dissertation. *Entrance requirements:* For master's, GRE or GMAT, minimum GPA of 3.0, active RN license, statement of purpose, 3 letters of reference, undergraduate level statistics class (minimum C grade), baccalaureate or graduate-level nursing degree, curriculum vitae/resume; for doctorate, GRE, minimum GPA of 3.0, transcripts, 3 letters of reference, interview, active unrestricted Ohio RN license, statement of purpose, writing sample, curriculum vitae/resume, baccalaureate and master's degrees in nursing or DNP, undergraduate or graduate level statistics course with a minimum C grade. Additional exam requirements/recommendations for international students: required—TOEFL (minimum score 83 iBT), IELTS (minimum score 6.5), PTE (minimum score 55), Michigan English Language Assessment Battery (minimum score 78). *Application deadline:* For fall admission, 3/1 for domestic and international students; for spring admission, 10/1 for domestic and international students. Applications are processed on a rolling basis. Application fee: $45 ($70 for international students). Electronic applications accepted. *Financial support:* Federal Work-Study and scholarships/grants available. Financial award application deadline: 2/1. *Unit head:* Dr. Barbara Broome, Ph.D., Dean, 330-672-3777, E-mail: bbroome1@kent.edu. *Application contact:* Dr. Wendy A. Umberger, Ph.D., Associate Dean for Graduate Programs/Professor, 330-672-8813, E-mail: wlewando@kent.edu.
Website: http://www.kent.edu/nursing/

**La Salle University,** School of Nursing and Health Sciences, Program in Nursing, Philadelphia, PA 19141-1199. Offers adult gerontology primary care nurse practitioner (MSN, Certificate); adult health and illness clinical nurse specialist (MSN); adult-gerontology clinical nurse specialist (MSN, Certificate); clinical nurse leader (MSN); family primary care nurse practitioner (MSN, Certificate); gerontology (Certificate); nurse anesthetist (MSN, Certificate); nursing (MSN, Certificate); nursing administration (MSN, Certificate); nursing education (Certificate); nursing practice (DNP); nursing service administration (MSN); public health nursing (MSN, Certificate); school nursing (Certificate); MSN/MBA; MSN/MPH. *Accreditation:* AACN. *Program availability:* Part-time, evening/weekend, 100% online. *Degree requirements:* For doctorate, minimum of 1,000 hours of post baccalaureate clinical practice supervised by preceptors. *Entrance*

*requirements:* For master's, GRE, MAT, or GMAT (for students with BSN GPA of less than 3.2), baccalaureate degree in nursing from ACEN- or CCNE-accredited program or an MSN Bridge program; Pennsylvania RN license; 2 letters of reference; resume; statement of philosophy articulating professional values and future educational goal; 1 year of work experience as a registered nurse; for doctorate, GRE (waived for applicants with MSN cumulative GPA of 3.7 or above), MSN, master's degree, MBA or MHA from nationally-accredited program; resume or curriculum vitae; 2 letters of reference; interview; for Certificate, GRE, MAT, or GMAT (for students with BSN GPA of less than 3.2, baccalaureate degree in nursing from ACEN- or CCNE-accredited program or an MSN Bridge program; Pennsylvania RN license; 2 letters of reference; resume; statement of philosophy articulating professional values and future educational goal; 1 year of work experience as a registered nurse. Additional exam requirements/recommendations for international students: required—TOEFL. Electronic applications accepted. Application fee is waived when completed online. *Expenses:* Contact institution.

**Lehman College of the City University of New York,** School of Health Sciences, Human Services and Nursing, Department of Nursing, Bronx, NY 10468-1589. Offers adult health nursing (MS); nursing of older adults (MS); parent-child nursing (MS); pediatric nurse practitioner (MS). *Accreditation:* AACN. *Program availability:* Part-time, evening/weekend. *Entrance requirements:* For master's, bachelor's degree in nursing, New York RN license. *Expenses: Tuition, area resident:* Full-time $5545; part-time $470 per credit. Tuition, nonresident: part-time $855 per credit. *Required fees:* $240.

**Lewis University,** College of Nursing and Health Sciences, Program in Nursing, Romeoville, IL 60446. Offers adult gerontology clinical nurse specialist (MSN); adult gerontology primary care nurse practitioner (MSN); family nurse practitioner (MSN); healthcare systems leadership (MSN); nursing education (MSN); school nurse (MSN). *Accreditation:* AACN. *Program availability:* Part-time, evening/weekend, 100% online, blended/hybrid learning. *Students:* 7 full-time (all women), 411 part-time (372 women); includes 113 minority (15 Black or African American, non-Hispanic/Latino; 43 Asian, non-Hispanic/Latino; 47 Hispanic/Latino; 8 Two or more races, non-Hispanic/Latino), 2 international. Average age 35. *Degree requirements:* For master's, clinical practicum. *Entrance requirements:* For master's, minimum undergraduate GPA of 3.0, degree in nursing, RN license, letter of recommendation, interview, resume or curriculum vitae. Additional exam requirements/recommendations for international students: required—TOEFL (minimum score 550 paper-based; 80 iBT), IELTS. *Application deadline:* For fall admission, 5/1 priority date for international students; for spring admission, 11/15 priority date for international students. Applications are processed on a rolling basis. Application fee: $40. Electronic applications accepted. *Financial support:* Federal Work-Study, scholarships/grants, tuition waivers (full and partial), and unspecified assistantships available. Financial award application deadline: 5/1; financial award applicants required to submit FAFSA. *Unit head:* Dr. Mary Desmond, Program Director. *Application contact:* Nancy Wiksten, Graduate Admission Counselor, 815-836-5610, E-mail: grad@lewisu.edu.

**Loma Linda University,** School of Nursing, Program in Nurse Educator, Loma Linda, CA 92350. Offers adult/gerontology (MS); obstetrics-pediatrics (MS). *Accreditation:* AACN. *Program availability:* Part-time. *Degree requirements:* For master's, thesis or alternative. *Entrance requirements:* For master's, GRE General Test, BSN, minimum GPA of 3.0, RN license. Additional exam requirements/recommendations for international students: required—TOEFL. Electronic applications accepted.

**Long Island University - Brooklyn,** Harriet Rothkopf Heilbrunn School of Nursing, Brooklyn, NY 11201-8423. Offers adult nurse practitioner (MS, Advanced Certificate); family nurse practitioner (MS, Advanced Certificate); nurse educator (MS). *Accreditation:* AACN. *Program availability:* Part-time, evening/weekend, blended/hybrid learning. *Entrance requirements:* Additional exam requirements/recommendations for international students: required—TOEFL or IELTS. Electronic applications accepted.

**Loyola University Chicago,** Graduate School, Marcella Niehoff School of Nursing, Maywood, IL 60153. Offers adult clinical nurse specialist (MSN, Certificate); adult nurse practitioner (Certificate); dietetics (MS); family nurse practitioner (Certificate); family, adult, and women's health nurse practitioner (MSN); health systems leadership (MSN); healthcare quality using education in safety and technology (DNP); infection prevention (MSN, DNP); nursing science (PhD); women's health clinical nurse specialist (Certificate). *Accreditation:* AACN. *Program availability:* Part-time, blended/hybrid learning. *Faculty:* 36 full-time (32 women), 18 part-time/adjunct (16 women). *Students:* 182 full-time (168 women), 198 part-time (175 women); includes 95 minority (26 Black or African American, non-Hispanic/Latino; 29 Asian, non-Hispanic/Latino; 37 Hispanic/Latino; 3 Two or more races, non-Hispanic/Latino), 7 international. Average age 35. 148 applicants, 59% accepted, 54 enrolled. In 2019, 84 master's, 16 doctorates, 27 other advanced degrees awarded. *Degree requirements:* For master's, comprehensive exam; for doctorate, thesis/dissertation, qualifying examination (for PhD); project (for DNP). *Entrance requirements:* For master's, BSN, minimum nursing GPA of 3.0, Illinois RN license, 3 letters of recommendation, 1000 hours of experience in area of specialty prior to starting clinical rotations, personal statement; for doctorate, BSN or MSN, minimum GPA of 3.0, professional nursing license, 3 letters of recommendation, personal statement. Additional exam requirements/recommendations for international students: required—TOEFL (minimum score 550 paper-based; 79 iBT), IELTS (minimum score 6), PTE (minimum score 53). *Application deadline:* For fall admission, 7/1 priority date for domestic and international students; for spring admission, 12/1 priority date for domestic and international students; for summer admission, 4/1 priority date for domestic and international students. Applications are processed on a rolling basis. Electronic applications accepted. Application fee is waived when completed online. *Expenses:* Contact institution. *Financial support:* In 2019–20, 53 students received support, including 3 research assistantships with full tuition reimbursements available (averaging $18,000 per year), 1 teaching assistantship with full tuition reimbursement available (averaging $18,000 per year); scholarships/grants, unspecified assistantships, and Nurse Faculty Loan Program also available. Financial award application deadline: 5/1; financial award applicants required to submit FAFSA. *Unit head:* Dr. Lorna Finnegan, Dean and Professor, 708-216-5448, Fax: 708-216-9555, E-mail: lornaf@luc.edu. *Application contact:* Glenda Runnels, Enrollment Advisor, 708-216-3751, Fax: 708-216-9555, E-mail: grunnels@luc.edu.
Website: http://www.luc.edu/nursing/

**Madonna University,** Program in Nursing, Livonia, MI 48150-1173. Offers adult health: chronic health conditions (MSN); adult nurse practitioner (MSN); nursing administration (MSN); MSN/MSBA. *Accreditation:* AACN. *Program availability:* Part-time. *Degree requirements:* For master's, thesis or alternative. *Entrance requirements:* For master's, GRE General Test, Michigan nursing license. Electronic applications accepted. *Expenses: Tuition:* Full-time $15,930; part-time $885 per credit hour. Tuition and fees vary according to degree level and program.

**Marian University,** School of Nursing and Health Professions, Fond du Lac, WI 54935-4699. Offers adult nurse practitioner (MSN); nurse educator (MSN); thanatology (MS). *Accreditation:* AACN. *Program availability:* Part-time, evening/weekend. *Degree requirements:* For master's, thesis, 675 clinical practicum hours. *Entrance requirements:* For master's, 3 letters of professional recommendation; undergraduate work in nursing research, statistics, health assessment. Additional exam requirements/recommendations for international students: required—TOEFL (minimum score 525 paper-based; 70 iBT). Electronic applications accepted. *Expenses:* Contact institution.

**Marquette University,** Graduate School, College of Nursing, Milwaukee, WI 53201-1881. Offers acute care nurse practitioner (Certificate); adult clinical nurse specialist (Certificate); adult nurse practitioner (Certificate); advanced practice nursing (MSN, DNP), including adult-older adult acute care (DNP), adults (MSN), adults-older adults (DNP), clinical nurse leader (MSN), health care systems leadership (DNP), nurse-midwifery (MSN), older adults (MSN), pediatrics-acute care, pediatrics-primary care, primary care (DNP), systems leadership and healthcare quality (MSN); family nurse practitioner (Certificate); nurse-midwifery (Certificate); nursing (PhD); pediatric acute care (Certificate); pediatric primary care (Certificate); systems leadership and healthcare quality (Certificate). *Accreditation:* AACN; AANA/CANAEP; ACNM/ACME. Terminal master's awarded for partial completion of doctoral program. *Degree requirements:* For master's, comprehensive exam, thesis or alternative. *Entrance requirements:* For master's, GRE General Test, BSN, Wisconsin RN license, official transcripts from all current and previous colleges/universities except Marquette, three completed recommendation forms, resume, written statement of professional goals; for doctorate, GRE General Test, official transcripts from all current and previous colleges/universities except Marquette, three letters of recommendation, resume, written statement of professional goals, sample of scholarly writing. Additional exam requirements/recommendations for international students: required—TOEFL (minimum score 530 paper-based). Electronic applications accepted.

**Maryville University of Saint Louis,** Myrtle E. and Earl E. Walker College of Health Professions, The Catherine McAuley School of Nursing, St. Louis, MO 63141-7299. Offers acute care nurse practitioner (MSN); adult gerontology nurse practitioner (MSN); advanced practice nursing (DNP); family nurse practitioner (MSN); pediatric nurse practitioner (MSN). *Accreditation:* AACN. *Program availability:* 100% online, blended/hybrid learning. *Faculty:* 14 full-time (all women), 131 part-time/adjunct (114 women). *Students:* 103 full-time (91 women), 3,493 part-time (3,050 women); includes 1,039 minority (530 Black or African American, non-Hispanic/Latino; 41 American Indian or Alaska Native, non-Hispanic/Latino; 157 Asian, non-Hispanic/Latino; 221 Hispanic/Latino; 90 Two or more races, non-Hispanic/Latino), 9 international. Average age 37. In 2019, 1,012 master's, 54 doctorates awarded. *Degree requirements:* For master's, practicum. *Entrance requirements:* For master's, BSN, current licensure, minimum GPA of 3.0, 3 letters of recommendation, curriculum vitae. Additional exam requirements/recommendations for international students: required—TOEFL (minimum score 550 paper-based). *Application deadline:* Applications are processed on a rolling basis. Electronic applications accepted. *Expenses:* Contact institution. *Financial support:* Federal Work-Study and campus employment available. Support available to part-time students. Financial award application deadline: 4/1; financial award applicants required to submit FAFSA. *Unit head:* Karla Larson, Assistant Dean Nursing, 314-529-6856, Fax: 314-529-9139, E-mail: klarson@maryville.edu. *Application contact:* Jeannie DeLuca, Director of Admissions and Advising, 314-929-9355, Fax: 314-529-9927, E-mail: jdeluca@maryville.edu.
Website: http://www.maryville.edu/hp/nursing/

**Medical University of South Carolina,** College of Nursing, Adult-Gerontology Health Nurse Practitioner Program, Charleston, SC 29425. Offers MSN, DNP. *Program availability:* Part-time, online learning. *Degree requirements:* For master's, comprehensive exam (for some programs), thesis optional; for doctorate, final project. *Entrance requirements:* For master's, BSN from nationally-accredited program, minimum nursing and cumulative GPA of 3.0, undergraduate-level statistics course, active RN License, 3 confidential references, current curriculum vitae or resume, essay; for doctorate, BSN from nationally-accredited program, minimum nursing and cumulative GPA of 3.0, undergraduate-level statistics course, active RN License, 3 confidential references, current curriculum vitae or resume, personal essay (for DNP). Additional exam requirements/recommendations for international students: required—TOEFL (minimum score 550 paper-based; 80 iBT). Electronic applications accepted.

**Monmouth University,** Graduate Studies, Marjorie K. Unterberg School of Nursing and Health Studies, West Long Branch, NJ 07764-1898. Offers adult-gerontological primary care nurse practitioner (Post-Master's Certificate); forensic nursing (MSN). *Accreditation:* AACN. *Program availability:* Part-time, evening/weekend, 100% online, blended/hybrid learning. *Faculty:* 13 full-time (all women), 9 part-time/adjunct (8 women). *Students:* 1 (woman) full-time, 284 part-time (261 women); includes 108 minority (37 Black or African American, non-Hispanic/Latino; 38 Asian, non-Hispanic/Latino; 32 Hispanic/Latino; 1 Two or more races, non-Hispanic/Latino). Average age 39. In 2019, 100 master's, 14 doctorates, 10 other advanced degrees awarded. *Degree requirements:* For master's, practicum (for some tracks); for doctorate, practicum, capstone course. *Entrance requirements:* For master's, GRE General Test (waived for MSN applicants with minimum B grade in each of the first four courses and for MS applicants with master's degree), BSN with minimum GPA of 2.75, current RN license, proof of liability and malpractice policy, personal statement, two letters of recommendation, college course work in health assessment, resume; CASPA application (for MS); for doctorate, accredited master's nursing program degree with minimum GPA of 3.2, active RN license, national certification as nurse practitioner or nurse administrator, working knowledge of statistics, statement of goals and vision for change, 2 letters of recommendation (professional or academic), resume, interview. Additional exam requirements/recommendations for international students: required—TOEFL (minimum score 550 paper-based; 79 iBT), IELTS (minimum score 6) or Michigan English Language Assessment Battery (minimum score 77). *Application deadline:* For fall admission, 7/15 priority date for domestic students, 6/1 for international students; for spring admission, 12/1 priority date for domestic students, 11/1 for international students; for summer admission, 5/1 for domestic students. Applications are processed on a rolling basis. Application fee: $50. Electronic applications accepted. *Expenses:* $1,233 per credit. *Financial support:* In 2019–20, 251 students received support. Research assistantships, teaching assistantships, scholarships/grants, and unspecified assistantships available. Support available to part-time students. Financial award applicants required to submit FAFSA. *Unit head:* Dr. Ann Marie Mauro, Dean, 732-571-3443, Fax: 732-263-5131, E-mail: amauro@monmouth.edu. *Application contact:* Laurie Kuhn, Associate Director of Graduate Admission, 732-571-3452, Fax: 732-263-5123, E-mail: gradadm@monmouth.edu.
Website: https://www.monmouth.edu/graduate/nursing-programs-of-study/

**Mount Carmel College of Nursing,** Nursing Program, Columbus, OH 43222. Offers adult gerontology acute care nurse practitioner (MS); adult health clinical nurse specialist (MS); family nurse practitioner (MS); nursing (DNP); nursing administration (MS); nursing education (MS). *Accreditation:* AACN. *Program availability:* Part-time. *Faculty:* 6 full-time (all women), 10 part-time/adjunct (9 women). *Students:* 101 full-time (82 women), 109 part-time (95 women); includes 43 minority (27 Black or African American, non-Hispanic/Latino; 4 Asian, non-Hispanic/Latino; 5 Hispanic/Latino; 7 Two or more races, non-Hispanic/Latino). Average age 32. 133 applicants, 84% accepted, 95 enrolled. In 2019, 66 master's, 2 doctorates awarded. *Degree requirements:* For master's, professional manuscript; for doctorate, practicum. *Entrance requirements:* For master's, letters of recommendation, statement of purpose, current resume, baccalaureate degree in nursing, current Ohio RN license, minimum cumulative GPA of

3.0; for doctorate, master's degree in nursing from program accredited by either ACEN or CCNE. Additional exam requirements/recommendations for international students: required—TOEFL (minimum score 550 paper-based; 80 iBT). *Application deadline:* For fall admission, 2/1 priority date for domestic students; for spring admission, 11/1 priority date for domestic students. Applications are processed on a rolling basis. Application fee: $30. Electronic applications accepted. *Expenses: Tuition:* Full-time $27,936; part-time $27,936 per year. *Required fees:* $360. *Financial support:* In 2019–20, 13 students received support. Institutionally sponsored loans and scholarships/grants available. Financial award application deadline: 3/1; financial award applicants required to submit FAFSA. *Unit head:* Dr. Jami Nininger, Interim Associate Dean Graduate Studies, 614-234-1777, Fax: 614-234-2875, E-mail: jnininger@mccn.edu. *Application contact:* Dr. Kim Campbell, Director of Recruitment and Admissions, 614-234-5144, Fax: 614-234-5427, E-mail: kcampbell@mccn.edu.
Website: www.mccn.edu

**Mount Saint Mary College,** School of Nursing, Newburgh, NY 12550. Offers adult nurse practitioner (MS, Advanced Certificate, including nursing education (MS); nursing management (MS); nursing education (Advanced Certificate). *Accreditation:* AACN. *Program availability:* Part-time, evening/weekend, blended/hybrid learning. *Faculty:* 6 full-time (all women), 11 part-time/adjunct (10 women). *Students:* 1 (woman) full-time, 186 part-time (171 women); includes 36 minority (16 Black or African American, non-Hispanic/Latino; 1 American Indian or Alaska Native, non-Hispanic/Latino; 5 Asian, non-Hispanic/Latino; 11 Hispanic/Latino; 1 Native Hawaiian or other Pacific Islander, non-Hispanic/Latino; 2 Two or more races, non-Hispanic/Latino), 1 international. Average age 37. 37 applicants, 84% accepted, 22 enrolled. In 2019, 33 master's, 4 other advanced degrees awarded. *Degree requirements:* For master's, research utilization project. *Entrance requirements:* For master's, BSN, minimum GPA of 3.0, RN license. Additional exam requirements/recommendations for international students: required—TOEFL (minimum score 80 iBT). *Application deadline:* For fall admission, 6/3 priority date for domestic students; for spring admission, 10/31 priority date for domestic students. Applications are processed on a rolling basis. Application fee: $45. Electronic applications accepted. Application fee is waived when completed online. *Expenses: Tuition:* Full-time $15,192; part-time $844 per credit. *Required fees:* $180; $90 per semester. *Financial support:* In 2019–20, 10 students received support. Scholarships/grants and unspecified assistantships available. Financial award application deadline: 4/15; financial award applicants required to submit FAFSA. *Unit head:* Christine Berte, Graduate Coordinator, 845-569-3141, Fax: 845-562-6762, E-mail: christine.berte@msmc.edu. *Application contact:* Eileen Bardney, Director of Admissions, 845-569-3254, Fax: 845-569-3438, E-mail: GraduateAdmissions@msmc.edu.
Website: http://www.msmc.edu/Academics/Graduate_Programs/Master_of_Science_in_Nursing

**Neumann University,** Graduate Program in Nursing, Aston, PA 19014-1298. Offers adult-gerontology nurse practitioner (MS, Certificate). *Accreditation:* ACEN. *Program availability:* Part-time, evening/weekend. *Entrance requirements:* For master's, official transcripts from all institutions attended, resume, letter of intent, current registered nursing license, two letters of reference; for Certificate, BSN, MSN, official transcripts from all institutions attended, resume, letter of intent, current registered nursing license, two official letters of reference. Additional exam requirements/recommendations for international students: required—TOEFL (minimum score 84 iBT). Electronic applications accepted.

**New York University,** Rory Meyers College of Nursing, Doctor of Nursing Practice Program, New York, NY 10012-1019. Offers nursing (DNP), including adult-gerontology acute care nurse practitioner, adult-gerontology primary care nurse practitioner, family nurse practitioner, nurse-midwifery, pediatrics nurse practitioner, psychiatric-mental health nurse practitioner. *Accreditation:* AACN. *Program availability:* Part-time, evening/weekend. *Degree requirements:* For doctorate, thesis/dissertation, project. *Entrance requirements:* For doctorate, MS, RN license, interview, Nurse Practitioner Certification, writing sample. Additional exam requirements/recommendations for international students: required—TOEFL (minimum score 100 iBT), IELTS (minimum score 7). Electronic applications accepted. *Expenses:* Contact institution.

**New York University,** Rory Meyers College of Nursing, Programs in Advanced Practice Nursing, New York, NY 10012-1019. Offers adult-gerontology acute care nurse practitioner (MS, Advanced Certificate); adult-gerontology primary care nurse practitioner (MS, Advanced Certificate); family nurse practitioner (MS, Advanced Certificate); gerontology nurse practitioner (Advanced Certificate); nurse-midwifery (MS, Advanced Certificate); nursing administration (MS, Advanced Certificate); nursing education (MS, Advanced Certificate); nursing informatics (MS, Advanced Certificate); pediatrics nurse practitioner (MS, Advanced Certificate); psychiatric-mental health nurse practitioner (MS, Advanced Certificate); MS/MPH. *Accreditation:* AACN; ACNM/ACME. *Program availability:* Part-time, evening/weekend. *Degree requirements:* For master's, thesis (for some programs), capstone. *Entrance requirements:* For master's, BS in nursing, AS in nursing with another BS/BA, interview, RN license, 1 year of clinical experience (3 for the MS in nursing education program); for Advanced Certificate, master's degree in nursing. Additional exam requirements/recommendations for international students: required—TOEFL (minimum score 100 iBT), IELTS (minimum score 7). Electronic applications accepted. *Expenses:* Contact institution.

**North Park University,** School of Nursing and Health Sciences, Chicago, IL 60625-4895. Offers advanced practice nursing (MS); leadership and management (MS); MBA/MS; MM/MSN; MS/MHR; MS/MNA. *Accreditation:* AACN. *Program availability:* Part-time, evening/weekend. *Degree requirements:* For master's, thesis. *Entrance requirements:* For master's, GMAT, MAT.

**Nova Southeastern University,** Ron and Kathy Assaf College of Nursing, Fort Lauderdale, FL 33314-7796. Offers advanced practice registered nurse (MSN), including adult-gerontology acute care nurse practitioner, family nurse practitioner, psychiatric mental health nurse practitioner; executive nurse leadership (MSN); nursing (PhD), including nursing education; nursing education (MSN); nursing informatics (MSN); nursing practice (DNP). *Accreditation:* AACN. *Program availability:* Part-time, evening/weekend, 100% online, blended/hybrid learning, annual one-week summer institute delivered face-to-face on main campus. *Faculty:* 32 full-time (29 women), 34 part-time/adjunct (31 women). *Students:* 4 full-time (3 women), 658 part-time (585 women); includes 427 minority (182 Black or African American, non-Hispanic/Latino; 35 Asian, non-Hispanic/Latino; 197 Hispanic/Latino; 13 Two or more races, non-Hispanic/Latino), 3 international. Average age 38. 157 applicants, 93% accepted, 146 enrolled. In 2019, 184 master's, 12 doctorates awarded. *Degree requirements:* For doctorate, comprehensive exam, thesis/dissertation. *Entrance requirements:* For master's, minimum GPA of 3.0, RN, BSN, BS or BA; for doctorate, minimum GPA of 3.5, MSN, RN. Additional exam requirements/recommendations for international students: recommended—TOEFL. *Application deadline:* For fall admission, 8/1 for domestic students, 3/1 for international students; for winter admission, 12/9 for domestic students, 11/1 for international students. Applications are processed on a rolling basis. Application fee: $50. Electronic applications accepted. *Expenses:* Contact institution. *Financial support:* Application deadline: 4/15; applicants required to submit FAFSA. *Unit head:* Dr. Marcella M. Rutherford, Dean, 954-262-1963, E-mail: rmarcell@nova.edu. *Application contact:* Dianna Murphey, Director of Operations, 954-262-1975, E-mail:

dgardner1@nova.edu.
Website: http://www.nova.edu/nursing/

**Old Dominion University,** College of Health Sciences, School of Nursing, Adult Gerontology Nursing Emphasis, Norfolk, VA 23529. Offers adult gerontology clinical nurse specialist/administrator (MSN); adult gerontology clinical nurse specialist/educator (MSN); advanced practice (DNP); neonatal clinical nurse specialist (MSN); pediatric clinical nurse specialist (MSN). *Program availability:* Part-time, online only, blended/hybrid learning. *Degree requirements:* For master's, comprehensive exam, internship, practicum. *Entrance requirements:* For master's, GRE or MAT (waived with a GPA above 3.5), undergraduate health/physical assessment course, statistics, 3 letters of recommendation, essay, resume, transcripts. Additional exam requirements/recommendations for international students: required—TOEFL. Electronic applications accepted. *Expenses:* Contact institution.

**Purdue University Fort Wayne,** College of Health and Human Services, Department of Nursing, Fort Wayne, IN 46805-1499. Offers adult-gerontology primary care nurse practitioner (MS); family nurse practitioner (MS); nurse executive (MS); nursing administration (Certificate); nursing education (MS). *Accreditation:* ACEN. *Program availability:* Part-time. *Entrance requirements:* For master's, GRE Writing Test (if GPA below 3.0), BS in nursing, eligibility for Indiana RN license, minimum GPA of 3.0, essay, copy of resume, three references, undergraduate course work in research and statistics within last 5 years. Additional exam requirements/recommendations for international students: required—TOEFL (minimum score 550 paper-based; 79 iBT); recommended—TWE. Electronic applications accepted.

**Purdue University Northwest,** Graduate Studies Office, School of Nursing, Hammond, IN 46323-2094. Offers adult health clinical nurse specialist (MS); critical care clinical nurse specialist (MS); family nurse practitioner (MS); nurse executive (MS). *Accreditation:* ACEN. *Program availability:* Part-time, online learning. *Entrance requirements:* For master's, BSN. Additional exam requirements/recommendations for international students: required—TOEFL. Electronic applications accepted.

**Quinnipiac University,** School of Nursing, Adult Nurse Practitioner Track, Hamden, CT 06518-1940. Offers DNP. *Accreditation:* ACEN. *Program availability:* Part-time. *Entrance requirements:* Additional exam requirements/recommendations for international students: required—TOEFL (minimum score 575 paper-based; 90 iBT), IELTS (minimum score 6.5). Electronic applications accepted. *Expenses: Tuition:* Part-time $1055 per credit. *Required fees:* $945 per semester. Tuition and fees vary according to course load and program.

**Rutgers University - Newark,** Rutgers School of Nursing, Newark, NJ 07107-3001. Offers adult health (MSN); adult occupational health (MSN); advanced practice nursing (MSN, Post Master's Certificate); family nurse practitioner (MSN); nurse anesthesia (MSN); nursing (MSN); nursing informatics (MSN); urban health (PhD); women's health practitioner (MSN). *Accreditation:* AANA/CANAEP. *Program availability:* Part-time. *Entrance requirements:* For master's, GRE, RN license; basic life support, statistics, and health assessment experience. Additional exam requirements/recommendations for international students: required—TOEFL. Electronic applications accepted. *Expenses:* Contact institution.

**St. Catherine University,** Graduate Programs, Program in Nursing, St. Paul, MN 55105. Offers adult-gerontological nurse practitioner (MS); nurse educator (MS); nursing (DNP); nursing: entry-level (MS); pediatric nurse practitioner (MS). *Accreditation:* ACEN. *Program availability:* Part-time, evening/weekend. *Degree requirements:* For master's, thesis; for doctorate, portfolio, systems change project. *Entrance requirements:* For master's, GRE General Test, bachelor's degree in nursing, current nursing license, 2 years of recent clinical practice; for doctorate, master's degree in nursing, RN license, advanced nursing position. Additional exam requirements/recommendations for international students: required—TOEFL (minimum score 600 paper-based; 100 iBT). *Expenses:* Contact institution.

**St. Joseph's College, Long Island Campus,** Program in Nursing, Patchogue, NY 11772-2399. Offers adult-gerontology clinical nurse specialist (MS); adult-gerontology primary care nurse practitioner (MS); nursing education (MS). *Program availability:* Part-time, evening/weekend. *Faculty:* 7 full-time (6 women), 1 (woman) part-time/adjunct. *Students:* 54 part-time (48 women); includes 18 minority (7 Black or African American, non-Hispanic/Latino; 2 Asian, non-Hispanic/Latino; 8 Hispanic/Latino; 1 Two or more races, non-Hispanic/Latino). Average age 38. 57 applicants, 51% accepted, 22 enrolled. In 2019, 14 master's awarded. *Entrance requirements:* For master's, Application, proof of New York State R.N. license, curriculum vitae, personal statement, 2 letters of reference, official transcripts, verification of employment form, proof of malpractice insurance. Additional exam requirements/recommendations for international students: required—TOEFL (minimum score 80 iBT). *Application deadline:* Applications are processed on a rolling basis. Application fee: $25. Electronic applications accepted. *Expenses: Tuition:* Full-time $19,350; part-time $1075 per credit. *Required fees:* $410. *Financial support:* In 2019–20, 33 students received support. *Unit head:* Dr. Maria Fletcher, RN, Director, Associate Professor, 631-687-5180, E-mail: mfletcher@sjcny.edu. *Application contact:* Dr. Maria Fletcher, RN, Director, Associate Professor, 631-687-5180, E-mail: mfletcher@sjcny.edu.
Website: https://www.sjcny.edu/nursingli

**St. Joseph's College, New York,** Program in Nursing, Brooklyn, NY 11205-3688. Offers adult-gerontology clinical nurse specialist (MS); adult-gerontology primary care nurse practitioner (MS); nursing education (MS). *Accreditation:* ACEN. *Program availability:* Part-time, evening/weekend. *Faculty:* 3 full-time (all women), 2 part-time/adjunct (both women). *Students:* 52 part-time (47 women); includes 43 minority (40 Black or African American, non-Hispanic/Latino; 2 Asian, non-Hispanic/Latino; 1 Two or more races, non-Hispanic/Latino). Average age 43. 49 applicants, 67% accepted, 21 enrolled. In 2019, 19 master's awarded. *Entrance requirements:* Additional exam requirements/recommendations for international students: required—TOEFL (minimum score 80 iBT). *Application deadline:* Applications are processed on a rolling basis. Application fee: $25. Electronic applications accepted. *Expenses: Tuition:* Full-time $19,350; part-time $1075 per credit. *Required fees:* $400. *Financial support:* In 2019–20, 9 students received support. *Unit head:* Maria Fletcher, Director, Associate Professor, 718-940-5891, E-mail: mfletcher@sjcny.edu. *Application contact:* Maria Fletcher, Director, Associate Professor, 718-940-5891, E-mail: mfletcher@sjcny.edu.
Website: https://www.sjcny.edu/brooklyn/academics/graduate/graduate-degrees/nursing-clinical-nurse-specialist/m.s.-in-nursing-major

**Saint Mary's College,** Graduate Studies, Doctor of Nursing Practice Program, Notre Dame, IN 46556. Offers adult - gerontology acute care nurse practitioner (DNP); adult - gerontology primary care nurse practitioner (DNP); family nurse practitioner (DNP). *Program availability:* Part-time-only, evening/weekend, online only, 100% online. *Faculty:* 11. *Students:* 58 part-time (53 women); includes 15 minority (8 Black or African American, non-Hispanic/Latino; 3 Asian, non-Hispanic/Latino; 4 Hispanic/Latino). Average age 30. 24 applicants, 75% accepted, 15 enrolled. In 2019, 1 doctorate awarded. *Degree requirements:* For doctorate, comprehensive exam, thesis/dissertation. *Entrance requirements:* For doctorate, BSN or MSN, unencumbered RN license or eligibility for RN licensure, official transcripts from previously-attended institutions, 3 letters of recommendation, personal statement, resume or curriculum

vitae. Additional exam requirements/recommendations for international students: recommended—TOEFL (minimum score 80 iBT), IELTS (minimum score 6.5). *Application deadline:* For fall admission, 3/31 priority date for domestic and international students. Applications are processed on a rolling basis. Application fee: $70. Electronic applications accepted. *Expenses:* $5765 per semester. *Financial support:* In 2019–20, 3 students received support. Scholarships/grants available. Financial award application deadline: 3/1; financial award applicants required to submit FAFSA. *Unit head:* Sue Anderson, Program Director, Doctor of Nursing Practice, 574-284-4682, E-mail: sanderson@saintmarys.edu. *Application contact:* Melissa Fruscione, Director, Graduate Studies, 574-284-5098, E-mail: graduateadmission@saintmarys.edu.
Website: https://grad.saintmarys.edu/academic-programs/doctor-nursing-practice

**Saint Peter's University,** School of Nursing, Nursing Program, Jersey City, NJ 07306-5997. Offers adult nurse practitioner (MSN, Certificate); advanced practice (DNP); case management (MSN, DNP). *Accreditation:* AACN. *Program availability:* Part-time, evening/weekend. *Entrance requirements:* Additional exam requirements/recommendations for international students: required—TOEFL. Electronic applications accepted.

**Seattle Pacific University,** MS in Nursing Program, Seattle, WA 98119-1997. Offers administration (MSN); adult/gerontology nurse practitioner (MSN); clinical nurse specialist (MSN); family nurse practitioner (MSN, Certificate); informatics (MSN); nurse educator (MSN). *Accreditation:* AACN. *Program availability:* Part-time. *Students:* 42 full-time (38 women), 18 part-time (16 women); includes 28 minority (5 Black or African American, non-Hispanic/Latino; 18 Asian, non-Hispanic/Latino; 5 Hispanic/Latino), 2 international. Average age 33. 59 applicants, 41% accepted. In 2019, 10 master's awarded. *Degree requirements:* For master's, thesis. *Entrance requirements:* For master's, personal statement, transcripts, undergraduate nursing degree, proof of undergraduate statistics course with minimum GPA of 2.0, 2 recommendations. *Application deadline:* For fall admission, 1/15 priority date for domestic students; for spring admission, 1/15 for domestic students. Applications are processed on a rolling basis. Application fee: $50. Electronic applications accepted. *Expenses:* Contact institution. *Financial support:* Fellowships and scholarships/grants available. Financial award applicants required to submit FAFSA. *Unit head:* Dr. Antwinett Lee, Associate Dean, 206-281-2607, E-mail: leea30@spu.edu. *Application contact:* Dr. Antwinett Lee, Associate Dean, 206-281-2607, E-mail: leea30@spu.edu.
Website: http://spu.edu/academics/school-of-health-sciences/undergraduate-programs/nursing

**Seton Hall University,** College of Nursing, South Orange, NJ 07079-2697. Offers advanced practice in primary health care (MSN, DNP), including adult/gerontological nurse practitioner, pediatric nurse practitioner; entry into practice (MSN); health systems administration (MSN, DNP); nursing (PhD); nursing case management (MSN); nursing education (MA); school nurse (MSN); MSN/MA. *Accreditation:* AACN. *Program availability:* Part-time, online learning. *Degree requirements:* For master's, research project; for doctorate, dissertation or scholarly project. *Entrance requirements:* For doctorate, GRE (waived for students with GPA of 3.5 or higher). Additional exam requirements/recommendations for international students: required—TOEFL. Electronic applications accepted.

**Shenandoah University,** Eleanor Wade Custer School of Nursing, Winchester, VA 22601. Offers adult gerontology primary care nurse practitioner (Graduate Certificate); adult-gerontology primary care nurse practitioner (MSN); family nurse practitioner (MSN, DNP, Graduate Certificate); general (MSN); health systems leadership (DNP); health systems management (MSN, Graduate Certificate); nurse midwifery (MSN); nurse-midwifery (Graduate Certificate); nursing education (Graduate Certificate); nursing practice (DNP); psychiatric mental health nurse practitioner (MSN, DNP, Graduate Certificate). *Accreditation:* AACN; ACNM/ACME. *Entrance requirements:* For master's, United States RN license; minimum GPA of 3.0; 2080 hours of clinical experience; curriculum vitae; 3 letters of recommendation from former dean, faculty member, or advisor familiar with the applicant, and a former or current supervisor; two-to-three-page essay on a specified topic; for doctorate, MSN, minimum GPA of 3.0, 3 letters of recommendation, interview, BSN, two-to-three page essay on a specific topic, 500-word statement of clinical practice research interest, resume, current U.S. RN license, 2080 clinical hours; for Graduate Certificate, MSN, minimum GPA of 3.0, 2 letters of recommendation, minimum of one year (2080 hours) of clinical nursing experience, interview, two-to-three page essay on a specific topic, resume, current United States RN license. Additional exam requirements/recommendations for international students: required—TOEFL (minimum score 558 paper-based; 83 iBT). Electronic applications accepted. *Expenses:* Contact institution.

**Southern Adventist University,** School of Nursing, Collegedale, TN 37315-0370. Offers acute care-adult/gerontology nurse practitioner (MSN, DNP); healthcare administration (MSN/MBA); lifestyle medicine (DNP); nurse educator (MSN, DNP); primary care-adult/gerontology nurse practitioner (MSN); primary care-family nurse practitioner (MSN, DNP); primary care-psychiatric mental health nurse practitioner (MSN, DNP); MSN/MBA. *Accreditation:* ACEN. *Program availability:* Part-time, 100% online. *Degree requirements:* For master's, thesis or project; for doctorate, scholarly project. *Entrance requirements:* For master's, RN license. Additional exam requirements/recommendations for international students: required—TOEFL (minimum score 100 iBT). Electronic applications accepted.

**South University - Tampa,** Program in Nursing, Tampa, FL 33614. Offers adult health nurse practitioner (MS); family nurse practitioner (MS); nurse educator (MS).

**Spalding University,** Graduate Studies, Kosair College of Health and Natural Sciences, School of Nursing, Louisville, KY 40203-2188. Offers adult nurse practitioner (MSN); family nurse practitioner (MSN); leadership in nursing and healthcare (MSN); nurse educator (Post-Master's Certificate); nurse practitioner (Post-Master's Certificate); pediatric nurse practitioner (MSN). *Accreditation:* AACN. *Program availability:* Part-time, evening/weekend. *Degree requirements:* For master's, comprehensive exam (for some programs), thesis. *Entrance requirements:* For master's, GRE General Test, BSN or bachelor's degree in related field, RN licensure, autobiographical statement, transcripts, letters of recommendation. Additional exam requirements/recommendations for international students: required—TOEFL (minimum score 535 paper-based).

**Stony Brook University, State University of New York,** Stony Brook Medicine, School of Nursing, Adult-Gerontology Primary Care Nurse Practitioner Program, Stony Brook, NY 11794. Offers adult health nurse practitioner (Certificate); adult health/primary care nursing (MS, DNP). *Accreditation:* AACN. *Program availability:* Part-time, blended/hybrid learning. *Students:* 11 full-time (all women), 151 part-time (128 women); includes 53 minority (20 Black or African American, non-Hispanic/Latino; 14 Asian, non-Hispanic/Latino; 17 Hispanic/Latino; 1 Native Hawaiian or other Pacific Islander, non-Hispanic/Latino; 1 Two or more races, non-Hispanic/Latino), 1 international. 148 applicants, 45% accepted, 59 enrolled. In 2019, 57 master's, 8 doctorates, 3 other advanced degrees awarded. *Entrance requirements:* For master's, BSN, minimum GPA of 3.0, course work in statistics. Additional exam requirements/recommendations for international students: required—TOEFL (minimum score 90 iBT). *Application deadline:* For fall admission, 12/5 for domestic students. Application fee: $100. *Expenses:* Contact institution. *Financial support:* Application deadline: 3/15. *Unit head:* Justin M. Waryold, Program Director, 631-444-3074, Fax: 631-444-3074, E-mail: justin.waryold@stonybrook.edu. *Application contact:* Dr. Dolores Bilges, Senior Staff Assistant, 631-444-2644, Fax: 631-444-3136, E-mail: anp.nursing@stonybrook.edu.
Website: https://nursing.stonybrookmedicine.edu/graduate

**Temple University,** College of Public Health, Department of Nursing, Philadelphia, PA 19122-6096. Offers adult-gerontology primary care (DNP); family-individual across the lifespan (DNP); nursing (DNP). *Accreditation:* AACN. *Program availability:* Part-time. *Faculty:* 15 full-time (13 women), 6 part-time/adjunct (5 women). *Students:* 3 full-time (1 woman), 55 part-time (50 women); includes 27 minority (13 Black or African American, non-Hispanic/Latino; 11 Asian, non-Hispanic/Latino; 2 Hispanic/Latino; 1 Two or more races, non-Hispanic/Latino). 26 applicants, 54% accepted, 14 enrolled. In 2019, 11 doctorates awarded. *Degree requirements:* For doctorate, evidence-based practice project. *Entrance requirements:* For doctorate, GRE/MAT (waived for those who enter post-master's), 2 letters of reference, statement of goals, RN license, interview, statement of purpose, resume. Additional exam requirements/recommendations for international students: required—TOEFL (minimum score 79 iBT), IELTS (minimum score 6.5), PTE (minimum score 53), one of three is required. *Application deadline:* For fall admission, 3/1 for domestic students. Application fee: $60. Electronic applications accepted. *Expenses:* Contact institution. *Financial support:* Federal Work-Study and scholarships/grants available. Support available to part-time students. Financial award applicants required to submit FAFSA. *Unit head:* Martha Y Kubik, Chairperson, 215-707-4687, E-mail: martha.kubik@temple.edu. *Application contact:* Amy Costik, Assistant Director of Admissions, 215-204-5229, E-mail: amy.costik@temple.edu.
Website: https://cph.temple.edu/nursing/home

**Texas Christian University,** Harris College of Nursing and Health Sciences, Master's Program in Nursing, Fort Worth, TX 76129-0002. Offers administration and leadership (MSN); clinical nurse leader (MSN, Certificate); clinical nurse specialist (MSN), including adult/gerontology nursing, pediatrics; nursing education (MSN). *Accreditation:* AACN. *Program availability:* Part-time, online only, 100% online. *Faculty:* 29 full-time (26 women), 1 (woman) part-time/adjunct. *Students:* 12 full-time (all women), 5 part-time (all women); includes 5 minority (1 Asian, non-Hispanic/Latino; 4 Hispanic/Latino). Average age 34. 41 applicants, 59% accepted, 8 enrolled. In 2019, 10 master's awarded. *Degree requirements:* For master's, thesis or alternative, practicum. *Entrance requirements:* For master's, 3 letters of reference, essay, resume, two official transcripts from every institution attended, current license to practice as a registered nurse. Additional exam requirements/recommendations for international students: required—TOEFL (minimum score 550 paper-based; 80 iBT). *Application deadline:* For spring admission, 8/15 for domestic and international students; for summer admission, 1/15 for domestic and international students. Application fee: $60. Electronic applications accepted. Full-time tuition and fees vary according to program. *Financial support:* In 2019–20, 15 students received support. Scholarships/grants available. Financial award application deadline: 2/15; financial award applicants required to submit FAFSA. *Unit head:* Dr. Kathy Ellis, Division Director, Graduate Nursing, 817-257-6726, Fax: 817-257-7944, E-mail: kathryn.ellis@tcu.edu. *Application contact:* Beth Janke, Academic Program Specialist, 817-257-6726, Fax: 817-257-7944, E-mail: graduatenursing@tcu.edu.
Website: http://www.nursing.tcu.edu/graduate.asp

**Texas Woman's University,** Graduate School, College of Nursing, Denton, TX 76204. Offers adult health clinical nurse specialist (MS); adult health nurse practitioner (MS); adult/gerontology acute care nurse practitioner (MS); child health clinical nurse specialist (MS); clinical nurse leader (MS); family nurse practitioner (MS); health systems management (MS); nursing education (MS); nursing practice (DNP); nursing science (PhD); pediatric nurse practitioner (MS); women's health clinical nurse specialist (MS); women's health nurse practitioner (MS). *Accreditation:* AACN. *Program availability:* Part-time, 100% online, blended/hybrid learning. *Faculty:* 48 full-time (47 women), 31 part-time/adjunct (24 women). *Students:* 42 full-time (40 women), 811 part-time (756 women); includes 481 minority (168 Black or African American, non-Hispanic/Latino; 2 American Indian or Alaska Native, non-Hispanic/Latino; 165 Asian, non-Hispanic/Latino; 118 Hispanic/Latino; 1 Native Hawaiian or other Pacific Islander, non-Hispanic/Latino; 27 Two or more races, non-Hispanic/Latino), 26 international. Average age 36. 435 applicants, 71% accepted, 172 enrolled. In 2019, 203 master's, 37 doctorates awarded. *Degree requirements:* For master's, comprehensive exam, thesis or alternative, 6-year time limit for completion of degree, professional or clinical project; for doctorate, comprehensive exam, thesis/dissertation, 10-year time limit for completion of degree; dissertation (PhD), assessment practicum (DPT). *Entrance requirements:* For master's, minimum GPA of 3.0 on last 60 hours in undergraduate nursing degree and overall, RN license, BS in nursing, basic statistics course; for doctorate, MS in nursing, minimum preferred GPA of 3.5, RN or APRN license, statistics course, 2 letters of reference, curriculum vitae, graduate nursing-theory course, graduate research course, statement of professional goals and research interests, 1 yr APRN experience. Additional exam requirements/recommendations for international students: required—TOEFL (minimum score 79 iBT); recommended—IELTS (minimum score 6.5), TSE (minimum score 53). *Application deadline:* For fall admission, 5/1 for domestic students, 3/1 priority date for international students; for spring admission, 9/15 for domestic students, 7/1 priority date for international students. Application fee: $50 ($75 for international students). Electronic applications accepted. *Expenses:* All are estimates. Tuition for 10 hours = $2,763; Fees for 10 hours = $1,342. Master's Nursing courses require additional $75/SCH; Doctoral Nursing courses require additional $80/SCH. *Financial support:* In 2019–20, 212 students received support, including 1 research assistantship, 6 teaching assistantships (averaging $12,029 per year); career-related internships or fieldwork, scholarships/grants, health care benefits, and unspecified assistantships also available. Support available to part-time students. Financial award application deadline: 3/1; financial award applicants required to submit FAFSA. *Unit head:* Dr. Rosalie Mainous, Dean, 940-898-2401, Fax: 940-898-2437, E-mail: nursing@twu.edu. *Application contact:* Korie Hawkins, Associate Director of Admissions, Graduate Recruitment, 940-898-3188, Fax: 940-898-3081, E-mail: admissions@twu.edu.
Website: http://www.twu.edu/nursing/

**Troy University,** Graduate School, College of Health and Human Services, Program in Nursing, Troy, AL 36082. Offers adult health (MSN); family nurse practitioner (DNP); maternal infant (MSN); nursing informatics specialist (MSN). *Accreditation:* ACEN. *Program availability:* Part-time, evening/weekend, online learning. *Faculty:* 14 full-time (all women). *Students:* 67 full-time (64 women), 160 part-time (139 women); includes 46 minority (37 Black or African American, non-Hispanic/Latino; 1 American Indian or Alaska Native, non-Hispanic/Latino; 1 Asian, non-Hispanic/Latino; 7 Hispanic/Latino). Average age 35. 64 applicants, 97% accepted, 59 enrolled. In 2019, 73 master's, 20 doctorates awarded. *Degree requirements:* For master's, comprehensive exam, minimum GPA of 3.0, candidacy; for doctorate, minimum GPA of 3.0, submission of approved comprehensive e-portfolio, completion of residency synthesis project, minimum of 1000 hours of clinical practice, qualifying exam. *Entrance requirements:* For master's, Score of 396 or higher on the Miller's Analogy Test (MAT) or score of 290 on Graduate Record Exam (850 on the old exam)(verbal plus quantitative); GRE or MAT required for every applicant, minimum GPA of 3.0, BSN, current RN licensure, 2 letters of reference, undergraduate health assessment course; for doctorate, GRE (minimum score of 850 on old exam or 294 on new exam), BSN or MSN, minimum GPA of 3.0, 2

letters of reference, current RN licensure, essay. Additional exam requirements/recommendations for international students: required—TOEFL (minimum score 523 paper-based; 70 iBT), IELTS (minimum score 6). *Application deadline:* For fall admission, 5/1 for domestic students; for spring admission, 10/1 for domestic students; for summer admission, 3/1 for domestic students. Applications are processed on a rolling basis. Application fee: $50. Electronic applications accepted. *Expenses: Tuition, area resident:* Full-time $7650; part-time $2550 per semester hour. Tuition, state resident: full-time $7650; part-time $2550 per semester hour. Tuition, nonresident: full-time $15,300; part-time $5100 per semester hour. *International tuition:* $15,300 full-time. *Required fees:* $856; $352 per semester hour. $176 per semester. *Financial support:* In 2019–20, 20 students received support. Fellowships, research assistantships, teaching assistantships, career-related internships or fieldwork, Federal Work-Study, scholarships/grants, traineeships, tuition waivers, and unspecified assistantships available. Support available to part-time students. Financial award application deadline: 3/1; financial award applicants required to submit FAFSA. *Unit head:* Dr. Wade Forehand, Professor, Director, School of Nursing, 334-670-3745, Fax: 334-670-3743, E-mail: jforehand@troy.edu. *Application contact:* Crystal G. Bishop, Director of Graduate Admissions, School of Nursing, 334-241-8631, E-mail: cdgodwin@troy.edu. Website: https://www.troy.edu/academics/academic-programs/college-health-human-services-programs.php

**Universidad del Turabo,** Graduate Programs, School of Health Sciences, Programs in Nursing, Program in Family Nurse Practitioner - Adult Nursing, Gurabo, PR 00778-3030. Offers MSN, Certificate. *Entrance requirements:* For master's, GRE, EXADEP or GMAT, interview, essay, official transcript, recommendation letters. Electronic applications accepted.

**University at Buffalo, the State University of New York,** Graduate School, School of Nursing, Buffalo, NY 14260. Offers adult gerontology nurse practitioner (DNP); family nurse practitioner (DNP); health care systems and leadership (MS); nurse anesthetist (DNP); nursing (PhD); nursing education (Certificate); psychiatric/mental health nurse practitioner (DNP). *Accreditation:* AACN; AANA/CANAEP (one or more programs are accredited). *Program availability:* Part-time, 100% online. *Degree requirements:* For master's, thesis optional; for doctorate, comprehensive exam (for some programs), capstone (for DNP), dissertation (for PhD). *Entrance requirements:* For master's, GRE or MAT; for doctorate, GRE or MAT, minimum GPA of 3.0 (for DNP), 3.25 (for PhD); RN license; BS or MS in nursing; 3 references; writing sample; resume; personal statement; for Certificate, interview, minimum GPA of 3.0 or GRE General Test, RN license, MS in nursing, professional certification. Additional exam requirements/recommendations for international students: required—TOEFL (minimum score 550 paper-based; 79 iBT), IELTS (minimum score 6.5). Electronic applications accepted. *Expenses:* Contact institution.

**The University of Alabama at Birmingham,** School of Nursing, Birmingham, AL 35294. Offers clinical nurse leader (MSN); nurse anesthesia (DNP); nurse practitioner (MSN, DNP), including adult-gerontology acute care (MSN), adult-gerontology primary care (MSN), family (MSN), pediatric (MSN), psychiatric/mental health (MSN), women's health (MSN); nursing (MSN, DNP, PhD); nursing health systems administration (MSN); nursing informatics (MSN). *Accreditation:* AACN; AANA/CANAEP. *Program availability:* Part-time, online only, blended/hybrid learning. *Faculty:* 86 full-time (79 women), 42 part-time/adjunct (35 women). *Students:* 228 full-time (165 women), 1,393 part-time (1,234 women); includes 398 minority (267 Black or African American, non-Hispanic/Latino; 4 American Indian or Alaska Native, non-Hispanic/Latino; 52 Asian, non-Hispanic/Latino; 41 Hispanic/Latino; 34 Two or more races, non-Hispanic/Latino), 3 international. Average age 33. 1,027 applicants, 55% accepted, 421 enrolled. In 2019, 557 master's, 19 doctorates awarded. Terminal master's awarded for partial completion of doctoral program. *Degree requirements:* For master's, comprehensive exam; for doctorate, comprehensive exam, thesis/dissertation, research mentorship experience (for PhD); scholarly project (for DNP). *Entrance requirements:* For master's, GRE, GMAT, or MAT, minimum cumulative undergraduate GPA of 3.0 or on last 60 semesters hours; letters of recommendation; for doctorate, GRE General Test, computer literacy, course work in statistics, interview, minimum GPA of 3.0, MS in nursing, references, writing sample. Additional exam requirements/recommendations for international students: required—TOEFL (minimum score 500 paper-based, 80 iBT) or IELTS (5.5). *Application deadline:* For fall admission, 2/24 for domestic students; for summer admission, 10/15 for domestic students. Application fee: $50. Electronic applications accepted. *Expenses:* Contact institution. *Financial support:* In 2019–20, 23 fellowships (averaging $34,685 per year), 12 research assistantships (averaging $9,042 per year), 2 teaching assistantships (averaging $22,000 per year) were awarded; scholarships/grants, traineeships, health care benefits, and unspecified assistantships also available. Support available to part-time students. *Unit head:* Dr. Doreen C. Harper, Dean, 205-934-5360, Fax: 205-934-1894, E-mail: dcharper@uab.edu. *Application contact:* John Updegraff, Director of Student Affairs, 205-975-3370, Fax: 205-934-5490, E-mail: jupde22@uab.edu. Website: http://www.uab.edu/nursing/home/

**University of Central Arkansas,** Graduate School, College of Health and Behavioral Sciences, Department of Nursing, Conway, AR 72035-0001. Offers adult nurse practitioner (PMC); clinical nurse leader (PMC); clinical nurse specialist (MSN); family nurse practitioner (PMC); nurse educator (PMC); nurse practitioner (MSN). *Accreditation:* AACN. *Program availability:* Part-time, evening/weekend, online learning. *Degree requirements:* For master's, comprehensive exam, thesis optional, clinicals. *Entrance requirements:* For master's, GRE General Test, minimum GPA of 2.7. Additional exam requirements/recommendations for international students: required—TOEFL (minimum score 550 paper-based; 80 iBT). Electronic applications accepted. *Expenses:* Contact institution.

**University of Cincinnati,** Graduate School, College of Nursing, Cincinnati, OH 45221-0038. Offers nurse midwifery (MSN); nurse practitioner (MSN, DNP), including acute care pediatrics (DNP), adult-gerontology acute care, adult-gerontology primary care, anesthesia (DNP), family (MSN), leadership (DNP), neonatal (MSN), women's health (MSN); nursing (MSN, PhD), including occupational health (MSN). *Accreditation:* AACN; AANA/CANAEP (one or more programs are accredited); ACNM/ACME. *Program availability:* Part-time, 100% online, blended/hybrid learning. *Faculty:* 62 full-time (55 women), 125 part-time/adjunct (114 women). *Students:* 429 full-time (355 women), 1,547 part-time (1,390 women); includes 453 minority (226 Black or African American, non-Hispanic/Latino; 5 American Indian or Alaska Native, non-Hispanic/Latino; 68 Asian, non-Hispanic/Latino; 103 Hispanic/Latino; 3 Native Hawaiian or other Pacific Islander, non-Hispanic/Latino; 48 Two or more races, non-Hispanic/Latino), 15 international. Average age 36. 779 applicants, 78% accepted, 464 enrolled. In 2019, 518 master's, 47 doctorates awarded. *Degree requirements:* For master's, thesis or alternative; for doctorate, comprehensive exam (for some programs), thesis/dissertation (for some programs). *Entrance requirements:* For master's, GRE required only for the Direct-Entry Accelerated Program. Additional exam requirements/recommendations for international students: required—TOEFL (minimum score 600 paper-based; 100 iBT); recommended—IELTS (minimum score 7). *Application deadline:* For fall admission, 4/1 priority date for domestic and international students; for spring admission, 9/1 priority date for domestic and international students; for summer admission, 2/1 priority date for

domestic and international students. Applications are processed on a rolling basis. Application fee: $135 ($140 for international students). Electronic applications accepted. *Expenses:* Contact institution. *Financial support:* In 2019–20, 103 students received support, including 9 fellowships with full tuition reimbursements available (averaging $18,595 per year), 7 research assistantships with full tuition reimbursements available (averaging $12,991 per year), 8 teaching assistantships with full tuition reimbursements available (averaging $12,991 per year); institutionally sponsored loans, scholarships/grants, traineeships, health care benefits, tuition waivers (partial), and unspecified assistantships also available. Support available to part-time students. Financial award application deadline: 4/1; financial award applicants required to submit FAFSA. *Unit head:* Dr. Greer Glazer, Dean, 513-558-5330, Fax: 513-558-9030, E-mail: greer.glazer@uc.edu. *Application contact:* Office of Student Affairs, 513-558-8400, E-mail: nursingbearcats@uc.edu. Website: https://nursing.uc.edu/

**University of Colorado Colorado Springs,** Helen and Arthur E. Johnson Beth-El College of Nursing and Health Sciences, Colorado Springs, CO 80918. Offers nursing practice (MSN, DNP). *Accreditation:* AACN. *Program availability:* Part-time, 100% online. *Faculty:* 62 full-time (47 women), 77 part-time/adjunct (68 women). *Students:* 20 full-time (18 women), 295 part-time (261 women); includes 74 minority (14 Black or African American, non-Hispanic/Latino; 2 American Indian or Alaska Native, non-Hispanic/Latino; 16 Asian, non-Hispanic/Latino; 26 Hispanic/Latino; 1 Native Hawaiian or other Pacific Islander, non-Hispanic/Latino; 15 Two or more races, non-Hispanic/Latino). Average age 36. 147 applicants, 44% accepted, 49 enrolled. In 2019, 63 master's, 4 doctorates awarded. *Degree requirements:* For master's, comprehensive exam, thesis optional; for doctorate, capstone project. *Entrance requirements:* For master's, completion of an accredited (programmatic) baccalaureate degree in nursing including undergraduate coursework in: Introduction to Statistics, nursing research, health assessment; curriculum vitae or resume; 3 letters of recommendation; minimum overall GPA of 2.75 for cumulative undergraduate course work and BSN GPA of 3.3 or higher; for doctorate, active RN license in state of practice; Master of Science Degree in Nursing from an accredited (CCNE/NLN) program; undergraduate cumulative GPA of 2.75 or higher and graduate cumulative GPA 3.3 or higher; National Certification* as NP or CNS; curriculum vitae; completion of application essay. Additional exam requirements/recommendations for international students: required—TOEFL (minimum score 80 iBT). *Application deadline:* For fall admission, 3/15 priority date for domestic students, 3/15 for international students; for spring admission, 8/15 for domestic and international students. Applications are processed on a rolling basis. Application fee: $60 ($100 for international students). Electronic applications accepted. *Expenses:* Contact institution. *Financial support:* In 2019–20, 14 students received support, including 1 research assistantship (averaging $20,800 per year), 9 teaching assistantships (averaging $3,000 per year); career-related internships or fieldwork, Federal Work-Study, and scholarships/grants also available. Support available to part-time students. Financial award application deadline: 3/1; financial award applicants required to submit FAFSA. *Unit head:* Dr. Deborah Pollard, Nursing Department Chair, 719-255-3577, Fax: 719-255-4416, E-mail: dpollard@uccs.edu. *Application contact:* Diane Busch, Program Assistant II, 719-255-4424, Fax: 719-255-4416, E-mail: dbusch@uccs.edu. Website: https://www.uccs.edu/johnsonbethel/

**University of Colorado Denver,** College of Nursing, Aurora, CO 80045. Offers adult clinical nurse specialist (MS); adult nurse practitioner (MS); family nurse practitioner (MS); family psychiatric mental health nurse practitioner (MS); health care informatics (MS); nurse-midwifery (MS); nursing (DNP, PhD); nursing leadership and health care systems (MS); pediatric nurse practitioner (MS); women's health (MS); MS/PhD. *Accreditation:* ACNM/ACME (one or more programs are accredited). *Program availability:* Part-time, evening/weekend, online learning. Terminal master's awarded for partial completion of doctoral program. *Degree requirements:* For master's, thesis optional; for doctorate, comprehensive exam, thesis/dissertation, 42 credits of coursework. *Entrance requirements:* For master's, GRE if cumulative undergraduate GPA is less than 3.0, undergraduate nursing degree from ACEN- or CCNE-accredited school or university; completion of research and statistics courses with minimum grade of C; copy of current and unencumbered nursing license; for doctorate, GRE, bachelor's and/or master's degrees in nursing from ACEN- or CCNE-accredited institution; portfolio; minimum undergraduate GPA of 3.0, graduate 3.5; graduate-level intermediate statistics and master's-level nursing theory courses with minimum B grade; interview. Additional exam requirements/recommendations for international students: required—TOEFL (minimum score 560 paper-based; 83 iBT). Electronic applications accepted. *Expenses:* Contact institution.

**University of Delaware,** College of Health Sciences, School of Nursing, Newark, DE 19716. Offers adult nurse practitioner (MSN, PMC); cardiopulmonary clinical nurse specialist (MSN, PMC); cardiopulmonary clinical nurse specialist/adult nurse practitioner (MSN, PMC); family nurse practitioner (MSN, PMC); gerontology clinical nurse specialist (MSN, PMC); gerontology clinical nurse specialist geriatric nurse practitioner (PMC); gerontology clinical nurse specialist/geriatric nurse practitioner (MSN); health services administration (MSN, PMC); nursing of children clinical nurse specialist (MSN, PMC); nursing of children clinical nurse specialist/pediatric nurse practitioner (MSN, PMC); oncology/immune deficiency clinical nurse specialist (MSN, PMC); oncology/immune deficiency clinical nurse specialist/adult nurse practitioner (MSN, PMC); perinatal/women's health clinical nurse specialist (MSN, PMC); perinatal/women's health clinical nurse specialist/women's health nurse practitioner (MSN, PMC); psychiatric nursing clinical nurse specialist (MSN, PMC). *Accreditation:* AACN. *Program availability:* Part-time, evening/weekend, online learning. *Degree requirements:* For master's, thesis optional. *Entrance requirements:* For master's, BSN, interview, RN license. Electronic applications accepted.

**University of Hawaii at Manoa,** Office of Graduate Education, School of Nursing and Dental Hygiene, Honolulu, HI 96822. Offers clinical nurse specialist (MS), including adult health, community mental health; nurse practitioner (MS), including adult health, community mental health, family nurse practitioner; nursing (PhD, Graduate Certificate); nursing administration (MS). *Accreditation:* AACN. *Program availability:* Part-time, online learning. *Degree requirements:* For master's, thesis optional; for doctorate, comprehensive exam, thesis/dissertation. *Entrance requirements:* For master's, Hawaii RN license. Additional exam requirements/recommendations for international students: required—TOEFL (minimum score 580 paper-based; 92 iBT), IELTS (minimum score 5). *Expenses:* Contact institution.

**University of Illinois at Chicago,** College of Nursing, Program in Nursing, Chicago, IL 60607-7128. Offers acute care clinical nurse specialist (MS); administrative nursing leadership (Certificate); adult nurse practitioner (MS); adult/geriatric nurse practitioner (MS); advanced community health nurse specialist (MS); family nurse practitioner (MS); geriatric clinical nurse specialist (MS); geriatric nurse practitioner (MS); nurse midwifery (MS); occupational health/advanced community health nurse specialist (MS); occupational health/family nurse practitioner (MS); pediatric nurse practitioner (MS); perinatal clinical nurse specialist (MS); school/advanced community health nurse specialist (MS); school/family nurse practitioner (MS); women's health nurse practitioner (MS). *Accreditation:* AACN. *Program availability:* Part-time. *Degree requirements:* For

## Adult Nursing

master's, thesis or alternative. *Entrance requirements:* For master's, GRE General Test, minimum GPA of 2.75. Additional exam requirements/recommendations for international students: required—TOEFL. Electronic applications accepted.

**The University of Kansas,** University of Kansas Medical Center, School of Nursing, Kansas City, KS 66045. Offers adult/gerontological clinical nurse specialist (PMC); adult/gerontological nurse practitioner (PMC); health care informatics (PMC); health professions educator (PMC); nurse midwife (PMC); nursing (MS, DNP, PhD); organizational leadership (PMC); psychiatric/mental health nurse practitioner (PMC); public health nursing (PMC). *Accreditation:* AACN; ACNM/ACME. *Program availability:* Part-time, 100% online, blended/hybrid learning. *Faculty:* 65. *Students:* 57 full-time (53 women), 267 part-time (242 women); includes 65 minority (14 Black or African American, non-Hispanic/Latino; 2 American Indian or Alaska Native, non-Hispanic/Latino; 21 Asian, non-Hispanic/Latino; 9 Hispanic/Latino; 1 Native Hawaiian or other Pacific Islander, non-Hispanic/Latino; 18 Two or more races, non-Hispanic/Latino), 2 international. Average age 35. In 2019, 26 master's, 48 doctorates, 5 other advanced degrees awarded. Terminal master's awarded for partial completion of doctoral program. *Degree requirements:* For master's, comprehensive exam, thesis (for some programs), general oral exam; for doctorate, thesis/dissertation or alternative, comprehensive oral exam (for DNP); comprehensive written and oral exam, or three publications (for PhD). *Entrance requirements:* For master's, bachelor's degree in nursing, minimum GPA of 3.0, 1 year of clinical experience, RN license in KS and MO; for doctorate, GRE General Test (for PhD only), bachelor's degree in nursing, minimum GPA of 3.5, RN license in KS and MO. Additional exam requirements/recommendations for international students: required—TOEFL. *Application deadline:* For fall admission, 4/1 for domestic and international students; for spring admission, 9/1 for domestic and international students. Application fee: $75. Electronic applications accepted. *Expenses:* Contact institution. *Financial support:* Research assistantships with tuition reimbursements, teaching assistantships with tuition reimbursements, scholarships/grants, and traineeships available. Financial award application deadline: 3/1; financial award applicants required to submit FAFSA. *Unit head:* Dr. Sally Maliski, Professor and Dean, 913-588-1601, Fax: 913-588-1660, E-mail: smaliski@kumc.edu. *Application contact:* Dr. Pamela K. Barnes, Associate Dean, Student Affairs and Enrollment Management, 913-588-1619, Fax: 913-588-1615, E-mail: pbarnes2@kumc.edu. Website: http://nursing.kumc.edu

**University of Massachusetts Amherst,** Graduate School, College of Nursing, Amherst, MA 01003. Offers adult gerontology primary care nurse practitioner (DNP); clinical nurse leader (MS); family nurse practitioner (DNP); nursing (PhD); public health nurse leader (DNP). *Accreditation:* AACN. *Program availability:* Part-time, online learning. Terminal master's awarded for partial completion of doctoral program. *Degree requirements:* For master's, thesis optional; for doctorate, comprehensive exam, thesis/dissertation. *Entrance requirements:* Additional exam requirements/recommendations for international students: required—TOEFL (minimum score 550 paper-based; 80 iBT), IELTS (minimum score 6.5). Electronic applications accepted.

**University of Massachusetts Medical School,** Graduate School of Nursing, Worcester, MA 01655. Offers adult gerontological acute care nurse practitioner (DNP, Post Master's Certificate); adult gerontological primary care nurse practitioner (DNP, Post Master's Certificate); family nursing practitioner (DNP); nurse administrator (DNP); nurse educator (MS); nursing (PhD); psychiatric mental health (Post Master's Certificate). *Accreditation:* AACN. *Program availability:* Blended/hybrid learning. *Faculty:* 26 full-time (22 women), 51 part-time/adjunct (40 women). *Students:* 176 full-time (152 women), 33 part-time (27 women); includes 61 minority (21 Black or African American, non-Hispanic/Latino; 1 American Indian or Alaska Native, non-Hispanic/Latino; 18 Asian, non-Hispanic/Latino; 20 Hispanic/Latino; 1 Native Hawaiian or other Pacific Islander, non-Hispanic/Latino). Average age 32. 131 applicants, 66% accepted, 58 enrolled. In 2019, 28 master's, 34 doctorates, 1 other advanced degree awarded. *Degree requirements:* For doctorate, thesis/dissertation (for some programs), comprehensive exam and manuscript (for PhD); scholarly project (for DNP). *Entrance requirements:* For master's, GRE General Test, bachelor's degree in nursing, course work in statistics, unrestricted Massachusetts license as registered nurse; for doctorate, GRE General Test, bachelor's or master's degree; for Post Master's Certificate, GRE General Test, MS in nursing. Additional exam requirements/recommendations for international students: required—TOEFL (minimum score 400 paper-based; 81 iBT). *Application deadline:* For fall admission, 12/1 priority date for domestic students. Applications are processed on a rolling basis. Application fee: $100. Electronic applications accepted. *Expenses:* Contact institution. *Financial support:* In 2019–20, 103 students received support. Scholarships/grants available. Support available to part-time students. Financial award application deadline: 5/15; financial award applicants required to submit FAFSA. *Unit head:* Dr. Joan Vitello-Cicciu, Dean, 508-856-5081, Fax: 508-856-6552, E-mail: joan.vitello@umassmed.edu. *Application contact:* Diane Brescia, Admissions Coordinator, 508-856-3488, Fax: 508-856-5851, E-mail: diane.brescia@umassmed.edu.
Website: http://www.umassmed.edu/gsn/

**University of Miami,** Graduate School, School of Nursing and Health Studies, Coral Gables, FL 33124. Offers acute care (MSN), including acute care nurse practitioner, nurse anesthesia; nursing (PhD); primary care (MSN), including adult nurse practitioner, family nurse practitioner, nurse midwifery, women's health practitioner. *Accreditation:* AACN; AANA/CANAEP; ACNM/ACME (one or more programs are accredited). *Program availability:* Part-time. *Degree requirements:* For master's, thesis optional; for doctorate, thesis/dissertation. *Entrance requirements:* For master's, GRE General Test, BSN, minimum GPA of 3.0, Florida RN license; for doctorate, GRE General Test, BSN or MSN, minimum GPA of 3.0. Additional exam requirements/recommendations for international students: required—TOEFL (minimum score 550 paper-based). Electronic applications accepted.

**University of Missouri,** Office of Research and Graduate Studies, Sinclair School of Nursing, Columbia, MO 65211. Offers adult-gerontology clinical nurse specialist (DNP, Certificate); family nurse practitioner (DNP); family psychiatric and mental health nurse practitioner (DNP); nursing (MS, PhD); nursing leadership and innovations in health care (DNP); pediatric clinical nurse specialist (DNP, Certificate); pediatric nurse practitioner (DNP). *Accreditation:* AACN. *Program availability:* Part-time. *Degree requirements:* For master's, thesis optional, oral exam; for doctorate, thesis/dissertation. *Entrance requirements:* For master's, GRE General Test, BSN, minimum GPA of 3.0 during last 60 hours, nursing license. Additional exam requirements/recommendations for international students: required—TOEFL, IELTS. Electronic applications accepted.

**University of Missouri–Kansas City,** School of Nursing and Health Studies, Kansas City, MO 64110-2499. Offers adult clinical nurse specialist (MSN), including adult nurse practitioner, women's health nurse practitioner (MSN, DNP); adult clinical nursing practice (DNP), including adult gerontology nurse practitioner, women's health nurse practitioner (MSN, DNP); clinical nursing practice (DNP), including family nurse practitioner; neonatal nurse practitioner (MSN); nurse educator (MSN); nurse executive (MSN); nursing practice (DNP); pediatric clinical nursing practice (DNP), including pediatric nurse practitioner; pediatric nurse practitioner (MSN). *Accreditation:* AACN. *Program availability:* Part-time, online learning. *Degree requirements:* For master's, thesis or alternative. *Entrance requirements:* For master's, minimum undergraduate

GPA of 3.2; for doctorate, GRE, 3 letters of reference. Additional exam requirements/recommendations for international students: required—TOEFL (minimum score 550 paper-based; 80 iBT).

**University of Missouri–St. Louis,** College of Nursing, St. Louis, MO 63121. Offers adult/geriatric nurse practitioner (Post Master's Certificate); family nurse practitioner (Post Master's Certificate); nursing (DNP, PhD); pediatric acute care nurse practitioner (Post Master's Certificate); pediatric nurse practitioner (Post Master's Certificate); psychiatric-mental health nurse practitioner (Post Master's Certificate); women's health nurse practitioner (Post Master's Certificate). *Accreditation:* AACN. *Program availability:* Part-time. *Degree requirements:* For doctorate, comprehensive exam, thesis/dissertation; for Post Master's Certificate, thesis. *Entrance requirements:* For doctorate, GRE, 2 letters of recommendation, MSN, minimum GPA of 3.2, course in differential/inferential statistics; for Post Master's Certificate, 2 recommendation letters; MSN; advanced practice certificate; minimum GPA of 3.0; essay. Additional exam requirements/recommendations for international students: recommended—TOEFL (minimum score 550 paper-based; 79 iBT), IELTS (minimum score 6.5). Electronic applications accepted. *Expenses: Tuition, area resident:* Full-time $9005.40; part-time $6003.60 per credit hour. Tuition, state resident: full-time $9005.40; part-time $6003.60 per credit hour. Tuition, nonresident: full-time $22,108; part-time $14,738.40 per credit hour. *International tuition:* $22,108 full-time. Tuition and fees vary according to course load.

**The University of North Carolina at Chapel Hill,** School of Nursing, Chapel Hill, NC 27599-7460. Offers advanced practice registered nurse (DNP); nursing (MSN, PhD, PMC), including administration (MSN), adult gerontology primary care nurse practitioner (MSN), clinical nurse leader (MSN), education (MSN), health care systems (PMC), informatics (MSN, PMC), nursing leadership (PMC), outcomes management (MSN), primary care family nurse practitioner (MSN), primary care pediatric nurse practitioner (MSN), psychiatric/mental health nurse practitioner (MSN, PMC). *Accreditation:* AACN; ACEN (one or more programs are accredited). *Program availability:* Part-time. *Degree requirements:* For master's, comprehensive exam, thesis; for doctorate, thesis/dissertation, 3 exams; for PMC, thesis. *Entrance requirements:* Additional exam requirements/recommendations for international students: required—TOEFL (minimum score 575 paper-based; 89 iBT), IELTS (minimum score 8). Electronic applications accepted.

**The University of North Carolina at Greensboro,** Graduate School, School of Nursing, Greensboro, NC 27412-5001. Offers adult clinical nurse specialist (MSN, PMC); adult/gerontological nurse practitioner (MSN, PMC); nurse anesthesia (MSN, PMC); nursing (PhD); nursing administration (MSN); nursing education (MSN); MSN/MBA. *Accreditation:* ACEN. *Degree requirements:* For master's, thesis or alternative. *Entrance requirements:* For master's, GRE General Test or MAT, BSN, clinical experience, liability insurance, RN license; for PMC, liability insurance, MSN, RN license. Additional exam requirements/recommendations for international students: required—TOEFL. Electronic applications accepted.

**University of Pennsylvania,** School of Nursing, Adult-Gerontology Acute Care Nurse Practitioner Program, Philadelphia, PA 19104. Offers MSN. *Accreditation:* AACN. *Program availability:* Part-time, online learning. *Students:* 26 full-time (25 women), 245 part-time (216 women); includes 69 minority (21 Black or African American, non-Hispanic/Latino; 29 Asian, non-Hispanic/Latino; 13 Hispanic/Latino; 6 Two or more races, non-Hispanic/Latino), 2 international. Average age 36. 193 applicants, 84% accepted, 143 enrolled. In 2019, 165 master's awarded. *Entrance requirements:* For master's, GRE General Test. Application fee: $80. *Financial support:* Application deadline: 4/1. *Unit head:* Assistant Dean of Admissions and Financial Aid, 866-867-6877, Fax: 215-573-8439, E-mail: admissions@nursing.upenn.edu. *Application contact:* Deborah Becker, Program Director, 215-898-0432, E-mail: debecker@nursing.upenn.edu.
Website: http://www.nursing.upenn.edu/

**University of Puerto Rico - Medical Sciences Campus,** School of Nursing, San Juan, PR 00936-5067. Offers adult and elderly nursing (MSN); child and adolescent nursing (MSN); critical care nursing (MSN); family and community nursing (MSN); family nurse practitioner (MSN); maternity nursing (MSN); mental health and psychiatric nursing (MSN). *Accreditation:* AACN; AANA/CANAEP. *Entrance requirements:* For master's, GRE or EXADEP, interview, Puerto Rico RN license or professional license for international students, general and specific point average, article analysis. Electronic applications accepted.

**University of Rhode Island,** Graduate School, College of Nursing, Kingston, RI 02881. Offers acute care nurse practitioner (adult-gerontology focus) (Post Master's Certificate); adult gerontology nurse practitioner/clinical nurse specialist (Post Master's Certificate); adult-gerontological acute care nurse practitioner (MS); adult-gerontological nurse practitioner/clinical nurse specialist (MS); family nurse practitioner (MS, Post Master's Certificate); nursing (DNP, PhD); nursing education (MS, Post Master's Certificate). *Accreditation:* AACN; ACNM/ACME (one or more programs are accredited). *Program availability:* Part-time, evening/weekend, 100% online, blended/hybrid learning. *Faculty:* 27 full-time (26 women). *Students:* 51 full-time (47 women), 72 part-time (65 women); includes 21 minority (9 Black or African American, non-Hispanic/Latino; 5 Asian, non-Hispanic/Latino; 4 Hispanic/Latino; 2 Native Hawaiian or other Pacific Islander, non-Hispanic/Latino; 1 Two or more races, non-Hispanic/Latino), 6 international. 32 applicants, 88% accepted, 21 enrolled. In 2019, 34 master's, 9 doctorates, 1 other advanced degree awarded. *Entrance requirements:* For master's, GRE or MAT, 2 letters of recommendation, scholarly papers; for doctorate, GRE, 3 letters of recommendation, scholarly papers. Additional exam requirements/recommendations for international students: required—TOEFL. *Application deadline:* For fall admission, 2/15 for domestic students, 2/1 for international students; for spring admission, 10/15 for domestic students, 7/15 for international students. Application fee: $65. Electronic applications accepted. *Expenses: Tuition, area resident:* Full-time $13,734; part-time $763 per credit. Tuition, state resident: full-time $13,734; part-time $763 per credit. Tuition, nonresident: full-time $26,512; part-time $1473 per credit. *International tuition:* $26,512 full-time. *Required fees:* $1780; $52 per credit. $35 per term. One-time fee: $165. *Financial support:* In 2019–20, 7 teaching assistantships with tuition reimbursements (averaging $13,376 per year) were awarded. Financial award application deadline: 2/1; financial award applicants required to submit FAFSA. *Unit head:* Dr. Barbara Wolfe, Dean, 401-874-5324, E-mail: bwolfe@uri.edu. *Application contact:* Dr. Denise Coppa, Associate Professor/Interim Associate Dean for Graduate Programs, 401-874-5036, E-mail: dcoppa@uri.edu.
Website: http://www.uri.edu/nursing/

**University of Rochester,** School of Nursing, Rochester, NY 14642. Offers adult gerontological acute care nurse practitioner (MS); adult gerontological primary care nurse practitioner (MS); clinical nurse leader (MS); family nurse practitioner (MS); family psychiatric mental health nurse practitioner (MS); health care organization management and leadership (MS); nursing (DNP); nursing and health science (PhD); nursing education (MS); pediatric nurse practitioner (MS); pediatric nurse practitioner/neonatal nurse practitioner (MS). *Accreditation:* AACN. *Program availability:* Part-time, 100% online, blended/hybrid learning. Terminal master's awarded for partial completion of doctoral program. *Degree requirements:* For master's, comprehensive exam; for

doctorate, thesis/dissertation. *Entrance requirements:* For master's, BS in nursing, RN license; for doctorate, GRE General Test (for PhD), B.S. degree, RN license most programs. Additional exam requirements/recommendations for international students: required—TOEFL (minimum score 560 paper-based; 88 iBT), TOEFL (minimum score 560 paper-based; 88 iBT) or IELTS (minimum score 6.5) recommended. Electronic applications accepted. *Expenses:* Contact institution.

**University of San Diego,** Hahn School of Nursing and Health Science, San Diego, CA 92110-2492. Offers adult-gerontology clinical nurse specialist (MSN); adult-gerontology nurse practitioner/family nurse practitioner (MSN); clinical nurse leader (MSN); executive nurse leader (MSN); family nurse practitioner (MSN); healthcare informatics (MS); master's entry program in clinical nursing (for non-rns) (MSN); nursing (PhD); nursing informatics (MSN); nursing practice (DNP); psychiatric-mental health nurse practitioner (MSN). *Accreditation:* AACN. *Program availability:* Part-time, evening/weekend. *Faculty:* 28 full-time (23 women), 43 part-time/adjunct (32 women). *Students:* 252 full-time (202 women), 288 part-time (227 women); includes 261 minority (53 Black or African American, non-Hispanic/Latino; 2 American Indian or Alaska Native, non-Hispanic/Latino; 106 Asian, non-Hispanic/Latino; 76 Hispanic/Latino; 24 Two or more races, non-Hispanic/Latino), 24 international. Average age 34. In 2019, 174 master's, 47 doctorates awarded. *Degree requirements:* For doctorate, thesis/dissertation (for some programs), residency (DNP). *Entrance requirements:* For master's, GRE General Test (for entry-level nursing), BSN, current California RN licensure (except for entry-level nursing), minimum GPA of 3.0; for doctorate, minimum GPA of 3.5, MSN, current California RN licensure. Additional exam requirements/recommendations for international students: required—TOEFL (minimum score 580 paper-based; 83 iBT), TWE. *Application deadline:* Applications are processed on a rolling basis. Application fee: $55. Electronic applications accepted. *Financial support:* In 2019–20, 284 students received support. Institutionally sponsored loans, scholarships/grants, and traineeships available. Support available to part-time students. Financial award application deadline: 4/1; financial award applicants required to submit FAFSA. *Unit head:* Dr. Jane Georges, Dean, Hahn School of Nursing and Health Science, 619-260-4550, Fax: 619-260-6814, E-mail: nursing@sandiego.edu. *Application contact:* Erika Garwood, Associate Director of Graduate Admissions, 619-260-4524, Fax: 619-260-4158, E-mail: grads@sandiego.edu.
Website: http://www.sandiego.edu/nursing/

**University of South Carolina,** The Graduate School, College of Nursing, Program in Health Nursing, Columbia, SC 29208. Offers adult nurse practitioner (MSN); community/public health clinical nurse specialist (MSN); family nurse practitioner (MSN); pediatric nurse practitioner (MSN). *Accreditation:* AACN. *Program availability:* Part-time. *Degree requirements:* For master's, thesis or alternative. *Entrance requirements:* For master's, GRE General Test or MAT, BS in nursing, nursing license. Additional exam requirements/recommendations for international students: required—TOEFL (minimum score 570 paper-based). Electronic applications accepted.

**University of Southern Maine,** College of Science, Technology, and Health, School of Nursing, Portland, ME 04103. Offers adult-gerontology primary care nurse practitioner (MS, PMC); education (MS); family nurse practitioner (MS, PMC); family psychiatric/mental health nurse practitioner (MS); management (MS); nursing (CAS, CGS); psychiatric-mental health nurse practitioner (PMC). *Accreditation:* AACN. *Program availability:* Part-time. *Degree requirements:* For master's, thesis optional. *Entrance requirements:* For master's, GRE General Test or MAT, minimum GPA of 3.0; for doctorate, GRE. Additional exam requirements/recommendations for international students: required—TOEFL (minimum score 550 paper-based). Electronic applications accepted. *Expenses:* Tuition, area resident: Full-time $864; part-time $432 per credit hour. Tuition, state resident: full-time $864; part-time $432 per credit hour. Tuition, nonresident: full-time $2372; part-time $1186 per credit hour. *Required fees:* $141; $108 per credit hour. Tuition and fees vary according to course load.

**University of South Florida,** College of Nursing, Tampa, FL 33612. Offers nurse anesthesia (DNP); nursing (MS, DNP), including adult-gerontology acute care nursing, adult-gerontology primary care nursing, family health nursing, nurse anesthesia (MS), nursing education (MS), occupational health nursing/adult-gerontology primary care nursing, oncology nursing/adult-gerontology primary care nursing (DNP), pediatric health nursing; nursing education (Post Master's Certificate); nursing science (PhD); simulation based academic fellowship in advanced pain management (Graduate Certificate). *Accreditation:* AACN; AANA/CANAEP. *Program availability:* Part-time. *Faculty:* 34 full-time (28 women), 2 part-time/adjunct (1 woman). *Students:* 265 full-time (207 women), 687 part-time (594 women); includes 343 minority (113 Black or African American, non-Hispanic/Latino; 1 American Indian or Alaska Native, non-Hispanic/Latino; 60 Asian, non-Hispanic/Latino; 141 Hispanic/Latino; 1 Native Hawaiian or other Pacific Islander, non-Hispanic/Latino; 27 Two or more races, non-Hispanic/Latino), 2 international. Average age 33. 955 applicants, 44% accepted, 343 enrolled. In 2019, 281 master's, 80 doctorates awarded. *Degree requirements:* For master's, comprehensive exam, thesis optional; for doctorate, comprehensive exam, thesis/dissertation (for some programs). *Entrance requirements:* For master's, GRE General Test, bachelor's in nursing or RN with Bachelor's in relevant field; current license as Registered Nurse; resume or CV; interview; pre-reqs may be required; for doctorate, GRE General Test (recommended), bachelor's degree in nursing from ACEN or CCNE regionally-accredited institution with minimum GPA of 3.0 in all coursework or in all upper-division coursework; current license as Registered Nurse in Florida; undergraduate statistics course with minimum B grade; 3 letters of recommendation; statement of goals; resume; interview. Additional exam requirements/recommendations for international students: required—TOEFL (minimum score 550 paper-based; 79 iBT). *Application deadline:* For fall admission, 12/15 for domestic and international students; for spring admission, 10/1 for domestic students, 9/15 for international students. Application fee: $30. Electronic applications accepted. *Financial support:* In 2019–20, 181 students received support, including 7 research assistantships with tuition reimbursements available (averaging $18,935 per year), 29 teaching assistantships with tuition reimbursements available (averaging $30,814 per year); tuition waivers (partial) and unspecified assistantships also available. Financial award application deadline: 2/1; financial award applicants required to submit FAFSA. *Unit head:* Dr. Victoria Rich, Dean, College of Nursing, 813-974-8939, Fax: 813-974-5418, E-mail: victoriarich@health.usf.edu. *Application contact:* Dr. Denise Maguire, Vice Dean, Graduate Programs, 813-396-9962, E-mail: dmaguire@health.usf.edu.
Website: http://health.usf.edu/nursing/index.htm

**The University of Tampa,** Program in Nursing, Tampa, FL 33606-1490. Offers adult nursing practitioner (MSN); family nursing practitioner (MSN); nursing (MS). *Accreditation:* ACEN. *Program availability:* Part-time, evening/weekend. *Degree requirements:* For master's, comprehensive exam, oral exam, practicum. *Entrance requirements:* For master's, GMAT or GRE, current licensure as registered nurse in state of Florida; minimum GPA of 3.0 in last 60 credit hours; minimum of one year of direct patient care experience within the past five years (recommended). Additional exam requirements/recommendations for international students: required—TOEFL (minimum score 577 paper-based; 90 iBT), IELTS (minimum score 7.5). Electronic applications accepted. *Expenses:* Contact institution.

**The University of Texas at Austin,** Graduate School, School of Nursing, Austin, TX 78712-1111. Offers adult - gerontology clinical nurse specialist (MSN); child health (MSN), including administration, public health nursing, teaching; family nurse practitioner (MSN); family psychiatric/mental health nurse practitioner (MSN); holistic adult health (MSN), including administration, teaching; maternity (MSN), including administration, public health nursing, teaching; nursing (PhD); nursing administration and healthcare systems management (MSN); nursing practice (DNP); pediatric nurse practitioner (MSN); public health nursing (MSN). *Accreditation:* AACN. *Program availability:* Part-time. *Degree requirements:* For master's, thesis optional; for doctorate, thesis/dissertation. *Entrance requirements:* For master's and doctorate, GRE General Test. Additional exam requirements/recommendations for international students: required—TOEFL (minimum score 550 paper-based). Electronic applications accepted.

**University of Wisconsin–Eau Claire,** College of Nursing and Health Sciences, Program in Nursing, Eau Claire, WI 54702-4004. Offers adult-gerontological administration (DNP); adult-gerontological clinical nurse specialist (DNP); adult-gerontological education (MSN); adult-gerontological primary care nurse practitioner (DNP); family health administration (DNP); family health in education (MSN); family health nurse practitioner (DNP); nursing (MSN); nursing practice (DNP). *Accreditation:* AACN. *Program availability:* Part-time. Terminal master's awarded for partial completion of doctoral program. *Degree requirements:* For master's, thesis optional, 500-600 hours clinical practicum, oral and written exams. *Entrance requirements:* For master's, Wisconsin RN license, minimum GPA of 3.0, undergraduate statistics, course work in health assessment. Additional exam requirements/recommendations for international students: required—TOEFL (minimum score 79 iBT). *Expenses:* Contact institution.

**University of Wisconsin–Madison,** School of Nursing, Madison, WI 53705. Offers adult/gerontology (DNP), including clinical nurse specialist; adult/gerontology acute care (DNP), including nurse practitioner; adult/gerontology primary care (DNP), including nurse practitioner; nursing (PhD); MS/MPH. *Accreditation:* AACN. *Program availability:* Part-time. *Degree requirements:* For doctorate, comprehensive exam, thesis/dissertation. *Entrance requirements:* For doctorate, GRE, bachelor's degree in nursing, undergraduate GPA of at least 3.0 on the last 60 credits, academic references, 2 original papers or other scholarly work, essay, RN license (for DNP), 1 year of professional nursing experience (for DNP). Additional exam requirements/recommendations for international students: required—TOEFL (minimum score 580 paper-based; 92 iBT), IELTS (minimum score 7). Electronic applications accepted. *Expenses:* Contact institution.

**University of Wisconsin–Oshkosh,** Graduate Studies, College of Nursing, Oshkosh, WI 54901. Offers adult health and illness (MSN); family nurse practitioner (MSN). *Accreditation:* AACN; AANA/CANAEP. *Program availability:* Part-time. *Degree requirements:* For master's, thesis or alternative, clinical paper. *Entrance requirements:* For master's, RN license, BSN, previous course work in statistics and health assessment, minimum undergraduate GPA of 3.0, letters of recommendation. Additional exam requirements/recommendations for international students: required—TOEFL (minimum score 550 paper-based; 79 iBT). Electronic applications accepted.

**Ursuline College,** School of Graduate and Professional Studies, Programs in Nursing, Pepper Pike, OH 44124-4398. Offers acute-care nurse practitioner (MSN); adult nurse practitioner (MSN); adult-gerontology acute care nurse practitioner (MSN); adult-gerontology clinical nurse specialist (MSN); adult-gerontology nurse practitioner (MSN); care management (MSN); clinical nurse specialist (MSN); family nurse practitioner (MSN); nursing (DNP); nursing education (MSN); palliative care (MSN). *Accreditation:* AACN. *Program availability:* Part-time, 100% online. *Faculty:* 6 full-time (all women), 25 part-time/adjunct (19 women). *Students:* 106 full-time (99 women), 117 part-time (105 women); includes 71 minority (46 Black or African American, non-Hispanic/Latino; 2 American Indian or Alaska Native, non-Hispanic/Latino; 12 Asian, non-Hispanic/Latino; 6 Hispanic/Latino; 5 Two or more races, non-Hispanic/Latino). Average age 38. 265 applicants, 98% accepted, 61 enrolled. In 2019, 68 master's, 2 doctorates awarded. *Degree requirements:* For master's, comprehensive exam; for doctorate, thesis/dissertation. *Entrance requirements:* For master's, minimum undergraduate GPA of 3.0, bachelor's degree in nursing, eligibility for or current Ohio RN license. Additional exam requirements/recommendations for international students: required—TOEFL (minimum score 500 paper-based). *Application deadline:* For fall admission, 8/1 priority date for domestic students. Applications are processed on a rolling basis. Application fee: $25. Electronic applications accepted. *Expenses: Tuition:* Full-time $18,784; part-time $1174 per credit hour. *Required fees:* $320; $240 per unit. One-time fee: $100. Tuition and fees vary according to course level and program. *Financial support:* In 2019–20, 10 students received support. Scholarships/grants, tuition waivers (partial), and College Free Credit available. Financial award application deadline: 3/1; financial award applicants required to submit FAFSA. *Unit head:* Dr. Janet Baker, Associate Dean of Graduate Nursing, 440-864-8172, Fax: 440-684-6053, E-mail: jbaker@ursuline.edu. *Application contact:* Melanie Steele, Director, Graduate Admission, 440-646-8119, Fax: 440-684-6138, E-mail: graduateadmissions@ursuline.edu.

**Villanova University,** M. Louise Fitzpatrick College of Nursing, Villanova, PA 19085. Offers adult-gerontology primary care nurse practitioner (MSN, Post Master's Certificate); family primary care nurse practitioner (MSN, Post Master's Certificate); nurse anesthesia (DNP); nursing (PhD); nursing education (MSN, Post Master's Certificate); nursing practice (DNP); pediatric primary care nurse practitioner (MSN, Post Master's Certificate). *Accreditation:* AACN; AANA/CANAEP. *Program availability:* Part-time, online learning. *Entrance requirements:* Additional exam requirements/recommendations for international students: required—TOEFL, IELTS. Electronic applications accepted.

**Virginia Commonwealth University,** Graduate School, School of Nursing, Richmond, VA 23284-9005. Offers adult health acute nursing (MS); adult health primary nursing (MS); biobehavioral clinical research (PhD); child health nursing (MS); clinical nurse leader (MS); family health nursing (MS); nurse educator (MS); nurse practitioner (MS); nursing (Certificate); nursing administration (MS), including clinical nurse manager; psychiatric-mental health nursing (MS); quality and safety in health care (DNP); women's health nursing (MS). *Accreditation:* AACN; ACEN (one or more programs are accredited). *Program availability:* Part-time, evening/weekend, online learning. *Degree requirements:* For master's, thesis optional; for doctorate, thesis/dissertation. *Entrance requirements:* For master's, GRE General Test, BSN, minimum GPA of 2.8; for doctorate, GRE General Test. Additional exam requirements/recommendations for international students: required—TOEFL (minimum score 600 paper-based; 100 iBT). Electronic applications accepted.

**Walden University,** Graduate Programs, School of Nursing, Minneapolis, MN 55401. Offers adult-gerontology acute care nurse practitioner (MSN); adult-gerontology nurse practitioner (MSN); education (MSN); family nurse practitioner (MSN); informatics (MSN); leadership and management (MSN); nursing (PhD, Post-Master's Certificate), including education (PhD), healthcare administration (PhD), interdisciplinary health (PhD), leadership (PhD), nursing education (Post-Master's Certificate), nursing informatics (Post-Master's Certificate), nursing leadership and management (Post-Master's Certificate), public health policy (PhD); nursing practice (DNP); psychiatric mental health (MSN). *Accreditation:* AACN. *Program availability:* Part-time, evening/weekend, online only, 100% online. *Degree requirements:* For doctorate, thesis/

dissertation (for some programs), residency (for some programs), field experience (for some programs). *Entrance requirements:* For master's, bachelor's degree or equivalent in related field or RN; minimum GPA of 2.5; official transcripts; goal statement (for some programs); access to computer and Internet; for doctorate, master's degree or higher; RN; three years of related professional or academic experience; goal statement; access to computer and Internet; for Post-Master's Certificate, relevant work experience; access to computer and Internet. Additional exam requirements/recommendations for international students: required—TOEFL (minimum score 550 paper-based, 79 iBT), IELTS (minimum score 6.5), Michigan English Language Assessment Battery (minimum score 82), or PTE (minimum score 53). Electronic applications accepted.

**Walsh University,** Master of Science in Nursing, North Canton, OH 44720-3396. Offers academic nurse educator (MSN); adult acute care nurse practitioner (MSN); clinical nurse leader (MSN); nursing practice (DNP). *Accreditation:* AACN. *Program availability:* Part-time, 100% online, blended/hybrid learning. *Faculty:* 5 full-time (4 women), 11 part-time/adjunct (10 women). *Students:* 80 full-time (68 women), 83 part-time (73 women); includes 12 minority (5 Black or African American, non-Hispanic/Latino; 1 Asian, non-Hispanic/Latino; 6 Two or more races, non-Hispanic/Latino). Average age 35. 76 applicants, 93% accepted, 55 enrolled. In 2019, 38 master's, 2 doctorates awarded. *Degree requirements:* For doctorate, scholarly project; residency practicum. *Entrance requirements:* For master's, Registered Nurse license(s), 1 year of experience as a Registered Nurse; Official transcripts documenting a baccalaureate degree in nursing from an accredited program, Minimum 3.0 cumulative GPA, completion of a statistics course, 2 letters of recommendation, resume or CV, personal statement. Additional exam requirements/recommendations for international students: required—TOEFL. *Application deadline:* Applications are processed on a rolling basis. Electronic applications accepted. *Expenses:* $725 per credit hour, $50 technology fee. *Financial support:* In 2019–20, 1 student received support. Research assistantships available. Financial award application deadline: 12/31; financial award applicants required to submit FAFSA. *Unit head:* Dr. Judy Kreye, Dean, Byers School of Nursing, 330-2444757, Fax: 330-4907206, E-mail: jkreye@walsh.edu. *Application contact:* Dr. Janet Finneran, Director of Graduate Nursing Programs, 330-2444759, Fax: 330-4907206, E-mail: jfinneran@walsh.edu.
Website: http://www.walsh.edu/master-of-science-in-nursing

**Wayne State University,** College of Nursing, Detroit, MI 48202. Offers adult gerontology acute care nurse practitioner (MSN); adult gerontology primary care nurse practitioner (MSN); advanced public health nursing (MSN); infant and mental health (DNP, PhD); neonatal nurse practitioner (MSN); nurse-midwifery (MSN); pediatric acute care nurse practitioner (MSN); pediatric primary care nurse practitioner (MSN); psychiatric mental health nurse practitioner (MSN); women's health nurse practitioner (MSN). *Accreditation:* AACN; ACNM/ACME. *Program availability:* Part-time. *Faculty:* 27. *Students:* 134 full-time (118 women), 216 part-time (187 women); includes 98 minority (51 Black or African American, non-Hispanic/Latino; 24 Asian, non-Hispanic/Latino; 6 Hispanic/Latino; 17 Two or more races, non-Hispanic/Latino), 18 international. Average age 33. 425 applicants, 37% accepted, 95 enrolled. In 2019, 58 master's, 31 doctorates awarded. *Degree requirements:* For doctorate, thesis/dissertation. *Entrance requirements:* For master's, Completed a Bachelor of Science in Nursing with a 3.0 or higher GPA. Official transcripts. Professional competence as documented by three references. Current Michigan Registered Nurse (RN) licensure. A personal statement of goals for graduate study; for doctorate, DNP: Minimum GPA of 3.0 or higher in BSN is required. Resume or Curriculum Vita that includes education, work and/or research experience. Two references, one from a doctorally prepared individual. RN license. PhD: BSN transcript; Two to three references from doctorally prepared individuals; goals statement; Resume or CV; Interview. Additional exam requirements/recommendations for international students: required—TOEFL (minimum score 101 iBT), TWE (minimum score 6), Michigan English Language Assessment Battery (minimum score 85); recommended—IELTS (minimum score 7). *Application deadline:* For fall admission, 1/31 for domestic students; for winter admission, 11/1 for domestic students. Applications are processed on a rolling basis. Application fee: $50. Electronic applications accepted. *Expenses:* $925.72 per credit hour in-state, $1,716.93 per credit hour out-of-state, $54.56 student service credit hour fee, $315.70 registration fee. *Financial support:* In 2019–20, 104 students received support, including 39 fellowships with tuition reimbursements available (averaging $6,456 per year), 1 research assistantship (averaging $24,950 per year), 5 teaching assistantships with tuition reimbursements available (averaging $25,000 per year); scholarships/grants, health care benefits, and unspecified assistantships also available. Support available to part-time students. Financial award application deadline: 3/1; financial award applicants required to submit FAFSA. *Unit head:* Dr. Laurie M Lauzon Clabo, Dean, College of Nursing, 313-577-4082, E-mail: laurie.lauzon.clabo@wayne.edu. *Application contact:* Dr. Laurie M Lauzon Clabo, Dean, College of Nursing, 313-577-4082, E-mail: laurie.lauzon.clabo@wayne.edu.
Website: http://nursing.wayne.edu/

**Western Connecticut State University,** Division of Graduate Studies, School of Professional Studies, Nursing Department, Danbury, CT 06810-6885. Offers adult gerontology clinical nurse specialist (MSN); adult gerontology nurse practitioner (MSN); nursing education (Ed D). *Accreditation:* AACN. *Program availability:* Part-time. *Entrance requirements:* For master's, MAT (if GPA less than 3.0), bachelor's degree in nursing, minimum GPA of 3.0, previous course work in statistics and nursing research, RN license. Additional exam requirements/recommendations for international students: recommended—TOEFL (minimum score 550 paper-based; 79 iBT), IELTS (minimum score 6). *Expenses:* Contact institution.

**Wilmington University,** College of Health Professions, New Castle, DE 19720-6491. Offers adult nurse practitioner (MSN); family nurse practitioner (MSN); gerontology nurse practitioner (MSN); nursing (MSN); nursing leadership (MSN); nursing practice (DNP). *Accreditation:* AACN. *Program availability:* Part-time. *Degree requirements:* For master's, thesis. *Entrance requirements:* For master's, BSN, RN license, interview, 3 letters of recommendation. Additional exam requirements/recommendations for international students: required—TOEFL (minimum score 500 paper-based). Electronic applications accepted.

**Winona State University,** College of Nursing and Health Sciences, Winona, MN 55987. Offers adult-gerontology acute care nurse practitioner (MS, DNP, Post Master's Certificate); adult-gerontology clinical nurse specialist (MS, DNP, Post Master's Certificate); adult-gerontology primary care nurse practitioner (MS, DNP, Post Master's Certificate); family nurse practitioner (MS, DNP, Post Master's Certificate); nurse educator (MS); nursing and organizational leadership (MS, DNP, Post Master's Certificate); practice and leadership innovations (DNP, Post Master's Certificate). *Accreditation:* AACN. *Program availability:* Part-time, online learning. *Degree requirements:* For master's, thesis; for doctorate, capstone. *Entrance requirements:* For master's, GRE (if GPA less than 3.0). Additional exam requirements/recommendations for international students: required—TOEFL (minimum score 550 paper-based).

**Wright State University,** Graduate School, College of Nursing and Health, Program in Nursing, Dayton, OH 45435. Offers administration of nursing and health care systems (MS); adult gerontology clinical nurse specialist (MS); adult-gerontology acute care nurse practitioner (MS); family nurse practitioner (MS); neonatal nurse practitioner (MS); pediatric nurse practitioner-acute care (MS); pediatric nurse practitioner-primary care (MS); psychiatric mental health nurse practitioner (MS); school nurse (MS). *Accreditation:* AACN. *Program availability:* Part-time, evening/weekend. *Degree requirements:* For master's, thesis or alternative. *Entrance requirements:* For master's, GRE General Test, BSN from ACEN-accredited college, Ohio RN license. Additional exam requirements/recommendations for international students: required—TOEFL.

# Community Health Nursing

**Allen College,** Graduate Programs, Waterloo, IA 50703. Offers adult-gerontology acute care nurse practitioner (MSN); community/public health nursing (MSN); education (MSN); family nurse practitioner (MSN); health sciences (Ed D); leadership in health care delivery (MSN); leadership in health care informatics (MSN); nursing (DNP); occupational therapy (MS); psychiatric mental health nurse practitioner (MSN). *Accreditation:* AACN; ACEN. *Faculty:* 27 full-time (23 women), 9 part-time/adjunct (8 women). *Students:* 193 full-time (175 women), 95 part-time (84 women); includes 22 minority (6 Black or African American, non-Hispanic/Latino; 1 American Indian or Alaska Native, non-Hispanic/Latino; 4 Asian, non-Hispanic/Latino; 5 Hispanic/Latino; 6 Two or more races, non-Hispanic/Latino). Average age 32. 376 applicants, 53% accepted, 122 enrolled. *Application deadline:* For fall admission, 2/1 priority date for domestic students; for spring admission, 9/1 priority date for domestic students. Applications are processed on a rolling basis. Application fee: $50. Electronic applications accepted. *Financial support:* In 2019–20, 78 students received support. Federal Work-Study, institutionally sponsored loans, and scholarships/grants available. Support available to part-time students. Financial award application deadline: 8/1; financial award applicants required to submit FAFSA. *Unit head:* Dr. Bob Loch, Provost, 319-226-2040, Fax: 319-226-2070, E-mail: bob.loch@allencollege.edu. *Application contact:* Molly Quinn, Director of Admissions, 319-226-2001, Fax: 319-226-2010, E-mail: molly.quinn@allencollege.edu.
Website: http://www.allencollege.edu/

**Binghamton University, State University of New York,** Graduate School, Decker School of Nursing, Binghamton, NY 13902-6000. Offers adult-gerontological nursing (MS, DNP, Certificate); community health nursing (MS, DNP, Certificate); family health nursing (MS, DNP, Certificate); family psychiatric mental health nursing (MS, DNP, Certificate); nursing (PhD). *Accreditation:* AACN. *Program availability:* Part-time, evening/weekend. Terminal master's awarded for partial completion of doctoral program. *Degree requirements:* For master's, comprehensive exam, thesis; for doctorate, comprehensive exam (for some programs), thesis/dissertation. *Entrance requirements:* For master's and doctorate, GRE General Test, nursing licensure. Additional exam requirements/recommendations for international students: required—TOEFL (minimum score 90 iBT). Electronic applications accepted. *Expenses:* Contact institution.

**Hampton University,** School of Nursing, Hampton, VA 23668. Offers community health nursing (MS); family nurse practitioner (MS); family research (PhD); nursing administration (MS); nursing education (MS). *Accreditation:* AACN. *Program availability:* Part-time, online learning. *Students:* 3 full-time (all women), 13 part-time (12 women); includes 15 minority (all Black or African American, non-Hispanic/Latino). Average age 49. 4 applicants, 25% accepted. In 2019, 3 master's, 5 doctorates awarded. *Degree requirements:* For master's, comprehensive exam, thesis optional; for doctorate, comprehensive exam, thesis/dissertation. *Entrance requirements:* For master's, GRE General Test. *Application deadline:* For fall admission, 6/1 priority date for domestic students, 4/1 priority date for international students; for spring admission, 11/1 priority date for domestic students, 9/1 priority date for international students; for summer admission, 4/1 priority date for domestic students, 2/1 priority date for international students. Applications are processed on a rolling basis. Application fee: $35. Electronic applications accepted. *Financial support:* In 2019–20, 2 students received support. Fellowships, research assistantships, teaching assistantships, career-related internships or fieldwork, Federal Work-Study, institutionally sponsored loans, and scholarships/grants available. Support available to part-time students. Financial award application deadline: 6/30; financial award applicants required to submit FAFSA. *Unit head:* Dr. Shevellanie Lott, Dean, 757-727-5654, E-mail: shevellanie.lott@hamptonu.edu. *Application contact:* Dr. Shevellanie Lott, Dean, 757-727-5654, E-mail: shevellanie.lott@hamptonu.edu.
Website: http://nursing.hamptonu.edu

**Hunter College of the City University of New York,** Graduate School, Hunter-Bellevue School of Nursing, Community/Public Health Nursing Program, New York, NY 10065-5085. Offers MS. *Accreditation:* AACN. *Program availability:* Part-time. *Degree requirements:* For master's, practicum. *Entrance requirements:* For master's, minimum GPA of 3.0, New York RN license, BSN. Additional exam requirements/recommendations for international students: required—TOEFL.

**Husson University,** Graduate Nursing Program, Bangor, ME 04401-2999. Offers educational leadership (MSN); family and community nurse practitioner (MSN, PMC); psychiatric mental health nurse practitioner (MSN, PMC). *Accreditation:* AACN. *Program availability:* Part-time, evening/weekend. *Degree requirements:* For master's, comprehensive exam (for some programs), research project. *Entrance requirements:* For master's, proof of RN licensure. Additional exam requirements/recommendations for international students: required—TOEFL (minimum score 550 paper-based; 80 iBT), IELTS (minimum score 6.5). Electronic applications accepted. *Expenses:* Contact institution.

**Independence University,** Program in Nursing, Salt Lake City, UT 84107. Offers community health (MSN); gerontology (MSN); nursing administration (MSN); wellness promotion (MSN).

**Johns Hopkins University,** School of Nursing and Bloomberg School of Public Health, MSN/MPH Public Health Nursing Program, Baltimore, MD 21218. Offers MSN/MPH. *Accreditation:* AACN; CEPH. *Program availability:* Part-time. *Faculty:* 4 full-time (all women). *Students:* 7 full-time (6 women), 2 part-time (both women); includes 2 minority

(1 Asian, non-Hispanic/Latino; 1 Hispanic/Latino). 13 applicants, 62% accepted, 6 enrolled. *Entrance requirements:* Additional exam requirements/recommendations for international students: required—No longer accepting applications to this program. *Expenses:* $1,742 per credit. *Financial support:* In 2019–20, 8 students received support. Federal Work-Study and scholarships/grants available. Support available to part-time students. Financial award application deadline: 3/1; financial award applicants required to submit FAFSA. *Unit head:* Dr. Joanne Flagg, 410-614-4082, E-mail: jsilber1@jhu.edu. *Application contact:* Cathy Wilson, Director of Admissions, 410-955-7548, Fax: 410-614-7086, E-mail: jhuson@jhu.edu.
Website: http://www.nursing.jhu.edu

**Kean University,** Nathan Weiss Graduate College, Program in Nursing, Union, NJ 07083. Offers clinical management (MSN); community health nursing (MSN). *Accreditation:* ACEN. *Program availability:* Part-time. *Faculty:* 5 full-time (all women). *Students:* 2 full-time (both women), 28 part-time (26 women); includes 15 minority (10 Black or African American, non-Hispanic/Latino; 2 Asian, non-Hispanic/Latino; 1 Hispanic/Latino; 2 Two or more races, non-Hispanic/Latino). Average age 45. 5 applicants, 100% accepted, 2 enrolled. In 2019, 10 master's awarded. *Degree requirements:* For master's, thesis or alternative, clinical field experience. *Entrance requirements:* For master's, minimum GPA of 3.0; BS in nursing; RN license; 2 letters of recommendation; interview; official transcripts from all institutions attended. Additional exam requirements/recommendations for international students: required—TOEFL (minimum score 550 paper-based; 79 iBT), IELTS (minimum score 6.5). *Application deadline:* For fall admission, 6/30 for domestic and international students; for spring admission, 12/1 for domestic and international students. Applications are processed on a rolling basis. Application fee: $75. Electronic applications accepted. *Expenses:* Tuition, state resident: full-time $15,326; part-time $748 per credit. Tuition, nonresident: full-time $20,288; part-time $902 per credit. *Required fees:* $2149.50; $91.25 per credit. Tuition and fees vary according to course level, course load, degree level and program. *Financial support:* Scholarships/grants and unspecified assistantships available. Financial award applicants required to submit FAFSA. *Unit head:* Dr. Joan Valas, Program Coordinator, 908-737-6210, E-mail: nursing@kean.edu. *Application contact:* Pedro Lopes, Admissions Counselor, 908-737-7100, E-mail: gradadmissions@kean.edu.
Website: http://grad.kean.edu/masters-programs/nursing-clinical-management

**La Salle University,** School of Nursing and Health Sciences, Program in Nursing, Philadelphia, PA 19141-1199. Offers adult gerontology primary care nurse practitioner (MSN, Certificate); adult health and illness clinical nurse specialist (MSN); adult-gerontology clinical nurse specialist (MSN, Certificate); clinical nurse leader (MSN); family primary care nurse practitioner (MSN, Certificate); gerontology (Certificate); nurse anesthetist (MSN, Certificate); nursing (MSN, Certificate); nursing administration (MSN, Certificate); nursing education (Certificate); nursing practice (DNP); nursing service administration (MSN); public health nursing (MSN, Certificate); school nursing (Certificate); MSN/MBA; MSN/MPH. *Accreditation:* AACN. *Program availability:* Part-time, evening/weekend, 100% online. *Degree requirements:* For doctorate, minimum of 1,000 hours of post baccalaureate clinical practice supervised by preceptors. *Entrance requirements:* For master's, GRE, MAT, or GMAT (for students with BSN GPA of less than 3.2), baccalaureate degree in nursing from ACEN- or CCNE-accredited program or an MSN Bridge program; Pennsylvania RN license; 2 letters of reference; resume; statement of philosophy articulating professional values and future educational goal; 1 year of work experience as a registered nurse; for doctorate, GRE (waived for applicants with MSN cumulative GPA of 3.7 or above), MSN, master's degree, MBA or MHA from nationally-accredited program; resume or curriculum vitae; 2 letters of reference; interview; for Certificate, GRE, MAT, or GMAT (for students with BSN GPA of less than 3.2, baccalaureate degree in nursing from ACEN- or CCNE-accredited program or an MSN Bridge program; Pennsylvania RN license; 2 letters of reference; resume; statement of philosophy articulating professional values and future educational goal; 1 year of work experience as a registered nurse. Additional exam requirements/recommendations for international students: required—TOEFL. Electronic applications accepted. Application fee is waived when completed online. *Expenses:* Contact institution.

**Louisiana State University Health Sciences Center,** School of Nursing, New Orleans, LA 70112. Offers adult gerontology acute care nurse practitioner (DNP, Post-Master's Certificate); adult gerontology clinical nurse specialist (DNP, Post-Master's Certificate); adult gerontology primary care nurse practitioner (DNP, Post-Master's Certificate); clinical nurse leader (MSN); executive nurse leader (DNP, Post-Master's Certificate); neonatal nurse practitioner (DNP, Post-Master's Certificate); nurse anesthesia (DNP, Post-Master's Certificate); nurse educator (MSN); nursing (DNS); primary care family nurse practitioner (DNP, Post-Master's Certificate); public/community health nursing (DNP, Post-Master's Certificate). *Accreditation:* AACN; AANA/CANAEP (one or more programs are accredited). *Program availability:* Part-time. *Faculty:* 25 full-time (21 women), 25 part-time/adjunct (13 women). *Students:* 182 full-time (127 women), 70 part-time (59 women); includes 82 minority (52 Black or African American, non-Hispanic/Latino; 2 American Indian or Alaska Native, non-Hispanic/Latino; 14 Asian, non-Hispanic/Latino; 14 Hispanic/Latino), 1 international. Average age 34. 34 applicants, 62% accepted, 21 enrolled. In 2019, 72 doctorates awarded. *Degree requirements:* For master's, thesis optional; for doctorate, thesis/dissertation. *Entrance requirements:* For master's, GRE, minimum GPA of 3.0; for doctorate, GRE, minimum GPA of 3.0 (for DNP), 3.5 (for DNS). Additional exam requirements/recommendations for international students: required—TOEFL (minimum score 550 paper-based; 79 iBT). *Application deadline:* For fall admission, 6/1 priority date for domestic and international students; for spring admission, 10/1 priority date for domestic and international students; for summer admission, 3/1 priority date for domestic and international students. Applications are processed on a rolling basis. Application fee: $100. Electronic applications accepted. *Expenses:* MSN and DNS: $13,354.50, $24,982.25 non-resident, $586 per hour (fall and spring), $467 per hour (summer), $1,102 per hour non-resident (fall and spring), $858 per hour non-resident (summer); DNP (Except Nurse Anethesia): $21,907.50, $38,262.23 non-resident, $973 per hour (fall and spring), $733 per hour (summer), $1,700 per hour non-resident (fall and spring), $1,278 per hour non-resident (summer); Nurse Anesthesia DNP: $26,407.50, $42,762.23 non-resident, $1,173 per hour (fall and spring), $883 per hour (summer), $1,900 per hour non-resident (fall and spring), $1,428 per hour non-resident (summer). *Financial support:* In 2019–20, 20 students received support. Institutionally sponsored loans, scholarships/grants, unspecified assistantships, and DNS Scholars Program available. Financial award application deadline: 4/15; financial award applicants required to submit FAFSA. *Unit head:* Dr. Demetrius James Porche, Dean, 504-568-4106, Fax: 504-599-0573, E-mail: dporch@lsuhsc.edu. *Application contact:* Tracie Gravolet, Director, Office of Student Affairs, 504-568-4114, Fax: 504-568-5711, E-mail: tgravo@lsuhsc.edu.
Website: http://nursing.lsuhsc.edu/

**Oregon Health & Science University,** School of Nursing, Program in Nursing Education, Portland, OR 97239-3098. Offers MN, Post Master's Certificate. *Program availability:* Part-time, online only, 100% online. *Entrance requirements:* For master's, minimum cumulative GPA of 3.0, 3 letters of recommendation, essay, RN license or eligibility, BS with major in nursing or BSN, statistics taken in last 5 years with minimum B- grade; for Post Master's Certificate, minimum cumulative GPA of 3.0, 3 letters of recommendation, essay, RN license or eligibility, master's degree in nursing, statistics taken in last 5 years with minimum B- grade. Additional exam requirements/recommendations for international students: required—TOEFL (minimum score 83 iBT). Electronic applications accepted. *Expenses:* Contact institution.

**San Francisco State University,** Division of Graduate Studies, College of Health and Social Sciences, School of Nursing, San Francisco, CA 94132-1722. Offers adult acute care (MS); clinical nurse specialist (MS); community/public health nursing (MS); family nurse practitioner (Certificate); nursing administration (MS); pediatrics (MS); women's health (MS). *Accreditation:* AACN. *Program availability:* Part-time. *Application deadline:* Applications are processed on a rolling basis. *Expenses: Tuition, area resident:* Full-time $7176; part-time $4164 per year. Tuition, state resident: full-time $7176; part-time $4164 per year. Tuition, nonresident: full-time $16,680; part-time $396 per unit. *International tuition:* $16,680 full-time. *Required fees:* $1524; $1524 per unit. $762 per semester. Tuition and fees vary according to degree level and program. *Financial support:* Career-related internships or fieldwork available. *Unit head:* Dr. Mary-Ann van Dam, 415-338-1802, Fax: 415-338-0555, E-mail: vandam@sfsu.edu. *Application contact:* Prof. Fang-yu Chou, Assistant Director of Graduate Programs, 415-338-6853, Fax: 415-338-0555, E-mail: fchou@sfsu.edu.
Website: http://nursing.sfsu.edu

**University of Hartford,** College of Education, Nursing, and Health Professions, Program in Nursing, West Hartford, CT 06117-1599. Offers community/public health nursing (MSN); nursing education (MSN); nursing management (MSN). *Accreditation:* AACN. *Program availability:* Part-time, evening/weekend. *Faculty:* 9 full-time (8 women), 5 part-time/adjunct (all women). *Students:* 7 full-time (all women), 100 part-time (94 women); includes 22 minority (12 Black or African American, non-Hispanic/Latino; 2 Asian, non-Hispanic/Latino; 6 Hispanic/Latino; 2 Two or more races, non-Hispanic/Latino), 9 international. Average age 39. 50 applicants, 96% accepted, 45 enrolled. In 2019, 65 master's awarded. *Entrance requirements:* For master's, BSN, Connecticut RN license. Additional exam requirements/recommendations for international students: required—TOEFL (minimum score 550 paper-based). *Application deadline:* For fall admission, 4/15 priority date for domestic students; for spring admission, 12/1 for domestic students. Application fee: $45. Electronic applications accepted. *Expenses:* Contact institution. *Financial support:* Teaching assistantships and Federal Work-Study available. Support available to part-time students. Financial award application deadline: 6/1; financial award applicants required to submit FAFSA. *Unit head:* Jane Williams, Chair, 860-768-4217, Fax: 860-768-5346. *Application contact:* Marlene Hall, Assistant Dean, 860-768-5116, E-mail: mhall@hartford.edu.
Website: http://www.hartford.edu/enhp/

**University of Hawaii at Manoa,** Office of Graduate Education, School of Nursing and Dental Hygiene, Honolulu, HI 96822. Offers clinical nurse specialist (MS), including adult health, community mental health; nurse practitioner (MS), including adult health, community mental health, family nurse practitioner; nursing (PhD, Graduate Certificate); nursing administration (MS). *Accreditation:* AACN. *Program availability:* Part-time, online learning. *Degree requirements:* For master's, thesis optional; for doctorate, comprehensive exam, thesis/dissertation. *Entrance requirements:* For master's, Hawaii RN license. Additional exam requirements/recommendations for international students: required—TOEFL (minimum score 580 paper-based; 92 iBT), IELTS (minimum score 5). *Expenses:* Contact institution.

**University of Illinois at Chicago,** College of Nursing, Program in Nursing, Chicago, IL 60607-7128. Offers acute care clinical nurse specialist (MS); administrative nursing leadership (Certificate); adult nurse practitioner (MS); adult/geriatric nurse practitioner (MS); advanced community health nurse specialist (MS); family nurse practitioner (MS); geriatric clinical nurse specialist (MS); geriatric nurse practitioner (MS); nurse midwifery (MS); occupational health/advanced community health nurse specialist (MS); occupational health/family nurse practitioner (MS); pediatric nurse practitioner (MS); perinatal clinical nurse specialist (MS); school/advanced community health nurse specialist (MS); school/family nurse practitioner (MS); women's health nurse practitioner (MS). *Accreditation:* AACN. *Program availability:* Part-time. *Degree requirements:* For master's, thesis or alternative. *Entrance requirements:* For master's, GRE General Test, minimum GPA of 2.75. Additional exam requirements/recommendations for international students: required—TOEFL. Electronic applications accepted.

**The University of Kansas,** University of Kansas Medical Center, School of Nursing, Kansas City, KS 66045. Offers adult/gerontological clinical nurse specialist (PMC); adult/gerontological nurse practitioner (PMC); health care informatics (PMC); health professions educator (PMC); nurse midwife (PMC); nursing (MS, DNP, PhD); organizational leadership (PMC); psychiatric/mental health nurse practitioner (PMC); public health nursing (PMC). *Accreditation:* AACN; ACNM/ACME. *Program availability:* Part-time, 100% online, blended/hybrid learning. *Faculty:* 65. *Students:* 57 full-time (53 women), 267 part-time (242 women); includes 65 minority (14 Black or African American, non-Hispanic/Latino; 2 American Indian or Alaska Native, non-Hispanic/Latino; 21 Asian, non-Hispanic/Latino; 9 Hispanic/Latino; 1 Native Hawaiian or other Pacific Islander, non-Hispanic/Latino; 18 Two or more races, non-Hispanic/Latino), 2 international. Average age 35. In 2019, 26 master's, 48 doctorates, 5 other advanced degrees awarded. Terminal master's awarded for partial completion of doctoral program. *Degree requirements:* For master's, comprehensive exam, thesis (for some programs), general oral exam; for doctorate, thesis/dissertation or alternative, comprehensive oral exam (for DNP); comprehensive written and oral exam, or three publications (for PhD). *Entrance requirements:* For master's, bachelor's degree in nursing, minimum GPA of 3.0, 1 year of clinical experience, RN license in KS and MO; for doctorate, GRE General Test (for PhD only), bachelor's degree in nursing, minimum GPA of 3.5, RN license in KS and MO. Additional exam requirements/recommendations for international students: required—TOEFL. *Application deadline:* For fall admission, 4/1 for domestic and international students; for spring admission, 9/1 for domestic and international students. Application fee: $75. Electronic applications accepted. *Expenses:* Contact institution. *Financial support:* Research assistantships with tuition reimbursements, teaching assistantships with tuition reimbursements, scholarships/grants, and traineeships available. Financial award application deadline: 3/1; financial award applicants required to submit FAFSA. *Unit head:* Dr. Sally Maliski, Professor and Dean, 913-588-1601, Fax: 913-588-1660, E-mail: smaliski@kumc.edu. *Application contact:* Dr. Pamela K. Barnes, Associate Dean, Student Affairs and Enrollment Management, 913-588-1619, Fax: 913-588-1615, E-mail: pbarnes2@kumc.edu.
Website: http://nursing.kumc.edu

**University of Maryland, Baltimore,** University of Maryland School of Nursing, Baltimore, MD 21201. Offers adult-gerontology acute care nurse practitioner (DNP); adult-gerontology primary care nurse practitioner (DNP); clinical nurse leader (MS); community/public health nursing (MS); family nurse practitioner (DNP); global health (Postbaccalaureate Certificate); health services leadership and management (MS); neonatal nurse practitioner (DNP); nurse anesthesia (DNP); nursing (PhD); nursing informatics (MS, Postbaccalaureate Certificate); pediatric acute/primary care nurse practitioner (DNP); psychiatric mental health nurse practitioner (DNP); teaching in nursing and health professions (Postbaccalaureate Certificate); MS/MBA. *Accreditation:* AANA/CANAEP. *Program availability:* Part-time. *Faculty:* 130 full-time (117 women), 125 part-time/adjunct (114 women). *Students:* 539 full-time (463 women), 586 part-time

(506 women); includes 485 minority (259 Black or African American, non-Hispanic/Latino; 3 American Indian or Alaska Native, non-Hispanic/Latino; 124 Asian, non-Hispanic/Latino; 66 Hispanic/Latino; 1 Native Hawaiian or other Pacific Islander, non-Hispanic/Latino; 32 Two or more races, non-Hispanic/Latino), 18 international. Average age 33. 964 applicants, 54% accepted, 347 enrolled. In 2019, 197 master's, 114 doctorates, 12 other advanced degrees awarded. *Degree requirements:* For master's and Postbaccalaureate Certificate, thesis (for some programs); for doctorate, comprehensive exam, thesis/dissertation. *Entrance requirements:* Additional exam requirements/recommendations for international students: required—TOEFL (minimum score 550 paper-based; 79 iBT); recommended—IELTS (minimum score 7). *Application deadline:* For fall admission, 11/1 priority date for domestic and international students; for spring admission, 12/15 for domestic and international students; for summer admission, 9/1 for domestic and international students. Applications are processed on a rolling basis. Application fee: $75. Electronic applications accepted. *Financial support:* In 2019–20, 257 students received support, including 31 research assistantships with full and partial tuition reimbursements available (averaging $25,000 per year), 21 teaching assistantships with full and partial tuition reimbursements available (averaging $19,000 per year); scholarships/grants, traineeships, and unspecified assistantships also available. Support available to part-time students. Financial award application deadline: 3/1; financial award applicants required to submit FAFSA. *Unit head:* Dr. Jane Kirschling, Dean, 410-706-4359, E-mail: kirschling@umaryland.edu. *Application contact:* Larry Fillian, Associate Dean of Student and Academic Services, 410-706-6298, E-mail: lfillian@umaryland.edu.
Website: http://www.nursing.umaryland.edu/

**University of Massachusetts Amherst,** Graduate School, College of Nursing, Amherst, MA 01003. Offers adult gerontology primary care nurse practitioner (DNP); clinical nurse leader (MS); family nurse practitioner (DNP); nursing (PhD); public health nurse leader (DNP). *Accreditation:* AACN. *Program availability:* Part-time, online learning. Terminal master's awarded for partial completion of doctoral program. *Degree requirements:* For master's, thesis optional; for doctorate, comprehensive exam, thesis/dissertation. *Entrance requirements:* Additional exam requirements/recommendations for international students: required—TOEFL (minimum score 550 paper-based; 80 iBT), IELTS (minimum score 6.5). Electronic applications accepted.

**University of Massachusetts Dartmouth,** Graduate School, College of Nursing and Health Sciences, North Dartmouth, MA 02747-2300. Offers MS, DNP, PhD. *Accreditation:* AACN. *Program availability:* Part-time, 100% online, blended/hybrid learning. *Faculty:* 26 full-time (all women), 45 part-time/adjunct (all women). *Students:* 2 full-time (both women), 122 part-time (111 women); includes 25 minority (10 Black or African American, non-Hispanic/Latino; 9 Asian, non-Hispanic/Latino; 4 Hispanic/Latino; 2 Two or more races, non-Hispanic/Latino), 1 international. Average age 38. 39 applicants, 95% accepted, 32 enrolled. In 2019, 1 master's, 12 doctorates awarded. *Degree requirements:* For master's, capstone project; for doctorate, comprehensive exam, thesis/dissertation, project (for DNP); dissertation (qualifying exam for PhD). *Entrance requirements:* For master's, statement of purpose (minimum of 300 words), resume, 2 letters of reference, official transcripts, BS Nursing, copy of RN license or license number; for doctorate, Personal statement, Current Mass registered Nurse license, 1 year professional Nursing experience, resume, official transcripts, scholarly writing samples (min 10 pages) and 3 letters of recommendation. Additional exam requirements/recommendations for international students: required—TOEFL. *Application deadline:* Applications are processed on a rolling basis. Application fee: $60. Electronic applications accepted. *Expenses: Tuition, area resident:* Full-time $16,390; part-time $682.92 per credit. Tuition, state resident: full-time $16,390; part-time $682.92 per credit. Tuition, nonresident: full-time $29,578; part-time $1232.42 per credit. *Required fees:* $575. *Financial support:* In 2019–20, 7 teaching assistantships (averaging $7,714 per year) were awarded; tuition waivers (partial) and doctoral support also available. Financial award application deadline: 3/1; financial award applicants required to submit FAFSA. *Unit head:* June Horowitz, Associate Dean for Graduate Programs and Research, 508-999-8251, E-mail: jhorowitz@umassd.edu. *Application contact:* Scott Webster, Director of Graduate Studies and Admissions, 508-999-8604, Fax: 508-999-8183, E-mail: graduate@umassd.edu.
Website: http://www.umassd.edu/nursing

**University of North Dakota,** Graduate School, College of Nursing and Professional Disciplines, Department of Nursing, Grand Forks, ND 58202. Offers adult-gerontological nurse practitioner (MS); advanced public health nurse (MS); family nurse practitioner (MS); nurse anesthesia (MS); nurse educator (MS); nursing (PhD, Post-Master's Certificate); nursing practice (DNP); psychiatric and mental health nurse practitioner (MS). *Accreditation:* AANA/CANAEP.

**University of Puerto Rico - Medical Sciences Campus,** School of Nursing, San Juan, PR 00936-5067. Offers adult and elderly nursing (MSN); child and adolescent nursing (MSN); critical care nursing (MSN); family and community nursing (MSN); family nurse practitioner (MSN); maternity nursing (MSN); mental health and psychiatric nursing (MSN). *Accreditation:* AACN; AANA/CANAEP. *Entrance requirements:* For master's, GRE or EXADEP, interview, Puerto Rico RN license or professional license for international students, general and specific point average, article analysis. Electronic applications accepted.

**University of South Carolina,** The Graduate School, College of Nursing, Program in Health Nursing, Columbia, SC 29208. Offers adult nurse practitioner (MSN); community/public health clinical nurse specialist (MSN); family nurse practitioner (MSN); pediatric nurse practitioner (MSN). *Accreditation:* AACN. *Program availability:* Part-time. *Degree requirements:* For master's, thesis or alternative. *Entrance requirements:* For master's, GRE General Test or MAT, BS in nursing, nursing license. Additional exam requirements/recommendations for international students: required—TOEFL (minimum score 570 paper-based). Electronic applications accepted.

**University of South Carolina,** The Graduate School, College of Nursing, Program in Nursing and Public Health, Columbia, SC 29208. Offers MPH/MSN. *Accreditation:* AACN; CEPH. *Program availability:* Part-time. *Entrance requirements:* Additional exam requirements/recommendations for international students: required—TOEFL (minimum score 570 paper-based). Electronic applications accepted.

**The University of Texas at Austin,** Graduate School, School of Nursing, Austin, TX 78712-1111. Offers adult - gerontology clinical nurse specialist (MSN); child health (MSN), including administration, public health nursing, teaching; family nurse practitioner (MSN); family psychiatric/mental health nurse practitioner (MSN); holistic adult health (MSN), including administration, teaching; maternity (MSN), including administration, public health nursing, teaching; nursing (PhD); nursing administration and healthcare systems management (MSN); nursing practice (DNP); pediatric nurse practitioner (MSN); public health nursing (MSN). *Accreditation:* AACN. *Program availability:* Part-time. *Degree requirements:* For master's, thesis optional; for doctorate, thesis/dissertation. *Entrance requirements:* For master's and doctorate, GRE General Test. Additional exam requirements/recommendations for international students: required—TOEFL (minimum score 550 paper-based). Electronic applications accepted.

**The University of Texas Health Science Center at San Antonio,** School of Nursing, San Antonio, TX 78229-3900. Offers administrative management (MSN); adult-gerontology acute care nurse practitioner (PGC); advanced practice leadership (DNP); clinical nurse leader (MSN); executive administrative management (DNP); family nurse practitioner (MSN, PGC); nursing (MSN, PhD); nursing education (MSN, PGC); pediatric nurse practitioner primary care (PGC); psychiatric mental health nurse practitioner (PGC); public health nurse leader (DNP). *Accreditation:* AACN. *Program availability:* Part-time. Terminal master's awarded for partial completion of doctoral program. *Degree requirements:* For master's, thesis optional; for doctorate, comprehensive exam, thesis/dissertation.

**The University of Toledo,** College of Graduate Studies, College of Nursing, Department of Population and Community Care, Toledo, OH 43606-3390. Offers clinical nurse leader (MSN); family nurse practitioner (MSN, Certificate); nurse educator (MSN, Certificate); pediatric nurse practitioner (MSN, Certificate). *Program availability:* Part-time. *Degree requirements:* For master's, thesis or alternative. *Entrance requirements:* For master's, GRE, BS in nursing, minimum undergraduate GPA of 3.0, statement of purpose, three letters of recommendation, transcripts from all prior institutions attended, Nursing CAS application, UT supplemental application; for Certificate, BS in nursing, minimum undergraduate GPA of 3.0, statement of purpose, three letters of recommendation, transcripts from all prior institutions attended. Additional exam requirements/recommendations for international students: required—TOEFL (minimum score 550 paper-based; 80 iBT). Electronic applications accepted.

**University of Washington, Tacoma,** Graduate Programs, Program in Nursing, Tacoma, WA 98402-3100. Offers communities, populations and health (MN); leadership in healthcare (MN); nurse educator (MN). *Program availability:* Part-time. *Degree requirements:* For master's, thesis (for some programs), advance fieldwork. *Entrance requirements:* For master's, Washington State NCLEX exam, minimum GPA of 3.0. Additional exam requirements/recommendations for international students: required—TOEFL (minimum score 580 paper-based; 70 iBT); recommended—IELTS (minimum score 7).

**Wayne State University,** College of Nursing, Detroit, MI 48202. Offers adult gerontology acute care nurse practitioner (MSN); adult gerontology primary care nurse practitioner (MSN); advanced public health nursing (MSN); infant and mental health (DNP, PhD); neonatal nurse practitioner (MSN); nurse-midwifery (MSN); pediatric acute care nurse practitioner (MSN); pediatric primary care nurse practitioner (MSN); psychiatric mental health nurse practitioner (MSN); women's health nurse practitioner (MSN). *Accreditation:* AACN; ACNM/ACME. *Program availability:* Part-time. *Faculty:* 27. *Students:* 134 full-time (118 women), 216 part-time (187 women); includes 98 minority (51 Black or African American, non-Hispanic/Latino; 24 Asian, non-Hispanic/Latino; 6 Hispanic/Latino; 17 Two or more races, non-Hispanic/Latino), 18 international. Average age 33. 425 applicants, 37% accepted, 95 enrolled. In 2019, 58 master's, 31 doctorates awarded. *Degree requirements:* For doctorate, thesis/dissertation. *Entrance requirements:* For master's, Completed a Bachelor of Science in Nursing with a 3.0 or higher GPA. Official transcripts. Professional competence as documented by three references. Current Michigan Registered Nurse (RN) licensure. A personal statement of goals for graduate study; for doctorate, DNP: Minimum GPA of 3.0 or higher in BSN is required. Resume or Curriculum Vita that includes education, work and/or research experience. Two references, one from a doctorally prepared individual. RN license. PhD: BSN transcript; Two to three references from doctorally prepared individuals; goals statement; Resume or CV; Interview. Additional exam requirements/recommendations for international students: required—TOEFL (minimum score 101 iBT), TWE (minimum score 6), Michigan English Language Assessment Battery (minimum score 85); recommended—IELTS (minimum score 7). *Application deadline:* For fall admission, 1/31 for domestic students; for winter admission, 11/1 for domestic students. Applications are processed on a rolling basis. Application fee: $50. Electronic applications accepted. *Expenses:* $925.72 per credit hour in-state, $1,716.93 per credit hour out-of-state, $54.56 student service credit hour fee, $315.70 registration fee. *Financial support:* In 2019–20, 104 students received support, including 39 fellowships with tuition reimbursements available (averaging $6,456 per year), 1 research assistantship (averaging $24,950 per year), 5 teaching assistantships with tuition reimbursements available (averaging $25,000 per year); scholarships/grants, health care benefits, and unspecified assistantships also available. Support available to part-time students. Financial award application deadline: 3/1; financial award applicants required to submit FAFSA. *Unit head:* Dr. Laurie M Lauzon Clabo, Dean, College of Nursing, 313-577-4082, E-mail: laurie.lauzon.clabo@wayne.edu. *Application contact:* Dr. Laurie M Lauzon Clabo, Dean, College of Nursing, 313-577-4082, E-mail: laurie.lauzon.clabo@wayne.edu.
Website: http://nursing.wayne.edu/

**Worcester State University,** Graduate School, Department of Nursing, Program in Community and Public Health Nursing, Worcester, MA 01602-2597. Offers MSN. *Accreditation:* AACN. *Program availability:* Part-time. *Faculty:* 4 full-time (all women), 4 part-time/adjunct (3 women). *Students:* 25 part-time (24 women); includes 6 minority (2 Black or African American, non-Hispanic/Latino; 1 Asian, non-Hispanic/Latino; 2 Hispanic/Latino; 1 Two or more races, non-Hispanic/Latino). Average age 39. 9 applicants, 100% accepted, 8 enrolled. In 2019, 13 master's awarded. *Degree requirements:* For master's, comprehensive exam (for some programs), thesis (for some programs), final project, practicum. For a detail list in Degree Completion requirements please see the graduate catalog at catalog.worcester.edu. *Entrance requirements:* For master's, Unencumbered license to practice as a Registered Nurse in Massachusetts. For a detail list of entrance requirements please see the graduate catalog at catalog.worcester.edu. Additional exam requirements/recommendations for international students: required—TOEFL (minimum score 500 paper-based; 79 iBT), IELTS (minimum score 6). *Application deadline:* For fall admission, 3/1 for domestic and international students; for spring admission, 11/1 for domestic and international students; for summer admission, 3/1 for domestic and international students. Applications are processed on a rolling basis. Application fee: $50. Electronic applications accepted. *Expenses: Tuition, area resident:* Full-time $3042; part-time $169 per credit hour. Tuition, state resident: full-time $3042; part-time $169 per credit hour. Tuition, nonresident: full-time $3042; part-time $169 per credit hour. *International tuition:* $3042 full-time. *Required fees:* $2754; $153 per credit hour. *Financial support:* Career-related internships or fieldwork, scholarships/grants, and unspecified assistantships available. Financial award application deadline: 3/1; financial award applicants required to submit FAFSA. *Unit head:* Dr. Stephanie Chalupka, Program Coordinator, 508-929-8680, Fax: 508-929-8168, E-mail: schalupka@worcester.edu. *Application contact:* Sara Grady, Associate Dean of Graduate Studies and Professional Development, 508-929-8130, Fax: 508-929-8100, E-mail: sara.grady@worcester.edu.

# Family Nurse Practitioner Studies

**Albany State University,** Darton College of Health Professions, Albany, GA 31705-2717. Offers nursing (MSN), including family nurse practitioner, nurse educator. *Accreditation:* ACEN. *Program availability:* Part-time, evening/weekend, online learning. *Degree requirements:* For master's, comprehensive exam, thesis. *Entrance requirements:* For master's, GRE or MAT, official transcript, letters of recommendation, pre-medical/certificate of immunizations. Electronic applications accepted.

**Allen College,** Graduate Programs, Waterloo, IA 50703. Offers adult-gerontology acute care nurse practitioner (MSN); community/public health nursing (MSN); education (MSN); family nurse practitioner (MSN); health sciences (Ed D); leadership in health care delivery (MSN); leadership in health care informatics (MSN); nursing (DNP); occupational therapy (MS); psychiatric mental health nurse practitioner (MSN). *Accreditation:* AACN; ACEN. *Faculty:* 27 full-time (23 women), 9 part-time/adjunct (8 women). *Students:* 193 full-time (175 women), 95 part-time (84 women); includes 22 minority (6 Black or African American, non-Hispanic/Latino; 1 American Indian or Alaska Native, non-Hispanic/Latino; 4 Asian, non-Hispanic/Latino; 5 Hispanic/Latino; 6 Two or more races, non-Hispanic/Latino). Average age 32. 376 applicants, 53% accepted, 122 enrolled. *Application deadline:* For fall admission, 2/1 priority date for domestic students; for spring admission, 9/1 priority date for domestic students. Applications are processed on a rolling basis. Application fee: $50. Electronic applications accepted. *Financial support:* In 2019–20, 78 students received support. Federal Work-Study, institutionally sponsored loans, and scholarships/grants available. Support available to part-time students. Financial award application deadline: 8/1; financial award applicants required to submit FAFSA. *Unit head:* Dr. Bob Loch, Provost, 319-226-2040, Fax: 319-226-2070, E-mail: bob.loch@allencollege.edu. *Application contact:* Molly Quinn, Director of Admissions, 319-226-2001, Fax: 319-226-2010, E-mail: molly.quinn@allencollege.edu.
Website: http://www.allencollege.edu/

**Alvernia University,** School of Graduate Studies, Department of Nursing, Reading, PA 19607-1799. Offers adult gerontology nurse practitioner (DNP); family nurse practitioner (DNP); nursing education (MSN); nursing leadership (Graduate Certificate); nursing leadership and healthcare administration (MSN).

**Alverno College,** JoAnn McGrath School of Nursing and Health Professions, Milwaukee, WI 53234-3922. Offers clinical nurse specialist (MSN); family nurse practitioner (MSN); nursing practice (DNP); psychiatric mental health nurse practitioner (MSN). *Accreditation:* AACN. *Program availability:* Part-time, evening/weekend, 100% online, blended/hybrid learning. *Faculty:* 7 full-time (all women), 10 part-time/adjunct (8 women). *Students:* 117 full-time (110 women), 139 part-time (129 women); includes 68 minority (32 Black or African American, non-Hispanic/Latino; 8 Asian, non-Hispanic/Latino; 24 Hispanic/Latino; 4 Two or more races, non-Hispanic/Latino), 1 international. Average age 36. 94 applicants, 95% accepted, 60 enrolled. In 2019, 51 master's, 3 doctorates awarded. *Degree requirements:* For master's, 500 clinical hours, capstone; for doctorate, 1,000 post-BSN clinical hours. *Entrance requirements:* For master's, BSN, current license; for doctorate, MSN, nursing license. Additional exam requirements/recommendations for international students: required—TOEFL. *Application deadline:* For fall admission, 7/15 priority date for domestic and international students; for spring admission, 12/15 priority date for domestic and international students. Applications are processed on a rolling basis. Electronic applications accepted. *Expenses:* $1098 per credit hour. *Financial support:* In 2019–20, 4 students received support. Federal Work-Study and scholarships/grants available. Support available to part-time students. Financial award applicants required to submit FAFSA. *Unit head:* Patti Varga, Dean, 414-382-6303, Fax: 414-382-6354, E-mail: patti.varga@alverno.edu. *Application contact:* Janet Stikel, Director of Admissions, 414-382-6112, Fax: 414-382-6354, E-mail: janet.stikel@alverno.edu.
Website: http://www.alverno.edu/academics/academicdepartments/joannmcgrathschoolofnursing/

**American International College,** School of Health Sciences, Springfield, MA 01109-3189. Offers exercise science (MS); family nurse practitioner (MSN, Post-Master's Certificate); nursing administrator (MSN); nursing educator (MSN); occupational therapy (MSOT, OTD); physical therapy (DPT). *Accreditation:* AOTA. *Program availability:* Part-time, 100% online. *Degree requirements:* For master's, practicum; for doctorate, thesis/dissertation, practicum. *Entrance requirements:* For master's, 3 letters of recommendation, personal goal statement; minimum GPA of 3.2, interview, BS or BA, and 2 clinical PT observations (for DPT); minimum GPA of 3.0, MSOT, OT licensen, and 2 clinical OT observations (for OTD); for doctorate, personal goal statement, 2 letters of recommendation; minimum GPA of 3.0, BS or BA, 2 clinical OT observations (for MSOT); RN license and minimum GPA of 3.0 (for MSN). Additional exam requirements/recommendations for international students: required—TOEFL (minimum score 577 paper-based; 91 iBT). Electronic applications accepted. *Expenses:* Contact institution.

**Anderson University,** College of Health Professions, Anderson, SC 29621. Offers advanced practice (DNP); executive leadership (MSN, DNP); family nurse practitioner (MSN, DNP); nurse educator (MSN); psychiatric mental health nurse practitioner (MSN, DNP). *Program availability:* Online learning. *Application deadline:* Applications are processed on a rolling basis. Electronic applications accepted. *Expenses:* Contact institution. *Financial support:* Scholarships/grants available. *Unit head:* Dr. Donald M. Peace, Dean, 864-231-5513, E-mail: dpeace@andersonuniversity.edu. *Application contact:* Dr. Donald M. Peace, Dean, 864-231-5513, E-mail: dpeace@andersonuniversity.edu.
Website: http://www.andersonuniversity.edu/health-professions

**Angelo State University,** College of Graduate Studies and Research, Archer College of Health and Human Services, Department of Nursing, San Angelo, TX 76909. Offers family nurse practitioner (MSN); nurse educator (MSN). *Accreditation:* AACN; ACEN. *Program availability:* Part-time, evening/weekend, online learning. *Entrance requirements:* For master's, essay, three letters of recommendation. Additional exam requirements/recommendations for international students: required—TOEFL or IELTS. Electronic applications accepted.

**Arizona State University at Tempe,** College of Nursing and Health Innovation, Phoenix, AZ 85004. Offers advanced nursing practice (DNP); clinical research management (MS); community and public health practice (Graduate Certificate); family mental health nurse practitioner (Graduate Certificate); family nurse practitioner (Graduate Certificate); geriatric nursing (Graduate Certificate); healthcare innovation (MHI); nurse education in academic and practice settings (Graduate Certificate); nurse educator (MS); nursing and healthcare innovation (PhD). *Accreditation:* AACN. *Program availability:* Online learning. *Degree requirements:* For master's, comprehensive exam (for some programs), thesis (for some programs), interactive Program of Study (iPOS) submitted before completing 50 percent of required credit hours; for doctorate, comprehensive exam, thesis/dissertation, interactive Program of Study (iPOS) submitted before completing 50 percent of required credit hours. *Entrance requirements:* For master's and doctorate, GRE, minimum GPA of 3.0 or equivalent in last 2 years of work leading to bachelor's degree. Additional exam requirements/recommendations for international students: required—TOEFL, IELTS, or PTE. Electronic applications accepted. *Expenses:* Contact institution.

**Ashland University,** Dwight Schar College of Nursing and Health Sciences, Department of Nursing, Ashland, OH 44805-3702. Offers family nurse practitioner (DNP). *Entrance requirements:* For doctorate, minimum GPA of 3.0, one year of clinical practice experience, 2-3 page paper, undergraduate- or graduate-level statistics course, interview. Additional exam requirements/recommendations for international students: recommended—TOEFL, IELTS, TSE. Electronic applications accepted. *Expenses: Tuition:* Full-time $10,800; part-time $5400 per credit hour. *Required fees:* $720; $360 per credit hour.

**Auburn University at Montgomery,** College of Nursing and Health Sciences, Montgomery, AL 36124. Offers family nurse practitioner (MSN); nurse educator for interprofessional practice (MSN). *Accreditation:* AACN. *Program availability:* Part-time, evening/weekend, 100% online, blended/hybrid learning. *Faculty:* 3 full-time (all women), 4 part-time/adjunct (all women). *Students:* 37 part-time (32 women); includes 13 minority (all Black or African American, non-Hispanic/Latino). Average age 36. 56 applicants, 46% accepted, 22 enrolled. *Entrance requirements:* Additional exam requirements/recommendations for international students: recommended—TOEFL (minimum score 500 paper-based; 61 iBT), IELTS (minimum score 5.5), TSE (minimum score 44). *Application deadline:* For fall admission, 7/1 for domestic students; for spring admission, 10/1 for domestic students; for summer admission, 3/1 for domestic students. Applications are processed on a rolling basis. Application fee: $25. Electronic applications accepted. *Expenses: Tuition, area resident:* Full-time $7578; part-time $421 per credit hour. Tuition, state resident: full-time $7578; part-time $421 per credit hour. Tuition, nonresident: full-time $17,046; part-time $947 per credit hour. *International tuition:* $17,046 full-time. *Required fees:* $868. *Financial support:* Application deadline: 3/1. *Unit head:* Dr. Jean Leuner, Dean, 334-244-3658, E-mail: jleuner@aum.edu. *Application contact:* Christy Dearden, Senior Administrative Associate, 334-244-3658, E-mail: cdearden@aum.edu.
Website: http://conhs.aum.edu/academic-programs/graduate-programs/msn

**Augsburg University,** Programs in Nursing, Minneapolis, MN 55454-1351. Offers MA, DNP. *Accreditation:* AACN. *Degree requirements:* For master's, thesis or alternative.

**Augusta University,** College of Nursing, Doctor of Nursing Practice Program, Augusta, GA 30912. Offers adult gerontology acute care nurse practitioner (DNP); family nurse practitioner (DNP); nurse executive (DNP); nursing (DNP); nursing anesthesia (DNP); pediatric nurse practitioner (DNP); psychiatric mental health nurse practitioner (DNP). *Accreditation:* AACN; AANA/CANAEP. *Degree requirements:* For doctorate, thesis/dissertation or alternative. *Entrance requirements:* For doctorate, GRE General Test or MAT, master's degree in nursing or related field, current professional nurse licensure. Additional exam requirements/recommendations for international students: required—TOEFL (minimum score 600 paper-based; 100 iBT). Electronic applications accepted.

**Austin Peay State University,** College of Graduate Studies, College of Behavioral and Health Sciences, School of Nursing, Clarksville, TN 37044. Offers family nurse practitioner (MSN); nursing administration (MSN); nursing education (MSN); nursing informatics (MSN). *Program availability:* Part-time, online learning. *Faculty:* 5 full-time (all women), 1 (woman) part-time/adjunct. *Students:* 12 full-time (11 women), 120 part-time (114 women); includes 25 minority (14 Black or African American, non-Hispanic/Latino; 3 Asian, non-Hispanic/Latino; 4 Hispanic/Latino; 4 Two or more races, non-Hispanic/Latino). Average age 34. 19 applicants, 84% accepted, 2 enrolled. In 2019, 51 master's awarded. *Degree requirements:* For master's, comprehensive exam. *Entrance requirements:* For master's, minimum GPA of 3.0, RN license eligibility, 3 letters of recommendation. Additional exam requirements/recommendations for international students: required—TOEFL (minimum score 500 paper-based). *Application deadline:* For fall admission, 8/5 priority date for domestic students. Applications are processed on a rolling basis. Application fee: $45 ($55 for international students). Electronic applications accepted. *Financial support:* Research assistantships with full tuition reimbursements, career-related internships or fieldwork, Federal Work-Study, institutionally sponsored loans, scholarships/grants, and unspecified assistantships available. Support available to part-time students. Financial award application deadline: 7/1; financial award applicants required to submit FAFSA. *Unit head:* Dr. Mary Rice, Interim Director of Nursing, 931-221-7483, Fax: 931-221-7595, E-mail: ricem@apsu.edu. *Application contact:* Megan Mitchell, Coordinator of Graduate Admissions, 931-221-6189, Fax: 931-221-7641, E-mail: mitchellm@apsu.edu.
Website: http://www.apsu.edu/nursing

**Azusa Pacific University,** School of Nursing, Azusa, CA 91702-7000. Offers adult clinical nurse specialist (MSN); adult-gerontology nurse practitioner (MSN); family nurse practitioner (MSN); healthcare administration and leadership (MSN); nursing (MSN, DNP, PhD); nursing education (MSN); parent-child clinical nurse specialist (MSN); psychiatric mental health nurse practitioner (MSN). *Accreditation:* AACN. *Program availability:* Part-time, evening/weekend. *Degree requirements:* For master's, thesis optional. *Entrance requirements:* For master's, BSN.

**Ball State University,** Graduate School, College of Health, School of Nursing, Muncie, IN 47304. Offers adult/gerontology nurse practitioner (Post Master's Certificate); evidence-based clinical practice (Postbaccalaureate Certificate); family nurse practitioner (Post Master's Certificate); nurse educator (Post Master's Certificate); nursing (MS), including family nurse practitioner, nurse administrator, nurse educator; nursing education (Postbaccalaureate Certificate); nursing practice (DNP). *Accreditation:* AACN. *Program availability:* Part-time-only, online only, 100% online. *Entrance requirements:* For master's, bachelor's degree in nursing, minimum GPA of 3.0, minimum C grade in at least 2 quarter or semester hours in an undergraduate research course, unencumbered license as a registered nurse in state of practice; for doctorate, advanced practice nurse (nurse practitioner, clinical nurse specialist, nurse midwife); master's degree in nursing from accredited program with minimum GPA of 3.2; graduate-level statistics, nursing research, and health assessment courses; unencumbered license as registered nurse in state of practice. Additional exam requirements/recommendations for international students: required—TOEFL (minimum score 550 paper-based; 79 iBT), IELTS (minimum score 6.5). Electronic applications accepted. *Expenses:* Contact institution.

**Barry University,** School of Adult and Continuing Education, Division of Nursing, Program in Nurse Practitioner, Miami Shores, FL 33161-6695. Offers acute care nurse practitioner (MSN); family nurse practitioner (MSN); nurse practitioner (Certificate). *Accreditation:* AACN. *Program availability:* Part-time, evening/weekend. *Degree requirements:* For master's, research project or thesis. *Entrance requirements:* For

master's, GRE General Test or MAT, BSN, minimum GPA of 3.0, course work in statistics. Electronic applications accepted.

**Bellarmine University,** College of Health Professions, Donna and Allan Lansing School of Nursing and Clinical Sciences, Louisville, KY 40205. Offers family nurse practitioner (MSN); health science (MHS); nursing administration (MSN); nursing education (MSN); nursing practice (DNP). *Accreditation:* AACN; APTA. *Program availability:* Part-time, evening/weekend. *Faculty:* 19 full-time (15 women), 7 part-time/adjunct (all women). *Students:* 142 full-time (104 women), 128 part-time (105 women); includes 55 minority (24 Black or African American, non-Hispanic/Latino; 1 American Indian or Alaska Native, non-Hispanic/Latino; 15 Asian, non-Hispanic/Latino; 10 Hispanic/Latino; 5 Two or more races, non-Hispanic/Latino), 10 international. Average age 30. 348 applicants, 82% accepted, 172 enrolled. In 2019, 29 master's, 4 doctorates awarded. *Degree requirements:* For master's, comprehensive exam, thesis (for some programs); for doctorate, comprehensive exam, thesis/dissertation. *Entrance requirements:* For master's, GRE General Test, minimum GPA of 3.0, interview, resume; BSN from CCNE- or ACEN-accredited program, professional references, goal statement, and RN license (for MSN); bachelor's degree with exposure to health issues and grade of C or better in math/science courses (for MHS); for doctorate, GRE General Test, MSN from CCNE- or ACEN-accredited program; minimum GPA of 3.5 in graduate coursework; professional references; goal statement; current curriculum vitae or resume; RN license; verification of post-baccalaureate clinical and practice hours. Additional exam requirements/recommendations for international students: required—TOEFL (minimum iBT score of 83, 26 on speaking test), IELTS (minimum score 7, speaking band score of 8), or language training at an approved center; recommended—TOEFL (minimum score 83 iBT), IELTS. *Application deadline:* Applications are processed on a rolling basis. Application fee: $40. Electronic applications accepted. *Expenses:* Accelerated BSN, May 2020 cohort: $905 per credit hour; Accelerated BSN, 2-yr. program, Summer 2020: $950 per credit hour; MHS: $770 per credit hour; MHS, Medical Lab Science: $665 per credit hour; MHS, Respiratory Therapy: $665 per credit hour; MSN, Education and Administration: $770 per credit hour; MSN, Family Nurse Practitioner: $770 per credit hour ($85 per credit hour fee for FNP specialty courses); Doctor of Nursing Practice: $855 per credit hour; Radiation Therapy Second Degree: $665 per credit hour. *Financial support:* Career-related internships or fieldwork and scholarships/grants available. Financial award applicants required to submit FAFSA. *Unit head:* Dr. Nancy York, Dean, 502-272-8639, E-mail: nyork@bellarmine.edu. *Application contact:* Julie Armstrong-Binnix, Health Science Recruiter, 800-274-4723 Ext. 8364, E-mail: julieab@bellarmine.edu.
Website: http://www.bellarmine.edu/lansing

**Bellin College,** School of Nursing, Green Bay, WI 54305. Offers family nurse practitioner (MSN); nurse educator (MSN). *Accreditation:* AACN.

**Binghamton University, State University of New York,** Graduate School, Decker School of Nursing, Binghamton, NY 13902-6000. Offers adult-gerontological nursing (MS, DNP, Certificate); community health nursing (MS, DNP, Certificate); family health nursing (MS, DNP, Certificate); family psychiatric mental health nursing (MS, DNP, Certificate); nursing (PhD). *Accreditation:* AACN. *Program availability:* Part-time, evening/weekend. Terminal master's awarded for partial completion of doctoral program. *Degree requirements:* For master's, comprehensive exam, thesis; for doctorate, comprehensive exam (for some programs), thesis/dissertation. *Entrance requirements:* For master's and doctorate, GRE General Test, nursing licensure. Additional exam requirements/recommendations for international students: required—TOEFL (minimum score 90 iBT). Electronic applications accepted. *Expenses:* Contact institution.

**Bloomsburg University of Pennsylvania,** School of Graduate Studies, College of Science and Technology, Department of Nursing, Bloomsburg, PA 17815-1301. Offers adult and family nurse practitioner (MSN); community health (MSN); nurse anesthesia (MSN); nursing (MSN, DNP); nursing administration (MSN). *Accreditation:* AACN. *Degree requirements:* For master's, thesis (for some programs), clinical experience. *Entrance requirements:* For master's, minimum QPA of 3.0, personal statement, 2 letters of recommendation, nursing license. Additional exam requirements/recommendations for international students: required—TOEFL, IELTS. Electronic applications accepted. *Expenses:* Contact institution.

**Bowie State University,** Graduate Programs, Department of Nursing, Bowie, MD 20715-9465. Offers administration of nursing services (MS); family nurse practitioner (MS); nursing education (MS). *Accreditation:* ACEN. *Program availability:* Part-time. *Degree requirements:* For master's, comprehensive exam, thesis, research paper. *Entrance requirements:* For master's, minimum GPA of 2.5. Electronic applications accepted. *Expenses: Tuition, area resident:* Full-time $11,942; part-time $423 per credit hour. Tuition, state resident: full-time $11,942; part-time $423 per credit hour. Tuition, nonresident: full-time $18,806; part-time $709 per credit hour. *International tuition:* $18,806 full-time. *Required fees:* $1106; $1106 per semester. $553 per semester.

**Bradley University,** The Graduate School, College of Education and Health Sciences, Department of Nursing, Peoria, IL 61625-0002. Offers family nurse practitioner (MSN, DNP, Certificate); leadership (DNP); nursing administration (MSN); nursing education (MSN, Certificate). *Accreditation:* AACN; ACEN. *Program availability:* Part-time, evening/weekend, 100% online. *Faculty:* 12 full-time (all women), 32 part-time/adjunct (28 women). *Students:* 91 full-time (79 women), 637 part-time (551 women); includes 253 minority (143 Black or African American, non-Hispanic/Latino; 13 American Indian or Alaska Native, non-Hispanic/Latino; 40 Asian, non-Hispanic/Latino; 45 Hispanic/Latino; 2 Native Hawaiian or other Pacific Islander, non-Hispanic/Latino; 10 Two or more races, non-Hispanic/Latino), 19 international. Average age 38. 229 applicants, 79% accepted, 114 enrolled. In 2019, 60 master's, 20 doctorates awarded. *Degree requirements:* For master's, comprehensive exam, thesis optional; for doctorate, comprehensive exam. *Entrance requirements:* For master's, GRE General Test or MAT, interview, Illinois RN license, advanced cardiac life support certification, pediatric advanced life support certification, 3 letters of recommendation. Additional exam requirements/recommendations for international students: required—TOEFL (minimum score 550 paper-based; 79 iBT), IELTS (minimum score 6.5), PTE (minimum score 58). *Application deadline:* For fall admission, 5/15 priority date for domestic and international students; for spring admission, 10/15 priority date for domestic and international students. Applications are processed on a rolling basis. Application fee: $40 ($50 for international students). Electronic applications accepted. *Expenses: Tuition:* Part-time $930 per credit hour. *Financial support:* Research assistantships, scholarships/grants, tuition waivers (partial), and unspecified assistantships available. Financial award application deadline: 4/1. *Unit head:* Jessica Clark, Associate Dean and Director of the Department of Nursing, 309-677-2547, E-mail: jclark@bradley.edu. *Application contact:* Rachel Webb, Director of On-Campus Graduate Admissions and International Student and Scholar Services, 309-677-2375, Fax: 309-677-3343, E-mail: rkwebb@bradley.edu.
Website: http://www.bradley.edu/academic/departments/nur/

**Brenau University,** Sydney O. Smith Graduate School, Ivester College of Health Sciences, Gainesville, GA 30501. Offers family nurse practitioner (MSN); general psychology (MS); nurse educator (MSN); nursing manager (MSN); occupational therapy (MS). *Accreditation:* AOTA. *Program availability:* Part-time, evening/weekend, 100% online, blended/hybrid learning. *Faculty:* 34 full-time (26 women), 11 part-time/adjunct (10 women). *Students:* 321 full-time (242 women), 209 part-time (197 women); includes 177 minority (104 Black or African American, non-Hispanic/Latino; 2 American Indian or Alaska Native, non-Hispanic/Latino; 24 Asian, non-Hispanic/Latino; 36 Hispanic/Latino; 2 Native Hawaiian or other Pacific Islander, non-Hispanic/Latino; 9 Two or more races, non-Hispanic/Latino), 3 international. Average age 29. 517 applicants, 47% accepted, 110 enrolled. In 2019, 174 master's awarded. *Entrance requirements:* For master's, GMAT, GRE, or MAT, minimum GPA 2.5. Additional exam requirements/recommendations for international students: required—TOEFL (minimum score 497 paper-based; 71 iBT); recommended—IELTS (minimum score 5.5). *Application deadline:* Applications are processed on a rolling basis. Application fee: $35. Electronic applications accepted. *Expenses:* $11,763 full-time tuition (average), $4,678 part-time tuition (average). *Financial support:* In 2019–20, 11 students received support. Scholarships/grants available. Financial award applicants required to submit FAFSA. *Unit head:* Dr. Gale Starich, Dean, 777-718-5305, Fax: 770-297-5929, E-mail: gstarich@brenau.edu. *Application contact:* Nathan Goss, Assistant Vice President for Recruitment, 770-534-6162, E-mail: ngoss@brenau.edu.
Website: http://www.brenau.edu/healthsciences/

**Brigham Young University,** Graduate Studies, College of Nursing, Provo, UT 84602. Offers family nurse practitioner (MS). *Accreditation:* AACN. *Faculty:* 16 full-time (9 women). *Students:* 30 full-time (26 women); includes 5 minority (1 Black or African American, non-Hispanic/Latino; 1 American Indian or Alaska Native, non-Hispanic/Latino; 2 Asian, non-Hispanic/Latino; 1 Hispanic/Latino), 1 international. Average age 33. 30 applicants, 50% accepted, 15 enrolled. In 2019, 15 master's awarded. *Degree requirements:* For master's, thesis or alternative. *Entrance requirements:* For master's, GRE, minimum cumulative undergraduate GPA of 3.0, baccalaureate degree in nursing from school with national nursing accreditation, interview, current RN license in Utah, pathophysiology and statistics classes, 3 letters of recommendation. Additional exam requirements/recommendations for international students: required—TOEFL (minimum score 580 paper-based; 85 iBT), IELTS (minimum score 7). *Application deadline:* For spring admission, 12/1 for domestic and international students. Application fee: $50. Electronic applications accepted. *Expenses:* $3,535 per semester. $8,838 per year. *Financial support:* In 2019–20, 30 students received support, including 1 research assistantship (averaging $6,000 per year); teaching assistantships, career-related internships or fieldwork, and scholarships/grants also available. Financial award application deadline: 8/13; financial award applicants required to submit FAFSA. *Unit head:* Dr. Beth Luthy, Dean, 801-422-6683, Fax: 801-422-0536, E-mail: beth-luthy@byu.edu. *Application contact:* Cherie Top, Graduate Secretary, 801-422-4142, Fax: 801-422-0538, E-mail: cherie-top@byu.edu.
Website: http://nursing.byu.edu/

**California Baptist University,** Program in Nursing, Riverside, CA 92504-3206. Offers clinical nurse specialist (MSN); family nurse practitioner (MSN); healthcare systems management (MSN); teaching-learning (MSN). *Accreditation:* AACN. *Program availability:* Part-time. *Degree requirements:* For master's, comprehensive exam or directed project thesis; capstone practicum. *Entrance requirements:* For master's, GRE or California Critical Thinking Skills Test; Test of Essential Academic Skills (TEAS), minimum undergraduate GPA of 3.0; completion of prerequisite courses with minimum grade of C; CPR certification; background check clearance; health clearance; drug testing; proof of health insurance; proof of motor vehicle insurance; three letters of recommendation; 1000-word essay; interview. Additional exam requirements/recommendations for international students: required—TOEFL (minimum score 80 iBT). Electronic applications accepted. *Expenses:* Contact institution.

**California State University, San Marcos,** College of Education, Health and Human Services, School of Nursing, San Marcos, CA 92096-0001. Offers advanced practice nursing (MSN), including clinical nurse specialist, family nurse practitioner, psychiatric mental health nurse practitioner; clinical nurse leader (MSN); nursing education (MSN). *Expenses: Tuition, area resident:* Full-time $7176. Tuition, state resident: full-time $7176. Tuition, nonresident: full-time $18,640. *International tuition:* $18,640 full-time. *Required fees:* $1960.

**Carlow University,** College of Health and Wellness, Program in Family Nurse Practitioner, Pittsburgh, PA 15213-3165. Offers MSN, Certificate. *Program availability:* Part-time. *Students:* 113 full-time (97 women), 46 part-time (44 women); includes 16 minority (9 Black or African American, non-Hispanic/Latino; 4 Asian, non-Hispanic/Latino; 1 Hispanic/Latino; 2 Two or more races, non-Hispanic/Latino). Average age 32. 52 applicants, 100% accepted, 34 enrolled. In 2019, 58 master's, 1 other advanced degree awarded. *Entrance requirements:* For master's, minimum undergraduate GPA of 3.0 from accredited BSN program; current license as RN in Pennsylvania; at least one year of recent clinical (bedside) nursing experience; course in statistics in past 6 years with a minimum grade of C; two recommendations; personal statement; personal interview. Additional exam requirements/recommendations for international students: required—TOEFL (minimum score 550 paper-based). *Application deadline:* Applications are processed on a rolling basis. Electronic applications accepted. *Expenses:* Contact institution. *Financial support:* Application deadline: 4/1; applicants required to submit FAFSA. *Unit head:* Dr. Deborah Mitchum, Director, Family Nurse Practitioner Program, 412-578-6586, Fax: 412-578-6114, E-mail: dlmitchum@carlow.edu. *Application contact:* Dr. Deborah Mitchum, Director, Family Nurse Practitioner Program, 412-578-6586, Fax: 412-578-6114, E-mail: dlmitchum@carlow.edu.
Website: http://www.carlow.edu/Master_of_Science_in_Nursing_Family_Nurse_Practitioner.aspx

**Case Western Reserve University,** Frances Payne Bolton School of Nursing, Master's Programs in Nursing, Nurse Practitioner Program, Cleveland, OH 44106. Offers acute care pediatric nurse practitioner (MSN); acute care/cardiovascular nursing (MSN); adult gerontology acute care nurse practitioner (MSN); adult gerontology primary care nurse practitioner (MSN); family nurse practitioner (MSN); family systems psychiatric mental health nursing (MSN); neonatal nurse practitioner (MSN); palliative care (MSN); pediatric nurse practitioner in acute care (MSN); pediatric primary care nurse practitioner (MSN); women's health nurse practitioner (MSN). *Accreditation:* ACEN. *Program availability:* Part-time. *Faculty:* 30 full-time (25 women), 6 part-time/adjunct (all women). *Students:* 47 full-time (36 women), 70 part-time (59 women); includes 34 minority (12 Black or African American, non-Hispanic/Latino; 11 Asian, non-Hispanic/Latino; 9 Hispanic/Latino; 2 Two or more races, non-Hispanic/Latino), 9 international. Average age 30. 45 applicants, 82% accepted, 22 enrolled. In 2019, 46 master's awarded. *Degree requirements:* For master's, thesis optional, minimum GPA of 3.0, clinical hours corresponding to requirements to sit for certification exam, portfolio. *Entrance requirements:* For master's, GRE/MAT (scores not required for application, but may be requested for an admission decision). Additional exam requirements/recommendations for international students: required—TOEFL (minimum score 577 paper-based; 90 iBT), IELTS (minimum score 7). *Application deadline:* For fall admission, 3/15 for domestic and international students; for spring admission, 10/1 for domestic and international students; for summer admission, 3/15 for domestic and international students. Applications are processed on a rolling basis. Application fee: $75. Electronic applications accepted. *Expenses:* Clinical placement $75; Activity fee $15 per semester; Graduate council fee $15 per semester; Tuition rate $2,133 per credit hour. *Financial support:* In 2019–20, 100 students received support, including 34 teaching

assistantships with partial tuition reimbursements available (averaging $19,197 per year); scholarships/grants and traineeships also available. Financial award application deadline: 5/15; financial award applicants required to submit FAFSA. *Unit head:* Dr. Latina Brooks, Director, 216-368-1196, Fax: 216-368-3542, E-mail: lmb3@case.edu. *Application contact:* Jackie Tepale, Admissions Coordinator, 216-368-5253, Fax: 216-368-3542, E-mail: yyd@case.edu.
Website: https://case.edu/nursing/programs/msn

**Cedarville University,** Graduate Programs, Cedarville, OH 45314. Offers business administration (MBA); family nurse practitioner (MSN); global ministry (M Div); global public health nursing (MSN); healthcare administration (MBA); ministry (M Min); nurse educator (MSN); operations management (MBA); pharmacy (Pharm D). *Program availability:* Part-time, evening/weekend, 100% online, blended/hybrid learning. *Faculty:* 52 full-time (19 women), 21 part-time/adjunct (13 women). *Students:* 378 full-time (221 women), 45 part-time (23 women); includes 76 minority (46 Black or African American, non-Hispanic/Latino; 2 American Indian or Alaska Native, non-Hispanic/Latino; 22 Asian, non-Hispanic/Latino; 1 Hispanic/Latino; 5 Two or more races, non-Hispanic/Latino), 2 international. Average age 26. 398 applicants, 70% accepted, 172 enrolled. In 2019, 74 master's, 34 doctorates awarded. *Degree requirements:* For master's, portfolio; for doctorate, comprehensive exam. *Entrance requirements:* For master's, GRE may be required, 2 professional recommendations; for doctorate, PCAT, professional recommendation from a practicing pharmacist or current employer/supervisor, resume, essay, interview. Additional exam requirements/recommendations for international students: required—TOEFL (minimum score 550 paper-based; 80 iBT). *Application deadline:* For fall admission, 5/1 priority date for domestic and international students; for spring admission, 11/1 priority date for domestic and international students. Applications are processed on a rolling basis. Electronic applications accepted. *Expenses: Tuition:* Full-time $12,594; part-time $566 per credit hour. One-time fee: $100. Tuition and fees vary according to course load and program. *Financial support:* Scholarships/grants and unspecified assistantships available. Support available to part-time students. Financial award application deadline: 1/30; financial award applicants required to submit FAFSA. *Unit head:* Dr. Janice Supplee, Dean of Graduate Studies, 937-766-8000, E-mail: suppleej@cedarville.edu. *Application contact:* Alexis McKay, Graduate Admissions Counselor, 937-766-8000, E-mail: amckay@cedarville.edu.
Website: https://www.cedarville.edu/offices/graduate-school

**Clarion University of Pennsylvania,** College of Health Sciences & Human Services, Master of Science in Nursing Program, Clarion, PA 16214. Offers family nurse practitioner (MSN). *Accreditation:* ACEN. *Program availability:* Part-time, online only, 100% online, blended/hybrid learning. *Faculty:* 5 full-time (all women), 3 part-time/adjunct (2 women). *Students:* 98 part-time (79 women); includes 8 minority (2 Black or African American, non-Hispanic/Latino; 2 Asian, non-Hispanic/Latino; 3 Hispanic/Latino; 1 Two or more races, non-Hispanic/Latino). Average age 34. 112 applicants, 41% accepted, 45 enrolled. In 2019, 39 master's awarded. *Degree requirements:* For master's, comprehensive exam, thesis, portfolio. *Entrance requirements:* For master's, Bachelor degree in nursing. 2.75 or above. 2000 hours of clinical practice. Additional exam requirements/recommendations for international students: required—TOEFL (minimum score 550 paper-based; 80 iBT). *Application deadline:* For fall admission, 8/1 for domestic students, 7/1 priority date for international students. Applications are processed on a rolling basis. Application fee: $40. Electronic applications accepted. *Expenses:* $736.40 per credit including fees. *Financial support:* Federal Work-Study and scholarships/grants available. Financial award application deadline: 3/1; financial award applicants required to submit FAFSA. *Unit head:* Dr. Deborah J. Kelly, Chair and Nurse Administrator, 814-393-1258, E-mail: dkelly@clarion.edu. *Application contact:* Susan Staub, Graduate Programs Counselor, 814-393-2337, Fax: 814-393-2722, E-mail: gradstudies@clarion.edu.
Website: http://www.clarion.edu/admissions/graduate/index.html

**Clarke University,** Department of Nursing and Health, Dubuque, IA 52001-3198. Offers family nurse practitioner (DNP); health leadership and practice (DNP); psychiatric mental health nurse practitioner (DNP). *Accreditation:* AACN. *Program availability:* Part-time. *Degree requirements:* For doctorate, comprehensive exam, thesis/dissertation. *Entrance requirements:* For doctorate, GRE (if GPA under 3.0), bachelor's degree from accredited nursing program and accredited college or university; minimum GPA of 3.0; minimum C grade on undergraduate prerequisite courses; three recommendation forms; curriculum vitae; statement of goals; transcripts; copy of nursing license; proof of health insurance; interview. Additional exam requirements/recommendations for international students: required—TOEFL (minimum score 550 paper-based; 80 iBT), IELTS (minimum score 6.5). Electronic applications accepted. *Expenses:* Contact institution.

**Clarkson College,** Master of Science in Nursing Program, Omaha, NE 68131. Offers adult nurse practitioner (MSN, Post-Master's Certificate); family nurse practitioner (MSN, Post-Master's Certificate); nursing education (MSN, Post-Master's Certificate); nursing health care leadership (MSN, Post-Master's Certificate). *Accreditation:* AANA/CANAEP; ACEN. *Program availability:* Part-time, evening/weekend, online learning. *Degree requirements:* For master's, on-campus skills assessment (family nurse practitioner, adult nurse practitioner), comprehensive exam or thesis. *Entrance requirements:* For master's, minimum GPA of 3.0, 2 references, resume. Additional exam requirements/recommendations for international students: required—TOEFL (minimum score 600 paper-based; 100 iBT). Electronic applications accepted.

**Clayton State University,** School of Graduate Studies, College of Health, Program in Nursing, Morrow, GA 30260-0285. Offers family nurse practitioner (MSN). *Accreditation:* AACN. *Degree requirements:* For master's, thesis. *Entrance requirements:* For master's, GRE, official transcript, 3 letters of recommendation, statement of purpose, on-campus interview, 1-2 years of clinical nursing experience (preferred). Additional exam requirements/recommendations for international students: required—TOEFL (minimum score 550 paper-based; 80 iBT). Electronic applications accepted. *Expenses:* Contact institution.

**Clemson University,** Graduate School, College of Behavioral, Social and Health Sciences, School of Nursing, Clemson, SC 29634. Offers clinical and translational research (PhD); global health (Certificate), including low resource countries; healthcare genetics (PhD); nursing (MS, DNP), including adult/gerontology nurse practitioner (MS), family nurse practitioner (MS). *Accreditation:* AACN. *Program availability:* Part-time, 100% online, blended/hybrid learning. *Faculty:* 47 full-time (45 women), 1 (woman) part-time/adjunct. *Students:* 67 full-time (59 women), 66 part-time (49 women); includes 18 minority (10 Black or African American, non-Hispanic/Latino; 4 Asian, non-Hispanic/Latino; 4 Two or more races, non-Hispanic/Latino), 7 international. Average age 35. 109 applicants, 62% accepted, 49 enrolled. In 2019, 56 master's, 8 doctorates awarded. *Degree requirements:* For master's, comprehensive exam, thesis or alternative; for doctorate, comprehensive exam, thesis/dissertation. *Entrance requirements:* For master's, GRE General Test, South Carolina RN license, unofficial transcripts, resume, letters of recommendation; for doctorate, GRE General Test, unofficial transcripts, MS/MA thesis or publications, curriculum vitae, statement of career goals, letters of recommendation. Additional exam requirements/recommendations for international students: required—TOEFL (minimum score 80 paper-based; 80 iBT); recommended—IELTS (minimum score 6.5), TSE (minimum score 54). *Application deadline:* For fall admission, 4/15 priority date for international students; for spring admission, 10/15

priority date for international students. Applications are processed on a rolling basis. Application fee: $80 ($90 for international students). Electronic applications accepted. *Expenses:* MS Nursing Full-Time Student per Semester: Tuition: $9075 (in-state), $16051 (out-of-state), Fees: $598; Graduate Assistant Per Semester: $1144; Part-Time Student Per Credit Hour: $1009 (in-state), $1784 (out-of-state), Fees: $46; other fees apply depending on program, credit hours, campus & residency. Doctoral Base Fee per Semester: $4938 (in-state), $10405 (out-of-state). *Financial support:* In 2019–20, 47 students received support, including 46 teaching assistantships with full and partial tuition reimbursements available (averaging $6,766 per year); career-related internships or fieldwork and unspecified assistantships also available. *Unit head:* Dr. Kathleen Valentine, Chief Academic Nursing Officer & Director, 864-656-4758, E-mail: klvalen@clemson.edu. *Application contact:* Dr. Stephanie Davis, Director of Graduate Programs, 864-656-2588, E-mail: stephad@clemson.edu.
Website: http://www.clemson.edu/cbshs/departments/nursing/

**College of Mount Saint Vincent,** School of Professional and Graduate Studies, Department of Nursing, Riverdale, NY 10471-1093. Offers family nurse practitioner (MSN, PMC); nurse educator (PMC); nursing administration (MSN); nursing education (MSN). *Accreditation:* AACN. *Program availability:* Part-time. *Entrance requirements:* For master's, BSN, interview, RN license, minimum GPA of 3.0, letters of reference. Additional exam requirements/recommendations for international students: required—TOEFL. *Expenses:* Contact institution.

**The College of New Rochelle,** Graduate School, Program in Nursing, New Rochelle, NY 10805-2308. Offers acute care nurse practitioner (MS, Certificate); clinical specialist in holistic nursing (MS, Certificate); family nurse practitioner (MS, Certificate); nursing and health care management (MS); nursing education (Certificate). *Accreditation:* AACN. *Program availability:* Part-time. *Entrance requirements:* For master's, GRE General Test or MAT, BSN, malpractice insurance, minimum GPA of 3.0, RN license. Electronic applications accepted.

**Colorado Mesa University,** Department of Health Sciences, Grand Junction, CO 81501-3122. Offers advanced nursing practice (MSN); family nurse practitioner (DNP); health information technology systems (Graduate Certificate); nursing education (MSN). *Accreditation:* AACN. *Program availability:* Part-time, evening/weekend, 100% online, blended/hybrid learning. *Degree requirements:* For master's and doctorate, capstone. *Entrance requirements:* For master's and doctorate, minimum GPA of 3.0 in BSN program. Additional exam requirements/recommendations for international students: required—TOEFL (minimum score 550 paper-based). Electronic applications accepted.

**Columbia University,** School of Nursing, Program in Family Nurse Practitioner, New York, NY 10032. Offers MS, Adv C. *Accreditation:* AACN. *Program availability:* Part-time. *Entrance requirements:* For master's, GRE General Test, NCLEX, BSN, 1 year of clinical experience (preferred); for Adv C, MSN. Additional exam requirements/recommendations for international students: required—TOEFL (minimum score 100 iBT). Electronic applications accepted. *Expenses: Tuition:* Full-time $47,600; part-time $1880 per credit. One-time fee: $105.

**Columbus State University,** Graduate Studies, College of Education and Health Professions, School of Nursing, Columbus, GA 31907-5645. Offers family nurse practitioner (MSN); nursing (MSN), including nurse educator, nurse informatics, nurse leader. *Program availability:* Part-time, online only, 100% online. *Entrance requirements:* For master's, GRE, BSN, minimum undergraduate GPA of 3.0. Additional exam requirements/recommendations for international students: required—TOEFL (minimum score 550 paper-based; 79 iBT). Electronic applications accepted. *Expenses:* Contact institution.

**Concordia University Wisconsin,** Graduate Programs, School of Nursing, Mequon, WI 53097-2402. Offers family nurse practitioner (MSN). *Accreditation:* AACN. *Program availability:* Online learning. *Degree requirements:* For master's, comprehensive exam, thesis or alternative. *Entrance requirements:* Additional exam requirements/recommendations for international students: required—TOEFL. *Expenses:* Contact institution.

**Coppin State University,** School of Graduate Studies, Helene Fuld School of Nursing, Baltimore, MD 21216-3698. Offers family nurse practitioner (PMC); nursing (MSN). *Accreditation:* AACN; ACEN. *Program availability:* Part-time, evening/weekend. *Degree requirements:* For master's, comprehensive exam, thesis, clinical internship. *Entrance requirements:* For master's, GRE, bachelor's degree in nursing, interview, minimum GPA of 3.0, RN license. Additional exam requirements/recommendations for international students: required—TOEFL (minimum score 550 paper-based).

**Cox College,** Programs in Nursing, Springfield, MO 65802. Offers clinical nurse leader (MSN); family nurse practitioner (MSN); nurse educator (MSN). *Accreditation:* AACN. *Entrance requirements:* For master's, RN license, essay, 2 letters of recommendation, official transcripts. Electronic applications accepted.

**Creighton University,** College of Nursing, Omaha, NE 68178-0001. Offers adult gerontology acute care nurse practitioner (DNP, Post-Master's Certificate); adult gerontology nurse practitioner (DNP); clinical nurse leader (MSN, Post-Graduate Certificate); clinical systems administration (MSN, DNP); family nurse practitioner (DNP, Post-Master's Certificate); neonatal nurse practitioner (DNP, Post-Master's Certificate); nursing (Post-Graduate Certificate); pediatric acute care nurse practitioner (DNP, Post-Master's Certificate); psychiatric mental health nurse practitioner (DNP). *Accreditation:* AACN. *Program availability:* Part-time, blended/hybrid learning. *Degree requirements:* For master's, capstone project; for doctorate, scholarly project. *Entrance requirements:* For master's and doctorate, BSN from ACEN- or CCNE-accredited nursing school, minimum cumulative GPA of 3.0, personal statement, active unencumbered RN license with NE eligibility, undergraduate statistics course, physical assessment course or equivalent, three recommendation letters; for other advanced degree, MSN or MS in nursing from ACEN- or CCNE-accredited nursing school, minimum cumulative GPA of 3.0, active unencumbered RN license with NE eligibility. Additional exam requirements/recommendations for international students: required—TOEFL (minimum score 600 paper-based, 100 iBT) or IELTS. Electronic applications accepted. *Expenses:* Contact institution.

**Delta State University,** Graduate Programs, Robert E. Smith School of Nursing, Cleveland, MS 38733. Offers family nurse practitioner (MSN); nurse administrator (MSN); nurse educator (MSN). *Accreditation:* AACN. *Program availability:* Part-time. *Degree requirements:* For master's, thesis optional. *Entrance requirements:* For master's, GRE General Test. Electronic applications accepted. *Expenses: Tuition, area resident:* Full-time $7501; part-time $417 per credit hour. Tuition, state resident: full-time $7501; part-time $417 per credit hour. Tuition, nonresident: full-time $7501; part-time $417 per credit hour. International tuition: $7501 full-time. *Required fees:* $170; $9.45 per credit hour. $9.45 per semester.

**DePaul University,** College of Science and Health, Chicago, IL 60604-2287. Offers applied mathematics (MS); applied statistics (MS); biological sciences (MA, MS); chemistry (MS); environmental science (MS); mathematics education (MA); mathematics for teaching (MS); nursing (MS); nursing practice (DNP); physics (MS); polymer and coatings science (MS); psychology (MS); pure mathematics (MS); science education (MS); MA/PhD. *Accreditation:* AACN. Electronic applications accepted.

### Family Nurse Practitioner Studies

**DeSales University,** Division of Healthcare, Center Valley, PA 18034-9568. Offers adult-gerontology acute care (Post Master's Certificate); adult-gerontology acute care nurse practitioner (MSN); adult-gerontology acute certified nurse practitioner (Post Master's Certificate); adult-gerontology clinical nurse specialist (MSN, Post Master's Certificate); clinical leadership (DNP); family nurse practitioner (MSN, Post Master's Certificate); general nursing practice (DNP); nurse anesthetist (MSN); nurse educator (Post Master's Certificate, Postbaccalaureate Certificate); nurse midwife (MSN); nurse practitioner (MSN); psychiatric-mental health nurse practitioner (MSN, Post Master's Certificate); DNP/MBA. *Accreditation:* ACEN. *Program availability:* Part-time. *Faculty:* 31 full-time (23 women), 12 part-time/adjunct (9 women). *Students:* 294 full-time (219 women), 128 part-time (109 women); includes 71 minority (20 Black or African American, non-Hispanic/Latino; 1 American Indian or Alaska Native, non-Hispanic/Latino; 15 Asian, non-Hispanic/Latino; 30 Hispanic/Latino; 5 Two or more races, non-Hispanic/Latino). Average age 28. 2,666 applicants, 6% accepted, 142 enrolled. In 2019, 115 master's, 30 doctorates awarded. *Degree requirements:* For master's, minimum GPA of 3.0, portfolio; for doctorate, minimum GPA of 3.0, scholarly capstone project. *Entrance requirements:* For master's, GRE or MAT (waived if applicant has an undergraduate GPA of 3.0 or higher), BSN from ACEN- or CCNE-accredited program, minimum undergraduate GPA of 3.0, active RN license or eligibility, two letters of recommendation, essay, health care experience, personal interview; for doctorate, BSN or MSN from ACEN- or CCNE-accredited institution, minimum GPA of 3.3 in graduate program, current licensure as an RN. Additional exam requirements/recommendations for international students: required—TOEFL (minimum score 104 iBT). *Application deadline:* Applications are processed on a rolling basis. Application fee: $50. Electronic applications accepted. *Expenses:* Contact institution. *Financial support:* Applicants required to submit FAFSA. *Unit head:* Ronald Nordone, Dean of Graduate Education, 610-282-1100 Ext. 1289, E-mail: ronald.nordone@desales.edu. *Application contact:* Julia Ferraro, Director of Graduate Admissions, 610-282-1100 Ext. 1768, E-mail: gradadmissions@desales.edu.

**Dominican College,** Division of Nursing, Orangeburg, NY 10962-1210. Offers MSN, DNP. *Accreditation:* AACN. *Program availability:* Part-time, evening/weekend. *Faculty:* 5 full-time (all women), 12 part-time/adjunct (8 women). *Students:* 29 full-time (24 women), 95 part-time (85 women); includes 71 minority (35 Black or African American, non-Hispanic/Latino; 17 Asian, non-Hispanic/Latino; 19 Hispanic/Latino). Average age 38. In 2019, 36 master's, 10 doctorates awarded. *Degree requirements:* For master's, guided research project, 750 hours of clinical practice with a final written project; for doctorate, Practicum hours: All students are required to have a minimum of 1,000 hours that will include hours from their Master's degree program and the DNP hours. 2 Capstone projects. *Entrance requirements:* For master's, RN license with 1 year of experience; minimum undergraduate GPA of 3.0; 3 letters of recommendation, personal essay including statement of career goals, submit official transcripts including baccalaureate health assessment course; introductory nursing research course; introductory statistical research course; for doctorate, 3.0 GPA in undergraduate work, 3.5 GPA in graduate work, MS in Nursing (FNP), 3 letters on official letterhead and physically signed, current licensure as a registered nurse and advanced practice nursing, interview, resume, case study. Additional exam requirements/recommendations for international students: required—TOEFL (minimum score 550 paper-based; 90 iBT). *Application deadline:* For fall admission, 3/29 priority date for domestic students; for summer admission, 12/15 priority date for domestic students. Applications are processed on a rolling basis. Application fee: $50. Electronic applications accepted. *Expenses:* Tuition: Part-time $965 per credit. *Required fees:* $200 per semester. One-time fee: $200. Tuition and fees vary according to course load, degree level and program. *Financial support:* Scholarships/grants available. Financial award application deadline: 1/1; financial award applicants required to submit FAFSA. *Unit head:* Dr. Lynne Weissman, Director, Master of Science FNP and DNP Programs, 845-848-6026, Fax: 845-398-4891, E-mail: lynne.weissman@dc.edu. *Application contact:* Ashley Scales, Assistant Director of Graduate Admissions, 845-848-7908, Fax: 845-365-3150, E-mail: admissions@dc.edu.

**Drexel University,** College of Nursing and Health Professions, Division of Graduate Nursing, Philadelphia, PA 19104-2875. Offers adult acute care (MSN); adult psychiatric/mental health (MSN); advanced practice nursing (MSN); clinical trials research (MSN); family nurse practitioner (MSN); leadership in health systems management (MSN); nursing education (MSN); pediatric primary care (MSN); women's health (MSN). *Accreditation:* AACN. Electronic applications accepted.

**Duke University,** School of Nursing, Durham, NC 27708. Offers acute care pediatric nurse practitioner (MSN, Post-Graduate Certificate); adult-gerontology nurse practitioner (MSN, Post-Graduate Certificate), including acute care, primary care; family nurse practitioner (MSN, Post-Graduate Certificate); neonatal nurse practitioner (MSN, Post-Graduate Certificate); nurse anesthesia (DNP); nurse practitioner (DNP); nursing (PhD); nursing and health care leadership (MSN, Post-Graduate Certificate); nursing education (MSN, Post-Graduate Certificate); nursing informatics (MSN, Post-Graduate Certificate); pediatric nurse practitioner (MSN, Post-Graduate Certificate), including primary care; psychiatric mental health nurse practitioner (MSN, Post-Graduate Certificate); women's health nurse practitioner (MSN, Post-Graduate Certificate). *Accreditation:* AACN; AANA/CANAEP. *Program availability:* Part-time, evening/weekend, online with on-campus intensives. *Faculty:* 48 full-time (40 women), 32 part-time/adjunct (28 women). *Students:* 666 full-time (601 women), 157 part-time (139 women); includes 193 minority (61 Black or African American, non-Hispanic/Latino; 4 American Indian or Alaska Native, non-Hispanic/Latino; 57 Asian, non-Hispanic/Latino; 49 Hispanic/Latino; 1 Native Hawaiian or other Pacific Islander, non-Hispanic/Latino; 21 Two or more races, non-Hispanic/Latino; 8 international). Average age 34. 761 applicants, 33% accepted, 149 enrolled. In 2019, 213 master's, 74 doctorates, 18 other advanced degrees awarded. Terminal master's awarded for partial completion of doctoral program. *Degree requirements:* For master's, thesis optional; for doctorate, capstone project. *Entrance requirements:* For master's, MSN applicants are no longer required to take the GRE, 1 year of nursing experience (recommended), BSN, minimum GPA of 3.0, previous course work in statistics; for doctorate, GRE is required for the DNP in Nurse Anesthesia, BSN or MSN, minimum GPA of 3.0, resume, personal statement, graduate statistics and research methods course, current licensure as a registered nurse, transcripts from all post-secondary institutions; for Post-Graduate Certificate, MSN, licensure or eligibility as a professional nurse, transcripts from all post-secondary institutions, previous course work in statistics. Additional exam requirements/recommendations for international students: required—TOEFL (minimum score 100 iBT), IELTS (minimum score 7). *Application deadline:* For fall admission, 12/1 for domestic and international students; for spring admission, 5/1 for domestic and international students. Application fee: $50. Electronic applications accepted. *Expenses:* Contact institution. *Financial support:* Institutionally sponsored loans, scholarships/grants, and traineeships available. Support available to part-time students. Financial award applicants required to submit FAFSA. *Unit head:* Dr. Marion E. Broome, Dean/Vice Chancellor for Nursing Affairs/Associate Vice President for Academic Affairs for Nursing, 919-684-9446, Fax: 919-684-9414, E-mail: marion.broome@duke.edu. *Application contact:* Dr. Ernie Rushing, Director of Admissions and Recruitment, 919-668-6274, Fax: 919-668-4693, E-mail: ernie.rushing@dm.duke.edu. Website: http://www.nursing.duke.edu/

**Duquesne University,** School of Nursing, Master of Science in Nursing Program, Pittsburgh, PA 15282-0001. Offers family (individual across the life span) nurse practitioner (MSN); forensic nursing (MSN); nursing education and faculty role (MSN). *Accreditation:* AACN. *Program availability:* Part-time, evening/weekend, minimal on-campus study. *Entrance requirements:* For master's, current RN license; BSN with minimum GPA of 3.0; minimum of 1 year of full-time work experience as RN prior to registration in clinical or specialty course. Additional exam requirements/recommendations for international students: required—TOEFL (minimum score 600 paper-based; 100 iBT). Electronic applications accepted. *Expenses:* Contact institution.

**Duquesne University,** School of Nursing, Post Master's Certificate Program, Pittsburgh, PA 15282-0001. Offers family (individual across the life span) nurse practitioner (Post-Master's Certificate); forensic nursing (Post-Master's Certificate); nursing education and faculty role (Post-Master's Certificate). *Program availability:* Part-time, evening/weekend, minimal on-campus study. *Entrance requirements:* For degree, current RN license, BSN, MSN. Additional exam requirements/recommendations for international students: required—TOEFL (minimum score 600 paper-based; 100 iBT). Electronic applications accepted. *Expenses:* Contact institution.

**D'Youville College,** School of Nursing, Buffalo, NY 14201-1084. Offers advanced practice nursing (DNP); family nurse practitioner (MSN, Certificate); nursing and health-related professions education (Certificate). *Accreditation:* AACN. *Program availability:* Part-time. *Degree requirements:* For master's, thesis or alternative. *Entrance requirements:* For master's, BS in nursing, minimum GPA of 3.0, course work in statistics and computers; for doctorate, BS in nursing, MS in advanced practice nursing specialty, minimum GPA of 3.25. Additional exam requirements/recommendations for international students: required—TOEFL (minimum score 500 paper-based). Electronic applications accepted.

**Eastern Kentucky University,** The Graduate School, College of Health Sciences, Department of Nursing, Richmond, KY 40475-3102. Offers rural community health care (MSN); rural health family nurse practitioner (MSN). *Accreditation:* AACN. *Entrance requirements:* For master's, GRE General Test, minimum GPA of 2.75.

**East Tennessee State University,** College of Graduate and Continuing Studies, College of Nursing, Johnson City, TN 37614. Offers acute care nurse practitioner (DNP); adult-gerontology primary care nurse practitioner (DNP); adult/gerontological nurse practitioner (Postbaccalaureate Certificate); executive leadership in nursing (DNP, Postbaccalaureate Certificate); family nurse practitioner (MSN, DNP, Post-Master's Certificate, Postbaccalaureate Certificate); nursing (PhD); nursing administration (MSN); nursing education (MSN); pediatric primary care nurse practitioner (DNP); psychiatric mental health nurse practitioner (Postbaccalaureate Certificate); psychiatric/mental health nurse practitioner (MSN, DNP, Post-Master's Certificate); women's health care nurse practitioner (DNP). *Accreditation:* AACN. *Program availability:* Part-time, evening/weekend, online learning. *Degree requirements:* For master's and other advanced degree, comprehensive exam, practicum; for doctorate, comprehensive exam, thesis/dissertation (for some programs), practicum, internship, evidence of professional malpractice insurance, CPR certification. *Entrance requirements:* For master's, bachelor's degree, minimum GPA of 3.0, current RN license and eligibility to practice, resume, three letters of recommendation; for doctorate, GRE General Test, MSN (for PhD), BSN or MSN (for DNP), current RN license and eligibility to practice, 2 years of full-time registered nurse work experience or equivalent, three letters of recommendation, resume or curriculum vitae, interview, writing sample; for other advanced degree, MSN, minimum GPA of 3.0, current RN license and eligibility to practice, three letters of recommendation, resume or curriculum vitae; DNP with designated concentration in advanced clinical practice or nursing administration (for select programs). Additional exam requirements/recommendations for international students: required—TOEFL (minimum score 600 paper-based; 79 iBT). Electronic applications accepted.

**Edinboro University of Pennsylvania,** Department of Nursing, Edinboro, PA 16444. Offers advanced practice nursing (DNP); family nurse practitioner (MSN); nurse educator (MSN). *Program availability:* Part-time, evening/weekend. *Faculty:* 6 full-time (5 women), 1 (woman) part-time/adjunct. *Students:* 105 part-time (85 women); includes 9 minority (4 Black or African American, non-Hispanic/Latino; 2 Asian, non-Hispanic/Latino; 3 Hispanic/Latino). Average age 37. 57 applicants, 100% accepted, 57 enrolled. *Degree requirements:* For master's, thesis, competency exam. *Entrance requirements:* For master's, GRE or MAT, minimum GPA 2.75; one year of recent full-time clinical practice or two years of part-time clinical practice; licensure as a registered nurse in the state where they plan to complete clinical practicum; for doctorate, minimum GPA 3.25; current unencumbered licenses as a Registered nurse. Additional exam requirements/recommendations for international students: required—TOEFL (minimum score 550 paper-based; 213 iBT), IELTS (minimum score 6.5). Application fee: $40. Electronic applications accepted. *Expenses:* Tuition & Fees: 889.8/credit for PA resident; 1025.24/credit for non-PA resident. *Financial support:* Application deadline: 2/15; applicants required to submit FAFSA. *Unit head:* Dr. Victoria Hedderick, Chair, 814-732-1655, E-mail: vhedderick@edinboro.edu. *Application contact:* Dr. Victoria Hedderick, Chair, 814-732-1655, E-mail: vhedderick@edinboro.edu. Website: https://www.edinboro.edu/academics/schools-and-departments/cshp/departments/nursing/

**Elms College,** School of Nursing, Chicopee, MA 01013-2839. Offers adult-gerontology acute care nurse practitioner (DNP); family nurse practitioner (DNP); health systems innovation and leadership (DNP); nursing and health services management (MSN); nursing education (MSN). *Accreditation:* AACN. *Program availability:* Part-time, evening/weekend. *Faculty:* 3 full-time (2 women), 2 part-time/adjunct (both women). *Students:* 13 full-time (11 women), 97 part-time (91 women); includes 8 minority (4 Black or African American, non-Hispanic/Latino; 2 Hispanic/Latino; 2 Two or more races, non-Hispanic/Latino). Average age 38. 39 applicants, 87% accepted, 27 enrolled. In 2019, 4 master's, 20 doctorates awarded. *Entrance requirements:* Additional exam requirements/recommendations for international students: required—TOEFL (minimum score 80 iBT). *Application deadline:* For fall admission, 7/1 priority date for domestic students; for spring admission, 11/1 priority date for domestic students. Applications are processed on a rolling basis. Electronic applications accepted. *Financial support:* Applicants required to submit FAFSA. *Unit head:* Dr. Kathleen Scoble, Dean, School of Nursing, 413-265-2204, E-mail: scoblek@elms.edu. *Application contact:* Nancy Davis, Director, Office of Graduate and Continuing Education Admissions, 413-265-2456, E-mail: grad@elms.edu.

**Emory University,** Nell Hodgson Woodruff School of Nursing, Atlanta, GA 30322-1100. Offers adult nurse practitioner (MSN); emergency nurse practitioner (MSN); family nurse practitioner (MSN); family nurse-midwife (MSN); health systems leadership (MSN); nurse-midwifery (MSN); pediatric nurse practitioner acute and primary care (MSN); women's health care (Title X) (MSN); women's health nurse practitioner (MSN); MSN/MPH. *Accreditation:* AACN; ACNM/ACME (one or more programs are accredited). *Program availability:* Part-time. *Entrance requirements:* For master's, GRE General Test or MAT, minimum GPA of 3.0, BS in nursing from an accredited institution, RN license and additional course work, 3 letters of recommendation. Additional exam requirements/recommendations for international students: required—TOEFL (minimum score 600 paper-based; 100 iBT). Electronic applications accepted. *Expenses:* Contact institution.

**Endicott College,** School of Nursing, Program in Nursing, Beverly, MA 01915. Offers family nurse practitioner (MSN, Post-Master's Certificate); global health (MSN); nursing administration (MSN); nursing administrator (Post-Master's Certificate); nursing educator (MSN, Post-Master's Certificate). *Program availability:* Part-time, evening/weekend, blended/hybrid learning. *Faculty:* 4 full-time (all women), 18 part-time/adjunct (13 women). *Students:* 20 full-time (19 women), 71 part-time (70 women); includes 11 minority (5 Black or African American, non-Hispanic/Latino; 3 Asian, non-Hispanic/Latino; 2 Hispanic/Latino; 1 Two or more races, non-Hispanic/Latino). Average age 37. 32 applicants, 41% accepted, 12 enrolled. In 2019, 34 master's, 6 other advanced degrees awarded. *Degree requirements:* For master's, thesis, Internship and Capstone portfolio (S); Minimum 600 faculty supervised clinical hours (S). *Entrance requirements:* Additional exam requirements/recommendations for international students: required—TOEFL. *Application deadline:* Applications are processed on a rolling basis. Application fee: $50. Electronic applications accepted. *Expenses:* Tuition varies by program. *Financial support:* Applicants required to submit FAFSA. *Unit head:* Nancy Meedzan, DNP, RN, CNE, Dean, School of Nursing, 978-232-2328, E-mail: nmeedzan@endicott.edu. *Application contact:* Ian Menchini, Director, Graduate Enrollment and Advising, 978-232-5292, Fax: 978-232-3000, E-mail: imenchin@endicott.edu.
Website: https://www.endicott.edu/academics/schools/nursing/graduate-programs

**Fairfield University,** Marion Peckham Egan School of Nursing and Health Studies, Fairfield, CT 06824. Offers advanced practice (DNP); family nurse practitioner (MSN, DNP); nurse anesthesia (DNP); nursing leadership (MSN); psychiatric nurse practitioner (MSN, DNP). *Accreditation:* AACN; AANA/CANAEP. *Program availability:* Part-time, evening/weekend. *Faculty:* 13 full-time (all women), 12 part-time/adjunct (9 women). *Students:* 56 full-time (49 women), 165 part-time (149 women); includes 62 minority (24 Black or African American, non-Hispanic/Latino; 12 Asian, non-Hispanic/Latino; 25 Hispanic/Latino; 1 Two or more races, non-Hispanic/Latino). Average age 33. 129 applicants, 56% accepted, 62 enrolled. In 2019, 26 master's, 36 doctorates awarded. *Degree requirements:* For master's, capstone project. *Entrance requirements:* For master's, minimum QPA of 3.0, RN license, resume, 2 recommendations; for doctorate, MSN (minimum QPA of 3.2) or BSN (minimum QPA of 3.0); critical care nursing experience (for nurse anesthesia DNP candidates). Additional exam requirements/recommendations for international students: required—TOEFL (minimum score 550 paper-based; 80 iBT), IELTS (minimum score 6.5), TOEFL (minimum score 550 paper-based; 80 iBT) or IELTS (minimum score 6.5). *Application deadline:* For fall admission, 5/15 for international students; for spring admission, 10/15 for international students. Applications are processed on a rolling basis. Application fee: $60. Electronic applications accepted. *Expenses:* $875 per credit hour tuition (for MS), $1,010 per credit hour tuition (for Master of Healthcare Administration), $1,025 per credit hour tuition (for Doctorate in Clinical Nutrition), $1,050 per credit hour tuition (for DNP Nurse Anesthesia), $1,000 per credit hour tuition (for all other DNP programs), $150 per semester clinical placement fee (applicable programs, fall and spring semesters), $50 per semester registration fee, $65 per semester graduate student activity fee (fall and spring). *Financial support:* In 2019–20, 45 students received support. Scholarships/grants and unspecified assistantships available. Financial award applicants required to submit FAFSA. *Unit head:* Dr. Meredith Wallace Kazer, Dean, 203-254-4000 Ext. 2701, Fax: 203-254-4126, E-mail: mkazer@fairfield.edu. *Application contact:* Melanie Rogers, Director of Graduate Admission, 203-254-4184, Fax: 203-254-4073, E-mail: gradadmis@fairfield.edu.
Website: http://fairfield.edu/son

**Felician University,** Master of Science in Nursing Program, Lodi, NJ 07644-2117. Offers adult-gerontology nurse practitioner (MSN, PMC); executive leadership (MSN, PMC); family nurse practitioner (MSN, PMC); nursing education (MSN, PMC). *Accreditation:* AACN. *Program availability:* Evening/weekend, online only, 100% online, blended/hybrid learning. *Degree requirements:* For master's, thesis, clinical presentation; for PMC, thesis, education project. *Entrance requirements:* For master's, BSN; minimum GPA of 3.0; 2 letters of recommendation; NJ RN license; personal statement; for PMC, RN license, minimum GPA of 3.0. Additional exam requirements/recommendations for international students: required—TOEFL (minimum score 550 paper-based; 79 iBT), IELTS (minimum score 6.5), PTE (minimum score 56). Electronic applications accepted. Application fee is waived when completed online. *Expenses:* Contact institution.

**Florida National University,** Program in Nursing, Hialeah, FL 33139. Offers family nurse practitioner (MSN); nurse educator (MSN); nurse leadership and management (MSN). *Program availability:* 100% online, blended/hybrid learning. *Faculty:* 6 full-time (4 women), 9 part-time/adjunct (7 women). *Students:* 14 full-time (10 women), 204 part-time (151 women); includes 213 minority (21 Black or African American, non-Hispanic/Latino; 1 Asian, non-Hispanic/Latino; 191 Hispanic/Latino). Average age 40. 54 applicants, 100% accepted, 54 enrolled. In 2019, 53 master's awarded. *Degree requirements:* For master's, practicum. *Entrance requirements:* For master's, active registered nurse license, BSN from accredited institution. Additional exam requirements/recommendations for international students: recommended—TOEFL. *Expenses:* Contact institution. *Financial support:* Scholarships/grants available. *Unit head:* Dr. Lydie Janvier, Master of Science in Nursing Program Director, 305-821-3333 Ext. 1056, Fax: 305-362-0595, E-mail: ljanvier@fnu.edu. *Application contact:* Dr. Lydie Janvier, Master of Science in Nursing Program Director, 305-821-3333 Ext. 1056, Fax: 305-362-0595, E-mail: ljanvier@fnu.edu.
Website: https://www.fnu.edu/prospective-students/our-programs/select-a-program/master-of-business-administration/nursing-msn-master/

**Florida Southern College,** School of Nursing and Health Sciences, Lakeland, FL 33801. Offers adult gerontology clinical nurse specialist (MSN); adult gerontology primary care nurse practitioner (MSN); family nurse practitioner (MSN); nurse educator (MSN); nursing administration (MSN). *Accreditation:* AACN. *Program availability:* Part-time, The Nurse Educator MSN degree concentration and NE postmasters certificate are fully online. The Nursing Administrative Leadership MSN degree concentration is delivered in blended/hybrid format. *Faculty:* 6 full-time (all women), 1 (woman) part-time/adjunct. *Students:* 145 full-time (131 women), 1 (woman) part-time; includes 70 minority (30 Black or African American, non-Hispanic/Latino; 11 Asian, non-Hispanic/Latino; 25 Hispanic/Latino; 4 Two or more races, non-Hispanic/Latino), 1 international. Average age 39. 81 applicants, 89% accepted, 50 enrolled. In 2019, 53 master's awarded. *Degree requirements:* For master's, comprehensive exam, 660 clinical hours (for Family Nurse Practitioner); 540 clinical hours (for Adult-Gerontology Primary Care Nurse Practitioner). *Entrance requirements:* For master's, Florida RN license, 3 letters of recommendation, professional statement, minimum GPA of 3.0 in the last 60 credit hours of BSN, BSN earned from a regionally accredited institution and a CCNE, CNEA, or ACEN accredited nursing program, resume, admission interview. Additional exam requirements/recommendations for international students: required—TOEFL (minimum score 550 paper-based; 79 iBT), IELTS (minimum score 6.5), International students from countries where English is not the standard for daily communication must submit either the TOEFL or IELTS. *Application deadline:* For fall admission, 6/1 for domestic and international students; for spring admission, 10/1 for domestic and international students. Applications are processed on a rolling basis. Electronic applications accepted. *Expenses:* DNP: $725 per credit hour tuition, $50 per semester technology fee (for 5-8 hours), $100 per semester technology fee (for 9-12 hours); MSN: $600 per credit hour tuition, $50 per semester technology fee (for 5-8 hours), $100 per semester technology fee (for 9-12 hours), $35 per semester insurance and lab supplies fees. *Financial support:* In 2019–20, 1 student received support. Employee tuition grants, athletic scholarships for students still eligible available. Financial award application deadline: 8/20; financial award applicants required to submit FAFSA. *Unit head:* Dr. Linda Comer, Dean, 863-680-3951, Fax: 863-680-3860, E-mail: lcomer@flsouthern.edu. *Application contact:* Kimberly Smith, Admission Counselor and Advisor for Nursing, 863-680-3090, Fax: 863-680-3872, E-mail: ksmith@flsouthern.edu.
Website: www.flsouthern.edu/sage

**Florida State University,** The Graduate School, College of Nursing, Tallahassee, FL 32306-4310. Offers family nurse practitioner (DNP); psychiatric mental health (Certificate). *Accreditation:* AACN; AANA/CANAEP. *Program availability:* Part-time, online only, 100% online. *Faculty:* 31 full-time (27 women), 10 part-time/adjunct (9 women). *Students:* 66 full-time (59 women), 72 part-time (63 women); includes 61 minority (32 Black or African American, non-Hispanic/Latino; 1 American Indian or Alaska Native, non-Hispanic/Latino; 5 Asian, non-Hispanic/Latino; 20 Hispanic/Latino; 3 Two or more races, non-Hispanic/Latino). Average age 40. 156 applicants, 39% accepted, 54 enrolled. In 2019, 24 doctorates awarded. *Degree requirements:* For doctorate, thesis/dissertation, evidence-based project. *Entrance requirements:* For doctorate, GRE General Test, MAT, minimum GPA of 3.0, BSN or MSN, Florida RN license. Additional exam requirements/recommendations for international students: required—TOEFL (minimum score 550 paper-based). *Application deadline:* For fall admission, 3/1 for domestic and international students. Application fee: $30. Electronic applications accepted. *Expenses:* Contact institution. *Financial support:* In 2019–20, 27 students received support, including fellowships with partial tuition reimbursements available (averaging $6,300 per year), research assistantships with partial tuition reimbursements available (averaging $3,000 per year), 3 teaching assistantships with partial tuition reimbursements available (averaging $3,000 per year); career-related internships or fieldwork, Federal Work-Study, institutionally sponsored loans, scholarships/grants, traineeships, and tuition waivers (partial) also available. Financial award application deadline: 4/1; financial award applicants required to submit FAFSA. *Unit head:* Dr. Laurie Grubbs, Interim Dean, 850-644-6846, Fax: 850-644-7660, E-mail: lgrubbs@fsu.edu. *Application contact:* Carlos Urrutia, Assistant Director for Student Services, 850-644-5638, Fax: 850-645-7249, E-mail: currutia@fsu.edu.
Website: http://nursing.fsu.edu/

**Franciscan Missionaries of Our Lady University,** School of Nursing, Program in Nursing, Baton Rouge, LA 70808. Offers family nurse practitioner (MSN). *Program availability:* Part-time. *Degree requirements:* For master's, capstone project. *Entrance requirements:* For master's, GRE within the last five years, BSN with minimum GPA of 3.0 during the last 60 hours of undergraduate work, 1 year of full-time experience as a registered nurse, current licensure or eligibility to practice as registered nurse in Louisiana, 3 professional letters of recommendation.

**Francis Marion University,** Graduate Programs, Department of Nursing, Florence, SC 29502-0547. Offers family nurse practitioner (MSN); family nurse practitioner with nurse educator certificate (MSN); nurse educator (MSN). *Program availability:* Part-time. *Entrance requirements:* For master's, GRE, official transcripts, two letters of recommendation from professional associates or former professors, written statement of applicant's career goals, current nursing license. Additional exam requirements/recommendations for international students: required—TOEFL (minimum score 550 paper-based; 79 iBT). Electronic applications accepted. *Expenses:* Contact institution.

**Fresno Pacific University,** Graduate Programs, Program in Nursing, Fresno, CA 93702-4709. Offers family nurse practitioner (MSN). *Entrance requirements:* For master's, official transcripts verifying BSN from accredited nursing program; minimum cumulative GPA of 3.0; three reference forms; statement of intent; resume or curriculum vitae; personal interview; active California RN license; completion of statistics, chemistry and upper-division writing. *Expenses:* Contact institution.

**Gannon University,** School of Graduate Studies, Morosky College of Health Professions and Sciences, Villa Maria School of Nursing, Program in Family Nurse Practitioner, Erie, PA 16541-0001. Offers MSN, Certificate. *Program availability:* Part-time, evening/weekend. *Degree requirements:* For master's, thesis (for some programs), practicum. *Entrance requirements:* For master's, GRE, BS with major in nursing from accredited program, transcripts, three letters of recommendation, evidence of fulfillment of legal requirements for practice of nursing in the United States; for Certificate, GRE, interview. Additional exam requirements/recommendations for international students: required—TOEFL (minimum score 79 iBT). Electronic applications accepted.

**Gardner-Webb University,** Graduate School, School of Nursing, Boiling Springs, NC 28017. Offers family nurse practitioner (MSN, DNP). *Accreditation:* ACEN. *Program availability:* Part-time, online learning. *Entrance requirements:* For master's, GRE or MAT, minimum undergraduate GPA of 2.7; unrestricted licensure to practice as an RN. *Expenses:* Contact institution.

**George Mason University,** College of Health and Human Services, School of Nursing, Fairfax, VA 22030. Offers adult gerontology (DNP); adult/gerontological nurse practitioner (MSN); family nurse practitioner (MSN, DNP); nurse educator (MSN); nursing (PhD); nursing administration (MSN, DNP); nursing education (Certificate); psychiatric mental health (DNP). *Accreditation:* AACN. *Program availability:* Part-time, evening/weekend, blended/hybrid learning. *Degree requirements:* For master's, comprehensive exam (for some programs), thesis in clinical classes; for doctorate, comprehensive exam (for some programs), thesis/dissertation (for some programs). *Entrance requirements:* For master's, 2 official transcripts; expanded goals statement; resume; BSN from accredited institution; minimum GPA of 3.0 in last 60 credits of undergraduate work; 2 letters of recommendation; completion of undergraduate statistics and graduate-level bivariate statistics; certification in professional CPR; for doctorate, GRE, 2 official transcripts; expanded goals statement; resume; 2 recommendation letters; nursing license; at least 1 year of work experience as an RN; interview; writing sample; evidence of graduate-level course in applied statistics; master's degree in nursing with minimum GPA of 3.5; for Certificate, 2 official transcripts; expanded goals statement; resume; master's degree from accredited institution or currently enrolled with minimum GPA of 3.0. Additional exam requirements/recommendations for international students: required—TOEFL (minimum score 570 paper-based; 88 iBT), IELTS (minimum score 6.5), PTE (minimum score 59). Electronic applications accepted. *Expenses:* Contact institution.

**Georgetown University,** Graduate School of Arts and Sciences, School of Nursing and Health Studies, Washington, DC 20057. Offers acute care nurse practitioner (MS); clinical nurse specialist (MS); family nurse practitioner (MS); health systems administration (MS); nurse anesthesia (MS); nurse-midwifery (MS); nursing (DNP); nursing education (MS). *Accreditation:* AACN; AANA/CANAEP (one or more programs are accredited); ACNM/ACME (one or more programs are accredited). *Degree requirements:* For master's, thesis optional. *Entrance requirements:* For master's, GRE General Test or MAT, bachelor's degree in nursing from ACEN-accredited school, minimum undergraduate GPA of 3.0. Additional exam requirements/recommendations for international students: required—TOEFL.

## Family Nurse Practitioner Studies

**The George Washington University,** School of Nursing, Washington, DC 20052. Offers adult nurse practitioner (MSN, DNP, Post-Master's Certificate); clinical research administration (MSN); family nurse practitioner (MSN, Post-Master's Certificate); health care quality (MSN, Post-Master's Certificate); nursing leadership and management (MSN); nursing practice (DNP); palliative care nurse practitioner (Post-Master's Certificate). *Accreditation:* AACN.

**Georgia Southern University,** Jack N. Averitt College of Graduate Studies, Waters College of Health Professions, School of Nursing, Program in Nurse Practitioner, Statesboro, GA 30458. Offers family nurse practitioner (MSN); psychiatric mental health nurse practitioner (MSN). *Program availability:* Part-time, blended/hybrid learning. *Students:* 19 part-time (all women); includes 6 minority (4 Black or African American, non-Hispanic/Latino; 1 Hispanic/Latino; 1 Two or more races, non-Hispanic/Latino). Average age 34. 4 applicants. In 2019, 47 master's awarded. *Entrance requirements:* For master's, minimum GPA of 3.0, Georgia nursing license, 2 years of clinical experience, CPR certification. Additional exam requirements/recommendations for international students: required—TOEFL (minimum score 550 paper-based; 80 iBT), IELTS (minimum score 6). *Application deadline:* For fall admission, 7/31 priority date for domestic and international students; for spring admission, 11/30 priority date for domestic students, 11/30 for international students; for summer admission, 3/31 for domestic and international students. Applications are processed on a rolling basis. Application fee: $50. Electronic applications accepted. *Expenses: Tuition, area resident:* Full-time $4986; part-time $277 per credit hour. Tuition, nonresident: full-time $19,890; part-time $1105 per credit hour. *International tuition:* $19,890 full-time. *Required fees:* $2114; $1057 per semester. $1057 per semester. Tuition and fees vary according to course load, campus/location and program. *Financial support:* In 2019–20, 27 students received support, including 5 fellowships with full tuition reimbursements available (averaging $7,750 per year); career-related internships or fieldwork, Federal Work-Study, scholarships/grants, traineeships, tuition waivers (full), and unspecified assistantships also available. Support available to part-time students. Financial award application deadline: 4/15; financial award applicants required to submit FAFSA. *Unit head:* Dr. Sharon Radzyminski, Department Chair, 912-478-5455, Fax: 912-478-5036, E-mail: sradzyminski@georgiasouthern.edu. *Application contact:* Dr. Sharon Radzyminski, Department Chair, 912-478-5455, Fax: 912-478-5036, E-mail: sradzyminski@georgiasouthern.edu.

**Georgia Southwestern State University,** College of Nursing and Health Sciences, Americus, GA 31709-4693. Offers family nurse practitioner (MSN); health informatics (Postbaccalaureate Certificate); nurse educator (Post Master's Certificate); nursing educator (MSN); nursing informatics (MSN); nursing leadership (MSN). *Program availability:* Part-time, online only, all theory courses are offered online. *Faculty:* 9 full-time (all women), 5 part-time/adjunct (all women). *Students:* 18 full-time (14 women), 104 part-time (91 women); includes 45 minority (31 Black or African American, non-Hispanic/Latino; 1 American Indian or Alaska Native, non-Hispanic/Latino; 4 Asian, non-Hispanic/Latino; 3 Hispanic/Latino; 6 Two or more races, non-Hispanic/Latino). Average age 36. 96 applicants, 45% accepted, 24 enrolled. In 2019, 53 master's awarded. *Degree requirements:* For master's, thesis (for some programs), minimum cumulative GPA of 3.0; maximum of 6 credit hours with C grade and no D grades; degree completed within 7 calendar years from initial enrollment date in graduate courses; for other advanced degree, minimum cumulative GPA of 3.0; maximum of 6 credit hours with C grade and no D grades; degree completed within 7 calendar years from initial enrollment date in graduate courses. *Entrance requirements:* For master's, baccalaureate degree in nursing from regionally-accredited institution and nationally-accredited nursing program with minimum GPA of 3.0; three completed recommendation forms from professional peer or clinical supervisor; current unencumbered RN license in state where clinical course requirements will be met; proof of immunizations; for other advanced degree, Baccalaureate or masters degree (depending upon certificate) in nursing; Minimum GPA of 3.0; 3 completed recommendation forms; current unencumbered RN license in state where clinical course requirements will be met. Application fee: $25. Electronic applications accepted. *Expenses:* $385.00 per credit hour tuition, plus fees, which vary according to enrolled credit hours. *Financial support:* Application deadline: 6/1; applicants required to submit FAFSA. *Unit head:* Dr. Sandra Daniel, Dean, 229-931-2275. *Application contact:* Office of Graduate Admissions, 800-338-0082, Fax: 229-931-2983, E-mail: graduateadmissions@gsw.edu.
Website: https://www.gsw.edu/academics/schools-and-departments/college-of-nursing-and-health-sciences/school-of-nursing/nursing-programs/graduate

**Georgia State University,** Byrdine F. Lewis School of Nursing, Atlanta, GA 30303. Offers adult health clinical nurse specialist/nurse practitioner (MS, Certificate); child health clinical nurse specialist/pediatric nurse practitioner (MS, Certificate); family nurse practitioner (MS, Certificate); family psychiatric mental health nurse practitioner (MS, Certificate); nursing (PhD); nursing leadership in healthcare innovations (MS), including nursing administration, nursing informatics; nutrition (MS); occupational therapy (MOT); perinatal clinical nurse specialist/women's health nurse practitioner (MS, Certificate); physical therapy (DPT); respiratory therapy (MS). *Accreditation:* AACN. *Program availability:* Part-time, blended/hybrid learning. *Faculty:* 57 full-time (40 women), 5 part-time/adjunct (4 women). *Students:* 388 full-time (290 women), 155 part-time (135 women); includes 217 minority (130 Black or African American, non-Hispanic/Latino; 47 Asian, non-Hispanic/Latino; 26 Hispanic/Latino; 14 Two or more races, non-Hispanic/Latino), 45 international. Average age 32. 480 applicants, 50% accepted, 164 enrolled. In 2019, 158 master's, 64 doctorates, 20 other advanced degrees awarded. *Degree requirements:* For doctorate, comprehensive exam, thesis/dissertation. *Entrance requirements:* For doctorate, GRE. Additional exam requirements/recommendations for international students: required—TOEFL. *Application deadline:* For fall admission, 2/1 priority date for domestic and international students; for spring admission, 9/15 for domestic and international students. Applications are processed on a rolling basis. Application fee: $50. Electronic applications accepted. *Expenses:* Contact institution. *Financial support:* In 2019–20, research assistantships with tuition reimbursements (averaging $1,666 per year), teaching assistantships with tuition reimbursements (averaging $1,920 per year) were awarded; scholarships/grants, tuition waivers (full and partial), and unspecified assistantships also available. Support available to part-time students. Financial award application deadline: 8/1; financial award applicants required to submit FAFSA. *Unit head:* Huanbiao Mo, Dean of Nursing. *Application contact:* Huanbiao Mo, Dean of Nursing.
Website: http://nursing.gsu.edu/

**Goshen College,** Graduate Program in Nursing, Goshen, IN 46526. Offers family nurse practitioner (MSN). *Accreditation:* AACN. *Program availability:* Part-time, evening/weekend. *Faculty:* 7 full-time (5 women). *Students:* 56 full-time (51 women), 5 part-time (all women); includes 11 minority (3 Black or African American, non-Hispanic/Latino; 2 Asian, non-Hispanic/Latino; 5 Hispanic/Latino; 1 Two or more races, non-Hispanic/Latino). Average age 35. 22 applicants, 100% accepted, 22 enrolled. In 2019, 21 master's awarded. *Degree requirements:* For master's, comprehensive exam (for some programs). *Entrance requirements:* For master's, minimum GPA of 3.0, curriculum vitae, bachelor's degree in nursing, active RN license in Indiana or Michigan, three professional references, essay, one year of clinical experience, statistics course, interview with program director. Additional exam requirements/recommendations for

international students: required—TOEFL (minimum score 600 paper-based; 100 iBT), IELTS (minimum score 6.5). *Application deadline:* For fall admission, 3/15 priority date for domestic students. Applications are processed on a rolling basis. Application fee: $25. Electronic applications accepted. *Expenses:* $650 per credit hour (master's); $780 per credit hour (doctorate). *Financial support:* In 2019–20, 7 students received support. Scholarships/grants available. *Unit head:* Ruth Stoltzfus, Director, 574-535-7973, E-mail: ruthas@goshen.edu. *Application contact:* Ruth Stoltzfus, Director, 574-535-7973, E-mail: ruthas@goshen.edu.
Website: http://www.goshen.edu/graduate/nursing/

**Graceland University,** School of Nursing, Independence, MO 64050-3434. Offers adult and gerontology acute care (MSN, PMC); family nurse practitioner (MSN, PMC); nurse educator (MSN, PMC); organizational leadership (DNP). *Accreditation:* AACN. *Program availability:* Part-time, online only, 100% online. *Degree requirements:* For master's, comprehensive exam (for some programs), thesis optional, scholarly project; for doctorate, capstone project. *Entrance requirements:* For master's, BSN from nationally-accredited program, RN license, minimum GPA of 3.0, satisfactory criminal background check, three professional reference letters, professional goals statement of 150 words or less; for doctorate, MSN from nationally-accredited program, RN license, minimum GPA of 3.0, criminal background check. Additional exam requirements/recommendations for international students: required—TOEFL (minimum score 550 paper-based; 80 iBT). Electronic applications accepted. *Expenses:* Contact institution.

**Grambling State University,** School of Graduate Studies and Research, College of Professional Studies, School of Nursing, Grambling, LA 71245. Offers family nurse practitioner (PMC); nursing (MSN). *Accreditation:* ACEN. *Program availability:* Part-time. *Degree requirements:* For master's, comprehensive exam (for some programs), thesis (for some programs). *Entrance requirements:* For master's, GRE, minimum GPA of 3.0 on last degree, interview, 2 years of experience as RN. Additional exam requirements/recommendations for international students: required—TOEFL (minimum score 500 paper-based; 62 iBT). Electronic applications accepted.

**Grand Canyon University,** College of Nursing and Health Care Professions, Phoenix, AZ 85017-1097. Offers acute care nurse practitioner (MSN, PMC); family nurse practitioner (MSN, PMC); health care administration (MS); health care informatics (MS, MSN); leadership in health care systems (MSN); nursing (DNP); nursing education (MSN, PMC); public health (MPH, MSN); MBA/MSN. *Accreditation:* AACN. *Program availability:* Part-time, evening/weekend, online learning. *Degree requirements:* For master's and PMC, comprehensive exam (for some programs). *Entrance requirements:* For master's, minimum cumulative and science course undergraduate GPA of 3.0. Additional exam requirements/recommendations for international students: required—TOEFL (minimum score 575 paper-based; 90 iBT), IELTS (minimum score 7).

**Gwynedd Mercy University,** Frances M. Maguire School of Nursing and Health Professions, Gwynedd Valley, PA 19437-0901. Offers clinical nurse specialist (MSN), including gerontology, oncology, pediatrics; nurse educator (MSN); nurse practitioner (MSN), including adult health, pediatric health; nursing (DNP). *Accreditation:* ACEN. *Program availability:* Part-time, blended/hybrid learning. *Faculty:* 4 full-time (all women), 1 (woman) part-time/adjunct. *Students:* 52 full-time (47 women), 58 part-time (52 women); includes 28 minority (17 Black or African American, non-Hispanic/Latino; 9 Asian, non-Hispanic/Latino; 2 Hispanic/Latino). Average age 33. 35 applicants, 43% accepted, 14 enrolled. In 2019, 26 master's awarded. *Degree requirements:* For master's, thesis optional; for doctorate, evidence-based scholarly project. *Entrance requirements:* For master's, current nursing experience, physical assessment, course work in statistics, BSN from ACEN-accredited program, 2 letters of recommendation, personal interview. *Application deadline:* For fall admission, 4/15 for domestic and international students. Applications are processed on a rolling basis. Electronic applications accepted. *Expenses:* Contact institution. *Financial support:* Scholarships/grants, traineeships, and unspecified assistantships available. Financial award application deadline: 4/15. *Unit head:* Dr. Ann Phalen, Dean, 215-646-7300 Ext. 539, Fax: 215-641-5517, E-mail: phalen.a@gmercyu.edu. *Application contact:* Mary Hermann, Associate Dean, 215-646-7300, E-mail: herman.m@gmercyu.edu.
Website: http://www.gmercyu.edu/academics/graduate-programs/nursing

**Hampton University,** School of Nursing, Hampton, VA 23668. Offers community health nursing (MS); family nurse practitioner (MS); family research (PhD); nursing administration (MS); nursing education (MS). *Accreditation:* AACN. *Program availability:* Part-time, online learning. *Students:* 3 full-time (all women), 13 part-time (12 women); includes 15 minority (all Black or African American, non-Hispanic/Latino). Average age 49. 4 applicants, 25% accepted. In 2019, 3 master's, 5 doctorates awarded. *Degree requirements:* For master's, comprehensive exam, thesis optional; for doctorate, comprehensive exam, thesis/dissertation. *Entrance requirements:* For master's, GRE General Test. *Application deadline:* For fall admission, 6/1 priority date for domestic students, 4/1 priority date for international students; for spring admission, 11/1 priority date for domestic students, 9/1 priority date for international students; for summer admission, 4/1 priority date for domestic students, 2/1 priority date for international students. Applications are processed on a rolling basis. Application fee: $35. Electronic applications accepted. *Financial support:* In 2019–20, 2 students received support. Fellowships, research assistantships, teaching assistantships, career-related internships or fieldwork, Federal Work-Study, institutionally sponsored loans, and scholarships/grants available. Support available to part-time students. Financial award application deadline: 6/30; financial award applicants required to submit FAFSA. *Unit head:* Dr. Shevellanie Lott, Dean, 757-727-5654, E-mail: shevellanie.lott@hamptonu.edu. *Application contact:* Dr. Shevellanie Lott, Dean, 757-727-5654, E-mail: shevellanie.lott@hamptonu.edu.
Website: http://nursing.hamptonu.edu

**Hardin-Simmons University,** Graduate School, Patty Hanks Shelton School of Nursing, Abilene, TX 79698-0001. Offers education (MSN); family nurse practitioner (MSN). *Accreditation:* AACN. *Program availability:* Part-time. *Degree requirements:* For master's, comprehensive exam, thesis or alternative. *Entrance requirements:* For master's, GRE, minimum undergraduate GPA of 3.0; interview; upper-level course work in statistics; CPR certification; letters of recommendation. Additional exam requirements/recommendations for international students: required—TOEFL (minimum score 550 paper-based; 79 iBT). Electronic applications accepted. *Expenses:* Contact institution.

**Hofstra University,** Hofstra Northwell School of Nursing and Physician Assistant Studies, Programs in Nursing, Hempstead, NY 11549. Offers adult-gerontology acute care nurse practitioner (MS); family nurse practitioner (MS); psychiatric-mental health np (MS). *Students:* 68 full-time (48 women), 159 part-time (138 women); includes 103 minority (24 Black or African American, non-Hispanic/Latino; 2 American Indian or Alaska Native, non-Hispanic/Latino; 41 Asian, non-Hispanic/Latino; 35 Hispanic/Latino; 1 Two or more races, non-Hispanic/Latino). Average age 33. 389 applicants, 32% accepted, 89 enrolled. In 2019, 44 master's awarded. *Degree requirements:* For master's, comprehensive exam, minimum GPA of 3.0. *Entrance requirements:* For master's, bachelor's degree in nursing, 3 letters of recommendation, essay, resume. Additional exam requirements/recommendations for international students: required—TOEFL (minimum score 550 paper-based; 80 iBT); recommended—IELTS (minimum score 6.5). Application fee: $75. Electronic applications accepted. *Expenses:* Tuition: Full-time $25,164; part-time $1398 per credit. *Required fees:* $580; $165 per semester.

Tuition and fees vary according to course load, degree level and program. *Financial support:* In 2019–20, 56 students received support, including 5 fellowships with full and partial tuition reimbursements available (averaging $10,870 per year); research assistantships with full and partial tuition reimbursements available, career-related internships or fieldwork, Federal Work-Study, institutionally sponsored loans, scholarships/grants, traineeships, tuition waivers (full and partial), unspecified assistantships, and scholarships and endowed scholarships also available. Support available to part-time students. Financial award applicants required to submit FAFSA. *Unit head:* Dr. Kathleen Gallo, Dean, 516-463-7475, Fax: 516-463-7495, E-mail: kathleen.gallo@hofstra.edu. *Application contact:* Sunil Samuel, Assistant Vice President of Admissions, 516-463-4723, Fax: 516-463-4664, E-mail: graduateadmission@hofstra.edu.

**Holy Names University,** Graduate Division, Department of Nursing, Oakland, CA 94619-1699. Offers administration/management (MSN, PMC); care transition management (MSN); family nurse practitioner (MSN, PMC); informatics (MSN); nurse educator (PMC); MSN/MBA. *Accreditation:* AACN. *Program availability:* Part-time, evening/weekend. *Entrance requirements:* For master's, bachelor's degree in nursing or related field; California RN license or eligibility; minimum cumulative GPA of 2.8, 3.0 in nursing courses from baccalaureate program; courses in pathophysiology, statistics, and research at the undergraduate level. Additional exam requirements/recommendations for international students: required—TOEFL (minimum score 550 paper-based; 79 iBT). Electronic applications accepted. Application fee is waived when completed online.

**Houston Baptist University,** School of Nursing and Allied Health, Program in Nursing, Houston, TX 77074-3298. Offers family nurse practitioner (MSN); pediatric nurse practitioner in primary care (MSN). *Program availability:* Part-time, evening/weekend, online only, 100% online. *Degree requirements:* For master's, comprehensive exam. *Entrance requirements:* For master's, GRE General Test, BSN from NLN or CCLE program, minimum GPA of 2.5, RN license in Texas; resume. Electronic applications accepted. Application fee is waived when completed online. *Expenses:* Contact institution.

**Howard University,** College of Nursing and Allied Health Sciences, Division of Nursing, Washington, DC 20059-0002. Offers family nurse practitioner (MSN); nurse educator (MSN). *Accreditation:* AACN. *Program availability:* Part-time. *Degree requirements:* For master's, comprehensive exam, thesis optional. *Entrance requirements:* For master's, RN license, minimum GPA of 3.0, BS in nursing.

**Hunter College of the City University of New York,** Graduate School, Hunter-Bellevue School of Nursing, Doctor of Nursing Practice Program, New York, NY 10065-5085. Offers adult-gerontology nurse practitioner (DNP); family nurse practitioner (DNP); psychiatric-mental health nurse practitioner (DNP).

**Husson University,** Graduate Nursing Program, Bangor, ME 04401-2999. Offers educational leadership (MSN); family and community nurse practitioner (MSN, PMC); psychiatric mental health nurse practitioner (MSN, PMC). *Accreditation:* AACN. *Program availability:* Part-time, evening/weekend. *Degree requirements:* For master's, comprehensive exam (for some programs), research project. *Entrance requirements:* For master's, proof of RN licensure. Additional exam requirements/recommendations for international students: required—TOEFL (minimum score 550 paper-based; 80 iBT), IELTS (minimum score 6.5). Electronic applications accepted. *Expenses:* Contact institution.

**Illinois State University,** Graduate School, Mennonite College of Nursing, Normal, IL 61790. Offers family nurse practitioner (PMC); nursing (MSN, PhD). *Accreditation:* AACN. *Faculty:* 41 full-time (39 women), 47 part-time/adjunct (40 women). *Students:* 12 full-time (9 women), 118 part-time (102 women). Average age 37. 46 applicants, 83% accepted, 16 enrolled. In 2019, 32 master's, 11 doctorates awarded. *Degree requirements:* For master's, variable foreign language requirement, comprehensive exam; for doctorate, residency. *Entrance requirements:* For master's and doctorate, GRE. Application fee: $50. *Expenses:* Contact institution. *Financial support:* In 2019–20, 5 teaching assistantships were awarded. *Unit head:* Dr. Judy Neubrander, Dean of Mennonite College of Nursing, 309-438-2174, E-mail: jlneubr@IllinoisState.edu. *Application contact:* Dr. Noelle Selkow, Interim Director of Graduate Studies, 309-438-2583, Fax: 309-438-7912, E-mail: gradinfor@ilstu.edu.
Website: http://www.mcn.ilstu.edu/

**Indiana State University,** College of Graduate and Professional Studies, College of Health and Human Services, Department of Advanced Practice Nursing, Terre Haute, IN 47809. Offers advanced practice nursing (DNP); family nurse practitioner (MS); nursing administration (MS); nursing education (MS). *Accreditation:* ACEN. *Program availability:* Part-time. *Degree requirements:* For master's, thesis or alternative. *Entrance requirements:* For master's, BSN, RN license, minimum undergraduate GPA of 3.0. Electronic applications accepted.

**Indiana University Kokomo,** School of Nursing, Kokomo, IN 46904. Offers family nurse practitioner (MSN); nurse administrator (MSN); nurse educator (MSN). Electronic applications accepted. *Expenses:* Contact institution.

**Indiana University-Purdue University Indianapolis,** School of Nursing, MSN Program in Nursing, Indianapolis, IN 46202. Offers adult/gerontology acute care nurse practitioner (MSN); adult/gerontology clinical nurse specialist (MSN); adult/gerontology primary care nurse practitioner (MSN); family nurse practitioner (MSN); nursing education (MSN); nursing leadership in health systems (MSN); pediatric clinical nurse specialist (MSN); pediatric nurse practitioner (MSN). *Accreditation:* AACN. *Program availability:* Part-time, blended/hybrid learning. *Degree requirements:* For master's, thesis. *Entrance requirements:* For master's, BSN from ACEN- or CCNE-accredited program, minimum undergraduate GPA of 3.0 (preferred), professional resume or curriculum vitae, essay stating career goals and objectives, current unencumbered RN license, three references from individuals with knowledge of ability to succeed in graduate program. Additional exam requirements/recommendations for international students: required—TOEFL (minimum score 550 paper-based; 79 iBT). Electronic applications accepted. *Expenses:* Contact institution.

**Indiana University South Bend,** Vera Z. Dwyer College of Health Sciences, School of Nursing, South Bend, IN 46615. Offers family nurse practitioner (MSN). *Accreditation:* AACN. *Program availability:* Part-time, evening/weekend. *Entrance requirements:* For master's, GRE General Test, minimum GPA of 3.0. *Expenses:* Contact institution.

**Jacksonville University,** Brooks Rehabilitation College of Healthcare Sciences, Keigwin School of Nursing, Master of Science in Nursing Program, Jacksonville, FL 32211. Offers clinical nurse educator (MSN); family nurse practitioner (MSN); family nurse practitioner/emergency nurse practitioner (MSN); leadership in the healthcare system (MSN); nursing informatics (MSN); psychiatric nurse practitioner (MSN); MSN/MBA. *Program availability:* Part-time, 100% online, blended/hybrid learning. In 2019, 215 master's awarded. *Degree requirements:* For master's, thesis. *Entrance requirements:* For master's, GRE General Test or undergraduate GPA above 3.0, BSN from ACEN- or CCNE-accredited program; course work in statistics and physical assessment within last 5 years; Florida nursing license; CPR/BLS certification; 3 recommendations, 2 of which are professional references; statement of intent; resume. Additional exam requirements/recommendations for international students: required—TOEFL (minimum score 650 paper-based; 114 iBT), IELTS (minimum score 8). *Application deadline:* Applications are processed on a rolling basis. Application fee: $50. Electronic applications accepted. *Expenses:* Contact institution. *Financial support:* Federal Work-Study, institutionally sponsored loans, scholarships/grants, and health care benefits available. Support available to part-time students. Financial award application deadline: 3/15; financial award applicants required to submit FAFSA. *Unit head:* Dr. Hilary Morgan, Director, Graduate Nursing Programs/Associate Professor, 904-256-7601, E-mail: hmorgan@ju.edu. *Application contact:* Kristen Kirkendall, Associate Director of Graduate Admissions and Communications, 904-256-7169, E-mail: kgreene8@ju.edu.
Website: https://www.ju.edu/nursing/graduate/master-science-nursing/index.php

**James Madison University,** The Graduate School, College of Health and Behavioral Studies, Program in Nursing, Harrisonburg, VA 22807. Offers adult/gerontology primary care nurse practitioner (MSN); clinical nurse leader (MSN); family nurse practitioner (MSN); nurse administrator (MSN); nurse midwifery (MSN); nursing (MSN, DNP); psychiatric mental health nurse practitioner (MSN). *Accreditation:* AACN. *Program availability:* Part-time, 100% online, blended/hybrid learning. *Students:* 15 full-time (14 women), 71 part-time (66 women); includes 10 minority (3 Black or African American, non-Hispanic/Latino; 6 Asian, non-Hispanic/Latino; 1 Hispanic/Latino). Average age 30. In 2019, 28 master's awarded. Application fee: $60. Electronic applications accepted. *Financial support:* In 2019–20, 2 students received support. Federal Work-Study and assistantships (averaging $7911) available. Financial award application deadline: 3/1; financial award applicants required to submit FAFSA. *Unit head:* Dr. Julie T. Sanford, Department Head, 540-568-6314, E-mail: sanforjt@jmu.edu. *Application contact:* Lynette D. Michael, Director of Graduate Admissions, 540-568-6131 Ext. 6395, Fax: 540-568-7860, E-mail: michaeld@jmu.edu.
Website: http://www.nursing.jmu.edu

**Johns Hopkins University,** School of Nursing, DNP Nurse Practitioner Track, Baltimore, MD 21218. Offers adult/gerontological acute care nurse practitioner (DNP); adult/gerontological primary care nurse practitioner (DNP); family primary care nurse practitioner (DNP); pediatric primary care nurse practitioner (DNP). *Accreditation:* AACN. *Students:* 176 applicants, 59% accepted, 64 enrolled. *Degree requirements:* For doctorate, thesis/dissertation, Preliminary justification; final justification. *Entrance requirements:* For doctorate, minimum GPA of 3.0, goal statement/essay, resume, letters of recommendation, official transcripts from all post-secondary institutions attended; BSN and RN license, work experience for some tracks. Additional exam requirements/recommendations for international students: required—TOEFL (minimum score 600 paper-based; 100 iBT), IELTS (minimum score 7). *Application deadline:* For fall admission, 11/1 priority date for domestic and international students. Application fee: $70. Electronic applications accepted. *Expenses:* Contact institution. *Financial support:* In 2019–20, 57 students received support. Federal Work-Study and scholarships/grants available. Support available to part-time students. Financial award application deadline: 3/1; financial award applicants required to submit FAFSA. *Unit head:* Dr. Kim McIltrot, Dean, Fax: 410-502-2247, E-mail: kmciltr1@jhmi.edu. *Application contact:* Cathy Wilson, Director of Admissions, 410-955-7548, Fax: 410-614-7086, E-mail: jhuson@jhu.edu.
Website: http://www.nursing.jhu.edu

**Keiser University,** Master of Science in Nursing Program, Fort Lauderdale, FL 33309. Offers family nurse practitioner (MSN); nursing (MSN). *Accreditation:* AANA/CANAEP.

**Kent State University,** College of Nursing, Kent, OH 44242. Offers advanced nursing practice (DNP), including adult/gerontology acute care nurse practitioner (MSN, DNP); nursing (MSN, PhD), including adult/gerontology acute care nurse practitioner (MSN, DNP), adult/gerontology clinical nurse specialist (MSN), adult/gerontology primary care nurse practitioner (MSN), family nurse practitioner (MSN), nurse educator (MSN), nursing and healthcare management (MSN), pediatric primary care nurse practitioner (MSN), psychiatric/mental health nurse practitioner (MSN); MBA/MSN. *Accreditation:* AACN. *Program availability:* Part-time, online learning. *Faculty:* 28 full-time (26 women), 15 part-time/adjunct (13 women). *Students:* 138 full-time (123 women), 522 part-time (464 women); includes 80 minority (41 Black or African American, non-Hispanic/Latino; 16 Asian, non-Hispanic/Latino; 9 Hispanic/Latino; 1 Native Hawaiian or other Pacific Islander, non-Hispanic/Latino; 13 Two or more races, non-Hispanic/Latino), 7 international. Average age 35. 303 applicants, 68% accepted, 154 enrolled. In 2019, 156 master's, 8 doctorates awarded. *Degree requirements:* For master's, practicum for master's degrees; for doctorate, comprehensive exam, thesis/dissertation. *Entrance requirements:* For master's, GRE or GMAT, minimum GPA of 3.0, active RN license, statement of purpose, 3 letters of reference, undergraduate level statistics class (minimum C grade), baccalaureate or graduate-level nursing degree, curriculum vitae/resume; for doctorate, GRE, minimum GPA of 3.0, transcripts, 3 letters of reference, interview, active unrestricted Ohio RN license, statement of purpose, writing sample, curriculum vitae/resume, baccalaureate and master's degrees in nursing or DNP, undergraduate or graduate level statistics course with a minimum C grade. Additional exam requirements/recommendations for international students: required—TOEFL (minimum score 83 iBT), IELTS (minimum score 6.5), PTE (minimum score 55), Michigan English Language Assessment Battery (minimum score 78). *Application deadline:* For fall admission, 3/1 for domestic and international students; for spring admission, 10/1 for domestic and international students. Applications are processed on a rolling basis. Application fee: $45 ($70 for international students). Electronic applications accepted. *Financial support:* Federal Work-Study and scholarships/grants available. Financial award application deadline: 2/1. *Unit head:* Dr. Barbara Broome, Ph.D., Dean, 330-672-3777, E-mail: bbroome1@kent.edu. *Application contact:* Dr. Wendy A. Umberger, Ph.D., Associate Dean for Graduate Programs/Professor, 330-672-8813, E-mail: wlewando@kent.edu.
Website: http://www.kent.edu/nursing/

**King University,** School of Nursing, Bristol, TN 37620-2699. Offers family nurse practitioner (MSN, Post-Master's Certificate); nurse educator (MSN, Post-Master's Certificate); nursing (DNP); nursing administration (MSN); pediatric nurse practitioner (MSN). *Program availability:* Part-time, evening/weekend, 100% online, blended/hybrid learning. *Faculty:* 13 full-time (12 women), 4 part-time/adjunct (2 women). *Students:* 115 full-time (103 women), 35 part-time (28 women); includes 12 minority (9 Black or African American, non-Hispanic/Latino; 1 Asian, non-Hispanic/Latino; 1 Hispanic/Latino; 1 Native Hawaiian or other Pacific Islander, non-Hispanic/Latino). Average age 37. 141 applicants, 96% accepted, 63 enrolled. In 2019, 89 master's, 1 doctorate, 6 other advanced degrees awarded. *Degree requirements:* For master's and Post-Master's Certificate, comprehensive exam (for some programs), thesis optional; for doctorate, comprehensive exam (for some programs), thesis/dissertation. *Entrance requirements:* For master's, Submit evidence of graduation from an accredited baccalaureate nursing program with a minimum cumulative undergraduate GPA of 3.0 on a 4.0 scale prior to enrolling; for doctorate, bachelor's and master's degree in nursing with a GPA of 3.25 or higher from a master's degree program accredited by the Accreditation Commission for Nursing Education (ACNE) or the Commission on Collegiate Nursing Education (CCNE); for Post-Master's Certificate, FNP and PNP applicants must complete an interview with the MSN Admissions Committee. Additional exam requirements/

recommendations for international students: required—TOEFL (minimum score 84 paper-based; 84 iBT). *Application deadline:* Applications are processed on a rolling basis. Application fee: $50. Electronic applications accepted. *Expenses: Tuition:* Full-time $10,890; part-time $605 per semester hour. *Required fees:* $100 per course. *Financial support:* Unspecified assistantships available. Financial award applicants required to submit FAFSA. *Unit head:* Dr. Tracy Slemp, Dean, School of Nursing, 423-652-6335, E-mail: tjslemp@king.edu. *Application contact:* Natalie Blankenship, Territory Manager/Enrollment Counselor, 652-652-4159, Fax: 652-652-4727, E-mail: nblankenship@king.edu.

**La Salle University,** School of Nursing and Health Sciences, Program in Nursing, Philadelphia, PA 19141-1199. Offers adult gerontology primary care nurse practitioner (MSN, Certificate); adult health and illness clinical nurse specialist (MSN); adult-gerontology clinical nurse specialist (MSN, Certificate); clinical nurse leader (MSN); family primary care nurse practitioner (MSN, Certificate); gerontology (Certificate); nurse anesthetist (MSN, Certificate); nursing (MSN, Certificate); nursing administration (MSN, Certificate); nursing education (Certificate); nursing practice (DNP); nursing service administration (MSN); public health nursing (MSN, Certificate); school nursing (Certificate); MSN/MBA; MSN/MPH. *Accreditation:* AACN. *Program availability:* Part-time, evening/weekend, 100% online. *Degree requirements:* For doctorate, minimum of 1,000 hours of post baccalaureate clinical practice supervised by preceptors. *Entrance requirements:* For master's, GRE, MAT, or GMAT (for students with BSN GPA of less than 3.2), baccalaureate degree in nursing from ACEN- or CCNE-accredited program or an MSN Bridge program; Pennsylvania RN license; 2 letters of reference; resume; statement of philosophy articulating professional values and future educational goal; 1 year of work experience as a registered nurse; for doctorate, GRE (waived for applicants with MSN cumulative GPA of 3.7 or above), MSN, master's degree, MBA or MHA from nationally-accredited program; resume or curriculum vitae; 2 letters of reference; interview; for Certificate, GRE, MAT, or GMAT (for students with BSN GPA of less than 3.2, baccalaureate degree in nursing from ACEN- or CCNE-accredited program or an MSN Bridge program; Pennsylvania RN license; 2 letters of reference; resume; statement of philosophy articulating professional values and future educational goal; 1 year of work experience as a registered nurse. Additional exam requirements/recommendations for international students: required—TOEFL. Electronic applications accepted. Application fee is waived when completed online. *Expenses:* Contact institution.

**Le Moyne College,** Department of Nursing, Syracuse, NY 13214. Offers family nurse practitioner (MS, CAS); informatics (MS, CAS); nursing administration (MS, CAS); nursing education (MS, CAS). *Accreditation:* AACN. *Program availability:* Part-time, evening/weekend. *Faculty:* 4 full-time (all women), 6 part-time/adjunct (4 women). *Students:* 18 full-time (17 women), 57 part-time (52 women); includes 7 minority (1 Black or African American, non-Hispanic/Latino; 1 Asian, non-Hispanic/Latino; 4 Hispanic/Latino; 1 Two or more races, non-Hispanic/Latino). Average age 31. 43 applicants, 84% accepted, 32 enrolled. In 2019, 33 master's, 3 other advanced degrees awarded. *Degree requirements:* For master's, 39-45 credit hours, varies by program, practicum, scholarly project; for CAS, Varies by experience or incoming degree. *Entrance requirements:* For master's, earned bachelor's degree transcripts, New York RN license, 2-3 letters of recommendation, personal statement, interview. Additional exam requirements/recommendations for international students: required—TOEFL (minimum score 79 iBT); recommended—IELTS (minimum score 6.5). *Application deadline:* For fall admission, 4/1 priority date for domestic students, 4/1 for international students; for spring admission, 11/1 priority date for domestic students, 11/1 for international students; for summer admission, 5/1 priority date for domestic students, 5/1 for international students. Applications are processed on a rolling basis. Electronic applications accepted. *Expenses:* $764-$951 per credit hour depending upon program, $75 fee per semester. *Financial support:* In 2019–20, 1 student received support. Career-related internships or fieldwork, Federal Work-Study, scholarships/grants, health care benefits, and unspecified assistantships available. Support available to part-time students. Financial award applicants required to submit FAFSA. *Unit head:* Catherine A. Brownell, Professor - Chair of Nursing, 315-445-5426, Fax: 315-445-6024, E-mail: nursing@lemoyne.edu. *Application contact:* Teresa M. Renn, Director of Graduate Admission, 315-445-5444, Fax: 315-445-6092, E-mail: GradAdmission@lemoyne.edu. Website: http://www.lemoyne.edu/nursing

**Lewis University,** College of Nursing and Health Sciences, Program in Nursing, Romeoville, IL 60446. Offers adult gerontology clinical nurse specialist (MSN); adult gerontology primary care nurse practitioner (MSN); family nurse practitioner (MSN); healthcare systems leadership (MSN); nursing education (MSN); school nurse (MSN). *Accreditation:* AACN. *Program availability:* Part-time, evening/weekend, 100% online, blended/hybrid learning. *Students:* 7 full-time (all women), 411 part-time (372 women); includes 113 minority (15 Black or African American, non-Hispanic/Latino; 43 Asian, non-Hispanic/Latino; 47 Hispanic/Latino; 8 Two or more races, non-Hispanic/Latino), 2 international. Average age 35. *Degree requirements:* For master's, clinical practicum. *Entrance requirements:* For master's, minimum undergraduate GPA of 3.0, degree in nursing, RN license, letter of recommendation, interview, resume or curriculum vitae. Additional exam requirements/recommendations for international students: required—TOEFL (minimum score 550 paper-based; 80 iBT), IELTS. *Application deadline:* For fall admission, 5/1 priority date for international students; for spring admission, 11/15 priority date for international students. Applications are processed on a rolling basis. Application fee: $40. Electronic applications accepted. *Financial support:* Federal Work-Study, scholarships/grants, tuition waivers (full and partial), and unspecified assistantships available. Financial award application deadline: 5/1; financial award applicants required to submit FAFSA. *Unit head:* Dr. Mary Desmond, Program Director. *Application contact:* Nancy Wiksten, Graduate Admission Counselor, 815-836-5610, E-mail: grad@lewisu.edu.

**Liberty University,** School of Nursing, Lynchburg, VA 24515. Offers family nurse practitioner (DNP); nurse educator (MSN); nursing administration (MSN); nursing informatics (MSN). *Accreditation:* AACN. *Program availability:* Part-time, online learning. *Students:* 279 full-time (257 women), 505 part-time (449 women); includes 170 minority (118 Black or African American, non-Hispanic/Latino; 2 American Indian or Alaska Native, non-Hispanic/Latino; 19 Asian, non-Hispanic/Latino; 25 Hispanic/Latino; 6 Two or more races, non-Hispanic/Latino), 11 international. Average age 39. 1,154 applicants, 27% accepted, 171 enrolled. In 2019, 138 master's, 26 doctorates awarded. *Entrance requirements:* For master's, minimum cumulative undergraduate GPA of 3.0; for doctorate, minimum GPA of 3.25 in most current nursing program completed. Additional exam requirements/recommendations for international students: recommended—TOEFL. *Application deadline:* Applications are processed on a rolling basis. Application fee: $50. Electronic applications accepted. *Expenses: Tuition:* Full-time $545; part-time $410 per credit hour. One-time fee: $50. *Financial support:* In 2019–20, 128 students received support. Federal Work-Study available. Financial award applicants required to submit FAFSA. *Unit head:* Dr. Shanna Akers, Dean, 434-592-3618, E-mail: lusondean@liberty.edu. *Application contact:* Jay Bridge, Director of Admissions, 800-424-9595, Fax: 800-628-7977, E-mail: gradadmissions@liberty.edu. Website: https://www.liberty.edu/nursing/

**Lincoln Memorial University,** Caylor School of Nursing, Harrogate, TN 37752-1901. Offers family nurse practitioner (MSN); nurse anesthesia (MSN); psychiatric mental health nurse practitioner (MSN). *Accreditation:* AANA/CANAEP; ACEN. *Program availability:* Part-time. *Entrance requirements:* For master's, GRE.

**Long Island University - Brentwood Campus,** Graduate Programs, Brentwood, NY 11717. Offers childhood education (MS), including grades 1-6; childhood education/literacy B-6 (MS); childhood education/special education (grades 1-6) (MS); clinical mental health counseling (MS, Advanced Certificate); criminal justice (MS); early childhood education (MS); educational leadership (MS Ed); family nurse practitioner (MS, Advanced Certificate); health administration (MPA); library and information science (MS); literacy (B-6) (MS Ed); school counselor (MS, Advanced Certificate); social work (MSW); special education (MS Ed); students with disabilities generalist (grades 7-12) (Advanced Certificate). *Program availability:* Part-time. *Entrance requirements:* For master's and Advanced Certificate, GRE. Additional exam requirements/recommendations for international students: required—TOEFL or IELTS. Electronic applications accepted.

**Long Island University - Brooklyn,** Harriet Rothkopf Heilbrunn School of Nursing, Brooklyn, NY 11201-8423. Offers adult nurse practitioner (MS, Advanced Certificate); family nurse practitioner (MS, Advanced Certificate); nurse educator (MS). *Accreditation:* AACN. *Program availability:* Part-time, evening/weekend, blended/hybrid learning. *Entrance requirements:* Additional exam requirements/recommendations for international students: required—TOEFL or IELTS. Electronic applications accepted.

**Long Island University - Post,** School of Health Professions and Nursing, Brookville, NY 11548-1300. Offers biomedical science (MS); cardiovascular perfusion (MS); clinical lab sciences (MS); clinical laboratory management (MS); dietetic internship (Advanced Certificate); family nurse practitioner (MS, Advanced Certificate); forensic social work (Advanced Certificate); gerontology (Advanced Certificate); health administration (MPA); non-profit management (Advanced Certificate); nursing education (MS); nutrition (MS); public administration (MPA); social work (MSW). *Program availability:* Part-time, blended/hybrid learning. *Degree requirements:* For master's, comprehensive exam (for some programs), thesis (for some programs). *Entrance requirements:* Additional exam requirements/recommendations for international students: required—TOEFL (minimum score 85 iBT) or IELTS (7.5). Electronic applications accepted.

**Louisiana State University Health Sciences Center,** School of Nursing, New Orleans, LA 70112. Offers adult gerontology acute care nurse practitioner (DNP, Post-Master's Certificate); adult gerontology clinical nurse specialist (DNP, Post-Master's Certificate); adult gerontology primary care nurse practitioner (DNP, Post-Master's Certificate); clinical nurse leader (MSN); executive nurse leader (DNP, Post-Master's Certificate); neonatal nurse practitioner (DNP, Post-Master's Certificate); nurse anesthesia (DNP, Post-Master's Certificate); nurse educator (MSN); nursing (DNS); primary care family nurse practitioner (DNP, Post-Master's Certificate); public/community health nursing (DNP, Post-Master's Certificate). *Accreditation:* AACN; AANA/CANAEP (one or more programs are accredited). *Program availability:* Part-time. *Faculty:* 25 full-time (21 women), 25 part-time/adjunct (13 women). *Students:* 182 full-time (127 women), 70 part-time (59 women); includes 82 minority (52 Black or African American, non-Hispanic/Latino; 2 American Indian or Alaska Native, non-Hispanic/Latino; 14 Asian, non-Hispanic/Latino; 14 Hispanic/Latino), 1 international. Average age 34. 34 applicants, 62% accepted, 21 enrolled. In 2019, 72 doctorates awarded. *Degree requirements:* For master's, thesis optional; for doctorate, thesis/dissertation. *Entrance requirements:* For master's, GRE, minimum GPA of 3.0; for doctorate, GRE, minimum GPA of 3.0 (for DNP), 3.5 (for DNS). Additional exam requirements/recommendations for international students: required—TOEFL (minimum score 550 paper-based; 79 iBT). *Application deadline:* For fall admission, 6/1 priority date for domestic and international students; for spring admission, 10/1 priority date for domestic and international students; for summer admission, 3/1 priority date for domestic and international students. Applications are processed on a rolling basis. Application fee: $100. Electronic applications accepted. *Expenses:* MSN and DNS: $13,354.50, $24,982.25 non-resident, $586 per hour (fall and spring), $467 per hour (summer), $1,102 per hour non-resident (fall and spring), $858 per hour non-resident (summer); DNP (Except Nurse Anethesia): $21,907.50, $38,262.23 non-resident, $973 per hour (fall and spring), $733 per hour (summer), $1,700 per hour non-resident (fall and spring), $1,278 per hour non-resident (summer); Nurse Anesthesia DNP: $26,407.50, $42,762.23 non-resident, $1,173 per hour (fall and spring), $883 per hour (summer), $1,900 per hour non-resident (fall and spring), $1,428 per hour non-resident (summer). *Financial support:* In 2019–20, 20 students received support. Institutionally sponsored loans, scholarships/grants, unspecified assistantships, and DNS Scholars Program available. Financial award application deadline: 4/15; financial award applicants required to submit FAFSA. *Unit head:* Dr. Demetrius James Porche, Dean, 504-568-4106, Fax: 504-599-0573, E-mail: dporch@lsuhsc.edu. *Application contact:* Tracie Gravolet, Director, Office of Student Affairs, 504-568-4114, Fax: 504-568-5711, E-mail: tgravo@lsuhsc.edu. Website: http://nursing.lsuhsc.edu/

**Loyola University Chicago,** Graduate School, Marcella Niehoff School of Nursing, Maywood, IL 60153. Offers adult clinical nurse specialist (MSN, Certificate); adult nurse practitioner (Certificate); dietetics (MS); family nurse practitioner (Certificate); family, adult, and women's health nurse practitioner (MSN); health systems leadership (MSN); healthcare quality using education in safety and technology (DNP); infection prevention (MSN, DNP); nursing science (PhD); women's health clinical nurse specialist (Certificate). *Accreditation:* AACN. *Program availability:* Part-time, blended/hybrid learning. *Faculty:* 36 full-time (32 women), 18 part-time/adjunct (16 women). *Students:* 182 full-time (168 women), 198 part-time (175 women); includes 95 minority (26 Black or African American, non-Hispanic/Latino; 29 Asian, non-Hispanic/Latino; 37 Hispanic/Latino; 3 Two or more races, non-Hispanic/Latino), 7 international. Average age 35. 148 applicants, 59% accepted, 54 enrolled. In 2019, 84 master's, 16 doctorates, 27 other advanced degrees awarded. *Degree requirements:* For master's, comprehensive exam; for doctorate, thesis/dissertation, qualifying examination (for PhD); project (for DNP). *Entrance requirements:* For master's, BSN, minimum nursing GPA of 3.0, Illinois RN license, 3 letters of recommendation, 1000 hours of experience in area of specialty prior to starting clinical rotations, personal statement; for doctorate, BSN or MSN, minimum GPA of 3.0, professional nursing license, 3 letters of recommendation, personal statement. Additional exam requirements/recommendations for international students: required—TOEFL (minimum score 550 paper-based; 79 iBT), IELTS (minimum score 6), PTE (minimum score 53). *Application deadline:* For fall admission, 7/1 priority date for domestic and international students; for spring admission, 12/1 priority date for domestic and international students; for summer admission, 4/1 priority date for domestic and international students. Applications are processed on a rolling basis. Electronic applications accepted. Application fee is waived when completed online. *Expenses:* Contact institution. *Financial support:* In 2019–20, 53 students received support, including 3 research assistantships with full tuition reimbursements available (averaging $18,000 per year), 1 teaching assistantship with full tuition reimbursement available (averaging $18,000 per year); scholarships/grants, unspecified assistantships, and Nurse Faculty Loan Program also available. Financial award application deadline: 5/1; financial award applicants required to submit FAFSA. *Unit head:* Dr. Lorna Finnegan, Dean and Professor, 708-216-5448, Fax: 708-216-9555, E-mail: lornaf@luc.edu.

*Application contact:* Glenda Runnels, Enrollment Advisor, 708-216-3751, Fax: 708-216-9555, E-mail: grunnels@luc.edu.
Website: http://www.luc.edu/nursing/

**Loyola University New Orleans,** College of Nursing and Health, School of Nursing, New Orleans, LA 70118. Offers family nurse practitioner (DNP); nursing (MSN). *Accreditation:* AACN; ACEN. *Program availability:* Part-time, online only, 100% online. *Faculty:* 15 full-time (13 women), 5 part-time/adjunct (4 women). *Students:* 78 full-time (74 women), 222 part-time (198 women); includes 86 minority (62 Black or African American, non-Hispanic/Latino; 3 American Indian or Alaska Native, non-Hispanic/Latino; 4 Asian, non-Hispanic/Latino; 15 Hispanic/Latino; 2 Native Hawaiian or other Pacific Islander, non-Hispanic/Latino). Average age 39. 209 applicants, 70% accepted, 60 enrolled. In 2019, 89 master's, 19 doctorates awarded. *Degree requirements:* For master's, Practicum 180-720 hours depending on track; for doctorate, DNP Scholarly Project with 1000+ graduate practicum hours. *Entrance requirements:* Additional exam requirements/recommendations for international students: recommended—TOEFL (minimum score 550 paper-based; 79 iBT). *Application deadline:* For fall admission, 7/15 priority date for domestic students; for spring admission, 11/15 priority date for domestic students; for summer admission, 4/15 priority date for domestic students. Applications are processed on a rolling basis. Electronic applications accepted. *Expenses:* MSN FNP (Most students) - $818/cr hr tution * 48 cr hrs + 4 * $850 practicum fee + $275/sem technology fee * 6 semesters (minimum) + $300 graduation fee = $44,614. MSN HSAL (36 cr & 1 practicum $500) $31,598. MSN NE (39 and 1 practicum $500) $34,052. BSN to DNP (78 credits, 7 practicum, 4 - $850, 3 - $500) $71,179. MSN to DNP (39 credits & 3 practicum $500) $35,052. *Financial support:* Traineeships and Incumbent Workers Training Program grants available. Financial award application deadline: 5/1; financial award applicants required to submit FAFSA. *Unit head:* Dr. Laurie Anne Ferguson, Dean and Director, 504-865-2880, Fax: 504-865-3254, E-mail: nursing@loyno.edu. *Application contact:* Jennifer Brackett, SON Office Manager & Admissions Coordinator, 504-865-2823, Fax: 504-865-3254, E-mail: edwadswo@loyno.edu.
Website: http://gps.loyno.edu/nursing

**Malone University,** Graduate Program in Nursing, Canton, OH 44709. Offers family nurse practitioner (MSN). *Accreditation:* AACN. *Program availability:* Part-time, evening/weekend. *Faculty:* 10 full-time (all women), 14 part-time/adjunct (13 women). *Students:* 30 part-time (24 women). Average age 30. In 2019, 26 master's awarded. *Degree requirements:* For master's, thesis. *Entrance requirements:* For master's, minimum GPA of 3.0 from BSN program, interview, Ohio RN license. Additional exam requirements/recommendations for international students: required—This program is not open to international students, because of course offerings and visa course requirements. *Application deadline:* Applications are processed on a rolling basis. *Financial support:* Unspecified assistantships available. *Unit head:* Dr. Sheri Hartman, Director, 330-471-8330, Fax: 330-471-8607, E-mail: shartman@malone.edu. *Application contact:* Dr. Sheri Hartman, Director, 330-471-8330, Fax: 330-471-8607, E-mail: shartman@malone.edu.
Website: http://www.malone.edu/admissions/graduate/nursing/

**Marian University,** Leighton School of Nursing, Indianapolis, IN 46222-1997. Offers family nurse practitioner (DNP); nurse anesthesia (DNP); nursing education (MSN). *Accreditation:* AANA/CANAEP. *Program availability:* Part-time. *Degree requirements:* For master's, 38 credits, designed to be completed in 2 years; 225-hour practicum including a culminating project; for doctorate, 70 credit hours (for family nurse practitioner track); 85 credits (for nurse anesthesia track); minimum of 1000 hours of supervised practice. *Entrance requirements:* For master's, degree in nursing from NLNAC- or CCNE-accredited program; current, valid RN license in State of Indiana; minimum undergraduate GPA of 3.0; 3 recommendations; interview with admissions committee; current resume; 500-word essay describing career goals; for doctorate, BSN from NSNAC- or CCNE-accredited program; minimum undergraduate GPA of 3.0; cureent, valid RN license; current resume or curriculum vitae; 500-word essay addressing career goals; 3 letters of recommendation; interview with Admissions Committee. Additional exam requirements/recommendations for international students: required—TOEFL (minimum score 550 paper-based; 79 iBT). Electronic applications accepted. Application fee is waived when completed online. *Expenses:* Contact institution.

**Marquette University,** Graduate School, College of Nursing, Milwaukee, WI 53201-1881. Offers acute care nurse practitioner (Certificate); adult clinical nurse specialist (Certificate); adult nurse practitioner (Certificate); advanced practice nursing (MSN, DNP), including adult-older adult acute care (DNP), adults (MSN), adults-older adults (DNP), clinical nurse leader (MSN), health care systems leadership (DNP), nurse-midwifery (MSN), older adults (MSN), pediatrics-acute care, pediatrics-primary care, primary care (DNP), systems leadership and healthcare quality (MSN); family nurse practitioner (Certificate); nurse-midwifery (Certificate); nursing (PhD); pediatric acute care (Certificate); pediatric primary care (Certificate); systems leadership and healthcare quality (Certificate). *Accreditation:* AACN; AANA/CANAEP; ACNM/ACME. Terminal master's awarded for partial completion of doctoral program. *Degree requirements:* For master's, comprehensive exam, thesis or alternative. *Entrance requirements:* For master's, GRE General Test, BSN, Wisconsin RN license, official transcripts from all current and previous colleges/universities except Marquette, three completed recommendation forms, resume, written statement of professional goals; for doctorate, GRE General Test, official transcripts from all current and previous colleges/universities except Marquette, three letters of recommendation, resume, written statement of professional goals, sample of scholarly writing. Additional exam requirements/recommendations for international students: required—TOEFL (minimum score 530 paper-based). Electronic applications accepted.

**Marymount University,** Malek School of Health Professions, Program in Nursing, Arlington, VA 22207-4299. Offers family nurse practitioner (MSN, DNP, Certificate). *Accreditation:* AACN. *Program availability:* Part-time, evening/weekend. *Faculty:* 3 full-time (all women), 2 part-time/adjunct (1 woman). *Students:* 14 full-time (13 women), 38 part-time (35 women); includes 15 minority (6 Black or African American, non-Hispanic/Latino; 5 Asian, non-Hispanic/Latino; 3 Hispanic/Latino; 1 Two or more races, non-Hispanic/Latino), 2 international. Average age 36. 30 applicants, 83% accepted, 16 enrolled. In 2019, 21 master's, 5 doctorates, 1 other advanced degree awarded. *Degree requirements:* For master's and Certificate, comprehensive exam, clinical practicum; for doctorate, thesis/dissertation, research presentation/residency. *Entrance requirements:* For master's, 2 letters of recommendation, interview, resume, current RN license, personal statement, minimum 3.0 GPA; for doctorate, 2 letters of recommendation, interview, resume, RN license, personal statement, APN licensure if applicable; for Certificate, interview, master's degree in nursing with a minimum of 3.3 GPA, current RN licensure, 2 letters of recommendation, personal statement, APN licnesure if applicable. Additional exam requirements/recommendations for international students: required—TOEFL (minimum score 600 paper-based; 96 iBT), IELTS (minimum score 6.5), PTE (minimum score 58). *Application deadline:* For fall admission, 3/1 priority date for domestic and international students; for spring admission, 11/1 priority date for domestic and international students. Application fee: $40. Electronic applications accepted. *Expenses: Tuition:* Part-time $1050 per credit. *Required fees:* $22 per credit. One-time fee: $270 part-time. Tuition and fees vary according to program. *Financial support:* In 2019–20, 11 students received support. Research assistantships, teaching assistantships, career-related internships or fieldwork, scholarships/grants, and unspecified assistantships available. Support available to part-time students. Financial award application deadline: 3/1; financial award applicants required to submit FAFSA. *Unit head:* Dr. Maureen Moriarty, Program Director, 703-284-1590, E-mail: maureen.moriarty@marymount.edu. *Application contact:* Fiona McDonnell, Administrative Assistant, 703-284-5901, E-mail: gadmissi@marymount.edu.
Website: https://www.marymount.edu/Academics/Malek-School-of-Health-Professions/Graduate-Programs

**Maryville University of Saint Louis,** Myrtle E. and Earl E. Walker College of Health Professions, The Catherine McAuley School of Nursing, St. Louis, MO 63141-7299. Offers acute care nurse practitioner (MSN); adult gerontology nurse practitioner (MSN); advanced practice nursing (DNP); family nurse practitioner (MSN); pediatric nurse practitioner (MSN). *Accreditation:* AACN. *Program availability:* 100% online, blended/hybrid learning. *Faculty:* 14 full-time (all women), 131 part-time/adjunct (114 women). *Students:* 103 full-time (91 women), 3,493 part-time (3,050 women); includes 1,039 minority (530 Black or African American, non-Hispanic/Latino; 41 American Indian or Alaska Native, non-Hispanic/Latino; 157 Asian, non-Hispanic/Latino; 221 Hispanic/Latino; 90 Two or more races, non-Hispanic/Latino), 9 international. Average age 37. In 2019, 1,012 master's, 54 doctorates awarded. *Degree requirements:* For master's, practicum. *Entrance requirements:* For master's, BSN, current licensure, minimum GPA of 3.0, 3 letters of recommendation, curriculum vitae. Additional exam requirements/recommendations for international students: required—TOEFL (minimum score 550 paper-based). *Application deadline:* Applications are processed on a rolling basis. Electronic applications accepted. *Expenses:* Contact institution. *Financial support:* Federal Work-Study and campus employment available. Support available to part-time students. Financial award application deadline: 4/1; financial award applicants required to submit FAFSA. *Unit head:* Karla Larson, Assistant Dean Nursing, 314-529-6856, Fax: 314-529-9139, E-mail: klarson@maryville.edu. *Application contact:* Jeannie DeLuca, Director of Admissions and Advising, 314-929-9355, Fax: 314-529-9927, E-mail: jdeluca@maryville.edu.
Website: http://www.maryville.edu/hp/nursing/

**McGill University,** Faculty of Graduate and Postdoctoral Studies, Faculty of Medicine, Ingram School of Nursing, Montréal, QC H3A 2T5, Canada. Offers nurse practitioner (Graduate Diploma); nursing (M Sc A, PhD).

**McMurry University,** Graduate Studies, Abilene, TX 79697. Offers education (MSN); family nurse practitioner (MSN).

**McNeese State University,** Doré School of Graduate Studies, College of Nursing and Health Professions, MSN Program, Lake Charles, LA 70609. Offers family nurse practitioner (MSN); nurse educator (MSN); psychiatric/mental health nurse practitioner (MSN). *Entrance requirements:* For master's, GRE, baccalaureate degree in nursing, minimum overall GPA of 2.7 for all undergraduate coursework, eligibility for unencumbered licensure as Registered Nurse in Louisiana or Texas, course in introductory statistics with minimum C grade, physical assessment skills, two letters of professional reference, 500-word essay, current resume.

**Medical University of South Carolina,** College of Nursing, Family Nurse Practitioner Program, Charleston, SC 29425. Offers MSN, DNP. *Program availability:* Part-time, online learning. *Degree requirements:* For master's, thesis optional; for doctorate, final project. *Entrance requirements:* For master's, BSN from nationally-accredited program, minimum nursing and cumulative GPA of 3.0, undergraduate-level statistics course, active RN License, 3 confidential references, current curriculum vitae or resume, essay; for doctorate, BSN from nationally-accredited program, minimum nursing and cumulative GPA of 3.0, undergraduate-level statistics course, active RN License, 3 confidential references, current curriculum vitae or resume, personal essay (for DNP). Additional exam requirements/recommendations for international students: required—TOEFL (minimum score 550 paper-based; 80 iBT). Electronic applications accepted.

**Mercer University,** Graduate Studies, Cecil B. Day Campus, Georgia Baptist College of Nursing, Atlanta, GA 30341. Offers adult gerontology acute care nurse practitioner (MSN, Certificate); family nurse practitioner (MSN, Certificate); nursing (PhD); nursing practice (DNP). *Accreditation:* AACN. *Program availability:* Part-time, blended/hybrid learning. *Faculty:* 26 full-time (23 women), 13 part-time/adjunct (11 women). *Students:* 69 full-time (64 women), 45 part-time (41 women); includes 61 minority (42 Black or African American, non-Hispanic/Latino; 12 Asian, non-Hispanic/Latino; 4 Hispanic/Latino; 1 Native Hawaiian or other Pacific Islander, non-Hispanic/Latino; 2 Two or more races, non-Hispanic/Latino), 1 international. Average age 35. 92 applicants, 75% accepted, 57 enrolled. In 2019, 14 master's, 10 doctorates awarded. *Degree requirements:* For master's, thesis or alternative, capstone project; for doctorate, comprehensive exam (for some programs), scholarly project (for DNP); dissertation (for PhD). *Entrance requirements:* For master's, bachelor's degree from accredited nursing program, minimum GPA 3.0, unencumbered license to practice as a Registered Nurse in Georgia, essay, three professional references; for doctorate, master's degree from accredited nursing program depending on program, unencumbered license to practice as a Registered Nurse, graduate statistics course, essay, three professional references; for Certificate, APRN license for post-master's certificate programs. Additional exam requirements/recommendations for international students: required—TOEFL (minimum score 100 iBT). *Application deadline:* For fall admission, 7/1 for domestic students; for spring admission, 12/1 for domestic students; for summer admission, 4/15 for domestic students. Applications are processed on a rolling basis. Application fee: $50. Electronic applications accepted. *Expenses:* Contact institution. *Financial support:* In 2019–20, 23 students received support, including 1 research assistantship with partial tuition reimbursement available (averaging $10,500 per year); scholarships/grants also available. Financial award application deadline: 6/30; financial award applicants required to submit FAFSA. *Unit head:* Dr. Linda Streit, Dean/Professor, 678-547-6793, Fax: 678-547-6796, E-mail: streit_la@mercer.edu. *Application contact:* Janda Anderson, Director of Admissions, 678-547-6700, Fax: 678-547-6794, E-mail: anderson_j@mercer.edu.
Website: http://www.nursing.mercer.edu

**Middle Tennessee State University,** College of Graduate Studies, College of Behavioral and Health Sciences, School of Nursing, Program in Family Nurse Practitioner, Murfreesboro, TN 37132. Offers MSN, Graduate Certificate. *Program availability:* Part-time, evening/weekend, online learning. *Entrance requirements:* Additional exam requirements/recommendations for international students: required—TOEFL (minimum score 525 paper-based; 71 iBT) or IELTS (minimum score 6). Electronic applications accepted.

**Midwestern State University,** Billie Doris McAda Graduate School, Robert D. and Carol Gunn College of Health Sciences and Human Services, Wilson School of Nursing, Wichita Falls, TX 76308. Offers family nurse practitioner (MSN); family psychiatric mental health nurse practitioner (MSN); nurse educator (MSN). *Accreditation:* AACN. *Program availability:* Part-time, evening/weekend. *Degree requirements:* For master's, comprehensive exam, thesis optional. *Entrance requirements:* For master's, GRE General Test or MAT. Additional exam requirements/recommendations for international students: required—TOEFL (minimum score 550 paper-based). Electronic applications accepted.

**Millersville University of Pennsylvania,** College of Graduate Studies and Adult Learning, College of Science and Technology, Department of Nursing, Millersville, PA 17551-0302. Offers family nurse practitioner (MSN, Post-Master's Certificate); nursing education (MSN, Post-Master's Certificate); nursing practice (DNP). *Accreditation:* ACEN. *Program availability:* Part-time. *Faculty:* 6 full-time (all women), 9 part-time/adjunct (8 women). *Students:* 122 part-time (100 women); includes 22 minority (8 Black or African American, non-Hispanic/Latino; 6 Asian, non-Hispanic/Latino; 7 Hispanic/Latino; 1 Two or more races, non-Hispanic/Latino). Average age 39. 44 applicants, 68% accepted, 26 enrolled. In 2019, 30 master's, 27 other advanced degrees awarded. *Entrance requirements:* For master's, resume, including minimum of 2 years of pertinent clinical experience (3-5 years preferred); copy of RN license; 3.0 GPA required; interview; minimum of one year of current clinical experience in nursing; for doctorate, goal statement, 3-5 page (APA 6th Ed.) Writing Sample Defining a Specific Issue or Problem in Nursing Practices, current resume/CV, verification of MSN Clinical Hours, completed MSN or MPH, with a minimum 3.5 GPA. Additional exam requirements/recommendations for international students: required—TOEFL, IELTS (minimum score 6), PTE (minimum score 60). Application fee: $40. Electronic applications accepted. *Expenses: Tuition, area resident:* Part-time $516 per credit. Tuition, state resident: part-time $516 per credit. Tuition, nonresident: part-time $774 per credit. *Required fees:* $118.75 per credit. Tuition and fees vary according to course load, degree level and program. *Financial support:* In 2019–20, 16 students received support. Scholarships/grants and unspecified assistantships available. Financial award application deadline: 3/15; financial award applicants required to submit FAFSA. *Unit head:* Dr. Kelly A. Kuhns, Chairperson, 717-871-5276, Fax: 717-871-4877, E-mail: kelly.kuhns@millersville.edu. *Application contact:* Dr. James A. Delle, Acting Dean of College of Graduate Studies and Adult Learning/Associate Provost, Academic Administration, 717-871-7462, E-mail: James.Delle@millersville.edu.
Website: https://www.millersville.edu/nursing/index.php

**Millersville University of Pennsylvania,** College of Graduate Studies and Adult Learning, College of Science and Technology, Department of Nursing, Program in Family Nurse Practitioner, Millersville, PA 17551-0302. Offers family nurse practitioner (MSN). *Program availability:* Part-time. *Students:* 92 part-time (76 women); includes 20 minority (7 Black or African American, non-Hispanic/Latino; 6 Asian, non-Hispanic/Latino; 6 Hispanic/Latino; 1 Two or more races, non-Hispanic/Latino). Average age 38. 33 applicants, 58% accepted, 16 enrolled. In 2019, 28 master's awarded. *Entrance requirements:* For master's, Resume, including minimum of 2 years of pertinent clinical experience (3-5 years preferred); Copy of RN license; 3.0 GPA required; Interview; Minimum of one year of current clinical experience in nursing. Additional exam requirements/recommendations for international students: required—TOEFL, IELTS (minimum score 6), PTE (minimum score 60). *Application deadline:* For fall admission, 2/15 for domestic students; for spring admission, 9/15 for domestic students. Application fee: $40. Electronic applications accepted. *Expenses: Tuition, area resident:* Part-time $516 per credit. Tuition, state resident: part-time $516 per credit. Tuition, nonresident: part-time $774 per credit. *Required fees:* $118.75 per credit. Tuition and fees vary according to course load, degree level and program. *Financial support:* In 2019–20, 12 students received support. Scholarships/grants and unspecified assistantships available. Financial award application deadline: 3/15; financial award applicants required to submit FAFSA. *Unit head:* Prof. Cayleigh Minter, Graduate Program Coordinator, 717-871-5341, E-mail: Cayleigh.Minter@millersville.edu. *Application contact:* Dr. James A. Delle, Acting Dean of College of Graduate Studies and Adult Learning/Associate Provost, Academic Administration, 717-871-7462, E-mail: James.Delle@millersville.edu.
Website: https://www.millersville.edu/programs/family-nurse-practitioner.php

**Minnesota State University Mankato,** College of Graduate Studies and Research, College of Allied Health and Nursing, School of Nursing, Mankato, MN 56001. Offers family nurse practitioner (MSN), including family nurse practitioner; nurse educator (MSN); nursing (DNP). *Accreditation:* AACN. *Degree requirements:* For master's, comprehensive exam, internships, research project or thesis; for doctorate, capstone project. *Entrance requirements:* For master's, GRE General Test or on-campus essay, minimum GPA of 3.0 during previous 2 years, BSN or equivalent references; for doctorate, master's degree in nursing. Additional exam requirements/recommendations for international students: required—TOEFL. Electronic applications accepted.

**Missouri State University,** Graduate College, College of Health and Human Services, School of Nursing, Springfield, MO 65897. Offers nursing (MSN), including family nurse practitioner, nurse educator; nursing practice (DNP). *Accreditation:* AACN. *Program availability:* 100% online, blended/hybrid learning. *Degree requirements:* For master's, comprehensive exam, thesis or alternative. *Entrance requirements:* For master's, GRE General Test, minimum GPA of 3.0, RN license (for MSN), 1 year of work experience (for MPH). Additional exam requirements/recommendations for international students: required—TOEFL (minimum score 550 paper-based; 79 iBT), IELTS (minimum score 6). Electronic applications accepted. *Expenses: Tuition, area resident:* Full-time $2600; part-time $1735 per credit hour. Tuition, nonresident: full-time $5240; part-time $3495 per credit hour. *International tuition:* $5240 full-time. *Required fees:* $530; $438 per credit hour. Tuition and fees vary according to class time, course level, course load, degree level, campus/location and program.

**Molloy College,** Graduate Nursing Program, Rockville Centre, NY 11571-5002. Offers adult-gerontology clinical nurse specialist (DNP); adult-gerontology nurse practitioner (MS, DNP); clinical nurse specialist: adult-gerontology (MS); family nurse practitioner (MS, DNP); family psychiatric/mental health nurse practitioner (MS, DNP); nursing (PhD, Advanced Certificate); nursing administration with informatics (MS); nursing education (MS); pediatric nurse practitioner (MS, DNP). *Accreditation:* AACN. *Program availability:* Part-time, evening/weekend. *Faculty:* 30 full-time (28 women), 10 part-time/adjunct (6 women). *Students:* 18 full-time (17 women), 573 part-time (520 women); includes 340 minority (181 Black or African American, non-Hispanic/Latino; 2 American Indian or Alaska Native, non-Hispanic/Latino; 100 Asian, non-Hispanic/Latino; 42 Hispanic/Latino; 5 Native Hawaiian or other Pacific Islander, non-Hispanic/Latino; 10 Two or more races, non-Hispanic/Latino), 3 international. Average age 38. 332 applicants, 60% accepted, 149 enrolled. In 2019, 136 master's, 12 doctorates, 22 other advanced degrees awarded. *Degree requirements:* For doctorate, clinical research residency and scholarly clinical project (for DNP); dissertation and comprehensive exam (for PhD). *Entrance requirements:* Additional exam requirements/recommendations for international students: required—TOEFL (minimum score 550 paper-based; 79 iBT). *Application deadline:* Applications are processed on a rolling basis. Application fee: $60. Electronic applications accepted. *Expenses: Tuition:* Full-time $21,510; part-time $1195 per credit hour. *Required fees:* $1100. Tuition and fees vary according to course load, degree level and program. *Financial support:* Application deadline: 3/1; applicants required to submit FAFSA. *Unit head:* Dr. Marcia R. Gardner, Dean, The Barbara H. Hagan School of Nursing, 516-323-3651, E-mail: mgardner@molloy.edu. *Application contact:* Faye Hood, Assistant Director for Admissions, 516-323-4009, E-mail: fhood@molloy.edu.
Website: https://www.molloy.edu/academics/graduate-programs/graduate-nursing-x25989

**Montana State University,** The Graduate School, College of Nursing, Bozeman, MT 59717. Offers clinical nurse leader (MN); family and individual nurse practitioner (DNP); family nurse practitioner (MN, Post-Master's Certificate); nursing education (Certificate, Post-Master's Certificate); psychiatric mental health nurse practitioner (MN); psychiatric/mental health nurse practitioner (DNP). *Accreditation:* AACN. *Program availability:* Part-time, online learning. *Degree requirements:* For master's, comprehensive exam, thesis (for some programs); for doctorate, thesis/dissertation, 1,125 hours in clinical settings. *Entrance requirements:* For master's, GRE General Test, minimum GPA of 3.0 for undergraduate and post-baccalaureate work. Additional exam requirements/recommendations for international students: required—TOEFL (minimum score 580 paper-based). Electronic applications accepted.

**Morningside College,** Graduate Programs, Nylen School of Nursing, Sioux City, IA 51106. Offers adult gerontology primary care nurse practitioner (MSN); clinical nurse leader (MSN); family primary care nurse practitioner (MSN). *Program availability:* Part-time, online only, 100% online. Electronic applications accepted. *Expenses:* Contact institution.

**Mount Carmel College of Nursing,** Nursing Program, Columbus, OH 43222. Offers adult gerontology acute care nurse practitioner (MS); adult health clinical nurse specialist (MS); family nurse practitioner (MS); nursing (DNP); nursing administration (MS); nursing education (MS). *Accreditation:* AACN. *Program availability:* Part-time. *Faculty:* 6 full-time (all women), 10 part-time/adjunct (9 women). *Students:* 101 full-time (82 women), 109 part-time (95 women); includes 43 minority (27 Black or African American, non-Hispanic/Latino; 4 Asian, non-Hispanic/Latino; 5 Hispanic/Latino; 7 Two or more races, non-Hispanic/Latino). Average age 32. 133 applicants, 84% accepted, 95 enrolled. In 2019, 66 master's, 2 doctorates awarded. *Degree requirements:* For master's, professional manuscript; for doctorate, practicum. *Entrance requirements:* For master's, letters of recommendation, statement of purpose, current resume, baccalaureate degree in nursing, current Ohio RN license, minimum cumulative GPA of 3.0; for doctorate, master's degree in nursing from program accredited by either ACEN or CCNE. Additional exam requirements/recommendations for international students: required—TOEFL (minimum score 550 paper-based; 80 iBT). *Application deadline:* For fall admission, 2/1 priority date for domestic students; for spring admission, 11/1 priority date for domestic students. Applications are processed on a rolling basis. Application fee: $30. Electronic applications accepted. *Expenses: Tuition:* Full-time $27,936; part-time $27,936 per year. *Required fees:* $360. *Financial support:* In 2019–20, 13 students received support. Institutionally sponsored loans and scholarships/grants available. Financial award application deadline: 3/1; financial award applicants required to submit FAFSA. *Unit head:* Dr. Jami Nininger, Interim Associate Dean Graduate Studies, 614-234-1777, Fax: 614-234-2875, E-mail: jnininger@mccn.edu. *Application contact:* Dr. Kim Campbell, Director of Recruitment and Admissions, 614-234-5144, Fax: 614-234-5427, E-mail: kcampbell@mccn.edu.
Website: www.mccn.edu

**Murray State University,** School of Nursing and Health Professions, Department of Nursing, Murray, KY 42071. Offers family nurse practitioner (DNP); nurse anesthetist (DNP). *Accreditation:* AACN; AANA/CANAEP. *Program availability:* Evening/weekend, 100% online, blended/hybrid learning. *Entrance requirements:* For doctorate, GRE, minimum university GPA of 2.75. Additional exam requirements/recommendations for international students: required—TOEFL (minimum score 527 paper-based; 71 iBT). Electronic applications accepted.

**National University,** School of Health and Human Services, La Jolla, CA 92037-1011. Offers clinical affairs (MS); clinical regulatory affairs (MS); complementary and integrative healthcare (MS); family nurse practitioner (MSN); health and life science analytics (MS); health informatics (MS, Certificate); healthcare administration (MHA); nurse anesthesia (MSNA); nursing administration (MSN); nursing informatics (MSN); psychiatric-mental health nurse practitioner (MSN); public health (MPH), including health promotion, healthcare administration, mental health. *Accreditation:* CEPH. *Program availability:* Part-time, evening/weekend, 100% online, blended/hybrid learning. *Degree requirements:* For master's, thesis (for some programs). *Entrance requirements:* For master's, interview, minimum GPA of 2.5. Additional exam requirements/recommendations for international students: required—TOEFL (minimum score 550 paper-based; 79 iBT), IELTS (minimum score 6). Electronic applications accepted. *Expenses: Tuition:* Full-time $442; part-time $442 per unit.

**New Mexico State University,** College of Health and Social Services, School of Nursing, Las Cruces, NM 88003. Offers family nurse practitioner (Graduate Certificate); nursing (MSN); nursing practice (DNP); nursing science (PhD); psychiatric/mental health nurse practitioner (Graduate Certificate). *Accreditation:* AACN. *Program availability:* Part-time, blended/hybrid learning. *Faculty:* 12 full-time (all women). *Students:* 29. 57 applicants, 98% accepted. In 2019, 4 master's, 20 doctorates, 5 other advanced degrees awarded. *Degree requirements:* For master's, comprehensive exam, thesis optional, clinical practicum; for doctorate, comprehensive exam, thesis/dissertation. *Entrance requirements:* For master's, NCLEX exam, BSN, minimum GPA of 3.0, course work in statistics, 3 letters of reference, writing sample, RN license, CPR certification, proof of liability, immunizations, criminal background check; for doctorate, NCLEX exam, MSN, minimum GPA of 3.0, 3 letters of reference, writing sample, RN license, CPR certification, proof of liability, immunizations, criminal background check, statistics course. Additional exam requirements/recommendations for international students: required—TOEFL (minimum score 550 paper-based; 79 iBT), IELTS (minimum score 6.5). *Application deadline:* For fall admission, 2/1 priority date for domestic students, 2/1 for international students. Application fee: $40 ($50 for international students). Electronic applications accepted. *Financial support:* In 2019–20, 7 teaching assistantships (averaging $10,499 per year) were awarded; career-related internships or fieldwork, Federal Work-Study, scholarships/grants, traineeships, health care benefits, and unspecified assistantships also available. Support available to part-time students. Financial award application deadline: 3/1. *Unit head:* Dr. Alexa Doig, Director, 575-646-3812, Fax: 575-646-2167, E-mail: adoig@nmsu.edu. *Application contact:* Alyce Kolenovsky, Academic Advisor, 575-646-3812, Fax: 575-646-2167, E-mail: nursing@nmsu.edu.
Website: http://schoolofnursing.nmsu.edu

**New York University,** Rory Meyers College of Nursing, Doctor of Nursing Practice Program, New York, NY 10012-1019. Offers nursing (DNP), including adult-gerontology acute care nurse practitioner, adult-gerontology primary care nurse practitioner, family nurse practitioner, nurse-midwifery, pediatrics nurse practitioner, psychiatric-mental health nurse practitioner. *Accreditation:* AACN. *Program availability:* Part-time, evening/weekend. *Degree requirements:* For doctorate, thesis/dissertation, project. *Entrance requirements:* For doctorate, MS, RN license, interview, Nurse Practitioner Certification, writing sample. Additional exam requirements/recommendations for international students: required—TOEFL (minimum score 100 iBT), IELTS (minimum score 7). Electronic applications accepted. *Expenses:* Contact institution.

**New York University,** Rory Meyers College of Nursing, Programs in Advanced Practice Nursing, New York, NY 10012-1019. Offers adult-gerontology acute care nurse practitioner (MS, Advanced Certificate); adult-gerontology primary care nurse practitioner (MS, Advanced Certificate); family nurse practitioner (MS, Advanced Certificate); gerontology nurse practitioner (Advanced Certificate); nurse-midwifery (MS, Advanced Certificate); nursing administration (MS, Advanced Certificate); nursing education (MS, Advanced Certificate); nursing informatics (MS, Advanced Certificate);

pediatrics nurse practitioner (MS, Advanced Certificate); psychiatric-mental health nurse practitioner (MS, Advanced Certificate); MS/MPH. *Accreditation:* AACN; ACNM/ACME. *Program availability:* Part-time, evening/weekend. *Degree requirements:* For master's, thesis (for some programs), capstone. *Entrance requirements:* For master's, BS in nursing, AS in nursing with another BS/BA, interview, RN license, 1 year of clinical experience (3 for the MS in nursing education program); for Advanced Certificate, master's degree in nursing. Additional exam requirements/recommendations for international students: required—TOEFL (minimum score 100 iBT), IELTS (minimum score 7). Electronic applications accepted. *Expenses:* Contact institution.

**Nicholls State University,** Graduate Studies, College of Nursing and Allied Health, Thibodaux, LA 70310. Offers family nurse practitioner (MSN); nurse executive (MSN); nursing education (MSN); psychiatric/mental health nurse practitioner (MSN).

**Northeastern University,** Bouvé College of Health Sciences, Boston, MA 02115-5096. Offers applied behavior analysis (MS); audiology (Au D); counseling psychology (MS, PhD, CAGS); exercise science (MS); nursing (MS, PhD, CAGS), including administration (MS), adult-gerontology acute care nurse practitioner (MS, CAGS), adult-gerontology primary care nurse practitioner (MS, CAGS), anesthesia (MS), family nurse practitioner (MS, CAGS), neonatal nurse practitioner (MS, CAGS), pediatric nurse practitioner (MS, CAGS), psychiatric mental health nurse practitioner (MS, CAGS); nursing practice (DNP); pharmaceutical sciences (MS, PhD), including interdisciplinary concentration, pharmaceutics and drug delivery systems; pharmacology (MS); pharmacy (Pharm D); school psychology (PhD); speech-language pathology (MS); urban health (MPH); MS/MBA. *Accreditation:* AANA/CANAEP; ACPE (one or more programs are accredited); ASHA; CEPH. *Program availability:* Part-time, evening/weekend, online learning. *Degree requirements:* For doctorate, thesis/dissertation (for some programs); for CAGS, comprehensive exam. Electronic applications accepted. *Expenses:* Contact institution.

**Northern Arizona University,** College of Health and Human Services, School of Nursing, Flagstaff, AZ 86011. Offers family nurse practitioner (Certificate); nursing (MS), including family nurse practitioner, generalist; nursing practice (DNP). *Accreditation:* AACN. *Program availability:* Part-time, 100% online, blended/hybrid learning. *Degree requirements:* For master's, variable foreign language requirement, comprehensive exam (for some programs), thesis (for some programs); for doctorate, variable foreign language requirement, comprehensive exam (for some programs), thesis/dissertation (for some programs), oral defense, individualized research. *Entrance requirements:* For master's, bachelor's degree in nursing from accredited program or associate's degree in nursing from accredited program with bachelor's degree in another field; minimum GPA of 3.0 in all nursing coursework; current RN license in good standing; for doctorate, master's degree in nursing from regionally-accredited university and nationally-accredited nursing program; minimum cumulative GPA of 3.0 in all nursing coursework of master's degree program; current RN license in good standing to practice. Additional exam requirements/recommendations for international students: required—TOEFL (minimum score 80 iBT), IELTS (minimum score 6.5). Electronic applications accepted.

**Nova Southeastern University,** Ron and Kathy Assaf College of Nursing, Fort Lauderdale, FL 33314-7796. Offers advanced practice registered nurse (MSN), including adult-gerontology acute care nurse practitioner, family nurse practitioner, psychiatric mental health nurse practitioner; executive nurse leadership (MSN); nursing (PhD), including nursing education; nursing education (MSN); nursing informatics (MSN); nursing practice (DNP). *Accreditation:* AACN. *Program availability:* Part-time, evening/weekend, 100% online, blended/hybrid learning, annual one-week summer institute delivered face-to-face on main campus. *Faculty:* 32 full-time (29 women), 34 part-time/adjunct (31 women). *Students:* 4 full-time (3 women), 658 part-time (585 women); includes 427 minority (182 Black or African American, non-Hispanic/Latino; 35 Asian, non-Hispanic/Latino; 197 Hispanic/Latino; 13 Two or more races, non-Hispanic/Latino), 3 international. Average age 38. 157 applicants, 93% accepted, 146 enrolled. In 2019, 184 master's, 12 doctorates awarded. *Degree requirements:* For doctorate, comprehensive exam, thesis/dissertation. *Entrance requirements:* For master's, minimum GPA of 3.0, RN, BSN, BS or BA; for doctorate, minimum GPA of 3.5, MSN, RN. Additional exam requirements/recommendations for international students: recommended—TOEFL. *Application deadline:* For fall admission, 8/1 for domestic students, 3/1 for international students; for winter admission, 12/9 for domestic students, 11/1 for international students. Applications are processed on a rolling basis. Application fee: $50. Electronic applications accepted. *Expenses:* Contact institution. *Financial support:* Application deadline: 4/15; applicants required to submit FAFSA. *Unit head:* Dr. Marcella M. Rutherford, Dean, 954-262-1963, E-mail: rmarcell@nova.edu. *Application contact:* Dianna Murphey, Director of Operations, 954-262-1975, E-mail: dgardner1@nova.edu.
Website: http://www.nova.edu/nursing/

**Oakland University,** Graduate Study and Lifelong Learning, School of Nursing, Program in Family Nurse Practitioner, Rochester, MI 48309-4401. Offers MSN, PMC. *Accreditation:* AACN. *Degree requirements:* For master's, thesis. *Entrance requirements:* Additional exam requirements/recommendations for international students: required—TOEFL (minimum score 550 paper-based; 79 iBT), IELTS (minimum score 6.5). Electronic applications accepted. *Expenses:* Contact institution.

**Ohio University,** Graduate College, College of Health Sciences and Professions, School of Nursing, Athens, OH 45701-2979. Offers advanced clinical practice (DNP); executive practice (DNP); family nurse practitioner (MSN); nurse educator (MSN). *Accreditation:* AACN. *Degree requirements:* For master's, capstone project. *Entrance requirements:* For master's, GRE, bachelor's degree in nursing from accredited college or university, minimum overall undergraduate GPA of 3.0, official transcripts, statement of goals and objectives, resume, 3 letters of recommendation. Additional exam requirements/recommendations for international students: required—TOEFL (minimum score 550 paper-based; 80 iBT) or IELTS (minimum score 6.5). Electronic applications accepted.

**Old Dominion University,** College of Health Sciences, School of Nursing, Family Nurse Practitioner Emphasis, Norfolk, VA 23529. Offers MSN. *Program availability:* Blended/hybrid learning. *Degree requirements:* For master's, comprehensive exam. *Entrance requirements:* For master's, GRE or MAT (waived with a GPA above 3.5), 3 letters of recommendation, essay, resume, transcripts. Additional exam requirements/recommendations for international students: required—TOEFL. Electronic applications accepted. *Expenses:* Contact institution.

**Olivet Nazarene University,** Graduate School, Department of Nursing, Bourbonnais, IL 60914. Offers family nurse practitioner (MSN); nursing (MSN).

**Oregon Health & Science University,** School of Nursing, Family Nurse Practitioner Program, Portland, OR 97239-2941. Offers MN. *Program availability:* Blended/hybrid learning. *Entrance requirements:* For master's, GRE General Test, bachelor's degree in nursing, minimum cumulative and science GPA of 3.0, 3 letters of recommendation, essay, statistics taken within last 5 years. Additional exam requirements/recommendations for international students: required—TOEFL (minimum score 83 iBT). Electronic applications accepted. *Expenses:* Contact institution.

**Otterbein University,** Department of Nursing, Westerville, OH 43081. Offers advanced practice nurse educator (Certificate); clinical nurse leader (MSN); family nurse practitioner (MSN, Certificate); nurse anesthesia (MSN, Certificate); nursing (DNP); nursing service administration (MSN). *Accreditation:* AACN; AANA/CANAEP; ACEN. *Program availability:* Part-time, evening/weekend, online learning. *Degree requirements:* For master's, comprehensive exam (for some programs), thesis (for some programs). *Entrance requirements:* For master's, 2 reference forms, resume; for Certificate, official transcripts, 2 reference forms, essay, resumé. Additional exam requirements/recommendations for international students: required—TOEFL (minimum score 550 paper-based; 79 iBT).

**Pace University,** College of Health Professions, Lienhard School of Nursing, New York, NY 10038. Offers adult acute care nurse practitioner (MS, CAGS); family nurse practitioner (MS, CAGS); nursing (DNP, PhD); professional nursing leadership (MS, CAGS). *Accreditation:* AACN. *Program availability:* Part-time. Terminal master's awarded for partial completion of doctoral program. *Entrance requirements:* For master's, RN license, resume, personal statement, 2 letters of recommendation, official transcripts, minimum GPA of 3.0, undergraduate statistics; for doctorate, RN license, resume, personal statement, 2 letters of recommendation, official transcripts, accredited master's degree in nursing, minimum GPA of 3.3, state certification and board eligibility as FNP or ANP; for CAGS, RN license, resume, personal statement, 2 letters of recommendation, official transcripts, minimum GPA of 3.0, undergraduate statistics, completion of 2nd degree in nursing. Additional exam requirements/recommendations for international students: required—TOEFL (minimum score 100 iBT), IELTS or PTE. Electronic applications accepted. *Expenses:* Contact institution.

**Pacific Lutheran University,** School of Nursing, DNP Program, Tacoma, WA 98447. Offers DNP. *Accreditation:* AACN. *Entrance requirements:* Additional exam requirements/recommendations for international students: required—TOEFL (minimum score 550 paper-based; 86 iBT). Electronic applications accepted. *Expenses:* Contact institution.

**Palm Beach Atlantic University,** School of Nursing, West Palm Beach, FL 33416-4708. Offers family nurse practitioner (DNP); health systems leadership (MSN). *Accreditation:* AACN. *Program availability:* Part-time. *Degree requirements:* For master's, capstone course. *Entrance requirements:* For master's, minimum GPA of 3.0; active RN license; personal interview; for doctorate, minimum GPA of 3.0; one year of experience as an RN; personal interview. Additional exam requirements/recommendations for international students: required—TOEFL (minimum score 550 paper-based; 79 iBT). Electronic applications accepted. *Expenses:* Contact institution.

**Point Loma Nazarene University,** School of Nursing, MS in Nursing Program, San Diego, CA 92106. Offers adult/gerontology (MSN); family/individual health (MSN); pediatrics (MSN). *Program availability:* Part-time. *Students:* 4 full-time (3 women), 49 part-time (41 women); includes 29 minority (5 Black or African American, non-Hispanic/Latino; 8 Asian, non-Hispanic/Latino; 14 Hispanic/Latino; 2 Two or more races, non-Hispanic/Latino). Average age 37. 30 applicants, 83% accepted, 14 enrolled. In 2019, 25 master's awarded. *Entrance requirements:* For master's, NCLEX exam, ADN or BSN in nursing, interview, RN license, essay, letters of recommendation, interview. *Application deadline:* For fall admission, 7/5 priority date for domestic students; for spring admission, 11/1 priority date for domestic students; for summer admission, 3/22 priority date for domestic students. Applications are processed on a rolling basis. Application fee: $50. Electronic applications accepted. *Expenses:* $820 per unit. *Financial support:* In 2019–20, 9 students received support. Scholarships/grants available. Financial award applicants required to submit FAFSA. *Unit head:* Dr. Larry Rankin, Associate Dean, 619-849-7813, E-mail: LarryRankin@pointloma.edu. *Application contact:* Dana Barger, Director of Recruitment and Admissions, Graduate and Professional Students, 619-329-6799, E-mail: gradinfo@pointloma.edu.
Website: https://www.pointloma.edu/graduate-studies/programs/nursing-ms

**Purdue University,** Graduate School, College of Health and Human Sciences, School of Nursing, West Lafayette, IN 47907. Offers adult gerontology primary care nurse practitioner (MS, Post Master's Certificate); nursing (DNP, PhD); primary care family nurse practitioner (MS, Post Master's Certificate); primary care pediatric nurse practitioner (MS, Post Master's Certificate). *Faculty:* 41 full-time (40 women), 9 part-time/adjunct (8 women). *Students:* 84 full-time (72 women), 46 part-time (43 women); includes 19 minority (7 Black or African American, non-Hispanic/Latino; 6 Asian, non-Hispanic/Latino; 4 Hispanic/Latino; 2 Two or more races, non-Hispanic/Latino), 1 international. Average age 33. 85 applicants, 80% accepted, 55 enrolled. In 2019, 29 master's, 7 doctorates, 2 other advanced degrees awarded. *Unit head:* Nancy E. Edwards, Head of the Graduate Program, 765-494-4015, E-mail: edwardsn@purdue.edu. *Application contact:* Reanne Hall, Graduate Contact, 765-494-9248, E-mail: gradnursing@purdue.edu.
Website: http://www.purdue.edu/hhs/nur/

**Purdue University Fort Wayne,** College of Health and Human Services, Department of Nursing, Fort Wayne, IN 46805-1499. Offers adult-gerontology primary care nurse practitioner (MS); family nurse practitioner (MS); nurse executive (MS); nursing administration (Certificate); nursing education (MS). *Accreditation:* ACEN. *Program availability:* Part-time. *Entrance requirements:* For master's, GRE Writing Test (if GPA below 3.0), BS in nursing, eligibility for Indiana RN license, minimum GPA of 3.0, essay, copy of resume, three references, undergraduate course work in research and statistics within last 5 years. Additional exam requirements/recommendations for international students: required—TOEFL (minimum score 550 paper-based; 79 iBT); recommended—TWE. Electronic applications accepted.

**Purdue University Northwest,** Graduate Studies Office, School of Nursing, Hammond, IN 46323-2094. Offers adult health clinical nurse specialist (MS); critical care clinical nurse specialist (MS); family nurse practitioner (MS); nurse executive (MS). *Accreditation:* ACEN. *Program availability:* Part-time, online learning. *Entrance requirements:* For master's, BSN. Additional exam requirements/recommendations for international students: required—TOEFL. Electronic applications accepted.

**Queen's University at Kingston,** School of Graduate Studies, Faculty of Health Sciences, School of Nursing, Kingston, ON K7L 3N6, Canada. Offers health and chronic illness (M Sc); nurse scientist (PhD); primary health care nurse practitioner (Certificate); women's and children's health (M Sc). *Degree requirements:* For master's, thesis. *Entrance requirements:* For master's, RN license. Additional exam requirements/recommendations for international students: required—TOEFL.

**Quinnipiac University,** School of Nursing, Family Nurse Practitioner Track, Hamden, CT 06518-1940. Offers DNP. *Accreditation:* ACEN. *Entrance requirements:* Additional exam requirements/recommendations for international students: required—TOEFL (minimum score 575 paper-based; 90 iBT), IELTS (minimum score 6.5). Electronic applications accepted. *Expenses: Tuition:* Part-time $1055 per credit. *Required fees:* $945 per semester. Tuition and fees vary according to course load and program.

**Ramapo College of New Jersey,** Master of Science in Nursing Program, Mahwah, NJ 07430. Offers family nurse practitioner (MSN); nursing administrator (MSN); nursing education (MSN). *Accreditation:* ACEN. *Program availability:* Part-time. *Degree requirements:* For master's, thesis or alternative. *Entrance requirements:* For master's, official transcript; personal statement; 2 letters of recommendation; resume; current licensure as a Registered Nurse, or eligibility for licensure; evidence of one year of recent experience as RN prior to entry into clinical practicum courses; evidence of

undergraduate statistics course; criminal background check. Additional exam requirements/recommendations for international students: required—TOEFL (minimum score 550 paper-based; 90 iBT); recommended—IELTS (minimum score 6). Electronic applications accepted. *Expenses:* Contact institution.

**Regis College,** Nursing and Health Sciences School, Weston, MA 02493. Offers applied behavior analysis (MS); counseling psychology (MA); health administration (MS); nurse practitioner (Certificate); nursing (MS, DNP); nursing education (Certificate); occupational therapy (MS). *Accreditation:* ACEN. *Program availability:* Part-time, evening/weekend, 100% online, blended/hybrid learning. *Degree requirements:* For doctorate, thesis/dissertation. *Entrance requirements:* For master's, minimum GPA of 3.0, official transcripts, recommendations, personal statement, resume/curriculum vitae, interview; for doctorate, GRE if GPA from master's lower than 3.5. Additional exam requirements/recommendations for international students: required—TOEFL (minimum score 560 paper-based; 79 iBT); recommended—IELTS (minimum score 6.5). *Application deadline:* Applications are processed on a rolling basis. Application fee: $75. Electronic applications accepted. *Financial support:* Federal Work-Study, scholarships/grants, and unspecified assistantships available. Support available to part-time students. Financial award applicants required to submit FAFSA. *Application contact:* Thomas May, Graduate Admission Counselor, 781-768-7162, E-mail: thomas.may@regiscollege.edu.

**Rivier University,** School of Graduate Studies, Division of Nursing and Health Professions, Nashua, NH 03060. Offers family nurse practitioner (MS); leadership in health systems management (MS); nursing education (MS); nursing practice (DNP); psychiatric/mental health nurse practitioner (MS); public health (MPH). *Accreditation:* ACEN. *Program availability:* Part-time, evening/weekend. *Entrance requirements:* For master's, GRE, MAT. Electronic applications accepted.

**Rocky Mountain University of Health Professions,** Doctor of Nursing Practice Program, Provo, UT 84606. Offers DNP. *Accreditation:* AACN.

**Rutgers University - Camden,** School of Nursing–Camden, Camden, NJ 08102-1401. Offers adult gerontology primary care nurse practitioner (DNP); family nurse practitioner (DNP). *Degree requirements:* For doctorate, minimum of 1,000 clinical residency hours, evidence-based clinical project.

**Rutgers University - Newark,** Rutgers School of Nursing, Newark, NJ 07107-3001. Offers adult health (MSN); adult occupational health (MSN); advanced practice nursing (MSN, Post Master's Certificate); family nurse practitioner (MSN); nurse anesthesia (MSN); nursing (MSN); nursing informatics (MSN); urban health (PhD); women's health practitioner (MSN). *Accreditation:* AANA/CANAEP. *Program availability:* Part-time. *Entrance requirements:* For master's, GRE, RN license; basic life support, statistics, and health assessment experience. Additional exam requirements/recommendations for international students: required—TOEFL. Electronic applications accepted. *Expenses:* Contact institution.

**Sacred Heart University,** Graduate Programs, College of Nursing, Fairfield, CT 06825. Offers clinical (DNP); clinical nurse leader (MSN); family nurse practitioner (MSN, Post-Master's Certificate); leadership (DNP); nursing education (MSN); nursing management and executive leadership (MSN). *Accreditation:* AACN. *Program availability:* Part-time, evening/weekend, 100% online, blended/hybrid learning. *Degree requirements:* For master's, thesis, 500 clinical hours; for doctorate, capstone. *Entrance requirements:* For master's, minimum GPA of 3.0, BSN or RN plus BS (for MSN); for doctorate, minimum GPA of 3.0, MSN or BSN plus MS in related field (for DNP). Additional exam requirements/recommendations for international students: required—TOEFL (minimum score 570 paper-based, 80 iBT), TWE, or IELTS (6.5). Electronic applications accepted. *Expenses:* Contact institution.

**Sage Graduate School,** School of Health Sciences, Department of Nursing, Program in Family Nurse Practitioner, Troy, NY 12180-4115. Offers MS. *Accreditation:* AACN. *Program availability:* Part-time, evening/weekend. *Faculty:* 8 full-time (all women), 13 part-time/adjunct (12 women). *Students:* 36 full-time (35 women), 102 part-time (92 women); includes 28 minority (10 Black or African American, non-Hispanic/Latino; 1 American Indian or Alaska Native, non-Hispanic/Latino; 10 Asian, non-Hispanic/Latino; 4 Hispanic/Latino; 3 Two or more races, non-Hispanic/Latino). Average age 33. 106 applicants, 33% accepted, 19 enrolled. In 2019, 26 master's awarded. *Degree requirements:* For master's, thesis or alternative. *Entrance requirements:* For master's, applicants must be currently licensed as a registered professional nurse in the state where they practice; bachelor's degree in nursing from a nationally accredited program; GPA of 3.0 or higher; official transcripts of all previous UG/GR study; 2 letters of reference; 1-2 page statement of professional goals; current resume. Additional exam requirements/recommendations for international students: required—TOEFL (minimum score 550 paper-based). *Application deadline:* Applications are processed on a rolling basis. Application fee: $40. Electronic applications accepted. *Expenses: Tuition:* Part-time $730 per credit hour. Tuition and fees vary according to course load, degree level and program. *Financial support:* Fellowships, research assistantships, scholarships/grants, and unspecified assistantships available. Financial award application deadline: 3/1; financial award applicants required to submit FAFSA. *Unit head:* Dr. Kathleen Kelly, Dean, School of Health Sciences, 518-244-2030, Fax: 518-244-2009, E-mail: kellyk5@sage.edu. *Application contact:* Erin Menzer, Associate Director of Transfer and Nursing Enrollment Management, 518-244-4565, Fax: 518-244-6880, E-mail: menzee@sage.edu.

**Saginaw Valley State University,** College of Health and Human Services, Program in Nurse Practitioner, University Center, MI 48710. Offers MSN, DNP. *Accreditation:* AACN. *Program availability:* Part-time, evening/weekend, online learning. *Students:* 3 full-time (all women), 69 part-time (56 women); includes 7 minority (4 Black or African American, non-Hispanic/Latino; 1 Asian, non-Hispanic/Latino; 2 Two or more races, non-Hispanic/Latino), 4 international. Average age 33. 28 applicants, 93% accepted, 21 enrolled. In 2019, 27 master's, 4 doctorates awarded. *Degree requirements:* For master's, thesis optional. *Entrance requirements:* For master's, GRE, minimum GPA of 3.0, license to practice nursing in MI; for doctorate, GRE, minimum GPA of 3.3, college chemistry with minimum C grade, college statistics with minimum B grade, employed as RN with current license in MI. Additional exam requirements/recommendations for international students: required—TOEFL (minimum score 580 paper-based; 92 iBT). *Application deadline:* For fall admission, 7/15 for international students; for winter admission, 11/15 for international students; for spring admission, 4/15 for international students. Applications are processed on a rolling basis. Application fee: $30 ($90 for international students). Electronic applications accepted. *Expenses: Tuition, area resident:* Full-time $11,212; part-time $622.90 per credit hour. Tuition, state resident: full-time $11,212; part-time $622.90 per credit hour. Tuition, nonresident: full-time $11,212; part-time $1253 per credit hour. *Required fees:* $263; $14.60 per credit hour. Tuition and fees vary according to course load, degree level and program. *Financial support:* Federal Work-Study and scholarships/grants available. Support available to part-time students. Financial award application deadline: 4/1; financial award applicants required to submit FAFSA. *Unit head:* Dr. Karen Brown-Fackler, Coordinator, 989-964-2185, Fax: 989-964-4925, E-mail: kmbrown4@svsu.edu. *Application contact:* Jenna Briggs, Director, Graduate and International Admissions, 989-964-6096, Fax: 989-964-2788, E-mail: gradadm@svsu.edu.

**Saint Francis Medical Center College of Nursing,** SFMC College of Nursing Graduate Programs, Peoria, IL 61603-3783. Offers adult gerontology (MSN); clinical nurse leader (MSN); family nurse practitioner (MSN, Post-Graduate Certificate); family psychiatric mental health nurse practitioner (MSN); neonatal nurse practitioner (MSN); nurse clinician (Post-Graduate Certificate); nurse educator (MSN, Post-Graduate Certificate); nursing (DNP), including leadership/ clinician; nursing management leadership (MSN). *Accreditation:* ACEN. *Program availability:* Part-time, online only, 100% online, blended/hybrid learning. *Faculty:* 12 full-time (all women), 10 part-time/adjunct (all women). *Students:* 1 (woman) full-time, 188 part-time (157 women); includes 20 minority (10 Black or African American, non-Hispanic/Latino; 3 Asian, non-Hispanic/Latino; 3 Hispanic/Latino; 4 Two or more races, non-Hispanic/Latino). Average age 40. 54 applicants, 91% accepted, 18 enrolled. In 2019, 51 master's, 11 doctorates awarded. *Degree requirements:* For master's, research experience, portfolio, practicum; for doctorate, practicum. *Entrance requirements:* For master's, Nursing research, health assessment, RN license; for doctorate, Master's degree in nursing, professional portfolio, graduate statistics, transcripts, RN license. Additional exam requirements/recommendations for international students: required—TOEFL (minimum score 550 paper-based; 79 iBT). *Application deadline:* For fall admission, 6/1 priority date for domestic and international students; for spring admission, 11/15 priority date for domestic and international students. Applications are processed on a rolling basis. Application fee: $50. *Expenses: Tuition:* Part-time $705 per credit hour. *Required fees:* $270 per unit. *Financial support:* In 2019–20, 13 students received support. Scholarships/grants available. Support available to part-time students. Financial award application deadline: 6/15; financial award applicants required to submit FAFSA. *Unit head:* Dr. Sandie S Soldwisch, President of OSF Colleges of Health Sciences, 815-282-7909, Fax: 309-624-8973, E-mail: Sandie.S.Soldwisch@osfhealthcare.org. *Application contact:* Dr. Kim A. Mitchell, Dean, Graduate Program, 309-655-2201, Fax: 309-624-8973, E-mail: kim.a.mitchell@osfhealthcare.org.
Website: http://www.sfmccon.edu/graduate-programs/

**Saint Joseph's College of Maine,** Master of Science in Nursing Program, Standish, ME 04084. Offers administration (MSN); education (MSN); family nurse practitioner (MSN); nursing administration and leadership (Certificate); nursing and health care education (Certificate). *Accreditation:* AACN. *Program availability:* Part-time, online learning. *Entrance requirements:* For master's, MAT. Electronic applications accepted.

**Saint Mary's College,** Graduate Studies, Doctor of Nursing Practice Program, Notre Dame, IN 46556. Offers adult - gerontology acute care nurse practitioner (DNP); adult - gerontology primary care nurse practitioner (DNP); family nurse practitioner (DNP). *Program availability:* Part-time-only, evening/weekend, online only, 100% online. *Faculty:* 11. *Students:* 58 part-time (53 women); includes 15 minority (8 Black or African American, non-Hispanic/Latino; 3 Asian, non-Hispanic/Latino; 4 Hispanic/Latino). Average age 30. 24 applicants, 75% accepted, 15 enrolled. In 2019, 1 doctorate awarded. *Degree requirements:* For doctorate, comprehensive exam, thesis/dissertation. *Entrance requirements:* For doctorate, BSN or MSN, unencumbered RN license or eligibility for RN licensure, official transcripts from previously-attended institutions, 3 letters of recommendation, personal statement, resume or curriculum vitae. Additional exam requirements/recommendations for international students: recommended—TOEFL (minimum score 80 iBT), IELTS (minimum score 6.5). *Application deadline:* For fall admission, 3/31 priority date for domestic and international students. Applications are processed on a rolling basis. Application fee: $70. Electronic applications accepted. *Expenses:* $5765 per semester. *Financial support:* In 2019–20, 3 students received support. Scholarships/grants available. Financial award application deadline: 3/1; financial award applicants required to submit FAFSA. *Unit head:* Sue Anderson, Program Director, Doctor of Nursing Practice, 574-284-4682, E-mail: sanderson@saintmarys.edu. *Application contact:* Melissa Fruscione, Director, Graduate Studies, 574-284-5098, E-mail: graduateadmission@saintmarys.edu.
Website: https://grad.saintmarys.edu/academic-programs/doctor-nursing-practice

**Salisbury University,** DNP Program, Salisbury, MD 21801. Offers family nurse practitioner (DNP); nursing leadership (DNP). *Accreditation:* AACN. *Program availability:* Part-time, evening/weekend, 100% online, blended/hybrid learning. *Faculty:* 14 full-time (13 women), 4 part-time/adjunct (all women). *Students:* 25 full-time (22 women), 8 part-time (all women); includes 8 minority (5 Black or African American, non-Hispanic/Latino; 1 Hispanic/Latino; 2 Two or more races, non-Hispanic/Latino). Average age 34. 17 applicants, 71% accepted, 8 enrolled. In 2019, 7 doctorates awarded. *Degree requirements:* For doctorate, Evidence based project. *Entrance requirements:* For doctorate, transcripts; resume or CV; personal statement; proof of certification or licensure; minimum GPA of 3.0; three letters of recommendation; undergraduate degree in nursing. *Application deadline:* For fall admission, 3/1 priority date for domestic and international students. Applications are processed on a rolling basis. Application fee: $65. Electronic applications accepted. *Expenses:* Contact institution. *Financial support:* Career-related internships or fieldwork and scholarships/grants available. Support available to part-time students. Financial award application deadline: 3/1; financial award applicants required to submit FAFSA. *Unit head:* Dr. Annette Barnes, Graduate Program Chair, 410-546-4380, E-mail: ahbarnes@salisbury.edu. *Application contact:* Kristi Jenkins, Administrative Assistant II, 410-548-2242, E-mail: kljenkins@salisbury.edu.
Website: https://www.salisbury.edu/explore-academics/programs/graduate-degree-programs/nursing-practice-doctor/

**Samford University,** Ida Moffett School of Nursing, Birmingham, AL 35229. Offers advanced practice (DNP), including emergency nurse practitioner, family nurse practitioner, transformation of care; family nurse practitioner (MSN, DNP), including emergency nurse practitioner specialty (MSN); nurse anesthesia (DNP); nursing administration (DNP); psychiatric mental health nurse practitioner (DNP). *Accreditation:* AACN; AANA/CANAEP. *Program availability:* Part-time, evening/weekend, blended/hybrid learning. *Faculty:* 16 full-time (all women), 3 part-time/adjunct (0 women). *Students:* 281 full-time (239 women), 39 part-time (38 women); includes 68 minority (39 Black or African American, non-Hispanic/Latino; 2 American Indian or Alaska Native, non-Hispanic/Latino; 10 Asian, non-Hispanic/Latino; 10 Hispanic/Latino; 1 Native Hawaiian or other Pacific Islander, non-Hispanic/Latino; 6 Two or more races, non-Hispanic/Latino). Average age 35. 59 applicants, 97% accepted, 29 enrolled. In 2019, 47 master's, 68 doctorates awarded. *Degree requirements:* For doctorate, DNP project with poster presentation. *Entrance requirements:* For doctorate, GRE is required for the Nurse Anesthesia Program. Additional exam requirements/recommendations for international students: required—TOEFL (minimum score 575 paper-based; 90 iBT), IELTS (minimum score 6.5). *Application deadline:* For fall admission, 4/1 for domestic and international students; for spring admission, 8/1 for domestic and international students; for summer admission, 1/1 for domestic and international students. Application fee: $50. Electronic applications accepted. *Expenses: Tuition:* Full-time $17,754; part-time $862 per credit hour. *Required fees:* $550; $550 per unit. Full-time tuition and fees vary according to course load, program and student level. *Financial support:* In 2019–20, 30 students received support. Application deadline: 2/15; applicants required to submit FAFSA. *Unit head:* Dr. Jane S. Martin, Interim Dean and Professor, Ida Moffett School of Nursing, 205-726-2760, E-mail: jsmartin@samford.edu. *Application contact:* Allyson Maddox, Director of Graduate Student Services, 205-726-2047, E-mail:

amaddox@samford.edu.
Website: http://samford.edu/nursing

**Samuel Merritt University,** School of Nursing, Oakland, CA 94609-3108. Offers case management (MSN); family nurse practitioner (MSN, DNP, Certificate); nurse anesthetist (MSN, Certificate); nursing (DNP). *Accreditation:* AACN; AANA/CANAEP (one or more programs are accredited). *Program availability:* Part-time, evening/weekend, 100% online, blended/hybrid learning. *Degree requirements:* For master's, thesis or alternative; for doctorate, project. *Entrance requirements:* For master's, GRE General Test (for nurse anesthetist program), minimum GPA of 2.5 in science, 3.0 overall; previous course work in statistics; current RN license; for doctorate and Certificate, minimum GPA of 2.5 in science, 3.0 overall; previous course work in statistics; current RN license. Additional exam requirements/recommendations for international students: required—TOEFL (minimum score 100 iBT). Electronic applications accepted. *Expenses:* Contact institution.

**San Francisco State University,** Division of Graduate Studies, College of Health and Social Sciences, School of Nursing, San Francisco, CA 94132-1722. Offers adult acute care (MS); clinical nurse specialist (MS); community/public health nursing (MS); family nurse practitioner (Certificate); nursing administration (MS); pediatrics (MS); women's health (MS). *Accreditation:* AACN. *Program availability:* Part-time. *Application deadline:* Applications are processed on a rolling basis. *Expenses: Tuition, area resident:* Full-time $7176; part-time $4164 per year. Tuition, state resident: full-time $7176; part-time $4164 per year. Tuition, nonresident: full-time $16,680; part-time $396 per unit. *International tuition:* $16,680 full-time. *Required fees:* $1524; $1524 per unit. $762 per semester. Tuition and fees vary according to degree level and program. *Financial support:* Career-related internships or fieldwork available. *Unit head:* Dr. Mary-Ann van Dam, 415-338-1802, Fax: 415-338-0555, E-mail: vandam@sfsu.edu. *Application contact:* Prof. Fang-yu Chou, Assistant Director of Graduate Programs, 415-338-6853, Fax: 415-338-0555, E-mail: fchou@sfsu.edu.
Website: http://nursing.sfsu.edu

**Seattle Pacific University,** MS in Nursing Program, Seattle, WA 98119-1997. Offers administration (MSN); adult/gerontology nurse practitioner (MSN); clinical nurse specialist (MSN); family nurse practitioner (MSN, Certificate); informatics (MSN); nurse educator (MSN). *Accreditation:* AACN. *Program availability:* Part-time. *Students:* 42 full-time (38 women), 18 part-time (16 women); includes 28 minority (5 Black or African American, non-Hispanic/Latino; 18 Asian, non-Hispanic/Latino; 5 Hispanic/Latino), 2 international. Average age 33. 59 applicants, 41% accepted. In 2019, 10 master's awarded. *Degree requirements:* For master's, thesis. *Entrance requirements:* For master's, personal statement, transcripts, undergraduate nursing degree, proof of undergraduate statistics course with minimum GPA of 2.0, 2 recommendations. *Application deadline:* For fall admission, 1/15 priority date for domestic students; for spring admission, 1/15 for domestic students. Applications are processed on a rolling basis. Application fee: $50. Electronic applications accepted. *Expenses:* Contact institution. *Financial support:* Fellowships and scholarships/grants available. Financial award applicants required to submit FAFSA. *Unit head:* Dr. Antwinett Lee, Associate Dean, 206-281-2607, E-mail: leea30@spu.edu. *Application contact:* Dr. Antwinett Lee, Associate Dean, 206-281-2607, E-mail: leea30@spu.edu.
Website: http://spu.edu/academics/school-of-health-sciences/undergraduate-programs/nursing

**Shenandoah University,** Eleanor Wade Custer School of Nursing, Winchester, VA 22601. Offers adult gerontology primary care nurse practitioner (Graduate Certificate); adult-gerontology primary care nurse practitioner (MSN); family nurse practitioner (MSN, DNP, Graduate Certificate); general (MSN); health systems leadership (DNP); health systems management (MSN, Graduate Certificate); nurse midwifery (MSN); nurse-midwifery (Graduate Certificate); nursing education (Graduate Certificate); nursing practice (DNP); psychiatric mental health nurse practitioner (MSN, DNP, Graduate Certificate). *Accreditation:* AACN; ACNM/ACME. *Entrance requirements:* For master's, United States RN license; minimum GPA of 3.0; 2080 hours of clinical experience; curriculum vitae; 3 letters of recommendation from former dean, faculty member, or advisor familiar with the applicant, and a former or current supervisor; two-to-three-page essay on a specified topic; for doctorate, MSN, minimum GPA of 3.0, 3 letters of recommendation, interview, BSN, two-to-three page essay on a specific topic, 500-word statement of clinical practice research interest, resume, current U.S. RN license, 2080 clinical hours; for Graduate Certificate, MSN, minimum GPA of 3.0, 2 letters of recommendation, minimum of one year (2080 hours) of clinical nursing experience, interview, two-to-three page essay on a specific topic, resume, current United States RN license. Additional exam requirements/recommendations for international students: required—TOEFL (minimum score 558 paper-based; 83 iBT). Electronic applications accepted. *Expenses:* Contact institution.

**Simmons University,** College of Natural, Behavioral, and Health Sciences, Boston, MA 02115. Offers nursing (MS, MSN), including family nurse practitioner (MS); nursing practice (DNP). *Accreditation:* AACN. *Program availability:* Part-time. *Faculty:* 39 full-time (33 women), 194 part-time/adjunct (180 women). *Students:* 418 full-time (374 women), 1,868 part-time (1,682 women); includes 477 minority (161 Black or African American, non-Hispanic/Latino; 4 American Indian or Alaska Native, non-Hispanic/Latino; 138 Asian, non-Hispanic/Latino; 124 Hispanic/Latino; 1 Native Hawaiian or other Pacific Islander, non-Hispanic/Latino; 49 Two or more races, non-Hispanic/Latino), 22 international. Average age 32. 1,442 applicants, 62% accepted, 501 enrolled. In 2019, 630 master's, 39 doctorates awarded. *Degree requirements:* For master's, thesis optional; for doctorate, thesis/dissertation (for some programs). *Entrance requirements:* For doctorate, GRE. Additional exam requirements/recommendations for international students: required—TOEFL (minimum score 570 paper-based; 88 iBT). *Application deadline:* For fall admission, 6/1 for international students. Applications are processed on a rolling basis. Application fee: $50. Electronic applications accepted. *Expenses:* Contact institution. *Financial support:* In 2019–20, 25 students received support, including 25 fellowships (averaging $3,015 per year); teaching assistantships and scholarships/grants also available. Financial award applicants required to submit FAFSA. *Unit head:* Dr. Lepaine Sharp-McHenry, Dean. *Application contact:* Brett DiMarzo, Director of Graduate Admission, 617-521-2651, Fax: 617-521-3137, E-mail: brett.dimarzo@simmons.edu.
Website: https://www.simmons.edu/academics/colleges-schools-departments/cnbhs

**Sonoma State University,** School of Science and Technology, Family Nurse Practitioner Program, Rohnert Park, CA 94928. Offers MSN. *Accreditation:* ACEN. *Program availability:* Part-time. *Degree requirements:* For master's, comprehensive exam, thesis or alternative, oral exams. *Entrance requirements:* For master's, GRE General Test, BSN, minimum GPA of 3.0, course work in statistics, physical assessment, RN license. Additional exam requirements/recommendations for international students: required—TOEFL (minimum score 500 paper-based).

**Southern Adventist University,** School of Nursing, Collegedale, TN 37315-0370. Offers acute care-adult/gerontology nurse practitioner (MSN, DNP); healthcare administration (MSN/MBA); lifestyle medicine (DNP); nurse educator (MSN, DNP); primary care-adult/gerontology nurse practitioner (MSN); primary care-family nurse practitioner (MSN, DNP); primary care-psychiatric mental health nurse practitioner (MSN, DNP); MSN/MBA. *Accreditation:* ACEN. *Program availability:* Part-time, 100% online. *Degree requirements:* For master's, thesis or project; for doctorate, scholarly project. *Entrance requirements:* For master's, RN license. Additional exam requirements/recommendations for international students: required—TOEFL (minimum score 100 iBT). Electronic applications accepted.

**Southern Connecticut State University,** School of Graduate Studies, School of Health and Human Services, Department of Nursing, New Haven, CT 06515-1355. Offers family nurse practitioner (MSN); nursing (Ed D); nursing education (MSN). *Accreditation:* AACN. *Program availability:* Part-time, evening/weekend. *Degree requirements:* For master's, thesis. *Entrance requirements:* For master's, GRE, MAT, interview, minimum QPA of 2.8, RN license, minimum 1 year of professional nursing experience. Electronic applications accepted.

**Southern Illinois University Edwardsville,** Graduate School, School of Nursing, Doctor of Nursing Practice Program, Edwardsville, IL 62026. Offers family nurse practitioner (DNP); nurse anesthesia (DNP); nursing (DNP). *Accreditation:* AACN. *Program availability:* Part-time, evening/weekend. *Degree requirements:* For doctorate, thesis/dissertation or alternative, project. *Entrance requirements:* Additional exam requirements/recommendations for international students: required—TOEFL (minimum score 550 paper-based; 79 iBT), IELTS (minimum score 6.5). Electronic applications accepted.

**Southern Illinois University Edwardsville,** Graduate School, School of Nursing, Program in Family Nurse Practitioner, Edwardsville, IL 62026. Offers MS, Post-Master's Certificate. *Accreditation:* AACN. *Program availability:* Part-time, evening/weekend. *Degree requirements:* For master's, comprehensive exam. *Entrance requirements:* For master's, appropriate bachelor's degree, RN license. Additional exam requirements/recommendations for international students: required—TOEFL (minimum score 550 paper-based; 79 iBT), IELTS (minimum score 6.5). Electronic applications accepted.

**Southern University and Agricultural and Mechanical College,** College of Nursing and Allied Health, School of Nursing, Baton Rouge, LA 70813. Offers educator/administrator (PhD); family health nursing (MSN); family nurse practitioner (Post Master's Certificate); geriatric nurse practitioner/gerontology (PhD); nursing (DNP). *Accreditation:* AACN. *Program availability:* Part-time. *Degree requirements:* For master's, comprehensive exam, thesis; for doctorate, comprehensive exam, thesis/dissertation. *Entrance requirements:* For master's, GRE General Test, BSN, minimum GPA of 2.7; for doctorate, GRE General Test; for Post Master's Certificate, MSN. Additional exam requirements/recommendations for international students: required—TOEFL (minimum score 525 paper-based).

**South University - Tampa,** Program in Nursing, Tampa, FL 33614. Offers adult health nurse practitioner (MS); family nurse practitioner (MS); nurse educator (MS).

**South University - Virginia Beach,** Program in Nursing, Virginia Beach, VA 23452. Offers family nurse practitioner (MSN).

**South University - West Palm Beach,** Program in Nursing, Royal Palm Beach, FL 33411. Offers family nurse practitioner (MS).

**Spalding University,** Graduate Studies, Kosair College of Health and Natural Sciences, School of Nursing, Louisville, KY 40203-2188. Offers adult nurse practitioner (MSN); family nurse practitioner (MSN); leadership in nursing and healthcare (MSN); nurse educator (Post-Master's Certificate); nurse practitioner (Post-Master's Certificate); pediatric nurse practitioner (MSN). *Accreditation:* AACN. *Program availability:* Part-time, evening/weekend. *Degree requirements:* For master's, comprehensive exam (for some programs), thesis. *Entrance requirements:* For master's, GRE General Test, BSN or bachelor's degree in related field, RN licensure, autobiographical statement, transcripts, letters of recommendation. Additional exam requirements/recommendations for international students: required—TOEFL (minimum score 535 paper-based).

**State University of New York Downstate Medical Center,** College of Nursing, Graduate Programs in Nursing, Nurse Practitioner Program, Brooklyn, NY 11203-2098. Offers MS, Post Master's Certificate. *Accreditation:* AACN. *Program availability:* Part-time. *Degree requirements:* For master's, thesis optional. *Entrance requirements:* For master's, GRE, BSN; minimum GPA of 3.0; previous undergraduate course work in statistics, health assessment, and nursing research; RN license; for Post Master's Certificate, BSN; minimum GPA of 3.0; RN license; previous undergraduate course work in statistics, health assessment, and nursing research.

**State University of New York Polytechnic Institute,** Program in Family Nurse Practitioner, Utica, NY 13502. Offers MS, CAS. *Accreditation:* AACN. *Program availability:* Part-time. *Degree requirements:* For master's, clinical hours. *Entrance requirements:* For master's, Bachelor of Science in Nursing, statistics, 2000 hours working exp RN.

**State University of New York Upstate Medical University,** College of Nursing, Syracuse, NY 13210. Offers nurse practitioner (Post Master's Certificate); nursing (MS). *Accreditation:* AACN. *Program availability:* Part-time, online learning. *Degree requirements:* For master's, thesis or alternative. *Entrance requirements:* For master's, 3 years of work experience. Electronic applications accepted.

**Stephen F. Austin State University,** Graduate School, College of Sciences and Mathematics, Richard and Lucille DeWitt School of Nursing, Nacogdoches, TX 75962. Offers family nurse practitioner (MSN).

**Stony Brook University, State University of New York,** Stony Brook Medicine, School of Nursing, Program in Family Nurse Practitioner, Stony Brook, NY 11794. Offers MS, DNP, Certificate. *Accreditation:* AACN. *Program availability:* Part-time, blended/hybrid learning. *Students:* 3 full-time (2 women), 170 part-time (149 women); includes 55 minority (19 Black or African American, non-Hispanic/Latino; 1 American Indian or Alaska Native, non-Hispanic/Latino; 16 Asian, non-Hispanic/Latino; 16 Hispanic/Latino; 3 Two or more races, non-Hispanic/Latino). 246 applicants, 30% accepted, 60 enrolled. In 2019, 66 master's, 2 doctorates, 1 other advanced degree awarded. *Entrance requirements:* For master's, BSN, minimum GPA of 3.0, course work in statistics. Additional exam requirements/recommendations for international students: required—TOEFL (minimum score 90 iBT). *Application deadline:* For fall admission, 12/5 for domestic students. Application fee: $100. *Expenses:* Contact institution. *Financial support:* Application deadline: 3/15. *Unit head:* Dr. Allyson Kornahrens, Program Director, 631-638-8538, Fax: 631-444-3136, E-mail: cheryl.meddles-torres@stonybrook.edu. *Application contact:* Staff Assistant, 631-444-3276, Fax: 631-444-3136, E-mail: fnp.nursing@stonybrook.edu.
Website: http://www.nursing.stonybrookmedicine.edu/about

**Stony Brook University, State University of New York,** Stony Brook Medicine, School of Nursing, Program in Perinatal Women's Health Nursing, Stony Brook, NY 11794. Offers MS, DNP, Certificate. *Accreditation:* AACN. *Program availability:* Blended/hybrid learning. *Students:* 2 part-time (both women); both minorities (both American Indian or Alaska Native, non-Hispanic/Latino). 2 applicants, 100% accepted, 2 enrolled. In 2019, 1 doctorate awarded. *Entrance requirements:* For master's, BSN, minimum GPA of 3.0, course work in statistics. Additional exam requirements/recommendations for international students: required—TOEFL (minimum score 90 iBT). *Application deadline:* For fall admission, 2/27 for domestic students. Application fee: $100. *Expenses:* Contact institution. *Financial support:* Application deadline: 3/15. *Unit head:* Dr. Elizabeth

Collins, Program Director, 631-444-3296, Fax: 631-444-3136, E-mail: elizabeth.collins@stonybrook.edu. *Application contact:* Linda Sacino, Staff Assistant, 631-632-3262, Fax: 631-444-3136, E-mail: elizabeth.collins@stonybrook.edu.
Website: http://www.nursing.stonybrookmedicine.edu/

**Temple University,** College of Public Health, Department of Nursing, Philadelphia, PA 19122-6096. Offers adult-gerontology primary care (DNP); family-individual across the lifespan (DNP); nursing (DNP). *Accreditation:* AACN. *Program availability:* Part-time. *Faculty:* 15 full-time (13 women), 6 part-time/adjunct (5 women). *Students:* 3 full-time (1 woman), 55 part-time (50 women); includes 27 minority (13 Black or African American, non-Hispanic/Latino; 11 Asian, non-Hispanic/Latino; 2 Hispanic/Latino; 1 Two or more races, non-Hispanic/Latino). 26 applicants, 54% accepted, 14 enrolled. In 2019, 11 doctorates awarded. *Degree requirements:* For doctorate, evidence-based practice project. *Entrance requirements:* For doctorate, GRE/MAT (waived for those who enter post-master's), 2 letters of reference, statement of goals, RN license, interview, statement of purpose, resume. Additional exam requirements/recommendations for international students: required—TOEFL (minimum score 79 iBT), IELTS (minimum score 6.5), PTE (minimum score 53), one of three is required. *Application deadline:* For fall admission, 3/1 for domestic students. Application fee: $60. Electronic applications accepted. *Expenses:* Contact institution. *Financial support:* Federal Work-Study and scholarships/grants available. Support available to part-time students. Financial award applicants required to submit FAFSA. *Unit head:* Martha Y Kubik, Chairperson, 215-707-4687, E-mail: martha.kubik@temple.edu. *Application contact:* Amy Costik, Assistant Director of Admissions, 215-204-5229, E-mail: amy.costik@temple.edu.
Website: https://cph.temple.edu/nursing/home

**Tennessee State University,** The School of Graduate Studies and Research, College of Health Sciences, School of Nursing, Nashville, TN 37209-1561. Offers family nurse practitioner (MSN, Certificate); holistic nurse practitioner (MSN); holistic nursing (Certificate); nursing education (MSN, Certificate). *Accreditation:* ACEN. *Entrance requirements:* For master's, GRE General Test or MAT, BSN, current RN license, minimum GPA of 3.0.

**Tennessee Technological University,** Whitson-Hester School of Nursing, DNP Program, Cookeville, TN 38505. Offers adult-gerontology acute care nurse practitioner (DNP); executive leadership in nursing (DNP); family nurse practitioner (DNP); pediatric nurse practitioner-primary care (DNP); psychiatric/mental health nurse practitioner (DNP); women's health care nurse practitioner (DNP). *Program availability:* Part-time. *Students:* 20 full-time (17 women), 12 part-time (all women); includes 3 minority (2 Black or African American, non-Hispanic/Latino; 1 Two or more races, non-Hispanic/Latino). 25 applicants, 60% accepted, 10 enrolled. *Application deadline:* For fall admission, 7/1 for domestic students, 5/1 for international students; for spring admission, 12/1 for domestic students, 10/1 for international students; for summer admission, 5/1 for domestic students, 2/1 for international students. Applications are processed on a rolling basis. Application fee: $35 ($40 for international students). Electronic applications accepted. *Expenses: Tuition, area resident:* Part-time $597 per credit hour. Tuition, state resident: part-time $597 per credit hour. Tuition, nonresident: part-time $1323 per credit hour. *Financial support:* Application deadline: 4/1; applicants required to submit FAFSA. *Unit head:* Dr. Kim Hanna, Dean, Fax: 931-372-6244, E-mail: khanna@tntech.edu. *Application contact:* Shelia K. Kendrick, Coordinator of Graduate Studies, 931-372-3808, Fax: 931-372-3497, E-mail: skendrick@tntech.edu.
Website: https://www.tntech.edu/nursing/doctor-of-nursing-practice/

**Tennessee Technological University,** Whitson-Hester School of Nursing, MSN Programs, Cookeville, TN 38505. Offers family nurse practitioner (MSN); nursing administration (MSN); nursing education (MSN). *Program availability:* Part-time. *Students:* 2 full-time (both women), 110 part-time (93 women); includes 7 minority (4 Black or African American, non-Hispanic/Latino; 1 Asian, non-Hispanic/Latino; 1 Hispanic/Latino; 1 Two or more races, non-Hispanic/Latino). 55 applicants, 73% accepted, 29 enrolled. In 2019, 29 master's awarded. *Application deadline:* For fall admission, 7/1 for domestic students, 5/1 for international students; for spring admission, 12/1 for domestic students, 10/1 for international students; for summer admission, 5/1 for domestic students, 2/1 for international students. Applications are processed on a rolling basis. Application fee: $35 ($40 for international students). Electronic applications accepted. *Expenses: Tuition, area resident:* Part-time $597 per credit hour. Tuition, state resident: part-time $597 per credit hour. Tuition, nonresident: part-time $1323 per credit hour. *Financial support:* Application deadline: 4/1; applicants required to submit FAFSA. *Unit head:* Dr. Kim Hanna, Dean, 931-372-3203, Fax: 931-372-6244, E-mail: khanna@tntech.edu. *Application contact:* Shelia K. Kendrick, Coordinator of Graduate Studies, 931-372-3808, Fax: 931-372-3497, E-mail: skendrick@tntech.edu.
Website: https://www.tntech.edu/nursing/masters/

**Texas A&M International University,** Office of Graduate Studies and Research, College of Nursing and Health Sciences, Laredo, TX 78041. Offers family nurse practitioner (MSN). *Accreditation:* ACEN. *Entrance requirements:* Additional exam requirements/recommendations for international students: required—TOEFL (minimum score 550 paper-based; 79 iBT).

**Texas A&M University,** College of Nursing, Bryan, TX 77843. Offers family nurse practitioner (MSN); forensic nursing (MSN); nursing education (MSN). *Expenses:* Contact institution.

**Texas A&M University–Corpus Christi,** College of Graduate Studies, College of Nursing and Health Sciences, Corpus Christi, TX 78412. Offers family nurse practitioner (MSN); leadership in nursing systems (MSN); nurse educator (MSN); nursing practice (DNP). *Accreditation:* AACN. *Program availability:* Part-time, evening/weekend, online only, 100% online. *Degree requirements:* For master's, clinical capstone; for doctorate, capstone/scholarly project. *Entrance requirements:* For master's, essay, resume, 3 letters of recommendation, minimum GPA of 3.0, current valid unencumbered Texas nursing license. Additional exam requirements/recommendations for international students: required—TOEFL (minimum score 550 paper-based; 79 iBT), IELTS (minimum score 6.5). Electronic applications accepted.

**Texas Christian University,** Harris College of Nursing and Health Sciences, Doctor of Nursing Practice Program, Fort Worth, TX 76129-0002. Offers clinical nurse specialist - adult/gerontology nursing (DNP); clinical nurse specialist - pediatrics (DNP); family nurse practitioner (DNP); general (DNP); nursing administration (DNP). *Accreditation:* AACN. *Program availability:* Part-time, 100% online, blended/hybrid learning. *Faculty:* 29 full-time (26 women), 1 (woman) part-time/adjunct. *Students:* 49 full-time (45 women), 13 part-time (10 women); includes 18 minority (9 Black or African American, non-Hispanic/Latino; 1 American Indian or Alaska Native, non-Hispanic/Latino; 3 Asian, non-Hispanic/Latino; 4 Hispanic/Latino; 1 Two or more races, non-Hispanic/Latino), 2 international. Average age 37. 57 applicants, 70% accepted, 24 enrolled. In 2019, 27 doctorates awarded. *Degree requirements:* For doctorate, thesis/dissertation or alternative, practicum. *Entrance requirements:* For doctorate, three reference letters, essay, resume, two official transcripts from each institution attended, APRN recognition or MSN with experience or certification in nursing administration, as applicable per track, current RN license, successful completion of interview. Additional exam requirements/recommendations for international students: required—TOEFL (minimum score 550 paper-based; 80 iBT). *Application deadline:* For summer admission, 1/15 for domestic and international students. Application fee: $60. Electronic applications accepted. Full-time tuition and fees vary according to program. *Financial support:* In 2019–20, 20 students received support. Scholarships/grants available. Financial award application deadline: 2/15; financial award applicants required to submit FAFSA. *Unit head:* Dr. Kathy Ellis, Division Director, Graduate Nursing, 817-257-6726, Fax: 817-257-7944, E-mail: kathryn.ellis@tcu.edu. *Application contact:* Beth Janke, Academic Program Specialist, 817-257-6726, Fax: 817-257-7944, E-mail: graduatenursing@tcu.edu.
Website: http://dnp.tcu.edu/

**Texas State University,** The Graduate College, College of Health Professions, Family Nurse Practitioner Program, San Marcos, TX 78666. Offers MSN. *Accreditation:* CAHME. *Program availability:* Part-time, evening/weekend, blended/hybrid learning. *Degree requirements:* For master's, comprehensive exam. *Entrance requirements:* For master's, BSN from institution accredited by nationally-recognized nursing education accrediting body (i.e., ACEN, CCNE) with minimum GPA of 3.0 in nursing courses and last 60 hours of undergraduate course work; current valid unencumbered RN license or multi-state privilege to practice as a registered nurse; resume, 3 letters of recommendations. Additional exam requirements/recommendations for international students: required—TOEFL (minimum score 550 paper-based; 78 iBT), IELTS (minimum score 6). Electronic applications accepted.

**Texas Tech University Health Sciences Center,** School of Nursing, Lubbock, TX 79430. Offers acute care nurse practitioner (MSN, Certificate); administration (MSN); advanced practice (DNP); education (MSN); executive leadership (DNP); family nurse practitioner (MSN, Certificate); geriatric nurse practitioner (MSN, Certificate); pediatric nurse practitioner (MSN, Certificate). *Accreditation:* AACN. *Program availability:* Part-time, online learning. *Degree requirements:* For master's, thesis optional. *Entrance requirements:* For master's, minimum GPA of 3.0, 3 letters of reference, BSN, RN license; for Certificate, minimum GPA of 3.0, 3 letters of reference, RN license. Additional exam requirements/recommendations for international students: required—TOEFL (minimum score 550 paper-based).

**Texas Woman's University,** Graduate School, College of Nursing, Denton, TX 76204. Offers adult health clinical nurse specialist (MS); adult health nurse practitioner (MS); adult/gerontology acute care nurse practitioner (MS); child health clinical nurse specialist (MS); clinical nurse leader (MS); family nurse practitioner (MS); health systems management (MS); nursing education (MS); nursing practice (DNP); nursing science (PhD); pediatric nurse practitioner (MS); women's health clinical nurse specialist (MS); women's health nurse practitioner (MS). *Accreditation:* AACN. *Program availability:* Part-time, 100% online, blended/hybrid learning. *Faculty:* 48 full-time (47 women), 31 part-time/adjunct (24 women). *Students:* 42 full-time (40 women), 811 part-time (756 women); includes 481 minority (168 Black or African American, non-Hispanic/Latino; 2 American Indian or Alaska Native, non-Hispanic/Latino; 165 Asian, non-Hispanic/Latino; 118 Hispanic/Latino; 1 Native Hawaiian or other Pacific Islander, non-Hispanic/Latino; 27 Two or more races, non-Hispanic/Latino), 26 international. Average age 36. 435 applicants, 71% accepted, 172 enrolled. In 2019, 203 master's, 37 doctorates awarded. *Degree requirements:* For master's, comprehensive exam, thesis or alternative, 6-year time limit for completion of degree, professional or clinical project; for doctorate, comprehensive exam, thesis/dissertation, 10-year time limit for completion of degree; dissertation (PhD), assessment practicum (DPT). *Entrance requirements:* For master's, minimum GPA of 3.0 on last 60 hours in undergraduate nursing degree and overall, RN license, BS in nursing, basic statistics course; for doctorate, MS in nursing, minimum preferred GPA of 3.5, RN or APRN license, statistics course, 2 letters of reference, curriculum vitae, graduate nursing-theory course, graduate research course, statement of professional goals and research interests, 1 yr APRN experience. Additional exam requirements/recommendations for international students: required—TOEFL (minimum score 79 iBT); recommended—IELTS (minimum score 6.5), TSE (minimum score 53). *Application deadline:* For fall admission, 5/1 for domestic students, 3/1 priority date for international students; for spring admission, 9/15 for domestic students, 7/1 priority date for international students. Application fee: $50 ($75 for international students). Electronic applications accepted. *Expenses:* All are estimates. Tuition for 10 hours = $2,763; Fees for 10 hours = $1,342. Master's Nursing courses require additional $75/SCH; Doctoral Nursing courses require additional $80/SCH. *Financial support:* In 2019–20, 212 students received support, including 1 research assistantship, 6 teaching assistantships (averaging $12,029 per year); career-related internships or fieldwork, scholarships/grants, health care benefits, and unspecified assistantships also available. Support available to part-time students. Financial award application deadline: 3/1; financial award applicants required to submit FAFSA. *Unit head:* Dr. Rosalie Mainous, Dean, 940-898-2401, Fax: 940-898-2437, E-mail: nursing@twu.edu. *Application contact:* Korie Hawkins, Associate Director of Admissions, Graduate Recruitment, 940-898-3188, Fax: 940-898-3081, E-mail: admissions@twu.edu.
Website: http://www.twu.edu/nursing/

**Troy University,** Graduate School, College of Health and Human Services, Program in Nursing, Troy, AL 36082. Offers adult health (MSN); family nurse practitioner (DNP); maternal infant (MSN); nursing informatics specialist (MSN). *Accreditation:* ACEN. *Program availability:* Part-time, evening/weekend, online learning. *Faculty:* 14 full-time (all women). *Students:* 67 full-time (64 women), 160 part-time (139 women); includes 46 minority (37 Black or African American, non-Hispanic/Latino; 1 American Indian or Alaska Native, non-Hispanic/Latino; 1 Asian, non-Hispanic/Latino; 7 Hispanic/Latino). Average age 35. 64 applicants, 97% accepted, 59 enrolled. In 2019, 73 master's, 20 doctorates awarded. *Degree requirements:* For master's, comprehensive exam, minimum GPA of 3.0, candidacy; for doctorate, minimum GPA of 3.0, submission of approved comprehensive e-portfolio, completion of residency synthesis project, minimum of 1000 hours of clinical practice, qualifying exam. *Entrance requirements:* For master's, Score of 396 or higher on the Miller's Analogy Test (MAT) or score of 290 on Graduate Record Exam (850 on the old exam)(verbal plus quantitative); GRE or MAT required for every applicant, minimum GPA of 3.0, BSN, current RN licensure, 2 letters of reference, undergraduate health assessment course; for doctorate, GRE (minimum score of 850 on old exam or 294 on new exam), BSN or MSN, minimum GPA of 3.0, 2 letters of reference, current RN licensure, essay. Additional exam requirements/recommendations for international students: required—TOEFL (minimum score 523 paper-based; 70 iBT), IELTS (minimum score 6). *Application deadline:* For fall admission, 5/1 for domestic students; for spring admission, 10/1 for domestic students; for summer admission, 3/1 for domestic students. Applications are processed on a rolling basis. Application fee: $50. Electronic applications accepted. *Expenses: Tuition, area resident:* Full-time $7650; part-time $2550 per semester hour. Tuition, state resident: full-time $7650; part-time $2550 per semester hour. Tuition, nonresident: full-time $15,300; part-time $5100 per semester hour. *International tuition:* $15,300 full-time. *Required fees:* $856; $352 per semester hour. $176 per semester. *Financial support:* In 2019–20, 20 students received support. Fellowships, research assistantships, teaching assistantships, career-related internships or fieldwork, Federal Work-Study, scholarships/grants, traineeships, tuition waivers, and unspecified assistantships available. Support available to part-time students. Financial award application deadline: 3/1; financial award applicants required to submit FAFSA. *Unit head:* Dr. Wade Forehand, Professor, Director, School of Nursing, 334-670-3745, Fax: 334-670-3743,

E-mail: jforehand@troy.edu. *Application contact:* Crystal G. Bishop, Director of Graduate Admissions, School of Nursing, 334-241-8631, E-mail: cdgodwin@troy.edu. Website: https://www.troy.edu/academics/academic-programs/college-health-human-services-programs.php

**Tusculum University,** Program in Nursing, Greeneville, TN 37743-9997. Offers family nurse practitioner (MSN). *Program availability:* Part-time. *Entrance requirements:* For master's, GRE. Additional exam requirements/recommendations for international students: required—TOEFL.

**Uniformed Services University of the Health Sciences,** Daniel K. Inouye Graduate School of Nursing, Bethesda, MD 20814. Offers adult-gerontology clinical nurse specialist (MSN, DNP); family nurse practitioner (DNP); nurse anesthesia (DNP); nursing science (PhD); psychiatric mental health nurse practitioner (DNP); women's health nurse practitioner (DNP). *Accreditation:* AACN; AANA/CANAEP. *Program availability:* Part-time. *Faculty:* 50 full-time (32 women), 1 part-time/adjunct (0 women). *Students:* 170 full-time (98 women); includes 51 minority (21 Black or African American, non-Hispanic/Latino; 17 Asian, non-Hispanic/Latino; 11 Hispanic/Latino; 2 Native Hawaiian or other Pacific Islander, non-Hispanic/Latino). Average age 34. 88 applicants, 75% accepted, 66 enrolled. In 2019, 2 master's, 42 doctorates awarded. *Degree requirements:* For master's, thesis, scholarly project; for doctorate, dissertation (for PhD); project (for DNP). *Entrance requirements:* For master's, GRE, BSN, clinical experience, minimum GPA of 3.0, previous course work in science; for doctorate, GRE, BSN, minimum GPA of 3.0, undergraduate/graduate science course within past 5 years, writing example, interview (for some programs), and 3 letters of reference (for DNP); master's degree, minimum GPA of 3.0 in nursing or related field, personal statement, 3 references, and interview (for PhD). *Application deadline:* For winter admission, 2/15 for domestic students; for summer admission, 8/15 for domestic students. Electronic applications accepted. *Financial support:* Robert Wood Johnson and Jonas scholars available. *Unit head:* Dr. Diane C. Seibert, Associate Dean for Academic Affairs, 301-295-1080, Fax: 301-295-1707, E-mail: diane.seibert@usuhs.edu. *Application contact:* Maureen Jackson, Student Admissions Program Manager, 301-295-1055, E-mail: maureen.jackson.ctr@usuhs.edu. Website: http://www.usuhs.edu/gsn/

**Union University,** School of Nursing, Jackson, TN 38305-3697. Offers executive leadership (DNP); nurse anesthesia (DNP); nurse practitioner (DNP); nursing education (MSN, PMC). *Accreditation:* AACN; AANA/CANAEP. *Degree requirements:* For master's, thesis or alternative. *Entrance requirements:* For master's, GRE, 3 letters of reference, bachelor's degree in nursing, minimum GPA of 3.0. Additional exam requirements/recommendations for international students: required—TOEFL (minimum score 560 paper-based). Electronic applications accepted.

**United States University,** Family Nurse Practitioner Program, San Diego, CA 92108. Offers MSN. *Degree requirements:* For master's, project. *Entrance requirements:* For master's, RN license, minimum cumulative undergraduate GPA of 2.5, background check, official transcripts, personal goal statement. Additional exam requirements/recommendations for international students: required—TOEFL (minimum score 550 paper-based; 80 iBT).

**Universidad del Turabo,** Graduate Programs, School of Health Sciences, Programs in Nursing, Program in Family Nurse Practitioner, Gurabo, PR 00778-3030. Offers MSN, Certificate. *Entrance requirements:* For master's, GMAT, EXADEP or GRE, interview, essay, official transcript, recommendation letters. Electronic applications accepted.

**University at Buffalo, the State University of New York,** Graduate School, School of Nursing, Buffalo, NY 14260. Offers adult gerontology nurse practitioner (DNP); family nurse practitioner (DNP); health care systems and leadership (MS); nurse anesthetist (DNP); nursing (PhD); nursing education (Certificate); psychiatric/mental health nurse practitioner (DNP). *Accreditation:* AACN; AANA/CANAEP (one or more programs are accredited). *Program availability:* Part-time, 100% online. *Degree requirements:* For master's, thesis optional; for doctorate, comprehensive exam (for some programs), capstone (for DNP), dissertation (for PhD). *Entrance requirements:* For master's, GRE or MAT; for doctorate, GRE or MAT, minimum GPA of 3.0 (for DNP), 3.25 (for PhD); RN license; BS or MS in nursing; 3 references; writing sample; resume; personal statement; for Certificate, interview, minimum GPA of 3.0 or GRE General Test, RN license, MS in nursing, professional certification. Additional exam requirements/recommendations for international students: required—TOEFL (minimum score 550 paper-based; 79 iBT), IELTS (minimum score 6.5). Electronic applications accepted. *Expenses:* Contact institution.

**The University of Alabama at Birmingham,** School of Nursing, Birmingham, AL 35294. Offers clinical nurse leader (MSN); nurse anesthesia (DNP); nurse practitioner (MSN, DNP), including adult-gerontology acute care (MSN), adult-gerontology primary care (MSN), family (MSN), pediatric (MSN), psychiatric/mental health (MSN), women's health (MSN); nursing (MSN, DNP, PhD); nursing health systems administration (MSN); nursing informatics (MSN). *Accreditation:* AACN; AANA/CANAEP. *Program availability:* Part-time, online only, blended/hybrid learning. *Faculty:* 86 full-time (79 women), 42 part-time/adjunct (35 women). *Students:* 228 full-time (165 women), 1,393 part-time (1,234 women); includes 398 minority (267 Black or African American, non-Hispanic/Latino; 4 American Indian or Alaska Native, non-Hispanic/Latino; 52 Asian, non-Hispanic/Latino; 41 Hispanic/Latino; 34 Two or more races, non-Hispanic/Latino), 3 international. Average age 33. 1,027 applicants, 55% accepted, 421 enrolled. In 2019, 557 master's, 19 doctorates awarded. Terminal master's awarded for partial completion of doctoral program. *Degree requirements:* For master's, comprehensive exam; for doctorate, comprehensive exam, thesis/dissertation, research mentorship experience (for PhD); scholarly project (for DNP). *Entrance requirements:* For master's, GRE, GMAT, or MAT, minimum cumulative undergraduate GPA of 3.0 or on last 60 semesters hours; letters of recommendation; for doctorate, GRE General Test, computer literacy, course work in statistics, interview, minimum GPA of 3.0, MS in nursing, references, writing sample. Additional exam requirements/recommendations for international students: required—TOEFL (minimum score 500 paper-based, 80 iBT) or IELTS (5.5). *Application deadline:* For fall admission, 2/24 for domestic students; for summer admission, 10/15 for domestic students. Application fee: $50. Electronic applications accepted. *Expenses:* Contact institution. *Financial support:* In 2019–20, 23 fellowships (averaging $34,685 per year), 12 research assistantships (averaging $9,042 per year), 2 teaching assistantships (averaging $22,000 per year) were awarded; scholarships/grants, traineeships, health care benefits, and unspecified assistantships also available. Support available to part-time students. *Unit head:* Dr. Doreen C. Harper, Dean, 205-934-5360, Fax: 205-934-1894, E-mail: dcharper@uab.edu. *Application contact:* John Updegraff, Director of Student Affairs, 205-975-3370, Fax: 205-934-5490, E-mail: jupde22@uab.edu. Website: http://www.uab.edu/nursing/home/

**The University of Alabama in Huntsville,** School of Graduate Studies, College of Nursing, Huntsville, AL 35899. Offers family nurse practitioner (Certificate); nursing (MSN, DNP), including adult-gerontology acute care nurse practitioner (MSN), adult-gerontology clinical nurse specialist (MSN), family nurse practitioner (MSN), leadership in health care systems (MSN); nursing education (Certificate). *Accreditation:* AACN. *Program availability:* Part-time. *Degree requirements:* For master's, comprehensive

exam, thesis or alternative, oral and written exams. *Entrance requirements:* For master's, MAT or GRE, Alabama RN license, BSN, minimum GPA of 3.0; for doctorate, master's degree in nursing in an advanced practice area; for Certificate, MAT or GRE, minimum GPA of 3.0. Additional exam requirements/recommendations for international students: required—TOEFL (minimum score 500 paper-based; 80 iBT), IELTS (minimum score 6.5). Electronic applications accepted.

**The University of Arizona,** College of Nursing, Tucson, AZ 85721. Offers health care informatics (Certificate); nurse practitioner (MS); nursing (DNP, PhD). *Accreditation:* AACN; AANA/CANAEP. *Program availability:* Part-time, online learning. Terminal master's awarded for partial completion of doctoral program. *Degree requirements:* For master's, thesis optional; for doctorate, comprehensive exam, thesis/dissertation. *Entrance requirements:* For master's, BSN, eligibility for RN license; for doctorate, BSN; for Certificate, GRE General Test, Arizona RN license, BSN, minimum GPA of 3.0. Additional exam requirements/recommendations for international students: required—TOEFL (minimum score 550 paper-based; 79 iBT). Electronic applications accepted. *Expenses:* Contact institution.

**University of Central Arkansas,** Graduate School, College of Health and Behavioral Sciences, Department of Nursing, Conway, AR 72035-0001. Offers adult nurse practitioner (PMC); clinical nurse leader (PMC); clinical nurse specialist (MSN); family nurse practitioner (PMC); nurse educator (PMC); nurse practitioner (MSN). *Accreditation:* AACN. *Program availability:* Part-time, evening/weekend, online learning. *Degree requirements:* For master's, comprehensive exam, thesis optional, clinicals. *Entrance requirements:* For master's, GRE General Test, minimum GPA of 2.7. Additional exam requirements/recommendations for international students: required—TOEFL (minimum score 550 paper-based; 80 iBT). Electronic applications accepted. *Expenses:* Contact institution.

**University of Colorado Denver,** College of Nursing, Aurora, CO 80045. Offers adult clinical nurse specialist (MS); adult nurse practitioner (MS); family nurse practitioner (MS); family psychiatric mental health nurse practitioner (MS); health care informatics (MS); nurse-midwifery (MS); nursing (DNP, PhD); nursing leadership and health care systems (MS); pediatric nurse practitioner (MS); women's health (MS); MS/PhD. *Accreditation:* ACNM/ACME (one or more programs are accredited). *Program availability:* Part-time, evening/weekend, online learning. Terminal master's awarded for partial completion of doctoral program. *Degree requirements:* For master's, thesis optional; for doctorate, comprehensive exam, thesis/dissertation, 42 credits of coursework. *Entrance requirements:* For master's, GRE if cumulative undergraduate GPA is less than 3.0, undergraduate nursing degree from ACEN or CCNE-accredited school or university; completion of research and statistics courses with minimum grade of C; copy of current and unencumbered nursing license; for doctorate, GRE, bachelor's and/or master's degrees in nursing from ACEN- or CCNE-accredited institution; portfolio; minimum undergraduate GPA of 3.0, graduate 3.5; graduate-level intermediate statistics and master's-level nursing theory courses with minimum B grade; interview. Additional exam requirements/recommendations for international students: required—TOEFL (minimum score 560 paper-based; 83 iBT). Electronic applications accepted. *Expenses:* Contact institution.

**University of Connecticut,** Graduate School, School of Nursing, MS Program in Nursing, Storrs, CT 06269. Offers adult gerontological acute care nurse practitioner (MS); adult gerontological primary care nurse practitioner (MS); family nurse practitioner (MS); neonatal nurse practitioner (MS). *Accreditation:* AACN. *Program availability:* Part-time, online learning. *Degree requirements:* For master's, comprehensive exam. *Entrance requirements:* For master's, official transcripts, Connecticut RN license, three letters of reference, curriculum vitae or resume, personal statement. Additional exam requirements/recommendations for international students: required—TOEFL (minimum score 550 paper-based). Electronic applications accepted.

**University of Delaware,** College of Health Sciences, School of Nursing, Newark, DE 19716. Offers adult nurse practitioner (MSN, PMC); cardiopulmonary clinical nurse specialist (MSN, PMC); cardiopulmonary clinical nurse specialist/adult nurse practitioner (MSN, PMC); family nurse practitioner (MSN, PMC); gerontology clinical nurse specialist (MSN, PMC); gerontology clinical nurse specialist geriatric nurse practitioner (PMC); gerontology clinical nurse specialist/geriatric nurse practitioner (MSN); health services administration (MSN, PMC); nursing of children clinical nurse specialist (MSN, PMC); nursing of children clinical nurse specialist/pediatric nurse practitioner (MSN, PMC); oncology/immune deficiency clinical nurse specialist (MSN, PMC); oncology/immune deficiency clinical nurse specialist/adult nurse practitioner (MSN, PMC); perinatal/women's health clinical nurse specialist (MSN, PMC); perinatal/women's health clinical nurse specialist/women's health nurse practitioner (MSN, PMC); psychiatric nursing clinical nurse specialist (MSN, PMC). *Accreditation:* AACN. *Program availability:* Part-time, evening/weekend, online learning. *Degree requirements:* For master's, thesis optional. *Entrance requirements:* For master's, BSN, interview, RN license. Electronic applications accepted.

**University of Detroit Mercy,** College of Health Professions, Detroit, MI 48221. Offers clinical nurse leader (MSN); family nurse practitioner (MSN); health services administration (MHSA); health systems management (MSN); nurse anesthesia (MS); nursing (DNP); nursing education (MSN, Certificate); nursing leadership and financial management (Certificate); outcomes performance management (Certificate); physician assistant (MS). *Accreditation:* AANA/CANAEP. *Entrance requirements:* For master's, GRE General Test, minimum GPA of 3.0.

**University of Hawaii at Manoa,** Office of Graduate Education, School of Nursing and Dental Hygiene, Honolulu, HI 96822. Offers clinical nurse specialist (MS), including adult health, community mental health; nurse practitioner (MS), including adult health, community mental health, family nurse practitioner; nursing (PhD, Graduate Certificate); nursing administration (MS). *Accreditation:* AACN. *Program availability:* Part-time, online learning. *Degree requirements:* For master's, thesis optional; for doctorate, comprehensive exam, thesis/dissertation. *Entrance requirements:* For master's, Hawaii RN license. Additional exam requirements/recommendations for international students: required—TOEFL (minimum score 580 paper-based; 92 iBT), IELTS (minimum score 5). *Expenses:* Contact institution.

**University of Houston,** College of Nursing, Sugar Land, TX 77479. Offers family nurse practitioner (MSN); nursing administration (MSN); nursing education (MSN). *Accreditation:* AACN. *Faculty:* 8 full-time (7 women). *Students:* 18 full-time (12 women), 33 part-time (32 women); includes 30 minority (13 Black or African American, non-Hispanic/Latino; 4 Asian, non-Hispanic/Latino; 12 Hispanic/Latino; 1 Native Hawaiian or other Pacific Islander, non-Hispanic/Latino). Average age 36. 38 applicants, 74% accepted, 20 enrolled. In 2019, 12 master's awarded. *Entrance requirements:* For master's, minimum GPA of 3.0, unencumbered Texas RN license, 2 letters of recommendation, essay, resume, interview required. Additional exam requirements/recommendations for international students: required—TOEFL. *Application deadline:* For fall admission, 6/1 for domestic and international students; for spring admission, 11/1 for domestic and international students; for summer admission, 4/1 for domestic and international students. Application fee: $75. Electronic applications accepted. *Financial support:* In 2019–20, 19 students received support. Federal Work-Study, scholarships/grants, and unspecified assistantships available. Support available to part-time students.

Financial award application deadline: 7/1; financial award applicants required to submit FAFSA. *Unit head:* Dr. Kathryn Tart, Dean, 832-842-8200, E-mail: kmtart@uh.edu. *Application contact:* Tammy N. Whatley, Student Affairs Director, 832-842-8220, E-mail: tnwhatley@uh.edu.
Website: http://www.uh.edu/nursing

**University of Illinois at Chicago,** College of Nursing, Program in Nursing, Chicago, IL 60607-7128. Offers acute care clinical nurse specialist (MS); administrative nursing leadership (Certificate); adult nurse practitioner (MS); adult/geriatric nurse practitioner (MS); advanced community health nurse specialist (MS); family nurse practitioner (MS); geriatric clinical nurse specialist (MS); geriatric nurse practitioner (MS); nurse midwifery (MS); occupational health/advanced community health nurse specialist (MS); occupational health/family nurse practitioner (MS); pediatric nurse practitioner (MS); perinatal clinical nurse specialist (MS); school/advanced community health nurse specialist (MS); school/family nurse practitioner (MS); women's health nurse practitioner (MS). *Accreditation:* AACN. *Program availability:* Part-time. *Degree requirements:* For master's, thesis or alternative. *Entrance requirements:* For master's, GRE General Test, minimum GPA of 2.75. Additional exam requirements/recommendations for international students: required—TOEFL. Electronic applications accepted.

**University of Indianapolis,** Graduate Programs, School of Nursing, Indianapolis, IN 46227-3697. Offers advanced practice nursing (DNP); family nurse practitioner (MSN); gerontological nurse practitioner (MSN); neonatal nurse practitioner (MSN); nurse-midwifery (MSN); nursing (MSN); nursing and health systems leadership (MSN); nursing education (MSN); women's health nurse practitioner (MSN); MBA/MSN. *Accreditation:* AACN. *Entrance requirements:* For master's, minimum GPA of 3.0, interview, letters of recommendation, resume, IN nursing license, 1 year of professional practice; for doctorate, graduate of ACEN- or CCNE-accredited nursing program; MSN or MA with nursing major and minimum cumulative GPA of 3.25; unencumbered RN license with eligibility for licensure in Indiana; completion of graduate-level statistics course within last 5 years with minimum grade of B; resume; essay; official transcripts from all academic institutions. Additional exam requirements/recommendations for international students: required—TOEFL (minimum score 550 paper-based). Electronic applications accepted.

**University of Louisiana at Lafayette,** College of Nursing and Allied Health Professions, Lafayette, LA 70504. Offers family nurse practitioner (MSN); nursing (DNP); nursing education (MSN). *Accreditation:* AACN. *Entrance requirements:* For master's, GRE General Test, minimum GPA of 2.75. Additional exam requirements/recommendations for international students: required—TOEFL (minimum score 550 paper-based). Electronic applications accepted. *Expenses: Tuition, area resident:* Full-time $5511; part-time $1630 per credit hour. Tuition, state resident: full-time $5511; part-time $1630 per credit hour. Tuition, nonresident: full-time $19,239; part-time $2409 per credit hour. *Required fees:* $46,637.

**University of Louisville,** Graduate School, School of Nursing, Louisville, KY 40202. Offers adult gerontology nurse practitioner (MSN, DNP); education and administration (MSN); family nurse practitioner (MSN, DNP); neonatal nurse practitioner (MSN, DNP); nursing research (PhD); psychiatric/mental health nurse practitioner (MSN, DNP); women's health nurse practitioner (MSN). *Accreditation:* AACN. *Program availability:* Part-time, blended/hybrid learning. *Faculty:* 49 full-time (46 women), 91 part-time/adjunct (86 women). *Students:* 164 full-time (140 women), 47 part-time (39 women); includes 45 minority (21 Black or African American, non-Hispanic/Latino; 5 Asian, non-Hispanic/Latino; 9 Hispanic/Latino; 10 Two or more races, non-Hispanic/Latino), 4 international. Average age 33. 84 applicants, 63% accepted, 48 enrolled. In 2019, 25 master's, 5 doctorates awarded. *Degree requirements:* For master's, varies; for doctorate, comprehensive exam (for some programs), thesis/dissertation (for some programs), varies. *Entrance requirements:* For master's, Our only master's degree is an accelerated program meant for students who have a bachelor's degree in another discipline who are transitioning into nursing. Thus, the main requirement is a bachelor's degree from a nationally-accredited college, and the completion of 6 prerequisite courses. Must have a minimum undergraduate GPA of 3.0; for doctorate, PhD program: GRE requirement omitted, DNP & PhD doctoral programs: 3 letters of professional reference. BSN applicants must have a 3.0 GPA. MSN applicants must have 3.25 GPA. Written statement of career goals, areas of expertise, reasons for pursuing doctoral degree, resume, and RN license. Additional exam requirements/recommendations for international students: recommended—TOEFL (minimum score 560 paper-based), IELTS (minimum score 6.5). *Application deadline:* For fall admission, 1/15 priority date for domestic and international students; for summer admission, 10/15 priority date for domestic students. Application fee: $60. Electronic applications accepted. *Expenses:* 17871. *Financial support:* In 2019–20, 47 students received support, including 2 fellowships with full tuition reimbursements available (averaging $20,000 per year), 9 research assistantships with full tuition reimbursements available (averaging $20,000 per year), 3 teaching assistantships with full tuition reimbursements available (averaging $15,000 per year); scholarships/grants, health care benefits, unspecified assistantships, and Jonas Nurse Leader Fellowships also available. Financial award application deadline: 10/1; financial award applicants required to submit FAFSA. *Unit head:* 502-852-8300, Fax: 502-852-5044, E-mail: sonya.hardin@louisville.edu. *Application contact:* Trish Hart, MA, Assistant Dean for Student Affairs, 502-852-5825, Fax: 502-852-8783, E-mail: trish.hart@louisville.edu.
Website: http://www.louisville.edu/nursing/

**University of Maine,** Graduate School, College of Natural Sciences, Forestry, and Agriculture, School of Nursing, Orono, ME 04469. Offers individualized (MS); nursing education (CGS); rural health family nurse practitioner (MS, CAS). *Accreditation:* AACN. *Faculty:* 6 full-time (all women), 6 part-time/adjunct (4 women). *Students:* 24 full-time (21 women), 20 part-time (18 women); includes 4 minority (2 American Indian or Alaska Native, non-Hispanic/Latino; 2 Hispanic/Latino). Average age 34. 14 applicants, 100% accepted, 10 enrolled. In 2019, 11 master's, 4 other advanced degrees awarded. *Entrance requirements:* For master's, GRE General Test; for other advanced degree, master's degree. Additional exam requirements/recommendations for international students: required—TOEFL. *Application deadline:* For fall admission, 7/1 for domestic students; for spring admission, 12/15 for domestic students; for summer admission, 4/15 for domestic students. Applications are processed on a rolling basis. Application fee: $65. Electronic applications accepted. *Expenses: Tuition, area resident:* Full-time $8100; part-time $450 per credit hour. Tuition, state resident: full-time $8100; part-time $450 per credit hour. Tuition, nonresident: full-time $26,388; part-time $1466 per credit hour. *International tuition:* $26,388 full-time. *Required fees:* $1257; $278 per semester. Tuition and fees vary according to course load. *Financial support:* Career-related internships or fieldwork, Federal Work-Study, institutionally sponsored loans, tuition waivers (full and partial), and unspecified assistantships available. Support available to part-time students. Financial award application deadline: 3/1. *Unit head:* Dr. Nancy Fishwick, Director, 207-581-2505, Fax: 207-581-2585. *Application contact:* Scott G. Delcourt, Assistant Vice President for Graduate Studies and Senior Associate Dean, 207-581-3291, Fax: 207-581-3232, E-mail: graduate@maine.edu.
Website: http://umaine.edu/nursing/

**University of Mary,** School of Health Sciences, Division of Nursing, Bismarck, ND 58504-9652. Offers family nurse practitioner (DNP); nurse administrator (MSN); nursing educator (MSN); MSN/MBA. *Accreditation:* AACN. *Program availability:* Part-time, evening/weekend, online learning. *Degree requirements:* For master's, comprehensive exam (for some programs), thesis (for some programs), internship (family nurse practitioner), teaching practice. *Entrance requirements:* For master's, minimum GPA of 2.75 in nursing, interview, letters of recommendation, criminal background check, immunizations, statement of professional goals. Additional exam requirements/recommendations for international students: required—TOEFL (minimum score 500 paper-based; 71 iBT). Electronic applications accepted.

**University of Mary Hardin-Baylor,** Graduate Studies in Nursing, Belton, TX 76513. Offers family nurse practitioner (MSN, Post-Master's Certificate); nursing education (MSN); nursing practice (DNP). *Accreditation:* AACN. *Program availability:* Evening/weekend. *Faculty:* 8 full-time (all women), 5 part-time/adjunct (3 women). *Students:* 22 full-time (20 women), 9 part-time (8 women); includes 15 minority (4 Black or African American, non-Hispanic/Latino; 3 Asian, non-Hispanic/Latino; 7 Hispanic/Latino; 1 Two or more races, non-Hispanic/Latino), 1 international. Average age 36. 26 applicants, 62% accepted, 15 enrolled. In 2019, 17 master's, 2 other advanced degrees awarded. *Degree requirements:* For master's, comprehensive exam, practicum; for doctorate, scholarly project. *Entrance requirements:* For master's, baccalaureate degree in nursing, current licensure as Registered Nurse in the state of Texas, minimum GPA of 3.0 in last 60 hours of undergraduate program, two letters of recommendation, full-time RN for 1 year, personal interview with director of MSN program; for doctorate, master's degree as an advanced practice nurse, nurse leader or nurse educator; three letters of recommendation; current RN license and approval to practice as an advanced practice nurse; essay; curriculum vitae; interview. Additional exam requirements/recommendations for international students: required—TOEFL (minimum score 60 iBT), IELTS (minimum score 4.5). *Application deadline:* For fall admission, 6/1 for domestic students, 4/30 priority date for international students; for spring admission, 11/1 for domestic students, 9/30 priority date for international students. Applications are processed on a rolling basis. Application fee: $35 ($135 for international students). Electronic applications accepted. *Expenses:* Contact institution. *Financial support:* In 2019–20, 24 students received support. Federal Work-Study, unspecified assistantships, and scholarships for some active duty military personnel available. Support available to part-time students. Financial award applicants required to submit FAFSA. *Unit head:* Dr. Elizabeth Jimenez, Director, Master of Science in Nursing Program & Assistant Professor, 254-295-4769, E-mail: ejimenez@umhb.edu. *Application contact:* Katherine Moore, Assistant Director, Graduate Admissions, 254-295-4924, E-mail: kmoore@umhb.edu.
Website: https://go.umhb.edu/graduate/nursing/home

**University of Maryland, Baltimore,** University of Maryland School of Nursing, Baltimore, MD 21201. Offers adult-gerontology acute care nurse practitioner (DNP); adult-gerontology primary care nurse practitioner (DNP); clinical nurse leader (MS); community/public health nursing (MS); family nurse practitioner (DNP); global health (Postbaccalaureate Certificate); health services leadership and management (MS); neonatal nurse practitioner (DNP); nurse anesthesia (DNP); nursing (PhD); nursing informatics (MS, Postbaccalaureate Certificate); pediatric acute/primary care nurse practitioner (DNP); psychiatric mental health nurse practitioner (DNP); teaching in nursing and health professions (Postbaccalaureate Certificate); MS/MBA. *Accreditation:* AANA/CANAEP. *Program availability:* Part-time. *Faculty:* 130 full-time (117 women), 125 part-time/adjunct (114 women). *Students:* 539 full-time (463 women), 586 part-time (506 women); includes 485 minority (259 Black or African American, non-Hispanic/Latino; 3 American Indian or Alaska Native, non-Hispanic/Latino; 124 Asian, non-Hispanic/Latino; 66 Hispanic/Latino; 1 Native Hawaiian or other Pacific Islander, non-Hispanic/Latino; 32 Two or more races, non-Hispanic/Latino), 18 international. Average age 33. 964 applicants, 54% accepted, 347 enrolled. In 2019, 197 master's, 114 doctorates, 12 other advanced degrees awarded. *Degree requirements:* For master's and Postbaccalaureate Certificate, thesis (for some programs); for doctorate, comprehensive exam, thesis/dissertation. *Entrance requirements:* Additional exam requirements/recommendations for international students: required—TOEFL (minimum score 550 paper-based; 79 iBT); recommended—IELTS (minimum score 7). *Application deadline:* For fall admission, 11/1 priority date for domestic and international students; for spring admission, 12/15 for domestic and international students; for summer admission, 9/1 for domestic and international students. Applications are processed on a rolling basis. Application fee: $75. Electronic applications accepted. *Financial support:* In 2019–20, 257 students received support, including 31 research assistantships with full and partial tuition reimbursements available (averaging $25,000 per year), 21 teaching assistantships with full and partial tuition reimbursements available (averaging $19,000 per year); scholarships/grants, traineeships, and unspecified assistantships also available. Support available to part-time students. Financial award application deadline: 3/1; financial award applicants required to submit FAFSA. *Unit head:* Dr. Jane Kirschling, Dean, 410-706-4359, E-mail: kirschling@umaryland.edu. *Application contact:* Larry Fillian, Associate Dean of Student and Academic Services, 410-706-6298, E-mail: lfillian@umaryland.edu.
Website: http://www.nursing.umaryland.edu/

**University of Massachusetts Amherst,** Graduate School, College of Nursing, Amherst, MA 01003. Offers adult gerontology primary care nurse practitioner (DNP); clinical nurse leader (MS); family nurse practitioner (DNP); nursing (PhD); public health nurse leader (DNP). *Accreditation:* AACN. *Program availability:* Part-time, online learning. Terminal master's awarded for partial completion of doctoral program. *Degree requirements:* For master's, thesis optional; for doctorate, comprehensive exam, thesis/dissertation. *Entrance requirements:* Additional exam requirements/recommendations for international students: required—TOEFL (minimum score 550 paper-based; 80 iBT), IELTS (minimum score 6.5). Electronic applications accepted.

**University of Massachusetts Lowell,** College of Health Sciences, School of Nursing, Program in Family Health Nursing, Lowell, MA 01854. Offers MS. *Accreditation:* AACN. *Degree requirements:* For master's, thesis optional. *Entrance requirements:* For master's, GRE General Test, minimum GPA of 3.0, MA nursing license, interview, 3 letters of recommendation.

**University of Massachusetts Medical School,** Graduate School of Nursing, Worcester, MA 01655. Offers adult gerontological acute care nurse practitioner (DNP, Post Master's Certificate); adult gerontological primary care nurse practitioner (DNP, Post Master's Certificate); family nursing practitioner (DNP); nurse administrator (DNP); nurse educator (MS); nursing (PhD); psychiatric mental health (Post Master's Certificate). *Accreditation:* AACN. *Program availability:* Blended/hybrid learning. *Faculty:* 26 full-time (22 women), 51 part-time/adjunct (40 women). *Students:* 176 full-time (152 women), 33 part-time (27 women); includes 61 minority (21 Black or African American, non-Hispanic/Latino; 1 American Indian or Alaska Native, non-Hispanic/Latino; 18 Asian, non-Hispanic/Latino; 20 Hispanic/Latino; 1 Native Hawaiian or other Pacific Islander, non-Hispanic/Latino). Average age 32. 131 applicants, 66% accepted, 58 enrolled. In 2019, 28 master's, 34 doctorates, 1 other advanced degree awarded. *Degree requirements:* For doctorate, thesis/dissertation (for some programs), comprehensive exam and manuscript (for PhD); scholarly project (for DNP). *Entrance requirements:* For master's, GRE General Test, bachelor's degree in nursing, course work in statistics, unrestricted Massachusetts license as registered nurse; for doctorate,

GRE General Test, bachelor's or master's degree; for Post Master's Certificate, GRE General Test, MS in nursing. Additional exam requirements/recommendations for international students: required—TOEFL (minimum score 400 paper-based; 81 iBT). *Application deadline:* For fall admission, 12/1 priority date for domestic students. Applications are processed on a rolling basis. Application fee: $100. Electronic applications accepted. *Expenses:* Contact institution. *Financial support:* In 2019–20, 103 students received support. Scholarships/grants available. Support available to part-time students. Financial award application deadline: 5/15; financial award applicants required to submit FAFSA. *Unit head:* Dr. Joan Vitello-Cicciu, Dean, 508-856-5081, Fax: 508-856-6552, E-mail: joan.vitello@umassmed.edu. *Application contact:* Diane Brescia, Admissions Coordinator, 508-856-3488, Fax: 508-856-5851, E-mail: diane.brescia@umassmed.edu.
Website: http://www.umassmed.edu/gsn/

**University of Memphis,** Loewenberg College of Nursing, Memphis, TN 38152. Offers advanced practice nursing (Graduate Certificate); executive leadership (MSN); family nurse practitioner (MSN); nursing administration (MSN, Graduate Certificate); nursing education (MSN, Graduate Certificate). *Accreditation:* AACN. *Program availability:* Part-time, evening/weekend, online learning. *Faculty:* 21 full-time (19 women), 11 part-time/adjunct (10 women). *Students:* 19 full-time (17 women), 281 part-time (254 women); includes 104 minority (87 Black or African American, non-Hispanic/Latino; 5 Asian, non-Hispanic/Latino; 7 Hispanic/Latino; 5 Two or more races, non-Hispanic/Latino), 2 international. Average age 34. 117 applicants, 79% accepted, 48 enrolled. In 2019, 71 master's, 3 other advanced degrees awarded. *Degree requirements:* For master's, comprehensive exam, thesis optional, scholarly project; clinical practicum hours. *Entrance requirements:* For master's, NCLEX exam, minimum undergraduate GPA of 2.8, letter of interest, letters of recommendation, interview, resume, nursing licensure; for Graduate Certificate, unrestricted license to practice as RN in TN, current CPR certification, evidence of vaccination, annual flu shot, evidence of current professional malpractice insurance, letters of recommendation, letter of intent, resume. Additional exam requirements/recommendations for international students: required—TOEFL (minimum score 550 paper-based; 79 iBT). *Application deadline:* For fall admission, 2/15 for domestic and international students; for spring admission, 10/1 for domestic and international students. Application fee: $35 ($60 for international students). *Expenses: Tuition, area resident:* Full-time $9216; part-time $512 per credit hour. Tuition, state resident: full-time $9216; part-time $512 per credit hour. Tuition, nonresident: full-time $12,672; part-time $704 per credit hour. *International tuition:* $16,128 full-time. *Required fees:* $1530; $85 per credit hour. Tuition and fees vary according to program. *Financial support:* Federal Work-Study and scholarships/grants available. Financial award application deadline: 2/1; financial award applicants required to submit FAFSA. *Unit head:* Dr. Lin Zhan, Dean, 901-678-2020, E-mail: lzhan@memphis.edu. *Application contact:* Dr. Lin Zhan, Dean, 901-678-2020, E-mail: lzhan@memphis.edu.
Website: http://www.memphis.edu/nursing

**University of Miami,** Graduate School, School of Nursing and Health Studies, Coral Gables, FL 33124. Offers acute care (MSN), including acute care nurse practitioner, nurse anesthesia; nursing (PhD); primary care (MSN), including adult nurse practitioner, family nurse practitioner, nurse midwifery, women's health practitioner. *Accreditation:* AACN; AANA/CANAEP; ACNM/ACME (one or more programs are accredited). *Program availability:* Part-time. *Degree requirements:* For master's, thesis optional; for doctorate, thesis/dissertation. *Entrance requirements:* For master's, GRE General Test, BSN, minimum GPA of 3.0, Florida RN license; for doctorate, GRE General Test, BSN or MSN, minimum GPA of 3.0. Additional exam requirements/recommendations for international students: required—TOEFL (minimum score 550 paper-based). Electronic applications accepted.

**University of Michigan–Flint,** School of Nursing, Flint, MI 48502-1950. Offers adult-gerontology acute care (DNP); adult-gerontology primary care (DNP); family nurse practitioner (DNP); nursing (MSN); psychiatric mental health (DNP); psychiatric mental health nurse practitioner (Certificate). *Accreditation:* AACN. *Program availability:* Part-time, evening/weekend, 100% online. *Faculty:* 32 full-time (31 women), 80 part-time/adjunct (71 women). *Students:* 198 full-time (174 women), 188 part-time (162 women); includes 55 minority (6 Black or African American, non-Hispanic/Latino; 3 American Indian or Alaska Native, non-Hispanic/Latino; 21 Asian, non-Hispanic/Latino; 18 Hispanic/Latino; 1 Native Hawaiian or other Pacific Islander, non-Hispanic/Latino; 6 Two or more races, non-Hispanic/Latino), 1 international. Average age 37. 140 applicants, 84% accepted, 75 enrolled. In 2019, 52 master's, 22 doctorates, 8 other advanced degrees awarded. *Entrance requirements:* For master's, BSN from regionally-accredited college; minimum GPA of 3.2; current unencumbered RN license in the United States; three or more credits in college-level chemistry or statistics with minimum C grade; for Certificate, completion of nurse practitioner program with MS from regionally-accredited college or university with minimum overall GPA of 3.2; current unencumbered RN license in the United States; current unencumbered license as nurse practitioner; current certification as nurse practitioner in specialty other than discipline of study. Additional exam requirements/recommendations for international students: required—TOEFL (minimum score 84 iBT), IELTS (minimum score 6.5). *Application deadline:* For fall admission, 7/1 for domestic students, 5/1 for international students; for winter admission, 11/15 for domestic students, 10/1 for international students; for spring admission, 3/15 for domestic students, 1/1 for international students; for summer admission, 5/15 for domestic students. Applications are processed on a rolling basis. Application fee: $55. Electronic applications accepted. *Expenses:* Contact institution. *Financial support:* Federal Work-Study, scholarships/grants, and unspecified assistantships available. Support available to part-time students. Financial award application deadline: 3/1; financial award applicants required to submit FAFSA. *Unit head:* Dr. Constance J. Creech, Director, 810-762-3420, Fax: 810-766-6851, E-mail: ccreech@umflint.edu. *Application contact:* Matt Bohlen, Director of Graduate Admissions, 810-762-3171, Fax: 810-766-6789, E-mail: mbohlen@umflint.edu.
Website: https://www.umflint.edu/nursing/graduate-nursing-programs

**University of Minnesota, Twin Cities Campus,** Graduate School, School of Nursing, Minneapolis, MN 55455-0213. Offers adult/gerontological clinical nurse specialist (DNP); adult/gerontological primary care nurse practitioner (DNP); family nurse practitioner (DNP); health innovation and leadership (DNP); integrative health and healing (DNP); nurse anesthesia (DNP); nurse midwifery (DNP); nursing (MN, PhD); nursing informatics (DNP); pediatric clinical nurse specialist (DNP); primary care certified pediatric nurse practitioner (DNP); psychiatric/mental health nurse practitioner (DNP); women's health nurse practitioner (DNP). *Accreditation:* AACN; AANA/CANAEP; ACNM/ACME (one or more programs are accredited). *Program availability:* Part-time, online learning. Terminal master's awarded for partial completion of doctoral program. *Degree requirements:* For master's, final oral exam, project or thesis; for doctorate, thesis/dissertation. *Entrance requirements:* For master's and doctorate, GRE General Test. Additional exam requirements/recommendations for international students: required—TOEFL (minimum score 586 paper-based). *Expenses:* Contact institution.

**University of Missouri,** Office of Research and Graduate Studies, Sinclair School of Nursing, Columbia, MO 65211. Offers adult-gerontology clinical nurse specialist (DNP, Certificate); family nurse practitioner (DNP); family psychiatric and mental health nurse practitioner (DNP); nursing (MS, PhD); nursing leadership and innovations in health care (DNP); pediatric clinical nurse specialist (DNP, Certificate); pediatric nurse practitioner (DNP). *Accreditation:* AACN. *Program availability:* Part-time. *Degree requirements:* For master's, thesis optional, oral exam; for doctorate, thesis/dissertation. *Entrance requirements:* For master's, GRE General Test, BSN, minimum GPA of 3.0 during last 60 hours, nursing license. Additional exam requirements/recommendations for international students: required—TOEFL, IELTS. Electronic applications accepted.

**University of Missouri–Kansas City,** School of Nursing and Health Studies, Kansas City, MO 64110-2499. Offers adult clinical nurse specialist (MSN), including adult nurse practitioner, women's health nurse practitioner (MSN, DNP); adult clinical nursing practice (DNP), including adult gerontology nurse practitioner, women's health nurse practitioner (MSN, DNP); clinical nursing practice (DNP), including family nurse practitioner; neonatal nurse practitioner (MSN); nurse educator (MSN); nurse executive (MSN); nursing practice (DNP); pediatric clinical nursing practice (DNP), including pediatric nurse practitioner; pediatric nurse practitioner (MSN). *Accreditation:* AACN. *Program availability:* Part-time, online learning. *Degree requirements:* For master's, thesis or alternative. *Entrance requirements:* For master's, minimum undergraduate GPA of 3.2; for doctorate, GRE, 3 letters of reference. Additional exam requirements/recommendations for international students: required—TOEFL (minimum score 550 paper-based; 80 iBT).

**University of Missouri–St. Louis,** College of Nursing, St. Louis, MO 63121. Offers adult/geriatric nurse practitioner (Post Master's Certificate); family nurse practitioner (Post Master's Certificate); nursing (DNP, PhD); pediatric acute care nurse practitioner (Post Master's Certificate); pediatric nurse practitioner (Post Master's Certificate); psychiatric-mental health nurse practitioner (Post Master's Certificate); women's health nurse practitioner (Post Master's Certificate). *Accreditation:* AACN. *Program availability:* Part-time. *Degree requirements:* For doctorate, comprehensive exam, thesis/dissertation; for Post Master's Certificate, thesis. *Entrance requirements:* For doctorate, GRE, 2 letters of recommendation, MSN, minimum GPA of 3.2, course in differential/inferential statistics; for Post Master's Certificate, 2 recommendation letters; MSN; advanced practice certificate; minimum GPA of 3.0; essay. Additional exam requirements/recommendations for international students: recommended—TOEFL (minimum score 550 paper-based; 79 iBT), IELTS (minimum score 6.5). Electronic applications accepted. *Expenses: Tuition, area resident:* Full-time $9005.40; part-time $6003.60 per credit hour. Tuition, state resident: full-time $9005.40; part-time $6003.60 per credit hour. Tuition, nonresident: full-time $22,108; part-time $14,738.40 per credit hour. *International tuition:* $22,108 full-time. Tuition and fees vary according to course load.

**University of Nevada, Las Vegas,** Graduate College, School of Nursing, Las Vegas, NV 89154-3018. Offers biobehavioral nursing (Advanced Certificate); family nurse practitioner (Advanced Certificate); nursing (MS, DNP, PhD); nursing education (Advanced Certificate). *Accreditation:* AACN. *Program availability:* Part-time, 100% online, blended/hybrid learning. *Faculty:* 15 full-time (13 women), 9 part-time/adjunct (8 women). *Students:* 44 full-time (41 women), 111 part-time (96 women); includes 48 minority (9 Black or African American, non-Hispanic/Latino; 16 Asian, non-Hispanic/Latino; 15 Hispanic/Latino; 1 Native Hawaiian or other Pacific Islander, non-Hispanic/Latino; 7 Two or more races, non-Hispanic/Latino), 1 international. Average age 38. 218 applicants, 33% accepted, 63 enrolled. In 2019, 19 master's, 14 doctorates, 2 other advanced degrees awarded. *Degree requirements:* For master's, comprehensive exam, thesis; for doctorate, comprehensive exam (for some programs), thesis/dissertation, project defense (for DNP). *Entrance requirements:* For master's, bachelor's degree with minimum GPA 3.0; 2 letters of recommendation; valid RN license; statement of purpose; for doctorate, GRE General Test, bachelor's degree; statement of purpose; 3 letters of recommendation; for Advanced Certificate, 2 letters of recommendation; statement of purpose; valid RN license. Additional exam requirements/recommendations for international students: recommended—TOEFL (minimum score 550 paper-based; 80 iBT), IELTS (minimum score 7). Application fee: $60 ($95 for international students). Electronic applications accepted. *Expenses:* Contact institution. *Financial support:* In 2019–20, 2 students received support, including 1 research assistantship with full tuition reimbursement available (averaging $20,250 per year), 1 teaching assistantship with full tuition reimbursement available (averaging $20,250 per year); institutionally sponsored loans, scholarships/grants, health care benefits, and unspecified assistantships also available. Financial award application deadline: 3/15; financial award applicants required to submit FAFSA. *Unit head:* Dr. Angela Amar, Dean/Professor, 702-895-3906, Fax: 702-895-4807, E-mail: nursing.dean@unlv.edu. *Application contact:* Dr. Angela Amar, Dean/Professor, 702-895-3906, Fax: 702-895-4807, E-mail: nursing.dean@unlv.edu.
Website: http://nursing.unlv.edu/

**University of New Hampshire,** Graduate School, College of Health and Human Services, Department of Nursing, Durham, NH 03824. Offers family nurse practitioner (Postbaccalaureate Certificate); nursing (MS, DNP); psychiatric mental health (Postbaccalaureate Certificate). *Accreditation:* AACN. *Program availability:* Part-time, online learning. *Students:* 46 full-time (27 women), 11 part-time (8 women); includes 6 minority (1 Black or African American, non-Hispanic/Latino; 1 Asian, non-Hispanic/Latino; 2 Hispanic/Latino; 2 Two or more races, non-Hispanic/Latino), 3 international. Average age 34. 17 applicants, 71% accepted, 10 enrolled. In 2019, 7 doctorates awarded. *Entrance requirements:* Additional exam requirements/recommendations for international students: required—TOEFL (minimum score 550 paper-based; 80 iBT), IELTS, PTE. *Application deadline:* For fall admission, 7/1 for domestic students; for spring admission, 11/1 for domestic students. Application fee: $65. Electronic applications accepted. *Financial support:* In 2019–20, 36 students received support, including 4 fellowships, 15 research assistantships, 13 teaching assistantships; Federal Work-Study, scholarships/grants, and tuition waivers (full and partial) also available. Financial award application deadline: 2/15. *Unit head:* Dr. Gene Harkless, Chair, 603-862-2285. *Application contact:* Pan DiNapoli, Administrative Assistant, 603-862-3976, E-mail: pam.dinapoli@unh.edu.
Website: https://chhs.unh.edu/nursing/graduate-program-nursing

**The University of North Carolina at Chapel Hill,** School of Nursing, Chapel Hill, NC 27599-7460. Offers advanced practice registered nurse (DNP); nursing (MSN, PhD, PMC), including administration (MSN), adult gerontology primary care nurse practitioner (MSN), clinical nurse leader (MSN), education (MSN), health care systems (PMC), informatics (MSN, PMC), nursing leadership (PMC), outcomes management (MSN), primary care family nurse practitioner (MSN), primary care pediatric nurse practitioner (MSN), psychiatric/mental health nurse practitioner (MSN, PMC). *Accreditation:* AACN; ACEN (one or more programs are accredited). *Program availability:* Part-time. *Degree requirements:* For master's, comprehensive exam, thesis; for doctorate, thesis/dissertation, 3 exams; for PMC, thesis. *Entrance requirements:* Additional exam requirements/recommendations for international students: required—TOEFL (minimum score 575 paper-based; 89 iBT), IELTS (minimum score 8). Electronic applications accepted.

**The University of North Carolina at Charlotte,** College of Health and Human Services, School of Nursing, Charlotte, NC 28223-0001. Offers adult-gerontology acute care nurse practitioner (Post-Master's Certificate); advanced clinical nursing (MSN), including adult psychiatric mental health, adult-gerontology acute care nurse practitioner, family nurse practitioner across the lifespan; family nurse practitioner

across the lifespan (Post-Master's Certificate); nurse anesthesia (MSN), including nurse anesthesia across the lifespan; nurse anesthesia across the lifespan (Post-Master's Certificate); nursing (DNP); nursing administrator (Graduate Certificate); nursing educator (Graduate Certificate); systems/population nursing (MSN), including community/public health nursing, nurse administrator, nurse educator. *Accreditation:* AACN; AANA/CANAEP. *Program availability:* Part-time, blended/hybrid learning. *Students:* 126 full-time (96 women), 142 part-time (127 women); includes 70 minority (48 Black or African American, non-Hispanic/Latino; 8 Asian, non-Hispanic/Latino; 9 Hispanic/Latino; 5 Two or more races, non-Hispanic/Latino), 1 international. Average age 35. 347 applicants, 37% accepted, 104 enrolled. In 2019, 102 master's, 10 doctorates, 10 other advanced degrees awarded. Terminal master's awarded for partial completion of doctoral program. *Entrance requirements:* For master's, GRE General Test, current unrestricted license as Registered Nurse in North Carolina; BSN from nationally-accredited program; one year of professional nursing practice in acute/critical care; minimum overall GPA of 3.0 in last degree; completion of undergraduate statistics course with minimum grade of C; statement of purpose; for doctorate, GRE or MAT, master's degree in nursing in an advanced nursing practice specialty from nationally-accredited program; minimum overall GPA of 3.5 in MSN program; current RN licensure in U.S. at time of application with eligibility for NC licensure; essay; resume/curriculum vitae; professional recommendations; clinical hours; for other advanced degree, GRE. Additional exam requirements/recommendations for international students: required—TOEFL (minimum score 557 paper-based; 83 iBT), IELTS (minimum score 6.5), TOEFL (minimum score 557 paper-based, 83 iBT) or IELTS (6.5). *Application deadline:* Applications are processed on a rolling basis. Application fee: $75. Electronic applications accepted. *Expenses:* Contact institution. *Financial support:* In 2019–20, 6 students received support, including 4 research assistantships (averaging $4,856 per year), 2 teaching assistantships (averaging $3,615 per year); career-related internships or fieldwork, institutionally sponsored loans, scholarships/grants, traineeships, and unspecified assistantships also available. Support available to part-time students. Financial award application deadline: 3/1; financial award applicants required to submit FAFSA. *Unit head:* Dr. Dena Evans, Director, 704-687-7974, E-mail: devans37@uncc.edu. *Application contact:* Kathy B. Giddings, Director of Graduate Admissions, 704-687-5503, Fax: 704-687-1668, E-mail: gradadm@uncc.edu.
Website: http://nursing.uncc.edu/

**The University of North Carolina Wilmington,** School of Nursing, Wilmington, NC 28403-3297. Offers clinical research and product development (MS); family nurse practitioner (Post-Master's Certificate); nurse educator (Post-Master's Certificate); nursing (MSN); nursing practice (DNP). *Accreditation:* AACN; ACEN. *Program availability:* Part-time, 100% online, blended/hybrid learning. *Faculty:* 51 full-time (46 women). *Students:* 171 full-time (156 women), 423 part-time (387 women); includes 117 minority (73 Black or African American, non-Hispanic/Latino; 6 American Indian or Alaska Native, non-Hispanic/Latino; 12 Asian, non-Hispanic/Latino; 16 Hispanic/Latino; 1 Native Hawaiian or other Pacific Islander, non-Hispanic/Latino; 9 Two or more races, non-Hispanic/Latino). Average age 38. 527 applicants, 57% accepted, 199 enrolled. In 2019, 149 master's, 9 doctorates awarded. *Degree requirements:* For master's, thesis or alternative, research/capstone project, presentation; for doctorate, comprehensive exam, clinical scholarly project, 1000 clinical hours. *Entrance requirements:* For master's, GRE General Test if overall Bachelor degree GPA under 3.0 (MSN degree); No tests for MCRD degree, 3 recommendations; statement of interest; resume; bachelor's degree, preferably in a life science, health care discipline, or mathematics/statistics; experience working in the biopharmaceutical or related field (MCRD degree); RN license in NC & must have 2.69 or higher Bachelor's GPA (for MSN); for doctorate, GRE General Test or MAT if Bachelor's GPA below 3.0 (FNP & Psychiatric Mental Health Nurse concentration), Varies based on concentration (Family Nurse Practitioner, Nurse Executive Leadership, Post APRN, and Psychiatric Mental Health Nurse); All require 3 professional references and an RN license. Additional exam requirements/recommendations for international students: required—TOEFL (minimum score 79 iBT), IELTS (minimum score 6.5). *Application deadline:* For fall admission, 4/15 for domestic students. Applications are processed on a rolling basis. Application fee: $75. Electronic applications accepted. *Expenses:* $324.70 per credit hour in-state (for DNP Program), $1,002.59 per credit hour out-of-state (for DNP Program), $259.01 per credit hour in-state (for the remaining online programs), $936.91 per credit hour out-of-state (for the remaining online programs), $3,728.47 entire year in-state (for main campus programs), $10,642.97 entire year out-of-state (for main campus programs). *Financial support:* Scholarships/grants available. Financial award application deadline: 1/1; financial award applicants required to submit FAFSA. *Unit head:* Dr. Linda Haddad, Director, 910-962-7410, Fax: 910-962-3723, E-mail: haddadl@uncw.edu. *Application contact:* Dr. Sarah Hubbell, MSN Graduate Coordinator, 910-962-0561, E-mail: hubbells@uncw.edu.
Website: https://uncw.edu/chhs/son/

**University of North Dakota,** Graduate School, College of Nursing and Professional Disciplines, Department of Nursing, Grand Forks, ND 58202. Offers adult-gerontological nurse practitioner (MS); advanced public health nurse (MS); family nurse practitioner (MS); nurse anesthesia (MS); nurse educator (MS); nursing (PhD, Post-Master's Certificate); nursing practice (DNP); psychiatric and mental health nurse practitioner (MS). *Accreditation:* AANA/CANAEP.

**University of Northern Colorado,** Graduate School, College of Natural and Health Sciences, School of Nursing, Greeley, CO 80639. Offers adult-gerontology acute care nurse practitioner (MSN, DNP); family nurse practitioner (MSN, DNP); nursing education (PhD); nursing practice (DNP). *Accreditation:* AACN. *Program availability:* Online learning. *Degree requirements:* For master's, comprehensive exam, thesis or alternative; for doctorate, comprehensive exam, thesis/dissertation. *Entrance requirements:* For master's and doctorate, GRE General Test, minimum GPA of 3.0 in last 60 hours, BS in nursing, 2 letters of recommendation. Electronic applications accepted.

**University of North Florida,** Brooks College of Health, School of Nursing, Jacksonville, FL 32224. Offers family nurse practitioner (Certificate); nurse anesthetist (MSN). *Accreditation:* AACN; AANA/CANAEP. *Program availability:* Part-time. *Degree requirements:* For master's, thesis optional. *Entrance requirements:* For master's, GRE General Test, minimum GPA of 3.0 in last 60 hours of course work, BSN, clinical experience, resume; for doctorate, GRE, master's degree in nursing specialty from nationally-accredited program; national certification in one of the following APRN roles: CNE, CNM, CNS, CRNA, CNP; minimum graduate GPA of 3.3; three letters of reference which address academic ability and clinical skills; active license as registered nurse or advanced practice registered nurse. Additional exam requirements/recommendations for international students: required—TOEFL (minimum score 500 paper-based; 61 iBT). Electronic applications accepted. *Expenses:* Contact institution.

**University of North Georgia,** Program in Family Nurse Practitioner, Dahlonega, GA 30597. Offers MS, Certificate. *Students:* 70 part-time (61 women); includes 17 minority (3 Black or African American, non-Hispanic/Latino; 8 Asian, non-Hispanic/Latino; 4 Hispanic/Latino; 1 Native Hawaiian or other Pacific Islander, non-Hispanic/Latino; 1 Two or more races, non-Hispanic/Latino). Average age 34. 3 applicants, 33% accepted. *Entrance requirements:* For master's, BSN with minimum GPA of 3.0, 1-2 years of post licensure clinical experience, GA registered nurse, professional resume. Additional exam requirements/recommendations for international students: required—TOEFL (minimum score 550 paper-based; 79 iBT), IELTS (minimum score 6.5). *Application deadline:* For summer admission, 2/28 for domestic students. Application fee: $40. Electronic applications accepted. *Expenses:* Contact institution. *Financial support:* Application deadline: 3/17; applicants required to submit FAFSA.
Website: https://ung.edu/graduate-admissions/programs/msn-family-nurse-practitioner.php

**University of Pennsylvania,** School of Nursing, Family Nurse Practitioner Program, Philadelphia, PA 19104. Offers MSN, Certificate. *Accreditation:* AACN. *Program availability:* Part-time. *Students:* 21 full-time (all women), 58 part-time (55 women); includes 28 minority (7 Black or African American, non-Hispanic/Latino; 14 Asian, non-Hispanic/Latino; 4 Hispanic/Latino; 3 Two or more races, non-Hispanic/Latino), 1 international. Average age 29. 39 applicants, 46% accepted, 13 enrolled. In 2019, 35 master's awarded. Application fee: $80. *Financial support:* Application deadline: 4/1.

**University of Phoenix - Hawaii Campus,** College of Nursing, Honolulu, HI 96813-3800. Offers education (MHA); family nurse practitioner (MSN); gerontology (MHA); health administration (MHA); nursing (MSN); nursing/health care education (MSN); MSN/MBA. *Program availability:* Evening/weekend. *Degree requirements:* For master's, thesis (for some programs). *Entrance requirements:* For master's, minimum undergraduate GPA of 2.5, 3 years of work experience, RN license. Additional exam requirements/recommendations for international students: required—TOEFL (minimum score 550 paper-based; 79 iBT). Electronic applications accepted.

**University of Phoenix–Online Campus,** College of Health Sciences and Nursing, Phoenix, AZ 85034-7209. Offers family nurse practitioner (Certificate); health care (Certificate); health care education (Certificate); health care informatics (Certificate); informatics (MSN); nursing (MSN); nursing and health care education (MSN); MSN/MBA; MSN/MHA. *Accreditation:* AACN. *Program availability:* Evening/weekend, online learning. *Entrance requirements:* Additional exam requirements/recommendations for international students: required—TOEFL, TOEIC (Test of English as an International Communication), Berlitz Online English Proficiency Exam, PTE, or IELTS. Electronic applications accepted. *Expenses:* Contact institution.

**University of Phoenix - Phoenix Campus,** College of Health Sciences and Nursing, Tempe, AZ 85282-2371. Offers family nurse practitioner (MSN, Certificate); gerontology health care (Certificate); health care education (MSN, Certificate); health care informatics (Certificate); informatics (MSN); nursing (MSN); MSN/MHA. *Program availability:* Evening/weekend, online learning. *Entrance requirements:* Additional exam requirements/recommendations for international students: required—TOEFL, TOEIC (Test of English as an International Communication), Berlitz Online English Proficiency Exam, PTE, or IELTS. Electronic applications accepted. *Expenses:* Contact institution.

**University of Phoenix - Sacramento Valley Campus,** College of Nursing, Sacramento, CA 95833-4334. Offers family nurse practitioner (MSN); health administration (MHA); health care education (MSN); nursing (MSN); MSN/MBA. *Program availability:* Evening/weekend. *Degree requirements:* For master's, thesis (for some programs). *Entrance requirements:* For master's, RN license, minimum undergraduate GPA of 2.5, 3 years work experience. Additional exam requirements/recommendations for international students: required—TOEFL (minimum score 550 paper-based; 79 iBT). Electronic applications accepted.

**University of Pittsburgh,** School of Nursing, Nurse Practitioner Program, Pittsburgh, PA 15261. Offers nurse practitioner (DNP), including adult gerontology acute care, adult gerontology primary care, family (individual across the lifespan), neonatal, pediatric primary care, psychiatric mental health. *Accreditation:* AACN. *Program availability:* Part-time. *Faculty:* 17 full-time (13 women), 3 part-time/adjunct (2 women). *Students:* 48 full-time (44 women), 31 part-time (27 women); includes 7 minority (2 Black or African American, non-Hispanic/Latino; 5 Asian, non-Hispanic/Latino). Average age 30. 70 applicants, 51% accepted, 26 enrolled. In 2019, 7 master's, 18 doctorates awarded. *Degree requirements:* For master's, comprehensive exam, thesis optional; for doctorate, comprehensive exam, thesis/dissertation, capstone project required. *Entrance requirements:* For doctorate, GRE (may be waived if GPA is 3.5 or greater), BSN, RN license, minimum GPA of 3.5, 3 letters of recommendation, resume/essay, course work in statistics, clinical experience for Neonatal. Additional exam requirements/recommendations for international students: required—TOEFL (minimum score 600 paper-based; 100 iBT), IELTS (minimum score 7), TOEFL (minimum score 600 paper-based; 100 IBT) or IELTS (minimum score 7.0). *Application deadline:* For fall admission, 6/1 priority date for domestic students, 2/15 priority date for international students. Application fee: $50. Electronic applications accepted. *Expenses:* $13,795 per term full-time resident tuition, $475 per term full-time resident fees, $1,122 per credit part-time resident tuition, $295 per term part-time resident fees, $16,474 per term full-time non-resident tuition, $475 per term full-time non-resident fees, $1,345 per credit part-time non-resident tuition, $295 per term part-time non-resident fees. *Financial support:* In 2019–20, 48 students received support, including 12 fellowships (averaging $10,969 per year), 21 teaching assistantships (averaging $12,964 per year); scholarships/grants, unspecified assistantships, and Matching Funds also available. Financial award application deadline: 6/1; financial award applicants required to submit FAFSA. *Unit head:* Dr. Sandra Engberg, Associate Dean for Clinical Education, 412-624-3835, Fax: 412-624-8521, E-mail: sje1@pitt.edu. *Application contact:* Laurie Lapsley, Graduate Administrator, 412-624-9670, Fax: 412-624-2409, E-mail: lapsleyl@pitt.edu.
Website: http://www.nursing.pitt.edu

**University of Portland,** School of Nursing, Portland, OR 97203-5798. Offers clinical nurse leader (MS); family nurse practitioner (DNP); nurse educator (MS). *Accreditation:* AACN. *Program availability:* Part-time, evening/weekend. *Entrance requirements:* For doctorate, RN license, BSN or MSN, 3 letters of recommendation, resume, writing sample, official transcripts. Additional exam requirements/recommendations for international students: required—TOEFL (minimum score 100 iBT), IELTS (minimum score 7.5). Electronic applications accepted. *Expenses:* Contact institution.

**University of Puerto Rico - Medical Sciences Campus,** School of Nursing, San Juan, PR 00936-5067. Offers adult and elderly nursing (MSN); child and adolescent nursing (MSN); critical care nursing (MSN); family and community nursing (MSN); family nurse practitioner (MSN); maternity nursing (MSN); mental health and psychiatric nursing (MSN). *Accreditation:* AACN; AANA/CANAEP. *Entrance requirements:* For master's, GRE or EXADEP, interview, Puerto Rico RN license or professional license for international students, general and specific point average, article analysis. Electronic applications accepted.

**University of Rhode Island,** Graduate School, College of Nursing, Kingston, RI 02881. Offers acute care nurse practitioner (adult-gerontology focus) (Post Master's Certificate); adult gerontology nurse practitioner/clinical nurse specialist (Post Master's Certificate); adult-gerontological acute care nurse practitioner (MS); adult-gerontological nurse practitioner/clinical nurse specialist (MS); family nurse practitioner (MS, Post Master's Certificate); nursing (DNP, PhD); nursing education (MS, Post Master's Certificate). *Accreditation:* AACN; ACNM/ACME (one or more programs are accredited). *Program availability:* Part-time, evening/weekend, 100% online, blended/hybrid learning. *Faculty:* 27 full-time (26 women). *Students:* 51 full-time (47 women), 72 part-time (65 women); includes 21 minority (9 Black or African American, non-Hispanic/Latino; 5 Asian, non-

Hispanic/Latino; 4 Hispanic/Latino; 2 Native Hawaiian or other Pacific Islander, non-Hispanic/Latino; 1 Two or more races, non-Hispanic/Latino), 6 international. 32 applicants, 88% accepted, 21 enrolled. In 2019, 34 master's, 9 doctorates, 1 other advanced degree awarded. *Entrance requirements:* For master's, GRE or MAT, 2 letters of recommendation, scholarly papers; for doctorate, GRE, 3 letters of recommendation, scholarly papers. Additional exam requirements/recommendations for international students: required—TOEFL. *Application deadline:* For fall admission, 2/15 for domestic students, 2/1 for international students; for spring admission, 10/15 for domestic students, 7/15 for international students. Application fee: $65. Electronic applications accepted. *Expenses: Tuition, area resident:* Full-time $13,734; part-time $763 per credit. Tuition, state resident: full-time $13,734; part-time $763 per credit. Tuition, nonresident: full-time $26,512; part-time $1473 per credit. *International tuition:* $26,512 full-time. *Required fees:* $1780; $52 per credit. $35 per term. One-time fee: $165. *Financial support:* In 2019–20, 7 teaching assistantships with tuition reimbursements (averaging $13,376 per year) were awarded. Financial award application deadline: 2/1; financial award applicants required to submit FAFSA. *Unit head:* Dr. Barbara Wolfe, Dean, 401-874-5324, E-mail: bwolfe@uri.edu. *Application contact:* Dr. Denise Coppa, Associate Professor/Interim Associate Dean for Graduate Programs, 401-874-5036, E-mail: dcoppa@uri.edu.
Website: http://www.uri.edu/nursing/

**University of Rochester,** School of Nursing, Rochester, NY 14642. Offers adult gerontological acute care nurse practitioner (MS); adult gerontological primary care nurse practitioner (MS); clinical nurse leader (MS); family nurse practitioner (MS); family psychiatric mental health nurse practitioner (MS); health care organization management and leadership (MS); nursing (DNP); nursing and health science (PhD); nursing education (MS); pediatric nurse practitioner (MS); pediatric nurse practitioner/neonatal nurse practitioner (MS). *Accreditation:* AACN. *Program availability:* Part-time, 100% online, blended/hybrid learning. Terminal master's awarded for partial completion of doctoral program. *Degree requirements:* For master's, comprehensive exam; for doctorate, thesis/dissertation. *Entrance requirements:* For master's, BS in nursing, RN license; for doctorate, GRE General Test (for PhD), B.S. degree, RN license most programs. Additional exam requirements/recommendations for international students: required—TOEFL (minimum score 560 paper-based; 88 iBT), TOEFL (minimum score 560 paper-based; 88 iBT) or IELTS (minimum score 6.5) recommended. Electronic applications accepted. *Expenses:* Contact institution.

**University of Saint Francis,** Graduate School, Division of Nursing, Fort Wayne, IN 46808. Offers family nurse practitioner (MSN, Post Master's Certificate); nurse anesthesia (DNP); nursing practice (DNP). *Accreditation:* AACN. *Program availability:* Part-time, blended/hybrid learning. *Faculty:* 12 full-time (10 women), 3 part-time/adjunct (2 women). *Students:* 67 full-time (45 women), 70 part-time (64 women); includes 22 minority (13 Black or African American, non-Hispanic/Latino; 1 Asian, non-Hispanic/Latino; 7 Hispanic/Latino; 1 Two or more races, non-Hispanic/Latino). Average age 32. 44 applicants, 98% accepted, 34 enrolled. In 2019, 37 master's, 1 other advanced degree awarded. *Entrance requirements:* Additional exam requirements/recommendations for international students: required—TOEFL (minimum score 550 paper-based), IELTS (minimum score 6.5). *Application deadline:* Applications are processed on a rolling basis. Electronic applications accepted. *Expenses:* MSN - $700 per semester hour; DNP - $1,055 per semester hour. *Financial support:* Applicants required to submit FAFSA. *Unit head:* Dr. Wendy Clark, Graduate Nursing Program Director, 260-399-7700 Ext. 8534, E-mail: wclark@sf.edu. *Application contact:* Kyle Richardson, Associate Director of Enrollment Management, 260-399-7700 Ext. 6310, Fax: 260-399-8152, E-mail: krichardson@sf.edu.

**University of St. Francis,** Leach College of Nursing, Joliet, IL 60435-6169. Offers family nurse practitioner (MSN, Post-Master's Certificate); nursing administration (MSN); nursing education (MSN); nursing practice (DNP); psychology/mental health nurse practitioner (MSN, Post-Master's Certificate); teaching in nursing (Certificate). *Accreditation:* AACN. *Program availability:* Part-time, evening/weekend, 100% online. *Degree requirements:* For master's, comprehensive exam. *Entrance requirements:* Additional exam requirements/recommendations for international students: required—TOEFL (minimum score 550 paper-based; 79 iBT), IELTS (minimum score 6). Electronic applications accepted. Application fee is waived when completed online. *Expenses:* Contact institution.

**University of Saint Joseph,** Department of Nursing, West Hartford, CT 06117-2700. Offers family nurse practitioner (MS); nurse educator (MS); nursing practice (DNP); psychiatric/mental health nurse practitioner (MS). *Accreditation:* AACN. *Program availability:* Part-time, evening/weekend. *Degree requirements:* For master's, thesis. *Entrance requirements:* For master's, 2 letters of recommendation. Electronic applications accepted. Application fee is waived when completed online.

**University of San Diego,** Hahn School of Nursing and Health Science, San Diego, CA 92110-2492. Offers adult-gerontology clinical nurse specialist (MSN); adult-gerontology nurse practitioner/family nurse practitioner (MSN); clinical nurse leader (MSN); executive nurse leader (MSN); family nurse practitioner (MSN); healthcare informatics (MS); master's entry program in clinical nursing (for non-rns) (MSN); nursing (PhD); nursing informatics (MSN); nursing practice (DNP); psychiatric-mental health nurse practitioner (MSN). *Accreditation:* AACN. *Program availability:* Part-time, evening/weekend. *Faculty:* 28 full-time (23 women), 43 part-time/adjunct (32 women). *Students:* 252 full-time (202 women), 288 part-time (227 women); includes 261 minority (53 Black or African American, non-Hispanic/Latino; 2 American Indian or Alaska Native, non-Hispanic/Latino; 106 Asian, non-Hispanic/Latino; 76 Hispanic/Latino; 24 Two or more races, non-Hispanic/Latino), 24 international. Average age 34. In 2019, 174 master's, 47 doctorates awarded. *Degree requirements:* For doctorate, thesis/dissertation (for some programs), residency (DNP). *Entrance requirements:* For master's, GRE General Test (for entry-level nursing), BSN, current California RN licensure (except for entry-level nursing), minimum GPA of 3.0; for doctorate, minimum GPA of 3.5, MSN, current California RN licensure. Additional exam requirements/recommendations for international students: required—TOEFL (minimum score 580 paper-based; 83 iBT), TWE. *Application deadline:* Applications are processed on a rolling basis. Application fee: $55. Electronic applications accepted. *Financial support:* In 2019–20, 284 students received support. Institutionally sponsored loans, scholarships/grants, and traineeships available. Support available to part-time students. Financial award application deadline: 4/1; financial award applicants required to submit FAFSA. *Unit head:* Dr. Jane Georges, Dean, Hahn School of Nursing and Health Science, 619-260-4550, Fax: 619-260-6814, E-mail: nursing@sandiego.edu. *Application contact:* Erika Garwood, Associate Director of Graduate Admissions, 619-260-4524, Fax: 619-260-4158, E-mail: grads@sandiego.edu.
Website: http://www.sandiego.edu/nursing/

**The University of Scranton,** Panuska College of Professional Studies, Department of Nursing, Scranton, PA 18510-4595. Offers family nurse practitioner (MSN, PMC); nurse anesthesia (MSN, PMC); nursing leadership (DNP). *Accreditation:* AACN; AANA/CANAEP. *Program availability:* Part-time, evening/weekend. *Degree requirements:* For master's, comprehensive exam (for some programs), thesis (for some programs), capstone experience. *Entrance requirements:* For master's, minimum GPA of 3.0, three letters of reference; for doctorate, RN licensure and evidence of certification in advanced

practice nursing specialty. Additional exam requirements/recommendations for international students: required—TOEFL (minimum score 500 paper-based; 80 iBT), IELTS (minimum score 6.5). Electronic applications accepted.

**University of South Carolina,** The Graduate School, College of Nursing, Program in Health Nursing, Columbia, SC 29208. Offers adult nurse practitioner (MSN); community/public health clinical nurse specialist (MSN); family nurse practitioner (MSN); pediatric nurse practitioner (MSN). *Accreditation:* AACN. *Program availability:* Part-time. *Degree requirements:* For master's, thesis or alternative. *Entrance requirements:* For master's, GRE General Test or MAT, BS in nursing, nursing license. Additional exam requirements/recommendations for international students: required—TOEFL (minimum score 570 paper-based). Electronic applications accepted.

**University of Southern Indiana,** Graduate Studies, College of Nursing and Health Professions, Program in Nursing, Evansville, IN 47712-3590. Offers adult-gerontology acute care nurse practitioner (MSN, PMC); adult-gerontology clinical nurse specialist (MSN, PMC); adult-gerontology primary care nurse practitioner (MSN, PMC); advanced nursing practice (DNP); family nurse practitioner (MSN, PMC); nursing education (MSN, PMC); nursing management and leadership (MSN, PMC); organizational and systems leadership (DNP); psychiatric mental health nurse practitioner (MSN, PMC). *Accreditation:* AACN. *Program availability:* Part-time, online learning. *Entrance requirements:* For master's, BSN from nationally-accredited school; minimum cumulative GPA of 3.0; satisfactory completion of a course in undergraduate statistics (minimum grade C); one year of full-time experience or 2,000 hours of clinical practice as an RN (recommended); unencumbered U.S. RN license; for doctorate, minimum GPA of 3.0, completion of graduate research course with minimum B grade, unencumbered RN license, resume/curriculum vitae, three professional references, 1-2 page narrative of practice experience and professional goals, Capstone Project Information form. Additional exam requirements/recommendations for international students: required—TOEFL (minimum score 550 paper-based; 79 iBT), IELTS (minimum score 6). Electronic applications accepted. *Expenses:* Contact institution.

**University of Southern Maine,** College of Science, Technology, and Health, School of Nursing, Portland, ME 04103. Offers adult-gerontology primary care nurse practitioner (MS, PMC); education (MS); family nurse practitioner (MS, PMC); family psychiatric/mental health nurse practitioner (MS); management (MS); nursing (CAS, CGS); psychiatric-mental health nurse practitioner (PMC). *Accreditation:* AACN. *Program availability:* Part-time. *Degree requirements:* For master's, thesis optional. *Entrance requirements:* For master's, GRE General Test or MAT, minimum GPA of 3.0; for doctorate, GRE. Additional exam requirements/recommendations for international students: required—TOEFL (minimum score 550 paper-based). Electronic applications accepted. *Expenses: Tuition, area resident:* Full-time $864; part-time $432 per credit hour. Tuition, state resident: full-time $864; part-time $432 per credit hour. Tuition, nonresident: full-time $2372; part-time $1186 per credit hour. *Required fees:* $141; $108 per credit hour. Tuition and fees vary according to course load.

**University of South Florida,** College of Nursing, Tampa, FL 33612. Offers nurse anesthesia (DNP); nursing (MS, DNP), including adult-gerontology acute care nursing, adult-gerontology primary care nursing, family health nursing, nurse anesthesia (MS), nursing education (MS), occupational health nursing/adult-gerontology primary care nursing, oncology nursing/adult-gerontology primary care nursing (DNP), pediatric health nursing; nursing education (Post Master's Certificate); nursing science (PhD); simulation based academic fellowship in advanced pain management (Graduate Certificate). *Accreditation:* AACN; AANA/CANAEP. *Program availability:* Part-time. *Faculty:* 34 full-time (28 women), 2 part-time/adjunct (1 woman). *Students:* 265 full-time (207 women), 687 part-time (594 women); includes 343 minority (113 Black or African American, non-Hispanic/Latino; 1 American Indian or Alaska Native, non-Hispanic/Latino; 60 Asian, non-Hispanic/Latino; 141 Hispanic/Latino; 1 Native Hawaiian or other Pacific Islander, non-Hispanic/Latino; 27 Two or more races, non-Hispanic/Latino), 2 international. Average age 33. 955 applicants, 44% accepted, 343 enrolled. In 2019, 281 master's, 80 doctorates awarded. *Degree requirements:* For master's, comprehensive exam, thesis optional; for doctorate, comprehensive exam, thesis/dissertation (for some programs). *Entrance requirements:* For master's, GRE General Test, bachelor's in nursing or RN with Bachelor's in relevant field; current license as Registered Nurse; resume or CV; interview; pre-reqs may be required; for doctorate, GRE General Test (recommended), bachelor's degree in nursing from ACEN or CCNE regionally-accredited institution with minimum GPA of 3.0 in all coursework or in all upper-division coursework; current license as Registered Nurse in Florida; undergraduate statistics course with minimum B grade; 3 letters of recommendation; statement of goals; resume; interview. Additional exam requirements/recommendations for international students: required—TOEFL (minimum score 550 paper-based; 79 iBT). *Application deadline:* For fall admission, 12/15 for domestic and international students; for spring admission, 10/1 for domestic students, 9/15 for international students. Application fee: $30. Electronic applications accepted. *Financial support:* In 2019–20, 181 students received support, including 7 research assistantships with tuition reimbursements available (averaging $18,935 per year), 29 teaching assistantships with tuition reimbursements available (averaging $30,814 per year); tuition waivers (partial) and unspecified assistantships also available. Financial award application deadline: 2/1; financial award applicants required to submit FAFSA. *Unit head:* Dr. Victoria Rich, Dean, College of Nursing, 813-974-8939, Fax: 813-974-5418, E-mail: victoriarich@health.usf.edu. *Application contact:* Dr. Denise Maguire, Vice Dean, Graduate Programs, 813-396-9962, E-mail: dmaguire@health.usf.edu.
Website: http://health.usf.edu/nursing/index.htm

**The University of Tampa,** Program in Nursing, Tampa, FL 33606-1490. Offers adult nursing practitioner (MSN); family nursing practitioner (MSN); nursing (MS). *Accreditation:* ACEN. *Program availability:* Part-time, evening/weekend. *Degree requirements:* For master's, comprehensive exam, oral exam, practicum. *Entrance requirements:* For master's, GMAT or GRE, current licensure as registered nurse in state of Florida; minimum GPA of 3.0 in last 60 credit hours; minimum of one year of direct patient care experience within the past five years (recommended). Additional exam requirements/recommendations for international students: required—TOEFL (minimum score 577 paper-based; 90 iBT), IELTS (minimum score 7.5). Electronic applications accepted. *Expenses:* Contact institution.

**The University of Tennessee at Chattanooga,** School of Nursing, Chattanooga, TN 37403. Offers certified nurse anesthetist (Post-Master's Certificate); family nurse practitioner (MSN, Post-Master's Certificate); gerontology acute care (MSN, Post-Master's Certificate); nurse anesthesia (MSN); nurse education (Post-Master's Certificate); nursing (DNP). *Accreditation:* AACN; AANA/CANAEP (one or more programs are accredited). *Program availability:* 100% online. *Faculty:* 32 full-time (29 women), 14 part-time/adjunct (10 women). *Students:* 78 full-time (49 women), 51 part-time (43 women); includes 24 minority (11 Black or African American, non-Hispanic/Latino; 2 American Indian or Alaska Native, non-Hispanic/Latino; 4 Asian, non-Hispanic/Latino; 5 Hispanic/Latino; 2 Two or more races, non-Hispanic/Latino). Average age 34. 50 applicants, 100% accepted, 46 enrolled. In 2019, 38 master's, 16 doctorates, 2 other advanced degrees awarded. *Degree requirements:* For master's, thesis optional, practicum; for doctorate, professional project; for Post-Master's Certificate, practicum. *Entrance requirements:* For master's, GRE General Test, MAT, BSN, minimum GPA of

3.0, eligibility for Tennessee RN license, 1 year of direct patient care experience; for doctorate, GRE General Test or MAT (if applicant does not have MSN), minimum GPA of 3.0 for highest degree earned; for Post-Master's Certificate, GRE General Test, MAT, MSN, minimum GPA of 3.0, eligibility for Tennessee RN license, one year of direct patient care experience. Additional exam requirements/recommendations for international students: required—TOEFL (minimum score 550 paper-based; 79 iBT), IELTS (minimum score 6). *Application deadline:* For fall admission, 6/15 priority date for domestic students, 7/1 for international students; for spring admission, 11/1 priority date for domestic students, 11/1 for international students. Applications are processed on a rolling basis. Application fee: $35 ($40 for international students). Electronic applications accepted. *Financial support:* Teaching assistantships, career-related internships or fieldwork, and scholarships/grants available. Support available to part-time students. Financial award application deadline: 7/1; financial award applicants required to submit FAFSA. *Unit head:* Dr. Chris Smith, Director, 423-425-4665, Fax: 423-425-4668, E-mail: chris-smith@utc.edu. *Application contact:* Dr. Joanne Romagni, Dean of the Graduate School, 423-425-4478, Fax: 423-425-5223, E-mail: joanne-romagni@utc.edu.
Website: http://www.utc.edu/nursing/

**The University of Tennessee Health Science Center,** College of Nursing, Memphis, TN 38163. Offers adult-gerontology acute care nurse practitioner (Post Master's Certificate); advance practice nursing (DNP); family nurse practitioner (Post-Doctoral Certificate); pediatric acute care nurse practitioner (Post-Doctoral Certificate); pediatric primary care nurse practitioner (Post-Doctoral Certificate); psychiatric/mental health nurse practitioner (Post-Doctoral Certificate); registered nurse first assistant (Certificate). *Accreditation:* AACN; AANA/CANAEP. *Program availability:* Part-time, blended/hybrid learning. *Faculty:* 62 full-time (55 women), 7 part-time/adjunct (2 women). *Students:* 226 full-time (187 women), 28 part-time (26 women); includes 80 minority (63 Black or African American, non-Hispanic/Latino; 15 Asian, non-Hispanic/Latino; 2 Hispanic/Latino). Average age 33. 652 applicants, 20% accepted, 104 enrolled. In 2019, 86 doctorates, 2 Certificates awarded. *Degree requirements:* For doctorate, project. *Entrance requirements:* For doctorate, RN license, minimum GPA of 3.0; http://www.uthsc.edu/nursing/dnp-admission-requirements.php; for other advanced degree, MSN, APN license, minimum GPA of 3.0; http://www.uthsc.edu/nursing/dnp-admission-requirements.php. Additional exam requirements/recommendations for international students: required—TOEFL (minimum score 550 paper-based; 80 iBT). *Application deadline:* For fall admission, 1/15 for domestic students; for spring admission, 8/15 for domestic students. Application fee: $70. Electronic applications accepted. *Expenses:* $5400 tuition, $450 fees, $110 loan fees, $5790 room/board, $2137 books/supplies, $1260 transportation, $2339 miscellaneous, $450 out-of-state tuition surcharge. *Financial support:* In 2019–20, 112 students received support, including 16 research assistantships (averaging $229,578 per year); Federal Work-Study, institutionally sponsored loans, scholarships/grants, and tuition waivers (partial) also available. Financial award application deadline: 3/15; financial award applicants required to submit FAFSA. *Unit head:* Dr. Wendy Likes, Dean, 901-448-6135, Fax: 901-448-4121, E-mail: wlikes@uthsc.edu. *Application contact:* Glynis Blackard, Assistant Dean for Student Affairs, 901-448-6139, Fax: 901-448-4121, E-mail: gblackar@uthsc.edu.
Website: http://uthsc.edu/nursing/

**The University of Texas at Arlington,** Graduate School, College of Nursing and Health Innovation, Arlington, TX 76019. Offers athletic training (MS); exercise science (MS); kinesiology (PhD); nurse practitioner (MSN); nursing (PhD); nursing administration (MSN); nursing education (MSN); nursing practice (DNP). *Accreditation:* AACN. *Program availability:* Part-time, evening/weekend, online learning. *Degree requirements:* For master's, practicum course; for doctorate, comprehensive exam (for some programs), thesis/dissertation (for some programs), proposal defense dissertation (for PhD); scholarship project (for DNP). *Entrance requirements:* For master's, GRE General Test if GPA less than 3.0, minimum GPA of 3.0, Texas nursing license, minimum C grade in undergraduate statistics course; for doctorate, GRE General Test (waived for MSN-to-PhD applicants), minimum undergraduate, graduate and statistics GPA of 3.0; Texas RN license; interview; written statement of goals. Additional exam requirements/recommendations for international students: required—TOEFL (minimum score 550 paper-based), IELTS (minimum score 7).

**The University of Texas at Austin,** Graduate School, School of Nursing, Austin, TX 78712-1111. Offers adult - gerontology clinical nurse specialist (MSN); child health (MSN), including administration, public health nursing, teaching; family nurse practitioner (MSN); family psychiatric/mental health nurse practitioner (MSN); holistic adult health (MSN), including administration, teaching; maternity (MSN), including administration, public health nursing, teaching; nursing (PhD); nursing administration and healthcare systems management (MSN); nursing practice (DNP); pediatric nurse practitioner (MSN); public health nursing (MSN). *Accreditation:* AACN. *Program availability:* Part-time. *Degree requirements:* For master's, thesis optional; for doctorate, thesis/dissertation. *Entrance requirements:* For master's and doctorate, GRE General Test. Additional exam requirements/recommendations for international students: required—TOEFL (minimum score 550 paper-based). Electronic applications accepted.

**The University of Texas at El Paso,** Graduate School, School of Nursing, El Paso, TX 79968-0001. Offers family nurse practitioner (MSN); health care leadership and management (Certificate); interdisciplinary health sciences (PhD); nursing (DNP); nursing education (MSN, Certificate); nursing systems management (MSN). *Accreditation:* AACN. *Program availability:* Online learning. *Degree requirements:* For master's, thesis optional; for doctorate, thesis/dissertation. *Entrance requirements:* For master's, minimum GPA of 3.0, resume; for doctorate, GRE, letters of reference, relevant personal/professional experience; master's degree in nursing (for DNP); for Certificate, bachelor's degree in nursing. Additional exam requirements/recommendations for international students: required—TOEFL; recommended—IELTS. Electronic applications accepted.

**The University of Texas at Tyler,** College of Nursing and Health Sciences, School of Nursing, Tyler, TX 75799. Offers nurse practitioner (MSN); nursing (PhD); nursing administration (MSN); nursing education (MSN); MSN/MBA. *Accreditation:* AACN. *Program availability:* Part-time, evening/weekend, online learning. *Faculty:* 27 full-time (all women), 4 part-time/adjunct (all women). *Students:* 101 full-time (83 women), 351 part-time (303 women); includes 149 minority (53 Black or African American, non-Hispanic/Latino; 1 American Indian or Alaska Native, non-Hispanic/Latino; 27 Asian, non-Hispanic/Latino; 51 Hispanic/Latino; 17 Two or more races, non-Hispanic/Latino), 5 international. Average age 37. 128 applicants, 67% accepted, 81 enrolled. In 2019, 86 master's, 21 doctorates awarded. *Degree requirements:* For master's, comprehensive exam (for some programs), thesis (for some programs); for doctorate, thesis/dissertation. *Entrance requirements:* For master's, GRE General Test or MAT, GMAT, minimum undergraduate GPA of 3.0, course work in statistics, RN license, BSN. Additional exam requirements/recommendations for international students: required—TOEFL. *Application deadline:* For fall admission, 8/17 priority date for domestic students, 7/1 priority date for international students; for spring admission, 12/21 priority date for domestic students, 11/1 priority date for international students. Applications are processed on a rolling basis. Application fee: $25 ($50 for international students). Electronic applications accepted. *Financial support:* In 2019–20, 15 students received support, including 1 fellowship (averaging $10,000 per year), 3 research assistantships (averaging $2,200 per year); institutionally sponsored loans and scholarships/grants also available. Financial award application deadline: 7/1; financial award applicants required to submit FAFSA. *Unit head:* Dr. Barbara Haas, Associate Dean, 903-566-7021, E-mail: bhaas@uttyler.edu. *Application contact:* Dr. Barbara Haas, Associate Dean, 903-566-7021, E-mail: bhaas@uttyler.edu.
Website: https://www.uttyler.edu/nursing/

**The University of Texas Health Science Center at San Antonio,** School of Nursing, San Antonio, TX 78229-3900. Offers administrative management (MSN); adult-gerontology acute care nurse practitioner (PGC); advanced practice leadership (DNP); clinical nurse leader (MSN); executive administrative management (DNP); family nurse practitioner (MSN, PGC); nursing (MSN, PhD); nursing education (MSN, PGC); pediatric nurse practitioner primary care (PGC); psychiatric mental health nurse practitioner (PGC); public health nurse leader (DNP). *Accreditation:* AACN. *Program availability:* Part-time. Terminal master's awarded for partial completion of doctoral program. *Degree requirements:* For master's, thesis optional; for doctorate, comprehensive exam, thesis/dissertation.

**The University of Toledo,** College of Graduate Studies, College of Nursing, Department of Population and Community Care, Toledo, OH 43606-3390. Offers clinical nurse leader (MSN); family nurse practitioner (MSN, Certificate); nurse educator (MSN, Certificate); pediatric nurse practitioner (MSN, Certificate). *Program availability:* Part-time. *Degree requirements:* For master's, thesis or alternative. *Entrance requirements:* For master's, GRE, BS in nursing, minimum undergraduate GPA of 3.0, statement of purpose, three letters of recommendation, transcripts from all prior institutions attended, Nursing CAS application, UT supplemental application; for Certificate, BS in nursing, minimum undergraduate GPA of 3.0, statement of purpose, three letters of recommendation, transcripts from all prior institutions attended. Additional exam requirements/recommendations for international students: required—TOEFL (minimum score 550 paper-based; 80 iBT). Electronic applications accepted.

**The University of Tulsa,** Graduate School, Oxley College of Health Sciences, School of Nursing, Tulsa, OK 74104-3189. Offers adult-gerontology acute care nurse practitioner (DNP); family nurse practitioner (DNP). *Degree requirements:* For doctorate, comprehensive exam, thesis/dissertation. *Entrance requirements:* Additional exam requirements/recommendations for international students: required—TOEFL (minimum score 550 paper-based; 91 iBT), IELTS (minimum score 6.5). Electronic applications accepted. *Expenses:* Contact institution.

**University of Victoria,** Faculty of Graduate Studies, Faculty of Human and Social Development, School of Nursing, Victoria, BC V8W 2Y2, Canada. Offers advanced nursing practice (advanced practice leadership option) (MN); advanced nursing practice (nurse educator option) (MN); advanced nursing practice (nurse practitioner option) (MN); nursing (PhD). *Program availability:* Part-time, online learning. *Entrance requirements:* Additional exam requirements/recommendations for international students: required—TOEFL (minimum score 575 paper-based), IELTS (minimum score 7). Electronic applications accepted.

**University of Wisconsin–Eau Claire,** College of Nursing and Health Sciences, Program in Nursing, Eau Claire, WI 54702-4004. Offers adult-gerontological administration (DNP); adult-gerontological clinical nurse specialist (DNP); adult-gerontological education (MSN); adult-gerontological primary care nurse practitioner (DNP); family health administration (DNP); family health in education (MSN); family health nurse practitioner (DNP); nursing (MSN); nursing practice (DNP). *Accreditation:* AACN. *Program availability:* Part-time. Terminal master's awarded for partial completion of doctoral program. *Degree requirements:* For master's, thesis optional, 500-600 hours clinical practicum, oral and written exams. *Entrance requirements:* For master's, Wisconsin RN license, minimum GPA of 3.0, undergraduate statistics, course work in health assessment. Additional exam requirements/recommendations for international students: required—TOEFL (minimum score 79 iBT). *Expenses:* Contact institution.

**University of Wisconsin–Milwaukee,** Graduate School, College of Nursing, Milwaukee, WI 53201. Offers clinical nurse specialist (Graduate Certificate); family nurse practitioner (Graduate Certificate); nursing (MN, DNP, PhD); sustainable peacebuilding (MSP). *Accreditation:* AACN. *Program availability:* Part-time. *Entrance requirements:* For master's, GRE General Test or MAT, autobiographical sketch; for doctorate, GRE, minimum GPA of 3.2. Additional exam requirements/recommendations for international students: required—TOEFL (minimum score 550 paper-based; 79 iBT), IELTS (minimum score 6.5). Electronic applications accepted.

**See Display on page 9999 and Close-Up on page 9999.**

**University of Wisconsin–Oshkosh,** Graduate Studies, College of Nursing, Oshkosh, WI 54901. Offers adult health and illness (MSN); family nurse practitioner (MSN). *Accreditation:* AACN; AANA/CANAEP. *Program availability:* Part-time. *Degree requirements:* For master's, thesis or alternative, clinical paper. *Entrance requirements:* For master's, RN license, BSN, previous course work in statistics and health assessment, minimum undergraduate GPA of 3.0, letters of recommendation. Additional exam requirements/recommendations for international students: required—TOEFL (minimum score 550 paper-based; 79 iBT). Electronic applications accepted.

**Ursuline College,** School of Graduate and Professional Studies, Programs in Nursing, Pepper Pike, OH 44124-4398. Offers acute-care nurse practitioner (MSN); adult nurse practitioner (MSN); adult-gerontology acute care nurse practitioner (MSN); adult-gerontology clinical nurse specialist (MSN); adult-gerontology nurse practitioner (MSN); care management (MSN); clinical nurse specialist (MSN); family nurse practitioner (MSN); nursing (DNP); nursing education (MSN); palliative care (MSN). *Accreditation:* AACN. *Program availability:* Part-time, 100% online. *Faculty:* 6 full-time (all women), 25 part-time/adjunct (19 women). *Students:* 106 full-time (99 women), 117 part-time (105 women); includes 71 minority (46 Black or African American, non-Hispanic/Latino; 2 American Indian or Alaska Native, non-Hispanic/Latino; 12 Asian, non-Hispanic/Latino; 6 Hispanic/Latino; 5 Two or more races, non-Hispanic/Latino). Average age 38. 265 applicants, 98% accepted, 61 enrolled. In 2019, 68 master's, 2 doctorates awarded. *Degree requirements:* For master's, comprehensive exam; for doctorate, thesis/dissertation. *Entrance requirements:* For master's, minimum undergraduate GPA of 3.0, bachelor's degree in nursing, eligibility for or current Ohio RN license. Additional exam requirements/recommendations for international students: required—TOEFL (minimum score 500 paper-based). *Application deadline:* For fall admission, 8/1 priority date for domestic students. Applications are processed on a rolling basis. Application fee: $25. Electronic applications accepted. *Expenses: Tuition:* Full-time $18,784; part-time $1174 per credit hour. *Required fees:* $320; $240 per unit. One-time fee: $100. Tuition and fees vary according to course level and program. *Financial support:* In 2019–20, 10 students received support. Scholarships/grants, tuition waivers (partial), and College Free Credit available. Financial award application deadline: 3/1; financial award applicants required to submit FAFSA. *Unit head:* Dr. Janet Baker, Associate Dean of Graduate Nursing, 440-864-8172, Fax: 440-684-6053, E-mail: jbaker@ursuline.edu. *Application contact:* Melanie Steele, Director, Graduate Admission, 440-646-8119, Fax: 440-684-6138, E-mail: graduateadmissions@ursuline.edu.

**Valdosta State University,** College of Nursing and Health Sciences, Valdosta, GA 31698. Offers adult gerontology nurse practitioner (MSN); exercise physiology (MS);

family nurse practitioner (MSN); family psychiatric mental health nurse practitioner (MSN). *Accreditation:* AACN. *Program availability:* Part-time, online learning. *Degree requirements:* For master's, thesis (for some programs), comprehensive written and/or oral exams. *Entrance requirements:* For master's, minimum GPA of 2.8. Additional exam requirements/recommendations for international students: required—TOEFL (minimum score 523 paper-based). Electronic applications accepted.

**Villanova University,** M. Louise Fitzpatrick College of Nursing, Villanova, PA 19085. Offers adult-gerontology primary care nurse practitioner (MSN, Post Master's Certificate); family primary care nurse practitioner (MSN, Post Master's Certificate); nurse anesthesia (DNP); nursing (PhD); nursing education (MSN, Post Master's Certificate; nursing practice (DNP); pediatric primary care nurse practitioner (MSN, Post Master's Certificate). *Accreditation:* AACN; AANA/CANAEP. *Program availability:* Part-time, online learning. *Entrance requirements:* Additional exam requirements/recommendations for international students: required—TOEFL, IELTS. Electronic applications accepted.

**Virginia Commonwealth University,** Graduate School, School of Nursing, Nurse Practitioner Program, Richmond, VA 23284-9005. Offers MS. *Program availability:* Part-time. *Entrance requirements:* For master's, GRE General Test, minimum GPA of 2.8. Additional exam requirements/recommendations for international students: required—TOEFL (minimum score 600 paper-based; 100 iBT). Electronic applications accepted.

**Wagner College,** Division of Graduate Studies, Evelyn L. Spiro School of Nursing, Staten Island, NY 10301-4495. Offers family nurse practitioner (MS, Certificate); nurse educator (MS); nursing (DNP). *Accreditation:* ACEN (one or more programs are accredited). *Program availability:* Part-time, evening/weekend. *Degree requirements:* For master's, thesis optional. *Entrance requirements:* For master's, BS in nursing, current clinical experience, minimum GPA of 3.3; for Certificate, master's degree in nursing from an NLN-accredited program, minimum GPA of 3.0. Additional exam requirements/recommendations for international students: required—TOEFL (minimum score 550 paper-based; 79 iBT), IELTS (minimum score 6.5). Electronic applications accepted.

**Walden University,** Graduate Programs, School of Nursing, Minneapolis, MN 55401. Offers adult-gerontology acute care nurse practitioner (MSN); adult-gerontology nurse practitioner (MSN); education (MSN); family nurse practitioner (MSN); informatics (MSN); leadership and management (MSN); nursing (PhD, Post-Master's Certificate), including education (PhD), healthcare administration (PhD), interdisciplinary health (PhD), leadership (PhD), nursing education (Post-Master's Certificate), nursing informatics (Post-Master's Certificate), nursing leadership and management (Post-Master's Certificate), public health policy (PhD); nursing practice (DNP); psychiatric mental health (MSN). *Accreditation:* AACN. *Program availability:* Part-time, evening/weekend, online only, 100% online. *Degree requirements:* For doctorate, thesis/dissertation (for some programs), residency (for some programs), field experience (for some programs). *Entrance requirements:* For master's, bachelor's degree or equivalent in related field or RN; minimum GPA of 2.5; official transcripts; goal statement (for some programs); access to computer and Internet; for doctorate, master's degree or higher; RN; three years of related professional or academic experience; goal statement; access to computer and Internet; for Post-Master's Certificate, relevant work experience; access to computer and Internet. Additional exam requirements/recommendations for international students: required—TOEFL (minimum score 550 paper-based, 79 iBT), IELTS (minimum score 6.5), Michigan English Language Assessment Battery (minimum score 82), or PTE (minimum score 53). Electronic applications accepted.

**Washington State University,** College of Nursing, Spokane, WA 99210. Offers advanced population health (MN, DNP); family nurse practitioner (MN, DNP); nursing (PhD); psychiatric/mental health nurse practitioner (DNP); psychiatric/mental health practitioner (MN). *Accreditation:* AACN. *Degree requirements:* For master's, comprehensive exam (for some programs), thesis (for some programs), oral exam, research project. *Entrance requirements:* For master's, minimum GPA of 3.0, Washington state RN license, physical assessment skills, course work in statistics, recommendations, written interview (for nurse practitioner).

**West Coast University,** Graduate Programs, North Hollywood, CA 91606. Offers advanced generalist (MSN); family nurse practitioner (MSN); health administration (MHA); occupational therapy (MS); pharmacy (Pharm D); physical therapy (DPT).

**Westminster College,** School of Nursing and Health Sciences, Salt Lake City, UT 84105-3697. Offers family nurse practitioner (MSN); nurse anesthesia (MSNA); public health (MPH). *Accreditation:* AACN; AANA/CANAEP; CEPH. *Degree requirements:* For master's, clinical practicum, 504 clinical practice hours. *Entrance requirements:* For master's, GRE (can be waived in select cases), personal statement, resume, 3 professional recommendations, copy of unrestricted Utah license to practice professional nursing, background check, minimum cumulative GPA of 3.0, documentation of current immunizations, physical and mental health certificate signed by primary care provider. Additional exam requirements/recommendations for international students: required—TOEFL (minimum score 84 iBT), IELTS (minimum score 7). Electronic applications accepted. *Expenses:* Contact institution.

**West Texas A&M University,** College of Nursing and Health Sciences, Department of Nursing, Canyon, TX 79015. Offers family nurse practitioner (MSN); nursing (MSN). *Accreditation:* AACN. *Program availability:* Part-time, online learning. *Degree requirements:* For master's, comprehensive exam, thesis optional. *Entrance requirements:* For master's, GRE General Test, bachelor's degree in nursing, minimum GPA of 3.0 in last 60 hours. Additional exam requirements/recommendations for international students: required—TOEFL (minimum score 550 paper-based). Electronic applications accepted.

**West Virginia Wesleyan College,** School of Nursing, Buckhannon, WV 26201. Offers family nurse practitioner (MS, Post Master's Certificate); nurse-midwifery (MS); nursing (DNP); nursing leadership (MS); psychiatric mental health nurse practitioner (MS); MSN/MBA. *Accreditation:* ACEN.

**Wilmington University,** College of Health Professions, New Castle, DE 19720-6491. Offers adult nurse practitioner (MSN); family nurse practitioner (MSN); gerontology nurse practitioner (MSN); nursing (MSN); nursing leadership (MSN); nursing practice (DNP). *Accreditation:* AACN. *Program availability:* Part-time. *Degree requirements:* For master's, thesis. *Entrance requirements:* For master's, BSN, RN license, interview, 3 letters of recommendation. Additional exam requirements/recommendations for international students: required—TOEFL (minimum score 500 paper-based). Electronic applications accepted.

**Winona State University,** College of Nursing and Health Sciences, Winona, MN 55987. Offers adult-gerontology acute care nurse practitioner (MS, DNP, Post Master's Certificate); adult-gerontology clinical nurse specialist (MS, DNP, Post Master's Certificate); adult-gerontology primary care nurse practitioner (MS, DNP, Post Master's Certificate); family nurse practitioner (MS, DNP, Post Master's Certificate); nurse educator (MS); nursing and organizational leadership (MS, DNP, Post Master's Certificate); practice and leadership innovations (DNP, Post Master's Certificate). *Accreditation:* AACN. *Program availability:* Part-time, online learning. *Degree requirements:* For master's, thesis; for doctorate, capstone. *Entrance requirements:* For master's, GRE (if GPA less than 3.0). Additional exam requirements/recommendations for international students: required—TOEFL (minimum score 550 paper-based).

**Winston-Salem State University,** Program in Nursing, Winston-Salem, NC 27110-0003. Offers advanced nurse educator (MSN); family nurse practitioner (MSN); nursing (DNP). *Accreditation:* AACN. *Program availability:* Part-time, evening/weekend, online learning. *Entrance requirements:* For master's, GRE, MAT, resume, NC or state compact license, 3 letters of recommendation. Electronic applications accepted.

**Wright State University,** Graduate School, College of Nursing and Health, Program in Nursing, Dayton, OH 45435. Offers administration of nursing and health care systems (MS); adult gerontology clinical nurse specialist (MS); adult-gerontology acute care nurse practitioner (MS); family nurse practitioner (MS); neonatal nurse practitioner (MS); pediatric nurse practitioner-acute care (MS); pediatric nurse practitioner-primary care (MS); psychiatric mental health nurse practitioner (MS); school nurse (MS). *Accreditation:* AACN. *Program availability:* Part-time, evening/weekend. *Degree requirements:* For master's, thesis or alternative. *Entrance requirements:* For master's, GRE General Test, BSN from ACEN-accredited college, Ohio RN license. Additional exam requirements/recommendations for international students: required—TOEFL.

# Forensic Nursing

**Aspen University,** Program in Nursing, Denver, CO 80246-1930. Offers forensic nursing (MSN); informatics (MSN); nursing (MSN); nursing administration and management (MSN); nursing education (MSN); public health (MSN). *Program availability:* Part-time, evening/weekend, online only, 100% online. *Degree requirements:* For master's, comprehensive exam. *Entrance requirements:* For master's, www.aspen.edu, www.aspen.edu. Electronic applications accepted.

**Duquesne University,** School of Nursing, Master of Science in Nursing Program, Pittsburgh, PA 15282-0001. Offers family (individual across the life span) nurse practitioner (MSN); forensic nursing (MSN); nursing education and faculty role (MSN). *Accreditation:* AACN. *Program availability:* Part-time, evening/weekend, minimal on-campus study. *Entrance requirements:* For master's, current RN license; BSN with minimum GPA of 3.0; minimum of 1 year of full-time work experience as RN prior to registration in clinical or specialty course. Additional exam requirements/recommendations for international students: required—TOEFL (minimum score 600 paper-based; 100 iBT). Electronic applications accepted. *Expenses:* Contact institution.

**Duquesne University,** School of Nursing, Post Master's Certificate Program, Pittsburgh, PA 15282-0001. Offers family (individual across the life span) nurse practitioner (Post-Master's Certificate); forensic nursing (Post-Master's Certificate); nursing education and faculty role (Post-Master's Certificate). *Program availability:* Part-time, evening/weekend, minimal on-campus study. *Entrance requirements:* For degree, current RN license, BSN, MSN. Additional exam requirements/recommendations for international students: required—TOEFL (minimum score 600 paper-based; 100 iBT). Electronic applications accepted. *Expenses:* Contact institution.

**Fitchburg State University,** Division of Graduate and Continuing Education, Program in Forensic Nursing, Fitchburg, MA 01420-2697. Offers MS, Certificate. *Accreditation:* AACN. *Program availability:* Part-time, evening/weekend, online only, 100% online. *Entrance requirements:* Additional exam requirements/recommendations for international students: required—TOEFL (minimum score 550 paper-based; 79 iBT). Electronic applications accepted. *Expenses:* Contact institution.

**Monmouth University,** Graduate Studies, Marjorie K. Unterberg School of Nursing and Health Studies, West Long Branch, NJ 07764-1898. Offers adult-gerontological primary care nurse practitioner (Post-Master's Certificate); forensic nursing (MSN). *Accreditation:* AACN. *Program availability:* Part-time, evening/weekend, 100% online, blended/hybrid learning. *Faculty:* 13 full-time (all women), 9 part-time/adjunct (8 women). *Students:* 1 (woman) full-time, 284 part-time (261 women); includes 108 minority (37 Black or African American, non-Hispanic/Latino; 38 Asian, non-Hispanic/Latino; 32 Hispanic/Latino; 1 Two or more races, non-Hispanic/Latino). Average age 39. In 2019, 100 master's, 14 doctorates, 10 other advanced degrees awarded. *Degree requirements:* For master's, practicum (for some tracks); for doctorate, practicum, capstone course. *Entrance requirements:* For master's, GRE General Test (waived for MSN applicants with minimum B grade in each of the first four courses and for MS applicants with master's degree), BSN with minimum GPA of 2.75, current RN license, proof of liability and malpractice policy, personal statement, two letters of recommendation, college course work in health assessment, resume; CASPA application (for MS); for doctorate, accredited master's nursing program degree with minimum GPA of 3.2, active RN license, national certification as nurse practitioner or nurse administrator, working knowledge of statistics, statement of goals and vision for change, 2 letters of recommendation (professional or academic), resume, interview. Additional exam requirements/recommendations for international students: required—TOEFL (minimum score 550 paper-based; 79 iBT), IELTS (minimum score 6) or Michigan English Language Assessment Battery (minimum score 77). *Application deadline:* For fall admission, 7/15 priority date for domestic students, 6/1 for international students; for spring admission, 12/1 priority date for domestic students, 11/1 for international students; for summer admission, 5/1 for domestic students. Applications are processed on a rolling basis. Application fee: $50. Electronic applications accepted. *Expenses:* $1,233 per credit. *Financial support:* In 2019–20, 251 students received support. Research assistantships, teaching assistantships, scholarships/grants, and unspecified assistantships available. Support available to part-time students. Financial award applicants required to submit FAFSA. *Unit head:* Dr. Ann Marie Mauro, Dean, 732-571-3443, Fax: 732-263-5131, E-mail: amauro@monmouth.edu. *Application contact:* Laurie Kuhn, Associate Director of Graduate Admission, 732-571-3452, Fax: 732-263-5123, E-mail: gradadm@monmouth.edu.
Website: https://www.monmouth.edu/graduate/nursing-programs-of-study/

*Forensic Nursing*

**Texas A&M University,** College of Nursing, Bryan, TX 77843. Offers family nurse practitioner (MSN); forensic nursing (MSN); nursing education (MSN). *Expenses:* Contact institution.

# Gerontological Nursing

**Allen College,** Graduate Programs, Waterloo, IA 50703. Offers adult-gerontology acute care nurse practitioner (MSN); community/public health nursing (MSN); education (MSN); family nurse practitioner (MSN); health sciences (Ed D); leadership in health care delivery (MSN); leadership in health care informatics (MSN); nursing (DNP); occupational therapy (MS); psychiatric mental health nurse practitioner (MSN). *Accreditation:* AACN; ACEN. *Faculty:* 27 full-time (23 women), 9 part-time/adjunct (8 women). *Students:* 193 full-time (175 women), 95 part-time (84 women); includes 22 minority (6 Black or African American, non-Hispanic/Latino; 1 American Indian or Alaska Native, non-Hispanic/Latino; 4 Asian, non-Hispanic/Latino; 5 Hispanic/Latino; 6 Two or more races, non-Hispanic/Latino). Average age 32. 376 applicants, 53% accepted, 122 enrolled. *Application deadline:* For fall admission, 2/1 priority date for domestic students; for spring admission, 9/1 priority date for domestic students. Applications are processed on a rolling basis. Application fee: $50. Electronic applications accepted. *Financial support:* In 2019–20, 78 students received support. Federal Work-Study, institutionally sponsored loans, and scholarships/grants available. Support available to part-time students. Financial award application deadline: 8/1; financial award applicants required to submit FAFSA. *Unit head:* Dr. Bob Loch, Provost, 319-226-2040, Fax: 319-226-2070, E-mail: bob.loch@allencollege.edu. *Application contact:* Molly Quinn, Director of Admissions, 319-226-2001, Fax: 319-226-2010, E-mail: molly.quinn@allencollege.edu.
Website: http://www.allencollege.edu/

**Alvernia University,** School of Graduate Studies, Department of Nursing, Reading, PA 19607-1799. Offers adult gerontology nurse practitioner (DNP); family nurse practitioner (DNP); nursing education (MSN); nursing leadership (Graduate Certificate); nursing leadership and healthcare administration (MSN).

**Arizona State University at Tempe,** College of Nursing and Health Innovation, Phoenix, AZ 85004. Offers advanced nursing practice (DNP); clinical research management (MS); community and public health practice (Graduate Certificate); family mental health nurse practitioner (Graduate Certificate); family nurse practitioner (Graduate Certificate); geriatric nursing (Graduate Certificate); healthcare innovation (MHI); nurse education in academic and practice settings (Graduate Certificate); nurse educator (MS); nursing and healthcare innovation (PhD). *Accreditation:* AACN. *Program availability:* Online learning. *Degree requirements:* For master's, comprehensive exam (for some programs), thesis (for some programs), interactive Program of Study (iPOS) submitted before completing 50 percent of required credit hours; for doctorate, comprehensive exam, thesis/dissertation, interactive Program of Study (iPOS) submitted before completing 50 percent of required credit hours. *Entrance requirements:* For master's and doctorate, GRE, minimum GPA of 3.0 or equivalent in last 2 years of work leading to bachelor's degree. Additional exam requirements/recommendations for international students: required—TOEFL, IELTS, or PTE. Electronic applications accepted. *Expenses:* Contact institution.

**Augusta University,** College of Nursing, Doctor of Nursing Practice Program, Augusta, GA 30912. Offers adult gerontology acute care nurse practitioner (DNP); family nurse practitioner (DNP); nurse executive (DNP); nursing (DNP); nursing anesthesia (DNP); pediatric nurse practitioner (DNP); psychiatric mental health nurse practitioner (DNP). *Accreditation:* AACN; AANA/CANAEP. *Degree requirements:* For doctorate, thesis/dissertation or alternative. *Entrance requirements:* For doctorate, GRE General Test or MAT, master's degree in nursing or related field, current professional nurse licensure. Additional exam requirements/recommendations for international students: required—TOEFL (minimum score 600 paper-based; 100 iBT). Electronic applications accepted.

**Azusa Pacific University,** School of Nursing, Azusa, CA 91702-7000. Offers adult clinical nurse specialist (MSN); adult-gerontology nurse practitioner (MSN); family nurse practitioner (MSN); healthcare administration and leadership (MSN); nursing (MSN, DNP, PhD); nursing education (MSN); parent-child clinical nurse specialist (MSN); psychiatric mental health nurse practitioner (MSN). *Accreditation:* AACN. *Program availability:* Part-time, evening/weekend. *Degree requirements:* For master's, thesis optional. *Entrance requirements:* For master's, BSN.

**Ball State University,** Graduate School, College of Health, School of Nursing, Muncie, IN 47304. Offers adult/gerontology nurse practitioner (Post Master's Certificate); evidence-based clinical practice (Postbaccalaureate Certificate); family nurse practitioner (Post Master's Certificate); nurse educator (Post Master's Certificate); nursing (MS), including family nurse practitioner, nurse administrator, nurse educator; nursing education (Postbaccalaureate Certificate); nursing practice (DNP). *Accreditation:* AACN. *Program availability:* Part-time-only, online only, 100% online. *Entrance requirements:* For master's, bachelor's degree in nursing, minimum GPA of 3.0, minimum C grade in at least 2 quarter or semester hours in an undergraduate research course, unencumbered license as a registered nurse in state of practice; for doctorate, advanced practice nurse (nurse practitioner, clinical nurse specialist, nurse midwife); master's degree in nursing from accredited program with minimum GPA of 3.2; graduate-level statistics, nursing research, and health assessment courses; unencumbered license as registered nurse in state of practice. Additional exam requirements/recommendations for international students: required—TOEFL (minimum score 550 paper-based; 79 iBT), IELTS (minimum score 6.5). Electronic applications accepted. *Expenses:* Contact institution.

**Binghamton University, State University of New York,** Graduate School, Decker School of Nursing, Binghamton, NY 13902-6000. Offers adult-gerontological nursing (MS, DNP, Certificate); community health nursing (MS, DNP, Certificate); family health nursing (MS, DNP, Certificate); family psychiatric mental health nursing (MS, DNP, Certificate); nursing (PhD). *Accreditation:* AACN. *Program availability:* Part-time, evening/weekend. Terminal master's awarded for partial completion of doctoral program. *Degree requirements:* For master's, comprehensive exam, thesis; for doctorate, comprehensive exam (for some programs), thesis/dissertation. *Entrance requirements:* For master's and doctorate, GRE General Test, nursing licensure. Additional exam requirements/recommendations for international students: required—TOEFL (minimum score 90 iBT). Electronic applications accepted. *Expenses:* Contact institution.

**Boise State University,** College of Health Sciences, School of Nursing, Boise, ID 83725-0399. Offers acute care adult gerontology (Graduate Certificate); adult gerontology acute care (MSN); adult gerontology primary care (MSN); healthcare simulation (Graduate Certificate); nursing practice (DNP); primary care adult gerontology (Graduate Certificate). *Accreditation:* AACN. *Students:* 1 (woman) full-time, 91 part-time (73 women); includes 8 minority (4 Black or African American, non-Hispanic/Latino; 3 Asian, non-Hispanic/Latino; 1 Native Hawaiian or other Pacific Islander, non-Hispanic/Latino). *Entrance requirements:* Additional exam requirements/recommendations for international students: required—TOEFL, IELTS. Electronic applications accepted. *Expenses: Tuition, area resident:* Full-time $7110; part-time $470 per credit hour. Tuition, state resident: full-time $7110; part-time $470 per credit hour. Tuition, nonresident: full-time $24,030; part-time $827 per credit hour. *International tuition:* $24,030 full-time. *Required fees:* $2536. Tuition and fees vary according to course load and program. *Financial support:* Applicants required to submit FAFSA. *Unit head:* Dr. Ann Hubbert, Director, 208-426-3404, E-mail: annhubbert@boisestate.edu. *Application contact:* Dr. Nancy Loftus, Program Coordinator, 208-426-3819, E-mail: nancyloftus@boisestate.edu.
Website: https://www.boisestate.edu/nursing/

**Boston College,** William F. Connell School of Nursing, Chestnut Hill, MA 02467. Offers adult-gerontology primary care nurse practitioner (MS); family health nursing (MS); nurse anesthesia (MS); nursing (PhD); pediatric primary care nurse practitioner (MS), including pediatric and women's health; psychiatric-mental health nursing (MS); women's health nursing (MS); MBA/MS; MS/MA; MS/PhD. *Accreditation:* AACN; AANA/CANAEP (one or more programs are accredited). *Program availability:* Part-time. *Faculty:* 56 full-time (50 women). *Students:* 228 full-time (200 women), 82 part-time (71 women); includes 54 minority (10 Black or African American, non-Hispanic/Latino; 18 Asian, non-Hispanic/Latino; 20 Hispanic/Latino; 6 Two or more races, non-Hispanic/Latino), 7 international. Average age 28. 360 applicants, 56% accepted, 93 enrolled. In 2019, 107 master's, 7 doctorates awarded. *Degree requirements:* For master's, comprehensive exam; for doctorate, comprehensive exam, thesis/dissertation, computer literacy exam or foreign language. *Entrance requirements:* For master's, bachelor's degree; for doctorate, GRE General Test, bachelor's in Nursing and master's degree in nursing or related field. Additional exam requirements/recommendations for international students: required—TOEFL (minimum score 600 paper-based; 100 iBT), IELTS (minimum score 7.5). *Application deadline:* For fall admission, 3/15 for domestic and international students; for spring admission, 9/30 for domestic and international students. Application fee: $40. Electronic applications accepted. *Expenses:* Contact institution. *Financial support:* In 2019–20, 135 students received support, including 12 fellowships with full tuition reimbursements available (averaging $24,504 per year), 29 teaching assistantships (averaging $4,380 per year); scholarships/grants, health care benefits, tuition waivers (partial), and unspecified assistantships also available. Support available to part-time students. Financial award application deadline: 4/18; financial award applicants required to submit FAFSA. *Unit head:* Dr. Susan Gennaro, Dean, 617-552-4251, Fax: 617-552-0931, E-mail: susan.gennaro@bc.edu. *Application contact:* Sean Sendall, Assistant Dean, Graduate Enrollment and Data Analytics, 617-552-4745, Fax: 617-552-2121, E-mail: sean.sendall@bc.edu.
Website: http://www.bc.edu/cson

**California State University, Stanislaus,** College of Science, Master's in Nursing Program, Turlock, CA 95382. Offers gerontological nursing (MS); nursing education (MS). *Accreditation:* AACN. *Program availability:* Part-time. *Degree requirements:* For master's, comprehensive exam, thesis or alternative. *Entrance requirements:* For master's, GRE or MAT, minimum GPA of 3.0, 3 letters of reference, RN. Additional exam requirements/recommendations for international students: required—TOEFL (minimum score 550 paper-based). Electronic applications accepted.

**Capella University,** School of Public Service Leadership, Master's Programs in Nursing, Minneapolis, MN 55402. Offers diabetes nursing (MSN); general nursing (MSN); gerontology nursing (MSN); health information management (MS); nurse educator (MSN); nursing leadership and administration (MSN). *Accreditation:* AACN.

**Caribbean University,** Graduate School, Bayamón, PR 00960-0493. Offers administration and supervision (MA Ed); criminal justice (MA); curriculum and instruction (MA Ed, PhD), including elementary education (MA Ed), English education (MA Ed), history education (MA Ed), mathematics education (MA Ed), primary education (MA Ed), science education (MA Ed), Spanish education (MA Ed); educational technology in instructional systems (MA Ed); gerontology (MSN); human resources (MBA); museology, archiving and art history (MA Ed); neonatal pediatrics (MSN); physical education (MA Ed); special education (MA Ed). *Entrance requirements:* For master's, interview, minimum GPA of 2.5.

**Case Western Reserve University,** Frances Payne Bolton School of Nursing, Master's Programs in Nursing, Nurse Practitioner Program, Cleveland, OH 44106. Offers acute care pediatric nurse practitioner (MSN); acute care/cardiovascular nursing (MSN); adult gerontology acute care nurse practitioner (MSN); adult gerontology primary care nurse practitioner (MSN); family nurse practitioner (MSN); family systems psychiatric mental health nursing (MSN); neonatal nurse practitioner (MSN); palliative care (MSN); pediatric nurse practitioner in acute care (MSN); pediatric primary care nurse practitioner (MSN); women's health nurse practitioner (MSN). *Accreditation:* ACEN. *Program availability:* Part-time. *Faculty:* 30 full-time (25 women), 6 part-time/adjunct (all women). *Students:* 47 full-time (36 women), 70 part-time (59 women); includes 34 minority (12 Black or African American, non-Hispanic/Latino; 11 Asian, non-Hispanic/Latino; 9 Hispanic/Latino; 2 Two or more races, non-Hispanic/Latino), 9 international. Average age 30. 45 applicants, 82% accepted, 22 enrolled. In 2019, 46 master's awarded. *Degree requirements:* For master's, thesis optional, minimum GPA of 3.0, clinical hours corresponding to requirements to sit for certification exam, portfolio. *Entrance requirements:* For master's, GRE/MAT (scores not required for application, but may be requested for an admission decision). Additional exam requirements/recommendations for international students: required—TOEFL (minimum score 577 paper-based; 90 iBT), IELTS (minimum score 7). *Application deadline:* For fall admission, 3/15 for domestic and international students; for spring admission, 10/1 for domestic and international students; for summer admission, 3/15 for domestic and international students. Applications are processed on a rolling basis. Application fee: $75. Electronic applications accepted. *Expenses:* Clinical placement $75; Activity fee $15 per semester; Graduate council fee $15 per semester; Tuition rate $2,133 per credit hour. *Financial support:* In 2019–20, 100 students received support, including 34 teaching assistantships with partial tuition reimbursements available (averaging $19,197 per year); scholarships/grants and traineeships also available. Financial award application

deadline: 5/15; financial award applicants required to submit FAFSA. *Unit head:* Dr. Latina Brooks, Director, 216-368-1196, Fax: 216-368-3542, E-mail: lmb3@case.edu. *Application contact:* Jackie Tepale, Admissions Coordinator, 216-368-5253, Fax: 216-368-3542, E-mail: yyd@case.edu.
Website: https://case.edu/nursing/programs/msn

**Clemson University,** Graduate School, College of Behavioral, Social and Health Sciences, School of Nursing, Clemson, SC 29634. Offers clinical and translational research (PhD); global health (Certificate), including low resource countries; healthcare genetics (PhD); nursing (MS, DNP), including adult/gerontology nurse practitioner (MS), family nurse practitioner (MS). *Accreditation:* AACN. *Program availability:* Part-time, 100% online, blended/hybrid learning. *Faculty:* 47 full-time (45 women), 1 (woman) part-time/adjunct. *Students:* 67 full-time (59 women), 66 part-time (49 women); includes 18 minority (10 Black or African American, non-Hispanic/Latino; 4 Asian, non-Hispanic/Latino; 4 Two or more races, non-Hispanic/Latino), 7 international. Average age 35. 109 applicants, 62% accepted, 49 enrolled. In 2019, 56 master's, 8 doctorates awarded. *Degree requirements:* For master's, comprehensive exam, thesis or alternative; for doctorate, comprehensive exam, thesis/dissertation. *Entrance requirements:* For master's, GRE General Test, South Carolina RN license, unofficial transcripts, resume, letters of recommendation; for doctorate, GRE General Test, unofficial transcripts, MS/MA thesis or publications, curriculum vitae, statement of career goals, letters of recommendation. Additional exam requirements/recommendations for international students: required—TOEFL (minimum score 80 paper-based; 80 iBT); recommended—IELTS (minimum score 6.5), TSE (minimum score 54). *Application deadline:* For fall admission, 4/15 priority date for international students; for spring admission, 10/15 priority date for international students. Applications are processed on a rolling basis. Application fee: $80 ($90 for international students). Electronic applications accepted. *Expenses:* MS Nursing Full-Time Student per Semester: Tuition: $9075 (in-state), $16051 (out-of-state), Fees: $598; Graduate Assistant Per Semester: $1144; Part-Time Student Per Credit Hour: $1009 (in-state), $1784 (out-of-state), Fees: $46; other fees apply depending on program, credit hours, campus & residency. Doctoral Base Fee per Semester: $4938 (in-state), $10405 (out-of-state). *Financial support:* In 2019–20, 47 students received support, including 46 teaching assistantships with full and partial tuition reimbursements available (averaging $6,766 per year); career-related internships or fieldwork and unspecified assistantships also available. *Unit head:* Dr. Kathleen Valentine, Chief Academic Nursing Officer & Director, 864-656-4758, E-mail: klvalen@clemson.edu. *Application contact:* Dr. Stephanie Davis, Director of Graduate Programs, 864-656-2588, E-mail: stephad@clemson.edu.
Website: http://www.clemson.edu/cbshs/departments/nursing/

**College of Staten Island of the City University of New York,** Graduate Programs, School of Health Sciences, Program in Adult-Gerontological Nursing, Staten Island, NY 10314-6600. Offers adult-gerontological nursing (MS, Post Master's Certificate), including clinical nurse specialist, nurse practitioner. *Program availability:* Part-time, evening/weekend. *Faculty:* 8. *Students:* 63. 43 applicants, 51% accepted, 13 enrolled. In 2019, 12 master's, 3 other advanced degrees awarded. *Degree requirements:* For master's, thesis optional, 42 credits with minimum of 500 supervised hours toward development of clinical competencies for primary care of the adult-gerontological population (15 core credits, advanced practice core of nine credits, specialty courses of 12 credits, and six credits of elective courses); for Post Master's Certificate, 12-21 credits with minimum of 500 supervised hours toward development of Clinical Nurse Specialist or Nurse Practitioner competencies. *Entrance requirements:* For master's, Bachelor's degree in nursing with minimum GPA of 3.0, 2 letters of recommendation, personal statement, current New York State RN license, minimum 1 year of full-time experience as registered nurse, 3 years of appropriate full-time clinical experience in nursing, completion of required nursing, science, and math courses; for Post Master's Certificate, master's degree in nursing; master's-level courses in pathophysiology, health assessment and pharmacology. Additional exam requirements/recommendations for international students: required—TOEFL (minimum score 550 paper-based; 79 iBT), IELTS (minimum score 6.5). *Application deadline:* For spring admission, 10/15 for domestic and international students. Applications are processed on a rolling basis. Application fee: $75. Electronic applications accepted. *Expenses:* For the Master's and Advanced Certificates, the tuition and fees are the same as for the majority of graduate programs. For the DNP $14,630 per year (Full Time NY State Resident); $620 per equated credit (part Time NY State Resident); $1,000 per equated credit Full/Part Time Non-State Resident). *Unit head:* Dr. Catherine Paradiso, 718-982-3838, E-mail: catherine.paradiso@csi.cuny.edu. *Application contact:* Sasha Spence, Associate Director for Graduate Admissions, 718-982-2019, Fax: 718-982-2500, E-mail: sasha.spence@csi.cuny.edu.
Website: http://www.csi.cuny.edu/nursing/graduate.html

**Columbia University,** School of Nursing, Program in Adult-Gerontology Primary Care Nurse Practitioner, New York, NY 10032. Offers MS, Adv C. *Accreditation:* AACN. *Program availability:* Part-time. *Entrance requirements:* For master's, GRE General Test, NCLEX, BSN, 1 year of clinical experience (preferred); for Adv C, MSN. Additional exam requirements/recommendations for international students: required—TOEFL (minimum score 100 iBT). Electronic applications accepted. *Expenses: Tuition:* Full-time $47,600; part-time $1880 per credit. One-time fee: $105.

**Creighton University,** College of Nursing, Omaha, NE 68178-0001. Offers adult gerontology acute care nurse practitioner (DNP, Post-Master's Certificate); adult gerontology nurse practitioner (DNP); clinical nurse leader (MSN, Post-Graduate Certificate); clinical systems administration (MSN, DNP); family nurse practitioner (DNP, Post-Master's Certificate); neonatal nurse practitioner (DNP, Post-Master's Certificate); nursing (Post-Graduate Certificate); pediatric acute care nurse practitioner (DNP, Post-Master's Certificate); psychiatric mental health nurse practitioner (DNP). *Accreditation:* AACN. *Program availability:* Part-time, blended/hybrid learning. *Degree requirements:* For master's, capstone project; for doctorate, scholarly project. *Entrance requirements:* For master's and doctorate, BSN from ACEN- or CCNE-accredited nursing school, minimum cumulative GPA of 3.0, personal statement, active unencumbered RN license with NE eligibility, undergraduate statistics course, physical assessment course or equivalent, three recommendation letters; for other advanced degree, MSN or MS in nursing from ACEN- or CCNE-accredited nursing school, minimum cumulative GPA of 3.0, active unencumbered RN license with NE eligibility. Additional exam requirements/recommendations for international students: required—TOEFL (minimum score 600 paper-based, 100 iBT) or IELTS. Electronic applications accepted. *Expenses:* Contact institution.

**Duke University,** School of Nursing, Durham, NC 27708. Offers acute care pediatric nurse practitioner (MSN, Post-Graduate Certificate); adult-gerontology nurse practitioner (MSN, Post-Graduate Certificate), including acute care, primary care; family nurse practitioner (MSN, Post-Graduate Certificate); neonatal nurse practitioner (MSN, Post-Graduate Certificate); nurse anesthesia (DNP); nurse practitioner (DNP); nursing (PhD); nursing and health care leadership (MSN, Post-Graduate Certificate); nursing education (MSN, Post-Graduate Certificate); nursing informatics (MSN, Post-Graduate Certificate); pediatric nurse practitioner (MSN, Post-Graduate Certificate), including primary care; psychiatric mental health nurse practitioner (MSN, Post-Graduate Certificate); women's health nurse practitioner (MSN, Post-Graduate Certificate). *Accreditation:* AACN; AANA/CANAEP. *Program availability:* Part-time, evening/weekend, online with on-campus intensives. *Faculty:* 48 full-time (40 women), 32 part-time/adjunct (28 women). *Students:* 666 full-time (601 women), 157 part-time (139 women); includes 193 minority (61 Black or African American, non-Hispanic/Latino; 4 American Indian or Alaska Native, non-Hispanic/Latino; 57 Asian, non-Hispanic/Latino; 49 Hispanic/Latino; 1 Native Hawaiian or other Pacific Islander, non-Hispanic/Latino; 21 Two or more races, non-Hispanic/Latino), 8 international. Average age 34. 761 applicants, 33% accepted, 149 enrolled. In 2019, 213 master's, 74 doctorates, 18 other advanced degrees awarded. Terminal master's awarded for partial completion of doctoral program. *Degree requirements:* For master's, thesis optional; for doctorate, capstone project. *Entrance requirements:* For master's, MSN applicants are no longer required to take the GRE, 1 year of nursing experience (recommended), BSN, minimum GPA of 3.0, previous course work in statistics; for doctorate, GRE is required for the DNP in Nurse Anesthesia, BSN or MSN, minimum GPA of 3.0, resume, personal statement, graduate statistics and research methods course, current licensure as a registered nurse, transcripts from all post-secondary institutions; for Post-Graduate Certificate, MSN, licensure or eligibility as a professional nurse, transcripts from all post-secondary institutions, previous course work in statistics. Additional exam requirements/recommendations for international students: required—TOEFL (minimum score 100 iBT), IELTS (minimum score 7). *Application deadline:* For fall admission, 12/1 for domestic and international students; for spring admission, 5/1 for domestic and international students. Application fee: $50. Electronic applications accepted. *Expenses:* Contact institution. *Financial support:* Institutionally sponsored loans, scholarships/grants, and traineeships available. Support available to part-time students. Financial award applicants required to submit FAFSA. *Unit head:* Dr. Marion E. Broome, Dean/Vice Chancellor for Nursing Affairs/Associate Vice President for Academic Affairs for Nursing, 919-684-9446, Fax: 919-684-9414, E-mail: marion.broome@duke.edu. *Application contact:* Dr. Ernie Rushing, Director of Admissions and Recruitment, 919-668-6274, Fax: 919-668-4693, E-mail: ernie.rushing@dm.duke.edu.
Website: http://www.nursing.duke.edu/

**East Tennessee State University,** College of Graduate and Continuing Studies, College of Nursing, Johnson City, TN 37614. Offers acute care nurse practitioner (DNP); adult-gerontology primary care nurse practitioner (DNP); adult/gerontological nurse practitioner (Postbaccalaureate Certificate); executive leadership in nursing (DNP, Postbaccalaureate Certificate); family nurse practitioner (MSN, DNP, Post-Master's Certificate, Postbaccalaureate Certificate); nursing (PhD); nursing administration (MSN); nursing education (MSN); pediatric primary care nurse practitioner (DNP); psychiatric mental health nurse practitioner (Postbaccalaureate Certificate); psychiatric/mental health nurse practitioner (MSN, DNP, Post-Master's Certificate); women's health care nurse practitioner (DNP). *Accreditation:* AACN. *Program availability:* Part-time, evening/weekend, online learning. *Degree requirements:* For master's and other advanced degree, comprehensive exam, practicum; for doctorate, comprehensive exam, thesis/dissertation (for some programs), practicum, internship, evidence of professional malpractice insurance, CPR certification. *Entrance requirements:* For master's, bachelor's degree, minimum GPA of 3.0, current RN license and eligibility to practice, resume, three letters of recommendation; for doctorate, GRE General Test, MSN (for PhD), BSN or MSN (for DNP), current RN license and eligibility to practice, 2 years of full-time registered nurse work experience or equivalent, three letters of recommendation, resume or curriculum vitae, interview, writing sample; for other advanced degree, MSN, minimum GPA of 3.0, current RN license and eligibility to practice, three letters of recommendation, resume or curriculum vitae; DNP with designated concentration in advanced clinical practice or nursing administration (for select programs). Additional exam requirements/recommendations for international students: required—TOEFL (minimum score 600 paper-based; 79 iBT). Electronic applications accepted.

**Elms College,** School of Nursing, Chicopee, MA 01013-2839. Offers adult-gerontology acute care nurse practitioner (DNP); family nurse practitioner (DNP); health systems innovation and leadership (DNP); nursing and health services management (MSN); nursing education (MSN). *Accreditation:* AACN. *Program availability:* Part-time, evening/weekend. *Faculty:* 3 full-time (2 women), 2 part-time/adjunct (both women). *Students:* 13 full-time (11 women), 97 part-time (91 women); includes 8 minority (4 Black or African American, non-Hispanic/Latino; 2 Hispanic/Latino; 2 Two or more races, non-Hispanic/Latino). Average age 38. 39 applicants, 87% accepted, 27 enrolled. In 2019, 4 master's, 20 doctorates awarded. *Entrance requirements:* Additional exam requirements/recommendations for international students: required—TOEFL (minimum score 80 iBT). *Application deadline:* For fall admission, 7/1 priority date for domestic students; for spring admission, 11/1 priority date for domestic students. Applications are processed on a rolling basis. Electronic applications accepted. *Financial support:* Applicants required to submit FAFSA. *Unit head:* Dr. Kathleen Scoble, Dean, School of Nursing, 413-265-2204, E-mail: scoblek@elms.edu. *Application contact:* Nancy Davis, Director, Office of Graduate and Continuing Education Admissions, 413-265-2456, E-mail: grad@elms.edu.

**Fairleigh Dickinson University, Florham Campus,** University College: Arts, Sciences, and Professional Studies, The Henry P. Becton School of Nursing and Allied Health, Madison, NJ 07940-1099. Offers adult gerontology primary care nurse practitioner (MSN); family psychiatric/mental health nurse practitioner (MSN). *Program availability:* Part-time, evening/weekend. *Entrance requirements:* For master's, BSN, minimum undergraduate GPA of 3.0, courses in statistics and nursing research at the undergraduate level, NJ Registered Nurse licensure, minimum of 1 year of clinical nursing experience, two letters of recommendation.

**Felician University,** Master of Science in Nursing Program, Lodi, NJ 07644-2117. Offers adult-gerontology nurse practitioner (MSN, PMC); executive leadership (MSN, PMC); family nurse practitioner (MSN, PMC); nursing education (MSN, PMC). *Accreditation:* AACN. *Program availability:* Evening/weekend, online only, 100% online, blended/hybrid learning. *Degree requirements:* For master's, thesis, clinical presentation; for PMC, thesis, education project. *Entrance requirements:* For master's, BSN; minimum GPA of 3.0; 2 letters of recommendation; NJ RN license; personal statement; for PMC, RN license, minimum GPA of 3.0. Additional exam requirements/recommendations for international students: required—TOEFL (minimum score 550 paper-based; 79 iBT), IELTS (minimum score 6.5), PTE (minimum score 56). Electronic applications accepted. Application fee is waived when completed online. *Expenses:* Contact institution.

**Florida Southern College,** School of Nursing and Health Sciences, Lakeland, FL 33801. Offers adult gerontology clinical nurse specialist (MSN); adult gerontology primary care nurse practitioner (MSN); family nurse practitioner (MSN); nurse educator (MSN); nursing administration (MSN). *Accreditation:* AACN. *Program availability:* Part-time, The Nurse Educator MSN degree concentration and NE postmasters certificate are fully online. The Nursing Administrative Leadership MSN degree concentration is delivered in blended/hybrid format. *Faculty:* 6 full-time (all women), 1 (woman) part-time/adjunct. *Students:* 145 full-time (131 women), 1 (woman) part-time; includes 70 minority (30 Black or African American, non-Hispanic/Latino; 11 Asian, non-Hispanic/Latino; 25 Hispanic/Latino; 4 Two or more races, non-Hispanic/Latino), 1 international. Average age 39. 81 applicants, 89% accepted, 50 enrolled. In 2019, 53 master's awarded.

*Degree requirements:* For master's, comprehensive exam, 660 clinical hours (for Family Nurse Practitioner); 540 clinical hours (for Adult-Gerontology Primary Care Nurse Practitioner). *Entrance requirements:* For master's, Florida RN license, 3 letters of recommendation, professional statement, minimum GPA of 3.0 in the last 60 credit hours of BSN, BSN earned from a regionally accredited institution and a CCNE, CNEA, or ACEN accredited nursing program, resume, admission interview. Additional exam requirements/recommendations for international students: required—TOEFL (minimum score 550 paper-based; 79 iBT), IELTS (minimum score 6.5), International students from countries where English is not the standard for daily communication must submit either the TOEFL or IELTS. *Application deadline:* For fall admission, 6/1 for domestic and international students; for spring admission, 10/1 for domestic and international students. Applications are processed on a rolling basis. Electronic applications accepted. *Expenses:* DNP: $725 per credit hour tuition, $50 per semester technology fee (for 5-8 hours), $100 per semester technology fee (for 9-12 hours); MSN: $600 per credit hour tuition, $50 per semester technology fee (for 5-8 hours), $100 per semester technology fee (for 9-12 hours), $35 per semester insurance and lab supplies fees. *Financial support:* In 2019–20, 1 student received support. Employee tuition grants, athletic scholarships for students still eligible available. Financial award application deadline: 8/20; financial award applicants required to submit FAFSA. *Unit head:* Dr. Linda Comer, Dean, 863-680-3951, Fax: 863-680-3860, E-mail: lcomer@flsouthern.edu. *Application contact:* Kimberly Smith, Admission Counselor and Advisor for Nursing, 863-680-3090, Fax: 863-680-3872, E-mail: ksmith@flsouthern.edu.
Website: www.flsouthern.edu/sage

**George Mason University,** College of Health and Human Services, School of Nursing, Fairfax, VA 22030. Offers adult gerontology (DNP); adult/gerontological nurse practitioner (MSN); family nurse practitioner (MSN, DNP); nurse educator (MSN); nursing (PhD); nursing administration (MSN, DNP); nursing education (Certificate); psychiatric mental health (DNP). *Accreditation:* AACN. *Program availability:* Part-time, evening/weekend, blended/hybrid learning. *Degree requirements:* For master's, comprehensive exam (for some programs), thesis in clinical classes; for doctorate, comprehensive exam (for some programs), thesis/dissertation (for some programs). *Entrance requirements:* For master's, 2 official transcripts; expanded goals statement; resume; BSN from accredited institution; minimum GPA of 3.0 in last 60 credits of undergraduate work; 2 letters of recommendation; completion of undergraduate statistics and graduate-level bivariate statistics; certification in professional CPR; for doctorate, GRE, 2 official transcripts; expanded goals statement; resume; 2 recommendation letters; nursing license; at least 1 year of work experience as an RN; interview; writing sample; evidence of graduate-level course in applied statistics; master's degree in nursing with minimum GPA of 3.5; for Certificate, 2 official transcripts; expanded goals statement; resume; master's degree from accredited institution or currently enrolled with minimum GPA of 3.0. Additional exam requirements/recommendations for international students: required—TOEFL (minimum score 570 paper-based; 88 iBT), IELTS (minimum score 6.5), PTE (minimum score 59). Electronic applications accepted. *Expenses:* Contact institution.

**Goldfarb School of Nursing at Barnes-Jewish College,** Graduate Programs, St. Louis, MO 63110. Offers adult-gerontology (MSN), including primary care nurse practitioner; adult-gerontology (MSN), including acute care nurse practitioner; health systems and population health leadership (MSN); nurse anesthesia (MSN). *Accreditation:* AACN; AANA/CANAEP. *Program availability:* Part-time, online learning. *Degree requirements:* For master's, thesis or alternative. *Entrance requirements:* For master's, 2 references, personal statement, curriculum vitae or resume. Additional exam requirements/recommendations for international students: required—TOEFL (minimum score 575 paper-based; 85 iBT).

**Graceland University,** School of Nursing, Independence, MO 64050-3434. Offers adult and gerontology acute care (MSN, PMC); family nurse practitioner (MSN, PMC); nurse educator (MSN, PMC); organizational leadership (DNP). *Accreditation:* AACN. *Program availability:* Part-time, online only, 100% online. *Degree requirements:* For master's, comprehensive exam (for some programs), thesis optional, scholarly project; for doctorate, capstone project. *Entrance requirements:* For master's, BSN from nationally-accredited program, RN license, minimum GPA of 3.0, satisfactory criminal background check, three professional reference letters, professional goals statement of 150 words or less; for doctorate, MSN from nationally-accredited program, RN license, minimum GPA of 3.0, criminal background check. Additional exam requirements/recommendations for international students: required—TOEFL (minimum score 550 paper-based; 80 iBT). Electronic applications accepted. *Expenses:* Contact institution.

**Gwynedd Mercy University,** Frances M. Maguire School of Nursing and Health Professions, Gwynedd Valley, PA 19437-0901. Offers clinical nurse specialist (MSN), including gerontology, oncology, pediatrics; nurse educator (MSN); nurse practitioner (MSN), including adult health, pediatric health; nursing (DNP). *Accreditation:* ACEN. *Program availability:* Part-time, blended/hybrid learning. *Faculty:* 4 full-time (all women), 1 (woman) part-time/adjunct. *Students:* 52 full-time (47 women), 58 part-time (52 women); includes 28 minority (17 Black or African American, non-Hispanic/Latino; 9 Asian, non-Hispanic/Latino; 2 Hispanic/Latino). Average age 33. 35 applicants, 43% accepted, 14 enrolled. In 2019, 26 master's awarded. *Degree requirements:* For master's, thesis optional; for doctorate, evidence-based scholarly project. *Entrance requirements:* For master's, current nursing experience, physical assessment, course work in statistics, BSN from ACEN-accredited program, 2 letters of recommendation, personal interview. *Application deadline:* For fall admission, 4/15 for domestic and international students. Applications are processed on a rolling basis. Electronic applications accepted. *Expenses:* Contact institution. *Financial support:* Scholarships/grants, traineeships, and unspecified assistantships available. Financial award application deadline: 4/15. *Unit head:* Dr. Ann Phalen, Dean, 215-646-7300 Ext. 539, Fax: 215-641-5517, E-mail: phalen.a@gmercyu.edu. *Application contact:* Mary Hermann, Associate Dean, 215-646-7300, E-mail: herman.m@gmercyu.edu.
Website: http://www.gmercyu.edu/academics/graduate-programs/nursing

**Hofstra University,** Hofstra Northwell School of Nursing and Physician Assistant Studies, Programs in Nursing, Hempstead, NY 11549. Offers adult-gerontology acute care nurse practitioner (MS); family nurse practitioner (MS); psychiatric-mental health np (MS). *Students:* 68 full-time (48 women), 159 part-time (138 women); includes 103 minority (24 Black or African American, non-Hispanic/Latino; 2 American Indian or Alaska Native, non-Hispanic/Latino; 41 Asian, non-Hispanic/Latino; 35 Hispanic/Latino; 1 Two or more races, non-Hispanic/Latino). Average age 33. 389 applicants, 32% accepted, 89 enrolled. In 2019, 44 master's awarded. *Degree requirements:* For master's, comprehensive exam, minimum GPA of 3.0. *Entrance requirements:* For master's, bachelor's degree in nursing, 3 letters of recommendation, essay, resume. Additional exam requirements/recommendations for international students: required—TOEFL (minimum score 550 paper-based; 80 iBT); recommended—IELTS (minimum score 6.5). Application fee: $75. Electronic applications accepted. *Expenses: Tuition:* Full-time $25,164; part-time $1398 per credit. *Required fees:* $580; $165 per semester. Tuition and fees vary according to course load, degree level and program. *Financial support:* In 2019–20, 56 students received support, including 5 fellowships with full and partial tuition reimbursements available (averaging $10,870 per year); research assistantships with full and partial tuition reimbursements available, career-related internships or fieldwork, Federal Work-Study, institutionally sponsored loans, scholarships/grants, traineeships, tuition waivers (full and partial), unspecified assistantships, and scholarships and endowed scholarships also available. Support available to part-time students. Financial award applicants required to submit FAFSA. *Unit head:* Dr. Kathleen Gallo, Dean, 516-463-7475, Fax: 516-463-7495, E-mail: kathleen.gallo@hofstra.edu. *Application contact:* Sunil Samuel, Assistant Vice President of Admissions, 516-463-4723, Fax: 516-463-4664, E-mail: graduateadmission@hofstra.edu.

**Hunter College of the City University of New York,** Graduate School, Hunter-Bellevue School of Nursing, Doctor of Nursing Practice Program, New York, NY 10065-5085. Offers adult-gerontology nurse practitioner (DNP); family nurse practitioner (DNP); psychiatric-mental health nurse practitioner (DNP).

**Hunter College of the City University of New York,** Graduate School, Hunter-Bellevue School of Nursing, Gerontological/Adult Nurse Practitioner Program, New York, NY 10065-5085. Offers MS. *Accreditation:* AACN. *Program availability:* Part-time. *Degree requirements:* For master's, practicum. *Entrance requirements:* For master's, minimum GPA of 3.0, New York RN license, 2 years of professional practice experience, BSN. Additional exam requirements/recommendations for international students: required—TOEFL.

**Hunter College of the City University of New York,** Graduate School, Hunter-Bellevue School of Nursing, Program in Adult-Gerontology Clinical Nurse Specialist, New York, NY 10065-5085. Offers MS. *Accreditation:* AACN. *Degree requirements:* For master's, practicum. *Entrance requirements:* For master's, minimum GPA of 3.0, New York RN license, 2 years of professional practice experience, BSN. Additional exam requirements/recommendations for international students: required—TOEFL.

**Independence University,** Program in Nursing, Salt Lake City, UT 84107. Offers community health (MSN); gerontology (MSN); nursing administration (MSN); wellness promotion (MSN).

**Indiana University-Purdue University Indianapolis,** School of Nursing, MSN Program in Nursing, Indianapolis, IN 46202. Offers adult/gerontology acute care nurse practitioner (MSN); adult/gerontology clinical nurse specialist (MSN); adult/gerontology primary care nurse practitioner (MSN); family nurse practitioner (MSN); nursing education (MSN); nursing leadership in health systems (MSN); pediatric clinical nurse specialist (MSN); pediatric nurse practitioner (MSN). *Accreditation:* AACN. *Program availability:* Part-time, blended/hybrid learning. *Degree requirements:* For master's, thesis. *Entrance requirements:* For master's, BSN from ACEN- or CCNE-accredited program, minimum undergraduate GPA of 3.0 (preferred), professional resume or curriculum vitae, essay stating career goals and objectives, current unencumbered RN license, three references from individuals with knowledge of ability to succeed in graduate program. Additional exam requirements/recommendations for international students: required—TOEFL (minimum score 550 paper-based; 79 iBT). Electronic applications accepted. *Expenses:* Contact institution.

**Jacksonville University,** Brooks Rehabilitation College of Healthcare Sciences, Keigwin School of Nursing, Jacksonville, FL 32211. Offers adult gerontology acute care nurse practitioner (MSN), including clinical nurse educator, family nurse practitioner, family nurse practitioner/emergency nurse practitioner, leadership in the healthcare system, nursing informatics, psychiatric nurse practitioner; adult-gerontology acute care nurse practitioner (Certificate); clinical nurse educator (Certificate); emergency nurse practitioner (Certificate); family nurse practitioner (Certificate); family nurse practitioner/emergency nurse practitioner (Certificate); leadership in healthcare systems (Certificate); nursing informatics (MSN, Certificate); nursing practice (DNP); psychiatric mental health nurse practitioner (Certificate); MSN/MBA. *Accreditation:* AACN. *Program availability:* Part-time, 100% online, blended/hybrid learning. *Students:* 49 full-time (39 women), 463 part-time (406 women); includes 153 minority (85 Black or African American, non-Hispanic/Latino; 2 American Indian or Alaska Native, non-Hispanic/Latino; 22 Asian, non-Hispanic/Latino; 32 Hispanic/Latino; 1 Native Hawaiian or other Pacific Islander, non-Hispanic/Latino; 11 Two or more races, non-Hispanic/Latino), 1 international. Average age 39. 203 applicants, 39% accepted, 67 enrolled. In 2019, 215 master's, 15 doctorates awarded. *Degree requirements:* For master's, thesis; for doctorate, thesis/dissertation. *Entrance requirements:* For master's, GRE General Test or undergraduate GPA above 3.0, BSN from ACEN- or CCNE-accredited program; course work in statistics and physical assessment within last 5 years; Florida nursing license; CPR/BLS certification; 3 recommendations, 2 of which are professional references; statement of intent; resume; for doctorate, official transcripts from all colleges/universities attended; MSN from ACEN- or CCNE-accredited program; licensure as RN or ARNP; 3 letters of reference (2 clinical, 1 professional/academic); curriculum vitae; graded essay; for Certificate, GRE (minimum score of 290, waived if undergraduate nursing GPA is 3.0 or higher), official transcripts from MSN; minimum graduate nursing GPA of 3.0; graduation from CCNE- or ACEN-accredited MSN program; 3 recommendations, 2 of which are professional references; 2 years of work experience in critical care setting; statement of intent; resume. Additional exam requirements/recommendations for international students: required—TOEFL (minimum score 650 paper-based; 114 iBT), IELTS (minimum score 8). *Application deadline:* Applications are processed on a rolling basis. Application fee: $50. Electronic applications accepted. *Expenses:* Contact institution. *Financial support:* Federal Work-Study, institutionally sponsored loans, scholarships/grants, and health care benefits available. Support available to part-time students. Financial award application deadline: 3/15; financial award applicants required to submit FAFSA. *Unit head:* Dr. Hilary Morgan, Director, Graduate Nursing Programs/Associate Professor, 904-256-7601, E-mail: hmorgan@ju.edu. *Application contact:* Kristen Kirkendall, Associate Director of Graduate Admissions and Communications, 904-256-7169, E-mail: kgreene8@ju.edu.
Website: http://www.ju.edu/chs/nursing/

**James Madison University,** The Graduate School, College of Health and Behavioral Studies, Program in Nursing, Harrisonburg, VA 22807. Offers adult/gerontology primary care nurse practitioner (MSN); clinical nurse leader (MSN); family nurse practitioner (MSN); nurse administrator (MSN); nurse midwifery (MSN); nursing (MSN, DNP); psychiatric mental health nurse practitioner (MSN). *Accreditation:* AACN. *Program availability:* Part-time, 100% online, blended/hybrid learning. *Students:* 15 full-time (14 women), 71 part-time (66 women); includes 10 minority (3 Black or African American, non-Hispanic/Latino; 6 Asian, non-Hispanic/Latino; 1 Hispanic/Latino). Average age 30. In 2019, 28 master's awarded. Application fee: $60. Electronic applications accepted. *Financial support:* In 2019–20, 2 students received support. Federal Work-Study and assistantships (averaging $7911) available. Financial award application deadline: 3/1; financial award applicants required to submit FAFSA. *Unit head:* Dr. Julie T. Sanford, Department Head, 540-568-6314, E-mail: sanforjt@jmu.edu. *Application contact:* Lynette D. Michael, Director of Graduate Admissions, 540-568-6131 Ext. 6395, Fax: 540-568-7860, E-mail: michaeld@jmu.edu.
Website: http://www.nursing.jmu.edu

**Johns Hopkins University,** School of Nursing, DNP Clinical Nurse Specialist Track, Baltimore, MD 21218. Offers adult/gerontological critical care clinical nurse specialist (DNP); adult/gerontological health clinical nurse specialist (DNP); pediatric critical care clinical nurse specialist (DNP). *Accreditation:* AACN. *Program availability:* Part-time,

100% online, blended/hybrid learning. *Faculty:* 22 full-time (20 women), 3 part-time/adjunct (2 women). *Students:* 22 full-time (21 women), 11 part-time (all women); includes 15 minority (3 Black or African American, non-Hispanic/Latino; 4 Asian, non-Hispanic/Latino; 6 Hispanic/Latino; 1 Native Hawaiian or other Pacific Islander, non-Hispanic/Latino; 1 Two or more races, non-Hispanic/Latino). 25 applicants, 88% accepted, 16 enrolled. In 2019, 3 doctorates awarded. *Entrance requirements:* For doctorate, GRE, Minimum GPA of 3.0, goal statement/essay, resume, letters of recommendation, official transcripts from all post-secondary institutions attended, BSN and RN license, prerequisite coursework. Additional exam requirements/recommendations for international students: required—TOEFL (minimum score 600 paper-based; 100 iBT), IELTS (minimum score 7). *Application deadline:* For fall admission, 11/1 priority date for domestic and international students. Application fee: $75. Electronic applications accepted. *Expenses:* $1,772 per credit. *Financial support:* In 2019–20, 23 students received support. Federal Work-Study and scholarships/grants available. Support available to part-time students. Financial award application deadline: 3/1; financial award applicants required to submit FAFSA. *Unit head:* Dr. Patricia M. Davidson, Dean, 410-955-7544, Fax: 410-955-4890, E-mail: sondeansoffice@jhu.edu. *Application contact:* Cathy Wilson, Director of Admissions, 410-955-7548, Fax: 410-614-7086, E-mail: jhuson@jhu.edu.
Website: http://www.nursing.jhu.edu

**Johns Hopkins University,** School of Nursing, DNP Nurse Practitioner Track, Baltimore, MD 21218. Offers adult/gerontological acute care nurse practitioner (DNP); adult/gerontological primary care nurse practitioner (DNP); family primary care nurse practitioner (DNP); pediatric primary care nurse practitioner (DNP). *Accreditation:* AACN. *Students:* 176 applicants, 59% accepted, 64 enrolled. *Degree requirements:* For doctorate, thesis/dissertation, Preliminary justification; final justification. *Entrance requirements:* For doctorate, minimum GPA of 3.0, goal statement/essay, resume, letters of recommendation, official transcripts from all post-secondary institutions attended; BSN and RN license, work experience for some tracks. Additional exam requirements/recommendations for international students: required—TOEFL (minimum score 600 paper-based; 100 iBT), IELTS (minimum score 7). *Application deadline:* For fall admission, 11/1 priority date for domestic and international students. Application fee: $70. Electronic applications accepted. *Expenses:* Contact institution. *Financial support:* In 2019–20, 57 students received support. Federal Work-Study and scholarships/grants available. Support available to part-time students. Financial award application deadline: 3/1; financial award applicants required to submit FAFSA. *Unit head:* Dr. Kim McIltrot, Dean, Fax: 410-502-2247, E-mail: kmciltr1@jhmi.edu. *Application contact:* Cathy Wilson, Director of Admissions, 410-955-7548, Fax: 410-614-7086, E-mail: jhuson@jhu.edu.
Website: http://www.nursing.jhu.edu

**Johns Hopkins University,** School of Nursing, Doctoral Program in Nursing, Baltimore, MD 21218. Offers adult/gerontological primary care nurse practitioner (PhD); nursing (PhD); nursing practice (DNP); DNP/PhD. *Faculty:* 39 full-time (35 women), 6 part-time/adjunct (5 women). *Students:* 9 full-time (all women), 1 (woman) part-time; includes 4 minority (2 Black or African American, non-Hispanic/Latino; 2 Asian, non-Hispanic/Latino). 7 applicants, 71% accepted, 3 enrolled. *Degree requirements:* For doctorate, comprehensive exam, thesis/dissertation, Preliminary and final oral exam. *Entrance requirements:* For doctorate, minimum GPA of 3.0, goal statement/essay, resume, letters of recommendation, official transcripts from all post-secondary institutions attended; BSN and RN license (for DNP); writing sample (for PhD), work experience for some tracks. Additional exam requirements/recommendations for international students: required—TOEFL (minimum score 600 paper-based; 100 iBT), IELTS (minimum score 7). *Application deadline:* For summer admission, 12/1 priority date for domestic and international students. Application fee: $75. Electronic applications accepted. *Expenses:* $2,053 per credit. *Financial support:* In 2019–20, 10 students received support. Federal Work-Study, scholarships/grants, and tuition waivers (partial) available. Support available to part-time students. Financial award application deadline: 3/1; financial award applicants required to submit FAFSA. *Unit head:* Dr. Jason Farley, 410-502-7563, E-mail: jfarley1@jhu.edu. *Application contact:* Cathy Wilson, Director of Admissions, 410-955-7548, Fax: 410-614-7086, E-mail: jhuson@jhu.edu.
Website: http://nursing.jhu.edu/

**Kent State University,** College of Nursing, Kent, OH 44242. Offers advanced nursing practice (DNP), including adult/gerontology acute care nurse practitioner (MSN, DNP); nursing (MSN, PhD), including adult/gerontology acute care nurse practitioner (MSN, DNP), adult/gerontology clinical nurse specialist (MSN), adult/gerontology primary care nurse practitioner (MSN), family nurse practitioner (MSN), nurse educator (MSN), nursing and healthcare management (MSN), pediatric primary care nurse practitioner (MSN), psychiatric/mental health nurse practitioner (MSN); MBA/MSN. *Accreditation:* AACN. *Program availability:* Part-time, online learning. *Faculty:* 28 full-time (26 women), 15 part-time/adjunct (13 women). *Students:* 138 full-time (123 women), 522 part-time (464 women); includes 80 minority (41 Black or African American, non-Hispanic/Latino; 16 Asian, non-Hispanic/Latino; 9 Hispanic/Latino; 1 Native Hawaiian or other Pacific Islander, non-Hispanic/Latino; 13 Two or more races, non-Hispanic/Latino), 7 international. Average age 35. 303 applicants, 68% accepted, 154 enrolled. In 2019, 156 master's, 8 doctorates awarded. *Degree requirements:* For master's, practicum for master's degrees; for doctorate, comprehensive exam, thesis/dissertation. *Entrance requirements:* For master's, GRE or GMAT, minimum GPA of 3.0, active RN license, statement of purpose, 3 letters of reference, undergraduate level statistics class (minimum C grade), baccalaureate or graduate-level nursing degree, curriculum vitae/resume; for doctorate, GRE, minimum GPA of 3.0, transcripts, 3 letters of reference, interview, active unrestricted Ohio RN license, statement of purpose, writing sample, curriculum vitae/resume, baccalaureate and master's degrees in nursing or DNP, undergraduate or graduate level statistics course with a minimum C grade. Additional exam requirements/recommendations for international students: required—TOEFL (minimum score 83 iBT), IELTS (minimum score 6.5), PTE (minimum score 55), Michigan English Language Assessment Battery (minimum score 78). *Application deadline:* For fall admission, 3/1 for domestic and international students; for spring admission, 10/1 for domestic and international students. Applications are processed on a rolling basis. Application fee: $45 ($70 for international students). Electronic applications accepted. *Financial support:* Federal Work-Study and scholarships/grants available. Financial award application deadline: 2/1. *Unit head:* Dr. Barbara Broome, Ph.D., Dean, 330-672-3777, E-mail: bbroome1@kent.edu. *Application contact:* Dr. Wendy A. Umberger, Ph.D., Associate Dean for Graduate Programs/Professor, 330-672-8813, E-mail: wlewando@kent.edu.
Website: http://www.kent.edu/nursing/

**Keuka College,** Program in Nursing, Keuka Park, NY 14478. Offers adult gerontology (MS); nursing education (MS). *Accreditation:* AACN. *Degree requirements:* For master's, exam or thesis. *Entrance requirements:* For master's, bachelor's degree from accredited institution, minimum GPA of 3.0, unencumbered NY State license, and current registration as RN (for nursing); currently full-time or part-time working RN and 2 clinical letters of recommendation (for adult gerontology nurse practitioner). Additional exam requirements/recommendations for international students: required—TOEFL (minimum score 550 paper-based). Electronic applications accepted. *Expenses:* Contact institution.

**La Salle University,** School of Nursing and Health Sciences, Program in Nursing, Philadelphia, PA 19141-1199. Offers adult gerontology primary care nurse practitioner (MSN, Certificate); adult health and illness clinical nurse specialist (MSN); adult-gerontology clinical nurse specialist (MSN, Certificate); clinical nurse leader (MSN); family primary care nurse practitioner (MSN, Certificate); gerontology (Certificate); nurse anesthetist (MSN, Certificate); nursing (MSN, Certificate); nursing administration (MSN, Certificate); nursing education (Certificate); nursing practice (DNP); nursing service administration (MSN); public health nursing (MSN, Certificate); school nursing (Certificate); MSN/MBA; MSN/MPH. *Accreditation:* AACN. *Program availability:* Part-time, evening/weekend, 100% online. *Degree requirements:* For doctorate, minimum of 1,000 hours of post baccalaureate clinical practice supervised by preceptors. *Entrance requirements:* For master's, GRE, MAT, or GMAT (for students with BSN GPA of less than 3.2), baccalaureate degree in nursing from ACEN- or CCNE-accredited program or an MSN Bridge program; Pennsylvania RN license; 2 letters of reference; resume; statement of philosophy articulating professional values and future educational goal; 1 year of work experience as a registered nurse; for doctorate, GRE (waived for applicants with MSN cumulative GPA of 3.7 or above), MSN, master's degree, MBA or MHA from nationally-accredited program; resume or curriculum vitae; 2 letters of reference; interview; for Certificate, GRE, MAT, or GMAT (for students with BSN GPA of less than 3.2, baccalaureate degree in nursing from ACEN- or CCNE-accredited program or an MSN Bridge program; Pennsylvania RN license; 2 letters of reference; resume; statement of philosophy articulating professional values and future educational goal; 1 year of work experience as a registered nurse. Additional exam requirements/recommendations for international students: required—TOEFL. Electronic applications accepted. Application fee is waived when completed online. *Expenses:* Contact institution.

**Lehman College of the City University of New York,** School of Health Sciences, Human Services and Nursing, Department of Nursing, Bronx, NY 10468-1589. Offers adult health nursing (MS); nursing of older adults (MS); parent-child nursing (MS); pediatric nurse practitioner (MS). *Accreditation:* AACN. *Program availability:* Part-time, evening/weekend. *Entrance requirements:* For master's, bachelor's degree in nursing, New York RN license. *Expenses: Tuition, area resident:* Full-time $5545; part-time $470 per credit. Tuition, nonresident: part-time $855 per credit. *Required fees:* $240.

**Loma Linda University,** School of Nursing, Program in Nurse Educator, Loma Linda, CA 92350. Offers adult/gerontology (MS); obstetrics-pediatrics (MS). *Accreditation:* AACN. *Program availability:* Part-time. *Degree requirements:* For master's, thesis or alternative. *Entrance requirements:* For master's, GRE General Test, BSN, minimum GPA of 3.0, RN license. Additional exam requirements/recommendations for international students: required—TOEFL. Electronic applications accepted.

**Louisiana State University Health Sciences Center,** School of Nursing, New Orleans, LA 70112. Offers adult gerontology acute care nurse practitioner (DNP, Post-Master's Certificate); adult gerontology clinical nurse specialist (DNP, Post-Master's Certificate); adult gerontology primary care nurse practitioner (DNP, Post-Master's Certificate); clinical nurse leader (MSN); executive nurse leader (DNP, Post-Master's Certificate); neonatal nurse practitioner (DNP, Post-Master's Certificate); nurse anesthesia (DNP, Post-Master's Certificate); nurse educator (MSN); nursing (DNS); primary care family nurse practitioner (DNP, Post-Master's Certificate); public/community health nursing (DNP, Post-Master's Certificate). *Accreditation:* AACN; AANA/CANAEP (one or more programs are accredited). *Program availability:* Part-time. *Faculty:* 25 full-time (21 women), 25 part-time/adjunct (13 women). *Students:* 182 full-time (127 women), 70 part-time (59 women); includes 82 minority (52 Black or African American, non-Hispanic/Latino; 2 American Indian or Alaska Native, non-Hispanic/Latino; 14 Asian, non-Hispanic/Latino; 14 Hispanic/Latino), 1 international. Average age 34. 34 applicants, 62% accepted, 21 enrolled. In 2019, 72 doctorates awarded. *Degree requirements:* For master's, thesis optional; for doctorate, thesis/dissertation. *Entrance requirements:* For master's, GRE, minimum GPA of 3.0; for doctorate, GRE, minimum GPA of 3.0 (for DNP), 3.5 (for DNS). Additional exam requirements/recommendations for international students: required—TOEFL (minimum score 550 paper-based; 79 iBT). *Application deadline:* For fall admission, 6/1 priority date for domestic and international students; for spring admission, 10/1 priority date for domestic and international students; for summer admission, 3/1 priority date for domestic and international students. Applications are processed on a rolling basis. Application fee: $100. Electronic applications accepted. *Expenses:* MSN and DNS: $13,354.50, $24,982.25 non-resident, $586 per hour (fall and spring), $467 per hour (summer), $1,102 per hour non-resident (fall and spring), $858 per hour non-resident (summer); DNP (Except Nurse Anethesia): $21,907.50, $38,262.23 non-resident, $973 per hour (fall and spring), $733 per hour (summer), $1,700 per hour non-resident (fall and spring), $1,278 per hour non-resident (summer); Nurse Anesthesia DNP: $26,407.50, $42,762.23 non-resident, $1,173 per hour (fall and spring), $883 per hour (summer), $1,900 per hour non-resident (fall and spring), $1,428 per hour non-resident (summer). *Financial support:* In 2019–20, 20 students received support. Institutionally sponsored loans, scholarships/grants, unspecified assistantships, and DNS Scholars Program available. Financial award application deadline: 4/15; financial award applicants required to submit FAFSA. *Unit head:* Dr. Demetrius James Porche, Dean, 504-568-4106, Fax: 504-599-0573, E-mail: dporch@lsuhsc.edu. *Application contact:* Tracie Gravolet, Director, Office of Student Affairs, 504-568-4114, Fax: 504-568-5711, E-mail: tgravo@lsuhsc.edu.
Website: http://nursing.lsuhsc.edu/

**Marquette University,** Graduate School, College of Nursing, Milwaukee, WI 53201-1881. Offers acute care nurse practitioner (Certificate); adult clinical nurse specialist (Certificate); adult nurse practitioner (Certificate); advanced practice nursing (MSN, DNP), including adult-older adult acute care (DNP), adults (MSN), adults-older adults (DNP), clinical nurse leader (MSN), health care systems leadership (DNP), nurse-midwifery (MSN), older adults (MSN), pediatrics-acute care, pediatrics-primary care, primary care (DNP), systems leadership and healthcare quality (MSN); family nurse practitioner (Certificate); nurse-midwifery (Certificate); nursing (PhD); pediatric acute care (Certificate); pediatric primary care (Certificate); systems leadership and healthcare quality (Certificate). *Accreditation:* AACN; AANA/CANAEP; ACNM/ACME. Terminal master's awarded for partial completion of doctoral program. *Degree requirements:* For master's, comprehensive exam, thesis or alternative. *Entrance requirements:* For master's, GRE General Test, BSN, Wisconsin RN license, official transcripts from all current and previous colleges/universities except Marquette, three completed recommendation forms, resume, written statement of professional goals; for doctorate, GRE General Test, official transcripts from all current and previous colleges/universities except Marquette, three letters of recommendation, resume, written statement of professional goals, sample of scholarly writing. Additional exam requirements/recommendations for international students: required—TOEFL (minimum score 530 paper-based). Electronic applications accepted.

**Maryville University of Saint Louis,** Myrtle E. and Earl E. Walker College of Health Professions, The Catherine McAuley School of Nursing, St. Louis, MO 63141-7299. Offers acute care nurse practitioner (MSN); adult gerontology nurse practitioner (MSN); advanced practice nursing (DNP); family nurse practitioner (MSN); pediatric nurse practitioner (MSN). *Accreditation:* AACN. *Program availability:* 100% online, blended/hybrid learning. *Faculty:* 14 full-time (all women), 131 part-time/adjunct (114 women).

## Gerontological Nursing

*Students:* 103 full-time (91 women), 3,493 part-time (3,050 women); includes 1,039 minority (530 Black or African American, non-Hispanic/Latino; 41 American Indian or Alaska Native, non-Hispanic/Latino; 157 Asian, non-Hispanic/Latino; 221 Hispanic/Latino; 90 Two or more races, non-Hispanic/Latino), 9 international. Average age 37. In 2019, 1,012 master's, 54 doctorates awarded. *Degree requirements:* For master's, practicum. *Entrance requirements:* For master's, BSN, current licensure, minimum GPA of 3.0, 3 letters of recommendation, curriculum vitae. Additional exam requirements/recommendations for international students: required—TOEFL (minimum score 550 paper-based). *Application deadline:* Applications are processed on a rolling basis. Electronic applications accepted. *Expenses:* Contact institution. *Financial support:* Federal Work-Study and campus employment available. Support available to part-time students. Financial award application deadline: 4/1; financial award applicants required to submit FAFSA. *Unit head:* Karla Larson, Assistant Dean Nursing, 314-529-6856, Fax: 314-529-9139, E-mail: klarson@maryville.edu. *Application contact:* Jeannie DeLuca, Director of Admissions and Advising, 314-929-9355, Fax: 314-529-9927, E-mail: jdeluca@maryville.edu.
Website: http://www.maryville.edu/hp/nursing/

**Medical University of South Carolina,** College of Nursing, Adult-Gerontology Health Nurse Practitioner Program, Charleston, SC 29425. Offers MSN, DNP. *Program availability:* Part-time, online learning. *Degree requirements:* For master's, comprehensive exam (for some programs), thesis optional; for doctorate, final project. *Entrance requirements:* For master's, BSN from nationally-accredited program, minimum nursing and cumulative GPA of 3.0, undergraduate-level statistics course, active RN License, 3 confidential references, current curriculum vitae or resume, essay; for doctorate, BSN from nationally-accredited program, minimum nursing and cumulative GPA of 3.0, undergraduate-level statistics course, active RN License, 3 confidential references, current curriculum vitae or resume, personal essay (for DNP). Additional exam requirements/recommendations for international students: required—TOEFL (minimum score 550 paper-based; 80 iBT). Electronic applications accepted.

**Mercer University,** Graduate Studies, Cecil B. Day Campus, Georgia Baptist College of Nursing, Atlanta, GA 30341. Offers adult gerontology acute care nurse practitioner (MSN, Certificate); family nurse practitioner (MSN; Certificate); nursing (PhD); nursing practice (DNP). *Accreditation:* AACN. *Program availability:* Part-time, blended/hybrid learning. *Faculty:* 26 full-time (23 women), 13 part-time/adjunct (11 women). *Students:* 69 full-time (64 women), 45 part-time (41 women); includes 61 minority (42 Black or African American, non-Hispanic/Latino; 12 Asian, non-Hispanic/Latino; 4 Hispanic/Latino; 1 Native Hawaiian or other Pacific Islander, non-Hispanic/Latino; 2 Two or more races, non-Hispanic/Latino), 1 international. Average age 35. 92 applicants, 75% accepted, 57 enrolled. In 2019, 14 master's, 10 doctorates awarded. *Degree requirements:* For master's, thesis or alternative, capstone project; for doctorate, comprehensive exam (for some programs), scholarly project (for DNP); dissertation (for PhD). *Entrance requirements:* For master's, bachelor's degree from accredited nursing program, minimum GPA 3.0, unencumbered license to practice as a Registered Nurse in Georgia, essay, three professional references; for doctorate, master's degree from accredited nursing program depending on program, unencumbered license to practice as a Registered Nurse, graduate statistics course, essay, three professional references; for Certificate, APRN license for post-master's certificate programs. Additional exam requirements/recommendations for international students: required—TOEFL (minimum score 100 iBT). *Application deadline:* For fall admission, 7/1 for domestic students; for spring admission, 12/1 for domestic students; for summer admission, 4/15 for domestic students. Applications are processed on a rolling basis. Application fee: $50. Electronic applications accepted. *Expenses:* Contact institution. *Financial support:* In 2019–20, 23 students received support, including 1 research assistantship with partial tuition reimbursement available (averaging $10,500 per year); scholarships/grants also available. Financial award application deadline: 6/30; financial award applicants required to submit FAFSA. *Unit head:* Dr. Linda Streit, Dean/Professor, 678-547-6793, Fax: 678-547-6796, E-mail: streit_la@mercer.edu. *Application contact:* Janda Anderson, Director of Admissions, 678-547-6700, Fax: 678-547-6794, E-mail: anderson_j@mercer.edu.
Website: http://www.nursing.mercer.edu.

**MGH Institute of Health Professions,** School of Nursing, Boston, MA 02129. Offers advanced practice nursing (MSN); gerontological nursing (MSN); nursing (DNP); pediatric nursing (MSN); psychiatric nursing (MSN); teaching and learning for health care education (Certificate); women's health nursing (MSN). *Accreditation:* AACN. *Degree requirements:* For master's, thesis or alternative. *Entrance requirements:* For master's, GRE General Test, bachelor's degree from regionally-accredited college or university. Additional exam requirements/recommendations for international students: required—TOEFL (minimum score 550 paper-based; 80 iBT). Electronic applications accepted.

**Middle Georgia State University,** Office of Graduate Studies, Macon, GA 31206. Offers adult/gerontology acute care nurse practitioner (MSN); information technology (MS), including health informatics, information security and digital forensics, software development. *Entrance requirements:* For master's, GRE. Additional exam requirements/recommendations for international students: required—TOEFL (minimum score 523 paper-based; 69 iBT). *Expenses:* Contact institution.

**Molloy College,** Graduate Nursing Program, Rockville Centre, NY 11571-5002. Offers adult-gerontology clinical nurse specialist (DNP); adult-gerontology nurse practitioner (MS, DNP); clinical nurse specialist: adult-gerontology (MS); family nurse practitioner (MS, DNP); family psychiatric/mental health nurse practitioner (MS, DNP); nursing (PhD, Advanced Certificate); nursing administration with informatics (MS); nursing education (MS); pediatric nurse practitioner (MS, DNP). *Accreditation:* AACN. *Program availability:* Part-time, evening/weekend. *Faculty:* 30 full-time (28 women), 10 part-time/adjunct (6 women). *Students:* 18 full-time (17 women), 573 part-time (520 women); includes 340 minority (181 Black or African American, non-Hispanic/Latino; 2 American Indian or Alaska Native, non-Hispanic/Latino; 100 Asian, non-Hispanic/Latino; 42 Hispanic/Latino; 5 Native Hawaiian or other Pacific Islander, non-Hispanic/Latino; 10 Two or more races, non-Hispanic/Latino), 3 international. Average age 38. 332 applicants, 60% accepted, 149 enrolled. In 2019, 136 master's, 12 doctorates, 22 other advanced degrees awarded. *Degree requirements:* For doctorate, clinical research residency and scholarly clinical project (for DNP); dissertation and comprehensive exam (for PhD). *Entrance requirements:* Additional exam requirements/recommendations for international students: required—TOEFL (minimum score 550 paper-based; 79 iBT). *Application deadline:* Applications are processed on a rolling basis. Application fee: $60. Electronic applications accepted. *Expenses: Tuition:* Full-time $21,510; part-time $1195 per credit hour. *Required fees:* $1100. Tuition and fees vary according to course load, degree level and program. *Financial support:* Application deadline: 3/1; applicants required to submit FAFSA. *Unit head:* Dr. Marcia R. Gardner, Dean, The Barbara H. Hagan School of Nursing, 516-323-3651, E-mail: mgardner@molloy.edu. *Application contact:* Faye Hood, Assistant Director for Admissions, 516-323-4009, E-mail: fhood@molloy.edu.
Website: https://www.molloy.edu/academics/graduate-programs/graduate-nursing-x25989

**Monmouth University,** Graduate Studies, Marjorie K. Unterberg School of Nursing and Health Studies, West Long Branch, NJ 07764-1898. Offers adult-gerontological primary care nurse practitioner (Post-Master's Certificate); forensic nursing (MSN).

*Accreditation:* AACN. *Program availability:* Part-time, evening/weekend, 100% online, blended/hybrid learning. *Faculty:* 13 full-time (all women), 9 part-time/adjunct (8 women). *Students:* 1 (woman) full-time, 284 part-time (261 women); includes 108 minority (37 Black or African American, non-Hispanic/Latino; 38 Asian, non-Hispanic/Latino; 32 Hispanic/Latino; 1 Two or more races, non-Hispanic/Latino). Average age 39. In 2019, 100 master's, 14 doctorates, 10 other advanced degrees awarded. *Degree requirements:* For master's, practicum (for some tracks); for doctorate, practicum, capstone course. *Entrance requirements:* For master's, GRE General Test (waived for MSN applicants with minimum B grade in each of the first four courses and for MS applicants with master's degree), BSN with minimum GPA of 2.75, current RN license, proof of liability and malpractice policy, personal statement, two letters of recommendation, college course work in health assessment, resume; CASPA application (for MS); for doctorate, accredited master's nursing program degree with minimum GPA of 3.2, active RN license, national certification as nurse practitioner or nurse administrator, working knowledge of statistics, statement of goals and vision for change, 2 letters of recommendation (professional or academic), resume, interview. Additional exam requirements/recommendations for international students: required—TOEFL (minimum score 550 paper-based; 79 iBT), IELTS (minimum score 6) or Michigan English Language Assessment Battery (minimum score 77). *Application deadline:* For fall admission, 7/15 priority date for domestic students, 6/1 for international students; for spring admission, 12/1 priority date for domestic students, 11/1 for international students; for summer admission, 5/1 for domestic students. Applications are processed on a rolling basis. Application fee: $50. Electronic applications accepted. *Expenses:* $1,233 per credit. *Financial support:* In 2019–20, 251 students received support. Research assistantships, teaching assistantships, scholarships/grants, and unspecified assistantships available. Support available to part-time students. Financial award applicants required to submit FAFSA. *Unit head:* Dr. Ann Marie Mauro, Dean, 732-571-3443, Fax: 732-263-5131, E-mail: amauro@monmouth.edu. *Application contact:* Laurie Kuhn, Associate Director of Graduate Admission, 732-571-3452, Fax: 732-263-5123, E-mail: gradadm@monmouth.edu.
Website: https://www.monmouth.edu/graduate/nursing-programs-of-study/

**Morningside College,** Graduate Programs, Nylen School of Nursing, Sioux City, IA 51106. Offers adult gerontology primary care nurse practitioner (MSN); clinical nurse leader (MSN); family primary care nurse practitioner (MSN). *Program availability:* Part-time, online only, 100% online. Electronic applications accepted. *Expenses:* Contact institution.

**Mount Carmel College of Nursing,** Nursing Program, Columbus, OH 43222. Offers adult gerontology acute care nurse practitioner (MS); adult health clinical nurse specialist (MS); family nurse practitioner (MS); nursing (DNP); nursing administration (MS); nursing education (MS). *Accreditation:* AACN. *Program availability:* Part-time. *Faculty:* 6 full-time (all women), 10 part-time/adjunct (9 women). *Students:* 101 full-time (82 women), 109 part-time (95 women); includes 43 minority (27 Black or African American, non-Hispanic/Latino; 4 Asian, non-Hispanic/Latino; 5 Hispanic/Latino; 7 Two or more races, non-Hispanic/Latino). Average age 32. 133 applicants, 84% accepted, 95 enrolled. In 2019, 66 master's, 2 doctorates awarded. *Degree requirements:* For master's, professional manuscript; for doctorate, practicum. *Entrance requirements:* For master's, letters of recommendation, statement of purpose, current resume, baccalaureate degree in nursing, current Ohio RN license, minimum cumulative GPA of 3.0; for doctorate, master's degree in nursing from program accredited by either ACEN or CCNE. Additional exam requirements/recommendations for international students: required—TOEFL (minimum score 550 paper-based; 80 iBT). *Application deadline:* For fall admission, 2/1 priority date for domestic students; for spring admission, 11/1 priority date for domestic students. Applications are processed on a rolling basis. Application fee: $30. Electronic applications accepted. *Expenses: Tuition:* Full-time $27,936; part-time $27,936 per year. *Required fees:* $360. *Financial support:* In 2019–20, 13 students received support. Institutionally sponsored loans and scholarships/grants available. Financial award application deadline: 3/1; financial award applicants required to submit FAFSA. *Unit head:* Dr. Jami Nininger, Interim Associate Dean Graduate Studies, 614-234-1777, Fax: 614-234-2875, E-mail: jnininger@mccn.edu. *Application contact:* Dr. Kim Campbell, Director of Recruitment and Admissions, 614-234-5144, Fax: 614-234-5427, E-mail: kcampbell@mccn.edu.
Website: www.mccn.edu

**Neumann University,** Graduate Program in Nursing, Aston, PA 19014-1298. Offers adult-gerontology nurse practitioner (MS, Certificate). *Accreditation:* ACEN. *Program availability:* Part-time, evening/weekend. *Entrance requirements:* For master's, official transcripts from all institutions attended, resume, letter of intent, current registered nursing license, two letters of reference; for Certificate, BSN, MSN, official transcripts from all institutions attended, resume, letter of intent, current registered nursing license, two official letters of reference. Additional exam requirements/recommendations for international students: required—TOEFL (minimum score 84 iBT). Electronic applications accepted.

**New York University,** Rory Meyers College of Nursing, Doctor of Nursing Practice Program, New York, NY 10012-1019. Offers nursing (DNP), including adult-gerontology acute care nurse practitioner, adult-gerontology primary care nurse practitioner, family nurse practitioner, nurse-midwifery, pediatrics nurse practitioner, psychiatric-mental health nurse practitioner. *Accreditation:* AACN. *Program availability:* Part-time, evening/weekend. *Degree requirements:* For doctorate, thesis/dissertation, project. *Entrance requirements:* For doctorate, MS, RN license, interview, Nurse Practitioner Certification, writing sample. Additional exam requirements/recommendations for international students: required—TOEFL (minimum score 100 iBT), IELTS (minimum score 7). Electronic applications accepted. *Expenses:* Contact institution.

**New York University,** Rory Meyers College of Nursing, Programs in Advanced Practice Nursing, New York, NY 10012-1019. Offers adult-gerontology acute care nurse practitioner (MS, Advanced Certificate); adult-gerontology primary care nurse practitioner (MS, Advanced Certificate); family nurse practitioner (MS, Advanced Certificate); gerontology nurse practitioner (Advanced Certificate); nurse-midwifery (MS, Advanced Certificate); nursing administration (MS, Advanced Certificate); nursing education (MS, Advanced Certificate); nursing informatics (MS, Advanced Certificate); pediatrics nurse practitioner (MS, Advanced Certificate); psychiatric-mental health nurse practitioner (MS, Advanced Certificate); MS/MPH. *Accreditation:* AACN; ACNM/ACME. *Program availability:* Part-time, evening/weekend. *Degree requirements:* For master's, thesis (for some programs), capstone. *Entrance requirements:* For master's, BS in nursing, AS in nursing with another BS/BA, interview, RN license, 1 year of clinical experience (3 for the MS in nursing education program); for Advanced Certificate, master's degree in nursing. Additional exam requirements/recommendations for international students: required—TOEFL (minimum score 100 iBT), IELTS (minimum score 7). Electronic applications accepted. *Expenses:* Contact institution.

**Northeastern University,** Bouvé College of Health Sciences, Boston, MA 02115-5096. Offers applied behavior analysis (MS); audiology (Au D); counseling psychology (MS, PhD, CAGS); exercise science (MS); nursing (MS, PhD, CAGS), including administration (MS), adult-gerontology acute care nurse practitioner (MS, CAGS), adult-gerontology primary care nurse practitioner (MS, CAGS), anesthesia (MS), family nurse practitioner (MS, CAGS), neonatal nurse practitioner (MS, CAGS), pediatric nurse

practitioner (MS, CAGS), psychiatric mental health nurse practitioner (MS, CAGS); nursing practice (DNP); pharmaceutical sciences (MS, PhD), including interdisciplinary concentration, pharmaceutics and drug delivery systems; pharmacology (MS); pharmacy (Pharm D); school psychology (PhD); speech-language pathology (MS); urban health (MPH); MS/MBA. *Accreditation:* AANA/CANAEP; ACPE (one or more programs are accredited); ASHA; CEPH. *Program availability:* Part-time, evening/weekend, online learning. *Degree requirements:* For doctorate, thesis/dissertation (for some programs); for CAGS, comprehensive exam. Electronic applications accepted. *Expenses:* Contact institution.

**Nova Southeastern University,** Ron and Kathy Assaf College of Nursing, Fort Lauderdale, FL 33314-7796. Offers advanced practice registered nurse (MSN), including adult-gerontology acute care nurse practitioner, family nurse practitioner, psychiatric mental health nurse practitioner; executive nurse leadership (MSN); nursing (PhD), including nursing education; nursing education (MSN); nursing informatics (MSN); nursing practice (DNP). *Accreditation:* AACN. *Program availability:* Part-time, evening/weekend, 100% online, blended/hybrid learning, annual one-week summer institute delivered face-to-face on main campus. *Faculty:* 32 full-time (29 women), 34 part-time/adjunct (31 women). *Students:* 4 full-time (3 women), 658 part-time (585 women); includes 427 minority (182 Black or African American, non-Hispanic/Latino; 35 Asian, non-Hispanic/Latino; 197 Hispanic/Latino; 13 Two or more races, non-Hispanic/Latino), 3 international. Average age 38. 157 applicants, 93% accepted, 146 enrolled. In 2019, 184 master's, 12 doctorates awarded. *Degree requirements:* For doctorate, comprehensive exam, thesis/dissertation. *Entrance requirements:* For master's, minimum GPA of 3.0, RN, BSN, BS or BA; for doctorate, minimum GPA of 3.5, MSN, RN. Additional exam requirements/recommendations for international students: recommended—TOEFL. *Application deadline:* For fall admission, 8/1 for domestic students, 3/1 for international students; for winter admission, 12/9 for domestic students, 11/1 for international students. Applications are processed on a rolling basis. Application fee: $50. Electronic applications accepted. *Expenses:* Contact institution. *Financial support:* Application deadline: 4/15; applicants required to submit FAFSA. *Unit head:* Dr. Marcella M. Rutherford, Dean, 954-262-1963, E-mail: rmarcell@nova.edu. *Application contact:* Dianna Murphey, Director of Operations, 954-262-1975, E-mail: dgardner1@nova.edu.
Website: http://www.nova.edu/nursing/

**Oakland University,** Graduate Study and Lifelong Learning, School of Nursing, Adult Gerontological Nurse Practitioner Program, Rochester, MI 48309-4401. Offers MSN, PMC. *Program availability:* Part-time. *Entrance requirements:* Additional exam requirements/recommendations for international students: required—TOEFL (minimum score 550 paper-based; 79 iBT), IELTS (minimum score 6.5). Electronic applications accepted. *Expenses: Tuition, area resident:* Full-time $12,328; part-time $770.50 per credit hour. Tuition, state resident: full-time $12,328; part-time $770.50 per credit hour. Tuition, nonresident: full-time $16,432; part-time $1027 per credit hour. *International tuition:* $16,432 full-time. Tuition and fees vary according to degree level and program.

**Old Dominion University,** College of Health Sciences, School of Nursing, Adult Gerontology Nursing Emphasis, Norfolk, VA 23529. Offers adult gerontology clinical nurse specialist/administrator (MSN); adult gerontology clinical nurse specialist/educator (MSN); advanced practice (DNP); neonatal clinical nurse specialist (MSN); pediatric clinical nurse specialist (MSN). *Program availability:* Part-time, online only, blended/hybrid learning. *Degree requirements:* For master's, comprehensive exam, internship, practicum. *Entrance requirements:* For master's, GRE or MAT (waived with a GPA above 3.5), undergraduate health/physical assessment course, statistics, 3 letters of recommendation, essay, resume, transcripts. Additional exam requirements/recommendations for international students: required—TOEFL. Electronic applications accepted. *Expenses:* Contact institution.

**Oregon Health & Science University,** School of Nursing, Program in Adult Gerontology Acute Care Nurse Practitioner, Portland, OR 97239-2941. Offers MN. *Entrance requirements:* For master's, minimum cumulative and science GPA of 3.0, 3 letters of recommendation, essay, statistics within last 5 years. Additional exam requirements/recommendations for international students: required—TOEFL (minimum score 83 iBT). Electronic applications accepted. *Expenses:* Contact institution.

**Point Loma Nazarene University,** School of Nursing, MS in Nursing Program, San Diego, CA 92106. Offers adult/gerontology (MSN); family/individual health (MSN); pediatrics (MSN). *Program availability:* Part-time. *Students:* 4 full-time (3 women), 49 part-time (41 women); includes 29 minority (5 Black or African American, non-Hispanic/Latino; 8 Asian, non-Hispanic/Latino; 14 Hispanic/Latino; 2 Two or more races, non-Hispanic/Latino). Average age 37. 30 applicants, 83% accepted, 14 enrolled. In 2019, 25 master's awarded. *Entrance requirements:* For master's, NCLEX exam, ADN or BSN in nursing, interview, RN license, essay, letters of recommendation, interview. *Application deadline:* For fall admission, 7/5 priority date for domestic students; for spring admission, 11/1 priority date for domestic students; for summer admission, 3/22 priority date for domestic students. Applications are processed on a rolling basis. Application fee: $50. Electronic applications accepted. *Expenses:* $820 per unit. *Financial support:* In 2019–20, 9 students received support. Scholarships/grants available. Financial award applicants required to submit FAFSA. *Unit head:* Dr. Larry Rankin, Associate Dean, 619-849-7813, E-mail: LarryRankin@pointloma.edu. *Application contact:* Dana Barger, Director of Recruitment and Admissions, Graduate and Professional Students, 619-329-6799, E-mail: gradinfo@pointloma.edu.
Website: https://www.pointloma.edu/graduate-studies/programs/nursing-ms

**Purdue University,** Graduate School, College of Health and Human Sciences, School of Nursing, West Lafayette, IN 47907. Offers adult gerontology primary care nurse practitioner (MS, Post Master's Certificate); nursing (DNP, PhD); primary care family nurse practitioner (MS, Post Master's Certificate); primary care pediatric nurse practitioner (MS, Post Master's Certificate). *Faculty:* 41 full-time (40 women), 9 part-time/adjunct (8 women). *Students:* 84 full-time (72 women), 46 part-time (43 women); includes 19 minority (7 Black or African American, non-Hispanic/Latino; 6 Asian, non-Hispanic/Latino; 4 Hispanic/Latino; 2 Two or more races, non-Hispanic/Latino), 1 international. Average age 33. 85 applicants, 80% accepted, 55 enrolled. In 2019, 29 master's, 7 doctorates, 2 other advanced degrees awarded. *Unit head:* Nancy E. Edwards, Head of the Graduate Program, 765-494-4015, E-mail: edwardsn@purdue.edu. *Application contact:* Reanne Hall, Graduate Contact, 765-494-9248, E-mail: gradnursing@purdue.edu.
Website: http://www.purdue.edu/hhs/nur/

**Purdue University Fort Wayne,** College of Health and Human Services, Department of Nursing, Fort Wayne, IN 46805-1499. Offers adult-gerontology primary care nurse practitioner (MS); family nurse practitioner (MS); nurse executive (MS); nursing administration (Certificate); nursing education (MS). *Accreditation:* ACEN. *Program availability:* Part-time. *Entrance requirements:* For master's, GRE Writing Test (if GPA below 3.0), BS in nursing, eligibility for Indiana RN license, minimum GPA of 3.0, essay, copy of resume, three references, undergraduate course work in research and statistics within last 5 years. Additional exam requirements/recommendations for international students: required—TOEFL (minimum score 550 paper-based; 79 iBT); recommended—TWE. Electronic applications accepted.

**Rutgers University - Camden,** School of Nursing–Camden, Camden, NJ 08102-1401. Offers adult gerontology primary care nurse practitioner (DNP); family nurse practitioner (DNP). *Degree requirements:* For doctorate, minimum of 1,000 clinical residency hours, evidence-based clinical project.

**Sage Graduate School,** School of Health Sciences, Department of Nursing, Program in Adult Gerontology Nurse Practitioner, Troy, NY 12180-4115. Offers MS, Certificate. *Program availability:* Part-time, evening/weekend. *Faculty:* 8 full-time (all women), 13 part-time/adjunct (12 women). *Students:* 7 full-time (4 women), 25 part-time (22 women); includes 8 minority (2 Black or African American, non-Hispanic/Latino; 5 Asian, non-Hispanic/Latino; 1 Two or more races, non-Hispanic/Latino). Average age 41. 16 applicants, 50% accepted, 7 enrolled. In 2019, 4 master's, 2 other advanced degrees awarded. *Entrance requirements:* For master's, Applicants must be currently licensed as a registered professional nurse in the state where they practice; a bachelor's degree in nursing from a nationally accredited program; a GPA of 3.0 or higher; official transcripts of all previous UG/GR study; 2 letters of reference; 1-2 page statement of professional goals; current resume. Additional exam requirements/recommendations for international students: required—TOEFL (minimum score 550 paper-based). *Application deadline:* Applications are processed on a rolling basis. Application fee: $40. Electronic applications accepted. *Expenses: Tuition:* Part-time $730 per credit hour. Tuition and fees vary according to course load, degree level and program. *Financial support:* Fellowships, research assistantships, scholarships/grants, and unspecified assistantships available. Financial award application deadline: 3/1; financial award applicants required to submit FAFSA. *Unit head:* Dr. Kathleen Kelly, Dean, School of Health Sciences, 518-244-2030, Fax: 518-244-2009, E-mail: kellyk5@sage.edu. *Application contact:* Erin Menzer, Associate Director of Transfer and Nursing Enrollment Management, 518-244-4565, Fax: 518-244-6880, E-mail: menzee@sage.edu.

**St. Catherine University,** Graduate Programs, Program in Nursing, St. Paul, MN 55105. Offers adult-gerontological nurse practitioner (MS); nurse educator (MS); nursing (DNP); nursing: entry-level (MS); pediatric nurse practitioner (MS). *Accreditation:* ACEN. *Program availability:* Part-time, evening/weekend. *Degree requirements:* For master's, thesis; for doctorate, portfolio, systems change project. *Entrance requirements:* For master's, GRE General Test, bachelor's degree in nursing, current nursing license, 2 years of recent clinical practice; for doctorate, master's degree in nursing, RN license, advanced nursing position. Additional exam requirements/recommendations for international students: required—TOEFL (minimum score 600 paper-based; 100 iBT). *Expenses:* Contact institution.

**Saint Francis Medical Center College of Nursing,** SFMC College of Nursing Graduate Programs, Peoria, IL 61603-3783. Offers adult gerontology (MSN); clinical nurse leader (MSN); family nurse practitioner (MSN, Post-Graduate Certificate); family psychiatric mental health nurse practitioner (MSN); neonatal nurse practitioner (MSN); nurse clinician (Post-Graduate Certificate); nurse educator (MSN, Post-Graduate Certificate); nursing (DNP), including leadership/ clinician; nursing management leadership (MSN). *Accreditation:* ACEN. *Program availability:* Part-time, online only, 100% online, blended/hybrid learning. *Faculty:* 12 full-time (all women), 10 part-time/adjunct (all women). *Students:* 1 (woman) full-time, 188 part-time (157 women); includes 20 minority (10 Black or African American, non-Hispanic/Latino; 3 Asian, non-Hispanic/Latino; 3 Hispanic/Latino; 4 Two or more races, non-Hispanic/Latino). Average age 40. 54 applicants, 91% accepted, 18 enrolled. In 2019, 51 master's, 11 doctorates awarded. *Degree requirements:* For master's, research experience, portfolio, practicum; for doctorate, practicum. *Entrance requirements:* For master's, Nursing research, health assessment, RN license; for doctorate, Master's degree in nursing, professional portfolio, graduate statistics, transcripts, RN license. Additional exam requirements/recommendations for international students: required—TOEFL (minimum score 550 paper-based; 79 iBT). *Application deadline:* For fall admission, 6/1 priority date for domestic and international students; for spring admission, 11/15 priority date for domestic and international students. Applications are processed on a rolling basis. Application fee: $50. *Expenses: Tuition:* Part-time $705 per credit hour. *Required fees:* $270 per unit. *Financial support:* In 2019–20, 13 students received support. Scholarships/grants available. Support available to part-time students. Financial award application deadline: 6/15; financial award applicants required to submit FAFSA. *Unit head:* Dr. Sandie S Soldwisch, President of OSF Colleges of Health Sciences, 815-282-7909, Fax: 309-624-8973, E-mail: Sandie.S.Soldwisch@osfhealthcare.org. *Application contact:* Dr. Kim A. Mitchell, Dean, Graduate Program, 309-655-2201, Fax: 309-624-8973, E-mail: kim.a.mitchell@osfhealthcare.org.
Website: http://www.sfmccon.edu/graduate-programs/

**St. Joseph's College, Long Island Campus,** Program in Nursing, Patchogue, NY 11772-2399. Offers adult-gerontology clinical nurse specialist (MS); adult-gerontology primary care nurse practitioner (MS); nursing education (MS). *Program availability:* Part-time, evening/weekend. *Faculty:* 7 full-time (6 women), 1 (woman) part-time/adjunct. *Students:* 54 part-time (48 women); includes 18 minority (7 Black or African American, non-Hispanic/Latino; 2 Asian, non-Hispanic/Latino; 8 Hispanic/Latino; 1 Two or more races, non-Hispanic/Latino). Average age 38. 57 applicants, 51% accepted, 22 enrolled. In 2019, 14 master's awarded. *Entrance requirements:* For master's, Application, proof of New York State R.N. license, curriculum vitae, personal statement, 2 letters of reference, official transcripts, verification of employment form, proof of malpractice insurance. Additional exam requirements/recommendations for international students: required—TOEFL (minimum score 80 iBT). *Application deadline:* Applications are processed on a rolling basis. Application fee: $25. Electronic applications accepted. *Expenses: Tuition:* Full-time $19,350; part-time $1075 per credit. *Required fees:* $410. *Financial support:* In 2019–20, 33 students received support. *Unit head:* Dr. Maria Fletcher, RN, Director, Associate Professor, 631-687-5180, E-mail: mfletcher@sjcny.edu. *Application contact:* Dr. Maria Fletcher, RN, Director, Associate Professor, 631-687-5180, E-mail: mfletcher@sjcny.edu.
Website: https://www.sjcny.edu/nursingli

**St. Joseph's College, New York,** Program in Nursing, Brooklyn, NY 11205-3688. Offers adult-gerontology clinical nurse specialist (MS); adult-gerontology primary care nurse practitioner (MS); nursing education (MS). *Accreditation:* ACEN. *Program availability:* Part-time, evening/weekend. *Faculty:* 3 full-time (all women), 2 part-time/adjunct (both women). *Students:* 52 part-time (47 women); includes 43 minority (40 Black or African American, non-Hispanic/Latino; 2 Asian, non-Hispanic/Latino; 1 Two or more races, non-Hispanic/Latino). Average age 43. 49 applicants, 67% accepted, 21 enrolled. In 2019, 19 master's awarded. *Entrance requirements:* Additional exam requirements/recommendations for international students: required—TOEFL (minimum score 80 iBT). *Application deadline:* Applications are processed on a rolling basis. Application fee: $25. Electronic applications accepted. *Expenses: Tuition:* Full-time $19,350; part-time $1075 per credit. *Required fees:* $400. *Financial support:* In 2019–20, 9 students received support. *Unit head:* Maria Fletcher, Director, Associate Professor, 718-940-5891, E-mail: mfletcher@sjcny.edu. *Application contact:* Maria Fletcher, Director, Associate Professor, 718-940-5891, E-mail: mfletcher@sjcny.edu.
Website: https://www.sjcny.edu/brooklyn/academics/graduate/graduate-degrees/nursing-clinical-nurse-specialist/m.s.-in-nursing-major

**Saint Mary's College,** Graduate Studies, Doctor of Nursing Practice Program, Notre Dame, IN 46556. Offers adult - gerontology acute care nurse practitioner (DNP); adult -

gerontology primary care nurse practitioner (DNP); family nurse practitioner (DNP). *Program availability:* Part-time-only, evening/weekend, online only, 100% online. *Faculty:* 11. *Students:* 58 part-time (53 women); includes 15 minority (8 Black or African American, non-Hispanic/Latino; 3 Asian, non-Hispanic/Latino; 4 Hispanic/Latino). Average age 30. 24 applicants, 75% accepted, 15 enrolled. In 2019, 1 doctorate awarded. *Degree requirements:* For doctorate, comprehensive exam, thesis/dissertation. *Entrance requirements:* For doctorate, BSN or MSN, unencumbered RN license or eligibility for RN licensure, official transcripts from previously-attended institutions, 3 letters of recommendation, personal statement, resume or curriculum vitae. Additional exam requirements/recommendations for international students: recommended—TOEFL (minimum score 80 iBT), IELTS (minimum score 6.5). *Application deadline:* For fall admission, 3/31 priority date for domestic and international students. Applications are processed on a rolling basis. Application fee: $70. Electronic applications accepted. *Expenses:* $5765 per semester. *Financial support:* In 2019–20, 3 students received support. Scholarships/grants available. Financial award application deadline: 3/1; financial award applicants required to submit FAFSA. *Unit head:* Sue Anderson, Program Director, Doctor of Nursing Practice, 574-284-4682, E-mail: sanderson@saintmarys.edu. *Application contact:* Melissa Fruscione, Director, Graduate Studies, 574-284-5098, E-mail: graduateadmission@saintmarys.edu.
Website: https://grad.saintmarys.edu/academic-programs/doctor-nursing-practice

**Salem State University,** School of Graduate Studies, Program in Nursing, Salem, MA 01970-5353. Offers adult-gerontology primary care nursing (MSN); nursing administration (MSN); nursing education (MSN); MBA/MSN. *Accreditation:* AACN. *Program availability:* Part-time, evening/weekend. *Entrance requirements:* For master's, GRE or MAT. Additional exam requirements/recommendations for international students: required—TOEFL (minimum score 550 paper-based; 80 iBT) or IELTS (minimum score 5.5).

**San Jose State University,** Program in Nursing, San Jose, CA 95192-0057. Offers gerontology nurse practitioner (MS); nursing (Certificate); nursing administration (MS); nursing education (MS). *Accreditation:* AACN. *Faculty:* 5 full-time (all women), 3 part-time/adjunct (all women). *Students:* 21 full-time (17 women), 52 part-time (49 women); includes 45 minority (4 Black or African American, non-Hispanic/Latino; 29 Asian, non-Hispanic/Latino; 12 Hispanic/Latino), 3 international. Average age 37. 30 applicants, 97% accepted, 23 enrolled. In 2019, 22 master's awarded. *Degree requirements:* For master's, comprehensive exam, thesis. *Entrance requirements:* For master's, BSN. *Application deadline:* For fall admission, 3/1 for domestic students. Applications are processed on a rolling basis. Application fee: $70. Electronic applications accepted. *Expenses:* Contact institution. *Financial support:* Application deadline: 5/1; applicants required to submit FAFSA. *Unit head:* Colleen O'Leary-Kelley, Department Chair, 408-924-1319, Fax: 408-924-3135, E-mail: colleen.oleary-kelley@sjsu.edu. *Application contact:* Karen Wilcox, FNP Program Analyst, 408-924-3153, Fax: 408-924-3135, E-mail: karen.wilcox@sjsu.edu.
Website: http://www.sjsu.edu/nursing/

**Seattle Pacific University,** MS in Nursing Program, Seattle, WA 98119-1997. Offers administration (MSN); adult/gerontology nurse practitioner (MSN); clinical nurse specialist (MSN); family nurse practitioner (MSN, Certificate); informatics (MSN); nurse educator (MSN). *Accreditation:* AACN. *Program availability:* Part-time. *Students:* 42 full-time (38 women), 18 part-time (16 women); includes 28 minority (5 Black or African American, non-Hispanic/Latino; 18 Asian, non-Hispanic/Latino; 5 Hispanic/Latino), 2 international. Average age 33. 59 applicants, 41% accepted. In 2019, 10 master's awarded. *Degree requirements:* For master's, thesis. *Entrance requirements:* For master's, personal statement, transcripts, undergraduate nursing degree, proof of undergraduate statistics course with minimum GPA of 2.0, 2 recommendations. *Application deadline:* For fall admission, 1/15 priority date for domestic students; for spring admission, 1/15 for domestic students. Applications are processed on a rolling basis. Application fee: $50. Electronic applications accepted. *Expenses:* Contact institution. *Financial support:* Fellowships and scholarships/grants available. Financial award applicants required to submit FAFSA. *Unit head:* Dr. Antwinett Lee, Associate Dean, 206-281-2607, E-mail: leea30@spu.edu. *Application contact:* Dr. Antwinett Lee, Associate Dean, 206-281-2607, E-mail: leea30@spu.edu.
Website: http://spu.edu/academics/school-of-health-sciences/undergraduate-programs/nursing

**Seton Hall University,** College of Nursing, South Orange, NJ 07079-2697. Offers advanced practice in primary health care (MSN, DNP), including adult/gerontological nurse practitioner, pediatric nurse practitioner; entry into practice (MSN); health systems administration (MSN, DNP); nursing (PhD); nursing case management (MSN); nursing education (MA); school nurse (MSN); MSN/MA. *Accreditation:* AACN. *Program availability:* Part-time, online learning. *Degree requirements:* For master's, research project; for doctorate, dissertation or scholarly project. *Entrance requirements:* For doctorate, GRE (waived for students with GPA of 3.5 or higher). Additional exam requirements/recommendations for international students: required—TOEFL. Electronic applications accepted.

**Shenandoah University,** Eleanor Wade Custer School of Nursing, Winchester, VA 22601. Offers adult gerontology primary care nurse practitioner (Graduate Certificate); adult-gerontology primary care nurse practitioner (MSN); family nurse practitioner (MSN, DNP, Graduate Certificate); general (MSN); health systems leadership (DNP); health systems management (MSN, Graduate Certificate); nurse midwifery (MSN); nurse-midwifery (Graduate Certificate); nursing education (Graduate Certificate); nursing practice (DNP); psychiatric mental health nurse practitioner (MSN, DNP, Graduate Certificate). *Accreditation:* AACN; ACNM/ACME. *Entrance requirements:* For master's, United States RN license; minimum GPA of 3.0; 2080 hours of clinical experience; curriculum vitae; 3 letters of recommendation from former dean, faculty member, or advisor familiar with the applicant, and a former or current supervisor; two-to-three-page essay on a specified topic; for doctorate, MSN, minimum GPA of 3.0, 3 letters of recommendation, interview, BSN, two-to-three page essay on a specific topic, 500-word statement of clinical practice research interest, resume, current U.S. RN license, 2080 clinical hours; for Graduate Certificate, MSN, minimum GPA of 3.0, 2 letters of recommendation, minimum of one year (2080 hours) of clinical nursing experience, interview, two-to-three page essay on a specific topic, resume, current United States RN license. Additional exam requirements/recommendations for international students: required—TOEFL (minimum score 558 paper-based; 83 iBT). Electronic applications accepted. *Expenses:* Contact institution.

**Southern Adventist University,** School of Nursing, Collegedale, TN 37315-0370. Offers acute care-adult/gerontology nurse practitioner (MSN, DNP); healthcare administration (MSN/MBA); lifestyle medicine (DNP); nurse educator (MSN, DNP); primary care-adult/gerontology nurse practitioner (MSN); primary care-family nurse practitioner (MSN, DNP); primary care-psychiatric mental health nurse practitioner (MSN, DNP); MSN/MBA. *Accreditation:* ACEN. *Program availability:* Part-time, 100% online. *Degree requirements:* For master's, thesis or project; for doctorate, scholarly project. *Entrance requirements:* For master's, RN license. Additional exam requirements/recommendations for international students: required—TOEFL (minimum score 100 iBT). Electronic applications accepted.

**Southern University and Agricultural and Mechanical College,** College of Nursing and Allied Health, School of Nursing, Baton Rouge, LA 70813. Offers educator/administrator (PhD); family health nursing (MSN); family nurse practitioner (Post Master's Certificate); geriatric nurse practitioner/gerontology (PhD); nursing (DNP). *Accreditation:* AACN. *Program availability:* Part-time. *Degree requirements:* For master's, comprehensive exam, thesis; for doctorate, comprehensive exam, thesis/dissertation. *Entrance requirements:* For master's, GRE General Test, BSN, minimum GPA of 2.7; for doctorate, GRE General Test; for Post Master's Certificate, MSN. Additional exam requirements/recommendations for international students: required—TOEFL (minimum score 525 paper-based).

**Stony Brook University, State University of New York,** Stony Brook Medicine, School of Nursing, Adult-Gerontology Primary Care Nurse Practitioner Program, Stony Brook, NY 11794. Offers adult health nurse practitioner (Certificate); adult health/primary care nursing (MS, DNP). *Accreditation:* AACN. *Program availability:* Part-time, blended/hybrid learning. *Students:* 11 full-time (all women), 151 part-time (128 women); includes 53 minority (20 Black or African American, non-Hispanic/Latino; 14 Asian, non-Hispanic/Latino; 17 Hispanic/Latino; 1 Native Hawaiian or other Pacific Islander, non-Hispanic/Latino; 1 Two or more races, non-Hispanic/Latino), 1 international. 148 applicants, 45% accepted, 59 enrolled. In 2019, 57 master's, 8 doctorates, 3 other advanced degrees awarded. *Entrance requirements:* For master's, BSN, minimum GPA of 3.0, course work in statistics. Additional exam requirements/recommendations for international students: required—TOEFL (minimum score 90 iBT). *Application deadline:* For fall admission, 12/5 for domestic students. Application fee: $100. *Expenses:* Contact institution. *Financial support:* Application deadline: 3/15. *Unit head:* Justin M. Waryold, Program Director, 631-444-3074, Fax: 631-444-3074, E-mail: justin.waryold@stonybrook.edu. *Application contact:* Dr. Dolores Bilges, Senior Staff Assistant, 631-444-2644, Fax: 631-444-3136, E-mail: anp.nursing@stonybrook.edu.
Website: https://nursing.stonybrookmedicine.edu/graduate

**Tennessee Technological University,** Whitson-Hester School of Nursing, DNP Program, Cookeville, TN 38505. Offers adult-gerontology acute care nurse practitioner (DNP); executive leadership in nursing (DNP); family nurse practitioner (DNP); pediatric nurse practitioner-primary care (DNP); psychiatric/mental health nurse practitioner (DNP); women's health care nurse practitioner (DNP). *Program availability:* Part-time. *Students:* 20 full-time (17 women), 12 part-time (all women); includes 3 minority (2 Black or African American, non-Hispanic/Latino; 1 Two or more races, non-Hispanic/Latino). 25 applicants, 60% accepted, 10 enrolled. *Application deadline:* For fall admission, 7/1 for domestic students, 5/1 for international students; for spring admission, 12/1 for domestic students, 10/1 for international students; for summer admission, 5/1 for domestic students, 2/1 for international students. Applications are processed on a rolling basis. Application fee: $35 ($40 for international students). Electronic applications accepted. *Expenses: Tuition, area resident:* Part-time $597 per credit hour. Tuition, state resident: part-time $597 per credit hour. Tuition, nonresident: part-time $1323 per credit hour. *Financial support:* Application deadline: 4/1; applicants required to submit FAFSA. *Unit head:* Dr. Kim Hanna, Dean, Fax: 931-372-6244, E-mail: khanna@tntech.edu. *Application contact:* Shelia K. Kendrick, Coordinator of Graduate Studies, 931-372-3808, Fax: 931-372-3497, E-mail: skendrick@tntech.edu.
Website: https://www.tntech.edu/nursing/doctor-of-nursing-practice/

**Texas Christian University,** Harris College of Nursing and Health Sciences, Master's Program in Nursing, Fort Worth, TX 76129-0002. Offers administration and leadership (MSN); clinical nurse leader (MSN, Certificate); clinical nurse specialist (MSN), including adult/gerontology nursing, pediatrics; nursing education (MSN). *Accreditation:* AACN. *Program availability:* Part-time, online only, 100% online. *Faculty:* 29 full-time (26 women), 1 (woman) part-time/adjunct. *Students:* 12 full-time (all women), 5 part-time (all women); includes 5 minority (1 Asian, non-Hispanic/Latino; 4 Hispanic/Latino). Average age 34. 41 applicants, 59% accepted, 8 enrolled. In 2019, 10 master's awarded. *Degree requirements:* For master's, thesis or alternative, practicum. *Entrance requirements:* For master's, 3 letters of reference, essay, resume, two official transcripts from every institution attended, current license to practice as a registered nurse. Additional exam requirements/recommendations for international students: required—TOEFL (minimum score 550 paper-based; 80 iBT). *Application deadline:* For spring admission, 8/15 for domestic and international students; for summer admission, 1/15 for domestic and international students. Application fee: $60. Electronic applications accepted. Full-time tuition and fees vary according to program. *Financial support:* In 2019–20, 15 students received support. Scholarships/grants available. Financial award application deadline: 2/15; financial award applicants required to submit FAFSA. *Unit head:* Dr. Kathy Ellis, Division Director, Graduate Nursing, 817-257-6726, Fax: 817-257-7944, E-mail: kathryn.ellis@tcu.edu. *Application contact:* Beth Janke, Academic Program Specialist, 817-257-6726, Fax: 817-257-7944, E-mail: graduatenursing@tcu.edu.
Website: http://www.nursing.tcu.edu/graduate.asp

**Texas Tech University Health Sciences Center,** School of Nursing, Lubbock, TX 79430. Offers acute care nurse practitioner (MSN, Certificate); administration (MSN); advanced practice (DNP); education (MSN); executive leadership (DNP); family nurse practitioner (MSN, Certificate); geriatric nurse practitioner (MSN, Certificate); pediatric nurse practitioner (MSN, Certificate). *Accreditation:* AACN. *Program availability:* Part-time, online learning. *Degree requirements:* For master's, thesis optional. *Entrance requirements:* For master's, minimum GPA of 3.0, 3 letters of reference, BSN, RN license; for Certificate, minimum GPA of 3.0, 3 letters of reference, RN license. Additional exam requirements/recommendations for international students: required—TOEFL (minimum score 550 paper-based).

**Texas Woman's University,** Graduate School, College of Nursing, Denton, TX 76204. Offers adult health clinical nurse specialist (MS); adult health nurse practitioner (MS); adult/gerontology acute care nurse practitioner (MS); child health clinical nurse specialist (MS); clinical nurse leader (MS); family nurse practitioner (MS); health systems management (MS); nursing education (MS); nursing practice (DNP); nursing science (PhD); pediatric nurse practitioner (MS); women's health clinical nurse specialist (MS); women's health nurse practitioner (MS). *Accreditation:* AACN. *Program availability:* Part-time, 100% online, blended/hybrid learning. *Faculty:* 48 full-time (47 women), 31 part-time/adjunct (24 women). *Students:* 42 full-time (40 women), 811 part-time (756 women); includes 481 minority (168 Black or African American, non-Hispanic/Latino; 2 American Indian or Alaska Native, non-Hispanic/Latino; 165 Asian, non-Hispanic/Latino; 118 Hispanic/Latino; 1 Native Hawaiian or other Pacific Islander, non-Hispanic/Latino; 27 Two or more races, non-Hispanic/Latino), 26 international. Average age 36. 435 applicants, 71% accepted, 172 enrolled. In 2019, 203 master's, 37 doctorates awarded. *Degree requirements:* For master's, comprehensive exam, thesis or alternative, 6-year time limit for completion of degree, professional or clinical project; for doctorate, comprehensive exam, thesis/dissertation, 10-year time limit for completion of degree; dissertation (PhD), assessment practicum (DPT). *Entrance requirements:* For master's, minimum GPA of 3.0 on last 60 hours in undergraduate nursing degree and overall, RN license, BS in nursing, basic statistics course; for doctorate, MS in nursing, minimum preferred GPA of 3.5, RN or APRN license, statistics course, 2 letters of reference, curriculum vitae, graduate nursing-theory course, graduate research course, statement of professional goals and research interests, 1 yr APRN experience. Additional exam requirements/recommendations for international students: required—

TOEFL (minimum score 79 iBT); recommended—IELTS (minimum score 6.5), TSE (minimum score 53). *Application deadline:* For fall admission, 5/1 for domestic students, 3/1 priority date for international students; for spring admission, 9/15 for domestic students, 7/1 priority date for international students. Application fee: $50 ($75 for international students). Electronic applications accepted. *Expenses:* All are estimates. Tuition for 10 hours = $2,763; Fees for 10 hours = $1,342. Master's Nursing courses require additional $75/SCH; Doctoral Nursing courses require additional $80/SCH. *Financial support:* In 2019–20, 212 students received support, including 1 research assistantship, 6 teaching assistantships (averaging $12,029 per year), career-related internships or fieldwork, scholarships/grants, health care benefits, and unspecified assistantships also available. Support available to part-time students. Financial award application deadline: 3/1; financial award applicants required to submit FAFSA. *Unit head:* Dr. Rosalie Mainous, Dean, 940-898-2401, Fax: 940-898-2437, E-mail: nursing@twu.edu. *Application contact:* Korie Hawkins, Associate Director of Admissions, Graduate Recruitment, 940-898-3188, Fax: 940-898-3081, E-mail: admissions@twu.edu.
Website: http://www.twu.edu/nursing/

**Uniformed Services University of the Health Sciences,** Daniel K. Inouye Graduate School of Nursing, Bethesda, MD 20814. Offers adult-gerontology clinical nurse specialist (MSN, DNP); family nurse practitioner (DNP); nurse anesthesia (DNP); nursing science (PhD); psychiatric mental health nurse practitioner (DNP); women's health nurse practitioner (DNP). *Accreditation:* AACN; AANA/CANAEP. *Program availability:* Part-time. *Faculty:* 50 full-time (32 women), 1 part-time/adjunct (0 women). *Students:* 170 full-time (98 women); includes 51 minority (21 Black or African American, non-Hispanic/Latino; 17 Asian, non-Hispanic/Latino; 11 Hispanic/Latino; 2 Native Hawaiian or other Pacific Islander, non-Hispanic/Latino). Average age 34. 88 applicants, 75% accepted, 66 enrolled. In 2019, 2 master's, 42 doctorates awarded. *Degree requirements:* For master's, thesis, scholarly project; for doctorate, dissertation (for PhD); project (for DNP). *Entrance requirements:* For master's, GRE, BSN, clinical experience, minimum GPA of 3.0, previous course work in science; for doctorate, GRE, BSN, minimum GPA of 3.0, undergraduate/graduate science course within past 5 years, writing example, interview (for some programs), and 3 letters of reference (for DNP); master's degree, minimum GPA of 3.0 in nursing or related field, personal statement, 3 references, and interview (for PhD). *Application deadline:* For winter admission, 2/15 for domestic students; for summer admission, 8/15 for domestic students. Electronic applications accepted. *Financial support:* Robert Wood Johnson and Jonas scholars available. *Unit head:* Dr. Diane C. Seibert, Associate Dean for Academic Affairs, 301-295-1080, Fax: 301-295-1707, E-mail: diane.seibert@usuhs.edu. *Application contact:* Maureen Jackson, Student Admissions Program Manager, 301-295-1055, E-mail: maureen.jackson.ctr@usuhs.edu.
Website: http://www.usuhs.edu/gsn/

**University at Buffalo, the State University of New York,** Graduate School, School of Nursing, Buffalo, NY 14260. Offers adult gerontology nurse practitioner (DNP); family nurse practitioner (DNP); health care systems and leadership (MS); nurse anesthetist (DNP); nursing (PhD); nursing education (Certificate); psychiatric/mental health nurse practitioner (DNP). *Accreditation:* AACN; AANA/CANAEP (one or more programs are accredited). *Program availability:* Part-time, 100% online. *Degree requirements:* For master's, thesis optional; for doctorate, comprehensive exam (for some programs), capstone (for DNP), dissertation (for PhD). *Entrance requirements:* For master's, GRE or MAT; for doctorate, GRE or MAT, minimum GPA of 3.0 (for DNP), 3.25 (for PhD); RN license; BS or MS in nursing; 3 references; writing sample; resume; personal statement; for Certificate, interview, minimum GPA of 3.0 or GRE General Test, RN license, MS in nursing, professional certification. Additional exam requirements/recommendations for international students: required—TOEFL (minimum score 550 paper-based; 79 iBT), IELTS (minimum score 6.5). Electronic applications accepted. *Expenses:* Contact institution.

**The University of Alabama at Birmingham,** School of Nursing, Birmingham, AL 35294. Offers clinical nurse leader (MSN); nurse anesthesia (DNP); nurse practitioner (MSN, DNP), including adult-gerontology acute care (MSN), adult-gerontology primary care (MSN), family (MSN), pediatric (MSN), psychiatric/mental health (MSN), women's health (MSN); nursing (MSN, DNP, PhD); nursing health systems administration (MSN); nursing informatics (MSN). *Accreditation:* AACN; AANA/CANAEP. *Program availability:* Part-time, online only, blended/hybrid learning. *Faculty:* 86 full-time (79 women), 42 part-time/adjunct (35 women). *Students:* 228 full-time (165 women), 1,393 part-time (1,234 women); includes 398 minority (267 Black or African American, non-Hispanic/Latino; 4 American Indian or Alaska Native, non-Hispanic/Latino; 52 Asian, non-Hispanic/Latino; 41 Hispanic/Latino; 34 Two or more races, non-Hispanic/Latino), 3 international. Average age 33. 1,027 applicants, 55% accepted, 421 enrolled. In 2019, 557 master's, 19 doctorates awarded. Terminal master's awarded for partial completion of doctoral program. *Degree requirements:* For master's, comprehensive exam; for doctorate, comprehensive exam, thesis/dissertation, research mentorship experience (for PhD); scholarly project (for DNP). *Entrance requirements:* For master's, GRE, GMAT, or MAT, minimum cumulative undergraduate GPA of 3.0 or on last 60 semesters hours; letters of recommendation; for doctorate, GRE General Test, computer literacy, course work in statistics, interview, minimum GPA of 3.0, MS in nursing, references, writing sample. Additional exam requirements/recommendations for international students: required—TOEFL (minimum score 500 paper-based, 80 iBT) or IELTS (5.5). *Application deadline:* For fall admission, 2/24 for domestic students; for summer admission, 10/15 for domestic students. Application fee: $50. Electronic applications accepted. *Expenses:* Contact institution. *Financial support:* In 2019–20, 23 fellowships (averaging $34,685 per year), 12 research assistantships (averaging $9,042 per year), 2 teaching assistantships (averaging $22,000 per year) were awarded; scholarships/grants, traineeships, health care benefits, and unspecified assistantships also available. Support available to part-time students. *Unit head:* Dr. Doreen C. Harper, Dean, 205-934-5360, Fax: 205-934-1894, E-mail: dcharper@uab.edu. *Application contact:* John Updegraff, Director of Student Affairs, 205-975-3370, Fax: 205-934-5490, E-mail: jupde22@uab.edu.
Website: http://www.uab.edu/nursing/home/

**The University of Alabama in Huntsville,** School of Graduate Studies, College of Nursing, Huntsville, AL 35899. Offers family nurse practitioner (Certificate); nursing (MSN, DNP), including adult-gerontology acute care nurse practitioner (MSN), adult-gerontology clinical nurse specialist (MSN), family nurse practitioner (MSN), leadership in health care systems (MSN); nursing education (Certificate). *Accreditation:* AACN. *Program availability:* Part-time. *Degree requirements:* For master's, comprehensive exam, thesis or alternative, oral and written exams. *Entrance requirements:* For master's, MAT or GRE, Alabama RN license, BSN, minimum GPA of 3.0; for doctorate, master's degree in nursing in an advanced practice area; for Certificate, MAT or GRE, minimum GPA of 3.0. Additional exam requirements/recommendations for international students: required—TOEFL (minimum score 500 paper-based; 80 iBT), IELTS (minimum score 6.5). Electronic applications accepted.

**University of Cincinnati,** Graduate School, College of Nursing, Cincinnati, OH 45221-0038. Offers nurse midwifery (MSN); nurse practitioner (MSN, DNP), including acute care pediatrics (DNP), adult-gerontology acute care, adult-gerontology primary care, anesthesia (DNP), family (MSN), leadership (DNP), neonatal (MSN), women's health (MSN); nursing (MSN, PhD), including occupational health (MSN). *Accreditation:* AACN; AANA/CANAEP (one or more programs are accredited); ACNM/ACME. *Program availability:* Part-time, 100% online, blended/hybrid learning. *Faculty:* 62 full-time (55 women), 125 part-time/adjunct (114 women). *Students:* 429 full-time (355 women), 1,547 part-time (1,390 women); includes 453 minority (226 Black or African American, non-Hispanic/Latino; 5 American Indian or Alaska Native, non-Hispanic/Latino; 68 Asian, non-Hispanic/Latino; 103 Hispanic/Latino; 3 Native Hawaiian or other Pacific Islander, non-Hispanic/Latino; 48 Two or more races, non-Hispanic/Latino), 15 international. Average age 36. 779 applicants, 78% accepted, 464 enrolled. In 2019, 518 master's, 47 doctorates awarded. *Degree requirements:* For master's, thesis or alternative; for doctorate, comprehensive exam (for some programs), thesis/dissertation (for some programs). *Entrance requirements:* For master's, GRE required only for the Direct-Entry Accelerated Program. Additional exam requirements/recommendations for international students: required—TOEFL (minimum score 600 paper-based; 100 iBT); recommended—IELTS (minimum score 7). *Application deadline:* For fall admission, 4/1 priority date for domestic and international students; for spring admission, 9/1 priority date for domestic and international students; for summer admission, 2/1 priority date for domestic and international students. Applications are processed on a rolling basis. Application fee: $135 ($140 for international students). Electronic applications accepted. *Expenses:* Contact institution. *Financial support:* In 2019–20, 103 students received support, including 9 fellowships with full tuition reimbursements available (averaging $18,595 per year), 7 research assistantships with full tuition reimbursements available (averaging $12,991 per year), 8 teaching assistantships with full tuition reimbursements available (averaging $12,991 per year); institutionally sponsored loans, scholarships/grants, traineeships, health care benefits, tuition waivers (partial), and unspecified assistantships also available. Support available to part-time students. Financial award application deadline: 4/1; financial award applicants required to submit FAFSA. *Unit head:* Dr. Greer Glazer, Dean, 513-558-5330, Fax: 513-558-9030, E-mail: greer.glazer@uc.edu. *Application contact:* Office of Student Affairs, 513-558-8400, E-mail: nursingbearcats@uc.edu.
Website: https://nursing.uc.edu/

**University of Colorado Colorado Springs,** Helen and Arthur E. Johnson Beth-El College of Nursing and Health Sciences, Colorado Springs, CO 80918. Offers nursing practice (MSN, DNP). *Accreditation:* AACN. *Program availability:* Part-time, 100% online. *Faculty:* 62 full-time (47 women), 77 part-time/adjunct (68 women). *Students:* 20 full-time (18 women), 295 part-time (261 women); includes 74 minority (14 Black or African American, non-Hispanic/Latino; 2 American Indian or Alaska Native, non-Hispanic/Latino; 16 Asian, non-Hispanic/Latino; 26 Hispanic/Latino; 1 Native Hawaiian or other Pacific Islander, non-Hispanic/Latino; 15 Two or more races, non-Hispanic/Latino). Average age 36. 147 applicants, 44% accepted, 49 enrolled. In 2019, 63 master's, 4 doctorates awarded. *Degree requirements:* For master's, comprehensive exam, thesis optional; for doctorate, capstone project. *Entrance requirements:* For master's, completion of an accredited (programmatic) baccalaureate degree in nursing including undergraduate coursework in: Introduction to Statistics, nursing research, health assessment; curriculum vitae or resume; 3 letters of recommendation; minimum overall GPA of 2.75 for cumulative undergraduate course work and BSN GPA of 3.3 or higher; for doctorate, active RN license in state of practice; Master of Science Degree in Nursing from an accredited (CCNE/NLN) program; undergraduate cumulative GPA of 2.75 or higher and graduate cumulative GPA 3.3 or higher; National Certification* as NP or CNS; curriculum vitae; completion of application essay. Additional exam requirements/recommendations for international students: required—TOEFL (minimum score 80 iBT). *Application deadline:* For fall admission, 3/15 priority date for domestic students, 3/15 for international students; for spring admission, 8/15 for domestic and international students. Applications are processed on a rolling basis. Application fee: $60 ($100 for international students). Electronic applications accepted. *Expenses:* Contact institution. *Financial support:* In 2019–20, 14 students received support, including 1 research assistantship (averaging $20,800 per year), 9 teaching assistantships (averaging $3,000 per year); career-related internships or fieldwork, Federal Work-Study, and scholarships/grants also available. Support available to part-time students. Financial award application deadline: 3/1; financial award applicants required to submit FAFSA. *Unit head:* Dr. Deborah Pollard, Nursing Department Chair, 719-255-3577, Fax: 719-255-4416, E-mail: dpollard@uccs.edu. *Application contact:* Diane Busch, Program Assistant II, 719-255-4424, Fax: 719-255-4416, E-mail: dbusch@uccs.edu.
Website: https://www.uccs.edu/johnsonbethel/

**University of Connecticut,** Graduate School, School of Nursing, MS Program in Nursing, Storrs, CT 06269. Offers adult gerontological acute care nurse practitioner (MS); adult gerontological primary care nurse practitioner (MS); family nurse practitioner (MS); neonatal nurse practitioner (MS). *Accreditation:* AACN. *Program availability:* Part-time, online learning. *Degree requirements:* For master's, comprehensive exam. *Entrance requirements:* For master's, official transcripts, Connecticut RN license, three letters of reference, curriculum vitae or resume, personal statement. Additional exam requirements/recommendations for international students: required—TOEFL (minimum score 550 paper-based). Electronic applications accepted.

**University of Connecticut,** Graduate School, School of Nursing, Post-Master's Certificate Programs, Storrs, CT 06269. Offers adult gerontology acute care nurse practitioner (Post-Master's Certificate); adult gerontology primary care nurse practitioner (Post-Master's Certificate); neonatal nurse practitioner (Post-Master's Certificate). *Entrance requirements:* For degree, minimum graduate GPA of 3.0, current Connecticut RN license, three letters of recommendation, current resume/curriculum vitae.

**University of Delaware,** College of Health Sciences, School of Nursing, Newark, DE 19716. Offers adult nurse practitioner (MSN, PMC); cardiopulmonary clinical nurse specialist (MSN, PMC); cardiopulmonary clinical nurse specialist/adult nurse practitioner (MSN, PMC); family nurse practitioner (MSN, PMC); gerontology clinical nurse specialist (MSN, PMC); gerontology clinical nurse specialist geriatric nurse practitioner (PMC); gerontology clinical nurse specialist/geriatric nurse practitioner (MSN); health services administration (MSN, PMC); nursing of children clinical nurse specialist (MSN, PMC); nursing of children clinical nurse specialist/pediatric nurse practitioner (MSN, PMC); oncology/immune deficiency clinical nurse specialist (MSN, PMC); oncology/immune deficiency clinical nurse specialist/adult nurse practitioner (MSN, PMC); perinatal/women's health clinical nurse specialist (MSN, PMC); perinatal/women's health clinical nurse specialist/women's health nurse practitioner (MSN, PMC); psychiatric nursing clinical nurse specialist (MSN, PMC). *Accreditation:* AACN. *Program availability:* Part-time, evening/weekend, online learning. *Degree requirements:* For master's, thesis optional. *Entrance requirements:* For master's, BSN, interview, RN license. Electronic applications accepted.

**University of Illinois at Chicago,** College of Nursing, Program in Nursing, Chicago, IL 60607-7128. Offers acute care clinical nurse specialist (MS); administrative nursing leadership (Certificate); adult nurse practitioner (MS); adult/geriatric nurse practitioner (MS); advanced community health nurse specialist (MS); family nurse practitioner (MS); geriatric clinical nurse specialist (MS); geriatric nurse practitioner (MS); nurse midwifery (MS); occupational health/advanced community health nurse specialist (MS);

occupational health/family nurse practitioner (MS); pediatric nurse practitioner (MS); perinatal clinical nurse specialist (MS); school/advanced community health nurse specialist (MS); school/family nurse practitioner (MS); women's health nurse practitioner (MS). *Accreditation:* AACN. *Program availability:* Part-time. *Degree requirements:* For master's, thesis or alternative. *Entrance requirements:* For master's, GRE General Test, minimum GPA of 2.75. Additional exam requirements/recommendations for international students: required—TOEFL. Electronic applications accepted.

**The University of Kansas,** University of Kansas Medical Center, School of Nursing, Kansas City, KS 66045. Offers adult/gerontological clinical nurse specialist (PMC); adult/gerontological nurse practitioner (PMC); health care informatics (PMC); health professions educator (PMC); nurse midwife (PMC); nursing (MS, DNP, PhD); organizational leadership (PMC); psychiatric/mental health nurse practitioner (PMC); public health nursing (PMC). *Accreditation:* AACN; ACNM/ACME. *Program availability:* Part-time, 100% online, blended/hybrid learning. *Faculty:* 65. *Students:* 57 full-time (53 women), 267 part-time (242 women); includes 65 minority (14 Black or African American, non-Hispanic/Latino; 2 American Indian or Alaska Native, non-Hispanic/Latino; 21 Asian, non-Hispanic/Latino; 9 Hispanic/Latino; 1 Native Hawaiian or other Pacific Islander, non-Hispanic/Latino; 18 Two or more races, non-Hispanic/Latino), 2 international. Average age 35. In 2019, 26 master's, 48 doctorates, 5 other advanced degrees awarded. Terminal master's awarded for partial completion of doctoral program. *Degree requirements:* For master's, comprehensive exam, thesis (for some programs), general oral exam; for doctorate, thesis/dissertation or alternative, comprehensive oral exam (for DNP); comprehensive written and oral exam, or three publications (for PhD). *Entrance requirements:* For master's, bachelor's degree in nursing, minimum GPA of 3.0, 1 year of clinical experience, RN license in KS and MO; for doctorate, GRE General Test (for PhD only), bachelor's degree in nursing, minimum GPA of 3.5, RN license in KS and MO. Additional exam requirements/recommendations for international students: required—TOEFL. *Application deadline:* For fall admission, 4/1 for domestic and international students; for spring admission, 9/1 for domestic and international students. Application fee: $75. Electronic applications accepted. *Expenses:* Contact institution. *Financial support:* Research assistantships with tuition reimbursements, teaching assistantships with tuition reimbursements, scholarships/grants, and traineeships available. Financial award application deadline: 3/1; financial award applicants required to submit FAFSA. *Unit head:* Dr. Sally Maliski, Professor and Dean, 913-588-1601, Fax: 913-588-1660, E-mail: smaliski@kumc.edu. *Application contact:* Dr. Pamela K. Barnes, Associate Dean, Student Affairs and Enrollment Management, 913-588-1619, Fax: 913-588-1615, E-mail: pbarnes2@kumc.edu. Website: http://nursing.kumc.edu

**University of Louisville,** Graduate School, School of Nursing, Louisville, KY 40202. Offers adult gerontology nurse practitioner (MSN, DNP); education and administration (MSN); family nurse practitioner (MSN, DNP); neonatal nurse practitioner (MSN, DNP); nursing research (PhD); psychiatric/mental health nurse practitioner (MSN, DNP); women's health nurse practitioner (MSN). *Accreditation:* AACN. *Program availability:* Part-time, blended/hybrid learning. *Faculty:* 49 full-time (46 women), 91 part-time/adjunct (86 women). *Students:* 164 full-time (140 women), 47 part-time (39 women); includes 45 minority (21 Black or African American, non-Hispanic/Latino; 5 Asian, non-Hispanic/Latino; 9 Hispanic/Latino; 10 Two or more races, non-Hispanic/Latino), 4 international. Average age 33. 84 applicants, 63% accepted, 48 enrolled. In 2019, 25 master's, 5 doctorates awarded. *Degree requirements:* For master's, varies; for doctorate, comprehensive exam (for some programs), thesis/dissertation (for some programs), varies. *Entrance requirements:* For master's, Our only master's degree is an accelerated program meant for students who have a bachelor's degree in another discipline who are transitioning into nursing. Thus, the main requirement is a bachelor's degree from a nationally-accredited college, and the completion of 6 prerequisite courses. Must have a minimum undergraduate GPA of 3.0; for doctorate, PhD program: GRE requirement omitted, DNP & PhD doctoral programs: 3 letters of professional reference. BSN applicants must have a 3.0 GPA. MSN applicants must have 3.25 GPA. Written statement of career goals, areas of expertise, reasons for pursuing doctoral degree, resume, and RN license. Additional exam requirements/recommendations for international students: recommended—TOEFL (minimum score 560 paper-based), IELTS (minimum score 6.5). *Application deadline:* For fall admission, 1/15 priority date for domestic and international students; for summer admission, 10/15 priority date for domestic students. Application fee: $60. Electronic applications accepted. *Expenses:* 17871. *Financial support:* In 2019–20, 47 students received support, including 2 fellowships with full tuition reimbursements available (averaging $20,000 per year), 9 research assistantships with full tuition reimbursements available (averaging $20,000 per year), 3 teaching assistantships with full tuition reimbursements available (averaging $15,000 per year); scholarships/grants, health care benefits, unspecified assistantships, and Jonas Nurse Leader Fellowships also available. Financial award application deadline: 10/1; financial award applicants required to submit FAFSA. *Unit head:* 502-852-8300, Fax: 502-852-5044, E-mail: sonya.hardin@louisville.edu. *Application contact:* Trish Hart, MA, Assistant Dean for Student Affairs, 502-852-5825, Fax: 502-852-8783, E-mail: trish.hart@louisville.edu.
Website: http://www.louisville.edu/nursing/

**University of Maryland, Baltimore,** University of Maryland School of Nursing, Baltimore, MD 21201. Offers adult-gerontology acute care nurse practitioner (DNP); adult-gerontology primary care nurse practitioner (DNP); clinical nurse leader (MS); community/public health nursing (MS); family nurse practitioner (DNP); global health (Postbaccalaureate Certificate); health services leadership and management (MS); neonatal nurse practitioner (DNP); nurse anesthesia (DNP); nursing (PhD); nursing informatics (MS, Postbaccalaureate Certificate); pediatric acute/primary care nurse practitioner (DNP); psychiatric mental health nurse practitioner (DNP); teaching in nursing and health professions (Postbaccalaureate Certificate); MS/MBA. *Accreditation:* AANA/CANAEP. *Program availability:* Part-time. *Faculty:* 130 full-time (117 women), 125 part-time/adjunct (114 women). *Students:* 539 full-time (463 women), 586 part-time (506 women); includes 485 minority (259 Black or African American, non-Hispanic/Latino; 3 American Indian or Alaska Native, non-Hispanic/Latino; 124 Asian, non-Hispanic/Latino; 66 Hispanic/Latino; 1 Native Hawaiian or other Pacific Islander, non-Hispanic/Latino; 32 Two or more races, non-Hispanic/Latino), 18 international. Average age 33. 964 applicants, 54% accepted, 347 enrolled. In 2019, 197 master's, 114 doctorates, 12 other advanced degrees awarded. *Degree requirements:* For master's and Postbaccalaureate Certificate, thesis (for some programs); for doctorate, comprehensive exam, thesis/dissertation. *Entrance requirements:* Additional exam requirements/recommendations for international students: required—TOEFL (minimum score 550 paper-based; 79 iBT); recommended—IELTS (minimum score 7). *Application deadline:* For fall admission, 11/1 priority date for domestic and international students; for spring admission, 12/15 for domestic and international students; for summer admission, 9/1 for domestic and international students. Applications are processed on a rolling basis. Application fee: $75. Electronic applications accepted. *Financial support:* In 2019–20, 257 students received support, including 31 research assistantships with full and partial tuition reimbursements available (averaging $25,000 per year), 21 teaching assistantships with full and partial tuition reimbursements available (averaging $19,000 per year); scholarships/grants, traineeships, and unspecified assistantships also available. Support available to part-time students. Financial award application

deadline: 3/1; financial award applicants required to submit FAFSA. *Unit head:* Dr. Jane Kirschling, Dean, 410-706-4359, E-mail: kirschling@umaryland.edu. *Application contact:* Larry Fillian, Associate Dean of Student and Academic Services, 410-706-6298, E-mail: lfillian@umaryland.edu.
Website: http://www.nursing.umaryland.edu/

**University of Massachusetts Amherst,** Graduate School, College of Nursing, Amherst, MA 01003. Offers adult gerontology primary care nurse practitioner (DNP); clinical nurse leader (MS); family nurse practitioner (DNP); nursing (PhD); public health nurse leader (DNP). *Accreditation:* AACN. *Program availability:* Part-time, online learning. Terminal master's awarded for partial completion of doctoral program. *Degree requirements:* For master's, thesis optional; for doctorate, comprehensive exam, thesis/dissertation. *Entrance requirements:* Additional exam requirements/recommendations for international students: required—TOEFL (minimum score 550 paper-based; 80 iBT), IELTS (minimum score 6.5). Electronic applications accepted.

**University of Massachusetts Lowell,** College of Health Sciences, School of Nursing, Program in Adult/Gerontological Nursing, Lowell, MA 01854. Offers MS. *Accreditation:* AACN. *Degree requirements:* For master's, thesis optional. *Entrance requirements:* For master's, GRE General Test, minimum GPA of 3.0, MA nursing license, interview, 3 letters of recommendation.

**University of Massachusetts Medical School,** Graduate School of Nursing, Worcester, MA 01655. Offers adult gerontological acute care nurse practitioner (DNP, Post Master's Certificate); adult gerontological primary care nurse practitioner (DNP, Post Master's Certificate); family nursing practitioner (DNP); nurse administrator (DNP); nurse educator (MS); nursing (PhD); psychiatric mental health (Post Master's Certificate). *Accreditation:* AACN. *Program availability:* Blended/hybrid learning. *Faculty:* 26 full-time (22 women), 51 part-time/adjunct (40 women). *Students:* 176 full-time (152 women), 33 part-time (27 women); includes 61 minority (21 Black or African American, non-Hispanic/Latino; 1 American Indian or Alaska Native, non-Hispanic/Latino; 18 Asian, non-Hispanic/Latino; 20 Hispanic/Latino; 1 Native Hawaiian or other Pacific Islander, non-Hispanic/Latino). Average age 32. 131 applicants, 66% accepted, 58 enrolled. In 2019, 28 master's, 34 doctorates, 1 other advanced degree awarded. *Degree requirements:* For doctorate, thesis/dissertation (for some programs), comprehensive exam and manuscript (for PhD); scholarly project (for DNP). *Entrance requirements:* For master's, GRE General Test, bachelor's degree in nursing, course work in statistics, unrestricted Massachusetts license as registered nurse; for doctorate, GRE General Test, bachelor's or master's degree; for Post Master's Certificate, GRE General Test, MS in nursing. Additional exam requirements/recommendations for international students: required—TOEFL (minimum score 400 paper-based; 81 iBT). *Application deadline:* For fall admission, 12/1 priority date for domestic students. Applications are processed on a rolling basis. Application fee: $100. Electronic applications accepted. *Expenses:* Contact institution. *Financial support:* In 2019–20, 103 students received support. Scholarships/grants available. Support available to part-time students. Financial award application deadline: 5/15; financial award applicants required to submit FAFSA. *Unit head:* Dr. Joan Vitello-Cicciu, Dean, 508-856-5081, Fax: 508-856-6552, E-mail: joan.vitello@umassmed.edu. *Application contact:* Diane Brescia, Admissions Coordinator, 508-856-3488, Fax: 508-856-5851, E-mail: diane.brescia@umassmed.edu.
Website: http://www.umassmed.edu/gsn/

**University of Minnesota, Twin Cities Campus,** Graduate School, School of Nursing, Minneapolis, MN 55455-0213. Offers adult/gerontological clinical nurse specialist (DNP); adult/gerontological primary care nurse practitioner (DNP); family nurse practitioner (DNP); health innovation and leadership (DNP); integrative health and healing (DNP); nurse anesthesia (DNP); nurse midwifery (DNP); nursing (MN, PhD); nursing informatics (DNP); pediatric clinical nurse specialist (DNP); primary care certified pediatric nurse practitioner (DNP); psychiatric/mental health nurse practitioner (DNP); women's health nurse practitioner (DNP). *Accreditation:* AACN; AANA/CANAEP; ACNM/ACME (one or more programs are accredited). *Program availability:* Part-time, online learning. Terminal master's awarded for partial completion of doctoral program. *Degree requirements:* For master's, final oral exam, project or thesis; for doctorate, thesis/dissertation. *Entrance requirements:* For master's and doctorate, GRE General Test. Additional exam requirements/recommendations for international students: required—TOEFL (minimum score 586 paper-based). *Expenses:* Contact institution.

**University of Missouri,** Office of Research and Graduate Studies, Sinclair School of Nursing, Columbia, MO 65211. Offers adult-gerontology clinical nurse specialist (DNP, Certificate); family nurse practitioner (DNP); family psychiatric and mental health nurse practitioner (DNP); nursing (MS, PhD); nursing leadership and innovations in health care (DNP); pediatric clinical nurse specialist (DNP, Certificate); pediatric nurse practitioner (DNP). *Accreditation:* AACN. *Program availability:* Part-time. *Degree requirements:* For master's, thesis optional, oral exam; for doctorate, thesis/dissertation. *Entrance requirements:* For master's, GRE General Test, BSN, minimum GPA of 3.0 during last 60 hours, nursing license. Additional exam requirements/recommendations for international students: required—TOEFL, IELTS. Electronic applications accepted.

**University of Missouri–Kansas City,** School of Nursing and Health Studies, Kansas City, MO 64110-2499. Offers adult clinical nurse specialist (MSN), including adult nurse practitioner, women's health nurse practitioner (MSN, DNP); adult clinical nursing practice (DNP), including adult gerontology nurse practitioner, women's health nurse practitioner (MSN, DNP); clinical nursing practice (DNP), including family nurse practitioner; neonatal nurse practitioner (MSN); nurse educator (MSN); nurse executive (MSN); nursing practice (DNP); pediatric clinical nursing practice (DNP), including pediatric nurse practitioner; pediatric nurse practitioner (MSN). *Accreditation:* AACN. *Program availability:* Part-time, online learning. *Degree requirements:* For master's, thesis or alternative. *Entrance requirements:* For master's, minimum undergraduate GPA of 3.2; for doctorate, GRE, 3 letters of reference. Additional exam requirements/recommendations for international students: required—TOEFL (minimum score 550 paper-based; 80 iBT).

**University of Missouri–St. Louis,** College of Nursing, St. Louis, MO 63121. Offers adult/geriatric nurse practitioner (Post Master's Certificate); family nurse practitioner (Post Master's Certificate); nursing (DNP, PhD); pediatric acute care nurse practitioner (Post Master's Certificate); pediatric nurse practitioner (Post Master's Certificate); psychiatric-mental health nurse practitioner (Post Master's Certificate); women's health nurse practitioner (Post Master's Certificate). *Accreditation:* AACN. *Program availability:* Part-time. *Degree requirements:* For doctorate, comprehensive exam, thesis/dissertation; for Post Master's Certificate, thesis. *Entrance requirements:* For doctorate, GRE, 2 letters of recommendation, MSN, minimum GPA of 3.2, course in differential/inferential statistics; for Post Master's Certificate, 2 recommendation letters; MSN; advanced practice certificate; minimum GPA of 3.0; essay. Additional exam requirements/recommendations for international students: recommended—TOEFL (minimum score 550 paper-based; 79 iBT), IELTS (minimum score 6.5). Electronic applications accepted. *Expenses:* Tuition, area resident: Full-time $9005.40; part-time $6003.60 per credit hour. Tuition, state resident: full-time $9005.40; part-time $6003.60 per credit hour. Tuition, nonresident: full-time $22,108; part-time $14,738.40 per credit hour. *International tuition:* $22,108 full-time. Tuition and fees vary according to course load.

**The University of North Carolina at Chapel Hill,** School of Nursing, Chapel Hill, NC 27599-7460. Offers advanced practice registered nurse (DNP); nursing (MSN, PhD, PMC), including administration (MSN), adult gerontology primary care nurse practitioner (MSN), clinical nurse leader (MSN), education (MSN), health care systems (PMC), informatics (MSN, PMC), nursing leadership (PMC), outcomes management (MSN), primary care family nurse practitioner (MSN), primary care pediatric nurse practitioner (MSN), psychiatric/mental health nurse practitioner (MSN, PMC). *Accreditation:* AACN; ACEN (one or more programs are accredited). *Program availability:* Part-time. *Degree requirements:* For master's, comprehensive exam, thesis; for doctorate, thesis/dissertation, 3 exams; for PMC, thesis. *Entrance requirements:* Additional exam requirements/recommendations for international students: required—TOEFL (minimum score 575 paper-based; 89 iBT), IELTS (minimum score 8). Electronic applications accepted.

**The University of North Carolina at Charlotte,** College of Health and Human Services, School of Nursing, Charlotte, NC 28223-0001. Offers adult-gerontology acute care nurse practitioner (Post-Master's Certificate); advanced clinical nursing (MSN), including adult psychiatric mental health, adult-gerontology acute care nurse practitioner, family nurse practitioner across the lifespan; family nurse practitioner across the lifespan (Post-Master's Certificate); nurse anesthesia (MSN), including nurse anesthesia across the lifespan; nurse anesthesia across the lifespan (Post-Master's Certificate); nursing (DNP); nursing administrator (Graduate Certificate); nursing educator (Graduate Certificate); systems/population nursing (MSN), including community/public health nursing, nurse administrator, nurse educator. *Accreditation:* AACN; AANA/CANAEP. *Program availability:* Part-time, blended/hybrid learning. *Students:* 126 full-time (96 women), 142 part-time (127 women); includes 70 minority (48 Black or African American, non-Hispanic/Latino; 8 Asian, non-Hispanic/Latino; 9 Hispanic/Latino; 5 Two or more races, non-Hispanic/Latino), 1 international. Average age 35. 347 applicants, 37% accepted, 104 enrolled. In 2019, 102 master's, 10 doctorates, 10 other advanced degrees awarded. Terminal master's awarded for partial completion of doctoral program. *Entrance requirements:* For master's, GRE General Test, current unrestricted license as Registered Nurse in North Carolina; BSN from nationally-accredited program; one year of professional nursing practice in acute/critical care; minimum overall GPA of 3.0 in last degree; completion of undergraduate statistics course with minimum grade of C; statement of purpose; for doctorate, GRE or MAT, master's degree in nursing in an advanced nursing practice specialty from nationally-accredited program; minimum overall GPA of 3.5 in MSN program; current RN licensure in U.S. at time of application with eligibility for NC licensure; essay; resume/curriculum vitae; professional recommendations; clinical hours; for other advanced degree, GRE. Additional exam requirements/recommendations for international students: required—TOEFL (minimum score 557 paper-based; 83 iBT), IELTS (minimum score 6.5), TOEFL (minimum score 557 paper-based, 83 iBT) or IELTS (6.5). *Application deadline:* Applications are processed on a rolling basis. Application fee: $75. Electronic applications accepted. *Expenses:* Contact institution. *Financial support:* In 2019–20, 6 students received support, including 4 research assistantships (averaging $4,856 per year), 2 teaching assistantships (averaging $3,615 per year); career-related internships or fieldwork, institutionally sponsored loans, scholarships/grants, traineeships, and unspecified assistantships also available. Support available to part-time students. Financial award application deadline: 3/1; financial award applicants required to submit FAFSA. *Unit head:* Dr. Dena Evans, Director, 704-687-7974, E-mail: devans37@uncc.edu. *Application contact:* Kathy B. Giddings, Director of Graduate Admissions, 704-687-5503, Fax: 704-687-1668, E-mail: gradadm@uncc.edu.
Website: http://nursing.uncc.edu/

**The University of North Carolina at Greensboro,** Graduate School, School of Nursing, Greensboro, NC 27412-5001. Offers adult clinical nurse specialist (MSN, PMC); adult/gerontological nurse practitioner (MSN, PMC); nurse anesthesia (MSN, PMC); nursing (PhD); nursing administration (MSN); nursing education (MSN); MSN/MBA. *Accreditation:* ACEN. *Degree requirements:* For master's, thesis or alternative. *Entrance requirements:* For master's, GRE General Test or MAT, BSN, clinical experience, liability insurance, RN license; for PMC, liability insurance, MSN, RN license. Additional exam requirements/recommendations for international students: required—TOEFL. Electronic applications accepted.

**University of North Dakota,** Graduate School, College of Nursing and Professional Disciplines, Department of Nursing, Grand Forks, ND 58202. Offers adult-gerontological nurse practitioner (MS); advanced public health nurse (MS); family nurse practitioner (MS); nurse anesthesia (MS); nurse educator (MS); nursing (PhD, Post-Master's Certificate); nursing practice (DNP); psychiatric and mental health nurse practitioner (MS). *Accreditation:* AANA/CANAEP.

**University of Pennsylvania,** School of Nursing, Adult Gerontology Clinical Nurse Specialist Program, Philadelphia, PA 19104. Offers MSN. *Students:* 5 part-time (4 women); includes 3 minority (1 Black or African American, non-Hispanic/Latino; 1 Hispanic/Latino; 1 Two or more races, non-Hispanic/Latino). Average age 30. In 2019, 6 master's awarded. Application fee: $80.
Website: http://www.nursing.upenn.edu/ahcns/

**University of Pennsylvania,** School of Nursing, Adult-Gerontology Primary Care Nurse Practitioner Program, Philadelphia, PA 19104. Offers MSN. *Program availability:* Part-time. *Students:* 17 full-time (all women), 62 part-time (58 women); includes 24 minority (8 Black or African American, non-Hispanic/Latino; 7 Asian, non-Hispanic/Latino; 7 Hispanic/Latino; 2 Two or more races, non-Hispanic/Latino), 1 international. Average age 29. In 2019, 16 master's awarded. Application fee: $80.

**University of Phoenix - Bay Area Campus,** College of Nursing, San Jose, CA 95134-1805. Offers education (MHA); gerontology (MHA); health administration (MHA, DHA); informatics (MHA, MSN); nursing (MSN, PhD); nursing/health care education (MSN); MSN/MBA. *Program availability:* Evening/weekend, online learning. *Degree requirements:* For master's, thesis (for some programs). *Entrance requirements:* For master's, minimum undergraduate GPA of 2.5, 3 years of work experience, RN license. Additional exam requirements/recommendations for international students: required—TOEFL (minimum score 550 paper-based; 79 iBT). Electronic applications accepted.

**University of Phoenix - Phoenix Campus,** College of Health Sciences and Nursing, Tempe, AZ 85282-2371. Offers family nurse practitioner (MSN, Certificate); gerontology health care (Certificate); health care education (MSN, Certificate); health care informatics (Certificate); informatics (MSN); nursing (MSN); MSN/MHA. *Program availability:* Evening/weekend, online learning. *Entrance requirements:* Additional exam requirements/recommendations for international students: required—TOEFL, TOEIC (Test of English as an International Communication), Berlitz Online English Proficiency Exam, PTE, or IELTS. Electronic applications accepted. *Expenses:* Contact institution.

**University of Pittsburgh,** School of Nursing, Clinical Nurse Specialist Program, Pittsburgh, PA 15260. Offers clinical nurse specialist (DNP), including adult gerontology. *Accreditation:* AACN. *Program availability:* Part-time. *Faculty:* 1 full-time (0 women). *Students:* 3 full-time (all women), 4 part-time (all women). Average age 39. 4 applicants, 100% accepted, 1 enrolled. In 2019, 2 doctorates awarded. *Degree requirements:* For doctorate, comprehensive exam, thesis/dissertation or alternative, capstone project required. *Entrance requirements:* For doctorate, GRE, BSN, RN license, course work in statistics, resume/essay, 3 letters of recommendation. Additional exam requirements/recommendations for international students: required—TOEFL (minimum score 600 paper-based; 100 iBT), IELTS (minimum score 7), TOEFL (minimum score 600 paper-based; 100 IBT) or IELTS (minimum score 7.0). *Application deadline:* For fall admission, 6/1 priority date for domestic students, 2/15 priority date for international students. Application fee: $50. Electronic applications accepted. *Expenses:* $13,795 per term full-time resident tuition, $475 per term full-time resident fees, $1,122 per credit part-time resident tuition, $295 per term part-time resident fees, $16,474 per term full-time non-resident tuition, $475 per term full-time non-resident fees, $1,345 per credit part-time non-resident tuition, $295 per term part-time non-resident fees. *Financial support:* In 2019–20, 7 students received support, including 4 fellowships (averaging $15,188 per year); scholarships/grants and Matching Funds also available. Financial award application deadline: 6/1; financial award applicants required to submit FAFSA. *Unit head:* Dr. Sandra Engberg, Associate Dean for Clinical Education, 412-624-3835, Fax: 412-624-8521, E-mail: sje1@pitt.edu. *Application contact:* Laurie Lapsley, Graduate Administrator, 412-624-9670, Fax: 412-624-2409, E-mail: lapsleyl@pitt.edu.

**University of Puerto Rico - Medical Sciences Campus,** School of Nursing, San Juan, PR 00936-5067. Offers adult and elderly nursing (MSN); child and adolescent nursing (MSN); critical care nursing (MSN); family and community nursing (MSN); family nurse practitioner (MSN); maternity nursing (MSN); mental health and psychiatric nursing (MSN). *Accreditation:* AACN; AANA/CANAEP. *Entrance requirements:* For master's, GRE or EXADEP, interview, Puerto Rico RN license or professional license for international students, general and specific point average, article analysis. Electronic applications accepted.

**University of Rhode Island,** Graduate School, College of Nursing, Kingston, RI 02881. Offers acute care nurse practitioner (adult-gerontology focus) (Post Master's Certificate); adult gerontology nurse practitioner/clinical nurse specialist (Post Master's Certificate); adult-gerontological acute care nurse practitioner (MS); adult-gerontological nurse practitioner/clinical nurse specialist (MS); family nurse practitioner (MS, Post Master's Certificate); nursing (DNP, PhD); nursing education (MS, Post Master's Certificate). *Accreditation:* AACN; ACNM/ACME (one or more programs are accredited). *Program availability:* Part-time, evening/weekend, 100% online, blended/hybrid learning. *Faculty:* 27 full-time (26 women). *Students:* 51 full-time (47 women), 72 part-time (65 women); includes 21 minority (9 Black or African American, non-Hispanic/Latino; 5 Asian, non-Hispanic/Latino; 4 Hispanic/Latino; 2 Native Hawaiian or other Pacific Islander, non-Hispanic/Latino; 1 Two or more races, non-Hispanic/Latino), 6 international. 32 applicants, 88% accepted, 21 enrolled. In 2019, 34 master's, 9 doctorates, 1 other advanced degree awarded. *Entrance requirements:* For master's, GRE or MAT, 2 letters of recommendation, scholarly papers; for doctorate, GRE, 3 letters of recommendation, scholarly papers. Additional exam requirements/recommendations for international students: required—TOEFL. *Application deadline:* For fall admission, 2/15 for domestic students, 2/1 for international students; for spring admission, 10/15 for domestic students, 7/15 for international students. Application fee: $65. Electronic applications accepted. *Expenses: Tuition, area resident:* Full-time $13,734; part-time $763 per credit. Tuition, state resident: full-time $13,734; part-time $763 per credit. Tuition, nonresident: full-time $26,512; part-time $1473 per credit. *International tuition:* $26,512 full-time. *Required fees:* $1780; $52 per credit. $35 per term. One-time fee: $165. *Financial support:* In 2019–20, 7 teaching assistantships with tuition reimbursements (averaging $13,376 per year) were awarded. Financial award application deadline: 2/1; financial award applicants required to submit FAFSA. *Unit head:* Dr. Barbara Wolfe, Dean, 401-874-5324, E-mail: bwolfe@uri.edu. *Application contact:* Dr. Denise Coppa, Associate Professor/Interim Associate Dean for Graduate Programs, 401-874-5036, E-mail: dcoppa@uri.edu.
Website: http://www.uri.edu/nursing/

**University of Rochester,** School of Nursing, Rochester, NY 14642. Offers adult gerontological acute care nurse practitioner (MS); adult gerontological primary care nurse practitioner (MS); clinical nurse leader (MS); family nurse practitioner (MS); family psychiatric mental health nurse practitioner (MS); health care organization management and leadership (MS); nursing (DNP); nursing and health science (PhD); nursing education (MS); pediatric nurse practitioner (MS); pediatric nurse practitioner/neonatal nurse practitioner (MS). *Accreditation:* AACN. *Program availability:* Part-time, 100% online, blended/hybrid learning. Terminal master's awarded for partial completion of doctoral program. *Degree requirements:* For master's, comprehensive exam; for doctorate, thesis/dissertation. *Entrance requirements:* For master's, BS in nursing, RN license; for doctorate, GRE General Test (for PhD), B.S. degree, RN license most programs. Additional exam requirements/recommendations for international students: required—TOEFL (minimum score 560 paper-based; 88 iBT), TOEFL (minimum score 560 paper-based; 88 iBT) or IELTS (minimum score 6.5) recommended. Electronic applications accepted. *Expenses:* Contact institution.

**University of San Diego,** Hahn School of Nursing and Health Science, San Diego, CA 92110-2492. Offers adult-gerontology clinical nurse specialist (MSN); adult-gerontology nurse practitioner/family nurse practitioner (MSN); clinical nurse leader (MSN); executive nurse leader (MSN); family nurse practitioner (MSN); healthcare informatics (MS); master's entry program in clinical nursing (for non-rns) (MSN); nursing (PhD); nursing informatics (MSN); nursing practice (DNP); psychiatric-mental health nurse practitioner (MSN). *Accreditation:* AACN. *Program availability:* Part-time, evening/weekend. *Faculty:* 28 full-time (23 women), 43 part-time/adjunct (32 women). *Students:* 252 full-time (202 women), 288 part-time (227 women); includes 261 minority (53 Black or African American, non-Hispanic/Latino; 2 American Indian or Alaska Native, non-Hispanic/Latino; 106 Asian, non-Hispanic/Latino; 76 Hispanic/Latino; 24 Two or more races, non-Hispanic/Latino), 24 international. Average age 34. In 2019, 174 master's, 47 doctorates awarded. *Degree requirements:* For doctorate, thesis/dissertation (for some programs), residency (DNP). *Entrance requirements:* For master's, GRE General Test (for entry-level nursing), BSN, current California RN licensure (except for entry-level nursing), minimum GPA of 3.0; for doctorate, minimum GPA of 3.5, MSN, current California RN licensure. Additional exam requirements/recommendations for international students: required—TOEFL (minimum score 580 paper-based; 83 iBT), TWE. *Application deadline:* Applications are processed on a rolling basis. Application fee: $55. Electronic applications accepted. *Financial support:* In 2019–20, 284 students received support. Institutionally sponsored loans, scholarships/grants, and traineeships available. Support available to part-time students. Financial award application deadline: 4/1; financial award applicants required to submit FAFSA. *Unit head:* Dr. Jane Georges, Dean, Hahn School of Nursing and Health Science, 619-260-4550, Fax: 619-260-6814, E-mail: nursing@sandiego.edu. *Application contact:* Erika Garwood, Associate Director of Graduate Admissions, 619-260-4524, Fax: 619-260-4158, E-mail: grads@sandiego.edu.
Website: http://www.sandiego.edu/nursing/

**University of Southern Maine,** College of Science, Technology, and Health, School of Nursing, Portland, ME 04103. Offers adult-gerontology primary care nurse practitioner (MS, PMC); education (MS); family nurse practitioner (MS, PMC); family psychiatric/mental health nurse practitioner (MS); management (MS); nursing (CAS, CGS); psychiatric-mental health nurse practitioner (PMC). *Accreditation:* AACN. *Program availability:* Part-time. *Degree requirements:* For master's, thesis optional. *Entrance*

*requirements:* For master's, GRE General Test or MAT, minimum GPA of 3.0; for doctorate, GRE. Additional exam requirements/recommendations for international students: required—TOEFL (minimum score 550 paper-based). Electronic applications accepted. *Expenses: Tuition, area resident:* Full-time $864; part-time $432 per credit hour. Tuition, state resident: full-time $864; part-time $432 per credit hour. Tuition, nonresident: full-time $2372; part-time $1186 per credit hour. *Required fees:* $141; $108 per credit hour. Tuition and fees vary according to course load.

**University of South Florida,** College of Nursing, Tampa, FL 33612. Offers nurse anesthesia (DNP); nursing (MS, DNP), including adult-gerontology acute care nursing, adult-gerontology primary care nursing, family health nursing, nurse anesthesia (MS), nursing education (MS), occupational health nursing/adult-gerontology primary care nursing, oncology nursing/adult-gerontology primary care nursing (DNP), pediatric health nursing; nursing education (Post Master's Certificate); nursing science (PhD); simulation based academic fellowship in advanced pain management (Graduate Certificate). *Accreditation:* AACN; AANA/CANAEP. *Program availability:* Part-time. *Faculty:* 34 full-time (28 women), 2 part-time/adjunct (1 woman). *Students:* 265 full-time (207 women), 687 part-time (594 women); includes 343 minority (113 Black or African American, non-Hispanic/Latino; 1 American Indian or Alaska Native, non-Hispanic/Latino; 60 Asian, non-Hispanic/Latino; 141 Hispanic/Latino; 1 Native Hawaiian or other Pacific Islander, non-Hispanic/Latino; 27 Two or more races, non-Hispanic/Latino), 2 international. Average age 33. 955 applicants, 44% accepted, 343 enrolled. In 2019, 281 master's, 80 doctorates awarded. *Degree requirements:* For master's, comprehensive exam, thesis optional; for doctorate, comprehensive exam, thesis/dissertation (for some programs). *Entrance requirements:* For master's, GRE General Test, bachelor's in nursing or RN with Bachelor's in relevant field; current license as Registered Nurse; resume or CV; interview; pre-reqs may be required; for doctorate, GRE General Test (recommended), bachelor's degree in nursing from ACEN or CCNE regionally-accredited institution with minimum GPA of 3.0 in all coursework or in all upper-division coursework; current license as Registered Nurse in Florida; undergraduate statistics course with minimum B grade; 3 letters of recommendation; statement of goals; resume; interview. Additional exam requirements/recommendations for international students: required—TOEFL (minimum score 550 paper-based; 79 iBT). *Application deadline:* For fall admission, 12/15 for domestic and international students; for spring admission, 10/1 for domestic students, 9/15 for international students. Application fee: $30. Electronic applications accepted. *Financial support:* In 2019–20, 181 students received support, including 7 research assistantships with tuition reimbursements available (averaging $18,935 per year), 29 teaching assistantships with tuition reimbursements available (averaging $30,814 per year); tuition waivers (partial) and unspecified assistantships also available. Financial award application deadline: 2/1; financial award applicants required to submit FAFSA. *Unit head:* Dr. Victoria Rich, Dean, College of Nursing, 813-974-8939, Fax: 813-974-5418, E-mail: victoriarich@health.usf.edu. *Application contact:* Dr. Denise Maguire, Vice Dean, Graduate Programs, 813-396-9962, E-mail: dmaguire@health.usf.edu.
Website: http://health.usf.edu/nursing/index.htm

**The University of Tennessee at Chattanooga,** School of Nursing, Chattanooga, TN 37403. Offers certified nurse anesthetist (Post-Master's Certificate); family nurse practitioner (MSN, Post-Master's Certificate); gerontology acute care (MSN, Post-Master's Certificate); nurse anesthesia (MSN); nurse education (Post-Master's Certificate); nursing (DNP). *Accreditation:* AACN; AANA/CANAEP (one or more programs are accredited). *Program availability:* 100% online. *Faculty:* 32 full-time (29 women), 14 part-time/adjunct (10 women). *Students:* 78 full-time (49 women), 51 part-time (43 women); includes 24 minority (11 Black or African American, non-Hispanic/Latino; 2 American Indian or Alaska Native, non-Hispanic/Latino; 4 Asian, non-Hispanic/Latino; 5 Hispanic/Latino; 2 Two or more races, non-Hispanic/Latino). Average age 34. 50 applicants, 100% accepted, 46 enrolled. In 2019, 38 master's, 16 doctorates, 2 other advanced degrees awarded. *Degree requirements:* For master's, thesis optional, practicum; for doctorate, professional project; for Post-Master's Certificate, practicum. *Entrance requirements:* For master's, GRE General Test, MAT, BSN, minimum GPA of 3.0, eligibility for Tennessee RN license, 1 year of direct patient care experience; for doctorate, GRE General Test or MAT (if applicant does not have MSN), minimum GPA of 3.0 for highest degree earned; for Post-Master's Certificate, GRE General Test, MAT, MSN, minimum GPA of 3.0, eligibility for Tennessee RN license, one year of direct patient care experience. Additional exam requirements/recommendations for international students: required—TOEFL (minimum score 550 paper-based; 79 iBT), IELTS (minimum score 6). *Application deadline:* For fall admission, 6/15 priority date for domestic students, 7/1 for international students; for spring admission, 11/1 priority date for domestic students, 11/1 for international students. Applications are processed on a rolling basis. Application fee: $35 ($40 for international students). Electronic applications accepted. *Financial support:* Teaching assistantships, career-related internships or fieldwork, and scholarships/grants available. Support available to part-time students. Financial award application deadline: 7/1; financial award applicants required to submit FAFSA. *Unit head:* Dr. Chris Smith, Director, 423-425-4665, Fax: 423-425-4668, E-mail: chris-smith@utc.edu. *Application contact:* Dr. Joanne Romagni, Dean of the Graduate School, 423-425-4478, Fax: 423-425-5223, E-mail: joanne-romagni@utc.edu.
Website: http://www.utc.edu/nursing/

**The University of Tennessee Health Science Center,** College of Nursing, Memphis, TN 38163. Offers adult-gerontology acute care nurse practitioner (Post Master's Certificate); advance practice nursing (DNP); family nurse practitioner (Post-Doctoral Certificate); pediatric acute care nurse practitioner (Post-Doctoral Certificate); pediatric primary care nurse practitioner (Post-Doctoral Certificate); psychiatric/mental health nurse practitioner (Post-Doctoral Certificate); registered nurse first assistant (Certificate). *Accreditation:* AACN; AANA/CANAEP. *Program availability:* Part-time, blended/hybrid learning. *Faculty:* 62 full-time (55 women), 7 part-time/adjunct (2 women). *Students:* 226 full-time (187 women), 28 part-time (26 women); includes 80 minority (63 Black or African American, non-Hispanic/Latino; 15 Asian, non-Hispanic/Latino; 2 Hispanic/Latino). Average age 33. 652 applicants, 20% accepted, 104 enrolled. In 2019, 86 doctorates, 2 Certificates awarded. *Degree requirements:* For doctorate, project. *Entrance requirements:* For doctorate, RN license, minimum GPA of 3.0; http://www.uthsc.edu/nursing/dnp-admission-requirements.php; for other advanced degree, MSN, APN license, minimum GPA of 3.0; http://www.uthsc.edu/nursing/dnp-admission-requirements.php. Additional exam requirements/recommendations for international students: required—TOEFL (minimum score 550 paper-based; 80 iBT). *Application deadline:* For fall admission, 1/15 for domestic students; for spring admission, 8/15 for domestic students. Application fee: $70. Electronic applications accepted. *Expenses:* $5400 tuition, $450 fees, $110 loan fees, $5790 room/board, $2137 books/supplies, $1260 transportation, $2339 miscellaneous, $450 out-of-state tuition surcharge. *Financial support:* In 2019–20, 112 students received support, including 16 research assistantships (averaging $229,578 per year); Federal Work-Study, institutionally sponsored loans, scholarships/grants, and tuition waivers (partial) also available. Financial award application deadline: 3/15; financial award applicants required to submit FAFSA. *Unit head:* Dr. Wendy Likes, Dean, 901-448-6135, Fax: 901-448-4121, E-mail: wlikes@uthsc.edu. *Application contact:* Glynis Blackard, Assistant Dean for Student Affairs, 901-448-6139, Fax: 901-448-4121, E-mail: gblackar@uthsc.edu.
Website: http://uthsc.edu/nursing/

**The University of Texas at Austin,** Graduate School, School of Nursing, Austin, TX 78712-1111. Offers adult - gerontology clinical nurse specialist (MSN); child health (MSN), including administration, public health nursing, teaching; family nurse practitioner (MSN); family psychiatric/mental health nurse practitioner (MSN); holistic adult health (MSN), including administration, teaching; maternity (MSN), including administration, public health nursing, teaching; nursing (PhD); nursing administration and healthcare systems management (MSN); nursing practice (DNP); pediatric nurse practitioner (MSN); public health nursing (MSN). *Accreditation:* AACN. *Program availability:* Part-time. *Degree requirements:* For master's, thesis optional; for doctorate, thesis/dissertation. *Entrance requirements:* For master's and doctorate, GRE General Test. Additional exam requirements/recommendations for international students: required—TOEFL (minimum score 550 paper-based). Electronic applications accepted.

**The University of Texas Health Science Center at San Antonio,** School of Nursing, San Antonio, TX 78229-3900. Offers administrative management (MSN); adult-gerontology acute care nurse practitioner (PGC); advanced practice leadership (DNP); clinical nurse leader (MSN); executive administrative management (DNP); family nurse practitioner (MSN, PGC); nursing (MSN, PhD); nursing education (MSN, PGC); pediatric nurse practitioner primary care (PGC); psychiatric mental health nurse practitioner (PGC); public health nurse leader (DNP). *Accreditation:* AACN. *Program availability:* Part-time. Terminal master's awarded for partial completion of doctoral program. *Degree requirements:* For master's, thesis optional; for doctorate, comprehensive exam, thesis/dissertation.

**The University of Tulsa,** Graduate School, Oxley College of Health Sciences, School of Nursing, Tulsa, OK 74104-3189. Offers adult-gerontology acute care nurse practitioner (DNP); family nurse practitioner (DNP). *Degree requirements:* For doctorate, comprehensive exam, thesis/dissertation. *Entrance requirements:* Additional exam requirements/recommendations for international students: required—TOEFL (minimum score 550 paper-based; 91 iBT), IELTS (minimum score 6.5). Electronic applications accepted. *Expenses:* Contact institution.

**University of Utah,** Graduate School, College of Nursing, Gerontology Program, Salt Lake City, UT 84112. Offers MS, Certificate. *Program availability:* Part-time, online only, 100% online. *Faculty:* 9 full-time (8 women), 1 (woman) part-time/adjunct. *Students:* 5 full-time (all women), 9 part-time (all women); includes 1 minority (Two or more races, non-Hispanic/Latino). Average age 41. 7 applicants, 100% accepted, 5 enrolled. In 2019, 2 master's awarded. *Degree requirements:* For master's, thesis optional, Colloquium Defense, Masters Project. *Entrance requirements:* For master's, Complete application for graduate admission; transcripts for all colleges and universities attended; evidence of bachelors degree from a regionally accredited university or college; minimum 3.0 cumulative GPA on a 4.0 scale; current resume or curriculum vitae; three professional references; goal statement. Additional exam requirements/recommendations for international students: required—TOEFL (minimum score 80 iBT), IELTS (minimum score 6.5). *Application deadline:* For fall admission, 12/1 for domestic and international students. Application fee: $55 ($65 for international students). Electronic applications accepted. *Expenses:* $22,975.43 for completion of three semester program (resident tuition rate); $52,735.55 for completion of three semester program (nonresident tuition rate). *Financial support:* In 2019–20, 8 students received support, including 8 fellowships with partial tuition reimbursements available (averaging $12,563 per year); research assistantships with partial tuition reimbursements available, teaching assistantships with partial tuition reimbursements available, Federal Work-Study, scholarships/grants, and unspecified assistantships also available. Support available to part-time students. Financial award application deadline: 1/20. *Unit head:* Dr. Jacqueline Eaton, Assistant Dean, 801-587-9638, Fax: 801-587-7697, E-mail: jacqueline.eaton@nurs.utah.edu. *Application contact:* Ashley Cadiz, Academic Program Manager, 801-581-8198, Fax: 801-585-2588, E-mail: ashley.cadiz@nurs.utah.edu.
Website: http://www.nursing.utah.edu/gerontology/

**University of Wisconsin–Eau Claire,** College of Nursing and Health Sciences, Program in Nursing, Eau Claire, WI 54702-4004. Offers adult-gerontological administration (DNP); adult-gerontological clinical nurse specialist (DNP); adult-gerontological education (MSN); adult-gerontological primary care nurse practitioner (DNP); family health administration (DNP); family health in eddcation (MSN); family health nurse practitioner (DNP); nursing (MSN); nursing practice (DNP). *Accreditation:* AACN. *Program availability:* Part-time. Terminal master's awarded for partial completion of doctoral program. *Degree requirements:* For master's, thesis optional, 500-600 hours clinical practicum, oral and written exams. *Entrance requirements:* For master's, Wisconsin RN license, minimum GPA of 3.0, undergraduate statistics, course work in health assessment. Additional exam requirements/recommendations for international students: required—TOEFL (minimum score 79 iBT). *Expenses:* Contact institution.

**University of Wisconsin–Madison,** School of Nursing, Madison, WI 53705. Offers adult/gerontology (DNP), including clinical nurse specialist; adult/gerontology acute care (DNP), including nurse practitioner; adult/gerontology primary care (DNP), including nurse practitioner; nursing (PhD); MS/MPH. *Accreditation:* AACN. *Program availability:* Part-time. *Degree requirements:* For doctorate, comprehensive exam, thesis/dissertation. *Entrance requirements:* For doctorate, GRE, bachelor's degree in nursing, undergraduate GPA of at least 3.0 on the last 60 credits, academic references, 2 original papers or other scholarly work, essay, RN license (for DNP), 1 year of professional nursing experience (for DNP). Additional exam requirements/recommendations for international students: required—TOEFL (minimum score 580 paper-based; 92 iBT), IELTS (minimum score 7). Electronic applications accepted. *Expenses:* Contact institution.

**Ursuline College,** School of Graduate and Professional Studies, Programs in Nursing, Pepper Pike, OH 44124-4398. Offers acute-care nurse practitioner (MSN); adult nurse practitioner (MSN); adult-gerontology acute care nurse practitioner (MSN); adult-gerontology clinical nurse specialist (MSN); adult-gerontology nurse practitioner (MSN); care management (MSN); clinical nurse specialist (MSN); family nurse practitioner (MSN); nursing (DNP); nursing education (MSN); palliative care (MSN). *Accreditation:* AACN. *Program availability:* Part-time, 100% online. *Faculty:* 6 full-time (all women), 25 part-time/adjunct (19 women). *Students:* 106 full-time (99 women), 117 part-time (105 women); includes 71 minority (46 Black or African American, non-Hispanic/Latino; 2 American Indian or Alaska Native, non-Hispanic/Latino; 12 Asian, non-Hispanic/Latino; 6 Hispanic/Latino; 5 Two or more races, non-Hispanic/Latino). Average age 38. 265 applicants, 98% accepted, 61 enrolled. In 2019, 68 master's, 2 doctorates awarded. *Degree requirements:* For master's, comprehensive exam; for doctorate, thesis/dissertation. *Entrance requirements:* For master's, minimum undergraduate GPA of 3.0, bachelor's degree in nursing, eligibility for or current Ohio RN license. Additional exam requirements/recommendations for international students: required—TOEFL (minimum score 500 paper-based). *Application deadline:* For fall admission, 8/1 priority date for domestic students. Applications are processed on a rolling basis. Application fee: $25. Electronic applications accepted. *Expenses: Tuition:* Full-time $18,784; part-time $1174 per credit hour. *Required fees:* $320; $240 per unit. One-time fee: $100. Tuition and fees vary according to course level and program. *Financial support:* In 2019–20, 10 students received support. Scholarships/grants, tuition waivers (partial), and College Free Credit available. Financial award application deadline: 3/1; financial award applicants required to submit FAFSA. *Unit head:* Dr. Janet Baker, Associate Dean of Graduate Nursing,

440-864-8172, Fax: 440-684-6053, E-mail: jbaker@ursuline.edu. *Application contact:* Melanie Steele, Director, Graduate Admission, 440-646-8119, Fax: 440-684-6138, E-mail: graduateadmissions@ursuline.edu.

**Valdosta State University,** College of Nursing and Health Sciences, Valdosta, GA 31698. Offers adult gerontology nurse practitioner (MSN); exercise physiology (MS); family nurse practitioner (MSN); family psychiatric mental health nurse practitioner (MSN). *Accreditation:* AACN. *Program availability:* Part-time, online learning. *Degree requirements:* For master's, thesis (for some programs), comprehensive written and/or oral exams. *Entrance requirements:* For master's, minimum GPA of 2.8. Additional exam requirements/recommendations for international students: required—TOEFL (minimum score 523 paper-based). Electronic applications accepted.

**Villanova University,** M. Louise Fitzpatrick College of Nursing, Villanova, PA 19085. Offers adult-gerontology primary care nurse practitioner (MSN, Post Master's Certificate); family primary care nurse practitioner (MSN, Post Master's Certificate); nurse anesthesia (DNP); nursing (PhD); nursing education (MSN, Post Master's Certificate); nursing practice (DNP); pediatric primary care nurse practitioner (MSN, Post Master's Certificate). *Accreditation:* AACN; AANA/CANAEP. *Program availability:* Part-time, online learning. *Entrance requirements:* Additional exam requirements/ recommendations for international students: required—TOEFL, IELTS. Electronic applications accepted.

**Walden University,** Graduate Programs, School of Nursing, Minneapolis, MN 55401. Offers adult-gerontology acute care nurse practitioner (MSN); adult-gerontology nurse practitioner (MSN); education (MSN); family nurse practitioner (MSN); informatics (MSN); leadership and management (MSN); nursing (PhD, Post-Master's Certificate), including education (PhD), healthcare administration (PhD), interdisciplinary health (PhD), leadership (PhD), nursing education (Post-Master's Certificate), nursing informatics (Post-Master's Certificate), nursing leadership and management (Post-Master's Certificate), public health policy (PhD); nursing practice (DNP); psychiatric mental health (MSN). *Accreditation:* AACN. *Program availability:* Part-time, evening/ weekend, online only, 100% online. *Degree requirements:* For doctorate, thesis/ dissertation (for some programs), residency (for some programs), field experience (for some programs). *Entrance requirements:* For master's, bachelor's degree or equivalent in related field or RN; minimum GPA of 2.5; official transcripts; goal statement (for some programs); access to computer and Internet; for doctorate, master's degree or higher; RN; three years of related professional or academic experience; goal statement; access to computer and Internet; for Post-Master's Certificate, relevant work experience; access to computer and Internet. Additional exam requirements/recommendations for international students: required—TOEFL (minimum score 550 paper-based, 79 iBT), IELTS (minimum score 6.5), Michigan English Language Assessment Battery (minimum score 82), or PTE (minimum score 53). Electronic applications accepted.

**Wayne State University,** College of Nursing, Detroit, MI 48202. Offers adult gerontology acute care nurse practitioner (MSN); adult gerontology primary care nurse practitioner (MSN); advanced public health nursing (MSN); infant and mental health (DNP, PhD); neonatal nurse practitioner (MSN); nurse-midwifery (MSN); pediatric acute care nurse practitioner (MSN); pediatric primary care nurse practitioner (MSN); psychiatric mental health nurse practitioner (MSN); women's health nurse practitioner (MSN). *Accreditation:* AACN; ACNM/ACME. *Program availability:* Part-time. *Faculty:* 27. *Students:* 134 full-time (118 women), 216 part-time (187 women); includes 98 minority (51 Black or African American, non-Hispanic/Latino; 24 Asian, non-Hispanic/Latino; 6 Hispanic/Latino; 17 Two or more races, non-Hispanic/Latino), 18 international. Average age 33. 425 applicants, 37% accepted, 95 enrolled. In 2019, 58 master's, 31 doctorates awarded. *Degree requirements:* For doctorate, thesis/dissertation. *Entrance requirements:* For master's, Completed a Bachelor of Science in Nursing with a 3.0 or higher GPA. Official transcripts. Professional competence as documented by three references. Current Michigan Registered Nurse (RN) licensure. A personal statement of goals for graduate study; for doctorate, DNP: Minimum GPA of 3.0 or higher in BSN is required. Resume or Curriculum Vita that includes education, work and/or research experience. Two references, one from a doctorally prepared individual. RN license. PhD: BSN transcript; Two to three references from doctorally prepared individuals; goals statement; Resume or CV; Interview. Additional exam requirements/recommendations for international students: required—TOEFL (minimum score 101 iBT), TWE (minimum score 6), Michigan English Language Assessment Battery (minimum score 85); recommended—IELTS (minimum score 7). *Application deadline:* For fall admission, 1/ 31 for domestic students; for winter admission, 11/1 for domestic students. Applications are processed on a rolling basis. Application fee: $50. Electronic applications accepted. *Expenses:* $925.72 per credit hour in-state, $1,716.93 per credit hour out-of-state, $54.56 student service credit hour fee, $315.70 registration fee. *Financial support:* In 2019–20, 104 students received support, including 39 fellowships with tuition reimbursements available (averaging $6,456 per year), 1 research assistantship (averaging $24,950 per year), 5 teaching assistantships with tuition reimbursements available (averaging $25,000 per year); scholarships/grants, health care benefits, and unspecified assistantships also available. Support available to part-time students. Financial award application deadline: 3/1; financial award applicants required to submit FAFSA. *Unit head:* Dr. Laurie M Lauzon Clabo, Dean, College of Nursing, 313-577-4082, E-mail: laurie.lauzon.clabo@wayne.edu. *Application contact:* Dr. Laurie M Lauzon Clabo, Dean, College of Nursing, 313-577-4082, E-mail: laurie.lauzon.clabo@wayne.edu.
Website: http://nursing.wayne.edu/

**Western Connecticut State University,** Division of Graduate Studies, School of Professional Studies, Nursing Department, Danbury, CT 06810-6885. Offers adult gerontology clinical nurse specialist (MSN); adult gerontology nurse practitioner (MSN); nursing education (Ed D). *Accreditation:* AACN. *Program availability:* Part-time. *Entrance requirements:* For master's, MAT (if GPA less than 3.0), bachelor's degree in nursing, minimum GPA of 3.0, previous course work in statistics and nursing research, RN license. Additional exam requirements/recommendations for international students: recommended—TOEFL (minimum score 550 paper-based; 79 iBT), IELTS (minimum score 6). *Expenses:* Contact institution.

**Wilmington University,** College of Health Professions, New Castle, DE 19720-6491. Offers adult nurse practitioner (MSN); family nurse practitioner (MSN); gerontology nurse practitioner (MSN); nursing (MSN); nursing leadership (MSN); nursing practice (DNP). *Accreditation:* AACN. *Program availability:* Part-time. *Degree requirements:* For master's, thesis. *Entrance requirements:* For master's, BSN, RN license, interview, 3 letters of recommendation. Additional exam requirements/recommendations for international students: required—TOEFL (minimum score 500 paper-based). Electronic applications accepted.

**Winona State University,** College of Nursing and Health Sciences, Winona, MN 55987. Offers adult-gerontology acute care nurse practitioner (MS, DNP, Post Master's Certificate); adult-gerontology clinical nurse specialist (MS, DNP, Post Master's Certificate); adult-gerontology primary care nurse practitioner (MS, DNP, Post Master's Certificate); family nurse practitioner (MS, DNP, Post Master's Certificate); nurse educator (MS); nursing and organizational leadership (MS, DNP, Post Master's Certificate); practice and leadership innovations (DNP, Post Master's Certificate). *Accreditation:* AACN. *Program availability:* Part-time, online learning. *Degree requirements:* For master's, thesis; for doctorate, capstone. *Entrance requirements:* For master's, GRE (if GPA less than 3.0). Additional exam requirements/recommendations for international students: required—TOEFL (minimum score 550 paper-based).

**Wright State University,** Graduate School, College of Nursing and Health, Program in Nursing, Dayton, OH 45435. Offers administration of nursing and health care systems (MS); adult gerontology clinical nurse specialist (MS); adult-gerontology acute care nurse practitioner (MS); family nurse practitioner (MS); neonatal nurse practitioner (MS); pediatric nurse practitioner-acute care (MS); pediatric nurse practitioner-primary care (MS); psychiatric mental health nurse practitioner (MS); school nurse (MS). *Accreditation:* AACN. *Program availability:* Part-time, evening/weekend. *Degree requirements:* For master's, thesis or alternative. *Entrance requirements:* For master's, GRE General Test, BSN from ACEN-accredited college, Ohio RN license. Additional exam requirements/recommendations for international students: required—TOEFL.

**York College of Pennsylvania,** The Stabler Department of Nursing, York, PA 17403-3651. Offers adult gerontology clinical nurse specialist (MS); nurse anesthetist (MS). *Accreditation:* AACN; AANA/CANAEP. *Program availability:* Part-time. *Faculty:* 6 full-time (all women), 5 part-time/adjunct (4 women). *Students:* 30 full-time (15 women), 36 part-time (30 women); includes 9 minority (1 Black or African American, non-Hispanic/ Latino; 6 Asian, non-Hispanic/Latino; 1 Hispanic/Latino; 1 Two or more races, non-Hispanic/Latino), 1 international. Average age 34. 61 applicants, 46% accepted, 23 enrolled. In 2019, 24 master's awarded. *Entrance requirements:* For master's, bachelor's degree in nursing, minimum GPA of 3.0. Additional exam requirements/ recommendations for international students: required—TOEFL (minimum score 530 paper-based; 72 iBT), IELTS. Electronic applications accepted. *Expenses:* Master's Programs (other than Psych/Mental Health NP): $820 per credit tuition; Master's Program, Psych/Mental Health NP: $775 per credit tuition; DNP Programs: $960 per credit tuition, $880 general fee. *Financial support:* In 2019–20, 1 student received support. Scholarships/grants available. Financial award applicants required to submit FAFSA. *Unit head:* Colleen Marshall-Fantaski, Director, Graduate Programs in Nursing, 717-815-1791, Fax: 717-849-1651, E-mail: cfantaski@ycp.edu. *Application contact:* Allison Malachosky, Administrative Assistant, 717-815-2290, Fax: 717-849-1651, E-mail: amalacho@ycp.edu.
Website: http://www.ycp.edu/academics/academic-departments/nursing/

# HIV/AIDS Nursing

**University of Delaware,** College of Health Sciences, School of Nursing, Newark, DE 19716. Offers adult nurse practitioner (MSN, PMC); cardiopulmonary clinical nurse specialist (MSN, PMC); cardiopulmonary clinical nurse specialist/adult nurse practitioner (MSN, PMC); family nurse practitioner (MSN, PMC); gerontology clinical nurse specialist (MSN, PMC); gerontology clinical nurse specialist geriatric nurse practitioner (PMC); gerontology clinical nurse specialist/geriatric nurse practitioner (MSN); health services administration (MSN, PMC); nursing of children clinical nurse specialist (MSN, PMC); nursing of children clinical nurse specialist/pediatric nurse practitioner (MSN, PMC); oncology/immune deficiency clinical nurse specialist (MSN, PMC); oncology/immune deficiency clinical nurse specialist/adult nurse practitioner (MSN, PMC); perinatal/ women's health clinical nurse specialist (MSN, PMC); perinatal/women's health clinical nurse specialist/women's health nurse practitioner (MSN, PMC); psychiatric nursing clinical nurse specialist (MSN, PMC). *Accreditation:* AACN. *Program availability:* Part-time, evening/weekend, online learning. *Degree requirements:* For master's, thesis optional. *Entrance requirements:* For master's, BSN, interview, RN license. Electronic applications accepted.

# Hospice Nursing

**Central Connecticut State University,** School of Graduate Studies, School of Education and Professional Studies, Department of Nursing, New Britain, CT 06050-4010. Offers hospice and palliative care (MSN). *Program availability:* Part-time, evening/ weekend. *Degree requirements:* For master's, thesis, nursing capstone. *Entrance requirements:* For master's, minimum undergraduate GPA of 2.7, essay, letter of reference, minimum grade of C+ in an undergraduate statistics course. Additional exam requirements/recommendations for international students: required—TOEFL (minimum score 550 paper-based; 79 iBT); recommended—IELTS (minimum score 6.5). Electronic applications accepted.

**Madonna University,** Program in Hospice, Livonia, MI 48150-1173. Offers MSH. *Program availability:* Part-time, evening/weekend. *Degree requirements:* For master's, thesis or alternative. *Entrance requirements:* For master's, GRE General Test, minimum

undergraduate GPA of 3.0, 2 letters of recommendation, interview. Electronic applications accepted. *Expenses: Tuition:* Full-time $15,930; part-time $885 per credit hour. Tuition and fees vary according to degree level and program.

# Maternal and Child/Neonatal Nursing

**Boston College,** William F. Connell School of Nursing, Chestnut Hill, MA 02467. Offers adult-gerontology primary care nurse practitioner (MS); family health nursing (MS); nurse anesthesia (MS); nursing (PhD); pediatric primary care nurse practitioner (MS), including pediatric and women's health; psychiatric-mental health nursing (MS); women's health nursing (MS); MBA/MS; MS/MA; MS/PhD. *Accreditation:* AACN; AANA/CANAEP (one or more programs are accredited). *Program availability:* Part-time. *Faculty:* 56 full-time (50 women). *Students:* 228 full-time (200 women), 82 part-time (71 women); includes 54 minority (10 Black or African American, non-Hispanic/Latino; 18 Asian, non-Hispanic/Latino; 20 Hispanic/Latino; 6 Two or more races, non-Hispanic/Latino), 7 international. Average age 28. 360 applicants, 56% accepted, 93 enrolled. In 2019, 107 master's, 7 doctorates awarded. *Degree requirements:* For master's, comprehensive exam; for doctorate, comprehensive exam, thesis/dissertation, computer literacy exam or foreign language. *Entrance requirements:* For master's, bachelor's degree; for doctorate, GRE General Test, bachelor's in Nursing and master's degree in nursing or related field. Additional exam requirements/recommendations for international students: required—TOEFL (minimum score 600 paper-based; 100 iBT), IELTS (minimum score 7.5). *Application deadline:* For fall admission, 3/15 for domestic and international students; for spring admission, 9/30 for domestic and international students. Application fee: $40. Electronic applications accepted. *Expenses:* Contact institution. *Financial support:* In 2019–20, 135 students received support, including 12 fellowships with full tuition reimbursements available (averaging $24,504 per year), 29 teaching assistantships (averaging $4,380 per year); scholarships/grants, health care benefits, tuition waivers (partial), and unspecified assistantships also available. Support available to part-time students. Financial award application deadline: 4/18; financial award applicants required to submit FAFSA. *Unit head:* Dr. Susan Gennaro, Dean, 617-552-4251, Fax: 617-552-0931, E-mail: susan.gennaro@bc.edu. *Application contact:* Sean Sendall, Assistant Dean, Graduate Enrollment and Data Analytics, 617-552-4745, Fax: 617-552-2121, E-mail: sean.sendall@bc.edu.
Website: http://www.bc.edu/cson

**Case Western Reserve University,** Frances Payne Bolton School of Nursing, Master's Programs in Nursing, Nurse Practitioner Program, Cleveland, OH 44106. Offers acute care pediatric nurse practitioner (MSN); acute care/cardiovascular nursing (MSN); adult gerontology acute care nurse practitioner (MSN); adult gerontology primary care nurse practitioner (MSN); family nurse practitioner (MSN); family systems psychiatric mental health nursing (MSN); neonatal nurse practitioner (MSN); palliative care (MSN); pediatric nurse practitioner in acute care (MSN); pediatric primary care nurse practitioner (MSN); women's health nurse practitioner (MSN). *Accreditation:* ACEN. *Program availability:* Part-time. *Faculty:* 30 full-time (25 women), 6 part-time/adjunct (all women). *Students:* 47 full-time (36 women), 70 part-time (59 women); includes 34 minority (12 Black or African American, non-Hispanic/Latino; 11 Asian, non-Hispanic/Latino; 9 Hispanic/Latino; 2 Two or more races, non-Hispanic/Latino), 9 international. Average age 30. 45 applicants, 82% accepted, 22 enrolled. In 2019, 46 master's awarded. *Degree requirements:* For master's, thesis optional, minimum GPA of 3.0, clinical hours corresponding to requirements to sit for certification exam, portfolio. *Entrance requirements:* For master's, GRE/MAT (scores not required for application, but may be requested for an admission decision). Additional exam requirements/recommendations for international students: required—TOEFL (minimum score 577 paper-based; 90 iBT), IELTS (minimum score 7). *Application deadline:* For fall admission, 3/15 for domestic and international students; for spring admission, 10/1 for domestic and international students; for summer admission, 3/15 for domestic and international students. Applications are processed on a rolling basis. Application fee: $75. Electronic applications accepted. *Expenses:* Clinical placement $75; Activity fee $15 per semester; Graduate council fee $15 per semester; Tuition rate $2,133 per credit hour. *Financial support:* In 2019–20, 100 students received support, including 34 teaching assistantships with partial tuition reimbursements available (averaging $19,197 per year); scholarships/grants and traineeships also available. Financial award application deadline: 5/15; financial award applicants required to submit FAFSA. *Unit head:* Dr. Latina Brooks, Director, 216-368-1196, Fax: 216-368-3542, E-mail: lmb3@case.edu. *Application contact:* Jackie Tepale, Admissions Coordinator, 216-368-5253, Fax: 216-368-3542, E-mail: yyd@case.edu.
Website: https://case.edu/nursing/programs/msn

**Creighton University,** College of Nursing, Omaha, NE 68178-0001. Offers adult gerontology acute care nurse practitioner (DNP, Post-Master's Certificate); adult gerontology nurse practitioner (DNP); clinical nurse leader (MSN, Post-Graduate Certificate); clinical systems administration (MSN, DNP); family nurse practitioner (DNP, Post-Master's Certificate); neonatal nurse practitioner (DNP, Post-Master's Certificate); nursing (Post-Graduate Certificate); pediatric acute care nurse practitioner (DNP, Post-Master's Certificate); psychiatric mental health nurse practitioner (DNP). *Accreditation:* AACN. *Program availability:* Part-time, blended/hybrid learning. *Degree requirements:* For master's, capstone project; for doctorate, scholarly project. *Entrance requirements:* For master's and doctorate, BSN from ACEN- or CCNE-accredited nursing school, minimum cumulative GPA of 3.0, personal statement, active unencumbered RN license with NE eligibility, undergraduate statistics course, physical assessment course or equivalent, three recommendation letters; for other advanced degree, MSN or MS in nursing from ACEN- or CCNE-accredited nursing school, minimum cumulative GPA of 3.0, active unencumbered RN license with NE eligibility. Additional exam requirements/recommendations for international students: required—TOEFL (minimum score 600 paper-based, 100 iBT) or IELTS. Electronic applications accepted. *Expenses:* Contact institution.

**Duke University,** School of Nursing, Durham, NC 27708. Offers acute care pediatric nurse practitioner (MSN, Post-Graduate Certificate); adult-gerontology nurse practitioner (MSN, Post-Graduate Certificate), including acute care, primary care; family nurse practitioner (MSN, Post-Graduate Certificate); neonatal nurse practitioner (MSN, Post-Graduate Certificate); nurse anesthesia (DNP); nurse practitioner (DNP); nursing (PhD); nursing and health care leadership (MSN, Post-Graduate Certificate); nursing education (MSN, Post-Graduate Certificate); nursing informatics (MSN, Post-Graduate Certificate); pediatric nurse practitioner (MSN, Post-Graduate Certificate), including primary care; psychiatric mental health nurse practitioner (MSN, Post-Graduate Certificate); women's health nurse practitioner (MSN, Post-Graduate Certificate). *Accreditation:* AACN; AANA/CANAEP. *Program availability:* Part-time, evening/weekend, online with on-campus intensives. *Faculty:* 48 full-time (40 women), 32 part-time/adjunct (28 women). *Students:*

666 full-time (601 women), 157 part-time (139 women); includes 193 minority (61 Black or African American, non-Hispanic/Latino; 4 American Indian or Alaska Native, non-Hispanic/Latino; 57 Asian, non-Hispanic/Latino; 49 Hispanic/Latino; 1 Native Hawaiian or other Pacific Islander, non-Hispanic/Latino; 21 Two or more races, non-Hispanic/Latino), 8 international. Average age 34. 761 applicants, 33% accepted, 149 enrolled. In 2019, 213 master's, 74 doctorates, 18 other advanced degrees awarded. Terminal master's awarded for partial completion of doctoral program. *Degree requirements:* For master's, thesis optional; for doctorate, capstone project. *Entrance requirements:* For master's, MSN applicants are no longer required to take the GRE, 1 year of nursing experience (recommended), BSN, minimum GPA of 3.0, previous course work in statistics; for doctorate, GRE is required for the DNP in Nurse Anesthesia, BSN or MSN, minimum GPA of 3.0, resume, personal statement, graduate statistics and research methods course, current licensure as a registered nurse, transcripts from all post-secondary institutions; for Post-Graduate Certificate, MSN, licensure or eligibility as a professional nurse, transcripts from all post-secondary institutions, previous course work in statistics. Additional exam requirements/recommendations for international students: required—TOEFL (minimum score 100 iBT), IELTS (minimum score 7). *Application deadline:* For fall admission, 12/1 for domestic and international students; for spring admission, 5/1 for domestic and international students. Application fee: $50. Electronic applications accepted. *Expenses:* Contact institution. *Financial support:* Institutionally sponsored loans, scholarships/grants, and traineeships available. Support available to part-time students. Financial award applicants required to submit FAFSA. *Unit head:* Dr. Marion E. Broome, Dean/Vice Chancellor for Nursing Affairs/Associate Vice President for Academic Affairs for Nursing, 919-684-9446, Fax: 919-684-9414, E-mail: marion.broome@duke.edu. *Application contact:* Dr. Ernie Rushing, Director of Admissions and Recruitment, 919-668-6274, Fax: 919-668-4693, E-mail: ernie.rushing@dm.duke.edu.
Website: http://www.nursing.duke.edu/

**Hardin-Simmons University,** Graduate School, Patty Hanks Shelton School of Nursing, Abilene, TX 79698-0001. Offers education (MSN); family nurse practitioner (MSN). *Accreditation:* AACN. *Program availability:* Part-time. *Degree requirements:* For master's, comprehensive exam, thesis or alternative. *Entrance requirements:* For master's, GRE, minimum undergraduate GPA of 3.0; interview; upper-level course work in statistics; CPR certification; letters of recommendation. Additional exam requirements/recommendations for international students: required—TOEFL (minimum score 550 paper-based; 79 iBT). Electronic applications accepted. *Expenses:* Contact institution.

**Lehman College of the City University of New York,** School of Health Sciences, Human Services and Nursing, Department of Nursing, Bronx, NY 10468-1589. Offers adult health nursing (MS); nursing of older adults (MS); parent-child nursing (MS); pediatric nurse practitioner (MS). *Accreditation:* AACN. *Program availability:* Part-time, evening/weekend. *Entrance requirements:* For master's, bachelor's degree in nursing, New York RN license. *Expenses: Tuition, area resident:* Full-time $5545; part-time $470 per credit. Tuition, nonresident: part-time $855 per credit. *Required fees:* $240.

**Louisiana State University Health Sciences Center,** School of Nursing, New Orleans, LA 70112. Offers adult gerontology acute care nurse practitioner (DNP, Post-Master's Certificate); adult gerontology clinical nurse specialist (DNP, Post-Master's Certificate); adult gerontology primary care nurse practitioner (DNP, Post-Master's Certificate); clinical nurse leader (MSN); executive nurse leader (DNP, Post-Master's Certificate); neonatal nurse practitioner (DNP, Post-Master's Certificate); nurse anesthesia (DNP, Post-Master's Certificate); nurse educator (MSN); nursing (DNS); primary care family nurse practitioner (DNP, Post-Master's Certificate); public/community health nursing (DNP, Post-Master's Certificate). *Accreditation:* AACN; AANA/CANAEP (one or more programs are accredited). *Program availability:* Part-time. *Faculty:* 25 full-time (21 women), 25 part-time/adjunct (13 women). *Students:* 182 full-time (127 women), 70 part-time (59 women); includes 82 minority (52 Black or African American, non-Hispanic/Latino; 2 American Indian or Alaska Native, non-Hispanic/Latino; 14 Asian, non-Hispanic/Latino; 14 Hispanic/Latino), 1 international. Average age 34. 34 applicants, 62% accepted, 21 enrolled. In 2019, 72 doctorates awarded. *Degree requirements:* For master's, thesis optional; for doctorate, thesis/dissertation. *Entrance requirements:* For master's, GRE, minimum GPA of 3.0; for doctorate, GRE, minimum GPA of 3.0 (for DNP), 3.5 (for DNS). Additional exam requirements/recommendations for international students: required—TOEFL (minimum score 550 paper-based; 79 iBT). *Application deadline:* For fall admission, 6/1 priority date for domestic and international students; for spring admission, 10/1 priority date for domestic and international students; for summer admission, 3/1 priority date for domestic and international students. Applications are processed on a rolling basis. Application fee: $100. Electronic applications accepted. *Expenses:* MSN and DNS: $13,354.50, $24,982.25 non-resident, $586 per hour (fall and spring), $467 per hour (summer), $1,102 per hour non-resident (fall and spring), $858 per hour non-resident (summer); DNP (Except Nurse Anethesia): $21,907.50, $38,262.23 non-resident, $973 per hour (fall and spring), $733 per hour (summer), $1,700 per hour non-resident (fall and spring), $1,278 per hour non-resident (summer); Nurse Anesthesia DNP: $26,407.50, $42,762.23 non-resident, $1,173 per hour (fall and spring), $883 per hour (summer), $1,900 per hour non-resident (fall and spring), $1,428 per hour non-resident (summer). *Financial support:* In 2019–20, 20 students received support. Institutionally sponsored loans, scholarships/grants, unspecified assistantships, and DNS Scholars Program available. Financial award application deadline: 4/15; financial award applicants required to submit FAFSA. *Unit head:* Dr. Demetrius James Porche, Dean, 504-568-4106, Fax: 504-599-0573, E-mail: dporch@lsuhsc.edu. *Application contact:* Tracie Gravolet, Director, Office of Student Affairs, 504-568-4114, Fax: 504-568-5711, E-mail: tgravo@lsuhsc.edu.
Website: http://nursing.lsuhsc.edu/

**Medical University of South Carolina,** College of Nursing, Pediatric Nurse Practitioner Program, Charleston, SC 29425. Offers MSN, DNP. *Accreditation:* AACN. *Program availability:* Part-time, online learning. *Degree requirements:* For master's, comprehensive exam (for some programs), thesis optional; for doctorate, final project. *Entrance requirements:* For master's, BSN from nationally-accredited program, minimum nursing and cumulative GPA of 3.0, undergraduate-level statistics course, active RN License, 3 confidential references, current curriculum vitae or resume, essay; for doctorate, BSN from nationally-accredited program, minimum nursing and cumulative GPA of 3.0, undergraduate-level statistics course, active RN License, 3

confidential references, current curriculum vitae or resume, personal essay (for DNP). Additional exam requirements/recommendations for international students: required—TOEFL (minimum score 550 paper-based; 80 iBT). Electronic applications accepted.

**Northeastern University,** Bouvé College of Health Sciences, Boston, MA 02115-5096. Offers applied behavior analysis (MS); audiology (Au D); counseling psychology (MS, PhD, CAGS); exercise science (MS); nursing (MS, PhD, CAGS), including administration (MS), adult-gerontology acute care nurse practitioner (MS, CAGS), adult-gerontology primary care nurse practitioner (MS, CAGS), anesthesia (MS), family nurse practitioner (MS, CAGS), neonatal nurse practitioner (MS, CAGS), pediatric nurse practitioner (MS, CAGS), psychiatric mental health nurse practitioner (MS, CAGS); nursing practice (DNP); pharmaceutical sciences (MS, PhD), including interdisciplinary concentration, pharmaceutics and drug delivery systems; pharmacology (MS); pharmacy (Pharm D); school psychology (PhD); speech-language pathology (MS); urban health (MPH); MS/MBA. *Accreditation:* AANA/CANAEP; ACPE (one or more programs are accredited); ASHA; CEPH. *Program availability:* Part-time, evening/weekend, online learning. *Degree requirements:* For doctorate, thesis/dissertation (for some programs); for CAGS, comprehensive exam. Electronic applications accepted. *Expenses:* Contact institution.

**Old Dominion University,** College of Health Sciences, School of Nursing, Adult Gerontology Nursing Emphasis, Norfolk, VA 23529. Offers adult gerontology clinical nurse specialist/administrator (MSN); adult gerontology clinical nurse specialist/educator (MSN); advanced practice (DNP); neonatal clinical nurse specialist (MSN); pediatric clinical nurse specialist (MSN). *Program availability:* Part-time, online only, blended/hybrid learning. *Degree requirements:* For master's, comprehensive exam, internship, practicum. *Entrance requirements:* For master's, GRE or MAT (waived with a GPA above 3.5), undergraduate health/physical assessment course, statistics, 3 letters of recommendation, essay, resume, transcripts. Additional exam requirements/recommendations for international students: required—TOEFL. Electronic applications accepted. *Expenses:* Contact institution.

**Old Dominion University,** College of Health Sciences, School of Nursing, Neonatal Nurse Practitioner Program, Norfolk, VA 23529. Offers advanced practice (DNP); neonatal clinical nurse specialist (MSN); neonatal nurse practitioner (MSN). *Program availability:* Part-time, online only, blended/hybrid learning. *Degree requirements:* For master's, comprehensive exam. *Entrance requirements:* For master's, current unencumbered license as a registered nurse (RN), baccalaureate degree in nursing or related science field with minimum GPA of 3.0, three letters of recommendation, undergraduate courses in statistics and health/physical assessment, two years' recent clinical practice experience working in an NICU. Additional exam requirements/recommendations for international students: required—TOEFL. Electronic applications accepted. *Expenses:* Contact institution.

**Regis University,** Rueckert-Hartman College for Health Professions, Denver, CO 80221-1099. Offers advanced practice nurse (DNP); counseling (MA); counseling children and adolescents (Post-Graduate Certificate); counseling military families (Post-Graduate Certificate); depth psychotherapy (Post-Graduate Certificate); fellowship in orthopedic manual physical therapy (Certificate); health care business management (Certificate); health care quality and patient safety (Certificate); health industry leadership (MBA); health services administration (MS); marriage and family therapy (MA, Post-Graduate Certificate); neonatal nurse practitioner (MSN); nursing education (MSN); nursing leadership (MSN); occupational therapy (OTD); pharmacy (Pharm D); physical therapy (DPT). *Accreditation:* ACPE. *Program availability:* Part-time, evening/weekend, 100% online, blended/hybrid learning. *Degree requirements:* For master's, thesis (for some programs), internship. *Entrance requirements:* For master's, official transcript reflecting baccalaureate degree awarded from regionally-accredited college or university. Additional exam requirements/recommendations for international students: required—TOEFL (minimum score 550 paper-based; 82 iBT). Electronic applications accepted. *Expenses:* Contact institution.

**Saint Francis Medical Center College of Nursing,** SFMC College of Nursing Graduate Programs, Peoria, IL 61603-3783. Offers adult gerontology (MSN); clinical nurse leader (MSN); family nurse practitioner (MSN, Post-Graduate Certificate); family psychiatric mental health nurse practitioner (MSN); neonatal nurse practitioner (MSN); nurse clinician (Post-Graduate Certificate); nurse educator (MSN, Post-Graduate Certificate); nursing (DNP), including leadership/ clinician; nursing management leadership (MSN). *Accreditation:* ACEN. *Program availability:* Part-time, online only, 100% online, blended/hybrid learning. *Faculty:* 12 full-time (all women), 10 part-time/adjunct (all women). *Students:* 1 (woman) full-time, 188 part-time (157 women); includes 20 minority (10 Black or African American, non-Hispanic/Latino; 3 Asian, non-Hispanic/Latino; 3 Hispanic/Latino; 4 Two or more races, non-Hispanic/Latino). Average age 40. 54 applicants, 91% accepted, 18 enrolled. In 2019, 51 master's, 11 doctorates awarded. *Degree requirements:* For master's, research experience, portfolio, practicum; for doctorate, practicum. *Entrance requirements:* For master's, Nursing research, health assessment, RN license; for doctorate, Master's degree in nursing, professional portfolio, graduate statistics, transcripts, RN license. Additional exam requirements/recommendations for international students: required—TOEFL (minimum score 550 paper-based; 79 iBT). *Application deadline:* For fall admission, 6/1 priority date for domestic and international students; for spring admission, 11/15 priority date for domestic and international students. Applications are processed on a rolling basis. Application fee: $50. *Expenses: Tuition:* Part-time $705 per credit hour. *Required fees:* $270 per unit. *Financial support:* In 2019–20, 13 students received support. Scholarships/grants available. Support available to part-time students. Financial award application deadline: 6/15; financial award applicants required to submit FAFSA. *Unit head:* Dr. Sandie S Soldwisch, President of OSF Colleges of Health Sciences, 815-282-7909, Fax: 309-624-8973, E-mail: Sandie.S.Soldwisch@osfhealthcare.org. *Application contact:* Dr. Kim A. Mitchell, Dean, Graduate Program, 309-655-2201, Fax: 309-624-8973, E-mail: kim.a.mitchell@osfhealthcare.org.
Website: http://www.sfmccon.edu/graduate-programs/

**Stony Brook University, State University of New York,** Stony Brook Medicine, School of Nursing, Program in Neonatal Nursing, Stony Brook, NY 11794. Offers neonatal nurse practitioner (Certificate); neonatal nursing (MS, DNP). *Accreditation:* AACN. *Program availability:* Part-time, blended/hybrid learning. *Students:* 14 part-time (all women); includes 6 minority (2 Black or African American, non-Hispanic/Latino; 2 Asian, non-Hispanic/Latino; 2 Hispanic/Latino). In 2019, 12 master's, 6 other advanced degrees awarded. *Entrance requirements:* For master's, BSN, minimum GPA of 3.0, course work in statistics. Additional exam requirements/recommendations for international students: required—TOEFL (minimum score 90 iBT). *Application deadline:* For fall admission, 2/27 for domestic students. Application fee: $100. *Expenses:* Contact institution. *Financial support:* Application deadline: 3/15. *Unit head:* Paula M. Timoney, Program Director, 631-444-3298, Fax: 631-444-3136, E-mail: paula.timoney@stonybrook.edu. *Application contact:* Linda Sacino, Staff Assistant, 631-632-3262, Fax: 631-444-3136, E-mail: nnp.nursing@stonybrook.edu.
Website: http://www.nursing.stonybrookmedicine.edu/

**Stony Brook University, State University of New York,** Stony Brook Medicine, School of Nursing, Program in Perinatal Women's Health Nursing, Stony Brook, NY 11794. Offers MS, DNP, Certificate. *Accreditation:* AACN. *Program availability:* Blended/hybrid

learning. *Students:* 2 part-time (both women); both minorities (both American Indian or Alaska Native, non-Hispanic/Latino). 2 applicants, 100% accepted, 2 enrolled. In 2019, 1 doctorate awarded. *Entrance requirements:* For master's, BSN, minimum GPA of 3.0, course work in statistics. Additional exam requirements/recommendations for international students: required—TOEFL (minimum score 90 iBT). *Application deadline:* For fall admission, 2/27 for domestic students. Application fee: $100. *Expenses:* Contact institution. *Financial support:* Application deadline: 3/15. *Unit head:* Dr. Elizabeth Collins, Program Director, 631-444-3296, Fax: 631-444-3136, E-mail: elizabeth.collins@stonybrook.edu. *Application contact:* Linda Sacino, Staff Assistant, 631-632-3262, Fax: 631-444-3136, E-mail: elizabeth.collins@stonybrook.edu.
Website: http://www.nursing.stonybrookmedicine.edu/

**University of Alberta,** Faculty of Medicine and Dentistry and Faculty of Graduate Studies and Research, Graduate Programs in Medicine, Department of Obstetrics and Gynecology, Edmonton, AB T6G 2E1, Canada. Offers MD. *Entrance requirements:* Additional exam requirements/recommendations for international students: required—TOEFL.

**University of Cincinnati,** Graduate School, College of Nursing, Cincinnati, OH 45221-0038. Offers nurse midwifery (MSN); nurse practitioner (MSN, DNP), including acute care pediatrics (DNP), adult-gerontology acute care, adult-gerontology primary care, anesthesia (DNP), family (MSN), leadership (DNP), neonatal (MSN), women's health (MSN); nursing (MSN, PhD), including occupational health (MSN). *Accreditation:* AACN; AANA/CANAEP (one or more programs are accredited); ACNM/ACME. *Program availability:* Part-time, 100% online, blended/hybrid learning. *Faculty:* 62 full-time (55 women), 125 part-time/adjunct (114 women). *Students:* 429 full-time (355 women), 1,547 part-time (1,390 women); includes 453 minority (226 Black or African American, non-Hispanic/Latino; 5 American Indian or Alaska Native, non-Hispanic/Latino; 68 Asian, non-Hispanic/Latino; 103 Hispanic/Latino; 3 Native Hawaiian or other Pacific Islander, non-Hispanic/Latino; 48 Two or more races, non-Hispanic/Latino), 15 international. Average age 36. 779 applicants, 78% accepted, 464 enrolled. In 2019, 518 master's, 47 doctorates awarded. *Degree requirements:* For master's, thesis or alternative; for doctorate, comprehensive exam (for some programs), thesis/dissertation (for some programs). *Entrance requirements:* For master's, GRE required only for the Direct-Entry Accelerated Program. Additional exam requirements/recommendations for international students: required—TOEFL (minimum score 600 paper-based; 100 iBT); recommended—IELTS (minimum score 7). *Application deadline:* For fall admission, 4/1 priority date for domestic and international students; for spring admission, 9/1 priority date for domestic and international students; for summer admission, 2/1 priority date for domestic and international students. Applications are processed on a rolling basis. Application fee: $135 ($140 for international students). Electronic applications accepted. *Expenses:* Contact institution. *Financial support:* In 2019–20, 103 students received support, including 9 fellowships with full tuition reimbursements available (averaging $18,595 per year), 7 research assistantships with full tuition reimbursements available (averaging $12,991 per year), 8 teaching assistantships with full tuition reimbursements available (averaging $12,991 per year); institutionally sponsored loans, scholarships/grants, traineeships, health care benefits, tuition waivers (partial), and unspecified assistantships also available. Support available to part-time students. Financial award application deadline: 4/1; financial award applicants required to submit FAFSA. *Unit head:* Dr. Greer Glazer, Dean, 513-558-5330, Fax: 513-558-9030, E-mail: greer.glazer@uc.edu. *Application contact:* Office of Student Affairs, 513-558-8400, E-mail: nursingbearcats@uc.edu.
Website: https://nursing.uc.edu/

**University of Connecticut,** Graduate School, School of Nursing, MS Program in Nursing, Storrs, CT 06269. Offers adult gerontological acute care nurse practitioner (MS); adult gerontological primary care nurse practitioner (MS); family nurse practitioner (MS); neonatal nurse practitioner (MS). *Accreditation:* AACN. *Program availability:* Part-time, online learning. *Degree requirements:* For master's, comprehensive exam. *Entrance requirements:* For master's, official transcripts, Connecticut RN license, three letters of reference, curriculum vitae or resume, personal statement. Additional exam requirements/recommendations for international students: required—TOEFL (minimum score 550 paper-based). Electronic applications accepted.

**University of Connecticut,** Graduate School, School of Nursing, Post-Master's Certificate Programs, Storrs, CT 06269. Offers adult gerontology acute care nurse practitioner (Post-Master's Certificate); adult gerontology primary care nurse practitioner (Post-Master's Certificate); neonatal nurse practitioner (Post-Master's Certificate). *Entrance requirements:* For degree, minimum graduate GPA of 3.0, current Connecticut RN license, three letters of recommendation, current resume/curriculum vitae.

**University of Delaware,** College of Health Sciences, School of Nursing, Newark, DE 19716. Offers adult nurse practitioner (MSN, PMC); cardiopulmonary clinical nurse specialist (MSN, PMC); cardiopulmonary clinical nurse specialist/adult nurse practitioner (MSN, PMC); family nurse practitioner (MSN, PMC); gerontology clinical nurse specialist (MSN, PMC); gerontology clinical nurse specialist geriatric nurse practitioner (PMC); gerontology clinical nurse specialist/geriatric nurse practitioner (MSN); health services administration (MSN, PMC); nursing of children clinical nurse specialist (MSN, PMC); nursing of children clinical nurse specialist/pediatric nurse practitioner (MSN, PMC); oncology/immune deficiency clinical nurse specialist (MSN, PMC); oncology/immune deficiency clinical nurse specialist/adult nurse practitioner (MSN, PMC); perinatal/women's health clinical nurse specialist (MSN, PMC); perinatal/women's health clinical nurse specialist/women's health nurse practitioner (MSN, PMC); psychiatric nursing clinical nurse specialist (MSN, PMC). *Accreditation:* AACN. *Program availability:* Part-time, evening/weekend, online learning. *Degree requirements:* For master's, thesis optional. *Entrance requirements:* For master's, BSN, interview, RN license. Electronic applications accepted.

**University of Illinois at Chicago,** College of Nursing, Program in Nursing, Chicago, IL 60607-7128. Offers acute care clinical nurse specialist (MS); administrative nursing leadership (Certificate); adult nurse practitioner (MS); adult/geriatric nurse practitioner (MS); advanced community health nurse specialist (MS); family nurse practitioner (MS); geriatric clinical nurse specialist (MS); geriatric nurse practitioner (MS); nurse midwifery (MS); occupational health/advanced community health nurse specialist (MS); occupational health/family nurse practitioner (MS); pediatric nurse practitioner (MS); perinatal clinical nurse specialist (MS); school/advanced community health nurse specialist (MS); school/family nurse practitioner (MS); women's health nurse practitioner (MS). *Accreditation:* AACN. *Program availability:* Part-time. *Degree requirements:* For master's, thesis or alternative. *Entrance requirements:* For master's, GRE General Test, minimum GPA of 2.75. Additional exam requirements/recommendations for international students: required—TOEFL. Electronic applications accepted.

**University of Indianapolis,** Graduate Programs, School of Nursing, Indianapolis, IN 46227-3697. Offers advanced practice nursing (DNP); family nurse practitioner (MSN); gerontological nurse practitioner (MSN); neonatal nurse practitioner (MSN); nurse-midwifery (MSN); nursing (MSN); nursing and health systems leadership (MSN); nursing education (MSN); women's health nurse practitioner (MSN); MBA/MSN. *Accreditation:* AACN. *Entrance requirements:* For master's, minimum GPA of 3.0, interview, letters of recommendation, resume, IN nursing license, 1 year of professional practice; for doctorate, graduate of ACEN- or CCNE-accredited nursing program; MSN or MA with

nursing major and minimum cumulative GPA of 3.25; unencumbered RN license with eligibility for licensure in Indiana; completion of graduate-level statistics course within last 5 years with minimum grade of B; resume; essay; official transcripts from all academic institutions. Additional exam requirements/recommendations for international students: required—TOEFL (minimum score 550 paper-based). Electronic applications accepted.

**University of Louisville,** Graduate School, School of Nursing, Louisville, KY 40202. Offers adult gerontology nurse practitioner (MSN, DNP); education and administration (MSN); family nurse practitioner (MSN, DNP); neonatal nurse practitioner (MSN, DNP); nursing research (PhD); psychiatric/mental health nurse practitioner (MSN, DNP); women's health nurse practitioner (MSN). *Accreditation:* AACN. *Program availability:* Part-time, blended/hybrid learning. *Faculty:* 49 full-time (46 women), 91 part-time/adjunct (86 women). *Students:* 164 full-time (140 women), 47 part-time (39 women); includes 45 minority (21 Black or African American, non-Hispanic/Latino; 5 Asian, non-Hispanic/Latino; 9 Hispanic/Latino; 10 Two or more races, non-Hispanic/Latino), 4 international. Average age 33. 84 applicants, 63% accepted, 48 enrolled. In 2019, 25 master's, 5 doctorates awarded. *Degree requirements:* For master's, varies; for doctorate, comprehensive exam (for some programs), thesis/dissertation (for some programs), varies. *Entrance requirements:* For master's, Our only master's degree is an accelerated program meant for students who have a bachelor's degree in another discipline who are transitioning into nursing. Thus, the main requirement is a bachelor's degree from a nationally-accredited college, and the completion of 6 prerequisite courses. Must have a minimum undergraduate GPA of 3.0; for doctorate, PhD program: GRE requirement omitted, DNP & PhD doctoral programs: 3 letters of professional reference. BSN applicants must have a 3.0 GPA. MSN applicants must have 3.25 GPA. Written statement of career goals, areas of expertise, reasons for pursuing doctoral degree, resume, and RN license. Additional exam requirements/recommendations for international students: recommended—TOEFL (minimum score 560 paper-based), IELTS (minimum score 6.5). *Application deadline:* For fall admission, 1/15 priority date for domestic and international students; for summer admission, 10/15 priority date for domestic students. Application fee: $60. Electronic applications accepted. *Expenses:* 17871. *Financial support:* In 2019–20, 47 students received support, including 2 fellowships with full tuition reimbursements available (averaging $20,000 per year), 9 research assistantships with full tuition reimbursements available (averaging $20,000 per year), 3 teaching assistantships with full tuition reimbursements available (averaging $15,000 per year); scholarships/grants, health care benefits, unspecified assistantships, and Jonas Nurse Leader Fellowships also available. Financial award application deadline: 10/1; financial award applicants required to submit FAFSA. *Unit head:* 502-852-8300, Fax: 502-852-5044, E-mail: sonya.hardin@louisville.edu. *Application contact:* Trish Hart, MA, Assistant Dean for Student Affairs, 502-852-5825, Fax: 502-852-8783, E-mail: trish.hart@louisville.edu.
Website: http://www.louisville.edu/nursing/

**University of Maryland, Baltimore,** University of Maryland School of Nursing, Baltimore, MD 21201. Offers adult-gerontology acute care nurse practitioner (DNP); adult-gerontology primary care nurse practitioner (DNP); clinical nurse leader (MS); community/public health nursing (MS); family nurse practitioner (DNP); global health (Postbaccalaureate Certificate); health services leadership and management (MS); neonatal nurse practitioner (DNP); nurse anesthesia (DNP); nursing (PhD); nursing informatics (MS, Postbaccalaureate Certificate); pediatric acute/primary care nurse practitioner (DNP); psychiatric mental health nurse practitioner (DNP); teaching in nursing and health professions (Postbaccalaureate Certificate); MS/MBA. *Accreditation:* AANA/CANAEP. *Program availability:* Part-time. *Faculty:* 130 full-time (117 women), 125 part-time/adjunct (114 women). *Students:* 539 full-time (463 women), 586 part-time (506 women); includes 485 minority (259 Black or African American, non-Hispanic/Latino; 3 American Indian or Alaska Native, non-Hispanic/Latino; 124 Asian, non-Hispanic/Latino; 66 Hispanic/Latino; 1 Native Hawaiian or other Pacific Islander, non-Hispanic/Latino; 32 Two or more races, non-Hispanic/Latino), 18 international. Average age 33. 964 applicants, 54% accepted, 347 enrolled. In 2019, 197 master's, 114 doctorates, 12 other advanced degrees awarded. *Degree requirements:* For master's and Postbaccalaureate Certificate, thesis (for some programs); for doctorate, comprehensive exam, thesis/dissertation. *Entrance requirements:* Additional exam requirements/recommendations for international students: required—TOEFL (minimum score 550 paper-based; 79 iBT); recommended—IELTS (minimum score 7). *Application deadline:* For fall admission, 11/1 priority date for domestic and international students; for spring admission, 12/15 for domestic and international students; for summer admission, 9/1 for domestic and international students. Applications are processed on a rolling basis. Application fee: $75. Electronic applications accepted. *Financial support:* In 2019–20, 257 students received support, including 31 research assistantships with full and partial tuition reimbursements available (averaging $25,000 per year), 21 teaching assistantships with full and partial tuition reimbursements available (averaging $19,000 per year); scholarships/grants, traineeships, and unspecified assistantships also available. Support available to part-time students. Financial award application deadline: 3/1; financial award applicants required to submit FAFSA. *Unit head:* Dr. Jane Kirschling, Dean, 410-706-4359, E-mail: kirschling@umaryland.edu. *Application contact:* Larry Fillian, Associate Dean of Student and Academic Services, 410-706-6298, E-mail: lfillian@umaryland.edu.
Website: http://www.nursing.umaryland.edu/

**University of Missouri–Kansas City,** School of Nursing and Health Studies, Kansas City, MO 64110-2499. Offers adult clinical nurse specialist (MSN), including adult nurse practitioner, women's health nurse practitioner (MSN, DNP); adult clinical nursing practice (DNP), including adult gerontology nurse practitioner, women's health nurse practitioner (MSN, DNP); clinical nursing practice (DNP), including family nurse practitioner; neonatal nurse practitioner (MSN); nurse educator (MSN); nurse executive (MSN); nursing practice (DNP); pediatric clinical nursing practice (DNP), including pediatric nurse practitioner; pediatric nurse practitioner (MSN). *Accreditation:* AACN. *Program availability:* Part-time, online learning. *Degree requirements:* For master's, thesis or alternative. *Entrance requirements:* For master's, minimum undergraduate GPA of 3.2; for doctorate, GRE, 3 letters of reference. Additional exam requirements/recommendations for international students: required—TOEFL (minimum score 550 paper-based; 80 iBT).

**University of Pennsylvania,** School of Nursing, Neonatal Clinical Nurse Specialist Program, Philadelphia, PA 19104. Offers MSN. *Program availability:* Part-time. *Students:* Average age 31. 18 applicants, 83% accepted, 13 enrolled. In 2019, 2 master's awarded. Application fee: $80.

**University of Pennsylvania,** School of Nursing, Neonatal Nurse Practitioner Program, Philadelphia, PA 19104. Offers MSN. *Accreditation:* AACN. *Program availability:* Part-time. *Students:* 5 part-time (all women); includes 1 minority (Asian, non-Hispanic/Latino). Average age 28. 3 applicants, 67% accepted, 2 enrolled. In 2019, 2 master's awarded. Application fee: $80.

**University of Puerto Rico - Medical Sciences Campus,** School of Nursing, San Juan, PR 00936-5067. Offers adult and elderly nursing (MSN); child and adolescent nursing (MSN); critical care nursing (MSN); family and community nursing (MSN); family nurse practitioner (MSN); maternity nursing (MSN); mental health and psychiatric nursing (MSN). *Accreditation:* AACN; AANA/CANAEP. *Entrance requirements:* For master's, GRE or EXADEP, interview, Puerto Rico RN license or professional license for international students, general and specific point average, article analysis. Electronic applications accepted.

**University of Rochester,** School of Nursing, Rochester, NY 14642. Offers adult gerontological acute care nurse practitioner (MS); adult gerontological primary care nurse practitioner (MS); clinical nurse leader (MS); family nurse practitioner (MS); family psychiatric mental health nurse practitioner (MS); health care organization management and leadership (MS); nursing (DNP); nursing and health science (PhD); nursing education (MS); pediatric nurse practitioner (MS); pediatric nurse practitioner/neonatal nurse practitioner (MS). *Accreditation:* AACN. *Program availability:* Part-time, 100% online, blended/hybrid learning. Terminal master's awarded for partial completion of doctoral program. *Degree requirements:* For master's, comprehensive exam; for doctorate, thesis/dissertation. *Entrance requirements:* For master's, BS in nursing, RN license; for doctorate, GRE General Test (for PhD), B.S. degree, RN license most programs. Additional exam requirements/recommendations for international students: required—TOEFL (minimum score 560 paper-based; 88 iBT), TOEFL (minimum score 560 paper-based; 88 iBT) or IELTS (minimum score 6.5) recommended. Electronic applications accepted. *Expenses:* Contact institution.

**University of South Africa,** College of Human Sciences, Pretoria, South Africa. Offers adult education (M Ed); African languages (MA, PhD); African politics (MA, PhD); Afrikaans (MA, PhD); ancient history (MA, PhD); ancient Near Eastern studies (MA, PhD); anthropology (MA, PhD); applied linguistics (MA); Arabic (MA, PhD); archaeology (MA); art history (MA); Biblical archaeology (MA); Biblical studies (M Th, D Th, PhD); Christian spirituality (M Th, D Th); church history (M Th, D Th); classical studies (MA, PhD); clinical psychology (MA); communication (MA, PhD); comparative education (M Ed, Ed D); consulting psychology (D Admin, D Com, PhD); curriculum studies (M Ed, Ed D); development studies (M Admin, MA, D Admin, PhD); didactics (M Ed, Ed D); education (M Tech); education management (M Ed, Ed D); educational psychology (M Ed); English (MA); environmental education (M Ed); French (MA, PhD); German (MA, PhD); Greek (MA); guidance and counseling (M Ed); health studies (MA, PhD), including health sciences education (MA), health services management (MA), medical and surgical nursing science (critical care general) (MA), midwifery and neonatal nursing science (MA), trauma and emergency care (MA); history (MA, PhD); history of education (Ed D); inclusive education (M Ed, Ed D); information and communications technology policy and regulation (MA); information science (MA, MIS, PhD); international politics (MA, PhD); Islamic studies (MA, PhD); Italian (MA, PhD); Judaica (MA, PhD); linguistics (MA, PhD); mathematical education (M Ed); mathematics education (MA); missiology (M Th, D Th); modern Hebrew (MA, PhD); musicology (MA, MMus, D Mus, PhD); natural science education (M Ed); New Testament (M Th, D Th); Old Testament (D Th); pastoral therapy (M Th, D Th); philosophy (MA); philosophy of education (M Ed, Ed D); politics (MA, PhD); Portuguese (MA, PhD); practical theology (M Th, D Th); psychology (MA, MS, PhD); psychology of education (M Ed, Ed D); public health (MA); religious studies (MA, D Th, PhD); Romance languages (MA); Russian (MA, PhD); Semitic languages (MA, PhD); social behavior studies in HIV/AIDS (MA); social science (mental health) (MA); social science in development studies (MA); social science in psychology (MA); social science in social work (MA); social science in sociology (MA); social work (MSW, DSW, PhD); socio-education (M Ed, Ed D); sociolinguistics (MA); sociology (MA, PhD); Spanish (MA, PhD); systematic theology (M Th, D Th); TESOL (teaching English to speakers of other languages) (MA); theological ethics (M Th, D Th); theory of literature (MA, PhD); urban ministries (D Th); urban ministry (M Th).

**The University of Texas at Austin,** Graduate School, School of Nursing, Austin, TX 78712-1111. Offers adult - gerontology clinical nurse specialist (MSN); child health (MSN), including administration, public health nursing, teaching; family nurse practitioner (MSN); family psychiatric/mental health nurse practitioner (MSN); holistic adult health (MSN), including administration, teaching; maternity (MSN), including administration, public health nursing, teaching; nursing (PhD); nursing administration and healthcare systems management (MSN); nursing practice (DNP); pediatric nurse practitioner (MSN); public health nursing (MSN). *Accreditation:* AACN. *Program availability:* Part-time. *Degree requirements:* For master's, thesis optional; for doctorate, thesis/dissertation. *Entrance requirements:* For master's and doctorate, GRE General Test. Additional exam requirements/recommendations for international students: required—TOEFL (minimum score 550 paper-based). Electronic applications accepted.

**Wayne State University,** College of Nursing, Detroit, MI 48202. Offers adult gerontology acute care nurse practitioner (MSN); adult gerontology primary care nurse practitioner (MSN); advanced public health nursing (MSN); infant and mental health (DNP, PhD); neonatal nurse practitioner (MSN); nurse-midwifery (MSN); pediatric acute care nurse practitioner (MSN); pediatric primary care nurse practitioner (MSN); psychiatric mental health nurse practitioner (MSN); women's health nurse practitioner (MSN). *Accreditation:* AACN; ACNM/ACME. *Program availability:* Part-time. *Faculty:* 27. *Students:* 134 full-time (118 women), 216 part-time (187 women); includes 98 minority (51 Black or African American, non-Hispanic/Latino; 24 Asian, non-Hispanic/Latino; 6 Hispanic/Latino; 17 Two or more races, non-Hispanic/Latino), 18 international. Average age 33. 425 applicants, 37% accepted, 95 enrolled. In 2019, 58 master's, 31 doctorates awarded. *Degree requirements:* For doctorate, thesis/dissertation. *Entrance requirements:* For master's, Completed a Bachelor of Science in Nursing with a 3.0 or higher GPA. Official transcripts. Professional competence as documented by three references. Current Michigan Registered Nurse (RN) licensure. A personal statement of goals for graduate study; for doctorate, DNP: Minimum GPA of 3.0 or higher in BSN is required. Resume or Curriculum Vita that includes education, work and/or research experience. Two references, one from a doctorally prepared individual. RN license. PhD: BSN transcript; Two to three references from doctorally prepared individuals; goals statement; Resume or CV; Interview. Additional exam requirements/recommendations for international students: required—TOEFL (minimum score 101 iBT), TWE (minimum score 6), Michigan English Language Assessment Battery (minimum score 85); recommended—IELTS (minimum score 7). *Application deadline:* For fall admission, 1/31 for domestic students; for winter admission, 11/1 for domestic students. Applications are processed on a rolling basis. Application fee: $50. Electronic applications accepted. *Expenses:* $925.72 per credit hour in-state, $1,716.93 per credit hour out-of-state, $54.56 student service credit hour fee, $315.70 registration fee. *Financial support:* In 2019–20, 104 students received support, including 39 fellowships with tuition reimbursements available (averaging $6,456 per year), 1 research assistantship (averaging $24,950 per year), 5 teaching assistantships with tuition reimbursements available (averaging $25,000 per year); scholarships/grants, health care benefits, and unspecified assistantships also available. Support available to part-time students. Financial award application deadline: 3/1; financial award applicants required to submit FAFSA. *Unit head:* Dr. Laurie M Lauzon Clabo, Dean, College of Nursing, 313-577-4082, E-mail: laurie.lauzon.clabo@wayne.edu. *Application contact:* Dr. Laurie M Lauzon Clabo, Dean, College of Nursing, 313-577-4082, E-mail: laurie.lauzon.clabo@wayne.edu.
Website: http://nursing.wayne.edu/

**Wright State University,** Graduate School, College of Nursing and Health, Program in Nursing, Dayton, OH 45435. Offers administration of nursing and health care systems

(MS); adult gerontology clinical nurse specialist (MS); adult-gerontology acute care nurse practitioner (MS); family nurse practitioner (MS); neonatal nurse practitioner (MS); pediatric nurse practitioner-acute care (MS); pediatric nurse practitioner-primary care (MS); psychiatric mental health nurse practitioner (MS); school nurse (MS).

*Accreditation:* AACN. *Program availability:* Part-time, evening/weekend. *Degree requirements:* For master's, thesis or alternative. *Entrance requirements:* For master's, GRE General Test, BSN from ACEN-accredited college, Ohio RN license. Additional exam requirements/recommendations for international students: required—TOEFL.

# Medical/Surgical Nursing

**Case Western Reserve University,** Frances Payne Bolton School of Nursing, Master's Programs in Nursing, Nurse Practitioner Program, Cleveland, OH 44106. Offers acute care pediatric nurse practitioner (MSN); acute care/cardiovascular nursing (MSN); adult gerontology acute care nurse practitioner (MSN); adult gerontology primary care nurse practitioner (MSN); family nurse practitioner (MSN); family systems psychiatric mental health nursing (MSN); neonatal nurse practitioner (MSN); palliative care (MSN); pediatric nurse practitioner in acute care (MSN); pediatric primary care nurse practitioner (MSN); women's health nurse practitioner (MSN). *Accreditation:* ACEN. *Program availability:* Part-time. *Faculty:* 30 full-time (25 women), 6 part-time/adjunct (all women). *Students:* 47 full-time (36 women), 70 part-time (59 women); includes 34 minority (12 Black or African American, non-Hispanic/Latino; 11 Asian, non-Hispanic/Latino; 9 Hispanic/Latino; 2 Two or more races, non-Hispanic/Latino), 9 international. Average age 30. 45 applicants, 82% accepted, 22 enrolled. In 2019, 46 master's awarded. *Degree requirements:* For master's, thesis optional, minimum GPA of 3.0, clinical hours corresponding to requirements to sit for certification exam, portfolio. *Entrance requirements:* For master's, GRE/MAT (scores not required for application, but may be requested for an admission decision). Additional exam requirements/recommendations for international students: required—TOEFL (minimum score 577 paper-based; 90 iBT), IELTS (minimum score 7). *Application deadline:* For fall admission, 3/15 for domestic and international students; for spring admission, 10/1 for domestic and international students; for summer admission, 3/15 for domestic and international students. Applications are processed on a rolling basis. Application fee: $75. Electronic applications accepted. *Expenses:* Clinical placement $75; Activity fee $15 per semester; Graduate council fee $15 per semester; Tuition rate $2,133 per credit hour. *Financial support:* In 2019–20, 100 students received support, including 34 teaching assistantships with partial tuition reimbursements available (averaging $19,197 per year); scholarships/grants and traineeships also available. Financial award application deadline: 5/15; financial award applicants required to submit FAFSA. *Unit head:* Dr. Latina Brooks, Director, 216-368-1196, Fax: 216-368-3542, E-mail: lmb3@case.edu. *Application contact:* Jackie Tepale, Admissions Coordinator, 216-368-5253, Fax: 216-368-3542, E-mail: yyd@case.edu.
Website: https://case.edu/nursing/programs/msn

**Daemen College,** Nursing Programs, Amherst, NY 14226-3592. Offers adult nurse practitioner (MS, Post Master's Certificate); nurse executive leadership (Post Master's Certificate); nursing education (MS, Post Master's Certificate); nursing executive leadership (MS); nursing practice (DNP); palliative care nursing (Post Master's Certificate). *Accreditation:* ACEN. *Program availability:* Part-time. *Degree requirements:* For master's, thesis, degree completed in 4 years; minimum GPA of 3.0 and a minimum grade of B in all courses; for doctorate, thesis/dissertation, degree completed in 5 years; minimum GPA of 3.0 and a minimum grade of B in all courses. *Entrance requirements:* For master's, bachelor's degree in nursing from a NLNAC or CCNE accredited program, 1 year medical-surgical clinical experience, resume, official transcripts, undergraduate or graduate statistics course (grade of C or better), GPA 3.25 or above (below may be accepted on provisional basis), NYS Nursing license, interview with nursing faculty. Additional exam requirements/recommendations for international students: required—TOEFL (minimum score 77 paper-based), IELTS (minimum score 6.5). Electronic applications accepted. Application fee is waived when completed online.

**Eastern Virginia Medical School,** Master of Surgical Assisting Program, Norfolk, VA 23501-1980. Offers MSA. Electronic applications accepted. *Expenses:* Contact institution.

**Inter American University of Puerto Rico, Arecibo Campus,** Program in Nursing, Arecibo, PR 00614-4050. Offers critical care nursing (MSN); surgical nursing (MSN). *Entrance requirements:* For master's, EXADEP or GRE General Test or MAT, 2 letters of recommendation, bachelor's degree in nursing, minimum GPA of 2.5 in last 60 credits, minimum 1 year nursing experience, nursing license.

**Inter American University of Puerto Rico, Barranquitas Campus,** Program in Nursing, Barranquitas, PR 00794. Offers critical care nursing (MSN); medical surgical nursing (MSN). *Program availability:* Part-time, evening/weekend. *Degree requirements:* For master's, 2 foreign languages, comprehensive exam (for some programs), thesis optional, minimum grade of B on all courses, integration seminar. *Entrance requirements:* For master's, bachelor's degree in nursing from accredited institution, minimum GPA of 2.5, provisional or permanent nursing license for practicing nursing in Puerto Rico, official academic transcript from institution that conferred bachelor's degree, two recommendations letters. Electronic applications accepted. *Expenses:* Contact institution.

**Pontifical Catholic University of Puerto Rico,** College of Sciences, Department of Nursing, Program in Medical-Surgical Nursing, Ponce, PR 00717-0777. Offers MSN. *Program availability:* Part-time, evening/weekend. *Degree requirements:* For master's, comprehensive exam (for some programs), thesis, clinical research paper. *Entrance requirements:* For master's, GRE General Test, 2 letters of recommendation, interview, minimum GPA of 2.75. Electronic applications accepted.

**Saint Francis Medical Center College of Nursing,** SFMC College of Nursing Graduate Programs, Peoria, IL 61603-3783. Offers adult gerontology (MSN); clinical nurse leader (MSN); family nurse practitioner (MSN, Post-Graduate Certificate); family psychiatric mental health nurse practitioner (MSN); neonatal nurse practitioner (MSN); nurse clinician (Post-Graduate Certificate); nurse educator (MSN, Post-Graduate Certificate); nursing (DNP), including leadership/ clinician; nursing management leadership (MSN). *Accreditation:* ACEN. *Program availability:* Part-time, online only, 100% online, blended/hybrid learning. *Faculty:* 12 full-time (all women), 10 part-time/adjunct (all women). *Students:* 1 (woman) full-time, 188 part-time (157 women); includes 20 minority (10 Black or African American, non-Hispanic/Latino; 3 Asian, non-Hispanic/Latino; 3 Hispanic/Latino; 4 Two or more races, non-Hispanic/Latino). Average age 40. 54 applicants, 91% accepted, 18 enrolled. In 2019, 51 master's, 11 doctorates awarded. *Degree requirements:* For master's, research experience, portfolio, practicum; for doctorate, practicum. *Entrance requirements:* For master's, Nursing research, health assessment, RN license; for doctorate, Master's degree in nursing, professional portfolio, graduate statistics, transcripts, RN license. Additional exam requirements/ recommendations for international students: required—TOEFL (minimum score 550

paper-based; 79 iBT). *Application deadline:* For fall admission, 6/1 priority date for domestic and international students; for spring admission, 11/15 priority date for domestic and international students. Applications are processed on a rolling basis. Application fee: $50. *Expenses: Tuition:* Part-time $705 per credit hour. *Required fees:* $270 per unit. *Financial support:* In 2019–20, 13 students received support. Scholarships/grants available. Support available to part-time students. Financial award application deadline: 6/15; financial award applicants required to submit FAFSA. *Unit head:* Dr. Sandie S Soldwisch, President of OSF Colleges of Health Sciences, 815-282-7909, Fax: 309-624-8973, E-mail: Sandie.S.Soldwisch@osfhealthcare.org. *Application contact:* Dr. Kim A. Mitchell, Dean, Graduate Program, 309-655-2201, Fax: 309-624-8973, E-mail: kim.a.mitchell@osfhealthcare.org.
Website: http://www.sfmccon.edu/graduate-programs/

**State University of New York Downstate Medical Center,** College of Nursing, Graduate Programs in Nursing, Program in Clinical Nurse Specialist, Brooklyn, NY 11203-2098. Offers MS, Post Master's Certificate.

**Universidad Adventista de las Antillas,** EGECED Department, Mayagüez, PR 00681-0118. Offers curriculum and instruction (M Ed); medical surgical nursing (MN); school administration and supervision (M Ed). *Degree requirements:* For master's, comprehensive exam (for some programs), thesis (for some programs). *Entrance requirements:* For master's, EXADEP or GRE General Test, recommendations. Electronic applications accepted.

**University of South Africa,** College of Human Sciences, Pretoria, South Africa. Offers adult education (M Ed); African languages (MA, PhD); African politics (MA, PhD); Afrikaans (MA, PhD); ancient history (MA, PhD); ancient Near Eastern studies (MA, PhD); anthropology (MA, PhD); applied linguistics (MA); Arabic (MA, PhD); archaeology (MA); art history (MA); Biblical archaeology (MA); Biblical studies (M Th, D Th, PhD); Christian spirituality (M Th, D Th); church history (M Th, D Th); classical studies (MA, PhD); clinical psychology (MA); communication (MA, PhD); comparative education (M Ed, Ed D); consulting psychology (D Admin, D Com, PhD); curriculum studies (M Ed, Ed D); development studies (M Admin, MA, D Admin, PhD); didactics (M Ed, Ed D); education (M Tech); education management (M Ed, Ed D); educational psychology (M Ed); English (MA); environmental education (M Ed); French (MA, PhD); German (MA, PhD); Greek (MA); guidance and counseling (M Ed); health studies (MA, PhD), including health sciences education (MA), health services management (MA), medical and surgical nursing science (critical care general) (MA), midwifery and neonatal nursing science (MA), trauma and emergency care (MA); history (MA, PhD); history of education (Ed D); inclusive education (M Ed, Ed D); information and communications technology policy and regulation (MA); information science (MA, MIS, PhD); international politics (MA, PhD); Islamic studies (MA, PhD); Italian (MA, PhD); Judaica (MA, PhD); linguistics (MA, PhD); mathematical education (M Ed); mathematics education (MA); missiology (M Th, D Th); modern Hebrew (MA, PhD); musicology (MA, MMus, D Mus, PhD); natural science education (M Ed); New Testament (M Th, D Th); Old Testament (D Th); pastoral therapy (M Th, D Th); philosophy (MA); philosophy of education (M Ed, Ed D); politics (MA, PhD); Portuguese (MA, PhD); practical theology (M Th, D Th); psychology (MA, MS, PhD); psychology of education (M Ed, Ed D); public health (MA); religious studies (MA, D Th, PhD); Romance languages (MA); Russian (MA, PhD); Semitic languages (MA, PhD); social behavior studies in HIV/AIDS (MA); social science (mental health) (MA); social science in development studies (MA); social science in psychology (MA); social science in social work (MA); social science in sociology (MA); social work (MSW, DSW, PhD); socio-education (M Ed, Ed D); sociolinguistics (MA); sociology (MA, PhD); Spanish (MA, PhD); systematic theology (M Th, D Th); TESOL (teaching English to speakers of other languages) (MA); theological ethics (M Th, D Th); theory of literature (MA, PhD); urban ministries (D Th); urban ministry (M Th).

**University of South Carolina,** The Graduate School, College of Nursing, Program in Clinical Nursing, Columbia, SC 29208. Offers acute care clinical specialist (MSN); acute care nurse practitioner (MSN); women's health nurse practitioner (MSN). *Accreditation:* AACN. *Program availability:* Part-time. *Degree requirements:* For master's, thesis or alternative. *Entrance requirements:* For master's, GRE General Test or MAT, BS in nursing, RN licensure. Additional exam requirements/recommendations for international students: required—TOEFL (minimum score 570 paper-based). Electronic applications accepted.

**Ursuline College,** School of Graduate and Professional Studies, Programs in Nursing, Pepper Pike, OH 44124-4398. Offers acute-care nurse practitioner (MSN); adult nurse practitioner (MSN); adult-gerontology acute care nurse practitioner (MSN); adult-gerontology clinical nurse specialist (MSN); adult-gerontology nurse practitioner (MSN); care management (MSN); clinical nurse specialist (MSN); family nurse practitioner (MSN); nursing (DNP); nursing education (MSN); palliative care (MSN). *Accreditation:* AACN. *Program availability:* Part-time, 100% online. *Faculty:* 6 full-time (all women), 25 part-time/adjunct (19 women). *Students:* 106 full-time (99 women), 117 part-time (105 women); includes 71 minority (46 Black or African American, non-Hispanic/Latino; 2 American Indian or Alaska Native, non-Hispanic/Latino; 12 Asian, non-Hispanic/Latino; 6 Hispanic/Latino; 5 Two or more races, non-Hispanic/Latino). Average age 38. 265 applicants, 98% accepted, 61 enrolled. In 2019, 68 master's, 2 doctorates awarded. *Degree requirements:* For master's, comprehensive exam; for doctorate, thesis/ dissertation. *Entrance requirements:* For master's, minimum undergraduate GPA of 3.0, bachelor's degree in nursing, eligibility for or current Ohio RN license. Additional exam requirements/recommendations for international students: required—TOEFL (minimum score 500 paper-based). *Application deadline:* For fall admission, 8/1 priority date for domestic students. Applications are processed on a rolling basis. Application fee: $25. Electronic applications accepted. *Expenses: Tuition:* Full-time $18,784; part-time $1174 per credit hour. *Required fees:* $320; $240 per unit. One-time fee: $100. Tuition and fees vary according to course level and program. *Financial support:* In 2019–20, 10 students received support. Scholarships/grants, tuition waivers (partial), and College Free Credit available. Financial award application deadline: 3/1; financial award applicants required to submit FAFSA. *Unit head:* Dr. Janet Baker, Associate Dean of Graduate Nursing, 440-864-8172, Fax: 440-684-6053, E-mail: jbaker@ursuline.edu. *Application contact:* Melanie Steele, Director, Graduate Admission, 440-646-8119, Fax: 440-684-6138, E-mail: graduateadmissions@ursuline.edu.

# Nurse Anesthesia

**AdventHealth University,** Program in Nurse Anesthesia, Orlando, FL 32803. Offers MS. *Accreditation:* AANA/CANAEP. *Entrance requirements:* For master's, GRE or MAT, minimum undergraduate cumulative GPA of 3.0, 1 year of intensive critical care nursing experience, 3 recommendations, interview.

**Albany Medical College,** Center for Nurse Anesthesiology, Albany, NY 12208. Offers anesthesia (MS). *Accreditation:* AANA/CANAEP. *Degree requirements:* For master's, thesis, thesis proposal/clinical research. *Entrance requirements:* For master's, GRE General Test, BSN or appropriate bachelor's degree, current RN license, critical care experience, organic chemistry, research methods. Electronic applications accepted. *Expenses:* Contact institution.

**Arkansas State University,** Graduate School, College of Nursing and Health Professions, School of Nursing, State University, AR 72467. Offers aging studies (Graduate Certificate); health care management (Graduate Certificate); health sciences (MS); health sciences education (Graduate Certificate); nurse anesthesia (MSN); nursing (MSN); nursing practice (DNP). *Accreditation:* AANA/CANAEP (one or more programs are accredited); ACEN. *Program availability:* Part-time. *Degree requirements:* For master's and Graduate Certificate, comprehensive exam, thesis or alternative; for doctorate, comprehensive exam, thesis/dissertation. *Entrance requirements:* For master's, GRE General Test or MAT, appropriate bachelor's degree, current Arkansas nursing license, CPR certification, physical examination, professional liability insurance, critical care experience, ACLS Certification, PALS Certification, interview, immunization records, personal goal statement, health assessment; for doctorate, GRE or MAT, NCLEX-RN Exam, appropriate master's degree, current Arkansas nursing license, CPR certification, physical examination, professional liability insurance, critical care experience, ACLS Certification, PALS Certification, interview, immunization records, personal goal statement, health assessment, TB skin test, background check; for Graduate Certificate, GRE or MAT, appropriate bachelor's degree, official transcripts, immunization records, proof of employment in healthcare, TB Skin Test, TB Mask Fit Test, CPR Certification. Additional exam requirements/recommendations for international students: required—TOEFL (minimum score 550 paper-based; 79 iBT), IELTS (minimum score 6), PTE (minimum score 56). Electronic applications accepted. *Expenses:* Contact institution.

**Augusta University,** College of Nursing, Doctor of Nursing Practice Program, Augusta, GA 30912. Offers adult gerontology acute care nurse practitioner (DNP); family nurse practitioner (DNP); nurse executive (DNP); nursing (DNP); nursing anesthesia (DNP); pediatric nurse practitioner (DNP); psychiatric mental health nurse practitioner (DNP). *Accreditation:* AACN; AANA/CANAEP. *Degree requirements:* For doctorate, thesis/dissertation or alternative. *Entrance requirements:* For doctorate, GRE General Test or MAT, master's degree in nursing or related field, current professional nurse licensure. Additional exam requirements/recommendations for international students: required—TOEFL (minimum score 600 paper-based; 100 iBT). Electronic applications accepted.

**Barry University,** College of Health Sciences, Program in Anesthesiology, Miami Shores, FL 33161-6695. Offers MS. *Accreditation:* AANA/CANAEP. *Degree requirements:* For master's, comprehensive exam. *Entrance requirements:* For master's, GRE General Test, minimum GPA of 3.0; 2 courses in chemistry (1 with lab); minimum 1 year critical care experience; BSN or RN; 4-year bachelor's degree in health sciences, nursing, biology, or chemistry. Electronic applications accepted.

**Baylor College of Medicine,** School of Health Professions, Graduate Program in Nurse Anesthesia, Houston, TX 77030-3498. Offers DNP. *Accreditation:* AANA/CANAEP. *Degree requirements:* For doctorate, comprehensive exam, thesis/dissertation. *Entrance requirements:* For doctorate, GRE General Test, Texas nursing license, 1 year of work experience in critical care nursing, minimum GPA of 3.0, BSN, statistics, organic chemistry. Electronic applications accepted. *Expenses:* Contact institution.

**Bloomsburg University of Pennsylvania,** School of Graduate Studies, College of Science and Technology, Department of Nursing, Bloomsburg, PA 17815-1301. Offers adult and family nurse practitioner (MSN); community health (MSN); nurse anesthesia (MSN); nursing (MSN, DNP); nursing administration (MSN). *Accreditation:* AACN. *Degree requirements:* For master's, thesis (for some programs), clinical experience. *Entrance requirements:* For master's, minimum QPA of 3.0, personal statement, 2 letters of recommendation, nursing license. Additional exam requirements/recommendations for international students: required—TOEFL, IELTS. Electronic applications accepted. *Expenses:* Contact institution.

**Boston College,** William F. Connell School of Nursing, Chestnut Hill, MA 02467. Offers adult-gerontology primary care nurse practitioner (MS); family health nursing (MS); nurse anesthesia (MS); nursing (PhD); pediatric primary care nurse practitioner (MS), including pediatric and women's health; psychiatric-mental health nursing (MS); women's health nursing (MS); MBA/MS; MS/MA; MS/PhD. *Accreditation:* AACN; AANA/CANAEP (one or more programs are accredited). *Program availability:* Part-time. *Faculty:* 56 full-time (50 women). *Students:* 228 full-time (200 women), 82 part-time (71 women); includes 54 minority (10 Black or African American, non-Hispanic/Latino; 18 Asian, non-Hispanic/Latino; 20 Hispanic/Latino; 6 Two or more races, non-Hispanic/Latino), 7 international. Average age 28. 360 applicants, 56% accepted, 93 enrolled. In 2019, 107 master's, 7 doctorates awarded. *Degree requirements:* For master's, comprehensive exam; for doctorate, comprehensive exam, thesis/dissertation, computer literacy exam or foreign language. *Entrance requirements:* For master's, bachelor's degree; for doctorate, GRE General Test, bachelor's in Nursing and master's degree in nursing or related field. Additional exam requirements/recommendations for international students: required—TOEFL (minimum score 600 paper-based; 100 iBT), IELTS (minimum score 7.5). *Application deadline:* For fall admission, 3/15 for domestic and international students; for spring admission, 9/30 for domestic and international students. Application fee: $40. Electronic applications accepted. *Expenses:* Contact institution. *Financial support:* In 2019–20, 135 students received support, including 12 fellowships with full tuition reimbursements available (averaging $24,504 per year), 29 teaching assistantships (averaging $4,380 per year); scholarships/grants, health care benefits, tuition waivers (partial), and unspecified assistantships also available. Support available to part-time students. Financial award application deadline: 4/18; financial award applicants required to submit FAFSA. *Unit head:* Dr. Susan Gennaro, Dean, 617-552-4251, Fax: 617-552-0931, E-mail: susan.gennaro@bc.edu. *Application contact:* Sean Sendall, Assistant Dean, Graduate Enrollment and Data Analytics, 617-552-4745, Fax: 617-552-2121, E-mail: sean.sendall@bc.edu.
Website: http://www.bc.edu/cson

**Bryan College of Health Sciences,** School of Nurse Anesthesia, Lincoln, NE 68506. Offers MS. *Accreditation:* AANA/CANAEP.

**California State University, Fullerton,** Graduate Studies, College of Health and Human Development, School of Nursing, Fullerton, CA 92831-3599. Offers leadership (MS); nurse anesthesia (MS); nurse educator (MS); nursing (DNP); school nursing (MS); women's health care (MS). *Accreditation:* AACN. *Program availability:* Part-time.

**Case Western Reserve University,** Frances Payne Bolton School of Nursing, Master's Programs in Nursing, Cleveland, OH 44106. Offers nurse anesthesia (MSN); nurse education (MSN); nurse midwifery (MSN); nurse practitioner (MSN), including acute care/cardiovascular nursing, adult gerontology nurse practitioner, palliative care; nursing (MN). *Accreditation:* ACEN. *Program availability:* Part-time. *Faculty:* 40 full-time (36 women), 8 part-time/adjunct (7 women). *Students:* 160 full-time (131 women), 141 part-time (108 women); includes 72 minority (26 Black or African American, non-Hispanic/Latino; 22 Asian, non-Hispanic/Latino; 16 Hispanic/Latino; 8 Two or more races, non-Hispanic/Latino), 13 international. Average age 29. 273 applicants, 64% accepted, 100 enrolled. In 2019, 122 master's awarded. *Degree requirements:* For master's, thesis optional, minimum GPA of 3.0, Typhon log of clinical hours corresponding to requirements to sit for certification exam. *Entrance requirements:* For master's, GRE/MAT (scores not required for application, but may be requested for an admission decision), CCRN certification and 2 years ICU experience (for nurse anesthesia). Additional exam requirements/recommendations for international students: required—TOEFL (minimum score 577 paper-based; 90 iBT), IELTS (minimum score 7). *Application deadline:* For fall admission, 3/1 for domestic and international students; for spring admission, 10/1 for domestic and international students; for summer admission, 3/1 for domestic and international students. Applications are processed on a rolling basis. Application fee: $75. Electronic applications accepted. *Expenses:* MSN $2,133 per credit hour; MN $25,596 per semester; Lab fee $215; NCLEX $300; ACEMAPP $50; Clinical placement $75; Activity fee $15; Graduate Council fee $15. *Financial support:* In 2019–20, 126 students received support, including 49 teaching assistantships with partial tuition reimbursements available (averaging $19,197 per year); scholarships/grants and traineeships also available. Financial award application deadline: 5/15; financial award applicants required to submit FAFSA. *Unit head:* Dr. Latina Brooks, Director, 216-368-1196, Fax: 216-368-3542, E-mail: lmb3@case.edu. *Application contact:* Jackie Tepale, Admissions Coordinator, 216-368-5253, Fax: 216-368-3542, E-mail: yyd@case.edu.
Website: https://case.edu/nursing/programs/msn

**Case Western Reserve University,** Frances Payne Bolton School of Nursing, Master's Programs in Nursing, Program in Nurse Anesthesia, Cleveland, OH 44106. Offers nurse anesthesia (MSN). *Accreditation:* AANA/CANAEP. *Faculty:* 19 full-time (17 women), 4 part-time/adjunct (3 women). *Students:* 31 full-time (23 women), 58 part-time (35 women); includes 17 minority (7 Black or African American, non-Hispanic/Latino; 4 Asian, non-Hispanic/Latino; 4 Hispanic/Latino; 2 Two or more races, non-Hispanic/Latino), 1 international. Average age 30. 90 applicants, 52% accepted, 34 enrolled. In 2019, 29 master's awarded. *Degree requirements:* For master's, minimum GPA of 3.0, cases/clinical hours corresponding to requirements to sit for certification exam, portfolio. *Entrance requirements:* For master's, GRE/MAT (scores not required for application, but may be requested for an admission decision), CCRN certification and 2 years of ICU experience. Additional exam requirements/recommendations for international students: required—TOEFL (minimum score 577 paper-based; 90 iBT), IELTS (minimum score 7). *Application deadline:* For summer admission, 6/1 for domestic and international students. Applications are processed on a rolling basis. Application fee: $75. Electronic applications accepted. *Expenses:* Lab fee $ 215; Examsoft fee $150; NSEE fee $250 (for first time entrants); Activity fee $15 per semester; Tuition rate $2,133 per credit hour. *Financial support:* In 2019–20, 96 students received support, including 2 teaching assistantships with partial tuition reimbursements available (averaging $19,197 per year); scholarships/grants and traineeships also available. Financial award application deadline: 5/15; financial award applicants required to submit FAFSA. *Unit head:* Dr. Sonya Moore, Director, 216-368-6659, Fax: 216-368-3542, E-mail: sdm37@case.edu. *Application contact:* Jackie Tepale, Admissions Coordinator, 216-368-5253, Fax: 216-368-3542, E-mail: yyd@case.edu.
Website: https://case.edu/nursing/programs/msn/msn-majors/nurse-anesthesia

**Columbia University,** School of Nursing, Program in Nurse Anesthesia, New York, NY 10032. Offers MS, Adv C. *Accreditation:* AACN; AANA/CANAEP. *Entrance requirements:* For master's, GRE General Test, NCLEX, BSN, 1 year of intensive care unit experience; for Adv C, MSN, 1 year of intensive care unit experience. Additional exam requirements/recommendations for international students: required—TOEFL (minimum score 100 iBT). Electronic applications accepted. *Expenses:* Tuition: Full-time $47,600; part-time $1880 per credit. One-time fee: $105.

**DeSales University,** Division of Healthcare, Center Valley, PA 18034-9568. Offers adult-gerontology acute care (Post Master's Certificate); adult-gerontology acute care nurse practitioner (MSN); adult-gerontology acute certified nurse practitioner (Post Master's Certificate); adult-gerontology clinical nurse specialist (MSN, Post Master's Certificate); clinical leadership (DNP); family nurse practitioner (MSN, Post Master's Certificate); general nursing practice (DNP); nurse anesthetist (MSN); nurse educator (Post Master's Certificate, Postbaccalaureate Certificate); nurse midwife (MSN); nurse practitioner (MSN); psychiatric-mental health nurse practitioner (MSN, Post Master's Certificate); DNP/MBA. *Accreditation:* ACEN. *Program availability:* Part-time. *Faculty:* 31 full-time (23 women), 12 part-time/adjunct (9 women). *Students:* 294 full-time (219 women), 128 part-time (109 women); includes 71 minority (20 Black or African American, non-Hispanic/Latino; 1 American Indian or Alaska Native, non-Hispanic/Latino; 15 Asian, non-Hispanic/Latino; 30 Hispanic/Latino; 5 Two or more races, non-Hispanic/Latino). Average age 28. 2,666 applicants, 6% accepted, 142 enrolled. In 2019, 115 master's, 30 doctorates awarded. *Degree requirements:* For master's, minimum GPA of 3.0, portfolio; for doctorate, minimum GPA of 3.0, scholarly capstone project. *Entrance requirements:* For master's, GRE or MAT (waived if applicant has an undergraduate GPA of 3.0 or higher), BSN from ACEN- or CCNE-accredited program, minimum undergraduate GPA of 3.0, active RN license or eligibility, two letters of recommendation, essay, health care experience, personal interview; for doctorate, BSN or MSN from ACEN- or CCNE-accredited institution, minimum GPA of 3.3 in graduate program, current licensure as an RN. Additional exam requirements/recommendations for international students: required—TOEFL (minimum score 104 iBT). *Application deadline:* Applications are processed on a rolling basis. Application fee: $50. Electronic applications accepted. *Expenses:* Contact institution. *Financial support:* Applicants required to submit FAFSA. *Unit head:* Ronald Nordone, Dean of Graduate Education, 610-282-1100 Ext. 1289, E-mail: ronald.nordone@desales.edu. *Application contact:* Julia Ferraro, Director of Graduate Admissions, 610-282-1100 Ext. 1768, E-mail: gradadmissions@desales.edu.

**Drexel University,** College of Nursing and Health Professions, Department of Nurse Anesthesia, Philadelphia, PA 19104-2875. Offers MSN. *Accreditation:* AACN; AANA/CANAEP. Electronic applications accepted.

**Duke University,** School of Nursing, Durham, NC 27708. Offers acute care pediatric nurse practitioner (MSN, Post-Graduate Certificate); adult-gerontology nurse practitioner (MSN, Post-Graduate Certificate), including acute care, primary care; family nurse practitioner (MSN, Post-Graduate Certificate); neonatal nurse practitioner (MSN, Post-Graduate Certificate); nurse anesthesia (DNP); nurse practitioner (DNP); nursing (PhD); nursing and health care leadership (MSN, Post-Graduate Certificate); nursing education (MSN, Post-Graduate Certificate); nursing informatics (MSN, Post-Graduate Certificate); pediatric nurse practitioner (MSN, Post-Graduate Certificate), including primary care; psychiatric mental health nurse practitioner (MSN, Post-Graduate Certificate); women's health nurse practitioner (MSN, Post-Graduate Certificate). *Accreditation:* AACN; AANA/CANAEP. *Program availability:* Part-time, evening/weekend, online with on-campus intensives. *Faculty:* 48 full-time (40 women), 32 part-time/adjunct (28 women). *Students:* 666 full-time (601 women), 157 part-time (139 women); includes 193 minority (61 Black or African American, non-Hispanic/Latino; 4 American Indian or Alaska Native, non-Hispanic/Latino; 57 Asian, non-Hispanic/Latino; 49 Hispanic/Latino; 1 Native Hawaiian or other Pacific Islander, non-Hispanic/Latino; 21 Two or more races, non-Hispanic/Latino), 8 international. Average age 34. 761 applicants, 33% accepted, 149 enrolled. In 2019, 213 master's, 74 doctorates, 18 other advanced degrees awarded. Terminal master's awarded for partial completion of doctoral program. *Degree requirements:* For master's, thesis optional; for doctorate, capstone project. *Entrance requirements:* For master's, MSN applicants are no longer required to take the GRE, 1 year of nursing experience (recommended), BSN, minimum GPA of 3.0, previous course work in statistics; for doctorate, GRE is required for the DNP in Nurse Anesthesia, BSN or MSN, minimum GPA of 3.0, resume, personal statement, graduate statistics and research methods course, current licensure as a registered nurse, transcripts from all post-secondary institutions; for Post-Graduate Certificate, MSN, licensure or eligibility as a professional nurse, transcripts from all post-secondary institutions, previous course work in statistics. Additional exam requirements/recommendations for international students: required—TOEFL (minimum score 100 iBT), IELTS (minimum score 7). *Application deadline:* For fall admission, 12/1 for domestic and international students; for spring admission, 5/1 for domestic and international students. Application fee: $50. Electronic applications accepted. *Expenses:* Contact institution. *Financial support:* Institutionally sponsored loans, scholarships/grants, and traineeships available. Support available to part-time students. Financial award applicants required to submit FAFSA. *Unit head:* Dr. Marion E. Broome, Dean/Vice Chancellor for Nursing Affairs/Associate Vice President for Academic Affairs for Nursing, 919-684-9446, Fax: 919-684-9414, E-mail: marion.broome@duke.edu. *Application contact:* Dr. Ernie Rushing, Director of Admissions and Recruitment, 919-668-6274, Fax: 919-668-4693, E-mail: ernie.rushing@dm.duke.edu.
Website: http://www.nursing.duke.edu/

**Fairfield University,** Marion Peckham Egan School of Nursing and Health Studies, Fairfield, CT 06824. Offers advanced practice (DNP); family nurse practitioner (MSN, DNP); nurse anesthesia (DNP); nursing leadership (MSN); psychiatric nurse practitioner (MSN, DNP). *Accreditation:* AACN; AANA/CANAEP. *Program availability:* Part-time, evening/weekend. *Faculty:* 13 full-time (all women), 12 part-time/adjunct (9 women). *Students:* 56 full-time (49 women), 165 part-time (149 women); includes 62 minority (24 Black or African American, non-Hispanic/Latino; 12 Asian, non-Hispanic/Latino; 25 Hispanic/Latino; 1 Two or more races, non-Hispanic/Latino). Average age 33. 129 applicants, 56% accepted, 62 enrolled. In 2019, 26 master's, 36 doctorates awarded. *Degree requirements:* For master's, capstone project. *Entrance requirements:* For master's, minimum QPA of 3.0, RN license, resume, 2 recommendations; for doctorate, MSN (minimum QPA of 3.2) or BSN (minimum QPA of 3.0); critical care nursing experience (for nurse anesthesia DNP candidates). Additional exam requirements/recommendations for international students: required—TOEFL (minimum score 550 paper-based; 80 iBT), IELTS (minimum score 6.5), TOEFL (minimum score 550 paper-based; 80 iBT) or IELTS (minimum score 6.5). *Application deadline:* For fall admission, 5/15 for international students; for spring admission, 10/15 for international students. Applications are processed on a rolling basis. Application fee: $60. Electronic applications accepted. *Expenses:* $875 per credit hour tuition (for MS), $1,010 per credit hour tuition (for Master of Healthcare Administration), $1,025 per credit hour tuition (for Doctorate in Clinical Nutrition), $1,050 per credit hour tuition (for DNP Nurse Anesthesia), $1,000 per credit hour tuition (for all other DNP programs), $150 per semester clinical placement fee (applicable programs, fall and spring semesters), $50 per semester registration fee, $65 per semester graduate student activity fee (fall and spring). *Financial support:* In 2019–20, 45 students received support. Scholarships/grants and unspecified assistantships available. Financial award applicants required to submit FAFSA. *Unit head:* Dr. Meredith Wallace Kazer, Dean, 203-254-4000 Ext. 2701, Fax: 203-254-4126, E-mail: mkazer@fairfield.edu. *Application contact:* Melanie Rogers, Director of Graduate Admission, 203-254-4184, Fax: 203-254-4073, E-mail: gradadmis@fairfield.edu.
Website: http://fairfield.edu/son

**Florida Gulf Coast University,** Elaine Nicpon Marieb College of Health and Human Services, Program in Nurse Anesthesia, Fort Myers, FL 33965-6565. Offers MSN. *Accreditation:* AACN; AANA/CANAEP. *Program availability:* Part-time. *Degree requirements:* For master's, thesis or alternative. *Entrance requirements:* For master's, GRE General Test, MAT, minimum GPA of 3.0. Additional exam requirements/recommendations for international students: required—TOEFL (minimum score 550 paper-based). Electronic applications accepted. *Expenses:* Tuition, area resident: Full-time $6974; part-time $4350 per credit hour. Tuition, state resident: full-time $6974; part-time $4350 per credit hour. Tuition, nonresident: full-time $28,169; part-time $17,595 per credit hour. *International tuition:* $28,169 full-time. *Required fees:* $2027; $1267 per credit hour. $507 per semester. Tuition and fees vary according to course load.

**Florida International University,** Nicole Wertheim College of Nursing and Health Sciences, Nursing Program, Miami, FL 33199. Offers adult health nursing (MSN); family health (MSN); nurse anesthetist (MSN); nursing practice (DNP); nursing science research (PhD); pediatric nurse (MSN); psychiatric and mental health nursing (MSN); registered nurse (MSN). *Accreditation:* AACN; AANA/CANAEP. *Program availability:* Part-time, evening/weekend. *Faculty:* 14 full-time (12 women), 19 part-time/adjunct (14 women). *Students:* 279 full-time (188 women), 109 part-time (87 women); includes 309 minority (110 Black or African American, non-Hispanic/Latino; 1 American Indian or Alaska Native, non-Hispanic/Latino; 29 Asian, non-Hispanic/Latino; 166 Hispanic/Latino; 2 Native Hawaiian or other Pacific Islander, non-Hispanic/Latino; 1 Two or more races, non-Hispanic/Latino), 6 international. Average age 35. 154 applicants, 61% accepted, 88 enrolled. In 2019, 167 master's, 46 doctorates awarded. *Degree requirements:* For master's, thesis or alternative; for doctorate, comprehensive exam, thesis/dissertation. *Entrance requirements:* For master's, bachelor's degree in nursing, minimum undergraduate GPA of 3.0 in upper-level coursework, letters of recommendation; for doctorate, GRE, letters of recommendation, minimum undergraduate GPA of 3.0 in upper-level coursework, interview. Additional exam requirements/recommendations for international students: required—TOEFL (minimum score 550 paper-based; 80 iBT). *Application deadline:* For fall admission, 6/1 for domestic students, 4/1 for international students; for spring admission, 10/1 for domestic students, 9/1 for international students. Applications are processed on a rolling basis. Application fee: $30. Electronic

applications accepted. *Expenses: Tuition, area resident:* Full-time $8912; part-time $446 per credit hour. Tuition, state resident: full-time $8912; part-time $446 per credit hour. Tuition, nonresident: full-time $21,393; part-time $992 per credit hour. *Required fees:* $2194. *Financial support:* Institutionally sponsored loans and scholarships/grants available. Financial award application deadline: 3/1; financial award applicants required to submit FAFSA. *Unit head:* Dr. Yhovana Gordon, Chair, 305-348-7733, Fax: 305-348-7051, E-mail: gordony@fiu.edu. *Application contact:* Nanett Rojas, Manager, Admissions Operations, 305-348-7464, Fax: 305-348-7441, E-mail: gradadm@fiu.edu. Website: http://cnhs.fiu.edu/

**Franciscan Missionaries of Our Lady University,** School of Nursing, Program in Nurse Anesthesia, Baton Rouge, LA 70808. Offers DNP. *Accreditation:* AANA/CANAEP. *Entrance requirements:* For doctorate, GRE, current RN license; baccalaureate degree in nursing; 1 year of full-time experience (2 years preferred) as RN in adult intensive care unit; minimum cumulative GPA of 3.0; three professional letters of recommendation. Additional exam requirements/recommendations for international students: required—TOEFL.

**Gannon University,** School of Graduate Studies, Morosky College of Health Professions and Sciences, Villa Maria School of Nursing, Program in Nurse Anesthesia, Erie, PA 16541-0001. Offers MSN, Certificate. *Program availability:* Part-time, evening/weekend. *Degree requirements:* For master's, thesis (for some programs), practicum. *Entrance requirements:* For master's and Certificate, GRE, BSN from accredited program, transcripts, evidence of fulfillment of legal requirements for practice of nursing in the United States, minimum cumulative GPA of 3.0 for undergraduate math and science courses and for last 60 hours of undergraduate nursing studies, four letters of recommendation, two years of clinical experience. Additional exam requirements/recommendations for international students: required—TOEFL (minimum score 79 iBT). Electronic applications accepted.

**Georgetown University,** Graduate School of Arts and Sciences, School of Nursing and Health Studies, Washington, DC 20057. Offers acute care nurse practitioner (MS); clinical nurse specialist (MS); family nurse practitioner (MS); health systems administration (MS); nurse anesthesia (MS); nurse-midwifery (MS); nursing (DNP); nursing education (MS). *Accreditation:* AACN; AANA/CANAEP (one or more programs are accredited); ACNM/ACME (one or more programs are accredited). *Degree requirements:* For master's, thesis optional. *Entrance requirements:* For master's, GRE General Test or MAT, bachelor's degree in nursing from ACEN-accredited school, minimum undergraduate GPA of 3.0. Additional exam requirements/recommendations for international students: required—TOEFL.

**Goldfarb School of Nursing at Barnes-Jewish College,** Graduate Programs, St. Louis, MO 63110. Offers adult-gerontology (MSN), including primary care nurse practitioner; adult-gerontology (MSN), including acute care nurse practitioner; health systems and population health leadership (MSN); nurse anesthesia (MSN). *Accreditation:* AACN; AANA/CANAEP. *Program availability:* Part-time, online learning. *Degree requirements:* For master's, thesis or alternative. *Entrance requirements:* For master's, 2 references, personal statement, curriculum vitae or resume. Additional exam requirements/recommendations for international students: required—TOEFL (minimum score 575 paper-based; 85 iBT).

**Inter American University of Puerto Rico, Arecibo Campus,** Program in Anesthesia, Arecibo, PR 00614-4050. Offers MS. *Accreditation:* AANA/CANAEP. *Degree requirements:* For master's, comprehensive exam, thesis optional. *Entrance requirements:* For master's, GRE, EXADEP, 2 letters of recommendation, bachelor's degree in nursing, interview, minimum GPA of 3.0 in last 60 credits, minimum 1 year experience.

**Keiser University,** Nurse Anesthesia Programs, Fort Lauderdale, FL 33309. Offers MSNA, DNAP.

**La Roche University,** School of Graduate Studies and Adult Education, Program in Nurse Anesthesia, Pittsburgh, PA 15237-5898. Offers MS, DNAP. *Accreditation:* AANA/CANAEP. *Faculty:* 6 part-time/adjunct (4 women). *Students:* 40 full-time (26 women). Average age 30. 22 applicants, 100% accepted, 21 enrolled. In 2019, 17 master's awarded. *Degree requirements:* For master's, thesis optional. *Entrance requirements:* For master's, GRE General Test, prior acceptance to the Allegheny Valley School of Anesthesia. *Application deadline:* For fall admission, 12/31 for domestic students. Application fee: $50. Electronic applications accepted. *Expenses:* Contact institution. *Financial support:* Application deadline: 3/31; applicants required to submit FAFSA. *Unit head:* Dr. Rosemary McCarthy, Associate Vice President for Academic Affairs and Dean of Graduate Studies and Adult Education, 412-536-1173, Fax: 412-536-1163, E-mail: rosemary.mccarthy@laroche.edu. *Application contact:* Erin Pottgen, Assistant Director, Graduate Admissions, 412-847-2509, Fax: 412-536-1283, E-mail: erin.pottgen@laroche.edu.

**La Salle University,** School of Nursing and Health Sciences, Program in Nursing, Philadelphia, PA 19141-1199. Offers adult gerontology primary care nurse practitioner (MSN, Certificate); adult health and illness clinical nurse specialist (MSN); adult-gerontology clinical nurse specialist (MSN, Certificate); clinical nurse leader (MSN); family primary care nurse practitioner (MSN, Certificate); gerontology (Certificate); nurse anesthetist (MSN, Certificate); nursing (MSN, Certificate); nursing administration (MSN, Certificate); nursing education (Certificate); nursing practice (DNP); nursing service administration (MSN); public health nursing (MSN, Certificate); school nursing (Certificate); MSN/MBA; MSN/MPH. *Accreditation:* AACN. *Program availability:* Part-time, evening/weekend, 100% online. *Degree requirements:* For doctorate, minimum of 1,000 hours of post baccalaureate clinical practice supervised by preceptors. *Entrance requirements:* For master's, GRE, MAT, or GMAT (for students with BSN GPA of less than 3.2), baccalaureate degree in nursing from ACEN- or CCNE-accredited program or an MSN Bridge program; Pennsylvania RN license; 2 letters of reference; resume; statement of philosophy articulating professional values and future educational goal; 1 year of work experience as a registered nurse; for doctorate, GRE (waived for applicants with MSN cumulative GPA of 3.7 or above), MSN, master's degree, MBA or MHA from nationally-accredited program; resume or curriculum vitae; 2 letters of reference; interview; for Certificate, GRE, MAT, or GMAT (for students with BSN GPA of less than 3.2, baccalaureate degree in nursing from ACEN- or CCNE-accredited program or an MSN Bridge program; Pennsylvania RN license; 2 letters of reference; resume; statement of philosophy articulating professional values and future educational goal; 1 year of work experience as a registered nurse. Additional exam requirements/recommendations for international students: required—TOEFL. Electronic applications accepted. Application fee is waived when completed online. *Expenses:* Contact institution.

**Lincoln Memorial University,** Caylor School of Nursing, Harrogate, TN 37752-1901. Offers family nurse practitioner (MSN); nurse anesthesia (MSN); psychiatric mental health nurse practitioner (MSN). *Accreditation:* AANA/CANAEP; ACEN. *Program availability:* Part-time. *Entrance requirements:* For master's, GRE.

**Louisiana State University Health Sciences Center,** School of Nursing, New Orleans, LA 70112. Offers adult gerontology acute care nurse practitioner (DNP, Post-Master's Certificate); adult gerontology clinical nurse specialist (DNP, Post-Master's Certificate); adult gerontology primary care nurse practitioner (DNP, Post-Master's Certificate);

clinical nurse leader (MSN); executive nurse leader (DNP, Post-Master's Certificate); neonatal nurse practitioner (DNP, Post-Master's Certificate); nurse anesthesia (DNP, Post-Master's Certificate); nurse educator (MSN); nursing (DNS); primary care family nurse practitioner (DNP, Post-Master's Certificate); public/community health nursing (DNP, Post-Master's Certificate). *Accreditation:* AACN; AANA/CANAEP (one or more programs are accredited). *Program availability:* Part-time. *Faculty:* 25 full-time (21 women), 25 part-time/adjunct (13 women). *Students:* 182 full-time (127 women), 70 part-time (59 women); includes 82 minority (52 Black or African American, non-Hispanic/Latino; 2 American Indian or Alaska Native, non-Hispanic/Latino; 14 Asian, non-Hispanic/Latino; 14 Hispanic/Latino), 1 international. Average age 34. 34 applicants, 62% accepted, 21 enrolled. In 2019, 72 doctorates awarded. *Degree requirements:* For master's, thesis optional; for doctorate, thesis/dissertation. *Entrance requirements:* For master's, GRE, minimum GPA of 3.0; for doctorate, GRE, minimum GPA of 3.0 (for DNP), 3.5 (for DNS). Additional exam requirements/recommendations for international students: required—TOEFL (minimum score 550 paper-based; 79 iBT). *Application deadline:* For fall admission, 6/1 priority date for domestic and international students; for spring admission, 10/1 priority date for domestic and international students; for summer admission, 3/1 priority date for domestic and international students. Applications are processed on a rolling basis. Application fee: $100. Electronic applications accepted. *Expenses:* MSN and DNS: $13,354.50, $24,982.25 non-resident, $586 per hour (fall and spring), $467 per hour (summer), $1,102 per hour non-resident (fall and spring), $858 per hour non-resident (summer); DNP (Except Nurse Anethesia): $21,907.50, $38,262.23 non-resident, $973 per hour (fall and spring), $733 per hour (summer), $1,700 per hour non-resident (fall and spring), $1,278 per hour non-resident (summer); Nurse Anesthesia DNP: $26,407.50, $42,762.23 non-resident, $1,173 per hour (fall and spring), $883 per hour (summer), $1,900 per hour non-resident (fall and spring), $1,428 per hour non-resident (summer). *Financial support:* In 2019–20, 20 students received support. Institutionally sponsored loans, scholarships/grants, unspecified assistantships, and DNS Scholars Program available. Financial award application deadline: 4/15; financial award applicants required to submit FAFSA. *Unit head:* Dr. Demetrius James Porche, Dean, 504-568-4106, Fax: 504-599-0573, E-mail: dporch@lsuhsc.edu. *Application contact:* Tracie Gravolet, Director, Office of Student Affairs, 504-568-4114, Fax: 504-568-5711, E-mail: tgravo@lsuhsc.edu.
Website: http://nursing.lsuhsc.edu/

**Lourdes University,** Graduate School, Sylvania, OH 43560-2898. Offers business (MBA); leadership (M Ed); nurse anesthesia (MSN); nurse educator (MSN); nurse leader (MSN); organizational leadership (MOL); reading (M Ed); teaching and curriculum (M Ed); theology (MA). *Accreditation:* AANA/CANAEP. *Program availability:* Evening/weekend. *Entrance requirements:* Additional exam requirements/recommendations for international students: required—TOEFL.

**Marian University,** Leighton School of Nursing, Indianapolis, IN 46222-1997. Offers family nurse practitioner (DNP); nurse anesthesia (DNP); nursing education (MSN). *Accreditation:* AANA/CANAEP. *Program availability:* Part-time. *Degree requirements:* For master's, 38 credits, designed to be completed in 2 years; 225-hour practicum including a culminating project; for doctorate, 70 credit hours (for family nurse practitioner track); 85 credits (for nurse anesthesia track); minimum of 1000 hours of supervised practice. *Entrance requirements:* For master's, degree in nursing from NLNAC- or CCNE-accredited program; current, valid RN license in State of Indiana; minimum undergraduate GPA of 3.0; 3 recommendations; interview with admissions committee; current resume; 500-word essay describing career goals; for doctorate, BSN from NSNAC- or CCNE-accredited program; minimum undergraduate GPA of 3.0; cureent, valid RN license; current resume or curriculum vitae; 500-word essay addressing career goals; 3 letters of recommendation; interview with Admissions Committee. Additional exam requirements/recommendations for international students: required—TOEFL (minimum score 550 paper-based; 79 iBT). Electronic applications accepted. Application fee is waived when completed online. *Expenses:* Contact institution.

**Marshall University,** Academic Affairs Division, College of Business, Program in Nurse Anesthesia, Huntington, WV 25755. Offers DMPNA.

**Mayo Clinic School of Health Sciences,** Doctor of Nurse Anesthesia Practice Program, Rochester, MN 55905. Offers DNAP. *Accreditation:* AANA/CANAEP. *Degree requirements:* For doctorate, comprehensive exam, research project. *Entrance requirements:* For doctorate, GRE General Test, official transcripts, three references, essay, RN license. Additional exam requirements/recommendations for international students: required—TOEFL. Electronic applications accepted. *Expenses:* Contact institution.

**Medical University of South Carolina,** College of Health Professions, Anesthesia for Nurses Program, Charleston, SC 29425. Offers MSNA. *Accreditation:* AANA/CANAEP. *Degree requirements:* For master's, comprehensive exam, research project, clinical practica. *Entrance requirements:* For master's, GRE General Test, interview, minimum GPA of 3.0, 2 years of RN (ICU) experience, RN license. Additional exam requirements/recommendations for international students: required—TOEFL (minimum score 600 paper-based). Electronic applications accepted.

**Midwestern University, Glendale Campus,** College of Health Sciences, Arizona Campus, Program in Nurse Anesthesia, Glendale, AZ 85308. Offers MS. *Accreditation:* AANA/CANAEP. *Expenses:* Contact institution.

**Missouri State University,** Graduate College, College of Health and Human Services, Department of Biomedical Sciences, School of Anesthesia, Springfield, MO 65897. Offers DNAP. *Accreditation:* AANA/CANAEP. *Entrance requirements:* Additional exam requirements/recommendations for international students: required—TOEFL (minimum score 550 paper-based; 79 iBT), IELTS (minimum score 6). Electronic applications accepted. *Expenses: Tuition, area resident:* Full-time $2600; part-time $1735 per credit hour. Tuition, nonresident: full-time $5240; part-time $3495 per credit hour. *International tuition:* $5240 full-time. *Required fees:* $530; $438 per credit hour. Tuition and fees vary according to class time, course level, course load, degree level, campus/location and program.

**Mount Marty University,** Graduate Studies Division, Yankton, SD 57078-3724. Offers business administration (MBA); nurse anesthesia (MS); nursing (MSN); pastoral ministries (MPM). *Accreditation:* AANA/CANAEP (one or more programs are accredited). *Degree requirements:* For master's, thesis or alternative. *Entrance requirements:* For master's, GRE General Test, minimum GPA of 3.0. Electronic applications accepted.

**Murray State University,** School of Nursing and Health Professions, Department of Nursing, Murray, KY 42071. Offers family nurse practitioner (DNP); nurse anesthetist (DNP). *Accreditation:* AACN; AANA/CANAEP. *Program availability:* Evening/weekend, 100% online, blended/hybrid learning. *Entrance requirements:* For doctorate, GRE, minimum university GPA of 2.75. Additional exam requirements/recommendations for international students: required—TOEFL (minimum score 527 paper-based; 71 iBT). Electronic applications accepted.

**National University,** School of Health and Human Services, La Jolla, CA 92037-1011. Offers clinical affairs (MS); clinical regulatory affairs (MS); complementary and integrative healthcare (MS); family nurse practitioner (MSN); health and life science analytics (MS); health informatics (MS, Certificate); healthcare administration (MHA); nurse anesthesia (MSNA); nursing administration (MSN); nursing informatics (MSN); psychiatric-mental health nurse practitioner (MSN); public health (MPH), including health promotion, healthcare administration, mental health. *Accreditation:* CEPH. *Program availability:* Part-time, evening/weekend, 100% online, blended/hybrid learning. *Degree requirements:* For master's, thesis (for some programs). *Entrance requirements:* For master's, interview, minimum GPA of 2.5. Additional exam requirements/recommendations for international students: required—TOEFL (minimum score 550 paper-based; 79 iBT), IELTS (minimum score 6). Electronic applications accepted. *Expenses: Tuition:* Full-time $442; part-time $442 per unit.

**Newman University,** School of Nursing and Allied Health, Wichita, KS 67213-2097. Offers nurse anesthesia (MS). *Accreditation:* AANA/CANAEP. *Degree requirements:* For master's, thesis optional. *Entrance requirements:* For master's, GRE General Test, registered professional nursing license in Kansas, 3 professional recommendations, 1-page letter detailing professional and educational goals, BSN, statistics course, 1 year of employment, interview. Additional exam requirements/recommendations for international students: required—TOEFL (minimum score 600 paper-based; 100 iBT). Electronic applications accepted. *Expenses:* Contact institution.

**Northeastern University,** Bouvé College of Health Sciences, Boston, MA 02115-5096. Offers applied behavior analysis (MS); audiology (Au D); counseling psychology (MS, PhD, CAGS); exercise science (MS); nursing (MS, PhD, CAGS), including administration (MS), adult-gerontology acute care nurse practitioner (MS, CAGS), adult-gerontology primary care nurse practitioner (MS, CAGS), anesthesia (MS), family nurse practitioner (MS, CAGS), neonatal nurse practitioner (MS, CAGS), pediatric nurse practitioner (MS, CAGS), psychiatric mental health nurse practitioner (MS, CAGS); nursing practice (DNP); pharmaceutical sciences (MS, PhD), including interdisciplinary concentration, pharmaceutics and drug delivery systems; pharmacology (MS); pharmacy (Pharm D); school psychology (PhD); speech-language pathology (MS); urban health (MPH); MS/MBA. *Accreditation:* AANA/CANAEP; ACPE (one or more programs are accredited); ASHA; CEPH. *Program availability:* Part-time, evening/weekend, online learning. *Degree requirements:* For doctorate, thesis/dissertation (for some programs); for CAGS, comprehensive exam. Electronic applications accepted. *Expenses:* Contact institution.

**Oakland University,** Graduate Study and Lifelong Learning, School of Nursing, Program in Nurse Anesthetist, Rochester, MI 48309-4401. Offers nurse anesthesia (MSN, PMC). *Accreditation:* AACN; AANA/CANAEP. *Degree requirements:* For master's, thesis (for some programs). *Entrance requirements:* Additional exam requirements/recommendations for international students: required—TOEFL (minimum score 550 paper-based; 79 iBT), IELTS (minimum score 6.5). Electronic applications accepted. *Expenses:* Contact institution.

**Old Dominion University,** College of Health Sciences, School of Nursing, Nurse Anesthesia Program, Virginia Beach, VA 23452. Offers DNP. *Accreditation:* AANA/CANAEP. *Degree requirements:* For doctorate, comprehensive exam, thesis/dissertation. *Entrance requirements:* For doctorate, GRE. Electronic applications accepted. *Expenses:* Contact institution.

**Oregon Health & Science University,** School of Nursing, Program in Nurse Anesthesia, Portland, OR 97239-3098. Offers MN. *Accreditation:* AANA/CANAEP. *Entrance requirements:* For master's, GRE, BS with major in nursing or BSN, licensed in state of Oregon, at least one year of adult or pediatric critical care ICU experience, statistics in last 5 years with minimum B- grade, three letters of reference. Additional exam requirements/recommendations for international students: required—TOEFL (minimum score 83 iBT). Electronic applications accepted. *Expenses:* Contact institution.

**Otterbein University,** Department of Nursing, Westerville, OH 43081. Offers advanced practice nurse educator (Certificate); clinical nurse leader (MSN); family nurse practitioner (MSN, Certificate); nurse anesthesia (MSN, Certificate); nursing (DNP); nursing service administration (MSN). *Accreditation:* AACN; AANA/CANAEP; ACEN. *Program availability:* Part-time, evening/weekend, online learning. *Degree requirements:* For master's, comprehensive exam (for some programs), thesis (for some programs). *Entrance requirements:* For master's, 2 reference forms, resume; for Certificate, official transcripts, 2 reference forms, essay, resumé. Additional exam requirements/recommendations for international students: required—TOEFL (minimum score 550 paper-based; 79 iBT).

**Quinnipiac University,** School of Nursing, Post-Bachelor's Nurse Anesthesia Track, Hamden, CT 06518-1940. Offers DNP. *Entrance requirements:* For doctorate, bachelor's degree in nursing or appropriate science, RN license, minimum GPA of 3.0, specific core science courses completed within the last 10 years, critical care experience within the last 5 years. Electronic applications accepted. *Expenses: Tuition:* Part-time $1055 per credit. *Required fees:* $945 per semester. Tuition and fees vary according to course load and program.

**Rosalind Franklin University of Medicine and Science,** College of Health Professions, Nurse Anesthesia Department, North Chicago, IL 60064-3095. Offers DNAP. *Accreditation:* AANA/CANAEP. *Entrance requirements:* For doctorate, interview. Additional exam requirements/recommendations for international students: required—TOEFL. Electronic applications accepted.

**Rutgers University - Newark,** Rutgers School of Nursing, Newark, NJ 07107-3001. Offers adult health (MSN); adult occupational health (MSN); advanced practice nursing (MSN, Post Master's Certificate); family nurse practitioner (MSN); nurse anesthesia (MSN); nursing (MSN); nursing informatics (MSN); urban health (PhD); women's health practitioner (MSN). *Accreditation:* AANA/CANAEP. *Program availability:* Part-time. *Entrance requirements:* For master's, GRE, RN license; basic life support, statistics, and health assessment experience. Additional exam requirements/recommendations for international students: required—TOEFL. Electronic applications accepted. *Expenses:* Contact institution.

**Saint Mary's University of Minnesota,** Schools of Graduate and Professional Programs, Graduate School of Health and Human Services, Nurse Anesthesia Program, Winona, MN 55987-1399. Offers MS. *Accreditation:* AANA/CANAEP. *Unit head:* Leah Gordon, Director, 612-728-5151, E-mail: lgordon@smumn.edu. *Application contact:* Laurie Roy, Director of Admission of Schools of Graduate and Professional Programs, 507-457-8606, Fax: 612-728-5121, E-mail: lroy@smumn.edu.
Website: http://www.smumn.edu/graduate-home/areas-of-study/graduate-school-of-health-human-services/ms-in-nurse-anesthesia

**Saint Vincent College,** Program in Health Science, Latrobe, PA 15650-2690. Offers nurse anesthesia (MS).

**Samford University,** Ida Moffett School of Nursing, Birmingham, AL 35229. Offers advanced practice (DNP), including emergency nurse practitioner, family nurse practitioner, transformation of care; family nurse practitioner (MSN, DNP), including emergency nurse practitioner specialty (MSN); nurse anesthesia (DNP); nursing administration (DNP); psychiatric mental health nurse practitioner (DNP). *Accreditation:* AACN; AANA/CANAEP. *Program availability:* Part-time, evening/weekend, blended/hybrid learning. *Faculty:* 16 full-time (all women), 3 part-time/adjunct (0 women).

*Students:* 281 full-time (239 women), 39 part-time (38 women); includes 68 minority (39 Black or African American, non-Hispanic/Latino; 2 American Indian or Alaska Native, non-Hispanic/Latino; 10 Asian, non-Hispanic/Latino; 10 Hispanic/Latino; 1 Native Hawaiian or other Pacific Islander, non-Hispanic/Latino; 6 Two or more races, non-Hispanic/Latino). Average age 35. 59 applicants, 97% accepted, 29 enrolled. In 2019, 47 master's, 68 doctorates awarded. *Degree requirements:* For doctorate, DNP project with poster presentation. *Entrance requirements:* For doctorate, GRE is required for the Nurse Anesthesia Program. Additional exam requirements/recommendations for international students: required—TOEFL (minimum score 575 paper-based; 90 iBT), IELTS (minimum score 6.5). *Application deadline:* For fall admission, 4/1 for domestic and international students; for spring admission, 8/1 for domestic and international students; for summer admission, 1/1 for domestic and international students. Application fee: $50. Electronic applications accepted. *Expenses: Tuition:* Full-time $17,754; part-time $862 per credit hour. *Required fees:* $550; $550 per unit. Full-time tuition and fees vary according to course load, program and student level. *Financial support:* In 2019–20, 30 students received support. Application deadline: 2/15; applicants required to submit FAFSA. *Unit head:* Dr. Jane S. Martin, Interim Dean and Professor, Ida Moffett School of Nursing, 205-726-2760, E-mail: jsmartin@samford.edu. *Application contact:* Allyson Maddox, Director of Graduate Student Services, 205-726-2047, E-mail: amaddox@samford.edu.
Website: http://samford.edu/nursing

**Samuel Merritt University,** School of Nursing, Oakland, CA 94609-3108. Offers case management (MSN); family nurse practitioner (MSN, DNP, Certificate); nurse anesthetist (MSN, Certificate); nursing (DNP). *Accreditation:* AACN; AANA/CANAEP (one or more programs are accredited). *Program availability:* Part-time, evening/weekend, 100% online, blended/hybrid learning. *Degree requirements:* For master's, thesis or alternative; for doctorate, project. *Entrance requirements:* For master's, GRE General Test (for nurse anesthetist program), minimum GPA of 2.5 in science, 3.0 overall; previous course work in statistics; current RN license; for doctorate and Certificate, minimum GPA of 2.5 in science, 3.0 overall; previous course work in statistics; current RN license. Additional exam requirements/recommendations for international students: required—TOEFL (minimum score 100 iBT). Electronic applications accepted. *Expenses:* Contact institution.

**Southern Illinois University Edwardsville,** Graduate School, School of Nursing, Doctor of Nursing Practice Program, Edwardsville, IL 62026. Offers family nurse practitioner (DNP); nurse anesthesia (DNP); nursing (DNP). *Accreditation:* AACN. *Program availability:* Part-time, evening/weekend. *Degree requirements:* For doctorate, thesis/dissertation or alternative, project. *Entrance requirements:* Additional exam requirements/recommendations for international students: required—TOEFL (minimum score 550 paper-based; 79 iBT), IELTS (minimum score 6.5). Electronic applications accepted.

**State University of New York Downstate Medical Center,** College of Nursing, Graduate Programs in Nursing, Program in Nurse Anesthesia, Brooklyn, NY 11203-2098. Offers MS. *Accreditation:* AACN. *Degree requirements:* For master's, thesis optional. *Entrance requirements:* For master's, GRE, BSN; minimum GPA of 3.0; previous undergraduate course work in statistics, health assessment, and nursing research; RN license.

**Texas Christian University,** Harris College of Nursing and Health Sciences, School of Nurse Anesthesia, Fort Worth, TX 76129-0002. Offers DNP-A. *Accreditation:* AANA/CANAEP. *Faculty:* 11 full-time (6 women), 2 part-time/adjunct (1 woman). *Students:* 208 full-time (135 women); includes 53 minority (7 Black or African American, non-Hispanic/Latino; 1 American Indian or Alaska Native, non-Hispanic/Latino; 19 Asian, non-Hispanic/Latino; 19 Hispanic/Latino; 7 Two or more races, non-Hispanic/Latino). Average age 31. 304 applicants, 35% accepted, 89 enrolled. In 2019, 50 doctorates awarded. *Entrance requirements:* For doctorate, GRE General Test, writing sample. Additional exam requirements/recommendations for international students: required—TOEFL (minimum score 600 paper-based; 94 iBT). *Application deadline:* For fall and spring admission, 7/1 for domestic and international students. Applications are processed on a rolling basis. Application fee: $70. Electronic applications accepted. *Expenses:* Contact institution. *Financial support:* In 2019–20, 3 students received support. Scholarships/grants available. Financial award application deadline: 7/1; financial award applicants required to submit FAFSA. *Unit head:* Dr. Robyn Ward, Director, 817-257-7887, Fax: 817-257-5472, E-mail: r.ward@tcu.edu. *Application contact:* Kimberly Bowen, Administrative Assistant, 817-257-7887, Fax: 817-257-5472, E-mail: k.k.bowen@tcu.edu.
Website: http://www.crna.tcu.edu/

**Texas Wesleyan University,** Graduate Programs, Programs in Nurse Anesthesia, Fort Worth, TX 76105. Offers MHS, MSNA, DNAP. *Accreditation:* AANA/CANAEP (one or more programs are accredited). *Entrance requirements:* For master's, GRE General Test, bachelor's degree, minimum GPA of 3.0, college-level chemistry within three years of start date, current unrestricted RN license valid in one of the 50 states or U.S. territories, minimum of one year of full-time critical care, current ACLS and PALS certifications; for doctorate, master's degree, RN license, CRNA certification/recertification, minimum GPA of 3.0 overall or on last 60 hours, graduate-level research course with minimum grade of B, current curriculum vitae. Electronic applications accepted. *Expenses:* Contact institution.

**Uniformed Services University of the Health Sciences,** Daniel K. Inouye Graduate School of Nursing, Bethesda, MD 20814. Offers adult-gerontology clinical nurse specialist (MSN, DNP); family nurse practitioner (DNP); nurse anesthesia (DNP); nursing science (PhD); psychiatric mental health nurse practitioner (DNP); women's health nurse practitioner (DNP). *Accreditation:* AACN; AANA/CANAEP. *Program availability:* Part-time. *Faculty:* 50 full-time (32 women), 1 part-time/adjunct (0 women). *Students:* 170 full-time (98 women); includes 51 minority (21 Black or African American, non-Hispanic/Latino; 17 Asian, non-Hispanic/Latino; 11 Hispanic/Latino; 2 Native Hawaiian or other Pacific Islander, non-Hispanic/Latino). Average age 34. 88 applicants, 75% accepted, 66 enrolled. In 2019, 2 master's, 42 doctorates awarded. *Degree requirements:* For master's, thesis, scholarly project; for doctorate, dissertation (for PhD); project (for DNP). *Entrance requirements:* For master's, GRE, BSN, clinical experience, minimum GPA of 3.0, previous course work in science; for doctorate, GRE, BSN, minimum GPA of 3.0, undergraduate/graduate science course within past 5 years, writing example, interview (for some programs), and 3 letters of reference (for DNP); master's degree, minimum GPA of 3.0 in nursing or related field, personal statement, 3 references, and interview (for PhD). *Application deadline:* For winter admission, 2/15 for domestic students; for summer admission, 8/15 for domestic students. Electronic applications accepted. *Financial support:* Robert Wood Johnson and Jonas scholars available. *Unit head:* Dr. Diane C. Seibert, Associate Dean for Academic Affairs, 301-295-1080, Fax: 301-295-1707, E-mail: diane.seibert@usuhs.edu. *Application contact:* Maureen Jackson, Student Admissions Program Manager, 301-295-1055, E-mail: maureen.jackson.ctr@usuhs.edu.
Website: http://www.usuhs.edu/gsn/

**Union University,** School of Nursing, Jackson, TN 38305-3697. Offers executive leadership (DNP); nurse anesthesia (DNP); nurse practitioner (DNP); nursing education (MSN, PMC). *Accreditation:* AACN; AANA/CANAEP. *Degree requirements:* For

master's, thesis or alternative. *Entrance requirements:* For master's, GRE, 3 letters of reference, bachelor's degree in nursing, minimum GPA of 3.0. Additional exam requirements/recommendations for international students: required—TOEFL (minimum score 560 paper-based). Electronic applications accepted.

**University at Buffalo, the State University of New York,** Graduate School, School of Nursing, Buffalo, NY 14260. Offers adult gerontology nurse practitioner (DNP); family nurse practitioner (DNP); health care systems and leadership (MS); nurse anesthetist (DNP); nursing (PhD); nursing education (Certificate); psychiatric/mental health nurse practitioner (DNP). *Accreditation:* AACN; AANA/CANAEP (one or more programs are accredited). *Program availability:* Part-time, 100% online. *Degree requirements:* For master's, thesis optional; for doctorate, comprehensive exam (for some programs), capstone (for DNP), dissertation (for PhD). *Entrance requirements:* For master's, GRE or MAT; for doctorate, GRE or MAT, minimum GPA of 3.0 (for DNP), 3.25 (for PhD); RN license; BS or MS in nursing; 3 references; writing sample; resume; personal statement; for Certificate, interview, minimum GPA of 3.0 or GRE General Test, RN license, MS in nursing, professional certification. Additional exam requirements/recommendations for international students: required—TOEFL (minimum score 550 paper-based; 79 iBT), IELTS (minimum score 6.5). Electronic applications accepted. *Expenses:* Contact institution.

**The University of Alabama at Birmingham,** School of Nursing, Birmingham, AL 35294. Offers clinical nurse leader (MSN); nurse anesthesia (DNP); nurse practitioner (MSN, DNP), including adult-gerontology acute care (MSN), adult-gerontology primary care (MSN), family (MSN), pediatric (MSN), psychiatric/mental health (MSN), women's health (MSN); nursing (MSN, DNP, PhD); nursing health systems administration (MSN); nursing informatics (MSN). *Accreditation:* AACN; AANA/CANAEP. *Program availability:* Part-time, online only, blended/hybrid learning. *Faculty:* 86 full-time (79 women), 42 part-time/adjunct (35 women). *Students:* 228 full-time (165 women), 1,393 part-time (1,234 women); includes 398 minority (267 Black or African American, non-Hispanic/Latino; 4 American Indian or Alaska Native, non-Hispanic/Latino; 52 Asian, non-Hispanic/Latino; 41 Hispanic/Latino; 34 Two or more races, non-Hispanic/Latino), 3 international. Average age 33. 1,027 applicants, 55% accepted, 421 enrolled. In 2019, 557 master's, 19 doctorates awarded. Terminal master's awarded for partial completion of doctoral program. *Degree requirements:* For master's, comprehensive exam; for doctorate, comprehensive exam, thesis/dissertation, research mentorship experience (for PhD); scholarly project (for DNP). *Entrance requirements:* For master's, GRE, GMAT, or MAT, minimum cumulative undergraduate GPA of 3.0 or on last 60 semesters hours; letters of recommendation; for doctorate, GRE General Test, computer literacy, course work in statistics, interview, minimum GPA of 3.0, MS in nursing, references, writing sample. Additional exam requirements/recommendations for international students: required—TOEFL (minimum score 500 paper-based, 80 iBT) or IELTS (5.5). *Application deadline:* For fall admission, 2/24 for domestic students; for summer admission, 10/15 for domestic students. Application fee: $50. Electronic applications accepted. *Expenses:* Contact institution. *Financial support:* In 2019–20, 23 fellowships (averaging $34,685 per year), 12 research assistantships (averaging $9,042 per year), 2 teaching assistantships (averaging $22,000 per year) were awarded; scholarships/grants, traineeships, health care benefits, and unspecified assistantships also available. Support available to part-time students. *Unit head:* Dr. Doreen C. Harper, Dean, 205-934-5360, Fax: 205-934-1894, E-mail: dcharper@uab.edu. *Application contact:* John Updegraff, Director of Student Affairs, 205-975-3370, Fax: 205-934-5490, E-mail: jupde22@uab.edu.
Website: http://www.uab.edu/nursing/home/

**University of Cincinnati,** Graduate School, College of Nursing, Cincinnati, OH 45221-0038. Offers nurse midwifery (MSN); nurse practitioner (MSN, DNP), including acute care pediatrics (DNP), adult-gerontology acute care, adult-gerontology primary care, anesthesia (DNP), family (MSN), leadership (DNP), neonatal (MSN), women's health (MSN); nursing (MSN, PhD), including occupational health (MSN). *Accreditation:* AACN; AANA/CANAEP (one or more programs are accredited); ACNM/ACME. *Program availability:* Part-time, 100% online, blended/hybrid learning. *Faculty:* 62 full-time (55 women), 125 part-time/adjunct (114 women). *Students:* 429 full-time (355 women), 1,547 part-time (1,390 women); includes 453 minority (226 Black or African American, non-Hispanic/Latino; 5 American Indian or Alaska Native, non-Hispanic/Latino; 68 Asian, non-Hispanic/Latino; 103 Hispanic/Latino; 3 Native Hawaiian or other Pacific Islander, non-Hispanic/Latino; 48 Two or more races, non-Hispanic/Latino), 15 international. Average age 36. 779 applicants, 78% accepted, 464 enrolled. In 2019, 518 master's, 47 doctorates awarded. *Degree requirements:* For master's, thesis or alternative; for doctorate, comprehensive exam (for some programs), thesis/dissertation (for some programs). *Entrance requirements:* For master's, GRE required only for the Direct-Entry Accelerated Program. Additional exam requirements/recommendations for international students: required—TOEFL (minimum score 600 paper-based; 100 iBT); recommended—IELTS (minimum score 7). *Application deadline:* For fall admission, 4/1 priority date for domestic and international students; for spring admission, 9/1 priority date for domestic and international students; for summer admission, 2/1 priority date for domestic and international students. Applications are processed on a rolling basis. Application fee: $135 ($140 for international students). Electronic applications accepted. *Expenses:* Contact institution. *Financial support:* In 2019–20, 103 students received support, including 9 fellowships with full tuition reimbursements available (averaging $18,595 per year), 7 research assistantships with full tuition reimbursements available (averaging $12,991 per year), 8 teaching assistantships with full tuition reimbursements available (averaging $12,991 per year); institutionally sponsored loans, scholarships/grants, traineeships, health care benefits, tuition waivers (partial), and unspecified assistantships also available. Support available to part-time students. Financial award application deadline: 4/1; financial award applicants required to submit FAFSA. *Unit head:* Dr. Greer Glazer, Dean, 513-558-5330, Fax: 513-558-9030, E-mail: greer.glazer@uc.edu. *Application contact:* Office of Student Affairs, 513-558-8400, E-mail: nursingbearcats@uc.edu.
Website: https://nursing.uc.edu/

**University of Detroit Mercy,** College of Health Professions, Detroit, MI 48221. Offers clinical nurse leader (MSN); family nurse practitioner (MSN); health services administration (MHSA); health systems management (MSN); nurse anesthesia (MS); nursing (DNP); nursing education (MSN, Certificate); nursing leadership and financial management (Certificate); outcomes performance management (Certificate); physician assistant (MS). *Accreditation:* AANA/CANAEP. *Entrance requirements:* For master's, GRE General Test, minimum GPA of 3.0.

**The University of Kansas,** University of Kansas Medical Center, School of Health Professions, Department of Nurse Anesthesia Education, Kansas City, KS 66045. Offers DNAP. *Accreditation:* AANA/CANAEP. *Faculty:* 17. *Students:* 86 full-time (51 women), 4 part-time (2 women); includes 16 minority (4 Black or African American, non-Hispanic/Latino; 2 American Indian or Alaska Native, non-Hispanic/Latino; 4 Asian, non-Hispanic/Latino; 4 Hispanic/Latino; 2 Two or more races, non-Hispanic/Latino). Average age 29. In 2019, 24 doctorates awarded. *Degree requirements:* For doctorate, comprehensive exam, thesis/dissertation or alternative. *Entrance requirements:* Additional exam requirements/recommendations for international students: required—TOEFL. *Application deadline:* For summer admission, 7/15 for domestic and

international students. Application fee: $60. Electronic applications accepted. *Expenses:* Contact institution. *Financial support:* Scholarships/grants available. Financial award application deadline: 3/1; financial award applicants required to submit FAFSA. *Unit head:* Dr. Donna S. Nyght, Chair, 913-588-6612, Fax: 913-588-3334, E-mail: dnyght@kumc.edu. *Application contact:* Joey Vincent, Program Coordinator, 913-588-6612, Fax: 913-588-3334, E-mail: na@kumc.edu.
Website: http://www.kumc.edu/school-of-health-professions/nurse-anesthesia-education.html

**University of Maryland, Baltimore,** University of Maryland School of Nursing, Baltimore, MD 21201. Offers adult-gerontology acute care nurse practitioner (DNP); adult-gerontology primary care nurse practitioner (DNP); clinical nurse leader (MS); community/public health nursing (MS); family nurse practitioner (DNP); global health (Postbaccalaureate Certificate); health services leadership and management (MS); neonatal nurse practitioner (DNP); nurse anesthesia (DNP); nursing (PhD); nursing informatics (MS, Postbaccalaureate Certificate); pediatric acute/primary care nurse practitioner (DNP); psychiatric mental health nurse practitioner (DNP); teaching in nursing and health professions (Postbaccalaureate Certificate); MS/MBA. *Accreditation:* AANA/CANAEP. *Program availability:* Part-time. *Faculty:* 130 full-time (117 women), 125 part-time/adjunct (114 women). *Students:* 539 full-time (463 women), 586 part-time (506 women); includes 485 minority (259 Black or African American, non-Hispanic/Latino; 3 American Indian or Alaska Native, non-Hispanic/Latino; 124 Asian, non-Hispanic/Latino; 66 Hispanic/Latino; 1 Native Hawaiian or other Pacific Islander, non-Hispanic/Latino; 32 Two or more races, non-Hispanic/Latino), 18 international. Average age 33. 964 applicants, 54% accepted, 347 enrolled. In 2019, 197 master's, 114 doctorates, 12 other advanced degrees awarded. *Degree requirements:* For master's and Postbaccalaureate Certificate, thesis (for some programs); for doctorate, comprehensive exam, thesis/dissertation. *Entrance requirements:* Additional exam requirements/recommendations for international students: required—TOEFL (minimum score 550 paper-based; 79 iBT); recommended—IELTS (minimum score 7). *Application deadline:* For fall admission, 11/1 priority date for domestic and international students; for spring admission, 12/15 for domestic and international students; for summer admission, 9/1 for domestic and international students. Applications are processed on a rolling basis. Application fee: $75. Electronic applications accepted. *Financial support:* In 2019–20, 257 students received support, including 31 research assistantships with full and partial tuition reimbursements available (averaging $25,000 per year), 21 teaching assistantships with full and partial tuition reimbursements available (averaging $19,000 per year); scholarships/grants, traineeships, and unspecified assistantships also available. Support available to part-time students. Financial award application deadline: 3/1; financial award applicants required to submit FAFSA. *Unit head:* Dr. Jane Kirschling, Dean, 410-706-4359, E-mail: kirschling@umaryland.edu. *Application contact:* Larry Fillian, Associate Dean of Student and Academic Services, 410-706-6298, E-mail: lfillian@umaryland.edu.
Website: http://www.nursing.umaryland.edu/

**University of Miami,** Graduate School, School of Nursing and Health Studies, Coral Gables, FL 33124. Offers acute care (MSN), including acute care nurse practitioner, nurse anesthesia; nursing (PhD); primary care (MSN), including adult nurse practitioner, family nurse practitioner, nurse midwifery, women's health practitioner. *Accreditation:* AACN; AANA/CANAEP; ACNM/ACME (one or more programs are accredited). *Program availability:* Part-time. *Degree requirements:* For master's, thesis optional; for doctorate, thesis/dissertation. *Entrance requirements:* For master's, GRE General Test, BSN, minimum GPA of 3.0, Florida RN license; for doctorate, GRE General Test, BSN or MSN, minimum GPA of 3.0. Additional exam requirements/recommendations for international students: required—TOEFL (minimum score 550 paper-based). Electronic applications accepted.

**University of Michigan–Flint,** College of Health Sciences, Program in Anesthesia, Flint, MI 48502-1950. Offers DNAP. *Accreditation:* AACN; AANA/CANAEP. *Program availability:* Part-time. *Faculty:* 17 full-time (12 women), 34 part-time/adjunct (18 women). *Students:* 48 full-time (26 women), 9 part-time (5 women); includes 8 minority (1 Black or African American, non-Hispanic/Latino; 2 Asian, non-Hispanic/Latino; 3 Hispanic/Latino; 2 Two or more races, non-Hispanic/Latino). Average age 33. 71 applicants, 37% accepted, 26 enrolled. In 2019, 9 doctorates awarded. *Entrance requirements:* For doctorate, Please refer to the DNAP website for admission requirements: https://www.umflint.edu/graduateprograms/anesthesia-entry-level-dnap#tab-admission. Additional exam requirements/recommendations for international students: required—TOEFL (minimum score 84 iBT), IELTS (minimum score 6.5). *Application deadline:* For fall admission, 2/1 for domestic students, 12/1 for international students. Applications are processed on a rolling basis. Application fee: $55. Electronic applications accepted. *Expenses:* Contact institution. *Financial support:* Federal Work-Study, scholarships/grants, and unspecified assistantships available. Support available to part-time students. Financial award application deadline: 3/1; financial award applicants required to submit FAFSA. *Unit head:* Dr. Shawn Fryzel, Director of Anesthesia Programs, 810-262-9264, Fax: 810-760-0839, E-mail: sfryzel@hurleymc.com. *Application contact:* Matt Bohlen, Associate Director of Graduate Programs, 810-762-3171, Fax: 810-766-6789, E-mail: mbohlen@umflint.edu.
Website: https://www.umflint.edu/graduateprograms/anesthesia-entry-level-dnap

**University of Minnesota, Twin Cities Campus,** Graduate School, School of Nursing, Minneapolis, MN 55455-0213. Offers adult/gerontological clinical nurse specialist (DNP); adult/gerontological primary care nurse practitioner (DNP); family nurse practitioner (DNP); health innovation and leadership (DNP); integrative health and healing (DNP); nurse anesthesia (DNP); nurse midwifery (DNP); nursing (MN, PhD); nursing informatics (DNP); pediatric clinical nurse specialist (DNP); primary care certified pediatric nurse practitioner (DNP); psychiatric/mental health nurse practitioner (DNP); women's health nurse practitioner (DNP). *Accreditation:* AACN; AANA/CANAEP; ACNM/ACME (one or more programs are accredited). *Program availability:* Part-time, online learning. Terminal master's awarded for partial completion of doctoral program. *Degree requirements:* For master's, final oral exam, project or thesis; for doctorate, thesis/dissertation. *Entrance requirements:* For master's and doctorate, GRE General Test. Additional exam requirements/recommendations for international students: required—TOEFL (minimum score 586 paper-based). *Expenses:* Contact institution.

**University of New England,** Westbrook College of Health Professions, Biddeford, ME 04005-9526. Offers nurse anesthesia (MSNA); occupational therapy (MS); physical therapy (DPT); physician assistant (MS); social work (MSW). *Accreditation:* AANA/CANAEP; AOTA. *Program availability:* Part-time. *Faculty:* 42 full-time (32 women), 23 part-time/adjunct (16 women). *Students:* 493 full-time (361 women), 8 part-time (7 women); includes 59 minority (3 Black or African American, non-Hispanic/Latino; 2 American Indian or Alaska Native, non-Hispanic/Latino; 36 Asian, non-Hispanic/Latino; 10 Hispanic/Latino; 2 Native Hawaiian or other Pacific Islander, non-Hispanic/Latino; 6 Two or more races, non-Hispanic/Latino), 2 international. Average age 27. In 2019, 154 master's, 58 doctorates awarded. *Application deadline:* Applications are processed on a rolling basis. Electronic applications accepted. *Financial support:* Application deadline: 5/1; applicants required to submit FAFSA. *Unit head:* Dr. Karen T. Pardue, Dean, Westbrook College of Health Professions, 207-221-4361, E-mail: kpardue@une.edu. *Application contact:* Scott Steinberg, Vice President of University Admissions, 207-221-4225, Fax: 207-523-1925, E-mail: ssteinberg@une.edu.
Website: http://www.une.edu/wchp/index.cfm

**The University of North Carolina at Charlotte,** College of Health and Human Services, School of Nursing, Charlotte, NC 28223-0001. Offers adult-gerontology acute care nurse practitioner (Post-Master's Certificate); advanced clinical nursing (MSN), including adult psychiatric mental health, adult-gerontology acute care nurse practitioner, family nurse practitioner across the lifespan; family nurse practitioner across the lifespan (Post-Master's Certificate); nurse anesthesia (MSN), including nurse anesthesia across the lifespan; nurse anesthesia across the lifespan (Post-Master's Certificate); nursing (DNP); nursing administrator (Graduate Certificate); nursing educator (Graduate Certificate); systems/population nursing (MSN), including community/public health nursing, nurse administrator, nurse educator. *Accreditation:* AACN; AANA/CANAEP. *Program availability:* Part-time, blended/hybrid learning. *Students:* 126 full-time (96 women), 142 part-time (127 women); includes 70 minority (48 Black or African American, non-Hispanic/Latino; 8 Asian, non-Hispanic/Latino; 9 Hispanic/Latino; 5 Two or more races, non-Hispanic/Latino), 1 international. Average age 35. 347 applicants, 37% accepted, 104 enrolled. In 2019, 102 master's, 10 doctorates, 10 other advanced degrees awarded. Terminal master's awarded for partial completion of doctoral program. *Entrance requirements:* For master's, GRE General Test, current unrestricted license as Registered Nurse in North Carolina; BSN from nationally-accredited program; one year of professional nursing practice in acute/critical care; minimum overall GPA of 3.0 in last degree; completion of undergraduate statistics course with minimum grade of C; statement of purpose; for doctorate, GRE or MAT, master's degree in nursing in an advanced nursing practice specialty from nationally-accredited program; minimum overall GPA of 3.5 in MSN program; current RN licensure in U.S. at time of application with eligibility for NC licensure; essay; resume/curriculum vitae; professional recommendations; clinical hours; for other advanced degree, GRE. Additional exam requirements/recommendations for international students: required—TOEFL (minimum score 557 paper-based; 83 iBT), IELTS (minimum score 6.5), TOEFL (minimum score 557 paper-based, 83 iBT) or IELTS (6.5). *Application deadline:* Applications are processed on a rolling basis. Application fee: $75. Electronic applications accepted. *Expenses:* Contact institution. *Financial support:* In 2019–20, 6 students received support, including 4 research assistantships (averaging $4,856 per year), 2 teaching assistantships (averaging $3,615 per year); career-related internships or fieldwork, institutionally sponsored loans, scholarships/grants, traineeships, and unspecified assistantships also available. Support available to part-time students. Financial award application deadline: 3/1; financial award applicants required to submit FAFSA. *Unit head:* Dr. Dena Evans, Director, 704-687-7974, E-mail: devans37@uncc.edu. *Application contact:* Kathy B. Giddings, Director of Graduate Admissions, 704-687-5503, Fax: 704-687-1668, E-mail: gradadm@uncc.edu.
Website: http://nursing.uncc.edu/

**The University of North Carolina at Greensboro,** Graduate School, School of Nursing, Greensboro, NC 27412-5001. Offers adult clinical nurse specialist (MSN, PMC); adult/gerontological nurse practitioner (MSN, PMC); nurse anesthesia (MSN, PMC); nursing (PhD); nursing administration (MSN); nursing education (MSN); MSN/MBA. *Accreditation:* ACEN. *Degree requirements:* For master's, thesis or alternative. *Entrance requirements:* For master's, GRE General Test or MAT, BSN, clinical experience, liability insurance, RN license; for PMC, liability insurance, MSN, RN license. Additional exam requirements/recommendations for international students: required—TOEFL. Electronic applications accepted.

**University of North Dakota,** Graduate School, College of Nursing and Professional Disciplines, Department of Nursing, Grand Forks, ND 58202. Offers adult-gerontological nurse practitioner (MS); advanced public health nurse (MS); family nurse practitioner (MS); nurse anesthesia (MS); nurse educator (MS); nursing (PhD, Post-Master's Certificate); nursing practice (DNP); psychiatric and mental health nurse practitioner (MS). *Accreditation:* AANA/CANAEP.

**University of North Florida,** Brooks College of Health, School of Nursing, Jacksonville, FL 32224. Offers family nurse practitioner (Certificate); nurse anesthetist (MSN). *Accreditation:* AACN; AANA/CANAEP. *Program availability:* Part-time. *Degree requirements:* For master's, thesis optional. *Entrance requirements:* For master's, GRE General Test, minimum GPA of 3.0 in last 60 hours of course work, BSN, clinical experience, resume; for doctorate, GRE, master's degree in nursing specialty from nationally-accredited program; national certification in one of the following APRN roles: CNE, CNM, CNS, CRNA, CNP; minimum graduate GPA of 3.3; three letters of reference which address academic ability and clinical skills; active license as registered nurse or advanced practice registered nurse. Additional exam requirements/recommendations for international students: required—TOEFL (minimum score 500 paper-based; 61 iBT). Electronic applications accepted. *Expenses:* Contact institution.

**University of Pennsylvania,** School of Nursing, Nurse Anesthesia Program, Philadelphia, PA 19104. Offers MSN. *Accreditation:* AANA/CANAEP. *Program availability:* Online learning. *Students:* 75 full-time (56 women), 4 part-time (all women); includes 31 minority (3 Black or African American, non-Hispanic/Latino; 15 Asian, non-Hispanic/Latino; 9 Hispanic/Latino; 4 Two or more races, non-Hispanic/Latino). Average age 30. 127 applicants, 46% accepted, 31 enrolled. Application fee: $80.

**University of Pittsburgh,** School of Nursing, Nurse Anesthesia Program, Pittsburgh, PA 15260. Offers anesthesia (DNP). *Accreditation:* AACN; AANA/CANAEP. *Faculty:* 4 full-time (1 woman), 2 part-time/adjunct (0 women). *Students:* 65 full-time (44 women), 71 part-time (43 women); includes 18 minority (6 Black or African American, non-Hispanic/Latino; 10 Asian, non-Hispanic/Latino; 2 Hispanic/Latino). Average age 28. 120 applicants, 38% accepted, 41 enrolled. In 2019, 1 doctorate awarded. *Degree requirements:* For doctorate, comprehensive exam, thesis/dissertation or alternative, capstone project required. *Entrance requirements:* For doctorate, GRE, BSN, RN license, course work in statistics, resume/essay, 3 letters of recommendation, clinical experience. Additional exam requirements/recommendations for international students: required—TOEFL (minimum score 600 paper-based; 100 iBT), IELTS (minimum score 7), TOEFL (minimum score 600 paper-based; 100 IBT) or IELTS (minimum score 7.0). Application fee: $50. Electronic applications accepted. *Expenses:* $13,795 per term full-time resident tuition, $475 per term full-time resident fees, $1,122 per credit part-time resident tuition, $295 per term part-time resident fees, $16,474 per term full-time non-resident tuition, $475 per term full-time non-resident fees, $1,345 per credit part-time non-resident tuition, $295 per term part-time non-resident fees. *Financial support:* In 2019–20, 82 students received support, including 1 fellowship (averaging $5,063 per year), 21 teaching assistantships (averaging $9,764 per year); scholarships/grants also available. Financial award application deadline: 6/1; financial award applicants required to submit FAFSA. *Unit head:* John O'Donnell, Director, 412-624-4860, Fax: 412-624-2401, E-mail: jod01@pitt.edu. *Application contact:* Laurie Lapsley, Graduate Administrator, 412-624-9670, Fax: 412-624-2409, E-mail: lapsleyl@pitt.edu.
Website: http://www.nursing.pitt.edu/

**University of Saint Francis,** Graduate School, Division of Nursing, Fort Wayne, IN 46808. Offers family nurse practitioner (MSN, Post Master's Certificate); nurse anesthesia (DNP); nursing practice (DNP). *Accreditation:* AACN. *Program availability:* Part-time, blended/hybrid learning. *Faculty:* 12 full-time (10 women), 3 part-time/adjunct (2 women). *Students:* 67 full-time (45 women), 70 part-time (64 women); includes 22

minority (13 Black or African American, non-Hispanic/Latino; 1 Asian, non-Hispanic/Latino; 7 Hispanic/Latino; 1 Two or more races, non-Hispanic/Latino). Average age 32. 44 applicants, 98% accepted, 34 enrolled. In 2019, 37 master's, 1 other advanced degree awarded. *Entrance requirements:* Additional exam requirements/recommendations for international students: required—TOEFL (minimum score 550 paper-based), IELTS (minimum score 6.5). *Application deadline:* Applications are processed on a rolling basis. Electronic applications accepted. *Expenses:* MSN - $700 per semester hour; DNP - $1,055 per semester hour. *Financial support:* Applicants required to submit FAFSA. *Unit head:* Dr. Wendy Clark, Graduate Nursing Program Director, 260-399-7700 Ext. 8534, E-mail: wclark@sf.edu. *Application contact:* Kyle Richardson, Associate Director of Enrollment Management, 260-399-7700 Ext. 6310, Fax: 260-399-8152, E-mail: krichardson@sf.edu.

**The University of Scranton,** Panuska College of Professional Studies, Department of Nursing, Scranton, PA 18510-4595. Offers family nurse practitioner (MSN, PMC); nurse anesthesia (MSN, PMC); nursing leadership (DNP). *Accreditation:* AACN; AANA/CANAEP. *Program availability:* Part-time, evening/weekend. *Degree requirements:* For master's, comprehensive exam (for some programs), thesis (for some programs), capstone experience. *Entrance requirements:* For master's, minimum GPA of 3.0, three letters of reference; for doctorate, RN licensure and evidence of certification in advanced practice nursing specialty. Additional exam requirements/recommendations for international students: required—TOEFL (minimum score 500 paper-based; 80 iBT), IELTS (minimum score 6.5). Electronic applications accepted.

**University of South Carolina,** School of Medicine and The Graduate School, Graduate Programs in Medicine, Program in Nurse Anesthesia, Columbia, SC 29208. Offers MNA. *Accreditation:* AACN; AANA/CANAEP. *Degree requirements:* For master's, comprehensive exam, practicum. *Entrance requirements:* For master's, GRE, 1 year of critical care experience, RN license. Electronic applications accepted. *Expenses:* Contact institution.

**University of Southern California,** Keck School of Medicine, Doctor of Nurse Anesthesia Practice Program, Los Angeles, CA 90089. Offers anesthesia (DNAP). *Accreditation:* AANA/CANAEP. *Faculty:* 3 full-time (2 women), 11 part-time/adjunct (7 women). *Students:* 39 full-time (26 women); includes 13 minority (9 Asian, non-Hispanic/Latino; 4 Hispanic/Latino). Average age 29. 84 applicants, 32% accepted, 20 enrolled. *Degree requirements:* For doctorate, comprehensive exam, thesis/dissertation, Capstone Scholarly Project. *Entrance requirements:* For doctorate, GRE, interview; minimum GPA of 3.0; minimum of two years of critical care nursing experience in a high acuity setting and shadow experience of CRNAs or anesthesiologists. *Application deadline:* For fall admission, 10/15 for domestic students, 9/15 for international students. Application fee: $75. Electronic applications accepted. *Financial support:* Applicants required to submit FAFSA. *Unit head:* Dr. Jeffrey R. Darna, Director, 323-4422037, E-mail: darna@usc.edu. *Application contact:* Marisela Zuniga, Department Business Administrator, 323-442-1607, Fax: 323-442-1199, E-mail: mzuniga@usc.edu. Website: http://keck.usc.edu/nurse-anesthesia-program/

**University of South Florida,** College of Nursing, Tampa, FL 33612. Offers nurse anesthesia (DNP); nursing (MS, DNP), including adult-gerontology acute care nursing, adult-gerontology primary care nursing, family health nursing, nurse anesthesia (MS), nursing education (MS), occupational health nursing/adult-gerontology primary care nursing, oncology nursing/adult-gerontology primary care nursing (DNP), pediatric health nursing; nursing education (Post Master's Certificate); nursing science (PhD); simulation based academic fellowship in advanced pain management (Graduate Certificate). *Accreditation:* AACN; AANA/CANAEP. *Program availability:* Part-time. *Faculty:* 34 full-time (28 women), 2 part-time/adjunct (1 woman). *Students:* 265 full-time (207 women), 687 part-time (594 women); includes 343 minority (113 Black or African American, non-Hispanic/Latino; 1 American Indian or Alaska Native, non-Hispanic/Latino; 60 Asian, non-Hispanic/Latino; 141 Hispanic/Latino; 1 Native Hawaiian or other Pacific Islander, non-Hispanic/Latino; 27 Two or more races, non-Hispanic/Latino), 2 international. Average age 33. 955 applicants, 44% accepted, 343 enrolled. In 2019, 281 master's, 80 doctorates awarded. *Degree requirements:* For master's, comprehensive exam, thesis optional; for doctorate, comprehensive exam, thesis/dissertation (for some programs). *Entrance requirements:* For master's, GRE General Test, bachelor's in nursing or RN with Bachelor's in relevant field; current license as Registered Nurse; resume or CV; interview; pre-reqs may be required; for doctorate, GRE General Test (recommended), bachelor's degree in nursing from ACEN or CCNE regionally-accredited institution with minimum GPA of 3.0 in all coursework or in all upper-division coursework; current license as Registered Nurse in Florida; undergraduate statistics course with minimum B grade; 3 letters of recommendation; statement of goals; resume; interview. Additional exam requirements/recommendations for international students: required—TOEFL (minimum score 550 paper-based; 79 iBT). *Application deadline:* For fall admission, 12/15 for domestic and international students; for spring admission, 10/1 for domestic students, 9/15 for international students. Application fee: $30. Electronic applications accepted. *Financial support:* In 2019–20, 181 students received support, including 7 research assistantships with tuition reimbursements available (averaging $18,935 per year), 29 teaching assistantships with tuition reimbursements available (averaging $30,814 per year); tuition waivers (partial) and unspecified assistantships also available. Financial award application deadline: 2/1; financial award applicants required to submit FAFSA. *Unit head:* Dr. Victoria Rich, Dean, College of Nursing, 813-974-8939, Fax: 813-974-5418, E-mail: victoriarich@health.usf.edu. *Application contact:* Dr. Denise Maguire, Vice Dean, Graduate Programs, 813-396-9962, E-mail: dmaguire@health.usf.edu. Website: http://health.usf.edu/nursing/index.htm

**The University of Tennessee at Chattanooga,** School of Nursing, Chattanooga, TN 37403. Offers certified nurse anesthetist (Post-Master's Certificate); family nurse practitioner (MSN, Post-Master's Certificate); gerontology acute care (MSN, Post-Master's Certificate); nurse anesthesia (MSN); nurse education (Post-Master's Certificate); nursing (DNP). *Accreditation:* AACN; AANA/CANAEP (one or more programs are accredited). *Program availability:* 100% online. *Faculty:* 32 full-time (29 women), 14 part-time/adjunct (10 women). *Students:* 78 full-time (49 women), 51 part-time (43 women); includes 24 minority (11 Black or African American, non-Hispanic/Latino; 2 American Indian or Alaska Native, non-Hispanic/Latino; 4 Asian, non-Hispanic/Latino; 5 Hispanic/Latino; 2 Two or more races, non-Hispanic/Latino). Average age 34. 50 applicants, 100% accepted, 46 enrolled. In 2019, 38 master's, 16 doctorates, 2 other advanced degrees awarded. *Degree requirements:* For master's, thesis optional, practicum; for doctorate, professional project; for Post-Master's Certificate, practicum. *Entrance requirements:* For master's, GRE General Test, MAT, BSN, minimum GPA of 3.0, eligibility for Tennessee RN license, 1 year of direct patient care experience; for doctorate, GRE General Test or MAT (if applicant does not have MSN), minimum GPA of 3.0 for highest degree earned; for Post-Master's Certificate, GRE General Test, MAT, MSN, minimum GPA of 3.0, eligibility for Tennessee RN license, one year of direct patient care experience. Additional exam requirements/recommendations for international students: required—TOEFL (minimum score 550 paper-based; 79 iBT), IELTS (minimum score 6). *Application deadline:* For fall admission, 6/15 priority date for domestic students, 7/1 for international students; for spring admission, 11/1 priority date for domestic students, 11/1 for international students. Applications are processed on a

rolling basis. Application fee: $35 ($40 for international students). Electronic applications accepted. *Financial support:* Teaching assistantships, career-related internships or fieldwork, and scholarships/grants available. Support available to part-time students. Financial award application deadline: 7/1; financial award applicants required to submit FAFSA. *Unit head:* Dr. Chris Smith, Director, 423-425-4665, Fax: 423-425-4668, E-mail: chris-smith@utc.edu. *Application contact:* Dr. Joanne Romagni, Dean of the Graduate School, 423-425-4478, Fax: 423-425-5223, E-mail: joanne-romagni@utc.edu. Website: http://www.utc.edu/nursing/

**University of Wisconsin–La Crosse,** College of Science and Health, Department of Biology, La Crosse, WI 54601. Offers aquatic sciences (MS); biology (MS); cellular and molecular biology (MS); clinical microbiology (MS); microbiology (MS); nurse anesthesia (MS); physiology (MS). *Accreditation:* AANA/CANAEP. *Program availability:* Part-time. *Faculty:* 19 full-time (7 women). *Students:* 12 full-time (6 women), 39 part-time (15 women); includes 2 minority (1 Black or African American, non-Hispanic/Latino; 1 Asian, non-Hispanic/Latino). Average age 28. 37 applicants, 68% accepted, 19 enrolled. In 2019, 19 master's awarded. *Degree requirements:* For master's, comprehensive exam, thesis. *Entrance requirements:* For master's, GRE General Test, minimum GPA of 2.85. Additional exam requirements/recommendations for international students: required—TOEFL (minimum score 550 paper-based; 79 iBT). *Application deadline:* For fall admission, 2/1 priority date for domestic and international students; for spring admission, 1/4 priority date for domestic and international students. Applications are processed on a rolling basis. Electronic applications accepted. *Financial support:* Research assistantships with partial tuition reimbursements, Federal Work-Study, scholarships/grants, health care benefits, and tuition waivers (partial) available. Support available to part-time students. Financial award application deadline: 3/15; financial award applicants required to submit FAFSA. *Unit head:* Dr. Michael Abler, Department Chair, 608-785-6962, E-mail: mabler@uwlax.edu. *Application contact:* Jennifer Weber, Senior Student Services Coordinator Graduate Admissions, 608-785-8939, E-mail: admissions@uwlax.edu. Website: http://uwlax.edu/biology/

**Villanova University,** M. Louise Fitzpatrick College of Nursing, Villanova, PA 19085. Offers adult-gerontology primary care nurse practitioner (MSN, Post Master's Certificate); family primary care nurse practitioner (MSN, Post Master's Certificate); nurse anesthesia (DNP); nursing (PhD); nursing education (MSN, Post Master's Certificate); nursing practice (DNP); pediatric primary care nurse practitioner (MSN, Post Master's Certificate). *Accreditation:* AACN; AANA/CANAEP. *Program availability:* Part-time, online learning. *Entrance requirements:* Additional exam requirements/recommendations for international students: required—TOEFL, IELTS. Electronic applications accepted.

**Virginia Commonwealth University,** Graduate School, School of Allied Health Professions, Department of Nurse Anesthesia, Richmond, VA 23284-9005. Offers MSNA, DNAP. *Accreditation:* AANA/CANAEP. *Degree requirements:* For master's, thesis. *Entrance requirements:* For master's, GRE General Test, 1 year of experience in acute critical care nursing, current state RN license, minimum GPA of 3.0; for doctorate, GRE General Test, accredited MSNA, CCNA certification, minimum GPA of 3.0. Additional exam requirements/recommendations for international students: required—TOEFL (minimum score 600 paper-based; 100 iBT); recommended—IELTS (minimum score 6.5). Electronic applications accepted.

**Virginia Commonwealth University,** Graduate School, School of Allied Health Professions, Doctoral Program in Health Related Sciences, Richmond, VA 23284-9005. Offers clinical laboratory sciences (PhD); gerontology (PhD); health administration (PhD); nurse anesthesia (PhD); occupational therapy (PhD); physical therapy (PhD); radiation sciences (PhD); rehabilitation leadership (PhD). *Entrance requirements:* For doctorate, GRE General Test or MAT, minimum GPA of 3.3 in master's degree. Additional exam requirements/recommendations for international students: required—TOEFL (minimum score 600 paper-based; 100 iBT); recommended—IELTS (minimum score 6.5). Electronic applications accepted.

**Wake Forest University,** School of Medicine and Graduate School of Arts and Sciences, Graduate Programs in Medicine, Nurse Anesthesia Program, Winston-Salem, NC 27109. Offers MS. *Accreditation:* AANA/CANAEP.

**Wayne State University,** Eugene Applebaum College of Pharmacy and Health Sciences, Department of Health Care Sciences, Detroit, MI 48201. Offers nurse anesthesia (MS, DNP-A, Certificate), including anesthesia (MS), nurse anesthesia practice (DNP-A), pediatric anesthesia (Certificate); occupational therapy (MOT); physical therapy (DPT); physician assistant studies (MS). *Faculty:* 5. *Students:* 310 full-time (209 women), 4 part-time (all women); includes 33 minority (7 Black or African American, non-Hispanic/Latino; 14 Asian, non-Hispanic/Latino; 8 Hispanic/Latino; 4 Two or more races, non-Hispanic/Latino), 4 international. Average age 26. 344 applicants, 20% accepted, 55 enrolled. In 2019, 97 master's, 36 doctorates awarded. *Entrance requirements:* Additional exam requirements/recommendations for international students: required—TOEFL (minimum score 550 paper-based; 79 iBT), Michigan English Language Assessment Battery (minimum score 85); recommended—IELTS (minimum score 6.5), TWE (minimum score 5.5). Application fee: $50. Electronic applications accepted. *Expenses:* Contact institution. *Financial support:* In 2019–20, 102 students received support. Fellowships and scholarships/grants available. Financial award applicants required to submit FAFSA. *Unit head:* Dr. Sara F Maher, Chair Department of Health Care Sciences, 313-577-5630, E-mail: sara.maher@wayne.edu. *Application contact:* Office of Student and Alumni Affairs, 313-577-1716, E-mail: cphsinfo@wayne.edu. Website: http://cphs.wayne.edu/hcs/

**Webster University,** College of Arts and Sciences, Department of Nurse Anesthesia, St. Louis, MO 63119-3194. Offers DNAP. *Accreditation:* AANA/CANAEP. *Program availability:* Online learning. *Entrance requirements:* Additional exam requirements/recommendations for international students: required—TOEFL.

**Westminster College,** School of Nursing and Health Sciences, Salt Lake City, UT 84105-3697. Offers family nurse practitioner (MSN); nurse anesthesia (MSNA); public health (MPH). *Accreditation:* AACN; AANA/CANAEP; CEPH. *Degree requirements:* For master's, clinical practicum, 504 clinical practice hours. *Entrance requirements:* For master's, GRE (can be waived in select cases), personal statement, resume, 3 professional recommendations, copy of unrestricted Utah license to practice professional nursing, background check, minimum cumulative GPA of 3.0, documentation of current immunizations, physical and mental health certificate signed by primary care provider. Additional exam requirements/recommendations for international students: required—TOEFL (minimum score 84 iBT), IELTS (minimum score 7). Electronic applications accepted. *Expenses:* Contact institution.

**York College of Pennsylvania,** The Stabler Department of Nursing, York, PA 17403-3651. Offers adult gerontology clinical nurse specialist (MS); nurse anesthetist (MS). *Accreditation:* AACN; AANA/CANAEP. *Program availability:* Part-time. *Faculty:* 6 full-time (all women), 5 part-time/adjunct (4 women). *Students:* 30 full-time (15 women), 36 part-time (30 women); includes 9 minority (1 Black or African American, non-Hispanic/Latino; 6 Asian, non-Hispanic/Latino; 1 Hispanic/Latino; 1 Two or more races, non-Hispanic/Latino), 1 international. Average age 34. 61 applicants, 46% accepted, 23

enrolled. In 2019, 24 master's awarded. *Entrance requirements:* For master's, bachelor's degree in nursing, minimum GPA of 3.0. Additional exam requirements/recommendations for international students: required—TOEFL (minimum score 530 paper-based; 72 iBT), IELTS. Electronic applications accepted. *Expenses:* Master's Programs (other than Psych/Mental Health NP): $820 per credit tuition; Master's Program, Psych/Mental Health NP: $775 per credit tuition; DNP Programs: $960 per credit tuition, $880 general fee. *Financial support:* In 2019–20, 1 student received support. Scholarships/grants available. Financial award applicants required to submit FAFSA. *Unit head:* Colleen Marshall-Fantaski, Director, Graduate Programs in Nursing, 717-815-1791, Fax: 717-849-1651, E-mail: cfantaski@ycp.edu. *Application contact:* Allison Malachosky, Administrative Assistant, 717-815-2290, Fax: 717-849-1651, E-mail: amalacho@ycp.edu.
Website: http://www.ycp.edu/academics/academic-departments/nursing/

# Nurse Midwifery

**Bastyr University,** School of Natural Health Arts and Sciences, Kenmore, WA 98028-4966. Offers counseling psychology (MA); maternal-child health systems (MA); midwifery (MS); nutrition (Certificate); nutrition and clinical health psychology (MS); nutrition and wellness (MS). *Accreditation:* AND; MEAC. *Program availability:* Part-time. *Degree requirements:* For master's, thesis optional. *Entrance requirements:* For master's, 1-2 years' basic sciences course work (depending on program). Additional exam requirements/recommendations for international students: required—TOEFL (minimum score 550 paper-based; 79 iBT).

**Bethel University,** Graduate School, St. Paul, MN 55112-6999. Offers business administration (MBA); classroom management (Certificate); counseling (MA); K-12 education (MA); leadership (Ed D); leadership foundations (Certificate); nurse educator (MS, Certificate); nurse-midwifery (MS); physician assistant (MS); special education (MA); strategic leadership (MA); teaching (MA); teaching and learning (Certificate). *Program availability:* Part-time, evening/weekend, 100% online, blended/hybrid learning. *Faculty:* 36 full-time (24 women), 112 part-time/adjunct (73 women). *Students:* 428 full-time (318 women), 825 part-time (482 women); includes 245 minority (95 Black or African American, non-Hispanic/Latino; 13 American Indian or Alaska Native, non-Hispanic/Latino; 52 Asian, non-Hispanic/Latino; 50 Hispanic/Latino; 2 Native Hawaiian or other Pacific Islander, non-Hispanic/Latino; 33 Two or more races, non-Hispanic/Latino), 28 international. Average age 38. 810 applicants, 45% accepted, 256 enrolled. In 2019, 320 master's, 34 doctorates, 112 other advanced degrees awarded. *Degree requirements:* For master's, comprehensive exam (for some programs), thesis (for some programs); for doctorate, comprehensive exam, thesis/dissertation. *Entrance requirements:* Additional exam requirements/recommendations for international students: required—TOEFL (minimum score 550 paper-based; 80 iBT), TOEFL (minimum score 550 paper-based, 80 iBT) or IELTS. *Application deadline:* Applications are processed on a rolling basis. Electronic applications accepted. *Expenses:* $420-$850/credit dependent on the program. *Financial support:* Teaching assistantships, career-related internships or fieldwork, and scholarships/grants available. Support available to part-time students. Financial award applicants required to submit FAFSA. *Unit head:* Dr. Randy Bergen, Associate Provost, 651-635-8000, Fax: 651-635-8004, E-mail: r-bergen@bethel.edu. *Application contact:* Director of Admissions, 651-635-8000, Fax: 651-635-8004, E-mail: gs@bethel.edu.
Website: https://www.bethel.edu/graduate/

**Case Western Reserve University,** Frances Payne Bolton School of Nursing, Master's Programs in Nursing, Cleveland, OH 44106. Offers nurse anesthesia (MSN); nurse education (MSN); nurse midwifery (MSN); nurse practitioner (MSN), including acute care/cardiovascular nursing, adult gerontology nurse practitioner, palliative care; nursing (MN). *Accreditation:* ACEN. *Program availability:* Part-time. *Faculty:* 40 full-time (36 women), 8 part-time/adjunct (7 women). *Students:* 160 full-time (131 women), 141 part-time (108 women); includes 72 minority (26 Black or African American, non-Hispanic/Latino; 22 Asian, non-Hispanic/Latino; 16 Hispanic/Latino; 8 Two or more races, non-Hispanic/Latino), 13 international. Average age 29. 273 applicants, 64% accepted, 100 enrolled. In 2019, 122 master's awarded. *Degree requirements:* For master's, thesis optional, minimum GPA of 3.0, Typhon log of clinical hours corresponding to requirements to sit for certification exam. *Entrance requirements:* For master's, GRE/MAT (scores not required for application, but may be requested for an admission decision), CCRN certification and 2 years ICU experience (for nurse anesthesia). Additional exam requirements/recommendations for international students: required—TOEFL (minimum score 577 paper-based; 90 iBT), IELTS (minimum score 7). *Application deadline:* For fall admission, 3/1 for domestic and international students; for spring admission, 10/1 for domestic and international students; for summer admission, 3/1 for domestic and international students. Applications are processed on a rolling basis. Application fee: $75. Electronic applications accepted. *Expenses:* MSN $2,133 per credit hour; MN $25,596 per semester; Lab fee $215; NCLEX $300; ACEMAPP $50; Clinical placement $75; Activity fee $15; Graduate Council fee $15. *Financial support:* In 2019–20, 126 students received support, including 49 teaching assistantships with partial tuition reimbursements available (averaging $19,197 per year); scholarships/grants and traineeships also available. Financial award application deadline: 5/15; financial award applicants required to submit FAFSA. *Unit head:* Dr. Latina Brooks, Director, 216-368-1196, Fax: 216-368-3542, E-mail: lmb3@case.edu. *Application contact:* Jackie Tepale, Admissions Coordinator, 216-368-5253, Fax: 216-368-3542, E-mail: yyd@case.edu.
Website: https://case.edu/nursing/programs/msn

**Case Western Reserve University,** Frances Payne Bolton School of Nursing, Master's Programs in Nursing, Program in Nurse Midwifery, Cleveland, OH 44106. Offers nurse midwifery (MSN). *Accreditation:* ACNM/ACME. *Program availability:* Part-time. *Faculty:* 14 full-time (13 women), 3 part-time/adjunct (all women). *Students:* 3 full-time (all women), 13 part-time (all women); includes 5 minority (4 Black or African American, non-Hispanic/Latino; 1 Two or more races, non-Hispanic/Latino). Average age 29. 6 applicants, 83% accepted, 4 enrolled. In 2019, 4 master's awarded. *Degree requirements:* For master's, minimum GPA of 3.0, cases/competencies clinical hours corresponding to requirements to sit for certification exam, portfolio. *Entrance requirements:* For master's, GRE/MAT (scores not required for application, but may be requested for an admission decision). Additional exam requirements/recommendations for international students: required—TOEFL (minimum score 577 paper-based; 90 iBT), IELTS (minimum score 7). *Application deadline:* For fall admission, 3/15 for domestic and international students; for spring admission, 10/1 for domestic and international students; for summer admission, 3/15 for domestic and international students. Applications are processed on a rolling basis. Application fee: $75. Electronic applications accepted. *Expenses:* Clinical placement fee $75; Activity fee $15 per semester; Student council fee $15 per semester; Tuition rate $2,133 per credit hour. *Financial support:* In 2019–20, 4 students received support, including 2 teaching assistantships with partial tuition reimbursements available (averaging $19,197 per year); scholarships/grants also available. Financial award application deadline: 5/15; financial award applicants required to submit FAFSA. *Unit head:* Dr. Mary Franklin, Director, 216-368-3198, Fax: 216-368-3542, E-mail: mrf19@case.edu. *Application contact:* Jackie Tepale, Admissions Coordinator, 216-368-5253, Fax: 216-368-3542, E-mail: yyd@case.edu.
Website: https://case.edu/nursing/programs/msn/msn-majors/nurse-midwifery-program-cnm

**Columbia University,** School of Nursing, Program in Nurse Midwifery, New York, NY 10032. Offers MS. *Accreditation:* AACN; ACNM/ACME. *Program availability:* Part-time. *Entrance requirements:* For master's, GRE General Test, NCLEX, BSN, 1 year of clinical experience (preferred). Additional exam requirements/recommendations for international students: required—TOEFL (minimum score 100 iBT). Electronic applications accepted. *Expenses: Tuition:* Full-time $47,600; part-time $1880 per credit. One-time fee: $105.

**DeSales University,** Division of Healthcare, Center Valley, PA 18034-9568. Offers adult-gerontology acute care (Post Master's Certificate); adult-gerontology acute care nurse practitioner (MSN); adult-gerontology acute certified nurse practitioner (Post Master's Certificate); adult-gerontology clinical nurse specialist (MSN, Post Master's Certificate); clinical leadership (DNP); family nurse practitioner (MSN, Post Master's Certificate); general nursing practice (DNP); nurse anesthetist (MSN); nurse educator (Post Master's Certificate, Postbaccalaureate Certificate); nurse midwife (MSN); nurse practitioner (MSN); psychiatric-mental health nurse practitioner (MSN, Post Master's Certificate); DNP/MBA. *Accreditation:* ACEN. *Program availability:* Part-time. *Faculty:* 31 full-time (23 women), 12 part-time/adjunct (9 women). *Students:* 294 full-time (219 women), 128 part-time (109 women); includes 71 minority (20 Black or African American, non-Hispanic/Latino; 1 American Indian or Alaska Native, non-Hispanic/Latino; 15 Asian, non-Hispanic/Latino; 30 Hispanic/Latino; 5 Two or more races, non-Hispanic/Latino). Average age 28. 2,666 applicants, 6% accepted, 142 enrolled. In 2019, 115 master's, 30 doctorates awarded. *Degree requirements:* For master's, minimum GPA of 3.0, portfolio; for doctorate, minimum GPA of 3.0, scholarly capstone project. *Entrance requirements:* For master's, GRE or MAT (waived if applicant has an undergraduate GPA of 3.0 or higher), BSN from ACEN- or CCNE-accredited program, minimum undergraduate GPA of 3.0, active RN license or eligibility, two letters of recommendation, essay, health care experience, personal interview; for doctorate, BSN or MSN from ACEN- or CCNE-accredited institution, minimum GPA of 3.3 in graduate program, current licensure as an RN. Additional exam requirements/recommendations for international students: required—TOEFL (minimum score 104 iBT). *Application deadline:* Applications are processed on a rolling basis. Application fee: $50. Electronic applications accepted. *Expenses:* Contact institution. *Financial support:* Applicants required to submit FAFSA. *Unit head:* Ronald Nordone, Dean of Graduate Education, 610-282-1100 Ext. 1289, E-mail: ronald.nordone@desales.edu. *Application contact:* Julia Ferraro, Director of Graduate Admissions, 610-282-1100 Ext. 1768, E-mail: gradadmissions@desales.edu.

**Emory University,** Nell Hodgson Woodruff School of Nursing, Atlanta, GA 30322-1100. Offers adult nurse practitioner (MSN); emergency nurse practitioner (MSN); family nurse practitioner (MSN); family nurse-midwife (MSN); health systems leadership (MSN); nurse-midwifery (MSN); pediatric nurse practitioner acute and primary care (MSN); women's health care (Title X) (MSN); women's health nurse practitioner (MSN); MSN/MPH. *Accreditation:* AACN; ACNM/ACME (one or more programs are accredited). *Program availability:* Part-time. *Entrance requirements:* For master's, GRE General Test or MAT, minimum GPA of 3.0, BS in nursing from an accredited institution, RN license and additional course work, 3 letters of recommendation. Additional exam requirements/recommendations for international students: required—TOEFL (minimum score 600 paper-based; 100 iBT). Electronic applications accepted. *Expenses:* Contact institution.

**Georgetown University,** Graduate School of Arts and Sciences, School of Nursing and Health Studies, Washington, DC 20057. Offers acute care nurse practitioner (MS); clinical nurse specialist (MS); family nurse practitioner (MS); health systems administration (MS); nurse anesthesia (MS); nurse-midwifery (MS); nursing (DNP); nursing education (MS). *Accreditation:* AACN; AANA/CANAEP (one or more programs are accredited); ACNM/ACME (one or more programs are accredited). *Degree requirements:* For master's, thesis optional. *Entrance requirements:* For master's, GRE General Test or MAT, bachelor's degree in nursing from ACEN-accredited school, minimum undergraduate GPA of 3.0. Additional exam requirements/recommendations for international students: required—TOEFL.

**James Madison University,** The Graduate School, College of Health and Behavioral Studies, Program in Nursing, Harrisonburg, VA 22807. Offers adult/gerontology primary care nurse practitioner (MSN); clinical nurse leader (MSN); family nurse practitioner (MSN); nurse administrator (MSN); nurse midwifery (MSN); nursing (MSN, DNP); psychiatric mental health nurse practitioner (MSN). *Accreditation:* AACN. *Program availability:* Part-time, 100% online, blended/hybrid learning. *Students:* 15 full-time (14 women), 71 part-time (66 women); includes 10 minority (3 Black or African American, non-Hispanic/Latino; 6 Asian, non-Hispanic/Latino; 1 Hispanic/Latino). Average age 30. In 2019, 28 master's awarded. Application fee: $60. Electronic applications accepted. *Financial support:* In 2019–20, 2 students received support. Federal Work-Study and assistantships (averaging $7911) available. Financial award application deadline: 3/1; financial award applicants required to submit FAFSA. *Unit head:* Dr. Julie T. Sanford, Department Head, 540-568-6314, E-mail: sanforjt@jmu.edu. *Application contact:* Lynette D. Michael, Director of Graduate Admissions, 540-568-6131 Ext. 6395, Fax: 540-568-7860, E-mail: michaeld@jmu.edu.
Website: http://www.nursing.jmu.edu

**Marquette University,** Graduate School, College of Nursing, Milwaukee, WI 53201-1881. Offers acute care nurse practitioner (Certificate); adult clinical nurse specialist (Certificate); adult nurse practitioner (Certificate); advanced practice nursing (MSN, DNP), including adult-older adult acute care (DNP), adults (MSN), adults-older adults (DNP), clinical nurse leader (MSN), health care systems leadership (DNP), nurse-midwifery (MSN), older adults (MSN), pediatrics-acute care, pediatrics-primary care, primary care (DNP), systems leadership and healthcare quality (MSN); family nurse practitioner (Certificate); nurse-midwifery (Certificate); nursing (PhD); pediatric acute care (Certificate); pediatric primary care (Certificate); systems leadership and healthcare

quality (Certificate). *Accreditation:* AACN; AANA/CANAEP; ACNM/ACME. Terminal master's awarded for partial completion of doctoral program. *Degree requirements:* For master's, comprehensive exam, thesis or alternative. *Entrance requirements:* For master's, GRE General Test, BSN, Wisconsin RN license, official transcripts from all current and previous colleges/universities except Marquette, three completed recommendation forms, resume, written statement of professional goals; for doctorate, GRE General Test, official transcripts from all current and previous colleges/universities except Marquette, three letters of recommendation, resume, written statement of professional goals, sample of scholarly writing. Additional exam requirements/recommendations for international students: required—TOEFL (minimum score 530 paper-based). Electronic applications accepted.

**Midwives College of Utah,** Graduate Program, Salt Lake City, UT 84106. Offers MS. *Accreditation:* MEAC. *Program availability:* Part-time. *Degree requirements:* For master's, comprehensive exam, thesis. *Entrance requirements:* Additional exam requirements/recommendations for international students: required—TOEFL (minimum score 88 iBT). Electronic applications accepted.

**National College of Midwifery,** Graduate Programs, Taos, NM 87571. Offers MS, PhD. *Accreditation:* MEAC. *Program availability:* Part-time, evening/weekend, online learning. *Degree requirements:* For master's, thesis, publication; for doctorate, thesis/dissertation, presentation, publication. *Entrance requirements:* For master's and doctorate, midwifery license or certification. Electronic applications accepted.

**New York University,** Rory Meyers College of Nursing, Doctor of Nursing Practice Program, New York, NY 10012-1019. Offers nursing (DNP), including adult-gerontology acute care nurse practitioner, adult-gerontology primary care nurse practitioner, family nurse practitioner, nurse-midwifery, pediatrics nurse practitioner, psychiatric-mental health nurse practitioner. *Accreditation:* AACN. *Program availability:* Part-time, evening/weekend. *Degree requirements:* For doctorate, thesis/dissertation, project. *Entrance requirements:* For doctorate, MS, RN license, interview, Nurse Practitioner Certification, writing sample. Additional exam requirements/recommendations for international students: required—TOEFL (minimum score 100 iBT), IELTS (minimum score 7). Electronic applications accepted. *Expenses:* Contact institution.

**New York University,** Rory Meyers College of Nursing, Programs in Advanced Practice Nursing, New York, NY 10012-1019. Offers adult-gerontology acute care nurse practitioner (MS, Advanced Certificate); adult-gerontology primary care nurse practitioner (MS, Advanced Certificate); family nurse practitioner (MS, Advanced Certificate); gerontology nurse practitioner (Advanced Certificate); nurse-midwifery (MS, Advanced Certificate); nursing administration (MS, Advanced Certificate); nursing education (MS, Advanced Certificate); nursing informatics (MS, Advanced Certificate); pediatrics nurse practitioner (MS, Advanced Certificate); psychiatric-mental health nurse practitioner (MS, Advanced Certificate); MS/MPH. *Accreditation:* AACN; ACNM/ACME. *Program availability:* Part-time, evening/weekend. *Degree requirements:* For master's, thesis (for some programs), capstone. *Entrance requirements:* For master's, BS in nursing, AS in nursing with another BS/BA, interview, RN license, 1 year of clinical experience (3 for the MS in nursing education program); for Advanced Certificate, master's degree in nursing. Additional exam requirements/recommendations for international students: required—TOEFL (minimum score 100 iBT), IELTS (minimum score 7). Electronic applications accepted. *Expenses:* Contact institution.

**Oregon Health & Science University,** School of Nursing, Program in Nurse Midwifery, Portland, OR 97239-3098. Offers MN. *Accreditation:* AACN; ACNM/ACME. *Degree requirements:* For master's, thesis optional. *Entrance requirements:* For master's, GRE General Test, minimum cumulative and science GPA of 3.0, 3 letters of recommendation, essay, statistics in last 5 years with minimum B- grade, BS with major in nursing or BSN. Additional exam requirements/recommendations for international students: required—TOEFL (minimum score 83 iBT). Electronic applications accepted. *Expenses:* Contact institution.

**Shenandoah University,** Eleanor Wade Custer School of Nursing, Winchester, VA 22601. Offers adult gerontology primary care nurse practitioner (Graduate Certificate); adult-gerontology primary care nurse practitioner (MSN); family nurse practitioner (MSN, DNP, Graduate Certificate); general (MSN); health systems leadership (DNP); health systems management (MSN, Graduate Certificate); nurse midwifery (MSN); nurse-midwifery (Graduate Certificate); nursing education (Graduate Certificate); nursing practice (DNP); psychiatric mental health nurse practitioner (MSN, DNP, Graduate Certificate). *Accreditation:* AACN; ACNM/ACME. *Entrance requirements:* For master's, United States RN license; minimum GPA of 3.0; 2080 hours of clinical experience; curriculum vitae; 3 letters of recommendation from former dean, faculty member, or advisor familiar with the applicant, and a former or current supervisor; two-to-three-page essay on a specified topic; for doctorate, MSN, minimum GPA of 3.0, 3 letters of recommendation, interview, BSN, two-to-three page essay on a specific topic, 500-word statement of clinical practice research interest, resume, current U.S. RN license, 2080 clinical hours; for Graduate Certificate, MSN, minimum GPA of 3.0, 2 letters of recommendation, minimum of one year (2080 hours) of clinical nursing experience, interview, two-to-three page essay on a specific topic, resume, current United States RN license. Additional exam requirements/recommendations for international students: required—TOEFL (minimum score 558 paper-based; 83 iBT). Electronic applications accepted. *Expenses:* Contact institution.

**State University of New York Downstate Medical Center,** College of Nursing, Graduate Programs in Nursing, Program in Nurse Midwifery, Brooklyn, NY 11203-2098. Offers MS, Post Master's Certificate. *Accreditation:* ACNM/ACME.

**Stony Brook University, State University of New York,** Stony Brook Medicine, School of Nursing, Program in Nurse Midwifery, Stony Brook, NY 11794. Offers MS, DNP, Certificate. *Accreditation:* AACN; ACNM/ACME. *Program availability:* Part-time, blended/hybrid learning. *Students:* 24 part-time (all women); includes 9 minority (5 Black or African American, non-Hispanic/Latino; 1 Asian, non-Hispanic/Latino; 1 Hispanic/Latino; 2 Two or more races, non-Hispanic/Latino). 32 applicants, 56% accepted, 11 enrolled. In 2019, 9 master's, 1 doctorate, 1 other advanced degree awarded. *Entrance requirements:* For master's, BSN, minimum GPA of 3.0, course work in statistics. Additional exam requirements/recommendations for international students: required—TOEFL (minimum score 90 iBT). *Application deadline:* For fall admission, 2/27 for domestic students. Application fee: $100. *Expenses:* Contact institution. *Financial support:* Fellowships, research assistantships, and teaching assistantships available. Financial award application deadline: 3/15. *Unit head:* Heather Findletar-Hines, Program Director, 631-444-1491, Fax: 631-444-3136, E-mail: heather.finlander@stonybrook.edu. *Application contact:* Linda Sacino, Staff Assistant, 631-632-3262, Fax: 631-444-3136, E-mail: cnm.nursing@stonybrook.edu. Website: http://www.nursing.stonybrookmedicine.edu/

**Thomas Jefferson University,** Jefferson College of Health Professions, Program in Midwifery, Philadelphia, PA 19107. Offers MS. *Accreditation:* ACNM/ACME. *Program availability:* Part-time, evening/weekend, online learning. *Entrance requirements:* For master's, GRE or MAT. Additional exam requirements/recommendations for international students: required—TOEFL (minimum score 550 paper-based; 79 iBT). Electronic applications accepted.

**University of Cincinnati,** Graduate School, College of Nursing, Cincinnati, OH 45221-0038. Offers nurse midwifery (MSN); nurse practitioner (MSN, DNP), including acute care pediatrics (DNP), adult-gerontology acute care, adult-gerontology primary care, anesthesia (DNP), family (MSN), leadership (DNP), neonatal (MSN), women's health (MSN); nursing (MSN, PhD), including occupational health (MSN). *Accreditation:* AACN; AANA/CANAEP (one or more programs are accredited); ACNM/ACME. *Program availability:* Part-time, 100% online, blended/hybrid learning. *Faculty:* 62 full-time (55 women), 125 part-time/adjunct (114 women). *Students:* 429 full-time (355 women), 1,547 part-time (1,390 women); includes 453 minority (226 Black or African American, non-Hispanic/Latino; 5 American Indian or Alaska Native, non-Hispanic/Latino; 68 Asian, non-Hispanic/Latino; 103 Hispanic/Latino; 3 Native Hawaiian or other Pacific Islander, non-Hispanic/Latino; 48 Two or more races, non-Hispanic/Latino), 15 international. Average age 36. 779 applicants, 78% accepted, 464 enrolled. In 2019, 518 master's, 47 doctorates awarded. *Degree requirements:* For master's, thesis or alternative; for doctorate, comprehensive exam (for some programs), thesis/dissertation (for some programs). *Entrance requirements:* For master's, GRE required only for the Direct-Entry Accelerated Program. Additional exam requirements/recommendations for international students: required—TOEFL (minimum score 600 paper-based; 100 iBT); recommended—IELTS (minimum score 7). *Application deadline:* For fall admission, 4/1 priority date for domestic and international students; for spring admission, 9/1 priority date for domestic and international students; for summer admission, 2/1 priority date for domestic and international students. Applications are processed on a rolling basis. Application fee: $135 ($140 for international students). Electronic applications accepted. *Expenses:* Contact institution. *Financial support:* In 2019–20, 103 students received support, including 9 fellowships with full tuition reimbursements available (averaging $18,595 per year), 7 research assistantships with full tuition reimbursements available (averaging $12,991 per year), 8 teaching assistantships with full tuition reimbursements available (averaging $12,991 per year); institutionally sponsored loans, scholarships/grants, traineeships, health care benefits, tuition waivers (partial), and unspecified assistantships also available. Support available to part-time students. Financial award application deadline: 4/1; financial award applicants required to submit FAFSA. *Unit head:* Dr. Greer Glazer, Dean, 513-558-5330, Fax: 513-558-9030, E-mail: greer.glazer@uc.edu. *Application contact:* Office of Student Affairs, 513-558-8400, E-mail: nursingbearcats@uc.edu. Website: https://nursing.uc.edu/

**University of Colorado Denver,** College of Nursing, Aurora, CO 80045. Offers adult clinical nurse specialist (MS); adult nurse practitioner (MS); family nurse practitioner (MS); family psychiatric mental health nurse practitioner (MS); health care informatics (MS); nurse-midwifery (MS); nursing (DNP, PhD); nursing leadership and health care systems (MS); pediatric nurse practitioner (MS); women's health (MS); MS/PhD. *Accreditation:* ACNM/ACME (one or more programs are accredited). *Program availability:* Part-time, evening/weekend, online learning. Terminal master's awarded for partial completion of doctoral program. *Degree requirements:* For master's, thesis optional; for doctorate, comprehensive exam, thesis/dissertation, 42 credits of coursework. *Entrance requirements:* For master's, GRE if cumulative undergraduate GPA is less than 3.0, undergraduate nursing degree from ACEN- or CCNE-accredited school or university; completion of research and statistics courses with minimum grade of C; copy of current and unencumbered nursing license; for doctorate, GRE, bachelor's and/or master's degrees in nursing from ACEN- or CCNE-accredited institution; portfolio; minimum undergraduate GPA of 3.0, graduate 3.5; graduate-level intermediate statistics and master's-level nursing theory courses with minimum B grade; interview. Additional exam requirements/recommendations for international students: required—TOEFL (minimum score 560 paper-based; 83 iBT). Electronic applications accepted. *Expenses:* Contact institution.

**University of Illinois at Chicago,** College of Nursing, Program in Nursing, Chicago, IL 60607-7128. Offers acute care clinical nurse specialist (MS); administrative nursing leadership (Certificate); adult nurse practitioner (MS); adult/geriatric nurse practitioner (MS); advanced community health nurse specialist (MS); family nurse practitioner (MS); geriatric clinical nurse specialist (MS); geriatric nurse practitioner (MS); nurse midwifery (MS); occupational health/advanced community health nurse specialist (MS); occupational health/family nurse practitioner (MS); pediatric nurse practitioner (MS); perinatal clinical nurse specialist (MS); school/advanced community health nurse specialist (MS); school/family nurse practitioner (MS); women's health nurse practitioner (MS). *Accreditation:* AACN. *Program availability:* Part-time. *Degree requirements:* For master's, thesis or alternative. *Entrance requirements:* For master's, GRE General Test, minimum GPA of 2.75. Additional exam requirements/recommendations for international students: required—TOEFL. Electronic applications accepted.

**University of Indianapolis,** Graduate Programs, School of Nursing, Indianapolis, IN 46227-3697. Offers advanced practice nursing (DNP); family nurse practitioner (MSN); gerontological nurse practitioner (MSN); neonatal nurse practitioner (MSN); nurse-midwifery (MSN); nursing (MSN); nursing and health systems leadership (MSN); nursing education (MSN); women's health nurse practitioner (MSN); MBA/MSN. *Accreditation:* AACN. *Entrance requirements:* For master's, minimum GPA of 3.0, interview, letters of recommendation, resume, IN nursing license, 1 year of professional practice; for doctorate, graduate of ACEN- or CCNE-accredited nursing program; MSN or MA with nursing major and minimum cumulative GPA of 3.25; unencumbered RN license with eligibility for licensure in Indiana; completion of graduate-level statistics course within last 5 years with minimum grade of B; resume; essay; official transcripts from all academic institutions. Additional exam requirements/recommendations for international students: required—TOEFL (minimum score 550 paper-based). Electronic applications accepted.

**The University of Kansas,** University of Kansas Medical Center, School of Nursing, Kansas City, KS 66045. Offers adult/gerontological clinical nurse specialist (PMC); adult/gerontological nurse practitioner (PMC); health care informatics (PMC); health professions educator (PMC); nurse midwife (PMC); nursing (MS, DNP, PhD); organizational leadership (PMC); psychiatric/mental health nurse practitioner (PMC); public health nursing (PMC). *Accreditation:* AACN; ACNM/ACME. *Program availability:* Part-time, 100% online, blended/hybrid learning. *Faculty:* 65. *Students:* 57 full-time (53 women), 267 part-time (242 women); includes 65 minority (14 Black or African American, non-Hispanic/Latino; 2 American Indian or Alaska Native, non-Hispanic/Latino; 21 Asian, non-Hispanic/Latino; 9 Hispanic/Latino; 1 Native Hawaiian or other Pacific Islander, non-Hispanic/Latino; 18 Two or more races, non-Hispanic/Latino), 2 international. Average age 35. In 2019, 26 master's, 48 doctorates, 5 other advanced degrees awarded. Terminal master's awarded for partial completion of doctoral program. *Degree requirements:* For master's, comprehensive exam, thesis (for some programs), general oral exam; for doctorate, thesis/dissertation or alternative, comprehensive oral exam (for DNP); comprehensive written and oral exam, or three publications (for PhD). *Entrance requirements:* For master's, bachelor's degree in nursing, minimum GPA of 3.0, 1 year of clinical experience, RN license in KS and MO; for doctorate, GRE General Test (for PhD only), bachelor's degree in nursing, minimum GPA of 3.5, RN license in KS and MO. Additional exam requirements/recommendations for international students: required—TOEFL. *Application deadline:* For fall admission, 4/1 for domestic and international students; for spring admission, 9/1 for domestic and international students. Application fee: $75. Electronic applications accepted. *Expenses:*

*Nurse Midwifery*

Contact institution. *Financial support:* Research assistantships with tuition reimbursements, teaching assistantships with tuition reimbursements, scholarships/grants, and traineeships available. Financial award application deadline: 3/1; financial award applicants required to submit FAFSA. *Unit head:* Dr. Sally Maliski, Professor and Dean, 913-588-1601, Fax: 913-588-1660, E-mail: smaliski@kumc.edu. *Application contact:* Dr. Pamela K. Barnes, Associate Dean, Student Affairs and Enrollment Management, 913-588-1619, Fax: 913-588-1615, E-mail: pbarnes2@kumc.edu.
Website: http://nursing.kumc.edu

**The University of Manchester,** School of Nursing, Midwifery and Social Work, Manchester, United Kingdom. Offers nursing (M Phil, PhD); social work (M Phil, PhD).

**University of Miami,** Graduate School, School of Nursing and Health Studies, Coral Gables, FL 33124. Offers acute care (MSN), including acute care nurse practitioner, nurse anesthesia; nursing (PhD); primary care (MSN), including adult nurse practitioner, family nurse practitioner, nurse midwifery, women's health practitioner. *Accreditation:* AACN; AANA/CANAEP; ACNM/ACME (one or more programs are accredited). *Program availability:* Part-time. *Degree requirements:* For master's, thesis optional; for doctorate, thesis/dissertation. *Entrance requirements:* For master's, GRE General Test, BSN, minimum GPA of 3.0, Florida RN license; for doctorate, GRE General Test, BSN or MSN, minimum GPA of 3.0. Additional exam requirements/recommendations for international students: required—TOEFL (minimum score 550 paper-based). Electronic applications accepted.

**University of Minnesota, Twin Cities Campus,** Graduate School, School of Nursing, Minneapolis, MN 55455-0213. Offers adult/gerontological clinical nurse specialist (DNP); adult/gerontological primary care nurse practitioner (DNP); family nurse practitioner (DNP); health innovation and leadership (DNP); integrative health and healing (DNP); nurse anesthesia (DNP); nurse midwifery (DNP); nursing (MN, PhD); nursing informatics (DNP); pediatric clinical nurse specialist (DNP); primary care certified pediatric nurse practitioner (DNP); psychiatric/mental health nurse practitioner (DNP); women's health nurse practitioner (DNP). *Accreditation:* AACN; AANA/CANAEP; ACNM/ACME (one or more programs are accredited). *Program availability:* Part-time, online learning. Terminal master's awarded for partial completion of doctoral program. *Degree requirements:* For master's, final oral exam, project or thesis; for doctorate, thesis/dissertation. *Entrance requirements:* For master's and doctorate, GRE General Test. Additional exam requirements/recommendations for international students: required—TOEFL (minimum score 586 paper-based). *Expenses:* Contact institution.

**University of Pennsylvania,** School of Nursing, Program in Nurse Midwifery, Philadelphia, PA 19104. Offers MSN. *Accreditation:* AACN; ACNM/ACME. *Program availability:* Part-time. *Students:* 26 full-time (all women), 14 part-time (all women); includes 12 minority (4 Black or African American, non-Hispanic/Latino; 3 Asian, non-Hispanic/Latino; 4 Hispanic/Latino; 1 Two or more races, non-Hispanic/Latino). Average age 29. 22 applicants, 23% accepted, 4 enrolled. In 2019, 23 master's awarded. Application fee: $80.

**University of Pittsburgh,** School of Nursing, Nurse-Midwife Program, Pittsburgh, PA 15260. Offers nurse midwife (DNP). *Accreditation:* ACNM/ACME. *Program availability:* Part-time. *Faculty:* 3 full-time (all women), 1 (woman) part-time/adjunct. *Students:* 5 full-time (all women), 1 (woman) part-time; includes 1 minority (Black or African American, non-Hispanic/Latino). Average age 26. 3 applicants, 67% accepted, 1 enrolled. *Degree requirements:* For doctorate, comprehensive exam, thesis/dissertation, capstone project required. *Entrance requirements:* For doctorate, GRE (may be waived if GPA is 3.5 or greater), BSN, RN license, minimum GPA of 3.5, 3 letters of recommendation, resume, personal essay, course work in statistics, clinical experience. Additional exam requirements/recommendations for international students: required—TOEFL (minimum score 600 paper-based; 100 iBT), IELTS (minimum score 7), TOEFL (minimum score 600 paper-based; 100 IBT) or IELTS (minimum score 7.0). *Application deadline:* For fall admission, 6/1 for domestic students, 2/15 for international students. Application fee: $50. Electronic applications accepted. *Expenses:* $13,795 per term full-time resident tuition, $475 per term full-time resident fees, $1,122 per credit part-time resident tuition, $295 per term part-time resident fees, $16,474 per term full-time non-resident tuition, $475 per term full-time non-resident fees, $1,345 per credit part-time non-resident tuition, $295 per term part-time non-resident fees. *Financial support:* In 2019–20, 3 students received support, including 2 teaching assistantships (averaging $9,740 per year); scholarships/grants and Matching Funds also available. Financial award application deadline: 6/1; financial award applicants required to submit FAFSA. *Unit head:* Dr. Sandra Engberg, Associate Dean for Clinical Education, 412-624-3835, Fax: 412-624-8521, E-mail: sje1@pitt.edu. *Application contact:* Laurie Lapsley, Administrator of Graduate Student Services, 412-624-9670, Fax: 412-624-2409, E-mail: lapsleyl@pitt.edu.

**University of Puerto Rico - Medical Sciences Campus,** Graduate School of Public Health, Department of Human Development, Program in Nurse Midwifery, San Juan, PR 00936-5067. Offers MPH, Certificate. *Program availability:* Part-time. *Entrance requirements:* For master's, GRE, previous course work in algebra.

**University of South Africa,** College of Human Sciences, Pretoria, South Africa. Offers adult education (M Ed); African languages (MA, PhD); African politics (MA, PhD); Afrikaans (MA, PhD); ancient history (MA, PhD); ancient Near Eastern studies (MA, PhD); anthropology (MA, PhD); applied linguistics (MA); Arabic (MA, PhD); archaeology (MA); art history (MA); Biblical archaeology (MA); Biblical studies (M Th, D Th, PhD); Christian spirituality (M Th, D Th); church history (M Th, D Th); classical studies (MA, PhD); clinical psychology (MA); communication (MA, PhD); comparative education (M Ed, Ed D); consulting psychology (D Admin, D Com, PhD); curriculum studies (M Ed, Ed D); development studies (M Admin, MA, D Admin, PhD); didactics (M Ed, Ed D); education (M Tech); education management (M Ed, Ed D); educational psychology (M Ed); English (MA); environmental education (M Ed); French (MA, PhD); German (MA, PhD); Greek (MA); guidance and counseling (M Ed); health studies (MA, PhD), including health sciences education (MA), health services management (MA), medical and surgical nursing science (critical care general) (MA), midwifery and neonatal nursing science (MA), trauma and emergency care (MA); history (MA, PhD); history of education (Ed D); inclusive education (M Ed, Ed D); information and communications technology policy and regulation (MA); information science (MA, MIS, PhD); international politics (MA, PhD); Islamic studies (MA, PhD); Italian (MA, PhD); Judaica (MA, PhD); linguistics (MA, PhD); mathematical education (M Ed); mathematics education (MA); missiology (M Th, D Th); modern Hebrew (MA, PhD); musicology (MA, MMus, D Mus, PhD); natural science education (M Ed); New Testament (M Th, D Th); Old Testament (D Th); pastoral therapy (M Th, D Th); philosophy (MA); philosophy of education (M Ed, Ed D); politics (MA, PhD); Portuguese (MA, PhD); practical theology (M Th, D Th); psychology (MA, MS, PhD); psychology of education (M Ed, Ed D); public health (MA); religious studies (MA, D Th, PhD); Romance languages (MA); Russian (MA, PhD); Semitic languages (MA, PhD); social behavior studies in HIV/AIDS (MA); social science (mental health) (MA); social science in development studies (MA); social science in psychology (MA); social science in social work (MA); social science in sociology (MA); social work (MSW, DSW, PhD); socio-education (M Ed, Ed D); sociolinguistics (MA); sociology (MA, PhD); Spanish (MA, PhD); systematic theology (M Th, D Th); TESOL (teaching English to speakers of other languages) (MA); theological ethics (M Th, D Th); theory of literature (MA, PhD); urban ministries (D Th); urban ministry (M Th).

**Wayne State University,** College of Nursing, Detroit, MI 48202. Offers adult gerontology acute care nurse practitioner (MSN); adult gerontology primary care nurse practitioner (MSN); advanced public health nursing (MSN); infant and mental health (DNP, PhD); neonatal nurse practitioner (MSN); nurse-midwifery (MSN); pediatric acute care nurse practitioner (MSN); pediatric primary care nurse practitioner (MSN); psychiatric mental health nurse practitioner (MSN); women's health nurse practitioner (MSN). *Accreditation:* AACN; ACNM/ACME. *Program availability:* Part-time. *Faculty:* 27. *Students:* 134 full-time (118 women), 216 part-time (187 women); includes 98 minority (51 Black or African American, non-Hispanic/Latino; 24 Asian, non-Hispanic/Latino; 6 Hispanic/Latino; 17 Two or more races, non-Hispanic/Latino), 18 international. Average age 33. 425 applicants, 37% accepted, 95 enrolled. In 2019, 58 master's, 31 doctorates awarded. *Degree requirements:* For doctorate, thesis/dissertation. *Entrance requirements:* For master's, Completed a Bachelor of Science in Nursing with a 3.0 or higher GPA. Official transcripts. Professional competence as documented by three references. Current Michigan Registered Nurse (RN) licensure. A personal statement of goals for graduate study; for doctorate, DNP: Minimum GPA of 3.0 or higher in BSN is required. Resume or Curriculum Vita that includes education, work and/or research experience. Two references, one from a doctorally prepared individual. RN license. PhD: BSN transcript; Two to three references from doctorally prepared individuals; goals statement; Resume or CV; Interview. Additional exam requirements/recommendations for international students: required—TOEFL (minimum score 101 iBT), TWE (minimum score 6), Michigan English Language Assessment Battery (minimum score 85); recommended—IELTS (minimum score 7). *Application deadline:* For fall admission, 1/31 for domestic students; for winter admission, 11/1 for domestic students. Applications are processed on a rolling basis. Application fee: $50. Electronic applications accepted. *Expenses:* $925.72 per credit hour in-state, $1,716.93 per credit hour out-of-state, $54.56 student service credit hour fee, $315.70 registration fee. *Financial support:* In 2019–20, 104 students received support, including 39 fellowships with tuition reimbursements available (averaging $6,456 per year), 1 research assistantship (averaging $24,950 per year), 5 teaching assistantships with tuition reimbursements available (averaging $25,000 per year); scholarships/grants, health care benefits, and unspecified assistantships also available. Support available to part-time students. Financial award application deadline: 3/1; financial award applicants required to submit FAFSA. *Unit head:* Dr. Laurie M Lauzon Clabo, Dean, College of Nursing, 313-577-4082, E-mail: laurie.lauzon.clabo@wayne.edu. *Application contact:* Dr. Laurie M Lauzon Clabo, Dean, College of Nursing, 313-577-4082, E-mail: laurie.lauzon.clabo@wayne.edu.
Website: http://nursing.wayne.edu/

**West Virginia Wesleyan College,** School of Nursing, Buckhannon, WV 26201. Offers family nurse practitioner (MS, Post Master's Certificate); nurse-midwifery (MS); nursing (DNP); nursing leadership (MS); psychiatric mental health nurse practitioner (MS); MSN/MBA. *Accreditation:* ACEN.

# Nursing and Healthcare Administration

**Abilene Christian University,** College of Graduate and Professional Studies, Program in Nursing Practice, Addison, TX 75001. Offers advanced practice nurse (DNP); executive nursing leadership (DNP); nursing education (DNP). *Program availability:* Part-time, online only, blended/hybrid learning. *Faculty:* 4 full-time (3 women), 1 (woman) part-time/adjunct. *Students:* 48 full-time (44 women), 64 part-time (55 women); includes 63 minority (35 Black or African American, non-Hispanic/Latino; 3 Asian, non-Hispanic/Latino; 24 Hispanic/Latino; 1 Two or more races, non-Hispanic/Latino), 2 international. 49 applicants, 100% accepted, 34 enrolled. In 2019, 10 doctorates awarded. *Entrance requirements:* For doctorate, master's degree in nursing, official transcripts, minimum graduate nursing cumulative GPA of 3.0, two recommendation letters, 500-word statement of purpose, professional curriculum vitae or resume. Additional exam requirements/recommendations for international students: required—TOEFL (minimum score 80 iBT), IELTS (minimum score 6). *Application deadline:* For fall admission, 10/7 for domestic students; for winter admission, 12/20 for domestic students; for spring admission, 2/24 for domestic students; for summer admission, 4/20 for domestic students. Applications are processed on a rolling basis. Application fee: $50. Electronic applications accepted. *Expenses:* $1000 per hour. *Financial support:* In 2019–20, 21 students received support. Scholarships/grants available. Financial award application deadline: 7/1; financial award applicants required to submit FAFSA. *Unit head:* Dr. Linda Gibson, Program Director, 214-305-9500, E-mail: lcg17a@acu.edu. *Application contact:* Graduate Advisor, 855-219-7300, E-mail: onlineadmissions@acu.edu.
Website: http://www.acu.edu/online/academics/doctor-of-nursing-practice.html

**Adelphi University,** College of Nursing and Public Health, Program in Nursing Administration, Garden City, NY 11530-0701. Offers MS, Certificate. *Entrance requirements:* Additional exam requirements/recommendations for international students: required—TOEFL (minimum score 550 paper-based; 80 iBT), IELTS (minimum score 6.5). *Expenses:* Contact institution.

**Allen College,** Graduate Programs, Waterloo, IA 50703. Offers adult-gerontology acute care nurse practitioner (MSN); community/public health nursing (MSN); education (MSN); family nurse practitioner (MSN); health sciences (Ed D); leadership in health care delivery (MSN); leadership in health care informatics (MSN); nursing (DNP); occupational therapy (MS); psychiatric mental health nurse practitioner (MSN). *Accreditation:* AACN; ACEN. *Faculty:* 27 full-time (23 women), 9 part-time/adjunct (8 women). *Students:* 193 full-time (175 women), 95 part-time (84 women); includes 22 minority (6 Black or African American, non-Hispanic/Latino; 1 American Indian or Alaska Native, non-Hispanic/Latino; 4 Asian, non-Hispanic/Latino; 5 Hispanic/Latino; 6 Two or more races, non-Hispanic/Latino). Average age 32. 376 applicants, 53% accepted, 122 enrolled. *Application deadline:* For fall admission, 2/1 priority date for domestic students;

for spring admission, 9/1 priority date for domestic students. Applications are processed on a rolling basis. Application fee: $50. Electronic applications accepted. *Financial support:* In 2019–20, 78 students received support. Federal Work-Study, institutionally sponsored loans, and scholarships/grants available. Support available to part-time students. Financial award application deadline: 8/1; financial award applicants required to submit FAFSA. *Unit head:* Dr. Bob Loch, Provost, 319-226-2040, Fax: 319-226-2070, E-mail: bob.loch@allencollege.edu. *Application contact:* Molly Quinn, Director of Admissions, 319-226-2001, Fax: 319-226-2010, E-mail: molly.quinn@allencollege.edu. Website: http://www.allencollege.edu/

**Alvernia University,** School of Graduate Studies, Department of Nursing, Reading, PA 19607-1799. Offers adult gerontology nurse practitioner (DNP); family nurse practitioner (DNP); nursing education (MSN); nursing leadership (Graduate Certificate); nursing leadership and healthcare administration (MSN).

**American International College,** School of Health Sciences, Springfield, MA 01109-3189. Offers exercise science (MS); family nurse practitioner (MSN, Post-Master's Certificate); nursing administrator (MSN); nursing educator (MSN); occupational therapy (MSOT, OTD); physical therapy (DPT). *Accreditation:* AOTA. *Program availability:* Part-time, 100% online. *Degree requirements:* For master's, practicum; for doctorate, thesis/dissertation, practicum, *Entrance requirements:* For master's, 3 letters of recommendation, personal goal statement; minimum GPA of 3.2, interview, BS or BA, and 2 clinical PT observations (for DPT); minimum GPA of 3.0, MSOT, OT licensen, and 2 clinical OT observations (for OTD); for doctorate, personal goal statement, 2 letters of recommendation; minimum GPA of 3.0, BS or BA, 2 clinical OT observations (for MSOT; RN license and minimum GPA of 3.0 (for MSN). Additional exam requirements/recommendations for international students: required—TOEFL (minimum score 577 paper-based; 91 iBT). Electronic applications accepted. *Expenses:* Contact institution.

**Anderson University,** College of Health Professions, Anderson, SC 29621. Offers advanced practice (DNP); executive leadership (MSN, DNP); family nurse practitioner (MSN, DNP); nurse educator (MSN); psychiatric mental health nurse practitioner (MSN, DNP). *Program availability:* Online learning. *Application deadline:* Applications are processed on a rolling basis. Electronic applications accepted. *Expenses:* Contact institution. *Financial support:* Scholarships/grants available. *Unit head:* Dr. Donald M. Peace, Dean, 864-231-5513, E-mail: dpeace@andersonuniversity.edu. *Application contact:* Dr. Donald M. Peace, Dean, 864-231-5513, E-mail: dpeace@andersonuniversity.edu.
Website: http://www.andersonuniversity.edu/health-professions

**Arizona State University at Tempe,** College of Nursing and Health Innovation, Phoenix, AZ 85004. Offers advanced nursing practice (DNP); clinical research management (MS); community and public health practice (Graduate Certificate); family mental health nurse practitioner (Graduate Certificate); family nurse practitioner (Graduate Certificate); geriatric nursing (Graduate Certificate); healthcare innovation (MHI); nurse education in academic and practice settings (Graduate Certificate); nurse educator (MS); nursing and healthcare innovation (PhD). *Accreditation:* AACN. *Program availability:* Online learning. *Degree requirements:* For master's, comprehensive exam (for some programs), thesis (for some programs), interactive Program of Study (iPOS) submitted before completing 50 percent of required credit hours; for doctorate, comprehensive exam, thesis/dissertation, interactive Program of Study (iPOS) submitted before completing 50 percent of required credit hours. *Entrance requirements:* For master's and doctorate, GRE, minimum GPA of 3.0 or equivalent in last 2 years of work leading to bachelor's degree. Additional exam requirements/recommendations for international students: required—TOEFL, IELTS, or PTE. Electronic applications accepted. *Expenses:* Contact institution.

**Aspen University,** Program in Nursing, Denver, CO 80246-1930. Offers forensic nursing (MSN); informatics (MSN); nursing (MSN); nursing administration and management (MSN); nursing education (MSN); public health (MSN). *Program availability:* Part-time, evening/weekend, online only, 100% online. *Degree requirements:* For master's, comprehensive exam. *Entrance requirements:* For master's, www.aspen.edu, www.aspen.edu. Electronic applications accepted.

**Athabasca University,** Faculty of Health Disciplines, Athabasca, AB T9S 3A3, Canada. Offers advanced nursing practice (MN, Advanced Diploma); generalist (MN); health studies (MHS). *Program availability:* Part-time, online learning. *Degree requirements:* For master's, comprehensive exam (for some programs). *Entrance requirements:* For master's, bachelor's degree in health-related field and 2 years of professional health service experience (MHS); bachelor's degree in nursing and 2 years' nursing experience (MN); minimum GPA of 3.0 in final 30 credits; for Advanced Diploma, RN license, 2 years of health care experience. Electronic applications accepted. *Expenses:* Contact institution.

**Augusta University,** College of Nursing, Clinical Nurse Leader Program, Augusta, GA 30912. Offers MSN. *Entrance requirements:* For master's, GRE (minimum score of 290 combined Verbal and Quantitative sections) or MAT (minimum score of 400) within last five years, bachelor's degree or higher in non-nursing discipline, minimum undergraduate cumulative GPA of 3.0. Additional exam requirements/recommendations for international students: required—TOEFL (minimum score 600 paper-based). Electronic applications accepted. *Expenses:* Contact institution.

**Augusta University,** College of Nursing, Doctor of Nursing Practice Program, Augusta, GA 30912. Offers adult gerontology acute care nurse practitioner (DNP); family nurse practitioner (DNP); nurse executive (DNP); nursing (DNP); nursing anesthesia (DNP); pediatric nurse practitioner (DNP); psychiatric mental health nurse practitioner (DNP). *Accreditation:* AACN; AANA/CANAEP. *Degree requirements:* For doctorate, thesis/dissertation or alternative. *Entrance requirements:* For doctorate, GRE General Test or MAT, master's degree in nursing or related field, current professional nurse licensure. Additional exam requirements/recommendations for international students: required—TOEFL (minimum score 600 paper-based; 100 iBT). Electronic applications accepted.

**Austin Peay State University,** College of Graduate Studies, College of Behavioral and Health Sciences, School of Nursing, Clarksville, TN 37044. Offers family nurse practitioner (MSN); nursing administration (MSN); nursing education (MSN); nursing informatics (MSN). *Program availability:* Part-time, online learning. *Faculty:* 5 full-time (all women), 1 (woman) part-time/adjunct. *Students:* 12 full-time (11 women), 120 part-time (114 women); includes 25 minority (14 Black or African American, non-Hispanic/Latino; 3 Asian, non-Hispanic/Latino; 4 Hispanic/Latino; 4 Two or more races, non-Hispanic/Latino). Average age 34. 19 applicants, 84% accepted, 2 enrolled. In 2019, 51 master's awarded. *Degree requirements:* For master's, comprehensive exam. *Entrance requirements:* For master's, minimum GPA of 3.0, RN license eligibility, 3 letters of recommendation. Additional exam requirements/recommendations for international students: required—TOEFL (minimum score 500 paper-based). *Application deadline:* For fall admission, 8/5 priority date for domestic students. Applications are processed on a rolling basis. Application fee: $45 ($55 for international students). Electronic applications accepted. *Financial support:* Research assistantships with full tuition reimbursements, career-related internships or fieldwork, Federal Work-Study, institutionally sponsored loans, scholarships/grants, and unspecified assistantships available. Support available to part-time students. Financial award application deadline: 7/1; financial award applicants required to submit FAFSA. *Unit head:* Dr. Mary Rice,

Interim Director of Nursing, 931-221-7483, Fax: 931-221-7595, E-mail: ricem@apsu.edu. *Application contact:* Megan Mitchell, Coordinator of Graduate Admissions, 931-221-6189, Fax: 931-221-7641, E-mail: mitchellm@apsu.edu.
Website: http://www.apsu.edu/nursing

**Azusa Pacific University,** School of Nursing, Azusa, CA 91702-7000. Offers adult clinical nurse specialist (MSN); adult-gerontology nurse practitioner (MSN); family nurse practitioner (MSN); healthcare administration and leadership (MSN); nursing (MSN, DNP, PhD); nursing education (MSN); parent-child clinical nurse specialist (MSN); psychiatric mental health nurse practitioner (MSN). *Accreditation:* AACN. *Program availability:* Part-time, evening/weekend. *Degree requirements:* For master's, thesis optional. *Entrance requirements:* For master's, BSN.

**Barry University,** School of Adult and Continuing Education, Division of Nursing, Program in Nursing Administration, Miami Shores, FL 33161-6695. Offers MSN, PhD, Certificate. *Accreditation:* AACN. *Program availability:* Part-time, evening/weekend. *Degree requirements:* For master's, research project or thesis. *Entrance requirements:* For master's, GRE General Test or MAT, BSN, minimum GPA of 3.0, course work in statistics. Electronic applications accepted.

**Barry University,** School of Adult and Continuing Education, Division of Nursing and Andreas School of Business, Program in Nursing Administration and Business Administration, Miami Shores, FL 33161-6695. Offers MSN/MBA. *Accreditation:* AACN. *Program availability:* Part-time, evening/weekend. Electronic applications accepted.

**Bellarmine University,** College of Health Professions, Donna and Allan Lansing School of Nursing and Clinical Sciences, Louisville, KY 40205. Offers family nurse practitioner (MSN); health science (MHS); nursing administration (MSN); nursing education (MSN); nursing practice (DNP). *Accreditation:* AACN; APTA. *Program availability:* Part-time, evening/weekend. *Faculty:* 19 full-time (15 women), 7 part-time/adjunct (all women). *Students:* 142 full-time (104 women), 128 part-time (105 women); includes 55 minority (24 Black or African American, non-Hispanic/Latino; 1 American Indian or Alaska Native, non-Hispanic/Latino; 15 Asian, non-Hispanic/Latino; 10 Hispanic/Latino; 5 Two or more races, non-Hispanic/Latino), 10 international. Average age 30. 348 applicants, 82% accepted, 172 enrolled. In 2019, 29 master's, 4 doctorates awarded. *Degree requirements:* For master's, comprehensive exam, thesis (for some programs); for doctorate, comprehensive exam, thesis/dissertation. *Entrance requirements:* For master's, GRE General Test, minimum GPA of 3.0, interview, resume; BSN from CCNE- or ACEN-accredited program, professional references, goal statement, and RN license (for MSN); bachelor's degree with exposure to health issues and grade of C or better in math/science courses (for MHS); for doctorate, GRE General Test, MSN from CCNE- or ACEN-accredited program; minimum GPA of 3.5 in graduate coursework; professional references; goal statement; current curriculum vitae or resume; RN license; verification of post-baccalaureate clinical and practice hours. Additional exam requirements/recommendations for international students: required—TOEFL (minimum iBT score of 83, 26 on speaking test), IELTS (minimum score 7, speaking band score of 8), or language training at an approved center; recommended—TOEFL (minimum score 83 iBT), IELTS. *Application deadline:* Applications are processed on a rolling basis. Application fee: $40. Electronic applications accepted. *Expenses:* Accelerated BSN, May 2020 cohort: $905 per credit hour; Accelerated BSN, 2-yr. program, Summer 2020: $950 per credit hour; MHS: $770 per credit hour; MHS, Medical Lab Science: $665 per credit hour; MHS, Respiratory Therapy: $665 per credit hour; MSN, Education and Administration: $770 per credit hour; MSN, Family Nurse Practitioner: $770 per credit hour ($85 per credit hour fee for FNP specialty courses); Doctor of Nursing Practice: $855 per credit hour; Radiation Therapy Second Degree: $665 per credit hour. *Financial support:* Career-related internships or fieldwork and scholarships/grants available. Financial award applicants required to submit FAFSA. *Unit head:* Dr. Nancy York, Dean, 502-272-8639, E-mail: nyork@bellarmine.edu. *Application contact:* Julie Armstrong-Binnix, Health Science Recruiter, 800-274-4723 Ext. 8364, E-mail: julieab@bellarmine.edu.
Website: http://www.bellarmine.edu/lansing

**Blessing-Rieman College of Nursing & Health Sciences,** Master of Science in Nursing Program, Quincy, IL 62305-7005. Offers nursing education (MSN); nursing leadership (MSN). *Program availability:* Part-time-only, evening/weekend, online only, 100% online. *Degree requirements:* For master's, thesis or project. *Entrance requirements:* Additional exam requirements/recommendations for international students: required—TOEFL (minimum score 500 paper-based; 80 iBT). Electronic applications accepted.

**Bloomsburg University of Pennsylvania,** School of Graduate Studies, College of Science and Technology, Department of Nursing, Bloomsburg, PA 17815-1301. Offers adult and family nurse practitioner (MSN); community health (MSN); nurse anesthesia (MSN); nursing (MSN, DNP); nursing administration (MSN). *Accreditation:* AACN. *Degree requirements:* For master's, thesis (for some programs), clinical experience. *Entrance requirements:* For master's, minimum QPA of 3.0, personal statement, 2 letters of recommendation, nursing license. Additional exam requirements/recommendations for international students: required—TOEFL, IELTS. Electronic applications accepted. *Expenses:* Contact institution.

**Bowie State University,** Graduate Programs, Department of Nursing, Bowie, MD 20715-9465. Offers administration of nursing services (MS); family nurse practitioner (MS); nursing education (MS). *Accreditation:* ACEN. *Program availability:* Part-time. *Degree requirements:* For master's, comprehensive exam, thesis, research paper. *Entrance requirements:* For master's, minimum GPA of 2.5. Electronic applications accepted. *Expenses:* Tuition, area resident: Full-time $11,942; part-time $423 per credit hour. Tuition, state resident: full-time $11,942; part-time $423 per credit hour. Tuition, nonresident: full-time $18,806; part-time $709 per credit hour. International tuition: $18,806 full-time. *Required fees:* $1106; $1106 per semester. $553 per semester.

**Bradley University,** The Graduate School, College of Education and Health Sciences, Department of Nursing, Peoria, IL 61625-0002. Offers family nurse practitioner (MSN, DNP, Certificate); leadership (DNP); nursing administration (MSN); nursing education (MSN, Certificate). *Accreditation:* AACN; ACEN. *Program availability:* Part-time, evening/weekend, 100% online. *Faculty:* 12 full-time (all women), 32 part-time/adjunct (28 women). *Students:* 91 full-time (79 women), 637 part-time (551 women); includes 253 minority (143 Black or African American, non-Hispanic/Latino; 13 American Indian or Alaska Native, non-Hispanic/Latino; 40 Asian, non-Hispanic/Latino; 45 Hispanic/Latino; 2 Native Hawaiian or other Pacific Islander, non-Hispanic/Latino; 10 Two or more races, non-Hispanic/Latino), 19 international. Average age 38. 229 applicants, 79% accepted, 114 enrolled. In 2019, 60 master's, 20 doctorates awarded. *Degree requirements:* For master's, comprehensive exam, thesis optional; for doctorate, comprehensive exam. *Entrance requirements:* For master's, GRE General Test or MAT, interview, Illinois RN license, advanced cardiac life support certification, pediatric advanced life support certification, 3 letters of recommendation. Additional exam requirements/recommendations for international students: required—TOEFL (minimum score 550 paper-based; 79 iBT), IELTS (minimum score 6.5), PTE (minimum score 58). *Application deadline:* For fall admission, 5/15 priority date for domestic and international students; for spring admission, 10/15 priority date for domestic and international students. Applications are processed on a rolling basis. Application fee: $40 ($50 for

international students). Electronic applications accepted. *Expenses: Tuition:* Part-time $930 per credit hour. *Financial support:* Research assistantships, scholarships/grants, tuition waivers (partial), and unspecified assistantships available. Financial award application deadline: 4/1. *Unit head:* Jessica Clark, Associate Dean and Director of the Department of Nursing, 309-677-2547, E-mail: jclark@bradley.edu. *Application contact:* Rachel Webb, Director of On-Campus Graduate Admissions and International Student and Scholar Services, 309-677-2375, Fax: 309-677-3343, E-mail: rkwebb@bradley.edu.
Website: http://www.bradley.edu/academic/departments/nur/

**Brenau University,** Sydney O. Smith Graduate School, Ivester College of Health Sciences, Gainesville, GA 30501. Offers family nurse practitioner (MSN); general psychology (MS); nurse educator (MSN); nursing manager (MSN); occupational therapy (MS). *Accreditation:* AOTA. *Program availability:* Part-time, evening/weekend, 100% online, blended/hybrid learning. *Faculty:* 34 full-time (26 women), 11 part-time/adjunct (10 women). *Students:* 321 full-time (242 women), 209 part-time (197 women); includes 177 minority (104 Black or African American, non-Hispanic/Latino; 2 American Indian or Alaska Native, non-Hispanic/Latino; 24 Asian, non-Hispanic/Latino; 36 Hispanic/Latino; 2 Native Hawaiian or other Pacific Islander, non-Hispanic/Latino; 9 Two or more races, non-Hispanic/Latino), 3 international. Average age 29. 517 applicants, 47% accepted, 110 enrolled. In 2019, 174 master's awarded. *Entrance requirements:* For master's, GMAT, GRE, or MAT, minimum GPA 2.5. Additional exam requirements/recommendations for international students: required—TOEFL (minimum score 497 paper-based; 71 iBT); recommended—IELTS (minimum score 5.5). *Application deadline:* Applications are processed on a rolling basis. Application fee: $35. Electronic applications accepted. *Expenses:* $11,763 full-time tuition (average), $4,678 part-time tuition (average). *Financial support:* In 2019–20, 11 students received support. Scholarships/grants available. Financial award applicants required to submit FAFSA. *Unit head:* Dr. Gale Starich, Dean, 777-718-5305, Fax: 770-297-5929, E-mail: gstarich@brenau.edu. *Application contact:* Nathan Goss, Assistant Vice President for Recruitment, 770-534-6162, E-mail: ngoss@brenau.edu.
Website: http://www.brenau.edu/healthsciences/

**Brookline College - Phoenix Campus,** Nursing Programs, Phoenix, AZ 85021. Offers health systems administration (MSN); nursing (MSN). *Program availability:* Part-time, online learning.

**California Baptist University,** Program in Nursing, Riverside, CA 92504-3206. Offers clinical nurse specialist (MSN); family nurse practitioner (MSN); healthcare systems management (MSN); teaching-learning (MSN). *Accreditation:* AACN. *Program availability:* Part-time. *Degree requirements:* For master's, comprehensive exam or directed project thesis; capstone practicum. *Entrance requirements:* For master's, GRE or California Critical Thinking Skills Test; Test of Essential Academic Skills (TEAS), minimum undergraduate GPA of 3.0; completion of prerequisite courses with minimum grade of C; CPR certification; background check clearance; health clearance; drug testing; proof of health insurance; proof of motor vehicle insurance; three letters of recommendation; 1000-word essay; interview. Additional exam requirements/recommendations for international students: required—TOEFL (minimum score 80 iBT). Electronic applications accepted. *Expenses:* Contact institution.

**California State University, Fullerton,** Graduate Studies, College of Health and Human Development, School of Nursing, Fullerton, CA 92831-3599. Offers leadership (MS); nurse anesthesia (MS); nurse educator (MS); nursing (DNP); school nursing (MS); women's health care (MS). *Accreditation:* AACN. *Program availability:* Part-time.

**California State University, San Marcos,** College of Education, Health and Human Services, School of Nursing, San Marcos, CA 92096-0001. Offers advanced practice nursing (MSN), including clinical nurse specialist, family nurse practitioner, psychiatric mental health nurse practitioner; clinical nurse leader (MSN); nursing education (MSN). *Expenses: Tuition, area resident:* Full-time $7176. Tuition, state resident: full-time $7176. Tuition, nonresident: full-time $18,640. *International tuition:* $18,640 full-time. *Required fees:* $1960.

**California University of Pennsylvania,** School of Graduate Studies and Research, Eberly College of Science and Technology, Department of Nursing, California, PA 15419-1394. Offers nursing administration and leadership (MSN); nursing education (MSN). *Expenses: Tuition, area resident:* Full-time $9288; part-time $516 per credit. Tuition, state resident: full-time $9288; part-time $516 per credit. Tuition, nonresident: full-time $13,932; part-time $774 per credit. *Required fees:* $3631; $291.13 per credit. Part-time tuition and fees vary according to course load.

**Capella University,** School of Public Service Leadership, Master's Programs in Nursing, Minneapolis, MN 55402. Offers diabetes nursing (MSN); general nursing (MSN); gerontology nursing (MSN); health information management (MS); nurse educator (MSN); nursing leadership and administration (MSN). *Accreditation:* AACN.

**Capital University,** School of Nursing, Columbus, OH 43209-2394. Offers administration (MSN); legal studies (MSN); theological studies (MSN); JD/MSN; MBA/MSN; MSN/MTS. *Accreditation:* AACN. *Program availability:* Part-time, evening/weekend. *Degree requirements:* For master's, thesis or alternative. *Entrance requirements:* For master's, BSN, current RN license, minimum GPA of 3.0, undergraduate courses in statistics and research. Additional exam requirements/recommendations for international students: required—TOEFL (minimum score 550 paper-based). *Expenses:* Contact institution.

**Carlow University,** College of Health and Wellness, Program in Nursing Leadership and Education, Pittsburgh, PA 15213-3165. Offers MSN. *Program availability:* Part-time, evening/weekend, 100% online, blended/hybrid learning. *Students:* 40 full-time (39 women), 10 part-time (all women); includes 6 minority (4 Black or African American, non-Hispanic/Latino; 1 Asian, non-Hispanic/Latino; 1 Two or more races, non-Hispanic/Latino). Average age 33. 20 applicants, 100% accepted, 15 enrolled. In 2019, 27 master's awarded. *Degree requirements:* For master's, internship. *Entrance requirements:* For master's, minimum undergraduate GPA of 3.0 from accredited BSN program; current license as RN in Pennsylvania; statistics class within past 6 years with minimum C grade; two professional recommendations; reflective essay of 300 words or less describing career goals and expectations for education. Additional exam requirements/recommendations for international students: required—TOEFL (minimum score 550 paper-based). *Application deadline:* Applications are processed on a rolling basis. Electronic applications accepted. *Expenses: Tuition:* Full-time $13,666; part-time $902 per credit hour. *Required fees:* $15; $15 per credit. Tuition and fees vary according to degree level and program. *Financial support:* Application deadline: 4/1; applicants required to submit FAFSA. *Unit head:* Dr. Renee Ingel, Director, Nursing Leadership and DNP Programs, 412-578-6103, Fax: 412-578-6114, E-mail: rmingel@carlow.edu. *Application contact:* Dr. Renee Ingel, Director, Nursing Leadership and DNP Programs, 412-578-6103, Fax: 412-578-6114, E-mail: rmingel@carlow.edu.
Website: http://www.carlow.edu/Master_of_Science_in_Nursing_Concentration_in_Education_and_Leadership.aspx

**Cedar Crest College,** School of Nursing, Allentown, PA 18104-6196. Offers nursing administration (MS); nursing education (MS). *Program availability:* Part-time. Electronic applications accepted. *Expenses:* Contact institution.

**Central Methodist University,** College of Graduate and Extended Studies, Fayette, MO 65248-1198. Offers clinical counseling (MS); clinical nurse leader (MSN); education (M Ed); music education (MME); nurse educator (MSN). *Program availability:* Part-time, evening/weekend, online learning. *Degree requirements:* For master's, thesis. *Entrance requirements:* For master's, GRE General Test, minimum GPA of 2.75. Electronic applications accepted.

**Chatham University,** Nursing Programs, Pittsburgh, PA 15232-2826. Offers education/leadership (MSN); nursing (DNP). *Accreditation:* AACN. *Program availability:* Online learning. *Entrance requirements:* For master's, RN license, BSN, minimum GPA of 3.0; for doctorate, RN license, MSN. Additional exam requirements/recommendations for international students: required—TOEFL (minimum score 600 paper-based; 100 iBT), IELTS (minimum score 6.5), TWE. Electronic applications accepted. Application fee is waived when completed online. *Expenses:* Contact institution.

**Clarke University,** Department of Nursing and Health, Dubuque, IA 52001-3198. Offers family nurse practitioner (DNP); health leadership and practice (DNP); psychiatric mental health nurse practitioner (DNP). *Accreditation:* AACN. *Program availability:* Part-time. *Degree requirements:* For doctorate, comprehensive exam, thesis/dissertation. *Entrance requirements:* For doctorate, GRE (if GPA under 3.0), bachelor's degree from accredited nursing program and accredited college or university; minimum GPA of 3.0; minimum C grade on undergraduate prerequisite courses; three recommendation forms; curriculum vitae; statement of goals; transcripts; copy of nursing license; proof of health insurance; interview. Additional exam requirements/recommendations for international students: required—TOEFL (minimum score 550 paper-based; 80 iBT), IELTS (minimum score 6.5). Electronic applications accepted. *Expenses:* Contact institution.

**Clarkson College,** Master of Science in Nursing Program, Omaha, NE 68131. Offers adult nurse practitioner (MSN, Post-Master's Certificate); family nurse practitioner (MSN, Post-Master's Certificate); nursing education (MSN, Post-Master's Certificate); nursing health care leadership (MSN, Post-Master's Certificate). *Accreditation:* AANA/CANAEP; ACEN. *Program availability:* Part-time, evening/weekend, online learning. *Degree requirements:* For master's, on-campus skills assessment (family nurse practitioner, adult nurse practitioner), comprehensive exam or thesis. *Entrance requirements:* For master's, minimum GPA of 3.0, 2 references, resume. Additional exam requirements/recommendations for international students: required—TOEFL (minimum score 600 paper-based; 100 iBT). Electronic applications accepted.

**Clarkson College,** Program in Health Care Administration, Omaha, NE 68131-2739. Offers MHCA. *Program availability:* Part-time, evening/weekend, online learning. *Entrance requirements:* For master's, minimum GPA of 3.0, resume, references. Additional exam requirements/recommendations for international students: required—TOEFL (minimum score 600 paper-based; 100 iBT). Electronic applications accepted.

**Clarkson University,** David D. Reh School of Business, Master's Programs in Healthcare Management and Leadership, Schenectady, NY 13699. Offers clinical leadership in healthcare management (MS); healthcare data analytics (MS); healthcare management (MBA, Advanced Certificate). *Program availability:* Part-time, evening/weekend, blended/hybrid learning. *Faculty:* 20 full-time (7 women), 6 part-time/adjunct (1 woman). *Students:* 36 full-time (22 women), 36 part-time (18 women); includes 12 minority (6 Black or African American, non-Hispanic/Latino; 4 Asian, non-Hispanic/Latino; 2 Hispanic/Latino), 7 international. 46 applicants, 70% accepted, 24 enrolled. In 2019, 28 master's awarded. *Entrance requirements:* For master's, GRE or GMAT. Additional exam requirements/recommendations for international students: required—TOEFL (minimum score 550 paper-based, 80 iBT) or IELTS (6.5). *Application deadline:* Applications are processed on a rolling basis. Application fee: $50. Electronic applications accepted. *Expenses: Tuition:* Full-time $24,984; part-time $1388 per credit hour. *Required fees:* $225. Tuition and fees vary according to campus/location and program. *Financial support:* Scholarships/grants available. *Unit head:* Dr. John Huppertz, Associate Professor / Director of Healthcare Management, 518-631-9892, E-mail: jhuppert@clarkson.edu. *Application contact:* Daniel Capogna, Director of Graduate Admissions & Recruitment, 518-631-9910, E-mail: graduate@clarkson.edu.

**College of Mount Saint Vincent,** School of Professional and Graduate Studies, Department of Nursing, Riverdale, NY 10471-1093. Offers family nurse practitioner (MSN, PMC); nurse educator (PMC); nursing administration (MSN); nursing education (MSN). *Accreditation:* AACN. *Program availability:* Part-time. *Entrance requirements:* For master's, BSN, interview, RN license, minimum GPA of 3.0, letters of reference. Additional exam requirements/recommendations for international students: required—TOEFL. *Expenses:* Contact institution.

**The College of New Rochelle,** Graduate School, Program in Nursing, New Rochelle, NY 10805-2308. Offers acute care nurse practitioner (MS, Certificate); clinical specialist in holistic nursing (MS, Certificate); family nurse practitioner (MS, Certificate); nursing and health care management (MS); nursing education (Certificate). *Accreditation:* AACN. *Program availability:* Part-time. *Entrance requirements:* For master's, GRE General Test or MAT, BSN, malpractice insurance, minimum GPA of 3.0, RN license. Electronic applications accepted.

**Columbus State University,** Graduate Studies, College of Education and Health Professions, School of Nursing, Columbus, GA 31907-5645. Offers family nurse practitioner (MSN); nursing (MSN), including nurse educator, nurse informatics, nurse leader. *Program availability:* Part-time, online only, 100% online. *Entrance requirements:* For master's, GRE, BSN, minimum undergraduate GPA of 3.0. Additional exam requirements/recommendations for international students: required—TOEFL (minimum score 550 paper-based; 79 iBT). Electronic applications accepted. *Expenses:* Contact institution.

**Cox College,** Programs in Nursing, Springfield, MO 65802. Offers clinical nurse leader (MSN); family nurse practitioner (MSN); nurse educator (MSN). *Accreditation:* AACN. *Entrance requirements:* For master's, RN license, essay, 2 letters of recommendation, official transcripts. Electronic applications accepted.

**Creighton University,** College of Nursing, Omaha, NE 68178-0001. Offers adult gerontology acute care nurse practitioner (DNP, Post-Master's Certificate); adult gerontology nurse practitioner (DNP); clinical nurse leader (MSN, Post-Graduate Certificate); clinical systems administration (MSN, DNP); family nurse practitioner (DNP, Post-Master's Certificate); neonatal nurse practitioner (DNP, Post-Master's Certificate); nursing (Post-Graduate Certificate); pediatric acute care nurse practitioner (DNP, Post-Master's Certificate); psychiatric mental health nurse practitioner (DNP). *Accreditation:* AACN. *Program availability:* Part-time, blended/hybrid learning. *Degree requirements:* For master's, capstone project; for doctorate, scholarly project. *Entrance requirements:* For master's and doctorate, BSN from ACEN- or CCNE-accredited nursing school, minimum cumulative GPA of 3.0, personal statement, active unencumbered RN license with NE eligibility, undergraduate statistics course, physical assessment course or equivalent, three recommendation letters; for other advanced degree, MSN or MS in nursing from ACEN- or CCNE-accredited nursing school, minimum cumulative GPA of 3.0, active unencumbered RN license with NE eligibility. Additional exam requirements/recommendations for international students: required—TOEFL (minimum score 600 paper-based, 100 iBT) or IELTS. Electronic applications accepted. *Expenses:* Contact institution.

**Daemen College,** Nursing Programs, Amherst, NY 14226-3592. Offers adult nurse practitioner (MS, Post Master's Certificate); nurse executive leadership (Post Master's Certificate); nursing education (MS, Post Master's Certificate); nursing executive leadership (MS); nursing practice (DNP); palliative care nursing (Post Master's Certificate). *Accreditation:* ACEN. *Program availability:* Part-time. *Degree requirements:* For master's, thesis, degree completed in 4 years; minimum GPA of 3.0 and a minimum grade of B in all courses; for doctorate, thesis/dissertation, degree completed in 5 years; minimum GPA of 3.0 and a minimum grade of B in all courses. *Entrance requirements:* For master's, bachelor's degree in nursing from a NLNAC or CCNE accredited program, 1 year medical-surgical clinical experience, resume, official transcripts, undergraduate or graduate statistics course (grade of C or better), GPA 3.25 or above (below may be accepted on provisional basis), NYS Nursing license, interview with nursing faculty. Additional exam requirements/recommendations for international students: required—TOEFL (minimum score 77 paper-based), IELTS (minimum score 6.5). Electronic applications accepted. Application fee is waived when completed online.

**DeSales University,** Division of Healthcare, Center Valley, PA 18034-9568. Offers adult-gerontology acute care (Post Master's Certificate); adult-gerontology acute care nurse practitioner (MSN); adult-gerontology acute certified nurse practitioner (Post Master's Certificate); adult-gerontology clinical nurse specialist (MSN, Post Master's Certificate); clinical leadership (DNP); family nurse practitioner (MSN, Post Master's Certificate); general nursing practice (DNP); nurse anesthetist (MSN); nurse educator (Post Master's Certificate, Postbaccalaureate Certificate); nurse midwife (MSN); nurse practitioner (MSN); psychiatric-mental health nurse practitioner (MSN, Post Master's Certificate); DNP/MBA. *Accreditation:* ACEN. *Program availability:* Part-time. *Faculty:* 31 full-time (23 women), 12 part-time/adjunct (9 women). *Students:* 294 full-time (219 women), 128 part-time (109 women); includes 71 minority (20 Black or African American, non-Hispanic/Latino; 1 American Indian or Alaska Native, non-Hispanic/Latino; 15 Asian, non-Hispanic/Latino; 30 Hispanic/Latino; 5 Two or more races, non-Hispanic/Latino). Average age 28. 2,666 applicants, 6% accepted, 142 enrolled. In 2019, 115 master's, 30 doctorates awarded. *Degree requirements:* For master's, minimum GPA of 3.0, portfolio; for doctorate, minimum GPA of 3.0, scholarly capstone project. *Entrance requirements:* For master's, GRE or MAT (waived if applicant has an undergraduate GPA of 3.0 or higher), BSN from ACEN- or CCNE-accredited program, minimum undergraduate GPA of 3.0, active RN license or eligibility, two letters of recommendation, essay, health care experience, personal interview; for doctorate, BSN or MSN from ACEN- or CCNE-accredited institution, minimum GPA of 3.3 in graduate program, current licensure as an RN. Additional exam requirements/recommendations for international students: required—TOEFL (minimum score 104 iBT). *Application deadline:* Applications are processed on a rolling basis. Application fee: $50. Electronic applications accepted. *Expenses:* Contact institution. *Financial support:* Applicants required to submit FAFSA. *Unit head:* Ronald Nordone, Dean of Graduate Education, 610-282-1100 Ext. 1289, E-mail: ronald.nordone@desales.edu. *Application contact:* Julia Ferraro, Director of Graduate Admissions, 610-282-1100 Ext. 1768, E-mail: gradadmissions@desales.edu.

**Drexel University,** College of Nursing and Health Professions, Division of Graduate Nursing, Philadelphia, PA 19104-2875. Offers adult acute care (MSN); adult psychiatric/mental health (MSN); advanced practice nursing (MSN); clinical trials research (MSN); family nurse practitioner (MSN); leadership in health systems management (MSN); nursing education (MSN); pediatric primary care (MSN); women's health (MSN). *Accreditation:* AACN. Electronic applications accepted.

**Duke University,** School of Nursing, Durham, NC 27708. Offers acute care pediatric nurse practitioner (MSN, Post-Graduate Certificate); adult-gerontology nurse practitioner (MSN, Post-Graduate Certificate), including acute care, primary care; family nurse practitioner (MSN, Post-Graduate Certificate); neonatal nurse practitioner (MSN, Post-Graduate Certificate); nurse anesthesia (DNP); nurse practitioner (DNP); nursing (PhD); nursing and health care leadership (MSN, Post-Graduate Certificate); nursing education (MSN, Post-Graduate Certificate); nursing informatics (MSN, Post-Graduate Certificate); pediatric nurse practitioner (MSN, Post-Graduate Certificate), including primary care; psychiatric mental health nurse practitioner (MSN, Post-Graduate Certificate); women's health nurse practitioner (MSN, Post-Graduate Certificate). *Accreditation:* AACN; AANA/CANAEP. *Program availability:* Part-time, evening/weekend, online with on-campus intensives. *Faculty:* 48 full-time (40 women), 32 part-time/adjunct (28 women). *Students:* 666 full-time (601 women), 157 part-time (139 women); includes 193 minority (61 Black or African American, non-Hispanic/Latino; 4 American Indian or Alaska Native, non-Hispanic/Latino; 57 Asian, non-Hispanic/Latino; 49 Hispanic/Latino; 1 Native Hawaiian or other Pacific Islander, non-Hispanic/Latino; 21 Two or more races, non-Hispanic/Latino), 8 international. Average age 34. 761 applicants, 33% accepted, 149 enrolled. In 2019, 213 master's, 74 doctorates, 18 other advanced degrees awarded. Terminal master's awarded for partial completion of doctoral program. *Degree requirements:* For master's, thesis optional; for doctorate, capstone project. *Entrance requirements:* For master's, MSN applicants are no longer required to take the GRE, 1 year of nursing experience (recommended), BSN, minimum GPA of 3.0, previous course work in statistics; for doctorate, GRE is required for the DNP in Nurse Anesthesia, BSN or MSN, minimum GPA of 3.0, resume, personal statement, graduate statistics and research methods course, current licensure as a registered nurse, transcripts from all post-secondary institutions; for Post-Graduate Certificate, MSN, licensure or eligibility as a professional nurse, transcripts from all post-secondary institutions, previous course work in statistics. Additional exam requirements/recommendations for international students: required—TOEFL (minimum score 100 iBT), IELTS (minimum score 7). *Application deadline:* For fall admission, 12/1 for domestic and international students; for spring admission, 5/1 for domestic and international students. Application fee: $50. Electronic applications accepted. *Expenses:* Contact institution. *Financial support:* Institutionally sponsored loans, scholarships/grants, and traineeships available. Support available to part-time students. Financial award applicants required to submit FAFSA. *Unit head:* Dr. Marion E. Broome, Dean/Vice Chancellor for Nursing Affairs/Associate Vice President for Academic Affairs for Nursing, 919-684-9446, Fax: 919-684-9414, E-mail: marion.broome@duke.edu. *Application contact:* Dr. Ernie Rushing, Director of Admissions and Recruitment, 919-668-6274, Fax: 919-668-4693, E-mail: ernie.rushing@dm.duke.edu.
Website: http://www.nursing.duke.edu/

**Eastern Mennonite University,** Program in Nursing, Harrisonburg, VA 22802-2462. Offers leadership and management (MSN); leadership and school nursing (MSN); nursing management (DNP). *Accreditation:* AACN. *Program availability:* Part-time, online learning. *Degree requirements:* For master's, leadership project. *Entrance requirements:* For master's, RN license, one year of full-time work experience as RN, minimum GPA of 3.0. Additional exam requirements/recommendations for international students: required—TOEFL. Application fee is waived when completed online.

**Eastern Michigan University,** Graduate School, College of Health and Human Services, School of Health Sciences, Programs in Clinical Research Administration, Ypsilanti, MI 48197. Offers MS, Graduate Certificate. *Program availability:* Part-time, evening/weekend, online learning. *Students:* 8 full-time (7 women), 21 part-time (19 women); includes 8 minority (2 Black or African American, non-Hispanic/Latino; 4 Asian, non-Hispanic/Latino; 2 Two or more races, non-Hispanic/Latino), 8 international. Average age 33. 34 applicants, 76% accepted, 14 enrolled. In 2019, 13 master's awarded. *Entrance requirements:* Additional exam requirements/recommendations for international students: required—TOEFL. *Application deadline:* Applications are processed on a rolling basis. Application fee: $45. *Financial support:* Fellowships, research assistantships with full tuition reimbursements, teaching assistantships with full tuition reimbursements, career-related internships or fieldwork, Federal Work-Study, institutionally sponsored loans, scholarships/grants, tuition waivers (partial), and unspecified assistantships available. Support available to part-time students. Financial award applicants required to submit FAFSA. *Application contact:* Dr. Jean Rowan, Program Director, 734-487-1238, Fax: 734-487-4095, E-mail: jrowan3@emich.edu.

**East Tennessee State University,** College of Graduate and Continuing Studies, College of Nursing, Johnson City, TN 37614. Offers acute care nurse practitioner (DNP); adult-gerontology primary care nurse practitioner (DNP); adult/gerontological nurse practitioner (Postbaccalaureate Certificate); executive leadership in nursing (DNP, Postbaccalaureate Certificate); family nurse practitioner (MSN, DNP, Post-Master's Certificate, Postbaccalaureate Certificate); nursing (PhD); nursing administration (MSN); nursing education (MSN); pediatric primary care nurse practitioner (DNP); psychiatric mental health nurse practitioner (Postbaccalaureate Certificate); psychiatric/mental health nurse practitioner (MSN, DNP, Post-Master's Certificate); women's health care nurse practitioner (DNP). *Accreditation:* AACN. *Program availability:* Part-time, evening/weekend, online learning. *Degree requirements:* For master's and other advanced degree, comprehensive exam, practicum; for doctorate, comprehensive exam, thesis/dissertation (for some programs), practicum, internship, evidence of professional malpractice insurance, CPR certification. *Entrance requirements:* For master's, bachelor's degree, minimum GPA of 3.0, current RN license and eligibility to practice, resume, three letters of recommendation; for doctorate, GRE General Test, MSN (for PhD), BSN or MSN (for DNP), current RN license and eligibility to practice, 2 years of full-time registered nurse work experience or equivalent, three letters of recommendation, resume or curriculum vitae, interview, writing sample; for other advanced degree, MSN, minimum GPA of 3.0, current RN license and eligibility to practice, three letters of recommendation, resume or curriculum vitae; DNP with designated concentration in advanced clinical practice or nursing administration (for select programs). Additional exam requirements/recommendations for international students: required—TOEFL (minimum score 600 paper-based; 79 iBT). Electronic applications accepted.

**Elms College,** School of Nursing, Chicopee, MA 01013-2839. Offers adult-gerontology acute care nurse practitioner (DNP); family nurse practitioner (DNP); health systems innovation and leadership (DNP); nursing and health services management (MSN); nursing education (MSN). *Accreditation:* AACN. *Program availability:* Part-time, evening/weekend. *Faculty:* 3 full-time (2 women), 2 part-time/adjunct (both women). *Students:* 13 full-time (11 women), 97 part-time (91 women); includes 8 minority (4 Black or African American, non-Hispanic/Latino; 2 Hispanic/Latino; 2 Two or more races, non-Hispanic/Latino). Average age 38. 39 applicants, 87% accepted, 27 enrolled. In 2019, 4 master's, 20 doctorates awarded. *Entrance requirements:* Additional exam requirements/recommendations for international students: required—TOEFL (minimum score 80 iBT). *Application deadline:* For fall admission, 7/1 priority date for domestic students; for spring admission, 11/1 priority date for domestic students. Applications are processed on a rolling basis. Electronic applications accepted. *Financial support:* Applicants required to submit FAFSA. *Unit head:* Dr. Kathleen Scoble, Dean, School of Nursing, 413-265-2204, E-mail: scoblek@elms.edu. *Application contact:* Nancy Davis, Director, Office of Graduate and Continuing Education Admissions, 413-265-2456, E-mail: grad@elms.edu.

**Emmanuel College,** Graduate and Professional Programs, Graduate Program in Nursing, Boston, MA 02115. Offers education (MSN, Graduate Certificate); management (MSN, Graduate Certificate). *Accreditation:* AACN. *Program availability:* Part-time, evening/weekend. *Faculty:* 2 full-time (both women), 3 part-time/adjunct (all women). *Students:* 27 part-time (all women); includes 7 minority (3 Black or African American, non-Hispanic/Latino; 1 Asian, non-Hispanic/Latino; 3 Hispanic/Latino). Average age 43. In 2019, 14 master's awarded. *Degree requirements:* For master's, 30 credits (eight 3 credit courses and 1 6 credit course); for Graduate Certificate, 12 credits (two 3 credit courses and 1 6 credit course). *Entrance requirements:* For degree, completed application, transcripts from all regionally-accredited institutions attended (showing proof of bachelor's degree completion), proof of current RN license, 2 letters of recommendation, admissions essay, current resume. Additional exam requirements/recommendations for international students: required—TOEFL. *Application deadline:* Applications are processed on a rolling basis. Electronic applications accepted. *Expenses:* $2,581 per course. *Financial support:* Application deadline: 2/15; applicants required to submit FAFSA. *Unit head:* Diane Shea, Associate Dean for Nursing/Professor of Nursing Practice, 617-732-1604, E-mail: shead@emmanuel.edu. *Application contact:* Helen Muterperl, Director of Graduate and Professional Programs, 617-735-9700, Fax: 617-507-0434, E-mail: gpp@emmanuel.edu.
Website: http://www.emmanuel.edu/graduate-professional-programs/academics/nursing.html

**Emory University,** Nell Hodgson Woodruff School of Nursing, Atlanta, GA 30322-1100. Offers adult nurse practitioner (MSN); emergency nurse practitioner (MSN); family nurse practitioner (MSN); family nurse-midwife (MSN); health systems leadership (MSN); nurse-midwifery (MSN); pediatric nurse practitioner acute and primary care (MSN); women's health care (Title X) (MSN); women's health nurse practitioner (MSN); MSN/MPH. *Accreditation:* AACN; ACNM/ACME (one or more programs are accredited). *Program availability:* Part-time. *Entrance requirements:* For master's, GRE General Test or MAT, minimum GPA of 3.0, BS in nursing from an accredited institution, RN license and additional course work, 3 letters of recommendation. Additional exam requirements/recommendations for international students: required—TOEFL (minimum score 600 paper-based; 100 iBT). Electronic applications accepted. *Expenses:* Contact institution.

**Endicott College,** School of Nursing, Program in Nursing, Beverly, MA 01915. Offers family nurse practitioner (MSN, Post-Master's Certificate); global health (MSN); nursing administration (MSN); nursing administrator (Post-Master's Certificate); nursing educator (MSN, Post-Master's Certificate). *Program availability:* Part-time, evening/weekend, blended/hybrid learning. *Faculty:* 4 full-time (all women), 18 part-time/adjunct (13 women). *Students:* 20 full-time (19 women), 71 part-time (70 women); includes 11 minority (5 Black or African American, non-Hispanic/Latino; 3 Asian, non-Hispanic/Latino; 2 Hispanic/Latino; 1 Two or more races, non-Hispanic/Latino). Average age 37. 32 applicants, 41% accepted, 12 enrolled. In 2019, 34 master's, 6 other advanced degrees awarded. *Degree requirements:* For master's, thesis, Internship and Capstone portfolio (S); Minimum 600 faculty supervised clinical hours (S). *Entrance requirements:* Additional exam requirements/recommendations for international students: required—TOEFL. *Application deadline:* Applications are processed on a rolling basis. Application fee: $50. Electronic applications accepted. *Expenses:* Tuition varies by program. *Financial support:* Applicants required to submit FAFSA. *Unit head:* Nancy Meedzan, DNP, RN, CNE, Dean, School of Nursing, 978-232-2328, E-mail: nmeedzan@endicott.edu. *Application contact:* Ian Menchini, Director, Graduate Enrollment and Advising, 978-232-5292, Fax: 978-232-3000, E-mail: imenchin@endicott.edu.
Website: https://www.endicott.edu/academics/schools/nursing/graduate-programs

## Nursing and Healthcare Administration

**Fairfield University,** Marion Peckham Egan School of Nursing and Health Studies, Fairfield, CT 06824. Offers advanced practice (DNP); family nurse practitioner (MSN, DNP); nurse anesthesia (DNP); nursing leadership (MSN); psychiatric nurse practitioner (MSN, DNP). *Accreditation:* AACN; AANA/CANAEP. *Program availability:* Part-time, evening/weekend. *Faculty:* 13 full-time (all women), 12 part-time/adjunct (9 women). *Students:* 56 full-time (49 women), 165 part-time (149 women); includes 62 minority (24 Black or African American, non-Hispanic/Latino; 12 Asian, non-Hispanic/Latino; 25 Hispanic/Latino; 1 Two or more races, non-Hispanic/Latino). Average age 33. 129 applicants, 56% accepted, 62 enrolled. In 2019, 26 master's, 36 doctorates awarded. *Degree requirements:* For master's, capstone project. *Entrance requirements:* For master's, minimum QPA of 3.0, RN license, resume, 2 recommendations; for doctorate, MSN (minimum QPA of 3.2) or BSN (minimum QPA of 3.0); critical care nursing experience (for nurse anesthesia DNP candidates). Additional exam requirements/recommendations for international students: required—TOEFL (minimum score 550 paper-based; 80 iBT), IELTS (minimum score 6.5), TOEFL (minimum score 550 paper-based; 80 iBT) or IELTS (minimum score 6.5). *Application deadline:* For fall admission, 5/15 for international students; for spring admission, 10/15 for international students. Applications are processed on a rolling basis. Application fee: $60. Electronic applications accepted. *Expenses:* $875 per credit hour tuition (for MS), $1,010 per credit hour tuition (for Master of Healthcare Administration), $1,025 per credit hour tuition (for Doctorate in Clinical Nutrition), $1,050 per credit hour tuition (for DNP Nurse Anesthesia), $1,000 per credit hour tuition (for all other DNP programs), $150 per semester clinical placement fee (applicable programs, fall and spring semesters), $50 per semester registration fee, $65 per semester graduate student activity fee (fall and spring). *Financial support:* In 2019–20, 45 students received support. Scholarships/grants and unspecified assistantships available. Financial award applicants required to submit FAFSA. *Unit head:* Dr. Meredith Wallace Kazer, Dean, 203-254-4000 Ext. 2701, Fax: 203-254-4126, E-mail: mkazer@fairfield.edu. *Application contact:* Melanie Rogers, Director of Graduate Admission, 203-254-4184, Fax: 203-254-4073, E-mail: gradadmis@fairfield.edu.
Website: http://fairfield.edu/son

**Felician University,** Doctor of Nursing Practice Program, Lodi, NJ 07644-2117. Offers advanced practice (DNP); executive leadership (DNP). *Accreditation:* AACN. *Program availability:* Evening/weekend, online only, 100% online, blended/hybrid learning. *Degree requirements:* For doctorate, thesis/dissertation, scholarly project. *Entrance requirements:* For doctorate, 2 letters of recommendation; national certification as nurse executive/administrator (preferred); interview; minimum GPA of 3.0. Additional exam requirements/recommendations for international students: required—TOEFL (minimum score 550 paper-based; 79 iBT), IELTS (minimum score 6.5), PTE (minimum score 56). Electronic applications accepted. Application fee is waived when completed online. *Expenses:* Contact institution.

**Felician University,** Master of Science in Nursing Program, Lodi, NJ 07644-2117. Offers adult-gerontology nurse practitioner (MSN, PMC); executive leadership (MSN, PMC); family nurse practitioner (MSN, PMC); nursing education (MSN, PMC). *Accreditation:* AACN. *Program availability:* Evening/weekend, online only, 100% online, blended/hybrid learning. *Degree requirements:* For master's, thesis, clinical presentation; for PMC, thesis, education project. *Entrance requirements:* For master's, BSN; minimum GPA of 3.0; 2 letters of recommendation; NJ RN license; personal statement; for PMC, RN license, minimum GPA of 3.0. Additional exam requirements/recommendations for international students: required—TOEFL (minimum score 550 paper-based; 79 iBT), IELTS (minimum score 6.5), PTE (minimum score 56). Electronic applications accepted. Application fee is waived when completed online. *Expenses:* Contact institution.

**Ferris State University,** College of Health Professions, School of Nursing, Big Rapids, MI 49307. Offers nursing (MSN); nursing administration (MSN); nursing education (MSN); nursing informatics (MSN). *Accreditation:* ACEN. *Program availability:* Part-time, evening/weekend, online only, 100% online. *Faculty:* 7 full-time (all women), 1 (woman) part-time/adjunct. *Students:* 103 part-time (95 women); includes 14 minority (2 Black or African American, non-Hispanic/Latino; 6 American Indian or Alaska Native, non-Hispanic/Latino; 4 Hispanic/Latino; 2 Two or more races, non-Hispanic/Latino). Average age 38. 31 applicants, 97% accepted, 24 enrolled. In 2019, 24 master's awarded. *Degree requirements:* For master's, practicum, practicum project. *Entrance requirements:* For master's, BS in nursing (for nursing education track); BS in nursing or related field (for nursing administration and nursing informatics tracks); registered nurse license, writing sample, letters of reference, 2 years' clinical experience (recommended). Additional exam requirements/recommendations for international students: required—TOEFL (minimum score 550 paper-based; 79 iBT). *Application deadline:* For fall admission, 4/15 priority date for domestic and international students; for spring admission, 10/15 for domestic and international students. Electronic applications accepted. Tuition and fees vary according to degree level, program and student level. *Financial support:* In 2019–20, 7 students received support. Career-related internships or fieldwork and scholarships/grants available. Financial award application deadline: 4/15; financial award applicants required to submit FAFSA. *Unit head:* Dr. Wendy Lenon, Chair, School of Nursing, 231-591-2267, Fax: 231-591-2325, E-mail: WendyLenon@ferris.edu. *Application contact:* Dr. Sharon Colley, MSN Program Coordinator, 231-591-2288, Fax: 231-591-2325, E-mail: colleys@ferris.edu.
Website: http://www.ferris.edu/htmls/colleges/alliedhe/Nursing/homepage.htm

**Florida Agricultural and Mechanical University,** Division of Graduate Studies, Research, and Continuing Education, School of Allied Health Sciences, Tallahassee, FL 32307-3200. Offers health administration (MS); occupational therapy (MOT); physical therapy (DPT). *Degree requirements:* For master's, thesis (for some programs). *Entrance requirements:* For master's, GRE General Test or GMAT, minimum GPA of 3.0. Additional exam requirements/recommendations for international students: required—TOEFL (minimum score 550 paper-based).

**Florida Atlantic University,** Christine E. Lynn College of Nursing, Boca Raton, FL 33431. Offers administrative and financial leadership in nursing and health care (Post Master's Certificate); nursing (MSN, PhD); nursing practice (DNP). *Accreditation:* AACN. *Program availability:* Part-time. *Faculty:* 37 full-time (35 women), 16 part-time/adjunct (15 women). *Students:* 75 full-time (66 women), 396 part-time (366 women); includes 272 minority (151 Black or African American, non-Hispanic/Latino; 24 Asian, non-Hispanic/Latino; 81 Hispanic/Latino; 16 Two or more races, non-Hispanic/Latino), 14 international. Average age 36. 515 applicants, 31% accepted, 131 enrolled. In 2019, 155 master's, 33 doctorates awarded. *Degree requirements:* For master's, thesis or alternative; for doctorate, comprehensive exam, thesis/dissertation. *Entrance requirements:* For master's, GRE General Test or MAT, bachelor's degree in nursing, Florida RN license, minimum GPA of 3.0, resume/curriculum vitae, letter of recommendation; for doctorate, GRE General Test or MAT, curriculum vitae, Florida RN license, minimum GPA of 3.5, master's degree in nursing, three letters of recommendation. *Application deadline:* For fall admission, 6/1 for domestic students, 2/15 for international students; for spring admission, 10/1 for domestic students, 7/15 for international students. Applications are processed on a rolling basis. Application fee: $30. *Expenses:* Tuition: Full-time $20,536; part-time $371.82 per credit hour. Tuition and fees vary according to program. *Financial support:* Research assistantships with partial

tuition reimbursements, teaching assistantships with partial tuition reimbursements, career-related internships or fieldwork, Federal Work-Study, institutionally sponsored loans, scholarships/grants, and traineeships available. Support available to part-time students. *Unit head:* Safiya A George Damida, Dean, 561-297-3206, E-mail: sgeorge@health.fau.edu. *Application contact:* Safiya A George Damida, Dean, 561-297-3206, E-mail: sgeorge@health.fau.edu.
Website: http://nursing.fau.edu/

**Florida National University,** Program in Nursing, Hialeah, FL 33139. Offers family nurse practitioner (MSN); nurse educator (MSN); nurse leadership and management (MSN). *Program availability:* 100% online, blended/hybrid learning. *Faculty:* 6 full-time (4 women), 9 part-time/adjunct (7 women). *Students:* 14 full-time (10 women), 204 part-time (151 women); includes 213 minority (21 Black or African American, non-Hispanic/Latino; 1 Asian, non-Hispanic/Latino; 191 Hispanic/Latino). Average age 40. 54 applicants, 100% accepted, 54 enrolled. In 2019, 53 master's awarded. *Degree requirements:* For master's, practicum. *Entrance requirements:* For master's, active registered nurse license, BSN from accredited institution. Additional exam requirements/recommendations for international students: recommended—TOEFL. *Expenses:* Contact institution. *Financial support:* Scholarships/grants available. *Unit head:* Dr. Lydie Janvier, Master of Science in Nursing Program Director, 305-821-3333 Ext. 1056, Fax: 305-362-0595, E-mail: ljanvier@fnu.edu. *Application contact:* Dr. Lydie Janvier, Master of Science in Nursing Program Director, 305-821-3333 Ext. 1056, Fax: 305-362-0595, E-mail: ljanvier@fnu.edu.
Website: https://www.fnu.edu/prospective-students/our-programs/select-a-program/master-of-business-administration/nursing-msn-master/

**Florida Southern College,** School of Nursing and Health Sciences, Lakeland, FL 33801. Offers adult gerontology clinical nurse specialist (MSN); adult gerontology primary care nurse practitioner (MSN); family nurse practitioner (MSN); nurse educator (MSN); nursing administration (MSN). *Accreditation:* AACN. *Program availability:* Part-time, The Nurse Educator MSN degree concentration and NE postmasters certificate are fully online. The Nursing Administrative Leadership MSN degree concentration is delivered in blended/hybrid format. *Faculty:* 6 full-time (all women), 1 (woman) part-time/adjunct. *Students:* 145 full-time (131 women), 1 (woman) part-time; includes 70 minority (30 Black or African American, non-Hispanic/Latino; 11 Asian, non-Hispanic/Latino; 25 Hispanic/Latino; 4 Two or more races, non-Hispanic/Latino), 1 international. Average age 39. 81 applicants, 89% accepted, 50 enrolled. In 2019, 53 master's awarded. *Degree requirements:* For master's, comprehensive exam, 660 clinical hours (for Family Nurse Practitioner); 540 clinical hours (for Adult-Gerontology Primary Care Nurse Practitioner). *Entrance requirements:* For master's, Florida RN license, 3 letters of recommendation, professional statement, minimum GPA of 3.0 in the last 60 credit hours of BSN, BSN earned from a regionally accredited institution and a CCNE, CNEA, or ACEN accredited nursing program, resume, admission interview. Additional exam requirements/recommendations for international students: required—TOEFL (minimum score 550 paper-based; 79 iBT), IELTS (minimum score 6.5), International students from countries where English is not the standard for daily communication must submit either the TOEFL or IELTS. *Application deadline:* For fall admission, 6/1 for domestic and international students; for spring admission, 10/1 for domestic and international students. Applications are processed on a rolling basis. Electronic applications accepted. *Expenses:* DNP: $725 per credit hour tuition, $50 per semester technology fee (for 5-8 hours), $100 per semester technology fee (for 9-12 hours); MSN: $600 per credit hour tuition, $50 per semester technology fee (for 5-8 hours), $100 per semester technology fee (for 9-12 hours), $35 per semester insurance and lab supplies fees. *Financial support:* In 2019–20, 1 student received support. Employee tuition grants, athletic scholarships for students still eligible available. Financial award application deadline: 8/20; financial award applicants required to submit FAFSA. *Unit head:* Dr. Linda Comer, Dean, 863-680-3951, Fax: 863-680-3860, E-mail: lcomer@flsouthern.edu. *Application contact:* Kimberly Smith, Admission Counselor and Advisor for Nursing, 863-680-3090, Fax: 863-680-3872, E-mail: ksmith@flsouthern.edu.
Website: www.flsouthern.edu/sage

**Framingham State University,** Graduate Studies, Program in Nursing, Framingham, MA 01701-9101. Offers nursing education (MSN); nursing leadership (MSN). *Accreditation:* AACN. *Entrance requirements:* For master's, BSN; minimum cumulative undergraduate GPA of 3.0, 3.25 in nursing courses; coursework in statistics; 2 letters of recommendation; interview. Electronic applications accepted.

**Franklin Pierce University,** Graduate and Professional Studies, Rindge, NH 03461-0060. Offers curriculum and instruction (M Ed); elementary education (MS Ed); emerging network technologies (Graduate Certificate); energy and sustainability studies (MBA, Graduate Certificate); health administration (MBA, Graduate Certificate); human resource management (MBA, Graduate Certificate); information technology (MBA); leadership (MBA); nursing education (MS); nursing leadership (MS); physical therapy (DPT); physician assistant studies (MPAS); special education (M Ed); sports management (MBA). *Accreditation:* APTA. *Program availability:* Part-time, 100% online, blended/hybrid learning. *Degree requirements:* For master's, concentrated original research projects; student teaching; fieldwork and/or internship; leadership project; PRAXIS I and II (for M Ed); for doctorate, concentrated original research projects, clinical fieldwork and/or internship, leadership project. *Entrance requirements:* For master's, minimum GPA of 2.5, 3 letters of recommendation; competencies in accounting, economics, statistics, and computer skills through life experience or undergraduate coursework (for MBA); certification/e-portfolio, minimum C grade in all education courses (for M Ed); license to practice as RN (for MS); for doctorate, GRE, 80 hours of observation/work in PT settings; completion of anatomy, chemistry, physics, and statistics; minimum GPA of 3.0. Additional exam requirements/recommendations for international students: required—TOEFL (minimum score 550 paper-based; 61 iBT). Electronic applications accepted.

**Frostburg State University,** College of Liberal Arts and Sciences, Department of Nursing, Frostburg, MD 21532-1099. Offers nursing administration (MSN); nursing education (MSN). *Program availability:* Part-time, online learning. *Entrance requirements:* For master's, current unrestricted RN license; BSN from a nursing program accredited by CCNE or ACEN. Additional exam requirements/recommendations for international students: required—TOEFL.

**Gannon University,** School of Graduate Studies, Morosky College of Health Professions and Sciences, Villa Maria School of Nursing, Program in Nursing Administration, Erie, PA 16541-0001. Offers MSN. *Program availability:* Part-time, evening/weekend. *Degree requirements:* For master's, thesis (for some programs), practicum. *Entrance requirements:* For master's, GRE, RN, transcripts, 3 letters of recommendation, evidence of the fulfillment of legal requirements for the practice of nursing in the United States. Additional exam requirements/recommendations for international students: required—TOEFL (minimum score 79 iBT). Electronic applications accepted.

**George Mason University,** College of Health and Human Services, School of Nursing, Fairfax, VA 22030. Offers adult gerontology (DNP); adult/gerontological nurse practitioner (MSN); family nurse practitioner (MSN, DNP); nurse educator (MSN); nursing (PhD); nursing administration (MSN, DNP); nursing education (Certificate); psychiatric mental health (DNP). *Accreditation:* AACN. *Program availability:* Part-time,

evening/weekend, blended/hybrid learning. *Degree requirements:* For master's, comprehensive exam (for some programs), thesis in clinical classes; for doctorate, comprehensive exam (for some programs), thesis/dissertation (for some programs). *Entrance requirements:* For master's, 2 official transcripts; expanded goals statement; resume; BSN from accredited institution; minimum GPA of 3.0 in last 60 credits of undergraduate work; 2 letters of recommendation; completion of undergraduate statistics and graduate-level bivariate statistics; certification in professional CPR; for doctorate, GRE, 2 official transcripts; expanded goals statement; resume; 2 recommendation letters; nursing license; at least 1 year of work experience as an RN; interview; writing sample; evidence of graduate-level course in applied statistics; master's degree in nursing with minimum GPA of 3.5; for Certificate, 2 official transcripts; expanded goals statement; resume; master's degree from accredited institution or currently enrolled with minimum GPA of 3.0. Additional exam requirements/recommendations for international students: required—TOEFL (minimum score 570 paper-based; 88 iBT), IELTS (minimum score 6.5), PTE (minimum score 59). Electronic applications accepted. *Expenses:* Contact institution.

**The George Washington University,** School of Nursing, Washington, DC 20052. Offers adult nurse practitioner (MSN, DNP, Post-Master's Certificate); clinical research administration (MSN); family nurse practitioner (MSN, Post-Master's Certificate); health care quality (MSN, Post-Master's Certificate); nursing leadership and management (MSN); nursing practice (DNP); palliative care nurse practitioner (Post-Master's Certificate). *Accreditation:* AACN.

**Georgia Southwestern State University,** College of Nursing and Health Sciences, Americus, GA 31709-4693. Offers family nurse practitioner (MSN); health informatics (Postbaccalaureate Certificate); nurse educator (Post Master's Certificate); nursing educator (MSN); nursing informatics (MSN); nursing leadership (MSN). *Program availability:* Part-time, online only, all theory courses are offered online. *Faculty:* 9 full-time (all women), 5 part-time/adjunct (all women). *Students:* 18 full-time (14 women), 104 part-time (91 women); includes 45 minority (31 Black or African American, non-Hispanic/Latino; 1 American Indian or Alaska Native, non-Hispanic/Latino; 4 Asian, non-Hispanic/Latino; 3 Hispanic/Latino; 6 Two or more races, non-Hispanic/Latino). Average age 36. 96 applicants, 45% accepted, 24 enrolled. In 2019, 53 master's awarded. *Degree requirements:* For master's, thesis (for some programs), minimum cumulative GPA of 3.0; maximum of 6 credit hours with C grade and no D grades; degree completed within 7 calendar years from initial enrollment date in graduate courses; for other advanced degree, minimum cumulative GPA of 3.0; maximum of 6 credit hours with C grade and no D grades; degree completed within 7 calendar years from initial enrollment date in graduate courses. *Entrance requirements:* For master's, baccalaureate degree in nursing from regionally-accredited institution and nationally-accredited nursing program with minimum GPA of 3.0; three completed recommendation forms from professional peer or clinical supervisor; current unencumbered RN license in state where clinical course requirements will be met; proof of immunizations; for other advanced degree, Baccalaureate or masters degree (depending upon certificate) in nursing; Minimum GPA of 3.0; 3 completed recommendation forms; current unencumbered RN license in state where clinical course requirements will be met. Application fee: $25. Electronic applications accepted. *Expenses:* $385.00 per credit hour tuition, plus fees, which vary according to enrolled credit hours. *Financial support:* Application deadline: 6/1; applicants required to submit FAFSA. *Unit head:* Dr. Sandra Daniel, Dean, 229-931-2275. *Application contact:* Office of Graduate Admissions, 800-338-0082, Fax: 229-931-2983, E-mail: graduateadmissions@gsw.edu.
Website: https://www.gsw.edu/academics/schools-and-departments/college-of-nursing-and-health-sciences/school-of-nursing/nursing-programs/graduate

**Georgia State University,** Byrdine F. Lewis School of Nursing, Atlanta, GA 30303. Offers adult health clinical nurse specialist/nurse practitioner (MS, Certificate); child health clinical nurse specialist/pediatric nurse practitioner (MS, Certificate); family nurse practitioner (MS, Certificate); family psychiatric mental health nurse practitioner (MS, Certificate); nursing (PhD); nursing leadership in healthcare innovations (MS), including nursing administration, nursing informatics; nutrition (MS); occupational therapy (MOT); perinatal clinical nurse specialist/women's health nurse practitioner (MS, Certificate); physical therapy (DPT); respiratory therapy (MS). *Accreditation:* AACN. *Program availability:* Part-time, blended/hybrid learning. *Faculty:* 57 full-time (40 women), 5 part-time/adjunct (4 women). *Students:* 388 full-time (290 women), 155 part-time (135 women); includes 217 minority (130 Black or African American, non-Hispanic/Latino; 47 Asian, non-Hispanic/Latino; 26 Hispanic/Latino; 14 Two or more races, non-Hispanic/Latino; 45 international. Average age 32. 480 applicants, 50% accepted, 164 enrolled. In 2019, 158 master's, 64 doctorates, 20 other advanced degrees awarded. *Degree requirements:* For doctorate, comprehensive exam, thesis/dissertation. *Entrance requirements:* For doctorate, GRE. Additional exam requirements/recommendations for international students: required—TOEFL. *Application deadline:* For fall admission, 2/1 priority date for domestic and international students; for spring admission, 9/15 for domestic and international students. Applications are processed on a rolling basis. Application fee: $50. Electronic applications accepted. *Expenses:* Contact institution. *Financial support:* In 2019–20, research assistantships with tuition reimbursements (averaging $1,666 per year), teaching assistantships with tuition reimbursements (averaging $1,920 per year) were awarded; scholarships/grants, tuition waivers (full and partial), and unspecified assistantships also available. Support available to part-time students. Financial award application deadline: 8/1; financial award applicants required to submit FAFSA. *Unit head:* Huanbiao Mo, Dean of Nursing. *Application contact:* Huanbiao Mo, Dean of Nursing.
Website: http://nursing.gsu.edu/

**Goldfarb School of Nursing at Barnes-Jewish College,** Graduate Programs, St. Louis, MO 63110. Offers adult-gerontology (MSN), including primary care nurse practitioner; adult-gerontology (MSN), including acute care nurse practitioner; health systems and population health leadership (MSN); nurse anesthesia (MSN). *Accreditation:* AACN; AANA/CANAEP. *Program availability:* Part-time, online learning. *Degree requirements:* For master's, thesis or alternative. *Entrance requirements:* For master's, 2 references, personal statement, curriculum vitae or resume. Additional exam requirements/recommendations for international students: required—TOEFL (minimum score 575 paper-based; 85 iBT).

**Grand Valley State University,** Kirkhof College of Nursing, Grand Rapids, MI 49503-3314. Offers case management (MSN); nursing practice (DNP); MSN/MBA. *Accreditation:* AACN. *Program availability:* Part-time. *Faculty:* 14 full-time (all women), 4 part-time/adjunct (3 women). *Students:* 55 full-time (47 women), 21 part-time (19 women); includes 12 minority (5 Black or African American, non-Hispanic/Latino; 4 Asian, non-Hispanic/Latino; 2 Hispanic/Latino; 1 Two or more races, non-Hispanic/Latino), 1 international. Average age 32. 33 applicants, 94% accepted, 21 enrolled. In 2019, 7 master's, 49 doctorates awarded. *Degree requirements:* For master's, thesis optional, thesis or project; for doctorate, thesis/dissertation optional, thesis or project. *Entrance requirements:* For master's, GRE, minimum upper-division GPA of 3.0, course work in statistics, Michigan RN license, writing sample, interview, criminal background check and drug screen, health records; for doctorate, minimum GPA of 3.0 in master's-level coursework, writing sample, interview, RN in Michigan, criminal background check

and drug screen, health records. Additional exam requirements/recommendations for international students: required—TOEFL (minimum iBT score of 80), IELTS (6.5), or Michigan English Language Assessment Battery (77). *Application deadline:* For fall admission, 3/15 priority date for domestic students. Applications are processed on a rolling basis. Application fee: $30. Electronic applications accepted. *Expenses:* $823 per credit hour, 75-77 credit hours. *Financial support:* In 2019–20, 39 students received support, including 14 fellowships, 20 research assistantships with partial tuition reimbursements available (averaging $4,000 per year); career-related internships or fieldwork, Federal Work-Study, institutionally sponsored loans, and traineeships also available. Financial award application deadline: 2/15. *Unit head:* Dr. Cynthia McCurren, Dean, 616-331-3558, Fax: 616-331-2510, E-mail: mccurrec@gvsu.edu. *Application contact:* Dr. Katherine Moran, Graduate Program Director, 616-331-5458, Fax: 616-331-2510, E-mail: morakath@gvsu.edu.
Website: http://www.gvsu.edu/kcon/

**Grand View University,** Graduate Studies, Des Moines, IA 50316-1599. Offers athletic training (MS); clinical nurse leader (MSN, Post Master's Certificate); nursing education (MSN, Post Master's Certificate); organizational leadership (MS); sport management (MS); teacher leadership (M Ed); urban education (M Ed). *Program availability:* Part-time, evening/weekend. *Degree requirements:* For master's, completion of all required coursework in common core and selected track with minimum cumulative GPA of 3.0 and no more than two grades of C. *Entrance requirements:* For master's, GRE, GMAT, or essay, minimum undergraduate GPA of 3.0, professional resume, 3 letters of recommendation, interview. Additional exam requirements/recommendations for international students: required—TOEFL (minimum score 550 paper-based). Electronic applications accepted.

**Grantham University,** College of Nursing and Allied Health, Lenexa, KS 66219. Offers case management (MSN); health systems management (MS); healthcare administration (MHA); nursing education (MSN); nursing informatics (MSN); nursing management and organizational leadership (MSN). *Program availability:* Part-time, evening/weekend, online only, 100% online. *Students:* 180 full-time (135 women), 61 part-time (47 women); includes 124 minority (71 Black or African American, non-Hispanic/Latino; 1 American Indian or Alaska Native, non-Hispanic/Latino; 17 Asian, non-Hispanic/Latino; 17 Hispanic/Latino; 1 Native Hawaiian or other Pacific Islander, non-Hispanic/Latino; 17 Two or more races, non-Hispanic/Latino). Average age 40. 53 applicants, 89% accepted, 37 enrolled. In 2019, 100 master's awarded. *Entrance requirements:* For master's, Graduate: A minimum score of 530 on the paper-based TOEFL, or 71 on the internet-based TOEFL, 6.5 on the IELTS, or 50 on the PTE Academic Score Report. Additional exam requirements/recommendations for international students: required—TOEFL (minimum score 530 paper-based; 71 iBT), IELTS (minimum score 6.5), PTE (minimum score 50). *Application deadline:* Applications are processed on a rolling basis. Electronic applications accepted. *Expenses:* Contact institution. *Financial support:* Scholarships/grants available. Financial award applicants required to submit FAFSA. *Unit head:* Dr. Cheryl Rules, Dean of the College of Nursing and the School of Allied Health changing to College of Health Professions, 913-309-4783, Fax: 844-897-6490, E-mail: crules@grantham.edu. *Application contact:* Adam Wright, Associate VP, Enrollment Services, 800-955-2527 Ext. 803, Fax: 877-304-4467, E-mail: admissions@grantham.edu.
Website: http://www.grantham.edu/nursing-and-allied-health/

**Hampton University,** School of Nursing, Hampton, VA 23668. Offers community health nursing (MS); family nurse practitioner (MS); family research (PhD); nursing administration (MS); nursing education (MS). *Accreditation:* AACN. *Program availability:* Part-time, online learning. *Students:* 3 full-time (all women), 13 part-time (12 women); includes 15 minority (all Black or African American, non-Hispanic/Latino). Average age 49. 4 applicants, 25% accepted. In 2019, 3 master's, 5 doctorates awarded. *Degree requirements:* For master's, comprehensive exam, thesis optional; for doctorate, comprehensive exam, thesis/dissertation. *Entrance requirements:* For master's, GRE General Test. *Application deadline:* For fall admission, 6/1 priority date for domestic students, 4/1 priority date for international students; for spring admission, 11/1 priority date for domestic students, 9/1 priority date for international students; for summer admission, 4/1 priority date for domestic students, 2/1 priority date for international students. Applications are processed on a rolling basis. Application fee: $35. Electronic applications accepted. *Financial support:* In 2019–20, 2 students received support. Fellowships, research assistantships, teaching assistantships, career-related internships or fieldwork, Federal Work-Study, institutionally sponsored loans, and scholarships/grants available. Support available to part-time students. Financial award application deadline: 6/30; financial award applicants required to submit FAFSA. *Unit head:* Dr. Shevellanie Lott, Dean, 757-727-5654, E-mail: shevellanie.lott@hamptonu.edu. *Application contact:* Dr. Shevellanie Lott, Dean, 757-727-5654, E-mail: shevellanie.lott@hamptonu.edu.
Website: http://nursing.hamptonu.edu

**Herzing University Online,** Program in Nursing, Menomonee Falls, WI 53051. Offers nursing (MSN); nursing education (MSN); nursing management (MSN). *Accreditation:* AACN. *Program availability:* Online learning.

**Hofstra University,** School of Education, Specialized Programs in Education, Hempstead, NY 11549. Offers applied behavior analysis (Advanced Certificate); childhood special education (MS Ed); early childhood special education (MS Ed, Advanced Certificate); educational and policy leadership (Ed D); educational leadership (Advanced Certificate); educational leadership and policy studies (MS Ed), including K-12; elementary special education (MS Ed); gifted education (Advanced Certificate); health education (MS); health professions pedagogy and leadership (MS); higher education leadership and policy studies (MS Ed); inclusive early childhood special education (MS Ed); inclusive elementary special education (MS Ed); inclusive secondary special education (MS Ed); literacy studies (MA, MS Ed, Ed D, Advanced Certificate); pedagogy for health professions (Advanced Certificate); physical education (MS); school district business leader (Advanced Certificate); secondary education generalist - students with disabilities 7-12 (MS Ed); secondary special education generalist - secondary education (MS Ed); special education (MS Ed, Advanced Certificate); special education assessment and diagnosis (Advanced Certificate); special education early childhood intervention (MS Ed); special education: international perspectives (MS Ed); teaching students with severe or multiple disabilities (Advanced Certificate). *Program availability:* Part-time, evening/weekend, online only, blended/hybrid learning. *Students:* 109 full-time (83 women), 209 part-time (155 women); includes 89 minority (41 Black or African American, non-Hispanic/Latino; 3 American Indian or Alaska Native, non-Hispanic/Latino; 8 Asian, non-Hispanic/Latino; 31 Hispanic/Latino; 6 Two or more races, non-Hispanic/Latino), 2 international. Average age 31. 194 applicants, 87% accepted, 108 enrolled. In 2019, 120 master's, 25 doctorates, 27 other advanced degrees awarded. *Degree requirements:* For master's, one foreign language, comprehensive exam (for some programs), thesis (for some programs), electronic portfolio, capstone course, internship, practicum, student teaching, seminars, minimum GPA of 3.0; for doctorate, one foreign language, comprehensive exam, thesis/dissertation, qualifying hearing. *Entrance requirements:* For master's, GRE, interview, letters of recommendation, portfolio, essay, certification; for doctorate, GRE or MAT, interview, resume, essay, master's degree, 3 letters of recommendation, writing sample;

for Advanced Certificate, GRE, interview, letters of recommendation, essay, professional experience, resume, master's degree. Additional exam requirements/recommendations for international students: required—TOEFL (minimum score 550 paper-based; 80 iBT); recommended—IELTS (minimum score 6.5). *Application deadline:* Applications are processed on a rolling basis. Application fee: $75. Electronic applications accepted. *Expenses: Tuition:* Full-time $25,164; part-time $1398 per credit. *Required fees:* $580; $165 per semester. Tuition and fees vary according to course load, degree level and program. *Financial support:* In 2019–20, 177 students received support, including 99 fellowships with full and partial tuition reimbursements available (averaging $4,221 per year), 12 research assistantships with full and partial tuition reimbursements available (averaging $5,577 per year); career-related internships or fieldwork, Federal Work-Study, institutionally sponsored loans, scholarships/grants, traineeships, tuition waivers (full and partial), unspecified assistantships, and scholarships and endowed scholarships also available. Support available to part-time students. Financial award applicants required to submit FAFSA. *Unit head:* Dr. Alan Flurkey, Chairperson, 516-463-5237, E-mail: alan.d.flurkey@hofstra.edu. *Application contact:* Sunil Samuel, Assistant Vice President of Admissions, 516-463-4723, Fax: 516-463-4664, E-mail: graduateadmission@hofstra.edu.
Website: http://www.hofstra.edu/education/

**Holy Family University,** Graduate and Professional Programs, School of Nursing and Allied Health Professions, Philadelphia, PA 19114. Offers nursing administration (MSN); nursing education (MSN). *Accreditation:* AACN. *Program availability:* Part-time, evening/weekend. *Degree requirements:* For master's, thesis or alternative, comprehensive portfolio, clinical practicum. *Entrance requirements:* For master's, BSN or RN from appropriately-accredited program, minimum GPA of 3.0, professional references, official transcripts of all college or university work, essay/personal statement, current resume, completion of one undergraduate statistics course with minimum grade of C. Additional exam requirements/recommendations for international students: required—TOEFL (minimum score 550 paper-based; 79 iBT), IELTS (minimum score 6), or PTE (minimum score 54). Electronic applications accepted.

**Holy Names University,** Graduate Division, Department of Nursing, Oakland, CA 94619-1699. Offers administration/management (MSN, PMC); care transition management (MSN); family nurse practitioner (MSN, PMC); informatics (MSN); nurse educator (PMC); MSN/MBA. *Accreditation:* AACN. *Program availability:* Part-time, evening/weekend. *Entrance requirements:* For master's, bachelor's degree in nursing or related field; California RN license or eligibility; minimum cumulative GPA of 2.8, 3.0 in nursing courses from baccalaureate program; courses in pathophysiology, statistics, and research at the undergraduate level. Additional exam requirements/recommendations for international students: required—TOEFL (minimum score 550 paper-based; 79 iBT). Electronic applications accepted. Application fee is waived when completed online.

**Immaculata University,** College of Graduate Studies, Division of Nursing, Immaculata, PA 19345. Offers nursing administration (MSN); nursing education (MSN). *Accreditation:* AACN. *Program availability:* Part-time, evening/weekend. *Entrance requirements:* For master's, MAT or GRE, BSN, minimum undergraduate GPA of 3.0. Additional exam requirements/recommendations for international students: required—TOEFL.

**Independence University,** Program in Nursing, Salt Lake City, UT 84107. Offers community health (MSN); gerontology (MSN); nursing administration (MSN); wellness promotion (MSN).

**Indiana State University,** College of Graduate and Professional Studies, College of Health and Human Services, Department of Advanced Practice Nursing, Terre Haute, IN 47809. Offers advanced practice nursing (DNP); family nurse practitioner (MS); nursing administration (MS); nursing education (MS). *Accreditation:* ACEN. *Program availability:* Part-time. *Degree requirements:* For master's, thesis or alternative. *Entrance requirements:* For master's, BSN, RN license, minimum undergraduate GPA of 3.0. Electronic applications accepted.

**Indiana University Kokomo,** School of Nursing, Kokomo, IN 46904. Offers family nurse practitioner (MSN); nurse administrator (MSN); nurse educator (MSN). Electronic applications accepted. *Expenses:* Contact institution.

**Indiana University of Pennsylvania,** School of Graduate Studies and Research, College of Health and Human Services, Department of Nursing and Allied Health Professions, Program in Nursing Administration, Indiana, PA 15705. Offers MS. *Accreditation:* AACN. *Program availability:* Part-time. *Faculty:* 7 full-time (6 women). *Students:* 13 part-time (10 women), 2 international. Average age 36. 6 applicants, 100% accepted, 3 enrolled. In 2019, 9 master's awarded. *Degree requirements:* For master's, thesis optional, practicum. *Entrance requirements:* For master's, goal statement, official transcripts, letters of recommendation. Additional exam requirements/recommendations for international students: required—TOEFL (minimum score 540 paper-based; 76 iBT), IELTS (minimum score 6). *Application deadline:* Applications are processed on a rolling basis. Application fee: $50. Electronic applications accepted. *Expenses:* Contact institution. *Financial support:* Research assistantships with tuition reimbursements, career-related internships or fieldwork, Federal Work-Study, scholarships/grants, and unspecified assistantships available. Financial award application deadline: 4/15; financial award applicants required to submit FAFSA. *Unit head:* Dr. Nashat Zuraikat, Graduate Coordinator, 724-357-3262, E-mail: zuraikat@iup.edu. *Application contact:* Dr. Nashat Zuraikat, Graduate Coordinator, 724-357-3262, E-mail: zuraikat@iup.edu.
Website: http://www.iup.edu/grad/nursing/default.aspx

**Indiana University-Purdue University Indianapolis,** School of Nursing, Doctor of Nursing Practice Program, Indianapolis, IN 46202. Offers executive leadership (DNP). *Accreditation:* AACN. *Program availability:* Blended/hybrid learning. *Entrance requirements:* For doctorate, MSN from ACEN- or CCNE-accredited program with minimum cumulative GPA of 3.3, documentation of supervised practice hours from accredited MSN program, unencumbered RN license, graduate-level course in statistics, three references indicating ability to succeed in DNP program. Additional exam requirements/recommendations for international students: required—TOEFL (minimum score 550 paper-based; 79 iBT). Electronic applications accepted. *Expenses:* Contact institution.

**Indiana University-Purdue University Indianapolis,** School of Nursing, MSN Program in Nursing, Indianapolis, IN 46202. Offers adult/gerontology acute care nurse practitioner (MSN); adult/gerontology clinical nurse specialist (MSN); adult/gerontology primary care nurse practitioner (MSN); family nurse practitioner (MSN); nursing education (MSN); nursing leadership in health systems (MSN); pediatric clinical nurse specialist (MSN); pediatric nurse practitioner (MSN). *Accreditation:* AACN. *Program availability:* Part-time, blended/hybrid learning. *Degree requirements:* For master's, thesis. *Entrance requirements:* For master's, BSN from ACEN- or CCNE-accredited program, minimum undergraduate GPA of 3.0 (preferred), professional resume or curriculum vitae, essay stating career goals and objectives, current unencumbered RN license, three references from individuals with knowledge of ability to succeed in graduate program. Additional exam requirements/recommendations for international students: required—TOEFL (minimum score 550 paper-based; 79 iBT). Electronic applications accepted. *Expenses:* Contact institution.

**Indiana Wesleyan University,** Graduate School, School of Nursing, Marion, IN 46953-4974. Offers nursing administration (MS); nursing education (MS); primary care nursing (MS); MSN/MBA. *Accreditation:* AACN. *Program availability:* Part-time, online learning. *Degree requirements:* For master's, capstone project or thesis. *Entrance requirements:* For master's, writing sample, RN license, 1 year of related experience, graduate statistics course. Additional exam requirements/recommendations for international students: required—TOEFL. *Expenses:* Contact institution.

**Jacksonville University,** Brooks Rehabilitation College of Healthcare Sciences, Keigwin School of Nursing, Master of Science in Nursing Program, Jacksonville, FL 32211. Offers clinical nurse educator (MSN); family nurse practitioner (MSN); family nurse practitioner/emergency nurse practitioner (MSN); leadership in the healthcare system (MSN); nursing informatics (MSN); psychiatric nurse practitioner (MSN); MSN/MBA. *Program availability:* Part-time, 100% online, blended/hybrid learning. In 2019, 215 master's awarded. *Degree requirements:* For master's, thesis. *Entrance requirements:* For master's, GRE General Test or undergraduate GPA above 3.0, BSN from ACEN- or CCNE-accredited program; course work in statistics and physical assessment within last 5 years; Florida nursing license; CPR/BLS certification; 3 recommendations, 2 of which are professional references; statement of intent; resume. Additional exam requirements/recommendations for international students: required—TOEFL (minimum score 650 paper-based; 114 iBT), IELTS (minimum score 8). *Application deadline:* Applications are processed on a rolling basis. Application fee: $50. Electronic applications accepted. *Expenses:* Contact institution. *Financial support:* Federal Work-Study, institutionally sponsored loans, scholarships/grants, and health care benefits available. Support available to part-time students. Financial award application deadline: 3/15; financial award applicants required to submit FAFSA. *Unit head:* Dr. Hilary Morgan, Director, Graduate Nursing Programs/Associate Professor, 904-256-7601, E-mail: hmorgan@ju.edu. *Application contact:* Kristen Kirkendall, Associate Director of Graduate Admissions and Communications, 904-256-7169, E-mail: kgreene8@ju.edu.
Website: https://www.ju.edu/nursing/graduate/master-science-nursing/index.php

**James Madison University,** The Graduate School, College of Health and Behavioral Studies, Program in Nursing, Harrisonburg, VA 22807. Offers adult/gerontology primary care nurse practitioner (MSN); clinical nurse leader (MSN); family nurse practitioner (MSN); nurse administrator (MSN); nurse midwifery (MSN); nursing (MSN, DNP); psychiatric mental health nurse practitioner (MSN). *Accreditation:* AACN. *Program availability:* Part-time, 100% online, blended/hybrid learning. *Students:* 15 full-time (14 women), 71 part-time (66 women); includes 10 minority (3 Black or African American, non-Hispanic/Latino; 6 Asian, non-Hispanic/Latino; 1 Hispanic/Latino). Average age 30. In 2019, 28 master's awarded. Application fee: $60. Electronic applications accepted. *Financial support:* In 2019–20, 2 students received support. Federal Work-Study and assistantships (averaging $7911) available. Financial award application deadline: 3/1; financial award applicants required to submit FAFSA. *Unit head:* Dr. Julie T. Sanford, Department Head, 540-568-6314, E-mail: sanforjt@jmu.edu. *Application contact:* Lynette D. Michael, Director of Graduate Admissions, 540-568-6131 Ext. 6395, Fax: 540-568-7860, E-mail: michaeld@jmu.edu.
Website: http://www.nursing.jmu.edu

**Jefferson College of Health Sciences,** Program in Nursing, Roanoke, VA 24013. Offers nursing education (MSN); nursing management (MSN). *Accreditation:* AACN. *Program availability:* Part-time. *Degree requirements:* For master's, project. *Entrance requirements:* For master's, MAT. Additional exam requirements/recommendations for international students: required—TOEFL (minimum score 550 paper-based; 80 iBT). Electronic applications accepted.

**Johns Hopkins University,** School of Nursing, DNP Clinical Nurse Specialist Track, Baltimore, MD 21218. Offers adult/gerontological critical care clinical nurse specialist (DNP); adult/gerontological health clinical nurse specialist (DNP); pediatric critical care clinical nurse specialist (DNP). *Accreditation:* AACN. *Program availability:* Part-time, 100% online, blended/hybrid learning. *Faculty:* 22 full-time (20 women), 3 part-time/adjunct (2 women). *Students:* 22 full-time (21 women), 11 part-time (all women); includes 15 minority (3 Black or African American, non-Hispanic/Latino; 4 Asian, non-Hispanic/Latino; 6 Hispanic/Latino; 1 Native Hawaiian or other Pacific Islander, non-Hispanic/Latino; 1 Two or more races, non-Hispanic/Latino). 25 applicants, 88% accepted, 16 enrolled. In 2019, 3 doctorates awarded. *Entrance requirements:* For doctorate, GRE, Minimum GPA of 3.0, goal statement/essay, resume, letters of recommendation, official transcripts from all post-secondary institutions attended, BSN, and RN license, prerequisite coursework. Additional exam requirements/recommendations for international students: required—TOEFL (minimum score 600 paper-based; 100 iBT), IELTS (minimum score 7). *Application deadline:* For fall admission, 11/1 priority date for domestic and international students. Application fee: $75. Electronic applications accepted. *Expenses:* $1,772 per credit. *Financial support:* In 2019–20, 23 students received support. Federal Work-Study and scholarships/grants available. Support available to part-time students. Financial award application deadline: 3/1; financial award applicants required to submit FAFSA. *Unit head:* Dr. Patricia M. Davidson, Dean, 410-955-7544, Fax: 410-955-4890, E-mail: sondeansoffice@jhu.edu. *Application contact:* Cathy Wilson, Director of Admissions, 410-955-7548, Fax: 410-614-7086, E-mail: jhuson@jhu.edu.
Website: http://www.nursing.jhu.edu

**Johns Hopkins University,** School of Nursing, DNP Executive Track, Baltimore, MD 21218. Offers DNP. *Program availability:* Part-time, online learning. *Faculty:* 14 full-time (12 women), 4 part-time/adjunct (3 women). *Students:* 12 full-time (11 women), 63 part-time (59 women); includes 44 minority (17 Black or African American, non-Hispanic/Latino; 1 American Indian or Alaska Native, non-Hispanic/Latino; 19 Asian, non-Hispanic/Latino; 4 Hispanic/Latino; 3 Two or more races, non-Hispanic/Latino). 76 applicants, 72% accepted, 49 enrolled. In 2019, 31 doctorates awarded. *Degree requirements:* For doctorate, thesis/dissertation, preliminary justification; final justification. *Entrance requirements:* For doctorate, GRE or GMAT for DNP/MBA, Minimum GPA of 3.0, goal statement/essay, resume, letters of recommendation, official transcripts from all post-secondary institutions attended, MSN and RN licensure, work experience for DNP/MBA, prerequisite coursework. Additional exam requirements/recommendations for international students: required—TOEFL (minimum score 600 paper-based; 100 iBT), IELTS (minimum score 7). *Application deadline:* For summer admission, 11/1 priority date for domestic students. Application fee: $75. Electronic applications accepted. *Expenses:* $1,772 per credit. *Financial support:* In 2019–20, 34 students received support. Federal Work-Study and scholarships/grants available. Support available to part-time students. Financial award application deadline: 3/1; financial award applicants required to submit FAFSA. *Unit head:* Dr. Kim McIltrot, 410-502-2247, E-mail: kmciltr1@jhmi.edu. *Application contact:* Cathy Wilson, Director of Admissions, 410-955-7548, E-mail: cathy.wilson@jhu.edu.

**Johns Hopkins University,** School of Nursing, MSN in Health Systems Management Program, Baltimore, MD 21218. Offers MSN. *Accreditation:* AACN. *Program availability:* Part-time, 100% online, blended/hybrid learning. *Faculty:* 12 full-time (10 women). *Students:* 3 full-time (2 women), 51 part-time (45 women); includes 18 minority (4 Black or African American, non-Hispanic/Latino; 8 Asian, non-Hispanic/Latino; 5 Hispanic/Latino; 1 Native Hawaiian or other Pacific Islander, non-Hispanic/Latino). 32 applicants,

88% accepted, 21 enrolled. In 2019, 18 master's awarded. *Entrance requirements:* For master's, GRE or GMAT for MSN/MBA, Minimum GPA of 3.0, goal statement/essay, resume, letters of recommendation, official transcripts from all post-secondary institutions attended, BSN and RN licensure, work experience for MSN/MBA, prerequisite coursework. Additional exam requirements/recommendations for international students: required—TOEFL (minimum score 600 paper-based; 100 iBT), IELTS (minimum score 7). *Application deadline:* For fall admission, 1/1 priority date for domestic students; for spring admission, 11/15 priority date for domestic students. Application fee: $75. Electronic applications accepted. *Expenses:* $1,688 per credit. *Financial support:* Federal Work-Study available. Financial award application deadline: 3/1; financial award applicants required to submit FAFSA. *Unit head:* Dr. Joanne Flagg, 410-614-4082, E-mail: jsilber1@jhu.edu. *Application contact:* Cathy Wilson, Director of Admissions, 410-955-7548, Fax: 410-614-7086, E-mail: jhuson@jhu.edu.
Website: http://www.nursing.jhu.edu

**Kean University,** Nathan Weiss Graduate College, Program in Nursing, Union, NJ 07083. Offers clinical management (MSN); community health nursing (MSN). *Accreditation:* ACEN. *Program availability:* Part-time. *Faculty:* 5 full-time (all women). *Students:* 2 full-time (both women), 28 part-time (26 women); includes 15 minority (10 Black or African American, non-Hispanic/Latino; 2 Asian, non-Hispanic/Latino; 1 Hispanic/Latino; 2 Two or more races, non-Hispanic/Latino). Average age 45. 5 applicants, 100% accepted, 2 enrolled. In 2019, 10 master's awarded. *Degree requirements:* For master's, thesis or alternative, clinical field experience. *Entrance requirements:* For master's, minimum GPA of 3.0; BS in nursing; RN license; 2 letters of recommendation; interview; official transcripts from all institutions attended. Additional exam requirements/recommendations for international students: required—TOEFL (minimum score 550 paper-based; 79 iBT), IELTS (minimum score 6.5). *Application deadline:* For fall admission, 6/30 for domestic and international students; for spring admission, 12/1 for domestic and international students. Applications are processed on a rolling basis. Application fee: $75. Electronic applications accepted. *Expenses:* Tuition, state resident: full-time $15,326; part-time $748 per credit. Tuition, nonresident: full-time $20,288; part-time $902 per credit. *Required fees:* $2149.50; $91.25 per credit. Tuition and fees vary according to course level, course load, degree level and program. *Financial support:* Scholarships/grants and unspecified assistantships available. Financial award applicants required to submit FAFSA. *Unit head:* Dr. Joan Valas, Program Coordinator, 908-737-6210, E-mail: nursing@kean.edu. *Application contact:* Pedro Lopes, Admissions Counselor, 908-737-7100, E-mail: gradadmissions@kean.edu.
Website: http://grad.kean.edu/masters-programs/nursing-clinical-management

**Kennesaw State University,** WellStar College of Health and Human Services, Program in Leadership in Nursing, Kennesaw, GA 30144. Offers nursing administration (MSN); nursing education (MSN). *Program availability:* Part-time, evening/weekend, online learning. *Students:* 27 full-time (26 women), 15 part-time (13 women); includes 12 minority (8 Black or African American, non-Hispanic/Latino; 2 Asian, non-Hispanic/Latino; 2 Two or more races, non-Hispanic/Latino), 1 international. Average age 34. 33 applicants, 91% accepted, 23 enrolled. In 2019, 1 master's awarded. *Entrance requirements:* For master's, minimum GPA of 3.0, RN license. Additional exam requirements/recommendations for international students: required—TOEFL (minimum score 80 iBT), IELTS (minimum score 6.5). *Application deadline:* For fall admission, 6/1 for domestic and international students. Application fee: $60. Electronic applications accepted. *Expenses: Tuition, area resident:* Full-time $7104; part-time $296 per credit hour. Tuition, state resident: full-time $7104; part-time $296 per credit hour. Tuition, nonresident: full-time $25,584; part-time $1066 per credit hour. *International tuition:* $25,584 full-time. *Required fees:* $2006; $1706 per unit. $853 per semester. *Financial support:* Applicants required to submit FAFSA. *Application contact:* Admissions Counselor, 470-578-4377, Fax: 470-578-9172, E-mail: ksugrad@kennesaw.edu.
Website: http://wellstarcollege.kennesaw.edu/nursing/master-science-nursing/leadership-in-nursing.php

**Kent State University,** College of Nursing, Kent, OH 44242. Offers advanced nursing practice (DNP), including adult/gerontology acute care nurse practitioner (MSN, DNP); nursing (MSN, PhD), including adult/gerontology acute care nurse practitioner (MSN, DNP), adult/gerontology clinical nurse specialist (MSN), adult/gerontology primary care nurse practitioner (MSN), family nurse practitioner (MSN), nurse educator (MSN), nursing and healthcare management (MSN), pediatric primary care nurse practitioner (MSN), psychiatric/mental health nurse practitioner (MSN); MBA/MSN. *Accreditation:* AACN. *Program availability:* Part-time, online learning. *Faculty:* 28 full-time (26 women), 15 part-time/adjunct (13 women). *Students:* 138 full-time (123 women), 522 part-time (464 women); includes 80 minority (41 Black or African American, non-Hispanic/Latino; 16 Asian, non-Hispanic/Latino; 9 Hispanic/Latino; 1 Native Hawaiian or other Pacific Islander, non-Hispanic/Latino; 13 Two or more races, non-Hispanic/Latino), 7 international. Average age 35. 303 applicants, 68% accepted, 154 enrolled. In 2019, 156 master's, 8 doctorates awarded. *Degree requirements:* For master's, practicum for master's degrees; for doctorate, comprehensive exam, thesis/dissertation. *Entrance requirements:* For master's, GRE or GMAT, minimum GPA of 3.0, active RN license, statement of purpose, 3 letters of reference, undergraduate level statistics class (minimum C grade), baccalaureate or graduate-level nursing degree, curriculum vitae/resume; for doctorate, GRE, minimum GPA of 3.0, transcripts, 3 letters of reference, interview, active unrestricted Ohio RN license, statement of purpose, writing sample, curriculum vitae/resume, baccalaureate and master's degrees in nursing or DNP, undergraduate or graduate level statistics course with a minimum C grade. Additional exam requirements/recommendations for international students: required—TOEFL (minimum score 83 iBT), IELTS (minimum score 6.5), PTE (minimum score 55), Michigan English Language Assessment Battery (minimum score 78). *Application deadline:* For fall admission, 3/1 for domestic and international students; for spring admission, 10/1 for domestic and international students. Applications are processed on a rolling basis. Application fee: $45 ($70 for international students). Electronic applications accepted. *Financial support:* Federal Work-Study and scholarships/grants available. Financial award application deadline: 2/1. *Unit head:* Dr. Barbara Broome, Ph.D., Dean, 330-672-3777, E-mail: bbroome1@kent.edu. *Application contact:* Dr. Wendy A. Umberger, Ph.D., Associate Dean for Graduate Programs/Professor, 330-672-8813, E-mail: wlewando@kent.edu.
Website: http://www.kent.edu/nursing/

**King University,** School of Nursing, Bristol, TN 37620-2699. Offers family nurse practitioner (MSN, Post-Master's Certificate); nurse educator (MSN, Post-Master's Certificate); nursing (DNP); nursing administration (MSN); pediatric nurse practitioner (MSN). *Program availability:* Part-time, evening/weekend, 100% online, blended/hybrid learning. *Faculty:* 13 full-time (12 women), 4 part-time/adjunct (2 women). *Students:* 115 full-time (103 women), 35 part-time (28 women); includes 12 minority (9 Black or African American, non-Hispanic/Latino; 1 Asian, non-Hispanic/Latino; 1 Hispanic/Latino; 1 Native Hawaiian or other Pacific Islander, non-Hispanic/Latino). Average age 37. 141 applicants, 96% accepted, 63 enrolled. In 2019, 89 master's, 1 doctorate, 6 other advanced degrees awarded. *Degree requirements:* For master's and post-master's certificate, comprehensive exam (for some programs), thesis optional; for doctorate, comprehensive exam (for some programs), thesis/dissertation. *Entrance requirements:* For master's, submit evidence of graduation from an accredited baccalaureate nursing program with a minimum cumulative undergraduate GPA of 3.0 on a 4.0 scale prior to enrolling; for doctorate, bachelor's and master's degree in nursing with a GPA of 3.25 or higher from a master's degree program accredited by the Accreditation Commission for Nursing Education (ACNE) or the Commission on Collegiate Nursing Education (CCNE); for Post-Master's Certificate, FNP and PNP applicants must complete an interview with the MSN Admissions Committee. Additional exam requirements/recommendations for international students: required—TOEFL (minimum score 84 paper-based; 84 iBT). *Application deadline:* Applications are processed on a rolling basis. Application fee: $50. Electronic applications accepted. *Expenses: Tuition:* Full-time $10,890; part-time $605 per semester hour. *Required fees:* $100 per course. *Financial support:* Unspecified assistantships available. Financial award applicants required to submit FAFSA. *Unit head:* Dr. Tracy Slemp, Dean, School of Nursing, 423-652-6335, E-mail: tjslemp@king.edu. *Application contact:* Natalie Blankenship, Territory Manager/Enrollment Counselor, 652-652-4159, Fax: 652-652-4727, E-mail: nblankenship@king.edu.

**Lamar University,** College of Graduate Studies, College of Arts and Sciences, JoAnne Gay Dishman Department of Nursing, Beaumont, TX 77710. Offers nursing administration (MSN); nursing education (MSN); MSN/MBA. *Accreditation:* ACEN. *Program availability:* Part-time, evening/weekend, online learning. *Faculty:* 33 full-time (30 women), 7 part-time/adjunct (6 women). *Students:* 1 (woman) full-time, 95 part-time (88 women); includes 42 minority (27 Black or African American, non-Hispanic/Latino; 2 American Indian or Alaska Native, non-Hispanic/Latino; 5 Asian, non-Hispanic/Latino; 8 Hispanic/Latino). Average age 40. 63 applicants, 79% accepted, 16 enrolled. In 2019, 29 master's awarded. *Degree requirements:* For master's, comprehensive exam, practicum project presentation, evidence-based project. *Entrance requirements:* For master's, GRE General Test, MAT, criminal background check, RN license, ACEN-accredited BSN, college course work in statistics in past 5 years, letters of recommendation, minimum undergraduate GPA of 3.0. Additional exam requirements/recommendations for international students: required—TOEFL (minimum score 550 paper-based; 79 iBT), IELTS (minimum score 6.5). *Application deadline:* Applications are processed on a rolling basis. Application fee: $25 ($50 for international students). Electronic applications accepted. *Expenses:* $13,098 total program cost. *Financial support:* In 2019–20, 3 students received support, including 2 teaching assistantships (averaging $24,000 per year); scholarships/grants and traineeships also available. Financial award applicants required to submit FAFSA. *Unit head:* Dr. Cynthia Stinson, School of Nursing Chair, 409-880-8817, Fax: 409-880-8698. *Application contact:* Celeste Contreas, Director, Admissions and Academic Services, 409-880-8888, Fax: 409-880-7419, E-mail: gradmissions@lamar.edu.
Website: http://artssciences.lamar.edu/nursing

**La Roche University,** School of Graduate Studies and Adult Education, Program in Nursing, Pittsburgh, PA 15237-5898. Offers clinical nurse leader (MSN); nursing education (MSN); nursing management (MSN). *Accreditation:* ACEN. *Program availability:* Part-time, evening/weekend, online only, 100% online. *Faculty:* 3 full-time (all women), 3 part-time/adjunct (all women). *Students:* 10 full-time (all women), 27 part-time (22 women); includes 4 minority (1 Black or African American, non-Hispanic/Latino; 2 Hispanic/Latino; 1 Native Hawaiian or other Pacific Islander, non-Hispanic/Latino). Average age 36. 9 applicants, 100% accepted, 7 enrolled. In 2019, 10 master's awarded. *Degree requirements:* For master's, thesis optional, internship, practicum. *Entrance requirements:* For master's, GRE General Test, BSN, nursing license, work experience. Additional exam requirements/recommendations for international students: recommended—TOEFL (minimum score 550 paper-based). *Application deadline:* For fall admission, 8/15 priority date for domestic students, 8/15 for international students; for spring admission, 12/15 priority date for domestic students, 12/15 for international students. Applications are processed on a rolling basis. Application fee: $50. Electronic applications accepted. *Expenses:* Contact institution. *Financial support:* Application deadline: 3/31; applicants required to submit FAFSA. *Unit head:* Dr. Terri Liberto, Professor, Master of Science in Nursing Department Chair, 412-847-1813, Fax: 412-536-1175, E-mail: terri.liberto@laroche.edu. *Application contact:* Erin Pottgen, Assistant Director, Graduate Admissions, 412-847-2509, Fax: 412-536-1283, E-mail: erin.pottgen@laroche.edu.

**La Salle University,** School of Nursing and Health Sciences, Program in Nursing, Philadelphia, PA 19141-1199. Offers adult gerontology primary care nurse practitioner (MSN, Certificate); adult health and illness clinical nurse specialist (MSN); adult-gerontology clinical nurse specialist (MSN, Certificate); clinical nurse leader (MSN); family primary care nurse practitioner (MSN, Certificate); gerontology (Certificate); nurse anesthetist (MSN, Certificate); nursing (MSN, Certificate); nursing administration (MSN, Certificate); nursing education (Certificate); nursing practice (DNP); nursing service administration (MSN); public health nursing (MSN, Certificate); school nursing (Certificate); MSN/MBA; MSN/MPH. *Accreditation:* AACN. *Program availability:* Part-time, evening/weekend, 100% online. *Degree requirements:* For doctorate, minimum of 1,000 hours of post baccalaureate clinical practice supervised by preceptors. *Entrance requirements:* For master's, GRE, MAT, or GMAT (for students with BSN GPA of less than 3.2), baccalaureate degree in nursing from ACEN- or CCNE-accredited program or an MSN Bridge program; Pennsylvania RN license; 2 letters of reference; resume; statement of philosophy articulating professional values and future educational goal; 1 year of work experience as a registered nurse; for doctorate, GRE (waived for applicants with MSN cumulative GPA of 3.7 or above), MSN, master's degree, MBA or MHA from nationally-accredited program; resume or curriculum vitae; 2 letters of reference; interview; for Certificate, GRE, MAT, or GMAT (for students with BSN GPA of less than 3.2, baccalaureate degree in nursing from ACEN- or CCNE-accredited program or an MSN Bridge program; Pennsylvania RN license; 2 letters of reference; resume; statement of philosophy articulating professional values and future educational goal; 1 year of work experience as a registered nurse. Additional exam requirements/recommendations for international students: required—TOEFL. Electronic applications accepted. Application fee is waived when completed online. *Expenses:* Contact institution.

**Le Moyne College,** Department of Nursing, Syracuse, NY 13214. Offers family nurse practitioner (MS, CAS); informatics (MS, CAS); nursing administration (MS, CAS); nursing education (MS, CAS). *Accreditation:* AACN. *Program availability:* Part-time, evening/weekend. *Faculty:* 4 full-time (all women), 6 part-time/adjunct (4 women). *Students:* 18 full-time (17 women), 57 part-time (52 women); includes 7 minority (1 Black or African American, non-Hispanic/Latino; 1 Asian, non-Hispanic/Latino; 4 Hispanic/Latino; 1 Two or more races, non-Hispanic/Latino). Average age 31. 43 applicants, 84% accepted, 32 enrolled. In 2019, 33 master's, 3 other advanced degrees awarded. *Degree requirements:* For master's, 39-45 credit hours, varies by program, practicum, scholarly project; for CAS, Varies by experience or incoming degree. *Entrance requirements:* For master's, earned bachelor's degree transcripts, New York RN license, 2-3 letters of recommendation, personal statement, interview. Additional exam requirements/recommendations for international students: required—TOEFL (minimum score 79 iBT); recommended—IELTS (minimum score 6.5). *Application deadline:* For fall admission, 4/1 priority date for domestic students, 4/1 for international students; for spring admission, 11/1 priority date for domestic students, 11/1 for international students; for summer admission, 5/1 priority date for domestic students, 5/1 for international students. Applications are processed on a rolling basis. Electronic

applications accepted. *Expenses:* $764-$951 per credit hour depending upon program, $75 fee per semester. *Financial support:* In 2019–20, 1 student received support. Career-related internships or fieldwork, Federal Work-Study, scholarships/grants, health care benefits, and unspecified assistantships available. Support available to part-time students. Financial award applicants required to submit FAFSA. *Unit head:* Catherine A. Brownell, Professor - Chair of Nursing, 315-445-5426, Fax: 315-445-6024, E-mail: nursing@lemoyne.edu. *Application contact:* Teresa M. Renn, Director of Graduate Admission, 315-445-5444, Fax: 315-445-6092, E-mail: GradAdmission@lemoyne.edu.
Website: http://www.lemoyne.edu/nursing

**Lenoir-Rhyne University,** Graduate Programs, School of Nursing, Program in Nursing, Hickory, NC 28601. Offers nursing administration (MSN); nursing education (MSN). *Accreditation:* AACN. *Program availability:* Online learning. *Degree requirements:* For master's, comprehensive exam, thesis optional. *Entrance requirements:* For master's, official transcripts, two recommendations, essay, resume, unrestricted RN license, criminal background check. Additional exam requirements/recommendations for international students: required—TOEFL (minimum score 600 paper-based). Electronic applications accepted. *Expenses:* Contact institution.

**Lewis University,** College of Nursing and Health Sciences, Program in Nursing, Romeoville, IL 60446. Offers adult gerontology clinical nurse specialist (MSN); adult gerontology primary care nurse practitioner (MSN); family nurse practitioner (MSN); healthcare systems leadership (MSN); nursing education (MSN); school nurse (MSN). *Accreditation:* AACN. *Program availability:* Part-time, evening/weekend, 100% online, blended/hybrid learning. *Students:* 7 full-time (all women), 411 part-time (372 women); includes 113 minority (15 Black or African American, non-Hispanic/Latino; 43 Asian, non-Hispanic/Latino; 47 Hispanic/Latino; 8 Two or more races, non-Hispanic/Latino), 2 international. Average age 35. *Degree requirements:* For master's, clinical practicum. *Entrance requirements:* For master's, minimum undergraduate GPA of 3.0, degree in nursing, RN license, letter of recommendation, interview, resume or curriculum vitae. Additional exam requirements/recommendations for international students: required—TOEFL (minimum score 550 paper-based; 80 iBT), IELTS. *Application deadline:* For fall admission, 5/1 priority date for international students; for spring admission, 11/15 priority date for international students. Applications are processed on a rolling basis. Application fee: $40. Electronic applications accepted. *Financial support:* Federal Work-Study, scholarships/grants, tuition waivers (full and partial), and unspecified assistantships available. Financial award application deadline: 5/1; financial award applicants required to submit FAFSA. *Unit head:* Dr. Mary Desmond, Program Director. *Application contact:* Nancy Wiksten, Graduate Admission Counselor, 815-836-5610, E-mail: grad@lewisu.edu.

**Liberty University,** Helms School of Government, Lynchburg, VA 24515. Offers criminal justice (MS), including forensic psychology, homeland security, public administration (MA, MS); international relations (MS); political science (MS); public administration (MPA), including business and government, healthcare, law and public policy, public and non-profit management; public policy (MA), including campaigns and elections, international affairs, Middle East affairs, public administration (MA, MS). *Program availability:* Part-time, online learning. *Students:* 1,143 full-time (565 women), 572 part-time (408 women); includes 795 minority (499 Black or African American, non-Hispanic/Latino; 16 American Indian or Alaska Native, non-Hispanic/Latino; 23 Asian, non-Hispanic/Latino; 162 Hispanic/Latino; 7 Native Hawaiian or other Pacific Islander, non-Hispanic/Latino; 88 Two or more races, non-Hispanic/Latino), 27 international. Average age 35. 3,017 applicants, 44% accepted, 728 enrolled. In 2019, 415 master's awarded. *Entrance requirements:* For master's, minimum undergraduate GPA of 3.0. Additional exam requirements/recommendations for international students: required—TOEFL (minimum score 600 paper-based; 100 iBT). *Application deadline:* Applications are processed on a rolling basis. Application fee: $50. Electronic applications accepted. *Expenses: Tuition:* Full-time $545; part-time $410 per credit hour. One-time fee: $50. *Financial support:* In 2019–20, 808 students received support. Teaching assistantships and Federal Work-Study available. *Unit head:* Ron Miller, Dean, 434-592-4986, E-mail: govtdean@liberty.edu. *Application contact:* Jay Bridge, Director of Admissions, 800-424-9595, Fax: 800-628-7977, E-mail: gradadmissions@liberty.edu.
Website: https://www.liberty.edu/government/

**Liberty University,** School of Nursing, Lynchburg, VA 24515. Offers family nurse practitioner (DNP); nurse educator (MSN); nursing administration (MSN); nursing informatics (MSN). *Accreditation:* AACN. *Program availability:* Part-time, online learning. *Students:* 279 full-time (257 women), 505 part-time (449 women); includes 170 minority (118 Black or African American, non-Hispanic/Latino; 2 American Indian or Alaska Native, non-Hispanic/Latino; 19 Asian, non-Hispanic/Latino; 25 Hispanic/Latino; 6 Two or more races, non-Hispanic/Latino), 11 international. Average age 39. 1,154 applicants, 27% accepted, 171 enrolled. In 2019, 138 master's, 26 doctorates awarded. *Entrance requirements:* For master's, minimum cumulative undergraduate GPA of 3.0; for doctorate, minimum GPA of 3.25 in most current nursing program completed. Additional exam requirements/recommendations for international students: recommended—TOEFL. *Application deadline:* Applications are processed on a rolling basis. Application fee: $50. Electronic applications accepted. *Expenses: Tuition:* Full-time $545; part-time $410 per credit hour. One-time fee: $50. *Financial support:* In 2019–20, 128 students received support. Federal Work-Study available. Financial award applicants required to submit FAFSA. *Unit head:* Dr. Shanna Akers, Dean, 434-592-3618, E-mail: lusondean@liberty.edu. *Application contact:* Jay Bridge, Director of Admissions, 800-424-9595, Fax: 800-628-7977, E-mail: gradadmissions@liberty.edu.
Website: https://www.liberty.edu/nursing/

**Loma Linda University,** School of Nursing, Program in Nursing Administration, Loma Linda, CA 92350. Offers MS. *Accreditation:* AACN. *Program availability:* Part-time. *Degree requirements:* For master's, thesis or alternative. *Entrance requirements:* For master's, GRE General Test, BSN, minimum GPA of 3.0, RN license. Additional exam requirements/recommendations for international students: required—TOEFL. Electronic applications accepted.

**Louisiana College,** Graduate Programs, Pineville, LA 71359-0001. Offers clinical nurse leadership (MSN); educational leadership (M Ed); social work (MSW); teaching (MAT).

**Louisiana State University Health Sciences Center,** School of Nursing, New Orleans, LA 70112. Offers adult gerontology acute care nurse practitioner (DNP, Post-Master's Certificate); adult gerontology clinical nurse specialist (DNP, Post-Master's Certificate); adult gerontology primary care nurse practitioner (DNP, Post-Master's Certificate); clinical nurse leader (MSN); executive nurse leader (DNP, Post-Master's Certificate); neonatal nurse practitioner (DNP, Post-Master's Certificate); nurse anesthesia (DNP, Post-Master's Certificate); nurse educator (MSN); nursing (DNS); primary care family nurse practitioner (DNP, Post-Master's Certificate); public/community health nursing (DNP, Post-Master's Certificate). *Accreditation:* AACN; AANA/CANAEP (one or more programs are accredited). *Program availability:* Part-time. *Faculty:* 25 full-time (21 women), 25 part-time/adjunct (13 women). *Students:* 182 full-time (127 women), 70 part-time (59 women); includes 82 minority (52 Black or African American, non-Hispanic/Latino; 2 American Indian or Alaska Native, non-Hispanic/Latino; 14 Asian, non-Hispanic/Latino; 14 Hispanic/Latino), 1 international. Average age 34. 34 applicants, 62% accepted, 21 enrolled. In 2019, 72 doctorates awarded. *Degree requirements:* For master's, thesis optional; for doctorate, thesis/dissertation. *Entrance requirements:* For master's, GRE, minimum GPA of 3.0; for doctorate, GRE, minimum GPA of 3.0 (for DNP), 3.5 (for DNS). Additional exam requirements/recommendations for international students: required—TOEFL (minimum score 550 paper-based; 79 iBT). *Application deadline:* For fall admission, 6/1 priority date for domestic and international students; for spring admission, 10/1 priority date for domestic and international students; for summer admission, 3/1 priority date for domestic and international students. Applications are processed on a rolling basis. Application fee: $100. Electronic applications accepted. *Expenses:* MSN and DNS: $13,354.50, $24,982.25 non-resident, $586 per hour (fall and spring), $467 per hour (summer), $1,102 per hour non-resident (fall and spring), $858 per hour non-resident (summer); DNP (Except Nurse Anethesia): $21,907.50, $38,262.23 non-resident, $973 per hour (fall and spring), $733 per hour (summer), $1,700 per hour non-resident (fall and spring), $1,278 per hour non-resident (summer); Nurse Anesthesia DNP: $26,407.50, $42,762.23 non-resident, $1,173 per hour (fall and spring), $883 per hour (summer), $1,900 per hour non-resident (fall and spring), $1,428 per hour non-resident (summer). *Financial support:* In 2019–20, 20 students received support. Institutionally sponsored loans, scholarships/grants, unspecified assistantships, and DNS Scholars Program available. Financial award application deadline: 4/15; financial award applicants required to submit FAFSA. *Unit head:* Dr. Demetrius James Porche, Dean, 504-568-4106, Fax: 504-599-0573, E-mail: dporch@lsuhsc.edu. *Application contact:* Tracie Gravolet, Director, Office of Student Affairs, 504-568-4114, Fax: 504-568-5711, E-mail: tgravo@lsuhsc.edu.
Website: http://nursing.lsuhsc.edu/

**Lourdes University,** Graduate School, Sylvania, OH 43560-2898. Offers business (MBA); leadership (M Ed); nurse anesthesia (MSN); nurse educator (MSN); nurse leader (MSN); organizational leadership (MOL); reading (M Ed); teaching and curriculum (M Ed); theology (MA). *Accreditation:* AANA/CANAEP. *Program availability:* Evening/weekend. *Entrance requirements:* Additional exam requirements/recommendations for international students: required—TOEFL.

**Loyola University Chicago,** Graduate School, Marcella Niehoff School of Nursing, Maywood, IL 60153. Offers adult clinical nurse specialist (MSN, Certificate); adult nurse practitioner (Certificate); dietetics (MS); family nurse practitioner (Certificate); family, adult, and women's health nurse practitioner (MSN); health systems leadership (MSN); healthcare quality using education in safety and technology (DNP); infection prevention (MSN, DNP); nursing science (PhD); women's health clinical nurse specialist (Certificate). *Accreditation:* AACN. *Program availability:* Part-time, blended/hybrid learning. *Faculty:* 36 full-time (32 women), 18 part-time/adjunct (16 women). *Students:* 182 full-time (168 women), 198 part-time (175 women); includes 95 minority (26 Black or African American, non-Hispanic/Latino; 29 Asian, non-Hispanic/Latino; 37 Hispanic/Latino; 3 Two or more races, non-Hispanic/Latino), 7 international. Average age 35. 148 applicants, 59% accepted, 54 enrolled. In 2019, 84 master's, 16 doctorates, 27 other advanced degrees awarded. *Degree requirements:* For master's, comprehensive exam; for doctorate, thesis/dissertation, qualifying examination (for PhD); project (for DNP). *Entrance requirements:* For master's, BSN, minimum nursing GPA of 3.0, Illinois RN license, 3 letters of recommendation, 1000 hours of experience in area of specialty prior to starting clinical rotations, personal statement; for doctorate, BSN or MSN, minimum GPA of 3.0, professional nursing license, 3 letters of recommendation, personal statement. Additional exam requirements/recommendations for international students: required—TOEFL (minimum score 550 paper-based; 79 iBT), IELTS (minimum score 6), PTE (minimum score 53). *Application deadline:* For fall admission, 7/1 priority date for domestic and international students; for spring admission, 12/1 priority date for domestic and international students; for summer admission, 4/1 priority date for domestic and international students. Applications are processed on a rolling basis. Electronic applications accepted. Application fee is waived when completed online. *Expenses:* Contact institution. *Financial support:* In 2019–20, 53 students received support, including 3 research assistantships with full tuition reimbursements available (averaging $18,000 per year), 1 teaching assistantship with full tuition reimbursement available (averaging $18,000 per year); scholarships/grants, unspecified assistantships, and Nurse Faculty Loan Program also available. Financial award application deadline: 5/1; financial award applicants required to submit FAFSA. *Unit head:* Dr. Lorna Finnegan, Dean and Professor, 708-216-5448, Fax: 708-216-9555, E-mail: lornaf@luc.edu. *Application contact:* Glenda Runnels, Enrollment Advisor, 708-216-3751, Fax: 708-216-9555, E-mail: grunnels@luc.edu.
Website: http://www.luc.edu/nursing/

**Madonna University,** Program in Nursing, Livonia, MI 48150-1173. Offers adult health: chronic health conditions (MSN); adult nurse practitioner (MSN); nursing administration (MSN); MSN/MSBA. *Accreditation:* AACN. *Program availability:* Part-time. *Degree requirements:* For master's, thesis or alternative. *Entrance requirements:* For master's, GRE General Test, Michigan nursing license. Electronic applications accepted. *Expenses: Tuition:* Full-time $15,930; part-time $885 per credit hour. Tuition and fees vary according to degree level and program.

**Marquette University,** Graduate School, College of Nursing, Milwaukee, WI 53201-1881. Offers acute care nurse practitioner (Certificate); adult clinical nurse specialist (Certificate); adult nurse practitioner (Certificate); advanced practice nursing (MSN, DNP), including adult-older adult acute care (DNP), adults (MSN), adults-older adults (DNP), clinical nurse leader (MSN), health care systems leadership (DNP), nurse-midwifery (MSN), older adults (MSN), pediatrics-acute care, pediatrics-primary care, primary care (DNP), systems leadership and healthcare quality (MSN); family nurse practitioner (Certificate); nurse-midwifery (Certificate); nursing (PhD); pediatric acute care (Certificate); pediatric primary care (Certificate); systems leadership and healthcare quality (Certificate). *Accreditation:* AACN; AANA/CANAEP; ACNM/ACME. Terminal master's awarded for partial completion of doctoral program. *Degree requirements:* For master's, comprehensive exam, thesis or alternative. *Entrance requirements:* For master's, GRE General Test, BSN, Wisconsin RN license, official transcripts from all current and previous colleges/universities except Marquette, three completed recommendation forms, resume, written statement of professional goals; for doctorate, GRE General Test, official transcripts from all current and previous colleges/universities except Marquette, three letters of recommendation, resume, written statement of professional goals, sample of scholarly writing. Additional exam requirements/recommendations for international students: required—TOEFL (minimum score 530 paper-based). Electronic applications accepted.

**McKendree University,** Graduate Programs, Master of Science in Nursing Program, Lebanon, IL 62254-1299. Offers nursing education (MSN); nursing management/administration (MSN). *Accreditation:* AACN. *Program availability:* Part-time, evening/weekend, online learning. *Degree requirements:* For master's, research project or thesis. *Entrance requirements:* For master's, resume, references, valid Professional Registered Nurse license. Additional exam requirements/recommendations for international students: required—TOEFL. Electronic applications accepted.

**Medical University of South Carolina,** College of Nursing, Nurse Administrator Program, Charleston, SC 29425. Offers MSN. *Accreditation:* AACN. *Program availability:* Part-time, online learning. *Degree requirements:* For master's, thesis optional. *Entrance requirements:* For master's, BSN, nursing license, minimum GPA of 3.0, current curriculum vitae, essay, three references. Additional exam requirements/

recommendations for international students: required—TOEFL (minimum score 600 paper-based). Electronic applications accepted.

**Mercer University,** Graduate Studies, Cecil B. Day Campus, College of Professional Advancement, Atlanta, GA 31207. Offers certified rehabilitation counseling (MS); clinical mental health (MS); counselor education and supervision (PhD); criminal justice and public safety leadership (MS); health informatics (MS); human services (MS), including child and adolescent services, gerontology services; organizational leadership (MS), including leadership for the health care professional, leadership for the nonprofit organization, organizational development and change; school counseling (MS). *Program availability:* Part-time, evening/weekend, 100% online, blended/hybrid learning. *Faculty:* 19 full-time (11 women), 34 part-time/adjunct (30 women). *Students:* 193 full-time (156 women), 277 part-time (225 women); includes 260 minority (211 Black or African American, non-Hispanic/Latino; 2 American Indian or Alaska Native, non-Hispanic/Latino; 23 Asian, non-Hispanic/Latino; 19 Hispanic/Latino; 5 Two or more races, non-Hispanic/Latino), 3 international. Average age 32. 300 applicants, 45% accepted, 114 enrolled. In 2019, 183 master's, 7 doctorates awarded. *Degree requirements:* For master's, comprehensive exam (for some programs), thesis (for some programs); for doctorate, thesis/dissertation. *Entrance requirements:* For master's, GRE or MAT, Georgia Professional Standards Commission (GPSC) Certification at the SC-5 level; for doctorate, GRE or MAT. Additional exam requirements/recommendations for international students: recommended—TOEFL (minimum score 550 paper-based; 80 iBT), IELTS (minimum score 6.5). *Application deadline:* For fall admission, 7/1 priority date for domestic and international students; for spring admission, 11/1 priority date for domestic and international students; for summer admission, 4/1 priority date for domestic and international students. Application fee: $35. Electronic applications accepted. Application fee is waived when completed online. *Expenses:* Contact institution. *Financial support:* In 2019–20, 32 students received support. Federal Work-Study, scholarships/grants, and unspecified assistantships available. Financial award applicants required to submit FAFSA. *Unit head:* Dr. Priscilla R. Danheiser, Dean, 678-547-6028, Fax: 678-547-6008, E-mail: danheiser_p@mercer.edu. *Application contact:* Theatis Anderson, Asst VP for Enrollment Management, 678-547-6421, E-mail: anderson_t@mercer.edu.
Website: https://professionaladvancement.mercer.edu/

**Mercy College,** School of Health and Natural Sciences, Programs in Nursing, Dobbs Ferry, NY 10522-1189. Offers nursing administration (MS); nursing education (MS). *Accreditation:* AACN. *Program availability:* Part-time, evening/weekend, 100% online, blended/hybrid learning. *Students:* 9 full-time (8 women), 208 part-time (196 women); includes 151 minority (89 Black or African American, non-Hispanic/Latino; 21 Asian, non-Hispanic/Latino; 32 Hispanic/Latino; 3 Native Hawaiian or other Pacific Islander, non-Hispanic/Latino; 6 Two or more races, non-Hispanic/Latino). Average age 40. 242 applicants, 73% accepted, 132 enrolled. In 2019, 67 master's awarded. *Degree requirements:* For master's, Capstone project and/or clinical practicum required for some programs. *Entrance requirements:* For master's, program application; transcript(s); RN registered in the U.S. Additional exam requirements/recommendations for international students: required—TOEFL (minimum score 80 iBT), IELTS (minimum score 6.5). *Application deadline:* Applications are processed on a rolling basis. Application fee: $40. Electronic applications accepted. *Expenses: Tuition:* Full-time $16,146; part-time $897 per credit. *Required fees:* $332; $166 per semester. Tuition and fees vary according to course load and program. *Financial support:* Career-related internships or fieldwork, Federal Work-Study, scholarships/grants, and unspecified assistantships available. Support available to part-time students. Financial award applicants required to submit FAFSA. *Unit head:* Dr. Joan Toglia, Dean, School of Health and Natural Sciences, 914-674-7746, E-mail: jtoglia@mercy.edu. *Application contact:* Allison Gurdineer, Executive Director of Admissions, 877-637-2946, Fax: 914-674-7382, E-mail: admissions@mercy.edu.
Website: https://www.mercy.edu/health-and-natural-sciences/graduate

**Metropolitan State University,** College of Nursing and Health Sciences, St. Paul, MN 55106-5000. Offers advanced dental therapy (MS); leadership and management (MSN); nurse educator (MSN); nursing (DNP). *Accreditation:* AACN. *Program availability:* Part-time. *Degree requirements:* For master's, thesis or alternative; for doctorate, thesis/dissertation or alternative. *Entrance requirements:* For master's, GRE General Test, minimum GPA of 3.0, RN license, BS/BA; for doctorate, minimum GPA of 3.0, RN license, MSN. Additional exam requirements/recommendations for international students: required—TOEFL (minimum score 550 paper-based).

**Miami Regional University,** School of Nursing and Health Sciences, Miami Springs, FL 33166. Offers nursing (MSN); nursing education (MSN); nursing leadership (MSN).

**MidAmerica Nazarene University,** School of Nursing and Health Science, Olathe, KS 66062. Offers healthcare administration (MSN); healthcare quality management (MSN); nursing education (MSN); public health (MSN); MSN/MBA. *Accreditation:* AACN. *Program availability:* Part-time, evening/weekend, 100% online. *Faculty:* 5 full-time (all women), 9 part-time/adjunct (7 women). *Students:* 14 full-time (12 women), 79 part-time (74 women); includes 12 minority (10 Black or African American, non-Hispanic/Latino; 1 American Indian or Alaska Native, non-Hispanic/Latino; 1 Hispanic/Latino), 2 international. Average age 38. 87 applicants, 39% accepted, 14 enrolled. In 2019, 39 master's awarded. *Entrance requirements:* For master's, BSN, minimum GPA of 3.0, active unencumbered RN license, undergraduate statistics course. Additional exam requirements/recommendations for international students: required—TOEFL (minimum score 81 iBT). *Application deadline:* Applications are processed on a rolling basis. Electronic applications accepted. *Expenses:* Tuition $499 per credit hour, technology fee $34.00 per credit hour, graduation fee $100, carrying fee $13 per course, other fee $215. *Financial support:* Unspecified assistantships available. Financial award applicants required to submit FAFSA. *Unit head:* Dr. Karen Wiegman, Dean, 913-971-3839, E-mail: kdwiegman@mnu.edu. *Application contact:* JoVonda Merrell, Compliance Coordinator, 913-971-3844, E-mail: jkmerrell@mnu.edu.
Website: http://www.mnu.edu/nursing.html

**Middle Tennessee State University,** College of Graduate Studies, University College, Murfreesboro, TN 37132. Offers advanced studies in teaching and learning (M Ed); human resources leadership (MPS); nursing administration (MSN); nursing education (MSN); strategic leadership (MPS); training and development (MPS). *Program availability:* Part-time, evening/weekend, online learning. *Entrance requirements:* Additional exam requirements/recommendations for international students: required—TOEFL (minimum score 525 paper-based; 71 iBT) or IELTS (minimum score 6).

**Milwaukee School of Engineering,** MS Program in Nursing - Leadership and Management, Milwaukee, WI 53202-3109. Offers MSN. *Program availability:* Part-time, evening/weekend, 100% online, blended/hybrid learning. *Entrance requirements:* For master's, GRE General Test or GMAT if undergraduate GPA less than 3.0, 2 letters of recommendation; BSN from accredited institution; current unrestricted licensure as a Registered Nurse. Additional exam requirements/recommendations for international students: required—TOEFL (minimum score 90 iBT), IELTS (minimum score 7). Electronic applications accepted.

**Missouri Western State University,** Program in Nursing, St. Joseph, MO 64507-2294. Offers health care leadership (MSN); nurse educator (MSN, Graduate Certificate). *Program availability:* Part-time. *Students:* 2 full-time (both women), 29 part-time (all women); includes 3 minority (1 Black or African American, non-Hispanic/Latino; 1 Asian, non-Hispanic/Latino; 1 Hispanic/Latino), 1 international. Average age 37. 13 applicants, 100% accepted, 12 enrolled. In 2019, 12 master's, 1 other advanced degree awarded. *Entrance requirements:* For master's, Minimum undergraduate GPA of 2.75 and nursing GPA 3.0 or higher. B.S.N. from a CCNE or NLNAC accredited college or university. Evidence of current, unencumbered RN license. Completion of undergraduate statistics and research methods courses with a minimum of "B" in each. Curriculum vitae/resume. A supporting statement of interest. Additional exam requirements/recommendations for international students: recommended—TOEFL (minimum score 79 iBT), IELTS (minimum score 6). *Application deadline:* For fall admission, 7/15 for domestic and international students; for spring admission, 11/1 for domestic and international students; for summer admission, 4/29 for domestic and international students. Applications are processed on a rolling basis. Application fee: $45 ($50 for international students). Electronic applications accepted. *Expenses:* Tuition, state resident: full-time $6469.02; part-time $359.39 per credit hour. Tuition, nonresident: full-time $11,581; part-time $643.39 per credit hour. *Required fees:* $345.20; $99.10 per credit hour. Tuition and fees vary according to course load, campus/location and program. *Financial support:* Scholarships/grants and unspecified assistantships available. Support available to part-time students. *Unit head:* Dr. Jacklyn Gentry, MSN Program Director and Assistant Professor, 816-271-4415, E-mail: jgentry8@missouriwestern.edu. *Application contact:* Dr. Jacklyn Gentry, MSN Program Director and Assistant Professor, 816-271-4415, E-mail: jgentry8@missouriwestern.edu.
Website: https://www.missouriwestern.edu/nursing/msn/

**Montana State University,** The Graduate School, College of Nursing, Bozeman, MT 59717. Offers clinical nurse leader (MN); family and individual nurse practitioner (DNP); family nurse practitioner (MN, Post-Master's Certificate); nursing education (Certificate, Post-Master's Certificate); psychiatric mental health nurse practitioner (MN); psychiatric/mental health nurse practitioner (DNP). *Accreditation:* AACN. *Program availability:* Part-time, online learning. *Degree requirements:* For master's, comprehensive exam, thesis (for some programs); for doctorate, thesis/dissertation, 1,125 hours in clinical settings. *Entrance requirements:* For master's, GRE General Test, minimum GPA of 3.0 for undergraduate and post-baccalaureate work. Additional exam requirements/recommendations for international students: required—TOEFL (minimum score 580 paper-based). Electronic applications accepted.

**Moravian College,** Graduate and Continuing Studies, Helen S. Breidegam School of Nursing, Bethlehem, PA 18018-6614. Offers clinical nurse leader (MS); nurse administrator (MS); nurse educator (MS); nurse practitioner - acute care (MS); nurse practitioner - primary care (MS). *Accreditation:* AACN. *Program availability:* Part-time, evening/weekend. *Faculty:* 2 full-time (both women), 3 part-time/adjunct (2 women). *Students:* 5 full-time (4 women), 103 part-time (95 women); includes 19 minority (4 Black or African American, non-Hispanic/Latino; 8 Asian, non-Hispanic/Latino; 7 Hispanic/Latino), 1 international. Average age 37. 131 applicants, 69% accepted, 85 enrolled. In 2019, 25 master's awarded. *Degree requirements:* For master's, comprehensive exam (for some programs), evidence-based practice project. *Entrance requirements:* For master's, BSN with minimum GPA of 3.0, active RN license, statistics course with minimum C grade, 2 professional references, written statement of goals, professional resume, interview, official transcripts. *Application deadline:* For fall admission, 8/1 priority date for domestic and international students; for spring admission, 1/1 priority date for domestic and international students; for summer admission, 5/1 priority date for domestic and international students. Applications are processed on a rolling basis. Electronic applications accepted. *Expenses:* Contact institution. *Financial support:* Applicants required to submit FAFSA. *Unit head:* Dr. Dawn Goodolf, 610-861-1412, Fax: 610-861-1466, E-mail: nursing@moravian.edu. *Application contact:* Caroline Bechtel, Student Experience Mentor, 610-861-1400, Fax: 610-861-1466, E-mail: graduate@moravian.edu.
Website: https://www.moravian.edu/graduate/programs/nursing#/

**Mount Carmel College of Nursing,** Nursing Program, Columbus, OH 43222. Offers adult gerontology acute care nurse practitioner (MS); adult health clinical nurse specialist (MS); family nurse practitioner (MS); nursing (DNP); nursing administration (MS); nursing education (MS). *Accreditation:* AACN. *Program availability:* Part-time. *Faculty:* 6 full-time (all women), 10 part-time/adjunct (9 women). *Students:* 101 full-time (82 women), 109 part-time (95 women); includes 43 minority (27 Black or African American, non-Hispanic/Latino; 4 Asian, non-Hispanic/Latino; 5 Hispanic/Latino; 7 Two or more races, non-Hispanic/Latino). Average age 32. 133 applicants, 84% accepted, 95 enrolled. In 2019, 66 master's, 2 doctorates awarded. *Degree requirements:* For master's, professional manuscript; for doctorate, practicum. *Entrance requirements:* For master's, letters of recommendation, statement of purpose, current resume, baccalaureate degree in nursing, current Ohio RN license, minimum cumulative GPA of 3.0; for doctorate, master's degree in nursing from program accredited by either ACEN or CCNE. Additional exam requirements/recommendations for international students: required—TOEFL (minimum score 550 paper-based; 80 iBT). *Application deadline:* For fall admission, 2/1 priority date for domestic students; for spring admission, 11/1 priority date for domestic students. Applications are processed on a rolling basis. Application fee: $30. Electronic applications accepted. *Expenses: Tuition:* Full-time $27,936; part-time $27,936 per year. *Required fees:* $360. *Financial support:* In 2019–20, 13 students received support. Institutionally sponsored loans and scholarships/grants available. Financial award application deadline: 3/1; financial award applicants required to submit FAFSA. *Unit head:* Dr. Jami Nininger, Interim Associate Dean Graduate Studies, 614-234-1777, Fax: 614-234-2875, E-mail: jnininger@mccn.edu. *Application contact:* Dr. Kim Campbell, Director of Recruitment and Admissions, 614-234-5144, Fax: 614-234-5427, E-mail: kcampbell@mccn.edu.
Website: www.mccn.edu

**Mount Mary University,** Graduate Programs, Program in Business Administration, Milwaukee, WI 53222-4597. Offers general management (MBA); health systems leadership (MBA). *Program availability:* Part-time, evening/weekend. *Degree requirements:* For master's, terminal project. *Entrance requirements:* For master's, minimum GPA of 2.75. Additional exam requirements/recommendations for international students: required—TOEFL (minimum score 550 paper-based; 80 iBT); recommended—IELTS (minimum score 6.5). Electronic applications accepted. *Expenses:* Contact institution.

**Mount Mercy University,** Program in Nursing, Cedar Rapids, IA 52402-4797. Offers health advocacy (MSN); nurse administration (MSN); nurse education (MSN). *Accreditation:* AACN. *Program availability:* Evening/weekend. *Degree requirements:* For master's, project/practicum.

**Mount St. Joseph University,** Master of Science in Nursing Program, Cincinnati, OH 45233-1670. Offers administration (MSN); clinical nurse leader (MSN); education (MSN). *Accreditation:* AACN. *Program availability:* Part-time. *Entrance requirements:* For master's, essay; BSN from regionally-accredited university; minimum undergraduate GPA of 3.25 or GRE; professional resume; three professional references; interview; 2 years of clinical nursing experience; active RN license; criminal background check. Additional exam requirements/recommendations for international students: required—

TOEFL (minimum score 560 paper-based; 83 iBT). Electronic applications accepted. *Expenses:* Contact institution.

**Mount Saint Mary College,** School of Nursing, Newburgh, NY 12550. Offers adult nurse practitioner (MS, Advanced Certificate), including nursing education (MS), nursing management (MS); nursing education (Advanced Certificate). *Accreditation:* AACN. *Program availability:* Part-time, evening/weekend, blended/hybrid learning. *Faculty:* 6 full-time (all women), 11 part-time/adjunct (10 women). *Students:* 1 (woman) full-time, 186 part-time (171 women); includes 36 minority (16 Black or African American, non-Hispanic/Latino; 1 American Indian or Alaska Native, non-Hispanic/Latino; 5 Asian, non-Hispanic/Latino; 11 Hispanic/Latino; 1 Native Hawaiian or other Pacific Islander, non-Hispanic/Latino; 2 Two or more races, non-Hispanic/Latino), 1 international. Average age 37. 37 applicants, 84% accepted, 22 enrolled. In 2019, 33 master's, 4 other advanced degrees awarded. *Degree requirements:* For master's, research utilization project. *Entrance requirements:* For master's, BSN, minimum GPA of 3.0, RN license. Additional exam requirements/recommendations for international students: required—TOEFL (minimum score 80 iBT). *Application deadline:* For fall admission, 6/3 priority date for domestic students; for spring admission, 10/31 priority date for domestic students. Applications are processed on a rolling basis. Application fee: $45. Electronic applications accepted. Application fee is waived when completed online. *Expenses: Tuition:* Full-time $15,192; part-time $844 per credit. *Required fees:* $180; $90 per semester. *Financial support:* In 2019–20, 10 students received support. Scholarships/grants and unspecified assistantships available. Financial award application deadline: 4/15; financial award applicants required to submit FAFSA. *Unit head:* Christine Berte, Graduate Coordinator, 845-569-3141, Fax: 845-562-6762, E-mail: christine.berte@msmc.edu. *Application contact:* Eileen Bardney, Director of Admissions, 845-569-3254, Fax: 845-569-3438, E-mail: GraduateAdmissions@msmc.edu.
Website: http://www.msmc.edu/Academics/Graduate_Programs/Master_of_Science_in_Nursing

**National American University,** Roueche Graduate Center, Austin, TX 78731. Offers accounting (MBA); aviation management (MBA, MM); care coordination (MSN); community college leadership (Ed D); criminal justice (MM); e-marketing (MBA, MM); health care administration (MBA, MM); higher education (MM); human resources management (MBA, MM); information technology management (MBA, MM); international business (MBA); leadership (EMBA); management (MBA); nursing administration (MSN); nursing education (MSN); nursing informatics (MSN); operations and configuration management (MBA, MM); project and process management (MBA, MM). *Program availability:* Part-time, evening/weekend, online learning. *Entrance requirements:* For master's, minimum undergraduate GPA of 2.75. Additional exam requirements/recommendations for international students: required—TOEFL, TWE. Electronic applications accepted.

**National University,** School of Health and Human Services, La Jolla, CA 92037-1011. Offers clinical affairs (MS); clinical regulatory affairs (MS); complementary and integrative healthcare (MS); family nurse practitioner (MSN); health and life science analytics (MS); health informatics (MS, Certificate); healthcare administration (MHA); nurse anesthesia (MSNA); nursing administration (MSN); nursing informatics (MSN); psychiatric-mental health nurse practitioner (MSN); public health (MPH), including health promotion, healthcare administration, mental health. *Accreditation:* CEPH. *Program availability:* Part-time, evening/weekend, 100% online, blended/hybrid learning. *Degree requirements:* For master's, thesis (for some programs). *Entrance requirements:* For master's, interview, minimum GPA of 2.5. Additional exam requirements/recommendations for international students: required—TOEFL (minimum score 550 paper-based; 79 iBT), IELTS (minimum score 6). Electronic applications accepted. *Expenses: Tuition:* Full-time $442; part-time $442 per unit.

**Nebraska Methodist College,** Program in Nursing, Omaha, NE 68114. Offers nurse educator (MSN); nurse executive (MSN). *Accreditation:* AACN. *Program availability:* Evening/weekend, online learning. *Degree requirements:* For master's, thesis or alternative, Evidence Based Practice (EBP) project. *Entrance requirements:* For master's, interview. Additional exam requirements/recommendations for international students: required—TOEFL (minimum score 550 paper-based; 80 iBT).

**New Mexico State University,** College of Health and Social Services, School of Nursing, Las Cruces, NM 88003. Offers family nurse practitioner (Graduate Certificate); nursing (MSN); nursing practice (DNP); nursing science (PhD); psychiatric/mental health nurse practitioner (Graduate Certificate). *Accreditation:* AACN. *Program availability:* Part-time, blended/hybrid learning. *Faculty:* 12 full-time (all women). *Students:* 29. 57 applicants, 98% accepted. In 2019, 4 master's, 20 doctorates, 5 other advanced degrees awarded. *Degree requirements:* For master's, comprehensive exam, thesis optional, clinical practicum; for doctorate, comprehensive exam, thesis/dissertation. *Entrance requirements:* For master's, NCLEX exam, BSN, minimum GPA of 3.0, course work in statistics, 3 letters of reference, writing sample, RN license, CPR certification, proof of liability, immunizations, criminal background check; for doctorate, NCLEX exam, MSN, minimum GPA of 3.0, 3 letters of reference, writing sample, RN license, CPR certification, proof of liability, immunizations, criminal background check, statistics course. Additional exam requirements/recommendations for international students: required—TOEFL (minimum score 550 paper-based; 79 iBT), IELTS (minimum score 6.5). *Application deadline:* For fall admission, 2/1 priority date for domestic students, 2/1 for international students. Application fee: $40 ($50 for international students). Electronic applications accepted. *Financial support:* In 2019–20, 7 teaching assistantships (averaging $10,499 per year) were awarded; career-related internships or fieldwork, Federal Work-Study, scholarships/grants, traineeships, health care benefits, and unspecified assistantships also available. Support available to part-time students. Financial award application deadline: 3/1. *Unit head:* Dr. Alexa Doig, Director, 575-646-3812, Fax: 575-646-2167, E-mail: adoig@nmsu.edu. *Application contact:* Alyce Kolenovsky, Academic Advisor, 575-646-3812, Fax: 575-646-2167, E-mail: nursing@nmsu.edu.
Website: http://schoolofnursing.nmsu.edu

**New York University,** Rory Meyers College of Nursing, Programs in Advanced Practice Nursing, New York, NY 10012-1019. Offers adult-gerontology acute care nurse practitioner (MS, Advanced Certificate); adult-gerontology primary care nurse practitioner (MS, Advanced Certificate); family nurse practitioner (MS, Advanced Certificate); gerontology nurse practitioner (Advanced Certificate); nurse-midwifery (MS, Advanced Certificate); nursing administration (MS, Advanced Certificate); nursing education (MS, Advanced Certificate); nursing informatics (MS, Advanced Certificate); pediatrics nurse practitioner (MS, Advanced Certificate); psychiatric-mental health nurse practitioner (MS, Advanced Certificate); MS/MPH. *Accreditation:* AACN; ACNM/ACME. *Program availability:* Part-time, evening/weekend. *Degree requirements:* For master's, thesis (for some programs), capstone. *Entrance requirements:* For master's, BS in nursing, AS in nursing with another BS/BA, interview, RN license, 1 year of clinical experience (3 for the MS in nursing education program); for Advanced Certificate, master's degree in nursing. Additional exam requirements/recommendations for international students: required—TOEFL (minimum score 100 iBT), IELTS (minimum score 7). Electronic applications accepted. *Expenses:* Contact institution.

**Nicholls State University,** Graduate Studies, College of Nursing and Allied Health, Thibodaux, LA 70310. Offers family nurse practitioner (MSN); nurse executive (MSN); nursing education (MSN); psychiatric/mental health nurse practitioner (MSN).

**Northeastern State University,** College of Science and Health Professions, Department of Health Professions, Program in Nursing, Muskogee, OK 74401. Offers nursing (MSN). *Faculty:* 2 full-time (both women), 4 part-time/adjunct (3 women). *Students:* 3 full-time (all women), 37 part-time (31 women); includes 17 minority (4 Black or African American, non-Hispanic/Latino; 7 American Indian or Alaska Native, non-Hispanic/Latino; 3 Hispanic/Latino; 3 Two or more races, non-Hispanic/Latino). Average age 42. In 2019, 4 master's awarded. *Application deadline:* Applications are processed on a rolling basis. Application fee: $25. Electronic applications accepted. *Expenses: Tuition, area resident:* Full-time $250; part-time $250 per credit hour. Tuition, state resident: full-time $250; part-time $250 per credit hour. Tuition, nonresident: full-time $556; part-time $555.50 per credit hour. *Required fees:* $33.40 per credit hour. *Unit head:* Dr. Heather Fenton, Program Coordinator, 918-444-5221, E-mail: fentonh@nsuok.edu. *Application contact:* Josh McCollum, Graduate Coordinator, 918-444-2093, E-mail: mccolluj@nsuok.edu.
Website: http://academics.nsuok.edu/healthprofessions/DegreePrograms/Graduate/NursingEducationMSN.aspx

**Northeastern University,** Bouvé College of Health Sciences, Boston, MA 02115-5096. Offers applied behavior analysis (MS); audiology (Au D); counseling psychology (MS, PhD, CAGS); exercise science (MS); nursing (MS, PhD, CAGS), including administration (MS), adult-gerontology acute care nurse practitioner (MS, CAGS), adult-gerontology primary care nurse practitioner (MS, CAGS), anesthesia (MS), family nurse practitioner (MS, CAGS), neonatal nurse practitioner (MS, CAGS), pediatric nurse practitioner (MS, CAGS), psychiatric mental health nurse practitioner (MS, CAGS); nursing practice (DNP); pharmaceutical sciences (MS, PhD), including interdisciplinary concentration, pharmaceutics and drug delivery systems; pharmacology (MS); pharmacy (Pharm D); school psychology (PhD); speech-language pathology (MS); urban health (MPH); MS/MBA. *Accreditation:* AANA/CANAEP; ACPE (one or more programs are accredited); ASHA; CEPH. *Program availability:* Part-time, evening/weekend, online learning. *Degree requirements:* For doctorate, thesis/dissertation (for some programs); for CAGS, comprehensive exam. Electronic applications accepted. *Expenses:* Contact institution.

**North Park University,** School of Nursing and Health Sciences, Chicago, IL 60625-4895. Offers advanced practice nursing (MS); leadership and management (MS); MBA/MS; MM/MSN; MS/MHR; MS/MNA. *Accreditation:* AACN. *Program availability:* Part-time, evening/weekend. *Degree requirements:* For master's, thesis. *Entrance requirements:* For master's, GMAT, MAT.

**Northwest Nazarene University,** Program in Nursing, Nampa, ID 83686-5897. Offers leadership/education (MSN). *Accreditation:* AACN. *Program availability:* Part-time, evening/weekend, online only, 100% online, And Residential LABS for FNP. *Entrance requirements:* For master's, bachelor degree from a regionally accredited school (for MSN Leadership/Education and FNP) or apply for admission to the RN-BSN program to complete general education prerequisites and required baccalaureate content courses, 3 professional recommendations, minimum GPA of 3.0 (for RN-MSN, FNP); currently employed as an RN. Additional exam requirements/recommendations for international students: required—TOEFL (minimum score 85 paper-based). Electronic applications accepted. *Expenses:* Contact institution.

**Norwich University,** College of Graduate and Continuing Studies, Master of Science in Nursing Program, Northfield, VT 05663. Offers nursing administration (MSN); nursing education (MSN). *Accreditation:* AACN. *Program availability:* Evening/weekend, online only, mostly all online with a week-long residency requirement. *Entrance requirements:* For master's, minimum undergraduate GPA of 3.0. Additional exam requirements/recommendations for international students: required—TOEFL (minimum score 550 paper-based; 80 iBT), IELTS (minimum score 6.5). Electronic applications accepted. *Expenses:* Contact institution.

**Ohio University,** Graduate College, College of Health Sciences and Professions, School of Nursing, Athens, OH 45701-2979. Offers advanced clinical practice (DNP); executive practice (DNP); family nurse practitioner (MSN); nurse educator (MSN). *Accreditation:* AACN. *Degree requirements:* For master's, capstone project. *Entrance requirements:* For master's, GRE, bachelor's degree in nursing from accredited college or university, minimum overall undergraduate GPA of 3.0, official transcripts, statement of goals and objectives, resume, 3 letters of recommendation. Additional exam requirements/recommendations for international students: required—TOEFL (minimum score 550 paper-based; 80 iBT) or IELTS (minimum score 6.5). Electronic applications accepted.

**Oklahoma Wesleyan University,** Professional Studies Division, Bartlesville, OK 74006-6299. Offers nursing administration (MSN); nursing education (MSN); strategic leadership (MS); theology and apologetics (MA).

**Old Dominion University,** College of Health Sciences, School of Nursing, Adult Gerontology Nursing Emphasis, Norfolk, VA 23529. Offers adult gerontology clinical nurse specialist/administrator (MSN); adult gerontology clinical nurse specialist/educator (MSN); advanced practice (DNP); neonatal clinical nurse specialist (MSN); pediatric clinical nurse specialist (MSN). *Program availability:* Part-time, online only, blended/hybrid learning. *Degree requirements:* For master's, comprehensive exam, internship, practicum. *Entrance requirements:* For master's, GRE or MAT (waived with a GPA above 3.5), undergraduate health/physical assessment course, statistics, 3 letters of recommendation, essay, resume, transcripts. Additional exam requirements/recommendations for international students: required—TOEFL. Electronic applications accepted. *Expenses:* Contact institution.

**Old Dominion University,** College of Health Sciences, School of Nursing, Nurse Administrator Emphasis, Norfolk, VA 23529. Offers nurse administrator (MSN); nurse executive (DNP). *Program availability:* Part-time, blended/hybrid learning. *Degree requirements:* For master's, comprehensive exam; for doctorate, capstone project. *Entrance requirements:* For master's, GRE or MAT if GPA is below 3.5, 3 letters of recommendation, essay, resume, transcripts. Additional exam requirements/recommendations for international students: required—TOEFL. Electronic applications accepted. *Expenses:* Contact institution.

**Oregon Health & Science University,** School of Nursing, Program in Health Systems and Organizational Leadership, Portland, OR 97239-3098. Offers MN. *Program availability:* Part-time, online only, 100% online. *Entrance requirements:* For master's, GRE General Test, 3 letters of recommendation, essay, statistics within last 5 years with minimum B- grade, BS in nursing, RN license. Additional exam requirements/recommendations for international students: required—TOEFL (minimum score 83 iBT). Electronic applications accepted. *Expenses:* Contact institution.

**Otterbein University,** Department of Nursing, Westerville, OH 43081. Offers advanced practice nurse educator (Certificate); clinical nurse leader (MSN); family nurse practitioner (MSN, Certificate); nurse anesthesia (MSN, Certificate); nursing (DNP); nursing service administration (MSN). *Accreditation:* AACN; AANA/CANAEP; ACEN. *Program availability:* Part-time, evening/weekend, online learning. *Degree requirements:*

For master's, comprehensive exam (for some programs), thesis (for some programs). *Entrance requirements:* For master's, 2 reference forms, resume; for Certificate, official transcripts, 2 reference forms, essay, resumé. Additional exam requirements/recommendations for international students: required—TOEFL (minimum score 550 paper-based; 79 iBT).

**Pace University,** College of Health Professions, Lienhard School of Nursing, New York, NY 10038. Offers adult acute care nurse practitioner (MS, CAGS); family nurse practitioner (MS, CAGS); nursing (DNP, PhD); professional nursing leadership (MS, CAGS). *Accreditation:* AACN. *Program availability:* Part-time. Terminal master's awarded for partial completion of doctoral program. *Entrance requirements:* For master's, RN license, resume, personal statement, 2 letters of recommendation, official transcripts, minimum GPA of 3.0, undergraduate statistics; for doctorate, RN license, resume, personal statement, 2 letters of recommendation, official transcripts, accredited master's degree in nursing, minimum GPA of 3.3, state certification and board eligibility as FNP or ANP; for CAGS, RN license, resume, personal statement, 2 letters of recommendation, official transcripts, minimum GPA of 3.0, undergraduate statistics, completion of 2nd degree in nursing. Additional exam requirements/recommendations for international students: required—TOEFL (minimum score 100 iBT), IELTS or PTE. Electronic applications accepted. *Expenses:* Contact institution.

**Palm Beach Atlantic University,** School of Nursing, West Palm Beach, FL 33416-4708. Offers family nurse practitioner (DNP); health systems leadership (MSN). *Accreditation:* AACN. *Program availability:* Part-time. *Degree requirements:* For master's, capstone course. *Entrance requirements:* For master's, minimum GPA of 3.0; active RN license; personal interview; for doctorate, minimum GPA of 3.0; one year of experience as an RN; personal interview. Additional exam requirements/recommendations for international students: required—TOEFL (minimum score 550 paper-based; 79 iBT). Electronic applications accepted. *Expenses:* Contact institution.

**Pennsylvania College of Health Sciences,** Graduate Programs, Lancaster, PA 17601. Offers administration (MSN); education (MSHS, MSN); healthcare administration (MHA). *Degree requirements:* For master's, internship (for MHA, MSN in administration); practicum (for MSHS, MSN in education).

**Purdue University Fort Wayne,** College of Health and Human Services, Department of Nursing, Fort Wayne, IN 46805-1499. Offers adult-gerontology primary care nurse practitioner (MS); family nurse practitioner (MS); nurse executive (MS); nursing administration (Certificate); nursing education (MS). *Accreditation:* ACEN. *Program availability:* Part-time. *Entrance requirements:* For master's, GRE Writing Test (if GPA below 3.0), BS in nursing, eligibility for Indiana RN license, minimum GPA of 3.0, essay, copy of resume, three references, undergraduate course work in research and statistics within last 5 years. Additional exam requirements/recommendations for international students: required—TOEFL (minimum score 550 paper-based; 79 iBT); recommended—TWE. Electronic applications accepted.

**Purdue University Global,** School of Nursing, Davenport, IA 52807. Offers nurse administrator (MS); nurse educator (MS). *Program availability:* Part-time, evening/weekend, online learning. *Entrance requirements:* For master's, RN. Additional exam requirements/recommendations for international students: required—TOEFL (minimum score 550 paper-based).

**Purdue University Northwest,** Graduate Studies Office, School of Nursing, Hammond, IN 46323-2094. Offers adult health clinical nurse specialist (MS); critical care clinical nurse specialist (MS); family nurse practitioner (MS); nurse executive (MS). *Accreditation:* ACEN. *Program availability:* Part-time, online learning. *Entrance requirements:* For master's, BSN. Additional exam requirements/recommendations for international students: required—TOEFL. Electronic applications accepted.

**Queens University of Charlotte,** Presbyterian School of Nursing, Charlotte, NC 28274-0002. Offers clinical nurse leader (MSN); nurse educator (MSN); nursing administrator (MSN). *Accreditation:* AACN. *Degree requirements:* For master's, research project. *Entrance requirements:* For master's, minimum GPA of 3.0. Additional exam requirements/recommendations for international students: required—TOEFL. Electronic applications accepted. *Expenses:* Contact institution.

**Quinnipiac University,** School of Nursing, Nursing Leadership Track, Hamden, CT 06518-1940. Offers DNP. *Program availability:* Part-time-only, evening/weekend, online only. Electronic applications accepted. *Expenses:* Contact institution.

**Ramapo College of New Jersey,** Master of Science in Nursing Program, Mahwah, NJ 07430. Offers family nurse practitioner (MSN); nursing administrator (MSN); nursing education (MSN). *Accreditation:* ACEN. *Program availability:* Part-time. *Degree requirements:* For master's, thesis or alternative. *Entrance requirements:* For master's, official transcript; personal statement; 2 letters of recommendation; resume; current licensure as a Registered Nurse, or eligibility for licensure; evidence of one year of recent experience as RN prior to entry into clinical practicum courses; evidence of undergraduate statistics course; criminal background check. Additional exam requirements/recommendations for international students: required—TOEFL (minimum score 550 paper-based; 90 iBT); recommended—IELTS (minimum score 6). Electronic applications accepted. *Expenses:* Contact institution.

**Regis University,** Rueckert-Hartman College for Health Professions, Denver, CO 80221-1099. Offers advanced practice nurse (DNP); counseling (MA); counseling children and adolescents (Post-Graduate Certificate); counseling military families (Post-Graduate Certificate); depth psychotherapy (Post-Graduate Certificate); fellowship in orthopedic manual physical therapy (Certificate); health care business management (Certificate); health care quality and patient safety (Certificate); health industry leadership (MBA); health services administration (MS); marriage and family therapy (MA, Post-Graduate Certificate); neonatal nurse practitioner (MSN); nursing education (MSN); nursing leadership (MSN); occupational therapy (OTD); pharmacy (Pharm D); physical therapy (DPT). *Accreditation:* ACPE. *Program availability:* Part-time, evening/weekend, 100% online, blended/hybrid learning. *Degree requirements:* For master's, thesis (for some programs), internship. *Entrance requirements:* For master's, official transcript reflecting baccalaureate degree awarded from regionally-accredited college or university. Additional exam requirements/recommendations for international students: required—TOEFL (minimum score 550 paper-based; 82 iBT). Electronic applications accepted. *Expenses:* Contact institution.

**Rivier University,** School of Graduate Studies, Division of Nursing and Health Professions, Nashua, NH 03060. Offers family nurse practitioner (MS); leadership in health systems management (MS); nursing education (MS); nursing practice (DNP); psychiatric/mental health nurse practitioner (MS); public health (MPH). *Accreditation:* ACEN. *Program availability:* Part-time, evening/weekend. *Entrance requirements:* For master's, GRE, MAT. Electronic applications accepted.

**Roberts Wesleyan College,** Department of Nursing, Rochester, NY 14624-1997. Offers nursing education (MSN); nursing informatics (MSN); nursing leadership and administration (MSN). *Accreditation:* AACN. *Program availability:* Evening/weekend, online learning. *Degree requirements:* For master's, thesis. *Entrance requirements:* For master's, minimum GPA of 3.0; BS in nursing; interview; RN license; resume; course work in statistics. Additional exam requirements/recommendations for international

students: required—TOEFL (minimum score 90 iBT), IELTS (minimum score 6.5). Electronic applications accepted.

**Sacred Heart University,** Graduate Programs, College of Nursing, Fairfield, CT 06825. Offers clinical (DNP); clinical nurse leader (MSN); family nurse practitioner (MSN, Post-Master's Certificate); leadership (DNP); nursing education (MSN); nursing management and executive leadership (MSN). *Accreditation:* AACN. *Program availability:* Part-time, evening/weekend, 100% online, blended/hybrid learning. *Degree requirements:* For master's, thesis, 500 clinical hours; for doctorate, capstone. *Entrance requirements:* For master's, minimum GPA of 3.0, BSN or RN plus BS (for MSN); for doctorate, minimum GPA of 3.0, MSN or BSN plus MS in related field (for DNP). Additional exam requirements/recommendations for international students: required—TOEFL (minimum score 570 paper-based, 80 iBT), TWE, or IELTS (6.5). Electronic applications accepted. *Expenses:* Contact institution.

**Saint Francis Medical Center College of Nursing,** SFMC College of Nursing Graduate Programs, Peoria, IL 61603-3783. Offers adult gerontology (MSN); clinical nurse leader (MSN); family nurse practitioner (MSN, Post-Graduate Certificate); family psychiatric mental health nurse practitioner (MSN); neonatal nurse practitioner (MSN); nurse clinician (Post-Graduate Certificate); nurse educator (MSN, Post-Graduate Certificate); nursing (DNP), including leadership/ clinician; nursing management leadership (MSN). *Accreditation:* ACEN. *Program availability:* Part-time, online only, 100% online, blended/hybrid learning. *Faculty:* 12 full-time (all women), 10 part-time/adjunct (all women). *Students:* 1 (woman) full-time, 188 part-time (157 women); includes 20 minority (10 Black or African American, non-Hispanic/Latino; 3 Asian, non-Hispanic/Latino; 3 Hispanic/Latino; 4 Two or more races, non-Hispanic/Latino). Average age 40. 54 applicants, 91% accepted, 18 enrolled. In 2019, 51 master's, 11 doctorates awarded. *Degree requirements:* For master's, research experience, portfolio, practicum; for doctorate, practicum. *Entrance requirements:* For master's, Nursing research, health assessment, RN license; for doctorate, Master's degree in nursing, professional portfolio, graduate statistics, transcripts, RN license. Additional exam requirements/recommendations for international students: required—TOEFL (minimum score 550 paper-based; 79 iBT). *Application deadline:* For fall admission, 6/1 priority date for domestic and international students; for spring admission, 11/15 priority date for domestic and international students. Applications are processed on a rolling basis. Application fee: $50. *Expenses: Tuition:* Part-time $705 per credit hour. *Required fees:* $270 per unit. *Financial support:* In 2019–20, 13 students received support. Scholarships/grants available. Support available to part-time students. Financial award application deadline: 6/15; financial award applicants required to submit FAFSA. *Unit head:* Dr. Sandie S Soldwisch, President of OSF Colleges of Health Sciences, 815-282-7909, Fax: 309-624-8973, E-mail: Sandie.S.Soldwisch@osfhealthcare.org. *Application contact:* Dr. Kim A. Mitchell, Dean, Graduate Program, 309-655-2201, Fax: 309-624-8973, E-mail: kim.a.mitchell@osfhealthcare.org.
Website: http://www.sfmccon.edu/graduate-programs/

**Saint Francis University,** Nursing Program, Loretto, PA 15940-0600. Offers leadership/education (MSN). *Program availability:* Part-time, online only, blended/hybrid learning. *Faculty:* 2 full-time (both women), 4 part-time/adjunct (all women). *Students:* 7 part-time (all women). Average age 44. 9 applicants, 78% accepted, 4 enrolled. In 2019, 10 master's awarded. *Entrance requirements:* Additional exam requirements/recommendations for international students: required—TOEFL. Application fee: $30. Electronic applications accepted. *Expenses:* 625 per credit, 48 credits. *Financial support:* Applicants required to submit FAFSA. *Unit head:* Dr. Camille Wendekier, RN, Coordinator, 814-472-2843, E-mail: cwendekier@francis.edu. *Application contact:* Dr. Peter Raymond Skoner.
Website: https://www.francis.edu/Nursing-Masters/

**Saint Joseph's College of Maine,** Master of Science in Nursing Program, Standish, ME 04084. Offers administration (MSN); education (MSN); family nurse practitioner (MSN); nursing administration and leadership (Certificate); nursing and health care education (Certificate). *Accreditation:* AACN. *Program availability:* Part-time, online learning. *Entrance requirements:* For master's, MAT. Electronic applications accepted.

**Saint Peter's University,** School of Nursing, Nursing Program, Jersey City, NJ 07306-5997. Offers adult nurse practitioner (MSN, Certificate); advanced practice (DNP); case management (MSN, DNP). *Accreditation:* AACN. *Program availability:* Part-time, evening/weekend. *Entrance requirements:* Additional exam requirements/recommendations for international students: required—TOEFL. Electronic applications accepted.

**Salem State University,** School of Graduate Studies, Program in Nursing, Salem, MA 01970-5353. Offers adult-gerontology primary care nursing (MSN); nursing administration (MSN); nursing education (MSN); MBA/MSN. *Accreditation:* AACN. *Program availability:* Part-time, evening/weekend. *Entrance requirements:* For master's, GRE or MAT. Additional exam requirements/recommendations for international students: required—TOEFL (minimum score 550 paper-based; 80 iBT) or IELTS (minimum score 5.5).

**Salisbury University,** DNP Program, Salisbury, MD 21801. Offers family nurse practitioner (DNP); nursing leadership (DNP). *Accreditation:* AACN. *Program availability:* Part-time, evening/weekend, 100% online, blended/hybrid learning. *Faculty:* 14 full-time (13 women), 4 part-time/adjunct (all women). *Students:* 25 full-time (22 women), 8 part-time (all women); includes 8 minority (5 Black or African American, non-Hispanic/Latino; 1 Hispanic/Latino; 2 Two or more races, non-Hispanic/Latino). Average age 34. 17 applicants, 71% accepted, 8 enrolled. In 2019, 7 doctorates awarded. *Degree requirements:* For doctorate, Evidence based project. *Entrance requirements:* For doctorate, transcripts; resume or CV; personal statement; proof of certification or licensure; minimum GPA of 3.0; three letters of recommendation; undergraduate degree in nursing. *Application deadline:* For fall admission, 3/1 priority date for domestic and international students. Applications are processed on a rolling basis. Application fee: $65. Electronic applications accepted. *Expenses:* Contact institution. *Financial support:* Career-related internships or fieldwork and scholarships/grants available. Support available to part-time students. Financial award application deadline: 3/1; financial award applicants required to submit FAFSA. *Unit head:* Dr. Annette Barnes, Graduate Program Chair, 410-546-4380, E-mail: ahbarnes@salisbury.edu. *Application contact:* Kristi Jenkins, Administrative Assistant II, 410-548-2242, E-mail: kljenkins@salisbury.edu.
Website: https://www.salisbury.edu/explore-academics/programs/graduate-degree-programs/nursing-practice-doctor/

**Salisbury University,** MS in Nursing Program, Salisbury, MD 21801-6837. Offers nursing (MS), including clinical nurse educator, health care leadership. *Accreditation:* AACN. *Program availability:* Part-time, evening/weekend, 100% online, blended/hybrid learning. *Faculty:* 14 full-time (13 women), 4 part-time/adjunct (all women). *Students:* 1 (woman) full-time, 4 part-time (all women); includes 2 minority (1 Asian, non-Hispanic/Latino; 1 Hispanic/Latino). Average age 27. 3 applicants, 100% accepted, 3 enrolled. *Degree requirements:* For master's, internship, capstone or thesis. *Entrance requirements:* For master's, transcripts; resume or CV; personal statement; proof of certification or licensure; minimum GPA of 3.0; two letters of recommendation; undergraduate degree in nursing; undergraduate statistics. *Application deadline:* For fall

admission, 3/1 priority date for domestic and international students. Application fee: $65. Electronic applications accepted. *Expenses:* Contact institution. *Financial support:* In 2019–20, 1 student received support, including 1 research assistantship with full tuition reimbursement available (averaging $8,000 per year), 1 teaching assistantship with full tuition reimbursement available (averaging $9,000 per year); career-related internships or fieldwork and scholarships/grants also available. Support available to part-time students. Financial award application deadline: 3/1; financial award applicants required to submit FAFSA. *Unit head:* Dr. Annette Barnes, Graduate Program Chair, 410-546-4380, E-mail: ahbarnes@salisbury.edu. *Application contact:* Kristi Jenkins, Administrative Assistant II, 410-548-2242, E-mail: kljenkins@salisbury.edu.
Website: https://www.salisbury.edu/explore-academics/programs/graduate-degree-programs/nursing-master/

**Samford University,** Ida Moffett School of Nursing, Birmingham, AL 35229. Offers advanced practice (DNP), including emergency nurse practitioner, family nurse practitioner, transformation of care; family nurse practitioner (MSN, DNP), including emergency nurse practitioner specialty (MSN); nurse anesthesia (DNP); nursing administration (DNP); psychiatric mental health nurse practitioner (DNP). *Accreditation:* AACN; AANA/CANAEP. *Program availability:* Part-time, evening/weekend, blended/hybrid learning. *Faculty:* 16 full-time (all women), 3 part-time/adjunct (0 women). *Students:* 281 full-time (239 women), 39 part-time (38 women); includes 68 minority (39 Black or African American, non-Hispanic/Latino; 2 American Indian or Alaska Native, non-Hispanic/Latino; 10 Asian, non-Hispanic/Latino; 10 Hispanic/Latino; 1 Native Hawaiian or other Pacific Islander, non-Hispanic/Latino; 6 Two or more races, non-Hispanic/Latino). Average age 35. 59 applicants, 97% accepted, 29 enrolled. In 2019, 47 master's, 68 doctorates awarded. *Degree requirements:* For doctorate, DNP project with poster presentation. *Entrance requirements:* For doctorate, GRE is required for the Nurse Anesthesia Program. Additional exam requirements/recommendations for international students: required—TOEFL (minimum score 575 paper-based; 90 iBT), IELTS (minimum score 6.5). *Application deadline:* For fall admission, 4/1 for domestic and international students; for spring admission, 8/1 for domestic and international students; for summer admission, 1/1 for domestic and international students. Application fee: $50. Electronic applications accepted. *Expenses: Tuition:* Full-time $17,754; part-time $862 per credit hour. *Required fees:* $550; $550 per unit. Full-time tuition and fees vary according to course load, program and student level. *Financial support:* In 2019–20, 30 students received support. Application deadline: 2/15; applicants required to submit FAFSA. *Unit head:* Dr. Jane S. Martin, Interim Dean and Professor, Ida Moffett School of Nursing, 205-726-2760, E-mail: jsmartin@samford.edu. *Application contact:* Allyson Maddox, Director of Graduate Student Services, 205-726-2047, E-mail: amaddox@samford.edu.
Website: http://samford.edu/nursing

**Samuel Merritt University,** School of Nursing, Oakland, CA 94609-3108. Offers case management (MSN); family nurse practitioner (MSN, DNP, Certificate); nurse anesthetist (MSN, Certificate); nursing (DNP). *Accreditation:* AACN; AANA/CANAEP (one or more programs are accredited). *Program availability:* Part-time, evening/weekend, 100% online, blended/hybrid learning. *Degree requirements:* For master's, thesis or alternative; for doctorate, project. *Entrance requirements:* For master's, GRE General Test (for nurse anesthetist program), minimum GPA of 2.5 in science, 3.0 overall; previous course work in statistics; current RN license; for doctorate and Certificate, minimum GPA of 2.5 in science, 3.0 overall; previous course work in statistics; current RN license. Additional exam requirements/recommendations for international students: required—TOEFL (minimum score 100 iBT). Electronic applications accepted. *Expenses:* Contact institution.

**San Francisco State University,** Division of Graduate Studies, College of Health and Social Sciences, School of Nursing, San Francisco, CA 94132-1722. Offers adult acute care (MS); clinical nurse specialist (MS); community/public health nursing (MS); family nurse practitioner (Certificate); nursing administration (MS); pediatrics (MS); women's health (MS). *Accreditation:* AACN. *Program availability:* Part-time. *Application deadline:* Applications are processed on a rolling basis. *Expenses: Tuition, area resident:* Full-time $7176; part-time $4164 per year. Tuition, state resident: full-time $7176; part-time $4164 per year. Tuition, nonresident: full-time $16,680; part-time $396 per unit. *International tuition:* $16,680 full-time. *Required fees:* $1524; $1524 per unit. $762 per semester. Tuition and fees vary according to degree level and program. *Financial support:* Career-related internships or fieldwork available. *Unit head:* Dr. Mary-Ann van Dam, 415-338-1802, Fax: 415-338-0555, E-mail: vandam@sfsu.edu. *Application contact:* Prof. Fang-yu Chou, Assistant Director of Graduate Programs, 415-338-6853, Fax: 415-338-0555, E-mail: fchou@sfsu.edu.
Website: http://nursing.sfsu.edu

**San Jose State University,** Program in Nursing, San Jose, CA 95192-0057. Offers gerontology nurse practitioner (MS); nursing (Certificate); nursing administration (MS); nursing education (MS). *Accreditation:* AACN. *Faculty:* 5 full-time (all women), 3 part-time/adjunct (all women). *Students:* 21 full-time (17 women), 52 part-time (49 women); includes 45 minority (4 Black or African American, non-Hispanic/Latino; 29 Asian, non-Hispanic/Latino; 12 Hispanic/Latino), 3 international. Average age 37. 30 applicants, 97% accepted, 23 enrolled. In 2019, 22 master's awarded. *Degree requirements:* For master's, comprehensive exam, thesis. *Entrance requirements:* For master's, BSN. *Application deadline:* For fall admission, 3/1 for domestic students. Applications are processed on a rolling basis. Application fee: $70. Electronic applications accepted. *Expenses:* Contact institution. *Financial support:* Application deadline: 5/1; applicants required to submit FAFSA. *Unit head:* Colleen O'Leary-Kelley, Department Chair, 408-924-1319, Fax: 408-924-3135, E-mail: colleen.oleary-kelley@sjsu.edu. *Application contact:* Karen Wilcox, FNP Program Analyst, 408-924-3153, Fax: 408-924-3135, E-mail: karen.wilcox@sjsu.edu.
Website: http://www.sjsu.edu/nursing/

**Seattle Pacific University,** MS in Nursing Program, Seattle, WA 98119-1997. Offers administration (MSN); adult/gerontology nurse practitioner (MSN); clinical nurse specialist (MSN); family nurse practitioner (MSN, Certificate); informatics (MSN); nurse educator (MSN). *Accreditation:* AACN. *Program availability:* Part-time. *Students:* 42 full-time (38 women), 18 part-time (16 women); includes 28 minority (5 Black or African American, non-Hispanic/Latino; 18 Asian, non-Hispanic/Latino; 5 Hispanic/Latino), 2 international. Average age 33. 59 applicants, 41% accepted. In 2019, 10 master's awarded. *Degree requirements:* For master's, thesis. *Entrance requirements:* For master's, personal statement, transcripts, undergraduate nursing degree, proof of undergraduate statistics course with minimum GPA of 2.0, 2 recommendations. *Application deadline:* For fall admission, 1/15 priority date for domestic students; for spring admission, 1/15 for domestic students. Applications are processed on a rolling basis. Application fee: $50. Electronic applications accepted. *Expenses:* Contact institution. *Financial support:* Fellowships and scholarships/grants available. Financial award applicants required to submit FAFSA. *Unit head:* Dr. Antwinett Lee, Associate Dean, 206-281-2607, E-mail: leea30@spu.edu. *Application contact:* Dr. Antwinett Lee, Associate Dean, 206-281-2607, E-mail: leea30@spu.edu.
Website: http://spu.edu/academics/school-of-health-sciences/undergraduate-programs/nursing

**Seton Hall University,** College of Nursing, South Orange, NJ 07079-2697. Offers advanced practice in primary health care (MSN, DNP), including adult/gerontological nurse practitioner, pediatric nurse practitioner; entry into practice (MSN); health systems administration (MSN, DNP); nursing (PhD); nursing case management (MSN); nursing education (MA); school nurse (MSN); MSN/MA. *Accreditation:* AACN. *Program availability:* Part-time, online learning. *Degree requirements:* For master's, research project; for doctorate, dissertation or scholarly project. *Entrance requirements:* For doctorate, GRE (waived for students with GPA of 3.5 or higher). Additional exam requirements/recommendations for international students: required—TOEFL. Electronic applications accepted.

**Shenandoah University,** Eleanor Wade Custer School of Nursing, Winchester, VA 22601. Offers adult gerontology primary care nurse practitioner (Graduate Certificate); adult-gerontology primary care nurse practitioner (MSN); family nurse practitioner (MSN, DNP, Graduate Certificate); general (MSN); health systems leadership (DNP); health systems management (MSN, Graduate Certificate); nurse midwifery (MSN); nurse-midwifery (Graduate Certificate); nursing education (Graduate Certificate); nursing practice (DNP); psychiatric mental health nurse practitioner (MSN, DNP, Graduate Certificate). *Accreditation:* AACN; ACNM/ACME. *Entrance requirements:* For master's, United States RN license; minimum GPA of 3.0; 2080 hours of clinical experience; curriculum vitae; 3 letters of recommendation from former dean, faculty member, or advisor familiar with the applicant, and a former or current supervisor; two-to-three-page essay on a specified topic; for doctorate, MSN, minimum GPA of 3.0, 3 letters of recommendation, interview, BSN, two-to-three page essay on a specific topic, 500-word statement of clinical practice research interest, resume, current U.S. RN license, 2080 clinical hours; for Graduate Certificate, MSN, minimum GPA of 3.0, 2 letters of recommendation, minimum of one year (2080 hours) of clinical nursing experience, interview, two-to-three page essay on a specific topic, resume, current United States RN license. Additional exam requirements/recommendations for international students: required—TOEFL (minimum score 558 paper-based; 83 iBT). Electronic applications accepted. *Expenses:* Contact institution.

**Southern Illinois University Edwardsville,** Graduate School, School of Nursing, Program in Health Care and Nursing Administration, Edwardsville, IL 62026. Offers MS, Post-Master's Certificate. *Program availability:* Part-time. *Degree requirements:* For master's, comprehensive exam. *Entrance requirements:* For master's, RN licensure, minimum undergraduate nursing GPA of 3.0, BS from CCNE- or ACEN-accredited program. Additional exam requirements/recommendations for international students: required—TOEFL (minimum score 550 paper-based; 79 iBT), IELTS (minimum score 6.5). Electronic applications accepted.

**Southern Nazarene University,** College of Professional and Graduate Studies, School of Nursing, Bethany, OK 73008. Offers nursing education (MS); nursing leadership (MS). *Accreditation:* AACN. *Program availability:* Part-time, evening/weekend. *Degree requirements:* For master's, thesis. *Entrance requirements:* For master's, minimum undergraduate cumulative GPA of 3.0; baccalaureate degree in nursing from nationally-accredited program; current unencumbered registered nurse licensure in Oklahoma or eligibility for same; documentation of basic computer skills; basic statistics course; statement of professional goals; three letters of recommendation. Additional exam requirements/recommendations for international students: required—TOEFL (minimum score 550 paper-based).

**Southern New Hampshire University,** Program in Nursing, Manchester, NH 03106-1045. Offers clinical nurse leader (MSN); nurse educator (MSN); nursing (MSN); patient safety and quality (MSN, Post Master's Certificate). *Program availability:* Online only, 100% online. *Entrance requirements:* For master's, undergraduate transcripts, active unencumbered license, bachelor's degree with minimum cumulative GPA of 3.0. Electronic applications accepted.

**Southern University and Agricultural and Mechanical College,** College of Nursing and Allied Health, School of Nursing, Baton Rouge, LA 70813. Offers educator/administrator (PhD); family health nursing (MSN); family nurse practitioner (Post Master's Certificate); geriatric nurse practitioner/gerontology (PhD); nursing (DNP). *Accreditation:* AACN. *Program availability:* Part-time. *Degree requirements:* For master's, comprehensive exam, thesis; for doctorate, comprehensive exam, thesis/dissertation. *Entrance requirements:* For master's, GRE General Test, BSN, minimum GPA of 2.7; for doctorate, GRE General Test; for Post Master's Certificate, MSN. Additional exam requirements/recommendations for international students: required—TOEFL (minimum score 525 paper-based).

**Spalding University,** Graduate Studies, Kosair College of Health and Natural Sciences, School of Nursing, Louisville, KY 40203-2188. Offers adult nurse practitioner (MSN); family nurse practitioner (MSN); leadership in nursing and healthcare (MSN); nurse educator (Post-Master's Certificate); nurse practitioner (Post-Master's Certificate); pediatric nurse practitioner (MSN). *Accreditation:* AACN. *Program availability:* Part-time, evening/weekend. *Degree requirements:* For master's, comprehensive exam (for some programs), thesis. *Entrance requirements:* For master's, GRE General Test, BSN or bachelor's degree in related field, RN licensure, autobiographical statement, transcripts, letters of recommendation. Additional exam requirements/recommendations for international students: required—TOEFL (minimum score 535 paper-based).

**Spring Hill College,** Graduate Programs, Program in Nursing, Mobile, AL 36608-1791. Offers MSN, Post-Master's Certificate. *Accreditation:* AACN. *Program availability:* Part-time, evening/weekend, online only, 100% online. *Degree requirements:* For master's, comprehensive exam, capstone courses, completion of program within 6 calendar years; for Post-Master's Certificate, 460 clinical integration hours. *Entrance requirements:* For master's, RN license in state where practicing nursing; 1 year of clinical nursing experience; work in clinical setting or access to health care facility for clinical integration/research; 3 written references; employer verification; resume; 500-word essay explaining how becoming a CNL will help applicant achieve personal and professional goals; for Post-Master's Certificate, RN license; master's degree in nursing. Additional exam requirements/recommendations for international students: required—TOEFL (minimum score 550 paper-based; 80 iBT), IELTS (minimum score 6.5), CPE or CAE (minimum score C), Michigan English Language Assessment Battery (minimum score 90). *Application deadline:* For fall admission, 8/1 priority date for domestic and international students; for spring admission, 12/1 priority date for domestic and international students. Applications are processed on a rolling basis. Application fee: $25 ($35 for international students). Electronic applications accepted. *Expenses:* Contact institution. *Financial support:* Fellowships, research assistantships, teaching assistantships, and tuition waivers available. Financial award applicants required to submit FAFSA. *Unit head:* Dr. Terran Mathers, Director, 251-380-4485, Fax: 251-460-4495, E-mail: tmathers@shc.edu. *Application contact:* Gary Bracken, Vice President of Enrollment Management, 251-380-3038, Fax: 251-460-2186, E-mail: gbracken@shc.edu.
Website: http://ug.shc.edu/graduate-degrees/master-science-nursing/

**State University of New York College of Technology at Delhi,** Program in Nursing, Delhi, NY 13753. Offers nursing administration (MS); nursing education (MS). *Program availability:* Part-time, online only, 100% online. *Faculty:* 6 full-time (all women), 2 part-time/adjunct (both women). *Students:* 10 full-time (7 women), 77 part-time (70 women);

includes 13 minority (7 Black or African American, non-Hispanic/Latino; 2 Asian, non-Hispanic/Latino; 4 Hispanic/Latino). Average age 38. 70 applicants, 71% accepted, 37 enrolled. In 2019, 15 master's awarded. *Application deadline:* For fall admission, 7/15 for domestic and international students; for spring admission, 11/15 for domestic and international students. Applications are processed on a rolling basis. Application fee: $75. Electronic applications accepted. *Expenses: Tuition, area resident:* Full-time $11,310; part-time $471 per credit hour. Tuition, state resident: full-time $11,310; part-time $471 per credit hour. Tuition, nonresident: full-time $13,570; part-time $565 per credit hour. *International tuition:* $13,570 full-time. *Required fees:* $420; $21.70 per credit hour. $21.70. *Financial support:* In 2019–20, 4 students received support. Scholarships/grants available. Financial award applicants required to submit FAFSA. *Unit head:* Susan Deane, Dean of the School of Nursing, 607-746-4550, Fax: 607-746-4104, E-mail: deanesg@delhi.edu. *Application contact:* Misty Fields, Associate Director of Admission, 607-746-4546, E-mail: fieldsmr@delhi.edu.

**Stevenson University,** Program in Nursing, Stevenson, MD 21153. Offers nursing education (MS); nursing leadership/management (MS); population-based care coordination (MS). *Accreditation:* AACN. *Program availability:* Part-time, blended/hybrid learning. *Faculty:* 2 full-time (both women), 5 part-time/adjunct (all women). *Students:* 144 part-time (138 women); includes 33 minority (24 Black or African American, non-Hispanic/Latino; 3 Asian, non-Hispanic/Latino; 4 Hispanic/Latino; 2 Two or more races, non-Hispanic/Latino). Average age 37. 56 applicants, 73% accepted, 30 enrolled. In 2019, 50 master's awarded. *Degree requirements:* For master's, capstone course. *Entrance requirements:* For master's, Personal statement; Official college transcript; Bachelor's degree in nursing; Cumulative GPA of 3.0; current registered nurse's license in good standing; 1 letter of recommendation; Professional Resume. *Application deadline:* For fall admission, 8/9 priority date for domestic students; for spring admission, 1/11 priority date for domestic students; for summer admission, 5/1 priority date for domestic students. Applications are processed on a rolling basis. Electronic applications accepted. *Expenses:* $625 per credit. *Financial support:* Unspecified assistantships available. Financial award applicants required to submit FAFSA. *Unit head:* Dr. Judith Feustle, Associate Dean, 443-394-9818, Fax: 443-394-0538, E-mail: jfeustle@stevenson.edu. *Application contact:* Amanda Millar, Director, Admissions, 443-352-4243, Fax: 443-394-0538, E-mail: amillar@stevenson.edu.
Website: https://www.stevenson.edu/online/academics/online-graduate-programs/nursing/

**Stony Brook University, State University of New York,** Stony Brook Medicine, School of Nursing, Program in Nursing Leadership, Stony Brook, NY 11794. Offers MS, Certificate. *Program availability:* Part-time, blended/hybrid learning. *Students:* 220 part-time (187 women); includes 73 minority (19 Black or African American, non-Hispanic/Latino; 25 Asian, non-Hispanic/Latino; 22 Hispanic/Latino; 1 Native Hawaiian or other Pacific Islander, non-Hispanic/Latino; 6 Two or more races, non-Hispanic/Latino), 1 international. 152 applicants, 97% accepted, 134 enrolled. In 2019, 98 master's awarded. *Entrance requirements:* Additional exam requirements/recommendations for international students: required—TOEFL (minimum score 90 iBT). *Application deadline:* For fall admission, 3/19 for domestic students. Application fee: $100. *Expenses:* Contact institution. *Unit head:* Paula M Timoney, Program Director, 631-444-3298, Fax: 631-444-3136, E-mail: paula.timoney@stonybrook.edu. *Application contact:* Silvana Jara, Staff Assistant, 631-444-3392, Fax: 631-444-3136, E-mail: silvana.jara@stonybrook.edu.

**Stony Brook University, State University of New York,** Stony Brook Medicine, School of Nursing, Program in Nursing Practice, Stony Brook, NY 11794. Offers DNP. *Program availability:* Part-time, blended/hybrid learning. *Students:* 12 full-time (11 women), 18 part-time (17 women); includes 13 minority (9 Black or African American, non-Hispanic/Latino; 3 Asian, non-Hispanic/Latino; 1 Hispanic/Latino). Average age 41. 34 applicants, 59% accepted, 15 enrolled. In 2019, 12 doctorates awarded. *Degree requirements:* For doctorate, thesis/dissertation, project. *Entrance requirements:* For doctorate, minimum GPA of 3.0. Additional exam requirements/recommendations for international students: required—TOEFL (minimum score 90 iBT). *Application deadline:* For fall admission, 2/27 for domestic students, 3/3 for international students. Application fee: $100. *Expenses:* Contact institution. *Unit head:* Patricia Bruckenthal, Program Director, 631-444-3236, Fax: 631-444-3136, E-mail: patricia.bruckenthal@stonybrook.edu. *Application contact:* Dr. Dolores Bilges, Senior Staff Assistant, 631-444-2644, Fax: 631-444-3136, E-mail: dnp.nursing@stonybrook.edu.
Website: http://www.nursing.stonybrookmedicine.edu/

**Tarleton State University,** College of Graduate Studies, College of Health Sciences and Human Services, School of Nursing, Stephenville, TX 76402. Offers nursing administration (MSN); nursing education (MSN). *Accreditation:* AACN. *Program availability:* Part-time, evening/weekend, 100% online, blended/hybrid learning. *Faculty:* 3 full-time (all women), 1 (woman) part-time/adjunct. *Students:* 5 part-time (4 women); includes 1 minority (Black or African American, non-Hispanic/Latino), 1 international. Average age 42. 7 applicants, 100% accepted, 1 enrolled. In 2019, 2 master's awarded. *Degree requirements:* For master's, comprehensive exam. *Entrance requirements:* For master's, GRE General Test, minimum GPA of 2.5. Additional exam requirements/recommendations for international students: required—TOEFL (minimum score 520 paper-based; 69 iBT); recommended—IELTS (minimum score 6), TSE (minimum score 50). *Application deadline:* For fall admission, 8/15 priority date for domestic students; for spring admission, 1/7 for domestic students. Applications are processed on a rolling basis. Application fee: $50 ($130 for international students). Electronic applications accepted. *Expenses:* Contact institution. *Financial support:* Career-related internships or fieldwork, Federal Work-Study, and institutionally sponsored loans available. Support available to part-time students. Financial award applicants required to submit FAFSA. *Unit head:* Dr. Jennifer Mundine, Department Head, 254-968-1827, E-mail: mundine@tarleton.edu. *Application contact:* Wendy Weiss, Graduate Admissions Coordinator, 254-968-9104, Fax: 254-968-9670, E-mail: weiss@tarleton.edu.
Website: https://www.tarleton.edu/nursing/index.html

**Teachers College, Columbia University,** Department of Organization and Leadership, New York, NY 10027-6696. Offers adult education guided intensive study (Ed D); adult learning and leadership (Ed M, MA, Ed D); educational leadership (Ed D); higher and postsecondary education (MA, Ed D); leadership, policy and politics (Ed D); nurse executive (MA, Ed D), including administration studies (MA), professorial studies (MA); private school leadership (Ed M, MA); public school building leadership (Ed M, MA); social and organizational psychology (MA); urban education leaders (Ed D); MA/MBA. *Faculty:* 24 full-time (12 women). *Students:* 272 full-time (178 women), 321 part-time (222 women); includes 239 minority (78 Black or African American, non-Hispanic/Latino; 70 Asian, non-Hispanic/Latino; 71 Hispanic/Latino; 1 Native Hawaiian or other Pacific Islander, non-Hispanic/Latino; 19 Two or more races, non-Hispanic/Latino), 73 international. 761 applicants, 65% accepted, 330 enrolled. *Unit head:* Prof. Bill Baldwin, Chair, 212-678-3043, E-mail: wjb12@tc.columbia.edu. *Application contact:* Kelly Sutton-Skinner, Director of Admission and New Student Enrollment, 212-678-3710, E-mail: kms2237@tc.columbia.edu.

**Tennessee Technological University,** College of Graduate Studies, College of Interdisciplinary Studies, School of Professional Studies, Cookeville, TN 38505. Offers health care administration (MPS); human resources leadership (MPS); public safety

(MPS); strategic leadership (MPS); teaching English to speakers of other languages (MPS); training and development (MPS). *Program availability:* Part-time, evening/weekend, online learning. *Students:* 9 full-time (7 women), 89 part-time (59 women); includes 14 minority (10 Black or African American, non-Hispanic/Latino; 1 Asian, non-Hispanic/Latino; 2 Hispanic/Latino; 1 Two or more races, non-Hispanic/Latino), 2 international. 30 applicants, 77% accepted, 16 enrolled. In 2019, 37 master's awarded. *Degree requirements:* For master's, comprehensive exam, thesis or alternative. *Entrance requirements:* For master's, GRE. Additional exam requirements/recommendations for international students: required—TOEFL (minimum score 527 paper-based; 71 iBT), IELTS (minimum score 5.5), PTE (minimum score 48), or TOEIC (Test of English as an International Communication). *Application deadline:* For fall admission, 7/1 for domestic students, 5/1 for international students; for spring admission, 11/1 for domestic students, 10/1 for international students; for summer admission, 5/1 for domestic students, 2/1 for international students. Applications are processed on a rolling basis. Application fee: $35 ($40 for international students). Electronic applications accepted. *Expenses: Tuition, area resident:* Part-time $597 per credit hour. Tuition, state resident: part-time $597 per credit hour. Tuition, nonresident: part-time $1323 per credit hour. *Financial support:* Application deadline: 4/1. *Unit head:* Dr. Mike Gotcher, Dean, 931-372-6223, E-mail: mgotcher@tntech.edu. *Application contact:* Shelia K. Kendrick, Coordinator of Graduate Studies, 931-372-3808, Fax: 931-372-3497, E-mail: skendrick@tntech.edu.
Website: https://www.tntech.edu/is/sps/

**Tennessee Technological University,** Whitson-Hester School of Nursing, DNP Program, Cookeville, TN 38505. Offers adult-gerontology acute care nurse practitioner (DNP); executive leadership in nursing (DNP); family nurse practitioner (DNP); pediatric nurse practitioner-primary care (DNP); psychiatric/mental health nurse practitioner (DNP); women's health care nurse practitioner (DNP). *Program availability:* Part-time. *Students:* 20 full-time (17 women), 12 part-time (all women); includes 3 minority (2 Black or African American, non-Hispanic/Latino; 1 Two or more races, non-Hispanic/Latino). 25 applicants, 60% accepted, 10 enrolled. *Application deadline:* For fall admission, 7/1 for domestic students, 5/1 for international students; for spring admission, 12/1 for domestic students, 10/1 for international students; for summer admission, 5/1 for domestic students, 2/1 for international students. Applications are processed on a rolling basis. Application fee: $35 ($40 for international students). Electronic applications accepted. *Expenses: Tuition, area resident:* Part-time $597 per credit hour. Tuition, state resident: part-time $597 per credit hour. Tuition, nonresident: part-time $1323 per credit hour. *Financial support:* Application deadline: 4/1; applicants required to submit FAFSA. *Unit head:* Dr. Kim Hanna, Dean, Fax: 931-372-6244, E-mail: khanna@tntech.edu. *Application contact:* Shelia K. Kendrick, Coordinator of Graduate Studies, 931-372-3808, Fax: 931-372-3497, E-mail: skendrick@tntech.edu.
Website: https://www.tntech.edu/nursing/doctor-of-nursing-practice/

**Tennessee Technological University,** Whitson-Hester School of Nursing, MSN Programs, Cookeville, TN 38505. Offers family nurse practitioner (MSN); nursing administration (MSN); nursing education (MSN). *Program availability:* Part-time. *Students:* 2 full-time (both women), 110 part-time (93 women); includes 7 minority (4 Black or African American, non-Hispanic/Latino; 1 Asian, non-Hispanic/Latino; 1 Hispanic/Latino; 1 Two or more races, non-Hispanic/Latino). 55 applicants, 73% accepted, 29 enrolled. In 2019, 29 master's awarded. *Application deadline:* For fall admission, 7/1 for domestic students, 5/1 for international students; for spring admission, 12/1 for domestic students, 10/1 for international students; for summer admission, 5/1 for domestic students, 2/1 for international students. Applications are processed on a rolling basis. Application fee: $35 ($40 for international students). Electronic applications accepted. *Expenses: Tuition, area resident:* Part-time $597 per credit hour. Tuition, state resident: part-time $597 per credit hour. Tuition, nonresident: part-time $1323 per credit hour. *Financial support:* Application deadline: 4/1; applicants required to submit FAFSA. *Unit head:* Dr. Kim Hanna, Dean, 931-372-3203, Fax: 931-372-6244, E-mail: khanna@tntech.edu. *Application contact:* Shelia K. Kendrick, Coordinator of Graduate Studies, 931-372-3808, Fax: 931-372-3497, E-mail: skendrick@tntech.edu.
Website: https://www.tntech.edu/nursing/masters/

**Texas A&M University–Corpus Christi,** College of Graduate Studies, College of Nursing and Health Sciences, Corpus Christi, TX 78412. Offers family nurse practitioner (MSN); leadership in nursing systems (MSN); nurse educator (MSN); nursing practice (DNP). *Accreditation:* AACN. *Program availability:* Part-time, evening/weekend, online only, 100% online. *Degree requirements:* For master's, clinical capstone; for doctorate, capstone/scholarly project. *Entrance requirements:* For master's, essay, resume, 3 letters of recommendation, minimum GPA of 3.0, current valid unencumbered Texas nursing license. Additional exam requirements/recommendations for international students: required—TOEFL (minimum score 550 paper-based; 79 iBT), IELTS (minimum score 6.5). Electronic applications accepted.

**Texas Christian University,** Harris College of Nursing and Health Sciences, Doctor of Nursing Practice Program, Fort Worth, TX 76129-0002. Offers clinical nurse specialist - adult/gerontology nursing (DNP); clinical nurse specialist - pediatrics (DNP); family nurse practitioner (DNP); general (DNP); nursing administration (DNP). *Accreditation:* AACN. *Program availability:* Part-time, 100% online, blended/hybrid learning. *Faculty:* 29 full-time (26 women), 1 (woman) part-time/adjunct. *Students:* 49 full-time (45 women), 13 part-time (10 women); includes 18 minority (9 Black or African American, non-Hispanic/Latino; 1 American Indian or Alaska Native, non-Hispanic/Latino; 3 Asian, non-Hispanic/Latino; 4 Hispanic/Latino; 1 Two or more races, non-Hispanic/Latino), 2 international. Average age 37. 57 applicants, 70% accepted, 24 enrolled. In 2019, 27 doctorates awarded. *Degree requirements:* For doctorate, thesis/dissertation or alternative, practicum. *Entrance requirements:* For doctorate, three reference letters, essay, resume, two official transcripts from each institution attended, APRN recognition or MSN with experience or certification in nursing administration, as applicable per track, current RN license, successful completion of interview. Additional exam requirements/recommendations for international students: required—TOEFL (minimum score 550 paper-based; 80 iBT). *Application deadline:* For summer admission, 1/15 for domestic and international students. Application fee: $60. Electronic applications accepted. Full-time tuition and fees vary according to program. *Financial support:* In 2019–20, 20 students received support. Scholarships/grants available. Financial award application deadline: 2/15; financial award applicants required to submit FAFSA. *Unit head:* Dr. Kathy Ellis, Division Director, Graduate Nursing, 817-257-6726, Fax: 817-257-7944, E-mail: kathryn.ellis@tcu.edu. *Application contact:* Beth Janke, Academic Program Specialist, 817-257-6726, Fax: 817-257-7944, E-mail: graduatenursing@tcu.edu.
Website: http://dnp.tcu.edu/

**Texas Christian University,** Harris College of Nursing and Health Sciences, Master's Program in Nursing, Fort Worth, TX 76129-0002. Offers administration and leadership (MSN); clinical nurse leader (MSN, Certificate); clinical nurse specialist (MSN), including adult/gerontology nursing, pediatrics; nursing education (MSN). *Accreditation:* AACN. *Program availability:* Part-time, online only, 100% online. *Faculty:* 29 full-time (26 women), 1 (woman) part-time/adjunct. *Students:* 12 full-time (all women), 5 part-time (all women); includes 5 minority (1 Asian, non-Hispanic/Latino; 4 Hispanic/Latino). Average age 34. 41 applicants, 59% accepted, 8 enrolled. In 2019, 10 master's awarded. *Degree*

*requirements:* For master's, thesis or alternative, practicum. *Entrance requirements:* For master's, 3 letters of reference, essay, resume, two official transcripts from every institution attended, current license to practice as a registered nurse. Additional exam requirements/recommendations for international students: required—TOEFL (minimum score 550 paper-based; 80 iBT). *Application deadline:* For spring admission, 8/15 for domestic and international students; for summer admission, 1/15 for domestic and international students. Application fee: $60. Electronic applications accepted. Full-time tuition and fees vary according to program. *Financial support:* In 2019–20, 15 students received support. Scholarships/grants available. Financial award application deadline: 2/15; financial award applicants required to submit FAFSA. *Unit head:* Dr. Kathy Ellis, Division Director, Graduate Nursing, 817-257-6726, Fax: 817-257-7944, E-mail: kathryn.ellis@tcu.edu. *Application contact:* Beth Janke, Academic Program Specialist, 817-257-6726, Fax: 817-257-7944, E-mail: graduatenursing@tcu.edu.
Website: http://www.nursing.tcu.edu/graduate.asp

**Texas Tech University Health Sciences Center,** School of Nursing, Lubbock, TX 79430. Offers acute care nurse practitioner (MSN, Certificate); administration (MSN); advanced practice (DNP); education (MSN); executive leadership (DNP); family nurse practitioner (MSN, Certificate); geriatric nurse practitioner (MSN, Certificate); pediatric nurse practitioner (MSN, Certificate). *Accreditation:* AACN. *Program availability:* Part-time, online learning. *Degree requirements:* For master's, thesis optional. *Entrance requirements:* For master's, minimum GPA of 3.0, 3 letters of reference, BSN, RN license; for Certificate, minimum GPA of 3.0, 3 letters of reference, RN license. Additional exam requirements/recommendations for international students: required—TOEFL (minimum score 550 paper-based).

**Texas Woman's University,** Graduate School, College of Nursing, Denton, TX 76204. Offers adult health clinical nurse specialist (MS); adult health nurse practitioner (MS); adult/gerontology acute care nurse practitioner (MS); child health clinical nurse specialist (MS); clinical nurse leader (MS); family nurse practitioner (MS); health systems management (MS); nursing education (MS); nursing practice (DNP); nursing science (PhD); pediatric nurse practitioner (MS); women's health clinical nurse specialist (MS); women's health nurse practitioner (MS). *Accreditation:* AACN. *Program availability:* Part-time, 100% online, blended/hybrid learning. *Faculty:* 48 full-time (47 women), 31 part-time/adjunct (24 women). *Students:* 42 full-time (40 women), 811 part-time (756 women); includes 481 minority (168 Black or African American, non-Hispanic/Latino; 2 American Indian or Alaska Native, non-Hispanic/Latino; 165 Asian, non-Hispanic/Latino; 118 Hispanic/Latino; 1 Native Hawaiian or other Pacific Islander, non-Hispanic/Latino; 27 Two or more races, non-Hispanic/Latino), 26 international. Average age 36. 435 applicants, 71% accepted, 172 enrolled. In 2019, 203 master's, 37 doctorates awarded. *Degree requirements:* For master's, comprehensive exam, thesis or alternative, 6-year time limit for completion of degree, professional or clinical project; for doctorate, comprehensive exam, thesis/dissertation, 10-year time limit for completion of degree; dissertation (PhD), assessment practicum (DPT). *Entrance requirements:* For master's, minimum GPA of 3.0 on last 60 hours in undergraduate nursing degree and overall, RN license, BS in nursing, basic statistics course; for doctorate, MS in nursing, minimum preferred GPA of 3.5, RN or APRN license, statistics course, 2 letters of reference, curriculum vitae, graduate nursing-theory course, graduate research course, statement of professional goals and research interests, 1 yr APRN experience. Additional exam requirements/recommendations for international students: required—TOEFL (minimum score 79 iBT); recommended—IELTS (minimum score 6.5), TSE (minimum score 53). *Application deadline:* For fall admission, 5/1 for domestic students, 3/1 priority date for international students; for spring admission, 9/15 for domestic students, 7/1 priority date for international students. Application fee: $50 ($75 for international students). Electronic applications accepted. *Expenses:* All are estimates. Tuition for 10 hours = $2,763; Fees for 10 hours = $1,342. Master's Nursing courses require additional $75/SCH; Doctoral Nursing courses require additional $80/SCH. *Financial support:* In 2019–20, 212 students received support, including 1 research assistantship, 6 teaching assistantships (averaging $12,029 per year); career-related internships or fieldwork, scholarships/grants, health care benefits, and unspecified assistantships also available. Support available to part-time students. Financial award application deadline: 3/1; financial award applicants required to submit FAFSA. *Unit head:* Dr. Rosalie Mainous, Dean, 940-898-2401, Fax: 940-898-2437, E-mail: nursing@twu.edu. *Application contact:* Korie Hawkins, Associate Director of Admissions, Graduate Recruitment, 940-898-3188, Fax: 940-898-3081, E-mail: admissions@twu.edu.
Website: http://www.twu.edu/nursing/

**Thomas Edison State University,** W. Cary Edwards School of Nursing, Master of Science in Nursing Program, Trenton, NJ 08608. Offers nurse educator (MSN); nursing administration (MSN); nursing informatics (MSN). *Accreditation:* AACN; ACEN. *Program availability:* Part-time, online learning. *Degree requirements:* For master's, nursing education seminar, onground practicum, online practicum. *Entrance requirements:* For master's, BSN. Additional exam requirements/recommendations for international students: required—TOEFL (minimum score 550 paper-based; 79 iBT). Electronic applications accepted.

**Union University,** School of Nursing, Jackson, TN 38305-3697. Offers executive leadership (DNP); nurse anesthesia (DNP); nurse practitioner (DNP); nursing education (MSN, PMC). *Accreditation:* AACN; AANA/CANAEP. *Degree requirements:* For master's, thesis or alternative. *Entrance requirements:* For master's, GRE, 3 letters of reference, bachelor's degree in nursing, minimum GPA of 3.0. Additional exam requirements/recommendations for international students: required—TOEFL (minimum score 560 paper-based). Electronic applications accepted.

**Universidad Metropolitana,** School of Health Sciences, Department of Nursing, San Juan, PR 00928-1150. Offers case management (Certificate); nursing (MSN); oncology nursing (Certificate). *Accreditation:* ACEN.

**University at Buffalo, the State University of New York,** Graduate School, School of Nursing, Buffalo, NY 14260. Offers adult gerontology nurse practitioner (DNP); family nurse practitioner (DNP); health care systems and leadership (MS); nurse anesthetist (DNP); nursing (PhD); nursing education (Certificate); psychiatric/mental health nurse practitioner (DNP). *Accreditation:* AACN; AANA/CANAEP (one or more programs are accredited). *Program availability:* Part-time, 100% online. *Degree requirements:* For master's, thesis optional; for doctorate, comprehensive exam (for some programs), capstone (for DNP), dissertation (for PhD). *Entrance requirements:* For master's, GRE or MAT; for doctorate, GRE or MAT, minimum GPA of 3.0 (for DNP), 3.25 (for PhD); RN license; BS or MS in nursing; 3 references; writing sample; resume; personal statement; for Certificate, interview, minimum GPA of 3.0 or GRE General Test, RN license, MS in nursing, professional certification. Additional exam requirements/recommendations for international students: required—TOEFL (minimum score 550 paper-based; 79 iBT), IELTS (minimum score 6.5). Electronic applications accepted. *Expenses:* Contact institution.

**The University of Alabama at Birmingham,** School of Nursing, Birmingham, AL 35294. Offers clinical nurse leader (MSN); nurse anesthesia (DNP); nurse practitioner (MSN, DNP), including adult-gerontology acute care (MSN), adult-gerontology primary care (MSN), family (MSN), pediatric (MSN), psychiatric/mental health (MSN), women's health (MSN); nursing (MSN, DNP, PhD); nursing health systems administration (MSN); nursing informatics (MSN). *Accreditation:* AACN; AANA/CANAEP. *Program availability:* Part-time, online only, blended/hybrid learning. *Faculty:* 86 full-time (79 women), 42 part-time/adjunct (35 women). *Students:* 228 full-time (165 women), 1,393 part-time (1,234 women); includes 398 minority (267 Black or African American, non-Hispanic/Latino; 4 American Indian or Alaska Native, non-Hispanic/Latino; 52 Asian, non-Hispanic/Latino; 41 Hispanic/Latino; 34 Two or more races, non-Hispanic/Latino), 3 international. Average age 33. 1,027 applicants, 55% accepted, 421 enrolled. In 2019, 557 master's, 19 doctorates awarded. Terminal master's awarded for partial completion of doctoral program. *Degree requirements:* For master's, comprehensive exam; for doctorate, comprehensive exam, thesis/dissertation, research mentorship experience (for PhD); scholarly project (for DNP). *Entrance requirements:* For master's, GRE, GMAT, or MAT, minimum cumulative undergraduate GPA of 3.0 or on last 60 semesters hours; letters of recommendation; for doctorate, GRE General Test, computer literacy, course work in statistics, interview, minimum GPA of 3.0, MS in nursing, references, writing sample. Additional exam requirements/recommendations for international students: required—TOEFL (minimum score 500 paper-based, 80 iBT) or IELTS (5.5). *Application deadline:* For fall admission, 2/24 for domestic students; for summer admission, 10/15 for domestic students. Application fee: $50. Electronic applications accepted. *Expenses:* Contact institution. *Financial support:* In 2019–20, 23 fellowships (averaging $34,685 per year), 12 research assistantships (averaging $9,042 per year), 2 teaching assistantships (averaging $22,000 per year) were awarded; scholarships/grants, traineeships, health care benefits, and unspecified assistantships also available. Support available to part-time students. *Unit head:* Dr. Doreen C. Harper, Dean, 205-934-5360, Fax: 205-934-1894, E-mail: dcharper@uab.edu. *Application contact:* John Updegraff, Director of Student Affairs, 205-975-3370, Fax: 205-934-5490, E-mail: jupde22@uab.edu.
Website: http://www.uab.edu/nursing/home/

**University of Central Arkansas,** Graduate School, College of Health and Behavioral Sciences, Department of Nursing, Conway, AR 72035-0001. Offers adult nurse practitioner (PMC); clinical nurse leader (PMC); clinical nurse specialist (MSN); family nurse practitioner (PMC); nurse educator (PMC); nurse practitioner (MSN). *Accreditation:* AACN. *Program availability:* Part-time, evening/weekend, online learning. *Degree requirements:* For master's, comprehensive exam, thesis optional, clinicals. *Entrance requirements:* For master's, GRE General Test, minimum GPA of 2.7. Additional exam requirements/recommendations for international students: required—TOEFL (minimum score 550 paper-based; 80 iBT). Electronic applications accepted. *Expenses:* Contact institution.

**University of Cincinnati,** Graduate School, College of Nursing, Cincinnati, OH 45221-0038. Offers nurse midwifery (MSN); nurse practitioner (MSN, DNP), including acute care pediatrics (DNP), adult-gerontology acute care, adult-gerontology primary care, anesthesia (DNP), family (MSN), leadership (DNP), neonatal (MSN), women's health (MSN); nursing (MSN, PhD), including occupational health (MSN). *Accreditation:* AACN; AANA/CANAEP (one or more programs are accredited); ACNM/ACME. *Program availability:* Part-time, 100% online, blended/hybrid learning. *Faculty:* 62 full-time (55 women), 125 part-time/adjunct (114 women). *Students:* 429 full-time (355 women), 1,547 part-time (1,390 women); includes 453 minority (226 Black or African American, non-Hispanic/Latino; 5 American Indian or Alaska Native, non-Hispanic/Latino; 68 Asian, non-Hispanic/Latino; 103 Hispanic/Latino; 3 Native Hawaiian or other Pacific Islander, non-Hispanic/Latino; 48 Two or more races, non-Hispanic/Latino), 15 international. Average age 36. 779 applicants, 78% accepted, 464 enrolled. In 2019, 518 master's, 47 doctorates awarded. *Degree requirements:* For master's, thesis or alternative; for doctorate, comprehensive exam (for some programs), thesis/dissertation (for some programs). *Entrance requirements:* For master's, GRE required only for the Direct-Entry Accelerated Program. Additional exam requirements/recommendations for international students: required—TOEFL (minimum score 600 paper-based; 100 iBT); recommended—IELTS (minimum score 7). *Application deadline:* For fall admission, 4/1 priority date for domestic and international students; for spring admission, 9/1 priority date for domestic and international students; for summer admission, 2/1 priority date for domestic and international students. Applications are processed on a rolling basis. Application fee: $135 ($140 for international students). Electronic applications accepted. *Expenses:* Contact institution. *Financial support:* In 2019–20, 103 students received support, including 9 fellowships with full tuition reimbursements available (averaging $18,595 per year), 7 research assistantships with full tuition reimbursements available (averaging $12,991 per year), 8 teaching assistantships with full tuition reimbursements available (averaging $12,991 per year); institutionally sponsored loans, scholarships/grants, traineeships, health care benefits, tuition waivers (partial), and unspecified assistantships also available. Support available to part-time students. Financial award application deadline: 4/1; financial award applicants required to submit FAFSA. *Unit head:* Dr. Greer Glazer, Dean, 513-558-5330, Fax: 513-558-9030, E-mail: greer.glazer@uc.edu. *Application contact:* Office of Student Affairs, 513-558-8400, E-mail: nursingbearcats@uc.edu.
Website: https://nursing.uc.edu/

**University of Colorado Denver,** College of Nursing, Aurora, CO 80045. Offers adult clinical nurse specialist (MS); adult nurse practitioner (MS); family nurse practitioner (MS); family psychiatric mental health nurse practitioner (MS); health care informatics (MS); nurse-midwifery (MS); nursing (DNP, PhD); nursing leadership and health care systems (MS); pediatric nurse practitioner (MS); women's health (MS); MS/PhD. *Accreditation:* ACNM/ACME (one or more programs are accredited). *Program availability:* Part-time, evening/weekend, online learning. Terminal master's awarded for partial completion of doctoral program. *Degree requirements:* For master's, thesis optional; for doctorate, comprehensive exam, thesis/dissertation, 42 credits of coursework. *Entrance requirements:* For master's, GRE if cumulative undergraduate GPA is less than 3.0, undergraduate nursing degree from ACEN- or CCNE-accredited school or university; completion of research and statistics courses with minimum grade of C; copy of current and unencumbered nursing license; for doctorate, GRE, bachelor's and/or master's degrees in nursing from ACEN- or CCNE-accredited institution; portfolio; minimum undergraduate GPA of 3.0, graduate 3.5; graduate-level intermediate statistics and master's-level nursing theory courses with minimum B grade; interview. Additional exam requirements/recommendations for international students: required—TOEFL (minimum score 560 paper-based; 83 iBT). Electronic applications accepted. *Expenses:* Contact institution.

**University of Delaware,** College of Health Sciences, School of Nursing, Newark, DE 19716. Offers adult nurse practitioner (MSN, PMC); cardiopulmonary clinical nurse specialist (MSN, PMC); cardiopulmonary clinical nurse specialist/adult nurse practitioner (MSN, PMC); family nurse practitioner (MSN, PMC); gerontology clinical nurse specialist (MSN, PMC); gerontology clinical nurse specialist geriatric nurse practitioner (PMC); gerontology clinical nurse specialist/geriatric nurse practitioner (MSN); health services administration (MSN, PMC); nursing of children clinical nurse specialist (MSN, PMC); nursing of children clinical nurse specialist/pediatric nurse practitioner (MSN, PMC); oncology/immune deficiency clinical nurse specialist (MSN, PMC); oncology/immune deficiency clinical nurse specialist/adult nurse practitioner (MSN, PMC); perinatal/women's health clinical nurse specialist (MSN, PMC); perinatal/women's health clinical nurse specialist/women's health nurse practitioner (MSN, PMC); psychiatric nursing clinical nurse specialist (MSN, PMC). *Accreditation:* AACN. *Program availability:* Part-

time, evening/weekend, online learning. *Degree requirements:* For master's, thesis optional. *Entrance requirements:* For master's, BSN, interview, RN license. Electronic applications accepted.

**University of Hawaii at Manoa,** Office of Graduate Education, School of Nursing and Dental Hygiene, Honolulu, HI 96822. Offers clinical nurse specialist (MS), including adult health, community mental health; nurse practitioner (MS), including adult health, community mental health, family nurse practitioner; nursing (PhD, Graduate Certificate); nursing administration (MS). *Accreditation:* AACN. *Program availability:* Part-time, online learning. *Degree requirements:* For master's, thesis optional; for doctorate, comprehensive exam, thesis/dissertation. *Entrance requirements:* For master's, Hawaii RN license. Additional exam requirements/recommendations for international students: required—TOEFL (minimum score 580 paper-based; 92 iBT), IELTS (minimum score 5). *Expenses:* Contact institution.

**University of Houston,** College of Nursing, Sugar Land, TX 77479. Offers family nurse practitioner (MSN); nursing administration (MSN); nursing education (MSN). *Accreditation:* AACN. *Faculty:* 8 full-time (7 women). *Students:* 18 full-time (12 women), 33 part-time (32 women); includes 30 minority (13 Black or African American, non-Hispanic/Latino; 4 Asian, non-Hispanic/Latino; 12 Hispanic/Latino; 1 Native Hawaiian or other Pacific Islander, non-Hispanic/Latino). Average age 36. 38 applicants, 74% accepted, 20 enrolled. In 2019, 12 master's awarded. *Entrance requirements:* For master's, minimum GPA of 3.0, unencumbered Texas RN license, 2 letters of recommendation, essay, resume, interview required. Additional exam requirements/recommendations for international students: required—TOEFL. *Application deadline:* For fall admission, 6/1 for domestic and international students; for spring admission, 11/1 for domestic and international students; for summer admission, 4/1 for domestic and international students. Application fee: $75. Electronic applications accepted. *Financial support:* In 2019–20, 19 students received support. Federal Work-Study, scholarships/grants, and unspecified assistantships available. Support available to part-time students. Financial award application deadline: 7/1; financial award applicants required to submit FAFSA. *Unit head:* Dr. Kathryn Tart, Dean, 832-842-8200, E-mail: kmtart@uh.edu. *Application contact:* Tammy N. Whatley, Student Affairs Director, 832-842-8220, E-mail: tnwhatley@uh.edu.
Website: http://www.uh.edu/nursing

**University of Illinois at Chicago,** College of Nursing, Program in Nursing, Chicago, IL 60607-7128. Offers acute care clinical nurse specialist (MS); administrative nursing leadership (Certificate); adult nurse practitioner (MS); adult/geriatric nurse practitioner (MS); advanced community health nurse specialist (MS); family nurse practitioner (MS); geriatric clinical nurse specialist (MS); geriatric nurse practitioner (MS); nurse midwifery (MS); occupational health/advanced community health nurse specialist (MS); occupational health/family nurse practitioner (MS); pediatric nurse practitioner (MS); perinatal clinical nurse specialist (MS); school/advanced community health nurse specialist (MS); school/family nurse practitioner (MS); women's health nurse practitioner (MS). *Accreditation:* AACN. *Program availability:* Part-time. *Degree requirements:* For master's, thesis or alternative. *Entrance requirements:* For master's, GRE General Test, minimum GPA of 2.75. Additional exam requirements/recommendations for international students: required—TOEFL. Electronic applications accepted.

**University of Indianapolis,** Graduate Programs, School of Nursing, Indianapolis, IN 46227-3697. Offers advanced practice nursing (DNP); family nurse practitioner (MSN); gerontological nurse practitioner (MSN); neonatal nurse practitioner (MSN); nurse-midwifery (MSN); nursing (MSN); nursing and health systems leadership (MSN); nursing education (MSN); women's health nurse practitioner (MSN); MBA/MSN. *Accreditation:* AACN. *Entrance requirements:* For master's, minimum GPA of 3.0, interview, letters of recommendation, resume, IN nursing license, 1 year of professional practice; for doctorate, graduate of ACEN- or CCNE-accredited nursing program; MSN or MA with nursing major and minimum cumulative GPA of 3.25; unencumbered RN license with eligibility for licensure in Indiana; completion of graduate-level statistics course within last 5 years with minimum grade of B; resume; essay; official transcripts from all academic institutions. Additional exam requirements/recommendations for international students: required—TOEFL (minimum score 550 paper-based). Electronic applications accepted.

**University of Louisiana at Lafayette,** BI Moody III College of Business Administration, Lafayette, LA 70504. Offers accounting (MS); business administration (MBA); entrepreneurship (MBA); finance (MBA); global management (MBA); health care administration (MBA); hospitality management (MBA); human resource management (MBA); project management (MBA); sales leadership (MBA). *Accreditation:* AACSB. *Program availability:* Part-time, evening/weekend. *Entrance requirements:* For master's, GRE General Test. Additional exam requirements/recommendations for international students: required—TOEFL (minimum score 550 paper-based). *Expenses: Tuition, area resident:* Full-time $5511; part-time $1630 per credit hour. Tuition, state resident: full-time $5511; part-time $1630 per credit hour. Tuition, nonresident: full-time $19,239; part-time $2409 per credit hour. *Required fees:* $46,637.

**University of Louisville,** Graduate School, School of Nursing, Louisville, KY 40202. Offers adult gerontology nurse practitioner (MSN, DNP); education and administration (MSN); family nurse practitioner (MSN, DNP); neonatal nurse practitioner (MSN, DNP); nursing research (PhD); psychiatric/mental health nurse practitioner (MSN, DNP); women's health nurse practitioner (MSN). *Accreditation:* AACN. *Program availability:* Part-time, blended/hybrid learning. *Faculty:* 49 full-time (46 women), 91 part-time/adjunct (86 women). *Students:* 164 full-time (140 women), 47 part-time (39 women); includes 45 minority (21 Black or African American, non-Hispanic/Latino; 5 Asian, non-Hispanic/Latino; 9 Hispanic/Latino; 10 Two or more races, non-Hispanic/Latino), 4 international. Average age 33. 84 applicants, 63% accepted, 48 enrolled. In 2019, 25 master's, 5 doctorates awarded. *Degree requirements:* For master's, varies; for doctorate, comprehensive exam (for some programs), thesis/dissertation (for some programs), varies. *Entrance requirements:* For master's, Our only master's degree is an accelerated program meant for students who have a bachelor's degree in another discipline who are transitioning into nursing. Thus, the main requirement is a bachelor's degree from a nationally-accredited college, and the completion of 6 prerequisite courses. Must have a minimum undergraduate GPA of 3.0; for doctorate, PhD program: GRE requirement omitted, DNP & PhD doctoral programs: 3 letters of professional reference. BSN applicants must have a 3.0 GPA. MSN applicants must have 3.25 GPA. Written statement of career goals, areas of expertise, reasons for pursuing doctoral degree, resume, and RN license. Additional exam requirements/recommendations for international students: recommended—TOEFL (minimum score 560 paper-based), IELTS (minimum score 6.5). *Application deadline:* For fall admission, 1/15 priority date for domestic and international students; for summer admission, 10/15 priority date for domestic students. Application fee: $60. Electronic applications accepted. *Expenses:* 17871. *Financial support:* In 2019–20, 47 students received support, including 2 fellowships with full tuition reimbursements available (averaging $20,000 per year), 9 research assistantships with full tuition reimbursements available (averaging $20,000 per year), 3 teaching assistantships with full tuition reimbursements available (averaging $15,000 per year); scholarships/grants, health care benefits, unspecified assistantships, and Jonas Nurse Leader Fellowships also available. Financial award application deadline: 10/1; financial award applicants required to submit FAFSA. *Unit head:* 502-852-8300, Fax: 502-852-5044, E-mail: sonya.hardin@louisville.edu. *Application contact:* Trish Hart, MA, Assistant Dean for Student Affairs, 502-852-5825, Fax: 502-852-8783, E-mail: trish.hart@louisville.edu.
Website: http://www.louisville.edu/nursing/

**University of Mary,** School of Health Sciences, Division of Nursing, Bismarck, ND 58504-9652. Offers family nurse practitioner (DNP); nurse administrator (MSN); nursing educator (MSN); MSN/MBA. *Accreditation:* AACN. *Program availability:* Part-time, evening/weekend, online learning. *Degree requirements:* For master's, comprehensive exam (for some programs), thesis (for some programs), internship (family nurse practitioner), teaching practice. *Entrance requirements:* For master's, minimum GPA of 2.75 in nursing, interview, letters of recommendation, criminal background check, immunizations, statement of professional goals. Additional exam requirements/recommendations for international students: required—TOEFL (minimum score 500 paper-based; 71 iBT). Electronic applications accepted.

**University of Maryland, Baltimore,** University of Maryland School of Nursing, Baltimore, MD 21201. Offers adult-gerontology acute care nurse practitioner (DNP); adult-gerontology primary care nurse practitioner (DNP); clinical nurse leader (MS); community/public health nursing (MS); family nurse practitioner (DNP); global health (Postbaccalaureate Certificate); health services leadership and management (MS); neonatal nurse practitioner (DNP); nurse anesthesia (DNP); nursing (PhD); nursing informatics (MS, Postbaccalaureate Certificate); pediatric acute/primary care nurse practitioner (DNP); psychiatric mental health nurse practitioner (DNP); teaching in nursing and health professions (Postbaccalaureate Certificate); MS/MBA. *Accreditation:* AANA/CANAEP. *Program availability:* Part-time. *Faculty:* 130 full-time (117 women), 125 part-time/adjunct (114 women). *Students:* 539 full-time (463 women), 586 part-time (506 women); includes 485 minority (259 Black or African American, non-Hispanic/Latino; 3 American Indian or Alaska Native, non-Hispanic/Latino; 124 Asian, non-Hispanic/Latino; 66 Hispanic/Latino; 1 Native Hawaiian or other Pacific Islander, non-Hispanic/Latino; 32 Two or more races, non-Hispanic/Latino), 18 international. Average age 33. 964 applicants, 54% accepted, 347 enrolled. In 2019, 197 master's, 114 doctorates, 12 other advanced degrees awarded. *Degree requirements:* For master's and Postbaccalaureate Certificate, thesis (for some programs); for doctorate, comprehensive exam, thesis/dissertation. *Entrance requirements:* Additional exam requirements/recommendations for international students: required—TOEFL (minimum score 550 paper-based; 79 iBT); recommended—IELTS (minimum score 7). *Application deadline:* For fall admission, 11/1 priority date for domestic and international students; for spring admission, 12/15 for domestic and international students; for summer admission, 9/1 for domestic and international students. Applications are processed on a rolling basis. Application fee: $75. Electronic applications accepted. *Financial support:* In 2019–20, 257 students received support, including 31 research assistantships with full and partial tuition reimbursements available (averaging $25,000 per year), 21 teaching assistantships with full and partial tuition reimbursements available (averaging $19,000 per year); scholarships/grants, traineeships, and unspecified assistantships also available. Support available to part-time students. Financial award application deadline: 3/1; financial award applicants required to submit FAFSA. *Unit head:* Dr. Jane Kirschling, Dean, 410-706-4359, E-mail: kirschling@umaryland.edu. *Application contact:* Larry Fillian, Associate Dean of Student and Academic Services, 410-706-6298, E-mail: lfillian@umaryland.edu.
Website: http://www.nursing.umaryland.edu/

**University of Massachusetts Amherst,** Graduate School, College of Nursing, Amherst, MA 01003. Offers adult gerontology primary care nurse practitioner (DNP); clinical nurse leader (MS); family nurse practitioner (DNP); nursing (PhD); public health nurse leader (DNP). *Accreditation:* AACN. *Program availability:* Part-time, online learning. Terminal master's awarded for partial completion of doctoral program. *Degree requirements:* For master's, thesis optional; for doctorate, comprehensive exam, thesis/dissertation. *Entrance requirements:* Additional exam requirements/recommendations for international students: required—TOEFL (minimum score 550 paper-based; 80 iBT), IELTS (minimum score 6.5). Electronic applications accepted.

**University of Massachusetts Medical School,** Graduate School of Nursing, Worcester, MA 01655. Offers adult gerontological acute care nurse practitioner (DNP, Post Master's Certificate); adult gerontological primary care nurse practitioner (DNP, Post Master's Certificate); family nursing practitioner (DNP); nurse administrator (DNP); nurse educator (MS); nursing (PhD); psychiatric mental health (Post Master's Certificate). *Accreditation:* AACN. *Program availability:* Blended/hybrid learning. *Faculty:* 26 full-time (22 women), 51 part-time/adjunct (40 women). *Students:* 176 full-time (152 women), 33 part-time (27 women); includes 61 minority (21 Black or African American, non-Hispanic/Latino; 1 American Indian or Alaska Native, non-Hispanic/Latino; 18 Asian, non-Hispanic/Latino; 20 Hispanic/Latino; 1 Native Hawaiian or other Pacific Islander, non-Hispanic/Latino). Average age 32. 131 applicants, 66% accepted, 58 enrolled. In 2019, 28 master's, 34 doctorates, 1 other advanced degree awarded. *Degree requirements:* For doctorate, thesis/dissertation (for some programs), comprehensive exam and manuscript (for PhD); scholarly project (for DNP). *Entrance requirements:* For master's, GRE General Test, bachelor's degree in nursing, course work in statistics, unrestricted Massachusetts license as registered nurse; for doctorate, GRE General Test, bachelor's or master's degree; for Post Master's Certificate, GRE General Test, MS in nursing. Additional exam requirements/recommendations for international students: required—TOEFL (minimum score 400 paper-based; 81 iBT). *Application deadline:* For fall admission, 12/1 priority date for domestic students. Applications are processed on a rolling basis. Application fee: $100. Electronic applications accepted. *Expenses:* Contact institution. *Financial support:* In 2019–20, 103 students received support. Scholarships/grants available. Support available to part-time students. Financial award application deadline: 5/15; financial award applicants required to submit FAFSA. *Unit head:* Dr. Joan Vitello-Cicciu, Dean, 508-856-5081, Fax: 508-856-6552, E-mail: joan.vitello@umassmed.edu. *Application contact:* Diane Brescia, Admissions Coordinator, 508-856-3488, Fax: 508-856-5851, E-mail: diane.brescia@umassmed.edu.
Website: http://www.umassmed.edu/gsn/

**University of Memphis,** Loewenberg College of Nursing, Memphis, TN 38152. Offers advanced practice nursing (Graduate Certificate); executive leadership (MSN); family nurse practitioner (MSN); nursing administration (MSN, Graduate Certificate); nursing education (MSN, Graduate Certificate). *Accreditation:* AACN. *Program availability:* Part-time, evening/weekend, online learning. *Faculty:* 21 full-time (19 women), 11 part-time/adjunct (10 women). *Students:* 19 full-time (17 women), 281 part-time (254 women); includes 104 minority (87 Black or African American, non-Hispanic/Latino; 5 Asian, non-Hispanic/Latino; 7 Hispanic/Latino; 5 Two or more races, non-Hispanic/Latino), 2 international. Average age 34. 117 applicants, 79% accepted, 48 enrolled. In 2019, 71 master's, 3 other advanced degrees awarded. *Degree requirements:* For master's, comprehensive exam, thesis optional, scholarly project; clinical practicum hours. *Entrance requirements:* For master's, NCLEX exam, minimum undergraduate GPA of 2.8, letter of interest, letters of recommendation, interview, resume, nursing licensure; for Graduate Certificate, unrestricted license to practice as RN in TN, current CPR certification, evidence of vaccination, annual flu shot, evidence of current professional malpractice insurance, letters of recommendation, letter of intent, resume. Additional

exam requirements/recommendations for international students: required—TOEFL (minimum score 550 paper-based; 79 iBT). *Application deadline:* For fall admission, 2/15 for domestic and international students; for spring admission, 10/1 for domestic and international students. Application fee: $35 ($60 for international students). *Expenses: Tuition, area resident:* Full-time $9216; part-time $512 per credit hour. Tuition, state resident: full-time $9216; part-time $512 per credit hour. Tuition, nonresident: full-time $12,672; part-time $704 per credit hour. *International tuition:* $16,128 full-time. *Required fees:* $1530; $85 per credit hour. Tuition and fees vary according to program. *Financial support:* Federal Work-Study and scholarships/grants available. Financial award application deadline: 2/1; financial award applicants required to submit FAFSA. *Unit head:* Dr. Lin Zhan, Dean, 901-678-2020, E-mail: lzhan@memphis.edu. *Application contact:* Dr. Lin Zhan, Dean, 901-678-2020, E-mail: lzhan@memphis.edu.
Website: http://www.memphis.edu/nursing

**University of Minnesota, Twin Cities Campus,** Graduate School, School of Nursing, Minneapolis, MN 55455-0213. Offers adult/gerontological clinical nurse specialist (DNP); adult/gerontological primary care nurse practitioner (DNP); family nurse practitioner (DNP); health innovation and leadership (DNP); integrative health and healing (DNP); nurse anesthesia (DNP); nurse midwifery (DNP); nursing (MN, PhD); nursing informatics (DNP); pediatric clinical nurse specialist (DNP); primary care certified pediatric nurse practitioner (DNP); psychiatric/mental health nurse practitioner (DNP); women's health nurse practitioner (DNP). *Accreditation:* AACN; AANA/CANAEP; ACNM/ACME (one or more programs are accredited). *Program availability:* Part-time, online learning. Terminal master's awarded for partial completion of doctoral program. *Degree requirements:* For master's, final oral exam, project or thesis; for doctorate, thesis/dissertation. *Entrance requirements:* For master's and doctorate, GRE General Test. Additional exam requirements/recommendations for international students: required—TOEFL (minimum score 586 paper-based). *Expenses:* Contact institution.

**University of Missouri,** Office of Research and Graduate Studies, Sinclair School of Nursing, Columbia, MO 65211. Offers adult-gerontology clinical nurse specialist (DNP, Certificate); family nurse practitioner (DNP); family psychiatric and mental health nurse practitioner (DNP); nursing (MS, PhD); nursing leadership and innovations in health care (DNP); pediatric clinical nurse specialist (DNP, Certificate); pediatric nurse practitioner (DNP). *Accreditation:* AACN. *Program availability:* Part-time. *Degree requirements:* For master's, thesis optional, oral exam; for doctorate, thesis/dissertation. *Entrance requirements:* For master's, GRE General Test, BSN, minimum GPA of 3.0 during last 60 hours, nursing license. Additional exam requirements/recommendations for international students: required—TOEFL, IELTS. Electronic applications accepted.

**University of Missouri–Kansas City,** School of Nursing and Health Studies, Kansas City, MO 64110-2499. Offers adult clinical nurse specialist (MSN), including adult nurse practitioner, women's health nurse practitioner (MSN, DNP); adult clinical nursing practice (DNP), including adult gerontology nurse practitioner, women's health nurse practitioner (MSN, DNP); clinical nursing practice (DNP), including family nurse practitioner; neonatal nurse practitioner (MSN); nurse educator (MSN); nurse executive (MSN); nursing practice (DNP); pediatric clinical nursing practice (DNP), including pediatric nurse practitioner; pediatric nurse practitioner (MSN). *Accreditation:* AACN. *Program availability:* Part-time, online learning. *Degree requirements:* For master's, thesis or alternative. *Entrance requirements:* For master's, minimum undergraduate GPA of 3.2; for doctorate, GRE, 3 letters of reference. Additional exam requirements/recommendations for international students: required—TOEFL (minimum score 550 paper-based; 80 iBT).

**University of Mobile,** Graduate Studies, School of Nursing, Mobile, AL 36613. Offers education/administration (MSN); nurse practitioner (DNP). *Accreditation:* AACN. *Program availability:* Part-time, evening/weekend. *Degree requirements:* For master's, comprehensive exam, thesis or alternative; for doctorate, comprehensive exam. *Entrance requirements:* For master's, minimum cumulative GPA of 2.5, unencumbered license to practice as a registered nurse. See catalog for additional requirements. Additional exam requirements/recommendations for international students: required—TOEFL (minimum score 550 paper-based; 80 iBT). Electronic applications accepted.

**The University of North Carolina at Chapel Hill,** School of Nursing, Chapel Hill, NC 27599-7460. Offers advanced practice registered nurse (DNP); nursing (MSN, PhD, PMC), including administration (MSN), adult gerontology primary care nurse practitioner (MSN), clinical nurse leader (MSN), education (MSN), health care systems (PMC), informatics (MSN, PMC), nursing leadership (PMC), outcomes management (MSN), primary care family nurse practitioner (MSN), primary care pediatric nurse practitioner (MSN), psychiatric/mental health nurse practitioner (MSN, PMC). *Accreditation:* AACN; ACEN (one or more programs are accredited). *Program availability:* Part-time. *Degree requirements:* For master's, comprehensive exam, thesis; for doctorate, thesis/dissertation, 3 exams; for PMC, thesis. *Entrance requirements:* Additional exam requirements/recommendations for international students: required—TOEFL (minimum score 575 paper-based; 89 iBT), IELTS (minimum score 8). Electronic applications accepted.

**The University of North Carolina at Charlotte,** College of Health and Human Services, School of Nursing, Charlotte, NC 28223-0001. Offers adult-gerontology acute care nurse practitioner (Post-Master's Certificate); advanced clinical nursing (MSN), including adult psychiatric mental health, adult-gerontology acute care nurse practitioner, family nurse practitioner across the lifespan; family nurse practitioner across the lifespan (Post-Master's Certificate); nurse anesthesia (MSN), including nurse anesthesia across the lifespan; nurse anesthesia across the lifespan (Post-Master's Certificate); nursing (DNP); nursing administrator (Graduate Certificate); nursing educator (Graduate Certificate); systems/population nursing (MSN), including community/public health nursing, nurse administrator, nurse educator. *Accreditation:* AACN; AANA/CANAEP. *Program availability:* Part-time, blended/hybrid learning. *Students:* 126 full-time (96 women), 142 part-time (127 women); includes 70 minority (48 Black or African American, non-Hispanic/Latino; 8 Asian, non-Hispanic/Latino; 9 Hispanic/Latino; 5 Two or more races, non-Hispanic/Latino), 1 international. Average age 35. 347 applicants, 37% accepted, 104 enrolled. In 2019, 102 master's, 10 doctorates, 10 other advanced degrees awarded. Terminal master's awarded for partial completion of doctoral program. *Entrance requirements:* For master's, GRE General Test, current unrestricted license as Registered Nurse in North Carolina; BSN from nationally-accredited program; one year of professional nursing practice in acute/critical care; minimum overall GPA of 3.0 in last degree; completion of undergraduate statistics course with minimum grade of C; statement of purpose; for doctorate, GRE or MAT, master's degree in nursing in an advanced nursing practice specialty from nationally-accredited program; minimum overall GPA of 3.5 in MSN program; current RN licensure in U.S. at time of application with eligibility for NC licensure; essay; resume/curriculum vitae; professional recommendations; clinical hours; for other advanced degree, GRE. Additional exam requirements/recommendations for international students: required—TOEFL (minimum score 557 paper-based; 83 iBT), IELTS (minimum score 6.5), TOEFL (minimum score 557 paper-based, 83 iBT) or IELTS (6.5). *Application deadline:* Applications are processed on a rolling basis. Application fee: $75. Electronic applications accepted. *Expenses:* Contact institution. *Financial support:* In 2019–20, 6 students received support, including 4 research assistantships (averaging $4,856 per year), 2 teaching assistantships (averaging $3,615 per year); career-related internships

or fieldwork, institutionally sponsored loans, scholarships/grants, traineeships, and unspecified assistantships also available. Support available to part-time students. Financial award application deadline: 3/1; financial award applicants required to submit FAFSA. *Unit head:* Dr. Dena Evans, Director, 704-687-7974, E-mail: devans37@uncc.edu. *Application contact:* Kathy B. Giddings, Director of Graduate Admissions, 704-687-5503, Fax: 704-687-1668, E-mail: gradadm@uncc.edu.
Website: http://nursing.uncc.edu/

**The University of North Carolina at Greensboro,** Graduate School, School of Nursing, Greensboro, NC 27412-5001. Offers adult clinical nurse specialist (MSN, PMC); adult/gerontological nurse practitioner (MSN, PMC); nurse anesthesia (MSN, PMC); nursing (PhD); nursing administration (MSN); nursing education (MSN); MSN/MBA. *Accreditation:* ACEN. *Degree requirements:* For master's, thesis or alternative. *Entrance requirements:* For master's, GRE General Test or MAT, BSN, clinical experience, liability insurance, RN license; for PMC, liability insurance, MSN, RN license. Additional exam requirements/recommendations for international students: required—TOEFL. Electronic applications accepted.

**The University of North Carolina at Pembroke,** The Graduate School, Department of Nursing, Pembroke, NC 28372-1510. Offers clinical nurse leader (MSN); nurse educator (MSN); rural case manager (MSN). *Accreditation:* AACN. *Program availability:* Part-time.

**University of Pennsylvania,** School of Nursing, Health Leadership Program, Philadelphia, PA 19104. Offers MSN. *Accreditation:* AACN. *Program availability:* Part-time. *Students:* 4 full-time (3 women), 16 part-time (14 women); includes 8 minority (2 Asian, non-Hispanic/Latino; 5 Hispanic/Latino; 1 Two or more races, non-Hispanic/Latino). Average age 32. 10 applicants, 80% accepted, 7 enrolled. In 2019, 10 master's awarded. Application fee: $80. *Financial support:* Application deadline: 4/1.

**University of Pennsylvania,** School of Nursing, Program in Nursing and Health Care Administration, Philadelphia, PA 19104. Offers MSN, PhD, MBA/MSN. *Accreditation:* AACN. *Program availability:* Part-time. *Students:* 1 (woman) full-time, 12 part-time (6 women); includes 3 minority (1 Asian, non-Hispanic/Latino; 1 Hispanic/Latino; 1 Two or more races, non-Hispanic/Latino). Average age 29. 7 applicants, 57% accepted, 2 enrolled. In 2019, 11 master's awarded. Terminal master's awarded for partial completion of doctoral program. Application fee: $80. *Application contact:* Sue Keim, Program Director, 215-573-9759, E-mail: skeim@nursing.upenn.edu.

**University of Phoenix - Bay Area Campus,** College of Nursing, San Jose, CA 95134-1805. Offers education (MHA); gerontology (MHA); health administration (MHA, DHA); informatics (MHA, MSN); nursing (MSN, PhD); nursing/health care education (MSN); MSN/MBA. *Program availability:* Evening/weekend, online learning. *Degree requirements:* For master's, thesis (for some programs). *Entrance requirements:* For master's, minimum undergraduate GPA of 2.5, 3 years of work experience, RN license. Additional exam requirements/recommendations for international students: required—TOEFL (minimum score 550 paper-based; 79 iBT). Electronic applications accepted.

**University of Pittsburgh,** School of Nursing, Nurse Specialty Role Program, Pittsburgh, PA 15260. Offers nurse specialty role (DNP), including clinical nurse leader, health systems executive leadership, nursing informatics. *Accreditation:* AACN. *Program availability:* Part-time. *Faculty:* 12 full-time (9 women), 1 part-time/adjunct (0 women). *Students:* 12 full-time (9 women), 1 part-time (0 women); includes 11 minority (4 Black or African American, non-Hispanic/Latino; 6 Asian, non-Hispanic/Latino; 1 Hispanic/Latino), 1 international. Average age 36. 38 applicants, 82% accepted, 25 enrolled. In 2019, 11 master's, 3 doctorates awarded. *Degree requirements:* For master's, comprehensive exam, thesis optional; for doctorate, comprehensive exam, thesis/dissertation or alternative, capstone project required. *Entrance requirements:* For doctorate, GRE (may be waived if GPA is 3.5 or greater), BSN/MSN, RN license, 3 letters of recommendation, personal essay, resume, course work in statistics, clinical experience. Additional exam requirements/recommendations for international students: required—TOEFL (minimum score 600 paper-based; 100 iBT), IELTS (minimum score 7), TOEFL (minimum score 600 paper-based; 100 iBT) or IELTS (minimum score 7.0). *Application deadline:* For fall admission, 6/1 priority date for domestic students, 2/15 priority date for international students. Application fee: $50. Electronic applications accepted. *Expenses:* $13,795 per term full-time resident tuition, $475 per term full-time resident fees, $1,122 per credit part-time resident tuition, $295 per term part-time resident fees, $16,474 per term full-time non-resident tuition, $475 per term full-time non-resident fees, $1,345 per credit part-time non-resident tuition, $295 per term part-time non-resident fees. *Financial support:* In 2019–20, 29 students received support. Scholarships/grants and Matching Funds available. Financial award application deadline: 6/1; financial award applicants required to submit FAFSA. *Unit head:* Dr. Sandra Engberg, Associate Dean for Clinical Education, 412-624-3835, Fax: 412-624-8521, E-mail: sje1@pitt.edu. *Application contact:* Laurie Lapsley, Graduate Administrator, 412-624-9670, Fax: 412-624-2409, E-mail: lapsleyl@pitt.edu.
Website: http://www.nursing.pitt.edu/

**University of Rochester,** School of Nursing, Rochester, NY 14642. Offers adult gerontological acute care nurse practitioner (MS); adult gerontological primary care nurse practitioner (MS); clinical nurse leader (MS); family nurse practitioner (MS); family psychiatric mental health nurse practitioner (MS); health care organization management and leadership (MS); nursing (DNP); nursing and health science (PhD); nursing education (MS); pediatric nurse practitioner (MS); pediatric nurse practitioner/neonatal nurse practitioner (MS). *Accreditation:* AACN. *Program availability:* Part-time, 100% online, blended/hybrid learning. Terminal master's awarded for partial completion of doctoral program. *Degree requirements:* For master's, comprehensive exam; for doctorate, thesis/dissertation. *Entrance requirements:* For master's, BS in nursing, RN license; for doctorate, GRE General Test (for PhD), B.S. degree, RN license most programs. Additional exam requirements/recommendations for international students: required—TOEFL (minimum score 560 paper-based; 88 iBT), TOEFL (minimum score 560 paper-based; 88 iBT) or IELTS (minimum score 6.5) recommended. Electronic applications accepted. *Expenses:* Contact institution.

**University of St. Augustine for Health Sciences,** Graduate Programs, Master of Science in Nursing Program, San Marcos, CA 92069. Offers nurse educator (MSN); nurse executive (MSN); nurse informatics (MSN). *Program availability:* Part-time, online learning.

**University of St. Francis,** Leach College of Nursing, Joliet, IL 60435-6169. Offers family nurse practitioner (MSN, Post-Master's Certificate); nursing administration (MSN); nursing education (MSN); nursing practice (DNP); psychology/mental health nurse practitioner (MSN, Post-Master's Certificate); teaching in nursing (Certificate). *Accreditation:* AACN. *Program availability:* Part-time, evening/weekend, 100% online. *Degree requirements:* For master's, comprehensive exam. *Entrance requirements:* Additional exam requirements/recommendations for international students: required—TOEFL (minimum score 550 paper-based; 79 iBT), IELTS (minimum score 6). Electronic applications accepted. Application fee is waived when completed online. *Expenses:* Contact institution.

**University of Saint Mary,** Graduate Programs, Program in Nursing, Leavenworth, KS 66048-5082. Offers nurse administrator (MSN); nurse educator (MSN). *Accreditation:* AACN. *Program availability:* Part-time, online only, 100% online. *Students:* 10 full-time (all women), 12 part-time (10 women); includes 2 minority (1 Hispanic/Latino; 1 Native

Hawaiian or other Pacific Islander, non-Hispanic/Latino). Average age 40. In 2019, 19 master's awarded. *Degree requirements:* For master's, practicum. *Entrance requirements:* For master's, BSN from CCNE- or ACEN-accredited baccalaureate nursing program at regionally-accredited institution. *Application deadline:* Applications are processed on a rolling basis. Application fee: $25. Electronic applications accepted. *Expenses:* $615 per credit hour. *Financial support:* Applicants required to submit FAFSA. *Unit head:* Michelle Birdashaw, Division Chair of Nursing, E-mail: michelle.birdashaw@stmary.edu. *Application contact:* Michelle Birdashaw, Division Chair of Nursing, E-mail: michelle.birdashaw@stmary.edu. Website: http://online.stmary.edu/msn

**University of San Diego,** Hahn School of Nursing and Health Science, San Diego, CA 92110-2492. Offers adult-gerontology clinical nurse specialist (MSN); adult-gerontology nurse practitioner/family nurse practitioner (MSN); clinical nurse leader (MSN); executive nurse leader (MSN); family nurse practitioner (MSN); healthcare informatics (MS); master's entry program in clinical nursing (for non-rns) (MSN); nursing (PhD); nursing informatics (MSN); nursing practice (DNP); psychiatric-mental health nurse practitioner (MSN). *Accreditation:* AACN. *Program availability:* Part-time, evening/weekend. *Faculty:* 28 full-time (23 women), 43 part-time/adjunct (32 women). *Students:* 252 full-time (202 women), 288 part-time (227 women); includes 261 minority (53 Black or African American, non-Hispanic/Latino; 2 American Indian or Alaska Native, non-Hispanic/Latino; 106 Asian, non-Hispanic/Latino; 76 Hispanic/Latino; 24 Two or more races, non-Hispanic/Latino), 24 international. Average age 34. In 2019, 174 master's, 47 doctorates awarded. *Degree requirements:* For doctorate, thesis/dissertation (for some programs), residency (DNP). *Entrance requirements:* For master's, GRE General Test (for entry-level nursing), BSN, current California RN licensure (except for entry-level nursing), minimum GPA of 3.0; for doctorate, minimum GPA of 3.5, MSN, current California RN licensure. Additional exam requirements/recommendations for international students: required—TOEFL (minimum score 580 paper-based; 83 iBT), TWE. *Application deadline:* Applications are processed on a rolling basis. Application fee: $55. Electronic applications accepted. *Financial support:* In 2019–20, 284 students received support. Institutionally sponsored loans, scholarships/grants, and traineeships available. Support available to part-time students. Financial award application deadline: 4/1; financial award applicants required to submit FAFSA. *Unit head:* Dr. Jane Georges, Dean, Hahn School of Nursing and Health Science, 619-260-4550, Fax: 619-260-6814, E-mail: nursing@sandiego.edu. *Application contact:* Erika Garwood, Associate Director of Graduate Admissions, 619-260-4524, Fax: 619-260-4158, E-mail: grads@sandiego.edu.
Website: http://www.sandiego.edu/nursing/

**The University of Scranton,** Panuska College of Professional Studies, Department of Nursing, Scranton, PA 18510-4595. Offers family nurse practitioner (MSN, PMC); nurse anesthesia (MSN, PMC); nursing leadership (DNP). *Accreditation:* AACN; AANA/CANAEP. *Program availability:* Part-time, evening/weekend. *Degree requirements:* For master's, comprehensive exam (for some programs), thesis (for some programs), capstone experience. *Entrance requirements:* For master's, minimum GPA of 3.0, three letters of reference; for doctorate, RN licensure and evidence of certification in advanced practice nursing specialty. Additional exam requirements/recommendations for international students: required—TOEFL (minimum score 500 paper-based; 80 iBT), IELTS (minimum score 6.5). Electronic applications accepted.

**University of South Alabama,** College of Nursing, Mobile, AL 36688-0002. Offers nursing (MSN, DNP); nursing administration (Certificate); nursing education (Certificate); nursing practice (Certificate). *Accreditation:* AACN. *Program availability:* Part-time, online learning. *Faculty:* 72 full-time (66 women), 116 part-time/adjunct (103 women). *Students:* 2,311 full-time (2,024 women), 716 part-time (636 women); includes 955 minority (613 Black or African American, non-Hispanic/Latino; 28 American Indian or Alaska Native, non-Hispanic/Latino; 121 Asian, non-Hispanic/Latino; 123 Hispanic/Latino; 4 Native Hawaiian or other Pacific Islander, non-Hispanic/Latino; 66 Two or more races, non-Hispanic/Latino). Average age 35. 884 applicants, 93% accepted, 624 enrolled. In 2019, 744 master's, 157 doctorates, 94 other advanced degrees awarded. *Degree requirements:* For master's, thesis optional. *Entrance requirements:* Additional exam requirements/recommendations for international students: required—TOEFL (minimum score 600 paper-based; 100 iBT). *Application deadline:* For fall admission, 2/15 priority date for domestic students, 1/15 priority date for international students; for spring admission, 7/15 priority date for domestic students, 6/15 priority date for international students; for summer admission, 11/15 priority date for domestic students, 10/15 priority date for international students. Applications are processed on a rolling basis. Application fee: $100. Electronic applications accepted. *Expenses:* Contact institution. *Financial support:* Fellowships, research assistantships, teaching assistantships, career-related internships or fieldwork, Federal Work-Study, institutionally sponsored loans, scholarships/grants, and unspecified assistantships available. Support available to part-time students. Financial award application deadline: 3/31; financial award applicants required to submit FAFSA. *Unit head:* Dr. Heather Hall, Dean, College of Nursing, 251-445-9400, Fax: 251-445-9416, E-mail: heatherhall@southalabama.edu. *Application contact:* Jennifer Bouvier, Academic Advisor II, 251-445-9400, Fax: 251-445-9416, E-mail: jcamp@southalabama.edu.
Website: http://www.southalabama.edu/colleges/con/index.html

**University of South Carolina,** The Graduate School, College of Nursing, Program in Nursing Administration, Columbia, SC 29208. Offers MSN. *Accreditation:* AACN. *Program availability:* Part-time. *Degree requirements:* For master's, thesis or alternative. *Entrance requirements:* For master's, GRE General Test or MAT, BS in nursing, nursing license. Additional exam requirements/recommendations for international students: required—TOEFL (minimum score 570 paper-based). Electronic applications accepted.

**University of Southern Indiana,** Graduate Studies, College of Nursing and Health Professions, Program in Nursing, Evansville, IN 47712-3590. Offers adult-gerontology acute care nurse practitioner (MSN, PMC); adult-gerontology clinical nurse specialist (MSN, PMC); adult-gerontology primary care nurse practitioner (MSN, PMC); advanced nursing practice (DNP); family nurse practitioner (MSN, PMC); nursing education (MSN, PMC); nursing management and leadership (MSN, PMC); organizational and systems leadership (DNP); psychiatric mental health nurse practitioner (MSN, PMC). *Accreditation:* AACN. *Program availability:* Part-time, online learning. *Entrance requirements:* For master's, BSN from nationally-accredited school; minimum cumulative GPA of 3.0; satisfactory completion of a course in undergraduate statistics (minimum grade C); one year of full-time experience or 2,000 hours of clinical practice as an RN (recommended); unencumbered U.S. RN license; for doctorate, minimum GPA of 3.0, completion of graduate research course with minimum B grade, unencumbered RN license, resume/curriculum vitae, three professional references, 1-2 page narrative of practice experience and professional goals, Capstone Project Information form. Additional exam requirements/recommendations for international students: required—TOEFL (minimum score 550 paper-based; 79 iBT), IELTS (minimum score 6). Electronic applications accepted. *Expenses:* Contact institution.

**University of Southern Maine,** College of Science, Technology, and Health, School of Nursing, Portland, ME 04103. Offers adult-gerontology primary care nurse practitioner (MS, PMC); education (MS); family nurse practitioner (MS, PMC); family psychiatric/mental health nurse practitioner (MS); management (MS); nursing (CAS, CGS);

psychiatric-mental health nurse practitioner (PMC). *Accreditation:* AACN. *Program availability:* Part-time. *Degree requirements:* For master's, thesis optional. *Entrance requirements:* For master's, GRE General Test or MAT, minimum GPA of 3.0; for doctorate, GRE. Additional exam requirements/recommendations for international students: required—TOEFL (minimum score 550 paper-based). Electronic applications accepted. *Expenses:* Tuition, area resident: Full-time $864; part-time $432 per credit hour. Tuition, state resident: full-time $864; part-time $432 per credit hour. Tuition, nonresident: full-time $2372; part-time $1186 per credit hour. *Required fees:* $141; $108 per credit hour. Tuition and fees vary according to course load.

**The University of Texas at Arlington,** Graduate School, College of Nursing and Health Innovation, Arlington, TX 76019. Offers athletic training (MS); exercise science (MS); kinesiology (PhD); nurse practitioner (MSN); nursing (PhD); nursing administration (MSN); nursing education (MSN); nursing practice (DNP). *Accreditation:* AACN. *Program availability:* Part-time, evening/weekend, online learning. *Degree requirements:* For master's, practicum course; for doctorate, comprehensive exam (for some programs), thesis/dissertation (for some programs), proposal defense dissertation (for PhD); scholarship project for DNP. *Entrance requirements:* For master's, GRE General Test if GPA less than 3.0, minimum GPA of 3.0, Texas nursing license, minimum C grade in undergraduate statistics course; for doctorate, GRE General Test (waived for MSN-to-PhD applicants), minimum undergraduate, graduate and statistics GPA of 3.0; Texas RN license; interview; written statement of goals. Additional exam requirements/recommendations for international students: required—TOEFL (minimum score 550 paper-based), IELTS (minimum score 7).

**The University of Texas at Austin,** Graduate School, School of Nursing, Austin, TX 78712-1111. Offers adult - gerontology clinical nurse specialist (MSN); child health (MSN), including administration, public health nursing, teaching; family nurse practitioner (MSN); family psychiatric/mental health nurse practitioner (MSN); holistic adult health (MSN), including administration, teaching; maternity (MSN), including administration, public health nursing, teaching; nursing (PhD); nursing administration and healthcare systems management (MSN); nursing practice (DNP); pediatric nurse practitioner (MSN); public health nursing (MSN). *Accreditation:* AACN. *Program availability:* Part-time. *Degree requirements:* For master's, thesis optional; for doctorate, thesis/dissertation. *Entrance requirements:* For master's and doctorate, GRE General Test. Additional exam requirements/recommendations for international students: required—TOEFL (minimum score 550 paper-based). Electronic applications accepted.

**The University of Texas at El Paso,** Graduate School, School of Nursing, El Paso, TX 79968-0001. Offers family nurse practitioner (MSN); health care leadership and management (Certificate); interdisciplinary health sciences (PhD); nursing (DNP); nursing education (MSN, Certificate); nursing systems management (MSN). *Accreditation:* AACN. *Program availability:* Online learning. *Degree requirements:* For master's, thesis optional; for doctorate, thesis/dissertation. *Entrance requirements:* For master's, minimum GPA of 3.0, resume; for doctorate, GRE, letters of reference, relevant personal/professional experience; master's degree in nursing (for DNP); for Certificate, bachelor's degree in nursing. Additional exam requirements/recommendations for international students: required—TOEFL; recommended—IELTS. Electronic applications accepted.

**The University of Texas at Tyler,** College of Nursing and Health Sciences, School of Nursing, Tyler, TX 75799. Offers nurse practitioner (MSN); nursing (PhD); nursing administration (MSN); nursing education (MSN); MSN/MBA. *Accreditation:* AACN. *Program availability:* Part-time, evening/weekend, online learning. *Faculty:* 27 full-time (all women), 4 part-time/adjunct (all women). *Students:* 101 full-time (83 women), 351 part-time (303 women); includes 149 minority (53 Black or African American, non-Hispanic/Latino; 1 American Indian or Alaska Native, non-Hispanic/Latino; 27 Asian, non-Hispanic/Latino; 51 Hispanic/Latino; 17 Two or more races, non-Hispanic/Latino), 5 international. Average age 37. 128 applicants, 67% accepted, 81 enrolled. In 2019, 86 master's, 21 doctorates awarded. *Degree requirements:* For master's, comprehensive exam (for some programs), thesis (for some programs); for doctorate, thesis/dissertation. *Entrance requirements:* For master's, GRE General Test or MAT, GMAT, minimum undergraduate GPA of 3.0, course work in statistics, RN license, BSN. Additional exam requirements/recommendations for international students: required—TOEFL. *Application deadline:* For fall admission, 8/17 priority date for domestic students, 7/1 priority date for international students; for spring admission, 12/21 priority date for domestic students, 11/1 priority date for international students. Applications are processed on a rolling basis. Application fee: $25 ($50 for international students). Electronic applications accepted. *Financial support:* In 2019–20, 15 students received support, including 1 fellowship (averaging $10,000 per year), 3 research assistantships (averaging $2,200 per year); institutionally sponsored loans and scholarships/grants also available. Financial award application deadline: 7/1; financial award applicants required to submit FAFSA. *Unit head:* Dr. Barbara Haas, Associate Dean, 903-566-7021, E-mail: bhaas@uttyler.edu. *Application contact:* Dr. Barbara Haas, Associate Dean, 903-566-7021, E-mail: bhaas@uttyler.edu.
Website: https://www.uttyler.edu/nursing/

**The University of Texas Health Science Center at San Antonio,** School of Nursing, San Antonio, TX 78229-3900. Offers administrative management (MSN); adult-gerontology acute care nurse practitioner (PGC); advanced practice leadership (DNP); clinical nurse leader (MSN); executive administrative management (DNP); family nurse practitioner (MSN, PGC); nursing (MSN, PhD); nursing education (MSN, PGC); pediatric nurse practitioner primary care (PGC); psychiatric mental health nurse practitioner (PGC); public health nurse leader (DNP). *Accreditation:* AACN. *Program availability:* Part-time. Terminal master's awarded for partial completion of doctoral program. *Degree requirements:* For master's, thesis optional; for doctorate, comprehensive exam, thesis/dissertation.

**The University of Toledo,** College of Graduate Studies, College of Nursing, Department of Population and Community Care, Toledo, OH 43606-3390. Offers clinical nurse leader (MSN); family nurse practitioner (MSN, Certificate); nurse educator (MSN, Certificate); pediatric nurse practitioner (MSN, Certificate). *Program availability:* Part-time. *Degree requirements:* For master's, thesis or alternative. *Entrance requirements:* For master's, GRE, BS in nursing, minimum undergraduate GPA of 3.0, statement of purpose, three letters of recommendation, transcripts from all prior institutions attended, Nursing CAS application, UT supplemental application; for Certificate, BS in nursing, minimum undergraduate GPA of 3.0, statement of purpose, three letters of recommendation, transcripts from all prior institutions attended. Additional exam requirements/recommendations for international students: required—TOEFL (minimum score 550 paper-based; 80 iBT). Electronic applications accepted.

**University of Victoria,** Faculty of Graduate Studies, Faculty of Human and Social Development, School of Nursing, Victoria, BC V8W 2Y2, Canada. Offers advanced nursing practice (advanced practice leadership option) (MN); advanced nursing practice (nurse educator option) (MN); advanced nursing practice (nurse practitioner option) (MN); nursing (PhD). *Program availability:* Part-time, online learning. *Entrance requirements:* Additional exam requirements/recommendations for international students: required—TOEFL (minimum score 575 paper-based), IELTS (minimum score 7). Electronic applications accepted.

## Nursing and Healthcare Administration

**University of Virginia,** School of Nursing, Charlottesville, VA 22903. Offers acute and specialty care (MSN); acute care nurse practitioner (MSN); clinical nurse leadership (MSN); community-public health leadership (MSN); nursing (DNP, PhD); psychiatric mental health counseling (MSN); MSN/MBA. *Accreditation:* AACN. *Program availability:* Part-time. *Degree requirements:* For doctorate, comprehensive exam (for some programs), capstone project (DNP), dissertation (PhD). *Entrance requirements:* For master's, GRE General Test, MAT; for doctorate, GRE General Test. Additional exam requirements/recommendations for international students: required—TOEFL, IELTS. Electronic applications accepted.

**University of Washington, Tacoma,** Graduate Programs, Program in Nursing, Tacoma, WA 98402-3100. Offers communities, populations and health (MN); leadership in healthcare (MN); nurse educator (MN). *Program availability:* Part-time. *Degree requirements:* For master's, thesis (for some programs), advance fieldwork. *Entrance requirements:* For master's, Washington State NCLEX exam, minimum GPA of 3.0. Additional exam requirements/recommendations for international students: required—TOEFL (minimum score 580 paper-based; 70 iBT); recommended—IELTS (minimum score 7).

**University of Wisconsin–Eau Claire,** College of Nursing and Health Sciences, Program in Nursing, Eau Claire, WI 54702-4004. Offers adult-gerontological administration (DNP); adult-gerontological clinical nurse specialist (DNP); adult-gerontological education (MSN); adult-gerontological primary care nurse practitioner (DNP); family health administration (DNP); family health in education (MSN); family health nurse practitioner (DNP); nursing (MSN); nursing practice (DNP). *Accreditation:* AACN. *Program availability:* Part-time. Terminal master's awarded for partial completion of doctoral program. *Degree requirements:* For master's, thesis optional, 500-600 hours clinical practicum, oral and written exams. *Entrance requirements:* For master's, Wisconsin RN license, minimum GPA of 3.0, undergraduate statistics, course work in health assessment. Additional exam requirements/recommendations for international students: required—TOEFL (minimum score 79 iBT). *Expenses:* Contact institution.

**University of Wisconsin–Green Bay,** Graduate Studies, Program in Nursing Leadership and Management in Health Systems, Green Bay, WI 54311-7001. Offers health and wellness management (MS); nursing (MSN). *Program availability:* Part-time, evening/weekend, online only, 100% online. *Degree requirements:* For master's, 9-credit practicum. *Entrance requirements:* For master's, baccalaureate degree in nursing with minimum GPA of 3.0; college-level inferential statistics course with minimum C grade (within past 5 years); statement of interest; official undergraduate and graduate transcripts; three letters of evaluation; curriculum vitae or resume; copy of current, unencumbered RN license; background check. Additional exam requirements/recommendations for international students: required—TOEFL. Electronic applications accepted.

**Virginia Commonwealth University,** Graduate School, School of Nursing, Richmond, VA 23284-9005. Offers adult health acute nursing (MS); adult health primary nursing (MS); biobehavioral clinical research (PhD); child health nursing (MS); clinical nurse leader (MS); family health nursing (MS); nurse educator (MS); nurse practitioner (MS); nursing (Certificate); nursing administration (MS), including clinical nurse manager; psychiatric-mental health nursing (MS); quality and safety in health care (DNP); women's health nursing (MS). *Accreditation:* AACN; ACEN (one or more programs are accredited). *Program availability:* Part-time, evening/weekend, online learning. *Degree requirements:* For master's, thesis optional; for doctorate, thesis/dissertation. *Entrance requirements:* For master's, GRE General Test, BSN, minimum GPA of 2.8; for doctorate, GRE General Test. Additional exam requirements/recommendations for international students: required—TOEFL (minimum score 600 paper-based; 100 iBT). Electronic applications accepted.

**Walden University,** Graduate Programs, School of Nursing, Minneapolis, MN 55401. Offers adult-gerontology acute care nurse practitioner (MSN); adult-gerontology nurse practitioner (MSN); education (MSN); family nurse practitioner (MSN); informatics (MSN); leadership and management (MSN); nursing (PhD, Post-Master's Certificate), including education (PhD), healthcare administration (PhD), interdisciplinary health (PhD), leadership (PhD), nursing education (Post-Master's Certificate), nursing informatics (Post-Master's Certificate), nursing leadership and management (Post-Master's Certificate), public health policy (PhD); nursing practice (DNP); psychiatric mental health (MSN). *Accreditation:* AACN. *Program availability:* Part-time, evening/weekend, online only, 100% online. *Degree requirements:* For doctorate, thesis/dissertation (for some programs), residency (for some programs), field experience (for some programs). *Entrance requirements:* For master's, bachelor's degree or equivalent in related field or RN; minimum GPA of 2.5; official transcripts; goal statement (for some programs); access to computer and Internet; for doctorate, master's degree or higher; RN; three years of related professional or academic experience; goal statement; access to computer and Internet; for Post-Master's Certificate, relevant work experience; access to computer and Internet. Additional exam requirements/recommendations for international students: required—TOEFL (minimum score 550 paper-based, 79 iBT), IELTS (minimum score 6.5), Michigan English Language Assessment Battery (minimum score 82), or PTE (minimum score 53). Electronic applications accepted.

**Walsh University,** Master of Science in Nursing, North Canton, OH 44720-3396. Offers academic nurse educator (MSN); adult acute care nurse practitioner (MSN); clinical nurse leader (MSN); nursing practice (DNP). *Accreditation:* AACN. *Program availability:* Part-time, 100% online, blended/hybrid learning. *Faculty:* 5 full-time (4 women), 11 part-time/adjunct (10 women). *Students:* 80 full-time (68 women), 83 part-time (73 women); includes 12 minority (5 Black or African American, non-Hispanic/Latino; 1 Asian, non-Hispanic/Latino; 6 Two or more races, non-Hispanic/Latino). Average age 35. 76 applicants, 93% accepted, 55 enrolled. In 2019, 38 master's, 2 doctorates awarded. *Degree requirements:* For doctorate, scholarly project; residency practicum. *Entrance requirements:* For master's, Registered Nurse license(s), 1 year of experience as a Registered Nurse; Official transcripts documenting a baccalaureate degree in nursing from an accredited program, Minimum 3.0 cumulative GPA, completion of a statistics course, 2 letters of recommendation, resume or CV, personal statement. Additional exam requirements/recommendations for international students: required—TOEFL. *Application deadline:* Applications are processed on a rolling basis. Electronic applications accepted. *Expenses:* $725 per credit hour, $50 technology fee. *Financial support:* In 2019–20, 1 student received support. Research assistantships available. Financial award application deadline: 12/31; financial award applicants required to submit FAFSA. *Unit head:* Dr. Judy Kreye, Dean, Byers School of Nursing, 330-2444757, Fax: 330-4907206, E-mail: jkreye@walsh.edu. *Application contact:* Dr. Janet Finneran, Director of Graduate Nursing Programs, 330-2444759, Fax: 330-4907206, E-mail: jfinneran@walsh.edu.
Website: http://www.walsh.edu/master-of-science-in-nursing

**Washburn University,** School of Nursing, Topeka, KS 66621. Offers clinical nurse leader (MSN); nursing (DNP); psychiatric mental health nurse practitioner (Post-Graduate Certificate). *Accreditation:* AACN. *Program availability:* Part-time. *Entrance requirements:* Additional exam requirements/recommendations for international students: required—TOEFL (minimum score 550 paper-based).

**Washington Adventist University,** Program in Nursing - Business Leadership, Takoma Park, MD 20912. Offers MSN. *Program availability:* Part-time. *Entrance requirements:* Additional exam requirements/recommendations for international students: required—TOEFL (minimum score 550 paper-based), IELTS (minimum score 5).

**Waynesburg University,** Graduate and Professional Studies, Canonsburg, PA 15370. Offers business (MBA), including energy management, finance, health systems, human resources, leadership, market development; counseling (MA), including addictions counseling, clinical mental health; counselor education and supervision (PhD); criminal investigation (MA); education (M Ed), including autism, curriculum and instruction, educational leadership, online teaching; nursing (MSN), including administration, education, informatics; nursing practice (DNP); special education (M Ed); technology (M Ed); MSN/MBA. *Accreditation:* AACN. *Program availability:* Part-time, evening/weekend. *Degree requirements:* For doctorate, thesis/dissertation. *Entrance requirements:* Additional exam requirements/recommendations for international students: required—TOEFL. Electronic applications accepted.

**Weber State University,** Dumke College of Health Professions, School of Nursing, Ogden, UT 84408-1001. Offers educator (MSN); executive (MSN); nurse practitioner (MSN). *Program availability:* Part-time, evening/weekend, online only, 100% online. *Faculty:* 14 full-time (13 women), 2 part-time/adjunct (both women). *Students:* 85 full-time (73 women), 18 part-time (16 women); includes 6 minority (1 Asian, non-Hispanic/Latino; 4 Hispanic/Latino; 1 Two or more races, non-Hispanic/Latino). Average age 38. In 2019, 52 master's awarded. *Entrance requirements:* For master's, bachelor's degree in nursing from ACEN- or CCNE-accredited program. *Application deadline:* For fall admission, 4/1 priority date for domestic students. Application fee: $60 ($90 for international students). Electronic applications accepted. *Expenses: Tuition, area resident:* full-time $7197; part-time $4981 per credit. Tuition, state resident: full-time $7197; part-time $4981 per credit. Tuition, nonresident: full-time $16,560; part-time $11,589 per credit. *Required fees:* $643 per semester. One-time fee: $60. Tuition and fees vary according to course load and program. *Financial support:* In 2019–20, 16 students received support. Scholarships/grants available. Financial award application deadline: 4/1; financial award applicants required to submit FAFSA. *Unit head:* Dr. Deborah Juff, MSN & DNP Program Director, 801-626-7833, Fax: 801-626-6397, E-mail: djudd@weber.edu. *Application contact:* Robert Holt, Director of Enrollment, 801-626-7774, Fax: 801-626-6397, E-mail: rholt@weber.edu.
Website: http://www.weber.edu/nursing

**Western Governors University,** College of Health Professions, Salt Lake City, UT 84107. Offers healthcare management (MBA); leadership and management (MSN); nursing education (MSN); nursing informatics (MSN). *Program availability:* Evening/weekend, online learning. *Degree requirements:* For master's, capstone project. *Entrance requirements:* For master's, transcripts. Additional exam requirements/recommendations for international students: required—TOEFL (minimum score 450 paper-based; 80 iBT). Electronic applications accepted. Application fee is waived when completed online.

**Western University of Health Sciences,** College of Graduate Nursing, Master of Science in Nursing Program, Pomona, CA 91766-1854. Offers administrative nurse leader (MSN); ambulatory care nurse (MSN); clinical nurse leader (MSN). *Accreditation:* AACN. *Faculty:* 19 full-time (16 women), 40 part-time/adjunct (31 women). *Students:* 231 full-time (182 women), 2 part-time (both women); includes 181 minority (8 Black or African American, non-Hispanic/Latino; 2 American Indian or Alaska Native, non-Hispanic/Latino; 82 Asian, non-Hispanic/Latino; 65 Hispanic/Latino; 1 Native Hawaiian or other Pacific Islander, non-Hispanic/Latino; 23 Two or more races, non-Hispanic/Latino), 3 international. Average age 29. 640 applicants, 23% accepted, 85 enrolled. In 2019, 77 master's awarded. *Degree requirements:* For master's, comprehensive exam (for some programs), project. *Entrance requirements:* For master's, Bachelor's degree, essay questions, Resume/Curriculum Vitae, 2 reference forms, Official transcripts of all schools attended, prerequisite worksheet, repeated courses work sheet. Additional exam requirements/recommendations for international students: required—TOEFL (minimum score 80 iBT). *Application deadline:* For fall admission, 11/2 for domestic and international students. Application fee: $60. Electronic applications accepted. *Expenses:* Contact institution. *Financial support:* In 2019–20, 17 students received support. Scholarships/grants available. Financial award application deadline: 3/2; financial award applicants required to submit FAFSA. *Unit head:* Dr. Mary Lopez, Dean, 909-706-3860, Fax: 909-469-5521, E-mail: mlopez@westernu.edu. *Application contact:* Daniell Mendoza, Assistant Director of Admissions, 909-469-5541, Fax: 909-469-5570, E-mail: dmendoza@westernu.edu.

**West Virginia Wesleyan College,** School of Nursing, Buckhannon, WV 26201. Offers family nurse practitioner (MS, Post Master's Certificate); nurse-midwifery (MS); nursing (DNP); nursing leadership (MS); psychiatric mental health nurse practitioner (MS); MSN/MBA. *Accreditation:* ACEN.

**Wilmington University,** College of Health Professions, New Castle, DE 19720-6491. Offers adult nurse practitioner (MSN); family nurse practitioner (MSN); gerontology nurse practitioner (MSN); nursing (MSN); nursing leadership (MSN); nursing practice (DNP). *Accreditation:* AACN. *Program availability:* Part-time. *Degree requirements:* For master's, thesis. *Entrance requirements:* For master's, BSN, RN license, interview, 3 letters of recommendation. Additional exam requirements/recommendations for international students: required—TOEFL (minimum score 500 paper-based). Electronic applications accepted.

**Wilson College,** Graduate Programs, Chambersburg, PA 17201-1285. Offers accounting (M Acc); choreography and visual art (MFA); education (M Ed); educational technology (MET); healthcare administration (MHA); humanities (MA), including art and culture, critical/cultural theory, English language and literature, women's studies; management (MSM); nursing (MSN), including nursing education, nursing leadership and management; special education (MSE). *Program availability:* Evening/weekend. *Degree requirements:* For master's, project. *Entrance requirements:* For master's, PRAXIS, minimum undergraduate cumulative GPA of 3.0, 2 letters of recommendation, current certification for eligibility to teach in grades K-12, resume, personal interview. Electronic applications accepted.

**Winona State University,** College of Nursing and Health Sciences, Winona, MN 55987. Offers adult-gerontology acute care nurse practitioner (MS, DNP, Post Master's Certificate); adult-gerontology clinical nurse specialist (MS, DNP, Post Master's Certificate); adult-gerontology primary care nurse practitioner (MS, DNP, Post Master's Certificate); family nurse practitioner (MS, DNP, Post Master's Certificate); nurse educator (MS); nursing and organizational leadership (MS, DNP, Post Master's Certificate); practice and leadership innovations (DNP, Post Master's Certificate). *Accreditation:* AACN. *Program availability:* Part-time, online learning. *Degree requirements:* For master's, thesis; for doctorate, capstone. *Entrance requirements:* For master's, GRE (if GPA less than 3.0). Additional exam requirements/recommendations for international students: required—TOEFL (minimum score 550 paper-based).

**Wright State University,** Graduate School, College of Nursing and Health, Program in Nursing, Dayton, OH 45435. Offers administration of nursing and health care systems (MS); adult gerontology clinical nurse specialist (MS); adult-gerontology acute care

nurse practitioner (MS); family nurse practitioner (MS); neonatal nurse practitioner (MS); pediatric nurse practitioner-acute care (MS); pediatric nurse practitioner-primary care (MS); psychiatric mental health nurse practitioner (MS); school nurse (MS). *Accreditation:* AACN. *Program availability:* Part-time, evening/weekend. *Degree*

*requirements:* For master's, thesis or alternative. *Entrance requirements:* For master's, GRE General Test, BSN from ACEN-accredited college, Ohio RN license. Additional exam requirements/recommendations for international students: required—TOEFL.

# Nursing Education

**Abilene Christian University,** College of Graduate and Professional Studies, Program in Nursing Practice, Addison, TX 75001. Offers advanced practice nurse (DNP); executive nursing leadership (DNP); nursing education (DNP). *Program availability:* Part-time, online only, blended/hybrid learning. *Faculty:* 4 full-time (3 women), 1 (woman) part-time/adjunct. *Students:* 48 full-time (44 women), 64 part-time (55 women); includes 63 minority (35 Black or African American, non-Hispanic/Latino; 3 Asian, non-Hispanic/Latino; 24 Hispanic/Latino; 1 Two or more races, non-Hispanic/Latino), 2 international. 49 applicants, 100% accepted, 34 enrolled. In 2019, 10 doctorates awarded. *Entrance requirements:* For doctorate, master's degree in nursing, official transcripts, minimum graduate nursing cumulative GPA of 3.0, two recommendation letters, 500-word statement of purpose, professional curriculum vitae or resume. Additional exam requirements/recommendations for international students: required—TOEFL (minimum score 80 iBT), IELTS (minimum score 6). *Application deadline:* For fall admission, 10/7 for domestic students; for winter admission, 12/20 for domestic students; for spring admission, 2/24 for domestic students; for summer admission, 4/20 for domestic students. Applications are processed on a rolling basis. Application fee: $50. Electronic applications accepted. *Expenses:* $1000 per hour. *Financial support:* In 2019–20, 21 students received support. Scholarships/grants available. Financial award application deadline: 7/1; financial award applicants required to submit FAFSA. *Unit head:* Dr. Linda Gibson, Program Director, 214-305-9500, E-mail: lcg17a@acu.edu. *Application contact:* Graduate Advisor, 855-219-7300, E-mail: onlineadmissions@acu.edu.
Website: http://www.acu.edu/online/academics/doctor-of-nursing-practice.html

**Adelphi University,** College of Nursing and Public Health, Program in Nursing Education, Garden City, NY 11530-0701. Offers MS, Certificate. *Entrance requirements:* Additional exam requirements/recommendations for international students: required—TOEFL (minimum score 550 paper-based; 80 iBT), IELTS (minimum score 6.5). *Expenses:* Contact institution.

**Albany State University,** Darton College of Health Professions, Albany, GA 31705-2717. Offers nursing (MSN), including family nurse practitioner, nurse educator. *Accreditation:* ACEN. *Program availability:* Part-time, evening/weekend, online learning. *Degree requirements:* For master's, comprehensive exam, thesis. *Entrance requirements:* For master's, GRE or MAT, official transcript, letters of recommendation, pre-medical/certificate of immunizations. Electronic applications accepted.

**Allen College,** Graduate Programs, Waterloo, IA 50703. Offers adult-gerontology acute care nurse practitioner (MSN); community/public health nursing (MSN); education (MSN); family nurse practitioner (MSN); health sciences (Ed D); leadership in health care delivery (MSN); leadership in health care informatics (MSN); nursing (DNP); occupational therapy (MS); psychiatric mental health nurse practitioner (MSN). *Accreditation:* AACN; ACEN. *Faculty:* 27 full-time (23 women), 9 part-time/adjunct (8 women). *Students:* 193 full-time (175 women), 95 part-time (84 women); includes 22 minority (6 Black or African American, non-Hispanic/Latino; 1 American Indian or Alaska Native, non-Hispanic/Latino; 4 Asian, non-Hispanic/Latino; 5 Hispanic/Latino; 6 Two or more races, non-Hispanic/Latino). Average age 32. 376 applicants, 53% accepted, 122 enrolled. *Application deadline:* For fall admission, 2/1 priority date for domestic students; for spring admission, 9/1 priority date for domestic students. Applications are processed on a rolling basis. Application fee: $50. Electronic applications accepted. *Financial support:* In 2019–20, 78 students received support. Federal Work-Study, institutionally sponsored loans, and scholarships/grants available. Support available to part-time students. Financial award application deadline: 8/1; financial award applicants required to submit FAFSA. *Unit head:* Dr. Bob Loch, Provost, 319-226-2040, Fax: 319-226-2070, E-mail: bob.loch@allencollege.edu. *Application contact:* Molly Quinn, Director of Admissions, 319-226-2001, Fax: 319-226-2010, E-mail: molly.quinn@allencollege.edu.
Website: http://www.allencollege.edu/

**Alvernia University,** School of Graduate Studies, Department of Nursing, Reading, PA 19607-1799. Offers adult gerontology nurse practitioner (DNP); family nurse practitioner (DNP); nursing education (MSN); nursing leadership (Graduate Certificate); nursing leadership and healthcare administration (MSN).

**American International College,** School of Health Sciences, Springfield, MA 01109-3189. Offers exercise science (MS); family nurse practitioner (MSN, Post-Master's Certificate); nursing administrator (MSN); nursing educator (MSN); occupational therapy (MSOT, OTD); physical therapy (DPT). *Accreditation:* AOTA. *Program availability:* Part-time, 100% online. *Degree requirements:* For master's, practicum; for doctorate, thesis/dissertation, practicum. *Entrance requirements:* For master's, 3 letters of recommendation, personal goal statement; minimum GPA of 3.2, interview, BS or BA, and 2 clinical PT observations (for DPT); minimum GPA of 3.0, MSOT, OT licensen, and 2 clinical OT observations (for OTD); for doctorate, personal goal statement, 2 letters of recommendation; minimum GPA of 3.0, BS or BA, 2 clinical OT observations (for MSOT); RN license and minimum GPA of 3.0 (for MSN). Additional exam requirements/recommendations for international students: required—TOEFL (minimum score 577 paper-based; 91 iBT). Electronic applications accepted. *Expenses:* Contact institution.

**Anderson University,** College of Health Professions, Anderson, SC 29621. Offers advanced practice (DNP); executive leadership (MSN, DNP); family nurse practitioner (MSN, DNP); nurse educator (MSN); psychiatric mental health nurse practitioner (MSN, DNP). *Program availability:* Online learning. *Application deadline:* Applications are processed on a rolling basis. Electronic applications accepted. *Expenses:* Contact institution. *Financial support:* Scholarships/grants available. *Unit head:* Dr. Donald M. Peace, Dean, 864-231-5513, E-mail: dpeace@andersonuniversity.edu. *Application contact:* Dr. Donald M. Peace, Dean, 864-231-5513, E-mail: dpeace@andersonuniversity.edu.
Website: http://www.andersonuniversity.edu/health-professions

**Angelo State University,** College of Graduate Studies and Research, Archer College of Health and Human Services, Department of Nursing, San Angelo, TX 76909. Offers family nurse practitioner (MSN); nurse educator (MSN). *Accreditation:* AACN; ACEN. *Program availability:* Part-time, evening/weekend, online learning. *Entrance requirements:* For master's, essay, three letters of recommendation. Additional exam requirements/recommendations for international students: required—TOEFL or IELTS. Electronic applications accepted.

**Arizona State University at Tempe,** College of Nursing and Health Innovation, Phoenix, AZ 85004. Offers advanced nursing practice (DNP); clinical research management (MS); community and public health practice (Graduate Certificate); family mental health nurse practitioner (Graduate Certificate); family nurse practitioner (Graduate Certificate); geriatric nursing (Graduate Certificate); healthcare innovation (MHI); nurse education in academic and practice settings (Graduate Certificate); nurse educator (MS); nursing and healthcare innovation (PhD). *Accreditation:* AACN. *Program availability:* Online learning. *Degree requirements:* For master's, comprehensive exam (for some programs), thesis (for some programs), interactive Program of Study (iPOS) submitted before completing 50 percent of required credit hours; for doctorate, comprehensive exam, thesis/dissertation, interactive Program of Study (iPOS) submitted before completing 50 percent of required credit hours. *Entrance requirements:* For master's and doctorate, GRE, minimum GPA of 3.0 or equivalent in last 2 years of work leading to bachelor's degree. Additional exam requirements/recommendations for international students: required—TOEFL, IELTS, or PTE. Electronic applications accepted. *Expenses:* Contact institution.

**Aspen University,** Program in Nursing, Denver, CO 80246-1930. Offers forensic nursing (MSN); informatics (MSN); nursing (MSN); nursing administration and management (MSN); nursing education (MSN); public health (MSN). *Program availability:* Part-time, evening/weekend, online only, 100% online. *Degree requirements:* For master's, comprehensive exam. *Entrance requirements:* For master's, www.aspen.edu, www.aspen.edu. Electronic applications accepted.

**Auburn University,** Graduate School, School of Nursing, Auburn, AL 36849. Offers nursing educator (MSN); primary care practitioner (MSN). *Accreditation:* AACN. *Program availability:* Part-time. *Faculty:* 30 full-time (27 women), 1 (woman) part-time/adjunct. *Students:* 13 full-time (all women), 132 part-time (117 women); includes 13 minority (7 Black or African American, non-Hispanic/Latino; 1 American Indian or Alaska Native, non-Hispanic/Latino; 2 Asian, non-Hispanic/Latino; 1 Hispanic/Latino; 2 Two or more races, non-Hispanic/Latino), 1 international. Average age 34. 88 applicants, 85% accepted, 58 enrolled. In 2019, 78 master's awarded. *Degree requirements:* For master's, Primary Care Practicum. *Entrance requirements:* For master's, BS in Nursing, license as a registered nurse in the US, C or better in undergraduate statistics course, BSN Nursing GPA of 3.0, Three professional references, Professional Goal Statement, resume or curriculum vitae. Additional exam requirements/recommendations for international students: required—TOEFL (minimum score 550 paper-based; 79 iBT). *Application deadline:* For fall admission, 6/1 priority date for domestic and international students; for spring admission, 10/1 priority date for domestic and international students; for summer admission, 3/1 priority date for domestic and international students. Application fee: $60 ($70 for international students). Electronic applications accepted. *Expenses:* $546 per credit hour state resident tuition, $1638 per credit hour nonresident tuition, $680 student services fee for GRA/GTA, $450 continuous enrollment fee, $450 clearing for graduation fee, $200 per clinical credit hour. *Financial support:* In 2019–20, 28 fellowships (averaging $28,714 per year), 2 teaching assistantships (averaging $9,696 per year) were awarded; scholarships/grants also available. Financial award application deadline: 3/15; financial award applicants required to submit FAFSA. *Unit head:* Dr. Gregg E. Newschwander, Dean, 334-844-3658, E-mail: gen0002@auburn.edu. *Application contact:* Dr. George Flowers, Dean of the Graduate School, 334-844-4700, E-mail: gradadm@auburn.edu.
Website: https://cws.auburn.edu/nursing/

**Auburn University at Montgomery,** College of Nursing and Health Sciences, Montgomery, AL 36124. Offers family nurse practitioner (MSN); nurse educator for interprofessional practice (MSN). *Accreditation:* AACN. *Program availability:* Part-time, evening/weekend, 100% online, blended/hybrid learning. *Faculty:* 3 full-time (all women), 4 part-time/adjunct (all women). *Students:* 37 part-time (32 women); includes 13 minority (all Black or African American, non-Hispanic/Latino). Average age 36. 56 applicants, 46% accepted, 22 enrolled. *Entrance requirements:* Additional exam requirements/recommendations for international students: recommended—TOEFL (minimum score 500 paper-based; 61 iBT), IELTS (minimum score 5.5), TSE (minimum score 44). *Application deadline:* For fall admission, 7/1 for domestic students; for spring admission, 10/1 for domestic students; for summer admission, 3/1 for domestic students. Applications are processed on a rolling basis. Application fee: $25. Electronic applications accepted. *Expenses: Tuition, area resident:* Full-time $7578; part-time $421 per credit hour. *Tuition, state resident:* full-time $7578; part-time $421 per credit hour. *Tuition, nonresident:* full-time $17,046; part-time $947 per credit hour. *International tuition:* $17,046 full-time. *Required fees:* $868. *Financial support:* Application deadline: 3/1. *Unit head:* Dr. Jean Leuner, Dean, 334-244-3658, E-mail: jleuner@aum.edu. *Application contact:* Christy Dearden, Senior Administrative Associate, 334-244-3658, E-mail: cdearden@aum.edu.
Website: http://conhs.aum.edu/academic-programs/graduate-programs/msn

**Austin Peay State University,** College of Graduate Studies, College of Behavioral and Health Sciences, School of Nursing, Clarksville, TN 37044. Offers family nurse practitioner (MSN); nursing administration (MSN); nursing education (MSN); nursing informatics (MSN). *Program availability:* Part-time, online learning. *Faculty:* 5 full-time (all women), 1 (woman) part-time/adjunct. *Students:* 12 full-time (11 women), 120 part-time (114 women); includes 25 minority (14 Black or African American, non-Hispanic/Latino; 3 Asian, non-Hispanic/Latino; 4 Hispanic/Latino; 4 Two or more races, non-Hispanic/Latino). Average age 34. 19 applicants, 84% accepted, 2 enrolled. In 2019, 51 master's awarded. *Degree requirements:* For master's, comprehensive exam. *Entrance requirements:* For master's, minimum GPA of 3.0, RN license eligibility, 3 letters of recommendation. Additional exam requirements/recommendations for international students: required—TOEFL (minimum score 500 paper-based). *Application deadline:* For fall admission, 8/5 priority date for domestic students. Applications are processed on a rolling basis. Application fee: $45 ($55 for international students). Electronic applications accepted. *Financial support:* Research assistantships with full tuition reimbursements, career-related internships or fieldwork, Federal Work-Study, institutionally sponsored loans, scholarships/grants, and unspecified assistantships available. Support available to part-time students. Financial award application deadline: 7/1; financial award applicants required to submit FAFSA. *Unit head:* Dr. Mary Rice, Interim Director of Nursing, 931-221-7483, Fax: 931-221-7595, E-mail: ricem@

apsu.edu. *Application contact:* Megan Mitchell, Coordinator of Graduate Admissions, 931-221-6189, Fax: 931-221-7641, E-mail: mitchellm@apsu.edu. Website: http://www.apsu.edu/nursing

**Azusa Pacific University,** School of Nursing, Azusa, CA 91702-7000. Offers adult clinical nurse specialist (MSN); adult-gerontology nurse practitioner (MSN); family nurse practitioner (MSN); healthcare administration and leadership (MSN); nursing (MSN, DNP, PhD); nursing education (MSN); parent-child clinical nurse specialist (MSN); psychiatric mental health nurse practitioner (MSN). *Accreditation:* AACN. *Program availability:* Part-time, evening/weekend. *Degree requirements:* For master's, thesis optional. *Entrance requirements:* For master's, BSN.

**Ball State University,** Graduate School, College of Health, School of Nursing, Muncie, IN 47304. Offers adult/gerontology nurse practitioner (Post Master's Certificate); evidence-based clinical practice (Postbaccalaureate Certificate); family nurse practitioner (Post Master's Certificate); nurse educator (Post Master's Certificate); nursing (MS), including family nurse practitioner, nurse administrator, nurse educator; nursing education (Postbaccalaureate Certificate); nursing practice (DNP). *Accreditation:* AACN. *Program availability:* Part-time-only, online only, 100% online. *Entrance requirements:* For master's, bachelor's degree in nursing, minimum GPA of 3.0, minimum C grade in at least 2 quarter or semester hours in an undergraduate research course, unencumbered license as a registered nurse in state of practice; for doctorate, advanced practice nurse (nurse practitioner, clinical nurse specialist, nurse midwife); master's degree in nursing from accredited program with minimum GPA of 3.2; graduate-level statistics, nursing research, and health assessment courses; unencumbered license as registered nurse in state of practice. Additional exam requirements/recommendations for international students: required—TOEFL (minimum score 550 paper-based; 79 iBT), IELTS (minimum score 6.5). Electronic applications accepted. *Expenses:* Contact institution.

**Barry University,** School of Adult and Continuing Education, Division of Nursing, Program in Nursing Education, Miami Shores, FL 33161-6695. Offers MSN, Certificate. *Accreditation:* AACN. *Program availability:* Part-time, evening/weekend. *Degree requirements:* For master's, research project or thesis. *Entrance requirements:* For master's, GRE General Test or MAT, BSN, minimum GPA of 3.0, course work in statistics. Electronic applications accepted.

**Bellarmine University,** College of Health Professions, Donna and Allan Lansing School of Nursing and Clinical Sciences, Louisville, KY 40205. Offers family nurse practitioner (MSN); health science (MHS); nursing administration (MSN); nursing education (MSN); nursing practice (DNP). *Accreditation:* AACN; APTA. *Program availability:* Part-time, evening/weekend. *Faculty:* 19 full-time (15 women), 7 part-time/adjunct (all women). *Students:* 142 full-time (104 women), 128 part-time (105 women); includes 55 minority (24 Black or African American, non-Hispanic/Latino; 1 American Indian or Alaska Native, non-Hispanic/Latino; 15 Asian, non-Hispanic/Latino; 10 Hispanic/Latino; 5 Two or more races, non-Hispanic/Latino), 10 international. Average age 30. 348 applicants, 82% accepted, 172 enrolled. In 2019, 29 master's, 4 doctorates awarded. *Degree requirements:* For master's, comprehensive exam, thesis (for some programs); for doctorate, comprehensive exam, thesis/dissertation. *Entrance requirements:* For master's, GRE General Test, minimum GPA of 3.0, interview, resume; BSN from CCNE- or ACEN-accredited program, professional references, goal statement, and RN license (for MSN); bachelor's degree with exposure to health issues and grade of C or better in math/science courses (for MHS); for doctorate, GRE General Test, MSN from CCNE- or ACEN-accredited program; minimum GPA of 3.5 in graduate coursework; professional references; goal statement; current curriculum vitae or resume; RN license; verification of post-baccalaureate clinical and practice hours. Additional exam requirements/recommendations for international students: required—TOEFL (minimum iBT score of 83, 26 on speaking test), IELTS (minimum score 7, speaking band score of 8), or language training at an approved center; recommended—TOEFL (minimum score 83 iBT), IELTS. *Application deadline:* Applications are processed on a rolling basis. Application fee: $40. Electronic applications accepted. *Expenses:* Accelerated BSN, May 2020 cohort: $905 per credit hour; Accelerated BSN, 2-yr. program, Summer 2020: $950 per credit hour; MHS: $770 per credit hour; MHS, Medical Lab Science: $665 per credit hour; MHS, Respiratory Therapy: $665 per credit hour; MSN, Education and Administration: $770 per credit hour; MSN, Family Nurse Practitioner: $770 per credit hour ($85 per credit hour fee for FNP specialty courses); Doctor of Nursing Practice: $855 per credit hour; Radiation Therapy Second Degree: $665 per credit hour. *Financial support:* Career-related internships or fieldwork and scholarships/grants available. Financial award applicants required to submit FAFSA. *Unit head:* Dr. Nancy York, Dean, 502-272-8639, E-mail: nyork@bellarmine.edu. *Application contact:* Julie Armstrong-Binnix, Health Science Recruiter, 800-274-4723 Ext. 8364, E-mail: julieab@bellarmine.edu. Website: http://www.bellarmine.edu/lansing

**Bellin College,** School of Nursing, Green Bay, WI 54305. Offers family nurse practitioner (MSN); nurse educator (MSN). *Accreditation:* AACN.

**Bethel University,** Graduate School, St. Paul, MN 55112-6999. Offers business administration (MBA); classroom management (Certificate); counseling (MA); K-12 education (MA); leadership (Ed D); leadership foundations (Certificate); nurse educator (MS, Certificate); nurse-midwifery (MS); physician assistant (MS); special education (MA); strategic leadership (MA); teaching (MA); teaching and learning (Certificate). *Program availability:* Part-time, evening/weekend, 100% online, blended/hybrid learning. *Faculty:* 36 full-time (24 women), 112 part-time/adjunct (73 women). *Students:* 428 full-time (318 women), 825 part-time (482 women); includes 245 minority (95 Black or African American, non-Hispanic/Latino; 13 American Indian or Alaska Native, non-Hispanic/Latino; 52 Asian, non-Hispanic/Latino; 50 Hispanic/Latino; 2 Native Hawaiian or other Pacific Islander, non-Hispanic/Latino; 33 Two or more races, non-Hispanic/Latino), 28 international. Average age 38. 810 applicants, 45% accepted, 256 enrolled. In 2019, 320 master's, 34 doctorates, 112 other advanced degrees awarded. *Degree requirements:* For master's, comprehensive exam (for some programs), thesis (for some programs); for doctorate, comprehensive exam, thesis/dissertation. *Entrance requirements:* Additional exam requirements/recommendations for international students: required—TOEFL (minimum score 550 paper-based; 80 iBT), TOEFL (minimum score 550 paper-based, 80 iBT) or IELTS. *Application deadline:* Applications are processed on a rolling basis. Electronic applications accepted. *Expenses:* $420-$850/credit dependent on the program. *Financial support:* Teaching assistantships, career-related internships or fieldwork, and scholarships/grants available. Support available to part-time students. Financial award applicants required to submit FAFSA. *Unit head:* Dr. Randy Bergen, Associate Provost, 651-635-8000, Fax: 651-635-8004, E-mail: r-bergen@bethel.edu. *Application contact:* Director of Admissions, 651-635-8000, Fax: 651-635-8004, E-mail: gs@bethel.edu. Website: https://www.bethel.edu/graduate/

**Blessing-Rieman College of Nursing & Health Sciences,** Master of Science in Nursing Program, Quincy, IL 62305-7005. Offers nursing education (MSN); nursing leadership (MSN). *Program availability:* Part-time-only, evening/weekend, online only, 100% online. *Degree requirements:* For master's, thesis or project. *Entrance requirements:* Additional exam requirements/recommendations for international

students: required—TOEFL (minimum score 500 paper-based; 80 iBT). Electronic applications accepted.

**Bowie State University,** Graduate Programs, Department of Nursing, Bowie, MD 20715-9465. Offers administration of nursing services (MS); family nurse practitioner (MS); nursing education (MS). *Accreditation:* ACEN. *Program availability:* Part-time. *Degree requirements:* For master's, comprehensive exam, thesis, research paper. *Entrance requirements:* For master's, minimum GPA of 2.5. Electronic applications accepted. *Expenses: Tuition, area resident:* Full-time $11,942; part-time $423 per credit hour. Tuition, state resident: full-time $11,942; part-time $423 per credit hour. Tuition, nonresident: full-time $18,806; part-time $709 per credit hour. *International tuition:* $18,806 full-time. *Required fees:* $1106; $1106 per semester. $553 per semester.

**Bradley University,** The Graduate School, College of Education and Health Sciences, Department of Nursing, Peoria, IL 61625-0002. Offers family nurse practitioner (MSN, DNP, Certificate); leadership (DNP); nursing administration (MSN); nursing education (MSN, Certificate). *Accreditation:* AACN; ACEN. *Program availability:* Part-time, evening/weekend, 100% online. *Faculty:* 12 full-time (all women), 32 part-time/adjunct (28 women). *Students:* 91 full-time (79 women), 637 part-time (551 women); includes 253 minority (143 Black or African American, non-Hispanic/Latino; 13 American Indian or Alaska Native, non-Hispanic/Latino; 40 Asian, non-Hispanic/Latino; 45 Hispanic/Latino; 2 Native Hawaiian or other Pacific Islander, non-Hispanic/Latino; 10 Two or more races, non-Hispanic/Latino), 19 international. Average age 38. 229 applicants, 79% accepted, 114 enrolled. In 2019, 60 master's, 20 doctorates awarded. *Degree requirements:* For master's, comprehensive exam, thesis optional; for doctorate, comprehensive exam. *Entrance requirements:* For master's, GRE General Test or MAT, interview, Illinois RN license, advanced cardiac life support certification, pediatric advanced life support certification, 3 letters of recommendation. Additional exam requirements/recommendations for international students: required—TOEFL (minimum score 550 paper-based; 79 iBT), IELTS (minimum score 6.5), PTE (minimum score 58). *Application deadline:* For fall admission, 5/15 priority date for domestic and international students; for spring admission, 10/15 priority date for domestic and international students. Applications are processed on a rolling basis. Application fee: $40 ($50 for international students). Electronic applications accepted. *Expenses: Tuition:* Part-time $930 per credit hour. *Financial support:* Research assistantships, scholarships/grants, tuition waivers (partial), and unspecified assistantships available. Financial award application deadline: 4/1. *Unit head:* Jessica Clark, Associate Dean and Director of the Department of Nursing, 309-677-2547, E-mail: jclark@bradley.edu. *Application contact:* Rachel Webb, Director of On-Campus Graduate Admissions and International Student and Scholar Services, 309-677-2375, Fax: 309-677-3343, E-mail: rkwebb@bradley.edu. Website: http://www.bradley.edu/academic/departments/nur/

**Brenau University,** Sydney O. Smith Graduate School, Ivester College of Health Sciences, Gainesville, GA 30501. Offers family nurse practitioner (MSN); general psychology (MS); nurse educator (MSN); nursing manager (MSN); occupational therapy (MS). *Accreditation:* AOTA. *Program availability:* Part-time, evening/weekend, 100% online, blended/hybrid learning. *Faculty:* 34 full-time (26 women), 11 part-time/adjunct (10 women). *Students:* 321 full-time (242 women), 209 part-time (197 women); includes 177 minority (104 Black or African American, non-Hispanic/Latino; 2 American Indian or Alaska Native, non-Hispanic/Latino; 24 Asian, non-Hispanic/Latino; 36 Hispanic/Latino; 2 Native Hawaiian or other Pacific Islander, non-Hispanic/Latino; 9 Two or more races, non-Hispanic/Latino), 3 international. Average age 29. 517 applicants, 47% accepted, 110 enrolled. In 2019, 174 master's awarded. *Entrance requirements:* For master's, GMAT, GRE, or MAT, minimum GPA 2.5. Additional exam requirements/recommendations for international students: required—TOEFL (minimum score 497 paper-based; 71 iBT); recommended—IELTS (minimum score 5.5). *Application deadline:* Applications are processed on a rolling basis. Application fee: $35. Electronic applications accepted. *Expenses:* $11,763 full-time tuition (average), $4,678 part-time tuition (average). *Financial support:* In 2019–20, 11 students received support. Scholarships/grants available. Financial award applicants required to submit FAFSA. *Unit head:* Dr. Gale Starich, Dean, 777-718-5305, Fax: 770-297-5929, E-mail: gstarich@brenau.edu. *Application contact:* Nathan Goss, Assistant Vice President for Recruitment, 770-534-6162, E-mail: ngoss@brenau.edu. Website: http://www.brenau.edu/healthsciences/

**California Baptist University,** Program in Nursing, Riverside, CA 92504-3206. Offers clinical nurse specialist (MSN); family nurse practitioner (MSN); healthcare systems management (MSN); teaching-learning (MSN). *Accreditation:* AACN. *Program availability:* Part-time. *Degree requirements:* For master's, comprehensive exam or directed project thesis; capstone practicum. *Entrance requirements:* For master's, GRE or California Critical Thinking Skills Test; Test of Essential Academic Skills (TEAS), minimum undergraduate GPA of 3.0; completion of prerequisite courses with minimum grade of C; CPR certification; background check clearance; health clearance; drug testing; proof of health insurance; proof of motor vehicle insurance; three letters of recommendation; 1000-word essay; interview. Additional exam requirements/recommendations for international students: required—TOEFL (minimum score 80 iBT). Electronic applications accepted. *Expenses:* Contact institution.

**California State University, Fullerton,** Graduate Studies, College of Health and Human Development, School of Nursing, Fullerton, CA 92831-3599. Offers leadership (MS); nurse anesthesia (MS); nurse educator (MS); nursing (DNP); school nursing (MS); women's health care (MS). *Accreditation:* AACN. *Program availability:* Part-time.

**California State University, San Marcos,** College of Education, Health and Human Services, School of Nursing, San Marcos, CA 92096-0001. Offers advanced practice nursing (MSN), including clinical nurse specialist, family nurse practitioner, psychiatric mental health nurse practitioner; clinical nurse leader (MSN); nursing education (MSN). *Expenses: Tuition, area resident:* Full-time $7176. Tuition, state resident: full-time $7176. Tuition, nonresident: full-time $18,640. *International tuition:* $18,640 full-time. *Required fees:* $1960.

**California State University, Stanislaus,** College of Science, Master's in Nursing Program, Turlock, CA 95382. Offers gerontological nursing (MS); nursing education (MS). *Accreditation:* AACN. *Program availability:* Part-time. *Degree requirements:* For master's, comprehensive exam, thesis or alternative. *Entrance requirements:* For master's, GRE or MAT, minimum GPA of 3.0, 3 letters of reference, RN. Additional exam requirements/recommendations for international students: required—TOEFL (minimum score 550 paper-based). Electronic applications accepted.

**California University of Pennsylvania,** School of Graduate Studies and Research, Eberly College of Science and Technology, Department of Nursing, California, PA 15419-1394. Offers nursing administration and leadership (MSN); nursing education (MSN). *Expenses: Tuition, area resident:* Full-time $9288; part-time $516 per credit. Tuition, state resident: full-time $9288; part-time $516 per credit. Tuition, nonresident: full-time $13,932; part-time $774 per credit. *Required fees:* $3631; $291.13 per credit. Part-time tuition and fees vary according to course load.

**Capella University,** School of Public Service Leadership, Doctoral Programs in Nursing, Minneapolis, MN 55402. Offers nursing education (PhD); nursing practice (DNP).

**Capella University,** School of Public Service Leadership, Master's Programs in Nursing, Minneapolis, MN 55402. Offers diabetes nursing (MSN); general nursing (MSN); gerontology nursing (MSN); health information management (MS); nurse educator (MSN); nursing leadership and administration (MSN). *Accreditation:* AACN.

**Carlow University,** College of Health and Wellness, Program in Nursing Leadership and Education, Pittsburgh, PA 15213-3165. Offers MSN. *Program availability:* Part-time, evening/weekend, 100% online, blended/hybrid learning. *Students:* 40 full-time (39 women), 10 part-time (all women); includes 6 minority (4 Black or African American, non-Hispanic/Latino; 1 Asian, non-Hispanic/Latino; 1 Two or more races, non-Hispanic/Latino). Average age 33. 20 applicants, 100% accepted, 15 enrolled. In 2019, 27 master's awarded. *Degree requirements:* For master's, internship. *Entrance requirements:* For master's, minimum undergraduate GPA of 3.0 from accredited BSN program; current license as RN in Pennsylvania; statistics class within past 6 years with minimum C grade; two professional recommendations; reflective essay of 300 words or less describing career goals and expectations for education. Additional exam requirements/recommendations for international students: required—TOEFL (minimum score 550 paper-based). *Application deadline:* Applications are processed on a rolling basis. Electronic applications accepted. *Expenses: Tuition:* Full-time $13,666; part-time $902 per credit hour. *Required fees:* $15; $15 per credit. Tuition and fees vary according to degree level and program. *Financial support:* Application deadline: 4/1; applicants required to submit FAFSA. *Unit head:* Dr. Renee Ingel, Director, Nursing Leadership and DNP Programs, 412-578-6103, Fax: 412-578-6114, E-mail: rmingel@carlow.edu. *Application contact:* Dr. Renee Ingel, Director, Nursing Leadership and DNP Programs, 412-578-6103, Fax: 412-578-6114, E-mail: rmingel@carlow.edu.
Website: http://www.carlow.edu/Master_of_Science_in_Nursing_Concentration_in_Education_and_Leadership.aspx

**Case Western Reserve University,** Frances Payne Bolton School of Nursing, Master's Programs in Nursing, Cleveland, OH 44106. Offers nurse anesthesia (MSN); nurse education (MSN); nurse midwifery (MSN); nurse practitioner (MSN), including acute care/cardiovascular nursing, adult gerontology nurse practitioner, palliative care; nursing (MN). *Accreditation:* ACEN. *Program availability:* Part-time. *Faculty:* 40 full-time (36 women), 8 part-time/adjunct (7 women). *Students:* 160 full-time (131 women), 141 part-time (108 women); includes 72 minority (26 Black or African American, non-Hispanic/Latino; 22 Asian, non-Hispanic/Latino; 16 Hispanic/Latino; 8 Two or more races, non-Hispanic/Latino), 13 international. Average age 29. 273 applicants, 64% accepted, 100 enrolled. In 2019, 122 master's awarded. *Degree requirements:* For master's, thesis optional, minimum GPA of 3.0, Typhon log of clinical hours corresponding to requirements to sit for certification exam. *Entrance requirements:* For master's, GRE/MAT (scores not required for application, but may be requested for an admission decision), CCRN certification and 2 years ICU experience (for nurse anesthesia). Additional exam requirements/recommendations for international students: required—TOEFL (minimum score 577 paper-based; 90 iBT), IELTS (minimum score 7). *Application deadline:* For fall admission, 3/1 for domestic and international students; for spring admission, 10/1 for domestic and international students; for summer admission, 3/1 for domestic and international students. Applications are processed on a rolling basis. Application fee: $75. Electronic applications accepted. *Expenses:* MSN $2,133 per credit hour; MN $25,596 per semester; Lab fee $215; NCLEX $300; ACEMAPP $50; Clinical placement $75; Activity fee $15; Graduate Council fee $15. *Financial support:* In 2019–20, 126 students received support, including 49 teaching assistantships with partial tuition reimbursements available (averaging $19,197 per year); scholarships/grants and traineeships also available. Financial award application deadline: 5/15; financial award applicants required to submit FAFSA. *Unit head:* Dr. Latina Brooks, Director, 216-368-1196, Fax: 216-368-3542, E-mail: lmb3@case.edu. *Application contact:* Jackie Tepale, Admissions Coordinator, 216-368-5253, Fax: 216-368-3542, E-mail: yyd@case.edu.
Website: https://case.edu/nursing/programs/msn

**Cedar Crest College,** School of Nursing, Allentown, PA 18104-6196. Offers nursing administration (MS); nursing education (MS). *Program availability:* Part-time. Electronic applications accepted. *Expenses:* Contact institution.

**Cedarville University,** Graduate Programs, Cedarville, OH 45314. Offers business administration (MBA); family nurse practitioner (MSN); global ministry (M Div); global public health nursing (MSN); healthcare administration (MBA); ministry (M Min); nurse educator (MSN); operations management (MBA); pharmacy (Pharm D). *Program availability:* Part-time, evening/weekend, 100% online, blended/hybrid learning. *Faculty:* 52 full-time (19 women), 21 part-time/adjunct (13 women). *Students:* 378 full-time (221 women), 45 part-time (23 women); includes 76 minority (46 Black or African American, non-Hispanic/Latino; 2 American Indian or Alaska Native, non-Hispanic/Latino; 22 Asian, non-Hispanic/Latino; 1 Hispanic/Latino; 5 Two or more races, non-Hispanic/Latino), 2 international. Average age 26. 398 applicants, 70% accepted, 172 enrolled. In 2019, 74 master's, 34 doctorates awarded. *Degree requirements:* For master's, portfolio; for doctorate, comprehensive exam. *Entrance requirements:* For master's, GRE may be required, 2 professional recommendations; for doctorate, PCAT, professional recommendation from a practicing pharmacist or current employer/supervisor, resume, essay, interview. Additional exam requirements/recommendations for international students: required—TOEFL (minimum score 550 paper-based; 80 iBT). *Application deadline:* For fall admission, 5/1 priority date for domestic and international students; for spring admission, 11/1 priority date for domestic and international students. Applications are processed on a rolling basis. Electronic applications accepted. *Expenses: Tuition:* Full-time $12,594; part-time $566 per credit hour. One-time fee: $100. Tuition and fees vary according to course load and program. *Financial support:* Scholarships/grants and unspecified assistantships available. Support available to part-time students. Financial award application deadline: 1/30; financial award applicants required to submit FAFSA. *Unit head:* Dr. Janice Supplee, Dean of Graduate Studies, 937-766-8000, E-mail: suppleej@cedarville.edu. *Application contact:* Alexis McKay, Graduate Admissions Counselor, 937-766-8000, E-mail: amckay@cedarville.edu.
Website: https://www.cedarville.edu/offices/graduate-school

**Central Methodist University,** College of Graduate and Extended Studies, Fayette, MO 65248-1198. Offers clinical counseling (MS); clinical nurse leader (MSN); education (M Ed); music education (MME); nurse educator (MSN). *Program availability:* Part-time, evening/weekend, online learning. *Degree requirements:* For master's, thesis. *Entrance requirements:* For master's, GRE General Test, minimum GPA of 2.75. Electronic applications accepted.

**Chatham University,** Nursing Programs, Pittsburgh, PA 15232-2826. Offers education/leadership (MSN); nursing (DNP). *Accreditation:* AACN. *Program availability:* Online learning. *Entrance requirements:* For master's, RN license, BSN, minimum GPA of 3.0; for doctorate, RN license, MSN. Additional exam requirements/recommendations for international students: required—TOEFL (minimum score 600 paper-based; 100 iBT), IELTS (minimum score 6.5), TWE. Electronic applications accepted. Application fee is waived when completed online. *Expenses:* Contact institution.

**Clarkson College,** Master of Science in Nursing Program, Omaha, NE 68131. Offers adult nurse practitioner (MSN, Post-Master's Certificate); family nurse practitioner (MSN, Post-Master's Certificate); nursing education (MSN, Post-Master's Certificate); nursing health care leadership (MSN, Post-Master's Certificate). *Accreditation:* AANA/CANAEP; ACEN. *Program availability:* Part-time, evening/weekend, online learning. *Degree requirements:* For master's, on-campus skills assessment (family nurse practitioner, adult nurse practitioner), comprehensive exam or thesis. *Entrance requirements:* For master's, minimum GPA of 3.0, 2 references, resume. Additional exam requirements/recommendations for international students: required—TOEFL (minimum score 600 paper-based; 100 iBT). Electronic applications accepted.

**Cleveland State University,** College of Graduate Studies, College of Education and Human Services, Doctoral Studies in Education, Specialization in Nursing Education, Cleveland, OH 44115. Offers PhD. *Program availability:* Part-time. *Entrance requirements:* For doctorate, GRE General Test (minimum score of 297 for combined Verbal and Quantitative exams, 4.0 preferred for Analytical Writing), MSN with minimum GPA of 3.25, curriculum vitae or resume, personal statement, 2 letters of recommendation. Additional exam requirements/recommendations for international students: required—TOEFL (minimum score 550 paper-based; 78 iBT), IELTS (minimum score 6). Electronic applications accepted. *Expenses:* Tuition, state resident: full-time $10,215; part-time $6810 per credit hour. Tuition, nonresident: full-time $17,496; part-time $11,664 per credit hour. *International tuition:* $19,316 full-time. Tuition and fees vary according to degree level and program.

**College of Mount Saint Vincent,** School of Professional and Graduate Studies, Department of Nursing, Riverdale, NY 10471-1093. Offers family nurse practitioner (MSN, PMC); nurse educator (PMC); nursing administration (MSN); nursing education (MSN). *Accreditation:* AACN. *Program availability:* Part-time. *Entrance requirements:* For master's, BSN, interview, RN license, minimum GPA of 3.0, letters of reference. Additional exam requirements/recommendations for international students: required—TOEFL. *Expenses:* Contact institution.

**The College of New Rochelle,** Graduate School, Program in Nursing, New Rochelle, NY 10805-2308. Offers acute care nurse practitioner (MS, Certificate); clinical specialist in holistic nursing (MS, Certificate); family nurse practitioner (MS, Certificate); nursing and health care management (MS); nursing education (Certificate). *Accreditation:* AACN. *Program availability:* Part-time. *Entrance requirements:* For master's, GRE General Test or MAT, BSN, malpractice insurance, minimum GPA of 3.0, RN license. Electronic applications accepted.

**Colorado Mesa University,** Department of Health Sciences, Grand Junction, CO 81501-3122. Offers advanced nursing practice (MSN); family nurse practitioner (DNP); health information technology systems (Graduate Certificate); nursing education (MSN). *Accreditation:* AACN. *Program availability:* Part-time, evening/weekend, 100% online, blended/hybrid learning. *Degree requirements:* For master's and doctorate, capstone. *Entrance requirements:* For master's and doctorate, minimum GPA of 3.0 in BSN program. Additional exam requirements/recommendations for international students: required—TOEFL (minimum score 550 paper-based). Electronic applications accepted.

**Columbus State University,** Graduate Studies, College of Education and Health Professions, School of Nursing, Columbus, GA 31907-5645. Offers family nurse practitioner (MSN); nursing (MSN), including nurse educator, nurse informatics, nurse leader. *Program availability:* Part-time, online only, 100% online. *Entrance requirements:* For master's, GRE, BSN, minimum undergraduate GPA of 3.0. Additional exam requirements/recommendations for international students: required—TOEFL (minimum score 550 paper-based; 79 iBT). Electronic applications accepted. *Expenses:* Contact institution.

**Cox College,** Programs in Nursing, Springfield, MO 65802. Offers clinical nurse leader (MSN); family nurse practitioner (MSN); nurse educator (MSN). *Accreditation:* AACN. *Entrance requirements:* For master's, RN license, essay, 2 letters of recommendation, official transcripts. Electronic applications accepted.

**Daemen College,** Nursing Programs, Amherst, NY 14226-3592. Offers adult nurse practitioner (MS, Post Master's Certificate); nurse executive leadership (Post Master's Certificate); nursing education (MS, Post Master's Certificate); nursing executive leadership (MS); nursing practice (DNP); palliative care nursing (Post Master's Certificate). *Accreditation:* ACEN. *Program availability:* Part-time. *Degree requirements:* For master's, thesis, degree completed in 4 years; minimum GPA of 3.0 and a minimum grade of B in all courses; for doctorate, thesis/dissertation, degree completed in 5 years; minimum GPA of 3.0 and a minimum grade of B in all courses. *Entrance requirements:* For master's, bachelor's degree in nursing from a NLNAC or CCNE accredited program, 1 year medical-surgical clinical experience, resume, official transcripts, undergraduate or graduate statistics course (grade of C or better), GPA 3.25 or above (below may be accepted on provisional basis), NYS Nursing license, interview with nursing faculty. Additional exam requirements/recommendations for international students: required—TOEFL (minimum score 77 paper-based), IELTS (minimum score 6.5). Electronic applications accepted. Application fee is waived when completed online.

**Delta State University,** Graduate Programs, Robert E. Smith School of Nursing, Cleveland, MS 38733. Offers family nurse practitioner (MSN); nurse administrator (MSN); nurse educator (MSN). *Accreditation:* AACN. *Program availability:* Part-time. *Degree requirements:* For master's, thesis optional. *Entrance requirements:* For master's, GRE General Test. Electronic applications accepted. *Expenses: Tuition, area resident:* Full-time $7501; part-time $417 per credit hour. Tuition, state resident: full-time $7501; part-time $417 per credit hour. Tuition, nonresident: full-time $7501; part-time $417 per credit hour. *International tuition:* $7501 full-time. *Required fees:* $170; $9.45 per credit hour. $9.45 per semester.

**DeSales University,** Division of Healthcare, Center Valley, PA 18034-9568. Offers adult-gerontology acute care (Post Master's Certificate); adult-gerontology acute care nurse practitioner (MSN); adult-gerontology acute certified nurse practitioner (Post Master's Certificate); adult-gerontology clinical nurse specialist (MSN, Post Master's Certificate); clinical leadership (DNP); family nurse practitioner (MSN, Post Master's Certificate); general nursing practice (DNP); nurse anesthetist (MSN); nurse educator (Post Master's Certificate, Postbaccalaureate Certificate); nurse midwife (MSN); nurse practitioner (MSN); psychiatric-mental health nurse practitioner (MSN, Post Master's Certificate); DNP/MBA. *Accreditation:* ACEN. *Program availability:* Part-time. *Faculty:* 31 full-time (23 women), 12 part-time/adjunct (9 women). *Students:* 294 full-time (219 women), 128 part-time (109 women); includes 71 minority (20 Black or African American, non-Hispanic/Latino; 1 American Indian or Alaska Native, non-Hispanic/Latino; 15 Asian, non-Hispanic/Latino; 30 Hispanic/Latino; 5 Two or more races, non-Hispanic/Latino). Average age 28. 2,666 applicants, 6% accepted, 142 enrolled. In 2019, 115 master's, 30 doctorates awarded. *Degree requirements:* For master's, minimum GPA of 3.0, portfolio; for doctorate, minimum GPA of 3.0, scholarly capstone project. *Entrance requirements:* For master's, GRE or MAT (waived if applicant has an undergraduate GPA of 3.0 or higher), BSN from ACEN- or CCNE-accredited program, minimum undergraduate GPA of 3.0, active RN license or eligibility, two letters of recommendation, essay, health care experience, personal interview; for doctorate, BSN or MSN from ACEN- or CCNE-accredited institution, minimum GPA of 3.3 in graduate program, current licensure as an RN. Additional exam requirements/recommendations for international students: required—TOEFL (minimum score 104 iBT). *Application deadline:* Applications are processed on a rolling basis. Application fee: $50. Electronic applications accepted. *Expenses:* Contact institution. *Financial support:* Applicants required to submit FAFSA. *Unit head:* Ronald Nordone, Dean of Graduate Education,

610-282-1100 Ext. 1289, E-mail: ronald.nordone@desales.edu. *Application contact:* Julia Ferraro, Director of Graduate Admissions, 610-282-1100 Ext. 1768, E-mail: gradadmissions@desales.edu.

**Drexel University,** College of Nursing and Health Professions, Division of Graduate Nursing, Philadelphia, PA 19104-2875. Offers adult acute care (MSN); adult psychiatric/mental health (MSN); advanced practice nursing (MSN); clinical trials research (MSN); family nurse practitioner (MSN); leadership in health systems management (MSN); nursing education (MSN); pediatric primary care (MSN); women's health (MSN). *Accreditation:* AACN. Electronic applications accepted.

**Duke University,** School of Nursing, Durham, NC 27708. Offers acute care pediatric nurse practitioner (MSN, Post-Graduate Certificate); adult-gerontology nurse practitioner (MSN, Post-Graduate Certificate), including acute care, primary care; family nurse practitioner (MSN, Post-Graduate Certificate); neonatal nurse practitioner (MSN, Post-Graduate Certificate); nurse anesthesia (DNP); nurse practitioner (DNP); nursing (PhD); nursing and health care leadership (MSN, Post-Graduate Certificate); nursing education (MSN, Post-Graduate Certificate); nursing informatics (MSN, Post-Graduate Certificate); pediatric nurse practitioner (MSN, Post-Graduate Certificate), including primary care; psychiatric mental health nurse practitioner (MSN, Post-Graduate Certificate); women's health nurse practitioner (MSN, Post-Graduate Certificate). *Accreditation:* AACN; AANA/CANAEP. *Program availability:* Part-time, evening/weekend, online with on-campus intensives. *Faculty:* 48 full-time (40 women), 32 part-time/adjunct (28 women). *Students:* 666 full-time (601 women), 157 part-time (139 women); includes 193 minority (61 Black or African American, non-Hispanic/Latino; 4 American Indian or Alaska Native, non-Hispanic/Latino; 57 Asian, non-Hispanic/Latino; 49 Hispanic/Latino; 1 Native Hawaiian or other Pacific Islander, non-Hispanic/Latino; 21 Two or more races, non-Hispanic/Latino), 8 international. Average age 34. 761 applicants, 33% accepted, 149 enrolled. In 2019, 213 master's, 74 doctorates, 18 other advanced degrees awarded. Terminal master's awarded for partial completion of doctoral program. *Degree requirements:* For master's, thesis optional; for doctorate, capstone project. *Entrance requirements:* For master's, MSN applicants are no longer required to take the GRE, 1 year of nursing experience (recommended), BSN, minimum GPA of 3.0, previous course work in statistics; for doctorate, GRE is required for the DNP in Nurse Anesthesia, BSN or MSN, minimum GPA of 3.0, resume, personal statement, graduate statistics and research methods course, current licensure as a registered nurse, transcripts from all post-secondary institutions; for Post-Graduate Certificate, MSN, licensure or eligibility as a professional nurse, transcripts from all post-secondary institutions, previous course work in statistics. Additional exam requirements/recommendations for international students: required—TOEFL (minimum score 100 iBT), IELTS (minimum score 7). *Application deadline:* For fall admission, 12/1 for domestic and international students; for spring admission, 5/1 for domestic and international students. Application fee: $50. Electronic applications accepted. *Expenses:* Contact institution. *Financial support:* Institutionally sponsored loans, scholarships/grants, and traineeships available. Support available to part-time students. Financial award applicants required to submit FAFSA. *Unit head:* Dr. Marion E. Broome, Dean/Vice Chancellor for Nursing Affairs/Associate Vice President for Academic Affairs for Nursing, 919-684-9446, Fax: 919-684-9414, E-mail: marion.broome@duke.edu. *Application contact:* Dr. Ernie Rushing, Director of Admissions and Recruitment, 919-668-6274, Fax: 919-668-4693, E-mail: ernie.rushing@dm.duke.edu.
Website: http://www.nursing.duke.edu/

**Duquesne University,** School of Nursing, Master of Science in Nursing Program, Pittsburgh, PA 15282-0001. Offers family (individual across the life span) nurse practitioner (MSN); forensic nursing (MSN); nursing education and faculty role (MSN). *Accreditation:* AACN. *Program availability:* Part-time, evening/weekend, minimal on-campus study. *Entrance requirements:* For master's, current RN license; BSN with minimum GPA of 3.0; minimum of 1 year of full-time work experience as RN prior to registration in clinical or specialty course. Additional exam requirements/recommendations for international students: required—TOEFL (minimum score 600 paper-based; 100 iBT). Electronic applications accepted. *Expenses:* Contact institution.

**Duquesne University,** School of Nursing, Post Master's Certificate Program, Pittsburgh, PA 15282-0001. Offers family (individual across the life span) nurse practitioner (Post-Master's Certificate); forensic nursing (Post-Master's Certificate); nursing education and faculty role (Post-Master's Certificate). *Program availability:* Part-time, evening/weekend, minimal on-campus study. *Entrance requirements:* For degree, current RN license, BSN, MSN. Additional exam requirements/recommendations for international students: required—TOEFL (minimum score 600 paper-based; 100 iBT). Electronic applications accepted. *Expenses:* Contact institution.

**Eastern Michigan University,** Graduate School, College of Health and Human Services, School of Nursing, Ypsilanti, MI 48197. Offers nursing (MSN); teaching in health care systems (MSN, Graduate Certificate). *Accreditation:* AACN. *Program availability:* Part-time, evening/weekend, online learning. *Faculty:* 27 full-time (24 women). *Students:* 23 full-time (17 women), 36 part-time (29 women); includes 19 minority (6 Black or African American, non-Hispanic/Latino; 5 Asian, non-Hispanic/Latino; 7 Hispanic/Latino; 1 Two or more races, non-Hispanic/Latino), 1 international. Average age 37. 27 applicants, 7% accepted. In 2019, 14 master's, 3 other advanced degrees awarded. *Entrance requirements:* For master's, GRE General Test, Michigan RN license. Additional exam requirements/recommendations for international students: required—TOEFL. *Application deadline:* Applications are processed on a rolling basis. Application fee: $45. *Financial support:* Fellowships, research assistantships with full tuition reimbursements, teaching assistantships with full tuition reimbursements, career-related internships or fieldwork, Federal Work-Study, institutionally sponsored loans, scholarships/grants, tuition waivers (partial), and unspecified assistantships available. Support available to part-time students. Financial award applicants required to submit FAFSA. *Unit head:* Dr. Michael Williams, Director, 734-487-2310, Fax: 734-487-6946, E-mail: mwilliams@emich.edu. *Application contact:* Deanna Kowaleski, Coordinator, School of Nursing, 734-487-6599, Fax: 734-487-6946, E-mail: dkowales@emich.edu.
Website: http://www.emich.edu/nursing

**East Tennessee State University,** College of Graduate and Continuing Studies, College of Nursing, Johnson City, TN 37614. Offers acute care nurse practitioner (DNP); adult-gerontology primary care nurse practitioner (DNP); adult/gerontological nurse practitioner (Postbaccalaureate Certificate); executive leadership in nursing (DNP, Postbaccalaureate Certificate); family nurse practitioner (MSN, DNP, Post-Master's Certificate, Postbaccalaureate Certificate); nursing (PhD); nursing administration (MSN); nursing education (MSN); pediatric primary care nurse practitioner (DNP); psychiatric mental health nurse practitioner (Postbaccalaureate Certificate); psychiatric/mental health nurse practitioner (MSN, DNP, Post-Master's Certificate); women's health care nurse practitioner (DNP). *Accreditation:* AACN. *Program availability:* Part-time, evening/weekend, online learning. *Degree requirements:* For master's and other advanced degree, comprehensive exam, practicum; for doctorate, comprehensive exam, thesis/dissertation (for some programs), practicum, internship, evidence of professional malpractice insurance, CPR certification. *Entrance requirements:* For master's, bachelor's degree, minimum GPA of 3.0, current RN license and eligibility to practice, resume, three letters of recommendation; for doctorate, GRE General Test, MSN (for PhD), BSN or MSN (for DNP), current RN license and eligibility to practice, 2 years of full-time registered nurse work experience or equivalent, three letters of recommendation, resume or curriculum vitae, interview, writing sample; for other advanced degree, MSN, minimum GPA of 3.0, current RN license and eligibility to practice, three letters of recommendation, resume or curriculum vitae; DNP with designated concentration in advanced clinical practice or nursing administration (for select programs). Additional exam requirements/recommendations for international students: required—TOEFL (minimum score 600 paper-based; 79 iBT). Electronic applications accepted.

**Edinboro University of Pennsylvania,** Department of Nursing, Edinboro, PA 16444. Offers advanced practice nursing (DNP); family nurse practitioner (MSN); nurse educator (MSN). *Program availability:* Part-time, evening/weekend. *Faculty:* 6 full-time (5 women), 1 (woman) part-time/adjunct. *Students:* 105 part-time (85 women); includes 9 minority (4 Black or African American, non-Hispanic/Latino; 2 Asian, non-Hispanic/Latino; 3 Hispanic/Latino). Average age 37. 57 applicants, 100% accepted, 57 enrolled. *Degree requirements:* For master's, thesis, competency exam. *Entrance requirements:* For master's, GRE or MAT, minimum GPA 2.75; one year of recent full-time clinical practice or two years of part-time clinical practice; licensure as a registered nurse in the state where they plan to complete clinical practicum; for doctorate, minimum GPA 3.25; current unencumbered licenses as a Registered nurse. Additional exam requirements/recommendations for international students: required—TOEFL (minimum score 550 paper-based; 213 iBT), IELTS (minimum score 6.5). Application fee: $40. Electronic applications accepted. *Expenses:* Tuition & Fees: 889.8/credit for PA resident; 1025.24/credit for non-PA resident. *Financial support:* Application deadline: 2/15; applicants required to submit FAFSA. *Unit head:* Dr. Victoria Hedderick, Chair, 814-732-1655, E-mail: vhedderick@edinboro.edu. *Application contact:* Dr. Victoria Hedderick, Chair, 814-732-1655, E-mail: vhedderick@edinboro.edu.
Website: https://www.edinboro.edu/academics/schools-and-departments/cshp/departments/nursing/

**Elms College,** School of Nursing, Chicopee, MA 01013-2839. Offers adult-gerontology acute care nurse practitioner (DNP); family nurse practitioner (DNP); health systems innovation and leadership (DNP); nursing and health services management (MSN); nursing education (MSN). *Accreditation:* AACN. *Program availability:* Part-time, evening/weekend. *Faculty:* 3 full-time (2 women), 2 part-time/adjunct (both women). *Students:* 13 full-time (11 women), 97 part-time (91 women); includes 8 minority (4 Black or African American, non-Hispanic/Latino; 2 Hispanic/Latino; 2 Two or more races, non-Hispanic/Latino). Average age 38. 39 applicants, 87% accepted, 27 enrolled. In 2019, 4 master's, 20 doctorates awarded. *Entrance requirements:* Additional exam requirements/recommendations for international students: required—TOEFL (minimum score 80 iBT). *Application deadline:* For fall admission, 7/1 priority date for domestic students; for spring admission, 11/1 priority date for domestic students. Applications are processed on a rolling basis. Electronic applications accepted. *Financial support:* Applicants required to submit FAFSA. *Unit head:* Dr. Kathleen Scoble, Dean, School of Nursing, 413-265-2204, E-mail: scoblek@elms.edu. *Application contact:* Nancy Davis, Director, Office of Graduate and Continuing Education Admissions, 413-265-2456, E-mail: grad@elms.edu.

**Emmanuel College,** Graduate and Professional Programs, Graduate Program in Nursing, Boston, MA 02115. Offers education (MSN, Graduate Certificate); management (MSN, Graduate Certificate). *Accreditation:* AACN. *Program availability:* Part-time, evening/weekend. *Faculty:* 2 full-time (both women), 3 part-time/adjunct (all women). *Students:* 27 part-time (all women); includes 7 minority (3 Black or African American, non-Hispanic/Latino; 1 Asian, non-Hispanic/Latino; 3 Hispanic/Latino). Average age 43. In 2019, 14 master's awarded. *Degree requirements:* For master's, 30 credits (eight 3 credit courses and 1 6 credit course); for Graduate Certificate, 12 credits (two 3 credit courses and 1 6 credit course). *Entrance requirements:* For degree, completed application, transcripts from all regionally-accredited institutions attended (showing proof of bachelor's degree completion), proof of current RN license, 2 letters of recommendation, admissions essay, current resume. Additional exam requirements/recommendations for international students: required—TOEFL. *Application deadline:* Applications are processed on a rolling basis. Electronic applications accepted. *Expenses:* $2,581 per course. *Financial support:* Application deadline: 2/15; applicants required to submit FAFSA. *Unit head:* Diane Shea, Associate Dean for Nursing/Professor of Nursing Practice, 617-732-1604, E-mail: shead@emmanuel.edu. *Application contact:* Helen Muterperl, Director of Graduate and Professional Programs, 617-735-9700, Fax: 617-507-0434, E-mail: gpp@emmanuel.edu.
Website: http://www.emmanuel.edu/graduate-professional-programs/academics/nursing.html

**Endicott College,** School of Nursing, Program in Nursing, Beverly, MA 01915. Offers family nurse practitioner (MSN, Post-Master's Certificate); global health (MSN); nursing administration (MSN); nursing administrator (Post-Master's Certificate); nursing educator (MSN, Post-Master's Certificate). *Program availability:* Part-time, evening/weekend, blended/hybrid learning. *Faculty:* 4 full-time (all women), 18 part-time/adjunct (13 women). *Students:* 20 full-time (19 women), 71 part-time (70 women); includes 11 minority (5 Black or African American, non-Hispanic/Latino; 3 Asian, non-Hispanic/Latino; 2 Hispanic/Latino; 1 Two or more races, non-Hispanic/Latino). Average age 37. 32 applicants, 41% accepted, 12 enrolled. In 2019, 34 master's, 6 other advanced degrees awarded. *Degree requirements:* For master's, thesis, Internship and Capstone portfolio (S); Minimum 600 faculty supervised clinical hours (S). *Entrance requirements:* Additional exam requirements/recommendations for international students: required—TOEFL. *Application deadline:* Applications are processed on a rolling basis. Application fee: $50. Electronic applications accepted. *Expenses:* Tuition varies by program. *Financial support:* Applicants required to submit FAFSA. *Unit head:* Nancy Meedzan, DNP, RN, CNE, Dean, School of Nursing, 978-232-2328, E-mail: nmeedzan@endicott.edu. *Application contact:* Ian Menchini, Director, Graduate Enrollment and Advising, 978-232-5292, Fax: 978-232-3000, E-mail: imenchin@endicott.edu.
Website: https://www.endicott.edu/academics/schools/nursing/graduate-programs

**Felician University,** Master of Science in Nursing Program, Lodi, NJ 07644-2117. Offers adult-gerontology nurse practitioner (MSN, PMC); executive leadership (MSN, PMC); family nurse practitioner (MSN, PMC); nursing education (MSN, PMC). *Accreditation:* AACN. *Program availability:* Evening/weekend, online only, 100% online, blended/hybrid learning. *Degree requirements:* For master's, thesis, clinical presentation; for PMC, thesis, education project. *Entrance requirements:* For master's, BSN; minimum GPA of 3.0; 2 letters of recommendation; NJ RN license; personal statement; for PMC, RN license, minimum GPA of 3.0. Additional exam requirements/recommendations for international students: required—TOEFL (minimum score 550 paper-based; 79 iBT), IELTS (minimum score 6.5), PTE (minimum score 56). Electronic applications accepted. Application fee is waived when completed online. *Expenses:* Contact institution.

**Ferris State University,** College of Health Professions, School of Nursing, Big Rapids, MI 49307. Offers nursing (MSN); nursing administration (MSN); nursing education (MSN); nursing informatics (MSN). *Accreditation:* ACEN. *Program availability:* Part-time, evening/weekend, online only, 100% online. *Faculty:* 7 full-time (all women), 1 (woman) part-time/adjunct. *Students:* 103 part-time (95 women); includes 14 minority (2 Black or African American, non-Hispanic/Latino; 6 American Indian or Alaska Native, non-

Hispanic/Latino; 4 Hispanic/Latino; 2 Two or more races, non-Hispanic/Latino). Average age 38. 31 applicants, 97% accepted, 24 enrolled. In 2019, 24 master's awarded. *Degree requirements:* For master's, practicum, practicum project. *Entrance requirements:* For master's, BS in nursing (for nursing education track); BS in nursing or related field (for nursing administration and nursing informatics tracks); registered nurse license, writing sample, letters of reference, 2 years' clinical experience (recommended). Additional exam requirements/recommendations for international students: required—TOEFL (minimum score 550 paper-based; 79 iBT). *Application deadline:* For fall admission, 4/15 priority date for domestic and international students; for spring admission, 10/15 for domestic and international students. Electronic applications accepted. Tuition and fees vary according to degree level, program and student level. *Financial support:* In 2019–20, 7 students received support. Career-related internships or fieldwork and scholarships/grants available. Financial award application deadline: 4/15; financial award applicants required to submit FAFSA. *Unit head:* Dr. Wendy Lenon, Chair, School of Nursing, 231-591-2267, Fax: 231-591-2325, E-mail: WendyLenon@ferris.edu. *Application contact:* Dr. Sharon Colley, MSN Program Coordinator, 231-591-2288, Fax: 231-591-2325, E-mail: colleys@ferris.edu.
Website: http://www.ferris.edu/htmls/colleges/alliedhe/Nursing/homepage.htm

**Florida Gulf Coast University,** Elaine Nicpon Marieb College of Health and Human Services, Program in Nurse Educator, Fort Myers, FL 33965-6565. Offers MSN. *Program availability:* Online learning. *Entrance requirements:* Additional exam requirements/recommendations for international students: required—TOEFL (minimum score 550 paper-based). Electronic applications accepted. *Expenses: Tuition, area resident:* Full-time $6974; part-time $4350 per credit hour. Tuition, state resident: full-time $6974; part-time $4350 per credit hour. Tuition, nonresident: full-time $28,169; part-time $17,595 per credit hour. *International tuition:* $28,169 full-time. *Required fees:* $2027; $1267 per credit hour. $507 per semester. Tuition and fees vary according to course load.

**Florida National University,** Program in Nursing, Hialeah, FL 33139. Offers family nurse practitioner (MSN); nurse educator (MSN); nurse leadership and management (MSN). *Program availability:* 100% online, blended/hybrid learning. *Faculty:* 6 full-time (4 women), 9 part-time/adjunct (7 women). *Students:* 14 full-time (10 women), 204 part-time (151 women); includes 213 minority (21 Black or African American, non-Hispanic/Latino; 1 Asian, non-Hispanic/Latino; 191 Hispanic/Latino). Average age 40. 54 applicants, 100% accepted, 54 enrolled. In 2019, 53 master's awarded. *Degree requirements:* For master's, practicum. *Entrance requirements:* For master's, active registered nurse license, BSN from accredited institution. Additional exam requirements/recommendations for international students: recommended—TOEFL. *Expenses:* Contact institution. *Financial support:* Scholarships/grants available. *Unit head:* Dr. Lydie Janvier, Master of Science in Nursing Program Director, 305-821-3333 Ext. 1056, Fax: 305-362-0595, E-mail: ljanvier@fnu.edu. *Application contact:* Dr. Lydie Janvier, Master of Science in Nursing Program Director, 305-821-3333 Ext. 1056, Fax: 305-362-0595, E-mail: ljanvier@fnu.edu.
Website: https://www.fnu.edu/prospective-students/our-programs/select-a-program/master-of-business-administration/nursing-msn-master/

**Florida Southern College,** School of Nursing and Health Sciences, Lakeland, FL 33801. Offers adult gerontology clinical nurse specialist (MSN); adult gerontology primary care nurse practitioner (MSN); family nurse practitioner (MSN); nurse educator (MSN); nursing administration (MSN). *Accreditation:* AACN. *Program availability:* Part-time, The Nurse Educator MSN degree concentration and NE postmasters certificate are fully online. The Nursing Administrative Leadership MSN degree concentration is delivered in blended/hybrid format. *Faculty:* 6 full-time (all women), 1 (woman) part-time/adjunct. *Students:* 145 full-time (131 women), 1 (woman) part-time; includes 70 minority (30 Black or African American, non-Hispanic/Latino; 11 Asian, non-Hispanic/Latino; 25 Hispanic/Latino; 4 Two or more races, non-Hispanic/Latino), 1 international. Average age 39. 81 applicants, 89% accepted, 50 enrolled. In 2019, 53 master's awarded. *Degree requirements:* For master's, comprehensive exam, 660 clinical hours (for Family Nurse Practitioner); 540 clinical hours (for Adult-Gerontology Primary Care Nurse Practitioner). *Entrance requirements:* For master's, Florida RN license, 3 letters of recommendation, professional statement, minimum GPA of 3.0 in the last 60 credit hours of BSN, BSN earned from a regionally accredited institution and a CCNE, CNEA, or ACEN accredited nursing program, resume, admission interview. Additional exam requirements/recommendations for international students: required—TOEFL (minimum score 550 paper-based; 79 iBT), IELTS (minimum score 6.5), International students from countries where English is not the standard for daily communication must submit either the TOEFL or IELTS. *Application deadline:* For fall admission, 6/1 for domestic and international students; for spring admission, 10/1 for domestic and international students. Applications are processed on a rolling basis. Electronic applications accepted. *Expenses:* DNP: $725 per credit hour tuition, $50 per semester technology fee (for 5-8 hours), $100 per semester technology fee (for 9-12 hours); MSN: $600 per credit hour tuition, $50 per semester technology fee (for 5-8 hours), $100 per semester technology fee (for 9-12 hours), $35 per semester insurance and lab supplies fees. *Financial support:* In 2019–20, 1 student received support. Employee tuition grants, athletic scholarships for students still eligible available. Financial award application deadline: 8/20; financial award applicants required to submit FAFSA. *Unit head:* Dr. Linda Comer, Dean, 863-680-3951, Fax: 863-680-3860, E-mail: lcomer@flsouthern.edu. *Application contact:* Kimberly Smith, Admission Counselor and Advisor for Nursing, 863-680-3090, Fax: 863-680-3872, E-mail: ksmith@flsouthern.edu.
Website: www.flsouthern.edu/sage

**Framingham State University,** Graduate Studies, Program in Nursing, Framingham, MA 01701-9101. Offers nursing education (MSN); nursing leadership (MSN). *Accreditation:* AACN. *Entrance requirements:* For master's, BSN; minimum cumulative undergraduate GPA of 3.0, 3.25 in nursing courses; coursework in statistics; 2 letters of recommendation; interview. Electronic applications accepted.

**Francis Marion University,** Graduate Programs, Department of Nursing, Florence, SC 29502-0547. Offers family nurse practitioner (MSN); family nurse practitioner with nurse educator certificate (MSN); nurse educator (MSN). *Program availability:* Part-time. *Entrance requirements:* For master's, GRE, official transcripts, two letters of recommendation from professional associates or former professors, written statement of applicant's career goals, current nursing license. Additional exam requirements/recommendations for international students: required—TOEFL (minimum score 550 paper-based; 79 iBT). Electronic applications accepted. *Expenses:* Contact institution.

**Franklin Pierce University,** Graduate and Professional Studies, Rindge, NH 03461-0060. Offers curriculum and instruction (M Ed); elementary education (MS Ed); emerging network technologies (Graduate Certificate); energy and sustainability studies (MBA, Graduate Certificate); health administration (MBA, Graduate Certificate); human resource management (MBA, Graduate Certificate); information technology (MBA); leadership (MBA); nursing education (MS); nursing leadership (MS); physical therapy (DPT); physician assistant studies (MPAS); special education (M Ed); sports management (MBA). *Accreditation:* APTA. *Program availability:* Part-time, 100% online, blended/hybrid learning. *Degree requirements:* For master's, concentrated original research projects; student teaching; fieldwork and/or internship; leadership project; PRAXIS I and II (for M Ed); for doctorate, concentrated original research projects, clinical fieldwork and/or internship, leadership project. *Entrance requirements:* For master's, minimum GPA of 2.5, 3 letters of recommendation; competencies in accounting, economics, statistics, and computer skills through life experience or undergraduate coursework (for MBA); certification/e-portfolio, minimum C grade in all education courses (for M Ed); license to practice as RN (for MS); for doctorate, GRE, 80 hours of observation/work in PT settings; completion of anatomy, chemistry, physics, and statistics; minimum GPA of 3.0. Additional exam requirements/recommendations for international students: required—TOEFL (minimum score 550 paper-based; 61 iBT). Electronic applications accepted.

**Frostburg State University,** College of Liberal Arts and Sciences, Department of Nursing, Frostburg, MD 21532-1099. Offers nursing administration (MSN); nursing education (MSN). *Program availability:* Part-time, online learning. *Entrance requirements:* For master's, current unrestricted RN license; BSN from a nursing program accredited by CCNE or ACEN. Additional exam requirements/recommendations for international students: required—TOEFL.

**George Mason University,** College of Health and Human Services, School of Nursing, Fairfax, VA 22030. Offers adult gerontology (DNP); adult/gerontological nurse practitioner (MSN); family nurse practitioner (MSN, DNP); nurse educator (MSN); nursing (PhD); nursing administration (MSN, DNP); nursing education (Certificate); psychiatric mental health (DNP). *Accreditation:* AACN. *Program availability:* Part-time, evening/weekend, blended/hybrid learning. *Degree requirements:* For master's, comprehensive exam (for some programs), thesis in clinical classes; for doctorate, comprehensive exam (for some programs), thesis/dissertation (for some programs). *Entrance requirements:* For master's, 2 official transcripts; expanded goals statement; resume; BSN from accredited institution; minimum GPA of 3.0 in last 60 credits of undergraduate work; 2 letters of recommendation; completion of undergraduate statistics and graduate-level bivariate statistics; certification in professional CPR; for doctorate, GRE, 2 official transcripts; expanded goals statement; resume; 2 recommendation letters; nursing license; at least 1 year of work experience as an RN; interview; writing sample; evidence of graduate-level course in applied statistics; master's degree in nursing with minimum GPA of 3.5; for Certificate, 2 official transcripts; expanded goals statement; resume; master's degree from accredited institution or currently enrolled with minimum GPA of 3.0. Additional exam requirements/recommendations for international students: required—TOEFL (minimum score 570 paper-based; 88 iBT), IELTS (minimum score 6.5), PTE (minimum score 59). Electronic applications accepted. *Expenses:* Contact institution.

**Georgetown University,** Graduate School of Arts and Sciences, School of Nursing and Health Studies, Washington, DC 20057. Offers acute care nurse practitioner (MS); clinical nurse specialist (MS); family nurse practitioner (MS); health systems administration (MS); nurse anesthesia (MS); nurse-midwifery (MS); nursing (DNP); nursing education (MS). *Accreditation:* AACN; AANA/CANAEP (one or more programs are accredited); ACNM/ACME (one or more programs are accredited). *Degree requirements:* For master's, thesis optional. *Entrance requirements:* For master's, GRE General Test or MAT, bachelor's degree in nursing from ACEN-accredited school, minimum undergraduate GPA of 3.0. Additional exam requirements/recommendations for international students: required—TOEFL.

**Georgia Southern University,** Jack N. Averitt College of Graduate Studies, Waters College of Health Professions, School of Nursing, Nurse Educator Certificate Program, Statesboro, GA 30458. Offers Certificate. *Students:* 6 part-time (5 women). Average age 42. 6 applicants, 17% accepted, 1 enrolled. In 2019, 4 Certificates awarded. *Entrance requirements:* For degree, master's degree in nursing, minimum GPA of 3.0, current RN license. Additional exam requirements/recommendations for international students: required—TOEFL (minimum score 80 iBT). *Application deadline:* For fall admission, 7/31 for domestic students; for spring admission, 11/30 for domestic students; for summer admission, 3/31 for domestic students. *Expenses: Tuition, area resident:* Full-time $4986; part-time $277 per credit hour. Tuition, nonresident: full-time $19,890; part-time $1105 per credit hour. *International tuition:* $19,890 full-time. *Required fees:* $2114; $1057 per semester. $1057 per semester. Tuition and fees vary according to course load, campus/location and program. *Financial support:* In 2019–20, 2 students received support. *Unit head:* Dr. Sharon Radzyminski, Department Chair, 912-478-5455, Fax: 912-478-0536, E-mail: sradzyminski@georgiasouthern.edu. *Application contact:* Dr. Sharon Radzyminski, Department Chair, 912-478-5455, Fax: 912-478-0536, E-mail: sradzyminski@georgiasouthern.edu.

**Georgia Southwestern State University,** College of Nursing and Health Sciences, Americus, GA 31709-4693. Offers family nurse practitioner (MSN); health informatics (Postbaccalaureate Certificate); nurse educator (Post Master's Certificate); nursing educator (MSN); nursing informatics (MSN); nursing leadership (MSN). *Program availability:* Part-time, online only, all theory courses are offered online. *Faculty:* 9 full-time (all women), 5 part-time/adjunct (all women). *Students:* 18 full-time (14 women), 104 part-time (91 women); includes 45 minority (31 Black or African American, non-Hispanic/Latino; 1 American Indian or Alaska Native, non-Hispanic/Latino; 4 Asian, non-Hispanic/Latino; 3 Hispanic/Latino; 6 Two or more races, non-Hispanic/Latino). Average age 36. 96 applicants, 45% accepted, 24 enrolled. In 2019, 53 master's awarded. *Degree requirements:* For master's, thesis (for some programs), minimum cumulative GPA of 3.0; maximum of 6 credit hours with C grade and no D grades; degree completed within 7 calendar years from initial enrollment date in graduate courses; for other advanced degree, minimum cumulative GPA of 3.0; maximum of 6 credit hours with C grade and no D grades; degree completed within 7 calendar years from initial enrollment date in graduate courses. *Entrance requirements:* For master's, baccalaureate degree in nursing from regionally-accredited institution and nationally-accredited nursing program with minimum GPA of 3.0; three completed recommendation forms from professional peer or clinical supervisor; current unencumbered RN license in state where clinical course requirements will be met; proof of immunizations; for other advanced degree, Baccalaureate or masters degree (depending upon certificate) in nursing; Minimum GPA of 3.0; 3 completed recommendation forms; current unencumbered RN license in state where clinical course requirements will be met. Application fee: $25. Electronic applications accepted. *Expenses:* $385.00 per credit hour tuition, plus fees, which vary according to enrolled credit hours. *Financial support:* Application deadline: 6/1; applicants required to submit FAFSA. *Unit head:* Dr. Sandra Daniel, Dean, 229-931-2275. *Application contact:* Office of Graduate Admissions, 800-338-0082, Fax: 229-931-2983, E-mail: graduateadmissions@gsw.edu.
Website: https://www.gsw.edu/academics/schools-and-departments/college-of-nursing-and-health-sciences/school-of-nursing/nursing-programs/graduate

**Graceland University,** School of Nursing, Independence, MO 64050-3434. Offers adult and gerontology acute care (MSN, PMC); family nurse practitioner (MSN, PMC); nurse educator (MSN, PMC); organizational leadership (DNP). *Accreditation:* AACN. *Program availability:* Part-time, online only, 100% online. *Degree requirements:* For master's, comprehensive exam (for some programs), thesis optional, scholarly project; for doctorate, capstone project. *Entrance requirements:* For master's, BSN from nationally-accredited program, RN license, minimum GPA of 3.0, satisfactory criminal background check, three professional reference letters, professional goals statement of 150 words or less; for doctorate, MSN from nationally-accredited program, RN license, minimum GPA

of 3.0, criminal background check. Additional exam requirements/recommendations for international students: required—TOEFL (minimum score 550 paper-based; 80 iBT). Electronic applications accepted. *Expenses:* Contact institution.

**Grand Canyon University,** College of Nursing and Health Care Professions, Phoenix, AZ 85017-1097. Offers acute care nurse practitioner (MSN, PMC); family nurse practitioner (MSN, PMC); health care administration (MS); health care informatics (MS, MSN); leadership in health care systems (MSN); nursing (DNP); nursing education (MSN, PMC); public health (MPH, MSN); MBA/MSN. *Accreditation:* AACN. *Program availability:* Part-time, evening/weekend, online learning. *Degree requirements:* For master's and PMC, comprehensive exam (for some programs). *Entrance requirements:* For master's, minimum cumulative and science course undergraduate GPA of 3.0. Additional exam requirements/recommendations for international students: required—TOEFL (minimum score 575 paper-based; 90 iBT), IELTS (minimum score 7).

**Grand View University,** Graduate Studies, Des Moines, IA 50316-1599. Offers athletic training (MS); clinical nurse leader (MSN, Post Master's Certificate); nursing education (MSN, Post Master's Certificate); organizational leadership (MS); sport management (MS); teacher leadership (M Ed); urban education (M Ed). *Program availability:* Part-time, evening/weekend. *Degree requirements:* For master's, completion of all required coursework in common core and selected track with minimum cumulative GPA of 3.0 and no more than two grades of C. *Entrance requirements:* For master's, GRE, GMAT, or essay, minimum undergraduate GPA of 3.0, professional resume, 3 letters of recommendation, interview. Additional exam requirements/recommendations for international students: required—TOEFL (minimum score 550 paper-based). Electronic applications accepted.

**Grantham University,** College of Nursing and Allied Health, Lenexa, KS 66219. Offers case management (MSN); health systems management (MS); healthcare administration (MHA); nursing education (MSN); nursing informatics (MSN); nursing management and organizational leadership (MSN). *Program availability:* Part-time, evening/weekend, online only, 100% online. *Students:* 180 full-time (135 women), 61 part-time (47 women); includes 124 minority (71 Black or African American, non-Hispanic/Latino; 1 American Indian or Alaska Native, non-Hispanic/Latino; 17 Asian, non-Hispanic/Latino; 17 Hispanic/Latino; 1 Native Hawaiian or other Pacific Islander, non-Hispanic/Latino; 17 Two or more races, non-Hispanic/Latino). Average age 40. 53 applicants, 89% accepted, 37 enrolled. In 2019, 100 master's awarded. *Entrance requirements:* For master's, Graduate: A minimum score of 530 on the paper-based TOEFL, or 71 on the internet-based TOEFL, 6.5 on the IELTS, or 50 on the PTE Academic Score Report. Additional exam requirements/recommendations for international students: required—TOEFL (minimum score 530 paper-based; 71 iBT), IELTS (minimum score 6.5), PTE (minimum score 50). *Application deadline:* Applications are processed on a rolling basis. Electronic applications accepted. *Expenses:* Contact institution. *Financial support:* Scholarships/grants available. Financial award applicants required to submit FAFSA. *Unit head:* Dr. Cheryl Rules, Dean of the College of Nursing and the School of Allied Health changing to College of Health Professions, 913-309-4783, Fax: 844-897-6490, E-mail: crules@grantham.edu. *Application contact:* Adam Wright, Associate VP, Enrollment Services, 800-955-2527 Ext. 803, Fax: 877-304-4467, E-mail: admissions@grantham.edu.
Website: http://www.grantham.edu/nursing-and-allied-health/

**Gwynedd Mercy University,** Frances M. Maguire School of Nursing and Health Professions, Gwynedd Valley, PA 19437-0901. Offers clinical nurse specialist (MSN), including gerontology, oncology, pediatrics; nurse educator (MSN); nurse practitioner (MSN), including adult health, pediatric health; nursing (DNP). *Accreditation:* ACEN. *Program availability:* Part-time, blended/hybrid learning. *Faculty:* 4 full-time (all women), 1 (woman) part-time/adjunct. *Students:* 52 full-time (47 women), 58 part-time (52 women); includes 28 minority (17 Black or African American, non-Hispanic/Latino; 9 Asian, non-Hispanic/Latino; 2 Hispanic/Latino). Average age 33. 35 applicants, 43% accepted, 14 enrolled. In 2019, 26 master's awarded. *Degree requirements:* For master's, thesis optional; for doctorate, evidence-based scholarly project. *Entrance requirements:* For master's, current nursing experience, physical assessment, course work in statistics, BSN from ACEN-accredited program, 2 letters of recommendation, personal interview. *Application deadline:* For fall admission, 4/15 for domestic and international students. Applications are processed on a rolling basis. Electronic applications accepted. *Expenses:* Contact institution. *Financial support:* Scholarships/grants, traineeships, and unspecified assistantships available. Financial award application deadline: 4/15. *Unit head:* Dr. Ann Phalen, Dean, 215-646-7300 Ext. 539, Fax: 215-641-5517, E-mail: phalen.a@gmercyu.edu. *Application contact:* Mary Hermann, Associate Dean, 215-646-7300, E-mail: herman.m@gmercyu.edu.
Website: http://www.gmercyu.edu/academics/graduate-programs/nursing

**Hampton University,** School of Nursing, Hampton, VA 23668. Offers community health nursing (MS); family nurse practitioner (MS); family research (PhD); nursing administration (MS); nursing education (MS). *Accreditation:* AACN. *Program availability:* Part-time, online learning. *Students:* 3 full-time (all women), 13 part-time (12 women); includes 15 minority (all Black or African American, non-Hispanic/Latino). Average age 49. 4 applicants, 25% accepted. In 2019, 3 master's, 5 doctorates awarded. *Degree requirements:* For master's, comprehensive exam, thesis optional; for doctorate, comprehensive exam, thesis/dissertation. *Entrance requirements:* For master's, GRE General Test. *Application deadline:* For fall admission, 6/1 priority date for domestic students, 4/1 priority date for international students; for spring admission, 11/1 priority date for domestic students, 9/1 priority date for international students; for summer admission, 4/1 priority date for domestic students, 2/1 priority date for international students. Applications are processed on a rolling basis. Application fee: $35. Electronic applications accepted. *Financial support:* In 2019–20, 2 students received support. Fellowships, research assistantships, teaching assistantships, career-related internships or fieldwork, Federal Work-Study, institutionally sponsored loans, and scholarships/grants available. Support available to part-time students. Financial award application deadline: 6/30; financial award applicants required to submit FAFSA. *Unit head:* Dr. Shevellanie Lott, Dean, 757-727-5654, E-mail: shevellanie.lott@hamptonu.edu. *Application contact:* Dr. Shevellanie Lott, Dean, 757-727-5654, E-mail: shevellanie.lott@hamptonu.edu.
Website: http://nursing.hamptonu.edu

**Hardin-Simmons University,** Graduate School, Patty Hanks Shelton School of Nursing, Abilene, TX 79698-0001. Offers education (MSN); family nurse practitioner (MSN). *Accreditation:* AACN. *Program availability:* Part-time. *Degree requirements:* For master's, comprehensive exam, thesis or alternative. *Entrance requirements:* For master's, GRE, minimum undergraduate GPA of 3.0; interview; upper-level course work in statistics; CPR certification; letters of recommendation. Additional exam requirements/recommendations for international students: required—TOEFL (minimum score 550 paper-based; 79 iBT). Electronic applications accepted. *Expenses:* Contact institution.

**Herzing University Online,** Program in Nursing, Menomonee Falls, WI 53051. Offers nursing (MSN); nursing education (MSN); nursing management (MSN). *Accreditation:* AACN. *Program availability:* Online learning.

**Holy Family University,** Graduate and Professional Programs, School of Nursing and Allied Health Professions, Philadelphia, PA 19114. Offers nursing administration (MSN); nursing education (MSN). *Accreditation:* AACN. *Program availability:* Part-time, evening/weekend. *Degree requirements:* For master's, thesis or alternative, comprehensive portfolio, clinical practicum. *Entrance requirements:* For master's, BSN or RN from appropriately-accredited program, minimum GPA of 3.0, professional references, official transcripts of all college or university work, essay/personal statement, current resume, completion of one undergraduate statistics course with minimum grade of C. Additional exam requirements/recommendations for international students: required—TOEFL (minimum score 550 paper-based; 79 iBT), IELTS (minimum score 6), or PTE (minimum score 54). Electronic applications accepted.

**Howard University,** College of Nursing and Allied Health Sciences, Division of Nursing, Washington, DC 20059-0002. Offers family nurse practitioner (MSN); nurse educator (MSN). *Accreditation:* AACN. *Program availability:* Part-time. *Degree requirements:* For master's, comprehensive exam, thesis optional. *Entrance requirements:* For master's, RN license, minimum GPA of 3.0, BS in nursing.

**Immaculata University,** College of Graduate Studies, Division of Nursing, Immaculata, PA 19345. Offers nursing administration (MSN); nursing education (MSN). *Accreditation:* AACN. *Program availability:* Part-time, evening/weekend. *Entrance requirements:* For master's, MAT or GRE, BSN, minimum undergraduate GPA of 3.0. Additional exam requirements/recommendations for international students: required—TOEFL.

**Indiana State University,** College of Graduate and Professional Studies, College of Health and Human Services, Department of Advanced Practice Nursing, Terre Haute, IN 47809. Offers advanced practice nursing (DNP); family nurse practitioner (MS); nursing administration (MS); nursing education (MS). *Accreditation:* ACEN. *Program availability:* Part-time. *Degree requirements:* For master's, thesis or alternative. *Entrance requirements:* For master's, BSN, RN license, minimum undergraduate GPA of 3.0. Electronic applications accepted.

**Indiana University Kokomo,** School of Nursing, Kokomo, IN 46904. Offers family nurse practitioner (MSN); nurse administrator (MSN); nurse educator (MSN). Electronic applications accepted. *Expenses:* Contact institution.

**Indiana University of Pennsylvania,** School of Graduate Studies and Research, College of Health and Human Services, Department of Nursing and Allied Health Professions, Program in Nursing Education, Indiana, PA 15705. Offers MS. *Program availability:* Part-time. *Faculty:* 7 full-time (6 women). *Students:* 31 part-time (28 women); includes 1 minority (American Indian or Alaska Native, non-Hispanic/Latino). Average age 37. 13 applicants, 100% accepted, 13 enrolled. In 2019, 9 master's awarded. *Degree requirements:* For master's, thesis optional, practicum. *Entrance requirements:* For master's, goal statement, official transcripts, letters of recommendation. Additional exam requirements/recommendations for international students: required—TOEFL (minimum score 540 paper-based; 76 iBT), IELTS (minimum score 6). *Application deadline:* Applications are processed on a rolling basis. Application fee: $50. Electronic applications accepted. *Expenses:* Contact institution. *Financial support:* In 2019–20, 13 research assistantships with tuition reimbursements (averaging $2,038 per year) were awarded; career-related internships or fieldwork, Federal Work-Study, scholarships/grants, and unspecified assistantships also available. Financial award application deadline: 4/15; financial award applicants required to submit FAFSA. *Unit head:* Dr. Nashat Zuraikat, Graduate Coordinator, 724-357-3262, E-mail: zuraikat@iup.edu. *Application contact:* Dr. Nashat Zuraikat, Graduate Coordinator, 724-357-3262, E-mail: zuraikat@iup.edu.
Website: http://www.iup.edu/grad/nursing/default.aspx

**Indiana University-Purdue University Indianapolis,** School of Nursing, MSN Program in Nursing, Indianapolis, IN 46202. Offers adult/gerontology acute care nurse practitioner (MSN); adult/gerontology clinical nurse specialist (MSN); adult/gerontology primary care nurse practitioner (MSN); family nurse practitioner (MSN); nursing education (MSN); nursing leadership in health systems (MSN); pediatric clinical nurse specialist (MSN); pediatric nurse practitioner (MSN). *Accreditation:* AACN. *Program availability:* Part-time, blended/hybrid learning. *Degree requirements:* For master's, thesis. *Entrance requirements:* For master's, BSN from ACEN- or CCNE-accredited program, minimum undergraduate GPA of 3.0 (preferred), professional resume or curriculum vitae, essay stating career goals and objectives, current unencumbered RN license, three references from individuals with knowledge of ability to succeed in graduate program. Additional exam requirements/recommendations for international students: required—TOEFL (minimum score 550 paper-based; 79 iBT). Electronic applications accepted. *Expenses:* Contact institution.

**Indiana Wesleyan University,** Graduate School, School of Nursing, Marion, IN 46953-4974. Offers nursing administration (MS); nursing education (MS); primary care nursing (MS); MSN/MBA. *Accreditation:* AACN. *Program availability:* Part-time, online learning. *Degree requirements:* For master's, capstone project or thesis. *Entrance requirements:* For master's, writing sample, RN license, 1 year of related experience, graduate statistics course. Additional exam requirements/recommendations for international students: required—TOEFL. *Expenses:* Contact institution.

**Jacksonville University,** Brooks Rehabilitation College of Healthcare Sciences, Keigwin School of Nursing, Master of Science in Nursing Program, Jacksonville, FL 32211. Offers clinical nurse educator (MSN); family nurse practitioner (MSN); family nurse practitioner/emergency nurse practitioner (MSN); leadership in the healthcare system (MSN); nursing informatics (MSN); psychiatric nurse practitioner (MSN); MSN/MBA. *Program availability:* Part-time, 100% online, blended/hybrid learning. In 2019, 215 master's awarded. *Degree requirements:* For master's, thesis. *Entrance requirements:* For master's, GRE General Test or undergraduate GPA above 3.0, BSN from ACEN- or CCNE-accredited program; course work in statistics and physical assessment within last 5 years; Florida nursing license; CPR/BLS certification; 3 recommendations, 2 of which are professional references; statement of intent; resume. Additional exam requirements/recommendations for international students: required—TOEFL (minimum score 650 paper-based; 114 iBT), IELTS (minimum score 8). *Application deadline:* Applications are processed on a rolling basis. Application fee: $50. Electronic applications accepted. *Expenses:* Contact institution. *Financial support:* Federal Work-Study, institutionally sponsored loans, scholarships/grants, and health care benefits available. Support available to part-time students. Financial award application deadline: 3/15; financial award applicants required to submit FAFSA. *Unit head:* Dr. Hilary Morgan, Director, Graduate Nursing Programs/Associate Professor, 904-256-7601, E-mail: hmorgan@ju.edu. *Application contact:* Kristen Kirkendall, Associate Director of Graduate Admissions and Communications, 904-256-7169, E-mail: kgreene8@ju.edu.
Website: https://www.ju.edu/nursing/graduate/master-science-nursing/index.php

**Jefferson College of Health Sciences,** Program in Nursing, Roanoke, VA 24013. Offers nursing education (MSN); nursing management (MSN). *Accreditation:* AACN. *Program availability:* Part-time. *Degree requirements:* For master's, project. *Entrance requirements:* For master's, MAT. Additional exam requirements/recommendations for international students: required—TOEFL (minimum score 550 paper-based; 80 iBT). Electronic applications accepted.

**Johns Hopkins University,** School of Nursing, Post Master's Certificate Program in Nursing, Baltimore, MD 21218. Offers nursing education (Certificate); pediatric acute

care nurse practitioner (Certificate); psychiatric mental health nurse practitioner (Certificate). *Program availability:* Part-time-only, online only, 100% online. *Faculty:* 4 full-time (all women), 2 part-time/adjunct (both women). *Students:* 47 part-time (44 women); includes 9 minority (3 Black or African American, non-Hispanic/Latino; 2 Asian, non-Hispanic/Latino; 3 Hispanic/Latino; 1 Two or more races, non-Hispanic/Latino). 127 applicants, 44% accepted, 47 enrolled. In 2019, 46 Certificates awarded. *Entrance requirements:* For degree, Minimum GPA of 3.0, goal statement/essay, resume, letters of recommendation, official transcripts from all post-secondary institutions attended, MSN and RN licensure, NP license for some tracks, work experience and prerequisite coursework for some tracks. Additional exam requirements/recommendations for international students: required—TOEFL (minimum score 600 paper-based; 100 iBT), IELTS (minimum score 7). *Application deadline:* For fall admission, 1/1 priority date for domestic students. Application fee: $75. Electronic applications accepted. *Expenses:* $1,688 per credit. *Financial support:* In 2019–20, 1 student received support. Federal Work-Study available. Financial award application deadline: 3/1; financial award applicants required to submit FAFSA. *Unit head:* Dr. Susan Renda, 410-955-7139, E-mail: srenda1@jhu.edu. *Application contact:* Cathy Wilson, Director of Admissions, 410-955-7548, Fax: 410-614-7086, E-mail: jhuson@jhu.edu.
Website: http://nursing.jhu.edu/

**Kennesaw State University,** WellStar College of Health and Human Services, Program in Leadership in Nursing, Kennesaw, GA 30144. Offers nursing administration (MSN); nursing education (MSN). *Program availability:* Part-time, evening/weekend, online learning. *Students:* 27 full-time (26 women), 15 part-time (13 women); includes 12 minority (8 Black or African American, non-Hispanic/Latino; 2 Asian, non-Hispanic/Latino; 2 Two or more races, non-Hispanic/Latino), 1 international. Average age 34. 33 applicants, 91% accepted, 23 enrolled. In 2019, 1 master's awarded. *Entrance requirements:* For master's, minimum GPA of 3.0, RN license. Additional exam requirements/recommendations for international students: required—TOEFL (minimum score 80 iBT), IELTS (minimum score 6.5). *Application deadline:* For fall admission, 6/1 for domestic and international students. Application fee: $60. Electronic applications accepted. *Expenses: Tuition, area resident:* Full-time $7104; part-time $296 per credit hour. Tuition, state resident: full-time $7104; part-time $296 per credit hour. Tuition, nonresident: full-time $25,584; part-time $1066 per credit hour. *International tuition:* $25,584 full-time. *Required fees:* $2006; $1706 per unit. $853 per semester. *Financial support:* Applicants required to submit FAFSA. *Application contact:* Admissions Counselor, 470-578-4377, Fax: 470-578-9172, E-mail: ksugrad@kennesaw.edu.
Website: http://wellstarcollege.kennesaw.edu/nursing/master-science-nursing/leadership-in-nursing.php

**Kent State University,** College of Nursing, Kent, OH 44242. Offers advanced nursing practice (DNP), including adult/gerontology acute care nurse practitioner (MSN, DNP); nursing (MSN, PhD), including adult/gerontology acute care nurse practitioner (MSN, DNP), adult/gerontology clinical nurse specialist (MSN), adult/gerontology primary care nurse practitioner (MSN), family nurse practitioner (MSN), nurse educator (MSN), nursing and healthcare management (MSN), pediatric primary care nurse practitioner (MSN), psychiatric/mental health nurse practitioner (MSN); MBA/MSN. *Accreditation:* AACN. *Program availability:* Part-time, online learning. *Faculty:* 28 full-time (26 women), 15 part-time/adjunct (13 women). *Students:* 138 full-time (123 women), 522 part-time (464 women); includes 80 minority (41 Black or African American, non-Hispanic/Latino; 16 Asian, non-Hispanic/Latino; 9 Hispanic/Latino; 1 Native Hawaiian or other Pacific Islander, non-Hispanic/Latino; 13 Two or more races, non-Hispanic/Latino), 7 international. Average age 35. 303 applicants, 68% accepted, 154 enrolled. In 2019, 156 master's, 8 doctorates awarded. *Degree requirements:* For master's, practicum for master's degrees; for doctorate, comprehensive exam, thesis/dissertation. *Entrance requirements:* For master's, GRE or GMAT, minimum GPA of 3.0, active RN license, statement of purpose, 3 letters of reference, undergraduate level statistics class (minimum C grade), baccalaureate or graduate-level nursing degree, curriculum vitae/resume; for doctorate, GRE, minimum GPA of 3.0, transcripts, 3 letters of reference, interview, active unrestricted Ohio RN license, statement of purpose, writing sample, curriculum vitae/resume, baccalaureate and master's degrees in nursing or DNP, undergraduate or graduate level statistics course with a minimum C grade. Additional exam requirements/recommendations for international students: required—TOEFL (minimum score 83 iBT), IELTS (minimum score 6.5), PTE (minimum score 55), Michigan English Language Assessment Battery (minimum score 78). *Application deadline:* For fall admission, 3/1 for domestic and international students; for spring admission, 10/1 for domestic and international students. Applications are processed on a rolling basis. Application fee: $45 ($70 for international students). Electronic applications accepted. *Financial support:* Federal Work-Study and scholarships/grants available. Financial award application deadline: 2/1. *Unit head:* Dr. Barbara Broome, Ph.D., Dean, 330-672-3777, E-mail: bbroome1@kent.edu. *Application contact:* Dr. Wendy A. Umberger, Ph.D., Associate Dean for Graduate Programs/Professor, 330-672-8813, E-mail: wlewando@kent.edu.
Website: http://www.kent.edu/nursing/

**Keuka College,** Program in Nursing, Keuka Park, NY 14478. Offers adult gerontology (MS); nursing education (MS). *Accreditation:* AACN. *Degree requirements:* For master's, exam or thesis. *Entrance requirements:* For master's, bachelor's degree from accredited institution, minimum GPA of 3.0, unencumbered NY State license, and current registration as RN (for nursing); currently full-time or part-time working RN and 2 clinical letters of recommendation (for adult gerontology nurse practitioner). Additional exam requirements/recommendations for international students: required—TOEFL (minimum score 550 paper-based). Electronic applications accepted. *Expenses:* Contact institution.

**King University,** School of Nursing, Bristol, TN 37620-2699. Offers family nurse practitioner (MSN, Post-Master's Certificate); nurse educator (MSN, Post-Master's Certificate); nursing (DNP); nursing administration (MSN); pediatric nurse practitioner (MSN). *Program availability:* Part-time, evening/weekend, 100% online, blended/hybrid learning. *Faculty:* 13 full-time (12 women), 4 part-time/adjunct (2 women). *Students:* 115 full-time (103 women), 35 part-time (28 women); includes 12 minority (9 Black or African American, non-Hispanic/Latino; 1 Asian, non-Hispanic/Latino; 1 Hispanic/Latino; 1 Native Hawaiian or other Pacific Islander, non-Hispanic/Latino). Average age 37. 141 applicants, 96% accepted, 63 enrolled. In 2019, 89 master's, 1 doctorate, 6 other advanced degrees awarded. *Degree requirements:* For master's and post-master's certificate, comprehensive exam (for some programs), thesis optional; for doctorate, comprehensive exam (for some programs), thesis/dissertation. *Entrance requirements:* For master's, submit evidence of graduation from an accredited baccalaureate nursing program with a minimum cumulative undergraduate GPA of 3.0 on a 4.0 scale prior to enrolling; for doctorate, bachelor's and master's degree in nursing with a GPA of 3.25 or higher from a master's degree program accredited by the Accreditation Commission for Nursing Education (ACNE) or the Commission on Collegiate Nursing Education (CCNE); for Post-Master's Certificate, FNP and PNP applicants must complete an interview with the MSN Admissions Committee. Additional exam requirements/recommendations for international students: required—TOEFL (minimum score 84 paper-based; 84 iBT). *Application deadline:* Applications are processed on a rolling basis. Application fee: $50. Electronic applications accepted. *Expenses: Tuition:* Full-time $10,890; part-time $605 per semester hour. *Required fees:* $100 per course. *Financial support:* Unspecified assistantships available. Financial award applicants required to submit FAFSA. *Unit head:* Dr. Tracy Slemp, Dean, School of Nursing, 423-652-6335, E-mail: tjslemp@king.edu. *Application contact:* Natalie Blankenship, Territory Manager/Enrollment Counselor, 652-652-4159, Fax: 652-652-4727, E-mail: nblankenship@king.edu.

**Lamar University,** College of Graduate Studies, College of Arts and Sciences, JoAnne Gay Dishman Department of Nursing, Beaumont, TX 77710. Offers nursing administration (MSN); nursing education (MSN); MSN/MBA. *Accreditation:* ACEN. *Program availability:* Part-time, evening/weekend, online learning. *Faculty:* 33 full-time (30 women), 7 part-time/adjunct (6 women). *Students:* 1 (woman) full-time, 95 part-time (88 women); includes 42 minority (27 Black or African American, non-Hispanic/Latino; 2 American Indian or Alaska Native, non-Hispanic/Latino; 5 Asian, non-Hispanic/Latino; 8 Hispanic/Latino). Average age 40. 63 applicants, 79% accepted, 16 enrolled. In 2019, 29 master's awarded. *Degree requirements:* For master's, comprehensive exam, practicum project presentation, evidence-based project. *Entrance requirements:* For master's, GRE General Test, MAT, criminal background check, RN license, ACEN-accredited BSN, college course work in statistics in past 5 years, letters of recommendation, minimum undergraduate GPA of 3.0. Additional exam requirements/recommendations for international students: required—TOEFL (minimum score 550 paper-based; 79 iBT), IELTS (minimum score 6.5). *Application deadline:* Applications are processed on a rolling basis. Application fee: $25 ($50 for international students). Electronic applications accepted. *Expenses:* $13,098 total program cost. *Financial support:* In 2019–20, 3 students received support, including 2 teaching assistantships (averaging $24,000 per year); scholarships/grants and traineeships also available. Financial award applicants required to submit FAFSA. *Unit head:* Dr. Cynthia Stinson, School of Nursing Chair, 409-880-8817, Fax: 409-880-8698. *Application contact:* Celeste Contreas, Director, Admissions and Academic Services, 409-880-8888, Fax: 409-880-7419, E-mail: gradmissions@lamar.edu.
Website: http://artssciences.lamar.edu/nursing

**La Roche University,** School of Graduate Studies and Adult Education, Program in Nursing, Pittsburgh, PA 15237-5898. Offers clinical nurse leader (MSN); nursing education (MSN); nursing management (MSN). *Accreditation:* ACEN. *Program availability:* Part-time, evening/weekend, online only, 100% online. *Faculty:* 3 full-time (all women), 3 part-time/adjunct (all women). *Students:* 10 full-time (all women), 27 part-time (22 women); includes 4 minority (1 Black or African American, non-Hispanic/Latino; 2 Hispanic/Latino; 1 Native Hawaiian or other Pacific Islander, non-Hispanic/Latino). Average age 36. 9 applicants, 100% accepted, 7 enrolled. In 2019, 10 master's awarded. *Degree requirements:* For master's, thesis optional, internship, practicum. *Entrance requirements:* For master's, GRE General Test, BSN, nursing license, work experience. Additional exam requirements/recommendations for international students: recommended—TOEFL (minimum score 550 paper-based). *Application deadline:* For fall admission, 8/15 priority date for domestic students, 8/15 for international students; for spring admission, 12/15 priority date for domestic students, 12/15 for international students. Applications are processed on a rolling basis. Application fee: $50. Electronic applications accepted. *Expenses:* Contact institution. *Financial support:* Application deadline: 3/31; applicants required to submit FAFSA. *Unit head:* Dr. Terri Liberto, Professor, Master of Science in Nursing Department Chair, 412-847-1813, Fax: 412-536-1175, E-mail: terri.liberto@laroche.edu. *Application contact:* Erin Pottgen, Assistant Director, Graduate Admissions, 412-847-2509, Fax: 412-536-1283, E-mail: erin.pottgen@laroche.edu.

**La Salle University,** School of Nursing and Health Sciences, Program in Nursing, Philadelphia, PA 19141-1199. Offers adult gerontology primary care nurse practitioner (MSN, Certificate); adult health and illness clinical nurse specialist (MSN); adult-gerontology clinical nurse specialist (MSN, Certificate); clinical nurse leader (MSN); family primary care nurse practitioner (MSN, Certificate); gerontology (Certificate); nurse anesthetist (MSN, Certificate); nursing (MSN, Certificate); nursing administration (MSN, Certificate); nursing education (Certificate); nursing practice (DNP); nursing service administration (MSN); public health nursing (MSN, Certificate); school nursing (Certificate); MSN/MBA; MSN/MPH. *Accreditation:* AACN. *Program availability:* Part-time, evening/weekend, 100% online. *Degree requirements:* For doctorate, minimum of 1,000 hours of post baccalaureate clinical practice supervised by preceptors. *Entrance requirements:* For master's, GRE, MAT, or GMAT (for students with BSN GPA of less than 3.2), baccalaureate degree in nursing from ACEN- or CCNE-accredited program or an MSN Bridge program; Pennsylvania RN license; 2 letters of reference; resume; statement of philosophy articulating professional values and future educational goal; 1 year of work experience as a registered nurse; for doctorate, GRE (waived for applicants with MSN cumulative GPA of 3.7 or above), MSN, master's degree, MBA or MHA from nationally-accredited program; resume or curriculum vitae; 2 letters of reference; interview; for Certificate, GRE, MAT, or GMAT (for students with BSN GPA of less than 3.2, baccalaureate degree in nursing from ACEN- or CCNE-accredited program or an MSN Bridge program; Pennsylvania RN license; 2 letters of reference; resume; statement of philosophy articulating professional values and future educational goal; 1 year of work experience as a registered nurse. Additional exam requirements/recommendations for international students: required—TOEFL. Electronic applications accepted. Application fee is waived when completed online. *Expenses:* Contact institution.

**Le Moyne College,** Department of Nursing, Syracuse, NY 13214. Offers family nurse practitioner (MS, CAS); informatics (MS, CAS); nursing administration (MS, CAS); nursing education (MS, CAS). *Accreditation:* AACN. *Program availability:* Part-time, evening/weekend. *Faculty:* 4 full-time (all women), 6 part-time/adjunct (4 women). *Students:* 18 full-time (17 women), 57 part-time (52 women); includes 7 minority (1 Black or African American, non-Hispanic/Latino; 1 Asian, non-Hispanic/Latino; 4 Hispanic/Latino; 1 Two or more races, non-Hispanic/Latino). Average age 31. 43 applicants, 84% accepted, 32 enrolled. In 2019, 33 master's, 3 other advanced degrees awarded. *Degree requirements:* For master's, 39-45 credit hours, varies by program, practicum, scholarly project; for CAS, Varies by experience or incoming degree. *Entrance requirements:* For master's, earned bachelor's degree transcripts, New York RN license, 2-3 letters of recommendation, personal statement, interview. Additional exam requirements/recommendations for international students: required—TOEFL (minimum score 79 iBT); recommended—IELTS (minimum score 6.5). *Application deadline:* For fall admission, 4/1 priority date for domestic students, 4/1 for international students; for spring admission, 11/1 priority date for domestic students, 11/1 for international students; for summer admission, 5/1 priority date for domestic students, 5/1 for international students. Applications are processed on a rolling basis. Electronic applications accepted. *Expenses:* $764-$951 per credit hour depending upon program, $75 fee per semester. *Financial support:* In 2019–20, 1 student received support. Career-related internships or fieldwork, Federal Work-Study, scholarships/grants, health care benefits, and unspecified assistantships available. Support available to part-time students. Financial award applicants required to submit FAFSA. *Unit head:* Catherine A. Brownell, Professor - Chair of Nursing, 315-445-5426, Fax: 315-445-6024, E-mail: nursing@lemoyne.edu. *Application contact:* Teresa M. Renn, Director of Graduate Admission, 315-445-5444, Fax: 315-445-6092, E-mail: GradAdmission@lemoyne.edu.
Website: http://www.lemoyne.edu/nursing

**Lenoir-Rhyne University,** Graduate Programs, School of Nursing, Program in Nursing, Hickory, NC 28601. Offers nursing administration (MSN); nursing education (MSN). *Accreditation:* AACN. *Program availability:* Online learning. *Degree requirements:* For master's, comprehensive exam, thesis optional. *Entrance requirements:* For master's, official transcripts, two recommendations, essay, resume, unrestricted RN license, criminal background check. Additional exam requirements/recommendations for international students: required—TOEFL (minimum score 600 paper-based). Electronic applications accepted. *Expenses:* Contact institution.

**Lewis University,** College of Nursing and Health Sciences, Program in Nursing, Romeoville, IL 60446. Offers adult gerontology clinical nurse specialist (MSN); adult gerontology primary care nurse practitioner (MSN); family nurse practitioner (MSN); healthcare systems leadership (MSN); nursing education (MSN); school nurse (MSN). *Accreditation:* AACN. *Program availability:* Part-time, evening/weekend, 100% online, blended/hybrid learning. *Students:* 7 full-time (all women), 411 part-time (372 women); includes 113 minority (15 Black or African American, non-Hispanic/Latino; 43 Asian, non-Hispanic/Latino; 47 Hispanic/Latino; 8 Two or more races, non-Hispanic/Latino), 2 international. Average age 35. *Degree requirements:* For master's, clinical practicum. *Entrance requirements:* For master's, minimum undergraduate GPA of 3.0, degree in nursing, RN license, letter of recommendation, interview, resume or curriculum vitae. Additional exam requirements/recommendations for international students: required—TOEFL (minimum score 550 paper-based; 80 iBT), IELTS. *Application deadline:* For fall admission, 5/1 priority date for international students; for spring admission, 11/15 priority date for international students. Applications are processed on a rolling basis. Application fee: $40. Electronic applications accepted. *Financial support:* Federal Work-Study, scholarships/grants, tuition waivers (full and partial), and unspecified assistantships available. Financial award application deadline: 5/1; financial award applicants required to submit FAFSA. *Unit head:* Dr. Mary Desmond, Program Director. *Application contact:* Nancy Wiksten, Graduate Admission Counselor, 815-836-5610, E-mail: grad@lewisu.edu.

**Liberty University,** School of Nursing, Lynchburg, VA 24515. Offers family nurse practitioner (DNP); nurse educator (MSN); nursing administration (MSN); nursing informatics (MSN). *Accreditation:* AACN. *Program availability:* Part-time, online learning. *Students:* 279 full-time (257 women), 505 part-time (449 women); includes 170 minority (118 Black or African American, non-Hispanic/Latino; 2 American Indian or Alaska Native, non-Hispanic/Latino; 19 Asian, non-Hispanic/Latino; 25 Hispanic/Latino; 6 Two or more races, non-Hispanic/Latino), 11 international. Average age 39. 1,154 applicants, 27% accepted, 171 enrolled. In 2019, 138 master's, 26 doctorates awarded. *Entrance requirements:* For master's, minimum cumulative undergraduate GPA of 3.0; for doctorate, minimum GPA of 3.25 in most current nursing program completed. Additional exam requirements/recommendations for international students: recommended—TOEFL. *Application deadline:* Applications are processed on a rolling basis. Application fee: $50. Electronic applications accepted. *Expenses: Tuition:* Full-time $545; part-time $410 per credit hour. One-time fee: $50. *Financial support:* In 2019–20, 128 students received support. Federal Work-Study available. Financial award applicants required to submit FAFSA. *Unit head:* Dr. Shanna Akers, Dean, 434-592-3618, E-mail: lusondean@liberty.edu. *Application contact:* Jay Bridge, Director of Admissions, 800-424-9595, Fax: 800-628-7977, E-mail: gradadmissions@liberty.edu.
Website: https://www.liberty.edu/nursing/

**Loma Linda University,** School of Nursing, Program in Nurse Educator, Loma Linda, CA 92350. Offers adult/gerontology (MS); obstetrics-pediatrics (MS). *Accreditation:* AACN. *Program availability:* Part-time. *Degree requirements:* For master's, thesis or alternative. *Entrance requirements:* For master's, GRE General Test, BSN, minimum GPA of 3.0, RN license. Additional exam requirements/recommendations for international students: required—TOEFL. Electronic applications accepted.

**Long Island University - Brooklyn,** Harriet Rothkopf Heilbrunn School of Nursing, Brooklyn, NY 11201-8423. Offers adult nurse practitioner (MS, Advanced Certificate); family nurse practitioner (MS, Advanced Certificate); nurse educator (MS). *Accreditation:* AACN. *Program availability:* Part-time, evening/weekend, blended/hybrid learning. *Entrance requirements:* Additional exam requirements/recommendations for international students: required—TOEFL or IELTS. Electronic applications accepted.

**Long Island University - Post,** School of Health Professions and Nursing, Brookville, NY 11548-1300. Offers biomedical science (MS); cardiovascular perfusion (MS); clinical lab sciences (MS); clinical laboratory management (MS); dietetic internship (Advanced Certificate); family nurse practitioner (MS, Advanced Certificate); forensic social work (Advanced Certificate); gerontology (Advanced Certificate); health administration (MPA); non-profit management (Advanced Certificate); nursing education (MS); nutrition (MS); public administration (MPA); social work (MSW). *Program availability:* Part-time, blended/hybrid learning. *Degree requirements:* For master's, comprehensive exam (for some programs), thesis (for some programs). *Entrance requirements:* Additional exam requirements/recommendations for international students: required—TOEFL (minimum score 85 iBT) or IELTS (7.5). Electronic applications accepted.

**Louisiana State University Health Sciences Center,** School of Nursing, New Orleans, LA 70112. Offers adult gerontology acute care nurse practitioner (DNP, Post-Master's Certificate); adult gerontology clinical nurse specialist (DNP, Post-Master's Certificate); adult gerontology primary care nurse practitioner (DNP, Post-Master's Certificate); clinical nurse leader (MSN); executive nurse leader (DNP, Post-Master's Certificate); neonatal nurse practitioner (DNP, Post-Master's Certificate); nurse anesthesia (DNP, Post-Master's Certificate); nurse educator (MSN); nursing (DNS); primary care family nurse practitioner (DNP, Post-Master's Certificate); public/community health nursing (DNP, Post-Master's Certificate). *Accreditation:* AACN; AANA/CANAEP (one or more programs are accredited). *Program availability:* Part-time. *Faculty:* 25 full-time (21 women), 25 part-time/adjunct (13 women). *Students:* 182 full-time (127 women), 70 part-time (59 women); includes 82 minority (52 Black or African American, non-Hispanic/Latino; 2 American Indian or Alaska Native, non-Hispanic/Latino; 14 Asian, non-Hispanic/Latino; 14 Hispanic/Latino), 1 international. Average age 34. 34 applicants, 62% accepted, 21 enrolled. In 2019, 72 doctorates awarded. *Degree requirements:* For master's, thesis optional; for doctorate, thesis/dissertation. *Entrance requirements:* For master's, GRE, minimum GPA of 3.0; for doctorate, GRE, minimum GPA of 3.0 (for DNP), 3.5 (for DNS). Additional exam requirements/recommendations for international students: required—TOEFL (minimum score 550 paper-based; 79 iBT). *Application deadline:* For fall admission, 6/1 priority date for domestic and international students; for spring admission, 10/1 priority date for domestic and international students; for summer admission, 3/1 priority date for domestic and international students. Applications are processed on a rolling basis. Application fee: $100. Electronic applications accepted. *Expenses:* MSN and DNS: $13,354.50, $24,982.25 non-resident, $586 per hour (fall and spring), $467 per hour (summer), $1,102 per hour non-resident (fall and spring), $858 per hour non-resident (summer); DNP (Except Nurse Anethesia): $21,907.50, $38,262.23 non-resident, $973 per hour (fall and spring), $733 per hour (summer), $1,700 per hour non-resident (fall and spring), $1,278 per hour non-resident (summer); Nurse Anesthesia DNP: $26,407.50, $42,762.23 non-resident, $1,173 per hour (fall and spring), $883 per hour (summer), $1,900 per hour non-resident (fall and spring), $1,428 per hour non-resident (summer). *Financial support:* In 2019–20, 20 students received support. Institutionally sponsored loans, scholarships/grants, unspecified assistantships, and DNS Scholars Program available. Financial award application deadline: 4/15; financial award applicants required to submit FAFSA. *Unit head:* Dr. Demetrius James Porche, Dean, 504-568-4106, Fax: 504-599-0573, E-mail: dporch@lsuhsc.edu. *Application contact:* Tracie Gravolet, Director, Office of Student Affairs, 504-568-4114, Fax: 504-568-5711, E-mail: tgravo@lsuhsc.edu.
Website: http://nursing.lsuhsc.edu/

**Lourdes University,** Graduate School, Sylvania, OH 43560-2898. Offers business (MBA); leadership (M Ed); nurse anesthesia (MSN); nurse educator (MSN); nurse leader (MSN); organizational leadership (MOL); reading (M Ed); teaching and curriculum (M Ed); theology (MA). *Accreditation:* AANA/CANAEP. *Program availability:* Evening/weekend. *Entrance requirements:* Additional exam requirements/recommendations for international students: required—TOEFL.

**Marian University,** Leighton School of Nursing, Indianapolis, IN 46222-1997. Offers family nurse practitioner (DNP); nurse anesthesia (DNP); nursing education (MSN). *Accreditation:* AANA/CANAEP. *Program availability:* Part-time. *Degree requirements:* For master's, 38 credits, designed to be completed in 2 years; 225-hour practicum including a culminating project; for doctorate, 70 credit hours (for family nurse practitioner track); 85 credits (for nurse anesthesia track); minimum of 1000 hours of supervised practice. *Entrance requirements:* For master's, degree in nursing from NLNAC- or CCNE-accredited program; current, valid RN license in State of Indiana; minimum undergraduate GPA of 3.0; 3 recommendations; interview with admissions committee; current resume; 500-word essay describing career goals; for doctorate, BSN from NSNAC- or CCNE-accredited program; minimum undergraduate GPA of 3.0; cureent, valid RN license; current resume or curriculum vitae; 500-word essay addressing career goals; 3 letters of recommendation; interview with Admissions Committee. Additional exam requirements/recommendations for international students: required—TOEFL (minimum score 550 paper-based; 79 iBT). Electronic applications accepted. Application fee is waived when completed online. *Expenses:* Contact institution.

**Marian University,** School of Nursing and Health Professions, Fond du Lac, WI 54935-4699. Offers adult nurse practitioner (MSN); nurse educator (MSN); thanatology (MS). *Accreditation:* AACN. *Program availability:* Part-time, evening/weekend. *Degree requirements:* For master's, thesis, 675 clinical practicum hours. *Entrance requirements:* For master's, 3 letters of professional recommendation; undergraduate work in nursing research, statistics, health assessment. Additional exam requirements/recommendations for international students: required—TOEFL (minimum score 525 paper-based; 70 iBT). Electronic applications accepted. *Expenses:* Contact institution.

**McKendree University,** Graduate Programs, Master of Science in Nursing Program, Lebanon, IL 62254-1299. Offers nursing education (MSN); nursing management/administration (MSN). *Accreditation:* AACN. *Program availability:* Part-time, evening/weekend, online learning. *Degree requirements:* For master's, research project or thesis. *Entrance requirements:* For master's, resume, references, valid Professional Registered Nurse license. Additional exam requirements/recommendations for international students: required—TOEFL. Electronic applications accepted.

**McMurry University,** Graduate Studies, Abilene, TX 79697. Offers education (MSN); family nurse practitioner (MSN).

**McNeese State University,** Doré School of Graduate Studies, College of Nursing and Health Professions, MSN Program, Lake Charles, LA 70609. Offers family nurse practitioner (MSN); nurse educator (MSN); psychiatric/mental health nurse practitioner (MSN). *Entrance requirements:* For master's, GRE, baccalaureate degree in nursing, minimum overall GPA of 2.7 for all undergraduate coursework, eligibility for unencumbered licensure as Registered Nurse in Louisiana or Texas, course in introductory statistics with minimum C grade, physical assessment skills, two letters of professional reference, 500-word essay, current resume.

**Medical University of South Carolina,** College of Nursing, Nurse Educator Program, Charleston, SC 29425. Offers MSN. *Program availability:* Part-time, evening/weekend, online learning. *Degree requirements:* For master's, thesis optional. *Entrance requirements:* For master's, BSN, course work in statistics, nursing license, minimum GPA of 3.0, current curriculum vitae, essay, three references. Additional exam requirements/recommendations for international students: required—TOEFL (minimum score 600 paper-based). Electronic applications accepted.

**Mercy College,** School of Health and Natural Sciences, Programs in Nursing, Dobbs Ferry, NY 10522-1189. Offers nursing administration (MS); nursing education (MS). *Accreditation:* AACN. *Program availability:* Part-time, evening/weekend, 100% online, blended/hybrid learning. *Students:* 9 full-time (8 women), 208 part-time (196 women); includes 151 minority (89 Black or African American, non-Hispanic/Latino; 21 Asian, non-Hispanic/Latino; 32 Hispanic/Latino; 3 Native Hawaiian or other Pacific Islander, non-Hispanic/Latino; 6 Two or more races, non-Hispanic/Latino). Average age 40. 242 applicants, 73% accepted, 132 enrolled. In 2019, 67 master's awarded. *Degree requirements:* For master's, Capstone project and/or clinical practicum required for some programs. *Entrance requirements:* For master's, program application; transcript(s); RN registered in the U.S. Additional exam requirements/recommendations for international students: required—TOEFL (minimum score 80 iBT), IELTS (minimum score 6.5). *Application deadline:* Applications are processed on a rolling basis. Application fee: $40. Electronic applications accepted. *Expenses: Tuition:* Full-time $16,146; part-time $897 per credit. *Required fees:* $332; $166 per semester. Tuition and fees vary according to course load and program. *Financial support:* Career-related internships or fieldwork, Federal Work-Study, scholarships/grants, and unspecified assistantships available. Support available to part-time students. Financial award applicants required to submit FAFSA. *Unit head:* Dr. Joan Toglia, Dean, School of Health and Natural Sciences, 914-674-7746, E-mail: jtoglia@mercy.edu. *Application contact:* Allison Gurdineer, Executive Director of Admissions, 877-637-2946, Fax: 914-674-7382, E-mail: admissions@mercy.edu.
Website: https://www.mercy.edu/health-and-natural-sciences/graduate

**Messiah University,** Program in Nursing, Mechanicsburg, PA 17055. Offers nurse educator (MSN).

**Metropolitan State University,** College of Nursing and Health Sciences, St. Paul, MN 55106-5000. Offers advanced dental therapy (MS); leadership and management (MSN); nurse educator (MSN); nursing (DNP). *Accreditation:* AACN. *Program availability:* Part-time. *Degree requirements:* For master's, thesis or alternative; for doctorate, thesis/dissertation or alternative. *Entrance requirements:* For master's, GRE General Test, minimum GPA of 3.0, RN license, BS/BA; for doctorate, minimum GPA of 3.0, RN license, MSN. Additional exam requirements/recommendations for international students: required—TOEFL (minimum score 550 paper-based).

**MGH Institute of Health Professions,** School of Nursing, Boston, MA 02129. Offers advanced practice nursing (MSN); gerontological nursing (MSN); nursing (DNP); pediatric nursing (MSN); psychiatric nursing (MSN); teaching and learning for health care education (Certificate); women's health nursing (MSN). *Accreditation:* AACN. *Degree requirements:* For master's, thesis or alternative. *Entrance requirements:* For master's, GRE General Test, bachelor's degree from regionally-accredited college or university. Additional exam requirements/recommendations for international students:

required—TOEFL (minimum score 550 paper-based; 80 iBT). Electronic applications accepted.

**Miami Regional University,** School of Nursing and Health Sciences, Miami Springs, FL 33166. Offers nursing (MSN); nursing education (MSN); nursing leadership (MSN).

**MidAmerica Nazarene University,** School of Nursing and Health Science, Olathe, KS 66062. Offers healthcare administration (MSN); healthcare quality management (MSN); nursing education (MSN); public health (MSN); MSN/MBA. *Accreditation:* AACN. *Program availability:* Part-time, evening/weekend, 100% online. *Faculty:* 5 full-time (all women), 9 part-time/adjunct (7 women). *Students:* 14 full-time (12 women), 79 part-time (74 women); includes 12 minority (10 Black or African American, non-Hispanic/Latino; 1 American Indian or Alaska Native, non-Hispanic/Latino; 1 Hispanic/Latino), 2 international. Average age 38. 87 applicants, 39% accepted, 14 enrolled. In 2019, 39 master's awarded. *Entrance requirements:* For master's, BSN, minimum GPA of 3.0, active unencumbered RN license, undergraduate statistics course. Additional exam requirements/recommendations for international students: required—TOEFL (minimum score 81 iBT). *Application deadline:* Applications are processed on a rolling basis. Electronic applications accepted. *Expenses:* Tuition $499 per credit hour, technology fee $34.00 per credit hour, graduation fee $100, carrying fee $13 per course, other fee $215. *Financial support:* Unspecified assistantships available. Financial award applicants required to submit FAFSA. *Unit head:* Dr. Karen Wiegman, Dean, 913-971-3839, E-mail: kdwiegman@mnu.edu. *Application contact:* JoVonda Merrell, Compliance Coordinator, 913-971-3844, E-mail: jkmerrell@mnu.edu.
Website: http://www.mnu.edu/nursing.html

**Middle Tennessee State University,** College of Graduate Studies, University College, Murfreesboro, TN 37132. Offers advanced studies in teaching and learning (M Ed); human resources leadership (MPS); nursing administration (MSN); nursing education (MSN); strategic leadership (MPS); training and development (MPS). *Program availability:* Part-time, evening/weekend, online learning. *Entrance requirements:* Additional exam requirements/recommendations for international students: required—TOEFL (minimum score 525 paper-based; 71 iBT) or IELTS (minimum score 6).

**Midwestern State University,** Billie Doris McAda Graduate School, Robert D. and Carol Gunn College of Health Sciences and Human Services, Wilson School of Nursing, Wichita Falls, TX 76308. Offers family nurse practitioner (MSN); family psychiatric/mental health nurse practitioner (MSN); nurse educator (MSN). *Accreditation:* AACN. *Program availability:* Part-time, evening/weekend. *Degree requirements:* For master's, comprehensive exam, thesis optional. *Entrance requirements:* For master's, GRE General Test or MAT. Additional exam requirements/recommendations for international students: required—TOEFL (minimum score 550 paper-based). Electronic applications accepted.

**Millersville University of Pennsylvania,** College of Graduate Studies and Adult Learning, College of Science and Technology, Department of Nursing, Millersville, PA 17551-0302. Offers family nurse practitioner (MSN, Post-Master's Certificate); nursing education (MSN, Post-Master's Certificate); nursing practice (DNP). *Accreditation:* ACEN. *Program availability:* Part-time. *Faculty:* 6 full-time (all women), 9 part-time/adjunct (8 women). *Students:* 122 part-time (100 women); includes 22 minority (8 Black or African American, non-Hispanic/Latino; 6 Asian, non-Hispanic/Latino; 7 Hispanic/Latino; 1 Two or more races, non-Hispanic/Latino). Average age 39. 44 applicants, 68% accepted, 26 enrolled. In 2019, 30 master's, 27 other advanced degrees awarded. *Entrance requirements:* For master's, resume, including minimum of 2 years of pertinent clinical experience (3-5 years preferred); copy of RN license; 3.0 GPA required; interview; minimum of one year of current clinical experience in nursing; for doctorate, goal statement, 3-5 page (APA 6th Ed.) Writing Sample Defining a Specific Issue or Problem in Nursing Practices, current resume/CV, verification of MSN Clinical Hours, completed MSN or MPH, with a minimum 3.5 GPA. Additional exam requirements/recommendations for international students: required—TOEFL, IELTS (minimum score 6), PTE (minimum score 60). Application fee: $40. Electronic applications accepted. *Expenses: Tuition, area resident:* Part-time $516 per credit. Tuition, state resident: part-time $516 per credit. Tuition, nonresident: part-time $774 per credit. *Required fees:* $118.75 per credit. Tuition and fees vary according to course load, degree level and program. *Financial support:* In 2019–20, 16 students received support. Scholarships/grants and unspecified assistantships available. Financial award application deadline: 3/15; financial award applicants required to submit FAFSA. *Unit head:* Dr. Kelly A. Kuhns, Chairperson, 717-871-5276, Fax: 717-871-4877, E-mail: kelly.kuhns@millersville.edu. *Application contact:* Dr. James A. Delle, Acting Dean of College of Graduate Studies and Adult Learning/Associate Provost, Academic Administration, 717-871-7462, E-mail: James.Delle@millersville.edu.
Website: https://www.millersville.edu/nursing/index.php

**Millersville University of Pennsylvania,** College of Graduate Studies and Adult Learning, College of Science and Technology, Department of Nursing, Program in Nursing Education, Millersville, PA 17551-0302. Offers nursing education (MSN). *Program availability:* Part-time. *Students:* 8 part-time (5 women). Average age 39. 3 applicants, 100% accepted, 3 enrolled. In 2019, 2 master's awarded. *Entrance requirements:* For master's, Resume, including minimum of 2 years of pertinent clinical experience (3-5 years preferred); Copy of RN license; 3.0 GPA required; Interview; Minimum of one year of current clinical experience in nursing. Additional exam requirements/recommendations for international students: required—TOEFL, IELTS (minimum score 6), PTE (minimum score 60). *Application deadline:* Applications are processed on a rolling basis. Application fee: $40. Electronic applications accepted. *Expenses: Tuition, area resident:* Part-time $516 per credit. Tuition, state resident: part-time $516 per credit. Tuition, nonresident: part-time $774 per credit. *Required fees:* $118.75 per credit. Tuition and fees vary according to course load, degree level and program. *Financial support:* In 2019–20, 2 students received support. Scholarships/grants and unspecified assistantships available. Financial award application deadline: 3/15; financial award applicants required to submit FAFSA. *Unit head:* Dr. Kelly A. Kuhns, Chairperson, 717-871-5276, Fax: 717-871-4877, E-mail: kelly.kuhns@millersville.edu. *Application contact:* Dr. James A. Delle, Acting Dean of College of Graduate Studies and Adult Learning/Associate Provost, Academic Administration, 717-871-7462, E-mail: James.Delle@millersville.edu.
Website: https://www.millersville.edu/nursing/msn/nursing-education.php

**Minnesota State University Mankato,** College of Graduate Studies and Research, College of Allied Health and Nursing, School of Nursing, Mankato, MN 56001. Offers family nurse practitioner (MSN), including family nurse practitioner; nurse educator (MSN); nursing (DNP). *Accreditation:* AACN. *Degree requirements:* For master's, comprehensive exam, internships, research project or thesis; for doctorate, capstone project. *Entrance requirements:* For master's, GRE General Test or on-campus essay, minimum GPA of 3.0 during previous 2 years, BSN or equivalent references; for doctorate, master's degree in nursing. Additional exam requirements/recommendations for international students: required—TOEFL. Electronic applications accepted.

**Missouri State University,** Graduate College, College of Health and Human Services, School of Nursing, Springfield, MO 65897. Offers nursing (MSN), including family nurse practitioner, nurse educator; nursing practice (DNP). *Accreditation:* AACN. *Program availability:* 100% online, blended/hybrid learning. *Degree requirements:* For master's,

comprehensive exam, thesis or alternative. *Entrance requirements:* For master's, GRE General Test, minimum GPA of 3.0, RN license (for MSN), 1 year of work experience (for MPH). Additional exam requirements/recommendations for international students: required—TOEFL (minimum score 550 paper-based; 79 iBT), IELTS (minimum score 6). Electronic applications accepted. *Expenses: Tuition, area resident:* Full-time $2600; part-time $1735 per credit hour. Tuition, nonresident: full-time $5240; part-time $3495 per credit hour. *International tuition:* $5240 full-time. *Required fees:* $530; $438 per credit hour. Tuition and fees vary according to class time, course level, course load, degree level, campus/location and program.

**Missouri Western State University,** Program in Nursing, St. Joseph, MO 64507-2294. Offers health care leadership (MSN); nurse educator (MSN, Graduate Certificate). *Program availability:* Part-time. *Students:* 2 full-time (both women), 29 part-time (all women); includes 3 minority (1 Black or African American, non-Hispanic/Latino; 1 Asian, non-Hispanic/Latino; 1 Hispanic/Latino), 1 international. Average age 37. 13 applicants, 100% accepted, 12 enrolled. In 2019, 12 master's, 1 other advanced degree awarded. *Entrance requirements:* For master's, Minimum undergraduate GPA of 2.75 and nursing GPA 3.0 or higher. B.S.N. from a CCNE or NLNAC accredited college or university. Evidence of current, unencumbered RN license. Completion of undergraduate statistics and research methods courses with a minimum of "B" in each. Curriculum vitae/resume. A supporting statement of interest. Additional exam requirements/recommendations for international students: recommended—TOEFL (minimum score 79 iBT), IELTS (minimum score 6). *Application deadline:* For fall admission, 7/15 for domestic and international students; for spring admission, 11/1 for domestic and international students; for summer admission, 4/29 for domestic and international students. Applications are processed on a rolling basis. Application fee: $45 ($50 for international students). Electronic applications accepted. *Expenses:* Tuition, state resident: full-time $6469.02; part-time $359.39 per credit hour. Tuition, nonresident: full-time $11,581; part-time $643.39 per credit hour. *Required fees:* $345.20; $99.10 per credit hour. Tuition and fees vary according to course load, campus/location and program. *Financial support:* Scholarships/grants and unspecified assistantships available. Support available to part-time students. *Unit head:* Dr. Jacklyn Gentry, MSN Program Director and Assistant Professor, 816-271-4415, E-mail: jgentry8@missouriwestern.edu. *Application contact:* Dr. Jacklyn Gentry, MSN Program Director and Assistant Professor, 816-271-4415, E-mail: jgentry8@missouriwestern.edu.
Website: https://www.missouriwestern.edu/nursing/msn/

**Molloy College,** Graduate Nursing Program, Rockville Centre, NY 11571-5002. Offers adult-gerontology clinical nurse specialist (DNP); adult-gerontology nurse practitioner (MS, DNP); clinical nurse specialist: adult-gerontology (MS); family nurse practitioner (MS, DNP); family psychiatric/mental health nurse practitioner (MS, DNP); nursing (PhD, Advanced Certificate); nursing administration with informatics (MS); nursing education (MS); pediatric nurse practitioner (MS, DNP). *Accreditation:* AACN. *Program availability:* Part-time, evening/weekend. *Faculty:* 30 full-time (28 women), 10 part-time/adjunct (6 women). *Students:* 18 full-time (17 women), 573 part-time (520 women); includes 340 minority (181 Black or African American, non-Hispanic/Latino; 2 American Indian or Alaska Native, non-Hispanic/Latino; 100 Asian, non-Hispanic/Latino; 42 Hispanic/Latino; 5 Native Hawaiian or other Pacific Islander, non-Hispanic/Latino; 10 Two or more races, non-Hispanic/Latino), 3 international. Average age 38. 332 applicants, 60% accepted, 149 enrolled. In 2019, 136 master's, 12 doctorates, 22 other advanced degrees awarded. *Degree requirements:* For doctorate, clinical research residency and scholarly clinical project (for DNP); dissertation and comprehensive exam (for PhD). *Entrance requirements:* Additional exam requirements/recommendations for international students: required—TOEFL (minimum score 550 paper-based; 79 iBT). *Application deadline:* Applications are processed on a rolling basis. Application fee: $60. Electronic applications accepted. *Expenses: Tuition:* Full-time $21,510; part-time $1195 per credit hour. *Required fees:* $1100. Tuition and fees vary according to course load, degree level and program. *Financial support:* Application deadline: 3/1; applicants required to submit FAFSA. *Unit head:* Dr. Marcia R. Gardner, Dean, The Barbara H. Hagan School of Nursing, 516-323-3651, E-mail: mgardner@molloy.edu. *Application contact:* Faye Hood, Assistant Director for Admissions, 516-323-4009, E-mail: fhood@molloy.edu.
Website: https://www.molloy.edu/academics/graduate-programs/graduate-nursing-x25989

**Montana State University,** The Graduate School, College of Nursing, Bozeman, MT 59717. Offers clinical nurse leader (MN); family and individual nurse practitioner (DNP); family nurse practitioner (MN, Post-Master's Certificate); nursing education (Certificate, Post-Master's Certificate); psychiatric mental health nurse practitioner (MN); psychiatric/mental health nurse practitioner (DNP). *Accreditation:* AACN. *Program availability:* Part-time, online learning. *Degree requirements:* For master's, comprehensive exam, thesis (for some programs); for doctorate, thesis/dissertation, 1,125 hours in clinical settings. *Entrance requirements:* For master's, GRE General Test, minimum GPA of 3.0 for undergraduate and post-baccalaureate work. Additional exam requirements/recommendations for international students: required—TOEFL (minimum score 580 paper-based). Electronic applications accepted.

**Moravian College,** Graduate and Continuing Studies, Helen S. Breidegam School of Nursing, Bethlehem, PA 18018-6614. Offers clinical nurse leader (MS); nurse administrator (MS); nurse educator (MS); nurse practitioner - acute care (MS); nurse practitioner - primary care (MS). *Accreditation:* AACN. *Program availability:* Part-time, evening/weekend. *Faculty:* 2 full-time (both women), 3 part-time/adjunct (2 women). *Students:* 5 full-time (4 women), 103 part-time (95 women); includes 19 minority (4 Black or African American, non-Hispanic/Latino; 8 Asian, non-Hispanic/Latino; 7 Hispanic/Latino), 1 international. Average age 37. 131 applicants, 69% accepted, 85 enrolled. In 2019, 25 master's awarded. *Degree requirements:* For master's, comprehensive exam (for some programs), evidence-based practice project. *Entrance requirements:* For master's, BSN with minimum GPA of 3.0, active RN license, statistics course with minimum C grade, 2 professional references, written statement of goals, professional resume, interview, official transcripts. *Application deadline:* For fall admission, 8/1 priority date for domestic and international students; for spring admission, 1/1 priority date for domestic and international students; for summer admission, 5/1 priority date for domestic and international students. Applications are processed on a rolling basis. Electronic applications accepted. *Expenses:* Contact institution. *Financial support:* Applicants required to submit FAFSA. *Unit head:* Dr. Dawn Goodolf, 610-861-1412, Fax: 610-861-1466, E-mail: nursing@moravian.edu. *Application contact:* Caroline Bechtel, Student Experience Mentor, 610-861-1400, Fax: 610-861-1466, E-mail: graduate@moravian.edu.
Website: https://www.moravian.edu/graduate/programs/nursing#/

**Mount Carmel College of Nursing,** Nursing Program, Columbus, OH 43222. Offers adult gerontology acute care nurse practitioner (MS); adult health clinical nurse specialist (MS); family nurse practitioner (MS); nursing (DNP); nursing administration (MS); nursing education (MS). *Accreditation:* AACN. *Program availability:* Part-time. *Faculty:* 6 full-time (all women), 10 part-time/adjunct (9 women). *Students:* 101 full-time (82 women), 109 part-time (95 women); includes 43 minority (27 Black or African American, non-Hispanic/Latino; 4 Asian, non-Hispanic/Latino; 5 Hispanic/Latino; 7 Two or more races, non-Hispanic/Latino). Average age 32. 133 applicants, 84% accepted, 95 enrolled. In 2019, 66 master's, 2 doctorates awarded. *Degree requirements:* For

master's, professional manuscript; for doctorate, practicum. *Entrance requirements:* For master's, letters of recommendation, statement of purpose, current resume, baccalaureate degree in nursing, current Ohio RN license, minimum cumulative GPA of 3.0; for doctorate, master's degree in nursing from program accredited by either ACEN or CCNE. Additional exam requirements/recommendations for international students: required—TOEFL (minimum score 550 paper-based; 80 iBT). *Application deadline:* For fall admission, 2/1 priority date for domestic students; for spring admission, 11/1 priority date for domestic students. Applications are processed on a rolling basis. Application fee: $30. Electronic applications accepted. *Expenses: Tuition:* Full-time $27,936; part-time $27,936 per year. *Required fees:* $360. *Financial support:* In 2019–20, 13 students received support. Institutionally sponsored loans and scholarships/grants available. Financial award application deadline: 3/1; financial award applicants required to submit FAFSA. *Unit head:* Dr. Jami Nininger, Interim Associate Dean Graduate Studies, 614-234-1777, Fax: 614-234-2875, E-mail: jnininger@mccn.edu. *Application contact:* Dr. Kim Campbell, Director of Recruitment and Admissions, 614-234-5144, Fax: 614-234-5427, E-mail: kcampbell@mccn.edu.
Website: www.mccn.edu

**Mount Mercy University,** Program in Nursing, Cedar Rapids, IA 52402-4797. Offers health advocacy (MSN); nurse administration (MSN); nurse education (MSN). *Accreditation:* AACN. *Program availability:* Evening/weekend. *Degree requirements:* For master's, project/practicum.

**Mount St. Joseph University,** Master of Science in Nursing Program, Cincinnati, OH 45233-1670. Offers administration (MSN); clinical nurse leader (MSN); education (MSN). *Accreditation:* AACN. *Program availability:* Part-time. *Entrance requirements:* For master's, essay; BSN from regionally-accredited university; minimum undergraduate GPA of 3.25 or GRE; professional resume; three professional references; interview; 2 years of clinical nursing experience; active RN license; criminal background check. Additional exam requirements/recommendations for international students: required—TOEFL (minimum score 560 paper-based; 83 iBT). Electronic applications accepted. *Expenses:* Contact institution.

**Mount Saint Mary College,** School of Nursing, Newburgh, NY 12550. Offers adult nurse practitioner (MS, Advanced Certificate), including nursing education (MS), nursing management (MS); nursing education (Advanced Certificate). *Accreditation:* AACN. *Program availability:* Part-time, evening/weekend, blended/hybrid learning. *Faculty:* 6 full-time (all women), 11 part-time/adjunct (10 women). *Students:* 1 (woman) full-time, 186 part-time (171 women); includes 36 minority (16 Black or African American, non-Hispanic/Latino; 1 American Indian or Alaska Native, non-Hispanic/Latino; 5 Asian, non-Hispanic/Latino; 11 Hispanic/Latino; 1 Native Hawaiian or other Pacific Islander, non-Hispanic/Latino; 2 Two or more races, non-Hispanic/Latino), 1 international. Average age 37. 37 applicants, 84% accepted, 22 enrolled. In 2019, 33 master's, 4 other advanced degrees awarded. *Degree requirements:* For master's, research utilization project. *Entrance requirements:* For master's, BSN, minimum GPA of 3.0, RN license. Additional exam requirements/recommendations for international students: required—TOEFL (minimum score 80 iBT). *Application deadline:* For fall admission, 6/3 priority date for domestic students; for spring admission, 10/31 priority date for domestic students. Applications are processed on a rolling basis. Application fee: $45. Electronic applications accepted. Application fee is waived when completed online. *Expenses: Tuition:* Full-time $15,192; part-time $844 per credit. *Required fees:* $180; $90 per semester. *Financial support:* In 2019–20, 10 students received support. Scholarships/grants and unspecified assistantships available. Financial award application deadline: 4/15; financial award applicants required to submit FAFSA. *Unit head:* Christine Berte, Graduate Coordinator, 845-569-3141, Fax: 845-562-6762, E-mail: christine.berte@msmc.edu. *Application contact:* Eileen Bardney, Director of Admissions, 845-569-3254, Fax: 845-569-3438, E-mail: GraduateAdmissions@msmc.edu.
Website: http://www.msmc.edu/Academics/Graduate_Programs/Master_of_Science_in_Nursing

**National American University,** Roueche Graduate Center, Austin, TX 78731. Offers accounting (MBA); aviation management (MBA, MM); care coordination (MSN); community college leadership (Ed D); criminal justice (MM); e-marketing (MBA, MM); health care administration (MBA, MM); higher education (MM); human resources management (MBA, MM); information technology management (MBA, MM); international business (MBA); leadership (EMBA); management (MBA); nursing administration (MSN); nursing education (MSN); nursing informatics (MSN); operations and configuration management (MBA, MM); project and process management (MBA, MM). *Program availability:* Part-time, evening/weekend, online learning. *Entrance requirements:* For master's, minimum undergraduate GPA of 2.75. Additional exam requirements/recommendations for international students: required—TOEFL, TWE. Electronic applications accepted.

**Nebraska Methodist College,** Program in Nursing, Omaha, NE 68114. Offers nurse educator (MSN); nurse executive (MSN). *Accreditation:* AACN. *Program availability:* Evening/weekend, online learning. *Degree requirements:* For master's, thesis or alternative, Evidence Based Practice (EBP) project. *Entrance requirements:* For master's, interview. Additional exam requirements/recommendations for international students: required—TOEFL (minimum score 550 paper-based; 80 iBT).

**New York University,** Rory Meyers College of Nursing, Programs in Advanced Practice Nursing, New York, NY 10012-1019. Offers adult-gerontology acute care nurse practitioner (MS, Advanced Certificate); adult-gerontology primary care nurse practitioner (MS, Advanced Certificate); family nurse practitioner (MS, Advanced Certificate); gerontology nurse practitioner (Advanced Certificate); nurse-midwifery (MS, Advanced Certificate); nursing administration (MS, Advanced Certificate); nursing education (MS, Advanced Certificate); nursing informatics (MS, Advanced Certificate); pediatrics nurse practitioner (MS, Advanced Certificate); psychiatric-mental health nurse practitioner (MS, Advanced Certificate); MS/MPH. *Accreditation:* AACN; ACNM/ACME. *Program availability:* Part-time, evening/weekend. *Degree requirements:* For master's, thesis (for some programs), capstone. *Entrance requirements:* For master's, BS in nursing, AS in nursing with another BS/BA, interview, RN license, 1 year of clinical experience (3 for the MS in nursing education program); for Advanced Certificate, master's degree in nursing. Additional exam requirements/recommendations for international students: required—TOEFL (minimum score 100 iBT), IELTS (minimum score 7). Electronic applications accepted. *Expenses:* Contact institution.

**Nicholls State University,** Graduate Studies, College of Nursing and Allied Health, Thibodaux, LA 70310. Offers family nurse practitioner (MSN); nurse executive (MSN); nursing education (MSN); psychiatric/mental health nurse practitioner (MSN).

**Northeastern State University,** College of Science and Health Professions, Department of Health Professions, Program in Nursing, Muskogee, OK 74401. Offers nursing (MSN). *Faculty:* 2 full-time (both women), 4 part-time/adjunct (3 women). *Students:* 3 full-time (all women), 37 part-time (31 women); includes 17 minority (4 Black or African American, non-Hispanic/Latino; 7 American Indian or Alaska Native, non-Hispanic/Latino; 3 Hispanic/Latino; 3 Two or more races, non-Hispanic/Latino). Average age 42. In 2019, 4 master's awarded. *Application deadline:* Applications are processed on a rolling basis. Application fee: $25. Electronic applications accepted. *Expenses: Tuition, area resident:* Full-time $250; part-time $250 per credit hour. Tuition, state resident: full-time $250; part-time $250 per credit hour. Tuition, nonresident: full-time $556; part-time $555.50 per credit hour. *Required fees:* $33.40 per credit hour. *Unit head:* Dr. Heather Fenton, Program Coordinator, 918-444-5221, E-mail: fentonh@nsuok.edu. *Application contact:* Josh McCollum, Graduate Coordinator, 918-444-2093, E-mail: mccolluj@nsuok.edu.
Website: http://academics.nsuok.edu/healthprofessions/DegreePrograms/Graduate/NursingEducationMSN.aspx

**Norwich University,** College of Graduate and Continuing Studies, Master of Science in Nursing Program, Northfield, VT 05663. Offers nursing administration (MSN); nursing education (MSN). *Accreditation:* AACN. *Program availability:* Evening/weekend, online only, mostly all online with a week-long residency requirement. *Entrance requirements:* For master's, minimum undergraduate GPA of 3.0. Additional exam requirements/recommendations for international students: required—TOEFL (minimum score 550 paper-based; 80 iBT), IELTS (minimum score 6.5). Electronic applications accepted. *Expenses:* Contact institution.

**Nova Southeastern University,** Ron and Kathy Assaf College of Nursing, Fort Lauderdale, FL 33314-7796. Offers advanced practice registered nurse (MSN), including adult-gerontology acute care nurse practitioner, family nurse practitioner, psychiatric mental health nurse practitioner; executive nurse leadership (MSN); nursing (PhD), including nursing education; nursing education (MSN); nursing informatics (MSN); nursing practice (DNP). *Accreditation:* AACN. *Program availability:* Part-time, evening/weekend, 100% online, blended/hybrid learning, annual one-week summer institute delivered face-to-face on main campus. *Faculty:* 32 full-time (29 women), 34 part-time/adjunct (31 women). *Students:* 4 full-time (3 women), 658 part-time (585 women); includes 427 minority (182 Black or African American, non-Hispanic/Latino; 35 Asian, non-Hispanic/Latino; 197 Hispanic/Latino; 13 Two or more races, non-Hispanic/Latino), 3 international. Average age 38. 157 applicants, 93% accepted, 146 enrolled. In 2019, 184 master's, 12 doctorates awarded. *Degree requirements:* For doctorate, comprehensive exam, thesis/dissertation. *Entrance requirements:* For master's, minimum GPA of 3.0, RN, BSN, BS or BA; for doctorate, minimum GPA of 3.5, MSN, RN. Additional exam requirements/recommendations for international students: recommended—TOEFL. *Application deadline:* For fall admission, 8/1 for domestic students, 3/1 for international students; for winter admission, 12/9 for domestic students, 11/1 for international students. Applications are processed on a rolling basis. Application fee: $50. Electronic applications accepted. *Expenses:* Contact institution. *Financial support:* Application deadline: 4/15; applicants required to submit FAFSA. *Unit head:* Dr. Marcella M. Rutherford, Dean, 954-262-1963, E-mail: rmarcell@nova.edu. *Application contact:* Dianna Murphey, Director of Operations, 954-262-1975, E-mail: dgardner1@nova.edu.
Website: http://www.nova.edu/nursing/

**Ohio University,** Graduate College, College of Health Sciences and Professions, School of Nursing, Athens, OH 45701-2979. Offers advanced clinical practice (DNP); executive practice (DNP); family nurse practitioner (MSN); nurse educator (MSN). *Accreditation:* AACN. *Degree requirements:* For master's, capstone project. *Entrance requirements:* For master's, GRE, bachelor's degree in nursing from accredited college or university, minimum overall undergraduate GPA of 3.0, official transcripts, statement of goals and objectives, resume, 3 letters of recommendation. Additional exam requirements/recommendations for international students: required—TOEFL (minimum score 550 paper-based; 80 iBT) or IELTS (minimum score 6.5). Electronic applications accepted.

**Oklahoma Baptist University,** Program in Nursing, Shawnee, OK 74804. Offers global nursing (MSN); nursing education (MSN). *Accreditation:* AACN.

**Oklahoma City University,** Kramer School of Nursing, Oklahoma City, OK 73106-1402. Offers clinical nurse leader (MSN); nursing (DNP, PhD); nursing education (MSN). *Accreditation:* ACEN. *Program availability:* Part-time, evening/weekend, online learning. *Degree requirements:* For master's, thesis, minimum GPA of 3.0; for doctorate, comprehensive exam, thesis/dissertation, minimum GPA of 3.0. *Entrance requirements:* For master's, registered nurse licensure, minimum undergraduate GPA of 3.0, BSN from nationally-accredited nursing program, completion of courses in health assessment and statistics; for doctorate, GRE, current RN licensure; bachelor's and master's degrees from accredited programs (at least one of which must be in nursing); minimum graduate GPA of 3.5; personal essay; approved scholarly paper or published article/paper in a refereed journal. Additional exam requirements/recommendations for international students: required—TOEFL (minimum score 550 paper-based; 80 iBT), IELTS (minimum score 6). Electronic applications accepted. *Expenses:* Contact institution.

**Oklahoma Wesleyan University,** Professional Studies Division, Bartlesville, OK 74006-6299. Offers nursing administration (MSN); nursing education (MSN); strategic leadership (MS); theology and apologetics (MA).

**Old Dominion University,** College of Health Sciences, School of Nursing, Adult Gerontology Nursing Emphasis, Norfolk, VA 23529. Offers adult gerontology clinical nurse specialist/administrator (MSN); adult gerontology clinical nurse specialist/educator (MSN); advanced practice (DNP); neonatal clinical nurse specialist (MSN); pediatric clinical nurse specialist (MSN). *Program availability:* Part-time, online only, blended/hybrid learning. *Degree requirements:* For master's, comprehensive exam, internship, practicum. *Entrance requirements:* For master's, GRE or MAT (waived with a GPA above 3.5), undergraduate health/physical assessment course, statistics, 3 letters of recommendation, essay, resume, transcripts. Additional exam requirements/recommendations for international students: required—TOEFL. Electronic applications accepted. *Expenses:* Contact institution.

**Oregon Health & Science University,** School of Nursing, Program in Nursing Education, Portland, OR 97239-3098. Offers MN, Post Master's Certificate. *Program availability:* Part-time, online only, 100% online. *Entrance requirements:* For master's, minimum cumulative GPA of 3.0, 3 letters of recommendation, essay, RN license or eligibility, BS with major in nursing or BSN, statistics taken in last 5 years with minimum B- grade; for Post Master's Certificate, minimum cumulative GPA of 3.0, 3 letters of recommendation, essay, RN license or eligibility, master's degree in nursing, statistics taken in last 5 years with minimum B- grade. Additional exam requirements/recommendations for international students: required—TOEFL (minimum score 83 iBT). Electronic applications accepted. *Expenses:* Contact institution.

**Otterbein University,** Department of Nursing, Westerville, OH 43081. Offers advanced practice nurse educator (Certificate); clinical nurse leader (MSN); family nurse practitioner (MSN, Certificate); nurse anesthesia (MSN, Certificate); nursing (DNP); nursing service administration (MSN). *Accreditation:* AACN; AANA/CANAEP; ACEN. *Program availability:* Part-time, evening/weekend, online learning. *Degree requirements:* For master's, comprehensive exam (for some programs), thesis (for some programs). *Entrance requirements:* For master's, 2 reference forms, resume; for Certificate, official transcripts, 2 reference forms, essay, resumé. Additional exam requirements/recommendations for international students: required—TOEFL (minimum score 550 paper-based; 79 iBT).

**Pennsylvania College of Health Sciences,** Graduate Programs, Lancaster, PA 17601. Offers administration (MSN); education (MSHS, MSN); healthcare administration

(MHA). *Degree requirements:* For master's, internship (for MHA, MSN in administration); practicum (for MSHS, MSN in education).

**Pittsburg State University,** Graduate School, College of Arts and Sciences, Irene Ransom Bailey School of Nursing, Pittsburg, KS 66762. Offers nursing (DNP); nursing education (MSN). *Accreditation:* AACN. *Program availability:* Part-time. *Degree requirements:* For master's, thesis optional; for doctorate, thesis/dissertation optional. *Entrance requirements:* For master's, GRE General Test. Additional exam requirements/recommendations for international students: required—TOEFL (minimum score 550 paper-based; 79 iBT), IELTS (minimum score 6.5), PTE (minimum score 53). Electronic applications accepted. *Expenses:* Contact institution.

**Purdue University Fort Wayne,** College of Health and Human Services, Department of Nursing, Fort Wayne, IN 46805-1499. Offers adult-gerontology primary care nurse practitioner (MS); family nurse practitioner (MS); nurse executive (MS); nursing administration (Certificate); nursing education (MS). *Accreditation:* ACEN. *Program availability:* Part-time. *Entrance requirements:* For master's, GRE Writing Test (if GPA below 3.0), BS in nursing, eligibility for Indiana RN license, minimum GPA of 3.0, essay, copy of resume, three references, undergraduate course work in research and statistics within last 5 years. Additional exam requirements/recommendations for international students: required—TOEFL (minimum score 550 paper-based; 79 iBT); recommended—TWE. Electronic applications accepted.

**Purdue University Global,** School of Nursing, Davenport, IA 52807. Offers nurse administrator (MS); nurse educator (MS). *Program availability:* Part-time, evening/weekend, online learning. *Entrance requirements:* For master's, RN. Additional exam requirements/recommendations for international students: required—TOEFL (minimum score 550 paper-based).

**Queens University of Charlotte,** Presbyterian School of Nursing, Charlotte, NC 28274-0002. Offers clinical nurse leader (MSN); nurse educator (MSN); nursing administrator (MSN). *Accreditation:* AACN. *Degree requirements:* For master's, research project. *Entrance requirements:* For master's, minimum GPA of 3.0. Additional exam requirements/recommendations for international students: required—TOEFL. Electronic applications accepted. *Expenses:* Contact institution.

**Ramapo College of New Jersey,** Master of Science in Nursing Program, Mahwah, NJ 07430. Offers family nurse practitioner (MSN); nursing administrator (MSN); nursing education (MSN). *Accreditation:* ACEN. *Program availability:* Part-time. *Degree requirements:* For master's, thesis or alternative. *Entrance requirements:* For master's, official transcript; personal statement; 2 letters of recommendation; resume; current licensure as a Registered Nurse, or eligibility for licensure; evidence of one year of recent experience as RN prior to entry into clinical practicum courses; evidence of undergraduate statistics course; criminal background check. Additional exam requirements/recommendations for international students: required—TOEFL (minimum score 550 paper-based; 90 iBT); recommended—IELTS (minimum score 6). Electronic applications accepted. *Expenses:* Contact institution.

**Regis College,** Nursing and Health Sciences School, Weston, MA 02493. Offers applied behavior analysis (MS); counseling psychology (MA); health administration (MS); nurse practitioner (Certificate); nursing (MS, DNP); nursing education (Certificate); occupational therapy (MS). *Accreditation:* ACEN. *Program availability:* Part-time, evening/weekend, 100% online, blended/hybrid learning. *Degree requirements:* For doctorate, thesis/dissertation. *Entrance requirements:* For master's, minimum GPA of 3.0, official transcripts, recommendations, personal statement, resume/curriculum vitae, interview; for doctorate, GRE if GPA from master's lower than 3.5. Additional exam requirements/recommendations for international students: required—TOEFL (minimum score 560 paper-based; 79 iBT); recommended—IELTS (minimum score 6.5). *Application deadline:* Applications are processed on a rolling basis. Application fee: $75. Electronic applications accepted. *Financial support:* Federal Work-Study, scholarships/grants, and unspecified assistantships available. Support available to part-time students. Financial award applicants required to submit FAFSA. *Application contact:* Thomas May, Graduate Admission Counselor, 781-768-7162, E-mail: thomas.may@regiscollege.edu.

**Regis University,** Rueckert-Hartman College for Health Professions, Denver, CO 80221-1099. Offers advanced practice nurse (DNP); counseling (MA); counseling children and adolescents (Post-Graduate Certificate); counseling military families (Post-Graduate Certificate); depth psychotherapy (Post-Graduate Certificate); fellowship in orthopedic manual physical therapy (Certificate); health care business management (Certificate); health care quality and patient safety (Certificate); health industry leadership (MBA); health services administration (MS); marriage and family therapy (MA, Post-Graduate Certificate); neonatal nurse practitioner (MSN); nursing education (MSN); nursing leadership (MSN); occupational therapy (OTD); pharmacy (Pharm D); physical therapy (DPT). *Accreditation:* ACPE. *Program availability:* Part-time, evening/weekend, 100% online, blended/hybrid learning. *Degree requirements:* For master's, thesis (for some programs), internship. *Entrance requirements:* For master's, official transcript reflecting baccalaureate degree awarded from regionally-accredited college or university. Additional exam requirements/recommendations for international students: required—TOEFL (minimum score 550 paper-based; 82 iBT). Electronic applications accepted. *Expenses:* Contact institution.

**Rivier University,** School of Graduate Studies, Division of Nursing and Health Professions, Nashua, NH 03060. Offers family nurse practitioner (MS); leadership in health systems management (MS); nursing education (MS); nursing practice (DNP); psychiatric/mental health nurse practitioner (MS); public health (MPH). *Accreditation:* ACEN. *Program availability:* Part-time, evening/weekend. *Entrance requirements:* For master's, GRE, MAT. Electronic applications accepted.

**Roberts Wesleyan College,** Department of Nursing, Rochester, NY 14624-1997. Offers nursing education (MSN); nursing informatics (MSN); nursing leadership and administration (MSN). *Accreditation:* AACN. *Program availability:* Evening/weekend, online learning. *Degree requirements:* For master's, thesis. *Entrance requirements:* For master's, minimum GPA of 3.0; BS in nursing; interview; RN license; resume; course work in statistics. Additional exam requirements/recommendations for international students: required—TOEFL (minimum score 90 iBT), IELTS (minimum score 6.5). Electronic applications accepted.

**Sacred Heart University,** Graduate Programs, College of Nursing, Fairfield, CT 06825. Offers clinical (DNP); clinical nurse leader (MSN); family nurse practitioner (MSN, Post-Master's Certificate); leadership (DNP); nursing education (MSN); nursing management and executive leadership (MSN). *Accreditation:* AACN. *Program availability:* Part-time, evening/weekend, 100% online, blended/hybrid learning. *Degree requirements:* For master's, thesis, 500 clinical hours; for doctorate, capstone. *Entrance requirements:* For master's, minimum GPA of 3.0, BSN or RN plus BS (for MSN); for doctorate, minimum GPA of 3.0, MSN or BSN plus MS in related field (for DNP). Additional exam requirements/recommendations for international students: required—TOEFL (minimum score 570 paper-based, 80 iBT), TWE, or IELTS (6.5). Electronic applications accepted. *Expenses:* Contact institution.

**Sage Graduate School,** School of Health Sciences, Department of Nursing, Program in Education and Leadership, Troy, NY 12180-4115. Offers DNS. *Program availability:* Part-time-only. *Faculty:* 8 full-time (all women), 13 part-time/adjunct (12 women). *Students:* 9 part-time (8 women), 2 international. Average age 49. In 2019, 4 doctorates awarded. *Degree requirements:* For doctorate, thesis/dissertation. *Entrance requirements:* For doctorate, master's degree in nursing from accredited institution; minimum GPA of 3.5; official transcripts; academic curriculum vitae; 3 letters of recommendation; 1-2 page personal essay; interview; current registered nurse license. Additional exam requirements/recommendations for international students: required—TOEFL (minimum score 550 paper-based). Application fee: $40. Electronic applications accepted. *Expenses:* Contact institution. *Unit head:* Dr. Kathleen Kelly, Dean, School of Health Sciences, 518-244-2030, Fax: 518-244-2009, E-mail: kellyk5@sage.edu. *Application contact:* Dr. Kathleen A. Kelly, Associate Professor/Director, Doctor of Nursing Science Program, 518-244-2030, Fax: 518-244-2009, E-mail: kelly5@sage.edu.

**St. Catherine University,** Graduate Programs, Program in Nursing, St. Paul, MN 55105. Offers adult-gerontological nurse practitioner (MS); nurse educator (MS); nursing (DNP); nursing; entry-level (MS); pediatric nurse practitioner (MS). *Accreditation:* ACEN. *Program availability:* Part-time, evening/weekend. *Degree requirements:* For master's, thesis; for doctorate, portfolio, systems change project. *Entrance requirements:* For master's, GRE General Test, bachelor's degree in nursing, current nursing license, 2 years of recent clinical practice; for doctorate, master's degree in nursing, RN license, advanced nursing position. Additional exam requirements/recommendations for international students: required—TOEFL (minimum score 600 paper-based; 100 iBT). *Expenses:* Contact institution.

**Saint Francis Medical Center College of Nursing,** SFMC College of Nursing Graduate Programs, Peoria, IL 61603-3783. Offers adult gerontology (MSN); clinical nurse leader (MSN); family nurse practitioner (MSN, Post-Graduate Certificate); family psychiatric mental health nurse practitioner (MSN); neonatal nurse practitioner (MSN); nurse clinician (Post-Graduate Certificate); nurse educator (MSN, Post-Graduate Certificate); nursing (DNP), including leadership/ clinician; nursing management leadership (MSN). *Accreditation:* ACEN. *Program availability:* Part-time, online only, 100% online, blended/hybrid learning. *Faculty:* 12 full-time (all women), 10 part-time/adjunct (all women). *Students:* 1 (woman) full-time, 188 part-time (157 women); includes 20 minority (10 Black or African American, non-Hispanic/Latino; 3 Asian, non-Hispanic/Latino; 3 Hispanic/Latino; 4 Two or more races, non-Hispanic/Latino). Average age 40. 54 applicants, 91% accepted, 18 enrolled. In 2019, 51 master's, 11 doctorates awarded. *Degree requirements:* For master's, research experience, portfolio, practicum; for doctorate, practicum. *Entrance requirements:* For master's, Nursing research, health assessment, RN license; for doctorate, Master's degree in nursing, professional portfolio, graduate statistics, transcripts, RN license. Additional exam requirements/recommendations for international students: required—TOEFL (minimum score 550 paper-based; 79 iBT). *Application deadline:* For fall admission, 6/1 priority date for domestic and international students; for spring admission, 11/15 priority date for domestic and international students. Applications are processed on a rolling basis. Application fee: $50. *Expenses: Tuition:* Part-time $705 per credit hour. *Required fees:* $270 per unit. *Financial support:* In 2019-20, 13 students received support. Scholarships/grants available. Support available to part-time students. Financial award application deadline: 6/15; financial award applicants required to submit FAFSA. *Unit head:* Dr. Sandie S Soldwisch, President of OSF Colleges of Health Sciences, 815-282-7909, Fax: 309-624-8973, E-mail: Sandie.S.Soldwisch@osfhealthcare.org. *Application contact:* Dr. Kim A. Mitchell, Dean, Graduate Program, 309-655-2201, Fax: 309-624-8973, E-mail: kim.a.mitchell@osfhealthcare.org.
Website: http://www.sfmccon.edu/graduate-programs/

**Saint Francis University,** Nursing Program, Loretto, PA 15940-0600. Offers leadership/education (MSN). *Program availability:* Part-time, online only, blended/hybrid learning. *Faculty:* 2 full-time (both women), 4 part-time/adjunct (all women). *Students:* 7 part-time (all women). Average age 44. 9 applicants, 78% accepted, 4 enrolled. In 2019, 10 master's awarded. *Entrance requirements:* Additional exam requirements/recommendations for international students: required—TOEFL. Application fee: $30. Electronic applications accepted. *Expenses:* 625 per credit, 48 credits. *Financial support:* Applicants required to submit FAFSA. *Unit head:* Dr. Camille Wendekier, RN, Coordinator, 814-472-2843, E-mail: cwendekier@francis.edu. *Application contact:* Dr. Peter Raymond Skoner.
Website: https://www.francis.edu/Nursing-Masters/

**St. Joseph's College, Long Island Campus,** Program in Nursing, Patchogue, NY 11772-2399. Offers adult-gerontology clinical nurse specialist (MS); adult-gerontology primary care nurse practitioner (MS); nursing education (MS). *Program availability:* Part-time, evening/weekend. *Faculty:* 7 full-time (6 women), 1 (woman) part-time/adjunct. *Students:* 54 part-time (48 women); includes 18 minority (7 Black or African American, non-Hispanic/Latino; 2 Asian, non-Hispanic/Latino; 8 Hispanic/Latino; 1 Two or more races, non-Hispanic/Latino). Average age 38. 57 applicants, 51% accepted, 22 enrolled. In 2019, 14 master's awarded. *Entrance requirements:* For master's, Application, proof of New York State R.N. license, curriculum vitae, personal statement, 2 letters of reference, official transcripts, verification of employment form, proof of malpractice insurance. Additional exam requirements/recommendations for international students: required—TOEFL (minimum score 80 iBT). *Application deadline:* Applications are processed on a rolling basis. Application fee: $25. Electronic applications accepted. *Expenses: Tuition:* Full-time $19,350; part-time $1075 per credit. *Required fees:* $410. *Financial support:* In 2019-20, 33 students received support. *Unit head:* Dr. Maria Fletcher, RN, Director, Associate Professor, 631-687-5180, E-mail: mfletcher@sjcny.edu. *Application contact:* Dr. Maria Fletcher, RN, Director, Associate Professor, 631-687-5180, E-mail: mfletcher@sjcny.edu.
Website: https://www.sjcny.edu/nursingli

**St. Joseph's College, New York,** Program in Nursing, Brooklyn, NY 11205-3688. Offers adult-gerontology clinical nurse specialist (MS); adult-gerontology primary care nurse practitioner (MS); nursing education (MS). *Accreditation:* ACEN. *Program availability:* Part-time, evening/weekend. *Faculty:* 3 full-time (all women), 2 part-time/adjunct (both women). *Students:* 52 part-time (47 women); includes 43 minority (40 Black or African American, non-Hispanic/Latino; 2 Asian, non-Hispanic/Latino; 1 Two or more races, non-Hispanic/Latino). Average age 43. 49 applicants, 67% accepted, 21 enrolled. In 2019, 19 master's awarded. *Entrance requirements:* Additional exam requirements/recommendations for international students: required—TOEFL (minimum score 80 iBT). *Application deadline:* Applications are processed on a rolling basis. Application fee: $25. Electronic applications accepted. *Expenses: Tuition:* Full-time $19,350; part-time $1075 per credit. *Required fees:* $400. *Financial support:* In 2019-20, 9 students received support. *Unit head:* Maria Fletcher, Director, Associate Professor, 718-940-5891, E-mail: mfletcher@sjcny.edu. *Application contact:* Maria Fletcher, Director, Associate Professor, 718-940-5891, E-mail: mfletcher@sjcny.edu.
Website: https://www.sjcny.edu/brooklyn/academics/graduate/graduate-degrees/nursing-clinical-nurse-specialist/m.s.-in-nursing-major

**Saint Joseph's College of Maine,** Master of Science in Nursing Program, Standish, ME 04084. Offers administration (MSN); education (MSN); family nurse practitioner (MSN); nursing administration and leadership (Certificate); nursing and health care

education (Certificate). *Accreditation:* AACN. *Program availability:* Part-time, online learning. *Entrance requirements:* For master's, MAT. Electronic applications accepted.

**Salem State University,** School of Graduate Studies, Program in Nursing, Salem, MA 01970-5353. Offers adult-gerontology primary care nursing (MSN); nursing administration (MSN); nursing education (MSN); MBA/MSN. *Accreditation:* AACN. *Program availability:* Part-time, evening/weekend. *Entrance requirements:* For master's, GRE or MAT. Additional exam requirements/recommendations for international students: required—TOEFL (minimum score 550 paper-based; 80 iBT) or IELTS (minimum score 5.5).

**Salisbury University,** MS in Nursing Program, Salisbury, MD 21801-6837. Offers nursing (MS), including clinical nurse educator, health care leadership. *Accreditation:* AACN. *Program availability:* Part-time, evening/weekend, 100% online, blended/hybrid learning. *Faculty:* 14 full-time (13 women), 4 part-time/adjunct (all women). *Students:* 1 (woman) full-time, 4 part-time (all women); includes 2 minority (1 Asian, non-Hispanic/Latino; 1 Hispanic/Latino). Average age 27. 3 applicants, 100% accepted, 3 enrolled. *Degree requirements:* For master's, internship, capstone or thesis. *Entrance requirements:* For master's, transcripts; resume or CV; personal statement; proof of certification or licensure; minimum GPA of 3.0; two letters of recommendation; undergraduate degree in nursing; undergraduate statistics. *Application deadline:* For fall admission, 3/1 priority date for domestic and international students. Application fee: $65. Electronic applications accepted. *Expenses:* Contact institution. *Financial support:* In 2019–20, 1 student received support, including 1 research assistantship with full tuition reimbursement available (averaging $8,000 per year), 1 teaching assistantship with full tuition reimbursement available (averaging $9,000 per year); career-related internships or fieldwork and scholarships/grants also available. Support available to part-time students. Financial award application deadline: 3/1; financial award applicants required to submit FAFSA. *Unit head:* Dr. Annette Barnes, Graduate Program Chair, 410-546-4380, E-mail: ahbarnes@salisbury.edu. *Application contact:* Kristi Jenkins, Administrative Assistant II, 410-548-2242, E-mail: kljenkins@salisbury.edu.
Website: https://www.salisbury.edu/explore-academics/programs/graduate-degree-programs/nursing-master/

**San Jose State University,** Program in Nursing, San Jose, CA 95192-0057. Offers gerontology nurse practitioner (MS); nursing (Certificate); nursing administration (MS); nursing education (MS). *Accreditation:* AACN. *Faculty:* 5 full-time (all women), 3 part-time/adjunct (all women). *Students:* 21 full-time (17 women), 52 part-time (49 women); includes 45 minority (4 Black or African American, non-Hispanic/Latino; 29 Asian, non-Hispanic/Latino; 12 Hispanic/Latino), 3 international. Average age 37. 30 applicants, 97% accepted, 23 enrolled. In 2019, 22 master's awarded. *Degree requirements:* For master's, comprehensive exam, thesis. *Entrance requirements:* For master's, BSN. *Application deadline:* For fall admission, 3/1 for domestic students. Applications are processed on a rolling basis. Application fee: $70. Electronic applications accepted. *Expenses:* Contact institution. *Financial support:* Application deadline: 5/1; applicants required to submit FAFSA. *Unit head:* Colleen O'Leary-Kelley, Department Chair, 408-924-1319, Fax: 408-924-3135, E-mail: colleen.oleary-kelley@sjsu.edu. *Application contact:* Karen Wilcox, FNP Program Analyst, 408-924-3153, Fax: 408-924-3135, E-mail: karen.wilcox@sjsu.edu.
Website: http://www.sjsu.edu/nursing/

**Seattle Pacific University,** MS in Nursing Program, Seattle, WA 98119-1997. Offers administration (MSN); adult/gerontology nurse practitioner (MSN); clinical nurse specialist (MSN); family nurse practitioner (MSN, Certificate); informatics (MSN); nurse educator (MSN). *Accreditation:* AACN. *Program availability:* Part-time. *Students:* 42 full-time (38 women), 18 part-time (16 women); includes 28 minority (5 Black or African American, non-Hispanic/Latino; 18 Asian, non-Hispanic/Latino; 5 Hispanic/Latino), 2 international. Average age 33. 59 applicants, 41% accepted. In 2019, 10 master's awarded. *Degree requirements:* For master's, thesis. *Entrance requirements:* For master's, personal statement, transcripts, undergraduate nursing degree, proof of undergraduate statistics course with minimum GPA of 2.0, 2 recommendations. *Application deadline:* For fall admission, 1/15 priority date for domestic students; for spring admission, 1/15 for domestic students. Applications are processed on a rolling basis. Application fee: $50. Electronic applications accepted. *Expenses:* Contact institution. *Financial support:* Fellowships and scholarships/grants available. Financial award applicants required to submit FAFSA. *Unit head:* Dr. Antwinett Lee, Associate Dean, 206-281-2607, E-mail: leea30@spu.edu. *Application contact:* Dr. Antwinett Lee, Associate Dean, 206-281-2607, E-mail: leea30@spu.edu.
Website: http://spu.edu/academics/school-of-health-sciences/undergraduate-programs/nursing

**Seton Hall University,** College of Nursing, South Orange, NJ 07079-2697. Offers advanced practice in primary health care (MSN, DNP), including adult/gerontological nurse practitioner, pediatric nurse practitioner; entry into practice (MSN); health systems administration (MSN, DNP); nursing (PhD); nursing case management (MSN); nursing education (MA); school nurse (MSN); MSN/MA. *Accreditation:* AACN. *Program availability:* Part-time, online learning. *Degree requirements:* For master's, research project; for doctorate, dissertation or scholarly project. *Entrance requirements:* For doctorate, GRE (waived for students with GPA of 3.5 or higher). Additional exam requirements/recommendations for international students: required—TOEFL. Electronic applications accepted.

**Shenandoah University,** Eleanor Wade Custer School of Nursing, Winchester, VA 22601. Offers adult gerontology primary care nurse practitioner (Graduate Certificate); adult-gerontology primary care nurse practitioner (MSN); family nurse practitioner (MSN, DNP, Graduate Certificate); general (MSN); health systems leadership (DNP); health systems management (MSN, Graduate Certificate); nurse midwifery (MSN); nurse-midwifery (Graduate Certificate); nursing education (Graduate Certificate); nursing practice (DNP); psychiatric mental health nurse practitioner (MSN, DNP, Graduate Certificate). *Accreditation:* AACN; ACNM/ACME. *Entrance requirements:* For master's, United States RN license; minimum GPA of 3.0; 2080 hours of clinical experience; curriculum vitae; 3 letters of recommendation from former dean, faculty member, or advisor familiar with the applicant, and a former or current supervisor; two-to-three-page essay on a specified topic; for doctorate, MSN, minimum GPA of 3.0, 3 letters of recommendation, interview, BSN, two-to-three page essay on a specific topic, 500-word statement of clinical practice research interest, resume, current U.S. RN license, 2080 clinical hours; for Graduate Certificate, MSN, minimum GPA of 3.0, 2 letters of recommendation, minimum of one year (2080 hours) of clinical nursing experience, interview, two-to-three page essay on a specific topic, resume, current United States RN license. Additional exam requirements/recommendations for international students: required—TOEFL (minimum score 558 paper-based; 83 iBT). Electronic applications accepted. *Expenses:* Contact institution.

**Southern Adventist University,** School of Nursing, Collegedale, TN 37315-0370. Offers acute care-adult/gerontology nurse practitioner (MSN, DNP); healthcare administration (MSN/MBA); lifestyle medicine (DNP); nurse educator (MSN, DNP); primary care-adult/gerontology nurse practitioner (MSN); primary care-family nurse practitioner (MSN, DNP); primary care-psychiatric mental health nurse practitioner (MSN, DNP); MSN/MBA. *Accreditation:* ACEN. *Program availability:* Part-time, 100% online. *Degree requirements:* For master's, thesis or project; for doctorate, scholarly project. *Entrance requirements:* For master's, RN license. Additional exam requirements/recommendations for international students: required—TOEFL (minimum score 100 iBT). Electronic applications accepted.

**Southern Connecticut State University,** School of Graduate Studies, School of Health and Human Services, Department of Nursing, New Haven, CT 06515-1355. Offers family nurse practitioner (MSN); nursing (Ed D); nursing education (MSN). *Accreditation:* AACN. *Program availability:* Part-time, evening/weekend. *Degree requirements:* For master's, thesis. *Entrance requirements:* For master's, GRE, MAT, interview, minimum QPA of 2.8, RN license, minimum 1 year of professional nursing experience. Electronic applications accepted.

**Southern Illinois University Edwardsville,** Graduate School, School of Nursing, Program in Nurse Educator, Edwardsville, IL 62026. Offers MS, Post-Master's Certificate. *Program availability:* Part-time, evening/weekend. *Degree requirements:* For master's, comprehensive exam. *Entrance requirements:* For master's, RN licensure, minimum undergraduate nursing GPA of 3.0. Additional exam requirements/recommendations for international students: required—TOEFL (minimum score 550 paper-based; 79 iBT), IELTS (minimum score 6.5). Electronic applications accepted.

**Southern Nazarene University,** College of Professional and Graduate Studies, School of Nursing, Bethany, OK 73008. Offers nursing education (MS); nursing leadership (MS). *Accreditation:* AACN. *Program availability:* Part-time, evening/weekend. *Degree requirements:* For master's, thesis. *Entrance requirements:* For master's, minimum undergraduate cumulative GPA of 3.0; baccalaureate degree in nursing from nationally-accredited program; current unencumbered registered nurse licensure in Oklahoma or eligibility for same; documentation of basic computer skills; basic statistics course; statement of professional goals; three letters of recommendation. Additional exam requirements/recommendations for international students: required—TOEFL (minimum score 550 paper-based).

**Southern New Hampshire University,** Program in Nursing, Manchester, NH 03106-1045. Offers clinical nurse leader (MSN); nurse educator (MSN); nursing (MSN); patient safety and quality (MSN, Post Master's Certificate). *Program availability:* Online only, 100% online. *Entrance requirements:* For master's, undergraduate transcripts, active unencumbered license, bachelor's degree with minimum cumulative GPA of 3.0. Electronic applications accepted.

**Southern University and Agricultural and Mechanical College,** College of Nursing and Allied Health, School of Nursing, Baton Rouge, LA 70813. Offers educator/administrator (PhD); family health nursing (MSN); family nurse practitioner (Post Master's Certificate); geriatric nurse practitioner/gerontology (PhD); nursing (DNP). *Accreditation:* AACN. *Program availability:* Part-time. *Degree requirements:* For master's, comprehensive exam, thesis; for doctorate, comprehensive exam, thesis/dissertation. *Entrance requirements:* For master's, GRE General Test, BSN, minimum GPA of 2.7; for doctorate, GRE General Test; for Post Master's Certificate, MSN. Additional exam requirements/recommendations for international students: required—TOEFL (minimum score 525 paper-based).

**South University - Savannah,** Graduate Programs, College of Nursing, Savannah, GA 31406. Offers nurse educator (MS). *Accreditation:* AACN.

**South University - Tampa,** Program in Nursing, Tampa, FL 33614. Offers adult health nurse practitioner (MS); family nurse practitioner (MS); nurse educator (MS).

**Spalding University,** Graduate Studies, Kosair College of Health and Natural Sciences, School of Nursing, Louisville, KY 40203-2188. Offers adult nurse practitioner (MSN); family nurse practitioner (MSN); leadership in nursing and healthcare (MSN); nurse educator (Post-Master's Certificate); nurse practitioner (Post-Master's Certificate); pediatric nurse practitioner (MSN). *Accreditation:* AACN. *Program availability:* Part-time, evening/weekend. *Degree requirements:* For master's, comprehensive exam (for some programs), thesis. *Entrance requirements:* For master's, GRE General Test, BSN or bachelor's degree in related field, RN licensure, autobiographical statement, transcripts, letters of recommendation. Additional exam requirements/recommendations for international students: required—TOEFL (minimum score 535 paper-based).

**State University of New York College of Technology at Delhi,** Program in Nursing, Delhi, NY 13753. Offers nursing administration (MS); nursing education (MS). *Program availability:* Part-time, online only, 100% online. *Faculty:* 6 full-time (all women), 2 part-time/adjunct (both women). *Students:* 10 full-time (7 women), 77 part-time (70 women); includes 13 minority (7 Black or African American, non-Hispanic/Latino; 2 Asian, non-Hispanic/Latino; 4 Hispanic/Latino). Average age 38. 70 applicants, 71% accepted, 37 enrolled. In 2019, 15 master's awarded. *Application deadline:* For fall admission, 7/15 for domestic and international students; for spring admission, 11/15 for domestic and international students. Applications are processed on a rolling basis. Application fee: $75. Electronic applications accepted. *Expenses: Tuition, area resident:* Full-time $11,310; part-time $471 per credit hour. Tuition, state resident: full-time $11,310; part-time $471 per credit hour. Tuition, nonresident: full-time $13,570; part-time $565 per credit hour. *International tuition:* $13,570 full-time. *Required fees:* $420; $21.70 per credit hour. $21.70. *Financial support:* In 2019–20, 4 students received support. Scholarships/grants available. Financial award applicants required to submit FAFSA. *Unit head:* Susan Deane, Dean of the School of Nursing, 607-746-4550, Fax: 607-746-4104, E-mail: deanesg@delhi.edu. *Application contact:* Misty Fields, Associate Director of Admission, 607-746-4546, E-mail: fieldsmr@delhi.edu.

**State University of New York Empire State College,** School for Graduate Studies, Program in Nursing Education, Saratoga Springs, NY 12866-4391. Offers MSN. *Accreditation:* AACN. *Program availability:* Online learning. *Degree requirements:* For master's, capstone.

**State University of New York Polytechnic Institute,** Program in Nursing Education, Utica, NY 13502. Offers MS, CAS. *Program availability:* Part-time, 100% online. *Degree requirements:* For master's, clinical hours; for CAS, project/internship. *Entrance requirements:* For master's, Bachelor of Science in Nursing and statistics course. Electronic applications accepted.

**Stevenson University,** Program in Nursing, Stevenson, MD 21153. Offers nursing education (MS); nursing leadership/management (MS); population-based care coordination (MS). *Accreditation:* AACN. *Program availability:* Part-time, blended/hybrid learning. *Faculty:* 2 full-time (both women), 5 part-time/adjunct (all women). *Students:* 144 part-time (138 women); includes 33 minority (24 Black or African American, non-Hispanic/Latino; 3 Asian, non-Hispanic/Latino; 4 Hispanic/Latino; 2 Two or more races, non-Hispanic/Latino). Average age 37. 56 applicants, 73% accepted, 30 enrolled. In 2019, 50 master's awarded. *Degree requirements:* For master's, capstone course. *Entrance requirements:* For master's, Personal statement; Official college transcript; Bachelor's degree in nursing; Cumulative GPA of 3.0; current registered nurse's license in good standing; 1 letter of recommendation; Professional Resume. *Application deadline:* For fall admission, 8/9 priority date for domestic students; for spring admission, 1/11 priority date for domestic students; for summer admission, 5/1 priority date for domestic students. Applications are processed on a rolling basis. Electronic applications accepted. *Expenses:* $625 per credit. *Financial support:* Unspecified assistantships available. Financial award applicants required to submit FAFSA. *Unit head:* Dr. Judith Feustle, Associate Dean, 443-394-9818, Fax: 443-394-0538, E-mail:

jfeustle@stevenson.edu. *Application contact:* Amanda Millar, Director, Admissions, 443-352-4243, Fax: 443-394-0538, E-mail: amillar@stevenson.edu.
Website: https://www.stevenson.edu/online/academics/online-graduate-programs/nursing/

**Stony Brook University, State University of New York,** Stony Brook Medicine, School of Nursing, Program in Nursing Education, Stony Brook, NY 11794. Offers MS, Certificate. *Program availability:* Part-time, blended/hybrid learning. *Students:* 144 part-time (142 women); includes 55 minority (13 Black or African American, non-Hispanic/Latino; 22 Asian, non-Hispanic/Latino; 19 Hispanic/Latino; 1 Two or more races, non-Hispanic/Latino). 111 applicants, 95% accepted, 95 enrolled. In 2019, 21 master's, 1 other advanced degree awarded. *Entrance requirements:* For master's, baccalaureate degree with major in nursing, minimum cumulative GPA of 3.0, current professional RN license, three letters of recommendation. Additional exam requirements/recommendations for international students: required—TOEFL (minimum score 90 iBT). *Application deadline:* For fall admission, 3/19 for domestic students. Application fee: $100. Electronic applications accepted. *Expenses:* Contact institution. *Unit head:* Lenore Lamanna, Program Director, 631-444-7640, Fax: 631-444-3136, E-mail: lenore.lamanna@stonybrook.edu. *Application contact:* Silvana Jara, Staff Assistant, 631-444-3392, Fax: 631-444-3136, E-mail: silvana.jara@stonybrook.edu.
Website: http://www.nursing.stonybrookmedicine.edu/nursingeducationmaster

**Tarleton State University,** College of Graduate Studies, College of Health Sciences and Human Services, School of Nursing, Stephenville, TX 76402. Offers nursing administration (MSN); nursing education (MSN). *Accreditation:* AACN. *Program availability:* Part-time, evening/weekend, 100% online, blended/hybrid learning. *Faculty:* 3 full-time (all women), 1 (woman) part-time/adjunct. *Students:* 5 part-time (4 women); includes 1 minority (Black or African American, non-Hispanic/Latino), 1 international. Average age 42. 7 applicants, 100% accepted, 1 enrolled. In 2019, 2 master's awarded. *Degree requirements:* For master's, comprehensive exam. *Entrance requirements:* For master's, GRE General Test, minimum GPA of 2.5. Additional exam requirements/recommendations for international students: required—TOEFL (minimum score 520 paper-based; 69 iBT); recommended—IELTS (minimum score 6), TSE (minimum score 50). *Application deadline:* For fall admission, 8/15 priority date for domestic students; for spring admission, 1/7 for domestic students. Applications are processed on a rolling basis. Application fee: $50 ($130 for international students). Electronic applications accepted. *Expenses:* Contact institution. *Financial support:* Career-related internships or fieldwork, Federal Work-Study, and institutionally sponsored loans available. Support available to part-time students. Financial award applicants required to submit FAFSA. *Unit head:* Dr. Jennifer Mundine, Department Head, 254-968-1827, E-mail: mundine@tarleton.edu. *Application contact:* Wendy Weiss, Graduate Admissions Coordinator, 254-968-9104, Fax: 254-968-9670, E-mail: weiss@tarleton.edu.
Website: https://www.tarleton.edu/nursing/index.html

**Teachers College, Columbia University,** Department of Health and Behavior Studies, New York, NY 10027-6696. Offers applied behavior analysis (MA, PhD); applied educational psychology: school psychology (Ed M, PhD); behavioral nutrition (PhD), including nutrition (Ed D, PhD); community health education (MS); community nutrition education (Ed M), including community nutrition education; education of deaf and hard of hearing (MA, PhD); health education (MA, Ed D); hearing impairment (Ed D); intellectual disability/autism (MA, Ed D, PhD); nursing education (Ed D, Advanced Certificate); nutrition and education (MS); nutrition and exercise physiology (MS); nutrition and public health (MS); nutrition education (Ed D), including nutrition (Ed D, PhD); physical disabilities (Ed D); reading specialist (MA); severe or multiple disabilities (MA); special education (Ed M, MA, Ed D); teaching of sign language (MA). *Faculty:* 17 full-time (11 women). *Students:* 243 full-time (225 women), 246 part-time (211 women); includes 172 minority (33 Black or African American, non-Hispanic/Latino; 2 American Indian or Alaska Native, non-Hispanic/Latino; 63 Asian, non-Hispanic/Latino; 63 Hispanic/Latino; 11 Two or more races, non-Hispanic/Latino), 67 international. 515 applicants, 68% accepted, 170 enrolled. *Unit head:* Dr. Dolores Perin, Chair, 212-678-3091, E-mail: dp111@tc.columbia.edu. *Application contact:* Kelly Sutton-Skinner, Director of Admission and New Student Enrollment, E-mail: kms2237@tc.columbia.edu.
Website: http://www.tc.columbia.edu/health-and-behavior-studies/

**Tennessee Technological University,** Whitson-Hester School of Nursing, MSN Programs, Cookeville, TN 38505. Offers family nurse practitioner (MSN); nursing administration (MSN); nursing education (MSN). *Program availability:* Part-time. *Students:* 2 full-time (both women), 110 part-time (93 women); includes 7 minority (4 Black or African American, non-Hispanic/Latino; 1 Asian, non-Hispanic/Latino; 1 Hispanic/Latino; 1 Two or more races, non-Hispanic/Latino). 55 applicants, 73% accepted, 29 enrolled. In 2019, 29 master's awarded. *Application deadline:* For fall admission, 7/1 for domestic students, 5/1 for international students; for spring admission, 12/1 for domestic students, 10/1 for international students; for summer admission, 5/1 for domestic students, 2/1 for international students. Applications are processed on a rolling basis. Application fee: $35 ($40 for international students). Electronic applications accepted. *Expenses: Tuition, area resident:* Part-time $597 per credit hour. Tuition, state resident: part-time $597 per credit hour. Tuition, nonresident: part-time $1323 per credit hour. *Financial support:* Application deadline: 4/1; applicants required to submit FAFSA. *Unit head:* Dr. Kim Hanna, Dean, 931-372-3203, Fax: 931-372-6244, E-mail: khanna@tntech.edu. *Application contact:* Shelia K. Kendrick, Coordinator of Graduate Studies, 931-372-3808, Fax: 931-372-3497, E-mail: skendrick@tntech.edu.
Website: https://www.tntech.edu/nursing/masters/

**Texas A&M University,** College of Nursing, Bryan, TX 77843. Offers family nurse practitioner (MSN); forensic nursing (MSN); nursing education (MSN). *Expenses:* Contact institution.

**Texas A&M University–Corpus Christi,** College of Graduate Studies, College of Nursing and Health Sciences, Corpus Christi, TX 78412. Offers family nurse practitioner (MSN); leadership in nursing systems (MSN); nurse educator (MSN); nursing practice (DNP). *Accreditation:* AACN. *Program availability:* Part-time, evening/weekend, online only, 100% online. *Degree requirements:* For master's, clinical capstone; for doctorate, capstone/scholarly project. *Entrance requirements:* For master's, essay, resume, 3 letters of recommendation, minimum GPA of 3.0, current valid unencumbered Texas nursing license. Additional exam requirements/recommendations for international students: required—TOEFL (minimum score 550 paper-based; 79 iBT), IELTS (minimum score 6.5). Electronic applications accepted.

**Texas Christian University,** Harris College of Nursing and Health Sciences, Master's Program in Nursing, Fort Worth, TX 76129-0002. Offers administration and leadership (MSN); clinical nurse leader (MSN, Certificate); clinical nurse specialist (MSN), including adult/gerontology nursing, pediatrics; nursing education (MSN). *Accreditation:* AACN. *Program availability:* Part-time, online only, 100% online. *Faculty:* 29 full-time (26 women), 1 (woman) part-time/adjunct. *Students:* 12 full-time (all women), 5 part-time (all women); includes 5 minority (1 Asian, non-Hispanic/Latino; 4 Hispanic/Latino). Average age 34. 41 applicants, 59% accepted, 8 enrolled. In 2019, 10 master's awarded. *Degree requirements:* For master's, thesis or alternative, practicum. *Entrance requirements:* For master's, 3 letters of reference, essay, resume, two official transcripts from every institution attended, current license to practice as a registered nurse. Additional exam

requirements/recommendations for international students: required—TOEFL (minimum score 550 paper-based; 80 iBT). *Application deadline:* For spring admission, 8/15 for domestic and international students; for summer admission, 1/15 for domestic and international students. Application fee: $60. Electronic applications accepted. Full-time tuition and fees vary according to program. *Financial support:* In 2019–20, 15 students received support. Scholarships/grants available. Financial award application deadline: 2/15; financial award applicants required to submit FAFSA. *Unit head:* Dr. Kathy Ellis, Division Director, Graduate Nursing, 817-257-6726, Fax: 817-257-7944, E-mail: kathryn.ellis@tcu.edu. *Application contact:* Beth Janke, Academic Program Specialist, 817-257-6726, Fax: 817-257-7944, E-mail: graduatenursing@tcu.edu.
Website: http://www.nursing.tcu.edu/graduate.asp

**Texas Tech University Health Sciences Center,** School of Nursing, Lubbock, TX 79430. Offers acute care nurse practitioner (MSN, Certificate); administration (MSN); advanced practice (DNP); education (MSN); executive leadership (DNP); family nurse practitioner (MSN, Certificate); geriatric nurse practitioner (MSN, Certificate); pediatric nurse practitioner (MSN, Certificate). *Accreditation:* AACN. *Program availability:* Part-time, online learning. *Degree requirements:* For master's, thesis optional. *Entrance requirements:* For master's, minimum GPA of 3.0, 3 letters of reference, BSN, RN license; for Certificate, minimum GPA of 3.0, 3 letters of reference, RN license. Additional exam requirements/recommendations for international students: required—TOEFL (minimum score 550 paper-based).

**Texas Woman's University,** Graduate School, College of Nursing, Denton, TX 76204. Offers adult health clinical nurse specialist (MS); adult health nurse practitioner (MS); adult/gerontology acute care nurse practitioner (MS); child health clinical nurse specialist (MS); clinical nurse leader (MS); family nurse practitioner (MS); health systems management (MS); nursing education (MS); nursing practice (DNP); nursing science (PhD); pediatric nurse practitioner (MS); women's health clinical nurse specialist (MS); women's health nurse practitioner (MS). *Accreditation:* AACN. *Program availability:* Part-time, 100% online, blended/hybrid learning. *Faculty:* 48 full-time (47 women), 31 part-time/adjunct (24 women). *Students:* 42 full-time (40 women), 811 part-time (756 women); includes 481 minority (168 Black or African American, non-Hispanic/Latino; 2 American Indian or Alaska Native, non-Hispanic/Latino; 165 Asian, non-Hispanic/Latino; 118 Hispanic/Latino; 1 Native Hawaiian or other Pacific Islander, non-Hispanic/Latino; 27 Two or more races, non-Hispanic/Latino), 26 international. Average age 36. 435 applicants, 71% accepted, 172 enrolled. In 2019, 203 master's, 37 doctorates awarded. *Degree requirements:* For master's, comprehensive exam, thesis or alternative, 6-year time limit for completion of degree, professional or clinical project; for doctorate, comprehensive exam, thesis/dissertation, 10-year time limit for completion of degree; dissertation (PhD), assessment practicum (DPT). *Entrance requirements:* For master's, minimum GPA of 3.0 on last 60 hours in undergraduate nursing degree and overall, RN license, BS in nursing, basic statistics course; for doctorate, MS in nursing, minimum preferred GPA of 3.5, RN or APRN license, statistics course, 2 letters of reference, curriculum vitae, graduate nursing-theory course, graduate research course, statement of professional goals and research interests, 1 yr APRN experience. Additional exam requirements/recommendations for international students: required—TOEFL (minimum score 79 iBT); recommended—IELTS (minimum score 6.5), TSE (minimum score 53). *Application deadline:* For fall admission, 5/1 for domestic students, 3/1 priority date for international students; for spring admission, 9/15 for domestic students, 7/1 priority date for international students. Application fee: $50 ($75 for international students). Electronic applications accepted. *Expenses:* All are estimates. Tuition for 10 hours = $2,763; Fees for 10 hours = $1,342. Master's Nursing courses require additional $75/SCH; Doctoral Nursing courses require additional $80/SCH. *Financial support:* In 2019–20, 212 students received support, including 1 research assistantship, 6 teaching assistantships (averaging $12,029 per year); career-related internships or fieldwork, scholarships/grants, health care benefits, and unspecified assistantships also available. Support available to part-time students. Financial award application deadline: 3/1; financial award applicants required to submit FAFSA. *Unit head:* Dr. Rosalie Mainous, Dean, 940-898-2401, Fax: 940-898-2437, E-mail: nursing@twu.edu. *Application contact:* Korie Hawkins, Associate Director of Admissions, Graduate Recruitment, 940-898-3188, Fax: 940-898-3081, E-mail: admissions@twu.edu.
Website: http://www.twu.edu/nursing/

**Thomas Edison State University,** W. Cary Edwards School of Nursing, Master of Science in Nursing Program, Trenton, NJ 08608. Offers nurse educator (MSN); nursing administration (MSN); nursing informatics (MSN). *Accreditation:* AACN; ACEN. *Program availability:* Part-time, online learning. *Degree requirements:* For master's, nursing education seminar, onground practicum, online practicum. *Entrance requirements:* For master's, BSN. Additional exam requirements/recommendations for international students: required—TOEFL (minimum score 550 paper-based; 79 iBT). Electronic applications accepted.

**UNB Fredericton,** School of Graduate Studies, Faculty of Nursing, Fredericton, NB E3B 5A3, Canada. Offers nurse educator (MN); nurse practitioner (MN); nursing (MN). *Program availability:* Part-time, online learning. *Faculty:* 41 full-time (37 women). *Students:* 14 full-time (13 women), 13 part-time (all women). Average age 36. In 2019, 10 master's awarded. *Degree requirements:* For master's, comprehensive exam (for some programs), thesis (for some programs). *Entrance requirements:* For master's, undergraduate coursework in statistics and nursing research, minimum GPA of 3.3, registration as a nurse (or eligibility) in New Brunswick. Additional exam requirements/recommendations for international students: required—TOEFL (minimum score 600 paper-based). *Application deadline:* For winter admission, 1/2 priority date for domestic students. Application fee: $50 Canadian dollars. Electronic applications accepted. *Expenses: Tuition, area resident:* Full-time $6975 Canadian dollars; part-time $3423 Canadian dollars per year. Tuition, state resident: full-time $6975 Canadian dollars; part-time $3423 Canadian dollars per year. Tuition, Canadian resident: full-time $6975 Canadian dollars; part-time $3423 Canadian dollars per year. *International tuition:* $12,435 Canadian dollars full-time. *Required fees:* $92.25 Canadian dollars per term. Full-time tuition and fees vary according to degree level, campus/location, program, reciprocity agreements and student level. *Financial support:* Fellowships and research assistantships available. Financial award application deadline: 1/15. *Unit head:* Lorna Butler, Dean, 506-458 7625, Fax: 506-447 3057, E-mail: Lorna.butler@unb.ca. *Application contact:* Tricia Canning, Graduate Secretary, 506-458 7650, Fax: 506-447-3057, E-mail: canningt@unb.ca.
Website: http://www.unb.ca/fredericton/nursing/graduate/

**Union University,** School of Nursing, Jackson, TN 38305-3697. Offers executive leadership (DNP); nurse anesthesia (DNP); nurse practitioner (DNP); nursing education (MSN, PMC). *Accreditation:* AACN; AANA/CANAEP. *Degree requirements:* For master's, thesis or alternative. *Entrance requirements:* For master's, GRE, 3 letters of reference, bachelor's degree in nursing, minimum GPA of 3.0. Additional exam requirements/recommendations for international students: required—TOEFL (minimum score 560 paper-based). Electronic applications accepted.

**The University of Alabama in Huntsville,** School of Graduate Studies, College of Nursing, Huntsville, AL 35899. Offers family nurse practitioner (Certificate); nursing (MSN, DNP), including adult-gerontology acute care nurse practitioner (MSN), adult-

gerontology clinical nurse specialist (MSN), family nurse practitioner (MSN), leadership in health care systems (MSN); nursing education (Certificate). *Accreditation:* AACN. *Program availability:* Part-time. *Degree requirements:* For master's, comprehensive exam, thesis or alternative, oral and written exams. *Entrance requirements:* For master's, MAT or GRE, Alabama RN license, BSN, minimum GPA of 3.0; for doctorate, master's degree in nursing in an advanced practice area; for Certificate, MAT or GRE, minimum GPA of 3.0. Additional exam requirements/recommendations for international students: required—TOEFL (minimum score 500 paper-based; 80 iBT), IELTS (minimum score 6.5). Electronic applications accepted.

**University of Central Arkansas,** Graduate School, College of Health and Behavioral Sciences, Department of Nursing, Conway, AR 72035-0001. Offers adult nurse practitioner (PMC); clinical nurse leader (PMC); clinical nurse specialist (MSN); family nurse practitioner (PMC); nurse educator (PMC); nurse practitioner (MSN). *Accreditation:* AACN. *Program availability:* Part-time, evening/weekend, online learning. *Degree requirements:* For master's, comprehensive exam, thesis optional, clinicals. *Entrance requirements:* For master's, GRE General Test, minimum GPA of 2.7. Additional exam requirements/recommendations for international students: required—TOEFL (minimum score 550 paper-based; 80 iBT). Electronic applications accepted. *Expenses:* Contact institution.

**University of Detroit Mercy,** College of Health Professions, Detroit, MI 48221. Offers clinical nurse leader (MSN); family nurse practitioner (MSN); health services administration (MHSA); health systems management (MSN); nurse anesthesia (MS); nursing (DNP); nursing education (MSN, Certificate); nursing leadership and financial management (Certificate); outcomes performance management (Certificate); physician assistant (MS). *Accreditation:* AANA/CANAEP. *Entrance requirements:* For master's, GRE General Test, minimum GPA of 3.0.

**University of Hartford,** College of Education, Nursing, and Health Professions, Program in Nursing, West Hartford, CT 06117-1599. Offers community/public health nursing (MSN); nursing education (MSN); nursing management (MSN). *Accreditation:* AACN. *Program availability:* Part-time, evening/weekend. *Faculty:* 9 full-time (8 women), 5 part-time/adjunct (all women). *Students:* 7 full-time (all women), 100 part-time (94 women); includes 22 minority (12 Black or African American, non-Hispanic/Latino; 2 Asian, non-Hispanic/Latino; 6 Hispanic/Latino; 2 Two or more races, non-Hispanic/Latino), 9 international. Average age 39. 50 applicants, 96% accepted, 45 enrolled. In 2019, 65 master's awarded. *Entrance requirements:* For master's, BSN, Connecticut RN license. Additional exam requirements/recommendations for international students: required—TOEFL (minimum score 550 paper-based). *Application deadline:* For fall admission, 4/15 priority date for domestic students; for spring admission, 12/1 for domestic students. Application fee: $45. Electronic applications accepted. *Expenses:* Contact institution. *Financial support:* Teaching assistantships and Federal Work-Study available. Support available to part-time students. Financial award application deadline: 6/1; financial award applicants required to submit FAFSA. *Unit head:* Jane Williams, Chair, 860-768-4217, Fax: 860-768-5346. *Application contact:* Marlene Hall, Assistant Dean, 860-768-5116, E-mail: mhall@hartford.edu.
Website: http://www.hartford.edu/enhp/

**University of Houston,** College of Nursing, Sugar Land, TX 77479. Offers family nurse practitioner (MSN); nursing administration (MSN); nursing education (MSN). *Accreditation:* AACN. *Faculty:* 8 full-time (7 women). *Students:* 18 full-time (12 women), 33 part-time (32 women); includes 30 minority (13 Black or African American, non-Hispanic/Latino; 4 Asian, non-Hispanic/Latino; 12 Hispanic/Latino; 1 Native Hawaiian or other Pacific Islander, non-Hispanic/Latino). Average age 36. 38 applicants, 74% accepted, 20 enrolled. In 2019, 12 master's awarded. *Entrance requirements:* For master's, minimum GPA of 3.0, unencumbered Texas RN license, 2 letters of recommendation, essay, resume, interview required. Additional exam requirements/recommendations for international students: required—TOEFL. *Application deadline:* For fall admission, 6/1 for domestic and international students; for spring admission, 11/1 for domestic and international students; for summer admission, 4/1 for domestic and international students. Application fee: $75. Electronic applications accepted. *Financial support:* In 2019–20, 19 students received support. Federal Work-Study, scholarships/grants, and unspecified assistantships available. Support available to part-time students. Financial award application deadline: 7/1; financial award applicants required to submit FAFSA. *Unit head:* Dr. Kathryn Tart, Dean, 832-842-8200, E-mail: kmtart@uh.edu. *Application contact:* Tammy N. Whatley, Student Affairs Director, 832-842-8220, E-mail: tnwhatley@uh.edu.
Website: http://www.uh.edu/nursing

**University of Indianapolis,** Graduate Programs, School of Nursing, Indianapolis, IN 46227-3697. Offers advanced practice nursing (DNP); family nurse practitioner (MSN); gerontological nurse practitioner (MSN); neonatal nurse practitioner (MSN); nurse-midwifery (MSN); nursing (MSN); nursing and health systems leadership (MSN); nursing education (MSN); women's health nurse practitioner (MSN); MBA/MSN. *Accreditation:* AACN. *Entrance requirements:* For master's, minimum GPA of 3.0, interview, letters of recommendation, resume, IN nursing license, 1 year of professional practice; for doctorate, graduate of ACEN- or CCNE-accredited nursing program; MSN or MA with nursing major and minimum cumulative GPA of 3.25; unencumbered RN license with eligibility for licensure in Indiana; completion of graduate-level statistics course within last 5 years with minimum grade of B; resume; essay; official transcripts from all academic institutions. Additional exam requirements/recommendations for international students: required—TOEFL (minimum score 550 paper-based). Electronic applications accepted.

**University of Louisiana at Lafayette,** College of Nursing and Allied Health Professions, Lafayette, LA 70504. Offers family nurse practitioner (MSN); nursing (DNP); nursing education (MSN). *Accreditation:* AACN. *Entrance requirements:* For master's, GRE General Test, minimum GPA of 2.75. Additional exam requirements/recommendations for international students: required—TOEFL (minimum score 550 paper-based). Electronic applications accepted. *Expenses: Tuition, area resident:* Full-time $5511; part-time $1630 per credit hour. Tuition, state resident: full-time $5511; part-time $1630 per credit hour. Tuition, nonresident: full-time $19,239; part-time $2409 per credit hour. *Required fees:* $46,637.

**University of Louisville,** Graduate School, School of Nursing, Louisville, KY 40202. Offers adult gerontology nurse practitioner (MSN, DNP); education and administration (MSN); family nurse practitioner (MSN, DNP); neonatal nurse practitioner (MSN, DNP); nursing research (PhD); psychiatric/mental health nurse practitioner (MSN, DNP); women's health nurse practitioner (MSN). *Accreditation:* AACN. *Program availability:* Part-time, blended/hybrid learning. *Faculty:* 49 full-time (46 women), 91 part-time/adjunct (86 women). *Students:* 164 full-time (140 women), 47 part-time (39 women); includes 45 minority (21 Black or African American, non-Hispanic/Latino; 5 Asian, non-Hispanic/Latino; 9 Hispanic/Latino; 10 Two or more races, non-Hispanic/Latino), 4 international. Average age 33. 84 applicants, 63% accepted, 48 enrolled. In 2019, 25 master's, 5 doctorates awarded. *Degree requirements:* For master's, varies; for doctorate, comprehensive exam (for some programs), thesis/dissertation (for some programs), varies. *Entrance requirements:* For master's, Our only master's degree is an accelerated program meant for students who have a bachelor's degree in another discipline who are transitioning into nursing. Thus, the main requirement is a bachelor's degree from a nationally-accredited college, and the completion of 6 prerequisite courses. Must have a minimum undergraduate GPA of 3.0; for doctorate, PhD program: GRE requirement omitted, DNP & PhD doctoral programs: 3 letters of professional reference. BSN applicants must have a 3.0 GPA. MSN applicants must have 3.25 GPA. Written statement of career goals, areas of expertise, reasons for pursuing doctoral degree, resume, and RN license. Additional exam requirements/recommendations for international students: recommended—TOEFL (minimum score 560 paper-based), IELTS (minimum score 6.5). *Application deadline:* For fall admission, 1/15 priority date for domestic and international students; for summer admission, 10/15 priority date for domestic students. Application fee: $60. Electronic applications accepted. *Expenses:* 17871. *Financial support:* In 2019–20, 47 students received support, including 2 fellowships with full tuition reimbursements available (averaging $20,000 per year), 9 research assistantships with full tuition reimbursements available (averaging $20,000 per year), 3 teaching assistantships with full tuition reimbursements available (averaging $15,000 per year); scholarships/grants, health care benefits, unspecified assistantships, and Jonas Nurse Leader Fellowships also available. Financial award application deadline: 10/1; financial award applicants required to submit FAFSA. *Unit head:* 502-852-8300, Fax: 502-852-5044, E-mail: sonya.hardin@louisville.edu. *Application contact:* Trish Hart, MA, Assistant Dean for Student Affairs, 502-852-5825, Fax: 502-852-8783, E-mail: trish.hart@louisville.edu.
Website: http://www.louisville.edu/nursing/

**University of Maine,** Graduate School, College of Natural Sciences, Forestry, and Agriculture, School of Nursing, Orono, ME 04469. Offers individualized (MS); nursing education (CGS); rural health family nurse practitioner (MS, CAS). *Accreditation:* AACN. *Faculty:* 6 full-time (all women), 6 part-time/adjunct (4 women). *Students:* 24 full-time (21 women), 20 part-time (18 women); includes 4 minority (2 American Indian or Alaska Native, non-Hispanic/Latino; 2 Hispanic/Latino). Average age 34. 14 applicants, 100% accepted, 10 enrolled. In 2019, 11 master's, 4 other advanced degrees awarded. *Entrance requirements:* For master's, GRE General Test; for other advanced degree, master's degree. Additional exam requirements/recommendations for international students: required—TOEFL. *Application deadline:* For fall admission, 7/1 for domestic students; for spring admission, 12/15 for domestic students; for summer admission, 4/15 for domestic students. Applications are processed on a rolling basis. Application fee: $65. Electronic applications accepted. *Expenses: Tuition, area resident:* Full-time $8100; part-time $450 per credit hour. Tuition, state resident: full-time $8100; part-time $450 per credit hour. Tuition, nonresident: full-time $26,388; part-time $1466 per credit hour. *International tuition:* $26,388 full-time. *Required fees:* $1257; $278 per semester. Tuition and fees vary according to course load. *Financial support:* Career-related internships or fieldwork, Federal Work-Study, institutionally sponsored loans, tuition waivers (full and partial), and unspecified assistantships available. Support available to part-time students. Financial award application deadline: 3/1. *Unit head:* Dr. Nancy Fishwick, Director, 207-581-2505, Fax: 207-581-2585. *Application contact:* Scott G. Delcourt, Assistant Vice President for Graduate Studies and Senior Associate Dean, 207-581-3291, Fax: 207-581-3232, E-mail: graduate@maine.edu.
Website: http://umaine.edu/nursing/

**University of Mary,** School of Health Sciences, Division of Nursing, Bismarck, ND 58504-9652. Offers family nurse practitioner (DNP); nurse administrator (MSN); nursing educator (MSN); MSN/MBA. *Accreditation:* AACN. *Program availability:* Part-time, evening/weekend, online learning. *Degree requirements:* For master's, comprehensive exam (for some programs), thesis (for some programs), internship (family nurse practitioner), teaching practice. *Entrance requirements:* For master's, minimum GPA of 2.75 in nursing, interview, letters of recommendation, criminal background check, immunizations, statement of professional goals. Additional exam requirements/recommendations for international students: required—TOEFL (minimum score 500 paper-based; 71 iBT). Electronic applications accepted.

**University of Mary Hardin-Baylor,** Graduate Studies in Education, Belton, TX 76513. Offers curriculum and instruction (M Ed); educational administration (M Ed, Ed D), including higher education (Ed D), leadership in nursing education (Ed D), P-12 (Ed D). *Program availability:* Part-time, evening/weekend. *Faculty:* 13 full-time (7 women), 6 part-time/adjunct (0 women). *Students:* 45 full-time (31 women), 81 part-time (59 women); includes 57 minority (38 Black or African American, non-Hispanic/Latino; 17 Hispanic/Latino; 2 Two or more races, non-Hispanic/Latino). Average age 41. 14 applicants, 86% accepted, 9 enrolled. In 2019, 20 master's, 18 doctorates awarded. *Degree requirements:* For master's, comprehensive exam; for doctorate, thesis/dissertation. *Entrance requirements:* For master's, minimum GPA of 3.0, interview; for doctorate, minimum GPA of 3.5, interview, essay, resume, employment verification, 3 letters of recommendation. Additional exam requirements/recommendations for international students: required—TOEFL (minimum score 60 iBT), IELTS (minimum score 4.5). *Application deadline:* For fall admission, 6/1 for domestic students, 4/30 priority date for international students; for spring admission, 11/1 for domestic students, 9/30 priority date for international students. Applications are processed on a rolling basis. Application fee: $35 ($135 for international students). Electronic applications accepted. *Expenses:* Contact institution. *Financial support:* In 2019–20, 126 students received support. Federal Work-Study and scholarships for some active duty military personnel available. Support available to part-time students. Financial award application deadline: 6/1; financial award applicants required to submit FAFSA. *Unit head:* Dr. Todd Kunders, Director, Graduate Programs in Education, 254-295-4579, E-mail: tkunders@umhb.edu. *Application contact:* Katherine Moore, Assistant Director, Graduate Admissions, 254-295-4924, E-mail: kmoore@umhb.edu.
Website: https://go.umhb.edu/graduate/education/home

**University of Mary Hardin-Baylor,** Graduate Studies in Nursing, Belton, TX 76513. Offers family nurse practitioner (MSN, Post-Master's Certificate); nursing education (MSN); nursing practice (DNP). *Accreditation:* AACN. *Program availability:* Evening/weekend. *Faculty:* 8 full-time (all women), 5 part-time/adjunct (3 women). *Students:* 22 full-time (20 women), 9 part-time (8 women); includes 15 minority (4 Black or African American, non-Hispanic/Latino; 3 Asian, non-Hispanic/Latino; 7 Hispanic/Latino; 1 Two or more races, non-Hispanic/Latino), 1 international. Average age 36. 26 applicants, 62% accepted, 15 enrolled. In 2019, 17 master's, 2 other advanced degrees awarded. *Degree requirements:* For master's, comprehensive exam, practicum; for doctorate, scholarly project. *Entrance requirements:* For master's, baccalaureate degree in nursing, current licensure as Registered Nurse in the state of Texas, minimum GPA of 3.0 in last 60 hours of undergraduate program, two letters of recommendation, full-time RN for 1 year, personal interview with director of MSN program; for doctorate, master's degree as an advanced practice nurse, nurse leader or nurse educator; three letters of recommendation; current RN license and approval to practice as an advanced practice nurse; essay; curriculum vitae; interview. Additional exam requirements/recommendations for international students: required—TOEFL (minimum score 60 iBT), IELTS (minimum score 4.5). *Application deadline:* For fall admission, 6/1 for domestic students, 4/30 priority date for international students; for spring admission, 11/1 for domestic students, 9/30 priority date for international students. Applications are processed on a rolling basis. Application fee: $35 ($135 for international students). Electronic applications accepted. *Expenses:* Contact institution. *Financial support:* In 2019–20, 24 students received support. Federal Work-Study, unspecified assistantships, and scholarships for some active duty military personnel available.

Support available to part-time students. Financial award applicants required to submit FAFSA. *Unit head:* Dr. Elizabeth Jimenez, Director, Master of Science in Nursing Program & Assistant Professor, 254-295-4769, E-mail: ejimenez@umhb.edu. *Application contact:* Katherine Moore, Assistant Director, Graduate Admissions, 254-295-4924, E-mail: kmoore@umhb.edu.
Website: https://go.umhb.edu/graduate/nursing/home

**University of Maryland, Baltimore,** University of Maryland School of Nursing, Baltimore, MD 21201. Offers adult-gerontology acute care nurse practitioner (DNP); adult-gerontology primary care nurse practitioner (DNP); clinical nurse leader (MS); community/public health nursing (MS); family nurse practitioner (DNP); global health (Postbaccalaureate Certificate); health services leadership and management (MS); neonatal nurse practitioner (DNP); nurse anesthesia (DNP); nursing (PhD); nursing informatics (MS, Postbaccalaureate Certificate); pediatric acute/primary care nurse practitioner (DNP); psychiatric mental health nurse practitioner (DNP); teaching in nursing and health professions (Postbaccalaureate Certificate); MS/MBA. *Accreditation:* AANA/CANAEP. *Program availability:* Part-time. *Faculty:* 130 full-time (117 women), 125 part-time/adjunct (114 women). *Students:* 539 full-time (463 women), 586 part-time (506 women); includes 485 minority (259 Black or African American, non-Hispanic/Latino; 3 American Indian or Alaska Native, non-Hispanic/Latino; 124 Asian, non-Hispanic/Latino; 66 Hispanic/Latino; 1 Native Hawaiian or other Pacific Islander, non-Hispanic/Latino; 32 Two or more races, non-Hispanic/Latino), 18 international. Average age 33. 964 applicants, 54% accepted, 347 enrolled. In 2019, 197 master's, 114 doctorates, 12 other advanced degrees awarded. *Degree requirements:* For master's and Postbaccalaureate Certificate, thesis (for some programs); for doctorate, comprehensive exam, thesis/dissertation. *Entrance requirements:* Additional exam requirements/recommendations for international students: required—TOEFL (minimum score 550 paper-based; 79 iBT); recommended—IELTS (minimum score 7). *Application deadline:* For fall admission, 11/1 priority date for domestic and international students; for spring admission, 12/15 for domestic and international students; for summer admission, 9/1 for domestic and international students. Applications are processed on a rolling basis. Application fee: $75. Electronic applications accepted. *Financial support:* In 2019–20, 257 students received support, including 31 research assistantships with full and partial tuition reimbursements available (averaging $25,000 per year), 21 teaching assistantships with full and partial tuition reimbursements available (averaging $19,000 per year); scholarships/grants, traineeships, and unspecified assistantships also available. Support available to part-time students. Financial award application deadline: 3/1; financial award applicants required to submit FAFSA. *Unit head:* Dr. Jane Kirschling, Dean, 410-706-4359, E-mail: kirschling@umaryland.edu. *Application contact:* Larry Fillian, Associate Dean of Student and Academic Services, 410-706-6298, E-mail: lfillian@umaryland.edu.
Website: http://www.nursing.umaryland.edu/

**University of Massachusetts Medical School,** Graduate School of Nursing, Worcester, MA 01655. Offers adult gerontological acute care nurse practitioner (DNP, Post Master's Certificate); adult gerontological primary care nurse practitioner (DNP, Post Master's Certificate); family nursing practitioner (DNP); nurse administrator (DNP); nurse educator (MS); nursing (PhD); psychiatric mental health (Post Master's Certificate). *Accreditation:* AACN. *Program availability:* Blended/hybrid learning. *Faculty:* 26 full-time (22 women), 51 part-time/adjunct (40 women). *Students:* 176 full-time (152 women), 33 part-time (27 women); includes 61 minority (21 Black or African American, non-Hispanic/Latino; 1 American Indian or Alaska Native, non-Hispanic/Latino; 18 Asian, non-Hispanic/Latino; 20 Hispanic/Latino; 1 Native Hawaiian or other Pacific Islander, non-Hispanic/Latino). Average age 32. 131 applicants, 66% accepted, 58 enrolled. In 2019, 28 master's, 34 doctorates, 1 other advanced degree awarded. *Degree requirements:* For doctorate, thesis/dissertation (for some programs), comprehensive exam and manuscript (for PhD); scholarly project (for DNP). *Entrance requirements:* For master's, GRE General Test, bachelor's degree in nursing, course work in statistics, unrestricted Massachusetts license as registered nurse; for doctorate, GRE General Test, bachelor's or master's degree; for Post Master's Certificate, GRE General Test, MS in nursing. Additional exam requirements/recommendations for international students: required—TOEFL (minimum score 400 paper-based; 81 iBT). *Application deadline:* For fall admission, 12/1 priority date for domestic students. Applications are processed on a rolling basis. Application fee: $100. Electronic applications accepted. *Expenses:* Contact institution. *Financial support:* In 2019–20, 103 students received support. Scholarships/grants available. Support available to part-time students. Financial award application deadline: 5/15; financial award applicants required to submit FAFSA. *Unit head:* Dr. Joan Vitello-Cicciu, Dean, 508-856-5081, Fax: 508-856-6552, E-mail: joan.vitello@umassmed.edu. *Application contact:* Diane Brescia, Admissions Coordinator, 508-856-3488, Fax: 508-856-5851, E-mail: diane.brescia@umassmed.edu.
Website: http://www.umassmed.edu/gsn/

**University of Memphis,** Loewenberg College of Nursing, Memphis, TN 38152. Offers advanced practice nursing (Graduate Certificate); executive leadership (MSN); family nurse practitioner (MSN); nursing administration (MSN, Graduate Certificate); nursing education (MSN, Graduate Certificate). *Accreditation:* AACN. *Program availability:* Part-time, evening/weekend, online learning. *Faculty:* 21 full-time (19 women), 11 part-time/adjunct (10 women). *Students:* 19 full-time (17 women), 281 part-time (254 women); includes 104 minority (87 Black or African American, non-Hispanic/Latino; 5 Asian, non-Hispanic/Latino; 7 Hispanic/Latino; 5 Two or more races, non-Hispanic/Latino), 2 international. Average age 34. 117 applicants, 79% accepted, 48 enrolled. In 2019, 71 master's, 3 other advanced degrees awarded. *Degree requirements:* For master's, comprehensive exam, thesis optional, scholarly project; clinical practicum hours. *Entrance requirements:* For master's, NCLEX exam, minimum undergraduate GPA of 2.8, letter of interest, letters of recommendation, interview, resume, nursing licensure; for Graduate Certificate, unrestricted license to practice as RN in TN, current CPR certification, evidence of vaccination, annual flu shot, evidence of current professional malpractice insurance, letters of recommendation, letter of intent, resume. Additional exam requirements/recommendations for international students: required—TOEFL (minimum score 550 paper-based; 79 iBT). *Application deadline:* For fall admission, 2/15 for domestic and international students; for spring admission, 10/1 for domestic and international students. Application fee: $35 ($60 for international students). *Expenses: Tuition, area resident:* Full-time $9216; part-time $512 per credit hour. *Tuition, state resident:* full-time $9216; part-time $512 per credit hour. *Tuition, nonresident:* full-time $12,672; part-time $704 per credit hour. *International tuition:* $16,128 full-time. *Required fees:* $1530; $85 per credit hour. Tuition and fees vary according to program. *Financial support:* Federal Work-Study and scholarships/grants available. Financial award application deadline: 2/1; financial award applicants required to submit FAFSA. *Unit head:* Dr. Lin Zhan, Dean, 901-678-2020, E-mail: lzhan@memphis.edu. *Application contact:* Dr. Lin Zhan, Dean, 901-678-2020, E-mail: lzhan@memphis.edu.
Website: http://www.memphis.edu/nursing

**University of Missouri–Kansas City,** School of Nursing and Health Studies, Kansas City, MO 64110-2499. Offers adult clinical nurse specialist (MSN), including adult nurse practitioner, women's health nurse practitioner (MSN, DNP); adult clinical nursing practice (DNP), including adult gerontology nurse practitioner, women's health nurse practitioner (MSN, DNP); clinical nursing practice (DNP), including family nurse

practitioner; neonatal nurse practitioner (MSN); nurse educator (MSN); nurse executive (MSN); nursing practice (DNP); pediatric clinical nursing practice (DNP), including pediatric nurse practitioner; pediatric nurse practitioner (MSN). *Accreditation:* AACN. *Program availability:* Part-time, online learning. *Degree requirements:* For master's, thesis or alternative. *Entrance requirements:* For master's, minimum undergraduate GPA of 3.2; for doctorate, GRE, 3 letters of reference. Additional exam requirements/recommendations for international students: required—TOEFL (minimum score 550 paper-based; 80 iBT).

**University of Mobile,** Graduate Studies, School of Nursing, Mobile, AL 36613. Offers education/administration (MSN); nurse practitioner (DNP). *Accreditation:* AACN. *Program availability:* Part-time, evening/weekend. *Degree requirements:* For master's, comprehensive exam, thesis or alternative; for doctorate, comprehensive exam. *Entrance requirements:* For master's, minimum cumulative GPA of 2.5, unencumbered license to practice as a registered nurse. See catalog for additional requirements. Additional exam requirements/recommendations for international students: required—TOEFL (minimum score 550 paper-based; 80 iBT). Electronic applications accepted.

**University of Nevada, Las Vegas,** Graduate College, School of Nursing, Las Vegas, NV 89154-3018. Offers biobehavioral nursing (Advanced Certificate); family nurse practitioner (Advanced Certificate); nursing (MS, DNP, PhD); nursing education (Advanced Certificate). *Accreditation:* AACN. *Program availability:* Part-time, 100% online, blended/hybrid learning. *Faculty:* 15 full-time (13 women), 9 part-time/adjunct (8 women). *Students:* 44 full-time (41 women), 111 part-time (96 women); includes 48 minority (9 Black or African American, non-Hispanic/Latino; 16 Asian, non-Hispanic/Latino; 15 Hispanic/Latino; 1 Native Hawaiian or other Pacific Islander, non-Hispanic/Latino; 7 Two or more races, non-Hispanic/Latino), 1 international. Average age 38. 218 applicants, 33% accepted, 63 enrolled. In 2019, 19 master's, 14 doctorates, 2 other advanced degrees awarded. *Degree requirements:* For master's, comprehensive exam, thesis; for doctorate, comprehensive exam (for some programs), thesis/dissertation, project defense (for DNP). *Entrance requirements:* For master's, bachelor's degree with minimum GPA 3.0; 2 letters of recommendation; valid RN license; statement of purpose; for doctorate, GRE General Test, bachelor's degree; statement of purpose; 3 letters of recommendation; for Advanced Certificate, 2 letters of recommendation; statement of purpose; valid RN license. Additional exam requirements/recommendations for international students: recommended—TOEFL (minimum score 550 paper-based; 80 iBT), IELTS (minimum score 7). Application fee: $60 ($95 for international students). Electronic applications accepted. *Expenses:* Contact institution. *Financial support:* In 2019–20, 2 students received support, including 1 research assistantship with full tuition reimbursement available (averaging $20,250 per year), 1 teaching assistantship with full tuition reimbursement available (averaging $20,250 per year); institutionally sponsored loans, scholarships/grants, health care benefits, and unspecified assistantships also available. Financial award application deadline: 3/15; financial award applicants required to submit FAFSA. *Unit head:* Dr. Angela Amar, Dean/Professor, 702-895-3906, Fax: 702-895-4807, E-mail: nursing.dean@unlv.edu. *Application contact:* Dr. Angela Amar, Dean/Professor, 702-895-3906, Fax: 702-895-4807, E-mail: nursing.dean@unlv.edu.
Website: http://nursing.unlv.edu/

**The University of North Carolina at Chapel Hill,** School of Nursing, Chapel Hill, NC 27599-7460. Offers advanced practice registered nurse (DNP); nursing (MSN, PhD, PMC), including administration (MSN), adult gerontology primary care nurse practitioner (MSN), clinical nurse leader (MSN), education (MSN), health care systems (PMC), informatics (MSN, PMC), nursing leadership (PMC), outcomes management (MSN), primary care family nurse practitioner (MSN), primary care pediatric nurse practitioner (MSN), psychiatric/mental health nurse practitioner (MSN, PMC). *Accreditation:* AACN; ACEN (one or more programs are accredited). *Program availability:* Part-time. *Degree requirements:* For master's, comprehensive exam, thesis; for doctorate, thesis/dissertation, 3 exams; for PMC, thesis. *Entrance requirements:* Additional exam requirements/recommendations for international students: required—TOEFL (minimum score 575 paper-based; 89 iBT), IELTS (minimum score 8). Electronic applications accepted.

**The University of North Carolina at Charlotte,** College of Health and Human Services, School of Nursing, Charlotte, NC 28223-0001. Offers adult-gerontology acute care nurse practitioner (Post-Master's Certificate); advanced clinical nursing (MSN), including adult psychiatric mental health, adult-gerontology acute care nurse practitioner, family nurse practitioner across the lifespan; family nurse practitioner across the lifespan (Post-Master's Certificate); nurse anesthesia (MSN), including nurse anesthesia across the lifespan; nurse anesthesia across the lifespan (Post-Master's Certificate); nursing (DNP); nursing administrator (Graduate Certificate); nursing educator (Graduate Certificate); systems/population nursing (MSN), including community/public health nursing, nurse administrator, nurse educator. *Accreditation:* AACN; AANA/CANAEP. *Program availability:* Part-time, blended/hybrid learning. *Students:* 126 full-time (96 women), 142 part-time (127 women); includes 70 minority (48 Black or African American, non-Hispanic/Latino; 8 Asian, non-Hispanic/Latino; 9 Hispanic/Latino; 5 Two or more races, non-Hispanic/Latino), 1 international. Average age 35. 347 applicants, 37% accepted, 104 enrolled. In 2019, 102 master's, 10 doctorates, 10 other advanced degrees awarded. Terminal master's awarded for partial completion of doctoral program. *Entrance requirements:* For master's, GRE General Test, current unrestricted license as Registered Nurse in North Carolina; BSN from nationally-accredited program; one year of professional nursing practice in acute/critical care; minimum overall GPA of 3.0 in last degree; completion of undergraduate statistics course with minimum grade of C; statement of purpose; for doctorate, GRE or MAT, master's degree in nursing in an advanced nursing practice specialty from nationally-accredited program; minimum overall GPA of 3.5 in MSN program; current RN licensure in U.S. at time of application with eligibility for NC licensure; essay; resume/curriculum vitae; professional recommendations; clinical hours; for other advanced degree, GRE. Additional exam requirements/recommendations for international students: required—TOEFL (minimum score 557 paper-based; 83 iBT), IELTS (minimum score 6.5), TOEFL (minimum score 557 paper-based, 83 iBT) or IELTS (6.5). *Application deadline:* Applications are processed on a rolling basis. Application fee: $75. Electronic applications accepted. *Expenses:* Contact institution. *Financial support:* In 2019–20, 6 students received support, including 4 research assistantships (averaging $4,856 per year), 2 teaching assistantships (averaging $3,615 per year); career-related internships or fieldwork, institutionally sponsored loans, scholarships/grants, traineeships, and unspecified assistantships also available. Support available to part-time students. Financial award application deadline: 3/1; financial award applicants required to submit FAFSA. *Unit head:* Dr. Dena Evans, Director, 704-687-7974, E-mail: devans37@uncc.edu. *Application contact:* Kathy B. Giddings, Director of Graduate Admissions, 704-687-5503, Fax: 704-687-1668, E-mail: gradadm@uncc.edu.
Website: http://nursing.uncc.edu/

**The University of North Carolina at Greensboro,** Graduate School, School of Nursing, Greensboro, NC 27412-5001. Offers adult clinical nurse specialist (MSN, PMC); adult/gerontological nurse practitioner (MSN, PMC); nurse anesthesia (MSN, PMC); nursing (PhD); nursing administration (MSN); nursing education (MSN); MSN/MBA. *Accreditation:* ACEN. *Degree requirements:* For master's, thesis or alternative. *Entrance requirements:* For master's, GRE General Test or MAT, BSN, clinical

experience, liability insurance, RN license; for PMC, liability insurance, MSN, RN license. Additional exam requirements/recommendations for international students: required—TOEFL. Electronic applications accepted.

**The University of North Carolina at Pembroke,** The Graduate School, Department of Nursing, Pembroke, NC 28372-1510. Offers clinical nurse leader (MSN); nurse educator (MSN); rural case manager (MSN). *Accreditation:* AACN. *Program availability:* Part-time.

**The University of North Carolina Wilmington,** School of Nursing, Wilmington, NC 28403-3297. Offers clinical research and product development (MS); family nurse practitioner (Post-Master's Certificate); nurse educator (Post-Master's Certificate); nursing (MSN); nursing practice (DNP). *Accreditation:* AACN; ACEN. *Program availability:* Part-time, 100% online, blended/hybrid learning. *Faculty:* 51 full-time (46 women). *Students:* 171 full-time (156 women), 423 part-time (387 women); includes 117 minority (73 Black or African American, non-Hispanic/Latino; 6 American Indian or Alaska Native, non-Hispanic/Latino; 12 Asian, non-Hispanic/Latino; 16 Hispanic/Latino; 1 Native Hawaiian or other Pacific Islander, non-Hispanic/Latino; 9 Two or more races, non-Hispanic/Latino). Average age 38. 527 applicants, 57% accepted, 199 enrolled. In 2019, 149 master's, 9 doctorates awarded. *Degree requirements:* For master's, thesis or alternative, research/capstone project, presentation; for doctorate, comprehensive exam, clinical scholarly project, 1000 clinical hours. *Entrance requirements:* For master's, GRE General Test if overall Bachelor degree GPA under 3.0 (MSN degree); No tests for MCRD degree, 3 recommendations; statement of interest; resume; bachelor's degree, preferably in a life science, health care discipline, or mathematics/statistics; experience working in the biopharmaceutical or related field (MCRD degree); RN license in NC & must have 2.69 or higher Bachelor's GPA (for MSN); for doctorate, GRE General Test or MAT if Bachelor's GPA below 3.0 (FNP & Psychiatric Mental Health Nurse concentration), Varies based on concentration (Family Nurse Practitioner, Nurse Executive Leadership, Post APRN, and Psychiatric Mental Health Nurse); All require 3 professional references and an RN license. Additional exam requirements/recommendations for international students: required—TOEFL (minimum score 79 iBT), IELTS (minimum score 6.5). *Application deadline:* For fall admission, 4/15 for domestic students. Applications are processed on a rolling basis. Application fee: $75. Electronic applications accepted. *Expenses:* $324.70 per credit hour in-state (for DNP Program), $1,002.59 per credit hour out-of-state (for DNP Program), $259.01 per credit hour in-state (for the remaining online programs), $936.91 per credit hour out-of-state (for the remaining online programs), $3,728.47 entire year in-state (for main campus programs), $10,642.97 entire year out-of-state (for main campus programs). *Financial support:* Scholarships/grants available. Financial award application deadline: 1/1; financial award applicants required to submit FAFSA. *Unit head:* Dr. Linda Haddad, Director, 910-962-7410, Fax: 910-962-3723, E-mail: haddadl@uncw.edu. *Application contact:* Dr. Sarah Hubbell, MSN Graduate Coordinator, 910-962-0561, E-mail: hubbells@uncw.edu.
Website: https://uncw.edu/chhs/son/

**University of North Dakota,** Graduate School, College of Nursing and Professional Disciplines, Department of Nursing, Grand Forks, ND 58202. Offers adult-gerontological nurse practitioner (MS); advanced public health nurse (MS); family nurse practitioner (MS); nurse anesthesia (MS); nurse educator (MS); nursing (PhD, Post-Master's Certificate); nursing practice (DNP); psychiatric and mental health nurse practitioner (MS). *Accreditation:* AANA/CANAEP.

**University of Northern Colorado,** Graduate School, College of Natural and Health Sciences, School of Nursing, Greeley, CO 80639. Offers adult-gerontology acute care nurse practitioner (MSN, DNP); family nurse practitioner (MSN, DNP); nursing education (PhD); nursing practice (DNP). *Accreditation:* AACN. *Program availability:* Online learning. *Degree requirements:* For master's, comprehensive exam, thesis or alternative; for doctorate, comprehensive exam, thesis/dissertation. *Entrance requirements:* For master's and doctorate, GRE General Test, minimum GPA of 3.0 in last 60 hours, BS in nursing, 2 letters of recommendation. Electronic applications accepted.

**University of North Georgia,** Program in Nursing Education, Dahlonega, GA 30597. Offers MS. *Program availability:* Part-time, evening/weekend, online only, Online program, with minimal campus visits required. *Students:* 16 part-time (all women); includes 1 minority (Black or African American, non-Hispanic/Latino). Average age 40. In 2019, 2 master's awarded. *Financial support:* Application deadline: 3/17; applicants required to submit FAFSA.
Website: https://ung.edu/graduate-admissions/programs/master-of-science-in-nursing-education.php

**University of Phoenix - Bay Area Campus,** College of Nursing, San Jose, CA 95134-1805. Offers education (MHA); gerontology (MHA); health administration (MHA, DHA); informatics (MHA, MSN); nursing (MSN, PhD); nursing/health care education (MSN); MSN/MBA. *Program availability:* Evening/weekend, online learning. *Degree requirements:* For master's, thesis (for some programs). *Entrance requirements:* For master's, minimum undergraduate GPA of 2.5, 3 years of work experience, RN license. Additional exam requirements/recommendations for international students: required—TOEFL (minimum score 550 paper-based; 79 iBT). Electronic applications accepted.

**University of Phoenix - Hawaii Campus,** College of Nursing, Honolulu, HI 96813-3800. Offers education (MHA); family nurse practitioner (MSN); gerontology (MHA); health administration (MHA); nursing (MSN); nursing/health care education (MSN); MSN/MBA. *Program availability:* Evening/weekend. *Degree requirements:* For master's, thesis (for some programs). *Entrance requirements:* For master's, minimum undergraduate GPA of 2.5, 3 years of work experience, RN license. Additional exam requirements/recommendations for international students: required—TOEFL (minimum score 550 paper-based; 79 iBT). Electronic applications accepted.

**University of Phoenix–Online Campus,** College of Health Sciences and Nursing, Phoenix, AZ 85034-7209. Offers family nurse practitioner (Certificate); health care (Certificate); health care education (Certificate); health care informatics (Certificate); informatics (MSN); nursing (MSN); nursing and health care education (MSN); MSN/MBA; MSN/MHA. *Accreditation:* AACN. *Program availability:* Evening/weekend, online learning. *Entrance requirements:* Additional exam requirements/recommendations for international students: required—TOEFL, TOEIC (Test of English as an International Communication), Berlitz Online English Proficiency Exam, PTE, or IELTS. Electronic applications accepted. *Expenses:* Contact institution.

**University of Phoenix - Phoenix Campus,** College of Health Sciences and Nursing, Tempe, AZ 85282-2371. Offers family nurse practitioner (MSN, Certificate); gerontology health care (Certificate); health care education (MSN, Certificate); health care informatics (Certificate); informatics (MSN); nursing (MSN); MSN/MHA. *Program availability:* Evening/weekend, online learning. *Entrance requirements:* Additional exam requirements/recommendations for international students: required—TOEFL, TOEIC (Test of English as an International Communication), Berlitz Online English Proficiency Exam, PTE, or IELTS. Electronic applications accepted. *Expenses:* Contact institution.

**University of Phoenix - Sacramento Valley Campus,** College of Nursing, Sacramento, CA 95833-4334. Offers family nurse practitioner (MSN); health administration (MHA); health care education (MSN); nursing (MSN); MSN/MBA. *Program availability:* Evening/weekend. *Degree requirements:* For master's, thesis (for some programs). *Entrance requirements:* For master's, RN license, minimum undergraduate GPA of 2.5, 3 years work experience. Additional exam requirements/recommendations for international students: required—TOEFL (minimum score 550 paper-based; 79 iBT). Electronic applications accepted.

**University of Phoenix - San Diego Campus,** College of Nursing, San Diego, CA 92123. Offers health care education (MSN); nursing (MSN); MSN/MBA. *Program availability:* Evening/weekend. *Degree requirements:* For master's, thesis (for some programs). *Entrance requirements:* For master's, minimum undergraduate GPA of 2.5, 3 years work experience, RN license. Additional exam requirements/recommendations for international students: required—TOEFL (minimum score 550 paper-based; 79 iBT). Electronic applications accepted.

**University of Portland,** School of Nursing, Portland, OR 97203-5798. Offers clinical nurse leader (MS); family nurse practitioner (DNP); nurse educator (MS). *Accreditation:* AACN. *Program availability:* Part-time, evening/weekend. *Entrance requirements:* For doctorate, RN license, BSN or MSN, 3 letters of recommendation, resume, writing sample, official transcripts. Additional exam requirements/recommendations for international students: required—TOEFL (minimum score 100 iBT), IELTS (minimum score 7.5). Electronic applications accepted. *Expenses:* Contact institution.

**University of Rhode Island,** Graduate School, College of Nursing, Kingston, RI 02881. Offers acute care nurse practitioner (adult-gerontology focus) (Post Master's Certificate); adult gerontology nurse practitioner/clinical nurse specialist (Post Master's Certificate); adult-gerontological acute care nurse practitioner (MS); adult-gerontological nurse practitioner/clinical nurse specialist (MS); family nurse practitioner (MS, Post Master's Certificate); nursing (DNP, PhD); nursing education (MS, Post Master's Certificate). *Accreditation:* AACN; ACNM/ACME (one or more programs are accredited). *Program availability:* Part-time, evening/weekend, 100% online, blended/hybrid learning. *Faculty:* 27 full-time (26 women). *Students:* 51 full-time (47 women), 72 part-time (65 women); includes 21 minority (9 Black or African American, non-Hispanic/Latino; 5 Asian, non-Hispanic/Latino; 4 Hispanic/Latino; 2 Native Hawaiian or other Pacific Islander, non-Hispanic/Latino; 1 Two or more races, non-Hispanic/Latino), 6 international. 32 applicants, 88% accepted, 21 enrolled. In 2019, 34 master's, 9 doctorates, 1 other advanced degree awarded. *Entrance requirements:* For master's, GRE or MAT, 2 letters of recommendation, scholarly papers; for doctorate, GRE, 3 letters of recommendation, scholarly papers. Additional exam requirements/recommendations for international students: required—TOEFL. *Application deadline:* For fall admission, 2/15 for domestic students, 2/1 for international students; for spring admission, 10/15 for domestic students, 7/15 for international students. Application fee: $65. Electronic applications accepted. *Expenses: Tuition, area resident:* Full-time $13,734; part-time $763 per credit. Tuition, state resident: full-time $13,734; part-time $763 per credit. Tuition, nonresident: full-time $26,512; part-time $1473 per credit. *International tuition:* $26,512 full-time. *Required fees:* $1780; $52 per credit. $35 per term. One-time fee: $165. *Financial support:* In 2019–20, 7 teaching assistantships with tuition reimbursements (averaging $13,376 per year) were awarded. Financial award application deadline: 2/1; financial award applicants required to submit FAFSA. *Unit head:* Dr. Barbara Wolfe, Dean, 401-874-5324, E-mail: bwolfe@uri.edu. *Application contact:* Dr. Denise Coppa, Associate Professor/Interim Associate Dean for Graduate Programs, 401-874-5036, E-mail: dcoppa@uri.edu.
Website: http://www.uri.edu/nursing/

**University of Rochester,** School of Nursing, Rochester, NY 14642. Offers adult gerontological acute care nurse practitioner (MS); adult gerontological primary care nurse practitioner (MS); clinical nurse leader (MS); family nurse practitioner (MS); family psychiatric mental health nurse practitioner (MS); health care organization management and leadership (MS); nursing (DNP); nursing and health science (PhD); nursing education (MS); pediatric nurse practitioner (MS); pediatric nurse practitioner/neonatal nurse practitioner (MS). *Accreditation:* AACN. *Program availability:* Part-time, 100% online, blended/hybrid learning. Terminal master's awarded for partial completion of doctoral program. *Degree requirements:* For master's, comprehensive exam; for doctorate, thesis/dissertation. *Entrance requirements:* For master's, BS in nursing, RN license; for doctorate, GRE General Test (for PhD), B.S. degree, RN license most programs. Additional exam requirements/recommendations for international students: required—TOEFL (minimum score 560 paper-based; 88 iBT), TOEFL (minimum score 560 paper-based; 88 iBT) or IELTS (minimum score 6.5) recommended. Electronic applications accepted. *Expenses:* Contact institution.

**University of St. Augustine for Health Sciences,** Graduate Programs, Master of Science in Nursing Program, San Marcos, CA 92069. Offers nurse educator (MSN); nurse executive (MSN); nurse informatics (MSN). *Program availability:* Part-time, online learning.

**University of St. Francis,** Leach College of Nursing, Joliet, IL 60435-6169. Offers family nurse practitioner (MSN, Post-Master's Certificate); nursing administration (MSN); nursing education (MSN); nursing practice (DNP); psychology/mental health nurse practitioner (MSN, Post-Master's Certificate); teaching in nursing (Certificate). *Accreditation:* AACN. *Program availability:* Part-time, evening/weekend, 100% online. *Degree requirements:* For master's, comprehensive exam. *Entrance requirements:* Additional exam requirements/recommendations for international students: required—TOEFL (minimum score 550 paper-based; 79 iBT), IELTS (minimum score 6). Electronic applications accepted. Application fee is waived when completed online. *Expenses:* Contact institution.

**University of Saint Joseph,** Department of Nursing, West Hartford, CT 06117-2700. Offers family nurse practitioner (MS); nurse educator (MS); nursing practice (DNP); psychiatric/mental health nurse practitioner (MS). *Accreditation:* AACN. *Program availability:* Part-time, evening/weekend. *Degree requirements:* For master's, thesis. *Entrance requirements:* For master's, 2 letters of recommendation. Electronic applications accepted. Application fee is waived when completed online.

**University of Saint Mary,** Graduate Programs, Program in Nursing, Leavenworth, KS 66048-5082. Offers nurse administrator (MSN); nurse educator (MSN). *Accreditation:* AACN. *Program availability:* Part-time, online only, 100% online. *Students:* 10 full-time (all women), 12 part-time (10 women); includes 2 minority (1 Hispanic/Latino; 1 Native Hawaiian or other Pacific Islander, non-Hispanic/Latino). Average age 40. In 2019, 19 master's awarded. *Degree requirements:* For master's, practicum. *Entrance requirements:* For master's, BSN from CCNE- or ACEN-accredited baccalaureate nursing program at regionally-accredited institution. *Application deadline:* Applications are processed on a rolling basis. Application fee: $25. Electronic applications accepted. *Expenses:* $615 per credit hour. *Financial support:* Applicants required to submit FAFSA. *Unit head:* Michelle Birdashaw, Division Chair of Nursing, E-mail: michelle.birdashaw@stmary.edu. *Application contact:* Michelle Birdashaw, Division Chair of Nursing, E-mail: michelle.birdashaw@stmary.edu.
Website: http://online.stmary.edu/msn

**University of South Alabama,** College of Nursing, Mobile, AL 36688-0002. Offers nursing (MSN, DNP); nursing administration (Certificate); nursing education (Certificate); nursing practice (Certificate). *Accreditation:* AACN. *Program availability:* Part-time, online learning. *Faculty:* 72 full-time (66 women), 116 part-time/adjunct (103 women). *Students:* 2,311 full-time (2,024 women), 716 part-time (636 women); includes 955 minority (613 Black or African American, non-Hispanic/Latino; 28 American Indian

or Alaska Native, non-Hispanic/Latino; 121 Asian, non-Hispanic/Latino; 123 Hispanic/Latino; 4 Native Hawaiian or other Pacific Islander, non-Hispanic/Latino; 66 Two or more races, non-Hispanic/Latino. Average age 35. 884 applicants, 93% accepted, 624 enrolled. In 2019, 744 master's, 157 doctorates, 94 other advanced degrees awarded. *Degree requirements:* For master's, thesis optional. *Entrance requirements:* Additional exam requirements/recommendations for international students: required—TOEFL (minimum score 600 paper-based; 100 iBT). *Application deadline:* For fall admission, 2/15 priority date for domestic students, 1/15 priority date for international students; for spring admission, 7/15 priority date for domestic students, 6/15 priority date for international students; for summer admission, 11/15 priority date for domestic students, 10/15 priority date for international students. Applications are processed on a rolling basis. Application fee: $100. Electronic applications accepted. *Expenses:* Contact institution. *Financial support:* Fellowships, research assistantships, teaching assistantships, career-related internships or fieldwork, Federal Work-Study, institutionally sponsored loans, scholarships/grants, and unspecified assistantships available. Support available to part-time students. Financial award application deadline: 3/31; financial award applicants required to submit FAFSA. *Unit head:* Dr. Heather Hall, Dean, College of Nursing, 251-445-9400, Fax: 251-445-9416, E-mail: heatherhall@southalabama.edu. *Application contact:* Jennifer Bouvier, Academic Advisor II, 251-445-9400, Fax: 251-445-9416, E-mail: jcamp@southalabama.edu.
Website: http://www.southalabama.edu/colleges/con/index.html

**University of Southern Indiana,** Graduate Studies, College of Nursing and Health Professions, Program in Nursing, Evansville, IN 47712-3590. Offers adult-gerontology acute care nurse practitioner (MSN, PMC); adult-gerontology clinical nurse specialist (MSN, PMC); adult-gerontology primary care nurse practitioner (MSN, PMC); advanced nursing practice (DNP); family nurse practitioner (MSN, PMC); nursing education (MSN, PMC); nursing management and leadership (MSN, PMC); organizational and systems leadership (DNP); psychiatric mental health nurse practitioner (MSN, PMC). *Accreditation:* AACN. *Program availability:* Part-time, online learning. *Entrance requirements:* For master's, BSN from nationally-accredited school; minimum cumulative GPA of 3.0; satisfactory completion of a course in undergraduate statistics (minimum grade C); one year of full-time experience or 2,000 hours of clinical practice as an RN (recommended); unencumbered U.S. RN license; for doctorate, minimum GPA of 3.0, completion of graduate research course with minimum B grade, unencumbered RN license, resume/curriculum vitae, three professional references, 1-2 page narrative of practice experience and professional goals, Capstone Project Information form. Additional exam requirements/recommendations for international students: required—TOEFL (minimum score 550 paper-based; 79 iBT), IELTS (minimum score 6). Electronic applications accepted. *Expenses:* Contact institution.

**University of Southern Maine,** College of Science, Technology, and Health, School of Nursing, Portland, ME 04103. Offers adult-gerontology primary care nurse practitioner (MS, PMC); education (MS); family nurse practitioner (MS, PMC); family psychiatric/mental health nurse practitioner (MS); management (MS); nursing (CAS, CGS); psychiatric-mental health nurse practitioner (PMC). *Accreditation:* AACN. *Program availability:* Part-time. *Degree requirements:* For master's, thesis optional. *Entrance requirements:* For master's, GRE General Test or MAT, minimum GPA of 3.0; for doctorate, GRE. Additional exam requirements/recommendations for international students: required—TOEFL (minimum score 550 paper-based). Electronic applications accepted. *Expenses:* Tuition, area resident: Full-time $864; part-time $432 per credit hour. Tuition, state resident: full-time $864; part-time $432 per credit hour. Tuition, nonresident: full-time $2372; part-time $1186 per credit hour. *Required fees:* $141; $108 per credit hour. Tuition and fees vary according to course load.

**University of South Florida,** College of Nursing, Tampa, FL 33612. Offers nurse anesthesia (DNP); nursing (MS, DNP), including adult-gerontology acute care nursing, adult-gerontology primary care nursing, family health nursing, nurse anesthesia (MS), nursing education (MS); occupational health nursing/adult-gerontology primary care nursing, oncology nursing/adult-gerontology primary care nursing (DNP), pediatric health nursing; nursing education (Post Master's Certificate); nursing science (PhD); simulation based academic fellowship in advanced pain management (Graduate Certificate). *Accreditation:* AACN; AANA/CANAEP. *Program availability:* Part-time. *Faculty:* 34 full-time (28 women), 2 part-time/adjunct (1 woman). *Students:* 265 full-time (207 women), 687 part-time (594 women); includes 343 minority (113 Black or African American, non-Hispanic/Latino; 1 American Indian or Alaska Native, non-Hispanic/Latino; 60 Asian, non-Hispanic/Latino; 141 Hispanic/Latino; 1 Native Hawaiian or other Pacific Islander, non-Hispanic/Latino; 27 Two or more races, non-Hispanic/Latino), 2 international. Average age 33. 955 applicants, 44% accepted, 343 enrolled. In 2019, 281 master's, 80 doctorates awarded. *Degree requirements:* For master's, comprehensive exam, thesis optional; for doctorate, comprehensive exam, thesis/dissertation (for some programs). *Entrance requirements:* For master's, GRE General Test, bachelor's in nursing or RN with Bachelor's in relevant field; current license as Registered Nurse; resume or CV; interview; pre-reqs may be required; for doctorate, GRE General Test (recommended), bachelor's degree in nursing from ACEN or CCNE regionally-accredited institution with minimum GPA of 3.0 in all coursework or in all upper-division coursework; current license as Registered Nurse in Florida; undergraduate statistics course with minimum B grade; 3 letters of recommendation; statement of goals; resume; interview. Additional exam requirements/recommendations for international students: required—TOEFL (minimum score 550 paper-based; 79 iBT). *Application deadline:* For fall admission, 12/15 for domestic and international students; for spring admission, 10/1 for domestic students, 9/15 for international students. Application fee: $30. Electronic applications accepted. *Financial support:* In 2019–20, 181 students received support, including 7 research assistantships with tuition reimbursements available (averaging $18,935 per year), 29 teaching assistantships with tuition reimbursements available (averaging $30,814 per year); tuition waivers (partial) and unspecified assistantships also available. Financial award application deadline: 2/1; financial award applicants required to submit FAFSA. *Unit head:* Dr. Victoria Rich, Dean, College of Nursing, 813-974-8939, Fax: 813-974-5418, E-mail: victoriarich@health.usf.edu. *Application contact:* Dr. Denise Maguire, Vice Dean, Graduate Programs, 813-396-9962, E-mail: dmaguire@health.usf.edu.
Website: http://health.usf.edu/nursing/index.htm

**The University of Tennessee at Chattanooga,** School of Nursing, Chattanooga, TN 37403. Offers certified nurse anesthetist (Post-Master's Certificate); family nurse practitioner (MSN, Post-Master's Certificate); gerontology acute care (MSN, Post-Master's Certificate); nurse anesthesia (MSN); nurse education (Post-Master's Certificate); nursing (DNP). *Accreditation:* AACN; AANA/CANAEP (one or more programs are accredited). *Program availability:* 100% online. *Faculty:* 32 full-time (29 women), 14 part-time/adjunct (10 women). *Students:* 78 full-time (49 women), 51 part-time (43 women); includes 24 minority (11 Black or African American, non-Hispanic/Latino; 2 American Indian or Alaska Native, non-Hispanic/Latino; 4 Asian, non-Hispanic/Latino; 5 Hispanic/Latino; 2 Two or more races, non-Hispanic/Latino). Average age 34. 50 applicants, 100% accepted, 46 enrolled. In 2019, 38 master's, 16 doctorates, 2 other advanced degrees awarded. *Degree requirements:* For master's, thesis optional, practicum; for doctorate, professional project; for Post-Master's Certificate, practicum. *Entrance requirements:* For master's, GRE General Test, MAT, BSN, minimum GPA of 3.0, eligibility for Tennessee RN license, 1 year of direct patient care experience; for

doctorate, GRE General Test or MAT (if applicant does not have MSN), minimum GPA of 3.0 for highest degree earned; for Post-Master's Certificate, GRE General Test, MAT, MSN, minimum GPA of 3.0, eligibility for Tennessee RN license, one year of direct patient care experience. Additional exam requirements/recommendations for international students: required—TOEFL (minimum score 550 paper-based; 79 iBT), IELTS (minimum score 6). *Application deadline:* For fall admission, 6/15 priority date for domestic students, 7/1 for international students; for spring admission, 11/1 priority date for domestic students, 11/1 for international students. Applications are processed on a rolling basis. Application fee: $35 ($40 for international students). Electronic applications accepted. *Financial support:* Teaching assistantships, career-related internships or fieldwork, and scholarships/grants available. Support available to part-time students. Financial award application deadline: 7/1; financial award applicants required to submit FAFSA. *Unit head:* Dr. Chris Smith, Director, 423-425-4665, Fax: 423-425-4668, E-mail: chris-smith@utc.edu. *Application contact:* Dr. Joanne Romagni, Dean of the Graduate School, 423-425-4478, Fax: 423-425-5223, E-mail: joanne-romagni@utc.edu.
Website: http://www.utc.edu/nursing/

**The University of Texas at Arlington,** Graduate School, College of Nursing and Health Innovation, Arlington, TX 76019. Offers athletic training (MS); exercise science (MS); kinesiology (PhD); nurse practitioner (MSN); nursing (PhD); nursing administration (MSN); nursing education (MSN); nursing practice (DNP). *Accreditation:* AACN. *Program availability:* Part-time, evening/weekend, online learning. *Degree requirements:* For master's, practicum course; for doctorate, comprehensive exam (for some programs), thesis/dissertation (for some programs), proposal defense dissertation (for PhD); scholarship project (for DNP). *Entrance requirements:* For master's, GRE General Test if GPA less than 3.0, minimum GPA of 3.0, Texas nursing license, minimum C grade in undergraduate statistics course; for doctorate, GRE General Test (waived for MSN-to-PhD applicants), minimum undergraduate, graduate and statistics GPA of 3.0; Texas RN license; interview; written statement of goals. Additional exam requirements/recommendations for international students: required—TOEFL (minimum score 550 paper-based), IELTS (minimum score 7).

**The University of Texas at Austin,** Graduate School, School of Nursing, Austin, TX 78712-1111. Offers adult - gerontology clinical nurse specialist (MSN); child health (MSN), including administration, public health nursing, teaching; family nurse practitioner (MSN); family psychiatric/mental health nurse practitioner (MSN); holistic adult health (MSN), including administration, teaching; maternity (MSN), including administration, public health nursing, teaching; nursing (PhD); nursing administration and healthcare systems management (MSN); nursing practice (DNP); pediatric nurse practitioner (MSN); public health nursing (MSN). *Accreditation:* AACN. *Program availability:* Part-time. *Degree requirements:* For master's, thesis optional; for doctorate, thesis/dissertation. *Entrance requirements:* For master's and doctorate, GRE General Test. Additional exam requirements/recommendations for international students: required—TOEFL (minimum score 550 paper-based). Electronic applications accepted.

**The University of Texas at El Paso,** Graduate School, School of Nursing, El Paso, TX 79968-0001. Offers family nurse practitioner (MSN); health care leadership and management (Certificate); interdisciplinary health sciences (PhD); nursing (DNP); nursing education (MSN, Certificate); nursing systems management (MSN). *Accreditation:* AACN. *Program availability:* Online learning. *Degree requirements:* For master's, thesis optional; for doctorate, thesis/dissertation. *Entrance requirements:* For master's, minimum GPA of 3.0, resume; for doctorate, GRE, letters of reference, relevant personal/professional experience; master's degree in nursing (for DNP); for Certificate, bachelor's degree in nursing. Additional exam requirements/recommendations for international students: required—TOEFL; recommended—IELTS. Electronic applications accepted.

**The University of Texas at Tyler,** College of Nursing and Health Sciences, School of Nursing, Tyler, TX 75799. Offers nurse practitioner (MSN); nursing (PhD); nursing administration (MSN); nursing education (MSN); MSN/MBA. *Accreditation:* AACN. *Program availability:* Part-time, evening/weekend, online learning. *Faculty:* 27 full-time (all women), 4 part-time/adjunct (all women). *Students:* 101 full-time (83 women), 351 part-time (303 women); includes 149 minority (53 Black or African American, non-Hispanic/Latino; 1 American Indian or Alaska Native, non-Hispanic/Latino; 27 Asian, non-Hispanic/Latino; 51 Hispanic/Latino; 17 Two or more races, non-Hispanic/Latino), 5 international. Average age 37. 128 applicants, 67% accepted, 81 enrolled. In 2019, 86 master's, 21 doctorates awarded. *Degree requirements:* For master's, comprehensive exam (for some programs), thesis (for some programs); for doctorate, thesis/dissertation. *Entrance requirements:* For master's, GRE General Test or MAT, GMAT, minimum undergraduate GPA of 3.0, course work in statistics, RN license, BSN. Additional exam requirements/recommendations for international students: required—TOEFL. *Application deadline:* For fall admission, 8/17 priority date for domestic students, 7/1 priority date for international students; for spring admission, 12/21 priority date for domestic students, 11/1 priority date for international students. Applications are processed on a rolling basis. Application fee: $25 ($50 for international students). Electronic applications accepted. *Financial support:* In 2019–20, 15 students received support, including 1 fellowship (averaging $10,000 per year), 3 research assistantships (averaging $2,200 per year); institutionally sponsored loans and scholarships/grants also available. Financial award application deadline: 7/1; financial award applicants required to submit FAFSA. *Unit head:* Dr. Barbara Haas, Associate Dean, 903-566-7021, E-mail: bhaas@uttyler.edu. *Application contact:* Dr. Barbara Haas, Associate Dean, 903-566-7021, E-mail: bhaas@uttyler.edu.
Website: https://www.uttyler.edu/nursing/

**The University of Texas Health Science Center at San Antonio,** School of Nursing, San Antonio, TX 78229-3900. Offers administrative management (MSN); adult-gerontology acute care nurse practitioner (PGC); advanced practice leadership (DNP); clinical nurse leader (MSN); executive administrative management (DNP); family nurse practitioner (MSN, PGC); nursing (MSN, PhD); nursing education (MSN, PGC); pediatric nurse practitioner primary care (PGC); psychiatric mental health nurse practitioner (PGC); public health nurse leader (DNP). *Accreditation:* AACN. *Program availability:* Part-time. Terminal master's awarded for partial completion of doctoral program. *Degree requirements:* For master's, thesis optional; for doctorate, comprehensive exam, thesis/dissertation.

**The University of Toledo,** College of Graduate Studies, College of Nursing, Department of Population and Community Care, Toledo, OH 43606-3390. Offers clinical nurse leader (MSN); family nurse practitioner (MSN, Certificate); nurse educator (MSN, Certificate); pediatric nurse practitioner (MSN, Certificate). *Program availability:* Part-time. *Degree requirements:* For master's, thesis or alternative. *Entrance requirements:* For master's, GRE, BS in nursing, minimum undergraduate GPA of 3.0, statement of purpose, three letters of recommendation, transcripts from all prior institutions attended, Nursing CAS application, UT supplemental application; for Certificate, BS in nursing, minimum undergraduate GPA of 3.0, statement of purpose, three letters of recommendation, transcripts from all prior institutions attended. Additional exam requirements/recommendations for international students: required—TOEFL (minimum score 550 paper-based; 80 iBT). Electronic applications accepted.

**University of Victoria,** Faculty of Graduate Studies, Faculty of Human and Social Development, School of Nursing, Victoria, BC V8W 2Y2, Canada. Offers advanced

nursing practice (advanced practice leadership option) (MN); advanced nursing practice (nurse educator option) (MN); advanced nursing practice (nurse practitioner option) (MN); nursing (PhD). *Program availability:* Part-time, online learning. *Entrance requirements:* Additional exam requirements/recommendations for international students: required—TOEFL (minimum score 575 paper-based), IELTS (minimum score 7). Electronic applications accepted.

**University of Washington, Tacoma,** Graduate Programs, Program in Nursing, Tacoma, WA 98402-3100. Offers communities, populations and health (MN); leadership in healthcare (MN); nurse educator (MN). *Program availability:* Part-time. *Degree requirements:* For master's, thesis (for some programs), advance fieldwork. *Entrance requirements:* For master's, Washington State NCLEX exam, minimum GPA of 3.0. Additional exam requirements/recommendations for international students: required—TOEFL (minimum score 580 paper-based; 70 iBT); recommended—IELTS (minimum score 7).

**University of Wisconsin–Eau Claire,** College of Nursing and Health Sciences, Program in Nursing, Eau Claire, WI 54702-4004. Offers adult-gerontological administration (DNP); adult-gerontological clinical nurse specialist (DNP); adult-gerontological education (MSN); adult-gerontological primary care nurse practitioner (DNP); family health administration (DNP); family health in education (MSN); family health nurse practitioner (DNP); nursing (MSN); nursing practice (DNP). *Accreditation:* AACN. *Program availability:* Part-time. Terminal master's awarded for partial completion of doctoral program. *Degree requirements:* For master's, thesis optional, 500-600 hours clinical practicum, oral and written exams. *Entrance requirements:* For master's, Wisconsin RN license, minimum GPA of 3.0, undergraduate statistics, course work in health assessment. Additional exam requirements/recommendations for international students: required—TOEFL (minimum score 79 iBT). *Expenses:* Contact institution.

**Ursuline College,** School of Graduate and Professional Studies, Programs in Nursing, Pepper Pike, OH 44124-4398. Offers acute-care nurse practitioner (MSN); adult nurse practitioner (MSN); adult-gerontology acute care nurse practitioner (MSN); adult-gerontology clinical nurse specialist (MSN); adult-gerontology nurse practitioner (MSN); care management (MSN); clinical nurse specialist (MSN); family nurse practitioner (MSN); nursing (DNP); nursing education (MSN); palliative care (MSN). *Accreditation:* AACN. *Program availability:* Part-time, 100% online. *Faculty:* 6 full-time (all women), 25 part-time/adjunct (19 women). *Students:* 106 full-time (99 women), 117 part-time (105 women); includes 71 minority (46 Black or African American, non-Hispanic/Latino; 2 American Indian or Alaska Native, non-Hispanic/Latino; 12 Asian, non-Hispanic/Latino; 6 Hispanic/Latino; 5 Two or more races, non-Hispanic/Latino). Average age 38. 265 applicants, 98% accepted, 61 enrolled. In 2019, 68 master's, 2 doctorates awarded. *Degree requirements:* For master's, comprehensive exam; for doctorate, thesis/dissertation. *Entrance requirements:* For master's, minimum undergraduate GPA of 3.0, bachelor's degree in nursing, eligibility for or current Ohio RN license. Additional exam requirements/recommendations for international students: required—TOEFL (minimum score 500 paper-based). *Application deadline:* For fall admission, 8/1 priority date for domestic students. Applications are processed on a rolling basis. Application fee: $25. Electronic applications accepted. *Expenses: Tuition:* Full-time $18,784; part-time $1174 per credit hour. *Required fees:* $320; $240 per unit. One-time fee: $100. Tuition and fees vary according to course level and program. *Financial support:* In 2019–20, 10 students received support. Scholarships/grants, tuition waivers (partial), and College Free Credit available. Financial award application deadline: 3/1; financial award applicants required to submit FAFSA. *Unit head:* Dr. Janet Baker, Associate Dean of Graduate Nursing, 440-864-8172, Fax: 440-684-6053, E-mail: jbaker@ursuline.edu. *Application contact:* Melanie Steele, Director, Graduate Admission, 440-646-8119, Fax: 440-684-6138, E-mail: graduateadmissions@ursuline.edu.

**Valparaiso University,** Graduate School and Continuing Education, College of Nursing and Health Professions, Valparaiso, IN 46383. Offers nursing (DNP); nursing education (MSN, Certificate); physician assistant (MSPA); public health (MPH); MSN/MHA. *Accreditation:* AACN. *Program availability:* Part-time, evening/weekend, online learning. *Entrance requirements:* For master's, minimum GPA of 3.0, undergraduate major in nursing, Indiana registered nursing license, undergraduate courses in research and statistics. Additional exam requirements/recommendations for international students: required—TOEFL (minimum score 550 paper-based; 80 iBT), IELTS (minimum score 6). Electronic applications accepted. *Expenses:* Contact institution.

**Villanova University,** M. Louise Fitzpatrick College of Nursing, Villanova, PA 19085. Offers adult-gerontology primary care nurse practitioner (MSN, Post Master's Certificate); family primary care nurse practitioner (MSN, Post Master's Certificate); nurse anesthesia (DNP); nursing (PhD); nursing education (MSN, Post Master's Certificate); nursing practice (DNP); pediatric primary care nurse practitioner (MSN, Post Master's Certificate). *Accreditation:* AACN; AANA/CANAEP. *Program availability:* Part-time, online learning. *Entrance requirements:* Additional exam requirements/recommendations for international students: required—TOEFL, IELTS. Electronic applications accepted.

**Virginia Commonwealth University,** Graduate School, School of Nursing, Richmond, VA 23284-9005. Offers adult health acute nursing (MS); adult health primary nursing (MS); biobehavioral clinical research (PhD); child health nursing (MS); clinical nurse leader (MS); family health nursing (MS); nurse educator (MS); nurse practitioner (MS); nursing (Certificate); nursing administration (MS), including clinical nurse manager; psychiatric-mental health nursing (MS); quality and safety in health care (DNP); women's health nursing (MS). *Accreditation:* AACN; ACEN (one or more programs are accredited). *Program availability:* Part-time, evening/weekend, online learning. *Degree requirements:* For master's, thesis optional; for doctorate, thesis/dissertation. *Entrance requirements:* For master's, GRE General Test, BSN, minimum GPA of 2.8; for doctorate, GRE General Test. Additional exam requirements/recommendations for international students: required—TOEFL (minimum score 600 paper-based; 100 iBT). Electronic applications accepted.

**Wagner College,** Division of Graduate Studies, Evelyn L. Spiro School of Nursing, Staten Island, NY 10301-4495. Offers family nurse practitioner (MS, Certificate); nurse educator (MS); nursing (DNP). *Accreditation:* ACEN (one or more programs are accredited). *Program availability:* Part-time, evening/weekend. *Degree requirements:* For master's, thesis optional. *Entrance requirements:* For master's, BS in nursing, current clinical experience, minimum GPA of 3.3; for Certificate, master's degree in nursing from an NLN-accredited program, minimum GPA of 3.0. Additional exam requirements/recommendations for international students: required—TOEFL (minimum score 550 paper-based; 79 iBT), IELTS (minimum score 6.5). Electronic applications accepted.

**Walden University,** Graduate Programs, School of Nursing, Minneapolis, MN 55401. Offers adult-gerontology acute care nurse practitioner (MSN); adult-gerontology nurse practitioner (MSN); education (MSN); family nurse practitioner (MSN); informatics (MSN); leadership and management (MSN); nursing (PhD, Post-Master's Certificate), including education (PhD), healthcare administration (PhD), interdisciplinary health (PhD), leadership (PhD), nursing education (Post-Master's Certificate), nursing informatics (Post-Master's Certificate), nursing leadership and management (Post-Master's Certificate), public health policy (PhD); nursing practice (DNP); psychiatric mental health (MSN). *Accreditation:* AACN. *Program availability:* Part-time, evening/weekend, online only, 100% online. *Degree requirements:* For doctorate, thesis/dissertation (for some programs), residency (for some programs), field experience (for some programs). *Entrance requirements:* For master's, bachelor's degree or equivalent in related field or RN; minimum GPA of 2.5; official transcripts; goal statement (for some programs); access to computer and Internet; for doctorate, master's degree or higher; RN; three years of related professional or academic experience; goal statement; access to computer and Internet; for Post-Master's Certificate, relevant work experience; access to computer and Internet. Additional exam requirements/recommendations for international students: required—TOEFL (minimum score 550 paper-based, 79 iBT), IELTS (minimum score 6.5), Michigan English Language Assessment Battery (minimum score 82), or PTE (minimum score 53). Electronic applications accepted.

**Walsh University,** Master of Science in Nursing, North Canton, OH 44720-3396. Offers academic nurse educator (MSN); adult acute care nurse practitioner (MSN); clinical nurse leader (MSN); nursing practice (DNP). *Accreditation:* AACN. *Program availability:* Part-time, 100% online, blended/hybrid learning. *Faculty:* 5 full-time (4 women), 11 part-time/adjunct (10 women). *Students:* 80 full-time (68 women), 83 part-time (73 women); includes 12 minority (5 Black or African American, non-Hispanic/Latino; 1 Asian, non-Hispanic/Latino; 6 Two or more races, non-Hispanic/Latino). Average age 35. 76 applicants, 93% accepted, 55 enrolled. In 2019, 38 master's, 2 doctorates awarded. *Degree requirements:* For doctorate, scholarly project; residency practicum. *Entrance requirements:* For master's, Registered Nurse license(s), 1 year of experience as a Registered Nurse; Official transcripts documenting a baccalaureate degree in nursing from an accredited program, Minimum 3.0 cumulative GPA, completion of a statistics course, 2 letters of recommendation, resume or CV, personal statement. Additional exam requirements/recommendations for international students: required—TOEFL. *Application deadline:* Applications are processed on a rolling basis. Electronic applications accepted. *Expenses:* $725 per credit hour, $50 technology fee. *Financial support:* In 2019–20, 1 student received support. Research assistantships available. Financial award application deadline: 12/31; financial award applicants required to submit FAFSA. *Unit head:* Dr. Judy Kreye, Dean, Byers School of Nursing, 330-2444757, Fax: 330-4907206, E-mail: jkreye@walsh.edu. *Application contact:* Dr. Janet Finneran, Director of Graduate Nursing Programs, 330-2444759, Fax: 330-4907206, E-mail: jfinneran@walsh.edu.
Website: http://www.walsh.edu/master-of-science-in-nursing

**Washington Adventist University,** Program in Nursing - Education, Takoma Park, MD 20912. Offers MS. *Program availability:* Part-time. *Entrance requirements:* Additional exam requirements/recommendations for international students: required—TOEFL (minimum score 550 paper-based), IELTS (minimum score 5).

**Waynesburg University,** Graduate and Professional Studies, Canonsburg, PA 15370. Offers business (MBA), including energy management, finance, health systems, human resources, leadership, market development; counseling (MA), including addictions counseling, clinical mental health; counselor education and supervision (PhD); criminal investigation (MA); education (M Ed), including autism, curriculum and instruction, educational leadership, online teaching; nursing (MSN), including administration, education, informatics; nursing practice (DNP); special education (M Ed); technology (M Ed); MSN/MBA. *Accreditation:* AACN. *Program availability:* Part-time, evening/weekend. *Degree requirements:* For doctorate, thesis/dissertation. *Entrance requirements:* Additional exam requirements/recommendations for international students: required—TOEFL. Electronic applications accepted.

**Weber State University,** Dumke College of Health Professions, School of Nursing, Ogden, UT 84408-1001. Offers educator (MSN); executive (MSN); nurse practitioner (MSN). *Program availability:* Part-time, evening/weekend, online only, 100% online. *Faculty:* 14 full-time (13 women), 2 part-time/adjunct (both women). *Students:* 85 full-time (73 women), 18 part-time (16 women); includes 6 minority (1 Asian, non-Hispanic/Latino; 4 Hispanic/Latino; 1 Two or more races, non-Hispanic/Latino). Average age 38. In 2019, 52 master's awarded. *Entrance requirements:* For master's, bachelor's degree in nursing from ACEN- or CCNE-accredited program. *Application deadline:* For fall admission, 4/1 priority date for domestic students. Application fee: $60 ($90 for international students). Electronic applications accepted. *Expenses: Tuition, area resident:* Full-time $7197; part-time $4981 per credit. Tuition, state resident: full-time $7197; part-time $4981 per credit. Tuition, nonresident: full-time $16,560; part-time $11,589 per credit. *Required fees:* $643 per semester. One-time fee: $60. Tuition and fees vary according to course load and program. *Financial support:* In 2019–20, 16 students received support. Scholarships/grants available. Financial award application deadline: 4/1; financial award applicants required to submit FAFSA. *Unit head:* Dr. Deborah Juff, MSN & DNP Program Director, 801-626-7833, Fax: 801-626-6397, E-mail: djudd@weber.edu. *Application contact:* Robert Holt, Director of Enrollment, 801-626-7774, Fax: 801-626-6397, E-mail: rholt@weber.edu.
Website: http://www.weber.edu/nursing

**Webster University,** College of Arts and Sciences, Department of Nursing, St. Louis, MO 63119-3194. Offers nurse educator (MSN). *Accreditation:* ACEN. *Degree requirements:* For master's, comprehensive exam. *Entrance requirements:* For master's, 1 year of clinical experience, BSN, interview, minimum C+ average in statistics and physical assessment, minimum GPA of 3.0, RN license. Additional exam requirements/recommendations for international students: required—TOEFL.

**Western Connecticut State University,** Division of Graduate Studies, School of Professional Studies, Nursing Department, Ed D in Nursing Education Program, Danbury, CT 06810-6885. Offers Ed D. *Program availability:* Online learning. *Entrance requirements:* For doctorate, GRE or MAT, official transcripts, current copy of RN license, three letters of reference, curriculum vitae or resume, personal statement.

**Western Governors University,** College of Health Professions, Salt Lake City, UT 84107. Offers healthcare management (MBA); leadership and management (MSN); nursing education (MSN); nursing informatics (MSN). *Program availability:* Evening/weekend, online learning. *Degree requirements:* For master's, capstone project. *Entrance requirements:* For master's, transcripts. Additional exam requirements/recommendations for international students: required—TOEFL (minimum score 450 paper-based; 80 iBT). Electronic applications accepted. Application fee is waived when completed online.

**Wilson College,** Graduate Programs, Chambersburg, PA 17201-1285. Offers accounting (M Acc); choreography and visual art (MFA); education (M Ed); educational technology (MET); healthcare administration (MHA); humanities (MA), including art and culture, critical/cultural theory, English language and literature, women's studies; management (MSM); nursing (MSN), including nursing education, nursing leadership and management; special education (MSE). *Program availability:* Evening/weekend. *Degree requirements:* For master's, project. *Entrance requirements:* For master's, PRAXIS, minimum undergraduate cumulative GPA of 3.0, 2 letters of recommendation, current certification for eligibility to teach in grades K-12, resume, personal interview. Electronic applications accepted.

**Winona State University,** College of Nursing and Health Sciences, Winona, MN 55987. Offers adult-gerontology acute care nurse practitioner (MS, DNP, Post Master's Certificate); adult-gerontology clinical nurse specialist (MS, DNP, Post Master's

Certificate); adult-gerontology primary care nurse practitioner (MS, DNP, Post Master's Certificate); family nurse practitioner (MS, DNP, Post Master's Certificate); nurse educator (MS); nursing and organizational leadership (MS, DNP, Post Master's Certificate); practice and leadership innovations (DNP, Post Master's Certificate). *Accreditation:* AACN. *Program availability:* Part-time, online learning. *Degree requirements:* For master's, thesis; for doctorate, capstone. *Entrance requirements:* For master's, GRE (if GPA less than 3.0). Additional exam requirements/recommendations for international students: required—TOEFL (minimum score 550 paper-based).

**Winston-Salem State University,** Program in Nursing, Winston-Salem, NC 27110-0003. Offers advanced nurse educator (MSN); family nurse practitioner (MSN); nursing (DNP). *Accreditation:* AACN. *Program availability:* Part-time, evening/weekend, online learning. *Entrance requirements:* For master's, GRE, MAT, resume, NC or state compact license, 3 letters of recommendation. Electronic applications accepted.

**Worcester State University,** Graduate School, Department of Nursing, Program in Nurse Educator, Worcester, MA 01602-2597. Offers MSN. *Accreditation:* AACN. *Program availability:* Part-time. *Faculty:* 4 full-time (all women), 4 part-time/adjunct (3 women). *Students:* 33 part-time (32 women); includes 7 minority (5 Black or African American, non-Hispanic/Latino; 1 Hispanic/Latino; 1 Two or more races, non-Hispanic/Latino), 1 international. Average age 44. 4 applicants, 100% accepted, 3 enrolled. In 2019, 11 master's awarded. *Degree requirements:* For master's, comprehensive exam (for some programs), thesis (for some programs), practicum. For a detail list in Degree Completion requirements please see the graduate catalog at catalog.worcester.edu. *Entrance requirements:* For master's, Unencumbered license to practice as a Registered Nurse in Massachusetts. For a detail list of entrance requirements please see the graduate catalog at catalog.worcester.edu. Additional exam requirements/recommendations for international students: required—TOEFL (minimum score 550 paper-based; 79 iBT), IELTS (minimum score 6). *Application deadline:* For fall admission, 3/1 for domestic and international students; for spring admission, 11/1 for domestic and international students; for summer admission, 3/1 for domestic and international students. Applications are processed on a rolling basis. Application fee: $50. Electronic applications accepted. *Expenses: Tuition, area resident:* Full-time $3042; part-time $169 per credit hour. Tuition, state resident: full-time $3042; part-time $169 per credit hour. Tuition, nonresident: full-time $3042; part-time $169 per credit hour. *International tuition:* $3042 full-time. *Required fees:* $2754; $153 per credit hour. *Financial support:* Career-related internships or fieldwork, scholarships/grants, and unspecified assistantships available. Financial award application deadline: 3/1; financial award applicants required to submit FAFSA. *Unit head:* Dr. Melissa Duprey, Program Coordinator, 508-929-8419, E-mail: mduprey1@worcester.edu. *Application contact:* Sara Grady, Associate Dean of Graduate Studies and Professional Development, 508-929-8130, Fax: 508-929-8100, E-mail: sara.grady@worcester.edu.

# Nursing Informatics

**Allen College,** Graduate Programs, Waterloo, IA 50703. Offers adult-gerontology acute care nurse practitioner (MSN); community/public health nursing (MSN); education (MSN); family nurse practitioner (MSN); health sciences (Ed D); leadership in health care delivery (MSN); leadership in health care informatics (MSN); nursing (DNP); occupational therapy (MS); psychiatric mental health nurse practitioner (MSN). *Accreditation:* AACN; ACEN. *Faculty:* 27 full-time (23 women), 9 part-time/adjunct (8 women). *Students:* 193 full-time (175 women), 95 part-time (84 women); includes 22 minority (6 Black or African American, non-Hispanic/Latino; 1 American Indian or Alaska Native, non-Hispanic/Latino; 4 Asian, non-Hispanic/Latino; 5 Hispanic/Latino; 6 Two or more races, non-Hispanic/Latino). Average age 32. 376 applicants, 53% accepted, 122 enrolled. *Application deadline:* For fall admission, 2/1 priority date for domestic students; for spring admission, 9/1 priority date for domestic students. Applications are processed on a rolling basis. Application fee: $50. Electronic applications accepted. *Financial support:* In 2019–20, 78 students received support. Federal Work-Study, institutionally sponsored loans, and scholarships/grants available. Support available to part-time students. Financial award application deadline: 8/1; financial award applicants required to submit FAFSA. *Unit head:* Dr. Bob Loch, Provost, 319-226-2040, Fax: 319-226-2070, E-mail: bob.loch@allencollege.edu. *Application contact:* Molly Quinn, Director of Admissions, 319-226-2001, Fax: 319-226-2010, E-mail: molly.quinn@allencollege.edu.
Website: http://www.allencollege.edu/

**Aspen University,** Program in Nursing, Denver, CO 80246-1930. Offers forensic nursing (MSN); informatics (MSN); nursing (MSN); nursing administration and management (MSN); nursing education (MSN); public health (MSN). *Program availability:* Part-time, evening/weekend, online only, 100% online. *Degree requirements:* For master's, comprehensive exam. *Entrance requirements:* For master's, www.aspen.edu, www.aspen.edu. Electronic applications accepted.

**Austin Peay State University,** College of Graduate Studies, College of Behavioral and Health Sciences, School of Nursing, Clarksville, TN 37044. Offers family nurse practitioner (MSN); nursing administration (MSN); nursing education (MSN); nursing informatics (MSN). *Program availability:* Part-time, online learning. *Faculty:* 5 full-time (all women), 1 (woman) part-time/adjunct. *Students:* 12 full-time (11 women), 120 part-time (114 women); includes 25 minority (14 Black or African American, non-Hispanic/Latino; 3 Asian, non-Hispanic/Latino; 4 Hispanic/Latino; 4 Two or more races, non-Hispanic/Latino). Average age 34. 19 applicants, 84% accepted, 2 enrolled. In 2019, 51 master's awarded. *Degree requirements:* For master's, comprehensive exam. *Entrance requirements:* For master's, minimum GPA of 3.0, RN license eligibility, 3 letters of recommendation. Additional exam requirements/recommendations for international students: required—TOEFL (minimum score 500 paper-based). *Application deadline:* For fall admission, 8/5 priority date for domestic students. Applications are processed on a rolling basis. Application fee: $45 ($55 for international students). Electronic applications accepted. *Financial support:* Research assistantships with full tuition reimbursements, career-related internships or fieldwork, Federal Work-Study, institutionally sponsored loans, scholarships/grants, and unspecified assistantships available. Support available to part-time students. Financial award application deadline: 7/1; financial award applicants required to submit FAFSA. *Unit head:* Dr. Mary Rice, Interim Director of Nursing, 931-221-7483, Fax: 931-221-7595, E-mail: ricem@apsu.edu. *Application contact:* Megan Mitchell, Coordinator of Graduate Admissions, 931-221-6189, Fax: 931-221-7641, E-mail: mitchellm@apsu.edu.
Website: http://www.apsu.edu/nursing

**Columbus State University,** Graduate Studies, College of Education and Health Professions, School of Nursing, Columbus, GA 31907-5645. Offers family nurse practitioner (MSN); nursing (MSN), including nurse educator, nurse informatics, nurse leader. *Program availability:* Part-time, online only, 100% online. *Entrance requirements:* For master's, GRE, BSN, minimum undergraduate GPA of 3.0. Additional exam requirements/recommendations for international students: required—TOEFL (minimum score 550 paper-based; 79 iBT). Electronic applications accepted. *Expenses:* Contact institution.

**Duke University,** School of Nursing, Durham, NC 27708. Offers acute care pediatric nurse practitioner (MSN, Post-Graduate Certificate); adult-gerontology nurse practitioner (MSN, Post-Graduate Certificate), including acute care, primary care; family nurse practitioner (MSN, Post-Graduate Certificate); neonatal nurse practitioner (MSN, Post-Graduate Certificate); nurse anesthesia (DNP); nurse practitioner (DNP); nursing (PhD); nursing and health care leadership (MSN, Post-Graduate Certificate); nursing education (MSN, Post-Graduate Certificate); nursing informatics (MSN, Post-Graduate Certificate); pediatric nurse practitioner (MSN, Post-Graduate Certificate), including primary care; psychiatric mental health nurse practitioner (MSN, Post-Graduate Certificate); women's health nurse practitioner (MSN, Post-Graduate Certificate). *Accreditation:* AACN; AANA/CANAEP. *Program availability:* Part-time, evening/weekend, online with on-campus intensives. *Faculty:* 48 full-time (40 women), 32 part-time/adjunct (28 women). *Students:* 666 full-time (601 women), 157 part-time (139 women); includes 193 minority (61 Black or African American, non-Hispanic/Latino; 4 American Indian or Alaska Native, non-Hispanic/Latino; 57 Asian, non-Hispanic/Latino; 49 Hispanic/Latino; 1 Native Hawaiian or other Pacific Islander, non-Hispanic/Latino; 21 Two or more races, non-Hispanic/Latino), 8 international. Average age 34. 761 applicants, 33% accepted, 149 enrolled. In 2019, 213 master's, 74 doctorates, 18 other advanced degrees awarded. Terminal master's awarded for partial completion of doctoral program. *Degree requirements:* For master's, thesis optional; for doctorate, capstone project. *Entrance requirements:* For master's, MSN applicants are no longer required to take the GRE, 1 year of nursing experience (recommended), BSN, minimum GPA of 3.0, previous course work in statistics; for doctorate, GRE is required for the DNP in Nurse Anesthesia, BSN or MSN, minimum GPA of 3.0, resume, personal statement, graduate statistics and research methods course, current licensure as a registered nurse, transcripts from all post-secondary institutions; for Post-Graduate Certificate, MSN, licensure or eligibility as a professional nurse, transcripts from all post-secondary institutions, previous course work in statistics. Additional exam requirements/recommendations for international students: required—TOEFL (minimum score 100 iBT), IELTS (minimum score 7). *Application deadline:* For fall admission, 12/1 for domestic and international students; for spring admission, 5/1 for domestic and international students. Application fee: $50. Electronic applications accepted. *Expenses:* Contact institution. *Financial support:* Institutionally sponsored loans, scholarships/grants, and traineeships available. Support available to part-time students. Financial award applicants required to submit FAFSA. *Unit head:* Dr. Marion E. Broome, Dean/Vice Chancellor for Nursing Affairs/Associate Vice President for Academic Affairs for Nursing, 919-684-9446, Fax: 919-684-9414, E-mail: marion.broome@duke.edu. *Application contact:* Dr. Ernie Rushing, Director of Admissions and Recruitment, 919-668-6274, Fax: 919-668-4693, E-mail: ernie.rushing@dm.duke.edu.
Website: http://www.nursing.duke.edu/

**Ferris State University,** College of Health Professions, School of Nursing, Big Rapids, MI 49307. Offers nursing (MSN); nursing administration (MSN); nursing education (MSN); nursing informatics (MSN). *Accreditation:* ACEN. *Program availability:* Part-time, evening/weekend, online only, 100% online. *Faculty:* 7 full-time (all women), 1 (woman) part-time/adjunct. *Students:* 103 part-time (95 women); includes 14 minority (2 Black or African American, non-Hispanic/Latino; 6 American Indian or Alaska Native, non-Hispanic/Latino; 4 Hispanic/Latino; 2 Two or more races, non-Hispanic/Latino). Average age 38. 31 applicants, 97% accepted, 24 enrolled. In 2019, 24 master's awarded. *Degree requirements:* For master's, practicum, practicum project. *Entrance requirements:* For master's, BS in nursing (for nursing education track); BS in nursing or related field (for nursing administration and nursing informatics tracks); registered nurse license, writing sample, letters of reference, 2 years' clinical experience (recommended). Additional exam requirements/recommendations for international students: required—TOEFL (minimum score 550 paper-based; 79 iBT). *Application deadline:* For fall admission, 4/15 priority date for domestic and international students; for spring admission, 10/15 for domestic and international students. Electronic applications accepted. Tuition and fees vary according to degree level, program and student level. *Financial support:* In 2019–20, 7 students received support. Career-related internships or fieldwork and scholarships/grants available. Financial award application deadline: 4/15; financial award applicants required to submit FAFSA. *Unit head:* Dr. Wendy Lenon, Chair, School of Nursing, 231-591-2267, Fax: 231-591-2325, E-mail: WendyLenon@ferris.edu. *Application contact:* Dr. Sharon Colley, MSN Program Coordinator, 231-591-2288, Fax: 231-591-2325, E-mail: colleys@ferris.edu.
Website: http://www.ferris.edu/htmls/colleges/alliedhe/Nursing/homepage.htm

**Georgia Southwestern State University,** College of Nursing and Health Sciences, Americus, GA 31709-4693. Offers family nurse practitioner (MSN); health informatics (Postbaccalaureate Certificate); nurse educator (Post Master's Certificate); nursing educator (MSN); nursing informatics (MSN); nursing leadership (MSN). *Program availability:* Part-time, online only, all theory courses are offered online. *Faculty:* 9 full-time (all women), 5 part-time/adjunct (all women). *Students:* 18 full-time (14 women), 104 part-time (91 women); includes 45 minority (31 Black or African American, non-Hispanic/Latino; 1 American Indian or Alaska Native, non-Hispanic/Latino; 4 Asian, non-Hispanic/Latino; 3 Hispanic/Latino; 6 Two or more races, non-Hispanic/Latino). Average age 36. 96 applicants, 45% accepted, 24 enrolled. In 2019, 53 master's awarded. *Degree requirements:* For master's, thesis (for some programs), minimum cumulative GPA of 3.0; maximum of 6 credit hours with C grade and no D grades; degree completed within 7 calendar years from initial enrollment date in graduate courses; for other advanced degree, minimum cumulative GPA of 3.0; maximum of 6 credit hours with C grade and no D grades; degree completed within 7 calendar years from initial enrollment date in graduate courses. *Entrance requirements:* For master's, baccalaureate degree in nursing from regionally-accredited institution and nationally-accredited nursing program with minimum GPA of 3.0; three completed recommendation forms from professional peer or clinical supervisor; current unencumbered RN license in state where clinical course requirements will be met; proof of immunizations; for other advanced degree, Baccalaureate or masters degree (depending upon certificate) in nursing; Minimum GPA of 3.0; 3 completed recommendation forms; current unencumbered RN license in state where clinical course requirements will be met. Application fee: $25. Electronic applications accepted. *Expenses:* $385.00 per credit hour tuition, plus fees, which vary according to enrolled

credit hours. *Financial support:* Application deadline: 6/1; applicants required to submit FAFSA. *Unit head:* Dr. Sandra Daniel, Dean, 229-931-2275. *Application contact:* Office of Graduate Admissions, 800-338-0082, Fax: 229-931-2983, E-mail: graduateadmissions@gsw.edu.
Website: https://www.gsw.edu/academics/schools-and-departments/college-of-nursing-and-health-sciences/school-of-nursing/nursing-programs/graduate

**Georgia State University,** Byrdine F. Lewis School of Nursing, Atlanta, GA 30303. Offers adult health clinical nurse specialist/nurse practitioner (MS, Certificate); child health clinical nurse specialist/pediatric nurse practitioner (MS, Certificate); family nurse practitioner (MS, Certificate); family psychiatric mental health nurse practitioner (MS, Certificate); nursing (PhD); nursing leadership in healthcare innovations (MS), including nursing administration, nursing informatics; nutrition (MS); occupational therapy (MOT); perinatal clinical nurse specialist/women's health nurse practitioner (MS, Certificate); physical therapy (DPT); respiratory therapy (MS). *Accreditation:* AACN. *Program availability:* Part-time, blended/hybrid learning. *Faculty:* 57 full-time (40 women), 5 part-time/adjunct (4 women). *Students:* 388 full-time (290 women), 155 part-time (135 women); includes 217 minority (130 Black or African American, non-Hispanic/Latino; 47 Asian, non-Hispanic/Latino; 26 Hispanic/Latino; 14 Two or more races, non-Hispanic/Latino), 45 international. Average age 32. 480 applicants, 50% accepted, 164 enrolled. In 2019, 158 master's, 64 doctorates, 20 other advanced degrees awarded. *Degree requirements:* For doctorate, comprehensive exam, thesis/dissertation. *Entrance requirements:* For doctorate, GRE. Additional exam requirements/recommendations for international students: required—TOEFL. *Application deadline:* For fall admission, 2/1 priority date for domestic and international students; for spring admission, 9/15 for domestic and international students. Applications are processed on a rolling basis. Application fee: $50. Electronic applications accepted. *Expenses:* Contact institution. *Financial support:* In 2019–20, research assistantships with tuition reimbursements (averaging $1,666 per year), teaching assistantships with tuition reimbursements (averaging $1,920 per year) were awarded; scholarships/grants, tuition waivers (full and partial), and unspecified assistantships also available. Support available to part-time students. Financial award application deadline: 8/1; financial award applicants required to submit FAFSA. *Unit head:* Huanbiao Mo, Dean of Nursing. *Application contact:* Huanbiao Mo, Dean of Nursing.
Website: http://nursing.gsu.edu/

**Grantham University,** College of Nursing and Allied Health, Lenexa, KS 66219. Offers case management (MSN); health systems management (MS); healthcare administration (MHA); nursing education (MSN); nursing informatics (MSN); nursing management and organizational leadership (MSN). *Program availability:* Part-time, evening/weekend, online only, 100% online. *Students:* 180 full-time (135 women), 61 part-time (47 women); includes 124 minority (71 Black or African American, non-Hispanic/Latino; 1 American Indian or Alaska Native, non-Hispanic/Latino; 17 Asian, non-Hispanic/Latino; 17 Hispanic/Latino; 1 Native Hawaiian or other Pacific Islander, non-Hispanic/Latino; 17 Two or more races, non-Hispanic/Latino). Average age 40. 53 applicants, 89% accepted, 37 enrolled. In 2019, 100 master's awarded. *Entrance requirements:* For master's, Graduate: A minimum score of 530 on the paper-based TOEFL, or 71 on the internet-based TOEFL, 6.5 on the IELTS, or 50 on the PTE Academic Score Report. Additional exam requirements/recommendations for international students: required—TOEFL (minimum score 530 paper-based; 71 iBT), IELTS (minimum score 6.5), PTE (minimum score 50). *Application deadline:* Applications are processed on a rolling basis. Electronic applications accepted. *Expenses:* Contact institution. *Financial support:* Scholarships/grants available. Financial award applicants required to submit FAFSA. *Unit head:* Dr. Cheryl Rules, Dean of the College of Nursing and the School of Allied Health changing to College of Health Professions, 913-309-4783, Fax: 844-897-6490, E-mail: crules@grantham.edu. *Application contact:* Adam Wright, Associate VP, Enrollment Services, 800-955-2527 Ext. 803, Fax: 877-304-4467, E-mail: admissions@grantham.edu.
Website: http://www.grantham.edu/nursing-and-allied-health/

**Holy Names University,** Graduate Division, Department of Nursing, Oakland, CA 94619-1699. Offers administration/management (MSN, PMC); care transition management (MSN); family nurse practitioner (MSN, PMC); informatics (MSN); nurse educator (PMC); MSN/MBA. *Accreditation:* AACN. *Program availability:* Part-time, evening/weekend. *Entrance requirements:* For master's, bachelor's degree in nursing or related field; California RN license or eligibility; minimum cumulative GPA of 2.8, 3.0 in nursing courses from baccalaureate program; courses in pathophysiology, statistics, and research at the undergraduate level. Additional exam requirements/recommendations for international students: required—TOEFL (minimum score 550 paper-based; 79 iBT). Electronic applications accepted. Application fee is waived when completed online.

**Jacksonville University,** Brooks Rehabilitation College of Healthcare Sciences, Keigwin School of Nursing, Master of Science in Nursing Program, Jacksonville, FL 32211. Offers clinical nurse educator (MSN); family nurse practitioner (MSN); family nurse practitioner/emergency nurse practitioner (MSN); leadership in the healthcare system (MSN); nursing informatics (MSN); psychiatric nurse practitioner (MSN); MSN/MBA. *Program availability:* Part-time, 100% online, blended/hybrid learning. In 2019, 215 master's awarded. *Degree requirements:* For master's, thesis. *Entrance requirements:* For master's, GRE General Test or undergraduate GPA above 3.0, BSN from ACEN- or CCNE-accredited program; course work in statistics and physical assessment within last 5 years; Florida nursing license; CPR/BLS certification; 3 recommendations, 2 of which are professional references; statement of intent; resume. Additional exam requirements/recommendations for international students: required—TOEFL (minimum score 650 paper-based; 114 iBT), IELTS (minimum score 8). *Application deadline:* Applications are processed on a rolling basis. Application fee: $50. Electronic applications accepted. *Expenses:* Contact institution. *Financial support:* Federal Work-Study, institutionally sponsored loans, scholarships/grants, and health care benefits available. Support available to part-time students. Financial award application deadline: 3/15; financial award applicants required to submit FAFSA. *Unit head:* Dr. Hilary Morgan, Director, Graduate Nursing Programs/Associate Professor, 904-256-7601, E-mail: hmorgan@ju.edu. *Application contact:* Kristen Kirkendall, Associate Director of Graduate Admissions and Communications, 904-256-7169, E-mail: kgreene8@ju.edu.
Website: https://www.ju.edu/nursing/graduate/master-science-nursing/index.php

**Le Moyne College,** Department of Nursing, Syracuse, NY 13214. Offers family nurse practitioner (MS, CAS); informatics (MS, CAS); nursing administration (MS, CAS); nursing education (MS, CAS). *Accreditation:* AACN. *Program availability:* Part-time, evening/weekend. *Faculty:* 4 full-time (all women), 6 part-time/adjunct (4 women). *Students:* 18 full-time (17 women), 57 part-time (52 women); includes 7 minority (1 Black or African American, non-Hispanic/Latino; 1 Asian, non-Hispanic/Latino; 4 Hispanic/Latino; 1 Two or more races, non-Hispanic/Latino). Average age 31. 43 applicants, 84% accepted, 32 enrolled. In 2019, 33 master's, 3 other advanced degrees awarded. *Degree requirements:* For master's, 39-45 credit hours, varies by program, practicum, scholarly project; for CAS, Varies by experience or incoming degree. *Entrance requirements:* For master's, earned bachelor's degree transcripts, New York RN license, 2-3 letters of recommendation, personal statement, interview. Additional exam requirements/recommendations for international students: required—TOEFL (minimum score 79 iBT); recommended—IELTS (minimum score 6.5). *Application deadline:* For fall admission, 4/1 priority date for domestic students, 4/1 for international students; for spring admission, 11/1 priority date for domestic students, 11/1 for international students; for summer admission, 5/1 priority date for domestic students, 5/1 for international students. Applications are processed on a rolling basis. Electronic applications accepted. *Expenses:* $764-$951 per credit hour depending upon program, $75 fee per semester. *Financial support:* In 2019–20, 1 student received support. Career-related internships or fieldwork, Federal Work-Study, scholarships/grants, health care benefits, and unspecified assistantships available. Support available to part-time students. Financial award applicants required to submit FAFSA. *Unit head:* Catherine A. Brownell, Professor - Chair of Nursing, 315-445-5426, Fax: 315-445-6024, E-mail: nursing@lemoyne.edu. *Application contact:* Teresa M. Renn, Director of Graduate Admission, 315-445-5444, Fax: 315-445-6092, E-mail: GradAdmission@lemoyne.edu.
Website: http://www.lemoyne.edu/nursing

**Liberty University,** School of Nursing, Lynchburg, VA 24515. Offers family nurse practitioner (DNP); nurse educator (MSN); nursing administration (MSN); nursing informatics (MSN). *Accreditation:* AACN. *Program availability:* Part-time, online learning. *Students:* 279 full-time (257 women), 505 part-time (449 women); includes 170 minority (118 Black or African American, non-Hispanic/Latino; 2 American Indian or Alaska Native, non-Hispanic/Latino; 19 Asian, non-Hispanic/Latino; 25 Hispanic/Latino; 6 Two or more races, non-Hispanic/Latino), 11 international. Average age 39. 1,154 applicants, 27% accepted, 171 enrolled. In 2019, 138 master's, 26 doctorates awarded. *Entrance requirements:* For master's, minimum cumulative undergraduate GPA of 3.0; for doctorate, minimum GPA of 3.25 in most current nursing program completed. Additional exam requirements/recommendations for international students: recommended—TOEFL. *Application deadline:* Applications are processed on a rolling basis. Application fee: $50. Electronic applications accepted. *Expenses: Tuition:* Full-time $545; part-time $410 per credit hour. One-time fee: $50. *Financial support:* In 2019–20, 128 students received support. Federal Work-Study available. Financial award applicants required to submit FAFSA. *Unit head:* Dr. Shanna Akers, Dean, 434-592-3618, E-mail: lusondean@liberty.edu. *Application contact:* Jay Bridge, Director of Admissions, 800-424-9595, Fax: 800-628-7977, E-mail: gradadmissions@liberty.edu.
Website: https://www.liberty.edu/nursing/

**National American University,** Roueche Graduate Center, Austin, TX 78731. Offers accounting (MBA); aviation management (MBA, MM); care coordination (MSN); community college leadership (Ed D); criminal justice (MM); e-marketing (MBA, MM); health care administration (MBA, MM); higher education (MM); human resources management (MBA, MM); information technology management (MBA, MM); international business (MBA); leadership (EMBA); management (MBA); nursing administration (MSN); nursing education (MSN); nursing informatics (MSN); operations and configuration management (MBA, MM); project and process management (MBA, MM). *Program availability:* Part-time, evening/weekend, online learning. *Entrance requirements:* For master's, minimum undergraduate GPA of 2.75. Additional exam requirements/recommendations for international students: required—TOEFL, TWE. Electronic applications accepted.

**National University,** School of Health and Human Services, La Jolla, CA 92037-1011. Offers clinical affairs (MS); clinical regulatory affairs (MS); complementary and integrative healthcare (MS); family nurse practitioner (MSN); health and life science analytics (MS); health informatics (MS, Certificate); healthcare administration (MHA); nurse anesthesia (MSNA); nursing administration (MSN); nursing informatics (MSN); psychiatric-mental health nurse practitioner (MSN); public health (MPH), including health promotion, healthcare administration, mental health. *Accreditation:* CEPH. *Program availability:* Part-time, evening/weekend, 100% online, blended/hybrid learning. *Degree requirements:* For master's, thesis (for some programs). *Entrance requirements:* For master's, interview, minimum GPA of 2.5. Additional exam requirements/recommendations for international students: required—TOEFL (minimum score 550 paper-based; 79 iBT), IELTS (minimum score 6). Electronic applications accepted. *Expenses: Tuition:* Full-time $442; part-time $442 per unit.

**New York University,** Rory Meyers College of Nursing, Programs in Advanced Practice Nursing, New York, NY 10012-1019. Offers adult-gerontology acute care nurse practitioner (MS, Advanced Certificate); adult-gerontology primary care nurse practitioner (MS, Advanced Certificate); family nurse practitioner (MS, Advanced Certificate); gerontology nurse practitioner (Advanced Certificate); nurse-midwifery (MS, Advanced Certificate); nursing administration (MS, Advanced Certificate); nursing education (MS, Advanced Certificate); nursing informatics (MS, Advanced Certificate); pediatrics nurse practitioner (MS, Advanced Certificate); psychiatric-mental health nurse practitioner (MS, Advanced Certificate); MS/MPH. *Accreditation:* AACN; ACNM/ACME. *Program availability:* Part-time, evening/weekend. *Degree requirements:* For master's, thesis (for some programs), capstone. *Entrance requirements:* For master's, BS in nursing, AS in nursing with another BS/BA, interview, RN license, 1 year of clinical experience (3 for the MS in nursing education program); for Advanced Certificate, master's degree in nursing. Additional exam requirements/recommendations for international students: required—TOEFL (minimum score 100 iBT), IELTS (minimum score 7). Electronic applications accepted. *Expenses:* Contact institution.

**Nova Southeastern University,** Ron and Kathy Assaf College of Nursing, Fort Lauderdale, FL 33314-7796. Offers advanced practice registered nurse (MSN), including adult-gerontology acute care nurse practitioner, family nurse practitioner, psychiatric mental health nurse practitioner; executive nurse leadership (MSN); nursing (PhD), including nursing education; nursing education (MSN); nursing informatics (MSN); nursing practice (DNP). *Accreditation:* AACN. *Program availability:* Part-time, evening/weekend, 100% online, blended/hybrid learning, annual one-week summer institute delivered face-to-face on main campus. *Faculty:* 32 full-time (29 women), 34 part-time/adjunct (31 women). *Students:* 4 full-time (3 women), 658 part-time (585 women); includes 427 minority (182 Black or African American, non-Hispanic/Latino; 35 Asian, non-Hispanic/Latino; 197 Hispanic/Latino; 13 Two or more races, non-Hispanic/Latino), 3 international. Average age 38. 157 applicants, 93% accepted, 146 enrolled. In 2019, 184 master's, 12 doctorates awarded. *Degree requirements:* For doctorate, comprehensive exam, thesis/dissertation. *Entrance requirements:* For master's, minimum GPA of 3.0, RN, BSN, BS or BA; for doctorate, minimum GPA of 3.5, MSN, RN. Additional exam requirements/recommendations for international students: recommended—TOEFL. *Application deadline:* For fall admission, 8/1 for domestic students, 3/1 for international students; for winter admission, 12/9 for domestic students, 11/1 for international students. Applications are processed on a rolling basis. Application fee: $50. Electronic applications accepted. *Expenses:* Contact institution. *Financial support:* Application deadline: 4/15; applicants required to submit FAFSA. *Unit head:* Dr. Marcella M. Rutherford, Dean, 954-262-1963, E-mail: rmarcell@nova.edu. *Application contact:* Dianna Murphey, Director of Operations, 954-262-1975, E-mail: dgardner1@nova.edu.
Website: http://www.nova.edu/nursing/

**Roberts Wesleyan College,** Department of Nursing, Rochester, NY 14624-1997. Offers nursing education (MSN); nursing informatics (MSN); nursing leadership and administration (MSN). *Accreditation:* AACN. *Program availability:* Evening/weekend,

online learning. *Degree requirements:* For master's, thesis. *Entrance requirements:* For master's, minimum GPA of 3.0; BS in nursing; interview; RN license; resume; course work in statistics. Additional exam requirements/recommendations for international students: required—TOEFL (minimum score 90 iBT), IELTS (minimum score 6.5). Electronic applications accepted.

**Rutgers University - Newark,** Rutgers School of Nursing, Program in Nursing Informatics - Newark, Newark, NJ 07102. Offers MSN. *Entrance requirements:* Additional exam requirements/recommendations for international students: required—TOEFL. Electronic applications accepted.

**Rutgers University - Newark,** Rutgers School of Nursing, Program in Nursing Informatics - Stratford, Newark, NJ 07102. Offers MSN. *Entrance requirements:* Additional exam requirements/recommendations for international students: required—TOEFL. Electronic applications accepted.

**Samford University,** Ida Moffett School of Nursing, Birmingham, AL 35229. Offers advanced practice (DNP), including emergency nurse practitioner, family nurse practitioner, transformation of care; family nurse practitioner (MSN, DNP), including emergency nurse practitioner specialty (MSN); nurse anesthesia (DNP); nursing administration (DNP); psychiatric mental health nurse practitioner (DNP). *Accreditation:* AACN; AANA/CANAEP. *Program availability:* Part-time, evening/weekend, blended/hybrid learning. *Faculty:* 16 full-time (all women), 3 part-time/adjunct (0 women). *Students:* 281 full-time (239 women), 39 part-time (38 women); includes 68 minority (39 Black or African American, non-Hispanic/Latino; 2 American Indian or Alaska Native, non-Hispanic/Latino; 10 Asian, non-Hispanic/Latino; 10 Hispanic/Latino; 1 Native Hawaiian or other Pacific Islander, non-Hispanic/Latino; 6 Two or more races, non-Hispanic/Latino). Average age 35. 59 applicants, 97% accepted, 29 enrolled. In 2019, 47 master's, 68 doctorates awarded. *Degree requirements:* For doctorate, DNP project with poster presentation. *Entrance requirements:* For doctorate, GRE is required for the Nurse Anesthesia Program. Additional exam requirements/recommendations for international students: required—TOEFL (minimum score 575 paper-based; 90 iBT), IELTS (minimum score 6.5). *Application deadline:* For fall admission, 4/1 for domestic and international students; for spring admission, 8/1 for domestic and international students; for summer admission, 1/1 for domestic and international students. Application fee: $50. Electronic applications accepted. *Expenses: Tuition:* Full-time $17,754; part-time $862 per credit hour. *Required fees:* $550; $550 per unit. Full-time tuition and fees vary according to course load, program and student level. *Financial support:* In 2019–20, 30 students received support. Application deadline: 2/15; applicants required to submit FAFSA. *Unit head:* Dr. Jane S. Martin, Interim Dean and Professor, Ida Moffett School of Nursing, 205-726-2760, E-mail: jsmartin@samford.edu. *Application contact:* Allyson Maddox, Director of Graduate Student Services, 205-726-2047, E-mail: amaddox@samford.edu.
Website: http://samford.edu/nursing

**Seattle Pacific University,** MS in Nursing Program, Seattle, WA 98119-1997. Offers administration (MSN); adult/gerontology nurse practitioner (MSN); clinical nurse specialist (MSN); family nurse practitioner (MSN, Certificate); informatics (MSN); nurse educator (MSN). *Accreditation:* AACN. *Program availability:* Part-time. *Students:* 42 full-time (38 women), 18 part-time (16 women); includes 28 minority (5 Black or African American, non-Hispanic/Latino; 18 Asian, non-Hispanic/Latino; 5 Hispanic/Latino), 2 international. Average age 33. 59 applicants, 41% accepted. In 2019, 10 master's awarded. *Degree requirements:* For master's, thesis. *Entrance requirements:* For master's, personal statement, transcripts, undergraduate nursing degree, proof of undergraduate statistics course with minimum GPA of 2.0, 2 recommendations. *Application deadline:* For fall admission, 1/15 priority date for domestic students; for spring admission, 1/15 for domestic students. Applications are processed on a rolling basis. Application fee: $50. Electronic applications accepted. *Expenses:* Contact institution. *Financial support:* Fellowships and scholarships/grants available. Financial award applicants required to submit FAFSA. *Unit head:* Dr. Antwinett Lee, Associate Dean, 206-281-2607, E-mail: leea30@spu.edu. *Application contact:* Dr. Antwinett Lee, Associate Dean, 206-281-2607, E-mail: leea30@spu.edu.
Website: http://spu.edu/academics/school-of-health-sciences/undergraduate-programs/nursing

**Thomas Edison State University,** W. Cary Edwards School of Nursing, Master of Science in Nursing Program, Trenton, NJ 08608. Offers nurse educator (MSN); nursing administration (MSN); nursing informatics (MSN). *Accreditation:* AACN; ACEN. *Program availability:* Part-time, online learning. *Degree requirements:* For master's, nursing education seminar, onground practicum, online practicum. *Entrance requirements:* For master's, BSN. Additional exam requirements/recommendations for international students: required—TOEFL (minimum score 550 paper-based; 79 iBT). Electronic applications accepted.

**Troy University,** Graduate School, College of Health and Human Services, Program in Nursing, Troy, AL 36082. Offers adult health (MSN); family nurse practitioner (DNP); maternal infant (MSN); nursing informatics specialist (MSN). *Accreditation:* ACEN. *Program availability:* Part-time, evening/weekend, online learning. *Faculty:* 14 full-time (all women). *Students:* 67 full-time (64 women), 160 part-time (139 women); includes 46 minority (37 Black or African American, non-Hispanic/Latino; 1 American Indian or Alaska Native, non-Hispanic/Latino; 1 Asian, non-Hispanic/Latino; 7 Hispanic/Latino). Average age 35. 64 applicants, 97% accepted, 59 enrolled. In 2019, 73 master's, 20 doctorates awarded. *Degree requirements:* For master's, comprehensive exam, minimum GPA of 3.0, candidacy; for doctorate, minimum GPA of 3.0, submission of approved comprehensive e-portfolio, completion of residency synthesis project, minimum of 1000 hours of clinical practice, qualifying exam. *Entrance requirements:* For master's, Score of 396 or higher on the Miller's Analogy Test (MAT) or score of 290 on Graduate Record Exam (850 on the old exam)(verbal plus quantitative); GRE or MAT required for every applicant, minimum GPA of 3.0, BSN, current RN licensure, 2 letters of reference, undergraduate health assessment course; for doctorate, GRE (minimum score of 850 on old exam or 294 on new exam), BSN or MSN, minimum GPA of 3.0, 2 letters of reference, current RN licensure, essay. Additional exam requirements/recommendations for international students: required—TOEFL (minimum score 523 paper-based; 70 iBT), IELTS (minimum score 6). *Application deadline:* For fall admission, 5/1 for domestic students; for spring admission, 10/1 for domestic students; for summer admission, 3/1 for domestic students. Applications are processed on a rolling basis. Application fee: $50. Electronic applications accepted. *Expenses: Tuition, area resident:* Full-time $7650; part-time $2550 per semester hour. Tuition, state resident: full-time $7650; part-time $2550 per semester hour. Tuition, nonresident: full-time $15,300; part-time $5100 per semester hour. *International tuition:* $15,300 full-time. *Required fees:* $856; $352 per semester hour. $176 per semester. *Financial support:* In 2019–20, 20 students received support. Fellowships, research assistantships, teaching assistantships, career-related internships or fieldwork, Federal Work-Study, scholarships/grants, traineeships, tuition waivers, and unspecified assistantships available. Support available to part-time students. Financial award application deadline: 3/1; financial award applicants required to submit FAFSA. *Unit head:* Dr. Wade Forehand, Professor, Director, School of Nursing, 334-670-3745, Fax: 334-670-3743, E-mail: jforehand@troy.edu. *Application contact:* Crystal G. Bishop, Director of Graduate Admissions, School of Nursing, 334-241-8631, E-mail: cdgodwin@troy.edu.

Website: https://www.troy.edu/academics/academic-programs/college-health-human-services-programs.php

**The University of Alabama at Birmingham,** School of Nursing, Birmingham, AL 35294. Offers clinical nurse leader (MSN); nurse anesthesia (DNP); nurse practitioner (MSN, DNP), including adult-gerontology acute care (MSN), adult-gerontology primary care (MSN), family (MSN), pediatric (MSN), psychiatric/mental health (MSN), women's health (MSN); nursing (MSN, DNP, PhD); nursing health systems administration (MSN); nursing informatics (MSN). *Accreditation:* AACN; AANA/CANAEP. *Program availability:* Part-time, online only, blended/hybrid learning. *Faculty:* 86 full-time (79 women), 42 part-time/adjunct (35 women). *Students:* 228 full-time (165 women), 1,393 part-time (1,234 women); includes 398 minority (267 Black or African American, non-Hispanic/Latino; 4 American Indian or Alaska Native, non-Hispanic/Latino; 52 Asian, non-Hispanic/Latino; 41 Hispanic/Latino; 34 Two or more races, non-Hispanic/Latino), 3 international. Average age 33. 1,027 applicants, 55% accepted, 421 enrolled. In 2019, 557 master's, 19 doctorates awarded. Terminal master's awarded for partial completion of doctoral program. *Degree requirements:* For master's, comprehensive exam; for doctorate, comprehensive exam, thesis/dissertation, research mentorship experience (for PhD); scholarly project (for DNP). *Entrance requirements:* For master's, GRE, GMAT, or MAT, minimum cumulative undergraduate GPA of 3.0 or on last 60 semesters hours; letters of recommendation; for doctorate, GRE General Test, computer literacy, course work in statistics, interview, minimum GPA of 3.0, MS in nursing, references, writing sample. Additional exam requirements/recommendations for international students: required—TOEFL (minimum score 500 paper-based, 80 iBT) or IELTS (5.5). *Application deadline:* For fall admission, 2/24 for domestic students; for summer admission, 10/15 for domestic students. Application fee: $50. Electronic applications accepted. *Expenses:* Contact institution. *Financial support:* In 2019–20, 23 fellowships (averaging $34,685 per year), 12 research assistantships (averaging $9,042 per year), 2 teaching assistantships (averaging $22,000 per year) were awarded; scholarships/grants, traineeships, health care benefits, and unspecified assistantships also available. Support available to part-time students. *Unit head:* Dr. Doreen C. Harper, Dean, 205-934-5360, Fax: 205-934-1894, E-mail: dcharper@uab.edu. *Application contact:* John Updegraff, Director of Student Affairs, 205-975-3370, Fax: 205-934-5490, E-mail: jupde22@uab.edu.
Website: http://www.uab.edu/nursing/home/

**University of Maryland, Baltimore,** University of Maryland School of Nursing, Baltimore, MD 21201. Offers adult-gerontology acute care nurse practitioner (DNP); adult-gerontology primary care nurse practitioner (DNP); clinical nurse leader (MS); community/public health nursing (MS); family nurse practitioner (DNP); global health (Postbaccalaureate Certificate); health services leadership and management (MS); neonatal nurse practitioner (DNP); nurse anesthesia (DNP); nursing (PhD); nursing informatics (MS, Postbaccalaureate Certificate); pediatric acute/primary care nurse practitioner (DNP); psychiatric mental health nurse practitioner (DNP); teaching in nursing and health professions (Postbaccalaureate Certificate); MS/MBA. *Accreditation:* AANA/CANAEP. *Program availability:* Part-time. *Faculty:* 130 full-time (117 women), 125 part-time/adjunct (114 women). *Students:* 539 full-time (463 women), 586 part-time (506 women); includes 485 minority (259 Black or African American, non-Hispanic/Latino; 3 American Indian or Alaska Native, non-Hispanic/Latino; 124 Asian, non-Hispanic/Latino; 66 Hispanic/Latino; 1 Native Hawaiian or other Pacific Islander, non-Hispanic/Latino; 32 Two or more races, non-Hispanic/Latino), 18 international. Average age 33. 964 applicants, 54% accepted, 347 enrolled. In 2019, 197 master's, 114 doctorates, 12 other advanced degrees awarded. *Degree requirements:* For master's and Postbaccalaureate Certificate, thesis (for some programs); for doctorate, comprehensive exam, thesis/dissertation. *Entrance requirements:* Additional exam requirements/recommendations for international students: required—TOEFL (minimum score 550 paper-based; 79 iBT); recommended—IELTS (minimum score 7). *Application deadline:* For fall admission, 11/1 priority date for domestic and international students; for spring admission, 12/15 for domestic and international students; for summer admission, 9/1 for domestic and international students. Applications are processed on a rolling basis. Application fee: $75. Electronic applications accepted. *Financial support:* In 2019–20, 257 students received support, including 31 research assistantships with full and partial tuition reimbursements available (averaging $25,000 per year), 21 teaching assistantships with full and partial tuition reimbursements available (averaging $19,000 per year); scholarships/grants, traineeships, and unspecified assistantships also available. Support available to part-time students. Financial award application deadline: 3/1; financial award applicants required to submit FAFSA. *Unit head:* Dr. Jane Kirschling, Dean, 410-706-4359, E-mail: kirschling@umaryland.edu. *Application contact:* Larry Fillian, Associate Dean of Student and Academic Services, 410-706-6298, E-mail: lfillian@umaryland.edu.
Website: http://www.nursing.umaryland.edu/

**University of Minnesota, Twin Cities Campus,** Graduate School, School of Nursing, Minneapolis, MN 55455-0213. Offers adult/gerontological clinical nurse specialist (DNP); adult/gerontological primary care nurse practitioner (DNP); family nurse practitioner (DNP); health innovation and leadership (DNP); integrative health and healing (DNP); nurse anesthesia (DNP); nurse midwifery (DNP); nursing (MN, PhD); nursing informatics (DNP); pediatric clinical nurse specialist (DNP); primary care certified pediatric nurse practitioner (DNP); psychiatric/mental health nurse practitioner (DNP); women's health nurse practitioner (DNP). *Accreditation:* AACN; AANA/CANAEP; ACNM/ACME (one or more programs are accredited). *Program availability:* Part-time, online learning. Terminal master's awarded for partial completion of doctoral program. *Degree requirements:* For master's, final oral exam, project or thesis; for doctorate, thesis/dissertation. *Entrance requirements:* For master's and doctorate, GRE General Test. Additional exam requirements/recommendations for international students: required—TOEFL (minimum score 586 paper-based). *Expenses:* Contact institution.

**The University of North Carolina at Chapel Hill,** School of Nursing, Chapel Hill, NC 27599-7460. Offers advanced practice registered nurse (DNP); nursing (MSN, PhD, PMC), including administration (MSN), adult gerontology primary care nurse practitioner (MSN), clinical nurse leader (MSN), education (MSN), health care systems (PMC), informatics (MSN, PMC), nursing leadership (PMC), outcomes management (MSN), primary care family nurse practitioner (MSN), primary care pediatric nurse practitioner (MSN), psychiatric/mental health nurse practitioner (MSN, PMC). *Accreditation:* AACN; ACEN (one or more programs are accredited). *Program availability:* Part-time. *Degree requirements:* For master's, comprehensive exam, thesis; for doctorate, thesis/dissertation, 3 exams; for PMC, thesis. *Entrance requirements:* Additional exam requirements/recommendations for international students: required—TOEFL (minimum score 575 paper-based; 89 iBT), IELTS (minimum score 8). Electronic applications accepted.

**University of Phoenix - Bay Area Campus,** College of Nursing, San Jose, CA 95134-1805. Offers education (MHA); gerontology (MHA); health administration (MHA, DHA); informatics (MHA, MSN); nursing (MSN, PhD); nursing/health care education (MSN); MSN/MBA. *Program availability:* Evening/weekend, online learning. *Degree requirements:* For master's, thesis (for some programs). *Entrance requirements:* For master's, minimum undergraduate GPA of 2.5, 3 years of work experience, RN license.

Additional exam requirements/recommendations for international students: required—TOEFL (minimum score 550 paper-based; 79 iBT). Electronic applications accepted.

**University of Phoenix - Phoenix Campus,** College of Health Sciences and Nursing, Tempe, AZ 85282-2371. Offers family nurse practitioner (MSN, Certificate); gerontology health care (Certificate); health care education (MSN, Certificate); health care informatics (Certificate); informatics (MSN); nursing (MSN); MSN/MHA. *Program availability:* Evening/weekend, online learning. *Entrance requirements:* Additional exam requirements/recommendations for international students: required—TOEFL, TOEIC (Test of English as an International Communication), Berlitz Online English Proficiency Exam, PTE, or IELTS. Electronic applications accepted. *Expenses:* Contact institution.

**University of St. Augustine for Health Sciences,** Graduate Programs, Master of Science in Nursing Program, San Marcos, CA 92069. Offers nurse educator (MSN); nurse executive (MSN); nurse informatics (MSN). *Program availability:* Part-time, online learning.

**Walden University,** Graduate Programs, School of Nursing, Minneapolis, MN 55401. Offers adult-gerontology acute care nurse practitioner (MSN); adult-gerontology nurse practitioner (MSN); education (MSN); family nurse practitioner (MSN); informatics (MSN); leadership and management (MSN); nursing (PhD, Post-Master's Certificate), including education (PhD), healthcare administration (PhD), interdisciplinary health (PhD), leadership (PhD), nursing education (Post-Master's Certificate), nursing informatics (Post-Master's Certificate), nursing leadership and management (Post-Master's Certificate), public health policy (PhD); nursing practice (DNP); psychiatric mental health (MSN). *Accreditation:* AACN. *Program availability:* Part-time, evening/weekend, online only, 100% online. *Degree requirements:* For doctorate, thesis/dissertation (for some programs), residency (for some programs), field experience (for some programs). *Entrance requirements:* For master's, bachelor's degree or equivalent in related field or RN; minimum GPA of 2.5; official transcripts; goal statement (for some programs); access to computer and Internet; for doctorate, master's degree or higher; RN; three years of related professional or academic experience; goal statement; access to computer and Internet; for Post-Master's Certificate, relevant work experience; access to computer and Internet. Additional exam requirements/recommendations for international students: required—TOEFL (minimum score 550 paper-based, 79 iBT), IELTS (minimum score 6.5), Michigan English Language Assessment Battery (minimum score 82), or PTE (minimum score 53). Electronic applications accepted.

**Waynesburg University,** Graduate and Professional Studies, Canonsburg, PA 15370. Offers business (MBA), including energy management, finance, health systems, human resources, leadership, market development; counseling (MA), including addictions counseling, clinical mental health; counselor education and supervision (PhD); criminal investigation (MA); education (M Ed), including autism, curriculum and instruction, educational leadership, online teaching; nursing (MSN), including administration, education, informatics; nursing practice (DNP); special education (M Ed); technology (M Ed); MSN/MBA. *Accreditation:* AACN. *Program availability:* Part-time, evening/weekend. *Degree requirements:* For doctorate, thesis/dissertation. *Entrance requirements:* Additional exam requirements/recommendations for international students: required—TOEFL. Electronic applications accepted.

**Western Governors University,** College of Health Professions, Salt Lake City, UT 84107. Offers healthcare management (MBA); leadership and management (MSN); nursing education (MSN); nursing informatics (MSN). *Program availability:* Evening/weekend, online learning. *Degree requirements:* For master's, capstone project. *Entrance requirements:* For master's, transcripts. Additional exam requirements/recommendations for international students: required—TOEFL (minimum score 450 paper-based; 80 iBT). Electronic applications accepted. Application fee is waived when completed online.

# Occupational Health Nursing

**Rutgers University - Newark,** Rutgers School of Nursing, Newark, NJ 07107-3001. Offers adult health (MSN); adult occupational health (MSN); advanced practice nursing (MSN, Post Master's Certificate); family nurse practitioner (MSN); nurse anesthesia (MSN); nursing (MSN); nursing informatics (MSN); urban health (PhD); women's health practitioner (MSN). *Accreditation:* AANA/CANAEP. *Program availability:* Part-time. *Entrance requirements:* For master's, GRE, RN license; basic life support, statistics, and health assessment experience. Additional exam requirements/recommendations for international students: required—TOEFL. Electronic applications accepted. *Expenses:* Contact institution.

**University of Cincinnati,** Graduate School, College of Nursing, Cincinnati, OH 45221-0038. Offers nurse midwifery (MSN); nurse practitioner (MSN, DNP), including acute care pediatrics (DNP), adult-gerontology acute care, adult-gerontology primary care, anesthesia (DNP), family (MSN), leadership (DNP), neonatal (MSN), women's health (MSN); nursing (MSN, PhD), including occupational health (MSN). *Accreditation:* AACN; AANA/CANAEP (one or more programs are accredited); ACNM/ACME. *Program availability:* Part-time, 100% online, blended/hybrid learning. *Faculty:* 62 full-time (55 women), 125 part-time/adjunct (114 women). *Students:* 429 full-time (355 women), 1,547 part-time (1,390 women); includes 453 minority (226 Black or African American, non-Hispanic/Latino; 5 American Indian or Alaska Native, non-Hispanic/Latino; 68 Asian, non-Hispanic/Latino; 103 Hispanic/Latino; 3 Native Hawaiian or other Pacific Islander, non-Hispanic/Latino; 48 Two or more races, non-Hispanic/Latino), 15 international. Average age 36. 779 applicants, 78% accepted, 464 enrolled. In 2019, 518 master's, 47 doctorates awarded. *Degree requirements:* For master's, thesis or alternative; for doctorate, comprehensive exam (for some programs), thesis/dissertation (for some programs). *Entrance requirements:* For master's, GRE required only for the Direct-Entry Accelerated Program. Additional exam requirements/recommendations for international students: required—TOEFL (minimum score 600 paper-based; 100 iBT); recommended—IELTS (minimum score 7). *Application deadline:* For fall admission, 4/1 priority date for domestic and international students; for spring admission, 9/1 priority date for domestic and international students; for summer admission, 2/1 priority date for domestic and international students. Applications are processed on a rolling basis. Application fee: $135 ($140 for international students). Electronic applications accepted. *Expenses:* Contact institution. *Financial support:* In 2019–20, 103 students received support, including 9 fellowships with full tuition reimbursements available (averaging $18,595 per year), 7 research assistantships with full tuition reimbursements available (averaging $12,991 per year), 8 teaching assistantships with full tuition reimbursements available (averaging $12,991 per year); institutionally sponsored loans, scholarships/grants, traineeships, health care benefits, tuition waivers (partial), and unspecified assistantships also available. Support available to part-time students. Financial award application deadline: 4/1; financial award applicants required to submit FAFSA. *Unit head:* Dr. Greer Glazer, Dean, 513-558-5330, Fax: 513-558-9030, E-mail: greer.glazer@uc.edu. *Application contact:* Office of Student Affairs, 513-558-8400, E-mail: nursingbearcats@uc.edu.
Website: https://nursing.uc.edu/

**University of Illinois at Chicago,** College of Nursing, Program in Nursing, Chicago, IL 60607-7128. Offers acute care clinical nurse specialist (MS); administrative nursing leadership (Certificate); adult nurse practitioner (MS); adult/geriatric nurse practitioner (MS); advanced community health nurse specialist (MS); family nurse practitioner (MS); geriatric clinical nurse specialist (MS); geriatric nurse practitioner (MS); nurse midwifery (MS); occupational health/advanced community health nurse specialist (MS); occupational health/family nurse practitioner (MS); pediatric nurse practitioner (MS); perinatal clinical nurse specialist (MS); school/advanced community health nurse specialist (MS); school/family nurse practitioner (MS); women's health nurse practitioner (MS). *Accreditation:* AACN. *Program availability:* Part-time. *Degree requirements:* For master's, thesis or alternative. *Entrance requirements:* For master's, GRE General Test, minimum GPA of 2.75. Additional exam requirements/recommendations for international students: required—TOEFL. Electronic applications accepted.

**University of Minnesota, Twin Cities Campus,** School of Public Health, Division of Environmental Health Sciences, Area in Occupational Health Nursing, Minneapolis, MN 55455-0213. Offers MPH, MS, PhD, MPH/MS. *Accreditation:* AACN. *Degree requirements:* For doctorate, thesis/dissertation. *Entrance requirements:* For master's and doctorate, GRE General Test. Electronic applications accepted.

**The University of North Carolina at Chapel Hill,** Graduate School, Gillings School of Global Public Health, Public Health Leadership Program, Chapel Hill, NC 27599. Offers health care and prevention (MPH); leadership (MPH); occupational health nursing (MPH). *Program availability:* Part-time, evening/weekend, 100% online, blended/hybrid learning. *Faculty:* 8 full-time (7 women), 48 part-time/adjunct (37 women). *Students:* 32 full-time (25 women), 17 part-time (12 women); includes 14 minority (2 Black or African American, non-Hispanic/Latino; 2 Asian, non-Hispanic/Latino; 6 Hispanic/Latino; 4 Two or more races, non-Hispanic/Latino), 2 international. Average age 36. 27 applicants, 78% accepted, 19 enrolled. In 2019, 80 master's awarded. *Degree requirements:* For master's, comprehensive exam, paper. *Entrance requirements:* For master's, three years of public health experience (recommended), three letters of recommendation (academic and/or professional; academic preferred). Additional exam requirements/recommendations for international students: required—TOEFL (minimum score 90 iBT), IELTS (minimum score 7). *Application deadline:* For fall admission, 2/1 for domestic and international students. Application fee: $90. Electronic applications accepted. *Financial support:* Research assistantships, teaching assistantships, career-related internships or fieldwork, institutionally sponsored loans, scholarships/grants, traineeships, and health care benefits available. Financial award application deadline: 12/10; financial award applicants required to submit FAFSA. *Unit head:* Dr. Anna P. Schenck, Director, 919-843-8580, E-mail: anna.schenck@unc.edu. *Application contact:* Joe Jacobs, Academic Coordinator, 919-962-3398, E-mail: mjj0216@email.unc.edu.
Website: https://sph.unc.edu/phlp/phlp/

**University of South Florida,** College of Nursing, Tampa, FL 33612. Offers nurse anesthesia (DNP); nursing (MS, DNP), including adult-gerontology acute care nursing, adult-gerontology primary care nursing, family health nursing, nurse anesthesia (MS), nursing education (MS), occupational health nursing/adult-gerontology primary care nursing, oncology nursing/adult-gerontology primary care nursing (DNP), pediatric health nursing; nursing education (Post Master's Certificate); nursing science (PhD); simulation based academic fellowship in advanced pain management (Graduate Certificate). *Accreditation:* AACN; AANA/CANAEP. *Program availability:* Part-time. *Faculty:* 34 full-time (28 women), 2 part-time/adjunct (1 woman). *Students:* 265 full-time (207 women), 687 part-time (594 women); includes 343 minority (113 Black or African American, non-Hispanic/Latino; 1 American Indian or Alaska Native, non-Hispanic/Latino; 60 Asian, non-Hispanic/Latino; 141 Hispanic/Latino; 1 Native Hawaiian or other Pacific Islander, non-Hispanic/Latino; 27 Two or more races, non-Hispanic/Latino), 2 international. Average age 33. 955 applicants, 44% accepted, 343 enrolled. In 2019, 281 master's, 80 doctorates awarded. *Degree requirements:* For master's, comprehensive exam, thesis optional; for doctorate, comprehensive exam, thesis/dissertation (for some programs). *Entrance requirements:* For master's, GRE General Test, bachelor's in nursing or RN with Bachelor's in relevant field; current license as Registered Nurse; resume or CV; interview; pre-reqs may be required; for doctorate, GRE General Test (recommended), bachelor's degree in nursing from ACEN or CCNE regionally-accredited institution with minimum GPA of 3.0 in all coursework or in all upper-division coursework; current license as Registered Nurse in Florida; undergraduate statistics course with minimum B grade; 3 letters of recommendation; statement of goals; resume; interview. Additional exam requirements/recommendations for international students: required—TOEFL (minimum score 550 paper-based; 79 iBT). *Application deadline:* For fall admission, 12/15 for domestic and international students; for spring admission, 10/1 for domestic students, 9/15 for international students. Application fee: $30. Electronic applications accepted. *Financial support:* In 2019–20, 181 students received support, including 7 research assistantships with tuition reimbursements available (averaging $18,935 per year), 29 teaching assistantships with tuition reimbursements available (averaging $30,814 per year); tuition waivers (partial) and unspecified assistantships also available. Financial award application deadline: 2/1; financial award applicants required to submit FAFSA. *Unit head:* Dr. Victoria Rich, Dean, College of Nursing, 813-974-8939, Fax: 813-974-5418, E-mail: victoriarich@health.usf.edu. *Application contact:* Dr. Denise Maguire, Vice Dean, Graduate Programs, 813-396-9962, E-mail: dmaguire@health.usf.edu.
Website: http://health.usf.edu/nursing/index.htm

**University of the Sacred Heart,** Graduate Programs, Department of Natural Sciences, San Juan, PR 00914-0383. Offers occupational health and safety (MS); occupational nursing (MSN). *Program availability:* Part-time, evening/weekend.

# Oncology Nursing

**Gwynedd Mercy University,** Frances M. Maguire School of Nursing and Health Professions, Gwynedd Valley, PA 19437-0901. Offers clinical nurse specialist (MSN), including gerontology, oncology, pediatrics; nurse educator (MSN); nurse practitioner (MSN), including adult health, pediatric health; nursing (DNP). *Accreditation:* ACEN. *Program availability:* Part-time, blended/hybrid learning. *Faculty:* 4 full-time (all women), 1 (woman) part-time/adjunct. *Students:* 52 full-time (47 women), 58 part-time (52 women); includes 28 minority (17 Black or African American, non-Hispanic/Latino; 9 Asian, non-Hispanic/Latino; 2 Hispanic/Latino). Average age 33. 35 applicants, 43% accepted, 14 enrolled. In 2019, 26 master's awarded. *Degree requirements:* For master's, thesis optional; for doctorate, evidence-based scholarly project. *Entrance requirements:* For master's, current nursing experience, physical assessment, course work in statistics, BSN from ACEN-accredited program, 2 letters of recommendation, personal interview. *Application deadline:* For fall admission, 4/15 for domestic and international students. Applications are processed on a rolling basis. Electronic applications accepted. *Expenses:* Contact institution. *Financial support:* Scholarships/grants, traineeships, and unspecified assistantships available. Financial award application deadline: 4/15. *Unit head:* Dr. Ann Phalen, Dean, 215-646-7300 Ext. 539, Fax: 215-641-5517, E-mail: phalen.a@gmercyu.edu. *Application contact:* Mary Hermann, Associate Dean, 215-646-7300, E-mail: herman.m@gmercyu.edu. Website: http://www.gmercyu.edu/academics/graduate-programs/nursing

**Universidad Metropolitana,** School of Health Sciences, Department of Nursing, San Juan, PR 00928-1150. Offers case management (Certificate); nursing (MSN); oncology nursing (Certificate). *Accreditation:* ACEN.

**University of Delaware,** College of Health Sciences, School of Nursing, Newark, DE 19716. Offers adult nurse practitioner (MSN, PMC); cardiopulmonary clinical nurse specialist (MSN, PMC); cardiopulmonary clinical nurse specialist/adult nurse practitioner (MSN, PMC); family nurse practitioner (MSN, PMC); gerontology clinical nurse specialist (MSN, PMC); gerontology clinical nurse specialist geriatric nurse practitioner (PMC); gerontology clinical nurse specialist/geriatric nurse practitioner (MSN); health services administration (MSN, PMC); nursing of children clinical nurse specialist (MSN, PMC); nursing of children clinical nurse specialist/pediatric nurse practitioner (MSN, PMC); oncology/immune deficiency clinical nurse specialist (MSN, PMC); oncology/immune deficiency clinical nurse specialist/adult nurse practitioner (MSN, PMC); perinatal/women's health clinical nurse specialist (MSN, PMC); perinatal/women's health clinical nurse specialist/women's health nurse practitioner (MSN, PMC); psychiatric nursing clinical nurse specialist (MSN, PMC). *Accreditation:* AACN. *Program availability:* Part-time, evening/weekend, online learning. *Degree requirements:* For master's, thesis optional. *Entrance requirements:* For master's, BSN, interview, RN license. Electronic applications accepted.

**University of South Florida,** College of Nursing, Tampa, FL 33612. Offers nurse anesthesia (DNP); nursing (MS, DNP), including adult-gerontology acute care nursing, adult-gerontology primary care nursing, family health nursing, nurse anesthesia (MS), nursing education (MS), occupational health nursing/adult-gerontology primary care nursing, oncology nursing/adult-gerontology primary care nursing (DNP), pediatric health nursing; nursing education (Post Master's Certificate); nursing science (PhD); simulation based academic fellowship in advanced pain management (Graduate Certificate). *Accreditation:* AACN; AANA/CANAEP. *Program availability:* Part-time. *Faculty:* 34 full-time (28 women), 2 part-time/adjunct (1 woman). *Students:* 265 full-time (207 women), 687 part-time (594 women); includes 343 minority (113 Black or African American, non-Hispanic/Latino; 1 American Indian or Alaska Native, non-Hispanic/Latino; 60 Asian, non-Hispanic/Latino; 141 Hispanic/Latino; 1 Native Hawaiian or other Pacific Islander, non-Hispanic/Latino; 27 Two or more races, non-Hispanic/Latino), 2 international. Average age 33. 955 applicants, 44% accepted, 343 enrolled. In 2019, 281 master's, 80 doctorates awarded. *Degree requirements:* For master's, comprehensive exam, thesis optional; for doctorate, comprehensive exam, thesis/dissertation (for some programs). *Entrance requirements:* For master's, GRE General Test, bachelor's in nursing or RN with Bachelor's in relevant field; current license as Registered Nurse; resume or CV; interview; pre-reqs may be required; for doctorate, GRE General Test (recommended), bachelor's degree in nursing from ACEN or CCNE regionally-accredited institution with minimum GPA of 3.0 in all coursework or in all upper-division coursework; current license as Registered Nurse in Florida; undergraduate statistics course with minimum B grade; 3 letters of recommendation; statement of goals; resume; interview. Additional exam requirements/recommendations for international students: required—TOEFL (minimum score 550 paper-based; 79 iBT). *Application deadline:* For fall admission, 12/15 for domestic and international students; for spring admission, 10/1 for domestic students, 9/15 for international students. Application fee: $30. Electronic applications accepted. *Financial support:* In 2019–20, 181 students received support, including 7 research assistantships with tuition reimbursements available (averaging $18,935 per year), 29 teaching assistantships with tuition reimbursements available (averaging $30,814 per year); tuition waivers (partial) and unspecified assistantships also available. Financial award application deadline: 2/1; financial award applicants required to submit FAFSA. *Unit head:* Dr. Victoria Rich, Dean, College of Nursing, 813-974-8939, Fax: 813-974-5418, E-mail: victoriarich@health.usf.edu. *Application contact:* Dr. Denise Maguire, Vice Dean, Graduate Programs, 813-396-9962, E-mail: dmaguire@health.usf.edu. Website: http://health.usf.edu/nursing/index.htm

# Pediatric Nursing

**Augusta University,** College of Nursing, Doctor of Nursing Practice Program, Augusta, GA 30912. Offers adult gerontology acute care nurse practitioner (DNP); family nurse practitioner (DNP); nurse executive (DNP); nursing (DNP); nursing anesthesia (DNP); pediatric nurse practitioner (DNP); psychiatric mental health nurse practitioner (DNP). *Accreditation:* AACN; AANA/CANAEP. *Degree requirements:* For doctorate, thesis/dissertation or alternative. *Entrance requirements:* For doctorate, GRE General Test or MAT, master's degree in nursing or related field, current professional nurse licensure. Additional exam requirements/recommendations for international students: required—TOEFL (minimum score 600 paper-based; 100 iBT). Electronic applications accepted.

**Azusa Pacific University,** School of Nursing, Azusa, CA 91702-7000. Offers adult clinical nurse specialist (MSN); adult-gerontology nurse practitioner (MSN); family nurse practitioner (MSN); healthcare administration and leadership (MSN); nursing (MSN, DNP, PhD); nursing education (MSN); parent-child clinical nurse specialist (MSN); psychiatric mental health nurse practitioner (MSN). *Accreditation:* AACN. *Program availability:* Part-time, evening/weekend. *Degree requirements:* For master's, thesis optional. *Entrance requirements:* For master's, BSN.

**Boston College,** William F. Connell School of Nursing, Chestnut Hill, MA 02467. Offers adult-gerontology primary care nurse practitioner (MS); family health nursing (MS); nurse anesthesia (MS); nursing (PhD); pediatric primary care nurse practitioner (MS), including pediatric and women's health; psychiatric-mental health nursing (MS); women's health nursing (MS); MBA/MS; MS/MA; MS/PhD. *Accreditation:* AACN; AANA/CANAEP (one or more programs are accredited). *Program availability:* Part-time. *Faculty:* 56 full-time (50 women). *Students:* 228 full-time (200 women), 82 part-time (71 women); includes 54 minority (10 Black or African American, non-Hispanic/Latino; 18 Asian, non-Hispanic/Latino; 20 Hispanic/Latino; 6 Two or more races, non-Hispanic/Latino), 7 international. Average age 28. 360 applicants, 56% accepted, 93 enrolled. In 2019, 107 master's, 7 doctorates awarded. *Degree requirements:* For master's, comprehensive exam; for doctorate, comprehensive exam, thesis/dissertation, computer literacy exam or foreign language. *Entrance requirements:* For master's, bachelor's degree; for doctorate, GRE General Test, bachelor's in Nursing and master's degree in nursing or related field. Additional exam requirements/recommendations for international students: required—TOEFL (minimum score 600 paper-based; 100 iBT), IELTS (minimum score 7.5). *Application deadline:* For fall admission, 3/15 for domestic and international students; for spring admission, 9/30 for domestic and international students. Application fee: $40. Electronic applications accepted. *Expenses:* Contact institution. *Financial support:* In 2019–20, 135 students received support, including 12 fellowships with full tuition reimbursements available (averaging $24,504 per year), 29 teaching assistantships (averaging $4,380 per year); scholarships/grants, health care benefits, tuition waivers (partial), and unspecified assistantships also available. Support available to part-time students. Financial award application deadline: 4/18; financial award applicants required to submit FAFSA. *Unit head:* Dr. Susan Gennaro, Dean, 617-552-4251, Fax: 617-552-0931, E-mail: susan.gennaro@bc.edu. *Application contact:* Sean Sendall, Assistant Dean, Graduate Enrollment and Data Analytics, 617-552-4745, Fax: 617-552-2121, E-mail: sean.sendall@bc.edu. Website: http://www.bc.edu/cson

**Caribbean University,** Graduate School, Bayamón, PR 00960-0493. Offers administration and supervision (MA Ed); criminal justice (MA); curriculum and instruction (MA Ed, PhD), including elementary education (MA Ed), English education (MA Ed), history education (MA Ed), mathematics education (MA Ed), primary education (MA Ed), science education (MA Ed), Spanish education (MA Ed); educational technology in instructional systems (MA Ed); gerontology (MSN); human resources (MBA); museology, archiving and art history (MA Ed); neonatal pediatrics (MSN); physical education (MA Ed); special education (MA Ed). *Entrance requirements:* For master's, interview, minimum GPA of 2.5.

**Case Western Reserve University,** Frances Payne Bolton School of Nursing, Master's Programs in Nursing, Nurse Practitioner Program, Cleveland, OH 44106. Offers acute care pediatric nurse practitioner (MSN); acute care/cardiovascular nursing (MSN); adult gerontology acute care nurse practitioner (MSN); adult gerontology primary care nurse practitioner (MSN); family nurse practitioner (MSN); family systems psychiatric mental health nursing (MSN); neonatal nurse practitioner (MSN); palliative care (MSN); pediatric nurse practitioner in acute care (MSN); pediatric primary care nurse practitioner (MSN); women's health nurse practitioner (MSN). *Accreditation:* ACEN. *Program availability:* Part-time. *Faculty:* 30 full-time (25 women), 6 part-time/adjunct (all women). *Students:* 47 full-time (36 women), 70 part-time (59 women); includes 34 minority (12 Black or African American, non-Hispanic/Latino; 11 Asian, non-Hispanic/Latino; 9 Hispanic/Latino; 2 Two or more races, non-Hispanic/Latino), 9 international. Average age 30. 45 applicants, 82% accepted, 22 enrolled. In 2019, 46 master's awarded. *Degree requirements:* For master's, thesis optional, minimum GPA of 3.0, clinical hours corresponding to requirements to sit for certification exam, portfolio. *Entrance requirements:* For master's, GRE/MAT (scores not required for application, but may be requested for an admission decision). Additional exam requirements/recommendations for international students: required—TOEFL (minimum score 577 paper-based; 90 iBT), IELTS (minimum score 7). *Application deadline:* For fall admission, 3/15 for domestic and international students; for spring admission, 10/1 for domestic and international students; for summer admission, 3/15 for domestic and international students. Applications are processed on a rolling basis. Application fee: $75. Electronic applications accepted. *Expenses:* Clinical placement $75; Activity fee $15 per semester; Graduate council fee $15 per semester; Tuition rate $2,133 per credit hour. *Financial support:* In 2019–20, 100 students received support, including 34 teaching assistantships with partial tuition reimbursements available (averaging $19,197 per year); scholarships/grants and traineeships also available. Financial award application deadline: 5/15; financial award applicants required to submit FAFSA. *Unit head:* Dr. Latina Brooks, Director, 216-368-1196, Fax: 216-368-3542, E-mail: lmb3@case.edu. *Application contact:* Jackie Tepale, Admissions Coordinator, 216-368-5253, Fax: 216-368-3542, E-mail: yyd@case.edu. Website: https://case.edu/nursing/programs/msn

**Columbia University,** School of Nursing, Program in Pediatric Nurse Practitioner, New York, NY 10032. Offers MS, Adv C. *Accreditation:* AACN. *Program availability:* Part-time. *Entrance requirements:* For master's, GRE General Test, NCLEX, BSN, 1 year of clinical experience (preferred); for Adv C, MSN. Additional exam requirements/recommendations for international students: required—TOEFL. Electronic applications accepted. *Expenses:* Tuition: Full-time $47,600; part-time $1880 per credit. One-time fee: $105.

**Creighton University,** College of Nursing, Omaha, NE 68178-0001. Offers adult gerontology acute care nurse practitioner (DNP, Post-Master's Certificate); adult gerontology nurse practitioner (DNP); clinical nurse leader (MSN, Post-Graduate

Certificate); clinical systems administration (MSN, DNP); family nurse practitioner (DNP, Post-Master's Certificate); neonatal nurse practitioner (DNP, Post-Master's Certificate); nursing (Post-Graduate Certificate); pediatric acute care nurse practitioner (DNP, Post-Master's Certificate); psychiatric mental health nurse practitioner (DNP). *Accreditation:* AACN. *Program availability:* Part-time, blended/hybrid learning. *Degree requirements:* For master's, capstone project; for doctorate, scholarly project. *Entrance requirements:* For master's and doctorate, BSN from ACEN- or CCNE-accredited nursing school, minimum cumulative GPA of 3.0, personal statement, active unencumbered RN license with NE eligibility, undergraduate statistics course, physical assessment course or equivalent, three recommendation letters; for other advanced degree, MSN or MS in nursing from ACEN- or CCNE-accredited nursing school, minimum cumulative GPA of 3.0, active unencumbered RN license with NE eligibility. Additional exam requirements/recommendations for international students: required—TOEFL (minimum score 600 paper-based, 100 iBT) or IELTS. Electronic applications accepted. *Expenses:* Contact institution.

**Drexel University,** College of Nursing and Health Professions, Division of Graduate Nursing, Philadelphia, PA 19104-2875. Offers adult acute care (MSN); adult psychiatric/mental health (MSN); advanced practice nursing (MSN); clinical trials research (MSN); family nurse practitioner (MSN); leadership in health systems management (MSN); nursing education (MSN); pediatric primary care (MSN); women's health (MSN). *Accreditation:* AACN. Electronic applications accepted.

**Duke University,** School of Nursing, Durham, NC 27708. Offers acute care pediatric nurse practitioner (MSN, Post-Graduate Certificate); adult-gerontology nurse practitioner (MSN, Post-Graduate Certificate), including acute care, primary care; family nurse practitioner (MSN, Post-Graduate Certificate); neonatal nurse practitioner (MSN, Post-Graduate Certificate); nurse anesthesia (DNP); nurse practitioner (DNP); nursing (PhD); nursing and health care leadership (MSN, Post-Graduate Certificate); nursing education (MSN, Post-Graduate Certificate); nursing informatics (MSN, Post-Graduate Certificate); pediatric nurse practitioner (MSN, Post-Graduate Certificate), including primary care; psychiatric mental health nurse practitioner (MSN, Post-Graduate Certificate); women's health nurse practitioner (MSN, Post-Graduate Certificate). *Accreditation:* AACN; AANA/CANAEP. *Program availability:* Part-time, evening/weekend, online with on-campus intensives. *Faculty:* 48 full-time (40 women), 32 part-time/adjunct (28 women). *Students:* 666 full-time (601 women), 157 part-time (139 women); includes 193 minority (61 Black or African American, non-Hispanic/Latino; 4 American Indian or Alaska Native, non-Hispanic/Latino; 57 Asian, non-Hispanic/Latino; 49 Hispanic/Latino; 1 Native Hawaiian or other Pacific Islander, non-Hispanic/Latino; 21 Two or more races, non-Hispanic/Latino), 8 international. Average age 34. 761 applicants, 33% accepted, 149 enrolled. In 2019, 213 master's, 74 doctorates, 18 other advanced degrees awarded. Terminal master's awarded for partial completion of doctoral program. *Degree requirements:* For master's, thesis optional; for doctorate, capstone project. *Entrance requirements:* For master's, MSN applicants are no longer required to take the GRE, 1 year of nursing experience (recommended), BSN, minimum GPA of 3.0, previous course work in statistics; for doctorate, GRE is required for the DNP in Nurse Anesthesia, BSN or MSN, minimum GPA of 3.0, resume, personal statement, graduate statistics and research methods course, current licensure as a registered nurse, transcripts from all post-secondary institutions; for Post-Graduate Certificate, MSN, licensure or eligibility as a professional nurse, transcripts from all post-secondary institutions, previous course work in statistics. Additional exam requirements/recommendations for international students: required—TOEFL (minimum score 100 iBT), IELTS (minimum score 7). *Application deadline:* For fall admission, 12/1 for domestic and international students; for spring admission, 5/1 for domestic and international students. Application fee: $50. Electronic applications accepted. *Expenses:* Contact institution. *Financial support:* Institutionally sponsored loans, scholarships/grants, and traineeships available. Support available to part-time students. Financial award applicants required to submit FAFSA. *Unit head:* Dr. Marion E. Broome, Dean/Vice Chancellor for Nursing Affairs/Associate Vice President for Academic Affairs for Nursing, 919-684-9446, Fax: 919-684-9414, E-mail: marion.broome@duke.edu. *Application contact:* Dr. Ernie Rushing, Director of Admissions and Recruitment, 919-668-6274, Fax: 919-668-4693, E-mail: ernie.rushing@dm.duke.edu.
Website: http://www.nursing.duke.edu/

**East Tennessee State University,** College of Graduate and Continuing Studies, College of Nursing, Johnson City, TN 37614. Offers acute care nurse practitioner (DNP); adult-gerontology primary care nurse practitioner (DNP); adult/gerontological nurse practitioner (Postbaccalaureate Certificate); executive leadership in nursing (DNP, Postbaccalaureate Certificate); family nurse practitioner (MSN, DNP, Post-Master's Certificate, Postbaccalaureate Certificate); nursing (PhD); nursing administration (MSN); nursing education (MSN); pediatric primary care nurse practitioner (DNP); psychiatric mental health nurse practitioner (Postbaccalaureate Certificate); psychiatric/mental health nurse practitioner (MSN, DNP, Post-Master's Certificate); women's health care nurse practitioner (DNP). *Accreditation:* AACN. *Program availability:* Part-time, evening/weekend, online learning. *Degree requirements:* For master's and other advanced degree, comprehensive exam, practicum; for doctorate, comprehensive exam, thesis/dissertation (for some programs), practicum, internship, evidence of professional malpractice insurance, CPR certification. *Entrance requirements:* For master's, bachelor's degree, minimum GPA of 3.0, current RN license and eligibility to practice, resume, three letters of recommendation; for doctorate, GRE General Test, MSN (for PhD), BSN or MSN (for DNP), current RN license and eligibility to practice, 2 years of full-time registered nurse work experience or equivalent, three letters of recommendation, resume or curriculum vitae, interview, writing sample; for other advanced degree, MSN, minimum GPA of 3.0, current RN license and eligibility to practice, three letters of recommendation, resume or curriculum vitae; DNP with designated concentration in advanced clinical practice or nursing administration (for select programs). Additional exam requirements/recommendations for international students: required—TOEFL (minimum score 600 paper-based; 79 iBT). Electronic applications accepted.

**Emory University,** Nell Hodgson Woodruff School of Nursing, Atlanta, GA 30322-1100. Offers adult nurse practitioner (MSN); emergency nurse practitioner (MSN); family nurse practitioner (MSN); family nurse-midwife (MSN); health systems leadership (MSN); nurse-midwifery (MSN); pediatric nurse practitioner acute and primary care (MSN); women's health care (Title X) (MSN); women's health nurse practitioner (MSN); MSN/MPH. *Accreditation:* AACN; ACNM/ACME (one or more programs are accredited). *Program availability:* Part-time. *Entrance requirements:* For master's, GRE General Test or MAT, minimum GPA of 3.0, BS in nursing from an accredited institution, RN license and additional course work, 3 letters of recommendation. Additional exam requirements/recommendations for international students: required—TOEFL (minimum score 600 paper-based; 100 iBT). Electronic applications accepted. *Expenses:* Contact institution.

**Florida International University,** Nicole Wertheim College of Nursing and Health Sciences, Nursing Program, Miami, FL 33199. Offers adult health nursing (MSN); family health (MSN); nurse anesthetist (MSN); nursing practice (DNP); nursing science research (PhD); pediatric nurse (MSN); psychiatric and mental health nursing (MSN); registered nurse (MSN). *Accreditation:* AACN; AANA/CANAEP. *Program availability:* Part-time, evening/weekend. *Faculty:* 14 full-time (12 women), 19 part-time/adjunct (14 women). *Students:* 279 full-time (188 women), 109 part-time (87 women); includes 309 minority (110 Black or African American, non-Hispanic/Latino; 1 American Indian or Alaska Native, non-Hispanic/Latino; 29 Asian, non-Hispanic/Latino; 166 Hispanic/Latino; 2 Native Hawaiian or other Pacific Islander, non-Hispanic/Latino; 1 Two or more races, non-Hispanic/Latino), 6 international. Average age 35. 154 applicants, 61% accepted, 88 enrolled. In 2019, 167 master's, 46 doctorates awarded. *Degree requirements:* For master's, thesis or alternative; for doctorate, comprehensive exam, thesis/dissertation. *Entrance requirements:* For master's, bachelor's degree in nursing, minimum undergraduate GPA of 3.0 in upper-level coursework, letters of recommendation; for doctorate, GRE, letters of recommendation, minimum undergraduate GPA of 3.0 in upper-level coursework, interview. Additional exam requirements/recommendations for international students: required—TOEFL (minimum score 550 paper-based; 80 iBT). *Application deadline:* For fall admission, 6/1 for domestic students, 4/1 for international students; for spring admission, 10/1 for domestic students, 9/1 for international students. Applications are processed on a rolling basis. Application fee: $30. Electronic applications accepted. *Expenses: Tuition, area resident:* Full-time $8912; part-time $446 per credit hour. Tuition, state resident: full-time $8912; part-time $446 per credit hour. Tuition, nonresident: full-time $21,393; part-time $992 per credit hour. *Required fees:* $2194. *Financial support:* Institutionally sponsored loans and scholarships/grants available. Financial award application deadline: 3/1; financial award applicants required to submit FAFSA. *Unit head:* Dr. Yhovana Gordon, Chair, 305-348-7733, Fax: 305-348-7051, E-mail: gordony@fiu.edu. *Application contact:* Nanett Rojas, Manager, Admissions Operations, 305-348-7464, Fax: 305-348-7441, E-mail: gradadm@fiu.edu.
Website: http://cnhs.fiu.edu/

**Georgia State University,** Byrdine F. Lewis School of Nursing, Atlanta, GA 30303. Offers adult health clinical nurse specialist/nurse practitioner (MS, Certificate); child health clinical nurse specialist/pediatric nurse practitioner (MS, Certificate); family nurse practitioner (MS, Certificate); family psychiatric mental health nurse practitioner (MS, Certificate); nursing (PhD); nursing leadership in healthcare innovations (MS), including nursing administration, nursing informatics; nutrition (MS); occupational therapy (MOT); perinatal clinical nurse specialist/women's health nurse practitioner (MS, Certificate); physical therapy (DPT); respiratory therapy (MS). *Accreditation:* AACN. *Program availability:* Part-time, blended/hybrid learning. *Faculty:* 57 full-time (40 women), 5 part-time/adjunct (4 women). *Students:* 388 full-time (290 women), 155 part-time (135 women); includes 217 minority (130 Black or African American, non-Hispanic/Latino; 47 Asian, non-Hispanic/Latino; 26 Hispanic/Latino; 14 Two or more races, non-Hispanic/Latino), 45 international. Average age 32. 480 applicants, 50% accepted, 164 enrolled. In 2019, 158 master's, 64 doctorates, 20 other advanced degrees awarded. *Degree requirements:* For doctorate, comprehensive exam, thesis/dissertation. *Entrance requirements:* For doctorate, GRE. Additional exam requirements/recommendations for international students: required—TOEFL. *Application deadline:* For fall admission, 2/1 priority date for domestic and international students; for spring admission, 9/15 for domestic and international students. Applications are processed on a rolling basis. Application fee: $50. Electronic applications accepted. *Expenses:* Contact institution. *Financial support:* In 2019–20, research assistantships with tuition reimbursements (averaging $1,666 per year), teaching assistantships with tuition reimbursements (averaging $1,920 per year) were awarded; scholarships/grants, tuition waivers (full and partial), and unspecified assistantships also available. Support available to part-time students. Financial award application deadline: 8/1; financial award applicants required to submit FAFSA. *Unit head:* Huanbiao Mo, Dean of Nursing. *Application contact:* Huanbiao Mo, Dean of Nursing.
Website: http://nursing.gsu.edu/

**Gwynedd Mercy University,** Frances M. Maguire School of Nursing and Health Professions, Gwynedd Valley, PA 19437-0901. Offers clinical nurse specialist (MSN), including gerontology, oncology, pediatrics; nurse educator (MSN); nurse practitioner (MSN), including adult health, pediatric health; nursing (DNP). *Accreditation:* ACEN. *Program availability:* Part-time, blended/hybrid learning. *Faculty:* 4 full-time (all women), 1 (woman) part-time/adjunct. *Students:* 52 full-time (47 women), 58 part-time (52 women); includes 28 minority (17 Black or African American, non-Hispanic/Latino; 9 Asian, non-Hispanic/Latino; 2 Hispanic/Latino). Average age 33. 35 applicants, 43% accepted, 14 enrolled. In 2019, 26 master's awarded. *Degree requirements:* For master's, thesis optional; for doctorate, evidence-based scholarly project. *Entrance requirements:* For master's, current nursing experience, physical assessment, course work in statistics, BSN from ACEN-accredited program, 2 letters of recommendation, personal interview. *Application deadline:* For fall admission, 4/15 for domestic and international students. Applications are processed on a rolling basis. Electronic applications accepted. *Expenses:* Contact institution. *Financial support:* Scholarships/grants, traineeships, and unspecified assistantships available. Financial award application deadline: 4/15. *Unit head:* Dr. Ann Phalen, Dean, 215-646-7300 Ext. 539, Fax: 215-641-5517, E-mail: phalen.a@gmercyu.edu. *Application contact:* Mary Hermann, Associate Dean, 215-646-7300, E-mail: herman.m@gmercyu.edu.
Website: http://www.gmercyu.edu/academics/graduate-programs/nursing

**Houston Baptist University,** School of Nursing and Allied Health, Program in Nursing, Houston, TX 77074-3298. Offers family nurse practitioner (MSN); pediatric nurse practitioner in primary care (MSN). *Program availability:* Part-time, evening/weekend, online only, 100% online. *Degree requirements:* For master's, comprehensive exam. *Entrance requirements:* For master's, GRE General Test, BSN from NLN or CCLE program, minimum GPA of 2.5, RN license in Texas; resume. Electronic applications accepted. Application fee is waived when completed online. *Expenses:* Contact institution.

**Indiana University-Purdue University Indianapolis,** School of Nursing, MSN Program in Nursing, Indianapolis, IN 46202. Offers adult/gerontology acute care nurse practitioner (MSN); adult/gerontology clinical nurse specialist (MSN); adult/gerontology primary care nurse practitioner (MSN); family nurse practitioner (MSN); nursing education (MSN); nursing leadership in health systems (MSN); pediatric clinical nurse specialist (MSN); pediatric nurse practitioner (MSN). *Accreditation:* AACN. *Program availability:* Part-time, blended/hybrid learning. *Degree requirements:* For master's, thesis. *Entrance requirements:* For master's, BSN from ACEN- or CCNE-accredited program, minimum undergraduate GPA of 3.0 (preferred), professional resume or curriculum vitae, essay stating career goals and objectives, current unencumbered RN license, three references from individuals with knowledge of ability to succeed in graduate program. Additional exam requirements/recommendations for international students: required—TOEFL (minimum score 550 paper-based; 79 iBT). Electronic applications accepted. *Expenses:* Contact institution.

**Johns Hopkins University,** School of Nursing, DNP Clinical Nurse Specialist Track, Baltimore, MD 21218. Offers adult/gerontological critical care clinical nurse specialist (DNP); adult/gerontological health clinical nurse specialist (DNP); pediatric critical care clinical nurse specialist (DNP). *Accreditation:* AACN. *Program availability:* Part-time, 100% online, blended/hybrid learning. *Faculty:* 22 full-time (20 women), 3 part-time/adjunct (2 women). *Students:* 22 full-time (21 women), 11 part-time (all women); includes 15 minority (3 Black or African American, non-Hispanic/Latino; 4 Asian, non-Hispanic/Latino; 6 Hispanic/Latino; 1 Native Hawaiian or other Pacific Islander, non-Hispanic/Latino; 1 Two or more races, non-Hispanic/Latino). 25 applicants, 88%

accepted, 16 enrolled. In 2019, 3 doctorates awarded. *Entrance requirements:* For doctorate, GRE, Minimum GPA of 3.0, goal statement/essay, resume, letters of recommendation, official transcripts from all post-secondary institutions attended, BSN, and RN license, prerequisite coursework. Additional exam requirements/recommendations for international students: required—TOEFL (minimum score 600 paper-based; 100 iBT), IELTS (minimum score 7). *Application deadline:* For fall admission, 11/1 priority date for domestic and international students. Application fee: $75. Electronic applications accepted. *Expenses:* $1,772 per credit. *Financial support:* In 2019–20, 23 students received support. Federal Work-Study and scholarships/grants available. Support available to part-time students. Financial award application deadline: 3/1; financial award applicants required to submit FAFSA. *Unit head:* Dr. Patricia M. Davidson, Dean, 410-955-7544, Fax: 410-955-4890, E-mail: sondeansoffice@jhu.edu. *Application contact:* Cathy Wilson, Director of Admissions, 410-955-7548, Fax: 410-614-7086, E-mail: jhuson@jhu.edu.
Website: http://www.nursing.jhu.edu

**Johns Hopkins University,** School of Nursing, DNP Nurse Practitioner Track, Baltimore, MD 21218. Offers adult/gerontological acute care nurse practitioner (DNP); adult/gerontological primary care nurse practitioner (DNP); family primary care nurse practitioner (DNP); pediatric primary care nurse practitioner (DNP). *Accreditation:* AACN. *Students:* 176 applicants, 59% accepted, 64 enrolled. *Degree requirements:* For doctorate, thesis/dissertation, Preliminary justification; final justification. *Entrance requirements:* For doctorate, minimum GPA of 3.0, goal statement/essay, resume, letters of recommendation, official transcripts from all post-secondary institutions attended; BSN and RN license, work experience for some tracks. Additional exam requirements/recommendations for international students: required—TOEFL (minimum score 600 paper-based; 100 iBT), IELTS (minimum score 7). *Application deadline:* For fall admission, 11/1 priority date for domestic and international students. Application fee: $70. Electronic applications accepted. *Expenses:* Contact institution. *Financial support:* In 2019–20, 57 students received support. Federal Work-Study and scholarships/grants available. Support available to part-time students. Financial award application deadline: 3/1; financial award applicants required to submit FAFSA. *Unit head:* Dr. Kim McIltrot, Dean, Fax: 410-502-2247, E-mail: kmciltr1@jhmi.edu. *Application contact:* Cathy Wilson, Director of Admissions, 410-955-7548, Fax: 410-614-7086, E-mail: jhuson@jhu.edu.
Website: http://www.nursing.jhu.edu

**Johns Hopkins University,** School of Nursing, Post Master's Certificate Program in Nursing, Baltimore, MD 21218. Offers nursing education (Certificate); pediatric acute care nurse practitioner (Certificate); psychiatric mental health nurse practitioner (Certificate). *Program availability:* Part-time-only, online only, 100% online. *Faculty:* 4 full-time (all women), 2 part-time/adjunct (both women). *Students:* 47 part-time (44 women); includes 9 minority (3 Black or African American, non-Hispanic/Latino; 2 Asian, non-Hispanic/Latino; 3 Hispanic/Latino; 1 Two or more races, non-Hispanic/Latino). 127 applicants, 44% accepted, 47 enrolled. In 2019, 46 Certificates awarded. *Entrance requirements:* For degree, Minimum GPA of 3.0, goal statement/essay, resume, letters of recommendation, official transcripts from all post-secondary institutions attended, MSN and RN licensure, NP license for some tracks, work experience and prerequisite coursework for some tracks. Additional exam requirements/recommendations for international students: required—TOEFL (minimum score 600 paper-based; 100 iBT), IELTS (minimum score 7). *Application deadline:* For fall admission, 1/1 priority date for domestic students. Application fee: $75. Electronic applications accepted. *Expenses:* $1,688 per credit. *Financial support:* In 2019–20, 1 student received support. Federal Work-Study available. Financial award application deadline: 3/1; financial award applicants required to submit FAFSA. *Unit head:* Dr. Susan Renda, 410-955-7139, E-mail: srenda1@jhu.edu. *Application contact:* Cathy Wilson, Director of Admissions, 410-955-7548, Fax: 410-614-7086, E-mail: jhuson@jhu.edu.
Website: http://nursing.jhu.edu/

**Kent State University,** College of Nursing, Kent, OH 44242. Offers advanced nursing practice (DNP), including adult/gerontology acute care nurse practitioner (MSN, DNP); nursing (MSN, PhD), including adult/gerontology acute care nurse practitioner (MSN, DNP); adult/gerontology clinical nurse specialist (MSN), adult/gerontology primary care nurse practitioner (MSN), family nurse practitioner (MSN), nurse educator (MSN), nursing and healthcare management (MSN), pediatric primary care nurse practitioner (MSN), psychiatric/mental health nurse practitioner (MSN); MBA/MSN. *Accreditation:* AACN. *Program availability:* Part-time, online learning. *Faculty:* 28 full-time (26 women), 15 part-time/adjunct (13 women). *Students:* 138 full-time (123 women), 522 part-time (464 women); includes 80 minority (41 Black or African American, non-Hispanic/Latino; 16 Asian, non-Hispanic/Latino; 9 Hispanic/Latino; 1 Native Hawaiian or other Pacific Islander, non-Hispanic/Latino; 13 Two or more races, non-Hispanic/Latino), 7 international. Average age 35. 303 applicants, 68% accepted, 154 enrolled. In 2019, 156 master's, 8 doctorates awarded. *Degree requirements:* For master's, practicum (for master's degrees; for doctorate, comprehensive exam, thesis/dissertation. *Entrance requirements:* For master's, GRE or GMAT, minimum GPA of 3.0, active RN license, statement of purpose, 3 letters of reference, undergraduate level statistics class (minimum C grade), baccalaureate or graduate-level nursing degree, curriculum vitae/resume; for doctorate, GRE, minimum GPA of 3.0, transcripts, 3 letters of reference, interview, active unrestricted Ohio RN license, statement of purpose, writing sample, curriculum vitae/resume, baccalaureate and master's degrees in nursing or DNP, undergraduate or graduate level statistics course with a minimum C grade. Additional exam requirements/recommendations for international students: required—TOEFL (minimum score 83 iBT), IELTS (minimum score 6.5), PTE (minimum score 55), Michigan English Language Assessment Battery (minimum score 78). *Application deadline:* For fall admission, 3/1 for domestic and international students; for spring admission, 10/1 for domestic and international students. Applications are processed on a rolling basis. Application fee: $45 ($70 for international students). Electronic applications accepted. *Financial support:* Federal Work-Study and scholarships/grants available. Financial award application deadline: 2/1. *Unit head:* Dr. Barbara Broome, Ph.D., Dean, 330-672-3777, E-mail: bbroome1@kent.edu. *Application contact:* Dr. Wendy A. Umberger, Ph.D., Associate Dean for Graduate Programs/Professor, 330-672-8813, E-mail: wlewando@kent.edu.
Website: http://www.kent.edu/nursing/

**King University,** School of Nursing, Bristol, TN 37620-2699. Offers family nurse practitioner (MSN, Post-Master's Certificate); nurse educator (MSN, Post-Master's Certificate); nursing (DNP); nursing administration (MSN); pediatric nurse practitioner (MSN). *Program availability:* Part-time, evening/weekend, 100% online, blended/hybrid learning. *Faculty:* 13 full-time (12 women), 4 part-time/adjunct (2 women). *Students:* 115 full-time (103 women), 35 part-time (28 women); includes 12 minority (9 Black or African American, non-Hispanic/Latino; 1 Asian, non-Hispanic/Latino; 1 Hispanic/Latino; 1 Native Hawaiian or other Pacific Islander, non-Hispanic/Latino). Average age 37. 141 applicants, 96% accepted, 63 enrolled. In 2019, 89 master's, 1 doctorate, 6 other advanced degrees awarded. *Degree requirements:* For master's and post-master's certificate, comprehensive exam (for some programs), thesis optional; for doctorate, comprehensive exam (for some programs), thesis/dissertation. *Entrance requirements:* For master's, submit evidence of graduation from an accredited baccalaureate nursing program with a minimum cumulative undergraduate GPA of 3.0 on a 4.0 scale prior to

enrolling; for doctorate, bachelor's and master's degree in nursing with a GPA of 3.25 or higher from a master's degree program accredited by the Accreditation Commission for Nursing Education (ACNE) or the Commission on Collegiate Nursing Education (CCNE); for Post-Master's Certificate, FNP and PNP applicants must complete an interview with the MSN Admissions Committee. Additional exam requirements/recommendations for international students: required—TOEFL (minimum score 84 paper-based; 84 iBT). *Application deadline:* Applications are processed on a rolling basis. Application fee: $50. Electronic applications accepted. *Expenses: Tuition:* Full-time $10,890; part-time $605 per semester hour. *Required fees:* $100 per course. *Financial support:* Unspecified assistantships available. Financial award applicants required to submit FAFSA. *Unit head:* Dr. Tracy Slemp, Dean, School of Nursing, 423-652-6335, E-mail: tjslemp@king.edu. *Application contact:* Natalie Blankenship, Territory Manager/Enrollment Counselor, 652-652-4159, Fax: 652-652-4727, E-mail: nblankenship@king.edu.

**Lehman College of the City University of New York,** School of Health Sciences, Human Services and Nursing, Department of Nursing, Bronx, NY 10468-1589. Offers adult health nursing (MS); nursing of older adults (MS); parent-child nursing (MS); pediatric nurse practitioner (MS). *Accreditation:* AACN. *Program availability:* Part-time, evening/weekend. *Entrance requirements:* For master's, bachelor's degree in nursing, New York RN license. *Expenses: Tuition, area resident:* Full-time $5545; part-time $470 per credit. Tuition, nonresident: part-time $855 per credit. *Required fees:* $240.

**Loma Linda University,** School of Nursing, Program in Nurse Educator, Loma Linda, CA 92350. Offers adult/gerontology (MS); obstetrics-pediatrics (MS). *Accreditation:* AACN. *Program availability:* Part-time. *Degree requirements:* For master's, thesis or alternative. *Entrance requirements:* For master's, GRE General Test, BSN, minimum GPA of 3.0, RN license. Additional exam requirements/recommendations for international students: required—TOEFL. Electronic applications accepted.

**Marquette University,** Graduate School, College of Nursing, Milwaukee, WI 53201-1881. Offers acute care nurse practitioner (Certificate); adult clinical nurse specialist (Certificate); adult nurse practitioner (Certificate); advanced practice nursing (MSN, DNP), including adult-older adult acute care (DNP), adults (MSN), adults-older adults (DNP), clinical nurse leader (MSN), health care systems leadership (DNP), nurse-midwifery (MSN), older adults (MSN), pediatrics-acute care, pediatrics-primary care, primary care (DNP), systems leadership and healthcare quality (MSN); family nurse practitioner (Certificate); nurse-midwifery (Certificate); nursing (PhD); pediatric acute care (Certificate); pediatric primary care (Certificate); systems leadership and healthcare quality (Certificate). *Accreditation:* AACN; AANA/CANAEP; ACNM/ACME. Terminal master's awarded for partial completion of doctoral program. *Degree requirements:* For master's, comprehensive exam, thesis or alternative. *Entrance requirements:* For master's, GRE General Test, BSN, Wisconsin RN license, official transcripts from all current and previous colleges/universities except Marquette, three completed recommendation forms, resume, written statement of professional goals; for doctorate, GRE General Test, official transcripts from all current and previous colleges/universities except Marquette, three letters of recommendation, resume, written statement of professional goals, sample of scholarly writing. Additional exam requirements/recommendations for international students: required—TOEFL (minimum score 530 paper-based). Electronic applications accepted.

**Maryville University of Saint Louis,** Myrtle E. and Earl E. Walker College of Health Professions, The Catherine McAuley School of Nursing, St. Louis, MO 63141-7299. Offers acute care nurse practitioner (MSN); adult gerontology nurse practitioner (MSN); advanced practice nursing (DNP); family nurse practitioner (MSN); pediatric nurse practitioner (MSN). *Accreditation:* AACN. *Program availability:* 100% online, blended/hybrid learning. *Faculty:* 14 full-time (all women), 131 part-time/adjunct (114 women). *Students:* 103 full-time (91 women), 3,493 part-time (3,050 women); includes 1,039 minority (530 Black or African American, non-Hispanic/Latino; 41 American Indian or Alaska Native, non-Hispanic/Latino; 157 Asian, non-Hispanic/Latino; 221 Hispanic/Latino; 90 Two or more races, non-Hispanic/Latino), 9 international. Average age 37. In 2019, 1,012 master's, 54 doctorates awarded. *Degree requirements:* For master's, practicum. *Entrance requirements:* For master's, BSN, current licensure, minimum GPA of 3.0, 3 letters of recommendation, curriculum vitae. Additional exam requirements/recommendations for international students: required—TOEFL (minimum score 550 paper-based). *Application deadline:* Applications are processed on a rolling basis. Electronic applications accepted. *Expenses:* Contact institution. *Financial support:* Federal Work-Study and campus employment available. Support available to part-time students. Financial award application deadline: 4/1; financial award applicants required to submit FAFSA. *Unit head:* Karla Larson, Assistant Dean Nursing, 314-529-6856, Fax: 314-529-9139, E-mail: klarson@maryville.edu. *Application contact:* Jeannie DeLuca, Director of Admissions and Advising, 314-929-9355, Fax: 314-529-9927, E-mail: jdeluca@maryville.edu.
Website: http://www.maryville.edu/hp/nursing/

**MGH Institute of Health Professions,** School of Nursing, Boston, MA 02129. Offers advanced practice nursing (MSN); gerontological nursing (MSN); nursing (DNP); pediatric nursing (MSN); psychiatric nursing (MSN); teaching and learning for health care education (Certificate); women's health nursing (MSN). *Accreditation:* AACN. *Degree requirements:* For master's, thesis or alternative. *Entrance requirements:* For master's, GRE General Test, bachelor's degree from regionally-accredited college or university. Additional exam requirements/recommendations for international students: required—TOEFL (minimum score 550 paper-based; 80 iBT). Electronic applications accepted.

**Molloy College,** Graduate Nursing Program, Rockville Centre, NY 11571-5002. Offers adult-gerontology clinical nurse specialist (DNP); adult-gerontology nurse practitioner (MS, DNP); clinical nurse specialist: adult-gerontology (MS); family nurse practitioner (MS, DNP); family psychiatric/mental health nurse practitioner (MS, DNP); nursing (PhD, Advanced Certificate); nursing administration with informatics (MS); nursing education (MS); pediatric nurse practitioner (MS, DNP). *Accreditation:* AACN. *Program availability:* Part-time, evening/weekend. *Faculty:* 30 full-time (28 women), 10 part-time/adjunct (6 women). *Students:* 18 full-time (17 women), 573 part-time (520 women); includes 340 minority (181 Black or African American, non-Hispanic/Latino; 2 American Indian or Alaska Native, non-Hispanic/Latino; 100 Asian, non-Hispanic/Latino; 42 Hispanic/Latino; 5 Native Hawaiian or other Pacific Islander, non-Hispanic/Latino; 10 Two or more races, non-Hispanic/Latino), 3 international. Average age 38. 332 applicants, 60% accepted, 149 enrolled. In 2019, 136 master's, 12 doctorates, 22 other advanced degrees awarded. *Degree requirements:* For doctorate, clinical research residency and scholarly clinical project (for DNP); dissertation and comprehensive exam (for PhD). *Entrance requirements:* Additional exam requirements/recommendations for international students: required—TOEFL (minimum score 550 paper-based; 79 iBT). *Application deadline:* Applications are processed on a rolling basis. Application fee: $60. Electronic applications accepted. *Expenses: Tuition:* Full-time $21,510; part-time $1195 per credit hour. *Required fees:* $1100. Tuition and fees vary according to course load, degree level and program. *Financial support:* Application deadline: 3/1; applicants required to submit FAFSA. *Unit head:* Dr. Marcia R. Gardner, Dean, The Barbara H. Hagan School of Nursing, 516-323-3651, E-mail: mgardner@molloy.edu. *Application contact:* Faye Hood, Assistant Director for Admissions, 516-323-4009, E-mail: fhood@molloy.edu.

*Pediatric Nursing*

Website: https://www.molloy.edu/academics/graduate-programs/graduate-nursing-x25989

**New York University,** Rory Meyers College of Nursing, Doctor of Nursing Practice Program, New York, NY 10012-1019. Offers nursing (DNP), including adult-gerontology acute care nurse practitioner, adult-gerontology primary care nurse practitioner, family nurse practitioner, nurse-midwifery, pediatrics nurse practitioner, psychiatric-mental health nurse practitioner. *Accreditation:* AACN. *Program availability:* Part-time, evening/weekend. *Degree requirements:* For doctorate, thesis/dissertation, project. *Entrance requirements:* For doctorate, MS, RN license, interview, Nurse Practitioner Certification, writing sample. Additional exam requirements/recommendations for international students: required—TOEFL (minimum score 100 iBT), IELTS (minimum score 7). Electronic applications accepted. *Expenses:* Contact institution.

**New York University,** Rory Meyers College of Nursing, Programs in Advanced Practice Nursing, New York, NY 10012-1019. Offers adult-gerontology acute care nurse practitioner (MS, Advanced Certificate); adult-gerontology primary care nurse practitioner (MS, Advanced Certificate); family nurse practitioner (MS, Advanced Certificate); gerontology nurse practitioner (Advanced Certificate); nurse-midwifery (MS, Advanced Certificate); nursing administration (MS, Advanced Certificate); nursing education (MS, Advanced Certificate); nursing informatics (MS, Advanced Certificate); pediatrics nurse practitioner (MS, Advanced Certificate); psychiatric-mental health nurse practitioner (MS, Advanced Certificate); MS/MPH. *Accreditation:* AACN; ACNM/ACME. *Program availability:* Part-time, evening/weekend. *Degree requirements:* For master's, thesis (for some programs), capstone. *Entrance requirements:* For master's, BS in nursing, AS in nursing with another BS/BA, interview, RN license, 1 year of clinical experience (3 for the MS in nursing education program); for Advanced Certificate, master's degree in nursing. Additional exam requirements/recommendations for international students: required—TOEFL (minimum score 100 iBT), IELTS (minimum score 7). Electronic applications accepted. *Expenses:* Contact institution.

**Northeastern University,** Bouvé College of Health Sciences, Boston, MA 02115-5096. Offers applied behavior analysis (MS); audiology (Au D); counseling psychology (MS, PhD, CAGS); exercise science (MS); nursing (MS, PhD, CAGS), including administration (MS), adult-gerontology acute care nurse practitioner (MS, CAGS), adult-gerontology primary care nurse practitioner (MS, CAGS), anesthesia (MS), family nurse practitioner (MS, CAGS), neonatal nurse practitioner (MS, CAGS), pediatric nurse practitioner (MS, CAGS), psychiatric mental health nurse practitioner (MS, CAGS); nursing practice (DNP); pharmaceutical sciences (MS, PhD), including interdisciplinary concentration, pharmaceutics and drug delivery systems; pharmacology (MS); pharmacy (Pharm D); school psychology (PhD); speech-language pathology (MS); urban health (MPH); MS/MBA. *Accreditation:* AANA/CANAEP; ACPE (one or more programs are accredited); ASHA; CEPH. *Program availability:* Part-time, evening/weekend, online learning. *Degree requirements:* For doctorate, thesis/dissertation (for some programs); for CAGS, comprehensive exam. Electronic applications accepted. *Expenses:* Contact institution.

**Old Dominion University,** College of Health Sciences, School of Nursing, Adult Gerontology Nursing Emphasis, Norfolk, VA 23529. Offers adult gerontology clinical nurse specialist/administrator (MSN); adult gerontology clinical nurse specialist/educator (MSN); advanced practice (DNP); neonatal clinical nurse specialist (MSN); pediatric clinical nurse specialist (MSN). *Program availability:* Part-time, online only, blended/hybrid learning. *Degree requirements:* For master's, comprehensive exam, internship, practicum. *Entrance requirements:* For master's, GRE or MAT (waived with a GPA above 3.5), undergraduate health/physical assessment course, statistics, 3 letters of recommendation, essay, resume, transcripts. Additional exam requirements/recommendations for international students: required—TOEFL. Electronic applications accepted. *Expenses:* Contact institution.

**Old Dominion University,** College of Health Sciences, School of Nursing, Pediatric Nursing Emphasis, Norfolk, VA 23529. Offers advanced practice (DNP); pediatric clinical nurse specialist (MSN); pediatric nurse practitioner (MSN). *Program availability:* Part-time, blended/hybrid learning. *Degree requirements:* For master's, comprehensive exam; for doctorate, capstone project. *Entrance requirements:* For master's, GRE or MAT if the undergraduate GPA is below 3.5, current unencumbered license as a registered nurse (RN) with 1 year of current experience in the role; undergraduate physical/health assessment course; undergraduate statistics course; baccalaureate degree in nursing or related science field with minimum GPA of 3.0; three letters of recommendation. Additional exam requirements/recommendations for international students: required—TOEFL. Electronic applications accepted. *Expenses:* Contact institution.

**Oregon Health & Science University,** School of Nursing, Program in Pediatric Nurse Practitioner, Portland, OR 97239-3098. Offers MN. *Program availability:* Blended/hybrid learning. *Entrance requirements:* For master's, GRE General Test, bachelor's degree in nursing, minimum cumulative and science GPA of 3.0, 3 letters of recommendation, essay, statistics within last 5 years. Additional exam requirements/recommendations for international students: required—TOEFL (minimum score 83 iBT). Electronic applications accepted. *Expenses:* Contact institution.

**Point Loma Nazarene University,** School of Nursing, MS in Nursing Program, San Diego, CA 92106. Offers adult/gerontology (MSN); family/individual health (MSN); pediatrics (MSN). *Program availability:* Part-time. *Students:* 4 full-time (3 women), 49 part-time (41 women); includes 29 minority (5 Black or African American, non-Hispanic/Latino; 8 Asian, non-Hispanic/Latino; 14 Hispanic/Latino; 2 Two or more races, non-Hispanic/Latino). Average age 37. 30 applicants, 83% accepted, 14 enrolled. In 2019, 25 master's awarded. *Entrance requirements:* For master's, NCLEX exam, ADN or BSN in nursing, interview, RN license, essay, letters of recommendation, interview. *Application deadline:* For fall admission, 7/5 priority date for domestic students; for spring admission, 11/1 priority date for domestic students; for summer admission, 3/22 priority date for domestic students. Applications are processed on a rolling basis. Application fee: $50. Electronic applications accepted. *Expenses:* $820 per unit. *Financial support:* In 2019–20, 9 students received support. Scholarships/grants available. Financial award applicants required to submit FAFSA. *Unit head:* Dr. Larry Rankin, Associate Dean, 619-849-7813, E-mail: LarryRankin@pointloma.edu. *Application contact:* Dana Barger, Director of Recruitment and Admissions, Graduate and Professional Students, 619-329-6799, E-mail: gradinfo@pointloma.edu.
Website: https://www.pointloma.edu/graduate-studies/programs/nursing-ms

**Purdue University,** Graduate School, College of Health and Human Sciences, School of Nursing, West Lafayette, IN 47907. Offers adult gerontology primary care nurse practitioner (MS, Post Master's Certificate); nursing (DNP, PhD); primary care family nurse practitioner (MS, Post Master's Certificate); primary care pediatric nurse practitioner (MS, Post Master's Certificate). *Faculty:* 41 full-time (40 women), 9 part-time/adjunct (8 women). *Students:* 84 full-time (72 women), 46 part-time (43 women); includes 19 minority (7 Black or African American, non-Hispanic/Latino; 6 Asian, non-Hispanic/Latino; 4 Hispanic/Latino; 2 Two or more races, non-Hispanic/Latino), 1 international. Average age 33. 85 applicants, 80% accepted, 55 enrolled. In 2019, 29 master's, 7 doctorates, 2 other advanced degrees awarded. *Unit head:* Nancy E. Edwards, Head of the Graduate Program, 765-494-4015, E-mail: edwardsn@purdue.edu. *Application contact:* Reanne Hall, Graduate Contact, 765-494-9248, E-mail: gradnursing@purdue.edu.
Website: http://www.purdue.edu/hhs/nur/

**Queen's University at Kingston,** School of Graduate Studies, Faculty of Health Sciences, School of Nursing, Kingston, ON K7L 3N6, Canada. Offers health and chronic illness (M Sc); nurse scientist (PhD); primary health care nurse practitioner (Certificate); women's and children's health (M Sc). *Degree requirements:* For master's, thesis. *Entrance requirements:* For master's, RN license. Additional exam requirements/recommendations for international students: required—TOEFL.

**St. Catherine University,** Graduate Programs, Program in Nursing, St. Paul, MN 55105. Offers adult-gerontological nurse practitioner (MS); nurse educator (MS); nursing (DNP); nursing: entry-level (MS); pediatric nurse practitioner (MS). *Accreditation:* ACEN. *Program availability:* Part-time, evening/weekend. *Degree requirements:* For master's, thesis; for doctorate, portfolio, systems change project. *Entrance requirements:* For master's, GRE General Test, bachelor's degree in nursing, current nursing license, 2 years of recent clinical practice; for doctorate, master's degree in nursing, RN license, advanced nursing position. Additional exam requirements/recommendations for international students: required—TOEFL (minimum score 600 paper-based; 100 iBT). *Expenses:* Contact institution.

**San Francisco State University,** Division of Graduate Studies, College of Health and Social Sciences, School of Nursing, San Francisco, CA 94132-1722. Offers adult acute care (MS); clinical nurse specialist (MS); community/public health nursing (MS); family nurse practitioner (Certificate); nursing administration (MS); pediatrics (MS); women's health (MS). *Accreditation:* AACN. *Program availability:* Part-time. *Application deadline:* Applications are processed on a rolling basis. *Expenses: Tuition, area resident:* Full-time $7176; part-time $4164 per year. Tuition, state resident: full-time $7176; part-time $4164 per year. Tuition, nonresident: full-time $16,680; part-time $396 per unit. *International tuition:* $16,680 full-time. *Required fees:* $1524; $1524 per unit. $762 per semester. Tuition and fees vary according to degree level and program. *Financial support:* Career-related internships or fieldwork available. *Unit head:* Dr. Mary-Ann van Dam, 415-338-1802, Fax: 415-338-0555, E-mail: vandam@sfsu.edu. *Application contact:* Prof. Fang-yu Chou, Assistant Director of Graduate Programs, 415-338-6853, Fax: 415-338-0555, E-mail: fchou@sfsu.edu.
Website: http://nursing.sfsu.edu

**Seton Hall University,** College of Nursing, South Orange, NJ 07079-2697. Offers advanced practice in primary health care (MSN, DNP), including adult/gerontological nurse practitioner, pediatric nurse practitioner; entry into practice (MSN); health systems administration (MSN, DNP); nursing (PhD); nursing case management (MSN); nursing education (MA); school nurse (MSN); MSN/MA. *Accreditation:* AACN. *Program availability:* Part-time, online learning. *Degree requirements:* For master's, research project; for doctorate, dissertation or scholarly project. *Entrance requirements:* For doctorate, GRE (waived for students with GPA of 3.5 or higher). Additional exam requirements/recommendations for international students: required—TOEFL. Electronic applications accepted.

**Spalding University,** Graduate Studies, Kosair College of Health and Natural Sciences, School of Nursing, Louisville, KY 40203-2188. Offers adult nurse practitioner (MSN); family nurse practitioner (MSN); leadership in nursing and healthcare (MSN); nurse educator (Post-Master's Certificate); nurse practitioner (Post-Master's Certificate); pediatric nurse practitioner (MSN). *Accreditation:* AACN. *Program availability:* Part-time, evening/weekend. *Degree requirements:* For master's, comprehensive exam (for some programs), thesis. *Entrance requirements:* For master's, GRE General Test, BSN or bachelor's degree in related field, RN licensure, autobiographical statement, transcripts, letters of recommendation. Additional exam requirements/recommendations for international students: required—TOEFL (minimum score 535 paper-based).

**Stony Brook University, State University of New York,** Stony Brook Medicine, School of Nursing, Pediatric Primary Care Nurse Practitioner Program, Stony Brook, NY 11794. Offers child health nurse practitioner (Certificate); child health nursing (MS, DNP). *Accreditation:* AACN. *Program availability:* Part-time, blended/hybrid learning. *Students:* 2 full-time (both women), 153 part-time (149 women); includes 44 minority (17 Black or African American, non-Hispanic/Latino; 13 Asian, non-Hispanic/Latino; 14 Hispanic/Latino). 92 applicants, 77% accepted, 66 enrolled. In 2019, 42 master's, 2 other advanced degrees awarded. *Entrance requirements:* For master's, BSN, minimum GPA of 3.0, course work in statistics. Additional exam requirements/recommendations for international students: required—TOEFL (minimum score 90 iBT). *Application deadline:* For fall admission, 1/9 for domestic students. Application fee: $100. *Expenses:* Contact institution. *Financial support:* Application deadline: 3/15. *Unit head:* Dr. Maria Mcilazzo, Program Director, 631-444-3264, Fax: 631-444-3130, E-mail: maria.milazzo@stonybrook.edu. *Application contact:* Linda Sacino, Staff Assist., 631-444-3262, Fax: 631-444-3136, E-mail: linda.sacino@stonybrook.edu.
Website: https://nursing.stonybrookmedicine.edu/graduate

**Texas Christian University,** Harris College of Nursing and Health Sciences, Doctor of Nursing Practice Program, Fort Worth, TX 76129-0002. Offers clinical nurse specialist - adult/gerontology nursing (DNP); clinical nurse specialist - pediatrics (DNP); family nurse practitioner (DNP); general (DNP); nursing administration (DNP). *Accreditation:* AACN. *Program availability:* Part-time, 100% online, blended/hybrid learning. *Faculty:* 29 full-time (26 women), 1 (woman) part-time/adjunct. *Students:* 49 full-time (45 women), 13 part-time (10 women); includes 18 minority (9 Black or African American, non-Hispanic/Latino; 1 American Indian or Alaska Native, non-Hispanic/Latino; 3 Asian, non-Hispanic/Latino; 4 Hispanic/Latino; 1 Two or more races, non-Hispanic/Latino), 2 international. Average age 37. 57 applicants, 70% accepted, 24 enrolled. In 2019, 27 doctorates awarded. *Degree requirements:* For doctorate, thesis/dissertation or alternative, practicum. *Entrance requirements:* For doctorate, three reference letters, essay, resume, two official transcripts from each institution attended, APRN recognition or MSN with experience or certification in nursing administration, as applicable per track, current RN license, successful completion of interview. Additional exam requirements/recommendations for international students: required—TOEFL (minimum score 550 paper-based; 80 iBT). *Application deadline:* For summer admission, 1/15 for domestic and international students. Application fee: $60. Electronic applications accepted. Full-time tuition and fees vary according to program. *Financial support:* In 2019–20, 20 students received support. Scholarships/grants available. Financial award application deadline: 2/15; financial award applicants required to submit FAFSA. *Unit head:* Dr. Kathy Ellis, Division Director, Graduate Nursing, 817-257-6726, Fax: 817-257-7944, E-mail: kathryn.ellis@tcu.edu. *Application contact:* Beth Janke, Academic Program Specialist, 817-257-6726, Fax: 817-257-7944, E-mail: graduatenursing@tcu.edu.
Website: http://dnp.tcu.edu/

**Texas Christian University,** Harris College of Nursing and Health Sciences, Master's Program in Nursing, Fort Worth, TX 76129-0002. Offers administration and leadership (MSN); clinical nurse leader (MSN, Certificate); clinical nurse specialist (MSN), including adult/gerontology nursing, pediatrics; nursing education (MSN). *Accreditation:* AACN. *Program availability:* Part-time, online only, 100% online. *Faculty:* 29 full-time (26 women), 1 (woman) part-time/adjunct. *Students:* 12 full-time (all women), 5 part-time (all women); includes 5 minority (1 Asian, non-Hispanic/Latino; 4 Hispanic/Latino). Average

age 34. 41 applicants, 59% accepted, 8 enrolled. In 2019, 10 master's awarded. *Degree requirements:* For master's, thesis or alternative, practicum. *Entrance requirements:* For master's, 3 letters of reference, essay, resume, two official transcripts from every institution attended, current license to practice as a registered nurse. Additional exam requirements/recommendations for international students: required—TOEFL (minimum score 550 paper-based; 80 iBT). *Application deadline:* For spring admission, 8/15 for domestic and international students; for summer admission, 1/15 for domestic and international students. Application fee: $60. Electronic applications accepted. Full-time tuition and fees vary according to program. *Financial support:* In 2019–20, 15 students received support. Scholarships/grants available. Financial award application deadline: 2/15; financial award applicants required to submit FAFSA. *Unit head:* Dr. Kathy Ellis, Division Director, Graduate Nursing, 817-257-6726, Fax: 817-257-7944, E-mail: kathryn.ellis@tcu.edu. *Application contact:* Beth Janke, Academic Program Specialist, 817-257-6726, Fax: 817-257-7944, E-mail: graduatenursing@tcu.edu.
Website: http://www.nursing.tcu.edu/graduate.asp

**Texas Tech University Health Sciences Center,** School of Nursing, Lubbock, TX 79430. Offers acute care nurse practitioner (MSN, Certificate); administration (MSN); advanced practice (DNP); education (MSN); executive leadership (DNP); family nurse practitioner (MSN, Certificate); geriatric nurse practitioner (MSN, Certificate); pediatric nurse practitioner (MSN, Certificate). *Accreditation:* AACN. *Program availability:* Part-time, online learning. *Degree requirements:* For master's, thesis optional. *Entrance requirements:* For master's, minimum GPA of 3.0, 3 letters of reference, BSN, RN license; for Certificate, minimum GPA of 3.0, 3 letters of reference, RN license. Additional exam requirements/recommendations for international students: required—TOEFL (minimum score 550 paper-based).

**Texas Woman's University,** Graduate School, College of Nursing, Denton, TX 76204. Offers adult health clinical nurse specialist (MS); adult health nurse practitioner (MS); adult/gerontology acute care nurse practitioner (MS); child health clinical nurse specialist (MS); clinical nurse leader (MS); family nurse practitioner (MS); health systems management (MS); nursing education (MS); nursing practice (DNP); nursing science (PhD); pediatric nurse practitioner (MS); women's health clinical nurse specialist (MS); women's health nurse practitioner (MS). *Accreditation:* AACN. *Program availability:* Part-time, 100% online, blended/hybrid learning. *Faculty:* 48 full-time (47 women), 31 part-time/adjunct (24 women). *Students:* 42 full-time (40 women), 811 part-time (756 women); includes 481 minority (168 Black or African American, non-Hispanic/Latino; 2 American Indian or Alaska Native, non-Hispanic/Latino; 165 Asian, non-Hispanic/Latino; 118 Hispanic/Latino; 1 Native Hawaiian or other Pacific Islander, non-Hispanic/Latino; 27 Two or more races, non-Hispanic/Latino), 26 international. Average age 36. 435 applicants, 71% accepted, 172 enrolled. In 2019, 203 master's, 37 doctorates awarded. *Degree requirements:* For master's, comprehensive exam, thesis or alternative, 6-year time limit for completion of degree, professional or clinical project; for doctorate, comprehensive exam, thesis/dissertation, 10-year time limit for completion of degree; dissertation (PhD), assessment practicum (DPT). *Entrance requirements:* For master's, minimum GPA of 3.0 on last 60 hours in undergraduate nursing degree and overall, RN license, BS in nursing, basic statistics course; for doctorate, MS in nursing, minimum preferred GPA of 3.5, RN or APRN license, statistics course, 2 letters of reference, curriculum vitae, graduate nursing-theory course, graduate research course, statement of professional goals and research interests, 1 yr APRN experience. Additional exam requirements/recommendations for international students: required—TOEFL (minimum score 79 iBT); recommended—IELTS (minimum score 6.5), TSE (minimum score 53). *Application deadline:* For fall admission, 5/1 for domestic students, 3/1 priority date for international students; for spring admission, 9/15 for domestic students, 7/1 priority date for international students. Application fee: $50 ($75 for international students). Electronic applications accepted. *Expenses:* All are estimates. Tuition for 10 hours = $2,763; Fees for 10 hours = $1,342. Master's Nursing courses require additional $75/SCH; Doctoral Nursing courses require additional $80/SCH. *Financial support:* In 2019–20, 212 students received support, including 1 research assistantship, 6 teaching assistantships (averaging $12,029 per year); career-related internships or fieldwork, scholarships/grants, health care benefits, and unspecified assistantships also available. Support available to part-time students. Financial award application deadline: 3/1; financial award applicants required to submit FAFSA. *Unit head:* Dr. Rosalie Mainous, Dean, 940-898-2401, Fax: 940-898-2437, E-mail: nursing@twu.edu. *Application contact:* Korie Hawkins, Associate Director of Admissions, Graduate Recruitment, 940-898-3188, Fax: 940-898-3081, E-mail: admissions@twu.edu.
Website: http://www.twu.edu/nursing/

**The University of Alabama at Birmingham,** School of Nursing, Birmingham, AL 35294. Offers clinical nurse leader (MSN); nurse anesthesia (DNP); nurse practitioner (MSN, DNP), including adult-gerontology acute care (MSN), adult-gerontology primary care (MSN), family (MSN), pediatric (MSN), psychiatric/mental health (MSN), women's health (MSN); nursing (MSN, DNP, PhD); nursing health systems administration (MSN); nursing informatics (MSN). *Accreditation:* AACN; AANA/CANAEP. *Program availability:* Part-time, online only, blended/hybrid learning. *Faculty:* 86 full-time (79 women), 42 part-time/adjunct (35 women). *Students:* 228 full-time (165 women), 1,393 part-time (1,234 women); includes 398 minority (267 Black or African American, non-Hispanic/Latino; 4 American Indian or Alaska Native, non-Hispanic/Latino; 52 Asian, non-Hispanic/Latino; 41 Hispanic/Latino; 34 Two or more races, non-Hispanic/Latino), 3 international. Average age 33. 1,027 applicants, 55% accepted, 421 enrolled. In 2019, 557 master's, 19 doctorates awarded. Terminal master's awarded for partial completion of doctoral program. *Degree requirements:* For master's, comprehensive exam; for doctorate, comprehensive exam, thesis/dissertation, research mentorship experience (for PhD); scholarly project (for DNP). *Entrance requirements:* For master's, GRE, GMAT, or MAT, minimum cumulative undergraduate GPA of 3.0 or on last 60 semesters hours; letters of recommendation; for doctorate, GRE General Test, computer literacy, course work in statistics, interview, minimum GPA of 3.0, MS in nursing, references, writing sample. Additional exam requirements/recommendations for international students: required—TOEFL (minimum score 500 paper-based, 80 iBT) or IELTS (5.5). *Application deadline:* For fall admission, 2/24 for domestic students; for summer admission, 10/15 for domestic students. Application fee: $50. Electronic applications accepted. *Expenses:* Contact institution. *Financial support:* In 2019–20, 23 fellowships (averaging $34,685 per year), 12 research assistantships (averaging $9,042 per year), 2 teaching assistantships (averaging $22,000 per year) were awarded; scholarships/grants, traineeships, health care benefits, and unspecified assistantships also available. Support available to part-time students. *Unit head:* Dr. Doreen C. Harper, Dean, 205-934-5360, Fax: 205-934-1894, E-mail: dcharper@uab.edu. *Application contact:* John Updegraff, Director of Student Affairs, 205-975-3370, Fax: 205-934-5490, E-mail: jupde22@uab.edu.
Website: http://www.uab.edu/nursing/home/

**University of Cincinnati,** Graduate School, College of Nursing, Cincinnati, OH 45221-0038. Offers nurse midwifery (MSN); nurse practitioner (MSN, DNP), including acute care pediatrics (DNP), adult-gerontology acute care, adult-gerontology primary care, anesthesia (DNP), family (MSN), leadership (DNP), neonatal (MSN), women's health (MSN); nursing (MSN, PhD), including occupational health (MSN). *Accreditation:* AACN; AANA/CANAEP (one or more programs are accredited); ACNM/ACME. *Program*

*availability:* Part-time, 100% online, blended/hybrid learning. *Faculty:* 62 full-time (55 women), 125 part-time/adjunct (114 women). *Students:* 429 full-time (355 women), 1,547 part-time (1,390 women); includes 453 minority (226 Black or African American, non-Hispanic/Latino; 5 American Indian or Alaska Native, non-Hispanic/Latino; 68 Asian, non-Hispanic/Latino; 103 Hispanic/Latino; 3 Native Hawaiian or other Pacific Islander, non-Hispanic/Latino; 48 Two or more races, non-Hispanic/Latino), 15 international. Average age 36. 779 applicants, 78% accepted, 464 enrolled. In 2019, 518 master's, 47 doctorates awarded. *Degree requirements:* For master's, thesis or alternative; for doctorate, comprehensive exam (for some programs), thesis/dissertation (for some programs). *Entrance requirements:* For master's, GRE required only for the Direct-Entry Accelerated Program. Additional exam requirements/recommendations for international students: required—TOEFL (minimum score 600 paper-based; 100 iBT); recommended—IELTS (minimum score 7). *Application deadline:* For fall admission, 4/1 priority date for domestic and international students; for spring admission, 9/1 priority date for domestic and international students; for summer admission, 2/1 priority date for domestic and international students. Applications are processed on a rolling basis. Application fee: $135 ($140 for international students). Electronic applications accepted. *Expenses:* Contact institution. *Financial support:* In 2019–20, 103 students received support, including 9 fellowships with full tuition reimbursements available (averaging $18,595 per year), 7 research assistantships with full tuition reimbursements available (averaging $12,991 per year), 8 teaching assistantships with full tuition reimbursements available (averaging $12,991 per year); institutionally sponsored loans, scholarships/grants, traineeships, health care benefits, tuition waivers (partial), and unspecified assistantships also available. Support available to part-time students. Financial award application deadline: 4/1; financial award applicants required to submit FAFSA. *Unit head:* Dr. Greer Glazer, Dean, 513-558-5330, Fax: 513-558-9030, E-mail: greer.glazer@uc.edu. *Application contact:* Office of Student Affairs, 513-558-8400, E-mail: nursingbearcats@uc.edu.
Website: https://nursing.uc.edu/

**University of Colorado Denver,** College of Nursing, Aurora, CO 80045. Offers adult clinical nurse specialist (MS); adult nurse practitioner (MS); family nurse practitioner (MS); family psychiatric mental health nurse practitioner (MS); health care informatics (MS); nurse-midwifery (MS); nursing (DNP, PhD); nursing leadership and health care systems (MS); pediatric nurse practitioner (MS); women's health (MS); MS/PhD. *Accreditation:* ACNM/ACME (one or more programs are accredited). *Program availability:* Part-time, evening/weekend, online learning. Terminal master's awarded for partial completion of doctoral program. *Degree requirements:* For master's, thesis optional; for doctorate, comprehensive exam, thesis/dissertation, 42 credits of coursework. *Entrance requirements:* For master's, GRE if cumulative undergraduate GPA is less than 3.0, undergraduate nursing degree from ACEN- or CCNE-accredited school or university; completion of research and statistics courses with minimum grade of C; copy of current and unencumbered nursing license; for doctorate, GRE, bachelor's and/or master's degrees in nursing from ACEN- or CCNE-accredited institution; portfolio; minimum undergraduate GPA of 3.0, graduate 3.5; graduate-level intermediate statistics and master's-level nursing theory courses with minimum B grade; interview. Additional exam requirements/recommendations for international students: required—TOEFL (minimum score 560 paper-based; 83 iBT). Electronic applications accepted. *Expenses:* Contact institution.

**University of Delaware,** College of Health Sciences, School of Nursing, Newark, DE 19716. Offers adult nurse practitioner (MSN, PMC); cardiopulmonary clinical nurse specialist (MSN, PMC); cardiopulmonary clinical nurse specialist/adult nurse practitioner (MSN, PMC); family nurse practitioner (MSN, PMC); gerontology clinical nurse specialist (MSN, PMC); gerontology clinical nurse specialist geriatric nurse practitioner (PMC); gerontology clinical nurse specialist/geriatric nurse practitioner (MSN); health services administration (MSN, PMC); nursing of children clinical nurse specialist (MSN, PMC); nursing of children clinical nurse specialist/pediatric nurse practitioner (MSN, PMC); oncology/immune deficiency clinical nurse specialist (MSN, PMC); oncology/immune deficiency clinical nurse specialist/adult nurse practitioner (MSN, PMC); perinatal/women's health clinical nurse specialist (MSN, PMC); perinatal/women's health clinical nurse specialist/women's health nurse practitioner (MSN, PMC); psychiatric nursing clinical nurse specialist (MSN, PMC). *Accreditation:* AACN. *Program availability:* Part-time, evening/weekend, online learning. *Degree requirements:* For master's, thesis optional. *Entrance requirements:* For master's, BSN, interview, RN license. Electronic applications accepted.

**University of Illinois at Chicago,** College of Nursing, Program in Nursing, Chicago, IL 60607-7128. Offers acute care clinical nurse specialist (MS); administrative nursing leadership (Certificate); adult nurse practitioner (MS); adult/geriatric nurse practitioner (MS); advanced community health nurse specialist (MS); family nurse practitioner (MS); geriatric clinical nurse specialist (MS); geriatric nurse practitioner (MS); nurse midwifery (MS); occupational health/advanced community health nurse specialist (MS); occupational health/family nurse practitioner (MS); pediatric nurse practitioner (MS); perinatal clinical nurse specialist (MS); school/advanced community health nurse specialist (MS); school/family nurse practitioner (MS); women's health nurse practitioner (MS). *Accreditation:* AACN. *Program availability:* Part-time. *Degree requirements:* For master's, thesis or alternative. *Entrance requirements:* For master's, GRE General Test, minimum GPA of 2.75. Additional exam requirements/recommendations for international students: required—TOEFL. Electronic applications accepted.

**University of Maryland, Baltimore,** University of Maryland School of Nursing, Baltimore, MD 21201. Offers adult-gerontology acute care nurse practitioner (DNP); adult-gerontology primary care nurse practitioner (DNP); clinical nurse leader (MS); community/public health nursing (MS); family nurse practitioner (DNP); global health (Postbaccalaureate Certificate); health services leadership and management (MS); neonatal nurse practitioner (DNP); nurse anesthesia (DNP); nursing (PhD); nursing informatics (MS, Postbaccalaureate Certificate); pediatric acute/primary care nurse practitioner (DNP); psychiatric mental health nurse practitioner (DNP); teaching in nursing and health professions (Postbaccalaureate Certificate); MS/MBA. *Accreditation:* AANA/CANAEP. *Program availability:* Part-time. *Faculty:* 130 full-time (117 women), 125 part-time/adjunct (114 women). *Students:* 539 full-time (463 women), 586 part-time (506 women); includes 485 minority (259 Black or African American, non-Hispanic/Latino; 3 American Indian or Alaska Native, non-Hispanic/Latino; 124 Asian, non-Hispanic/Latino; 66 Hispanic/Latino; 1 Native Hawaiian or other Pacific Islander, non-Hispanic/Latino; 32 Two or more races, non-Hispanic/Latino), 18 international. Average age 33. 964 applicants, 54% accepted, 347 enrolled. In 2019, 197 master's, 114 doctorates, 12 other advanced degrees awarded. *Degree requirements:* For master's and Postbaccalaureate Certificate, thesis (for some programs); for doctorate, comprehensive exam, thesis/dissertation. *Entrance requirements:* Additional exam requirements/recommendations for international students: required—TOEFL (minimum score 550 paper-based; 79 iBT); recommended—IELTS (minimum score 7). *Application deadline:* For fall admission, 11/1 priority date for domestic and international students; for spring admission, 12/15 for domestic and international students; for summer admission, 9/1 for domestic and international students. Applications are processed on a rolling basis. Application fee: $75. Electronic applications accepted. *Financial support:* In 2019–20, 257 students received support, including 31 research assistantships with full and partial tuition reimbursements available (averaging $25,000 per year), 21

teaching assistantships with full and partial tuition reimbursements available (averaging $19,000 per year); scholarships/grants, traineeships, and unspecified assistantships also available. Support available to part-time students. Financial award application deadline: 3/1; financial award applicants required to submit FAFSA. *Unit head:* Dr. Jane Kirschling, Dean, 410-706-4359, E-mail: kirschling@umaryland.edu. *Application contact:* Larry Fillian, Associate Dean of Student and Academic Services, 410-706-6298, E-mail: lfillian@umaryland.edu.
Website: http://www.nursing.umaryland.edu/

**University of Michigan,** Rackham Graduate School, School of Nursing, Ann Arbor, MI 48109. Offers acute care pediatric nurse practitioner (MS); nursing (DNP, PhD, Post Master's Certificate). *Accreditation:* AACN; ACNM/ACME (one or more programs are accredited). *Program availability:* Part-time, online learning. Terminal master's awarded for partial completion of doctoral program. *Degree requirements:* For doctorate, thesis/dissertation.

**University of Minnesota, Twin Cities Campus,** Graduate School, School of Nursing, Minneapolis, MN 55455-0213. Offers adult/gerontological clinical nurse specialist (DNP); adult/gerontological primary care nurse practitioner (DNP); family nurse practitioner (DNP); health innovation and leadership (DNP); integrative health and healing (DNP); nurse anesthesia (DNP); nurse midwifery (DNP); nursing (MN, PhD); nursing informatics (DNP); pediatric clinical nurse specialist (DNP); primary care certified pediatric nurse practitioner (DNP); psychiatric/mental health nurse practitioner (DNP); women's health nurse practitioner (DNP). *Accreditation:* AACN; AANA/CANAEP; ACNM/ACME (one or more programs are accredited). *Program availability:* Part-time, online learning. Terminal master's awarded for partial completion of doctoral program. *Degree requirements:* For master's, final oral exam, project or thesis; for doctorate, thesis/dissertation. *Entrance requirements:* For master's and doctorate, GRE General Test. Additional exam requirements/recommendations for international students: required—TOEFL (minimum score 586 paper-based). *Expenses:* Contact institution.

**University of Missouri,** Office of Research and Graduate Studies, Sinclair School of Nursing, Columbia, MO 65211. Offers adult-gerontology clinical nurse specialist (DNP, Certificate); family nurse practitioner (DNP); family psychiatric and mental health nurse practitioner (DNP); nursing (MS, PhD); nursing leadership and innovations in health care (DNP); pediatric clinical nurse specialist (DNP, Certificate); pediatric nurse practitioner (DNP). *Accreditation:* AACN. *Program availability:* Part-time. *Degree requirements:* For master's, thesis optional, oral exam; for doctorate, thesis/dissertation. *Entrance requirements:* For master's, GRE General Test, BSN, minimum GPA of 3.0 during last 60 hours, nursing license. Additional exam requirements/recommendations for international students: required—TOEFL, IELTS. Electronic applications accepted.

**University of Missouri–Kansas City,** School of Nursing and Health Studies, Kansas City, MO 64110-2499. Offers adult clinical nurse specialist (MSN), including adult nurse practitioner, women's health nurse practitioner (MSN, DNP); adult clinical nursing practice (DNP), including adult gerontology nurse practitioner, women's health nurse practitioner (MSN, DNP); clinical nursing practice (DNP), including family nurse practitioner; neonatal nurse practitioner (MSN); nurse educator (MSN); nurse executive (MSN); nursing practice (DNP); pediatric clinical nursing practice (DNP), including pediatric nurse practitioner; pediatric nurse practitioner (MSN). *Accreditation:* AACN. *Program availability:* Part-time, online learning. *Degree requirements:* For master's, thesis or alternative. *Entrance requirements:* For master's, minimum undergraduate GPA of 3.2; for doctorate, GRE, 3 letters of reference. Additional exam requirements/recommendations for international students: required—TOEFL (minimum score 550 paper-based; 80 iBT).

**University of Missouri–St. Louis,** College of Nursing, St. Louis, MO 63121. Offers adult/geriatric nurse practitioner (Post Master's Certificate); family nurse practitioner (Post Master's Certificate); nursing (DNP, PhD); pediatric acute care nurse practitioner (Post Master's Certificate); pediatric nurse practitioner (Post Master's Certificate); psychiatric-mental health nurse practitioner (Post Master's Certificate); women's health nurse practitioner (Post Master's Certificate). *Accreditation:* AACN. *Program availability:* Part-time. *Degree requirements:* For doctorate, comprehensive exam, thesis/dissertation; for Post Master's Certificate, thesis. *Entrance requirements:* For doctorate, GRE, 2 letters of recommendation, MSN, minimum GPA of 3.2, course in differential/inferential statistics; for Post Master's Certificate, 2 recommendation letters; MSN; advanced practice certificate; minimum GPA of 3.0; essay. Additional exam requirements/recommendations for international students: recommended—TOEFL (minimum score 550 paper-based; 79 iBT), IELTS (minimum score 6.5). Electronic applications accepted. *Expenses: Tuition, area resident:* Full-time $9005.40; part-time $6003.60 per credit hour. Tuition, state resident: full-time $9005.40; part-time $6003.60 per credit hour. Tuition, nonresident: full-time $22,108; part-time $14,738.40 per credit hour. *International tuition:* $22,108 full-time. Tuition and fees vary according to course load.

**The University of North Carolina at Chapel Hill,** School of Nursing, Chapel Hill, NC 27599-7460. Offers advanced practice registered nurse (DNP); nursing (MSN, PhD, PMC), including administration (MSN), adult gerontology primary care nurse practitioner (MSN), clinical nurse leader (MSN), education (MSN), health care systems (PMC), informatics (MSN, PMC), nursing leadership (PMC), outcomes management (MSN), primary care family nurse practitioner (MSN), primary care pediatric nurse practitioner (MSN), psychiatric/mental health nurse practitioner (MSN, PMC). *Accreditation:* AACN; ACEN (one or more programs are accredited). *Program availability:* Part-time. *Degree requirements:* For master's, comprehensive exam, thesis; for doctorate, thesis/dissertation, 3 exams; for PMC, thesis. *Entrance requirements:* Additional exam requirements/recommendations for international students: required—TOEFL (minimum score 575 paper-based; 89 iBT), IELTS (minimum score 8). Electronic applications accepted.

**University of Pennsylvania,** School of Nursing, Pediatric Acute Care Nurse Practitioner Program, Philadelphia, PA 19104. Offers MSN. *Accreditation:* AACN. *Program availability:* Part-time, online learning. *Students:* 8 full-time (all women), 51 part-time (48 women); includes 8 minority (2 Black or African American, non-Hispanic/Latino; 5 Asian, non-Hispanic/Latino; 1 Two or more races, non-Hispanic/Latino), 1 international. Average age 27. 46 applicants, 74% accepted, 30 enrolled. In 2019, 34 master's awarded. Application fee: $80.

**University of Pennsylvania,** School of Nursing, Pediatric Clinical Nurse Specialist Program, Philadelphia, PA 19104. Offers MSN. *Accreditation:* AACN. *Students:* 11 full-time (all women), 12 part-time (11 women); includes 2 minority (1 Asian, non-Hispanic/Latino; 1 Hispanic/Latino). Average age 28. 26 applicants, 50% accepted, 8 enrolled. In 2019, 17 master's awarded. Application fee: $80. *Financial support:* Application deadline: 4/1. *Unit head:* Assistant Dean of Admissions and Financial Aid, 866-867-6877, Fax: 215-573-8439, E-mail: admissions@nursing.upenn.edu. *Application contact:* Judy Verger, Senior Lecturer, 215-898-4271, E-mail: jtv@nursing.upenn.edu.
Website: http://www.nursing.upenn.edu/peds/

**University of Pennsylvania,** School of Nursing, Pediatric Primary Care Nurse Practitioner Program, Philadelphia, PA 19104. Offers MSN. *Accreditation:* AACN. *Program availability:* Part-time. *Students:* 7 part-time (6 women). Average age 32. 10 applicants, 50% accepted, 4 enrolled. In 2019, 4 master's awarded. Application fee: $80.

**University of Puerto Rico - Medical Sciences Campus,** School of Nursing, San Juan, PR 00936-5067. Offers adult and elderly nursing (MSN); child and adolescent nursing (MSN); critical care nursing (MSN); family and community nursing (MSN); family nurse practitioner (MSN); maternity nursing (MSN); mental health and psychiatric nursing (MSN). *Accreditation:* AACN; AANA/CANAEP. *Entrance requirements:* For master's, GRE or EXADEP, interview, Puerto Rico RN license or professional license for international students, general and specific point average, article analysis. Electronic applications accepted.

**University of Rochester,** School of Nursing, Rochester, NY 14642. Offers adult gerontological acute care nurse practitioner (MS); adult gerontological primary care nurse practitioner (MS); clinical nurse leader (MS); family nurse practitioner (MS); family psychiatric mental health nurse practitioner (MS); health care organization management and leadership (MS); nursing (DNP); nursing and health science (PhD); nursing education (MS); pediatric nurse practitioner (MS); pediatric nurse practitioner/neonatal nurse practitioner (MS). *Accreditation:* AACN. *Program availability:* Part-time, 100% online, blended/hybrid learning. Terminal master's awarded for partial completion of doctoral program. *Degree requirements:* For master's, comprehensive exam; for doctorate, thesis/dissertation. *Entrance requirements:* For master's, BS in nursing, RN license; for doctorate, GRE General Test (for PhD), B.S. degree, RN license most programs. Additional exam requirements/recommendations for international students: required—TOEFL (minimum score 560 paper-based; 88 iBT), TOEFL (minimum score 560 paper-based; 88 iBT) or IELTS (minimum score 6.5) recommended. Electronic applications accepted. *Expenses:* Contact institution.

**University of San Diego,** Hahn School of Nursing and Health Science, San Diego, CA 92110-2492. Offers adult-gerontology clinical nurse specialist (MSN); adult-gerontology nurse practitioner/family nurse practitioner (MSN); clinical nurse leader (MSN); executive nurse leader (MSN); family nurse practitioner (MSN); healthcare informatics (MS); master's entry program in clinical nursing (for non-rns) (MSN); nursing (PhD); nursing informatics (MSN); nursing practice (DNP); psychiatric-mental health nurse practitioner (MSN). *Accreditation:* AACN. *Program availability:* Part-time, evening/weekend. *Faculty:* 28 full-time (23 women), 43 part-time/adjunct (32 women). *Students:* 252 full-time (202 women), 288 part-time (227 women); includes 261 minority (53 Black or African American, non-Hispanic/Latino; 2 American Indian or Alaska Native, non-Hispanic/Latino; 106 Asian, non-Hispanic/Latino; 76 Hispanic/Latino; 24 Two or more races, non-Hispanic/Latino), 24 international. Average age 34. In 2019, 174 master's, 47 doctorates awarded. *Degree requirements:* For doctorate, thesis/dissertation (for some programs), residency (DNP). *Entrance requirements:* For master's, GRE General Test (for entry-level nursing), BSN, current California RN licensure (except for entry-level nursing), minimum GPA of 3.0; for doctorate, minimum GPA of 3.5, MSN, current California RN licensure. Additional exam requirements/recommendations for international students: required—TOEFL (minimum score 580 paper-based; 83 iBT), TWE. *Application deadline:* Applications are processed on a rolling basis. Application fee: $55. Electronic applications accepted. *Financial support:* In 2019–20, 284 students received support. Institutionally sponsored loans, scholarships/grants, and traineeships available. Support available to part-time students. Financial award application deadline: 4/1; financial award applicants required to submit FAFSA. *Unit head:* Dr. Jane Georges, Dean, Hahn School of Nursing and Health Science, 619-260-4550, Fax: 619-260-6814, E-mail: nursing@sandiego.edu. *Application contact:* Erika Garwood, Associate Director of Graduate Admissions, 619-260-4524, Fax: 619-260-4158, E-mail: grads@sandiego.edu.
Website: http://www.sandiego.edu/nursing/

**University of South Carolina,** The Graduate School, College of Nursing, Program in Health Nursing, Columbia, SC 29208. Offers adult nurse practitioner (MSN); community/public health clinical nurse specialist (MSN); family nurse practitioner (MSN); pediatric nurse practitioner (MSN). *Accreditation:* AACN. *Program availability:* Part-time. *Degree requirements:* For master's, thesis or alternative. *Entrance requirements:* For master's, GRE General Test or MAT, BS in nursing, nursing license. Additional exam requirements/recommendations for international students: required—TOEFL (minimum score 570 paper-based). Electronic applications accepted.

**University of South Florida,** College of Nursing, Tampa, FL 33612. Offers nurse anesthesia (DNP); nursing (MS, DNP), including adult-gerontology acute care nursing, adult-gerontology primary care nursing, family health nursing, nurse anesthesia (MS), nursing education (MS), occupational health nursing/adult-gerontology primary care nursing, oncology nursing/adult-gerontology primary care nursing (DNP), pediatric health nursing; nursing education (Post Master's Certificate); nursing science (PhD); simulation based academic fellowship in advanced pain management (Graduate Certificate). *Accreditation:* AACN; AANA/CANAEP. *Program availability:* Part-time. *Faculty:* 34 full-time (28 women), 2 part-time/adjunct (1 woman). *Students:* 265 full-time (207 women), 687 part-time (594 women); includes 343 minority (113 Black or African American, non-Hispanic/Latino; 1 American Indian or Alaska Native, non-Hispanic/Latino; 60 Asian, non-Hispanic/Latino; 141 Hispanic/Latino; 1 Native Hawaiian or other Pacific Islander, non-Hispanic/Latino; 27 Two or more races, non-Hispanic/Latino), 2 international. Average age 33. 955 applicants, 44% accepted, 343 enrolled. In 2019, 281 master's, 80 doctorates awarded. *Degree requirements:* For master's, comprehensive exam, thesis optional; for doctorate, comprehensive exam, thesis/dissertation (for some programs). *Entrance requirements:* For master's, GRE General Test, bachelor's in nursing or RN with Bachelor's in relevant field; current license as Registered Nurse; resume or CV; interview; pre-reqs may be required; for doctorate, GRE General Test (recommended), bachelor's degree in nursing from ACEN or CCNE regionally-accredited institution with minimum GPA of 3.0 in all coursework or in all upper-division coursework; current license as Registered Nurse in Florida; undergraduate statistics course with minimum B grade; 3 letters of recommendation; statement of goals; resume; interview. Additional exam requirements/recommendations for international students: required—TOEFL (minimum score 550 paper-based; 79 iBT). *Application deadline:* For fall admission, 12/15 for domestic and international students; for spring admission, 10/1 for domestic students, 9/15 for international students. Application fee: $30. Electronic applications accepted. *Financial support:* In 2019–20, 181 students received support, including 7 research assistantships with tuition reimbursements available (averaging $18,935 per year), 29 teaching assistantships with tuition reimbursements available (averaging $30,814 per year); tuition waivers (partial) and unspecified assistantships also available. Financial award application deadline: 2/1; financial award applicants required to submit FAFSA. *Unit head:* Dr. Victoria Rich, Dean, College of Nursing, 813-974-8939, Fax: 813-974-5418, E-mail: victoriarich@health.usf.edu. *Application contact:* Dr. Denise Maguire, Vice Dean, Graduate Programs, 813-396-9962, E-mail: dmaguire@health.usf.edu.
Website: http://health.usf.edu/nursing/index.htm

**The University of Tennessee Health Science Center,** College of Nursing, Memphis, TN 38163. Offers adult-gerontology acute care nurse practitioner (Post Master's Certificate); advance practice nursing (DNP); family nurse practitioner (Post-Doctoral Certificate); pediatric acute care nurse practitioner (Post-Doctoral Certificate); pediatric primary care nurse practitioner (Post-Doctoral Certificate); psychiatric/mental health nurse practitioner (Post-Doctoral Certificate); registered nurse first assistant (Certificate). *Accreditation:* AACN; AANA/CANAEP. *Program availability:* Part-time,

blended/hybrid learning. *Faculty:* 62 full-time (55 women), 7 part-time/adjunct (2 women). *Students:* 226 full-time (187 women), 28 part-time (26 women); includes 80 minority (63 Black or African American, non-Hispanic/Latino; 15 Asian, non-Hispanic/Latino; 2 Hispanic/Latino). Average age 33. 652 applicants, 20% accepted, 104 enrolled. In 2019, 86 doctorates, 2 Certificates awarded. *Degree requirements:* For doctorate, project. *Entrance requirements:* For doctorate, RN license, minimum GPA of 3.0; http://www.uthsc.edu/nursing/dnp-admission-requirements.php; for other advanced degree, MSN, APN license, minimum GPA of 3.0; http://www.uthsc.edu/nursing/dnp-admission-requirements.php. Additional exam requirements/recommendations for international students: required—TOEFL (minimum score 550 paper-based; 80 iBT). *Application deadline:* For fall admission, 1/15 for domestic students; for spring admission, 8/15 for domestic students. Application fee: $70. Electronic applications accepted. *Expenses:* $5400 tuition, $450 fees, $110 loan fees, $5790 room/board, $2137 books/supplies, $1260 transportation, $2339 miscellaneous, $450 out-of-state tuition surcharge. *Financial support:* In 2019–20, 112 students received support, including 16 research assistantships (averaging $229,578 per year); Federal Work-Study, institutionally sponsored loans, scholarships/grants, and tuition waivers (partial) also available. Financial award application deadline: 3/15; financial award applicants required to submit FAFSA. *Unit head:* Dr. Wendy Likes, Dean, 901-448-6135, Fax: 901-448-4121, E-mail: wlikes@uthsc.edu. *Application contact:* Glynis Blackard, Assistant Dean for Student Affairs, 901-448-6139, Fax: 901-448-4121, E-mail: gblackar@uthsc.edu.
Website: http://uthsc.edu/nursing/

**The University of Texas at Austin,** Graduate School, School of Nursing, Austin, TX 78712-1111. Offers adult - gerontology clinical nurse specialist (MSN); child health (MSN), including administration, public health nursing, teaching; family nurse practitioner (MSN); family psychiatric/mental health nurse practitioner (MSN); holistic adult health (MSN), including administration, teaching; maternity (MSN), including administration, public health nursing, teaching; nursing (PhD); nursing administration and healthcare systems management (MSN); nursing practice (DNP); pediatric nurse practitioner (MSN); public health nursing (MSN). *Accreditation:* AACN. *Program availability:* Part-time. *Degree requirements:* For master's, thesis optional; for doctorate, thesis/dissertation. *Entrance requirements:* For master's and doctorate, GRE General Test. Additional exam requirements/recommendations for international students: required—TOEFL (minimum score 550 paper-based). Electronic applications accepted.

**The University of Texas Health Science Center at San Antonio,** School of Nursing, San Antonio, TX 78229-3900. Offers administrative management (MSN); adult-gerontology acute care nurse practitioner (PGC); advanced practice leadership (DNP); clinical nurse leader (MSN); executive administrative management (DNP); family nurse practitioner (MSN, PGC); nursing (MSN, PhD); nursing education (MSN, PGC); pediatric nurse practitioner primary care (PGC); psychiatric mental health nurse practitioner (PGC); public health nurse leader (DNP). *Accreditation:* AACN. *Program availability:* Part-time. Terminal master's awarded for partial completion of doctoral program. *Degree requirements:* For master's, thesis optional; for doctorate, comprehensive exam, thesis/dissertation.

**The University of Toledo,** College of Graduate Studies, College of Nursing, Department of Population and Community Care, Toledo, OH 43606-3390. Offers clinical nurse leader (MSN); family nurse practitioner (MSN, Certificate); nurse educator (MSN, Certificate); pediatric nurse practitioner (MSN, Certificate). *Program availability:* Part-time. *Degree requirements:* For master's, thesis or alternative. *Entrance requirements:* For master's, GRE, BS in nursing, minimum undergraduate GPA of 3.0, statement of purpose, three letters of recommendation, transcripts from all prior institutions attended, Nursing CAS application, UT supplemental application; for Certificate, BS in nursing, minimum undergraduate GPA of 3.0, statement of purpose, three letters of recommendation, transcripts from all prior institutions attended. Additional exam requirements/recommendations for international students: required—TOEFL (minimum score 550 paper-based; 80 iBT). Electronic applications accepted.

**University of Wisconsin–Madison,** School of Nursing, Madison, WI 53705. Offers adult/gerontology (DNP), including clinical nurse specialist; adult/gerontology acute care (DNP), including nurse practitioner; adult/gerontology primary care (DNP), including nurse practitioner; nursing (PhD); MS/MPH. *Accreditation:* AACN. *Program availability:* Part-time. *Degree requirements:* For doctorate, comprehensive exam, thesis/dissertation. *Entrance requirements:* For doctorate, GRE, bachelor's degree in nursing, undergraduate GPA of at least 3.0 on the last 60 credits, academic references, 2 original papers or other scholarly work, essay, RN license (for DNP), 1 year of professional nursing experience (for DNP). Additional exam requirements/recommendations for international students: required—TOEFL (minimum score 580 paper-based; 92 iBT), IELTS (minimum score 7). Electronic applications accepted. *Expenses:* Contact institution.

**Villanova University,** M. Louise Fitzpatrick College of Nursing, Villanova, PA 19085. Offers adult-gerontology primary care nurse practitioner (MSN, Post Master's Certificate); family primary care nurse practitioner (MSN, Post Master's Certificate); nurse anesthesia (DNP); nursing (PhD); nursing education (MSN, Post Master's Certificate); nursing practice (DNP); pediatric primary care nurse practitioner (MSN, Post Master's Certificate). *Accreditation:* AACN; AANA/CANAEP. *Program availability:* Part-time, online learning. *Entrance requirements:* Additional exam requirements/recommendations for international students: required—TOEFL, IELTS. Electronic applications accepted.

**Virginia Commonwealth University,** Graduate School, School of Nursing, Richmond, VA 23284-9005. Offers adult health acute nursing (MS); adult health primary nursing (MS); biobehavioral clinical research (PhD); child health nursing (MS); clinical nurse leader (MS); family health nursing (MS); nurse educator (MS); nurse practitioner (MS); nursing (Certificate); nursing administration (MS), including clinical nurse manager; psychiatric-mental health nursing (MS); quality and safety in health care (DNP); women's health nursing (MS). *Accreditation:* AACN; ACEN (one or more programs are accredited). *Program availability:* Part-time, evening/weekend, online learning. *Degree requirements:* For master's, thesis optional; for doctorate, thesis/dissertation. *Entrance requirements:* For master's, GRE General Test, BSN, minimum GPA of 2.8; for doctorate, GRE General Test. Additional exam requirements/recommendations for international students: required—TOEFL (minimum score 600 paper-based; 100 iBT). Electronic applications accepted.

**Wayne State University,** College of Nursing, Detroit, MI 48202. Offers adult gerontology acute care nurse practitioner (MSN); adult gerontology primary care nurse practitioner (MSN); advanced public health nursing (MSN); infant and mental health (DNP, PhD); neonatal nurse practitioner (MSN); nurse-midwifery (MSN); pediatric acute care nurse practitioner (MSN); pediatric primary care nurse practitioner (MSN); psychiatric mental health nurse practitioner (MSN); women's health nurse practitioner (MSN). *Accreditation:* AACN; ACNM/ACME. *Program availability:* Part-time. *Faculty:* 27. *Students:* 134 full-time (118 women), 216 part-time (187 women); includes 98 minority (51 Black or African American, non-Hispanic/Latino; 24 Asian, non-Hispanic/Latino; 6 Hispanic/Latino; 17 Two or more races, non-Hispanic/Latino), 18 international. Average age 33. 425 applicants, 37% accepted, 95 enrolled. In 2019, 58 master's, 31 doctorates awarded. *Degree requirements:* For doctorate, thesis/dissertation. *Entrance requirements:* For master's, Completed a Bachelor of Science in Nursing with a 3.0 or higher GPA. Official transcripts. Professional competence as documented by three references. Current Michigan Registered Nurse (RN) licensure. A personal statement of goals for graduate study; for doctorate, DNP: Minimum GPA of 3.0 or higher in BSN is required. Resume or Curriculum Vita that includes education, work and/or research experience. Two references, one from a doctorally prepared individual. RN license. PhD: BSN transcript; Two to three references from doctorally prepared individuals; goals statement; Resume or CV; Interview. Additional exam requirements/recommendations for international students: required—TOEFL (minimum score 101 iBT), TWE (minimum score 6), Michigan English Language Assessment Battery (minimum score 85); recommended—IELTS (minimum score 7). *Application deadline:* For fall admission, 1/31 for domestic students; for winter admission, 11/1 for domestic students. Applications are processed on a rolling basis. Application fee: $50. Electronic applications accepted. *Expenses:* $925.72 per credit hour in-state, $1,716.93 per credit hour out-of-state, $54.56 student service credit hour fee, $315.70 registration fee. *Financial support:* In 2019–20, 104 students received support, including 39 fellowships with tuition reimbursements available (averaging $6,456 per year), 1 research assistantship (averaging $24,950 per year), 5 teaching assistantships with tuition reimbursements available (averaging $25,000 per year); scholarships/grants, health care benefits, and unspecified assistantships also available. Support available to part-time students. Financial award application deadline: 3/1; financial award applicants required to submit FAFSA. *Unit head:* Dr. Laurie M Lauzon Clabo, Dean, College of Nursing, 313-577-4082, E-mail: laurie.lauzon.clabo@wayne.edu. *Application contact:* Dr. Laurie M Lauzon Clabo, Dean, College of Nursing, 313-577-4082, E-mail: laurie.lauzon.clabo@wayne.edu.
Website: http://nursing.wayne.edu/

**Wayne State University,** Eugene Applebaum College of Pharmacy and Health Sciences, Department of Health Care Sciences, Detroit, MI 48201. Offers nurse anesthesia (MS, DNP-A, Certificate), including anesthesia (MS), nurse anesthesia practice (DNP-A), pediatric anesthesia (Certificate); occupational therapy (MOT); physical therapy (DPT); physician assistant studies (MS). *Faculty:* 5. *Students:* 310 full-time (209 women), 4 part-time (all women); includes 33 minority (7 Black or African American, non-Hispanic/Latino; 14 Asian, non-Hispanic/Latino; 8 Hispanic/Latino; 4 Two or more races, non-Hispanic/Latino), 4 international. Average age 26. 344 applicants, 20% accepted, 55 enrolled. In 2019, 97 master's, 36 doctorates awarded. *Entrance requirements:* Additional exam requirements/recommendations for international students: required—TOEFL (minimum score 550 paper-based; 79 iBT), Michigan English Language Assessment Battery (minimum score 85); recommended—IELTS (minimum score 6.5), TWE (minimum score 5.5). Application fee: $50. Electronic applications accepted. *Expenses:* Contact institution. *Financial support:* In 2019–20, 102 students received support. Fellowships and scholarships/grants available. Financial award applicants required to submit FAFSA. *Unit head:* Dr. Sara F Maher, Chair Department of Health Care Sciences, 313-577-5630, E-mail: sara.maher@wayne.edu. *Application contact:* Office of Student and Alumni Affairs, 313-577-1716, E-mail: cphsinfo@wayne.edu.
Website: http://cphs.wayne.edu/hcs/

**Wright State University,** Graduate School, College of Nursing and Health, Program in Nursing, Dayton, OH 45435. Offers administration of nursing and health care systems (MS); adult gerontology clinical nurse specialist (MS); adult-gerontology acute care nurse practitioner (MS); family nurse practitioner (MS); neonatal nurse practitioner (MS); pediatric nurse practitioner-acute care (MS); pediatric nurse practitioner-primary care (MS); psychiatric mental health nurse practitioner (MS); school nurse (MS). *Accreditation:* AACN. *Program availability:* Part-time, evening/weekend. *Degree requirements:* For master's, thesis or alternative. *Entrance requirements:* For master's, GRE General Test, BSN from ACEN-accredited college, Ohio RN license. Additional exam requirements/recommendations for international students: required—TOEFL.

# Psychiatric Nursing

**Allen College,** Graduate Programs, Waterloo, IA 50703. Offers adult-gerontology acute care nurse practitioner (MSN); community/public health nursing (MSN); education (MSN); family nurse practitioner (MSN); health sciences (Ed D); leadership in health care delivery (MSN); leadership in health care informatics (MSN); nursing (DNP); occupational therapy (MS); psychiatric mental health nurse practitioner (MSN). *Accreditation:* AACN; ACEN. *Faculty:* 27 full-time (23 women), 9 part-time/adjunct (8 women). *Students:* 193 full-time (175 women), 95 part-time (84 women); includes 22 minority (6 Black or African American, non-Hispanic/Latino; 1 American Indian or Alaska Native, non-Hispanic/Latino; 4 Asian, non-Hispanic/Latino; 5 Hispanic/Latino; 6 Two or more races, non-Hispanic/Latino). Average age 32. 376 applicants, 53% accepted, 122 enrolled. *Application deadline:* For fall admission, 2/1 priority date for domestic students; for spring admission, 9/1 priority date for domestic students. Applications are processed on a rolling basis. Application fee: $50. Electronic applications accepted. *Financial support:* In 2019–20, 78 students received support. Federal Work-Study, institutionally sponsored loans, and scholarships/grants available. Support available to part-time students. Financial award application deadline: 8/1; financial award applicants required to submit FAFSA. *Unit head:* Dr. Bob Loch, Provost, 319-226-2040, Fax: 319-226-2070, E-mail: bob.loch@allencollege.edu. *Application contact:* Molly Quinn, Director of Admissions, 319-226-2001, Fax: 319-226-2010, E-mail: molly.quinn@allencollege.edu.
Website: http://www.allencollege.edu/

**Alverno College,** JoAnn McGrath School of Nursing and Health Professions, Milwaukee, WI 53234-3922. Offers clinical nurse specialist (MSN); family nurse practitioner (MSN); nursing practice (DNP); psychiatric mental health nurse practitioner (MSN). *Accreditation:* AACN. *Program availability:* Part-time, evening/weekend, 100% online, blended/hybrid learning. *Faculty:* 7 full-time (all women), 10 part-time/adjunct (8 women). *Students:* 117 full-time (110 women), 139 part-time (129 women); includes 68 minority (32 Black or African American, non-Hispanic/Latino; 8 Asian, non-Hispanic/

Latino; 24 Hispanic/Latino; 4 Two or more races, non-Hispanic/Latino), 1 international. Average age 36. 94 applicants, 95% accepted, 60 enrolled. In 2019, 51 master's, 3 doctorates awarded. *Degree requirements:* For master's, 500 clinical hours, capstone; for doctorate, 1,000 post-BSN clinical hours. *Entrance requirements:* For master's, BSN, current license; for doctorate, MSN, nursing license. Additional exam requirements/recommendations for international students: required—TOEFL. *Application deadline:* For fall admission, 7/15 priority date for domestic and international students; for spring admission, 12/15 priority date for domestic and international students. Applications are processed on a rolling basis. Electronic applications accepted. *Expenses:* $1098 per credit hour. *Financial support:* In 2019–20, 4 students received support. Federal Work-Study and scholarships/grants available. Support available to part-time students. Financial award applicants required to submit FAFSA. *Unit head:* Patti Varga, Dean, 414-382-6303, Fax: 414-382-6354, E-mail: patti.varga@alverno.edu. *Application contact:* Janet Stikel, Director of Admissions, 414-382-6112, Fax: 414-382-6354, E-mail: janet.stikel@alverno.edu.
Website: http://www.alverno.edu/academics/academicdepartments/joannmcgrathschoolofnursing/

**Anderson University,** College of Health Professions, Anderson, SC 29621. Offers advanced practice (DNP); executive leadership (MSN, DNP); family nurse practitioner (MSN, DNP); nurse educator (MSN); psychiatric mental health nurse practitioner (MSN, DNP). *Program availability:* Online learning. *Application deadline:* Applications are processed on a rolling basis. Electronic applications accepted. *Expenses:* Contact institution. *Financial support:* Scholarships/grants available. *Unit head:* Dr. Donald M. Peace, Dean, 864-231-5513, E-mail: dpeace@andersonuniversity.edu. *Application contact:* Dr. Donald M. Peace, Dean, 864-231-5513, E-mail: dpeace@andersonuniversity.edu.
Website: http://www.andersonuniversity.edu/health-professions

**Arizona State University at Tempe,** College of Nursing and Health Innovation, Phoenix, AZ 85004. Offers advanced nursing practice (DNP); clinical research management (MS); community and public health practice (Graduate Certificate); family mental health nurse practitioner (Graduate Certificate); family nurse practitioner (Graduate Certificate); geriatric nursing (Graduate Certificate); healthcare innovation (MHI); nurse education in academic and practice settings (Graduate Certificate); nurse educator (MS); nursing and healthcare innovation (PhD). *Accreditation:* AACN. *Program availability:* Online learning. *Degree requirements:* For master's, comprehensive exam (for some programs), thesis (for some programs), interactive Program of Study (iPOS) submitted before completing 50 percent of required credit hours; for doctorate, comprehensive exam, thesis/dissertation, interactive Program of Study (iPOS) submitted before completing 50 percent of required credit hours. *Entrance requirements:* For master's and doctorate, GRE, minimum GPA of 3.0 or equivalent in last 2 years of work leading to bachelor's degree. Additional exam requirements/recommendations for international students: required—TOEFL, IELTS, or PTE. Electronic applications accepted. *Expenses:* Contact institution.

**Augusta University,** College of Nursing, Doctor of Nursing Practice Program, Augusta, GA 30912. Offers adult gerontology acute care nurse practitioner (DNP); family nurse practitioner (DNP); nurse executive (DNP); nursing (DNP); nursing anesthesia (DNP); pediatric nurse practitioner (DNP); psychiatric mental health nurse practitioner (DNP). *Accreditation:* AACN; AANA/CANAEP. *Degree requirements:* For doctorate, thesis/dissertation or alternative. *Entrance requirements:* For doctorate, GRE General Test or MAT, master's degree in nursing or related field, current professional nurse licensure. Additional exam requirements/recommendations for international students: required—TOEFL (minimum score 600 paper-based; 100 iBT). Electronic applications accepted.

**Azusa Pacific University,** School of Nursing, Azusa, CA 91702-7000. Offers adult clinical nurse specialist (MSN); adult-gerontology nurse practitioner (MSN); family nurse practitioner (MSN); healthcare administration and leadership (MSN); nursing (MSN, DNP, PhD); nursing education (MSN); parent-child clinical nurse specialist (MSN); psychiatric mental health nurse practitioner (MSN). *Accreditation:* AACN. *Program availability:* Part-time, evening/weekend. *Degree requirements:* For master's, thesis optional. *Entrance requirements:* For master's, BSN.

**Binghamton University, State University of New York,** Graduate School, Decker School of Nursing, Binghamton, NY 13902-6000. Offers adult-gerontological nursing (MS, DNP, Certificate); community health nursing (MS, DNP, Certificate); family health nursing (MS, DNP, Certificate); family psychiatric mental health nursing (MS, DNP, Certificate); nursing (PhD). *Accreditation:* AACN. *Program availability:* Part-time, evening/weekend. Terminal master's awarded for partial completion of doctoral program. *Degree requirements:* For master's, comprehensive exam, thesis; for doctorate, comprehensive exam (for some programs), thesis/dissertation. *Entrance requirements:* For master's and doctorate, GRE General Test, nursing licensure. Additional exam requirements/recommendations for international students: required—TOEFL (minimum score 90 iBT). Electronic applications accepted. *Expenses:* Contact institution.

**Boston College,** William F. Connell School of Nursing, Chestnut Hill, MA 02467. Offers adult-gerontology primary care nurse practitioner (MS); family health nursing (MS); nurse anesthesia (MS); nursing (PhD); pediatric primary care nurse practitioner (MS), including pediatric and women's health; psychiatric-mental health nursing (MS); women's health nursing (MS); MBA/MS; MS/MA; MS/PhD. *Accreditation:* AACN; AANA/CANAEP (one or more programs are accredited). *Program availability:* Part-time. *Faculty:* 56 full-time (50 women). *Students:* 228 full-time (200 women), 82 part-time (71 women); includes 54 minority (10 Black or African American, non-Hispanic/Latino; 18 Asian, non-Hispanic/Latino; 20 Hispanic/Latino; 6 Two or more races, non-Hispanic/Latino), 7 international. Average age 28. 360 applicants, 56% accepted, 93 enrolled. In 2019, 107 master's, 7 doctorates awarded. *Degree requirements:* For master's, comprehensive exam; for doctorate, comprehensive exam, thesis/dissertation, computer literacy exam or foreign language. *Entrance requirements:* For master's, bachelor's degree; for doctorate, GRE General Test, bachelor's in Nursing and master's degree in nursing or related field. Additional exam requirements/recommendations for international students: required—TOEFL (minimum score 600 paper-based; 100 iBT), IELTS (minimum score 7.5). *Application deadline:* For fall admission, 3/15 for domestic and international students; for spring admission, 9/30 for domestic and international students. Application fee: $40. Electronic applications accepted. *Expenses:* Contact institution. *Financial support:* In 2019–20, 135 students received support, including 12 fellowships with full tuition reimbursements available (averaging $24,504 per year), 29 teaching assistantships (averaging $4,380 per year); scholarships/grants, health care benefits, tuition waivers (partial), and unspecified assistantships also available. Support available to part-time students. Financial award application deadline: 4/18; financial award applicants required to submit FAFSA. *Unit head:* Dr. Susan Gennaro, Dean, 617-552-4251, Fax: 617-552-0931, E-mail: susan.gennaro@bc.edu. *Application contact:* Sean Sendall, Assistant Dean, Graduate Enrollment and Data Analytics, 617-552-4745, Fax: 617-552-2121, E-mail: sean.sendall@bc.edu.
Website: http://www.bc.edu/cson

**California State University, San Marcos,** College of Education, Health and Human Services, School of Nursing, San Marcos, CA 92096-0001. Offers advanced practice nursing (MSN), including clinical nurse specialist, family nurse practitioner, psychiatric mental health nurse practitioner; clinical nurse leader (MSN); nursing education (MSN). *Expenses: Tuition, area resident:* Full-time $7176. Tuition, state resident: full-time $7176. Tuition, nonresident: full-time $18,640. *International tuition:* $18,640 full-time. *Required fees:* $1960.

**Case Western Reserve University,** Frances Payne Bolton School of Nursing, Master's Programs in Nursing, Nurse Practitioner Program, Cleveland, OH 44106. Offers acute care pediatric nurse practitioner (MSN); acute care/cardiovascular nursing (MSN); adult gerontology acute care nurse practitioner (MSN); adult gerontology primary care nurse practitioner (MSN); family nurse practitioner (MSN); family systems psychiatric mental health nursing (MSN); neonatal nurse practitioner (MSN); palliative care (MSN); pediatric nurse practitioner in acute care (MSN); pediatric primary care nurse practitioner (MSN); women's health nurse practitioner (MSN). *Accreditation:* ACEN. *Program availability:* Part-time. *Faculty:* 30 full-time (25 women), 6 part-time/adjunct (all women). *Students:* 47 full-time (36 women), 70 part-time (59 women); includes 34 minority (12 Black or African American, non-Hispanic/Latino; 11 Asian, non-Hispanic/Latino; 9 Hispanic/Latino; 2 Two or more races, non-Hispanic/Latino), 9 international. Average age 30. 45 applicants, 82% accepted, 22 enrolled. In 2019, 46 master's awarded. *Degree requirements:* For master's, thesis optional, minimum GPA of 3.0, clinical hours corresponding to requirements to sit for certification exam, portfolio. *Entrance requirements:* For master's, GRE/MAT (scores not required for application, but may be requested for an admission decision). Additional exam requirements/recommendations for international students: required—TOEFL (minimum score 577 paper-based; 90 iBT), IELTS (minimum score 7). *Application deadline:* For fall admission, 3/15 for domestic and international students; for spring admission, 10/1 for domestic and international students; for summer admission, 3/15 for domestic and international students. Applications are processed on a rolling basis. Application fee: $75. Electronic applications accepted. *Expenses:* Clinical placement $75; Activity fee $15 per semester; Graduate council fee $15 per semester; Tuition rate $2,133 per credit hour. *Financial support:* In 2019–20, 100 students received support, including 34 teaching assistantships with partial tuition reimbursements available (averaging $19,197 per year); scholarships/grants and traineeships also available. Financial award application deadline: 5/15; financial award applicants required to submit FAFSA. *Unit head:* Dr. Latina Brooks, Director, 216-368-1196, Fax: 216-368-3542, E-mail: lmb3@case.edu. *Application contact:* Jackie Tepale, Admissions Coordinator, 216-368-5253, Fax: 216-368-3542, E-mail: yyd@case.edu.
Website: https://case.edu/nursing/programs/msn

**Clarke University,** Department of Nursing and Health, Dubuque, IA 52001-3198. Offers family nurse practitioner (DNP); health leadership and practice (DNP); psychiatric mental health nurse practitioner (DNP). *Accreditation:* AACN. *Program availability:* Part-time. *Degree requirements:* For doctorate, comprehensive exam, thesis/dissertation. *Entrance requirements:* For doctorate, GRE (if GPA under 3.0), bachelor's degree from accredited nursing program and accredited college or university; minimum GPA of 3.0; minimum C grade on undergraduate prerequisite courses; three recommendation forms; curriculum vitae; statement of goals; transcripts; copy of nursing license; proof of health insurance; interview. Additional exam requirements/recommendations for international students: required—TOEFL (minimum score 550 paper-based; 80 iBT), IELTS (minimum score 6.5). Electronic applications accepted. *Expenses:* Contact institution.

**Columbia University,** School of Nursing, Program in Psychiatric Mental Health Nursing, New York, NY 10032. Offers MS, Adv C. *Accreditation:* AACN. *Program availability:* Part-time. *Entrance requirements:* For master's, GRE General Test, NCLEX, BSN, 1 year of clinical experience (preferred); for Adv C, MSN. Additional exam requirements/recommendations for international students: required—TOEFL (minimum score 100 iBT). Electronic applications accepted. *Expenses: Tuition:* Full-time $47,600; part-time $1880 per credit. One-time fee: $105.

**Creighton University,** College of Nursing, Omaha, NE 68178-0001. Offers adult gerontology acute care nurse practitioner (DNP, Post-Master's Certificate); adult gerontology nurse practitioner (DNP); clinical nurse leader (MSN, Post-Graduate Certificate); clinical systems administration (MSN, DNP); family nurse practitioner (DNP, Post-Master's Certificate); neonatal nurse practitioner (DNP, Post-Master's Certificate); nursing (Post-Graduate Certificate); pediatric acute care nurse practitioner (DNP, Post-Master's Certificate); psychiatric mental health nurse practitioner (DNP). *Accreditation:* AACN. *Program availability:* Part-time, blended/hybrid learning. *Degree requirements:* For master's, capstone project; for doctorate, scholarly project. *Entrance requirements:* For master's and doctorate, BSN from ACEN- or CCNE-accredited nursing school, minimum cumulative GPA of 3.0, personal statement, active unencumbered RN license with NE eligibility, undergraduate statistics course, physical assessment course or equivalent, three recommendation letters; for other advanced degree, MSN or MS in nursing from ACEN- or CCNE-accredited nursing school, minimum cumulative GPA of 3.0, active unencumbered RN license with NE eligibility. Additional exam requirements/recommendations for international students: required—TOEFL (minimum score 600 paper-based, 100 iBT) or IELTS. Electronic applications accepted. *Expenses:* Contact institution.

**Drexel University,** College of Nursing and Health Professions, Division of Graduate Nursing, Philadelphia, PA 19104-2875. Offers adult acute care (MSN); adult psychiatric/mental health (MSN); advanced practice nursing (MSN); clinical trials research (MSN); family nurse practitioner (MSN); leadership in health systems management (MSN); nursing education (MSN); pediatric primary care (MSN); women's health (MSN). *Accreditation:* AACN. Electronic applications accepted.

**East Tennessee State University,** College of Graduate and Continuing Studies, College of Nursing, Johnson City, TN 37614. Offers acute care nurse practitioner (DNP); adult-gerontology primary care nurse practitioner (DNP); adult/gerontological nurse practitioner (Postbaccalaureate Certificate); executive leadership in nursing (DNP, Postbaccalaureate Certificate); family nurse practitioner (MSN, DNP, Post-Master's Certificate, Postbaccalaureate Certificate); nursing (PhD); nursing administration (MSN); nursing education (MSN); pediatric primary care nurse practitioner (DNP); psychiatric mental health nurse practitioner (Postbaccalaureate Certificate); psychiatric/mental health nurse practitioner (MSN, DNP, Post-Master's Certificate); women's health care nurse practitioner (DNP). *Accreditation:* AACN. *Program availability:* Part-time, evening/weekend, online learning. *Degree requirements:* For master's and other advanced degree, comprehensive exam, practicum; for doctorate, comprehensive exam, thesis/dissertation (for some programs), practicum, internship, evidence of professional malpractice insurance, CPR certification. *Entrance requirements:* For master's, bachelor's degree, minimum GPA of 3.0, current RN license and eligibility to practice, resume, three letters of recommendation; for doctorate, GRE General Test, MSN (for PhD), BSN or MSN (for DNP), current RN license and eligibility to practice, 2 years of full-time registered nurse work experience or equivalent, three letters of recommendation, resume or curriculum vitae, interview, writing sample; for other advanced degree, MSN, minimum GPA of 3.0, current RN license and eligibility to practice, three letters of recommendation, resume or curriculum vitae; DNP with designated concentration in advanced clinical practice or nursing administration (for select programs). Additional exam requirements/recommendations for international students: required—TOEFL (minimum score 600 paper-based; 79 iBT). Electronic applications accepted.

**Fairfield University,** Marion Peckham Egan School of Nursing and Health Studies, Fairfield, CT 06824. Offers advanced practice (DNP); family nurse practitioner (MSN, DNP); nurse anesthesia (DNP); nursing leadership (MSN); psychiatric nurse practitioner (MSN, DNP). *Accreditation:* AACN; AANA/CANAEP. *Program availability:* Part-time, evening/weekend. *Faculty:* 13 full-time (all women), 12 part-time/adjunct (9 women). *Students:* 56 full-time (49 women), 165 part-time (149 women); includes 62 minority (24 Black or African American, non-Hispanic/Latino; 12 Asian, non-Hispanic/Latino; 25 Hispanic/Latino; 1 Two or more races, non-Hispanic/Latino). Average age 33. 129 applicants, 56% accepted, 62 enrolled. In 2019, 26 master's, 36 doctorates awarded. *Degree requirements:* For master's, capstone project. *Entrance requirements:* For master's, minimum QPA of 3.0, RN license, resume, 2 recommendations; for doctorate, MSN (minimum QPA of 3.2) or BSN (minimum QPA of 3.0); critical care nursing experience (for nurse anesthesia DNP candidates). Additional exam requirements/ recommendations for international students: required—TOEFL (minimum score 550 paper-based; 80 iBT), IELTS (minimum score 6.5), TOEFL (minimum score 550 paper-based; 80 iBT) or IELTS (minimum score 6.5). *Application deadline:* For fall admission, 5/15 for international students; for spring admission, 10/15 for international students. Applications are processed on a rolling basis. Application fee: $60. Electronic applications accepted. *Expenses:* $875 per credit hour tuition (for MS), $1,010 per credit hour tuition (for Master of Healthcare Administration), $1,025 per credit hour tuition (for Doctorate in Clinical Nutrition), $1,050 per credit hour tuition (for DNP Nurse Anesthesia), $1,000 per credit hour tuition (for all other DNP programs), $150 per semester clinical placement fee (applicable programs, fall and spring semesters), $50 per semester registration fee, $65 per semester graduate student activity fee (fall and spring). *Financial support:* In 2019–20, 45 students received support. Scholarships/ grants and unspecified assistantships available. Financial award applicants required to submit FAFSA. *Unit head:* Dr. Meredith Wallace Kazer, Dean, 203-254-4000 Ext. 2701, Fax: 203-254-4126, E-mail: mkazer@fairfield.edu. *Application contact:* Melanie Rogers, Director of Graduate Admission, 203-254-4184, Fax: 203-254-4073, E-mail: gradadmis@fairfield.edu.
Website: http://fairfield.edu/son

**Fairleigh Dickinson University, Florham Campus,** University College: Arts, Sciences, and Professional Studies, The Henry P. Becton School of Nursing and Allied Health, Madison, NJ 07940-1099. Offers adult gerontology primary care nurse practitioner (MSN); family psychiatric/mental health nurse practitioner (MSN). *Program availability:* Part-time, evening/weekend. *Entrance requirements:* For master's, BSN, minimum undergraduate GPA of 3.0, courses in statistics and nursing research at the undergraduate level, NJ Registered Nurse licensure, minimum of 1 year of clinical nursing experience, two letters of recommendation.

**Florida International University,** Nicole Wertheim College of Nursing and Health Sciences, Nursing Program, Miami, FL 33199. Offers adult health nursing (MSN); family health (MSN); nurse anesthetist (MSN); nursing practice (DNP); nursing science research (PhD); pediatric nurse (MSN); psychiatric and mental health nursing (MSN); registered nurse (MSN). *Accreditation:* AACN; AANA/CANAEP. *Program availability:* Part-time, evening/weekend. *Faculty:* 14 full-time (12 women), 19 part-time/adjunct (14 women). *Students:* 279 full-time (188 women), 109 part-time (87 women); includes 309 minority (110 Black or African American, non-Hispanic/Latino; 1 American Indian or Alaska Native, non-Hispanic/Latino; 29 Asian, non-Hispanic/Latino; 166 Hispanic/Latino; 2 Native Hawaiian or other Pacific Islander, non-Hispanic/Latino; 1 Two or more races, non-Hispanic/Latino), 6 international. Average age 35. 154 applicants, 61% accepted, 88 enrolled. In 2019, 167 master's, 46 doctorates awarded. *Degree requirements:* For master's, thesis or alternative; for doctorate, comprehensive exam, thesis/dissertation. *Entrance requirements:* For master's, bachelor's degree in nursing, minimum undergraduate GPA of 3.0 in upper-level coursework, letters of recommendation; for doctorate, GRE, letters of recommendation, minimum undergraduate GPA of 3.0 in upper-level coursework, interview. Additional exam requirements/recommendations for international students: required—TOEFL (minimum score 550 paper-based; 80 iBT). *Application deadline:* For fall admission, 6/1 for domestic students, 4/1 for international students; for spring admission, 10/1 for domestic students, 9/1 for international students. Applications are processed on a rolling basis. Application fee: $30. Electronic applications accepted. *Expenses: Tuition, area resident:* Full-time $8912; part-time $446 per credit hour. Tuition, state resident: full-time $8912; part-time $446 per credit hour. Tuition, nonresident: full-time $21,393; part-time $992 per credit hour. *Required fees:* $2194. *Financial support:* Institutionally sponsored loans and scholarships/grants available. Financial award application deadline: 3/1; financial award applicants required to submit FAFSA. *Unit head:* Dr. Yhovana Gordon, Chair, 305-348-7733, Fax: 305-348-7051, E-mail: gordony@fiu.edu. *Application contact:* Nanett Rojas, Manager, Admissions Operations, 305-348-7464, Fax: 305-348-7441, E-mail: gradadm@fiu.edu.
Website: http://cnhs.fiu.edu/

**Florida State University,** The Graduate School, College of Nursing, Tallahassee, FL 32306-4310. Offers family nurse practitioner (DNP); psychiatric mental health (Certificate). *Accreditation:* AACN; AANA/CANAEP. *Program availability:* Part-time, online only, 100% online. *Faculty:* 31 full-time (27 women), 10 part-time/adjunct (9 women). *Students:* 66 full-time (59 women), 72 part-time (63 women); includes 61 minority (32 Black or African American, non-Hispanic/Latino; 1 American Indian or Alaska Native, non-Hispanic/Latino; 5 Asian, non-Hispanic/Latino; 20 Hispanic/Latino; 3 Two or more races, non-Hispanic/Latino). Average age 40. 156 applicants, 39% accepted, 54 enrolled. In 2019, 24 doctorates awarded. *Degree requirements:* For doctorate, thesis/dissertation, evidence-based project. *Entrance requirements:* For doctorate, GRE General Test, MAT, minimum GPA of 3.0, BSN or MSN, Florida RN license. Additional exam requirements/recommendations for international students: required—TOEFL (minimum score 550 paper-based). *Application deadline:* For fall admission, 3/1 for domestic and international students. Application fee: $30. Electronic applications accepted. *Expenses:* Contact institution. *Financial support:* In 2019–20, 27 students received support, including fellowships with partial tuition reimbursements available (averaging $6,300 per year), research assistantships with partial tuition reimbursements available (averaging $3,000 per year), 3 teaching assistantships with partial tuition reimbursements available (averaging $3,000 per year); career-related internships or fieldwork, Federal Work-Study, institutionally sponsored loans, scholarships/grants, traineeships, and tuition waivers (partial) also available. Financial award application deadline: 4/1; financial award applicants required to submit FAFSA. *Unit head:* Dr. Laurie Grubbs, Interim Dean, 850-644-6846, Fax: 850-644-7660, E-mail: lgrubbs@fsu.edu. *Application contact:* Carlos Urrutia, Assistant Director for Student Services, 850-644-5638, Fax: 850-645-7249, E-mail: currutia@fsu.edu.
Website: http://nursing.fsu.edu/

**George Mason University,** College of Health and Human Services, School of Nursing, Fairfax, VA 22030. Offers adult gerontology (DNP); adult/gerontological nurse practitioner (MSN); family nurse practitioner (MSN, DNP); nurse educator (MSN); nursing (PhD); nursing administration (MSN, DNP); nursing education (Certificate); psychiatric mental health (DNP). *Accreditation:* AACN. *Program availability:* Part-time, evening/weekend, blended/hybrid learning. *Degree requirements:* For master's, comprehensive exam (for some programs), thesis in clinical classes; for doctorate, comprehensive exam (for some programs), thesis/dissertation (for some programs). *Entrance requirements:* For master's, 2 official transcripts; expanded goals statement;

resume; BSN from accredited institution; minimum GPA of 3.0 in last 60 credits of undergraduate work; 2 letters of recommendation; completion of undergraduate statistics and graduate-level bivariate statistics; certification in professional CPR; for doctorate, GRE, 2 official transcripts; expanded goals statement; resume; 2 recommendation letters; nursing license; at least 1 year of work experience as an RN; interview; writing sample; evidence of graduate-level course in applied statistics; master's degree in nursing with minimum GPA of 3.5; for Certificate, 2 official transcripts; expanded goals statement; resume; master's degree from accredited institution or currently enrolled with minimum GPA of 3.0. Additional exam requirements/recommendations for international students: required—TOEFL (minimum score 570 paper-based; 88 iBT), IELTS (minimum score 6.5), PTE (minimum score 59). Electronic applications accepted. *Expenses:* Contact institution.

**Georgia Southern University,** Jack N. Averitt College of Graduate Studies, Waters College of Health Professions, School of Nursing, Program in Nurse Practitioner, Statesboro, GA 30458. Offers family nurse practitioner (MSN); psychiatric mental health nurse practitioner (MSN). *Program availability:* Part-time, blended/hybrid learning. *Students:* 19 part-time (all women); includes 6 minority (4 Black or African American, non-Hispanic/Latino; 1 Hispanic/Latino; 1 Two or more races, non-Hispanic/Latino). Average age 34. 4 applicants. In 2019, 47 master's awarded. *Entrance requirements:* For master's, minimum GPA of 3.0, Georgia nursing license, 2 years of clinical experience, CPR certification. Additional exam requirements/recommendations for international students: required—TOEFL (minimum score 550 paper-based; 80 iBT), IELTS (minimum score 6). *Application deadline:* For fall admission, 7/31 priority date for domestic and international students; for spring admission, 11/30 priority date for domestic students, 11/30 for international students; for summer admission, 3/31 for domestic and international students. Applications are processed on a rolling basis. Application fee: $50. Electronic applications accepted. *Expenses: Tuition, area resident:* Full-time $4986; part-time $277 per credit hour. Tuition, nonresident: full-time $19,890; part-time $1105 per credit hour. *International tuition:* $19,890 full-time. *Required fees:* $2114; $1057 per semester. $1057 per semester. Tuition and fees vary according to course load, campus/location and program. *Financial support:* In 2019–20, 27 students received support, including 5 fellowships with full tuition reimbursements available (averaging $7,750 per year); career-related internships or fieldwork, Federal Work-Study, scholarships/grants, traineeships, tuition waivers (full), and unspecified assistantships also available. Support available to part-time students. Financial award application deadline: 4/15; financial award applicants required to submit FAFSA. *Unit head:* Dr. Sharon Radzyminski, Department Chair, 912-478-5455, Fax: 912-478-5036, E-mail: sradzyminski@georgiasouthern.edu. *Application contact:* Dr. Sharon Radzyminski, Department Chair, 912-478-5455, Fax: 912-478-5036, E-mail: sradzyminski@georgiasouthern.edu.

**Georgia State University,** Byrdine F. Lewis School of Nursing, Atlanta, GA 30303. Offers adult health clinical nurse specialist/nurse practitioner (MS, Certificate); child health clinical nurse specialist/pediatric nurse practitioner (MS, Certificate); family nurse practitioner (MS, Certificate); family psychiatric mental health nurse practitioner (MS, Certificate); nursing (PhD); nursing leadership in healthcare innovations (MS), including nursing administration, nursing informatics; nutrition (MS); occupational therapy (MOT); perinatal clinical nurse specialist/women's health nurse practitioner (MS, Certificate); physical therapy (DPT); respiratory therapy (MS). *Accreditation:* AACN. *Program availability:* Part-time, blended/hybrid learning. *Faculty:* 57 full-time (40 women), 5 part-time/adjunct (4 women). *Students:* 388 full-time (290 women), 155 part-time (135 women); includes 217 minority (130 Black or African American, non-Hispanic/Latino; 47 Asian, non-Hispanic/Latino; 26 Hispanic/Latino; 14 Two or more races, non-Hispanic/Latino), 45 international. Average age 32. 480 applicants, 50% accepted, 164 enrolled. In 2019, 158 master's, 64 doctorates, 20 other advanced degrees awarded. *Degree requirements:* For doctorate, comprehensive exam, thesis/dissertation. *Entrance requirements:* For doctorate, GRE. Additional exam requirements/recommendations for international students: required—TOEFL. *Application deadline:* For fall admission, 2/1 priority date for domestic and international students; for spring admission, 9/15 for domestic and international students. Applications are processed on a rolling basis. Application fee: $50. Electronic applications accepted. *Expenses:* Contact institution. *Financial support:* In 2019–20, research assistantships with tuition reimbursements (averaging $1,666 per year), teaching assistantships with tuition reimbursements (averaging $1,920 per year) were awarded; scholarships/grants, tuition waivers (full and partial), and unspecified assistantships also available. Support available to part-time students. Financial award application deadline: 8/1; financial award applicants required to submit FAFSA. *Unit head:* Huanbiao Mo, Dean of Nursing. *Application contact:* Huanbiao Mo, Dean of Nursing.
Website: http://nursing.gsu.edu/

**Hofstra University,** Hofstra Northwell School of Nursing and Physician Assistant Studies, Programs in Nursing, Hempstead, NY 11549. Offers adult-gerontology acute care nurse practitioner (MS); family nurse practitioner (MS); psychiatric-mental health np (MS). *Students:* 68 full-time (48 women), 159 part-time (138 women); includes 103 minority (24 Black or African American, non-Hispanic/Latino; 2 American Indian or Alaska Native, non-Hispanic/Latino; 41 Asian, non-Hispanic/Latino; 35 Hispanic/Latino; 1 Two or more races, non-Hispanic/Latino). Average age 33. 389 applicants, 32% accepted, 89 enrolled. In 2019, 44 master's awarded. *Degree requirements:* For master's, comprehensive exam, minimum GPA of 3.0. *Entrance requirements:* For master's, bachelor's degree in nursing, 3 letters of recommendation, essay, resume. Additional exam requirements/recommendations for international students: required—TOEFL (minimum score 550 paper-based; 80 iBT); recommended—IELTS (minimum score 6.5). Application fee: $75. Electronic applications accepted. *Expenses: Tuition:* Full-time $25,164; part-time $1398 per credit. *Required fees:* $580; $165 per semester. Tuition and fees vary according to course load, degree level and program. *Financial support:* In 2019–20, 56 students received support, including 5 fellowships with full and partial tuition reimbursements available (averaging $10,870 per year); research assistantships with full and partial tuition reimbursements available, career-related internships or fieldwork, Federal Work-Study, institutionally sponsored loans, scholarships/grants, traineeships, tuition waivers (full and partial), unspecified assistantships, and scholarships and endowed scholarships also available. Support available to part-time students. Financial award applicants required to submit FAFSA. *Unit head:* Dr. Kathleen Gallo, Dean, 516-463-7475, Fax: 516-463-7495, E-mail: kathleen.gallo@hofstra.edu. *Application contact:* Sunil Samuel, Assistant Vice President of Admissions, 516-463-4723, Fax: 516-463-4664, E-mail: graduateadmission@hofstra.edu.

**Hunter College of the City University of New York,** Graduate School, Hunter-Bellevue School of Nursing, Doctor of Nursing Practice Program, New York, NY 10065-5085. Offers adult-gerontology nurse practitioner (DNP); family nurse practitioner (DNP); psychiatric-mental health nurse practitioner (DNP).

**Hunter College of the City University of New York,** Graduate School, Hunter-Bellevue School of Nursing, Program in Psychiatric-Mental Health Nurse Practitioner, New York, NY 10065-5085. Offers MS, AC. *Accreditation:* AACN. *Program availability:* Part-time. *Degree requirements:* For master's, practicum. *Entrance requirements:* For

master's, minimum GPA of 3.0, New York RN license, BSN. Additional exam requirements/recommendations for international students: required—TOEFL.

**Husson University,** Graduate Nursing Program, Bangor, ME 04401-2999. Offers educational leadership (MSN); family and community nurse practitioner (MSN, PMC); psychiatric mental health nurse practitioner (MSN, PMC). *Accreditation:* AACN. *Program availability:* Part-time, evening/weekend. *Degree requirements:* For master's, comprehensive exam (for some programs), research project. *Entrance requirements:* For master's, proof of RN licensure. Additional exam requirements/recommendations for international students: required—TOEFL (minimum score 550 paper-based; 80 iBT), IELTS (minimum score 6.5). Electronic applications accepted. *Expenses:* Contact institution.

**Jacksonville University,** Brooks Rehabilitation College of Healthcare Sciences, Keigwin School of Nursing, Master of Science in Nursing Program, Jacksonville, FL 32211. Offers clinical nurse educator (MSN); family nurse practitioner (MSN); family nurse practitioner/emergency nurse practitioner (MSN); leadership in the healthcare system (MSN); nursing informatics (MSN); psychiatric nurse practitioner (MSN); MSN/MBA. *Program availability:* Part-time, 100% online, blended/hybrid learning. In 2019, 215 master's awarded. *Degree requirements:* For master's, thesis. *Entrance requirements:* For master's, GRE General Test or undergraduate GPA above 3.0, BSN from ACEN- or CCNE-accredited program; course work in statistics and physical assessment within last 5 years; Florida nursing license; CPR/BLS certification; 3 recommendations, 2 of which are professional references; statement of intent; resume. Additional exam requirements/recommendations for international students: required—TOEFL (minimum score 650 paper-based; 114 iBT), IELTS (minimum score 8). *Application deadline:* Applications are processed on a rolling basis. Application fee: $50. Electronic applications accepted. *Expenses:* Contact institution. *Financial support:* Federal Work-Study, institutionally sponsored loans, scholarships/grants, and health care benefits available. Support available to part-time students. Financial award application deadline: 3/15; financial award applicants required to submit FAFSA. *Unit head:* Dr. Hilary Morgan, Director, Graduate Nursing Programs/Associate Professor, 904-256-7601, E-mail: hmorgan@ju.edu. *Application contact:* Kristen Kirkendall, Associate Director of Graduate Admissions and Communications, 904-256-7169, E-mail: kgreene8@ju.edu.
Website: https://www.ju.edu/nursing/graduate/master-science-nursing/index.php

**James Madison University,** The Graduate School, College of Health and Behavioral Studies, Program in Nursing, Harrisonburg, VA 22807. Offers adult/gerontology primary care nurse practitioner (MSN); clinical nurse leader (MSN); family nurse practitioner (MSN); nurse administrator (MSN); nurse midwifery (MSN); nursing (MSN, DNP); psychiatric mental health nurse practitioner (MSN). *Accreditation:* AACN. *Program availability:* Part-time, 100% online, blended/hybrid learning. *Students:* 15 full-time (14 women), 71 part-time (66 women); includes 10 minority (3 Black or African American, non-Hispanic/Latino; 6 Asian, non-Hispanic/Latino; 1 Hispanic/Latino). Average age 30. In 2019, 28 master's awarded. Application fee: $60. Electronic applications accepted. *Financial support:* In 2019–20, 2 students received support. Federal Work-Study and assistantships (averaging $7911) available. Financial award application deadline: 3/1; financial award applicants required to submit FAFSA. *Unit head:* Dr. Julie T. Sanford, Department Head, 540-568-6314, E-mail: sanforjt@jmu.edu. *Application contact:* Lynette D. Michael, Director of Graduate Admissions, 540-568-6131 Ext. 6395, Fax: 540-568-7860, E-mail: michaeld@jmu.edu.
Website: http://www.nursing.jmu.edu

**Johns Hopkins University,** School of Nursing, Post Master's Certificate Program in Nursing, Baltimore, MD 21218. Offers nursing education (Certificate); pediatric acute care nurse practitioner (Certificate); psychiatric mental health nurse practitioner (Certificate). *Program availability:* Part-time-only, online only, 100% online. *Faculty:* 4 full-time (all women), 2 part-time/adjunct (both women). *Students:* 47 part-time (44 women); includes 9 minority (3 Black or African American, non-Hispanic/Latino; 2 Asian, non-Hispanic/Latino; 3 Hispanic/Latino; 1 Two or more races, non-Hispanic/Latino). 127 applicants, 44% accepted, 47 enrolled. In 2019, 46 Certificates awarded. *Entrance requirements:* For degree, Minimum GPA of 3.0, goal statement/essay, resume, letters of recommendation, official transcripts from all post-secondary institutions attended, MSN and RN licensure, NP license for some tracks, work experience and prerequisite coursework for some tracks. Additional exam requirements/recommendations for international students: required—TOEFL (minimum score 600 paper-based; 100 iBT), IELTS (minimum score 7). *Application deadline:* For fall admission, 1/1 priority date for domestic students. Application fee: $75. Electronic applications accepted. *Expenses:* $1,688 per credit. *Financial support:* In 2019–20, 1 student received support. Federal Work-Study available. Financial award application deadline: 3/1; financial award applicants required to submit FAFSA. *Unit head:* Dr. Susan Renda, 410-955-7139, E-mail: srenda1@jhu.edu. *Application contact:* Cathy Wilson, Director of Admissions, 410-955-7548, Fax: 410-614-7086, E-mail: jhuson@jhu.edu.
Website: http://nursing.jhu.edu/

**Kent State University,** College of Nursing, Kent, OH 44242. Offers advanced nursing practice (DNP), including adult/gerontology acute care nurse practitioner (MSN, DNP); nursing (MSN, PhD), including adult/gerontology acute care nurse practitioner (MSN, DNP), adult/gerontology clinical nurse specialist (MSN), adult/gerontology primary care nurse practitioner (MSN), family nurse practitioner (MSN), nurse educator (MSN), nursing and healthcare management (MSN), pediatric primary care nurse practitioner (MSN), psychiatric/mental health nurse practitioner (MSN); MBA/MSN. *Accreditation:* AACN. *Program availability:* Part-time, online learning. *Faculty:* 28 full-time (26 women), 15 part-time/adjunct (13 women). *Students:* 138 full-time (123 women), 522 part-time (464 women); includes 80 minority (41 Black or African American, non-Hispanic/Latino; 16 Asian, non-Hispanic/Latino; 9 Hispanic/Latino; 1 Native Hawaiian or other Pacific Islander, non-Hispanic/Latino; 13 Two or more races, non-Hispanic/Latino), 7 international. Average age 35. 303 applicants, 68% accepted, 154 enrolled. In 2019, 156 master's, 8 doctorates awarded. *Degree requirements:* For master's, practicum for master's degrees; for doctorate, comprehensive exam, thesis/dissertation. *Entrance requirements:* For master's, GRE or GMAT, minimum GPA of 3.0, active RN license, statement of purpose, 3 letters of reference, undergraduate level statistics class (minimum C grade), baccalaureate or graduate-level nursing degree, curriculum vitae/resume; for doctorate, GRE, minimum GPA of 3.0, transcripts, 3 letters of reference, interview, active unrestricted Ohio RN license, statement of purpose, writing sample, curriculum vitae/resume, baccalaureate and master's degrees in nursing or DNP, undergraduate or graduate level statistics course with a minimum C grade. Additional exam requirements/recommendations for international students: required—TOEFL (minimum score 83 iBT), IELTS (minimum score 6.5), PTE (minimum score 55), Michigan English Language Assessment Battery (minimum score 78). *Application deadline:* For fall admission, 3/1 for domestic and international students; for spring admission, 10/1 for domestic and international students. Applications are processed on a rolling basis. Application fee: $45 ($70 for international students). Electronic applications accepted. *Financial support:* Federal Work-Study and scholarships/grants available. Financial award application deadline: 2/1. *Unit head:* Dr. Barbara Broome, Ph.D., Dean, 330-672-3777, E-mail: bbroome1@kent.edu. *Application contact:* Dr. Wendy A. Umberger, Ph.D., Associate Dean for Graduate Programs/Professor, 330-672-8813, E-mail: wlewando@kent.edu.
Website: http://www.kent.edu/nursing/

**Lincoln Memorial University,** Caylor School of Nursing, Harrogate, TN 37752-1901. Offers family nurse practitioner (MSN); nurse anesthesia (MSN); psychiatric mental health nurse practitioner (MSN). *Accreditation:* AANA/CANAEP; ACEN. *Program availability:* Part-time. *Entrance requirements:* For master's, GRE.

**McNeese State University,** Doré School of Graduate Studies, College of Nursing and Health Professions, MSN Program, Lake Charles, LA 70609. Offers family nurse practitioner (MSN); nurse educator (MSN); psychiatric/mental health nurse practitioner (MSN). *Entrance requirements:* For master's, GRE, baccalaureate degree in nursing, minimum overall GPA of 2.7 for all undergraduate coursework, eligibility for unencumbered licensure as Registered Nurse in Louisiana or Texas, course in introductory statistics with minimum C grade, physical assessment skills, two letters of professional reference, 500-word essay, current resume.

**McNeese State University,** Doré School of Graduate Studies, College of Nursing and Health Professions, Post Master's Psychiatric/Mental Health Nurse Practitioner Program, Lake Charles, LA 70609. Offers PMC. *Entrance requirements:* For degree, GRE, MSN, eligible for unencumbered licensure as RN in Louisiana.

**MGH Institute of Health Professions,** School of Nursing, Boston, MA 02129. Offers advanced practice nursing (MSN); gerontological nursing (MSN); nursing (DNP); pediatric nursing (MSN); psychiatric nursing (MSN); teaching and learning for health care education (Certificate); women's health nursing (MSN). *Accreditation:* AACN. *Degree requirements:* For master's, thesis or alternative. *Entrance requirements:* For master's, GRE General Test, bachelor's degree from regionally-accredited college or university. Additional exam requirements/recommendations for international students: required—TOEFL (minimum score 550 paper-based; 80 iBT). Electronic applications accepted.

**Midwestern State University,** Billie Doris McAda Graduate School, Robert D. and Carol Gunn College of Health Sciences and Human Services, Wilson School of Nursing, Wichita Falls, TX 76308. Offers family nurse practitioner (MSN); family psychiatric mental health nurse practitioner (MSN); nurse educator (MSN). *Accreditation:* AACN. *Program availability:* Part-time, evening/weekend. *Degree requirements:* For master's, comprehensive exam, thesis optional. *Entrance requirements:* For master's, GRE General Test or MAT. Additional exam requirements/recommendations for international students: required—TOEFL (minimum score 550 paper-based). Electronic applications accepted.

**Molloy College,** Graduate Nursing Program, Rockville Centre, NY 11571-5002. Offers adult-gerontology clinical nurse specialist (DNP); adult-gerontology nurse practitioner (MS, DNP); clinical nurse specialist: adult-gerontology (MS); family nurse practitioner (MS, DNP); family psychiatric/mental health nurse practitioner (MS, DNP); nursing (PhD, Advanced Certificate); nursing administration with informatics (MS); nursing education (MS); pediatric nurse practitioner (MS, DNP). *Accreditation:* AACN. *Program availability:* Part-time, evening/weekend. *Faculty:* 30 full-time (28 women), 10 part-time/adjunct (6 women). *Students:* 18 full-time (17 women), 573 part-time (520 women); includes 340 minority (181 Black or African American, non-Hispanic/Latino; 2 American Indian or Alaska Native, non-Hispanic/Latino; 100 Asian, non-Hispanic/Latino; 42 Hispanic/Latino; 5 Native Hawaiian or other Pacific Islander, non-Hispanic/Latino; 10 Two or more races, non-Hispanic/Latino), 3 international. Average age 38. 332 applicants, 60% accepted, 149 enrolled. In 2019, 136 master's, 12 doctorates, 22 other advanced degrees awarded. *Degree requirements:* For doctorate, clinical research residency and scholarly clinical project (for DNP); dissertation and comprehensive exam (for PhD). *Entrance requirements:* Additional exam requirements/recommendations for international students: required—TOEFL (minimum score 550 paper-based; 79 iBT). *Application deadline:* Applications are processed on a rolling basis. Application fee: $60. Electronic applications accepted. *Expenses: Tuition:* Full-time $21,510; part-time $1195 per credit hour. *Required fees:* $1100. Tuition and fees vary according to course load, degree level and program. *Financial support:* Application deadline: 3/1; applicants required to submit FAFSA. *Unit head:* Dr. Marcia R. Gardner, Dean, The Barbara H. Hagan School of Nursing, 516-323-3651, E-mail: mgardner@molloy.edu. *Application contact:* Faye Hood, Assistant Director for Admissions, 516-323-4009, E-mail: fhood@molloy.edu.
Website: https://www.molloy.edu/academics/graduate-programs/graduate-nursing-x25989

**Montana State University,** The Graduate School, College of Nursing, Bozeman, MT 59717. Offers clinical nurse leader (MN); family and individual nurse practitioner (DNP); family nurse practitioner (MN, Post-Master's Certificate); nursing education (Certificate, Post-Master's Certificate); psychiatric mental health nurse practitioner (MN); psychiatric/mental health nurse practitioner (DNP). *Accreditation:* AACN. *Program availability:* Part-time, online learning. *Degree requirements:* For master's, comprehensive exam, thesis (for some programs); for doctorate, thesis/dissertation, 1,125 hours in clinical settings. *Entrance requirements:* For master's, GRE General Test, minimum GPA of 3.0 for undergraduate and post-baccalaureate work. Additional exam requirements/recommendations for international students: required—TOEFL (minimum score 580 paper-based). Electronic applications accepted.

**National University,** School of Health and Human Services, La Jolla, CA 92037-1011. Offers clinical affairs (MS); clinical regulatory affairs (MS); complementary and integrative healthcare (MS); family nurse practitioner (MSN); health and life science analytics (MS); health informatics (MS, Certificate); healthcare administration (MHA); nurse anesthesia (MSNA); nursing administration (MSN); nursing informatics (MSN); psychiatric-mental health nurse practitioner (MSN); public health (MPH), including health promotion, healthcare administration, mental health. *Accreditation:* CEPH. *Program availability:* Part-time, evening/weekend, 100% online, blended/hybrid learning. *Degree requirements:* For master's, thesis (for some programs). *Entrance requirements:* For master's, interview, minimum GPA of 2.5. Additional exam requirements/recommendations for international students: required—TOEFL (minimum score 550 paper-based; 79 iBT), IELTS (minimum score 6). Electronic applications accepted. *Expenses: Tuition:* Full-time $442; part-time $442 per unit.

**New Mexico State University,** College of Health and Social Services, School of Nursing, Las Cruces, NM 88003. Offers family nurse practitioner (Graduate Certificate); nursing (MSN); nursing practice (DNP); nursing science (PhD); psychiatric/mental health nurse practitioner (Graduate Certificate). *Accreditation:* AACN. *Program availability:* Part-time, blended/hybrid learning. *Faculty:* 12 full-time (all women). *Students:* 29. 57 applicants, 98% accepted. In 2019, 4 master's, 20 doctorates, 5 other advanced degrees awarded. *Degree requirements:* For master's, comprehensive exam, thesis optional, clinical practicum; for doctorate, comprehensive exam, thesis/dissertation. *Entrance requirements:* For master's, NCLEX exam, BSN, minimum GPA of 3.0, course work in statistics, 3 letters of reference, writing sample, RN license, CPR certification, proof of liability, immunizations, criminal background check; for doctorate, NCLEX exam, MSN, minimum GPA of 3.0, 3 letters of reference, writing sample, RN license, CPR certification, proof of liability, immunizations, criminal background check, statistics course. Additional exam requirements/recommendations for international students: required—TOEFL (minimum score 550 paper-based; 79 iBT), IELTS (minimum score 6.5). *Application deadline:* For fall admission, 2/1 priority date for domestic students, 2/1

for international students. Application fee: $40 ($50 for international students). Electronic applications accepted. *Financial support:* In 2019–20, 7 teaching assistantships (averaging $10,499 per year) were awarded; career-related internships or fieldwork, Federal Work-Study, scholarships/grants, traineeships, health care benefits, and unspecified assistantships also available. Support available to part-time students. Financial award application deadline: 3/1. *Unit head:* Dr. Alexa Doig, Director, 575-646-3812, Fax: 575-646-2167, E-mail: adoig@nmsu.edu. *Application contact:* Alyce Kolenovsky, Academic Advisor, 575-646-3812, Fax: 575-646-2167, E-mail: nursing@nmsu.edu.
Website: http://schoolofnursing.nmsu.edu

**New York University,** Rory Meyers College of Nursing, Doctor of Nursing Practice Program, New York, NY 10012-1019. Offers nursing (DNP), including adult-gerontology acute care nurse practitioner, adult-gerontology primary care nurse practitioner, family nurse practitioner, nurse-midwifery, pediatrics nurse practitioner, psychiatric-mental health nurse practitioner. *Accreditation:* AACN. *Program availability:* Part-time, evening/weekend. *Degree requirements:* For doctorate, thesis/dissertation, project. *Entrance requirements:* For doctorate, MS, RN license, interview, Nurse Practitioner Certification, writing sample. Additional exam requirements/recommendations for international students: required—TOEFL (minimum score 100 iBT), IELTS (minimum score 7). Electronic applications accepted. *Expenses:* Contact institution.

**New York University,** Rory Meyers College of Nursing, Programs in Advanced Practice Nursing, New York, NY 10012-1019. Offers adult-gerontology acute care nurse practitioner (MS, Advanced Certificate); adult-gerontology primary care nurse practitioner (MS, Advanced Certificate); family nurse practitioner (MS, Advanced Certificate); gerontology nurse practitioner (Advanced Certificate); nurse-midwifery (MS, Advanced Certificate); nursing administration (MS, Advanced Certificate); nursing education (MS, Advanced Certificate); nursing informatics (MS, Advanced Certificate); pediatrics nurse practitioner (MS, Advanced Certificate); psychiatric-mental health nurse practitioner (MS, Advanced Certificate); MS/MPH. *Accreditation:* AACN; ACNM/ACME. *Program availability:* Part-time, evening/weekend. *Degree requirements:* For master's, thesis (for some programs), capstone. *Entrance requirements:* For master's, BS in nursing, AS in nursing with another BS/BA, interview, RN license, 1 year of clinical experience (3 for the MS in nursing education program); for Advanced Certificate, master's degree in nursing. Additional exam requirements/recommendations for international students: required—TOEFL (minimum score 100 iBT), IELTS (minimum score 7). Electronic applications accepted. *Expenses:* Contact institution.

**Nicholls State University,** Graduate Studies, College of Nursing and Allied Health, Thibodaux, LA 70310. Offers family nurse practitioner (MSN); nurse executive (MSN); nursing education (MSN); psychiatric/mental health nurse practitioner (MSN).

**Northeastern University,** Bouvé College of Health Sciences, Boston, MA 02115-5096. Offers applied behavior analysis (MS); audiology (Au D); counseling psychology (MS, PhD, CAGS); exercise science (MS); nursing (MS, PhD, CAGS), including administration (MS), adult-gerontology acute care nurse practitioner (MS, CAGS), adult-gerontology primary care nurse practitioner (MS, CAGS), anesthesia (MS), family nurse practitioner (MS, CAGS), neonatal nurse practitioner (MS, CAGS), pediatric nurse practitioner (MS, CAGS), psychiatric mental health nurse practitioner (MS, CAGS); nursing practice (DNP); pharmaceutical sciences (MS, PhD), including interdisciplinary concentration, pharmaceutics and drug delivery systems; pharmacology (MS); pharmacy (Pharm D); school psychology (PhD); speech-language pathology (MS); urban health (MPH); MS/MBA. *Accreditation:* AANA/CANAEP; ACPE (one or more programs are accredited); ASHA; CEPH. *Program availability:* Part-time, evening/weekend, online learning. *Degree requirements:* For doctorate, thesis/dissertation (for some programs); for CAGS, comprehensive exam. Electronic applications accepted. *Expenses:* Contact institution.

**Nova Southeastern University,** Ron and Kathy Assaf College of Nursing, Fort Lauderdale, FL 33314-7796. Offers advanced practice registered nurse (MSN), including adult-gerontology acute care nurse practitioner, family nurse practitioner, psychiatric mental health nurse practitioner; executive nurse leadership (MSN); nursing (PhD), including nursing education; nursing education (MSN); nursing informatics (MSN); nursing practice (DNP). *Accreditation:* AACN. *Program availability:* Part-time, evening/weekend, 100% online, blended/hybrid learning, annual one-week summer institute delivered face-to-face on main campus. *Faculty:* 32 full-time (29 women), 34 part-time/adjunct (31 women). *Students:* 4 full-time (3 women), 658 part-time (585 women); includes 427 minority (182 Black or African American, non-Hispanic/Latino; 35 Asian, non-Hispanic/Latino; 197 Hispanic/Latino; 13 Two or more races, non-Hispanic/Latino), 3 international. Average age 38. 157 applicants, 93% accepted, 146 enrolled. In 2019, 184 master's, 12 doctorates awarded. *Degree requirements:* For doctorate, comprehensive exam, thesis/dissertation. *Entrance requirements:* For master's, minimum GPA of 3.0, RN, BSN, BS or BA; for doctorate, minimum GPA of 3.5, MSN, RN. Additional exam requirements/recommendations for international students: recommended—TOEFL. *Application deadline:* For fall admission, 8/1 for domestic students, 3/1 for international students; for winter admission, 12/9 for domestic students, 11/1 for international students. Applications are processed on a rolling basis. Application fee: $50. Electronic applications accepted. *Expenses:* Contact institution. *Financial support:* Application deadline: 4/15; applicants required to submit FAFSA. *Unit head:* Dr. Marcella M. Rutherford, Dean, 954-262-1963, E-mail: rmarcell@nova.edu. *Application contact:* Dianna Murphey, Director of Operations, 954-262-1975, E-mail: dgardner1@nova.edu.
Website: http://www.nova.edu/nursing/

**Oregon Health & Science University,** School of Nursing, Program in Psychiatric Mental Health Nurse Practitioner, Portland, OR 97239-3098. Offers MN. *Accreditation:* AACN. *Degree requirements:* For master's, thesis optional. *Entrance requirements:* For master's, GRE General Test, bachelor's degree in nursing, minimum cumulative and science GPA of 3.0, 3 letters of recommendation, essays, statistics within last 5 years. Additional exam requirements/recommendations for international students: required—TOEFL (minimum score 83 iBT). Electronic applications accepted. *Expenses:* Contact institution.

**Pontifical Catholic University of Puerto Rico,** College of Sciences, Department of Nursing, Program in Mental Health and Psychiatric Nursing, Ponce, PR 00717-0777. Offers MSN. *Program availability:* Part-time, evening/weekend. *Degree requirements:* For master's, comprehensive exam (for some programs), thesis, clinical research paper. *Entrance requirements:* For master's, GRE General Test, 2 letters of recommendation, interview, minimum GPA of 2.75. Electronic applications accepted.

**Rivier University,** School of Graduate Studies, Division of Nursing and Health Professions, Nashua, NH 03060. Offers family nurse practitioner (MS); leadership in health systems management (MS); nursing education (MS); nursing practice (DNP); psychiatric/mental health nurse practitioner (MS); public health (MPH). *Accreditation:* ACEN. *Program availability:* Part-time, evening/weekend. *Entrance requirements:* For master's, GRE, MAT. Electronic applications accepted.

**Sage Graduate School,** School of Health Sciences, Department of Nursing, Program in Psychiatric Mental Health Nurse Practitioner, Troy, NY 12180-4115. Offers MS, Post Master's Certificate. *Accreditation:* AACN. *Program availability:* Part-time, evening/weekend. *Faculty:* 8 full-time (all women), 13 part-time/adjunct (12 women). *Students:* 8 full-time (7 women), 36 part-time (34 women); includes 11 minority (3 Black or African American, non-Hispanic/Latino; 1 American Indian or Alaska Native, non-Hispanic/Latino; 3 Asian, non-Hispanic/Latino; 4 Hispanic/Latino). Average age 40. 38 applicants, 37% accepted, 7 enrolled. In 2019, 11 master's, 7 other advanced degrees awarded. *Degree requirements:* For master's, thesis or alternative. *Entrance requirements:* For master's, applicants must be currently licensed as a registered professional nurse in the state where they practice; bachelor's degree in nursing from a nationally accredited program; GPA of 3.0 or higher; official transcripts of all previous UG/GR study; 2 letters of reference; 1-2 page statement of professional goals; current resume. Additional exam requirements/recommendations for international students: required—TOEFL (minimum score 550 paper-based). *Application deadline:* Applications are processed on a rolling basis. Application fee: $40. Electronic applications accepted. *Expenses:* Tuition: Part-time $730 per credit hour. Tuition and fees vary according to course load, degree level and program. *Financial support:* Fellowships, research assistantships, scholarships/grants, and unspecified assistantships available. Financial award application deadline: 3/1; financial award applicants required to submit FAFSA. *Unit head:* Dr. Kathleen Kelly, Dean, School of Health Sciences, 518-244-2030, Fax: 518-244-2009, E-mail: kellyk5@sage.edu. *Application contact:* Erin Menzer, Associate Director of Transfer and Nursing Enrollment Management, 518-244-4565, Fax: 518-244-6880, E-mail: menzee@sage.edu.

**Saint Francis Medical Center College of Nursing,** SFMC College of Nursing Graduate Programs, Peoria, IL 61603-3783. Offers adult gerontology (MSN); clinical nurse leader (MSN); family nurse practitioner (MSN, Post-Graduate Certificate); family psychiatric mental health nurse practitioner (MSN); neonatal nurse practitioner (MSN); nurse clinician (Post-Graduate Certificate); nurse educator (MSN, Post-Graduate Certificate); nursing (DNP), including leadership/ clinician; nursing management leadership (MSN). *Accreditation:* ACEN. *Program availability:* Part-time, online only, 100% online, blended/hybrid learning. *Faculty:* 12 full-time (all women), 10 part-time/adjunct (all women). *Students:* 1 (woman) full-time, 188 part-time (157 women); includes 20 minority (10 Black or African American, non-Hispanic/Latino; 3 Asian, non-Hispanic/Latino; 3 Hispanic/Latino; 4 Two or more races, non-Hispanic/Latino). Average age 40. 54 applicants, 91% accepted, 18 enrolled. In 2019, 51 master's, 11 doctorates awarded. *Degree requirements:* For master's, research experience, portfolio, practicum; for doctorate, practicum. *Entrance requirements:* For master's, Nursing research, health assessment, RN license; for doctorate, Master's degree in nursing, professional portfolio, graduate statistics, transcripts, RN license. Additional exam requirements/recommendations for international students: required—TOEFL (minimum score 550 paper-based; 79 iBT). *Application deadline:* For fall admission, 6/1 priority date for domestic and international students; for spring admission, 11/15 priority date for domestic and international students. Applications are processed on a rolling basis. Application fee: $50. *Expenses:* Tuition: Part-time $705 per credit hour. *Required fees:* $270 per unit. *Financial support:* In 2019–20, 13 students received support. Scholarships/grants available. Support available to part-time students. Financial award application deadline: 6/15; financial award applicants required to submit FAFSA. *Unit head:* Dr. Sandie S Soldwisch, President of OSF Colleges of Health Sciences, 815-282-7909, Fax: 309-624-8973, E-mail: Sandie.S.Soldwisch@osfhealthcare.org. *Application contact:* Dr. Kim A. Mitchell, Dean, Graduate Program, 309-655-2201, Fax: 309-624-8973, E-mail: kim.a.mitchell@osfhealthcare.org.
Website: http://www.sfmccon.edu/graduate-programs/

**Shenandoah University,** Eleanor Wade Custer School of Nursing, Winchester, VA 22601. Offers adult gerontology primary care nurse practitioner (Graduate Certificate); adult-gerontology primary care nurse practitioner (MSN); family nurse practitioner (MSN, DNP, Graduate Certificate); general (MSN); health systems leadership (DNP); health systems management (MSN, Graduate Certificate); nurse midwifery (MSN); nurse-midwifery (Graduate Certificate); nursing education (Graduate Certificate); nursing practice (DNP); psychiatric mental health nurse practitioner (MSN, DNP, Graduate Certificate). *Accreditation:* AACN; ACNM/ACME. *Entrance requirements:* For master's, United States RN license; minimum GPA of 3.0; 2080 hours of clinical experience; curriculum vitae; 3 letters of recommendation from former dean, faculty member, or advisor familiar with the applicant, and a former or current supervisor; two-to-three-page essay on a specified topic; for doctorate, MSN, minimum GPA of 3.0, 3 letters of recommendation, interview, BSN, two-to-three page essay on a specific topic, 500-word statement of clinical practice research interest, resume, current U.S. RN license, 2080 clinical hours; for Graduate Certificate, MSN, minimum GPA of 3.0, 2 letters of recommendation, minimum of one year (2080 hours) of clinical nursing experience, interview, two-to-three page essay on a specific topic, resume, current United States RN license. Additional exam requirements/recommendations for international students: required—TOEFL (minimum score 558 paper-based; 83 iBT). Electronic applications accepted. *Expenses:* Contact institution.

**Southern Adventist University,** School of Nursing, Collegedale, TN 37315-0370. Offers acute care-adult/gerontology nurse practitioner (MSN, DNP); healthcare administration (MSN/MBA); lifestyle medicine (DNP); nurse educator (MSN, DNP); primary care-adult/gerontology nurse practitioner (MSN); primary care-family nurse practitioner (MSN, DNP); primary care-psychiatric mental health nurse practitioner (MSN, DNP); MSN/MBA. *Accreditation:* ACEN. *Program availability:* Part-time, 100% online. *Degree requirements:* For master's, thesis or project; for doctorate, scholarly project. *Entrance requirements:* For master's, RN license. Additional exam requirements/recommendations for international students: required—TOEFL (minimum score 100 iBT). Electronic applications accepted.

**Southern Arkansas University–Magnolia,** School of Graduate Studies, Magnolia, AR 71753. Offers agriculture (MS); business administration (MBA), including agribusiness, social entrepreneurship, supply chain management; clinical and mental health counseling (MS); computer and information sciences (MS), including cyber security and privacy, data science, information technology; gifted and talented (M Ed), including curriculum and instruction, educational administration and supervision, gifted and talented P-8/7-12, instructional specialist P-4; higher, adult and lifelong education (M Ed); kinesiology (M Ed), including coaching; library media and information specialist (M Ed); public administration (MPA); school counseling K-12 (M Ed); student affairs and college counseling (M Ed); teaching (MAT). *Accreditation:* NCATE. *Program availability:* Part-time, 100% online, blended/hybrid learning. *Faculty:* 33 full-time (18 women), 29 part-time/adjunct (17 women). *Students:* 134 full-time (80 women), 704 part-time (471 women); includes 223 minority (158 Black or African American, non-Hispanic/Latino; 5 American Indian or Alaska Native, non-Hispanic/Latino; 19 Asian, non-Hispanic/Latino; 6 Hispanic/Latino; 1 Native Hawaiian or other Pacific Islander, non-Hispanic/Latino; 34 Two or more races, non-Hispanic/Latino), 135 international. Average age 28. 290 applicants, 99% accepted, 149 enrolled. In 2019, 177 master's awarded. *Degree requirements:* For master's, comprehensive exam (for some programs), thesis optional. *Entrance requirements:* For master's, GRE, MAT or GMAT, minimum GPA of 2.5. Additional exam requirements/recommendations for international students: required—TOEFL (minimum score 550 paper-based), IELTS (minimum score 6). *Application deadline:* For fall admission, 8/1 for domestic and international students; for spring admission, 12/1 for domestic students, 11/15 for international students; for summer admission, 5/1 for domestic students, 5/10 for international students. Applications are

processed on a rolling basis. Application fee: $25 ($90 for international students). Electronic applications accepted. *Expenses: Tuition, area resident:* Full-time $6720; part-time $3360 per semester. Tuition, state resident: full-time $6720; part-time $3360 per semester. Tuition, nonresident: full-time $10,560; part-time $5280 per semester. *International tuition:* $10,560 full-time. *Required fees:* $2046; $1023 $267. One-time fee: $25. Tuition and fees vary according to course load. *Financial support:* Career-related internships or fieldwork, Federal Work-Study, scholarships/grants, tuition waivers (full), and unspecified assistantships available. Financial award applicants required to submit FAFSA. *Unit head:* Dr. Kim Bloss, Dean, School of Graduate Studies, 870-235-4150, Fax: 870-235-5227, E-mail: kkbloss@saumag.edu. *Application contact:* Talia Jett, Admissions Coordinator, 870-2355450, Fax: 870-235-5227, E-mail: taliajett@saumag.edu.
Website: http://www.saumag.edu/graduate

**Stony Brook University, State University of New York,** Stony Brook Medicine, School of Nursing, Psychiatric-Mental Health Nurse Practitioner Program, Stony Brook, NY 11794. Offers MS, DNP, Certificate. *Accreditation:* AACN. *Program availability:* Part-time, blended/hybrid learning. *Students:* 150 part-time (118 women); includes 67 minority (33 Black or African American, non-Hispanic/Latino; 12 Asian, non-Hispanic/Latino; 14 Hispanic/Latino; 1 Native Hawaiian or other Pacific Islander, non-Hispanic/Latino; 7 Two or more races, non-Hispanic/Latino). 180 applicants, 37% accepted, 61 enrolled. In 2019, 31 master's, 9 other advanced degrees awarded. *Degree requirements:* For master's, thesis; for doctorate, thesis/dissertation. *Entrance requirements:* For master's, BSN, minimum GPA of 3.0, course work in statistics. Additional exam requirements/recommendations for international students: required—TOEFL (minimum score 90 iBT). *Application deadline:* For fall admission, 2/27 for domestic students. Application fee: $100. Electronic applications accepted. *Expenses:* Contact institution. *Financial support:* Application deadline: 3/15. *Unit head:* Dr. Barbara Sprung, Program Director, 631-444-3292, Fax: 631-444-3136, E-mail: barbara.sprung@stonybrook.edu. *Application contact:* Staff Assistant, 631-444-3276, Fax: 631-444-3136, E-mail: pmhnp_nursing@stonybrook.edu.
Website: http://www.nursing.stonybrookmedicine.edu/

**Tennessee Technological University,** Whitson-Hester School of Nursing, DNP Program, Cookeville, TN 38505. Offers adult-gerontology acute care nurse practitioner (DNP); executive leadership in nursing (DNP); family nurse practitioner (DNP); pediatric nurse practitioner-primary care (DNP); psychiatric/mental health nurse practitioner (DNP); women's health care nurse practitioner (DNP). *Program availability:* Part-time. *Students:* 20 full-time (17 women), 12 part-time (all women); includes 3 minority (2 Black or African American, non-Hispanic/Latino; 1 Two or more races, non-Hispanic/Latino). 25 applicants, 60% accepted, 10 enrolled. *Application deadline:* For fall admission, 7/1 for domestic students, 5/1 for international students; for spring admission, 12/1 for domestic students, 10/1 for international students; for summer admission, 5/1 for domestic students, 2/1 for international students. Applications are processed on a rolling basis. Application fee: $35 ($40 for international students). Electronic applications accepted. *Expenses: Tuition, area resident:* Part-time $597 per credit hour. Tuition, state resident: part-time $597 per credit hour. Tuition, nonresident: part-time $1323 per credit hour. *Financial support:* Application deadline: 4/1; applicants required to submit FAFSA. *Unit head:* Dr. Kim Hanna, Dean, Fax: 931-372-6244, E-mail: khanna@tntech.edu. *Application contact:* Shelia K. Kendrick, Coordinator of Graduate Studies, 931-372-3808, Fax: 931-372-3497, E-mail: skendrick@tntech.edu.
Website: https://www.tntech.edu/nursing/doctor-of-nursing-practice/

**Uniformed Services University of the Health Sciences,** Daniel K. Inouye Graduate School of Nursing, Bethesda, MD 20814. Offers adult-gerontology clinical nurse specialist (MSN, DNP); family nurse practitioner (DNP); nurse anesthesia (DNP); nursing science (PhD); psychiatric mental health nurse practitioner (DNP); women's health nurse practitioner (DNP). *Accreditation:* AACN; AANA/CANAEP. *Program availability:* Part-time. *Faculty:* 50 full-time (32 women), 1 part-time/adjunct (0 women). *Students:* 170 full-time (98 women); includes 51 minority (21 Black or African American, non-Hispanic/Latino; 17 Asian, non-Hispanic/Latino; 11 Hispanic/Latino; 2 Native Hawaiian or other Pacific Islander, non-Hispanic/Latino). Average age 34. 88 applicants, 75% accepted, 66 enrolled. In 2019, 2 master's, 42 doctorates awarded. *Degree requirements:* For master's, thesis, scholarly project; for doctorate, dissertation (for PhD); project (for DNP). *Entrance requirements:* For master's, GRE, BSN, clinical experience, minimum GPA of 3.0, previous course work in science; for doctorate, GRE, BSN, minimum GPA of 3.0, undergraduate/graduate science course within past 5 years, writing example, interview (for some programs), and 3 letters of reference (for DNP); master's degree, minimum GPA of 3.0 in nursing or related field, personal statement, 3 references, and interview (for PhD). *Application deadline:* For winter admission, 2/15 for domestic students; for summer admission, 8/15 for domestic students. Electronic applications accepted. *Financial support:* Robert Wood Johnson and Jonas scholars available. *Unit head:* Dr. Diane C. Seibert, Associate Dean for Academic Affairs, 301-295-1080, Fax: 301-295-1707, E-mail: diane.seibert@usuhs.edu. *Application contact:* Maureen Jackson, Student Admissions Program Manager, 301-295-1055, E-mail: maureen.jackson.ctr@usuhs.edu.
Website: http://www.usuhs.edu/gsn/

**University at Buffalo, the State University of New York,** Graduate School, School of Nursing, Buffalo, NY 14260. Offers adult gerontology nurse practitioner (DNP); family nurse practitioner (DNP); health care systems and leadership (MS); nurse anesthetist (DNP); nursing (PhD); nursing education (Certificate); psychiatric/mental health nurse practitioner (DNP). *Accreditation:* AACN; AANA/CANAEP (one or more programs are accredited). *Program availability:* Part-time, 100% online. *Degree requirements:* For master's, thesis optional; for doctorate, comprehensive exam (for some programs), capstone (for DNP), dissertation (for PhD). *Entrance requirements:* For master's, GRE or MAT; for doctorate, GRE or MAT, minimum GPA of 3.0 (for DNP), 3.25 (for PhD); RN license; BS or MS in nursing; 3 references; writing sample; resume; personal statement; for Certificate, interview, minimum GPA of 3.0 or GRE General Test, RN license, MS in nursing, professional certification. Additional exam requirements/recommendations for international students: required—TOEFL (minimum score 550 paper-based; 79 iBT), IELTS (minimum score 6.5). Electronic applications accepted. *Expenses:* Contact institution.

**The University of Alabama at Birmingham,** School of Nursing, Birmingham, AL 35294. Offers clinical nurse leader (MSN); nurse anesthesia (DNP); nurse practitioner (MSN, DNP), including adult-gerontology acute care (MSN), adult-gerontology primary care (MSN), family (MSN), pediatric (MSN), psychiatric/mental health (MSN), women's health (MSN); nursing (MSN, DNP, PhD); nursing health systems administration (MSN); nursing informatics (MSN). *Accreditation:* AACN; AANA/CANAEP. *Program availability:* Part-time, online only, blended/hybrid learning. *Faculty:* 86 full-time (79 women), 42 part-time/adjunct (35 women). *Students:* 228 full-time (165 women), 1,393 part-time (1,234 women); includes 398 minority (267 Black or African American, non-Hispanic/Latino; 4 American Indian or Alaska Native, non-Hispanic/Latino; 52 Asian, non-Hispanic/Latino; 41 Hispanic/Latino; 34 Two or more races, non-Hispanic/Latino), 3 international. Average age 33. 1,027 applicants, 55% accepted, 421 enrolled. In 2019, 557 master's, 19 doctorates awarded. Terminal master's awarded for partial completion of doctoral program. *Degree requirements:* For master's, comprehensive exam; for doctorate, comprehensive exam, thesis/dissertation, research mentorship experience (for PhD); scholarly project (for DNP). *Entrance requirements:* For master's, GRE, GMAT, or MAT, minimum cumulative undergraduate GPA of 3.0 or on last 60 semesters hours; letters of recommendation; for doctorate, GRE General Test, computer literacy, course work in statistics, interview, minimum GPA of 3.0, MS in nursing, references, writing sample. Additional exam requirements/recommendations for international students: required—TOEFL (minimum score 500 paper-based, 80 iBT) or IELTS (5.5). *Application deadline:* For fall admission, 2/24 for domestic students; for summer admission, 10/15 for domestic students. Application fee: $50. Electronic applications accepted. *Expenses:* Contact institution. *Financial support:* In 2019–20, 23 fellowships (averaging $34,685 per year), 12 research assistantships (averaging $9,042 per year), 2 teaching assistantships (averaging $22,000 per year) were awarded; scholarships/grants, traineeships, health care benefits, and unspecified assistantships also available. Support available to part-time students. *Unit head:* Dr. Doreen C. Harper, Dean, 205-934-5360, Fax: 205-934-1894, E-mail: dcharper@uab.edu. *Application contact:* John Updegraff, Director of Student Affairs, 205-975-3370, Fax: 205-934-5490, E-mail: jupde22@uab.edu.
Website: http://www.uab.edu/nursing/home/

**University of Colorado Denver,** College of Nursing, Aurora, CO 80045. Offers adult clinical nurse specialist (MS); adult nurse practitioner (MS); family nurse practitioner (MS); family psychiatric mental health nurse practitioner (MS); health care informatics (MS); nurse-midwifery (MS); nursing (DNP, PhD); nursing leadership and health care systems (MS); pediatric nurse practitioner (MS); women's health (MS); MS/PhD. *Accreditation:* ACNM/ACME (one or more programs are accredited). *Program availability:* Part-time, evening/weekend, online learning. Terminal master's awarded for partial completion of doctoral program. *Degree requirements:* For master's, thesis optional; for doctorate, comprehensive exam, thesis/dissertation, 42 credits of coursework. *Entrance requirements:* For master's, GRE if cumulative undergraduate GPA is less than 3.0, undergraduate nursing degree from ACEN- or CCNE-accredited school or university; completion of research and statistics courses with minimum grade of C; copy of current and unencumbered nursing license; for doctorate, GRE, bachelor's and/or master's degrees in nursing from ACEN- or CCNE-accredited institution; portfolio; minimum undergraduate GPA of 3.0, graduate 3.5; graduate-level intermediate statistics and master's-level nursing theory courses with minimum B grade; interview. Additional exam requirements/recommendations for international students: required—TOEFL (minimum score 560 paper-based; 83 iBT). Electronic applications accepted. *Expenses:* Contact institution.

**University of Delaware,** College of Health Sciences, School of Nursing, Newark, DE 19716. Offers adult nurse practitioner (MSN, PMC); cardiopulmonary clinical nurse specialist (MSN, PMC); cardiopulmonary clinical nurse specialist/adult nurse practitioner (MSN, PMC); family nurse practitioner (MSN, PMC); gerontology clinical nurse specialist (MSN, PMC); gerontology clinical nurse specialist geriatric nurse practitioner (PMC); gerontology clinical nurse specialist/geriatric nurse practitioner (MSN); health services administration (MSN, PMC); nursing of children clinical nurse specialist (MSN, PMC); nursing of children clinical nurse specialist/pediatric nurse practitioner (MSN, PMC); oncology/immune deficiency clinical nurse specialist (MSN, PMC); oncology/immune deficiency clinical nurse specialist/adult nurse practitioner (MSN, PMC); perinatal/women's health clinical nurse specialist (MSN, PMC); perinatal/women's health clinical nurse specialist/women's health nurse practitioner (MSN, PMC); psychiatric nursing clinical nurse specialist (MSN, PMC). *Accreditation:* AACN. *Program availability:* Part-time, evening/weekend, online learning. *Degree requirements:* For master's, thesis optional. *Entrance requirements:* For master's, BSN, interview, RN license. Electronic applications accepted.

**The University of Kansas,** University of Kansas Medical Center, School of Nursing, Kansas City, KS 66045. Offers adult/gerontological clinical nurse specialist (PMC); adult/gerontological nurse practitioner (PMC); health care informatics (PMC); health professions educator (PMC); nurse midwife (PMC); nursing (MS, DNP, PhD); organizational leadership (PMC); psychiatric/mental health nurse practitioner (PMC); public health nursing (PMC). *Accreditation:* AACN; ACNM/ACME. *Program availability:* Part-time, 100% online, blended/hybrid learning. *Faculty:* 65. *Students:* 57 full-time (53 women), 267 part-time (242 women); includes 65 minority (14 Black or African American, non-Hispanic/Latino; 2 American Indian or Alaska Native, non-Hispanic/Latino; 21 Asian, non-Hispanic/Latino; 9 Hispanic/Latino; 1 Native Hawaiian or other Pacific Islander, non-Hispanic/Latino; 18 Two or more races, non-Hispanic/Latino), 2 international. Average age 35. In 2019, 26 master's, 48 doctorates, 5 other advanced degrees awarded. Terminal master's awarded for partial completion of doctoral program. *Degree requirements:* For master's, comprehensive exam, thesis (for some programs), general oral exam; for doctorate, thesis/dissertation or alternative, comprehensive oral exam (for DNP); comprehensive written and oral exam, or three publications (for PhD). *Entrance requirements:* For master's, bachelor's degree in nursing, minimum GPA of 3.0, 1 year of clinical experience, RN license in KS and MO; for doctorate, GRE General Test (for PhD only), bachelor's degree in nursing, minimum GPA of 3.5, RN license in KS and MO. Additional exam requirements/recommendations for international students: required—TOEFL. *Application deadline:* For fall admission, 4/1 for domestic and international students; for spring admission, 9/1 for domestic and international students. Application fee: $75. Electronic applications accepted. *Expenses:* Contact institution. *Financial support:* Research assistantships with tuition reimbursements, teaching assistantships with tuition reimbursements, scholarships/grants, and traineeships available. Financial award application deadline: 3/1; financial award applicants required to submit FAFSA. *Unit head:* Dr. Sally Maliski, Professor and Dean, 913-588-1601, Fax: 913-588-1660, E-mail: smaliski@kumc.edu. *Application contact:* Dr. Pamela K. Barnes, Associate Dean, Student Affairs and Enrollment Management, 913-588-1619, Fax: 913-588-1615, E-mail: pbarnes2@kumc.edu.
Website: http://nursing.kumc.edu

**University of Louisville,** Graduate School, School of Nursing, Louisville, KY 40202. Offers adult gerontology nurse practitioner (MSN, DNP); education and administration (MSN); family nurse practitioner (MSN, DNP); neonatal nurse practitioner (MSN, DNP); nursing research (PhD); psychiatric/mental health nurse practitioner (MSN, DNP); women's health nurse practitioner (MSN). *Accreditation:* AACN. *Program availability:* Part-time, blended/hybrid learning. *Faculty:* 49 full-time (46 women), 91 part-time/adjunct (86 women). *Students:* 164 full-time (140 women), 47 part-time (39 women); includes 45 minority (21 Black or African American, non-Hispanic/Latino; 5 Asian, non-Hispanic/Latino; 9 Hispanic/Latino; 10 Two or more races, non-Hispanic/Latino), 4 international. Average age 33. 84 applicants, 63% accepted, 48 enrolled. In 2019, 25 master's, 5 doctorates awarded. *Degree requirements:* For master's, varies; for doctorate, comprehensive exam (for some programs), thesis/dissertation (for some programs), varies. *Entrance requirements:* For master's, Our only master's degree is an accelerated program meant for students who have a bachelor's degree in another discipline who are transitioning into nursing. Thus, the main requirement is a bachelor's degree from a nationally-accredited college, and the completion of 6 prerequisite courses. Must have a minimum undergraduate GPA of 3.0; for doctorate, PhD program: GRE requirement omitted, DNP & PhD doctoral programs: 3 letters of professional reference. BSN applicants must have a 3.0 GPA. MSN applicants must have 3.25 GPA. Written statement of career goals, areas of expertise, reasons for pursuing doctoral

degree, resume, and RN license. Additional exam requirements/recommendations for international students: recommended—TOEFL (minimum score 560 paper-based), IELTS (minimum score 6.5). *Application deadline:* For fall admission, 1/15 priority date for domestic and international students; for summer admission, 10/15 priority date for domestic students. Application fee: $60. Electronic applications accepted. *Expenses:* 17871. *Financial support:* In 2019–20, 47 students received support, including 2 fellowships with full tuition reimbursements available (averaging $20,000 per year), 9 research assistantships with full tuition reimbursements available (averaging $20,000 per year), 3 teaching assistantships with full tuition reimbursements available (averaging $15,000 per year); scholarships/grants, health care benefits, unspecified assistantships, and Jonas Nurse Leader Fellowships also available. Financial award application deadline: 10/1; financial award applicants required to submit FAFSA. *Unit head:* 502-852-8300, Fax: 502-852-5044, E-mail: sonya.hardin@louisville.edu. *Application contact:* Trish Hart, MA, Assistant Dean for Student Affairs, 502-852-5825, Fax: 502-852-8783, E-mail: trish.hart@louisville.edu.
Website: http://www.louisville.edu/nursing/

**University of Maryland, Baltimore,** University of Maryland School of Nursing, Baltimore, MD 21201. Offers adult-gerontology acute care nurse practitioner (DNP); adult-gerontology primary care nurse practitioner (DNP); clinical nurse leader (MS); community/public health nursing (MS); family nurse practitioner (DNP); global health (Postbaccalaureate Certificate); health services leadership and management (MS); neonatal nurse practitioner (DNP); nurse anesthesia (DNP); nursing (PhD); nursing informatics (MS, Postbaccalaureate Certificate); pediatric acute/primary care nurse practitioner (DNP); psychiatric mental health nurse practitioner (DNP); teaching in nursing and health professions (Postbaccalaureate Certificate); MS/MBA. *Accreditation:* AANA/CANAEP. *Program availability:* Part-time. *Faculty:* 130 full-time (117 women), 125 part-time/adjunct (114 women). *Students:* 539 full-time (463 women), 586 part-time (506 women); includes 485 minority (259 Black or African American, non-Hispanic/Latino; 3 American Indian or Alaska Native, non-Hispanic/Latino; 124 Asian, non-Hispanic/Latino; 66 Hispanic/Latino; 1 Native Hawaiian or other Pacific Islander, non-Hispanic/Latino; 32 Two or more races, non-Hispanic/Latino), 18 international. Average age 33. 964 applicants, 54% accepted, 347 enrolled. In 2019, 197 master's, 114 doctorates, 12 other advanced degrees awarded. *Degree requirements:* For master's and Postbaccalaureate Certificate, thesis (for some programs); for doctorate, comprehensive exam, thesis/dissertation. *Entrance requirements:* Additional exam requirements/recommendations for international students: required—TOEFL (minimum score 550 paper-based; 79 iBT); recommended—IELTS (minimum score 7). *Application deadline:* For fall admission, 11/1 priority date for domestic and international students; for spring admission, 12/15 for domestic and international students; for summer admission, 9/1 for domestic and international students. Applications are processed on a rolling basis. Application fee: $75. Electronic applications accepted. *Financial support:* In 2019–20, 257 students received support, including 31 research assistantships with full and partial tuition reimbursements available (averaging $25,000 per year), 21 teaching assistantships with full and partial tuition reimbursements available (averaging $19,000 per year); scholarships/grants, traineeships, and unspecified assistantships also available. Support available to part-time students. Financial award application deadline: 3/1; financial award applicants required to submit FAFSA. *Unit head:* Dr. Jane Kirschling, Dean, 410-706-4359, E-mail: kirschling@umaryland.edu. *Application contact:* Larry Fillian, Associate Dean of Student and Academic Services, 410-706-6298, E-mail: lfillian@umaryland.edu.
Website: http://www.nursing.umaryland.edu/

**University of Michigan–Flint,** School of Nursing, Flint, MI 48502-1950. Offers adult-gerontology acute care (DNP); adult-gerontology primary care (DNP); family nurse practitioner (DNP); nursing (MSN); psychiatric mental health (DNP); psychiatric mental health nurse practitioner (Certificate). *Accreditation:* AACN. *Program availability:* Part-time, evening/weekend, 100% online. *Faculty:* 32 full-time (31 women), 80 part-time/adjunct (71 women). *Students:* 198 full-time (174 women), 188 part-time (162 women); includes 55 minority (6 Black or African American, non-Hispanic/Latino; 3 American Indian or Alaska Native, non-Hispanic/Latino; 21 Asian, non-Hispanic/Latino; 18 Hispanic/Latino; 1 Native Hawaiian or other Pacific Islander, non-Hispanic/Latino; 6 Two or more races, non-Hispanic/Latino), 1 international. Average age 37. 140 applicants, 84% accepted, 75 enrolled. In 2019, 52 master's, 22 doctorates, 8 other advanced degrees awarded. *Entrance requirements:* For master's, BSN from regionally-accredited college; minimum GPA of 3.2; current unencumbered RN license in the United States; three or more credits in college-level chemistry or statistics with minimum C grade; for Certificate, completion of nurse practitioner program with MS from regionally-accredited college or university with minimum overall GPA of 3.2; current unencumbered RN license in the United States; current unencumbered license as nurse practitioner; current certification as nurse practitioner in specialty other than discipline of study. Additional exam requirements/recommendations for international students: required—TOEFL (minimum score 84 iBT), IELTS (minimum score 6.5). *Application deadline:* For fall admission, 7/1 for domestic students, 5/1 for international students; for winter admission, 11/15 for domestic students, 10/1 for international students; for spring admission, 3/15 for domestic students, 1/1 for international students; for summer admission, 5/15 for domestic students. Applications are processed on a rolling basis. Application fee: $55. Electronic applications accepted. *Expenses:* Contact institution. *Financial support:* Federal Work-Study, scholarships/grants, and unspecified assistantships available. Support available to part-time students. Financial award application deadline: 3/1; financial award applicants required to submit FAFSA. *Unit head:* Dr. Constance J. Creech, Director, 810-762-3420, Fax: 810-766-6851, E-mail: ccreech@umflint.edu. *Application contact:* Matt Bohlen, Director of Graduate Admissions, 810-762-3171, Fax: 810-766-6789, E-mail: mbohlen@umflint.edu.
Website: https://www.umflint.edu/nursing/graduate-nursing-programs

**University of Minnesota, Twin Cities Campus,** Graduate School, School of Nursing, Minneapolis, MN 55455-0213. Offers adult/gerontological clinical nurse specialist (DNP); adult/gerontological primary care nurse practitioner (DNP); family nurse practitioner (DNP); health innovation and leadership (DNP); integrative health and healing (DNP); nurse anesthesia (DNP); nurse midwifery (DNP); nursing (MN, PhD); nursing informatics (DNP); pediatric clinical nurse specialist (DNP); primary care certified pediatric nurse practitioner (DNP); psychiatric/mental health nurse practitioner (DNP); women's health nurse practitioner (DNP). *Accreditation:* AACN; AANA/CANAEP; ACNM/ACME (one or more programs are accredited). *Program availability:* Part-time, online learning. Terminal master's awarded for partial completion of doctoral program. *Degree requirements:* For master's, final oral exam, project or thesis; for doctorate, thesis/dissertation. *Entrance requirements:* For master's and doctorate, GRE General Test. Additional exam requirements/recommendations for international students: required—TOEFL (minimum score 586 paper-based). *Expenses:* Contact institution.

**University of Missouri,** Office of Research and Graduate Studies, Sinclair School of Nursing, Columbia, MO 65211. Offers adult-gerontology clinical nurse specialist (DNP, Certificate); family nurse practitioner (DNP); family psychiatric and mental health nurse practitioner (DNP); nursing (MS, PhD); nursing leadership and innovations in health care (DNP); pediatric clinical nurse specialist (DNP, Certificate); pediatric nurse practitioner (DNP). *Accreditation:* AACN. *Program availability:* Part-time. *Degree requirements:* For master's, thesis optional, oral exam; for doctorate, thesis/dissertation. *Entrance requirements:* For master's, GRE General Test, BSN, minimum GPA of 3.0 during last 60 hours, nursing license. Additional exam requirements/recommendations for international students: required—TOEFL, IELTS. Electronic applications accepted.

**University of Missouri–St. Louis,** College of Nursing, St. Louis, MO 63121. Offers adult/geriatric nurse practitioner (Post Master's Certificate); family nurse practitioner (Post Master's Certificate); nursing (DNP, PhD); pediatric acute care nurse practitioner (Post Master's Certificate); pediatric nurse practitioner (Post Master's Certificate); psychiatric-mental health nurse practitioner (Post Master's Certificate); women's health nurse practitioner (Post Master's Certificate). *Accreditation:* AACN. *Program availability:* Part-time. *Degree requirements:* For doctorate, comprehensive exam, thesis/dissertation; for Post Master's Certificate, thesis. *Entrance requirements:* For doctorate, GRE, 2 letters of recommendation, MSN, minimum GPA of 3.2, course in differential/inferential statistics; for Post Master's Certificate, 2 recommendation letters; MSN; advanced practice certificate; minimum GPA of 3.0; essay. Additional exam requirements/recommendations for international students: recommended—TOEFL (minimum score 550 paper-based; 79 iBT), IELTS (minimum score 6.5). Electronic applications accepted. *Expenses: Tuition, area resident:* Full-time $9005.40; part-time $6003.60 per credit hour. Tuition, state resident: full-time $9005.40; part-time $6003.60 per credit hour. Tuition, nonresident: full-time $22,108; part-time $14,738.40 per credit hour. *International tuition:* $22,108 full-time. Tuition and fees vary according to course load.

**University of New Hampshire,** Graduate School, College of Health and Human Services, Department of Nursing, Durham, NH 03824. Offers family nurse practitioner (Postbaccalaureate Certificate); nursing (MS, DNP); psychiatric mental health (Postbaccalaureate Certificate). *Accreditation:* AACN. *Program availability:* Part-time, online learning. *Students:* 46 full-time (27 women), 11 part-time (8 women); includes 6 minority (1 Black or African American, non-Hispanic/Latino; 1 Asian, non-Hispanic/Latino; 2 Hispanic/Latino; 2 Two or more races, non-Hispanic/Latino), 3 international. Average age 34. 17 applicants, 71% accepted, 10 enrolled. In 2019, 7 doctorates awarded. *Entrance requirements:* Additional exam requirements/recommendations for international students: required—TOEFL (minimum score 550 paper-based; 80 iBT), IELTS, PTE. *Application deadline:* For fall admission, 7/1 for domestic students; for spring admission, 11/1 for domestic students. Application fee: $65. Electronic applications accepted. *Financial support:* In 2019–20, 36 students received support, including 4 fellowships, 15 research assistantships, 13 teaching assistantships; Federal Work-Study, scholarships/grants, and tuition waivers (full and partial) also available. Financial award application deadline: 2/15. *Unit head:* Dr. Gene Harkless, Chair, 603-862-2285. *Application contact:* Pan DiNapoli, Administrative Assistant, 603-862-3976, E-mail: pam.dinapoli@unh.edu.
Website: https://chhs.unh.edu/nursing/graduate-program-nursing

**The University of North Carolina at Chapel Hill,** School of Nursing, Chapel Hill, NC 27599-7460. Offers advanced practice registered nurse (DNP); nursing (MSN, PhD, PMC), including administration (MSN), adult gerontology primary care nurse practitioner (MSN), clinical nurse leader (MSN), education (MSN), health care systems (PMC), informatics (MSN, PMC), nursing leadership (PMC), outcomes management (MSN), primary care family nurse practitioner (MSN), primary care pediatric nurse practitioner (MSN), psychiatric/mental health nurse practitioner (MSN, PMC). *Accreditation:* AACN; ACEN (one or more programs are accredited). *Program availability:* Part-time. *Degree requirements:* For master's, comprehensive exam, thesis; for doctorate, thesis/dissertation, 3 exams; for PMC, thesis. *Entrance requirements:* Additional exam requirements/recommendations for international students: required—TOEFL (minimum score 575 paper-based; 89 iBT), IELTS (minimum score 8). Electronic applications accepted.

**University of North Dakota,** Graduate School, College of Nursing and Professional Disciplines, Department of Nursing, Grand Forks, ND 58202. Offers adult-gerontological nurse practitioner (MS); advanced public health nurse (MS); family nurse practitioner (MS); nurse anesthesia (MS); nurse educator (MS); nursing (PhD, Post-Master's Certificate); nursing practice (DNP); psychiatric and mental health nurse practitioner (MS). *Accreditation:* AANA/CANAEP.

**University of Pennsylvania,** School of Nursing, Psychiatric Mental Health Advanced Practice Nurse Program, Philadelphia, PA 19104. Offers adult and special populations (MSN); child and family (MSN); geropsychiatrics (MSN). *Accreditation:* AACN. *Program availability:* Part-time. *Students:* 22 full-time (17 women), 21 part-time (17 women); includes 18 minority (7 Black or African American, non-Hispanic/Latino; 5 Asian, non-Hispanic/Latino; 5 Hispanic/Latino; 1 Two or more races, non-Hispanic/Latino). Average age 34. 52 applicants, 50% accepted, 17 enrolled. In 2019, 15 master's awarded. Application fee: $80. *Financial support:* Application deadline: 4/1.

**University of Puerto Rico - Medical Sciences Campus,** School of Nursing, San Juan, PR 00936-5067. Offers adult and elderly nursing (MSN); child and adolescent nursing (MSN); critical care nursing (MSN); family and community nursing (MSN); family nurse practitioner (MSN); maternity nursing (MSN); mental health and psychiatric nursing (MSN). *Accreditation:* AACN; AANA/CANAEP. *Entrance requirements:* For master's, GRE or EXADEP, interview, Puerto Rico RN license or professional license for international students, general and specific point average, article analysis. Electronic applications accepted.

**University of Rochester,** School of Nursing, Rochester, NY 14642. Offers adult gerontological acute care nurse practitioner (MS); adult gerontological primary care nurse practitioner (MS); clinical nurse leader (MS); family nurse practitioner (MS); family psychiatric mental health nurse practitioner (MS); health care organization management and leadership (MS); nursing (DNP); nursing and health science (PhD); nursing education (MS); pediatric nurse practitioner (MS); pediatric nurse practitioner/neonatal nurse practitioner (MS). *Accreditation:* AACN. *Program availability:* Part-time, 100% online, blended/hybrid learning. Terminal master's awarded for partial completion of doctoral program. *Degree requirements:* For master's, comprehensive exam; for doctorate, thesis/dissertation. *Entrance requirements:* For master's, BS in nursing, RN license; for doctorate, GRE General Test (for PhD), B.S. degree, RN license most programs. Additional exam requirements/recommendations for international students: required—TOEFL (minimum score 560 paper-based; 88 iBT), TOEFL (minimum score 560 paper-based; 88 iBT) or IELTS (minimum score 6.5) recommended. Electronic applications accepted. *Expenses:* Contact institution.

**University of St. Francis,** Leach College of Nursing, Joliet, IL 60435-6169. Offers family nurse practitioner (MSN, Post-Master's Certificate); nursing administration (MSN); nursing education (MSN); nursing practice (DNP); psychology/mental health nurse practitioner (MSN, Post-Master's Certificate); teaching in nursing (Certificate). *Accreditation:* AACN. *Program availability:* Part-time, evening/weekend, 100% online. *Degree requirements:* For master's, comprehensive exam. *Entrance requirements:* Additional exam requirements/recommendations for international students: required—TOEFL (minimum score 550 paper-based; 79 iBT), IELTS (minimum score 6). Electronic applications accepted. Application fee is waived when completed online. *Expenses:* Contact institution.

**University of Saint Joseph,** Department of Nursing, West Hartford, CT 06117-2700. Offers family nurse practitioner (MS); nurse educator (MS); nursing practice (DNP);

psychiatric/mental health nurse practitioner (MS). *Accreditation:* AACN. *Program availability:* Part-time, evening/weekend. *Degree requirements:* For master's, thesis. *Entrance requirements:* For master's, 2 letters of recommendation. Electronic applications accepted. Application fee is waived when completed online.

**University of San Diego,** Hahn School of Nursing and Health Science, San Diego, CA 92110-2492. Offers adult-gerontology clinical nurse specialist (MSN); adult-gerontology nurse practitioner/family nurse practitioner (MSN); clinical nurse leader (MSN); executive nurse leader (MSN); family nurse practitioner (MSN); healthcare informatics (MS); master's entry program in clinical nursing (for non-rns) (MSN); nursing (PhD); nursing informatics (MSN); nursing practice (DNP); psychiatric-mental health nurse practitioner (MSN). *Accreditation:* AACN. *Program availability:* Part-time, evening/weekend. *Faculty:* 28 full-time (23 women), 43 part-time/adjunct (32 women). *Students:* 252 full-time (202 women), 288 part-time (227 women); includes 261 minority (53 Black or African American, non-Hispanic/Latino; 2 American Indian or Alaska Native, non-Hispanic/Latino; 106 Asian, non-Hispanic/Latino; 76 Hispanic/Latino; 24 Two or more races, non-Hispanic/Latino), 24 international. Average age 34. In 2019, 174 master's, 47 doctorates awarded. *Degree requirements:* For doctorate, thesis/dissertation (for some programs), residency (DNP). *Entrance requirements:* For master's, GRE General Test (for entry-level nursing), BSN, current California RN licensure (except for entry-level nursing), minimum GPA of 3.0; for doctorate, minimum GPA of 3.5, MSN, current California RN licensure. Additional exam requirements/recommendations for international students: required—TOEFL (minimum score 580 paper-based; 83 iBT), TWE. *Application deadline:* Applications are processed on a rolling basis. Application fee: $55. Electronic applications accepted. *Financial support:* In 2019–20, 284 students received support. Institutionally sponsored loans, scholarships/grants, and traineeships available. Support available to part-time students. Financial award application deadline: 4/1; financial award applicants required to submit FAFSA. *Unit head:* Dr. Jane Georges, Dean, Hahn School of Nursing and Health Science, 619-260-4550, Fax: 619-260-6814, E-mail: nursing@sandiego.edu. *Application contact:* Erika Garwood, Associate Director of Graduate Admissions, 619-260-4524, Fax: 619-260-4158, E-mail: grads@sandiego.edu.
Website: http://www.sandiego.edu/nursing/

**University of South Carolina,** The Graduate School, College of Nursing, Program in Advanced Practice Nursing in Psychiatric Mental Health, Columbia, SC 29208. Offers MSN, Certificate. *Program availability:* Part-time, online learning. *Entrance requirements:* For master's, master's degree in nursing, RN license; for Certificate, MSN. Additional exam requirements/recommendations for international students: required—TOEFL (minimum score 570 paper-based). Electronic applications accepted.

**University of South Carolina,** The Graduate School, College of Nursing, Program in Community Mental Health and Psychiatric Health Nursing, Columbia, SC 29208. Offers psychiatric/mental health nurse practitioner (MSN); psychiatric/mental health specialist (MSN). *Accreditation:* AACN. *Program availability:* Part-time. *Degree requirements:* For master's, thesis or alternative. *Entrance requirements:* For master's, GRE General Test, MAT, BS in nursing, nursing license. Additional exam requirements/recommendations for international students: required—TOEFL (minimum score 570 paper-based). Electronic applications accepted.

**University of Southern Indiana,** Graduate Studies, College of Nursing and Health Professions, Program in Nursing, Evansville, IN 47712-3590. Offers adult-gerontology acute care nurse practitioner (MSN, PMC); adult-gerontology clinical nurse specialist (MSN, PMC); adult-gerontology primary care nurse practitioner (MSN, PMC); advanced nursing practice (DNP); family nurse practitioner (MSN, PMC); nursing education (MSN, PMC); nursing management and leadership (MSN, PMC); organizational and systems leadership (DNP); psychiatric mental health nurse practitioner (MSN, PMC). *Accreditation:* AACN. *Program availability:* Part-time, online learning. *Entrance requirements:* For master's, BSN from nationally-accredited school; minimum cumulative GPA of 3.0; satisfactory completion of a course in undergraduate statistics (minimum grade C); one year of full-time experience or 2,000 hours of clinical practice as an RN (recommended); unencumbered U.S. RN license; for doctorate, minimum GPA of 3.0, completion of graduate research course with minimum B grade, unencumbered RN license, resume/curriculum vitae, three professional references, 1-2 page narrative of practice experience and professional goals, Capstone Project Information form. Additional exam requirements/recommendations for international students: required—TOEFL (minimum score 550 paper-based; 79 iBT), IELTS (minimum score 6). Electronic applications accepted. *Expenses:* Contact institution.

**University of Southern Maine,** College of Science, Technology, and Health, School of Nursing, Portland, ME 04103. Offers adult-gerontology primary care nurse practitioner (MS, PMC); education (MS); family nurse practitioner (MS, PMC); family psychiatric/mental health nurse practitioner (MS); management (MS); nursing (CAS, CGS); psychiatric-mental health nurse practitioner (PMC). *Accreditation:* AACN. *Program availability:* Part-time. *Degree requirements:* For master's, thesis optional. *Entrance requirements:* For master's, GRE General Test or MAT, minimum GPA of 3.0; for doctorate, GRE. Additional exam requirements/recommendations for international students: required—TOEFL (minimum score 550 paper-based). Electronic applications accepted. *Expenses: Tuition, area resident:* Full-time $864; part-time $432 per credit hour. Tuition, state resident: full-time $864; part-time $432 per credit hour. Tuition, nonresident: full-time $2372; part-time $1186 per credit hour. *Required fees:* $141; $108 per credit hour. Tuition and fees vary according to course load.

**The University of Tennessee Health Science Center,** College of Nursing, Memphis, TN 38163. Offers adult-gerontology acute care nurse practitioner (Post Master's Certificate); advance practice nursing (DNP); family nurse practitioner (Post-Doctoral Certificate); pediatric acute care nurse practitioner (Post-Doctoral Certificate); pediatric primary care nurse practitioner (Post-Doctoral Certificate); psychiatric/mental health nurse practitioner (Post-Doctoral Certificate); registered nurse first assistant (Certificate). *Accreditation:* AACN; AANA/CANAEP. *Program availability:* Part-time, blended/hybrid learning. *Faculty:* 62 full-time (55 women), 7 part-time/adjunct (2 women). *Students:* 226 full-time (187 women), 28 part-time (26 women); includes 80 minority (63 Black or African American, non-Hispanic/Latino; 15 Asian, non-Hispanic/Latino; 2 Hispanic/Latino). Average age 33. 652 applicants, 20% accepted, 104 enrolled. In 2019, 86 doctorates, 2 Certificates awarded. *Degree requirements:* For doctorate, project. *Entrance requirements:* For doctorate, RN license, minimum GPA of 3.0; http://www.uthsc.edu/nursing/dnp-admission-requirements.php; for other advanced degree, MSN, APN license, minimum GPA of 3.0; http://www.uthsc.edu/nursing/dnp-admission-requirements.php. Additional exam requirements/recommendations for international students: required—TOEFL (minimum score 550 paper-based; 80 iBT). *Application deadline:* For fall admission, 1/15 for domestic students; for spring admission, 8/15 for domestic students. Application fee: $70. Electronic applications accepted. *Expenses:* $5400 tuition, $450 fees, $110 loan fees, $5790 room/board, $2137 books/supplies, $1260 transportation, $2339 miscellaneous, $450 out-of-state tuition surcharge. *Financial support:* In 2019–20, 112 students received support, including 16 research assistantships (averaging $229,578 per year); Federal Work-Study, institutionally sponsored loans, scholarships/grants, and tuition waivers (partial) also available. Financial award application deadline: 3/15; financial award applicants required to submit FAFSA. *Unit head:* Dr. Wendy Likes, Dean, 901-448-6135, Fax: 901-448-4121, E-mail: wlikes@uthsc.edu. *Application contact:* Glynis Blackard, Assistant Dean for Student Affairs, 901-448-6139, Fax: 901-448-4121, E-mail: gblackar@uthsc.edu.
Website: http://uthsc.edu/nursing/

**The University of Texas at Austin,** Graduate School, School of Nursing, Austin, TX 78712-1111. Offers adult - gerontology clinical nurse specialist (MSN); child health (MSN), including administration, public health nursing, teaching; family nurse practitioner (MSN); family psychiatric/mental health nurse practitioner (MSN); holistic adult health (MSN), including administration, teaching; maternity (MSN), including administration, public health nursing, teaching; nursing (PhD); nursing administration and healthcare systems management (MSN); nursing practice (DNP); pediatric nurse practitioner (MSN); public health nursing (MSN). *Accreditation:* AACN. *Program availability:* Part-time. *Degree requirements:* For master's, thesis optional; for doctorate, thesis/dissertation. *Entrance requirements:* For master's and doctorate, GRE General Test. Additional exam requirements/recommendations for international students: required—TOEFL (minimum score 550 paper-based). Electronic applications accepted.

**The University of Texas Health Science Center at San Antonio,** School of Nursing, San Antonio, TX 78229-3900. Offers administrative management (MSN); adult-gerontology acute care nurse practitioner (PGC); advanced practice leadership (DNP); clinical nurse leader (MSN); executive administrative management (DNP); family nurse practitioner (MSN, PGC); nursing (MSN, PhD); nursing education (MSN, PGC); pediatric nurse practitioner primary care (PGC); psychiatric mental health nurse practitioner (PGC); public health nurse leader (DNP). *Accreditation:* AACN. *Program availability:* Part-time. Terminal master's awarded for partial completion of doctoral program. *Degree requirements:* For master's, thesis optional; for doctorate, comprehensive exam, thesis/dissertation.

**University of Virginia,** School of Nursing, Charlottesville, VA 22903. Offers acute and specialty care (MSN); acute care nurse practitioner (MSN); clinical nurse leadership (MSN); community-public health leadership (MSN); nursing (DNP, PhD); psychiatric mental health counseling (MSN); MSN/MBA. *Accreditation:* AACN. *Program availability:* Part-time. *Degree requirements:* For doctorate, comprehensive exam (for some programs), capstone project (DNP), dissertation (PhD). *Entrance requirements:* For master's, GRE General Test, MAT; for doctorate, GRE General Test. Additional exam requirements/recommendations for international students: required—TOEFL, IELTS. Electronic applications accepted.

**University of Wisconsin–Madison,** School of Nursing, Madison, WI 53705. Offers adult/gerontology (DNP), including clinical nurse specialist; adult/gerontology acute care (DNP), including nurse practitioner; adult/gerontology primary care (DNP), including nurse practitioner; nursing (PhD); MS/MPH. *Accreditation:* AACN. *Program availability:* Part-time. *Degree requirements:* For doctorate, comprehensive exam, thesis/dissertation. *Entrance requirements:* For doctorate, GRE, bachelor's degree in nursing, undergraduate GPA of at least 3.0 on the last 60 credits, academic references, 2 original papers or other scholarly work, essay, RN license (for DNP), 1 year of professional nursing experience (for DNP). Additional exam requirements/recommendations for international students: required—TOEFL (minimum score 580 paper-based; 92 iBT), IELTS (minimum score 7). Electronic applications accepted. *Expenses:* Contact institution.

**Valdosta State University,** College of Nursing and Health Sciences, Valdosta, GA 31698. Offers adult gerontology nurse practitioner (MSN); exercise physiology (MS); family nurse practitioner (MSN); family psychiatric mental health nurse practitioner (MSN). *Accreditation:* AACN. *Program availability:* Part-time, online learning. *Degree requirements:* For master's, thesis (for some programs), comprehensive written and/or oral exams. *Entrance requirements:* For master's, minimum GPA of 2.8. Additional exam requirements/recommendations for international students: required—TOEFL (minimum score 523 paper-based). Electronic applications accepted.

**Virginia Commonwealth University,** Graduate School, School of Nursing, Richmond, VA 23284-9005. Offers adult health acute nursing (MS); adult health primary nursing (MS); biobehavioral clinical research (PhD); child health nursing (MS); clinical nurse leader (MS); family health nursing (MS); nurse educator (MS); nurse practitioner (MS); nursing (Certificate); nursing administration (MS), including clinical nurse manager; psychiatric-mental health nursing (MS); quality and safety in health care (DNP); women's health nursing (MS). *Accreditation:* AACN; ACEN (one or more programs are accredited). *Program availability:* Part-time, evening/weekend, online learning. *Degree requirements:* For master's, thesis optional; for doctorate, thesis/dissertation. *Entrance requirements:* For master's, GRE General Test, BSN, minimum GPA of 2.8; for doctorate, GRE General Test. Additional exam requirements/recommendations for international students: required—TOEFL (minimum score 600 paper-based; 100 iBT). Electronic applications accepted.

**Washington State University,** College of Nursing, Spokane, WA 99210. Offers advanced population health (MN, DNP); family nurse practitioner (MN, DNP); nursing (PhD); psychiatric/mental health nurse practitioner (DNP); psychiatric/mental health practitioner (MN). *Accreditation:* AACN. *Degree requirements:* For master's, comprehensive exam (for some programs), thesis (for some programs), oral exam, research project. *Entrance requirements:* For master's, minimum GPA of 3.0, Washington state RN license, physical assessment skills, course work in statistics, recommendations, written interview (for nurse practitioner).

**Wayne State University,** College of Nursing, Detroit, MI 48202. Offers adult gerontology acute care nurse practitioner (MSN); adult gerontology primary care nurse practitioner (MSN); advanced public health nursing (MSN); infant and mental health (DNP, PhD); neonatal nurse practitioner (MSN); nurse-midwifery (MSN); pediatric acute care nurse practitioner (MSN); pediatric primary care nurse practitioner (MSN); psychiatric mental health nurse practitioner (MSN); women's health nurse practitioner (MSN). *Accreditation:* AACN; ACNM/ACME. *Program availability:* Part-time. *Faculty:* 27. *Students:* 134 full-time (118 women), 216 part-time (187 women); includes 98 minority (51 Black or African American, non-Hispanic/Latino; 24 Asian, non-Hispanic/Latino; 6 Hispanic/Latino; 17 Two or more races, non-Hispanic/Latino), 18 international. Average age 33. 425 applicants, 37% accepted, 95 enrolled. In 2019, 58 master's, 31 doctorates awarded. *Degree requirements:* For doctorate, thesis/dissertation. *Entrance requirements:* For master's, Completed a Bachelor of Science in Nursing with a 3.0 or higher GPA. Official transcripts. Professional competence as documented by three references. Current Michigan Registered Nurse (RN) licensure. A personal statement of goals for graduate study; for doctorate, DNP: Minimum GPA of 3.0 or higher in BSN is required. Resume or Curriculum Vita that includes education, work and/or research experience. Two references, one from a doctorally prepared individual. RN license. PhD: BSN transcript; Two to three references from doctorally prepared individuals; goals statement; Resume or CV; Interview. Additional exam requirements/recommendations for international students: required—TOEFL (minimum score 101 iBT), TWE (minimum score 6), Michigan English Language Assessment Battery (minimum score 85); recommended—IELTS (minimum score 7). *Application deadline:* For fall admission, 1/31 for domestic students; for winter admission, 11/1 for domestic students. Applications are processed on a rolling basis. Application fee: $50. Electronic applications accepted. *Expenses:* $925.72 per credit hour in-state, $1,716.93 per credit hour out-of-state, $54.56 student service credit hour fee, $315.70 registration fee. *Financial support:* In

2019–20, 104 students received support, including 39 fellowships with tuition reimbursements available (averaging $6,456 per year), 1 research assistantship (averaging $24,950 per year), 5 teaching assistantships with tuition reimbursements available (averaging $25,000 per year); scholarships/grants, health care benefits, and unspecified assistantships also available. Support available to part-time students. Financial award application deadline: 3/1; financial award applicants required to submit FAFSA. *Unit head:* Dr. Laurie M Lauzon Clabo, Dean, College of Nursing, 313-577-4082, E-mail: laurie.lauzon.clabo@wayne.edu. *Application contact:* Dr. Laurie M Lauzon Clabo, Dean, College of Nursing, 313-577-4082, E-mail: laurie.lauzon.clabo@wayne.edu.
Website: http://nursing.wayne.edu/

**West Virginia Wesleyan College,** School of Nursing, Buckhannon, WV 26201. Offers family nurse practitioner (MS, Post Master's Certificate); nurse-midwifery (MS); nursing (DNP); nursing leadership (MS); psychiatric mental health nurse practitioner (MS); MSN/MBA. *Accreditation:* ACEN.

**Wright State University,** Graduate School, College of Nursing and Health, Program in Nursing, Dayton, OH 45435. Offers administration of nursing and health care systems (MS); adult gerontology clinical nurse specialist (MS); adult-gerontology acute care nurse practitioner (MS); family nurse practitioner (MS); neonatal nurse practitioner (MS); pediatric nurse practitioner-acute care (MS); pediatric nurse practitioner-primary care (MS); psychiatric mental health nurse practitioner (MS); school nurse (MS). *Accreditation:* AACN. *Program availability:* Part-time, evening/weekend. *Degree requirements:* For master's, thesis or alternative. *Entrance requirements:* For master's, GRE General Test, BSN from ACEN-accredited college, Ohio RN license. Additional exam requirements/recommendations for international students: required—TOEFL.

# School Nursing

**California State University, Fullerton,** Graduate Studies, College of Health and Human Development, School of Nursing, Fullerton, CA 92831-3599. Offers leadership (MS); nurse anesthesia (MS); nurse educator (MS); nursing (DNP); school nursing (MS); women's health care (MS). *Accreditation:* AACN. *Program availability:* Part-time.

**Cambridge College,** School of Education, Boston, MA 02129. Offers autism specialist (M Ed); autism/behavior analyst (M Ed); behavior analyst (Post-Master's Certificate); curriculum and instruction (CAGS); early childhood teacher (M Ed); educational leadership (M Ed, Ed D); elementary teacher (M Ed); English as a second language (M Ed, Certificate); general science (M Ed); health education (Post-Master's Certificate); interdisciplinary studies (M Ed); library teacher (M Ed); mathematics education (M Ed); mathematics specialist (Certificate); school administration (M Ed, CAGS); school nurse education (M Ed); teacher of students with moderate disabilities (M Ed); teaching skills and methodologies (M Ed). *Program availability:* Part-time, evening/weekend, online learning. *Degree requirements:* For master's, thesis, internship/practicum (licensure program only); for doctorate, thesis/dissertation; for other advanced degree, thesis. *Entrance requirements:* For master's, interview, resume, documentation of licensure, 2 professional references; for doctorate, official transcripts, interview, resume, written personal statement/essay, portfolio of scholarly and professional work, 2 professional references, health insurance, immunizations form; for other advanced degree, official transcripts, interview, resume, written personal statement/essay, 2 professional references, health insurance, immunizations form. Additional exam requirements/recommendations for international students: required—TOEFL (minimum score 550 paper-based; 79 iBT), Michigan English Language Assessment Battery (minimum score 85); recommended—IELTS (minimum score 6). Electronic applications accepted. *Expenses:* Contact institution.

**Eastern Mennonite University,** Program in Nursing, Harrisonburg, VA 22802-2462. Offers leadership and management (MSN); leadership and school nursing (MSN); nursing management (DNP). *Accreditation:* AACN. *Program availability:* Part-time, online learning. *Degree requirements:* For master's, leadership project. *Entrance requirements:* For master's, RN license, one year of full-time work experience as RN, minimum GPA of 3.0. Additional exam requirements/recommendations for international students: required—TOEFL. Application fee is waived when completed online.

**La Salle University,** School of Nursing and Health Sciences, Program in Nursing, Philadelphia, PA 19141-1199. Offers adult gerontology primary care nurse practitioner (MSN, Certificate); adult health and illness clinical nurse specialist (MSN); adult-gerontology clinical nurse specialist (MSN, Certificate); clinical nurse leader (MSN); family primary care nurse practitioner (MSN, Certificate); gerontology (Certificate); nurse anesthetist (MSN, Certificate); nursing (MSN, Certificate); nursing administration (MSN, Certificate); nursing education (Certificate); nursing practice (DNP); nursing service administration (MSN); public health nursing (MSN, Certificate); school nursing (Certificate); MSN/MBA; MSN/MPH. *Accreditation:* AACN. *Program availability:* Part-time, evening/weekend, 100% online. *Degree requirements:* For doctorate, minimum of 1,000 hours of post baccalaureate clinical practice supervised by preceptors. *Entrance requirements:* For master's, GRE, MAT, or GMAT (for students with BSN GPA of less than 3.2), baccalaureate degree in nursing from ACEN- or CCNE-accredited program or an MSN Bridge program; Pennsylvania RN license; 2 letters of reference; resume; statement of philosophy articulating professional values and future educational goal; 1 year of work experience as a registered nurse; for doctorate, GRE (waived for applicants with MSN cumulative GPA of 3.7 or above), MSN, master's degree, MBA or MHA from nationally-accredited program; resume or curriculum vitae; 2 letters of reference; interview; for Certificate, GRE, MAT, or GMAT (for students with BSN GPA of less than 3.2, baccalaureate degree in nursing from ACEN- or CCNE-accredited program or an MSN Bridge program; Pennsylvania RN license; 2 letters of reference; resume; statement of philosophy articulating professional values and future educational goal; 1 year of work experience as a registered nurse. Additional exam requirements/recommendations for international students: required—TOEFL. Electronic applications accepted. Application fee is waived when completed online. *Expenses:* Contact institution.

**Lewis University,** College of Nursing and Health Sciences, Program in Nursing, Romeoville, IL 60446. Offers adult gerontology clinical nurse specialist (MSN); adult gerontology primary care nurse practitioner (MSN); family nurse practitioner (MSN); healthcare systems leadership (MSN); nursing education (MSN); school nurse (MSN). *Accreditation:* AACN. *Program availability:* Part-time, evening/weekend, 100% online, blended/hybrid learning. *Students:* 7 full-time (all women), 411 part-time (372 women); includes 113 minority (15 Black or African American, non-Hispanic/Latino; 43 Asian, non-Hispanic/Latino; 47 Hispanic/Latino; 8 Two or more races, non-Hispanic/Latino), 2 international. Average age 35. *Degree requirements:* For master's, clinical practicum. *Entrance requirements:* For master's, minimum undergraduate GPA of 3.0, degree in nursing, RN license, letter of recommendation, interview, resume or curriculum vitae. Additional exam requirements/recommendations for international students: required—TOEFL (minimum score 550 paper-based; 80 iBT), IELTS. *Application deadline:* For fall admission, 5/1 priority date for international students; for spring admission, 11/15 priority date for international students. Applications are processed on a rolling basis. Application fee: $40. Electronic applications accepted. *Financial support:* Federal Work-Study, scholarships/grants, tuition waivers (full and partial), and unspecified assistantships available. Financial award application deadline: 5/1; financial award applicants required to submit FAFSA. *Unit head:* Dr. Mary Desmond, Program Director. *Application contact:* Nancy Wiksten, Graduate Admission Counselor, 815-836-5610, E-mail: grad@lewisu.edu.

**Rowan University,** Graduate School, College of Education, Department of Educational Services and Leadership, Glassboro, NJ 08028-1701. Offers counseling in educational settings (MA); educational leadership (Ed D, CAGS); higher education administration (MA); principal preparation (CAGS); school administration (MA); school and public librarianship (MA); school nursing (Postbaccalaureate Certificate); school psychology (MA, Ed S); supervisor (CAGS). *Accreditation:* NCATE. *Program availability:* Part-time, evening/weekend. *Degree requirements:* For master's, comprehensive exam, thesis; for other advanced degree, thesis or alternative. *Entrance requirements:* For master's and other advanced degree, GRE General Test. Additional exam requirements/recommendations for international students: required—TOEFL. Electronic applications accepted. *Expenses: Tuition, area resident:* Part-time $715.50 per semester hour. Tuition, state resident: part-time $715.50 per semester hour. Tuition, nonresident: part-time $715.50 per semester hour. *Required fees:* $161.55 per semester hour.

**Seton Hall University,** College of Nursing, South Orange, NJ 07079-2697. Offers advanced practice in primary health care (MSN, DNP), including adult/gerontological nurse practitioner, pediatric nurse practitioner; entry into practice (MSN); health systems administration (MSN, DNP); nursing (PhD); nursing case management (MSN); nursing education (MA); school nurse (MSN); MSN/MA. *Accreditation:* AACN. *Program availability:* Part-time, online learning. *Degree requirements:* For master's, research project; for doctorate, dissertation or scholarly project. *Entrance requirements:* For doctorate, GRE (waived for students with GPA of 3.5 or higher). Additional exam requirements/recommendations for international students: required—TOEFL. Electronic applications accepted.

**University of Illinois at Chicago,** College of Nursing, Program in Nursing, Chicago, IL 60607-7128. Offers acute care clinical nurse specialist (MS); administrative nursing leadership (Certificate); adult nurse practitioner (MS); adult/geriatric nurse practitioner (MS); advanced community health nurse specialist (MS); family nurse practitioner (MS); geriatric clinical nurse specialist (MS); geriatric nurse practitioner (MS); nurse midwifery (MS); occupational health/advanced community health nurse specialist (MS); occupational health/family nurse practitioner (MS); pediatric nurse practitioner (MS); perinatal clinical nurse specialist (MS); school/advanced community health nurse specialist (MS); school/family nurse practitioner (MS); women's health nurse practitioner (MS). *Accreditation:* AACN. *Program availability:* Part-time. *Degree requirements:* For master's, thesis or alternative. *Entrance requirements:* For master's, GRE General Test, minimum GPA of 2.75. Additional exam requirements/recommendations for international students: required—TOEFL. Electronic applications accepted.

**Wright State University,** Graduate School, College of Nursing and Health, Program in Nursing, Dayton, OH 45435. Offers administration of nursing and health care systems (MS); adult gerontology clinical nurse specialist (MS); adult-gerontology acute care nurse practitioner (MS); family nurse practitioner (MS); neonatal nurse practitioner (MS); pediatric nurse practitioner-acute care (MS); pediatric nurse practitioner-primary care (MS); psychiatric mental health nurse practitioner (MS); school nurse (MS). *Accreditation:* AACN. *Program availability:* Part-time, evening/weekend. *Degree requirements:* For master's, thesis or alternative. *Entrance requirements:* For master's, GRE General Test, BSN from ACEN-accredited college, Ohio RN license. Additional exam requirements/recommendations for international students: required—TOEFL.

# Transcultural Nursing

**Augsburg University,** Programs in Nursing, Minneapolis, MN 55454-1351. Offers MA, DNP. *Accreditation:* AACN. *Degree requirements:* For master's, thesis or alternative.

**Rutgers University - Newark,** Rutgers School of Nursing, Newark, NJ 07107-3001. Offers adult health (MSN); adult occupational health (MSN); advanced practice nursing (MSN, Post Master's Certificate); family nurse practitioner (MSN); nurse anesthesia (MSN); nursing (MSN); nursing informatics (MSN); urban health (PhD); women's health practitioner (MSN). *Accreditation:* AANA/CANAEP. *Program availability:* Part-time. *Entrance requirements:* For master's, GRE, RN license; basic life support, statistics, and health assessment experience. Additional exam requirements/recommendations for international students: required—TOEFL. Electronic applications accepted. *Expenses:* Contact institution.

# Women's Health Nursing

**Boston College,** William F. Connell School of Nursing, Chestnut Hill, MA 02467. Offers adult-gerontology primary care nurse practitioner (MS); family health nursing (MS); nurse anesthesia (MS); nursing (PhD); pediatric primary care nurse practitioner (MS), including pediatric and women's health; psychiatric-mental health nursing (MS); women's health nursing (MS); MBA/MS; MS/MA; MS/PhD. *Accreditation:* AACN; AANA/CANAEP (one or more programs are accredited). *Program availability:* Part-time. *Faculty:* 56 full-time (50 women). *Students:* 228 full-time (200 women), 82 part-time (71 women); includes 54 minority (10 Black or African American, non-Hispanic/Latino; 18 Asian, non-Hispanic/Latino; 20 Hispanic/Latino; 6 Two or more races, non-Hispanic/Latino), 7 international. Average age 28. 360 applicants, 56% accepted, 93 enrolled. In 2019, 107 master's, 7 doctorates awarded. *Degree requirements:* For master's, comprehensive exam; for doctorate, comprehensive exam, thesis/dissertation, computer literacy exam or foreign language. *Entrance requirements:* For master's, bachelor's degree; for doctorate, GRE General Test, bachelor's in Nursing and master's degree in nursing or related field. Additional exam requirements/recommendations for international students: required—TOEFL (minimum score 600 paper-based; 100 iBT), IELTS (minimum score 7.5). *Application deadline:* For fall admission, 3/15 for domestic and international students; for spring admission, 9/30 for domestic and international students. Application fee: $40. Electronic applications accepted. *Expenses:* Contact institution. *Financial support:* In 2019–20, 135 students received support, including 12 fellowships with full tuition reimbursements available (averaging $24,504 per year), 29 teaching assistantships (averaging $4,380 per year); scholarships/grants, health care benefits, tuition waivers (partial), and unspecified assistantships also available. Support available to part-time students. Financial award application deadline: 4/18; financial award applicants required to submit FAFSA. *Unit head:* Dr. Susan Gennaro, Dean, 617-552-4251, Fax: 617-552-0931, E-mail: susan.gennaro@bc.edu. *Application contact:* Sean Sendall, Assistant Dean, Graduate Enrollment and Data Analytics, 617-552-4745, Fax: 617-552-2121, E-mail: sean.sendall@bc.edu.
Website: http://www.bc.edu/cson

**California State University, Fullerton,** Graduate Studies, College of Health and Human Development, School of Nursing, Fullerton, CA 92831-3599. Offers leadership (MS); nurse anesthesia (MS); nurse educator (MS); nursing (DNP); school nursing (MS); women's health care (MS). *Accreditation:* AACN. *Program availability:* Part-time.

**Carlow University,** College of Health and Wellness, Program in Women's Health Nurse Practitioner, Pittsburgh, PA 15213-3165. Offers MSN, Certificate. *Program availability:* Part-time, evening/weekend. *Students:* 6 full-time (all women), 6 part-time (all women); includes 1 minority (Black or African American, non-Hispanic/Latino). Average age 30. 8 applicants, 100% accepted, 4 enrolled. In 2019, 6 master's, 1 other advanced degree awarded. *Entrance requirements:* For master's, minimum undergraduate GPA of 3.0 from accredited BSN program; current license as RN in Pennsylvania; course in statistics with minimum C grade in past 6 years; two recommendations; personal statement; personal interview. Additional exam requirements/recommendations for international students: required—TOEFL (minimum score 550 paper-based). *Application deadline:* Applications are processed on a rolling basis. *Expenses: Tuition:* Full-time $13,666; part-time $902 per credit hour. *Required fees:* $15; $15 per credit. Tuition and fees vary according to degree level and program. *Financial support:* Application deadline: 4/1; applicants required to submit FAFSA. *Unit head:* Dr. Lynn George, Dean, 412-578-6115, Fax: 412-578-6114. *Application contact:* Dr. Lynn George, Dean, 412-578-6115, Fax: 412-578-6114.
Website: http://www.carlow.edu/Master_of_Science_in_Nursing_Womens_Health_Nurse_Practitioner.aspx

**Case Western Reserve University,** Frances Payne Bolton School of Nursing, Master's Programs in Nursing, Nurse Practitioner Program, Cleveland, OH 44106. Offers acute care pediatric nurse practitioner (MSN); acute care/cardiovascular nursing (MSN); adult gerontology acute care nurse practitioner (MSN); adult gerontology primary care nurse practitioner (MSN); family nurse practitioner (MSN); family systems psychiatric mental health nursing (MSN); neonatal nurse practitioner (MSN); palliative care (MSN); pediatric nurse practitioner in acute care (MSN); pediatric primary care nurse practitioner (MSN); women's health nurse practitioner (MSN). *Accreditation:* ACEN. *Program availability:* Part-time. *Faculty:* 30 full-time (25 women), 6 part-time/adjunct (all women). *Students:* 47 full-time (36 women), 70 part-time (59 women); includes 34 minority (12 Black or African American, non-Hispanic/Latino; 11 Asian, non-Hispanic/Latino; 9 Hispanic/Latino; 2 Two or more races, non-Hispanic/Latino), 9 international. Average age 30. 45 applicants, 82% accepted, 22 enrolled. In 2019, 46 master's awarded. *Degree requirements:* For master's, thesis optional, minimum GPA of 3.0, clinical hours corresponding to requirements to sit for certification exam, portfolio. *Entrance requirements:* For master's, GRE/MAT (scores not required for application, but may be requested for an admission decision). Additional exam requirements/recommendations for international students: required—TOEFL (minimum score 577 paper-based; 90 iBT), IELTS (minimum score 7). *Application deadline:* For fall admission, 3/15 for domestic and international students; for spring admission, 10/1 for domestic and international students; for summer admission, 3/15 for domestic and international students. Applications are processed on a rolling basis. Application fee: $75. Electronic applications accepted. *Expenses:* Clinical placement $75; Activity fee $15 per semester; Graduate council fee $15 per semester; Tuition rate $2,133 per credit hour. *Financial support:* In 2019–20, 100 students received support, including 34 teaching assistantships with partial tuition reimbursements available (averaging $19,197 per year); scholarships/grants and traineeships also available. Financial award application deadline: 5/15; financial award applicants required to submit FAFSA. *Unit head:* Dr. Latina Brooks, Director, 216-368-1196, Fax: 216-368-3542, E-mail: lmb3@case.edu. *Application contact:* Jackie Tepale, Admissions Coordinator, 216-368-5253, Fax: 216-368-3542, E-mail: yyd@case.edu.
Website: https://case.edu/nursing/programs/msn

**Drexel University,** College of Nursing and Health Professions, Division of Graduate Nursing, Philadelphia, PA 19104-2875. Offers adult acute care (MSN); adult psychiatric/mental health (MSN); advanced practice nursing (MSN); clinical trials research (MSN); family nurse practitioner (MSN); leadership in health systems management (MSN); nursing education (MSN); pediatric primary care (MSN); women's health (MSN). *Accreditation:* AACN. Electronic applications accepted.

**Duke University,** School of Nursing, Durham, NC 27708. Offers acute care pediatric nurse practitioner (MSN, Post-Graduate Certificate); adult-gerontology nurse practitioner (MSN, Post-Graduate Certificate), including acute care, primary care; family nurse practitioner (MSN, Post-Graduate Certificate); neonatal nurse practitioner (MSN, Post-Graduate Certificate); nurse anesthesia (DNP); nurse practitioner (DNP); nursing (PhD); nursing and health care leadership (MSN, Post-Graduate Certificate); nursing education (MSN, Post-Graduate Certificate); nursing informatics (MSN, Post-Graduate Certificate); pediatric nurse practitioner (MSN, Post-Graduate Certificate), including primary care; psychiatric mental health nurse practitioner (MSN, Post-Graduate Certificate); women's health nurse practitioner (MSN, Post-Graduate Certificate). *Accreditation:* AACN; AANA/CANAEP. *Program availability:* Part-time, evening/weekend, online with on-campus intensives. *Faculty:* 48 full-time (40 women), 32 part-time/adjunct (28 women). *Students:* 666 full-time (601 women), 157 part-time (139 women); includes 193 minority (61 Black or African American, non-Hispanic/Latino; 4 American Indian or Alaska Native, non-Hispanic/Latino; 57 Asian, non-Hispanic/Latino; 49 Hispanic/Latino; 1 Native Hawaiian or other Pacific Islander, non-Hispanic/Latino; 21 Two or more races, non-Hispanic/Latino), 8 international. Average age 34. 761 applicants, 33% accepted, 149 enrolled. In 2019, 213 master's, 74 doctorates, 18 other advanced degrees awarded. Terminal master's awarded for partial completion of doctoral program. *Degree requirements:* For master's, thesis optional; for doctorate, capstone project. *Entrance requirements:* For master's, MSN applicants are no longer required to take the GRE, 1 year of nursing experience (recommended), BSN, minimum GPA of 3.0, previous course work in statistics; for doctorate, GRE is required for the DNP in Nurse Anesthesia, BSN or MSN, minimum GPA of 3.0, resume, personal statement, graduate statistics and research methods course, current licensure as a registered nurse, transcripts from all post-secondary institutions; for Post-Graduate Certificate, MSN, licensure or eligibility as a professional nurse, transcripts from all post-secondary institutions, previous course work in statistics. Additional exam requirements/recommendations for international students: required—TOEFL (minimum score 100 iBT), IELTS (minimum score 7). *Application deadline:* For fall admission, 12/1 for domestic and international students; for spring admission, 5/1 for domestic and international students. Application fee: $50. Electronic applications accepted. *Expenses:* Contact institution. *Financial support:* Institutionally sponsored loans, scholarships/grants, and traineeships available. Support available to part-time students. Financial award applicants required to submit FAFSA. *Unit head:* Dr. Marion E. Broome, Dean/Vice Chancellor for Nursing Affairs/Associate Vice President for Academic Affairs for Nursing, 919-684-9446, Fax: 919-684-9414, E-mail: marion.broome@duke.edu. *Application contact:* Dr. Ernie Rushing, Director of Admissions and Recruitment, 919-668-6274, Fax: 919-668-4693, E-mail: ernie.rushing@dm.duke.edu.
Website: http://www.nursing.duke.edu/

**East Tennessee State University,** College of Graduate and Continuing Studies, College of Nursing, Johnson City, TN 37614. Offers acute care nurse practitioner (DNP); adult-gerontology primary care nurse practitioner (DNP); adult/gerontological nurse practitioner (Postbaccalaureate Certificate); executive leadership in nursing (DNP, Postbaccalaureate Certificate); family nurse practitioner (MSN, DNP, Post-Master's Certificate, Postbaccalaureate Certificate); nursing (PhD); nursing administration (MSN); nursing education (MSN); pediatric primary care nurse practitioner (DNP); psychiatric mental health nurse practitioner (Postbaccalaureate Certificate); psychiatric/mental health nurse practitioner (MSN, DNP, Post-Master's Certificate); women's health care nurse practitioner (DNP). *Accreditation:* AACN. *Program availability:* Part-time, evening/weekend, online learning. *Degree requirements:* For master's and other advanced degree, comprehensive exam, practicum; for doctorate, comprehensive exam, thesis/dissertation (for some programs), practicum, internship, evidence of professional malpractice insurance, CPR certification. *Entrance requirements:* For master's, bachelor's degree, minimum GPA of 3.0, current RN license and eligibility to practice, resume, three letters of recommendation; for doctorate, GRE General Test, MSN (for PhD), BSN or MSN (for DNP), current RN license and eligibility to practice, 2 years of full-time registered nurse work experience or equivalent, three letters of recommendation, resume or curriculum vitae, interview, writing sample; for other advanced degree, MSN, minimum GPA of 3.0, current RN license and eligibility to practice, three letters of recommendation, resume or curriculum vitae; DNP with designated concentration in advanced clinical practice or nursing administration (for select programs). Additional exam requirements/recommendations for international students: required—TOEFL (minimum score 600 paper-based; 79 iBT). Electronic applications accepted.

**Emory University,** Nell Hodgson Woodruff School of Nursing, Atlanta, GA 30322-1100. Offers adult nurse practitioner (MSN); emergency nurse practitioner (MSN); family nurse practitioner (MSN); family nurse-midwife (MSN); health systems leadership (MSN); nurse-midwifery (MSN); pediatric nurse practitioner acute and primary care (MSN); women's health care (Title X) (MSN); women's health nurse practitioner (MSN); MSN/MPH. *Accreditation:* AACN; ACNM/ACME (one or more programs are accredited). *Program availability:* Part-time. *Entrance requirements:* For master's, GRE General Test or MAT, minimum GPA of 3.0, BS in nursing from an accredited institution, RN license and additional course work, 3 letters of recommendation. Additional exam requirements/recommendations for international students: required—TOEFL (minimum score 600 paper-based; 100 iBT). Electronic applications accepted. *Expenses:* Contact institution.

**Georgia State University,** Byrdine F. Lewis School of Nursing, Atlanta, GA 30303. Offers adult health clinical nurse specialist/nurse practitioner (MS, Certificate); child health clinical nurse specialist/pediatric nurse practitioner (MS, Certificate); family nurse practitioner (MS, Certificate); family psychiatric mental health nurse practitioner (MS, Certificate); nursing (PhD); nursing leadership in healthcare innovations (MS), including nursing administration, nursing informatics; nutrition (MS); occupational therapy (MOT); perinatal clinical nurse specialist/women's health nurse practitioner (MS, Certificate); physical therapy (DPT); respiratory therapy (MS). *Accreditation:* AACN. *Program availability:* Part-time, blended/hybrid learning. *Faculty:* 57 full-time (40 women), 5 part-time/adjunct (4 women). *Students:* 388 full-time (290 women), 155 part-time (135 women); includes 217 minority (130 Black or African American, non-Hispanic/Latino; 47 Asian, non-Hispanic/Latino; 26 Hispanic/Latino; 14 Two or more races, non-Hispanic/Latino), 45 international. Average age 32. 480 applicants, 50% accepted, 164 enrolled. In 2019, 158 master's, 64 doctorates, 20 other advanced degrees awarded. *Degree requirements:* For doctorate, comprehensive exam, thesis/dissertation. *Entrance requirements:* For doctorate, GRE. Additional exam requirements/recommendations for international students: required—TOEFL. *Application deadline:* For fall admission, 2/1 priority date for domestic and international students; for spring admission, 9/15 for domestic and international students. Applications are processed on a rolling basis. Application fee: $50. Electronic applications accepted. *Expenses:* Contact institution. *Financial support:* In 2019–20, research assistantships with tuition reimbursements (averaging $1,666 per year), teaching assistantships with tuition reimbursements (averaging $1,920 per year) were awarded; scholarships/grants, tuition waivers (full and partial), and unspecified assistantships also available. Support available to part-time students. Financial award application deadline: 8/1; financial award applicants required to submit FAFSA. *Unit head:* Huanbiao Mo, Dean of Nursing. *Application contact:* Huanbiao Mo, Dean of Nursing.
Website: http://nursing.gsu.edu/

**Loyola University Chicago,** Graduate School, Marcella Niehoff School of Nursing, Maywood, IL 60153. Offers adult clinical nurse specialist (MSN, Certificate); adult nurse practitioner (Certificate); dietetics (MS); family nurse practitioner (Certificate); family, adult, and women's health nurse practitioner (MSN); health systems leadership (MSN); healthcare quality using education in safety and technology (DNP); infection prevention (MSN, DNP); nursing science (PhD); women's health clinical nurse specialist (Certificate). *Accreditation:* AACN. *Program availability:* Part-time, blended/hybrid learning. *Faculty:* 36 full-time (32 women), 18 part-time/adjunct (16 women). *Students:* 182 full-time (168 women), 198 part-time (175 women); includes 95 minority (26 Black or African American, non-Hispanic/Latino; 29 Asian, non-Hispanic/Latino; 37 Hispanic/Latino; 3 Two or more races, non-Hispanic/Latino), 7 international. Average age 35. 148 applicants, 59% accepted, 54 enrolled. In 2019, 84 master's, 16 doctorates, 27 other advanced degrees awarded. *Degree requirements:* For master's, comprehensive exam; for doctorate, thesis/dissertation, qualifying examination (for PhD); project (for DNP). *Entrance requirements:* For master's, BSN, minimum nursing GPA of 3.0, Illinois RN license, 3 letters of recommendation, 1000 hours of experience in area of specialty prior to starting clinical rotations, personal statement; for doctorate, BSN or MSN, minimum GPA of 3.0, professional nursing license, 3 letters of recommendation, personal statement. Additional exam requirements/recommendations for international students: required—TOEFL (minimum score 550 paper-based; 79 iBT), IELTS (minimum score 6), PTE (minimum score 53). *Application deadline:* For fall admission, 7/1 priority date for domestic and international students; for spring admission, 12/1 priority date for domestic and international students; for summer admission, 4/1 priority date for domestic and international students. Applications are processed on a rolling basis. Electronic applications accepted. Application fee is waived when completed online. *Expenses:* Contact institution. *Financial support:* In 2019–20, 53 students received support, including 3 research assistantships with full tuition reimbursements available (averaging $18,000 per year), 1 teaching assistantship with full tuition reimbursement available (averaging $18,000 per year); scholarships/grants, unspecified assistantships, and Nurse Faculty Loan Program also available. Financial award application deadline: 5/1; financial award applicants required to submit FAFSA. *Unit head:* Dr. Lorna Finnegan, Dean and Professor, 708-216-5448, Fax: 708-216-9555, E-mail: lornaf@luc.edu. *Application contact:* Glenda Runnels, Enrollment Advisor, 708-216-3751, Fax: 708-216-9555, E-mail: grunnels@luc.edu.
Website: http://www.luc.edu/nursing/

**MGH Institute of Health Professions,** School of Nursing, Boston, MA 02129. Offers advanced practice nursing (MSN); gerontological nursing (MSN); nursing (DNP); pediatric nursing (MSN); psychiatric nursing (MSN); teaching and learning for health care education (Certificate); women's health nursing (MSN). *Accreditation:* AACN. *Degree requirements:* For master's, thesis or alternative. *Entrance requirements:* For master's, GRE General Test, bachelor's degree from regionally-accredited college or university. Additional exam requirements/recommendations for international students: required—TOEFL (minimum score 550 paper-based; 80 iBT). Electronic applications accepted.

**Queen's University at Kingston,** School of Graduate Studies, Faculty of Health Sciences, School of Nursing, Kingston, ON K7L 3N6, Canada. Offers health and chronic illness (M Sc); nurse scientist (PhD); primary health care nurse practitioner (Certificate); women's and children's health (M Sc). *Degree requirements:* For master's, thesis. *Entrance requirements:* For master's, RN license. Additional exam requirements/recommendations for international students: required—TOEFL.

**Rutgers University - Newark,** Rutgers School of Nursing, Newark, NJ 07107-3001. Offers adult health (MSN); adult occupational health (MSN); advanced practice nursing (MSN, Post Master's Certificate); family nurse practitioner (MSN); nurse anesthesia (MSN); nursing (MSN); nursing informatics (MSN); urban health (PhD); women's health practitioner (MSN). *Accreditation:* AANA/CANAEP. *Program availability:* Part-time. *Entrance requirements:* For master's, GRE, RN license; basic life support, statistics, and health assessment experience. Additional exam requirements/recommendations for international students: required—TOEFL. Electronic applications accepted. *Expenses:* Contact institution.

**San Francisco State University,** Division of Graduate Studies, College of Health and Social Sciences, School of Nursing, San Francisco, CA 94132-1722. Offers adult acute care (MS); clinical nurse specialist (MS); community/public health nursing (MS); family nurse practitioner (Certificate); nursing administration (MS); pediatrics (MS); women's health (MS). *Accreditation:* AACN. *Program availability:* Part-time. *Application deadline:* Applications are processed on a rolling basis. *Expenses: Tuition, area resident:* Full-time $7176; part-time $4164 per year. Tuition, state resident: full-time $7176; part-time $4164 per year. Tuition, nonresident: full-time $16,680; part-time $396 per unit. International tuition: $16,680 full-time. *Required fees:* $1524; $1524 per unit. $762 per semester. Tuition and fees vary according to degree level and program. *Financial support:* Career-related internships or fieldwork available. *Unit head:* Dr. Mary-Ann van Dam, 415-338-1802, Fax: 415-338-0555, E-mail: vandam@sfsu.edu. *Application contact:* Prof. Fang-yu Chou, Assistant Director of Graduate Programs, 415-338-6853, Fax: 415-338-0555, E-mail: fchou@sfsu.edu.
Website: http://nursing.sfsu.edu

**Stony Brook University, State University of New York,** Stony Brook Medicine, School of Nursing, Program in Perinatal Women's Health Nursing, Stony Brook, NY 11794. Offers MS, DNP, Certificate. *Accreditation:* AACN. *Program availability:* Blended/hybrid learning. *Students:* 2 part-time (both women); both minorities (both American Indian or Alaska Native, non-Hispanic/Latino). 2 applicants, 100% accepted, 2 enrolled. In 2019, 1 doctorate awarded..*Entrance requirements:* For master's, BSN, minimum GPA of 3.0, course work in statistics. Additional exam requirements/recommendations for international students: required—TOEFL (minimum score 90 iBT). *Application deadline:* For fall admission, 2/27 for domestic students. Application fee: $100. *Expenses:* Contact institution. *Financial support:* Application deadline: 3/15. *Unit head:* Dr. Elizabeth Collins, Program Director, 631-444-3296, Fax: 631-444-3136, E-mail: elizabeth.collins@stonybrook.edu. *Application contact:* Linda Sacino, Staff Assistant, 631-632-3262, Fax: 631-444-3136, E-mail: elizabeth.collins@stonybrook.edu.
Website: http://www.nursing.stonybrookmedicine.edu/

**Tennessee Technological University,** Whitson-Hester School of Nursing, DNP Program, Cookeville, TN 38505. Offers adult-gerontology acute care nurse practitioner (DNP); executive leadership in nursing (DNP); family nurse practitioner (DNP); pediatric nurse practitioner-primary care (DNP); psychiatric/mental health nurse practitioner (DNP); women's health care nurse practitioner (DNP). *Program availability:* Part-time. *Students:* 20 full-time (17 women), 12 part-time (all women); includes 3 minority (2 Black or African American, non-Hispanic/Latino; 1 Two or more races, non-Hispanic/Latino). 25 applicants, 60% accepted, 10 enrolled. *Application deadline:* For fall admission, 7/1 for domestic students, 5/1 for international students; for spring admission, 12/1 for domestic students, 10/1 for international students; for summer admission, 5/1 for domestic students, 2/1 for international students. Applications are processed on a rolling basis. Application fee: $35 ($40 for international students). Electronic applications accepted. *Expenses: Tuition, area resident:* Part-time $597 per credit hour. Tuition, state resident: part-time $597 per credit hour. Tuition, nonresident: part-time $1323 per credit hour. *Financial support:* Application deadline: 4/1; applicants required to submit FAFSA. *Unit head:* Dr. Kim Hanna, Dean, Fax: 931-372-6244, E-mail: khanna@tntech.edu. *Application contact:* Shelia K. Kendrick, Coordinator of Graduate Studies, 931-372-3808, Fax: 931-372-3497, E-mail: skendrick@tntech.edu.
Website: https://www.tntech.edu/nursing/doctor-of-nursing-practice/

**Texas Woman's University,** Graduate School, College of Nursing, Denton, TX 76204. Offers adult health clinical nurse specialist (MS); adult health nurse practitioner (MS); adult/gerontology acute care nurse practitioner (MS); child health clinical nurse specialist (MS); clinical nurse leader (MS); family nurse practitioner (MS); health systems management (MS); nursing education (MS); nursing practice (DNP); nursing science (PhD); pediatric nurse practitioner (MS); women's health clinical nurse specialist (MS); women's health nurse practitioner (MS). *Accreditation:* AACN. *Program availability:* Part-time, 100% online, blended/hybrid learning. *Faculty:* 48 full-time (47 women), 31 part-time/adjunct (24 women). *Students:* 42 full-time (40 women), 811 part-time (756 women); includes 481 minority (168 Black or African American, non-Hispanic/Latino; 2 American Indian or Alaska Native, non-Hispanic/Latino; 165 Asian, non-Hispanic/Latino; 118 Hispanic/Latino; 1 Native Hawaiian or other Pacific Islander, non-Hispanic/Latino; 27 Two or more races, non-Hispanic/Latino), 26 international. Average age 36. 435 applicants, 71% accepted, 172 enrolled. In 2019, 203 master's, 37 doctorates awarded. *Degree requirements:* For master's, comprehensive exam, thesis or alternative, 6-year time limit for completion of degree, professional or clinical project; for doctorate, comprehensive exam, thesis/dissertation, 10-year time limit for completion of degree; dissertation (PhD), assessment practicum (DPT). *Entrance requirements:* For master's, minimum GPA of 3.0 on last 60 hours in undergraduate nursing degree and overall, RN license, BS in nursing, basic statistics course; for doctorate, MS in nursing, minimum preferred GPA of 3.5, RN or APRN license, statistics course, 2 letters of reference, curriculum vitae, graduate nursing-theory course, graduate research course, statement of professional goals and research interests, 1 yr APRN experience. Additional exam requirements/recommendations for international students: required—TOEFL (minimum score 79 iBT); recommended—IELTS (minimum score 6.5), TSE (minimum score 53). *Application deadline:* For fall admission, 5/1 for domestic students, 3/1 priority date for international students; for spring admission, 9/15 for domestic students, 7/1 priority date for international students. Application fee: $50 ($75 for international students). Electronic applications accepted. *Expenses:* All are estimates. Tuition for 10 hours = $2,763; Fees for 10 hours = $1,342. Master's Nursing courses require additional $75/SCH; Doctoral Nursing courses require additional $80/SCH. *Financial support:* In 2019–20, 212 students received support, including 1 research assistantship, 6 teaching assistantships (averaging $12,029 per year); career-related internships or fieldwork, scholarships/grants, health care benefits, and unspecified assistantships also available. Support available to part-time students. Financial award application deadline: 3/1; financial award applicants required to submit FAFSA. *Unit head:* Dr. Rosalie Mainous, Dean, 940-898-2401, Fax: 940-898-2437, E-mail: nursing@twu.edu. *Application contact:* Korie Hawkins, Associate Director of Admissions, Graduate Recruitment, 940-898-3188, Fax: 940-898-3081, E-mail: admissions@twu.edu.
Website: http://www.twu.edu/nursing/

**Uniformed Services University of the Health Sciences,** Daniel K. Inouye Graduate School of Nursing, Bethesda, MD 20814. Offers adult-gerontology clinical nurse specialist (MSN, DNP); family nurse practitioner (DNP); nurse anesthesia (DNP); nursing science (PhD); psychiatric mental health nurse practitioner (DNP); women's health nurse practitioner (DNP). *Accreditation:* AACN; AANA/CANAEP. *Program availability:* Part-time. *Faculty:* 50 full-time (32 women), 1 part-time/adjunct (0 women). *Students:* 170 full-time (98 women); includes 51 minority (21 Black or African American, non-Hispanic/Latino; 17 Asian, non-Hispanic/Latino; 11 Hispanic/Latino; 2 Native Hawaiian or other Pacific Islander, non-Hispanic/Latino). Average age 34. 88 applicants, 75% accepted, 66 enrolled. In 2019, 2 master's, 42 doctorates awarded. *Degree requirements:* For master's, thesis, scholarly project; for doctorate, dissertation (for PhD); project (for DNP). *Entrance requirements:* For master's, GRE, BSN, clinical experience, minimum GPA of 3.0, previous course work in science; for doctorate, GRE, BSN, minimum GPA of 3.0, undergraduate/graduate science course within past 5 years, writing example, interview (for some programs), and 3 letters of reference (for DNP); master's degree, minimum GPA of 3.0 in nursing or related field, personal statement, 3 references, and interview (for PhD). *Application deadline:* For winter admission, 2/15 for domestic students; for summer admission, 8/15 for domestic students. Electronic applications accepted. *Financial support:* Robert Wood Johnson and Jonas scholars available. *Unit head:* Dr. Diane C. Seibert, Associate Dean for Academic Affairs, 301-295-1080, Fax: 301-295-1707, E-mail: diane.seibert@usuhs.edu. *Application contact:* Maureen Jackson, Student Admissions Program Manager, 301-295-1055, E-mail: maureen.jackson.ctr@usuhs.edu.
Website: http://www.usuhs.edu/gsn/

**The University of Alabama at Birmingham,** School of Nursing, Birmingham, AL 35294. Offers clinical nurse leader (MSN); nurse anesthesia (DNP); nurse practitioner (MSN, DNP), including adult-gerontology acute care (MSN), adult-gerontology primary care (MSN), family (MSN), pediatric (MSN), psychiatric/mental health (MSN), women's health (MSN); nursing (MSN, DNP, PhD); nursing health systems administration (MSN); nursing informatics (MSN). *Accreditation:* AACN; AANA/CANAEP. *Program availability:* Part-time, online only, blended/hybrid learning. *Faculty:* 86 full-time (79 women), 42 part-time/adjunct (35 women). *Students:* 228 full-time (165 women), 1,393 part-time (1,234 women); includes 398 minority (267 Black or African American, non-Hispanic/Latino; 4 American Indian or Alaska Native, non-Hispanic/Latino; 52 Asian, non-Hispanic/Latino; 41 Hispanic/Latino; 34 Two or more races, non-Hispanic/Latino), 3 international. Average age 33. 1,027 applicants, 55% accepted, 421 enrolled. In 2019, 557 master's, 19 doctorates awarded. Terminal master's awarded for partial completion of doctoral program. *Degree requirements:* For master's, comprehensive exam; for doctorate, comprehensive exam, thesis/dissertation, research mentorship experience (for PhD); scholarly project (for DNP). *Entrance requirements:* For master's, GRE, GMAT, or MAT, minimum cumulative undergraduate GPA of 3.0 or on last 60 semesters hours; letters of recommendation; for doctorate, GRE General Test, computer literacy, course work in statistics, interview, minimum GPA of 3.0, MS in nursing, references, writing sample. Additional exam requirements/recommendations for international students: required—TOEFL (minimum score 500 paper-based, 80 iBT) or IELTS (5.5). *Application deadline:* For fall admission, 2/24 for domestic students; for summer admission, 10/15 for domestic students. Application fee: $50. Electronic applications accepted. *Expenses:* Contact institution. *Financial support:* In 2019–20, 23 fellowships (averaging $34,685 per year), 12 research assistantships (averaging $9,042 per year), 2 teaching assistantships (averaging $22,000 per year) were awarded; scholarships/grants, traineeships, health care benefits, and unspecified assistantships also available. Support available to part-time students. *Unit head:* Dr. Doreen C. Harper, Dean, 205-934-5360, Fax: 205-934-1894, E-mail: dcharper@uab.edu. *Application contact:* John Updegraff, Director of Student Affairs, 205-975-3370, Fax: 205-934-5490, E-mail: jupde22@uab.edu.
Website: http://www.uab.edu/nursing/home/

**University of Cincinnati,** Graduate School, College of Nursing, Cincinnati, OH 45221-0038. Offers nurse midwifery (MSN); nurse practitioner (MSN, DNP), including acute care pediatrics (DNP), adult-gerontology acute care, adult-gerontology primary care,

anesthesia (DNP), family (MSN), leadership (DNP), neonatal (MSN), women's health (MSN); nursing (MSN, PhD), including occupational health (MSN). *Accreditation:* AACN; AANA/CANAEP (one or more programs are accredited); ACNM/ACME. *Program availability:* Part-time, 100% online, blended/hybrid learning. *Faculty:* 62 full-time (55 women), 125 part-time/adjunct (114 women). *Students:* 429 full-time (355 women), 1,547 part-time (1,390 women); includes 453 minority (226 Black or African American, non-Hispanic/Latino; 5 American Indian or Alaska Native, non-Hispanic/Latino; 68 Asian, non-Hispanic/Latino; 103 Hispanic/Latino; 3 Native Hawaiian or other Pacific Islander, non-Hispanic/Latino; 48 Two or more races, non-Hispanic/Latino), 15 international. Average age 36. 779 applicants, 78% accepted, 464 enrolled. In 2019, 518 master's, 47 doctorates awarded. *Degree requirements:* For master's, thesis or alternative; for doctorate, comprehensive exam (for some programs), thesis/dissertation (for some programs). *Entrance requirements:* For master's, GRE required only for the Direct-Entry Accelerated Program. Additional exam requirements/recommendations for international students: required—TOEFL (minimum score 600 paper-based; 100 iBT); recommended—IELTS (minimum score 7). *Application deadline:* For fall admission, 4/1 priority date for domestic and international students; for spring admission, 9/1 priority date for domestic and international students; for summer admission, 2/1 priority date for domestic and international students. Applications are processed on a rolling basis. Application fee: $135 ($140 for international students). Electronic applications accepted. *Expenses:* Contact institution. *Financial support:* In 2019–20, 103 students received support, including 9 fellowships with full tuition reimbursements available (averaging $18,595 per year), 7 research assistantships with full tuition reimbursements available (averaging $12,991 per year), 8 teaching assistantships with full tuition reimbursements available (averaging $12,991 per year); institutionally sponsored loans, scholarships/grants, traineeships, health care benefits, tuition waivers (partial), and unspecified assistantships also available. Support available to part-time students. Financial award application deadline: 4/1; financial award applicants required to submit FAFSA. *Unit head:* Dr. Greer Glazer, Dean, 513-558-5330, Fax: 513-558-9030, E-mail: greer.glazer@uc.edu. *Application contact:* Office of Student Affairs, 513-558-8400, E-mail: nursingbearcats@uc.edu.
Website: https://nursing.uc.edu/

**University of Colorado Denver,** College of Nursing, Aurora, CO 80045. Offers adult clinical nurse specialist (MS); adult nurse practitioner (MS); family nurse practitioner (MS); family psychiatric mental health nurse practitioner (MS); health care informatics (MS); nurse-midwifery (MS); nursing (DNP, PhD); nursing leadership and health care systems (MS); pediatric nurse practitioner (MS); women's health (MS); MS/PhD. *Accreditation:* ACNM/ACME (one or more programs are accredited). *Program availability:* Part-time, evening/weekend, online learning. Terminal master's awarded for partial completion of doctoral program. *Degree requirements:* For master's, thesis optional; for doctorate, comprehensive exam, thesis/dissertation, 42 credits of coursework. *Entrance requirements:* For master's, GRE if cumulative undergraduate GPA is less than 3.0, undergraduate nursing degree from ACEN- or CCNE-accredited school or university; completion of research and statistics courses with minimum grade of C; copy of current and unencumbered nursing license; for doctorate, GRE, bachelor's and/or master's degrees in nursing from ACEN- or CCNE-accredited institution; portfolio; minimum undergraduate GPA of 3.0, graduate 3.5; graduate-level intermediate statistics and master's-level nursing theory courses with minimum B grade; interview. Additional exam requirements/recommendations for international students: required—TOEFL (minimum score 560 paper-based; 83 iBT). Electronic applications accepted. *Expenses:* Contact institution.

**University of Delaware,** College of Health Sciences, School of Nursing, Newark, DE 19716. Offers adult nurse practitioner (MSN, PMC); cardiopulmonary clinical nurse specialist (MSN, PMC); cardiopulmonary clinical nurse specialist/adult nurse practitioner (MSN, PMC); family nurse practitioner (MSN, PMC); gerontology clinical nurse specialist (MSN, PMC); gerontology clinical nurse specialist geriatric nurse practitioner (PMC); gerontology clinical nurse specialist/geriatric nurse practitioner (MSN); health services administration (MSN, PMC); nursing of children clinical nurse specialist (MSN, PMC); nursing of children clinical nurse specialist/pediatric nurse practitioner (MSN, PMC); oncology/immune deficiency clinical nurse specialist (MSN, PMC); oncology/immune deficiency clinical nurse specialist/adult nurse practitioner (MSN, PMC); perinatal/women's health clinical nurse specialist (MSN, PMC); perinatal/women's health clinical nurse specialist/women's health nurse practitioner (MSN, PMC); psychiatric nursing clinical nurse specialist (MSN, PMC). *Accreditation:* AACN. *Program availability:* Part-time, evening/weekend, online learning. *Degree requirements:* For master's, thesis optional. *Entrance requirements:* For master's, BSN, interview, RN license. Electronic applications accepted.

**University of Illinois at Chicago,** College of Nursing, Program in Nursing, Chicago, IL 60607-7128. Offers acute care clinical nurse specialist (MS); administrative nursing leadership (Certificate); adult nurse practitioner (MS); adult/geriatric nurse practitioner (MS); advanced community health nurse specialist (MS); family nurse practitioner (MS); geriatric clinical nurse specialist (MS); geriatric nurse practitioner (MS); nurse midwifery (MS); occupational health/advanced community health nurse specialist (MS); occupational health/family nurse practitioner (MS); pediatric nurse practitioner (MS); perinatal clinical nurse specialist (MS); school/advanced community health nurse specialist (MS); school/family nurse practitioner (MS); women's health nurse practitioner (MS). *Accreditation:* AACN. *Program availability:* Part-time. *Degree requirements:* For master's, thesis or alternative. *Entrance requirements:* For master's, GRE General Test, minimum GPA of 2.75. Additional exam requirements/recommendations for international students: required—TOEFL. Electronic applications accepted.

**University of Indianapolis,** Graduate Programs, School of Nursing, Indianapolis, IN 46227-3697. Offers advanced practice nursing (DNP); family nurse practitioner (MSN); gerontological nurse practitioner (MSN); neonatal nurse practitioner (MSN); nurse-midwifery (MSN); nursing (MSN); nursing and health systems leadership (MSN); nursing education (MSN); women's health nurse practitioner (MSN); MBA/MSN. *Accreditation:* AACN. *Entrance requirements:* For master's, minimum GPA of 3.0, interview, letters of recommendation, resume, IN nursing license, 1 year of professional practice; for doctorate, graduate of ACEN- or CCNE-accredited nursing program; MSN or MA with nursing major and minimum cumulative GPA of 3.25; unencumbered RN license with eligibility for licensure in Indiana; completion of graduate-level statistics course within last 5 years with minimum grade of B; resume; essay; official transcripts from all academic institutions. Additional exam requirements/recommendations for international students: required—TOEFL (minimum score 550 paper-based). Electronic applications accepted.

**University of Louisville,** Graduate School, School of Nursing, Louisville, KY 40202. Offers adult gerontology nurse practitioner (MSN, DNP); education and administration (MSN); family nurse practitioner (MSN, DNP); neonatal nurse practitioner (MSN, DNP); nursing research (PhD); psychiatric/mental health nurse practitioner (MSN, DNP); women's health nurse practitioner (MSN). *Accreditation:* AACN. *Program availability:* Part-time, blended/hybrid learning. *Faculty:* 49 full-time (46 women), 91 part-time/adjunct (86 women). *Students:* 164 full-time (140 women), 47 part-time (39 women); includes 45 minority (21 Black or African American, non-Hispanic/Latino; 5 Asian, non-Hispanic/Latino; 9 Hispanic/Latino; 10 Two or more races, non-Hispanic/Latino), 4 international. Average age 33. 84 applicants, 63% accepted, 48 enrolled. In 2019, 25 master's, 5 doctorates awarded. *Degree requirements:* For master's, varies; for doctorate, comprehensive exam (for some programs), thesis/dissertation (for some programs), varies. *Entrance requirements:* For master's, Our only master's degree is an accelerated program meant for students who have a bachelor's degree in another discipline who are transitioning into nursing. Thus, the main requirement is a bachelor's degree from a nationally-accredited college, and the completion of 6 prerequisite courses. Must have a minimum undergraduate GPA of 3.0; for doctorate, PhD program: GRE requirement omitted, DNP & PhD doctoral programs: 3 letters of professional reference. BSN applicants must have a 3.0 GPA. MSN applicants must have 3.25 GPA. Written statement of career goals, areas of expertise, reasons for pursuing doctoral degree, resume, and RN license. Additional exam requirements/recommendations for international students: recommended—TOEFL (minimum score 560 paper-based), IELTS (minimum score 6.5). *Application deadline:* For fall admission, 1/15 priority date for domestic and international students; for summer admission, 10/15 priority date for domestic students. Application fee: $60. Electronic applications accepted. *Expenses:* 17871. *Financial support:* In 2019–20, 47 students received support, including 2 fellowships with full tuition reimbursements available (averaging $20,000 per year), 9 research assistantships with full tuition reimbursements available (averaging $20,000 per year), 3 teaching assistantships with full tuition reimbursements available (averaging $15,000 per year); scholarships/grants, health care benefits, unspecified assistantships, and Jonas Nurse Leader Fellowships also available. Financial award application deadline: 10/1; financial award applicants required to submit FAFSA. *Unit head:* 502-852-8300, Fax: 502-852-5044, E-mail: sonya.hardin@louisville.edu. *Application contact:* Trish Hart, MA, Assistant Dean for Student Affairs, 502-852-5825, Fax: 502-852-8783, E-mail: trish.hart@louisville.edu.
Website: http://www.louisville.edu/nursing/

**University of Minnesota, Twin Cities Campus,** Graduate School, School of Nursing, Minneapolis, MN 55455-0213. Offers adult/gerontological clinical nurse specialist (DNP); adult/gerontological primary care nurse practitioner (DNP); family nurse practitioner (DNP); health innovation and leadership (DNP); integrative health and healing (DNP); nurse anesthesia (DNP); nurse midwifery (DNP); nursing (MN, PhD); nursing informatics (DNP); pediatric clinical nurse specialist (DNP); primary care certified pediatric nurse practitioner (DNP); psychiatric/mental health nurse practitioner (DNP); women's health nurse practitioner (DNP). *Accreditation:* AACN; AANA/CANAEP; ACNM/ACME (one or more programs are accredited). *Program availability:* Part-time, online learning. Terminal master's awarded for partial completion of doctoral program. *Degree requirements:* For master's, final oral exam, project or thesis; for doctorate, thesis/dissertation. *Entrance requirements:* For master's and doctorate, GRE General Test. Additional exam requirements/recommendations for international students: required—TOEFL (minimum score 586 paper-based). *Expenses:* Contact institution.

**University of Missouri–Kansas City,** School of Nursing and Health Studies, Kansas City, MO 64110-2499. Offers adult clinical nurse specialist (MSN), including adult nurse practitioner, women's health nurse practitioner (MSN, DNP); adult clinical nursing practice (DNP), including adult gerontology nurse practitioner, women's health nurse practitioner (MSN, DNP); clinical nursing practice (DNP), including family nurse practitioner; neonatal nurse practitioner (MSN); nurse educator (MSN); nurse executive (MSN); nursing practice (DNP); pediatric clinical nursing practice (DNP), including pediatric nurse practitioner; pediatric nurse practitioner (MSN). *Accreditation:* AACN. *Program availability:* Part-time, online learning. *Degree requirements:* For master's, thesis or alternative. *Entrance requirements:* For master's, minimum undergraduate GPA of 3.2; for doctorate, GRE, 3 letters of reference. Additional exam requirements/recommendations for international students: required—TOEFL (minimum score 550 paper-based; 80 iBT).

**University of Missouri–St. Louis,** College of Nursing, St. Louis, MO 63121. Offers adult/geriatric nurse practitioner (Post Master's Certificate); family nurse practitioner (Post Master's Certificate); nursing (DNP, PhD); pediatric acute care nurse practitioner (Post Master's Certificate); pediatric nurse practitioner (Post Master's Certificate); psychiatric-mental health nurse practitioner (Post Master's Certificate); women's health nurse practitioner (Post Master's Certificate). *Accreditation:* AACN. *Program availability:* Part-time. *Degree requirements:* For doctorate, comprehensive exam, thesis/dissertation; for Post Master's Certificate, thesis. *Entrance requirements:* For doctorate, GRE, 2 letters of recommendation, MSN, minimum GPA of 3.2, course in differential/inferential statistics; for Post Master's Certificate, 2 recommendation letters; MSN; advanced practice certificate; minimum GPA of 3.0; essay. Additional exam requirements/recommendations for international students: recommended—TOEFL (minimum score 550 paper-based; 79 iBT), IELTS (minimum score 6.5). Electronic applications accepted. *Expenses: Tuition, area resident:* Full-time $9005.40; part-time $6003.60 per credit hour. Tuition, state resident: full-time $9005.40; part-time $6003.60 per credit hour. Tuition, nonresident: full-time $22,108; part-time $14,738.40 per credit hour. *International tuition:* $22,108 full-time. Tuition and fees vary according to course load.

**University of Pennsylvania,** School of Nursing, Women's Health/Gender Related Nurse Practitioner Program, Philadelphia, PA 19104. Offers MSN. *Accreditation:* AACN. *Program availability:* Part-time, online learning. *Students:* 8 full-time (all women), 20 part-time (all women); includes 10 minority (5 Black or African American, non-Hispanic/Latino; 4 Hispanic/Latino; 1 Two or more races, non-Hispanic/Latino). Average age 28. In 2019, 2 master's awarded. *Financial support:* Application deadline: 4/1.

**University of South Carolina,** The Graduate School, College of Nursing, Program in Clinical Nursing, Columbia, SC 29208. Offers acute care clinical specialist (MSN); acute care nurse practitioner (MSN); women's health nurse practitioner (MSN). *Accreditation:* AACN. *Program availability:* Part-time. *Degree requirements:* For master's, thesis or alternative. *Entrance requirements:* For master's, GRE General Test or MAT, BS in nursing, RN licensure. Additional exam requirements/recommendations for international students: required—TOEFL (minimum score 570 paper-based). Electronic applications accepted.

**Virginia Commonwealth University,** Graduate School, School of Nursing, Richmond, VA 23284-9005. Offers adult health acute nursing (MS); adult health primary nursing (MS); biobehavioral clinical research (PhD); child health nursing (MS); clinical nurse leader (MS); family health nursing (MS); nurse educator (MS); nurse practitioner (MS); nursing (Certificate); nursing administration (MS), including clinical nurse manager; psychiatric-mental health nursing (MS); quality and safety in health care (DNP); women's health nursing (MS). *Accreditation:* AACN; ACEN (one or more programs are accredited). *Program availability:* Part-time, evening/weekend, online learning. *Degree requirements:* For master's, thesis optional; for doctorate, thesis/dissertation. *Entrance requirements:* For master's, GRE General Test, BSN, minimum GPA of 2.8; for doctorate, GRE General Test. Additional exam requirements/recommendations for international students: required—TOEFL (minimum score 600 paper-based; 100 iBT). Electronic applications accepted.

**Wayne State University,** College of Nursing, Detroit, MI 48202. Offers adult gerontology acute care nurse practitioner (MSN); adult gerontology primary care nurse practitioner (MSN); advanced public health nursing (MSN); infant and mental health (DNP, PhD); neonatal nurse practitioner (MSN); nurse-midwifery (MSN); pediatric acute

care nurse practitioner (MSN); pediatric primary care nurse practitioner (MSN); psychiatric mental health nurse practitioner (MSN); women's health nurse practitioner (MSN). *Accreditation:* AACN; ACNM/ACME. *Program availability:* Part-time. *Faculty:* 27. *Students:* 134 full-time (118 women), 216 part-time (187 women); includes 98 minority (51 Black or African American, non-Hispanic/Latino; 24 Asian, non-Hispanic/Latino; 6 Hispanic/Latino; 17 Two or more races, non-Hispanic/Latino), 18 international. Average age 33. 425 applicants, 37% accepted, 95 enrolled. In 2019, 58 master's, 31 doctorates awarded. *Degree requirements:* For doctorate, thesis/dissertation. *Entrance requirements:* For master's, Completed a Bachelor of Science in Nursing with a 3.0 or higher GPA. Official transcripts. Professional competence as documented by three references. Current Michigan Registered Nurse (RN) licensure. A personal statement of goals for graduate study; for doctorate, DNP: Minimum GPA of 3.0 or higher in BSN is required. Resume or Curriculum Vita that includes education, work and/or research experience. Two references, one from a doctorally prepared individual. RN license. PhD: BSN transcript; Two to three references from doctorally prepared individuals; goals statement; Resume or CV; Interview. Additional exam requirements/recommendations for international students: required—TOEFL (minimum score 101 iBT), TWE (minimum score 6), Michigan English Language Assessment Battery (minimum score 85); recommended—IELTS (minimum score 7). *Application deadline:* For fall admission, 1/31 for domestic students; for winter admission, 11/1 for domestic students. Applications are processed on a rolling basis. Application fee: $50. Electronic applications accepted. *Expenses:* $925.72 per credit hour in-state, $1,716.93 per credit hour out-of-state, $54.56 student service credit hour fee, $315.70 registration fee. *Financial support:* In 2019–20, 104 students received support, including 39 fellowships with tuition reimbursements available (averaging $6,456 per year), 1 research assistantship (averaging $24,950 per year), 5 teaching assistantships with tuition reimbursements available (averaging $25,000 per year); scholarships/grants, health care benefits, and unspecified assistantships also available. Support available to part-time students. Financial award application deadline: 3/1; financial award applicants required to submit FAFSA. *Unit head:* Dr. Laurie M Lauzon Clabo, Dean, College of Nursing, 313-577-4082, E-mail: laurie.lauzon.clabo@wayne.edu. *Application contact:* Dr. Laurie M Lauzon Clabo, Dean, College of Nursing, 313-577-4082, E-mail: laurie.lauzon.clabo@wayne.edu.
Website: http://nursing.wayne.edu/

# FRONTIER NURSING UNIVERSITY
*School of Nursing*

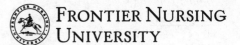

## Programs of Study

Established in 1939, Frontier Nursing University is a pioneer in graduate-level nursing and midwifery education. Today, with more than 2,000 enrolled students, it provides innovative distance education that allows students from around the world to complete didactic courses online and receive clinical education in their communities. The university has received national recognition for its long tradition of providing innovation and excellence in education. U.S. News & World Report ranks Frontier Nursing University in the top 100 online graduate nursing programs.

Frontier Nursing University offers evidence-based Master of Science in Nursing (MSN) degree programs, post-graduate certificates, and Doctor of Nursing Practice (DNP) programs. Its curriculum includes four specialties: nurse-midwife, family nurse practitioner, women's health care nurse practitioner and psychiatric-mental health nurse practitioner.

The MSN degree program allows students to complete a Master of Science in Nursing degree with the option to continue and complete a Doctor of Nursing Practice degree via a direct admissions process. The program begins with a four-day "Frontier Bound" orientation that takes place on FNU's campus, then all coursework and clinicals are completed in the student's own community. The MSN program takes approximately two years to complete full-time (a part-time option is also available) with the optional DNP consisting of 21 additional credit hours. Online coursework involves frequent interaction between faculty members and students via e-mail, forums, and telephone. A five-day Clinical Bound session at FNU is where students demonstrate their ability to begin community-based clinical practice. After the Clinical Bound-, students have Clinical Practicum in their own communities. Once the MSN degree is conferred, a student can complete three to five additional terms of DNP coursework and clinical education if the student chooses to continue to complete the DNP

The practice-focused Post-Master's Doctor of Nursing (DNP) degree program is for current nurse-midwives and nurse practitioners and builds on the MSN curriculum by providing additional training in evidence-based practice, quality improvement, systems leadership, and other essential areas of advanced practice. The curriculum also includes 360 hours planning, implementing, and disseminating the results of a rapid cycle quality improvement initiatives. Students become highly-skilled clinicians with competencies in evaluating evidence, translating research into practice, and using research findings in decision-making. They also become adept at using clinical innovations to change practice.

The Nurse-Midwife Specialty curriculum trains students to become outstanding clinicians as well as leaders and entrepreneurs in maternal and infant health care. The program's strong primary care component ensures that students also gain the skills needed to care for women across their life spans. The MSN program consists of 49 didactic credits and 15 clinical credits. It can be completed in about two years full-time (a part-time option is also available). Students also have the option to exit the program once the MSN is conferred.

Students who choose the Family Nurse Practitioner Specialty receive the training needed to become well-rounded clinicians, leaders, and entrepreneurs in primary health care. The MSN program contains 46 didactic credits and 15 clinical credits. It can be completed in about two years full-time (a part-time option is also

available). Students also have the option to exit the program once the MSN is conferred.

The Women's Health Care Nurse Practitioner Specialty program prepares students for advanced nursing practice as well as leadership and entrepreneurial roles in women's health care. The curriculum's solid primary care component ensures that students receive the skills needed to care for women in all stages of life. The complete MSN program consists of 43 didactic credits and 15 clinical credits. It can be completed in about two years full-time (a part-time option is also available). Students also have the option to exit the program once the MSN is conferred.

The Psychiatric-Mental Health Nurse Practitioner Specialty program educates students for advanced practice to improve mental health care and overall health status of communities with a focus on individuals across the lifespan. The MSN program consists of 42 didactic credits and 15 clinical credits. It can be completed in about two years full time (a part-time option is also available). Students have the option to exit the program once the MSN is conferred.

## How Distance Education Works

After attending an orientation on the FNU campus in Kentucky, students return to their communities to study online. FNU courses are taught in eleven-week terms. All courses are taught each term and designed with flexibility that allows adult learners to develop their own study schedule. Students can choose the number of credits to take based on their other life responsibilities. Advisers assist students in developing individualized timelines that will meet their specific needs.

Faculty teach and guide using a variety of modalities such as computer forums, e-mail, chats, video or audio lectures, interactive sessions using BigBlueButton, Google Suites, and the telephone. Assignments are designed to promote student engagement in the courses and within the community in which the student lives. Interaction with the school community is fostered through a dynamic web portal and Frontier Community Connection forums. Support, explanations, and information are readily available.

After completing the majority of their didactic course work, students begin their clinical learning experience. Clinical preceptors are sought within the student's own community whenever possible, allowing students to learn in their home area. While the goal is to keep the student as close to their home as possible, if appropriate clinical practice sites are not available, students may be required to travel to a clinical site for part or all of their clinical experiences.

## Financial Aid

FNU students may qualify for Federal Stafford Unsubsidized Loans, private loans, and external scholarships. In addition, Frontier offers several scholarships including the Kitty Ernst Scholarship, Alumni Scholarship, Family Nurse Practitioner Scholarship, and Student Scholarship.

## Cost of Study

Tuition is $618 per credit hour for all programs of study. The most current information regarding tuition and other fees associated with each program is available at https://www.frontier.edu/tuition.

*Frontier Nursing University*

### The University

Frontier Nursing University is located in Kentucky in the southeastern region of the United States. Its campus provides a tranquil, picturesque environment in which to learn and connect with faculty and fellow students during the brief two to three brief required visits to campus.

### Faculty

FNU has more than 100 faculty members who are accomplished teachers, expert clinicians, and dedicated mentors. They create mutually respectful relationships with students and support them in achieving their academic and professional goals.

They are also pioneers in distance nursing education who are highly accessible and skilled at supporting students in a virtual learning environment.

### Applying

Frontier strives to make the admissions process easy. Complete admissions criteria and application forms for each program are available online at https://www.frontier.edu/admissions. Application deadlines and admission calendars for each program can be found at https://www.frontier.edu/admissions/admissions-calendar.

Frontier Nursing University
2050 Lexington Road
Versailles, Kentucky 40383
Phone: 859-251-4700
E-mail: FNU@frontier.edu
Website: https://www.frontier.edu

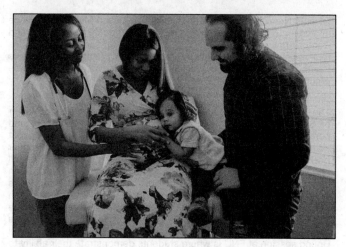

# UNIVERSITY OF WISCONSIN MILWAUKEE
## College of Nursing

## Program of Study

An innovative, academic nursing community, the University of Wisconsin-Milwaukee College of Nursing faculty, staff, students and alumni are renowned leaders in creating bold and effective solutions for advancing local, national and global health. The College is also home to the Master of Sustainable Peacebuilding program.

UW-Milwaukee's nursing program is valued for its ability to prepare science-based, compassionate nurse leaders through innovative, superior educational programs. The College is a vibrant, innovative environment for teaching, research, practice, and service to the community and the profession. The College is one of three universities in the state to offer students the full range of nursing degrees including: Bachelor of Science in Nursing, Master of Nursing, Doctor of Philosophy in Nursing, and Doctor of Nursing Practice.

The College offers a Masters in Nursing (M.N.) program with two entry options. The Master of Nursing degree is for nurses and non-nurses who hold a bachelor's degree and wish to pursue an advanced degree in nursing. The program provides the framework for practice as a clinical nurse leader, public health nurse, clinical research manager, health informatics specialist or nurse manager. The M.N. Direct Entry option admits students as a cohort which allows relationships among peers and faculty to develop through the program. After 16 months, students are eligible to sit for the NCLEX-RN examination, allowing students to work as Registered Nurses while completing the remaining MN credits. Through the curriculum and time spent in the Nursing Learning Resource Center (NLRC), students will have a variety of clinical experiences providing a broad overview of all of the major specialties in which nurses work, as well as a variety of settings across the health care. Students also have volunteer opportunities to expand their education.

The Master of Sustainable Peacebuilding (M.S.P.) is new to the College of Nursing and prepares practitioners, from any academic background, with skills and concepts required to engage and change issues at a global or local level. The interacting forces of urbanization, climate change, economic inequity and ideological polarization intertwine to generate complex pressures on the environment, society, and culture. Figuring out where to start requires transdisciplinary systems-based approaches and new ways of thinking about solutions and fixes. The M.S.P. provides the conceptual foundation and instills the practical skills for engaging complex problems with methods for building peace. The M.S.P.'s premise is that healthy and sustainable communities lead to long-term positive change. M.S.P. students learn techniques for grappling with complexity and developing strategies for effective change, while building critical leadership skills in facilitation, strategic planning, and evaluation. These skills can be applied across diverse employment sectors, such as population and community health, natural resources stewardship, conflict transformation, global security, education and nonprofit management.

In addition to the Masters programs, the College offers two doctoral programs: Doctor of Nursing Practice (D.N.P.) and Doctor of Philosophy in Nursing (Ph.D.) in face-to-face and online formats. Students in the doctoral programs work closely with faculty mentors to define success early and develop into key clinical and research partners.

The D.N.P. is a practice-focused doctoral program that prepares advanced-practice nurses for the highest level of clinical nursing practice beyond the initial preparation in the discipline. The program prepares students to develop clinical, organizational, economic, and leadership skills to design and implement programs of care delivery that will significantly impact health care outcomes and transform health care delivery. Graduates with this terminal practice degree will be prepared for roles in direct care or indirect, systems-focused care. Students who enter from a bachelor's degree to D.N.P. can specialize as: family nurse practitioner, psychiatric-mental health nurse practitioner, clinical nurse specialist, leadership/systems, and community/public health.

The College of Nursing's Ph.D. program integrates science, theory, and research to educate the next generation of nurse scientists and educators. Students strive to advance nursing knowledge and translate research into practice that promotes the health and care of patients. This research-intensive program prepares doctoral students as scientists who generate knowledge to advance nursing. For maximum flexibility, the program is offered in-person and online, both full-time (9 credits) and part-time (6 credits), and structured so that the required courses are offered only one day per week. What students accomplish in the college's traditional Ph.D. program depends on their focus area, personal interests and long-term research and career preferences. Faculty mentors help Ph.D. candidates define their success early, and plan and conduct cutting-edge research. These research and mentorship experiences prepare doctoral students for successful careers as scientists, as educators and for other opportunities in the rapidly evolving nursing professions.

## Research Facilities

UW-Milwaukee is one of only 131 universities (out of 4,600) in the country to receive the "highest research activity" (R-1 status) designated by the Carnegie Classification of Institutions of Higher Education. The College of Nursing is one of the most robust scientific research ventures on campus. The global and national perspectives expand the reach of the College's work in key areas, including community-engaged health research, geriatric health care, global health, healthcare delivery and system development and self-management. Removed the last sentence

The College pioneered and is home to two nurse-managed Community Nursing Centers, serving the uninsured and underinsured communities and providing healthcare solutions aligned with their needs. The Self-Management Science Center, originally funded by the National Institutes of Health (P20NR015339), expands research aimed at enhancing the science of self-management in individuals and families. Faculty members and students have also extended the scope of international research to health care in rural Malawi, Thailand, Ecuador and Kenya.

Research support is provided through the Harriet H. Werley Center for Nursing Research and Evaluation (WCNRE). The WCNRE was established in 1977 under a federal Faculty Research Development Grant and continues to offer support to faculty and nursing community.

## Financial Aid

A variety of options are available to help students finance their education, including over $500,000 in scholarships annually, as well as loans, grants, student employment, fellowships, military education benefits, and more.

## Cost of Study

Graduate-level tuition and fees are $12,050 for Wisconsin residents, $17,321 for Midwest Student Exchange Rate students, and $25,282 for nonresidents.

## Location

Milwaukee offers students a vibrant city on the shores of beautiful Lake Michigan, just 90 minutes north of Chicago. Milwaukee boasts a beautiful lakefront, a world-class art museum, hundreds of parks and recreational opportunities, major-league sports, a range of unique restaurants, and exciting events all year round. Big enough to offer urban amenities, small enough that it's possible to get most places within 20 minutes.

## University of Wisconsin Milwaukee

UW–Milwaukee students can use UPASS for unlimited free rides on the county bus system.

### The University and The College

As Wisconsin's largest nursing program, the University of Wisconsin–Milwaukee College of Nursing has made its home in the commercial, cultural, and economic capital of Wisconsin for over 50 years. The College of Nursing has an enrollment of over 1,200 undergraduate and 300 graduate students. The College of Nursing is a premier, urban, academic, collegial, nursing community that acts collaboratively with partners to:

- Prepare a diverse population of students to become science-based, compassionate, nurse leaders through innovative, quality, educational programs for all settings and levels of practice.
- Conduct research and scholarship that advance science in nursing and health.
- Address emerging health needs through evidence-based practice and consultation; and
- Develop leaders who transform health care delivery.

UW-Milwaukee is a community inspired by history and motivated by vision. It offers a uniquely relevant learning experience, educating more Wisconsin residents than any university in the world and recruiting a growing population of international students and faculty. As the most diverse institution in the University of Wisconsin System, it's a learning destination for about 24,000 students. The campus occupies 104 acres and offers 199 degree programs.

### Faculty

The College of Nursing faculty challenges students, creating innovative classroom environments using the latest technology while maintaining over 130 clinical and research partnerships throughout Southeast Wisconsin. Faculty members embrace practice by engaging regional and global communities in the development of solutions to improve health care. The College is consistently ranked in the top 15 percent for academic excellence among colleges with graduate nursing programs by *U.S. News & World Report*. Faculty members embrace practice by engaging regional and global communities in the development of solutions to improve health care.

### Applying

The UW–Milwaukee College of Nursing offers a priority deadline for application to its programs. For fall admission, February 1 is the priority deadline for master's-level programs and January 1 is the priority deadline for Ph.D. programs. For spring admission, October 1 is the priority deadline for master's-level programs and September 1 is the priority deadline for Ph.D. programs. All materials should be sent in by the deadline for full consideration of admission and funding opportunities. After the priority deadline has passed, admission of applicants to the graduate programs will be made on a space available basis.

More information about the UW–Milwaukee College of Nursing can be found at www.nursing.uwm.edu.

### Correspondence and Information

Office of Student Affairs
University of Wisconsin—Milwaukee College of Nursing
1921 East Hartford Avenue
Milwaukee, Wisconsin 53201
Phone: 414-229-5047
Fax: 414-229-5554
E-mail: uwmnurse@uwm.edu

Ph.D. in Nursing students discuss complex issues facing nursing science.

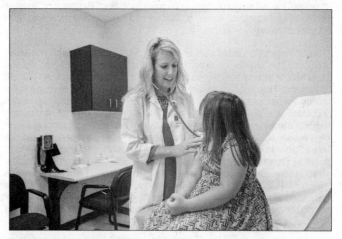

DNP students apply evidence-based research to practice.

Students and faculty work together to impact health care quality and delivery.

# Section 24
# Public Health

This section contains a directory of institutions offering graduate work in public health, followed by an in-depth entry submitted by an institution that chose to prepare a detailed program description. Additional information about programs listed in the directory but not augmented by an in-depth entry may be obtained by writing directly to the dean of a graduate school or chair of a department at the address given in the directory.

For programs offering related work, see also in this book *Allied Health; Biological and Biomedical Sciences; Ecology, Environmental Biology, and Evolutionary Biology; Health Services; Microbiological Sciences; Nursing;* and *Nutrition.* In the other guides in this series:

**Graduate Programs in the Humanities, Arts & Social Sciences**

See *Family and Consumer Sciences (Gerontology)* and *Sociology, Anthropology, and Archaeology (Demography and Population Studies)*

**Graduate Programs in the Physical Sciences, Mathematics, Agricultural Sciences, the Environment & Natural Resources**

See *Mathematical Sciences* and *Environmental Sciences and Management*

**Graduate Programs in Engineering & Applied Sciences**

See *Biomedical Engineering and Biotechnology, Civil and Environmental Engineering, Industrial Engineering, Energy and Power Engineering (Nuclear Engineering),* and *Management of Engineering and Technology*

**Graduate Programs in Business, Education, Information Studies, Law & Social Work**

See *Education.*

## CONTENTS

### Program Directories

### Featured School: Display and Close-Up

# Public Health—General

**Adelphi University,** College of Nursing and Public Health, Program in Public Health, Garden City, NY 11530-0701. Offers MPH. *Entrance requirements:* Additional exam requirements/recommendations for international students: required—TOEFL (minimum score 550 paper-based; 80 iBT), IELTS (minimum score 6.5). *Expenses:* Contact institution.

**Allen College,** Graduate Programs, Waterloo, IA 50703. Offers adult-gerontology acute care nurse practitioner (MSN); community/public health nursing (MSN); education (MSN); family nurse practitioner (MSN); health sciences (Ed D); leadership in health care delivery (MSN); leadership in health care informatics (MSN); nursing (DNP); occupational therapy (MS); psychiatric mental health nurse practitioner (MSN). *Accreditation:* AACN; ACEN. *Faculty:* 27 full-time (23 women), 9 part-time/adjunct (8 women). *Students:* 193 full-time (175 women), 95 part-time (84 women); includes 22 minority (6 Black or African American, non-Hispanic/Latino; 1 American Indian or Alaska Native, non-Hispanic/Latino; 4 Asian, non-Hispanic/Latino; 5 Hispanic/Latino; 6 Two or more races, non-Hispanic/Latino). Average age 32. 376 applicants, 53% accepted, 122 enrolled. *Application deadline:* For fall admission, 2/1 priority date for domestic students; for spring admission, 9/1 priority date for domestic students. Applications are processed on a rolling basis. Application fee: $50. Electronic applications accepted. *Financial support:* In 2019–20, 78 students received support. Federal Work-Study, institutionally sponsored loans, and scholarships/grants available. Support available to part-time students. Financial award application deadline: 8/1; financial award applicants required to submit FAFSA. *Unit head:* Dr. Bob Loch, Provost, 319-226-2040, Fax: 319-226-2070, E-mail: bob.loch@allencollege.edu. *Application contact:* Molly Quinn, Director of Admissions, 319-226-2001, Fax: 319-226-2010, E-mail: molly.quinn@allencollege.edu.
Website: http://www.allencollege.edu/

**American University of Armenia,** Graduate Programs, Yerevan, Armenia. Offers business administration (MBA); computer and information science (MS), including business management, design and manufacturing, energy (ME, MS), industrial engineering and systems management; economics (MS); industrial engineering and systems management (ME), including business, computer aided design/manufacturing, energy (ME, MS), information technology; law (LL M); political science and international affairs (MPSIA); public health (MPH); teaching English as a foreign language (MA). *Program availability:* Part-time, evening/weekend. *Degree requirements:* For master's, thesis (for some programs), capstone/project. *Entrance requirements:* For master's, GRE, GMAT, or LSAT. Additional exam requirements/recommendations for international students: recommended—TOEFL (minimum score 79 iBT), IELTS (minimum score 6.5). *Expenses: Tuition:* Full-time $3100; part-time $165 per credit. Tuition and fees vary according to program.

**Andrews University,** College of Health and Human Services, School of Population Health, Nutrition & Wellness, Berrien Springs, MI 49104. Offers nutrition (MS); nutrition and dietetics (Certificate); public health (MPH). *Accreditation:* CEPH. *Program availability:* Part-time. *Faculty:* 1 (woman) full-time, 7 part-time/adjunct (2 women). *Students:* 20 full-time (19 women), 41 part-time (31 women); includes 24 minority (15 Black or African American, non-Hispanic/Latino; 2 Asian, non-Hispanic/Latino; 6 Hispanic/Latino; 1 Two or more races, non-Hispanic/Latino), 12 international. Average age 33. In 2019, 6 master's, 14 other advanced degrees awarded. *Entrance requirements:* For master's, GRE. Additional exam requirements/recommendations for international students: required—TOEFL (minimum score 550 paper-based). *Application deadline:* Applications are processed on a rolling basis. Application fee: $60. Electronic applications accepted. *Financial support:* Research assistantships, teaching assistantships, Federal Work-Study, institutionally sponsored loans, and scholarships/grants available. *Unit head:* Dr. Padma Tadiupala, Chairperson, 269-471-3370. *Application contact:* Jillian Panigot, Director, University Admissions, 800-253-2874, Fax: 269-471-6321, E-mail: graduate@andrews.edu.
Website: https://www.andrews.edu/shp/publichealth/

**Arcadia University,** College of Health Sciences, Department of Public Health, Program in Public Health, Glenside, PA 19038-3295. Offers MPH. *Accreditation:* CEPH. *Students:* 25 full-time (22 women), 4 part-time (all women); includes 7 minority (4 Black or African American, non-Hispanic/Latino; 2 Asian, non-Hispanic/Latino; 1 Hispanic/Latino), 1 international. In 2019, 24 master's awarded. *Entrance requirements:* For master's, Test scores for the Graduate Record Examination (GRE) or Medical College Admission Test (MCAT) taken within the last five years. Test scores are not required for students with an earned graduate degree in a related field per the department's review and approval. Additional exam requirements/recommendations for international students: required—TOEFL/IELTS results are required for all students for whom English is a second language. *Expenses:* Contact institution. *Financial support:* Unspecified assistantships available. *Unit head:* Dr. Katie DiSantis, Chair, 215-517-2680, E-mail: DiSantisK@arcadia.edu. *Application contact:* 215-572-2910, Fax: 215-572-4049, E-mail: admiss@arcadia.edu.
Website: http://www.arcadia.edu/academic/public-health/

**Argosy University, Atlanta,** College of Health Sciences, Atlanta, GA 30328. Offers public health (MPH).

**Argosy University, Chicago,** College of Health Sciences, Chicago, IL 60601. Offers public health (MPH).

**Argosy University, Hawaii,** College of Health Sciences, Honolulu, HI 96813. Offers public health (MPH).

**Argosy University, Los Angeles,** College of Health Sciences, Los Angeles, CA 90045. Offers public health (MPH).

**Argosy University, Northern Virginia,** College of Health Sciences, Arlington, VA 22209. Offers public health (MPH).

**Argosy University, Orange County,** College of Health Sciences, Orange, CA 92868. Offers public health (MPH).

**Argosy University, Phoenix,** College of Health Sciences, Phoenix, AZ 85021. Offers public health (MPH).

**Argosy University, Seattle,** College of Health Sciences, Seattle, WA 98121. Offers public health (MPH).

**Argosy University, Tampa,** College of Health Sciences, Tampa, FL 33607. Offers public health (MPH).

**Argosy University, Twin Cities,** College of Health Sciences, Eagan, MN 55121. Offers health services management (MS); public health (MPH).

**Arizona State University at Tempe,** College of Nursing and Health Innovation, Phoenix, AZ 85004. Offers advanced nursing practice (DNP); clinical research management (MS); community and public health practice (Graduate Certificate); family mental health nurse practitioner (Graduate Certificate); family nurse practitioner (Graduate Certificate); geriatric nursing (Graduate Certificate); healthcare innovation (MHI); nurse education in academic and practice settings (Graduate Certificate); nurse educator (MS); nursing and healthcare innovation (PhD). *Accreditation:* AACN. *Program availability:* Online learning. *Degree requirements:* For master's, comprehensive exam (for some programs), thesis (for some programs), interactive Program of Study (iPOS) submitted before completing 50 percent of required credit hours; for doctorate, comprehensive exam, thesis/dissertation, interactive Program of Study (iPOS) submitted before completing 50 percent of required credit hours. *Entrance requirements:* For master's and doctorate, GRE, minimum GPA of 3.0 or equivalent in last 2 years of work leading to bachelor's degree. Additional exam requirements/recommendations for international students: required—TOEFL, IELTS, or PTE. Electronic applications accepted. *Expenses:* Contact institution.

**A.T. Still University,** College of Graduate Health Studies, Kirksville, MO 63501. Offers dental public health (MPH); exercise and sport psychology (Certificate); fundamentals of education (Certificate); geriatric exercise science (Certificate); global health (Certificate); health administration (MHA, DHA); health professions (Ed D); health sciences (DH Sc); kinesiology (MS); leadership and organizational behavior (Certificate); public health (MPH); sports conditioning (Certificate). *Accreditation:* CEPH. *Program availability:* Part-time, evening/weekend, online only, 100% online, blended/hybrid learning. *Faculty:* 49 full-time (36 women), 109 part-time/adjunct (66 women). *Students:* 601 full-time (406 women), 532 part-time (331 women); includes 457 minority (197 Black or African American, non-Hispanic/Latino; 15 American Indian or Alaska Native, non-Hispanic/Latino; 114 Asian, non-Hispanic/Latino; 105 Hispanic/Latino; 3 Native Hawaiian or other Pacific Islander, non-Hispanic/Latino; 23 Two or more races, non-Hispanic/Latino), 30 international. Average age 36. 339 applicants, 73% accepted, 217 enrolled. In 2019, 175 master's, 100 doctorates, 118 other advanced degrees awarded. *Degree requirements:* For master's, thesis, integrated terminal project, practicum; for doctorate, thesis/dissertation. *Entrance requirements:* For master's, minimum GPA of 2.5, bachelor's degree or equivalent, essay, resume, English proficiency; for doctorate, minimum GPA of 2.5, master's or terminal degree, essay, past experience in relevant field, resume, English proficiency. Additional exam requirements/recommendations for international students: required—TOEFL (minimum score 550 paper-based; 80 iBT). *Application deadline:* For fall admission, 6/24 for domestic and international students; for winter admission, 9/9 for domestic and international students; for spring admission, 12/9 for domestic and international students; for summer admission, 3/2 for domestic and international students. Applications are processed on a rolling basis. Application fee: $70. Electronic applications accepted. *Financial support:* In 2019–20, 13 students received support. Scholarships/grants available. Financial award applicants required to submit FAFSA. *Unit head:* Dr. Donald Altman, Dean, 480-219-6008, Fax: 660-626-2826, E-mail: daltman@atsu.edu. *Application contact:* Amie Waldemer, Associate Director, Online Admissions, 480-219-6146, E-mail: awaldemer@atsu.edu.
Website: http://www.atsu.edu/college-of-graduate-health-studies

**Augusta University,** College of Allied Health Sciences, Program in Public Health, Augusta, GA 30912. Offers environmental health (MPH); health informatics (MPH); health management (MPH); social and behavioral sciences (MPH). *Accreditation:* CEPH. *Program availability:* Part-time. *Degree requirements:* For master's, thesis (for some programs). *Entrance requirements:* For master's, GRE General Test, three letters of recommendation. Additional exam requirements/recommendations for international students: required—TOEFL. Electronic applications accepted.

**Austin Peay State University,** College of Graduate Studies, College of Behavioral and Health Sciences, Department of Health and Human Performance, Clarksville, TN 37044. Offers public health education (MS); sports and wellness leadership (MS). *Program availability:* Part-time, evening/weekend, online learning. *Faculty:* 6 full-time (3 women), 2 part-time/adjunct (1 woman). *Students:* 13 full-time (11 women), 57 part-time (38 women); includes 22 minority (10 Black or African American, non-Hispanic/Latino; 1 Asian, non-Hispanic/Latino; 5 Hispanic/Latino; 6 Two or more races, non-Hispanic/Latino), 2 international. Average age 30. 51 applicants, 88% accepted, 39 enrolled. In 2019, 28 master's awarded. *Degree requirements:* For master's, comprehensive exam, thesis optional. *Entrance requirements:* For master's, GRE General Test, 3 letters of recommendation, minimum undergraduate GPA of 2.5. Additional exam requirements/recommendations for international students: required—TOEFL (minimum score 500 paper-based). *Application deadline:* For fall admission, 8/5 priority date for domestic students. Applications are processed on a rolling basis. Application fee: $45 ($55 for international students). Electronic applications accepted. *Financial support:* Research assistantships with full tuition reimbursements, career-related internships or fieldwork, Federal Work-Study, institutionally sponsored loans, scholarships/grants, and unspecified assistantships available. Support available to part-time students. Financial award application deadline: 7/1; financial award applicants required to submit FAFSA. *Unit head:* Dr. Marcy Maurer, Chair, 931-221-6105, Fax: 931-221-7040, E-mail: maurerm@apsu.edu. *Application contact:* Megan Mitchell, Coordinator of Graduate Admissions, 931-221-6189, Fax: 931-221-7641, E-mail: mitchellm@apsu.edu.
Website: http://www.apsu.edu/hhp/index.php

**Azusa Pacific University,** University College, Azusa, CA 91702-7000. Offers leadership and organizational studies (MA); public health (MPH). *Program availability:* Online learning.

**Baldwin Wallace University,** Graduate Programs, Public Health Program, Berea, OH 44017-2088. Offers health education and disease prevention (MPH); population health leadership and management (MPH). *Program availability:* Part-time, evening/weekend. *Faculty:* 4 full-time (1 woman). *Students:* 23 full-time (19 women), 12 part-time (10 women); includes 15 minority (9 Black or African American, non-Hispanic/Latino; 3 Asian, non-Hispanic/Latino; 2 Hispanic/Latino; 1 Two or more races, non-Hispanic/Latino), 1 international. Average age 36. 20 applicants, 75% accepted, 14 enrolled. In 2019, 9 master's awarded. *Entrance requirements:* For master's, GRE. Additional exam requirements/recommendations for international students: required—TOEFL (minimum score 550 paper-based; 100 iBT). *Application deadline:* For fall admission, 7/15 for domestic students. Applications are processed on a rolling basis. *Expenses:* Non-partners total program - $48,000; Partners total program - $43,200; MetroHealth employees total program - $36,000. *Financial support:* Unspecified assistantships available. Financial award applicants required to submit FAFSA. *Unit head:* Stephen D. Stahl, Provost, Academic Affairs, 440-826-2251, Fax: 440-826-2329, E-mail: sstahl@bw.edu. *Application contact:* Kate Glaser, Associate Director of Admission, Graduate and Professional Studies, 440-826-8016, E-mail: kglaser@bw.edu.
Website: http://www.bw.edu/mph

**Barry University,** School of Podiatric Medicine, Podiatric Medicine and Surgery Program, Podiatric Medicine/Public Health Option, Miami Shores, FL 33161-6695. Offers DPM/MPH.

**Baylor University,** Graduate School, Robbins College of Health and Human Sciences, Department of Public Health, Waco, TX 76798. Offers community health (MPH). *Program availability:* Part-time, 100% online, blended/hybrid learning. *Faculty:* 9 full-time (6 women). *Students:* 174 full-time (153 women); includes 126 minority (56 Black or African American, non-Hispanic/Latino; 2 American Indian or Alaska Native, non-Hispanic/Latino; 14 Asian, non-Hispanic/Latino; 28 Hispanic/Latino; 1 Native Hawaiian or other Pacific Islander, non-Hispanic/Latino; 25 Two or more races, non-Hispanic/Latino), 1 international. 161 applicants, 92% accepted, 174 enrolled. In 2019, 10 master's awarded. Terminal master's awarded for partial completion of doctoral program. *Degree requirements:* For master's, thesis optional. *Entrance requirements:* Additional exam requirements/recommendations for international students: required—TOEFL, PTE, GRE. *Application deadline:* For fall admission, 12/15 for domestic and international students. Applications are processed on a rolling basis. Application fee: $180. Electronic applications accepted. *Financial support:* Research assistantships and unspecified assistantships available. Financial award application deadline: 2/15. *Unit head:* Dr. Eva I. Doyle, Chair, 254-710-4023, E-mail: eva_doyle@baylor.edu. *Application contact:* Dr. Renee Umstattd Meyer, Graduate Program Director, 254-710-4029, E-mail: renee_umstattd@baylor.edu.
Website: https://www.baylor.edu/publichealth/

**Belmont University,** College of Pharmacy, Nashville, TN 37212. Offers advanced pharmacotherapy (Pharm D); health care informatics (Pharm D); management (Pharm D); missions/public health (Pharm D); Pharm D/MBA. *Accreditation:* ACPE. *Faculty:* 29 full-time (16 women), 4 part-time/adjunct (2 women). *Students:* 354 full-time (242 women); includes 120 minority (50 Black or African American, non-Hispanic/Latino; 1 American Indian or Alaska Native, non-Hispanic/Latino; 41 Asian, non-Hispanic/Latino; 18 Hispanic/Latino; 10 Two or more races, non-Hispanic/Latino), 3 international. Average age 25. In 2019, 67 doctorates awarded. *Degree requirements:* For doctorate, comprehensive exam. *Entrance requirements:* For doctorate, PCAT. Additional exam requirements/recommendations for international students: required—TOEFL. *Application deadline:* For fall admission, 8/31 priority date for domestic students; for spring admission, 3/1 for domestic students. Applications are processed on a rolling basis. Application fee: $50. Electronic applications accepted. *Expenses:* Contact institution. *Financial support:* In 2019–20, 112 students received support. Career-related internships or fieldwork and scholarships/grants available. Financial award application deadline: 12/1; financial award applicants required to submit FAFSA. *Unit head:* Dr. David Gregory, Dean, 615-460-6746, Fax: 615-460-6741, E-mail: david.gregory@belmont.edu. *Application contact:* Dr. David Gregory, Dean, 615-460-6746, Fax: 615-460-6741, E-mail: david.gregory@belmont.edu.
Website: http://www.belmont.edu/pharmacy/index.html

**Benedictine University,** Graduate Programs, Program in Public Health, Lisle, IL 60532. Offers administration of health care institutions (MPH); dietetics (MPH); disaster management (MPH); health education (MPH); health information systems (MPH); management information systems (MPH/MS); MBA/MPH; MPH/MS. *Accreditation:* CEPH. *Program availability:* Part-time, evening/weekend, 100% online. *Entrance requirements:* For master's, GRE, MAT, GMAT, LSAT, DAT or other graduate professional exams, official transcript; 2 letters of recommendation from individuals familiar with the applicant's professional or academic work, excluding family or personal friends; essay describing the candidate's career path. Additional exam requirements/recommendations for international students: required—TOEFL (minimum score 600 paper-based; 79 iBT), IELTS (minimum score 6.5). Electronic applications accepted.

**Boise State University,** College of Health Sciences, Boise, ID 83725-0399. Offers MAL, MHS, MK, MS, MSN, MSW, DNP, Graduate Certificate. *Students:* 12 full-time (10 women); includes 1 minority (Black or African American, non-Hispanic/Latino). Average age 35. *Entrance requirements:* Additional exam requirements/recommendations for international students: required—TOEFL, IELTS. Electronic applications accepted. *Expenses: Tuition, area resident:* Full-time $7110; part-time $470 per credit hour. Tuition, state resident: full-time $7110; part-time $470 per credit hour. Tuition, nonresident: full-time $24,030; part-time $827 per credit hour. *International tuition:* $24,030 full-time. *Required fees:* $2536. Tuition and fees vary according to course load and program. *Financial support:* Applicants required to submit FAFSA. *Unit head:* Dr. Tim Dunnagan, Dean, 208-426-4150, E-mail: timdunnagan@boisestate.edu. *Application contact:* Alicia Anderson, Project Director, 208-426-2425, E-mail: aliciaanderson@boisestate.edu.
Website: https://www.boisestate.edu/healthsciences/

**Boston University,** School of Public Health, Boston, MA 02118. Offers MA, MPH, MS, Dr PH, PhD, JD/MPH, MBA/MPH, MD/MPH, MPH/MS, MSW/MPH. *Accreditation:* CEPH. *Program availability:* Part-time, evening/weekend, 100% online, blended/hybrid learning. *Faculty:* 115 full-time, 190 part-time/adjunct. *Students:* 540 full-time (455 women), 327 part-time (265 women); includes 280 minority (69 Black or African American, non-Hispanic/Latino; 1 American Indian or Alaska Native, non-Hispanic/Latino; 111 Asian, non-Hispanic/Latino; 73 Hispanic/Latino; 26 Two or more races, non-Hispanic/Latino), 116 international. Average age 26. 2,298 applicants, 65% accepted, 266 enrolled. In 2019, 542 master's, 13 doctorates awarded. *Degree requirements:* For master's, Some require practicum or other practical training; for doctorate, comprehensive exam, thesis/dissertation, DrPH requires practicum, research training, some require teaching assistantships. *Entrance requirements:* For master's, U.S. bachelor's degree or international equivalent; most programs require standardized test scores, transcripts, proof of English proficiency (for international students), letters of recommendation, a statement of purpose, and a CV or résumé; for doctorate, MPH or equivalent; most programs require standardized test scores, transcripts, proof of English proficiency (for international students), letters of recommendation, a statement of purpose, and a CV or résumé. Additional exam requirements/recommendations for international students: required—TOEFL (minimum score 600 paper-based; 100 iBT), IELTS (minimum score 7). *Application deadline:* For fall admission, 1/15 priority date for domestic and international students; for spring admission, 1/1 priority date for domestic students, 10/15 priority date for international students. Applications are processed on a rolling basis. Application fee: $140. Electronic applications accepted. *Financial support:* In 2019–20, 871 students received support. Federal Work-Study, institutionally sponsored loans, and scholarships/grants available. Financial award application deadline: 5/1; financial award applicants required to submit FAFSA. *Unit head:* Dr. Sandro Galea, Dean, 617-358-3301, E-mail: asksph@bu.edu. *Application contact:* Ann Marie Larese, Senior Director of Admissions, 617-358-2470, Fax: 617-358-3248, E-mail: asksph@bu.edu.
Website: http://www.bu.edu/sph

**Bowling Green State University,** Graduate College, College of Health and Human Services, Program in Public Health, Bowling Green, OH 43403. Offers MPH. *Program availability:* Part-time. *Degree requirements:* For master's, thesis or alternative. *Entrance requirements:* For master's, GRE General Test, minimum GPA of 3.0. Additional exam requirements/recommendations for international students: required—TOEFL. Electronic applications accepted.

**Brigham Young University,** Graduate Studies, College of Life Sciences, Department of Public Health, Provo, UT 84602. Offers MPH. *Accreditation:* CEPH. *Faculty:* 19 full-time (6 women). *Students:* 29 full-time (26 women), 1 (woman) part-time; includes 3 minority (1 Asian, non-Hispanic/Latino; 1 Hispanic/Latino; 1 Native Hawaiian or other Pacific Islander, non-Hispanic/Latino), 1 international. Average age 30. 38 applicants, 63% accepted, 21 enrolled. In 2019, 15 master's awarded. *Degree requirements:* For master's, comprehensive exam, thesis or alternative, CPH exam. *Entrance requirements:* For master's, GRE General Test (minimum score of 300), minimum cumulative GPA of 3.2. Additional exam requirements/recommendations for international students: required—TOEFL (minimum score 580 paper-based; 85 iBT), IELTS (minimum score 7). *Application deadline:* For fall admission, 2/1 for domestic and international students. Application fee: $50. Electronic applications accepted. *Expenses:* LDS: $7,290 per year tuition ($14,580 to complete degree); Non-LDS: $14,580 per year tuition ($29,160 to complete degree). *Financial support:* In 2019–20, 32 students received support, including 16 research assistantships (averaging $1,300 per year), 16 teaching assistantships (averaging $1,550 per year); career-related internships or fieldwork and scholarships/grants also available. Financial award application deadline: 6/15. *Unit head:* Benjamin T. Crookston, Chair, 801-422-3143, Fax: 801-422-0004, E-mail: benjamin_crookston@byu.edu. *Application contact:* Ruth Ann Riggs, MPH Director, 801-422-3082, Fax: 801-422-0004, E-mail: ruth_riggs@byu.edu.
Website: http://ph.byu.edu/mph

**Brooklyn College of the City University of New York,** School of Natural and Behavioral Sciences, Department of Health and Nutrition Sciences, Program in Public Health, Brooklyn, NY 11210-2889. Offers general public health (MPH); health care policy and administration (MPH). *Degree requirements:* For master's, thesis or alternative, 46 credits. *Entrance requirements:* For master's, GRE, 2 letters of recommendation, essay, interview. Electronic applications accepted.

**Brown University,** Graduate School, Division of Biology and Medicine, School of Public Health, Program in Public Health, Providence, RI 02912. Offers MPH. *Entrance requirements:* For master's, GRE General Test or MCAT. Additional exam requirements/recommendations for international students: required—TOEFL.

**California Baptist University,** Program in Public Health, Riverside, CA 92504-3206. Offers health education and promotion (MPH); health policy and administration (MPH). *Accreditation:* CEPH. *Program availability:* Part-time, evening/weekend, 100% online, blended/hybrid learning. *Degree requirements:* For master's, capstone project; practicum. *Entrance requirements:* For master's, minimum undergraduate GPA of 2.75, two recommendations, 500-word essay, resume. Additional exam requirements/recommendations for international students: required—TOEFL (minimum score 80 iBT). Electronic applications accepted. *Expenses:* Contact institution.

**California State University, Fresno,** Division of Research and Graduate Studies, College of Health and Human Services, Department of Public Health, Fresno, CA 93740-8027. Offers health policy and management (MPH); health promotion (MPH). *Accreditation:* CEPH. *Program availability:* Part-time, evening/weekend. *Degree requirements:* For master's, thesis or alternative. *Entrance requirements:* For master's, GRE General Test, minimum GPA of 2.5. Additional exam requirements/recommendations for international students: required—TOEFL. Electronic applications accepted. *Expenses:* Tuition, state resident: full-time $4012; part-time $2506 per semester.

**California State University, Fullerton,** Graduate Studies, College of Health and Human Development, Department of Public Health, Fullerton, CA 92831-3599. Offers environmental and occupational health and safety (MPH); gerontological health (MPH); health promotion and disease (MPH). *Accreditation:* CEPH. *Program availability:* Part-time. *Entrance requirements:* For master's, minimum GPA of 3.0 in last 60 units attempted.

**California State University, Long Beach,** Graduate Studies, College of Health and Human Services, Department of Health Science, Long Beach, CA 90840. Offers MPH. *Accreditation:* CEPH; NCATE. *Program availability:* Part-time. *Degree requirements:* For master's, thesis optional. *Entrance requirements:* For master's, GRE, minimum GPA of 3.0 in last 60 units. Electronic applications accepted.

**California State University, Northridge,** Graduate Studies, College of Health and Human Development, Department of Health Sciences, Northridge, CA 91330. Offers health administration (MS); public health (MPH), including applied epidemiology, community health education. *Accreditation:* CAHME; CEPH. *Entrance requirements:* For master's, GRE General Test or minimum GPA of 3.0. Additional exam requirements/recommendations for international students: required—TOEFL.

**California State University, San Bernardino,** Graduate Studies, College of Natural Sciences, Program in Public Health, San Bernardino, CA 92407. Offers MPH. *Accreditation:* CEPH. *Students:* 8 full-time (all women), 27 part-time (8 women); includes 22 minority (2 Black or African American, non-Hispanic/Latino; 3 Asian, non-Hispanic/Latino; 16 Hispanic/Latino; 1 Two or more races, non-Hispanic/Latino), 4 international. Average age 29. 51 applicants, 59% accepted, 20 enrolled. In 2019, 21 master's awarded. *Entrance requirements:* Additional exam requirements/recommendations for international students: required—TOEFL. *Application deadline:* For fall admission, 5/5 for domestic students. Application fee: $55. *Unit head:* Dr. Salome Mshigeni, Program Coordinator, 909-537-4337, E-mail: Salome.Mshigeni@csusb.edu. *Application contact:* Dr. Dorota Huizinga, Dean of Graduate Studies, 909-537-3064, E-mail: dorota.huizinga@csusb.edu.

**California State University, San Marcos,** College of Education, Health and Human Services, Program in Public Health, San Marcos, CA 92096-0001. Offers MPH. *Expenses: Tuition, area resident:* Full-time $7176. Tuition, state resident: full-time $7176. Tuition, nonresident: full-time $18,640. *International tuition:* $18,640 full-time. *Required fees:* $1960.

**Campbell University,** Graduate and Professional Programs, College of Pharmacy and Health Sciences, Buies Creek, NC 27506. Offers athletic training (MAT); clinical research (MS); pharmaceutical sciences (MS); pharmacy (Pharm D); physical therapy (DPT); physician assistant (MPAP); public health (MS). *Accreditation:* ACPE; CEPH. *Program availability:* Part-time, evening/weekend. *Entrance requirements:* For master's, MCAT, PCAT, GRE, bachelor's degree in health sciences or related field; for doctorate, PCAT. Additional exam requirements/recommendations for international students: required—TOEFL (minimum score 550 paper-based; 79 iBT). Electronic applications accepted. *Expenses:* Contact institution.

**Case Western Reserve University,** School of Medicine and School of Graduate Studies, Graduate Programs in Medicine, Department of Population and Quantitative Health Sciences, Program in Public Health, Cleveland, OH 44106. Offers MPH. *Accreditation:* CEPH. *Program availability:* Part-time. *Degree requirements:* For master's, essay, field experience, presentation. *Entrance requirements:* For master's, GRE General Test or MCAT, 3 letters of recommendation. Additional exam requirements/recommendations for international students: required—TOEFL. Electronic applications accepted.

**Charles R. Drew University of Medicine and Science,** College of Science and Health, Los Angeles, CA 90059. Offers urban public health (MPH). *Accreditation:* CEPH.

**Chicago State University,** School of Graduate and Professional Studies, College of Health Sciences, Department of Health Studies, Chicago, IL 60628. Offers public health (MPH).

## Public Health—General

**Claremont Graduate University,** Graduate Programs, School of Community and Global Health, Claremont, CA 91773. Offers health promotion science (PhD); public health (MPH). *Accreditation:* CEPH. *Entrance requirements:* For master's and doctorate, GRE. Additional exam requirements/recommendations for international students: required—TOEFL (minimum score 75 iBT). Electronic applications accepted.

**Clemson University,** Graduate School, College of Behavioral, Social and Health Sciences, Department of Public Health Sciences, Clemson, SC 29634. Offers applied health research and evaluation (MS, PhD); biomedical data science and informatics (PhD); clinical and translational research (Certificate). *Faculty:* 23 full-time (13 women). *Students:* 20 full-time (13 women), 41 part-time (31 women); includes 11 minority (2 Black or African American, non-Hispanic/Latino; 6 Asian, non-Hispanic/Latino; 2 Hispanic/Latino; 1 Two or more races, non-Hispanic/Latino), 3 international. Average age 32. 50 applicants, 84% accepted, 36 enrolled. In 2019, 11 master's, 3 other advanced degrees awarded. *Expenses:* Full-Time Student per Semester: Tuition: $6225 (in-state), $13425 (out-of-state), Fees: $598; Graduate Assistant per Semester: $1144; Part-Time Student Per Credit Hour: $833 (in-state), $1731 (out-of-state), Fees: $617; other fees apply depending on program, credit hours, campus & residency. Doctoral Base Fee per Semester: $4938 (in-state), $10405 (out-of-state). *Financial support:* In 2019–20, 24 students received support, including 2 fellowships with full and partial tuition reimbursements available (averaging $5,000 per year), 9 research assistantships with full and partial tuition reimbursements available (averaging $18,428 per year), 7 teaching assistantships with full and partial tuition reimbursements available (averaging $17,325 per year); career-related internships or fieldwork and unspecified assistantships also available. *Application contact:* Dr. Sarah Griffin, Graduate Program Director, 864-656-1622, E-mail: sgriffi@clemson.edu. Website: http://www.clemson.edu/cbshs/departments/public-health/index.html

**Cleveland State University,** College of Graduate Studies, College of Education and Human Services, Department of Health and Human Performance, Cleveland, OH 44115. Offers physical education pedagogy (M Ed); public health (MPH). *Program availability:* Part-time. *Faculty:* 7 full-time (4 women), 3 part-time/adjunct (2 women). *Students:* 94 full-time (30 women), 40 part-time (12 women); includes 31 minority (23 Black or African American, non-Hispanic/Latino; 1 Asian, non-Hispanic/Latino; 1 Hispanic/Latino; 6 Two or more races, non-Hispanic/Latino), 2 international. Average age 29. 103 applicants, 72% accepted, 43 enrolled. In 2019, 36 master's awarded. *Degree requirements:* For master's, comprehensive exam, thesis optional. *Entrance requirements:* For master's, GRE General Test or MAT (if undergraduate GPA less than 2.75), minimum undergraduate GPA of 2.75. Additional exam requirements/ recommendations for international students: required—TOEFL (minimum score 550 paper-based; 78 iBT), IELTS (minimum score 6). *Application deadline:* For fall admission, 7/15 priority date for domestic students; for spring admission, 12/15 priority date for domestic students. Applications are processed on a rolling basis. Application fee: $30. Electronic applications accepted. *Expenses:* Tuition, state resident: full-time $10,215; part-time $6810 per credit hour. Tuition, nonresident: full-time $17,496; part-time $11,664 per credit hour. *International tuition:* $19,316 full-time. Tuition and fees vary according to degree level and program. *Financial support:* In 2019–20, 6 research assistantships with tuition reimbursements (averaging $3,480 per year), 1 teaching assistantship with tuition reimbursement (averaging $3,480 per year) were awarded; career-related internships or fieldwork, tuition waivers (full), and unspecified assistantships also available. Financial award application deadline: 3/15; financial award applicants required to submit FAFSA. *Unit head:* Dr. Mike Loovis, Associate Professor/ Department Chairperson, 216-687-3665, Fax: 216-687-5410, E-mail: e.loovis@ csuohio.edu. *Application contact:* David Easler, Director, Graduate Recruitment, 216-687-5047, Fax: 216-687-5400, E-mail: d.easler@csuohio.edu. Website: http://www.csuohio.edu/cehs/departments/HPERD/hperd_dept.html

**The College of New Jersey,** Office of Graduate and Advancing Education, School of Nursing, Health, and Exercise Science, Program in Public Health, Ewing, NJ 08628. Offers global health (MPH); health communications (MPH); precision health (MPH).

**College of Saint Elizabeth,** Program in Public Health, Morristown, NJ 07960-6989. Offers MPH. *Program availability:* Part-time. *Degree requirements:* For master's, thesis. *Entrance requirements:* Additional exam requirements/recommendations for international students: required—TOEFL (minimum score 550 paper-based; 79 iBT), IELTS (minimum score 6.5). Electronic applications accepted. Application fee is waived when completed online.

**Columbia University,** Columbia University Mailman School of Public Health, New York, NY 10032. Offers Exec MHA, Exec MPH, MHA, MPH, MS, Dr PH, PhD, DDS/MPH, MBA/MPH, MD/MPH, MPA/MPH, MPH/MIA, MPH/MOT, MPH/MS, MPH/MSN, MPH/ MSSW. *Accreditation:* CEPH (one or more programs are accredited). *Program availability:* Part-time, evening/weekend. *Students:* 1,055 full-time (833 women), 511 part-time (366 women); includes 585 minority (94 Black or African American, non-Hispanic/Latino; 4 American Indian or Alaska Native, non-Hispanic/Latino; 298 Asian, non-Hispanic/Latino; 141 Hispanic/Latino; 2 Native Hawaiian or other Pacific Islander, non-Hispanic/Latino; 46 Two or more races, non-Hispanic/Latino), 354 international. Average age 27. 3,081 applicants, 65% accepted, 730 enrolled. In 2019, 597 master's, 29 doctorates awarded. *Degree requirements:* For master's, thesis (for some programs); for doctorate, comprehensive exam, thesis/dissertation. *Entrance requirements:* For master's, GRE General Test; for doctorate, GRE General Test, MPH or equivalent (for Dr PH). Additional exam requirements/recommendations for international students: required—TOEFL (minimum score 600 paper-based; 100 iBT). *Application deadline:* For fall admission, 12/1 priority date for domestic and international students. Application fee: $120. Electronic applications accepted. *Expenses:* Contact institution. *Financial support:* Fellowships, research assistantships, teaching assistantships, career-related internships or fieldwork, Federal Work-Study, and traineeships available. Support available to part-time students. Financial award application deadline: 2/1; financial award applicants required to submit FAFSA. *Unit head:* Dr. Linda P. Fried, Dean/ Professor, 212-305-9300, Fax: 212-305-9342, E-mail: lpfried@columbia.edu. *Application contact:* Clare Norton, Associate Dean for Enrollment Management, 212-305-8698, Fax: 212-342-1861, E-mail: ph-admit@columbia.edu. Website: https://www.mailman.columbia.edu/

**Creighton University,** Graduate School, Department of Interdisciplinary Studies, Master of Public Health Program, Omaha, NE 68178-0001. Offers MPH. *Program availability:* Part-time. *Degree requirements:* For master's, practicum. *Entrance requirements:* For master's, resume, essay. Additional exam requirements/ recommendations for international students: required—TOEFL (minimum score 90 iBT), IELTS (minimum score 6.5). Electronic applications accepted. *Expenses:* Contact institution.

**Daemen College,** Public Health Programs, Amherst, NY 14226-3592. Offers community health education (MPH); epidemiology (MPH); generalist (MPH). *Program availability:* Part-time, evening/weekend. *Degree requirements:* For master's, successful completion of a practicum and capstone; minimum grade of B- in any course; maximum of 2 repeated courses is allowed; students must maintain an overall minimum cumulative GPA of 3.0. *Entrance requirements:* For master's, bachelor's degree, official transcripts, GPA 3.0 or above (under 3.0 may be submitted on a conditional basis), 2 letters of

recommendation, personal statement, interview with MPH faculty. Additional exam requirements/recommendations for international students: required—TOEFL (minimum score 85 paper-based), IELTS (minimum score 6.5). Electronic applications accepted. Application fee is waived when completed online.

**Dartmouth College,** The Dartmouth Institute, Program in Public Health, Hanover, NH 03755. Offers MPH. *Accreditation:* CEPH. *Program availability:* Part-time. *Degree requirements:* For master's, research project or practicum. *Entrance requirements:* For master's, GRE or MCAT, 3 letters of recommendation. Additional exam requirements/ recommendations for international students: required—TOEFL. Electronic applications accepted.

**Davenport University,** Sneden Graduate School, Grand Rapids, MI 49512. Offers accounting (MBA); business administration (EMBA); finance (MBA); health care management (MBA); human resources (MBA); information assurance (MS); occupational therapy (MSOT); public health (MPH); strategic management (MBA). *Program availability:* Evening/weekend. *Entrance requirements:* For master's, GMAT, minimum undergraduate GPA of 2.75. Additional exam requirements/recommendations for international students: required—TOEFL. Electronic applications accepted.

**DePaul University,** College of Liberal Arts and Social Sciences, Chicago, IL 60614. Offers Arabic (MA); Chinese (MA); critical ethnic studies (MA); English (MA); French (MA); German (MA); history (MA); interdisciplinary studies (MA, MS); international public service (MS); international studies (MA); Italian (MA); Japanese (MA); liberal studies (MA); nonprofit management (MNM); public administration (MPA); public health (MPH); public policy (MPP); public service management (MS); refugee and forced migration studies (MS); social work (MSW); sociology (MA); Spanish (MA); sustainable urban development (MA); women's and gender studies (MA); writing and publishing (MA); writing, rhetoric and discourse (MA); MA/PhD. *Accreditation:* CEPH. *Program availability:* Part-time, evening/weekend, online learning. Terminal master's awarded for partial completion of doctoral program. *Degree requirements:* For master's, variable foreign language requirement, comprehensive exam (for some programs), thesis (for some programs). Electronic applications accepted.

**Des Moines University,** College of Health Sciences, Program in Public Health, Des Moines, IA 50312-4104. Offers MPH. *Accreditation:* CEPH. *Program availability:* Part-time, evening/weekend. *Entrance requirements:* For master's, minimum GPA of 3.0. Additional exam requirements/recommendations for international students: required— TOEFL (minimum score 600 paper-based). Electronic applications accepted. *Expenses:* Contact institution.

**Drexel University,** Dornsife School of Public Health, Philadelphia, PA 19104-2875. Offers MPH, MS, PhD, Certificate. *Accreditation:* CEPH. *Entrance requirements:* For master's, GMAT, GRE, LSAT, or MCAT, previous course work in statistics and word processing. Additional exam requirements/recommendations for international students: required—TOEFL. Electronic applications accepted. *Expenses:* Contact institution.

**East Carolina University,** Brody School of Medicine, Department of Public Health, Greenville, NC 27858-4353. Offers public health (Dr PH); MD/MPH. *Accreditation:* CEPH. *Program availability:* Part-time, online learning. *Entrance requirements:* For master's, GRE. Additional exam requirements/recommendations for international students: recommended—TOEFL, IELTS. *Application deadline:* For fall admission, 4/15 for domestic and international students; for spring admission, 10/15 for domestic and international students. Electronic applications accepted. *Expenses: Tuition, area resident:* Full-time $4749; part-time $185 per credit hour. Tuition, state resident: full-time $4749; part-time $185 per credit hour. Tuition, nonresident: full-time $17,898; part-time $864 per credit hour. *International tuition:* $17,898 full-time. *Required fees:* $2787. *Financial support:* Research assistantships and unspecified assistantships available. Financial award applicants required to submit FAFSA. *Unit head:* Dr. Ronny Bell, Chair, 252-744-4065, E-mail: mph@ecu.edu. *Application contact:* Graduate School Admissions, 252-328-6012, Fax: 252-328-6071, E-mail: gradschool@ecu.edu.

**East Carolina University,** Graduate School, College of Fine Arts and Communication, School of Communication, Greenville, NC 27858-4353. Offers communication (MA); health communication (Certificate). *Application deadline:* For fall admission, 6/1 priority date for domestic students; for spring admission, 10/15 for domestic students. *Expenses: Tuition, area resident:* Full-time $4749; part-time $185 per credit hour. Tuition, state resident: full-time $4749; part-time $185 per credit hour. Tuition, nonresident: full-time $17,898; part-time $864 per credit hour. *International tuition:* $17,898 full-time. *Required fees:* $2787. *Unit head:* Dr. Linda Kean, Director, 252-328-4227, E-mail: keanl@ecu.edu. *Application contact:* Graduate School Admissions, 252-328-6012, Fax: 252-328-6071, E-mail: gradschool@ecu.edu. Website: https://communication.ecu.edu/

**Eastern Virginia Medical School,** Master of Public Health Program, Norfolk, VA 23501-1980. Offers MPH. *Accreditation:* CEPH. *Program availability:* Evening/weekend. *Degree requirements:* For master's, field practicum. *Entrance requirements:* For master's, GRE General Test. Additional exam requirements/recommendations for international students: required—TOEFL (minimum score 650 paper-based). Electronic applications accepted. *Expenses:* Contact institution.

**Eastern Washington University,** Graduate Studies, College of Health Science and Public Health, Program in Public Health, Cheney, WA 99004-2431. Offers MPH. *Faculty:* 8 full-time (4 women). *Students:* 23 full-time (17 women), 23 part-time (12 women); includes 5 minority (2 Black or African American, non-Hispanic/Latino; 2 American Indian or Alaska Native, non-Hispanic/Latino; 1 Hispanic/Latino), 3 international. Average age 32. 25 applicants, 84% accepted, 15 enrolled. In 2019, 16 master's awarded. *Degree requirements:* For master's, comprehensive exam (for some programs), thesis (for some programs). *Entrance requirements:* For master's, minimum cumulative GPA of 3.0 in last 90 quarter or 60 semester credits of post-secondary coursework; current resume; three short career plan essays. Additional exam requirements/recommendations for international students: required—TOEFL (minimum score 580 paper-based; 92 iBT), IELTS (minimum score 7), PTE (minimum score 6). *Application deadline:* For fall admission, 8/1 for domestic students; for spring admission, 12/15 for domestic students. Application fee: $75. Electronic applications accepted. *Financial support:* Application deadline: 2/15; applicants required to submit FAFSA. *Unit head:* Dr. Donna Mann, OTD, MEd, OT/L, Interim Chair, 509-828-1489, E-mail: Dmann@ewu.edu. *Application contact:* Kathy White, Advisor/Recruiter for Graduate Studies, 509-359-2491, Fax: 509-359-6044, E-mail: gradprograms@ewu.edu. Website: http://www.ewu.edu/chsph/programs/public-health

**East Stroudsburg University of Pennsylvania,** Graduate and Extended Studies, College of Health Sciences, Department of Health Studies, East Stroudsburg, PA 18301-2999. Offers MPH, MS. *Accreditation:* CEPH (one or more programs are accredited). *Program availability:* Part-time, evening/weekend, online learning. *Degree requirements:* For master's, oral comprehensive exam. *Entrance requirements:* For master's, GRE General Test, minimum GPA of 3.0 in major, 2.8 overall; undergraduate prerequisites in anatomy and physiology; 3 verifiable letters of recommendation; professional resume. Additional exam requirements/recommendations for international students: recommended—TOEFL (minimum score 560 paper-based; 83 iBT), IELTS. Electronic applications accepted.

**East Tennessee State University,** College of Graduate and Continuing Studies, College of Public Health, Johnson City, TN 37614. Offers MPH, MSEH, DPH, PhD, Postbaccalaureate Certificate. *Accreditation:* CEPH. *Program availability:* Part-time, online learning. *Degree requirements:* For master's, comprehensive exam, field experience; research project or thesis; environmental health practice; seminar; for doctorate, comprehensive exam, thesis/dissertation, practicum; seminar. *Entrance requirements:* For master's, GRE General Test, SOPHAS application, three letters of recommendation; for doctorate, GRE General Test, SOPHAS application, three letters of recommendation, curriculum vitae or resume; for Postbaccalaureate Certificate, minimum GPA of 2.5, three letters of recommendation, resume. Additional exam requirements/recommendations for international students: required—TOEFL (minimum score 550 paper-based; 79 iBT), IELTS (minimum score 6.5). Electronic applications accepted.

**Elmhurst University,** Graduate Programs, Program in Public Health, Elmhurst, IL 60126-3296. Offers MPH. *Program availability:* Part-time, evening/weekend, online learning. *Students:* Average age 31. 2 applicants, 100% accepted. In 2019, 12 master's awarded. *Entrance requirements:* For master's, 3 recommendations, resume, statement of purpose. Additional exam requirements/recommendations for international students: required—TOEFL (minimum score 550 paper-based; 79 iBT). *Application deadline:* Applications are processed on a rolling basis. Electronic applications accepted. *Expenses:* Contact institution. *Financial support:* In 2019–20, 15 students received support. Scholarships/grants available. Support available to part-time students. Financial award application deadline: 3/1; financial award applicants required to submit FAFSA. *Unit head:* Dr. Terry Johnson, Associate Professor, 630-617-3510, E-mail: terryj@elmhurst.edu. *Application contact:* Timothy J. Panfil, Director of Enrollment Management, 630-617-3300 Ext. 3256, Fax: 630-617-6471, E-mail: panfilt@elmhurst.edu.

**Emory University,** Rollins School of Public Health, Atlanta, GA 30322. Offers MPH, MSPH, PhD, JD/MPH, MBA/MPH, MD/MPH, MM Sc/MPH, MSN/MPH. *Accreditation:* CEPH (one or more programs are accredited). *Program availability:* Part-time, evening/weekend, online learning. *Degree requirements:* For master's, variable foreign language requirement, comprehensive exam (for some programs), thesis (for some programs), practicum. *Entrance requirements:* For master's, GRE General Test. Additional exam requirements/recommendations for international students: required—TOEFL (minimum score 550 paper-based; 80 iBT). Electronic applications accepted. *Expenses:* Contact institution.

**Everglades University,** Graduate Programs, Program in Public Health Administration, Boca Raton, FL 33431. Offers complementary and alternative medicine (MPH). *Program availability:* Part-time, evening/weekend, 100% online. *Degree requirements:* For master's, capstone course. *Entrance requirements:* For master's, GMAT (minimum score of 400) or GRE (minimum score of 290), bachelor's or graduate degree from college accredited by an agency recognized by the U.S. Department of Education; minimum cumulative GPA of 2.0 at the baccalaureate level, 3.0 at the master's level. Additional exam requirements/recommendations for international students: recommended—TOEFL (minimum score 500 paper-based). Electronic applications accepted. *Expenses:* Contact institution.

**Ferris State University,** College of Health Professions, Program in Public Health, Big Rapids, MI 49307. Offers MPH. *Program availability:* Part-time, evening/weekend, 100% online. *Faculty:* 4 full-time (2 women). *Students:* 6 full-time (4 women), 20 part-time (18 women); includes 7 minority (5 Black or African American, non-Hispanic/Latino; 1 Asian, non-Hispanic/Latino; 1 Two or more races, non-Hispanic/Latino). Average age 33. 7 applicants, 100% accepted, 6 enrolled. In 2019, 4 master's awarded. *Degree requirements:* For master's, comprehensive exam, capstone project. *Entrance requirements:* For master's, GRE (if GPA is below a 3.5 or does not have a health related certification), minimum GPA of 3.0. Additional exam requirements/recommendations for international students: recommended—TOEFL (minimum score 550 paper-based). *Application deadline:* For fall admission, 7/1 for domestic and international students; for spring admission, 12/1 for domestic and international students; for summer admission, 4/1 for domestic and international students. Applications are processed on a rolling basis. Electronic applications accepted. Tuition and fees vary according to degree level, program and student level. *Financial support:* In 2019–20, 4 students received support. Scholarships/grants available. Financial award applicants required to submit FAFSA. *Unit head:* Dr. Michael Reger, Coordinator, 231-591-3132, E-mail: michaelreger@ferris.edu. *Application contact:* Dr. Michael Reger, Coordinator, 231-591-3132, E-mail: michaelreger@ferris.edu.
Website: https://ferris.edu/HTMLS/colleges/alliedhe/PublicHealth/MSPH/homepage.htm

**Florida Agricultural and Mechanical University,** Division of Graduate Studies, Research, and Continuing Education, College of Pharmacy and Pharmaceutical Sciences, Institute of Public Health, Tallahassee, FL 32307-3200. Offers MPH, DPH. *Accreditation:* CEPH. *Entrance requirements:* Additional exam requirements/recommendations for international students: required—TOEFL.

**Florida International University,** Robert Stempel College of Public Health and Social Work, Programs in Public Health, Miami, FL 33199. Offers biostatistics (MPH); environmental and occupational health (MPH, PhD); epidemiology (MPH, PhD); health policy and management (MPH); health promotion and disease prevention (MPH, PhD). *Accreditation:* CEPH. *Program availability:* Part-time, evening/weekend, online learning. *Faculty:* 31 full-time (15 women), 8 part-time/adjunct (6 women). *Students:* 176 full-time (117 women), 58 part-time (42 women); includes 170 minority (57 Black or African American, non-Hispanic/Latino; 1 American Indian or Alaska Native, non-Hispanic/Latino; 14 Asian, non-Hispanic/Latino; 95 Hispanic/Latino; 3 Two or more races, non-Hispanic/Latino), 32 international. Average age 29. 260 applicants, 68% accepted, 68 enrolled. In 2019, 70 master's, 16 doctorates awarded. *Degree requirements:* For master's, thesis optional; for doctorate, comprehensive exam, thesis/dissertation. *Entrance requirements:* For master's, minimum GPA of 3.0, letters of recommendation; for doctorate, GRE, resume, minimum GPA of 3.0, letters of recommendation, letter of intent. Additional exam requirements/recommendations for international students: required—TOEFL (minimum score 550 paper-based; 80 iBT). *Application deadline:* For fall admission, 6/1 for domestic students, 4/1 for international students; for spring admission, 10/1 for domestic students, 9/1 for international students. Applications are processed on a rolling basis. Application fee: $30. Electronic applications accepted. *Expenses:* Contact institution. *Financial support:* Institutionally sponsored loans, scholarships/grants, and tuition waivers (full) available. Financial award application deadline: 3/1; financial award applicants required to submit FAFSA. *Unit head:* Dr. Kim Tieu, Chair, 305-348-0371, E-mail: kim.tieu@fiu.edu. *Application contact:* Nanett Rojas, Manager, Admissions Operations, 305-348-7464, Fax: 305-348-7441, E-mail: gradadm@fiu.edu.

**Florida State University,** The Graduate School, College of Social Sciences and Public Policy, Public Health Program, Tallahassee, FL 32306. Offers MPH, MPH/MSP. *Accreditation:* CEPH. *Program availability:* Part-time. *Faculty:* 9 full-time (2 women). *Students:* 48 full-time (32 women), 23 part-time (15 women); includes 45 minority (24 Black or African American, non-Hispanic/Latino; 5 Asian, non-Hispanic/Latino; 13 Hispanic/Latino; 3 Two or more races, non-Hispanic/Latino), 4 international. Average age 27. 94 applicants, 55% accepted, 28 enrolled. In 2019, 33 master's awarded. *Degree requirements:* For master's, internship, research paper. *Entrance requirements:* For master's, GRE General Test, minimum GPA of 3.0. Additional exam requirements/recommendations for international students: required—TOEFL (minimum score 550 paper-based; 80 iBT). *Application deadline:* For fall admission, 7/1 priority date for domestic students, 7/1 for international students; for spring admission, 11/1 for domestic and international students. Applications are processed on a rolling basis. Application fee: $30. Electronic applications accepted. *Financial support:* In 2019–20, research assistantships with full tuition reimbursements (averaging $5,000 per year) were awarded; fellowships with tuition reimbursements, career-related internships or fieldwork, Federal Work-Study, institutionally sponsored loans, and unspecified assistantships also available. Financial award application deadline: 2/15. *Unit head:* Dr. William G. Weissert, Director, 850-644-4418, Fax: 850-644-1367, E-mail: wweissert@fsu.edu. *Application contact:* Sabrina Smith, Academic Program Specialist, 850-644-4418, E-mail: ssmith9@fsu.edu.
Website: http://www.coss.fsu.edu/publichealth/

**Fort Valley State University,** College of Graduate Studies and Extended Education, Program in Public Health, Fort Valley, GA 31030. Offers environmental health (MPH). *Degree requirements:* For master's, thesis. *Entrance requirements:* For master's, GRE General Test. Additional exam requirements/recommendations for international students: recommended—TOEFL.

**George Mason University,** College of Health and Human Services, Department of Global and Community Health, Fairfax, VA 22030. Offers global and community health (Certificate); global health (MS); public health (MPH, Certificate), including epidemiology (MPH), leadership and management (Certificate). *Accreditation:* CEPH. *Program availability:* Part-time, evening/weekend. *Degree requirements:* For master's, thesis, 200-hour practicum. *Entrance requirements:* For master's, GRE, GMAT (depending on program), 2 official transcripts; expanded goals statement; 3 letters of recommendation; resume; 1 completed course in health science, statistics, natural sciences and social science (for MPH); 6 credits of foreign language if not fluent (for MS); minimum undergraduate GPA of 3.0; for Certificate, 2 official transcripts; expanded goals statement; 3 letters of recommendation; resume; bachelor's degree from regionally-accredited institution with minimum GPA of 3.0. Additional exam requirements/recommendations for international students: required—TOEFL (minimum score 570 paper-based; 88 iBT), IELTS (minimum score 6.5), PTE (minimum score 59). Electronic applications accepted. *Expenses:* Contact institution.

**Georgetown University,** Graduate School of Arts and Sciences, Department of Microbiology and Immunology, Washington, DC 20057. Offers biohazardous threat agents and emerging infectious diseases (MS); biomedical science policy and advocacy (MS); general microbiology and immunology (MS); global infectious diseases (PhD); microbiology and immunology (PhD). *Program availability:* Part-time. *Degree requirements:* For master's, 30 credit hours of coursework; for doctorate, comprehensive exam, thesis/dissertation. *Entrance requirements:* For master's, GRE General Test, 3 letters of reference, bachelor's degree in related field; for doctorate, GRE General Test, 3 letters of reference, MS/BS in related field. Additional exam requirements/recommendations for international students: required—TOEFL (minimum score 505 paper-based). Electronic applications accepted.

**The George Washington University,** Milken Institute School of Public Health, Department of Global Health, Washington, DC 20052. Offers global health (Dr PH); global health communication (MPH). *Entrance requirements:* For master's, GMAT, GRE General Test, or MCAT. Additional exam requirements/recommendations for international students: required—TOEFL.

**Georgia Southern University,** Jack N. Averitt College of Graduate Studies, Jiann-Ping Hsu College of Public Health, Program in Public Health, Statesboro, GA 30460. Offers biostatistics (MPH, Dr PH); community health behavior and education (Dr PH); community health education (MPH); environmental health sciences (MPH); epidemiology (MPH); health policy and management (MPH, Dr PH). *Program availability:* Part-time. *Faculty:* 42 full-time (22 women), 1 (woman) part-time/adjunct. *Students:* 142 full-time (105 women), 88 part-time (62 women); includes 132 minority (100 Black or African American, non-Hispanic/Latino; 10 Asian, non-Hispanic/Latino; 8 Hispanic/Latino; 14 Two or more races, non-Hispanic/Latino), 46 international. Average age 32. 195 applicants, 85% accepted, 59 enrolled. In 2019, 90 master's, 14 doctorates awarded. *Degree requirements:* For master's, thesis optional, practicum; for doctorate, comprehensive exam, thesis/dissertation, preceptorship. *Entrance requirements:* For master's, GRE General Test, minimum GPA of 2.75, 3 letters of recommendation, statement of purpose, resume or curriculum vitae; for doctorate, GRE, GMAT, MCAT, LSAT, minimum GPA of 3.0, 3 letters of recommendation, statement of purpose, resume or curriculum vitae. Additional exam requirements/recommendations for international students: required—TOEFL (minimum score 537 paper-based; 75 iBT), IELTS (minimum score 6). *Application deadline:* For fall admission, 6/1 for domestic students, 5/1 for international students. Applications are processed on a rolling basis. Application fee: $135. Electronic applications accepted. *Expenses:* Contact institution. *Financial support:* In 2019–20, 94 students received support, including 1 research assistantship with full tuition reimbursement available (averaging $12,350 per year), 6 teaching assistantships with full tuition reimbursements available (averaging $12,350 per year); scholarships/grants, tuition waivers (full), and unspecified assistantships also available. Financial award application deadline: 4/15; financial award applicants required to submit FAFSA. *Unit head:* Dr. Robert Greg Evans, Dean, 912-478-2674, E-mail: rgevans@georgiasouthern.edu. *Application contact:* Shamia Garrett, Coordinator, Office of Student Services, 912-478-2674, Fax: 912-478-5811, E-mail: jphcoph-gradadvisor@georgiasouthern.edu.
Website: http://jphcoph.georgiasouthern.edu/

**Georgia State University,** Andrew Young School of Policy Studies, Department of Public Management and Policy, Atlanta, GA 30303. Offers criminal justice (MPA); disaster management (Certificate); disaster policy (MPA); environmental policy (PhD); health policy (PhD); management and finance (MPA); nonprofit management (MPA, Certificate); nonprofit policy (MPA); planning and economic development (MPP, Certificate); policy analysis and evaluation (MPA), including planning and economic development; public and nonprofit management (PhD); public finance and budgeting (PhD), including science and technology policy, urban and regional economic development; public finance policy (MPA), including social policy; public health (MPA). *Accreditation:* NASPAA (one or more programs are accredited). *Program availability:* Part-time. *Faculty:* 13 full-time (7 women), 3 part-time/adjunct (1 woman). *Students:* 125 full-time (81 women), 91 part-time (66 women); includes 103 minority (78 Black or African American, non-Hispanic/Latino; 3 Asian, non-Hispanic/Latino; 14 Hispanic/Latino; 8 Two or more races, non-Hispanic/Latino), 31 international. Average age 32. 298 applicants, 60% accepted, 82 enrolled. In 2019, 70 master's, 8 other advanced degrees awarded. Terminal master's awarded for partial completion of doctoral program. *Degree requirements:* For master's, thesis optional; for doctorate, comprehensive exam, thesis/dissertation. *Entrance requirements:* For master's and doctorate, GRE. Additional exam requirements/recommendations for international students: required—TOEFL (minimum score 603 paper-based; 100 iBT) or IELTS (minimum score 7). *Application deadline:* For fall admission, 1/15 for domestic and international students. Application fee: $50. Electronic applications accepted. *Expenses:*

## Public Health—General

*Tuition, area resident:* Full-time $7164; part-time $398 per credit hour. *Tuition, state resident:* full-time $7164; part-time $398 per credit hour. *Tuition, nonresident:* full-time $22,662; part-time $1259 per credit hour. *International tuition:* $22,662 full-time. *Required fees:* $2128; $312 per credit hour. Tuition and fees vary according to course load and program. *Financial support:* In 2019–20, fellowships (averaging $8,194 per year), research assistantships (averaging $8,068 per year), teaching assistantships (averaging $3,600 per year) were awarded; institutionally sponsored loans, scholarships/grants, health care benefits, and unspecified assistantships also available. Financial award application deadline: 2/1. *Unit head:* Dr. Cathy Yang Liu, Chair and Professor, 404-413-0102, Fax: 404-413-0104, E-mail: cyliu@gsu.edu. *Application contact:* Dr. Cathy Yang Liu, Chair and Professor, 404-413-0102, Fax: 404-413-0104, E-mail: cyliu@gsu.edu.
Website: https://aysps.gsu.edu/public-management-policy/

**Georgia State University,** School of Public Health, Atlanta, GA 30302-3995. Offers MPH, Dr PH, PhD, Certificate. *Accreditation:* CEPH. *Program availability:* Part-time. *Faculty:* 30 full-time (16 women), 7 part-time/adjunct (3 women). *Students:* 233 full-time (175 women), 101 part-time (80 women); includes 196 minority (126 Black or African American, non-Hispanic/Latino; 31 Asian, non-Hispanic/Latino; 24 Hispanic/Latino; 15 Two or more races, non-Hispanic/Latino), 38 international. Average age 29. 405 applicants, 60% accepted, 122 enrolled. In 2019, 105 master's, 9 doctorates, 9 other advanced degrees awarded. *Degree requirements:* For master's, thesis, applied practicum; for doctorate, comprehensive exam, thesis/dissertation, applied, research or teaching practicum. *Entrance requirements:* For master's, doctorate, and Certificate, GRE or GMAT. Additional exam requirements/recommendations for international students: required—TOEFL (minimum score 550 paper-based; 80 iBT). *Application deadline:* For fall admission, 2/1 for domestic and international students; for spring admission, 10/1 for domestic and international students. Application fee: $50. Electronic applications accepted. *Expenses:* Contact institution. *Financial support:* In 2019–20, fellowships (averaging $2,500 per year), research assistantships with full tuition reimbursements (averaging $22,000 per year), teaching assistantships with full tuition reimbursements (averaging $22,000 per year) were awarded; career-related internships or fieldwork, scholarships/grants, health care benefits, unspecified assistantships, and out-of-state tuition waivers also available. *Unit head:* Dr. Rodney Lyn. *Application contact:* Dr. Rodney Lyn.
Website: http://publichealth.gsu.edu/

**Grand Canyon University,** College of Nursing and Health Care Professions, Phoenix, AZ 85017-1097. Offers acute care nurse practitioner (MSN, PMC); family nurse practitioner (MSN, PMC); health care administration (MS); health care informatics (MS, MSN); leadership in health care systems (MSN); nursing (DNP); nursing education (MSN, PMC); public health (MPH, MSN); MBA/MSN. *Accreditation:* AACN. *Program availability:* Part-time, evening/weekend, online learning. *Degree requirements:* For master's and PMC, comprehensive exam (for some programs). *Entrance requirements:* For master's, minimum cumulative and science course undergraduate GPA of 3.0. Additional exam requirements/recommendations for international students: required—TOEFL (minimum score 575 paper-based; 90 iBT), IELTS (minimum score 7).

**Grand Valley State University,** College of Health Professions, Public Health Program, Allendale, MI 49401-9403. Offers MPH. *Program availability:* Part-time. *Faculty:* 7 full-time (6 women). *Students:* 74 full-time (59 women), 14 part-time (12 women); includes 21 minority (7 Black or African American, non-Hispanic/Latino; 4 Asian, non-Hispanic/Latino; 7 Hispanic/Latino; 3 Two or more races, non-Hispanic/Latino), 7 international. Average age 26. 85 applicants, 92% accepted, 37 enrolled. In 2019, 42 master's awarded. *Degree requirements:* For master's, thesis optional, thesis or project. *Entrance requirements:* For master's, baccalaureate degree and official transcripts with minimum GPA of 3.0, 2 letters of recommendation, personal essay. Additional exam

requirements/recommendations for international students: required—TOEFL (minimum iBT score of 80), IELTS (6.5), or Michigan English Language Assessment Battery (77). *Application deadline:* For fall admission, 2/1 for domestic students. Application fee: $30. *Expenses:* $733 per credit hour, 51-54 credit hours. *Financial support:* In 2019–20, 24 students received support, including 13 fellowships, 2 research assistantships with full and partial tuition reimbursements available (averaging $8,000 per year); unspecified assistantships also available. *Unit head:* Dr. Ranelle Brew, Director, 616-331-5570, Fax: 616-331-5550, E-mail: brewr@gvsu.edu. *Application contact:* Darlene Zwart, Student Services Coordinator, 616-331-3958, Fax: 616-331-5643, E-mail: zwartda@gvsu.edu.
Website: http://www.gvsu.edu/grad/mph/

**Harvard University,** Cyprus International Institute for the Environment and Public Health in Association with Harvard School of Public Health, Cambridge, MA 02138. Offers environmental health (MS); environmental/public health (PhD); epidemiology and biostatistics (MS). *Entrance requirements:* For master's and doctorate, GRE, resume/curriculum vitae, 3 letters of recommendation, BA or BS (including diploma and official transcripts). Additional exam requirements/recommendations for international students: required—TOEFL, IELTS (minimum score 7). Electronic applications accepted.

**Harvard University,** Harvard T.H. Chan School of Public Health, Doctor of Public Health Program, Cambridge, MA 02138. Offers Dr PH. *Students:* 48 full-time (29 women); includes 16 minority (6 Black or African American, non-Hispanic/Latino; 7 Asian, non-Hispanic/Latino; 3 Hispanic/Latino), 22 international. Average age 29. 175 applicants, 7% accepted, 9 enrolled. In 2019, 15 doctorates awarded. *Entrance requirements:* Additional exam requirements/recommendations for international students: recommended—TOEFL (minimum score 600 paper-based; 100 iBT), IELTS (minimum score 7). *Application deadline:* For fall admission, 12/1 for domestic students. Application fee: $140. Electronic applications accepted. *Unit head:* Richard Siegrist, Director. *Application contact:* Vincent W. James, Director of Admissions, 617-432-1031, Fax: 617-432-7080, E-mail: admissions@hsph.harvard.edu.
Website: http://www.hsph.harvard.edu/drph/

**Harvard University,** Harvard T.H. Chan School of Public Health, Master of Public Health Program, Boston, MA 02115-6096. Offers clinical effectiveness (MPH); global health (MPH); health and social behavior (MPH); health management (MPH); health policy (MPH); occupational and environmental health (MPH); quantitative methods (MPH); JD/MPH; MD/MPH. *Accreditation:* CEPH. *Program availability:* Part-time. *Students:* 346 full-time (216 women), 249 part-time (136 women); includes 156 minority (24 Black or African American, non-Hispanic/Latino; 1 American Indian or Alaska Native, non-Hispanic/Latino; 85 Asian, non-Hispanic/Latino; 32 Hispanic/Latino; 14 Two or more races, non-Hispanic/Latino), 239 international. Average age 29. 1,212 applicants, 49% accepted, 402 enrolled. In 2019, 393 master's awarded. *Entrance requirements:* For master's, GRE, MCAT, GMAT, DAT, LSAT. Additional exam requirements/recommendations for international students: recommended—TOEFL (minimum score 600 paper-based; 100 iBT), IELTS (minimum score 7). *Application deadline:* For fall admission, 12/1 priority date for domestic and international students. Application fee: $140. Electronic applications accepted. *Financial support:* Federal Work-Study, scholarships/grants, and unspecified assistantships available. Support available to part-time students. Financial award application deadline: 2/15; financial award applicants required to submit FAFSA. *Unit head:* Dr. Murray Mittleman, Chair of the MPH Steering Committee, 617-432-0090, Fax: 617-432-3365, E-mail: mmittlem@hsph.harvard.edu. *Application contact:* Vincent W. James, Director of Admissions, 617-432-1031, Fax: 617-432-7080, E-mail: admissions@hsph.harvard.edu.
Website: http://www.hsph.harvard.edu/master-of-public-health-program/

See Display below and Close-Up on page 655.

**Harvard University,** Harvard T.H. Chan School of Public Health, PhD Program in Biological Sciences in Public Health, Boston, MA 02115. Offers PhD. *Students:* 49 full-time (0 women). Average age 29. In 2019, 9 doctorates awarded. *Degree requirements:* For doctorate, qualifying examination, dissertation/defense. *Entrance requirements:* For doctorate, GRE General Test. Additional exam requirements/recommendations for international students: recommended—TOEFL (minimum score 600 paper-based; 100 iBT), IELTS (minimum score 7). Electronic applications accepted. *Financial support:* Fellowships, research assistantships, teaching assistantships, institutionally sponsored loans, health care benefits, and tuition waivers (full) available. Financial award application deadline: 1/1. *Unit head:* Tatevik Holmgren, Assistant Director, 617-432-4397, E-mail: bph@hsph.harvard.edu. *Application contact:* Tatevik Holmgren, Assistant Director, 617-432-4397, E-mail: bph@hsph.harvard.edu.
Website: http://www.hsph.harvard.edu/admissions/degree-programs/doctor-of-philosophy/phd-in-biological-sciences-and-public-health/

**See Display below and Close-Up on page 9999.**

**Hawaii Pacific University,** College of Health and Society, Program in Public Health, Honolulu, HI 96813. Offers MPH. *Program availability:* Part-time, evening/weekend, 100% online, blended/hybrid learning. *Entrance requirements:* For master's, transcripts; baccalaureate degree; personal statement; minimum overall GPA of 3.0; 3 letters of reference; current curriculum vitae/resume; one college-level course in each of the following areas: general biology, statistics, and a health-related science course (anatomy, physiology, nutrition, microbiology). Additional exam requirements/recommendations for international students: recommended—TOEFL (minimum score 550 paper-based; 80 iBT), IELTS (minimum score 6), TWE (minimum score 5). Electronic applications accepted. *Expenses: Tuition:* Full-time $18,000; part-time $1125 per credit. *Required fees:* $213; $38 per semester.

**Hofstra University,** School of Health Professions and Human Services, Programs in Health, Hempstead, NY 11549. Offers foundations of public health (Advanced Certificate); health administration (MHA); health informatics (MS); occupational therapy (MS); public health (MPH); security and privacy in health information systems (Advanced Certificate); sports science (MS); teacher of students with speech-language disabilities (Advanced Certificate). *Program availability:* Part-time, evening/weekend. *Students:* 291 full-time (220 women), 128 part-time (88 women); includes 192 minority (69 Black or African American, non-Hispanic/Latino; 3 American Indian or Alaska Native, non-Hispanic/Latino; 72 Asian, non-Hispanic/Latino; 37 Hispanic/Latino; 4 Native Hawaiian or other Pacific Islander, non-Hispanic/Latino; 7 Two or more races, non-Hispanic/Latino), 25 international. Average age 29. 676 applicants, 52% accepted, 132 enrolled. In 2019, 170 master's, 1 other advanced degree awarded. *Degree requirements:* For master's, internship, minimum GPA of 3.0. *Entrance requirements:* For master's, interview, 2 letters of recommendation, essay, resume. Additional exam requirements/recommendations for international students: required—TOEFL (minimum score 550 paper-based; 80 iBT); recommended—IELTS (minimum score 6.5). *Application deadline:* Applications are processed on a rolling basis. Application fee: $75. Electronic applications accepted. *Expenses: Tuition:* Full-time $25,164; part-time $1398 per credit. *Required fees:* $580; $165 per semester. Tuition and fees vary according to course load, degree level and program. *Financial support:* In 2019–20, 181 students received support, including 104 fellowships with full and partial tuition reimbursements available (averaging $3,465 per year), 5 research assistantships with full and partial tuition reimbursements available (averaging $7,172 per year); career-related internships or fieldwork, Federal Work-Study, institutionally sponsored loans, scholarships/grants, traineeships, tuition waivers (full and partial), unspecified assistantships, and scholarships and endowed scholarships also available. Support available to part-time students. Financial award applicants required to submit FAFSA. *Unit head:* Dr. Corinne Kyriacou, Chairperson, 516-463-4553, E-mail: corinne.m.kyriacou@hofstra.edu. *Application contact:* Sunil Samuel, Assistant Vice President of Admissions, 516-463-4723, Fax: 516-463-4664, E-mail: graduateadmission@hofstra.edu.
Website: http://www.hofstra.edu/academics/colleges/healthscienceshumanservices/

**Howard University,** College of Medicine, Program in Public Health, Washington, DC 20059-0002. Offers MPH.

**Hunter College of the City University of New York,** Graduate School, Hunter-Bellevue School of Nursing, Community/Public Health Nursing Program, New York, NY 10065-5085. Offers MS. *Accreditation:* AACN. *Program availability:* Part-time. *Degree requirements:* For master's, practicum. *Entrance requirements:* For master's, minimum GPA of 3.0, New York RN license, BSN. Additional exam requirements/recommendations for international students: required—TOEFL.

**Hunter College of the City University of New York,** Graduate School, School of Urban Public Health, New York, NY 10065-5085. Offers nutrition (MS). *Program availability:* Part-time. *Degree requirements:* For master's, comprehensive exam. *Entrance requirements:* For master's, GRE General Test. Additional exam requirements/recommendations for international students: required—TOEFL.

**Icahn School of Medicine at Mount Sinai,** Graduate School of Biomedical Sciences, New York, NY 10029-6504. Offers biomedical sciences (MS, PhD); clinical research education (MS, PhD); community medicine (MPH); genetic counseling (MS); neurosciences (PhD); MD/PhD. Terminal master's awarded for partial completion of doctoral program. *Degree requirements:* For master's, thesis; for doctorate, comprehensive exam, thesis/dissertation. *Entrance requirements:* For master's, GRE General Test; for doctorate, GRE General Test, GRE Subject Test, 3 years of college pre-med course work. Additional exam requirements/recommendations for international students: required—TOEFL. Electronic applications accepted.

**Idaho State University,** Graduate School, College of Health Professions, Department of Community and Public Health, Program in Public Health, Pocatello, ID 83209-8109. Offers MPH. *Accreditation:* CEPH. *Program availability:* Part-time. *Degree requirements:* For master's, comprehensive exam, thesis. *Entrance requirements:* For master's, GRE General Test, minimum GPA of 3.0 for upper division classes, 2 letters of recommendation. Additional exam requirements/recommendations for international students: required—TOEFL (minimum score 600 paper-based). Electronic applications accepted.

**Independence University,** Program in Public Health, Salt Lake City, UT 84107. Offers MPH. *Program availability:* Part-time, evening/weekend, online learning. *Degree requirements:* For master's, final project or thesis.

**Indiana University Bloomington,** School of Public Health, Department of Applied Health Science, Bloomington, IN 47405. Offers behavioral, social, and community health (MPH); family health (MPH); health behavior (PhD); nutrition science (MS); professional health education (MPH); public health administration (MPH); safety management (MS); school and college health education (MS). *Degree requirements:* For master's, thesis optional; for doctorate, comprehensive exam, thesis/dissertation. *Entrance requirements:* For master's, GRE (for MS in nutrition science), 3 recommendations; for doctorate, GRE, 3 recommendations. Additional exam requirements/recommendations for international students: required—TOEFL (minimum score 550 paper-based; 80 iBT). Electronic applications accepted.

**Indiana University-Purdue University Indianapolis,** Richard M. Fairbanks School of Public Health, Indianapolis, IN 46202. Offers biostatistics (MS, PhD); environmental health (MPH); epidemiology (MPH, PhD); global health leadership (Dr PH); health administration (MHA); health policy (Graduate Certificate); health policy and management (MPH, PhD); health systems management (Graduate Certificate); product stewardship (MS); public health (Graduate Certificate); social and behavioral sciences (MPH). *Accreditation:* CAHME; CEPH. *Expenses:* Contact institution.

**Indiana University-Purdue University Indianapolis,** School of Physical Education and Tourism Management, Indianapolis, IN 46202-5193. Offers event tourism (MS), including sport event tourism; kinesiology (MS), including clinical exercise science; public health (Graduate Certificate). *Degree requirements:* For master's, comprehensive exam (for some programs), thesis (for some programs). *Entrance requirements:* For master's, GRE. Additional exam requirements/recommendations for international students: required—TOEFL. Electronic applications accepted. *Expenses:* Contact institution.

**Indiana Wesleyan University,** Graduate School, School of Health Sciences, Marion, IN 46953-4974. Offers athletic training (MS); occupational therapy (OTD); public health (MPH).

**Jackson State University,** Graduate School, School of Public Health, Public Health Program, Jackson, MS 39217. Offers MPH, Dr PH. *Accreditation:* CEPH.

**Johns Hopkins University,** Bloomberg School of Public Health, Baltimore, MD 21205. Offers MAS, MBE, MHA, MHS, MPH, MSPH, Sc M, Dr PH, PhD, JD/MPH, MBA/MPH, MSN/MPH, MSW/MPH. *Accreditation:* CEPH. *Program availability:* Part-time, 100% online, blended/hybrid learning. *Degree requirements:* For master's, comprehensive exam (for some programs), thesis (for some programs); for doctorate, comprehensive exam, thesis/dissertation. *Entrance requirements:* For master's and doctorate, Official transcripts from every college-level institution attended (academic records from institutions outside the U.S. must undergo a credentials evaluation), SOPHAS application, Three Letters of Recommendation, Statement of Purpose and Objectives, CV/Resume, Entrance Exam. Additional exam requirements/recommendations for international students: required—TOEFL (minimum score 100 iBT), IELTS (minimum score 7). Electronic applications accepted. *Expenses:* Contact institution.

**Kansas State University,** Graduate School, College of Human Ecology, Department of Food, Nutrition, Dietetics and Health, Manhattan, KS 66506. Offers dietetics (MS); human nutrition (PhD); nutrition, dietetics and sensory sciences (MS); nutritional sciences (PhD); public health nutrition (PhD); public health physical activity (PhD); sensory analysis and consumer behavior (PhD). *Program availability:* Part-time. *Degree requirements:* For master's, thesis or alternative, residency; for doctorate, thesis/dissertation, residency. *Entrance requirements:* For master's, GRE General Test, minimum undergraduate GPA of 3.0; for doctorate, GRE General Test, minimum graduate GPA of 3.0. Additional exam requirements/recommendations for international students: required—TOEFL (minimum score 550 paper-based; 79 iBT), IELTS (minimum score 6.5). Electronic applications accepted.

**Kansas State University,** Graduate School, College of Veterinary Medicine, Department of Clinical Sciences, Manhattan, KS 66506. Offers MPH, Graduate Certificate. *Degree requirements:* For master's, thesis. *Entrance requirements:* For master's, GRE, DVM. Additional exam requirements/recommendations for international students: required—TOEFL (minimum score 550 paper-based). Electronic applications accepted. *Expenses:* Contact institution.

**Kent State University,** College of Public Health, Kent, OH 44242-0001. Offers public health (MPH, PhD), including biostatistics (MPH), environmental health sciences (MPH), epidemiology, health policy and management, prevention science (PhD), social and behavioral sciences (MPH). *Accreditation:* CEPH. *Program availability:* Part-time, 100% online. *Faculty:* 23 full-time (12 women), 4 part-time/adjunct (1 woman). *Students:* 136 full-time (98 women), 158 part-time (129 women); includes 71 minority (45 Black or African American, non-Hispanic/Latino; 12 Asian, non-Hispanic/Latino; 8 Hispanic/Latino; 6 Two or more races, non-Hispanic/Latino), 40 international. Average age 31. 187 applicants, 79% accepted, 85 enrolled. In 2019, 93 master's, 7 doctorates awarded. *Degree requirements:* For master's, comprehensive exam, between 150 - 300 hours' placement at public health agency, final portfolio and presentation; for doctorate, comprehensive exam, thesis/dissertation. *Entrance requirements:* For master's, GRE or other standardized graduate admission exam (GMAT, MCAT, LSAT or PCAT), minimum GPA of 3.0, transcripts, goal statement, 3 letters of recommendation; for doctorate, GRE or other standardized graduate admission exam with a quantitative component, Master's degree in related discipline, minimum GPA of 3.0, personal statement, resume, interview with faculty, 3 letters of recommendation, transcript(s). Additional exam requirements/recommendations for international students: required—TOEFL (minimum score 94 iBT), IELTS (minimum score 7), PTE (minimum score 65), For MPH: TOEFL iBT 79, Michigan English Language Assessment Battery (minimum score of 77), IELTS 6.5, PTE 58; For Ph.D.: see below and min MELAB 82. *Application deadline:* For fall admission, 6/15 for domestic and international students; for spring admission, 10/15 for domestic and international students; for summer admission, 3/15 for domestic and international students. Applications are processed on a rolling basis. Application fee: $45 ($70 for international students). Electronic applications accepted. *Financial support:* Career-related internships or fieldwork, Federal Work-Study, scholarships/grants, and unspecified assistantships available. *Unit head:* Dr. Sonia Alemagno, Dean and Professor of Health Policy and Management, 330-672-6500, E-mail: salemagn@kent.edu. *Application contact:* Dr. Jeffrey S. Hallam, Professor/Associate Dean for Research and Graduate Studies, 330-672-0679, E-mail: jhallam1@kent.edu.
Website: http://www.kent.edu/publichealth/

**La Salle University,** School of Nursing and Health Sciences, Program in Public Health, Philadelphia, PA 19141-1199. Offers MPH, MPH/MSN. *Accreditation:* CEPH. *Program availability:* Part-time, evening/weekend. *Degree requirements:* For master's, capstone project. *Entrance requirements:* For master's, minimum undergraduate GPA of 3.0; curriculum vitae/resume; personal statement; 2 letters of reference; interview; prior academic and professional experience in healthcare (recommended). Additional exam requirements/recommendations for international students: required—TOEFL. Electronic applications accepted. Application fee is waived when completed online. *Expenses:* Contact institution.

**Laurentian University,** School of Graduate Studies and Research, Interdisciplinary Program in Rural and Northern Health, Sudbury, ON P3E 2C6, Canada. Offers PhD.

**Lenoir-Rhyne University,** Graduate Programs, School of Health, Exercise and Sport Science, Program in Public Health, Hickory, NC 28601. Offers MPH. *Accreditation:* CEPH. *Entrance requirements:* For master's, GRE General Test or MAT, essay; resume; minimum GPA of 2.7 undergraduate, 3.0 graduate. Additional exam requirements/recommendations for international students: required—TOEFL (minimum score 600 paper-based). Electronic applications accepted. *Expenses:* Contact institution.

**Liberty University,** School of Health Sciences, Lynchburg, VA 24515. Offers anatomy and cell biology (PhD); biomedical sciences (MS); epidemiology (MPH); exercise science (MS), including clinical, community physical activity, human performance,

nutrition; global health (MPH); health promotion (MPH); medical sciences (MA), including biopsychology, business management, health informatics, molecular medicine, public health; nutrition (MPH). *Program availability:* Part-time, online learning. *Students:* 820 full-time (588 women), 889 part-time (612 women); includes 611 minority (402 Black or African American, non-Hispanic/Latino; 10 American Indian or Alaska Native, non-Hispanic/Latino; 43 Asian, non-Hispanic/Latino; 85 Hispanic/Latino; 1 Native Hawaiian or other Pacific Islander, non-Hispanic/Latino; 70 Two or more races, non-Hispanic/Latino), 67 international. Average age 32. 2,610 applicants, 33% accepted, 406 enrolled. In 2019, 445 master's awarded. *Degree requirements:* For master's, thesis (for some programs); for doctorate, thesis/dissertation. *Entrance requirements:* For doctorate, MAT or GRE, minimum GPA of 3.25 in master's program, 2-3 recommendations, writing samples (for some programs), letter of intent, professional vitae. Additional exam requirements/recommendations for international students: required—TOEFL (minimum score 600 paper-based; 100 iBT). *Application fee:* $50. *Expenses:* Tuition: Full-time $545; part-time $410 per credit hour. One-time fee: $50. *Financial support:* In 2019–20, 918 students received support. Federal Work-Study available. Financial award applicants required to submit FAFSA. *Unit head:* Dr. Ralph Linstra, Dean. *Application contact:* Jay Bridge, Director of Admissions, 800-424-9595, Fax: 800-628-7977, E-mail: gradadmissions@liberty.edu.
Website: https://www.liberty.edu/health-sciences/

**Loma Linda University,** School of Public Health, Loma Linda, CA 92350. Offers MBA, MPH, MS, Dr PH, PhD. *Accreditation:* CEPH. *Program availability:* Part-time. *Degree requirements:* For doctorate, thesis/dissertation. *Entrance requirements:* For master's, GRE General Test, baccalaureate degree, minimum GPA of 3.0; for doctorate, GRE General Test, minimum GPA of 3.2. Additional exam requirements/recommendations for international students: required—TOEFL (minimum score 550 paper-based) or Michigan English Language Assessment Battery. Electronic applications accepted.

**London Metropolitan University,** Graduate Programs, London, United Kingdom. Offers applied psychology (M Sc); architecture (MA); biomedical science (M Sc); blood science (M Sc); cancer pharmacology (M Sc); computer networking and cyber security (M Sc); computing and information systems (M Sc); conference interpreting (MA); counter-terrorism studies (M Sc); creative, digital and professional writing (MA); crime, violence and prevention (M Sc); criminology (M Sc); curating contemporary art (MA); data analytics (M Sc); digital media (MA); early childhood studies (MA); education (MA, Ed D); financial services law, regulation and compliance (LL M); food science (M Sc); forensic psychology (M Sc); health and social care management and policy (M Sc); human nutrition (M Sc); human resource management (MA); human rights and international conflict (MA); information technology (M Sc); intelligence and security studies (M Sc); international oil, gas and energy law (LL M); international relations (MA); interpreting (MA); learning and teaching in higher education (MA); legal practice (LL M); media and entertainment law (LL M); organizational and consumer psychology (M Sc); psychological therapy (M Sc); psychology of mental health (M Sc); public health (M Sc); public policy and management (MPA); security studies (M Sc); social work (M Sc); spatial planning and urban design (MA); sports therapy (M Sc); supporting older children and young people with dyslexia (MA); teaching languages (MA), including Arabic, English; translation (MA); woman and child abuse (MA).

**Long Island University - Brooklyn,** School of Health Professions, Brooklyn, NY 11201-8423. Offers athletic training and sport sciences (MS); community health (MS Ed); exercise science (MS); forensic social work (Advanced Certificate); occupational therapy (MS); physical therapy (DPT); physician assistant (MS); public health (MPH); social work (MSW); speech-language pathology (MS). *Accreditation:* AOTA; CEPH. *Degree requirements:* For master's, comprehensive exam (for some programs), thesis (for some programs); for doctorate, comprehensive exam (for some programs). *Entrance requirements:* For master's and doctorate, GRE. Additional exam requirements/recommendations for international students: required—TOEFL (minimum score 550 paper-based; 79 iBT). Electronic applications accepted.

**Louisiana State University Health Sciences Center,** School of Public Health, New Orleans, LA 70112. Offers behavioral and community health sciences (MPH); biostatistics (MPH, MS, PhD); community health sciences (PhD); environmental and occupational health sciences (MPH); epidemiology (MPH, PhD); health policy and systems management (MPH). *Accreditation:* CEPH. *Program availability:* Part-time. *Degree requirements:* For doctorate, thesis/dissertation. *Entrance requirements:* For master's, GRE General Test. Additional exam requirements/recommendations for international students: recommended—TOEFL (minimum score 550 paper-based; 79 iBT), IELTS. Electronic applications accepted.

**Louisiana State University in Shreveport,** College of Business, Education, and Human Development, Program in Public Health, Shreveport, LA 71115-2399. Offers MPH. *Accreditation:* CEPH. *Program availability:* Part-time, evening/weekend. *Degree requirements:* For master's, thesis optional, practicum. *Entrance requirements:* For master's, GRE or MCAT, 3 letters of recommendation, personal interview. Additional exam requirements/recommendations for international students: required—TOEFL (minimum score 550 paper-based; 61 iBT). Electronic applications accepted.

**Loyola University Chicago,** Graduate School, Master of Public Health (MPH) Program, Maywood, IL 60660. Offers epidemiology (MPH). *Accreditation:* CEPH. *Program availability:* Part-time, evening/weekend, 100% online, blended/hybrid learning. *Students:* 146 applicants, 68% accepted, 38 enrolled. In 2019, 15 master's awarded. *Entrance requirements:* For master's, GRE, MCAT, or other graduate entrance exam (waived for GPA above 3.0). Students complete WES evaluation as part of the SOPHAS application, Apply through SOPHAS at sophas.org (search for Loyola in the keyword box). Additional exam requirements/recommendations for international students: required—TOEFL (minimum score 550 paper-based; 79 iBT). *Application deadline:* For fall admission, 5/15 for domestic students, 5/15 priority date for international students; for spring admission, 11/15 for domestic students, 11/15 priority date for international students. Applications are processed on a rolling basis. Application fee: $135. Electronic applications accepted. *Expenses:* Tuition: Full-time $18,540; part-time $1033 per credit hour. Required fees: $904; $230 per credit hour. *Financial support:* In 2019–20, 8 students received support, including 2 research assistantships (averaging $4,500 per year), 6 teaching assistantships (averaging $4,500 per year); career-related internships or fieldwork also available. Financial award applicants required to submit FAFSA. *Unit head:* Dr. David Shoham, MPH Program Director, 708-327-9224, E-mail: dshoham@luc.edu. *Application contact:* Briana Lemon, Student Services Administrator, 708-327-9224, E-mail: blemon@luc.edu.
Website: luc.edu/publichealth

**Marshall University,** Academic Affairs Division, College of Health Professions, Department of Public Health, Huntington, WV 25755. Offers MPH.

**McGill University,** Faculty of Graduate and Postdoctoral Studies, Faculty of Medicine, Department of Epidemiology, Biostatistics and Occupational Health, Montréal, QC H3A 2T5, Canada. Offers biostatistics (M Sc, PhD); epidemiology (M Sc, PhD); occupational health (M Sc A); public health (MSPH). *Program availability:* Part-time, online learning. *Degree requirements:* For doctorate, thesis/dissertation. *Entrance requirements:* For master's, B Sc in chemistry, engineering physics, environmental sciences, medicine, nursing, or other health science (for occupational health); MD or B Sc in nursing (for

distance education); minimum GPA of 3.0; for doctorate, TOEFL, M Sc in environmental health, chemistry, engineering, community health, physics, epidemiology, medicine, nursing, or occupational health.

**MCPHS University,** Graduate Studies, Program in Public Health, Boston, MA 02115-5896. Offers MPH.

**Medical College of Wisconsin,** Graduate School, Program in Public and Community Health, Milwaukee, WI 53226. Offers PhD, MD/PhD. *Accreditation:* CEPH. *Students:* 12 full-time (7 women), 5 part-time (4 women); includes 5 minority (4 Black or African American, non-Hispanic/Latino; 1 American Indian or Alaska Native, non-Hispanic/Latino), 5 international. Average age 33. 19 applicants, 26% accepted, 5 enrolled. In 2019, 5 doctorates awarded. *Degree requirements:* For doctorate, comprehensive exam, thesis/dissertation. *Entrance requirements:* For doctorate, GRE, official transcripts, three letters of recommendation. Additional exam requirements/recommendations for international students: required—TOEFL (minimum score 580 paper-based; 100 iBT). *Application deadline:* For fall admission, 12/1 for domestic and international students. Applications are processed on a rolling basis. Application fee: $50. Electronic applications accepted. *Expenses:* $1250 per credit PhD students; $1056 per credit Masters students; $155 per year full time students fees. *Financial support:* In 2019–20, 12 students received support, including fellowships with full tuition reimbursements available (averaging $30,000 per year); scholarships/grants, health care benefits, and tuition waivers (full) also available. Financial award application deadline: 2/15; financial award applicants required to submit FAFSA. *Unit head:* Dr. Laura D. Cassidy, Director, 414-955-4517, Fax: 414-955-6555, E-mail: phdpch@mcw.edu. *Application contact:* Recruitment Office, 414-955-4402, Fax: 414-955-6555, E-mail: gradschoolrecruit@mcw.edu.
Website: http://www.mcw.edu/Graduate-School/Programs/Public-Health/Public-and-Community-Health.htm

**Medical College of Wisconsin,** Graduate School, Program in Public Health, Milwaukee, WI 53226. Offers MPH, Graduate Certificate. *Accreditation:* CEPH. *Program availability:* Part-time, evening/weekend, online only, 100% online. *Students:* 5 full-time (all women), 24 part-time (17 women); includes 5 minority (1 Black or African American, non-Hispanic/Latino; 2 Asian, non-Hispanic/Latino; 1 Hispanic/Latino; 1 Two or more races, non-Hispanic/Latino), 3 international. Average age 37. 28 applicants, 64% accepted, 15 enrolled. In 2019, 14 master's, 1 other advanced degree awarded. *Entrance requirements:* For master's and Graduate Certificate, GRE, official transcripts, three letters of recommendation. Additional exam requirements/recommendations for international students: required—TOEFL. *Application deadline:* For fall admission, 7/1 for domestic and international students; for spring admission, 11/1 for domestic and international students; for summer admission, 4/1 for domestic and international students. Application fee: $50. Electronic applications accepted. *Expenses:* $950 per credit for MPH students; $1,056 per credit for certificate students. *Financial support:* Applicants required to submit FAFSA. *Unit head:* Terry Brandenburg, Director, 414-955-8218, Fax: 414-955-6555, E-mail: gradschool@mcw.edu. *Application contact:* Recruitment Office, 414-955-4402, Fax: 414-955-6555, E-mail: gradschoolrecruit@mcw.edu.
Website: https://www.mcw.edu/MPH-Program.htm

**Meharry Medical College,** School of Graduate Studies, Division of Public Health Practice, Nashville, TN 37208-9989. Offers occupational medicine (MSPH); public health administration (MSPH). *Accreditation:* CEPH. *Program availability:* Part-time, evening/weekend. *Degree requirements:* For master's, thesis, externship. *Entrance requirements:* For master's, GRE General Test, GMAT. Additional exam requirements/recommendations for international students: required—TOEFL. *Application deadline:* For fall admission, 6/1 for domestic students. Applications are processed on a rolling basis. Application fee: $65. *Expenses:* Contact institution. *Financial support:* Career-related internships or fieldwork, Federal Work-Study, institutionally sponsored loans, and scholarships/grants available. Support available to part-time students. Financial award application deadline: 7/15; financial award applicants required to submit FAFSA. *Unit head:* Stephanie Bailey, MD, Senior Associate Dean, 615-327-6069, E-mail: sbailey@mmc.edu. *Application contact:* Kimberlee Wyche-Etheridge, MD,MPH, Interim Program Director, 615-327-6675, E-mail: ketheridge@mmc.edu.
Website: https://home.mmc.edu/school-of-graduate-studies-research/the-m-s-p-h-program/

**Mercer University,** Graduate Studies, Cecil B. Day Campus, College of Health Professions, Atlanta, GA 31207. Offers athletic training (MAT); clinical medical psychology (Psy D); physical therapy (DPT); physician assistant studies (MM Sc); public health (MPH); DPT/MBA; DPT/MPH; MM Sc/MPH; Pharm D/MPH. *Accreditation:* CEPH. *Faculty:* 17 full-time (13 women), 17 part-time/adjunct (10 women). *Students:* 360 full-time (292 women), 74 part-time (58 women); includes 171 minority (100 Black or African American, non-Hispanic/Latino; 36 Asian, non-Hispanic/Latino; 31 Hispanic/Latino; 4 Two or more races, non-Hispanic/Latino), 10 international. Average age 26. In 2019, 141 master's, 51 doctorates awarded. *Expenses:* Contact institution. *Financial support:* Federal Work-Study, traineeships, and unspecified assistantships available. *Unit head:* Dr. Lisa Lundquist, Dean/Clinical Professor, 678-547-6308, E-mail: lundquist_lm@mercer.edu. *Application contact:* Laura Ellison, Director of Admissions and Student Affairs, 678-547-6391, E-mail: ellison_la@mercer.edu.
Website: http://chp.mercer.edu/

**Michigan State University,** College of Human Medicine and The Graduate School, Graduate Programs in Human Medicine, Program in Public Health, East Lansing, MI 48824. Offers MPH.

**MidAmerica Nazarene University,** School of Nursing and Health Science, Olathe, KS 66062. Offers healthcare administration (MSN); healthcare quality management (MSN); nursing education (MSN); public health (MSN); MSN/MBA. *Accreditation:* AACN. *Program availability:* Part-time, evening/weekend, 100% online. *Faculty:* 5 full-time (all women), 9 part-time/adjunct (7 women). *Students:* 14 full-time (12 women), 79 part-time (74 women); includes 12 minority (10 Black or African American, non-Hispanic/Latino; 1 American Indian or Alaska Native, non-Hispanic/Latino; 1 Hispanic/Latino), 2 international. Average age 38. 87 applicants, 39% accepted, 14 enrolled. In 2019, 39 master's awarded. *Entrance requirements:* For master's, BSN, minimum GPA of 3.0, active unencumbered RN license, undergraduate statistics course. Additional exam requirements/recommendations for international students: required—TOEFL (minimum score 81 iBT). *Application deadline:* Applications are processed on a rolling basis. Electronic applications accepted. *Expenses:* Tuition $499 per credit hour, technology fee $34.00 per credit hour, graduation fee $100, carrying fee $13 per course, other fee $215. *Financial support:* Unspecified assistantships available. Financial award applicants required to submit FAFSA. *Unit head:* Dr. Karen Wiegman, Dean, 913-971-3839, E-mail: kdwiegman@mnu.edu. *Application contact:* JoVonda Merrell, Compliance Coordinator, 913-971-3844, E-mail: jkmerrell@mnu.edu.
Website: http://www.mnu.edu/nursing.html

**Mississippi University for Women,** Graduate School, College of Nursing and Health Sciences, Columbus, MS 39701-9998. Offers nursing (MSN, DNP, PMC); public health education (MPH); speech-language pathology (MS). *Accreditation:* AACN; ASHA. *Program availability:* Part-time. *Degree requirements:* For master's, comprehensive

exam, thesis. *Entrance requirements:* For master's, GRE General Test, bachelor's degree in nursing, previous course work in statistics, proficiency in English.

**Missouri State University,** Graduate College, College of Health and Human Services, Program in Public Health, Springfield, MO 65897. Offers MPH. *Accreditation:* CEPH. *Degree requirements:* For master's, comprehensive exam, thesis or alternative. *Entrance requirements:* For master's, GRE, minimum GPA of 3.0, 1 year of work experience. Additional exam requirements/recommendations for international students: required—TOEFL (minimum score 550 paper-based; 79 iBT), IELTS (minimum score 6). Electronic applications accepted. *Expenses: Tuition, area resident:* Full-time $2600; part-time $1735 per credit hour. Tuition, nonresident: full-time $5240; part-time $3495 per credit hour. *International tuition:* $5240 full-time. *Required fees:* $530; $438 per credit hour. Tuition and fees vary according to class time, course level, course load, degree level, campus/location and program.

**Monroe College,** King Graduate School, Bronx, NY 10468. Offers accounting (MS); business administration (MBA), including entrepreneurship, finance, general business administration, healthcare management, human resources, information technology, marketing; computer science (MS); criminal justice (MS); hospitality management (MS); public health (MPH), including biostatistics and epidemiology, community health, health administration and leadership. *Program availability:* Online learning.

**Montclair State University,** The Graduate School, College of Education and Human Services, Program in Public Health, Montclair, NJ 07043-1624. Offers MPH. *Accreditation:* CEPH. *Program availability:* Part-time, evening/weekend. *Degree requirements:* For master's, comprehensive exam, thesis or alternative. *Entrance requirements:* For master's, GRE General Test, essay, 2 letters of recommendation. Additional exam requirements/recommendations for international students: required—TOEFL (minimum score 83 iBT), IELTS (minimum score 6.5). Electronic applications accepted.

**Morehouse School of Medicine,** Master of Public Health Program, Atlanta, GA 30310-1495. Offers MPH. *Accreditation:* CEPH. *Program availability:* Part-time. *Degree requirements:* For master's, thesis, practicum, public health leadership seminar. *Entrance requirements:* For master's, GRE General Test, writing test, public health or human service experience. Additional exam requirements/recommendations for international students: required—TOEFL (minimum score 550 paper-based). Electronic applications accepted. *Expenses:* Contact institution.

**Morgan State University,** School of Graduate Studies, School of Community Health and Policy, Program in Public Health, Baltimore, MD 21251. Offers MPH, Dr PH. *Accreditation:* CEPH. *Program availability:* Part-time, evening/weekend, 100% online. *Faculty:* 23 full-time (14 women), 8 part-time/adjunct (6 women). *Students:* 87 full-time (74 women), 21 part-time (15 women); includes 91 minority (86 Black or African American, non-Hispanic/Latino; 2 Asian, non-Hispanic/Latino; 1 Hispanic/Latino; 2 Two or more races, non-Hispanic/Latino), 12 international. Average age 35. 35 applicants, 63% accepted, 7 enrolled. In 2019, 14 master's awarded. *Degree requirements:* For master's, comprehensive exam; for doctorate, comprehensive exam, thesis/dissertation. *Entrance requirements:* For master's and doctorate, Minimum GPA 3.0, GRE. Additional exam requirements/recommendations for international students: required—TOEFL (minimum score 550 paper-based; 70 iBT). *Application deadline:* For fall admission, 5/1 for domestic students, 4/1 for international students. Applications are processed on a rolling basis. Application fee: $50 ($70 for international students). Electronic applications accepted. *Expenses:* Tuition, state resident: full-time $455; part-time $455 per credit hour. Tuition, nonresident: full-time $894; part-time $894 per credit hour. *Required fees:* $82; $82 per credit hour. *Financial support:* In 2019–20, 24 students received support. Fellowships with full and partial tuition reimbursements available, research assistantships with full and partial tuition reimbursements available, teaching assistantships with full and partial tuition reimbursements available, career-related internships or fieldwork, Federal Work-Study, scholarships/grants, tuition waivers (full and partial), and unspecified assistantships available. Support available to part-time students. Financial award application deadline: 5/1. *Unit head:* Dr. Kim Dobson Sydnor, Dean, 443-885-3560, E-mail: kim.sydnor@morgan.edu. *Application contact:* Dr. Jahmaine Smith, Director of Admissions, 443-885-3185, Fax: 443-885-8226, E-mail: gradapply@morgan.edu.
Website: https://www.morgan.edu/schp/publichealth

**National University,** School of Health and Human Services, La Jolla, CA 92037-1011. Offers clinical affairs (MS); clinical regulatory affairs (MS); complementary and integrative healthcare (MS); family nurse practitioner (MSN); health and life science analytics (MS); health informatics (MS, Certificate); healthcare administration (MHA); nurse anesthesia (MSNA); nursing administration (MSN); nursing informatics (MSN); psychiatric-mental health nurse practitioner (MSN); public health (MPH), including health promotion, healthcare administration, mental health. *Accreditation:* CEPH. *Program availability:* Part-time, evening/weekend, 100% online, blended/hybrid learning. *Degree requirements:* For master's, thesis (for some programs). *Entrance requirements:* For master's, interview, minimum GPA of 2.5. Additional exam requirements/recommendations for international students: required—TOEFL (minimum score 550 paper-based; 79 iBT), IELTS (minimum score 6). Electronic applications accepted. *Expenses: Tuition:* Full-time $442; part-time $442 per unit.

**New England Institute of Technology,** Program in Public Health, East Greenwich, RI 02818. Offers MPH. *Program availability:* Part-time, evening/weekend, online only, 100% online, blended/hybrid learning. *Students:* 15 full-time (11 women), 6 part-time (all women); includes 5 minority (3 Black or African American, non-Hispanic/Latino; 1 Hispanic/Latino; 1 Two or more races, non-Hispanic/Latino). Average age 32. In 2019, 2 master's awarded. *Entrance requirements:* For master's, Minimum GPA of 2.5 awarded Bachelor's degree in related field from an accredited institution plus personal statement and a processional resume. Additional exam requirements/recommendations for international students: required—TOEFL. *Application deadline:* Applications are processed on a rolling basis. Application fee: $50. Electronic applications accepted. *Unit head:* Dr. Douglas H. Sherman, Senior Vice President and Provost, 401-739-5000 Ext. 3481, Fax: 401-886-0859, E-mail: dsherman@neit.edu. *Application contact:* Tim Reardon, Vice President for Enrollment Management and Marketing, 401-739-5000, Fax: 401-886-0859, E-mail: treardon@neit.edu.
Website: https://www.neit.edu/Programs/Online-and-Hybrid-Degree-Programs/Master-of-Public-Health-Degree-Online

**New Mexico State University,** College of Health and Social Services, Department of Public Health Sciences, Las Cruces, NM 88003-8001. Offers public health (MPH, Graduate Certificate). *Accreditation:* CEPH. *Program availability:* Part-time, blended/hybrid learning. *Faculty:* 13 full-time (9 women), 4 part-time/adjunct (3 women). *Students:* 40 full-time (29 women), 66 part-time (55 women); includes 54 minority (4 Black or African American, non-Hispanic/Latino; 6 American Indian or Alaska Native, non-Hispanic/Latino; 4 Asian, non-Hispanic/Latino; 36 Hispanic/Latino; 4 Two or more races, non-Hispanic/Latino), 9 international. Average age 33. 109 applicants, 87% accepted, 56 enrolled. In 2019, 23 master's, 4 other advanced degrees awarded. *Degree requirements:* For master's, thesis optional. *Entrance requirements:* For master's, GRE. Additional exam requirements/recommendations for international students: required—TOEFL (minimum score 550 paper-based; 79 iBT), IELTS (minimum score 6.5). *Application deadline:* For fall admission, 2/15 for domestic and international students. Application fee: $40 ($50 for international students). Electronic applications accepted. *Financial support:* In 2019–20, 42 students received support, including 1 fellowship (averaging $4,844 per year), 4 research assistantships (averaging $11,285 per year), 10 teaching assistantships (averaging $11,806 per year); career-related internships or fieldwork, Federal Work-Study, health care benefits, and unspecified assistantships also available. Financial award application deadline: 3/1. *Unit head:* Dr. Satyapriya Rao, Department Head, 575-646-4300, Fax: 575-646-4343, E-mail: sakishn@nmsu.edu. *Application contact:* Dr. Joe Tomaka, Graduate Coordinator, 575-646-7431, Fax: 575-646-4343, E-mail: tomaka@nmsu.edu.
Website: http://publichealth.nmsu.edu

**New York Medical College,** School of Health Sciences and Practice, Valhalla, NY 10595. Offers behavioral sciences and health promotion (MPH); biostatistics (MS); children with special health care (Graduate Certificate); emergency preparedness (Graduate Certificate); environmental health science (MPH); epidemiology (MPH, MS); global health (Graduate Certificate); health education (Graduate Certificate); health policy and management (MPH, Dr PH); industrial hygiene (Graduate Certificate); pediatric dysphagia (Post-Graduate Certificate); physical therapy (DPT); public health (Graduate Certificate); speech-language pathology (MS). *Accreditation:* ASHA; CEPH. *Program availability:* Part-time, evening/weekend, 100% online, blended/hybrid learning. *Faculty:* 47 full-time (34 women), 203 part-time/adjunct (125 women). *Students:* 230 full-time (171 women), 292 part-time (207 women); includes 204 minority (73 Black or African American, non-Hispanic/Latino; 4 American Indian or Alaska Native, non-Hispanic/Latino; 59 Asian, non-Hispanic/Latino; 54 Hispanic/Latino; 1 Native Hawaiian or other Pacific Islander, non-Hispanic/Latino; 13 Two or more races, non-Hispanic/Latino), 35 international. Average age 29. 790 applicants, 61% accepted, 162 enrolled. In 2019, 113 master's, 47 doctorates awarded. *Degree requirements:* For master's, comprehensive exam (for some programs), thesis (for some programs); for doctorate, thesis/dissertation. *Entrance requirements:* For master's, GRE (for MS in speech-language pathology); for doctorate, GRE (for Doctor of Physical Therapy and Doctor of Public Health). Additional exam requirements/recommendations for international students: required—TOEFL (minimum score 96 paper-based; 24 iBT), IELTS (minimum score 7). *Application deadline:* For fall admission, 8/1 for domestic students, 4/15 for international students; for spring admission, 12/1 for domestic students; for summer admission, 5/1 for domestic students, 4/15 for international students. Applications are processed on a rolling basis. Application fee: $128 ($120 for international students). Electronic applications accepted. *Expenses:* $1195 credit fee, academic support fee $200, Student activities fee $140 per year, technology fee $150. *Financial support:* In 2019–20, 18 students received support. Federal Work-Study, scholarships/grants, unspecified assistantships, and Federal student loans available. Financial award application deadline: 4/30; financial award applicants required to submit FAFSA. *Unit head:* Ben Johnson, PhD, Vice Dean, 914-594-4531, E-mail: bjohnson23@nymc.edu. *Application contact:* Irene Bundziak, Assistant to Director of Admissions, 914-594-4905, E-mail: irene_bundziak@nymc.edu.
Website: http://www.nymc.edu/school-of-health-sciences-and-practice-shsp/

**New York University,** College of Global Public Health, New York, NY 10012. Offers biological basis of public health (PhD); community and international health (MPH); global health leadership (MPH); health systems and health services research (PhD); population and community health (PhD); public health nutrition (MPH); social and behavioral sciences (MPH); socio-behavioral health (PhD). *Accreditation:* CEPH. *Program availability:* Part-time, online learning. *Degree requirements:* For master's, thesis (for some programs); for doctorate, thesis/dissertation. *Entrance requirements:* For master's and doctorate, GRE. Additional exam requirements/recommendations for international students: required—TOEFL. Electronic applications accepted. *Expenses:* Contact institution.

**North Dakota State University,** College of Graduate and Interdisciplinary Studies, College of Health Professions, Department of Public Health, Fargo, ND 58102. Offers American Indian public health (MPH); community health sciences (MPH); management of infectious diseases (MPH); Pharm D/MPH. *Accreditation:* CEPH. *Program availability:* Online learning. Tuition and fees vary according to program and reciprocity agreements.

**Northeastern University,** Bouvé College of Health Sciences, Boston, MA 02115-5096. Offers applied behavior analysis (MS); audiology (Au D); counseling psychology (MS, PhD, CAGS); exercise science (MS); nursing (MS, PhD, CAGS), including administration (MS), adult-gerontology acute care nurse practitioner (MS, CAGS), adult-gerontology primary care nurse practitioner (MS, CAGS), anesthesia (MS), family nurse practitioner (MS, CAGS), neonatal nurse practitioner (MS, CAGS), pediatric nurse practitioner (MS, CAGS), psychiatric mental health nurse practitioner (MS, CAGS); nursing practice (DNP); pharmaceutical sciences (MS, PhD), including interdisciplinary concentration, pharmaceutics and drug delivery systems; pharmacology (MS); pharmacy (Pharm D); school psychology (PhD); speech-language pathology (MS); urban health (MPH); MS/MBA. *Accreditation:* AANA/CANAEP; ACPE (one or more programs are accredited); ASHA; CEPH. *Program availability:* Part-time, evening/weekend, online learning. *Degree requirements:* For doctorate, thesis/dissertation (for some programs); for CAGS, comprehensive exam. Electronic applications accepted. *Expenses:* Contact institution.

**Northeast Ohio Medical University,** College of Graduate Studies, Rootstown, OH 44272-0095. Offers health-system pharmacy administration (MS); integrated pharmaceutical medicine (MS, PhD); medical ethics and humanities (MS, Certificate); public health (MPH). *Program availability:* Part-time, evening/weekend, 100% online, blended/hybrid learning. *Faculty:* 126 part-time/adjunct (62 women). *Students:* 24 full-time (12 women), 28 part-time (15 women); includes 21 minority (2 Black or African American, non-Hispanic/Latino; 10 Asian, non-Hispanic/Latino; 5 Hispanic/Latino; 4 Two or more races, non-Hispanic/Latino). Average age 26. 31 applicants, 97% accepted, 21 enrolled. In 2019, 15 master's, 13 other advanced degrees awarded. *Degree requirements:* For master's, thesis (for some programs), thesis (for MS in medical ethics and humanities, integrated pharmaceutical medicine, MS in MAS); for doctorate, thesis/dissertation, For IPM Ph.D Program. *Entrance requirements:* Additional exam requirements/recommendations for international students: recommended—TOEFL (minimum score 550 paper-based). *Application deadline:* For fall admission, 7/17 for domestic students. Applications are processed on a rolling basis. Application fee: $95. Electronic applications accepted. *Expenses:* Student health and fitness, student activities. *Financial support:* In 2019–20, 6 students received support. Scholarships/grants and tuition waivers (full and partial) available. Financial award application deadline: 3/15; financial award applicants required to submit FAFSA. *Unit head:* Dr. Steven Schmidt, Dean, 330-325-6290. *Application contact:* Dr. Steven Schmidt, Dean, 330-325-6290.
Website: https://www.neomed.edu/graduatestudies/

**Northern Illinois University,** Graduate School, College of Health and Human Sciences, Ph.D Health Sciences, De Kalb, IL 60115-2854. Offers nutrition and dietetics (MS); public health (MPH). *Accreditation:* CEPH. *Students:* 4 full-time (3 women), 42 part-time (28 women); includes 13 minority (5 Black or African American, non-Hispanic/Latino; 4 Asian, non-Hispanic/Latino; 2 Hispanic/Latino; 2 Two or more races, non-Hispanic/Latino), 2 international. Average age 40. 38 applicants, 37% accepted, 4

enrolled. In 2019, 4 master's awarded. *Entrance requirements:* Additional exam requirements/recommendations for international students: required—TOEFL (minimum score 550 paper-based). *Application deadline:* Applications are processed on a rolling basis. Electronic applications accepted. *Unit head:* Daniel Boutin, Chair, 815-753-1384. *Application contact:* Graduate School Office, 815-753-0395, E-mail: gradsch@niu.edu.
Website: http://chhs.niu.edu/health-studies/

**Northwestern University,** Feinberg School of Medicine, Program in Public Health, Evanston, IL 60208. Offers MPH. *Accreditation:* CEPH. *Program availability:* Part-time, evening/weekend. *Entrance requirements:* For master's, GRE General Test. Additional exam requirements/recommendations for international students: required—TOEFL.

**Nova Southeastern University,** Dr. Kiran C. Patel College of Osteopathic Medicine, Fort Lauderdale, FL 33314-7796. Offers biomedical informatics (MS, Graduate Certificate), including biomedical informatics (MS), clinical informatics (Graduate Certificate), public health informatics (Graduate Certificate); disaster and emergency management (MS); medical education (MS); nutrition (MS, Graduate Certificate), including functional nutrition and herbal therapy (Graduate Certificate); osteopathic medicine (DO); public health (MPH, Graduate Certificate), including health education (Graduate Certificate); social medicine (Graduate Certificate); DO/DMD. *Accreditation:* AOsA; CEPH. *Program availability:* Part-time, 100% online, blended/hybrid learning. *Faculty:* 73 full-time (43 women), 35 part-time/adjunct (14 women). *Students:* 1,410 full-time (740 women), 182 part-time (118 women); includes 895 minority (126 Black or African American, non-Hispanic/Latino; 1 American Indian or Alaska Native, non-Hispanic/Latino; 416 Asian, non-Hispanic/Latino; 309 Hispanic/Latino; 1 Native Hawaiian or other Pacific Islander, non-Hispanic/Latino; 42 Two or more races, non-Hispanic/Latino), 70 international. Average age 26. 5,078 applicants, 10% accepted, 495 enrolled. In 2019, 117 master's, 233 doctorates, 3 other advanced degrees awarded. *Degree requirements:* For master's, comprehensive exam (for MPH); field/special projects; for doctorate, comprehensive exam, COMLEX Board Exams; for Graduate Certificate, thesis or alternative. *Entrance requirements:* For master's, GRE; for doctorate, MCAT, coursework in biology, chemistry, organic chemistry, physics (all with labs), biochemistry, and English. *Application deadline:* For fall admission, 1/15 for domestic students. Applications are processed on a rolling basis. Application fee: $50. Electronic applications accepted. *Expenses:* Contact institution. *Financial support:* In 2019–20, 83 students received support, including 24 fellowships with tuition reimbursements available; Federal Work-Study and scholarships/grants also available. Financial award application deadline: 6/1; financial award applicants required to submit FAFSA. *Unit head:* Elaine M. Wallace, Dean, 954-262-1457, Fax: 954-262-2250, E-mail: ewallace@nova.edu. *Application contact:* HPD Admissions, 877-640-0218, E-mail: hpdinfo@nova.edu.
Website: https://www.osteopathic.nova.edu/

**Oakland University,** Graduate Study and Lifelong Learning, School of Health Sciences, Program in Public Health, Rochester, MI 48309-4401. Offers MPH. *Program availability:* Part-time, evening/weekend, blended/hybrid learning. *Entrance requirements:* For master's, Personal statement of no more than 1000 words. Additional exam requirements/recommendations for international students: required—TOEFL (minimum score 550 paper-based; 79 iBT), IELTS (minimum score 6.5). Electronic applications accepted. *Expenses: Tuition, area resident:* Full-time $12,328; part-time $770.50 per credit hour. Tuition, state resident: full-time $12,328; part-time $770.50 per credit hour. Tuition, nonresident: full-time $16,432; part-time $1027 per credit hour. *International tuition:* $16,432 full-time. Tuition and fees vary according to degree level and program.

**The Ohio State University,** College of Public Health, Columbus, OH 43210. Offers MHA, MPH, MS, PhD, DVM/MPH, JD/MHA, MHA/MBA, MHA/MD, MHA/MPA, MHA/MS, MPH/MBA, MPH/MD, MPH/MSW. *Accreditation:* CAHME; CEPH. *Program availability:* Part-time. Terminal master's awarded for partial completion of doctoral program. *Degree requirements:* For master's, thesis optional, practicum; for doctorate, thesis/dissertation. *Entrance requirements:* For master's and doctorate, GRE. Additional exam requirements/recommendations for international students: required—TOEFL (minimum score 550 paper-based; 79 iBT); recommended—IELTS (minimum score 7). Electronic applications accepted.

**Ohio University,** Graduate College, College of Health Sciences and Professions, Department of Social and Public Health, Athens, OH 45701-2979. Offers early child development and family life (MS); family studies (MS); health administration (MHA); public health (MPH); social work (MSW). *Program availability:* Part-time, evening/weekend, online learning. *Degree requirements:* For master's, capstone (MPH). *Entrance requirements:* For master's, GMAT, GRE General Test, previous course work in accounting, management, and statistics; previous public health background (MHA, MPH). Additional exam requirements/recommendations for international students: required—TOEFL (minimum score 550 paper-based; 80 iBT) or IELTS (minimum score 6.5). Electronic applications accepted. *Expenses:* Contact institution.

**Old Dominion University,** College of Health Sciences, School of Dental Hygiene, Norfolk, VA 23529. Offers dental hygiene (MS), including community/public health, education, generalist, global health, marketing, modeling and simulation, research. *Program availability:* Part-time, evening/weekend, blended/hybrid learning. *Degree requirements:* For master's, comprehensive exam, thesis optional, writing proficiency exam, responsible conduct of research training. *Entrance requirements:* For master's, Dental Hygiene National Board Examination or copy of license to practice dental hygiene, BS or certificate in dental hygiene or related area, minimum GPA of 2.8 (3.0 in major), 4 letters of recommendation. Additional exam requirements/recommendations for international students: required—TOEFL (minimum score 550 paper-based, 79 iBT) or IELTS (minimum score 6.5). Electronic applications accepted. *Expenses:* Contact institution.

**Oregon State University,** College of Public Health and Human Sciences, Program in Public Health, Corvallis, OR 97331. Offers biostatistics (MPH); environmental and occupational health (MPH, PhD); epidemiology (MPH, PhD); global health (MPH, PhD). *Accreditation:* CEPH. Terminal master's awarded for partial completion of doctoral program. *Entrance requirements:* For master's and doctorate, GRE, minimum GPA of 3.0 in last 90 hours. Additional exam requirements/recommendations for international students: required—TOEFL (minimum score 80 iBT), IELTS (minimum score 6.5). Electronic applications accepted. *Expenses:* Contact institution.

**Penn State Hershey Medical Center,** College of Medicine, Graduate School Programs in the Biomedical Sciences, Graduate Program in Public Health, Hershey, PA 17033. Offers MPH, Dr PH. *Accreditation:* CEPH. *Program availability:* Part-time, evening/weekend. *Degree requirements:* For master's, thesis or alternative; for doctorate, comprehensive exam, thesis/dissertation. *Entrance requirements:* For master's, GRE General Test; for doctorate, GRE General Test, master's degree. Additional exam requirements/recommendations for international students: required—TOEFL (minimum score 81 iBT). Electronic applications accepted.

**Penn State Hershey Medical Center,** College of Medicine, Graduate School Programs in the Biomedical Sciences, Graduate Program in Public Health Sciences, Hershey, PA 17033. Offers MS. *Accreditation:* CEPH. *Program availability:* Part-time. *Entrance requirements:* For master's, GRE General Test. Additional exam requirements/recommendations for international students: required—TOEFL (minimum score 81 iBT). Electronic applications accepted.

**Philadelphia College of Osteopathic Medicine,** Graduate and Professional Programs, School of Professional and Applied Psychology, Philadelphia, PA 19131. Offers applied behavior analysis (Certificate); clinical health psychology (Post-Doctoral Certificate); clinical neuropsychology (Post-Doctoral Certificate); clinical psychology (Psy D); educational psychology (PhD); mental health counseling (MS); organizational development and leadership (MS); psychology (Certificate); public health management and administration (MS); school psychology (MS, Psy D, Ed S). *Accreditation:* APA. *Faculty:* 19 full-time (11 women), 122 part-time/adjunct (58 women). *Students:* 342 (285 women); includes 108 minority (65 Black or African American, non-Hispanic/Latino; 1 American Indian or Alaska Native, non-Hispanic/Latino; 10 Asian, non-Hispanic/Latino; 14 Hispanic/Latino; 18 Two or more races, non-Hispanic/Latino). Average age 25. 357 applicants, 51% accepted, 113 enrolled. In 2019, 79 master's, 38 doctorates, 16 other advanced degrees awarded. Terminal master's awarded for partial completion of doctoral program. *Degree requirements:* For master's, comprehensive exam (for some programs), thesis (for some programs); for doctorate, comprehensive exam, thesis/dissertation. *Entrance requirements:* For master's, GRE or MAT, minimum GPA of 3.0; bachelor's degree from regionally-accredited college or university; for doctorate, PRAXIS II (for Psy D in school psychology), minimum undergraduate GPA of 3.0; for other advanced degree, GRE (for Ed S). Additional exam requirements/recommendations for international students: required—TOEFL (minimum score 79 iBT). *Application deadline:* Applications are processed on a rolling basis. Application fee: $50. Electronic applications accepted. *Financial support:* In 2019–20, 28 teaching assistantships were awarded; Federal Work-Study, institutionally sponsored loans, and scholarships/grants also available. Financial award application deadline: 3/15; financial award applicants required to submit FAFSA. *Unit head:* Dr. Robert DiTomasso, Chairman, 215-871-6442, Fax: 215-871-6458, E-mail: robertd@pcom.edu. *Application contact:* Johnathan Cox, Associate Director of Admissions, 215-871-6700, Fax: 215-871-6719, E-mail: johnathancox@pcom.edu.
Website: pcom.edu

**Ponce Health Sciences University,** Masters Program in Public Health, Ponce, PR 00732-7004. Offers epidemiology (Dr PH); public health (MPH). *Accreditation:* CEPH. *Degree requirements:* For master's, one foreign language, comprehensive exam, thesis. *Entrance requirements:* For master's, GRE General Test or EXADEP, proficiency in Spanish and English, minimum GPA of 2.7, 3 letters of recommendation; for doctorate, GRE, proficiency in Spanish and English, minimum GPA of 3.0, letter of recommendation.

**Portland State University,** Graduate Studies, OHSU-PSU School of Public Health, Portland, OR 97207-0751. Offers MA, MPH, PhD. *Accreditation:* CEPH. *Program availability:* Part-time. *Faculty:* 26 full-time (19 women), 15 part-time/adjunct (10 women). *Students:* 2 full-time (both women), 13 part-time (11 women); includes 4 minority (1 Asian, non-Hispanic/Latino; 1 Native Hawaiian or other Pacific Islander, non-Hispanic/Latino; 2 Two or more races, non-Hispanic/Latino). Average age 40. In 2019, 15 master's, 1 doctorate awarded. *Degree requirements:* For master's, comprehensive exam, field experience, CPH exam (for MPH); for doctorate, thesis/dissertation. *Entrance requirements:* For master's, GRE General Test, SOPHAS application, background check, personal statement, 3 letters of recommendation, curriculum vitae/resume. Additional exam requirements/recommendations for international students: required—TOEFL (minimum score 550 paper-based; 90 iBT). *Application deadline:* For fall admission, 4/1 for domestic students. Application fee: $165. *Expenses: Tuition, area resident:* Full-time $13,020; part-time $6510 per year. Tuition, state resident: full-time $13,020; part-time $6510 per year. Tuition, nonresident: full-time $19,830; part-time $9915 per year. *International tuition:* $19,830 full-time. *Required fees:* $1226. One-time fee: $350. Tuition and fees vary according to course load, program and reciprocity agreements. *Financial support:* In 2019–20, 15 students received support, including 8 research assistantships with full and partial tuition reimbursements available (averaging $11,578 per year); teaching assistantships with full and partial tuition reimbursements available, Federal Work-Study, and unspecified assistantships also available. Financial award applicants required to submit FAFSA. *Unit head:* Dr. David Bangsberg, Dean, 503-494-8257. *Application contact:* Kelly Doherty, Director of Graduate Admissions, 503-725-5391, Fax: 503-725-3416, E-mail: dohertyk@pdx.edu.
Website: http://ohsu-psu-sph.org/

**Purdue University,** Graduate School, College of Health and Human Sciences, Department of Nutrition Science, West Lafayette, IN 47907. Offers animal health (MS, PhD); biochemical and molecular nutrition (MS, PhD); growth and development (MS, PhD); human and clinical nutrition (MS, PhD); public health and education (MS, PhD). *Faculty:* 19 full-time (13 women), 1 part-time/adjunct (0 women). *Students:* 41 full-time (34 women), 2 part-time (both women); includes 2 minority (1 Black or African American, non-Hispanic/Latino; 1 Two or more races, non-Hispanic/Latino), 17 international. Average age 26. 43 applicants, 35% accepted, 10 enrolled. In 2019, 2 master's, 9 doctorates awarded. *Degree requirements:* For master's, thesis; for doctorate, thesis/dissertation. *Entrance requirements:* For master's and doctorate, GRE General Test (minimum scores in verbal and quantitative areas of 1000 or 300 on new scoring), minimum undergraduate GPA of 3.0 or equivalent. Additional exam requirements/recommendations for international students: required—TOEFL (minimum score 600 paper-based; 77 iBT). *Application deadline:* For fall admission, 1/10 for domestic and international students. Applications are processed on a rolling basis. Application fee: $60 ($75 for international students). Electronic applications accepted. *Financial support:* Fellowships, research assistantships, and teaching assistantships available. Support available to part-time students. Financial award applicants required to submit FAFSA. *Unit head:* Amanda Siedl, Interim Head, 765-496-3570, E-mail: asiedl@purdue.edu. *Application contact:* Kim Buhman, Graduate Contact for Admissions, 765-496-6872, E-mail: kbuhman@purdue.edu.
Website: http://www.cfs.purdue.edu/fn/

**Purdue University,** School of Veterinary Medicine and Graduate School, Graduate Programs in Veterinary Medicine, Department of Comparative Pathobiology, West Lafayette, IN 47907-2027. Offers comparative epidemiology and public health (MS); comparative epidemiology and public heath (PhD); comparative microbiology and immunology (MS, PhD); comparative pathobiology (MS, PhD); interdisciplinary studies (PhD), including microbial pathogenesis, molecular signaling and cancer biology, molecular virology; lab animal medicine (MS); veterinary anatomic pathology (MS); veterinary clinical pathology (MS). Terminal master's awarded for partial completion of doctoral program. *Degree requirements:* For master's, thesis (for some programs); for doctorate, thesis/dissertation. *Entrance requirements:* For master's and doctorate, GRE General Test. Additional exam requirements/recommendations for international students: required—TOEFL (minimum score 575 paper-based), IELTS (minimum score 6.5), TWE (minimum score 4). Electronic applications accepted.

**Queen's University at Kingston,** School of Graduate Studies, Faculty of Health Sciences, Department of Community Health and Epidemiology, Kingston, ON K7L 3N6, Canada. Offers epidemiology (M Sc, PhD); policy research and clinical epidemiology (M Sc); public health (MPH). *Program availability:* Part-time. *Degree requirements:* For master's, thesis. *Entrance requirements:* For master's, GRE General Test (strongly

recommended). Additional exam requirements/recommendations for international students: required—TOEFL (minimum score 600 paper-based).

**Rivier University,** School of Graduate Studies, Division of Nursing and Health Professions, Nashua, NH 03060. Offers family nurse practitioner (MS); leadership in health systems management (MS); nursing education (MS); nursing practice (DNP); psychiatric/mental health nurse practitioner (MS); public health (MPH). *Accreditation:* ACEN. *Program availability:* Part-time, evening/weekend. *Entrance requirements:* For master's, GRE, MAT. Electronic applications accepted.

**Rollins College,** Hamilton Holt School, Master of Public Health Program, Winter Park, FL 32789-4499. Offers MPH. *Program availability:* Part-time. *Faculty:* 3 full-time (2 women). *Students:* 29 full-time (25 women); includes 11 minority (4 Black or African American, non-Hispanic/Latino; 7 Hispanic/Latino), 3 international. Average age 34. In 2019, 11 master's awarded. Application fee: $50. *Expenses: Tuition:* Part-time $2700 per credit hour. Tuition and fees vary according to program. *Unit head:* Dr. Allen Johnson, Director, E-mail: jajohnson@rollins.edu. *Application contact:* Nick Georgoudiou, Director of Admission, 407-691-1781, Fax: 407-646-1551, E-mail: ngeorgoudiou@rollins.edu.
Website: https://www.rollins.edu/evening/academics/graduate/master-of-public-health.html

**Rutgers University - Camden,** School of Public Health, Stratford, NJ 08084. Offers general public health (Certificate); health systems and policy (MPH); DO/MPH. *Program availability:* Part-time, evening/weekend. *Degree requirements:* For master's, thesis, internship. *Entrance requirements:* For master's, GRE General Test. Additional exam requirements/recommendations for international students: required—TOEFL. Electronic applications accepted.

**Rutgers University - Newark,** School of Public Health, Newark, NJ 07107-1709. Offers clinical epidemiology (Certificate); dental public health (MPH); general public health (Certificate); public policy and oral health services administration (Certificate); quantitative methods (MPH); urban health (MPH); DMD/MPH; MD/MPH; MS/MPH. *Program availability:* Part-time, evening/weekend. *Degree requirements:* For master's, thesis, internship. *Entrance requirements:* For master's, GRE General Test. Additional exam requirements/recommendations for international students: required—TOEFL. Electronic applications accepted.

**Rutgers University - New Brunswick,** School of Public Health, Program in Public Health, Piscataway, NJ 08854-8097. Offers MPH, Dr PH, PhD, MBA/MPH, MD/MPH. *Accreditation:* CEPH. *Program availability:* Part-time, evening/weekend. *Degree requirements:* For master's, internship; for doctorate, thesis/dissertation. *Entrance requirements:* For master's, GMAT, GRE General Test; for doctorate, GRE General Test, MPH (for Dr PH). Additional exam requirements/recommendations for international students: required—TOEFL. *Expenses:* Contact institution.

**Sacred Heart University,** Graduate Programs, College of Health Professions, Department of Public Health, Fairfield, CT 06825. Offers MPH. *Program availability:* Part-time. *Entrance requirements:* For master's, bachelor's degree with minimum cumulative GPA of 3.0.

**St. Ambrose University,** College of Health and Human Services, Program in Public Health, Davenport, IA 52803-2898. Offers MPH. *Program availability:* Online learning.

**St. Catherine University,** Graduate Programs, Program in Holistic Health Studies, St. Paul, MN 55105. Offers MA. *Program availability:* Part-time. *Degree requirements:* For master's, thesis optional. *Entrance requirements:* For master's, 1 course in anatomy, physiology and psychology. Additional exam requirements/recommendations for international students: required—TOEFL (minimum score 600 paper-based; 100 iBT). *Expenses:* Contact institution.

**St. John's University,** College of Pharmacy and Health Sciences, Graduate Programs in Pharmaceutical Sciences, Master of Public Health Program, Queens, NY 11439. Offers MPH. *Entrance requirements:* For master's, GRE General Test, letters of recommendation, transcripts, resume, personal statement. Additional exam requirements/recommendations for international students: required—TOEFL (minimum score 100 iBT), IELTS (minimum score 7). Electronic applications accepted.

**Saint Louis University,** Graduate Programs, College for Public Health and Social Justice, Department of Health Management and Policy, St. Louis, MO 63103. Offers health administration (MHA); health policy (MPH); public health studies (PhD). *Accreditation:* CAHME. *Program availability:* Part-time. *Degree requirements:* For master's, comprehensive exam, internship. *Entrance requirements:* For master's, GMAT or GRE General Test, LSAT, MCAT, letters of recommendation, resume. Additional exam requirements/recommendations for international students: required—TOEFL (minimum score 525 paper-based).

**Salus University,** College of Health Sciences, Elkins Park, PA 19027-1598. Offers physician assistant (MMS); public health (MPH). *Accreditation:* ARC-PA. *Entrance requirements:* For master's, GRE (recommended). Additional exam requirements/recommendations for international students: required—TOEFL. Electronic applications accepted.

**Samford University,** School of Public Health, Birmingham, AL 35229. Offers health informatics (MSHI); healthcare administration (MHA); nutrition (MS); public health (MPH); social work (MSW). *Accreditation:* CSWE. *Program availability:* Part-time, online only, 100% online. *Faculty:* 16 full-time (9 women), 5 part-time/adjunct (4 women). *Students:* 76 full-time (71 women), 16 part-time (14 women); includes 19 minority (14 Black or African American, non-Hispanic/Latino; 1 Asian, non-Hispanic/Latino; 1 Hispanic/Latino; 3 Two or more races, non-Hispanic/Latino). Average age 28. 74 applicants, 78% accepted, 39 enrolled. In 2019, 51 master's awarded. *Degree requirements:* For master's, capstone course. *Entrance requirements:* For master's, GRE, MAT, recommendations, resume, personal statement, transcripts, application. Additional exam requirements/recommendations for international students: required—TOEFL (minimum score 590 paper-based; 90 iBT), IELTS (minimum score 6.5). *Application deadline:* For fall admission, 10/1 for domestic students; for winter admission, 12/1 for domestic students; for spring admission, 5/1 for domestic students. Applications are processed on a rolling basis. Application fee: $75. Electronic applications accepted. *Expenses: Tuition:* Full-time $17,754; part-time $862 per credit hour. *Required fees:* $550; $550 per unit. Full-time tuition and fees vary according to course load, program and student level. *Financial support:* In 2019–20, 30 students received support. Scholarships/grants available. Financial award application deadline: 5/1; financial award applicants required to submit FAFSA. *Unit head:* Dr. Keith Elder, Ph.D., Dean, School of Public Health, 205-726-4655, E-mail: kelder@samford.edu. *Application contact:* Dr. Marian Carter, Ed.D, Assistant Dean of Enrollment Management, 205-726-2611, E-mail: mwcarter@samford.edu.
Website: http://www.samford.edu/publichealth

**San Diego State University,** Graduate and Research Affairs, College of Health and Human Services, School of Public Health, San Diego, CA 92182. Offers environmental health (MPH); epidemiology (MPH, PhD), including biostatistics (MPH); global emergency preparedness and response (MS); global health (PhD); health behavior (PhD); health promotion (MPH); health services administration (MPH); toxicology (MS); MPH/MA; MSW/MPH. *Accreditation:* CAHME (one or more programs are accredited); CEPH. *Program availability:* Part-time. *Degree requirements:* For master's, comprehensive exam (for some programs), thesis (for some programs); for doctorate, thesis/dissertation. *Entrance requirements:* For master's, GMAT (MPH in health services administration), GRE General Test; for doctorate, GRE General Test. Additional exam requirements/recommendations for international students: required—TOEFL.

**San Francisco State University,** Division of Graduate Studies, College of Health and Social Sciences, Department of Health Education, San Francisco, CA 94132-1722. Offers community health education (MPH). *Accreditation:* CEPH. *Program availability:* Part-time. *Students:* Average age 36. *Application deadline:* Applications are processed on a rolling basis. *Expenses: Tuition, area resident:* Full-time $7176; part-time $4164 per year. Tuition, state resident: full-time $7176; part-time $4164 per year. Tuition, nonresident: full-time $16,680; part-time $396 per unit. *International tuition:* $16,680 full-time. *Required fees:* $1524; $1524 per unit. $762 per semester. Tuition and fees vary according to degree level and program. *Unit head:* Dr. Marty Martinson, Chair, 415-338-1413, Fax: 415-338-0570, E-mail: martym@sfsu.edu. *Application contact:* Vincent Lam, Graduate Coordinator, 415-338-1413, Fax: 415-338-0570, E-mail: vlam@sfsu.edu.
Website: http://healthed.sfsu.edu/graduate

**San Juan Bautista School of Medicine,** Graduate and Professional Programs, Caguas, PR 00726-4968. Offers MPH, MD. *Accreditation:* LCME/AMA. *Degree requirements:* For doctorate, comprehensive exam, United States Medical Licensing Exam Steps I and II. *Entrance requirements:* For master's, bachelor's degree from university or college accredited by the Council of Higher Education of Puerto Rico or by a renowned accrediting agency that is registered at the Federal Education Department; minimum GPA of 2.5; for doctorate, MCAT, interview.

**Sarah Lawrence College,** Graduate Studies, Program in Health Advocacy, Bronxville, NY 10708-5999. Offers MA. *Program availability:* Part-time. *Degree requirements:* For master's, thesis, fieldwork. *Entrance requirements:* For master's, previous course work in biology and microeconomics, minimum B average in undergraduate course work. Additional exam requirements/recommendations for international students: required—TOEFL (minimum score 600 paper-based). Electronic applications accepted.

**Shenandoah University,** School of Health Professions, Winchester, VA 22601. Offers athletic training (MSAT); occupational therapy (MS); performing arts medicine (Certificate); physical therapy (DPT); physician assistant studies (MS); public health (MPH, Certificate). *Program availability:* Part-time, 100% online. *Faculty:* 1 (woman) full-time, 2 part-time/adjunct (both women). *Students:* 3 full-time (2 women), 25 part-time (20 women); includes 8 minority (4 Black or African American, non-Hispanic/Latino; 2 Asian, non-Hispanic/Latino; 2 Hispanic/Latino). Average age 34. 35 applicants, 97% accepted, 6 enrolled. In 2019, 1 other advanced degree awarded. *Degree requirements:* For master's, Practicum experience. *Entrance requirements:* For master's, Minimum GPA: 3.0 cumulative; Prerequisites: Bachelor's Degree or higher. Additional exam requirements/recommendations for international students: required—TOEFL (minimum score 83 iBT). *Application deadline:* For fall admission, 8/1 for domestic students; for spring admission, 12/1 for domestic students. Applications are processed on a rolling basis. Application fee: $30. Electronic applications accepted. *Expenses:* $700 per credit hour; 32 credit hours for program completion. *Financial support:* In 2019–20, 17 students received support, including 1 fellowship (averaging $210 per year); scholarships/grants and Faculty staff grant Public Health Discount (graduate) Valley Health SU Discretionary Award Anatomy and physiology graduate also available. Financial award application deadline: 8/1; financial award applicants required to submit FAFSA. *Unit head:* Michelle Gamber, DrPH, MA, Director, 540-665-5560, Fax: 540-665-5519, E-mail: mgamber@su.edu. *Application contact:* Katie Olivo, Associate Director of Admission, 540-665-5441, Fax: 540-665-4627, E-mail: kolivo@su.edu.
Website: su.edu/public-health/

**Simmons University,** Gwen Ifill College of Media, Arts, and Humanities, Boston, MA 02115. Offers behavior analysis (MS, PhD, Ed S); children's literature (MA); dietetics (Certificate); elementary education (MAT); English (MA); gender/cultural studies (MA); history (MA); nutrition and health promotion (MS); physical therapy (DPT); public health (MPH); public policy (MPP); special education: moderate and severe disabilities (MS Ed); sports nutrition (Certificate); writing for children (MFA). *Program availability:* Part-time. *Faculty:* 10 full-time (9 women), 7 part-time/adjunct (6 women). *Students:* 2 full-time (both women), 67 part-time (57 women); includes 13 minority (3 Black or African American, non-Hispanic/Latino; 4 Asian, non-Hispanic/Latino; 3 Hispanic/Latino; 3 Two or more races, non-Hispanic/Latino), 1 international. Average age 31. 42 applicants, 62% accepted, 23 enrolled. In 2019, 24 master's awarded. *Degree requirements:* For master's, thesis optional. *Entrance requirements:* For master's, GRE, bachelor's degree from accredited college or university; minimum B average (preferred). Additional exam requirements/recommendations for international students: required—TOEFL (minimum score 600 paper-based; 100 iBT). *Application deadline:* For fall admission, 8/1 for domestic and international students; for spring admission, 12/15 for domestic and international students; for summer admission, 5/1 for domestic and international students. Applications are processed on a rolling basis. Application fee: $35. Electronic applications accepted. *Expenses:* Contact institution. *Financial support:* In 2019–20, 14 students received support, including 1 fellowship (averaging $15,360 per year), 13 teaching assistantships (averaging $2,000 per year); scholarships/grants also available. Financial award applicants required to submit FAFSA. *Unit head:* Dr. Brian Norman, Dean, 617-521-2472, E-mail: brian.norman@simmons.edu. *Application contact:* Patricia Flaherty, Director, Graduate Studies Admission, 617-521-3902, Fax: 617-521-3058, E-mail: gsa@simmons.edu.
Website: https://www.simmons.edu/academics/colleges-schools-departments/ifill

**Simon Fraser University,** Office of Graduate Studies and Postdoctoral Fellows, Faculty of Health Sciences, Burnaby, BC V5A 1S6, Canada. Offers global health (Graduate Diploma); health sciences (M Sc, PhD); public health (MPH). *Accreditation:* CEPH. *Degree requirements:* For master's, thesis (for some programs); for doctorate, comprehensive exam, thesis/dissertation. *Entrance requirements:* For master's, minimum GPA of 3.0 (on scale of 4.33) or 3.33 based on last 60 credits of undergraduate courses; for doctorate, minimum GPA of 3.5 (on scale of 4.33); for Graduate Diploma, minimum GPA of 2.5 (on scale of 4.33) or 2.67 based on last 60 credits of undergraduate courses. Additional exam requirements/recommendations for international students: recommended—TOEFL (minimum score 580 paper-based; 93 iBT), IELTS (minimum score 7), TWE (minimum score 5). Electronic applications accepted.

**Slippery Rock University of Pennsylvania,** Graduate Studies (Recruitment), College of Health, Engineering, and Science, Department of Public Health and Social Work, Slippery Rock, PA 16057-1383. Offers public health (MPH). *Program availability:* Part-time, blended/hybrid learning. *Faculty:* 4 full-time (1 woman), 1 (woman) part-time/adjunct. *Students:* 31 full-time (23 women), 16 part-time (14 women); includes 7 minority (4 Black or African American, non-Hispanic/Latino; 3 Two or more races, non-Hispanic/Latino). Average age 27. 46 applicants, 67% accepted, 26 enrolled. In 2019, 21 master's awarded. *Degree requirements:* For master's, thesis. *Entrance requirements:* For master's, personal statement, letter of recommendation, official transcripts, minimum GPA of 3.0, statistics course, natural or social science course. Additional exam requirements/recommendations for international students: required—TOEFL (minimum score 550 paper-based; 80 iBT). *Application deadline:* For fall admission, 5/1 priority

date for domestic students, 3/1 priority date for international students; for spring admission, 9/1 priority date for domestic students, 10/1 priority date for international students. Applications are processed on a rolling basis. Application fee: $25 ($30 for international students). Electronic applications accepted. *Expenses:* $516 per credit in-state tuition, $173.61 per credit in-state fees; $774 per credit out-of-state tuition, $224.31 per credit out-of-state fees; $516 per credit in-state tuition, $105.40 per credit in-state fees (for distance education); $526 per credit out-of-state tuition, $118.90 per credit out-of-state fees (for distance education). *Financial support:* In 2019–20, 10 students received support. Career-related internships or fieldwork, Federal Work-Study, institutionally sponsored loans, scholarships/grants, tuition waivers (partial), and unspecified assistantships available. Support available to part-time students. Financial award application deadline: 5/1; financial award applicants required to submit FAFSA. *Unit head:* Dr. Joseph Robare, Graduate Coordinator, 724-738-2943, Fax: 724-738-4032, E-mail: joseph.robare@sru.edu. *Application contact:* Brandi Weber-Mortimer, Director of Graduate Admissions, 724-738-4340, E-mail: graduate.admissions@sru.edu.
Website: http://www.sru.edu/academics/colleges-and-departments/ches/departments/public-health

**Southern Connecticut State University,** School of Graduate Studies, School of Health and Human Services, Department of Public Health, New Haven, CT 06515-1355. Offers MPH. *Accreditation:* CEPH. *Program availability:* Part-time, evening/weekend. *Degree requirements:* For master's, thesis or alternative. *Entrance requirements:* For master's, minimum undergraduate QPA of 3.0 in graduate major field or 2.5 overall, interview. Electronic applications accepted.

**State University of New York Downstate Medical Center,** College of Medicine, Program in Public Health, Brooklyn, NY 11203-2098. Offers urban and immigrant health (MPH); MD/MPH. *Program availability:* Part-time. *Degree requirements:* For master's, practicum. *Entrance requirements:* For master's, GRE, MCAT or OAT, 2 letters of recommendation, minimum undergraduate GPA of 3.0. Additional exam requirements/recommendations for international students: required—TOEFL (minimum score 550 paper-based).

**State University of New York Upstate Medical University,** College of Graduate Studies, Central New York Master of Public Health Program, Syracuse, NY 13210. Offers MPH.

**Stony Brook University, State University of New York,** Stony Brook Medicine, Renaissance School of Medicine, Program in Public Health, Stony Brook, NY 11794. Offers community health (MPH); evaluation sciences (MPH); family violence (MPH); health communication (Certificate); health economics (MPH); health education and promotion (Certificate); population health (MPH); substance abuse (MPH). *Accreditation:* CEPH. *Program availability:* Part-time, evening/weekend. *Students:* 39 full-time (30 women), 17 part-time (12 women); includes 24 minority (3 Black or African American, non-Hispanic/Latino; 13 Asian, non-Hispanic/Latino; 7 Hispanic/Latino; 1 Two or more races, non-Hispanic/Latino), 2 international. Average age 28. 174 applicants, 67% accepted, 70 enrolled. In 2019, 22 master's awarded. *Entrance requirements:* For master's, GRE, 3 references, bachelor's degree from accredited college or university with minimum GPA of 3.0, essays, interview. Additional exam requirements/recommendations for international students: required—TOEFL (minimum score 90 iBT). *Application deadline:* For fall admission, 7/15 for domestic students. Application fee: $100. Electronic applications accepted. *Expenses:* Contact institution. *Financial support:* In 2019–20, 4 research assistantships were awarded; fellowships also available. *Unit head:* Dr. Lisa A. Benz Scott, Director, 631-444-9396, E-mail: publichealth@stonybrookmedicine.edu. *Application contact:* Joanie Maniaci, Assistant Director for Student Affairs, 631-444-2074, Fax: 631-444-6035, E-mail: joanmarie.maniaci@stonybrook.edu.
Website: https://publichealth.stonybrookmedicine.edu/

**SUNY Brockport,** School of Education, Health, and Human Services, Department of Public Health and Health Education, Brockport, NY 14420-2997. Offers community health education (MS Ed); health education (MS Ed), including health education K-12. *Faculty:* 4 full-time (1 woman), 4 part-time/adjunct (3 women). *Students:* 14 full-time (4 women), 108 part-time (49 women); includes 3 minority (1 Black or African American, non-Hispanic/Latino; 1 Asian, non-Hispanic/Latino; 1 Hispanic/Latino). 51 applicants, 65% accepted, 27 enrolled. In 2019, 18 master's awarded. *Entrance requirements:* For master's, minimum GPA of 3.0, letters of recommendation. Additional exam requirements/recommendations for international students: required—TOEFL (minimum score 550 paper-based; 79 iBT), IELTS (minimum score 6.5). *Application deadline:* For fall admission, 3/1 priority date for domestic and international students; for spring admission, 10/1 priority date for domestic and international students; for summer admission, 3/1 priority date for domestic and international students. Application fee: $80. Electronic applications accepted. *Expenses: Tuition, area resident:* Part-time $471 per credit hour. Tuition, nonresident: part-time $963 per credit hour. *Financial support:* In 2019–20, 1 teaching assistantship with full tuition reimbursement (averaging $6,000 per year) was awarded; Federal Work-Study, scholarships/grants, and unspecified assistantships also available. Support available to part-time students. Financial award application deadline: 3/15; financial award applicants required to submit FAFSA. *Unit head:* Dr. Darson Rhodes, Graduate Director, 585-395-5901, Fax: 585-395-5246, E-mail: drhodes@brockport.edu. *Application contact:* Danielle A. Welch, Graduate Admissions Counselor, 585-395-5465, Fax: 585-395-2515.
Website: https://www.brockport.edu/academics/public_health/

**Tarleton State University,** College of Graduate Studies, College of Health Sciences and Human Services, Department of Medical Laboratory Sciences and Public Health, Fort Worth, TX 76402. Offers medical laboratory sciences (MS). *Accreditation:* NAACLS. *Program availability:* Part-time. *Faculty:* 6 full-time (5 women), 1 (woman) part-time/adjunct. *Students:* 10 full-time (8 women), 13 part-time (9 women); includes 12 minority (3 Black or African American, non-Hispanic/Latino; 1 American Indian or Alaska Native, non-Hispanic/Latino; 4 Asian, non-Hispanic/Latino; 4 Hispanic/Latino), 2 international. Average age 30. 24 applicants, 71% accepted, 13 enrolled. In 2019, 1 master's awarded. *Degree requirements:* For master's, comprehensive exam, thesis optional. *Entrance requirements:* For master's, GRE, minimum GPA of 2.5. Additional exam requirements/recommendations for international students: required—TOEFL (minimum score 520 paper-based; 69 iBT); recommended—IELTS (minimum score 6), TSE (minimum score 50). *Application deadline:* For fall admission, 8/15 for domestic students; for spring admission, 1/7 for domestic students. Applications are processed on a rolling basis. Application fee: $50 ($130 for international students). Electronic applications accepted. *Expenses:* Tuition, state resident: part-time $221.73 per credit hour. Tuition, nonresident: part-time $636.73 per credit hour. *Required fees:* $198 per credit hour. $100 per semester. Tuition and fees vary according to degree level. *Financial support:* Career-related internships or fieldwork, Federal Work-Study, and scholarships/grants available. Support available to part-time students. Financial award application deadline: 5/1; financial award applicants required to submit FAFSA. *Unit head:* Sally Lewis, Head, 817-926-1101, E-mail: slewis@tarleton.edu. *Application contact:* Wendy Weiss, Graduate Admissions Coordinator, 254-968-9104, Fax: 254-968-9670, E-mail: weiss@tarleton.edu.
Website: http://www.tarleton.edu/degrees/masters/ms-medical-laboratory-science/

**Temple University,** College of Public Health, Department of Social and Behavioral Sciences, Philadelphia, PA 19122-6096. Offers MPH, PhD. *Accreditation:* CEPH (one or more programs are accredited). *Program availability:* Part-time, evening/weekend, online learning. *Faculty:* 17 full-time (13 women). *Students:* 40 full-time (27 women), 52 part-time (46 women); includes 31 minority (13 Black or African American, non-Hispanic/Latino; 5 Asian, non-Hispanic/Latino; 11 Hispanic/Latino; 2 Two or more races, non-Hispanic/Latino), 6 international. 108 applicants, 58% accepted, 28 enrolled. In 2019, 22 master's, 2 doctorates awarded. *Degree requirements:* For master's, fieldwork practicum with final paper; for doctorate, thesis/dissertation, area paper. *Entrance requirements:* For master's, GRE, DAT, GMAT, LSAT, MCAT, OAT, or PCAT, statement of goals, clearances for clinical/field education, resume, 3 letters of recommendation; for doctorate, GRE, coursework in the natural, social, or behavioral sciences related to health, statement of goals, resume, writing sample, 3 letters of recommendation. Additional exam requirements/recommendations for international students: required—TOEFL (minimum score 79 iBT), IELTS (minimum score 6.5), PTE (minimum score 53), one of three is required. Application fee: $60. Electronic applications accepted. *Expenses:* Contact institution. *Financial support:* Fellowships, research assistantships, teaching assistantships, Federal Work-Study, scholarships/grants, health care benefits, and unspecified assistantships available. Financial award applicants required to submit FAFSA. *Unit head:* Stephen Lepore, Department Chair/Professor, 215-204-8726, E-mail: slepore@temple.edu. *Application contact:* Annemarie Szambelak, Assistant Director of Admissions, 215-204-4526, E-mail: aszambelak@temple.edu.
Website: https://cph.temple.edu/socialbehavioral/home

**Tennessee State University,** The School of Graduate Studies and Research, College of Health Sciences, Department of Public Health, Health Administration and Health Sciences, Nashville, TN 37209-1561. Offers public health (MPH). *Accreditation:* CEPH. *Degree requirements:* For master's, capstone project.

**Texas A&M University,** School of Public Health, College Station, TX 77843. Offers biostatistics (MPH, MSPH); environmental health (MPH, MSPH); epidemiology (MPH, MSPH); health administration (MHA); health policy and management (MPH); health services research (PhD); occupational safety and health (MPH). *Accreditation:* CAHME; CEPH. *Program availability:* Part-time, blended/hybrid learning. *Entrance requirements:* For master's, GRE General Test, 3 letters of recommendation; statement of purpose; current curriculum vitae or resume; official transcripts; for doctorate, GRE General Test, 3 letters of recommendation; statement of purpose; current curriculum vitae or resume; official transcripts; interview (in some cases). Additional exam requirements/recommendations for international students: required—TOEFL (minimum score 597 paper-based, 95 iBT) or GRE (minimum verbal score 153). Electronic applications accepted. *Expenses:* Contact institution.

**Thomas Edison State University,** John S. Watson School of Public Service and Continuing Studies, Trenton, NJ 08608. Offers community and economic development (MSM); environmental policy/environmental justice (MSM); homeland security (MSHS, MSM); information and technology for public service (MSM); nonprofit management (MSM); public and municipal finance (MSM); public health (MSM); public service administration and leadership (MSM); public service leadership (MPSL). *Program availability:* Part-time, online learning. *Entrance requirements:* Additional exam requirements/recommendations for international students: required—TOEFL (minimum score 550 paper-based; 79 iBT). Electronic applications accepted.

**Thomas Jefferson University,** Jefferson College of Population Health, Program in Public Health, Philadelphia, PA 19107. Offers MPH, Certificate. *Accreditation:* CEPH. *Program availability:* Part-time, evening/weekend, online learning. Terminal master's awarded for partial completion of doctoral program. *Degree requirements:* For master's, capstone project or thesis. *Entrance requirements:* For master's, GRE or other graduate examination, 2 letters of recommendation, interview, curriculum vitae. Additional exam requirements/recommendations for international students: required—TOEFL (minimum score 100 iBT). Electronic applications accepted.

**Touro University California,** Graduate Programs, Vallejo, CA 94592. Offers education (MA); medical health sciences (MS); osteopathic medicine (DO); pharmacy (Pharm D); public health (MPH). *Accreditation:* ACPE; AOsA; ARC-PA; CEPH. *Program availability:* Part-time, evening/weekend. *Degree requirements:* For master's, comprehensive exam, thesis; for doctorate, comprehensive exam. *Entrance requirements:* For doctorate, BS/BA. Electronic applications accepted.

**Trinity Washington University,** School of Business and Graduate Studies, Washington, DC 20017-1094. Offers business administration (MBA); communication (MA); international security studies (MA); organizational management (MSA), including federal program management, human resource management, nonprofit management, organizational development, public and community health. *Program availability:* Part-time, evening/weekend. *Degree requirements:* For master's, thesis (for some programs), capstone project (MSA). *Entrance requirements:* For master's, minimum GPA of 2.5. Additional exam requirements/recommendations for international students: required—TOEFL (minimum score 550 paper-based).

**Tufts University,** School of Medicine, Public Health and Professional Degree Programs, Boston, MA 02111. Offers biomedical sciences (MS); health communication (MS, Certificate); pain research, education and policy (MS, Certificate); physician assistant (MS); public health (MPH, Dr PH), including behavioral science (MPH), biostatistics (MPH), epidemiology (MPH), health communication (MPH), health services (MPH), management and policy (MPH), nutrition (MPH); DMD/MPH; DVM/MPH; JD/MPH; MD/MPH; MMS/MPH; MS/MBA; MS/MPH. *Accreditation:* CEPH (one or more programs are accredited). *Program availability:* Part-time, evening/weekend. *Students:* 450 full-time (291 women), 68 part-time (58 women); includes 201 minority (34 Black or African American, non-Hispanic/Latino; 1 American Indian or Alaska Native, non-Hispanic/Latino; 106 Asian, non-Hispanic/Latino; 41 Hispanic/Latino; 1 Native Hawaiian or other Pacific Islander, non-Hispanic/Latino; 18 Two or more races, non-Hispanic/Latino), 16 international. Average age 27. 1,076 applicants, 70% accepted, 213 enrolled. In 2019, 268 master's, 2 doctorates awarded. Terminal master's awarded for partial completion of doctoral program. *Degree requirements:* For master's, thesis (for some programs); for doctorate, thesis/dissertation. *Entrance requirements:* For master's, GRE General Test, MCAT, or GMAT; LSAT for applicants to the JD/MPH combined degree; for doctorate, GRE General Test or MCAT. Additional exam requirements/recommendations for international students: required—TOEFL (minimum score 100 iBT); recommended—IELTS (minimum score 7), TSE. *Application deadline:* For fall admission, 1/15 priority date for domestic and international students; for spring admission, 10/25 priority date for domestic and international students. Applications are processed on a rolling basis. Application fee: $70. Electronic applications accepted. *Expenses:* Contact institution. *Financial support:* In 2019–20, 13 students received support, including 1 fellowship (averaging $3,000 per year), 50 research assistantships (averaging $1,000 per year), 65 teaching assistantships (averaging $2,000 per year); Federal Work-Study and scholarships/grants also available. Financial award application deadline: 2/23; financial award applicants required to submit FAFSA. *Unit head:* Dr. Aviva Must, Dean, 617-636-0935, Fax: 617-636-0898, E-mail: aviva.must@tufts.edu. *Application contact:* Emily Keily, Director of Admissions, 617-636-0935, Fax: 617-636-0898, E-mail: med-phpd@tufts.edu.
Website: http://publichealth.tufts.edu

**Tulane University,** School of Public Health and Tropical Medicine, New Orleans, LA 70112. Offers MHA, MPH, MPHTM, MS, MSPH, Dr PH, PhD, JD/MHA, JD/MPH, MBA/MHA, MD/MPH, MD/MPHTM, MD/MSPH, MSW/MPH. *Accreditation:* CAHME (one or more programs are accredited); CEPH. *Program availability:* Part-time, evening/weekend, 100% online, synchronous sessions. *Degree requirements:* For master's, comprehensive exam (for some programs); for doctorate, comprehensive exam, thesis/dissertation. *Entrance requirements:* For master's and doctorate, GRE General Test, career statement; letters of recommendation. Additional exam requirements/recommendations for international students: required—TOEFL, IELTS. Electronic applications accepted. *Expenses:* Contact institution.

**Uniformed Services University of the Health Sciences,** F. Edward Hebert School of Medicine, Graduate Programs in the Biomedical Sciences and Public Health, Bethesda, MD 20814. Offers emerging infectious diseases (PhD); medical and clinical psychology (PhD), including clinical psychology, medical psychology; medicine (MS, PhD), including health professions education; molecular and cell biology (MS, PhD); neuroscience (PhD); preventive medicine and biometrics (MPH, MS, MSPH, MTMH, PhD), including environmental health sciences (PhD), healthcare administration and policy (MS), medical zoology (PhD), public health (MPH, MSPH), tropical medicine and hygiene (MTMH). Terminal master's awarded for partial completion of doctoral program. *Degree requirements:* For master's, comprehensive exam, thesis or alternative; for doctorate, comprehensive exam, thesis/dissertation, qualifying exam. *Entrance requirements:* For master's, GRE General Test; for doctorate, GRE General Test, minimum GPA of 3.0. Electronic applications accepted. *Expenses:* Contact institution.

**Uniformed Services University of the Health Sciences,** F. Edward Hebert School of Medicine, Graduate Programs in the Biomedical Sciences and Public Health, Department of Preventive Medicine and Biostatistics, Program in Public Health, Bethesda, MD 20814-4799. Offers MPH, MSPH. *Accreditation:* CEPH (one or more programs are accredited). *Degree requirements:* For master's, comprehensive exam. *Entrance requirements:* For master's, GRE General Test. Additional exam requirements/recommendations for international students: required—TOEFL.

**Université de Montréal,** Faculty of Arts and Sciences, Program in Societies, Public Policies and Health, Montréal, QC H3C 3J7, Canada. Offers DESS.

**Université de Montréal,** Faculty of Medicine, Program in Communal and Public Health, Montréal, QC H3C 3J7, Canada. Offers community health (M Sc, DESS); public health (PhD). *Accreditation:* CEPH. *Program availability:* Part-time. Terminal master's awarded for partial completion of doctoral program. *Degree requirements:* For master's, thesis; for doctorate, thesis/dissertation, general exam. *Entrance requirements:* For master's and doctorate, proficiency in French, knowledge of English; for DESS, proficiency in French. Electronic applications accepted.

**University at Albany, State University of New York,** School of Public Health, Program in Public Health, Rensselaer, NY 12144. Offers MPH, Dr PH. *Accreditation:* CEPH. *Program availability:* Part-time, evening/weekend, online only, 100% online, blended/hybrid learning. *Faculty:* 10 full-time (3 women), 8 part-time/adjunct (5 women). *Students:* 123 full-time (95 women), 220 part-time (167 women); includes 124 minority (46 Black or African American, non-Hispanic/Latino; 40 Asian, non-Hispanic/Latino; 24 Hispanic/Latino; 14 Two or more races, non-Hispanic/Latino), 17 international. 295 applicants, 77% accepted, 113 enrolled. In 2019, 106 master's, 5 doctorates awarded. *Entrance requirements:* For master's, GPA of 3.0 or higher; transcripts of all schools attended; statement of background and goals; departmental questionnaire; resume; names and contact information for 3 recommenders; for doctorate, GRE General Test. Additional exam requirements/recommendations for international students: required—TOEFL (minimum score 550 paper-based; 98 iBT). *Application deadline:* For fall admission, 4/1 for domestic students, 5/1 for international students; for spring admission, 10/31 for domestic students, 11/1 for international students. Applications are processed on a rolling basis. Application fee: $75. Electronic applications accepted. *Expenses: Tuition, area resident:* Full-time $11,530; part-time $480 per credit hour. Tuition, nonresident: full-time $23,530; part-time $980 per credit hour. *International tuition:* $23,530 full-time. *Required fees:* $2185; $96 per credit hour. Part-time tuition and fees vary according to course load and program. *Financial support:* Application deadline: 5/30. *Unit head:* Dr. David Holtgrave, Dean, 518-402-0281, E-mail: dholtgrave@albany.edu. *Application contact:* Michael DeRensis, Director, Graduate Admissions, 518-442-3980, Fax: 518-442-3922, E-mail: graduate@albany.edu. Website: https://www.albany.edu/sph/programs/mph-public-health

**University at Buffalo, the State University of New York,** Graduate School, School of Public Health and Health Professions, Department of Epidemiology and Environmental Health, Buffalo, NY 14214. Offers epidemiology (MS, PhD); public health (MPH). *Accreditation:* CEPH. *Program availability:* Part-time. Terminal master's awarded for partial completion of doctoral program. *Entrance requirements:* For master's and doctorate, GRE General Test. Additional exam requirements/recommendations for international students: required—TOEFL (minimum score 600 paper-based; 100 iBT). Electronic applications accepted. *Expenses: Tuition, area resident:* Full-time $11,310; part-time $471 per credit hour. Tuition, state resident: full-time $11,310; part-time $471 per credit hour. Tuition, nonresident: full-time $23,100; part-time $963 per credit hour. *International tuition:* $23,100 full-time. *Required fees:* $2820.

**The University of Alabama at Birmingham,** School of Public Health, Program in Health Care Organization and Policy, Birmingham, AL 35294. Offers applied epidemiology and pharmacoepidemiology (MSPH); biostatistics (MPH); clinical and translational science (MSPH); environmental health (MPH); environmental health and toxicology (MSPH); epidemiology (MPH); general theory and practice (MPH); health behavior (MPH); health care organization (MPH, Dr PH); health policy (MPH); industrial hygiene (MPH, MSPH); maternal and child health policy (Dr PH); maternal and child health policy and leadership (MPH); occupational health and safety (MPH); outcomes research (MSPH, Dr PH); public health (PhD); public health preparedness management (MPH). *Accreditation:* CEPH. *Program availability:* Part-time, 100% online, blended/hybrid learning. *Faculty:* 14 full-time (6 women). *Students:* 53 full-time (37 women), 61 part-time (45 women); includes 37 minority (12 Black or African American, non-Hispanic/Latino; 20 Asian, non-Hispanic/Latino; 1 Hispanic/Latino; 4 Two or more races, non-Hispanic/Latino), 17 international. Average age 31. 136 applicants, 59% accepted, 44 enrolled. In 2019, 36 master's, 4 doctorates awarded. *Degree requirements:* For master's, comprehensive exam (for some programs), thesis (for some programs); for doctorate, comprehensive exam, thesis/dissertation. *Entrance requirements:* For doctorate, GRE. Additional exam requirements/recommendations for international students: required—TOEFL (minimum score 80 iBT), IELTS (minimum score 6.5). *Application deadline:* For fall admission, 4/1 priority date for domestic students, 4/1 for international students; for spring admission, 11/1 for domestic students; for summer admission, 4/1 for domestic students. Application fee: $50 ($60 for international students). Electronic applications accepted. *Financial support:* Fellowships, research assistantships, teaching assistantships, scholarships/grants, traineeships, and unspecified assistantships available. Financial award application deadline: 3/1; financial award applicants required to submit FAFSA. *Unit head:* Dr. Martha Wingate, Program Director, 205-934-6783, Fax: 205-975-5484, E-mail: mslay@uab.edu. *Application contact:* Dustin Shaw, Coordinator, Student Admissions and Record, 205-934-3939,

E-mail: bcampbel@uab.edu.
Website: http://www.soph.uab.edu

**University of Alaska Anchorage,** College of Health, Department of Health Sciences, Anchorage, AK 99508. Offers physician assistant (MS); public health practice (MPH); MSW/MPH. *Accreditation:* CEPH. *Program availability:* Part-time. *Degree requirements:* For master's, comprehensive exam, thesis. *Entrance requirements:* For master's, writing sample. Additional exam requirements/recommendations for international students: required—TOEFL (minimum score 550 paper-based).

**University of Alberta,** School of Public Health, Department of Public Health Sciences, Edmonton, AB T6G 2E1, Canada. Offers clinical epidemiology (M Sc, MPH); environmental and occupational health (MPH); environmental health sciences (M Sc); epidemiology (M Sc); global health (M Sc, MPH); health policy and management (MPH); health policy research (M Sc); health technology assessment (MPH); occupational health (M Sc); population health (M Sc); public health leadership (MPH); public health sciences (PhD); quantitative methods (MPH). *Accreditation:* CEPH. Terminal master's awarded for partial completion of doctoral program. *Degree requirements:* For master's, thesis (for some programs); for doctorate, thesis/dissertation. *Entrance requirements:* For master's, GMAT or GRE General Test. Additional exam requirements/recommendations for international students: required—TOEFL (minimum score 550 paper-based) or IELTS (minimum score 6). Electronic applications accepted.

**The University of Arizona,** Mel and Enid Zuckerman College of Public Health, Program in Public Health, Tucson, AZ 85721. Offers MPH, Dr PH, PhD. *Accreditation:* CEPH. *Entrance requirements:* Additional exam requirements/recommendations for international students: required—TOEFL (minimum score 550 paper-based; 79 iBT). Electronic applications accepted.

**University of Arkansas for Medical Sciences,** Fay W. Boozman College of Public Health, Little Rock, AR 72205-7199. Offers biostatistics (MPH); environmental and occupational health (MPH, Certificate); epidemiology (MPH, PhD); health behavior and health education (MPH); health policy and management (MPH); health promotion and prevention research (PhD); health services administration (MHSA); health systems research (PhD); public health (Certificate); public health leadership (Dr PH). *Accreditation:* CAHME; CEPH. *Program availability:* Part-time. *Degree requirements:* For master's, preceptorship, culminating experience, internship; for doctorate, comprehensive exam, capstone. *Entrance requirements:* For master's, GRE, GMAT, LSAT, PCAT, MCAT, DAT; for doctorate, GRE. Additional exam requirements/recommendations for international students: required—TOEFL (minimum score 80 iBT), IELTS. Electronic applications accepted. *Expenses:* Contact institution.

**The University of British Columbia,** Faculty of Medicine, School of Population and Public Health, Vancouver, BC V6T 1Z3, Canada. Offers health administration (MHA); health sciences (MH Sc); occupational and environmental hygiene (M Sc); population and public health (M Sc, MPH, PhD); MPH/MSN. *Program availability:* Online learning. *Degree requirements:* For master's, thesis (for some programs), major paper (MH Sc), research project (MHA); for doctorate, thesis/dissertation. *Entrance requirements:* For master's, GRE General Test or GMAT, PCAT, MCAT (for MHA), MD or equivalent (for MH Sc); 4-year undergraduate degree from accredited university with minimum B+ overall academic average and in math or statistics course at undergraduate level (for MPH); 4-year undergraduate degree from accredited university with minimum B+ overall academic average plus work experience (for MHA); for doctorate, master's degree from accredited university with minimum B+ overall academic average and in math or statistics course at undergraduate level. Additional exam requirements/recommendations for international students: required—TOEFL. Electronic applications accepted. *Expenses:* Contact institution.

**University of California, Berkeley,** Graduate Division, Haas School of Business and School of Public Health, Concurrent MBA/MPH Program, Berkeley, CA 94720. Offers MBA/MPH. *Accreditation:* AACSB. *Entrance requirements:* Additional exam requirements/recommendations for international students: required—TOEFL (minimum score 570 paper-based; 90 iBT); recommended—IELTS (minimum score 7). Electronic applications accepted. *Expenses:* Contact institution.

**University of California, Berkeley,** Graduate Division, School of Public Health, Programs in Public Health, Berkeley, CA 94720. Offers MPH, Dr PH. *Accreditation:* CEPH. *Program availability:* Blended/hybrid learning. *Degree requirements:* For doctorate, thesis/dissertation, exam. *Entrance requirements:* For doctorate, GRE General Test, minimum GPA of 3.0. Electronic applications accepted.

**University of California, Irvine,** Programs in Health Sciences, Program in Public Health, Irvine, CA 92697. Offers MPH, PhD. *Accreditation:* CEPH. *Students:* 75 full-time (52 women), 8 part-time (5 women); includes 55 minority (4 Black or African American, non-Hispanic/Latino; 24 Asian, non-Hispanic/Latino; 22 Hispanic/Latino; 1 Native Hawaiian or other Pacific Islander, non-Hispanic/Latino; 4 Two or more races, non-Hispanic/Latino), 9 international. Average age 28. 214 applicants, 57% accepted, 32 enrolled. In 2019, 23 master's, 3 doctorates awarded. Application fee: $120 ($140 for international students). *Unit head:* Bernadette Boden-Albala, Director and Founding Dean, 949-824-5735, E-mail: bbodenal@uci.edu. *Application contact:* Jacqueline Barruga, Director of Student Affairs, 949-824-0546, E-mail: barrugaj@exchange.uci.edu.
Website: http://publichealth.uci.edu/

**University of California, Irvine,** School of Social Ecology, Programs in Social Ecology, Irvine, CA 92697. Offers environmental analysis and design (PhD); epidemiology and public health (PhD); social ecology (PhD). *Students:* 19 full-time (15 women); includes 7 minority (3 Black or African American, non-Hispanic/Latino; 1 Asian, non-Hispanic/Latino; 2 Hispanic/Latino; 1 Two or more races, non-Hispanic/Latino), 2 international. Average age 29. 36 applicants, 28% accepted, 6 enrolled. In 2019, 1 doctorate awarded. Application fee: $120 ($140 for international students). *Unit head:* Tim-Allen Bruckner, Professor, 949-824-5797, Fax: 949-824-1845, E-mail: tim.bruckner@uci.edu. *Application contact:* Jennifer Craig, Director of Graduate Student Services, 949-824-5918, Fax: 949-824-1845, E-mail: craigj@uci.edu.
Website: http://socialecology.uci.edu/core/graduate-se-core-programs

**University of California, Los Angeles,** Graduate Division, Fielding School of Public Health, Los Angeles, CA 90095. Offers MPH, MS, D Env, Dr PH, PhD, JD/MPH, MA/MPH, MBA/MPH, MD/MPH, MD/PhD, MSW/MPH. *Accreditation:* CEPH (one or more programs are accredited). *Degree requirements:* For doctorate, thesis/dissertation, oral and written qualifying exams. *Entrance requirements:* For master's, GRE General Test, minimum GPA of 3.0; for doctorate, GRE General Test, minimum undergraduate GPA of 3.0. Electronic applications accepted.

**University of California, San Diego,** Graduate Division, Program in Public Health, La Jolla, CA 92093. Offers epidemiology (PhD); global health (PhD); health behavior (PhD). *Students:* 19 full-time (13 women), 16 part-time (12 women). In 2019, 9 doctorates awarded. *Degree requirements:* For doctorate, thesis/dissertation, 2 semesters/quarters of teaching assistantship. *Entrance requirements:* For doctorate, GRE General Test, minimum GPA of 3.0, curriculum vitae or resume, letters of recommendation, statement of purpose. Additional exam requirements/recommendations for international students: required—TOEFL (minimum score 550 paper-based; 80 iBT), IELTS (minimum score 7).

Electronic applications accepted. *Financial support:* Teaching assistantships available. Financial award applicants required to submit FAFSA. *Unit head:* David Strong, Faculty Director, 858-657-5241, E-mail: dstrong@ucsd.edu. *Application contact:* Carrie Goldsmith, Graduate Coordinator, 858-246-5423, E-mail: publichealthjdp@ucsd.edu. Website: http://publichealth.ucsd.edu/jdp/

**University of Cincinnati,** Graduate School, College of Education, Criminal Justice, and Human Services, School of Human Services, Health Promotion and Education Program, Cincinnati, OH 45221. Offers exercise and fitness (MS); health education (PhD); public and community health (MS); public health (MPH). *Accreditation:* NCATE. *Program availability:* Part-time, evening/weekend. *Degree requirements:* For master's, thesis or alternative; for doctorate, thesis/dissertation. *Entrance requirements:* For master's and doctorate, GRE General Test. Additional exam requirements/recommendations for international students: required—TOEFL (minimum score 580 paper-based). Electronic applications accepted.

**University of Colorado Denver,** Colorado School of Public Health, Program in Public Health, Aurora, CO 80045. Offers community and behavioral health (MPH, Dr PH). *Accreditation:* CEPH. *Program availability:* Part-time, evening/weekend. *Degree requirements:* For master's, thesis or alternative, 42 credit hours; for doctorate, comprehensive exam, thesis/dissertation, 67 credit hours. *Entrance requirements:* For master's, GRE, MCAT, DAT, LSAT, PCAT, GMAT or master's degree from accredited institution, baccalaureate degree or equivalent; minimum GPA of 3.0; transcripts; references; resume; essay; for doctorate, GRE, MCAT, DAT, LSAT, PCAT or GMAT, MPH or master's or higher degree in related field or equivalent; 2 years of previous work experience in public health; essay; resume. Additional exam requirements/ recommendations for international students: required—TOEFL (minimum score 550 paper-based; 80 iBT). Tuition and fees vary according to course load, program and reciprocity agreements.

**University of Connecticut Health Center,** Graduate School, Program in Public Health, Farmington, CT 06030. Offers MPH, DMD/MPH, MD/MPH. *Accreditation:* CEPH. *Program availability:* Part-time, evening/weekend. *Degree requirements:* For master's, thesis optional. *Entrance requirements:* For master's, GRE. Additional exam requirements/recommendations for international students: required—TOEFL (minimum score 600 paper-based). Electronic applications accepted.

**University of Florida,** College of Medicine, Program in Clinical Investigation, Gainesville, FL 32611. Offers clinical investigation (MS); epidemiology (MS); public health (MPH). *Program availability:* Part-time. *Entrance requirements:* For master's, GRE, MD, PhD, DMD/DDS or Pharm D.

**University of Florida,** Graduate School, College of Public Health and Health Professions, Programs in Public Health, Gainesville, FL 32611. Offers biostatistics (MPH); clinical and translational science (PhD); environmental health (MPH); epidemiology (MPH); health management and policy (MPH); public health (MPH, PhD, Certificate); public health practice (MPH); rehabilitation science (PhD); social and behavioral sciences (MPH); DPT/MPH; DVM/MPH; JD/MPH; MD/MPH; Pharm D/MPH. *Accreditation:* CEPH. *Program availability:* Online learning. *Degree requirements:* For master's, internship. *Entrance requirements:* For master's, GRE General Test, minimum GPA of 3.0. Additional exam requirements/recommendations for international students: required—TOEFL (minimum score 550 paper-based; 80 iBT), IELTS (minimum score 6).

**University of Georgia,** College of Public Health, Doctor of Public Health Program, Athens, GA 30602. Offers Dr PH.

**University of Hawaii at Manoa,** John A. Burns School of Medicine, Department of Public Health Sciences and Epidemiology, Honolulu, HI 96822. Offers epidemiology (PhD); global health and population studies (Graduate Certificate); public health (MPH, MS, Dr PH). *Accreditation:* CEPH. *Program availability:* Part-time. *Entrance requirements:* Additional exam requirements/recommendations for international students: required—TOEFL (minimum score 550 paper-based; 79 iBT), IELTS (minimum score 5).

**University of Illinois at Chicago,** School of Public Health, Chicago, IL 60607-7128. Offers MHA, MPH, MS, Dr PH, PhD, DDS/MPH, MBA/MPH, MD/PhD, MPH/MS. *Accreditation:* CEPH. *Program availability:* Part-time. Terminal master's awarded for partial completion of doctoral program. *Degree requirements:* For master's, thesis, field practicum; for doctorate, thesis/dissertation, independent research, internship. *Entrance requirements:* For master's and doctorate, GRE General Test, minimum GPA of 2.75. Additional exam requirements/recommendations for international students: required—TOEFL. Electronic applications accepted. *Expenses:* Contact institution.

**University of Illinois at Springfield,** Graduate Programs, College of Public Affairs and Administration, Program in Public Health, Springfield, IL 62703-5407. Offers community health education (Graduate Certificate); emergency preparedness and homeland security (Graduate Certificate); environmental health (MPH, Graduate Certificate); environmental risk assessment (Graduate Certificate); epidemiology (Graduate Certificate); public health (MPH). *Program availability:* Part-time, 100% online. *Faculty:* 7 full-time (5 women). *Students:* 31 full-time (24 women), 36 part-time (27 women); includes 13 minority (9 Black or African American, non-Hispanic/Latino; 1 Asian, non-Hispanic/Latino; 1 Hispanic/Latino; 2 Two or more races, non-Hispanic/Latino), 27 international. Average age 30. 90 applicants, 54% accepted, 12 enrolled. In 2019, 13 master's, 10 other advanced degrees awarded. *Degree requirements:* For master's, comprehensive exam, internship. *Entrance requirements:* For master's, GRE, minimum undergraduate GPA of 3.0, 3 letters of recommendation, essay addressing the areas outlined on the department application form. Additional exam requirements/ recommendations for international students: required—TOEFL (minimum score 500 paper-based; 61 iBT). *Application deadline:* Applications are processed on a rolling basis. Application fee: $60 ($75 for international students). Electronic applications accepted. *Expenses:* $33.25 per credit hour (online fee). *Financial support:* In 2019–20, research assistantships with full tuition reimbursements (averaging $10,562 per year), teaching assistantships with full tuition reimbursements (averaging $10,652 per year) were awarded; fellowships, career-related internships or fieldwork, Federal Work-Study, scholarships/grants, health care benefits, and unspecified assistantships also available. Support available to part-time students. Financial award application deadline: 11/15; financial award applicants required to submit FAFSA. *Unit head:* Dr. Josiah Alamu, Program Administrator, 217-206-7874, Fax: 217-206-7279, E-mail: jalam3@uis.edu. *Application contact:* Dr. Josiah Alamu, Program Administrator, 217-206-7874, Fax: 217-206-7279, E-mail: jalam3@uis.edu.
Website: http://www.uis.edu/publichealth/

**University of Illinois at Urbana-Champaign,** Graduate College, College of Applied Health Sciences, Department of Kinesiology and Community Health, Champaign, IL 61820. Offers community health (MS, MSPH, PhD); kinesiology (MS, PhD); public health (MPH); rehabilitation (MS); PhD/MPH.

**University of Indianapolis,** Graduate Programs, College of Health Sciences, Program in Public Health, Indianapolis, IN 46227-3697. Offers MPH. *Degree requirements:* For master's, capstone.

**The University of Iowa,** College of Dentistry and Graduate College, Graduate Programs in Dentistry, Department of Preventive and Community Dentistry, Iowa City, IA 52242-1316. Offers dental public health (MS). *Degree requirements:* For master's, thesis. *Entrance requirements:* For master's, GRE, DDS. Additional exam requirements/ recommendations for international students: required—TOEFL.

**The University of Iowa,** Graduate College, College of Public Health, Iowa City, IA 52242-1316. Offers MHA, MPH, MS, PhD, Certificate, DVM/MPH, JD/MHA, JD/MPH, MBA/MHA, MD/MPH, MHA/MA, MS/MA, MS/MS, Pharm D/MPH. *Accreditation:* CEPH. *Degree requirements:* For master's, exam; for doctorate, comprehensive exam, thesis/ dissertation. *Entrance requirements:* For master's and doctorate, GRE General Test, minimum GPA of 3.0. Additional exam requirements/recommendations for international students: required—TOEFL. Electronic applications accepted. *Expenses:* Contact institution.

**The University of Kansas,** University of Kansas Medical Center, School of Medicine, Department of Population Health, Kansas City, KS 66160. Offers clinical research (MS); epidemiology (MPH); public health management (MPH); social and behavioral health (MPH); MD/MPH; PhD/MPH. *Accreditation:* CEPH. *Program availability:* Part-time. *Faculty:* 100. *Students:* 73 full-time (54 women), 49 part-time (35 women); includes 37 minority (9 Black or African American, non-Hispanic/Latino; 3 American Indian or Alaska Native, non-Hispanic/Latino; 9 Asian, non-Hispanic/Latino; 11 Hispanic/Latino; 5 Two or more races, non-Hispanic/Latino), 5 international. Average age 30. In 2019, 52 master's awarded. *Degree requirements:* For master's, thesis, capstone practicum defense. *Entrance requirements:* For master's, GRE for MHSA Program; GRE for MPH Program; GRE, MCAT, LSAT, GMAT or other equivalent graduate professional exam for MS Clinical Research Program. Additional exam requirements/recommendations for international students: required—TOEFL. *Application deadline:* For fall admission, 3/1 for domestic and international students; for spring admission, 11/1 for domestic and international students. Applications are processed on a rolling basis. Application fee: $60. Electronic applications accepted. *Expenses:* Tuition, state resident: full-time $9989. Tuition, nonresident: full-time $23,950. *International tuition:* $23,950 full-time. *Required fees:* $984; $81.99 per credit hour. Tuition and fees vary according to course load, campus/location and program. *Financial support:* Research assistantships, career-related internships or fieldwork, Federal Work-Study, scholarships/grants, and unspecified assistantships available. Support available to part-time students. Financial award application deadline: 3/1; financial award applicants required to submit FAFSA. *Unit head:* Dr. Edward F. Ellerbeck, Professor and Chair, 913-588-2775, Fax: 913-588-2780, E-mail: eellerbe@kumc.edu. *Application contact:* Dr. Edward F. Ellerbeck, Professor and Chair, 913-588-2775, Fax: 913-588-2780, E-mail: eellerbe@kumc.edu.
Website: http://www.kumc.edu/school-of-medicine/population-health.html

**University of Kentucky,** Graduate School, College of Public Health, Program in Public Health, Lexington, KY 40506-0032. Offers MPH, Dr PH. *Accreditation:* CEPH. *Entrance requirements:* For master's, GRE General Test, minimum undergraduate GPA of 2.75. Additional exam requirements/recommendations for international students: required—TOEFL (minimum score 550 paper-based). Electronic applications accepted.

**University of La Verne,** College of Business and Public Management, Master's Program in Public Administration, La Verne, CA 91750-4443. Offers gerontology (MPA); nonprofit (MPA); public health (MPA); urban management and affairs (MPA). *Accreditation:* NASPAA. *Program availability:* Part-time. *Entrance requirements:* For master's, minimum undergraduate GPA of 3.0, statement of purpose, 2 letters of recommendation, resume. Additional exam requirements/recommendations for international students: required—TOEFL (minimum score 550 paper-based). *Expenses:* Contact institution.

**University of Louisville,** Graduate School, School of Public Health and Information Sciences, Department of Environmental and Occupational Health Sciences, Louisville, KY 40202. Offers environmental and occupational health sciences (MPH); public health (PhD), including environmental health. *Accreditation:* CEPH. *Faculty:* 3 full-time (1 woman), 2 part-time/adjunct (0 women). *Students:* 4 full-time (2 women), 2 international. Average age 33. 2 applicants, 50% accepted, 1 enrolled. *Degree requirements:* For doctorate, comprehensive exam, thesis/dissertation. *Entrance requirements:* For doctorate, bachelor's degree from an accredited institution or its equivalent with emphasis in sciences. Recommended minimum GPA of 3.0 on a 4.0 scale. Three letters of recommendation (professional or academic) written within the last twelve months. Official transcripts of all degrees. One-page personal statement. Additional exam requirements/recommendations for international students: required—TOEFL (minimum score 90 iBT). *Application deadline:* For fall admission, 5/1 for domestic and international students. Applications are processed on a rolling basis. Application fee: $65. Electronic applications accepted. *Expenses: Tuition, area resident:* Full-time $13,000; part-time $723 per credit hour. Tuition, state resident: full-time $13,000; part-time $723 per credit hour. Tuition, nonresident: full-time $27,114; part-time $1507 per credit hour. *International tuition:* $27,114 full-time. *Required fees:* $196. Tuition and fees vary according to program and reciprocity agreements. *Financial support:* In 2019–20, 2 students received support, including 1 research assistantship with full tuition reimbursement available (averaging $20,000 per year); fellowships, scholarships/grants, and unspecified assistantships also available. Financial award application deadline: 1/ 15; financial award applicants required to submit FAFSA. *Unit head:* Dr. Gary W. Hoyle, Professor & Acting Chair, 502-852-7337, Fax: 502-852-3291, E-mail: gary.hoyle@ louisville.edu. *Application contact:* Barbara Parker, Administrative Specialist, 502-852-3290, Fax: 502-852-3291, E-mail: barbara.parker@louisville.edu.
Website: http://louisville.edu/sphis/departments/environmental-occupational-health-sciences

**University of Louisville,** Graduate School, School of Public Health and Information Sciences, Department of Epidemiology and Population Health, Louisville, KY 40292-0001. Offers epidemiology (MPH, MS); public health sciences (PhD), including epidemiology. *Faculty:* 7 full-time (5 women). *Students:* 1 (woman) full-time, 29 part-time (23 women); includes 5 minority (1 Black or African American, non-Hispanic/Latino; 1 Asian, non-Hispanic/Latino; 1 Hispanic/Latino; 2 Two or more races, non-Hispanic/ Latino), 5 international. Average age 36. 13 applicants, 92% accepted, 8 enrolled. In 2019, 8 master's awarded. *Degree requirements:* For master's, thesis; for doctorate, thesis/dissertation. *Entrance requirements:* For master's, GRE (taken within past 5 years), bachelor's degree from an accredited institution or its equivalent, recommended minimum GPA of 3.0 on a 4.0 scale, 2 letters of recommendation written within the last twelve months, official transcripts of all degrees, one-page personal statement. Additional exam requirements/recommendations for international students: required—TOEFL (minimum score 90 iBT). *Application deadline:* For fall admission, 4/1 for domestic students, 1/2 priority date for international students. Applications are processed on a rolling basis. Application fee: $65. Electronic applications accepted. *Expenses: Tuition, area resident:* Full-time $13,000; part-time $723 per credit hour. Tuition, state resident: full-time $13,000; part-time $723 per credit hour. Tuition, nonresident: full-time $27,114; part-time $1507 per credit hour. *International tuition:* $27,114 full-time. *Required fees:* $196. Tuition and fees vary according to program and reciprocity agreements. *Financial support:* In 2019–20, 29 students received support, including 1 fellowship with full tuition reimbursement available (averaging $20,000 per year), 3 research assistantships with full tuition reimbursements available (averaging $20,000 per year); tuition waivers (partial) also available. Financial award application deadline: 3/1; financial award applicants required to submit FAFSA. *Unit head:* Dr.

Richard N Baumgartner, PhD, Professor and Chair, 502-852-3003, Fax: 502-852-3291, E-mail: rnbaum01@gwise.louisville.edu. *Application contact:* Robin Newlon, Administrative Specialist, 502-852-3003, Fax: 502-852-3294, E-mail: robin.newlon@louisville.edu.
Website: http://louisville.edu/sphis/departments/epidemiology-population-health

**University of Louisville,** Graduate School, School of Public Health and Information Sciences, Department of Health Management and Systems Sciences, Louisville, KY 40202. Offers health policy (MPH); population health management (MPH); public health sciences (PhD), including health management and policy. *Program availability:* Part-time, evening/weekend. *Faculty:* 11 full-time (4 women), 5 part-time/adjunct (3 women). *Students:* 20 full-time (16 women), 6 part-time (5 women); includes 6 minority (3 Black or African American, non-Hispanic/Latino; 1 Asian, non-Hispanic/Latino; 1 Hispanic/Latino; 1 Two or more races, non-Hispanic/Latino), 1 international. Average age 31. 21 applicants, 76% accepted, 12 enrolled. In 2019, 10 master's awarded. *Degree requirements:* For master's, comprehensive exam (for some programs); for doctorate, comprehensive exam, thesis/dissertation. *Entrance requirements:* For master's, GRE, GMAT, MCAT, LSAT, or DAT, bachelor's degree from an accredited institution or its equivalent, recommended minimum GPA of 3.0 on a 4.0 scale; for doctorate, Graduate Record Examination (GRE), Medical College Admission Test (MCAT), Dental Admissions Test (DAT), minimum of 3.0 on 4.0 scale for both undergraduate and graduate GPA. Additional exam requirements/recommendations for international students: required—TOEFL (minimum score 90 iBT). *Application deadline:* For fall admission, 7/1 for domestic students, 3/1 priority date for international students. Applications are processed on a rolling basis. Application fee: $65. Electronic applications accepted. *Expenses: Tuition, area resident:* Full-time $13,000; part-time $723 per credit hour. Tuition, state resident: full-time $13,000; part-time $723 per credit hour. Tuition, nonresident: full-time $27,114; part-time $1507 per credit hour. *International tuition:* $27,114 full-time. *Required fees:* $196. Tuition and fees vary according to program and reciprocity agreements. *Financial support:* In 2019–20, 7 students received support, including 1 fellowship with full tuition reimbursement available (averaging $20,000 per year), 5 research assistantships with full tuition reimbursements available (averaging $20,000 per year); scholarships/grants and unspecified assistantships also available. Financial award application deadline: 3/1; financial award applicants required to submit FAFSA. *Unit head:* Dr. Christopher Elliot Johnson, Ph.D., Professor and Chair, 502-852-3987, Fax: 502-852-3294, E-mail: christopher-e.johnson@lousiville.edu. *Application contact:* Darla Dale Samuelsen, Program Coordinator, Sr., 502-852-2797, Fax: 502-852-3294, E-mail: darla.samuelsen@louisville.edu.
Website: http://louisville.edu/sphis/departments/health-management-systems-science

**University of Lynchburg,** Graduate Studies, Master of Public Health Program, Lynchburg, VA 24501-3199. Offers public health (MPH), including health promotion. *Program availability:* Part-time. *Degree requirements:* For master's, internship, capstone project. *Entrance requirements:* For master's, GRE. Additional exam requirements/recommendations for international students: required—TOEFL (minimum score 550 paper-based; 80 iBT), IELTS (minimum score 6). Electronic applications accepted. Application fee is waived when completed online. *Expenses:* Contact institution.

**The University of Manchester,** School of Dentistry, Manchester, United Kingdom. Offers basic dental sciences (cancer studies) (M Phil, PhD); basic dental sciences (molecular genetics) (M Phil, PhD); basic dental sciences (stem cell biology) (M Phil, PhD); biomaterials sciences and dental technology (M Phil, PhD); dental public health/community dentistry (M Phil, PhD); dental science (clinical) (PhD); endodontology (M Phil, PhD); fixed and removable prosthodontics (M Phil, PhD); operative dentistry (M Phil, PhD); oral and maxillofacial surgery (M Phil, PhD); oral radiology (M Phil, PhD); orthodontics (M Phil, PhD); restorative dentistry (M Phil, PhD).

**University of Maryland, College Park,** Academic Affairs, School of Public Health, College Park, MD 20742. Offers MA, MHA, MPH, MS, PhD. *Accreditation:* CEPH. *Program availability:* Part-time, evening/weekend. *Degree requirements:* For doctorate, thesis/dissertation. *Entrance requirements:* For master's and doctorate, GRE General Test, minimum GPA of 3.0, 3 letters of recommendation. Additional exam requirements/recommendations for international students: required—TOEFL. Electronic applications accepted.

**University of Massachusetts Amherst,** Graduate School, Interdisciplinary Programs, Dual Degree Program in Public Policy and Administration and Public Health, Amherst, MA 01003. Offers MPH/MPPA. *Entrance requirements:* Additional exam requirements/recommendations for international students: required—TOEFL (minimum score 550 paper-based; 80 iBT), IELTS (minimum score 6.5). Electronic applications accepted.

**University of Massachusetts Amherst,** Graduate School, School of Public Health and Health Sciences, Department of Public Health, Amherst, MA 01003. Offers biostatistics (MPH, MS, PhD); community health education (MPH, MS, PhD); environmental health sciences (MPH, MS, PhD); epidemiology (MPH, MS, PhD); health policy and management (MPH, MS, PhD); nutrition (MPH, PhD); public health practice (MPH); MPH/MPPA. *Accreditation:* CEPH. *Program availability:* Part-time, evening/weekend, online learning. Terminal master's awarded for partial completion of doctoral program. *Degree requirements:* For master's, thesis (for some programs); for doctorate, comprehensive exam, thesis/dissertation. *Entrance requirements:* For master's and doctorate, GRE General Test. Additional exam requirements/recommendations for international students: required—TOEFL (minimum score 550 paper-based; 80 iBT), IELTS (minimum score 6.5). Electronic applications accepted.

**University of Memphis,** Graduate School, School of Public Health, Memphis, TN 38152. Offers biostatistics (MPH); environmental health (MPH); epidemiology (MPH, PhD); health systems and policy (PhD); health systems management (MPH); public health (MHA); social and behavioral sciences (MPH, PhD). *Accreditation:* CAHME; CEPH. *Program availability:* Part-time, evening/weekend, online learning. *Faculty:* 20 full-time (7 women), 10 part-time/adjunct (4 women). *Students:* 126 full-time (80 women), 77 part-time (60 women); includes 70 minority (40 Black or African American, non-Hispanic/Latino; 17 Asian, non-Hispanic/Latino; 9 Hispanic/Latino; 4 Two or more races, non-Hispanic/Latino), 29 international. Average age 30. 105 applicants, 97% accepted, 67 enrolled. In 2019, 47 master's, 9 doctorates awarded. *Degree requirements:* For master's, comprehensive exam, thesis (for some programs), practicum/field experience; for doctorate, comprehensive exam, thesis/dissertation, residency. *Entrance requirements:* For master's, GRE or GMAT, letters of recommendation; letter of intent; for doctorate, GRE, letters of recommendation; personal statement. Additional exam requirements/recommendations for international students: required—TOEFL (minimum score 550 paper-based; 79 iBT). *Application deadline:* For fall admission, 4/1 for domestic students; for spring admission, 11/1 for domestic students. Application fee: $35 ($60 for international students). Electronic applications accepted. *Expenses: Tuition, area resident:* Full-time $9216; part-time $512 per credit hour. Tuition, state resident: full-time $9216; part-time $512 per credit hour. Tuition, nonresident: full-time $12,672; part-time $704 per credit hour. *International tuition:* $16,128 full-time. *Required fees:* $1530; $85 per credit hour. Tuition and fees vary according to program. *Financial support:* Research assistantships with full tuition reimbursements, Federal Work-Study, scholarships/grants, and unspecified assistantships available. Financial award application deadline: 2/1; financial award applicants required to submit FAFSA. *Unit head:* Dr. James Gurney, Dean, 901-678-1673, E-mail: jggurney@memphis.edu. *Application contact:* Dr. Marian Levy, Associate Dean, 901-678-4514, E-mail: mlevy@memphis.edu.
Website: http://www.memphis.edu/sph/

**University of Miami,** Graduate School, Miller School of Medicine, Graduate Programs in Medicine, Department of Public Health Sciences, Miami, FL 33124. Offers biostatistics (MS, PhD); climate and health (MS); epidemiology (PhD); epidemiology, biostatistics, prevention science and community health (MD/PhD); generalist (MPH, MSPH); prevention science and community health (MS, PhD); JD/MPH; MD/MPH; MD/PhD; MPA/MPH; MPH/MAIA. *Accreditation:* CEPH (one or more programs are accredited). *Faculty:* 35 full-time (15 women), 24 part-time/adjunct (14 women). *Students:* 328 full-time (216 women), 30 part-time (25 women); includes 169 minority (35 Black or African American, non-Hispanic/Latino; 1 American Indian or Alaska Native, non-Hispanic/Latino; 40 Asian, non-Hispanic/Latino; 68 Hispanic/Latino; 7 Native Hawaiian or other Pacific Islander, non-Hispanic/Latino; 18 Two or more races, non-Hispanic/Latino), 41 international. In 2019, 109 master's, 9 doctorates awarded. *Degree requirements:* For master's, thesis (for some programs), project, practicum; for doctorate, comprehensive exam, thesis/dissertation. *Entrance requirements:* For master's, GRE General Test, MCAT, LSAT (for joint MPH/JD applicants), minimum GPA of 3.0, official transcripts, statement of purpose, 3 letters of recommendation, resume/CV; for doctorate, GRE General Test, minimum GPA of 3.0, pre-requisite coursework, 3 letters of recommendation, official transcripts, resume/CV. Additional exam requirements/recommendations for international students: required—TOEFL (minimum score 550 paper-based; 80 iBT). Application fee: $135. Electronic applications accepted. *Unit head:* Dr. David Lee, Chair, E-mail: dlee@med.miami.edu. *Application contact:* Andria Williams, Director of Admissions, 305-243-0291, E-mail: alw157@med.miami.edu.
Website: https://www.publichealth.med.miami.edu/

**University of Michigan,** School of Public Health, Ann Arbor, MI 48109. Offers MHSA, MPH, MS, PhD, JD/MHSA, MD/MPH, MHSA/MBA, MHSA/MPP, MPH/MSIOE, MPH/JD, MPH/MA, MPH/MBA, MPH/MPP, MPH/MS, MPH/MSW. *Accreditation:* CAHME (one or more programs are accredited); CEPH (one or more programs are accredited). *Program availability:* Evening/weekend. Terminal master's awarded for partial completion of doctoral program. *Degree requirements:* For master's, internship; for doctorate, oral defense of dissertation, preliminary exam. *Entrance requirements:* For master's and doctorate, GRE General Test. Additional exam requirements/recommendations for international students: required—TOEFL (minimum score 100 iBT). Electronic applications accepted.

**University of Michigan–Flint,** College of Health Sciences, Program in Public Health, Flint, MI 48502-1950. Offers health administration (MPH); health education (MPH). *Program availability:* Part-time. *Faculty:* 15 full-time (11 women), 29 part-time/adjunct (15 women). *Students:* 19 full-time (16 women), 23 part-time (20 women); includes 15 minority (9 Black or African American, non-Hispanic/Latino; 2 Asian, non-Hispanic/Latino; 4 Hispanic/Latino), 5 international. Average age 32. 43 applicants, 65% accepted, 9 enrolled. In 2019, 22 master's awarded. *Entrance requirements:* For master's, bachelor's degree from accredited institution with sufficient preparation in algebra to succeed in epidemiology and biostatistics; minimum overall undergraduate GPA of 3.0; completion of BIO 104 or an equivalent course in anatomy and physiology. Additional exam requirements/recommendations for international students: required—TOEFL (minimum score 84 iBT), IELTS (minimum score 6.5). *Application deadline:* For fall admission, 8/1 for domestic students, 5/1 for international students; for winter admission, 11/15 for domestic students, 10/1 for international students; for spring admission, 3/15 for domestic students, 1/1 for international students. Applications are processed on a rolling basis. Application fee: $55. Electronic applications accepted. *Expenses:* Contact institution. *Financial support:* Federal Work-Study, scholarships/grants, and unspecified assistantships available. Support available to part-time students. Financial award application deadline: 3/1; financial award applicants required to submit FAFSA. *Unit head:* Dr. Shan Parker, Director, 810-762-3172, E-mail: shanpark@umflint.edu. *Application contact:* Matt Bohlen, Director of Graduate Admissions, 810-762-3171, Fax: 810-766-6789, E-mail: mbohlen@umflint.edu.
Website: http://www.umflint.edu/graduateprograms/public-health-mph

**University of Minnesota, Twin Cities Campus,** School of Public Health, Minneapolis, MN 55455. Offers MHA, MPH, MS, PhD, Certificate, DVM/MPH, JD/MS, JD/PhD, MD/MPH, MD/PhD, MPH/JD, MPH/MS, MPH/MSN, MPP/MS. *Accreditation:* CEPH (one or more programs are accredited). *Program availability:* Part-time, online learning. Terminal master's awarded for partial completion of doctoral program. *Degree requirements:* For doctorate, thesis/dissertation. *Entrance requirements:* For master's and doctorate, GRE General Test. Additional exam requirements/recommendations for international students: required—TOEFL. Electronic applications accepted. *Expenses:* Contact institution.

**University of Missouri,** School of Health Professions, Master of Public Health Program, Columbia, MO 65211. Offers global public health (Graduate Certificate); health promotion and policy (MPH); public health (Graduate Certificate); veterinary public health (MPH); DVM/MPH; MPH/MA; MPH/MPA. *Accreditation:* CEPH. *Entrance requirements:* Additional exam requirements/recommendations for international students: required—TOEFL (minimum score 550 paper-based; 80 iBT), IELTS (minimum score 6.5). Electronic applications accepted.

**University of Montana,** Graduate School, College of Health Professions and Biomedical Sciences, School of Public and Community Health Sciences, Missoula, MT 59812. Offers public health (MPH, CPH). *Accreditation:* CEPH. *Program availability:* Part-time, online learning.

**University of Nebraska Medical Center,** College of Public Health, Omaha, NE 68198-4355. Offers MPH. *Accreditation:* CEPH. *Program availability:* Part-time, online learning. *Degree requirements:* For master's, service-learning capstone course. *Entrance requirements:* Additional exam requirements/recommendations for international students: required—TOEFL (minimum score 550 paper-based). Electronic applications accepted.

**University of Nevada, Las Vegas,** Graduate College, School of Public Health, Department of Environmental and Occupational Health, Las Vegas, NV 89154-3064. Offers infection prevention (Certificate); public health (MPH, PhD, Certificate). *Program availability:* Part-time. *Faculty:* 8 full-time (3 women), 3 part-time/adjunct (1 woman). *Students:* 54 full-time (42 women), 43 part-time (36 women); includes 46 minority (14 Black or African American, non-Hispanic/Latino; 9 Asian, non-Hispanic/Latino; 13 Hispanic/Latino; 2 Native Hawaiian or other Pacific Islander, non-Hispanic/Latino; 8 Two or more races, non-Hispanic/Latino), 11 international. Average age 32. 46 applicants, 74% accepted, 24 enrolled. In 2019, 15 master's, 4 doctorates, 2 other advanced degrees awarded. *Degree requirements:* For master's, thesis; for doctorate, comprehensive exam, thesis/dissertation. *Entrance requirements:* For master's, GRE General Test, bachelor's degree with minimum GPA 3.0; personal essay; 3 letters of recommendation; for doctorate, GRE General Test, bachelor's degree; master's degree with minimum GPA of 3.0; 3 letters of recommendation; personal interview. Additional exam requirements/recommendations for international students: required—TOEFL

(minimum score 550 paper-based; 85 iBT), IELTS (minimum score 7). *Application deadline:* For fall admission, 3/1 for domestic students, 4/1 for international students; for spring admission, 10/1 for domestic and international students. Application fee: $60 ($95 for international students). Electronic applications accepted. *Expenses:* Contact institution. *Financial support:* In 2019–20, 31 students received support, including 1 fellowship with full tuition reimbursement available (averaging $20,000 per year), 22 research assistantships with full tuition reimbursements available (averaging $14,409 per year), 8 teaching assistantships with full tuition reimbursements available (averaging $12,323 per year); institutionally sponsored loans, scholarships/grants, health care benefits, and unspecified assistantships also available. Financial award application deadline: 3/15; financial award applicants required to submit FAFSA. *Unit head:* Dr. Francisco Sy, Chair, 702-895-5420, Fax: 702-895-5184, E-mail: eoh.chair@unlv.edu. *Application contact:* Dr. Jennifer Pharr, Graduate Coordinator, 702-895-2006, Fax: 702-895-5184, E-mail: eoh.gradcoord@unlv.edu.

**University of Nevada, Reno,** Graduate School, Division of Health Sciences, School of Community Health Sciences, Reno, NV 89557. Offers MPH, PhD, MPH/MSN. *Accreditation:* CEPH. Terminal master's awarded for partial completion of doctoral program. *Degree requirements:* For master's, thesis optional; for doctorate, thesis/dissertation. *Entrance requirements:* For master's, GRE General Test, GMAT, LSAT, MCAT or DAT, minimum GPA of 2.75; for doctorate, GRE General Test, GMAT, LSAT, MCAT or DAT, minimum GPA of 3.0. Additional exam requirements/recommendations for international students: required—TOEFL (minimum score 500 paper-based; 61 iBT), IELTS (minimum score 6). Electronic applications accepted.

**University of New England,** College of Graduate and Professional Studies, Portland, ME 04005-9526. Offers advanced educational leadership (CAGS); applied nutrition (MS); career and technical education (MS Ed); curriculum and instruction (MS Ed); education (CAGS, Post-Master's Certificate); educational leadership (MS Ed, Ed D); generalist (MS Ed); health informatics (MS, Graduate Certificate); inclusion education (MS Ed); literacy K-12 (MS Ed); medical education leadership (MMEL); public health (MPH, Graduate Certificate); reading specialist (MS Ed); social work (MSW). *Program availability:* Part-time, evening/weekend, online only, 100% online. *Faculty:* 2 full-time (1 woman), 63 part-time/adjunct (44 women). *Students:* 1,001 full-time (795 women), 470 part-time (378 women); includes 306 minority (211 Black or African American, non-Hispanic/Latino; 12 American Indian or Alaska Native, non-Hispanic/Latino; 61 Asian, non-Hispanic/Latino; 14 Hispanic/Latino; 4 Native Hawaiian or other Pacific Islander, non-Hispanic/Latino; 4 Two or more races, non-Hispanic/Latino). Average age 36. In 2019, 614 master's, 85 doctorates, 79 other advanced degrees awarded. *Application deadline:* Applications are processed on a rolling basis. Electronic applications accepted. *Financial support:* Application deadline: 5/1; applicants required to submit FAFSA. *Unit head:* Dr. Martha Wilson, Dean of the College of Graduate and Professional Studies, 207-221-4985, E-mail: mwilson13@une.edu. *Application contact:* Nicole Lindsay, Director of Online Admissions, 207-221-4966, E-mail: nlindsay1@une.edu.
Website: http://online.une.edu

**University of New Hampshire,** Graduate School, College of Health and Human Services, Department of Health Management and Policy, Durham, NH 03824. Offers public health (MPH, Postbaccalaureate Certificate). *Accreditation:* CEPH. *Program availability:* Part-time, evening/weekend. *Students:* 12 full-time (6 women), 9 part-time (7 women); includes 4 minority (1 Black or African American, non-Hispanic/Latino; 3 Hispanic/Latino). Average age 32. 19 applicants, 47% accepted, 5 enrolled. In 2019, 10 master's, 3 other advanced degrees awarded. *Entrance requirements:* Additional exam requirements/recommendations for international students: required—TOEFL (minimum score 550 paper-based; 80 iBT), IELTS, PTE. *Application deadline:* For fall admission, 7/1 for domestic students; for spring admission, 10/15 for domestic students. Application fee: $65. Electronic applications accepted. *Financial support:* Fellowships, research assistantships, teaching assistantships, and scholarships/grants available. Financial award application deadline: 2/15. *Unit head:* Rosemary M. Caron, Chair, 603-862-3653. *Application contact:* Pamela Thomas, Academic Coordinator, 603-862-2733, E-mail: pamela.thomas@unh.edu.
Website: http://chhs.unh.edu/hmp

**University of New Hampshire,** Graduate School Manchester Campus, Manchester, NH 03101. Offers business administration (MBA); cybersecurity policy and risk management (MS); educational administration and supervision (Ed S); educational studies (M Ed); elementary education (M Ed); information technology (MS); public administration (MPA); public health (MPH, Certificate); secondary education (M Ed, MAT); social work (MSW); substance use disorders (Certificate). *Program availability:* Part-time, evening/weekend. *Students:* 118 full-time (56 women), 110 part-time (47 women); includes 23 minority (4 Black or African American, non-Hispanic/Latino; 5 Asian, non-Hispanic/Latino; 13 Hispanic/Latino; 1 Two or more races, non-Hispanic/Latino), 39 international. Average age 32. 231 applicants, 78% accepted, 64 enrolled. In 2019, 47 master's, 3 other advanced degrees awarded. *Entrance requirements:* Additional exam requirements/recommendations for international students: required—TOEFL (minimum score 550 paper-based; 80 iBT), IELTS, PTE. *Application deadline:* For fall admission, 6/1 for domestic students, 4/1 for international students; for spring admission, 12/1 for domestic students. Application fee: $65. Electronic applications accepted. *Financial support:* In 2019–20, 11 students received support, including 1 teaching assistantship; fellowships, research assistantships, Federal Work-Study, scholarships/grants, health care benefits, and unspecified assistantships also available. Support available to part-time students. Financial award application deadline: 2/15; financial award applicants required to submit FAFSA. *Unit head:* Candice Morey, Educational Programs Coordinator, 603-641-4313, E-mail: unhm.gradcenter@unh.edu. *Application contact:* Candice Morey, Educational Programs Coordinator, 603-641-4313, E-mail: unhm.gradcenter@unh.edu.
Website: http://www.gradschool.unh.edu/manchester/

**University of New Mexico,** Graduate Studies, Health Sciences Center, Program in Public Health, Albuquerque, NM 87131-5196. Offers community health (MPH); epidemiology (MPH); health systems, services and policy (MPH). *Accreditation:* CEPH. *Program availability:* Part-time, online learning. *Entrance requirements:* For master's, GRE, MCAT, 2 years of experience in health field. Additional exam requirements/recommendations for international students: required—TOEFL. *Expenses:* Tuition, state resident: full-time $7633; part-time $972 per year. Tuition, nonresident: full-time $22,586; part-time $3840 per year. *International tuition:* $23,292 full-time. *Required fees:* $8608. Tuition and fees vary according to course level, course load, degree level, program and student level.

**The University of North Carolina at Chapel Hill,** Graduate School, Gillings School of Global Public Health, Chapel Hill, NC 27599. Offers MHA, MPH, MS, MSCR, MSEE, MSPH, Dr PH, PhD, JD/MPH, MBA/MSPH, MD/MPH, MD/MSPH, MHA/MBA, MHA/MCRP, MHA/MSIS, MHA/MSLS, MPH/MCRP, MPH/MSW, MS/MCRP, MSPH/M Ed, MSPH/MCRP, MSPH/MSIS, MSPH/MSLS, MSPH/MSW, MSPH/PhD, PhD/MD, Pharm D/MPH. *Accreditation:* CAHME (one or more programs are accredited); CEPH. *Program availability:* Part-time, 100% online, blended/hybrid learning. *Faculty:* 234 full-time (140 women), 476 part-time/adjunct (274 women). *Students:* 1,204 full-time (884 women), 212 part-time (148 women); includes 391 minority (113 Black or African American, non-Hispanic/Latino; 130 Asian, non-Hispanic/Latino; 86 Hispanic/Latino; 62 Two or more races, non-Hispanic/Latino), 190 international. Average age 29. 2,442 applicants, 47% accepted, 524 enrolled. In 2019, 272 master's, 88 doctorates awarded. Terminal master's awarded for partial completion of doctoral program. *Degree requirements:* For master's, comprehensive exam (for some programs), thesis (for some programs); for doctorate, comprehensive exam, thesis/dissertation. *Entrance requirements:* Additional exam requirements/recommendations for international students: required—TOEFL (minimum score 90 iBT), IELTS (minimum score 7). *Application deadline:* For fall admission, 2/1 for domestic and international students. Application fee: $90. Electronic applications accepted. *Expenses:* Contact institution. *Financial support:* Fellowships, research assistantships, teaching assistantships, career-related internships or fieldwork, Federal Work-Study, scholarships/grants, traineeships, health care benefits, and unspecified assistantships available. Financial award application deadline: 12/11; financial award applicants required to submit FAFSA. *Unit head:* Dr. Barbara K. Rimer, Dean, 919-966-3215, Fax: 919-966-7678. *Application contact:* Johnston King, Enrollment Management Coordinator, 919-962-6314, Fax: 919-966-6352, E-mail: sph-osa@unc.edu.
Website: https://sph.unc.edu/

**The University of North Carolina at Charlotte,** College of Health and Human Services, Department of Public Health Sciences, Charlotte, NC 28223-0001. Offers community health (Certificate); health administration (MHA); public health (MPH), including community health practice, epidemiology, and population health analytics; public health core concepts (Graduate Certificate); public health sciences (PhD). *Accreditation:* CAHME; CEPH. *Program availability:* Part-time. *Faculty:* 30 full-time (18 women), 4 part-time/adjunct (2 women). *Students:* 103 full-time (85 women), 13 part-time (9 women); includes 43 minority (28 Black or African American, non-Hispanic/Latino; 8 Asian, non-Hispanic/Latino; 3 Hispanic/Latino; 1 Native Hawaiian or other Pacific Islander, non-Hispanic/Latino; 3 Two or more races, non-Hispanic/Latino), 10 international. Average age 26. 154 applicants, 77% accepted, 47 enrolled. In 2019, 49 master's, 3 doctorates, 1 other advanced degree awarded. *Degree requirements:* For master's, capstone; for doctorate, thesis/dissertation. *Entrance requirements:* For master's, GRE or MCAT (for MSPH); GRE or GMAT (for MHA), career goal statement, current resume, letters of recommendation, undergraduate major or coursework that prepares students for graduate work; for doctorate, GRE, master's degree in public health or a related field with minimum GPA of 3.5 in all graduate work; statement of purpose detailing why applicant wants to pursue a PhD in public health sciences in the specified concentration at UNC Charlotte; three letters of recommendation (including at least two letters from former professors); for other advanced degree, bachelor's degree from regionally-accredited university; minimum GPA of 2.75 on all post-secondary work attempted; transcripts; personal statement outlining why the applicant seeks admission to the program. Additional exam requirements/recommendations for international students: required—TOEFL (minimum score 557 paper-based; 83 iBT), IELTS (minimum score 6.5), TOEFL (minimum score 557 paper-based,83 iBT) or IELTS (6.5). *Application deadline:* Applications are processed on a rolling basis. Application fee: $75. Electronic applications accepted. *Expenses:* Contact institution. *Financial support:* In 2019–20, 27 students received support, including 4 research assistantships (averaging $14,323 per year), 15 teaching assistantships (averaging $7,966 per year); fellowships, career-related internships or fieldwork, Federal Work-Study, institutionally sponsored loans, scholarships/grants, and unspecified assistantships also available. Support available to part-time students. Financial award application deadline: 3/1; financial award applicants required to submit FAFSA. *Unit head:* Dr. Jan Warren-Findlow, Professor and Interim Chair, 704-687-7908, E-mail: jwarren1@uncc.edu. *Application contact:* Kathy B. Giddings, Director of Graduate Admissions, 704-687-5503, Fax: 704-687-1668, E-mail: gradadm@uncc.edu.
Website: http://publichealth.uncc.edu/

**University of North Dakota,** School of Medicine and Health Sciences, Program in Public Health, Grand Forks, ND 58202. Offers MPH. *Accreditation:* CEPH.

**University of Northern Colorado,** Graduate School, College of Natural and Health Sciences, School of Human Sciences, Program in Public Health, Greeley, CO 80639. Offers community health education (MPH); global health and community health education (MPH); healthy aging and community health education (MPH). *Degree requirements:* For master's, comprehensive exam, thesis or alternative. *Entrance requirements:* For master's, GRE General Test, 2 letters of recommendation. Electronic applications accepted.

**University of North Florida,** Brooks College of Health, Department of Public Health, Jacksonville, FL 32224. Offers aging services (Certificate); public health (MPH). *Accreditation:* CEPH. *Program availability:* Part-time, evening/weekend. *Degree requirements:* For master's, thesis optional. *Entrance requirements:* For master's, GRE General Test (MSH, MS, MPH); GMAT or GRE General Test (MHA), minimum GPA of 3.0 in last 60 hours. Additional exam requirements/recommendations for international students: required—TOEFL (minimum score 500 paper-based). Electronic applications accepted.

**University of North Texas Health Science Center at Fort Worth,** School of Public Health, Fort Worth, TX 76107-2699. Offers biostatistics (MS); epidemiology (MPH, MS, PhD); food security and public health (Graduate Certificate); GIS in public health (Graduate Certificate); global health (Graduate Certificate); global health for medical professionals (Graduate Certificate); health administration (MHA); health behavior research (MS, PhD); maternal and child health (MPH); public health (Graduate Certificate); public health practice (MPH); DO/MPH; MS/MPH. *Accreditation:* CAHME; CEPH. *Program availability:* Part-time, evening/weekend, 100% online. *Degree requirements:* For master's, thesis or alternative, supervised internship; for doctorate, thesis/dissertation, supervised internship. *Entrance requirements:* For master's, GRE General Test. Additional exam requirements/recommendations for international students: required—TOEFL. Electronic applications accepted. *Expenses:* Contact institution.

**University of Oklahoma Health Sciences Center,** Graduate College, Hudson College of Public Health, Program in General Public Health, Oklahoma City, OK 73190. Offers MPH, Dr PH. *Accreditation:* CEPH.

**University of Oklahoma Health Sciences Center,** Graduate College, Hudson College of Public Health, Program in Preparedness and Terrorism, Oklahoma City, OK 73190. Offers MPH.

**University of Ottawa,** Faculty of Graduate and Postdoctoral Studies, Interdisciplinary Programs, Program in Population Health, Ottawa, ON K1N 6N5, Canada. Offers PhD. *Degree requirements:* For doctorate, comprehensive exam, thesis/dissertation. Electronic applications accepted.

**University of Pennsylvania,** Perelman School of Medicine, Master of Public Health Program, Philadelphia, PA 19104. Offers environmental health (MPH); generalist (MPH); global health (MPH); DMD/MPH; JD/MPH; MD/MPH; MES/MPH; MPH/MBE; MPH/MPA; MPH/MS; MSN/MPH; MSSP/MPH; MSW/MPH; PhD/MPH. *Accreditation:* CEPH. *Program availability:* Part-time, evening/weekend. *Financial support:* Application deadline: 4/1. *Unit head:* Dr. Jennifer Pinto-Martin, Director, 898-4726. *Application*

*contact:* Moriah Hall, Associate Director, MPH program, 573-8841.
Website: http://www.cphi.upenn.edu/mph

**University of Pittsburgh,** Graduate School of Public Health, Pittsburgh, PA 15261. Offers MHA, MPH, MS, Dr PH, PhD, Certificate, JD/MPH, MD/MPH, MD/PhD, MID/MPH, MPH/MPA, MPH/MSW, MPH/PhD, MS/MPH. *Accreditation:* CEPH (one or more programs are accredited). *Program availability:* Part-time, evening/weekend. *Faculty:* 154 full-time (81 women), 37 part-time/adjunct (23 women). *Students:* 428 full-time (308 women), 129 part-time (96 women); includes 131 minority (34 Black or African American, non-Hispanic/Latino; 44 Asian, non-Hispanic/Latino; 31 Hispanic/Latino; 1 Native Hawaiian or other Pacific Islander, non-Hispanic/Latino; 21 Two or more races, non-Hispanic/Latino), 110 international. Average age 28. 1,494 applicants, 52% accepted, 210 enrolled. In 2019, 180 master's, 39 doctorates awarded. Terminal master's awarded for partial completion of doctoral program. *Degree requirements:* For master's, comprehensive exam (for some programs), thesis; for doctorate, comprehensive exam, thesis/dissertation. *Entrance requirements:* For master's, 3 cr. of human biology; 3 cr. algebra or higher math; Bachelor's degree from accredited institution; substantial knowledge is discipline relevant to public health through study, experience, or both; GRE quantitative score at or above 70th percentile; for doctorate, GRE. MCAT, DAT, GMAT, LSAT sometimes accepted by department, 3 cr of human biology, 3 cr. algebra or higher math* U grad degree or bachelor's degree or equivalent degree from foreign school in a field relevant to the PhD program applied to. See also department requirements. Additional exam requirements/recommendations for international students: required—TOEFL (minimum score 90 iBT), WES evaluation for foreign education. *Application deadline:* For fall admission, 1/15 for domestic and international students. Applications are processed on a rolling basis. Application fee: $135. Electronic applications accepted. *Expenses:* $13,379 per term full-time resident, $23,407 per term full-time non-resident, $1122 per credit part-time resident, $1916 per credit part-time non-resident, $500 per term for full-time dissertation research, $475 per term full-time fees, $295 per term part-time fees. *Financial support:* In 2019–20, 200 students received support, including 118 research assistantships (averaging $20,500 per year), 5 teaching assistantships (averaging $18,500 per year); career-related internships or fieldwork, institutionally sponsored loans, scholarships/grants, traineeships, health care benefits, and unspecified assistantships also available. Support available to part-time students. Financial award applicants required to submit FAFSA. *Unit head:* A, Everette James, III, Interim Dean, Graduate School of Public Health, 412-624-3001, Fax: 412-624-3013. *Application contact:* Karrie A. Lukin, Admissions Manager, 412-624-3003, Fax: 412-624-3755, E-mail: presutti@pitt.edu.
Website: http://www.publichealth.pitt.edu/

**University of Rochester,** School of Medicine and Dentistry, Graduate Programs in Medicine and Dentistry, Department of Community and Preventive Medicine, Programs in Public Health and Clinical Investigation, Rochester, NY 14627. Offers clinical investigation (MS); public health (MPH); MBA/MPH; MD/MPH; MPH/MS; MPH/PhD. *Accreditation:* CEPH. *Entrance requirements:* For master's, GRE General Test.

**University of Saint Joseph,** Department of Nutrition and Public Health, West Hartford, CT 06117-2700. Offers nutrition (MS); public health (MPH). *Program availability:* Part-time, evening/weekend, online learning. *Entrance requirements:* For master's, 2 letters of recommendation, letter of intent. Electronic applications accepted. Application fee is waived when completed online.

**University of San Francisco,** School of Nursing and Health Professions, Program in Public Health, San Francisco, CA 94117. Offers MPH. *Accreditation:* CEPH. *Program availability:* Part-time, evening/weekend, online learning. *Faculty:* 11 full-time (8 women), 2 part-time/adjunct (both women). *Students:* 125 full-time (104 women), 11 part-time (all women); includes 90 minority (15 Black or African American, non-Hispanic/Latino; 28 Asian, non-Hispanic/Latino; 36 Hispanic/Latino; 1 Native Hawaiian or other Pacific Islander, non-Hispanic/Latino; 10 Two or more races, non-Hispanic/Latino), 5 international. Average age 31. 272 applicants, 56% accepted, 68 enrolled. In 2019, 86 master's awarded. *Entrance requirements:* Additional exam requirements/recommendations for international students: required—TOEFL (minimum score 600 paper-based; 90 iBT), IELTS. *Application deadline:* For fall admission, 5/15 for domestic students. Applications are processed on a rolling basis. Application fee: $55. Electronic applications accepted. *Financial support:* Scholarships/grants available. *Unit head:* Dr. Taryn Vian, Program Director, 415-422-6681, E-mail: nursing@usfca.edu. *Application contact:* Carolyn Arroyo, Graduate Enrollment Manager, 415-422-2806, E-mail: carroyo2@usfca.edu.
Website: http://www.usfca.edu/nursing/mph/

**University of South Africa,** College of Human Sciences, Pretoria, South Africa. Offers adult education (M Ed); African languages (MA, PhD); African politics (MA, PhD); Afrikaans (MA, PhD); ancient history (MA, PhD); ancient Near Eastern studies (MA, PhD); anthropology (MA, PhD); applied linguistics (MA); Arabic (MA, PhD); archaeology (MA); art history (MA); Biblical archaeology (MA); Biblical studies (M Th, D Th, PhD); Christian spirituality (M Th, D Th); church history (M Th, D Th); classical studies (MA, PhD); clinical psychology (MA); communication (MA, PhD); comparative education (M Ed, Ed D); consulting psychology (D Admin, D Com, PhD); curriculum studies (M Ed, Ed D); development studies (M Admin, MA, D Admin, PhD); didactics (M Ed, Ed D); education (M Tech); education management (M Ed, Ed D); educational psychology (M Ed); English (MA); environmental education (M Ed); French (MA, PhD); German (MA, PhD); Greek (MA); guidance and counseling (M Ed); health studies (MA, PhD), including health sciences education (MA), health services management (MA), medical and surgical nursing science (critical care general) (MA), midwifery and neonatal nursing science (MA), trauma and emergency care (MA); history (MA, PhD); history of education (Ed D); inclusive education (M Ed, Ed D); information and communications technology policy and regulation (MA); information science (MA, MIS, PhD); international politics (MA, PhD); Islamic studies (MA, PhD); Italian (MA, PhD); Judaica (MA, PhD); linguistics (MA, PhD); mathematical education (M Ed); mathematics education (MA); missiology (M Th, D Th); modern Hebrew (MA, PhD); musicology (MA, MMus, D Mus, PhD); natural science education (M Ed); New Testament (M Th, D Th); Old Testament (D Th); pastoral therapy (M Th, D Th); philosophy (MA); philosophy of education (M Ed, Ed D); politics (MA, PhD); Portuguese (MA, PhD); practical theology (M Th, D Th); psychology (MA, MS, PhD); psychology of education (M Ed, Ed D); public health (MA); religious studies (MA, D Th, PhD); Romance languages (MA); Russian (MA, PhD); Semitic languages (MA, PhD); social behavior studies in HIV/AIDS (MA); social science (mental health) (MA); social science in development studies (MA); social science in psychology (MA); social science in social work (MA); social science in sociology (MA); social work (MSW, DSW, PhD); socio-education (M Ed, Ed D); sociolinguistics (MA); sociology (MA, PhD); Spanish (MA, PhD); systematic theology (M Th, D Th); TESOL (teaching English to speakers of other languages) (MA); theological ethics (M Th, D Th); theory of literature (MA, PhD); urban ministries (D Th); urban ministry (M Th).

**University of South Carolina,** The Graduate School, Arnold School of Public Health, Program in General Public Health, Columbia, SC 29208. Offers MPH. *Accreditation:* CEPH. *Program availability:* Part-time. *Degree requirements:* For master's, comprehensive exam, practicum. *Entrance requirements:* For master's, DAT or MCAT, GRE General Test, previously earned MD or doctoral degree. Additional exam requirements/recommendations for international students: required—TOEFL (minimum score 570 paper-based). Electronic applications accepted.

**University of South Carolina,** The Graduate School, Arnold School of Public Health, Program in Physical Activity and Public Health, Columbia, SC 29208. Offers MPH. *Accreditation:* CEPH. *Program availability:* Part-time. *Degree requirements:* For master's, comprehensive exam, practicum. *Entrance requirements:* For master's, GRE. Additional exam requirements/recommendations for international students: required—TOEFL (minimum score 570 paper-based). Electronic applications accepted.

**University of South Carolina,** The Graduate School, College of Nursing, Program in Nursing and Public Health, Columbia, SC 29208. Offers MPH/MSN. *Accreditation:* AACN; CEPH. *Program availability:* Part-time. *Entrance requirements:* Additional exam requirements/recommendations for international students: required—TOEFL (minimum score 570 paper-based). Electronic applications accepted.

**University of South Dakota,** Graduate School, School of Health Sciences, Program in Public Health, Vermillion, SD 57069. Offers MPH. *Program availability:* Part-time, evening/weekend, 100% online. *Entrance requirements:* For master's, official transcript, two letters of recommendation, statement of purpose, criminal background check. Additional exam requirements/recommendations for international students: required—TOEFL (minimum score 550 paper-based; 79 iBT), IELTS (minimum score 6).

**University of Southern California,** Keck School of Medicine and Graduate School, Graduate Programs in Medicine, Department of Preventive Medicine, Master of Public Health Program, Los Angeles, CA 90032. Offers biostatistics and epidemiology (MPH); child and family health (MPH); community health promotion (MPH); environmental health (MPH); geohealth (MPH); global health leadership (MPH); health communication (MPH); health services and policy (MPH). *Accreditation:* CEPH. *Program availability:* Part-time, evening/weekend, 100% online. *Faculty:* 37 full-time (28 women), 8 part-time/adjunct (6 women). *Students:* 261 full-time (201 women), 74 part-time (55 women); includes 224 minority (46 Black or African American, non-Hispanic/Latino; 2 American Indian or Alaska Native, non-Hispanic/Latino; 79 Asian, non-Hispanic/Latino; 56 Hispanic/Latino; 6 Native Hawaiian or other Pacific Islander, non-Hispanic/Latino; 35 Two or more races, non-Hispanic/Latino), 21 international. Average age 28. 420 applicants, 76% accepted, 94 enrolled. In 2019, 123 master's awarded. *Degree requirements:* For master's, practicum, final report, oral presentation. *Entrance requirements:* For master's, GRE General Test, MCAT, GMAT, minimum GPA of 3.0. Additional exam requirements/recommendations for international students: required—TOEFL (minimum score 600 paper-based; 90 iBT). *Application deadline:* For fall admission, 12/1 priority date for domestic students, 5/1 priority date for international students; for spring admission, 9/1 priority date for domestic and international students; for summer admission, 3/1 for domestic and international students. Applications are processed on a rolling basis. Application fee: $135. Electronic applications accepted. *Financial support:* Career-related internships or fieldwork, Federal Work-Study, institutionally sponsored loans, and scholarships/grants available. Support available to part-time students. Financial award application deadline: 5/4; financial award applicants required to submit CSS PROFILE or FAFSA. *Unit head:* Dr. Louise A. Rohrbach, Director, 323-442-8237, Fax: 323-442-8297, E-mail: rohrbac@usc.edu. *Application contact:* Valerie Burris, Admissions Counselor, 323-442-7257, Fax: 323-442-8297, E-mail: valeriem@usc.edu.
Website: https://preventivemedicine.usc.edu/education/graduate-programs/mph/

**University of Southern Maine,** College of Management and Human Service, Muskie School of Public Service, Program in Health Policy and Management, Portland, ME 04103. Offers MPH, CGS, MBA/MPH. *Program availability:* Part-time, evening/weekend, online learning. *Degree requirements:* For master's, thesis, capstone project, field experience. *Entrance requirements:* For master's, GRE General Test. Additional exam requirements/recommendations for international students: required—TOEFL. Electronic applications accepted. *Expenses: Tuition, area resident:* Full-time $864; part-time $432 per credit hour. Tuition, state resident: full-time $864; part-time $432 per credit hour. Tuition, nonresident: full-time $2372; part-time $1186 per credit hour. *Required fees:* $141; $108 per credit hour. Tuition and fees vary according to course load.

**University of Southern Mississippi,** College of Nursing and Health Professions, School of Health Professions, Hattiesburg, MS 39406-0001. Offers epidemiology and biostatistics (MPH); health policy and administration (MPH). *Accreditation:* CEPH. *Program availability:* Part-time, evening/weekend. *Students:* 58 full-time (41 women), 8 part-time (3 women); includes 25 minority (18 Black or African American, non-Hispanic/Latino; 2 Asian, non-Hispanic/Latino; 2 Hispanic/Latino; 3 Two or more races, non-Hispanic/Latino), 22 international. 125 applicants, 32% accepted, 23 enrolled. In 2019, 19 master's awarded. *Degree requirements:* For master's, comprehensive exam, thesis (for some programs). *Entrance requirements:* For master's, GRE General Test, minimum GPA of 2.75 in last 60 hours. Additional exam requirements/recommendations for international students: required—TOEFL, IELTS. *Application deadline:* For fall admission, 3/1 priority date for domestic and international students; for spring admission, 1/10 priority date for domestic and international students. Applications are processed on a rolling basis. Application fee: $60. Electronic applications accepted. *Expenses: Tuition, area resident:* Full-time $4393; part-time $488 per credit hour. Tuition, nonresident: full-time $5393; part-time $600 per credit hour. *Required fees:* $6 per semester. *Financial support:* Research assistantships with full tuition reimbursements, teaching assistantships with full tuition reimbursements, career-related internships or fieldwork, Federal Work-Study, institutionally sponsored loans, scholarships/grants, health care benefits, and unspecified assistantships available. Financial award application deadline: 3/15; financial award applicants required to submit FAFSA. *Unit head:* Hwanseok Choi, Director, 601-266-5435, Fax: 601-266-5043, E-mail: hwanseok.choi@usm.edu. *Application contact:* Hwanseok Choi, Director, 601-266-5435, Fax: 601-266-5043, E-mail: hwanseok.choi@usm.edu.
Website: http://www.usm.edu/community-public-health-sciences

**University of South Florida,** College of Public Health, Tampa, FL 33612. Offers MHA, MPH, MSPH, Dr PH, PhD. *Accreditation:* CEPH (one or more programs are accredited). *Program availability:* Part-time, evening/weekend, 100% online, blended/hybrid learning. *Degree requirements:* For master's, comprehensive exam, thesis (for some programs); for doctorate, comprehensive exam, thesis/dissertation. *Entrance requirements:* For master's, GRE General Test, minimum GPA of 3.0 in upper-level course work, 3 professional letters of recommendation, resume/curriculum vitae; for doctorate, GRE General Test, minimum GPA of 3.0 in upper-level course work, goal statement, three professional letters of recommendation, resume/curriculum vitae, writing sample. Additional exam requirements/recommendations for international students: required—TOEFL (minimum score 550 paper-based; 79 iBT). Electronic applications accepted. *Expenses:* Contact institution.

**University of South Florida,** Innovative Education, Tampa, FL 33620-9951. Offers adult, career and higher education (Graduate Certificate), including college teaching, leadership in developing human resources, leadership in higher education; Africana studies (Graduate Certificate), including diasporas and health disparities, genocide and human rights; aging studies (Graduate Certificate), including gerontology; art research (Graduate Certificate), including museum studies; business foundations (Graduate Certificate); chemical and biomedical engineering (Graduate Certificate), including

materials science and engineering, water, health and sustainability; child and family studies (Graduate Certificate), including positive behavior support; civil and industrial engineering (Graduate Certificate), including transportation systems analysis; community and family health (Graduate Certificate), including maternal and child health, social marketing and public health, violence and injury: prevention and intervention, women's health; criminology (Graduate Certificate), including criminal justice administration; data science for public administration (Graduate Certificate); digital humanities (Graduate Certificate); educational measurement and research (Graduate Certificate), including evaluation; English (Graduate Certificate), including comparative literary studies, creative writing, professional and technical communication; entrepreneurship (Graduate Certificate); environmental health (Graduate Certificate), including safety management; epidemiology and biostatistics (Graduate Certificate), including applied biostatistics, biostatistics, concepts and tools of epidemiology, epidemiology, epidemiology of infectious diseases; geography, environment and planning (Graduate Certificate), including community development, environmental policy and management, geographical information systems; geology (Graduate Certificate), including hydrogeology; global health (Graduate Certificate), including disaster management, global health and Latin American and Caribbean studies, global health practice, humanitarian assistance, infection control; government and international affairs (Graduate Certificate), including Cuban studies, globalization studies; health policy and management (Graduate Certificate), including health management and leadership, public health policy and programs; hearing specialist: early intervention (Graduate Certificate); industrial and management systems engineering (Graduate Certificate), including systems engineering, technology management; information studies (Graduate Certificate), including school library media specialist; information systems/decision sciences (Graduate Certificate), including analytics and business intelligence; instructional technology (Graduate Certificate), including distance education, Florida digital/virtual educator, instructional design, multimedia design, Web design; internal medicine, bioethics and medical humanities (Graduate Certificate), including biomedical ethics; Latin American and Caribbean studies (Graduate Certificate); leadership for coastal resiliency planning (Graduate Certificate); mass communications (Graduate Certificate), including multimedia journalism; mathematics and statistics (Graduate Certificate), including mathematics; medicine (Graduate Certificate), including aging and neuroscience, bioinformatics, biotechnology, brain fitness and memory management, clinical investigation, hand and upper limb rehabilitation, health informatics, health sciences, integrative weight management, intellectual property, medicine and gender, metabolic and nutritional medicine, metabolic cardiology, pharmacy sciences; national and competitive intelligence (Graduate Certificate); nursing (Graduate Certificate), including simulation based academic fellowship in advanced pain management; psychological and social foundations (Graduate Certificate), including career counseling, college teaching, diversity in education, mental health counseling, school counseling; public affairs (Graduate Certificate), including nonprofit management, public management, research administration; public health (Graduate Certificate), including assessing chemical toxicity and public health risks, health equity, pharmacoepidemiology, public health generalist, toxicology, translational research in adolescent behavioral health; public health practices (Graduate Certificate), including planning for healthy communities; rehabilitation and mental health counseling (Graduate Certificate), including integrative mental health care, marriage and family therapy, rehabilitation technology; secondary education (Graduate Certificate), including ESOL, foreign language education: culture and content, foreign language education: professional; social work (Graduate Certificate), including geriatric social work/clinical gerontology; special education (Graduate Certificate), including autism spectrum disorder, disabilities education: severe/profound; world languages (Graduate Certificate), including teaching English as a second language (TESL) or foreign language. *Unit head:* Dr. Cynthia DeLuca, Associate Vice President and Assistant Vice Provost, 813-974-3077, Fax: 813-974-7061, E-mail: deluca@usf.edu. *Application contact:* Owen Hooper, Director, Summer and Alternative Calendar Programs, 813-974-6917, E-mail: hooper@usf.edu.
Website: http://www.usf.edu/innovative-education/

**The University of Tennessee,** Graduate School, College of Education, Health and Human Sciences, Program in Public Health, Knoxville, TN 37996. Offers community health education (MPH); gerontology (MPH); health planning/administration (MPH); MS/MPH. *Accreditation:* CEPH. *Degree requirements:* For master's, thesis optional. *Entrance requirements:* For master's, minimum GPA of 2.7. Additional exam requirements/recommendations for international students: required—TOEFL. Electronic applications accepted.

**The University of Texas at El Paso,** Graduate School, College of Health Sciences, Department of Public Health Sciences, El Paso, TX 79968-0001. Offers MPH, Graduate Certificate. *Accreditation:* CEPH. *Program availability:* Part-time, evening/weekend. *Degree requirements:* For master's, thesis optional. *Entrance requirements:* For master's, GRE, minimum GPA of 3.0, resume, letters of recommendation. Additional exam requirements/recommendations for international students: required—TOEFL; recommended—IELTS. Electronic applications accepted.

**The University of Texas Health Science Center at Houston,** School of Public Health, Houston, TX 77030. Offers behavioral science (PhD); biostatistics (MPH, MS, PhD); environmental health (MPH); epidemiology (MPH, MS, PhD); general public health (Certificate); genomics and bioinformatics (Certificate); health disparities (Certificate); health promotion/health education (MPH, Dr PH); healthcare management (Certificate); management, policy and community health (MPH, Dr PH, PhD); maternal and child health (Certificate); public health informatics (Certificate); DDS/MPH; JD/MPH; MBA/MPH; MD/MPH; MGPS/MPH; MP Aff/MPH; MS/MPH; MSN/MPH; MSW/MPH; PhD/MPH. *Accreditation:* CAHME; CEPH. *Program availability:* Part-time. *Degree requirements:* For master's, thesis (for some programs); for doctorate, comprehensive exam, thesis/dissertation. *Entrance requirements:* For master's and doctorate, GRE General Test. Additional exam requirements/recommendations for international students: required—TOEFL (minimum score 600 paper-based, 100 iBT) or IELTS (7.5). Electronic applications accepted. *Expenses:* Contact institution.

**The University of Texas Health Science Center at Tyler,** School of Community and Rural Health, Tyler, TX 75708. Offers health administration (MHA); public health (MPH).

**The University of Texas Medical Branch,** Graduate School of Biomedical Sciences, Program in Public Health, Galveston, TX 77555. Offers MPH. *Accreditation:* CEPH. *Degree requirements:* For master's, thesis. *Entrance requirements:* For master's, GRE, United States Medical Licensing Exam (USMLE) or NBE, preventive medicine residency. Additional exam requirements/recommendations for international students: required—TOEFL (minimum score 550 paper-based). Electronic applications accepted.

**University of the Sciences,** Program in Public Health, Philadelphia, PA 19104-4495. Offers MPH. *Program availability:* Part-time, evening/weekend, online learning. *Entrance requirements:* Additional exam requirements/recommendations for international students: required—TOEFL, TWE.

**The University of Toledo,** College of Graduate Studies, College of Health and Human Services, School of Population Health, Toledo, OH 43606-3390. Offers health education (PhD); occupational health-industrial hygiene (MS); public health (MPH).

**The University of Toledo,** College of Graduate Studies, College of Medicine and Life Sciences, Department of Public Health and Preventative Medicine, Toledo, OH 43606-3390. Offers biostatistics and epidemiology (Certificate); contemporary gerontological practice (Certificate); environmental and occupational health and safety (MPH); epidemiology (Certificate); global public health (Certificate); health promotion and education (MPH); industrial hygiene (MSOH); medical and health science teaching and learning (Certificate); occupational health (Certificate); public health administration (MPH); public health and emergency response (Certificate); public health epidemiology (MPH); public health nutrition (MPH); MD/MPH. *Program availability:* Part-time, evening/weekend. *Degree requirements:* For master's, thesis or alternative. *Entrance requirements:* For master's, GRE, minimum undergraduate GPA of 3.0, three letters of recommendation, statement of purpose, transcripts from all prior institutions attended, resume; for Certificate, minimum undergraduate GPA of 3.0, three letters of recommendation, statement of purpose, transcripts from all prior institutions attended, resume. Additional exam requirements/recommendations for international students: required—TOEFL (minimum score 550 paper-based; 80 iBT), IELTS (minimum score 6.5). Electronic applications accepted.

**University of Toronto,** School of Graduate Studies, Department of Public Health Sciences, Toronto, ON M5S 1A1, Canada. Offers biostatistics (M Sc, PhD); community health (M Sc); community nutrition (MPH), including nutrition and dietetics; epidemiology (MPH, PhD); family and community medicine (MPH); occupational and environmental health (MPH); social and behavioral health science (PhD); social and behavioral health sciences (MPH), including health promotion. *Accreditation:* CAHME (one or more programs are accredited). *Program availability:* Part-time. *Degree requirements:* For master's, thesis (for some programs), practicum; for doctorate, comprehensive exam, thesis/dissertation, oral thesis defense. *Entrance requirements:* For master's, 2 letters of reference, relevant professional/research experience, minimum B average in final year; for doctorate, 2 letters of reference, relevant professional/research experience, minimum B+ average. Additional exam requirements/recommendations for international students: required—TOEFL (minimum score 580 paper-based; 93 iBT), TWE (minimum score 5). Electronic applications accepted. *Expenses:* Contact institution.

**University of Utah,** School of Medicine and Graduate School, Graduate Programs in Medicine, Department of Family and Preventive Medicine, Programs in Public Health, Salt Lake City, UT 84112-1107. Offers biostatistics (M Stat); public health (MPH, MSPH, PhD). *Accreditation:* CEPH (one or more programs are accredited). *Program availability:* Part-time. *Degree requirements:* For master's, comprehensive exam, thesis or project (MSPH); for doctorate, comprehensive exam, thesis/dissertation. *Entrance requirements:* For master's and doctorate, GRE General Test, 3 letters of reference, in-person interviews, minimum GPA of 3.0. Additional exam requirements/recommendations for international students: required—TOEFL (minimum score 550 paper-based). Electronic applications accepted. *Expenses:* Tuition, state resident: full-time $7085; part-time $272.51 per credit hour. Tuition, nonresident: full-time $24,937; part-time $959.12 per credit hour. *Required fees:* $880.52; $880.52 per semester. Tuition and fees vary according to degree level, program and student level.

**University of Vermont,** The Robert Larner, MD College of Medicine and Graduate College, Graduate Programs in Medicine, Program in Public Health, Burlington, VT 05405. Offers epidemiology (Graduate Certificate); global and environmental health (Graduate Certificate); healthcare management and policy (Graduate Certificate); public health (MPH). *Program availability:* Online only, 100% online. *Entrance requirements:* For master's and Graduate Certificate, resume/curriculum vitae. Additional exam requirements/recommendations for international students: required—TOEFL (minimum iBT score of 90) or IELTS (6.5). Electronic applications accepted. *Expenses:* Contact institution.

**University of Virginia,** School of Medicine, Department of Public Health Sciences, Program in Public Health, Charlottesville, VA 22903. Offers MPH, MPP/MPH. *Accreditation:* CEPH. *Degree requirements:* For master's, written or oral comprehensive exam or thesis. *Entrance requirements:* For master's, GRE, MCAT, LSAT or GMAT, 2 letters of recommendation. Additional exam requirements/recommendations for international students: required—TOEFL. Electronic applications accepted.

**University of Virginia,** School of Nursing, Charlottesville, VA 22903. Offers acute and specialty care (MSN); acute care nurse practitioner (MSN); clinical nurse leadership (MSN); community-public health leadership (MSN); nursing (DNP, PhD); psychiatric mental health counseling (MSN); MSN/MBA. *Accreditation:* AACN. *Program availability:* Part-time. *Degree requirements:* For doctorate, comprehensive exam (for some programs), capstone project (DNP), dissertation (PhD). *Entrance requirements:* For master's, GRE General Test, MAT; for doctorate, GRE General Test. Additional exam requirements/recommendations for international students: required—TOEFL, IELTS. Electronic applications accepted.

**University of Washington,** Graduate School, School of Public Health, Online Executive MPH, Seattle, WA 98195. Offers MPH. *Accreditation:* CEPH. *Program availability:* Evening/weekend, online learning. *Students:* 47 full-time (35 women), 24 part-time (16 women); includes 28 minority (8 Black or African American, non-Hispanic/Latino; 15 Asian, non-Hispanic/Latino; 5 Hispanic/Latino), 3 international. Average age 36. 63 applicants, 90% accepted, 41 enrolled. In 2019, 20 master's awarded. *Entrance requirements:* Additional exam requirements/recommendations for international students: required—TOEFL. Electronic applications accepted. *Expenses:* 57,456. *Unit head:* Dr. Miruna Petrescu-Prahova, Director, 206-221-3349. *Application contact:* Angela Cross, Student Services Coordinator, 206-685-7580, Fax: 206-543-3964, E-mail: uwemph@uw.edu.
Website: https://www.executivemph.uw.edu/

**University of Waterloo,** Graduate Studies and Postdoctoral Affairs, Faculty of Applied Health Sciences, School of Public Health and Health Systems, Waterloo, ON N2L 3G1, Canada. Offers health evaluation (MHE); health informatics (MHI); health studies and gerontology (M Sc, PhD); public health (MPH). *Program availability:* Part-time. *Degree requirements:* For master's, thesis; for doctorate, comprehensive exam, thesis/dissertation. *Entrance requirements:* For master's, honors degree, minimum B average, resume, writing sample; for doctorate, GRE (recommended), master's degree, minimum B average, resume, writing sample. Additional exam requirements/recommendations for international students: required—TOEFL, IELTS, PTE. Electronic applications accepted.

**University of West Florida,** Usha Kundu, MD College of Health, Department of Public Health, Pensacola, FL 32514-5750. Offers MPH. *Accreditation:* CEPH. *Program availability:* Part-time, evening/weekend. *Entrance requirements:* For master's, GRE (minimum score: verbal 450, quantitative 550), GMAT (minimum score 465), or MCAT (minimum score 25), official transcripts; two personal writing samples (e.g., written reports completed by applicant or other representative samples of professional writing skills); basic computer competency; three letters of recommendation. Additional exam requirements/recommendations for international students: required—TOEFL (minimum score 550 paper-based).

**University of Wisconsin–La Crosse,** College of Science and Health, Department of Health Education and Health Promotion, Program in Community Health Education, La Crosse, WI 54601-3742. Offers community health education (MS); public health (MPH). *Accreditation:* CEPH. *Faculty:* 4 full-time (2 women). *Students:* 2 full-time (both women),

5 part-time (3 women); includes 2 minority (1 Asian, non-Hispanic/Latino; 1 Two or more races, non-Hispanic/Latino). Average age 36. In 2019, 9 master's awarded. *Degree requirements:* For master's, thesis. *Entrance requirements:* For master's, GRE General Test, GRE Subject Test (for MPH), 3 letters of recommendation. Additional exam requirements/recommendations for international students: required—TOEFL (minimum score 550 paper-based; 79 iBT). Electronic applications accepted. *Financial support:* Research assistantships with partial tuition reimbursements, Federal Work-Study, scholarships/grants, health care benefits, and tuition waivers (partial) available. Support available to part-time students. Financial award applicants required to submit FAFSA. *Unit head:* Dr. Gary Gilmore, Director, 608-785-8163, E-mail: gilmore.gary@uwlax.edu. *Application contact:* Dr. Gary Gilmore, Director, 608-785-8163, E-mail: gilmore.gary@uwlax.edu.

**University of Wisconsin–Madison,** School of Medicine and Public Health, Master of Public Health Program, Madison, WI 53706-1380. Offers MPH. *Accreditation:* CEPH.

**University of Wisconsin–Milwaukee,** Graduate School, Joseph J. Zilber School of Public Health, Milwaukee, WI 53201-0413. Offers MPH, PhD, Graduate Certificate. *Accreditation:* CEPH. *Program availability:* Part-time. Electronic applications accepted.

**Utah State University,** School of Graduate Studies, Emma Eccles Jones College of Education and Human Services, Department of Kinesiology and Health Science, Logan, UT 84322. Offers fitness promotion (MS); health and human movement (MS); pathokinesiology (PhD); physical and sport education (M Ed); public health (MPH). *Program availability:* Part-time, evening/weekend, online learning. *Degree requirements:* For master's, thesis (for some programs). *Entrance requirements:* For master's, GRE General Test or MAT, minimum GPA of 3.0. Additional exam requirements/recommendations for international students: required—TOEFL.

**Valparaiso University,** Graduate School and Continuing Education, College of Nursing and Health Professions, Valparaiso, IN 46383. Offers nursing (DNP); nursing education (MSN, Certificate); physician assistant (MSPA); public health (MPH); MSN/MHA. *Accreditation:* AACN. *Program availability:* Part-time, evening/weekend, online learning. *Entrance requirements:* For master's, minimum GPA of 3.0, undergraduate major in nursing, Indiana registered nursing license, undergraduate courses in research and statistics. Additional exam requirements/recommendations for international students: required—TOEFL (minimum score 550 paper-based; 80 iBT), IELTS (minimum score 6). Electronic applications accepted. *Expenses:* Contact institution.

**Vanderbilt University,** Center for Medicine, Health, and Society, Nashville, TN 37240-1001. Offers MA. *Faculty:* 8 full-time (5 women). *Students:* 9 full-time (7 women), 3 part-time (2 women); includes 5 minority (3 Black or African American, non-Hispanic/Latino; 2 Two or more races, non-Hispanic/Latino). Average age 23. 21 applicants, 86% accepted, 9 enrolled. In 2019, 15 master's awarded. *Degree requirements:* For master's, comprehensive exam (for some programs), thesis (for some programs). *Entrance requirements:* Additional exam requirements/recommendations for international students: required—TOEFL (minimum score 570 paper-based; 88 iBT). *Application deadline:* For fall admission, 1/15 for domestic and international students. Electronic applications accepted. *Expenses: Tuition:* Full-time $51,018; part-time $2087 per hour. *Required fees:* $542. Tuition and fees vary according to program. *Financial support:* Federal Work-Study, scholarships/grants, and health care benefits available. Financial award application deadline: 1/15; financial award applicants required to submit CSS PROFILE or FAFSA. *Unit head:* Dr. Jonathan Metzl, Director, 615-343-2504, Fax: 615-343-8889, E-mail: jonathan.metzl@vanderbilt.edu. *Application contact:* JuLeigh Petty, Acting Director/Director of Graduate Studies, 615-322-6725, Fax: 615-322-2731, E-mail: juleigh.petty@vanderbilt.edu.
Website: http://www.vanderbilt.edu/mhs/

**Virginia Commonwealth University,** Medical College of Virginia-Professional Programs, School of Medicine, Graduate Programs in Medicine, Department of Family Medicine and Population Health, Richmond, VA 23284-9005. Offers epidemiology (MPH, PhD); public health practice (MPH); social and behavioral science (MPH); MD/MPH. *Accreditation:* CEPH. *Program availability:* Part-time. *Degree requirements:* For doctorate, comprehensive exam, thesis/dissertation. *Entrance requirements:* For master's, GRE; for doctorate, GRE General Test, interview, 3 letters of recommendation, minimum graduate GPA of 3.0, master's degree in public health or related field including epidemiology and biostatistics. Additional exam requirements/recommendations for international students: required—TOEFL (minimum score 600 paper-based; 100 iBT). Electronic applications accepted.

**Virginia Polytechnic Institute and State University,** Virginia-Maryland College of Veterinary Medicine, Blacksburg, VA 24061. Offers biomedical and veterinary sciences (MS, PhD); public health (MPH); veterinary medicine (DVM). *Accreditation:* AVMA (one or more programs are accredited); CEPH. *Faculty:* 132 full-time (79 women), 6 part-time/adjunct (5 women). *Students:* 583 full-time (422 women), 34 part-time (26 women); includes 142 minority (28 Black or African American, non-Hispanic/Latino; 3 American Indian or Alaska Native, non-Hispanic/Latino; 23 Asian, non-Hispanic/Latino; 35 Hispanic/Latino; 53 Two or more races, non-Hispanic/Latino), 28 international. Average age 26. 85 applicants, 87% accepted, 54 enrolled. In 2019, 33 master's, 137 doctorates awarded. *Degree requirements:* For master's, comprehensive exam (for some programs), thesis (for some programs); for doctorate, comprehensive exam (for some programs), thesis/dissertation (for some programs). *Entrance requirements:* For master's and doctorate, GRE/GMAT. Additional exam requirements/recommendations for international students: required—TOEFL (minimum score 90 iBT). *Application deadline:* For fall admission, 8/1 for domestic students, 4/1 for international students; for spring admission, 1/1 for domestic students, 9/1 for international students. Applications are processed on a rolling basis. Application fee: $75. Electronic applications accepted. *Expenses:* Tuition, state resident: full-time $13,700; part-time $761.25 per credit hour. Tuition, nonresident: full-time $27,614; part-time $1534 per credit hour. *Required fees:* $886.50 per term. Tuition and fees vary according to campus/location and program. *Financial support:* In 2019–20, 3 fellowships with full and partial tuition reimbursements (averaging $2,668 per year), 33 research assistantships with full tuition reimbursements (averaging $19,301 per year), 30 teaching assistantships with full tuition reimbursements (averaging $21,932 per year) were awarded; scholarships/grants also available. Financial award application deadline: 3/1; financial award applicants required to submit FAFSA. *Unit head:* Dr. Daniel Givens, Dean, 540-231-7910, Fax: 540-231-3505, E-mail: gdaniel@vt.edu. *Application contact:* Sheila Steele, Executive Assistant, 540-231-7910, Fax: 540-231-3505, E-mail: ssteele@vt.edu.
Website: http://www.vetmed.vt.edu

**Walden University,** Graduate Programs, School of Counseling, Minneapolis, MN 55401. Offers addiction counseling (MS), including addictions and public health, child and adolescent counseling, family studies and interventions, forensic counseling, general program, military families and culture, trauma and crisis counseling; clinical mental health counseling (MS), including addiction counseling, forensic counseling, military families and culture, trauma and crisis counseling; counselor education and supervision (PhD), including consultation, counseling and social change, forensic mental health counseling, leadership and program evaluation, trauma and crisis; marriage, couple, and family counseling (MS), including addiction counseling, career counseling, forensic counseling, military families and culture, trauma and crisis counseling; school

counseling (MS), including addiction counseling, career counseling, crisis and trauma, military families and culture. *Accreditation:* ACA. *Program availability:* Part-time, evening/weekend, online only, 100% online. *Degree requirements:* For master's, residency, field experience, professional development plan, licensure plan; for doctorate, thesis/dissertation, residency, practicum, internship. *Entrance requirements:* For master's, bachelor's degree or higher; minimum GPA of 2.5; official transcripts; goal statement (for some programs); access to computer and Internet; for doctorate, master's degree or higher; three years of related professional or academic experience (preferred); minimum GPA of 3.0; goal statement and current resume (for select programs); official transcripts; access to computer and Internet. Additional exam requirements/recommendations for international students: required—TOEFL (minimum score 550 paper-based, 79 iBT), IELTS (minimum score 6.5), Michigan English Language Assessment Battery (minimum score 82), or PTE (minimum score 53). Electronic applications accepted.

**Walden University,** Graduate Programs, School of Health Sciences, Minneapolis, MN 55401. Offers clinical research administration (MS, Graduate Certificate); health education and promotion (MS, PhD), including behavioral health (PhD), disease surveillance (PhD), emergency preparedness (MS), general (MHA, MS), global health (PhD), health policy (PhD), health policy and advocacy (MS), population health (PhD); health informatics (MS); health services (PhD), including community health, healthcare administration, leadership, public health policy, self-designed; healthcare administration (MHA, DHA), including general (MHA, MS); leadership and organizational development (MHA); public health (MPH, Dr PH, PhD, Graduate Certificate), including community health education (PhD), epidemiology (PhD); systems policy (MHA). *Program availability:* Part-time, evening/weekend, online only, 100% online. *Degree requirements:* For doctorate, thesis/dissertation, residency. *Entrance requirements:* For master's, bachelor's degree or higher; minimum GPA of 2.5; official transcripts; goal statement (for some programs); access to computer and Internet; for doctorate, master's degree or higher; three years of related professional or academic experience (preferred); minimum GPA of 3.0; goal statement and current resume (for select programs); official transcripts; access to computer and Internet; for Graduate Certificate, relevant work experience; access to computer and Internet. Additional exam requirements/recommendations for international students: required—TOEFL (minimum score 550 paper-based, 79 iBT), IELTS (minimum score 6.5), Michigan English Language Assessment Battery (minimum score 82), or PTE (minimum score 53). Electronic applications accepted.

**Walden University,** Graduate Programs, School of Nursing, Minneapolis, MN 55401. Offers adult-gerontology acute care nurse practitioner (MSN); adult-gerontology nurse practitioner (MSN); education (MSN); family nurse practitioner (MSN); informatics (MSN); leadership and management (MSN); nursing (PhD, Post-Master's Certificate), including education (PhD), healthcare administration (PhD), interdisciplinary health (PhD), leadership (PhD), nursing education (Post-Master's Certificate), nursing informatics (Post-Master's Certificate), nursing leadership and management (Post-Master's Certificate), public health policy (PhD); nursing practice (DNP); psychiatric mental health (MSN). *Accreditation:* AACN. *Program availability:* Part-time, evening/weekend, online only, 100% online. *Degree requirements:* For doctorate, thesis/dissertation (for some programs), residency (for some programs), field experience (for some programs). *Entrance requirements:* For master's, bachelor's degree or equivalent in related field or RN; minimum GPA of 2.5; official transcripts; goal statement (for some programs); access to computer and Internet; for doctorate, master's degree or higher; RN; three years of related professional or academic experience; goal statement; access to computer and Internet; for Post-Master's Certificate, relevant work experience; access to computer and Internet. Additional exam requirements/recommendations for international students: required—TOEFL (minimum score 550 paper-based, 79 iBT), IELTS (minimum score 6.5), Michigan English Language Assessment Battery (minimum score 82), or PTE (minimum score 53). Electronic applications accepted.

**Washington University in St. Louis,** Brown School, St. Louis, MO 63130-4899. Offers American Indian/Alaska native (MSW); children, youth and families (MSW); epidemiology/biostatistics (MPH); generalist (MPH); global health (MPH); health (MSW); health policy analysis (MPH); individualized (MSW), including health; mental health (MSW); older adults and aging societies (MSW); public health sciences (PhD); social and economic development (MSW), including domestic, international; social work (PhD); urban design (MPH); violence and injury prevention (MSW); JD/MSW; M Arch/MSW; MPH/MBA; MSW/M Div; MSW/M Ed; MSW/MAPS; MSW/MBA; MSW/MPH; MUD/MSW. *Accreditation:* CEPH, CSWE (one or more programs are accredited). *Faculty:* 54 full-time (31 women), 87 part-time/adjunct (61 women). *Students:* 282 full-time (226 women); includes 90 minority (40 Black or African American, non-Hispanic/Latino; 10 American Indian or Alaska Native, non-Hispanic/Latino; 26 Asian, non-Hispanic/Latino; 13 Hispanic/Latino; 1 Native Hawaiian or other Pacific Islander, non-Hispanic/Latino). Average age 24. *Degree requirements:* For master's, 60 credit hours (for MSW); 52 credit hours (for MPH); practicum; for doctorate, comprehensive exam, thesis/dissertation. *Entrance requirements:* For master's, GRE (preferred), GMAT, LSAT, MCAT, PCAT, or United States Medical Licensing Exam (for MPH); for doctorate, GRE. Additional exam requirements/recommendations for international students: required—TOEFL (minimum score 100 iBT), IELTS (minimum score 7). *Application deadline:* For fall admission, 12/15 priority date for domestic and international students; for winter admission, 3/1 priority date for domestic and international students. Applications are processed on a rolling basis. Electronic applications accepted. *Expenses:* Contact institution. *Financial support:* In 2019–20, 90 research assistantships were awarded; fellowships, teaching assistantships, career-related internships or fieldwork, Federal Work-Study, scholarships/grants, and unspecified assistantships also available. Support available to part-time students. Financial award applicants required to submit FAFSA. *Unit head:* Jamie L. Adkisson-Hennessey, Director of Admissions and Recruitment, 314-935-3524, Fax: 314-935-4859, E-mail: jadkisson@wustl.edu. *Application contact:* Office of Admissions and Recruitment, 314-935-6676, Fax: 314-935-4859, E-mail: brownadmissions@wustl.edu.
Website: http://brownschool.wustl.edu

**Washington University in St. Louis,** School of Medicine, Master of Population Health Sciences Program, St. Louis, MO 63110. Offers clinical epidemiology (MPHS); health services (MPHS); psychiatric and behavioral health sciences (MPHS); quantitative methods (MPHS). *Program availability:* Part-time. *Entrance requirements:* For master's, possess or currently be in pursuit of a clinical doctorate degree (including but not limited to: MD, PhD, PharmD, DPH, DO, DPT, DNP, OTD, etc.). Additional exam requirements/recommendations for international students: required—TOEFL.

**Western Illinois University,** School of Graduate Studies, College of Education and Human Services, Department of Health Sciences and Social Work, Macomb, IL 61455-1390. Offers health sciences (MS), including public health, school health. *Accreditation:* NCATE. *Program availability:* Part-time. *Degree requirements:* For master's, comprehensive exam, thesis or alternative. *Entrance requirements:* Additional exam requirements/recommendations for international students: required—TOEFL (minimum score 550 paper-based; 80 iBT). Electronic applications accepted.

**Western Kentucky University,** Graduate School, College of Health and Human Services, Department of Public Health, Bowling Green, KY 42101. Offers healthcare

administration (MHA); public health (MPH). *Accreditation:* CEPH. *Program availability:* Part-time, evening/weekend. *Degree requirements:* For master's, comprehensive exam, thesis or alternative. *Entrance requirements:* For master's, GRE General Test, minimum GPA of 2.75. Additional exam requirements/recommendations for international students: required—TOEFL (minimum score 555 paper-based; 79 iBT).

**Westminster College,** School of Nursing and Health Sciences, Salt Lake City, UT 84105-3697. Offers family nurse practitioner (MSN); nurse anesthesia (MSNA); public health (MPH). *Accreditation:* AACN; AANA/CANAEP; CEPH. *Degree requirements:* For master's, clinical practicum, 504 clinical practice hours. *Entrance requirements:* For master's, GRE (can be waived in select cases), personal statement, resume, 3 professional recommendations, copy of unrestricted Utah license to practice professional nursing, background check, minimum cumulative GPA of 3.0, documentation of current immunizations, physical and mental health certificate signed by primary care provider. Additional exam requirements/recommendations for international students: required—TOEFL (minimum score 84 iBT), IELTS (minimum score 7). Electronic applications accepted. *Expenses:* Contact institution.

**West Virginia University,** School of Public Health, Morgantown, WV 26506. Offers biostatistics (MPH, MS, PhD); epidemiology (MPH, PhD); health policy (MPH); occupational and environmental health sciences (MPH, PhD); public health (MPH); school health education (MS); social and behavioral science (MPH, PhD). *Accreditation:* CEPH. *Program availability:* Part-time, online learning. *Degree requirements:* For master's, practicum, project. *Entrance requirements:* For master's, GRE General Test, MCAT, medical degree, medical internship. Additional exam requirements/recommendations for international students: required—TOEFL (minimum score 550 paper-based; 80 iBT). *Expenses:* Contact institution.

**Wright State University,** Boonshoft School of Medicine, Department of Population and Public Health Sciences, Dayton, OH 45435. Offers health promotion and education (MPH). *Accreditation:* CEPH.

**Yale University,** Yale School of Medicine, Yale School of Public Health, New Haven, CT 06520. Offers applied biostatistics and epidemiology (APMPH); biostatistics (MPH, MS, PhD), including global health (MPH); chronic disease epidemiology (MPH, PhD), including global health (MPH); environmental health sciences (MPH, PhD), including global health (MPH); epidemiology of microbial diseases (MPH, PhD), including global health (MPH); global health (APMPH); health management (MPH), including global health; health policy (MPH), including global health; health policy and administration (APMPH, PhD); occupational and environmental medicine (APMPH); preventive medicine (APMPH); social and behavioral sciences (APMPH, MPH), including global health (MPH); JD/MPH; M Div/MPH; MBA/MPH; MD/MPH; MEM/MPH; MFS/MPH; MM Sc/MPH; MPH/MA; MSN/MPH. *Accreditation:* CEPH. *Faculty:* 161 full-time (71 women), 121 part-time/adjunct (57 women). *Students:* 534 full-time (386 women); includes 156 minority (24 Black or African American, non-Hispanic/Latino; 83 Asian, non-Hispanic/Latino; 30 Hispanic/Latino; 19 Two or more races, non-Hispanic/Latino), 220 international. Average age 25. 1,300 applicants, 220 enrolled. In 2019, 250 master's, 12 doctorates awarded. *Degree requirements:* For master's, thesis; for doctorate, comprehensive exam, thesis/dissertation. *Entrance requirements:* For master's, GMAT, GRE, or MCAT; for doctorate, GRE General Test. Additional exam requirements/recommendations for international students: required—TOEFL (minimum score 100 iBT). *Application deadline:* For fall admission, 12/15 for domestic and international students; for summer admission, 12/15 for domestic and international students. Applications are processed on a rolling basis. Application fee: $135. Electronic applications accepted. *Expenses:* Contact institution. *Financial support:* Fellowships with full tuition reimbursements, research assistantships with full tuition reimbursements, teaching assistantships with full tuition reimbursements, career-related internships or fieldwork, institutionally sponsored loans, scholarships/grants, and tuition waivers available. Support available to part-time students. Financial award application deadline: 3/1; financial award applicants required to submit FAFSA. *Unit head:* Dr. Sten Vermund, Dean and Anna M.R. Lauder Professor of Public Health, E-mail: sten.vermund@yale.edu. *Application contact:* Mary Keefe, Director of Admissions, 203-785-2844, E-mail: ysph.admissions@yale.edu.
Website: http://publichealth.yale.edu/

**Youngstown State University,** College of Graduate Studies, Bitonte College of Health and Human Services, Department of Health Professions, Youngstown, OH 44555-0001. Offers health and human services (MHHS); public health (MPH). *Accreditation:* NAACLS. *Program availability:* Part-time, evening/weekend. *Degree requirements:* For master's, thesis optional. *Entrance requirements:* For master's, GRE General Test, minimum GPA of 3.0. Additional exam requirements/recommendations for international students: required—TOEFL.

# Community Health

**Adler University,** Master of Public Policy Program, Chicago, IL 60602. Offers community health (MPP); human rights advocacy (MPP). *Program availability:* Part-time, evening/weekend. In 2019, 1 master's awarded. *Degree requirements:* For master's, Social Justice Practicum; Capstone Project. *Unit head:* Phyllis Horton, Director of Admissions, 312-662-4100, E-mail: admissions@adler.edu. *Application contact:* Phyllis Horton, Director of Admissions, 312-662-4100, E-mail: admissions@adler.edu.

**Arizona State University at Tempe,** College of Nursing and Health Innovation, Phoenix, AZ 85004. Offers advanced nursing practice (DNP); clinical research management (MS); community and public health practice (Graduate Certificate); family mental health nurse practitioner (Graduate Certificate); family nurse practitioner (Graduate Certificate); geriatric nursing (Graduate Certificate); healthcare innovation (MHI); nurse education in academic and practice settings (Graduate Certificate); nurse educator (MS); nursing and healthcare innovation (PhD). *Accreditation:* AACN. *Program availability:* Online learning. *Degree requirements:* For master's, comprehensive exam (for some programs), thesis (for some programs), interactive Program of Study (iPOS) submitted before completing 50 percent of required credit hours; for doctorate, comprehensive exam, thesis/dissertation, interactive Program of Study (iPOS) submitted before completing 50 percent of required credit hours. *Entrance requirements:* For master's and doctorate, GRE, minimum GPA of 3.0 or equivalent in last 2 years of work leading to bachelor's degree. Additional exam requirements/recommendations for international students: required—TOEFL, IELTS, or PTE. Electronic applications accepted. *Expenses:* Contact institution.

**Baylor University,** Graduate School, Robbins College of Health and Human Sciences, Department of Public Health, Waco, TX 76798. Offers community health (MPH). *Program availability:* Part-time, 100% online, blended/hybrid learning. *Faculty:* 9 full-time (6 women). *Students:* 174 full-time (153 women); includes 126 minority (56 Black or African American, non-Hispanic/Latino; 2 American Indian or Alaska Native, non-Hispanic/Latino; 14 Asian, non-Hispanic/Latino; 28 Hispanic/Latino; 1 Native Hawaiian or other Pacific Islander, non-Hispanic/Latino; 25 Two or more races, non-Hispanic/Latino), 1 international. 161 applicants, 92% accepted, 174 enrolled. In 2019, 10 master's awarded. Terminal master's awarded for partial completion of doctoral program. *Degree requirements:* For master's, thesis optional. *Entrance requirements:* Additional exam requirements/recommendations for international students: required—TOEFL, PTE, GRE. *Application deadline:* For fall admission, 12/15 for domestic and international students. Applications are processed on a rolling basis. Application fee: $180. Electronic applications accepted. *Financial support:* Research assistantships and unspecified assistantships available. Financial award application deadline: 2/15. *Unit head:* Dr. Eva I. Doyle, Chair, 254-710-4023, E-mail: eva_doyle@baylor.edu. *Application contact:* Dr. Renee Umstattd Meyer, Graduate Program Director, 254-710-4029, E-mail: renee_umstattd@baylor.edu.
Website: https://www.baylor.edu/publichealth/

**Bloomsburg University of Pennsylvania,** School of Graduate Studies, College of Science and Technology, Department of Nursing, Bloomsburg, PA 17815-1301. Offers adult and family nurse practitioner (MSN); community health (MSN); nurse anesthesia (MSN); nursing (MSN, DNP); nursing administration (MSN). *Accreditation:* AACN. *Degree requirements:* For master's, thesis (for some programs), clinical experience. *Entrance requirements:* For master's, minimum QPA of 3.0, personal statement, 2 letters of recommendation, nursing license. Additional exam requirements/recommendations for international students: required—TOEFL, IELTS. Electronic applications accepted. *Expenses:* Contact institution.

**Brooklyn College of the City University of New York,** School of Natural and Behavioral Sciences, Department of Health and Nutrition Sciences, Program in Community Health, Brooklyn, NY 11210-2889. Offers community health education (MA); thanatology (MA). *Accreditation:* CEPH. *Degree requirements:* For master's, thesis or alternative. *Entrance requirements:* For master's, 2 letters of recommendation, essay. Additional exam requirements/recommendations for international students: required—TOEFL. Electronic applications accepted.

**Brown University,** Graduate School, Division of Biology and Medicine, School of Public Health, Providence, RI 02912. Offers behavioral and social sciences intervention (M Sc); biostatistics (AM, Sc M, PhD); epidemiology (Sc M); health services, policy and practice (PhD); public health (MPH); MD/PhD. *Accreditation:* CEPH. *Degree requirements:* For doctorate, thesis/dissertation, preliminary exam. *Entrance requirements:* For master's and doctorate, GRE General Test. Additional exam requirements/recommendations for international students: required—TOEFL.

**Canisius College,** Graduate Division, School of Education and Human Services, Office of Professional Studies, Buffalo, NY 14208-1098. Offers applied nutrition (MS, Certificate); community and school health (MS); health and human performance (MS); health information technology (MS); respiratory care (MS). *Program availability:* Part-time, evening/weekend, 100% online, blended/hybrid learning. *Faculty:* 1 full-time (0 women), 20 part-time/adjunct (11 women). *Students:* 12 full-time (8 women), 28 part-time (17 women); includes 9 minority (3 Black or African American, non-Hispanic/Latino; 1 Asian, non-Hispanic/Latino; 3 Hispanic/Latino; 2 Two or more races, non-Hispanic/Latino). Average age 33. 24 applicants, 88% accepted, 11 enrolled. In 2019, 27 master's awarded. *Degree requirements:* For master's, thesis (for some programs), Programs require Thesis/Project or Internship. *Entrance requirements:* For master's, GRE recommended, bachelor's degree transcript, two letters of recommendation, current licensure (for applied nutrition), minimum GPA of 2.7, current resume. Additional exam requirements/recommendations for international students: required—TOEFL (550+ PBT or 79+ IBT), IELTS (6.5+), or CAEL (70+). *Application deadline:* Applications are processed on a rolling basis. Electronic applications accepted. *Expenses: Tuition:* Part-time $900 per credit. *Required fees:* $25 per credit hour. $65 per term. Part-time tuition and fees vary according to course load and program. *Financial support:* Career-related internships or fieldwork, Federal Work-Study, scholarships/grants, tuition waivers (partial), and unspecified assistantships available. Support available to part-time students. Financial award application deadline: 4/30; financial award applicants required to submit FAFSA. *Unit head:* Dennis W. Koch, Director, Office of Professional Studies, 716-888-8292, E-mail: koch5@canisius.edu. *Application contact:* Dennis W. Koch, Director, Office of Professional Studies, 716-888-8292, E-mail: koch5@canisius.edu.
Website: http://www.canisius.edu/graduate/

**Clark University,** Graduate School, Department of International Development, Community, and Environment, Program in Community and Global Health, Worcester, MA 01610-1477. Offers MHS. *Degree requirements:* For master's, project; capstone, practicum, or internship. *Entrance requirements:* Additional exam requirements/recommendations for international students: required—TOEFL (minimum score 90 iBT), IELTS (minimum score 6.5). Electronic applications accepted. *Expenses:* Contact institution.

**Columbia University,** Columbia University Mailman School of Public Health, Department of Sociomedical Sciences, New York, NY 10032. Offers MPH, MS, Dr PH, PhD. *Accreditation:* CEPH (one or more programs are accredited). *Program availability:* Part-time. *Students:* 157 full-time (141 women), 59 part-time (49 women); includes 86 minority (22 Black or African American, non-Hispanic/Latino; 1 American Indian or Alaska Native, non-Hispanic/Latino; 37 Asian, non-Hispanic/Latino; 20 Hispanic/Latino; 6 Two or more races, non-Hispanic/Latino), 23 international. Average age 26. 514 applicants, 61% accepted, 102 enrolled. In 2019, 88 master's, 5 doctorates awarded. *Degree requirements:* For master's, thesis; for doctorate, thesis/dissertation. *Entrance requirements:* For master's, GRE General Test; for doctorate, GRE General Test, MPH or equivalent (for Dr PH). Additional exam requirements/recommendations for international students: required—TOEFL (minimum score 600 paper-based; 100 iBT). *Application deadline:* For fall admission, 12/1 priority date for domestic and international students. Application fee: $120. Electronic applications accepted. *Expenses: Tuition:* Full-time $47,600; part-time $1880 per credit. One-time fee: $105. *Financial support:* Research assistantships, teaching assistantships, career-related internships or fieldwork, and Federal Work-Study available. Support available to part-time students. Financial award application deadline: 2/1; financial award applicants required to submit FAFSA. *Unit head:* Dr. Kathleen Sikkema, Chairperson, 212-305-8236. *Application*

*contact:* Clare Norton, Associate Dean for Enrollment Management, 212-305-8698, Fax: 212-342-1861, E-mail: ph-admit@columbia.edu.
Website: https://www.mailman.columbia.edu/become-student/departments/sociomedical-sciences

**Daemen College,** Public Health Programs, Amherst, NY 14226-3592. Offers community health education (MPH); epidemiology (MPH); generalist (MPH). *Program availability:* Part-time, evening/weekend. *Degree requirements:* For master's, successful completion of a practicum and capstone; minimum grade of B- in any course; maximum of 2 repeated courses is allowed; students must maintain an overall minimum cumulative GPA of 3.0. *Entrance requirements:* For master's, bachelor's degree, official transcripts, GPA 3.0 or above (under 3.0 may be submitted on a conditional basis), 2 letters of recommendation, personal statement, interview with MPH faculty. Additional exam requirements/recommendations for international students: required—TOEFL (minimum score 85 paper-based), IELTS (minimum score 6.5). Electronic applications accepted. Application fee is waived when completed online.

**Dalhousie University,** Faculty of Medicine, Department of Community Health and Epidemiology, Halifax, NS B3H 4R2, Canada. Offers M Sc. *Degree requirements:* For master's, thesis. *Entrance requirements:* Additional exam requirements/recommendations for international students: required—1 of 5 approved tests: TOEFL, IELTS, CANTEST, CAEL, Michigan English Language Assessment Battery. Electronic applications accepted. *Expenses:* Contact institution.

**Eastern Kentucky University,** The Graduate School, College of Health Sciences, Program in Public Health, Richmond, KY 40475-3102. Offers community health education (MPH); environmental health science (MPH); industrial hygiene (MPH); public health nutrition (MPH). *Accreditation:* CEPH. *Degree requirements:* For master's, comprehensive exam, thesis optional, practicum, capstone course. *Entrance requirements:* For master's, GRE.

**East Tennessee State University,** College of Graduate and Continuing Studies, College of Public Health, Program in Public Health, Johnson City, TN 37614. Offers biostatistics (MPH, Postbaccalaureate Certificate); community health (MPH, DPH); environmental health (MPH); epidemiology (MPH, DPH, Postbaccalaureate Certificate); gerontology (Postbaccalaureate Certificate); global health (Postbaccalaureate Certificate); health care management (Postbaccalaureate Certificate); health management and policy (DPH); public health (Postbaccalaureate Certificate); public health services administration (MPH); rural health (Postbaccalaureate Certificate). *Accreditation:* CEPH. *Program availability:* Part-time, online learning. *Degree requirements:* For master's, comprehensive exam, field experience; for doctorate, thesis/dissertation, practicum. *Entrance requirements:* For master's, GRE General Test, minimum GPA of 2.75, SOPHAS application, three letters of recommendation; for doctorate, GRE General Test, SOPHAS application, three letters of recommendation; for Postbaccalaureate Certificate, minimum GPA of 2.5, three letters of recommendation, resume. Additional exam requirements/recommendations for international students: required—TOEFL (minimum score 550 paper-based; 79 iBT), IELTS (minimum score 6.5). Electronic applications accepted.

**George Mason University,** College of Health and Human Services, Department of Global and Community Health, Fairfax, VA 22030. Offers global and community health (Certificate); global health (MS); public health (MPH, Certificate), including epidemiology (MPH), leadership and management (Certificate). *Accreditation:* CEPH. *Program availability:* Part-time, evening/weekend. *Degree requirements:* For master's, thesis, 200-hour practicum. *Entrance requirements:* For master's, GRE, GMAT (depending on program), 2 official transcripts; expanded goals statement; 3 letters of recommendation; resume; 1 completed course in health science, statistics, natural sciences and social science (for MPH); 6 credits of foreign language if not fluent (for MS); minimum undergraduate GPA of 3.0; for Certificate, 2 official transcripts; expanded goals statement; 3 letters of recommendation; resume; bachelor's degree from regionally-accredited institution with minimum GPA of 3.0. Additional exam requirements/recommendations for international students: required—TOEFL (minimum score 570 paper-based; 88 iBT), IELTS (minimum score 6.5), PTE (minimum score 59). Electronic applications accepted. *Expenses:* Contact institution.

**The George Washington University,** Milken Institute School of Public Health, Department of Prevention and Community Health, Washington, DC 20052. Offers MPH, Dr PH.

**Georgia Southern University,** Jack N. Averitt College of Graduate Studies, Jiann-Ping Hsu College of Public Health, Program in Public Health, Statesboro, GA 30460. Offers biostatistics (MPH, Dr PH); community health behavior and education (Dr PH); community health education (MPH); environmental health sciences (MPH); epidemiology (MPH); health policy and management (MPH, Dr PH). *Program availability:* Part-time. *Faculty:* 42 full-time (22 women), 1 (woman) part-time/adjunct. *Students:* 142 full-time (105 women), 88 part-time (62 women); includes 132 minority (100 Black or African American, non-Hispanic/Latino; 10 Asian, non-Hispanic/Latino; 8 Hispanic/Latino; 14 Two or more races, non-Hispanic/Latino), 46 international. Average age 32. 195 applicants, 85% accepted, 59 enrolled. In 2019, 90 master's, 14 doctorates awarded. *Degree requirements:* For master's, thesis optional, practicum; for doctorate, comprehensive exam, thesis/dissertation, preceptorship. *Entrance requirements:* For master's, GRE General Test, minimum GPA of 2.75, 3 letters of recommendation, statement of purpose, resume or curriculum vitae; for doctorate, GRE, GMAT, MCAT, LSAT, minimum GPA of 3.0, 3 letters of recommendation, statement of purpose, resume or curriculum vitae. Additional exam requirements/recommendations for international students: required—TOEFL (minimum score 537 paper-based; 75 iBT), IELTS (minimum score 6). *Application deadline:* For fall admission, 6/1 for domestic students, 5/1 for international students. Applications are processed on a rolling basis. Application fee: $135. Electronic applications accepted. *Expenses:* Contact institution. *Financial support:* In 2019–20, 94 students received support, including 1 research assistantship with full tuition reimbursement available (averaging $12,350 per year), 6 teaching assistantships with full tuition reimbursements available (averaging $12,350 per year); scholarships/grants, tuition waivers (full), and unspecified assistantships also available. Financial award application deadline: 4/15; financial award applicants required to submit FAFSA. *Unit head:* Dr. Robert Greg Evans, Dean, 912-478-2674, E-mail: rgevans@georgiasouthern.edu. *Application contact:* Shamia Garrett, Coordinator, Office of Student Services, 912-478-2674, Fax: 912-478-5811, E-mail: jphcoph-gradadvisor@georgiasouthern.edu.
Website: http://jphcoph.georgiasouthern.edu/

**Icahn School of Medicine at Mount Sinai,** Graduate School of Biomedical Sciences, New York, NY 10029-6504. Offers biomedical sciences (MS, PhD); clinical research education (MS, PhD); community medicine (MPH); genetic counseling (MS); neurosciences (PhD); MD/PhD. Terminal master's awarded for partial completion of doctoral program. *Degree requirements:* For master's, thesis; for doctorate, comprehensive exam, thesis/dissertation. *Entrance requirements:* For master's, GRE General Test; for doctorate, GRE General Test, GRE Subject Test, 3 years of college pre-med course work. Additional exam requirements/recommendations for international students: required—TOEFL. Electronic applications accepted.

**Idaho State University,** Graduate School, College of Health Professions, Department of Family Medicine, Pocatello, ID 83209-8357. Offers Post-Master's Certificate. *Degree requirements:* For Post-Master's Certificate, comprehensive exam, thesis optional, 3 year residency program. *Entrance requirements:* For degree, GRE General Test, MD or DO. Additional exam requirements/recommendations for international students: required—TOEFL (minimum score 600 paper-based). Electronic applications accepted.

**Independence University,** Program in Health Services, Salt Lake City, UT 84107. Offers community health (MSHS); wellness promotion (MSHS). *Program availability:* Part-time, evening/weekend, online learning. *Degree requirements:* For master's, fieldwork, internship, final project (wellness promotion). *Entrance requirements:* For master's, previous course work in psychology.

**Indiana University Bloomington,** School of Public Health, Department of Applied Health Science, Bloomington, IN 47405. Offers behavioral, social, and community health (MPH); family health (MPH); health behavior (PhD); nutrition science (MS); professional health education (MPH); public health administration (MPH); safety management (MS); school and college health education (MS). *Degree requirements:* For master's, thesis optional; for doctorate, comprehensive exam, thesis/dissertation. *Entrance requirements:* For master's, GRE (for MS in nutrition science), 3 recommendations; for doctorate, GRE, 3 recommendations. Additional exam requirements/recommendations for international students: required—TOEFL (minimum score 550 paper-based; 80 iBT). Electronic applications accepted.

**Indiana University-Purdue University Indianapolis,** Richard M. Fairbanks School of Public Health, Indianapolis, IN 46202. Offers biostatistics (MS, PhD); environmental health (MPH); epidemiology (MPH, PhD); global health leadership (Dr PH); health administration (MHA); health policy (Graduate Certificate); health policy and management (MPH, PhD); health systems management (Graduate Certificate); product stewardship (MS); public health (Graduate Certificate); social and behavioral sciences (MPH). *Accreditation:* CAHME; CEPH. *Expenses:* Contact institution.

**Johns Hopkins University,** Bloomberg School of Public Health, Department of Health, Behavior and Society, Baltimore, MD 21218. Offers genetic counseling (Sc M); health education and health communication (MSPH); social and behavioral sciences (PhD); social factors in health (MHS). *Degree requirements:* For master's, comprehensive exam (for some programs), thesis (for some programs); for doctorate, comprehensive exam, thesis/dissertation. *Entrance requirements:* For master's, GRE, curriculum vitae, 3 letters of recommendation; for doctorate, GRE, transcripts, curriculum vitae, 3 recommendation letters. Additional exam requirements/recommendations for international students: required—TOEFL (minimum score 100 iBT), IELTS (minimum score 7). Electronic applications accepted.

**Long Island University - Brooklyn,** School of Health Professions, Brooklyn, NY 11201-8423. Offers athletic training and sport sciences (MS); community health (MS Ed); exercise science (MS); forensic social work (Advanced Certificate); occupational therapy (MS); physical therapy (DPT); physician assistant (MS); public health (MPH); social work (MSW); speech-language pathology (MS). *Accreditation:* AOTA; CEPH. *Degree requirements:* For master's, comprehensive exam (for some programs), thesis (for some programs); for doctorate, comprehensive exam (for some programs). *Entrance requirements:* For master's and doctorate, GRE. Additional exam requirements/recommendations for international students: required—TOEFL (minimum score 550 paper-based; 79 iBT). Electronic applications accepted.

**Louisiana State University Health Sciences Center,** School of Public Health, New Orleans, LA 70112. Offers behavioral and community health sciences (MPH); biostatistics (MPH, MS, PhD); community health sciences (PhD); environmental and occupational health sciences (MPH); epidemiology (MPH, PhD); health policy and systems management (MPH). *Accreditation:* CEPH. *Program availability:* Part-time. *Degree requirements:* For doctorate, thesis/dissertation. *Entrance requirements:* For master's, GRE General Test. Additional exam requirements/recommendations for international students: recommended—TOEFL (minimum score 550 paper-based; 79 iBT), IELTS. Electronic applications accepted.

**Medical College of Wisconsin,** Graduate School, Program in Public and Community Health, Milwaukee, WI 53226. Offers PhD, MD/PhD. *Accreditation:* CEPH. *Students:* 12 full-time (7 women), 5 part-time (4 women); includes 5 minority (4 Black or African American, non-Hispanic/Latino; 1 American Indian or Alaska Native, non-Hispanic/Latino), 5 international. Average age 33. 19 applicants, 26% accepted, 5 enrolled. In 2019, 5 doctorates awarded. *Degree requirements:* For doctorate, comprehensive exam, thesis/dissertation. *Entrance requirements:* For doctorate, GRE, official transcripts, three letters of recommendation. Additional exam requirements/recommendations for international students: required—TOEFL (minimum score 580 paper-based; 100 iBT). *Application deadline:* For fall admission, 12/1 for domestic and international students. Applications are processed on a rolling basis. Application fee: $50. Electronic applications accepted. *Expenses:* $1250 per credit PhD students; $1056 per credit Masters students; $155 per year full time students fees. *Financial support:* In 2019–20, 12 students received support, including fellowships with full tuition reimbursements available (averaging $30,000 per year); scholarships/grants, health care benefits, and tuition waivers (full) also available. Financial award application deadline: 2/15; financial award applicants required to submit FAFSA. *Unit head:* Dr. Laura D. Cassidy, Director, 414-955-4517, Fax: 414-955-6555, E-mail: phdpch@mcw.edu. *Application contact:* Recruitment Office, 414-955-4402, Fax: 414-955-6555, E-mail: gradschoolrecruit@mcw.edu.
Website: http://www.mcw.edu/Graduate-School/Programs/Public-Health/Public-and-Community-Health.htm

**Memorial University of Newfoundland,** Faculty of Medicine and School of Graduate Studies, Graduate Programs in Medicine, Division of Community Health and Humanities, St. John's, NL A1C 5S7, Canada. Offers community health (M Sc, PhD, Diploma). *Program availability:* Part-time. *Degree requirements:* For master's, thesis; for doctorate, comprehensive exam, thesis/dissertation, oral defense of thesis. *Entrance requirements:* For master's, MD or B Sc; for doctorate, MD or M Sc; for Diploma, bachelor's degree in health-related field. Additional exam requirements/recommendations for international students: required—TOEFL.

**Midwestern State University,** Billie Doris McAda Graduate School, Robert D. and Carol Gunn College of Health Sciences and Human Services, Department of Criminal Justice and Health Services Administration, Wichita Falls, TX 76308. Offers criminal justice (MA); health information management (MHA); health services administration (Graduate Certificate); medical practice management (MHA); public and community sector health care management (MHA); rural and urban hospital management (MHA). *Program availability:* Part-time, evening/weekend. *Degree requirements:* For master's, comprehensive exam, thesis. *Entrance requirements:* For master's, GRE. Additional exam requirements/recommendations for international students: required—TOEFL (minimum score 550 paper-based). Electronic applications accepted.

**Minnesota State University Mankato,** College of Graduate Studies and Research, College of Allied Health and Nursing, Department of Health Science, Mankato, MN 56001. Offers community health education (MS); public health education (Postbaccalaureate Certificate); school health education (MS, Postbaccalaureate Certificate). *Program availability:* Part-time. *Degree requirements:* For master's,

comprehensive exam, thesis or alternative. *Entrance requirements:* For master's, minimum GPA of 3.0 during previous 2 years; for Postbaccalaureate Certificate, teaching license. Additional exam requirements/recommendations for international students: required—TOEFL (minimum score 500 paper-based; 61 iBT). Electronic applications accepted.

**Monroe College,** King Graduate School, Bronx, NY 10468. Offers accounting (MS); business administration (MBA), including entrepreneurship, finance, general business administration, healthcare management, human resources, information technology, marketing; computer science (MS); criminal justice (MS); hospitality management (MS); public health (MPH), including biostatistics and epidemiology, community health, health administration and leadership. *Program availability:* Online learning.

**New Jersey City University,** College of Professional Studies, Department of Health Sciences, Jersey City, NJ 07305-1597. Offers community health education (MS); health administration (MS); school health education (MS). *Program availability:* Part-time, evening/weekend. *Degree requirements:* For master's, thesis or alternative, internship. *Entrance requirements:* Additional exam requirements/recommendations for international students: required—TOEFL (minimum score 79 iBT).

**New York University,** College of Global Public Health, New York, NY 10012. Offers biological basis of public health (PhD); community and international health (MPH); global health leadership (MPH); health systems and health services research (PhD); population and community health (PhD); public health nutrition (MPH); social and behavioral sciences (MPH); socio-behavioral health (PhD). *Accreditation:* CEPH. *Program availability:* Part-time, online learning. *Degree requirements:* For master's, thesis (for some programs); for doctorate, thesis/dissertation. *Entrance requirements:* For master's and doctorate, GRE. Additional exam requirements/recommendations for international students: required—TOEFL. Electronic applications accepted. *Expenses:* Contact institution.

**North Dakota State University,** College of Graduate and Interdisciplinary Studies, College of Health Professions, Department of Public Health, Fargo, ND 58102. Offers American Indian public health (MPH); community health sciences (MPH); management of infectious diseases (MPH); Pharm D/MPH. *Accreditation:* CEPH. *Program availability:* Online learning. Tuition and fees vary according to program and reciprocity agreements.

**Old Dominion University,** College of Health Sciences, School of Community and Environmental Health, Norfolk, VA 23529. Offers general environmental health (MS); industrial hygiene (MS). *Degree requirements:* For master's, comprehensive exam, oral exam, written exam, practicum or thesis. *Entrance requirements:* For master's, GRE General Test, minimum GPA of 2.75. Additional exam requirements/recommendations for international students: required—TOEFL (minimum score 650 paper-based). Electronic applications accepted. *Expenses:* Contact institution.

**Old Dominion University,** College of Health Sciences, School of Dental Hygiene, Norfolk, VA 23529. Offers dental hygiene (MS), including community/public health, education, generalist, global health, marketing, modeling and simulation, research. *Program availability:* Part-time, evening/weekend, blended/hybrid learning. *Degree requirements:* For master's, comprehensive exam, thesis optional, writing proficiency exam, responsible conduct of research training. *Entrance requirements:* For master's, Dental Hygiene National Board Examination or copy of license to practice dental hygiene, BS or certificate in dental hygiene or related area, minimum GPA of 2.8 (3.0 in major), 4 letters of recommendation. Additional exam requirements/recommendations for international students: required—TOEFL (minimum score 550 paper-based, 79 iBT) or IELTS (minimum score 6.5). Electronic applications accepted. *Expenses:* Contact institution.

**Quinnipiac University,** School of Nursing, Care of Populations Track, Hamden, CT 06518-1940. Offers DNP. *Program availability:* Part-time-only, evening/weekend, online only. *Entrance requirements:* For doctorate, minimum GPA of 3.0; RN or NCLEX-eligible nurse with bachelor's degree in nursing or another field; master's degree in relevant field; minimum of 1000 hours of field work observation. Additional exam requirements/recommendations for international students: required—TOEFL (minimum score 575 paper-based; 90 iBT), IELTS (minimum score 6.5). Electronic applications accepted. *Expenses:* Contact institution.

**Saint Louis University,** Graduate Programs, College for Public Health and Social Justice, Department of Community Health, St. Louis, MO 63103. Offers MPH, MS, MSPH. *Program availability:* Part-time, online learning. *Degree requirements:* For master's, comprehensive exam. *Entrance requirements:* For master's, GRE General Test, LSAT, GMAT or MCAT, letters of recommendation, resume. Additional exam requirements/recommendations for international students: required—TOEFL (minimum score 525 paper-based). Electronic applications accepted.

**San Francisco State University,** Division of Graduate Studies, College of Health and Social Sciences, Department of Health Education, San Francisco, CA 94132-1722. Offers community health education (MPH). *Accreditation:* CEPH. *Program availability:* Part-time. *Students:* Average age 36. *Application deadline:* Applications are processed on a rolling basis. *Expenses: Tuition, area resident:* Full-time $7176; part-time $4164 per year. Tuition, state resident: full-time $7176; part-time $4164 per year. Tuition, nonresident: full-time $16,680; part-time $396 per unit. *International tuition:* $16,680 full-time. *Required fees:* $1524; $1524 per unit. $762 per semester. Tuition and fees vary according to degree level and program. *Unit head:* Dr. Marty Martinson, Chair, 415-338-1413, Fax: 415-338-0570, E-mail: martym@sfsu.edu. *Application contact:* Vincent Lam, Graduate Coordinator, 415-338-1413, Fax: 415-338-0570, E-mail: vlam@sfsu.edu.
Website: http://healthed.sfsu.edu/graduate

**Southern Illinois University Carbondale,** Graduate School, College of Education and Human Services, Department of Health Education and Recreation, Program in Community Health Education, Carbondale, IL 62901-4701. Offers MPH, MD/MPH, PhD/MPH. *Accreditation:* CEPH. *Entrance requirements:* Additional exam requirements/recommendations for international students: required—TOEFL (minimum score 550 paper-based; 80 iBT).

**State University of New York College at Cortland,** Graduate Studies, School of Professional Studies, Department of Health, Cortland, NY 13045. Offers community health (MS); health education (MST). *Accreditation:* NCATE. *Program availability:* Part-time, evening/weekend. *Entrance requirements:* Additional exam requirements/recommendations for international students: required—TOEFL.

**State University of New York College at Potsdam,** School of Education and Professional Studies, Program in Community Health, Potsdam, NY 13676. Offers MS. *Entrance requirements:* For master's, baccalaureate degree from accredited institution, minimum GPA of 3.0 for final 60 credits of baccalaureate work, statement of professional and educational goals, three letters of recommendation, resume or curriculum vitae.

**State University of New York Downstate Medical Center,** College of Medicine, Program in Public Health, Brooklyn, NY 11203-2098. Offers urban and immigrant health (MPH); MD/MPH. *Program availability:* Part-time. *Degree requirements:* For master's, practicum. *Entrance requirements:* For master's, GRE, MCAT or OAT, 2 letters of recommendation, minimum undergraduate GPA of 3.0. Additional exam requirements/recommendations for international students: required—TOEFL (minimum score 550 paper-based).

**Stony Brook University, State University of New York,** Stony Brook Medicine, Renaissance School of Medicine, Program in Population Health and Clinical Outcomes Research, Stony Brook, NY 11794. Offers PhD. *Students:* 2 full-time (both women), 3 part-time (all women); includes 1 minority (Asian, non-Hispanic/Latino), 1 international. Average age 29. 21 applicants. *Degree requirements:* For doctorate, thesis/dissertation. *Entrance requirements:* For doctorate, GRE (verbal, quantitative, and analytical), personal or telephone interview, minimum GPA of 3.0 in undergraduate work, cover letter, 3.0 GPA or better. Additional exam requirements/recommendations for international students: required—TOEFL (minimum score 90 iBT). *Application deadline:* For fall admission, 1/15 for domestic students. Electronic applications accepted. *Expenses:* Contact institution. *Financial support:* In 2019–20, 1 research assistantship was awarded. *Unit head:* Dr. Dylan Smith, Director, Ph.D. Program, 631-444-3074, E-mail: dylan.m.smith@stonybrook.edu. *Application contact:* Joanie Maniaci, Assistant Director for Student Affairs, 631-632-2074, Fax: 631-444-6035, E-mail: joanmarie.maniaci@stonybrook.edu.
Website: https://publichealth.stonybrookmedicine.edu/phcor

**Stony Brook University, State University of New York,** Stony Brook Medicine, Renaissance School of Medicine, Program in Public Health, Stony Brook, NY 11794. Offers community health (MPH); evaluation sciences (MPH); family violence (MPH); health communication (Certificate); health economics (MPH); health education and promotion (Certificate); population health (MPH); substance abuse (MPH). *Accreditation:* CEPH. *Program availability:* Part-time, evening/weekend. *Students:* 39 full-time (30 women), 17 part-time (12 women); includes 24 minority (3 Black or African American, non-Hispanic/Latino; 13 Asian, non-Hispanic/Latino; 7 Hispanic/Latino; 1 Two or more races, non-Hispanic/Latino), 2 international. Average age 28. 174 applicants, 67% accepted, 70 enrolled. In 2019, 22 master's awarded. *Entrance requirements:* For master's, GRE, 3 references, bachelor's degree from accredited college or university with minimum GPA of 3.0, essays, interview. Additional exam requirements/recommendations for international students: required—TOEFL (minimum score 90 iBT). *Application deadline:* For fall admission, 7/15 for domestic students. Application fee: $100. Electronic applications accepted. *Expenses:* Contact institution. *Financial support:* In 2019–20, 4 research assistantships were awarded; fellowships also available. *Unit head:* Dr. Lisa A. Benz Scott, Director, 631-444-9396, E-mail: publichealth@stonybrookmedicine.edu. *Application contact:* Joanie Maniaci, Assistant Director for Student Affairs, 631-444-2074, Fax: 631-444-6035, E-mail: joanmarie.maniaci@stonybrook.edu.
Website: https://publichealth.stonybrookmedicine.edu/

**Suffolk University,** Sawyer Business School, Department of Public Administration, Boston, MA 02108-2770. Offers community health (MPA); information systems, performance management, and big data analytics (MPA); nonprofit management (MPA); state and local government (MPA); JD/MPA; MPA/MS; MPA/MSCJ; MPA/MSMHC; MPA/MSPS. *Accreditation:* NASPAA (one or more programs are accredited). *Program availability:* Part-time, evening/weekend. *Faculty:* 12 full-time (7 women), 4 part-time/adjunct (3 women). *Students:* 13 full-time (5 women), 72 part-time (55 women); includes 35 minority (21 Black or African American, non-Hispanic/Latino; 3 Asian, non-Hispanic/Latino; 9 Hispanic/Latino; 2 Two or more races, non-Hispanic/Latino), 2 international. Average age 35. 89 applicants, 85% accepted, 30 enrolled. In 2019, 40 master's awarded. *Entrance requirements:* Additional exam requirements/recommendations for international students: required—TOEFL (minimum score 550 paper-based; 80 iBT). *Application deadline:* For fall admission, 3/15 priority date for domestic and international students; for spring admission, 10/15 priority date for domestic and international students. Applications are processed on a rolling basis. Application fee: $50. Electronic applications accepted. *Expenses:* Contact institution. *Financial support:* In 2019–20, 47 students received support, including 2 fellowships (averaging $2,657 per year); career-related internships or fieldwork, Federal Work-Study, institutionally sponsored loans, and scholarships/grants also available. Support available to part-time students. Financial award application deadline: 4/1; financial award applicants required to submit FAFSA. *Unit head:* Brenda Bond, Director/Department Chair, 617-305-1768, E-mail: bbond@suffolk.edu. *Application contact:* Mara Marzocchi, Associate Director of Graduate Admissions, 617-573-8302, Fax: 617-305-1733, E-mail: grad.admission@suffolk.edu.
Website: http://www.suffolk.edu/mpa

**Suffolk University,** Sawyer Business School, Program in Healthcare Administration, Boston, MA 02108-2770. Offers community health (MPA); health (MBAH); healthcare administration (MHA). *Accreditation:* CAHME. *Program availability:* Part-time, evening/weekend. *Faculty:* 4 full-time (1 woman), 3 part-time/adjunct (1 woman). *Students:* 22 full-time (17 women), 32 part-time (26 women); includes 19 minority (7 Black or African American, non-Hispanic/Latino; 7 Asian, non-Hispanic/Latino; 3 Hispanic/Latino; 2 Two or more races, non-Hispanic/Latino), 9 international. Average age 28. 56 applicants, 80% accepted, 23 enrolled. In 2019, 41 master's awarded. *Entrance requirements:* Additional exam requirements/recommendations for international students: required—TOEFL (minimum score 550 paper-based; 80 iBT). *Application deadline:* For fall admission, 3/15 priority date for domestic and international students; for spring admission, 10/15 priority date for domestic and international students. Applications are processed on a rolling basis. Application fee: $50. Electronic applications accepted. *Expenses:* Contact institution. *Financial support:* In 2019–20, 31 students received support. Fellowships, career-related internships or fieldwork, Federal Work-Study, institutionally sponsored loans, scholarships/grants, and health care benefits available. Support available to part-time students. Financial award application deadline: 4/1; financial award applicants required to submit FAFSA. *Unit head:* Richard Gregg, Director of Programs in Healthcare Administration/Chair of Healthcare Department, 617-994-4246, E-mail: rgregg@suffolk.edu. *Application contact:* Mara Marzocchi, Associate Director of Graduate Admissions, 617-573-8302, Fax: 617-305-1733, E-mail: grad.admission@suffolk.edu.
Website: http://www.suffolk.edu/business/graduate/62398.php

**SUNY Brockport,** School of Education, Health, and Human Services, Department of Public Health and Health Education, Brockport, NY 14420-2997. Offers community health education (MS Ed); health education (MS Ed), including health education K-12. *Faculty:* 4 full-time (1 woman), 4 part-time/adjunct (3 women). *Students:* 14 full-time (4 women), 108 part-time (49 women); includes 3 minority (1 Black or African American, non-Hispanic/Latino; 1 Asian, non-Hispanic/Latino; 1 Hispanic/Latino). 51 applicants, 65% accepted, 27 enrolled. In 2019, 18 master's awarded. *Entrance requirements:* For master's, minimum GPA of 3.0, letters of recommendation. Additional exam requirements/recommendations for international students: required—TOEFL (minimum score 550 paper-based; 79 iBT), IELTS (minimum score 6.5). *Application deadline:* For fall admission, 3/1 priority date for domestic and international students; for spring admission, 10/1 priority date for domestic and international students; for summer admission, 3/1 priority date for domestic and international students. Application fee: $80. Electronic applications accepted. *Expenses: Tuition, area resident:* Part-time $471 per credit hour. Tuition, nonresident: part-time $963 per credit hour. *Financial support:* In 2019–20, 1 teaching assistantship with full tuition reimbursement (averaging $6,000 per year) was awarded; Federal Work-Study, scholarships/grants, and unspecified assistantships also available. Support available to part-time students. Financial award application deadline: 3/15; financial award applicants required to submit FAFSA. *Unit*

*head:* Dr. Darson Rhodes, Graduate Director, 585-395-5901, Fax: 585-395-5246, E-mail: drhodes@brockport.edu. *Application contact:* Danielle A. Welch, Graduate Admissions Counselor, 585-395-5465, Fax: 585-395-2515.
Website: https://www.brockport.edu/academics/public_health/

**Teachers College, Columbia University,** Department of Health and Behavior Studies, New York, NY 10027-6696. Offers applied behavior analysis (MA, PhD); applied educational psychology: school psychology (Ed M, PhD); behavioral nutrition (PhD), including nutrition (Ed D, PhD); community health education (MS); community nutrition education (Ed M), including community nutrition education; education of deaf and hard of hearing (MA, PhD); health education (MA, Ed D); hearing impairment (Ed D); intellectual disability/autism (MA, Ed D, PhD); nursing education (Ed D, Advanced Certificate); nutrition and education (MS); nutrition and exercise physiology (MS); nutrition and public health (MS); nutrition education (Ed D), including nutrition (Ed D, PhD); physical disabilities (Ed D); reading specialist (MA); severe or multiple disabilities (MA); special education (Ed M, MA, Ed D); teaching of sign language (MA). *Faculty:* 17 full-time (11 women). *Students:* 243 full-time (225 women), 246 part-time (211 women); includes 172 minority (33 Black or African American, non-Hispanic/Latino; 2 American Indian or Alaska Native, non-Hispanic/Latino; 63 Asian, non-Hispanic/Latino; 63 Hispanic/Latino; 11 Two or more races, non-Hispanic/Latino), 67 international. 515 applicants, 68% accepted, 170 enrolled. *Unit head:* Dr. Dolores Perin, Chair, 212-678-3091, E-mail: dp111@tc.columbia.edu. *Application contact:* Kelly Sutton-Skinner, Director of Admission and New Student Enrollment, E-mail: kms2237@tc.columbia.edu.
Website: http://www.tc.columbia.edu/health-and-behavior-studies/

**Tulane University,** School of Public Health and Tropical Medicine, Department of Global Community Health and Behavioral Sciences, New Orleans, LA 70118-5669. Offers community health sciences (MPH); global community health and behavioral sciences (Dr PH, PhD); JD/MPH; MD/MPH; MSW/MPH. *Program availability:* Part-time. *Degree requirements:* For doctorate, comprehensive exam, thesis/dissertation. *Entrance requirements:* For master's and doctorate, GRE General Test. Additional exam requirements/recommendations for international students: required—TOEFL. Electronic applications accepted. *Expenses: Tuition:* Full-time $57,004; part-time $3167 per credit hour. *Required fees:* $2086; $44.50 per credit hour. $80 per term. Tuition and fees vary according to course load, degree level and program.

**Universidad de Ciencias Medicas,** Graduate Programs, San Jose, Costa Rica. Offers dermatology (SP); family health (MS); health service center administration (MHA); human anatomy (MS); medical and surgery (MD); occupational medicine (MS); pharmacy (Pharm D). *Program availability:* Part-time. *Degree requirements:* For master's, thesis; for doctorate and SP, comprehensive exam. *Entrance requirements:* For master's, MD or bachelor's degree; for doctorate, admissions test; for SP, admissions test, MD.

**Université de Montréal,** Faculty of Medicine, Program in Communal and Public Health, Montréal, QC H3C 3J7, Canada. Offers community health (M Sc, DESS); public health (PhD). *Accreditation:* CEPH. *Program availability:* Part-time. Terminal master's awarded for partial completion of doctoral program. *Degree requirements:* For master's, thesis; for doctorate, thesis/dissertation, general exam. *Entrance requirements:* For master's and doctorate, proficiency in French, knowledge of English; for DESS, proficiency in French. Electronic applications accepted.

**University at Buffalo, the State University of New York,** Graduate School, School of Architecture and Planning, Department of Urban and Regional Planning, Buffalo, NY 14214. Offers economic development (MUP); environment/land use (MUP); health and food systems (MUP); historic preservation (MUP, Certificate); neighborhood/community development (MUP); real estate development (MSRED); urban and regional planning (PhD); urban design (MUP); JD/MUP; M Arch/MUP. *Accreditation:* ACSP. *Program availability:* Part-time. *Faculty:* 11 full-time (4 women), 15 part-time/adjunct (6 women). *Students:* 88 full-time (40 women), 25 part-time (10 women); includes 32 minority (16 Black or African American, non-Hispanic/Latino; 2 Asian, non-Hispanic/Latino; 7 Hispanic/Latino; 7 Two or more races, non-Hispanic/Latino), 13 international. Average age 26. 146 applicants, 40% accepted, 40 enrolled. In 2019, 31 master's, 1 doctorate, 4 other advanced degrees awarded. *Degree requirements:* For master's, thesis or alternative, project; for doctorate, comprehensive exam, thesis/dissertation, dissertation. *Entrance requirements:* For master's, resume, two letters of recommendation, personal statement, transcripts; for doctorate, GRE, transcripts, three letters of recommendation, resume, research statement, writing sample. Additional exam requirements/recommendations for international students: required—TOEFL (minimum score 79 iBT), IELTS (minimum score 6.5). *Application deadline:* For fall admission, 3/1 priority date for domestic and international students; for spring admission, 10/31 priority date for domestic students, 10/1 priority date for international students. Applications are processed on a rolling basis. Application fee: $75. Electronic applications accepted. *Expenses: Tuition, area resident:* Full-time $11,310; part-time $471 per credit hour. Tuition, state resident: full-time $11,310; part-time $471 per credit hour. Tuition, nonresident: full-time $23,100; part-time $963 per credit hour. *International tuition:* $23,100 full-time. *Required fees:* $2820. *Financial support:* In 2019–20, 54 students received support, including 5 fellowships with full tuition reimbursements available (averaging $22,560 per year), 1 research assistantship with partial tuition reimbursement available (averaging $16,027 per year), 20 teaching assistantships with partial tuition reimbursements available (averaging $6,912 per year); career-related internships or fieldwork, Federal Work-Study, institutionally sponsored loans, scholarships/grants, health care benefits, tuition waivers (full and partial), and unspecified assistantships also available. Financial award application deadline: 3/1; financial award applicants required to submit FAFSA. *Unit head:* Dr. Daniel B. Hess, Professor and Chair, 716-829-5326, Fax: 716-829-3256, E-mail: dbhess@buffalo.edu. *Application contact:* Norma Everett, Graduate Programs Coordinator, 716-829-3283, Fax: 716-829-3256, E-mail: norma.everett@buffalo.edu.
Website: http://www.ap.buffalo.edu/planning/

**University at Buffalo, the State University of New York,** Graduate School, School of Public Health and Health Professions, Department of Community Health and Health Behavior, Buffalo, NY 14260. Offers MPH, PhD. *Accreditation:* CEPH. *Program availability:* Part-time. *Entrance requirements:* For master's and doctorate, GRE. Additional exam requirements/recommendations for international students: required—TOEFL (minimum score 79 iBT). Electronic applications accepted. *Expenses: Tuition, area resident:* Full-time $11,310; part-time $471 per credit hour. Tuition, state resident: full-time $11,310; part-time $471 per credit hour. Tuition, nonresident: full-time $23,100; part-time $963 per credit hour. *International tuition:* $23,100 full-time. *Required fees:* $2820.

**The University of Alabama,** Graduate School, College of Human Environmental Sciences, Department of General Human Environmental Sciences, Tuscaloosa, AL 35487. Offers interactive technology (MS); quality management (MS); restaurant and meeting management (MS); rural community health (MS); sport management (MS). *Program availability:* Part-time, evening/weekend, online learning. *Faculty:* 2 full-time (both women). *Students:* 61 full-time (42 women), 108 part-time (54 women); includes 45 minority (26 Black or African American, non-Hispanic/Latino; 1 American Indian or Alaska Native, non-Hispanic/Latino; 2 Asian, non-Hispanic/Latino; 8 Hispanic/Latino; 8 Two or more races, non-Hispanic/Latino), 1 international. Average age 33. 89 applicants, 89% accepted, 61 enrolled. In 2019, 130 master's awarded. *Degree requirements:* For master's, comprehensive exam. *Entrance requirements:* For master's, GRE (for some specializations), minimum GPA of 3.0. Additional exam requirements/recommendations for international students: required—TOEFL. *Application deadline:* For fall admission, 7/1 for domestic students; for spring admission, 11/1 for domestic students; for summer admission, 4/15 for domestic students. Applications are processed on a rolling basis. Application fee: $50 ($60 for international students). Electronic applications accepted. *Expenses: Tuition, area resident:* Full-time $10,780; part-time $440 per credit hour. Tuition, nonresident: full-time $30,250; part-time $1550 per credit hour. *Financial support:* Teaching assistantships with full tuition reimbursements available. Financial award application deadline: 7/1. *Unit head:* Dr. Stuart L. Usdan, Dean, 205-348-6250, Fax: 205-348-3789, E-mail: susdan@ches.ua.edu. *Application contact:* Dr. Stuart Usdan, Associate Dean, 205-348-6150, Fax: 205-348-3789, E-mail: susdan@ches.ua.edu.
Website: http://www.ches.ua.edu/programs-of-study.html

**The University of Alabama at Birmingham,** School of Education, Community Health and Human Services Program, Birmingham, AL 35294. Offers MA Ed. *Accreditation:* NCATE. *Faculty:* 4 full-time (2 women). *Students:* 12 full-time (11 women), 12 part-time (9 women); includes 14 minority (13 Black or African American, non-Hispanic/Latino; 1 Hispanic/Latino), 1 international. Average age 33. 19 applicants, 84% accepted, 9 enrolled. In 2019, 14 master's awarded. *Degree requirements:* For master's, comprehensive exam (for some programs), thesis optional. *Entrance requirements:* For master's, GRE General Test or MAT, minimum GPA of 3.0, references. *Application deadline:* Applications are processed on a rolling basis. Application fee: $35 ($60 for international students). Electronic applications accepted. *Unit head:* Dr. Kristi Menear, Chair, 205-975-7409, Fax: 205-975-8040, E-mail: kmenear@uab.edu. *Application contact:* Dr. Retta R. Evans, Program Coordinator, 205-996-2701, Fax: 205-975-8040, E-mail: rrevans@uab.edu.

**University of Alberta,** School of Public Health, Department of Public Health Sciences, Edmonton, AB T6G 2E1, Canada. Offers clinical epidemiology (M Sc, MPH); environmental and occupational health (MPH); environmental health sciences (M Sc); epidemiology (M Sc); global health (M Sc, MPH); health policy and management (MPH); health policy research (M Sc); health technology assessment (MPH); occupational health (M Sc); population health (M Sc); public health leadership (MPH); public health sciences (PhD); quantitative methods (MPH). *Accreditation:* CEPH. Terminal master's awarded for partial completion of doctoral program. *Degree requirements:* For master's, thesis (for some programs); for doctorate, thesis/dissertation. *Entrance requirements:* For master's, GMAT or GRE General Test. Additional exam requirements/recommendations for international students: required—TOEFL (minimum score 550 paper-based) or IELTS (minimum score 6). Electronic applications accepted.

**University of Arkansas,** Graduate School, College of Education and Health Professions, Department of Health, Human Performance and Recreation, Program in Community Health Promotion, Fayetteville, AR 72701. Offers MS, PhD. *Students:* 9 full-time (7 women), 8 part-time (7 women), 4 international. 15 applicants, 53% accepted. In 2019, 4 master's, 1 doctorate awarded. *Application deadline:* For fall admission, 8/1 for domestic students, 4/1 for international students; for spring admission, 12/1 for domestic students, 10/1 for international students; for summer admission, 4/15 for domestic students, 3/1 for international students. Application fee: $60. *Unit head:* Dr. Matthew Ganio, Department Head, 479-575-2956, E-mail: msganio@uark.edu. *Application contact:* Dr. Paul Calleja, Assistant Dept. Head - HHPR, Graduate Coordinator, 479-575-2854, Fax: 479-575-5778, E-mail: pcallej@uark.edu.
Website: https://hhpr.uark.edu

**University of Calgary,** Cumming School of Medicine and Faculty of Graduate Studies, Program in Community Health Sciences, Calgary, AB T2N 1N4, Canada. Offers M Sc, PhD. *Degree requirements:* For master's, thesis; for doctorate, thesis/dissertation, candidacy exam. *Entrance requirements:* For master's and doctorate, minimum GPA of 3.2. Additional exam requirements/recommendations for international students: required—TOEFL (minimum score 600 paper-based). Electronic applications accepted.

**University of California, Los Angeles,** Graduate Division, Fielding School of Public Health, Department of Community Health Sciences, Los Angeles, CA 90095. Offers public health (MPH, MS, Dr PH, PhD); JD/MPH; MA/MPH; MD/MPH; MSW/MPH. *Accreditation:* CEPH. *Degree requirements:* For master's, comprehensive exam or thesis; for doctorate, thesis/dissertation, oral and written qualifying exams. *Entrance requirements:* For master's, GRE General Test, minimum GPA of 3.0; for doctorate, GRE General Test, minimum undergraduate GPA of 3.0. Electronic applications accepted.

**University of Colorado Denver,** College of Liberal Arts and Sciences, Program in Humanities, Denver, CO 80217. Offers community health (MSS); ethnic studies (MH, MSS); humanities (MH, Graduate Certificate); international studies (MSS); philosophy and theory (MH); social justice (MH, MSS); society and the environment (MSS); visual studies (MH); women's and gender studies (MH, MSS). *Program availability:* Part-time, evening/weekend. *Degree requirements:* For master's, 36 credit hours, project or thesis. *Entrance requirements:* For master's, writing sample, statement of purpose/letter of intent, three letters of recommendation. Additional exam requirements/recommendations for international students: required—TOEFL (minimum score 537 paper-based; 75 iBT); recommended—IELTS (minimum score 6.5). Electronic applications accepted. Tuition and fees vary according to course load, program and reciprocity agreements.

**University of Colorado Denver,** Colorado School of Public Health, Program in Public Health, Aurora, CO 80045. Offers community and behavioral health (MPH, Dr PH). *Accreditation:* CEPH. *Program availability:* Part-time, evening/weekend. *Degree requirements:* For master's, thesis or alternative, 42 credit hours; for doctorate, comprehensive exam, thesis/dissertation, 67 credit hours. *Entrance requirements:* For master's, GRE, MCAT, DAT, LSAT, PCAT, GMAT or master's degree from accredited institution, baccalaureate degree or equivalent; minimum GPA of 3.0; transcripts; references; resume; essay; for doctorate, GRE, MCAT, DAT, LSAT, PCAT or GMAT, MPH or master's or higher degree in related field or equivalent; 2 years of previous work experience in public health; essay; resume. Additional exam requirements/recommendations for international students: required—TOEFL (minimum score 550 paper-based; 80 iBT). Tuition and fees vary according to course load, program and reciprocity agreements.

**University of Colorado Denver,** School of Medicine, Physician Assistant Program, Aurora, CO 80045. Offers child health associate (MPAS), including global health, leadership, education, advocacy, development, and scholarship, pediatric critical and acute care, rural health, urban/underserved populations. *Accreditation:* ARC-PA. *Degree requirements:* For master's, comprehensive exam. *Entrance requirements:* For master's, GRE General Test, minimum GPA of 2.8; 3 letters of recommendation; prerequisite courses in chemistry, biology, general genetics, psychology and statistics; interview. Additional exam requirements/recommendations for international students: required—TOEFL (minimum score 550 paper-based; 80 iBT). Electronic applications accepted. Tuition and fees vary according to course load, program and reciprocity agreements.

*Community Health*

**University of Illinois at Chicago,** School of Public Health, Division of Community Health Sciences, Chicago, IL 60607-7128. Offers MPH, MS, Dr PH, PhD. *Program availability:* Part-time. Terminal master's awarded for partial completion of doctoral program. *Degree requirements:* For master's, thesis, field practicum; for doctorate, thesis/dissertation, independent research, internship. *Entrance requirements:* For master's and doctorate, GRE General Test, minimum GPA of 2.75. Additional exam requirements/recommendations for international students: required—TOEFL. Electronic applications accepted. *Expenses:* Contact institution.

**University of Illinois at Springfield,** Graduate Programs, College of Public Affairs and Administration, Program in Public Health, Springfield, IL 62703-5407. Offers community health education (Graduate Certificate); emergency preparedness and homeland security (Graduate Certificate); environmental health (MPH, Graduate Certificate); environmental risk assessment (Graduate Certificate); epidemiology (Graduate Certificate); public health (MPH). *Program availability:* Part-time, 100% online. *Faculty:* 7 full-time (5 women). *Students:* 31 full-time (24 women), 36 part-time (27 women); includes 13 minority (9 Black or African American, non-Hispanic/Latino; 1 Asian, non-Hispanic/Latino; 1 Hispanic/Latino; 2 Two or more races, non-Hispanic/Latino), 27 international. Average age 30. 90 applicants, 54% accepted, 12 enrolled. In 2019, 13 master's, 10 other advanced degrees awarded. *Degree requirements:* For master's, comprehensive exam, internship. *Entrance requirements:* For master's, GRE, minimum undergraduate GPA of 3.0, 3 letters of recommendation, essay addressing the areas outlined on the department application form. Additional exam requirements/recommendations for international students: required—TOEFL (minimum score 500 paper-based; 61 iBT). *Application deadline:* Applications are processed on a rolling basis. Application fee: $60 ($75 for international students). Electronic applications accepted. *Expenses:* $33.25 per credit hour (online fee). *Financial support:* In 2019–20, research assistantships with full tuition reimbursements (averaging $10,562 per year), teaching assistantships with full tuition reimbursements (averaging $10,652 per year) were awarded; fellowships, career-related internships or fieldwork, Federal Work-Study, scholarships/grants, health care benefits, and unspecified assistantships also available. Support available to part-time students. Financial award application deadline: 11/15; financial award applicants required to submit FAFSA. *Unit head:* Dr. Josiah Alamu, Program Administrator, 217-206-7874, Fax: 217-206-7279, E-mail: jalam3@uis.edu. *Application contact:* Dr. Josiah Alamu, Program Administrator, 217-206-7874, Fax: 217-206-7279, E-mail: jalam3@uis.edu.
Website: http://www.uis.edu/publichealth/

**University of Illinois at Urbana-Champaign,** Graduate College, College of Applied Health Sciences, Department of Kinesiology and Community Health, Champaign, IL 61820. Offers community health (MS, MSPH, PhD); kinesiology (MS, PhD); public health (MPH); rehabilitation (MS); PhD/MPH.

**The University of Iowa,** Graduate College, College of Public Health, Department of Community and Behavioral Health, Iowa City, IA 52242-1316. Offers MPH, MS, PhD. *Degree requirements:* For master's, thesis; for doctorate, comprehensive exam, thesis/dissertation. *Entrance requirements:* For master's and doctorate, GRE General Test, minimum GPA of 3.0. Additional exam requirements/recommendations for international students: required—TOEFL (minimum score 600 paper-based; 100 iBT). Electronic applications accepted.

**The University of Kansas,** Graduate Studies, College of Liberal Arts and Sciences, Department of Applied Behavioral Science, Lawrence, KS 66045. Offers applied behavioral science (MA); behavioral psychology (PhD); community health and development (Graduate Certificate); PhD/MPH. *Program availability:* Part-time. *Students:* 42 full-time (29 women), 45 part-time (40 women); includes 10 minority (2 Black or African American, non-Hispanic/Latino; 3 Asian, non-Hispanic/Latino; 2 Hispanic/Latino; 1 Native Hawaiian or other Pacific Islander, non-Hispanic/Latino; 2 Two or more races, non-Hispanic/Latino). Average age 35. 110 applicants, 42% accepted, 32 enrolled. In 2019, 7 master's, 4 doctorates, 12 other advanced degrees awarded. Terminal master's awarded for partial completion of doctoral program. *Entrance requirements:* For master's, GRE, curriculum vitae; 3 letters of recommendation; personal statement; all academic transcripts; copies of pertinent written work, published or not, as well as presented papers; for doctorate, GRE, curriculum vitae; 3 letters of recommendation; personal statement; copies of pertinent written work, published or not, as well as presented papers. Additional exam requirements/recommendations for international students: required—TOEFL, IELTS. *Application deadline:* For fall admission, 12/15 priority date for domestic students, 12/15 for international students. Application fee: $65 ($85 for international students). Electronic applications accepted. *Expenses:* Tuition, state resident: full-time $9989. Tuition, nonresident: full-time $23,950. *International tuition:* $23,950 full-time. *Required fees:* $984; $81.99 per credit hour. Tuition and fees vary according to course load, campus/location and program. *Financial support:* Fellowships, research assistantships, teaching assistantships, career-related internships or fieldwork, traineeships, tuition waivers (full), and unspecified assistantships available. Financial award application deadline: 12/15; financial award applicants required to submit CSS PROFILE or FAFSA. *Unit head:* Dr. Florence DiGennaro Reed, Chairperson, 785-864-0521, E-mail: fdreed@ku.edu. *Application contact:* Brittney Tyler-Milholland, Graduate Representative, 785-864-3625, E-mail: tylermil@ku.edu.
Website: http://absc.ku.edu

**University of Louisville,** Graduate School, College of Education and Human Development, Department of Health and Sport Sciences, Louisville, KY 40292-0001. Offers community health education (M Ed); exercise physiology (MS), including health and sport sciences, strength and conditioning; health and physical education (MAT); sport administration (MS). *Program availability:* Part-time, evening/weekend. *Faculty:* 24 full-time (14 women), 37 part-time/adjunct (22 women). *Students:* 85 full-time (30 women), 12 part-time (4 women); includes 20 minority (14 Black or African American, non-Hispanic/Latino; 1 Asian, non-Hispanic/Latino; 5 Two or more races, non-Hispanic/Latino), 9 international. Average age 26. 92 applicants, 80% accepted, 53 enrolled. In 2019, 51 master's awarded. *Degree requirements:* For master's, comprehensive exam (for some programs), thesis optional. *Entrance requirements:* For master's, GRE (for most programs), PRAXIS (for educator preparation programs), professional statement, recommendation letters, resume, transcripts. Additional exam requirements/recommendations for international students: required—TOEFL (minimum score 550 paper-based; 79 iBT); recommended—IELTS (minimum score 6.5). *Application deadline:* For fall admission, 3/1 priority date for domestic and international students; for spring admission, 11/1 priority date for domestic and international students; for summer admission, 4/1 priority date for domestic and international students. Application fee: $65. Electronic applications accepted. *Expenses: Tuition, area resident:* Full-time $13,000; part-time $723 per credit hour. Tuition, state resident: full-time $13,000; part-time $723 per credit hour. Tuition, nonresident: full-time $27,114; part-time $1507 per credit hour. *International tuition:* $27,114 full-time. *Required fees:* $196. Tuition and fees vary according to program and reciprocity agreements. *Financial support:* In 2019–20, 56 students received support, including 7 research assistantships with full tuition reimbursements available (averaging $21,024 per year), 6 teaching assistantships with full tuition reimbursements available (averaging $21,024 per year); fellowships, scholarships/grants, traineeships, health care benefits, and unspecified assistantships also available. Financial award application deadline: 2/1; financial award applicants required to submit FAFSA. *Unit head:* Dr. Dylan Naeger, Interim Chair, 502-852-6645, E-mail: hss@louisville.edu. *Application contact:* Dr. Margaret Pentecost, Director of Grad Assistant Dean for Graduate Student Success Graduate Student Services, 502-852-6437, Fax: 502-852-1465, E-mail: gedadm@louisville.edu.
Website: http://www.louisville.edu/education/departments/hss

**University of Manitoba,** Max Rady College of Medicine and Faculty of Graduate Studies, Graduate Programs in Medicine, Department of Community Health Sciences, Winnipeg, MB R3T 2N2, Canada. Offers M Sc, MPH, PhD, G Dip. *Program availability:* Part-time. *Degree requirements:* For master's, thesis; for doctorate, thesis/dissertation. *Entrance requirements:* For master's and doctorate, minimum GPA of 3.0.

**University of Massachusetts Amherst,** Graduate School, School of Public Health and Health Sciences, Department of Public Health, Amherst, MA 01003. Offers biostatistics (MPH, MS, PhD); community health education (MPH, MS, PhD); environmental health sciences (MPH, MS, PhD); epidemiology (MPH, MS, PhD); health policy and management (MPH, MS, PhD); nutrition (MPH, PhD); public health practice (MPH); MPH/MPPA. *Accreditation:* CEPH. *Program availability:* Part-time, evening/weekend, online learning. Terminal master's awarded for partial completion of doctoral program. *Degree requirements:* For master's, thesis (for some programs); for doctorate, comprehensive exam, thesis/dissertation. *Entrance requirements:* For master's and doctorate, GRE General Test. Additional exam requirements/recommendations for international students: required—TOEFL (minimum score 550 paper-based; 80 iBT), IELTS (minimum score 6.5). Electronic applications accepted.

**University of Miami,** Graduate School, Miller School of Medicine, Graduate Programs in Medicine, Department of Public Health Sciences, Miami, FL 33124. Offers biostatistics (MS, PhD); climate and health (MS); epidemiology (PhD); epidemiology, biostatistics, prevention science and community health (MD/PhD); generalist (MPH, MSPH); prevention science and community health (MS, PhD); JD/MPH; MD/MPH; MD/PhD; MPA/MPH; MPH/MAIA. *Accreditation:* CEPH (one or more programs are accredited). *Faculty:* 35 full-time (15 women), 24 part-time/adjunct (14 women). *Students:* 328 full-time (216 women), 30 part-time (25 women); includes 169 minority (35 Black or African American, non-Hispanic/Latino; 1 American Indian or Alaska Native, non-Hispanic/Latino; 40 Asian, non-Hispanic/Latino; 68 Hispanic/Latino; 7 Native Hawaiian or other Pacific Islander, non-Hispanic/Latino; 18 Two or more races, non-Hispanic/Latino), 41 international. In 2019, 109 master's, 9 doctorates awarded. *Degree requirements:* For master's, thesis (for some programs), project, practicum; for doctorate, comprehensive exam, thesis/dissertation. *Entrance requirements:* For master's, GRE General Test, MCAT, LSAT (for joint MPH/JD applicants), minimum GPA of 3.0, official transcripts, statement of purpose, 3 letters of recommendation, resume/CV; for doctorate, GRE General Test, minimum GPA of 3.0, pre-requisite coursework, 3 letters of recommendation, official transcripts, resume/CV. Additional exam requirements/recommendations for international students: required—TOEFL (minimum score 550 paper-based; 80 iBT). Application fee: $135. Electronic applications accepted. *Unit head:* Dr. David Lee, Chair, E-mail: dlee@med.miami.edu. *Application contact:* Andria Williams, Director of Admissions, 305-243-0291, E-mail: alw157@med.miami.edu.
Website: https://www.publichealth.med.miami.edu/

**University of Miami,** Graduate School, School of Education and Human Development, Department of Educational and Psychological Studies, Program in Community Well-Being, Coral Gables, FL 33124. Offers PhD. *Students:* 10 full-time (8 women); includes 4 minority (3 Black or African American, non-Hispanic/Latino; 1 Hispanic/Latino), 2 international. Average age 32. 19 applicants, 26% accepted, 4 enrolled. In 2019, 3 doctorates awarded. *Degree requirements:* For doctorate, thesis/dissertation, qualifying exam. *Entrance requirements:* For doctorate, GRE General Test. Additional exam requirements/recommendations for international students: required—TOEFL (minimum score 550 paper-based; 80 iBT); recommended—IELTS (minimum score 6.5). *Application deadline:* For fall admission, 1/1 priority date for domestic students, 10/1 priority date for international students. Application fee: $85. Electronic applications accepted. *Financial support:* Fellowships and tuition waivers (full) available. Financial award application deadline: 3/1; financial award applicants required to submit FAFSA. *Unit head:* Dr. Dina Birman, Professor and Program Director, 305-284-3460, E-mail: d.birman@miami.edu. *Application contact:* Dr. Dina Birman, Professor and Program Director, 305-284-3460, E-mail: d.birman@miami.edu.
Website: https://sites.education.miami.edu/community-well-being/

**University of Minnesota, Twin Cities Campus,** School of Public Health, Major in Community Health Education, Minneapolis, MN 55455-0213. Offers MPH. *Accreditation:* CEPH. *Program availability:* Part-time. *Degree requirements:* For master's, fieldwork, project. *Entrance requirements:* For master's, GRE General Test. Additional exam requirements/recommendations for international students: required—TOEFL. Electronic applications accepted.

**University of Montana,** Graduate School, Phyllis J. Washington College of Education and Human Sciences, Department of Health and Human Performance, Missoula, MT 59812. Offers community health (MS); exercise science (MS); health and human performance generalist (MS). *Program availability:* Part-time. *Entrance requirements:* For master's, GRE General Test. Additional exam requirements/recommendations for international students: required—TOEFL.

**University of Nevada, Las Vegas,** Graduate College, School of Public Health, Las Vegas, NV 89154-3063. Offers Exec MHA, MHA, MPH, PhD, Certificate. *Accreditation:* CEPH. *Program availability:* Part-time. *Faculty:* 26 full-time (11 women), 10 part-time/adjunct (5 women). *Students:* 100 full-time (66 women), 54 part-time (40 women); includes 77 minority (22 Black or African American, non-Hispanic/Latino; 1 American Indian or Alaska Native, non-Hispanic/Latino; 17 Asian, non-Hispanic/Latino; 21 Hispanic/Latino; 2 Native Hawaiian or other Pacific Islander, non-Hispanic/Latino; 14 Two or more races, non-Hispanic/Latino), 13 international. Average age 32. 74 applicants, 77% accepted, 39 enrolled. In 2019, 38 master's, 4 doctorates, 2 other advanced degrees awarded. *Degree requirements:* For master's, thesis (for some programs); for doctorate, comprehensive exam, thesis/dissertation. *Entrance requirements:* For master's and doctorate, GRE General Test. Additional exam requirements/recommendations for international students: required—TOEFL (minimum score 550 paper-based; 85 iBT), IELTS (minimum score 7). Application fee: $60 ($95 for international students). Electronic applications accepted. *Expenses:* Contact institution. *Financial support:* In 2019–20, 38 students received support, including 1 fellowship with full tuition reimbursement available (averaging $20,000 per year), 24 research assistantships with full tuition reimbursements available (averaging $14,146 per year), 10 teaching assistantships with full tuition reimbursements available (averaging $12,135 per year); institutionally sponsored loans, scholarships/grants, health care benefits, and unspecified assistantships also available. Financial award application deadline: 3/15; financial award applicants required to submit FAFSA. *Unit head:* Dr. Shawn Gerstenberger, Dean, 702-895-5090, Fax: 702-895-5184, E-mail: sph.dean@unlv.edu. *Application contact:* Dr. Shawn Gerstenberger, Dean, 702-895-5090, Fax: 702-895-5184, E-mail: sph.dean@unlv.edu.
Website: http://publichealth.unlv.edu/

**University of New Mexico,** Graduate Studies, College of Education and Human Sciences, Program in Health Education, Albuquerque, NM 87131-2039. Offers community health education (MS). *Accreditation:* NCATE. *Program availability:* Part-time. *Degree requirements:* For master's, comprehensive exam, thesis optional. *Entrance requirements:* For master's, 3 letters of reference, resume, minimum cumulative GPA of 3.0 in last 2 years of bachelor's degree, letter of intent. Additional exam requirements/recommendations for international students: required—TOEFL (minimum score 550 paper-based). Electronic applications accepted. *Expenses:* Tuition, state resident: full-time $7633; part-time $972 per year. Tuition, nonresident: full-time $22,586; part-time $3840 per year. *International tuition:* $23,292 full-time. *Required fees:* $8608. Tuition and fees vary according to course level, course load, degree level, program and student level.

**University of New Mexico,** Graduate Studies, Health Sciences Center, Program in Public Health, Albuquerque, NM 87131-5196. Offers community health (MPH); epidemiology (MPH); health systems, services and policy (MPH). *Accreditation:* CEPH. *Program availability:* Part-time, online learning. *Entrance requirements:* For master's, GRE, MCAT, 2 years of experience in health field. Additional exam requirements/recommendations for international students: required—TOEFL. *Expenses:* Tuition, state resident: full-time $7633; part-time $972 per year. Tuition, nonresident: full-time $22,586; part-time $3840 per year. *International tuition:* $23,292 full-time. *Required fees:* $8608. Tuition and fees vary according to course level, course load, degree level, program and student level.

**The University of North Carolina at Charlotte,** College of Health and Human Services, Department of Public Health Sciences, Charlotte, NC 28223-0001. Offers community health (Certificate); health administration (MHA); public health (MPH), including community health practice, epidemiology, and population health analytics; public health core concepts (Graduate Certificate); public health sciences (PhD). *Accreditation:* CAHME; CEPH. *Program availability:* Part-time. *Faculty:* 30 full-time (18 women), 4 part-time/adjunct (2 women). *Students:* 103 full-time (85 women), 13 part-time (9 women); includes 43 minority (28 Black or African American, non-Hispanic/Latino; 8 Asian, non-Hispanic/Latino; 3 Hispanic/Latino; 1 Native Hawaiian or other Pacific Islander, non-Hispanic/Latino; 3 Two or more races, non-Hispanic/Latino), 10 international. Average age 26. 154 applicants, 77% accepted, 47 enrolled. In 2019, 49 master's, 3 doctorates, 1 other advanced degree awarded. *Degree requirements:* For master's, capstone; for doctorate, thesis/dissertation. *Entrance requirements:* For master's, GRE or MCAT (for MSPH); GRE or GMAT (for MHA), career goal statement, current resume, letters of recommendation, undergraduate major or coursework that prepares students for graduate work; for doctorate, GRE, master's degree in public health or a related field with minimum GPA of 3.5 in all graduate work; statement of purpose detailing why applicant wants to pursue a PhD in public health sciences in the specified concentration at UNC Charlotte; three letters of recommendation (including at least two letters from former professors); for other advanced degree, bachelor's degree from regionally-accredited university; minimum GPA of 2.75 on all post-secondary work attempted; transcripts; personal statement outlining why the applicant seeks admission to the program. Additional exam requirements/recommendations for international students: required—TOEFL (minimum score 557 paper-based; 83 iBT), IELTS (minimum score 6.5), TOEFL (minimum score 557 paper-based,83 iBT) or IELTS (6.5). *Application deadline:* Applications are processed on a rolling basis. Application fee: $75. Electronic applications accepted. *Expenses:* Contact institution. *Financial support:* In 2019–20, 27 students received support, including 4 research assistantships (averaging $14,323 per year), 15 teaching assistantships (averaging $7,966 per year); fellowships, career-related internships or fieldwork, Federal Work-Study, institutionally sponsored loans, scholarships/grants, and unspecified assistantships also available. Support available to part-time students. Financial award application deadline: 3/1; financial award applicants required to submit FAFSA. *Unit head:* Dr. Jan Warren-Findlow, Professor and Interim Chair, 704-687-7908, E-mail: jwarren1@uncc.edu. *Application contact:* Kathy B. Giddings, Director of Graduate Admissions, 704-687-5503, Fax: 704-687-1668, E-mail: gradadm@uncc.edu.
Website: http://publichealth.uncc.edu/

**The University of North Carolina at Greensboro,** Graduate School, School of Health and Human Sciences, Department of Public Health Education, Greensboro, NC 27412-5001. Offers community health education (MPH, Dr PH). *Accreditation:* CEPH; NCATE. *Degree requirements:* For master's, comprehensive exam, thesis or alternative. *Entrance requirements:* For master's, GRE General Test or MAT. Additional exam requirements/recommendations for international students: required—TOEFL. Electronic applications accepted.

**University of Northern British Columbia,** Office of Graduate Studies, Prince George, BC V2N 4Z9, Canada. Offers business administration (Diploma); community health science (M Sc); disability management (MA); education (M Ed); first nations studies (MA); gender studies (MA); history (MA); interdisciplinary studies (MA); international studies (MA); mathematical, computer and physical sciences (M Sc); natural resources and environmental studies (M Sc, MA, MNRES, PhD); political science (MA); psychology (M Sc, PhD); social work (MSW). *Program availability:* Part-time, evening/weekend, online learning. *Degree requirements:* For master's, thesis; for doctorate, thesis/dissertation. *Entrance requirements:* For master's, GRE, minimum B average in undergraduate course work; for doctorate, candidacy exam, minimum A average in graduate course work.

**University of Northern Colorado,** Graduate School, College of Natural and Health Sciences, School of Human Sciences, Program in Public Health, Greeley, CO 80639. Offers community health education (MPH); global health and community health education (MPH); healthy aging and community health education (MPH). *Degree requirements:* For master's, comprehensive exam, thesis or alternative. *Entrance requirements:* For master's, GRE General Test, 2 letters of recommendation. Electronic applications accepted.

**University of Northern Iowa,** Graduate College, College of Education, School of Kinesiology, Allied Health and Human Services, MA Program in Health Education, Cedar Falls, IA 50614. Offers community health education (MA); health promotion/fitness management (MA); school health education (MA). *Program availability:* Part-time, evening/weekend. *Degree requirements:* For master's, comprehensive exam, thesis or alternative. *Entrance requirements:* For master's, minimum GPA of 3.0. Additional exam requirements/recommendations for international students: required—TOEFL (minimum score 500 paper-based; 61 iBT). Electronic applications accepted.

**University of North Florida,** Brooks College of Health, Department of Public Health, Jacksonville, FL 32224. Offers aging services (Certificate); public health (MPH). *Accreditation:* CEPH. *Program availability:* Part-time, evening/weekend. *Degree requirements:* For master's, thesis optional. *Entrance requirements:* For master's, GRE General Test (MSH, MS, MPH); GMAT or GRE General Test (MHA), minimum GPA of 3.0 in last 60 hours. Additional exam requirements/recommendations for international students: required—TOEFL (minimum score 500 paper-based). Electronic applications accepted.

**University of Ottawa,** Faculty of Graduate and Postdoctoral Studies, Interdisciplinary Programs, Ottawa, ON K1N 6N5, Canada. Offers e-business (Certificate); e-commerce (Certificate); finance (Certificate); health services and policies research (Diploma); population health (PhD); population health risk assessment and management (Certificate); public management and governance (Certificate); systems science (Certificate).

**University of Phoenix - Central Valley Campus,** College of Nursing, Fresno, CA 93720-1552. Offers education (MHA); gerontology (MHA); health administration (MHA); nursing (MSN); MSN/MBA.

**University of Phoenix - Hawaii Campus,** College of Nursing, Honolulu, HI 96813-3800. Offers education (MHA); family nurse practitioner (MSN); gerontology (MHA); health administration (MHA); nursing (MSN); nursing/health care education (MSN); MSN/MBA. *Program availability:* Evening/weekend. *Degree requirements:* For master's, thesis (for some programs). *Entrance requirements:* For master's, minimum undergraduate GPA of 2.5, 3 years of work experience, RN license. Additional exam requirements/recommendations for international students: required—TOEFL (minimum score 550 paper-based; 79 iBT). Electronic applications accepted.

**University of Pittsburgh,** Graduate School of Public Health, Department of Behavioral and Community Health Sciences, Pittsburgh, PA 15261. Offers applied research and leadership in behavioral and community health sciences (Dr PH); applied social and behavioral concepts in public health (MPH); community-based participatory research (Certificate); evaluation of public health programs (Certificate); global health (Certificate); health equity (Certificate); LGBT health and wellness (Certificate); maternal and child health (MPH); MID/MPH; MPH/MPA; MPH/MSW; MPH/PhD. *Accreditation:* CEPH. *Program availability:* Part-time. *Faculty:* 7 full-time (5 women), 8 part-time/adjunct (4 women). *Students:* 98 full-time (85 women), 8 part-time (5 women); includes 18 minority (7 Black or African American, non-Hispanic/Latino; 5 Asian, non-Hispanic/Latino; 6 Hispanic/Latino), 4 international. Average age 28. 153 applicants, 48% accepted, 21 enrolled. In 2019, 42 master's, 10 doctorates awarded. *Degree requirements:* For master's, thesis or alternative, Master's students can either complete an Essay or a Thesis; for doctorate, comprehensive exam, thesis/dissertation. *Entrance requirements:* For master's, GRE, applicants must have completed and earned a C or better in a three-credit math or statistics class taken in a math or statistics department. They must also have completed six credits of social sciences (anthropology, economics, geography, political science, psychology, social psychology); for doctorate, GRE, PhD applicants must hold a post-baccalaureate degree e.g. a Master of Science degree in a discipline relevant to public health such as social work or anthropology or an MD or JD. Additional exam requirements/recommendations for international students: required—TOEFL (minimum score 100 iBT), TOEFL or IELTS, WES evaluation for foreign education. *Application deadline:* For fall admission, 7/15 for domestic students, 4/15 for international students; for spring admission, 10/15 for domestic students, 8/1 for international students. Applications are processed on a rolling basis. Application fee: $135. *Expenses:* $13,379 per term full-time resident, $23,407 per term full-time non-resident, $1122 per credit part-time resident, $1916 per credit part-time non-resident, $500 per term for full-time dissertation research, $475 per term full-time fees, $295 per term part-time fees. *Financial support:* In 2019–20, 1 fellowship with full tuition reimbursement (averaging $24,816 per year), 11 research assistantships with full tuition reimbursements (averaging $16,386 per year) were awarded; traineeships also available. Financial award application deadline: 10/1; financial award applicants required to submit FAFSA. *Unit head:* Susan Cotter, Department Administrator, 412-624-9594, Fax: 412-624-5510, E-mail: suecot@pitt.edu. *Application contact:* Paul J. Markgraf, Recruitment and Academic Affairs Administrator, 412-624-3107, Fax: 412-624-5510, E-mail: pjm111@pitt.edu.
Website: http://www.bchs.pitt.edu/

**University of Pittsburgh,** Graduate School of Public Health, Department of Infectious Diseases and Microbiology, Pittsburgh, PA 15261. Offers infectious diseases and microbiology (MS, PhD); management, intervention, and community practice (MPH); pathogenesis, eradication, and laboratory practice (MPH). *Program availability:* Part-time. *Faculty:* 17 full-time (7 women), 4 part-time/adjunct (0 women). *Students:* 56 full-time (44 women), 20 part-time (10 women); includes 19 minority (6 Black or African American, non-Hispanic/Latino; 5 Asian, non-Hispanic/Latino; 3 Hispanic/Latino; 5 Two or more races, non-Hispanic/Latino), 6 international. Average age 26. 146 applicants, 80% accepted, 38 enrolled. In 2019, 24 master's, 2 doctorates awarded. Terminal master's awarded for partial completion of doctoral program. *Degree requirements:* For master's, comprehensive exam (for some programs), thesis; for doctorate, comprehensive exam, thesis/dissertation, preliminary exam, dissertation defense. *Entrance requirements:* Additional exam requirements/recommendations for international students: required—TOEFL (minimum score 550 paper-based; 80 iBT), IELTS (minimum score 6.5), TOEFL or IELTS, WES evaluation for foreign education. *Application deadline:* For fall admission, 1/15 for domestic students, 3/15 priority date for international students. Applications are processed on a rolling basis. Application fee: $135. Electronic applications accepted. *Expenses:* $13,379 state resident per term full-time, $23,407 non-state resident per term full-time, $1122 state resident per credit part-time, $1916 non-state resident per credit part-time, $500 per term for full-time dissertation research, $475 per term full-time fees, $295 per term part-time fees. *Financial support:* In 2019–20, 38 students received support. Scholarships/grants, traineeships, health care benefits, and unspecified assistantships available. Financial award applicants required to submit FAFSA. *Unit head:* Robin Tierno, Department Administrator, 412-624-3105, Fax: 412-624-4953, E-mail: rtierno@pitt.edu. *Application contact:* Chelsea Yonash, Student Services Coordinator, 412-624-3331, E-mail: cry8@pitt.edu.
Website: http://www.publichealth.pitt.edu/idm

**University of Saskatchewan,** College of Medicine, Department of Community Health and Epidemiology, Saskatoon, SK S7N 5A2, Canada. Offers M Sc, PhD. *Degree requirements:* For master's, thesis; for doctorate, thesis/dissertation. *Entrance requirements:* Additional exam requirements/recommendations for international students: required—TOEFL.

**University of South Florida,** Innovative Education, Tampa, FL 33620-9951. Offers adult, career and higher education (Graduate Certificate), including college teaching, leadership in developing human resources, leadership in higher education; Africana studies (Graduate Certificate), including diasporas and health disparities, genocide and human rights; aging studies (Graduate Certificate), including gerontology; art research (Graduate Certificate), including museum studies; business foundations (Graduate Certificate); chemical and biomedical engineering (Graduate Certificate), including materials science and engineering, water, health and sustainability; child and family studies (Graduate Certificate), including positive behavior support; civil and industrial engineering (Graduate Certificate), including transportation systems analysis; community and family health (Graduate Certificate), including maternal and child health, social marketing and public health, violence and injury: prevention and intervention, women's health; criminology (Graduate Certificate), including criminal justice administration; data science for public administration (Graduate Certificate); digital humanities (Graduate Certificate); educational measurement and research (Graduate Certificate), including evaluation; English (Graduate Certificate), including comparative literary studies, creative writing, professional and technical communication; entrepreneurship (Graduate Certificate); environmental health (Graduate Certificate),

including safety management; epidemiology and biostatistics (Graduate Certificate), including applied biostatistics, biostatistics, concepts and tools of epidemiology, epidemiology, epidemiology of infectious diseases; geography, environment and planning (Graduate Certificate), including community development, environmental policy and management, geographical information systems; geology (Graduate Certificate), including hydrogeology; global health (Graduate Certificate), including disaster management, global health and Latin American and Caribbean studies, global health practice, humanitarian assistance, infection control; government and international affairs (Graduate Certificate), including Cuban studies, globalization studies; health policy and management (Graduate Certificate), including health management and leadership, public health policy and programs; hearing specialist: early intervention (Graduate Certificate); industrial and management systems engineering (Graduate Certificate), including systems engineering, technology management; information studies (Graduate Certificate), including school library media specialist; information systems/decision sciences (Graduate Certificate), including analytics and business intelligence; instructional technology (Graduate Certificate), including distance education, Florida digital/virtual educator, instructional design, multimedia design, Web design; internal medicine, bioethics and medical humanities (Graduate Certificate), including biomedical ethics; Latin American and Caribbean studies (Graduate Certificate); leadership for coastal resiliency planning (Graduate Certificate); mass communications (Graduate Certificate), including multimedia journalism; mathematics and statistics (Graduate Certificate), including mathematics; medicine (Graduate Certificate), including aging and neuroscience, bioinformatics, biotechnology, brain fitness and memory management, clinical investigation, hand and upper limb rehabilitation, health informatics, health sciences, integrative weight management, intellectual property, medicine and gender, metabolic and nutritional medicine, metabolic cardiology, pharmacy sciences; national and competitive intelligence (Graduate Certificate); nursing (Graduate Certificate), including simulation based academic fellowship in advanced pain management; psychological and social foundations (Graduate Certificate), including career counseling, college teaching, diversity in education, mental health counseling, school counseling; public affairs (Graduate Certificate), including nonprofit management, public management, research administration; public health (Graduate Certificate), including assessing chemical toxicity and public health risks, health equity, pharmacoepidemiology, public health generalist, toxicology, translational research in adolescent behavioral health; public health practices (Graduate Certificate), including planning for healthy communities; rehabilitation and mental health counseling (Graduate Certificate), including integrative mental health care, marriage and family therapy, rehabilitation technology; secondary education (Graduate Certificate), including ESOL, foreign language education: culture and content, foreign language education: professional; social work (Graduate Certificate), including geriatric social work/clinical gerontology; special education (Graduate Certificate), including autism spectrum disorder, disabilities education: severe/profound; world languages (Graduate Certificate), including teaching English as a second language (TESL) or foreign language. *Unit head:* Dr. Cynthia DeLuca, Associate Vice President and Assistant Vice Provost, 813-974-3077, Fax: 813-974-7061, E-mail: deluca@usf.edu. *Application contact:* Owen Hooper, Director, Summer and Alternative Calendar Programs, 813-974-6917, E-mail: hooper@usf.edu.
Website: http://www.usf.edu/innovative-education/

**The University of Tennessee,** Graduate School, College of Education, Health and Human Sciences, Program in Human Ecology, Knoxville, TN 37996. Offers child and family studies (PhD); community health (PhD); nutrition science (PhD); retailing and consumer sciences (PhD); textile science (PhD). *Degree requirements:* For doctorate, thesis/dissertation. *Entrance requirements:* For doctorate, GRE General Test, minimum GPA of 2.7. Additional exam requirements/recommendations for international students: required—TOEFL. Electronic applications accepted.

**The University of Tennessee,** Graduate School, College of Education, Health and Human Sciences, Program in Public Health, Knoxville, TN 37996. Offers community health education (MPH); gerontology (MPH); health planning/administration (MPH); MS/MPH. *Accreditation:* CEPH. *Degree requirements:* For master's, thesis optional. *Entrance requirements:* For master's, minimum GPA of 2.7. Additional exam requirements/recommendations for international students: required—TOEFL. Electronic applications accepted.

**The University of Texas Health Science Center at Houston,** School of Public Health, Houston, TX 77030. Offers behavioral science (PhD); biostatistics (MPH, MS, PhD); environmental health (MPH); epidemiology (MPH, MS, PhD); general public health (Certificate); genomics and bioinformatics (Certificate); health disparities (Certificate); health promotion/health education (MPH, Dr PH); healthcare management (Certificate); management, policy and community health (MPH, Dr PH, PhD); maternal and child health (Certificate); public health informatics (Certificate); DDS/MPH; JD/MPH; MBA/MPH; MD/MPH; MGPS/MPH; MP Aff/MPH; MS/MPH; MSN/MPH; MSW/MPH; PhD/MPH. *Accreditation:* CAHME; CEPH. *Program availability:* Part-time. *Degree requirements:* For master's, thesis (for some programs); for doctorate, comprehensive exam, thesis/dissertation. *Entrance requirements:* For master's and doctorate, GRE General Test. Additional exam requirements/recommendations for international students: required—TOEFL (minimum score 600 paper-based, 100 iBT) or IELTS (7.5). Electronic applications accepted. *Expenses:* Contact institution.

**University of Toronto,** School of Graduate Studies, Department of Public Health Sciences, Toronto, ON M5S 1A1, Canada. Offers biostatistics (M Sc, PhD); community health (M Sc); community nutrition (MPH), including nutrition and dietetics; epidemiology (MPH, PhD); family and community medicine (MPH); occupational and environmental health (MPH); social and behavioral health science (PhD); social and behavioral health sciences (MPH), including health promotion. *Accreditation:* CAHME (one or more programs are accredited). *Program availability:* Part-time. *Degree requirements:* For master's, thesis (for some programs), practicum; for doctorate, comprehensive exam, thesis/dissertation, oral thesis defense. *Entrance requirements:* For master's, 2 letters of reference, relevant professional/research experience, minimum B average in final year; for doctorate, 2 letters of reference, relevant professional/research experience, minimum B+ average. Additional exam requirements/recommendations for international students: required—TOEFL (minimum score 580 paper-based; 93 iBT), TWE (minimum score 5). Electronic applications accepted. *Expenses:* Contact institution.

**University of Vermont,** Graduate College, College of Agriculture and Life Sciences, Program in Dietetics, Burlington, VT 05405-0086. Offers dietetics (MS), including community health and nutrition. *Entrance requirements:* For master's, GRE General Test. Additional exam requirements/recommendations for international students: required—TOEFL (minimum score 550 paper-based, 90 iBT) or IELTS (6.5). Electronic applications accepted.

**University of Virginia,** School of Nursing, Charlottesville, VA 22903. Offers acute and specialty care (MSN); acute care nurse practitioner (MSN); clinical nurse leadership (MSN); community-public health leadership (MSN); nursing (DNP, PhD); psychiatric mental health counseling (MSN); MSN/MBA. *Accreditation:* AACN. *Program availability:* Part-time. *Degree requirements:* For doctorate, comprehensive exam (for some programs), capstone project (DNP), dissertation (PhD). *Entrance requirements:* For master's, GRE General Test, MAT; for doctorate, GRE General Test. Additional exam requirements/recommendations for international students: required—TOEFL, IELTS. Electronic applications accepted.

**University of Washington,** Graduate School, School of Public Health, Department of Health Services, Seattle, WA 98195. Offers community-oriented public health practice (MPH); health services (MPH, MS, PhD); health systems and policy (MPH); maternal and child health (MPH); social and behavioral sciences (MPH); MPH/JD; MPH/MD; MPH/MN; MPH/MPA; MPH/MS; MPH/MSD; MPH/MSW; MPH/PhD. *Program availability:* Blended/hybrid learning. *Faculty:* 50 full-time (26 women), 71 part-time/adjunct (36 women). *Students:* 136 full-time (109 women), 16 part-time (all women); includes 62 minority (12 Black or African American, non-Hispanic/Latino; 6 American Indian or Alaska Native, non-Hispanic/Latino; 28 Asian, non-Hispanic/Latino; 14 Hispanic/Latino; 2 Native Hawaiian or other Pacific Islander, non-Hispanic/Latino), 9 international. Average age 31. 236 applicants, 62% accepted, 56 enrolled. In 2019, 63 master's, 10 doctorates awarded. Terminal master's awarded for partial completion of doctoral program. *Degree requirements:* For doctorate, comprehensive exam, thesis/dissertation. *Entrance requirements:* Additional exam requirements/recommendations for international students: required—TOEFL (minimum score 80 iBT). Application fee: $85. Electronic applications accepted. *Expenses:* MPH resident $22,476, MPH non-resident $38,316, resident MS & PhD $19,389, non-resident MS & PhD $32,775. *Financial support:* Fellowships, research assistantships, teaching assistantships, Federal Work-Study, institutionally sponsored loans, scholarships/grants, traineeships, health care benefits, and unspecified assistantships available. Financial award applicants required to submit FAFSA. *Unit head:* Dr. Jeffrey Harris, Chair, 206-616-2930, E-mail: hschair@uw.edu. *Application contact:* Marketing & Recruitment Specialist, 206-616-1397, E-mail: hservask@uw.edu.
Website: http://depts.washington.edu/hserv/

**University of Wisconsin–La Crosse,** College of Science and Health, Department of Health Education and Health Promotion, Program in Community Health Education, La Crosse, WI 54601-3742. Offers community health education (MS); public health (MPH). *Accreditation:* CEPH. *Faculty:* 4 full-time (2 women). *Students:* 2 full-time (both women), 5 part-time (3 women); includes 2 minority (1 Asian, non-Hispanic/Latino; 1 Two or more races, non-Hispanic/Latino). Average age 36. In 2019, 9 master's awarded. *Degree requirements:* For master's, thesis. *Entrance requirements:* For master's, GRE General Test, GRE Subject Test (for MPH), 3 letters of recommendation. Additional exam requirements/recommendations for international students: required—TOEFL (minimum score 550 paper-based; 79 iBT). Electronic applications accepted. *Financial support:* Research assistantships with partial tuition reimbursements, Federal Work-Study, scholarships/grants, health care benefits, and tuition waivers (partial) available. Support available to part-time students. Financial award applicants required to submit FAFSA. *Unit head:* Dr. Gary Gilmore, Director, 608-785-8163, E-mail: gilmore.gary@uwlax.edu. *Application contact:* Dr. Gary Gilmore, Director, 608-785-8163, E-mail: gilmore.gary@uwlax.edu.

**University of Wisconsin–Milwaukee,** Graduate School, College of Health Sciences, Program in Health Sciences, Milwaukee, WI 53201-0413. Offers health sciences (PhD), including diagnostic and biomedical sciences, disability and rehabilitation, health administration and policy, human movement sciences, population health. *Degree requirements:* For doctorate, comprehensive exam, thesis/dissertation. *Entrance requirements:* For doctorate, GRE. Additional exam requirements/recommendations for international students: required—TOEFL (minimum score 600 paper-based), IELTS (minimum score 6.5).

**University of Wyoming,** College of Education, Programs in Counselor Education, Laramie, WY 82071. Offers community mental health (MS); counselor education and supervision (PhD); school counseling (MS); student affairs (MS). *Accreditation:* ACA (one or more programs are accredited). *Degree requirements:* For master's, comprehensive exam (for some programs), thesis optional; for doctorate, thesis/dissertation, video demonstration. *Entrance requirements:* For master's, interview, background check; for doctorate, video tape session, interview, writing sample, master's degree, background check. Additional exam requirements/recommendations for international students: required—TOEFL.

**Université Laval,** Faculty of Medicine, Graduate Programs in Medicine, Department of Social and Preventive Medicine, Program in Community Health, Québec, QC G1K 7P4, Canada. Offers M Sc, PhD. *Program availability:* Part-time. Terminal master's awarded for partial completion of doctoral program. *Degree requirements:* For master's, thesis (for some programs); for doctorate, comprehensive exam, thesis/dissertation. *Entrance requirements:* For master's, knowledge of French, comprehension of written English; for doctorate, French exam, comprehension of French, written comprehension of English. Electronic applications accepted.

**Université Laval,** Faculty of Medicine, Post-Professional Programs in Medical Studies, Québec, QC G1K 7P4, Canada. Offers anatomy–pathology (DESS); anesthesiology (DESS); cardiology (DESS); care of older people (Diploma); clinical research (DESS); community health (DESS); dermatology (DESS); diagnostic radiology (DESS); emergency medicine (Diploma); family medicine (DESS); general surgery (DESS); geriatrics (DESS); hematology (DESS); internal medicine (DESS); maternal and fetal medicine (Diploma); medical biochemistry (DESS); medical microbiology and infectious diseases (DESS); medical oncology (DESS); nephrology (DESS); neurology (DESS); neurosurgery (DESS); obstetrics and gynecology (DESS); ophthalmology (DESS); orthopedic surgery (DESS); oto-rhino-laryngology (DESS); palliative medicine (Diploma); pediatrics (DESS); plastic surgery (DESS); psychiatry (DESS); pulmonary medicine (DESS); radiology–oncology (DESS); thoracic surgery (DESS); urology (DESS). *Degree requirements:* For other advanced degree, comprehensive exam. *Entrance requirements:* For degree, knowledge of French. Electronic applications accepted.

**Virginia Commonwealth University,** Medical College of Virginia-Professional Programs, School of Medicine, Graduate Programs in Medicine, Department of Family Medicine and Population Health, Richmond, VA 23284-9005. Offers epidemiology (MPH, PhD); public health practice (MPH); social and behavioral science (MPH); MD/MPH. *Accreditation:* CEPH. *Program availability:* Part-time. *Degree requirements:* For doctorate, comprehensive exam, thesis/dissertation. *Entrance requirements:* For master's, GRE; for doctorate, GRE General Test, interview, 3 letters of recommendation, minimum graduate GPA of 3.0, master's degree in public health or related field including epidemiology and biostatistics. Additional exam requirements/recommendations for international students: required—TOEFL (minimum score 600 paper-based; 100 iBT). Electronic applications accepted.

**Virginia State University,** College of Graduate Studies, College of Natural and Health Sciences, Department of Psychology, Petersburg, VA 23806-0001. Offers behavioral and community health sciences (PhD); clinical health psychology (PhD); clinical psychology (MS); general psychology (MS). *Degree requirements:* For master's, one foreign language, thesis. *Entrance requirements:* For master's, GRE General Test.

**Walden University,** Graduate Programs, School of Health Sciences, Minneapolis, MN 55401. Offers clinical research administration (MS, Graduate Certificate); health education and promotion (MS, PhD), including behavioral health (PhD), disease surveillance (PhD), emergency preparedness (MS), general (MHA, MS), global health

(PhD), health policy (PhD), health policy and advocacy (MS), population health (PhD); health informatics (MS); health services (PhD), including community health, healthcare administration, leadership, public health policy, self-designed; healthcare administration (MHA, DHA), including general (MHA, MS); leadership and organizational development (MHA); public health (MPH, Dr PH, PhD, Graduate Certificate), including community health education (PhD), epidemiology (PhD); systems policy (MHA). *Program availability:* Part-time, evening/weekend, online only, 100% online. *Degree requirements:* For doctorate, thesis/dissertation, residency. *Entrance requirements:* For master's, bachelor's degree or higher; minimum GPA of 2.5; official transcripts; goal statement (for some programs); access to computer and Internet; for doctorate, master's degree or higher; three years of related professional or academic experience (preferred); minimum GPA of 3.0; goal statement and current resume (for select programs); official transcripts; access to computer and Internet; for Graduate Certificate, relevant work experience; access to computer and Internet. Additional exam requirements/recommendations for international students: required—TOEFL (minimum score 550 paper-based, 79 iBT), IELTS (minimum score 6.5), Michigan English Language Assessment Battery (minimum score 82), or PTE (minimum score 53). Electronic applications accepted.

**Washington State University,** College of Nursing, Spokane, WA 99210. Offers advanced population health (MN, DNP); family nurse practitioner (MN, DNP); nursing (PhD); psychiatric/mental health nurse practitioner (DNP); psychiatric/mental health practitioner (MN). *Accreditation:* AACN. *Degree requirements:* For master's, comprehensive exam (for some programs), thesis (for some programs), oral exam, research project. *Entrance requirements:* For master's, minimum GPA of 3.0, Washington state RN license, physical assessment skills, course work in statistics, recommendations, written interview (for nurse practitioner).

**William James College,** Graduate Programs, Newton, MA 02459. Offers applied psychology in higher education student personnel administration (MA); clinical psychology (Psy D); counseling psychology (MA); counseling psychology and community mental health (MA); counseling psychology and global mental health (MA); executive coaching (Graduate Certificate); forensic and counseling psychology (MA); leadership psychology (Psy D); organizational psychology (MA); primary care psychology (MA); respecialization in clinical psychology (Certificate); school psychology (Psy D); MA/CAGS. *Accreditation:* APA. *Degree requirements:* For master's, comprehensive exam (for some programs); for doctorate, thesis/dissertation (for some programs). Electronic applications accepted.

# Environmental and Occupational Health

**Augusta University,** College of Allied Health Sciences, Program in Public Health, Augusta, GA 30912. Offers environmental health (MPH); health informatics (MPH); health management (MPH); social and behavioral sciences (MPH). *Accreditation:* CEPH. *Program availability:* Part-time. *Degree requirements:* For master's, thesis (for some programs). *Entrance requirements:* For master's, GRE General Test, three letters of recommendation. Additional exam requirements/recommendations for international students: required—TOEFL. Electronic applications accepted.

**Boise State University,** College of Health Sciences, Department of Community and Environmental Health, Boise, ID 83725-0399. Offers community and environmental health (MHS); health science (MHS), including health policy, health promotion, health services leadership; health services leadership (Graduate Certificate). *Students:* 20 full-time (18 women), 38 part-time (33 women); includes 7 minority (1 Asian, non-Hispanic/Latino; 5 Hispanic/Latino; 1 Two or more races, non-Hispanic/Latino). Average age 36. 38 applicants, 50% accepted, 11 enrolled. In 2019, 21 master's, 13 Graduate Certificates awarded. *Entrance requirements:* For master's, writing assessment, minimum GPA of 3.0. Additional exam requirements/recommendations for international students: required—TOEFL (minimum score 550 paper-based; 80 iBT), IELTS (minimum score 6). *Application deadline:* For fall admission, 3/15 for domestic and international students; for spring admission, 10/15 for domestic and international students. Application fee: $65 ($95 for international students). Electronic applications accepted. *Expenses: Tuition, area resident:* Full-time $7110; part-time $470 per credit hour. Tuition, state resident: full-time $7110; part-time $470 per credit hour. Tuition, nonresident: full-time $24,030; part-time $827 per credit hour. *International tuition:* $24,030 full-time. *Required fees:* $2536. Tuition and fees vary according to course load and program. *Financial support:* Research assistantships, scholarships/grants, and unspecified assistantships available. Financial award application deadline: 3/15; financial award applicants required to submit FAFSA. *Unit head:* Dr. Lillian Smith, Department Head, 208-426-3795, E-mail: lilliansmith@boisestate.edu. *Application contact:* Dr. Sarah Toevs, Director, Master of Health Science Program, 208-426-2452, E-mail: stoevs@boisestate.edu.
Website: https://www.boisestate.edu/healthsciences/

**California State University, Fullerton,** Graduate Studies, College of Health and Human Development, Department of Public Health, Fullerton, CA 92831-3599. Offers environmental and occupational health and safety (MPH); gerontological health (MPH); health promotion and disease (MPH). *Accreditation:* CEPH. *Program availability:* Part-time. *Entrance requirements:* For master's, minimum GPA of 3.0 in last 60 units attempted.

**California State University, Northridge,** Graduate Studies, College of Health and Human Development, Department of Environmental and Occupational Health, Northridge, CA 91330. Offers environmental and occupational health (MS); industrial hygiene (MS). *Degree requirements:* For master's, seminar, field experience, comprehensive exam or thesis. *Entrance requirements:* For master's, GRE General Test or minimum GPA of 3.0. Additional exam requirements/recommendations for international students: required—TOEFL.

**Capella University,** School of Public Service Leadership, Doctoral Programs in Healthcare, Minneapolis, MN 55402. Offers criminal justice (PhD); emergency management (PhD); epidemiology (Dr PH); general health administration (DHA); general public administration (DPA); health advocacy and leadership (Dr PH); health care administration (PhD); health care leadership (DHA); health policy advocacy (DHA); multidisciplinary human services (PhD); nonprofit management and leadership (PhD); public safety leadership (PhD); social and community services (PhD).

**Capella University,** School of Public Service Leadership, Master's Programs in Healthcare, Minneapolis, MN 55402. Offers criminal justice (MS); emergency management (MS); general public health (MPH); gerontology (MS); health administration (MHA); health care operations (MHA); health management policy (MPH); health policy (MHA); homeland security (MS); multidisciplinary human services (MS); public administration (MPA); public safety leadership (MS); social and community services (MS); social behavioral sciences (MPH); MS/MPA.

**Clemson University,** Graduate School, College of Engineering, Computing and Applied Sciences, Department of Environmental Engineering and Earth Sciences, Anderson, SC 29625. Offers biosystems engineering (MS, PhD); environmental engineering and science (MS, PhD); environmental health physics (MS); hydrogeology (MS). *Program availability:* Part-time. *Faculty:* 30 full-time (9 women), 2 part-time/adjunct (1 woman). *Students:* 80 full-time (31 women), 12 part-time (4 women); includes 5 minority (1 Black or African American, non-Hispanic/Latino; 1 Hispanic/Latino; 1 Native Hawaiian or other Pacific Islander, non-Hispanic/Latino; 2 Two or more races, non-Hispanic/Latino), 34 international. Average age 25. 108 applicants, 65% accepted, 30 enrolled. In 2019, 21 master's, 5 doctorates awarded. *Degree requirements:* For master's, thesis or alternative; for doctorate, comprehensive exam, thesis/dissertation. *Entrance requirements:* For master's and doctorate, GRE General Test, unofficial transcripts, letters of recommendation. Additional exam requirements/recommendations for international students: required—TOEFL (minimum score 80 paper-based; 80 iBT); recommended—IELTS (minimum score 6.5), TSE (minimum score 54). *Application deadline:* For fall admission, 2/15 for domestic and international students. Applications are processed on a rolling basis. Application fee: $80 ($90 for international students). Electronic applications accepted. *Expenses: Tuition, area resident:* Full-time $10,600; part-time $8688 per semester. Tuition, state resident: full-time $10,600; part-time $8688 per semester. Tuition, nonresident: full-time $22,050; part-time $17,412 per semester. *International tuition:* $22,050 full-time. *Required fees:* $1196; $617 per semester. $617 per semester. Tuition and fees vary according to course load, degree level, campus/location and program. *Financial support:* In 2019–20, 47 students received support, including 3 fellowships with full and partial tuition reimbursements available (averaging $16,000 per year), 15 research assistantships with full and partial tuition reimbursements available (averaging $22,327 per year), 24 teaching assistantships with full and partial tuition reimbursements available (averaging $21,681 per year); career-related internships or fieldwork and unspecified assistantships also available. Financial award application deadline: 2/15. *Unit head:* Dr. David Freedman, Department Chair, 864-656-5566, E-mail: dfreedm@clemson.edu. *Application contact:* Dr. Mark Schlautman, Graduate Program Coordinator, 864-656-4059, E-mail: mschlau@clemson.edu.
Website: https://www.clemson.edu/cecas/departments/eees/

**Colorado State University,** College of Veterinary Medicine and Biomedical Sciences, Department of Environmental and Radiological Health Sciences, Fort Collins, CO 80523-1681. Offers environmental health (MS, PhD), including environmental health and safety (MS), epidemiology (PhD). Terminal master's awarded for partial completion of doctoral program. *Degree requirements:* For master's, comprehensive exam (for some programs), thesis (for some programs); for doctorate, comprehensive exam (for some programs), thesis/dissertation (for some programs). *Entrance requirements:* For master's, GRE, minimum GPA of 3.0, bachelor's degree, resume or curriculum vitae, official transcripts, written statement, 3 letters of recommendation; for doctorate, GRE, minimum GPA of 3.0, MS or proof of research, resume or curriculum vitae, official transcripts, written statement, 3 letters of recommendation. Additional exam requirements/recommendations for international students: required—TOEFL (minimum score 80 iBT), IELTS (minimum score 6.5). Electronic applications accepted. *Expenses:* Contact institution.

**Columbia Southern University,** College of Safety and Emergency Services, Orange Beach, AL 36561. Offers criminal justice administration (MS); emergency services management (MS); occupational safety and health (MS), including environmental management. *Program availability:* Part-time, evening/weekend, online learning. *Entrance requirements:* For master's, bachelor's degree from accredited/approved institution. Additional exam requirements/recommendations for international students: required—TOEFL. Electronic applications accepted.

**Columbia University,** Columbia University Mailman School of Public Health, Department of Environmental Health Sciences, New York, NY 10032. Offers environmental health sciences (MPH, Dr PH, PhD); radiological sciences (MS); toxicology (MS). *Accreditation:* CEPH (one or more programs are accredited). *Program availability:* Part-time. *Students:* 45 full-time (37 women), 27 part-time (17 women); includes 27 minority (1 Black or African American, non-Hispanic/Latino; 1 American Indian or Alaska Native, non-Hispanic/Latino; 12 Asian, non-Hispanic/Latino; 7 Hispanic/Latino; 1 Native Hawaiian or other Pacific Islander, non-Hispanic/Latino; 5 Two or more races, non-Hispanic/Latino), 12 international. Average age 27. 161 applicants, 54% accepted, 33 enrolled. In 2019, 28 master's, 2 doctorates awarded. *Degree requirements:* For master's, thesis optional; for doctorate, thesis/dissertation. *Entrance requirements:* For master's, GRE General Test, 1 year of course work in biology, general chemistry, organic chemistry, and mathematics; for doctorate, GRE General Test, MPH or equivalent (for Dr PH). Additional exam requirements/recommendations for international students: required—TOEFL (minimum score 600 paper-based; 100 iBT). *Application deadline:* For fall admission, 12/1 priority date for domestic and international students. Applications are processed on a rolling basis. Application fee: $120. Electronic applications accepted. *Expenses: Tuition:* Full-time $47,600; part-time $1880 per credit. One-time fee: $105. *Financial support:* Research assistantships, teaching assistantships, career-related internships or fieldwork, and Federal Work-Study available. Support available to part-time students. Financial award application deadline: 2/1; financial award applicants required to submit FAFSA. *Unit head:* Dr. Andrea Baccarelli, Chair, 212-305-3466, Fax: 212-305-4012. *Application contact:* Clare Norton, Associate Dean for Enrollment Management, 212-305-8698, Fax: 212-342-1861, E-mail: ph-admit@columbia.edu.
Website: https://www.mailman.columbia.edu/become-student/departments/environmental-health-sciences

**Duke University,** Graduate School, Integrated Toxicology and Environmental Health Program, Durham, NC 27708. Offers Certificate. *Entrance requirements:* Additional exam requirements/recommendations for international students: required—TOEFL (minimum score 577 paper-based; 90 iBT) or IELTS (minimum score 7). Electronic applications accepted.

**East Carolina University,** Graduate School, College of Health and Human Performance, Department of Health Education and Promotion, Greenville, NC 27858-4353. Offers environmental health (MS); health education (MA Ed); health education and promotion (MA). *Accreditation:* NCATE. *Application deadline:* For fall admission, 6/1 priority date for domestic students. *Expenses: Tuition, area resident:* Full-time $4749;

part-time $185 per credit hour. Tuition, state resident: full-time $4749; part-time $185 per credit hour. Tuition, nonresident: full-time $17,898; part-time $864 per credit hour. *International tuition:* $17,898 full-time. *Required fees:* $2787. *Financial support:* Application deadline: 6/1. *Unit head:* Vic Aeby, Associate Professor, 252-328-6000, E-mail: aeby@ecu.edu. *Application contact:* Graduate School Admissions, 252-328-6012, Fax: 252-328-6071, E-mail: gradschool@ecu.edu.
Website: https://hhp.ecu.edu/hep/

**East Carolina University,** Graduate School, Thomas Harriot College of Arts and Sciences, Department of Psychology, Greenville, NC 27858-4353. Offers health psychology (PhD), including clinical health psychology, occupational health psychology, pediatric school psychology; industrial and organizational psychology (MA); quantitative methods for the social and behavioral sciences (Certificate); MA/CAS. *Program availability:* Part-time, evening/weekend. *Application deadline:* For fall admission, 12/1 priority date for domestic and international students. *Expenses: Tuition, area resident:* Full-time $4749; part-time $185 per credit hour. Tuition, state resident: full-time $4749; part-time $185 per credit hour. Tuition, nonresident: full-time $17,898; part-time $864 per credit hour. *International tuition:* $17,898 full-time. *Required fees:* $2787. *Financial support:* Application deadline: 6/1. *Unit head:* Dr. Alan Christensen, Chair, E-mail: christensenal19@ecu.edu. *Application contact:* Graduate School Admissions, 252-328-6012, Fax: 252-328-6071, E-mail: gradschool@ecu.edu.
Website: https://psychology.ecu.edu/

**Eastern Kentucky University,** The Graduate School, College of Health Sciences, Program in Public Health, Richmond, KY 40475-3102. Offers community health education (MPH); environmental health science (MPH); industrial hygiene (MPH); public health nutrition (MPH). *Accreditation:* CEPH. *Degree requirements:* For master's, comprehensive exam, thesis optional, practicum, capstone course. *Entrance requirements:* For master's, GRE.

**East Tennessee State University,** College of Graduate and Continuing Studies, College of Public Health, Department of Environmental Health, Johnson City, TN 37614. Offers MSEH, PhD. *Program availability:* Part-time. *Degree requirements:* For master's, comprehensive exam, research project or thesis; environmental health practice; seminar; for doctorate, comprehensive exam, thesis/dissertation, environmental health practice, seminar. *Entrance requirements:* For master's, GRE General Test, 30 hours of course work in natural and physical sciences, minimum GPA of 2.75, SOPHAS application, three letters of recommendation; for doctorate, GRE General Test, MPH or MS in related field of study with research-based thesis, SOPHAS application, three letters of recommendation, curriculum vitae or resume. Additional exam requirements/recommendations for international students: required—TOEFL (minimum score 550 paper-based; 79 iBT). Electronic applications accepted.

**East Tennessee State University,** College of Graduate and Continuing Studies, College of Public Health, Program in Public Health, Johnson City, TN 37614. Offers biostatistics (MPH, Postbaccalaureate Certificate); community health (MPH, DPH); environmental health (MPH); epidemiology (MPH, DPH, Postbaccalaureate Certificate); gerontology (Postbaccalaureate Certificate); global health (Postbaccalaureate Certificate); health care management (Postbaccalaureate Certificate); health management and policy (DPH); public health (Postbaccalaureate Certificate); public health services administration (MPH); rural health (Postbaccalaureate Certificate). *Accreditation:* CEPH. *Program availability:* Part-time, online learning. *Degree requirements:* For master's, comprehensive exam, field experience; for doctorate, thesis/dissertation, practicum. *Entrance requirements:* For master's, GRE General Test, minimum GPA of 2.75, SOPHAS application, three letters of recommendation; for doctorate, GRE General Test, SOPHAS application, three letters of recommendation; for Postbaccalaureate Certificate, minimum GPA of 2.5, three letters of recommendation, resume. Additional exam requirements/recommendations for international students: required—TOEFL (minimum score 550 paper-based; 79 iBT), IELTS (minimum score 6.5). Electronic applications accepted.

**Embry-Riddle Aeronautical University–Worldwide,** Department of Aeronautics, Graduate Studies, Daytona Beach, FL 32114-3900. Offers aeronautics (MSA); aeronautics and design (MS); aviation & aerospace sustainability (MS); aviation maintenance (MAM); aviation/aerospace research (MS); education (MS); human factors (MSHFS); occupational safety management (MS); operations (MS); safety/emergency response (MS); space systems (MS); unmanned systems (MS). *Program availability:* Part-time, evening/weekend, 100% online. *Degree requirements:* For master's, comprehensive exam, thesis (for some programs), capstone or thesis dependent on degree program. *Entrance requirements:* For master's, GRE required for MSHF. Additional exam requirements/recommendations for international students: required—TOEFL (minimum score 550 paper-based; 79 iBT), IELTS (minimum score 6), TOEFL or IELTS required for Applicants for whom English is not the primary language. Electronic applications accepted.

**Emory University,** Rollins School of Public Health, Department of Environmental Health, Atlanta, GA 30322-1100. Offers environmental health (MPH); environmental health and epidemiology (MSPH); environmental health sciences (PhD); global environmental health (MPH). *Program availability:* Part-time. *Degree requirements:* For master's, thesis, practicum. *Entrance requirements:* For master's, GRE General Test. Additional exam requirements/recommendations for international students: required—TOEFL. Electronic applications accepted.

**Florida International University,** Robert Stempel College of Public Health and Social Work, Programs in Public Health, Miami, FL 33199. Offers biostatistics (MPH); environmental and occupational health (MPH, PhD); epidemiology (MPH, PhD); health policy and management (MPH); health promotion and disease prevention (MPH, PhD). *Accreditation:* CEPH. *Program availability:* Part-time, evening/weekend, online learning. *Faculty:* 31 full-time (15 women), 8 part-time/adjunct (6 women). *Students:* 176 full-time (117 women), 58 part-time (42 women); includes 170 minority (57 Black or African American, non-Hispanic/Latino; 1 American Indian or Alaska Native, non-Hispanic/Latino; 14 Asian, non-Hispanic/Latino; 95 Hispanic/Latino; 3 Two or more races, non-Hispanic/Latino), 32 international. Average age 29. 260 applicants, 68% accepted, 68 enrolled. In 2019, 70 master's, 16 doctorates awarded. *Degree requirements:* For master's, thesis optional; for doctorate, comprehensive exam, thesis/dissertation. *Entrance requirements:* For master's, minimum GPA of 3.0, letters of recommendation; for doctorate, GRE, resume, minimum GPA of 3.0, letters of recommendation, letter of intent. Additional exam requirements/recommendations for international students: required—TOEFL (minimum score 550 paper-based; 80 iBT). *Application deadline:* For fall admission, 6/1 for domestic students, 4/1 for international students; for spring admission, 10/1 for domestic students, 9/1 for international students. Applications are processed on a rolling basis. Application fee: $30. Electronic applications accepted. *Expenses:* Contact institution. *Financial support:* Institutionally sponsored loans, scholarships/grants, and tuition waivers (full) available. Financial award application deadline: 3/1; financial award applicants required to submit FAFSA. *Unit head:* Dr. Kim Tieu, Chair, 305-348-0371, E-mail: kim.tieu@fiu.edu. *Application contact:* Nanett Rojas, Manager, Admissions Operations, 305-348-7464, Fax: 305-348-7441, E-mail: gradadm@fiu.edu.

**Fort Valley State University,** College of Graduate Studies and Extended Education, Program in Public Health, Fort Valley, GA 31030. Offers environmental health (MPH). *Degree requirements:* For master's, thesis. *Entrance requirements:* For master's, GRE General Test. Additional exam requirements/recommendations for international students: recommended—TOEFL.

**Gannon University,** School of Graduate Studies, College of Engineering and Business, School of Engineering and Computer Science, Program in Environmental Science and Engineering, Erie, PA 16541-0001. Offers environmental health (MSEH); environmental health and engineering (MS). *Program availability:* Part-time, evening/weekend. *Degree requirements:* For master's, thesis (for some programs), research paper or project (for some programs). *Entrance requirements:* For master's, GRE, bachelor's degree in science or engineering from an accredited college or university. Additional exam requirements/recommendations for international students: required—TOEFL (minimum score 79 iBT), GRE. Electronic applications accepted. Application fee is waived when completed online.

**The George Washington University,** Milken Institute School of Public Health, Department of Environmental and Occupational Health, Washington, DC 20052. Offers environ-occupational health (Dr PH). *Entrance requirements:* Additional exam requirements/recommendations for international students: required—TOEFL.

**Georgia Southern University,** Jack N. Averitt College of Graduate Studies, Allen E. Paulson College of Engineering and Computing, Department of Manufacturing Engineering, Program in Occupational Safety and Environmental Compliance, Statesboro, GA 30458. Offers Graduate Certificate. *Students:* 1 applicant. In 2019, 1 Graduate Certificate awarded. *Entrance requirements:* Additional exam requirements/recommendations for international students: required—TOEFL (minimum score 550 paper-based; 80 iBT), IELTS (minimum score 6). *Application deadline:* For fall admission, 3/1 priority date for domestic and international students. Applications are processed on a rolling basis. Application fee: $50. Electronic applications accepted. *Expenses: Tuition, area resident:* Full-time $4986; part-time $277 per credit hour. Tuition, nonresident: full-time $19,890; part-time $1105 per credit hour. *International tuition:* $19,890 full-time. *Required fees:* $2114; $1057 per semester. $1057 per semester. Tuition and fees vary according to course load, campus/location and program. *Financial support:* Applicants required to submit FAFSA. *Unit head:* Dr. Biswanath Samanta, Program Coordinator, 912-478-0334, E-mail: bsamanta@georgiasouthern.edu. *Application contact:* Dr. Biswanath Samanta, Program Coordinator, 912-478-0334, E-mail: bsamanta@georgiasouthern.edu.

**Georgia Southern University,** Jack N. Averitt College of Graduate Studies, Allen E. Paulson College of Engineering and Computing, Department of Mechanical Engineering, Statesboro, GA 30460. Offers engineering and information technology (MSAE), including engineering and information technology; engineering and manufacturing management (Graduate Certificate); engineering/energy science (MSAE); engineering/engineering management (MSAE); engineering/mechatronics (MSAE); occupational safety and environmental compliance (Graduate Certificate). *Program availability:* Part-time, evening/weekend. *Faculty:* 24 full-time (1 woman), 1 part-time/adjunct (0 women). *Students:* 13 full-time (0 women), 3 part-time (1 woman); includes 5 minority (1 Black or African American, non-Hispanic/Latino; 3 Asian, non-Hispanic/Latino; 1 Hispanic/Latino), 4 international. Average age 25. 24 applicants, 71% accepted, 11 enrolled. In 2019, 23 master's, 1 Graduate Certificate awarded. *Degree requirements:* For master's, comprehensive exam, thesis optional. *Entrance requirements:* For master's, GRE, undergraduate major or equivalent in proposed study area. Additional exam requirements/recommendations for international students: required—TOEFL (minimum score 550 paper-based; 80 iBT), IELTS (minimum score 6). *Application deadline:* For fall admission, 3/1 priority date for domestic and international students; for spring admission, 10/1 priority date for domestic students, 10/1 for international students. Applications are processed on a rolling basis. Application fee: $50. Electronic applications accepted. *Expenses: Tuition, area resident:* Full-time $4986; part-time $277 per credit hour. Tuition, nonresident: full-time $19,890; part-time $1105 per credit hour. *International tuition:* $19,890 full-time. *Required fees:* $2114; $1057 per semester. $1057 per semester. Tuition and fees vary according to course load, campus/location and program. *Financial support:* In 2019–20, 17 students received support, including 4 research assistantships with partial tuition reimbursements available (averaging $7,200 per year), teaching assistantships with partial tuition reimbursements available (averaging $7,200 per year); Federal Work-Study, scholarships/grants, tuition waivers (partial), and unspecified assistantships also available. Financial award application deadline: 4/15; financial award applicants required to submit FAFSA. *Unit head:* Dr. Brian Vlcek, Chair, 912-478-5761, Fax: 912-478-1455, E-mail: bvlcek@georgiasouthern.edu.

**Georgia Southern University,** Jack N. Averitt College of Graduate Studies, Jiann-Ping Hsu College of Public Health, Program in Public Health, Statesboro, GA 30460. Offers biostatistics (MPH, Dr PH); community health behavior and education (Dr PH); community health education (MPH); environmental health sciences (MPH); epidemiology (MPH); health policy and management (MPH, Dr PH). *Program availability:* Part-time. *Faculty:* 42 full-time (22 women), 1 (woman) part-time/adjunct. *Students:* 142 full-time (105 women), 88 part-time (62 women); includes 132 minority (100 Black or African American, non-Hispanic/Latino; 10 Asian, non-Hispanic/Latino; 8 Hispanic/Latino; 14 Two or more races, non-Hispanic/Latino), 46 international. Average age 32. 195 applicants, 85% accepted, 59 enrolled. In 2019, 90 master's, 14 doctorates awarded. *Degree requirements:* For master's, thesis optional, practicum; for doctorate, comprehensive exam, thesis/dissertation, preceptorship. *Entrance requirements:* For master's, GRE General Test, minimum GPA of 2.75, 3 letters of recommendation, statement of purpose, resume or curriculum vitae; for doctorate, GRE, GMAT, MCAT, LSAT, minimum GPA of 3.0, 3 letters of recommendation, statement of purpose, resume or curriculum vitae. Additional exam requirements/recommendations for international students: required—TOEFL (minimum score 537 paper-based; 75 iBT), IELTS (minimum score 6). *Application deadline:* For fall admission, 6/1 for domestic students, 5/1 for international students. Applications are processed on a rolling basis. Application fee: $135. Electronic applications accepted. *Expenses:* Contact institution. *Financial support:* In 2019–20, 94 students received support, including 1 research assistantship with full tuition reimbursement available (averaging $12,350 per year), 6 teaching assistantships with full tuition reimbursements available (averaging $12,350 per year); scholarships/grants, tuition waivers (full), and unspecified assistantships also available. Financial award application deadline: 4/15; financial award applicants required to submit FAFSA. *Unit head:* Dr. Robert Greg Evans, Dean, 912-478-2674, E-mail: rgevans@georgiasouthern.edu. *Application contact:* Shamia Garrett, Coordinator, Office of Student Services, 912-478-2674, Fax: 912-478-5811, E-mail: jphcoph-gradadvisor@georgiasouthern.edu.
Website: http://jphcoph.georgiasouthern.edu/

**Harvard University,** Cyprus International Institute for the Environment and Public Health in Association with Harvard School of Public Health, Cambridge, MA 02138. Offers environmental health (MS); environmental/public health (PhD); epidemiology and biostatistics (MS). *Entrance requirements:* For master's and doctorate, GRE, resume/curriculum vitae, 3 letters of recommendation, BA or BS (including diploma and official

transcripts). Additional exam requirements/recommendations for international students: required—TOEFL, IELTS (minimum score 7). Electronic applications accepted.

**Harvard University,** Harvard T.H. Chan School of Public Health, Department of Environmental Health, Boston, MA 02115-6096. Offers environmental epidemiology (SM); environmental exposure assessment (SM); ergonomics and safety (SM); occupational health (SM); occupational hygiene (SM); population health sciences (PhD); risk and decision science (SM). *Program availability:* Part-time. *Faculty:* 42 full-time (13 women), 16 part-time/adjunct (4 women). *Students:* 39 full-time (29 women); includes 9 minority (3 Black or African American, non-Hispanic/Latino; 3 Asian, non-Hispanic/Latino; 1 Hispanic/Latino; 2 Two or more races, non-Hispanic/Latino), 20 international. Average age 29. 51 applicants, 55% accepted, 20 enrolled. In 2019, 10 master's, 8 doctorates awarded. *Degree requirements:* For doctorate, thesis/dissertation, qualifying exam. *Entrance requirements:* For master's, GRE, MCAT; for doctorate, GRE. Additional exam requirements/recommendations for international students: recommended—TOEFL (minimum score 600 paper-based; 100 iBT), IELTS (minimum score 7). *Application deadline:* For fall admission, 12/1 for domestic and international students. Application fee: $140. Electronic applications accepted. *Financial support:* Fellowships, research assistantships, teaching assistantships, career-related internships or fieldwork, Federal Work-Study, scholarships/grants, traineeships, and unspecified assistantships available. Support available to part-time students. Financial award application deadline: 2/15; financial award applicants required to submit FAFSA. *Unit head:* Dr. Russ Hauser, Chairman, 617-432-1270, Fax: 617-432-6913. *Application contact:* Vincent W. James, Director of Admissions, 617-432-1031, Fax: 617-432-7080, E-mail: admissions@hsph.harvard.edu.
Website: http://www.hsph.harvard.edu/environmental-health/

**Harvard University,** Harvard T.H. Chan School of Public Health, PhD Program in Population Health Sciences, Boston, MA 02138. Offers environmental health (PhD); epidemiology (PhD); global health and population (PhD); nutrition (PhD); social and behavioral sciences (PhD). *Students:* 159 full-time (0 women). Average age 29. In 2019, 5 doctorates awarded. *Entrance requirements:* Additional exam requirements/recommendations for international students: recommended—TOEFL, IELTS. *Application deadline:* For fall admission, 12/1 for domestic and international students. Electronic applications accepted. *Financial support:* Application deadline: 2/15; applicants required to submit FAFSA. *Unit head:* Bruce Villineau, Assistant Director, 617-432-6076, E-mail: phdphs@hsph.harvard.edu. *Application contact:* Bruce Villineau, Assistant Director, 617-432-6076, E-mail: phdphs@hsph.harvard.edu.

**Indiana State University,** College of Graduate and Professional Studies, College of Technology, Department of Built Environment, Terre Haute, IN 47809. Offers occupational safety management (MS).

**Indiana University Bloomington,** School of Public Health, Department of Environmental Health, Bloomington, IN 47405. Offers MPH, PhD. *Degree requirements:* For doctorate, comprehensive exam, thesis/dissertation. *Entrance requirements:* For master's, GRE if cumulative GPA less than 2.8; for doctorate, GRE. Additional exam requirements/recommendations for international students: required—TOEFL (minimum score 550 paper-based; 80 iBT). Electronic applications accepted.

**Indiana University of Pennsylvania,** School of Graduate Studies and Research, College of Health and Human Services, Department of Safety Sciences, MS Program in Safety Sciences, Indiana, PA 15705. Offers MS. *Program availability:* Part-time, blended/hybrid learning. *Faculty:* 5 full-time (2 women). *Students:* 10 full-time (5 women), 30 part-time (8 women); includes 4 minority (3 Black or African American, non-Hispanic/Latino; 1 Hispanic/Latino), 1 international. Average age 30. 23 applicants, 100% accepted, 16 enrolled. In 2019, 26 master's awarded. *Degree requirements:* For master's, thesis optional. *Entrance requirements:* For master's, 2 letters of recommendation, official transcripts, goal statement. Additional exam requirements/recommendations for international students: required—TOEFL (minimum score 540 paper-based; 76 iBT), IELTS (minimum score 6). *Application deadline:* For fall admission, 4/1 priority date for domestic students. Applications are processed on a rolling basis. Application fee: $50. Electronic applications accepted. *Expenses:* Contact institution. *Financial support:* In 2019–20, 3 fellowships with tuition reimbursements (averaging $667 per year), 5 research assistantships with tuition reimbursements (averaging $5,800 per year) were awarded; teaching assistantships, career-related internships or fieldwork, Federal Work-Study, scholarships/grants, and unspecified assistantships also available. Financial award application deadline: 4/15; financial award applicants required to submit FAFSA. *Unit head:* Dr. Wanda Minnick, Graduate Coordinator, 724-357-3276, E-mail: Wanda.Minnick@iup.edu. *Application contact:* Dr. Wanda Minnick, Graduate Coordinator, 724-357-3276, E-mail: Wanda.Minnick@iup.edu.
Website: http://www.iup.edu/grad/safety/default.aspx

**Indiana University of Pennsylvania,** School of Graduate Studies and Research, College of Health and Human Services, Department of Safety Sciences, PhD Program in Safety Sciences, Indiana, PA 15705. Offers PhD. *Program availability:* Part-time, blended/hybrid learning. *Faculty:* 5 full-time (2 women). *Students:* 56 part-time (21 women); includes 15 minority (12 Black or African American, non-Hispanic/Latino; 3 Hispanic/Latino), 3 international. Average age 46. 40 applicants, 78% accepted, 23 enrolled. In 2019, 4 doctorates awarded. *Degree requirements:* For doctorate, thesis/dissertation. *Entrance requirements:* For doctorate, GRE, master's degree in safety sciences or closely-related field such as industrial hygiene, environmental health, or ergonomics; minimum graduate GPA of 3.0; official transcripts; three letters of recommendation; statement of goals; resume; sample of written work. Additional exam requirements/recommendations for international students: required—TOEFL (minimum score 540 paper-based; 76 iBT), IELTS (minimum score 6). *Application deadline:* For fall admission, 4/1 priority date for domestic students. Applications are processed on a rolling basis. Application fee: $50. Electronic applications accepted. *Expenses:* Contact institution. *Financial support:* In 2019–20, 1 fellowship (averaging $2,100 per year), 4 research assistantships with tuition reimbursements (averaging $3,500 per year) were awarded; teaching assistantships with partial tuition reimbursements and unspecified assistantships also available. Financial award application deadline: 4/15; financial award applicants required to submit FAFSA. *Unit head:* Dr. Jan Wachter, Coordinator, 724-357-3275, E-mail: jan.wachter@iup.edu. *Application contact:* Dr. Jan Wachter, Coordinator, 724-357-3275, E-mail: jan.wachter@iup.edu.
Website: http://www.iup.edu/safetysciences/grad/safety-sciences-phd/

**Indiana University-Purdue University Indianapolis,** Richard M. Fairbanks School of Public Health, Indianapolis, IN 46202. Offers biostatistics (MS, PhD); environmental health (MPH); epidemiology (MPH, PhD); global health leadership (Dr PH); health administration (MHA); health policy (Graduate Certificate); health policy and management (MPH, PhD); health systems management (Graduate Certificate); product stewardship (MS); public health (Graduate Certificate); social and behavioral sciences (MPH). *Accreditation:* CAHME; CEPH. *Expenses:* Contact institution.

**Indiana University-Purdue University Indianapolis,** School of Public and Environmental Affairs, Indianapolis, IN 46202. Offers criminal justice and public safety (MS); homeland security and emergency management (Graduate Certificate); library management (Graduate Certificate); nonprofit management (Graduate Certificate); public affairs (MPA); public management (Graduate Certificate); social entrepreneurship: nonprofit and public benefit organizations (Graduate Certificate); JD/MPA; MLS/NMC; MLS/PMC; MPA/MA. *Accreditation:* CAHME (one or more programs are accredited); NASPAA. *Program availability:* Part-time, evening/weekend, online learning. *Entrance requirements:* For master's, GRE General Test, GMAT or LSAT, minimum GPA of 3.0 (preferred). Additional exam requirements/recommendations for international students: required—TOEFL (minimum score 93 iBT), IELTS (minimum score 6.5). Electronic applications accepted.

**Johns Hopkins University,** Bloomberg School of Public Health, Department of Environmental Health and Engineering, Baltimore, MD 21218. Offers environmental health (MHS, Sc M, Dr PH, PhD); occupational and environmental hygiene (MSPH); toxicity testing and human health risk assessment of environmental agents (MSPH). *Degree requirements:* For master's, essay, presentation; for doctorate, comprehensive exam, thesis/dissertation, 1-year full-time residency, oral and written exams. *Entrance requirements:* For master's, GRE General Test or MCAT, 3 letters of recommendation, transcripts; for doctorate, GRE General Test or MCAT, 3 letters of recommendation. Additional exam requirements/recommendations for international students: required—TOEFL (minimum score 100 iBT), IELTS (minimum score 7). Electronic applications accepted.

**Johns Hopkins University,** G. W. C. Whiting School of Engineering, Department of Environmental Health and Engineering, Baltimore, MD 21218. Offers MA, MS, MSE, PhD. Terminal master's awarded for partial completion of doctoral program. *Degree requirements:* For master's, thesis optional, 1-year full-time residency; for doctorate, comprehensive exam, thesis/dissertation, oral exam, 2-year full-time residency. *Entrance requirements:* For master's and doctorate, GRE General Test, 3 letters of recommendation, statement of purpose, transcripts. Additional exam requirements/recommendations for international students: required—TOEFL (minimum score 600 paper-based, 100 iBT) or IELTS (7). Electronic applications accepted.

**Kent State University,** College of Public Health, Kent, OH 44242-0001. Offers public health (MPH, PhD), including biostatistics (MPH), environmental health sciences (MPH), epidemiology, health policy and management, prevention science (PhD), social and behavioral sciences (MPH). *Accreditation:* CEPH. *Program availability:* Part-time, 100% online. *Faculty:* 23 full-time (12 women), 4 part-time/adjunct (1 woman). *Students:* 136 full-time (98 women), 158 part-time (129 women); includes 71 minority (45 Black or African American, non-Hispanic/Latino; 12 Asian, non-Hispanic/Latino; 8 Hispanic/Latino; 6 Two or more races, non-Hispanic/Latino), 40 international. Average age 31. 187 applicants, 79% accepted, 85 enrolled. In 2019, 93 master's, 7 doctorates awarded. *Degree requirements:* For master's, comprehensive exam, between 150 - 300 hours' placement at public health agency, final portfolio and presentation; for doctorate, comprehensive exam, thesis/dissertation. *Entrance requirements:* For master's, GRE or other standardized graduate admission exam (GMAT, MCAT, LSAT or PCAT), minimum GPA of 3.0, transcripts, goal statement, 3 letters of recommendation; for doctorate, GRE or other standardized graduate admission exam with a quantitative component, Master's degree in related discipline, minimum GPA of 3.0, personal statement, resume, interview with faculty, 3 letters of recommendation, transcript(s). Additional exam requirements/recommendations for international students: required—TOEFL (minimum score 94 iBT), IELTS (minimum score 7), PTE (minimum score 65), For MPH: TOEFL iBT 79, Michigan English Language Assessment Battery (minimum score of 77), IELTS 6.5, PTE 58; For Ph.D.: see below and min MELAB 82. *Application deadline:* For fall admission, 6/15 for domestic and international students; for spring admission, 10/15 for domestic and international students; for summer admission, 3/15 for domestic and international students. Applications are processed on a rolling basis. Application fee: $45 ($70 for international students). Electronic applications accepted. *Financial support:* Career-related internships or fieldwork, Federal Work-Study, scholarships/grants, and unspecified assistantships available. *Unit head:* Dr. Sonia Alemagno, Dean and Professor of Health Policy and Management, 330-672-6500, E-mail: salemagn@kent.edu. *Application contact:* Dr. Jeffrey S. Hallam, Professor/Associate Dean for Research and Graduate Studies, 330-672-0679, E-mail: jhallam1@kent.edu.
Website: http://www.kent.edu/publichealth/

**Lehigh University,** College of Arts and Sciences, Environmental Policy Program, Bethlehem, PA 18015. Offers environmental health (Graduate Certificate); environmental justice (Graduate Certificate); environmental policy and law (Graduate Certificate); environmental policy design (MA); sustainable development (Graduate Certificate); urban environmental policy (Graduate Certificate). *Faculty:* 8 full-time (3 women). *Students:* 12 full-time (10 women), 4 part-time (3 women); includes 3 minority (1 Asian, non-Hispanic/Latino; 1 Hispanic/Latino; 1 Two or more races, non-Hispanic/Latino), 2 international. Average age 26. 10 applicants, 80% accepted, 6 enrolled. In 2019, 5 master's awarded. *Degree requirements:* For master's, thesis or additional course work. *Entrance requirements:* For master's, GRE, minimum GPA of 2.75, 3.0 for last two undergraduate semesters; essay; 2 letters of recommendation. Additional exam requirements/recommendations for international students: required—TOEFL (minimum score 85 iBT), IELTS (minimum score 6.5). *Application deadline:* For fall admission, 1/1 for domestic and international students; for spring admission, 12/1 for domestic and international students. Application fee: $75. *Financial support:* In 2019–20, 6 students received support. Fellowships, teaching assistantships, career-related internships or fieldwork, scholarships/grants, health care benefits, and unspecified assistantships available. Financial award application deadline: 1/1. *Unit head:* Dr. Karen B. Pooley, Director, 610-758-2637, E-mail: kbp312@lehigh.edu. *Application contact:* Mandy Fraley, Academic Coordinator, 610-758-5837, Fax: 610-758-6232, E-mail: amf518@lehigh.edu.
Website: http://ei.cas2.lehigh.edu/

**Lewis University,** College of Education and Social Sciences, Program in Public Safety Administration, Romeoville, IL 60446. Offers MS. *Program availability:* Part-time, evening/weekend, 100% online, blended/hybrid learning. *Students:* 3 full-time (0 women), 53 part-time (18 women); includes 9 minority (2 Black or African American, non-Hispanic/Latino; 7 Hispanic/Latino). Average age 35. *Entrance requirements:* For master's, bachelor's degree, 2 letters of recommendation, personal statement. Additional exam requirements/recommendations for international students: required—TOEFL (minimum score 550 paper-based; 79 iBT), IELTS (minimum score 6). *Application deadline:* For fall admission, 5/1 priority date for international students; for spring admission, 11/15 priority date for international students. Applications are processed on a rolling basis. Application fee: $40. Electronic applications accepted. *Financial support:* Federal Work-Study and unspecified assistantships available. Financial award application deadline: 5/1; financial award applicants required to submit FAFSA. *Unit head:* Dr. Raymond Garritano, Director of the Public Safety Administration Graduate Program. *Application contact:* Sheri Vilcek, Graduate Admission Counselor, 815-838-5610, E-mail: grad@lewisu.edu.

**Loma Linda University,** School of Public Health, Program in Environmental and Occupational Health, Loma Linda, CA 92350. Offers MPH. *Entrance requirements:* Additional exam requirements/recommendations for international students: required—Michigan English Language Assessment Battery or TOEFL.

**Louisiana State University Health Sciences Center,** School of Public Health, New Orleans, LA 70112. Offers behavioral and community health sciences (MPH); biostatistics (MPH, MS, PhD); community health sciences (PhD); environmental and

occupational health sciences (MPH); epidemiology (MPH, PhD); health policy and systems management (MPH). *Accreditation:* CEPH. *Program availability:* Part-time. *Degree requirements:* For doctorate, thesis/dissertation. *Entrance requirements:* For master's, GRE General Test. Additional exam requirements/recommendations for international students: recommended—TOEFL (minimum score 550 paper-based; 79 iBT), IELTS. Electronic applications accepted.

**McGill University,** Faculty of Graduate and Postdoctoral Studies, Faculty of Medicine, Department of Epidemiology, Biostatistics and Occupational Health, Montréal, QC H3A 2T5, Canada. Offers biostatistics (M Sc, PhD); epidemiology (M Sc, PhD); occupational health (M Sc A); public health (MSPH). *Program availability:* Part-time, online learning. *Degree requirements:* For doctorate, thesis/dissertation. *Entrance requirements:* For master's, B Sc in chemistry, engineering physics, environmental sciences, medicine, nursing, or other health science (for occupational health); MD or B Sc in nursing (for distance education); minimum GPA of 3.0; for doctorate, TOEFL, M Sc in environmental health, chemistry, engineering, community health, physics, epidemiology, medicine, nursing, or occupational health.

**Meharry Medical College,** School of Graduate Studies, Division of Public Health Practice, Nashville, TN 37208-9989. Offers occupational medicine (MSPH); public health administration (MSPH). *Accreditation:* CEPH. *Program availability:* Part-time, evening/weekend. *Degree requirements:* For master's, thesis, externship. *Entrance requirements:* For master's, GRE General Test, GMAT. Additional exam requirements/ recommendations for international students: required—TOEFL. *Application deadline:* For fall admission, 6/1 for domestic students. Applications are processed on a rolling basis. Application fee: $65. *Expenses:* Contact institution. *Financial support:* Career-related internships or fieldwork, Federal Work-Study, institutionally sponsored loans, and scholarships/grants available. Support available to part-time students. Financial award application deadline: 7/15; financial award applicants required to submit FAFSA. *Unit head:* Stephanie Bailey, MD, Senior Associate Dean, 615-327-6069, E-mail: sbailey@mmc.edu. *Application contact:* Kimberlee Wyche-Etheridge, MD,MPH, Interim Program Director, 615-327-6675, E-mail: ketheridge@mmc.edu.
Website: https://home.mmc.edu/school-of-graduate-studies-research/the-m-s-p-h-program/

**Mercer University,** Graduate Studies, Cecil B. Day Campus, College of Professional Advancement, Atlanta, GA 31207. Offers certified rehabilitation counseling (MS); clinical mental health (MS); counselor education and supervision (PhD); criminal justice and public safety leadership (MS); health informatics (MS); human services (MS), including child and adolescent services, gerontology services; organizational leadership (MS), including leadership for the health care professional, leadership for the nonprofit organization, organizational development and change; school counseling (MS). *Program availability:* Part-time, evening/weekend, 100% online, blended/hybrid learning. *Faculty:* 19 full-time (11 women), 34 part-time/adjunct (30 women). *Students:* 193 full-time (156 women), 277 part-time (225 women); includes 260 minority (211 Black or African American, non-Hispanic/Latino; 2 American Indian or Alaska Native, non-Hispanic/Latino; 23 Asian, non-Hispanic/Latino; 19 Hispanic/Latino; 5 Two or more races, non-Hispanic/Latino), 3 international. Average age 32. 300 applicants, 45% accepted, 114 enrolled. In 2019, 183 master's, 7 doctorates awarded. *Degree requirements:* For master's, comprehensive exam (for some programs), thesis (for some programs); for doctorate, thesis/dissertation. *Entrance requirements:* For master's, GRE or MAT, Georgia Professional Standards Commission (GPSC) Certification at the SC-5 level; for doctorate, GRE or MAT. Additional exam requirements/recommendations for international students: recommended—TOEFL (minimum score 550 paper-based; 80 iBT), IELTS (minimum score 6.5). *Application deadline:* For fall admission, 7/1 priority date for domestic and international students; for spring admission, 11/1 priority date for domestic and international students; for summer admission, 4/1 priority date for domestic and international students. Application fee: $35. Electronic applications accepted. Application fee is waived when completed online. *Expenses:* Contact institution. *Financial support:* In 2019–20, 32 students received support. Federal Work-Study, scholarships/grants, and unspecified assistantships available. Financial award applicants required to submit FAFSA. *Unit head:* Dr. Priscilla R. Danheiser, Dean, 678-547-6028, Fax: 678-547-6008, E-mail: danheiser_p@mercer.edu. *Application contact:* Theatis Anderson, Asst VP for Enrollment Management, 678-547-6421, E-mail: anderson_t@mercer.edu.
Website: https://professionaladvancement.mercer.edu/

**Mississippi Valley State University,** Department of Natural Sciences and Environmental Health, Itta Bena, MS 38941-1400. Offers environmental health (MS). *Program availability:* Part-time, evening/weekend. *Degree requirements:* For master's, comprehensive exam, thesis optional. *Entrance requirements:* For master's, GRE, minimum GPA of 3.0. Additional exam requirements/recommendations for international students: recommended—TOEFL (minimum score 525 paper-based). *Expenses:* Contact institution.

**Murray State University,** Jesse D. Jones College of Science, Engineering and Technology, Department of Occupational Safety and Health, Murray, KY 42071. Offers environmental science (MS). *Program availability:* Part-time, evening/weekend, 100% online, blended/hybrid learning. *Entrance requirements:* For master's, GRE or GMAT, minimum university GPA of 2.75. Additional exam requirements/recommendations for international students: required—TOEFL (minimum score 527 paper-based; 71 iBT). Electronic applications accepted.

**New York Medical College,** School of Health Sciences and Practice, Valhalla, NY 10595. Offers behavioral sciences and health promotion (MPH); biostatistics (MS); children with special health care (Graduate Certificate); emergency preparedness (Graduate Certificate); environmental health science (MPH); epidemiology (MPH, MS); global health (Graduate Certificate); health education (Graduate Certificate); health policy and management (MPH, Dr PH); industrial hygiene (Graduate Certificate); pediatric dysphagia (Post-Graduate Certificate); physical therapy (DPT); public health (Graduate Certificate); speech-language pathology (MS). *Accreditation:* ASHA; CEPH. *Program availability:* Part-time, evening/weekend, 100% online, blended/hybrid learning. *Faculty:* 47 full-time (34 women), 203 part-time/adjunct (125 women). *Students:* 230 full-time (171 women), 292 part-time (207 women); includes 204 minority (73 Black or African American, non-Hispanic/Latino; 4 American Indian or Alaska Native, non-Hispanic/Latino; 59 Asian, non-Hispanic/Latino; 54 Hispanic/Latino; 1 Native Hawaiian or other Pacific Islander, non-Hispanic/Latino; 13 Two or more races, non-Hispanic/ Latino), 35 international. Average age 29. 790 applicants, 61% accepted, 162 enrolled. In 2019, 113 master's, 47 doctorates awarded. *Degree requirements:* For master's, comprehensive exam (for some programs), thesis (for some programs); for doctorate, thesis/dissertation. *Entrance requirements:* For master's, GRE (for MS in speech-language pathology); for doctorate, GRE (for Doctor of Physical Therapy and Doctor of Public Health). Additional exam requirements/recommendations for international students: required—TOEFL (minimum score 96 paper-based; 24 iBT), IELTS (minimum score 7). *Application deadline:* For fall admission, 8/1 for domestic students, 4/15 for international students; for spring admission, 12/1 for domestic students; for summer admission, 5/1 for domestic students, 4/15 for international students. Applications are processed on a rolling basis. Application fee: $128 ($120 for international students). Electronic applications accepted. *Expenses:* $1195 credit fee, academic support fee $200, Student activities fee $140 per year, technology fee $150. *Financial support:* In 2019–20, 18 students received support. Federal Work-Study, scholarships/grants, unspecified assistantships, and Federal student loans available. Financial award application deadline: 4/30; financial award applicants required to submit FAFSA. *Unit head:* Ben Johnson, PhD, Vice Dean, 914-594-4531, E-mail: bjohnson23@nymc.edu. *Application contact:* Irene Bundziak, Assistant to Director of Admissions, 914-594-4905, E-mail: irene_bundziak@nymc.edu.
Website: http://www.nymc.edu/school-of-health-sciences-and-practice-shsp/

**Oakland University,** Graduate Study and Lifelong Learning, School of Health Sciences, Program in Safety Management, Rochester, MI 48309-4401. Offers safety management (MS). *Entrance requirements:* Additional exam requirements/recommendations for international students: required—TOEFL (minimum score 550 paper-based; 79 iBT), IELTS (minimum score 6.5). Electronic applications accepted. *Expenses: Tuition, area resident:* Full-time $12,328; part-time $770.50 per credit hour. Tuition, state resident: full-time $12,328; part-time $770.50 per credit hour. Tuition, nonresident: full-time $16,432; part-time $1027 per credit hour. *International tuition:* $16,432 full-time. Tuition and fees vary according to degree level and program.

**Old Dominion University,** College of Health Sciences, School of Community and Environmental Health, Norfolk, VA 23529. Offers general environmental health (MS); industrial hygiene (MS). *Degree requirements:* For master's, comprehensive exam, oral exam, written exam, practicum or thesis. *Entrance requirements:* For master's, GRE General Test, minimum GPA of 2.75. Additional exam requirements/recommendations for international students: required—TOEFL (minimum score 650 paper-based). Electronic applications accepted. *Expenses:* Contact institution.

**Oregon State University,** College of Public Health and Human Sciences, Program in Public Health, Corvallis, OR 97331. Offers biostatistics (MPH); environmental and occupational health (MPH, PhD); epidemiology (MPH, PhD); global health (MPH, PhD). *Accreditation:* CEPH. Terminal master's awarded for partial completion of doctoral program. *Entrance requirements:* For master's and doctorate, GRE, minimum GPA of 3.0 in last 90 hours. Additional exam requirements/recommendations for international students: required—TOEFL (minimum score 80 iBT), IELTS (minimum score 6.5). Electronic applications accepted. *Expenses:* Contact institution.

**Purdue University,** Graduate School, College of Health and Human Sciences, School of Health Sciences, West Lafayette, IN 47907. Offers health physics (MS, PhD); medical physics (MS, PhD); occupational and environmental health science (MS, PhD), including aerosol deposition and lung disease, ergonomics, exposure and risk assessment, indoor air quality and bioaerosols (PhD), liver/lung toxicology; radiological health (PhD); toxicology (PhD); MS/PhD. *Program availability:* Part-time. *Faculty:* 15 full-time (6 women), 1 part-time/adjunct (0 women). *Students:* 39 full-time (22 women), 6 part-time (3 women); includes 12 minority (2 Black or African American, non-Hispanic/Latino; 1 American Indian or Alaska Native, non-Hispanic/Latino; 3 Asian, non-Hispanic/Latino; 1 Hispanic/Latino; 5 Two or more races, non-Hispanic/Latino), 15 international. Average age 28. 61 applicants, 43% accepted, 14 enrolled. In 2019, 15 master's, 6 doctorates awarded. *Degree requirements:* For master's, thesis optional; for doctorate, one foreign language, thesis/dissertation. *Entrance requirements:* For master's and doctorate, GRE General Test, minimum undergraduate GPA of 3.0 or equivalent. Additional exam requirements/recommendations for international students: required—TOEFL (minimum score 550 paper-based; 77 iBT); recommended—TWE. *Application deadline:* For fall admission, 5/15 for domestic and international students; for spring admission, 10/15 for domestic and international students. Applications are processed on a rolling basis. Application fee: $60 ($75 for international students). Electronic applications accepted. *Financial support:* In 2019–20, fellowships with tuition reimbursements (averaging $14,400 per year), research assistantships with tuition reimbursements (averaging $12,000 per year), teaching assistantships with tuition reimbursements (averaging $12,000 per year) were awarded; career-related internships or fieldwork and traineeships also available. Support available to part-time students. Financial award applicants required to submit FAFSA. *Unit head:* Aaron Bowman, Head of the Graduate Program, 765-494-2684, E-mail: bowma117@purdue.edu. *Application contact:* Karen E. Walker, Graduate Contact, 765-494-1419, E-mail: kwalker@purdue.edu.
Website: https://www.purdue.edu/hhs/hsci/

**Rochester Institute of Technology,** Graduate Enrollment Services, College of Applied Science and Technology, School of Engineering Technology, MS Program in Environmental, Health and Safety Management, Rochester, NY 14623-5603. Offers MS. *Program availability:* Part-time, evening/weekend, 100% online, blended/hybrid learning. *Degree requirements:* For master's, thesis or alternative. *Entrance requirements:* For master's, minimum GPA of 3.0 (recommended). Additional exam requirements/ recommendations for international students: required—TOEFL (minimum score 88 iBT), IELTS (minimum score 6.5), PTE (minimum score 61). Electronic applications accepted. *Expenses:* Contact institution.

**Rutgers University - New Brunswick,** School of Public Health, Piscataway, NJ 08854. Offers biostatistics (MPH, MS, Dr PH, PhD); clinical epidemiology (Certificate); environmental and occupational health (MPH, Dr PH, PhD, Certificate); epidemiology (MPH, Dr PH, PhD); general public health (Certificate); health education and behavioral science (MPH, Dr PH, PhD); health systems and policy (MPH, PhD); public health (MPH, Dr PH, PhD); public health preparedness (Certificate); DO/MPH; JD/MPH; MBA/ MPH; MD/MPH; MPH/MBA; MPH/MSPA; MS/MPH; Psy D/MPH. *Accreditation:* CEPH. *Program availability:* Part-time, evening/weekend. *Degree requirements:* For master's, thesis, internship; for doctorate, comprehensive exam, thesis/dissertation. *Entrance requirements:* For master's, GRE General Test; for doctorate, GRE General Test, MPH (Dr PH); MA, MPH, or MS (PhD). Additional exam requirements/recommendations for international students: required—TOEFL. Electronic applications accepted.

**San Diego State University,** Graduate and Research Affairs, College of Health and Human Services, School of Public Health, San Diego, CA 92182. Offers environmental health (MPH); epidemiology (MPH, PhD), including biostatistics (MPH); global emergency preparedness and response (MS); global health (PhD); health behavior (PhD); health promotion (MPH); health services administration (MPH); toxicology (MS); MPH/MA; MSW/MPH. *Accreditation:* CAHME (one or more programs are accredited); CEPH. *Program availability:* Part-time. *Degree requirements:* For master's, comprehensive exam (for some programs), thesis (for some programs); for doctorate, thesis/dissertation. *Entrance requirements:* For master's, GMAT (MPH in health services administration), GRE General Test; for doctorate, GRE General Test. Additional exam requirements/recommendations for international students: required—TOEFL.

**Southeastern Oklahoma State University,** School of Arts and Sciences, Durant, OK 74701-0609. Offers biology (MT); computer information systems (MT); occupational safety and health (MT). *Program availability:* Part-time, evening/weekend. *Degree requirements:* For master's, thesis optional. *Entrance requirements:* For master's, minimum GPA of 3.0 in last 60 hours or 2.75 overall. Additional exam requirements/ recommendations for international students: required—TOEFL (minimum score 550 paper-based; 79 iBT). Electronic applications accepted.

**Syracuse University,** College of Engineering and Computer Science, CAS Program in Environmental Health, Syracuse, NY 13244. Offers CAS. *Program availability:* Part-time.

*Entrance requirements:* For degree, three letters of recommendation, resume, personal statement, official transcripts. Electronic applications accepted.

**Temple University,** College of Public Health, Department of Epidemiology and Biostatistics, Philadelphia, PA 19122-6096. Offers applied biostatistics (MPH); environmental health (MPH); epidemiology (MPH, MS, PhD). *Accreditation:* CEPH. *Program availability:* Part-time, evening/weekend, online learning. *Faculty:* 9 full-time (7 women), 5 part-time/adjunct (1 woman). *Students:* 38 full-time (26 women), 28 part-time (16 women); includes 19 minority (9 Black or African American, non-Hispanic/Latino; 1 American Indian or Alaska Native, non-Hispanic/Latino; 3 Asian, non-Hispanic/Latino; 5 Hispanic/Latino; 1 Two or more races, non-Hispanic/Latino), 19 international. 173 applicants, 46% accepted, 19 enrolled. In 2019, 12 master's, 2 doctorates awarded. *Degree requirements:* For doctorate, thesis/dissertation, area paper. *Entrance requirements:* For master's, GRE, statement of goals, resume, clearances for clinical/field education (M.P.H. programs); for doctorate, GRE, writing sample, resume, relevant coursework, statement of goals. Additional exam requirements/recommendations for international students: required—TOEFL (minimum score 79 iBT), IELTS (minimum score 6.5), PTE (minimum score 53), one of three required. Application fee: $50. Electronic applications accepted. *Expenses:* Contact institution. *Financial support:* Fellowships, research assistantships, teaching assistantships, Federal Work-Study, scholarships/grants, and health care benefits available. Financial award applicants required to submit FAFSA. *Unit head:* Resa M Jones, Department Chair and Assistant Professor, 215-204-8726, E-mail: resa.jones@temple.edu. *Application contact:* Tre Grue, Assistant Director of Admissions, 215-204-5806, E-mail: tre@temple.edu. Website: https://cph.temple.edu/epibio/

**Texas A&M University,** School of Public Health, College Station, TX 77843. Offers biostatistics (MPH, MSPH); environmental health (MPH, MSPH); epidemiology (MPH, MSPH); health administration (MHA); health policy and management (MPH); health services research (PhD); occupational safety and health (MPH). *Accreditation:* CAHME; CEPH. *Program availability:* Part-time, blended/hybrid learning. *Entrance requirements:* For master's, GRE General Test, 3 letters of recommendation; statement of purpose; current curriculum vitae or resume; official transcripts; for doctorate, GRE General Test, 3 letters of recommendation; statement of purpose; current curriculum vitae or resume; official transcripts; interview (in some cases). Additional exam requirements/recommendations for international students: required—TOEFL (minimum score 597 paper-based, 95 iBT) or GRE (minimum verbal score 153). Electronic applications accepted. *Expenses:* Contact institution.

**Towson University,** College of Health Professions, Program in Occupational Science, Towson, MD 21252-0001. Offers Sc D. *Program availability:* Part-time, evening/weekend. *Students:* 5 full-time (4 women), 4 part-time (all women); includes 2 minority (both Black or African American, non-Hispanic/Latino). *Entrance requirements:* For doctorate, master's degree with minimum GPA of 3.25, interview, 3 letters of recommendation, letter of intent. Additional exam requirements/recommendations for international students: required—TOEFL (minimum score 600 paper-based). *Application deadline:* For fall admission, 1/17 for domestic students, 5/15 for international students; for spring admission, 10/15 for domestic students, 12/1 for international students. Applications are processed on a rolling basis. Application fee: $45. Electronic applications accepted. *Expenses: Tuition, area resident:* Full-time $7920; part-time $439 per credit. Tuition, nonresident: full-time $16,344; part-time $908 per credit. *International tuition:* $16,344 full-time. *Required fees:* $2628; $146 per credit. $876 per term. *Financial support:* Application deadline: 4/1. *Unit head:* Dr. Beth Merryman, Department Chair, 410-704-2762, E-mail: otadmissions@towson.edu. *Application contact:* Coverley Beidleman, Assistant Director of Graduate Admissions, 410-704-5630, Fax: 410-704-3030, E-mail: grads@towson.edu. Website: https://www.towson.edu/chp/departments/occutherapy/programs/

**Trident University International,** College of Health Sciences, Program in Health Sciences, Cypress, CA 90630. Offers clinical research administration (MS, Certificate); emergency and disaster management (MS, Certificate); environmental health science (Certificate); health care administration (PhD); health care management (MS), including health informatics; health education (MS, Certificate); health informatics (Certificate); health sciences (PhD); international health (MS); international health: educator or researcher option (PhD); international health: practitioner option (PhD); law and expert witness studies (MS, Certificate); public health (MS); quality assurance (Certificate). *Program availability:* Part-time, evening/weekend, online learning. *Degree requirements:* For doctorate, comprehensive exam, thesis/dissertation, defense of dissertation. *Entrance requirements:* For master's, minimum GPA of 2.5 (students with GPA 3.0 or greater may transfer up to 30% of graduate level credits); for doctorate, minimum GPA of 3.4, curriculum vitae, course work in research methods or statistics. Additional exam requirements/recommendations for international students: required—TOEFL. Electronic applications accepted.

**Tufts University,** Cummings School of Veterinary Medicine, Program in Conservation Medicine, Medford, MA 02155. Offers MS. *Degree requirements:* For master's, case study, preceptorship. *Entrance requirements:* For master's, GRE, official transcripts, curriculum vitae. Additional exam requirements/recommendations for international students: required—TOEFL or IELTS. Electronic applications accepted. *Expenses: Tuition:* Part-time $1799 per credit hour. Full-time tuition and fees vary according to degree level, program and student level. Part-time tuition and fees vary according to course load.

**Tufts University,** School of Engineering, Department of Civil and Environmental Engineering, Medford, MA 02155. Offers bioengineering (MS), including environmental biotechnology; civil and environmental engineering (MS, PhD), including applied data science, environmental and water resources engineering, environmental health, geosystems engineering, structural engineering and mechanics; PhD/PhD. *Program availability:* Part-time. Terminal master's awarded for partial completion of doctoral program. *Degree requirements:* For master's, thesis (for some programs); for doctorate, thesis/dissertation. *Entrance requirements:* For master's and doctorate, GRE General Test. Additional exam requirements/recommendations for international students: required—TOEFL (minimum score 550 paper-based; 80 iBT), IELTS (minimum score 6.5). Electronic applications accepted. *Expenses: Tuition:* Part-time $1799 per credit hour. Full-time tuition and fees vary according to degree level, program and student level. Part-time tuition and fees vary according to course load.

**Tulane University,** School of Public Health and Tropical Medicine, Department of Global Environmental Health Sciences, New Orleans, LA 70118-5669. Offers MPH, MSPH, PhD, JD/MPH, MD/MPH, MSW/MPH. *Accreditation:* ABET (one or more programs are accredited). *Degree requirements:* For doctorate, comprehensive exam, thesis/dissertation. *Entrance requirements:* For master's and doctorate, GRE General Test. Additional exam requirements/recommendations for international students: required—TOEFL. Electronic applications accepted. *Expenses: Tuition:* Full-time $57,004; part-time $3167 per credit hour. *Required fees:* $2086; $44.50 per credit hour. $80 per term. Tuition and fees vary according to course load, degree level and program.

**Uniformed Services University of the Health Sciences,** F. Edward Hebert School of Medicine, Graduate Programs in the Biomedical Sciences and Public Health, Bethesda, MD 20814. Offers emerging infectious diseases (PhD); medical and clinical psychology (PhD), including clinical psychology, medical psychology; medicine (MS, PhD), including health professions education; molecular and cell biology (MS, PhD); neuroscience (PhD); preventive medicine and biometrics (MPH, MS, MSPH, MTMH, PhD), including environmental health sciences (PhD), healthcare administration and policy (MS), medical zoology (PhD), public health (MPH, MSPH), tropical medicine and hygiene (MTMH). Terminal master's awarded for partial completion of doctoral program. *Degree requirements:* For master's, comprehensive exam, thesis or alternative; for doctorate, comprehensive exam, thesis/dissertation, qualifying exam. *Entrance requirements:* For master's, GRE General Test; for doctorate, GRE General Test, minimum GPA of 3.0. Electronic applications accepted. *Expenses:* Contact institution.

**Uniformed Services University of the Health Sciences,** F. Edward Hebert School of Medicine, Graduate Programs in the Biomedical Sciences and Public Health, Department of Preventive Medicine and Biostatistics, Program in Environmental Health Sciences, Bethesda, MD 20814-4799. Offers PhD. *Accreditation:* CEPH. *Degree requirements:* For doctorate, comprehensive exam, thesis/dissertation, qualifying exam. *Entrance requirements:* For doctorate, GRE, minimum GPA of 3.0. Additional exam requirements/recommendations for international students: required—TOEFL.

**Universidad Autonoma de Guadalajara,** Graduate Programs, Guadalajara, Mexico. Offers administrative law and justice (LL M); advertising and corporate communications (MA); architecture (M Arch); business (MBA); computational science (MCC); education (Ed M, Ed D); English-Spanish translation (MA); entrepreneurship and management (MBA); integrated management of digital animation (MA); international business (MIB); international corporate law (LL M); Internet technologies (MS); manufacturing systems (MMS); occupational health (MS); philosophy (MA, PhD); power electronics (MS); quality systems (MQS); renewable energy (MS); social evaluation of projects (MBA); strategic market research (MBA); tax law (MA); teaching mathematics (MA).

**Universidad de Ciencias Medicas,** Graduate Programs, San Jose, Costa Rica. Offers dermatology (SP); family health (MS); health service center administration (MHA); human anatomy (MS); medical and surgery (MD); occupational medicine (MS); pharmacy (Pharm D). *Program availability:* Part-time. *Degree requirements:* For master's, thesis; for doctorate and SP, comprehensive exam. *Entrance requirements:* For master's, MD or bachelor's degree; for doctorate, admissions test; for SP, admissions test, MD.

**Université de Montréal,** Faculty of Medicine, Department of Environmental and Occupational Health, Montréal, QC H3C 3J7, Canada. Offers M Sc. *Accreditation:* CEPH. *Degree requirements:* For master's, thesis. *Entrance requirements:* For master's, proficiency in French, knowledge of English. Electronic applications accepted.

**Université du Québec à Montréal,** Graduate Programs, Program in Ergonomics in Occupational Health and Safety, Montréal, QC H3C 3P8, Canada. Offers Diploma. *Program availability:* Part-time. *Entrance requirements:* For degree, appropriate bachelor's degree or equivalent, proficiency in French.

**University at Albany, State University of New York,** School of Public Health, Department of Environmental Health Sciences, Albany, NY 12222-0001. Offers environmental and occupational health (MS, PhD); environmental chemistry (MS, PhD); toxicology (MS, PhD). *Program availability:* Blended/hybrid learning. *Faculty:* 8 full-time (6 women), 1 (woman) part-time/adjunct. *Students:* 15 full-time (8 women), 8 part-time (7 women); includes 7 minority (5 Black or African American, non-Hispanic/Latino; 2 Asian, non-Hispanic/Latino), 7 international. 19 applicants, 74% accepted, 7 enrolled. In 2019, 2 doctorates awarded. *Degree requirements:* For master's, thesis; for doctorate, comprehensive exam, thesis/dissertation. *Entrance requirements:* For master's and doctorate, transcripts of all schools attended; statement of background and goals; departmental questionnaire; resume; names and contact information for 3 recommenders. Additional exam requirements/recommendations for international students: required—TOEFL (minimum score 600 paper-based). *Application deadline:* For fall admission, 1/15 for domestic and international students; for winter admission, 4/1 for domestic and international students; for spring admission, 11/15 for domestic and international students. Applications are processed on a rolling basis. Application fee: $75. Electronic applications accepted. *Expenses: Tuition, area resident:* Full-time $11,530; part-time $480 per credit hour. Tuition, nonresident: full-time $23,530; part-time $980 per credit hour. *International tuition:* $23,530 full-time. *Required fees:* $2185; $96 per credit hour. Part-time tuition and fees vary according to course load and program. *Financial support:* Fellowships, research assistantships with full tuition reimbursements, teaching assistantships with full tuition reimbursements, scholarships/grants, health care benefits, tuition waivers (partial), and unspecified assistantships available. Financial award application deadline: 1/15. *Unit head:* Dr. David Lawrence, Chair, 518-474-7161, E-mail: dalawrence@albany.edu. *Application contact:* Dr. David Lawrence, Chair, 518-474-7161, E-mail: dalawrence@albany.edu. Website: https://www.albany.edu/sph/programs/ms-environmental-health

**The University of Alabama at Birmingham,** School of Public Health, Program in Environmental Health Sciences, Birmingham, AL 35294. Offers environmental health sciences (PhD); industrial hygiene (PhD). *Program availability:* Part-time, 100% online, blended/hybrid learning. *Faculty:* 7 full-time (5 women). *Students:* 28 full-time (18 women), 18 part-time (12 women); includes 5 minority (3 Black or African American, non-Hispanic/Latino; 1 Asian, non-Hispanic/Latino; 1 Hispanic/Latino), 8 international. Average age 40. 50 applicants, 52% accepted, 13 enrolled. In 2019, 1 doctorate awarded. *Degree requirements:* For doctorate, comprehensive exam, thesis/dissertation. *Entrance requirements:* For doctorate, GRE General Test. Additional exam requirements/recommendations for international students: required—TOEFL (minimum score 80 iBT), IELTS (minimum score 6.5). *Application deadline:* For fall admission, 4/1 priority date for domestic students, 4/1 for international students; for spring admission, 11/1 for domestic students; for summer admission, 4/1 for domestic students. Application fee: $50 ($60 for international students). Electronic applications accepted. *Financial support:* Fellowships, teaching assistantships, career-related internships or fieldwork, scholarships/grants, and unspecified assistantships available. Financial award application deadline: 3/1; financial award applicants required to submit FAFSA. *Unit head:* Dr. Peter Ginter, Graduate Program Director, 205-975-8970, Fax: 205-975-6341, E-mail: pginter@uab.edu. *Application contact:* Dustin Shaw, Coordinator, Student Admissions and Records, 205-934-2684, E-mail: dshaw84@uab.edu. Website: http://www.soph.uab.edu/ehs

**The University of Alabama at Birmingham,** School of Public Health, Program in Health Care Organization and Policy, Birmingham, AL 35294. Offers applied epidemiology and pharmacoepidemiology (MSPH); biostatistics (MPH); clinical and translational science (MSPH); environmental health (MPH); environmental health and toxicology (MSPH); epidemiology (MPH); general theory and practice (MPH); health behavior (MPH); health care organization (MPH, Dr PH); health policy (MPH); industrial hygiene (MPH, MSPH); maternal and child health policy (Dr PH); maternal and child health policy and leadership (MPH); occupational health and safety (MPH); outcomes research (MSPH, Dr PH); public health (PhD); public health preparedness management (MPH). *Accreditation:* CEPH. *Program availability:* Part-time, 100% online, blended/hybrid learning. *Faculty:* 14 full-time (6 women). *Students:* 53 full-time (37 women), 61 part-time (45 women); includes 37 minority (12 Black or African American, non-Hispanic/Latino; 20 Asian, non-Hispanic/Latino; 1 Hispanic/Latino; 4 Two or more races, non-

Hispanic/Latino), 17 international. Average age 31. 136 applicants, 59% accepted, 44 enrolled. In 2019, 36 master's, 4 doctorates awarded. *Degree requirements:* For master's, comprehensive exam (for some programs), thesis (for some programs); for doctorate, comprehensive exam, thesis/dissertation. *Entrance requirements:* For doctorate, GRE. Additional exam requirements/recommendations for international students: required—TOEFL (minimum score 80 iBT), IELTS (minimum score 6.5). *Application deadline:* For fall admission, 4/1 priority date for domestic students, 4/1 for international students; for spring admission, 11/1 for domestic students; for summer admission, 4/1 for domestic students. Application fee: $50 ($60 for international students). Electronic applications accepted. *Financial support:* Fellowships, research assistantships, teaching assistantships, scholarships/grants, traineeships, and unspecified assistantships available. Financial award application deadline: 3/1; financial award applicants required to submit FAFSA. *Unit head:* Dr. Martha Wingate, Program Director, 205-934-6783, Fax: 205-975-5484, E-mail: mslay@uab.edu. *Application contact:* Dustin Shaw, Coordinator, Student Admissions and Record, 205-934-3939, E-mail: bcampbel@uab.edu.
Website: http://www.soph.uab.edu

**University of Alberta,** School of Public Health, Department of Public Health Sciences, Edmonton, AB T6G 2E1, Canada. Offers clinical epidemiology (M Sc, MPH); environmental and occupational health (MPH); environmental health sciences (M Sc); epidemiology (M Sc); global health (M Sc, MPH); health policy and management (MPH); health policy research (M Sc); health technology assessment (MPH); occupational health (M Sc); population health (M Sc); public health leadership (MPH); public health sciences (PhD); quantitative methods (MPH). *Accreditation:* CEPH. Terminal master's awarded for partial completion of doctoral program. *Degree requirements:* For master's, thesis (for some programs); for doctorate, thesis/dissertation. *Entrance requirements:* For master's, GMAT or GRE General Test. Additional exam requirements/recommendations for international students: required—TOEFL (minimum score 550 paper-based) or IELTS (minimum score 6). Electronic applications accepted.

**University of Arkansas for Medical Sciences,** Fay W. Boozman College of Public Health, Little Rock, AR 72205-7199. Offers biostatistics (MPH); environmental and occupational health (MPH, Certificate); epidemiology (MPH, PhD); health behavior and health education (MPH); health policy and management (MPH); health promotion and prevention research (PhD); health services administration (MHSA); health systems research (PhD); public health (Certificate); public health leadership (Dr PH). *Accreditation:* CAHME; CEPH. *Program availability:* Part-time. *Degree requirements:* For master's, preceptorship, culminating experience, internship; for doctorate, comprehensive exam, capstone. *Entrance requirements:* For master's, GRE, GMAT, LSAT, PCAT, MCAT, DAT; for doctorate, GRE. Additional exam requirements/recommendations for international students: required—TOEFL (minimum score 80 iBT), IELTS. Electronic applications accepted. *Expenses:* Contact institution.

**University of California, Berkeley,** Graduate Division, School of Public Health, Group in Environmental Health Sciences, Berkeley, CA 94720. Offers MS, PhD. *Degree requirements:* For master's, comprehensive exam (MPH), project or thesis (MS); for doctorate, thesis/dissertation, departmental and qualifying exams. *Entrance requirements:* For master's, GRE General Test, minimum GPA of 3.0; previous course work in biology, calculus, and chemistry; 3 letters of recommendation; for doctorate, GRE General Test, master's degree in relevant scientific discipline or engineering; minimum GPA of 3.0; previous course work in biology, calculus, and chemistry; 3 letters of recommendation. Additional exam requirements/recommendations for international students: required—TOEFL (minimum score 570 paper-based; 90 iBT). Electronic applications accepted.

**University of California, Irvine,** School of Medicine, Program in Environmental Health Sciences, Irvine, CA 92697. Offers environmental health sciences (MS); environmental toxicology (PhD); exposure sciences and risk assessment (PhD). *Students:* 19 full-time (11 women); includes 6 minority (1 Black or African American, non-Hispanic/Latino; 2 Asian, non-Hispanic/Latino; 2 Hispanic/Latino; 1 Two or more races, non-Hispanic/Latino), 3 international. Average age 30. 17 applicants, 53% accepted, 4 enrolled. In 2019, 2 master's, 1 doctorate awarded. Terminal master's awarded for partial completion of doctoral program. *Degree requirements:* For master's, comprehensive exam; for doctorate, comprehensive exam, thesis/dissertation. *Entrance requirements:* For master's and doctorate, GRE General Test, GRE Subject Test, minimum GPA of 3.0. Additional exam requirements/recommendations for international students: required—TOEFL (minimum score 550 paper-based). *Application deadline:* For fall admission, 1/15 for domestic students. Applications are processed on a rolling basis. Application fee: $120 ($140 for international students). Electronic applications accepted. *Financial support:* Fellowships, research assistantships with full tuition reimbursements, teaching assistantships, institutionally sponsored loans, traineeships, health care benefits, and unspecified assistantships available. Financial award application deadline: 12/15; financial award applicants required to submit FAFSA. *Unit head:* Dr. Ulrike Luderer, Director, 949-824-8848, E-mail: uluderer@uci.edu. *Application contact:* Armando Villalpando, Student Affairs Officer, 949-824-8848, E-mail: afvillal@uci.edu.
Website: http://www.medicine.uci.edu/occupational/graduate.asp

**University of California, Los Angeles,** Graduate Division, Fielding School of Public Health, Department of Environmental Health Sciences, Los Angeles, CA 90095. Offers environmental health sciences (MS, PhD); environmental science and engineering (D Env); molecular toxicology (PhD); JD/MPH. *Accreditation:* ABET (one or more programs are accredited); CEPH. *Degree requirements:* For master's, comprehensive exam or thesis; for doctorate, thesis/dissertation, oral and written qualifying exams. *Entrance requirements:* For master's, GRE General Test, minimum GPA of 3.0; for doctorate, GRE General Test, minimum undergraduate GPA of 3.0. Electronic applications accepted.

**University of Central Missouri,** The Graduate School, Warrensburg, MO 64093. Offers accountancy (MA); accounting (MBA); applied mathematics (MS); aviation safety (MA); biology (MS); business administration (MBA); career and technology education (MS); college student personnel administration (MS); communication (MA); computer information systems and information technology (MS); computer science (MS); counseling (MS); criminal justice and criminology (MS); educational leadership (Ed S); educational leadership and policy analysis (Ed D); educational technology (MS, Ed S); elementary and early childhood education (MSE); English (MA); english language learners - teaching english as a second language (MA); environmental studies (MA); finance (MBA); history (MA); industrial hygiene (MS); industrial management (MS); information systems (MBA); kinesiology (MS); library science and information services (MS); literacy education (MSE); marketing (MBA); mathematics (MS); music (MA); occupational safety management (MS); professional leadership - adult, career, and technical education (Ed S); professional leadership - counseling (Ed S); psychology (MS); rural family nursing (MS); school administration (MSE); social gerontology (MS); sociology (MA); special education (MSE); speech language pathology (MS); teaching (MAT); technology (MS); technology management (PhD); theatre (MA). *Accreditation:* ASHA. *Program availability:* Part-time, 100% online, blended/hybrid learning. *Faculty:* 236 full-time (113 women), 97 part-time/adjunct (61 women). *Students:* 787 full-time (448 women), 1,459 part-time (997 women); includes 213 minority (72 Black or African American, non-Hispanic/Latino; 5 American Indian or Alaska Native, non-Hispanic/Latino; 27 Asian, non-Hispanic/Latino; 59 Hispanic/Latino; 50 Two or more races, non-Hispanic/Latino), 574 international. Average age 30. 1,477 applicants, 68% accepted, 664 enrolled. In 2019, 831 master's, 93 other advanced degrees awarded. *Degree requirements:* For master's and Ed S, comprehensive exam (for some programs), thesis (for some programs). *Entrance requirements:* For master's, A GRE or GMAT test score may be required by some of the programs, A minimum GPA, letters of recommendation, a statement of purpose may be required by some of the programs; for Ed S, A master's degree is required for the application of an Education Specialist's degree program. Additional exam requirements/recommendations for international students: required—TOEFL (minimum score 550 paper-based; 79 iBT). *Application deadline:* For fall admission, 6/1 priority date for domestic and international students; for spring admission, 10/15 priority date for domestic and international students; for summer admission, 4/1 priority date for domestic and international students. Applications are processed on a rolling basis. Application fee: $30 ($75 for international students). Electronic applications accepted. *Expenses: Tuition, area resident:* Full-time $7524; part-time $313.50 per credit hour. Tuition, state resident: full-time $7524; part-time $313.50 per credit hour. Tuition, nonresident: full-time $15,048; part-time $627 per credit hour. *International tuition:* $15,048 full-time. *Required fees:* $915; $30.50 per credit hour. *Financial support:* In 2019–20, 89 students received support. Research assistantships, teaching assistantships, career-related internships or fieldwork, Federal Work-Study, scholarships/grants, unspecified assistantships, and administrative and laboratory assistantships available. Support available to part-time students. Financial award application deadline: 4/1; financial award applicants required to submit FAFSA. *Unit head:* Shellie Hewitt, Director of Graduate and International Student Services, 660-543-4621, Fax: 660-543-4778, E-mail: hewitt@ucmo.edu. *Application contact:* Shellie Hewitt, Director of Graduate and International Student Services, 660-543-4621, Fax: 660-543-4778, E-mail: hewitt@ucmo.edu.
Website: http://www.ucmo.edu/graduate/

**University of Cincinnati,** Graduate School, College of Medicine, Graduate Programs in Biomedical Sciences, Department of Environmental Health, Cincinnati, OH 45221. Offers environmental and industrial hygiene (MS, PhD); environmental and occupational medicine (MS); environmental genetics and molecular toxicology (MS, PhD); epidemiology and biostatistics (MS, PhD); occupational safety and ergonomics (MS, PhD). *Accreditation:* ABET (one or more programs are accredited); CEPH. Terminal master's awarded for partial completion of doctoral program. *Degree requirements:* For master's, thesis; for doctorate, thesis/dissertation, qualifying exam. *Entrance requirements:* For master's, GRE General Test, bachelor's degree in science; for doctorate, GRE General Test. Additional exam requirements/recommendations for international students: required—TOEFL (minimum score 600 paper-based; 100 iBT). Electronic applications accepted.

**University of Colorado Denver,** College of Liberal Arts and Sciences, Department of Geography and Environmental Sciences, Denver, CO 80217. Offers environmental sciences (MS), including air quality, ecosystems, environmental health, geospatial analysis, hazardous waste, water quality. *Program availability:* Part-time, evening/weekend. *Degree requirements:* For master's, thesis or alternative, 30 credits including 21 of core requirements and 9 of environmental science electives. *Entrance requirements:* For master's, GRE General Test, BA in one of the natural/physical sciences or engineering (or equivalent background); prerequisite coursework in calculus and physics (one semester each); general chemistry with lab and general biology with lab (two semesters each); three letters of recommendation. Additional exam requirements/recommendations for international students: required—TOEFL (minimum score 537 paper-based; 75 iBT); recommended—IELTS (minimum score 6.5). Electronic applications accepted. Tuition and fees vary according to course load, program and reciprocity agreements.

**University of Connecticut,** Graduate School, eCampus, Program in Occupational Safety and Health Management, Storrs, CT 06269. Offers Certificate.

**University of Florida,** Graduate School, College of Public Health and Health Professions, Department of Environmental and Global Health, Gainesville, FL 32611. Offers environmental health (PhD); one health (MHS, PhD). *Entrance requirements:* For master's and doctorate, GRE, minimum GPA of 3.0. Additional exam requirements/recommendations for international students: required—TOEFL (minimum score 550 paper-based; 80 iBT), IELTS (minimum score 6).

**University of Florida,** Graduate School, College of Public Health and Health Professions, Programs in Public Health, Gainesville, FL 32611. Offers biostatistics (MPH); clinical and translational science (PhD); environmental health (MPH); epidemiology (MPH); health management and policy (MPH); public health (MPH, PhD, Certificate); public health practice (MPH); rehabilitation science (PhD); social and behavioral sciences (MPH); DPT/MPH; DVM/MPH; JD/MPH; MD/MPH; Pharm D/MPH. *Accreditation:* CEPH. *Program availability:* Online learning. *Degree requirements:* For master's, internship. *Entrance requirements:* For master's, GRE General Test, minimum GPA of 3.0. Additional exam requirements/recommendations for international students: required—TOEFL (minimum score 550 paper-based; 80 iBT), IELTS (minimum score 6).

**University of Georgia,** College of Public Health, Department of Environmental Health Science, Athens, GA 30602. Offers MPH, MS, PhD. Terminal master's awarded for partial completion of doctoral program. *Degree requirements:* For master's, thesis; for doctorate, comprehensive exam, thesis/dissertation. *Entrance requirements:* For master's and doctorate, GRE General Test. Additional exam requirements/recommendations for international students: required—TOEFL. Electronic applications accepted.

**University of Illinois at Chicago,** School of Public Health, Division of Environmental and Occupational Health Sciences, Chicago, IL 60607-7128. Offers MPH, MS, Dr PH, PhD. *Accreditation:* ABET (one or more programs are accredited). *Program availability:* Part-time. Terminal master's awarded for partial completion of doctoral program. *Degree requirements:* For master's, thesis, field practicum; for doctorate, thesis/dissertation, independent research, internship. *Entrance requirements:* For master's and doctorate, GRE General Test, minimum GPA of 2.75. Additional exam requirements/recommendations for international students: required—TOEFL. Electronic applications accepted. *Expenses:* Contact institution.

**University of Illinois at Springfield,** Graduate Programs, College of Public Affairs and Administration, Program in Public Health, Springfield, IL 62703-5407. Offers community health education (Graduate Certificate); emergency preparedness and homeland security (Graduate Certificate); environmental health (MPH, Graduate Certificate); environmental risk assessment (Graduate Certificate); epidemiology (Graduate Certificate); public health (MPH). *Program availability:* Part-time, 100% online. *Faculty:* 7 full-time (5 women). *Students:* 31 full-time (24 women), 36 part-time (27 women); includes 13 minority (9 Black or African American, non-Hispanic/Latino; 1 Asian, non-Hispanic/Latino; 1 Hispanic/Latino; 2 Two or more races, non-Hispanic/Latino), 27 international. Average age 30. 90 applicants, 54% accepted, 12 enrolled. In 2019, 13 master's, 10 other advanced degrees awarded. *Degree requirements:* For master's, comprehensive exam, internship. *Entrance requirements:* For master's, GRE, minimum undergraduate GPA of 3.0, 3 letters of recommendation, essay addressing the areas outlined on the department application form. Additional exam requirements/

recommendations for international students: required—TOEFL (minimum score 500 paper-based; 61 iBT). *Application deadline:* Applications are processed on a rolling basis. Application fee: $60 ($75 for international students). Electronic applications accepted. *Expenses:* $33.25 per credit hour (online fee). *Financial support:* In 2019–20, research assistantships with full tuition reimbursements (averaging $10,562 per year), teaching assistantships with full tuition reimbursements (averaging $10,652 per year) were awarded; fellowships, career-related internships or fieldwork, Federal Work-Study, scholarships/grants, health care benefits, and unspecified assistantships also available. Support available to part-time students. Financial award application deadline: 11/15; financial award applicants required to submit FAFSA. *Unit head:* Dr. Josiah Alamu, Program Administrator, 217-206-7874, Fax: 217-206-7279, E-mail: jalam3@uis.edu. *Application contact:* Dr. Josiah Alamu, Program Administrator, 217-206-7874, Fax: 217-206-7279, E-mail: jalam3@uis.edu.
Website: http://www.uis.edu/publichealth/

**The University of Iowa,** Graduate College, College of Public Health, Department of Occupational and Environmental Health, Iowa City, IA 52242-1316. Offers agricultural safety and health (MS, PhD); ergonomics (MPH); industrial hygiene (MS, PhD); occupational and environmental health (MPH, MS, PhD, Certificate); MS/MA; MS/MS. *Accreditation:* ABET (one or more programs are accredited). *Degree requirements:* For master's, thesis optional, exam; for doctorate, comprehensive exam, thesis/dissertation. *Entrance requirements:* For master's and doctorate, GRE General Test, minimum GPA of 3.0. Additional exam requirements/recommendations for international students: required—TOEFL (minimum score 600 paper-based; 100 iBT). Electronic applications accepted.

**University of Louisville,** Graduate School, School of Public Health and Information Sciences, Department of Environmental and Occupational Health Sciences, Louisville, KY 40202. Offers environmental and occupational health sciences (MPH); public health (PhD), including environmental health. *Accreditation:* CEPH. *Faculty:* 3 full-time (1 woman), 2 part-time/adjunct (0 women). *Students:* 4 full-time (2 women), 2 international. Average age 33. 2 applicants, 50% accepted, 1 enrolled. *Degree requirements:* For doctorate, comprehensive exam, thesis/dissertation. *Entrance requirements:* For doctorate, bachelor's degree from an accredited institution or its equivalent with emphasis in sciences. Recommended minimum GPA of 3.0 on a 4.0 scale. Three letters of recommendation (professional or academic) written within the last twelve months. Official transcripts of all degrees. One-page personal statement. Additional exam requirements/recommendations for international students: required—TOEFL (minimum score 90 iBT). *Application deadline:* For fall admission, 5/1 for domestic and international students. Applications are processed on a rolling basis. Application fee: $65. Electronic applications accepted. *Expenses: Tuition, area resident:* Full-time $13,000; part-time $723 per credit hour. Tuition, state resident: full-time $13,000; part-time $723 per credit hour. Tuition, nonresident: full-time $27,114; part-time $1507 per credit hour. *International tuition:* $27,114 full-time. *Required fees:* $196. Tuition and fees vary according to program and reciprocity agreements. *Financial support:* In 2019–20, 2 students received support, including 1 research assistantship with full tuition reimbursement available (averaging $20,000 per year); fellowships, scholarships/grants, and unspecified assistantships also available. Financial award application deadline: 1/15; financial award applicants required to submit FAFSA. *Unit head:* Dr. Gary W. Hoyle, Professor & Acting Chair, 502-852-7337, Fax: 502-852-3291, E-mail: gary.hoyle@louisville.edu. *Application contact:* Barbara Parker, Administrative Specialist, 502-852-3290, Fax: 502-852-3291, E-mail: barbara.parker@louisville.edu.
Website: http://louisville.edu/sphis/departments/environmental-occupational-health-sciences

**University of Maryland, College Park,** Academic Affairs, School of Public Health, Maryland Institute for Applied Environmental Health, College Park, MD 20742. Offers environmental health sciences (MPH). *Entrance requirements:* For master's, GRE General Test, 3 letters of recommendation, minimum undergraduate GPA of 3.0, undergraduate transcripts, statement of goals and interests. Electronic applications accepted.

**University of Massachusetts Amherst,** Graduate School, School of Public Health and Health Sciences, Department of Public Health, Amherst, MA 01003. Offers biostatistics (MPH, MS, PhD); community health education (MPH, MS, PhD); environmental health sciences (MPH, MS, PhD); epidemiology (MPH, MS, PhD); health policy and management (MPH, MS, PhD); nutrition (MPH, PhD); public health practice (MPH); MPH/MPPA. *Accreditation:* CEPH. *Program availability:* Part-time, evening/weekend, online learning. Terminal master's awarded for partial completion of doctoral program. *Degree requirements:* For master's, thesis (for some programs); for doctorate, comprehensive exam, thesis/dissertation. *Entrance requirements:* For master's and doctorate, GRE General Test. Additional exam requirements/recommendations for international students: required—TOEFL (minimum score 550 paper-based; 80 iBT), IELTS (minimum score 6.5). Electronic applications accepted.

**University of Memphis,** Graduate School, School of Public Health, Memphis, TN 38152. Offers biostatistics (MPH); environmental health (MPH); epidemiology (MPH, PhD); health systems and policy (PhD); health systems management (MPH); public health (MHA); social and behavioral sciences (MPH, PhD). *Accreditation:* CAHME; CEPH. *Program availability:* Part-time, evening/weekend, online learning. *Faculty:* 20 full-time (7 women), 10 part-time/adjunct (4 women). *Students:* 126 full-time (80 women), 77 part-time (60 women); includes 70 minority (40 Black or African American, non-Hispanic/Latino; 17 Asian, non-Hispanic/Latino; 9 Hispanic/Latino; 4 Two or more races, non-Hispanic/Latino), 29 international. Average age 30. 105 applicants, 97% accepted, 67 enrolled. In 2019, 47 master's, 9 doctorates awarded. *Degree requirements:* For master's, comprehensive exam, thesis (for some programs), practicum/field experience; for doctorate, comprehensive exam, thesis/dissertation, residency. *Entrance requirements:* For master's, GRE or GMAT, letters of recommendation; letter of intent; for doctorate, GRE, letters of recommendation; personal statement. Additional exam requirements/recommendations for international students: required—TOEFL (minimum score 550 paper-based; 79 iBT). *Application deadline:* For fall admission, 4/1 for domestic students; for spring admission, 11/1 for domestic students. Application fee: $35 ($60 for international students). Electronic applications accepted. *Expenses: Tuition, area resident:* Full-time $9216; part-time $512 per credit hour. Tuition, state resident: full-time $9216; part-time $512 per credit hour. Tuition, nonresident: full-time $12,672; part-time $704 per credit hour. *International tuition:* $16,128 full-time. *Required fees:* $1530; $85 per credit hour. Tuition and fees vary according to program. *Financial support:* Research assistantships with full tuition reimbursements, Federal Work-Study, scholarships/grants, and unspecified assistantships available. Financial award application deadline: 2/1; financial award applicants required to submit FAFSA. *Unit head:* Dr. James Gurney, Dean, 901-678-1673, E-mail: jggurney@memphis.edu. *Application contact:* Dr. Marian Levy, Associate Dean, 901-678-4514, E-mail: mlevy@memphis.edu.
Website: http://www.memphis.edu/sph/

**University of Miami,** Graduate School, College of Engineering, Department of Industrial Engineering, Program in Occupational Ergonomics and Safety, Coral Gables, FL 33124. Offers environmental health and safety (MS); occupational ergonomics and safety (MSOES). *Program availability:* Part-time. *Degree requirements:* For master's,

thesis optional. *Entrance requirements:* For master's, GRE General Test, minimum GPA of 3.0. Additional exam requirements/recommendations for international students: required—TOEFL (minimum score 550 paper-based). Electronic applications accepted.

**University of Michigan,** School of Public Health, Department of Environmental Health Sciences, Ann Arbor, MI 48109. Offers environmental health policy and promotion (MPH); environmental health sciences (MS, PhD); environmental quality, sustainability and health (MPH); industrial hygiene (MPH, MS); occupational and environmental epidemiology (MPH); toxicology (MPH, MS, PhD). *Accreditation:* CEPH (one or more programs are accredited). Terminal master's awarded for partial completion of doctoral program. *Degree requirements:* For master's, thesis (for some programs); for doctorate, thesis/dissertation, preliminary exam, oral defense of dissertation. *Entrance requirements:* For master's and doctorate, GRE General Test and/or MCAT. Additional exam requirements/recommendations for international students: required—TOEFL (minimum score 100 iBT). Electronic applications accepted.

**University of Minnesota, Twin Cities Campus,** School of Public Health, Division of Environmental Health Sciences, Area in Environmental Health Policy, Minneapolis, MN 55455-0213. Offers MPH, MS, PhD. *Accreditation:* CEPH (one or more programs are accredited). *Degree requirements:* For doctorate, thesis/dissertation. *Entrance requirements:* For master's and doctorate, GRE General Test. Electronic applications accepted.

**University of Minnesota, Twin Cities Campus,** School of Public Health, Division of Environmental Health Sciences, Area in Occupational Medicine, Minneapolis, MN 55455-0213. Offers MPH. *Accreditation:* CEPH. *Entrance requirements:* For master's, GRE General Test. Electronic applications accepted.

**University of Minnesota, Twin Cities Campus,** School of Public Health, Major in Public Health Practice, Minneapolis, MN 55455-0213. Offers core concepts (Certificate); food safety and biosecurity (Certificate); occupational health and safety (Certificate); preparedness, response and recovery (Certificate); public health practice (MPH); DVM/MPH; MD/MPH. *Program availability:* Part-time, online learning. *Degree requirements:* For master's, thesis. *Entrance requirements:* For master's, GRE, MCAT, United States Medical Licensing Exam. Additional exam requirements/recommendations for international students: required—TOEFL (minimum score 600 paper-based). Electronic applications accepted.

**University of Nebraska Medical Center,** Environmental Health, Occupational Health and Toxicology Graduate Program, Omaha, NE 68198-4388. Offers PhD. *Degree requirements:* For doctorate, comprehensive exam, thesis/dissertation. *Entrance requirements:* For doctorate, GRE General Test, BS in chemistry, biology, biochemistry or related area. Additional exam requirements/recommendations for international students: required—TOEFL (minimum score 550 paper-based; 80 iBT). Electronic applications accepted.

**University of Nevada, Reno,** Graduate School, Interdisciplinary Program in Environmental Sciences and Health, Reno, NV 89557. Offers MS, PhD. Terminal master's awarded for partial completion of doctoral program. *Degree requirements:* For master's, thesis; for doctorate, thesis/dissertation. *Entrance requirements:* For master's, GRE General Test, minimum GPA of 2.75; for doctorate, GRE General Test, minimum GPA of 3.0. Additional exam requirements/recommendations for international students: required—TOEFL (minimum score 500 paper-based; 61 iBT), IELTS (minimum score 6). Electronic applications accepted.

**University of New Haven,** Graduate School, College of Arts and Sciences, Program in Environmental Science, West Haven, CT 06516. Offers environmental ecology (MS); environmental geoscience (MS); environmental health and management (MS); environmental science (MS); geographical information systems (MS). *Program availability:* Part-time, evening/weekend. *Students:* 14 full-time (8 women), 13 part-time (6 women); includes 7 minority (3 Black or African American, non-Hispanic/Latino; 3 Hispanic/Latino; 1 Native Hawaiian or other Pacific Islander, non-Hispanic/Latino), 4 international. Average age 29. 59 applicants, 86% accepted, 10 enrolled. In 2019, 17 master's awarded. *Entrance requirements:* Additional exam requirements/recommendations for international students: required—TOEFL (minimum score 80 iBT), IELTS, PTE. *Application deadline:* Applications are processed on a rolling basis. Application fee: $50. Electronic applications accepted. Application fee is waived when completed online. *Financial support:* Research assistantships with partial tuition reimbursements, teaching assistantships with partial tuition reimbursements, Federal Work-Study, scholarships/grants, and unspecified assistantships available. Support available to part-time students. Financial award applicants required to submit FAFSA. *Unit head:* Dr. Christian Conroy, Assistant Professor, 203-932-7436, E-mail: CWConroy@newhaven.edu. *Application contact:* Selina O'Toole, Senior Associate Director of Graduate Admissions, 203-932-7337, E-mail: SOToole@newhaven.edu.
Website: https://www.newhaven.edu/arts-sciences/graduate-programs/environmental-science/

**The University of North Carolina at Chapel Hill,** Graduate School, Gillings School of Global Public Health, Department of Environmental Sciences and Engineering, Chapel Hill, NC 27599. Offers environmental engineering (MPH, MS, MSEE, MSPH); environmental health sciences (MPH, MS, MSPH, PhD); MPH/MCRP; MS/MCRP; MSPH/MCRP. *Faculty:* 26 full-time (10 women), 38 part-time/adjunct (10 women). *Students:* 87 full-time (53 women); includes 10 minority (2 Black or African American, non-Hispanic/Latino; 3 Asian, non-Hispanic/Latino; 1 Hispanic/Latino; 4 Two or more races, non-Hispanic/Latino), 19 international. Average age 28. 101 applicants, 47% accepted, 19 enrolled. In 2019, 20 master's, 16 doctorates awarded. Terminal master's awarded for partial completion of doctoral program. *Degree requirements:* For master's, comprehensive exam, thesis (for some programs), research paper; for doctorate, comprehensive exam, thesis/dissertation. *Entrance requirements:* For master's and doctorate, GRE General Test, 3 letters of recommendation (academic and/or professional; at least one academic). Additional exam requirements/recommendations for international students: required—TOEFL (minimum score 90 iBT), IELTS (minimum score 7). *Application deadline:* For fall admission, 4/9 for domestic and international students. Application fee: $90. Electronic applications accepted. *Financial support:* Fellowships with tuition reimbursements, research assistantships with tuition reimbursements, teaching assistantships with tuition reimbursements, career-related internships or fieldwork, Federal Work-Study, scholarships/grants, traineeships, health care benefits, and unspecified assistantships available. Support available to part-time students. Financial award application deadline: 12/10; financial award applicants required to submit FAFSA. *Unit head:* Dr. Barbara J. Turpin, Professor and Chair, 919-966-1024, Fax: 919-966-7911, E-mail: esechair@unc.edu. *Application contact:* Adia Ware, Academic Coordinator, 919-966-3844, Fax: 919-966-7911, E-mail: aware@unc.edu.
Website: https://sph.unc.edu/envr/environmental-sciences-and-engineering-home/

**University of Oklahoma Health Sciences Center,** Graduate College, Hudson College of Public Health, Department of Occupational and Environmental Health, Oklahoma City, OK 73190. Offers MPH, MS, Dr PH, PhD, JD/MPH, JD/MS. *Accreditation:* ABET (one or more programs are accredited); CEPH (one or more programs are accredited). *Program availability:* Part-time. *Degree requirements:* For master's, comprehensive exam, thesis (for some programs); for doctorate, comprehensive exam, thesis/

dissertation. *Entrance requirements:* For master's, GRE General Test (for all except occupational medicine), 3 letters of recommendation, resume; for doctorate, GRE (for all except occupational medicine), 3 letters of recommendation, resume. Additional exam requirements/recommendations for international students: required—TOEFL (minimum score 570 paper-based).

**University of Pennsylvania,** Perelman School of Medicine, Master of Public Health Program, Philadelphia, PA 19104. Offers environmental health (MPH); generalist (MPH); global health (MPH); DMD/MPH; JD/MPH; MD/MPH; MES/MPH; MPH/MBE; MPH/MPA; MPH/MS; MSN/MPH; MSSP/MPH; MSW/MPH; PhD/MPH. *Accreditation:* CEPH. *Program availability:* Part-time, evening/weekend. *Financial support:* Application deadline: 4/1. *Unit head:* Dr. Jennifer Pinto-Martin, Director, 898-4726. *Application contact:* Moriah Hall, Associate Director, MPH program, 573-8841.
Website: http://www.cphi.upenn.edu/mph

**University of Pittsburgh,** Graduate School of Public Health, Department of Environmental and Occupational Health, Pittsburgh, PA 15260. Offers MPH, MS, PhD. *Accreditation:* CEPH (one or more programs are accredited). *Faculty:* 12 full-time (3 women). *Students:* 27 full-time (19 women), 2 part-time (both women); includes 4 minority (1 Black or African American, non-Hispanic/Latino; 3 Hispanic/Latino), 13 international. Average age 29. 54 applicants, 57% accepted, 10 enrolled. In 2019, 4 master's, 4 doctorates awarded. Terminal master's awarded for partial completion of doctoral program. *Degree requirements:* For master's, comprehensive exam, thesis; for doctorate, comprehensive exam, thesis/dissertation. *Entrance requirements:* For master's, GRE General Test, transcripts, recommendation letters, personal statement, bachelor's degree; for doctorate, GRE General Test, minimum GPA of 3.4; 2 courses each in physics, chemistry and math; bachelor's or master's degree. Additional exam requirements/recommendations for international students: required—TOEFL (minimum score 80 iBT), IELTS (minimum score 6.5), TOEFL or IELTS, WES evaluation for foreign education. *Application deadline:* For fall admission, 7/15 for domestic students, 4/15 for international students; for spring admission, 10/15 for domestic students, 8/1 for international students. Application fee: $135. Electronic applications accepted. *Expenses:* $13,379 per term full-time resident, $23,407 per term full-time non-resident, $1122 per credit part-time resident, $1916 per credit part-time non-resident, $500 per term for full-time dissertation research, $475 per term full-time fees, $295 per term part-time fees. *Financial support:* In 2019–20, 17 students received support, including 1 teaching assistantship with full tuition reimbursement available (averaging $28,800 per year); scholarships/grants, traineeships, and unspecified assistantships also available. Financial award application deadline: 4/1; financial award applicants required to submit FAFSA. *Unit head:* Matthew Weaver, Department Administrator, 412-383-6900, E-mail: msweaver@pitt.edu. *Application contact:* Bryanna Snyder, Associate Administrator, 412-383-7297, E-mail: bms85@pitt.edu.
Website: https://www.publichealth.pitt.edu/eoh/_rdr

**University of Puerto Rico - Medical Sciences Campus,** Graduate School of Public Health, Department of Environmental Health, Doctoral Program in Environmental Health, San Juan, PR 00936-5067. Offers MS, Dr PH. *Program availability:* Part-time. *Expenses:* Contact institution.

**University of Saint Francis,** Graduate School, Keith Busse School of Business and Entrepreneurial Leadership, Fort Wayne, IN 46808-3994. Offers business administration (MBA), including sustainability; environmental health (MEH); healthcare administration (MHA); organizational leadership (MOL). *Accreditation:* ACBSP. *Program availability:* Part-time, evening/weekend, online only, 100% online. *Faculty:* 1 full-time (0 women), 19 part-time/adjunct (6 women). *Students:* 59 full-time (40 women), 105 part-time (63 women); includes 43 minority (24 Black or African American, non-Hispanic/Latino; 2 American Indian or Alaska Native, non-Hispanic/Latino; 4 Asian, non-Hispanic/Latino; 7 Hispanic/Latino; 6 Two or more races, non-Hispanic/Latino), 1 international. Average age 36. 90 applicants, 100% accepted, 56 enrolled. In 2019, 98 master's awarded. *Entrance requirements:* Additional exam requirements/recommendations for international students: required—TOEFL (minimum score 550 paper-based), IELTS (minimum score 6.5). *Application deadline:* Applications are processed on a rolling basis. Electronic applications accepted. *Expenses: Tuition:* Full-time $9450; part-time $525 per semester hour. *Required fees:* $330 per semester. Tuition and fees vary according to course load, degree level, campus/location and program. *Financial support:* Applicants required to submit FAFSA. *Unit head:* Eye-Lynn Clarke, KBSOBEL Division Director, 260-399-7700 Ext. 8315, E-mail: eclarke@sf.edu. *Application contact:* Kyle Richardson, Associate Director of Enrollment Management, 260-399-7700 Ext. 6310, Fax: 260-399-8152, E-mail: krichardson@sf.edu.
Website: https://admissions.sf.edu/graduate/

**University of South Alabama,** Graduate School, Program in Environmental Toxicology, Mobile, AL 36688-0002. Offers basic medical sciences (MS); biology (MS); chemistry (MS); environmental toxicology (MS); exposure route and chemical transport (MS). *Faculty:* 4 full-time (0 women). *Students:* 7 full-time (5 women), 4 part-time (1 woman); includes 1 minority (Black or African American, non-Hispanic/Latino), 1 international. Average age 26. 2 applicants, 50% accepted, 1 enrolled. In 2019, 3 master's awarded. *Degree requirements:* For master's, comprehensive exam, thesis optional, research project or thesis. *Entrance requirements:* For master's, GRE. Additional exam requirements/recommendations for international students: required—TOEFL (minimum score 525 paper-based; 71 iBT). *Application deadline:* For fall admission, 7/1 for domestic students, 3/1 for international students; for spring admission, 12/1 for domestic students, 11/1 for international students. Application fee: $50. Electronic applications accepted. *Expenses: Tuition, area resident:* Part-time $442 per credit hour. Tuition, state resident: full-time $10,608; part-time $442 per credit hour. Tuition, nonresident: full-time $21,216; part-time $884 per credit hour. *Financial support:* Fellowships, research assistantships, teaching assistantships, career-related internships or fieldwork, Federal Work-Study, institutionally sponsored loans, scholarships/grants, and unspecified assistantships available. Support available to part-time students. Financial award application deadline: 3/31; financial award applicants required to submit FAFSA. *Unit head:* Dr. Sean Powers, Chair, Marine Sciences, 251-460-7136, E-mail: spowers@disl.org. *Application contact:* Dr. David Forbes, Graduate Coordinator/Director, Environmental Toxicology, 251-460-6181, E-mail: dforbes@southalabama.edu.
Website: https://www.southalabama.edu/colleges/graduateschool/etox/

**University of South Carolina,** The Graduate School, Arnold School of Public Health, Department of Environmental Health Sciences, Program in Environmental Quality, Columbia, SC 29208. Offers MPH, MS, MSPH, PhD. *Accreditation:* CEPH (one or more programs are accredited). *Program availability:* Part-time. *Degree requirements:* For master's, comprehensive exam, thesis (for some programs), practicum (MPH); for doctorate, one foreign language, comprehensive exam, thesis/dissertation. *Entrance requirements:* For master's and doctorate, GRE General Test. Additional exam requirements/recommendations for international students: required—TOEFL (minimum score 570 paper-based). Electronic applications accepted.

**University of Southern California,** Keck School of Medicine and Graduate School, Graduate Programs in Medicine, Department of Preventive Medicine, Master of Public Health Program, Los Angeles, CA 90032. Offers biostatistics and epidemiology (MPH); child and family health (MPH); community health promotion (MPH); environmental health (MPH); geohealth (MPH); global health leadership (MPH); health communication (MPH); health services and policy (MPH). *Accreditation:* CEPH. *Program availability:* Part-time, evening/weekend, 100% online. *Faculty:* 37 full-time (28 women), 8 part-time/adjunct (6 women). *Students:* 261 full-time (201 women), 74 part-time (55 women); includes 224 minority (46 Black or African American, non-Hispanic/Latino; 2 American Indian or Alaska Native, non-Hispanic/Latino; 79 Asian, non-Hispanic/Latino; 56 Hispanic/Latino; 6 Native Hawaiian or other Pacific Islander, non-Hispanic/Latino; 35 Two or more races, non-Hispanic/Latino), 21 international. Average age 28. 420 applicants, 76% accepted, 94 enrolled. In 2019, 123 master's awarded. *Degree requirements:* For master's, practicum, final report, oral presentation. *Entrance requirements:* For master's, GRE General Test, MCAT, GMAT, minimum GPA of 3.0. Additional exam requirements/recommendations for international students: required—TOEFL (minimum score 600 paper-based; 90 iBT). *Application deadline:* For fall admission, 12/1 priority date for domestic students, 5/1 priority date for international students; for spring admission, 9/1 priority date for domestic and international students; for summer admission, 3/1 for domestic and international students. Applications are processed on a rolling basis. Application fee: $135. Electronic applications accepted. *Financial support:* Career-related internships or fieldwork, Federal Work-Study, institutionally sponsored loans, and scholarships/grants available. Support available to part-time students. Financial award application deadline: 5/4; financial award applicants required to submit CSS PROFILE or FAFSA. *Unit head:* Dr. Louise A. Rohrbach, Director, 323-442-8237, Fax: 323-442-8297, E-mail: rohrbac@usc.edu. *Application contact:* Valerie Burris, Admissions Counselor, 323-442-7257, Fax: 323-442-8297, E-mail: valeriem@usc.edu.
Website: https://preventivemedicine.usc.edu/education/graduate-programs/mph/

**University of South Florida,** Innovative Education, Tampa, FL 33620-9951. Offers adult, career and higher education (Graduate Certificate), including college teaching, leadership in developing human resources, leadership in higher education; Africana studies (Graduate Certificate), including diasporas and health disparities, genocide and human rights; aging studies (Graduate Certificate), including gerontology; art research (Graduate Certificate), including museum studies; business foundations (Graduate Certificate); chemical and biomedical engineering (Graduate Certificate), including materials science and engineering, water, health and sustainability; child and family studies (Graduate Certificate), including positive behavior support; civil and industrial engineering (Graduate Certificate), including transportation systems analysis; community and family health (Graduate Certificate), including maternal and child health, social marketing and public health, violence and injury: prevention and intervention, women's health; criminology (Graduate Certificate), including criminal justice administration; data science for public administration (Graduate Certificate); digital humanities (Graduate Certificate); educational measurement and research (Graduate Certificate), including evaluation; English (Graduate Certificate), including comparative literary studies, creative writing, professional and technical communication; entrepreneurship (Graduate Certificate); environmental health (Graduate Certificate), including safety management; epidemiology and biostatistics (Graduate Certificate), including applied biostatistics, biostatistics, concepts and tools of epidemiology, epidemiology, epidemiology of infectious diseases; geography, environment and planning (Graduate Certificate), including community development, environmental policy and management, geographical information systems; geology (Graduate Certificate), including hydrogeology; global health (Graduate Certificate), including disaster management, global health and Latin American and Caribbean studies, global health practice, humanitarian assistance, infection control; government and international affairs (Graduate Certificate), including Cuban studies, globalization studies; health policy and management (Graduate Certificate), including health management and leadership, public health policy and programs; hearing specialist: early intervention (Graduate Certificate); industrial and management systems engineering (Graduate Certificate), including systems engineering, technology management; information studies (Graduate Certificate), including school library media specialist; information systems/decision sciences (Graduate Certificate), including analytics and business intelligence; instructional technology (Graduate Certificate), including distance education, Florida digital/virtual educator, instructional design, multimedia design, Web design; internal medicine, bioethics and medical humanities (Graduate Certificate), including biomedical ethics; Latin American and Caribbean studies (Graduate Certificate); leadership for coastal resiliency planning (Graduate Certificate); mass communications (Graduate Certificate), including multimedia journalism; mathematics and statistics (Graduate Certificate), including mathematics; medicine (Graduate Certificate), including aging and neuroscience, bioinformatics, biotechnology, brain fitness and memory management, clinical investigation, hand and upper limb rehabilitation, health informatics, health sciences, integrative weight management, intellectual property, medicine and gender, metabolic and nutritional medicine, metabolic cardiology, pharmacy sciences; national and competitive intelligence (Graduate Certificate); nursing (Graduate Certificate), including simulation based academic fellowship in advanced pain management; psychological and social foundations (Graduate Certificate), including career counseling, college teaching, diversity in education, mental health counseling, school counseling; public affairs (Graduate Certificate), including nonprofit management, public management, research administration; public health (Graduate Certificate), including assessing chemical toxicity and public health risks, health equity, pharmacoepidemiology, public health generalist, toxicology, translational research in adolescent behavioral health; public health practices (Graduate Certificate), including planning for healthy communities; rehabilitation and mental health counseling (Graduate Certificate), including integrative mental health care, marriage and family therapy, rehabilitation technology; secondary education (Graduate Certificate), including ESOL, foreign language education: culture and content, foreign language education: professional; social work (Graduate Certificate), including geriatric social work/clinical gerontology; special education (Graduate Certificate), including autism spectrum disorder, disabilities education: severe/profound; world languages (Graduate Certificate), including teaching English as a second language (TESL) or foreign language. *Unit head:* Dr. Cynthia DeLuca, Associate Vice President and Assistant Vice Provost, 813-974-3077, Fax: 813-974-7061, E-mail: deluca@usf.edu. *Application contact:* Owen Hooper, Director, Summer and Alternative Calendar Programs, 813-974-6917, E-mail: hooper@usf.edu.
Website: http://www.usf.edu/innovative-education/

**The University of Texas at Tyler,** College of Engineering, Department of Civil Engineering, Tyler, TX 75799-0001. Offers environmental engineering (MS); industrial safety (MS); structural engineering (MS); transportation engineering (MS); water resources engineering (MS). *Program availability:* Part-time, evening/weekend. *Faculty:* 5 full-time. *Students:* 7 full-time (0 women), 8 part-time (6 women); includes 4 minority (1 Asian, non-Hispanic/Latino; 3 Hispanic/Latino), 4 international. Average age 28. 14 applicants, 79% accepted, 4 enrolled. In 2019, 6 master's awarded. *Entrance requirements:* For master's, GRE General Test, bachelor's degree in engineering, associated science degree. Additional exam requirements/recommendations for international students: required—TOEFL. *Application deadline:* For fall admission, 8/17 priority date for domestic students, 7/1 priority date for international students; for spring admission, 12/21 priority date for domestic students, 11/1 priority date for international students. Application fee: $25 ($50 for international students). *Financial support:*

Application deadline: 7/1. *Unit head:* Dr. Torey Nalbone, Chair, 903-565-5520, E-mail: tnalbone@uttyler.edu. *Application contact:* Dr. Torey Nalbone, Chair, 903-565-5520, E-mail: tnalbone@uttyler.edu.
Website: https://www.uttyler.edu/ce/

**The University of Texas Health Science Center at Houston,** School of Public Health, Houston, TX 77030. Offers behavioral science (PhD); biostatistics (MPH, MS, PhD); environmental health (MPH); epidemiology (MPH, MS, PhD); general public health (Certificate); genomics and bioinformatics (Certificate); health disparities (Certificate); health promotion/health education (MPH, Dr PH); healthcare management (Certificate); management, policy and community health (MPH, Dr PH, PhD); maternal and child health (Certificate); public health informatics (Certificate); DDS/MPH; JD/MPH; MBA/MPH; MD/MPH; MGPS/MPH; MP Aff/MPH; MS/MPH; MSN/MPH; MSW/MPH; PhD/MPH. *Accreditation:* CAHME; CEPH. *Program availability:* Part-time. *Degree requirements:* For master's, thesis (for some programs); for doctorate, comprehensive exam, thesis/dissertation. *Entrance requirements:* For master's and doctorate, GRE General Test. Additional exam requirements/recommendations for international students: required—TOEFL (minimum score 600 paper-based, 100 iBT) or IELTS (7.5). Electronic applications accepted. *Expenses:* Contact institution.

**University of the Sacred Heart,** Graduate Programs, Department of Natural Sciences, Program in Occupational Health and Safety, San Juan, PR 00914-0383. Offers MS.

**The University of Toledo,** College of Graduate Studies, College of Health and Human Services, School of Population Health, Toledo, OH 43606-3390. Offers health education (PhD); occupational health-industrial hygiene (MS); public health (MPH).

**The University of Toledo,** College of Graduate Studies, College of Medicine and Life Sciences, Department of Public Health and Preventative Medicine, Toledo, OH 43606-3390. Offers biostatistics and epidemiology (Certificate); contemporary gerontological practice (Certificate); environmental and occupational health and safety (MPH); epidemiology (Certificate); global public health (Certificate); health promotion and education (MPH); industrial hygiene (MSOH); medical and health science teaching and learning (Certificate); occupational health (Certificate); public health administration (MPH); public health and emergency response (Certificate); public health epidemiology (MPH); public health nutrition (MPH); MD/MPH. *Program availability:* Part-time, evening/weekend. *Degree requirements:* For master's, thesis or alternative. *Entrance requirements:* For master's, GRE, minimum undergraduate GPA of 3.0, three letters of recommendation, statement of purpose, transcripts from all prior institutions attended, resume; for Certificate, minimum undergraduate GPA of 3.0, three letters of recommendation, statement of purpose, transcripts from all prior institutions attended, resume. Additional exam requirements/recommendations for international students: required—TOEFL (minimum score 550 paper-based; 80 iBT), IELTS (minimum score 6.5). Electronic applications accepted.

**University of Toronto,** School of Graduate Studies, Department of Public Health Sciences, Toronto, ON M5S 1A1, Canada. Offers biostatistics (M Sc, PhD); community health (M Sc); community nutrition (MPH), including nutrition and dietetics; epidemiology (MPH, PhD); family and community medicine (MPH); occupational and environmental health (MPH); social and behavioral health science (PhD); social and behavioral health sciences (MPH), including health promotion. *Accreditation:* CAHME (one or more programs are accredited). *Program availability:* Part-time. *Degree requirements:* For master's, thesis (for some programs), practicum; for doctorate, comprehensive exam, thesis/dissertation, oral thesis defense. *Entrance requirements:* For master's, 2 letters of reference, relevant professional/research experience, minimum B average in final year; for doctorate, 2 letters of reference, relevant professional/research experience, minimum B+ average. Additional exam requirements/recommendations for international students: required—TOEFL (minimum score 580 paper-based; 93 iBT), TWE (minimum score 5). Electronic applications accepted. *Expenses:* Contact institution.

**University of Vermont,** The Robert Larner, MD College of Medicine and Graduate College, Graduate Programs in Medicine, Program in Public Health, Burlington, VT 05405. Offers epidemiology (Graduate Certificate); global and environmental health (Graduate Certificate); healthcare management and policy (Graduate Certificate); public health (MPH). *Program availability:* Online only, 100% online. *Entrance requirements:* For master's and Graduate Certificate, resume/curriculum vitae. Additional exam requirements/recommendations for international students: required—TOEFL (minimum iBT score of 90) or IELTS (6.5). Electronic applications accepted. *Expenses:* Contact institution.

**University of Washington,** Graduate School, School of Public Health, Department of Environmental and Occupational Health Sciences, Seattle, WA 98195. Offers applied toxicology (MS); environmental and occupational health (MPH); environmental and occupational hygiene (PhD); environmental health (MS); environmental toxicology (MS, PhD); occupational and environmental exposure sciences (MS); occupational and environmental medicine (MPH). *Accreditation:* CEPH. *Program availability:* Part-time. *Faculty:* 35 full-time (16 women), 14 part-time/adjunct (5 women). *Students:* 61 full-time (39 women), 8 part-time (6 women); includes 24 minority (3 Black or African American, non-Hispanic/Latino; 13 Asian, non-Hispanic/Latino; 6 Hispanic/Latino; 2 Native Hawaiian or other Pacific Islander, non-Hispanic/Latino), 6 international. Average age 32. 106 applicants, 66% accepted, 40 enrolled. In 2019, 27 master's, 6 doctorates awarded. Terminal master's awarded for partial completion of doctoral program. *Entrance requirements:* For master's and doctorate, GRE General Test. Additional exam requirements/recommendations for international students: required—TOEFL. *Application deadline:* For fall admission, 12/1 for domestic and international students. Application fee: $85. Electronic applications accepted. *Expenses:* Contact institution. *Financial support:* Fellowships, research assistantships, teaching assistantships, career-related internships or fieldwork, institutionally sponsored loans, scholarships/grants, traineeships, health care benefits, and unspecified assistantships available. *Unit head:* Dr. Michael Yost, Chair, 206-543-3199, Fax: 206-543-9616. *Application contact:* Trina Sterry, Manager of Student and Academic Services, 206-543-3199, E-mail: ehgrad@uw.edu.
Website: http://deohs.washington.edu/

**University of Wisconsin–Milwaukee,** Graduate School, Joseph J. Zilber School of Public Health, Program in Environmental Health Sciences, Milwaukee, WI 53201-0413. Offers PhD. Electronic applications accepted.

**University of Wisconsin–Milwaukee,** Graduate School, Joseph J. Zilber School of Public Health, Program in Public Health, Milwaukee, WI 53201-0413. Offers biostatistics (MPH); community and behavioral health promotion (MPH); environmental health sciences (MPH); epidemiology (MPH, PhD); public and population health (Graduate Certificate); public health policy and administration (MPH); public health: biostatistics (PhD); public health: community and behavioral health promotion (PhD). Electronic applications accepted.

**University of Wisconsin–Whitewater,** School of Graduate Studies, College of Education and Professional Studies, Department of Occupational and Environmental Safety, Whitewater, WI 53190-1790. Offers safety (MS). *Program availability:* Part-time, evening/weekend, online learning. *Degree requirements:* For master's, thesis or alternative. *Entrance requirements:* For master's, 2 letters of recommendation. Additional exam requirements/recommendations for international students: required—TOEFL (minimum score 550 paper-based; 80 iBT), IELTS (minimum score 6). Electronic applications accepted.

**Université Laval,** Faculty of Medicine, Graduate Programs in Medicine, Department of Social and Preventive Medicine, Program in Accident Prevention and Occupational Health and Safety Management, Québec, QC G1K 7P4, Canada. Offers Diploma. *Program availability:* Part-time. *Entrance requirements:* For degree, knowledge of French. Electronic applications accepted.

**West Virginia University,** School of Public Health, Morgantown, WV 26506. Offers biostatistics (MPH, MS, PhD); epidemiology (MPH, PhD); health policy (MPH); occupational and environmental health sciences (MPH, PhD); public health (MPH); school health education (MS); social and behavioral science (MPH, PhD). *Accreditation:* CEPH. *Program availability:* Part-time, online learning. *Degree requirements:* For master's, practicum, project. *Entrance requirements:* For master's, GRE General Test, MCAT, medical degree, medical internship. Additional exam requirements/recommendations for international students: required—TOEFL (minimum score 550 paper-based; 80 iBT). *Expenses:* Contact institution.

**Yale University,** Yale School of Medicine, Yale School of Public Health, New Haven, CT 06520. Offers applied biostatistics and epidemiology (APMPH); biostatistics (MPH, MS, PhD), including global health (MPH); chronic disease epidemiology (MPH, PhD), including global health (MPH); environmental health sciences (MPH, PhD), including global health (MPH); epidemiology of microbial diseases (MPH, PhD), including global health (MPH); global health (APMPH); health management (MPH), including global health; health policy (MPH), including global health; health policy and administration (APMPH, PhD); occupational and environmental medicine (APMPH); preventive medicine (APMPH); social and behavioral sciences (APMPH, MPH), including global health (MPH); JD/MPH; M Div/MPH; MBA/MPH; MD/MPH; MEM/MPH; MFS/MPH; MM Sc/MPH; MPH/MA; MSN/MPH. *Accreditation:* CEPH. *Faculty:* 161 full-time (71 women), 121 part-time/adjunct (57 women). *Students:* 534 full-time (386 women); includes 156 minority (24 Black or African American, non-Hispanic/Latino; 83 Asian, non-Hispanic/Latino; 30 Hispanic/Latino; 19 Two or more races, non-Hispanic/Latino), 220 international. Average age 25. 1,300 applicants, 220 enrolled. In 2019, 250 master's, 12 doctorates awarded. *Degree requirements:* For master's, thesis; for doctorate, comprehensive exam, thesis/dissertation. *Entrance requirements:* For master's, GMAT, GRE, or MCAT; for doctorate, GRE General Test. Additional exam requirements/recommendations for international students: required—TOEFL (minimum score 100 iBT). *Application deadline:* For fall admission, 12/15 for domestic and international students; for summer admission, 12/15 for domestic and international students. Applications are processed on a rolling basis. Application fee: $135. Electronic applications accepted. *Expenses:* Contact institution. *Financial support:* Fellowships with full tuition reimbursements, research assistantships with full tuition reimbursements, teaching assistantships with full tuition reimbursements, career-related internships or fieldwork, institutionally sponsored loans, scholarships/grants, and tuition waivers available. Support available to part-time students. Financial award application deadline: 3/1; financial award applicants required to submit FAFSA. *Unit head:* Dr. Sten Vermund, Dean and Anna M.R. Lauder Professor of Public Health, E-mail: sten.vermund@yale.edu. *Application contact:* Mary Keefe, Director of Admissions, 203-785-2844, E-mail: ysph.admissions@yale.edu.
Website: http://publichealth.yale.edu/

# Epidemiology

**Brown University,** Graduate School, Division of Biology and Medicine, School of Public Health, Department of Epidemiology, Providence, RI 02912. Offers Sc M, PhD. *Degree requirements:* For doctorate, thesis/dissertation, preliminary exam. *Entrance requirements:* For master's and doctorate, GRE General Test.

**California State University, Northridge,** Graduate Studies, College of Health and Human Development, Department of Health Sciences, Northridge, CA 91330. Offers health administration (MS); public health (MPH), including applied epidemiology, community health education. *Accreditation:* CAHME; CEPH. *Entrance requirements:* For master's, GRE General Test or minimum GPA of 3.0. Additional exam requirements/recommendations for international students: required—TOEFL.

**Capella University,** School of Public Service Leadership, Doctoral Programs in Healthcare, Minneapolis, MN 55402. Offers criminal justice (PhD); emergency management (PhD); epidemiology (Dr PH); general health administration (DHA); general public administration (DPA); health advocacy and leadership (Dr PH); health care administration (PhD); health care leadership (DHA); health policy advocacy (DHA); multidisciplinary human services (PhD); nonprofit management and leadership (PhD); public safety leadership (PhD); social and community services (PhD).

**Case Western Reserve University,** School of Medicine and School of Graduate Studies, Graduate Programs in Medicine, Department of Population and Quantitative Health Sciences, Program in Epidemiology and Biostatistics, Cleveland, OH 44106. Offers PhD. *Program availability:* Part-time. Terminal master's awarded for partial completion of doctoral program. *Degree requirements:* For doctorate, comprehensive exam, thesis/dissertation. *Entrance requirements:* For doctorate, GRE General Test, 3 recommendations. Additional exam requirements/recommendations for international students: required—TOEFL (minimum score 550 paper-based). Electronic applications accepted.

**Colorado State University,** College of Veterinary Medicine and Biomedical Sciences, Department of Environmental and Radiological Health Sciences, Fort Collins, CO 80523-1681. Offers environmental health (MS, PhD), including environmental health and safety (MS), epidemiology (PhD). Terminal master's awarded for partial completion of doctoral program. *Degree requirements:* For master's, comprehensive exam (for some programs), thesis (for some programs); for doctorate, comprehensive exam (for some programs), thesis/dissertation (for some programs). *Entrance requirements:* For master's, GRE, minimum GPA of 3.0, bachelor's degree, resume or curriculum vitae,

official transcripts, written statement, 3 letters of recommendation; for doctorate, GRE, minimum GPA of 3.0, MS or proof of research, resume or curriculum vitae, official transcripts, written statement, 3 letters of recommendation. Additional exam requirements/recommendations for international students: required—TOEFL (minimum score 80 iBT), IELTS (minimum score 6.5). Electronic applications accepted. *Expenses:* Contact institution.

**Columbia University,** Columbia University Mailman School of Public Health, Department of Epidemiology, New York, NY 10032. Offers MPH, MS, Dr PH, PhD. *Accreditation:* CEPH (one or more programs are accredited). *Program availability:* Part-time, evening/weekend. *Students:* 244 full-time (183 women), 147 part-time (105 women); includes 159 minority (26 Black or African American, non-Hispanic/Latino; 1 American Indian or Alaska Native, non-Hispanic/Latino; 82 Asian, non-Hispanic/Latino; 36 Hispanic/Latino; 14 Two or more races, non-Hispanic/Latino), 72 international. Average age 28. 712 applicants, 64% accepted, 170 enrolled. In 2019, 139 master's, 10 doctorates awarded. *Degree requirements:* For master's, thesis; for doctorate, thesis/dissertation. *Entrance requirements:* For master's, GRE General Test; for doctorate, GRE General Test, MPH or equivalent (for Dr PH). Additional exam requirements/recommendations for international students: required—TOEFL (minimum score 600 paper-based; 100 iBT). *Application deadline:* For fall admission, 12/1 priority date for domestic and international students. Application fee: $120. Electronic applications accepted. *Expenses: Tuition:* Full-time $47,600; part-time $1880 per credit. One-time fee: $105. *Financial support:* Research assistantships, teaching assistantships, career-related internships or fieldwork, and Federal Work-Study available. Support available to part-time students. Financial award application deadline: 2/1; financial award applicants required to submit FAFSA. *Unit head:* Dr. Charles Branas, Chairperson, 212-305-8755. *Application contact:* Clare Norton, Associate Dean for Enrollment Management, 212-305-8698, Fax: 212-342-1861, E-mail: ph-admit@columbia.edu.
Website: https://www.mailman.columbia.edu/become-student/departments/epidemiology

**Daemen College,** Public Health Programs, Amherst, NY 14226-3592. Offers community health education (MPH); epidemiology (MPH); generalist (MPH). *Program availability:* Part-time, evening/weekend. *Degree requirements:* For master's, successful completion of a practicum and capstone; minimum grade of B- in any course; maximum of 2 repeated courses is allowed; students must maintain an overall minimum cumulative GPA of 3.0. *Entrance requirements:* For master's, bachelor's degree, official transcripts, GPA 3.0 or above (under 3.0 may be submitted on a conditional basis), 2 letters of recommendation, personal statement, interview with MPH faculty. Additional exam requirements/recommendations for international students: required—TOEFL (minimum score 85 paper-based), IELTS (minimum score 6.5). Electronic applications accepted. Application fee is waived when completed online.

**Dalhousie University,** Faculty of Medicine, Department of Community Health and Epidemiology, Halifax, NS B3H 4R2, Canada. Offers M Sc. *Degree requirements:* For master's, thesis. *Entrance requirements:* Additional exam requirements/recommendations for international students: required—1 of 5 approved tests: TOEFL, IELTS, CANTEST, CAEL, Michigan English Language Assessment Battery. Electronic applications accepted. *Expenses:* Contact institution.

**Dartmouth College,** Guarini School of Graduate and Advanced Studies, Institute for Quantitative Biomedical Sciences, Hanover, NH 03755. Offers epidemiology (MS); health data science (MS); quantitative biomedical sciences (PhD). *Entrance requirements:* For doctorate, GRE (minimum scores: 1200 old scoring, 308 new scoring verbal and quantitative; analytical writing 4.5; verbal 500 old scoring, 153 new scoring). Electronic applications accepted.

**Drexel University,** Dornsife School of Public Health, Department of Epidemiology and Biostatistics, Philadelphia, PA 19104-2875. Offers biostatistics (MS); epidemiology (PhD); epidemiology and biostatistics (Certificate).

**East Tennessee State University,** College of Graduate and Continuing Studies, College of Public Health, Program in Public Health, Johnson City, TN 37614. Offers biostatistics (MPH, Postbaccalaureate Certificate); community health (MPH, DPH); environmental health (MPH); epidemiology (MPH, DPH, Postbaccalaureate Certificate); gerontology (Postbaccalaureate Certificate); global health (Postbaccalaureate Certificate); health care management (Postbaccalaureate Certificate); health management and policy (DPH); public health (Postbaccalaureate Certificate); public health services administration (MPH); rural health (Postbaccalaureate Certificate). *Accreditation:* CEPH. *Program availability:* Part-time, online learning. *Degree requirements:* For master's, comprehensive exam, field experience; for doctorate, thesis/dissertation, practicum. *Entrance requirements:* For master's, GRE General Test, minimum GPA of 2.75, SOPHAS application, three letters of recommendation; for doctorate, GRE General Test, SOPHAS application, three letters of recommendation; for Postbaccalaureate Certificate, minimum GPA of 2.5, three letters of recommendation, resume. Additional exam requirements/recommendations for international students: required—TOEFL (minimum score 550 paper-based; 79 iBT), IELTS (minimum score 6.5). Electronic applications accepted.

**Emory University,** Rollins School of Public Health, Department of Environmental Health, Atlanta, GA 30322-1100. Offers environmental health (MPH); environmental health and epidemiology (MSPH); environmental health sciences (PhD); global environmental health (MPH). *Program availability:* Part-time. *Degree requirements:* For master's, thesis, practicum. *Entrance requirements:* For master's, GRE General Test. Additional exam requirements/recommendations for international students: required—TOEFL. Electronic applications accepted.

**Emory University,** Rollins School of Public Health, Department of Epidemiology, Atlanta, GA 30322-1100. Offers MPH, MSPH, PhD. *Program availability:* Part-time. *Degree requirements:* For master's, thesis, practicum. *Entrance requirements:* For master's, GRE General Test. Additional exam requirements/recommendations for international students: required—TOEFL (minimum score 550 paper-based; 80 iBT). Electronic applications accepted. *Expenses:* Contact institution.

**Emory University,** Rollins School of Public Health, Online Program in Public Health, Atlanta, GA 30322-1100. Offers applied epidemiology (MPH); applied public health informatics (MPH); prevention science (MPH). *Program availability:* Part-time, evening/weekend, online learning. *Degree requirements:* For master's, thesis, practicum. *Entrance requirements:* For master's, GRE. Additional exam requirements/recommendations for international students: required—TOEFL (minimum score 550 paper-based; 80 iBT). Electronic applications accepted.

**Florida International University,** Robert Stempel College of Public Health and Social Work, Programs in Public Health, Miami, FL 33199. Offers biostatistics (MPH); environmental and occupational health (MPH, PhD); epidemiology (MPH, PhD); health policy and management (MPH); health promotion and disease prevention (MPH, PhD). *Accreditation:* CEPH. *Program availability:* Part-time, evening/weekend, online learning. *Faculty:* 31 full-time (15 women), 8 part-time/adjunct (6 women). *Students:* 176 full-time (117 women), 58 part-time (42 women); includes 170 minority (57 Black or African American, non-Hispanic/Latino; 1 American Indian or Alaska Native, non-Hispanic/Latino; 14 Asian, non-Hispanic/Latino; 95 Hispanic/Latino; 3 Two or more races, non-Hispanic/Latino), 32 international. Average age 29. 260 applicants, 68% accepted, 68 enrolled. In 2019, 70 master's, 16 doctorates awarded. *Degree requirements:* For master's, thesis optional; for doctorate, comprehensive exam, thesis/dissertation. *Entrance requirements:* For master's, minimum GPA of 3.0, letters of recommendation; for doctorate, GRE, resume, minimum GPA of 3.0, letters of recommendation, letter of intent. Additional exam requirements/recommendations for international students: required—TOEFL (minimum score 550 paper-based; 80 iBT). *Application deadline:* For fall admission, 6/1 for domestic students, 4/1 for international students; for spring admission, 10/1 for domestic students, 9/1 for international students. Applications are processed on a rolling basis. Application fee: $30. Electronic applications accepted. *Expenses:* Contact institution. *Financial support:* Institutionally sponsored loans, scholarships/grants, and tuition waivers (full) available. Financial award application deadline: 3/1; financial award applicants required to submit FAFSA. *Unit head:* Dr. Kim Tieu, Chair, 305-348-0371, E-mail: kim.tieu@fiu.edu. *Application contact:* Nanett Rojas, Manager, Admissions Operations, 305-348-7464, Fax: 305-348-7441, E-mail: gradadm@fiu.edu.

**George Mason University,** College of Health and Human Services, Department of Global and Community Health, Fairfax, VA 22030. Offers global and community health (Certificate); global health (MS); public health (MPH, Certificate), including epidemiology (MPH), leadership and management (Certificate). *Accreditation:* CEPH. *Program availability:* Part-time, evening/weekend. *Degree requirements:* For master's, thesis, 200-hour practicum. *Entrance requirements:* For master's, GRE, GMAT (depending on program), 2 official transcripts; expanded goals statement; 3 letters of recommendation; resume; 1 completed course in health science, statistics, natural sciences and social science (for MPH); 6 credits of foreign language if not fluent (for MS); minimum undergraduate GPA of 3.0; for Certificate, 2 official transcripts; expanded goals statement; 3 letters of recommendation; resume; bachelor's degree from regionally-accredited institution with minimum GPA of 3.0. Additional exam requirements/recommendations for international students: required—TOEFL (minimum score 570 paper-based; 88 iBT), IELTS (minimum score 6.5), PTE (minimum score 59). Electronic applications accepted. *Expenses:* Contact institution.

**Georgetown University,** Graduate School of Arts and Sciences, Department of Biostatistics, Bioinformatics and Biomathematics, Washington, DC 20057-1484. Offers biostatistics (MS, Certificate), including bioinformatics (MS), epidemiology (MS); epidemiology (Certificate). *Entrance requirements:* For master's, GRE General Test. Additional exam requirements/recommendations for international students: required—TOEFL.

**The George Washington University,** Milken Institute School of Public Health, Department of Epidemiology and Biostatistics, Washington, DC 20052. Offers biostatistics (MPH); epidemiology (MPH); microbiology and emerging infectious diseases (MSPH). *Entrance requirements:* For master's, GMAT, GRE General Test, or MCAT. Additional exam requirements/recommendations for international students: required—TOEFL.

**Georgia Southern University,** Jack N. Averitt College of Graduate Studies, Jiann-Ping Hsu College of Public Health, Program in Public Health, Statesboro, GA 30460. Offers biostatistics (MPH, Dr PH); community health behavior and education (Dr PH); community health education (MPH); environmental health sciences (MPH); epidemiology (MPH); health policy and management (MPH, Dr PH). *Program availability:* Part-time. *Faculty:* 42 full-time (22 women), 1 (woman) part-time/adjunct. *Students:* 142 full-time (105 women), 88 part-time (62 women); includes 132 minority (100 Black or African American, non-Hispanic/Latino; 10 Asian, non-Hispanic/Latino; 8 Hispanic/Latino; 14 Two or more races, non-Hispanic/Latino), 46 international. Average age 32. 195 applicants, 85% accepted, 59 enrolled. In 2019, 90 master's, 14 doctorates awarded. *Degree requirements:* For master's, thesis optional, practicum; for doctorate, comprehensive exam, thesis/dissertation, preceptorship. *Entrance requirements:* For master's, GRE General Test, minimum GPA of 2.75, 3 letters of recommendation, statement of purpose, resume or curriculum vitae; for doctorate, GRE, GMAT, MCAT, LSAT, minimum GPA of 3.0, 3 letters of recommendation, statement of purpose, resume or curriculum vitae. Additional exam requirements/recommendations for international students: required—TOEFL (minimum score 537 paper-based; 75 iBT), IELTS (minimum score 6). *Application deadline:* For fall admission, 6/1 for domestic students, 5/1 for international students. Applications are processed on a rolling basis. Application fee: $135. Electronic applications accepted. *Expenses:* Contact institution. *Financial support:* In 2019–20, 94 students received support, including 1 research assistantship with full tuition reimbursement available (averaging $12,350 per year), 6 teaching assistantships with full tuition reimbursements available (averaging $12,350 per year); scholarships/grants, tuition waivers (full), and unspecified assistantships also available. Financial award application deadline: 4/15; financial award applicants required to submit FAFSA. *Unit head:* Dr. Robert Greg Evans, Dean, 912-478-2674, E-mail: rgevans@georgiasouthern.edu. *Application contact:* Shamia Garrett, Coordinator, Office of Student Services, 912-478-2674, Fax: 912-478-5811, E-mail: jphcoph-gradadvisor@georgiasouthern.edu.
Website: http://jphcoph.georgiasouthern.edu/

**Harvard University,** Cyprus International Institute for the Environment and Public Health in Association with Harvard School of Public Health, Cambridge, MA 02138. Offers environmental health (MS); environmental/public health (PhD); epidemiology and biostatistics (MS). *Entrance requirements:* For master's and doctorate, GRE, resume/curriculum vitae, 3 letters of recommendation, BA or BS (including diploma and official transcripts). Additional exam requirements/recommendations for international students: required—TOEFL, IELTS (minimum score 7). Electronic applications accepted.

**Harvard University,** Harvard T.H. Chan School of Public Health, Department of Epidemiology, Boston, MA 02115-6096. Offers cancer epidemiology (SM); cardiovascular epidemiology (SM); clinical epidemiology (SM); environmental and occupational epidemiology (SM); epidemiologic methods (SM); epidemiology of aging (SM); genetic epidemiology and statistical genetics (SM); infectious disease epidemiology (SM); neuro-psychiatric epidemiology (SM); nutritional epidemiology (SM); pharmacoepidemiology (SM); population health sciences (PhD); reproductive epidemiology (SM). *Program availability:* Part-time. *Faculty:* 100 full-time (44 women), 39 part-time/adjunct (16 women). *Students:* 80 full-time (64 women), 7 part-time (4 women); includes 9 minority (3 Black or African American, non-Hispanic/Latino; 3 Asian, non-Hispanic/Latino; 1 Hispanic/Latino; 2 Two or more races, non-Hispanic/Latino), 20 international. Average age 29. 261 applicants, 28% accepted, 46 enrolled. In 2019, 42 master's, 11 doctorates awarded. *Entrance requirements:* For master's, GRE, MCAT. Additional exam requirements/recommendations for international students: recommended—TOEFL (minimum score 600 paper-based; 100 iBT), IELTS (minimum score 7). *Application deadline:* For fall admission, 12/1 for domestic and international students. Application fee: $140. Electronic applications accepted. *Financial support:* Fellowships, research assistantships, teaching assistantships, Federal Work-Study, scholarships/grants, traineeships, and unspecified assistantships available. Support available to part-time students. Financial award application deadline: 2/15; financial award applicants required to submit FAFSA. *Unit head:* Dr. Albert Hofman, Chair, 617-432-6477. *Application contact:* Vincent W. James, Director of Admissions, 617-432-1031, Fax: 617-432-7080, E-mail: admissions@hsph.harvard.edu.
Website: http://www.hsph.harvard.edu/epidemiology/

**Harvard University,** Harvard T.H. Chan School of Public Health, PhD Program in Population Health Sciences, Boston, MA 02138. Offers environmental health (PhD); epidemiology (PhD); global health and population (PhD); nutrition (PhD); social and behavioral sciences (PhD). *Students:* 159 full-time (0 women). Average age 29. In 2019, 5 doctorates awarded. *Entrance requirements:* Additional exam requirements/recommendations for international students: recommended—TOEFL, IELTS. *Application deadline:* For fall admission, 12/1 for domestic and international students. Electronic applications accepted. *Financial support:* Application deadline: 2/15; applicants required to submit FAFSA. *Unit head:* Bruce Villineau, Assistant Director, 617-432-6076, E-mail: phdphs@hsph.harvard.edu. *Application contact:* Bruce Villineau, Assistant Director, 617-432-6076, E-mail: phdphs@hsph.harvard.edu.

**Indiana University Bloomington,** School of Public Health, Department of Epidemiology and Biostatistics, Bloomington, IN 47405. Offers biostatistics (MPH); epidemiology (MPH, PhD). *Degree requirements:* For master's, thesis or alternative; for doctorate, comprehensive exam, thesis/dissertation. *Entrance requirements:* For master's, GRE (for applicants with cumulative undergraduate GPA less than 2.8); for doctorate, GRE. Additional exam requirements/recommendations for international students: required—TOEFL (minimum score 550 paper-based; 80 iBT). Electronic applications accepted.

**Indiana University-Purdue University Indianapolis,** Richard M. Fairbanks School of Public Health, Indianapolis, IN 46202. Offers biostatistics (MS, PhD); environmental health (MPH); epidemiology (MPH, PhD); global health leadership (Dr PH); health administration (MHA); health policy (Graduate Certificate); health policy and management (MPH, PhD); health systems management (Graduate Certificate); product stewardship (MS); public health (Graduate Certificate); social and behavioral sciences (MPH). *Accreditation:* CAHME; CEPH. *Expenses:* Contact institution.

**Johns Hopkins University,** Bloomberg School of Public Health, Department of Epidemiology, Baltimore, MD 21205. Offers cancer epidemiology (MHS, Sc M, PhD, Sc D); cardiovascular disease and clinical epidemiology (MHS, Sc M, PhD, Sc D); clinical trials (PhD, Sc D); clinical trials and evidence synthesis (MHS, Sc M, PhD, Sc D); environmental epidemiology (MHS, Sc M, PhD, Sc D); epidemiology of aging (MHS, Sc M, PhD, Sc D); general epidemiology and methodology (MHS, Sc M); genetic epidemiology (MHS, Sc M, PhD, Sc D); infectious disease epidemiology (MHS, Sc M, PhD, Sc D). *Degree requirements:* For master's, comprehensive exam, thesis, 1-year full-time residency; for doctorate, comprehensive exam, thesis/dissertation, 2 years' full-time residency, oral and written exams, student teaching. *Entrance requirements:* For master's, GRE General Test or MCAT, 3 letters of recommendation, curriculum vitae; for doctorate, GRE General Test, minimum 1 year of work experience, 3 letters of recommendation, curriculum vitae, academic records from all schools. Additional exam requirements/recommendations for international students: required—TOEFL (minimum score 100 iBT), IELTS (minimum score 7.5). Electronic applications accepted.

**Johns Hopkins University,** Bloomberg School of Public Health, Department of International Health, Baltimore, MD 21205. Offers global disease epidemiology and control (MSPH, PhD); global health economics (MHS); health systems (MSPH, PhD); human nutrition (MSPH, PhD); social and behavioral interventions (MSPH, PhD). *Degree requirements:* For master's, comprehensive exam, thesis (for some programs), 1-year full-time residency, 4-9 month internship; for doctorate, comprehensive exam, thesis/dissertation or alternative, 1.5 years' full-time residency, oral and written exams. *Entrance requirements:* For master's, GRE General Test or MCAT, 3 letters of recommendation, resume; for doctorate, GRE General Test or MCAT, 3 letters of recommendation, resume, transcripts. Additional exam requirements/recommendations for international students: required—TOEFL (minimum score 600 paper-based; 100 iBT); recommended—IELTS (minimum score 7). Electronic applications accepted.

**Kent State University,** College of Public Health, Kent, OH 44242-0001. Offers public health (MPH, PhD), including biostatistics (MPH), environmental health sciences (MPH), epidemiology, health policy and management, prevention science (PhD), social and behavioral sciences (MPH). *Accreditation:* CEPH. *Program availability:* Part-time, 100% online. *Faculty:* 23 full-time (12 women), 4 part-time/adjunct (1 woman). *Students:* 136 full-time (98 women), 158 part-time (129 women); includes 71 minority (45 Black or African American, non-Hispanic/Latino; 12 Asian, non-Hispanic/Latino; 8 Hispanic/Latino; 6 Two or more races, non-Hispanic/Latino), 40 international. Average age 31. 187 applicants, 79% accepted, 85 enrolled. In 2019, 93 master's, 7 doctorates awarded. *Degree requirements:* For master's, comprehensive exam, between 150 - 300 hours' placement at public health agency, final portfolio and presentation; for doctorate, comprehensive exam, thesis/dissertation. *Entrance requirements:* For master's, GRE or other standardized graduate admission exam (GMAT, MCAT, LSAT or PCAT), minimum GPA of 3.0, transcripts, goal statement, 3 letters of recommendation; for doctorate, GRE or other standardized graduate admission exam with a quantitative component, Master's degree in related discipline, minimum GPA of 3.0, personal statement, resume, interview with faculty, 3 letters of recommendation, transcript(s). Additional exam requirements/recommendations for international students: required—TOEFL (minimum score 94 iBT), IELTS (minimum score 7), PTE (minimum score 65), For MPH: TOEFL iBT 79, Michigan English Language Assessment Battery (minimum score of 77), IELTS 6.5, PTE 58; For Ph.D.: see below and min MELAB 82. *Application deadline:* For fall admission, 6/15 for domestic and international students; for spring admission, 10/15 for domestic and international students; for summer admission, 3/15 for domestic and international students. Applications are processed on a rolling basis. Application fee: $45 ($70 for international students). Electronic applications accepted. *Financial support:* Career-related internships or fieldwork, Federal Work-Study, scholarships/grants, and unspecified assistantships available. *Unit head:* Dr. Sonia Alemagno, Dean and Professor of Health Policy and Management, 330-672-6500, E-mail: salemagn@kent.edu. *Application contact:* Dr. Jeffrey S. Hallam, Professor/Associate Dean for Research and Graduate Studies, 330-672-0679, E-mail: jhallam1@kent.edu. Website: http://www.kent.edu/publichealth/

**Liberty University,** School of Health Sciences, Lynchburg, VA 24515. Offers anatomy and cell biology (PhD); biomedical sciences (MS); epidemiology (MPH); exercise science (MS), including clinical, community physical activity, human performance, nutrition; global health (MPH); health promotion (MPH); medical sciences (MA), including biopsychology, business management, health informatics, molecular medicine, public health; nutrition (MPH). *Program availability:* Part-time, online learning. *Students:* 820 full-time (588 women), 889 part-time (612 women); includes 611 minority (402 Black or African American, non-Hispanic/Latino; 10 American Indian or Alaska Native, non-Hispanic/Latino; 43 Asian, non-Hispanic/Latino; 85 Hispanic/Latino; 1 Native Hawaiian or other Pacific Islander, non-Hispanic/Latino; 70 Two or more races, non-Hispanic/Latino), 67 international. Average age 32. 2,610 applicants, 33% accepted, 406 enrolled. In 2019, 445 master's awarded. *Degree requirements:* For master's, thesis (for some programs); for doctorate, thesis/dissertation. *Entrance requirements:* For doctorate, MAT or GRE, minimum GPA of 3.25 in master's program, 2-3 recommendations, writing samples (for some programs), letter of intent, professional vitae. Additional exam requirements/recommendations for international students: required—TOEFL (minimum score 600 paper-based; 100 iBT). Application fee: $50. *Expenses:* Tuition: Full-time $545; part-time $410 per credit hour. One-time fee: $50. *Financial support:* In 2019–20, 918 students received support. Federal Work-Study available. Financial award

applicants required to submit FAFSA. *Unit head:* Dr. Ralph Linstra, Dean. *Application contact:* Jay Bridge, Director of Admissions, 800-424-9595, Fax: 800-628-7977, E-mail: gradadmissions@liberty.edu. Website: https://www.liberty.edu/health-sciences/

**Loma Linda University,** School of Public Health, Programs in Epidemiology and Biostatistics, Loma Linda, CA 92350. Offers biostatistics (MPH); epidemiology (MPH, Dr PH, PhD). *Entrance requirements:* Additional exam requirements/recommendations for international students: required—Michigan English Language Assessment Battery or TOEFL.

**Louisiana State University Health Sciences Center,** School of Public Health, New Orleans, LA 70112. Offers behavioral and community health sciences (MPH); biostatistics (MPH, MS, PhD); community health sciences (PhD); environmental and occupational health sciences (MPH); epidemiology (MPH, PhD); health policy and systems management (MPH). *Accreditation:* CEPH. *Program availability:* Part-time. *Degree requirements:* For doctorate, thesis/dissertation. *Entrance requirements:* For master's, GRE General Test. Additional exam requirements/recommendations for international students: recommended—TOEFL (minimum score 550 paper-based; 79 iBT), IELTS. Electronic applications accepted.

**McGill University,** Faculty of Graduate and Postdoctoral Studies, Faculty of Medicine, Department of Epidemiology, Biostatistics and Occupational Health, Montréal, QC H3A 2T5, Canada. Offers biostatistics (M Sc, PhD); epidemiology (M Sc, PhD); occupational health (M Sc A); public health (MSPH). *Program availability:* Part-time, online learning. *Degree requirements:* For doctorate, thesis/dissertation. *Entrance requirements:* For master's, B Sc in chemistry, engineering physics, environmental sciences, medicine, nursing, or other health science (for occupational health); MD or B Sc in nursing (for distance education); minimum GPA of 3.0; for doctorate, TOEFL, M Sc in environmental health, chemistry, engineering, community health, physics, epidemiology, medicine, nursing, or occupational health.

**Medical University of South Carolina,** College of Graduate Studies, Division of Biostatistics and Epidemiology, Charleston, SC 29425. Offers biostatistics (MS, PhD); epidemiology (MS, PhD); DMD/PhD; MD/PhD. Terminal master's awarded for partial completion of doctoral program. *Degree requirements:* For master's, comprehensive exam, thesis (for some programs); for doctorate, comprehensive exam, oral and written exams. *Entrance requirements:* For master's, GRE General Test, two semesters of college-level calculus; for doctorate, GRE General Test, interview, minimum GPA of 3.0, two semesters of college-level calculus. Additional exam requirements/recommendations for international students: required—TOEFL (minimum score 600 paper-based; 100 iBT). Electronic applications accepted.

**Memorial University of Newfoundland,** Faculty of Medicine and School of Graduate Studies, Graduate Programs in Medicine, Division of Clinical Epidemiology, St. John's, NL A1C 5S7, Canada. Offers M Sc, PhD, Diploma.

**Michigan State University,** College of Human Medicine and The Graduate School, Graduate Programs in Human Medicine, Department of Epidemiology, East Lansing, MI 48824. Offers MS, PhD. *Degree requirements:* For master's, oral thesis defense. *Entrance requirements:* Additional exam requirements/recommendations for international students: required—TOEFL. Electronic applications accepted.

**Monroe College,** King Graduate School, Bronx, NY 10468. Offers accounting (MS); business administration (MBA), including entrepreneurship, finance, general business administration, healthcare management, human resources, information technology, marketing; computer science (MS); criminal justice (MS); hospitality management (MS); public health (MPH), including biostatistics and epidemiology, community health, health administration and leadership. *Program availability:* Online learning.

**New York Medical College,** School of Health Sciences and Practice, Valhalla, NY 10595. Offers behavioral sciences and health promotion (MPH); biostatistics (MS); children with special health care (Graduate Certificate); emergency preparedness (Graduate Certificate); environmental health science (MPH); epidemiology (MPH, MS); global health (Graduate Certificate); health education (Graduate Certificate); health policy and management (MPH, Dr PH); industrial hygiene (Graduate Certificate); pediatric dysphagia (Post-Graduate Certificate); physical therapy (DPT); public health (Graduate Certificate); speech-language pathology (MS). *Accreditation:* ASHA; CEPH. *Program availability:* Part-time, evening/weekend, 100% online, blended/hybrid learning. *Faculty:* 47 full-time (34 women), 203 part-time/adjunct (125 women). *Students:* 230 full-time (171 women), 292 part-time (207 women); includes 204 minority (73 Black or African American, non-Hispanic/Latino; 4 American Indian or Alaska Native, non-Hispanic/Latino; 59 Asian, non-Hispanic/Latino; 54 Hispanic/Latino; 1 Native Hawaiian or other Pacific Islander, non-Hispanic/Latino; 13 Two or more races, non-Hispanic/Latino), 35 international. Average age 29. 790 applicants, 61% accepted, 162 enrolled. In 2019, 113 master's, 47 doctorates awarded. *Degree requirements:* For master's, comprehensive exam (for some programs), thesis (for some programs); for doctorate, thesis/dissertation. *Entrance requirements:* For master's, GRE (for MS in speech-language pathology); for doctorate, GRE (for Doctor of Physical Therapy and Doctor of Public Health). Additional exam requirements/recommendations for international students: required—TOEFL (minimum score 96 paper-based; 24 iBT), IELTS (minimum score 7). *Application deadline:* For fall admission, 8/1 for domestic students, 4/15 for international students; for spring admission, 12/1 for domestic students; for summer admission, 5/1 for domestic students, 4/15 for international students. Applications are processed on a rolling basis. Application fee: $128 ($120 for international students). Electronic applications accepted. *Expenses:* $1195 credit fee, academic support fee $200, Student activities fee $140 per year, technology fee $150. *Financial support:* In 2019–20, 18 students received support. Federal Work-Study, scholarships/grants, unspecified assistantships, and Federal student loans available. Financial award application deadline: 4/30; financial award applicants required to submit FAFSA. *Unit head:* Ben Johnson, PhD, Vice Dean, 914-594-4531, E-mail: bjohnson23@nymc.edu. *Application contact:* Irene Bundziak, Assistant to Director of Admissions, 914-594-4905, E-mail: irene_bundziak@nymc.edu. Website: http://www.nymc.edu/school-of-health-sciences-and-practice-shsp/

**North Carolina State University,** College of Veterinary Medicine, Program in Comparative Biomedical Sciences, Raleigh, NC 27695. Offers cell biology (MS, PhD); infectious disease (MS, PhD); pathology (MS, PhD); pharmacology (MS, PhD); population medicine (MS, PhD). *Program availability:* Part-time. *Degree requirements:* For master's, thesis; for doctorate, thesis/dissertation. *Entrance requirements:* For master's and doctorate, GRE General Test. Additional exam requirements/recommendations for international students: required—TOEFL (minimum score 550 paper-based). Electronic applications accepted. *Expenses:* Contact institution.

**Northwestern University,** Feinberg School of Medicine, Driskill Graduate Program in Life Sciences, Chicago, IL 60611. Offers biostatistics (PhD); epidemiology (PhD); health and biomedical informatics (PhD); health services and outcomes research (PhD); healthcare quality and patient safety (PhD); translational outcomes in science (PhD). *Degree requirements:* For doctorate, comprehensive exam, thesis/dissertation, written and oral qualifying exams. *Entrance requirements:* For doctorate, GRE General Test. Additional exam requirements/recommendations for international students: required—TOEFL (minimum score 600 paper-based). Electronic applications accepted.

**Oregon State University,** College of Public Health and Human Sciences, Program in Public Health, Corvallis, OR 97331. Offers biostatistics (MPH); environmental and occupational health (MPH, PhD); epidemiology (MPH, PhD); global health (MPH, PhD). *Accreditation:* CEPH. Terminal master's awarded for partial completion of doctoral program. *Entrance requirements:* For master's and doctorate, GRE, minimum GPA of 3.0 in last 90 hours. Additional exam requirements/recommendations for international students: required—TOEFL (minimum score 80 iBT), IELTS (minimum score 6.5). Electronic applications accepted. *Expenses:* Contact institution.

**Ponce Health Sciences University,** Masters Program in Public Health, Ponce, PR 00732-7004. Offers epidemiology (Dr PH); public health (MPH). *Accreditation:* CEPH. *Degree requirements:* For master's, one foreign language, comprehensive exam, thesis. *Entrance requirements:* For master's, GRE General Test or EXADEP, proficiency in Spanish and English, minimum GPA of 2.7, 3 letters of recommendation; for doctorate, GRE, proficiency in Spanish and English, minimum GPA of 3.0, letter of recommendation.

**Purdue University,** School of Veterinary Medicine and Graduate School, Graduate Programs in Veterinary Medicine, Department of Comparative Pathobiology, West Lafayette, IN 47907-2027. Offers comparative epidemiology and public health (MS); comparative epidemiology and public heath (PhD); comparative microbiology and immunology (MS, PhD); comparative pathobiology (MS, PhD); interdisciplinary studies (PhD), including microbial pathogenesis, molecular signaling and cancer biology, molecular virology; lab animal medicine (MS); veterinary anatomic pathology (MS); veterinary clinical pathology (MS). Terminal master's awarded for partial completion of doctoral program. *Degree requirements:* For master's, thesis (for some programs); for doctorate, thesis/dissertation. *Entrance requirements:* For master's and doctorate, GRE General Test. Additional exam requirements/recommendations for international students: required—TOEFL (minimum score 575 paper-based), IELTS (minimum score 6.5), TWE (minimum score 4). Electronic applications accepted.

**Queen's University at Kingston,** School of Graduate Studies, Faculty of Health Sciences, Department of Community Health and Epidemiology, Kingston, ON K7L 3N6, Canada. Offers epidemiology (M Sc, PhD); policy research and clinical epidemiology (M Sc); public health (MPH). *Program availability:* Part-time. *Degree requirements:* For master's, thesis. *Entrance requirements:* For master's, GRE General Test (strongly recommended). Additional exam requirements/recommendations for international students: required—TOEFL (minimum score 600 paper-based).

**Rutgers University - Newark,** School of Public Health, Newark, NJ 07107-1709. Offers clinical epidemiology (Certificate); dental public health (MPH); general public health (Certificate); public policy and oral health services administration (Certificate); quantitative methods (MPH); urban health (MPH); DMD/MPH; MD/MPH; MS/MPH. *Program availability:* Part-time, evening/weekend. *Degree requirements:* For master's, thesis, internship. *Entrance requirements:* For master's, GRE General Test. Additional exam requirements/recommendations for international students: required—TOEFL. Electronic applications accepted.

**Rutgers University - New Brunswick,** School of Public Health, Piscataway, NJ 08854. Offers biostatistics (MPH, MS, Dr PH, PhD); clinical epidemiology (Certificate); environmental and occupational health (MPH, Dr PH, PhD, Certificate); epidemiology (MPH, Dr PH, PhD); general public health (Certificate); health education and behavioral science (MPH, Dr PH, PhD); health systems and policy (MPH, PhD); public health (MPH, Dr PH, PhD); public health preparedness (Certificate); DO/MPH; JD/MPH; MBA/MPH; MD/MPH; MPH/MBA; MPH/MSPA; MS/MPH; Psy D/MPH. *Accreditation:* CEPH. *Program availability:* Part-time, evening/weekend. *Degree requirements:* For master's, thesis, internship; for doctorate, comprehensive exam, thesis/dissertation. *Entrance requirements:* For master's, GRE General Test; for doctorate, GRE General Test, MPH (Dr PH); MA, MPH, or MS (PhD). Additional exam requirements/recommendations for international students: required—TOEFL. Electronic applications accepted.

**San Diego State University,** Graduate and Research Affairs, College of Health and Human Services, School of Public Health, San Diego, CA 92182. Offers environmental health (MPH); epidemiology (MPH, PhD), including biostatistics (MPH); global emergency preparedness and response (MS); global health (PhD); health behavior (PhD); health promotion (MPH); health services administration (MPH); toxicology (MS); MPH/MA; MSW/MPH. *Accreditation:* CAHME (one or more programs are accredited); CEPH. *Program availability:* Part-time. *Degree requirements:* For master's, comprehensive exam (for some programs), thesis (for some programs); for doctorate, thesis/dissertation. *Entrance requirements:* For master's, GMAT (MPH in health services administration), GRE General Test; for doctorate, GRE General Test. Additional exam requirements/recommendations for international students: required—TOEFL.

**Stanford University,** School of Medicine, Graduate Programs in Medicine, Department of Health Research and Policy, Program in Epidemiology and Clinical Research, Stanford, CA 94305-2004. Offers MS, PhD. *Expenses: Tuition:* Full-time $52,479; part-time $34,110 per unit. *Required fees:* $672; $224 per quarter. Tuition and fees vary according to program and student level.
Website: http://med.stanford.edu/epidemiology/

**Temple University,** College of Public Health, Department of Epidemiology and Biostatistics, Philadelphia, PA 19122-6096. Offers applied biostatistics (MPH); environmental health (MPH); epidemiology (MPH, MS, PhD). *Accreditation:* CEPH. *Program availability:* Part-time, evening/weekend, online learning. *Faculty:* 9 full-time (7 women), 5 part-time/adjunct (1 woman). *Students:* 38 full-time (26 women), 28 part-time (16 women); includes 19 minority (9 Black or African American, non-Hispanic/Latino; 1 American Indian or Alaska Native, non-Hispanic/Latino; 3 Asian, non-Hispanic/Latino; 5 Hispanic/Latino; 1 Two or more races, non-Hispanic/Latino), 19 international. 173 applicants, 46% accepted, 19 enrolled. In 2019, 12 master's, 2 doctorates awarded. *Degree requirements:* For doctorate, thesis/dissertation, area paper. *Entrance requirements:* For master's, GRE, statement of goals, resume, clearances for clinical/field education (M.P.H. programs); for doctorate, GRE, writing sample, resume, relevant coursework, statement of goals. Additional exam requirements/recommendations for international students: required—TOEFL (minimum score 79 iBT), IELTS (minimum score 6.5), PTE (minimum score 53), one of three required. Application fee: $50. Electronic applications accepted. *Expenses:* Contact institution. *Financial support:* Fellowships, research assistantships, teaching assistantships, Federal Work-Study, scholarships/grants, and health care benefits available. Financial award applicants required to submit FAFSA. *Unit head:* Resa M Jones, Department Chair and Assistant Professor, 215-204-8726, E-mail: resa.jones@temple.edu. *Application contact:* Tre Grue, Assistant Director of Admissions, 215-204-5806, E-mail: tre@temple.edu.
Website: https://cph.temple.edu/epibio/

**Texas A&M University,** School of Public Health, College Station, TX 77843. Offers biostatistics (MPH, MSPH); environmental health (MPH, MSPH); epidemiology (MPH, MSPH); health administration (MHA); health policy and management (MPH); health services research (PhD); occupational safety and health (MPH). *Accreditation:* CAHME; CEPH. *Program availability:* Part-time, blended/hybrid learning. *Entrance requirements:* For master's, GRE General Test, 3 letters of recommendation; statement of purpose; current curriculum vitae or resume; official transcripts; for doctorate, GRE General Test, 3 letters of recommendation; statement of purpose; current curriculum vitae or resume; official transcripts; interview (in some cases). Additional exam requirements/recommendations for international students: required—TOEFL (minimum score 597 paper-based, 95 iBT) or GRE (minimum verbal score 153). Electronic applications accepted. *Expenses:* Contact institution.

**Tufts University,** Graduate School of Arts and Sciences, Graduate Certificate Programs, Program in Epidemiology, Medford, MA 02155. Offers Certificate. Electronic applications accepted. *Expenses: Tuition:* Part-time $1799 per credit hour. Full-time tuition and fees vary according to degree level, program and student level. Part-time tuition and fees vary according to course load.

**Tufts University,** School of Medicine, Public Health and Professional Degree Programs, Boston, MA 02111. Offers biomedical sciences (MS); health communication (MS, Certificate); pain research, education and policy (MS, Certificate); physician assistant (MS); public health (MPH, Dr PH), including behavioral science (MPH), biostatistics (MPH), epidemiology (MPH), health communication (MPH), health services (MPH), management and policy (MPH), nutrition (MPH); DMD/MPH; DVM/MPH; JD/MPH; MD/MPH; MMS/MPH; MS/MBA; MS/MPH. *Accreditation:* CEPH (one or more programs are accredited). *Program availability:* Part-time, evening/weekend. *Students:* 450 full-time (291 women), 68 part-time (58 women); includes 201 minority (34 Black or African American, non-Hispanic/Latino; 1 American Indian or Alaska Native, non-Hispanic/Latino; 106 Asian, non-Hispanic/Latino; 41 Hispanic/Latino; 1 Native Hawaiian or other Pacific Islander, non-Hispanic/Latino; 18 Two or more races, non-Hispanic/Latino), 16 international. Average age 27. 1,076 applicants, 70% accepted, 213 enrolled. In 2019, 268 master's, 2 doctorates awarded. Terminal master's awarded for partial completion of doctoral program. *Degree requirements:* For master's, thesis (for some programs); for doctorate, thesis/dissertation. *Entrance requirements:* For master's, GRE General Test, MCAT, or GMAT; LSAT for applicants to the JD/MPH combined degree; for doctorate, GRE General Test or MCAT. Additional exam requirements/recommendations for international students: required—TOEFL (minimum score 100 iBT); recommended—IELTS (minimum score 7), TSE. *Application deadline:* For fall admission, 1/15 priority date for domestic and international students; for spring admission, 10/25 priority date for domestic and international students. Applications are processed on a rolling basis. Application fee: $70. Electronic applications accepted. *Expenses:* Contact institution. *Financial support:* In 2019–20, 13 students received support, including 1 fellowship (averaging $3,000 per year), 50 research assistantships (averaging $1,000 per year), 65 teaching assistantships (averaging $2,000 per year); Federal Work-Study and scholarships/grants also available. Financial award application deadline: 2/23; financial award applicants required to submit FAFSA. *Unit head:* Dr. Aviva Must, Dean, 617-636-0935, Fax: 617-636-0898, E-mail: aviva.must@tufts.edu. *Application contact:* Emily Keily, Director of Admissions, 617-636-0935, Fax: 617-636-0898, E-mail: med-phpd@tufts.edu.
Website: http://publichealth.tufts.edu

**Tulane University,** School of Public Health and Tropical Medicine, Department of Epidemiology, New Orleans, LA 70118-5669. Offers MPH, MS, Dr PH, PhD, MD/MPH. *Program availability:* Part-time. *Degree requirements:* For doctorate, comprehensive exam, thesis/dissertation. *Entrance requirements:* For master's and doctorate, GRE General Test. Additional exam requirements/recommendations for international students: required—TOEFL. Electronic applications accepted. *Expenses: Tuition:* Full-time $57,004; part-time $3167 per credit hour. *Required fees:* $2086; $44.50 per credit hour. $80 per term. Tuition and fees vary according to course load, degree level and program.

**University at Albany, State University of New York,** School of Public Health, Department of Epidemiology and Biostatistics, Albany, NY 12222-0001. Offers epidemiology and biostatistics (MS, PhD). *Program availability:* Blended/hybrid learning. *Faculty:* 11 full-time (5 women), 2 part-time/adjunct (1 woman). *Students:* 25 full-time (14 women), 41 part-time (27 women); includes 6 minority (5 Asian, non-Hispanic/Latino; 1 Hispanic/Latino), 25 international. 49 applicants, 53% accepted, 13 enrolled. In 2019, 114 master's, 8 doctorates awarded. *Degree requirements:* For master's, thesis; for doctorate, thesis/dissertation. *Entrance requirements:* For master's, GPA of 3.0 or higher; transcripts of all schools attended; statement of background and goals; departmental questionnaire; tesume; names and contact information for 3 recommenders; for doctorate, GRE General Test. Additional exam requirements/recommendations for international students: required—TOEFL (minimum score 550 paper-based; 98 iBT). *Application deadline:* For fall admission, 6/30 for domestic students, 5/1 for international students; for spring admission, 11/30 for domestic students, 11/1 for international students. Applications are processed on a rolling basis. Application fee: $75. Electronic applications accepted. *Expenses: Tuition, area resident:* Full-time $11,530; part-time $480 per credit hour. Tuition, nonresident: full-time $23,530; part-time $980 per credit hour. *International tuition:* $23,530 full-time. *Required fees:* $2185; $96 per credit hour. Part-time tuition and fees vary according to course load and program. *Financial support:* Application deadline: 4/1. *Unit head:* Dr. Recai Ycel, Chair, 518-402-0372, E-mail: rycel@albany.edu. *Application contact:* Dr. Recai Ycel, Chair, 518-402-0372, E-mail: rycel@albany.edu.
Website: https://www.albany.edu/sph/programs/phd-epidemiology

**University at Buffalo, the State University of New York,** Graduate School, School of Public Health and Health Professions, Department of Epidemiology and Environmental Health, Buffalo, NY 14214. Offers epidemiology (MS, PhD); public health (MPH). *Accreditation:* CEPH. *Program availability:* Part-time. Terminal master's awarded for partial completion of doctoral program. *Entrance requirements:* For master's and doctorate, GRE General Test. Additional exam requirements/recommendations for international students: required—TOEFL (minimum score 600 paper-based; 100 iBT). Electronic applications accepted. *Expenses: Tuition, area resident:* Full-time $11,310; part-time $471 per credit hour. Tuition, state resident: full-time $11,310; part-time $471 per credit hour. Tuition, nonresident: full-time $23,100; part-time $963 per credit hour. *International tuition:* $23,100 full-time. *Required fees:* $2820.

**The University of Alabama at Birmingham,** School of Public Health, Program in Epidemiology, Birmingham, AL 35294. Offers epidemiology (PhD). *Program availability:* Part-time, 100% online, blended/hybrid learning. *Students:* Average age 29. 166 applicants, 66% accepted, 46 enrolled. In 2019, 6 doctorates awarded. *Degree requirements:* For doctorate, comprehensive exam, thesis/dissertation. *Entrance requirements:* For doctorate, GRE General Test, MPH or MSPH. Additional exam requirements/recommendations for international students: required—TOEFL (minimum score 80 iBT), IELTS (minimum score 6.5). *Application deadline:* For fall admission, 4/1 priority date for domestic and international students; for spring admission, 11/1 for domestic students; for summer admission, 4/1 for domestic students. Application fee: $50 ($60 for international students). Electronic applications accepted. *Financial support:* Fellowships, career-related internships or fieldwork, scholarships/grants, and unspecified assistantships available. Financial award application deadline: 3/1; financial award applicants required to submit FAFSA. *Unit head:* Dr. Cora E. Lewis, Graduate Program Director, 205-974-6736, E-mail: celewis@uabmc.edu. *Application contact:* Dustin Shaw, Coordinator, Student Admissions and Records, 205-934-2684, E-mail: dshaw84@uab.edu.
Website: http://www.soph.uab.edu/epi

**The University of Alabama at Birmingham,** School of Public Health, Program in Health Care Organization and Policy, Birmingham, AL 35294. Offers applied epidemiology and pharmacoepidemiology (MSPH); biostatistics (MPH); clinical and translational science (MSPH); environmental health (MPH); environmental health and toxicology (MSPH); epidemiology (MPH); general theory and practice (MPH); health behavior (MPH); health care organization (MPH, Dr PH); health policy (MPH); industrial hygiene (MPH, MSPH); maternal and child health policy (Dr PH); maternal and child health policy and leadership (MPH); occupational health and safety (MPH); outcomes research (MSPH, Dr PH); public health (PhD); public health preparedness management (MPH). *Accreditation:* CEPH. *Program availability:* Part-time, 100% online, blended/hybrid learning. *Faculty:* 14 full-time (6 women). *Students:* 53 full-time (37 women), 61 part-time (45 women); includes 37 minority (12 Black or African American, non-Hispanic/Latino; 20 Asian, non-Hispanic/Latino; 1 Hispanic/Latino; 4 Two or more races, non-Hispanic/Latino), 17 international. Average age 31. 136 applicants, 59% accepted, 44 enrolled. In 2019, 36 master's, 4 doctorates awarded. *Degree requirements:* For master's, comprehensive exam (for some programs), thesis (for some programs); for doctorate, comprehensive exam, thesis/dissertation. *Entrance requirements:* For doctorate, GRE. Additional exam requirements/recommendations for international students: required—TOEFL (minimum score 80 iBT), IELTS (minimum score 6.5). *Application deadline:* For fall admission, 4/1 priority date for domestic students, 4/1 for international students; for spring admission, 11/1 for domestic students; for summer admission, 4/1 for domestic students. Application fee: $50 ($60 for international students). Electronic applications accepted. *Financial support:* Fellowships, research assistantships, teaching assistantships, scholarships/grants, traineeships, and unspecified assistantships available. Financial award application deadline: 3/1; financial award applicants required to submit FAFSA. *Unit head:* Dr. Martha Wingate, Program Director, 205-934-6783, Fax: 205-975-5484, E-mail: mslay@uab.edu. *Application contact:* Dustin Shaw, Coordinator, Student Admissions and Record, 205-934-3939, E-mail: bcampbel@uab.edu.
Website: http://www.soph.uab.edu

**University of Alberta,** School of Public Health, Department of Public Health Sciences, Edmonton, AB T6G 2E1, Canada. Offers clinical epidemiology (M Sc, MPH); environmental and occupational health (MPH); environmental health sciences (M Sc); epidemiology (M Sc); global health (M Sc, MPH); health policy and management (MPH); health policy research (M Sc); health technology assessment (MPH); occupational health (M Sc); population health (M Sc); public health leadership (MPH); public health sciences (PhD); quantitative methods (MPH). *Accreditation:* CEPH. Terminal master's awarded for partial completion of doctoral program. *Degree requirements:* For master's, thesis (for some programs); for doctorate, thesis/dissertation. *Entrance requirements:* For master's, GMAT or GRE General Test. Additional exam requirements/recommendations for international students: required—TOEFL (minimum score 550 paper-based) or IELTS (minimum score 6). Electronic applications accepted.

**The University of Arizona,** Mel and Enid Zuckerman College of Public Health, Program in Epidemiology, Tucson, AZ 85721. Offers MS, PhD. *Entrance requirements:* Additional exam requirements/recommendations for international students: required—TOEFL (minimum score 550 paper-based; 79 iBT). Electronic applications accepted.

**University of Arkansas for Medical Sciences,** Fay W. Boozman College of Public Health, Little Rock, AR 72205-7199. Offers biostatistics (MPH); environmental and occupational health (MPH, Certificate); epidemiology (MPH, PhD); health behavior and health education (MPH); health policy and management (MPH); health promotion and prevention research (PhD); health services administration (MHSA); health systems research (PhD); public health (Certificate); public health leadership (Dr PH). *Accreditation:* CAHME; CEPH. *Program availability:* Part-time. *Degree requirements:* For master's, preceptorship, culminating experience, internship; for doctorate, comprehensive exam, capstone. *Entrance requirements:* For master's, GRE, GMAT, LSAT, PCAT, MCAT, DAT; for doctorate, GRE. Additional exam requirements/recommendations for international students: required—TOEFL (minimum score 80 iBT), IELTS. Electronic applications accepted. *Expenses:* Contact institution.

**University of California, Berkeley,** Graduate Division, School of Public Health, Group in Epidemiology, Berkeley, CA 94720. Offers epidemiology (MS, PhD); infectious diseases (PhD). *Degree requirements:* For master's, comprehensive exam; for doctorate, thesis/dissertation, oral and written exam. *Entrance requirements:* For master's, GRE General Test, minimum GPA of 3.0; MD, DDS, DVM, or PhD in biomedical science (MPH); for doctorate, GRE General Test, minimum GPA of 3.0. Electronic applications accepted.

**University of California, Davis,** Graduate Studies, Graduate Group in Epidemiology, Davis, CA 95616. Offers MS, PhD. Terminal master's awarded for partial completion of doctoral program. *Degree requirements:* For master's, comprehensive exam (for some programs), thesis (for some programs); for doctorate, thesis/dissertation. *Entrance requirements:* For master's and doctorate, GRE General Test, GRE Subject Test (biology), minimum GPA of 3.25. Additional exam requirements/recommendations for international students: required—TOEFL (minimum score 550 paper-based). Electronic applications accepted.

**University of California, Irvine,** School of Medicine, Department of Epidemiology, Irvine, CA 92697. Offers MS, PhD. *Students:* 8 full-time (7 women); includes 4 minority (2 Black or African American, non-Hispanic/Latino; 1 Asian, non-Hispanic/Latino; 1 Hispanic/Latino), 2 international. Average age 29. 27 applicants, 37% accepted, 4 enrolled. In 2019, 5 master's, 2 doctorates awarded. Terminal master's awarded for partial completion of doctoral program. *Degree requirements:* For master's, comprehensive exam, thesis; for doctorate, comprehensive exam, thesis/dissertation, 72 quarter units. *Entrance requirements:* For master's, GRE, minimum GPA of 3.0, letters of recommendation; for doctorate, GRE, minimum GPA of 3.0, personal statement, letters of recommendation. Additional exam requirements/recommendations for international students: required—TOEFL (minimum score 550 paper-based; 80 iBT), IELTS (minimum score 7). *Application deadline:* For fall admission, 1/15 priority date for domestic and international students. Application fee: $120 ($140 for international students). Electronic applications accepted. *Financial support:* In 2019–20, fellowships with full tuition reimbursements (averaging $25,000 per year), research assistantships with full tuition reimbursements (averaging $46,000 per year), teaching assistantships with full tuition reimbursements (averaging $33,000 per year) were awarded; Federal Work-Study, institutionally sponsored loans, scholarships/grants, traineeships, health care benefits, and unspecified assistantships also available. Financial award application deadline: 1/15; financial award applicants required to submit FAFSA. *Unit head:* Dr. Hoda Anton-Culver, Chair, 949-824-7401, Fax: 949-824-4773, E-mail: hantoncu@uci.edu. *Application contact:* Julie Strope, Departmental Administrator, 949-824-0306, Fax: 949-824-4773, E-mail: jstrope@uci.edu.
Website: http://www.epi.uci.edu/

**University of California, Irvine,** School of Social Ecology, Programs in Social Ecology, Irvine, CA 92697. Offers environmental analysis and design (PhD); epidemiology and public health (PhD); social ecology (PhD). *Students:* 19 full-time (15 women); includes 7 minority (3 Black or African American, non-Hispanic/Latino; 1 Asian, non-Hispanic/Latino; 2 Hispanic/Latino; 1 Two or more races, non-Hispanic/Latino), 2 international. Average age 29. 36 applicants, 28% accepted, 6 enrolled. In 2019, 1 doctorate awarded.

Application fee: $120 ($140 for international students). *Unit head:* Tim-Allen Bruckner, Professor, 949-824-5797, Fax: 949-824-1845, E-mail: tim.bruckner@uci.edu. *Application contact:* Jennifer Craig, Director of Graduate Student Services, 949-824-5918, Fax: 949-824-1845, E-mail: craigj@uci.edu.
Website: http://socialecology.uci.edu/core/graduate-se-core-programs

**University of California, Los Angeles,** Graduate Division, Fielding School of Public Health, Department of Epidemiology, Los Angeles, CA 90095. Offers MPH, MS, Dr PH, PhD, MD/MPH. *Accreditation:* CEPH. *Degree requirements:* For master's, comprehensive exam or thesis; for doctorate, thesis/dissertation, oral and written qualifying exams. *Entrance requirements:* For master's, GRE General Test, minimum GPA of 3.0; for doctorate, GRE General Test, minimum undergraduate GPA of 3.0. Electronic applications accepted.

**University of California, San Diego,** Graduate Division, Program in Public Health, La Jolla, CA 92093. Offers epidemiology (PhD); global health (PhD); health behavior (PhD). *Students:* 19 full-time (13 women), 16 part-time (12 women). In 2019, 9 doctorates awarded. *Degree requirements:* For doctorate, thesis/dissertation, 2 semesters/quarters of teaching assistantship. *Entrance requirements:* For doctorate, GRE General Test, minimum GPA of 3.0, curriculum vitae or resume, letters of recommendation, statement of purpose. Additional exam requirements/recommendations for international students: required—TOEFL (minimum score 550 paper-based; 80 iBT), IELTS (minimum score 7). Electronic applications accepted. *Financial support:* Teaching assistantships available. Financial award applicants required to submit FAFSA. *Unit head:* David Strong, Faculty Director, 858-657-5241, E-mail: dstrong@ucsd.edu. *Application contact:* Carrie Goldsmith, Graduate Coordinator, 858-246-5423, E-mail: publichealthjdp@ucsd.edu.
Website: http://publichealth.ucsd.edu/jdp/

**University of Cincinnati,** Graduate School, College of Medicine, Graduate Programs in Biomedical Sciences, Department of Environmental Health, Cincinnati, OH 45221. Offers environmental and industrial hygiene (MS, PhD); environmental and occupational medicine (MS); environmental genetics and molecular toxicology (MS, PhD); epidemiology and biostatistics (MS, PhD); occupational safety and ergonomics (MS, PhD). *Accreditation:* ABET (one or more programs are accredited); CEPH. Terminal master's awarded for partial completion of doctoral program. *Degree requirements:* For master's, thesis; for doctorate, thesis/dissertation, qualifying exam. *Entrance requirements:* For master's, GRE General Test, bachelor's degree in science; for doctorate, GRE General Test. Additional exam requirements/recommendations for international students: required—TOEFL (minimum score 600 paper-based; 100 iBT). Electronic applications accepted.

**University of Colorado Denver,** Colorado School of Public Health, Department of Epidemiology, Aurora, CO 80045. Offers MS, PhD. *Program availability:* Part-time. *Degree requirements:* For master's, thesis, 38 credit hours; for doctorate, comprehensive exam, thesis/dissertation, 67 credit hours. *Entrance requirements:* For master's, GRE General Test, baccalaureate degree in scientific field, minimum GPA of 3.0, math course work through integral calculus, two official copies of all academic transcripts, four letters of recommendation/reference, essays describing the applicant's career goals and reasons for applying to the program, resume; for doctorate, GRE or MCAT, bachelor's, master's, or higher degree; minimum undergraduate and graduate GPA of 3.0; coursework in calculus, organic chemistry, epidemiology, biological sciences, and public health; 2 official copies of all academic transcripts; 4 letters of reference; essays. Additional exam requirements/recommendations for international students: required—TOEFL (minimum score 550 paper-based; 80 iBT). Electronic applications accepted. Tuition and fees vary according to course load, program and reciprocity agreements.

**University of Florida,** College of Medicine, Program in Clinical Investigation, Gainesville, FL 32611. Offers clinical investigation (MS); epidemiology (MS); public health (MPH). *Program availability:* Part-time. *Entrance requirements:* For master's, GRE, MD, PhD, DMD/DDS or Pharm D.

**University of Florida,** Graduate School, College of Public Health and Health Professions, Department of Epidemiology, Gainesville, FL 32611. Offers clinical and translational science (PhD); epidemiology (MS, PhD). *Degree requirements:* For master's, thesis; for doctorate, thesis/dissertation. *Entrance requirements:* For master's and doctorate, GRE (minimum score verbal/quantitative combined 300), minimum GPA of 3.0. Additional exam requirements/recommendations for international students: required—TOEFL (minimum score 550 paper-based; 80 iBT), IELTS (minimum score 6).

**University of Florida,** Graduate School, College of Public Health and Health Professions, Programs in Public Health, Gainesville, FL 32611. Offers biostatistics (MPH); clinical and translational science (PhD); environmental health (MPH); epidemiology (MPH); health management and policy (MPH); public health (MPH, PhD, Certificate); public health practice (MPH); rehabilitation science (PhD); social and behavioral sciences (MPH); DPT/MPH; DVM/MPH; JD/MPH; MD/MPH; Pharm D/MPH. *Accreditation:* CEPH. *Program availability:* Online learning. *Degree requirements:* For master's, internship. *Entrance requirements:* For master's, GRE General Test, minimum GPA of 3.0. Additional exam requirements/recommendations for international students: required—TOEFL (minimum score 550 paper-based; 80 iBT), IELTS (minimum score 6).

**University of Guelph,** Ontario Veterinary College and Office of Graduate and Postdoctoral Studies, Graduate Programs in Veterinary Sciences, Department of Population Medicine, Guelph, ON N1G 2W1, Canada. Offers epidemiology (M Sc, DV Sc, PhD); health management (DV Sc); population medicine and health management (M Sc); swine health management (M Sc); theriogenology (M Sc, DV Sc). *Degree requirements:* For master's, thesis; for doctorate, comprehensive exam, thesis/dissertation. *Entrance requirements:* Additional exam requirements/recommendations for international students: required—TOEFL.

**University of Hawaii at Manoa,** John A. Burns School of Medicine, Department of Public Health Sciences and Epidemiology, Program in Epidemiology, Honolulu, HI 96822. Offers PhD. *Program availability:* Part-time. *Degree requirements:* For doctorate, comprehensive exam, thesis/dissertation. *Entrance requirements:* For doctorate, GRE General Test. Additional exam requirements/recommendations for international students: required—TOEFL (minimum score 600 paper-based; 100 iBT), IELTS (minimum score 7).

**University of Illinois at Chicago,** School of Public Health, Epidemiology and Biostatistics Division, Chicago, IL 60607-7128. Offers biostatistics (MPH, MS, PhD); epidemiology (MPH, MS, PhD). *Program availability:* Part-time. Terminal master's awarded for partial completion of doctoral program. *Degree requirements:* For master's, thesis, field practicum; for doctorate, thesis/dissertation, independent research, internship. *Entrance requirements:* For master's and doctorate, GRE General Test, minimum GPA of 2.75. Additional exam requirements/recommendations for international students: required—TOEFL. Electronic applications accepted. *Expenses:* Contact institution.

**University of Illinois at Springfield,** Graduate Programs, College of Public Affairs and Administration, Program in Public Health, Springfield, IL 62703-5407. Offers community health education (Graduate Certificate); emergency preparedness and homeland security (Graduate Certificate); environmental health (MPH, Graduate Certificate);

environmental risk assessment (Graduate Certificate); epidemiology (Graduate Certificate); public health (MPH). *Program availability:* Part-time, 100% online. *Faculty:* 7 full-time (5 women). *Students:* 31 full-time (24 women), 36 part-time (27 women); includes 13 minority (9 Black or African American, non-Hispanic/Latino; 1 Asian, non-Hispanic/Latino; 1 Hispanic/Latino; 2 Two or more races, non-Hispanic/Latino), 27 international. Average age 30. 90 applicants, 54% accepted, 12 enrolled. In 2019, 13 master's, 10 other advanced degrees awarded. *Degree requirements:* For master's, comprehensive exam, internship. *Entrance requirements:* For master's, GRE, minimum undergraduate GPA of 3.0, 3 letters of recommendation, essay addressing the areas outlined on the department application form. Additional exam requirements/recommendations for international students: required—TOEFL (minimum score 500 paper-based; 61 iBT). *Application deadline:* Applications are processed on a rolling basis. Application fee: $60 ($75 for international students). Electronic applications accepted. *Expenses:* $33.25 per credit hour (online fee). *Financial support:* In 2019–20, research assistantships with full tuition reimbursements (averaging $10,562 per year), teaching assistantships with full tuition reimbursements (averaging $10,652 per year) were awarded; fellowships, career-related internships or fieldwork, Federal Work-Study, scholarships/grants, health care benefits, and unspecified assistantships also available. Support available to part-time students. Financial award application deadline: 11/15; financial award applicants required to submit FAFSA. *Unit head:* Dr. Josiah Alamu, Program Administrator, 217-206-7874, Fax: 217-206-7279, E-mail: jalam3@uis.edu. *Application contact:* Dr. Josiah Alamu, Program Administrator, 217-206-7874, Fax: 217-206-7279, E-mail: jalam3@uis.edu.
Website: http://www.uis.edu/publichealth/

**The University of Iowa,** Graduate College, College of Public Health, Department of Epidemiology, Iowa City, IA 52242-1316. Offers clinical investigation (MS); epidemiology (MPH, MS, PhD). *Degree requirements:* For master's, thesis optional, exam; for doctorate, comprehensive exam, thesis/dissertation. *Entrance requirements:* For master's and doctorate, GRE General Test, minimum GPA of 3.0. Additional exam requirements/recommendations for international students: required—TOEFL (minimum score 600 paper-based; 100 iBT). Electronic applications accepted.

**The University of Kansas,** University of Kansas Medical Center, School of Medicine, Department of Population Health, Kansas City, KS 66160. Offers clinical research (MS); epidemiology (MPH); public health management (MPH); social and behavioral health (MPH); MD/MPH; PhD/MPH. *Accreditation:* CEPH. *Program availability:* Part-time. *Faculty:* 100. *Students:* 73 full-time (54 women), 49 part-time (35 women); includes 37 minority (9 Black or African American, non-Hispanic/Latino; 3 American Indian or Alaska Native, non-Hispanic/Latino; 9 Asian, non-Hispanic/Latino; 11 Hispanic/Latino; 5 Two or more races, non-Hispanic/Latino), 5 international. Average age 30. In 2019, 52 master's awarded. *Degree requirements:* For master's, thesis, capstone practicum defense. *Entrance requirements:* For master's, GRE for MHSA Program; GRE for MPH Program; GRE, MCAT, LSAT, GMAT or other equivalent graduate professional exam for MS Clinical Research Program. Additional exam requirements/recommendations for international students: required—TOEFL. *Application deadline:* For fall admission, 3/1 for domestic and international students; for spring admission, 11/1 for domestic and international students. Applications are processed on a rolling basis. Application fee: $60. Electronic applications accepted. *Expenses:* Tuition, state resident: full-time $9989. Tuition, nonresident: full-time $23,950. *International tuition:* $23,950 full-time. *Required fees:* $984; $81.99 per credit hour. Tuition and fees vary according to course load, campus/location and program. *Financial support:* Research assistantships, career-related internships or fieldwork, Federal Work-Study, scholarships/grants, and unspecified assistantships available. Support available to part-time students. Financial award application deadline: 3/1; financial award applicants required to submit FAFSA. *Unit head:* Dr. Edward F. Ellerbeck, Professor and Chair, 913-588-2775, Fax: 913-588-2780, E-mail: eellerbe@kumc.edu. *Application contact:* Dr. Edward F. Ellerbeck, Professor and Chair, 913-588-2775, Fax: 913-588-2780, E-mail: eellerbe@kumc.edu.
Website: http://www.kumc.edu/school-of-medicine/population-health.html

**University of Kentucky,** Graduate School, College of Public Health, Program in Epidemiology and Biostatistics, Lexington, KY 40506-0032. Offers PhD.

**University of Louisville,** Graduate School, School of Public Health and Information Sciences, Department of Epidemiology and Population Health, Louisville, KY 40292-0001. Offers epidemiology (MPH, MS); public health sciences (PhD), including epidemiology. *Faculty:* 7 full-time (5 women). *Students:* 1 (woman) full-time, 29 part-time (23 women); includes 5 minority (1 Black or African American, non-Hispanic/Latino; 1 Asian, non-Hispanic/Latino; 1 Hispanic/Latino; 2 Two or more races, non-Hispanic/Latino), 5 international. Average age 36. 13 applicants, 92% accepted, 8 enrolled. In 2019, 8 master's awarded. *Degree requirements:* For master's, thesis; for doctorate, thesis/dissertation. *Entrance requirements:* For master's, GRE (taken within past 5 years), bachelor's degree from an accredited institution or its equivalent, recommended minimum GPA of 3.0 on a 4.0 scale, 2 letters of recommendation written within the last twelve months, official transcripts of all degrees, one-page personal statement. Additional exam requirements/recommendations for international students: required—TOEFL (minimum score 90 iBT). *Application deadline:* For fall admission, 4/1 for domestic students, 1/2 priority date for international students. Applications are processed on a rolling basis. Application fee: $65. Electronic applications accepted. *Expenses: Tuition, area resident:* Full-time $13,000; part-time $723 per credit hour. Tuition, state resident: full-time $13,000; part-time $723 per credit hour. Tuition, nonresident: full-time $27,114; part-time $1507 per credit hour. *International tuition:* $27,114 full-time. *Required fees:* $196. Tuition and fees vary according to program and reciprocity agreements. *Financial support:* In 2019–20, 29 students received support, including 1 fellowship with full tuition reimbursement available (averaging $20,000 per year), 3 research assistantships with full tuition reimbursements available (averaging $20,000 per year); tuition waivers (partial) also available. Financial award application deadline: 3/1; financial award applicants required to submit FAFSA. *Unit head:* Dr. Richard N Baumgartner, PhD, Professor and Chair, 502-852-3003, Fax: 502-852-3291, E-mail: rnbaum01@gwise.louisville.edu. *Application contact:* Robin Newlon, Administrative Specialist, 502-852-3003, Fax: 502-852-3294, E-mail: robin.newlon@louisville.edu.
Website: http://louisville.edu/sphis/departments/epidemiology-population-health

**University of Maryland, Baltimore,** Graduate School, Graduate Program in Life Sciences, Baltimore, MD 21201. Offers biochemistry and molecular biology (MS, PhD), including biochemistry; cellular and molecular biomedical science (MS); clinical research (Postbaccalaureate Certificate); epidemiology (PhD); gerontology (PhD); molecular medicine (PhD), including applied pharmacology and toxicology, cancer biology, genome biology, molecular and cellular physiology; molecular microbiology and immunology (PhD); neuroscience (PhD); physical rehabilitation science (PhD); toxicology (MS, PhD); MD/MS; MD/PhD. *Degree requirements:* For master's, comprehensive exam (for some programs), thesis (for some programs); for doctorate, comprehensive exam, thesis/dissertation. *Entrance requirements:* For master's and doctorate, GRE. Additional exam requirements/recommendations for international students: required—TOEFL (minimum score 80 iBT); recommended—IELTS (minimum score 7). Electronic applications accepted.

**University of Maryland, Baltimore,** Graduate School, Graduate Programs in Pharmacy, Department of Pharmaceutical Health Service Research, Baltimore, MD 21201. Offers epidemiology (MS); pharmacy administration (PhD); Pharm D/PhD. *Degree requirements:* For doctorate, comprehensive exam, thesis/dissertation. *Entrance requirements:* For doctorate, GRE General Test. Additional exam requirements/recommendations for international students: required—TOEFL, IELTS. Electronic applications accepted.

**University of Maryland, Baltimore,** School of Medicine, Department of Epidemiology and Public Health, Baltimore, MD 21201. Offers biostatistics (MS); clinical research (MS); epidemiology and preventive medicine (MPH, MS, PhD); gerontology (PhD); human genetics and genomic medicine (MS, PhD); molecular epidemiology (MS, PhD); toxicology (MS, PhD); JD/MS; MD/PhD; MS/PhD. *Accreditation:* CEPH. *Program availability:* Part-time. *Students:* 75 full-time (51 women), 32 part-time (28 women); includes 29 minority (11 Black or African American, non-Hispanic/Latino; 11 Asian, non-Hispanic/Latino; 5 Hispanic/Latino; 2 Two or more races, non-Hispanic/Latino), 24 international. Average age 31. In 2019, 27 master's, 9 doctorates awarded. *Degree requirements:* For doctorate, comprehensive exam, thesis/dissertation. *Entrance requirements:* For master's and doctorate, GRE General Test. Additional exam requirements/recommendations for international students: required—TOEFL (minimum score 550 paper-based; 80 iBT); recommended—IELTS (minimum score 7). *Application deadline:* For fall admission, 1/15 for domestic and international students. Application fee: $75. Electronic applications accepted. *Expenses:* Contact institution. *Financial support:* In 2019–20, research assistantships with partial tuition reimbursements (averaging $26,000 per year) were awarded; fellowships, Federal Work-Study, scholarships/grants, and unspecified assistantships also available. Financial award application deadline: 3/1; financial award applicants required to submit FAFSA. *Unit head:* Dr. Laura Hungerford, Program Director, 410-706-8492, Fax: 410-706-4225. *Application contact:* Jessica Kelley, Program Coordinator, 410-706-8492, Fax: 410-706-4225, E-mail: jkelley@som.umaryland.edu.
Website: http://lifesciences.umaryland.edu/epidemiology/

**University of Maryland, Baltimore County,** The Graduate School, College of Arts, Humanities and Social Sciences, Department of Emergency Health Services, Baltimore, MD 21250. Offers emergency health services (MS), including administration, planning, and policy, preventive medicine and epidemiology; emergency management (Postbaccalaureate Certificate); public policy (PhD), including emergency health, emergency management. *Program availability:* Part-time, evening/weekend, 100% online, blended/hybrid learning. *Faculty:* 4 full-time (2 women), 8 part-time/adjunct (3 women). *Students:* 5 full-time (4 women), 9 part-time (5 women); includes 5 minority (2 Black or African American, non-Hispanic/Latino; 1 Asian, non-Hispanic/Latino; 2 Hispanic/Latino), 2 international. Average age 37. 19 applicants, 68% accepted, 3 enrolled. In 2019, 5 master's, 2 other advanced degrees awarded. Terminal master's awarded for partial completion of doctoral program. *Degree requirements:* For master's, comprehensive exam (for some programs), capstone project or thesis. *Entrance requirements:* For master's, GRE General Test if GPA is below 3.2, minimum GPA of 3.2. Additional exam requirements/recommendations for international students: required—TOEFL (minimum score 80 iBT), IELTS, or PTE. *Application deadline:* For fall admission, 6/15 for domestic students, 3/1 for international students; for spring admission, 12/1 for domestic students, 10/1 for international students. Applications are processed on a rolling basis. Application fee: $50. Electronic applications accepted. *Expenses:* $14,382 per year. *Financial support:* In 2019–20, 1 student received support, including 1 research assistantship with full tuition reimbursement available (averaging $16,875 per year); career-related internships or fieldwork, Federal Work-Study, health care benefits, and unspecified assistantships also available. Financial award application deadline: 5/30; financial award applicants required to submit FAFSA. *Unit head:* Dr. J. Lee Jenkins, Department Chair, 410-455-3216, Fax: 410-455-3045, E-mail: jleejenkins@umbc.edu. *Application contact:* Dr. Rick Bissell, Program Director, 410-455-3776, Fax: 410-455-3045, E-mail: bissell@umbc.edu.
Website: http://ehs.umbc.edu/

**University of Maryland, College Park,** Academic Affairs, School of Public Health, Department of Epidemiology and Biostatistics, College Park, MD 20742. Offers biostatistics (MPH); epidemiology (MPH, PhD).

**University of Massachusetts Amherst,** Graduate School, School of Public Health and Health Sciences, Department of Public Health, Amherst, MA 01003. Offers biostatistics (MPH, MS, PhD); community health education (MPH, MS, PhD); environmental health sciences (MPH, MS, PhD); epidemiology (MPH, MS, PhD); health policy and management (MPH, MS, PhD); nutrition (MPH, PhD); public health practice (MPH); MPH/MPPA. *Accreditation:* CEPH. *Program availability:* Part-time, evening/weekend, online learning. Terminal master's awarded for partial completion of doctoral program. *Degree requirements:* For master's, thesis (for some programs); for doctorate, comprehensive exam, thesis/dissertation. *Entrance requirements:* For master's and doctorate, GRE General Test. Additional exam requirements/recommendations for international students: required—TOEFL (minimum score 550 paper-based; 80 iBT), IELTS (minimum score 6.5). Electronic applications accepted.

**University of Memphis,** Graduate School, School of Public Health, Memphis, TN 38152. Offers biostatistics (MPH); environmental health (MPH); epidemiology (MPH, PhD); health systems and policy (PhD); health systems management (MPH); public health (MHA); social and behavioral sciences (MPH, PhD). *Accreditation:* CAHME; CEPH. *Program availability:* Part-time, evening/weekend, online learning. *Faculty:* 20 full-time (7 women), 10 part-time/adjunct (4 women). *Students:* 126 full-time (80 women), 77 part-time (60 women); includes 70 minority (40 Black or African American, non-Hispanic/Latino; 17 Asian, non-Hispanic/Latino; 9 Hispanic/Latino; 4 Two or more races, non-Hispanic/Latino), 29 international. Average age 30. 105 applicants, 97% accepted, 67 enrolled. In 2019, 47 master's, 9 doctorates awarded. *Degree requirements:* For master's, comprehensive exam, thesis (for some programs), practicum/field experience; for doctorate, comprehensive exam, thesis/dissertation, residency. *Entrance requirements:* For master's, GRE or GMAT, letters of recommendation; letter of intent; for doctorate, GRE, letters of recommendation; personal statement. Additional exam requirements/recommendations for international students: required—TOEFL (minimum score 550 paper-based; 79 iBT). *Application deadline:* For fall admission, 4/1 for domestic students; for spring admission, 11/1 for domestic students. Application fee: $35 ($60 for international students). Electronic applications accepted. *Expenses: Tuition, area resident:* Full-time $9216; part-time $512 per credit hour. Tuition, state resident: full-time $9216; part-time $512 per credit hour. Tuition, nonresident: full-time $12,672; part-time $704 per credit hour. *International tuition:* $16,128 full-time. *Required fees:* $1530; $85 per credit hour. Tuition and fees vary according to program. *Financial support:* Research assistantships with full tuition reimbursements, Federal Work-Study, scholarships/grants, and unspecified assistantships available. Financial award application deadline: 2/1; financial award applicants required to submit FAFSA. *Unit head:* Dr. James Gurney, Dean, 901-678-1673, E-mail: jggurney@memphis.edu. *Application contact:* Dr. Marian Levy, Associate Dean, 901-678-4514, E-mail: mlevy@memphis.edu.
Website: http://www.memphis.edu/sph/

**University of Miami,** Graduate School, Miller School of Medicine, Graduate Programs in Medicine, Department of Public Health Sciences, Miami, FL 33124. Offers biostatistics (MS, PhD); climate and health (MS); epidemiology (PhD); epidemiology, biostatistics, prevention science and community health (MD/PhD); generalist (MPH, MSPH); prevention science and community health (MS, PhD); JD/MPH; MD/MPH; MD/PhD; MPA/MPH; MPH/MAIA. *Accreditation:* CEPH (one or more programs are accredited). *Faculty:* 35 full-time (15 women), 24 part-time/adjunct (14 women). *Students:* 328 full-time (216 women), 30 part-time (25 women); includes 169 minority (35 Black or African American, non-Hispanic/Latino; 1 American Indian or Alaska Native, non-Hispanic/Latino; 40 Asian, non-Hispanic/Latino; 68 Hispanic/Latino; 7 Native Hawaiian or other Pacific Islander, non-Hispanic/Latino; 18 Two or more races, non-Hispanic/Latino), 41 international. In 2019, 109 master's, 9 doctorates awarded. *Degree requirements:* For master's, thesis (for some programs), project, practicum; for doctorate, comprehensive exam, thesis/dissertation. *Entrance requirements:* For master's, GRE General Test, MCAT, LSAT (for joint MPH/JD applicants), minimum GPA of 3.0, official transcripts, statement of purpose, 3 letters of recommendation, resume/CV; for doctorate, GRE General Test, minimum GPA of 3.0, pre-requisite coursework, 3 letters of recommendation, official transcripts, resume/CV. Additional exam requirements/recommendations for international students: required—TOEFL (minimum score 550 paper-based; 80 iBT). Application fee: $135. Electronic applications accepted. *Unit head:* Dr. David Lee, Chair, E-mail: dlee@med.miami.edu. *Application contact:* Andria Williams, Director of Admissions, 305-243-0291, E-mail: alw157@med.miami.edu.
Website: https://www.publichealth.med.miami.edu/

**University of Michigan,** School of Public Health, Department of Epidemiology, Ann Arbor, MI 48109-2029. Offers epidemiological science (PhD); general epidemiology (MPH); global health epidemiology (MPH); hospital and molecular epidemiology (MPH); occupational and environmental epidemiology (MPH). *Accreditation:* CEPH (one or more programs are accredited). Terminal master's awarded for partial completion of doctoral program. *Degree requirements:* For master's, thesis (for some programs); for doctorate, comprehensive exam, thesis/dissertation, oral defense of dissertation, preliminary exam. *Entrance requirements:* For master's and doctorate, GRE General Test, MCAT. Additional exam requirements/recommendations for international students: required—TOEFL (minimum score 100 iBT). Electronic applications accepted.

**University of Minnesota, Twin Cities Campus,** School of Public Health, Division of Environmental Health Sciences, Area in Environmental and Occupational Epidemiology, Minneapolis, MN 55455-0213. Offers MPH, MS, PhD. *Accreditation:* CEPH (one or more programs are accredited). *Degree requirements:* For doctorate, thesis/dissertation. *Entrance requirements:* For master's and doctorate, GRE General Test. Electronic applications accepted.

**University of Minnesota, Twin Cities Campus,** School of Public Health, Major in Epidemiology, Minneapolis, MN 55455-0213. Offers MPH, PhD. *Accreditation:* CEPH (one or more programs are accredited). *Program availability:* Part-time. Terminal master's awarded for partial completion of doctoral program. *Degree requirements:* For master's, fieldwork, project; for doctorate, comprehensive exam, thesis/dissertation. *Entrance requirements:* For master's, GRE General Test; for doctorate, GRE General Test, master's degree in related field. Additional exam requirements/recommendations for international students: required—TOEFL. Electronic applications accepted. *Expenses:* Contact institution.

**University of Nebraska Medical Center,** Department of Epidemiology, Omaha, NE 68198-4395. Offers PhD. *Program availability:* Part-time. *Degree requirements:* For doctorate, comprehensive exam, thesis/dissertation. *Entrance requirements:* For doctorate, GRE, master's degree in epidemiology or related field. Additional exam requirements/recommendations for international students: required—TOEFL (minimum score 550 paper-based; 80 iBT). Electronic applications accepted.

**University of New Mexico,** Graduate Studies, Health Sciences Center, Program in Public Health, Albuquerque, NM 87131-5196. Offers community health (MPH); epidemiology (MPH); health systems, services and policy (MPH). *Accreditation:* CEPH. *Program availability:* Part-time, online learning. *Entrance requirements:* For master's, GRE, MCAT, 2 years of experience in health field. Additional exam requirements/recommendations for international students: required—TOEFL. *Expenses:* Tuition, state resident: full-time $7633; part-time $972 per year. Tuition, nonresident: full-time $22,586; part-time $3840 per year. International tuition: $23,292 full-time. *Required fees:* $8608. Tuition and fees vary according to course level, course load, degree level, program and student level.

**The University of North Carolina at Chapel Hill,** Graduate School, Gillings School of Global Public Health, Department of Epidemiology, Chapel Hill, NC 27599. Offers clinical research (MSCR); epidemiology (MPH, PhD); veterinary epidemiology (MPH); Pharm D/MPH. *Faculty:* 54 full-time (34 women), 81 part-time/adjunct (42 women). *Students:* 160 full-time (121 women), 20 part-time (9 women); includes 61 minority (17 Black or African American, non-Hispanic/Latino; 26 Asian, non-Hispanic/Latino; 9 Hispanic/Latino; 9 Two or more races, non-Hispanic/Latino), 23 international. Average age 30. 232 applicants, 28% accepted, 34 enrolled. In 2019, 21 master's, 31 doctorates awarded. Terminal master's awarded for partial completion of doctoral program. *Degree requirements:* For master's, comprehensive exam, major paper; for doctorate, comprehensive exam, thesis/dissertation. *Entrance requirements:* For master's, GRE General Test or MCAT, doctoral degree (completed or in-progress); for doctorate, GRE General Test, strong quantitative and biological preparation, 3 letters of recommendation (academic and/or professional). Additional exam requirements/recommendations for international students: required—TOEFL (minimum score 90 iBT), IELTS (minimum score 7). *Application deadline:* For fall admission, 12/11 for domestic and international students. Application fee: $90. Electronic applications accepted. *Financial support:* Fellowships with tuition reimbursements, research assistantships with tuition reimbursements, teaching assistantships with tuition reimbursements, career-related internships or fieldwork, Federal Work-Study, institutionally sponsored loans, scholarships/grants, traineeships, health care benefits, and unspecified assistantships available. Support available to part-time students. Financial award application deadline: 12/10; financial award applicants required to submit FAFSA. *Unit head:* Dr. Til Sturmer, Chair, 919-966-7433, Fax: 919-966-2089, E-mail: sturmer@unc.edu. *Application contact:* Valerie Hudock, Academic Coordinator, 919-966-7459, E-mail: vhudock@email.unc.edu.
Website: https://sph.unc.edu/epid/epidemiology-landing/

**The University of North Carolina at Chapel Hill,** School of Dentistry and Graduate School, Graduate Programs in Dentistry, Chapel Hill, NC 27599. Offers dental hygiene (MS); endodontics (MS); epidemiology (PhD); operative dentistry (MS); oral and maxillofacial pathology (MS); oral and maxillofacial radiology (MS); oral biology (PhD); orthodontics (MS); pediatric dentistry (MS); periodontology (MS); prosthodontics (MS). *Degree requirements:* For master's, thesis; for doctorate, thesis/dissertation. *Entrance requirements:* For master's, GRE General Test (for orthodontics and oral biology only); National Dental Board Part I (Part II if available), dental degree (for all except dental hygiene); for doctorate, GRE General Test. Additional exam requirements/recommendations for international students: required—TOEFL (minimum score 550 paper-based; 79 iBT). Electronic applications accepted. *Expenses:* Contact institution.

**University of North Texas Health Science Center at Fort Worth,** School of Public Health, Fort Worth, TX 76107-2699. Offers biostatistics (MS); epidemiology (MPH, MS, PhD); food security and public health (Graduate Certificate); GIS in public health (Graduate Certificate); global health (Graduate Certificate); global health for medical professionals (Graduate Certificate); health administration (MHA); health behavior research (MS, PhD); maternal and child health (MPH); public health (Graduate Certificate); public health practice (MPH); DO/MPH; MS/MPH. *Accreditation:* CAHME; CEPH. *Program availability:* Part-time, evening/weekend, 100% online. *Degree requirements:* For master's, thesis or alternative, supervised internship; for doctorate, thesis/dissertation, supervised internship. *Entrance requirements:* For master's, GRE General Test. Additional exam requirements/recommendations for international students: required—TOEFL. Electronic applications accepted. *Expenses:* Contact institution.

**University of Oklahoma Health Sciences Center,** Graduate College, Hudson College of Public Health, Department of Biostatistics and Epidemiology, Oklahoma City, OK 73190. Offers biostatistics (MPH, MS, Dr PH, PhD); epidemiology (MPH, MS, Dr PH, PhD). *Accreditation:* CEPH (one or more programs are accredited). *Program availability:* Part-time. *Degree requirements:* For master's, comprehensive exam, thesis (for some programs); for doctorate, comprehensive exam, thesis/dissertation. *Entrance requirements:* For master's, 3 letters of recommendation, resume; for doctorate, GRE General Test, letters of recommendation. Additional exam requirements/recommendations for international students: required—TOEFL (minimum score 570 paper-based), TWE.

**University of Ottawa,** Faculty of Graduate and Postdoctoral Studies, Faculty of Medicine, Department of Epidemiology and Community Medicine, Ottawa, ON K1N 6N5, Canada. Offers epidemiology (M Sc), including health technology assessment. *Degree requirements:* For master's, thesis. *Entrance requirements:* For master's, honors degree or equivalent, minimum B average. Electronic applications accepted.

**University of Pennsylvania,** Perelman School of Medicine, Center for Clinical Epidemiology and Biostatistics, Philadelphia, PA 19104. Offers clinical epidemiology (MSCE), including bioethics, clinical trials, human genetics, patient centered outcome research, pharmacoepidemiology. *Program availability:* Part-time. *Faculty:* 102 full-time (49 women), 39 part-time/adjunct (25 women). *Students:* 92 full-time (59 women), 2 part-time (1 woman); includes 42 minority (15 Black or African American, non-Hispanic/Latino; 21 Asian, non-Hispanic/Latino; 5 Hispanic/Latino; 1 Two or more races, non-Hispanic/Latino). Average age 35. 40 applicants, 90% accepted, 31 enrolled. In 2019, 27 master's awarded. *Degree requirements:* For master's, comprehensive exam, thesis. *Entrance requirements:* For master's, GRE or MCAT, advanced degree in medicine or another health field, clinical experience (MD, DO,PharmD, DMD, DDS, VMD). Additional exam requirements/recommendations for international students: required—TOEFL. *Application deadline:* For fall admission, 12/1 priority date for domestic students, 12/1 for international students. Electronic applications accepted. *Expenses:* Contact institution. *Financial support:* In 2019–20, 50 students received support, including 50 fellowships with tuition reimbursements available (averaging $57,000 per year); research assistantships, teaching assistantships, and tuition waivers also available. Financial award application deadline: 12/1. *Unit head:* Dr. Harold Feldman, Director, 215-573-0901. *Application contact:* Jennifer Kuklinski, Program Coordinator, 215-573-2382, E-mail: jkuklins@pennmedicine.upenn.edu.
Website: http://www.cceb.med.upenn.edu/

**University of Pittsburgh,** Graduate School of Public Health, Department of Epidemiology, Pittsburgh, PA 15261. Offers epidemiology (MPH, MS, PhD); theory and research methods (Dr PH); MD/PhD. *Accreditation:* CEPH (one or more programs are accredited). *Faculty:* 40 full-time (25 women), 2 part-time/adjunct (1 woman). *Students:* 85 full-time (64 women), 84 part-time (21 women); includes 26 minority (4 Black or African American, non-Hispanic/Latino; 8 Asian, non-Hispanic/Latino; 8 Hispanic/Latino; 6 Two or more races, non-Hispanic/Latino), 23 international. Average age 28. 414 applicants, 50% accepted, 38 enrolled. In 2019, 34 master's, 9 doctorates awarded. Terminal master's awarded for partial completion of doctoral program. *Degree requirements:* For master's, comprehensive exam (for some programs), thesis (for some programs); for doctorate, comprehensive exam, thesis/dissertation. *Entrance requirements:* For master's, 3 credits Human Biology, 3 credits Algebra or higher math. Applicants must possess a U.S. bachelor's degree from an accredited institution or the equivalent degree from a foreign school and substantial knowledge in a discipline relevant to public health, either through study, experience, or both; for doctorate, 3 credits Human Biology, 3 credits Algebra or higher math. Prospective students must also possess a U.S. graduate or bachelor's degree, or the equivalent degree from a foreign school, in a field relevant to the PhD program to which they are applying, and must have had sufficient prerequisite courses in the field to which they are applying. Additional exam requirements/recommendations for international students: required—TOEFL (minimum score 90 iBT), IELTS (minimum score 7), TOEFL or IELTS, WES evaluation for foreign education. *Application deadline:* For fall admission, 1/15 for domestic and international students. Applications are processed on a rolling basis. Application fee: $135. Electronic applications accepted. *Expenses:* $13,379 per term full-time resident, $23,407 per term full-time non-resident, $1122 per credit part-time resident, $1916 per credit part-time non-resident, $500 per term for full-time dissertation research, $475 per term full-time fees, $295 per term part-time fees. *Financial support:* In 2019–20, 22 research assistantships with full tuition reimbursements (averaging $24,000 per year), 2 teaching assistantships with full tuition reimbursements (averaging $29,000 per year) were awarded; career-related internships or fieldwork, institutionally sponsored loans, scholarships/grants, traineeships, and health care benefits also available. Support available to part-time students. Financial award applicants required to submit FAFSA. *Unit head:* Dr. Anne B. Newman, Chair, 412-624-3056, Fax: 412-624-3737, E-mail: newmana@edc.pitt.edu. *Application contact:* Lori Sarracino Smith, Student Services Manager/Program Administrator, 412-383-5269, Fax: 412-383-5325, E-mail: smithl@edc.pitt.edu.
Website: http://www.epidemiology.pitt.edu/

**University of Prince Edward Island,** Atlantic Veterinary College, Graduate Program in Veterinary Medicine, Charlottetown, PE C1A 4P3, Canada. Offers anatomy (M Sc, PhD); bacteriology (M Sc, PhD); clinical pharmacology (M Sc, PhD); clinical sciences (M Sc, PhD); epidemiology (M Sc, PhD), including reproduction; fish health (M Sc, PhD); food animal nutrition (M Sc, PhD); immunology (M Sc, PhD); microanatomy (M Sc, PhD); parasitology (M Sc, PhD); pathology (M Sc, PhD); pharmacology (M Sc, PhD); physiology (M Sc, PhD); toxicology (M Sc, PhD); veterinary science (M Vet Sc); virology (M Sc, PhD). *Program availability:* Part-time. *Degree requirements:* For master's, thesis; for doctorate, thesis/dissertation. *Entrance requirements:* For master's, DVM, B Sc honors degree, or equivalent; for doctorate, M Sc. Additional exam requirements/recommendations for international students: required—TOEFL (minimum score 550 paper-based; 80 iBT). *Expenses:* Contact institution.

**University of Puerto Rico - Medical Sciences Campus,** Graduate School of Public Health, Department of Social Sciences, Program in Epidemiology, San Juan, PR 00936-5067. Offers MPH, MS. *Accreditation:* CEPH (one or more programs are accredited). *Program availability:* Part-time. *Entrance requirements:* For master's, GRE, previous

course work in biology, chemistry, physics, mathematics, and social sciences. *Expenses:* Contact institution.

**University of Rochester,** School of Medicine and Dentistry, Graduate Programs in Medicine and Dentistry, Department of Community and Preventive Medicine, Program in Epidemiology, Rochester, NY 14627. Offers PhD. *Degree requirements:* For doctorate, thesis/dissertation, qualifying exam. *Entrance requirements:* For doctorate, GRE General Test.

**University of Saskatchewan,** College of Medicine, Department of Community Health and Epidemiology, Saskatoon, SK S7N 5A2, Canada. Offers M Sc, PhD. *Degree requirements:* For master's, thesis; for doctorate, thesis/dissertation. *Entrance requirements:* Additional exam requirements/recommendations for international students: required—TOEFL.

**University of South Carolina,** The Graduate School, Arnold School of Public Health, Department of Epidemiology and Biostatistics, Program in Epidemiology, Columbia, SC 29208. Offers MPH, MSPH, Dr PH, PhD. *Accreditation:* CEPH (one or more programs are accredited). *Program availability:* Part-time. *Degree requirements:* For master's, comprehensive exam, thesis (for some programs), practicum (MPH); for doctorate, comprehensive exam, thesis/dissertation (for some programs), practicum. *Entrance requirements:* For master's, GRE General Test; for doctorate, GRE General Test, master's degree. Additional exam requirements/recommendations for international students: required—TOEFL (minimum score 570 paper-based; 88 iBT). Electronic applications accepted.

**University of Southern California,** Keck School of Medicine and Graduate School, Graduate Programs in Medicine, Department of Preventive Medicine, Division of Biostatistics, Los Angeles, CA 90032. Offers applied biostatistics and epidemiology (MS); biostatistics (MS, PhD); epidemiology (PhD); molecular epidemiology (MS). *Program availability:* Part-time. *Faculty:* 47 full-time (8 women), 7 part-time/adjunct (3 women). *Students:* 151 full-time (99 women); includes 48 minority (5 Black or African American, non-Hispanic/Latino; 6 American Indian or Alaska Native, non-Hispanic/Latino; 31 Asian, non-Hispanic/Latino; 4 Hispanic/Latino; 2 Two or more races, non-Hispanic/Latino), 64 international. Average age 32. 237 applicants, 51% accepted, 40 enrolled. In 2019, 21 master's, 15 doctorates awarded. Terminal master's awarded for partial completion of doctoral program. *Degree requirements:* For master's, thesis; for doctorate, thesis/dissertation. *Entrance requirements:* For master's, GRE General Test (minimum scores of 150 each on Verbal and Quantitative sections), minimum GPA of 3.0; for doctorate, GRE General Test (minimum scores of 160 each on Verbal and Quantitative sections), minimum GPA of 3.5. Additional exam requirements/recommendations for international students: required—TOEFL (minimum score 600 paper-based; 100 iBT), IELTS (minimum score 7). *Application deadline:* For fall admission, 12/1 priority date for domestic and international students; for winter admission, 5/1 priority date for domestic and international students; for spring admission, 10/1 priority date for domestic and international students; for summer admission, 3/1 priority date for domestic and international students. Applications are processed on a rolling basis. Application fee: $85. Electronic applications accepted. *Expenses:* Contact institution. *Financial support:* In 2019–20, 38 students received support, including 10 fellowships with full tuition reimbursements available (averaging $35,000 per year), 36 research assistantships with tuition reimbursements available (averaging $35,000 per year), 15 teaching assistantships with tuition reimbursements available (averaging $35,000 per year); career-related internships or fieldwork, Federal Work-Study, institutionally sponsored loans, scholarships/grants, traineeships, health care benefits, and unspecified assistantships also available. Financial award application deadline: 12/1; financial award applicants required to submit CSS PROFILE or FAFSA. *Unit head:* Dr. Kimberley Siegmund, Director, Graduate Programs in Biostatistics and Epidemiology, 323-442-1994, Fax: 323-442-2993, E-mail: kims@usc.edu. *Application contact:* Renee Stanley, Student Program Advisor, 323-442-1810, Fax: 323-442-2993, E-mail: reneesta@usc.edu.

**University of Southern California,** Keck School of Medicine and Graduate School, Graduate Programs in Medicine, Department of Preventive Medicine, Master of Public Health Program, Los Angeles, CA 90032. Offers biostatistics and epidemiology (MPH); child and family health (MPH); community health promotion (MPH); environmental health (MPH); geohealth (MPH); global health leadership (MPH); health communication (MPH); health services and policy (MPH). *Accreditation:* CEPH. *Program availability:* Part-time, evening/weekend, 100% online. *Faculty:* 37 full-time (28 women), 8 part-time/adjunct (6 women). *Students:* 261 full-time (201 women), 74 part-time (55 women); includes 224 minority (46 Black or African American, non-Hispanic/Latino; 2 American Indian or Alaska Native, non-Hispanic/Latino; 79 Asian, non-Hispanic/Latino; 56 Hispanic/Latino; 6 Native Hawaiian or other Pacific Islander, non-Hispanic/Latino; 35 Two or more races, non-Hispanic/Latino), 21 international. Average age 28. 420 applicants, 76% accepted, 94 enrolled. In 2019, 123 master's awarded. *Degree requirements:* For master's, practicum, final report, oral presentation. *Entrance requirements:* For master's, GRE General Test, MCAT, GMAT, minimum GPA of 3.0. Additional exam requirements/recommendations for international students: required—TOEFL (minimum score 600 paper-based; 90 iBT). *Application deadline:* For fall admission, 12/1 priority date for domestic students, 5/1 priority date for international students; for spring admission, 9/1 priority date for domestic and international students; for summer admission, 3/1 for domestic and international students. Applications are processed on a rolling basis. Application fee: $135. Electronic applications accepted. *Financial support:* Career-related internships or fieldwork, Federal Work-Study, institutionally sponsored loans, and scholarships/grants available. Support available to part-time students. Financial award application deadline: 5/4; financial award applicants required to submit CSS PROFILE or FAFSA. *Unit head:* Dr. Louise A. Rohrbach, Director, 323-442-8237, Fax: 323-442-8297, E-mail: rohrbac@usc.edu. *Application contact:* Valerie Burris, Admissions Counselor, 323-442-7257, Fax: 323-442-8297, E-mail: valeriem@usc.edu.
Website: https://preventivemedicine.usc.edu/education/graduate-programs/mph/

**University of Southern Mississippi,** College of Nursing and Health Professions, School of Health Professions, Hattiesburg, MS 39406-0001. Offers epidemiology and biostatistics (MPH); health policy and administration (MPH). *Accreditation:* CEPH. *Program availability:* Part-time, evening/weekend. *Students:* 58 full-time (41 women), 8 part-time (3 women); includes 25 minority (18 Black or African American, non-Hispanic/Latino; 2 Asian, non-Hispanic/Latino; 2 Hispanic/Latino; 3 Two or more races, non-Hispanic/Latino), 22 international. 125 applicants, 32% accepted, 23 enrolled. In 2019, 19 master's awarded. *Degree requirements:* For master's, comprehensive exam, thesis (for some programs). *Entrance requirements:* For master's, GRE General Test, minimum GPA of 2.75 in last 60 hours. Additional exam requirements/recommendations for international students: required—TOEFL, IELTS. *Application deadline:* For fall admission, 3/1 priority date for domestic and international students; for spring admission, 1/10 priority date for domestic and international students. Applications are processed on a rolling basis. Application fee: $60. Electronic applications accepted. *Expenses: Tuition, area resident:* Full-time $4393; part-time $488 per credit hour. Tuition, nonresident: full-time $5393; part-time $600 per credit hour. *Required fees:* $6 per semester. *Financial support:* Research assistantships with full tuition reimbursements, teaching assistantships with full tuition reimbursements, career-related internships or fieldwork, Federal Work-Study, institutionally sponsored loans, scholarships/grants, health care benefits, and unspecified assistantships available. Financial award application deadline: 3/15; financial award applicants required to submit FAFSA. *Unit head:* Hwanseok Choi, Director, 601-266-5435, Fax: 601-266-5043, E-mail: hwanseok.choi@usm.edu. *Application contact:* Hwanseok Choi, Director, 601-266-5435, Fax: 601-266-5043, E-mail: hwanseok.choi@usm.edu.
Website: http://www.usm.edu/community-public-health-sciences

**University of South Florida,** Innovative Education, Tampa, FL 33620-9951. Offers adult, career and higher education (Graduate Certificate), including college teaching, leadership in developing human resources, leadership in higher education; Africana studies (Graduate Certificate), including diasporas and health disparities, genocide and human rights; aging studies (Graduate Certificate), including gerontology; art research (Graduate Certificate), including museum studies; business foundations (Graduate Certificate); chemical and biomedical engineering (Graduate Certificate), including materials science and engineering, water, health and sustainability; child and family studies (Graduate Certificate), including positive behavior support; civil and industrial engineering (Graduate Certificate), including transportation systems analysis; community and family health (Graduate Certificate), including maternal and child health, social marketing and public health, violence and injury: prevention and intervention, women's health; criminology (Graduate Certificate), including criminal justice administration; data science for public administration (Graduate Certificate); digital humanities (Graduate Certificate); educational measurement and research (Graduate Certificate), including evaluation; English (Graduate Certificate), including comparative literary studies, creative writing, professional and technical communication; entrepreneurship (Graduate Certificate); environmental health (Graduate Certificate), including safety management; epidemiology and biostatistics (Graduate Certificate), including applied biostatistics, biostatistics, concepts and tools of epidemiology, epidemiology, epidemiology of infectious diseases; geography, environment and planning (Graduate Certificate), including community development, environmental policy and management, geographical information systems; geology (Graduate Certificate), including hydrogeology; global health (Graduate Certificate), including disaster management, global health and Latin American and Caribbean studies, global health practice, humanitarian assistance, infection control; government and international affairs (Graduate Certificate), including Cuban studies, globalization studies; health policy and management (Graduate Certificate), including health management and leadership, public health policy and programs; hearing specialist: early intervention (Graduate Certificate); industrial and management systems engineering (Graduate Certificate), including systems engineering, technology management; information studies (Graduate Certificate), including school library media specialist; information systems/decision sciences (Graduate Certificate), including analytics and business intelligence; instructional technology (Graduate Certificate), including distance education, Florida digital/virtual educator, instructional design, multimedia design, Web design; internal medicine, bioethics and medical humanities (Graduate Certificate), including biomedical ethics; Latin American and Caribbean studies (Graduate Certificate); leadership for coastal resiliency planning (Graduate Certificate); mass communications (Graduate Certificate), including multimedia journalism; mathematics and statistics (Graduate Certificate), including mathematics; medicine (Graduate Certificate), including aging and neuroscience, bioinformatics, biotechnology, brain fitness and memory management, clinical investigation, hand and upper limb rehabilitation, health informatics, health sciences, integrative weight management, intellectual property, medicine and gender, metabolic and nutritional medicine, metabolic cardiology, pharmacy sciences; national and competitive intelligence (Graduate Certificate); nursing (Graduate Certificate), including simulation based academic fellowship in advanced pain management; psychological and social foundations (Graduate Certificate), including career counseling, college teaching, diversity in education, mental health counseling, school counseling; public affairs (Graduate Certificate), including nonprofit management, public management, research administration; public health (Graduate Certificate), including assessing chemical toxicity and public health risks, health equity, pharmacoepidemiology, public health generalist, toxicology, translational research in adolescent behavioral health; public health practices (Graduate Certificate), including planning for healthy communities; rehabilitation and mental health counseling (Graduate Certificate), including integrative mental health care, marriage and family therapy, rehabilitation technology; secondary education (Graduate Certificate), including ESOL, foreign language education: culture and content, foreign language education: professional; social work (Graduate Certificate), including geriatric social work/clinical gerontology; special education (Graduate Certificate), including autism spectrum disorder, disabilities education: severe/profound; world languages (Graduate Certificate), including teaching English as a second language (TESL) or foreign language. *Unit head:* Dr. Cynthia DeLuca, Associate Vice President and Assistant Vice Provost, 813-974-3077, Fax: 813-974-7061, E-mail: deluca@usf.edu. *Application contact:* Owen Hooper, Director, Summer and Alternative Calendar Programs, 813-974-6917, E-mail: hooper@usf.edu.
Website: http://www.usf.edu/innovative-education/

**The University of Tennessee Health Science Center,** College of Graduate Health Sciences, Memphis, TN 38163. Offers biomedical engineering (MS, PhD); biomedical sciences (PhD); dental sciences (MDS); epidemiology (MS); health outcomes and policy research (PhD); laboratory research and management (MS); nursing science (PhD); pharmaceutical sciences (PhD); pharmacology (MS); speech and hearing science (PhD); DDS/PhD; DNP/PhD; MD/PhD; Pharm D/PhD. Terminal master's awarded for partial completion of doctoral program. *Degree requirements:* For master's, comprehensive exam, thesis; for doctorate, thesis/dissertation, oral and written preliminary and comprehensive exams. *Entrance requirements:* For master's and doctorate, GRE General Test, minimum GPA of 3.0. Additional exam requirements/recommendations for international students: recommended—TOEFL (minimum score 79 iBT), IELTS (minimum score 6.5). Electronic applications accepted. *Expenses:* Contact institution.

**The University of Texas Health Science Center at Houston,** School of Public Health, Houston, TX 77030. Offers behavioral science (PhD); biostatistics (MPH, MS, PhD); environmental health (MPH); epidemiology (MPH, MS, PhD); general public health (Certificate); genomics and bioinformatics (Certificate); health disparities (Certificate); health promotion/health education (MPH, Dr PH); healthcare management (Certificate); management, policy and community health (MPH, Dr PH, PhD); maternal and child health (Certificate); public health informatics (Certificate); DDS/MPH; JD/MPH; MBA/MPH; MD/MPH; MGPS/MPH; MP Aff/MPH; MS/MPH; MSN/MPH; MSW/MPH; PhD/MPH. *Accreditation:* CAHME; CEPH. *Program availability:* Part-time. *Degree requirements:* For master's, thesis (for some programs); for doctorate, comprehensive exam, thesis/dissertation. *Entrance requirements:* For master's and doctorate, GRE General Test. Additional exam requirements/recommendations for international students: required—TOEFL (minimum score 600 paper-based, 100 iBT) or IELTS (7.5). Electronic applications accepted. *Expenses:* Contact institution.

**The University of Toledo,** College of Graduate Studies, College of Medicine and Life Sciences, Department of Public Health and Preventative Medicine, Toledo, OH 43606-3390. Offers biostatistics and epidemiology (Certificate); contemporary gerontological practice (Certificate); environmental and occupational health and safety (MPH);

epidemiology (Certificate); global public health (Certificate); health promotion and education (MPH); industrial hygiene (MSOH); medical and health science teaching and learning (Certificate); occupational health (Certificate); public health administration (MPH); public health and emergency response (Certificate); public health epidemiology (MPH); public health nutrition (MPH); MD/MPH. *Program availability:* Part-time, evening/weekend. *Degree requirements:* For master's, thesis or alternative. *Entrance requirements:* For master's, GRE, minimum undergraduate GPA of 3.0, three letters of recommendation, statement of purpose, transcripts from all prior institutions attended, resume; for Certificate, minimum undergraduate GPA of 3.0, three letters of recommendation, statement of purpose, transcripts from all prior institutions attended, resume. Additional exam requirements/recommendations for international students: required—TOEFL (minimum score 550 paper-based; 80 iBT), IELTS (minimum score 6.5). Electronic applications accepted.

**University of Toronto,** School of Graduate Studies, Department of Public Health Sciences, Toronto, ON M5S 1A1, Canada. Offers biostatistics (M Sc, PhD); community health (M Sc); community nutrition (MPH), including nutrition and dietetics; epidemiology (MPH, PhD); family and community medicine (MPH); occupational and environmental health (MPH); social and behavioral health science (PhD); social and behavioral health sciences (MPH), including health promotion. *Accreditation:* CAHME (one or more programs are accredited). *Program availability:* Part-time. *Degree requirements:* For master's, thesis (for some programs), practicum; for doctorate, comprehensive exam, thesis/dissertation, oral thesis defense. *Entrance requirements:* For master's, 2 letters of reference, relevant professional/research experience, minimum B average in final year; for doctorate, 2 letters of reference, relevant professional/research experience, minimum B+ average. Additional exam requirements/recommendations for international students: required—TOEFL (minimum score 580 paper-based; 93 iBT), TWE (minimum score 5). Electronic applications accepted. *Expenses:* Contact institution.

**University of Vermont,** The Robert Larner, MD College of Medicine and Graduate College, Graduate Programs in Medicine, Program in Public Health, Burlington, VT 05405. Offers epidemiology (Graduate Certificate); global and environmental health (Graduate Certificate); healthcare management and policy (Graduate Certificate); public health (MPH). *Program availability:* Online only, 100% online. *Entrance requirements:* For master's and Graduate Certificate, resume/curriculum vitae. Additional exam requirements/recommendations for international students: required—TOEFL (minimum iBT score of 90) or IELTS (6.5). Electronic applications accepted. *Expenses:* Contact institution.

**University of Washington,** Graduate School, School of Public Health, Department of Epidemiology, Seattle, WA 98195. Offers clinical and translational research methods (MS); epidemiology (PhD); general epidemiology (MPH, MS); global health (MPH); maternal and child health (MPH); MPH/MPA. *Accreditation:* CEPH (one or more programs are accredited). *Program availability:* Part-time. *Faculty:* 54 full-time (36 women), 60 part-time/adjunct (27 women). *Students:* 161 full-time (116 women), 43 part-time (33 women); includes 54 minority (8 Black or African American, non-Hispanic/Latino; 4 American Indian or Alaska Native, non-Hispanic/Latino; 34 Asian, non-Hispanic/Latino; 8 Hispanic/Latino), 30 international. Average age 32. 393 applicants, 56% accepted, 91 enrolled. In 2019, 37 master's, 21 doctorates awarded. *Degree requirements:* For master's, thesis; for doctorate, comprehensive exam, thesis/dissertation. *Entrance requirements:* For master's, GRE (except for MDs from US institutions), Earned Bachelor's degree; for doctorate, GRE, Earned Master's degree. Additional exam requirements/recommendations for international students: required—TOEFL (minimum score 80 iBT). *Application deadline:* For fall admission, 12/1 for domestic and international students. Application fee: $85. Electronic applications accepted. *Financial support:* In 2019–20, 135 students received support, including 55 fellowships with full and partial tuition reimbursements available (averaging $38,000 per year), 50 research assistantships with full and partial tuition reimbursements available (averaging $30,000 per year), 15 teaching assistantships with full and partial tuition reimbursements available (averaging $24,000 per year); career-related internships or fieldwork, Federal Work-Study, institutionally sponsored loans, scholarships/grants, traineeships, health care benefits, tuition waivers (full and partial), and unspecified assistantships also available. Support available to part-time students. Financial award application deadline: 12/1. *Unit head:* Dr. Stephen E. Hawes, Professor and Chair, 206-685-0146, E-mail: epiadmin@uw.edu. *Application contact:* John Paulson, Assistant Director of Student Academic Services, 206-685-1762, E-mail: epi@uw.edu.
Website: https://epi.washington.edu/

**The University of Western Ontario,** Schulich School of Medicine and Dentistry, Department of Epidemiology and Biostatistics, London, ON N6A 3K7, Canada. Offers M Sc, PhD. *Program availability:* Part-time. *Degree requirements:* For master's, thesis; for doctorate, comprehensive exam, thesis proposal defense. *Entrance requirements:* For master's, BA or B Sc honors degree, minimum B+ average in last 10 courses; for doctorate, M Sc or equivalent, minimum B+ average in last 10 courses.

**University of Wisconsin–Madison,** School of Medicine and Public Health, Population Health and Epidemiology Graduate Program, Madison, WI 53726. Offers epidemiology (MS, PhD); population health (MS, PhD), including epidemiology. *Program availability:* Part-time. Terminal master's awarded for partial completion of doctoral program. *Degree requirements:* For master's, thesis, thesis defense; for doctorate, comprehensive exam, thesis/dissertation, qualifying exam, preliminary exam, dissertation defense. *Entrance requirements:* For master's and doctorate, GRE taken within the last 5 years (MCAT or LSAT acceptable for those with doctoral degrees), minimum GPA of 3.0, quantitative preparation (calculus, statistics, or other) with minimum B average. Additional exam requirements/recommendations for international students: required—TOEFL (minimum score 580 paper-based; 92 iBT). Electronic applications accepted. *Expenses:* Contact institution.

**University of Wisconsin–Milwaukee,** Graduate School, Joseph J. Zilber School of Public Health, Program in Public Health, Milwaukee, WI 53201-0413. Offers biostatistics (MPH); community and behavioral health promotion (MPH); environmental health sciences (MPH); epidemiology (MPH, PhD); public and population health (Graduate Certificate); public health policy and administration (MPH); public health: biostatistics (PhD); public health: community and behavioral health promotion (PhD). Electronic applications accepted.

**Université Laval,** Faculty of Medicine, Graduate Programs in Medicine, Department of Medicine, Programs in Epidemiology, Québec, QC G1K 7P4, Canada. Offers M Sc, PhD. Terminal master's awarded for partial completion of doctoral program. *Degree requirements:* For master's, thesis; for doctorate, comprehensive exam, thesis/dissertation. *Entrance requirements:* For master's and doctorate, knowledge of French, comprehension of written English. Electronic applications accepted.

**Virginia Commonwealth University,** Medical College of Virginia-Professional Programs, School of Medicine, Graduate Programs in Medicine, Department of Family Medicine and Population Health, Richmond, VA 23284-9005. Offers epidemiology (MPH, PhD); public health practice (MPH); social and behavioral science (MPH); MD/MPH. *Accreditation:* CEPH. *Program availability:* Part-time. *Degree requirements:* For doctorate, comprehensive exam, thesis/dissertation. *Entrance requirements:* For master's, GRE; for doctorate, GRE General Test, interview, 3 letters of recommendation, minimum graduate GPA of 3.0, master's degree in public health or related field including epidemiology and biostatistics. Additional exam requirements/recommendations for international students: required—TOEFL (minimum score 600 paper-based; 100 iBT). Electronic applications accepted.

**Walden University,** Graduate Programs, School of Health Sciences, Minneapolis, MN 55401. Offers clinical research administration (MS, Graduate Certificate); health education and promotion (MS, PhD), including behavioral health (PhD), disease surveillance (PhD), emergency preparedness (MS), general (MHA, MS), global health (PhD), health policy (PhD), health policy and advocacy (MS), population health (PhD); health informatics (MS); health services (PhD), including community health, healthcare administration, leadership, public health policy, self-designed; healthcare administration (MHA, DHA), including general (MHA, MS); leadership and organizational development (MHA); public health (MPH, Dr PH, PhD, Graduate Certificate), including community health education (PhD), epidemiology (PhD); systems policy (MHA). *Program availability:* Part-time, evening/weekend, online only, 100% online. *Degree requirements:* For doctorate, thesis/dissertation, residency. *Entrance requirements:* For master's, bachelor's degree or higher; minimum GPA of 2.5; official transcripts; goal statement (for some programs); access to computer and Internet; for doctorate, master's degree or higher; three years of related professional or academic experience (preferred); minimum GPA of 3.0; goal statement and current resume (for select programs); official transcripts; access to computer and Internet; for Graduate Certificate, relevant work experience; access to computer and Internet. Additional exam requirements/recommendations for international students: required—TOEFL (minimum score 550 paper-based, 79 iBT), IELTS (minimum score 6.5), Michigan English Language Assessment Battery (minimum score 82), or PTE (minimum score 53). Electronic applications accepted.

**Washington University in St. Louis,** Brown School, St. Louis, MO 63130-4899. Offers American Indian/Alaska native (MSW); children, youth and families (MSW); epidemiology/biostatistics (MPH); generalist (MPH); global health (MPH); health (MSW); health policy analysis (MPH); individualized (MSW), including health; mental health (MSW); older adults and aging societies (MSW); public health sciences (PhD); social and economic development (MSW), including domestic, international; social work (PhD); urban design (MPH); violence and injury prevention (MSW); JD/MSW; M Arch/MSW; MPH/MBA; MSW/M Div; MSW/M Ed; MSW/MAPS; MSW/MBA; MSW/MPH; MUD/MSW. *Accreditation:* CEPH; CSWE (one or more programs are accredited). *Faculty:* 54 full-time (31 women), 87 part-time/adjunct (61 women). *Students:* 282 full-time (226 women); includes 90 minority (40 Black or African American, non-Hispanic/Latino; 10 American Indian or Alaska Native, non-Hispanic/Latino; 26 Asian, non-Hispanic/Latino; 13 Hispanic/Latino; 1 Native Hawaiian or other Pacific Islander, non-Hispanic/Latino). Average age 24. *Degree requirements:* For master's, 60 credit hours (for MSW); 52 credit hours (for MPH); practicum; for doctorate, comprehensive exam, thesis/dissertation. *Entrance requirements:* For master's, GRE (preferred), GMAT, LSAT, MCAT, PCAT, or United States Medical Licensing Exam (for MPH); for doctorate, GRE. Additional exam requirements/recommendations for international students: required—TOEFL (minimum score 100 iBT), IELTS (minimum score 7). *Application deadline:* For fall admission, 12/15 priority date for domestic and international students; for winter admission, 3/1 priority date for domestic and international students. Applications are processed on a rolling basis. Electronic applications accepted. *Expenses:* Contact institution. *Financial support:* In 2019–20, 90 research assistantships were awarded; fellowships, teaching assistantships, career-related internships or fieldwork, Federal Work-Study, scholarships/grants, and unspecified assistantships also available. Support available to part-time students. Financial award applicants required to submit FAFSA. *Unit head:* Jamie L. Adkisson-Hennessey, Director of Admissions and Recruitment, 314-935-3524, Fax: 314-935-4859, E-mail: jadkisson@wustl.edu. *Application contact:* Office of Admissions and Recruitment, 314-935-6676, Fax: 314-935-4859, E-mail: brownadmissions@wustl.edu.
Website: http://brownschool.wustl.edu

**Weill Cornell Medicine,** Weill Cornell Graduate School of Medical Sciences, Program in Clinical Epidemiology and Health Services Research, New York, NY 10021. Offers MS. *Degree requirements:* For master's, thesis. *Entrance requirements:* For master's, 3 years of work experience, MD or RN certificate.

**West Virginia University,** School of Public Health, Morgantown, WV 26506. Offers biostatistics (MPH, MS, PhD); epidemiology (MPH, PhD); health policy (MPH); occupational and environmental health sciences (MPH, PhD); public health (MPH); school health education (MS); social and behavioral science (MPH, PhD). *Accreditation:* CEPH. *Program availability:* Part-time, online learning. *Degree requirements:* For master's, practicum, project. *Entrance requirements:* For master's, GRE General Test, MCAT, medical degree, medical internship. Additional exam requirements/recommendations for international students: required—TOEFL (minimum score 550 paper-based; 80 iBT). *Expenses:* Contact institution.

**Yale University,** Yale School of Medicine, Yale School of Public Health, New Haven, CT 06520. Offers applied biostatistics and epidemiology (APMPH); biostatistics (MPH, MS, PhD), including global health (MPH); chronic disease epidemiology (MPH, PhD), including global health (MPH); environmental health sciences (MPH, PhD), including global health (MPH); epidemiology of microbial diseases (MPH, PhD), including global health (MPH); global health (APMPH); health management (MPH), including global health; health policy (MPH), including global health; health policy and administration (APMPH, PhD); occupational and environmental medicine (APMPH); preventive medicine (APMPH); social and behavioral sciences (APMPH, MPH), including global health (MPH); JD/MPH; M Div/MPH; MBA/MPH; MD/MPH; MEM/MPH; MFS/MPH; MM Sc/MPH; MPH/MA; MSN/MPH. *Accreditation:* CEPH. *Faculty:* 161 full-time (71 women), 121 part-time/adjunct (57 women). *Students:* 534 full-time (386 women); includes 156 minority (24 Black or African American, non-Hispanic/Latino; 83 Asian, non-Hispanic/Latino; 30 Hispanic/Latino; 19 Two or more races, non-Hispanic/Latino), 220 international. Average age 25. 1,300 applicants, 220 enrolled. In 2019, 250 master's, 12 doctorates awarded. *Degree requirements:* For master's, thesis; for doctorate, comprehensive exam, thesis/dissertation. *Entrance requirements:* For master's, GMAT, GRE, or MCAT; for doctorate, GRE General Test. Additional exam requirements/recommendations for international students: required—TOEFL (minimum score 100 iBT). *Application deadline:* For fall admission, 12/15 for domestic and international students; for summer admission, 12/15 for domestic and international students. Applications are processed on a rolling basis. Application fee: $135. Electronic applications accepted. *Expenses:* Contact institution. *Financial support:* Fellowships with full tuition reimbursements, research assistantships with full tuition reimbursements, teaching assistantships with full tuition reimbursements, career-related internships or fieldwork, institutionally sponsored loans, scholarships/grants, and tuition waivers available. Support available to part-time students. Financial award application deadline: 3/1; financial award applicants required to submit FAFSA. *Unit head:* Dr. Sten Vermund, Dean and Anna M.R. Lauder Professor of Public Health, E-mail: sten.vermund@yale.edu. *Application contact:* Mary Keefe, Director of Admissions, 203-785-2844, E-mail: ysph.admissions@yale.edu.
Website: http://publichealth.yale.edu/

# Health Promotion

**American College of Healthcare Sciences,** Graduate Programs, Portland, OR 97239-3719. Offers anatomy and physiology (Graduate Certificate); aromatherapy (MS, Graduate Certificate); botanical safety (Graduate Certificate); complementary alternative medicine (MS, Graduate Certificate); health and wellness (MS); herbal medicine (MS, Graduate Certificate); holistic nutrition (MS, Graduate Certificate); wellness coaching (Graduate Certificate). *Program availability:* Part-time, evening/weekend, online learning. *Degree requirements:* For master's, capstone project. *Entrance requirements:* For master's, interview, letters of recommendation, essay.

**American University,** College of Arts and Sciences, Department of Health Studies, Washington, DC 20016. Offers health promotion management (MS), including health promotion management; nutrition education (MS, Certificate). *Program availability:* 100% online, blended/hybrid learning. *Degree requirements:* For master's, comprehensive exam (for some programs), thesis or alternative. *Entrance requirements:* For master's, Please visit the website: https://www.american.edu/cas/health/, statement of purpose, transcripts, 2 letters of recommendation, resume. Additional exam requirements/recommendations for international students: required—TOEFL. Electronic applications accepted. *Expenses:* Contact institution.

**Arizona State University at Tempe,** College of Health Solutions, School of Nutrition and Health Promotion, Tempe, AZ 85287. Offers clinical exercise physiology (MS); exercise and wellness (MS); nutrition (MS), including dietetics, human nutrition; obesity prevention and management (MS); physical activity, nutrition and wellness (PhD).

**Ball State University,** Graduate School, College of Health, School of Kinesiology, Interdepartmental Program in Wellness Management, Muncie, IN 47306. Offers MA, MS. *Entrance requirements:* For master's, GRE General Test, interview. *Expenses: Tuition, area resident:* Full-time $7506; part-time $417 per credit hour. Tuition, nonresident: full-time $20,610; part-time $1145 per credit hour. *Required fees:* $2126. Tuition and fees vary according to course load, campus/location and program.

**Boise State University,** College of Health Sciences, Department of Community and Environmental Health, Boise, ID 83725-0399. Offers community and environmental health (MHS); health science (MHS), including health policy, health promotion, health services leadership; health services leadership (Graduate Certificate). *Students:* 20 full-time (18 women), 38 part-time (33 women); includes 7 minority (1 Asian, non-Hispanic/Latino; 5 Hispanic/Latino; 1 Two or more races, non-Hispanic/Latino). Average age 36. 38 applicants, 50% accepted, 11 enrolled. In 2019, 21 master's, 13 Graduate Certificates awarded. *Entrance requirements:* For master's, writing assessment, minimum GPA of 3.0. Additional exam requirements/recommendations for international students: required—TOEFL (minimum score 550 paper-based; 80 iBT), IELTS (minimum score 6). *Application deadline:* For fall admission, 3/15 for domestic and international students; for spring admission, 10/15 for domestic and international students. Application fee: $65 ($95 for international students). Electronic applications accepted. *Expenses: Tuition, area resident:* Full-time $7110; part-time $470 per credit hour. Tuition, state resident: full-time $7110; part-time $470 per credit hour. Tuition, nonresident: full-time $24,030; part-time $827 per credit hour. *International tuition:* $24,030 full-time. *Required fees:* $2536. Tuition and fees vary according to course load and program. *Financial support:* Research assistantships, scholarships/grants, and unspecified assistantships available. Financial award application deadline: 3/15; financial award applicants required to submit FAFSA. *Unit head:* Dr. Lillian Smith, Department Head, 208-426-3795, E-mail: lilliansmith@boisestate.edu. *Application contact:* Dr. Sarah Toevs, Director, Master of Health Science Program, 208-426-2452, E-mail: stoevs@boisestate.edu.
Website: https://www.boisestate.edu/healthsciences/

**Bridgewater State University,** College of Graduate Studies, College of Education and Allied Studies, Department of Movement Arts, Health Promotion, and Leisure Studies, Program in Health Promotion, Bridgewater, MA 02325. Offers M Ed. *Program availability:* Part-time, evening/weekend. *Entrance requirements:* For master's, GRE General Test.

**Brigham Young University,** Graduate Studies, College of Life Sciences, Department of Exercise Sciences, Provo, UT 84602. Offers athletic training (MS); exercise physiology (MS, PhD); exercise sciences (MS); health promotion (MS, PhD); physical medicine and rehabilitation (PhD). *Faculty:* 21 full-time (2 women). *Students:* 14 full-time (8 women), 12 part-time (7 women); includes 4 minority (1 Black or African American, non-Hispanic/Latino; 3 Asian, non-Hispanic/Latino). Average age 23. 21 applicants, 52% accepted, 9 enrolled. In 2019, 1 master's, 2 doctorates awarded. *Degree requirements:* For master's, thesis, oral defense; for doctorate, comprehensive exam, thesis/dissertation, oral defense, oral and written exams. *Entrance requirements:* For master's, GRE General Test (minimum score of 300, 4.0 on analytic writing portion), minimum GPA of 3.2 in last 60 hours of course work; for doctorate, GRE General Test (minimum score of 300, 4.0 on analytic writing portion), minimum GPA of 3.5 in last 60 hours of course work. Additional exam requirements/recommendations for international students: required—TOEFL (minimum score 580 paper-based; 85 iBT), IELTS (minimum score 7). *Application deadline:* For fall admission, 2/1 for domestic and international students. Application fee: $50. Electronic applications accepted. *Financial support:* In 2019–20, 20 students received support. Scholarships/grants, unspecified assistantships, and 5 PhD full-tuition scholarships available. Financial award application deadline: 4/15. *Unit head:* Dr. Allen Parcell, Chair, 801-422-4450, Fax: 801-422-0555, E-mail: allenparcell@gmail.com. *Application contact:* Dr. J. Ty Hopkins, Graduate Coordinator, 801-422-1573, Fax: 801-422-0555, E-mail: tyhopkins@byu.edu.
Website: http://exsc.byu.edu/

**California Baptist University,** Program in Public Health, Riverside, CA 92504-3206. Offers health education and promotion (MPH); health policy and administration (MPH). *Accreditation:* CEPH. *Program availability:* Part-time, evening/weekend, 100% online, blended/hybrid learning. *Degree requirements:* For master's, capstone project; practicum. *Entrance requirements:* For master's, minimum undergraduate GPA of 2.75, two recommendations, 500-word essay, resume. Additional exam requirements/recommendations for international students: required—TOEFL (minimum score 80 iBT). Electronic applications accepted. *Expenses:* Contact institution.

**California State University, Fresno,** Division of Research and Graduate Studies, College of Health and Human Services, Department of Public Health, Fresno, CA 93740-8027. Offers health policy and management (MPH); health promotion (MPH). *Accreditation:* CEPH. *Program availability:* Part-time, evening/weekend. *Degree requirements:* For master's, thesis or alternative. *Entrance requirements:* For master's, GRE General Test, minimum GPA of 2.5. Additional exam requirements/recommendations for international students: required—TOEFL. Electronic applications accepted. *Expenses:* Tuition, state resident: full-time $4012; part-time $2506 per semester.

**California State University, Fullerton,** Graduate Studies, College of Health and Human Development, Department of Public Health, Fullerton, CA 92831-3599. Offers environmental and occupational health and safety (MPH); gerontological health (MPH); health promotion and disease (MPH). *Accreditation:* CEPH. *Program availability:* Part-time. *Entrance requirements:* For master's, minimum GPA of 3.0 in last 60 units attempted.

**Claremont Graduate University,** Graduate Programs, School of Community and Global Health, Claremont, CA 91773. Offers health promotion science (PhD); public health (MPH). *Accreditation:* CEPH. *Entrance requirements:* For master's and doctorate, GRE. Additional exam requirements/recommendations for international students: required—TOEFL (minimum score 75 iBT). Electronic applications accepted.

**Cleveland University–Kansas City,** Program in Health Education and Promotion, Overland Park, KS 66210. Offers MS. *Program availability:* Part-time. *Entrance requirements:* For master's, professional statement. Additional exam requirements/recommendations for international students: required—TOEFL (minimum score 550 paper-based; 79 iBT). Electronic applications accepted. *Expenses:* Contact institution.

**Concord University,** Graduate Studies, Athens, WV 24712-1000. Offers educational leadership and supervision (M Ed); health promotion (MA); reading specialist (M Ed); social work (MSW); special education (M Ed); teaching (MAT). *Program availability:* Part-time, evening/weekend, 100% online. *Degree requirements:* For master's, thesis (for some programs). *Entrance requirements:* For master's, GRE or MAT, baccalaureate degree with minimum GPA of 2.5 from regionally-accredited institution; teaching license; 2 letters of recommendation; completed disposition assessment form. Electronic applications accepted. *Expenses: Tuition, area resident:* Full-time $481; part-time $481 per credit hour. Tuition, state resident: full-time $481; part-time $481 per credit hour. Tuition, nonresident: full-time $481; part-time $481 per credit hour.

**Creighton University,** Graduate School, Department of Interdisciplinary Studies, MS Program in Health and Wellness Coaching, Omaha, NE 68178-0001. Offers MS. *Program availability:* Part-time, online only, 100% online. *Entrance requirements:* Additional exam requirements/recommendations for international students: required—TOEFL (minimum score 90 iBT). Electronic applications accepted. *Expenses:* Contact institution.

**East Carolina University,** Graduate School, College of Health and Human Performance, Department of Health Education and Promotion, Greenville, NC 27858-4353. Offers environmental health (MS); health education (MA Ed); health education and promotion (MA). *Accreditation:* NCATE. *Application deadline:* For fall admission, 6/1 priority date for domestic students. *Expenses: Tuition, area resident:* Full-time $4749; part-time $185 per credit hour. Tuition, state resident: full-time $4749; part-time $185 per credit hour. Tuition, nonresident: full-time $17,898; part-time $864 per credit hour. *International tuition:* $17,898 full-time. *Required fees:* $2787. *Financial support:* Application deadline: 6/1. *Unit head:* Vic Aeby, Associate Professor, 252-328-6000, E-mail: aeby@ecu.edu. *Application contact:* Graduate School Admissions, 252-328-6012, Fax: 252-328-6071, E-mail: gradschool@ecu.edu.
Website: https://hhp.ecu.edu/hep/

**Eastern Kentucky University,** The Graduate School, College of Health Sciences, Department of Exercise and Sport Science, Richmond, KY 40475-3102. Offers exercise and sport science (MS); exercise and wellness (MS); sports administration (MS). *Program availability:* Part-time. *Entrance requirements:* For master's, GRE General Test (minimum score 700 verbal and quantitative), minimum GPA of 2.5 (for most), minimum GPA of 3.0 (analytical writing).

**Eastern Michigan University,** Graduate School, College of Health and Human Services, School of Health Promotion and Human Performance, Ypsilanti, MI 48197. Offers MS, Graduate Certificate. *Program availability:* Part-time, evening/weekend, online learning. *Faculty:* 32 full-time (15 women). *Students:* 150 full-time (89 women), 41 part-time (19 women); includes 33 minority (9 Black or African American, non-Hispanic/Latino; 1 American Indian or Alaska Native, non-Hispanic/Latino; 7 Asian, non-Hispanic/Latino; 13 Hispanic/Latino; 3 Two or more races, non-Hispanic/Latino), 7 international. Average age 26. 241 applicants, 49% accepted, 59 enrolled. In 2019, 89 master's awarded. *Entrance requirements:* For master's, MAT (for orthotics and prosthetics). Additional exam requirements/recommendations for international students: required—TOEFL. *Application deadline:* For fall admission, 8/1 for domestic students, 5/1 for international students; for winter admission, 12/1 for domestic students, 10/1 for international students; for spring admission, 4/15 for domestic students, 3/1 for international students. Applications are processed on a rolling basis. Application fee: $45. *Financial support:* Fellowships, research assistantships with full tuition reimbursements, teaching assistantships with full tuition reimbursements, career-related internships or fieldwork, Federal Work-Study, institutionally sponsored loans, scholarships/grants, tuition waivers (partial), and unspecified assistantships available. Support available to part-time students. Financial award applicants required to submit FAFSA. *Unit head:* Dr. Christopher Herman, Director, 734-487-2185, Fax: 734-487-2024, E-mail: cherman2@emich.edu. *Application contact:* Linda Jermone, HPHP Academic Advisor, 734-487-0092, Fax: 734-487-2024, E-mail: ljerme@emich.edu.

**Emory University,** Rollins School of Public Health, Online Program in Public Health, Atlanta, GA 30322-1100. Offers applied epidemiology (MPH); applied public health informatics (MPH); prevention science (MPH). *Program availability:* Part-time, evening/weekend, online learning. *Degree requirements:* For master's, thesis, practicum. *Entrance requirements:* For master's, GRE. Additional exam requirements/recommendations for international students: required—TOEFL (minimum score 550 paper-based; 80 iBT). Electronic applications accepted.

**Fairmont State University,** Programs in Education, Fairmont, WV 26554. Offers digital media, new literacies and learning (M Ed); education (MAT); exercise science, fitness and wellness (M Ed); professional studies (M Ed); reading (M Ed); special education (M Ed). *Accreditation:* NCATE. *Program availability:* Part-time, evening/weekend, 100% online. *Entrance requirements:* For master's, GRE. Additional exam requirements/recommendations for international students: required—TOEFL (minimum score 80 iBT), IELTS (minimum score 6.5). Electronic applications accepted.

**Florida Atlantic University,** Charles E. Schmidt College of Science, Department of Exercise Science and Health Promotion, Boca Raton, FL 33431-0991. Offers MS. *Program availability:* Part-time, evening/weekend. *Faculty:* 8 full-time (2 women). *Students:* 20 full-time (8 women), 22 part-time (12 women); includes 10 minority (4 Black or African American, non-Hispanic/Latino; 4 Hispanic/Latino; 2 Two or more races, non-Hispanic/Latino), 3 international. Average age 28. 32 applicants, 56% accepted, 13 enrolled. In 2019, 18 master's awarded. *Degree requirements:* For master's, comprehensive exam, thesis optional. *Entrance requirements:* For master's, GRE General Test, minimum GPA of 3.0 during last 60 hours of course work. Additional exam

requirements/recommendations for international students: required—TOEFL (minimum score 500 paper-based; 61 iBT), IELTS (minimum score 6). *Application deadline:* For fall admission, 7/1 priority date for domestic students, 2/15 for international students; for spring admission, 11/1 priority date for domestic students, 7/15 for international students. Applications are processed on a rolling basis. Application fee: $30. *Expenses: Tuition:* Full-time $20,536; part-time $371.82 per credit hour. Tuition and fees vary according to program. *Financial support:* Research assistantships with partial tuition reimbursements, teaching assistantships with partial tuition reimbursements, and career-related internships or fieldwork available. *Unit head:* Dr. Michael Whitehurst, 561-297-2317, E-mail: eshpinfo@fau.edu. *Application contact:* Dr. Michael Whitehurst, 561-297-2317, E-mail: eshpinfo@fau.edu.
Website: http://www.coe.fau.edu/academicdepartments/eshp/

**Florida International University,** Robert Stempel College of Public Health and Social Work, Programs in Public Health, Miami, FL 33199. Offers biostatistics (MPH); environmental and occupational health (MPH, PhD); epidemiology (MPH, PhD); health policy and management (MPH); health promotion and disease prevention (MPH, PhD). *Accreditation:* CEPH. *Program availability:* Part-time, evening/weekend, online learning. *Faculty:* 31 full-time (15 women), 8 part-time/adjunct (6 women). *Students:* 176 full-time (117 women), 58 part-time (42 women); includes 170 minority (57 Black or African American, non-Hispanic/Latino; 1 American Indian or Alaska Native, non-Hispanic/Latino; 14 Asian, non-Hispanic/Latino; 95 Hispanic/Latino; 3 Two or more races, non-Hispanic/Latino), 32 international. Average age 29. 260 applicants, 68% accepted, 68 enrolled. In 2019, 70 master's, 16 doctorates awarded. *Degree requirements:* For master's, thesis optional; for doctorate, comprehensive exam, thesis/dissertation. *Entrance requirements:* For master's, minimum GPA of 3.0, letters of recommendation; for doctorate, GRE, resume, minimum GPA of 3.0, letters of recommendation, letter of intent. Additional exam requirements/recommendations for international students: required—TOEFL (minimum score 550 paper-based; 80 iBT). *Application deadline:* For fall admission, 6/1 for domestic students, 4/1 for international students; for spring admission, 10/1 for domestic students, 9/1 for international students. Applications are processed on a rolling basis. Application fee: $30. Electronic applications accepted. *Expenses:* Contact institution. *Financial support:* Institutionally sponsored loans, scholarships/grants, and tuition waivers (full) available. Financial award application deadline: 3/1; financial award applicants required to submit FAFSA. *Unit head:* Dr. Kim Tieu, Chair, 305-348-0371, E-mail: kim.tieu@fiu.edu. *Application contact:* Nanett Rojas, Manager, Admissions Operations, 305-348-7464, Fax: 305-348-7441, E-mail: gradadm@fiu.edu.

**George Mason University,** College of Education and Human Development, School of Recreation, Health and Tourism, Manassas, VA 20110. Offers athletic training (MS); exercise, fitness, and health promotion (MS), including advanced practitioner, wellness practitioner; international sport management (Certificate); recreation, health and tourism (Certificate); sport management (MS), including sport and recreation studies. *Program availability:* Part-time, evening/weekend. *Entrance requirements:* Additional exam requirements/recommendations for international students: required—TOEFL (minimum score 575 paper-based; 88 iBT), IELTS (minimum score 6.5), PTE (minimum score 59). Electronic applications accepted.

**Georgetown University,** Graduate School of Arts and Sciences, Department of Microbiology and Immunology, Washington, DC 20057. Offers biohazardous threat agents and emerging infectious diseases (MS); biomedical science policy and advocacy (MS); general microbiology and immunology (MS); global infectious diseases (PhD); microbiology and immunology (PhD). *Program availability:* Part-time. *Degree requirements:* For master's, 30 credit hours of coursework; for doctorate, comprehensive exam, thesis/dissertation. *Entrance requirements:* For master's, GRE General Test, 3 letters of reference, bachelor's degree in related field; for doctorate, GRE General Test, 3 letters of reference, MS/BS in related field. Additional exam requirements/recommendations for international students: required—TOEFL (minimum score 505 paper-based). Electronic applications accepted.

**Georgia College & State University,** The Graduate School, College of Health Sciences, School of Health and Human Performance, Milledgeville, GA 31061. Offers health and human performance (MS), including health performance, health promotion; kinesiology/health education (MAT). *Accreditation:* NCATE (one or more programs are accredited). *Program availability:* Part-time. *Students:* 44 full-time (24 women), 22 part-time (14 women); includes 19 minority (13 Black or African American, non-Hispanic/Latino; 1 Asian, non-Hispanic/Latino; 5 Hispanic/Latino), 2 international. Average age 26. 38 applicants, 100% accepted, 32 enrolled. In 2019, 21 master's awarded. *Degree requirements:* For master's, thesis or alternative, completed in 6 years with minimum GPA of 3.0 and electronic teaching portfolio (for MAT), capstone (MSAT), thesis option (MS), GACE 360 Ethics Exam & GACE content assessment (MAT). *Entrance requirements:* For master's, for the MSAT program, GACE Basic Skills Test minimum score of 250 on each of the three sections unless official copies of exemption scores are submitted either the ACT, SAT or GRE, resume, 3 professional references; letter of application/personal statement, minimum GPA of 2.75 in upper-level undergraduate major courses(MAT), undergraduate statistics course (for MS); completion of Human Anatomy & Physiology or two integrated courses in Anatomy & Physiology (MS). *Application deadline:* Applications are processed on a rolling basis. Application fee: $40. Electronic applications accepted. *Expenses:* See program page. *Financial support:* In 2019–20, 21 students received support. Unspecified assistantships available. Financial award application deadline: 7/1; financial award applicants required to submit FAFSA. *Unit head:* Dr. Lisa Griffin, Director, School of Health and Human Performance, 478-445-4072, Fax: 478-445-4074, E-mail: lisa.griffin@gcsu.edu. *Application contact:* Dr. Lisa Griffin, Director, School of Health and Human Performance, 478-445-4072, Fax: 478-445-4074, E-mail: lisa.griffin@gcsu.edu.
Website: http://www.gcsu.edu/health/shhp

**Goddard College,** Graduate Division, Master of Arts in Health Arts and Sciences Program, Plainfield, VT 05667-9432. Offers MA. *Degree requirements:* For master's, thesis. *Entrance requirements:* For master's, 3 letters of recommendation, interview. Electronic applications accepted.

**Harvard University,** Harvard T.H. Chan School of Public Health, Department of Social and Behavioral Sciences, Boston, MA 02115-6096. Offers population health sciences (PhD). *Program availability:* Part-time. *Faculty:* 33 full-time (18 women), 10 part-time/adjunct (5 women). *Students:* 6 full-time (3 women), 3 international. Average age 29. In 2019, 1 master's, 10 doctorates awarded. *Entrance requirements:* For master's, GRE, MCAT. Additional exam requirements/recommendations for international students: recommended—TOEFL (minimum score 600 paper-based; 100 iBT), IELTS (minimum score 7). *Application deadline:* For fall admission, 12/1 for domestic and international students. Application fee: $140. Electronic applications accepted. *Financial support:* Fellowships, research assistantships, teaching assistantships, Federal Work-Study, scholarships/grants, traineeships, and unspecified assistantships available. Support available to part-time students. Financial award application deadline: 2/15; financial award applicants required to submit FAFSA. *Unit head:* Dr. David Williams, Chair, E-mail: dwilliam@hsph.harvard.edu. *Application contact:* Vincent W. James, Director of Admissions, 617-432-1031, Fax: 617-432-7080, E-mail: admissions@hsph.harvard.edu.
Website: http://www.hsph.harvard.edu/social-and-behavioral-sciences/

**Immaculata University,** College of Graduate Studies, Program in Nutrition Education, Immaculata, PA 19345. Offers nutrition education for the registered dietitian (MA); nutrition education with dietetic internship (MA); nutrition education with wellness promotion (MA). *Program availability:* Part-time, evening/weekend. *Degree requirements:* For master's, comprehensive exam, thesis optional. *Entrance requirements:* For master's, GRE or MAT, minimum GPA of 3.0. Additional exam requirements/recommendations for international students: required—TOEFL. Electronic applications accepted.

**Independence University,** Program in Health Services, Salt Lake City, UT 84107. Offers community health (MSHS); wellness promotion (MSHS). *Program availability:* Part-time, evening/weekend, online learning. *Degree requirements:* For master's, fieldwork, internship, final project (wellness promotion). *Entrance requirements:* For master's, previous course work in psychology.

**Independence University,** Program in Nursing, Salt Lake City, UT 84107. Offers community health (MSN); gerontology (MSN); nursing administration (MSN); wellness promotion (MSN).

**Indiana University Bloomington,** School of Public Health, Department of Kinesiology, Bloomington, IN 47405. Offers applied sport science (MS); athletic administration/sport management (MS); athletic training (MS); biomechanics (MS); ergonomics (MS); exercise physiology (MS); human performance (PhD), including biomechanics, exercise physiology, motor learning/control, sport management; motor learning/control (MS); physical activity (MPH); physical activity, fitness and wellness (MS). *Program availability:* Part-time. Terminal master's awarded for partial completion of doctoral program. *Degree requirements:* For master's, thesis optional; for doctorate, variable foreign language requirement, comprehensive exam, thesis/dissertation. *Entrance requirements:* For master's, GRE General Test, minimum GPA of 2.8; for doctorate, GRE General Test, minimum graduate GPA of 3.5, undergraduate 3.0. Additional exam requirements/recommendations for international students: required—TOEFL (minimum score 80 iBT).

**Instituto Tecnologico de Santo Domingo,** Graduate School, Area of Health Sciences, Santo Domingo, Dominican Republic. Offers bioethics (M Bioethics); clinical bioethics (Certificate); clinical nutrition (Certificate); comprehensive adolescent health (MS); comprehensive health and the adolescent (Certificate); health and social security (M Mgmt).

**Kent State University,** College of Education, Health and Human Services, School of Health Sciences, Program in Health Education and Promotion, Kent, OH 44242-0001. Offers M Ed, PhD. *Accreditation:* NCATE. *Degree requirements:* For doctorate, comprehensive exam, thesis/dissertation. *Entrance requirements:* For master's, 2 letters of reference, goals statement; for doctorate, goals statement, resume, interview. Additional exam requirements/recommendations for international students: required—TOEFL (minimum score 550 paper-based; 80 iBT). Electronic applications accepted.

**Lehman College of the City University of New York,** School of Health Sciences, Human Services and Nursing, Department of Health Sciences, Program in Health Education and Promotion, Bronx, NY 10468-1589. Offers MA. *Accreditation:* NCATE. *Program availability:* Part-time, evening/weekend. *Degree requirements:* For master's, thesis or alternative. *Entrance requirements:* For master's, minimum GPA of 2.7. *Expenses: Tuition, area resident:* Full-time $5545; part-time $470 per credit. Tuition, nonresident: part-time $855 per credit. *Required fees:* $240.

**Liberty University,** School of Behavioral Sciences, Lynchburg, VA 24515. Offers applied psychology (MA), including developmental psychology (MA, MS), industrial/organizational psychology (MA, MS); clinical mental health counseling (MA); community care and counseling (Ed D), including marriage and family counseling, pastoral care and counseling, traumatology; counselor education and supervision (PhD); human services counseling (MA), including addictions and recovery, business, child and family law, Christian ministries, criminal justice, crisis response and trauma, executive leadership, health and wellness, life coaching, marriage and family, military resilience; marriage and family counseling (MA); marriage and family therapy (MA); military resilience (Certificate); pastoral counseling (MA), including addictions and recovery, community chaplaincy, crisis response and trauma, discipleship and church ministry, leadership, life coaching, marriage and family, marriage and family studies, military resilience, parenting and child/adolescent, pastoral counseling, theology; professional counseling (MA); psychology (MS), including developmental psychology (MA, MS), industrial/organizational psychology (MA, MS); school counseling (M Ed). *Program availability:* Part-time, online learning. *Students:* 3,786 full-time (3,065 women), 5,193 part-time (4,081 women); includes 2,733 minority (1,967 Black or African American, non-Hispanic/Latino; 48 American Indian or Alaska Native, non-Hispanic/Latino; 103 Asian, non-Hispanic/Latino; 349 Hispanic/Latino; 19 Native Hawaiian or other Pacific Islander, non-Hispanic/Latino; 247 Two or more races, non-Hispanic/Latino), 133 international. Average age 38. 13,324 applicants, 28% accepted, 2,163 enrolled. In 2019, 2,322 master's, 19 doctorates, 112 other advanced degrees awarded. *Entrance requirements:* For master's, Official bachelor's degree transcripts with a 2.0 GPA or higher. *Application deadline:* Applications are processed on a rolling basis. Application fee: $50. Electronic applications accepted. *Expenses: Tuition:* Full-time $545; part-time $410 per credit hour. One-time fee: $50. *Financial support:* In 2019–20, 1,003 students received support. Teaching assistantships and Federal Work-Study available. Financial award applicants required to submit FAFSA. *Unit head:* Dr. Kenyon Knapp, Dean, School of Behavioral Services, E-mail: kcknapp@liberty.edu. *Application contact:* Jay Bridge, Director of Admissions, 800-424-9595, Fax: 800-628-7977, E-mail: gradadmissions@liberty.edu.
Website: https://www.liberty.edu/behavioral-sciences/

**Liberty University,** School of Health Sciences, Lynchburg, VA 24515. Offers anatomy and cell biology (PhD); biomedical sciences (MS); epidemiology (MPH); exercise science (MS), including clinical, community physical activity, human performance, nutrition; global health (MPH); health promotion (MPH); medical sciences (MA), including biopsychology, business management, health informatics, molecular medicine, public health; nutrition (MPH). *Program availability:* Part-time, online learning. *Students:* 820 full-time (588 women), 889 part-time (612 women); includes 611 minority (402 Black or African American, non-Hispanic/Latino; 10 American Indian or Alaska Native, non-Hispanic/Latino; 43 Asian, non-Hispanic/Latino; 85 Hispanic/Latino; 1 Native Hawaiian or other Pacific Islander, non-Hispanic/Latino; 70 Two or more races, non-Hispanic/Latino), 67 international. Average age 32. 2,610 applicants, 33% accepted, 406 enrolled. In 2019, 445 master's awarded. *Degree requirements:* For master's, thesis (for some programs); for doctorate, thesis/dissertation. *Entrance requirements:* For doctorate, MAT or GRE, minimum GPA of 3.25 in master's program, 2-3 recommendations, writing samples (for some programs), letter of intent, professional vitae. Additional exam requirements/recommendations for international students: required—TOEFL (minimum score 600 paper-based; 100 iBT). Application fee: $50. *Expenses: Tuition:* Full-time $545; part-time $410 per credit hour. One-time fee: $50. *Financial support:* In 2019–20, 918 students received support. Federal Work-Study available. Financial award applicants required to submit FAFSA. *Unit head:* Dr. Ralph Linstra, Dean. *Application contact:* Jay Bridge, Director of Admissions, 800-424-9595, Fax: 800-628-7977, E-mail: gradadmissions@liberty.edu.
Website: https://www.liberty.edu/health-sciences/

## Health Promotion

**Lindenwood University,** Graduate Programs, School of Health Sciences, St. Charles, MO 63301-1695. Offers human performance (MS); nursing (MS). *Program availability:* Part-time, blended/hybrid learning. *Faculty:* 8 full-time (3 women), 8 part-time/adjunct (5 women). *Students:* 22 full-time (11 women), 25 part-time (18 women); includes 5 minority (3 Black or African American, non-Hispanic/Latino; 1 Hispanic/Latino; 1 Native Hawaiian or other Pacific Islander, non-Hispanic/Latino), 6 international. Average age 30. 43 applicants, 37% accepted, 12 enrolled. In 2019, 31 master's awarded. *Degree requirements:* For master's, minimum cumulative GPA of 3.0. *Entrance requirements:* For master's, minimum cumulative GPA of 3.0. Additional exam requirements/recommendations for international students: required—TOEFL (minimum score 553 paper-based; 81 iBT); recommended—IELTS (minimum score 6.5). *Application deadline:* For fall admission, 8/9 priority date for domestic students, 6/1 priority date for international students; for spring admission, 12/20 priority date for domestic students, 11/1 priority date for international students; for summer admission, 5/15 priority date for domestic students, 3/27 priority date for international students. Applications are processed on a rolling basis. Application fee: $0 ($100 for international students). Electronic applications accepted. *Expenses: Tuition:* Full-time $8910; part-time $495 per credit. Tuition and fees vary according to course load, degree level and program. *Financial support:* In 2019–20, 25 students received support. Career-related internships or fieldwork, Federal Work-Study, institutionally sponsored loans, scholarships/grants, tuition waivers (partial), and unspecified assistantships available. Financial award application deadline: 6/30; financial award applicants required to submit FAFSA. *Unit head:* Dr. Cynthia Schroeder, Dean, School of Health Sciences, 636-949-4318, E-mail: cschroeder@lindenwood.edu. *Application contact:* Kara Schilli, Assistant Vice President, University Admissions, 636-949-4349, Fax: 636-949-4109, E-mail: adultadmissions@lindenwood.edu.
Website: https://www.lindenwood.edu/academics/academic-schools/school-of-health-sciences/

**Lock Haven University of Pennsylvania,** College of Natural, Behavioral and Health Sciences, Lock Haven, PA 17745-2390. Offers actuarial science (PSM); athletic training (MS); health promotion/education (MHS); healthcare management (MHS); physician assistant (MHS). *Accreditation:* ARC-PA. *Entrance requirements:* For master's, minimum undergraduate GPA of 3.0. Additional exam requirements/recommendations for international students: required—TOEFL. Electronic applications accepted.

**Manhattanville College,** School of Education, Program in Physical Education and Sports Pedagogy, Purchase, NY 10577-2132. Offers health and wellness specialist (Advanced Certificate); physical education and sport pedagogy (MAT). *Program availability:* Part-time, evening/weekend. *Faculty:* 2 full-time (both women), 10 part-time/adjunct (3 women). *Students:* 48 full-time (12 women), 55 part-time (15 women); includes 17 minority (9 Black or African American, non-Hispanic/Latino; 1 American Indian or Alaska Native, non-Hispanic/Latino; 2 Asian, non-Hispanic/Latino; 5 Hispanic/Latino). Average age 29. 31 applicants, 87% accepted, 26 enrolled. In 2019, 33 master's awarded. *Degree requirements:* For master's, comprehensive exam (for some programs), student teaching, research seminars, portfolios, internships, writing assessment; for Advanced Certificate, comprehensive exam (for some programs). *Entrance requirements:* For master's, for programs leading to certification, candidates must submit scores from GRE or MAT(Miller Analogies Test), minimum undergraduate GPA of 3.0, all transcripts from all colleges and universities attended, 2 letters of recommendation, interview, essay (2-3 page personal statement that describes reasons for choosing education as profession and personal philosophy of education), proof of immunization (for those born after 1957). Additional exam requirements/recommendations for international students: required—TOEFL or IELTS are required. Manhattanville College now accepts the Duolingo English Test with a required score of 105; recommended—TOEFL (minimum score 600 paper-based; 110 iBT), IELTS (minimum score 8). *Application deadline:* Applications are processed on a rolling basis. Application fee: $75. Electronic applications accepted. *Expenses:* $935 per credit, $45 technology fee, and $60 registration fee. *Financial support:* In 2019–20, 71 students received support. Teaching assistantships, scholarships/grants, tuition waivers, and unspecified assistantships available. Support available to part-time students. Financial award application deadline: 3/15; financial award applicants required to submit FAFSA. *Unit head:* Dr. Shelley Wepner, Dean, 914-323-3153, Fax: 914-323-5493, E-mail: Shelley.Wepner@mville.edu. *Application contact:* Alissa Wilson, Director, SOE Graduate Enrollment Management, 914-323-3150, Fax: 914-694-1732, E-mail: Alissa.Wilson@mville.edu.
Website: http://www.mville.edu/programs/physical-education-and-sports-pedagogy

**Maryland University of Integrative Health,** Programs in Health and Wellness Coaching, Laurel, MD 20723. Offers MA, Postbaccalaureate Certificate.

**Maryland University of Integrative Health,** Programs in Health Promotion and Yoga Therapy, Laurel, MD 20723. Offers health promotion (MS); yoga therapy (MS).

**Marymount University,** Malek School of Health Professions, Program in Health Education and Promotion, Arlington, VA 22207-4299. Offers health education and promotion (MS). *Program availability:* Part-time, evening/weekend. *Faculty:* 4 full-time (all women), 1 (woman) part-time/adjunct. *Students:* 43 full-time (33 women), 12 part-time (7 women); includes 5 minority (1 Black or African American, non-Hispanic/Latino; 1 Asian, non-Hispanic/Latino; 2 Hispanic/Latino; 1 Two or more races, non-Hispanic/Latino), 35 international. Average age 29. 54 applicants, 96% accepted, 27 enrolled. In 2019, 6 master's awarded. *Degree requirements:* For master's, thesis or alternative, Students have the option to complete an internship, research project, or capstone as the culminating experience for the program. *Entrance requirements:* For master's, GRE or MAT or Cumulative GPA of 3.0 or significant related experience, 2 letters of recommendation, resume, personal statement. Additional exam requirements/recommendations for international students: required—TOEFL (minimum score 600 paper-based; 96 iBT), IELTS (minimum score 6.5), PTE (minimum score 58). *Application deadline:* Applications are processed on a rolling basis. Application fee: $40. Electronic applications accepted. *Expenses: Tuition:* Part-time $1050 per credit. *Required fees:* $22 per credit. One-time fee: $270 part-time. Tuition and fees vary according to program. *Financial support:* In 2019–20, 6 students received support. Research assistantships, teaching assistantships, career-related internships or fieldwork, scholarships/grants, and unspecified assistantships available. Support available to part-time students. Financial award application deadline: 3/1; financial award applicants required to submit FAFSA. *Unit head:* Dr. Michael Nordvall, Chair, Health and Human Performance, 703-526-6876, E-mail: michael.nordvall@marymount.edu. *Application contact:* Fiona McDonnell, Administrative Assistant, 703-284-5901, E-mail: gadmissi@marymount.edu.
Website: https://www.marymount.edu/Academics/Malek-School-of-Health-Professions/Graduate-Programs/Health-Education-Promotion-(M-S)

**McNeese State University,** Doré School of Graduate Studies, Burton College of Education, Department of Health and Human Performance, Lake Charles, LA 70609. Offers exercise physiology (MS); health promotion (MS); nutrition and wellness (MS). *Accreditation:* NCATE. *Program availability:* Evening/weekend. *Entrance requirements:* For master's, GRE, undergraduate major or minor in health and human performance or related field of study.

**Merrimack College,** School of Health Sciences, North Andover, MA 01845-5800. Offers athletic training (MS); community health education (MS); exercise and sport science (MS); health and wellness management (MS). *Program availability:* Part-time, evening/weekend. *Degree requirements:* For master's, capstone (for community health education, exercise and sport science, and health and wellness management). *Entrance requirements:* For master's, resume, official college transcripts, personal statement, 2 recommendations. Additional exam requirements/recommendations for international students: required—TOEFL (minimum score 84 iBT), IELTS (minimum score 6.5), PTE (minimum score 56). Electronic applications accepted. Application fee is waived when completed online. *Expenses:* Contact institution.

**Morehead State University,** Graduate School, College of Science, Department of Kinesiology, Health, and Imaging Sciences, Morehead, KY 40351. Offers wellness promotion (MA). *Accreditation:* NCATE. *Program availability:* Part-time, evening/weekend. *Faculty:* 3 full-time (2 women), 1 (woman) part-time/adjunct. *Students:* 12 full-time (8 women), 6 part-time (5 women); includes 5 minority (3 Black or African American, non-Hispanic/Latino; 2 Two or more races, non-Hispanic/Latino). 7 applicants, 86% accepted, 6 enrolled. In 2019, 5 master's awarded. *Degree requirements:* For master's, comprehensive exam, thesis, minimum 3.0 GPA. *Entrance requirements:* For master's, Minimum 2.75 UG GPA. *Application deadline:* Applications are processed on a rolling basis. Application fee: $30. Electronic applications accepted. *Expenses: Tuition, area resident:* Part-time $570 per credit hour. Tuition, state resident: part-time $570 per credit hour. Tuition, nonresident: part-time $570 per credit hour. *Required fees:* $14 per credit hour. *Financial support:* Research assistantships, teaching assistantships, career-related internships or fieldwork, and unspecified assistantships available. Financial award applicants required to submit FAFSA. *Unit head:* Dr. Manuel Probst, Department of Kinesiology, Health and Imaging Sciences, 606-783-2462, E-mail: m.probst@moreheadstate.edu. *Application contact:* Dr. Manuel Probst, Department of Kinesiology, Health and Imaging Sciences, 606-783-2462, E-mail: m.probst@moreheadstate.edu.
Website: https://www.moreheadstate.edu/College-of-Science/Kinesiology,-Health,-and-Imaging-Sciences

**Mount St. Joseph University,** Graduate Program in Religious Studies, Cincinnati, OH 45233-1670. Offers religious studies (MA); spirituality and wellness (Certificate). *Program availability:* Part-time, evening/weekend. *Degree requirements:* For master's, comprehensive exam, 36 hours of credit, pastoral PRAXIS component (3 credit hours), integrating project (3 credit hours). *Entrance requirements:* For master's, undergraduate transcript with minimum overall GPA of 3.0, 3 letters of recommendation from professional colleagues, 3-page essay, interview with the Graduate Admissions Committee, current work resume. Additional exam requirements/recommendations for international students: required—TOEFL (minimum score 560 paper-based; 83 iBT). Electronic applications accepted. *Expenses:* Contact institution.

**National University,** School of Health and Human Services, La Jolla, CA 92037-1011. Offers clinical affairs (MS); clinical regulatory affairs (MS); complementary and integrative healthcare (MS); family nurse practitioner (MSN); health and life science analytics (MS); health informatics (MS, Certificate); healthcare administration (MHA); nurse anesthesia (MSNA); nursing administration (MSN); nursing informatics (MSN); psychiatric-mental health nurse practitioner (MSN); public health (MPH), including health promotion, healthcare administration, mental health. *Accreditation:* CEPH. *Program availability:* Part-time, evening/weekend, 100% online, blended/hybrid learning. *Degree requirements:* For master's, thesis (for some programs). *Entrance requirements:* For master's, interview, minimum GPA of 2.5. Additional exam requirements/recommendations for international students: required—TOEFL (minimum score 550 paper-based; 79 iBT), IELTS (minimum score 6). Electronic applications accepted. *Expenses: Tuition:* Full-time $442; part-time $442 per unit.

**Nebraska Methodist College,** Program in Health Promotion Management, Omaha, NE 68114. Offers MS. *Program availability:* Part-time, evening/weekend, online learning. *Degree requirements:* For master's, thesis or alternative, capstone project. *Entrance requirements:* For master's, interview. Additional exam requirements/recommendations for international students: required—TOEFL (minimum score 550 paper-based; 80 iBT).

**New York University,** Steinhardt School of Culture, Education, and Human Development, Department of Applied Psychology, Programs in Counseling, New York, NY 10012. Offers counseling and guidance (MA, Advanced Certificate), including bilingual school counseling K-12 (MA), school counseling K-12 (MA); counseling for mental health and wellness (MA); counseling psychology (PhD); LGBT health, education, and social services (Advanced Certificate); Advanced Certificate/MPH; MA/Advanced Certificate. *Accreditation:* APA (one or more programs are accredited). *Program availability:* Part-time. *Entrance requirements:* For doctorate, GRE General Test, interview. Additional exam requirements/recommendations for international students: required—TOEFL (minimum score 100 iBT). Electronic applications accepted.

**Old Dominion University,** Darden College of Education, Program in Physical Education, Exercise Science and Wellness Emphasis, Norfolk, VA 23529. Offers physical education (MS Ed), including exercise science and wellness. *Program availability:* Part-time, evening/weekend. *Degree requirements:* For master's, comprehensive exam, thesis or alternative, internship, research project. *Entrance requirements:* For master's, GRE (minimum score of 291 for combined verbal and quantitative), minimum GPA of 2.8 overall, 3.0 in major. Additional exam requirements/recommendations for international students: required—TOEFL (minimum score 550 paper-based; 79 iBT). Electronic applications accepted.

**Oregon State University,** College of Public Health and Human Sciences, Program in Public Health, Corvallis, OR 97331. Offers biostatistics (MPH); environmental and occupational health (MPH, PhD); epidemiology (MPH, PhD); global health (MPH, PhD). *Accreditation:* CEPH. Terminal master's awarded for partial completion of doctoral program. *Entrance requirements:* For master's and doctorate, GRE, minimum GPA of 3.0 in last 90 hours. Additional exam requirements/recommendations for international students: required—TOEFL (minimum score 80 iBT), IELTS (minimum score 6.5). Electronic applications accepted. *Expenses:* Contact institution.

**Plymouth State University,** College of Graduate Studies, Graduate Studies in Education, Program in Health Education, Plymouth, NH 03264-1595. Offers eating disorders (M Ed); health education (M Ed); health promotion (MS). *Program availability:* Part-time, evening/weekend. *Entrance requirements:* For master's, MAT, minimum GPA of 3.0.

**Plymouth State University,** Program in Personal and Organizational Wellness, Plymouth, NH 03264-1595. Offers MA, Graduate Certificate.

**Portland State University,** Graduate Studies, OHSU-PSU School of Public Health, Health Promotion Program, Portland, OR 97207-0751. Offers community health (PhD); health promotion (MPH); health studies (MA). *Program availability:* Part-time. *Students:* 1 (woman) full-time, 4 part-time (all women); includes 2 minority (1 Asian, non-Hispanic/Latino; 1 Two or more races, non-Hispanic/Latino). Average age 38. In 2019, 9 master's awarded. *Degree requirements:* For master's, comprehensive exam (for some programs), thesis (for some programs), internship/practicum, oral and written exams (depending on program); for doctorate, comprehensive exam, thesis/dissertation. *Entrance requirements:* For master's, GRE General Test (minimum scores: Verbal 153;

Quantitative 148; Analytic Writing 4.5), personal statement, 3 letters of recommendation, minimum GPA of 3.0, resume, background check; for doctorate, GRE General Test (minimum scores: Verbal 153; Quantitative 148; Analytic Writing 4.5), transcripts, personal statement, resume, writing sample, 3 letters of recommendation, background check. Additional exam requirements/recommendations for international students: required—TOEFL (minimum score 550 paper-based; 80 iBT). *Application deadline:* For fall admission, 2/1 for domestic and international students. Applications are processed on a rolling basis. Application fee: $65. *Expenses: Tuition, area resident:* Full-time $13,020; part-time $6510 per year. Tuition, state resident: full-time $13,020; part-time $6510 per year. Tuition, nonresident: full-time $19,830; part-time $9915 per year. *International tuition:* $19,830 full-time. *Required fees:* $1226. One-time fee: $350. Tuition and fees vary according to course load, program and reciprocity agreements. *Financial support:* Research assistantships with full and partial tuition reimbursements, teaching assistantships, career-related internships or fieldwork, Federal Work-Study, scholarships/grants, and unspecified assistantships available. Support available to part-time students. Financial award application deadline: 3/1; financial award applicants required to submit FAFSA. *Unit head:* Dr. David Bangsberg, Founding Dean, 503-282-7537. *Application contact:* Dr. Jill Rissi, Associate Dean for Academic Affairs, 503-725-8217, E-mail: jrissi@pdx.edu.
Website: https://ohsu-psu-sph.org/

**Queen's University at Kingston,** School of Graduate Studies, School of Kinesiology and Health Studies, Kingston, ON K7L 3N6, Canada. Offers biomechanics and ergonomics (M Sc, PhD); exercise physiology (M Sc, PhD); health promotion (M Sc, PhD); physical activity epidemiology (M Sc, PhD); sociocultural studies of sport, health and the body (MA, PhD); sport psychology (M Sc, PhD). *Program availability:* Part-time. *Degree requirements:* For master's, thesis (for some programs); for doctorate, comprehensive exam, thesis/dissertation. *Entrance requirements:* For master's and doctorate, minimum B+ average. Additional exam requirements/recommendations for international students: required—TOEFL. Electronic applications accepted.

**Rosalind Franklin University of Medicine and Science,** College of Health Professions, Department of Nutrition, North Chicago, IL 60064-3095. Offers clinical nutrition (MS); health promotion and wellness (MS); nutrition education (MS). *Program availability:* Part-time, evening/weekend, online learning. *Degree requirements:* For master's, thesis optional, portfolio. *Entrance requirements:* For master's, minimum GPA of 2.75, registered dietitian (RD), professional certificate or license. Additional exam requirements/recommendations for international students: required—TOEFL. *Expenses:* Contact institution.

**Rowan University,** Graduate School, School of Biomedical Science and Health Professions, Department of Health and Exercise Science, Glassboro, NJ 08028-1701. Offers wellness and lifestyle management (MA). *Degree requirements:* For master's, comprehensive exam, thesis. *Entrance requirements:* For master's, GRE General Test, GRE Subject Test, interview, minimum GPA of 2.8. Additional exam requirements/recommendations for international students: required—TOEFL. Electronic applications accepted. *Expenses: Tuition, area resident:* Part-time $715.50 per semester hour. Tuition, state resident: part-time $715.50 per semester hour. Tuition, nonresident: part-time $715.50 per semester hour. *Required fees:* $161.55 per semester hour.

**San Diego State University,** Graduate and Research Affairs, College of Health and Human Services, School of Public Health, San Diego, CA 92182. Offers environmental health (MPH); epidemiology (MPH, PhD), including biostatistics (MPH); global emergency preparedness and response (MS); global health (PhD); health behavior (PhD); health promotion (MPH); health services administration (MPH); toxicology (MS); MPH/MA; MSW/MPH. *Accreditation:* CAHME (one or more programs are accredited); CEPH. *Program availability:* Part-time. *Degree requirements:* For master's, comprehensive exam (for some programs), thesis (for some programs); for doctorate, thesis/dissertation. *Entrance requirements:* For master's, GMAT (MPH in health services administration), GRE General Test; for doctorate, GRE General Test. Additional exam requirements/recommendations for international students: required—TOEFL.

**Simmons University,** Gwen Ifill College of Media, Arts, and Humanities, Boston, MA 02115. Offers behavior analysis (MS, PhD, Ed S); children's literature (MA); dietetics (Certificate); elementary education (MAT); English (MA); gender/cultural studies (MA); history (MA); nutrition and health promotion (MS); physical therapy (DPT); public health (MPH); public policy (MPP); special education: moderate and severe disabilities (MS Ed); sports nutrition (Certificate); writing for children (MFA). *Program availability:* Part-time. *Faculty:* 10 full-time (9 women), 7 part-time/adjunct (6 women). *Students:* 2 full-time (both women), 67 part-time (57 women); includes 13 minority (3 Black or African American, non-Hispanic/Latino; 4 Asian, non-Hispanic/Latino; 3 Hispanic/Latino; 3 Two or more races, non-Hispanic/Latino), 1 international. Average age 31. 42 applicants, 62% accepted, 23 enrolled. In 2019, 24 master's awarded. *Degree requirements:* For master's, thesis optional. *Entrance requirements:* For master's, GRE, bachelor's degree from accredited college or university; minimum B average (preferred). Additional exam requirements/recommendations for international students: required—TOEFL (minimum score 600 paper-based; 100 iBT). *Application deadline:* For fall admission, 8/1 for domestic and international students; for spring admission, 12/15 for domestic and international students; for summer admission, 5/1 for domestic and international students. Applications are processed on a rolling basis. Application fee: $35. Electronic applications accepted. *Expenses:* Contact institution. *Financial support:* In 2019-20, 14 students received support, including 1 fellowship (averaging $15,360 per year), 13 teaching assistantships (averaging $2,000 per year); scholarships/grants also available. Financial award applicants required to submit FAFSA. *Unit head:* Dr. Brian Norman, Dean, 617-521-2472, E-mail: brian.norman@simmons.edu. *Application contact:* Patricia Flaherty, Director, Graduate Studies Admission, 617-521-3902, Fax: 617-521-3058, E-mail: gsa@simmons.edu.
Website: https://www.simmons.edu/academics/colleges-schools-departments/ifill

**Sonoma State University,** School of Science and Technology, Department of Kinesiology, Rohnert Park, CA 94928. Offers exercise science/pre-physical therapy (MA); interdisciplinary (MA); interdisciplinary pre-occupational therapy (MA); lifetime physical activity (MA), including coach education, fitness and wellness. *Program availability:* Part-time. *Degree requirements:* For master's, thesis, oral exam. *Entrance requirements:* For master's, minimum GPA of 2.8. Additional exam requirements/recommendations for international students: required—TOEFL (minimum score 500 paper-based).

**Southern Methodist University,** Simmons School of Education and Human Development, Department of Allied Physiology and Wellness, Dallas, TX 75275. Offers applied physiology (PhD); health promotion management (MS); sport management (MS). *Entrance requirements:* For master's, GMAT, resume, essays, transcripts from all colleges and universities attended, two references. Additional exam requirements/recommendations for international students: required—TOEFL or PTE.

**Springfield College,** Graduate Programs, Programs in Physical Education, Springfield, MA 01109-3797. Offers adapted physical education (MS); advanced-level coaching (M Ed); athletic administration (MS); exercise physiology (PhD); health promotion and disease prevention (MS); physical education initial licensure (CAGS); sport and exercise psychology (PhD); teaching and administration (PhD). *Program availability:* Part-time.

*Degree requirements:* For master's, comprehensive exam, thesis (for some programs). *Entrance requirements:* For master's and doctorate, GRE General Test. Additional exam requirements/recommendations for international students: required—TOEFL (minimum score 550 paper-based); recommended—IELTS (minimum score 7). Electronic applications accepted.

**Stony Brook University, State University of New York,** Stony Brook Medicine, Renaissance School of Medicine, Program in Public Health, Stony Brook, NY 11794. Offers community health (MPH); evaluation sciences (MPH); family violence (MPH); health communication (Certificate); health economics (MPH); health education and promotion (Certificate); population health (MPH); substance abuse (MPH). *Accreditation:* CEPH. *Program availability:* Part-time, evening/weekend. *Students:* 39 full-time (30 women), 17 part-time (12 women); includes 24 minority (3 Black or African American, non-Hispanic/Latino; 13 Asian, non-Hispanic/Latino; 7 Hispanic/Latino; 1 Two or more races, non-Hispanic/Latino), 2 international. Average age 28. 174 applicants, 67% accepted, 70 enrolled. In 2019, 22 master's awarded. *Entrance requirements:* For master's, GRE, 3 references, bachelor's degree from accredited college or university with minimum GPA of 3.0, essays, interview. Additional exam requirements/recommendations for international students: required—TOEFL (minimum score 90 iBT). *Application deadline:* For fall admission, 7/15 for domestic students. Application fee: $100. Electronic applications accepted. *Expenses:* Contact institution. *Financial support:* In 2019-20, 4 research assistantships were awarded; fellowships also available. *Unit head:* Dr. Lisa A. Benz Scott, Director, 631-444-9396, E-mail: publichealth@stonybrookmedicine.edu. *Application contact:* Joanie Maniaci, Assistant Director for Student Affairs, 631-444-2074, Fax: 631-444-6035, E-mail: joanmarie.maniaci@stonybrook.edu.
Website: https://publichealth.stonybrookmedicine.edu/

**Tennessee Technological University,** College of Graduate Studies, College of Education, Department of Exercise Science, Physical Education and Wellness, Cookeville, TN 38505. Offers adapted physical education (MA); elementary/middle school physical education (MA); lifetime wellness (MA); sport management (MA). *Accreditation:* NCATE. *Program availability:* Part-time, online learning. *Faculty:* 7 full-time (0 women). *Students:* 12 full-time (5 women), 39 part-time (20 women); includes 5 minority (2 Black or African American, non-Hispanic/Latino; 1 Hispanic/Latino; 2 Two or more races, non-Hispanic/Latino), 2 international. 28 applicants, 64% accepted, 14 enrolled. In 2019, 20 master's awarded. *Degree requirements:* For master's, comprehensive exam, thesis or alternative. *Entrance requirements:* For master's, MAT or GRE. Additional exam requirements/recommendations for international students: required—TOEFL (minimum score 527 paper-based; 71 iBT), IELTS (minimum score 5.5), PTE (minimum score 48), or TOEIC (Test of English as an International Communication). *Application deadline:* For fall admission, 8/1 for domestic students, 5/1 for international students; for spring admission, 12/1 for domestic students, 10/1 for international students; for summer admission, 5/1 for domestic students, 2/1 for international students. Applications are processed on a rolling basis. Application fee: $35 ($40 for international students). Electronic applications accepted. *Expenses: Tuition, area resident:* Part-time $597 per credit hour. Tuition, state resident: part-time $597 per credit hour. Tuition, nonresident: part-time $1323 per credit hour. *Financial support:* Fellowships, research assistantships, teaching assistantships, and career-related internships or fieldwork available. Financial award application deadline: 4/1. *Unit head:* Dr. Christy Killman, Chairperson, 931-372-3467, Fax: 931-372-6319, E-mail: ckillman@tntech.edu. *Application contact:* Shelia K. Kendrick, Coordinator of Graduate Studies, 931-372-3808, Fax: 931-372-3497, E-mail: skendrick@tntech.edu.

**Tulane University,** School of Professional Advancement, New Orleans, LA 70118-5669. Offers health and wellness management (MPS); homeland security studies (MPS); information technology management (MPS); liberal arts (MLA). *Program availability:* Part-time. *Degree requirements:* For master's, thesis. *Entrance requirements:* For master's, GRE General Test, minimum B average in undergraduate course work. Additional exam requirements/recommendations for international students: required—TOEFL. *Expenses: Tuition:* Full-time $57,004; part-time $3167 per credit hour. *Required fees:* $2086; $44.50 per credit hour. $80 per term. Tuition and fees vary according to course load, degree level and program.

**Union Institute & University,** Master of Arts Program, Cincinnati, OH 45206-1925. Offers creativity studies (MA); health and wellness (MA); history and culture (MA); leadership, public policy, and social issues (MA); literature and writing (MA). *Program availability:* Part-time, online only, 100% online. *Degree requirements:* For master's, thesis. *Entrance requirements:* For master's, transcript, essay, 3 letters of recommendation, resume. Additional exam requirements/recommendations for international students: recommended—TOEFL. Electronic applications accepted. *Expenses:* Contact institution.

**Universidad del Turabo,** Graduate Programs, Programs in Education, Program in Wellness, Gurabo, PR 00778-3030. Offers MPHE. *Entrance requirements:* For master's, GRE, EXADEP, GMAT, interview, official transcript, essay, recommendation letters. Electronic applications accepted.

**The University of Alabama,** Graduate School, College of Human Environmental Sciences, Department of Health Science, Tuscaloosa, AL 35487-0311. Offers health education and promotion (PhD); health studies (MA). *Program availability:* Part-time, online learning. *Faculty:* 12 full-time (6 women). *Students:* 41 full-time (30 women), 70 part-time (57 women); includes 47 minority (31 Black or African American, non-Hispanic/Latino; 1 American Indian or Alaska Native, non-Hispanic/Latino; 5 Asian, non-Hispanic/Latino; 7 Hispanic/Latino; 3 Two or more races, non-Hispanic/Latino), 3 international. Average age 34. 67 applicants, 64% accepted, 26 enrolled. In 2019, 47 master's, 3 doctorates awarded. *Degree requirements:* For master's, comprehensive exam, thesis optional; for doctorate, one foreign language, comprehensive exam, thesis/dissertation. *Entrance requirements:* For master's, minimum GPA of 3.0; for doctorate, GRE General Test, minimum GPA of 3.0, prerequisites in health education. Additional exam requirements/recommendations for international students: required—TOEFL. *Application deadline:* For fall admission, 3/15 priority date for domestic students, 3/15 for international students. Applications are processed on a rolling basis. Application fee: $50 ($60 for international students). Electronic applications accepted. *Expenses: Tuition, area resident:* Full-time $10,780; part-time $440 per credit hour. Tuition, nonresident: full-time $30,250; part-time $1550 per credit hour. *Financial support:* In 2019-20, 10 students received support. Research assistantships with full tuition reimbursements available, teaching assistantships with full tuition reimbursements available, career-related internships or fieldwork, Federal Work-Study, institutionally sponsored loans, health care benefits, and unspecified assistantships available. Financial award application deadline: 4/15; financial award applicants required to submit FAFSA. *Unit head:* Dr. Don Chaney, Department Head and Professor, 205-348-9087, Fax: 205-348-7568, E-mail: dchaney@ches.ua.edu. *Application contact:* Dr. Angelia Paschal, Associate Professor and Doctoral Program Coordinator, 205-348-5708, Fax: 205-348-7568, E-mail: apaschal@ches.ua.edu.
Website: http://ches.ua.edu/

**The University of Alabama at Birmingham,** School of Public Health, Health Behavior, Birmingham, AL 35294. Offers health education and health promotion (PhD). *Program availability:* Part-time, 100% online, blended/hybrid learning. *Faculty:* 8 full-time (5

women). *Students:* 45 full-time (37 women), 31 part-time (30 women); includes 30 minority (20 Black or African American, non-Hispanic/Latino; 4 American Indian or Alaska Native, non-Hispanic/Latino; 1 Asian, non-Hispanic/Latino; 2 Hispanic/Latino; 3 Two or more races, non-Hispanic/Latino), 5 international. Average age 32. 62 applicants, 61% accepted, 21 enrolled. In 2019, 5 doctorates awarded. *Degree requirements:* For doctorate, comprehensive exam, thesis/dissertation, research internship. *Entrance requirements:* For doctorate, GRE, 3 letters of recommendation, transcripts, personal statement, curriculum vitae/resume. Additional exam requirements/recommendations for international students: required—TOEFL (minimum score 80 iBT), IELTS (minimum score 6.5). *Application deadline:* For fall admission, 4/1 priority date for domestic and international students; for spring admission, 11/1 for domestic students; for summer admission, 4/1 for domestic students. Application fee: $50 ($60 for international students). Electronic applications accepted. *Financial support:* Fellowships, research assistantships, teaching assistantships, career-related internships or fieldwork, Federal Work-Study, scholarships/grants, traineeships, health care benefits, and full-time employee tuition coverage available. Financial award application deadline: 3/1; financial award applicants required to submit FAFSA. *Unit head:* Dr. Robin G. Lanzi, Graduate Program Director, 205-975-8071, Fax: 205-934-9325, E-mail: rlanzi@uab.edu. *Application contact:* Dustin Shaw, Coordinator, Student Admissions and Record, 205-934-2684, E-mail: dshaw84@uab.edu.
Website: http://www.soph.uab.edu/hb

**University of Alberta,** School of Public Health, Centre for Health Promotion Studies, Edmonton, AB T6G 2E1, Canada. Offers health promotion (M Sc, Postgraduate Diploma). *Program availability:* Part-time, online learning.

**University of Arkansas,** Graduate School, College of Education and Health Professions, Department of Health, Human Performance and Recreation, Program in Community Health Promotion, Fayetteville, AR 72701. Offers MS, PhD. *Students:* 9 full-time (7 women), 8 part-time (7 women), 4 international. 15 applicants, 53% accepted. In 2019, 4 master's, 1 doctorate awarded. *Application deadline:* For fall admission, 8/1 for domestic students, 4/1 for international students; for spring admission, 12/1 for domestic students, 10/1 for international students; for summer admission, 4/15 for domestic students, 3/1 for international students. Application fee: $60. *Unit head:* Dr. Matthew Ganio, Department Head, 479-575-2956, E-mail: msganio@uark.edu. *Application contact:* Dr. Paul Calleja, Assistant Dept. Head - HHPR, Graduate Coordinator, 479-575-2854, Fax: 479-575-5778, E-mail: pcallej@uark.edu.
Website: https://hhpr.uark.edu

**University of Arkansas for Medical Sciences,** Fay W. Boozman College of Public Health, Little Rock, AR 72205-7199. Offers biostatistics (MPH); environmental and occupational health (MPH, Certificate); epidemiology (MPH, PhD); health behavior and health education (MPH); health policy and management (MPH); health promotion and prevention research (PhD); health services administration (MHSA); health systems research (PhD); public health (Certificate); public health leadership (Dr PH). *Accreditation:* CAHME; CEPH. *Program availability:* Part-time. *Degree requirements:* For master's, preceptorship, culminating experience, internship; for doctorate, comprehensive exam, capstone. *Entrance requirements:* For master's, GRE, GMAT, LSAT, PCAT, MCAT, DAT; for doctorate, GRE. Additional exam requirements/recommendations for international students: required—TOEFL (minimum score 80 iBT), IELTS. Electronic applications accepted. *Expenses:* Contact institution.

**University of Central Oklahoma,** The Jackson College of Graduate Studies, College of Education and Professional Studies, Department of Kinesiology and Health Studies, Edmond, OK 73034-5209. Offers athletic training (MS); wellness management (MS), including exercise science, health promotion. *Degree requirements:* For master's, comprehensive exam (for some programs), thesis (for some programs). *Entrance requirements:* Additional exam requirements/recommendations for international students: required—TOEFL (minimum score 550 paper-based; 79 iBT), IELTS (minimum score 6.5). Electronic applications accepted.

**University of Chicago,** Division of the Biological Sciences, Department of Public Health Sciences, Chicago, IL 60637. Offers MS, PhD. *Program availability:* Part-time. Terminal master's awarded for partial completion of doctoral program. *Degree requirements:* For master's, thesis; for doctorate, comprehensive exam, thesis/dissertation, ethics class, 2 teaching assistantships. *Entrance requirements:* For master's, MCAT or GRE, doctoral-level clinical degree or completed pre-clinical training at accredited medical school, transcripts, statement of purpose, 3 letters of recommendation; for doctorate, GRE General Test, transcripts, statement of purpose, 3 letters of recommendation. Additional exam requirements/recommendations for international students: required—TOEFL (minimum score 600 paper-based; 104 iBT), IELTS (minimum score 7). Electronic applications accepted.

**University of Cincinnati,** Graduate School, College of Education, Criminal Justice, and Human Services, School of Human Services, Health Promotion and Education Program, Cincinnati, OH 45221. Offers exercise and fitness (MS); health education (PhD); public and community health (MS); public health (MPH). *Accreditation:* NCATE. *Program availability:* Part-time, evening/weekend. *Degree requirements:* For master's, thesis or alternative; for doctorate, thesis/dissertation. *Entrance requirements:* For master's and doctorate, GRE General Test. Additional exam requirements/recommendations for international students: required—TOEFL (minimum score 580 paper-based). Electronic applications accepted.

**University of Delaware,** College of Health Sciences, Department of Behavioral Health and Nutrition, Newark, DE 19716. Offers health promotion (MS); human nutrition (MS). *Program availability:* Part-time. *Degree requirements:* For master's, thesis. *Entrance requirements:* For master's, GRE General Test, interview, minimum GPA of 3.0. Additional exam requirements/recommendations for international students: required—TOEFL (minimum score 550 paper-based). Electronic applications accepted.

**University of Georgia,** College of Public Health, Department of Health Promotion and Behavior, Athens, GA 30602. Offers MA, MPH, Dr PH, PhD. *Accreditation:* NCATE (one or more programs are accredited). *Degree requirements:* For master's, thesis (MA); for doctorate, thesis/dissertation. *Entrance requirements:* For master's, GRE General Test or MAT; for doctorate, GRE General Test. Electronic applications accepted.

**The University of Kansas,** Graduate Studies, School of Architecture and Design, Department of Architecture, Lawrence, KS 66045. Offers architectural acoustics (Certificate); architecture (M Arch, PhD); health and wellness (Certificate); historic preservation (Certificate); urban design (Certificate). *Students:* 93 full-time (45 women), 23 part-time (13 women); includes 20 minority (4 Black or African American, non-Hispanic/Latino; 5 Asian, non-Hispanic/Latino; 4 Hispanic/Latino; 7 Two or more races, non-Hispanic/Latino), 23 international. Average age 25. 91 applicants, 59% accepted, 30 enrolled. In 2019, 70 master's, 2 doctorates, 8 other advanced degrees awarded. Terminal master's awarded for partial completion of doctoral program. *Entrance requirements:* For master's, GRE, transcript; resume, minimum GPA of 3.0; statement of purpose; letters of recommendation; portfolio of design work, or samples of written work or other creative artifacts produced if previous degree was not in a design-related discipline; for doctorate, GRE, transcript, resume, minimum GPA of 3.0, statement of purpose, letters of recommendation, research-informed writing sample, exhibit of work illustrating applicant's interests and abilities in areas related to the design disciplines. Additional exam requirements/recommendations for international students: required—TOEFL, IELTS. *Application deadline:* For fall admission, 1/15 priority date for domestic and international students; for summer admission, 1/15 priority date for domestic and international students. Application fee: $65 ($85 for international students). Electronic applications accepted. *Expenses:* Tuition, state resident: full-time $9989. Tuition, nonresident: full-time $23,950. *International tuition:* $23,950 full-time. *Required fees:* $984; $81.99 per credit hour. Tuition and fees vary according to course load, campus/location and program. *Financial support:* Fellowships, research assistantships, teaching assistantships, scholarships/grants, health care benefits, and unspecified assistantships available. Financial award application deadline: 1/15; financial award applicants required to submit FAFSA. *Unit head:* Frank Zilm, Dean, 816-561-7186, E-mail: frankzilm@ku.edu. *Application contact:* Joan Weaver, Graduate Admissions Contact, 785-864-3709, Fax: 785-864-5185, E-mail: jweaver@ku.edu.
Website: http://architecture.ku.edu/

**University of Kentucky,** Graduate School, College of Education, Program in Kinesiology and Health Promotion, Lexington, KY 40506-0032. Offers biomechanics (MS); exercise physiology (MS, PhD); exercise science (PhD); health promotion (MS, Ed D); physical education training (Ed D); sport leadership (MS); teaching and coaching (MS). Terminal master's awarded for partial completion of doctoral program. *Degree requirements:* For master's, comprehensive exam, thesis optional; for doctorate, comprehensive exam, thesis/dissertation. *Entrance requirements:* For master's, GRE General Test, minimum undergraduate GPA of 2.75; for doctorate, GRE General Test, minimum graduate GPA of 3.0. Additional exam requirements/recommendations for international students: required—TOEFL (minimum score 550 paper-based). Electronic applications accepted.

**University of Louisville,** Graduate School, School of Public Health and Information Sciences, Department of Health Promotion and Behavioral Sciences, Louisville, KY 40202. Offers health promotion (PhD). *Accreditation:* CEPH. *Program availability:* Part-time. *Faculty:* 9 full-time (5 women). *Students:* 20 full-time (9 women), 8 part-time (3 women); includes 12 minority (5 Black or African American, non-Hispanic/Latino; 4 Asian, non-Hispanic/Latino; 1 Hispanic/Latino; 2 Two or more races, non-Hispanic/Latino), 9 international. Average age 38. 11 applicants, 45% accepted, 4 enrolled. In 2019, 1 doctorate awarded. *Degree requirements:* For doctorate, comprehensive exam, thesis/dissertation. *Entrance requirements:* For doctorate, Recommended minimum GPA of 3.0 on a 4.0 scale. Three letters of recommendation (professional or academic) written within the last twelve months. Official transcripts of all degrees. One-page personal statement. Additional exam requirements/recommendations for international students: required—TOEFL (minimum score 90 iBT). *Application deadline:* For fall admission, 12/31 priority date for domestic students, 3/1 for international students. Applications are processed on a rolling basis. Application fee: $65. Electronic applications accepted. *Expenses: Tuition, area resident:* Full-time $13,000; part-time $723 per credit hour. Tuition, state resident: full-time $13,000; part-time $723 per credit hour. Tuition, nonresident: full-time $27,114; part-time $1507 per credit hour. *International tuition:* $27,114 full-time. *Required fees:* $196. Tuition and fees vary according to program and reciprocity agreements. *Financial support:* In 2019–20, 12 students received support, including 3 fellowships with full tuition reimbursements available (averaging $20,000 per year), 7 research assistantships with full tuition reimbursements available (averaging $20,000 per year); scholarships/grants, health care benefits, and unspecified assistantships also available. Support available to part-time students. Financial award application deadline: 12/31; financial award applicants required to submit FAFSA. *Unit head:* Dr. Monica Lynn Wendel, DrPH, MA, Professor and Chair, 502-852-2305, Fax: 502-852-3291, E-mail: monica.wendel@louisville.edu. *Application contact:* Barbara Parker, Administrative Specialist, 502-852-3290, Fax: 502-852-3291, E-mail: barbara.parker@louisville.edu.
Website: http://louisville.edu/sphis/departments/health-promotion-behavioral-sciences

**University of Lynchburg,** Graduate Studies, Master of Public Health Program, Lynchburg, VA 24501-3199. Offers public health (MPH), including health promotion. *Program availability:* Part-time. *Degree requirements:* For master's, internship, capstone project. *Entrance requirements:* For master's, GRE. Additional exam requirements/recommendations for international students: required—TOEFL (minimum score 550 paper-based; 80 iBT), IELTS (minimum score 6). Electronic applications accepted. Application fee is waived when completed online. *Expenses:* Contact institution.

**University of Massachusetts Lowell,** College of Health Sciences, School of Nursing, PhD Program in Nursing, Lowell, MA 01854. Offers PhD. *Accreditation:* AACN. *Degree requirements:* For doctorate, thesis/dissertation, qualifying examination. *Entrance requirements:* For doctorate, GRE General Test, master's degree in nursing with minimum GPA of 3.3, current MA RN license, 2 years of professional nursing experience, 3 letters of recommendation.

**University of Memphis,** Graduate School, School of Health Studies, Memphis, TN 38152. Offers faith and health (Graduate Certificate); health studies (MS), including exercise, sport and movement sciences, health promotion, physical education teacher education; nutrition (MS), including clinical nutrition, environmental nutrition, nutrition science; sport nutrition and dietary supplementation (Graduate Certificate). *Program availability:* 100% online. *Faculty:* 19 full-time (11 women), 2 part-time/adjunct (1 woman). *Students:* 56 full-time (44 women), 42 part-time (33 women); includes 39 minority (24 Black or African American, non-Hispanic/Latino; 4 Asian, non-Hispanic/Latino; 4 Hispanic/Latino; 2 Native Hawaiian or other Pacific Islander, non-Hispanic/Latino; 5 Two or more races, non-Hispanic/Latino), 6 international. Average age 29. 63 applicants, 84% accepted, 37 enrolled. In 2019, 38 master's, 2 other advanced degrees awarded. *Degree requirements:* For master's, comprehensive exam, thesis or alternative, culminating experience; for Graduate Certificate, practicum. *Entrance requirements:* For master's, GRE or PRAXIS II, letters of recommendation, statement of goals, minimum undergraduate GPA of 2.5; for Graduate Certificate, minimum undergraduate GPA of 2.5. Additional exam requirements/recommendations for international students: required—TOEFL (minimum score 550 paper-based; 79 iBT). *Application deadline:* For fall admission, 4/15 priority date for domestic students; for spring admission, 10/15 priority date for domestic students; for summer admission, 4/15 priority date for domestic students. Application fee: $35 ($60 for international students). *Expenses: Tuition, area resident:* Full-time $9216; part-time $512 per credit hour. Tuition, state resident: full-time $9216; part-time $512 per credit hour. Tuition, nonresident: full-time $12,672; part-time $704 per credit hour. *International tuition:* $16,128 full-time. *Required fees:* $1530; $85 per credit hour. Tuition and fees vary according to program. *Financial support:* Research assistantships, teaching assistantships, career-related internships or fieldwork, Federal Work-Study, scholarships/grants, and unspecified assistantships available. Financial award application deadline: 2/1; financial award applicants required to submit FAFSA. *Unit head:* Dr. Richard Bloomer, Dean, 901-678-4316, Fax: 901-678-3591, E-mail: rbloomer@memphis.edu. *Application contact:* Dr. Richard Bloomer, Dean, 901-678-4316, Fax: 901-678-3591, E-mail: rbloomer@memphis.edu.
Website: http://www.memphis.edu/shs/

**University of Michigan,** School of Public Health, Department of Health Behavior and Health Education, Ann Arbor, MI 48109. Offers MPH, PhD, MPH/MSW. *Accreditation:* CEPH (one or more programs are accredited). Terminal master's awarded for partial

completion of doctoral program. *Degree requirements:* For doctorate, oral defense of dissertation, preliminary exam. *Entrance requirements:* For master's, GRE General Test (preferred); MCAT; for doctorate, GRE General Test. Additional exam requirements/ recommendations for international students: required—TOEFL (minimum score 100 iBT). Electronic applications accepted.

**University of Mississippi,** Graduate School, School of Applied Sciences, University, MS 38677. Offers communicative disorders (MS); criminal justice (MCJ); exercise science (MS); food and nutrition services (MS); health and kinesiology (PhD); health promotion (MS); nutrition and hospitality management (PhD); park and recreation management (MA); social welfare (PhD); social work (MSW). *Students:* 188 full-time (149 women), 37 part-time (18 women); includes 47 minority (35 Black or African American, non-Hispanic/Latino; 2 American Indian or Alaska Native, non-Hispanic/ Latino; 1 Asian, non-Hispanic/Latino; 5 Hispanic/Latino; 1 Native Hawaiian or other Pacific Islander, non-Hispanic/Latino; 3 Two or more races, non-Hispanic/Latino), 23 international. Average age 26. *Expenses:* Tuition, state resident: full-time $8718; part-time $484.25 per credit hour. Tuition, nonresident: full-time $24,990; part-time $1388.25 per credit hour. *Required fees:* $100; $4.16 per credit hour. *Unit head:* Dr. Peter Grandjean, Dean of Applied Sciences, 662-915-7900, Fax: 662-915-7901, E-mail: applsci@olemiss.edu. *Application contact:* Temeka Smith, Graduate Activities Specialist for Admissions, 662-915-7474, Fax: 662-915-7577, E-mail: gschool@olemiss.edu.
Website: applsci@olemiss.edu

**University of Missouri,** School of Health Professions, Master of Public Health Program, Columbia, MO 65211. Offers global public health (Graduate Certificate); health promotion and policy (MPH); public health (Graduate Certificate); veterinary public health (MPH); DVM/MPH; MPH/MA; MPH/MPA. *Accreditation:* CEPH. *Entrance requirements:* Additional exam requirements/recommendations for international students: required—TOEFL (minimum score 550 paper-based; 80 iBT), IELTS (minimum score 6.5). Electronic applications accepted.

**University of Nebraska–Lincoln,** Graduate College, College of Education and Human Sciences, Department of Nutrition and Health Sciences, Lincoln, NE 68588. Offers community nutrition and health promotion (MS); nutrition (MS, PhD); nutrition and exercise (MS); nutrition and health sciences (MS, PhD). *Degree requirements:* For master's, thesis optional. *Entrance requirements:* For master's, GRE General Test. Additional exam requirements/recommendations for international students: required—TOEFL (minimum score 550 paper-based). Electronic applications accepted.

**University of Nebraska Medical Center,** Department of Health Promotion, Social and Behavioral Health, Omaha, NE 68198. Offers health promotion and disease prevention research (PhD). *Program availability:* Part-time. *Degree requirements:* For doctorate, comprehensive exam, thesis/dissertation, teaching experience. *Entrance requirements:* For doctorate, GRE, official transcripts, master's or other advanced degree, written statement of career goals, three letters of recommendation. Additional exam requirements/recommendations for international students: required—TOEFL (minimum score 550 paper-based; 80 iBT). Electronic applications accepted.

**University of North Alabama,** College of Education, Department of Health, Physical Education, and Recreation, Florence, AL 35632-0001. Offers health and human performance (MS), including exercise science, kinesiology, wellness and health promotion. *Program availability:* Part-time. *Degree requirements:* For master's, comprehensive exam (for some programs), thesis optional. *Entrance requirements:* For master's, MAT or GRE, 3 letters of recommendation, essay. Additional exam requirements/recommendations for international students: required—TOEFL (minimum score 79 iBT), IELTS (minimum score 6), PTE (minimum score 54). Electronic applications accepted.

**The University of North Carolina at Chapel Hill,** Graduate School, Gillings School of Global Public Health, Public Health Leadership Program, Chapel Hill, NC 27599. Offers health care and prevention (MPH); leadership (MPH); occupational health nursing (MPH). *Program availability:* Part-time, evening/weekend, 100% online, blended/hybrid learning. *Faculty:* 8 full-time (7 women), 48 part-time/adjunct (37 women). *Students:* 32 full-time (25 women), 17 part-time (12 women); includes 14 minority (2 Black or African American, non-Hispanic/Latino; 2 Asian, non-Hispanic/Latino; 6 Hispanic/Latino; 4 Two or more races, non-Hispanic/Latino), 2 international. Average age 36. 27 applicants, 78% accepted, 19 enrolled. In 2019, 80 master's awarded. *Degree requirements:* For master's, comprehensive exam, paper. *Entrance requirements:* For master's, three years of public health experience (recommended), three letters of recommendation (academic and/or professional; academic preferred). Additional exam requirements/ recommendations for international students: required—TOEFL (minimum score 90 iBT), IELTS (minimum score 7). *Application deadline:* For fall admission, 2/1 for domestic and international students. Application fee: $90. Electronic applications accepted. *Financial support:* Research assistantships, teaching assistantships, career-related internships or fieldwork, institutionally sponsored loans, scholarships/grants, traineeships, and health care benefits available. Financial award application deadline: 12/10; financial award applicants required to submit FAFSA. *Unit head:* Dr. Anna P. Schenck, Director, 919-843-8580, E-mail: anna.schenck@unc.edu. *Application contact:* Joe Jacobs, Academic Coordinator, 919-962-3398, E-mail: mjj0216@email.unc.edu.
Website: https://sph.unc.edu/phlp/phlp/

**University of Northern Iowa,** Graduate College, College of Education, School of Kinesiology, Allied Health and Human Services, MA Program in Health Education, Cedar Falls, IA 50614. Offers community health education (MA); health promotion/ fitness management (MA); school health education (MA). *Program availability:* Part-time, evening/weekend. *Degree requirements:* For master's, comprehensive exam, thesis or alternative. *Entrance requirements:* For master's, minimum GPA of 3.0. Additional exam requirements/recommendations for international students: required—TOEFL (minimum score 500 paper-based; 61 iBT). Electronic applications accepted.

**University of Oklahoma,** College of Arts and Sciences, Department of Health and Exercise Science, Norman, OK 73019. Offers exercise physiology (MS, PhD); health and exercise science (MS); health promotion (MS, PhD). *Degree requirements:* For master's, comprehensive exam (for some programs), thesis; for doctorate, comprehensive exam, thesis/dissertation. *Entrance requirements:* For master's and doctorate, GRE. Additional exam requirements/recommendations for international students: required—TOEFL (minimum score 79 iBT) or IELTS (minimum score 6.5). Electronic applications accepted. *Expenses:* Tuition, state resident: full-time $6583.20; part-time $274.30 per credit hour. Tuition, nonresident: full-time $21,242; part-time $885.10 per credit hour. *International tuition:* $21,242.40 full-time. *Required fees:* $1994.20; $72.55 per credit hour. $126.50 per semester. Tuition and fees vary according to course load and degree level.

**University of Oklahoma Health Sciences Center,** Graduate College, Hudson College of Public Health, Department of Health Promotion Sciences, Oklahoma City, OK 73190. Offers MPH, MS, Dr PH, PhD. *Accreditation:* CEPH (one or more programs are accredited). *Program availability:* Part-time. *Degree requirements:* For master's, comprehensive exam, thesis (for some programs); for doctorate, 2 foreign languages, comprehensive exam, thesis/dissertation. *Entrance requirements:* For master's, letters of recommendation, resume; for doctorate, GRE, letters of recommendation. Additional exam requirements/recommendations for international students: required—TOEFL (minimum score 570 paper-based).

**University of Puerto Rico - Medical Sciences Campus,** Graduate School of Public Health, Department of Human Development, Program in School Health Promotion, San Juan, PR 00936-5067. Offers Certificate.

**University of South Carolina,** The Graduate School, Arnold School of Public Health, Department of Health Promotion, Education, and Behavior, Columbia, SC 29208. Offers health education (MAT); health promotion, education, and behavior (MPH, MS, MSPH, Dr PH, PhD); school health education (Certificate); MSW/MPH. *Accreditation:* CEPH (one or more programs are accredited); NCATE (one or more programs are accredited). *Program availability:* Part-time. *Degree requirements:* For master's, comprehensive exam, thesis or alternative, practicum (MPH), project (MS); for doctorate, comprehensive exam, thesis/dissertation. *Entrance requirements:* For master's and doctorate, GRE General Test. Additional exam requirements/recommendations for international students: required—TOEFL (minimum score 570 paper-based; 75 iBT). Electronic applications accepted.

**University of South Carolina,** The Graduate School, Arnold School of Public Health, Program in Physical Activity and Public Health, Columbia, SC 29208. Offers MPH. *Accreditation:* CEPH. *Program availability:* Part-time. *Degree requirements:* For master's, comprehensive exam, practicum. *Entrance requirements:* For master's, GRE. Additional exam requirements/recommendations for international students: required—TOEFL (minimum score 570 paper-based). Electronic applications accepted.

**University of Southern California,** Keck School of Medicine and Graduate School, Graduate Programs in Medicine, Department of Preventive Medicine, Master of Public Health Program, Los Angeles, CA 90032. Offers biostatistics and epidemiology (MPH); child and family health (MPH); community health promotion (MPH); environmental health (MPH); geohealth (MPH); global health leadership (MPH); health communication (MPH); health services and policy (MPH). *Accreditation:* CEPH. *Program availability:* Part-time, evening/weekend, 100% online. *Faculty:* 37 full-time (28 women), 8 part-time/ adjunct (6 women). *Students:* 261 full-time (201 women), 74 part-time (55 women); includes 224 minority (46 Black or African American, non-Hispanic/Latino; 2 American Indian or Alaska Native, non-Hispanic/Latino; 79 Asian, non-Hispanic/Latino; 56 Hispanic/Latino; 6 Native Hawaiian or other Pacific Islander, non-Hispanic/Latino; 35 Two or more races, non-Hispanic/Latino), 21 international. Average age 28. 420 applicants, 76% accepted, 94 enrolled. In 2019, 123 master's awarded. *Degree requirements:* For master's, practicum, final report, oral presentation. *Entrance requirements:* For master's, GRE General Test, MCAT, GMAT, minimum GPA of 3.0. Additional exam requirements/recommendations for international students: required—TOEFL (minimum score 600 paper-based; 90 iBT). *Application deadline:* For fall admission, 12/1 priority date for domestic students, 5/1 priority date for international students; for spring admission, 9/1 priority date for domestic and international students; for summer admission, 3/1 for domestic and international students. Applications are processed on a rolling basis. Application fee: $135. Electronic applications accepted. *Financial support:* Career-related internships or fieldwork, Federal Work-Study, institutionally sponsored loans, and scholarships/grants available. Support available to part-time students. Financial award application deadline: 5/4; financial award applicants required to submit CSS PROFILE or FAFSA. *Unit head:* Dr. Louise A. Rohrbach, Director, 323-442-8237, Fax: 323-442-8297, E-mail: rohrbac@usc.edu. *Application contact:* Valerie Burris, Admissions Counselor, 323-442-7257, Fax: 323-442-8297, E-mail: valeriem@usc.edu.
Website: https://preventivemedicine.usc.edu/education/graduate-programs/mph/

**The University of Tennessee,** Graduate School, College of Education, Health and Human Sciences, Program in Health Promotion and Health Education, Knoxville, TN 37996. Offers MS. *Program availability:* Part-time. *Degree requirements:* For master's, thesis optional. *Entrance requirements:* For master's, minimum GPA of 2.7. Additional exam requirements/recommendations for international students: required—TOEFL. Electronic applications accepted.

**The University of Texas Health Science Center at Houston,** School of Public Health, Houston, TX 77030. Offers behavioral science (PhD); biostatistics (MPH, MS, PhD); environmental health (MPH); epidemiology (MPH, MS, PhD); general public health (Certificate); genomics and bioinformatics (Certificate); health disparities (Certificate); health promotion/health education (MPH, Dr PH); healthcare management (Certificate); management, policy and community health (MPH, Dr PH, PhD); maternal and child health (Certificate); public health informatics (Certificate); DDS/MPH; JD/MPH; MBA/ MPH; MD/MPH; MGPS/MPH; MP Aff/MPH; MS/MPH; MSN/MPH; MSW/MPH; PhD/ MPH. *Accreditation:* CAHME; CEPH. *Program availability:* Part-time. *Degree requirements:* For master's, thesis (for some programs); for doctorate, comprehensive exam, thesis/dissertation. *Entrance requirements:* For master's and doctorate, GRE General Test. Additional exam requirements/recommendations for international students: required—TOEFL (minimum score 600 paper-based, 100 iBT) or IELTS (7.5). Electronic applications accepted. *Expenses:* Contact institution.

**The University of Toledo,** College of Graduate Studies, College of Medicine and Life Sciences, Department of Public Health and Preventative Medicine, Toledo, OH 43606-3390. Offers biostatistics and epidemiology (Certificate); contemporary gerontological practice (Certificate); environmental and occupational health and safety (MPH); epidemiology (Certificate); global public health (Certificate); health promotion and education (MPH); industrial hygiene (MSOH); medical and health science teaching and learning (Certificate); occupational health (Certificate); public health administration (MPH); public health and emergency response (Certificate); public health epidemiology (MPH); public health nutrition (MPH); MD/MPH. *Program availability:* Part-time, evening/ weekend. *Degree requirements:* For master's, thesis or alternative. *Entrance requirements:* For master's, GRE, minimum undergraduate GPA of 3.0, three letters of recommendation, statement of purpose, transcripts from all prior institutions attended, resume; for Certificate, minimum undergraduate GPA of 3.0, three letters of recommendation, statement of purpose, transcripts from all prior institutions attended, resume. Additional exam requirements/recommendations for international students: required—TOEFL (minimum score 550 paper-based; 80 iBT), IELTS (minimum score 6.5). Electronic applications accepted.

**The University of Toledo,** College of Graduate Studies, College of Nursing, Department of Health Promotions, Outcomes, Systems, and Policy, Toledo, OH 43606-3390. Offers MSN, DNP. *Program availability:* Online learning. *Degree requirements:* For doctorate, thesis/dissertation or alternative, evidence-based project. *Entrance requirements:* For doctorate, GRE (taken within the past 5 years), personal statement, resume/curriculum vitae, letters of recommendation, documented supervised clinical hours in master's program, Nursing CAS application, UT supplemental application. Additional exam requirements/recommendations for international students: required—TOEFL (minimum score 550 paper-based; 80 iBT). Electronic applications accepted.

**University of Toronto,** School of Graduate Studies, Department of Public Health Sciences, Toronto, ON M5S 1A1, Canada. Offers biostatistics (M Sc, PhD); community health (M Sc); community nutrition (MPH), including nutrition and dietetics; epidemiology (MPH, PhD); family and community medicine (MPH); occupational and environmental health (MPH); social and behavioral health science (PhD); social and behavioral health

sciences (MPH), including health promotion. *Accreditation:* CAHME (one or more programs are accredited). *Program availability:* Part-time. *Degree requirements:* For master's, thesis (for some programs), practicum; for doctorate, comprehensive exam, thesis/dissertation, oral thesis defense. *Entrance requirements:* For master's, 2 letters of reference, relevant professional/research experience, minimum B average in final year; for doctorate, 2 letters of reference, relevant professional/research experience, minimum B+ average. Additional exam requirements/recommendations for international students: required—TOEFL (minimum score 580 paper-based; 93 iBT), TWE (minimum score 5). Electronic applications accepted. *Expenses:* Contact institution.

**University of Vermont,** Graduate College, College of Nursing and Health Sciences, Program in Physical Activity and Wellness Science, Burlington, VT 05405. Offers MS. *Entrance requirements:* Additional exam requirements/recommendations for international students: required—TOEFL (minimum iBT score of 90) or IELTS (6.5). Electronic applications accepted.

**University of West Florida,** Usha Kundu, MD College of Health, Department of Exercise Science and Community Health, Pensacola, FL 32514-5750. Offers health promotion (MS); health, leisure, and exercise science (MS), including exercise science, physical education. *Program availability:* Part-time, evening/weekend. *Degree requirements:* For master's, thesis or alternative. *Entrance requirements:* For master's, GRE or MAT, official transcripts; minimum GPA of 3.0; letter of intent; three personal references; work experience as reflected in resume. Additional exam requirements/ recommendations for international students: required—TOEFL (minimum score 550 paper-based).

**University of Wisconsin–Milwaukee,** Graduate School, Joseph J. Zilber School of Public Health, Program in Public Health, Milwaukee, WI 53201-0413. Offers biostatistics (MPH); community and behavioral health promotion (MPH); environmental health sciences (MPH); epidemiology (MPH, PhD); public and population health (Graduate Certificate); public health policy and administration (MPH); public health: biostatistics (PhD); public health: community and behavioral health promotion (PhD). Electronic applications accepted.

**University of Wisconsin–Parkside,** College of Natural and Health Sciences, Program in Health and Wellness Management, Kenosha, WI 53141-2000. Offers MS. *Program availability:* Online learning. *Entrance requirements:* For master's, bachelor's degree with minimum GPA of 3.0. *Expenses: Tuition, area resident:* Full-time $9173; part-time $509.64 per credit. Tuition, state resident: full-time $9173; part-time $509.64 per credit. Tuition, nonresident: full-time $18,767; part-time $1042.64 per credit. *International tuition:* $18,767 full-time. *Required fees:* $1123.20; $63.64 per credit. Tuition and fees vary according to campus/location, program and reciprocity agreements.

**University of Wisconsin–Stevens Point,** College of Professional Studies, School of Health Promotion and Human Development, Program in Health and Wellness Management, Stevens Point, WI 54481-3897. Offers MS.

**University of Wyoming,** College of Health Sciences, Division of Kinesiology and Health, Laramie, WY 82071. Offers MS. *Accreditation:* NCATE. *Program availability:* Part-time, online learning. *Degree requirements:* For master's, comprehensive exam (for some programs), thesis (for some programs). *Entrance requirements:* For master's, GRE General Test, minimum GPA of 3.0. Additional exam requirements/ recommendations for international students: required—TOEFL. Electronic applications accepted.

**Utah State University,** School of Graduate Studies, Emma Eccles Jones College of Education and Human Services, Department of Kinesiology and Health Science, Logan, UT 84322. Offers fitness promotion (MS); health and human movement (MS); pathokinesiology (PhD); physical and sport education (M Ed); public health (MPH). *Program availability:* Part-time, evening/weekend, online learning. *Degree requirements:* For master's, thesis (for some programs). *Entrance requirements:* For master's, GRE General Test or MAT, minimum GPA of 3.0. Additional exam requirements/ recommendations for international students: required—TOEFL.

**Walden University,** Graduate Programs, School of Health Sciences, Minneapolis, MN 55401. Offers clinical research administration (MS, Graduate Certificate); health education and promotion (MS, PhD), including behavioral health (PhD), disease surveillance (PhD), emergency preparedness (MS), general (MHA, MS), global health (PhD), health policy (PhD), health policy and advocacy (MS), population health (PhD); health informatics (MS); health services (PhD), including community health, healthcare administration, leadership, public health policy, self-designed; healthcare administration (MHA, DHA), including general (MHA, MS); leadership and organizational development (MHA); public health (MPH, Dr PH, PhD, Graduate Certificate), including community health education (PhD), epidemiology (PhD); systems policy (MHA). *Program availability:* Part-time, evening/weekend, online only, 100% online. *Degree requirements:* For doctorate, thesis/dissertation, residency. *Entrance requirements:* For master's, bachelor's degree or higher; minimum GPA of 2.5; official transcripts; goal statement (for some programs); access to computer and Internet; for doctorate, master's degree or higher; three years of related professional or academic experience (preferred); minimum GPA of 3.0; goal statement and current resume (for select programs); official transcripts; access to computer and Internet; for Graduate Certificate, relevant work experience; access to computer and Internet. Additional exam requirements/recommendations for international students: required—TOEFL (minimum score 550 paper-based, 79 iBT), IELTS (minimum score 6.5), Michigan English Language Assessment Battery (minimum score 82), or PTE (minimum score 53). Electronic applications accepted.

**Wilfrid Laurier University,** Faculty of Graduate and Postdoctoral Studies, Faculty of Science, Department of Kinesiology and Physical Education, Waterloo, ON N2L 3C5, Canada. Offers physical activity and health (M Sc). *Degree requirements:* For master's, thesis. *Entrance requirements:* For master's, honours degree in kinesiology, health, physical education with a minimum B+ in kinesiology and health-related courses. Additional exam requirements/recommendations for international students: required—TOEFL (minimum score 89 iBT). Electronic applications accepted.

**Wright State University,** Boonshoft School of Medicine, Department of Population and Public Health Sciences, Dayton, OH 45435. Offers health promotion and education (MPH). *Accreditation:* CEPH.

# Industrial Hygiene

**California State University, Northridge,** Graduate Studies, College of Health and Human Development, Department of Environmental and Occupational Health, Northridge, CA 91330. Offers environmental and occupational health (MS); industrial hygiene (MS). *Degree requirements:* For master's, seminar, field experience, comprehensive exam or thesis. *Entrance requirements:* For master's, GRE General Test or minimum GPA of 3.0. Additional exam requirements/recommendations for international students: required—TOEFL.

**Eastern Kentucky University,** The Graduate School, College of Health Sciences, Program in Public Health, Richmond, KY 40475-3102. Offers community health education (MPH); environmental health science (MPH); industrial hygiene (MPH); public health nutrition (MPH). *Accreditation:* CEPH. *Degree requirements:* For master's, comprehensive exam, thesis optional, practicum, capstone course. *Entrance requirements:* For master's, GRE.

**Montana Technological University,** Department of Industrial Hygiene, Butte, MT 59701-8997. Offers MS. *Accreditation:* ABET. *Program availability:* Part-time, online learning. *Faculty:* 9 full-time (4 women). *Students:* 19 full-time (13 women), 90 part-time (34 women); includes 15 minority (4 Black or African American, non-Hispanic/Latino; 1 American Indian or Alaska Native, non-Hispanic/Latino; 1 Asian, non-Hispanic/Latino; 8 Hispanic/Latino; 1 Native Hawaiian or other Pacific Islander, non-Hispanic/Latino), 4 international. 30 applicants, 70% accepted, 19 enrolled. In 2019, 23 master's awarded. *Degree requirements:* For master's, comprehensive exam (for some programs), thesis. *Entrance requirements:* For master's, GRE or 5 years' work experience (for online program), minimum GPA of 3.0. Additional exam requirements/recommendations for international students: required—TOEFL (minimum score 545 paper-based; 78 iBT), IELTS (minimum score 6.5). *Application deadline:* For fall admission, 4/1 priority date for domestic students; for spring admission, 10/1 priority date for domestic students. Applications are processed on a rolling basis. Application fee: $50. Electronic applications accepted. *Financial support:* In 2019–20, 15 students received support, including 9 teaching assistantships with partial tuition reimbursements available (averaging $2,400 per year); research assistantships with partial tuition reimbursements available, career-related internships or fieldwork, institutionally sponsored loans, and tuition waivers (full and partial) also available. Financial award application deadline: 4/1; financial award applicants required to submit FAFSA. *Unit head:* Dr. Terry Spear, Head, 406-496-4445, Fax: 406-496-4650, E-mail: tspear@mtech.edu. *Application contact:* Daniel Stirling, Administrator, Graduate School, 406-496-4304, Fax: 406-496-4710, E-mail: gradschool@mtech.edu.
Website: http://www.mtech.edu/academics/gradschool/degreeprograms/degrees-industrial-hygiene.htm

**New York Medical College,** School of Health Sciences and Practice, Valhalla, NY 10595. Offers behavioral sciences and health promotion (MPH); biostatistics (MS); children with special health care (Graduate Certificate); emergency preparedness (Graduate Certificate); environmental health science (MPH); epidemiology (MPH, MS); global health (Graduate Certificate); health education (Graduate Certificate); health policy and management (MPH, Dr PH); industrial hygiene (Graduate Certificate); pediatric dysphagia (Post-Graduate Certificate); physical therapy (DPT); public health (Graduate Certificate); speech-language pathology (MS). *Accreditation:* ASHA; CEPH. *Program availability:* Part-time, evening/weekend, 100% online, blended/hybrid learning. *Faculty:* 47 full-time (34 women), 203 part-time/adjunct (125 women). *Students:* 230 full-time (171 women), 292 part-time (207 women); includes 204 minority (73 Black or African American, non-Hispanic/Latino; 4 American Indian or Alaska Native, non-Hispanic/Latino; 59 Asian, non-Hispanic/Latino; 54 Hispanic/Latino; 1 Native Hawaiian or other Pacific Islander, non-Hispanic/Latino; 13 Two or more races, non-Hispanic/ Latino), 35 international. Average age 29. 790 applicants, 61% accepted, 162 enrolled. In 2019, 113 master's, 47 doctorates awarded. *Degree requirements:* For master's, comprehensive exam (for some programs), thesis (for some programs); for doctorate, thesis/dissertation. *Entrance requirements:* For master's, GRE (for MS in speech-language pathology); for doctorate, GRE (for Doctor of Physical Therapy and Doctor of Public Health). Additional exam requirements/recommendations for international students: required—TOEFL (minimum score 96 paper-based; 24 iBT), IELTS (minimum score 7). *Application deadline:* For fall admission, 8/1 for domestic students, 4/15 for international students; for spring admission, 12/1 for domestic students; for summer admission, 5/1 for domestic students, 4/15 for international students. Applications are processed on a rolling basis. Application fee: $128 ($120 for international students). Electronic applications accepted. *Expenses:* $1195 credit fee, academic support fee $200, Student activities fee $140 per year, technology fee $150. *Financial support:* In 2019–20, 18 students received support. Federal Work-Study, scholarships/grants, unspecified assistantships, and Federal student loans available. Financial award application deadline: 4/30; financial award applicants required to submit FAFSA. *Unit head:* Ben Johnson, PhD, Vice Dean, 914-594-4531, E-mail: bjohnson23@nymc.edu. *Application contact:* Irene Bundziak, Assistant to Director of Admissions, 914-594-4905, E-mail: irene_bundziak@nymc.edu.
Website: http://www.nymc.edu/school-of-health-sciences-and-practice-shsp/

**Old Dominion University,** College of Health Sciences, School of Community and Environmental Health, Norfolk, VA 23529. Offers general environmental health (MS); industrial hygiene (MS). *Degree requirements:* For master's, comprehensive exam, oral exam, written exam, practicum or thesis. *Entrance requirements:* For master's, GRE General Test, minimum GPA of 2.75. Additional exam requirements/recommendations for international students: required—TOEFL (minimum score 650 paper-based). Electronic applications accepted. *Expenses:* Contact institution.

**The University of Alabama at Birmingham,** School of Public Health, Program in Environmental Health Sciences, Birmingham, AL 35294. Offers environmental health sciences (PhD); industrial hygiene (PhD). *Program availability:* Part-time, 100% online, blended/hybrid learning. *Faculty:* 7 full-time (5 women). *Students:* 28 full-time (18 women), 18 part-time (12 women); includes 5 minority (3 Black or African American, non-Hispanic/Latino; 1 Asian, non-Hispanic/Latino; 1 Hispanic/Latino), 8 international. Average age 40. 50 applicants, 52% accepted, 13 enrolled. In 2019, 1 doctorate awarded. *Degree requirements:* For doctorate, comprehensive exam, thesis/ dissertation. *Entrance requirements:* For doctorate, GRE General Test. Additional exam requirements/recommendations for international students: required—TOEFL (minimum score 80 iBT), IELTS (minimum score 6.5). *Application deadline:* For fall admission, 4/1 priority date for domestic students, 4/1 for international students; for spring admission, 11/1 for domestic students; for summer admission, 4/1 for domestic students. Application fee: $50 ($60 for international students). Electronic applications accepted. *Financial support:* Fellowships, teaching assistantships, career-related internships or fieldwork, scholarships/grants, and unspecified assistantships available. Financial award application deadline: 3/1; financial award applicants required to submit FAFSA. *Unit*

*head:* Dr. Peter Ginter, Graduate Program Director, 205-975-8970, Fax: 205-975-6341, E-mail: pginter@uab.edu. *Application contact:* Dustin Shaw, Coordinator, Student Admissions and Records, 205-934-2684, E-mail: dshaw84@uab.edu. Website: http://www.soph.uab.edu/ehs

**The University of Alabama at Birmingham,** School of Public Health, Program in Health Care Organization and Policy, Birmingham, AL 35294. Offers applied epidemiology and pharmacoepidemiology (MSPH); biostatistics (MPH); clinical and translational science (MSPH); environmental health (MPH); environmental health and toxicology (MSPH); epidemiology (MPH); general theory and practice (MPH); health behavior (MPH); health care organization (MPH, Dr PH); health policy (MPH); industrial hygiene (MPH, MSPH); maternal and child health policy (Dr PH); maternal and child health policy and leadership (MPH); occupational health and safety (MPH); outcomes research (MSPH, Dr PH); public health (PhD); public health preparedness management (MPH). *Accreditation:* CEPH. *Program availability:* Part-time, 100% online, blended/hybrid learning. *Faculty:* 14 full-time (6 women). *Students:* 53 full-time (37 women), 61 part-time (45 women); includes 37 minority (12 Black or African American, non-Hispanic/Latino; 20 Asian, non-Hispanic/Latino; 1 Hispanic/Latino; 4 Two or more races, non-Hispanic/Latino), 17 international. Average age 31. 136 applicants, 59% accepted, 44 enrolled. In 2019, 36 master's, 4 doctorates awarded. *Degree requirements:* For master's, comprehensive exam (for some programs), thesis (for some programs); for doctorate, comprehensive exam, thesis/dissertation. *Entrance requirements:* For doctorate, GRE. Additional exam requirements/recommendations for international students: required—TOEFL (minimum score 80 iBT), IELTS (minimum score 6.5). *Application deadline:* For fall admission, 4/1 priority date for domestic students, 4/1 for international students; for spring admission, 11/1 for domestic students; for summer admission, 4/1 for domestic students. Application fee: $50 ($60 for international students). Electronic applications accepted. *Financial support:* Fellowships, research assistantships, teaching assistantships, scholarships/grants, traineeships, and unspecified assistantships available. Financial award application deadline: 3/1; financial award applicants required to submit FAFSA. *Unit head:* Dr. Martha Wingate, Program Director, 205-934-6783, Fax: 205-975-5484, E-mail: mslay@uab.edu. *Application contact:* Dustin Shaw, Coordinator, Student Admissions and Record, 205-934-3939, E-mail: bcampbel@uab.edu. Website: http://www.soph.uab.edu

**University of Central Missouri,** The Graduate School, Warrensburg, MO 64093. Offers accountancy (MA); accounting (MBA); applied mathematics (MS); aviation safety (MA); biology (MS); business administration (MBA); career and technology education (MS); college student personnel administration (MS); communication (MA); computer information systems and information technology (MS); computer science (MS); counseling (MS); criminal justice and criminology (MS); educational leadership (Ed S); educational leadership and policy analysis (Ed D); educational technology (MS, Ed S); elementary and early childhood education (MSE); English (MA); english language learners - teaching english as a second language (MA); environmental studies (MA); finance (MBA); history (MA); industrial hygiene (MS); industrial management (MS); information systems (MBA); kinesiology (MS); library science and information services (MS); literacy education (MSE); marketing (MBA); mathematics (MS); music (MA); occupational safety management (MS); professional leadership - adult, career, and technical education (Ed S); professional leadership - counseling (Ed S); psychology (MS); rural family nursing (MS); school administration (MSE); social gerontology (MS); sociology (MA); special education (MSE); speech language pathology (MS); teaching (MAT); technology (MS); technology management (PhD); theatre (MA). *Accreditation:* ASHA. *Program availability:* Part-time, 100% online, blended/hybrid learning. *Faculty:* 236 full-time (113 women), 97 part-time/adjunct (61 women). *Students:* 787 full-time (448 women), 1,459 part-time (997 women); includes 213 minority (72 Black or African American, non-Hispanic/Latino; 5 American Indian or Alaska Native, non-Hispanic/Latino; 27 Asian, non-Hispanic/Latino; 59 Hispanic/Latino; 50 Two or more races, non-Hispanic/Latino), 574 international. Average age 30. 1,477 applicants, 68% accepted, 664 enrolled. In 2019, 831 master's, 93 other advanced degrees awarded. *Degree requirements:* For master's and Ed S, comprehensive exam (for some programs), thesis (for some programs). *Entrance requirements:* For master's, A GRE or GMAT test score may be required by some of the programs, A minimum GPA, letters of recommendation, a statement of purpose may be required by some of the programs; for Ed S, A master's degree is required for the application of an Education Specialist's degree program. Additional exam requirements/recommendations for international students: required—TOEFL (minimum score 550 paper-based; 79 iBT). *Application deadline:* For fall admission, 6/1 priority date for domestic and international students; for spring admission, 10/15 priority date for domestic and international students; for summer admission, 4/1 priority date for domestic and international students. Applications are processed on a rolling basis. Application fee: $30 ($75 for international students). Electronic applications accepted. *Expenses:* Tuition, area resident: Full-time $7524; part-time $313.50 per credit hour. Tuition, state resident: full-time $7524; part-time $313.50 per credit hour. Tuition, nonresident: full-time $15,048; part-time $627 per credit hour. International tuition: $15,048 full-time. Required fees: $915; $30.50 per credit hour. *Financial support:* In 2019–20, 89 students received support. Research assistantships, teaching assistantships, career-related internships or fieldwork, Federal Work-Study, scholarships/grants, unspecified assistantships, and administrative and laboratory assistantships available. Support available to part-time students. Financial award application deadline: 4/1; financial award applicants required to submit FAFSA. *Unit head:* Shellie Hewitt, Director of Graduate and International Student Services, 660-543-4621, Fax: 660-543-4778, E-mail: hewitt@ucmo.edu. *Application contact:* Shellie Hewitt, Director of Graduate and International Student Services, 660-543-4621, Fax: 660-543-4778, E-mail: hewitt@ucmo.edu. Website: http://www.ucmo.edu/graduate/

**University of Cincinnati,** Graduate School, College of Medicine, Graduate Programs in Biomedical Sciences, Department of Environmental Health, Cincinnati, OH 45221. Offers environmental and industrial hygiene (MS, PhD); environmental and occupational medicine (MS); environmental genetics and molecular toxicology (MS, PhD); epidemiology and biostatistics (MS, PhD); occupational safety and ergonomics (MS, PhD). *Accreditation:* ABET (one or more programs are accredited); CEPH. Terminal

master's awarded for partial completion of doctoral program. *Degree requirements:* For master's, thesis; for doctorate, thesis/dissertation, qualifying exam. *Entrance requirements:* For master's, GRE General Test, bachelor's degree in science; for doctorate, GRE General Test. Additional exam requirements/recommendations for international students: required—TOEFL (minimum score 600 paper-based; 100 iBT). Electronic applications accepted.

**The University of Iowa,** Graduate College, College of Public Health, Department of Occupational and Environmental Health, Iowa City, IA 52242-1316. Offers agricultural safety and health (MS, PhD); ergonomics (MPH); industrial hygiene (MS, PhD); occupational and environmental health (MPH, MS, PhD, Certificate); MS/MA; MS/MS. *Accreditation:* ABET (one or more programs are accredited). *Degree requirements:* For master's, thesis optional, exam; for doctorate, comprehensive exam, thesis/dissertation. *Entrance requirements:* For master's and doctorate, GRE General Test, minimum GPA of 3.0. Additional exam requirements/recommendations for international students: required—TOEFL (minimum score 600 paper-based; 100 iBT). Electronic applications accepted.

**University of Michigan,** School of Public Health, Department of Environmental Health Sciences, Ann Arbor, MI 48109. Offers environmental health policy and promotion (MPH); environmental health sciences (MS, PhD); environmental quality, sustainability and health (MPH); industrial hygiene (MPH, MS); occupational and environmental epidemiology (MPH); toxicology (MPH, MS, PhD). *Accreditation:* CEPH (one or more programs are accredited). Terminal master's awarded for partial completion of doctoral program. *Degree requirements:* For master's, thesis (for some programs); for doctorate, thesis/dissertation, preliminary exam, oral defense of dissertation. *Entrance requirements:* For master's and doctorate, GRE General Test and/or MCAT. Additional exam requirements/recommendations for international students: required—TOEFL (minimum score 100 iBT). Electronic applications accepted.

**University of Minnesota, Twin Cities Campus,** School of Public Health, Division of Environmental Health Sciences, Area in Industrial Hygiene, Minneapolis, MN 55455-0213. Offers MPH, MS, PhD. *Accreditation:* ABET (one or more programs are accredited); CEPH (one or more programs are accredited). *Degree requirements:* For doctorate, thesis/dissertation. *Entrance requirements:* For master's and doctorate, GRE General Test. Electronic applications accepted.

**University of Puerto Rico - Medical Sciences Campus,** Graduate School of Public Health, Department of Environmental Health, Program in Industrial Hygiene, San Juan, PR 00936-5067. Offers MS. *Program availability:* Part-time. *Degree requirements:* For master's, thesis. *Entrance requirements:* For master's, GRE, previous course work in biology, chemistry, mathematics, and physics. *Expenses:* Contact institution.

**University of South Carolina,** The Graduate School, Arnold School of Public Health, Department of Environmental Health Sciences, Program in Industrial Hygiene, Columbia, SC 29208. Offers MPH, MSPH, PhD. *Accreditation:* CEPH (one or more programs are accredited). *Degree requirements:* For master's, comprehensive exam, thesis (for some programs), practicum (MPH); for doctorate, one foreign language, comprehensive exam, thesis/dissertation. *Entrance requirements:* Additional exam requirements/recommendations for international students: required—TOEFL (minimum score 570 paper-based). Electronic applications accepted.

**The University of Toledo,** College of Graduate Studies, College of Health and Human Services, School of Population Health, Toledo, OH 43606-3390. Offers health education (PhD); occupational health-industrial hygiene (MS); public health (MPH).

**The University of Toledo,** College of Graduate Studies, College of Medicine and Life Sciences, Department of Public Health and Preventative Medicine, Toledo, OH 43606-3390. Offers biostatistics and epidemiology (Certificate); contemporary gerontological practice (Certificate); environmental and occupational health and safety (MPH); epidemiology (Certificate); global public health (Certificate); health promotion and education (MPH); industrial hygiene (MSOH); medical and health science teaching and learning (Certificate); occupational health (Certificate); public health administration (MPH); public health and emergency response (Certificate); public health epidemiology (MPH); public health nutrition (MPH); MD/MPH. *Program availability:* Part-time, evening/weekend. *Degree requirements:* For master's, thesis or alternative. *Entrance requirements:* For master's, GRE, minimum undergraduate GPA of 3.0, three letters of recommendation, statement of purpose, transcripts from all prior institutions attended, resume; for Certificate, minimum undergraduate GPA of 3.0, three letters of recommendation, statement of purpose, transcripts from all prior institutions attended, resume. Additional exam requirements/recommendations for international students: required—TOEFL (minimum score 550 paper-based; 80 iBT), IELTS (minimum score 6.5). Electronic applications accepted.

**University of Wisconsin–Stout,** Graduate School, College of Management, Program in Risk Control, Menomonie, WI 54751. Offers MS. *Program availability:* Part-time. *Degree requirements:* For master's, thesis. *Entrance requirements:* For master's, minimum GPA of 3.0. Additional exam requirements/recommendations for international students: required—TOEFL (minimum score 500 paper-based; 61 iBT). Electronic applications accepted.

**West Virginia University,** Statler College of Engineering and Mineral Resources, Morgantown, WV 26506. Offers aerospace engineering (MSAE, PhD); chemical engineering (MS Ch E, PhD); civil engineering (MSCE, PhD); computer engineering (PhD); computer science (MSCS, PhD); electrical engineering (MSEE, PhD); energy systems engineering (MSESE); engineering (MSE); industrial engineering (MSIE, PhD); industrial hygiene (MS); material science and engineering (MSMSE, PhD); mechanical engineering (MSME, PhD); mining engineering (MS Min E, PhD); petroleum and natural gas engineering (MSPNGE, PhD); safety management (MS); software engineering (MSSE). *Program availability:* Part-time. Terminal master's awarded for partial completion of doctoral program. *Degree requirements:* For master's, thesis optional; for doctorate, comprehensive exam, thesis/dissertation. *Entrance requirements:* Additional exam requirements/recommendations for international students: required—TOEFL (minimum score 550 paper-based). Electronic applications accepted. *Expenses:* Contact institution.

# International Health

**Arizona State University at Tempe,** College of Liberal Arts and Sciences, School of Human Evolution and Social Change, Tempe, AZ 85287-2402. Offers anthropology (MA, PhD), including anthropology (PhD), archaeology (PhD), bioarchaeology (PhD), evolutionary (PhD), museum studies (MA), sociocultural (PhD); applied mathematics for the life and social sciences (PhD); environmental social science (PhD), including environmental social science, urbanism; global health (MA, PhD), including complex adaptive systems science (PhD), evolutionary global health sciences (PhD), health and culture (PhD), urbanism (PhD); immigration studies (Graduate Certificate). Terminal master's awarded for partial completion of doctoral program. *Degree requirements:* For master's, thesis or alternative, interactive Program of Study (iPOS) submitted before

completing 50 percent of required credit hours; for doctorate, comprehensive exam, thesis/dissertation, interactive Program of Study (iPOS) submitted before completing 50 percent of required credit hours. *Entrance requirements:* For master's and doctorate, GRE, minimum GPA of 3.0 or equivalent in last 2 years of work leading to bachelor's degree. Additional exam requirements/recommendations for international students: required—TOEFL, IELTS, or PTE. Electronic applications accepted.

**A.T. Still University,** College of Graduate Health Studies, Kirksville, MO 63501. Offers dental public health (MPH); exercise and sport psychology (Certificate); fundamentals of education (Certificate); geriatric exercise science (Certificate); global health (Certificate); health administration (MHA, DHA); health professions (Ed D); health sciences (DH Sc); kinesiology (MS); leadership and organizational behavior (Certificate); public health (MPH); sports conditioning (Certificate). *Accreditation:* CEPH. *Program availability:* Part-time, evening/weekend, online only, 100% online, blended/hybrid learning. *Faculty:* 49 full-time (36 women), 109 part-time/adjunct (66 women). *Students:* 601 full-time (406 women), 532 part-time (331 women); includes 457 minority (197 Black or African American, non-Hispanic/Latino; 15 American Indian or Alaska Native, non-Hispanic/Latino; 114 Asian, non-Hispanic/Latino; 105 Hispanic/Latino; 3 Native Hawaiian or other Pacific Islander, non-Hispanic/Latino; 23 Two or more races, non-Hispanic/Latino), 30 international. Average age 36. 339 applicants, 73% accepted, 217 enrolled. In 2019, 175 master's, 100 doctorates, 118 other advanced degrees awarded. *Degree requirements:* For master's, thesis, integrated terminal project, practicum; for doctorate, thesis/dissertation. *Entrance requirements:* For master's, minimum GPA of 2.5, bachelor's degree or equivalent, essay, resume, English proficiency; for doctorate, minimum GPA of 2.5, master's or terminal degree, essay, past experience in relevant field, resume, English proficiency. Additional exam requirements/recommendations for international students: required—TOEFL (minimum score 550 paper-based; 80 iBT). *Application deadline:* For fall admission, 6/24 for domestic and international students; for winter admission, 9/9 for domestic and international students; for spring admission, 12/9 for domestic and international students; for summer admission, 3/2 for domestic and international students. Applications are processed on a rolling basis. Application fee: $70. Electronic applications accepted. *Financial support:* In 2019–20, 13 students received support. Scholarships/grants available. Financial award applicants required to submit FAFSA. *Unit head:* Dr. Donald Altman, Dean, 480-219-6008, Fax: 660-626-2826, E-mail: daltman@atsu.edu. *Application contact:* Amie Waldemer, Associate Director, Online Admissions, 480-219-6146, E-mail: awaldemer@atsu.edu.
Website: http://www.atsu.edu/college-of-graduate-health-studies

**Brandeis University,** The Heller School for Social Policy and Management, Program in International Health Policy and Management, Waltham, MA 02454-9110. Offers MS. *Entrance requirements:* For master's, 3 letters of recommendation, curriculum vitae or resume, 5 years of international health experience. Additional exam requirements/recommendations for international students: required—TOEFL (minimum score 600 paper-based; 100 iBT). Electronic applications accepted.

**Brandeis University,** The Heller School for Social Policy and Management, Program in Social Policy, Waltham, MA 02454-9110. Offers assets and inequalities (PhD); children, youth and families (PhD); global health and development (PhD); health and behavioral health (PhD). *Degree requirements:* For doctorate, comprehensive exam, thesis/dissertation, qualifying paper, 2-year residency. *Entrance requirements:* For doctorate, GRE General Test, 3 letters of recommendation, statement of purpose, writing sample, at least 3-5 years of professional experience. Additional exam requirements/recommendations for international students: required—TOEFL (minimum score 600 paper-based; 100 iBT). Electronic applications accepted.

**Cedarville University,** Graduate Programs, Cedarville, OH 45314. Offers business administration (MBA); family nurse practitioner (MSN); global ministry (M Div); global public health nursing (MSN); healthcare administration (MBA); ministry (M Min); nurse educator (MSN); operations management (MBA); pharmacy (Pharm D). *Program availability:* Part-time, evening/weekend, 100% online, blended/hybrid learning. *Faculty:* 52 full-time (19 women), 21 part-time/adjunct (13 women). *Students:* 378 full-time (221 women), 45 part-time (23 women); includes 76 minority (46 Black or African American, non-Hispanic/Latino; 2 American Indian or Alaska Native, non-Hispanic/Latino; 22 Asian, non-Hispanic/Latino; 1 Hispanic/Latino; 5 Two or more races, non-Hispanic/Latino), 2 international. Average age 26. 398 applicants, 70% accepted, 172 enrolled. In 2019, 74 master's, 34 doctorates awarded. *Degree requirements:* For master's, portfolio; for doctorate, comprehensive exam. *Entrance requirements:* For master's, GRE may be required, 2 professional recommendations; for doctorate, PCAT, professional recommendation from a practicing pharmacist or current employer/supervisor, resume, essay, interview. Additional exam requirements/recommendations for international students: required—TOEFL (minimum score 550 paper-based; 80 iBT). *Application deadline:* For fall admission, 5/1 priority date for domestic and international students; for spring admission, 11/1 priority date for domestic and international students. Applications are processed on a rolling basis. Electronic applications accepted. *Expenses: Tuition:* Full-time $12,594; part-time $566 per credit hour. One-time fee: $100. Tuition and fees vary according to course load and program. *Financial support:* Scholarships/grants and unspecified assistantships available. Support available to part-time students. Financial award application deadline: 1/30; financial award applicants required to submit FAFSA. *Unit head:* Dr. Janice Supplee, Dean of Graduate Studies, 937-766-8000, E-mail: suppleej@cedarville.edu. *Application contact:* Alexis McKay, Graduate Admissions Counselor, 937-766-8000, E-mail: amckay@cedarville.edu.
Website: https://www.cedarville.edu/offices/graduate-school

**Central Michigan University,** Central Michigan University Global Campus, Program in Health Administration, Mount Pleasant, MI 48859. Offers health administration (DHA); international health (Certificate); nutrition and dietetics (MS). *Program availability:* Part-time, evening/weekend, online learning. Electronic applications accepted. *Expenses: Tuition, area resident:* Full-time $12,267; part-time $8178 per year. Tuition, state resident: full-time $12,267; part-time $8178 per year. Tuition, nonresident: full-time $12,267; part-time $8178 per year. *International tuition:* $16,110 full-time. *Required fees:* $225 per semester. Tuition and fees vary according to degree level and program.

**Clark University,** Graduate School, Department of International Development, Community, and Environment, Program in Community and Global Health, Worcester, MA 01610-1477. Offers MHS. *Degree requirements:* For master's, project; capstone, practicum, or internship. *Entrance requirements:* Additional exam requirements/recommendations for international students: required—TOEFL (minimum score 90 iBT), IELTS (minimum score 6.5). Electronic applications accepted. *Expenses:* Contact institution.

**Clemson University,** Graduate School, College of Behavioral, Social and Health Sciences, School of Nursing, Clemson, SC 29634. Offers clinical and translational research (PhD); global health (Certificate), including low resource countries; healthcare genetics (PhD); nursing (MS, DNP), including adult/gerontology nurse practitioner (MS), family nurse practitioner (MS). *Accreditation:* AACN. *Program availability:* Part-time, 100% online, blended/hybrid learning. *Faculty:* 47 full-time (45 women), 1 (woman) part-time/adjunct. *Students:* 67 full-time (59 women), 66 part-time (49 women); includes 18 minority (10 Black or African American, non-Hispanic/Latino; 4 Asian, non-Hispanic/Latino; 4 Two or more races, non-Hispanic/Latino), 7 international. Average age 35. 109 applicants, 62% accepted, 49 enrolled. In 2019, 56 master's, 8 doctorates awarded. *Degree requirements:* For master's, comprehensive exam, thesis or alternative; for doctorate, comprehensive exam, thesis/dissertation. *Entrance requirements:* For master's, GRE General Test, South Carolina RN license, unofficial transcripts, resume, letters of recommendation; for doctorate, GRE General Test, unofficial transcripts, MS/MA thesis or publications, curriculum vitae, statement of career goals, letters of recommendation. Additional exam requirements/recommendations for international students: required—TOEFL (minimum score 80 paper-based; 80 iBT); recommended—IELTS (minimum score 6.5), TSE (minimum score 54). *Application deadline:* For fall admission, 4/15 priority date for international students; for spring admission, 10/15 priority date for international students. Applications are processed on a rolling basis. Application fee: $80 ($90 for international students). Electronic applications accepted. *Expenses:* MS Nursing Full-Time Student per Semester: Tuition: $9075 (in-state), $16051 (out-of-state), Fees: $598; Graduate Assistant Per Semester: $1144; Part-Time Student Per Credit Hour: $1009 (in-state), $1784 (out-of-state), Fees: $46; other fees apply depending on program, credit hours, campus & residency. Doctoral Base Fee per Semester: $4938 (in-state), $10405 (out-of-state). *Financial support:* In 2019–20, 47 students received support, including 46 teaching assistantships with full and partial tuition reimbursements available (averaging $6,766 per year); career-related internships or fieldwork and unspecified assistantships also available. *Unit head:* Dr. Kathleen Valentine, Chief Academic Nursing Officer & Director, 864-656-4758, E-mail: klvalen@clemson.edu. *Application contact:* Dr. Stephanie Davis, Director of Graduate Programs, 864-656-2588, E-mail: stephad@clemson.edu.
Website: http://www.clemson.edu/cbshs/departments/nursing/

**The College of New Jersey,** Office of Graduate and Advancing Education, School of Nursing, Health, and Exercise Science, Program in Public Health, Ewing, NJ 08628. Offers global health (MPH); health communications (MPH); precision health (MPH).

**Duke University,** Graduate School, Duke Global Health Institute, Durham, NC 27708. Offers MS. *Degree requirements:* For master's, thesis. *Entrance requirements:* For master's, GRE General Test or MCAT. Additional exam requirements/recommendations for international students: required—TOEFL (minimum score 577 paper-based; 90 iBT) or IELTS (minimum score 7).

**East Tennessee State University,** College of Graduate and Continuing Studies, College of Public Health, Program in Public Health, Johnson City, TN 37614. Offers biostatistics (MPH, Postbaccalaureate Certificate); community health (MPH, DPH); environmental health (MPH); epidemiology (MPH, DPH, Postbaccalaureate Certificate); gerontology (Postbaccalaureate Certificate); global health (Postbaccalaureate Certificate); health care management (Postbaccalaureate Certificate); health management and policy (DPH); public health (Postbaccalaureate Certificate); public health services administration (MPH); rural health (Postbaccalaureate Certificate). *Accreditation:* CEPH. *Program availability:* Part-time, online learning. *Degree requirements:* For master's, comprehensive exam, field experience; for doctorate, thesis/dissertation, practicum. *Entrance requirements:* For master's, GRE General Test, minimum GPA of 2.75, SOPHAS application, three letters of recommendation; for doctorate, GRE General Test, SOPHAS application, three letters of recommendation; for Postbaccalaureate Certificate, minimum GPA of 2.5, three letters of recommendation, resume. Additional exam requirements/recommendations for international students: required—TOEFL (minimum score 550 paper-based; 79 iBT), IELTS (minimum score 6.5). Electronic applications accepted.

**Emory University,** Rollins School of Public Health, Hubert Department of Global Health, Atlanta, GA 30322-1100. Offers global health (MPH); public nutrition (MSPH). *Degree requirements:* For master's, thesis, practicum. *Entrance requirements:* For master's, GRE General Test. Additional exam requirements/recommendations for international students: required—TOEFL (minimum score 550 paper-based; 80 iBT). Electronic applications accepted.

**Endicott College,** School of Nursing, Program in Nursing, Beverly, MA 01915. Offers family nurse practitioner (MSN, Post-Master's Certificate); global health (MSN); nursing administration (MSN); nursing administrator (Post-Master's Certificate); nursing educator (MSN, Post-Master's Certificate). *Program availability:* Part-time, evening/weekend, blended/hybrid learning. *Faculty:* 4 full-time (all women), 18 part-time/adjunct (13 women). *Students:* 20 full-time (19 women), 71 part-time (70 women); includes 11 minority (5 Black or African American, non-Hispanic/Latino; 3 Asian, non-Hispanic/Latino; 2 Hispanic/Latino; 1 Two or more races, non-Hispanic/Latino). Average age 37. 32 applicants, 41% accepted, 12 enrolled. In 2019, 34 master's, 6 other advanced degrees awarded. *Degree requirements:* For master's, thesis, Internship and Capstone portfolio (S); Minimum 600 faculty supervised clinical hours (S). *Entrance requirements:* Additional exam requirements/recommendations for international students: required—TOEFL. *Application deadline:* Applications are processed on a rolling basis. Application fee: $50. Electronic applications accepted. *Expenses:* Tuition varies by program. *Financial support:* Applicants required to submit FAFSA. *Unit head:* Nancy Meedzan, DNP, RN, CNE, Dean, School of Nursing, 978-232-2328, E-mail: nmeedzan@endicott.edu. *Application contact:* Ian Menchini, Director, Graduate Enrollment and Advising, 978-232-5292, Fax: 978-232-3000, E-mail: imenchin@endicott.edu.
Website: https://www.endicott.edu/academics/schools/nursing/graduate-programs

**George Mason University,** College of Health and Human Services, Department of Global and Community Health, Fairfax, VA 22030. Offers global and community health (Certificate); global health (MS); public health (MPH, Certificate), including epidemiology (MPH), leadership and management (Certificate). *Accreditation:* CEPH. *Program availability:* Part-time, evening/weekend. *Degree requirements:* For master's, thesis, 200-hour practicum. *Entrance requirements:* For master's, GRE, GMAT (depending on program), 2 official transcripts; expanded goals statement; 3 letters of recommendation; resume; 1 completed course in health science, statistics, natural sciences and social science (for MPH); 6 credits of foreign language if not fluent (for MS); minimum undergraduate GPA of 3.0; for Certificate, 2 official transcripts; expanded goals statement; 3 letters of recommendation; resume; bachelor's degree from regionally-accredited institution with minimum GPA of 3.0. Additional exam requirements/recommendations for international students: required—TOEFL (minimum score 570 paper-based; 88 iBT), IELTS (minimum score 6.5), PTE (minimum score 59). Electronic applications accepted. *Expenses:* Contact institution.

**Georgetown University,** Law Center, Washington, DC 20001. Offers environmental law (LL M); global health law (LL M); global health law and international institutions (LL M); individualized study (LL M); international business and economic law (LL M); law (JD, SJD); national security law (LL M); securities and financial regulation (LL M); taxation (LL M); JD/LL M; JD/MA; JD/MBA; JD/MPH; JD/PhD. *Accreditation:* ABA. *Program availability:* Part-time, evening/weekend. *Degree requirements:* For master's, thesis; for doctorate, thesis/dissertation (for some programs). *Entrance requirements:* For master's, JD, LL B, or first law degree earned in country of origin; for doctorate, LSAT (for JD). Additional exam requirements/recommendations for international students: required—TOEFL. *Expenses:* Contact institution.

**The George Washington University,** Milken Institute School of Public Health, Department of Global Health, Washington, DC 20052. Offers global health (Dr PH); global health communication (MPH). *Entrance requirements:* For master's, GMAT, GRE

General Test, or MCAT. Additional exam requirements/recommendations for international students: required—TOEFL.

**Harvard University,** Harvard T.H. Chan School of Public Health, Department of Global Health and Population, Boston, MA 02115-6096. Offers global health and population (SM); population health sciences (PhD). *Program availability:* Part-time. *Faculty:* 48 full-time (18 women), 16 part-time/adjunct (5 women). *Students:* 39 full-time (30 women); includes 17 minority (8 Asian, non-Hispanic/Latino; 4 Hispanic/Latino; 1 Native Hawaiian or other Pacific Islander, non-Hispanic/Latino; 4 Two or more races, non-Hispanic/Latino), 15 international. Average age 29. 66 applicants, 48% accepted, 18 enrolled. In 2019, 17 master's, 8 doctorates awarded. *Degree requirements:* For master's, thesis; for doctorate, thesis/dissertation, qualifying exam. *Entrance requirements:* For master's, GRE, MCAT; for doctorate, GRE. Additional exam requirements/recommendations for international students: recommended—TOEFL (minimum score 600 paper-based; 100 iBT), IELTS (minimum score 7). *Application deadline:* For fall admission, 12/1 for domestic and international students. Application fee: $140. Electronic applications accepted. *Financial support:* Fellowships, research assistantships, teaching assistantships, Federal Work-Study, scholarships/grants, traineeships, and unspecified assistantships available. Support available to part-time students. Financial award application deadline: 2/15; financial award applicants required to submit FAFSA. *Unit head:* Dr. Marcia Castro, Chair, E-mail: mcastro@hsph.harvard.edu. *Application contact:* Vincent W. James, Director of Admissions, 617-432-1031, Fax: 617-432-7080, E-mail: admissions@hsph.harvard.edu.
Website: http://www.hsph.harvard.edu/global-health-and-population/

**Harvard University,** Harvard T.H. Chan School of Public Health, PhD Program in Population Health Sciences, Boston, MA 02138. Offers environmental health (PhD); epidemiology (PhD); global health and population (PhD); nutrition (PhD); social and behavioral sciences (PhD). *Students:* 159 full-time (0 women). Average age 29. In 2019, 5 doctorates awarded. *Entrance requirements:* Additional exam requirements/recommendations for international students: recommended—TOEFL, IELTS. *Application deadline:* For fall admission, 12/1 for domestic and international students. Electronic applications accepted. *Financial support:* Application deadline: 2/15; applicants required to submit FAFSA. *Unit head:* Bruce Villineau, Assistant Director, 617-432-6076, E-mail: phdphs@hsph.harvard.edu. *Application contact:* Bruce Villineau, Assistant Director, 617-432-6076, E-mail: phdphs@hsph.harvard.edu.

**Indiana University-Purdue University Indianapolis,** Richard M. Fairbanks School of Public Health, Indianapolis, IN 46202. Offers biostatistics (MS, PhD); environmental health (MPH); epidemiology (MPH, PhD); global health leadership (Dr PH); health administration (MHA); health policy (Graduate Certificate); health policy and management (MPH, PhD); health systems management (Graduate Certificate); product stewardship (MS); public health (Graduate Certificate); social and behavioral sciences (MPH). *Accreditation:* CAHME; CEPH. *Expenses:* Contact institution.

**Johns Hopkins University,** Bloomberg School of Public Health, Department of International Health, Baltimore, MD 21205. Offers global disease epidemiology and control (MSPH, PhD); global health economics (MHS); health systems (MSPH, PhD); human nutrition (MSPH, PhD); social and behavioral interventions (MSPH, PhD). *Degree requirements:* For master's, comprehensive exam, thesis (for some programs), 1-year full-time residency, 4-9 month internship; for doctorate, comprehensive exam, thesis/dissertation or alternative, 1.5 years' full-time residency, oral and written exams. *Entrance requirements:* For master's, GRE General Test or MCAT, 3 letters of recommendation, resume; for doctorate, GRE General Test or MCAT, 3 letters of recommendation, resume, transcripts. Additional exam requirements/recommendations for international students: required—TOEFL (minimum score 600 paper-based; 100 iBT); recommended—IELTS (minimum score 7). Electronic applications accepted.

**Liberty University,** School of Health Sciences, Lynchburg, VA 24515. Offers anatomy and cell biology (PhD); biomedical sciences (MS); epidemiology (MPH); exercise science (MS), including clinical, community physical activity, human performance, nutrition; global health (MPH); health promotion (MPH); medical sciences (MA), including biopsychology, business management, health informatics, molecular medicine, public health; nutrition (MPH). *Program availability:* Part-time, online learning. *Students:* 820 full-time (588 women), 889 part-time (612 women); includes 611 minority (402 Black or African American, non-Hispanic/Latino; 10 American Indian or Alaska Native, non-Hispanic/Latino; 43 Asian, non-Hispanic/Latino; 85 Hispanic/Latino; 1 Native Hawaiian or other Pacific Islander, non-Hispanic/Latino; 70 Two or more races, non-Hispanic/Latino), 67 international. Average age 32. 2,610 applicants, 33% accepted, 406 enrolled. In 2019, 445 master's awarded. *Degree requirements:* For master's, thesis (for some programs); for doctorate, thesis/dissertation. *Entrance requirements:* For doctorate, MAT or GRE, minimum GPA of 3.25 in master's program, 2-3 recommendations, writing samples (for some programs), letter of intent, professional vitae. Additional exam requirements/recommendations for international students: required—TOEFL (minimum score 600 paper-based; 100 iBT). Application fee: $50. *Expenses: Tuition:* Full-time $545; part-time $410 per credit hour. One-time fee: $50. *Financial support:* In 2019–20, 918 students received support. Federal Work-Study available. Financial award applicants required to submit FAFSA. *Unit head:* Dr. Ralph Linstra, Dean. *Application contact:* Jay Bridge, Director of Admissions, 800-424-9595, Fax: 800-628-7977, E-mail: gradadmissions@liberty.edu.
Website: https://www.liberty.edu/health-sciences/

**Loma Linda University,** School of Public Health, Program in Global Health, Loma Linda, CA 92350. Offers MPH. *Entrance requirements:* Additional exam requirements/recommendations for international students: required—Michigan English Language Assessment Battery or TOEFL. *Expenses:* Contact institution.

**Medical University of South Carolina,** College of Health Professions, Program in Health Administration-Global, Charleston, SC 29425. Offers MHA. *Entrance requirements:* Additional exam requirements/recommendations for international students: required—TOEFL.

**National University of Natural Medicine,** School of Undergraduate and Graduate Studies, Portland, OR 97201. Offers Ayurveda (MS); global health (MS); integrative medicine research (MS); integrative mental health (MS); nutrition (MS). *Program availability:* 100% online. *Students:* 92 full-time (83 women), 6 part-time (all women); includes 13 minority (1 Black or African American, non-Hispanic/Latino; 4 Asian, non-Hispanic/Latino; 3 Hispanic/Latino; 5 Two or more races, non-Hispanic/Latino). Average age 31. 114 applicants, 88% accepted, 60 enrolled. In 2019, 72 master's awarded. *Degree requirements:* For master's, thesis. *Entrance requirements:* For master's, Bachelor's degree from a regionally accredited institution and prerequisite courses. Additional exam requirements/recommendations for international students: required—TOEFL (minimum score 550 paper-based; 80 iBT), We accept IETS and PTE. *Application deadline:* For fall admission, 5/1 for domestic and international students. Applications are processed on a rolling basis. Application fee: $75. Electronic applications accepted. *Expenses: Tuition:* Part-time $464 per credit hour. *Financial support:* Federal Work-Study and scholarships/grants available. Financial award application deadline: 2/15; financial award applicants required to submit FAFSA. *Unit head:* Dr. Tim Irving, Program Director - School of Undergraduate and Graduate Studies, 503-552-1660, Fax: 503-499-0027, E-mail: admission@nunm.edu. *Application contact:* Ryan Hollister, Director of Admissions, 503-552-1665, Fax: 503-499-0027, E-mail: admissions@numn.edu.
Website: http://nunm.edu/academics/school-of-research-graduate-studies/

**New York Institute of Technology,** College of Osteopathic Medicine, Old Westbury, NY 11568. Offers global health (Certificate); DO/MS. *Accreditation:* AOsA. *Faculty:* 94 full-time (44 women), 36 part-time/adjunct (16 women). *Students:* 1,734 full-time (827 women); includes 814 minority (68 Black or African American, non-Hispanic/Latino; 627 Asian, non-Hispanic/Latino; 81 Hispanic/Latino; 38 Two or more races, non-Hispanic/Latino). Average age 27. 7,140 applicants, 13% accepted, 435 enrolled. *Entrance requirements:* Additional exam requirements/recommendations for international students: required—TOEFL, IELTS, PTE. *Application deadline:* For fall admission, 3/1 for domestic students. Applications are processed on a rolling basis. Application fee: $80. Electronic applications accepted. *Expenses:* Annual tuition $59,350 plus fees. *Financial support:* In 2019–20, 690 students received support. Federal Work-Study and scholarships/grants available. Financial award application deadline: 2/15; financial award applicants required to submit FAFSA. *Unit head:* Dr. Jerry Balentine, Dean, 516-686-3999, Fax: 516-686-3830, E-mail: Jerry.Balentine@nyit.edu. *Application contact:* Carol Zerah, Director, Admissions, 516-686-3997, E-mail: comadm@nyit.edu.
Website: https://www.nyit.edu/medicine

**New York Medical College,** School of Health Sciences and Practice, Valhalla, NY 10595. Offers behavioral sciences and health promotion (MPH); biostatistics (MS); children with special health care (Graduate Certificate); emergency preparedness (Graduate Certificate); environmental health science (MPH); epidemiology (MPH, MS); global health (Graduate Certificate); health education (Graduate Certificate); health policy and management (MPH, Dr PH); industrial hygiene (Graduate Certificate); pediatric dysphagia (Post-Graduate Certificate); physical therapy (DPT); public health (Graduate Certificate); speech-language pathology (MS). *Accreditation:* ASHA; CEPH. *Program availability:* Part-time, evening/weekend, 100% online, blended/hybrid learning. *Faculty:* 47 full-time (34 women), 203 part-time/adjunct (125 women). *Students:* 230 full-time (171 women), 292 part-time (207 women); includes 204 minority (73 Black or African American, non-Hispanic/Latino; 4 American Indian or Alaska Native, non-Hispanic/Latino; 59 Asian, non-Hispanic/Latino; 54 Hispanic/Latino; 1 Native Hawaiian or other Pacific Islander, non-Hispanic/Latino; 13 Two or more races, non-Hispanic/Latino), 35 international. Average age 29. 790 applicants, 61% accepted, 162 enrolled. In 2019, 113 master's, 47 doctorates awarded. *Degree requirements:* For master's, comprehensive exam (for some programs), thesis (for some programs); for doctorate, thesis/dissertation. *Entrance requirements:* For master's, GRE (for MS in speech-language pathology); for doctorate, GRE (for Doctor of Physical Therapy and Doctor of Public Health). Additional exam requirements/recommendations for international students: required—TOEFL (minimum score 96 paper-based; 24 iBT), IELTS (minimum score 7). *Application deadline:* For fall admission, 8/1 for domestic students, 4/15 for international students; for spring admission, 12/1 for domestic students; for summer admission, 5/1 for domestic students, 4/15 for international students. Applications are processed on a rolling basis. Application fee: $128 ($120 for international students). Electronic applications accepted. *Expenses:* $1195 credit fee, academic support fee $200, Student activities fee $140 per year, technology fee $150. *Financial support:* In 2019–20, 18 students received support. Federal Work-Study, scholarships/grants, unspecified assistantships, and Federal student loans available. Financial award application deadline: 4/30; financial award applicants required to submit FAFSA. *Unit head:* Ben Johnson, PhD, Vice Dean, 914-594-4531, E-mail: bjohnson23@nymc.edu. *Application contact:* Irene Bundziak, Assistant to Director of Admissions, 914-594-4905, E-mail: irene_bundziak@nymc.edu.
Website: http://www.nymc.edu/school-of-health-sciences-and-practice-shsp/

**New York University,** College of Global Public Health, New York, NY 10012. Offers biological basis of public health (PhD); community and international health (MPH); global health leadership (MPH); health systems and health services research (PhD); population and community health (PhD); public health nutrition (MPH); social and behavioral sciences (MPH); socio-behavioral health (PhD). *Accreditation:* CEPH. *Program availability:* Part-time, online learning. *Degree requirements:* For master's, thesis (for some programs); for doctorate, thesis/dissertation. *Entrance requirements:* For master's and doctorate, GRE. Additional exam requirements/recommendations for international students: required—TOEFL. Electronic applications accepted. *Expenses:* Contact institution.

**Northwestern University,** School of Professional Studies, Program in Global Health, Evanston, IL 60208. Offers MS. *Program availability:* Part-time, evening/weekend, online learning. *Degree requirements:* For master's, practicum.

**Oregon State University,** College of Public Health and Human Sciences, Program in Public Health, Corvallis, OR 97331. Offers biostatistics (MPH); environmental and occupational health (MPH, PhD); epidemiology (MPH, PhD); global health (MPH, PhD). *Accreditation:* CEPH. Terminal master's awarded for partial completion of doctoral program. *Entrance requirements:* For master's and doctorate, GRE, minimum GPA of 3.0 in last 90 hours. Additional exam requirements/recommendations for international students: required—TOEFL (minimum score 80 iBT), IELTS (minimum score 6.5). Electronic applications accepted. *Expenses:* Contact institution.

**Park University,** School of Graduate and Professional Studies, Kansas City, MO 54105. Offers adult education (M Ed); business and government leadership (Graduate Certificate); business, government, and global society (MPA); communication and leadership (MA); creative and life writing (Graduate Certificate); disaster and emergency management (MPA, Graduate Certificate); educational leadership (M Ed); finance (MBA, Graduate Certificate); general business (MBA); global business (Graduate Certificate); healthcare administration (MHA); healthcare services management and leadership (Graduate Certificate); international business (MBA); language and literacy (M Ed), including English for speakers of other languages, special reading teacher/literacy coach; leadership of international healthcare organizations (Graduate Certificate); management information systems (MBA, Graduate Certificate); music performance (ADP, Graduate Certificate), including cello (MM, ADP), piano (MM, ADP), viola (MM, ADP), violin (MM, ADP); nonprofit and community services management (MPA); nonprofit leadership (Graduate Certificate); performance (MM), including cello (MM, ADP), piano (MM, ADP), viola (MM, ADP), violin (MM, ADP); public management (MPA); social work (MSW); teacher leadership (M Ed), including curriculum and assessment, instructional leader. *Program availability:* Part-time, evening/weekend, online learning. *Degree requirements:* For master's, comprehensive exam (for some programs), thesis (for some programs), internship (for some programs); exam (for some programs). *Entrance requirements:* For master's, GRE or GMAT (for some programs), teacher certification (for some M Ed programs), letters of recommendation, essay, resume (for some programs). Additional exam requirements/recommendations for international students: required—TOEFL (minimum score 550 paper-based; 79 iBT), IELTS (minimum score 6). Electronic applications accepted.

**St. Catherine University,** Graduate Programs, Program in Global Health, St. Paul, MN 55105. Offers MPH.

**San Diego State University,** Graduate and Research Affairs, College of Health and Human Services, School of Public Health, San Diego, CA 92182. Offers environmental

health (MPH); epidemiology (MPH, PhD), including biostatistics (MPH); global emergency preparedness and response (MS); global health (PhD); health behavior (PhD); health promotion (MPH); health services administration (MPH); toxicology (MS); MPH/MA; MSW/MPH. *Accreditation:* CAHME (one or more programs are accredited); CEPH. *Program availability:* Part-time. *Degree requirements:* For master's, comprehensive exam (for some programs), thesis (for some programs); for doctorate, thesis/dissertation. *Entrance requirements:* For master's, GMAT (MPH in health services administration), GRE General Test; for doctorate, GRE General Test. Additional exam requirements/recommendations for international students: required—TOEFL.

**Seton Hall University,** School of Diplomacy and International Relations, South Orange, NJ 07079-2697. Offers diplomacy and international relations (MA); global health management (Graduate Certificate); post-conflict state reconstruction and sustainability (Graduate Certificate); United Nations studies (Graduate Certificate); JD/MA; MA/MA; MBA/MA; MPA/MA. *Program availability:* Part-time, evening/weekend, 100% online, blended/hybrid learning. *Degree requirements:* For master's, thesis (for some programs), 45 credits; for Graduate Certificate, 15 credits. *Entrance requirements:* For master's, GRE, GMAT, or LSAT. Additional exam requirements/recommendations for international students: required—TOEFL. Electronic applications accepted. *Expenses:* Contact institution.

**Simon Fraser University,** Office of Graduate Studies and Postdoctoral Fellows, Faculty of Health Sciences, Burnaby, BC V5A 1S6, Canada. Offers global health (Graduate Diploma); health sciences (M Sc, PhD); public health (MPH). *Accreditation:* CEPH. *Degree requirements:* For master's, thesis (for some programs); for doctorate, comprehensive exam, thesis/dissertation. *Entrance requirements:* For master's, minimum GPA of 3.0 (on scale of 4.33) or 3.33 based on last 60 credits of undergraduate courses; for doctorate, minimum GPA of 3.5 (on scale of 4.33); for Graduate Diploma, minimum GPA of 2.5 (on scale of 4.33) or 2.67 based on last 60 credits of undergraduate courses. Additional exam requirements/recommendations for international students: recommended—TOEFL (minimum score 580 paper-based; 93 iBT), IELTS (minimum score 7), TWE (minimum score 5). Electronic applications accepted.

**Syracuse University,** David B. Falk College of Sport and Human Dynamics, MS Programs in Public Health, Syracuse, NY 13244. Offers MS. *Program availability:* Part-time. *Entrance requirements:* For master's, GRE, personal statement, official transcripts, three letters of recommendation, resume. Additional exam requirements/recommendations for international students: required—TOEFL (minimum score 100 iBT). Electronic applications accepted.

**Trident University International,** College of Health Sciences, Program in Health Sciences, Cypress, CA 90630. Offers clinical research administration (MS, Certificate); emergency and disaster management (MS, Certificate); environmental health science (Certificate); health care administration (PhD); health care management (MS), including health informatics; health education (MS, Certificate); health informatics (Certificate); health sciences (PhD); international health (MS); international health: educator or researcher option (PhD); international health: practitioner option (PhD); law and expert witness studies (MS, Certificate); public health (MS); quality assurance (Certificate). *Program availability:* Part-time, evening/weekend, online learning. *Degree requirements:* For doctorate, comprehensive exam, thesis/dissertation, defense of dissertation. *Entrance requirements:* For master's, minimum GPA of 2.5 (students with GPA 3.0 or greater may transfer up to 30% of graduate level credits); for doctorate, minimum GPA of 3.4, curriculum vitae, course work in research methods or statistics. Additional exam requirements/recommendations for international students: required—TOEFL. Electronic applications accepted.

**Tulane University,** School of Public Health and Tropical Medicine, Department of Global Community Health and Behavioral Sciences, New Orleans, LA 70118-5669. Offers community health sciences (MPH); global community health and behavioral sciences (Dr PH, PhD); JD/MPH; MD/MPH; MSW/MPH. *Program availability:* Part-time. *Degree requirements:* For doctorate, comprehensive exam, thesis/dissertation. *Entrance requirements:* For master's and doctorate, GRE General Test. Additional exam requirements/recommendations for international students: required—TOEFL. Electronic applications accepted. *Expenses: Tuition:* Full-time $57,004; part-time $3167 per credit hour. *Required fees:* $2086; $44.50 per credit hour. $80 per term. Tuition and fees vary according to course load, degree level and program.

**Tulane University,** School of Public Health and Tropical Medicine, Department of Global Environmental Health Sciences, New Orleans, LA 70118-5669. Offers MPH, MSPH, PhD, JD/MPH, MD/MPH, MSW/MPH. *Accreditation:* ABET (one or more programs are accredited). *Degree requirements:* For doctorate, comprehensive exam, thesis/dissertation. *Entrance requirements:* For master's and doctorate, GRE General Test. Additional exam requirements/recommendations for international students: required—TOEFL. Electronic applications accepted. *Expenses: Tuition:* Full-time $57,004; part-time $3167 per credit hour. *Required fees:* $2086; $44.50 per credit hour. $80 per term. Tuition and fees vary according to course load, degree level and program.

**Tulane University,** School of Public Health and Tropical Medicine, Department of Health Policy and Management, New Orleans, LA 70118-5669. Offers MHA, MPH, PhD, Sc D, JD/MHA, MBA/MHA, MD/MPH, MSW/MPH. *Accreditation:* CAHME (one or more programs are accredited). *Degree requirements:* For doctorate, comprehensive exam, thesis/dissertation. *Entrance requirements:* For master's, GMAT, GRE General Test; for doctorate, GRE General Test. Additional exam requirements/recommendations for international students: required—TOEFL. Electronic applications accepted. *Expenses: Tuition:* Full-time $57,004; part-time $3167 per credit hour. *Required fees:* $2086; $44.50 per credit hour. $80 per term. Tuition and fees vary according to course load, degree level and program.

**Uniformed Services University of the Health Sciences,** F. Edward Hebert School of Medicine, Graduate Programs in the Biomedical Sciences and Public Health, Bethesda, MD 20814. Offers emerging infectious diseases (PhD); medical and clinical psychology (PhD), including clinical psychology, medical psychology; medicine (MS, PhD), including health professions education; molecular and cell biology (MS, PhD); neuroscience (PhD); preventive medicine and biometrics (MPH, MS, MSPH, MTMH, PhD), including environmental health sciences (PhD), healthcare administration and policy (MS), medical zoology (PhD), public health (MPH, MSPH), tropical medicine and hygiene (MTMH). Terminal master's awarded for partial completion of doctoral program. *Degree requirements:* For master's, comprehensive exam, thesis or alternative; for doctorate, comprehensive exam, thesis/dissertation, qualifying exam. *Entrance requirements:* For master's, GRE General Test; for doctorate, GRE General Test, minimum GPA of 3.0. Electronic applications accepted. *Expenses:* Contact institution.

**Uniformed Services University of the Health Sciences,** F. Edward Hebert School of Medicine, Graduate Programs in the Biomedical Sciences and Public Health, Department of Preventive Medicine and Biostatistics, Program in Tropical Medicine and Hygiene, Bethesda, MD 20814-4799. Offers MTMH. *Accreditation:* CEPH. *Degree requirements:* For master's, comprehensive exam. *Entrance requirements:* For master's, GRE General Test, MD, U.S. citizenship.

**University of Alberta,** School of Public Health, Department of Public Health Sciences, Edmonton, AB T6G 2E1, Canada. Offers clinical epidemiology (M Sc, MPH); environmental and occupational health (MPH); environmental health sciences (M Sc); epidemiology (M Sc); global health (M Sc, MPH); health policy and management (MPH); health policy research (M Sc); health technology assessment (MPH); occupational health (M Sc); population health (M Sc); public health leadership (MPH); public health sciences (PhD); quantitative methods (MPH). *Accreditation:* CEPH. Terminal master's awarded for partial completion of doctoral program. *Degree requirements:* For master's, thesis (for some programs); for doctorate, thesis/dissertation. *Entrance requirements:* For master's, GMAT or GRE General Test. Additional exam requirements/recommendations for international students: required—TOEFL (minimum score 550 paper-based) or IELTS (minimum score 6). Electronic applications accepted.

**University of California, Riverside,** Graduate Division, School of Public Policy, Riverside, CA 92521-0102. Offers global health (MS); public policy (MPP, PhD); MD/MPP.

**University of California, San Diego,** Graduate Division, Program in Public Health, La Jolla, CA 92093. Offers epidemiology (PhD); global health (PhD); health behavior (PhD). *Students:* 19 full-time (13 women), 16 part-time (12 women). In 2019, 9 doctorates awarded. *Degree requirements:* For doctorate, thesis/dissertation, 2 semesters/quarters of teaching assistantship. *Entrance requirements:* For doctorate, GRE General Test, minimum GPA of 3.0, curriculum vitae or resume, letters of recommendation, statement of purpose. Additional exam requirements/recommendations for international students: required—TOEFL (minimum score 550 paper-based; 80 iBT), IELTS (minimum score 7). Electronic applications accepted. *Financial support:* Teaching assistantships available. Financial award applicants required to submit FAFSA. *Unit head:* David Strong, Faculty Director, 858-657-5241, E-mail: dstrong@ucsd.edu. *Application contact:* Carrie Goldsmith, Graduate Coordinator, 858-246-5423, E-mail: publichealthjdp@ucsd.edu. Website: http://publichealth.ucsd.edu/jdp/

**University of Colorado Denver,** School of Medicine, Physician Assistant Program, Aurora, CO 80045. Offers child health associate (MPAS), including global health, leadership, education, advocacy, development, and scholarship, pediatric critical and acute care, rural health, urban/underserved populations. *Accreditation:* ARC-PA. *Degree requirements:* For master's, comprehensive exam. *Entrance requirements:* For master's, GRE General Test, minimum GPA of 2.8; 3 letters of recommendation; prerequisite courses in chemistry, biology, general genetics, psychology and statistics; interview. Additional exam requirements/recommendations for international students: required—TOEFL (minimum score 550 paper-based; 80 iBT). Electronic applications accepted. Tuition and fees vary according to course load, program and reciprocity agreements.

**University of Denver,** Josef Korbel School of International Studies, Denver, CO 80208. Offers conflict resolution (MA); global business and corporate social responsibility (Certificate); global finance, trade and economic integration (MA); global health affairs (Certificate); homeland security (Certificate); humanitarian assistance (Certificate); international administration (MA); international development (MA); international human rights (MA); international security (MA); international studies (MA, PhD); public policy studies (MPP); religion and international affairs (Certificate). *Program availability:* Part-time. *Faculty:* 41 full-time (15 women), 14 part-time/adjunct (2 women). *Students:* 208 full-time (112 women), 24 part-time (13 women); includes 50 minority (11 Black or African American, non-Hispanic/Latino; 10 Asian, non-Hispanic/Latino; 15 Hispanic/Latino; 14 Two or more races, non-Hispanic/Latino), 20 international. Average age 27. 718 applicants, 70% accepted, 88 enrolled. In 2019, 134 master's, 2 doctorates, 26 other advanced degrees awarded. *Degree requirements:* For master's, variable foreign language requirement, thesis (for some programs); for doctorate, one foreign language, comprehensive exam, thesis/dissertation, one extended research paper. *Entrance requirements:* For master's, GRE General Test, bachelor's degree, transcripts, two letters of recommendation, personal statement, resume or curriculum vitae; for doctorate, GRE General Test, bachelor's degree (most have a master's degree), transcripts, personal statement, resume or curriculum vitae, writing sample. Additional exam requirements/recommendations for international students: required—TOEFL (minimum score 587 paper-based; 95 iBT). *Application deadline:* For fall admission, 1/23 priority date for domestic and international students; for winter admission, 11/1 for domestic and international students. Applications are processed on a rolling basis. Application fee: $65. Electronic applications accepted. *Expenses:* Contact institution. *Financial support:* In 2019–20, 161 students received support, including 4 teaching assistantships with tuition reimbursements available (averaging $16,875 per year); research assistantships with tuition reimbursements available, career-related internships or fieldwork, Federal Work-Study, institutionally sponsored loans, scholarships/grants, and unspecified assistantships also available. Support available to part-time students. Financial award application deadline: 2/15; financial award applicants required to submit FAFSA. *Unit head:* Dr. Fritz Mayer, Dean, 303-871-6338, E-mail: frederick.mayer@du.edu. *Application contact:* Admissions Contact, 303-871-2324, E-mail: korbeladm@du.edu.
Website: http://www.du.edu/korbel

**University of Florida,** Graduate School, College of Public Health and Health Professions, Department of Environmental and Global Health, Gainesville, FL 32611. Offers environmental health (PhD); one health (MHS, PhD). *Entrance requirements:* For master's and doctorate, GRE, minimum GPA of 3.0. Additional exam requirements/recommendations for international students: required—TOEFL (minimum score 550 paper-based; 80 iBT), IELTS (minimum score 6).

**University of Maryland, Baltimore,** University of Maryland School of Nursing, Baltimore, MD 21201. Offers adult-gerontology acute care nurse practitioner (DNP); adult-gerontology primary care nurse practitioner (DNP); clinical nurse leader (MS); community/public health nursing (MS); family nurse practitioner (DNP); global health (Postbaccalaureate Certificate); health services leadership and management (MS); neonatal nurse practitioner (DNP); nurse anesthesia (DNP); nursing (PhD); nursing informatics (MS, Postbaccalaureate Certificate); pediatric acute/primary care nurse practitioner (DNP); psychiatric mental health nurse practitioner (DNP); teaching in nursing and health professions (Postbaccalaureate Certificate); MS/MBA. *Accreditation:* AANA/CANAEP. *Program availability:* Part-time. *Faculty:* 130 full-time (117 women), 125 part-time/adjunct (114 women). *Students:* 539 full-time (463 women), 586 part-time (506 women); includes 485 minority (259 Black or African American, non-Hispanic/Latino; 3 American Indian or Alaska Native, non-Hispanic/Latino; 124 Asian, non-Hispanic/Latino; 66 Hispanic/Latino; 1 Native Hawaiian or other Pacific Islander, non-Hispanic/Latino; 32 Two or more races, non-Hispanic/Latino), 18 international. Average age 33. 964 applicants, 54% accepted, 347 enrolled. In 2019, 197 master's, 114 doctorates, 12 other advanced degrees awarded. *Degree requirements:* For master's and Postbaccalaureate Certificate, thesis (for some programs); for doctorate, comprehensive exam, thesis/dissertation. *Entrance requirements:* Additional exam requirements/recommendations for international students: required—TOEFL (minimum score 550 paper-based; 79 iBT); recommended—IELTS (minimum score 7). *Application deadline:* For fall admission, 11/1 priority date for domestic and international students; for spring admission, 12/15 for domestic and international students; for summer admission, 9/1 for domestic and international students. Applications are processed on a rolling basis. Application fee: $75. Electronic applications accepted. *Financial support:* In 2019–20, 257 students received support, including 31 research assistantships with

full and partial tuition reimbursements available (averaging $25,000 per year), 21 teaching assistantships with full and partial tuition reimbursements available (averaging $19,000 per year); scholarships/grants, traineeships, and unspecified assistantships also available. Support available to part-time students. Financial award application deadline: 3/1; financial award applicants required to submit FAFSA. *Unit head:* Dr. Jane Kirschling, Dean, 410-706-4359, E-mail: kirschling@umaryland.edu. *Application contact:* Larry Fillian, Associate Dean of Student and Academic Services, 410-706-6298, E-mail: lfillian@umaryland.edu.
Website: http://www.nursing.umaryland.edu/

**University of Michigan,** School of Public Health, Department of Epidemiology, Ann Arbor, MI 48109-2029. Offers epidemiological science (PhD); general epidemiology (MPH); global health epidemiology (MPH); hospital and molecular epidemiology (MPH); occupational and environmental epidemiology (MPH). *Accreditation:* CEPH (one or more programs are accredited). Terminal master's awarded for partial completion of doctoral program. *Degree requirements:* For master's, thesis (for some programs); for doctorate, comprehensive exam, thesis/dissertation, oral defense of dissertation, preliminary exam. *Entrance requirements:* For master's and doctorate, GRE General Test, MCAT. Additional exam requirements/recommendations for international students: required—TOEFL (minimum score 100 iBT). Electronic applications accepted.

**University of Minnesota, Twin Cities Campus,** School of Public Health, Division of Environmental Health Sciences, Minneapolis, MN 55455-0213. Offers environmental and occupational epidemiology (MPH, MS, PhD); environmental chemistry (MS, PhD); environmental health policy (MPH, MS, PhD); environmental infectious diseases (MPH, MS, PhD); environmental toxicology (MPH, MS, PhD); exposure sciences (MS); general environmental health (MPH, MS); global environmental health (MPH, MS, PhD); industrial hygiene (MPH, MS, PhD); occupational health nursing (MPH, MS, PhD); occupational medicine (MPH); MPH/MS. *Accreditation:* CEPH (one or more programs are accredited). *Program availability:* Part-time. *Degree requirements:* For master's, thesis optional; for doctorate, thesis/dissertation. *Entrance requirements:* For master's and doctorate, GRE General Test. Additional exam requirements/recommendations for international students: required—TOEFL (minimum score 600 paper-based; 100 iBT). Electronic applications accepted.

**University of Missouri,** School of Health Professions, Master of Public Health Program, Columbia, MO 65211. Offers global public health (Graduate Certificate); health promotion and policy (MPH); public health (Graduate Certificate); veterinary public health (MPH); DVM/MPH; MPH/MA; MPH/MPA. *Accreditation:* CEPH. *Entrance requirements:* Additional exam requirements/recommendations for international students: required—TOEFL (minimum score 550 paper-based; 80 iBT), IELTS (minimum score 6.5). Electronic applications accepted.

**University of Northern Colorado,** Graduate School, College of Natural and Health Sciences, School of Human Sciences, Program in Public Health, Greeley, CO 80639. Offers community health education (MPH); global health and community health education (MPH); healthy aging and community health education (MPH). *Degree requirements:* For master's, comprehensive exam, thesis or alternative. *Entrance requirements:* For master's, GRE General Test, 2 letters of recommendation. Electronic applications accepted.

**University of North Texas Health Science Center at Fort Worth,** School of Public Health, Fort Worth, TX 76107-2699. Offers biostatistics (MS); epidemiology (MPH, MS, PhD); food security and public health (Graduate Certificate); GIS in public health (Graduate Certificate); global health (Graduate Certificate); global health for medical professionals (Graduate Certificate); health administration (MHA); health behavior research (MS, PhD); maternal and child health (MPH); public health (Graduate Certificate); public health practice (MPH); DO/MPH; MS/MPH. *Accreditation:* CAHME; CEPH. *Program availability:* Part-time, evening/weekend, 100% online. *Degree requirements:* For master's, thesis or alternative, supervised internship; for doctorate, thesis/dissertation, supervised internship. *Entrance requirements:* For master's, GRE General Test. Additional exam requirements/recommendations for international students: required—TOEFL. Electronic applications accepted. *Expenses:* Contact institution.

**University of Pennsylvania,** Perelman School of Medicine, Master of Public Health Program, Philadelphia, PA 19104. Offers environmental health (MPH); generalist (MPH); global health (MPH); DMD/MPH; JD/MPH; MD/MPH; MES/MPH; MPH/MBE; MPH/MPA; MPH/MS; MSN/MPH; MSSP/MPH; MSW/MPH; PhD/MPH. *Accreditation:* CEPH. *Program availability:* Part-time, evening/weekend. *Financial support:* Application deadline: 4/1. *Unit head:* Dr. Jennifer Pinto-Martin, Director, 898-4726. *Application contact:* Moriah Hall, Associate Director, MPH program, 573-8841.
Website: http://www.cphi.upenn.edu/mph

**University of Pittsburgh,** Graduate School of Public Health, Department of Behavioral and Community Health Sciences, Pittsburgh, PA 15261. Offers applied research and leadership in behavioral and community health sciences (Dr PH); applied social and behavioral concepts in public health (MPH); community-based participatory research (Certificate); evaluation of public health programs (Certificate); global health (Certificate); health equity (Certificate); LGBT health and wellness (Certificate); maternal and child health (MPH); MID/MPH; MPH/MPA; MPH/MSW; MPH/PhD. *Accreditation:* CEPH. *Program availability:* Part-time. *Faculty:* 7 full-time (5 women), 8 part-time/adjunct (4 women). *Students:* 98 full-time (85 women), 8 part-time (5 women); includes 18 minority (7 Black or African American, non-Hispanic/Latino; 5 Asian, non-Hispanic/Latino; 6 Hispanic/Latino), 4 international. Average age 28. 153 applicants, 48% accepted, 21 enrolled. In 2019, 42 master's, 10 doctorates awarded. *Degree requirements:* For master's, thesis or alternative, Master's students can either complete an Essay or a Thesis; for doctorate, comprehensive exam, thesis/dissertation. *Entrance requirements:* For master's, GRE, applicants must have completed and earned a C or better in a three-credit math or statistics class taken in a math or statistics department. They must also have completed six credits of social sciences (anthropology, economics, geography, political science, psychology, social psychology); for doctorate, GRE, PhD applicants must hold a post-baccalaureate degree e.g. a Master of Science degree in a discipline relevant to public health such as social work or anthropology or an MD or JD. Additional exam requirements/recommendations for international students: required—TOEFL (minimum score 100 iBT), TOEFL or IELTS, WES evaluation for foreign education. *Application deadline:* For fall admission, 7/15 for domestic students, 4/15 for international students; for spring admission, 10/15 for domestic students, 8/1 for international students. Applications are processed on a rolling basis. Application fee: $135. *Expenses:* $13,379 per term full-time resident, $23,407 per term full-time non-resident, $1122 per credit part-time resident, $1916 per credit part-time non-resident, $500 per term for full-time dissertation research, $475 per term full-time fees, $295 per term part-time fees. *Financial support:* In 2019–20, 1 fellowship with full tuition reimbursement (averaging $24,816 per year), 11 research assistantships with full tuition reimbursements (averaging $16,386 per year) were awarded; traineeships also available. Financial award application deadline: 10/1; financial award applicants required to submit FAFSA. *Unit head:* Susan Cotter, Department Administrator, 412-624-9594, Fax: 412-624-5510, E-mail: suecot@pitt.edu. *Application contact:* Paul J. Markgraf, Recruitment and Academic Affairs Administrator, 412-624-3107, Fax: 412-624-5510, E-mail: pjm111@pitt.edu.
Website: http://www.bchs.pitt.edu/

**University of Pittsburgh,** School of Pharmacy, Professional Program in Pharmacy, Pittsburgh, PA 15261. Offers community, leadership, innovation, and practice (Pharm D); global health (Pharm D); pediatrics (Pharm D); pharmacotherapy (Pharm D); pharmacy business administration (Pharm D). *Accreditation:* ACPE. *Entrance requirements:* For doctorate, PCAT. Electronic applications accepted. *Expenses:* Contact institution.

**University of Southern California,** Keck School of Medicine and Graduate School, Graduate Programs in Medicine, Department of Preventive Medicine, Master of Public Health Program, Los Angeles, CA 90032. Offers biostatistics and epidemiology (MPH); child and family health (MPH); community health promotion (MPH); environmental health (MPH); geohealth (MPH); global health leadership (MPH); health communication (MPH); health services and policy (MPH). *Accreditation:* CEPH. *Program availability:* Part-time, evening/weekend, 100% online. *Faculty:* 37 full-time (28 women), 8 part-time/adjunct (6 women). *Students:* 261 full-time (201 women), 74 part-time (55 women); includes 224 minority (46 Black or African American, non-Hispanic/Latino; 2 American Indian or Alaska Native, non-Hispanic/Latino; 79 Asian, non-Hispanic/Latino; 56 Hispanic/Latino; 6 Native Hawaiian or other Pacific Islander, non-Hispanic/Latino; 35 Two or more races, non-Hispanic/Latino), 21 international. Average age 28. 420 applicants, 76% accepted, 94 enrolled. In 2019, 123 master's awarded. *Degree requirements:* For master's, practicum, final report, oral presentation. *Entrance requirements:* For master's, GRE General Test, MCAT, GMAT, minimum GPA of 3.0. Additional exam requirements/recommendations for international students: required—TOEFL (minimum score 600 paper-based; 90 iBT). *Application deadline:* For fall admission, 12/1 priority date for domestic students, 5/1 priority date for international students; for spring admission, 9/1 priority date for domestic and international students; for summer admission, 3/1 for domestic and international students. Applications are processed on a rolling basis. Application fee: $135. Electronic applications accepted. *Financial support:* Career-related internships or fieldwork, Federal Work-Study, institutionally sponsored loans, and scholarships/grants available. Support available to part-time students. Financial award application deadline: 5/4; financial award applicants required to submit CSS PROFILE or FAFSA. *Unit head:* Dr. Louise A. Rohrbach, Director, 323-442-8237, Fax: 323-442-8297, E-mail: rohrbac@usc.edu. *Application contact:* Valerie Burris, Admissions Counselor, 323-442-7257, Fax: 323-442-8297, E-mail: valeriem@usc.edu.
Website: https://preventivemedicine.usc.edu/education/graduate-programs/mph/

**University of Southern California,** Keck School of Medicine and Graduate School, Graduate Programs in Medicine, Master of Science Program in Global Medicine, Los Angeles, CA 90033. Offers MS, Certificate. *Program availability:* Part-time. *Faculty:* 1 (woman) full-time, 17 part-time/adjunct (9 women). *Students:* 105 full-time (77 women), 5 part-time (4 women); includes 67 minority (5 Black or African American, non-Hispanic/Latino; 34 Asian, non-Hispanic/Latino; 14 Hispanic/Latino; 2 Native Hawaiian or other Pacific Islander, non-Hispanic/Latino; 12 Two or more races, non-Hispanic/Latino). Average age 24. 72 applicants, 65% accepted, 32 enrolled. In 2019, 114 master's awarded. *Entrance requirements:* For master's, Minimum cumulative undergraduate GPA 3.0; Minimum cumulative undergraduate science GPA 3.0; for Certificate, GRE, MCAT, or DAT. Additional exam requirements/recommendations for international students: required—TOEFL (minimum score 100 iBT), IELTS (minimum score 6.5), TOEFL (minimum score 100 iBT), IELTS (6.5), or PTE. *Application deadline:* For fall admission, 6/15 for domestic and international students; for spring admission, 10/31 for domestic and international students. Applications are processed on a rolling basis. Application fee: $90. Electronic applications accepted. *Financial support:* Application deadline: 5/8; applicants required to submit FAFSA. *Unit head:* Dr. Elahe Nezami, Program Director, 323-442-3141, E-mail: nezami@usc.edu. *Application contact:* Dr. Elahe Nezami, Director, 323-442-3141, E-mail: msgm@med.usc.edu.
Website: https://msgm.usc.edu

**University of South Florida,** Innovative Education, Tampa, FL 33620-9951. Offers adult, career and higher education (Graduate Certificate), including college teaching, leadership in developing human resources, leadership in higher education; Africana studies (Graduate Certificate), including diasporas and health disparities, genocide and human rights; aging studies (Graduate Certificate), including gerontology; art research (Graduate Certificate), including museum studies; business foundations (Graduate Certificate); chemical and biomedical engineering (Graduate Certificate), including materials science and engineering, water, health and sustainability; child and family studies (Graduate Certificate), including positive behavior support; civil and industrial engineering (Graduate Certificate), including transportation systems analysis; community and family health (Graduate Certificate), including maternal and child health, social marketing and public health, violence and injury: prevention and intervention, women's health; criminology (Graduate Certificate), including criminal justice administration; data science for public administration (Graduate Certificate); digital humanities (Graduate Certificate); educational measurement and research (Graduate Certificate), including evaluation; English (Graduate Certificate), including comparative literary studies, creative writing, professional and technical communication; entrepreneurship (Graduate Certificate); environmental health (Graduate Certificate), including safety management; epidemiology and biostatistics (Graduate Certificate), including applied biostatistics, biostatistics, concepts and tools of epidemiology, epidemiology, epidemiology of infectious diseases; geography, environment and planning (Graduate Certificate), including community development, environmental policy and management, geographical information systems; geology (Graduate Certificate), including hydrogeology; global health (Graduate Certificate), including disaster management, global health and Latin American and Caribbean studies, global health practice, humanitarian assistance, infection control; government and international affairs (Graduate Certificate), including Cuban studies, globalization studies; health policy and management (Graduate Certificate), including health management and leadership, public health policy and programs; hearing specialist: early intervention (Graduate Certificate); industrial and management systems engineering (Graduate Certificate), including systems engineering, technology management; information studies (Graduate Certificate), including school library media specialist; information systems/decision sciences (Graduate Certificate), including analytics and business intelligence; instructional technology (Graduate Certificate), including distance education, Florida digital/virtual educator, instructional design, multimedia design, Web design; internal medicine, bioethics and medical humanities (Graduate Certificate), including biomedical ethics; Latin American and Caribbean studies (Graduate Certificate); leadership for coastal resiliency planning (Graduate Certificate); mass communications (Graduate Certificate), including multimedia journalism; mathematics and statistics (Graduate Certificate), including mathematics; medicine (Graduate Certificate), including aging and neuroscience, bioinformatics, biotechnology, brain fitness and memory management, clinical investigation, hand and upper limb rehabilitation, health informatics, health sciences, integrative weight management, intellectual property, medicine and gender, metabolic and nutritional medicine, metabolic cardiology, pharmacy sciences; national and competitive intelligence (Graduate Certificate); nursing (Graduate Certificate), including simulation based academic fellowship in advanced pain management; psychological and social foundations (Graduate Certificate), including career

counseling, college teaching, diversity in education, mental health counseling, school counseling; public affairs (Graduate Certificate), including nonprofit management, public management, research administration; public health (Graduate Certificate), including assessing chemical toxicity and public health risks, health equity, pharmacoepidemiology, public health generalist, toxicology, translational research in adolescent behavioral health; public health practices (Graduate Certificate), including planning for healthy communities; rehabilitation and mental health counseling (Graduate Certificate), including integrative mental health care, marriage and family therapy, rehabilitation technology; secondary education (Graduate Certificate), including ESOL, foreign language education: culture and content, foreign language education: professional; social work (Graduate Certificate), including geriatric social work/clinical gerontology; special education (Graduate Certificate), including autism spectrum disorder, disabilities education: severe/profound; world languages (Graduate Certificate), including teaching English as a second language (TESL) or foreign language. *Unit head:* Dr. Cynthia DeLuca, Associate Vice President and Assistant Vice Provost, 813-974-3077, Fax: 813-974-7061, E-mail: deluca@usf.edu. *Application contact:* Owen Hooper, Director, Summer and Alternative Calendar Programs, 813-974-6917, E-mail: hooper@usf.edu.
Website: http://www.usf.edu/innovative-education/

**The University of Toledo,** College of Graduate Studies, College of Medicine and Life Sciences, Department of Public Health and Preventative Medicine, Toledo, OH 43606-3390. Offers biostatistics and epidemiology (Certificate); contemporary gerontological practice (Certificate); environmental and occupational health and safety (MPH); epidemiology (Certificate); global public health (Certificate); health promotion and education (MPH); industrial hygiene (MSOH); medical and health science teaching and learning (Certificate); occupational health (Certificate); public health administration (MPH); public health and emergency response (Certificate); public health epidemiology (MPH); public health nutrition (MPH); MD/MPH. *Program availability:* Part-time, evening/weekend. *Degree requirements:* For master's, thesis or alternative. *Entrance requirements:* For master's, GRE, minimum undergraduate GPA of 3.0, three letters of recommendation, statement of purpose, transcripts from all prior institutions attended, resume; for Certificate, minimum undergraduate GPA of 3.0, three letters of recommendation, statement of purpose, transcripts from all prior institutions attended, resume. Additional exam requirements/recommendations for international students: required—TOEFL (minimum score 550 paper-based; 80 iBT), IELTS (minimum score 6.5). Electronic applications accepted.

**University of Vermont,** The Robert Larner, MD College of Medicine and Graduate College, Graduate Programs in Medicine, Program in Public Health, Burlington, VT 05405. Offers epidemiology (Graduate Certificate); global and environmental health (Graduate Certificate); healthcare management and policy (Graduate Certificate); public health (MPH). *Program availability:* Online only, 100% online. *Entrance requirements:* For master's and Graduate Certificate, resume/curriculum vitae. Additional exam requirements/recommendations for international students: required—TOEFL (minimum iBT score of 90) or IELTS (6.5). Electronic applications accepted. *Expenses:* Contact institution.

**University of Washington,** Graduate School, School of Public Health, Department of Epidemiology, Seattle, WA 98195. Offers clinical and translational research methods (MS); epidemiology (PhD); general epidemiology (MPH, MS); global health (MPH); maternal and child health (MPH); MPH/MPA. *Accreditation:* CEPH (one or more programs are accredited). *Program availability:* Part-time. *Faculty:* 54 full-time (36 women), 60 part-time/adjunct (27 women). *Students:* 161 full-time (116 women), 43 part-time (33 women); includes 54 minority (8 Black or African American, non-Hispanic/Latino; 4 American Indian or Alaska Native, non-Hispanic/Latino; 34 Asian, non-Hispanic/Latino; 8 Hispanic/Latino), 30 international. Average age 32. 393 applicants, 56% accepted, 91 enrolled. In 2019, 37 master's, 21 doctorates awarded. *Degree requirements:* For master's, thesis; for doctorate, comprehensive exam, thesis/dissertation. *Entrance requirements:* For master's, GRE (except for MDs from US institutions), Earned Bachelor's degree; for doctorate, GRE, Earned Master's degree. Additional exam requirements/recommendations for international students: required—TOEFL (minimum score 80 iBT). *Application deadline:* For fall admission, 12/1 for domestic and international students. Application fee: $85. Electronic applications accepted. *Financial support:* In 2019–20, 135 students received support, including 55 fellowships with full and partial tuition reimbursements available (averaging $38,000 per year), 50 research assistantships with full and partial tuition reimbursements available (averaging $30,000 per year), 15 teaching assistantships with full and partial tuition reimbursements available (averaging $24,000 per year); career-related internships or fieldwork, Federal Work-Study, institutionally sponsored loans, scholarships/grants, traineeships, health care benefits, tuition waivers (full and partial), and unspecified assistantships also available. Support available to part-time students. Financial award application deadline: 12/1. *Unit head:* Dr. Stephen E. Hawes, Professor and Chair, 206-685-0146, E-mail: epiadmin@uw.edu. *Application contact:* John Paulson, Assistant Director of Student Academic Services, 206-685-1762, E-mail: epi@uw.edu.
Website: https://epi.washington.edu/

**University of Washington,** Graduate School, School of Public Health, Department of Global Health, Seattle, WA 98195. Offers global health (MPH); global health metrics and implementation science (PhD); health metrics and evaluation (MPH); leadership, policy and management (MPH); pathobiology (PhD). *Accreditation:* CEPH. *Program availability:* Part-time. *Faculty:* 75 full-time (41 women), 86 part-time/adjunct (38 women). *Students:* 118 full-time (81 women), 47 part-time (33 women); includes 49 minority (14 Black or African American, non-Hispanic/Latino; 3 American Indian or Alaska Native, non-Hispanic/Latino; 24 Asian, non-Hispanic/Latino; 7 Hispanic/Latino; 1 Native Hawaiian or other Pacific Islander, non-Hispanic/Latino), 43 international. Average age 31. 386 applicants, 25% accepted, 67 enrolled. In 2019, 58 master's, 10 doctorates awarded. Terminal master's awarded for partial completion of doctoral program. *Entrance requirements:* Additional exam requirements/recommendations for international students: required—TOEFL (minimum score 500 paper-based; 80 iBT). *Application deadline:* For fall admission, 12/1 for domestic and international students. Application fee: $85. Electronic applications accepted. *Financial support:* In 2019–20, 22 students received support, including 6 fellowships with partial tuition reimbursements available (averaging $5,000 per year), 7 research assistantships with full tuition reimbursements available (averaging $21,492 per year), 2 teaching assistantships with full tuition reimbursements available (averaging $4,776 per year); career-related internships or fieldwork, scholarships/grants, tuition waivers (full and partial), and unspecified assistantships also available. Financial award application deadline: 12/1; financial award applicants required to submit FAFSA. *Unit head:* Dr. Judith Wasserheit, Chair, 206-221-4970, Fax: 206-685-8519, E-mail: jwasserh@uw.edu. *Application contact:* Noura Youssoufa, Academic Program Coordinator, 206-685-1292, E-mail: ghprog@uw.edu.
Website: http://globalhealth.washington.edu/

**Walden University,** Graduate Programs, School of Health Sciences, Minneapolis, MN 55401. Offers clinical research administration (MS, Graduate Certificate); health education and promotion (MS, PhD), including behavioral health (PhD), disease surveillance (PhD), emergency preparedness (MS), general (MHA, MS), global health (PhD), health policy (PhD), health policy and advocacy (MS), population health (PhD); health informatics (MS); health services (PhD), including community health, healthcare administration, leadership, public health policy, self-designed; healthcare administration (MHA, DHA), including general (MHA, MS); leadership and organizational development (MHA); public health (MPH, Dr PH, PhD, Graduate Certificate), including community health education (PhD), epidemiology (PhD); systems policy (MHA). *Program availability:* Part-time, evening/weekend, online only, 100% online. *Degree requirements:* For doctorate, thesis/dissertation, residency. *Entrance requirements:* For master's, bachelor's degree or higher; minimum GPA of 2.5; official transcripts; goal statement (for some programs); access to computer and Internet; for doctorate, master's degree or higher; three years of related professional or academic experience (preferred); minimum GPA of 3.0; goal statement and current resume (for select programs); official transcripts; access to computer and Internet; for Graduate Certificate, relevant work experience; access to computer and Internet. Additional exam requirements/recommendations for international students: required—TOEFL (minimum score 550 paper-based, 79 iBT), IELTS (minimum score 6.5), Michigan English Language Assessment Battery (minimum score 82), or PTE (minimum score 53). Electronic applications accepted.

**Washington University in St. Louis,** Brown School, St. Louis, MO 63130-4899. Offers American Indian/Alaska native (MSW); children, youth and families (MSW); epidemiology/biostatistics (MPH); generalist (MPH); global health (MPH); health (MSW); health policy analysis (MPH); individualized (MSW), including health; mental health (MSW); older adults and aging societies (MSW); public health sciences (PhD); social and economic development (MSW), including domestic, international; social work (PhD); urban design (MPH); violence and injury prevention (MSW); JD/MSW; M Arch/MSW; MPH/MBA; MSW/M Div; MSW/M Ed; MSW/MAPS; MSW/MBA; MSW/MPH; MUD/MSW. *Accreditation:* CEPH; CSWE (one or more programs are accredited). *Faculty:* 54 full-time (31 women), 87 part-time/adjunct (61 women). *Students:* 282 full-time (226 women); includes 90 minority (40 Black or African American, non-Hispanic/Latino; 10 American Indian or Alaska Native, non-Hispanic/Latino; 26 Asian, non-Hispanic/Latino; 13 Hispanic/Latino; 1 Native Hawaiian or other Pacific Islander, non-Hispanic/Latino). Average age 24. *Degree requirements:* For master's, 60 credit hours (for MSW); 52 credit hours (for MPH); practicum; for doctorate, comprehensive exam, thesis/dissertation. *Entrance requirements:* For master's, GRE (preferred), GMAT, LSAT, MCAT, PCAT, or United States Medical Licensing Exam (for MPH); for doctorate, GRE. Additional exam requirements/recommendations for international students: required—TOEFL (minimum score 100 iBT), IELTS (minimum score 7). *Application deadline:* For fall admission, 12/15 priority date for domestic and international students; for winter admission, 3/1 priority date for domestic and international students. Applications are processed on a rolling basis. Electronic applications accepted. *Expenses:* Contact institution. *Financial support:* In 2019–20, 90 research assistantships were awarded; fellowships, teaching assistantships, career-related internships or fieldwork, Federal Work-Study, scholarships/grants, and unspecified assistantships also available. Support available to part-time students. Financial award applicants required to submit FAFSA. *Unit head:* Jamie L. Adkisson-Hennessey, Director of Admissions and Recruitment, 314-935-3524, Fax: 314-935-4859, E-mail: jadkisson@wustl.edu. *Application contact:* Office of Admissions and Recruitment, 314-935-6676, Fax: 314-935-4859, E-mail: brownadmissions@wustl.edu.
Website: http://brownschool.wustl.edu

**William James College,** Graduate Programs, Newton, MA 02459. Offers applied psychology in higher education student personnel administration (MA); clinical psychology (Psy D); counseling psychology (MA); counseling psychology and community mental health (MA); counseling psychology and global mental health (MA); executive coaching (Graduate Certificate); forensic and counseling psychology (MA); leadership psychology (Psy D); organizational psychology (MA); primary care psychology (MA); respecialization in clinical psychology (Certificate); school psychology (Psy D); MA/CAGS. *Accreditation:* APA. *Degree requirements:* For master's, comprehensive exam (for some programs); for doctorate, thesis/dissertation (for some programs). Electronic applications accepted.

**Yale University,** Yale School of Medicine, Yale School of Public Health, New Haven, CT 06520. Offers applied biostatistics and epidemiology (APMPH); biostatistics (MPH, MS, PhD), including global health (MPH); chronic disease epidemiology (MPH, PhD), including global health (MPH); environmental health sciences (MPH, PhD), including global health (MPH); epidemiology of microbial diseases (MPH, PhD), including global health (MPH); global health (APMPH); health management (MPH), including global health; health policy (MPH), including global health; health policy and administration (APMPH, PhD); occupational and environmental medicine (APMPH); preventive medicine (APMPH); social and behavioral sciences (APMPH, MPH), including global health (MPH); JD/MPH; M Div/MPH; MBA/MPH; MD/MPH; MEM/MPH; MFS/MPH; MM Sc/MPH; MPH/MA; MSN/MPH. *Accreditation:* CEPH. *Faculty:* 161 full-time (71 women), 121 part-time/adjunct (57 women). *Students:* 534 full-time (386 women); includes 156 minority (24 Black or African American, non-Hispanic/Latino; 83 Asian, non-Hispanic/Latino; 30 Hispanic/Latino; 19 Two or more races, non-Hispanic/Latino), 220 international. Average age 25. 1,300 applicants, 220 enrolled. In 2019, 250 master's, 12 doctorates awarded. *Degree requirements:* For master's, thesis; for doctorate, comprehensive exam, thesis/dissertation. *Entrance requirements:* For master's, GMAT, GRE, or MCAT; for doctorate, GRE General Test. Additional exam requirements/recommendations for international students: required—TOEFL (minimum score 100 iBT). *Application deadline:* For fall admission, 12/15 for domestic and international students; for summer admission, 12/15 for domestic and international students. Applications are processed on a rolling basis. Application fee: $135. Electronic applications accepted. *Expenses:* Contact institution. *Financial support:* Fellowships with full tuition reimbursements, research assistantships with full tuition reimbursements, teaching assistantships with full tuition reimbursements, career-related internships or fieldwork, institutionally sponsored loans, scholarships/grants, and tuition waivers available. Support available to part-time students. Financial award application deadline: 3/1; financial award applicants required to submit FAFSA. *Unit head:* Dr. Sten Vermund, Dean and Anna M.R. Lauder Professor of Public Health, E-mail: sten.vermund@yale.edu. *Application contact:* Mary Keefe, Director of Admissions, 203-785-2844, E-mail: ysph.admissions@yale.edu.
Website: http://publichealth.yale.edu/

# Maternal and Child Health

**Bank Street College of Education,** Graduate School, Program in Child Life, New York, NY 10025. Offers MS. *Degree requirements:* For master's, thesis. *Entrance requirements:* For master's, interview, essays, 100 hours of volunteer experience in a child life setting. Additional exam requirements/recommendations for international students: required—TOEFL (minimum score 600 paper-based; 100 iBT), IELTS (minimum score 7).

**Bank Street College of Education,** Graduate School, Program in Infant and Family Development and Early Intervention, New York, NY 10025. Offers infant and family development (MS Ed); infant and family early childhood special and general education (MS Ed); infant and family/early childhood special education (Ed M). *Degree requirements:* For master's, thesis. *Entrance requirements:* For master's, interview, essays. Additional exam requirements/recommendations for international students: required—TOEFL (minimum score 600 paper-based; 100 iBT), IELTS (minimum score 7). Electronic applications accepted.

**Bastyr University,** School of Natural Health Arts and Sciences, Kenmore, WA 98028-4966. Offers counseling psychology (MA); maternal-child health systems (MA); midwifery (MS); nutrition (Certificate); nutrition and clinical health psychology (MS); nutrition and wellness (MS). *Accreditation:* AND; MEAC. *Program availability:* Part-time. *Degree requirements:* For master's, thesis optional. *Entrance requirements:* For master's, 1-2 years' basic sciences course work (depending on program). Additional exam requirements/recommendations for international students: required—TOEFL (minimum score 550 paper-based; 79 iBT).

**Columbia University,** Columbia University Mailman School of Public Health, Department of Population and Family Health, New York, NY 10032. Offers MPH, Dr PH. *Accreditation:* CEPH (one or more programs are accredited). *Program availability:* Part-time. *Students:* 142 full-time (122 women), 31 part-time (27 women); includes 68 minority (11 Black or African American, non-Hispanic/Latino; 1 American Indian or Alaska Native, non-Hispanic/Latino; 23 Asian, non-Hispanic/Latino; 27 Hispanic/Latino; 6 Two or more races, non-Hispanic/Latino), 16 international. Average age 27. 316 applicants, 78% accepted, 82 enrolled. In 2019, 46 master's, 4 doctorates awarded. *Entrance requirements:* For master's, GRE General Test; for doctorate, GRE General Test, MPH or equivalent (for Dr PH). Additional exam requirements/recommendations for international students: required—TOEFL (minimum score 600 paper-based; 100 iBT). *Application deadline:* For fall admission, 12/1 priority date for domestic and international students. Application fee: $120. *Expenses: Tuition:* Full-time $47,600; part-time $1880 per credit. One-time fee: $105. *Financial support:* Research assistantships, career-related internships or fieldwork, and Federal Work-Study available. Financial award application deadline: 2/1; financial award applicants required to submit FAFSA. *Unit head:* Terry McGovern, Professor and Interim Chairperson, 212-304-5200. *Application contact:* Clare Norton, Associate Dean for Enrollment Management, 212-305-8698, Fax: 212-342-1861, E-mail: ph-admit@columbia.edu.
Website: https://www.mailman.columbia.edu/become-student/departments/population-and-family-health

**East Carolina University,** Graduate School, Thomas Harriot College of Arts and Sciences, Department of Psychology, Greenville, NC 27858-4353. Offers health psychology (PhD), including clinical health psychology, occupational health psychology, pediatric school psychology; industrial and organizational psychology (MA); quantitative methods for the social and behavioral sciences (Certificate); MA/CAS. *Program availability:* Part-time, evening/weekend. *Application deadline:* For fall admission, 12/1 priority date for domestic and international students. *Expenses: Tuition, area resident:* Full-time $4749; part-time $185 per credit hour. Tuition, state resident: full-time $4749; part-time $185 per credit hour. Tuition, nonresident: full-time $17,898; part-time $864 per credit hour. *International tuition:* $17,898 full-time. *Required fees:* $2787. *Financial support:* Application deadline: 6/1. *Unit head:* Dr. Alan Christensen, Chair, E-mail: christensenal19@ecu.edu. *Application contact:* Graduate School Admissions, 252-328-6012, Fax: 252-328-6071, E-mail: gradschool@ecu.edu.
Website: https://psychology.ecu.edu/

**Instituto Tecnologico de Santo Domingo,** Graduate School, Area of Health Sciences, Santo Domingo, Dominican Republic. Offers bioethics (M Bioethics); clinical bioethics (Certificate); clinical nutrition (Certificate); comprehensive adolescent health (MS); comprehensive health and the adolescent (Certificate); health and social security (M Mgmt).

**Troy University,** Graduate School, College of Health and Human Services, Program in Nursing, Troy, AL 36082. Offers adult health (MSN); family nurse practitioner (DNP); maternal infant (MSN); nursing informatics specialist (MSN). *Accreditation:* ACEN. *Program availability:* Part-time, evening/weekend, online learning. *Faculty:* 14 full-time (all women). *Students:* 67 full-time (64 women), 160 part-time (139 women); includes 46 minority (37 Black or African American, non-Hispanic/Latino; 1 American Indian or Alaska Native, non-Hispanic/Latino; 1 Asian, non-Hispanic/Latino; 7 Hispanic/Latino). Average age 35. 64 applicants, 97% accepted, 59 enrolled. In 2019, 73 master's, 20 doctorates awarded. *Degree requirements:* For master's, comprehensive exam, minimum GPA of 3.0, candidacy; for doctorate, minimum GPA of 3.0, submission of approved comprehensive e-portfolio, completion of residency synthesis project, minimum of 1000 hours of clinical practice, qualifying exam. *Entrance requirements:* For master's, Score of 396 or higher on the Miller's Analogy Test (MAT) or score of 290 on Graduate Record Exam (850 on the old exam)(verbal plus quantitative); GRE or MAT required for every applicant, minimum GPA of 3.0, BSN, current RN licensure, 2 letters of reference, undergraduate health assessment course; for doctorate, GRE (minimum score of 850 on old exam or 294 on new exam), BSN or MSN, minimum GPA of 3.0, 2 letters of reference, current RN licensure, essay. Additional exam requirements/recommendations for international students: required—TOEFL (minimum score 523 paper-based; 70 iBT), IELTS (minimum score 6). *Application deadline:* For fall admission, 5/1 for domestic students; for spring admission, 10/1 for domestic students; for summer admission, 3/1 for domestic students. Applications are processed on a rolling basis. Application fee: $50. Electronic applications accepted. *Expenses: Tuition, area resident:* Full-time $7650; part-time $2550 per semester hour. Tuition, state resident: full-time $7650; part-time $2550 per semester hour. Tuition, nonresident: full-time $15,300; part-time $5100 per semester hour. *International tuition:* $15,300 full-time. *Required fees:* $856; $352 per semester hour. $176 per semester. *Financial support:* In 2019–20, 20 students received support. Fellowships, research assistantships, teaching assistantships, career-related internships or fieldwork, Federal Work-Study, scholarships/grants, traineeships, tuition waivers, and unspecified assistantships available. Support available to part-time students. Financial award application deadline: 3/1; financial award applicants required to submit FAFSA. *Unit head:* Dr. Wade Forehand, Professor, Director, School of Nursing, 334-670-3745, Fax: 334-670-3743, E-mail: jforehand@troy.edu. *Application contact:* Crystal G. Bishop, Director of Graduate

Admissions, School of Nursing, 334-241-8631, E-mail: cdgodwin@troy.edu.
Website: https://www.troy.edu/academics/academic-programs/college-health-human-services-programs.php

**The University of Alabama at Birmingham,** School of Public Health, Program in Health Care Organization and Policy, Birmingham, AL 35294. Offers applied epidemiology and pharmacoepidemiology (MSPH); biostatistics (MPH); clinical and translational science (MSPH); environmental health (MPH); environmental health and toxicology (MSPH); epidemiology (MPH); general theory and practice (MPH); health behavior (MPH); health care organization (MPH, Dr PH); health policy (MPH); industrial hygiene (MPH, MSPH); maternal and child health policy (Dr PH); maternal and child health policy and leadership (MPH); occupational health and safety (MPH); outcomes research (MSPH, Dr PH); public health (PhD); public health preparedness management (MPH). *Accreditation:* CEPH. *Program availability:* Part-time, 100% online, blended/hybrid learning. *Faculty:* 14 full-time (6 women). *Students:* 53 full-time (37 women), 61 part-time (45 women); includes 37 minority (12 Black or African American, non-Hispanic/Latino; 20 Asian, non-Hispanic/Latino; 1 Hispanic/Latino; 4 Two or more races, non-Hispanic/Latino), 17 international. Average age 31. 136 applicants, 59% accepted, 44 enrolled. In 2019, 36 master's, 4 doctorates awarded. *Degree requirements:* For master's, comprehensive exam (for some programs), thesis (for some programs); for doctorate, comprehensive exam, thesis/dissertation. *Entrance requirements:* For doctorate, GRE. Additional exam requirements/recommendations for international students: required—TOEFL (minimum score 80 iBT), IELTS (minimum score 6.5). *Application deadline:* For fall admission, 4/1 priority date for domestic students, 4/1 for international students; for spring admission, 11/1 for domestic students; for summer admission, 4/1 for domestic students. Application fee: $50 ($60 for international students). Electronic applications accepted. *Financial support:* Fellowships, research assistantships, teaching assistantships, scholarships/grants, traineeships, and unspecified assistantships available. Financial award application deadline: 3/1; financial award applicants required to submit FAFSA. *Unit head:* Dr. Martha Wingate, Program Director, 205-934-6783, Fax: 205-975-5484, E-mail: mslay@uab.edu. *Application contact:* Dustin Shaw, Coordinator, Student Admissions and Record, 205-934-3939, E-mail: bcampbel@uab.edu.
Website: http://www.soph.uab.edu

**University of California, Davis,** Graduate Studies, Program in Maternal and Child Nutrition, Davis, CA 95616. Offers MAS. *Degree requirements:* For master's, comprehensive exam. *Entrance requirements:* Additional exam requirements/recommendations for international students: required—TOEFL (minimum score 550 paper-based).

**University of Manitoba,** Max Rady College of Medicine and Faculty of Graduate Studies, Graduate Programs in Medicine, Department of Pediatrics and Child Health, Winnipeg, MB R3T 2N2, Canada. Offers M Sc.

**University of Maryland, College Park,** Academic Affairs, School of Public Health, Department of Family Science, College Park, MD 20742. Offers family studies (PhD); marriage and family therapy (MS); maternal and child health (PhD). *Accreditation:* AAMFT/COAMFTE. *Program availability:* Part-time, evening/weekend. *Degree requirements:* For master's, thesis or alternative; for doctorate, comprehensive exam, thesis/dissertation, oral defense. *Entrance requirements:* For master's, GRE General Test, minimum GPA of 3.0, 3 letters of recommendation; for doctorate, GRE General Test, minimum GPA of 3.0, 3 letters of recommendation, research sample. Electronic applications accepted.

**University of Minnesota, Twin Cities Campus,** School of Public Health, Major in Maternal and Child Health, Minneapolis, MN 55455-0213. Offers MPH. *Accreditation:* CEPH. *Program availability:* Part-time. *Degree requirements:* For master's, fieldwork, project. *Entrance requirements:* For master's, GRE General Test, 1 year of relevant experience. Additional exam requirements/recommendations for international students: required—TOEFL. Electronic applications accepted. *Expenses:* Contact institution.

**The University of North Carolina at Chapel Hill,** Graduate School, Gillings School of Global Public Health, Department of Maternal and Child Health, Chapel Hill, NC 27599. Offers MPH, MSPH, Dr PH, PhD, MD/MSPH, MPH/MSW, MSPH/M Ed, MSPH/MSW. *Faculty:* 17 full-time (14 women), 57 part-time/adjunct (40 women). *Students:* 57 full-time (54 women), 1 (woman) part-time; includes 14 minority (6 Black or African American, non-Hispanic/Latino; 2 Asian, non-Hispanic/Latino; 2 Hispanic/Latino; 4 Two or more races, non-Hispanic/Latino), 6 international. Average age 29. 57 applicants, 23% accepted, 7 enrolled. In 2019, 33 master's, 7 doctorates awarded. *Degree requirements:* For master's, comprehensive exam, major paper; for doctorate, comprehensive exam, thesis/dissertation. *Entrance requirements:* For master's, GRE General Test or MCAT, at least one year of post-BA maternal health/child health-related work experience, interview, 3 letters of recommendation (academic and/or professional; academic preferred); for doctorate, GRE General Test, graduate-level degree, at least one year of post-BA maternal health/child health-related work experience, interview, 3 letters of recommendation (academic and/or professional; academic preferred). Additional exam requirements/recommendations for international students: required—TOEFL (minimum score 90 iBT), IELTS (minimum score 7). *Application deadline:* For fall admission, 2/1 for domestic and international students. Application fee: $90. Electronic applications accepted. *Financial support:* Fellowships with tuition reimbursements, research assistantships with tuition reimbursements, teaching assistantships with tuition reimbursements, career-related internships or fieldwork, Federal Work-Study, institutionally sponsored loans, scholarships/grants, traineeships, health care benefits, and unspecified assistantships available. Financial award application deadline: 12/10; financial award applicants required to submit FAFSA. *Unit head:* Dr. Carolyn Halpern, Chair, 919-966-5981, E-mail: carolyn_halpern@unc.edu. *Application contact:* Cindy Reilly, Academic Coordinator, 919-843-2385, E-mail: cindy_reilly@unc.edu.
Website: https://sph.unc.edu/mch/maternal-and-child-health/

**University of Puerto Rico - Medical Sciences Campus,** Graduate School of Public Health, Department of Human Development, Program in Maternal and Child Health, San Juan, PR 00936-5067. Offers MPH. *Accreditation:* CEPH. *Program availability:* Part-time, evening/weekend. *Entrance requirements:* For master's, GRE, previous course work in algebra.

**University of South Florida,** Innovative Education, Tampa, FL 33620-9951. Offers adult, career and higher education (Graduate Certificate), including college teaching, leadership in developing human resources, leadership in higher education; Africana studies (Graduate Certificate), including diasporas and health disparities, genocide and human rights; aging studies (Graduate Certificate), including gerontology; art research (Graduate Certificate), including museum studies; business foundations (Graduate Certificate); chemical and biomedical engineering (Graduate Certificate), including materials science and engineering, water, health and sustainability; child and family

*Maternal and Child Health*

studies (Graduate Certificate), including positive behavior support; civil and industrial engineering (Graduate Certificate), including transportation systems analysis; community and family health (Graduate Certificate), including maternal and child health, social marketing and public health, violence and injury: prevention and intervention, women's health; criminology (Graduate Certificate), including criminal justice administration; data science for public administration (Graduate Certificate); digital humanities (Graduate Certificate); educational measurement and research (Graduate Certificate), including evaluation; English (Graduate Certificate), including comparative literary studies, creative writing, professional and technical communication; entrepreneurship (Graduate Certificate); environmental health (Graduate Certificate), including safety management; epidemiology and biostatistics (Graduate Certificate), including applied biostatistics, biostatistics, concepts and tools of epidemiology, epidemiology, epidemiology of infectious diseases; geography, environment and planning (Graduate Certificate), including community development, environmental policy and management, geographical information systems; geology (Graduate Certificate), including hydrogeology; global health (Graduate Certificate), including disaster management, global health and Latin American and Caribbean studies, global health practice, humanitarian assistance, infection control; government and international affairs (Graduate Certificate), including Cuban studies, globalization studies; health policy and management (Graduate Certificate), including health management and leadership, public health policy and programs; hearing specialist: early intervention (Graduate Certificate); industrial and management systems engineering (Graduate Certificate), including systems engineering, technology management; information studies (Graduate Certificate), including school library media specialist; information systems/decision sciences (Graduate Certificate), including analytics and business intelligence; instructional technology (Graduate Certificate), including distance education, Florida digital/virtual educator, instructional design, multimedia design, Web design; internal medicine, bioethics and medical humanities (Graduate Certificate), including biomedical ethics; Latin American and Caribbean studies (Graduate Certificate); leadership for coastal resiliency planning (Graduate Certificate); mass communications (Graduate Certificate), including multimedia journalism; mathematics and statistics (Graduate Certificate), including mathematics; medicine (Graduate Certificate), including aging and neuroscience, bioinformatics, biotechnology, brain fitness and memory management, clinical investigation, hand and upper limb rehabilitation, health informatics, health sciences, integrative weight management, intellectual property, medicine and gender, metabolic and nutritional medicine, metabolic cardiology, pharmacy sciences; national and competitive intelligence (Graduate Certificate); nursing (Graduate Certificate), including simulation based academic fellowship in advanced pain management; psychological and social foundations (Graduate Certificate), including career counseling, college teaching, diversity in education, mental health counseling, school counseling; public affairs (Graduate Certificate), including nonprofit management, public management, research administration; public health (Graduate Certificate), including assessing chemical toxicity and public health risks, health equity, pharmacoepidemiology, public health generalist, toxicology, translational research in adolescent behavioral health; public health practices (Graduate Certificate), including planning for healthy communities; rehabilitation and mental health counseling (Graduate Certificate), including integrative mental health care, marriage and family therapy, rehabilitation technology; secondary education (Graduate Certificate), including ESOL, foreign language education: culture and content, foreign language education; professional; social work (Graduate Certificate), including geriatric social work/clinical gerontology; special education (Graduate Certificate), including autism spectrum disorder, disabilities education: severe/profound; world languages (Graduate Certificate), including teaching English as a second language (TESL) or foreign language. *Unit head:* Dr. Cynthia DeLuca, Associate Vice President and Assistant Vice Provost, 813-974-3077, Fax: 813-974-7061, E-mail: deluca@usf.edu. *Application contact:* Owen Hooper, Director, Summer and Alternative Calendar Programs, 813-974-6917, E-mail: hooper@usf.edu.
Website: http://www.usf.edu/innovative-education/

**The University of Texas Health Science Center at Houston,** School of Public Health, Houston, TX 77030. Offers behavioral science (PhD); biostatistics (MPH, MS, PhD); environmental health (MPH); epidemiology (MPH, MS, PhD); general public health (Certificate); genomics and bioinformatics (Certificate); health disparities (Certificate); health promotion/health education (MPH, Dr PH); healthcare management (Certificate);

management, policy and community health (MPH, Dr PH, PhD); maternal and child health (Certificate); public health informatics (Certificate); DDS/MPH; JD/MPH; MBA/MPH; MD/MPH; MGPS/MPH; MP Aff/MPH; MS/MPH; MSN/MPH; MSW/MPH; PhD/MPH. *Accreditation:* CAHME; CEPH. *Program availability:* Part-time. *Degree requirements:* For master's, thesis (for some programs); for doctorate, comprehensive exam, thesis/dissertation. *Entrance requirements:* For master's and doctorate, GRE General Test. Additional exam requirements/recommendations for international students: required—TOEFL (minimum score 600 paper-based, 100 iBT) or IELTS (7.5). Electronic applications accepted. *Expenses:* Contact institution.

**University of Washington,** School of Public Health, Department of Epidemiology, Seattle, WA 98195. Offers clinical and translational research methods (MS); epidemiology (PhD); general epidemiology (MPH, MS); global health (MPH); maternal and child health (MPH); MPH/MPA. *Accreditation:* CEPH (one or more programs are accredited). *Program availability:* Part-time. *Faculty:* 54 full-time (36 women), 60 part-time/adjunct (27 women). *Students:* 161 full-time (116 women), 43 part-time (33 women); includes 54 minority (8 Black or African American, non-Hispanic/Latino; 4 American Indian or Alaska Native, non-Hispanic/Latino; 34 Asian, non-Hispanic/Latino; 8 Hispanic/Latino), 30 international. Average age 32. 393 applicants, 56% accepted, 91 enrolled. In 2019, 37 master's, 21 doctorates awarded. *Degree requirements:* For master's, thesis; for doctorate, comprehensive exam, thesis/dissertation. *Entrance requirements:* For master's, GRE (except for MDs from US institutions), Earned Bachelor's degree; for doctorate, GRE, Earned Master's degree. Additional exam requirements/recommendations for international students: required—TOEFL (minimum score 80 iBT). *Application deadline:* For fall admission, 12/1 for domestic and international students. Application fee: $85. Electronic applications accepted. *Financial support:* In 2019–20, 135 students received support, including 55 fellowships with full and partial tuition reimbursements available (averaging $38,000 per year), 50 research assistantships with full and partial tuition reimbursements available (averaging $30,000 per year), 15 teaching assistantships with full and partial tuition reimbursements available (averaging $24,000 per year); career-related internships or fieldwork, Federal Work-Study, institutionally sponsored loans, scholarships/grants, traineeships, health care benefits, tuition waivers (full and partial), and unspecified assistantships also available. Support available to part-time students. Financial award application deadline: 12/1. *Unit head:* Dr. Stephen E. Hawes, Professor and Chair, 206-685-0146, E-mail: epiadmin@uw.edu. *Application contact:* John Paulson, Assistant Director of Student Academic Services, 206-685-1762, E-mail: epi@uw.edu.
Website: https://epi.washington.edu/

**University of Washington,** Graduate School, School of Public Health, Department of Health Services, Seattle, WA 98195. Offers community-oriented public health practice (MPH); health services (MPH, MS, PhD); health systems and policy (MPH); maternal and child health (MPH); social and behavioral sciences (MPH); MPH/JD; MPH/MD; MPH/MN; MPH/MPA; MPH/MS; MPH/MSD; MPH/MSW; MPH/PhD. *Program availability:* Blended/hybrid learning. *Faculty:* 50 full-time (26 women), 71 part-time/adjunct (36 women). *Students:* 136 full-time (109 women), 16 part-time (all women); includes 62 minority (12 Black or African American, non-Hispanic/Latino; 6 American Indian or Alaska Native, non-Hispanic/Latino; 28 Asian, non-Hispanic/Latino; 14 Hispanic/Latino; 2 Native Hawaiian or other Pacific Islander, non-Hispanic/Latino), 9 international. Average age 31. 236 applicants, 62% accepted, 56 enrolled. In 2019, 63 master's, 10 doctorates awarded. Terminal master's awarded for partial completion of doctoral program. *Degree requirements:* For doctorate, comprehensive exam, thesis/dissertation. *Entrance requirements:* Additional exam requirements/recommendations for international students: required—TOEFL (minimum score 80 iBT). Application fee: $85. Electronic applications accepted. *Expenses:* MPH resident $22,476, MPH non-resident $38,316, resident MS & PhD $19,389, non-resident MS & PhD $32,775. *Financial support:* Fellowships, research assistantships, teaching assistantships, Federal Work-Study, institutionally sponsored loans, scholarships/grants, traineeships, health care benefits, and unspecified assistantships available. Financial award applicants required to submit FAFSA. *Unit head:* Dr. Jeffrey Harris, Chair, 206-616-2930, E-mail: hschair@uw.edu. *Application contact:* Marketing & Recruitment Specialist, 206-616-1397, E-mail: hservask@uw.edu.
Website: http://depts.washington.edu/hserv/

# HARVARD UNIVERSITY
## T. H. Chan School of Public Health

**HARVARD T.H. CHAN** | **SCHOOL OF PUBLIC HEALTH**
Powerful ideas for a healthier world

## Programs of Study

The Harvard T. H. Chan School of Public Health offers programs leading to the graduate degrees of Master of Public Health (M.P.H.), Master in Health Care Management (M.H.C.M.), Doctor of Public Health (Dr.P.H.), and Master of Science in a specified field (S.M. in that field). Doctor of Philosophy (Ph.D.) degrees are offered in specific fields of study through the Harvard Graduate School of Arts and Sciences. Programs are offered in biostatistics; computational biology and quantitative genetics; environmental health; epidemiology; genetics and complex diseases; global health and population; health data science; health policy and management; immunology and infectious diseases; nutrition; population health sciences, and social and behavioral sciences. Some programs are designed for physicians, lawyers, managers, and other health-care professionals; some for college graduates who wish to train for health careers; and others for individuals who hold graduate degrees in medicine, law, business, government, education, and other fields who wish to apply their special skills to public health problems. Degrees offered jointly with other Harvard University Schools include the M.U.P. (Master of Urban Planning)/M.P.H. with Harvard Graduate School of Design, the M.D. or D.M.D./M.P.H. for Harvard Medical School and Harvard School of Dental Medicine students post-primary clinical year, and the J.D./M.P.H. for Harvard Law School students. Degrees offered jointly with other institutions include the M.D., D.O., D.M.D., or D.D.S/M.P.H. for medical and dental students enrolled in U.S.-based programs post-primary clinical year. The School offers residency training leading to certification by the American Board of Preventive Medicine in occupational medicine.

## Research Facilities

The main buildings of the School are the Sebastian S. Kresge Educational Facilities Building at 677 Huntington Avenue, the François-Xavier Bagnoud Building at 651 Huntington Avenue, and the Health Sciences Laboratories at 665 Huntington Avenue. The School maintains well-equipped research laboratories containing sophisticated instrumentation and supporting animal facilities. Computing and data processing resources are also available to students through the Instructional Computing Facility. The Francis A. Countway Library serves the library needs of the School. It holds more than 630,000 volumes, subscribes to 3,500 current journal titles, and houses over 10,000 noncurrent biomedical journal titles in addition to its extensive collection of historical materials, making it the largest library in the country serving a medical and health-related school.

## Financial Aid

Financial aid at the Harvard Chan School can come from a variety of sources. Some departments have training grants that offer students full tuition plus a stipend. Through need-based and merit-based programs at the School and University levels, other students are offered grants that range from quarter to full tuition. To supplement other aid, many students borrow through one or more of the federal student loan programs and work at part-time jobs at Harvard and in the community.

## Cost of Study

Master's program students are assessed a program-specific flat tuition rate. The full-time rate for the Master of Public Health 45 Credit (1 year) Program is $64,998. The full-time rate for the Master of Public Health 65 Credit (1.5 year) program is $57,100. The full-time rate for the Master of Science 42.5 Credit (1 year) program is $61,446. The full-time rate for both the Master of Science 80 Credit (2 year) and 60 Credit (1.5 year) program is $49,020.

Doctoral students are assessed a flat tuition rate. The full-time rate for 2020–21 for students in their first or second year is $49,020.

Health insurance and health services fee are required, which total $5,128. Books and supplies are estimated to be $1,386 in 2020–21.

## Living and Housing Costs

For the academic year 2020–21, it is estimated that a single student in a master's program needs a minimum of $23,004 for housing and living costs: $14,238 for rent and utilities and $8,766 for other expenses. If a master's student elects to start their program in the summer, an additional $6,498 should be added to that estimate.

Limited housing is available in the Shattuck International House, with preference given to international students. Most students arrange for housing in the adjacent communities.

## Student Group

There were 1,316 graduate students enrolled in 2019–20. Forty-seven nations were represented in the incoming 2019 class.

## Student Outcomes

Graduates of the Harvard T. H. Chan School of Public Health find employment in a variety of settings. It depends in part upon their previous experience and in part upon department and degree programs from which they graduate. Recent graduates have found positions in research institutes, with pharmaceutical companies and governmental and nongovernmental agencies, within the health-care industry, and as faculty members of universities.

## Location

Boston is a heterogeneous metropolis rich in history and charm. Athletic, cultural, and recreational activities are abundant. The School is within walking distance of museums, colleges and universities, waterways, and parks.

## The University and The School

Harvard College was founded in 1636; until the establishment of professorships in medicine in 1782, it composed the whole of the institution now called Harvard University. In addition to the college, eleven graduate schools are now part of the University.

The Harvard T. H. Chan School of Public Health traces its roots to public health activism at the beginning of the last century, a time of energetic social reform. The School began as the Harvard-MIT School for Health Officers, founded in 1913 as the first professional public health training program in the United States. In 1922, the School split off from MIT; in 1946, the Harvard School of Public Health became an independent, degree-granting body. In 2014, the Harvard School of Public Health was renamed the Harvard T. H. Chan School of Public Health in recognition of an extraordinary gift from The Morningside Foundation. The primary mission of the School is to carry out teaching and research aimed at improving the health of population groups throughout the world. The School emphasizes not only the development and implementation of disease prevention and treatment programs but also the planning and management of systems involved in the delivery of health services in this country and abroad. The School cooperates with the Medical School in teaching and research and has close ties with other Harvard faculties. The School has more than 480 full-time and part-time faculty members and nine academic departments representing major biomedical and social disciplines.

## Applying

Harvard Chan School participates in SOPHAS, which is the centralized application service for schools and programs of public health. Applicants should visit the SOPHAS website at http://www.sophas.org for more specific information and for access to the application for admission. All applicants to the School are required to submit scores from the GRE (ETS school code: 3456); applicants are urged to take the test no later than November, since applications are not considered without the scores. Applicants may submit the DAT, GMAT, LSAT, or MCAT, as appropriate to the applicant's background, in lieu of the GRE. In addition, applicants must demonstrate to the Committee on Admissions and Degrees of their ability to meet academic standards and of their overall qualifications to undertake advanced study at a graduate level. Students should visit the School's website (http://www.hsph.harvard.edu/admissions) for information concerning the deadline to apply for admission and to apply online.

As a matter of policy, law, and commitment, the Harvard Chan School does not discriminate against any person on the basis of race, color, sex, sexual orientation, gender identity, religion, age, national or ethnic origin, political beliefs, veteran status, or disability in admission to, access to, treatment in, or employment in its programs and activities. Members of minority groups are strongly encouraged to apply.

## Correspondence and Information

Harvard T. H. Chan School of Public Health Admissions Office
158 Longwood Avenue
Boston, Massachusetts 02115-5810
United States
Phone: 617-432-1031
Fax: 617-432-7080
E-mail: admissions@hsph.harvard.edu
Website: http://www.hsph.harvard.edu/admissions

**Counseling and program information:**
Vincent W. James, Director
Kerri Noonan, Associate Director
Elizabeth Anderson, Assistant Director
Charlie Dill, Assistant Director
Ruth Thompson, Admissions Coordinator
Andy Lopez-Lara, Admissions Assistant

*Harvard University*

# FACULTY CHAIRS AND DEPARTMENTAL ACTIVITIES

### Biostatistics
(617-432-1087, biostat_admissions@hsph.harvard.edu)

Chair: John Quackenbush, Ph.D., M.S. Advancing health science research, education, and practice by turning data into knowledge to address the greatest public health challenges of the 21st century. The program combines both theory and application of statistical science to analyze public health problems and further biomedical research. Students are prepared for academic and private-sector research careers. Current departmental research on statistical and computing methods for observational studies and clinical trials includes survival analysis, missing-data problems, and causal inference. Other areas of investigation include environmental research; statistical aspects of the study of AIDS and cancer; quantitative problems in health-risk analysis, technology assessment, and clinical decision making; statistical methodology in psychiatric research and in genetic studies, and statistical genetics and computational biology.

### Environmental Health
(617-432-1270, envhlth@hsph.harvard.edu)

Chair: Russ Hauser, M.D., Sc.D., M.P.H. The mission of the Department of Environmental Health is to address critical environmental and public health challenges through national and global leadership in research and training. The department emphasizes the role of air, water, the built environment, and the workplace as critical determinants of health. Teaching and research activities of the department are carried out through three concentrations: exposure, epidemiology, and risk; occupational health; and molecular and integrative physiological sciences.

### Epidemiology
(617-432-1328, edigiova@hsph.harvard.edu)

Chair: Albert Hofman, M.D., Ph.D. Epidemiology, the study of the frequency, distribution, and determinants of disease in humans, is a fundamental science of public health. Epidemiologists use many approaches, but the ultimate aim of epidemiologic research is the prevention or effective control of human disease. The department has a long tradition of teaching and research in the epidemiology of cancer, cardiovascular disease, and other chronic diseases as well as in epidemiologic methodology. Areas of interest include: cancer epidemiology; cardiovascular epidemiology; clinical epidemiology; environmental and occupational epidemiology; epidemiologic methods; epidemiology of aging; infectious disease epidemiology; genetic epidemiology and statistical genetics; neuro-psychiatric epidemiology; nutritional epidemiology; pharmacoepidemiology; and reproductive, perinatal, and pediatric epidemiology.

### Genetics and Complex Diseases
Chair: Robert Farese, M.D. The complex interplay of biological processes with environmental factors as they apply to chronic, multigenic, and multifactorial diseases, with special attention to metabolism, is the emphasis of the Department of Genetics and Complex Diseases. Research programs in the department focus on molecular mechanisms of adaptive responses to environmental signals to elucidate the mechanisms underlying the intricate interaction between genetic determinants and their divergent responses to stress signals.

### Global Health and Population
(617-432-1179, bheil@hsph.harvard.edu)

Chair: Marcia Castro, M.A., Ph.D. The department seeks to improve global health through education, research, and service from a population-based perspective. Research interests span a wide spectrum of topics, including social and economic development, health policy, and demography; design and financing of health care systems; women's and children's health; global nutritional epidemiology and practice; prevention and control of infectious and chronic diseases; program evaluation; and humanitarian assistance and ethics. The department has a special concern with questions of health equity and human rights, particularly in relation to health and population issues in developing countries.

### Health Policy and Management
(617-432-4324, jmoltoni@hsph.harvard.edu)

Chair: Arnold Epstein, M.D. The department is committed to training and inspiring the next generation of health care leaders. Academic programs focus on developing the critical thinking and applied problem-solving skills needed to address a wide variety of challenges throughout the health care delivery, public policy, and public health systems.

### Immunology and Infectious Diseases
(617-432-1023, asabarof@hsph.harvard.edu)

Chair: Sarah Fortune, M.D. The department focuses on the biological, immunological, epidemiological, and ecological aspects of viral, bacterial, and protozoan diseases, primarily in developing countries. Emphasis is on research identifying basic pathogenic mechanisms that may lead to better diagnostic tools and the development of vaccines as well as the identification of new targets for antiviral and antiparasitic drugs.

### Nutrition
(617-432-1528, sdean@hsph.harvard.edu)

Chair: Frank B. Hu, M.D., M.P.H., Ph.D. The department's mission is to improve human health through better nutrition and lifestyle. The department strives to accomplish this goal through research aimed at an increased understanding of how diet influences health at molecular and population levels, the development of nutritional strategies, informing policy, the education of researchers and practitioners, and the dissemination of nutrition information to health professionals and the public. Department research ranges from molecular biology to human studies of cancer and heart disease, including the conduct of population-based intervention trials.

### Social and Behavioral Sciences
(617-432-3689, wwaddell@hsph.harvard.edu)

Chair: David Williams, M.P.H., Ph.D. The mission of the Department of Social and Behavioral Sciences is to understand and intervene on the social determinants of health and health equity across the life-course. This mission is achieved through research to identify the social and behavioral determinants of health, development and evaluation of interventions and policies leading to the improvement of population health, and the preparation of professionals and researchers who fill leadership positions in advocacy and public service.

### Master of Public Health Program
(617-432-0090, mph@hsph.harvard.edu)

Director: Murray Mittleman, M.D.C.M., M.P.H., D.P.H. The program is designed to provide both a general background and flexibility of specialization in public health. The fields of study are clinical effectiveness, global health, health and social behavior, health management, health policy, nutrition, occupational and environmental health, and quantitative methods. There is also an online and on-campus M.P.H. in Epidemiology.

### Doctor of Public Health Program
(617-432-5008, drph@hsph.harvard.edu)

Director: Rick Siegrist, M.B.A., M.S., CPA. The Doctor of Public Health degree is for exceptional individuals with proven potential who want to accelerate their careers, lead organizations, and have an important impact on people's health and lives. Students will enjoy unique opportunities to engage with Harvard's world-renowned faculty through rigorous teaching, interactive learning, case discussions, simulations, and field experiences in a variety of major public health organizations. This innovative, transformative educational experience has been designed so that no prior public health degree is required.

### Division of Biological Sciences
(617-432-4397, bph@hsph.harvard.edu)

Director: Brendan Manning, Ph.D. The Division of Biological Sciences is an umbrella organization encompassing the Harvard Chan School Departments of Environmental Health, Genetics and Complex Diseases, Immunology and Infectious Diseases, and Nutrition. The Ph.D. program in Biological Sciences in Public Health trains students in individual fields of biological research with a focus on understanding, preventing, and treating diseases affecting large populations. The Ph.D. programs are offered under the aegis of the Harvard Graduate School of Arts and Sciences and administered by the Harvard Chan School Division of Biological Sciences.

### Population Health Sciences
(617-432-4397, bph@hsph.harvard.edu)

Director: Lisa Berkman, Ph.D. The program offers advanced doctoral-level research training that builds on multiple disciplinary perspectives to understand origins and determinants of health and disease across populations. Population Health Sciences is an umbrella organization encompassing the Departments of Environmental Health, Epidemiology, Global Health and Population, Nutrition, and Social and Behavioral Sciences. In these departments, the doctoral degree offered is the Doctor of Philosophy (Ph.D.). The Ph.D. programs are offered under the aegis of the Harvard Graduate School of Arts and Sciences and administered by the Harvard Chan School Program in Population Health Sciences.

# ACADEMIC AND PROFESSIONAL PROGRAMS IN THE MEDICAL PROFESSIONS AND SCIENCES

# Section 25
# Acupuncture and Oriental Medicine

This section contains a directory of institutions offering graduate work in acupuncture and oriental medicine. Additional information about programs listed in the directory but not augmented by an in-depth entry may be obtained by writing directly to the dean of a graduate school or chair of a department at the address given in the directory.

## CONTENTS

### Program Directory

# Acupuncture and Oriental Medicine

**Academy for Five Element Acupuncture,** Graduate Program, Gainesville, FL 32601. Offers M Ac. *Accreditation:* ACAOM.

**Academy of Chinese Culture and Health Sciences,** Program in Traditional Chinese Medicine, Oakland, CA 94612. Offers MS. *Accreditation:* ACAOM. *Program availability:* Part-time, evening/weekend. *Degree requirements:* For master's, comprehensive exam, thesis. *Entrance requirements:* Additional exam requirements/recommendations for international students: required—TOEFL (minimum score 500 paper-based).

**Acupuncture & Integrative Medicine College, Berkeley,** Master of Science in Oriental Medicine Program, Berkeley, CA 94704. Offers MS. *Accreditation:* ACAOM. *Program availability:* Part-time. *Degree requirements:* For master's, comprehensive exam, 350 clinic treatments. *Entrance requirements:* For master's, interview, minimum GPA of 3.0, 60 semester units of course work at the baccalaureate level. Additional exam requirements/recommendations for international students: required—TOEFL (minimum score 61 iBT). Electronic applications accepted. *Expenses:* Contact institution.

**Acupuncture and Massage College,** Program in Oriental Medicine, Miami, FL 33176. Offers MOM. *Accreditation:* ACAOM.

**American Academy of Acupuncture and Oriental Medicine,** Graduate Programs, Roseville, MN 55113. Offers MAOM, DAOM. *Accreditation:* ACAOM.

**American College of Acupuncture and Oriental Medicine,** Graduate Studies, Houston, TX 77063. Offers MAOM. *Accreditation:* ACAOM. *Program availability:* Part-time. *Entrance requirements:* For master's, 60 undergraduate credit hours. Additional exam requirements/recommendations for international students: required—TOEFL.

**American Institute of Alternative Medicine,** School of Acupuncture, Columbus, OH 43229. Offers M Ac.

**AOMA Graduate School of Integrative Medicine,** Doctor of Acupuncture and Oriental Medicine Program, Austin, TX 78757. Offers DAOM. *Degree requirements:* For doctorate, comprehensive exam, clinical internship, clinical externship, capstone research project, portfolio. *Entrance requirements:* For doctorate, master's degree from ACAOM-accredited program in acupuncture and Oriental medicine; minimum GPA of 3.0 in master's studies; current license or eligibility to obtain a license to practice acupuncture in the state of Texas. Additional exam requirements/recommendations for international students: required—TOEFL (minimum score 508 paper-based; 87 iBT), IELTS (minimum score 6.5). Electronic applications accepted.

**AOMA Graduate School of Integrative Medicine,** Master of Acupuncture and Oriental Medicine Program, Austin, TX 78757. Offers MAcOM. *Accreditation:* ACAOM. *Degree requirements:* For master's, comprehensive exam, clinical rotations (40.5 credits), portfolio. *Entrance requirements:* For master's, BA or higher or minimum of 90 credits at baccalaureate level from regionally-accredited institution with 30 credits of general education coursework; minimum GPA of 2.5. Additional exam requirements/recommendations for international students: required—TOEFL (minimum score 508 paper-based; 87 iBT), IELTS. Electronic applications accepted.

**Arizona School of Acupuncture and Oriental Medicine,** Graduate Programs, Tucson, AZ 85712. Offers M Ac, M Ac OM. *Accreditation:* ACAOM.

**Atlantic Institute of Oriental Medicine,** Graduate Program, Fort Lauderdale, FL 33301. Offers MS, DAOM. *Accreditation:* ACAOM. *Program availability:* Evening/weekend. *Degree requirements:* For master's, comprehensive exam; for doctorate, comprehensive exam, thesis/dissertation. *Entrance requirements:* For master's, official transcripts, professional resume, essay, two letters of reference. Additional exam requirements/recommendations for international students: required—TOEFL (minimum score 500 paper-based). *Expenses: Tuition:* Full-time $17,000; part-time $15,000 per year. *Required fees:* $250. One-time fee: $150.

**Bastyr University,** School of Traditional World Medicines, Kenmore, WA 98028-4966. Offers acupuncture and Oriental medicine (MS, DAOM); Ayurvedic sciences (MS). *Accreditation:* ACAOM. *Program availability:* Evening/weekend. *Entrance requirements:* For master's, course work in biology, chemistry, intermediate algebra and psychology; for doctorate, MS in acupuncture or certificate and 10 years of clinical experience. Additional exam requirements/recommendations for international students: required—TOEFL (minimum score 550 paper-based; 79 iBT). Electronic applications accepted.

**Canadian Memorial Chiropractic College,** Certificate Programs, Toronto, ON M2H 3J1, Canada. Offers chiropractic clinical sciences (Certificate); chiropractic radiology (Certificate); chiropractic sports sciences (Certificate); clinical acupuncture (Certificate). *Degree requirements:* For Certificate, thesis. *Entrance requirements:* For degree, DC, board certification.

**Colorado School of Traditional Chinese Medicine,** Graduate Programs, Denver, CO 80206-2127. Offers acupuncture (MS); traditional Chinese medicine (MS). *Accreditation:* ACAOM. *Entrance requirements:* Additional exam requirements/recommendations for international students: required—TOEFL (minimum score 80 iBT), IELTS (minimum score 6.5). *Expenses:* Contact institution.

**Daoist Traditions College of Chinese Medical Arts,** Graduate Programs, Asheville, NC 28801. Offers acupuncture and Chinese medicine (DACM); acupuncture and Oriental medicine (MAOM).

**Dongguk University Los Angeles,** Program in Oriental Medicine, Los Angeles, CA 90020. Offers MS. *Accreditation:* ACAOM. *Program availability:* Part-time, evening/weekend.

**Dragon Rises College of Oriental Medicine,** Graduate Program, Gainesville, FL 32601. Offers MAOM. *Accreditation:* ACAOM. *Entrance requirements:* For master's, two letters of recommendation, official transcripts. Electronic applications accepted. *Expenses: Tuition:* Full-time $11,200. *Required fees:* $460.

**Eastern School of Acupuncture and Traditional Medicine,** Acupuncture Program, Montclair, NJ 07042-3551. Offers MSAC.

**East West College of Natural Medicine,** Graduate Programs, Sarasota, FL 34234. Offers MSOM. *Accreditation:* ACAOM.

**Emperor's College of Traditional Oriental Medicine,** Graduate Programs, Santa Monica, CA 90403. Offers MTOM, DAOM. *Accreditation:* ACAOM. *Program availability:* Part-time, evening/weekend. *Entrance requirements:* For master's, minimum 2 years of undergraduate course work, interview; for doctorate, CA acupuncture licensure.

**Five Branches University,** Graduate School of Traditional Chinese Medicine, Santa Cruz, CA 95062. Offers acupuncture (M Ac); acupuncture and Oriental medicine (DAOM); traditional Chinese medicine (MTCM, PhD). *Accreditation:* ACAOM. *Degree requirements:* For master's, comprehensive exam. *Entrance requirements:* For master's, 6 units in anatomy and physiology, 9 units in basic sciences, minimum GPA of 2.5. Additional exam requirements/recommendations for international students: required—TOEFL, IELTS. Electronic applications accepted.

**Florida College of Integrative Medicine,** Graduate Program, Orlando, FL 32809. Offers MSOM. *Accreditation:* ACAOM. *Program availability:* Evening/weekend. *Entrance requirements:* For master's, minimum 60 semester hours of undergraduate coursework. Electronic applications accepted.

**Institute of Clinical Acupuncture and Oriental Medicine,** Program in Oriental Medicine, Honolulu, HI 96817. Offers MSOM. *Accreditation:* ACAOM.

**Institute of Taoist Education and Acupuncture,** Graduate Program, Louisville, CO 80027. Offers classical five-element acupuncture (M Ac). *Accreditation:* ACAOM.

**Maryland University of Integrative Health,** Program in Herbal Medicine, Laurel, MD 20723. Offers clinical herbalism (Certificate); herbal studies (Certificate); therapeutic herbalism (MS). *Entrance requirements:* Additional exam requirements/recommendations for international students: required—TOEFL.

**Maryland University of Integrative Health,** Programs in Acupuncture and Oriental Medicine, Laurel, MD 20723. Offers acupuncture (M Ac, D Ac); Chinese herbs (Certificate); Oriental medicine (MOM, DOM). *Accreditation:* ACAOM. *Degree requirements:* For master's, comprehensive exam, 500 clinical hours, oral exams. *Entrance requirements:* Additional exam requirements/recommendations for international students: required—TOEFL.

**MCPHS University,** New England School of Acupuncture, Boston, MA 02115-5896. Offers acupuncture (M Ac); acupuncture and Oriental medicine (MAOM). *Accreditation:* ACAOM (one or more programs are accredited). *Program availability:* Part-time. *Degree requirements:* For master's, comprehensive exam. *Entrance requirements:* For master's, previous course work in anatomy, biology, physiology, and psychology. Additional exam requirements/recommendations for international students: required—TOEFL (minimum score 550 paper-based).

**Midwest College of Oriental Medicine,** Graduate Programs, Racine, WI 53403-9747. Offers acupuncture (Certificate); Oriental medicine (MSOM). *Accreditation:* ACAOM. *Program availability:* Part-time, evening/weekend. *Degree requirements:* For master's and Certificate, comprehensive exam, thesis. *Entrance requirements:* For master's and Certificate, 60 semester credit hours from accredited school, 2 letters of recommendation, interview. Additional exam requirements/recommendations for international students: required—TOEFL. *Expenses: Tuition:* Full-time $1160; part-time $1160 per course. *Required fees:* $570; $570 per course. $190 per quarter. One-time fee: $65.

**Midwest College of Oriental Medicine,** Graduate Programs-Chicago, Chicago, IL 60613. Offers acupuncture (Certificate); oriental medicine (MSOM). *Accreditation:* ACAOM. *Program availability:* Part-time, evening/weekend. *Degree requirements:* For master's and Certificate, comprehensive exam, thesis. *Entrance requirements:* For master's and Certificate, 60 semester credit hours from accredited school, 2 letters of recommendation, interview. Additional exam requirements/recommendations for international students: required—TOEFL. *Expenses: Tuition:* Full-time $1160; part-time $1160 per course. *Required fees:* $570; $570 per course. $190 per quarter. One-time fee: $65.

**National University of Health Sciences,** Graduate Programs, Lombard, IL 60148-4583. Offers acupuncture (MSAC); chiropractic (DC); diagnostic imaging (MS); naturopathic medicine (ND); Oriental medicine (MSOM). *Accreditation:* ACAOM; CCE; CNME.

**National University of Natural Medicine,** College of Classical Chinese Medicine, Portland, OR 97201. Offers M Ac, MSOM, DOM. *Accreditation:* ACAOM. *Students:* 70 full-time (55 women), 22 part-time (15 women); includes 21 minority (4 Black or African American, non-Hispanic/Latino; 7 Asian, non-Hispanic/Latino; 5 Hispanic/Latino; 5 Two or more races, non-Hispanic/Latino), 2 international. Average age 33. 45 applicants, 78% accepted, 23 enrolled. In 2019, 21 master's, 13 doctorates awarded. *Degree requirements:* For master's, thesis. *Entrance requirements:* Additional exam requirements/recommendations for international students: required—TOEFL (minimum score 550 paper-based; 80 iBT), IELTS and PTE are also accepted. *Application deadline:* For fall and winter admission, 5/1 priority date for domestic and international students. Applications are processed on a rolling basis. Application fee: $75. Electronic applications accepted. *Expenses: Tuition:* Part-time $464 per credit hour. *Financial support:* Federal Work-Study and scholarships/grants available. Financial award application deadline: 2/15; financial award applicants required to submit FAFSA. *Unit head:* Andrew McIntyre, LAc, Program Director of Chinese Medicine, 503-552-1775, Fax: 503-499-0027, E-mail: admissions@nunm.edu. *Application contact:* Ryan Hollister, Director of Admissions, 503-552-1665, Fax: 503-499-0027, E-mail: admissions@nunm.edu.
Website: http://nunm.edu/academics/school-of-classical-chinese-medicine/

**New York Chiropractic College,** Finger Lakes School of Acupuncture and Oriental Medicine, Seneca Falls, NY 13148-0800. Offers acupuncture (MS); acupuncture and Oriental medicine (MS). *Accreditation:* ACAOM. *Degree requirements:* For master's, clinical internship. *Entrance requirements:* For master's, interview, three written references. Additional exam requirements/recommendations for international students: recommended—TOEFL (minimum score 550 paper-based). Electronic applications accepted.

**New York College of Health Professions,** Graduate School of Oriental Medicine, Syosset, NY 11791-4413. Offers acupuncture (MS); Oriental medicine (MS). *Accreditation:* ACAOM. *Program availability:* Part-time. *Degree requirements:* For master's, thesis. *Entrance requirements:* For master's, minimum GPA of 2.5, 60 semester credits in undergraduate course work. Additional exam requirements/recommendations for international students: required—TOEFL.

**New York College of Traditional Chinese Medicine,** Graduate Programs, Mineola, NY 11501. Offers Oriental medicine (MAOM). *Accreditation:* ACAOM. *Entrance requirements:* For master's, statement of purpose, official transcript, three recommendation letters, immunizations. Additional exam requirements/recommendations for international students: required—TOEFL (minimum score 61 iBT), IELTS (minimum score 6).

**Northwestern Health Sciences University,** College of Health and Wellness, Bloomington, MN 55431-1599. Offers acupuncture (M Ac); applied clinical nutrition (MHS); Oriental medicine (MOM). *Accreditation:* ACAOM. *Entrance requirements:* For master's, 60 semester credits of course work with minimum GPA of 2.5. Additional exam requirements/recommendations for international students: required—TOEFL (minimum score 540 paper-based; 76 iBT). Electronic applications accepted.

**Oregon College of Oriental Medicine,** Graduate Program in Acupuncture and Oriental Medicine, Portland, OR 97216. Offers M Ac OM, MAcOM, DAOM. *Accreditation:* ACAOM. *Program availability:* Part-time. *Entrance requirements:* For master's, minimum 3 years of college; course work in chemistry, biology, and psychology; for doctorate, documentation of clinical practice, 3 years of clinical experience. Additional exam requirements/recommendations for international students: required—TOEFL (minimum score 550 paper-based).

**Pacific College of Oriental Medicine,** Graduate Program, San Diego, CA 92108. Offers MSTOM, DAOM. *Accreditation:* ACAOM. *Program availability:* Part-time, evening/weekend. *Entrance requirements:* For master's, 2 letters of reference, interviews, minimum GPA of 3.0.

**Pacific College of Oriental Medicine–Chicago,** Graduate Program, Chicago, IL 60601. Offers MTOM. *Accreditation:* ACAOM. *Program availability:* Part-time, evening/weekend. *Entrance requirements:* For master's, 2 letters of reference, interview, minimum GPA of 3.0.

**Pacific College of Oriental Medicine-New York,** Graduate Program, New York, NY 10010. Offers MSTOM. *Accreditation:* ACAOM. *Program availability:* Part-time, evening/weekend. *Entrance requirements:* For master's, 2 letters of reference, interview, minimum GPA of 3.0.

**Phoenix Institute of Herbal Medicine & Acupuncture,** Graduate Programs, Phoenix, AZ 85018. Offers acupuncture (MSAC); Oriental medicine (MSOM). *Accreditation:* ACAOM. *Entrance requirements:* For master's, baccalaureate degree, personal statement, resume, 2 letters of recommendation, official transcripts.

**Seattle Institute of East Asian Medicine,** Graduate Program, Seattle, WA 98115. Offers M Ac OM. *Accreditation:* ACAOM. *Degree requirements:* For master's, one foreign language, comprehensive exam. *Entrance requirements:* For master's, course work in biology, psychology, chemistry, anatomy, physiology; CPR/first aid certification; 3 years (90 semester credits) post secondary coursework. Additional exam requirements/recommendations for international students: recommended—TOEFL (minimum score 500 paper-based).

**South Baylo University,** Program in Oriental Medicine and Acupuncture, Anaheim, CA 92801-1701. Offers MS. *Accreditation:* ACAOM. *Program availability:* Evening/weekend. *Degree requirements:* For master's, 3 foreign languages, comprehensive exam. *Entrance requirements:* Additional exam requirements/recommendations for international students: required—TOEFL (minimum score 500 paper-based). Electronic applications accepted.

**Southern California University of Health Sciences,** College of Eastern Medicine, Whittier, CA 90609-1166. Offers MAOM, DAOM. *Accreditation:* ACAOM. *Program availability:* Part-time, evening/weekend. *Degree requirements:* For master's and doctorate, comprehensive exam. *Entrance requirements:* For master's, 60 semester hours or 90 quarter credits of undergraduate course work, interview. Additional exam requirements/recommendations for international students: required—TOEFL (minimum score 500 paper-based). Electronic applications accepted.

**Southwest Acupuncture College,** Master in Acupuncture & Chinese Herbal Medicine, Santa Fe, NM 87505. Offers MS. *Accreditation:* ACAOM. *Program availability:* Part-time. *Entrance requirements:* For master's, minimum 2 years of college general education. Additional exam requirements/recommendations for international students: required—TOEFL (minimum score 500 paper-based). *Application deadline:* For fall admission, 8/1 priority date for domestic and international students; for spring admission, 12/1 priority date for domestic and international students; for summer admission, 4/1 priority date for domestic and international students. Applications are processed on a rolling basis. Application fee: $50. Electronic applications accepted. *Expenses: Tuition:* Full-time $19,500; part-time $9450 per credit hour. *Required fees:* $300; $300 per semester. Tuition and fees vary according to course load. *Financial support:* Scholarships/grants available. Financial award applicants required to submit FAFSA. *Unit head:* Paul Rossignol, Campus Director, 505-438-8884, Fax: 505-438-8883. *Application contact:* Susan Chaney, Academic Dean, 505-438-8884, Fax: 505-438-8883.
Website: http://www.acupuncturecollege.edu

**Southwest Acupuncture College,** Master in Acupuncture with a Chinese Herbal Medicine Specilization, Boulder, CO 80301. Offers MS. *Accreditation:* ACAOM. *Program availability:* Part-time. In 2019, 2 master's awarded. *Entrance requirements:* For master's, minimum 2 years of college general education. Additional exam requirements/recommendations for international students: required—TOEFL (minimum score 500 paper-based). *Application deadline:* For fall admission, 8/1 priority date for domestic students; for spring admission, 12/1 priority date for domestic students; for summer admission, 4/1 priority date for domestic students. Applications are processed on a rolling basis. Application fee: $50. Electronic applications accepted. *Expenses: Tuition:* Full-time $19,500; part-time $9450 per credit hour. *Required fees:* $300; $300 per semester. Tuition and fees vary according to course load. *Financial support:* Scholarships/grants available. Financial award applicants required to submit FAFSA. *Unit head:* Heather Lang, Campus Director, 303-581-9955, Fax: 303-581-9944, E-mail: boulder@acupuncturecollege.edu. *Application contact:* Nate Mohler, Academic Dean, 303-581-9955, Fax: 303-581-9944, E-mail: nate@acupuncturecollege.edu.

**Swedish Institute, College of Health Sciences,** Graduate Program, New York, NY 10001-6700. Offers acupuncture (MS). *Program availability:* Part-time, evening/weekend. *Entrance requirements:* Additional exam requirements/recommendations for international students: required—TOEFL (minimum score 72 iBT).

**Texas Health and Science University,** Graduate Programs, Austin, TX 78704. Offers acupuncture and Oriental medicine (MS, DAOM); business administration (MBA); healthcare management (MBA). *Accreditation:* ACAOM. *Entrance requirements:* For master's, 60 hours applicable to bachelor's degree. Additional exam requirements/recommendations for international students: required—TOEFL (minimum score 500 paper-based), TWE. Electronic applications accepted. *Expenses: Tuition:* Full-time $11,780; part-time $3440 per credit. *Required fees:* $292; $146 per credit. $220 per trimester. One-time fee: $72. Tuition and fees vary according to course load and program.

**University of Bridgeport,** Acupuncture Institute, Bridgeport, CT 06604. Offers MS. *Accreditation:* ACAOM. *Program availability:* Part-time. *Entrance requirements:* Additional exam requirements/recommendations for international students: recommended—TOEFL (minimum score 550 paper-based; 80 iBT), IELTS (minimum score 6.5). Electronic applications accepted. *Expenses:* Contact institution.

**University of East-West Medicine,** Graduate Programs, Sunnyvale, CA 94085-3922. Offers acupuncture and Oriental medicine (DAOM); Tai Chi (MS); traditional Chinese medicine (MSTCM). *Accreditation:* ACAOM.

**Virginia University of Integrative Medicine,** Graduate Programs, Fairfax, VA 22031. Offers acupuncture (MS, D Ac); acupuncture and Oriental medicine (DAOM); East Asian nutrition (Certificate); Oriental medicine (MSOM, DOM). *Expenses: Tuition:* Part-time $300 per credit.

**Wongu University of Oriental Medicine,** Graduate Program, Las Vegas, NV 89123. Offers MSOM. *Program availability:* Part-time. *Degree requirements:* For master's, comprehensive exam, Comprehensive Graduation Exam. *Entrance requirements:* For master's, Bachelor's Degree from and Accredited University with a minimum 2.75 GPA. Additional exam requirements/recommendations for international students: required—TOEFL (minimum score 80 iBT), IELTS (minimum score 6.5). Electronic applications accepted. *Expenses: Tuition:* Full-time $11,320; part-time $2830 per quarter. *Required fees:* $520; $520 per quarter. $130 per quarter. One-time fee: $150. Tuition and fees vary according to course load, program and student level.

**Wongu University of Oriental Medicine,** Graduate Program, Program in Acupuncture, Las Vegas, NV 89123. Offers MSOM. *Program availability:* Part-time. *Degree requirements:* For master's, comprehensive exam, Completion of Graduation Exam. *Entrance requirements:* For master's, Bachelor's Degree from an Accredited University; Minimum of 2.75 GPA. Additional exam requirements/recommendations for international students: required—TOEFL (minimum score 80 iBT), IELTS (minimum score 6.5). Electronic applications accepted. *Expenses: Tuition:* Full-time $11,320; part-time $2830 per quarter. *Required fees:* $520; $520 per quarter. $130 per quarter. One-time fee: $150. Tuition and fees vary according to course load, program and student level.

**Wongu University of Oriental Medicine,** Graduate Program, Program in Herbology, Las Vegas, NV 89123. Offers MSOM. *Program availability:* Part-time. *Degree requirements:* For master's, comprehensive exam, Comprehensive Graduation Exam. *Entrance requirements:* For master's, Bachelor's Degree from an Accredited University with a minimum 2.75 GPA. Additional exam requirements/recommendations for international students: required—TOEFL (minimum score 80 iBT), IELTS (minimum score 6.5). Electronic applications accepted. *Expenses: Tuition:* Full-time $11,320; part-time $2830 per quarter. *Required fees:* $520; $520 per quarter. $130 per quarter. One-time fee: $150. Tuition and fees vary according to course load, program and student level.

**Wongu University of Oriental Medicine,** Graduate Program, Program in Oriental Medicine, Las Vegas, NV 89123. Offers MSOM. *Program availability:* Part-time. *Degree requirements:* For master's, comprehensive exam, Comprehensive Graduation Exam. *Entrance requirements:* For master's, Bachelor's Degree from an Accredited University with a minimum 2.75 GPA. Additional exam requirements/recommendations for international students: required—TOEFL (minimum score 80 iBT), IELTS (minimum score 6.5). Electronic applications accepted. *Expenses: Tuition:* Full-time $11,320; part-time $2830 per quarter. *Required fees:* $520; $520 per quarter. $130 per quarter. One-time fee: $150. Tuition and fees vary according to course load, program and student level.

**Wongu University of Oriental Medicine,** Graduate Program, Program in Western Medicine, Las Vegas, NV 89123. Offers MSOM. *Program availability:* Part-time. *Degree requirements:* For master's, comprehensive exam, Comprehensive Graduation Exam. *Entrance requirements:* For master's, Bachelor's Degree from an Accredited University with a minimum 2.75 GPA. Additional exam requirements/recommendations for international students: required—TOEFL (minimum score 80 iBT); recommended—IELTS (minimum score 6.5). Electronic applications accepted. *Expenses: Tuition:* Full-time $11,320; part-time $2830 per quarter. *Required fees:* $520; $520 per quarter. $130 per quarter. One-time fee: $150. Tuition and fees vary according to course load, program and student level.

**Won Institute of Graduate Studies,** Acupuncture Studies Program, Glenside, PA 19038. Offers M Ac. *Accreditation:* ACAOM. *Entrance requirements:* For master's, 6 prerequisite credits in anatomy and physiology, 2 letters of recommendation, essay, bachelor's degree, 3 credits of basic science (chemistry, biology, physics or botany). Additional exam requirements/recommendations for international students: required—TOEFL (minimum score 550 paper-based; 79 iBT). Electronic applications accepted. *Expenses: Tuition:* Full-time $15,000; part-time $7500 per credit. *Required fees:* $750; $600 per credit. Tuition and fees vary according to degree level and program.

**Won Institute of Graduate Studies,** Program in Chinese Herbal Medicine, Glenside, PA 19038. Offers Certificate. *Entrance requirements:* For degree, licensed acupuncturist with bachelor's degree, graduate of ACAOM-approved acupuncture program, or currently enrolled in ACAOM-approved acupuncture program. Additional exam requirements/recommendations for international students: required—TOEFL (minimum score 550 paper-based; 79 iBT). Electronic applications accepted. *Expenses:* Contact institution.

**Yo San University of Traditional Chinese Medicine,** Program in Acupuncture and Traditional Chinese Medicine, Los Angeles, CA 90066. Offers MATCM. *Accreditation:* ACAOM. *Program availability:* Part-time, online learning. *Degree requirements:* For master's, observation and practice internships, exam. *Entrance requirements:* For master's, minimum 2 years of college, interview, minimum GPA of 2.5.

# Section 26
# Chiropractic

This section contains a directory of institutions offering graduate work in chiropractic. Additional information about programs listed in the directory but not augmented by an in-depth entry may be obtained by writing directly to the dean of a graduate school or chair of a department at the address given in the directory.

## CONTENTS

### Program Directory

# Chiropractic

**Canadian Memorial Chiropractic College,** Certificate Programs, Toronto, ON M2H 3J1, Canada. Offers chiropractic clinical sciences (Certificate); chiropractic radiology (Certificate); chiropractic sports sciences (Certificate); clinical acupuncture (Certificate). *Degree requirements:* For Certificate, thesis. *Entrance requirements:* For degree, DC, board certification.

**Canadian Memorial Chiropractic College,** Professional Program, Toronto, ON M2H 3J1, Canada. Offers DC. *Entrance requirements:* For doctorate, 3 full years of university (15 full courses or 90 hours).

**Cleveland University–Kansas City,** Doctor of Chiropractic Program, Overland Park, KS 66210. Offers DC. *Accreditation:* CCE. *Program availability:* Part-time. *Degree requirements:* For doctorate, comprehensive exam. *Entrance requirements:* For doctorate, 90 semester hours of pre-professional study, college transcripts, minimum cumulative college GPA of 3.0. Additional exam requirements/recommendations for international students: required—TOEFL (minimum score 550 paper-based; 79 iBT). Electronic applications accepted.

**D'Youville College,** Department of Chiropractic, Buffalo, NY 14201-1084. Offers DC. *Accreditation:* CCE. *Entrance requirements:* For doctorate, minimum GPA of 2.5, 90 undergraduate credits. Electronic applications accepted. *Expenses:* Contact institution.

**Institut Franco-EuropÃ©en de Chiropraxie,** Professional Program, Ivry-sur-Seine, France. Offers DC.

**Life Chiropractic College West,** Professional Program, Hayward, CA 94545. Offers DC. *Accreditation:* CCE. *Entrance requirements:* For doctorate, minimum GPA of 3.0. Additional exam requirements/recommendations for international students: required—TOEFL (minimum score 550 paper-based). Electronic applications accepted.

**Life University,** College of Chiropractic, Marietta, GA 30060. Offers DC. *Accreditation:* CCE. *Faculty:* 83 full-time (32 women), 22 part-time/adjunct (6 women). *Students:* 1,552 full-time (712 women), 99 part-time (50 women); includes 576 minority (207 Black or African American, non-Hispanic/Latino; 17 American Indian or Alaska Native, non-Hispanic/Latino; 62 Asian, non-Hispanic/Latino; 290 Hispanic/Latino), 66 international. Average age 28. In 2019, 353 doctorates awarded. *Degree requirements:* For doctorate, comprehensive exam, thesis/dissertation or alternative. *Entrance requirements:* For doctorate, minimum of 3 years of college; course work in biology, chemistry, physics, humanities, psychology, and English; minimum GPA of 2.75. Additional exam requirements/recommendations for international students: required—TOEFL (minimum score 500 paper-based). *Application deadline:* For fall admission, 8/1 for domestic students; for winter admission, 11/1 for domestic students; for spring admission, 3/1 for domestic students; for summer admission, 7/1 for domestic students. Applications are processed on a rolling basis. Application fee: $50. Electronic applications accepted. *Expenses:* Contact institution. *Financial support:* Research assistantships, Federal Work-Study, institutionally sponsored loans, scholarships/grants, and tuition waivers (partial) available. Support available to part-time students. Financial award application deadline: 9/1; financial award applicants required to submit FAFSA. *Unit head:* Dr. Leslie King, Dean, 770-426-2713, E-mail: lesliek@life.edu. *Application contact:* Charmaine Townsend, Director of Chiropractic Enrollment, 678-331 4382, Fax: 770-426-2895, E-mail: charmaine.edwards@life.edu.
Website: https://www.life.edu/academic-pages/chiropractic-program/

**Logan University,** College of Chiropractic, Chesterfield, MO 63017. Offers DC. *Accreditation:* CCE. *Degree requirements:* For doctorate, comprehensive exam, preceptorship. *Entrance requirements:* For doctorate, 90 hours of pre-chiropractic including biology, chemistry, physics, and social sciences; minimum GPA of 3.0. Additional exam requirements/recommendations for international students: required—TOEFL (minimum score 500 paper-based; 79 iBT); recommended—IELTS. Electronic applications accepted. *Expenses:* Contact institution.

**National University of Health Sciences,** Graduate Programs, Lombard, IL 60148-4583. Offers acupuncture (MSAC); chiropractic (DC); diagnostic imaging (MS); naturopathic medicine (ND); Oriental medicine (MSOM). *Accreditation:* ACAOM; CCE; CNME.

**New York Chiropractic College,** Doctor of Chiropractic Program, Seneca Falls, NY 13148-0800. Offers DC. *Accreditation:* CCE. *Degree requirements:* For doctorate, internship in health center. *Entrance requirements:* For doctorate, 24 credit hours of course work in science; 90 credit hours with minimum GPA of 2.5; references; interview. Additional exam requirements/recommendations for international students: recommended—TOEFL (minimum score 550 paper-based). Electronic applications accepted.

**Northwestern Health Sciences University,** College of Chiropractic, Bloomington, MN 55431-1599. Offers DC. *Accreditation:* CCE. *Entrance requirements:* For doctorate, 90 semester hours of course work in health or science, minimum GPA of 2.75. Additional exam requirements/recommendations for international students: required—TOEFL (minimum score 540 paper-based; 76 iBT). Electronic applications accepted.

**Palmer College of Chiropractic,** Professional Program, Davenport, IA 52803-5287. Offers DC. *Accreditation:* CCE. *Program availability:* Part-time. *Entrance requirements:* For doctorate, minimum GPA of 2.5, 90 hours of prerequisite coursework. Additional exam requirements/recommendations for international students: required—TOEFL (minimum score 500 paper-based; 61 iBT). Electronic applications accepted. *Expenses:* Contact institution.

**Palmer College of Chiropractic,** Professional Program–Florida Campus, Port Orange, FL 32129. Offers DC. *Program availability:* Part-time. *Degree requirements:* For doctorate, clinical internship. *Entrance requirements:* For doctorate, minimum GPA of 2.5, 90 hours of prerequisite coursework. Additional exam requirements/recommendations for international students: recommended—TOEFL (minimum score 500 paper-based; 61 iBT). *Expenses:* Contact institution.

**Palmer College of Chiropractic,** Professional Program–West Campus, San Jose, CA 95134-1617. Offers DC. *Accreditation:* CCE. *Program availability:* Part-time. *Degree requirements:* For doctorate, clinical internship. *Entrance requirements:* For doctorate, minimum GPA of 2.5. Additional exam requirements/recommendations for international students: required—TOEFL. Electronic applications accepted. *Expenses:* Contact institution.

**Parker University,** Doctor of Chiropractic Program, Dallas, TX 75229-5668. Offers DC. *Accreditation:* CCE. *Program availability:* Part-time. *Entrance requirements:* For doctorate, minimum GPA of 2.65. Additional exam requirements/recommendations for international students: required—TOEFL (minimum score 550 paper-based). Electronic applications accepted.

**Sherman College of Chiropractic,** Professional Program, Spartanburg, SC 29304-1452. Offers DC. *Accreditation:* CCE. *Entrance requirements:* For doctorate, two letters of recommendation, official transcripts. Electronic applications accepted.

**Southern California University of Health Sciences,** Los Angeles College of Chiropractic, Whittier, CA 90609-1166. Offers DC. *Accreditation:* CCE. *Degree requirements:* For doctorate, comprehensive exam. *Entrance requirements:* For doctorate, minimum GPA of 2.5, 90 incoming units in prerequisite coursework. Additional exam requirements/recommendations for international students: required—TOEFL (minimum score 500 paper-based). Electronic applications accepted.

**Texas Chiropractic College,** Professional Program, Pasadena, TX 77505-1699. Offers DC. *Accreditation:* CCE. *Entrance requirements:* For doctorate, 90 semester hours at regionally-accredited college or university, minimum GPA of 3.0 (24 hours of life and physical sciences, half of which have a lab component). Additional exam requirements/recommendations for international students: required—TOEFL.

**Université du Québec à Trois-Rivières,** Graduate Programs, Program in Chiropractic, Trois-Rivières, QC G9A 5H7, Canada. Offers DC.

**University of Bridgeport,** College of Chiropractic, Bridgeport, CT 06604. Offers DC. *Accreditation:* CCE. *Degree requirements:* For doctorate, thesis/dissertation, National Board of Chiropractic Exam Parts I and II. *Entrance requirements:* Additional exam requirements/recommendations for international students: recommended—TOEFL (minimum score 550 paper-based; 80 iBT), IELTS (minimum score 6.5). Electronic applications accepted. *Expenses:* Contact institution.

**University of Western States,** Professional Program, Portland, OR 97230-3099. Offers DC. *Accreditation:* CCE. *Degree requirements:* For doctorate, comprehensive exam, internship. *Entrance requirements:* For doctorate, 3 years of pre-chiropractic study in biological sciences, minimum GPA of 2.5.

# Section 27
# Dentistry and Dental Sciences

This section contains a directory of institutions offering graduate work in dentistry and dental sciences, followed by an in-depth entry submitted by an institution that chose to prepare a detailed program description. Additional information about programs listed in the directory but not augmented by an in-depth entry may be obtained by writing directly to the dean of a graduate school or chair of a department at the address given in the directory.

For programs offering related work, see also in this book *Allied Health*.

## CONTENTS

### Program Directories

# Dentistry

**A.T. Still University,** Arizona School of Dentistry & Oral Health, Mesa, AZ 85206. Offers dental medicine (DMD); orthodontics (MS, Certificate). *Accreditation:* ADA. *Faculty:* 130 full-time (87 women), 90 part-time/adjunct (32 women). *Students:* 314 full-time (169 women); includes 163 minority (9 Black or African American, non-Hispanic/Latino; 2 American Indian or Alaska Native, non-Hispanic/Latino; 107 Asian, non-Hispanic/Latino; 17 Hispanic/Latino; 1 Native Hawaiian or other Pacific Islander, non-Hispanic/Latino; 27 Two or more races, non-Hispanic/Latino), 3 international. Average age 28. 2,323 applicants, 7% accepted, 77 enrolled. In 2019, 5 master's, 74 doctorates, 1 other advanced degree awarded. *Entrance requirements:* For doctorate, Dental Admissions Test, A formal minimum of three years (90 semester hours or 135 quarter hours); baccalaureate degree is preferred. Minimum cumulative and science GPA of 2.5 on a four-point scale (3.0 recommended). The overall and science GPA, the school(s) attended, and the rigor of the academic course load are all assessed on an individual basis. Additional exam requirements/recommendations for international students: recommended—TOEFL. *Application deadline:* For fall admission, 11/15 for domestic and international students; for summer admission, 11/15 for domestic and international students. Applications are processed on a rolling basis. Application fee: $70. Electronic applications accepted. *Financial support:* In 2019–20, 61 students received support. Federal Work-Study and scholarships/grants available. Financial award application deadline: 6/1; financial award applicants required to submit FAFSA. *Unit head:* Dr. Robert Trombly, Dean, 480-248-8105, Fax: 623-223-7063, E-mail: rtrombly@atsu.edu. *Application contact:* Donna Sparks, Director, Admissions Processing, 660-626-2117, Fax: 660-626-2969, E-mail: admissions@atsu.edu.
Website: http://www.atsu.edu/asdoh

**A.T. Still University,** Missouri School of Dentistry & Oral Health, Kirksville, MO 63501. Offers dental medicine (DMD). *Accreditation:* ADA. *Faculty:* 48 full-time (23 women), 35 part-time/adjunct (10 women). *Students:* 185 full-time (87 women); includes 57 minority (1 Black or African American, non-Hispanic/Latino; 38 Asian, non-Hispanic/Latino; 11 Hispanic/Latino; 7 Two or more races, non-Hispanic/Latino). Average age 27. 1,308 applicants, 13% accepted, 62 enrolled. In 2019, 42 doctorates awarded. *Degree requirements:* For doctorate, National Board exams 1 and 2. *Application deadline:* For fall admission, 12/1 for domestic students; for summer admission, 12/1 for domestic students. Applications are processed on a rolling basis. Application fee: $70. Electronic applications accepted. *Financial support:* In 2019–20, 37 students received support. Federal Work-Study and scholarships/grants available. Financial award application deadline: 6/1; financial award applicants required to submit FAFSA. *Unit head:* Dr. Dwight McLeod, Dean, 660-626-2842, Fax: 660-626-2969, E-mail: dmcleod@atsu.edu. *Application contact:* Donna Sparks, Director, Admissions Processing, 660-626-2237, Fax: 660-626-2969, E-mail: admissions@atsu.edu.
Website: http://www.atsu.edu/mosdoh/

**Augusta University,** The Dental College of Georgia, Augusta, GA 30912. Offers DMD, DMD/MS, DMD/PhD. *Accreditation:* ADA. *Degree requirements:* For doctorate, comprehensive exam. *Entrance requirements:* For doctorate, DAT, previous course work in biology, English, organic chemistry, and general chemistry; 1 semester of course work in physics. Additional exam requirements/recommendations for international students: required—TOEFL (minimum score 100 iBT). Electronic applications accepted. *Expenses:* Contact institution.

**Case Western Reserve University,** School of Dental Medicine, Professional Program in Dentistry, Cleveland, OH 44106. Offers DMD. *Accreditation:* ADA. *Degree requirements:* For doctorate, thesis/dissertation. *Entrance requirements:* For doctorate, DAT. Additional exam requirements/recommendations for international students: required—TOEFL (minimum score 550 paper-based). *Expenses:* Contact institution.

**Columbia University,** College of Dental Medicine, Professional Program in Dental and Oral Surgery, New York, NY 10032. Offers DDS, DDS/MBA, DDS/MPH. *Accreditation:* ADA. *Entrance requirements:* For doctorate, DAT, previous course work in biology, organic chemistry, inorganic chemistry, physics, and English. *Expenses: Tuition:* Full-time $47,600; part-time $1880 per credit. One-time fee: $105.

**Creighton University,** School of Dentistry, Omaha, NE 68178-0001. Offers DDS. *Accreditation:* ADA. *Entrance requirements:* For doctorate, DAT. *Expenses:* Contact institution.

**East Carolina University,** School of Dental Medicine, Greenville, NC 27858-4353. Offers DMD. *Accreditation:* ADA. *Entrance requirements:* For doctorate, DAT. *Application deadline:* For fall admission, 6/30 for domestic students. *Expenses: Tuition, area resident:* Full-time $4749; part-time $185 per credit hour. Tuition, state resident: full-time $4749; part-time $185 per credit hour. Tuition, nonresident: full-time $17,898; part-time $864 per credit hour. *International tuition:* $17,898 full-time. *Required fees:* $2787. *Unit head:* Dr. Greg Chadwick, Dean, 252-737-7703. *Application contact:* Graduate School Admissions, 252-328-6012, Fax: 252-328-6071, E-mail: gradschool@ecu.edu.
Website: http://www.ecu.edu/dental/

**Harvard University,** School of Dental Medicine, Advanced Graduate Programs in Dentistry, Cambridge, MA 02138. Offers advanced general dentistry (Certificate); dental public health (Certificate); endodontics (Certificate); general practice residency (Certificate); oral biology (M Med Sc, D Med Sc); oral implantology (Certificate); oral medicine (Certificate); oral pathology (Certificate); oral surgery (Certificate); orthodontics (Certificate); pediatric dentistry (Certificate); periodontics (Certificate); prosthodontics (Certificate). *Degree requirements:* For master's, comprehensive exam, thesis optional; for doctorate, comprehensive exam, thesis/dissertation. *Entrance requirements:* Additional exam requirements/recommendations for international students: required—TOEFL (minimum iBT score of 95; subcategory score minimums of Reading 21, Listening 17, Speaking 24, and Writing 25).

**Harvard University,** School of Dental Medicine, Professional Program in Dental Medicine, Cambridge, MA 02138. Offers DMD. *Accreditation:* ADA. *Degree requirements:* For doctorate, comprehensive exam, thesis/dissertation. *Entrance requirements:* For doctorate, DAT, 1 semester of biochemistry; 2 semesters each of biology, inorganic/general chemistry, organic chemistry, physics, English, and calculus or one semester each of calculus and statistics, preferably biostatistics. Electronic applications accepted.

**Howard University,** College of Dentistry, Washington, DC 20059-0002. Offers advanced education in general dentistry (Certificate); dentistry (DDS); general dentistry practice (Certificate); oral and maxillofacial surgery (Certificate); orthodontics (Certificate); pediatric dentistry (Certificate). *Accreditation:* ADA (one or more programs are accredited). *Degree requirements:* For doctorate, comprehensive exam, didactic and clinical exams. *Entrance requirements:* For doctorate, DAT, 8 semester hours of course

work each in biology, inorganic chemistry, and organic chemistry. *Expenses:* Contact institution.

**Idaho State University,** Graduate School, College of Health Professions, Department of Dental Sciences, Pocatello, ID 83209-8088. Offers advanced general dentistry (Post-Doctoral Certificate). *Degree requirements:* For Post-Doctoral Certificate, comprehensive exam, thesis optional, 1-year residency. *Entrance requirements:* For degree, DAT, 3 dental application forms. Additional exam requirements/recommendations for international students: required—TOEFL (minimum score 600 paper-based). Electronic applications accepted. *Expenses:* Contact institution.

**Indiana University-Purdue University Indianapolis,** School of Dentistry, Indianapolis, IN 46202. Offers cariology and operative dentistry (MSD); dental materials (MS, MSD); dental sciences (PhD); dentistry (DDS, Certificate); endodontics (MSD); oral and maxillofacial surgery (MSD); orthodontics (MSD); pediatric dentistry (MSD); periodontics (MSD); prosthodontics (MSD). *Accreditation:* ADA (one or more programs are accredited). *Degree requirements:* For master's, thesis or manuscript, qualifying exam; for doctorate, thesis/dissertation, minimum GPA of 3.0 and qualifying examination (for PhD); minimum GPA of 2.0 and Part I and II of National Board of Dental Examinations (for DDS); for Certificate, thesis, minimum GPA of 3.0. *Entrance requirements:* For master's, GRE (orthodontics); National Board Dental Exam Part I (periodontics), Parts I and II (endodontics); ADAT (pediatric dentistry); for doctorate, GRE (for PhD); DAT (for DDS). Additional exam requirements/recommendations for international students: required—TOEFL (minimum iBT score 90; 79 for MDS) or IELTS (6.5). Electronic applications accepted. *Expenses:* Contact institution.

**Jacksonville University,** Brooks Rehabilitation College of Healthcare Sciences, School of Orthodontics, Jacksonville, FL 32211. Offers dentistry (MS); orthodontics (Certificate). *Students:* 44 full-time (18 women), 6 part-time (3 women); includes 14 minority (1 Black or African American, non-Hispanic/Latino; 2 Asian, non-Hispanic/Latino; 10 Hispanic/Latino; 1 Two or more races, non-Hispanic/Latino), 5 international. Average age 34. In 2019, 8 other advanced degrees awarded. *Degree requirements:* For master's and Certificate, thesis. *Entrance requirements:* For master's, DDS/DMD or equivalent; for Certificate, American Board of Orthodontics written exam; U.S. National Dental Boards (part 1 and 2), curriculum vitae, official transcripts, 3 professional evaluations, 3 professional recommendations (dean of dental school or faculty, or other professional colleagues), statement of intent, clinical competencies through delivering evidence-based patient care, DDS/DMD or equivalent. Additional exam requirements/recommendations for international students: required—TOEFL (minimum score 610 paper-based). *Application deadline:* For fall admission, 9/14 priority date for domestic students, 9/14 for international students. Applications are processed on a rolling basis. Application fee: $175. Electronic applications accepted. *Expenses:* Contact institution. *Financial support:* Fellowships, scholarships/grants, and health care benefits available. Financial award application deadline: 3/15; financial award applicants required to submit FAFSA. *Unit head:* Dr. James Toruten, Program Director & Clinical Associate Professor, 904-256-7850, E-mail: jtroute@ju.edu. *Application contact:* Sharon Frazier, Executive Operations Coordinator, 904-256-7847, Fax: 904-256-7847, E-mail: juorthoadmissions@ju.edu.
Website: https://www.ju.edu/orthodontics/index.php

**Loma Linda University,** School of Dentistry, Loma Linda, CA 92350. Offers MS, DDS, Certificate, DDS/MS, DDS/PhD, MS/Certificate. *Accreditation:* ADA. *Entrance requirements:* For master's, GRE, minimum GPA of 3.0; for doctorate, DAT. Additional exam requirements/recommendations for international students: required—TOEFL (minimum score 550 paper-based). *Expenses:* Contact institution.

**Louisiana State University Health Sciences Center,** School of Dentistry, New Orleans, LA 70112-2223. Offers DDS. *Accreditation:* ADA. *Entrance requirements:* For doctorate, DAT, interview. *Expenses:* Contact institution.

**Marquette University,** School of Dentistry, Professional Program in Dentistry, Milwaukee, WI 53201-1881. Offers DDS. *Accreditation:* ADA. *Degree requirements:* For doctorate, National Board Dental Exam Part 1 and 2, regional licensure exam. *Entrance requirements:* For doctorate, DAT, 1 year of course work each in biology, inorganic chemistry, organic chemistry, physics, and English. Additional exam requirements/recommendations for international students: required—TOEFL. *Expenses:* Contact institution.

**McGill University,** Faculty of Graduate and Postdoctoral Studies, Faculty of Dentistry, Montréal, QC H3A 2T5, Canada. Offers forensic dentistry (Certificate); oral and maxillofacial surgery (M Sc, PhD). *Accreditation:* ADA.

**McGill University,** Professional Program in Dentistry, Montréal, QC H3A 2T5, Canada. Offers DMD. *Accreditation:* ADA. Electronic applications accepted.

**Medical University of South Carolina,** College of Dental Medicine, Charleston, SC 29425. Offers DMD, DMD/PhD. *Accreditation:* ADA. *Degree requirements:* For doctorate, National Board of Dental Examinations Part I and II. *Entrance requirements:* For doctorate, DAT, interview, 52 hours of specific pre-dental course work. Additional exam requirements/recommendations for international students: required—TOEFL (minimum score 600 paper-based). Electronic applications accepted. *Expenses:* Contact institution.

**Meharry Medical College,** School of Dentistry, Nashville, TN 37208-9989. Offers DDS, PhD. *Accreditation:* ADA. *Entrance requirements:* For doctorate, DAT. *Application deadline:* For winter admission, 1/15 for domestic and international students. Applications are processed on a rolling basis. Application fee: $65. *Financial support:* Career-related internships or fieldwork, Federal Work-Study, and institutionally sponsored loans available. Financial award application deadline: 4/15; financial award applicants required to submit FAFSA. *Unit head:* Cherae M. Farmer-Dixon, DDS, Dean, 615-327-6207, E-mail: cdixon@mmc.edu. *Application contact:* Cherae M. Farmer-Dixon, DDS, Dean, 615-327-6207, E-mail: cdixon@mmc.edu.
Website: https://home.mmc.edu/school-of-dentistry/

**Midwestern University, Downers Grove Campus,** College of Dental Medicine-Illinois, Downers Grove, IL 60515-1235. Offers DMD. *Accreditation:* ADA. *Entrance requirements:* For doctorate, DAT, bachelor's degree, minimum overall GPA of 2.75, three letters of recommendation.

**Midwestern University, Glendale Campus,** College of Dental Medicine, Glendale, AZ 85308. Offers DMD. *Accreditation:* ADA.

**New York University,** College of Dentistry, Advanced Standing DDS Program, New York, NY 10010. Offers DDS. *Accreditation:* ADA. *Degree requirements:* For doctorate, one foreign language. *Entrance requirements:* For doctorate, National Board Dental Exam Parts I and II, official ECE course-by-course evaluation, notarized copies of dental diploma, three letters of evaluation, letter of evaluation from dean of dental school from

which applicant graduated, two other letters of evaluation from faculty members. Additional exam requirements/recommendations for international students: required—TOEFL (minimum score 603 paper-based; 100 iBT). Electronic applications accepted. *Expenses:* Contact institution.

**Nova Southeastern University,** College of Dental Medicine, Fort Lauderdale, FL 33314-7796. Offers dental medicine (DMD); dentistry (MS). *Accreditation:* ADA. *Faculty:* 82 full-time (34 women), 10 part-time/adjunct (1 woman). *Students:* 598 full-time (330 women), 8 part-time (3 women); includes 312 minority (15 Black or African American, non-Hispanic/Latino; 84 Asian, non-Hispanic/Latino; 197 Hispanic/Latino; 16 Two or more races, non-Hispanic/Latino), 66 international. Average age 28. 3,207 applicants, 5% accepted, 155 enrolled. In 2019, 21 master's, 125 doctorates awarded. *Entrance requirements:* For doctorate, DAT, minimum GPA of 3.25. Additional exam requirements/recommendations for international students: required—TOEFL (minimum score 550 paper-based), IELTS (minimum score 6), PTE (minimum score 54). *Application deadline:* Applications are processed on a rolling basis. Application fee: $50. Electronic applications accepted. *Expenses:* Contact institution. *Financial support:* Application deadline: 4/15; applicants required to submit FAFSA. *Unit head:* Dr. Steven I. Kaltman, Interim Dean and Professor, 954-262-7332, Fax: 954-262-3293, E-mail: skaltman@nova.edu. *Application contact:* Audrey Levitt Galga, Assistant Dean, Admissions, Student Affairs and Services, 954-262-7318, E-mail: agalka@nova.edu. Website: http://dental.nova.edu/

**The Ohio State University,** College of Dentistry, Columbus, OH 43210. Offers dental anesthesiology (MS); dental hygiene (MDH); dentistry (DDS); endodontics (MS); oral and maxillofacial pathology (MS); oral and maxillofacial surgery (MS); oral biology (PhD); orthodontics (MS); pediatric dentistry (MS); periodontology (MS); prosthodontics (MS); DDS/PhD. *Accreditation:* ADA (one or more programs are accredited). Terminal master's awarded for partial completion of doctoral program. *Degree requirements:* For master's, thesis; for doctorate, thesis/dissertation (for some programs). *Entrance requirements:* For master's, GRE General Test (for all applicants with cumulative GPA below 3.0); for doctorate, DAT (for DDS); GRE General Test, GRE Subject Test in biology recommended (for PhD). Additional exam requirements/recommendations for international students: required—TOEFL (minimum score 550 paper-based; 79 iBT), IELTS (minimum score 7), Michigan English Language Assessment Battery (minimum score 82). Electronic applications accepted. *Expenses:* Contact institution.

**Oregon Health & Science University,** School of Dentistry, Professional Program in Dentistry, Portland, OR 97239-3098. Offers dentistry (DMD); oral and maxillofacial surgery (Certificate); MD/DMD. *Accreditation:* ADA. *Entrance requirements:* For doctorate, DAT. Electronic applications accepted.

**Roseman University of Health Sciences,** College of Dental Medicine - Henderson Campus, Henderson, NV 89014. Offers business administration (MBA); dental medicine (Post-Doctoral Certificate). *Degree requirements:* For master's, comprehensive exam, thesis or alternative. *Entrance requirements:* For master's, National Board Dental Examination 1 and 2, graduation from U.S. or Canadian dental school, Nevada dental license. *Expenses:* Contact institution.

**Roseman University of Health Sciences,** College of Dental Medicine - South Jordan, Utah Campus, South Jordan, UT 84095. Offers DMD. *Accreditation:* ADA. *Degree requirements:* For doctorate, comprehensive exam, thesis/dissertation or alternative, National Board Dental Examinations (NBDE). *Entrance requirements:* For doctorate, DAT. Additional exam requirements/recommendations for international students: recommended—TOEFL. Electronic applications accepted. *Expenses:* Contact institution.

**Rutgers University - Newark,** Rutgers School of Dental Medicine, Newark, NJ 07101-1709. Offers dental science (MS); dentistry (DMD); endodontics (Certificate); oral medicine (Certificate); orthodontics (Certificate); pediatric dentistry (Certificate); periodontics (Certificate); prosthodontics (Certificate); DMD/MPH; DMD/PhD; MD/Certificate; MS/Certificate. *Accreditation:* ADA (one or more programs are accredited). *Entrance requirements:* For doctorate, DAT. Electronic applications accepted. *Expenses:* Contact institution.

**Saint Louis University,** Graduate Programs, Center for Advanced Dental Education, St. Louis, MO 63103. Offers endodontics (MSD); orthodontics (MSD); periodontics (MSD). *Degree requirements:* For master's, comprehensive exam, thesis, teaching practicum. *Entrance requirements:* For master's, GRE General Test, NBDE (National Board Dental Exam), DDS or DMD, interview, letters of recommendation. Additional exam requirements/recommendations for international students: required—TOEFL (minimum score 525 paper-based). Electronic applications accepted.

**Southern Illinois University Edwardsville,** School of Dental Medicine, Alton, IL 62002. Offers DMD. *Accreditation:* ADA. *Entrance requirements:* For doctorate, DAT. Electronic applications accepted. *Expenses:* Contact institution.

**Stony Brook University, State University of New York,** Stony Brook Medicine, School of Dental Medicine, Professional Program in Dental Medicine, Stony Brook, NY 11794. Offers dental medicine (DDS); endodontics (Certificate); orthodontics (Certificate); periodontics (Certificate). *Accreditation:* ADA (one or more programs are accredited). *Faculty:* 33 full-time (15 women), 75 part-time/adjunct (20 women). *Students:* 201 full-time (107 women); includes 81 minority (3 Black or African American, non-Hispanic/Latino; 63 Asian, non-Hispanic/Latino; 10 Hispanic/Latino; 5 Two or more races, non-Hispanic/Latino), 3 international. Average age 25. 1,065 applicants, 12% accepted, 46 enrolled. In 2019, 45 doctorates, 8 Certificates awarded. *Entrance requirements:* For doctorate, DAT (minimum score of 17 preferred in all subsections), minimum GPA of 3.0 (preferred). Additional exam requirements/recommendations for international students: required—TOEFL. *Application deadline:* For fall admission, 12/1 for domestic students. Application fee: $100. *Expenses:* Contact institution. *Financial support:* Research assistantships, teaching assistantships, and Federal Work-Study available. Support available to part-time students. *Unit head:* Dr. Mary R. Truhlar, Dean, 631-632-6985, Fax: 631-632-6621, E-mail: mary.truhlar@stonybrook.edu. *Application contact:* Marcia Simon, Director, 631-632-8922, Fax: 631-632-7130. Website: http://dentistry.stonybrookmedicine.edu/

**Temple University,** Kornberg School of Dentistry, Professional Program in Dentistry, Philadelphia, PA 19122-6096. Offers DMD, DMD/MBA. *Accreditation:* ADA. *Entrance requirements:* For doctorate, DAT, 6 credits of course work in each biology, chemistry, organic chemistry, physics, and English. *Expenses:* Contact institution.

**Texas A&M University,** College of Dentistry, Dallas, TX 75266-0677. Offers maxillofacial surgery (Certificate); pediatric dentistry (Certificate). *Accreditation:* ADA; SACS/CC. *Entrance requirements:* Additional exam requirements/recommendations for international students: required—TOEFL (minimum score 550 paper-based; 79 iBT). Electronic applications accepted. *Expenses:* Contact institution.

**Tufts University,** School of Dental Medicine, International Student Program in Dental Medicine, Medford, MA 02155. Offers DMD. *Accreditation:* ADA. *Entrance requirements:* For doctorate, National Dental Hygiene Board Exam Part I, BDS, DDS, or equivalent. Additional exam requirements/recommendations for international students: required—TOEFL. *Expenses: Tuition:* Part-time $1799 per credit hour. Full-time tuition and fees

vary according to degree level, program and student level. Part-time tuition and fees vary according to course load.

**Tufts University,** School of Dental Medicine, Professional Program in Dental Medicine, Medford, MA 02155. Offers DMD, DMD/PhD. *Accreditation:* ADA. *Entrance requirements:* For doctorate, DAT. *Expenses: Tuition:* Part-time $1799 per credit hour. Full-time tuition and fees vary according to degree level, program and student level. Part-time tuition and fees vary according to course load.

**Universidad Central del Este,** School of Dentistry, San Pedro de Macoris, Dominican Republic. Offers DMD.

**Universidad Iberoamericana,** Graduate School, Santo Domingo D.N., Dominican Republic. Offers business administration (MBA, PMBA); constitutional law (LL M); dentistry (DMD); educational management (MA); integrated marketing communication (MA); psychopedagogical intervention (M Ed); real estate law (LL M); strategic management of human talent (MM).

**Universidad Nacional Pedro Henriquez Urena,** School of Dentistry, Santo Domingo, Dominican Republic. Offers DDS.

**University at Buffalo, the State University of New York,** Graduate School, School of Dental Medicine, Professional Program in Dental Medicine, Buffalo, NY 14260. Offers DDS. *Accreditation:* ADA. *Degree requirements:* For doctorate, National Dental Board Exams. *Entrance requirements:* For doctorate, DAT. Additional exam requirements/recommendations for international students: required—TOEFL (minimum score 550 paper-based; 79 iBT), IELTS (minimum score 6.5), PTE (minimum score 55). Electronic applications accepted. *Expenses:* Contact institution.

**The University of Alabama at Birmingham,** School of Dentistry, Professional Program in Dentistry, Birmingham, AL 35294. Offers DMD. *Accreditation:* ADA. *Faculty:* 56 full-time (23 women), 18 part-time/adjunct (7 women). *Students:* 282 full-time (159 women); includes 83 minority (14 Black or African American, non-Hispanic/Latino; 48 Asian, non-Hispanic/Latino; 17 Hispanic/Latino; 4 Two or more races, non-Hispanic/Latino), 1 international. Average age 25. 825 applicants, 11% accepted, 60 enrolled. In 2019, 53 doctorates awarded. *Degree requirements:* For doctorate, comprehensive exam. *Entrance requirements:* For doctorate, DAT, letters of recommendation, interview. Additional exam requirements/recommendations for international students: required—TOEFL (minimum score 94 iBT), National Boards Part I. *Application deadline:* For fall admission, 11/1 for domestic students; for spring admission, 5/31 for international students. Application fee: $75 ($175 for international students). Electronic applications accepted. *Expenses:* Contact institution. *Financial support:* In 2019–20, 13 students received support. Scholarships/grants available. Financial award application deadline: 6/30; financial award applicants required to submit FAFSA. *Unit head:* Dr. Michael S. Reddy, Dean, 205-934-4720, Fax: 205-934-9283. *Application contact:* Dr. Steven J. Filler, Director of Dentistry Admissions, 205-934-3387, Fax: 205-934-0209, E-mail: sfiller@uab.edu. Website: https://www.dental.uab.edu

**University of Alberta,** Faculty of Medicine and Dentistry, School of Dentistry, Professional Program in Dentistry, Edmonton, AB T6G 2E1, Canada. Offers DDS. *Accreditation:* ADA. *Entrance requirements:* For doctorate, DAT (Canadian version), interview. Additional exam requirements/recommendations for international students: required—TOEFL. Electronic applications accepted.

**The University of British Columbia,** Faculty of Dentistry, Professional Program in Dentistry, Vancouver, BC V6T 1Z1, Canada. Offers DMD. *Accreditation:* ADA. *Entrance requirements:* For doctorate, DAT, ACFD Eligibility Exam, interview, psychomotor assessment. Additional exam requirements/recommendations for international students: required—IELTS. Electronic applications accepted. *Expenses:* Contact institution.

**University of California, Los Angeles,** School of Dentistry, Professional Program in Dentistry, Los Angeles, CA 90095. Offers DDS, Certificate, DDS/MS, DDS/PhD, MS/Certificate, PhD/Certificate. *Accreditation:* ADA (one or more programs are accredited). *Entrance requirements:* For doctorate, DAT, interview. Additional exam requirements/recommendations for international students: required—TOEFL. Electronic applications accepted. *Expenses:* Contact institution.

**University of California, San Francisco,** School of Dentistry, San Francisco, CA 94143-0150. Offers DDS. *Accreditation:* ADA. *Entrance requirements:* For doctorate, DAT. *Expenses:* Contact institution.

**University of Colorado Denver,** School of Dental Medicine, Aurora, CO 80045. Offers dental surgery (DDS); orthodontics (Certificate); periodontics (Certificate). *Accreditation:* ADA. *Entrance requirements:* For doctorate, DAT, prerequisite courses in microbiology, general biochemistry and English composition (1 semester each); general chemistry/lab, organic chemistry/lab, general biology/lab and general physics/lab (2 semesters each); interview; letters of recommendation; essay. Additional exam requirements/recommendations for international students: required—TOEFL (minimum score 580 paper-based; 80 iBT); recommended—IELTS (minimum score 6.8). Electronic applications accepted. Tuition and fees vary according to course load, program and reciprocity agreements.

**University of Connecticut Health Center,** School of Dental Medicine, Professional Program in Dental Medicine, Farmington, CT 06030. Offers DMD, Certificate. *Accreditation:* ADA. *Entrance requirements:* For doctorate, National Board Dental Examination. Additional exam requirements/recommendations for international students: required—TOEFL (minimum score 550 paper-based).

**University of Detroit Mercy,** School of Dentistry, Detroit, MI 48208. Offers MS, DDS, Certificate. *Accreditation:* ADA (one or more programs are accredited). *Degree requirements:* For master's, thesis. *Entrance requirements:* For master's, DDS or DMD; for doctorate, DAT; for Certificate, DAT, DDS or DMD. *Expenses:* Contact institution.

**University of Florida,** College of Dentistry, Professional Programs in Dentistry, Gainesville, FL 32611. Offers dentistry (DMD); foreign trained dentistry (Certificate). *Accreditation:* ADA. *Degree requirements:* For Certificate, National Dental Boards Parts I and II. *Entrance requirements:* For doctorate, DAT, interview; for Certificate, interview. Additional exam requirements/recommendations for international students: required—TOEFL (minimum score 550 paper-based).

**University of Illinois at Chicago,** College of Dentistry, Professional Program in Dentistry, Chicago, IL 60607-7128. Offers DDS, DDS/MPH, DDS/PhD. *Accreditation:* ADA. *Entrance requirements:* For doctorate, DAT. Additional exam requirements/recommendations for international students: required—TOEFL. Electronic applications accepted. *Expenses:* Contact institution.

**The University of Iowa,** College of Dentistry and Graduate College, Graduate Programs in Dentistry, Iowa City, IA 52242-1316. Offers endodontics (MS, Certificate); operative dentistry (MS, Certificate); oral and maxillofacial surgery (MS, PhD, Certificate); oral pathology, radiology and medicine (MS, PhD, Certificate); oral science (MS, PhD); orthodontics (MS, Certificate); pediatric dentistry (Certificate); periodontics (MS, Certificate); preventive and community dentistry (MS), including dental public health; prosthodontics (MS, Certificate). *Accreditation:* ADA. *Degree requirements:* For master's, thesis; for doctorate, thesis/dissertation. *Entrance requirements:* For master's,

GRE, DDS; for Certificate, DDS. Additional exam requirements/recommendations for international students: required—TOEFL. *Expenses:* Contact institution.

**The University of Iowa,** College of Dentistry, Professional Program in Dentistry, Iowa City, IA 52242-1316. Offers DDS. *Accreditation:* ADA. *Entrance requirements:* For doctorate, DAT, minimum 90 semester hours with minimum GPA of 2.5.

**University of Kentucky,** College of Dentistry, Lexington, KY 40506-0032. Offers DMD. *Accreditation:* ADA. *Degree requirements:* For doctorate, comprehensive exam. *Entrance requirements:* For doctorate, DAT. Electronic applications accepted. *Expenses:* Contact institution.

**University of Louisville,** School of Dentistry, Louisville, KY 40202. Offers dentistry (DMD); oral biology (MS). *Accreditation:* ADA (one or more programs are accredited). *Faculty:* 74 full-time (32 women), 67 part-time/adjunct (22 women). *Students:* 523 full-time (255 women), 3 part-time (1 woman); includes 144 minority (29 Black or African American, non-Hispanic/Latino; 61 Asian, non-Hispanic/Latino; 37 Hispanic/Latino; 17 Two or more races, non-Hispanic/Latino), 21 international. Average age 27. 196 applicants, 94% accepted, 143 enrolled. In 2019, 24 master's, 115 doctorates awarded. *Degree requirements:* For master's, thesis; for doctorate, NBDE Pt 1 and 2. *Entrance requirements:* For master's, DAT, GRE General Test, or National Board Dental Exam, minimum GPA of 2.75; for doctorate, DAT, 38 hours of coursework in science (biology, chemistry, physics, and biochemistry). Additional exam requirements/recommendations for international students: required—TOEFL (minimum score 100 iBT). *Application deadline:* For fall admission, 1/1 for domestic and international students. Applications are processed on a rolling basis. Application fee: $65. Electronic applications accepted. *Expenses: Tuition, area resident:* Full-time $13,000; part-time $723 per credit hour. Tuition, state resident: full-time $13,000; part-time $723 per credit hour. Tuition, nonresident: full-time $27,114; part-time $1507 per credit hour. *International tuition:* $27,114 full-time. *Required fees:* $196. Tuition and fees vary according to program and reciprocity agreements. *Financial support:* In 2019–20, 15 students received support, including 1 fellowship with full tuition reimbursement available (averaging $15,000 per year); scholarships/grants also available. Financial award application deadline: 3/15; financial award applicants required to submit FAFSA. *Unit head:* Dr. T. Gerry Bradley, Dean, 502-852-5295, E-mail: t0brad03@exchange.louisville.edu. *Application contact:* Jami Campbell, Assistant Director of Admissions, 502-852-5081, Fax: 502-852-1210, E-mail: dmdadms@louisville.edu.
Website: http://louisville.edu/dental/

**The University of Manchester,** School of Dentistry, Manchester, United Kingdom. Offers basic dental sciences (cancer studies) (M Phil, PhD); basic dental sciences (molecular genetics) (M Phil, PhD); basic dental sciences (stem cell biology) (M Phil, PhD); biomaterials sciences and dental technology (M Phil, PhD); dental public health/community dentistry (M Phil, PhD); dental science (clinical) (PhD); endodontology (M Phil, PhD); fixed and removable prosthodontics (M Phil, PhD); operative dentistry (M Phil, PhD); oral and maxillofacial surgery (M Phil, PhD); oral radiology (M Phil, PhD); orthodontics (M Phil, PhD); restorative dentistry (M Phil, PhD).

**University of Manitoba,** Dr. Gerald Niznick College of Dentistry, Professional Program in Dentistry, Winnipeg, MB R3T 2N2, Canada. Offers DMD. *Accreditation:* ADA. *Entrance requirements:* For doctorate, DAT, interview.

**University of Maryland, Baltimore,** Professional and Advanced Education Programs in Dentistry, Baltimore, MD 21201-1627. Offers advanced general dentistry (Certificate); dentistry (DDS); endodontics (Certificate); oral-maxillofacial surgery (Certificate); orthodontics (Certificate); pediatric dentistry (Certificate); periodontics (Certificate); prosthodontics (Certificate); DDS/MBA; DDS/PhD. *Accreditation:* ADA. *Students:* 582 full-time (301 women), 4 part-time (2 women); includes 282 minority (58 Black or African American, non-Hispanic/Latino; 140 Asian, non-Hispanic/Latino; 54 Hispanic/Latino; 30 Two or more races, non-Hispanic/Latino), 28 international. Average age 27. 1,322 applicants, 75% accepted, 159 enrolled. In 2019, 132 doctorates, 23 Certificates awarded. *Entrance requirements:* For doctorate, DAT, coursework in science; for Certificate, National Dental Board Exams, DDS. Additional exam requirements/recommendations for international students: required—TOEFL (minimum score 550 paper-based; 80 iBT). *Application deadline:* Applications are processed on a rolling basis. Application fee: $85. Electronic applications accepted. *Expenses:* Contact institution. *Financial support:* Career-related internships or fieldwork, Federal Work-Study, scholarships/grants, and traineeships available. Financial award application deadline: 3/1; financial award applicants required to submit FAFSA. *Unit head:* Dr. Mark A. Reynolds, Dean, 410-706-7461. *Application contact:* Dr. Judith A. Porter, Assistant Dean for Admissions and Recruitment, 410-706-7472, Fax: 410-706-0945, E-mail: ddsadmissions@umaryland.edu.
Website: http://www.dental.umaryland.edu/

**University of Michigan,** School of Dentistry, Professional Program in Dentistry, Ann Arbor, MI 48109. Offers DDS. *Accreditation:* ADA. *Entrance requirements:* For doctorate, DAT, 6 credits of course work in English; 8 credits of course work each in chemistry, organic chemistry, biology, and physics; 3 credits each of biochemistry, microbiology, psychology, and sociology. Electronic applications accepted. *Expenses:* Contact institution.

**University of Minnesota, Twin Cities Campus,** School of Dentistry, Professional Program in Dentistry, Minneapolis, MN 55455-0213. Offers DDS. *Accreditation:* ADA. *Entrance requirements:* For doctorate, DAT. Additional exam requirements/recommendations for international students: required—TOEFL.

**University of Mississippi Medical Center,** School of Dentistry, Jackson, MS 39216-4505. Offers MS, DMD, PhD. *Accreditation:* ADA. *Entrance requirements:* For doctorate, DAT (for DMD). *Expenses:* Contact institution.

**University of Missouri–Kansas City,** School of Dentistry, Kansas City, MO 64110-2499. Offers advanced education in dentistry (Graduate Dental Certificate); dental hygiene education (MS); endodontics (Graduate Dental Certificate); oral and maxillofacial surgery (Graduate Dental Certificate); oral biology (MS, PhD); orthodontics and dentofacial orthopedics (Graduate Dental Certificate); periodontics (Graduate Dental Certificate). *Accreditation:* ADA (one or more programs are accredited). *Degree requirements:* For master's, thesis; for doctorate, thesis/dissertation (for some programs). *Entrance requirements:* For master's, DAT, letters of evaluation, personal interview; for doctorate, DAT (for DDS); for Graduate Dental Certificate, DDS. Additional exam requirements/recommendations for international students: required—TOEFL (minimum score 550 paper-based; 80 iBT). *Expenses:* Contact institution.

**University of Nebraska Medical Center,** College of Dentistry, Lincoln, NE 68583-0740. Offers MS, DDS, PhD, Certificate. *Accreditation:* ADA (one or more programs are accredited). *Degree requirements:* For Certificate, thesis or alternative. *Entrance requirements:* For doctorate, DAT (for DDS). Additional exam requirements/recommendations for international students: required—TOEFL. Electronic applications accepted. *Expenses:* Contact institution.

**University of Nevada, Las Vegas,** School of Dental Medicine, Las Vegas, NV 89154. Offers dental medicine (DMD); dental surgery (DDS); dentistry (DMD); oral biology (MS); orthodontics and dentofacial orthopedics (Certificate). *Accreditation:* ADA. *Program availability:* Part-time, evening/weekend, online learning. *Students:* 369 full-time (154 women), 1 (woman) part-time; includes 154 minority (7 Black or African American, non-Hispanic/Latino; 1 American Indian or Alaska Native, non-Hispanic/Latino; 89 Asian, non-Hispanic/Latino; 36 Hispanic/Latino; 1 Native Hawaiian or other Pacific Islander, non-Hispanic/Latino; 20 Two or more races, non-Hispanic/Latino), 3 international. Average age 29. 1,543 applicants, 11% accepted, 80 enrolled. In 2019, 6 master's, 93 doctorates, 5 other advanced degrees awarded. *Entrance requirements:* For doctorate, DAT; for Certificate, National Board Dental Exam part 1 and 2. Additional exam requirements/recommendations for international students: required—TOEFL (minimum score 550 paper-based; 80 iBT), IELTS (minimum score 7). *Application deadline:* For fall admission, 1/1 for domestic and international students; for summer admission, 3/1 for domestic students. Applications are processed on a rolling basis. Application fee: $75. Electronic applications accepted. *Expenses:* Contact institution. *Financial support:* Federal Work-Study, institutionally sponsored loans, scholarships/grants, health care benefits, and unspecified assistantships available. Support available to part-time students. Financial award application deadline: 3/15; financial award applicants required to submit FAFSA. *Unit head:* Dr. Christine C. Ancajas, Assistant Dean of Admissions and Student Affairs, 702-774-2522, Fax: 702-774-2521, E-mail: christine.ancajas@unlv.edu. *Application contact:* Dr. Christine C. Ancajas, Assistant Dean of Admissions and Student Affairs, 702-774-2522, Fax: 702-774-2521, E-mail: christine.ancajas@unlv.edu.
Website: http://www.unlv.edu/dental

**University of New England,** College of Dental Medicine, Biddeford, ME 04005-9526. Offers DMD. *Accreditation:* ADA. *Faculty:* 28 full-time (14 women), 27 part-time/adjunct (4 women). *Students:* 250 full-time (137 women); includes 73 minority (12 Black or African American, non-Hispanic/Latino; 4 American Indian or Alaska Native, non-Hispanic/Latino; 38 Asian, non-Hispanic/Latino; 10 Hispanic/Latino; 2 Native Hawaiian or other Pacific Islander, non-Hispanic/Latino; 7 Two or more races, non-Hispanic/Latino), 4 international. Average age 27. In 2019, 63 doctorates awarded. *Entrance requirements:* For doctorate, DAT, minimum 30 hours of clinical experience in dental setting. *Application deadline:* For fall admission, 11/1 for domestic and international students. Electronic applications accepted. *Financial support:* Application deadline: 5/1; applicants required to submit FAFSA. *Unit head:* Dr. Jon Ryder, Dean, College of Dental Medicine, 207-221-4702, Fax: 207-523-1915, E-mail: jryder2@une.edu. *Application contact:* Scott Steinberg, Vice President of University Admissions, 207-221-4225, Fax: 207-523-1925, E-mail: ssteinberg@une.edu.
Website: http://www.une.edu/dentalmedicine/

**The University of North Carolina at Chapel Hill,** School of Dentistry, Professional Program in Dentistry, Chapel Hill, NC 27599-7450. Offers DDS, DDS/PhD. *Accreditation:* ADA. *Entrance requirements:* For doctorate, DAT, interview. Additional exam requirements/recommendations for international students: required—TOEFL (minimum score 550 paper-based). Electronic applications accepted. *Expenses:* Contact institution.

**University of Oklahoma Health Sciences Center,** College of Dentistry, Advanced Education in General Dentistry Program, Oklahoma City, OK 73190. Offers Certificate. *Accreditation:* ADA. Electronic applications accepted.

**University of Oklahoma Health Sciences Center,** College of Dentistry, Professional Program in Dentistry, Oklahoma City, OK 73190. Offers DDS. *Accreditation:* ADA. *Degree requirements:* For doctorate, National Board Dental Exam Part I and Part II. *Entrance requirements:* For doctorate, DAT, minimum GPA of 2.5; course work in English, general psychology, biology, general chemistry, organic chemistry, physics, and biochemistry. Additional exam requirements/recommendations for international students: required—TOEFL (minimum score 570 paper-based). Electronic applications accepted.

**University of Pennsylvania,** School of Dental Medicine, Philadelphia, PA 19104. Offers DMD, DMD/MS Ed. *Accreditation:* ADA. *Entrance requirements:* For doctorate, DAT. *Expenses:* Contact institution.

**University of Pittsburgh,** School of Dental Medicine, Advanced Education Program in General Practice, Pittsburgh, PA 15213. Offers Certificate. *Accreditation:* ADA. *Faculty:* 2 full-time (1 woman), 5 part-time/adjunct (1 woman). *Students:* 3 full-time (2 women); includes 1 minority (Asian, non-Hispanic/Latino). Average age 28. 20 applicants, 45% accepted, 3 enrolled. In 2019, 3 Certificates awarded. *Degree requirements:* For Certificate, comprehensive exam, DMD or DDS from accredited US or Canadian Dental School. *Entrance requirements:* Additional exam requirements/recommendations for international students: required—TOEFL (minimum score 70 paper-based). *Application deadline:* For fall admission, 10/15 for domestic and international students. Electronic applications accepted. *Expenses:* Contact institution. *Unit head:* Dr. Elizabeth Clark Pawlowicz, DMD, Program Director, 412-648-6328, Fax: 412-648-6505, E-mail: pawlowiczec2@upmc.edu. *Application contact:* Andrea M. Ford, Residency Coordinator, 412-648-6801, Fax: 412-648-6835, E-mail: fordam@upmc.edu.
Website: http://www.dental.pitt.edu/students/general-practice-residency-program

**University of Pittsburgh,** School of Dental Medicine, Department of Pediatric Dentistry, Pittsburgh, PA 15261. Offers dental science (MDS); multidisciplinary public health (MPH); pediatric dentistry (Certificate). *Accreditation:* ADA. *Faculty:* 1 (woman) full-time, 10 part-time/adjunct (5 women). *Students:* 6 full-time (all women); includes 1 minority (Asian, non-Hispanic/Latino), 1 international. Average age 30. 28 applicants, 7% accepted, 2 enrolled. In 2019, 1 master's, 4 other advanced degrees awarded. *Degree requirements:* For master's, thesis; for Certificate, completed research project and maintenance of a B or greater GPA. *Entrance requirements:* For master's, qualification exam for the master's degree is given at the end of fall term, the first year. *Application deadline:* For fall admission, 9/15 for domestic and international students. Electronic applications accepted. *Expenses:* In-state tuition is $54,128 and out-of state tuition is $66,370. The additional fees (instruments, departmental, and University fees total $4,540. *Financial support:* In 2019–20, 4 students received support. Each resident receives an annual $24,000 stipend. available. Financial award application deadline: 9/15. *Unit head:* Dr. Deborah Studen-Pavlovich, Professor and Graduate Program Director, 412-648-8183, Fax: 412-648-8435, E-mail: das12@pitt.edu. *Application contact:* Sharon A. Hohman, Departmental Secretary, 412-648-8416, Fax: 412-648-8435.
Website: http://www.dental.pitt.edu

**University of Pittsburgh,** School of Dental Medicine, Predoctoral Program in Dental Medicine, Pittsburgh, PA 15261. Offers DMD. *Accreditation:* ADA. *Entrance requirements:* For doctorate, DAT, minimum GPA of 3.2 (science and non-science). Additional exam requirements/recommendations for international students: required—TOEFL (minimum score 100 iBT). Electronic applications accepted. *Expenses:* Contact institution.

**University of Puerto Rico - Medical Sciences Campus,** School of Dental Medicine, Professional Program in Dentistry, San Juan, PR 00936-5067. Offers DMD. *Accreditation:* ADA. *Entrance requirements:* For doctorate, DAT, interview. *Expenses:* Contact institution.

**University of Saskatchewan,** College of Dentistry, Saskatoon, SK S7N 5A2, Canada. Offers DMD. *Accreditation:* ADA. *Entrance requirements:* For doctorate, DAT. Additional exam requirements/recommendations for international students: required—TOEFL

(minimum score 550 paper-based; 80 iBT), IELTS (minimum score 6.5), Michigan English Language Assessment Battery (85); CanTEST (4.0); CAEL (60); CPE (C). Electronic applications accepted. *Expenses:* Contact institution.

**University of Southern California,** Graduate School, Herman Ostrow School of Dentistry, Professional Program in Dentistry, Los Angeles, CA 90089. Offers DDS, DDS/MBA, DDS/MS. *Accreditation:* ADA (one or more programs are accredited).

**The University of Tennessee Health Science Center,** College of Dentistry, Memphis, TN 38163-0002. Offers DDS. *Accreditation:* ADA. *Entrance requirements:* For doctorate, DAT, interview, pre-professional evaluation. Additional exam requirements/recommendations for international students: required—TOEFL. Electronic applications accepted. *Expenses:* Contact institution.

**The University of Texas Health Science Center at Houston,** School of Dentistry, Houston, TX 77225-0036. Offers MS, DDS. *Accreditation:* ADA. *Entrance requirements:* For doctorate, DAT, 90 semester hours of prerequisite courses. Electronic applications accepted.

**The University of Texas Health Science Center at San Antonio,** Graduate School of Biomedical Sciences, Program in Dental Science, San Antonio, TX 78229-3900. Offers MS. *Degree requirements:* For master's, thesis.

**The University of Texas Health Science Center at San Antonio,** UT Health San Antonio School of Dentistry, San Antonio, TX 78229-3900. Offers MS, DDS, Certificate, DDS/PhD. *Accreditation:* ADA (one or more programs are accredited). *Faculty:* 100 full-time (41 women), 83 part-time/adjunct (20 women). *Students:* 509 full-time (272 women), 27 part-time (13 women); includes 268 minority (15 Black or African American, non-Hispanic/Latino; 108 Asian, non-Hispanic/Latino; 126 Hispanic/Latino; 7 Native Hawaiian or other Pacific Islander, non-Hispanic/Latino; 12 Two or more races, non-Hispanic/Latino), 27 international. Average age 27. 1,448 applicants, 15% accepted, 100 enrolled. In 2019, 25 master's, 100 doctorates, 44 other advanced degrees awarded. *Degree requirements:* For master's, thesis; for doctorate, comprehensive exam. *Entrance requirements:* For master's, GRE General Test; for doctorate, DAT; for Certificate, National Board Part 1 and Part 2, DDS. Additional exam requirements/recommendations for international students: required—TOEFL (minimum score 92 iBT). *Application deadline:* For fall admission, 10/1 for domestic students. Applications are processed on a rolling basis. Application fee: $100. Electronic applications accepted. *Expenses:* Statuatory tuition, Designated Tuition, Instructional Technology, Liability Insurance, Library Fee, Student Services Fee, Medical Services Fee, Fitness Center Fee, Health Insurance, Implantation Materials Fee, Instrument Kit Rental Fee, Electronic Media Bundle, Clinic Usage, Microscope Fee, Lab Fee. *Financial support:* In 2019–20, 90 students received support, including 1 fellowship (averaging $50,000 per year), 1 research assistantship (averaging $6,156 per year), 86 teaching assistantships (averaging $15,434 per year); Federal Work-Study also available. Financial award application deadline: 7/15; financial award applicants required to submit FAFSA. *Unit head:* Dr. Kay Malone, Director of Admissions, 210-567-3180, Fax: 210-567-6721, E-mail: dsadmissions@uthscsa.edu. *Application contact:* Dr. Kay Malone, Director of Admissions, 210-567-3180, Fax: 210-567-6721, E-mail: dsadmissions@uthscsa.edu.
Website: dental.uthscsa.edu

**University of the Pacific,** Arthur A. Dugoni School of Dentistry, Stockton, CA 95211-0197. Offers MSD, DDS, Certificate. *Accreditation:* ADA (one or more programs are accredited). *Degree requirements:* For master's, comprehensive exam, thesis. *Entrance requirements:* For master's, GRE General Test; for doctorate, National Board Dental Exam Part I, DAT, foreign dental degree (for international students); for Certificate, DDS/DMD. Additional exam requirements/recommendations for international students: required—TOEFL. Electronic applications accepted. *Expenses:* Contact institution.

**University of Toronto,** School of Graduate Studies, Faculty of Dentistry, Professional Program in Dentistry, Toronto, ON M5S 1A1, Canada. Offers DDS. *Accreditation:* ADA. *Entrance requirements:* For doctorate, Canadian DAT or equivalent, minimum GPA of 3.0; completion of at least 2 courses in life sciences and 1 course in humanities or social sciences. Additional exam requirements/recommendations for international students: required—TOEFL (minimum score 600 paper-based; 100 iBT), TWE (minimum score 5). Electronic applications accepted. *Expenses:* Contact institution.

**University of Utah,** School of Dentistry, Salt Lake City, UT 84112-1107. Offers DDS. *Accreditation:* ADA. *Faculty:* 12 full-time (2 women), 1 part-time/adjunct (0 women). *Students:* 194 full-time (54 women); includes 42 minority (2 Black or African American, non-Hispanic/Latino; 16 Asian, non-Hispanic/Latino; 17 Hispanic/Latino; 7 Two or more races, non-Hispanic/Latino). Average age 27. 503 applicants, 10% accepted, 51 enrolled. In 2019, 27 doctorates awarded. *Degree requirements:* For doctorate, comprehensive exam, Competencies. *Entrance requirements:* For doctorate, DAT. *Application deadline:* For fall admission, 10/1 for domestic students. Application fee: $90. *Expenses:* 40,537 Yearly Resident Tuition; 76,745 Yearly Non-resident Tuition; $1,879 Yearly Mandatory General Fees, $7,725 Yearly Instrument Rental, $761 Yearly Instructional Materials. *Financial support:* In 2019–20, 13 students received support. Scholarships/grants available. Financial award application deadline: 5/15; financial award applicants required to submit FAFSA. *Unit head:* Dr. Wyatt R. Hume, DDS, Dean, 801-587-1208, E-mail: wyatt.hume@hsc.utah.edu. *Application contact:* Julie Oyler, Office of Admissions, 801-585-0718, Fax: 801-585-6485, E-mail: julie.oyler@hsc.utah.edu.
Website: http://dentistry.utah.edu/

**University of Washington,** Graduate School, School of Dentistry and Graduate School, Graduate Programs in Dentistry, Department of Pediatric Dentistry, Seattle, WA 98195. Offers MSD, Certificate.

**University of Washington,** Graduate School, School of Dentistry and Graduate School, Graduate Programs in Dentistry, Department of Restorative Dentistry, Seattle, WA 98195. Offers prosthodontics (MSD, Certificate).

**University of Washington,** Graduate School, School of Dentistry, Program in Dental Surgery, Seattle, WA 98195. Offers DDS. *Accreditation:* ADA. *Entrance requirements:* For doctorate, DAT.

**The University of Western Ontario,** Schulich School of Medicine and Dentistry, Graduate and Professional Programs in Dentistry, Professional Program in Dentistry, London, ON N6A 3K7, Canada. Offers DDS. *Accreditation:* ADA. *Entrance requirements:* For doctorate, DAT (Canadian version), minimum B average.

**Université Laval,** Faculty of Dentistry, Professional Programs in Dentistry, Québec, QC G1K 7P4, Canada. Offers DMD. *Accreditation:* ADA. *Entrance requirements:* For doctorate, visual perception exam, manual dexterity exam, interview, knowledge of French. Electronic applications accepted.

**Virginia Commonwealth University,** Medical College of Virginia-Professional Programs, School of Dentistry, Richmond, VA 23284-9005. Offers MS, DDS. *Accreditation:* ADA. *Entrance requirements:* For master's, National Board Dental Exam; for doctorate, DAT. Electronic applications accepted. *Expenses:* Contact institution.

**Western University of Health Sciences,** College of Dental Medicine, Pomona, CA 91766-1854. Offers DMD. *Accreditation:* ADA. *Faculty:* 45 full-time (21 women), 21 part-time/adjunct (7 women). *Students:* 283 full-time (147 women); includes 185 minority (7 Black or African American, non-Hispanic/Latino; 2 American Indian or Alaska Native, non-Hispanic/Latino; 105 Asian, non-Hispanic/Latino; 43 Hispanic/Latino; 28 Two or more races, non-Hispanic/Latino), 7 international. Average age 28. 2,548 applicants, 8% accepted, 74 enrolled. In 2019, 68 doctorates awarded. *Degree requirements:* For doctorate, comprehensive exam. *Entrance requirements:* For doctorate, DAT scores are valid for three years, minimum of 90 semester or 135 quarter units of undergraduate/graduate course work; minimum 30 hours of dental-related work experience or shadowing; complete all prerequisite coursework with minimum grade of C; the letters of recommendation. Additional exam requirements/recommendations for international students: required—TOEFL (minimum score 79 iBT), or 6 semesters of English classes. *Application deadline:* For fall admission, 12/1 for domestic and international students. Applications are processed on a rolling basis. Application fee: $60. Electronic applications accepted. Application fee is waived when completed online. *Expenses:* Tuition is about 76325 per year. Other fees included student body fees, vital source, dental instrument and supply fee and other fees are about 8000 per year. and other one time fee such as graduation fee, Mobil livescan, CPR, Exam for CDC, ipad, Henry Schein, eHuman/Interactive tool, and Kilgore cost about $1600. *Financial support:* In 2019–20, 8 students received support. Scholarships/grants available. Financial award application deadline: 3/2; financial award applicants required to submit FAFSA. *Unit head:* Dr. Steven Friedrichsen, Dean, 909-706-3911, E-mail: sfriedrichsen@westernu.edu. *Application contact:* Marie Anderson, Admissions Counselor, 909-469-5290, Fax: 909-469-5570, E-mail: mesparza@westernu.edu.
Website: http://www.westernu.edu/dentistry/

**West Virginia University,** School of Dentistry, Morgantown, WV 26506. Offers dental hygiene (MS); dentistry (DDS); endodontics (MS); orthodontics (MS); periodontics (MS); prosthodontics (MS). *Accreditation:* ADA (one or more programs are accredited). *Degree requirements:* For master's, thesis; for doctorate, comprehensive exam. *Entrance requirements:* For doctorate, DAT, letters of recommendation, interview, minimum of 50 semester credit hours. Additional exam requirements/recommendations for international students: required—TOEFL (minimum score 500 paper-based). Electronic applications accepted. *Expenses:* Contact institution.

# Oral and Dental Sciences

**A.T. Still University,** Arizona School of Dentistry & Oral Health, Mesa, AZ 85206. Offers dental medicine (DMD); orthodontics (MS, Certificate). *Accreditation:* ADA. *Faculty:* 130 full-time (87 women), 90 part-time/adjunct (32 women). *Students:* 314 full-time (169 women); includes 163 minority (9 Black or African American, non-Hispanic/Latino; 2 American Indian or Alaska Native, non-Hispanic/Latino; 107 Asian, non-Hispanic/Latino; 17 Hispanic/Latino; 1 Native Hawaiian or other Pacific Islander, non-Hispanic/Latino; 27 Two or more races, non-Hispanic/Latino), 3 international. Average age 28. 2,323 applicants, 7% accepted, 77 enrolled. In 2019, 5 master's, 74 doctorates, 1 other advanced degree awarded. *Entrance requirements:* For doctorate, Dental Admissions Test, A formal minimum of three years (90 semester hours or 135 quarter hours); baccalaureate degree is preferred. Minimum cumulative and science GPA of 2.5 on a four-point scale (3.0 recommended). The overall and science GPA, the school(s) attended, and the rigor of the academic course load are all assessed on an individual basis. Additional exam requirements/recommendations for international students: recommended—TOEFL. *Application deadline:* For fall admission, 11/15 for domestic and international students; for summer admission, 11/15 for domestic and international students. Applications are processed on a rolling basis. Application fee: $70. Electronic applications accepted. *Financial support:* In 2019–20, 61 students received support. Federal Work-Study and scholarships/grants available. Financial award application deadline: 6/1; financial award applicants required to submit FAFSA. *Unit head:* Dr. Robert Trombly, Dean, 480-248-8105, Fax: 623-223-7063, E-mail: rtrombly@atsu.edu. *Application contact:* Donna Sparks, Director, Admissions Processing, 660-626-2117, Fax: 660-626-2969, E-mail: admissions@atsu.edu.
Website: http://www.atsu.edu/asdoh

**A.T. Still University,** College of Graduate Health Studies, Kirksville, MO 63501. Offers dental public health (MPH); exercise and sport psychology (Certificate); fundamentals of education (Certificate); geriatric exercise science (Certificate); global health (Certificate); health administration (MHA, DHA); health professions (Ed D); health sciences (DH Sc); kinesiology (MS); leadership and organizational behavior (Certificate); public health (MPH); sports conditioning (Certificate). *Accreditation:* CEPH. *Program availability:* Part-time, evening/weekend, online only, 100% online, blended/hybrid learning. *Faculty:* 49 full-time (36 women), 109 part-time/adjunct (66 women). *Students:* 601 full-time (406 women), 532 part-time (331 women); includes 457 minority (197 Black or African American, non-Hispanic/Latino; 15 American Indian or Alaska Native, non-Hispanic/Latino; 114 Asian, non-Hispanic/Latino; 105 Hispanic/Latino; 3 Native Hawaiian or other Pacific Islander, non-Hispanic/Latino; 23 Two or more races, non-Hispanic/Latino), 30 international. Average age 36. 339 applicants, 73% accepted, 217 enrolled. In 2019, 175 master's, 100 doctorates, 118 other advanced degrees awarded. *Degree requirements:* For master's, thesis, integrated terminal project, practicum; for doctorate, thesis/dissertation. *Entrance requirements:* For master's, minimum GPA of 2.5, bachelor's degree or equivalent, essay, resume, English proficiency; for doctorate, minimum GPA of 2.5, master's or terminal degree, essay, past experience in relevant field, resume, English proficiency. Additional exam requirements/recommendations for international students: required—TOEFL (minimum score 550 paper-based; 80 iBT). *Application deadline:* For fall admission, 6/24 for domestic and international students; for winter admission, 9/9 for domestic and international students; for spring admission, 12/9 for domestic and international students; for summer admission, 3/2 for domestic and international students. Applications are processed on a rolling basis. Application fee: $70. Electronic applications accepted. *Financial support:* In 2019–20, 13 students received support. Scholarships/grants available. Financial award applicants required to submit FAFSA. *Unit head:* Dr. Donald Altman, Dean, 480-219-6008, Fax: 660-626-2826, E-mail: daltman@atsu.edu. *Application contact:* Amie Waldemer, Associate Director,

Online Admissions, 480-219-6146, E-mail: awaldemer@atsu.edu.
Website: http://www.atsu.edu/college-of-graduate-health-studies

**Augusta University,** Program in Oral Biology, Augusta, GA 30912. Offers MS, PhD. *Program availability:* Part-time. *Degree requirements:* For master's, thesis; for doctorate, thesis/dissertation. *Entrance requirements:* For master's and doctorate, GRE General Test or DAT, DDS, DMD, or equivalent degree. Additional exam requirements/recommendations for international students: required—TOEFL (minimum score 550 paper-based; 79 iBT). Electronic applications accepted.

**Boston University,** School of Medicine, Graduate Medical Sciences, Program in Oral Biology, Boston, MA 02215. Offers PhD. *Degree requirements:* For doctorate, thesis/dissertation. *Application deadline:* For fall admission, 12/1 priority date for domestic students. Application fee: $95. Electronic applications accepted. *Unit head:* Dr. Phillip Trackman, Director, 617-358-4440, E-mail: trackman@bu.edu. *Application contact:* GMS Admissions Office, 617-358-9518, Fax: 617-358-2913, E-mail: gmsbusm@bu.edu.
Website: http://www.bu.edu/dental-research/student-research/phd-in-oral-biology/

**Boston University,** School of Medicine, Graduate Medical Sciences, Program in Oral Health Sciences, Boston, MA 02215. Offers MS. *Degree requirements:* For master's, capstone project or thesis. *Entrance requirements:* For master's, DAT. *Application deadline:* Applications are processed on a rolling basis. Electronic applications accepted. *Financial support:* Scholarships/grants available. Financial award applicants required to submit FAFSA. *Unit head:* Dr. Theresa A. Davies, Director, 617-358-9546, E-mail: tdavies@bu.edu. *Application contact:* GMS Office of Admissions, 617-358-9518, Fax: 617-358-2913, E-mail: ohs@bu.edu.
Website: http://www.bumc.bu.edu/gms/ohs/

**Case Western Reserve University,** School of Dental Medicine and School of Graduate Studies, Advanced Specialty Education Programs in Dentistry, Cleveland, OH 44106. Offers advanced general dentistry (Certificate); endodontics (MSD, Certificate); oral surgery (Certificate); orthodontics (MSD, Certificate); pedodontics (MSD, Certificate); periodontics (MSD, Certificate). *Degree requirements:* For master's, thesis. *Entrance requirements:* For master's, National Dental Board Exam, DDS, minimum GPA of 3.0; for Certificate, DDS. Additional exam requirements/recommendations for international students: required—TOEFL (minimum score 550 paper-based; 79 iBT). *Expenses:* Contact institution.

**Columbia University,** College of Dental Medicine and Graduate School of Arts and Sciences, Programs in Dental Specialties, New York, NY 10027. Offers advanced education in general dentistry (Certificate); biomedical informatics (MA, PhD); endodontics (Certificate); orthodontics (MS, Certificate); periodontics (MS, Certificate); prosthodontics (MS, Certificate); science education (MA). *Degree requirements:* For master's, thesis, presentation of seminar. *Entrance requirements:* For master's, GRE General Test, DDS or equivalent. *Expenses:* Contact institution.

**Dalhousie University,** Faculty of Dentistry, Department of Oral and Maxillofacial Surgery, Halifax, NS B3H 3J5, Canada. Offers MD/M Sc. Electronic applications accepted. *Expenses:* Contact institution.

**Harvard University,** Graduate School of Arts and Sciences, Program in Biological Sciences in Dental Medicine, Cambridge, MA 02138. Offers PhD.

**Harvard University,** School of Dental Medicine, Advanced Graduate Programs in Dentistry, Cambridge, MA 02138. Offers advanced general dentistry (Certificate); dental public health (Certificate); endodontics (Certificate); general practice residency (Certificate); oral biology (M Med Sc, D Med Sc); oral implantology (Certificate); oral medicine (Certificate); oral pathology (Certificate); oral surgery (Certificate); orthodontics (Certificate); pediatric dentistry (Certificate); periodontics (Certificate); prosthodontics (Certificate). *Degree requirements:* For master's, comprehensive exam, thesis optional; for doctorate, comprehensive exam, thesis/dissertation. *Entrance requirements:* Additional exam requirements/recommendations for international students: required—TOEFL (minimum iBT score of 95; subcategory score minimums of Reading 21, Listening 17, Speaking 24, and Writing 25).

**Howard University,** College of Dentistry, Washington, DC 20059-0002. Offers advanced education in general dentistry (Certificate); dentistry (DDS); general dentistry practice (Certificate); oral and maxillofacial surgery (Certificate); orthodontics (Certificate); pediatric dentistry (Certificate). *Accreditation:* ADA (one or more programs are accredited). *Degree requirements:* For doctorate, comprehensive exam, didactic and clinical exams. *Entrance requirements:* For doctorate, DAT, 8 semester hours of course work each in biology, inorganic chemistry, and organic chemistry. *Expenses:* Contact institution.

**Idaho State University,** Graduate School, College of Health Professions, Department of Dental Sciences, Pocatello, ID 83209-8088. Offers advanced general dentistry (Post-Doctoral Certificate). *Degree requirements:* For Post-Doctoral Certificate, comprehensive exam, thesis optional, 1-year residency. *Entrance requirements:* For degree, DAT, 3 dental application forms. Additional exam requirements/recommendations for international students: required—TOEFL (minimum score 600 paper-based). Electronic applications accepted. *Expenses:* Contact institution.

**Jacksonville University,** Brooks Rehabilitation College of Healthcare Sciences, School of Orthodontics, Jacksonville, FL 32211. Offers dentistry (MS); orthodontics (Certificate). *Students:* 44 full-time (18 women), 6 part-time (3 women); includes 14 minority (1 Black or African American, non-Hispanic/Latino; 2 Asian, non-Hispanic/Latino; 10 Hispanic/Latino; 1 Two or more races, non-Hispanic/Latino), 5 international. Average age 34. In 2019, 8 other advanced degrees awarded. *Degree requirements:* For master's and Certificate, thesis. *Entrance requirements:* For master's, DDS/DMD or equivalent; for Certificate, American Board of Orthodontics written exam; U.S. National Dental Boards (part 1 and 2), curriculum vitae, official transcripts, 3 professional evaluations, 3 professional recommendations (dean of dental school or faculty, or other professional colleagues), statement of intent, clinical competencies through delivering evidence-based patient care, DDS/DMD or equivalent. Additional exam requirements/recommendations for international students: required—TOEFL (minimum score 610 paper-based). *Application deadline:* For fall admission, 9/14 priority date for domestic students, 9/14 for international students. Applications are processed on a rolling basis. Application fee: $175. Electronic applications accepted. *Expenses:* Contact institution. *Financial support:* Fellowships, scholarships/grants, and health care benefits available. Financial award application deadline: 3/15; financial award applicants required to submit FAFSA. *Unit head:* Dr. James Toruten, Program Director & Clinical Associate Professor, 904-256-7850, E-mail: jtroute@ju.edu. *Application contact:* Sharon Frazier, Executive Operations Coordinator, 904-256-7847, Fax: 904-256-7847, E-mail: juorthoadmissions@ju.edu.
Website: https://www.ju.edu/orthodontics/index.php

**Loma Linda University,** School of Dentistry, Program in Endodontics, Loma Linda, CA 92350. Offers MS, Certificate, MS/Certificate. *Degree requirements:* For master's, thesis. *Entrance requirements:* For master's, GRE General Test, DDS or DMD, minimum GPA of 3.0, National Boards. Additional exam requirements/recommendations for international students: required—TOEFL (minimum score 550 paper-based).

**Loma Linda University,** School of Dentistry, Program in Implant Dentistry, Loma Linda, CA 92350. Offers MS, Certificate, MS/Certificate. *Degree requirements:* For master's, thesis. *Entrance requirements:* For master's, GRE General Test, DDS or DMD, minimum GPA of 3.0.

**Loma Linda University,** School of Dentistry, Program in Oral and Maxillofacial Surgery, Loma Linda, CA 92350. Offers MS, Certificate, MS/Certificate. *Degree requirements:* For master's, thesis. *Entrance requirements:* For master's, GRE General Test, DDS or DMD, minimum GPA of 3.0.

**Loma Linda University,** School of Dentistry, Program in Orthodontics and Dentofacial Orthopedics, Loma Linda, CA 92350. Offers MS, Certificate, MS/Certificate. *Degree requirements:* For master's, thesis. *Entrance requirements:* For master's, GRE General Test, DDS or DMD, minimum GPA of 3.0. Additional exam requirements/recommendations for international students: required—TOEFL (minimum score 550 paper-based).

**Loma Linda University,** School of Dentistry, Program in Periodontics, Loma Linda, CA 92350. Offers MS. *Degree requirements:* For master's, thesis. *Entrance requirements:* For master's, GRE General Test, DDS or DMD, minimum GPA of 3.0. Additional exam requirements/recommendations for international students: required—TOEFL (minimum score 550 paper-based).

**Marquette University,** School of Dentistry and Graduate School, Graduate Programs in Dentistry, Program in Advanced Training in General Dentistry, Milwaukee, WI 53201-1881. Offers MS, Certificate. *Entrance requirements:* For master's, National Board Dental Exams I and II, DDS or equivalent. Additional exam requirements/recommendations for international students: required—TOEFL.

**Marquette University,** School of Dentistry and Graduate School, Graduate Programs in Dentistry, Program in Dental Biomaterials, Milwaukee, WI 53201-1881. Offers MS. *Program availability:* Part-time. *Degree requirements:* For master's, thesis. *Entrance requirements:* For master's, GRE General Test. Additional exam requirements/recommendations for international students: required—TOEFL.

**Marquette University,** School of Dentistry and Graduate School, Graduate Programs in Dentistry, Program in Endodontics, Milwaukee, WI 53201-1881. Offers MS, Certificate. *Degree requirements:* For master's, research thesis or acceptance of a paper in a peer-reviewed journal. *Entrance requirements:* For master's, National Board Dental Exams I and II, DDS or equivalent. Additional exam requirements/recommendations for international students: required—TOEFL. *Expenses:* Contact institution.

**Marquette University,** School of Dentistry and Graduate School, Graduate Programs in Dentistry, Program in Orthodontics, Milwaukee, WI 53201-1881. Offers MS, Certificate. *Degree requirements:* For master's, thesis. *Entrance requirements:* For master's, National Board Dental Exams I and II, DDS or equivalent. Additional exam requirements/recommendations for international students: required—TOEFL. *Expenses:* Contact institution.

**Marquette University,** School of Dentistry and Graduate School, Graduate Programs in Dentistry, Program in Periodontics, Milwaukee, WI 53201-1881. Offers MS, Certificate.

**Marquette University,** School of Dentistry and Graduate School, Graduate Programs in Dentistry, Program in Prosthodontics, Milwaukee, WI 53201-1881. Offers MS, Certificate. *Degree requirements:* For master's, thesis or alternative. *Entrance requirements:* For master's, National Board Dental Exams I and II, DDS or equivalent. Additional exam requirements/recommendations for international students: required—TOEFL.

**McGill University,** Faculty of Graduate and Postdoctoral Studies, Faculty of Dentistry, Montréal, QC H3A 2T5, Canada. Offers forensic dentistry (Certificate); oral and maxillofacial surgery (M Sc, PhD). *Accreditation:* ADA.

**Metropolitan State University,** College of Nursing and Health Sciences, St. Paul, MN 55106-5000. Offers advanced dental therapy (MS); leadership and management (MSN); nurse educator (MSN); nursing (DNP). *Accreditation:* AACN. *Program availability:* Part-time. *Degree requirements:* For master's, thesis or alternative; for doctorate, thesis/dissertation or alternative. *Entrance requirements:* For master's, GRE General Test, minimum GPA of 3.0, RN license, BS/BA; for doctorate, minimum GPA of 3.0, RN license, MSN. Additional exam requirements/recommendations for international students: required—TOEFL (minimum score 550 paper-based).

**New York University,** College of Dentistry, Department of Biomaterials, New York, NY 10012-1019. Offers biomaterials science (MS). *Degree requirements:* For master's, thesis optional. *Entrance requirements:* For master's, GRE or another standardized test (such as DAT, CDAT, National Dental Board Part I and National Dental Board Part II), academic transcripts, personal statement, resume or curriculum vitae, three letters of recommendation. Additional exam requirements/recommendations for international students: required—TOEFL (minimum score 600 paper-based; 100 iBT). Electronic applications accepted. *Expenses:* Contact institution.

**New York University,** College of Dentistry, Post-Graduate Programs, New York, NY 10010. Offers endodontics (Advanced Certificate); oral and maxillofacial surgery (Advanced Certificate); orthodontics (Advanced Certificate); pediatric dentistry (Advanced Certificate); periodontics (Advanced Certificate); prosthodontics (Advanced Certificate). *Degree requirements:* For Advanced Certificate, one foreign language. *Entrance requirements:* For degree, National Dental Board Exam Part I and II, three sealed letters of recommendation, including the dean's letter; official dental school transcript noting degree; personal essay. Additional exam requirements/recommendations for international students: required—TOEFL (minimum score 603 paper-based; 100 iBT). Electronic applications accepted. *Expenses:* Contact institution.

**New York University,** Graduate School of Arts and Science, Department of Biology, New York, NY 10012-1019. Offers biology (PhD); biomedical journalism (MS); cancer and molecular biology (PhD); computational biology (PhD); computers in biological research (MS); developmental genetics (PhD); general biology (MS); immunology and microbiology (PhD); molecular genetics (PhD); neurobiology (PhD); oral biology (MS); plant biology (PhD); recombinant DNA technology (MS); MS/MBA. *Program availability:* Part-time. Terminal master's awarded for partial completion of doctoral program. *Degree requirements:* For master's, thesis or alternative, qualifying paper; for doctorate, comprehensive exam, thesis/dissertation. *Entrance requirements:* For master's and doctorate, GRE General Test. Additional exam requirements/recommendations for international students: required—TOEFL, IELTS.

**The Ohio State University,** College of Dentistry, Columbus, OH 43210. Offers dental anesthesiology (MS); dental hygiene (MDH); dentistry (DDS); endodontics (MS); oral and maxillofacial pathology (MS); oral and maxillofacial surgery (MS); oral biology (PhD); orthodontics (MS); pediatric dentistry (MS); periodontology (MS); prosthodontics (MS); DDS/PhD. *Accreditation:* ADA (one or more programs are accredited). Terminal master's awarded for partial completion of doctoral program. *Degree requirements:* For master's, thesis; for doctorate, thesis/dissertation (for some programs). *Entrance requirements:* For master's, GRE General Test (for all applicants with cumulative GPA below 3.0); for doctorate, DAT (for DDS); GRE General Test, GRE Subject Test in biology recommended (for PhD). Additional exam requirements/recommendations for international students: required—TOEFL (minimum score 550 paper-based; 79 iBT), IELTS (minimum score 7), Michigan English Language Assessment Battery (minimum score 82). Electronic applications accepted. *Expenses:* Contact institution.

**Oregon Health & Science University,** School of Dentistry, Graduate Programs in Dentistry, Department of Endodontics, Portland, OR 97239-3098. Offers Certificate. *Entrance requirements:* For degree, GRE General Test. Additional exam requirements/recommendations for international students: required—TOEFL.

**Oregon Health & Science University,** School of Dentistry, Graduate Programs in Dentistry, Department of Orthodontics, Portland, OR 97239-3098. Offers MS, Certificate. *Degree requirements:* For master's, thesis. *Entrance requirements:* For master's and Certificate, GRE General Test, DMD/DDS. Additional exam requirements/recommendations for international students: required—TOEFL.

**Oregon Health & Science University,** School of Dentistry, Graduate Programs in Dentistry, Department of Pediatric Dentistry, Portland, OR 97239-3098. Offers Certificate.

**Oregon Health & Science University,** School of Dentistry, Graduate Programs in Dentistry, Department of Periodontology, Portland, OR 97239-3098. Offers MS, Certificate. *Degree requirements:* For master's, thesis. *Entrance requirements:* For master's and Certificate, GRE General Test, DMD/DDS. Additional exam requirements/recommendations for international students: required—TOEFL.

**Oregon Health & Science University,** School of Dentistry, Graduate Programs in Dentistry, Department of Restorative Dentistry, Division of Biomaterials and Biomechanics, Portland, OR 97239-3098. Offers MS.

**Oregon Health & Science University,** School of Dentistry, Graduate Programs in Dentistry, Program in Oral Molecular Biology, Portland, OR 97239-3098. Offers MS.

**Oregon Health & Science University,** School of Dentistry, Professional Program in Dentistry, Portland, OR 97239-3098. Offers dentistry (DMD); oral and maxillofacial surgery (Certificate); MD/DMD. *Accreditation:* ADA. *Entrance requirements:* For doctorate, DAT. Electronic applications accepted.

**Rutgers University - Newark,** Rutgers School of Dental Medicine, Newark, NJ 07101-1709. Offers dental science (MS); dentistry (DMD); endodontics (Certificate); oral medicine (Certificate); orthodontics (Certificate); pediatric dentistry (Certificate); periodontics (Certificate); prosthodontics (Certificate); DMD/MPH; DMD/PhD; MD/Certificate; MS/Certificate. *Accreditation:* ADA (one or more programs are accredited). *Entrance requirements:* For doctorate, DAT. Electronic applications accepted. *Expenses:* Contact institution.

**Saint Louis University,** Graduate Programs, Center for Advanced Dental Education, St. Louis, MO 63103. Offers endodontics (MSD); orthodontics (MSD); periodontics (MSD). *Degree requirements:* For master's, comprehensive exam, thesis, teaching practicum. *Entrance requirements:* For master's, GRE General Test, NBDE (National Board Dental Exam), DDS or DMD, interview, letters of recommendation. Additional exam requirements/recommendations for international students: required—TOEFL (minimum score 525 paper-based). Electronic applications accepted.

**Seton Hill University,** Master's and Certificate Program in Orthodontics, Greensburg, PA 15601. Offers MS, Certificate. *Students:* 27. *Entrance requirements:* For degree, U.S. National Dental Board Exams (Part 1 and Part 2), eligibility for PA licensure, DDS/DMD, minimum GPA of 3.0, transcripts, personal statement. Additional exam requirements/recommendations for international students: required—TOEFL (minimum score 650 paper-based; 114 iBT), IELTS (minimum score 7). *Application deadline:* Applications are processed on a rolling basis. Electronic applications accepted. *Expenses: Tuition:* Full-time $29,196; part-time $811 per credit. *Required fees:* $550; $100 per unit. $25 per semester. Tuition and fees vary according to class time, course level, course load, degree level, campus/location, program, reciprocity agreements, student level and student's religious affiliation. *Financial support:* Application deadline: 5/15; applicants required to submit FAFSA. Website: http://www.setonhill.edu/academics/graduate_programs/orthodontics

**Stony Brook University, State University of New York,** Stony Brook Medicine, School of Dental Medicine and Graduate School, Department of Oral Biology and Pathology, Stony Brook, NY 11794. Offers MS, PhD. *Faculty:* 7 full-time (3 women), 1 (woman) part-time/adjunct. *Students:* 1 (woman) full-time, 3 part-time (all women), 2 international. Average age 32. 1 applicant. In 2019, 1 doctorate awarded. Terminal master's awarded for partial completion of doctoral program. *Entrance requirements:* For doctorate, GRE General Test. Additional exam requirements/recommendations for international students: required—TOEFL. *Application deadline:* For fall admission, 1/15 for domestic students; for spring admission, 10/1 for domestic students. Application fee: $100. *Expenses:* Contact institution. *Financial support:* Fellowships, research assistantships, teaching assistantships, and Federal Work-Study available. Financial award application deadline: 3/15. *Unit head:* Dr. Lucille London, Interim, 631-632-8615, E-mail: Lucille.London@stonybrook.edu. *Application contact:* Marguerite Baldwin, Graduate Program Coordinator, 631-632-9189, Fax: 631-632-9704, E-mail: marguerite.baldwin@stonybrook.edu. Website: https://dentistry.stonybrookmedicine.edu/oralbiology

**Stony Brook University, State University of New York,** Stony Brook Medicine, School of Dental Medicine, Professional Program in Dental Medicine, Stony Brook, NY 11794. Offers dental medicine (DDS); endodontics (Certificate); orthodontics (Certificate); periodontics (Certificate). *Accreditation:* ADA (one or more programs are accredited). *Faculty:* 33 full-time (15 women), 75 part-time/adjunct (20 women). *Students:* 201 full-time (107 women); includes 81 minority (3 Black or African American, non-Hispanic/Latino; 63 Asian, non-Hispanic/Latino; 10 Hispanic/Latino; 5 Two or more races, non-Hispanic/Latino), 3 international. Average age 25. 1,065 applicants, 12% accepted, 46 enrolled. In 2019, 45 doctorates, 8 Certificates awarded. *Entrance requirements:* For doctorate, DAT (minimum score of 17 preferred in all subsections), minimum GPA of 3.0 (preferred). Additional exam requirements/recommendations for international students: required—TOEFL. *Application deadline:* For fall admission, 12/1 for domestic students. Application fee: $100. *Expenses:* Contact institution. *Financial support:* Research assistantships, teaching assistantships, and Federal Work-Study available. Support available to part-time students. *Unit head:* Dr. Mary R. Truhlar, Dean, 631-632-6985, Fax: 631-632-6621, E-mail: mary.truhlar@stonybrook.edu. *Application contact:* Marcia Simon, Director, 631-632-8922, Fax: 631-632-7130. Website: http://dentistry.stonybrookmedicine.edu/

**Temple University,** Kornberg School of Dentistry, Graduate Programs in Dentistry, Philadelphia, PA 19122-6096. Offers advanced education in general dentistry (Certificate); endodontology (Certificate); oral biology (MS); orthodontics (Certificate); periodontology (Certificate). *Degree requirements:* For master's, thesis; for Certificate, comprehensive exam. *Entrance requirements:* For master's, GRE; for Certificate, National Boards Parts I and II, DMD or DDS, 3 letters of recommendation. Additional exam requirements/recommendations for international students: required—TOEFL (minimum score 650 paper-based). *Expenses:* Contact institution.

**Texas A&M University,** College of Dentistry, Dallas, TX 75266-0677. Offers maxillofacial surgery (Certificate); pediatric dentistry (Certificate). *Accreditation:* ADA; SACS/CC. *Entrance requirements:* Additional exam requirements/recommendations for international students: required—TOEFL (minimum score 550 paper-based; 79 iBT). Electronic applications accepted. *Expenses:* Contact institution.

**Tufts University,** School of Dental Medicine, Advanced Education Programs in Dental Medicine, Medford, MA 02155. Offers dentistry (Certificate), including endodontics, oral and maxillofacial surgery, orthodontics, pediatric dentistry, periodontology, prosthodontics. *Entrance requirements:* Additional exam requirements/recommendations for international students: required—TOEFL. *Expenses:* Contact institution.

**Tufts University,** School of Dental Medicine, Graduate Programs in Dental Medicine, Medford, MA 02155. Offers MS. *Degree requirements:* For master's, thesis. *Entrance requirements:* For master's, DDS, DMD, or equivalent; minimum B average. Additional exam requirements/recommendations for international students: required—TOEFL. *Expenses:* Contact institution.

**Université de Montréal,** Faculty of Dental Medicine, Program in Multidisciplinary Residency, Montréal, QC H3C 3J7, Canada. Offers Certificate. Electronic applications accepted.

**Université de Montréal,** Faculty of Dental Medicine, Program in Oral and Dental Sciences, Montréal, QC H3C 3J7, Canada. Offers M Sc. Electronic applications accepted.

**Université de Montréal,** Faculty of Dental Medicine, Program in Orthodontics, Montréal, QC H3C 3J7, Canada. Offers M Sc. Electronic applications accepted.

**Université de Montréal,** Faculty of Dental Medicine, Program in Pediatric Dentistry, Montréal, QC H3C 3J7, Canada. Offers M Sc. Electronic applications accepted.

**Université de Montréal,** Faculty of Dental Medicine, Program in Prosthodontics Rehabilitation, Montréal, QC H3C 3J7, Canada. Offers M Sc. Electronic applications accepted.

**University at Buffalo, the State University of New York,** Graduate School, School of Dental Medicine, Graduate Programs in Dental Medicine, Department of Oral Biology, Buffalo, NY 14260. Offers oral biology (PhD). *Degree requirements:* For doctorate, thesis/dissertation. *Entrance requirements:* For doctorate, GRE General Test. Additional exam requirements/recommendations for international students: required—TOEFL (minimum score 550 paper-based; 79 iBT), IELTS (minimum score 6.5), PTE (minimum score 55). Electronic applications accepted. *Expenses: Tuition, area resident:* Full-time $11,310; part-time $471 per credit hour. Tuition, state resident: full-time $11,310; part-time $471 per credit hour. Tuition, nonresident: full-time $23,100; part-time $963 per credit hour. *International tuition:* $23,100 full-time. *Required fees:* $2820.

**University at Buffalo, the State University of New York,** Graduate School, School of Dental Medicine, Graduate Programs in Dental Medicine, Department of Orthodontics, Buffalo, NY 14260. Offers orthodontics (Certificate). *Degree requirements:* For master's, thesis. *Entrance requirements:* For master's, GRE General Test, National Board Dental Exam, DDS or equivalent. Additional exam requirements/recommendations for international students: required—TOEFL (minimum score 550 paper-based; 79 iBT), IELTS (minimum score 6.5), PTE (minimum score 55). Electronic applications accepted. *Expenses:* Contact institution.

**University at Buffalo, the State University of New York,** Graduate School, School of Dental Medicine, Graduate Programs in Dental Medicine, Program in Biomaterials, Buffalo, NY 14260. Offers biomaterials (MS). *Program availability:* Part-time. *Degree requirements:* For master's, thesis. *Entrance requirements:* For master's, GRE General Test. Additional exam requirements/recommendations for international students: required—TOEFL (minimum score 550 paper-based; 79 iBT), IELTS (minimum score 6.5), PTE (minimum score 55). Electronic applications accepted. *Expenses: Tuition, area resident:* Full-time $11,310; part-time $471 per credit hour. Tuition, state resident: full-time $11,310; part-time $471 per credit hour. Tuition, nonresident: full-time $23,100; part-time $963 per credit hour. *International tuition:* $23,100 full-time. *Required fees:* $2820.

**University at Buffalo, the State University of New York,** Graduate School, School of Dental Medicine, Graduate Programs in Dental Medicine, Program in Oral Sciences, Buffalo, NY 14260. Offers oral sciences (MS). *Degree requirements:* For master's, thesis. *Entrance requirements:* Additional exam requirements/recommendations for international students: required—TOEFL (minimum score 550 paper-based; 79 iBT), IELTS (minimum score 6.5), PTE (minimum score 55). Electronic applications accepted. *Expenses: Tuition, area resident:* Full-time $11,310; part-time $471 per credit hour. Tuition, state resident: full-time $11,310; part-time $471 per credit hour. Tuition, nonresident: full-time $23,100; part-time $963 per credit hour. *International tuition:* $23,100 full-time. *Required fees:* $2820.

**The University of Alabama at Birmingham,** School of Dentistry, Graduate Programs in Dentistry, Birmingham, AL 35294. Offers MS. *Students:* 1 (woman) part-time; minority (Two or more races, non-Hispanic/Latino). Average age 44. In 2019, 12 master's awarded. *Degree requirements:* For master's, thesis. *Unit head:* Dr. Amjad Javed, Program Director, 205-934-5407, Fax: 205-934-0208, E-mail: javeda@uab.edu. *Application contact:* Dr. Steven J. Filler, Director of Dentistry Admissions, 205-934-3387, Fax: 205-934-0209. Website: http://www.dental.uab.edu/

**University of Alberta,** Faculty of Medicine and Dentistry, School of Dentistry, Program in Orthodontics, Edmonton, AB T6G 2E1, Canada. Offers M Sc, PhD. *Degree requirements:* For master's, thesis; for doctorate, thesis/dissertation. *Entrance requirements:* Additional exam requirements/recommendations for international students: required—TOEFL (minimum score 580 paper-based). Electronic applications accepted.

**The University of British Columbia,** Faculty of Dentistry, Research Training Programs in Dentistry, Vancouver, BC V6T 1Z1, Canada. Offers craniofacial science (M Sc, PhD). *Degree requirements:* For master's, thesis; for doctorate, comprehensive exam, thesis/dissertation. *Entrance requirements:* Additional exam requirements/recommendations for international students: required—TOEFL (minimum score 580 paper-based). Electronic applications accepted. *Expenses:* Contact institution.

**University of California, Los Angeles,** Graduate Division, College of Letters and Science and David Geffen School of Medicine, UCLA ACCESS to Programs in the Molecular, Cellular and Integrative Life Sciences, Los Angeles, CA 90095. Offers biochemistry and molecular biology (PhD); biological chemistry (PhD); cellular and molecular pathology (PhD); human genetics (PhD); microbiology, immunology, and molecular genetics (PhD); molecular biology (PhD); molecular toxicology (PhD); molecular, cellular and integrative physiology (PhD); neurobiology (PhD); oral biology (PhD); physiology (PhD). *Degree requirements:* For doctorate, thesis/dissertation, oral and written qualifying exams. *Entrance requirements:* For doctorate, GRE General Test, bachelor's degree; minimum undergraduate GPA of 3.0 (or its equivalent if letter grade system not used). Additional exam requirements/recommendations for international students: required—TOEFL. Electronic applications accepted.

**University of California, Los Angeles,** School of Dentistry and Graduate Division, Graduate Programs in Dentistry, Program in Oral Biology, Los Angeles, CA 90095. Offers MS, PhD, DDS/MS, DDS/PhD, MD/PhD, MS/Certificate, PhD/Certificate. *Degree requirements:* For master's, thesis; for doctorate, thesis/dissertation, oral and written qualifying exams; 1 quarter of teaching experience. *Entrance requirements:* For

master's and doctorate, GRE General Test, bachelor's degree; minimum undergraduate GPA of 3.0 (or its equivalent if letter grade system not used). Additional exam requirements/recommendations for international students: required—TOEFL. Electronic applications accepted.

**University of California, San Francisco,** Graduate Division, Program in Oral and Craniofacial Sciences, San Francisco, CA 94143. Offers MS, PhD. Terminal master's awarded for partial completion of doctoral program. *Degree requirements:* For master's, thesis; for doctorate, thesis/dissertation. *Entrance requirements:* For master's and doctorate, GRE General Test.

**University of Colorado Denver,** School of Dental Medicine, Aurora, CO 80045. Offers dental surgery (DDS); orthodontics (Certificate); periodontics (Certificate). *Accreditation:* ADA. *Entrance requirements:* For doctorate, DAT, prerequisite courses in microbiology, general biochemistry and English composition (1 semester each); general chemistry/lab, organic chemistry/lab, general biology/lab and general physics/lab (2 semesters each); interview; letters of recommendation; essay. Additional exam requirements/recommendations for international students: required—TOEFL (minimum score 580 paper-based; 80 iBT); recommended—IELTS (minimum score 6.8). Electronic applications accepted. Tuition and fees vary according to course load, program and reciprocity agreements.

**University of Connecticut Health Center,** Graduate School, Programs in Biomedical Sciences, Combined Degree Programs in Oral Biology, Farmington, CT 06030. Offers DMD/PhD. *Entrance requirements:* Additional exam requirements/recommendations for international students: required—TOEFL (minimum score 600 paper-based).

**University of Connecticut Health Center,** School of Dental Medicine, Program in Dental Science, Farmington, CT 06030. Offers MDS. *Program availability:* Part-time. *Degree requirements:* For master's, comprehensive exam, thesis. *Entrance requirements:* For master's, National Board Dental Examination Parts I and II. *Expenses:* Contact institution.

**University of Detroit Mercy,** School of Dentistry, Detroit, MI 48208. Offers MS, DDS, Certificate. *Accreditation:* ADA (one or more programs are accredited). *Degree requirements:* For master's, thesis. *Entrance requirements:* For master's, DDS or DMD; for doctorate, DAT; for Certificate, DAT, DDS or DMD. *Expenses:* Contact institution.

**University of Florida,** College of Dentistry and Graduate School, Graduate Programs in Dentistry, Department of Endodontics, Gainesville, FL 32611. Offers MS, Certificate. *Entrance requirements:* For master's, DAT, GRE General Test, National Board Dental Examination Parts I and II, minimum GPA of 3.0, interview; for Certificate, DAT. Additional exam requirements/recommendations for international students: required—TOEFL (minimum score 550 paper-based).

**University of Florida,** College of Dentistry and Graduate School, Graduate Programs in Dentistry, Department of Oral Biology, Gainesville, FL 32611. Offers PhD. *Degree requirements:* For doctorate, thesis/dissertation. *Entrance requirements:* For doctorate, GRE General Test, minimum GPA of 3.0. Additional exam requirements/recommendations for international students: required—TOEFL. Electronic applications accepted.

**University of Florida,** College of Dentistry and Graduate School, Graduate Programs in Dentistry, Department of Orthodontics, Gainesville, FL 32611. Offers MS, Certificate. *Degree requirements:* For master's, thesis. *Entrance requirements:* For master's, DAT, GRE General Test, National Board Dental Examination Parts I and II, minimum GPA of 3.0, interview. Additional exam requirements/recommendations for international students: required—TOEFL (minimum score 550 paper-based).

**University of Florida,** College of Dentistry and Graduate School, Graduate Programs in Dentistry, Department of Periodontology, Gainesville, FL 32611. Offers MS, Certificate. *Degree requirements:* For master's, thesis. *Entrance requirements:* For master's, DAT, GRE General Test, National Board Dental Examination Parts I and II, minimum GPA of 3.0, interview. Additional exam requirements/recommendations for international students: required—TOEFL (minimum score 550 paper-based).

**University of Florida,** College of Dentistry and Graduate School, Graduate Programs in Dentistry, Department of Prosthodontics, Gainesville, FL 32611. Offers MS, Certificate. *Degree requirements:* For master's, thesis. *Entrance requirements:* For master's, DAT, GRE General Test, National Board Dental Examination Parts I and II, minimum GPA of 3.0, interview. Additional exam requirements/recommendations for international students: required—TOEFL (minimum score 550 paper-based).

**University of Illinois at Chicago,** College of Dentistry, Graduate Programs in Oral Sciences, Chicago, IL 60607-7128. Offers MS, PhD. *Degree requirements:* For master's, thesis. *Entrance requirements:* For master's, GRE General Test, DDS, DVM, or MD. Additional exam requirements/recommendations for international students: required—TOEFL. Electronic applications accepted. *Expenses:* Contact institution.

**The University of Iowa,** College of Dentistry and Graduate College, Graduate Programs in Dentistry, Department of Endodontics, Iowa City, IA 52242-1316. Offers MS, Certificate. *Degree requirements:* For master's, thesis. *Entrance requirements:* For master's, GRE, DDS; for Certificate, DDS. Additional exam requirements/recommendations for international students: required—TOEFL.

**The University of Iowa,** College of Dentistry and Graduate College, Graduate Programs in Dentistry, Department of Operative Dentistry, Iowa City, IA 52242-1316. Offers MS, Certificate. *Degree requirements:* For master's, thesis. *Entrance requirements:* For master's, GRE, DDS; for Certificate, DDS. Additional exam requirements/recommendations for international students: required—TOEFL.

**The University of Iowa,** College of Dentistry and Graduate College, Graduate Programs in Dentistry, Department of Oral and Maxillofacial Surgery, Iowa City, IA 52242-1316. Offers MS, PhD, Certificate. *Degree requirements:* For master's, thesis. *Entrance requirements:* For master's, GRE, DDS; for Certificate, DDS.

**The University of Iowa,** College of Dentistry and Graduate College, Graduate Programs in Dentistry, Department of Oral Pathology, Radiology and Medicine, Iowa City, IA 52242-1316. Offers MS, PhD, Certificate. *Degree requirements:* For master's, thesis. *Entrance requirements:* For master's, GRE, DDS, minimum GPA of 2.7. Additional exam requirements/recommendations for international students: required—TOEFL.

**The University of Iowa,** College of Dentistry and Graduate College, Graduate Programs in Dentistry, Department of Orthodontics, Iowa City, IA 52242-1316. Offers MS, Certificate. *Degree requirements:* For master's, thesis. *Entrance requirements:* For master's, GRE, DDS; for Certificate, DDS. Additional exam requirements/recommendations for international students: required—TOEFL.

**The University of Iowa,** College of Dentistry and Graduate College, Graduate Programs in Dentistry, Department of Pediatric Dentistry, Iowa City, IA 52242-1316. Offers Certificate. *Entrance requirements:* For degree, DDS. Additional exam requirements/recommendations for international students: required—TOEFL.

**The University of Iowa,** College of Dentistry and Graduate College, Graduate Programs in Dentistry, Department of Periodontics, Iowa City, IA 52242-1316. Offers MS, Certificate. *Degree requirements:* For master's, thesis. *Entrance requirements:* For master's, GRE, DDS; for Certificate, DDS. Additional exam requirements/recommendations for international students: required—TOEFL.

**The University of Iowa,** College of Dentistry and Graduate College, Graduate Programs in Dentistry, Department of Preventive and Community Dentistry, Iowa City, IA 52242-1316. Offers dental public health (MS). *Degree requirements:* For master's, thesis. *Entrance requirements:* For master's, GRE, DDS. Additional exam requirements/recommendations for international students: required—TOEFL.

**The University of Iowa,** College of Dentistry and Graduate College, Graduate Programs in Dentistry, Department of Prosthodontics, Iowa City, IA 52242-1316. Offers MS, Certificate. *Degree requirements:* For master's, thesis. *Entrance requirements:* For master's, GRE, DDS; for Certificate, DDS. Additional exam requirements/recommendations for international students: required—TOEFL.

**The University of Iowa,** College of Dentistry and Graduate College, Graduate Programs in Dentistry, Oral Science Graduate Program, Iowa City, IA 52242-1316. Offers MS, PhD. *Degree requirements:* For master's, thesis; for doctorate, thesis/dissertation. *Entrance requirements:* For master's, GRE, DDS. Additional exam requirements/recommendations for international students: required—TOEFL.

**University of Kentucky,** Graduate School, Graduate Program in Dentistry, Lexington, KY 40506-0032. Offers MS. *Degree requirements:* For master's, comprehensive exam, thesis. *Entrance requirements:* For master's, GRE General Test, minimum undergraduate GPA of 2.5. Additional exam requirements/recommendations for international students: required—TOEFL (minimum score 550 paper-based). Electronic applications accepted.

**University of Louisville,** School of Dentistry, Louisville, KY 40202. Offers dentistry (DMD); oral biology (MS). *Accreditation:* ADA (one or more programs are accredited). *Faculty:* 74 full-time (32 women), 67 part-time/adjunct (22 women). *Students:* 523 full-time (255 women), 3 part-time (1 woman); includes 144 minority (29 Black or African American, non-Hispanic/Latino; 61 Asian, non-Hispanic/Latino; 37 Hispanic/Latino; 17 Two or more races, non-Hispanic/Latino), 21 international. Average age 27. 196 applicants, 94% accepted, 143 enrolled. In 2019, 24 master's, 115 doctorates awarded. *Degree requirements:* For master's, thesis; for doctorate, NBDE Pt 1 and 2. *Entrance requirements:* For master's, DAT, GRE General Test, or National Board Dental Exam, minimum GPA of 2.75; for doctorate, DAT, 38 hours of coursework in science (biology, chemistry, physics, and biochemistry). Additional exam requirements/recommendations for international students: required—TOEFL (minimum score 100 iBT). *Application deadline:* For fall admission, 1/1 for domestic and international students. Applications are processed on a rolling basis. Application fee: $65. Electronic applications accepted. *Expenses: Tuition, area resident:* Full-time $13,000; part-time $723 per credit hour. Tuition, state resident: full-time $13,000; part-time $723 per credit hour. Tuition, nonresident: full-time $27,114; part-time $1507 per credit hour. *International tuition:* $27,114 full-time. *Required fees:* $196. Tuition and fees vary according to program and reciprocity agreements. *Financial support:* In 2019–20, 15 students received support, including 1 fellowship with full tuition reimbursement available (averaging $15,000 per year); scholarships/grants also available. Financial award application deadline: 3/15; financial award applicants required to submit FAFSA. *Unit head:* Dr. T. Gerry Bradley, Dean, 502-852-5295, E-mail: t0brad03@exchange.louisville.edu. *Application contact:* Jami Campbell, Assistant Director of Admissions, 502-852-5081, Fax: 502-852-1210, E-mail: dmdadms@louisville.edu.
Website: http://louisville.edu/dental/

**The University of Manchester,** School of Dentistry, Manchester, United Kingdom. Offers basic dental sciences (cancer studies) (M Phil, PhD); basic dental sciences (molecular genetics) (M Phil, PhD); basic dental sciences (stem cell biology) (M Phil, PhD); biomaterials sciences and dental technology (M Phil, PhD); dental public health/community dentistry (M Phil, PhD); dental science (clinical) (PhD); endodontology (M Phil, PhD); fixed and removable prosthodontics (M Phil, PhD); operative dentistry (M Phil, PhD); oral and maxillofacial surgery (M Phil, PhD); oral radiology (M Phil, PhD); orthodontics (M Phil, PhD); restorative dentistry (M Phil, PhD).

**University of Manitoba,** Dr. Gerald Niznick College of Dentistry and Faculty of Graduate Studies, Graduate Programs in Dentistry, Department of Dental Diagnostic and Surgical Sciences, Winnipeg, MB R3T 2N2, Canada. Offers oral and maxillofacial surgery (M Dent); periodontology (M Dent). *Entrance requirements:* For master's, dental degree.

**University of Manitoba,** Dr. Gerald Niznick College of Dentistry and Faculty of Graduate Studies, Graduate Programs in Dentistry, Department of Oral Biology, Winnipeg, MB R3T 2N2, Canada. Offers M Sc, PhD. *Degree requirements:* For master's, thesis; for doctorate, comprehensive exam, thesis/dissertation. *Entrance requirements:* For master's, B Sc or pre-M Sc. Additional exam requirements/recommendations for international students: required—TOEFL.

**University of Manitoba,** Dr. Gerald Niznick College of Dentistry and Faculty of Graduate Studies, Graduate Programs in Dentistry, Department of Preventive Dental Science, Winnipeg, MB R3T 2N2, Canada. Offers orthodontics (M Sc). *Degree requirements:* For master's, thesis. *Entrance requirements:* For master's, dental degree. Electronic applications accepted.

**University of Maryland, Baltimore,** Graduate School, Graduate Programs in Dentistry, Department of Oral Pathology, Baltimore, MD 21201. Offers PhD. *Degree requirements:* For doctorate, comprehensive exam, thesis/dissertation. *Entrance requirements:* For doctorate, GRE General Test, DDS, DMD, minimum GPA of 3.0, curriculum vitae, essay, 3 letters of recommendation. Additional exam requirements/recommendations for international students: required—TOEFL (minimum score 80 iBT); recommended—IELTS (minimum score 7). Electronic applications accepted.

**University of Maryland, Baltimore,** Graduate School, Graduate Programs in Dentistry, Graduate Program in Biomedical Sciences, Baltimore, MD 21201. Offers MS, PhD, DDS/PhD. *Degree requirements:* For doctorate, comprehensive exam, thesis/dissertation. *Entrance requirements:* For doctorate, GRE General Test, minimum GPA of 3.0, curriculum vitae, essay, 3 letters of recommendation. Additional exam requirements/recommendations for international students: required—TOEFL (minimum score 80 iBT); recommended—IELTS (minimum score 7). Electronic applications accepted.

**University of Maryland, Baltimore,** Professional and Advanced Education Programs in Dentistry, Baltimore, MD 21201-1627. Offers advanced general dentistry (Certificate); dentistry (DDS); endodontics (Certificate); oral-maxillofacial surgery (Certificate); orthodontics (Certificate); pediatric dentistry (Certificate); periodontics (Certificate); prosthodontics (Certificate); DDS/MBA; DDS/PhD. *Accreditation:* ADA. *Students:* 582 full-time (301 women), 4 part-time (2 women); includes 282 minority (58 Black or African American, non-Hispanic/Latino; 140 Asian, non-Hispanic/Latino; 54 Hispanic/Latino; 30 Two or more races, non-Hispanic/Latino), 28 international. Average age 27. 1,322 applicants, 75% accepted, 159 enrolled. In 2019, 132 doctorates, 23 Certificates awarded. *Entrance requirements:* For doctorate, DAT, coursework in science; for Certificate, National Dental Board Exams, DDS. Additional exam requirements/recommendations for international students: required—TOEFL (minimum score 550 paper-based; 80 iBT). *Application deadline:* Applications are processed on a rolling

basis. Application fee: $85. Electronic applications accepted. *Expenses:* Contact institution. *Financial support:* Career-related internships or fieldwork, Federal Work-Study, scholarships/grants, and traineeships available. Financial award application deadline: 3/1; financial award applicants required to submit FAFSA. *Unit head:* Dr. Mark A. Reynolds, Dean, 410-706-7461. *Application contact:* Dr. Judith A. Porter, Assistant Dean for Admissions and Recruitment, 410-706-7472, Fax: 410-706-0945, E-mail: ddsadmissions@umaryland.edu.
Website: http://www.dental.umaryland.edu/

**University of Michigan,** School of Dentistry and Rackham Graduate School, Graduate Programs in Dentistry, Endodontics Program, Ann Arbor, MI 48109-1078. Offers MS. *Degree requirements:* For master's, thesis. *Entrance requirements:* For master's, DDS. Additional exam requirements/recommendations for international students: required—TOEFL (minimum score 84 iBT). Electronic applications accepted. *Expenses:* Contact institution.

**University of Michigan,** School of Dentistry and Rackham Graduate School, Graduate Programs in Dentistry, Orthodontics Program, Ann Arbor, MI 48109-1078. Offers MS. *Degree requirements:* For master's, thesis. *Entrance requirements:* For master's, GRE, National Dental Board Exam, DDS. Additional exam requirements/recommendations for international students: required—TOEFL (minimum score 84 iBT). Electronic applications accepted. *Expenses:* Contact institution.

**University of Michigan,** School of Dentistry and Rackham Graduate School, Graduate Programs in Dentistry, Pediatric Dentistry Program, Ann Arbor, MI 48109-1078. Offers MS. *Degree requirements:* For master's, thesis. *Entrance requirements:* For master's, National Dental Board Exam (for domestic applicants; not required of international applicants), DDS. Additional exam requirements/recommendations for international students: required—TOEFL (minimum score 84 iBT). Electronic applications accepted. *Expenses:* Contact institution.

**University of Michigan,** School of Dentistry and Rackham Graduate School, Graduate Programs in Dentistry, Periodontics Program, Ann Arbor, MI 48109-1078. Offers MS. *Degree requirements:* For master's, thesis. *Entrance requirements:* For master's, DDS. Additional exam requirements/recommendations for international students: required—TOEFL (minimum score 84 iBT). Electronic applications accepted. *Expenses:* Contact institution.

**University of Michigan,** School of Dentistry and Rackham Graduate School, Graduate Programs in Dentistry, Prosthodontics Program, Ann Arbor, MI 48109-1078. Offers MS. *Degree requirements:* For master's, thesis. *Entrance requirements:* For master's, DDS. Additional exam requirements/recommendations for international students: required—TOEFL (minimum score 84 iBT). Electronic applications accepted. *Expenses:* Contact institution.

**University of Michigan,** School of Dentistry and Rackham Graduate School, Graduate Programs in Dentistry, Restorative Dentistry Program, Ann Arbor, MI 48109-1078. Offers MS. *Degree requirements:* For master's, thesis. *Entrance requirements:* For master's, DDS. Additional exam requirements/recommendations for international students: required—TOEFL (minimum score 84 iBT). Electronic applications accepted. *Expenses:* Contact institution.

**University of Michigan,** School of Dentistry, Oral Health Sciences PhD Program, Ann Arbor, MI 48109-1078. Offers oral health sciences (PhD). *Degree requirements:* For doctorate, thesis/dissertation, preliminary exam, oral defense of dissertation. *Entrance requirements:* For doctorate, GRE. Additional exam requirements/recommendations for international students: required—TOEFL (minimum score 560 paper-based, 84 iBT) or IELTS (6.5). Electronic applications accepted. *Expenses:* Contact institution.

**University of Minnesota, Twin Cities Campus,** School of Dentistry and Graduate School, Graduate Programs in Dentistry, Advanced Education Program in Periodontology, Minneapolis, MN 55455-0213. Offers MS. *Degree requirements:* For master's, comprehensive exam, thesis. *Entrance requirements:* For master's, DDS/DMD, letter from Dental Dean, specific GGP/class rank, two letters of recommendation. Additional exam requirements/recommendations for international students: required—TOEFL (minimum score 590 paper-based).

**University of Minnesota, Twin Cities Campus,** School of Dentistry and Graduate School, Graduate Programs in Dentistry, Division of Endodontics, Minneapolis, MN 55455-0213. Offers MS, Certificate. *Degree requirements:* For master's, thesis. *Entrance requirements:* Additional exam requirements/recommendations for international students: required—TOEFL.

**University of Minnesota, Twin Cities Campus,** School of Dentistry and Graduate School, Graduate Programs in Dentistry, Division of Orthodontics, Minneapolis, MN 55455-0213. Offers MS. *Degree requirements:* For master's, thesis. *Entrance requirements:* Additional exam requirements/recommendations for international students: required—TOEFL (minimum score 587 paper-based).

**University of Minnesota, Twin Cities Campus,** School of Dentistry and Graduate School, Graduate Programs in Dentistry, Division of Pediatric Dentistry, Minneapolis, MN 55455-0213. Offers MS. *Degree requirements:* For master's, thesis. *Entrance requirements:* Additional exam requirements/recommendations for international students: required—TOEFL.

**University of Minnesota, Twin Cities Campus,** School of Dentistry and Graduate School, Graduate Programs in Dentistry, Division of Prosthodontics, Minneapolis, MN 55455-0213. Offers MS. *Degree requirements:* For master's, thesis, clinical. *Entrance requirements:* Additional exam requirements/recommendations for international students: required—TOEFL.

**University of Minnesota, Twin Cities Campus,** School of Dentistry and Graduate School, Graduate Programs in Dentistry, Program in Oral Biology, Minneapolis, MN 55455-0213. Offers MS, PhD. *Degree requirements:* For master's, thesis.

**University of Minnesota, Twin Cities Campus,** School of Dentistry and Graduate School, Graduate Programs in Dentistry, Program in Oral Health Services for Older Adults (Geriatrics), Minneapolis, MN 55455-0213. Offers MS, Certificate. *Degree requirements:* For master's, thesis (for some programs). *Entrance requirements:* For master's, DDS degree or equivalent. Additional exam requirements/recommendations for international students: required—TOEFL (minimum score 560 paper-based). Electronic applications accepted.

**University of Minnesota, Twin Cities Campus,** School of Dentistry and Graduate School, Graduate Programs in Dentistry, Program in Temporomandibular Joint Disorders, Minneapolis, MN 55455-0213. Offers MS. *Degree requirements:* For master's, comprehensive exam, thesis. *Entrance requirements:* Additional exam requirements/recommendations for international students: required—TOEFL. Electronic applications accepted.

**University of Mississippi Medical Center,** School of Dentistry, Department of Craniofacial and Dental Research, Jackson, MS 39216-4505. Offers MS, PhD.

**University of Missouri–Kansas City,** School of Dentistry, Kansas City, MO 64110-2499. Offers advanced education in dentistry (Graduate Dental Certificate); dental hygiene education (MS); endodontics (Graduate Dental Certificate); oral and maxillofacial surgery (Graduate Dental Certificate); oral biology (MS, PhD); orthodontics and dentofacial orthopedics (Graduate Dental Certificate); periodontics (Graduate Dental Certificate). *Accreditation:* ADA (one or more programs are accredited). *Degree requirements:* For master's, thesis; for doctorate, thesis/dissertation (for some programs). *Entrance requirements:* For master's, DAT, letters of evaluation, personal interview; for doctorate, DAT (for DDS); for Graduate Dental Certificate, DDS. Additional exam requirements/recommendations for international students: required—TOEFL (minimum score 550 paper-based; 80 iBT). *Expenses:* Contact institution.

**University of Missouri–Kansas City,** School of Graduate Studies, Kansas City, MO 64110-2499. Offers interdisciplinary studies (PhD), including art history, cell biology and biophysics, chemistry, computer and electrical engineering, computer science and informatics, economics, education, engineering, English, entrepreneurship and innovation, geosciences, history, mathematics and statistics, molecular biology and biochemistry, music education, oral and craniofacial sciences, pharmaceutical sciences, pharmacology, physics, political science, public affairs and administration, religious studies, social science, telecommunications and computer networking; PMBA/MHA. *Degree requirements:* For doctorate, comprehensive exam, thesis/dissertation, residency. *Entrance requirements:* For doctorate, GRE General Test, minimum GPA of 2.75 (undergraduate), 3.0 (graduate). Additional exam requirements/recommendations for international students: required—TOEFL (minimum score 550 paper-based; 80 iBT), TWE (minimum score 4). Electronic applications accepted.

**University of Nebraska Medical Center,** Medical Sciences Interdepartmental Area, Omaha, NE 68198. Offers applied behavior analysis (PhD); clinical translational research (MS, PhD); health practice and medical education research (MS); oral biology (MS, PhD). *Program availability:* Part-time. Terminal master's awarded for partial completion of doctoral program. *Degree requirements:* For master's, comprehensive exam, thesis; for doctorate, comprehensive exam, thesis/dissertation. *Entrance requirements:* For master's, GRE General Test; for doctorate, GRE General Test, MCAT, DAT, LSAT. Additional exam requirements/recommendations for international students: required—TOEFL (minimum score 550 paper-based; 80 iBT), IELTS. Electronic applications accepted. *Expenses:* Contact institution.

**University of Nevada, Las Vegas,** School of Dental Medicine, Las Vegas, NV 89154. Offers dental medicine (DMD); dental surgery (DDS); dentistry (DMD); oral biology (MS); orthodontics and dentofacial orthopedics (Certificate). *Accreditation:* ADA. *Program availability:* Part-time, evening/weekend, online learning. *Students:* 369 full-time (154 women), 1 (woman) part-time; includes 154 minority (7 Black or African American, non-Hispanic/Latino; 1 American Indian or Alaska Native, non-Hispanic/Latino; 89 Asian, non-Hispanic/Latino; 36 Hispanic/Latino; 1 Native Hawaiian or other Pacific Islander, non-Hispanic/Latino; 20 Two or more races, non-Hispanic/Latino), 3 international. Average age 29. 1,543 applicants, 11% accepted, 80 enrolled. In 2019, 6 master's, 93 doctorates, 5 other advanced degrees awarded. *Entrance requirements:* For doctorate, DAT; for Certificate, National Board Dental Exam part 1 and 2. Additional exam requirements/recommendations for international students: required—TOEFL (minimum score 550 paper-based; 80 iBT), IELTS (minimum score 7). *Application deadline:* For fall admission, 1/1 for domestic and international students; for summer admission, 3/1 for domestic students. Applications are processed on a rolling basis. Application fee: $75. Electronic applications accepted. *Expenses:* Contact institution. *Financial support:* Federal Work-Study, institutionally sponsored loans, scholarships/grants, health care benefits, and unspecified assistantships available. Support available to part-time students. Financial award application deadline: 3/15; financial award applicants required to submit FAFSA. *Unit head:* Dr. Christine C. Ancajas, Assistant Dean of Admissions and Student Affairs, 702-774-2522, Fax: 702-774-2521, E-mail: christine.ancajas@unlv.edu. *Application contact:* Dr. Christine C. Ancajas, Assistant Dean of Admissions and Student Affairs, 702-774-2522, Fax: 702-774-2521, E-mail: christine.ancajas@unlv.edu.
Website: http://www.unlv.edu/dental

**The University of North Carolina at Chapel Hill,** School of Dentistry and Graduate School, Graduate Programs in Dentistry, Chapel Hill, NC 27599. Offers dental hygiene (MS); endodontics (MS); epidemiology (PhD); operative dentistry (MS); oral and maxillofacial pathology (MS); oral and maxillofacial radiology (MS); oral biology (PhD); orthodontics (MS); pediatric dentistry (MS); periodontology (MS); prosthodontics (MS). *Degree requirements:* For master's, thesis; for doctorate, thesis/dissertation. *Entrance requirements:* For master's, GRE General Test (for orthodontics and oral biology only); National Dental Board Part I (Part II if available), dental degree (for all except dental hygiene); for doctorate, GRE General Test. Additional exam requirements/recommendations for international students: required—TOEFL (minimum score 550 paper-based; 79 iBT). Electronic applications accepted. *Expenses:* Contact institution.

**University of Oklahoma Health Sciences Center,** College of Dentistry and Graduate College, Graduate Programs in Dentistry, Department of Orthodontics, Oklahoma City, OK 73190. Offers MS. *Degree requirements:* For master's, thesis. *Entrance requirements:* For master's, minimum GPA of 3.0, DDS/DMD. Additional exam requirements/recommendations for international students: required—TOEFL. Electronic applications accepted.

**University of Oklahoma Health Sciences Center,** College of Dentistry and Graduate College, Graduate Programs in Dentistry, Department of Periodontics, Oklahoma City, OK 73190. Offers MS. *Degree requirements:* For master's, thesis. *Entrance requirements:* For master's, DDS/DMD, minimum GPA of 3.0. Additional exam requirements/recommendations for international students: required—TOEFL (minimum score 550 paper-based). Electronic applications accepted.

**University of Pittsburgh,** School of Dental Medicine, Advanced Education Program in Oral and Maxillofacial Pathology, Pittsburgh, PA 15261. Offers Certificate. *Faculty:* 2 full-time (1 woman), 1 (woman) part-time/adjunct. *Students:* 2 full-time (1 woman). Average age 35. 5 applicants, 20% accepted, 1 enrolled. In 2019, 1 Certificate awarded. *Entrance requirements:* For degree, National Board of Dental Examiners I and II. *Application deadline:* For fall admission, 10/1 for domestic students. Applications are processed on a rolling basis. Application fee: $50. Electronic applications accepted. Application fee is waived when completed online. *Financial support:* In 2019–20, 2 students received support. CMS GME funding available. *Unit head:* Dr. Kurt F. Summersgill, Program Director, 412-648-8635, Fax: 412-383-9142, E-mail: kfs8@pitt.edu. *Application contact:* Erin King, Coordinator, 412-648-8636, Fax: 412-383-9142, E-mail: emk74@pitt.edu.
Website: https://www.dental.pitt.edu/residency-program-oral-and-maxillofacial-pathology

**University of Pittsburgh,** School of Dental Medicine, Department of Dental Anesthesiology, Pittsburgh, PA 15261. Offers Certificate. *Faculty:* 4 full-time (0 women), 5 part-time/adjunct (0 women). *Students:* 12 full-time (4 women). Average age 28. 38 applicants, 11% accepted, 4 enrolled. In 2019, 4 Certificates awarded. *Degree requirements:* For Certificate, comprehensive exam. *Entrance requirements:* Additional exam requirements/recommendations for international students: required—TOEFL (minimum score 85 paper-based). *Application deadline:* For fall admission, 9/15 for domestic students. Application fee: $95. Electronic applications accepted. *Unit head:* Dr. Michael A. Cuddy, Program Director, 412-648-9901, Fax: 412-648-2591, E-mail: mc2@

pitt.edu. *Application contact:* Lisa Lehman, Residency Coordinator, 412-648-8609, Fax: 412-648-2591, E-mail: lrl12@pitt.edu.

**University of Pittsburgh,** School of Dental Medicine, Department of Endodontics, Pittsburgh, PA 15260. Offers Certificate. *Faculty:* 3 full-time (0 women), 11 part-time/adjunct (3 women). *Students:* 8 full-time (2 women); includes 3 minority (2 Black or African American, non-Hispanic/Latino; 1 Asian, non-Hispanic/Latino). Average age 30. 120 applicants, 3% accepted, 4 enrolled. In 2019, 4 Certificates awarded. *Degree requirements:* For Certificate, 350 Root Canals, 15 surgery cases. *Entrance requirements:* For degree, Part 1, Part 2 National Dental Board Examination, DMD/DDS degree. Additional exam requirements/recommendations for international students: required—TOEFL. Application fee: $50. Electronic applications accepted. *Unit head:* Dr. Herbert L. Ray, Chair, Department of Endodontics, Director of Endodontic Residency Program, 412-648-8647, Fax: 412-383-9478, E-mail: hlr21@pitt.edu. *Application contact:* Rosann Donahoe, Department Administrator, 412-648-8647, Fax: 412-383-9478, E-mail: rod8@pitt.edu.

**University of Pittsburgh,** School of Dental Medicine, Department of Oral and Maxillofacial Surgery, Pittsburgh, PA 15213. Offers oral and maxillofacial surgery (Certificate); pediatric cranio-maxillofacial surgery (Certificate). *Faculty:* 7 full-time (0 women). *Students:* 17 full-time (3 women); includes 2 minority (both Asian, non-Hispanic/Latino). Average age 25. 250 applicants, 1% accepted, 3 enrolled. In 2019, 4 Certificates awarded. *Degree requirements:* For Certificate, comprehensive exam. *Entrance requirements:* For degree, National Boards, Part 1, CBSE, US or Canadien. Dental Degree (DDS or DMD). Additional exam requirements/recommendations for international students: required—TOEFL. *Application deadline:* For fall admission, 9/1 for domestic students. Applications are processed on a rolling basis. Electronic applications accepted. *Financial support:* Scholarships/grants and health care benefits available. *Unit head:* Dr. Larry Cunningham, Interim Program Director/Chair, 412-648-6801, Fax: 412-648-6835, E-mail: lac229@pitt.edu. *Application contact:* Andrea M. Ford, Residency Coordinator, 412-648-6801, Fax: 412-648-6835, E-mail: fordam@upmc.edu.
Website: http://www.dental.pitt.edu/

**University of Pittsburgh,** School of Dental Medicine, Department of Oral Biology, Pittsburgh, PA 15260. Offers oral biology (MS, PhD), including craniofacial genetics (PhD), craniofacial regeneration (PhD). *Faculty:* 8 full-time (4 women), 2 part-time/adjunct (0 women). *Students:* 12 full-time (9 women); includes 4 minority (all Asian, non-Hispanic/Latino), 8 international. 13 applicants, 38% accepted, 5 enrolled. In 2019, 2 master's, 3 doctorates awarded. Terminal master's awarded for partial completion of doctoral program. *Degree requirements:* For master's, thesis; for doctorate, thesis/dissertation. *Entrance requirements:* For master's, Baccalaureate degree in a natural or physical science or engineering program; Minimum GPA of 3.0; Minimum 3 letters of recommendation. Additional exam requirements/recommendations for international students: required—TOEFL (minimum score 600 paper-based; 100 iBT), Dulingo; recommended—IELTS (minimum score 7). *Application deadline:* For fall admission, 1/15 for domestic and international students. Application fee: $50. *Expenses:* Contact institution. *Financial support:* In 2019–20, 4 research assistantships with tuition reimbursements (averaging $28,000 per year), 1 teaching assistantship with full tuition reimbursement (averaging $19,480 per year) were awarded; unspecified assistantships also available. Financial award applicants required to submit FAFSA. *Unit head:* Dr. Elia Beniash, Interim Department Chair/Graduate Program Director, 412-648-0108, Fax: 412-624-6685, E-mail: ebeniash@pitt.edu. *Application contact:* Alycia Maltony, Graduate Programs Administrator, 412-648-5096, Fax: 412-648-9571, E-mail: aam111@pitt.edu.
Website: http://www.dental.pitt.edu/oral-biology-academic-programs

**University of Pittsburgh,** School of Dental Medicine, Department of Orthodontics and Dentofacial Orthopedics, Pittsburgh, PA 15261. Offers orthodontics (MDS, Certificate). *Faculty:* 2 full-time (0 women), 5 part-time/adjunct (0 women). *Students:* 11 full-time (7 women); includes 7 minority (all Asian, non-Hispanic/Latino). Average age 28. 177 applicants, 2% accepted, 3 enrolled. In 2019, 2 master's awarded. *Degree requirements:* For master's, comprehensive exam, thesis. *Entrance requirements:* For degree, Part 1, Part 2 National Dental Board Examination, DMD/DDS. *Application deadline:* For fall admission, 10/1 for domestic and international students. Electronic applications accepted. *Unit head:* Dr. Joseph F. A. Petrone, BA, DDS, MSD, MPH, Chair, 412-648-8638, Fax: 412-648-8817, E-mail: jfap@pitt.edu. *Application contact:* E. Dawson Baloga, 412-648-8419, Fax: 412-648-8817, E-mail: edb38@pitt.edu.
Website: http://www.dental.pitt.edu/department/orthodontics-and-dentofacial-orthopedics

**University of Pittsburgh,** School of Dental Medicine, Department of Pediatric Dentistry, Pittsburgh, PA 15261. Offers dental science (MDS); multidisciplinary public health (MPH); pediatric dentistry (Certificate). *Accreditation:* ADA. *Faculty:* 1 (woman) full-time, 10 part-time/adjunct (5 women). *Students:* 6 full-time (all women); includes 1 minority (Asian, non-Hispanic/Latino), 1 international. Average age 30. 28 applicants, 7% accepted, 2 enrolled. In 2019, 1 master's, 4 other advanced degrees awarded. *Degree requirements:* For master's, thesis; for Certificate, Completed research project and maintenance of a B or greater GPA. *Entrance requirements:* For master's, The qualification exam for the Master's Degree is given at the end of fall term, the first year. *Application deadline:* For fall admission, 9/15 for domestic and international students. Electronic applications accepted. *Expenses:* In-state tuition is $54,128 and out-of state tuition is $66,370, The additional fees (instruments, departmental, and University fees total $4,540. *Financial support:* In 2019–20, 4 students received support. Each resident receives an annual $24,000 stipend. available. Financial award application deadline: 9/15. *Unit head:* Dr. Deborah Studen-Pavlovich, Professor and Graduate Program Director, 412-648-8183, Fax: 412-648-8435, E-mail: das12@pitt.edu. *Application contact:* Sharon A. Hohman, Departmental Secretary, 412-648-8416, Fax: 412-648-8435.
Website: http://www.dental.pitt.edu

**University of Pittsburgh,** School of Dental Medicine, Department of Periodontics and Preventive Dentistry, Pittsburgh, PA 15261. Offers periodontics (MDS, Certificate). *Faculty:* 4 full-time (2 women), 8 part-time/adjunct (0 women). *Students:* 8 full-time (3 women); includes 4 minority (1 American Indian or Alaska Native, non-Hispanic/Latino; 1 Asian, non-Hispanic/Latino; 1 Hispanic/Latino; 1 Two or more races, non-Hispanic/Latino). Average age 30. 38 applicants, 8% accepted, 3 enrolled. In 2019, 3 Certificates awarded. *Degree requirements:* For master's, thesis. *Entrance requirements:* For degree, Part 1, Part 2 National Dental Board Examination, DMD, DDS. Additional exam requirements/recommendations for international students: recommended—TOEFL. *Application deadline:* For fall admission, 8/15 for domestic and international students. Application fee: $50. Electronic applications accepted. *Expenses:* Tuition, instrument fees, university fees, and professional fees. *Financial support:* Stipends (averaging $25,000 per year) available. *Unit head:* Dr. Kelly Williams, Residency Program Director, 412-648-8837, Fax: 412-648-8594, E-mail: KellyWilliams@pitt.edu. *Application contact:* Alycia Maltony, Alumni Affairs/Development and Residency Education Administrator, 412-648-5096, Fax: 412-648-8637, E-mail: aam111@pitt.edu.
Website: http://www.dental.pitt.edu/department/periodontics-and-preventive-dentistry

**University of Pittsburgh,** School of Dental Medicine, Department of Prosthodontics, Pittsburgh, PA 15261. Offers MDS, Certificate. *Faculty:* 4 full-time (2 women), 5 part-time/adjunct (0 women). *Students:* 8 full-time (3 women); includes 2 minority (both Asian, non-Hispanic/Latino), 3 international. Average age 30. 62 applicants, 5% accepted, 3 enrolled. In 2019, 2 Certificates awarded. *Degree requirements:* For master's, thesis. *Entrance requirements:* For degree, Part 1, Part 2 National Dental Board Examination, DMD/DDS degree. *Application deadline:* For fall admission, 11/1 for domestic and international students. Application fee: $50. Electronic applications accepted. *Financial support:* Stipend available. *Unit head:* Dr. Thomas Craig Kunkel, Chair and Program Director, 412-648-8674, Fax: 412-648-8850, E-mail: tck14@pit.edu. *Application contact:* Mary Katherine Minnick, Administrator, 412-648-8840, Fax: 412-648-8850, E-mail: mkm94@pitt.edu.

**University of Puerto Rico - Medical Sciences Campus,** School of Dental Medicine, Graduate Programs in Dentistry, San Juan, PR 00936-5067. Offers general dentistry (Certificate); oral and maxillofacial surgery (Certificate); orthodontics (Certificate); pediatric dentistry (Certificate); prosthodontics (Certificate). *Degree requirements:* For Certificate, comprehensive exam (for some programs). *Entrance requirements:* For degree, National Board Dental Exam I, National Board Dental Exam II, DDS or DMD, interview. Electronic applications accepted. *Expenses:* Contact institution.

**University of Rochester,** School of Medicine and Dentistry, Graduate Programs in Medicine and Dentistry, Center for Oral Biology, Rochester, NY 14627. Offers dental science (MS). *Degree requirements:* For master's, thesis. *Entrance requirements:* For master's, GRE General Test, DDS or equivalent.

**University of Southern California,** Graduate School, Herman Ostrow School of Dentistry and Graduate School, Department of Craniofacial Biology, Los Angeles, CA 90089. Offers MS, PhD, Graduate Certificate. Terminal master's awarded for partial completion of doctoral program. *Degree requirements:* For master's, comprehensive exam, thesis; for doctorate, comprehensive exam, thesis/dissertation. *Entrance requirements:* For master's and doctorate, GRE, undergraduate degree. Additional exam requirements/recommendations for international students: required—TOEFL. Electronic applications accepted.

**The University of Tennessee Health Science Center,** College of Graduate Health Sciences, Memphis, TN 38163. Offers biomedical engineering (MS, PhD); biomedical sciences (PhD); dental sciences (MDS); epidemiology (MS); health outcomes and policy research (PhD); laboratory research and management (MS); nursing science (PhD); pharmaceutical sciences (PhD); pharmacology (MS); speech and hearing science (PhD); DDS/PhD; DNP/PhD; MD/PhD; Pharm D/PhD. Terminal master's awarded for partial completion of doctoral program. *Degree requirements:* For master's, comprehensive exam, thesis; for doctorate, thesis/dissertation, oral and written preliminary and comprehensive exams. *Entrance requirements:* For master's and doctorate, GRE General Test, minimum GPA of 3.0. Additional exam requirements/recommendations for international students: recommended—TOEFL (minimum score 79 iBT), IELTS (minimum score 6.5). Electronic applications accepted. *Expenses:* Contact institution.

**The University of Toledo,** College of Graduate Studies, College of Medicine and Life Sciences, Department of Surgery, Toledo, OH 43606-3390. Offers oral biology (MSBS). *Degree requirements:* For master's, thesis or alternative. *Entrance requirements:* For master's, DAT, minimum undergraduate GPA of 3.0, three letters of recommendation, statement of purpose, transcripts from all prior institutions attended, acceptance into Pediatric Dental Residency Program at UT. Additional exam requirements/recommendations for international students: required—TOEFL (minimum score 550 paper-based; 80 iBT). Electronic applications accepted.

**University of Toronto,** School of Graduate Studies, Faculty of Dentistry, Graduate Programs in Dentistry, Toronto, ON M5S 1A1, Canada. Offers M Sc, PhD. *Program availability:* Part-time. Terminal master's awarded for partial completion of doctoral program. *Degree requirements:* For master's, thesis; for doctorate, thesis/dissertation. *Entrance requirements:* For master's, honors B Sc, minimum B average, 2 letters of reference; for doctorate, M Sc, minimum B+ average. Additional exam requirements/recommendations for international students: required—Michigan English Language Assessment Battery, IELTS, TOEFL, or COPE. Electronic applications accepted. *Expenses:* Contact institution.

**University of Toronto,** School of Graduate Studies, Faculty of Dentistry, Specialty Master's Programs, Toronto, ON M5S 1A1, Canada. Offers dental public health (M Sc); endodontics (M Sc); oral and maxillofacial radiology (M Sc); oral and maxillofacial surgery (M Sc); oral medicine (M Sc); orthodontics and dentofacial orthopedics (M Sc); pediatric dentistry (M Sc); periodontology (M Sc). *Degree requirements:* For master's, thesis. *Entrance requirements:* For master's, completion of professional degree of DDS/BDS, DMD, minimum B average, 2 letters of reference. Additional exam requirements/recommendations for international students: required—TOEFL (minimum score 600 paper-based; 100 iBT), TWE (minimum score 5). *Expenses:* Contact institution.

**University of Washington,** Graduate School, School of Dentistry and Graduate School, Graduate Programs in Dentistry, Department of Endodontics, Seattle, WA 98195. Offers MSD, Certificate.

**University of Washington,** Graduate School, School of Dentistry and Graduate School, Graduate Programs in Dentistry, Department of Oral Biology, Seattle, WA 98195. Offers MS, MSD, PhD.

**University of Washington,** Graduate School, School of Dentistry and Graduate School, Graduate Programs in Dentistry, Department of Oral Medicine, Seattle, WA 98195. Offers MSD.

**University of Washington,** Graduate School, School of Dentistry and Graduate School, Graduate Programs in Dentistry, Department of Orthodontics, Seattle, WA 98195. Offers MSD, Certificate.

**University of Washington,** Graduate School, School of Dentistry and Graduate School, Graduate Programs in Dentistry, Department of Periodontics, Seattle, WA 98195. Offers MSD, PhD, Certificate.

**University of Washington,** Graduate School, School of Dentistry, Program in Dental Surgery, Seattle, WA 98195. Offers DDS. *Accreditation:* ADA. *Entrance requirements:* For doctorate, DAT.

**The University of Western Ontario,** Schulich School of Medicine and Dentistry, Graduate and Professional Programs in Dentistry, Program in Graduate Orthodontics, London, ON N6A 3K7, Canada. Offers M Cl D. *Degree requirements:* For master's, thesis. *Entrance requirements:* For master's, GRE General Test, minimum B average, 1 year of general practice preferred. Additional exam requirements/recommendations for international students: required—TOEFL (minimum score 600 paper-based).

**Université Laval,** Faculty of Dentistry, Diploma Program in Buccal and Maxillofacial Surgery, Québec, QC G1K 7P4, Canada. Offers DESS. *Degree requirements:* For DESS, comprehensive exam. *Entrance requirements:* For degree, interview, knowledge of French. Electronic applications accepted.

**Université Laval,** Faculty of Dentistry, Diploma Program in Gerodontology, Québec, QC G1K 7P4, Canada. Offers DESS. *Program availability:* Part-time. *Entrance*

*requirements:* For degree, interview, good knowledge of French. Electronic applications accepted.

**Université Laval,** Faculty of Dentistry, Diploma Program in Multidisciplinary Dentistry, Québec, QC G1K 7P4, Canada. Offers DESS. *Entrance requirements:* For degree, interview, knowledge of French. Electronic applications accepted.

**Université Laval,** Faculty of Dentistry, Diploma Program in Periodontics, Québec, QC G1K 7P4, Canada. Offers DESS. *Entrance requirements:* For degree, interview, knowledge of French. Electronic applications accepted.

**Université Laval,** Faculty of Dentistry, Graduate Program in Dentistry, Québec, QC G1K 7P4, Canada. Offers M Sc. *Degree requirements:* For master's, thesis (for some programs). Electronic applications accepted.

**West Virginia University,** School of Dentistry, Morgantown, WV 26506. Offers dental hygiene (MS); dentistry (DDS); endodontics (MS); orthodontics (MS); periodontics (MS); prosthodontics (MS). *Accreditation:* ADA (one or more programs are accredited). *Degree requirements:* For master's, thesis; for doctorate, comprehensive exam. *Entrance requirements:* For doctorate, DAT, letters of recommendation, interview, minimum of 50 semester credit hours. Additional exam requirements/recommendations for international students: required—TOEFL (minimum score 500 paper-based). Electronic applications accepted. *Expenses:* Contact institution.

# Section 28
# Medicine

This section contains a directory of institutions offering graduate work in medicine, followed by an in-depth entry submitted by an institution that chose to prepare a detailed program description. Additional information about programs listed in the directory but not augmented by an in-depth entry may be obtained by writing directly to the dean of a graduate school or chair of a department at the address given in the directory.

## CONTENTS

### Program Directories

# Allopathic Medicine

**Albany Medical College,** Professional Program, Albany, NY 12208-3479. Offers MD. *Accreditation:* LCME/AMA. *Degree requirements:* For doctorate, United States Medical Licensing Exam Steps 1 and 2, clinical skills. *Entrance requirements:* For doctorate, MCAT, letters of recommendation, interview. Electronic applications accepted. *Expenses:* Contact institution.

**Albert Einstein College of Medicine,** Professional Program in Medicine, Bronx, NY 10461. Offers MD, MD/PhD. *Accreditation:* LCME/AMA. *Degree requirements:* For doctorate, independent scholars project. *Entrance requirements:* For doctorate, MCAT, interview.

**Augusta University,** Medical College of Georgia, Augusta, GA 30912. Offers MD, MD/PhD. *Accreditation:* LCME/AMA. *Degree requirements:* For doctorate, comprehensive exam. *Entrance requirements:* For doctorate, MCAT (minimum score of 509). *Expenses:* Contact institution.

**Baylor College of Medicine,** Medical School, Professional Program in Medicine, Houston, TX 77030-3498. Offers MD. *Accreditation:* LCME/AMA. *Entrance requirements:* For doctorate, MCAT, 90 hours of pre-med course work. Electronic applications accepted. *Expenses:* Contact institution.

**Boston University,** School of Medicine, Professional Program in Medicine, Boston, MA 02215. Offers MD, MD/Certificate, MD/JD, MD/MA, MD/MBA, MD/MPH, MD/MSCI, MD/PhD. *Accreditation:* LCME/AMA. *Students:* 700 full-time (361 women), 29 part-time (17 women); includes 344 minority (30 Black or African American, non-Hispanic/Latino; 190 Asian, non-Hispanic/Latino; 88 Hispanic/Latino; 3 Native Hawaiian or other Pacific Islander, non-Hispanic/Latino; 33 Two or more races, non-Hispanic/Latino), 46 international. Average age 24. 9,238 applicants, 5% accepted, 160 enrolled. In 2019, 144 doctorates awarded. *Entrance requirements:* For doctorate, MCAT, 1 year each of English literature/composition, humanities, biology with lab, and physics; 2 semesters of chemistry or biochemistry with lab; minimum 3 letters of recommendation. *Application deadline:* For fall admission, 11/1 for domestic and international students. Applications are processed on a rolling basis. Application fee: $110. Electronic applications accepted. *Expenses:* Contact institution. *Financial support:* Federal Work-Study available. Support available to part-time students. *Unit head:* Dr. Karen H. Antman, Dean/Provost, 617-358-9600. *Application contact:* Dr. Kristen Goodell, Associate Dean for Admissions, 617-358-9640, E-mail: kgoodell@bu.edu.

**Brown University,** Graduate School, Division of Biology and Medicine, Program in Medicine, Providence, RI 02912. Offers MD, MD/PhD. *Accreditation:* LCME/AMA. *Expenses:* Contact institution.

**California Northstate University,** College of Medicine, Elk Grove, CA 95757. Offers MD. *Entrance requirements:* For doctorate, MCAT, three letters of recommendation.

**Case Western Reserve University,** School of Medicine, Professional Program in Medicine, Cleveland, OH 44106. Offers MD, MD/JD, MD/MA, MD/MBA, MD/MPH, MD/MS, MD/PhD. *Accreditation:* LCME/AMA. *Entrance requirements:* For doctorate, MCAT, interview. Electronic applications accepted.

**Central Michigan University,** College of Graduate Studies, College of Medicine, Mount Pleasant, MI 48859. Offers MD. *Expenses: Tuition,* area resident: Full-time $12,267; part-time $8178 per year. Tuition, state resident: full-time $12,267; part-time $8178 per year. Tuition, nonresident: full-time $12,267; part-time $8178 per year. *International tuition:* $16,110 full-time. *Required fees:* $225 per semester. Tuition and fees vary according to degree level and program.

**Charles R. Drew University of Medicine and Science,** Professional Program in Medicine, Los Angeles, CA 90059. Offers MD. *Entrance requirements:* For doctorate, MCAT.

**Columbia University,** College of Physicians and Surgeons, Professional Program in Medicine, New York, NY 10032. Offers MD, MD/DDS, MD/MPH, MD/MS, MD/PhD. *Accreditation:* LCME/AMA. *Program availability:* Part-time. *Entrance requirements:* For doctorate, MCAT. *Expenses: Tuition:* Full-time $47,600; part-time $1880 per credit. One-time fee: $105.

**Columbia University,** School of Professional Studies, Program in Narrative Medicine, New York, NY 10027. Offers MS. Electronic applications accepted. *Expenses: Tuition:* Full-time $47,600; part-time $1880 per credit. One-time fee: $105.

**Creighton University,** School of Medicine, Professional Program in Medicine, Omaha, NE 68178-0001. Offers MD, MD/PhD. *Accreditation:* LCME/AMA. *Entrance requirements:* For doctorate, MCAT. Electronic applications accepted.

**Dalhousie University,** Faculty of Medicine, Halifax, NS B3H 4H7, Canada. Offers M Sc, MD, PhD, M Sc/PhD, MD/M Sc, MD/PhD. *Accreditation:* LCME/AMA. *Entrance requirements:* For master's, MCAT; for doctorate, MCAT (for MD). Electronic applications accepted.

**Dartmouth College,** Geisel School of Medicine, Hanover, NH 03755. Offers MD, MD/MBA, MD/MPH, MD/MS, MD/PhD. *Accreditation:* LCME/AMA. *Entrance requirements:* For doctorate, one year (8 semester hours or equivalent) of general biology and general physics; two years (16 semester hours or equivalent) of chemistry, which must include one semester each or equivalent of organic chemistry and biochemistry; one half-year (3 semester hours or equivalent) of college-level mathematics. Electronic applications accepted.

**Drexel University,** College of Medicine, Professional Program in Medicine, Philadelphia, PA 19104-2875. Offers MD, MD/PhD. *Accreditation:* LCME/AMA. *Degree requirements:* For doctorate, National Board Exam Parts I and II. *Entrance requirements:* For doctorate, MCAT. Electronic applications accepted.

**Duke University,** School of Medicine, Doctor of Medicine, Durham, NC 27708. Offers MD, MD/JD, MD/MA, MD/MALS, MD/MBA, MD/MHS, MD/MLS, MD/MMCi, MD/MPH, MD/MPP, MD/MS, MD/MSE, MD/MSIS, MD/PhD. *Accreditation:* LCME/AMA. *Faculty:* 1,524 full-time (537 women). *Students:* 504 full-time (275 women); includes 250 minority (59 Black or African American, non-Hispanic/Latino; 12 American Indian or Alaska Native, non-Hispanic/Latino; 152 Asian, non-Hispanic/Latino; 25 Hispanic/Latino; 2 Native Hawaiian or other Pacific Islander, non-Hispanic/Latino), 7 international. Average age 25. 8,141 applicants, 3% accepted, 129 enrolled. In 2019, 119 doctorates awarded. *Degree requirements:* For doctorate, thesis for third-year scholarly experience. *Entrance requirements:* For doctorate, MCAT. *Application deadline:* For fall admission, 10/15 for domestic students. Application fee: $85. Electronic applications accepted. *Financial support:* In 2019–20, 340 students received support. Scholarships/grants available. Financial award application deadline: 5/1; financial award applicants required to submit CSS PROFILE or FAFSA. *Unit head:* Dr. Edward G. Buckley, Vice Dean of Medical Education, 919-668-3381, Fax: 919-660-7040, E-mail: buckl002@mc.duke.edu. *Application contact:* Andrea Liu, Director of Admissions, 919-684-2985, Fax: 919-684-

8893, E-mail: medadm@mc.duke.edu. Website: http://www.dukemed.duke.edu/

**East Carolina University,** Brody School of Medicine, Professional Program in Medicine, Greenville, NC 27858-4353. Offers MD. *Accreditation:* LCME/AMA. *Entrance requirements:* For doctorate, MCAT, pre-med courses, interviews, faculty evaluations. *Application deadline:* For fall admission, 11/1 for domestic students. Applications are processed on a rolling basis. Electronic applications accepted. *Expenses:* Contact institution. *Financial support:* Institutionally sponsored loans and scholarships/grants available. *Unit head:* Dr. Mark Stacy, Vice Chancellor and Dean, 252-744-2201. *Application contact:* Office of Admissions Brody School of Medicine, 252-744-2202, Fax: 252-744-1926, E-mail: somadmissions@ecu.edu. Website: http://medicine.ecu.edu

**Eastern Virginia Medical School,** Professional Program in Medicine, Norfolk, VA 23501-1980. Offers MD, MD/MPH. *Accreditation:* LCME/AMA. *Entrance requirements:* For doctorate, MCAT, bachelor's degree or equivalent, course work in sciences. Electronic applications accepted.

**East Tennessee State University,** Quillen College of Medicine, Professional Program in Medicine, Johnson City, TN 37614. Offers MD. *Accreditation:* LCME/AMA. *Entrance requirements:* For doctorate, MCAT. Additional exam requirements/recommendations for international students: required—TOEFL (minimum score 550 paper-based).

**Emory University,** School of Medicine, Professional Program in Medicine, Atlanta, GA 30322-4510. Offers MD, MD/MA, MD/MPH, MD/MSCR, MD/PhD. *Accreditation:* LCME/AMA. *Degree requirements:* For doctorate, United States Medical Licensing Exam Step 1 and 2. *Entrance requirements:* For doctorate, MCAT, AMCAS application, supplemental application, interview (by invitation only). Electronic applications accepted. *Expenses:* Contact institution.

**Florida Atlantic University,** Charles E. Schmidt College of Medicine, Boca Raton, FL 33431-0991. Offers biomedical science (MS); medicine (MD). *Program availability:* Part-time. *Faculty:* 35 full-time (13 women), 1 part-time/adjunct (0 women). *Students:* 286 full-time (146 women), 31 part-time (18 women); includes 139 minority (27 Black or African American, non-Hispanic/Latino; 1 American Indian or Alaska Native, non-Hispanic/Latino; 53 Asian, non-Hispanic/Latino; 52 Hispanic/Latino; 6 Two or more races, non-Hispanic/Latino), 2 international. Average age 25. 3,233 applicants, 4% accepted, 87 enrolled. In 2019, 30 master's, 55 doctorates awarded. *Degree requirements:* For master's, thesis (for some programs); for doctorate, comprehensive exam. *Entrance requirements:* For master's, GRE, minimum GPA of 3.0; for doctorate, MCAT, AMCAS application, letters of recommendation, interview. *Application deadline:* For fall admission, 5/1 for domestic students, 3/15 for international students; for spring admission, 10/1 for domestic and international students. Application fee: $30. Electronic applications accepted. *Expenses:* Contact institution. *Financial support:* Fellowships and research assistantships available. Financial award applicants required to submit FAFSA. *Unit head:* Marc Kantorow, Assistant Dean, Graduate Programs, 561-297-2142, E-mail: mkantoro@health.fau.edu. *Application contact:* Marc Kantorow, Assistant Dean, Graduate Programs, 561-297-2142, E-mail: mkantoro@health.fau.edu. Website: http://med.fau.edu/

**Florida International University,** Herbert Wertheim College of Medicine, Miami, FL 33199. Offers biomedical sciences (PhD); medicine (MD); physician assistant studies (MPAS). *Accreditation:* LCME/AMA. *Faculty:* 75 full-time (36 women), 76 part-time/adjunct (23 women). *Students:* 632 full-time (366 women), 1 (woman) part-time; includes 416 minority (41 Black or African American, non-Hispanic/Latino; 112 Asian, non-Hispanic/Latino; 235 Hispanic/Latino; 28 Two or more races, non-Hispanic/Latino), 7 international. Average age 26. 5,124 applicants, 4% accepted, 171 enrolled. In 2019, 44 master's, 124 doctorates awarded. *Entrance requirements:* For doctorate, MCAT (minimum score of 25), minimum overall GPA of 3.0; 3 letters of recommendation, 2 from basic science faculty (biology, chemistry, physics, math) and 1 from any other faculty member. *Application deadline:* For fall admission, 12/15 for domestic students. Application fee: $160. Electronic applications accepted. *Expenses:* Contact institution. *Financial support:* Institutionally sponsored loans and scholarships/grants available. Financial award application deadline: 3/1; financial award applicants required to submit FAFSA. *Unit head:* Dr. Robert Sackstein, Dean, E-mail: med.admissions@fiu.edu. *Application contact:* Cristina M. Arabatzis, Assistant Director of Admissions, 305-348-0639, Fax: 305-348-0650, E-mail: carabatz@fiu.edu. Website: http://medicine.fiu.edu/

**Florida State University,** College of Medicine, Tallahassee, FL 32306. Offers MD, PhD. *Accreditation:* LCME/AMA. *Faculty:* 177 full-time (93 women), 68 part-time/adjunct (26 women). *Students:* 472 full-time (269 women), 8 part-time (6 women); includes 202 minority (51 Black or African American, non-Hispanic/Latino; 60 Asian, non-Hispanic/Latino; 38 Hispanic/Latino; 53 Two or more races, non-Hispanic/Latino). Average age 26. 7,313 applicants, 2% accepted, 120 enrolled. *Degree requirements:* For doctorate, comprehensive exam. *Entrance requirements:* For doctorate, MCAT (for MD), baccalaureate degree, letters of recommendation (for MD). *Application deadline:* Applications are processed on a rolling basis. Application fee: $30. Electronic applications accepted. *Expenses:* $1,120.41 student financial aid fee, $190.38 capital improvement trust fund fee, $284.40 athletics fee, $462.96 activity and service fee, $502.92 student health fee, $132.00 (first 2 years only) student facility use fee, $320.40 transportation fee, $189 technology fee, $690 equipment use fee, $347.81 material and supply fee, $10 FSUCard term fee (fall and spring only). *Financial support:* In 2019–20, 136 students received support. Scholarships/grants and tuition waivers (partial) available. Financial award application deadline: 6/30; financial award applicants required to submit FAFSA. *Unit head:* Dr. John Patrick Fogarty, MD, Dean, 850-644-1346, Fax: 850-645-1420, E-mail: john.fogarty@med.fsu.edu. *Application contact:* Davalda Bellot, Admissions Officer, 850-644-7904, Fax: 850-645-2846, E-mail: medadmissions@med.fsu.edu. Website: http://www.med.fsu.edu/

**Geisinger Commonwealth School of Medicine,** Professional Program in Medicine, Scranton, PA 18509. Offers MD, MD/MHA, MD/MPH. *Accreditation:* LCME/AMA. *Entrance requirements:* For doctorate, MCAT, bachelor's degree.

**Georgetown University,** School of Medicine, Washington, DC 20057. Offers MD, MD/MBA, MD/PhD. *Accreditation:* LCME/AMA. *Entrance requirements:* For doctorate, MCAT, minimum 90 credit hours with 1 year of course work in biology, organic chemistry, inorganic chemistry, physics, mathematics, and English. *Expenses:* Contact institution.

**The George Washington University,** School of Medicine and Health Sciences, Professional Program in Medicine, Washington, DC 20052. Offers MD. *Accreditation:*

LCME/AMA. *Entrance requirements:* For doctorate, MCAT, minimum of 90 undergraduate semester hours, specific pre-med courses equal to 38 semester hours.

**Harvard University,** Harvard Medical School, Professional Program in Medicine, Cambridge, MA 02138. Offers MD, PhD, MD/MBA, MD/MM Sc, MD/MPH, MD/MPP, MD/PhD. *Accreditation:* LCME/AMA. Electronic applications accepted.

**Hofstra University,** Donald and Barbara Zucker School of Medicine at Hofstra/Northwell, Hempstead, NY 11549. Offers medicine (MD); molecular basis of medicine (PhD); MD/MPH; MD/PhD. *Accreditation:* LCME/AMA. *Faculty:* 20 full-time (13 women), 15 part-time/adjunct (10 women). *Students:* 429 full-time (197 women); includes 195 minority (26 Black or African American, non-Hispanic/Latino; 108 Asian, non-Hispanic/Latino; 46 Hispanic/Latino; 4 Native Hawaiian or other Pacific Islander, non-Hispanic/Latino; 11 Two or more races, non-Hispanic/Latino), 2 international. Average age 25. 5,330 applicants, 7% accepted, 104 enrolled. In 2019, 98 doctorates awarded. *Entrance requirements:* For doctorate, MCAT, CASPER, Pre-med committee letter or 3 letters of recommendation. *Application deadline:* For fall admission, 12/1 priority date for domestic students. Applications are processed on a rolling basis. Application fee: $100. Electronic applications accepted. *Expenses:* $26,595 per term (tuition and fees) for MD rate. $13,250 per term (tuition and fees) for PHD rate. *Financial support:* In 2019–20, 352 students received support, including 347 fellowships with full and partial tuition reimbursements available (averaging $26,261 per year); research assistantships with full and partial tuition reimbursements available, career-related internships or fieldwork, Federal Work-Study, institutionally sponsored loans, scholarships/grants, tuition waivers (full and partial), unspecified assistantships, and scholarships and endowed scholarships also available. Support available to part-time students. Financial award applicants required to submit FAFSA. *Unit head:* Dr. Lawrence Smith, Dean, 516-463-7517, Fax: 516-463-7543, E-mail: lawrence.smith@hofstra.edu. *Application contact:* Sunil Samuel, Assistant Vice President of Admissions, 516-463-4723, Fax: 516-463-4664.
Website: http://medicine.hofstra.edu/index.html

**Howard University,** College of Medicine, Professional Program in Medicine, Washington, DC 20059-0002. Offers MD, PhD, MD/PhD. *Accreditation:* LCME/AMA.

**Icahn School of Medicine at Mount Sinai,** Department of Medical Education, New York, NY 10029-6504. Offers MD, MD/PhD. *Accreditation:* LCME/AMA. *Degree requirements:* For doctorate, comprehensive exam, United States Medical Licensing Examination Steps 1 and 2. *Entrance requirements:* For doctorate, MCAT. Additional exam requirements/recommendations for international students: required—TOEFL. Electronic applications accepted. *Expenses:* Contact institution.

**Indiana University-Purdue University Indianapolis,** Indiana University School of Medicine, Indianapolis, IN 46202-5114. Offers MS, MD, PhD, MD/MA, MD/MBA, MD/MS, MD/PhD. *Accreditation:* LCME/AMA. *Degree requirements:* For doctorate, thesis/dissertation (for some programs). *Entrance requirements:* For master's, GRE General Test; for doctorate, GRE General Test (for PhD); MCAT (for MD). Additional exam requirements/recommendations for international students: required—TOEFL. *Expenses:* Contact institution.

**Instituto Tecnologico de Santo Domingo,** School of Medicine, Santo Domingo, Dominican Republic. Offers M Bioethics, MD.

**Johns Hopkins University,** School of Medicine, Professional Program in Medicine, Baltimore, MD 21218. Offers MD, MD/PhD. *Accreditation:* LCME/AMA. *Entrance requirements:* For doctorate, MCAT. Electronic applications accepted.

**Loma Linda University,** School of Medicine, Loma Linda, CA 92350. Offers MS, MD, PhD. *Accreditation:* LCME/AMA. *Degree requirements:* For master's, thesis optional; for doctorate, thesis/dissertation (for some programs). *Entrance requirements:* For doctorate, MCAT (for MD). Additional exam requirements/recommendations for international students: required—TOEFL (minimum score 550 paper-based). *Expenses:* Contact institution.

**Louisiana State University Health Sciences Center,** School of Medicine in New Orleans, New Orleans, LA 70112-2223. Offers MPH, MD, MD/PhD. *Accreditation:* LCME/AMA. *Entrance requirements:* For doctorate, MCAT. Electronic applications accepted. *Expenses:* Contact institution.

**Louisiana State University Health Sciences Center at Shreveport,** School of Medicine, Shreveport, LA 71130-3932. Offers MD, MD/PhD. *Accreditation:* LCME/AMA. *Entrance requirements:* For doctorate, MCAT. *Expenses:* Contact institution.

**Marshall University,** Joan C. Edwards School of Medicine, MD Program, Huntington, WV 25701. Offers MD. *Accreditation:* LCME/AMA. *Degree requirements:* For doctorate, U. S. Medical Licensing Exam, Steps 1 and 2. *Entrance requirements:* For doctorate, MCAT, 1 year of course work in biology, physics, chemistry, organic chemistry, English, and social or behavioral sciences; 1 semester of biochemistry. Electronic applications accepted. *Expenses:* Contact institution.

**Mayo Clinic Alix School of Medicine,** Professional Program, Rochester, MN 55905. Offers MD, MD/Certificate, MD/PhD. *Accreditation:* LCME/AMA. *Entrance requirements:* For doctorate, MCAT, previous undergraduate course work in biology, chemistry, physics, and biochemistry. Electronic applications accepted.

**McGill University,** Faculty of Graduate and Postdoctoral Studies, Faculty of Medicine, Department of Surgery, Montréal, QC H3A 2T5, Canada. Offers M Sc, PhD.

**McGill University,** Professional Program in Medicine, Montréal, QC H3A 2T5, Canada. Offers MD/CM, MD/MBA, MD/PhD. *Accreditation:* LCME/AMA.

**Medical College of Wisconsin,** Medical School, Professional Program in Medicine, Milwaukee, WI 53226. Offers MD, MD/MPH, MD/MS, MD/PhD. *Accreditation:* LCME/AMA. *Students:* 977 full-time (484 women), 3 part-time (1 woman); includes 284 minority (42 Black or African American, non-Hispanic/Latino; 1 American Indian or Alaska Native, non-Hispanic/Latino; 124 Asian, non-Hispanic/Latino; 78 Hispanic/Latino; 3 Native Hawaiian or other Pacific Islander, non-Hispanic/Latino; 36 Two or more races, non-Hispanic/Latino), 34 international. Average age 25. 5,712 applicants, 9% accepted, 252 enrolled. In 2019, 229 doctorates awarded. *Entrance requirements:* For doctorate, GRE, MCAT, official transcripts, three letters of recommendation. Additional exam requirements/recommendations for international students: required—TOEFL. *Application deadline:* For fall admission, 11/1 for domestic students. Applications are processed on a rolling basis. Application fee: $100. Electronic applications accepted. *Expenses:* Tuition: Full-time $55,130; part-time $1056 per credit. *Required fees:* $555.50. One-time fee: $72 full-time; $50 part-time. Tuition and fees vary according to degree level and program. *Financial support:* In 2019–20, 27 fellowships with full tuition reimbursements (averaging $55,130 per year) were awarded. Financial award application deadline: 2/1; financial award applicants required to submit FAFSA. *Unit head:* Joseph E. Kerschner, MD, Provost/Executive Vice President/Dean, 414-955-8739. *Application contact:* Alexis C Meyer, Director of Recruitment and Admissions, 414-456-8246, E-mail: medschool@mcw.edu.
Website: https://www.mcw.edu/education/medical-school

**Medical University of South Carolina,** College of Medicine, Charleston, SC 29425. Offers MD, MD/MBA, MD/MHA, MD/MPH, MD/MSCR, MD/PhD. *Accreditation:* LCME/AMA. *Degree requirements:* For doctorate, Steps 1 and 2 of Clinical Performance Exam

and U.S. Medical Licensing Examination. *Entrance requirements:* For doctorate, MCAT, interview. Electronic applications accepted. *Expenses:* Contact institution.

**Meharry Medical College,** School of Medicine, Nashville, TN 37208-9989. Offers MD. *Accreditation:* LCME/AMA. *Entrance requirements:* For doctorate, MCAT. *Application deadline:* For fall admission, 12/15 for domestic students. Applications are processed on a rolling basis. Application fee: $65. Electronic applications accepted. *Financial support:* Federal Work-Study, institutionally sponsored loans, and tuition waivers (partial) available. Financial award applicants required to submit FAFSA. *Unit head:* Dr. Digna Forbes, Interim Dean, 615-327-6204, E-mail: dforbes@mmc.edu. *Application contact:* Dr. Theodora Pinnock, Associate Dean of Student Affairs & Admissions, 615-327-6057, E-mail: tpinnock@mmc.edu.
Website: https://home.mmc.edu/school-of-medicine/

**Mercer University,** School of Medicine, Macon, GA 31207. Offers MFT, MPH, MSA, MD. *Accreditation:* AAMFT/COAMFTE; LCME/AMA (one or more programs are accredited). *Students:* 586 full-time (307 women), 11 part-time (9 women); includes 193 minority (59 Black or African American, non-Hispanic/Latino; 1 American Indian or Alaska Native, non-Hispanic/Latino; 93 Asian, non-Hispanic/Latino; 29 Hispanic/Latino; 11 Two or more races, non-Hispanic/Latino). Average age 25. 1,060 applicants, 24% accepted, 174 enrolled. In 2019, 63 master's, 108 doctorates awarded. *Entrance requirements:* For master's, Varies by program. Please see https://medicine.mercer.edu/, Varies by program. Please see https://medicine.mercer.edu/; for doctorate, Varies by program. Please see https://medicine.mercer.edu/. Additional exam requirements/recommendations for international students: required—TOEFL. *Application deadline:* For fall admission, 1/15 for domestic students, 10/1 for international students. Applications are processed on a rolling basis. Application fee: $50 ($150 for international students). Tuition and fees vary according to degree level, campus/location and program. *Financial support:* Institutionally sponsored loans available. Financial award application deadline: 4/1; financial award applicants required to submit FAFSA. *Unit head:* Dr. Jean Sumner, Dean, 478-301-5571, Fax: 478-301-2547, E-mail: sumner_jr@mercer.edu. *Application contact:* Ariel Morgan, Assistant Director for Admission, 478-301-5425, Fax: 478-301-2547, E-mail: morgan_ac@mercer.edu.
Website: http://medicine.mercer.edu

**Michigan State University,** College of Human Medicine, Professional Program in Human Medicine, East Lansing, MI 48824. Offers human medicine (MD); human medicine/medical scientist training program (MD). *Accreditation:* LCME/AMA. *Entrance requirements:* Additional exam requirements/recommendations for international students: required—TOEFL, Michigan State University ELT ( minimum score 85), Michigan Michigan English Language Assessment Battery (minimum score 83). Electronic applications accepted.

**Morehouse School of Medicine,** Professional Program, Atlanta, GA 30310-1495. Offers MD, MD/MPH. *Accreditation:* LCME/AMA. *Degree requirements:* For doctorate, U.S. Medical Licensing Exam Steps 1 and 2. *Entrance requirements:* For doctorate, MCAT. Electronic applications accepted. *Expenses:* Contact institution.

**New York Medical College,** School of Medicine, Valhalla, NY 10595-1691. Offers MD, MD/MPH, MD/PhD. *Accreditation:* LCME/AMA. *Faculty:* 1,077 full-time (439 women), 1,023 part-time/adjunct (373 women). *Students:* 862 full-time (493 women); includes 376 minority (54 Black or African American, non-Hispanic/Latino; 220 Asian, non-Hispanic/Latino; 77 Hispanic/Latino; 25 Two or more races, non-Hispanic/Latino), 8 international. Average age 26. 12,845 applicants, 4% accepted, 215 enrolled. In 2019, 200 doctorates awarded. *Entrance requirements:* For doctorate, MCAT, 2 semesters of course work in general biology, general chemistry, organic chemistry, physics, and English. *Application deadline:* For fall admission, 1/31 for domestic and international students. Applications are processed on a rolling basis. Application fee: $130. Electronic applications accepted. *Expenses:* MD Tuition is $54,580. MD Fees are $3,447. *Financial support:* In 2019–20, 404 students received support. Federal Work-Study, institutionally sponsored loans, scholarships/grants, unspecified assistantships, and Federal Student Loans available. Financial award application deadline: 4/30; financial award applicants required to submit FAFSA. *Unit head:* Jennifer Koestler, MD, Senior Associate Dean for Medical Education, 914-594-4500, E-mail: jennifer_koestler@nymc.edu. *Application contact:* James DeMaio, Director of Admissions, 914-594-4507, Fax: 914-594-4613, E-mail: mdadmit@nymc.edu.
Website: http://www.nymc.edu/

**New York University,** School of Medicine, New York, NY 10012. Offers MS, MD, PhD, MD/MA, MD/MBA, MD/MPA, MD/MPH, MD/PhD. *Accreditation:* LCME/AMA (one or more programs are accredited). *Entrance requirements:* For doctorate, MCAT (for MD). Electronic applications accepted. *Expenses:* Contact institution.

**Northeast Ohio Medical University,** College of Medicine, Rootstown, OH 44272-0095. Offers MD. *Accreditation:* LCME/AMA. *Faculty:* 137 full-time (53 women), 1,984 part-time/adjunct (652 women). *Students:* 586 full-time (313 women); includes 286 minority (19 Black or African American, non-Hispanic/Latino; 224 Asian, non-Hispanic/Latino; 15 Hispanic/Latino; 28 Two or more races, non-Hispanic/Latino). Average age 24. 4,069 applicants, 5% accepted, 151 enrolled. In 2019, 154 doctorates awarded. *Degree requirements:* For doctorate, U. S. Medical Licensing Exam Step 2. *Entrance requirements:* For doctorate, MCAT, two semesters each of organic chemistry and lab, physics and lab, and biology and lab; one semester of biochemistry. *Application deadline:* For fall admission, 8/1 priority date for domestic students; for winter admission, 10/1 for domestic students. Applications are processed on a rolling basis. Application fee: $95. Electronic applications accepted. *Expenses:* Student Health and Fitness, Student Activities, Matriculation Fee, Academic Software/Hardware, Credentialing, Testing, Lab fees. *Financial support:* In 2019–20, 185 students received support. Institutionally sponsored loans, scholarships/grants, tuition waivers, and Service Scholarships/Forgivable Loans available. Financial award application deadline: 3/15; financial award applicants required to submit FAFSA. *Unit head:* Dr. Elisabeth H. Young, Dean, 330-325-6122, Fax: 330-325-5941, E-mail: eyoung1@neomed.edu. *Application contact:* James Barrett, Sr. Executive Director, Strategic Enrollment Initiative, 330-325-6274, E-mail: admission@neomed.edu.
Website: https://www.neomed.edu/medicine/

**Northwestern University,** Feinberg School of Medicine, Combined MD/PhD Medical Scientist Training Program, Evanston, IL 60208. Offers MD/PhD. *Accreditation:* LCME/AMA. Electronic applications accepted.

**Nova Southeastern University,** Dr. Kiran C. Patel College of Allopathic Medicine, Fort Lauderdale, FL 33314-7796. Offers MD. *Faculty:* 18 full-time (11 women), 3 part-time/adjunct (2 women). *Students:* 104 full-time (41 women); includes 42 minority (1 Black or African American, non-Hispanic/Latino; 30 Asian, non-Hispanic/Latino; 8 Hispanic/Latino; 3 Two or more races, non-Hispanic/Latino). Average age 25. Electronic applications accepted. Tuition and fees vary according to course load, degree level and program. *Financial support:* Applicants required to submit FAFSA. *Unit head:* Dr. Johannes Vieweg, MD, Dean, 954-262-1501, E-mail: jvieweg@nova.edu. *Application contact:* Paula Wales, Executive Associate Dean, Academic and Student Affairs/Professor, 954-262-1074, E-mail: pwales@nova.edu.
Website: http://md.nova.edu/

## Allopathic Medicine

**The Ohio State University,** College of Medicine, Professional Program in Medicine, Columbus, OH 43210. Offers MD, MD/PhD. *Accreditation:* LCME/AMA. *Entrance requirements:* For doctorate, MCAT. Electronic applications accepted.

**Oregon Health & Science University,** School of Medicine, Professional Program in Medicine, Portland, OR 97239-3098. Offers MD, MD/MPH, MD/PhD. *Accreditation:* LCME/AMA. *Degree requirements:* For doctorate, thesis/dissertation (for some programs), National Board Exam Parts I and II. *Entrance requirements:* For doctorate, MCAT, 1 year of course work in biology, English, social science and physics; 2 years of course work in chemistry and genetics. Electronic applications accepted.

**Penn State Hershey Medical Center,** College of Medicine, Hershey, PA 17033. Offers MPAS, MPH, MS, Dr PH, MD, PhD, MD/PhD, PhD/MBA. *Accreditation:* LCME/AMA. Terminal master's awarded for partial completion of doctoral program. *Degree requirements:* For master's, thesis optional; for doctorate, comprehensive exam, thesis/dissertation, minimum GPA of 3.0 (for PhD). *Entrance requirements:* For master's, GRE; for doctorate, GRE (for PhD); MCAT (for MD). Additional exam requirements/recommendations for international students: required—TOEFL (minimum score 560 paper-based; 81 iBT). Electronic applications accepted. *Expenses:* Contact institution.

**Pontificia Universidad Catolica Madre y Maestra,** Department of Medicine, Santiago, Dominican Republic. Offers MD.

**Queen's University at Kingston,** School of Medicine, Professional Program in Medicine, Kingston, ON K7L 3N6, Canada. Offers MD. *Accreditation:* LCME/AMA. *Entrance requirements:* For doctorate, MCAT.

**Quinnipiac University,** Frank H. Netter MD School of Medicine, MD Program, Hamden, CT 06518. Offers MD. *Accreditation:* LCME/AMA. *Faculty:* 28 full-time (12 women). *Students:* 387 full-time (221 women); includes 166 minority (37 Black or African American, non-Hispanic/Latino; 1 American Indian or Alaska Native, non-Hispanic/Latino; 94 Asian, non-Hispanic/Latino; 33 Hispanic/Latino; 1 Native Hawaiian or other Pacific Islander, non-Hispanic/Latino). Average age 27. 7,701 applicants, 4% accepted, 94 enrolled. In 2019, 85 doctorates awarded. *Degree requirements:* For doctorate, capstone project. *Entrance requirements:* For doctorate, MCAT. *Application deadline:* For fall admission, 12/1 for domestic students. Applications are processed on a rolling basis. Application fee: $100. Electronic applications accepted. *Expenses:* $60,610. *Financial support:* In 2019–20, 220 students received support. Institutionally sponsored loans and scholarships/grants available. Financial award application deadline: 3/1; financial award applicants required to submit FAFSA. *Unit head:* Dr. Bruce Koeppen, Dean, 203-582-5301, E-mail: brucedean.koeppen@quinnipiac.edu. *Application contact:* Michael Cole, Director of Admissions Operations, 203-582-6562, E-mail: michael.cole@quinnipiac.edu.
Website: https://www.qu.edu/schools/medicine/academics/md-program.html

**Rosalind Franklin University of Medicine and Science,** Chicago Medical School, North Chicago, IL 60064-3095. Offers MD, MD/MS, MD/PhD. *Accreditation:* LCME/AMA. *Degree requirements:* For doctorate, clerkship, step 1 and step 2 exams. *Entrance requirements:* For doctorate, MCAT, 3 years of course work with lab in biology, physics, inorganic chemistry, and organic chemistry. *Expenses:* Contact institution.

**Rowan University,** Cooper Medical School, Glassboro, NJ 08028-1701. Offers MD. *Accreditation:* LCME/AMA. *Expenses: Tuition, area resident:* Part-time $715.50 per semester hour. Tuition, state resident: part-time $715.50 per semester hour. Tuition, nonresident: part-time $715.50 per semester hour. *Required fees:* $161.55 per semester hour.

**Rush University,** Rush Medical College, Chicago, IL 60612. Offers MD. *Accreditation:* LCME/AMA. *Faculty:* 1,634. *Students:* 553 full-time (276 women); includes 221 minority (35 Black or African American, non-Hispanic/Latino; 112 Asian, non-Hispanic/Latino; 50 Hispanic/Latino; 24 Two or more races, non-Hispanic/Latino). Average age 26. 9,099 applicants, 3% accepted, 144 enrolled. In 2019, 120 doctorates awarded. *Degree requirements:* For doctorate, USMLE Step 1, Step 2 CK, Step 2 CS. *Entrance requirements:* For doctorate, MCAT, on-campus interview. *Application deadline:* For fall admission, 11/1 for domestic students. Applications are processed on a rolling basis. Application fee: $100. Electronic applications accepted. *Expenses:* Contact institution. *Financial support:* In 2019–20, 317 students received support. Federal Work-Study, institutionally sponsored loans, and scholarships/grants available. Financial award applicants required to submit FAFSA. *Unit head:* Dr. Cynthia E. Boyd, Assistant Dean, Admissions and Recruitment, 312-942-6915, E-mail: rmc_admissions@rush.edu. *Application contact:* Dr. Cynthia E. Boyd, Assistant Dean, Admissions and Recruitment, 312-942-6915, E-mail: rmc_admissions@rush.edu.
Website: https://www.rushu.rush.edu/rush-medical-college

**Rutgers University - Newark,** New Jersey Medical School, Newark, NJ 07101-1709. Offers MD, MD/Certificate, MD/JD, MD/MBA, MD/MPH, MD/PhD. *Accreditation:* LCME/AMA. *Entrance requirements:* For doctorate, MCAT. Additional exam requirements/recommendations for international students: required—TOEFL. Electronic applications accepted. *Expenses:* Contact institution.

**Rutgers University - New Brunswick,** Robert Wood Johnson Medical School, Piscataway, NJ 08822. Offers MD, MD/JD, MD/MBA, MD/MPH, MD/MS, MD/MSJ, MD/PhD. *Accreditation:* LCME/AMA (one or more programs are accredited). *Entrance requirements:* For doctorate, MCAT. Additional exam requirements/recommendations for international students: required—TOEFL. Electronic applications accepted. *Expenses:* Contact institution.

**Saint Louis University,** Graduate Programs, School of Medicine, Professional Program in Medicine, St. Louis, MO 63103. Offers MD. *Accreditation:* LCME/AMA. *Degree requirements:* For doctorate, U.S. Medical Licensing Exam Steps 1 and 2. *Entrance requirements:* For doctorate, MCAT, photograph, letters of recommendation, interview. Additional exam requirements/recommendations for international students: required—TOEFL (minimum score 525 paper-based). Electronic applications accepted. *Expenses:* Contact institution.

**San Juan Bautista School of Medicine,** Graduate and Professional Programs, Caguas, PR 00726-4968. Offers MPH, MD. *Accreditation:* LCME/AMA. *Degree requirements:* For doctorate, comprehensive exam, United States Medical Licensing Exam Steps I and II. *Entrance requirements:* For master's, bachelor's degree from university or college accredited by the Council of Higher Education of Puerto Rico or by a renowned accrediting agency that is registered at the Federal Education Department; minimum GPA of 2.5; for doctorate, MCAT, interview.

**Seton Hall University,** School of Medicine, Nutley, NJ 07110. Offers MD.

**Stanford University,** School of Medicine, Professional Program in Medicine, Stanford, CA 94305-2004. Offers MD, MD/PhD. *Accreditation:* LCME/AMA. *Expenses: Tuition:* Full-time $52,479; part-time $34,110 per unit. *Required fees:* $672; $224 per quarter. Tuition and fees vary according to program and student level.

**State University of New York Downstate Medical Center,** College of Medicine, Brooklyn, NY 11203-2098. Offers MPH, MD, MD/MPH, MD/PhD. *Accreditation:* LCME/AMA. *Entrance requirements:* For doctorate, MCAT. *Expenses:* Contact institution.

**State University of New York Downstate Medical Center,** School of Graduate Studies, MD/PhD Program, Brooklyn, NY 11203-2098. Offers MD/PhD. *Accreditation:*

LCME/AMA. *Entrance requirements:* Additional exam requirements/recommendations for international students: recommended—TOEFL.

**State University of New York Upstate Medical University,** College of Medicine, Syracuse, NY 13210. Offers MD, MD/PhD. *Accreditation:* LCME/AMA. *Degree requirements:* For doctorate, comprehensive exam. *Entrance requirements:* For doctorate, MCAT. Additional exam requirements/recommendations for international students: required—TOEFL. Electronic applications accepted. *Expenses:* Contact institution.

**Stony Brook University, State University of New York,** Stony Brook Medicine, Renaissance School of Medicine, Medical Scientist Training Program, Stony Brook, NY 11794-8651. Offers MD/PhD. *Entrance requirements:* Additional exam requirements/recommendations for international students: required—TOEFL. *Application deadline:* For fall admission, 12/1 for domestic students. *Expenses: Tuition, area resident:* Full-time $11,310; part-time $471 per credit. Tuition, state resident: full-time $11,310; part-time $471 per credit. Tuition, nonresident: full-time $23,100; part-time $963 per credit. *International tuition:* $23,100 full-time. *Required fees:* $2247.50. *Financial support:* Tuition waivers (full) available. *Unit head:* Dr. Michael A. Frohman, Director, 631-444-3050, Fax: 631-444-9749, E-mail: michael.frohman@stonybrook.edu. *Application contact:* Alison Gibbons, Program Administrator, 631-444-3051, Fax: 631-444-3492, E-mail: alison.gibbons@stonybrook.edu.
Website: https://renaissance.stonybrookmedicine.edu/mstp/program

**Stony Brook University, State University of New York,** Stony Brook Medicine, Renaissance School of Medicine, Professional Program in Medicine, Stony Brook, NY 11794. Offers MD, MD/PhD. *Accreditation:* LCME/AMA. *Faculty:* 964 full-time (465 women), 137 part-time/adjunct (96 women). *Students:* 564 full-time (273 women); includes 264 minority (24 Black or African American, non-Hispanic/Latino; 1 American Indian or Alaska Native, non-Hispanic/Latino; 180 Asian, non-Hispanic/Latino; 46 Hispanic/Latino; 13 Two or more races, non-Hispanic/Latino), 26 international. Average age 25. 5,241 applicants, 8% accepted, 136 enrolled. In 2019, 130 doctorates awarded. *Entrance requirements:* For doctorate, MCAT, interview. Additional exam requirements/recommendations for international students: required—TOEFL. *Application deadline:* For fall admission, 12/1 for domestic students. Application fee: $100. Electronic applications accepted. *Expenses:* Contact institution. *Financial support:* Fellowships available. *Unit head:* Dr. Kenneth Kaushansky, Dean & Senior Vice President, Health Sciences, 631-444-2121, Fax: 631-444-6621, E-mail: kenneth.kaushansky@stonybrook.edu. *Application contact:* Committee on Admissions, 631-444-2113, Fax: 631-444-6032, E-mail: somadmissions@stonybrookmedicine.edu.
Website: https://medicine.stonybrookmedicine.edu/

**Temple University,** Lewis Katz School of Medicine, Doctor of Medicine Program, Philadelphia, PA 19140. Offers MD, MD/MA, MD/MBA, MD/MPH, MD/PhD. *Accreditation:* LCME/AMA. *Degree requirements:* For doctorate, United States Medical Licensing Exam Step 1, Step 2CK, Step 2CS. *Entrance requirements:* For doctorate, MCAT. Electronic applications accepted. *Expenses:* Contact institution.

**Texas A&M University,** College of Medicine, Bryan, TX 77843. Offers medical sciences (PhD); medicine (MD). *Accreditation:* LCME/AMA. *Degree requirements:* For doctorate, comprehensive exam (for some programs), thesis/dissertation (for some programs), United States Medical Licensing Exam Steps 1 and 2 (for MD). *Entrance requirements:* For doctorate, GRE General Test (for PhD); MCAT (for MD), TMDSAS Application; letters of recommendation; official transcripts. Electronic applications accepted. *Expenses:* Contact institution.

**Texas Tech University Health Sciences Center,** School of Medicine, Lubbock, TX 79430-0002. Offers MD, JD/MD, MD/MBA, MD/PhD. *Accreditation:* LCME/AMA. *Entrance requirements:* For doctorate, MCAT. Additional exam requirements/recommendations for international students: required—TOEFL. Electronic applications accepted. *Expenses:* Contact institution.

**Texas Tech University Health Sciences Center El Paso,** Paul L. Foster School of Medicine, El Paso, TX 79905. Offers MD. *Accreditation:* LCME/AMA.

**Thomas Jefferson University,** Jefferson College of Life Sciences, MD/PhD Program, Philadelphia, PA 19107. Offers MD/PhD. *Entrance requirements:* Additional exam requirements/recommendations for international students: required—TOEFL (minimum score 100 iBT) or IELTS (7.0). Electronic applications accepted.

**Thomas Jefferson University,** Sidney Kimmel Medical College, Philadelphia, PA 19107. Offers MD, MD/PhD. *Accreditation:* LCME/AMA. *Entrance requirements:* For doctorate, MCAT. Electronic applications accepted. *Expenses:* Contact institution.

**Tufts University,** School of Medicine, Professional Program in Medicine, Medford, MA 02155. Offers MD, MD/MA, MD/MBA, MD/MPH, MD/PhD. *Accreditation:* LCME/AMA. *Entrance requirements:* For doctorate, MCAT. Electronic applications accepted. *Expenses:* Contact institution.

**Tulane University,** School of Medicine, Professional Programs in Medicine, New Orleans, LA 70118-5669. Offers MD, MD/MBA, MD/MPH, MD/MPHTM, MD/MSPH, MD/PhD. *Accreditation:* LCME/AMA. *Entrance requirements:* For doctorate, MCAT. *Expenses: Tuition:* Full-time $57,004; part-time $3167 per credit hour. *Required fees:* $2086; $44.50 per credit hour. $80 per term. Tuition and fees vary according to course load, degree level and program.

**Uniformed Services University of the Health Sciences,** F. Edward Hebert School of Medicine, Bethesda, MD 20814. Offers MPH, MS, MSPH, MTMH, Dr PH, MD, PhD. *Accreditation:* LCME/AMA. Terminal master's awarded for partial completion of doctoral program. *Degree requirements:* For master's, comprehensive exam, thesis or alternative; for doctorate, comprehensive exam (for some programs), thesis/dissertation (for some programs). *Entrance requirements:* For master's, GRE General Test. Additional exam requirements/recommendations for international students: required—TOEFL.

**Universidad Autonoma de Guadalajara,** School of Medicine, Guadalajara, Mexico. Offers MD.

**Universidad Central del Caribe,** School of Medicine, Bayamón, PR 00960-6032. Offers MA, MS, MD, PhD. *Accreditation:* LCME/AMA. *Degree requirements:* For doctorate, variable foreign language requirement. *Entrance requirements:* For doctorate, MCAT (for MD).

**Universidad Central del Este,** Medical School, San Pedro de Macoris, Dominican Republic. Offers MD.

**Universidad de Ciencias Medicas,** Graduate Programs, San Jose, Costa Rica. Offers dermatology (SP); family health (MS); health service center administration (MHA); human anatomy (MS); medical and surgery (MD); occupational medicine (MS); pharmacy (Pharm D). *Program availability:* Part-time. *Degree requirements:* For master's, thesis; for doctorate and SP, comprehensive exam. *Entrance requirements:* For master's, MD or bachelor's degree; for doctorate, admissions test; for SP, admissions test, MD.

**Universidad de Iberoamerica,** Graduate School, San Jose, Costa Rica. Offers clinical neuropsychology (PhD); clinical psychology (M Psych); educational psychology

(M Psych); forensic psychology (M Psych); hospital management (MHA); intensive care nursing (MN); medicine (MD).

**Universidad Iberoamericana,** School of Medicine, Santo Domingo D.N., Dominican Republic. Offers MD.

**Universidad Nacional Pedro Henriquez Urena,** School of Medicine, Santo Domingo, Dominican Republic. Offers MD.

**Université de Montréal,** Faculty of Medicine, Professional Program in Medicine, Montréal, QC H3C 3J7, Canada. Offers MD. *Accreditation:* LCME/AMA. *Entrance requirements:* For doctorate, proficiency in French. Electronic applications accepted.

**Université de Sherbrooke,** Faculty of Medicine and Health Sciences, Professional Program in Medicine, Sherbrooke, QC J1K 2R1, Canada. Offers MD. *Accreditation:* LCME/AMA. Electronic applications accepted.

**University at Buffalo, the State University of New York,** Graduate School, Jacobs School of Medicine and Biomedical Sciences, Professional Program in Medicine, Buffalo, NY 14203-1121. Offers MD, MD/MBA, MD/MPH, MD/PhD. *Accreditation:* LCME/AMA. *Students:* 619 full-time (308 women); includes 215 minority (15 Black or African American, non-Hispanic/Latino; 1 American Indian or Alaska Native, non-Hispanic/Latino; 110 Asian, non-Hispanic/Latino; 56 Hispanic/Latino; 33 Two or more races, non-Hispanic/Latino). Average age 24. 3,823 applicants, 10% accepted, 180 enrolled. In 2019, 140 doctorates awarded. *Entrance requirements:* For doctorate, MCAT. *Application deadline:* For fall admission, 11/15 for domestic students. Applications are processed on a rolling basis. Application fee: $65. Electronic applications accepted. Application fee is waived when completed online. *Expenses: Tuition, area resident:* Full-time $11,310; part-time $471 per credit hour. Tuition, state resident: full-time $11,310; part-time $471 per credit hour. Tuition, nonresident: full-time $23,100; part-time $963 per credit hour. *International tuition:* $23,100 full-time. *Required fees:* $2820. *Financial support:* Application deadline: 6/15; applicants required to submit FAFSA. *Unit head:* Dr. David A. Milling, Senior Associate Dean for Student and Academic Affairs, 716-829-2802 Ext. 2381, Fax: 716-829-2798, E-mail: dmilling@buffalo.edu. *Application contact:* Dr. David A. Milling, Senior Associate Dean for Student and Academic Affairs, 716-829-2802 Ext. 2381, Fax: 716-829-2798, E-mail: dmilling@buffalo.edu.
Website: http://medicine.buffalo.edu/education/md.html

**The University of Alabama at Birmingham,** School of Medicine, Birmingham, AL 35294. Offers MD, MD/PhD. *Accreditation:* LCME/AMA (one or more programs are accredited). *Faculty:* 107 full-time (54 women), 47 part-time/adjunct (24 women). *Students:* 780 full-time (346 women); includes 177 minority (33 Black or African American, non-Hispanic/Latino; 6 American Indian or Alaska Native, non-Hispanic/Latino; 71 Asian, non-Hispanic/Latino; 3 Hispanic/Latino; 64 Two or more races, non-Hispanic/Latino). Average age 25. 3,768 applicants, 7% accepted, 186 enrolled. In 2019, 181 doctorates awarded. *Entrance requirements:* For doctorate, MCAT (minimum score of 24), AMCAS application, letters of recommendation, interview, U.S. citizenship or permanent residency. *Application deadline:* For fall admission, 11/1 for domestic students. Application fee: $80. Electronic applications accepted. *Expenses:* Contact institution. *Financial support:* In 2019–20, 233 students received support. Career-related internships or fieldwork and scholarships/grants available. Financial award application deadline: 5/1; financial award applicants required to submit FAFSA. *Unit head:* Dr. Selwyn M. Vickers, Senior Vice President/Dean, School of Medicine, 205-934-1111, Fax: 205-934-0333. *Application contact:* Dr. Selwyn M. Vickers, Senior Vice President/Dean, School of Medicine, 205-934-1111, Fax: 205-934-0333.
Website: http://www.uab.edu/medicine/home/

**University of Alberta,** Faculty of Medicine and Dentistry, Professional Program in Medicine, Edmonton, AB T6G 2E1, Canada. Offers MD. *Accreditation:* LCME/AMA. Electronic applications accepted.

**The University of Arizona,** College of Medicine, Professional Programs in Medicine, Tucson, AZ 85721. Offers MD, PhD. *Accreditation:* LCME/AMA. *Entrance requirements:* For doctorate, MCAT, previous course work in general chemistry, organic chemistry, biology/zoology, physics, and English.

**The University of Arizona,** College of Medicine, Program in Medical Sciences, Tucson, AZ 85721. Offers MS, PhD. *Accreditation:* LCME/AMA. *Degree requirements:* For doctorate, comprehensive exam, thesis/dissertation.

**University of Arkansas for Medical Sciences,** College of Medicine, Little Rock, AR 72205-7199. Offers MD, MD/PhD. *Accreditation:* LCME/AMA. *Entrance requirements:* For doctorate, MCAT. Electronic applications accepted. *Expenses:* Contact institution.

**The University of British Columbia,** Faculty of Medicine, Department of Surgery, Vancouver, BC V5Z 1M9, Canada. Offers M Sc. *Program availability:* Part-time. *Degree requirements:* For master's, thesis. *Entrance requirements:* Additional exam requirements/recommendations for international students: required—TOEFL. Electronic applications accepted. *Expenses:* Contact institution.

**The University of British Columbia,** Faculty of Medicine, MD/PhD Program, Vancouver, BC V6T 1Z3, Canada. Offers MD/PhD. *Entrance requirements:* Additional exam requirements/recommendations for international students: required—TOEFL. Electronic applications accepted. *Expenses:* Contact institution.

**The University of British Columbia,** Faculty of Medicine, Professional Program in Medicine, Vancouver, BC V6T 1Z1, Canada. Offers MD, MD/PhD. *Accreditation:* LCME/AMA. *Entrance requirements:* For doctorate, MCAT.

**University of Calgary,** Cumming School of Medicine, Program in Community Medicine, Calgary, AB T2N 4N1, Canada. Offers MD. *Accreditation:* LCME/AMA. *Entrance requirements:* For doctorate, MCAT. Electronic applications accepted.

**University of California, Berkeley,** Graduate Division, School of Public Health, Group in Health and Medical Sciences, Berkeley, CA 94720. Offers MD/MS. Electronic applications accepted.

**University of California, Davis,** School of Medicine, Sacramento, CA 95817. Offers MD, MD/MBA, MD/MPH, MD/MS, MD/PhD. *Accreditation:* LCME/AMA. *Degree requirements:* For doctorate, comprehensive exam. *Entrance requirements:* For doctorate, MCAT, 1 year each of English, biological science (lower-division with lab), general chemistry (with lab), organic chemistry (with lab), physics and college-level math, plus 1/2 year upper-division biology. Electronic applications accepted. *Expenses:* Contact institution.

**University of California, Irvine,** School of Medicine, Professional Program in Medicine, Irvine, CA 92697. Offers MD, MD/MBA, MD/MPH, MD/PhD. *Accreditation:* LCME/AMA. *Students:* 414 full-time (217 women), 30 part-time (11 women); includes 40 minority (3 Black or African American, non-Hispanic/Latino; 21 Asian, non-Hispanic/Latino; 16 Hispanic/Latino). Average age 26. In 2019, 110 doctorates awarded. *Entrance requirements:* For doctorate, MCAT. Additional exam requirements/recommendations for international students: required—TOEFL (minimum score 550 paper-based). *Application deadline:* For fall admission, 11/1 for domestic students. Application fee: $120 ($140 for international students). Electronic applications accepted. *Financial support:* Fellowships, institutionally sponsored loans, traineeships, health care benefits, and unspecified assistantships available. Financial award application deadline: 3/1;

financial award applicants required to submit FAFSA. *Unit head:* Ellena Peterson, Associate Dean, 949-824-4169, Fax: 949-824-2160, E-mail: ellena.peterson@uci.edu. *Application contact:* Frances Stephens, Admissions Counselor, 949-824-4614, E-mail: fran.stephens@uci.edu.
Website: http://www.som.uci.edu/graduate-studies/education/md-degree.asp

**University of California, Los Angeles,** David Geffen School of Medicine, Professional Program in Medicine, Los Angeles, CA 90095. Offers MD, MD/MBA, MD/PhD. *Accreditation:* LCME/AMA. *Entrance requirements:* For doctorate, MCAT, interview. *Expenses:* Contact institution.

**University of California, Riverside,** School of Medicine, Riverside, CA 92521-0102. Offers MD. *Accreditation:* LCME/AMA.

**University of California, San Diego,** School of Medicine, Professional Program in Medicine, La Jolla, CA 92093. Offers MD, MD/PhD. *Accreditation:* LCME/AMA. *Students:* 528. *Entrance requirements:* For doctorate, MCAT. *Application deadline:* For fall admission, 11/1 for domestic students. Application fee: $90. *Expenses:* Contact institution. *Unit head:* Dr. Carolyn J. Kelly, MD, Associate Dean, Admissions and Student Affairs. *Application contact:* 858-534-3880, E-mail: somadmissions@ucsd.edu.

**University of California, San Francisco,** School of Medicine, San Francisco, CA 94143-0410. Offers MD, PhD, MD/MPH, MD/MS, MD/PhD. *Accreditation:* LCME/AMA (one or more programs are accredited). *Entrance requirements:* For doctorate, MCAT (for MD), interview (for MD). Electronic applications accepted. *Expenses:* Contact institution.

**University of Central Florida,** College of Medicine, Orlando, FL 32816. Offers MS, MD, PhD. *Accreditation:* LCME/AMA. *Faculty:* 143 full-time (66 women), 22 part-time/adjunct (10 women). *Students:* 130 full-time (80 women), 14 part-time (9 women); includes 57 minority (14 Black or African American, non-Hispanic/Latino; 11 Asian, non-Hispanic/Latino; 30 Hispanic/Latino; 2 Two or more races, non-Hispanic/Latino), 32 international. Average age 26. 293 applicants, 35% accepted, 61 enrolled. In 2019, 42 master's, 5 doctorates awarded. *Financial support:* In 2019–20, 85 students received support, including 13 fellowships (averaging $17,508 per year), 84 research assistantships (averaging $5,909 per year), 43 teaching assistantships (averaging $6,320 per year). *Unit head:* Dr. Deborah C. German, Vice President for Medical Affairs/Dean, 407-266-1000, E-mail: deb@ucf.edu. *Application contact:* Associate Director, Graduate Admissions, 407-823-2766, Fax: 407-823-6442, E-mail: gradadmissions@ucf.edu.
Website: http://www.med.ucf.edu

**University of Chicago,** Pritzker School of Medicine, Chicago, IL 60637. Offers MD, MD/PhD. *Accreditation:* LCME/AMA. *Entrance requirements:* For doctorate, MCAT, competency requirements in the following areas: biology, chemistry, physics, mathematics, humanities, writing and analysis, interpersonal skills, and clinical exploration. Electronic applications accepted. *Expenses:* Contact institution.

**University of Cincinnati,** Graduate School, College of Medicine, Medical Scientist Training Program, Cincinnati, OH 45221. Offers MD/PhD. Electronic applications accepted.

**University of Cincinnati,** Graduate School, College of Medicine, Professional Program in Medicine, Cincinnati, OH 45221. Offers MD. *Accreditation:* LCME/AMA. *Entrance requirements:* For doctorate, MCAT. Electronic applications accepted.

**University of Colorado Denver,** School of Medicine, Professional Program in Medicine, Aurora, CO 80045. Offers MD, MD/MBA, MD/PhD. *Accreditation:* LCME/AMA. *Entrance requirements:* For doctorate, MCAT, AMCAS application, essay, interviews, prerequisite coursework in biology (with lab), general chemistry (with lab), organic chemistry (with lab), general physics (with lab), English literature/composition, college-level mathematics (algebra and above). Additional exam requirements/recommendations for international students: required—TOEFL (minimum score 550 paper-based; 80 iBT). Electronic applications accepted. Tuition and fees vary according to course load, program and reciprocity agreements.

**University of Connecticut Health Center,** School of Medicine, Farmington, CT 06030. Offers MD, MD/MBA, MD/MPH, MD/PhD. *Accreditation:* LCME/AMA. *Entrance requirements:* For doctorate, MCAT. Electronic applications accepted. *Expenses:* Contact institution.

**University of Florida,** College of Medicine, Professional Program in Medicine, Gainesville, FL 32611. Offers MD, MD/PhD. *Accreditation:* LCME/AMA. *Entrance requirements:* For doctorate, MCAT, 8 semester hours of course work in biology, general chemistry, and general physics; 4 semester hours of course work in geochemistry and organic chemistry. Electronic applications accepted.

**University of Hawaii at Manoa,** John A. Burns School of Medicine, Professional Program in Medicine, Honolulu, HI 96822. Offers MD. *Accreditation:* LCME/AMA. *Entrance requirements:* For doctorate, MCAT. Electronic applications accepted. *Expenses:* Contact institution.

**University of Illinois at Chicago,** College of Medicine, Professional Program in Medicine, Chicago, IL 60607-7128. Offers MD, MD/MS, MD/PhD. *Accreditation:* LCME/AMA. *Program availability:* Part-time. *Entrance requirements:* For doctorate, MCAT. Electronic applications accepted.

**The University of Iowa,** Roy J. and Lucille A. Carver College of Medicine and Graduate College, Medical Scientist Training Program, Iowa City, IA 52242. Offers MD/PhD. *Faculty:* 87 full-time (28 women). *Students:* 73 full-time (31 women); includes 24 minority (3 Black or African American, non-Hispanic/Latino; 1 American Indian or Alaska Native, non-Hispanic/Latino; 10 Asian, non-Hispanic/Latino; 9 Hispanic/Latino; 1 Two or more races, non-Hispanic/Latino). Average age 28. 202 applicants, 9% accepted, 8 enrolled. *Application deadline:* For fall admission, 12/15 priority date for domestic students. Applications are processed on a rolling basis. Application fee: $60. Electronic applications accepted. *Expenses:* Contact institution. *Financial support:* In 2019–20, 73 students received support, including 29 fellowships with full tuition reimbursements available (averaging $30,500 per year), 40 research assistantships with full tuition reimbursements available (averaging $30,500 per year); scholarships/grants, traineeships, health care benefits, unspecified assistantships, and travel awards also available. *Unit head:* Dr. Steven R. Lentz, Director, 319-356-4048, Fax: 319-335-6634, E-mail: steven-lentz@uiowa.edu. *Application contact:* Jessica Jensen, Administrative Coordinator, 319-335-8303, Fax: 319-335-6634, E-mail: mstp@uiowa.edu.
Website: https://medicine.uiowa.edu/mstp/

**The University of Iowa,** Roy J. and Lucille A. Carver College of Medicine, Professional Program in Medicine, Iowa City, IA 52242-1316. Offers MD, MD/JD, MD/MBA, MD/MPH, MD/PhD. *Accreditation:* LCME/AMA. *Degree requirements:* For doctorate, U.S. Medical Licensing Examination Steps 1 and 2. *Entrance requirements:* For doctorate, MCAT, course work in biology, chemistry, organic chemistry, biochemistry, physics, mathematics, English, and social sciences; bachelor's degree. Electronic applications accepted. Application fee is waived when completed online. *Expenses:* Contact institution.

**The University of Kansas,** University of Kansas Medical Center, School of Medicine, MD/PhD Program, Kansas City, KS 66160. Offers MD/PhD. *Students:* 26 full-time (9 women); includes 4 minority (2 Asian, non-Hispanic/Latino; 1 Hispanic/Latino; 1 Two or

more races, non-Hispanic/Latino). Average age 27. *Application deadline:* For fall admission, 10/15 priority date for domestic students. Applications are processed on a rolling basis. Application fee: $50. Electronic applications accepted. *Expenses:* Contact institution. *Financial support:* Fellowships with full tuition reimbursements, research assistantships with full tuition reimbursements, and teaching assistantships with full tuition reimbursements available. Financial award application deadline: 3/1; financial award applicants required to submit FAFSA. *Unit head:* Dr. Timothy A. Fields, Director, 913-588-7169, E-mail: tfields@kumc.edu. *Application contact:* Janice Fletcher, Administrative Manager, 913-588-5241, Fax: 913-945-6848, E-mail: jfletcher@kumc.edu.
Website: http://www.kumc.edu/md-phd-program.html

**The University of Kansas,** University of Kansas Medical Center, School of Medicine, MD Program, Kansas City, KS 66045. Offers MD. *Accreditation:* LCME/AMA. *Students:* 851 full-time (405 women); includes 228 minority (6 Black or African American, non-Hispanic/Latino; 1 American Indian or Alaska Native, non-Hispanic/Latino; 96 Asian, non-Hispanic/Latino; 61 Hispanic/Latino; 64 Two or more races, non-Hispanic/Latino). Average age 26. 3,254 applicants, 8% accepted, 211 enrolled. In 2019, 203 doctorates awarded. *Degree requirements:* For doctorate, comprehensive exam. *Entrance requirements:* For doctorate, MCAT, bachelor's degree. *Application deadline:* For fall admission, 10/15 for domestic students. Applications are processed on a rolling basis. Application fee: $50. Electronic applications accepted. *Expenses:* Contact institution. *Financial support:* Scholarships/grants available. Financial award application deadline: 3/1; financial award applicants required to submit FAFSA. *Unit head:* Dr. Akinlolu Ojo, Executive Dean. *Application contact:* Jason Edwards, Director of Premedical Programs, 913-588-5280, Fax: 913-588-5259, E-mail: premedinfo@kumc.edu.
Website: http://www.kumc.edu/school-of-medicine.html

**University of Kentucky,** College of Medicine, Lexington, KY 40536. Offers MD, MD/MBA, MD/MPH, MD/PhD. *Accreditation:* LCME/AMA. *Degree requirements:* For doctorate, comprehensive exam (for some programs), thesis/dissertation (for some programs). *Entrance requirements:* For doctorate, MCAT (for MD). Electronic applications accepted. *Expenses:* Contact institution.

**University of Louisville,** School of Medicine, Professional Programs in Medicine, Louisville, KY 40292-0001. Offers MD, MD/MBA, MD/MS, MD/PhD. *Accreditation:* LCME/AMA. *Faculty:* 675 full-time (400 women), 85 part-time/adjunct (47 women). *Students:* 645 full-time (290 women), 3 part-time (0 women); includes 150 minority (41 Black or African American, non-Hispanic/Latino; 1 American Indian or Alaska Native, non-Hispanic/Latino; 63 Asian, non-Hispanic/Latino; 19 Hispanic/Latino; 26 Two or more races, non-Hispanic/Latino). Average age 26. 3,805 applicants, 8% accepted, 170 enrolled. In 2019, 147 doctorates awarded. *Degree requirements:* For doctorate, Pass all courses and pass USMLE Step 1 and USMLE Step 2 Clinical Knowledge and USMLE Step 2 Clinical Skills Exams. *Entrance requirements:* For doctorate, MCAT. *Application deadline:* For fall admission, 11/1 priority date for domestic and international students. Applications are processed on a rolling basis. Application fee: $75. Electronic applications accepted. *Expenses:* 42366.00. *Financial support:* In 2019–20, 41 students received support. Scholarships/grants available. Financial award applicants required to submit FAFSA. *Unit head:* Dr. Toni M. Ganzel, Dean, 502-852-1499, Fax: 502-852-1484, E-mail: mlmuck01@louisville.edu. *Application contact:* Dr. Stephen F. Wheeler, Director of Admissions, 502-852-5793, Fax: 502-852-6849, E-mail: sfwhee01@louisville.edu.
Website: http://louisville.edu/medicine/departments

**University of Lynchburg,** Graduate Studies, Doctor of Medical Science Program, Lynchburg, VA 24501-3199. Offers physician assisted medicine (D Med Sc). *Program availability:* Online learning. *Degree requirements:* For doctorate, scholarly project and practicum. *Entrance requirements:* For doctorate, graduate-level research course, minimum overall graduate cumulative GPA of 3.0; all official transcripts prior to matriculation; 300-word essay describing areas of interest and scholarly project; intended discipline and plan for completing clinical or PA education; master's or doctoral degree from regionally-accredited institution. Additional exam requirements/recommendations for international students: required—TOEFL (minimum score 550 paper-based; 80 iBT), IELTS (minimum score 6). Electronic applications accepted. *Expenses:* Contact institution.

**University of Manitoba,** Max Rady College of Medicine and Faculty of Graduate Studies, Graduate Programs in Medicine, Department of Surgery, Winnipeg, MB R3T 2N2, Canada. Offers M Sc.

**University of Maryland, Baltimore,** School of Medicine, Professional Program in Medicine, Baltimore, MD 21201. Offers MD, MD/PhD. *Accreditation:* LCME/AMA. *Students:* 624 full-time (375 women), 5 part-time (3 women); includes 289 minority (37 Black or African American, non-Hispanic/Latino; 195 Asian, non-Hispanic/Latino; 38 Hispanic/Latino; 19 Two or more races, non-Hispanic/Latino), 7 international. Average age 25. 5,192 applicants, 6% accepted, 161 enrolled. In 2019, 166 doctorates awarded. *Entrance requirements:* For doctorate, MCAT, AMCAS application, science coursework. *Application deadline:* For fall admission, 11/1 for domestic students. Applications are processed on a rolling basis. Application fee: $70. Electronic applications accepted. *Expenses:* Contact institution. *Financial support:* Federal Work-Study and scholarships/grants available. Financial award application deadline: 3/15; financial award applicants required to submit FAFSA. *Unit head:* Dr. E. Albert Reece, Dean and Vice President for Medical Affairs, 410-706-7410, Fax: 410-706-0235, E-mail: deanmed@som.umaryland.edu. *Application contact:* Dr. Milford M. Foxwell, Jr., Associate Dean for Admissions, 410-706-7478, Fax: 410-706-0467, E-mail: admissions@som.umaryland.edu.

**University of Massachusetts Medical School,** School of Medicine, Worcester, MA 01655. Offers MD. *Accreditation:* LCME/AMA. *Faculty:* 1,258 full-time (525 women), 372 part-time/adjunct (238 women). *Students:* 643 full-time (369 women); includes 204 minority (28 Black or African American, non-Hispanic/Latino; 2 American Indian or Alaska Native, non-Hispanic/Latino; 153 Asian, non-Hispanic/Latino; 20 Hispanic/Latino; 1 Native Hawaiian or other Pacific Islander, non-Hispanic/Latino), 2 international. Average age 26. 4,094 applicants, 9% accepted, 162 enrolled. In 2019, 125 doctorates awarded. *Degree requirements:* For doctorate, U.S. Medical Licensing Examination Step 1 and Step 2 (CS and CK). *Entrance requirements:* For doctorate, MCAT, bachelor's degree. *Application deadline:* For fall admission, 12/1 for domestic students. Applications are processed on a rolling basis. Application fee: $100. Electronic applications accepted. *Expenses:* Contact institution. *Financial support:* In 2019–20, 197 students received support, including 14 fellowships with full tuition reimbursements available (averaging $33,061 per year), 57 research assistantships with full tuition reimbursements available (averaging $32,850 per year); institutionally sponsored loans, scholarships/grants, and tuition waivers (partial) also available. Financial award application deadline: 3/31; financial award applicants required to submit CSS PROFILE or FAFSA. *Unit head:* Dr. Terence R. Flotte, Dean/Provost/Executive Deputy Chancellor, 508-856-8000, E-mail: terry.flotte@umassmed.edu. *Application contact:* Jennifer Lee Shea, Admissions Coordinator, 508-856-2323, Fax: 508-856-3629, E-mail: admissions@umassmed.edu.
Website: http://www.umassmed.edu/som

**University of Miami,** Graduate School, Miller School of Medicine, Professional Program in Medicine, Coral Gables, FL 33124. Offers MD. *Accreditation:* LCME/AMA. *Faculty:* 907 full-time (376 women), 62 part-time/adjunct (46 women). *Students:* 798 full-time (448 women), 10 part-time (7 women); includes 435 minority (44 Black or African American, non-Hispanic/Latino; 122 Asian, non-Hispanic/Latino; 162 Hispanic/Latino; 107 Two or more races, non-Hispanic/Latino), 4 international. Average age 25. 9,164 applicants, 4% accepted, 207 enrolled. In 2019, 179 doctorates awarded. *Entrance requirements:* For doctorate, MCAT, 90 pre-med semester hours. *Application deadline:* For fall admission, 12/1 for domestic students. Applications are processed on a rolling basis. Application fee: $75. Electronic applications accepted. *Financial support:* In 2019–20, 570 students received support. Federal Work-Study, institutionally sponsored loans, and scholarships/grants available. Financial award application deadline: 4/1; financial award applicants required to submit FAFSA. *Unit head:* Dr. Henri Ford, Dean and Chief Academic Officer, 305-243-3234, Fax: 305-243-6548, E-mail: hford@med.miami.edu. *Application contact:* Agnes Murphy, Director of Admissions, 305-243-3234, Fax: 305-243-6548, E-mail: med.admissions@miami.edu.
Website: http://www.miami.edu/medical-admissions/

**University of Michigan,** Medical School, Ann Arbor, MI 48109. Offers MD, MD/MA Edu, MD/MBA, MD/MPH, MD/MPP, MD/MS, MD/MSI, MD/PhD. *Accreditation:* LCME/AMA. *Entrance requirements:* For doctorate, MCAT. Electronic applications accepted. *Expenses:* Contact institution.

**University of Minnesota, Duluth,** Medical School, Professional Program in Medicine, Duluth, MN 55812-2496. Offers MD. *Entrance requirements:* For doctorate, MCAT. Electronic applications accepted.

**University of Minnesota, Twin Cities Campus,** Medical School, Minneapolis, MN 55455-0213. Offers MA, MS, DPT, MD, PhD, JD/MD, MD/MBA, MD/MHI, MD/MPH, MD/MS, MD/PhD. *Accreditation:* LCME/AMA. *Program availability:* Part-time, evening/weekend. *Expenses:* Contact institution.

**University of Mississippi Medical Center,** School of Medicine, Jackson, MS 39216-4505. Offers MD, MD/PhD. *Accreditation:* LCME/AMA. *Program availability:* Part-time. *Entrance requirements:* For doctorate, MCAT. Electronic applications accepted.

**University of Missouri,** School of Medicine, Professional Program in Medicine, Columbia, MO 65211. Offers MD, MD/PhD. *Accreditation:* LCME/AMA. *Entrance requirements:* For doctorate, MCAT, minimum GPA of 3.49.

**University of Missouri–Kansas City,** School of Medicine, Kansas City, MO 64110-2499. Offers health professions education (MS); MD/PhD. *Accreditation:* LCME/AMA. *Degree requirements:* For doctorate, one foreign language, United States Medical Licensing Exam Step 1 and 2. *Entrance requirements:* For doctorate, interview. *Expenses:* Contact institution.

**University of Nebraska Medical Center,** College of Medicine, Omaha, NE 68198-5527. Offers MD, Certificate, MD/MPH, MD/PhD. *Accreditation:* LCME/AMA. *Entrance requirements:* For doctorate, MCAT. Electronic applications accepted.

**University of Nevada, Reno,** School of Medicine, Reno, NV 89557. Offers MD, MD/PhD. *Accreditation:* LCME/AMA. *Expenses:* Contact institution.

**University of New Mexico,** School of Medicine, Professional Program in Medicine, Albuquerque, NM 87131-2039. Offers MD. *Accreditation:* LCME/AMA. *Degree requirements:* For doctorate, comprehensive exam, research. *Entrance requirements:* For doctorate, MCAT, general biology, general chemistry, organic chemistry, biochemistry and physics; minimum GPA of 3.0. Electronic applications accepted. *Expenses:* Contact institution.

**The University of North Carolina at Chapel Hill,** School of Medicine, Professional Program in Medicine, Chapel Hill, NC 27599. Offers MD, MD/MPH, MD/PhD. *Accreditation:* LCME/AMA. *Entrance requirements:* For doctorate, MCAT.

**University of Oklahoma Health Sciences Center,** College of Medicine, Professional Program in Medicine, Oklahoma City, OK 73190. Offers MD, MD/PhD. *Accreditation:* LCME/AMA. *Entrance requirements:* For doctorate, MCAT.

**University of Ottawa,** Faculty of Graduate and Postdoctoral Studies, Faculty of Medicine, Ottawa, ON K1N 6N5, Canada. Offers M Sc, MD, PhD. *Accreditation:* LCME/AMA. *Degree requirements:* For master's, thesis; for doctorate, thesis/dissertation (for some programs). *Entrance requirements:* For master's, honors degree or equivalent, minimum B average. Electronic applications accepted.

**University of Pennsylvania,** Perelman School of Medicine, Professional Program in Medicine, Philadelphia, PA 19104. Offers MD, MD/JD, MD/MBA, MD/MPH, MD/MSCE, MD/MSHP, MD/MSME, MD/MTR, MD/PhD. *Accreditation:* LCME/AMA. *Faculty:* 3,309 full-time (1,408 women), 624 part-time/adjunct (271 women). *Students:* 777 full-time (388 women); includes 395 minority (54 Black or African American, non-Hispanic/Latino; 194 Asian, non-Hispanic/Latino; 103 Hispanic/Latino; 1 Native Hawaiian or other Pacific Islander, non-Hispanic/Latino; 43 Two or more races, non-Hispanic/Latino), 24 international. Average age 28. 6,578 applicants, 4% accepted, 150 enrolled. *Entrance requirements:* For doctorate, MCAT. Additional exam requirements/recommendations for international students: required—TOEFL. *Financial support:* Scholarships/grants available. Financial award applicants required to submit FAFSA. *Unit head:* Dr. Suzanne Rose, Senior Vice Dean for Education, 215-898-8034, E-mail: suzirose@upenn.edu. *Application contact:* Laura Harlan, Director, Admissions, 215-898-8000, E-mail: lharlan@pennmedicine.upenn.edu.

**University of Pittsburgh,** School of Medicine, Professional Program in Medicine, Pittsburgh, PA 15261. Offers MD. *Accreditation:* LCME/AMA. *Entrance requirements:* For doctorate, MCAT, undergraduate degree including at least one year of post secondary education in the United States or Canada; one year of course work each in biology (with lab), general or inorganic chemistry (with lab), organic chemistry (with lab), physics (with lab), and English. Additional exam requirements/recommendations for international students: required—TOEFL (minimum score 600 paper-based; 100 iBT), IELTS (minimum score 7). Electronic applications accepted. *Expenses:* Contact institution.

**University of Puerto Rico - Medical Sciences Campus,** School of Medicine, Professional Program in Medicine, San Juan, PR 00936-5067. Offers MD. *Accreditation:* LCME/AMA. *Degree requirements:* For doctorate, one foreign language. *Entrance requirements:* For doctorate, MCAT, minimum GPA of 2.5, computer literacy.

**University of Rochester,** School of Medicine and Dentistry, Professional Program in Medicine, Rochester, NY 14627. Offers MD, MD/MPH, MD/MS, MD/PhD. *Accreditation:* LCME/AMA. *Entrance requirements:* For doctorate, MCAT.

**University of Saskatchewan,** College of Medicine, Professional Program in Medicine, Saskatoon, SK S7N 5A2, Canada. Offers MD. *Accreditation:* LCME/AMA.

**University of South Alabama,** College of Medicine, Doctor of Medicine Program, Mobile, AL 36688-0002. Offers MD. *Accreditation:* LCME/AMA. *Students:* 291 full-time (141 women); includes 85 minority (30 Black or African American, non-Hispanic/Latino; 6 American Indian or Alaska Native, non-Hispanic/Latino; 37 Asian, non-Hispanic/Latino; 8 Hispanic/Latino; 1 Native Hawaiian or other Pacific Islander, non-Hispanic/Latino; 3 Two or more races, non-Hispanic/Latino). Average age 24. In 2019, 80

doctorates awarded. *Entrance requirements:* For doctorate, MCAT. Additional exam requirements/recommendations for international students: required—TOEFL (minimum score 600 paper-based; 100 iBT). *Application deadline:* For fall admission, 11/15 for domestic and international students. Application fee: $75. Electronic applications accepted. *Expenses:* Contact institution. *Financial support:* Fellowships, research assistantships, teaching assistantships, career-related internships or fieldwork, institutionally sponsored loans, scholarships/grants, and unspecified assistantships available. Support available to part-time students. Financial award application deadline: 3/31; financial award applicants required to submit FAFSA. *Unit head:* Dr. T.J. Hundley, Associate Dean for Medical Education; Associate Professor, Internal Medicine, 251-460-7176, Fax: 251-460-6278, E-mail: tjhundley@health.southalabama.edu. *Application contact:* Mark Scott, Director of Admissions, College of Medicine, 251-460-7176, Fax: 251-460-6278, E-mail: mscott@southalabama.edu.
Website: https://www.southalabama.edu/colleges/com/doctoral-program/

**University of South Carolina,** School of Medicine, Professional Program in Medicine, Columbia, SC 29208. Offers MD, MD/MPH, MD/PhD. *Accreditation:* LCME/AMA. *Entrance requirements:* For doctorate, MCAT. Electronic applications accepted.

**University of South Dakota,** Graduate School, Sanford School of Medicine, Professional Program in Medicine, Vermillion, SD 57069. Offers bioethics (Certificate); medicine (MD). *Accreditation:* LCME/AMA. *Degree requirements:* For doctorate, U. S. Medical Licensing Exam-Step 1 and 2. *Entrance requirements:* For doctorate, MCAT, previous course work in biology, chemistry, organic chemistry, mathematics and physics. Electronic applications accepted.

**University of Southern California,** Keck School of Medicine, Professional Program in Medicine, Los Angeles, CA 90089. Offers MD, MD/MBA, MD/MPH, MD/PhD. *Accreditation:* LCME/AMA. *Students:* Average age 24. 8,041 applicants, 5% accepted, 186 enrolled. In 2019, 196 doctorates awarded. *Entrance requirements:* For doctorate, MCAT, baccalaureate degree, or its equivalent, from accredited college or university. *Application deadline:* For fall admission, 11/1 for domestic and international students. Applications are processed on a rolling basis. Application fee: $100. Electronic applications accepted. Application fee is waived when completed online. *Expenses:* Contact institution. *Financial support:* In 2019–20, 333 students received support, including 19 research assistantships (averaging $23,000 per year); institutionally sponsored loans and scholarships/grants also available. Financial award application deadline: 4/3; financial award applicants required to submit FAFSA. *Unit head:* Dr. Raquel Arias, Associate Dean for Admissions, 323-442-2552, Fax: 323-442-2433, E-mail: medadmit@usc.edu. *Application contact:* Susan Wong, Associate Director of Admissions, 323-442-2552, Fax: 323-442-2433, E-mail: medadmit@usc.edu.
Website: https://keck.usc.edu/education/md-program/

**University of South Florida,** Morsani College of Medicine, Tampa, FL 33620-9951. Offers MS, MSB, MSBCB, MSHI, MSMS, DPT, MD, PhD. *Accreditation:* LCME/AMA. *Program availability:* Part-time. *Faculty:* 200 full-time (85 women), 39 part-time/adjunct (17 women). *Students:* 1,314 full-time (694 women), 272 part-time (172 women); includes 634 minority (112 Black or African American, non-Hispanic/Latino; 7 American Indian or Alaska Native, non-Hispanic/Latino; 289 Asian, non-Hispanic/Latino; 194 Hispanic/Latino; 2 Native Hawaiian or other Pacific Islander, non-Hispanic/Latino; 30 Two or more races, non-Hispanic/Latino), 50 international. Average age 26. 8,974 applicants, 11% accepted, 567 enrolled. In 2019, 362 master's, 226 doctorates awarded. Terminal master's awarded for partial completion of doctoral program. *Degree requirements:* For master's, comprehensive exam, thesis; for doctorate, comprehensive exam (for some programs), thesis/dissertation (for some programs). *Entrance requirements:* For master's, GRE General Test or GMAT, BA or equivalent degree from regionally-accredited university with minimum GPA of 3.0 in upper-division coursework; for doctorate, GRE General Test, BA or equivalent degree from regionally-accredited university with minimum GPA of 3.0 in upper-division sciences coursework; three letters of recommendation; personal interview; one- to two-page personal statement. Additional exam requirements/recommendations for international students: required—TOEFL (minimum score 550 paper-based; 79 iBT). *Application deadline:* For fall admission, 2/1 priority date for domestic students, 2/1 for international students. Application fee: $30. Electronic applications accepted. *Financial support:* In 2019–20, 749 students received support. *Unit head:* Dr. Charles J. Lockwood, Dean, 813-974-0533, Fax: 813-974-4990, E-mail: cjlockwood@health.usf.edu. *Application contact:* Dr. Bob Deschenes, Vice Dean, Educational Affairs, 813-974-6393, E-mail: rdeschen@health.usf.edu.
Website: http://health.usf.edu/medicine/index.htm

**The University of Tennessee Health Science Center,** College of Medicine, Memphis, TN 38163-0002. Offers MD, MD/PhD. *Accreditation:* LCME/AMA. *Entrance requirements:* For doctorate, MCAT. Electronic applications accepted. *Expenses:* Contact institution.

**The University of Texas at Austin,** Dell Medical School, Austin, TX 78712-1111. Offers MD.

**The University of Texas Health Science Center at Houston,** McGovern Medical School, Houston, TX 77225-0036. Offers MD, MD/MPH, MD/PhD. *Accreditation:* LCME/AMA. *Entrance requirements:* For doctorate, MCAT. Electronic applications accepted. *Expenses:* Contact institution.

**The University of Texas Health Science Center at San Antonio,** Joe R. and Teresa Lozano Long School of Medicine, San Antonio, TX 78229-3900. Offers deaf education and hearing (MS); medicine (MD); MPH/MD. *Accreditation:* LCME/AMA. *Degree requirements:* For master's, comprehensive exam, practicum assignments. *Entrance requirements:* For master's, minimum GPA of 3.0, interview, 3 professional letters of recommendation; for doctorate, MCAT. Electronic applications accepted. *Expenses:* Contact institution.

**The University of Texas Medical Branch,** School of Medicine, Galveston, TX 77555. Offers MD. *Accreditation:* LCME/AMA. *Entrance requirements:* For doctorate, MCAT. *Expenses:* Contact institution.

**The University of Texas Rio Grande Valley,** School of Medicine, Edinburg, TX 78539. Offers MD. *Students:* 204 full-time (103 women); includes 135 minority (22 Black or African American, non-Hispanic/Latino; 25 Asian, non-Hispanic/Latino; 76 Hispanic/Latino; 12 Native Hawaiian or other Pacific Islander, non-Hispanic/Latino). Average age 26. *Expenses: Tuition, area resident:* Full-time $5959; part-time $440 per credit hour. Tuition, state resident: full-time $5959. Tuition, nonresident: full-time $5959. *International tuition:* $13,321 full-time. *Required fees:* $1169; $185 per credit hour.
Website: utrgv.edu/school-of-medicine/index.htm

**The University of Texas Southwestern Medical Center,** Southwestern Medical School, Dallas, TX 75390. Offers MD, MD/PhD. *Accreditation:* LCME/AMA. *Entrance requirements:* For doctorate, MCAT. Electronic applications accepted. *Expenses:* Contact institution.

**The University of Toledo,** College of Graduate Studies, College of Medicine and Life Sciences, Toledo, OH 43606-3390. Offers MPH, MS, MSBS, MSOH, MD, PhD, Certificate, MD/MPH, MD/MSBS, MD/PhD, PhD/MSBS. *Accreditation:* LCME/AMA. *Program availability:* Part-time, evening/weekend. Terminal master's awarded for partial completion of doctoral program. *Degree requirements:* For master's, thesis/scholarly

project; for doctorate, thesis/dissertation. *Entrance requirements:* For master's, doctorate, and Certificate, GRE/MCAT (varies by program), minimum GPA of 3.0 from institution granting baccalaureate degree; two or three letters of recommendation (depending on program), statement of purpose, transcripts from all prior institutions attended. Additional exam requirements/recommendations for international students: required—TOEFL (minimum score 550 paper-based; 80 iBT). Electronic applications accepted. *Expenses:* Contact institution.

**University of Toronto,** Faculty of Medicine, Toronto, ON M5S 1A1, Canada. Offers M Sc, M Sc BMC, M Sc OT, M Sc PT, MH Sc, MD, PhD, MD/PhD. *Accreditation:* LCME/AMA. *Entrance requirements:* For doctorate, MCAT (for MD). Electronic applications accepted. *Expenses:* Contact institution.

**University of Utah,** School of Medicine, MD/PhD Program in Medicine, Salt Lake City, UT 84112-1107. Offers MD/PhD. *Program availability:* Part-time. Electronic applications accepted. *Expenses:* Tuition, state resident: full-time $7085; part-time $272.51 per credit hour. Tuition, nonresident: full-time $24,937; part-time $959.12 per credit hour. *Required fees:* $880.52; $880.52 per semester. Tuition and fees vary according to degree level, program and student level.

**University of Utah,** School of Medicine, Professional Program in Medicine, Salt Lake City, UT 84112-1107. Offers MD. *Accreditation:* LCME/AMA. *Entrance requirements:* For doctorate, MCAT, 2 years chemistry with lab, 1 year physics with lab, writing/speech, 2 courses biology, 1 course cell biology or biochemistry, 1 course humanities, 1 course diversity, 1 course social science. Electronic applications accepted. *Expenses:* Contact institution.

**University of Vermont,** The Robert Larner, MD College of Medicine, Burlington, VT 05405. Offers MPH, MS, MD, PhD, Certificate, Graduate Certificate, MD/MS, MD/PhD. *Accreditation:* LCME/AMA. *Degree requirements:* For master's, thesis; for doctorate, thesis/dissertation (for some programs). *Entrance requirements:* For master's, GRE General Test; for doctorate, GRE General Test (for PhD); MCAT (for MD). Electronic applications accepted. *Expenses:* Contact institution.

**University of Virginia,** School of Medicine, Charlottesville, VA 22903. Offers MPH, MS, MD, PhD, JD/MD, JD/MPH, MD/JD, MD/MBA, MD/PhD, MPP/MPH. *Accreditation:* LCME/AMA. *Entrance requirements:* For doctorate, MCAT (for MD). Additional exam requirements/recommendations for international students: required—TOEFL. Electronic applications accepted.

**University of Washington,** Graduate School, School of Medicine, Professional Program in Medicine, Seattle, WA 98195. Offers MD, MD/MPH, MD/PhD. *Accreditation:* LCME/AMA. *Entrance requirements:* For doctorate, MCAT or GRE, minimum 3 years of college. Electronic applications accepted.

**The University of Western Ontario,** Schulich School of Medicine and Dentistry, Department of Family Medicine, London, ON N6A 3K7, Canada. Offers M Cl Sc. *Accreditation:* LCME/AMA. *Program availability:* Part-time, online learning. *Degree requirements:* For master's, thesis. *Entrance requirements:* For master's, medical degree, minimum B average. Additional exam requirements/recommendations for international students: required—TOEFL.

**The University of Western Ontario,** Schulich School of Medicine and Dentistry, Professional Program in Medicine, London, ON N6A 3K7, Canada. Offers MD. *Accreditation:* LCME/AMA.

**University of Wisconsin–Madison,** School of Medicine and Public Health, Doctor of Medicine Program, Madison, WI 53705. Offers MD, MD/MPH, MD/PhD. *Accreditation:* LCME/AMA. *Degree requirements:* For doctorate, comprehensive exam. *Entrance requirements:* For doctorate, MCAT. Electronic applications accepted. *Expenses:* Contact institution.

**Université Laval,** Faculty of Medicine, Post-Professional Programs in Medical Studies, Québec, QC G1K 7P4, Canada. Offers anatomy–pathology (DESS); anesthesiology (DESS); cardiology (DESS); care of older people (Diploma); clinical research (DESS); community health (DESS); dermatology (DESS); diagnostic radiology (DESS); emergency medicine (Diploma); family medicine (DESS); general surgery (DESS); geriatrics (DESS); hematology (DESS); internal medicine (DESS); maternal and fetal medicine (Diploma); medical biochemistry (DESS); medical microbiology and infectious diseases (DESS); medical oncology (DESS); nephrology (DESS); neurology (DESS); neurosurgery (DESS); obstetrics and gynecology (DESS); ophthalmology (DESS); orthopedic surgery (DESS); oto-rhino-laryngology (DESS); palliative medicine (Diploma); pediatrics (DESS); plastic surgery (DESS); psychiatry (DESS); pulmonary medicine (DESS); radiology–oncology (DESS); thoracic surgery (DESS); urology (DESS). *Degree requirements:* For other advanced degree, comprehensive exam. *Entrance requirements:* For degree, knowledge of French. Electronic applications accepted.

**Université Laval,** Faculty of Medicine, Professional Program in Medicine, Québec, QC G1K 7P4, Canada. Offers MD. *Accreditation:* LCME/AMA. *Entrance requirements:* For doctorate, interview, proficiency in French. Electronic applications accepted.

**Vanderbilt University,** School of Medicine, Nashville, TN 37240-1001. Offers MDE, MMP, MS, MSCI, Au D, DMP, MD, PhD, MD/PhD. *Accreditation:* LCME/AMA (one or more programs are accredited). *Faculty:* 115 full-time (44 women), 2 part-time/adjunct (0 women). *Entrance requirements:* For doctorate, MCAT (for MD). *Application deadline:* For fall admission, 11/15 for domestic and international students. Application fee: $50. *Expenses:* Contact institution. *Financial support:* Institutionally sponsored loans and scholarships/grants available. Financial award application deadline: 3/1; financial award applicants required to submit FAFSA. *Unit head:* Dr. Jeffrey R. Balser, Dean, School of Medicine, 615-936-3030, E-mail: jeffrey.balser@vanderbilt.edu. *Application contact:* Dr. Jeffrey R. Balser, Dean, School of Medicine, 615-936-3030, E-mail: jeffrey.balser@vanderbilt.edu.
Website: http://www.mc.vanderbilt.edu/medschool/

**Virginia Commonwealth University,** Medical College of Virginia-Professional Programs, School of Medicine, Professional Program in Medicine, Richmond, VA 23284-9005. Offers MD, MD/MHA, MD/MPH, MD/PhD. *Accreditation:* LCME/AMA. *Entrance requirements:* For doctorate, MCAT. Electronic applications accepted. *Expenses:* Contact institution.

**Virginia Polytechnic Institute and State University,** Virginia Tech Carilion School of Medicine and Research Institute, Blacksburg, VA 24061. Offers MD. *Accreditation:* LCME/AMA. *Faculty:* 10 full-time (6 women), 1 (woman) part-time/adjunct. *Students:* 169 full-time (69 women), 1 part-time (0 women); includes 20 minority (4 Black or African American, non-Hispanic/Latino; 15 Asian, non-Hispanic/Latino; 1 Hispanic/Latino). Average age 26. In 2019, 37 doctorates awarded. *Application deadline:* For fall admission, 12/1 for domestic students. Electronic applications accepted. *Expenses:* Contact institution. *Financial support:* Scholarships/grants available. *Unit head:* Lee Learman, MD, Dean, 540-526-2559. *Application contact:* Lee Learman, MD, Dean, 540-526-2559.
Website: https://www.vtc.vt.edu/

**Wake Forest University,** School of Medicine, Professional Program in Medicine, Winston-Salem, NC 27109. Offers MD, MD/MA, MD/MBA, MD/MS, MD/PhD.

*Accreditation:* LCME/AMA. *Entrance requirements:* For doctorate, MCAT, 32 hours of course work in science. Electronic applications accepted.

**Washington State University,** Elson S. Floyd College of Medicine, Pullman, WA 99164. Offers MS, MD.

**Washington University in St. Louis,** School of Medicine, Professional Program in Medicine, St. Louis, MO 63130-4899. Offers MD, MD/MA, MD/MS, MD/PhD. *Accreditation:* LCME/AMA. *Degree requirements:* For doctorate, thesis/dissertation (for some programs). *Entrance requirements:* For doctorate, MCAT (for MD). Electronic applications accepted.

**Western Michigan University Homer Stryker MD School of Medicine,** MD Program, . Offers MD.

**West Virginia University,** School of Medicine, Morgantown, WV 26506. Offers biochemistry and molecular biology (PhD); biomedical science (MS); cancer cell biology (PhD); cellular and integrative physiology (PhD); exercise physiology (MS, PhD); health sciences (MS); immunology (PhD); medicine (MD); occupational therapy (MOT); pathologists assistant' (MHS); physical therapy (DPT). *Accreditation:* AOTA; LCME/AMA. *Program availability:* Part-time, evening/weekend. *Entrance requirements:* Additional exam requirements/recommendations for international students: required—TOEFL. Electronic applications accepted. *Expenses:* Contact institution.

**Wright State University,** Boonshoft School of Medicine, Professional Program in Medicine, Dayton, OH 45435. Offers MD. *Accreditation:* LCME/AMA. *Entrance requirements:* For doctorate, MCAT.

**Yale University,** Yale School of Medicine, Professional Program in Medicine, New Haven, CT 06510. Offers MD. *Accreditation:* LCME/AMA. *Degree requirements:* For doctorate, thesis/dissertation. *Entrance requirements:* For doctorate, MCAT. Electronic applications accepted.

# Bioethics

**Albany Medical College,** Alden March Bioethics Institute, Albany, NY 12208. Offers bioethics (MS, DPS); clinical ethics (Certificate); clinical ethics consultation (Certificate). *Program availability:* Part-time, evening/weekend, online learning. *Degree requirements:* For master's, thesis. *Entrance requirements:* For master's and Certificate, GRE, GMAT, LSAT, or MCAT (if no graduate degree), essay, official transcripts, 2 letters of reference. Additional exam requirements/recommendations for international students: recommended—TOEFL. Electronic applications accepted. *Expenses:* Contact institution.

**Case Western Reserve University,** School of Medicine and School of Graduate Studies, Graduate Programs in Medicine, Department of Bioethics, Cleveland, OH 44106. Offers MA, JD/MA, MA/MD, MA/MPH, MA/MSN, MSSA/MA. *Entrance requirements:* For master's, GRE General Test or MCAT or MAT or LSAT or GMAT. Additional exam requirements/recommendations for international students: required—TOEFL (minimum score 550 paper-based). Electronic applications accepted.

**Clarkson University,** Department of Bioethics, Schenectady, NY 13699. Offers bioethics (MS, Advanced Certificate), including bioethics policy (MS), clinical ethics, health, policy, and law (Advanced Certificate), research ethics. *Program availability:* Part-time, evening/weekend, 100% online, blended/hybrid learning. *Faculty:* 5 part-time/adjunct (2 women). *Students:* 3 full-time (2 women), 26 part-time (19 women); includes 6 minority (1 Black or African American, non-Hispanic/Latino; 2 Asian, non-Hispanic/Latino; 2 Hispanic/Latino; 1 Two or more races, non-Hispanic/Latino), 14 international. 20 applicants, 90% accepted, 15 enrolled. In 2019, 18 master's, 6 other advanced degrees awarded. *Degree requirements:* For master's, project. *Entrance requirements:* Additional exam requirements/recommendations for international students: required—TOEFL (minimum score 550 paper-based, 80 iBT) or IELTS (6.5). *Application deadline:* Applications are processed on a rolling basis. Application fee: $50. Electronic applications accepted. *Expenses:* Contact institution. *Financial support:* Scholarships/grants available. *Unit head:* Jane Oppenlander, Assistant Professor of Operations & Information Systems, 518-631-9905, E-mail: joppenla@clarkson.edu. *Application contact:* Daniel Capogna, Director of Graduate Admissions and Recruitment, 518-631-9910, E-mail: dcapogna@clarkson.edu.
Website: https://www.clarkson.edu/academics/graduate

**Cleveland State University,** College of Graduate Studies, College of Liberal Arts and Social Sciences, Department of Philosophy and Comparative Religion, Cleveland, OH 44115. Offers bioethics (MA, Certificate), including bioethics (MA); philosophy (MA), including philosophy. *Program availability:* Part-time, evening/weekend. *Faculty:* 4 full-time (all women), 2 part-time/adjunct (1 woman). *Students:* 2 part-time (1 woman). Average age 39. 11 applicants, 100% accepted, 4 enrolled. In 2019, 1 master's awarded. *Degree requirements:* For master's, comprehensive exam, thesis optional, 32 credit hours of coursework; for Certificate, 12 credit hours of coursework. *Entrance requirements:* For master's and Certificate, BA, BS, or equivalent degree with minimum GPA of 2.75. Additional exam requirements/recommendations for international students: required—TOEFL (minimum score 550 paper-based; 78 iBT). *Application deadline:* For fall admission, 7/1 priority date for domestic students, 5/15 priority date for international students; for spring admission, 11/15 for domestic students, 11/1 for international students; for summer admission, 4/1 for domestic students, 3/15 for international students. Applications are processed on a rolling basis. Application fee: $40. Electronic applications accepted. *Expenses:* Tuition, state resident: full-time $10,215; part-time $6810 per credit hour. Tuition, nonresident: full-time $17,496; part-time $11,664 per credit hour. *International tuition:* $19,316 full-time. Tuition and fees vary according to degree level and program. *Financial support:* In 2019–20, 5 students received support, including 5 teaching assistantships with full tuition reimbursements available (averaging $4,000 per year); health care benefits, tuition waivers (full), and unspecified assistantships also available. Support available to part-time students. *Unit head:* Dr. Mary Ellen Waithe, Chairperson, 216-687-3900, Fax: 216-523-7482, E-mail: m.waithe@csuohio.edu. *Application contact:* Deborah L. Brown, Interim Assistant Director, Graduate Admissions, 216-523-7572, Fax: 216-687-5400, E-mail: d.l.brown@csuohio.edu.
Website: http://www.csuohio.edu/class/philosophy-religion/philosophy-religion

**Columbia University,** School of Professional Studies, Program in Bioethics, New York, NY 10027. Offers MS. *Program availability:* Part-time. *Degree requirements:* For master's, thesis. Electronic applications accepted. *Expenses: Tuition:* Full-time $47,600; part-time $1880 per credit. One-time fee: $105.

**Creighton University,** Graduate School, Department of Interdisciplinary Studies, MS Program in Health Care Ethics, Omaha, NE 68178-0001. Offers MS. *Program availability:* Part-time. *Degree requirements:* For master's, practicum, capstone. *Entrance requirements:* For master's, resume, essay. Additional exam requirements/recommendations for international students: required—TOEFL (minimum score 90 iBT), IELTS (minimum score 6.5). Electronic applications accepted.

**Duke University,** Graduate School, Program in Bioethics and Science Policy, Durham, NC 27708-0141. Offers MA. *Entrance requirements:* For master's, GRE General Test. Additional exam requirements/recommendations for international students: required—TOEFL (minimum score 577 paper-based; 90 iBT) or IELTS (minimum score 7).

**Duquesne University,** Graduate School of Liberal Arts, Center for Healthcare Ethics, Pittsburgh, PA 15282-0001. Offers MA, DHCE, PhD, Certificate. *Program availability:* Part-time, 100% online. Terminal master's awarded for partial completion of doctoral program. *Degree requirements:* For doctorate, 2 foreign languages, comprehensive exam, thesis/dissertation. *Entrance requirements:* For master's, GRE General Test; for doctorate, GRE General Test, master's degree in health care ethics. Additional exam requirements/recommendations for international students: required—TOEFL. Electronic applications accepted.

**Emory University,** Laney Graduate School, Emory Center for Ethics, Atlanta, GA 30322-1100. Offers bioethics (MA). Terminal master's awarded for partial completion of doctoral program. *Degree requirements:* For master's, practicum experience, capstone project. *Entrance requirements:* Additional exam requirements/recommendations for international students: recommended—TOEFL. Electronic applications accepted.

**Hofstra University,** Maurice A. Deane School of Law, Hempstead, NY 11549. Offers alternative dispute resolution (JD); American legal studies (LL M); business law honors (JD); clinical bioethics (Certificate); corporate compliance (JD); criminal law and procedure (JD); family law (LL M, JD); health law (JD); health law and policy (LL M, MA); intellectual property law honors (JD); international law honors (JD); JD/MBA; JD/MPH. *Accreditation:* ABA. *Program availability:* Part-time, 100% online. *Faculty:* 45 full-time (24 women), 86 part-time/adjunct (34 women). *Students:* 768 full-time (401 women), 119 part-time (83 women); includes 200 minority (56 Black or African American, non-Hispanic/Latino; 3 American Indian or Alaska Native, non-Hispanic/Latino; 42 Asian, non-Hispanic/Latino; 91 Hispanic/Latino; 4 Native Hawaiian or other Pacific Islander, non-Hispanic/Latino; 4 Two or more races, non-Hispanic/Latino), 14 international. Average age 27. 2,993 applicants, 49% accepted, 312 enrolled. In 2019, 48 master's, 217 doctorates awarded. *Entrance requirements:* For doctorate, LSAT, letter of recommendation, personal statement, undergraduate transcripts; for Certificate, 2 letters of recommendation, JD or LLM, personal statement, law school transcripts. Additional exam requirements/recommendations for international students: recommended—TOEFL (minimum score 600 paper-based; 100 iBT). *Application deadline:* For fall admission, 4/15 priority date for domestic and international students. Applications are processed on a rolling basis. Electronic applications accepted. *Expenses:* $30,127 per term for Full-time (tuition and fees). *Financial support:* In 2019–20, 690 students received support, including 669 fellowships with full and partial tuition reimbursements available (averaging $33,308 per year), 1 research assistantship with full and partial tuition reimbursement available (averaging $6,750 per year); career-related internships or fieldwork, Federal Work-Study, institutionally sponsored loans, scholarships/grants, tuition waivers (full and partial), unspecified assistantships, and scholarships and endowed scholarships also available. Support available to part-time students. Financial award applicants required to submit FAFSA. *Unit head:* Gail Prudenti, Dean, 516-463-4068, E-mail: gail.prudenti@hofstra.edu. *Application contact:* Sunil Samuel, Assistant Vice President of Admissions, 516-463-4723, Fax: 516-463-4664.
Website: http://law.hofstra.edu/

**Icahn School of Medicine at Mount Sinai,** The Bioethics Program, New York, NY 10029-6504. Offers MS.

**Indiana University-Purdue University Indianapolis,** Robert H. McKinney School of Law, Indianapolis, IN 46202. Offers advocacy skills (Certificate); American law for foreign lawyers (LL M); civil and human rights (Certificate); corporate and commercial law (LL M, Certificate); criminal law (Certificate); environmental and natural resources (Certificate); health law (Certificate); health law, policy and bioethics (LL M); intellectual property law (LL M, Certificate); international and comparative law (LL M, Certificate); international human rights law (LL M); law (MJ, JD, SJD); JD/M Phil; JD/MBA; JD/MD; JD/MHA; JD/MLS; JD/MPA; JD/MPH; JD/MSW. *Accreditation:* ABA. *Program availability:* Part-time. *Entrance requirements:* For doctorate, LSAT. Additional exam requirements/recommendations for international students: required—TOEFL (minimum score 79 iBT), IELTS (minimum score 6.5). Electronic applications accepted. *Expenses:* Contact institution.

**Indiana University-Purdue University Indianapolis,** School of Liberal Arts, Department of Philosophy, Indianapolis, IN 46202. Offers American philosophy (Certificate); bioethics (Certificate); philosophy (MA); philosophy/bioethics (MA); JD/MA; MD/MA. *Program availability:* Part-time. *Degree requirements:* For master's, thesis optional. *Entrance requirements:* For master's, GRE, writing sample, transcripts, three letters of recommendation, personal statement; for Certificate, letter of recommendation, transcripts, statement of purpose. Additional exam requirements/recommendations for international students: required—TOEFL, PTE, IUPUI ESL Exam. Electronic applications accepted. *Expenses:* Contact institution.

**Instituto Tecnologico de Santo Domingo,** Graduate School, Area of Health Sciences, Santo Domingo, Dominican Republic. Offers bioethics (M Bioethics); clinical bioethics (Certificate); clinical nutrition (Certificate); comprehensive adolescent health (MS); comprehensive health and the adolescent (Certificate); health and social security (M Mgmt).

**Johns Hopkins University,** Bloomberg School of Public Health, Department of Health Policy and Management, Baltimore, MD 21205-1996. Offers bioethics and policy (PhD); health administration (MHA); health and public policy (PhD); health economics (MHS); health economics and policy (PhD); health finance and management (MHS); health policy (MSPH); health policy and management (Dr PH); health services research and policy (PhD); public policy (MPP). *Accreditation:* CAHME (one or more programs are accredited). *Program availability:* Part-time. *Degree requirements:* For master's, thesis (for some programs), internship (for some programs); for doctorate, comprehensive exam, thesis/dissertation, 1-year full-time residency (for some programs), oral and written exams. *Entrance requirements:* For master's, GRE General Test or GMAT, 3 letters of recommendation, curriculum vitae/resume; for doctorate, GRE General Test or

GMAT, 3 letters of recommendation, curriculum vitae, transcripts. Additional exam requirements/recommendations for international students: required—TOEFL (minimum score 100 iBT), IELTS (minimum score 7). Electronic applications accepted.

**Johns Hopkins University,** Bloomberg School of Public Health, Master of Bioethics Program, Baltimore, MD 21218. Offers MBE. *Program availability:* Part-time. *Degree requirements:* For master's, thesis, practicum. *Entrance requirements:* Additional exam requirements/recommendations for international students: required—TOEFL, IELTS. Electronic applications accepted.

**Kansas City University of Medicine and Biosciences,** College of Biosciences, Kansas City, MO 64106-1453. Offers bioethics (MA); biomedical sciences (MS). *Program availability:* Part-time. *Degree requirements:* For master's, comprehensive exam, thesis (for some programs). *Entrance requirements:* For master's, MCAT, GRE.

**Loma Linda University,** School of Religion, Program in Bioethics, Loma Linda, CA 92350. Offers MA, Certificate. *Degree requirements:* For master's, comprehensive exam, thesis optional. *Entrance requirements:* For master's, GRE General Test, baccalaureate degree. Additional exam requirements/recommendations for international students: required—TOEFL. Electronic applications accepted.

**Loyola Marymount University,** Bellarmine College of Liberal Arts, Program in Bioethics, Los Angeles, CA 90045. Offers MA. *Entrance requirements:* For master's, completed bachelor degree; graduate admissions application; undergraduate GPA of at least 3.0; 2 letters of recommendation; short essay; personal statement; 1 official transcript; personal interview. *Unit head:* Dr. Roberto Dell'Oro, Director, Bioethics Institute, 310-338-2752, E-mail: rdelloro@lmu.edu. *Application contact:* Ammar Dalal, Assistant Vice Provost for Graduate Enrollment, 310-338-2721, Fax: 310-338-6086, E-mail: graduateadmission@lmu.edu.
Website: http://bellarmine.lmu.edu/bioethics/academics/gradprograms

**Loyola University Chicago,** Graduate School, Neiswanger Institute for Bioethics, Maywood, IL 60660. Offers clinical bioethics, bioethics and health policy, catholic health care ethics (Certificate); clinical bioethics, catholic bioethics, organizational ethics, research ethics, public health ethics (D Be); MD/MA. *Program availability:* Part-time, online only, 100% online, blended/hybrid learning. *Faculty:* 8 full-time (5 women), 6 part-time/adjunct (2 women). *Students:* 26 full-time (17 women), 91 part-time (53 women); includes 21 minority (7 Black or African American, non-Hispanic/Latino; 2 American Indian or Alaska Native, non-Hispanic/Latino; 4 Asian, non-Hispanic/Latino; 7 Hispanic/Latino; 1 Two or more races, non-Hispanic/Latino). Average age 47. 43 applicants, 72% accepted, 25 enrolled. In 2019, 33 master's, 11 doctorates, 8 other advanced degrees awarded. *Degree requirements:* For master's, thesis; for doctorate, comprehensive exam, thesis/dissertation. *Entrance requirements:* For master's, advanced degree; for doctorate, masters degree in bioethics or health care ethics preferred. Additional exam requirements/recommendations for international students: required—TOEFL (minimum score 550 paper-based). *Application deadline:* For fall admission, 8/1 for domestic and international students; for spring admission, 1/5 for domestic and international students; for summer admission, 5/1 for domestic and international students. *Expenses:* Contact institution. *Financial support:* In 2019–20, 93 students received support. Institutionally sponsored loans and scholarships/grants available. Financial award applicants required to submit FAFSA. *Unit head:* Robbin Hiller, Coordinator, Bioethics Education, 708-327-9212, Fax: 708-327-9209, E-mail: rhiller@luc.edu. *Application contact:* Robbin Hiller, Coordinator, Bioethics Education, 708-321-9219, Fax: 708-327-9209, E-mail: rhiller@luc.edu.
Website: http://bioethics.luc.edu

**McGill University,** Faculty of Graduate and Postdoctoral Studies, Faculty of Arts, Department of Philosophy, Montréal, QC H3A 2T5, Canada. Offers bioethics (MA); philosophy (PhD).

**McGill University,** Faculty of Graduate and Postdoctoral Studies, Faculty of Law, Montréal, QC H3A 2T5, Canada. Offers air and space law (LL M, DCL, Graduate Certificate); bioethics (LL M); comparative law (LL M, DCL, Graduate Certificate); law (LL M, DCL).

**McGill University,** Faculty of Graduate and Postdoctoral Studies, Faculty of Medicine, Department of Medicine, Montréal, QC H3A 2T5, Canada. Offers experimental medicine (M Sc, PhD), including bioethics (M Sc), experimental medicine.

**Medical College of Wisconsin,** Graduate School, Center for Bioethics and Medical Humanities, Milwaukee, WI 53226. Offers bioethics (MA); clinical bioethics (Graduate Certificate); research ethics (Graduate Certificate). *Program availability:* Part-time. *Students:* 5 full-time (2 women), 12 part-time (all women); includes 2 minority (1 Black or African American, non-Hispanic/Latino; 1 Two or more races, non-Hispanic/Latino). Average age 35. 16 applicants, 63% accepted, 8 enrolled. In 2019, 6 master's, 3 other advanced degrees awarded. *Degree requirements:* For master's, thesis. *Entrance requirements:* For master's and Graduate Certificate, GRE, official transcripts, three letters of recommendation. Additional exam requirements/recommendations for international students: required—TOEFL. *Application deadline:* For fall admission, 1/15 priority date for domestic students. Applications are processed on a rolling basis. Application fee: $50. Electronic applications accepted. *Expenses:* $1,056 per credit for masters and certificate students; $155 per year fees for full time students. *Financial support:* Available to part-time students. Application deadline: 2/15; applicants required to submit FAFSA. *Application contact:* Recruitment Office, 414-955-4402, Fax: 414-955-6555, E-mail: gradschoolrecruit@mcw.edu.
Website: http://www.mcw.edu/Graduate-School/Programs/Bioethics.htm

**Northeast Ohio Medical University,** College of Graduate Studies, Rootstown, OH 44272-0095. Offers health-system pharmacy administration (MS); integrated pharmaceutical medicine (MS, PhD); medical ethics and humanities (MS, Certificate); public health (MPH). *Program availability:* Part-time, evening/weekend, 100% online, blended/hybrid learning. *Faculty:* 126 part-time/adjunct (62 women). *Students:* 24 full-time (12 women), 28 part-time (15 women); includes 21 minority (2 Black or African American, non-Hispanic/Latino; 10 Asian, non-Hispanic/Latino; 5 Hispanic/Latino; 4 Two or more races, non-Hispanic/Latino). Average age 26. 31 applicants, 97% accepted, 21 enrolled. In 2019, 15 master's, 13 other advanced degrees awarded. *Degree requirements:* For master's, thesis (for some programs), thesis (for MS in medical ethics and humanities, integrated pharmaceutical medicine, MS in MAS); for doctorate, thesis/dissertation, For IPM Ph.D Program. *Entrance requirements:* Additional exam requirements/recommendations for international students: recommended—TOEFL (minimum score 550 paper-based). *Application deadline:* For fall admission, 7/17 for domestic students. Applications are processed on a rolling basis. Application fee: $95. Electronic applications accepted. *Expenses:* Student health and fitness, student activities. *Financial support:* In 2019–20, 6 students received support. Scholarships/grants and tuition waivers (full and partial) available. Financial award application deadline: 3/15; financial award applicants required to submit FAFSA. *Unit head:* Dr. Steven Schmidt, Dean, 330-325-6290. *Application contact:* Dr. Steven Schmidt, Dean, 330-325-6290.
Website: https://www.neomed.edu/graduatestudies/

**Saint Louis University,** Graduate Programs, Center for Health Care Ethics, St. Louis, MO 63103. Offers clinical health care ethics (Certificate); health care ethics (PhD). *Degree requirements:* For doctorate, comprehensive exam, thesis/dissertation. *Entrance requirements:* For doctorate, GRE General Test, master's degree in ethics or a field related to health care, basic competencies in philosophical and applied ethics, transcripts. Additional exam requirements/recommendations for international students: required—TOEFL (minimum score 525 paper-based). Electronic applications accepted.

**Stony Brook University, State University of New York,** Stony Brook Medicine, Renaissance School of Medicine, Center for Medical Humanities, Compassionate Care, and Bioethics, Stony Brook, NY 11794. Offers MD/MA. *Students:* 6 full-time (5 women), 5 part-time (all women); includes 2 minority (1 Hispanic/Latino; 1 Two or more races, non-Hispanic/Latino), 1 international. Average age 33. 8 applicants, 100% accepted, 6 enrolled. *Entrance requirements:* Additional exam requirements/recommendations for international students: required—TOEFL. *Application deadline:* For fall admission, 7/1 for domestic students, 4/1 for international students; for spring admission, 11/1 for domestic students, 10/1 for international students. Application fee: $100. *Expenses:* Contact institution. *Financial support:* Fellowships available. *Unit head:* Dr. Stephen G. Post, Director, 631-444-9797, E-mail: stephen.post@stonybrookmedicine.edu. *Application contact:* April Bortzfield, Graduate Program Coordinator, 631-444-8029, Fax: 631-444-9744, E-mail: april.bortzfield@stonybrookmedicine.edu.
Website: https://www.stonybrook.edu/bioethics/

**Trinity International University,** Trinity Graduate School, Deerfield, IL 60015-1284. Offers athletic training (MA); bioethics (MA); counseling psychology (MA); diverse learning (M Ed); leadership (MA); teaching (MA). *Program availability:* Part-time, evening/weekend, online learning. *Degree requirements:* For master's, comprehensive exam. *Entrance requirements:* For master's, GRE General Test or MAT, minimum undergraduate GPA of 3.0. Additional exam requirements/recommendations for international students: required—TOEFL (minimum score 580 paper-based), TWE (minimum score 4). Electronic applications accepted.

**Trinity International University,** Trinity Law School, Santa Ana, CA 92705. Offers bioethics (MLS); church and ministry management (MLS); general legal studies (MLS); human resources management (MLS); human rights (MLS); law (JD); nonprofit organizations (MLS). *Program availability:* Part-time, evening/weekend. *Entrance requirements:* For doctorate, LSAT. Additional exam requirements/recommendations for international students: required—TOEFL (minimum score 580 paper-based). *Expenses:* Contact institution.

**Université de Montréal,** Faculty of Medicine, Programs in Bioethics, Montréal, QC H3C 3J7, Canada. Offers MA, DESS. Electronic applications accepted.

**Université de Montréal,** Faculty of Theology and Sciences of Religions, Montréal, QC H3C 3J7, Canada. Offers health, spirituality and bioethics (DESS); practical theology (MA, PhD); religious sciences (MA, PhD); theology (MA, D Th, PhD, L Th); theology-Biblical studies (PhD). *Degree requirements:* For master's, one foreign language; for doctorate, 2 foreign languages, thesis/dissertation, general exam. Electronic applications accepted.

**University of Louisville,** School of Interdisciplinary and Graduate Studies, Louisville, KY 40292. Offers interdisciplinary studies (MA, MS, PhD), including bioethics and medical humanities (MA), bioinformatics (PhD), sustainability (MA, MS), translational bioengineering (PhD), translational neuroscience (PhD). *Program availability:* Part-time. *Students:* 36 full-time (21 women), 14 part-time (5 women); includes 5 minority (1 Black or African American, non-Hispanic/Latino; 3 Hispanic/Latino; 1 Two or more races, non-Hispanic/Latino), 10 international. Average age 32. 27 applicants, 70% accepted, 14 enrolled. In 2019, 3 master's, 1 doctorate awarded. *Degree requirements:* For master's, variable foreign language requirement, comprehensive exam (for some programs), thesis (for some programs); for doctorate, variable foreign language requirement, comprehensive exam, thesis/dissertation. *Entrance requirements:* For master's and doctorate, GRE General Test, 2 letters of recommendation, transcripts from previous post-secondary educational institutions. Additional exam requirements/recommendations for international students: required—TOEFL (minimum score 550 paper-based; 79 iBT), IELTS (minimum score 6.5). *Application deadline:* For fall admission, 7/1 priority date for domestic students, 5/1 priority date for international students; for winter admission, 7/1 priority date for domestic students, 5/1 for international students; for spring admission, 12/1 priority date for domestic students, 11/1 for international students; for summer admission, 4/1 priority date for domestic students, 4/1 for international students. Applications are processed on a rolling basis. Application fee: $65. Electronic applications accepted. *Expenses: Tuition, area resident:* Full-time $13,000; part-time $723 per credit hour. Tuition, state resident: full-time $13,000; part-time $723 per credit hour. Tuition, nonresident: full-time $27,114; part-time $1507 per credit hour. *International tuition:* $27,114 full-time. *Required fees:* $196. Tuition and fees vary according to program and reciprocity agreements. *Financial support:* In 2019–20, 35 students received support, including 120 fellowships with full tuition reimbursements available (averaging $20,000 per year); scholarships/grants, health care benefits, unspecified assistantships, and Diversity scholarships also available. Financial award application deadline: 1/1; financial award applicants required to submit FAFSA. *Unit head:* Dr. Paul J. DeMarco, Acting Vice Provost for Graduate Affairs, Acting Dean of the Graduate School, 502-852-0788, Fax: 502-852-2365, E-mail: paul.demarco@louisville.edu. *Application contact:* Dr. Barbara Clark, Acting Associate Dean of the Graduate School, 502-852-6498, Fax: 502-852-3111, E-mail: gradadm@louisville.edu.
Website: http://www.graduate.louisville.edu

**University of Mary,** School of Health Sciences, Program in Bioethics, Bismarck, ND 58504-9652. Offers MS. *Degree requirements:* For master's, practicum, capstone project.

**University of Pennsylvania,** Perelman School of Medicine, Department of Medical Ethics and Health Policy, Philadelphia, PA 19104. Offers MBE, MSME, DMD/MBE, JD/MBE, LL M/MBE, MBE/MSME, MD/MBE, MPA/MBE, MRA/MBE, MS Ed/MBE, MSN/MBE, MSW/MBE, PhD/MBE. *Program availability:* Part-time, evening/weekend. *Faculty:* 12 full-time (4 women). *Students:* 37 full-time (22 women), 74 part-time (44 women); includes 31 minority (10 Black or African American, non-Hispanic/Latino; 1 American Indian or Alaska Native, non-Hispanic/Latino; 16 Asian, non-Hispanic/Latino; 4 Hispanic/Latino). Average age 34. 54 applicants, 59% accepted, 15 enrolled. In 2019, 44 master's awarded. *Degree requirements:* For master's, thesis, capstone project must be of publishable quality. *Entrance requirements:* Additional exam requirements/recommendations for international students: required—TOEFL. *Application deadline:* Applications are processed on a rolling basis. Application fee: $70. Electronic applications accepted. *Expenses:* Tuition, general fees, tech fees. *Financial support:* In 2019–20, 3 fellowships with full tuition reimbursements (averaging $90,000 per year) were awarded; research assistantships, teaching assistantships, and tuition waivers also available. *Unit head:* Dr. Autumn Fiester, Assistant Chair of Education and Training, 573-2602. *Application contact:* AJ Roholt, Program Coordinator, 898-3837, E-mail: arroholt@pennmedicine.upenn.edu.
Website: http://www.mbe.org

**University of Pittsburgh,** Kenneth P. Dietrich School of Arts and Sciences, Center for Bioethics and Health Law, Pittsburgh, PA 15213. Offers bioethics (MA). *Program availability:* Part-time. *Faculty:* 11 full-time (4 women), 4 part-time/adjunct (1 woman).

*Students:* 5 full-time (all women), 5 part-time (4 women); includes 1 minority (Asian, non-Hispanic/Latino), 1 international. Average age 32. 6 applicants, 67% accepted, 4 enrolled. In 2019, 7 master's awarded. *Entrance requirements:* Additional exam requirements/recommendations for international students: required—TOEFL (minimum score 550 paper-based); recommended—IELTS (minimum score 7). *Application deadline:* For fall admission, 3/1 priority date for domestic and international students. Applications are processed on a rolling basis. Application fee: $50. Electronic applications accepted. *Financial support:* Scholarships/grants available. Financial award application deadline: 3/1. *Unit head:* Dr. Lisa S. Parker, PhD, Director, 412-648-7007, Fax: 412-648-2649, E-mail: lisap@pitt.edu. *Application contact:* Jody Stockdill, Administrative Assistant, 412-648-7007, Fax: 412-648-2649, E-mail: joc10@pitt.edu.
Website: http://www.bioethics.pitt.edu

**University of South Dakota,** Graduate School, Sanford School of Medicine, Professional Program in Medicine, Vermillion, SD 57069. Offers bioethics (Certificate); medicine (MD). *Accreditation:* LCME/AMA. *Degree requirements:* For doctorate, U. S. Medical Licensing Exam-Step 1 and 2. *Entrance requirements:* For doctorate, MCAT, previous course work in biology, chemistry, organic chemistry, mathematics and physics. Electronic applications accepted.

**University of South Florida,** Innovative Education, Tampa, FL 33620-9951. Offers adult, career and higher education (Graduate Certificate), including college teaching, leadership in developing human resources, leadership in higher education; Africana studies (Graduate Certificate), including diasporas and health disparities, genocide and human rights; aging studies (Graduate Certificate), including gerontology; art research (Graduate Certificate), including museum studies; business foundations (Graduate Certificate); chemical and biomedical engineering (Graduate Certificate), including materials science and engineering, water, health and sustainability; child and family studies (Graduate Certificate), including positive behavior support; civil and industrial engineering (Graduate Certificate), including transportation systems analysis; community and family health (Graduate Certificate), including maternal and child health, social marketing and public health, violence and injury: prevention and intervention, women's health; criminology (Graduate Certificate), including criminal justice administration; data science for public administration (Graduate Certificate); digital humanities (Graduate Certificate); educational measurement and research (Graduate Certificate), including evaluation; English (Graduate Certificate), including comparative literary studies, creative writing, professional and technical communication; entrepreneurship (Graduate Certificate); environmental health (Graduate Certificate), including safety management; epidemiology and biostatistics (Graduate Certificate), including applied biostatistics, biostatistics, concepts and tools of epidemiology, epidemiology, epidemiology of infectious diseases; geography, environment and planning (Graduate Certificate), including community development, environmental policy and management, geographical information systems; geology (Graduate Certificate), including hydrogeology; global health (Graduate Certificate), including disaster management, global health and Latin American and Caribbean studies, global health practice, humanitarian assistance, infection control; government and international affairs (Graduate Certificate), including Cuban studies, globalization studies; health policy and management (Graduate Certificate), including health management and leadership, public health policy and programs; hearing specialist: early intervention (Graduate Certificate); industrial and management systems engineering (Graduate Certificate), including systems engineering, technology management; information studies (Graduate Certificate), including school library media specialist; information systems/decision sciences (Graduate Certificate), including analytics and business intelligence; instructional technology (Graduate Certificate), including distance education, Florida digital/virtual educator, instructional design, multimedia design, Web design; internal medicine, bioethics and medical humanities (Graduate Certificate), including biomedical ethics; Latin American and Caribbean studies (Graduate Certificate); leadership for coastal resiliency planning (Graduate Certificate); mass communications (Graduate Certificate), including multimedia journalism; mathematics and statistics (Graduate Certificate), including mathematics; medicine (Graduate Certificate), including aging and neuroscience, bioinformatics, biotechnology, brain fitness and memory management, clinical investigation, hand and upper limb rehabilitation, health informatics, health sciences, integrative weight management, intellectual property, medicine and gender, metabolic and nutritional medicine, metabolic cardiology, pharmacy sciences; national and competitive intelligence (Graduate Certificate); nursing (Graduate Certificate), including simulation based academic fellowship in advanced pain management; psychological and social foundations (Graduate Certificate), including career counseling, college teaching, diversity in education, mental health counseling, school counseling; public affairs (Graduate Certificate), including nonprofit management, public management, research administration; public health (Graduate Certificate), including assessing chemical toxicity and public health risks, health equity, pharmacoepidemiology, public health generalist, toxicology, translational research in adolescent behavioral health; public health practices (Graduate Certificate), including planning for healthy communities; rehabilitation and mental health counseling (Graduate Certificate), including integrative mental health care, marriage and family therapy, rehabilitation technology; secondary education (Graduate Certificate), including ESOL, foreign language education: culture and content, foreign language education: professional; social work (Graduate Certificate), including geriatric social work/clinical gerontology; special education (Graduate Certificate), including autism spectrum disorder, disabilities education: severe/profound; world languages (Graduate Certificate), including teaching English as a second language (TESL) or foreign language. *Unit head:* Dr. Cynthia DeLuca, Associate Vice President and Assistant Vice Provost, 813-974-3077, Fax: 813-974-7061, E-mail: deluca@usf.edu. *Application contact:* Owen Hooper, Director, Summer and Alternative Calendar Programs, 813-974-6917, E-mail: hooper@usf.edu.
Website: http://www.usf.edu/innovative-education/

**The University of Tennessee,** Graduate School, College of Arts and Sciences, Department of Philosophy, Knoxville, TN 37996. Offers medical ethics (MA, PhD); philosophy (MA, PhD); religious studies (MA). *Program availability:* Part-time. *Degree requirements:* For master's, thesis or alternative; for doctorate, one foreign language, thesis/dissertation. *Entrance requirements:* For master's and doctorate, GRE General Test, minimum GPA of 2.7. Additional exam requirements/recommendations for international students: required—TOEFL. Electronic applications accepted.

**University of Toronto,** Faculty of Medicine, Institute of Medical Science, Toronto, ON M5S 1A1, Canada. Offers bioethics (MH Sc); biomedical communications (M Sc BMC); medical radiation science (MH Sc); medical science (PhD). *Degree requirements:* For master's, thesis; for doctorate, thesis/dissertation, thesis defense. *Entrance requirements:* For master's, minimum GPA of 3.7 in 3 of 4 years (M Sc), interview; for doctorate, M Sc or equivalent, defended thesis, minimum A- average, interview. Additional exam requirements/recommendations for international students: required—TOEFL (minimum score 600 paper-based; 93 iBT), TWE (minimum score 5). Electronic applications accepted.

**University of Washington,** Graduate School, School of Medicine, Graduate Programs in Medicine, Department of Medical History and Ethics, Seattle, WA 98195. Offers bioethics (MA).

**Washington State University,** College of Arts and Sciences, School of Politics, Philosophy and Public Affairs, Pullman, WA 99164-4880. Offers bioethics (Graduate Certificate); political science (MA, PhD); public affairs (MPA). *Accreditation:* NASPAA. *Program availability:* Online learning. Terminal master's awarded for partial completion of doctoral program. *Degree requirements:* For master's, comprehensive exam (for some programs), thesis, oral exam; for doctorate, comprehensive exam, thesis/dissertation, oral exam, written exam. *Entrance requirements:* For master's, GRE General Test, minimum GPA of 3.0; for doctorate, GRE General Test, minimum GPA of 3.5. Additional exam requirements/recommendations for international students: required—TOEFL. Electronic applications accepted.

**Washington University in St. Louis,** School of Medicine, Program in Clinical Investigation, St. Louis, MO 63130-4899. Offers clinical investigation (MS), including bioethics, entrepreneurship, genetics/genomics, translational medicine. *Program availability:* Part-time, evening/weekend. *Degree requirements:* For master's, thesis. *Entrance requirements:* For master's, doctoral-level degree or in process of obtaining doctoral-level degree. Electronic applications accepted.

# Naturopathic Medicine

**Bastyr University,** School of Naturopathic Medicine, Kenmore, WA 98028-4966. Offers ND, Postbaccalaureate Certificate. *Accreditation:* CNME; MEAC. *Program availability:* Part-time. *Degree requirements:* For doctorate, comprehensive exam. *Entrance requirements:* For doctorate, 1 year of course work each in biology, chemistry, organic chemistry and physics; for Postbaccalaureate Certificate, BS or BA with 1 year of course work each in biology, chemistry, organic chemistry and physics. Additional exam requirements/recommendations for international students: required—TOEFL (minimum score 550 paper-based; 79 iBT). Electronic applications accepted.

**Canadian College of Naturopathic Medicine,** Doctor of Naturopathy Program, Toronto, ON M2K 1E2, Canada. Offers ND. *Accreditation:* CNME. *Entrance requirements:* Additional exam requirements/recommendations for international students: recommended—TOEFL (minimum score 580 paper-based; 86 iBT), IELTS (minimum score 6.5). Electronic applications accepted.

**Maryland University of Integrative Health,** Program in Naturopathic Medicine, Laurel, MD 20723. Offers ND.

**National University of Health Sciences,** Graduate Programs, Lombard, IL 60148-4583. Offers acupuncture (MSAC); chiropractic (DC); diagnostic imaging (MS); naturopathic medicine (ND); Oriental medicine (MSOM). *Accreditation:* ACAOM; CCE; CNME.

**National University of Natural Medicine,** College of Naturopathic Medicine, Portland, OR 97201. Offers integrative medicine research (MS); naturopathic medicine (ND). *Accreditation:* CNME. *Students:* 247 full-time (210 women), 16 part-time (12 women); includes 67 minority (3 Black or African American, non-Hispanic/Latino; 3 American Indian or Alaska Native, non-Hispanic/Latino; 21 Asian, non-Hispanic/Latino; 22 Hispanic/Latino; 1 Native Hawaiian or other Pacific Islander, non-Hispanic/Latino; 17 Two or more races, non-Hispanic/Latino), 5 international. Average age 30. 113 applicants, 79% accepted, 55 enrolled. In 2019, 89 doctorates awarded. *Degree requirements:* For doctorate, comprehensive exam. *Entrance requirements:* For doctorate, Bachelor's Degree from a regionally accredited institution and specific prerequisite coursework. Additional exam requirements/recommendations for international students: required—TOEFL (minimum score 550 paper-based; 80 iBT), IELTS and PTE are accepted. *Application deadline:* For fall admission, 5/1 priority date for domestic and international students. Applications are processed on a rolling basis. Application fee: $75. Electronic applications accepted. *Expenses: Tuition:* Part-time $464 per credit hour. *Financial support:* Federal Work-Study and scholarships/grants available. Financial award application deadline: 2/15; financial award applicants required to submit FAFSA. *Unit head:* Kelly Baltazar, ND, DC, MS, Interim Program Director of Naturopathic Medicine, 503-503.552.1696, Fax: 503-499-0027, E-mail: admissions@nunm.edu. *Application contact:* Ryan Hollister, Director of Admissions, 503-552-1665, Fax: 503-499-0027, E-mail: admissions@numn.edu.
Website: http://nunm.edu/academics/school-of-naturopathic-medicine/

**National University of Natural Medicine,** School of Undergraduate and Graduate Studies, Portland, OR 97201. Offers Ayurveda (MS); global health (MS); integrative medicine research (MS); integrative mental health (MS); nutrition (MS). *Program availability:* 100% online. *Students:* 92 full-time (83 women), 6 part-time (all women); includes 13 minority (1 Black or African American, non-Hispanic/Latino; 4 Asian, non-Hispanic/Latino; 3 Hispanic/Latino; 5 Two or more races, non-Hispanic/Latino). Average age 31. 114 applicants, 88% accepted, 60 enrolled. In 2019, 72 master's awarded. *Degree requirements:* For master's, thesis. *Entrance requirements:* For master's, Bachelor's degree from a regionally accredited institution and prerequisite courses. Additional exam requirements/recommendations for international students: required—TOEFL (minimum score 550 paper-based; 80 iBT), We accept IETS and PTE. *Application deadline:* For fall admission, 5/1 for domestic and international students. Applications are processed on a rolling basis. Application fee: $75. Electronic applications accepted. *Expenses: Tuition:* Part-time $464 per credit hour. *Financial support:* Federal Work-Study and scholarships/grants available. Financial award application deadline: 2/15; financial award applicants required to submit FAFSA. *Unit head:* Dr. Tim Irving, Program Director - School of Undergraduate and Graduate Studies, 503-552-1660, Fax: 503-499-0027, E-mail: admission@nunm.edu. *Application contact:* Ryan Hollister, Director of Admissions, 503-552-1665, Fax: 503-499-0027, E-mail: admissions@numn.edu.
Website: http://nunm.edu/academics/school-of-research-graduate-studies/

**Southwest College of Naturopathic Medicine and Health Sciences,** Doctor of Naturopathic Medicine Program, Tempe, AZ 85282. Offers ND. *Accreditation:* CNME. *Entrance requirements:* For doctorate, minimum GPA of 3.0, letters of recommendation, in-person interview. Additional exam requirements/recommendations for international

students: required—TOEFL (minimum score 637 paper-based; 110 iBT). Electronic applications accepted. *Expenses:* Contact institution.

**Universidad del Turabo,** Graduate Programs, School of Health Sciences, Program in Naturopathy, Gurabo, PR 00778-3030. Offers ND. *Entrance requirements:* For doctorate, GRE, EXADEP or GMAT, official transcript, recommendation letters, essay, curriculum vitae, interview. Electronic applications accepted.

**University of Bridgeport,** College of Naturopathic Medicine, Bridgeport, CT 06604. Offers ND. *Accreditation:* CNME. *Degree requirements:* For doctorate, NPLEX Part I. *Entrance requirements:* For doctorate, minimum GPA of 2.5. Additional exam requirements/recommendations for international students: recommended—TOEFL (minimum score 550 paper-based; 80 iBT), IELTS. Electronic applications accepted.

# Osteopathic Medicine

**Alabama College of Osteopathic Medicine,** Graduate Program, Dothan, AL 36303. Offers DO. *Accreditation:* AOsA.

**Arkansas Colleges of Health Education,** Arkansas College of Osteopathic Medicine, Fort Smith, AR 72916. Offers DO.

**A.T. Still University,** Kirksville College of Osteopathic Medicine, Kirksville, MO 63501. Offers biomedical sciences (MS); osteopathic medicine (DO). *Accreditation:* AOsA. *Faculty:* 147 full-time (95 women), 61 part-time/adjunct (23 women). *Students:* 710 full-time (311 women), 10 part-time (3 women); includes 143 minority (17 Black or African American, non-Hispanic/Latino; 46 Asian, non-Hispanic/Latino; 41 Hispanic/Latino; 1 Native Hawaiian or other Pacific Islander, non-Hispanic/Latino; 38 Two or more races, non-Hispanic/Latino). Average age 27. 4,388 applicants, 9% accepted, 180 enrolled. In 2019, 7 master's, 173 doctorates awarded. *Degree requirements:* For master's, thesis; for doctorate, Level 1 and 2 COMLEX-PE and CE exams. *Entrance requirements:* For master's, GRE, MCAT, or DAT, minimum undergraduate GPA of 2.65 (cumulative and science); for doctorate, MCAT, bachelor's degree with minimum GPA of 2.8 (cumulative and science) or 90 semester hours with minimum GPA of 3.5 (cumulative and science) and MCAT (minimum score 500). *Application deadline:* For fall admission, 2/1 for domestic students; for summer admission, 2/1 for domestic students. Applications are processed on a rolling basis. Application fee: $70. Electronic applications accepted. *Financial support:* In 2019–20, 194 students received support, including 10 fellowships with full tuition reimbursements available (averaging $58,290 per year); Federal Work-Study and scholarships/grants also available. Financial award application deadline: 6/1; financial award applicants required to submit FAFSA. *Unit head:* Dr. Margaret Wilson, Dean, 660-626-2354, Fax: 660-626-2080, E-mail: mwilson@atsu.edu. *Application contact:* Donna Sparks, Director, Admissions Processing, 660-626-2117, Fax: 660-626-2969, E-mail: admissions@atsu.edu.
Website: http://www.atsu.edu/kcom/

**A.T. Still University,** School of Osteopathic Medicine in Arizona, Mesa, AZ 85206. Offers osteopathic medicine (DO). *Accreditation:* AOsA. *Faculty:* 49 full-time (26 women), 74 part-time/adjunct (21 women). *Students:* 480 full-time (276 women); includes 249 minority (9 Black or African American, non-Hispanic/Latino; 163 Asian, non-Hispanic/Latino; 33 Hispanic/Latino; 3 Native Hawaiian or other Pacific Islander, non-Hispanic/Latino; 41 Two or more races, non-Hispanic/Latino). Average age 27. 5,597 applicants, 7% accepted, 161 enrolled. In 2019, 104 doctorates awarded. *Degree requirements:* For doctorate, Level 1 and 2 COMLEX-PE and CE exams. *Entrance requirements:* For doctorate, MCAT, minimum undergraduate GPA of 2.8 (cumulative and science) with bachelor's degree. *Application deadline:* For fall admission, 3/1 for domestic students; for summer admission, 3/1 for domestic students. Applications are processed on a rolling basis. Application fee: $70. Electronic applications accepted. *Financial support:* In 2019–20, 71 students received support, including 1 fellowship with full tuition reimbursement available (averaging $59,802 per year); Federal Work-Study and scholarships/grants also available. Financial award application deadline: 6/1; financial award applicants required to submit FAFSA. *Unit head:* Dr. Jeffrey Morgan, Dean, 480-265-8017, Fax: 480-219-6159, E-mail: jeffreymorgan@atsu.edu. *Application contact:* Donna Sparks, Director, Admissions Processing, 660-626-2117, Fax: 660-626-2969, E-mail: admissions@atsu.edu.
Website: http://www.atsu.edu/soma

**Burrell College of Osteopathic Medicine,** Graduate Program, Las Cruces, NM 88001. Offers DO.

**Campbell University,** Graduate and Professional Programs, Jerry M. Wallace School of Osteopathic Medicine, Buies Creek, NC 27506. Offers DO. *Accreditation:* AOsA.

**Des Moines University,** College of Osteopathic Medicine, Des Moines, IA 50312-4104. Offers DO. *Accreditation:* AOsA. *Degree requirements:* For doctorate, National Board of Osteopathic Medical Examiners Exam Level 1 and 2. *Entrance requirements:* For doctorate, MCAT, minimum GPA of 3.0; 8 hours of course work in biology, chemistry, organic chemistry, and physics; 3 hours of biochemistry; 6 hours of course work in English; interview. Electronic applications accepted. *Expenses:* Contact institution.

**Edward Via College of Osteopathic Medicine–Carolinas Campus,** Graduate Program, Spartanburg, SC 29303. Offers DO. *Accreditation:* AOsA.

**Edward Via College of Osteopathic Medicine–Virginia Campus,** Graduate Program, Blacksburg, VA 24060. Offers DO. *Accreditation:* AOsA. *Degree requirements:* For doctorate, thesis/dissertation. *Entrance requirements:* For doctorate, MCAT, 8 hours of biology, general chemistry, and organic chemistry; 6 hours each of additional science and English; minimum overall science GPA of 2.75.

**Georgia Campus–Philadelphia College of Osteopathic Medicine,** Doctor of Osteopathic Medicine Program, Suwanee, GA 30024. Offers DO. *Accreditation:* AOsA. *Degree requirements:* For doctorate, comprehensive exam. *Entrance requirements:* For doctorate, MCAT. Additional exam requirements/recommendations for international students: required—TOEFL (minimum score 79 iBT). Electronic applications accepted. *Expenses:* Contact institution.

**Kansas City University of Medicine and Biosciences,** College of Osteopathic Medicine, Kansas City, MO 64106-1453. Offers DO, DO/MA, DO/MBA. *Accreditation:* AOsA. *Degree requirements:* For doctorate, comprehensive exam, National Board Exam - COMLEX. *Entrance requirements:* For doctorate, MCAT, on-campus interview.

**Lake Erie College of Osteopathic Medicine,** Professional Programs, Erie, PA 16509-1025. Offers biomedical sciences (Postbaccalaureate Certificate); medical education (MS); osteopathic medicine (DO); pharmacy (Pharm D). *Accreditation:* ACPE; AOsA. *Degree requirements:* For doctorate, comprehensive exam, National Osteopathic Medical Licensing Exam, Levels 1 and 2; for Postbaccalaureate Certificate, comprehensive exam, North American Pharmacist Licensure Examination (NAPLEX). *Entrance requirements:* For doctorate, MCAT, minimum GPA of 3.2, letters of recommendation; for Postbaccalaureate Certificate, PCAT, letters of recommendation, minimum GPA of 3.5. Electronic applications accepted.

**Liberty University,** College of Osteopathic Medicine, Lynchburg, VA 24515. Offers DO. *Accreditation:* AOsA. *Students:* 604 full-time (280 women), 6 part-time (1 woman); includes 135 minority (14 Black or African American, non-Hispanic/Latino; 1 American Indian or Alaska Native, non-Hispanic/Latino; 82 Asian, non-Hispanic/Latino; 22 Hispanic/Latino; 16 Two or more races, non-Hispanic/Latino), 23 international. Average age 27. 2,282 applicants, 7% accepted, 152 enrolled. In 2019, 126 doctorates awarded. *Entrance requirements:* For doctorate, MCAT (minimum cumulative score of 22). *Application deadline:* Applications are processed on a rolling basis. Electronic applications accepted. *Expenses:* Contact institution. *Financial support:* In 2019–20, 167 students received support. Teaching assistantships and Federal Work-Study available. *Unit head:* Dr. Peter A. Bell, Dean, 434-592-6515. *Application contact:* Jay Bridge, Director of Admissions, 800-424-9595, Fax: 800-628-7977, E-mail: gradadmissions@liberty.edu.
Website: http://www.liberty.edu/lucom/

**Lincoln Memorial University,** DeBusk College of Osteopathic Medicine, Harrogate, TN 37752-1901. Offers DO. *Accreditation:* AOsA. *Entrance requirements:* For doctorate, MCAT. Additional exam requirements/recommendations for international students: required—TOEFL (minimum score 600 paper-based; 100 iBT).

**Marian University,** College of Osteopathic Medicine, Indianapolis, IN 46222-1997. Offers MS, DO. *Accreditation:* AOsA. *Degree requirements:* For master's, thesis; for doctorate, comprehensive exam, COMLEX licensing exam. *Entrance requirements:* For master's, MCAT or GRE; for doctorate, MCAT. Additional exam requirements/recommendations for international students: required—TOEFL. Electronic applications accepted. *Expenses:* Contact institution.

**Michigan State University,** College of Osteopathic Medicine, Professional Program in Osteopathic Medicine, East Lansing, MI 48824. Offers DO. *Accreditation:* AOsA. Electronic applications accepted.

**Midwestern University, Downers Grove Campus,** Chicago College of Osteopathic Medicine, Downers Grove, IL 60515-1235. Offers DO. *Accreditation:* AOsA. *Entrance requirements:* For doctorate, MCAT, 1 year course work each in organic chemistry, general chemistry, biology, physics, and English. *Expenses:* Contact institution.

**Midwestern University, Glendale Campus,** Arizona College of Osteopathic Medicine, Glendale, AZ 85308. Offers DO. *Accreditation:* AOsA. *Entrance requirements:* For doctorate, MCAT. Electronic applications accepted. *Expenses:* Contact institution.

**New York Institute of Technology,** College of Osteopathic Medicine, Old Westbury, NY 11568. Offers global health (Certificate); DO/MS. *Accreditation:* AOsA. *Faculty:* 94 full-time (44 women), 36 part-time/adjunct (16 women). *Students:* 1,734 full-time (827 women); includes 814 minority (68 Black or African American, non-Hispanic/Latino; 627 Asian, non-Hispanic/Latino; 81 Hispanic/Latino; 38 Two or more races, non-Hispanic/Latino). Average age 27. 7,140 applicants, 13% accepted, 435 enrolled. *Entrance requirements:* Additional exam requirements/recommendations for international students: required—TOEFL, IELTS, PTE. *Application deadline:* For fall admission, 3/1 for domestic students. Applications are processed on a rolling basis. Application fee: $80. Electronic applications accepted. *Expenses:* Annual tuition $59,350 plus fees. *Financial support:* In 2019–20, 690 students received support. Federal Work-Study and scholarships/grants available. Financial award application deadline: 2/15; financial award applicants required to submit FAFSA. *Unit head:* Dr. Jerry Balentine, Dean, 516-686-3999, Fax: 516-686-3830, E-mail: Jerry.Balentine@nyit.edu. *Application contact:* Carol Zerah, Director, Admissions, 516-686-3997, E-mail: comadm@nyit.edu.
Website: https://www.nyit.edu/medicine

**Nova Southeastern University,** Dr. Kiran C. Patel College of Osteopathic Medicine, Fort Lauderdale, FL 33314-7796. Offers biomedical informatics (MS, Graduate Certificate), including biomedical informatics (MS), clinical informatics (Graduate Certificate), public health informatics (Graduate Certificate); disaster and emergency management (MS); medical education (MS); nutrition (MS, Graduate Certificate), including functional nutrition and herbal therapy (Graduate Certificate); osteopathic medicine (DO); public health (MPH, Graduate Certificate), including health education (Graduate Certificate); social medicine (Graduate Certificate); DO/DMD. *Accreditation:* AOsA; CEPH. *Program availability:* Part-time, 100% online, blended/hybrid learning. *Faculty:* 73 full-time (43 women), 35 part-time/adjunct (14 women). *Students:* 1,410 full-time (740 women), 182 part-time (118 women); includes 895 minority (126 Black or African American, non-Hispanic/Latino; 1 American Indian or Alaska Native, non-Hispanic/Latino; 416 Asian, non-Hispanic/Latino; 309 Hispanic/Latino; 1 Native Hawaiian or other Pacific Islander, non-Hispanic/Latino; 42 Two or more races, non-Hispanic/Latino), 70 international. Average age 26. 5,078 applicants, 10% accepted, 495 enrolled. In 2019, 117 master's, 233 doctorates, 3 other advanced degrees awarded. *Degree requirements:* For master's, comprehensive exam (for MPH); field/special projects; for doctorate, comprehensive exam, COMLEX Board Exams; for Graduate Certificate, thesis or alternative. *Entrance requirements:* For master's, GRE; for doctorate, MCAT, coursework in biology, chemistry, organic chemistry, physics (all with labs), biochemistry, and English. *Application deadline:* For fall admission, 1/15 for domestic students. Applications are processed on a rolling basis. Application fee: $50. Electronic applications accepted. *Expenses:* Contact institution. *Financial support:* In 2019–20, 83 students received support, including 24 fellowships with tuition reimbursements available; Federal Work-Study and scholarships/grants also available. Financial award application deadline: 6/1; financial award applicants required to submit FAFSA. *Unit head:* Elaine M. Wallace, Dean, 954-262-1457, Fax: 954-262-2250, E-mail: ewallace@nova.edu. *Application contact:* HPD Admissions, 877-640-0218, E-mail: hpdinfo@nova.edu.
Website: https://www.osteopathic.nova.edu/

**Ohio University,** Heritage College of Osteopathic Medicine, Athens, OH 45701. Offers DO, DO/MBA, DO/MGH, DO/MPH, DO/MS, DO/PhD. *Accreditation:* AOsA. *Degree requirements:* For doctorate, comprehensive exam, National Board Exam Parts I and II, COMLEX-PE. *Entrance requirements:* For doctorate, MCAT, interview; course work in English, physics, biology, general chemistry, organic chemistry, and behavioral sciences

with minimum grade of C. Electronic applications accepted. *Expenses:* Contact institution.

**Oklahoma State University Center for Health Sciences,** College of Osteopathic Medicine, Tulsa, OK 74114. Offers DO, DO/MBA, DO/MPH, DO/MS, DO/PhD. *Accreditation:* AOsA. *Degree requirements:* For doctorate, COMLEX Board exams. *Entrance requirements:* For doctorate, MCAT (minimum score 492), interview; minimum 90 hours of college course work; minimum cumulative GPA of 3.0, science 2.75. Electronic applications accepted.

**Pacific Northwest University of Health Sciences,** College of Osteopathic Medicine, Yakima, WA 98901. Offers DO. *Accreditation:* AOsA. *Degree requirements:* For doctorate, COMLEX-USA licensure exams. *Entrance requirements:* For doctorate, MCAT. Electronic applications accepted. *Expenses:* Contact institution.

**Philadelphia College of Osteopathic Medicine,** Graduate and Professional Programs, Doctor of Osteopathic Medicine Program, Philadelphia, PA 19131. Offers DO, DO/MA, DO/MBA, DO/MPH, DO/MS, DO/PhD. *Accreditation:* AOsA. *Faculty:* 77 full-time (38 women), 1,293 part-time/adjunct (257 women). *Students:* 1,091 full-time (566 women); includes 363 minority (96 Black or African American, non-Hispanic/Latino; 1 American Indian or Alaska Native, non-Hispanic/Latino; 114 Asian, non-Hispanic/Latino; 24 Hispanic/Latino; 128 Two or more races, non-Hispanic/Latino), 2 international. Average age 27. 9,185 applicants, 6% accepted, 270 enrolled. In 2019, 258 doctorates awarded. *Entrance requirements:* For doctorate, MCAT, minimum GPA of 3.2; premedical prerequisite coursework; biochemistry (recommended). Additional exam requirements/recommendations for international students: required—TOEFL (minimum score 79 iBT). *Application deadline:* For fall admission, 2/1 for domestic students. Applications are processed on a rolling basis. Application fee: $75. Electronic applications accepted. *Expenses:* Contact institution. *Financial support:* In 2019–20, 870 students received support, including 14 fellowships with partial tuition reimbursements available; Federal Work-Study, institutionally sponsored loans, and scholarships/grants also available. Financial award application deadline: 3/15; financial award applicants required to submit FAFSA. *Unit head:* Dr. Kenneth J. Veit, Dean, 215-871-6770, Fax: 215-871-6781, E-mail: kenv@pcom.edu. *Application contact:* Kari A. Shotwell, Director of Admissions, 215-871-6700, Fax: 215-871-6719, E-mail: karis@pcom.edu. Website: http://www.pcom.edu

**Rocky Vista University,** College of Osteopathic Medicine, Parker, CO 80134. Offers DO. *Accreditation:* AOsA. *Expenses:* Contact institution.

**Rowan University,** School of Osteopathic Medicine, Stratford, NJ 08084-1501. Offers DO, DO/MA, DO/MBA, DO/MPH, DO/MS, DO/PhD, JD/DO. *Accreditation:* AOsA. *Degree requirements:* For doctorate, comprehensive exam. *Entrance requirements:* For doctorate, MCAT. Electronic applications accepted. *Expenses:* Contact institution.

**Touro University California,** Graduate Programs, Vallejo, CA 94592. Offers education (MA); medical health sciences (MS); osteopathic medicine (DO); pharmacy (Pharm D); public health (MPH). *Accreditation:* ACPE; AOsA; ARC-PA; CEPH. *Program availability:* Part-time, evening/weekend. *Degree requirements:* For master's, comprehensive exam, thesis; for doctorate, comprehensive exam. *Entrance requirements:* For doctorate, BS/BA. Electronic applications accepted.

**University of New England,** College of Osteopathic Medicine, Biddeford, ME 04005-9526. Offers DO, DO/MPH. *Accreditation:* AOsA. *Faculty:* 46 full-time (22 women), 27 part-time/adjunct (11 women). *Students:* 710 full-time (391 women); includes 135 minority (3 Black or African American, non-Hispanic/Latino; 1 American Indian or Alaska Native, non-Hispanic/Latino; 113 Asian, non-Hispanic/Latino; 5 Hispanic/Latino; 13 Two or more races, non-Hispanic/Latino), 20 international. Average age 27. In 2019, 180 doctorates awarded. *Entrance requirements:* For doctorate, MCAT. *Application deadline:* For fall admission, 3/1 for domestic students. *Financial support:* Application deadline: 5/1; applicants required to submit FAFSA. *Unit head:* Dr. Jane Carreiro, Dean, College of Osteopathic Medicine, 207-602-2460, E-mail: jcarreiro@une.edu. *Application contact:* Scott Steinberg, Vice President of University Admissions, 207-221-4225, Fax: 207-523-1925, E-mail: ssteinberg@une.edu. Website: http://www.une.edu/com/index.cfm

**University of North Texas Health Science Center at Fort Worth,** Texas College of Osteopathic Medicine, Fort Worth, TX 76107-2699. Offers DO, DO/MPH, DO/MS, DO/PhD. *Accreditation:* AOsA. *Entrance requirements:* For doctorate, MCAT, 1 year of course work each in biology, physics and English; 2 years' course work in chemistry. Electronic applications accepted.

**University of Pikeville,** Kentucky College of Osteopathic Medicine, Pikeville, KY 41501. Offers DO. *Accreditation:* AOsA. *Faculty:* 24 full-time (9 women), 35 part-time/adjunct (13 women). *Students:* 551 full-time (267 women); includes 131 minority (5

Black or African American, non-Hispanic/Latino; 1 American Indian or Alaska Native, non-Hispanic/Latino; 105 Asian, non-Hispanic/Latino; 15 Hispanic/Latino; 5 Native Hawaiian or other Pacific Islander, non-Hispanic/Latino). Average age 25. 3,763 applicants, 6% accepted, 134 enrolled. In 2019, 119 doctorates awarded. *Degree requirements:* For doctorate, COMLEX Level 1 and COMLEX Level 2CE and 2PE. *Entrance requirements:* For doctorate, MCAT. *Application deadline:* For fall admission, 5/1 for domestic students. Applications are processed on a rolling basis. Application fee: $75. *Expenses:* $47,420 tuition. *Financial support:* In 2019–20, 11 students received support, including 11 fellowships with full and partial tuition reimbursements available (averaging $28,169 per year); scholarships/grants also available. Financial award application deadline: 8/1; financial award applicants required to submit FAFSA. *Unit head:* Dr. Dana Shaffer, Dean, 606-218-5410, E-mail: danashaffer@upike.edu. *Application contact:* Michael Kennedy, Senior Recruiter, 606-218-5257, E-mail: michaelkennedy@upike.edu. Website: https://www.upike.edu/osteopathic-medicine/

**University of the Incarnate Word,** School of Osteopathic Medicine, San Antonio, TX 78209-6397. Offers MBS, DO. *Faculty:* 9 full-time (5 women), 1 part-time/adjunct (0 women). *Students:* 513 full-time (304 women), 2 part-time (both women); includes 323 minority (33 Black or African American, non-Hispanic/Latino; 1 American Indian or Alaska Native, non-Hispanic/Latino; 122 Asian, non-Hispanic/Latino; 145 Hispanic/Latino; 22 Two or more races, non-Hispanic/Latino). 574 applicants, 75% accepted, 207 enrolled. In 2019, 31 master's awarded. *Degree requirements:* For master's, thesis or alternative; for doctorate, comprehensive exam. *Entrance requirements:* For master's, GRE or MCAT, courses in biology, general chemistry, anatomy and physiology, biochemistry, and mathematics; for doctorate, MCAT, courses in biology, inorganic chemistry, organic chemistry, physics, and English; three letters of recommendation. *Application deadline:* For fall admission, 9/1 for domestic students; for spring admission, 3/15 for domestic students. Applications are processed on a rolling basis. Application fee: $50. Electronic applications accepted. *Expenses:* $56,000 annual tuition, plus annual fees from $1,000 - $2,000. *Financial support:* Research assistantships, career-related internships or fieldwork, scholarships/grants, and unspecified assistantships available. Financial award applicants required to submit FAFSA. *Unit head:* Dr. Robyn Phillips-Madson, Dean, E-mail: rmadson@uiwtx.edu. *Application contact:* Sonia Winney, Admissions Coordinator, 210-283-6998, E-mail: winney@uiwtx.edu. Website: https://osteopathic-medicine.uiw.edu/index.html

**Western University of Health Sciences,** College of Osteopathic Medicine of the Pacific, Pomona, CA 91766-1854. Offers DO. *Accreditation:* AOsA. *Faculty:* 71 full-time (32 women), 18 part-time/adjunct (5 women). *Students:* 1,321 full-time (632 women); includes 678 minority (21 Black or African American, non-Hispanic/Latino; 2 American Indian or Alaska Native, non-Hispanic/Latino; 466 Asian, non-Hispanic/Latino; 90 Hispanic/Latino; 2 Native Hawaiian or other Pacific Islander, non-Hispanic/Latino; 97 Two or more races, non-Hispanic/Latino), 24 international. Average age 27. 5,235 applicants, 14% accepted, 318 enrolled. In 2019, 328 doctorates awarded. *Degree requirements:* For doctorate, comprehensive exam (for some programs). *Entrance requirements:* For doctorate, MCAT, minimum GPA of 3.3, interview, 2 letters of recommendation, confirmation of a baccalaureate degree as a requirement for matriculation, completion of the majority of prerequisite courses listed, completion of a minimum of 90 semester units from a regionally accredited US institution or its equivalent abroad at time of application. *Application deadline:* For fall admission, 2/1 for domestic and international students. Applications are processed on a rolling basis. Application fee: $65. Electronic applications accepted. *Expenses:* Contact institution. *Financial support:* In 2019–20, 139 students received support. Career-related internships or fieldwork and scholarships/grants available. Financial award application deadline: 3/2; financial award applicants required to submit FAFSA. *Unit head:* Dr. Paula Crone, Dean, 541-259-0206, Fax: 541-259-0201, E-mail: pcrone@westernu.edu. *Application contact:* Martha Alfaro, Assistant Director of Admissions, 909-469-5332, Fax: 909-469-5570, E-mail: mhuizar@westernu.edu. Website: http://www.westernu.edu/osteopathy/

**West Virginia School of Osteopathic Medicine,** Professional Program, Lewisburg, WV 24901-1196. Offers DO. *Accreditation:* AOsA. *Degree requirements:* For doctorate, comprehensive exam, Comlex Level 1 and 2 (PE and CE). *Entrance requirements:* For doctorate, MCAT, 6 semester hours each of biology/zoology, physics, English, and behavioral sciences; 9 semester hours in chemistry; 3 semester hours in biochemistry. Electronic applications accepted. *Expenses: Tuition, area resident:* Full-time $22,472. Tuition, nonresident: full-time $53,710. *Required fees:* $1200.

**William Carey University,** College of Osteopathic Medicine, Hattiesburg, MS 39401. Offers DO. *Accreditation:* AOsA.

# Podiatric Medicine

---

**Barry University,** School of Podiatric Medicine, Podiatric Medicine and Surgery Program, Miami Shores, FL 33161-6695. Offers DPM, DPM/MBA, DPM/MPH. *Accreditation:* APMA. *Entrance requirements:* For doctorate, MCAT, GRE General Test, previous course work in science and English. Additional exam requirements/recommendations for international students: required—TOEFL. Electronic applications accepted. *Expenses:* Contact institution.

**Des Moines University,** College of Podiatric Medicine and Surgery, Des Moines, IA 50312-4104. Offers DPM. *Accreditation:* APMA. *Entrance requirements:* For doctorate, MCAT, interview; minimum GPA of 2.5; 1 year of organic chemistry, inorganic chemistry, physics, biology, and English. Electronic applications accepted. *Expenses:* Contact institution.

**Kent State University,** College of Podiatric Medicine, Kent, OH 44131. Offers DPM. *Accreditation:* APMA. *Entrance requirements:* For doctorate, MCAT, satisfactory course work in biology, chemistry, English and physics; background check, drug test. Additional exam requirements/recommendations for international students: recommended—TOEFL (minimum score 81 iBT). Electronic applications accepted. *Expenses:* Contact institution.

**Midwestern University, Glendale Campus,** College of Health Sciences, Arizona Campus, Program in Podiatric Medicine, Glendale, AZ 85308. Offers DPM. *Accreditation:* APMA. *Entrance requirements:* For doctorate, MCAT or PCAT, 90 semester hours at an accredited college or university, minimum GPA of 2.75. *Expenses:* Contact institution.

**New York College of Podiatric Medicine,** Professional Program, New York, NY 10035. Offers DPM, DPM/MPH. *Accreditation:* APMA. *Degree requirements:* For doctorate,

comprehensive exam. *Entrance requirements:* For doctorate, MCAT or DAT, 1 year course work in biology, physics, English, and general and organic chemistry. Additional exam requirements/recommendations for international students: required—TOEFL.

**Rosalind Franklin University of Medicine and Science,** Dr. William M. Scholl College of Podiatric Medicine, North Chicago, IL 60064-3095. Offers DPM. *Accreditation:* APMA. *Entrance requirements:* For doctorate, MCAT (or GRE on approval), 12 semester hours of biology; 8 semester hours of inorganic chemistry, organic chemistry and physics; 6 semester hours of English. Additional exam requirements/recommendations for international students: required—TOEFL.

**Samuel Merritt University,** California School of Podiatric Medicine, Oakland, CA 94609-3108. Offers DPM. *Accreditation:* APMA. *Entrance requirements:* For doctorate, MCAT (less than 3 years old), at least 90 semester hours of undergraduate course work; 1 year of course work in organic chemistry or biochemistry, inorganic chemistry, physics, biological sciences (all courses must come with a lab), and English/communications. Additional exam requirements/recommendations for international students: required—TOEFL (minimum score 100 iBT). Electronic applications accepted. *Expenses:* Contact institution.

**Temple University,** School of Podiatric Medicine, Philadelphia, PA 19107-2496. Offers DPM, DPM/MBA, DPM/PhD. *Accreditation:* APMA. *Degree requirements:* For doctorate, National Board Exam. *Entrance requirements:* For doctorate, MCAT, GRE, or DAT, interview, 8 hours of organic chemistry, inorganic chemistry, physics, biology.

**Western University of Health Sciences,** College of Podiatric Medicine, Pomona, CA 91766-1854. Offers DPM. *Accreditation:* APMA. *Faculty:* 11 full-time (7 women), 5 part-time/adjunct (1 woman). *Students:* 153 full-time (53 women); includes 96 minority (7

Black or African American, non-Hispanic/Latino; 60 Asian, non-Hispanic/Latino; 15 Hispanic/Latino; 1 Native Hawaiian or other Pacific Islander, non-Hispanic/Latino; 13 Two or more races, non-Hispanic/Latino), 1 international. Average age 27. 454 applicants, 27% accepted, 49 enrolled. In 2019, 27 doctorates awarded. *Degree requirements:* For doctorate, comprehensive exam (for some programs). *Entrance requirements:* For doctorate, MCAT or DAT, letters of recommendation from a podiatric physician; BS or BA (recommended); transcripts from all colleges, universities and professional schools attended. Additional exam requirements/recommendations for international students: required—TOEFL (minimum score 79 iBT), or 6 semesters of English courses in the States. *Application deadline:* For fall admission, 6/30 for domestic and international students. Applications are processed on a rolling basis. Electronic applications accepted. *Expenses:* Tuition is average about $39820 per year, Student body fees is $40 per year, APMSA membership fee is $75 per year and one time SEP/Medical Equipment fee is $1147. *Financial support:* In 2019–20, 28 students received support. Career-related internships or fieldwork, scholarships/grants, and traineeships available. Financial award application deadline: 3/2; financial award applicants required to submit FAFSA. *Unit head:* Dr. Kathleen Satterfield, Dean, 909-706-3933, E-mail: vsatterfield@westernu.edu. *Application contact:* Marie Anderson, Director of Admissions, 909-469-5485, Fax: 909-469-5570, E-mail: admissions@westernu.edu. Website: http://www.westernu.edu/podiatry/

# Section 29
# Optometry and Vision Sciences

This section contains a directory of institutions offering graduate work in optometry and vision sciences. Additional information about programs listed in the directory may be obtained by writing directly to the dean of a graduate school or chair of a department at the address given in the directory.

In the other guides in this series:

**Graduate Programs in the Humanities, Arts & Social Sciences**
See *Psychology and Counseling*

**Graduate Programs in the Physical Sciences, Mathematics, Agricultural Sciences, the Environment & Natural Resources**
See *Physics*

**Graduate Programs in Engineering & Applied Sciences**
See *Biomedical Engineering* and *Biotechnology*

## CONTENTS

### Program Directories

# Optometry

**Ferris State University,** Michigan College of Optometry, Big Rapids, MI 49307. Offers OD. *Accreditation:* AOA. *Faculty:* 19 full-time (9 women), 115 part-time/adjunct (52 women). *Students:* 146 full-time (90 women); includes 6 minority (1 Asian, non-Hispanic/Latino; 4 Hispanic/Latino; 1 Two or more races, non-Hispanic/Latino), 10 international. Average age 24. 225 applicants, 30% accepted, 38 enrolled. In 2019, 35 doctorates awarded. *Degree requirements:* For doctorate, comprehensive exam, Research project. *Entrance requirements:* For doctorate, OAT, OPTOMCAS application. Additional exam requirements/recommendations for international students: recommended—TOEFL (minimum score 550 paper-based; 80 iBT). *Application deadline:* For fall admission, 2/1 for domestic and international students. Applications are processed on a rolling basis. Application fee: $175. Electronic applications accepted. *Expenses:* $30,704 for 1st year, $30,704 for 2nd year, $42,016 for 3rd year, $35,552 for 4th year. *Financial support:* In 2019–20, 13 students received support. Career-related internships or fieldwork, Federal Work-Study, and scholarships/grants available. Financial award application deadline: 2/1; financial award applicants required to submit FAFSA. *Unit head:* Dr. David Damari, Dean, 231-591-3706, Fax: 231-591-2394, E-mail: damarid@ferris.edu. *Application contact:* Amy Parks, Health College Administrative Specialist, 231-591-3703, Fax: 231-591-2394, E-mail: amyparks@ferris.edu.
Website: http://www.ferris.edu/mco/

**Illinois College of Optometry,** Professional Program, Chicago, IL 60616-3878. Offers OD. *Accreditation:* AOA. *Entrance requirements:* For doctorate, OAT. Electronic applications accepted.

**Indiana University Bloomington,** School of Optometry, Bloomington, IN 47405-3680. Offers MS, OD, PhD. *Accreditation:* AOA (one or more programs are accredited). Terminal master's awarded for partial completion of doctoral program. *Degree requirements:* For master's, thesis; for doctorate, comprehensive exam, thesis/dissertation. *Entrance requirements:* For master's, GRE, BA in science; for doctorate, GRE; OAT (for OD), BA in science (master's degree preferred). Additional exam requirements/recommendations for international students: required—TOEFL (minimum score 550 paper-based; 80 iBT). Electronic applications accepted. *Expenses:* Contact institution.

**Inter American University of Puerto Rico School of Optometry,** Professional Program, Bayamón, PR 00957. Offers OD. *Accreditation:* AOA. *Degree requirements:* For doctorate, thesis/dissertation, research project. *Entrance requirements:* For doctorate, OAT, interview, minimum GPA of 2.5, 2 letters of recommendation. Electronic applications accepted. *Expenses:* Contact institution.

**Marshall B. Ketchum University,** Graduate and Professional Programs, Fullerton, CA 92831-1615. Offers optometry (OD); pharmacy (Pharm D); vision science (MS). *Degree requirements:* For doctorate, thesis/dissertation. *Entrance requirements:* For doctorate, OAT. Electronic applications accepted.

**MCPHS University,** School of Optometry, Boston, MA 02115-5896. Offers OD. *Accreditation:* AOA.

**Midwestern University, Downers Grove Campus,** Chicago College of Optometry, Downers Grove, IL 60515-1235. Offers OD. *Entrance requirements:* For doctorate, OAT, bachelor's degree, minimum overall cumulative and science GPA of 2.75, two letters of recommendation.

**Midwestern University, Glendale Campus,** Arizona College of Optometry, Glendale, AZ 85308. Offers OD. *Accreditation:* AOA. *Entrance requirements:* For doctorate, OAT, bachelor's degree, minimum overall cumulative and science GPA of 2.75, 2 letters of recommendation.

**New England College of Optometry,** Graduate and Professional Programs, Boston, MA 02115-1100. Offers optometry (OD); vision science (MS). *Accreditation:* AOA. *Students:* 815 applicants, 40% accepted, 138 enrolled. In 2019, 115 doctorates awarded. *Entrance requirements:* For doctorate, OAT, GRE. *Application deadline:* For fall admission, 3/31 for domestic students. Applications are processed on a rolling basis. Application fee: $40. Electronic applications accepted. *Financial support:* In 2019–20, 357 students received support, including 12 research assistantships (averaging $5,193 per year); career-related internships or fieldwork, Federal Work-Study, institutionally sponsored loans, and scholarships/grants also available. Financial award application deadline: 4/1; financial award applicants required to submit FAFSA. *Application contact:* Kristen Tobin, Director of Admissions, 617-587-5580, Fax: 617-587-5550, E-mail: tobink@neco.edu.

**Northeastern State University,** Oklahoma College of Optometry, Tahlequah, OK 74464. Offers OD. *Accreditation:* AOA. *Faculty:* 15 full-time (6 women). *Students:* 113 full-time (64 women); includes 28 minority (1 Black or African American, non-Hispanic/Latino; 4 American Indian or Alaska Native, non-Hispanic/Latino; 8 Asian, non-Hispanic/Latino; 3 Hispanic/Latino; 12 Two or more races, non-Hispanic/Latino). Average age 25. In 2019, 27 doctorates awarded. *Degree requirements:* For doctorate, research project. *Entrance requirements:* For doctorate, OAT. *Application deadline:* For fall admission, 2/1 for domestic students. Applications are processed on a rolling basis. Application fee: $45. Electronic applications accepted. *Expenses:* Contact institution. *Financial support:* Federal Work-Study, institutionally sponsored loans, scholarships/grants, tuition waivers (partial), and residencies available. Financial award application deadline: 5/1; financial award applicants required to submit FAFSA. *Unit head:* Dr. Douglas Penisten, Dean of Oklahoma College of Optometry, 918-444-4025, E-mail: penisten@nsuok.edu. *Application contact:* Sandy Medearis, Optometric Student and Alumni Services Director, 918-444-4006, Fax: 918-458-2104, E-mail: medearis@nsuok.edu.
Website: http://optometry.nsuok.edu

**Nova Southeastern University,** College of Optometry, Fort Lauderdale, FL 33328. Offers MS, OD. *Accreditation:* AOA. *Program availability:* Part-time. *Faculty:* 41 full-time (30 women), 4 part-time/adjunct (2 women). *Students:* 435 full-time (292 women), 5 part-time (all women); includes 228 minority (25 Black or African American, non-Hispanic/Latino; 90 Asian, non-Hispanic/Latino; 90 Hispanic/Latino; 23 Two or more races, non-Hispanic/Latino), 41 international. Average age 28. 636 applicants, 17% accepted, 110 enrolled. In 2019, 3 master's, 104 doctorates awarded. *Degree requirements:* For master's, thesis. *Entrance requirements:* For master's, OAT, MCAT or GRE, BA; for doctorate, OAT, minimum GPA of 3.0. Additional exam requirements/recommendations for international students: required—TOEFL (minimum score 79 iBT). *Application deadline:* For fall admission, 10/1 for domestic students; for winter admission, 1/1 for domestic students; for spring admission, 4/1 for domestic students; for summer admission, 7/1 for domestic students. Applications are processed on a rolling basis. Application fee: $50. Electronic applications accepted. *Expenses:* Contact institution. *Financial support:* Federal Work-Study, institutionally sponsored loans, and scholarships/grants available. Support available to part-time students. Financial award application deadline: 4/15; financial award applicants required to submit FAFSA. Unit

*head:* Dr. David Loshin, Dean, 954-262-1404, Fax: 954-262-1818, E-mail: loshin@nova.edu. *Application contact:* Nicole Patterson, Assistant Dean for Student Affairs & Admissions, 954-262-1410, Fax: 954-262-1818, E-mail: npatters@nova.edu.
Website: http://optometry.nova.edu/

**The Ohio State University,** College of Optometry, Columbus, OH 43210. Offers optometry (OD); vision science (MS, PhD); OD/MS. *Accreditation:* AOA (one or more programs are accredited). *Degree requirements:* For master's, thesis; for doctorate, thesis/dissertation. *Entrance requirements:* For master's, GRE; for doctorate, GRE (for PhD); OAT (for OD). Additional exam requirements/recommendations for international students: required—TOEFL minimum score 550 paper-based, 79 iBT, Michigan English Language Assessment Battery minimum score 82, IELTS minimum score 7 (for MS and PhD); TOEFL minimum score 577 paper-based; 90 iBT, Michigan English Language Assessment Battery minimum score 84, IELTS minimum score 7.5 (for OD). Electronic applications accepted. *Expenses:* Contact institution.

**Pacific University,** College of Optometry, Forest Grove, OR 97116-1797. Offers optometry (OD); vision science (MS, PhD). *Accreditation:* AOA (one or more programs are accredited). *Degree requirements:* For doctorate, thesis/dissertation optional. *Entrance requirements:* For master's, GRE General Test, course work in natural sciences; for doctorate, OAT, 30 hours OD observation; course work in natural sciences, math, psychology, English, letters of recommendation. Additional exam requirements/recommendations for international students: required—TOEFL (minimum score 600 paper-based). Electronic applications accepted. *Expenses:* Contact institution.

**Salus University,** Pennsylvania College of Optometry, Elkins Park, PA 19027-1598. Offers OD, OD/MS. *Accreditation:* AOA. *Degree requirements:* For doctorate, comprehensive exam (for some programs). *Entrance requirements:* For doctorate, OAT, interview. Additional exam requirements/recommendations for international students: required—TOEFL. Electronic applications accepted.

**Southern College of Optometry,** Professional Program, Memphis, TN 38104-2222. Offers OD. *Accreditation:* AOA. *Degree requirements:* For doctorate, clinical experience. *Entrance requirements:* For doctorate, OAT, 3 years of undergraduate pre-optometry course work.

**State University of New York College of Optometry,** Professional Program, New York, NY 10036. Offers OD, OD/MS, OD/PhD. *Accreditation:* AOA. *Entrance requirements:* For doctorate, OAT. Additional exam requirements/recommendations for international students: required—TOEFL (minimum score 550 paper-based; 80 iBT). Electronic applications accepted.

**Université de Montréal,** School of Optometry, Professional Program in Optometry, Montréal, QC H3C 3J7, Canada. Offers OD. *Accreditation:* AOA. *Degree requirements:* For doctorate, thesis/dissertation. Electronic applications accepted.

**The University of Alabama at Birmingham,** School of Optometry, Professional Program in Optometry, Birmingham, AL 35294. Offers OD. *Accreditation:* AOA. *Students:* 190 full-time (138 women); includes 47 minority (9 Black or African American, non-Hispanic/Latino; 2 American Indian or Alaska Native, non-Hispanic/Latino; 29 Asian, non-Hispanic/Latino; 6 Hispanic/Latino; 1 Two or more races, non-Hispanic/Latino), 2 international. Average age 25. 323 applicants, 35% accepted, 49 enrolled. In 2019, 45 doctorates awarded. *Degree requirements:* For doctorate, National board Examinations I and II. *Entrance requirements:* For doctorate, OAT, composite evaluation or letters of recommendation, interview, optometric shadowing experience. Additional exam requirements/recommendations for international students: required—TOEFL (minimum score 500 paper-based; 61 iBT). *Application deadline:* For fall admission, 4/1 for domestic students. Applications are processed on a rolling basis. Application fee: $75. Electronic applications accepted. *Financial support:* In 2019–20, 57 students received support. Scholarships/grants and out-of-state tuition offsets available. Financial award application deadline: 5/1; financial award applicants required to submit FAFSA. *Unit head:* Dr. Gerald Simon, Director, Optometry Student Affairs, 205-975-0739, Fax: 205-934-6758, E-mail: gsimonod@uab.edu. *Application contact:* Dr. Gerald Simon, Director, Optometry Student Affairs, 205-975-0739, Fax: 205-934-6758, E-mail: gsimonod@uab.edu.

**University of California, Berkeley,** School of Optometry, Berkeley, CA 94720. Offers OD, Certificate. *Accreditation:* AOA. *Entrance requirements:* For doctorate, OAT. Additional exam requirements/recommendations for international students: required—TOEFL (minimum score 570 paper-based; 90 iBT). Electronic applications accepted.

**University of Houston,** College of Optometry, Professional Program in Optometry, Houston, TX 77204. Offers OD. *Accreditation:* AOA.

**The University of Manchester,** School of Biological Sciences, Manchester, United Kingdom. Offers adaptive organismal biology (M Phil, PhD); animal biology (M Phil, PhD); biochemistry (M Phil, PhD); bioinformatics (M Phil, PhD); biomolecular sciences (M Phil, PhD); biotechnology (M Phil, PhD); cell biology (M Phil, PhD); cell matrix research (M Phil, PhD); channels and transporters (M Phil, PhD); developmental biology (M Phil, PhD); environmental biology (M Phil, PhD); evolutionary biology (M Phil, PhD); gene expression (M Phil, PhD); genetics (M Phil, PhD); history of science, technology and medicine (M Phil, PhD); immunology (M Phil, PhD); integrative neurobiology and behavior (M Phil, PhD); membrane trafficking (M Phil, PhD); microbiology (M Phil, PhD); molecular and cellular neuroscience (M Phil, PhD); molecular biology (M Phil, PhD); molecular cancer studies (M Phil, PhD); neuroscience (M Phil, PhD); ophthalmology (M Phil, PhD); optometry (M Phil, PhD); organelle function (M Phil, PhD); pharmacology (M Phil, PhD); physiology (M Phil, PhD); plant sciences (M Phil, PhD); stem cell research (M Phil, PhD); structural biology (M Phil, PhD); systems neuroscience (M Phil, PhD); toxicology (M Phil, PhD).

**University of Pikeville,** Kentucky College of Optometry, Pikeville, KY 41501. Offers OD. *Faculty:* 15 full-time (5 women). *Students:* 236 full-time (155 women); includes 43 minority (10 Black or African American, non-Hispanic/Latino; 2 American Indian or Alaska Native, non-Hispanic/Latino; 19 Asian, non-Hispanic/Latino; 12 Hispanic/Latino). Average age 25. 460 applicants, 38% accepted, 62 enrolled. *Degree requirements:* For doctorate, comprehensive exam. *Entrance requirements:* For doctorate, OAT. *Application deadline:* For fall admission, 3/31 for domestic students. *Expenses:* $42,200 tuition. *Financial support:* Fellowships available. Financial award application deadline: 7/1; financial award applicants required to submit FAFSA. *Unit head:* Dr. Michael Bacigalupi, Dean, 606-218-5510, E-mail: mbacigalupi@upike.edu. *Application contact:* Casey Price, Coordinator of Admissions, 606-218-5517, E-mail: caseyprice@upike.edu.
Website: https://www.upike.edu/optometry/

**University of the Incarnate Word,** Rosenberg School of Optometry, San Antonio, TX 78209-6397. Offers OD. *Accreditation:* AOA. *Faculty:* 17 full-time (5 women). *Students:* 258 full-time (187 women); includes 158 minority (8 Black or African American, non-

Hispanic/Latino; 2 American Indian or Alaska Native, non-Hispanic/Latino; 89 Asian, non-Hispanic/Latino; 58 Hispanic/Latino; 1 Two or more races, non-Hispanic/Latino), 4 international. 91 applicants, 99% accepted, 69 enrolled. In 2019, 65 doctorates awarded. *Degree requirements:* For doctorate, clinical contact hours. *Entrance requirements:* For doctorate, OAT, 90 credit hours of prerequisite course work; letters of recommendation; interview. Additional exam requirements/recommendations for international students: required—TOEFL (minimum score 560 paper-based; 83 iBT). *Application deadline:* For fall admission, 5/1 for domestic students. Application fee: $50. Electronic applications accepted. *Expenses:* $39,000 annual tuition; fees vary by year. *Financial support:* Fellowships, Federal Work-Study, and scholarships/grants available. Financial award applicants required to submit FAFSA. *Unit head:* Dr. Timothy Wingert, Dean, 210-883-1195, Fax: 210-283-6890, E-mail: twingert@uiwtx.edu. *Application contact:* Jill Mohr, Director of Admissions and Student Services, 210-883-1190, Fax: 210-883-1191, E-mail: mohr@uiwtx.edu.
Website: https://optometry.uiw.edu/index.html

**University of Waterloo,** Graduate Studies and Postdoctoral Affairs, Faculty of Science, School of Optometry and Vision Science, Waterloo, ON N2L 3G1, Canada. Offers optometry (OD); vision science (M Sc, PhD). *Accreditation:* AOA. *Program availability:* Part-time. *Degree requirements:* For master's, thesis; for doctorate, thesis/dissertation. *Entrance requirements:* For master's, honors degree, minimum B average; for doctorate, master's degree, minimum B average. Additional exam requirements/recommendations for international students: required—TOEFL, IELTS, PTE. Electronic applications accepted.

**Western University of Health Sciences,** College of Optometry, Pomona, CA 91766-1854. Offers OD. *Accreditation:* AOA. *Faculty:* 30 full-time (15 women), 4 part-time/adjunct (2 women). *Students:* 315 full-time (231 women); includes 216 minority (7 Black or African American, non-Hispanic/Latino; 1 American Indian or Alaska Native, non-Hispanic/Latino; 124 Asian, non-Hispanic/Latino; 46 Hispanic/Latino; 2 Native Hawaiian or other Pacific Islander, non-Hispanic/Latino; 36 Two or more races, non-Hispanic/Latino), 14 international. Average age 27. 416 applicants, 38% accepted, 69 enrolled. In 2019, 86 doctorates awarded. *Degree requirements:* For doctorate, comprehensive exam (for some programs), thesis/dissertation (for some programs). *Entrance requirements:* For doctorate, 3 letters of recommendation; BS or BA (recommended); must meet the functional guidelines; established by the Association of Schools and Colleges of Optometry (ASCO). Additional exam requirements/recommendations for international students: required—TOEFL (minimum score 79 iBT), or 6 semesters of English classes. *Application deadline:* For fall admission, 5/1 for domestic and international students. Applications are processed on a rolling basis. Application fee: $65. Electronic applications accepted. *Expenses:* Tuition is about $40,850 per year and other fees such as AOSA membership fee, top hat and other fees are about $3000 per year. Other one time fees including, SEP first year Optometry kit, vital source and Livescan Finger Printing fee are $4100. *Financial support:* In 2019–20, 31 students received support. Career-related internships or fieldwork, scholarships/grants, and traineeships available. Financial award application deadline: 3/2; financial award applicants required to submit FAFSA. *Unit head:* Dr. Elizabeth Hoppe, Dean, 909-706-3497, E-mail: ehoppe@westernu.edu. *Application contact:* Marie Anderson, Director of Admissions, 909-469-5485, Fax: 909-469-5570, E-mail: admissions@westernu.edu.
Website: http://www.westernu.edu/optometry/

# Vision Sciences

**Eastern Virginia Medical School,** Ophthalmic Technology Program, Norfolk, VA 23501-1980. Offers Certificate. Electronic applications accepted. *Expenses:* Contact institution.

**Marshall B. Ketchum University,** Graduate and Professional Programs, Fullerton, CA 92831-1615. Offers optometry (OD); pharmacy (Pharm D); vision science (MS). *Degree requirements:* For doctorate, thesis/dissertation. *Entrance requirements:* For doctorate, OAT. Electronic applications accepted.

**New England College of Optometry,** Graduate and Professional Programs, Boston, MA 02115-1100. Offers optometry (OD); vision science (MS). *Accreditation:* AOA. *Students:* 815 applicants, 40% accepted, 138 enrolled. In 2019, 115 doctorates awarded. *Entrance requirements:* For doctorate, OAT, GRE. *Application deadline:* For fall admission, 3/31 for domestic students. Applications are processed on a rolling basis. Application fee: $40. Electronic applications accepted. *Financial support:* In 2019–20, 357 students received support, including 12 research assistantships (averaging $5,193 per year); career-related internships or fieldwork, Federal Work-Study, institutionally sponsored loans, and scholarships/grants also available. Financial award application deadline: 4/1; financial award applicants required to submit FAFSA. *Application contact:* Kristen Tobin, Director of Admissions, 617-587-5580, Fax: 617-587-5550, E-mail: tobink@neco.edu.

**Pacific University,** College of Optometry, Forest Grove, OR 97116-1797. Offers optometry (OD); vision science (MS, PhD). *Accreditation:* AOA (one or more programs are accredited). *Degree requirements:* For doctorate, thesis/dissertation optional. *Entrance requirements:* For master's, GRE General Test, course work in natural sciences; for doctorate, OAT, 30 hours OD observation; course work in natural sciences, math, psychology, English, letters of recommendation. Additional exam requirements/recommendations for international students: required—TOEFL (minimum score 600 paper-based). Electronic applications accepted. *Expenses:* Contact institution.

**Salus University,** College of Education and Rehabilitation, Elkins Park, PA 19027-1598. Offers education of children and youth with visual and multiple impairments (M Ed, Certificate); low vision rehabilitation (MS, Certificate); occupational therapy (MS); orientation and mobility therapy (MS, Certificate); speech-language pathology (MS); vision rehabilitation therapy (MS, Certificate); OD/MS. *Accreditation:* AOTA. *Program availability:* Part-time, online learning. *Entrance requirements:* For master's, GRE or MAT, 3 letters of reference, 2 interviews. Additional exam requirements/recommendations for international students: required—TOEFL, TWE. *Expenses:* Contact institution.

**State University of New York College of Optometry,** Graduate Programs, New York, NY 10036. Offers PhD, OD/MS, OD/PhD. *Program availability:* Part-time. Terminal master's awarded for partial completion of doctoral program. *Degree requirements:* For doctorate, comprehensive exam, thesis/dissertation, specialty exam. *Entrance requirements:* For doctorate, GRE General Test. Additional exam requirements/recommendations for international students: required—TOEFL (minimum score 550 paper-based; 80 iBT). *Expenses:* Contact institution.

**Université de Montréal,** School of Optometry, Graduate Programs in Optometry, Montréal, QC H3C 3J7, Canada. Offers vision sciences (M Sc); visual impairment intervention-orientation and mobility (DESS); visual impairment intervention-readaptation (DESS). *Program availability:* Part-time. *Degree requirements:* For master's, thesis. *Entrance requirements:* For master's, OD or appropriate bachelor's degree, minimum GPA of 2.7. Electronic applications accepted.

**The University of Alabama at Birmingham,** School of Optometry, Graduate Program in Vision Science, Birmingham, AL 35294. Offers sensory impairment (PhD); vision science (MS, PhD). *Faculty:* 15 full-time (3 women). *Students:* 21 full-time (9 women), 10 part-time (8 women); includes 3 minority (1 Black or African American, non-Hispanic/Latino; 2 Asian, non-Hispanic/Latino), 10 international. Average age 33. 19 applicants, 26% accepted, 3 enrolled. In 2019, 3 master's, 5 doctorates awarded. Terminal master's awarded for partial completion of doctoral program. *Degree requirements:* For master's, thesis; for doctorate, thesis/dissertation. *Entrance requirements:* For master's, minimum GPA of 3.00, letters of recommendation, interview; for doctorate, interview, minimum GPA of 3.00, 3 letters of recommendations. Additional exam requirements/recommendations for international students: required—TOEFL (minimum score 570 paper-based; 80 iBT), IELTS (minimum score 6.5). *Application deadline:* For fall admission, 1/15 priority date for domestic and international students. Applications are processed on a rolling basis. Application fee: $50. Electronic applications accepted. *Financial support:* In 2019–20, 21 students received support, including 9 fellowships (averaging $23,805 per year); scholarships/grants and health care benefits also available. *Unit head:* Dr. Lawrence C Sincich, Interim Director of the Graduate Program, E-mail: sincich@uab.edu. *Application contact:* Dr. Stefanie B. Varghese, Program Manager, 205-934-6743, Fax: 205-934-5725, E-mail: sbvarghese@uab.edu.
Website: http://www.uab.edu/vsgp/

**University of Alberta,** Faculty of Medicine and Dentistry and Faculty of Graduate Studies and Research, Graduate Programs in Medicine, Department of Ophthalmology, Edmonton, AB T6G 2E1, Canada. Offers M Sc, PhD. *Program availability:* Part-time. Terminal master's awarded for partial completion of doctoral program. *Degree requirements:* For master's, thesis; for doctorate, comprehensive exam, thesis/dissertation.

**University of California, Berkeley,** Graduate Division, Group in Vision Science, Berkeley, CA 94720. Offers MS, PhD. *Degree requirements:* For master's, thesis; for doctorate, thesis/dissertation. *Entrance requirements:* For master's and doctorate, GRE General Test, GRE Subject Test, minimum GPA of 3.0, 3 letters of recommendation. Electronic applications accepted.

**University of Guelph,** Ontario Veterinary College and Office of Graduate and Postdoctoral Studies, Graduate Programs in Veterinary Sciences, Department of Clinical Studies, Guelph, ON N1G 2W1, Canada. Offers anesthesiology (M Sc, DV Sc); cardiology (DV Sc, Diploma); clinical studies (Diploma); dermatology (M Sc); diagnostic imaging (M Sc, DV Sc); emergency/critical care (M Sc, DV Sc, Diploma); medicine (M Sc, DV Sc); neurology (M Sc, DV Sc); ophthalmology (M Sc, DV Sc); surgery (M Sc, DV Sc). *Degree requirements:* For master's, thesis; for doctorate, comprehensive exam, thesis/dissertation. *Entrance requirements:* Additional exam requirements/recommendations for international students: required—TOEFL (minimum score 550 paper-based), IELTS (minimum score 6.5). Electronic applications accepted.

**University of Houston,** College of Optometry, Program in Physiological Optics/Vision Science, Houston, TX 77204-2020. Offers physiological optics (MS, PhD). *Faculty:* 24 full-time (10 women), 1 part-time/adjunct (0 women). *Students:* 49 full-time (30 women), 3 part-time (1 woman); includes 40 minority (7 Black or African American, non-Hispanic/Latino; 31 Asian, non-Hispanic/Latino; 2 Hispanic/Latino). Average age 27. 38 applicants, 34% accepted, 12 enrolled. In 2019, 4 master's, 2 doctorates awarded. Terminal master's awarded for partial completion of doctoral program. *Degree requirements:* For master's, thesis; for doctorate, comprehensive exam, thesis/dissertation. *Entrance requirements:* For master's, GRE but not in 21-22 waived; for doctorate, GRE but not in 21-22 waived. Additional exam requirements/recommendations for international students: recommended—TOEFL (minimum score 550 paper-based; 79 iBT), IELTS (minimum score 6.5). *Application deadline:* For fall admission, 1/31 for domestic and international students; for spring admission, 10/15 for domestic and international students. Application fee: $50 ($25 for international students). Electronic applications accepted. *Financial support:* In 2019–20, 50 students received support, including 7 fellowships with full tuition reimbursements available (averaging $2,500 per year), 8 research assistantships with full tuition reimbursements available (averaging $25,000 per year), 20 teaching assistantships with full tuition reimbursements available (averaging $25,000 per year); career-related internships or fieldwork, Federal Work-Study, scholarships/grants, health care benefits, tuition waivers (full), and unspecified assistantships also available. Support available to part-time students. Financial award application deadline: 1/31; financial award applicants required to submit FAFSA. *Unit head:* Dr. Laura D Frishman, Associate Dean, 713-743-1972, E-mail: Lfrishman@uh.edu. *Application contact:* Dr. Laura D Frishman, Associate Dean, 713-743-1972, E-mail: Lfrishman@uh.edu.
Website: https://www.opt.uh.edu/future-students-residents/programs/graduate-program/

**The University of Manchester,** School of Biological Sciences, Manchester, United Kingdom. Offers adaptive organismal biology (M Phil, PhD); animal biology (M Phil, PhD); biochemistry (M Phil, PhD); bioinformatics (M Phil, PhD); biomolecular sciences (M Phil, PhD); biotechnology (M Phil, PhD); cell biology (M Phil, PhD); cell matrix research (M Phil, PhD); channels and transporters (M Phil, PhD); developmental biology (M Phil, PhD); environmental biology (M Phil, PhD); evolutionary biology (M Phil, PhD); gene expression (M Phil, PhD); genetics (M Phil, PhD); history of science, technology and medicine (M Phil, PhD); immunology (M Phil, PhD); integrative neurobiology and behavior (M Phil, PhD); membrane trafficking (M Phil, PhD); microbiology (M Phil, PhD); molecular and cellular neuroscience (M Phil, PhD); molecular biology (M Phil, PhD); molecular cancer studies (M Phil, PhD); neuroscience (M Phil, PhD); ophthalmology (M Phil, PhD); optometry (M Phil, PhD); organelle function (M Phil, PhD); pharmacology (M Phil, PhD); physiology (M Phil, PhD); plant sciences (M Phil, PhD); stem cell research (M Phil, PhD); structural biology (M Phil, PhD); systems neuroscience (M Phil, PhD); toxicology (M Phil, PhD).

**University of Massachusetts Boston,** Graduate School of Global Inclusion and Social Development, Program in Vision Studies, Boston, MA 02125-3393. Offers M Ed.

*Vision Sciences*

**University of Waterloo,** Graduate Studies and Postdoctoral Affairs, Faculty of Science, School of Optometry and Vision Science, Waterloo, ON N2L 3G1, Canada. Offers optometry (OD); vision science (M Sc, PhD). *Accreditation:* AOA. *Program availability:* Part-time. *Degree requirements:* For master's, thesis; for doctorate, thesis/dissertation. *Entrance requirements:* For master's, honors degree, minimum B average; for doctorate, master's degree, minimum B average. Additional exam requirements/ recommendations for international students: required—TOEFL, IELTS, PTE. Electronic applications accepted.

**Western Michigan University,** Graduate College, College of Health and Human Services, Department of Blindness and Low Vision Studies, Kalamazoo, MI 49008. Offers orientation and mobility (MA); orientation and mobility of children (MA); vision rehabilitation therapy (MA). *Accreditation:* CORE.

# Section 30
# Pharmacy and Pharmaceutical Sciences

This section contains a directory of institutions offering graduate work in pharmacy and pharmaceutical sciences, followed by in-depth entries submitted by institutions that chose to prepare detailed program descriptions. Additional information about programs listed in the directory but not augmented by an in-depth entry may be obtained by writing directly to the dean of a graduate school or chair of a department at the address given in the directory.

For programs offering related work, see also in this book *Allied Health, Biochemistry, Biological and Biomedical Sciences, Nutrition, Pharmacology and Toxicology,* and *Physiology.* In the other guides in this series:

**Graduate Programs in the Physical Sciences, Mathematics, Agricultural Sciences, the Environment & Natural Resources**
See *Chemistry*

**Graduate Programs in Engineering & Applied Sciences**
See *Biomedical Engineering and Biotechnology,* and *Chemical Engineering*

## CONTENTS

### Program Directories

# Medicinal and Pharmaceutical Chemistry

**Duquesne University,** School of Pharmacy, Graduate School of Pharmaceutical Sciences, Program in Medicinal Chemistry, Pittsburgh, PA 15282-0001. Offers MS, PhD. *Degree requirements:* For master's, thesis; for doctorate, comprehensive exam, thesis/dissertation. *Entrance requirements:* For master's and doctorate, GRE General Test. Additional exam requirements/recommendations for international students: required—TOEFL (minimum score 100 iBT). Electronic applications accepted. *Expenses:* Contact institution.

**Florida Agricultural and Mechanical University,** Division of Graduate Studies, Research, and Continuing Education, College of Pharmacy and Pharmaceutical Sciences, Graduate Programs in Pharmaceutical Sciences, Tallahassee, FL 32307-3200. Offers environmental toxicology (PhD); health outcomes research and pharmacoeconomics (PhD); medicinal chemistry (MS, PhD); pharmaceutics (MS, PhD); pharmacology/toxicology (MS, PhD); pharmacy administration (MS). *Accreditation:* CEPH. *Degree requirements:* For master's, comprehensive exam, thesis, publishable paper; for doctorate, comprehensive exam, thesis/dissertation, publishable paper. *Entrance requirements:* For master's and doctorate, GRE General Test, minimum GPA of 3.0 in last 60 hours. Additional exam requirements/recommendations for international students: required—TOEFL.

**Idaho State University,** Graduate School, College of Pharmacy, Department of Biomedical and Pharmaceutical Sciences, Pocatello, ID 83209-8334. Offers biopharmaceutical analysis (PhD); drug delivery (PhD); medicinal chemistry (PhD); pharmaceutical sciences (MS); pharmacology (PhD). *Program availability:* Part-time. *Degree requirements:* For master's, one foreign language, comprehensive exam, thesis, thesis research, classes in speech and technical writing; for doctorate, comprehensive exam, thesis/dissertation, written and oral exams, classes in speech and technical writing. *Entrance requirements:* For master's, GRE General Test, minimum GPA of 3.0, 3 letters of recommendation; for doctorate, GRE General Test, BS in pharmacy or related field, minimum GPA of 3.0, 3 letters of recommendation. Additional exam requirements/recommendations for international students: required—TOEFL (minimum score 550 paper-based; 80 iBT). Electronic applications accepted. *Expenses:* Contact institution.

**Medical University of South Carolina,** College of Graduate Studies, Department of Pharmaceutical and Biomedical Sciences, Charleston, SC 29425. Offers cell injury and repair (PhD); drug discovery (PhD); medicinal chemistry (PhD); toxicology (PhD); DMD/PhD; MD/PhD; Pharm D/PhD. *Degree requirements:* For doctorate, thesis/dissertation, oral and written exams, teaching and research seminar. *Entrance requirements:* For doctorate, GRE General Test, interview, minimum GPA of 3.0. Additional exam requirements/recommendations for international students: required—TOEFL (minimum score 600 paper-based; 100 iBT). Electronic applications accepted.

**New Jersey Institute of Technology,** College of Science and Liberal Arts, Newark, NJ 07102. Offers applied mathematics (MS); applied physics (MS, PhD); applied statistics (MS, Certificate); biology (MS, PhD); biostatistics (MS); chemistry (MS, PhD); environmental and sustainability policy (MS); environmental science (MS, PhD); history (MA, MAT); materials science and engineering (MS, PhD); mathematical and computational finance (MS); mathematical sciences (PhD); pharmaceutical chemistry (MS); professional and technical communications (MS); technical communication essentials (Certificate). *Program availability:* Part-time, evening/weekend. *Faculty:* 159 full-time (42 women), 156 part-time/adjunct (61 women). *Students:* 197 full-time (80 women), 58 part-time (14 women); includes 58 minority (18 Black or African American, non-Hispanic/Latino; 22 Asian, non-Hispanic/Latino; 16 Hispanic/Latino; 2 Two or more races, non-Hispanic/Latino), 130 international. Average age 29. 401 applicants, 63% accepted, 73 enrolled. In 2019, 54 master's, 10 doctorates, 1 other advanced degree awarded. Terminal master's awarded for partial completion of doctoral program. *Degree requirements:* For master's, thesis (for some programs); for doctorate, thesis/dissertation. *Entrance requirements:* For master's and doctorate, GRE General Test, Minimum GPA of 3.0, personal statement, three (3) letters of recommendation, and transcripts. Additional exam requirements/recommendations for international students: required—TOEFL (minimum score 550 paper-based; 79 iBT), IELTS (minimum score 6.5). *Application deadline:* For fall admission, 6/1 priority date for domestic students, 5/1 priority date for international students; for spring admission, 11/15 priority date for domestic and international students. Applications are processed on a rolling basis. Application fee: $75. Electronic applications accepted. *Expenses:* $23,828 per year (in-state), $33,744 per year (out-of-state). *Financial support:* In 2019–20, 147 students received support, including 13 fellowships with full tuition reimbursements available (averaging $24,000 per year), 41 research assistantships with full tuition reimbursements available (averaging $24,000 per year), 87 teaching assistantships with full tuition reimbursements available (averaging $24,000 per year); scholarships/grants, traineeships, health care benefits, and unspecified assistantships also available. Financial award application deadline: 1/15. *Unit head:* Dr. Kevin Belfield, Dean, 973-596-3676, Fax: 973-565-0586, E-mail: kevin.d.belfield@njit.edu. *Application contact:* Stephen Eck, Director of Admissions, 973-596-3300, Fax: 973-596-3461, E-mail: admissions@njit.edu.
Website: http://csla.njit.edu/

**Purdue University,** College of Pharmacy and Graduate School, Graduate Programs in Pharmacy and Pharmacal Sciences, Department of Medicinal Chemistry and Molecular Pharmacology, West Lafayette, IN 47907. Offers biophysical and computational chemistry (PhD); cancer research (PhD); immunology and infectious disease (PhD); medicinal biochemistry and molecular biology (PhD); medicinal chemistry and chemical biology (PhD); molecular pharmacology (PhD); neuropharmacology, neurodegeneration, and neurotoxicity (PhD); systems biology and functional genomics (PhD). *Faculty:* 20 full-time (5 women), 7 part-time/adjunct (2 women). *Students:* 80 full-time (40 women), 2 part-time (0 women); includes 9 minority (5 Asian, non-Hispanic/Latino; 2 Hispanic/Latino; 2 Two or more races, non-Hispanic/Latino), 44 international. Average age 26. 162 applicants, 20% accepted, 15 enrolled. In 2019, 11 doctorates awarded. *Degree requirements:* For doctorate, thesis/dissertation. *Entrance requirements:* For doctorate, GRE General Test; GRE Subject Test in biology, biochemistry, and chemistry (recommended), minimum undergraduate GPA of 3.0. Additional exam requirements/recommendations for international students: required—TOEFL (minimum score 550 paper-based; 77 iBT); recommended—TWE. *Application deadline:* For fall admission, 2/1 for domestic and international students. Applications are processed on a rolling basis. Application fee: $60 ($75 for international students). Electronic applications accepted. *Financial support:* Fellowships, research assistantships, teaching assistantships, and traineeships available. Support available to part-time students. Financial award applicants required to submit FAFSA. *Unit head:* Zhong-Yin Zhang, Head, 765-494-1403, E-mail: zhang-yn@purdue.edu. *Application contact:* Delayne Graham, Graduate Contact, 765-494-1362, E-mail: dkgraham@purdue.edu.

**Rutgers University - New Brunswick,** Ernest Mario School of Pharmacy, Program in Medicinal Chemistry, Piscataway, NJ 08854-8097. Offers MS, PhD. *Program availability:* Part-time. *Degree requirements:* For master's, comprehensive exam, thesis; for doctorate, comprehensive exam, thesis/dissertation. *Entrance requirements:* For master's and doctorate, GRE General Test. Additional exam requirements/recommendations for international students: required—TOEFL (minimum score 600 paper-based; 90 iBT). Electronic applications accepted.

**Temple University,** School of Pharmacy, Department of Pharmaceutical Sciences, Philadelphia, PA 19122-6096. Offers medicinal chemistry (MS, PhD); pharmaceutics (MS, PhD); pharmacodynamics (MS, PhD); regulatory affairs and quality assurance (MS). *Program availability:* Part-time, evening/weekend, online learning. *Faculty:* 11 full-time (2 women), 36 part-time/adjunct (14 women). *Students:* 30 full-time (12 women), 222 part-time (153 women); includes 37 minority (10 Black or African American, non-Hispanic/Latino; 22 Asian, non-Hispanic/Latino; 3 Hispanic/Latino; 2 Two or more races, non-Hispanic/Latino), 28 international. 78 applicants, 77% accepted, 45 enrolled. In 2019, 89 master's, 7 doctorates awarded. *Entrance requirements:* For master's and doctorate, GRE, bachelor's degree in related discipline, statement of goals, 3 letters of recommendation. Additional exam requirements/recommendations for international students: required—TOEFL (minimum score 82 iBT), IELTS (minimum score 6.5), PTE (minimum score 58). *Application deadline:* For fall admission, 12/15 for domestic students. Application fee: $60. Electronic applications accepted. *Expenses:* Contact institution. *Financial support:* Fellowships, research assistantships, teaching assistantships, Federal Work-Study, health care benefits, and unspecified assistantships available. Financial award applicants required to submit FAFSA. *Unit head:* Michael Borenstein, Interim Dean, 215-707-2976, E-mail: michael.borenstein@temple.edu. *Application contact:* Sophon Din, Administrative Assistant, 215-204-4948, E-mail: tuspgrad@temple.edu.
Website: https://pharmacy.temple.edu/academics/department-pharmaceutical-science

**University at Buffalo, the State University of New York,** Graduate School, College of Arts and Sciences, Department of Chemistry, Buffalo, NY 14260. Offers chemistry (MA, PhD); medicinal chemistry (MS, PhD). *Program availability:* Part-time. *Faculty:* 27 full-time (5 women), 3 part-time/adjunct (2 women). *Students:* 149 full-time (71 women); includes 29 minority (6 Black or African American, non-Hispanic/Latino; 10 Asian, non-Hispanic/Latino; 10 Hispanic/Latino; 3 Two or more races, non-Hispanic/Latino), 40 international. Average age 26. 163 applicants, 28% accepted, 18 enrolled. In 2019, 16 master's, 28 doctorates awarded. Terminal master's awarded for partial completion of doctoral program. *Degree requirements:* For master's, thesis or alternative, project; for doctorate, thesis/dissertation, synopsis and proposal and 8th semester presentation. *Entrance requirements:* For master's and doctorate, GRE General Test, 3.0 GPA, letters of recommendation, baccalaureate degree or its equivalent. Additional exam requirements/recommendations for international students: required—TOEFL. *Application deadline:* For fall admission, 3/1 for domestic and international students; for spring admission, 11/1 for domestic and international students. Applications are processed on a rolling basis. Application fee: $75. Electronic applications accepted. *Expenses:* Contact institution. *Financial support:* In 2019–20, 17 students received support, including 3 fellowships with full tuition reimbursements available (averaging $27,000 per year), 38 research assistantships with full tuition reimbursements available (averaging $23,000 per year), 88 teaching assistantships with full tuition reimbursements available (averaging $23,000 per year); Federal Work-Study, institutionally sponsored loans, scholarships/grants, health care benefits, and unspecified assistantships also available. Financial award application deadline: 3/1. *Unit head:* Dr. David F. Watson, Chairman, 716-645-6824, Fax: 716-645-6963, E-mail: chechair@buffalo.edu. *Application contact:* Dr. Jason B. Benedict, Director of Graduate Studies, 716-645-4276, Fax: 716-645-6963, E-mail: jbb6@buffalo.edu.
Website: https://arts-sciences.buffalo.edu/chemistry.html

**University of California, Irvine,** Programs in Health Sciences, Program in Medicinal Chemistry and Pharmacology, Irvine, CA 92697. Offers PhD.

**University of California, San Francisco,** School of Pharmacy and Graduate Division, Chemistry and Chemical Biology Graduate Program, San Francisco, CA 94143. Offers PhD. *Degree requirements:* For doctorate, thesis/dissertation. *Entrance requirements:* For doctorate, GRE General Test, minimum GPA of 3.0, bachelor's degree. Additional exam requirements/recommendations for international students: required—TOEFL (minimum score 550 paper-based; 80 iBT). Electronic applications accepted.

**University of Connecticut,** Graduate School, School of Pharmacy, Department of Pharmaceutical Sciences, Program in Medicinal Chemistry, Storrs, CT 06269. Offers MS, PhD. Terminal master's awarded for partial completion of doctoral program. *Degree requirements:* For master's, comprehensive exam, thesis; for doctorate, thesis/dissertation. *Entrance requirements:* Additional exam requirements/recommendations for international students: required—TOEFL (minimum score 550 paper-based). Electronic applications accepted.

**University of Florida,** Graduate School, College of Pharmacy, Graduate Programs in Pharmacy, Department of Medicinal Chemistry, Gainesville, FL 32611. Offers clinical toxicology (MSP); forensic DNA and serology (MSP); forensic drug chemistry (MSP); forensic science (MSP); medicinal chemistry (MSP, PhD); pharmaceutical chemistry (MSP). *Program availability:* Part-time, evening/weekend, online learning. Terminal master's awarded for partial completion of doctoral program. *Degree requirements:* For master's, thesis optional; for doctorate, comprehensive exam, thesis/dissertation. *Entrance requirements:* For master's and doctorate, GRE General Test, minimum GPA of 3.0. Additional exam requirements/recommendations for international students: required—TOEFL (minimum score 550 paper-based; 80 iBT), IELTS (minimum score 6). Electronic applications accepted.

**University of Illinois at Chicago,** College of Pharmacy, Graduate Programs in Pharmacy, Chicago, IL 60607-7128. Offers comparative effectiveness research (MS); forensic science (MS); forensic toxicology (MS); medicinal chemistry (MS, PhD); pharmacognosy (MS, PhD); pharmacy (PhD). Terminal master's awarded for partial completion of doctoral program. *Degree requirements:* For master's, variable foreign language requirement, thesis; for doctorate, variable foreign language requirement, thesis/dissertation. *Entrance requirements:* For master's and doctorate, GRE General Test. Additional exam requirements/recommendations for international students: required—TOEFL. Electronic applications accepted.

**The University of Iowa,** College of Pharmacy, Iowa City, IA 52242-1316. Offers clinical pharmaceutical sciences (PhD); medicinal and natural products chemistry (PhD); pharmaceutical socioeconomics (PhD); pharmaceutics (MS, PhD); pharmacy (Pharm D); Pharm D/MPH. *Accreditation:* ACPE (one or more programs are accredited). *Degree requirements:* For master's, thesis optional, exam; for doctorate, comprehensive exam, thesis/dissertation. *Entrance requirements:* For master's and doctorate, GRE

General Test, minimum GPA of 3.0. Additional exam requirements/recommendations for international students: required—TOEFL (minimum score 550 paper-based; 81 iBT). Electronic applications accepted.

**The University of Kansas,** Graduate Studies, School of Pharmacy, Department of Medicinal Chemistry, Lawrence, KS 66045. Offers MS, PhD. *Students:* 19 full-time (7 women); includes 2 minority (1 Black or African American, non-Hispanic/Latino; 1 Hispanic/Latino), 8 international. Average age 26. 36 applicants, 33% accepted, 6 enrolled. In 2019, 2 master's, 3 doctorates awarded. Terminal master's awarded for partial completion of doctoral program. *Entrance requirements:* For master's, GRE General Test, BS in pharmacy, medicinal chemistry, chemistry, biochemistry, or closely-related field; minimum undergraduate GPA of 3.0; one year of organic chemistry with laboratory; for doctorate, GRE General Test, BS or MS in pharmacy, medicinal chemistry, chemistry, biochemistry, or closely-related field; minimum undergraduate GPA of 3.0; one year of organic chemistry with laboratory. Additional exam requirements/recommendations for international students: required—TOEFL, IELTS. *Application deadline:* For fall admission, 12/15 for domestic and international students. Application fee: $65 ($85 for international students). Electronic applications accepted. *Expenses:* Tuition, state resident: full-time $9989. Tuition, nonresident: full-time $23,950. *International tuition:* $23,950 full-time. *Required fees:* $984; $81.99 per credit hour. Tuition and fees vary according to course load, campus/location and program. *Financial support:* Fellowships, research assistantships, teaching assistantships, health care benefits, and unspecified assistantships available. Financial award application deadline: 2/1. *Unit head:* Robert Hanzlik, Chair, 785-864-3750, E-mail: rhanzlik@ku.edu. *Application contact:* Norma Henley, Graduate Admission Contact, 785-864-4495, E-mail: medchem@ku.edu.
Website: http://www.medchem.ku.edu/

**The University of Kansas,** Graduate Studies, School of Pharmacy, Department of Pharmaceutical Chemistry, Lawrence, KS 66047. Offers MS, PhD. *Program availability:* Part-time, evening/weekend, online learning. *Students:* 35 full-time (19 women), 6 part-time (1 woman); includes 7 minority (4 Asian, non-Hispanic/Latino; 1 Hispanic/Latino; 2 Two or more races, non-Hispanic/Latino), 21 international. Average age 28. 46 applicants, 35% accepted, 7 enrolled. In 2019, 11 master's, 8 doctorates awarded. Terminal master's awarded for partial completion of doctoral program. *Entrance requirements:* For master's, GRE General Test, bachelor's degree in biological sciences, chemical engineering, chemistry, or pharmacy; official transcripts from all universities/institutions in which the applicant has studied; personal statement; resume; three letters of recommendation; for doctorate, GRE General Test, official transcripts from all universities/institutions in which the applicant has studied, personal statement, resume, three letters of recommendation. Additional exam requirements/recommendations for international students: required—TOEFL, IELTS. *Application deadline:* For fall admission, 7/1 for domestic and international students; for spring admission, 12/15 for domestic and international students; for summer admission, 5/1 for domestic and international students. Application fee: $65 ($85 for international students). Electronic applications accepted. *Expenses:* Tuition, state resident: full-time $9989. Tuition, nonresident: full-time $23,950. *International tuition:* $23,950 full-time. *Required fees:* $984; $81.99 per credit hour. Tuition and fees vary according to course load, campus/location and program. *Financial support:* Fellowships, research assistantships, career-related internships or fieldwork, scholarships/grants, traineeships, and unspecified assistantships available. Financial award application deadline: 1/15. *Unit head:* Ken Audus, Dean, 785-864-3550, E-mail: audus@ku.edu. *Application contact:* Michelle Husling, Graduate Admissions Contact, 785-864-4822, E-mail: mrhuslig@ku.edu.
Website: http://www.pharmchem.ku.edu/

**University of Michigan,** College of Pharmacy and Rackham Graduate School, Department of Medicinal Chemistry, Ann Arbor, MI 48109. Offers PhD. *Degree requirements:* For doctorate, thesis/dissertation, oral defense of dissertation, preliminary exam. *Entrance requirements:* For doctorate, GRE. Additional exam requirements/recommendations for international students: required—TOEFL (minimum score 560 paper-based; 84 iBT) or IELTS (minimum score 6.5). Electronic applications accepted.

**University of Minnesota, Twin Cities Campus,** College of Pharmacy and Graduate School, Graduate Programs in Pharmacy, Graduate Program in Medicinal Chemistry, Minneapolis, MN 55455. Offers MS, PhD. *Faculty:* 28 full-time (4 women), 8 part-time/adjunct (4 women). *Students:* 51 full-time (18 women); includes 6 minority (1 Black or African American, non-Hispanic/Latino; 3 Asian, non-Hispanic/Latino; 2 Hispanic/Latino), 15 international. Average age 26. 63 applicants, 30% accepted, 11 enrolled. In 2019, 1 master's, 4 doctorates awarded. Terminal master's awarded for partial completion of doctoral program. *Degree requirements:* For master's, comprehensive exam, thesis; for doctorate, comprehensive exam, thesis/dissertation. *Entrance requirements:* For doctorate, GRE General Test, BS in biology, chemistry, biochemistry or pharmacy. Additional exam requirements/recommendations for international students: required—TOEFL (minimum score 550 paper-based; 100 iBT), IELTS (minimum score 7.5). *Application deadline:* For fall admission, 1/3 for domestic and international students. Application fee: $75 ($95 for international students). Electronic applications accepted. *Financial support:* In 2019–20, 46 students received support, including 30 fellowships with full tuition reimbursements available (averaging $9,500 per year), 24 research assistantships with full tuition reimbursements available (averaging $26,750 per year), 10 teaching assistantships with full tuition reimbursements available (averaging $16,669 per year); traineeships, health care benefits, and unspecified assistantships also available. Financial award application deadline: 1/3. *Unit head:* Dr. Gunda I. Georg, Department Head of Medicinal Chemistry, 612-626-6320, Fax: 612-626-3114, E-mail: georg@umn.edu. *Application contact:* Information Contact, 612-625-3014, Fax: 612-625-6002, E-mail: gsquest@umn.edu.
Website: https://z.umn.edu/medchemgrad

**University of Mississippi,** Graduate School, School of Pharmacy, University, MS 38677. Offers environmental toxicology (MS, PhD); industrial pharmacy (MS); medicinal chemistry (MS, PhD); pharmaceutics (MS, PhD); pharmacognosy (MS, PhD); pharmacology (MS, PhD); pharmacy (Pharm D); pharmacy administration (MS, PhD). *Accreditation:* ACPE (one or more programs are accredited). *Program availability:* Part-time. *Faculty:* 68 full-time (33 women), 13 part-time/adjunct (5 women). *Students:* 223 full-time (137 women), 215 part-time (137 women); includes 71 minority (29 Black or African American, non-Hispanic/Latino; 1 American Indian or Alaska Native, non-Hispanic/Latino; 31 Asian, non-Hispanic/Latino; 4 Hispanic/Latino; 6 Two or more races, non-Hispanic/Latino), 90 international. Average age 25. In 2019, 29 master's, 13 doctorates awarded. Terminal master's awarded for partial completion of doctoral program. *Degree requirements:* For master's, thesis; for doctorate, thesis/dissertation (for some programs). *Entrance requirements:* For master's, GRE General Test, minimum GPA of 3.0; for doctorate, GRE General Test (for PhD). Additional exam requirements/recommendations for international students: required—TOEFL. *Application deadline:* Applications are processed on a rolling basis. Application fee: $50. Electronic applications accepted. *Expenses:* Tuition, state resident: full-time $8718; part-time $484.25 per credit hour. Tuition, nonresident: full-time $24,990; part-time $1388.25 per credit hour. *Required fees:* $100; $4.16 per credit hour. *Financial support:* Fellowships, research assistantships, teaching assistantships, career-related internships or fieldwork, Federal Work-Study, institutionally sponsored loans, scholarships/grants, tuition waivers (full), and unspecified assistantships available. Financial award application deadline: 3/1; financial award applicants required to submit FAFSA. *Unit head:* Dr. David Allen, Dean, School of Pharmacy, 662-915-7265, Fax: 662-9155704, E-mail: sopdean@olemiss.edu. *Application contact:* Temeka Smith, Graduate Activities Specialist for Admissions, 662-915-7474, Fax: 662-915-7577, E-mail: gschool@olemiss.edu.
Website: http://www.pharmacy.olemiss.edu/

**University of Montana,** Graduate School, College of Health Professions and Biomedical Sciences, Skaggs School of Pharmacy, Department of Biomedical and Pharmaceutical Sciences, Missoula, MT 59812. Offers biomedical sciences (PhD); medicinal chemistry (MS, PhD); molecular and cellular toxicology (MS, PhD); neuroscience (PhD); pharmaceutical sciences (MS). *Accreditation:* ACPE. *Degree requirements:* For master's, oral defense of thesis; for doctorate, research dissertation defense. *Entrance requirements:* For master's and doctorate, GRE General Test. Additional exam requirements/recommendations for international students: required—TOEFL (minimum score 540 paper-based). Electronic applications accepted.

**University of Rhode Island,** Graduate School, College of Pharmacy, Department of Biomedical and Pharmaceutical Sciences, Kingston, RI 02881. Offers health outcomes (MS, PhD); medicinal chemistry and pharmacognosy (MS, PhD); pharmaceutics and pharmacokinetics (MS, PhD); pharmacology and toxicology (MS, PhD). *Program availability:* Part-time. *Faculty:* 23 full-time (11 women). *Students:* 42 full-time (20 women), 11 part-time (6 women); includes 8 minority (1 American Indian or Alaska Native, non-Hispanic/Latino; 5 Asian, non-Hispanic/Latino; 2 Hispanic/Latino), 19 international. In 2019, 4 master's, 11 doctorates awarded. *Entrance requirements:* Additional exam requirements/recommendations for international students: required—TOEFL. *Application deadline:* For fall admission, 7/15 for domestic students, 2/1 for international students. Application fee: $65. Electronic applications accepted. *Expenses:* Tuition, area resident: Full-time $13,734; part-time $763 per credit. Tuition, state resident: full-time $13,734; part-time $763 per credit. Tuition, nonresident: full-time $26,512; part-time $1473 per credit. *International tuition:* $26,512 full-time. *Required fees:* $1780; $52 per credit. $35 per term. One-time fee: $165. *Financial support:* In 2019–20, 112 research assistantships with tuition reimbursements (averaging $8,040 per year), 17 teaching assistantships with tuition reimbursements (averaging $11,829 per year) were awarded. Financial award application deadline: 2/1; financial award applicants required to submit FAFSA. *Unit head:* Dr. Navindra Seeram, Chair, E-mail: nseeram@uri.edu. *Application contact:* Dr. Navindra Seeram, Chair, E-mail: nseeram@uri.edu.
Website: http://www.uri.edu/pharmacy/departments/bps/index.shtml

**The University of Texas at Austin,** Graduate School, College of Pharmacy, Graduate Programs in Pharmacy, Austin, TX 78712-1111. Offers health outcomes and pharmacy practice (MS, PhD); medicinal chemistry (PhD); pharmaceutics (PhD); pharmacology and toxicology (PhD); pharmacotherapy (MS, PhD); translational science (PhD). *Degree requirements:* For master's, thesis; for doctorate, thesis/dissertation. *Entrance requirements:* For master's and doctorate, GRE General Test. Electronic applications accepted.

**University of the Sciences,** Program in Chemistry, Biochemistry and Pharmacognosy, Philadelphia, PA 19104-4495. Offers biochemistry (MS, PhD); chemistry (MS, PhD); pharmacognosy (MS, PhD). *Program availability:* Part-time. *Degree requirements:* For master's, thesis, qualifying exams; for doctorate, comprehensive exam, thesis/dissertation, qualifying exams. *Entrance requirements:* For master's and doctorate, GRE General Test, GRE Subject Test. Additional exam requirements/recommendations for international students: required—TOEFL, TWE. *Expenses:* Contact institution.

**The University of Toledo,** College of Graduate Studies, College of Pharmacy and Pharmaceutical Sciences, Program in Medicinal and Biological Chemistry, Toledo, OH 43606-3390. Offers MS, PhD. Terminal master's awarded for partial completion of doctoral program. *Degree requirements:* For master's, thesis; for doctorate, thesis/dissertation. *Entrance requirements:* For master's and doctorate, GRE General Test. Additional exam requirements/recommendations for international students: required—TOEFL (minimum score 550 paper-based; 80 iBT). Electronic applications accepted.

**University of Utah,** Graduate School, College of Pharmacy, Department of Medicinal Chemistry, Salt Lake City, UT 84112-5820. Offers MS, PhD. *Faculty:* 5 full-time (2 women). *Students:* 9 full-time (7 women), 5 part-time (3 women); includes 2 minority (both Asian, non-Hispanic/Latino), 8 international. Average age 27. In 2019, 3 doctorates awarded. Terminal master's awarded for partial completion of doctoral program. *Degree requirements:* For master's, comprehensive exam, thesis, end of first-year capstone exam; for doctorate, comprehensive exam, thesis/dissertation, end of first-year capstone exam. *Entrance requirements:* For doctorate, minimum GPA of 3.0. Additional exam requirements/recommendations for international students: required—TOEFL (minimum score 550 paper-based; 80 iBT), IELTS (minimum score 6.5). *Application deadline:* For fall admission, 12/15 for domestic and international students. Application fee: $55 ($65 for international students). *Expenses:* Contact institution. *Financial support:* In 2019–20, 13 students received support, including 8 research assistantships (averaging $16,375 per year); unspecified assistantships also available. Financial award application deadline: 12/15. *Unit head:* Dr. Darrell R. Davis, Chair, 801-581-7063, Fax: 801-585-6208, E-mail: darrell.davis@utah.edu. *Application contact:* Dr. Thomas E. Cheatham, Director of Graduate Studies, 801-587-9652, Fax: 801-585-6208, E-mail: tom.cheatham@pharm.utah.edu.
Website: http://www.pharmacy.utah.edu/medchem/

**University of Utah,** Graduate School, College of Pharmacy, Department of Pharmaceutics and Pharmaceutical Chemistry, Salt Lake City, UT 84112. Offers PhD. *Faculty:* 8 full-time (1 woman). *Students:* 10 full-time (5 women); includes 2 minority (1 Black or African American, non-Hispanic/Latino; 1 Asian, non-Hispanic/Latino), 5 international. Average age 29. 28 applicants, 4% accepted, 1 enrolled. In 2019, 3 doctorates awarded. Terminal master's awarded for partial completion of doctoral program. *Degree requirements:* For doctorate, comprehensive exam, thesis/dissertation. *Entrance requirements:* For doctorate, B.S. degree in Pharmacy,Chemistry, Biology, Chemical Engineering and/or related areas. Additional exam requirements/recommendations for international students: required—TOEFL (minimum score 550 paper-based; 100 iBT), GRE; recommended—IELTS. *Application deadline:* For fall admission, 12/1 for domestic and international students. Application fee: $55. Electronic applications accepted. *Expenses:* Tuition Benefit Plan is offered for the first 8 semesters (entering with a Masters Degree) or 10 semesters (entering with a Bachelor Degree) to cover tuition, fees & some portion of insurance if student maintains standards of the program. Tuition pricing differs based on International Student, Domestic and In-state. *Financial support:* In 2019–20, 10 students received support, including 10 research assistantships (averaging $27,000 per year); unspecified assistantships also available. *Unit head:* James Herron, Associate Professor, 801-581-7307, E-mail: james.herron@utah.edu. *Application contact:* Dalynn Bergund, Manager, Administration, 801-585-0070, E-mail: dalynn.berglund@utah.edu.
Website: http://www.pharmacy.utah.edu/pharmaceutics/

## Medicinal and Pharmaceutical Chemistry

**University of Washington,** School of Pharmacy, Department of Medicinal Chemistry, Seattle, WA 98195. Offers PhD. *Faculty:* 9 full-time (1 woman). *Students:* 27 full-time (11 women); includes 7 minority (1 American Indian or Alaska Native, non-Hispanic/Latino; 5 Asian, non-Hispanic/Latino; 1 Hispanic/Latino), 3 international. Average age 27. 45 applicants, 22% accepted, 3 enrolled. In 2019, 4 doctorates awarded. *Degree requirements:* For doctorate, thesis/dissertation, cumulative exams, general oral exam, final defense exam. *Entrance requirements:* For doctorate, GRE General Test, minimum GPA of 3.0, 3 letters of recommendation, statement of purpose, transcripts, resume. Additional exam requirements/recommendations for international students: required—TOEFL (minimum score 580 paper-based; 92 iBT). *Application deadline:* For fall admission, 12/14 for domestic and international students. Electronic applications accepted. *Financial support:* Fellowships, research assistantships with full tuition reimbursements, and scholarships/grants available. *Unit head:* Dr. William M. Atkins, Professor and Chair, 206-543-2224, Fax: 206-685-3252, E-mail: winky@uw.edu. *Application contact:* Caryl Corsi, Graduate Program Operations Specialist, 206-543-2224, Fax: 206-685-3252, E-mail: medchem@uw.edu.
Website: https://sop.washington.edu/department-of-medicinal-chemistry/

**Virginia Commonwealth University,** Medical College of Virginia-Professional Programs, School of Pharmacy, Department of Pharmaceutics, Richmond, VA 23284-9005. Offers medicinal chemistry (MS); pharmaceutical sciences (PhD); pharmaceutics (MS); pharmacotherapy and pharmacy administration (MS). Terminal master's awarded for partial completion of doctoral program. *Degree requirements:* For master's, thesis; for doctorate, thesis/dissertation. *Entrance requirements:* For master's and doctorate, GRE General Test. Additional exam requirements/recommendations for international students: required—TOEFL. Electronic applications accepted.

**Wayne State University,** Eugene Applebaum College of Pharmacy and Health Sciences, Applied Health Sciences, Detroit, MI 48202. Offers medicinal chemistry (MS, PhD); pharmaceutics (MS, PhD), including medicinal chemistry (PhD); pharmacology and toxicology (MS, PhD). *Entrance requirements:* For master's, GRE General Test, bachelor's degree; adequate background in biology, physics, calculus, and chemistry; three letters of recommendation; personal statement; for doctorate, GRE General Test, bachelor's or master's degree in one of the behavioral, biological, pharmaceutical or physical sciences; three letters of recommendation. Additional exam requirements/recommendations for international students: required—TOEFL (minimum score 550 paper-based; 79 iBT), Michigan English Language Assessment Battery (minimum score 85); recommended—IELTS (minimum score 6.5), TWE (minimum score 5.5). Electronic applications accepted. *Expenses:* Contact institution.

# Pharmaceutical Administration

**Belmont University,** College of Pharmacy, Nashville, TN 37212. Offers advanced pharmacotherapy (Pharm D); health care informatics (Pharm D); management (Pharm D); missions/public health (Pharm D); Pharm D/MBA. *Accreditation:* ACPE. *Faculty:* 29 full-time (16 women), 4 part-time/adjunct (2 women). *Students:* 354 full-time (242 women); includes 120 minority (50 Black or African American, non-Hispanic/Latino; 1 American Indian or Alaska Native, non-Hispanic/Latino; 41 Asian, non-Hispanic/Latino; 18 Hispanic/Latino; 10 Two or more races, non-Hispanic/Latino), 3 international. Average age 25. In 2019, 67 doctorates awarded. *Degree requirements:* For doctorate, comprehensive exam. *Entrance requirements:* For doctorate, PCAT. Additional exam requirements/recommendations for international students: required—TOEFL. *Application deadline:* For fall admission, 8/31 priority date for domestic students; for spring admission, 3/1 for domestic students. Applications are processed on a rolling basis. Application fee: $50. Electronic applications accepted. *Expenses:* Contact institution. *Financial support:* In 2019–20, 112 students received support. Career-related internships or fieldwork and scholarships/grants available. Financial award application deadline: 12/1; financial award applicants required to submit FAFSA. *Unit head:* Dr. David Gregory, Dean, 615-460-6746, Fax: 615-460-6741, E-mail: david.gregory@belmont.edu. *Application contact:* Dr. David Gregory, Dean, 615-460-6746, Fax: 615-460-6741, E-mail: david.gregory@belmont.edu.
Website: http://www.belmont.edu/pharmacy/index.html

**Columbia University,** Graduate School of Business, MBA Program, New York, NY 10027. Offers accounting (MBA); decision, risk, and operations (MBA); entrepreneurship (MBA); finance and economics (MBA); healthcare and pharmaceutical management (MBA); human resource management (MBA); international business (MBA); leadership and ethics (MBA); management (MBA); marketing (MBA); media (MBA); private equity (MBA); real estate (MBA); social enterprise (MBA); value investing (MBA); DDS/MBA; JD/MBA; MBA/MIA; MBA/MPH; MBA/MS; MD/MBA. *Entrance requirements:* For master's, GMAT, 2 letters of recommendation. Additional exam requirements/recommendations for international students: required—TOEFL. Electronic applications accepted. *Expenses:* Contact institution.

**Duquesne University,** School of Pharmacy, Graduate School of Pharmaceutical Sciences, Program in Pharmacy Administration, Pittsburgh, PA 15282-0001. Offers MS. *Entrance requirements:* For master's, GRE General Test. Additional exam requirements/recommendations for international students: required—TOEFL (minimum score 100 iBT). Electronic applications accepted. *Expenses:* Contact institution.

**Fairleigh Dickinson University, Metropolitan Campus,** Silberman College of Business, Program in Pharmaceutical Studies, Teaneck, NJ 07666-1914. Offers chemical studies (Certificate); pharmaceutical studies (MBA, Certificate).

**Florida Agricultural and Mechanical University,** Division of Graduate Studies, Research, and Continuing Education, College of Pharmacy and Pharmaceutical Sciences, Graduate Programs in Pharmaceutical Sciences, Tallahassee, FL 32307-3200. Offers environmental toxicology (PhD); health outcomes research and pharmacoeconomics (PhD); medicinal chemistry (MS, PhD); pharmaceutics (MS, PhD); pharmacology/toxicology (MS, PhD); pharmacy administration (MS). *Accreditation:* CEPH. *Degree requirements:* For master's, comprehensive exam, thesis, publishable paper; for doctorate, comprehensive exam, thesis/dissertation, publishable paper. *Entrance requirements:* For master's and doctorate, GRE General Test, minimum GPA of 3.0 in last 60 hours. Additional exam requirements/recommendations for international students: required—TOEFL.

**Idaho State University,** Graduate School, College of Pharmacy, Department of Pharmacy Practice and Administrative Sciences, Pocatello, ID 83209-8333. Offers pharmacy (Pharm D); pharmacy administration (MS, PhD). *Accreditation:* ACPE (one or more programs are accredited). *Program availability:* Part-time. *Degree requirements:* For master's, one foreign language, comprehensive exam, thesis, thesis research, speech and technical writing classes; for doctorate, comprehensive exam, thesis/dissertation, oral and written exams, speech and technical writing classes. *Entrance requirements:* For master's, GRE General Test, minimum GPA of 3.0, 3 letters of recommendation; for doctorate, GRE General Test, BS in pharmacy or related field, minimum GPA of 3.0, 3 letters of recommendation. Additional exam requirements/recommendations for international students: required—TOEFL (minimum score 550 paper-based; 80 iBT). Electronic applications accepted. *Expenses:* Contact institution.

**New Jersey Institute of Technology,** Newark College of Engineering, Newark, NJ 07102. Offers biomedical engineering (MS, PhD); biopharmaceutical engineering (MS); chemical engineering (MS, PhD); civil engineering (MS, PhD); computer engineering (MS); critical infrastructure systems (MS); electrical engineering (MS, PhD); engineering management (MS); engineering science (MS); environmental engineering (MS, PhD); healthcare systems management (MS); industrial engineering (MS, PhD); internet engineering (MS); manufacturing systems engineering (MS); materials science & engineering (PhD); materials science and engineering (MS); mechanical engineering (MS, PhD); occupational safety and health engineering (MS). *Program availability:* Part-time, evening/weekend. *Faculty:* 151 full-time (29 women), 135 part-time/adjunct (15 women). *Students:* 576 full-time (161 women), 528 part-time (111 women); includes 366 minority (61 Black or African American, non-Hispanic/Latino; 1 American Indian or Alaska Native, non-Hispanic/Latino; 166 Asian, non-Hispanic/Latino; 115 Hispanic/Latino; 23 Two or more races, non-Hispanic/Latino), 450 international. Average age 28. 2,053 applicants, 67% accepted, 338 enrolled. In 2019, 474 master's, 30 doctorates awarded. Terminal master's awarded for partial completion of doctoral program. *Degree requirements:* For master's, thesis (for some programs); for doctorate, thesis/dissertation. *Entrance requirements:* For master's, GRE General Test, minimum GPA 2.8, personal statement, 1 letter of recommendation, transcripts; for doctorate, GRE General Test, minimum GPA of 3.5, personal statement, 3 letters of recommendation, transcripts. Additional exam requirements/recommendations for international students: required—TOEFL (minimum score 550 paper-based; 79 iBT), IELTS (minimum score 6.5). *Application deadline:* For fall admission, 6/1 priority date for domestic students, 5/1 priority date for international students; for spring admission, 11/15 priority date for domestic and international students. Applications are processed on a rolling basis. Application fee: $75. Electronic applications accepted. *Expenses:* $23,828 per year (in-state), $33,744 per year (out-of-state). *Financial support:* In 2019–20, 352 students received support, including 33 fellowships with full tuition reimbursements available (averaging $24,000 per year), 89 research assistantships with full tuition reimbursements available (averaging $24,000 per year), 112 teaching assistantships with full tuition reimbursements available (averaging $24,000 per year); career-related internships or fieldwork, Federal Work-Study, scholarships/grants, and unspecified assistantships also available. Financial award application deadline: 1/15. *Unit head:* Dr. Moshe Kam, Dean, 973-596-5534, Fax: 973-596-2316, E-mail: moshe.kam@njit.edu. *Application contact:* Stephen Eck, Executive Director of University Admissions, 973-596-3300, Fax: 973-596-3461, E-mail: admissions@njit.edu.
Website: http://engineering.njit.edu/

**Northeast Ohio Medical University,** College of Graduate Studies, Rootstown, OH 44272-0095. Offers health-system pharmacy administration (MS); integrated pharmaceutical medicine (MS, PhD); medical ethics and humanities (MS, Certificate); public health (MPH). *Program availability:* Part-time, evening/weekend, 100% online, blended/hybrid learning. *Faculty:* 126 part-time/adjunct (62 women). *Students:* 24 full-time (12 women), 28 part-time (15 women); includes 21 minority (2 Black or African American, non-Hispanic/Latino; 10 Asian, non-Hispanic/Latino; 5 Hispanic/Latino; 4 Two or more races, non-Hispanic/Latino). Average age 26. 31 applicants, 97% accepted, 21 enrolled. In 2019, 15 master's, 13 other advanced degrees awarded. *Degree requirements:* For master's, thesis (for some programs), thesis (for MS in medical ethics and humanities, integrated pharmaceutical medicine, MS in MAS); for doctorate, thesis/dissertation, For IPM Ph.D Program. *Entrance requirements:* Additional exam requirements/recommendations for international students: recommended—TOEFL (minimum score 550 paper-based). *Application deadline:* For fall admission, 7/17 for domestic students. Applications are processed on a rolling basis. Application fee: $95. Electronic applications accepted. *Expenses:* Student health and fitness, student activities. *Financial support:* In 2019–20, 6 students received support. Scholarships/grants and tuition waivers (full and partial) available. Financial award application deadline: 3/15; financial award applicants required to submit FAFSA. *Unit head:* Dr. Steven Schmidt, Dean, 330-325-6290. *Application contact:* Dr. Steven Schmidt, Dean, 330-325-6290.
Website: https://www.neomed.edu/graduatestudies/

**The Ohio State University,** College of Pharmacy, Columbus, OH 43210. Offers MS, PhD, Pharm D, Pharm D/MBA, Pharm D/MPH, Pharm D/PhD. *Accreditation:* ACPE (one or more programs are accredited). Terminal master's awarded for partial completion of doctoral program. *Degree requirements:* For doctorate, comprehensive exam (for some programs), thesis/dissertation (for some programs). *Entrance requirements:* For master's, GRE General Test, minimum GPA of 3.0; for doctorate, GRE General Test; PCAT (for PharmD), minimum GPA of 3.0. Additional exam requirements/recommendations for international students: required—TOEFL minimum score 600 paper-based, 100 iBT (for MS and PhD); TOEFL minimum score 577 paper-based; 90 iBT, Michigan English Language Assessment Battery minimum score 84, IELTS minimum score 7.5 (for PharmD). Electronic applications accepted. *Expenses:* Contact institution.

**Purdue University,** College of Pharmacy and Graduate School, Graduate Programs in Pharmacy and Pharmacal Sciences, Department of Industrial and Physical Pharmacy, West Lafayette, IN 47907. Offers pharmaceutics (PhD); regulatory quality compliance (MS, Certificate). *Faculty:* 9 full-time (3 women), 1 part-time/adjunct (0 women). *Students:* 37 full-time (18 women); includes 3 minority (1 Asian, non-Hispanic/Latino; 2 Two or more races, non-Hispanic/Latino), 25 international. Average age 28. 55 applicants, 25% accepted, 5 enrolled. In 2019, 6 doctorates awarded. *Degree requirements:* For doctorate, thesis/dissertation. *Entrance requirements:* For master's, minimum GPA of 3.0; for doctorate, GRE General Test, minimum GPA of 3.0. Additional exam requirements/recommendations for international students: required—TOEFL (minimum score 580 paper-based; 77 iBT). *Application deadline:* For fall admission, 1/1 for domestic and international students. Applications are processed on a rolling basis. Application fee: $60 ($75 for international students). Electronic applications accepted. *Financial support:* Fellowships, research assistantships, teaching assistantships, and traineeships available. Support available to part-time students. Financial award

applicants required to submit FAFSA. *Unit head:* Eric J. Munson, Head of the Graduate Program, 765-494-1450, E-mail: munsone@purdue.edu. *Application contact:* Delayne Graham, Graduate Contact, 765-494-1362, E-mail: dkgraham@purdue.edu.

**Rutgers University - Newark,** Rutgers Business School–Newark and New Brunswick, Program in Pharmaceutical Management, Newark, NJ 07102. Offers MBA.

**St. John's University,** College of Pharmacy and Health Sciences, Graduate Programs in Pharmaceutical Sciences, Program in Pharmacy Administration, Queens, NY 11439. Offers MS. *Entrance requirements:* For master's, GRE General Test, letters of recommendation, transcripts, resume, personal statement. Additional exam requirements/recommendations for international students: required—TOEFL (minimum score 100 iBT), IELTS (minimum score 7). Electronic applications accepted. *Expenses:* Contact institution.

**San Diego State University,** Graduate and Research Affairs, College of Sciences, Program in Regulatory Affairs, San Diego, CA 92182. Offers MS. *Degree requirements:* For master's, thesis. *Entrance requirements:* For master's, GRE General Test, 3 letters of recommendation, employment/volunteer experience list. Additional exam requirements/recommendations for international students: required—TOEFL. Electronic applications accepted.

**Southwestern Oklahoma State University,** College of Pharmacy, Weatherford, OK 73096-3098. Offers pharmacy (Pharm D); pharmacy leadership (Pharm D). *Accreditation:* ACPE. *Entrance requirements:* For doctorate, PCAT.

**Temple University,** Fox School of Business, MBA Programs, Philadelphia, PA 19122-6096. Offers accounting (MBA); business management (MBA); financial management (MBA); healthcare and life sciences innovation (MBA); human resource management (MBA); international business (IMBA); IT management (MBA); marketing management (MBA); pharmaceutical management (MBA); strategic management (EMBA, MBA). *Accreditation:* AACSB. *Program availability:* Part-time, evening/weekend, online learning. *Entrance requirements:* For master's, GMAT, minimum undergraduate GPA of 3.0. Additional exam requirements/recommendations for international students: required—TOEFL (minimum score 600 paper-based; 100 iBT), IELTS (minimum score 7.5).

**University of Florida,** Graduate School, College of Pharmacy, Graduate Programs in Pharmacy, Department of Pharmaceutical Outcomes and Policy, Gainesville, FL 32611. Offers MSP, PhD. *Program availability:* Part-time, online learning. *Degree requirements:* For doctorate, thesis/dissertation. *Entrance requirements:* For master's and doctorate, GRE General Test, minimum GPA of 3.0. Additional exam requirements/recommendations for international students: required—TOEFL (minimum score 550 paper-based; 80 iBT), IELTS (minimum score 6). Electronic applications accepted.

**University of Georgia,** College of Pharmacy, Department of Clinical and Administrative Pharmacy, Athens, GA 30602. Offers clinical and experimental therapeutics (PhD); pharmacy care administration (PhD).

**University of Houston,** College of Pharmacy, Houston, TX 77204. Offers pharmaceutics (MSPHR, PhD); pharmacology (MSPHR, PhD); pharmacy (Pharm D); pharmacy administration (MSPHR, PhD). *Accreditation:* ACPE. *Program availability:* Part-time. Terminal master's awarded for partial completion of doctoral program. *Entrance requirements:* For doctorate, PCAT (for Pharm D). Additional exam requirements/recommendations for international students: required—TOEFL. Electronic applications accepted.

**University of Illinois at Chicago,** College of Pharmacy, Graduate Programs in Pharmacy, Chicago, IL 60607-7128. Offers comparative effectiveness research (MS); forensic science (MS); forensic toxicology (MS); medicinal chemistry (MS, PhD); pharmacognosy (MS, PhD); pharmacy (PhD). Terminal master's awarded for partial completion of doctoral program. *Degree requirements:* For master's, variable foreign language requirement, thesis; for doctorate, variable foreign language requirement, thesis/dissertation. *Entrance requirements:* For master's and doctorate, GRE General Test. Additional exam requirements/recommendations for international students: required—TOEFL. Electronic applications accepted.

**University of Maryland, Baltimore,** Graduate School, Graduate Programs in Pharmacy, Department of Pharmaceutical Health Service Research, Baltimore, MD 21201. Offers epidemiology (MS); pharmacy administration (PhD); Pharm D/PhD. *Degree requirements:* For doctorate, comprehensive exam, thesis/dissertation. *Entrance requirements:* For doctorate, GRE General Test. Additional exam requirements/recommendations for international students: required—TOEFL, IELTS. Electronic applications accepted.

**University of Maryland, Baltimore,** Graduate School, Graduate Programs in Pharmacy, Program in Regulatory Science, Baltimore, MD 21201. Offers MS.

**University of Michigan,** College of Pharmacy and Rackham Graduate School, Department of Clinical Pharmacy, Ann Arbor, MI 48109. Offers PhD. Terminal master's awarded for partial completion of doctoral program. *Degree requirements:* For doctorate, thesis/dissertation, oral defense of dissertation, preliminary exam. *Entrance requirements:* For doctorate, GRE. Additional exam requirements/recommendations for international students: required—TOEFL (minimum score 560 paper-based; 84 iBT) or IELTS (minimum score 6.5). *Expenses:* Contact institution.

**University of Minnesota, Twin Cities Campus,** College of Pharmacy and Graduate School, Graduate Programs in Pharmacy, Graduate Program in Social and Administrative Pharmacy, Minneapolis, MN 55455-0213. Offers MS, PhD. *Program availability:* Part-time. Terminal master's awarded for partial completion of doctoral program. *Degree requirements:* For master's, thesis (for some programs); for doctorate, thesis/dissertation. *Entrance requirements:* For master's, GRE General Test, BS in science; for doctorate, GRE General Test or Pharm D. Additional exam requirements/recommendations for international students: required—TOEFL (minimum score 100 iBT). Electronic applications accepted.

**University of Mississippi,** Graduate School, School of Pharmacy, University, MS 38677. Offers environmental toxicology (MS, PhD); industrial pharmacy (MS); medicinal chemistry (MS, PhD); pharmaceutics (MS, PhD); pharmacognosy (MS, PhD); pharmacology (MS, PhD); pharmacy (Pharm D); pharmacy administration (MS, PhD). *Accreditation:* ACPE (one or more programs are accredited). *Program availability:* Part-time. *Faculty:* 68 full-time (33 women), 13 part-time/adjunct (5 women). *Students:* 223 full-time (137 women), 215 part-time (137 women); includes 71 minority (29 Black or African American, non-Hispanic/Latino; 1 American Indian or Alaska Native, non-Hispanic/Latino; 31 Asian, non-Hispanic/Latino; 4 Hispanic/Latino; 6 Two or more races, non-Hispanic/Latino), 90 international. Average age 25. In 2019, 29 master's, 13

doctorates awarded. Terminal master's awarded for partial completion of doctoral program. *Degree requirements:* For master's, thesis; for doctorate, thesis/dissertation (for some programs). *Entrance requirements:* For master's, GRE General Test, minimum GPA of 3.0; for doctorate, GRE General Test (for PhD). Additional exam requirements/recommendations for international students: required—TOEFL. *Application deadline:* Applications are processed on a rolling basis. Application fee: $50. Electronic applications accepted. *Expenses:* Tuition, state resident: full-time $8718; part-time $484.25 per credit hour. Tuition, nonresident: full-time $24,990; part-time $1388.25 per credit hour. *Required fees:* $100; $4.16 per credit hour. *Financial support:* Fellowships, research assistantships, teaching assistantships, career-related internships or fieldwork, Federal Work-Study, institutionally sponsored loans, scholarships/grants, tuition waivers (full), and unspecified assistantships available. Financial award application deadline: 3/1; financial award applicants required to submit FAFSA. *Unit head:* Dr. David Allen, Dean, School of Pharmacy, 662-915-7265, Fax: 662-9155704, E-mail: sopdean@olemiss.edu. *Application contact:* Temeka Smith, Graduate Activities Specialist for Admissions, 662-915-7474, Fax: 662-915-7577, E-mail: gschool@olemiss.edu.
Website: http://www.pharmacy.olemiss.edu/

**The University of North Carolina at Chapel Hill,** Eshelman School of Pharmacy, Chapel Hill, NC 27599. Offers pharmaceutical sciences (PhD); pharmaceutical sciences - health system pharmacy administration (MS); pharmacy (Pharm D). *Accreditation:* ACPE (one or more programs are accredited). Terminal master's awarded for partial completion of doctoral program. *Degree requirements:* For master's, comprehensive exam, thesis; for doctorate, comprehensive exam, thesis/dissertation. *Entrance requirements:* For master's and doctorate, GRE General Test, minimum GPA of 3.0. Additional exam requirements/recommendations for international students: required—TOEFL (minimum score 550 paper-based; 90 iBT), IELTS (minimum score 7). Electronic applications accepted. *Expenses:* Contact institution.

**University of Pittsburgh,** School of Pharmacy, Program in Pharmacy Business Administration, Pittsburgh, PA 15261. Offers MS. *Program availability:* Part-time, evening/weekend. *Entrance requirements:* For master's, GMAT (recommended), Pharm D, BS in pharmacy, or equivalent undergraduate degree from accredited U.S. institution; minimum of 2 years' professional experience; 2 professional letters of reference. Additional exam requirements/recommendations for international students: required—TOEFL (minimum score 80 iBT) or IELTS (minimum score 6.5). *Expenses:* Contact institution.

**University of Southern California,** Graduate School, School of Pharmacy, Program in Healthcare Decision Analysis, Los Angeles, CA 90089. Offers MS. *Program availability:* Part-time, online learning.

**University of the Sciences,** Program in Pharmaceutical and Healthcare Business, Philadelphia, PA 19104-4495. Offers MBA. *Program availability:* Part-time, evening/weekend, online learning. *Entrance requirements:* Additional exam requirements/recommendations for international students: required—TOEFL, TWE. *Expenses:* Contact institution.

**University of the Sciences,** Program in Pharmacy Administration, Philadelphia, PA 19104-4495. Offers MS. *Program availability:* Part-time. *Entrance requirements:* Additional exam requirements/recommendations for international students: required—TOEFL, TWE. *Expenses:* Contact institution.

**The University of Toledo,** College of Graduate Studies, College of Pharmacy and Pharmaceutical Sciences, Program in Pharmaceutical Sciences, Toledo, OH 43606-3390. Offers administrative pharmacy (MSPS); industrial pharmacy (MSPS); pharmacology toxicology (MSPS). *Degree requirements:* For master's, thesis. *Entrance requirements:* For master's, GRE General Test. Additional exam requirements/recommendations for international students: required—TOEFL (minimum score 550 paper-based; 80 iBT). Electronic applications accepted.

**University of Utah,** Graduate School, College of Pharmacy, Department of Pharmacotherapy, Salt Lake City, UT 84112. Offers health system pharmacy administration (MS); outcomes research and health policy (PhD). *Faculty:* 19 full-time (12 women). *Students:* 6 full-time (3 women), 7 part-time (1 woman); includes 1 minority (Asian, non-Hispanic/Latino), 4 international. Average age 33. 14 applicants, 43% accepted, 6 enrolled. In 2019, 1 master's, 1 doctorate awarded. Terminal master's awarded for partial completion of doctoral program. *Degree requirements:* For master's, comprehensive exam, thesis or alternative, project; for doctorate, comprehensive exam, thesis/dissertation. *Entrance requirements:* Additional exam requirements/recommendations for international students: required—TOEFL (minimum score 550 paper-based; 80 iBT), GRE. *Application deadline:* For fall admission, 1/10 for domestic students, 12/15 for international students. Application fee: $55 ($65 for international students). *Expenses:* Tuition, state resident: full-time $7085; part-time $272.51 per credit hour. Tuition, nonresident: full-time $24,937; part-time $959.12 per credit hour. *Required fees:* $880.52; $880.52 per semester. Tuition and fees vary according to degree level, program and student level. *Financial support:* In 2019–20, 1 research assistantship (averaging $4,000 per year) was awarded. Financial award applicants required to submit CSS PROFILE or FAFSA. *Unit head:* Daniel Malone, Professor, 801-581-8054, Fax: 801-587-7923, E-mail: dan.malone@utah.edu. *Application contact:* Linda O'Connor, Education Coordinator, 801-585-1065, E-mail: linda.oconner@pharm.utah.edu.
Website: http://www.pharmacy.utah.edu/pharmacotherapy/

**University of Wisconsin–Madison,** School of Pharmacy and Graduate School, Graduate Programs in Pharmacy, Madison, WI 53706-1380. Offers pharmaceutical sciences (PhD); social and administrative sciences in pharmacy (MS, PhD). Terminal master's awarded for partial completion of doctoral program. *Degree requirements:* For master's, thesis (for some programs); for doctorate, comprehensive exam (for some programs), thesis/dissertation. *Entrance requirements:* For master's and doctorate, GRE. Additional exam requirements/recommendations for international students: required—TOEFL. Electronic applications accepted. *Expenses:* Contact institution.

**Virginia Commonwealth University,** Medical College of Virginia-Professional Programs, School of Pharmacy, Department of Pharmaceutics, Richmond, VA 23284-9005. Offers medicinal chemistry (MS); pharmaceutical sciences (PhD); pharmaceutics (MS); pharmacotherapy and pharmacy administration (MS). Terminal master's awarded for partial completion of doctoral program. *Degree requirements:* For master's, thesis; for doctorate, thesis/dissertation. *Entrance requirements:* For master's and doctorate, GRE General Test. Additional exam requirements/recommendations for international students: required—TOEFL. Electronic applications accepted.

# Pharmaceutical Sciences

**Albany College of Pharmacy and Health Sciences,** School of Pharmacy and Pharmaceutical Sciences, Albany, NY 12208. Offers health outcomes research (MS); pharmaceutical sciences (MS), including pharmaceutics, pharmacology; pharmacy (Pharm D). *Accreditation:* ACPE. *Degree requirements:* For master's, thesis; for doctorate, practice experience. *Entrance requirements:* For master's, GRE, minimum GPA of 3.0; for doctorate, PCAT, minimum GPA of 2.5. Additional exam requirements/recommendations for international students: required—TOEFL (minimum score 84 iBT). Electronic applications accepted.

**Auburn University,** Harrison School of Pharmacy and Graduate School, Graduate Program in Pharmacy, Auburn University, AL 36849. Offers pharmacal sciences (MS, PhD); pharmaceutical sciences (PhD); pharmacy care systems (MS, PhD). *Program availability:* Part-time. *Faculty:* 58 full-time (34 women), 1 (woman) part-time/adjunct. *Students:* 50 full-time (27 women), 15 part-time (7 women); includes 4 minority (2 Black or African American, non-Hispanic/Latino; 1 American Indian or Alaska Native, non-Hispanic/Latino; 1 Asian, non-Hispanic/Latino), 44 international. Average age 30. 102 applicants, 16% accepted, 10 enrolled. In 2019, 3 master's, 9 doctorates awarded. *Degree requirements:* For master's, thesis; for doctorate, thesis/dissertation. *Entrance requirements:* For master's and doctorate, GRE General Test. *Application deadline:* For fall admission, 1/15 for domestic and international students. Application fee: $60 ($70 for international students). Electronic applications accepted. *Expenses:* $546 per credit hour state resident tuition, $1638 per credit hour nonresident tuition, $680 student services fee for GRA/GTA, $838 student services fee, $5283 per semester. *Financial support:* Fellowships, research assistantships, and teaching assistantships available. Financial award application deadline: 3/15. *Unit head:* Dr. Richard Hansen, Dean/Professor, Harrison School of Pharmacy, 334-844-8348, Fax: 334-844-8307. *Application contact:* Dr. George Flowers, Dean of the Graduate School, 334-844-2125.

**Boston University,** School of Medicine, Graduate Medical Sciences, Department of Pharmacology and Experimental Therapeutics, Boston, MA 02118. Offers PhD, MD/PhD. Terminal master's awarded for partial completion of doctoral program. *Application deadline:* For fall admission, 1/15 for domestic students; for spring admission, 10/15 for domestic students. *Unit head:* Dr. David H. Farb, Chairman, E-mail: dfarb@bu.edu. *Application contact:* GMS Admissions Office, 617-358-9518, Fax: 617-358-2913, E-mail: gmsbusm@bu.edu.
Website: http://www.bumc.bu.edu/busm-pm/

**Butler University,** College of Pharmacy and Health Sciences, Indianapolis, IN 46208-3485. Offers pharmaceutical science (MS); pharmacy (Pharm D), including medical Spanish, research; physician assistant studies (MS). *Accreditation:* ACPE (one or more programs are accredited). *Program availability:* Part-time, evening/weekend, 100% online. *Faculty:* 14 full-time (8 women). *Students:* 358 full-time (245 women), 2 part-time (0 women); includes 42 minority (1 Black or African American, non-Hispanic/Latino; 23 Asian, non-Hispanic/Latino; 12 Hispanic/Latino; 6 Two or more races, non-Hispanic/Latino), 4 international. Average age 24. 441 applicants, 17% accepted, 76 enrolled. In 2019, 77 master's, 106 doctorates awarded. *Degree requirements:* For master's, comprehensive exam (for some programs), thesis (for some programs), research paper or thesis; for doctorate, thesis/dissertation (for some programs). *Entrance requirements:* For master's, GRE General Test, CASPA application, official transcripts, baccalaureate degree from accredited institution (for physician assistant studies). Additional exam requirements/recommendations for international students: required—TOEFL (minimum score 550 paper-based; 79 iBT), IELTS (minimum score 6). *Application deadline:* For fall admission, 4/1 for domestic and international students. Electronic applications accepted. *Expenses:* Pharmacy: Pharmacy year 1 &2 (pre-Pharmacy) $20,685 per semester Pharmacy year 3-5 (P1-P3) $22,000 per semester; Pharm D (6th year only) (P4) $47,00 per year, billed summer ($4,780), fall* ($21,510), spring* ($21,510) Note: Rate is NOT based on number of hours enrolled. *Each hour above 20 hours is $1,830 for P1-P3. Master's of Science in Pharmaceutical Science: $760 per credit hour; Doctor of Medical Science: $800 per credit hour; PA Master's Program: $44,820 per year, billed summer ($4,482), fall* ($20,169), spring* ($20,169) Note: Rate is NOT based on number of hours enrolled. *each hour above 20 hours is $1,830 per credit hour. *Financial support:* In 2019–20, 4 students received support. Scholarships/grants, tuition waivers (full and partial), and unspecified assistantships available. Financial award applicants required to submit FAFSA. *Unit head:* Dr. Robert Soltis, Dean, 317-940-9322, E-mail: rsoltis@butler.edu. *Application contact:* Katie Clarizio, Academic Program Coordinator, 317-940-9297, E-mail: kclarizio@butler.edu.
Website: https://www.butler.edu/pharmacy-pa/about

**Campbell University,** Graduate and Professional Programs, College of Pharmacy and Health Sciences, Buies Creek, NC 27506. Offers athletic training (MAT); clinical research (MS); pharmaceutical sciences (MS); pharmacy (Pharm D); physical therapy (DPT); physician assistant (MPAP); public health (MS). *Accreditation:* ACPE; CEPH. *Program availability:* Part-time, evening/weekend. *Entrance requirements:* For master's, MCAT, PCAT, GRE, bachelor's degree in health sciences or related field; for doctorate, PCAT. Additional exam requirements/recommendations for international students: required—TOEFL (minimum score 550 paper-based; 79 iBT). Electronic applications accepted. *Expenses:* Contact institution.

**Chapman University,** School of Pharmacy, Irvine, CA 92618. Offers pharmaceutical sciences (MS, PhD); pharmacy (Pharm D). *Accreditation:* ACPE. *Faculty:* 44 full-time (22 women), 5 part-time/adjunct (1 woman). *Students:* 310 full-time (196 women), 6 part-time (5 women); includes 234 minority (14 Black or African American, non-Hispanic/Latino; 1 American Indian or Alaska Native, non-Hispanic/Latino; 187 Asian, non-Hispanic/Latino; 24 Hispanic/Latino; 8 Two or more races, non-Hispanic/Latino), 17 international. Average age 26. In 2019, 17 master's, 72 doctorates awarded. *Degree requirements:* For master's, thesis or alternative; for doctorate, dissertation for PhD. *Entrance requirements:* For doctorate, PCAT (PharmD), GRE (PhD). Additional exam requirements/recommendations for international students: required—TOEFL (minimum score 80 iBT), IELTS (minimum score 6.5), PTE (minimum score 53). *Application deadline:* Applications are processed on a rolling basis. Electronic applications accepted. *Expenses:* Contact institution. *Financial support:* Fellowships, research assistantships, Federal Work-Study, and scholarships/grants available. *Unit head:* Ronald P. Jordan, Dean, 714-516-5486, E-mail: rpjordan@chapman.edu. *Application contact:* Rocke DeMark, Associate Dean of Student and Academic Affairs, 714-516-516-5460, E-mail: pharmacyadmissions@chapman.edu.
Website: https://www.chapman.edu/pharmacy/index.aspx

**Creighton University,** School of Medicine and Graduate School, Graduate Programs in Medicine, Department of Pharmacology, Omaha, NE 68178-0001. Offers pharmaceutical sciences (MS); pharmacology (MS, PhD); Pharm D/MS. Terminal master's awarded for partial completion of doctoral program. *Degree requirements:* For master's, comprehensive exam, thesis; for doctorate, comprehensive exam, thesis/

dissertation, oral and written preliminary exams. *Entrance requirements:* For master's and doctorate, GRE General Test, minimum GPA of 3.0, undergraduate degree in sciences. Additional exam requirements/recommendations for international students: required—TOEFL. Electronic applications accepted.

**Creighton University,** School of Pharmacy and Health Professions, Program in Pharmaceutical Sciences, Omaha, NE 68178-0001. Offers MS, Pharm D/MS. *Degree requirements:* For master's, thesis. *Entrance requirements:* For master's, GRE, three recommendations. Additional exam requirements/recommendations for international students: required—TOEFL (minimum score 550 paper-based; 80 iBT). Electronic applications accepted.

**Drexel University,** College of Medicine, Biomedical Graduate Programs, Program in Drug Discovery and Development, Philadelphia, PA 19104-2875. Offers MS. *Degree requirements:* For master's, thesis.

**Duquesne University,** School of Pharmacy, Graduate School of Pharmaceutical Sciences, Program in Pharmaceutics, Pittsburgh, PA 15282-0001. Offers MS, PhD, MBA/MS. *Degree requirements:* For master's, thesis; for doctorate, comprehensive exam, thesis/dissertation. *Entrance requirements:* For master's and doctorate, GRE General Test. Additional exam requirements/recommendations for international students: required—TOEFL (minimum score 100 iBT). Electronic applications accepted. *Expenses:* Contact institution.

**East Tennessee State University,** Quillen College of Medicine, Department of Biomedical Sciences, Johnson City, TN 37614. Offers anatomy (PhD); biochemistry (PhD); microbiology (PhD); pharmaceutical sciences (PhD); pharmacology (PhD); physiology (PhD); quantitative biosciences (PhD). *Degree requirements:* For doctorate, comprehensive exam, thesis/dissertation, comprehensive qualifying exam; one-year residency. *Entrance requirements:* For doctorate, GRE General Test, GRE Subject Test, 3 letters of recommendation, minimum of 60 credit hours beyond the baccalaureate degree. Additional exam requirements/recommendations for international students: required—TOEFL (minimum score 550 paper-based; 79 iBT). Electronic applications accepted. *Expenses:* Contact institution.

**Florida Agricultural and Mechanical University,** Division of Graduate Studies, Research, and Continuing Education, College of Pharmacy and Pharmaceutical Sciences, Graduate Programs in Pharmaceutical Sciences, Tallahassee, FL 32307-3200. Offers environmental toxicology (PhD); health outcomes research and pharmacoeconomics (PhD); medicinal chemistry (MS, PhD); pharmaceutics (MS, PhD); pharmacology/toxicology (MS, PhD); pharmacy administration (MS). *Accreditation:* CEPH. *Degree requirements:* For master's, comprehensive exam, thesis, publishable paper; for doctorate, comprehensive exam, thesis/dissertation, publishable paper. *Entrance requirements:* For master's and doctorate, GRE General Test, minimum GPA of 3.0 in last 60 hours. Additional exam requirements/recommendations for international students: required—TOEFL.

**Idaho State University,** Graduate School, College of Pharmacy, Department of Biomedical and Pharmaceutical Sciences, Pocatello, ID 83209-8334. Offers biopharmaceutical analysis (PhD); drug delivery (PhD); medicinal chemistry (PhD); pharmaceutical sciences (MS); pharmacology (PhD). *Program availability:* Part-time. *Degree requirements:* For master's, one foreign language, comprehensive exam, thesis, thesis research, classes in speech and technical writing; for doctorate, comprehensive exam, thesis/dissertation, written and oral exams, classes in speech and technical writing. *Entrance requirements:* For master's, GRE General Test, minimum GPA of 3.0, 3 letters of recommendation; for doctorate, GRE General Test, BS in pharmacy or related field, minimum GPA of 3.0, 3 letters of recommendation. Additional exam requirements/recommendations for international students: required—TOEFL (minimum score 550 paper-based; 80 iBT). Electronic applications accepted. *Expenses:* Contact institution.

**Irell & Manella Graduate School of Biological Sciences,** Graduate Program, Duarte, CA 91010. Offers brain metastatic cancer (PhD); cancer and stem cell metabolism (PhD); cancer biology (PhD); cancer biology and developmental therapeutics (PhD); cell biology (PhD); chemical biology (PhD); chromosomal break repair (PhD); diabetes and pancreatic progenitor cell biology (PhD); DNA repair and cancer biology (PhD); germline epigenetic remodeling and endocrine disruptors (PhD); hematology and hematopoietic cell transplantation (PhD); hematology and immunology (PhD); inflammation and cancer (PhD); micrornas and gene regulation in cardiovascular disease (PhD); mixed chimerism for reversal of autoimmunity (PhD); molecular and cellular biology (PhD); molecular biology and genetics (PhD); nanoparticle mediated twist1 silencing in metastatic cancer (PhD); neuro-oncology and stem cell biology (PhD); neuroscience (PhD); RNA directed therapies for HIV-1 (PhD); small RNA-induced transcriptional gene activation (PhD); stem cell regulation by the microenvironment (PhD); translational oncology and pharmaceutical sciences (PhD); tumor biology (PhD). *Degree requirements:* For doctorate, comprehensive exam, thesis/dissertation, qualifying exams, two advanced courses. *Entrance requirements:* For doctorate, GRE General Test; GRE Subject Test (recommended), 2 years of course work in chemistry (general and organic); 1 year of course work each in biochemistry, general biology, and general physics; 2 semesters of course work in mathematics; significant research laboratory experience. Additional exam requirements/recommendations for international students: required—TOEFL. Electronic applications accepted.

**Johns Hopkins University,** Advanced Academic Programs, Program in Regulatory Science, Washington, DC 21218. Offers MS. *Program availability:* Part-time, evening/weekend, online learning. *Entrance requirements:* For master's, undergraduate degree in the life sciences or engineering with minimum GPA of 3.0 from a four-year college. Additional exam requirements/recommendations for international students: required—TOEFL (minimum score 100 iBT).

**Long Island University - Brooklyn,** Arnold and Marie Schwartz College of Pharmacy and Health Sciences, Brooklyn, NY 11201-8423. Offers drug regulatory affairs (MS); pharmaceutics (MS, PhD), including cosmetic science (MS), industrial pharmacy (MS); pharmacology and toxicology (MS); pharmacy (Pharm D). *Accreditation:* ACPE. *Program availability:* Part-time. Terminal master's awarded for partial completion of doctoral program. *Degree requirements:* For master's, comprehensive exam, thesis; for doctorate, comprehensive exam, thesis/dissertation. *Entrance requirements:* For master's and doctorate, GRE. Additional exam requirements/recommendations for international students: required—TOEFL (minimum score 550 paper-based, 79 iBT) or IELTS. Electronic applications accepted. *Expenses:* Contact institution.

**Long Island University - Hudson,** Graduate School, Purchase, NY 10577. Offers autism (Advanced Certificate); bilingual education (Advanced Certificate); childhood education (MS Ed); crisis management (Advanced Certificate); early childhood education (MS Ed); educational leadership (MS Ed); health administration (MPA);

literacy (MS Ed); marriage and family therapy (MS); mental health counseling (MS, Advanced Certificate), including credentialed alcoholism and substance abuse counselor (MS); middle childhood and adolescence education (MS Ed); pharmaceutics (MS), including cosmetic science, industrial pharmacy; public administration (MPA); school counseling (MS Ed, Advanced Certificate); school psychology (MS Ed); special education (MS Ed); TESOL (MS Ed); TESOL (all grades) (Advanced Certificate). *Program availability:* Part-time, evening/weekend. *Entrance requirements:* Additional exam requirements/recommendations for international students: required—TOEFL. Electronic applications accepted. *Expenses:* Contact institution.

**MCPHS University,** Graduate Studies, Program in Pharmaceutics/Industrial Pharmacy, Boston, MA 02115-5896. Offers MS, PhD. Terminal master's awarded for partial completion of doctoral program. *Degree requirements:* For master's, thesis, oral defense of thesis; for doctorate, one foreign language, comprehensive exam, thesis/dissertation, oral defense of dissertation, qualifying exam. *Entrance requirements:* For master's and doctorate, GRE General Test, minimum QPA of 3.0. Additional exam requirements/recommendations for international students: required—TOEFL (minimum score 550 paper-based; 79 iBT).

**Memorial University of Newfoundland,** School of Graduate Studies, School of Pharmacy, St. John's, NL A1C 5S7, Canada. Offers MSCPharm, PhD. *Program availability:* Part-time. *Degree requirements:* For master's, thesis, seminar; for doctorate, comprehensive exam, thesis/dissertation, oral defense of thesis. *Entrance requirements:* For master's, B Sc in pharmacy or related area; for doctorate, master's degree in pharmacy or closely-related field. Electronic applications accepted.

**Mercer University,** Graduate Studies, Cecil B. Day Campus, College of Pharmacy, Atlanta, GA 31207. Offers pharmaceutical sciences (PhD); pharmacy (Pharm D); Pharm D/MBA; Pharm D/MPH; Pharm D/PhD. *Accreditation:* ACPE (one or more programs are accredited). *Faculty:* 22 full-time (16 women), 15 part-time/adjunct (6 women). *Students:* 573 full-time (388 women), 3 part-time (2 women); includes 366 minority (164 Black or African American, non-Hispanic/Latino; 168 Asian, non-Hispanic/Latino; 22 Hispanic/Latino; 12 Two or more races, non-Hispanic/Latino), 49 international. Average age 26. 677 applicants, 48% accepted, 152 enrolled. In 2019, 144 doctorates awarded. *Degree requirements:* For doctorate, comprehensive exam (for some programs), thesis/dissertation (for some programs). *Entrance requirements:* For doctorate, GRE (for PhD); PCAT, MCAT, DAT, OAT, GRE (for Pharm D), Pharm D or BS in pharmacy or science and minimum GPA of 3.0 (for PhD); 66 hours of undergraduate pre-pharmacy coursework (for PharmD). Additional exam requirements/recommendations for international students: required—TOEFL (minimum score 100 iBT). *Application deadline:* For fall admission, 6/3 for domestic and international students. Applications are processed on a rolling basis. Electronic applications accepted. *Expenses:* Contact institution. *Financial support:* In 2019–20, 238 students received support, including 10 research assistantships with full tuition reimbursements available (averaging $15,000 per year), 35 teaching assistantships with full tuition reimbursements available (averaging $15,000 per year); Federal Work-Study, scholarships/grants, and tuition waivers (full) also available. Financial award application deadline: 5/1; financial award applicants required to submit FAFSA. *Unit head:* Dr. Brian L. Crabtree, Dean, 678-547-6306, Fax: 678-547-6315, E-mail: crabtree_bl@mercer.edu. *Application contact:* Jordana S. Berry, Director of Admissions, 678-547-6182, Fax: 678-547-6518, E-mail: berry_js@mercer.edu.
Website: http://pharmacy.mercer.edu/

**Northeastern University,** Bouvé College of Health Sciences, Boston, MA 02115-5096. Offers applied behavior analysis (MS); audiology (Au D); counseling psychology (MS, PhD, CAGS); exercise science (MS); nursing (MS, PhD, CAGS), including administration (MS), adult-gerontology acute care nurse practitioner (MS, CAGS), adult-gerontology primary care nurse practitioner (MS, CAGS), anesthesia (MS), family nurse practitioner (MS, CAGS), neonatal nurse practitioner (MS, CAGS), pediatric nurse practitioner (MS, CAGS), psychiatric mental health nurse practitioner (MS, CAGS); nursing practice (DNP); pharmaceutical sciences (MS, PhD), including interdisciplinary concentration, pharmaceutics and drug delivery systems; pharmacology (MS); pharmacy (Pharm D); school psychology (PhD); speech-language pathology (MS); urban health (MPH); MS/MBA. *Accreditation:* AANA/CANAEP; ACPE (one or more programs are accredited); ASHA; CEPH. *Program availability:* Part-time, evening/weekend, online learning. *Degree requirements:* For doctorate, thesis/dissertation (for some programs); for CAGS, comprehensive exam. Electronic applications accepted. *Expenses:* Contact institution.

**Northeast Ohio Medical University,** College of Graduate Studies, Rootstown, OH 44272-0095. Offers health-system pharmacy administration (MS); integrated pharmaceutical medicine (MS, PhD); medical ethics and humanities (MS, Certificate); public health (MPH). *Program availability:* Part-time, evening/weekend, 100% online, blended/hybrid learning. *Faculty:* 126 part-time/adjunct (62 women). *Students:* 24 full-time (12 women), 28 part-time (15 women); includes 21 minority (2 Black or African American, non-Hispanic/Latino; 10 Asian, non-Hispanic/Latino; 5 Hispanic/Latino; 4 Two or more races, non-Hispanic/Latino). Average age 26. 31 applicants, 97% accepted, 21 enrolled. In 2019, 15 master's, 13 other advanced degrees awarded. *Degree requirements:* For master's, thesis (for some programs), thesis (for MS in medical ethics and humanities, integrated pharmaceutical medicine, MS in MAS); for doctorate, thesis/dissertation, For IPM Ph.D Program. *Entrance requirements:* Additional exam requirements/recommendations for international students: recommended—TOEFL (minimum score 550 paper-based). *Application deadline:* For fall admission, 7/17 for domestic students. Applications are processed on a rolling basis. Application fee: $95. Electronic applications accepted. *Expenses:* Student health and fitness, student activities. *Financial support:* In 2019–20, 6 students received support. Scholarships/grants and tuition waivers (full and partial) available. Financial award application deadline: 3/15; financial award applicants required to submit FAFSA. *Unit head:* Dr. Steven Schmidt, Dean, 330-325-6290. *Application contact:* Dr. Steven Schmidt, Dean, 330-325-6290.
Website: https://www.neomed.edu/graduatestudies/

**Oregon State University,** College of Pharmacy, Program in Pharmaceutical Sciences, Corvallis, OR 97331. Offers biopharmaceutics (MS, PhD). *Entrance requirements:* For master's and doctorate, GRE. Additional exam requirements/recommendations for international students: required—TOEFL (minimum score 80 iBT), IELTS (minimum score 6.5).

**Purdue University,** College of Pharmacy and Graduate School, Graduate Programs in Pharmacy and Pharmacal Sciences, West Lafayette, IN 47907. Offers industrial and physical pharmacy (PhD, Certificate), including pharmaceutics (PhD), regulatory quality compliance (Certificate); pharmacy practice (MS), including clinical pharmacy, pharmacy administration. *Program availability:* Part-time. *Faculty:* 65 full-time (28 women), 16 part-time/adjunct (7 women). *Students:* 128 full-time (64 women), 6 part-time (3 women); includes 13 minority (1 Black or African American, non-Hispanic/Latino; 6 Asian, non-Hispanic/Latino; 2 Hispanic/Latino; 4 Two or more races, non-Hispanic/Latino), 80 international. Average age 27. 282 applicants, 20% accepted, 21 enrolled. In 2019, 4 master's, 19 doctorates awarded. Terminal master's awarded for partial completion of doctoral program. *Degree requirements:* For doctorate, thesis/dissertation. *Entrance requirements:* For master's and doctorate, GRE General Test, minimum undergraduate GPA of 3.0. Additional exam requirements/recommendations for international students: required—TOEFL. *Application deadline:* Applications are processed on a rolling basis. Application fee: $60 ($75 for international students). Electronic applications accepted. *Financial support:* Fellowships, research assistantships, teaching assistantships, career-related internships or fieldwork, and traineeships available. Support available to part-time students. Financial award applicants required to submit FAFSA. *Unit head:* Eric L. Barker, Dean, 765-494-1368, E-mail: barkerel@purdue.edu. *Application contact:* Danzhou Yang, Associate Dean for Graduate Programs, 765-494-1362.

**Purdue University,** College of Pharmacy and Graduate School, Graduate Programs in Pharmacy and Pharmacal Sciences, Department of Pharmacy Practice, West Lafayette, IN 47907. Offers clinical pharmacy (PhD); pharmacy administration (MS, PhD). *Faculty:* 35 full-time (20 women), 8 part-time/adjunct (5 women). *Students:* 11 full-time (6 women), 4 part-time (3 women); includes 1 minority (Black or African American, non-Hispanic/Latino), 11 international. Average age 29. 65 applicants, 12% accepted, 1 enrolled. In 2019, 3 master's, 2 doctorates awarded. Terminal master's awarded for partial completion of doctoral program. *Degree requirements:* For master's, thesis optional; for doctorate, thesis/dissertation. *Entrance requirements:* For master's, GRE General Test, minimum undergraduate GPA of 3.0 or equivalent; for doctorate, GRE General Test, minimum undergraduate GPA of 3.0 or equivalent; master's degree with minimum GPA of 3.0 or equivalent. Additional exam requirements/recommendations for international students: required—TOEFL (minimum score 550 paper-based; 77 iBT), TWE (recommended for MS, required for PhD). *Application deadline:* Applications are processed on a rolling basis. Application fee: $60 ($75 for international students). Electronic applications accepted. *Financial support:* In 2019–20, teaching assistantships with tuition reimbursements (averaging $20,000 per year) were awarded; fellowships, research assistantships, career-related internships or fieldwork, and traineeships also available. Support available to part-time students. Financial award applicants required to submit FAFSA. *Unit head:* Alan J. Zillich, Head of the Graduate Program, 317-880-5430, E-mail: azillich@purdue.edu. *Application contact:* Delayne Graham, Graduate Contact, 765-494-1362, E-mail: dkgraham@purdue.edu.

**Rowan University,** Graduate School, College of Science and Mathematics, Program in Pharmaceutical Sciences, Glassboro, NJ 08028-1701. Offers MS. Electronic applications accepted. *Expenses: Tuition, area resident:* Part-time $715.50 per semester hour. Tuition, state resident: part-time $715.50 per semester hour. Tuition, nonresident: part-time $715.50 per semester hour. *Required fees:* $161.55 per semester hour.

**Rush University,** Graduate College, Division of Pharmacology, Chicago, IL 60612-3832. Offers clinical research (MS); pharmacology (MS, PhD); MD/PhD. Terminal master's awarded for partial completion of doctoral program. *Degree requirements:* For master's, thesis; for doctorate, thesis/dissertation. *Entrance requirements:* For master's and doctorate, GRE General Test, interview. Additional exam requirements/recommendations for international students: required—TOEFL (minimum score 550 paper-based).

**Rutgers University - New Brunswick,** Ernest Mario School of Pharmacy, Program in Pharmaceutical Science, Piscataway, NJ 08854-8097. Offers MS, PhD. *Program availability:* Part-time. Terminal master's awarded for partial completion of doctoral program. *Degree requirements:* For master's, thesis; for doctorate, thesis/dissertation. *Entrance requirements:* For master's and doctorate, GRE General Test, 3 letters of recommendation. Additional exam requirements/recommendations for international students: required—TOEFL (minimum score 550 paper-based; 83 iBT). Electronic applications accepted.

**St. John's University,** College of Pharmacy and Health Sciences, Graduate Programs in Pharmaceutical Sciences, Program in Pharmaceutical Sciences, Queens, NY 11439. Offers MS, PhD. *Program availability:* Part-time. Terminal master's awarded for partial completion of doctoral program. *Degree requirements:* For master's, comprehensive exam (for some programs), thesis (for some programs); for doctorate, comprehensive exam, thesis/dissertation, residency requirement: 24 credits in first two academic years. *Entrance requirements:* For master's and doctorate, GRE General Test, letters of recommendation, transcripts, resume, personal statement. Additional exam requirements/recommendations for international students: required—TOEFL (minimum score 100 iBT), IELTS (minimum score 7). Electronic applications accepted. *Expenses:* Contact institution.

**South Dakota State University,** Graduate School, College of Pharmacy and Allied Health Professions, Department of Pharmaceutical Sciences, Brookings, SD 57007. Offers biological science (MS); pharmaceutical sciences (PhD). *Degree requirements:* For master's, thesis, oral exam; for doctorate, comprehensive exam, thesis/dissertation, oral exam. *Entrance requirements:* For master's and doctorate, GRE General Test. Additional exam requirements/recommendations for international students: required—TOEFL (minimum score 550 paper-based).

**Stevens Institute of Technology,** Graduate School, Charles V. Schaefer Jr. School of Engineering and Science, Department of Mechanical Engineering, Program in Pharmaceutical Manufacturing, Hoboken, NJ 07030. Offers M Eng, MS, Certificate. *Program availability:* Part-time, evening/weekend. *Faculty:* 29 full-time (3 women), 11 part-time/adjunct (0 women). *Students:* 8 full-time (3 women), 27 part-time (14 women); includes 8 minority (1 Black or African American, non-Hispanic/Latino; 7 Asian, non-Hispanic/Latino), 5 international. Average age 29. In 2019, 27 master's, 30 other advanced degrees awarded. *Degree requirements:* For master's, thesis optional, minimum B average in major field and overall; for Certificate, minimum B average. *Entrance requirements:* For master's, International applicants must submit TOEFL/IELTS scores and fulfill the English Language Proficiency Requirement. Applicants to full-time programs who do not qualify for a score waiver are required to submit GRE/GMAT scores. Additional exam requirements/recommendations for international students: required—TOEFL (minimum score 74 iBT), IELTS (minimum score 6). *Application deadline:* For fall admission, 4/15 for domestic and international students; for spring admission, 11/1 for domestic and international students; for summer admission, 5/1 for domestic students. Applications are processed on a rolling basis. Application fee: $60. Electronic applications accepted. *Expenses: Tuition:* Full-time $52,134. *Required fees:* $1880. Tuition and fees vary according to course load. *Financial support:* Fellowships, research assistantships, teaching assistantships, career-related internships or fieldwork, Federal Work-Study, scholarships/grants, and unspecified assistantships available. Financial award application deadline: 2/15; financial award applicants required to submit FAFSA. *Unit head:* Dr. Jean Zu, Dean of SES, 201-216.8233, Fax: 201-216.8372, E-mail: Jean.Zu@stevens.edu. *Application contact:* Graduate Admissions, 888-783-8367, Fax: 888-511-1306, E-mail: graduate@stevens.edu.

**Stevens Institute of Technology,** Graduate School, School of Business, Program in Business Administration, Hoboken, NJ 07030. Offers business intelligence and analytics (MBA); engineering management (MBA); finance (MBA); information systems (MBA); innovation and entrepreneurship (MBA); marketing (MBA); pharmaceutical management (MBA); project management (MBA, Certificate); technology management (MBA); telecommunications management (MBA). *Accreditation:* AACSB. *Program availability:*

Part-time, evening/weekend. *Faculty:* 59 full-time (11 women), 30 part-time/adjunct (5 women). *Students:* 50 full-time (21 women), 242 part-time (112 women); includes 68 minority (13 Black or African American, non-Hispanic/Latino; 2 American Indian or Alaska Native, non-Hispanic/Latino; 51 Asian, non-Hispanic/Latino; 2 Hispanic/Latino), 55 international. Average age 36. In 2019, 60 master's awarded. Terminal master's awarded for partial completion of doctoral program. *Degree requirements:* For master's, thesis optional, minimum B average in major field and overall; for Certificate, minimum B average. *Entrance requirements:* For master's, International applicants must submit TOEFL/IELTS scores and fulfill the English Language Proficiency Requirement. Applicants to full-time programs who do not qualify for a score waiver are required to submit GRE/GMAT scores. Additional exam requirements/recommendations for international students: required—TOEFL (minimum score 74 iBT), IELTS (minimum score 6). *Application deadline:* For fall admission, 4/1 for domestic and international students; for spring admission, 11/1 for domestic and international students; for summer admission, 5/1 for domestic students. Applications are processed on a rolling basis. Application fee: $60. Electronic applications accepted. *Expenses: Tuition:* Full-time $52,134. *Required fees:* $1880. Tuition and fees vary according to course load. *Financial support:* Fellowships, research assistantships, teaching assistantships, career-related internships or fieldwork, Federal Work-Study, scholarships/grants, and unspecified assistantships available. Financial award application deadline: 2/15; financial award applicants required to submit FAFSA. *Unit head:* Dr. Gregory Prastacos, Dean, 201-216-8366, E-mail: gprastac@stevens.edu. *Application contact:* Graduate Admissions, 888-783-8367, Fax: 888-511-1306, E-mail: graduate@stevens.edu.
Website: https://www.stevens.edu/school-business/masters-programs/mbaemba

**Temple University,** School of Pharmacy, Department of Pharmaceutical Sciences, Philadelphia, PA 19122-6096. Offers medicinal chemistry (MS, PhD); pharmaceutics (MS, PhD); pharmacodynamics (MS, PhD); regulatory affairs and quality assurance (MS). *Program availability:* Part-time, evening/weekend, online learning. *Faculty:* 11 full-time (2 women), 36 part-time/adjunct (14 women). *Students:* 30 full-time (12 women), 222 part-time (153 women); includes 37 minority (10 Black or African American, non-Hispanic/Latino; 22 Asian, non-Hispanic/Latino; 3 Hispanic/Latino; 2 Two or more races, non-Hispanic/Latino), 28 international. 78 applicants, 77% accepted, 45 enrolled. In 2019, 89 master's, 7 doctorates awarded. *Entrance requirements:* For master's and doctorate, GRE, bachelor's degree in related discipline, statement of goals, 3 letters of recommendation. Additional exam requirements/recommendations for international students: required—TOEFL (minimum score 82 iBT), IELTS (minimum score 6.5), PTE (minimum score 58). *Application deadline:* For fall admission, 12/15 for domestic students. Application fee: $60. Electronic applications accepted. *Expenses:* Contact institution. *Financial support:* Fellowships, research assistantships, teaching assistantships, Federal Work-Study, health care benefits, and unspecified assistantships available. Financial award applicants required to submit FAFSA. *Unit head:* Michael Borenstein, Interim Dean, 215-707-2976, E-mail: michael.borenstein@temple.edu. *Application contact:* Sophon Din, Administrative Assistant, 215-204-4948, E-mail: tuspgrad@temple.edu.
Website: https://pharmacy.temple.edu/academics/department-pharmaceutical-science

**Texas Southern University,** College of Pharmacy and Health Sciences, Department of Pharmaceutical Sciences, Houston, TX 77004-4584. Offers MS, PhD. *Program availability:* Online learning. *Entrance requirements:* For master's, PCAT; for doctorate, GRE General Test. Electronic applications accepted.

**Texas Tech University Health Sciences Center,** Graduate School of Biomedical Sciences, Program in Pharmaceutical Sciences, Lubbock, TX 79430. Offers MS, PhD. *Accreditation:* ACPE. Terminal master's awarded for partial completion of doctoral program. *Degree requirements:* For master's, thesis; for doctorate, thesis/dissertation. *Entrance requirements:* For master's and doctorate, GRE General Test, minimum GPA of 3.0. Additional exam requirements/recommendations for international students: required—TOEFL (minimum score 550 paper-based; 79 iBT). Electronic applications accepted.

**Université de Montréal,** Faculty of Pharmacy, Montréal, QC H3C 3J7, Canada. Offers drugs development (DESS); pharmaceutical care (DESS); pharmaceutical practice (M Sc); pharmaceutical sciences (M Sc, PhD); pharmacist-supervisor teacher (DESS). *Program availability:* Part-time. Terminal master's awarded for partial completion of doctoral program. *Degree requirements:* For master's, thesis; for doctorate, thesis/dissertation. *Entrance requirements:* For master's and doctorate, proficiency in French. Electronic applications accepted.

**University at Buffalo, the State University of New York,** Graduate School, School of Pharmacy and Pharmaceutical Sciences, Department of Pharmaceutical Sciences, Buffalo, NY 14260. Offers pharmaceutical sciences (MS); Pharm D/MS; Pharm D/PhD. *Faculty:* 18 full-time (4 women), 2 part-time/adjunct (1 woman). *Students:* 93 full-time (45 women), 16 part-time (9 women); includes 33 minority (2 Black or African American, non-Hispanic/Latino; 28 Asian, non-Hispanic/Latino; 3 Hispanic/Latino), 43 international. Average age 26. 344 applicants, 11% accepted, 36 enrolled. In 2019, 13 master's, 10 doctorates awarded. Terminal master's awarded for partial completion of doctoral program. *Degree requirements:* For master's, comprehensive exam (for some programs), thesis optional, project; for doctorate, comprehensive exam, thesis/dissertation. *Entrance requirements:* For master's, GRE, BS, B Eng, or Pharm D; for doctorate, GRE, BS, MS, B Eng, M Eng, or Pharm D. Additional exam requirements/recommendations for international students: required—TOEFL (minimum score 550 paper-based; 79 iBT), IELTS (minimum score 6.5); recommended—TSE. *Application deadline:* For fall admission, 2/15 for domestic and international students. Applications are processed on a rolling basis. Application fee: $50. Electronic applications accepted. *Expenses:* Contact institution. *Financial support:* In 2019–20, 43 students received support, including 35 research assistantships with full tuition reimbursements available (averaging $26,000 per year); fellowships also available. Financial award application deadline: 3/1; financial award applicants required to submit FAFSA. *Unit head:* Dr. Marilyn E. Morris, Chair, 716-645-4839, Fax: 716-829-6569, E-mail: memorris@buffalo.edu. *Application contact:* Dr. Murali Ramanathan, Director of Graduate Studies, 716-645-4846, Fax: 716-645-3690, E-mail: murali@buffalo.edu.
Website: http://pharmacy.buffalo.edu/departments-offices/pharmaceutical-sciences.html

**University of Alberta,** Faculty of Pharmacy and Pharmaceutical Sciences, Edmonton, AB T6G 2E1, Canada. Offers M Sc, PhD. Terminal master's awarded for partial completion of doctoral program. *Degree requirements:* For master's, thesis; for doctorate, thesis/dissertation. *Entrance requirements:* Additional exam requirements/recommendations for international students: required—Michigan English Language Assessment Battery or IELTS. Electronic applications accepted.

**The University of Arizona,** College of Pharmacy, Program in Pharmaceutical Sciences, Tucson, AZ 85721. Offers medicinal and natural products chemistry (MS, PhD); pharmaceutical economics (MS, PhD); pharmaceutics and pharmacokinetics (MS, PhD). *Degree requirements:* For master's, thesis; for doctorate, one foreign language, thesis/dissertation. *Entrance requirements:* For master's, GRE General Test, 3 letters of recommendation, bachelor's degree in related field; for doctorate, GRE General Test, 3 letters of recommendation, statement of purpose, bachelor's degree in related field. Additional exam requirements/recommendations for international students: required—TOEFL (minimum score 550 paper-based; 79 iBT). Electronic applications accepted.

**The University of British Columbia,** Faculty of Pharmaceutical Sciences, Vancouver, BC V6T 1Z3, Canada. Offers M Sc, PhD, Pharm D. *Degree requirements:* For master's, thesis, seminar; for doctorate, comprehensive exam, thesis/dissertation, seminar. *Entrance requirements:* Additional exam requirements/recommendations for international students: required—TOEFL (minimum score 600 paper-based; 100 iBT), IELTS (minimum score 6.5). Electronic applications accepted. *Expenses:* Contact institution.

**University of California, Irvine,** School of Medicine, Program in Pharmacological Sciences, Irvine, CA 92697. Offers PhD, MD/PhD. *Students:* 44 full-time (26 women); includes 20 minority (1 Black or African American, non-Hispanic/Latino; 10 Asian, non-Hispanic/Latino; 9 Hispanic/Latino), 7 international. Average age 28. 93 applicants, 29% accepted, 13 enrolled. In 2019, 5 doctorates awarded. *Entrance requirements:* For doctorate, GRE General Test, GRE Subject Test, minimum GPA of 3.0. Additional exam requirements/recommendations for international students: required—TOEFL (minimum score 550 paper-based). *Application deadline:* For fall admission, 1/15 priority date for domestic students, 1/15 for international students. Applications are processed on a rolling basis. Application fee: $120 ($140 for international students). Electronic applications accepted. *Financial support:* Fellowships, research assistantships, teaching assistantships, institutionally sponsored loans, traineeships, and unspecified assistantships available. Financial award application deadline: 3/1; financial award applicants required to submit FAFSA. *Unit head:* Dr. Jan Hirsch, Dean, 949-924-0505, E-mail: jdhirsch@uci.edu. *Application contact:* Jill Richardson, Director of Student Affairs, 949-824-9708, E-mail: jillkr@uci.edu.
Website: https://pharmsci.uci.edu/

**University of California, San Francisco,** School of Pharmacy and Graduate Division, Pharmaceutical Sciences and Pharmacogenomics Program, San Francisco, CA 94158-0775. Offers PhD. *Degree requirements:* For doctorate, comprehensive exam, thesis/dissertation. *Entrance requirements:* For doctorate, GRE General Test, bachelor's degree, 3 letters of recommendation, personal statement. Additional exam requirements/recommendations for international students: required—TOEFL. Electronic applications accepted.

**University of Cincinnati,** James L. Winkle College of Pharmacy, Division of Pharmaceutical Sciences, Cincinnati, OH 45237. Offers biomembrane science (MS), including cosmetic science (MS, PhD); biomembrane sciences (PhD), including cosmetic science (MS, PhD); experiential therapeutics (MS). *Program availability:* Part-time, evening/weekend, 100% online, blended/hybrid learning. *Degree requirements:* For master's, thesis; for doctorate, thesis/dissertation. *Entrance requirements:* For master's and doctorate, GRE General Test, minimum GPA of 3.0. Additional exam requirements/recommendations for international students: required—TOEFL (minimum score 90 iBT); recommended—IELTS (minimum score 6.5). Electronic applications accepted.

**University of Colorado Denver,** Skaggs School of Pharmacy and Pharmaceutical Sciences, Program in Pharmaceutical Sciences, Aurora, CO 80045. Offers clinical pharmaceutical sciences (PhD). *Entrance requirements:* For doctorate, GRE, minimum undergraduate GPA of 3.0; prior coursework in general chemistry, organic chemistry, calculus, biology, and physics. Tuition and fees vary according to course load, program and reciprocity agreements.

**University of Connecticut,** Graduate School, School of Pharmacy, Department of Pharmaceutical Sciences, Program in Pharmaceutics, Storrs, CT 06269. Offers MS, PhD. Terminal master's awarded for partial completion of doctoral program. *Degree requirements:* For master's, comprehensive exam, thesis; for doctorate, thesis/dissertation. *Entrance requirements:* For master's and doctorate, GRE General Test. Additional exam requirements/recommendations for international students: required—TOEFL (minimum score 550 paper-based). Electronic applications accepted.

**University of Florida,** Graduate School, College of Pharmacy, Graduate Programs in Pharmacy, Department of Pharmaceutics, Gainesville, FL 32611. Offers clinical and translational sciences (PhD); pharmaceutical sciences (MSP, PhD); pharmacy (MSP, PhD). *Degree requirements:* For doctorate, comprehensive exam, thesis/dissertation. *Entrance requirements:* For master's and doctorate, GRE General Test, minimum GPA of 3.0. Additional exam requirements/recommendations for international students: required—TOEFL (minimum score 550 paper-based; 80 iBT), IELTS (minimum score 6). Electronic applications accepted.

**University of Florida,** Graduate School, College of Pharmacy, Graduate Programs in Pharmacy, Department of Pharmacotherapy and Translational Research, Gainesville, FL 32611. Offers clinical pharmaceutical sciences (PhD); clinical pharmacy (MSP). *Entrance requirements:* For master's and doctorate, GRE General Test, minimum GPA of 3.0. Additional exam requirements/recommendations for international students: required—TOEFL (minimum score 550 paper-based; 80 iBT), IELTS (minimum score 6). Electronic applications accepted.

**University of Georgia,** College of Pharmacy, Department of Pharmaceutical and Biomedical Sciences, Athens, GA 30602. Offers MS, PhD. *Degree requirements:* For master's, thesis; for doctorate, one foreign language, thesis/dissertation. *Entrance requirements:* For master's and doctorate, GRE General Test, minimum GPA of 3.0. Additional exam requirements/recommendations for international students: required—TOEFL. Electronic applications accepted.

**University of Hawaii at Hilo,** Program in Pharmaceutical Sciences, Hilo, HI 96720-4091. Offers PhD. *Entrance requirements:* Additional exam requirements/recommendations for international students: required—TOEFL. Electronic applications accepted.

**University of Houston,** College of Pharmacy, Houston, TX 77204. Offers pharmaceutics (MSPHR, PhD); pharmacology (MSPHR, PhD); pharmacy (Pharm D); pharmacy administration (MSPHR, PhD). *Accreditation:* ACPE. *Program availability:* Part-time. Terminal master's awarded for partial completion of doctoral program. *Entrance requirements:* For doctorate, PCAT (for Pharm D). Additional exam requirements/recommendations for international students: required—TOEFL. Electronic applications accepted.

**University of Illinois at Chicago,** College of Pharmacy, Department of Biopharmaceutical Sciences, Chicago, IL 60607-7173. Offers PhD.

**University of Illinois at Chicago,** College of Pharmacy, Graduate Programs in Pharmacy, Chicago, IL 60607-7128. Offers comparative effectiveness research (MS); forensic science (MS); forensic toxicology (MS); medicinal chemistry (MS, PhD); pharmacognosy (MS, PhD); pharmacy (PhD). Terminal master's awarded for partial completion of doctoral program. *Degree requirements:* For master's, variable foreign language requirement, thesis; for doctorate, variable foreign language requirement, thesis/dissertation. *Entrance requirements:* For master's and doctorate, GRE General Test. Additional exam requirements/recommendations for international students: required—TOEFL. Electronic applications accepted.

**The University of Iowa,** College of Pharmacy, Iowa City, IA 52242-1316. Offers clinical pharmaceutical sciences (PhD); medicinal and natural products chemistry (PhD); pharmaceutical socioeconomics (PhD); pharmaceutics (MS, PhD); pharmacy (Pharm D); Pharm D/MPH. *Accreditation:* ACPE (one or more programs are accredited). *Degree requirements:* For master's, thesis optional, exam; for doctorate, comprehensive exam, thesis/dissertation. *Entrance requirements:* For master's and doctorate, GRE General Test, minimum GPA of 3.0. Additional exam requirements/recommendations for international students: required—TOEFL (minimum score 550 paper-based; 81 iBT). Electronic applications accepted.

**University of Kentucky,** Graduate School, Graduate Programs in Pharmaceutical Sciences, Lexington, KY 40506-0032. Offers MS, PhD. Terminal master's awarded for partial completion of doctoral program. *Degree requirements:* For master's, thesis optional; for doctorate, comprehensive exam, thesis/dissertation. *Entrance requirements:* For master's, GRE General Test, minimum undergraduate GPA of 3.2; for doctorate, GRE General Test, minimum graduate GPA of 3.2. Additional exam requirements/recommendations for international students: required—TOEFL (minimum score 550 paper-based; 79 iBT). Electronic applications accepted.

**The University of Manchester,** School of Pharmacy and Pharmaceutical Sciences, Manchester, United Kingdom. Offers M Phil, PhD.

**University of Manitoba,** Faculty of Graduate Studies, College of Pharmacy, Winnipeg, MB R3T 2N2, Canada. Offers M Sc, PhD. *Degree requirements:* For master's, one foreign language, thesis.

**University of Maryland, Baltimore,** Graduate School, Graduate Programs in Pharmacy, Department of Pharmaceutical Sciences, Baltimore, MD 21201. Offers PhD. *Degree requirements:* For doctorate, comprehensive exam, thesis/dissertation. *Entrance requirements:* For doctorate, GRE General Test. Additional exam requirements/recommendations for international students: required—TOEFL (minimum score 600 paper-based), IELTS. Electronic applications accepted.

**University of Maryland Eastern Shore,** Graduate Programs, School of Pharmacy, Princess Anne, MD 21853. Offers pharmaceutical sciences (MS, PhD); pharmacy (Pharm D). *Accreditation:* ACPE.

**University of Michigan,** College of Pharmacy and Rackham Graduate School, Department of Pharmaceutical Sciences, Ann Arbor, MI 48109. Offers PhD. Terminal master's awarded for partial completion of doctoral program. *Degree requirements:* For doctorate, thesis/dissertation, oral defense of dissertation, preliminary exam. *Entrance requirements:* For doctorate, GRE. Additional exam requirements/recommendations for international students: required—TOEFL (minimum score 560 paper-based; 84 iBT) or IELTS (minimum score 6.5). Electronic applications accepted. *Expenses:* Contact institution.

**University of Minnesota, Twin Cities Campus,** College of Pharmacy and Graduate School, Graduate Programs in Pharmacy, Graduate Program in Pharmaceutics, Minneapolis, MN 55455. Offers MS, PhD. *Faculty:* 9 full-time (1 woman), 21 part-time/adjunct (5 women). *Students:* 37 full-time (21 women); includes 17 minority (1 Black or African American, non-Hispanic/Latino; 15 Asian, non-Hispanic/Latino; 1 Two or more races, non-Hispanic/Latino). Average age 25. 86 applicants, 19% accepted, 10 enrolled. In 2019, 6 master's, 5 doctorates awarded. Terminal master's awarded for partial completion of doctoral program. *Degree requirements:* For master's, comprehensive exam, thesis; for doctorate, comprehensive exam, thesis/dissertation. *Entrance requirements:* For master's and doctorate, GRE General Test (preferred minimum scores: Quantitative Reasoning 80%, Analytical Writing 3.5), Bachelor's degree. Additional exam requirements/recommendations for international students: required—TOEFL (minimum score 100 iBT), IELTS (minimum score 6.5). *Application deadline:* For fall admission, 11/30 for domestic and international students. Application fee: $75 ($95 for international students). Electronic applications accepted. *Financial support:* In 2019–20, 25 students received support, including 5 fellowships (averaging $5,000 per year), 19 research assistantships with full tuition reimbursements available (averaging $25,000 per year), 7 teaching assistantships with full tuition reimbursements available (averaging $25,000 per year); career-related internships or fieldwork and health care benefits also available. Financial award application deadline: 2/15. *Unit head:* Dr. Ronald A. Siegel, Professor and Interim Department Head, 612-624-6164, Fax: 612-626-2125, E-mail: siege017@umn.edu. *Application contact:* Katie M. James, Graduate Program Coordinator, 612-624-5153, Fax: 612-626-2125, E-mail: kmjames@umn.edu. Website: http://www.pharmacy.umn.edu/pharmaceutics/

**University of Mississippi,** Graduate School, School of Pharmacy, University, MS 38677. Offers environmental toxicology (MS, PhD); industrial pharmacy (MS); medicinal chemistry (MS, PhD); pharmaceutics (MS, PhD); pharmacognosy (MS, PhD); pharmacology (MS, PhD); pharmacy (Pharm D); pharmacy administration (MS, PhD). *Accreditation:* ACPE (one or more programs are accredited). *Program availability:* Part-time. *Faculty:* 68 full-time (33 women), 13 part-time/adjunct (5 women). *Students:* 223 full-time (137 women), 215 part-time (137 women); includes 71 minority (29 Black or African American, non-Hispanic/Latino; 1 American Indian or Alaska Native, non-Hispanic/Latino; 31 Asian, non-Hispanic/Latino; 4 Hispanic/Latino; 6 Two or more races, non-Hispanic/Latino), 90 international. Average age 25. In 2019, 29 master's, 13 doctorates awarded. Terminal master's awarded for partial completion of doctoral program. *Degree requirements:* For master's, thesis; for doctorate, thesis/dissertation (for some programs). *Entrance requirements:* For master's, GRE General Test, minimum GPA of 3.0; for doctorate, GRE General Test (for PhD). Additional exam requirements/recommendations for international students: required—TOEFL. *Application deadline:* Applications are processed on a rolling basis. Application fee: $50. Electronic applications accepted. *Expenses:* Tuition, state resident: full-time $8718; part-time $484.25 per credit hour. Tuition, nonresident: full-time $24,990; part-time $1388.25 per credit hour. *Required fees:* $100; $4.16 per credit hour. *Financial support:* Fellowships, research assistantships, teaching assistantships, career-related internships or fieldwork, Federal Work-Study, institutionally sponsored loans, scholarships/grants, tuition waivers (full), and unspecified assistantships available. Financial award application deadline: 3/1; financial award applicants required to submit FAFSA. *Unit head:* Dr. David Allen, Dean, School of Pharmacy, 662-915-7265, Fax: 662-9155704, E-mail: sopdean@olemiss.edu. *Application contact:* Temeka Smith, Graduate Activities Specialist for Admissions, 662-915-7474, Fax: 662-915-7577, E-mail: gschool@olemiss.edu. Website: http://www.pharmacy.olemiss.edu/

**University of Montana,** Graduate School, College of Health Professions and Biomedical Sciences, Skaggs School of Pharmacy, Department of Biomedical and Pharmaceutical Sciences, Missoula, MT 59812. Offers biomedical sciences (PhD); medicinal chemistry (MS, PhD); molecular and cellular toxicology (MS, PhD); neuroscience (PhD); pharmaceutical sciences (MS). *Accreditation:* ACPE. *Degree requirements:* For master's, oral defense of thesis; for doctorate, research dissertation defense. *Entrance requirements:* For master's and doctorate, GRE General Test. Additional exam requirements/recommendations for international students: required—TOEFL (minimum score 540 paper-based). Electronic applications accepted.

**University of Nebraska Medical Center,** Department of Pharmaceutical Sciences, Omaha, NE 68198. Offers MS, PhD, MD/PhD. Terminal master's awarded for partial

completion of doctoral program. *Degree requirements:* For master's, comprehensive exam, thesis; for doctorate, comprehensive exam, thesis/dissertation. *Entrance requirements:* For master's, GRE General Test; for doctorate, GRE. Additional exam requirements/recommendations for international students: required—TOEFL (minimum score 550 paper-based; 80 iBT). Electronic applications accepted. *Expenses:* Contact institution.

**University of New Mexico,** Graduate Studies, College of Pharmacy, Graduate Programs in Pharmaceutical Sciences, Albuquerque, NM 87131-2039. Offers MS, PhD. *Program availability:* Part-time. *Degree requirements:* For master's, comprehensive exam, thesis; for doctorate, comprehensive exam, thesis/dissertation. *Entrance requirements:* For master's and doctorate, GRE General Test (for some concentrations), 3 letters of recommendation, letter of intent, resume. Additional exam requirements/recommendations for international students: required—TOEFL (minimum score 580 paper-based; 93 iBT). Electronic applications accepted. *Expenses:* Tuition, state resident: full-time $7633; part-time $972 per year. Tuition, nonresident: full-time $22,586; part-time $3840 per year. *International tuition:* $23,292 full-time. *Required fees:* $8608. Tuition and fees vary according to course level, course load, degree level, program and student level.

**The University of North Carolina at Chapel Hill,** Eshelman School of Pharmacy, Chapel Hill, NC 27599. Offers pharmaceutical sciences (PhD); pharmaceutical sciences - health system pharmacy administration (MS); pharmacy (Pharm D). *Accreditation:* ACPE (one or more programs are accredited). Terminal master's awarded for partial completion of doctoral program. *Degree requirements:* For master's, comprehensive exam, thesis; for doctorate, comprehensive exam, thesis/dissertation. *Entrance requirements:* For master's and doctorate, GRE General Test, minimum GPA of 3.0. Additional exam requirements/recommendations for international students: required—TOEFL (minimum score 550 paper-based; 90 iBT), IELTS (minimum score 7). Electronic applications accepted. *Expenses:* Contact institution.

**University of North Texas Health Science Center at Fort Worth,** Graduate School of Biomedical Sciences, Fort Worth, TX 76107-2699. Offers biochemistry and cancer biology (MS, PhD); biotechnology (MS); cell biology, immunology and microbiology (MS, PhD); clinical research management (MS); forensic genetics (MS); genetics (MS, PhD); integrative physiology (MS, PhD); medical sciences (MS); pharmaceutical sciences and pharmacotherapy (MS, PhD); pharmacology and neuroscience (MS, PhD); structural anatomy and rehabilitation sciences (MS, PhD); DO/MS; DO/PhD. Terminal master's awarded for partial completion of doctoral program. *Degree requirements:* For master's, thesis; for doctorate, thesis/dissertation. *Entrance requirements:* For master's and doctorate, GRE General Test. Additional exam requirements/recommendations for international students: required—TOEFL. *Expenses:* Contact institution.

**University of Oklahoma Health Sciences Center,** College of Pharmacy and Graduate College, Graduate Programs in Pharmacy, Oklahoma City, OK 73190. Offers MS, PhD, MS/MBA. Terminal master's awarded for partial completion of doctoral program. *Degree requirements:* For master's, comprehensive exam, thesis; for doctorate, comprehensive exam, thesis/dissertation. *Entrance requirements:* For master's and doctorate, GRE General Test. Additional exam requirements/recommendations for international students: required—TOEFL.

**University of Pittsburgh,** School of Pharmacy, Graduate Programs in Pharmaceutical Sciences, Pittsburgh, PA 15261. Offers pharmaceutical sciences (MS, PhD), including biochemical pharmacology, clinical pharmaceutical scientist, medicinal chemistry, pharmaceutical outcomes and policy research, pharmaceutics. *Program availability:* Part-time. Terminal master's awarded for partial completion of doctoral program. *Degree requirements:* For master's, comprehensive exam (for some programs), thesis (for some programs), 34 credits (for non-thesis), 30 credits (for thesis); for doctorate, comprehensive exam, thesis/dissertation, 72 credits. *Entrance requirements:* For master's, GRE General Test, bachelor's degree; for doctorate, GRE General Test, bachelor's degree, research experience. Additional exam requirements/recommendations for international students: required—TOEFL (minimum score 100 iBT), IELTS (minimum score 7). Electronic applications accepted. *Expenses:* Contact institution.

**University of Puerto Rico - Medical Sciences Campus,** School of Pharmacy, San Juan, PR 00936-5067. Offers industrial pharmacy (MS); pharmaceutical sciences (MS); pharmacy (Pharm D). *Accreditation:* ACPE. *Program availability:* Part-time, evening/weekend. *Degree requirements:* For master's, thesis; for doctorate, portfolio, research project. *Entrance requirements:* For master's, GRE, interview; for doctorate, PCAT, interview. Electronic applications accepted. *Expenses:* Contact institution.

**University of Rhode Island,** Graduate School, College of Pharmacy, Department of Biomedical and Pharmaceutical Sciences, Kingston, RI 02881. Offers health outcomes (MS, PhD); medicinal chemistry and pharmacognosy (MS, PhD); pharmaceutics and pharmacokinetics (MS, PhD); pharmacology and toxicology (MS, PhD). *Program availability:* Part-time. *Faculty:* 23 full-time (11 women). *Students:* 42 full-time (20 women), 11 part-time (6 women); includes 8 minority (1 American Indian or Alaska Native, non-Hispanic/Latino; 5 Asian, non-Hispanic/Latino; 2 Hispanic/Latino), 19 international. In 2019, 4 master's, 11 doctorates awarded. *Entrance requirements:* Additional exam requirements/recommendations for international students: required—TOEFL. *Application deadline:* For fall admission, 7/15 for domestic students, 2/1 for international students. Application fee: $65. Electronic applications accepted. *Expenses:* Tuition, area resident: Full-time $13,734; part-time $763 per credit. Tuition, state resident: full-time $13,734; part-time $763 per credit. Tuition, nonresident: full-time $26,512; part-time $1473 per credit. *International tuition:* $26,512 full-time. *Required fees:* $1780; $52 per credit. $35 per term. One-time fee: $165. *Financial support:* In 2019–20, 112 research assistantships with tuition reimbursements (averaging $8,040 per year), 17 teaching assistantships with tuition reimbursements (averaging $11,829 per year) were awarded. Financial award application deadline: 2/1; financial award applicants required to submit FAFSA. *Unit head:* Dr. Navindra Seeram, Chair, E-mail: nseeram@uri.edu. *Application contact:* Dr. Navindra Seeram, Chair, E-mail: nseeram@uri.edu. Website: http://www.uri.edu/pharmacy/departments/bps/index.shtml

**University of South Carolina,** South Carolina College of Pharmacy and The Graduate School, Department of Basic Pharmaceutical Sciences, Columbia, SC 29208. Offers MS, PhD. *Program availability:* Part-time. Terminal master's awarded for partial completion of doctoral program. *Degree requirements:* For master's, one foreign language, comprehensive exam, thesis; for doctorate, one foreign language, comprehensive exam, thesis/dissertation. *Entrance requirements:* For master's, GRE General Test, BS in biology, chemistry, pharmacy, or related field; for doctorate, GRE General Test, BS in biology, chemistry, or related field. Additional exam requirements/recommendations for international students: required—TOEFL. Electronic applications accepted.

**University of Southern California,** Graduate School, School of Pharmacy, Graduate Programs in Pharmaceutical Economics and Policy, Los Angeles, CA 90033. Offers MS, PhD. Terminal master's awarded for partial completion of doctoral program. *Degree requirements:* For master's, comprehensive exam, thesis, 24 units of formal course work, excluding research and seminar courses; for doctorate, comprehensive exam,

thesis/dissertation, 24 units of formal course work, excluding research and seminar courses. *Entrance requirements:* For master's and doctorate, GRE. Additional exam requirements/recommendations for international students: required—TOEFL (minimum score 603 paper-based; 100 iBT). Electronic applications accepted.

**University of Southern California,** Graduate School, School of Pharmacy, Graduate Programs in Pharmaceutical Sciences, Los Angeles, CA 90089. Offers MS, PhD. Terminal master's awarded for partial completion of doctoral program. *Degree requirements:* For master's, comprehensive exam, thesis, 24 units of formal course work, excluding research and seminar courses; for doctorate, comprehensive exam, thesis/dissertation, 24 units of formal course work, excluding research and seminar courses. *Entrance requirements:* For master's and doctorate, GRE. Additional exam requirements/recommendations for international students: required—TOEFL (minimum score 603 paper-based; 100 iBT). Electronic applications accepted.

**University of Southern California,** Graduate School, School of Pharmacy, Program in Clinical and Experimental Therapeutics, Los Angeles, CA 90089. Offers PhD. Terminal master's awarded for partial completion of doctoral program. *Degree requirements:* For doctorate, comprehensive exam, thesis/dissertation, 24 units of course work, excluding research and dissertation courses. *Entrance requirements:* For doctorate, GRE, minimum overall GPA of 3.0, three letters of recommendation. Additional exam requirements/recommendations for international students: required—TOEFL (minimum score 625 paper-based; 100 iBT). Electronic applications accepted.

**University of Southern California,** Graduate School, School of Pharmacy, Regulatory Science Programs, Los Angeles, CA 90089. Offers clinical research design and management (Graduate Certificate); food safety (Graduate Certificate); patient and product safety (Graduate Certificate); preclinical drug development (Graduate Certificate); regulatory and clinical affairs (Graduate Certificate); regulatory science (MS, DRSc). *Program availability:* Part-time, evening/weekend, online learning. Terminal master's awarded for partial completion of doctoral program. *Degree requirements:* For master's, thesis optional; for doctorate, comprehensive exam, thesis/dissertation. *Entrance requirements:* For master's, GRE. Additional exam requirements/recommendations for international students: required—TOEFL (minimum score 603 paper-based; 100 iBT). Electronic applications accepted.

**University of South Florida,** USF Health Taneja College of Pharmacy, Tampa, FL 33612. Offers pharmaceutical nanotechnology (MS), including biomedical engineering, drug discovery, delivery, development and manufacturing; pharmacy (Pharm D), including pharmacy and health education. *Accreditation:* ACPE. *Program availability:* Part-time, 100% online, blended/hybrid learning. *Faculty:* 32 full-time (18 women), 1 part-time/adjunct (0 women). *Students:* 398 full-time (234 women), 7 part-time (3 women); includes 180 minority (33 Black or African American, non-Hispanic/Latino; 72 Asian, non-Hispanic/Latino; 59 Hispanic/Latino; 2 Native Hawaiian or other Pacific Islander, non-Hispanic/Latino; 14 Two or more races, non-Hispanic/Latino), 13 international. Average age 25. 465 applicants, 44% accepted, 112 enrolled. In 2019, 11 master's, 91 doctorates awarded. *Degree requirements:* For master's, comprehensive exam, thesis optional, capstone or thesis; for doctorate, internship/field experience. *Entrance requirements:* For master's, GRE, MCAT or DAT, Bachelor's preferably in biomedical, biological, chemical sciences or engineering; 2 letters of recommendation; resume; professional statement; interview; for doctorate, PCAT, minimum GPA of 2.75 overall (preferred); completion of 72 prerequisite credit hours; U.S. citizenship or permanent resident; interviews; criminal background check and drug screen. Additional exam requirements/recommendations for international students: required—TOEFL (minimum score 550 paper-based; 79 iBT), IELTS (minimum score 6.5). *Application deadline:* For fall admission, 6/1 for domestic and international students; for spring admission, 10/15 for domestic students, 9/15 for international students; for summer admission, 2/15 for domestic and international students. Applications are processed on a rolling basis. Application fee: $30. Electronic applications accepted. *Financial support:* In 2019–20, 159 students received support. Scholarships/grants available. *Unit head:* James Lambert, 813-974-4562, E-mail: jlambert2@usf.edu. *Application contact:* Dr. Amy Schwartz, Admissions Recruiter, 813-974-4652, E-mail: jlambert2@usf.edu.
Website: https://health.usf.edu/pharmacy

**The University of Tennessee Health Science Center,** College of Graduate Health Sciences, Memphis, TN 38163. Offers biomedical engineering (MS, PhD); biomedical sciences (PhD); dental sciences (MDS); epidemiology (MS); health outcomes and policy research (PhD); laboratory research and management (MS); nursing science (PhD); pharmaceutical sciences (PhD); pharmacology (MS); speech and hearing science (PhD); DDS/PhD; DNP/PhD; MD/PhD; Pharm D/PhD. Terminal master's awarded for partial completion of doctoral program. *Degree requirements:* For master's, comprehensive exam, thesis; for doctorate, thesis/dissertation, oral and written preliminary and comprehensive exams. *Entrance requirements:* For master's and doctorate, GRE General Test, minimum GPA of 3.0. Additional exam requirements/recommendations for international students: recommended—TOEFL (minimum score 79 iBT), IELTS (minimum score 6.5). Electronic applications accepted. *Expenses:* Contact institution.

**The University of Texas at Austin,** Graduate School, College of Pharmacy, Graduate Programs in Pharmacy, Austin, TX 78712-1111. Offers health outcomes and pharmacy practice (MS, PhD); medicinal chemistry (PhD); pharmaceutics (PhD); pharmacology and toxicology (PhD); pharmacotherapy (MS, PhD); translational science (PhD). *Degree requirements:* For master's, thesis; for doctorate, thesis/dissertation. *Entrance requirements:* For master's and doctorate, GRE General Test. Electronic applications accepted.

**University of the Pacific,** Thomas J. Long School of Pharmacy and Health Sciences, Pharmaceutical and Chemical Sciences Graduate Program, Stockton, CA 95211-0197. Offers MS, PhD. *Entrance requirements:* Additional exam requirements/recommendations for international students: required—TOEFL.

**University of the Sciences,** Program in Pharmaceutics, Philadelphia, PA 19104-4495. Offers MS, PhD. *Program availability:* Part-time. Terminal master's awarded for partial completion of doctoral program. *Degree requirements:* For master's, thesis (for some programs); for doctorate, comprehensive exam, thesis/dissertation, oral defense. *Entrance requirements:* For master's and doctorate, GRE General Test. Additional exam requirements/recommendations for international students: required—TOEFL, TWE.

**The University of Toledo,** College of Graduate Studies, College of Pharmacy and Pharmaceutical Sciences, Program in Pharmaceutical Sciences, Toledo, OH 43606-3390. Offers administrative pharmacy (MSPS); industrial pharmacy (MSPS); pharmacology toxicology (MSPS). *Degree requirements:* For master's, thesis. *Entrance requirements:* For master's, GRE General Test. Additional exam requirements/recommendations for international students: required—TOEFL (minimum score 550 paper-based; 80 iBT). Electronic applications accepted.

**University of Toronto,** School of Graduate Studies, Leslie Dan Faculty of Pharmacy, Toronto, ON M5S 1A1, Canada. Offers M Sc, PhD, Pharm D. *Program availability:* Part-time. *Degree requirements:* For master's, thesis, poster presentation, oral thesis defense; for doctorate, thesis/dissertation (for some programs). *Entrance requirements:* For master's, minimum B average in last 2 years of full-time study, 3 letters of reference, resume. Additional exam requirements/recommendations for international students: required—TOEFL (minimum score 600 paper-based), Michigan English Language Assessment Battery (minum score 88) or IELTS (minimum score 7). Electronic applications accepted.

**University of Utah,** Graduate School, College of Pharmacy, Department of Pharmacotherapy, Salt Lake City, UT 84112. Offers health system pharmacy administration (MS); outcomes research and health policy (PhD). *Faculty:* 19 full-time (12 women). *Students:* 6 full-time (3 women), 7 part-time (1 woman); includes 1 minority (Asian, non-Hispanic/Latino), 4 international. Average age 33. 14 applicants, 43% accepted, 6 enrolled. In 2019, 1 master's, 1 doctorate awarded. Terminal master's awarded for partial completion of doctoral program. *Degree requirements:* For master's, comprehensive exam, thesis or alternative, project; for doctorate, comprehensive exam, thesis/dissertation. *Entrance requirements:* Additional exam requirements/recommendations for international students: required—TOEFL (minimum score 550 paper-based; 80 iBT), GRE. *Application deadline:* For fall admission, 1/10 for domestic students, 12/15 for international students. Application fee: $55 ($65 for international students). *Expenses:* Tuition, state resident: full-time $7085; part-time $272.51 per credit hour. Tuition, nonresident: full-time $24,937; part-time $959.12 per credit hour. *Required fees:* $880.52; $880.52 per semester. Tuition and fees vary according to degree level, program and student level. *Financial support:* In 2019–20, 1 research assistantship (averaging $4,000 per year) was awarded. Financial award applicants required to submit CSS PROFILE or FAFSA. *Unit head:* Daniel Malone, Professor, 801-581-8054, Fax: 801-587-7923, E-mail: dan.malone@utah.edu. *Application contact:* Linda O'Connor, Education Coordinator, 801-585-1065, E-mail: linda.oconner@pharm.utah.edu.
Website: http://www.pharmacy.utah.edu/pharmacotherapy/

**University of Washington,** School of Pharmacy, Department of Pharmaceutics, Seattle, WA 98195. Offers MS, PhD, Pharm D/PhD. *Faculty:* 10 full-time (4 women), 2 part-time/adjunct (1 woman). *Students:* 23 full-time (10 women); includes 10 minority (2 Black or African American, non-Hispanic/Latino; 1 American Indian or Alaska Native, non-Hispanic/Latino; 5 Asian, non-Hispanic/Latino; 2 Hispanic/Latino), 7 international. Average age 30. 83 applicants, 16% accepted, 4 enrolled. In 2019, 1 master's, 5 doctorates awarded. Terminal master's awarded for partial completion of doctoral program. *Degree requirements:* For master's, thesis; for doctorate, thesis/dissertation. *Entrance requirements:* For master's and doctorate, GRE General Test. *Application deadline:* For fall admission, 12/31 for domestic and international students. Application fee: $85. Electronic applications accepted. *Financial support:* In 2019–20, 23 students received support, including 4 fellowships with full tuition reimbursements available (averaging $31,800 per year), 23 research assistantships with full tuition reimbursements available (averaging $31,800 per year); career-related internships or fieldwork, institutionally sponsored loans, scholarships/grants, traineeships, health care benefits, tuition waivers (full), and unspecified assistantships also available. *Unit head:* Dr. Nina Isoherranen, Chair, 206-543-2517, Fax: 206-543-3204, E-mail: ni2@u.washington.edu. *Application contact:* Heidi Hannah, Graduate Program Advisor, 206-616-2797, Fax: 206-543-3204, E-mail: hmhannah@u.washington.edu.
Website: http://sop.washington.edu/pharmaceutics

**University of Wisconsin–Madison,** School of Pharmacy and Graduate School, Graduate Programs in Pharmacy, Pharmaceutical Sciences Division, Madison, WI 53705. Offers PhD. Terminal master's awarded for partial completion of doctoral program. *Degree requirements:* For doctorate, comprehensive exam, thesis/dissertation. *Entrance requirements:* For doctorate, GRE. Additional exam requirements/recommendations for international students: required—TOEFL. Electronic applications accepted.

**University of Wisconsin–Madison,** School of Pharmacy and Graduate School, Graduate Programs in Pharmacy, Social and Administrative Sciences in Pharmacy Division, Madison, WI 53706-1380. Offers MS, PhD. Terminal master's awarded for partial completion of doctoral program. *Degree requirements:* For master's, comprehensive exam (for some programs), thesis optional; for doctorate, comprehensive exam, thesis/dissertation. *Entrance requirements:* For master's and doctorate, GRE. Additional exam requirements/recommendations for international students: required—TOEFL. Electronic applications accepted.

**Université Laval,** Faculty of Pharmacy, Program in Hospital Pharmacy, Québec, QC G1K 7P4, Canada. Offers M Sc. *Entrance requirements:* For master's, knowledge of French, interview. Electronic applications accepted.

**Université Laval,** Faculty of Pharmacy, Programs in Community Pharmacy, Québec, QC G1K 7P4, Canada. Offers DESS. *Program availability:* Part-time. *Entrance requirements:* For degree, knowledge of French. Electronic applications accepted.

**Université Laval,** Faculty of Pharmacy, Programs in Pharmacy, Québec, QC G1K 7P4, Canada. Offers M Sc, PhD. *Program availability:* Part-time. Terminal master's awarded for partial completion of doctoral program. *Degree requirements:* For master's, thesis; for doctorate, comprehensive exam, thesis/dissertation. *Entrance requirements:* For master's and doctorate, knowledge of French. Electronic applications accepted.

**Virginia Commonwealth University,** Medical College of Virginia-Professional Programs, School of Pharmacy, Department of Pharmaceutics, Richmond, VA 23284-9005. Offers medicinal chemistry (MS); pharmaceutical sciences (PhD); pharmaceutics (MS); pharmacotherapy and pharmacy administration (MS). Terminal master's awarded for partial completion of doctoral program. *Degree requirements:* For master's, thesis; for doctorate, thesis/dissertation. *Entrance requirements:* For master's and doctorate, GRE General Test. Additional exam requirements/recommendations for international students: required—TOEFL. Electronic applications accepted.

**Wayne State University,** Eugene Applebaum College of Pharmacy and Health Sciences, Applied Health Sciences, Detroit, MI 48202. Offers medicinal chemistry (MS, PhD); pharmaceutics (MS, PhD), including medicinal chemistry (PhD); pharmacology and toxicology (MS, PhD). *Entrance requirements:* For master's, GRE General Test, bachelor's degree; adequate background in biology, physics, calculus, and chemistry; three letters of recommendation; personal statement; for doctorate, GRE General Test, bachelor's or master's degree in one of the behavioral, biological, pharmaceutical or physical sciences; three letters of recommendation. Additional exam requirements/recommendations for international students: required—TOEFL (minimum score 550 paper-based; 79 iBT), Michigan English Language Assessment Battery (minimum score 85); recommended—IELTS (minimum score 6.5), TWE (minimum score 5.5). Electronic applications accepted. *Expenses:* Contact institution.

**Western University of Health Sciences,** College of Pharmacy, Program in Pharmaceutical Sciences, Pomona, CA 91766-1854. Offers pharmaceutical sciences (MS). *Faculty:* 12 full-time (4 women). *Students:* 7 full-time (4 women), 7 part-time (5 women); includes 5 minority (4 Asian, non-Hispanic/Latino; 1 Hispanic/Latino), 7 international. Average age 28. 26 applicants, 19% accepted, 5 enrolled. In 2019, 9 master's awarded. *Degree requirements:* For master's, comprehensive exam (for some programs), thesis. *Entrance requirements:* For master's, GRE, minimum overall GPA of 2.5; BS in pharmacy, chemistry, biology or related scientific area; 3 letters of recommendation; curriculum vitae. Additional exam requirements/recommendations for international students: required—TOEFL (minimum score 89 iBT), IELTS (minimum score 6.5). *Application deadline:* For fall admission, 4/1 for domestic and international

students; for spring admission, 9/1 for domestic and international students. Applications are processed on a rolling basis. Application fee: $40. Electronic applications accepted. *Expenses:* Tuition is $15480 per year. *Financial support:* In 2019–20, 15 students received support, including 15 teaching assistantships with full tuition reimbursements available (averaging $21,000 per year); scholarships/grants also available. Financial award application deadline: 3/2; financial award applicants required to submit FAFSA. *Unit head:* Stephen O'Barr, Chair, 909-469-5643, E-mail: sobarr@westernu.edu. *Application contact:* Elaine Gonzalez, Admissions Counselo, 909-469-5337, Fax: 909-469-5570, E-mail: egonzalez@westernu.edu.
Website: http://www.westernu.edu/pharmacy-dpp_message

**West Virginia University,** School of Pharmacy, Morgantown, WV 26506. Offers health services and outcomes research (PhD); pharmaceutical and pharmacological sciences (PhD); professional pharmacy (Pharm D). *Accreditation:* ACPE. Terminal master's awarded for partial completion of doctoral program. *Degree requirements:* For doctorate, variable foreign language requirement, comprehensive exam (for some programs), thesis/dissertation (for some programs). *Entrance requirements:* For doctorate, GRE General Test (for PhD), minimum GPA of 2.75 (for PhD). Additional exam requirements/recommendations for international students: required—TOEFL (minimum score 500 paper-based). Electronic applications accepted. *Expenses:* Contact institution.

**York College of the City University of New York,** School of Arts and Sciences, Jamaica, NY 11451. Offers pharmaceutcal science and business (MS).

# Pharmacy

**Albany College of Pharmacy and Health Sciences,** School of Pharmacy and Pharmaceutical Sciences, Albany, NY 12208. Offers health outcomes research (MS); pharmaceutical sciences (MS), including pharmaceutics, pharmacology; pharmacy (Pharm D). *Accreditation:* ACPE. *Degree requirements:* For master's, thesis; for doctorate, practice experience. *Entrance requirements:* For master's, GRE, minimum GPA of 3.0; for doctorate, PCAT, minimum GPA of 2.5. Additional exam requirements/recommendations for international students: required—TOEFL (minimum score 84 iBT). Electronic applications accepted.

**Appalachian College of Pharmacy,** Doctor of Pharmacy Program, Oakwood, VA 24631. Offers Pharm D. *Accreditation:* ACPE.

**Auburn University,** Harrison School of Pharmacy, Professional Program in Pharmacy, Auburn University, AL 36849. Offers Pharm D. *Accreditation:* ACPE. *Program availability:* Part-time. *Faculty:* 58 full-time (34 women), 1 (woman) part-time/adjunct. *Students:* 588 full-time (392 women); includes 126 minority (56 Black or African American, non-Hispanic/Latino; 1 American Indian or Alaska Native, non-Hispanic/Latino; 48 Asian, non-Hispanic/Latino; 13 Hispanic/Latino; 1 Native Hawaiian or other Pacific Islander, non-Hispanic/Latino; 7 Two or more races, non-Hispanic/Latino), 1 international. Average age 25. 421 applicants, 65% accepted, 148 enrolled. In 2019, 145 doctorates awarded. *Application deadline:* For fall admission, 1/15 for domestic and international students. Application fee: $60 ($70 for international students). Electronic applications accepted. *Expenses:* $546 per credit hour state resident tuition, $1638 per credit hour nonresident tuition, $680 student services fee for GRA/GTA, $838 student services fee, $5283 per semester. *Financial support:* Federal Work-Study available. Support available to part-time students. Financial award application deadline: 3/15; financial award applicants required to submit FAFSA. *Unit head:* Dr. Richard Hansen, Dean/Professor, Harrison School of Pharmacy, 334-844-8348, Fax: 334-844-8307. *Application contact:* Dr. George Flowers, Dean of the Graduate School, 334-844-2125.

**Belmont University,** College of Pharmacy, Nashville, TN 37212. Offers advanced pharmacotherapy (Pharm D); health care informatics (Pharm D); management (Pharm D); missions/public health (Pharm D); Pharm D/MBA. *Accreditation:* ACPE. *Faculty:* 29 full-time (16 women), 4 part-time/adjunct (2 women). *Students:* 354 full-time (242 women); includes 120 minority (50 Black or African American, non-Hispanic/Latino; 1 American Indian or Alaska Native, non-Hispanic/Latino; 41 Asian, non-Hispanic/Latino; 18 Hispanic/Latino; 10 Two or more races, non-Hispanic/Latino), 3 international. Average age 25. In 2019, 67 doctorates awarded. *Degree requirements:* For doctorate, comprehensive exam. *Entrance requirements:* For doctorate, PCAT. Additional exam requirements/recommendations for international students: required—TOEFL. *Application deadline:* For fall admission, 8/31 priority date for domestic students; for spring admission, 3/1 for domestic students. Applications are processed on a rolling basis. Application fee: $50. Electronic applications accepted. *Expenses:* Contact institution. *Financial support:* In 2019–20, 112 students received support. Career-related internships or fieldwork and scholarships/grants available. Financial award application deadline: 12/1; financial award applicants required to submit FAFSA. *Unit head:* Dr. David Gregory, Dean, 615-460-6746, Fax: 615-460-6741, E-mail: david.gregory@belmont.edu. *Application contact:* Dr. David Gregory, Dean, 615-460-6746, Fax: 615-460-6741, E-mail: david.gregory@belmont.edu.
Website: http://www.belmont.edu/pharmacy/index.html

**Binghamton University, State University of New York,** Graduate School, School of Pharmacy and Pharmaceutical Sciences, Binghamton, NY 13902-6000. Offers pharmacy (Pharm D).

**Butler University,** College of Pharmacy and Health Sciences, Indianapolis, IN 46208-3485. Offers pharmaceutical science (MS); pharmacy (Pharm D), including medical Spanish, research; physician assistant studies (MS). *Accreditation:* ACPE (one or more programs are accredited). *Program availability:* Part-time, evening/weekend, 100% online. *Faculty:* 14 full-time (8 women). *Students:* 358 full-time (245 women), 2 part-time (0 women); includes 42 minority (1 Black or African American, non-Hispanic/Latino; 23 Asian, non-Hispanic/Latino; 12 Hispanic/Latino; 6 Two or more races, non-Hispanic/Latino), 4 international. Average age 24. 441 applicants, 17% accepted, 76 enrolled. In 2019, 77 master's, 106 doctorates awarded. *Degree requirements:* For master's, comprehensive exam (for some programs), thesis (for some programs), research paper or thesis; for doctorate, thesis/dissertation (for some programs). *Entrance requirements:* For master's, GRE General Test, CASPA application, official transcripts, baccalaureate degree from accredited institution (for physician assistant studies). Additional exam requirements/recommendations for international students: required—TOEFL (minimum score 550 paper-based; 79 iBT), IELTS (minimum score 6). *Application deadline:* For fall admission, 4/1 for domestic and international students. Electronic applications accepted. *Expenses:* Pharmacy: Pharmacy year 1 &2 (pre-Pharmacy) $20,685 per semester Pharmacy year 3-5 (P1-P3) $22,000 per semester; Pharm D (6th year only) (P4) $47,00 per year, billed summer ($4,780), fall* ($21,510), spring* ($21,510) Note: Rate is NOT based on number of hours enrolled. *Each hour above 20 hours is $1,830 for P1-P3. Master's of Science in Pharmaceutical Science: $760 per credit hour; Doctor of Medical Science: $800 per credit hour; PA Master's Program: $44,820 per year, billed summer ($4,482), fall* ($20,169), spring* ($20,169) Note: Rate is NOT based on number of hours enrolled. *each hour above 20 hours is $1,830 per credit hour. *Financial support:* In 2019–20, 4 students received support. Scholarships/grants, tuition waivers (full and partial), and unspecified assistantships available. Financial award applicants required to submit FAFSA. *Unit head:* Dr. Robert Soltis, Dean, 317-940-9322, E-mail: rsoltis@butler.edu. *Application contact:* Katie Clarizio, Academic Program Coordinator, 317-940-9297, E-mail: kclarizio@butler.edu.
Website: https://www.butler.edu/pharmacy-pa/about

**California Health Sciences University,** College of Pharmacy, Clovis, CA 93612. Offers Pharm D. *Accreditation:* ACPE.

**California Northstate University,** College of Pharmacy, Elk Grove, CA 95757. Offers Pharm D. *Accreditation:* ACPE.

**Campbell University,** Graduate and Professional Programs, College of Pharmacy and Health Sciences, Buies Creek, NC 27506. Offers athletic training (MAT); clinical research (MS); pharmaceutical sciences (MS); pharmacy (Pharm D); physical therapy (DPT); physician assistant (MPAP); public health (MS). *Accreditation:* ACPE; CEPH. *Program availability:* Part-time, evening/weekend. *Entrance requirements:* For master's, MCAT, PCAT, GRE, bachelor's degree in health sciences or related field; for doctorate, PCAT. Additional exam requirements/recommendations for international students: required—TOEFL (minimum score 550 paper-based; 79 iBT). Electronic applications accepted. *Expenses:* Contact institution.

**Cedarville University,** Graduate Programs, Cedarville, OH 45314. Offers business administration (MBA); family nurse practitioner (MSN); global ministry (M Div); global public health nursing (MSN); healthcare administration (MBA); ministry (M Min); nurse educator (MSN); operations management (MBA); pharmacy (Pharm D). *Program availability:* Part-time, evening/weekend, 100% online, blended/hybrid learning. *Faculty:* 52 full-time (19 women), 21 part-time/adjunct (13 women). *Students:* 378 full-time (221 women), 45 part-time (23 women); includes 76 minority (46 Black or African American, non-Hispanic/Latino; 2 American Indian or Alaska Native, non-Hispanic/Latino; 22 Asian, non-Hispanic/Latino; 1 Hispanic/Latino; 5 Two or more races, non-Hispanic/Latino), 2 international. Average age 26. 398 applicants, 70% accepted, 172 enrolled. In 2019, 74 master's, 34 doctorates awarded. *Degree requirements:* For master's, portfolio; for doctorate, comprehensive exam. *Entrance requirements:* For master's, GRE may be required, 2 professional recommendations; for doctorate, PCAT, professional recommendation from a practicing pharmacist or current employer/supervisor, resume, essay, interview. Additional exam requirements/recommendations for international students: required—TOEFL (minimum score 550 paper-based; 80 iBT). *Application deadline:* For fall admission, 5/1 priority date for domestic and international students; for spring admission, 11/1 priority date for domestic and international students. Applications are processed on a rolling basis. Electronic applications accepted. *Expenses:* Tuition: Full-time $12,594; part-time $566 per credit hour. One-time fee: $100. Tuition and fees vary according to course load and program. *Financial support:* Scholarships/grants and unspecified assistantships available. Support available to part-time students. Financial award application deadline: 1/30; financial award applicants required to submit FAFSA. *Unit head:* Dr. Janice Supplee, Dean of Graduate Studies, 937-766-8000, E-mail: suppleej@cedarville.edu. *Application contact:* Alexis McKay, Graduate Admissions Counselor, 937-766-8000, E-mail: amckay@cedarville.edu.
Website: https://www.cedarville.edu/offices/graduate-school

**Chapman University,** School of Pharmacy, Irvine, CA 92618. Offers pharmaceutical sciences (MS, PhD); pharmacy (Pharm D). *Accreditation:* ACPE. *Faculty:* 44 full-time (22 women), 5 part-time/adjunct (1 woman). *Students:* 310 full-time (196 women), 6 part-time (5 women); includes 234 minority (14 Black or African American, non-Hispanic/Latino; 1 American Indian or Alaska Native, non-Hispanic/Latino; 187 Asian, non-Hispanic/Latino; 24 Hispanic/Latino; 8 Two or more races, non-Hispanic/Latino), 17 international. Average age 26. In 2019, 17 master's, 72 doctorates awarded. *Degree requirements:* For master's, thesis or alternative; for doctorate, dissertation for PhD. *Entrance requirements:* For doctorate, PCAT (PharmD), GRE (PhD). Additional exam requirements/recommendations for international students: required—TOEFL (minimum score 80 iBT), IELTS (minimum score 6.5), PTE (minimum score 53). *Application deadline:* Applications are processed on a rolling basis. Electronic applications accepted. *Expenses:* Contact institution. *Financial support:* Fellowships, research assistantships, Federal Work-Study, and scholarships/grants available. *Unit head:* Ronald P. Jordan, Dean, 714-516-5486, E-mail: rpjordan@chapman.edu. *Application contact:* Rocke DeMark, Associate Dean of Student and Academic Affairs, 714-516-516-5460, E-mail: pharmacyadmissions@chapman.edu.
Website: https://www.chapman.edu/pharmacy/index.aspx

**Chicago State University,** College of Pharmacy, Chicago, IL 60628. Offers Pharm D. *Accreditation:* ACPE. *Entrance requirements:* For doctorate, PCAT, minimum cumulative GPA of 2.5.

**Concordia University Wisconsin,** Graduate Programs, School of Pharmacy, Mequon, WI 53097-2402. Offers pharmaceutical/chemical product development (MPD); pharmacy (Pharm D). *Accreditation:* ACPE.

**Creighton University,** School of Pharmacy and Health Professions, Professional Program in Pharmacy, Omaha, NE 68178-0001. Offers Pharm D. *Accreditation:* ACPE. *Program availability:* Online learning. *Entrance requirements:* For doctorate, PCAT. Additional exam requirements/recommendations for international students: required—TOEFL. Electronic applications accepted.

**Drake University,** College of Pharmacy and Health Sciences, Des Moines, IA 50311-4516. Offers athletic training (MAT); Pharm D/JD; Pharm D/MBA; Pharm D/MPA. *Accreditation:* ACPE. *Students:* 464 full-time (337 women), 3 part-time (1 woman); includes 74 minority (3 Black or African American, non-Hispanic/Latino; 46 Asian, non-Hispanic/Latino; 17 Hispanic/Latino; 8 Two or more races, non-Hispanic/Latino), 7 international. Average age 23. In 2019, 130 doctorates awarded. *Degree requirements:* For doctorate, rotations. *Entrance requirements:* For doctorate, PCAT, interview. Additional exam requirements/recommendations for international students: required—TOEFL. *Application deadline:* For fall admission, 2/1 priority date for domestic students. Application fee: $135. Electronic applications accepted. *Expenses:* Contact institution. *Financial support:* Teaching assistantships, career-related internships or fieldwork, Federal Work-Study, institutionally sponsored loans, and scholarships/grants available.

Support available to part-time students. Financial award application deadline: 3/1; financial award applicants required to submit FAFSA. *Unit head:* Dr. Renae Chesnut, Dean, 515-271-3018, Fax: 515-271-4171, E-mail: renae.chesnut@drake.edu. *Application contact:* Dr. Renae Chesnut, Dean, 515-271-3018, Fax: 515-271-4171, E-mail: renae.chesnut@drake.edu.
Website: http://www.drake.edu/cphs/

**Duquesne University,** School of Pharmacy, Pharm D Program, Pittsburgh, PA 15282. Offers Pharm D. *Accreditation:* ACPE. *Program availability:* Blended/hybrid learning. *Degree requirements:* For doctorate, comprehensive exam, Pharmacy Curriculum Outcomes Assessment Exam (PCOA) and Capstone Skills Assessment. *Entrance requirements:* For doctorate, PCAT. Additional exam requirements/recommendations for international students: required—TOEFL. Electronic applications accepted. *Expenses:* Contact institution.

**D'Youville College,** School of Pharmacy, Buffalo, NY 14201-1084. Offers Pharm D. *Accreditation:* ACPE. *Entrance requirements:* For doctorate, PCAT, PharmCAS application, official transcripts from all colleges previously attended, three letters of recommendation. Electronic applications accepted. *Expenses:* Contact institution.

**East Tennessee State University,** Bill Gatton College of Pharmacy, Johnson City, TN 37614. Offers Pharm D. *Accreditation:* ACPE. *Program availability:* Part-time. *Degree requirements:* For doctorate, comprehensive exam. *Entrance requirements:* Additional exam requirements/recommendations for international students: required—TOEFL (minimum score 550 paper-based; 79 iBT). Electronic applications accepted.

**Fairleigh Dickinson University, Florham Campus,** School of Pharmacy, Madison, NJ 07940-1099. Offers Pharm D. *Accreditation:* ACPE.

**Ferris State University,** College of Pharmacy, Big Rapids, MI 49307. Offers Pharm D. *Accreditation:* ACPE. *Faculty:* 43 full-time (26 women), 3 part-time/adjunct (2 women). *Students:* 517 full-time (285 women), 16 part-time (10 women); includes 50 minority (4 Black or African American, non-Hispanic/Latino; 2 American Indian or Alaska Native, non-Hispanic/Latino; 21 Asian, non-Hispanic/Latino; 16 Hispanic/Latino; 7 Two or more races, non-Hispanic/Latino), 11 international. Average age 24. 280 applicants, 62% accepted, 119 enrolled. In 2019, 149 doctorates awarded. *Degree requirements:* For doctorate, 6 clerkships during 4th professional year which equals 1,740 hours of clerkship. *Entrance requirements:* For doctorate, PCAT, 3 years or more of pre-pharmacy course work. *Application deadline:* For fall admission, 3/1 for domestic and international students. Applications are processed on a rolling basis. Application fee: $175. Electronic applications accepted. *Expenses:* Contact institution. *Financial support:* In 2019–20, 150 students received support. Career-related internships or fieldwork, Federal Work-Study, institutionally sponsored loans, and scholarships/grants available. Financial award application deadline: 4/15; financial award applicants required to submit FAFSA. *Unit head:* Dr. Stephen Durst, Dean, 231-591-2254, Fax: 231-591-3829, E-mail: dursts@ferris.edu. *Application contact:* Tara M. Lee, Director of Admissions, 231-591-2249, Fax: 231-591-3829, E-mail: leet@ferris.edu.
Website: http://www.ferris.edu/colleges/pharmacy/

**Florida Agricultural and Mechanical University,** Division of Graduate Studies, Research, and Continuing Education, College of Pharmacy and Pharmaceutical Sciences, Professional Program in Pharmacy and Pharmaceutical Sciences, Tallahassee, FL 32307-3200. Offers Pharm D. *Accreditation:* ACPE. *Entrance requirements:* Additional exam requirements/recommendations for international students: required—TOEFL.

**Georgia Campus–Philadelphia College of Osteopathic Medicine,** School of Pharmacy, Suwanee, GA 30024. Offers Pharm D. *Accreditation:* ACPE. *Degree requirements:* For doctorate, capstone. *Entrance requirements:* For doctorate, PCAT. Additional exam requirements/recommendations for international students: required—TOEFL (minimum score 79 iBT). Electronic applications accepted. *Expenses:* Contact institution.

**Harding University,** College of Pharmacy, Searcy, AR 72147-2230. Offers Pharm D. *Accreditation:* ACPE. *Faculty:* 16 full-time (11 women). *Students:* 172 full-time (119 women), 9 part-time (5 women); includes 41 minority (22 Black or African American, non-Hispanic/Latino; 16 Asian, non-Hispanic/Latino; 3 Hispanic/Latino), 2 international. Average age 27. 143 applicants, 24% accepted, 35 enrolled. In 2019, 48 doctorates awarded. *Degree requirements:* For doctorate, licensure as a pharmacy intern in AR, completion of 300 hours of introductory pharmacy practice experience and 1,440 hours of advanced pharmacy practice experience. *Entrance requirements:* For doctorate, PCAT, 90 semester hours of undergraduate work. Additional exam requirements/recommendations for international students: required—TOEFL (minimum score 550 paper-based). *Application deadline:* For fall admission, 3/1 priority date for domestic and international students. Applications are processed on a rolling basis. Application fee: $50. Electronic applications accepted. *Expenses:* Contact institution. *Financial support:* In 2019–20, 35 students received support. Scholarships/grants available. Financial award applicants required to submit FAFSA. *Unit head:* Dr. Jeff Mercer, Dean, 501-279-5205, Fax: 501-279-5525, E-mail: jmercer@harding.edu. *Application contact:* Carol Jones, Director of Admissions, 501-279-5523, Fax: 501-279-5525, E-mail: ccjones@harding.edu.
Website: http://www.harding.edu/pharmacy/

**High Point University,** Norcross Graduate School, High Point, NC 27268. Offers athletic training (MSAT); business administration (MBA); educational leadership (M Ed, Ed D); elementary education (M Ed, MAT); pharmacy (Pharm D); physical therapy (DPT); physician assistant studies (MPAS); secondary mathematics (M Ed, MAT); special education (M Ed); strategic communication (MA). *Accreditation:* NCATE. *Program availability:* Part-time, evening/weekend. *Degree requirements:* For master's, comprehensive exam (for some programs), thesis (for some programs). *Entrance requirements:* For master's, GMAT (MBA), GRE, MAT, minimum GPA of 3.0. Additional exam requirements/recommendations for international students: required—TOEFL (minimum score 550 paper-based). Electronic applications accepted.

**Howard University,** College of Pharmacy, Washington, DC 20059-0002. Offers Pharm D, Pharm D/MBA. *Accreditation:* ACPE. *Program availability:* Online learning. *Degree requirements:* For doctorate, comprehensive exam. *Entrance requirements:* For doctorate, PCAT, minimum GPA of 2.5. Electronic applications accepted. *Expenses:* Contact institution.

**Husson University,** School of Pharmacy, Bangor, ME 04401-2999. Offers pharmacology (MS); pharmacy (Pharm D). *Accreditation:* ACPE. *Entrance requirements:* For doctorate, PCAT, PharmCAS application. Additional exam requirements/recommendations for international students: required—TOEFL (minimum score 550 paper-based; 80 iBT), IELTS (minimum score 6.5). Electronic applications accepted. *Expenses:* Contact institution.

**Idaho State University,** Graduate School, College of Pharmacy, Department of Pharmacy Practice and Administrative Sciences, Pocatello, ID 83209-8333. Offers pharmacy (Pharm D); pharmacy administration (MS, PhD). *Accreditation:* ACPE (one or more programs are accredited). *Program availability:* Part-time. *Degree requirements:* For master's, one foreign language, comprehensive exam, thesis, thesis research, speech and technical writing classes; for doctorate, comprehensive exam, thesis/dissertation, oral and written exams, speech and technical writing classes. *Entrance requirements:* For master's, GRE General Test, minimum GPA of 3.0, 3 letters of recommendation; for doctorate, GRE General Test, BS in pharmacy or related field, minimum GPA of 3.0, 3 letters of recommendation. Additional exam requirements/recommendations for international students: required—TOEFL (minimum score 550 paper-based; 80 iBT). Electronic applications accepted. *Expenses:* Contact institution.

**Lake Erie College of Osteopathic Medicine,** Professional Programs, Erie, PA 16509-1025. Offers biomedical sciences (Postbaccalaureate Certificate); medical education (MS); osteopathic medicine (DO); pharmacy (Pharm D). *Accreditation:* ACPE; AOsA. *Degree requirements:* For doctorate, comprehensive exam, National Osteopathic Medical Licensing Exam, Levels 1 and 2; for Postbaccalaureate Certificate, comprehensive exam, North American Pharmacist Licensure Examination (NAPLEX). *Entrance requirements:* For doctorate, MCAT, minimum GPA of 3.2, letters of recommendation; for Postbaccalaureate Certificate, PCAT, letters of recommendation, minimum GPA of 3.5. Electronic applications accepted.

**Lebanese American University,** School of Pharmacy, Beirut, Lebanon. Offers Pharm D. *Accreditation:* ACPE.

**Lipscomb University,** College of Pharmacy, Nashville, TN 37204-3951. Offers healthcare informatics (MS); pharmacy (Pharm D); Pharm D/MM; Pharm D/MS. *Accreditation:* ACPE. *Degree requirements:* For master's, capstone project; for doctorate, comprehensive exam. *Entrance requirements:* For master's, GRE, 2 references, transcripts, resume, personal statement, eligibility documentation (degree and/or experience in related area); for doctorate, PCAT (minimum 45th percentile), 66 pre-professional semester hours, minimum GPA of 2.5, interview, PharmCAS application (for international students). Additional exam requirements/recommendations for international students: required—TOEFL (minimum score 550 paper-based; 80 iBT). Electronic applications accepted. *Expenses:* Contact institution.

**Loma Linda University,** School of Pharmacy, Loma Linda, CA 92350. Offers Pharm D. *Accreditation:* ACPE. *Degree requirements:* For doctorate, intern pharmacist license.

**Long Island University - Brooklyn,** Arnold and Marie Schwartz College of Pharmacy and Health Sciences, Brooklyn, NY 11201-8423. Offers drug regulatory affairs (MS); pharmaceutics (MS, PhD), including cosmetic science (MS), industrial pharmacy (MS); pharmacology and toxicology (MS); pharmacy (Pharm D). *Accreditation:* ACPE. *Program availability:* Part-time. Terminal master's awarded for partial completion of doctoral program. *Degree requirements:* For master's, comprehensive exam, thesis; for doctorate, comprehensive exam, thesis/dissertation. *Entrance requirements:* For master's and doctorate, GRE. Additional exam requirements/recommendations for international students: required—TOEFL (minimum score 550 paper-based, 79 iBT) or IELTS. Electronic applications accepted. *Expenses:* Contact institution.

**Long Island University - Hudson,** Graduate School, Purchase, NY 10577. Offers autism (Advanced Certificate); bilingual education (Advanced Certificate); childhood education (MS Ed); crisis management (Advanced Certificate); early childhood education (MS Ed); educational leadership (MS Ed); health administration (MPA); literacy (MS Ed); marriage and family therapy (MS); mental health counseling (MS, Advanced Certificate), including credentialed alcoholism and substance abuse counselor (MS); middle childhood and adolescence education (MS Ed); pharmaceutics (MS), including cosmetic science, industrial pharmacy; public administration (MPA); school counseling (MS Ed, Advanced Certificate); school psychology (MS Ed); special education (MS Ed); TESOL (MS Ed); TESOL (all grades) (Advanced Certificate). *Program availability:* Part-time, evening/weekend. *Entrance requirements:* Additional exam requirements/recommendations for international students: required—TOEFL. Electronic applications accepted. *Expenses:* Contact institution.

**Manchester University,** Doctor of Pharmacy Program, Fort Wayne, IN 46962-1225. Offers Pharm D. *Accreditation:* ACPE. *Degree requirements:* For doctorate, service learning, portfolio, competency assessments. *Entrance requirements:* For doctorate, minimum GPA of 2.5 (cumulative and prerequisites), minimum C grade on all prerequisite courses, U.S. citizenship or permanent residency, PharmCAS and supplemental application, 3 letters of recommendation. Electronic applications accepted. *Expenses:* Contact institution.

**Marshall B. Ketchum University,** Graduate and Professional Programs, Fullerton, CA 92831-1615. Offers optometry (OD); pharmacy (Pharm D); vision science (MS). *Degree requirements:* For doctorate, thesis/dissertation. *Entrance requirements:* For doctorate, OAT. Electronic applications accepted.

**Marshall University,** Academic Affairs Division, School of Pharmacy, Huntington, WV 25755. Offers Pharm D. *Accreditation:* ACPE.

**MCPHS University,** Graduate Studies, Doctoral Programs in Pharmacy–Boston, Doctor of Pharmacy Program - Boston, Boston, MA 02115-5896. Offers Pharm D. *Accreditation:* ACPE. *Program availability:* Online learning. *Entrance requirements:* For doctorate, SAT (if fewer than 30 semester hours completed), minimum GPA of 2.5, interview. Additional exam requirements/recommendations for international students: required—TOEFL (minimum score 550 paper-based; 79 iBT). Electronic applications accepted.

**MCPHS University,** Graduate Studies, Doctoral Programs in Pharmacy–Boston, Postbaccalaureate Doctor of Pharmacy Pathway Program, Boston, MA 02115-5896. Offers Pharm D. *Program availability:* Part-time, online learning. *Entrance requirements:* For doctorate, registered pharmacist status in the U.S.; working at or have access to a site that provides opportunities to practice pharmaceutical care; curriculum vitae; letter of recommendation. Additional exam requirements/recommendations for international students: required—TOEFL (minimum score 550 paper-based; 79 iBT). Electronic applications accepted.

**MCPHS University,** School of Pharmacy–Worcester/Manchester, Boston, MA 02115-5896. Offers Pharm D. *Accreditation:* ACPE. *Entrance requirements:* Additional exam requirements/recommendations for international students: required—TOEFL (minimum score 550 paper-based; 79 iBT).

**Medical College of Wisconsin,** Pharmacy School, Milwaukee, WI 53226. Offers Pharm D. *Students:* 142 full-time (79 women), 1 part-time (0 women); includes 33 minority (2 Black or African American, non-Hispanic/Latino; 21 Asian, non-Hispanic/Latino; 5 Hispanic/Latino; 1 Native Hawaiian or other Pacific Islander, non-Hispanic/Latino; 4 Two or more races, non-Hispanic/Latino), 1 international. Average age 26. 156 applicants, 51% accepted, 49 enrolled. *Entrance requirements:* For doctorate, interview. *Application deadline:* For fall admission, 6/1 for domestic students. Applications are processed on a rolling basis. Application fee: $175. Electronic applications accepted. *Expenses:* $44,880 per year tuition; $996 per year fees. *Financial support:* Applicants required to submit FAFSA. *Unit head:* Dr. George E. MacKinnon, III, Dean, 414-955-7476, E-mail: gmackinnon@mcw.edu. *Application contact:* Dr. George E. MacKinnon, III, Dean, 414-955-7476, E-mail: gmackinnon@mcw.edu.
Website: http://www.mcw.edu/Pharmacy-School.htm

**Medical University of South Carolina,** South Carolina College of Pharmacy, Charleston, SC 29425. Offers Pharm D. *Accreditation:* ACPE. *Entrance requirements:* For doctorate, PCAT, 2 years of pre-professional course work, interview, minimum GPA

of 2.5. Additional exam requirements/recommendations for international students: required—TOEFL (minimum score 550 paper-based). Electronic applications accepted. *Expenses:* Contact institution.

**Mercer University,** Graduate Studies, Cecil B. Day Campus, College of Pharmacy, Atlanta, GA 31207. Offers pharmaceutical sciences (PhD); pharmacy (Pharm D); Pharm D/MBA; Pharm D/MPH; Pharm D/PhD. *Accreditation:* ACPE (one or more programs are accredited). *Faculty:* 22 full-time (16 women), 15 part-time/adjunct (6 women). *Students:* 573 full-time (388 women), 3 part-time (2 women); includes 366 minority (164 Black or African American, non-Hispanic/Latino; 168 Asian, non-Hispanic/Latino; 22 Hispanic/Latino; 12 Two or more races, non-Hispanic/Latino), 49 international. Average age 26. 677 applicants, 48% accepted, 152 enrolled. In 2019, 144 doctorates awarded. *Degree requirements:* For doctorate, comprehensive exam (for some programs), thesis/dissertation (for some programs). *Entrance requirements:* For doctorate, GRE (for PhD); PCAT, MCAT, DAT, OAT, GRE (for Pharm D), Pharm D or BS in pharmacy or science and minimum GPA of 3.0 (for PhD); 66 hours of undergraduate pre-pharmacy coursework (for PharmD). Additional exam requirements/recommendations for international students: required—TOEFL (minimum score 100 iBT). *Application deadline:* For fall admission, 6/3 for domestic and international students. Applications are processed on a rolling basis. Electronic applications accepted. *Expenses:* Contact institution. *Financial support:* In 2019–20, 238 students received support, including 10 research assistantships with full tuition reimbursements available (averaging $15,000 per year), 35 teaching assistantships with full tuition reimbursements available (averaging $15,000 per year); Federal Work-Study, scholarships/grants, and tuition waivers (full) also available. Financial award application deadline: 5/1; financial award applicants required to submit FAFSA. *Unit head:* Dr. Brian L. Crabtree, Dean, 678-547-6306, Fax: 678-547-6315, E-mail: crabtree_bl@mercer.edu. *Application contact:* Jordana S. Berry, Director of Admissions, 678-547-6182, Fax: 678-547-6518, E-mail: berry_js@mercer.edu.
Website: http://pharmacy.mercer.edu/

**Midwestern University, Downers Grove Campus,** Chicago College of Pharmacy, Downers Grove, IL 60515-1235. Offers Pharm D. *Accreditation:* ACPE. *Program availability:* Part-time, online learning. *Entrance requirements:* For doctorate, PCAT. *Expenses:* Contact institution.

**Midwestern University, Glendale Campus,** College of Pharmacy-Glendale, Glendale, AZ 85308. Offers Pharm D. *Accreditation:* ACPE. *Entrance requirements:* For doctorate, PCAT. *Expenses:* Contact institution.

**North Dakota State University,** College of Graduate and Interdisciplinary Studies, College of Health Professions, School of Pharmacy, Fargo, ND 58102. Offers MS, PhD, Pharm D, Pharm D/MBA, Pharm D/MPH, Pharm D/PhD. *Accreditation:* ACPE. *Program availability:* Part-time. Terminal master's awarded for partial completion of doctoral program. *Entrance requirements:* For master's and doctorate, GRE General Test. Additional exam requirements/recommendations for international students: required—TOEFL. Electronic applications accepted. Tuition and fees vary according to program and reciprocity agreements.

**Northeastern University,** Bouvé College of Health Sciences, Boston, MA 02115-5096. Offers applied behavior analysis (MS); audiology (Au D); counseling psychology (MS, PhD, CAGS); exercise science (MS); nursing (MS, PhD, CAGS), including administration (MS), adult-gerontology acute care nurse practitioner (MS, CAGS), adult-gerontology primary care nurse practitioner (MS, CAGS), anesthesia (MS), family nurse practitioner (MS, CAGS), neonatal nurse practitioner (MS, CAGS), pediatric nurse practitioner (MS, CAGS), psychiatric mental health nurse practitioner (MS, CAGS); nursing practice (DNP); pharmaceutical sciences (MS, PhD), including interdisciplinary concentration, pharmaceutics and drug delivery systems; pharmacology (MS); pharmacy (Pharm D); school psychology (PhD); speech-language pathology (MS); urban health (MPH); MS/MBA. *Accreditation:* AANA/CANAEP; ACPE (one or more programs are accredited); ASHA; CEPH. *Program availability:* Part-time, evening/weekend, online learning. *Degree requirements:* For doctorate, thesis/dissertation (for some programs); for CAGS, comprehensive exam. Electronic applications accepted. *Expenses:* Contact institution.

**Northeast Ohio Medical University,** College of Pharmacy, Rootstown, OH 44272-0095. Offers Pharm D. *Accreditation:* ACPE. *Faculty:* 45 full-time (21 women), 620 part-time/adjunct (356 women). *Students:* 340 full-time (202 women); includes 88 minority (32 Black or African American, non-Hispanic/Latino; 36 Asian, non-Hispanic/Latino; 10 Hispanic/Latino; 10 Two or more races, non-Hispanic/Latino). Average age 26. 479 applicants, 35% accepted, 92 enrolled. In 2019, 67 doctorates awarded. *Entrance requirements:* For doctorate, Pharmacy College Application Service (PharmCAS) application. *Application deadline:* For fall admission, 6/1 for domestic students. Applications are processed on a rolling basis. Application fee: $175. Electronic applications accepted. *Expenses:* Tuition, student health & fitness, student activities, academic software/hardware fee, credentialing, testing, course fees. *Financial support:* In 2019–20, 100 students received support. Scholarships/grants available. Financial award application deadline: 3/15; financial award applicants required to submit FAFSA. *Unit head:* Dr. Richard Kasmer, Pharm.D., J.D., Dean, 330-325-6461, Fax: 330-325-5951, E-mail: rkasmer@neomed.edu. *Application contact:* James Barrett, Sr. Executive Director, Strategic Enrollment Initiative, 330-325-6274, E-mail: admission@neomed.edu.
Website: https://www.neomed.edu/pharmacy/academics/

**Notre Dame of Maryland University,** Graduate Studies, Program in Pharmacy, Baltimore, MD 21210-2476. Offers Pharm D. *Accreditation:* ACPE.

**Nova Southeastern University,** College of Pharmacy, Fort Lauderdale, FL 33314-7796. Offers pharmaceutical affairs (MS); pharmaceutical sciences (MS, PhD), including drug development, molecular medicine and pharmacogenomics, social and administrative pharmacy; pharmacy (Pharm D); Pharm D/MBA; Pharm D/MPH; Pharm D/MSBI. *Accreditation:* ACPE. *Faculty:* 51 full-time (29 women), 9 part-time/adjunct (3 women). *Students:* 969 full-time (663 women), 16 part-time (11 women); includes 763 minority (64 Black or African American, non-Hispanic/Latino; 114 Asian, non-Hispanic/Latino; 564 Hispanic/Latino; 1 Native Hawaiian or other Pacific Islander, non-Hispanic/Latino; 20 Two or more races, non-Hispanic/Latino), 72 international. Average age 27. 723 applicants, 32% accepted, 230 enrolled. In 2019, 254 doctorates awarded. Terminal master's awarded for partial completion of doctoral program. *Degree requirements:* For master's, thesis or alternative; for doctorate, comprehensive exam, thesis/dissertation. *Entrance requirements:* For master's, PCAT or GRE (for pharmaceutical affairs); GRE (for pharmaceutical sciences); for doctorate, PCAT (for Pharm D); GRE (for PhD). *Application deadline:* For fall admission, 3/15 for international students. Applications are processed on a rolling basis. Application fee: $50. Electronic applications accepted. Tuition and fees vary according to course load, degree level and program. *Financial support:* In 2019–20, 62 students received support, including 12 teaching assistantships with full tuition reimbursements available (averaging $45,465 per year); career-related internships or fieldwork, Federal Work-Study, scholarships/grants, tuition waivers (full), and unspecified assistantships also available. Financial award application deadline: 4/15; financial award applicants required to submit FAFSA. *Unit head:* Dr. Michelle Clark, Dean, 954-262-1384, Fax: 954-262-2282, E-mail: miclark@nova.edu. *Application contact:* Rose Llanos-Almeida, Assistant Director II, Graduate Admissions, 954-262-1193, Fax: 954-262-2282, E-mail: rllanos@nova.edu.
Website: http://pharmacy.nova.edu/

**Ohio Northern University,** Raabe College of Pharmacy, Ada, OH 45810-1599. Offers Pharm D. *Accreditation:* ACPE. *Degree requirements:* For doctorate, 9 clinical rotations, capstone course. *Entrance requirements:* For doctorate, ACT or SAT. Additional exam requirements/recommendations for international students: required—TOEFL (minimum score 550 paper-based; 80 iBT). *Expenses:* Contact institution.

**The Ohio State University,** College of Pharmacy, Columbus, OH 43210. Offers MS, PhD, Pharm D, Pharm D/MBA, Pharm D/MPH, Pharm D/PhD. *Accreditation:* ACPE (one or more programs are accredited). Terminal master's awarded for partial completion of doctoral program. *Degree requirements:* For doctorate, comprehensive exam (for some programs), thesis/dissertation (for some programs). *Entrance requirements:* For master's, GRE General Test, minimum GPA of 3.0; for doctorate, GRE General Test; PCAT (for PharmD), minimum GPA of 3.0. Additional exam requirements/recommendations for international students: required—TOEFL minimum score 600 paper-based, 100 iBT (for MS and PhD); TOEFL minimum score 577 paper-based; 90 iBT, Michigan English Language Assessment Battery minimum score 84, IELTS minimum score 7.5 (for PharmD). Electronic applications accepted. *Expenses:* Contact institution.

**Oregon State University,** College of Pharmacy, Pharmacy Doctoral Program, Corvallis, OR 97331. Offers Pharm D. *Accreditation:* ACPE. *Expenses:* Contact institution.

**Pacific University,** School of Pharmacy, Forest Grove, OR 97116-1797. Offers Pharm D. *Accreditation:* ACPE. *Entrance requirements:* Additional exam requirements/recommendations for international students: required—TOEFL (minimum score 600 paper-based). Electronic applications accepted. *Expenses:* Contact institution.

**Palm Beach Atlantic University,** Gregory School of Pharmacy, West Palm Beach, FL 33416-4708. Offers Pharm D, Pharm D/MBA. *Accreditation:* ACPE. *Entrance requirements:* For doctorate, PCAT, minimum GPA of 2.75. Additional exam requirements/recommendations for international students: required—TOEFL (minimum score 550 paper-based; 79 iBT). Electronic applications accepted. *Expenses:* Contact institution.

**Presbyterian College,** Presbyterian College School of Pharmacy (PCSP), Clinton, SC 29325. Offers Pharm D. *Accreditation:* ACPE. *Degree requirements:* For doctorate, comprehensive exam. *Entrance requirements:* For doctorate, PCAT, PharmD. Electronic applications accepted.

**Purdue University,** College of Pharmacy, Professional Program in Pharmacy and Pharmacal Sciences, West Lafayette, IN 47907. Offers Pharm D. *Accreditation:* ACPE. *Students:* 604 full-time (400 women), 7 part-time (3 women); includes 179 minority (26 Black or African American, non-Hispanic/Latino; 3 American Indian or Alaska Native, non-Hispanic/Latino; 110 Asian, non-Hispanic/Latino; 24 Hispanic/Latino; 16 Two or more races, non-Hispanic/Latino), 16 international. Average age 22. 364 applicants, 46% accepted, 150 enrolled. *Entrance requirements:* For doctorate, minimum 2 years of pre-pharmacy course work, interview. *Application deadline:* For fall admission, 12/2 for domestic and international students. Application fee: $60 ($75 for international students). *Expenses:* Contact institution. *Financial support:* Career-related internships or fieldwork, Federal Work-Study, and scholarships/grants available. Financial award application deadline: 3/15; financial award applicants required to submit FAFSA. *Unit head:* Eric L. Barker, Dean, 765-494-1368, Fax: 765-494-7880, E-mail: barkerel@purdue.edu. *Application contact:* Danzhou Yang, Associate Dean for Research and Graduate Programs, 765-494-1362, E-mail: yangdz@purdue.edu.

**Regis University,** Rueckert-Hartman College for Health Professions, Denver, CO 80221-1099. Offers advanced practice nurse (DNP); counseling (MA); counseling children and adolescents (Post-Graduate Certificate); counseling military families (Post-Graduate Certificate); depth psychotherapy (Post-Graduate Certificate); fellowship in orthopedic manual physical therapy (Certificate); health care business management (Certificate); health care quality and patient safety (Certificate); health industry leadership (MBA); health services administration (MS); marriage and family therapy (MA, Post-Graduate Certificate); neonatal nurse practitioner (MSN); nursing education (MSN); nursing leadership (MSN); occupational therapy (OTD); pharmacy (Pharm D); physical therapy (DPT). *Accreditation:* ACPE. *Program availability:* Part-time, evening/weekend, 100% online, blended/hybrid learning. *Degree requirements:* For master's, thesis (for some programs), internship. *Entrance requirements:* For master's, official transcript reflecting baccalaureate degree awarded from regionally-accredited college or university. Additional exam requirements/recommendations for international students: required—TOEFL (minimum score 550 paper-based; 82 iBT). Electronic applications accepted. *Expenses:* Contact institution.

**Roosevelt University,** Graduate Division, College of Pharmacy, Chicago, IL 60605. Offers Pharm D. *Accreditation:* ACPE. Electronic applications accepted. *Expenses:* Contact institution.

**Rosalind Franklin University of Medicine and Science,** College of Pharmacy, North Chicago, IL 60064-3095. Offers Pharm D. *Accreditation:* ACPE.

**Roseman University of Health Sciences,** College of Pharmacy, Henderson, NV 89014. Offers Pharm D. *Accreditation:* ACPE. *Degree requirements:* For doctorate, comprehensive exam. *Entrance requirements:* For doctorate, PCAT or bachelor's degree. Electronic applications accepted. *Expenses:* Contact institution.

**Rutgers University - New Brunswick,** Ernest Mario School of Pharmacy, Piscataway, NJ 08854-8097. Offers medicinal chemistry (MS, PhD); pharmaceutical science (MS, PhD); pharmacy (Pharm D). *Accreditation:* ACPE. *Degree requirements:* For doctorate, variable foreign language requirement. *Entrance requirements:* For doctorate, SAT or PCAT (for Pharm D), interview, criminal background check (for Pharm D). Additional exam requirements/recommendations for international students: recommended—TOEFL (minimum score 550 paper-based). Electronic applications accepted. *Expenses:* Contact institution.

**St. John Fisher College,** Wegmans School of Pharmacy, Doctor of Pharmacy Program, Rochester, NY 14618-3597. Offers Pharm D. *Accreditation:* ACPE. *Faculty:* 21 full-time (12 women). *Students:* 278 full-time (170 women), 11 part-time (4 women); includes 60 minority (8 Black or African American, non-Hispanic/Latino; 38 Asian, non-Hispanic/Latino; 6 Hispanic/Latino; 8 Two or more races, non-Hispanic/Latino), 3 international. Average age 24. 269 applicants, 43% accepted, 67 enrolled. In 2019, 79 doctorates awarded. *Degree requirements:* For doctorate, advanced pharmacy practice experience. *Entrance requirements:* For doctorate, PCAT, 2 letters of recommendation, interview, minimum of 62 credit hours of specific undergraduate courses. Additional exam requirements/recommendations for international students: required—TOEFL (minimum score 575 paper-based; 80 iBT). *Application deadline:* For fall admission, 3/1 for domestic students. Applications are processed on a rolling basis. Application fee: $30. Electronic applications accepted. *Expenses:* Contact institution. *Financial support:* Scholarships/grants available. Financial award applicants required to submit FAFSA. *Unit head:* Dr. Christine Birnie, Dean of the School of Pharmacy, 585-385-7202, E-mail: cbirnie@sjfc.edu. *Application contact:* Michelle Gosier, Director of Transfer and

Graduate Admissions, 585-385-8064, E-mail: mgosier@sjfc.edu.
Website: https://www.sjfc.edu/graduate-programs/doctor-of-pharmacy-pharmd/

**St. John's University,** College of Pharmacy and Health Sciences, Queens, NY 11439. Offers MPH, MS, PhD. *Accreditation:* ACPE (one or more programs are accredited). *Program availability:* Part-time, evening/weekend. Terminal master's awarded for partial completion of doctoral program. *Degree requirements:* For master's, comprehensive exam (for some programs), thesis (for some programs); for doctorate, comprehensive exam, thesis/dissertation, residency requirement: 24 credits in first two academic years. *Entrance requirements:* For master's and doctorate, GRE General Test, letters of recommendation, transcripts, resume, personal statement. Additional exam requirements/recommendations for international students: required—TOEFL (minimum score 100 iBT), IELTS (minimum score 7). Electronic applications accepted. *Expenses:* Contact institution.

**St. Louis College of Pharmacy,** School of Pharmacy, St. Louis, MO 63110. Offers Pharm D. *Accreditation:* ACPE. *Faculty:* 37 full-time (23 women), 43 part-time/adjunct (31 women). *Students:* 679 full-time (427 women), 25 part-time (14 women); includes 248 minority (72 Black or African American, non-Hispanic/Latino; 1 American Indian or Alaska Native, non-Hispanic/Latino; 150 Asian, non-Hispanic/Latino; 15 Hispanic/Latino; 10 Two or more races, non-Hispanic/Latino), 28 international. Average age 25. 292 applicants, 59% accepted, 154 enrolled. In 2019, 241 doctorates awarded. *Entrance requirements:* For doctorate, PCAT. Additional exam requirements/recommendations for international students: required—TOEFL (minimum score 550 paper-based); recommended—IELTS. *Application deadline:* For fall admission, 3/1 for domestic and international students. Applications are processed on a rolling basis. Application fee: $55. Electronic applications accepted. Application fee is waived when completed online. *Expenses: Tuition:* Full-time $37,153; part-time $1161 per credit hour. *Required fees:* $600; $600. Part-time tuition and fees vary according to course load. *Financial support:* In 2019–20, 389 students received support. Federal Work-Study and scholarships/grants available. Financial award application deadline: 3/15; financial award applicants required to submit FAFSA. *Unit head:* Dr. Brenda Gleason, Interim Dean of Pharmacy, 314-446-8184. *Application contact:* Jill Gebke, Director of Admissions, 314-446-8140, Fax: 314-446-8309, E-mail: jill.gebke@stlcop.edu.
Website: www.stlcop.edu

**Samford University,** McWhorter School of Pharmacy, Birmingham, AL 35229. Offers Pharm D, Pharm D/MBA, Pharm D/MPH. *Accreditation:* ACPE. *Faculty:* 34 full-time (23 women), 1 part-time/adjunct (0 women). *Students:* 461 full-time (300 women), 8 part-time (6 women); includes 102 minority (50 Black or African American, non-Hispanic/Latino; 3 American Indian or Alaska Native, non-Hispanic/Latino; 27 Asian, non-Hispanic/Latino; 18 Hispanic/Latino; 4 Two or more races, non-Hispanic/Latino), 2 international. Average age 24. 331 applicants, 38% accepted, 125 enrolled. In 2019, 123 doctorates awarded. *Degree requirements:* For doctorate, thesis/dissertation. *Entrance requirements:* For doctorate, overall GPA greater than or equal to 2.75 plus overall GPA of at least 2.0 in the math/science prerequisite courses to be considered for an admissions interview. Additional exam requirements/recommendations for international students: required—TOEFL (minimum score 575 paper-based; 90 iBT). *Application deadline:* For fall admission, 6/1 priority date for domestic and international students. Applications are processed on a rolling basis. Electronic applications accepted. *Expenses:* 2019-20 tuition $38,521 ($16,853 spring, $4,815 May IPPE) 2019-20 Fees $550. *Financial support:* In 2019–20, 243 students received support. Institutionally sponsored loans and scholarships/grants available. Financial award application deadline: 2/15; financial award applicants required to submit FAFSA. *Unit head:* Dr. Michael Crouch, PharmD, BCPS, Dean/Professor, 205-726-4475, E-mail: mcrouch@samford.edu. *Application contact:* Jonathan Parker, MA, EdS, Director of Pharmacy Admissions, 205-726-4242, E-mail: jmparker@samford.edu.
Website: https://www.samford.edu/pharmacy

**Shenandoah University,** Doctor of Pharmacy, Winchester, VA 22601-5195. Offers Pharm D. *Accreditation:* ACPE. *Program availability:* Online only, 100% online. *Faculty:* 30 full-time (19 women), 6 part-time/adjunct (3 women). *Students:* 317 full-time (219 women), 2 part-time (both women); includes 54 minority (25 Black or African American, non-Hispanic/Latino; 1 American Indian or Alaska Native, non-Hispanic/Latino; 16 Asian, non-Hispanic/Latino; 7 Hispanic/Latino; 1 Native Hawaiian or other Pacific Islander, non-Hispanic/Latino; 4 Two or more races, non-Hispanic/Latino), 15 international. Average age 26. 260 applicants, 73% accepted, 76 enrolled. In 2019, 63 doctorates awarded. *Entrance requirements:* For doctorate, PCAT, 63 credits of prerequisites, essay, interview, minimum GPA of 2.5, 3 letters of recommendation. Additional exam requirements/recommendations for international students: required—TOEFL (minimum score 21 paper-based; 79 iBT), TOEFL (minimum score 21 paper-based, 79 iBT) OR IELTS (6.5). *Application deadline:* For fall admission, 6/1 for domestic and international students. Applications are processed on a rolling basis. Application fee: $30. Electronic applications accepted. *Expenses:* 165 per term full-time student services fee (fall and spring only), $175 per term full-time technology fee, $305 per term iMLearning fee, curriculum fees, $260 per term Pharmacy Clinical Fee (charged to 1st through 3rd year students). *Financial support:* In 2019–20, 18 students received support. Scholarships/grants available. Financial award application deadline: 7/1; financial award applicants required to submit FAFSA. *Unit head:* Robert DiCenzo, PhD, Dean of Pharmacy, 540-665-1280, Fax: 540-665-1283, E-mail: rdicenzo@su.edu. *Application contact:* Katelyn M Sanders, Pharm.D., Director Admissions Pharmacy Practice, 540-678-4377, Fax: 540-665-1283, E-mail: ksanders@su.edu.
Website: http://www.pharmacy.su.edu

**South College,** Program in Pharmacy, Knoxville, TN 37917. Offers Pharm D. *Accreditation:* ACPE. *Entrance requirements:* For doctorate, PharmCAS application.

**South Dakota State University,** Graduate School, College of Pharmacy and Allied Health Professions, Professional Program in Pharmacy, Brookings, SD 57007. Offers Pharm D. *Accreditation:* ACPE. *Entrance requirements:* For doctorate, ACT or PCAT, bachelor's degree in pharmacy. Additional exam requirements/recommendations for international students: required—TOEFL (minimum score 550 paper-based).

**Southern Illinois University Edwardsville,** School of Pharmacy, Edwardsville, IL 62026. Offers pharmacy education (Pharm D); pharmacy pediatrics (Pharm D). *Accreditation:* ACPE. *Entrance requirements:* For doctorate, PCAT. Electronic applications accepted.

**South University - Columbia,** Program in Pharmacy, Columbia, SC 29203. Offers Pharm D.

**South University - Savannah,** Graduate Programs, School of Pharmacy, Savannah, GA 31406. Offers Pharm D/MBA. *Accreditation:* ACPE.

**Southwestern Oklahoma State University,** College of Pharmacy, Weatherford, OK 73096-3098. Offers pharmacy (Pharm D); pharmacy leadership (Pharm D). *Accreditation:* ACPE. *Entrance requirements:* For doctorate, PCAT.

**Sullivan University,** College of Pharmacy, Louisville, KY 40205. Offers Pharm D. *Accreditation:* ACPE. *Expenses: Tuition:* Full-time $21,120; part-time $660 per quarter hour. One-time fee: $30 full-time. Tuition and fees vary according to course load and degree level.

**Temple University,** School of Pharmacy, Philadelphia, PA 19122-6096. Offers MS, PhD, Pharm D. *Accreditation:* ACPE (one or more programs are accredited). *Program availability:* Part-time, evening/weekend, online learning. *Faculty:* 33 full-time (16 women), 38 part-time/adjunct (15 women). *Students:* 596 full-time (331 women), 222 part-time (153 women); includes 369 minority (62 Black or African American, non-Hispanic/Latino; 173 Asian, non-Hispanic/Latino; 23 Hispanic/Latino; 111 Two or more races, non-Hispanic/Latino), 49 international. 550 applicants, 55% accepted, 199 enrolled. In 2019, 89 master's, 139 doctorates awarded. Terminal master's awarded for partial completion of doctoral program. *Entrance requirements:* For master's, GRE General Test, minimum undergraduate GPA of 3.0; for doctorate, GRE General Test, PCAT, minimum GPA of 3.0. Additional exam requirements/recommendations for international students: required—TOEFL (minimum score 550 paper-based; 82 iBT), IELTS, PTE, one of three is required. Application fee: $60. Electronic applications accepted. *Expenses:* Contact institution. *Financial support:* Fellowships, research assistantships, teaching assistantships, Federal Work-Study, and unspecified assistantships available. Financial award application deadline: 3/1; financial award applicants required to submit FAFSA. *Unit head:* Michael Borenstein, Interim Dean, 215-707-2976, E-mail: michael.borenstein@temple.edu. *Application contact:* Joan Hankins, Director of Admissions, 215-707-4900, E-mail: joan.hankins@temple.edu.
Website: http://www.temple.edu/pharmacy/

**Texas A&M University,** Irma Lerma Rangel College of Pharmacy, Kingsville, TX 77843. Offers Pharm D. *Accreditation:* ACPE. *Entrance requirements:* For doctorate, PCAT, transcripts from each college/university attended; 3 PharmCAS recommendations. Additional exam requirements/recommendations for international students: required—TOEFL (minimum score 550 paper-based; 80 iBT). Electronic applications accepted. *Expenses:* Contact institution.

**Texas Southern University,** College of Pharmacy and Health Sciences, Department of Pharmacy Practice, Houston, TX 77004-4584. Offers Pharm D. *Accreditation:* ACPE. *Program availability:* Online learning. *Entrance requirements:* For doctorate, GRE General Test, PCAT. Electronic applications accepted.

**Texas Tech University Health Sciences Center,** Pharm D Program, Lubbock, TX 79430. Offers Pharm D.

**Thomas Jefferson University,** Jefferson College of Pharmacy, Philadelphia, PA 19107. Offers Pharm D. *Accreditation:* ACPE. *Degree requirements:* For doctorate, 141 semester credits. *Entrance requirements:* For doctorate, PCAT. Additional exam requirements/recommendations for international students: required—TOEFL (minimum score 87 iBT), PCAT. Electronic applications accepted.

**Touro University California,** Graduate Programs, Vallejo, CA 94592. Offers education (MA); medical health sciences (MS); osteopathic medicine (DO); pharmacy (Pharm D); public health (MPH). *Accreditation:* ACPE; AOsA; ARC-PA; CEPH. *Program availability:* Part-time, evening/weekend. *Degree requirements:* For master's, comprehensive exam, thesis; for doctorate, comprehensive exam. *Entrance requirements:* For doctorate, BS/BA. Electronic applications accepted.

**Union University,** College of Pharmacy, Jackson, TN 38305-3697. Offers Pharm D. *Accreditation:* ACPE. *Entrance requirements:* For doctorate, PCAT. Additional exam requirements/recommendations for international students: required—TOEFL (minimum score 80 paper-based). Electronic applications accepted. *Expenses:* Contact institution.

**Universidad de Ciencias Medicas,** Graduate Programs, San Jose, Costa Rica. Offers dermatology (SP); family health (MS); health service center administration (MHA); human anatomy (MS); medical and surgery (MD); occupational medicine (MS); pharmacy (Pharm D). *Program availability:* Part-time. *Degree requirements:* For master's, thesis; for doctorate and SP, comprehensive exam. *Entrance requirements:* For master's, MD or bachelor's degree; for doctorate, admissions test; for SP, admissions test, MD.

**University at Buffalo, the State University of New York,** Graduate School, School of Pharmacy and Pharmaceutical Sciences, Professional Program in Pharmacy, Buffalo, NY 14260. Offers Pharm D, Pharm D/JD, Pharm D/MBA, Pharm D/MPH, Pharm D/MS, Pharm D/PhD. *Accreditation:* ACPE. *Faculty:* 30 full-time (12 women), 4 part-time/adjunct (3 women). *Students:* 488 full-time (289 women), 10 part-time (3 women); includes 184 minority (24 Black or African American, non-Hispanic/Latino; 158 Asian, non-Hispanic/Latino; 2 Hispanic/Latino), 40 international. Average age 24. 376 applicants, 35% accepted, 132 enrolled. In 2019, 131 doctorates awarded. *Degree requirements:* For doctorate, project. *Entrance requirements:* For doctorate, PCAT, GRE, LSAT, MCAT, GMAT, DAT. Additional exam requirements/recommendations for international students: required—TOEFL (minimum score 550 paper-based; 79 iBT); recommended—IELTS, TSE. *Application deadline:* For fall admission, 2/1 priority date for domestic and international students. Applications are processed on a rolling basis. Application fee: $50. Electronic applications accepted. *Expenses:* Contact institution. *Financial support:* In 2019–20, 232 students received support. Scholarships/grants available. Financial award application deadline: 3/1; financial award applicants required to submit FAFSA. *Unit head:* Dr. William Prescott, Interim Chair, 716-645-4780, Fax: 716-829-6568, E-mail: prescott@buffalo.edu. *Application contact:* Dr. Jennifer M. Rosenberg, Associate Dean, 716-645-2825 Ext. 1, Fax: 716-829-6568, E-mail: prepharm@buffalo.edu.
Website: http://pharmacy.buffalo.edu/departments-offices/pharmacy-practice.html

**University of Alberta,** Faculty of Pharmacy and Pharmaceutical Sciences, Edmonton, AB T6G 2E1, Canada. Offers M Sc, PhD. Terminal master's awarded for partial completion of doctoral program. *Degree requirements:* For master's, thesis; for doctorate, thesis/dissertation. *Entrance requirements:* Additional exam requirements/recommendations for international students: required—Michigan English Language Assessment Battery or IELTS. Electronic applications accepted.

**The University of Arizona,** College of Pharmacy, Pharmacy Professional Program, Tucson, AZ 85721. Offers Pharm D. *Accreditation:* ACPE. *Program availability:* Part-time. *Entrance requirements:* For doctorate, PCAT, 4-6 months of pharmacy experience. Additional exam requirements/recommendations for international students: required—TOEFL (minimum score 550 paper-based; 79 iBT). Electronic applications accepted.

**University of Arkansas for Medical Sciences,** College of Pharmacy, Little Rock, AR 72205-7199. Offers MS, Pharm D. *Accreditation:* ACPE (one or more programs are accredited). *Degree requirements:* For master's, thesis. *Entrance requirements:* For master's, GRE; for doctorate, PCAT. Additional exam requirements/recommendations for international students: recommended—TOEFL. Electronic applications accepted. *Expenses:* Contact institution.

**The University of British Columbia,** Faculty of Pharmaceutical Sciences, Vancouver, BC V6T 1Z3, Canada. Offers M Sc, PhD, Pharm D. *Degree requirements:* For master's, thesis, seminar; for doctorate, comprehensive exam, thesis/dissertation, seminar. *Entrance requirements:* Additional exam requirements/recommendations for international students: required—TOEFL (minimum score 600 paper-based; 100 iBT), IELTS (minimum score 6.5). Electronic applications accepted. *Expenses:* Contact institution.

**University of California, San Diego,** Skaggs School of Pharmacy and Pharmaceutical Sciences, La Jolla, CA 92093. Offers Pharm D, Pharm D/PhD. *Accreditation:* ACPE.

*Students:* 252. *Unit head:* Dr. James McKerrow, Dean, 858-822-7801. *Application contact:* Dr. James McKerrow, Dean, 858-822-7801.
Website: http://www.pharmacy.ucsd.edu/

**University of California, San Francisco,** School of Pharmacy, Program in Pharmacy, San Francisco, CA 94143. Offers Pharm D. *Accreditation:* ACPE. *Degree requirements:* For doctorate, comprehensive exam, supervised practice experience. *Entrance requirements:* For doctorate, 2 years of preparatory course work in basic sciences. Electronic applications accepted.

**University of Charleston,** School of Pharmacy, Charleston, WV 25304-1099. Offers Pharm D. *Accreditation:* ACPE. *Degree requirements:* For doctorate, minimum cumulative GPA of 2.3 for all courses. *Entrance requirements:* For doctorate, PCAT (taken within 3 years of the date of application), criminal background check, proof of health insurance, immunizations and health clearance, minimum undergraduate GPA of 2.75, two letters of recommendation, interview. Additional exam requirements/recommendations for international students: required—TOEFL. Electronic applications accepted.

**University of Cincinnati,** James L. Winkle College of Pharmacy, Division of Pharmacy Practice, Cincinnati, OH 45221. Offers Pharm D. *Accreditation:* ACPE. *Entrance requirements:* For doctorate, GRE General Test, BS in pharmacy or equivalent, minimum GPA of 3.0. Additional exam requirements/recommendations for international students: required—TOEFL.

**University of Colorado Denver,** Skaggs School of Pharmacy and Pharmaceutical Sciences, Doctor of Pharmacy Program, Aurora, CO 80045. Offers Pharm D. *Accreditation:* ACPE. *Program availability:* Online learning. Tuition and fees vary according to course load, program and reciprocity agreements.

**University of Connecticut,** Graduate School, School of Pharmacy, Professional Program in Pharmacy, Storrs, CT 06269. Offers Pharm D. *Accreditation:* ACPE.

**The University of Findlay,** Office of Graduate Admissions, Findlay, OH 45840. Offers applied security and analytics (MSAS); athletic training (MAT); business (MBA), including certified management accountant, certified public accountant, health care management, hospitality management; education (MA Ed, Ed D), including children's literature (MA Ed), curriculum and teaching (MA Ed), education (MA Ed), educational administration (MA Ed), human resource development (MA Ed), mathematics (MA Ed), reading (MA Ed), science education (MA Ed), superintendent (Ed D), teaching (Ed D), technology (MA Ed); environmental, safety, and health management (MSEM); health informatics (MS); occupational therapy (MOT); pharmacy (Pharm D); physical therapy (DPT); physician assistant (MPA); rhetoric and writing (MA); teaching English to speakers of other languages (TESOL) and applied linguistics (MA). *Program availability:* Part-time, evening/weekend, 100% online, blended/hybrid learning. *Students:* 688 full-time (430 women), 553 part-time (308 women), 170 international. Average age 28. 865 applicants, 31% accepted, 235 enrolled. In 2019, 363 master's, 141 doctorates awarded. *Degree requirements:* For master's, comprehensive exam (for some programs), thesis (for some programs), cumulative project, capstone project; for doctorate, thesis/dissertation (for some programs). *Entrance requirements:* For master's, GRE/GMAT, bachelor's degree from accredited institution, minimum undergraduate GPA of 2.5 in last 64 hours of course work; for doctorate, GRE, MAT, minimum cumulative GPA of 3.0. Additional exam requirements/recommendations for international students: required—TOEFL (minimum score 79 iBT), IELTS (minimum score 7), PTE (minimum score 61). *Application deadline:* Applications are processed on a rolling basis. Electronic applications accepted. *Financial support:* In 2019–20, 10 research assistantships with partial tuition reimbursements (averaging $7,200 per year), 35 teaching assistantships with partial tuition reimbursements (averaging $7,200 per year) were awarded; Federal Work-Study, institutionally sponsored loans, and unspecified assistantships also available. Financial award applicants required to submit FAFSA. *Unit head:* Dave M. Emsweller, Director of Admissions, Interim, 419-434-4578, E-mail: emsweller@findlay.edu. *Application contact:* Amber Feehan, Graduate Admissions Counselor, 419-434-6933, Fax: 419-434-4898, E-mail: feehan@findlay.edu. Website: http://www.findlay.edu/admissions/graduate/Pages/default.aspx

**University of Florida,** Graduate School, College of Pharmacy, Graduate Programs in Pharmacy, Department of Pharmaceutics, Gainesville, FL 32611. Offers clinical and translational sciences (PhD); pharmaceutical sciences (MSP, PhD); pharmacy (MSP, PhD). *Degree requirements:* For doctorate, comprehensive exam, thesis/dissertation. *Entrance requirements:* For master's and doctorate, GRE General Test, minimum GPA of 3.0. Additional exam requirements/recommendations for international students: required—TOEFL (minimum score 550 paper-based; 80 iBT), IELTS (minimum score 6). Electronic applications accepted.

**University of Florida,** Graduate School, College of Pharmacy, Professional Program in Pharmacy, Gainesville, FL 32611. Offers Pharm D, MBA/Pharm D, Pharm D/MPH, Pharm D/PhD. *Accreditation:* ACPE. *Program availability:* Part-time, online learning. *Entrance requirements:* For doctorate, PCAT, minimum GPA of 2.5. Additional exam requirements/recommendations for international students: required—TOEFL. Electronic applications accepted.

**University of Georgia,** College of Pharmacy, Athens, GA 30602. Offers MS, PhD, Pharm D, Certificate. *Accreditation:* ACPE (one or more programs are accredited). *Degree requirements:* For doctorate, variable foreign language requirement, thesis/dissertation (for some programs). *Entrance requirements:* For master's, GRE General Test, minimum GPA of 3.0; for doctorate, GRE General Test (for PhD), minimum GPA of 3.0 (for PhD). Additional exam requirements/recommendations for international students: required—TOEFL (minimum score 80 iBT). Electronic applications accepted. *Expenses:* Contact institution.

**University of Hawaii at Hilo,** Program in Pharmacy, Hilo, HI 96720-4091. Offers Pharm D. *Accreditation:* ACPE. Electronic applications accepted.

**University of Houston,** College of Pharmacy, Houston, TX 77204. Offers pharmaceutics (MSPHR, PhD); pharmacology (MSPHR, PhD); pharmacy (Pharm D); pharmacy administration (MSPHR, PhD). *Accreditation:* ACPE. *Program availability:* Part-time. Terminal master's awarded for partial completion of doctoral program. *Entrance requirements:* For doctorate, PCAT (for Pharm D). Additional exam requirements/recommendations for international students: required—TOEFL. Electronic applications accepted.

**University of Illinois at Chicago,** College of Pharmacy, Professional Program in Pharmacy, Chicago, IL 60607-7128. Offers Pharm D. *Accreditation:* ACPE. *Entrance requirements:* For doctorate, PCAT. *Expenses:* Contact institution.

**The University of Iowa,** College of Pharmacy, Iowa City, IA 52242-1316. Offers clinical pharmaceutical sciences (PhD); medicinal and natural products chemistry (PhD); pharmaceutical socioeconomics (PhD); pharmaceutics (MS, PhD); pharmacy (Pharm D); Pharm D/MPH. *Accreditation:* ACPE (one or more programs are accredited). *Degree requirements:* For master's, thesis optional, exam; for doctorate, comprehensive exam, thesis/dissertation. *Entrance requirements:* For master's and doctorate, GRE General Test, minimum GPA of 3.0. Additional exam requirements/recommendations for international students: required—TOEFL (minimum score 550 paper-based; 81 iBT). Electronic applications accepted.

**The University of Kansas,** Graduate Studies, School of Pharmacy, Lawrence, KS 66045. Offers MS, PhD. *Accreditation:* ACPE (one or more programs are accredited). *Students:* 75 full-time (37 women), 16 part-time (6 women); includes 12 minority (1 Black or African American, non-Hispanic/Latino; 5 Asian, non-Hispanic/Latino; 4 Hispanic/Latino; 2 Two or more races, non-Hispanic/Latino), 39 international. Average age 28. 149 applicants, 28% accepted, 23 enrolled. In 2019, 18 master's, 15 doctorates awarded. *Entrance requirements:* For master's and doctorate, GRE General Test, curriculum vitae, personal statement, official transcripts. Additional exam requirements/recommendations for international students: required—TOEFL, IELTS, TOEFL or IELTS. Application fee: $65 ($85 for international students). Electronic applications accepted. *Expenses:* Tuition, state resident: full-time $9989. Tuition, nonresident: full-time $23,950. *International tuition:* $23,950 full-time. *Required fees:* $984; $81.99 per credit hour. Tuition and fees vary according to course load, campus/location and program. *Financial support:* Fellowships, research assistantships, teaching assistantships, career-related internships or fieldwork, scholarships/grants, traineeships, and unspecified assistantships available. *Unit head:* Kenneth L. Audus, Dean, 785-864-3591, E-mail: audus@ku.edu. *Application contact:* Patti Steffan, Graduate Admissions Contact, 785-864-3893, E-mail: psteffan@ku.edu.
Website: http://pharmacy.ku.edu/

**University of Kentucky,** Graduate School, Professional Program in Pharmacy, Lexington, KY 40506-0032. Offers Pharm D. *Accreditation:* ACPE. *Entrance requirements:* For doctorate, PCAT, interview, minimum GPA of 2.5. Additional exam requirements/recommendations for international students: required—TOEFL (minimum score 527 paper-based). Electronic applications accepted. *Expenses:* Contact institution.

**University of Louisiana at Monroe,** Graduate School, College of Pharmacy, Monroe, LA 71209-0001. Offers pharmacy (PhD); toxicology (PhD). *Accreditation:* ACPE. *Faculty:* 19 full-time (10 women). *Students:* 371 full-time (228 women), 1 part-time (0 women); includes 91 minority (42 Black or African American, non-Hispanic/Latino; 2 American Indian or Alaska Native, non-Hispanic/Latino; 32 Asian, non-Hispanic/Latino; 6 Hispanic/Latino; 9 Two or more races, non-Hispanic/Latino), 29 international. Average age 24. 147 applicants, 66% accepted, 86 enrolled. In 2019, 104 doctorates awarded. *Degree requirements:* For doctorate, comprehensive exam, thesis/dissertation (for some programs). *Entrance requirements:* For doctorate, GRE General Test; PCAT, minimum undergraduate GPA of 2.5. Additional exam requirements/recommendations for international students: required—TOEFL (minimum score 500 paper-based; 61 iBT); recommended—IELTS (minimum score 5.5). *Application deadline:* For fall admission, 3/1 for domestic and international students; for spring admission, 9/1 for domestic and international students. Applications are processed on a rolling basis. Electronic applications accepted. *Expenses:* Contact institution. *Financial support:* In 2019–20, 130 students received support. Research assistantships with full tuition reimbursements available, career-related internships or fieldwork, Federal Work-Study, scholarships/grants, and unspecified assistantships available. Financial award application deadline: 2/15; financial award applicants required to submit FAFSA. *Unit head:* Dr. Glenn Anderson, Dean, 318-342-1600, E-mail: ganderson@ulm.edu. *Application contact:* Dr. Kevin Baer, Director of Graduate Studies and Research, 318-342-1698, E-mail: baer@ulm.edu.
Website: http://www.ulm.edu/pharmacy/

**The University of Manchester,** School of Pharmacy and Pharmaceutical Sciences, Manchester, United Kingdom. Offers M Phil, PhD.

**University of Maryland, Baltimore,** Graduate School, Graduate Programs in Pharmacy, Baltimore, MD 21201. Offers pharmaceutical health service research (MS, PhD), including epidemiology (MS), pharmacy administration (PhD); pharmaceutical sciences (PhD); Pharm D/PhD. *Degree requirements:* For doctorate, comprehensive exam, thesis/dissertation. *Entrance requirements:* For doctorate, GRE General Test. Additional exam requirements/recommendations for international students: required—TOEFL (minimum score 550 paper-based), IELTS. Electronic applications accepted.

**University of Maryland, Baltimore,** Professional Program in Pharmacy, Baltimore, MD 21201. Offers Pharm D, JD/Pharm D, Pharm D/MBA, Pharm D/MPH, Pharm D/PhD. *Accreditation:* ACPE. *Entrance requirements:* For doctorate, PCAT, 65 hours in pre-pharmacy course work, on-site interview. Additional exam requirements/recommendations for international students: required—TOEFL (minimum score 550 paper-based; 80 iBT). Electronic applications accepted.

**University of Maryland Eastern Shore,** Graduate Programs, School of Pharmacy, Princess Anne, MD 21853. Offers pharmaceutical sciences (MS, PhD); pharmacy (Pharm D). *Accreditation:* ACPE.

**University of Michigan,** College of Pharmacy, Professional Program in Pharmacy, Ann Arbor, MI 48109. Offers Pharm D, Pharm D/PhD. *Accreditation:* ACPE. *Entrance requirements:* For doctorate, PCAT. *Expenses:* Contact institution.

**University of Minnesota, Duluth,** Medical School, Department of Biochemistry, Molecular Biology and Biophysics, Duluth, MN 55812-2496. Offers biochemistry, molecular biology and biophysics (MS); biology and biophysics (PhD); social, administrative, and clinical pharmacy (MS, PhD); toxicology (MS, PhD). Terminal master's awarded for partial completion of doctoral program. *Degree requirements:* For master's, comprehensive exam, thesis; for doctorate, comprehensive exam, thesis/dissertation. *Entrance requirements:* For master's and doctorate, GRE General Test. Additional exam requirements/recommendations for international students: required—TOEFL. Electronic applications accepted.

**University of Minnesota, Twin Cities Campus,** College of Pharmacy, Professional Program in Pharmacy, Minneapolis, MN 55455-0213. Offers Pharm D. *Accreditation:* ACPE. *Degree requirements:* For doctorate, paper and seminar presentation. *Entrance requirements:* For doctorate, 2 years of pharmacy-related course work.

**University of Mississippi,** Graduate School, School of Pharmacy, University, MS 38677. Offers environmental toxicology (MS, PhD); industrial pharmacy (MS); medicinal chemistry (MS, PhD); pharmaceutics (MS, PhD); pharmacognosy (MS, PhD); pharmacology (MS, PhD); pharmacy (Pharm D); pharmacy administration (MS, PhD). *Accreditation:* ACPE (one or more programs are accredited). *Program availability:* Part-time. *Faculty:* 68 full-time (33 women), 13 part-time/adjunct (5 women). *Students:* 223 full-time (137 women), 215 part-time (137 women); includes 71 minority (29 Black or African American, non-Hispanic/Latino; 1 American Indian or Alaska Native, non-Hispanic/Latino; 31 Asian, non-Hispanic/Latino; 4 Hispanic/Latino; 6 Two or more races, non-Hispanic/Latino), 90 international. Average age 25. In 2019, 29 master's, 13 doctorates awarded. Terminal master's awarded for partial completion of doctoral program. *Degree requirements:* For master's, thesis; for doctorate, thesis/dissertation (for some programs). *Entrance requirements:* For master's, GRE General Test, minimum GPA of 3.0; for doctorate, GRE General Test (for PhD). Additional exam requirements/recommendations for international students: required—TOEFL. *Application deadline:* Applications are processed on a rolling basis. Application fee: $50. Electronic applications accepted. *Expenses:* Tuition, state resident: full-time $8718; part-time $484.25 per credit hour. Tuition, nonresident: full-time $24,990; part-time $1388.25 per credit hour. *Required fees:* $100; $4.16 per credit hour. *Financial support:* Fellowships, research assistantships, teaching assistantships, career-related

internships or fieldwork, Federal Work-Study, institutionally sponsored loans, scholarships/grants, tuition waivers (full), and unspecified assistantships available. Financial award application deadline: 3/1; financial award applicants required to submit FAFSA. *Unit head:* Dr. David Allen, Dean, School of Pharmacy, 662-915-7265, Fax: 662-9155704, E-mail: sopdean@olemiss.edu. *Application contact:* Temeka Smith, Graduate Activities Specialist for Admissions, 662-915-7474, Fax: 662-915-7577, E-mail: gschool@olemiss.edu.
Website: http://www.pharmacy.olemiss.edu/

**University of Missouri–Kansas City,** School of Pharmacy, Kansas City, MO 64110-2499. Offers PhD, Pharm D. *Accreditation:* ACPE (one or more programs are accredited). *Program availability:* Online learning. *Degree requirements:* For doctorate, comprehensive exam (for some programs), thesis/dissertation (for some programs). *Entrance requirements:* For doctorate, PCAT (for Pharm D). Additional exam requirements/recommendations for international students: required—TOEFL (minimum score 550 paper-based; 80 iBT). Electronic applications accepted. *Expenses:* Contact institution.

**University of Montana,** Graduate School, College of Health Professions and Biomedical Sciences, Skaggs School of Pharmacy, Missoula, MT 59812. Offers biomedical and pharmaceutical sciences (MS, PhD), including biomedical sciences (PhD), medicinal chemistry, molecular and cellular toxicology, neuroscience (PhD), pharmaceutical sciences (MS); pharmacy (Pharm D). *Accreditation:* ACPE. Electronic applications accepted.

**University of Nebraska Medical Center,** College of Pharmacy, Omaha, NE 68198-6000. Offers Pharm D. *Accreditation:* ACPE. *Entrance requirements:* For doctorate, PCAT, 90 semester hours of pre-pharmacy work. Electronic applications accepted. *Expenses:* Contact institution.

**University of New England,** College of Pharmacy, Portland, ME 04005-9526. Offers Pharm D. *Accreditation:* ACPE. *Faculty:* 22 full-time (13 women), 2 part-time/adjunct (1 woman). *Students:* 219 full-time (147 women); includes 45 minority (21 Black or African American, non-Hispanic/Latino; 19 Asian, non-Hispanic/Latino; 4 Hispanic/Latino; 1 Two or more races, non-Hispanic/Latino), 1 international. Average age 25. In 2019, 91 doctorates awarded. *Entrance requirements:* For doctorate, PCAT. *Application deadline:* For fall admission, 3/1 for domestic students. Applications are processed on a rolling basis. Electronic applications accepted. *Financial support:* Application deadline: 5/1; applicants required to submit FAFSA. *Unit head:* Dr. Robert L. McCarthy, Dean, College of Pharmacy, 207-221-4365, E-mail: rmccarthy2@une.edu. *Application contact:* Scott Steinberg, Vice President of University Admissions, 207-221-4225, Fax: 207-523-1925, E-mail: ssteinberg@une.edu.
Website: http://www.une.edu/pharmacy/

**University of New Mexico,** Graduate Studies, College of Pharmacy, Professional Program in Pharmacy, Albuquerque, NM 87131-2039. Offers Pharm D. *Accreditation:* ACPE. *Entrance requirements:* For doctorate, PCAT, 3 letters of recommendation, interview, 91 credit hours of prerequisites, letter of intent, Pharmcas application. Electronic applications accepted. *Expenses:* Contact institution.

**The University of North Carolina at Chapel Hill,** Eshelman School of Pharmacy, Chapel Hill, NC 27599. Offers pharmaceutical sciences (PhD); pharmaceutical sciences - health system pharmacy administration (MS); pharmacy (Pharm D). *Accreditation:* ACPE (one or more programs are accredited). Terminal master's awarded for partial completion of doctoral program. *Degree requirements:* For master's, comprehensive exam, thesis; for doctorate, comprehensive exam, thesis/dissertation. *Entrance requirements:* For master's and doctorate, GRE General Test, minimum GPA of 3.0. Additional exam requirements/recommendations for international students: required—TOEFL (minimum score 550 paper-based; 90 iBT), IELTS (minimum score 7). Electronic applications accepted. *Expenses:* Contact institution.

**University of Oklahoma Health Sciences Center,** College of Pharmacy, Professional Program in Pharmacy, Oklahoma City, OK 73190. Offers Pharm D. *Accreditation:* ACPE.

**University of Pittsburgh,** School of Pharmacy, Professional Program in Pharmacy, Pittsburgh, PA 15261. Offers community, leadership, innovation, and practice (Pharm D); global health (Pharm D); pediatrics (Pharm D); pharmacotherapy (Pharm D); pharmacy business administration (Pharm D). *Accreditation:* ACPE. *Entrance requirements:* For doctorate, PCAT. Electronic applications accepted. *Expenses:* Contact institution.

**University of Puerto Rico - Medical Sciences Campus,** School of Pharmacy, San Juan, PR 00936-5067. Offers industrial pharmacy (MS); pharmaceutical sciences (MS); pharmacy (Pharm D). *Accreditation:* ACPE. *Program availability:* Part-time, evening/weekend. *Degree requirements:* For master's, thesis; for doctorate, portfolio, research project. *Entrance requirements:* For master's, GRE, interview; for doctorate, PCAT, interview. Electronic applications accepted. *Expenses:* Contact institution.

**University of Rhode Island,** Graduate School, College of Pharmacy, Department of Pharmacy Practice, Kingston, RI 02881. Offers pharmacy practice (Pharm D); Pharm D/MBA; Pharm D/MPAS; Pharm D/MS. *Accreditation:* ACPE. *Faculty:* 30 full-time (23 women). *Students:* 765 full-time (536 women), 2 part-time (1 woman); includes 135 minority (14 Black or African American, non-Hispanic/Latino; 1 American Indian or Alaska Native, non-Hispanic/Latino; 65 Asian, non-Hispanic/Latino; 39 Hispanic/Latino; 16 Two or more races, non-Hispanic/Latino), 35 international. In 2019, 110 doctorates awarded. *Entrance requirements:* Additional exam requirements/recommendations for international students: required—TOEFL. *Application deadline:* For fall admission, 12/1 for domestic and international students. Application fee: $65. Electronic applications accepted. *Expenses: Tuition, area resident:* Full-time $13,734; part-time $763 per credit. Tuition, state resident: full-time $13,734; part-time $763 per credit. Tuition, nonresident: full-time $26,512; part-time $1473 per credit. *International tuition:* $26,512 full-time. *Required fees:* $1780; $52 per credit. $35 per term. One-time fee: $165. *Financial support:* In 2019–20, 4 research assistantships with tuition reimbursements (averaging $13,826 per year) were awarded. Financial award application deadline: 12/1; financial award applicants required to submit FAFSA. *Unit head:* Dr. Marilyn Barbour, Chair, 401-874-5842, Fax: 401-874-2181, E-mail: mbarbourri@aol.com. *Application contact:* Dr. Marilyn Barbour, Chair, 401-874-5842, Fax: 401-874-2181, E-mail: mbarbourri@aol.com.
Website: http://www.uri.edu/pharmacy/departments/php/index.shtml

**University of Saint Joseph,** School of Pharmacy and Physician Assistant Studies, West Hartford, CT 06117-2700. Offers pharmacy (Pharm D). *Accreditation:* ACPE. Electronic applications accepted.

**University of Saskatchewan,** College of Graduate and Postdoctoral Studies, College of Pharmacy and Nutrition, Saskatoon, SK S7N 5A2, Canada. Offers nutrition (M Sc, PhD); pharmacy (M Sc, PhD). *Degree requirements:* For master's, thesis; for doctorate, thesis/dissertation. *Entrance requirements:* Additional exam requirements/recommendations for international students: required—TOEFL.

**University of South Carolina,** South Carolina College of Pharmacy, Professional Program in Pharmacy, Columbia, SC 29208. Offers Pharm D. *Accreditation:* ACPE. *Degree requirements:* For doctorate, one foreign language. *Entrance requirements:* For doctorate, PCAT, 2 years of preprofessional study, interview. Electronic applications accepted.

**University of Southern California,** Graduate School, School of Pharmacy, Professional Program in Pharmacy, Los Angeles, CA 90089. Offers Pharm D, Pharm D/MBA, Pharm D/MS, Pharm D/PhD. *Accreditation:* ACPE. Electronic applications accepted.

**University of South Florida,** Innovative Education, Tampa, FL 33620-9951. Offers adult, career and higher education (Graduate Certificate), including college teaching, leadership in developing human resources, leadership in higher education; Africana studies (Graduate Certificate), including diasporas and health disparities, genocide and human rights; aging studies (Graduate Certificate), including gerontology; art research (Graduate Certificate), including museum studies; business foundations (Graduate Certificate); chemical and biomedical engineering (Graduate Certificate), including materials science and engineering, water, health and sustainability; child and family studies (Graduate Certificate), including positive behavior support; civil and industrial engineering (Graduate Certificate), including transportation systems analysis; community and family health (Graduate Certificate), including maternal and child health, social marketing and public health, violence and injury: prevention and intervention, women's health; criminology (Graduate Certificate), including criminal justice administration; data science for public administration (Graduate Certificate); digital humanities (Graduate Certificate); educational measurement and research (Graduate Certificate), including evaluation; English (Graduate Certificate), including comparative literary studies, creative writing, professional and technical communication; entrepreneurship (Graduate Certificate); environmental health (Graduate Certificate), including safety management; epidemiology and biostatistics (Graduate Certificate), including applied biostatistics, biostatistics, concepts and tools of epidemiology, epidemiology, epidemiology of infectious diseases; geography, environment and planning (Graduate Certificate), including community development, environmental policy and management, geographical information systems; geology (Graduate Certificate), including hydrogeology; global health (Graduate Certificate), including disaster management, global health and Latin American and Caribbean studies, global health practice, humanitarian assistance, infection control; government and international affairs (Graduate Certificate), including Cuban studies, globalization studies; health policy and management (Graduate Certificate), including health management and leadership, public health policy and programs; hearing specialist: early intervention (Graduate Certificate); industrial and management systems engineering (Graduate Certificate), including systems engineering, technology management; information studies (Graduate Certificate), including school library media specialist; information systems/decision sciences (Graduate Certificate), including analytics and business intelligence; instructional technology (Graduate Certificate), including distance education, Florida digital/virtual educator, instructional design, multimedia design, Web design; internal medicine, bioethics and medical humanities (Graduate Certificate), including biomedical ethics; Latin American and Caribbean studies (Graduate Certificate); leadership for coastal resiliency planning (Graduate Certificate); mass communications (Graduate Certificate), including multimedia journalism; mathematics and statistics (Graduate Certificate), including mathematics; medicine (Graduate Certificate), including aging and neuroscience, bioinformatics, biotechnology, brain fitness and memory management, clinical investigation, hand and upper limb rehabilitation, health informatics, health sciences, integrative weight management, intellectual property, medicine and gender, metabolic and nutritional medicine, metabolic cardiology, pharmacy sciences; national and competitive intelligence (Graduate Certificate); nursing (Graduate Certificate), including simulation based academic fellowship in advanced pain management; psychological and social foundations (Graduate Certificate), including career counseling, college teaching, diversity in education, mental health counseling, school counseling; public affairs (Graduate Certificate), including nonprofit management, public management, research administration; public health (Graduate Certificate), including assessing chemical toxicity and public health risks, health equity, pharmacoepidemiology, public health generalist, toxicology, translational research in adolescent behavioral health; public health practices (Graduate Certificate), including planning for healthy communities; rehabilitation and mental health counseling (Graduate Certificate), including integrative mental health care, marriage and family therapy, rehabilitation technology; secondary education (Graduate Certificate), including ESOL, foreign language education: culture and content, foreign language education: professional; social work (Graduate Certificate), including geriatric social work/clinical gerontology; special education (Graduate Certificate), including autism spectrum disorder, disabilities education: severe/profound; world languages (Graduate Certificate), including teaching English as a second language (TESL) or foreign language. *Unit head:* Dr. Cynthia DeLuca, Associate Vice President and Assistant Vice Provost, 813-974-3077, Fax: 813-974-7061, E-mail: deluca@usf.edu. *Application contact:* Owen Hooper, Director, Summer and Alternative Calendar Programs, 813-974-6917, E-mail: hooper@usf.edu.
Website: http://www.usf.edu/innovative-education/

**University of South Florida,** USF Health Taneja College of Pharmacy, Tampa, FL 33612. Offers pharmaceutical nanotechnology (MS), including biomedical engineering, drug discovery, delivery, development and manufacturing; pharmacy (Pharm D), including pharmacy and health education. *Accreditation:* ACPE. *Program availability:* Part-time, 100% online, blended/hybrid learning. *Faculty:* 32 full-time (18 women), 1 part-time/adjunct (0 women). *Students:* 398 full-time (234 women), 7 part-time (3 women); includes 180 minority (33 Black or African American, non-Hispanic/Latino; 72 Asian, non-Hispanic/Latino; 59 Hispanic/Latino; 2 Native Hawaiian or other Pacific Islander, non-Hispanic/Latino; 14 Two or more races, non-Hispanic/Latino), 13 international. Average age 25. 465 applicants, 44% accepted, 112 enrolled. In 2019, 11 master's, 91 doctorates awarded. *Degree requirements:* For master's, comprehensive exam, thesis optional, capstone or thesis; for doctorate, internship/field experience. *Entrance requirements:* For master's, GRE, MCAT or DAT, Bachelor's preferably in biomedical, biological, chemical sciences or engineering; 2 letters of recommendation; resume; professional statement; interview; for doctorate, PCAT, minimum GPA of 2.75 overall (preferred); completion of 72 prerequisite credit hours; U.S. citizenship or permanent resident; interviews; criminal background check and drug screen. Additional exam requirements/recommendations for international students: required—TOEFL (minimum score 550 paper-based; 79 iBT), IELTS (minimum score 6.5). *Application deadline:* For fall admission, 6/1 for domestic and international students; for spring admission, 10/15 for domestic students, 9/15 for international students; for summer admission, 2/15 for domestic and international students. Applications are processed on a rolling basis. Application fee: $30. Electronic applications accepted. *Financial support:* In 2019–20, 159 students received support. Scholarships/grants available. *Unit head:* James Lambert, 813-974-4562, E-mail: jlambert2@usf.edu. *Application contact:* Dr. Amy Schwartz, Admissions Recruiter, 813-974-4652, E-mail: jlambert2@usf.edu.
Website: https://health.usf.edu/pharmacy

**The University of Tennessee Health Science Center,** College of Pharmacy, Memphis, TN 38163. Offers MS, PhD, Pharm D, Pharm D/PhD. *Accreditation:* ACPE (one or more programs are accredited). Terminal master's awarded for partial completion of doctoral program. *Degree requirements:* For master's, thesis; for doctorate, thesis/dissertation (for some programs). *Entrance requirements:* For

master's, GRE; for doctorate, PCAT (for Pharm D); GRE (for PhD). Additional exam requirements/recommendations for international students: required—TOEFL. Electronic applications accepted. *Expenses:* Contact institution.

**The University of Texas at Austin,** Graduate School, College of Pharmacy, Professional Program in Pharmacy, Austin, TX 78712-1111. Offers Pharm D, Pharm D/PhD. *Accreditation:* ACPE. *Entrance requirements:* For doctorate, GRE General Test.

**The University of Texas at Tyler,** Ben and Maytee Fisch College of Pharmacy, Tyler, TX 75799. Offers Pharm D. *Faculty:* 22 full-time (9 women), 3 part-time/adjunct (1 woman). *Students:* 313 full-time (191 women), 18 part-time (10 women); includes 214 minority (95 Black or African American, non-Hispanic/Latino; 64 Asian, non-Hispanic/Latino; 48 Hispanic/Latino; 7 Two or more races, non-Hispanic/Latino), 4 international. Average age 27. 133 applicants, 57% accepted, 75 enrolled. In 2019, 64 doctorates awarded. *Unit head:* Dr. Lane J. Brunner, Dean, 903-566-6153, E-mail: lbrunner@uttyler.edu. *Application contact:* Jennifer Engel, Admissions Representative, 903-565-5777, E-mail: pharmacy@uttyler.edu.
Website: http://www.uttyler.edu/pharmacy/

**University of the Incarnate Word,** Feik School of Pharmacy, San Antonio, TX 78209-6397. Offers Pharm D. *Accreditation:* ACPE. *Faculty:* 21 full-time (15 women), 1 (woman) part-time/adjunct. *Students:* 365 full-time (254 women), 8 part-time (7 women); includes 273 minority (26 Black or African American, non-Hispanic/Latino; 79 Asian, non-Hispanic/Latino; 160 Hispanic/Latino; 1 Native Hawaiian or other Pacific Islander, non-Hispanic/Latino; 7 Two or more races, non-Hispanic/Latino), 17 international. 108 applicants, 97% accepted, 92 enrolled. In 2019, 91 doctorates awarded. *Entrance requirements:* For doctorate, PCAT, 80 hours of documented pharmacy observational experience; minimum GPA of 2.5; 64 hours (71 hours for financial aid) in accredited pre-pharmacy course. Additional exam requirements/recommendations for international students: required—TOEFL (minimum score 560 paper-based; 83 iBT). *Application deadline:* For fall admission, 12/1 for domestic and international students. Application fee: $50. Electronic applications accepted. *Expenses:* $38,000 tuition per year; $705 fees per year. *Financial support:* Research assistantships, Federal Work-Study, scholarships/grants, and unspecified assistantships available. Financial award applicants required to submit FAFSA. *Unit head:* Dr. David Maize, Dean, 210-883-1000, Fax: 210-822-1516, E-mail: maize@uiwtx.edu. *Application contact:* Dr. Amy Diepenbrock, Assistant Dean, Student Affairs, 210-883-1060, Fax: 210-822-1521, E-mail: diepenbr@uiwtx.edu.
Website: https://pharmacy.uiw.edu/index.html

**University of the Pacific,** Thomas J. Long School of Pharmacy and Health Sciences, Professional Program in Pharmacy, Stockton, CA 95211-0197. Offers Pharm D. *Accreditation:* ACPE. *Entrance requirements:* Additional exam requirements/recommendations for international students: required—TOEFL.

**University of the Sciences,** Philadelphia College of Pharmacy, Philadelphia, PA 19104-4495. Offers Pharm D. *Accreditation:* ACPE. *Entrance requirements:* Additional exam requirements/recommendations for international students: required—TOEFL, TWE.

**The University of Toledo,** College of Graduate Studies, College of Pharmacy and Pharmaceutical Sciences, Toledo, OH 43606-3390. Offers MS, MSPS, PhD, Pharm D. *Accreditation:* ACPE. Terminal master's awarded for partial completion of doctoral program. *Degree requirements:* For master's, thesis; for doctorate, thesis/dissertation. *Entrance requirements:* For master's and doctorate, GRE General Test. Additional exam requirements/recommendations for international students: required—TOEFL (minimum score 550 paper-based; 80 iBT). Electronic applications accepted.

**University of Utah,** Graduate School, College of Pharmacy and Graduate School, Department of Pharmacy, Salt Lake City, UT 84112-1107. Offers MS. *Degree requirements:* For master's, thesis optional. *Entrance requirements:* For master's, GRE, undergraduate degree in pharmacy. *Expenses:* Tuition, state resident: full-time $7085; part-time $272.51 per credit hour. Tuition, nonresident: full-time $24,937; part-time $959.12 per credit hour. *Required fees:* $880.52; $880.52 per semester. Tuition and fees vary according to degree level, program and student level.

**University of Utah,** Graduate School, College of Pharmacy, Professional Program in Pharmacy, Salt Lake City, UT 84112-5820. Offers Pharm D. *Accreditation:* ACPE. *Faculty:* 42 full-time (19 women), 141 part-time/adjunct (63 women). *Students:* 217 full-time (127 women), 4 part-time (2 women); includes 75 minority (5 Black or African American, non-Hispanic/Latino; 43 Asian, non-Hispanic/Latino; 14 Hispanic/Latino; 13 Two or more races, non-Hispanic/Latino), 3 international. Average age 26. 228 applicants, 32% accepted, 53 enrolled. In 2019, 61 doctorates awarded. *Degree requirements:* For doctorate, Capstone Pharm.D. research project. *Entrance requirements:* For doctorate, PCAT required for applicants who don't have a bachelor's degree, prerequisite undergraduate coursework including: 1 semester each of human anatomy, human physiology, calculus, physics, statistics, microbiology, professional/technical writing (or public speaking; 2 semesters each of general chemistry with labs and organic chemistry with labs. Additional exam requirements/recommendations for international students: required—TOEFL (minimum score 80 paper-based) or IELTS (minimum score 6.5). *Application deadline:* For fall admission, 6/1 for domestic and international students. Applications are processed on a rolling basis. Application fee: $175 ($65 for international students). Electronic applications accepted. *Expenses:* $30,418 first professional year, $30,556 second professional year, $34,183 third professional year (includes experiential rotations during summer semester), $36,009 fourth professional year (experiential rotations summer, fall and spring semesters). *Financial support:* In 2019–20, 71 students received support, including 90 teaching assistantships (averaging $1,500 per year); scholarships/grants also available. Financial award application deadline: 1/20; financial award applicants required to submit FAFSA. *Unit head:* Dean Randall T. Peterson, PhD, Professor and Dean, 801-581-6731, Fax: 801-581-3716, E-mail: randall.peterson@pharm.utah.edu. *Application contact:* Shawna Webster, Associate Director of Student Services, 801-585-1848, Fax: 801-581-3716, E-mail: randall.peterson@pharm.utah.edu.
Website: http://www.pharmacy.utah.edu/

**University of Washington,** School of Pharmacy and Graduate School, Department of Pharmacy, Seattle, WA 98195-7630. Offers biomedical regulatory affairs (MS); pharmaceutical outcomes research and policy (PhD). *Program availability:* Part-time. *Faculty:* 12 full-time (4 women), 9 part-time/adjunct (1 woman). *Students:* 29 full-time (21 women), 35 part-time (27 women); includes 22 minority (1 Black or African American, non-Hispanic/Latino; 1 American Indian or Alaska Native, non-Hispanic/Latino; 17 Asian, non-Hispanic/Latino; 2 Hispanic/Latino; 1 Native Hawaiian or other Pacific Islander, non-Hispanic/Latino), 21 international. 84 applicants, 44% accepted, 26 enrolled. In 2019, 17 master's, 3 doctorates awarded. *Degree requirements:* For master's, thesis; for doctorate, comprehensive exam, thesis/dissertation. *Entrance requirements:* For master's and doctorate, GRE General Test. Additional exam requirements/recommendations for international students: required—TOEFL (minimum score 100 iBT). *Application deadline:* For fall admission, 12/15 priority date for domestic and international students. Application fee: $85. Electronic applications accepted. *Expenses:* Contact institution. *Financial support:* Fellowships with full tuition reimbursements, research assistantships with full tuition reimbursements, teaching assistantships with full tuition reimbursements, institutionally sponsored loans, scholarships/grants, health care benefits, tuition waivers (full), and unspecified assistantships available. *Unit head:* Dr. H. Steve White, Chair, 206-543-3782, Fax: 206-543-3835, E-mail: hswhite@uw.edu. *Application contact:* Dr. Josh Carlson, Associate Professor, 206-543-9649, Fax: 206-543-3835, E-mail: carlsojj@uw.edu.
Website: https://sop.washington.edu/department-of-pharmacy/

**University of Washington,** School of Pharmacy, Doctor of Pharmacy Program, Seattle, WA 98195-7631. Offers Pharm D, Pharm D/Certificate, Pharm D/MS. *Accreditation:* ACPE. *Faculty:* 108. *Students:* 433 full-time (309 women); includes 310 minority (13 Black or African American, non-Hispanic/Latino; 2 American Indian or Alaska Native, non-Hispanic/Latino; 255 Asian, non-Hispanic/Latino; 15 Hispanic/Latino; 1 Native Hawaiian or other Pacific Islander, non-Hispanic/Latino; 24 Two or more races, non-Hispanic/Latino). Average age 26. 344 applicants, 44% accepted, 105 enrolled. In 2019, 85 doctorates awarded. *Entrance requirements:* Additional exam requirements/recommendations for international students: required—TOEFL (minimum score 100 iBT). *Application deadline:* For fall admission, 12/1 for domestic and international students. Applications are processed on a rolling basis. Application fee: $175. Electronic applications accepted. *Financial support:* In 2019–20, 348 students received support. Career-related internships or fieldwork and scholarships/grants available. Financial award application deadline: 6/30. *Unit head:* Dr. Peggy Odegard, Associate Dean, Office of Professional Pharmacy Education, 206-543-6100, Fax: 206-685-9297. *Application contact:* Mike Spielman, Director of Admissions, 206-543-6100, Fax: 206-685-9297, E-mail: mspiel@uw.edu.
Website: https://sop.washington.edu/pharmd/

**University of Wisconsin–Madison,** School of Pharmacy, Professional Program in Pharmacy, Madison, WI 53706-1380. Offers Pharm D. *Accreditation:* ACPE.

**University of Wyoming,** College of Health Sciences, School of Pharmacy, Laramie, WY 82071. Offers health services administration (MS); pharmacy (Pharm D). *Accreditation:* ACPE (one or more programs are accredited). *Program availability:* Online learning. *Entrance requirements:* For doctorate, PCAT. Additional exam requirements/recommendations for international students: required—TOEFL.

**Virginia Commonwealth University,** Medical College of Virginia-Professional Programs, School of Pharmacy, Professional Program in Pharmacy, Richmond, VA 23284-9005. Offers Pharm D. *Accreditation:* ACPE. *Program availability:* Part-time. *Degree requirements:* For doctorate, research project. *Entrance requirements:* For doctorate, PCAT. Electronic applications accepted.

**Washington State University,** College of Pharmacy and Pharmaceutical Sciences, Spokane, WA 99210-1495. Offers health policy and administration (MHPA); nutrition and exercise physiology (MS); pharmacy (Pharm D). *Accreditation:* ACPE (one or more programs are accredited). *Degree requirements:* For master's, comprehensive exam, thesis, oral exam; for doctorate, comprehensive exam, thesis/dissertation, oral exam (for PhD). *Entrance requirements:* For master's, GRE General Test, minimum GPA of 3.0, interview; for doctorate, GRE General Test, minimum GPA of 3.0, interview, minimum 60 hours of documented pharmacy experience.

**Wayne State University,** Eugene Applebaum College of Pharmacy and Health Sciences, Pharmacy, Detroit, MI 48202. Offers Pharm D, Pharm D/PhD. *Accreditation:* ACPE. *Entrance requirements:* For doctorate, PCAT, PharmCAS application, interview, criminal background check, minimum GPA of 3.0 in required preprofessional courses and overall, work experience, community service, leadership abilities. Additional exam requirements/recommendations for international students: required—TOEFL (minimum score 550 paper-based; 79 iBT), Michigan English Language Assessment Battery (minimum score 85); recommended—IELTS (minimum score 6.5), TWE (minimum score 5.5). Electronic applications accepted. *Expenses:* Contact institution.

**West Coast University,** Graduate Programs, North Hollywood, CA 91606. Offers advanced generalist (MSN); family nurse practitioner (MSN); health administration (MHA); occupational therapy (MS); pharmacy (Pharm D); physical therapy (DPT).

**Western New England University,** College of Pharmacy and Health Sciences, Pharm D Program, Springfield, MA 01119. Offers Pharm D, Pharm D/MBA, Pharm D/MS. *Accreditation:* ACPE. *Entrance requirements:* For doctorate, PCAT, two letters of recommendation, completion of all pre-pharmacy course requirements at accredited college or university. Additional exam requirements/recommendations for international students: required—TOEFL (minimum score 80 iBT). Electronic applications accepted. *Expenses:* Contact institution.

**Western University of Health Sciences,** College of Pharmacy, Program in Pharmacy, Pomona, CA 91766-1854. Offers Pharm D. *Accreditation:* ACPE. *Faculty:* 26 full-time (12 women), 7 part-time/adjunct (3 women). *Students:* 519 full-time (355 women); includes 380 minority (18 Black or African American, non-Hispanic/Latino; 276 Asian, non-Hispanic/Latino; 39 Hispanic/Latino; 47 Two or more races, non-Hispanic/Latino), 23 international. Average age 28. 497 applicants, 63% accepted, 129 enrolled. In 2019, 137 doctorates awarded. *Degree requirements:* For doctorate, comprehensive exam (for some programs). *Entrance requirements:* For doctorate, minimum GPA of 2.75, interview, PharmCAS letters of recommendation; BS in pharmacy or equivalent (recommended), official transcripts, 60 semester hours or 90 quarter hours of coursework from a regionally accredited US institution at the time of application. Additional exam requirements/recommendations for international students: required—TOEFL (minimum score 79 iBT). *Application deadline:* For fall admission, 3/1 for domestic and international students. Application fee: $65. Electronic applications accepted. *Expenses:* Tuition is $50,675 per year. *Financial support:* In 2019–20, 38 students received support. Research assistantships and scholarships/grants available. Financial award application deadline: 3/2; financial award applicants required to submit FAFSA. *Unit head:* Dr. Daniel Robinson, Dean, 909-469-5533, Fax: 909-469-5539, E-mail: drobinson@westernu.edu. *Application contact:* Elaine Gonzalez, Admission Counselor, 909-469-5337, Fax: 909-469-5570, E-mail: egonzalez@westernu.edu.
Website: http://www.westernu.edu/pharmacy-dpp_message

**West Virginia University,** School of Pharmacy, Morgantown, WV 26506. Offers health services and outcomes research (PhD); pharmaceutical and pharmacological sciences (PhD); professional pharmacy (Pharm D). *Accreditation:* ACPE. Terminal master's awarded for partial completion of doctoral program. *Degree requirements:* For doctorate, variable foreign language requirement, comprehensive exam (for some programs), thesis/dissertation (for some programs). *Entrance requirements:* For doctorate, GRE General Test (for PhD), minimum GPA of 2.75 (for PhD). Additional exam requirements/recommendations for international students: required—TOEFL (minimum score 500 paper-based). Electronic applications accepted. *Expenses:* Contact institution.

**William Carey University,** School of Pharmacy, Hattiesburg, MS 39401. Offers Pharm D.

**Wingate University,** School of Pharmacy, Wingate, NC 28174. Offers Pharm D. *Accreditation:* ACPE. *Degree requirements:* For doctorate, comprehensive exam. *Entrance requirements:* For doctorate, PCAT. Electronic applications accepted. *Expenses:* Contact institution.

**Xavier University of Louisiana,** College of Pharmacy, New Orleans, LA 70125. Offers Pharm D. *Accreditation:* ACPE. *Entrance requirements:* Additional exam requirements/

recommendations for international students: required—TOEFL. Electronic applications accepted. *Expenses:* Contact institution.

# Section 31
# Veterinary Medicine and Sciences

This section contains a directory of institutions offering graduate work in veterinary medicine and sciences. Additional information about programs listed in the directory may be obtained by writing directly to the dean of a graduate school or chair of a department at the address given in the directory.

For programs offering related work, see also in this book *Biological and Biomedical Sciences* and *Zoology*. In the other guides in this series:

**Graduate Programs in the Humanities, Arts & Social Sciences**
See *Economics (Agricultural Economics and Agribusiness)*

**Graduate Programs in the Physical Sciences, Mathematics, Agricultural Sciences, the Environment & Natural Resources**
See *Agricultural and Food Sciences, Marine Sciences and Oceanography,* and *Natural Resources*

**Graduate Programs in Engineering & Applied Sciences**
See *Agricultural Engineering and Bioengineering* and *Biomedical Engineering and Biotechnology*

## CONTENTS

### Program Directories

# Veterinary Medicine

**Auburn University,** College of Veterinary Medicine, Professional Program in Veterinary Medicine, Auburn University, AL 36849. Offers DVM, DVM/MS. *Accreditation:* AVMA. *Faculty:* 2 full-time (1 woman), 1 (woman) part-time/adjunct. *Students:* 482 full-time (397 women), 31 part-time (24 women); includes 48 minority (9 Black or African American, non-Hispanic/Latino; 1 American Indian or Alaska Native, non-Hispanic/Latino; 8 Asian, non-Hispanic/Latino; 25 Hispanic/Latino; 5 Two or more races, non-Hispanic/Latino). Average age 26. 139 applicants, 99% accepted, 130 enrolled. In 2019, 123 doctorates awarded. *Degree requirements:* For doctorate, preceptorship. *Entrance requirements:* Additional exam requirements/recommendations for international students: recommended—TOEFL (minimum score 550 paper-based; 79 iBT). Application fee: $60 ($70 for international students). Electronic applications accepted. *Expenses:* $546 per credit hour state resident tuition, $1638 per credit hour nonresident tuition, $680 student services fee for GRA/GTA, $838 student services fee, $691 clinical rotation fee, $4542 professional and program fees per semester. *Financial support:* In 2019–20, 47 fellowships with tuition reimbursements were awarded; research assistantships also available. Financial award application deadline: 3/15; financial award applicants required to submit FAFSA. *Unit head:* Dr. Calvin Johnson, Dean, 334-844-4546. *Application contact:* Dr. George Flowers, Interim Dean of the Graduate School, 334-844-2125.

**Colorado State University,** College of Veterinary Medicine and Biomedical Sciences, Doctor of Veterinary Medicine Program, Fort Collins, CO 80523-1601. Offers DVM, DVM/MPH, DVM/MS, DVM/MST, DVM/PhD, MBA/DVM. *Accreditation:* AVMA. *Students:* 590 full-time (497 women); includes 122 minority (3 Black or African American, non-Hispanic/Latino; 30 Asian, non-Hispanic/Latino; 61 Hispanic/Latino; 28 Two or more races, non-Hispanic/Latino), 3 international. Average age 26. 2,258 applicants, 7% accepted, 147 enrolled. *Entrance requirements:* For doctorate, GRE, interview by invitation; CSA supplemental application; transcripts; VMCAS application; letters of recommendation. Additional exam requirements/recommendations for international students: required—TOEFL (minimum score 550 paper-based; 80 iBT), IELTS (minimum score 6.5). *Application deadline:* For fall admission, 9/17 for domestic and international students. Application fee: $60 ($70 for international students). Electronic applications accepted. *Expenses:* Tuition, state resident: full-time $10,520; part-time $5844 per credit hour. Tuition, nonresident: full-time $25,791; part-time $14,328 per credit hour. *International tuition:* $25,791 full-time. *Required fees:* $2512.80. Part-time tuition and fees vary according to course level, course load, degree level, program and student level. *Financial support:* Scholarships/grants and unspecified assistantships available. *Unit head:* Gretchen Delcambre, Director, Veterinary Admissions, 970-491-6163, E-mail: gh.delcambre@colostate.edu. *Application contact:* Janet Janke, Director, DVM Admissions Operations, 970-491-7052, E-mail: janet.janke@colostate.edu.
Website: https://vetmedbiosci.colostate.edu/dvm/

**Cornell University,** College of Veterinary Medicine, Ithaca, NY 14853. Offers DVM. *Accreditation:* AVMA. *Faculty:* 212 full-time (105 women). *Students:* 442 full-time (362 women); includes 136 minority (11 Black or African American, non-Hispanic/Latino; 5 American Indian or Alaska Native, non-Hispanic/Latino; 48 Asian, non-Hispanic/Latino; 47 Hispanic/Latino; 2 Native Hawaiian or other Pacific Islander, non-Hispanic/Latino; 23 Two or more races, non-Hispanic/Latino), 8 international. Average age 25. 1,147 applicants, 16% accepted, 110 enrolled. In 2019, 96 doctorates awarded. *Entrance requirements:* For doctorate, GRE General Test or MCAT required through Fall 2019. Starting Fall 2020 application cycle GRE/MCAT no longer required to apply, veterinary experience with letter(s) of recommendation. Additional exam requirements/recommendations for international students: required—TOEFL (minimum score 600 paper-based; 100 iBT). *Application deadline:* For fall admission, 9/15 for domestic and international students. Electronic applications accepted. *Expenses:* Contact institution. *Financial support:* In 2019–20, 296 students received support. Federal Work-Study, institutionally sponsored loans, and scholarships/grants available. Financial award application deadline: 2/15; financial award applicants required to submit CSS PROFILE or FAFSA. *Unit head:* Dr. Lorin Warnick, Dean, 607-253-3771, Fax: 607-253-3701. *Application contact:* Jennifer A. Mailey, Director of Admissions, 607-253-3700, Fax: 607-253-3709, E-mail: jam333@cornell.edu.
Website: http://www.vet.cornell.edu/

**Iowa State University of Science and Technology,** Department of Veterinary Diagnostic and Production Animal Medicine, Ames, IA 50011. Offers veterinary preventative medicine (MS). *Accreditation:* AVMA. *Degree requirements:* For master's, thesis or alternative. *Entrance requirements:* For master's, GRE General Test. Additional exam requirements/recommendations for international students: required—TOEFL (minimum score 550 paper-based; 79 iBT), IELTS (minimum score 6.5). Electronic applications accepted.

**Kansas State University,** Graduate School, College of Veterinary Medicine, Professional Program in Veterinary Medicine, Manhattan, KS 66506. Offers DVM. *Accreditation:* AVMA. *Entrance requirements:* Additional exam requirements/recommendations for international students: required—TOEFL. *Expenses:* Contact institution.

**Lincoln Memorial University,** College of Veterinary Medicine, Harrogate, TN 37752-1901. Offers DVM.

**Louisiana State University and Agricultural & Mechanical College,** School of Veterinary Medicine, Professional Program in Veterinary Medicine, Baton Rouge, LA 70803. Offers DVM. *Accreditation:* AVMA.

**Michigan State University,** College of Veterinary Medicine, Professional Program in Veterinary Medicine, East Lansing, MI 48824. Offers veterinary medicine (DVM); veterinary medicine/medical scientist training program (DVM). *Accreditation:* AVMA. *Entrance requirements:* Additional exam requirements/recommendations for international students: required—TOEFL. Electronic applications accepted. *Expenses:* Contact institution.

**Midwestern University, Glendale Campus,** College of Veterinary Medicine, Glendale, AZ 85308. Offers DVM.

**Mississippi State University,** College of Veterinary Medicine, College of Veterinary Medicine, Mississippi State, MS 39762. Offers DVM. *Accreditation:* AVMA. *Faculty:* 85 full-time (35 women), 26 part-time/adjunct (4 women). *Students:* 373 full-time (316 women); includes 34 minority (4 Black or African American, non-Hispanic/Latino; 1 American Indian or Alaska Native, non-Hispanic/Latino; 8 Asian, non-Hispanic/Latino; 19 Hispanic/Latino; 2 Two or more races, non-Hispanic/Latino). Average age 25. 1,464 applicants, 7% accepted, 96 enrolled. *Entrance requirements:* For doctorate, minimum overall GPA of 2.8. Additional exam requirements/recommendations for international students: required—TOEFL (minimum score 79 iBT). *Application deadline:* For fall admission, 9/17 for domestic and international students. Application fee: $60. Electronic

applications accepted. *Expenses:* Base Tuition: CVM $24,938.44/year; Technology Fee $70.68/year; University Fees; $2,238.88/year; Total Charge to Student - Resident $27,248/year; Base Tuition CVM $24,938.44/year; Non-Resident Surcharge; $21,200/year; Technology Fee $70.68/year; University Fees $2,238.88/year; Total Charge to Student - Non Resident $48,448/year. *Financial support:* In 2019–20, 209 students received support. Scholarships/grants available. Financial award applicants required to submit FAFSA. *Unit head:* Dr. Jack D Smith, Associate Dean for Academic Affairs, 662-325-4401, Fax: 662-325-1027, E-mail: smith@cvm.msstate.edu. *Application contact:* Dr. Brittany S Moore-Henderson, Director of Admissions, 662-325-4401, Fax: 662-325-1027, E-mail: admit@vetmed.msstate.edu.
Website: http://www.vetmed.msstate.edu/

**Oklahoma State University,** Center for Veterinary Health Sciences, Professional Program in Veterinary Medicine, Stillwater, OK 74078. Offers DVM. *Entrance requirements:* For doctorate, GRE General Test, GRE Subject Test (biology). Electronic applications accepted. *Expenses: Tuition, area resident:* Full-time $4148.10; part-time $2765.40 per credit hour. Tuition, state resident: full-time $4148.10; part-time $2765.40 per credit hour. Tuition, nonresident: full-time $15,775; part-time $10,516.80 per credit hour. *International tuition:* $15,775.20 full-time. *Required fees:* $2196.90; $122.05 per credit hour. Tuition and fees vary according to course load, campus/location and program.

**Oregon State University,** College of Veterinary Medicine, Veterinary Medicine Professional Program, Corvallis, OR 97331. Offers DVM. *Accreditation:* AVMA. *Entrance requirements:* For doctorate, GRE. *Expenses:* Contact institution.

**Purdue University,** School of Veterinary Medicine, Professional Program in Veterinary Medicine, West Lafayette, IN 47907. Offers DVM, DVM/MS, DVM/PhD. *Accreditation:* AVMA. *Entrance requirements:* For doctorate, GRE General Test. Additional exam requirements/recommendations for international students: required—TOEFL. Electronic applications accepted.

**Texas A&M University,** College of Veterinary Medicine and Biomedical Sciences, College Station, TX 77843. Offers MS, DVM, PhD. *Accreditation:* AVMA. *Program availability:* Part-time. Terminal master's awarded for partial completion of doctoral program. *Entrance requirements:* For master's and doctorate, GRE General Test. Additional exam requirements/recommendations for international students: required—TOEFL (minimum score 550 paper-based; 80 iBT), IELTS (minimum score 6), PTE (minimum score 53). *Expenses:* Contact institution.

**Tufts University,** Cummings School of Veterinary Medicine, North Grafton, MA 01536. Offers animals and public policy (MS); biomedical sciences (PhD), including digestive diseases, infectious diseases, neuroscience and reproductive biology, pathology; conservation medicine (MS); veterinary medicine (DVM); DVM/MPH; DVM/MS. *Accreditation:* AVMA (one or more programs are accredited). *Degree requirements:* For master's, thesis (for some programs); for doctorate, comprehensive exam, thesis/dissertation (for some programs). *Entrance requirements:* For master's and doctorate, GRE General Test. Additional exam requirements/recommendations for international students: required—TOEFL or IELTS. Electronic applications accepted. *Expenses:* Contact institution.

**Tuskegee University,** Graduate Programs, College of Veterinary Medicine, Nursing and Allied Health, School of Veterinary Medicine, Tuskegee, AL 36088. Offers MS, DVM. *Accreditation:* AVMA. *Degree requirements:* For master's, thesis. *Entrance requirements:* For master's, GRE General Test; for doctorate, VCAT. Additional exam requirements/recommendations for international students: required—TOEFL (minimum score 500 paper-based).

**Université de Montréal,** Faculty of Veterinary Medicine, Professional Program in Veterinary Medicine, Montréal, QC H3C 3J7, Canada. Offers DES. *Accreditation:* AVMA. *Program availability:* Part-time. Electronic applications accepted.

**University of California, Davis,** School of Veterinary Medicine, Program in Veterinary Medicine, Davis, CA 95616. Offers DVM, DVM/MPVM. *Accreditation:* AVMA. *Entrance requirements:* For doctorate, GRE General Test. Additional exam requirements/recommendations for international students: required—TOEFL. Electronic applications accepted.

**University of Florida,** College of Veterinary Medicine, Professional Program in Veterinary Medicine, Gainesville, FL 32611. Offers DVM. *Accreditation:* AVMA. *Entrance requirements:* For doctorate, GRE General Test.

**University of Georgia,** College of Veterinary Medicine, Athens, GA 30602. Offers MS, DVM, PhD. *Accreditation:* AVMA (one or more programs are accredited). *Degree requirements:* For doctorate, variable foreign language requirement, thesis/dissertation (for some programs). *Entrance requirements:* For master's, GRE General Test; for doctorate, GRE General Test; GRE Subject Test in biology (for DVM). Electronic applications accepted. *Expenses:* Contact institution.

**University of Guelph,** Ontario Veterinary College and Office of Graduate and Postdoctoral Studies, Graduate Programs in Veterinary Sciences, Department of Clinical Studies, Guelph, ON N1G 2W1, Canada. Offers anesthesiology (M Sc, DV Sc); cardiology (DV Sc, Diploma); clinical studies (Diploma); dermatology (M Sc); diagnostic imaging (M Sc, DV Sc); emergency/critical care (M Sc, DV Sc, Diploma); medicine (M Sc, DV Sc); neurology (M Sc, DV Sc); ophthalmology (M Sc, DV Sc); surgery (M Sc, DV Sc). *Degree requirements:* For master's, thesis; for doctorate, comprehensive exam, thesis/dissertation. *Entrance requirements:* Additional exam requirements/recommendations for international students: required—TOEFL (minimum score 550 paper-based), IELTS (minimum score 6.5). Electronic applications accepted.

**University of Illinois at Urbana-Champaign,** College of Veterinary Medicine, Professional Program in Veterinary Medicine, Champaign, IL 61820. Offers veterinary medical science (DVM). *Accreditation:* AVMA. *Expenses:* Contact institution.

**University of Maryland, College Park,** Academic Affairs, College of Agriculture and Natural Resources, Maryland Campus of VA/MD Regional College of Veterinary Medicine, Professional Program in Veterinary Medicine, College Park, MD 20742. Offers DVM. *Degree requirements:* For doctorate, thesis/dissertation, oral exam, public seminar.

**University of Minnesota, Twin Cities Campus,** College of Veterinary Medicine, Professional Program in Veterinary Medicine, Minneapolis, MN 55455-0213. Offers DVM, DVM/PhD. *Accreditation:* AVMA. *Entrance requirements:* For doctorate, GRE General Test. Electronic applications accepted. *Expenses:* Contact institution.

**University of Missouri,** College of Veterinary Medicine and Office of Research and Graduate Studies, Graduate Programs in Veterinary Medicine, Department of Biomedical Sciences, Columbia, MO 65211. Offers biomedical sciences (MS, PhD); comparative medicine (MS); veterinary medicine and surgery (MS); DVM/PhD. *Entrance*

*requirements:* For master's and doctorate, GRE General Test, minimum GPA of 3.0; 10 hours each of biology and chemistry; 3 hours each of physics, biochemistry, and calculus.

**University of Missouri,** College of Veterinary Medicine, Professional Program in Veterinary Medicine, Columbia, MO 65211. Offers DVM. *Accreditation:* AVMA. *Entrance requirements:* For doctorate, VCAT, minimum GPA of 2.5 (for state residents), 3.0 (for nonresidents). Electronic applications accepted.

**University of Pennsylvania,** School of Veterinary Medicine, Philadelphia, PA 19104. Offers VMD, VMD/MBA, VMD/PhD. *Faculty:* 110 full-time (54 women), 58 part-time/adjunct (41 women). *Students:* 476 full-time (400 women), 5 part-time (4 women); includes 79 minority (5 Black or African American, non-Hispanic/Latino; 28 Asian, non-Hispanic/Latino; 34 Hispanic/Latino; 12 Two or more races, non-Hispanic/Latino), 6 international. Average age 26. 1,238 applicants, 10% accepted, 121 enrolled. In 2019, 121 doctorates awarded. Application fee: $75. *Unit head:* Andrew M. Hoffman, Dean. *Application contact:* Andrew M. Hoffman, Dean.
Website: http://www.vet.upenn.edu/

**University of Prince Edward Island,** Atlantic Veterinary College, Professional Program in Veterinary Medicine, Charlottetown, PE C1A 4P3, Canada. Offers DVM. *Accreditation:* AVMA. *Entrance requirements:* For doctorate, GRE. Additional exam requirements/recommendations for international students: required—TOEFL (minimum score 550 paper-based; 80 iBT), Canadian Academic English Language Assessment, Michigan English Language Assessment Battery, Canadian Test of English for Scholars and Trainees.

**University of Saskatchewan,** Western College of Veterinary Medicine and College of Graduate and Postdoctoral Studies, Graduate Programs in Veterinary Medicine, Department of Large Animal Clinical Sciences, Saskatoon, SK S7N 5A2, Canada. Offers M Sc, M Vet Sc, PhD. *Degree requirements:* For master's, thesis (for some programs); for doctorate, comprehensive exam (for some programs), thesis/dissertation. *Entrance requirements:* Additional exam requirements/recommendations for international students: required—TOEFL (minimum score 80 iBT); recommended—IELTS (minimum score 6.5). Electronic applications accepted.

**University of Saskatchewan,** Western College of Veterinary Medicine and College of Graduate and Postdoctoral Studies, Graduate Programs in Veterinary Medicine, Department of Small Animal Clinical Sciences, Saskatoon, SK S7N 5A2, Canada. Offers small animal clinical sciences (M Sc, PhD); veterinary anesthesiology, radiology and surgery (M Vet Sc); veterinary internal medicine (M Vet Sc). *Degree requirements:* For master's, thesis (for some programs); for doctorate, comprehensive exam (for some programs), thesis/dissertation. *Entrance requirements:* Additional exam requirements/recommendations for international students: required—TOEFL (minimum score 80 iBT); recommended—IELTS (minimum score 6.5). Electronic applications accepted.

**University of Saskatchewan,** Western College of Veterinary Medicine, Professional Program in Veterinary Medicine, Saskatoon, SK S7N 5A2, Canada. Offers DVM. *Accreditation:* AVMA. *Degree requirements:* For doctorate, thesis/dissertation.

**The University of Tennessee,** Graduate School, College of Veterinary Medicine, Knoxville, TN 37996. Offers DVM. *Accreditation:* AVMA. *Entrance requirements:* For doctorate, VCAT, interview, minimum GPA of 2.7. Additional exam requirements/recommendations for international students: required—TOEFL. *Expenses:* Contact institution.

**University of Wisconsin–Madison,** School of Veterinary Medicine, Madison, WI 53706-1380. Offers MS, DVM, PhD. *Accreditation:* AVMA (one or more programs are accredited). Terminal master's awarded for partial completion of doctoral program. *Degree requirements:* For master's, thesis; for doctorate, thesis/dissertation (for some programs). *Entrance requirements:* For doctorate, GRE General Test (for DVM). *Expenses:* Contact institution.

**Virginia Polytechnic Institute and State University,** Virginia-Maryland College of Veterinary Medicine, Blacksburg, VA 24061. Offers biomedical and veterinary sciences (MS, PhD); public health (MPH); veterinary medicine (DVM). *Accreditation:* AVMA (one or more programs are accredited); CEPH. *Faculty:* 132 full-time (79 women), 6 part-time/adjunct (5 women). *Students:* 583 full-time (422 women), 34 part-time (26 women); includes 142 minority (28 Black or African American, non-Hispanic/Latino; 3 American Indian or Alaska Native, non-Hispanic/Latino; 23 Asian, non-Hispanic/Latino; 35 Hispanic/Latino; 53 Two or more races, non-Hispanic/Latino), 28 international. Average age 26. 85 applicants, 87% accepted, 54 enrolled. In 2019, 33 master's, 137 doctorates awarded. *Degree requirements:* For master's, comprehensive exam (for some programs), thesis (for some programs); for doctorate, comprehensive exam (for some programs), thesis/dissertation (for some programs). *Entrance requirements:* For

master's and doctorate, GRE/GMAT. Additional exam requirements/recommendations for international students: required—TOEFL (minimum score 90 iBT). *Application deadline:* For fall admission, 8/1 for domestic students, 4/1 for international students; for spring admission, 1/1 for domestic students, 9/1 for international students. Applications are processed on a rolling basis. Application fee: $75. Electronic applications accepted. *Expenses:* Tuition, state resident: full-time $13,700; part-time $761.25 per credit hour. Tuition, nonresident: full-time $27,614; part-time $1534 per credit hour. *Required fees:* $886.50 per term. Tuition and fees vary according to campus/location and program. *Financial support:* In 2019–20, 3 fellowships with full and partial tuition reimbursements (averaging $2,668 per year), 33 research assistantships with full tuition reimbursements (averaging $19,301 per year), 30 teaching assistantships with full tuition reimbursements (averaging $21,932 per year) were awarded; scholarships/grants also available. Financial award application deadline: 3/1; financial award applicants required to submit FAFSA. *Unit head:* Dr. Daniel Givens, Dean, 540-231-7910, Fax: 540-231-3505, E-mail: gdaniel@vt.edu. *Application contact:* Sheila Steele, Executive Assistant, 540-231-7910, Fax: 540-231-3505, E-mail: ssteele@vt.edu.
Website: http://www.vetmed.vt.edu

**Washington State University,** College of Veterinary Medicine, Professional Program in Veterinary Medicine, Pullman, WA 99164. Offers DVM, DVM/MS, DVM/PhD. *Accreditation:* AVMA. *Faculty:* 24 full-time (5 women), 50 part-time/adjunct (12 women). *Students:* 530 full-time (405 women); includes 79 minority (1 American Indian or Alaska Native, non-Hispanic/Latino; 16 Asian, non-Hispanic/Latino; 4 Hispanic/Latino; 58 Two or more races, non-Hispanic/Latino), 3 international. Average age 24. 1,499 applicants, 14% accepted, 135 enrolled. In 2019, 126 doctorates awarded. Terminal master's awarded for partial completion of doctoral program. *Degree requirements:* For doctorate, written exam, oral exam. *Entrance requirements:* For doctorate, GRE General Test. Additional exam requirements/recommendations for international students: required—TOEFL (minimum score 550 paper-based; 79 iBT). *Application deadline:* For fall admission, 9/15 for domestic and international students. Application fee: $65. Electronic applications accepted. *Expenses:* Contact institution. *Financial support:* In 2019–20, 446 students received support, including 28 fellowships with full tuition reimbursements available, 87 research assistantships with full tuition reimbursements available (averaging $23,000 per year), 34 teaching assistantships with full tuition reimbursements available (averaging $22,000 per year); career-related internships or fieldwork, Federal Work-Study, institutionally sponsored loans, scholarships/grants, traineeships, health care benefits, and unspecified assistantships also available. Support available to part-time students. Financial award application deadline: 1/15; financial award applicants required to submit FAFSA. *Unit head:* Dr. Patricia Talcott, Director of Admissions, 509-355-1532. *Application contact:* Stacey Poler, Recruitment Officer, 509-335-1532, Fax: 509-335-6133, E-mail: s.poler@wsu.edu.
Website: http://www.vetmed.wsu.edu/

**Western University of Health Sciences,** College of Veterinary Medicine, Pomona, CA 91766-1854. Offers DVM. *Accreditation:* AVMA. *Faculty:* 55 full-time (26 women), 10 part-time/adjunct (5 women). *Students:* 414 full-time (323 women); includes 200 minority (11 Black or African American, non-Hispanic/Latino; 1 American Indian or Alaska Native, non-Hispanic/Latino; 56 Asian, non-Hispanic/Latino; 92 Hispanic/Latino; 1 Native Hawaiian or other Pacific Islander, non-Hispanic/Latino; 39 Two or more races, non-Hispanic/Latino), 3 international. Average age 27. 817 applicants, 33% accepted, 108 enrolled. In 2019, 103 doctorates awarded. *Degree requirements:* For doctorate, comprehensive exam (for some programs). *Entrance requirements:* For doctorate, MCAT or GRE General Test (within 5 years of matriculation) (Required), minimum GPA of 2.75; 3 letters of recommendation; BA or BS (recommended); 500 hours of hands-on animal-related experience; transcripts from all colleges or universities attended (Required). TOFEL and proof of legal US residency are required for international students. Additional exam requirements/recommendations for international students: required—TOEFL (minimum score 550 paper-based; 79 iBT). *Application deadline:* For fall admission, 9/15 for domestic and international students. Electronic applications accepted. *Expenses:* Tuition is about $55535 per year, Other fees such as Student body fees, SAVMA fee and SEP/Medical equipment cost about $500 per year. One time graduation fee is $350. *Financial support:* In 2019–20, 20 students received support. Career-related internships or fieldwork, institutionally sponsored loans, scholarships/grants, and veterans' educational benefits available. Financial award application deadline: 3/2; financial award applicants required to submit FAFSA. *Unit head:* Dr. Phil Nelson, Dean, 909-469-5661, Fax: 909-469-5635, E-mail: pnelson@westernu.edu. *Application contact:* Karen Hutton-Lopez, Director of Admissions, 909-469-5650, Fax: 909-469-5570, E-mail: admissions@westernu.edu.
Website: http://www.westernu.edu/veterinary

# Veterinary Sciences

**Clemson University,** Graduate School, College of Agriculture, Forestry and Life Sciences, Department of Animal and Veterinary Sciences, Clemson, SC 29634. Offers MS, PhD. *Program availability:* Part-time. *Students:* Average age 28. 17 applicants, 94% accepted, 12 enrolled. In 2019, 8 master's, 3 doctorates awarded. *Degree requirements:* For master's, thesis optional; for doctorate, comprehensive exam, thesis/dissertation. *Entrance requirements:* For master's and doctorate, GRE General Test, unofficial transcripts, letters of recommendation. Additional exam requirements/recommendations for international students: required—TOEFL (minimum score 80 paper-based; 80 iBT); recommended—IELTS (minimum score 6.5), TSE (minimum score 54). *Application deadline:* For fall admission, 4/15 for international students; for spring admission, 10/15 for international students. Applications are processed on a rolling basis. Application fee: $80 ($90 for international students). Electronic applications accepted. *Expenses:* Contact institution. *Financial support:* In 2019–20, 21 students received support, including 2 fellowships with full and partial tuition reimbursements available (averaging $7,000 per year), 10 research assistantships with full and partial tuition reimbursements available (averaging $12,938 per year), 9 teaching assistantships with full and partial tuition reimbursements available (averaging $12,931 per year); career-related internships or fieldwork also available. *Unit head:* Dr. James Strickland, Department Chair, 864-656-3138, E-mail: jrstric@clemson.edu. *Application contact:* Dr. Jeryl Jones, Graduate Program Coordinator, 864-656-2142, E-mail: jerylj@clemson.edu.
Website: http://www.clemson.edu/cafls/departments/animal_vet_science/

**Colorado State University,** College of Veterinary Medicine and Biomedical Sciences, Department of Clinical Sciences, Fort Collins, CO 80523-1678. Offers MS, PhD. *Program availability:* Part-time. *Faculty:* 89 full-time (53 women), 12 part-time/adjunct (7 women). *Students:* 13 full-time (8 women), 49 part-time (32 women); includes 1 minority

(Two or more races, non-Hispanic/Latino), 20 international. Average age 32. 24 applicants, 96% accepted, 23 enrolled. In 2019, 15 master's, 4 doctorates awarded. *Degree requirements:* For master's, comprehensive exam, thesis (for some programs); for doctorate, comprehensive exam, thesis/dissertation. *Entrance requirements:* For master's and doctorate, minimum overall GPA of 3.0; transcripts; 3 letters of recommendation; statement of purpose. Additional exam requirements/recommendations for international students: required—TOEFL (minimum score 550 paper-based; 80 iBT), IELTS (minimum score 6.5). *Application deadline:* For fall admission, 6/30 for domestic students, 4/1 for international students; for winter admission, 6/30 for domestic students, 4/1 for international students; for spring admission, 10/31 for domestic students, 9/1 for international students; for summer admission, 4/29 for domestic students, 5/1 for international students. Application fee: $70. *Expenses:* Tuition, state resident: full-time $10,520; part-time $5844 per credit hour. Tuition, nonresident: full-time $25,791; part-time $14,328 per credit hour. *International tuition:* $25,791 full-time. *Required fees:* $2512.80. Part-time tuition and fees vary according to course level, course load, degree level, program and student level. *Financial support:* In 2019–20, 19 students received support, including 16 fellowships (averaging $32,500 per year), 7 research assistantships (averaging $23,049 per year); career-related internships or fieldwork, institutionally sponsored loans, scholarships/grants, health care benefits, and unspecified assistantships also available. Financial award application deadline: 4/1; financial award applicants required to submit FAFSA. *Unit head:* Dr. Wayne Jensen, Professor and Department Head, 970-297-1274, Fax: 970-297-1275, E-mail: wayne.jensen@colostate.edu. *Application contact:* Morna Mynard, Graduate Coordinator, 970-297-4030, Fax: 970-297-1275, E-mail: mmynard@colostate.edu.
Website: https://vetmedbiosci.colostate.edu/cs/

### Veterinary Sciences

**Drexel University,** College of Medicine, Biomedical Graduate Programs, Program in Laboratory Animal Science, Philadelphia, PA 19104-2875. Offers MLAS. *Program availability:* Part-time. *Degree requirements:* For master's, comprehensive exam. *Entrance requirements:* For master's, GRE General Test, minimum GPA of 3.0. Additional exam requirements/recommendations for international students: required—TOEFL. Electronic applications accepted.

**Iowa State University of Science and Technology,** Department of Veterinary Clinical Sciences, Ames, IA 50011. Offers MS. *Degree requirements:* For master's, thesis or alternative. *Entrance requirements:* For master's, GRE. Additional exam requirements/recommendations for international students: required—TOEFL (minimum score 550 paper-based; 79 iBT), IELTS (minimum score 6.5). Electronic applications accepted.

**Iowa State University of Science and Technology,** Department of Veterinary Microbiology and Preventive Medicine, Ames, IA 50011. Offers veterinary microbiology (MS, PhD). *Entrance requirements:* For master's and doctorate, GRE General Test. Additional exam requirements/recommendations for international students: required—TOEFL (minimum score 550 paper-based; 79 iBT), IELTS (minimum score 6.5). Electronic applications accepted.

**Kansas State University,** Graduate School, College of Veterinary Medicine, Department of Clinical Sciences, Manhattan, KS 66506. Offers MPH, Graduate Certificate. *Degree requirements:* For master's, thesis. *Entrance requirements:* For master's, GRE, DVM. Additional exam requirements/recommendations for international students: required—TOEFL (minimum score 550 paper-based). Electronic applications accepted. *Expenses:* Contact institution.

**Louisiana State University and Agricultural & Mechanical College,** School of Veterinary Medicine and Graduate School, Department of Comparative Biomedical Sciences, Baton Rouge, LA 70803. Offers MS, PhD.

**Louisiana State University and Agricultural & Mechanical College,** School of Veterinary Medicine and Graduate School, Department of Pathobiological Sciences, Baton Rouge, LA 70803. Offers MS, PhD.

**Louisiana State University and Agricultural & Mechanical College,** School of Veterinary Medicine and Graduate School, Department of Veterinary Clinical Sciences, Baton Rouge, LA 70803. Offers MS, PhD.

**Michigan State University,** College of Veterinary Medicine and The Graduate School, Graduate Programs in Veterinary Medicine, East Lansing, MI 48824. Offers comparative medicine and integrative biology (MS, PhD), including comparative medicine and integrative biology, comparative medicine and integrative biology–environmental toxicology (PhD); food safety and toxicology (MS), including food safety; integrative toxicology (PhD), including animal science–environmental toxicology, biochemistry and molecular biology–environmental toxicology, chemistry–environmental toxicology, crop and soil sciences–environmental toxicology, environmental engineering–environmental toxicology, environmental geosciences–environmental toxicology, fisheries and wildlife–environmental toxicology, food science–environmental toxicology, forestry–environmental toxicology, genetics–environmental toxicology, human nutrition–environmental toxicology, microbiology–environmental toxicology, pharmacology and toxicology–environmental toxicology, zoology–environmental toxicology; large animal clinical sciences (MS, PhD); microbiology and molecular genetics (MS, PhD), including industrial microbiology, microbiology, microbiology and molecular genetics, microbiology–environmental toxicology (PhD); pathobiology and diagnostic investigation (MS, PhD), including pathology, pathology–environmental toxicology (PhD); pharmacology and toxicology (MS, PhD); pharmacology and toxicology–environmental toxicology (PhD); physiology (MS, PhD); small animal clinical sciences (MS). Electronic applications accepted.

**Mississippi State University,** College of Veterinary Medicine, Office of Research and Graduate Studies, Mississippi State, MS 39762. Offers MS, PhD. *Program availability:* Part-time. *Faculty:* 85 full-time (35 women), 26 part-time/adjunct (4 women). *Students:* 25 full-time (16 women), 27 part-time (18 women); includes 5 minority (2 Black or African American, non-Hispanic/Latino; 1 Hispanic/Latino; 2 Two or more races, non-Hispanic/Latino), 11 international. Average age 31. 16 applicants, 44% accepted, 7 enrolled. In 2019, 12 master's, 10 doctorates awarded. Terminal master's awarded for partial completion of doctoral program. *Degree requirements:* For master's, comprehensive exam (for some programs), thesis (for some programs); for doctorate, comprehensive exam, thesis/dissertation. *Entrance requirements:* For master's, minimum undergraduate GPA of 3.0, bachelor's degree; for doctorate, minimum undergraduate GPA of 3.0. Additional exam requirements/recommendations for international students: required—TOEFL (minimum score 550 paper-based; 79 iBT); recommended—IELTS (minimum score 6.5). *Application deadline:* For fall admission, 7/1 priority date for domestic students, 5/1 priority date for international students; for spring admission, 11/1 priority date for domestic students, 10/1 priority date for international students; for summer admission, 5/1 priority date for domestic students, 3/1 priority date for international students. Applications are processed on a rolling basis. Application fee: $60 ($80 for international students). Electronic applications accepted. *Expenses:* Tuition, area resident: Full-time $8880; part-time $456 per credit hour. Tuition, state resident: full-time $8880. Tuition, nonresident: full-time $23,840; part-time $1236 per credit hour. *Required fees:* $110; $11.12 per credit hour. Tuition and fees vary according to course load. *Financial support:* In 2019–20, 21 students received support, including 21 research assistantships with full tuition reimbursements available (averaging $19,000 per year); career-related internships or fieldwork, institutionally sponsored loans, scholarships/grants, and unspecified assistantships also available. Financial award application deadline: 4/1; financial award applicants required to submit FAFSA. *Unit head:* Dr. Stephen B. Pruett, Interim Associate Dean of Research and Graduate Studies, 662-325-1205, Fax: 662-325-1193, E-mail: Pruett@cvm.msstate.edu. *Application contact:* Tia H. Perkins, Coordinator, Graduate Studies, 662-325-1417, Fax: 662-325-1193, E-mail: tia.perkins@msstate.edu.
Website: http://www.cvm.msstate.edu/index.php/academics/degree-programs-research/office-of-research-graduate-studies-orgs

**North Carolina State University,** College of Veterinary Medicine, Program in Comparative Biomedical Sciences, Raleigh, NC 27695. Offers cell biology (MS, PhD); infectious disease (MS, PhD); pathology (MS, PhD); pharmacology (MS, PhD); population medicine (MS, PhD). *Program availability:* Part-time. *Degree requirements:* For master's, thesis; for doctorate, thesis/dissertation. *Entrance requirements:* For master's and doctorate, GRE General Test. Additional exam requirements/recommendations for international students: required—TOEFL (minimum score 550 paper-based). Electronic applications accepted. *Expenses:* Contact institution.

**The Ohio State University,** College of Veterinary Medicine, Program In Comparative and Veterinary Medicine, Columbus, OH 43210. Offers MS, PhD. *Entrance requirements:* For master's and doctorate, GRE. Additional exam requirements/recommendations for international students: required—TOEFL (minimum score 550 paper-based; 79 iBT), Michigan English Language Assessment Battery (minimum score 82); recommended—IELTS (minimum score 7). Electronic applications accepted.

**Oklahoma State University,** Center for Veterinary Health Sciences and Graduate College, Graduate Program in Veterinary Biomedical Sciences, Stillwater, OK 74078.

Offers MS, PhD. *Program availability:* Online learning. Terminal master's awarded for partial completion of doctoral program. *Degree requirements:* For master's, thesis; for doctorate, comprehensive exam, thesis/dissertation. *Entrance requirements:* For master's and doctorate, GRE General Test. Additional exam requirements/recommendations for international students: required—TOEFL (minimum score 80 iBT). Electronic applications accepted. *Expenses:* Contact institution.

**Penn State Hershey Medical Center,** College of Medicine, Graduate School Programs in the Biomedical Sciences, Graduate Program in Laboratory Animal Medicine, Hershey, PA 17033. Offers MS. *Degree requirements:* For master's, thesis or alternative. *Entrance requirements:* For master's, GRE, DVM. Additional exam requirements/recommendations for international students: required—TOEFL (minimum score 550 paper-based). Electronic applications accepted.

**Purdue University,** School of Veterinary Medicine and Graduate School, Graduate Programs in Veterinary Medicine, Department of Basic Medical Sciences, West Lafayette, IN 47907. Offers anatomy (MS, PhD); pharmacology (MS, PhD); physiology (MS, PhD). *Program availability:* Part-time. Terminal master's awarded for partial completion of doctoral program. *Degree requirements:* For master's, thesis; for doctorate, thesis/dissertation. *Entrance requirements:* For master's and doctorate, GRE General Test. Additional exam requirements/recommendations for international students: required—TOEFL. Electronic applications accepted.

**Purdue University,** School of Veterinary Medicine and Graduate School, Graduate Programs in Veterinary Medicine, Department of Comparative Pathobiology, West Lafayette, IN 47907-2027. Offers comparative epidemiology and public health (MS); comparative epidemiology and public heath (PhD); comparative microbiology and immunology (MS, PhD); comparative pathobiology (MS, PhD); interdisciplinary studies (PhD), including microbial pathogenesis, molecular signaling and cancer biology, molecular virology; lab animal medicine (MS); veterinary anatomic pathology (MS); veterinary clinical pathology (MS). Terminal master's awarded for partial completion of doctoral program. *Degree requirements:* For master's, thesis (for some programs); for doctorate, thesis/dissertation. *Entrance requirements:* For master's and doctorate, GRE General Test. Additional exam requirements/recommendations for international students: required—TOEFL (minimum score 575 paper-based), IELTS (minimum score 6.5), TWE (minimum score 4). Electronic applications accepted.

**Purdue University,** School of Veterinary Medicine and Graduate School, Graduate Programs in Veterinary Medicine, Department of Veterinary Clinical Sciences, West Lafayette, IN 47907. Offers MS, PhD. Terminal master's awarded for partial completion of doctoral program. *Degree requirements:* For master's, thesis (for some programs); for doctorate, thesis/dissertation. *Entrance requirements:* For master's and doctorate, DVM.

**South Dakota State University,** Graduate School, College of Agriculture, Food and Environmental Sciences, Department of Veterinary and Biomedical Sciences, Brookings, SD 57007. Offers biological sciences (MS, PhD). *Program availability:* Part-time, evening/weekend. *Degree requirements:* For master's, thesis (for some programs), oral exam; for doctorate, comprehensive exam, thesis/dissertation, preliminary oral and written exams. *Entrance requirements:* Additional exam requirements/recommendations for international students: required—TOEFL (minimum score 525 paper-based; 71 iBT).

**Texas A&M University,** College of Veterinary Medicine and Biomedical Sciences, College Station, TX 77843. Offers MS, DVM, PhD. *Accreditation:* AVMA. *Program availability:* Part-time. Terminal master's awarded for partial completion of doctoral program. *Entrance requirements:* For master's and doctorate, GRE General Test. Additional exam requirements/recommendations for international students: required—TOEFL (minimum score 550 paper-based; 80 iBT), IELTS (minimum score 6), PTE (minimum score 53). *Expenses:* Contact institution.

**Tuskegee University,** Graduate Programs, College of Veterinary Medicine, Nursing and Allied Health, School of Veterinary Medicine, Tuskegee, AL 36088. Offers MS, DVM. *Accreditation:* AVMA. *Degree requirements:* For master's, thesis. *Entrance requirements:* For master's, GRE General Test; for doctorate, VCAT. Additional exam requirements/recommendations for international students: required—TOEFL (minimum score 500 paper-based).

**Université de Montréal,** Faculty of Veterinary Medicine, Graduate Programs in Veterinary Sciences, Montréal, QC H3C 3J7, Canada. Offers M Sc, PhD. *Degree requirements:* For master's, one foreign language, thesis optional. Electronic applications accepted.

**University of California, Davis,** School of Veterinary Medicine and Graduate Studies, Program in Preventive Veterinary Medicine, Davis, CA 95616. Offers MPVM, DVM/MPVM. *Program availability:* Part-time. *Degree requirements:* For master's, thesis. *Entrance requirements:* For master's, DVM or equivalent. Additional exam requirements/recommendations for international students: required—TOEFL (minimum score 550 paper-based).

**University of California, Davis,** School of Veterinary Medicine, Residency Training Program, Davis, CA 95616. Offers Certificate. *Entrance requirements:* For degree, DVM or equivalent, 1 year of related experience.

**University of Florida,** College of Veterinary Medicine, Graduate Program in Veterinary Medical Sciences, Gainesville, FL 32611. Offers forensic toxicology (Certificate); veterinary medical sciences (MS, PhD), including forensic toxicology (MS). *Program availability:* Online learning. Terminal master's awarded for partial completion of doctoral program. *Degree requirements:* For master's, thesis; for doctorate, thesis/dissertation. *Entrance requirements:* For master's and doctorate, GRE General Test, minimum GPA of 3.0. Additional exam requirements/recommendations for international students: required—TOEFL (minimum score 550 paper-based). Electronic applications accepted. *Expenses:* Contact institution.

**University of Guelph,** Ontario Veterinary College and Office of Graduate and Postdoctoral Studies, Graduate Programs in Veterinary Sciences, Guelph, ON N1G 2W1, Canada. Offers M Sc, DV Sc, PhD, Diploma. *Accreditation:* AVMA (one or more programs are accredited). *Degree requirements:* For master's, thesis; for doctorate, comprehensive exam, thesis/dissertation. *Entrance requirements:* Additional exam requirements/recommendations for international students: required—TOEFL.

**University of Idaho,** College of Graduate Studies, College of Agricultural and Life Sciences, Department of Animal and Veterinary Science, Moscow, ID 83844-2282. Offers MS, PhD. *Faculty:* 5 full-time. *Students:* 24 full-time, 7 part-time. Average age 27. In 2019, 8 master's, 2 doctorates awarded. *Degree requirements:* For doctorate, thesis/dissertation. *Entrance requirements:* For master's and doctorate, minimum GPA of 3.0. Additional exam requirements/recommendations for international students: required—TOEFL (minimum score 79 iBT). *Application deadline:* For fall admission, 7/30 for domestic students; for spring admission, 12/1 for domestic students. Applications are processed on a rolling basis. Application fee: $60. Electronic applications accepted. *Expenses:* Tuition, state resident: full-time $7753.80; part-time $502 per credit hour. Tuition, nonresident: full-time $26,990; part-time $1571 per credit hour. *Required fees:* $2122.20; $47 per credit hour. *Financial support:* Research assistantships and teaching assistantships available. Financial award applicants required to submit FAFSA. *Unit head:* Dr. Amin Ahmadzadeh, Department Head, 208-885-6345, E-mail: avs@

uidaho.edu. *Application contact:* Dr. Amin Ahmadzadeh, Department Head, 208-885-6345, E-mail: avs@uidaho.edu.
Website: https://www.uidaho.edu/cals/animal-and-veterinary-science

**University of Illinois at Urbana-Champaign,** College of Veterinary Medicine, Department of Comparative Biosciences, Urbana, IL 61802. Offers MS, PhD, DVM/PhD. *Degree requirements:* For doctorate, thesis/dissertation.

**University of Illinois at Urbana-Champaign,** College of Veterinary Medicine, Department of Pathobiology, Urbana, IL 61802. Offers MS, PhD, DVM/PhD. Terminal master's awarded for partial completion of doctoral program. *Degree requirements:* For doctorate, thesis/dissertation.

**University of Illinois at Urbana-Champaign,** College of Veterinary Medicine, Department of Veterinary Clinical Medicine, Urbana, IL 61801. Offers MS, PhD, DVM/PhD. *Degree requirements:* For doctorate, thesis/dissertation.

**University of Kentucky,** Graduate School, College of Agriculture, Food and Environment, Program in Veterinary Science, Lexington, KY 40506-0032. Offers MS, PhD. *Degree requirements:* For master's, comprehensive exam, thesis; for doctorate, comprehensive exam, thesis/dissertation. *Entrance requirements:* For master's, GRE General Test, minimum undergraduate GPA of 2.75; for doctorate, GRE General Test, minimum graduate GPA of 3.0. Additional exam requirements/recommendations for international students: required—TOEFL (minimum score 550 paper-based). Electronic applications accepted.

**University of Maryland, College Park,** Academic Affairs, College of Agriculture and Natural Resources, Maryland Campus of VA/MD Regional College of Veterinary Medicine, Veterinary Medical Sciences Program, College Park, MD 20742. Offers MS, PhD. *Degree requirements:* For master's, thesis, oral exam; for doctorate, thesis/dissertation, oral exam, public seminar. *Entrance requirements:* For doctorate, GRE General Test. Electronic applications accepted.

**University of Minnesota, Twin Cities Campus,** College of Veterinary Medicine and Graduate School, Graduate Programs in Veterinary Medicine, Program in Comparative and Molecular Bioscience, Minneapolis, MN 55455-0213. Offers MS, PhD, DVM/PhD. Terminal master's awarded for partial completion of doctoral program. *Degree requirements:* For master's, comprehensive exam, thesis; for doctorate, comprehensive exam, thesis/dissertation. *Entrance requirements:* For master's and doctorate, GRE. Additional exam requirements/recommendations for international students: required—TOEFL (minimum score 550 paper-based; 79 iBT). Electronic applications accepted.

**University of Minnesota, Twin Cities Campus,** College of Veterinary Medicine and Graduate School, Graduate Programs in Veterinary Medicine, Program in Veterinary Medicine, Minneapolis, MN 55455-0213. Offers MS, PhD, DVM/PhD. Terminal master's awarded for partial completion of doctoral program. *Degree requirements:* For master's, comprehensive exam, thesis; for doctorate, comprehensive exam, thesis/dissertation. *Entrance requirements:* Additional exam requirements/recommendations for international students: required—TOEFL (minimum score 550 paper-based; 79 iBT). Electronic applications accepted.

**University of Missouri,** College of Veterinary Medicine and Office of Research and Graduate Studies, Graduate Programs in Veterinary Medicine, Department of Veterinary Medicine and Surgery, Columbia, MO 65211. Offers MS. *Entrance requirements:* For master's, GRE General Test, minimum GPA of 3.0; 2 letters of recommendation.

**University of Nebraska–Lincoln,** Graduate College, College of Agricultural Sciences and Natural Resources, School of Veterinary Medicine and Biomedical Sciences, Lincoln, NE 68588. Offers veterinary science (MS). *Program availability:* Online learning. *Degree requirements:* For master's, thesis optional; for doctorate, comprehensive exam, thesis/dissertation. *Entrance requirements:* For master's, GRE General Test; for doctorate, GRE General Test, MCAT, or VCAT. Additional exam requirements/recommendations for international students: required—TOEFL (minimum score 550 paper-based). Electronic applications accepted.

**University of Prince Edward Island,** Atlantic Veterinary College, Graduate Program in Veterinary Medicine, Charlottetown, PE C1A 4P3, Canada. Offers anatomy (M Sc, PhD); bacteriology (M Sc, PhD); clinical pharmacology (M Sc, PhD); clinical sciences (M Sc, PhD); epidemiology (M Sc, PhD), including reproduction; fish health (M Sc, PhD); food animal nutrition (M Sc, PhD); immunology (M Sc, PhD); microanatomy (M Sc, PhD); parasitology (M Sc, PhD); pathology (M Sc, PhD); pharmacology (M Sc, PhD); physiology (M Sc, PhD); toxicology (M Sc, PhD); veterinary science (M Vet Sc); virology (M Sc, PhD). *Program availability:* Part-time. *Degree requirements:* For master's, thesis; for doctorate, thesis/dissertation. *Entrance requirements:* For master's, DVM, B Sc honors degree, or equivalent; for doctorate, M Sc. Additional exam requirements/recommendations for international students: required—TOEFL (minimum score 550 paper-based; 80 iBT). *Expenses:* Contact institution.

**University of Saskatchewan,** Western College of Veterinary Medicine and College of Graduate and Postdoctoral Studies, Graduate Programs in Veterinary Medicine, Saskatoon, SK S7N 5A2, Canada. Offers large animal clinical sciences (M Sc, M Vet Sc, PhD); small animal clinical sciences (M Sc, M Vet Sc, PhD), including small animal clinical sciences (M Sc, PhD), veterinary anesthesiology, radiology and surgery (M Vet Sc), veterinary internal medicine (M Vet Sc); veterinary biomedical sciences (M Sc, M Vet Sc, PhD), including veterinary anatomy (M Sc), veterinary biomedical sciences (M Vet Sc), veterinary physiological sciences (M Sc, PhD); veterinary medicine (M Sc, PhD); veterinary microbiology (M Sc, M Vet Sc, PhD); veterinary pathology

(M Sc, M Vet Sc, PhD). *Degree requirements:* For master's, comprehensive exam, thesis (for some programs); for doctorate, comprehensive exam, thesis/dissertation. *Entrance requirements:* Additional exam requirements/recommendations for international students: required—TOEFL (minimum score 80 iBT) or IELTS (minimum score 6.5). Electronic applications accepted. *Expenses:* Contact institution.

**University of Vermont,** Graduate College, College of Agriculture and Life Sciences, Department of Animal and Veterinary Sciences, Burlington, VT 05405-0148. Offers animal science (MS); animal, nutrition and food sciences (PhD). *Degree requirements:* For master's, thesis; for doctorate, one foreign language, thesis/dissertation. *Entrance requirements:* For master's and doctorate, GRE General Test. Additional exam requirements/recommendations for international students: required—TOEFL (minimum score 550 paper-based, 90 iBT) or IELTS (6.5). Electronic applications accepted.

**University of Washington,** Graduate School, School of Medicine, Graduate Programs in Medicine, Department of Comparative Medicine, Seattle, WA 98195. Offers MS.

**University of Wisconsin–Madison,** School of Veterinary Medicine, Madison, WI 53706-1380. Offers MS, DVM, PhD. *Accreditation:* AVMA (one or more programs are accredited). Terminal master's awarded for partial completion of doctoral program. *Degree requirements:* For master's, thesis; for doctorate, thesis/dissertation (for some programs). *Entrance requirements:* For doctorate, GRE General Test (for DVM). *Expenses:* Contact institution.

**Utah State University,** School of Graduate Studies, College of Agriculture and Applied Sciences, Department of Animal, Dairy and Veterinary Sciences, Logan, UT 84322. Offers animal science (MS, PhD); bioveterinary science (MS, PhD); dairy science (MS). *Program availability:* Part-time. *Degree requirements:* For master's, thesis (for some programs); for doctorate, comprehensive exam, thesis/dissertation. *Entrance requirements:* For master's and doctorate, GRE General Test, minimum GPA of 3.0. Additional exam requirements/recommendations for international students: required—TOEFL. Electronic applications accepted.

**Virginia Polytechnic Institute and State University,** Virginia-Maryland College of Veterinary Medicine, Blacksburg, VA 24061. Offers biomedical and veterinary sciences (MS, PhD); public health (MPH); veterinary medicine (DVM). *Accreditation:* AVMA (one or more programs are accredited); CEPH. *Faculty:* 132 full-time (79 women), 6 part-time/adjunct (5 women). *Students:* 583 full-time (422 women), 34 part-time (26 women); includes 142 minority (28 Black or African American, non-Hispanic/Latino; 3 American Indian or Alaska Native, non-Hispanic/Latino; 23 Asian, non-Hispanic/Latino; 35 Hispanic/Latino; 53 Two or more races, non-Hispanic/Latino), 28 international. Average age 26. 85 applicants, 87% accepted, 54 enrolled. In 2019, 33 master's, 137 doctorates awarded. *Degree requirements:* For master's, comprehensive exam (for some programs), thesis (for some programs); for doctorate, comprehensive exam (for some programs), thesis/dissertation (for some programs). *Entrance requirements:* For master's and doctorate, GRE/GMAT. Additional exam requirements/recommendations for international students: required—TOEFL (minimum score 90 iBT). *Application deadline:* For fall admission, 8/1 for domestic students, 4/1 for international students; for spring admission, 1/1 for domestic students, 9/1 for international students. Applications are processed on a rolling basis. Application fee: $75. Electronic applications accepted. *Expenses:* Tuition, state resident: full-time $13,700; part-time $761.25 per credit hour. Tuition, nonresident: full-time $27,614; part-time $1534 per credit hour. *Required fees:* $886.50 per term. Tuition and fees vary according to campus/location and program. *Financial support:* In 2019–20, 3 fellowships with full and partial tuition reimbursements (averaging $2,668 per year), 33 research assistantships with full tuition reimbursements (averaging $19,301 per year), 30 teaching assistantships with full tuition reimbursements (averaging $21,932 per year) were awarded; scholarships/grants also available. Financial award application deadline: 3/1; financial award applicants required to submit FAFSA. *Unit head:* Dr. Daniel Givens, Dean, 540-231-7910, Fax: 540-231-3505, E-mail: gdaniel@vt.edu. *Application contact:* Sheila Steele, Executive Assistant, 540-231-7910, Fax: 540-231-3505, E-mail: ssteele@vt.edu.
Website: http://www.vetmed.vt.edu

**Washington State University,** College of Veterinary Medicine, Program in Veterinary Clinical Sciences, Pullman, WA 99164. Offers clinical and translational science (MS, PhD). *Program availability:* Part-time. *Faculty:* 41 full-time (22 women). *Students:* 14 full-time (6 women), 21 part-time (16 women); includes 11 minority (3 Asian, non-Hispanic/Latino; 8 Hispanic/Latino), 8 international. Average age 30. 10 applicants, 100% accepted, 10 enrolled. In 2019, 7 master's awarded. *Degree requirements:* For master's, thesis, oral exam; for doctorate, thesis/dissertation, oral exam. *Entrance requirements:* For master's and doctorate, minimum GPA of 3.0, DVM or equivalent. Additional exam requirements/recommendations for international students: required—TOEFL (minimum score 550 paper-based; 80 iBT), IELTS (minimum score 7). *Application deadline:* For fall admission, 3/31 for domestic and international students. Application fee: $75. Electronic applications accepted. *Financial support:* In 2019–20, 35 students received support, including 34 research assistantships with full tuition reimbursements available (averaging $33,024 per year), 1 teaching assistantship (averaging $33,126 per year); fellowships and health care benefits also available. Financial award application deadline: 3/1. *Unit head:* Dr. Robert Mealey, Chair, 509-335-0738, Fax: 509-335-0880, E-mail: rmealey@wsu.edu. *Application contact:* Kathy L. Dahmen, Administrative Manager, 509-335-4156, Fax: 509-335-0880, E-mail: dahmen@wsu.edu.
Website: http://graduate.vetmed.wsu.edu/

# APPENDIXES

# Institutional Changes
# Since the 2020 Edition (Graduate)

Following is an alphabetical listing of institutions that have recently closed, merged with other institutions, or changed their names or status. In the case of a name change, the former name appears first, followed by the new name.

Antioch University (Midwest Yellow Springs, OH): *closed.*

Argosy University, Atlanta (Atlanta, GA): *closed.*

Argosy University, Chicago (Chicago, IL): *closed.*

Argosy University, Hawaii (Honolulu, HI): *closed.*

Argosy University, Los Angeles (Los Angeles, CA): *closed.*

Argosy University, Northern Virginia (Arlington, VA): *closed.*

Argosy University, Orange County (Orange, CA): *closed.*

Argosy University, Phoenix (Phoenix, AZ): *closed.*

Argosy University, Seattle (Seattle, WA): *closed.*

Argosy University, Tampa (Tampa, FL): *closed.*

Argosy University, Twin Cities (Eagan, MN): *closed.*

College of Saint Elizabeth (Morristown, NJ): *name changed to Saint Elizabeth University.*

College of St. Joseph (Rutland, VT): *closed.*

Concordia University (Portland, OR): *closed.*

Elmhurst College (Elmhurst, IL): *name changed to Elmhurst University.*

The John Marshall Law School (Chicago, IL): *closed; acquired by University of Illinois at Chicago; name changed to UIC John Marshall Law School.*

Marygrove College (Detroit, MI): *closed.*

Nebraska Christian College of Hope International University (Papillion, NE): *closed.*

Northwest Christian University (Eugene, OR): *name changed to Bushnell University.*

Notre Dame de Namur University (Belmont, CA): *closed.*

Silver Lake College of the Holy Family (Manitowoc, WI): *closed.*

University of South Florida Sarasota-Manatee (Sarasota, FL): *to merge with University of South Florida Main Campus.*

University of South Florida, St. Petersburg (St. Petersburg, FL): *to merge with University of South Florida Main Campus.*

Watkins College of Art, Design, and Film (Nashville, TN): *to merge with Belmont University.*

# Abbreviations Used in the Guides

The following list includes abbreviations of degree names used in the profiles in the 2020 edition of the guides. Because some degrees (e.g., Doctor of Education) can be abbreviated in more than one way (e.g., D.Ed. or Ed.D.), and because the abbreviations used in the guides reflect the preferences of the individual colleges and universities, the list may include two or more abbreviations for a single degree.

## DEGREES

| | |
|---|---|
| A Mus D | Doctor of Musical Arts |
| AC | Advanced Certificate |
| AD | Artist's Diploma |
| | Doctor of Arts |
| ADP | Artist's Diploma |
| Adv C | Advanced Certificate |
| AGC | Advanced Graduate Certificate |
| AGSC | Advanced Graduate Specialist Certificate |
| ALM | Master of Liberal Arts |
| AM | Master of Arts |
| AMBA | Accelerated Master of Business Administration |
| APC | Advanced Professional Certificate |
| APMPH | Advanced Professional Master of Public Health |
| App Sc | Applied Scientist |
| App Sc D | Doctor of Applied Science |
| AstE | Astronautical Engineer |
| ATC | Advanced Training Certificate |
| Au D | Doctor of Audiology |
| B Th | Bachelor of Theology |
| CAES | Certificate of Advanced Educational Specialization |
| CAGS | Certificate of Advanced Graduate Studies |
| CAL | Certificate in Applied Linguistics |
| CAPS | Certificate of Advanced Professional Studies |
| CAS | Certificate of Advanced Studies |
| CATS | Certificate of Achievement in Theological Studies |
| CE | Civil Engineer |
| CEM | Certificate of Environmental Management |
| CET | Certificate in Educational Technologies |
| CGS | Certificate of Graduate Studies |
| Ch E | Chemical Engineer |
| Clin Sc D | Doctor of Clinical Science |
| CM | Certificate in Management |
| CMH | Certificate in Medical Humanities |
| CMM | Master of Church Ministries |
| CMS | Certificate in Ministerial Studies |
| CNM | Certificate in Nonprofit Management |
| CPC | Certificate in Publication and Communication |
| CPH | Certificate in Public Health |
| CPS | Certificate of Professional Studies |
| CScD | Doctor of Clinical Science |
| CSD | Certificate in Spiritual Direction |
| CSS | Certificate of Special Studies |
| CTS | Certificate of Theological Studies |
| D Ac | Doctor of Acupuncture |
| D Admin | Doctor of Administration |
| D Arch | Doctor of Architecture |
| D Be | Doctor in Bioethics |
| D Com | Doctor of Commerce |
| D Couns | Doctor of Counseling |
| D Des | Doctorate of Design |
| D Div | Doctor of Divinity |
| D Ed | Doctor of Education |
| D Ed Min | Doctor of Educational Ministry |
| D Eng | Doctor of Engineering |
| D Engr | Doctor of Engineering |

| | |
|---|---|
| D Ent | Doctor of Enterprise |
| D Env | Doctor of Environment |
| D Law | Doctor of Law |
| D Litt | Doctor of Letters |
| D Med Sc | Doctor of Medical Science |
| D Mgt | Doctor of Management |
| D Min | Doctor of Ministry |
| D Miss | Doctor of Missiology |
| D Mus | Doctor of Music |
| D Mus A | Doctor of Musical Arts |
| D Phil | Doctor of Philosophy |
| D Prof | Doctor of Professional Studies |
| D Ps | Doctor of Psychology |
| D Sc | Doctor of Science |
| D Sc D | Doctor of Science in Dentistry |
| D Sc IS | Doctor of Science in Information Systems |
| D Sc PA | Doctor of Science in Physician Assistant Studies |
| D Th | Doctor of Theology |
| D Th P | Doctor of Practical Theology |
| DA | Doctor of Accounting |
| | Doctor of Arts |
| DACM | Doctor of Acupuncture and Chinese Medicine |
| DAIS | Doctor of Applied Intercultural Studies |
| DAOM | Doctorate in Acupuncture and Oriental Medicine |
| DAT | Doctorate of Athletic Training |
| | Professional Doctor of Art Therapy |
| DBA | Doctor of Business Administration |
| DBH | Doctor of Behavioral Health |
| DBL | Doctor of Business Leadership |
| DC | Doctor of Chiropractic |
| DCC | Doctor of Computer Science |
| DCD | Doctor of Communications Design |
| DCE | Doctor of Computer Engineering |
| DCJ | Doctor of Criminal Justice |
| DCL | Doctor of Civil Law |
| | Doctor of Comparative Law |
| DCM | Doctor of Church Music |
| DCN | Doctor of Clinical Nutrition |
| DCS | Doctor of Computer Science |
| DDN | Diplôme du Droit Notarial |
| DDS | Doctor of Dental Surgery |
| DE | Doctor of Education |
| | Doctor of Engineering |
| DED | Doctor of Economic Development |
| DEIT | Doctor of Educational Innovation and Technology |
| DEL | Doctor of Executive Leadership |
| DEM | Doctor of Educational Ministry |
| DEPD | Diplôme Études Spécialisées |
| DES | Doctor of Engineering Science |
| DESS | Diplôme Études Supérieures Spécialisées |
| DET | Doctor of Educational Technology |
| DFA | Doctor of Fine Arts |
| DGP | Diploma in Graduate and Professional Studies |
| DGS | Doctor of Global Security |
| DH Sc | Doctor of Health Sciences |
| DHA | Doctor of Health Administration |
| DHCE | Doctor of Health Care Ethics |
| DHL | Doctor of Hebrew Letters |
| DHPE | Doctorate of Health Professionals Education |
| DHS | Doctor of Health Science |
| DHSc | Doctor of Health Science |
| DIT | Doctor of Industrial Technology |

| | |
|---|---|
| | Doctor of Information Technology |
| DJS | Doctor of Jewish Studies |
| DLS | Doctor of Liberal Studies |
| DM | Doctor of Management |
| | Doctor of Music |
| DMA | Doctor of Musical Arts |
| DMD | Doctor of Dental Medicine |
| DME | Doctor of Manufacturing Management |
| | Doctor of Music Education |
| DMFT | Doctor of Marital and Family Therapy |
| DMH | Doctor of Medical Humanities |
| DML | Doctor of Modern Languages |
| DMP | Doctorate in Medical Physics |
| DMPNA | Doctor of Management Practice in Nurse Anesthesia |
| DN Sc | Doctor of Nursing Science |
| DNAP | Doctor of Nurse Anesthesia Practice |
| DNP | Doctor of Nursing Practice |
| DNP-A | Doctor of Nursing Practice - Anesthesia |
| DNS | Doctor of Nursing Science |
| DO | Doctor of Osteopathy |
| DOL | Doctorate of Organizational Leadership |
| DOM | Doctor of Oriental Medicine |
| DOT | Doctor of Occupational Therapy |
| DPA | Diploma in Public Administration |
| | Doctor of Public Administration |
| DPDS | Doctor of Planning and Development Studies |
| DPH | Doctor of Public Health |
| DPM | Doctor of Plant Medicine |
| | Doctor of Podiatric Medicine |
| DPPD | Doctor of Policy, Planning, and Development |
| DPS | Doctor of Professional Studies |
| DPT | Doctor of Physical Therapy |
| DPTSc | Doctor of Physical Therapy Science |
| Dr DES | Doctor of Design |
| Dr NP | Doctor of Nursing Practice |
| Dr OT | Doctor of Occupational Therapy |
| Dr PH | Doctor of Public Health |
| Dr Sc PT | Doctor of Science in Physical Therapy |
| DRSc | Doctor of Regulatory Science |
| DS | Doctor of Science |
| DS Sc | Doctor of Social Science |
| DScPT | Doctor of Science in Physical Therapy |
| DSI | Doctor of Strategic Intelligence |
| DSJS | Doctor of Science in Jewish Studies |
| DSL | Doctor of Strategic Leadership |
| DSNS | Doctorate of Statecraft and National Security |
| DSS | Doctor of Strategic Security |
| DSW | Doctor of Social Work |
| DTL | Doctor of Talmudic Law |
| | Doctor of Transformational Leadership |
| DV Sc | Doctor of Veterinary Science |
| DVM | Doctor of Veterinary Medicine |
| DWS | Doctor of Worship Studies |
| EAA | Engineer in Aeronautics and Astronautics |
| EASPh D | Engineering and Applied Science Doctor of Philosophy |
| ECS | Engineer in Computer Science |
| Ed D | Doctor of Education |
| Ed DCT | Doctor of Education in College Teaching |
| Ed L D | Doctor of Education Leadership |
| Ed M | Master of Education |
| Ed S | Specialist in Education |
| Ed Sp | Specialist in Education |
| EDB | Executive Doctorate in Business |
| EDM | Executive Doctorate in Management |
| EE | Electrical Engineer |
| EJD | Executive Juris Doctor |
| EMBA | Executive Master of Business Administration |

| | |
|---|---|
| EMFA | Executive Master of Forensic Accounting |
| EMHA | Executive Master of Health Administration |
| EMHCL | Executive Master in Healthcare Leadership |
| EMIB | Executive Master of International Business |
| EMIR | Executive Master in International Relations |
| EML | Executive Master of Leadership |
| EMPA | Executive Master of Public Administration |
| EMPL | Executive Master in Policy Leadership |
| | Executive Master in Public Leadership |
| EMS | Executive Master of Science |
| EMTM | Executive Master of Technology Management |
| Eng | Engineer |
| Eng Sc D | Doctor of Engineering Science |
| Engr | Engineer |
| Exec MHA | Executive Master of Health Administration |
| Exec Ed D | Executive Doctor of Education |
| Exec MBA | Executive Master of Business Administration |
| Exec MPA | Executive Master of Public Administration |
| Exec MPH | Executive Master of Public Health |
| Exec MS | Executive Master of Science |
| Executive MA | Executive Master of Arts |
| G Dip | Graduate Diploma |
| GBC | Graduate Business Certificate |
| GDM | Graduate Diploma in Management |
| GDPA | Graduate Diploma in Public Administration |
| GEMBA | Global Executive Master of Business Administration |
| GM Acc | Graduate Master of Accountancy |
| GMBA | Global Master of Business Administration |
| GP LL M | Global Professional Master of Laws |
| GPD | Graduate Performance Diploma |
| GSS | Graduate Special Certificate for Students in Special Situations |
| IEMBA | International Executive Master of Business Administration |
| IMA | Interdisciplinary Master of Arts |
| IMBA | International Master of Business Administration |
| IMES | International Master's in Environmental Studies |
| Ingeniero | Engineer |
| JCD | Doctor of Canon Law |
| JCL | Licentiate in Canon Law |
| JD | Juris Doctor |
| JM | Juris Master |
| JSD | Doctor of Juridical Science |
| | Doctor of Jurisprudence |
| | Doctor of the Science of Law |
| JSM | Master of the Science of Law |
| L Th | Licentiate in Theology |
| LL B | Bachelor of Laws |
| LL CM | Master of Comparative Law |
| LL D | Doctor of Laws |
| LL M | Master of Laws |
| LL M in Tax | Master of Laws in Taxation |
| LL M CL | Master of Laws in Common Law |
| M Ac | Master of Accountancy |
| | Master of Accounting |
| | Master of Acupuncture |
| M Ac OM | Master of Acupuncture and Oriental Medicine |
| M Acc | Master of Accountancy |
| | Master of Accounting |
| M Acct | Master of Accountancy |
| | Master of Accounting |
| M Accy | Master of Accountancy |
| M Actg | Master of Accounting |
| M Acy | Master of Accountancy |
| M Ad | Master of Administration |
| M Ad Ed | Master of Adult Education |
| M Adm | Master of Administration |

| | |
|---|---|
| M Adm Mgt | Master of Administrative Management |
| M Admin | Master of Administration |
| M ADU | Master of Architectural Design and Urbanism |
| M Adv | Master of Advertising |
| M Ag | Master of Agriculture |
| M Ag Ed | Master of Agricultural Education |
| M Agr | Master of Agriculture |
| M App Comp Sc | Master of Applied Computer Science |
| M App St | Master of Applied Statistics |
| M Appl Stat | Master of Applied Statistics |
| M Aq | Master of Aquaculture |
| M Ar | Master of Architecture |
| M Arch | Master of Architecture |
| M Arch I | Master of Architecture I |
| M Arch II | Master of Architecture II |
| M Arch E | Master of Architectural Engineering |
| M Arch H | Master of Architectural History |
| M Bioethics | Master in Bioethics |
| M Cat | Master of Catechesis |
| M Ch E | Master of Chemical Engineering |
| M Cl D | Master of Clinical Dentistry |
| M Cl Sc | Master of Clinical Science |
| M Comm | Master of Communication |
| M Comp | Master of Computing |
| M Comp Sc | Master of Computer Science |
| M Coun | Master of Counseling |
| M Dent | Master of Dentistry |
| M Dent Sc | Master of Dental Sciences |
| M Des | Master of Design |
| M Des S | Master of Design Studies |
| M Div | Master of Divinity |
| M E Sci | Master of Earth Science |
| M Ec | Master of Economics |
| M Econ | Master of Economics |
| M Ed | Master of Education |
| M Ed T | Master of Education in Teaching |
| M En | Master of Engineering |
| M En S | Master of Environmental Sciences |
| M Eng | Master of Engineering |
| M Eng Mgt | Master of Engineering Management |
| M Engr | Master of Engineering |
| M Ent | Master of Enterprise |
| M Env | Master of Environment |
| M Env Des | Master of Environmental Design |
| M Env E | Master of Environmental Engineering |
| M Env Sc | Master of Environmental Science |
| M Ext Ed | Master of Extension Education |
| M Fin | Master of Finance |
| M Geo E | Master of Geological Engineering |
| M Geoenv E | Master of Geoenvironmental Engineering |
| M Geog | Master of Geography |
| M Hum | Master of Humanities |
| M IDST | Master's in Interdisciplinary Studies |
| M Jur | Master of Jurisprudence |
| M Kin | Master of Kinesiology |
| M Land Arch | Master of Landscape Architecture |
| M Litt | Master of Letters |
| M Mark | Master of Marketing |
| M Mat SE | Master of Material Science and Engineering |
| M Math | Master of Mathematics |
| M Mech E | Master of Mechanical Engineering |
| M Med Sc | Master of Medical Science |
| M Mgmt | Master of Management |
| M Mgt | Master of Management |
| M Min | Master of Ministries |
| M Mtl E | Master of Materials Engineering |
| M Mu | Master of Music |
| M Mus | Master of Music |
| M Mus Ed | Master of Music Education |
| M Music | Master of Music |
| M Pet E | Master of Petroleum Engineering |
| M Pharm | Master of Pharmacy |
| M Phil | Master of Philosophy |
| M Phil F | Master of Philosophical Foundations |
| M Pl | Master of Planning |
| M Plan | Master of Planning |
| M Pol | Master of Political Science |
| M Pr Met | Master of Professional Meteorology |
| M Prob S | Master of Probability and Statistics |
| M Psych | Master of Psychology |
| M Pub | Master of Publishing |
| M Rel | Master of Religion |
| M Sc | Master of Science |
| M Sc A | Master of Science (Applied) |
| M Sc AC | Master of Science in Applied Computing |
| M Sc AHN | Master of Science in Applied Human Nutrition |
| M Sc BMC | Master of Science in Biomedical Communications |
| M Sc CS | Master of Science in Computer Science |
| M Sc E | Master of Science in Engineering |
| M Sc Eng | Master of Science in Engineering |
| M Sc Engr | Master of Science in Engineering |
| M Sc F | Master of Science in Forestry |
| M Sc FE | Master of Science in Forest Engineering |
| M Sc Geogr | Master of Science in Geography |
| M Sc N | Master of Science in Nursing |
| M Sc OT | Master of Science in Occupational Therapy |
| M Sc P | Master of Science in Planning |
| M Sc Pl | Master of Science in Planning |
| M Sc PT | Master of Science in Physical Therapy |
| M Sc T | Master of Science in Teaching |
| M SEM | Master of Sustainable Environmental Management |
| M Serv Soc | Master of Social Service |
| M Soc | Master of Sociology |
| M Sp Ed | Master of Special Education |
| M Stat | Master of Statistics |
| M Sys E | Master of Systems Engineering |
| M Sys Sc | Master of Systems Science |
| M Tax | Master of Taxation |
| M Tech | Master of Technology |
| M Th | Master of Theology |
| M Trans E | Master of Transportation Engineering |
| M U Ed | Master of Urban Education |
| M Urb | Master of Urban Planning |
| M Vet Sc | Master of Veterinary Science |
| MA | Master of Accounting |
| | Master of Administration |
| | Master of Arts |
| MA Comm | Master of Arts in Communication |
| MA Ed | Master of Arts in Education |
| MA Ed/HD | Master of Arts in Education and Human Development |
| MA Islamic | Master of Arts in Islamic Studies |
| MA Min | Master of Arts in Ministry |
| MA Miss | Master of Arts in Missiology |
| MA Past St | Master of Arts in Pastoral Studies |
| MA Ph | Master of Arts in Philosophy |
| MA Psych | Master of Arts in Psychology |
| MA Sc | Master of Applied Science |
| MA Sp | Master of Arts (Spirituality) |
| MA Th | Master of Arts in Theology |
| MA-R | Master of Arts (Research) |
| MAA | Master of Applied Anthropology |
| | Master of Applied Arts |
| | Master of Arts in Administration |
| MAAA | Master of Arts in Arts Administration |

| | |
|---|---|
| MAAD | Master of Advanced Architectural Design |
| MAAE | Master of Arts in Art Education |
| MAAPPS | Master of Arts in Asia Pacific Policy Studies |
| MAAS | Master of Arts in Aging and Spirituality |
| MAASJ | Master of Arts in Applied Social Justice |
| MAAT | Master of Arts in Applied Theology |
| MAB | Master of Agribusiness |
| | Master of Applied Bioengineering |
| | Master of Arts in Business |
| MABA | Master's in Applied Behavior Analysis |
| MABC | Master of Arts in Biblical Counseling |
| MABE | Master of Arts in Bible Exposition |
| MABL | Master of Arts in Biblical Languages |
| MABM | Master of Agribusiness Management |
| MABS | Master of Arts in Biblical Studies |
| MABT | Master of Arts in Bible Teaching |
| MAC | Master of Accountancy |
| | Master of Accounting |
| | Master of Arts in Communication |
| | Master of Arts in Counseling |
| MACC | Master of Arts in Christian Counseling |
| MACCT | Master of Accounting |
| MACD | Master of Arts in Christian Doctrine |
| MACE | Master of Arts in Christian Education |
| MACH | Master of Arts in Church History |
| MACI | Master of Arts in Curriculum and Instruction |
| MACIS | Master of Accounting and Information Systems |
| MACJ | Master of Arts in Criminal Justice |
| MACL | Master of Arts in Christian Leadership |
| | Master of Arts in Community Leadership |
| MACM | Master of Arts in Christian Ministries |
| | Master of Arts in Christian Ministry |
| | Master of Arts in Church Music |
| | Master of Arts in Counseling Ministries |
| MACML | Master of Arts in Christian Ministry and Leadership |
| MACN | Master of Arts in Counseling |
| MACO | Master of Arts in Counseling |
| MAcOM | Master of Acupuncture and Oriental Medicine |
| MACP | Master of Arts in Christian Practice |
| | Master of Arts in Church Planting |
| | Master of Arts in Counseling Psychology |
| MACS | Master of Applied Computer Science |
| | Master of Arts in Catholic Studies |
| | Master of Arts in Christian Studies |
| MACSE | Master of Arts in Christian School Education |
| MACT | Master of Arts in Communications and Technology |
| MAD | Master in Educational Institution Administration |
| | Master of Art and Design |
| MADR | Master of Arts in Dispute Resolution |
| MADS | Master of Applied Disability Studies |
| MAE | Master of Aerospace Engineering |
| | Master of Agricultural Economics |
| | Master of Agricultural Education |
| | Master of Applied Economics |
| | Master of Architectural Engineering |
| | Master of Art Education |
| | Master of Arts in Education |
| | Master of Arts in English |
| MAEd | Master of Arts Education |
| MAEE | Master of Agricultural and Extension Education |
| MAEL | Master of Arts in Educational Leadership |
| MAEM | Master of Arts in Educational Ministries |
| MAEP | Master of Arts in Economic Policy |
| | Master of Arts in Educational Psychology |
| MAES | Master of Arts in Environmental Sciences |
| MAET | Master of Arts in English Teaching |

| | |
|---|---|
| MAF | Master of Arts in Finance |
| MAFE | Master of Arts in Financial Economics |
| MAFM | Master of Accounting and Financial Management |
| MAFS | Master of Arts in Family Studies |
| MAG | Master of Applied Geography |
| MAGU | Master of Urban Analysis and Management |
| MAH | Master of Arts in Humanities |
| MAHA | Master of Arts in Humanitarian Assistance |
| MAHCM | Master of Arts in Health Care Mission |
| MAHG | Master of American History and Government |
| MAHL | Master of Arts in Hebrew Letters |
| MAHN | Master of Applied Human Nutrition |
| MAHR | Master of Applied Historical Research |
| MAHS | Master of Arts in Human Services |
| MAHSR | Master in Applied Health Services Research |
| MAIA | Master of Arts in International Administration |
| | Master of Arts in International Affairs |
| MAICS | Master of Arts in Intercultural Studies |
| MAIDM | Master of Arts in Interior Design and Merchandising |
| MAIH | Master of Arts in Interdisciplinary Humanities |
| MAIOP | Master of Applied Industrial/Organizational Psychology |
| MAIS | Master of Arts in Intercultural Studies |
| | Master of Arts in Interdisciplinary Studies |
| | Master of Arts in International Studies |
| MAIT | Master of Administration in Information Technology |
| MAJ | Master of Arts in Journalism |
| MAJCS | Master of Arts in Jewish Communal Service |
| MAJPS | Master of Arts in Jewish Professional Studies |
| MAJS | Master of Arts in Jewish Studies |
| MAL | Master of Athletic Leadership |
| MALA | Master of Arts in Liberal Arts |
| MALCM | Master in Arts Leadership and Cultural Management |
| MALD | Master of Arts in Law and Diplomacy |
| MALER | Master of Arts in Labor and Employment Relations |
| MALL | Master of Arts in Language Learning |
| MALLT | Master of Arts in Language, Literature, and Translation |
| MALP | Master of Arts in Language Pedagogy |
| MALS | Master of Arts in Liberal Studies |
| MAM | Master of Acquisition Management |
| | Master of Agriculture and Management |
| | Master of Applied Mathematics |
| | Master of Arts in Management |
| | Master of Arts in Ministry |
| | Master of Arts Management |
| | Master of Aviation Management |
| MAMC | Master of Arts in Mass Communication |
| | Master of Arts in Ministry and Culture |
| | Master of Arts in Ministry for a Multicultural Church |
| MAME | Master of Arts in Missions/Evangelism |
| MAMFC | Master of Arts in Marriage and Family Counseling |
| MAMFT | Master of Arts in Marriage and Family Therapy |
| MAMHC | Master of Arts in Mental Health Counseling |
| MAMS | Master of Applied Mathematical Sciences |
| | Master of Arts in Ministerial Studies |
| | Master of Arts in Ministry and Spirituality |
| MAMT | Master of Arts in Mathematics Teaching |
| MAN | Master of Applied Nutrition |
| MANT | Master of Arts in New Testament |
| MAOL | Master of Arts in Organizational Leadership |
| MAOM | Master of Acupuncture and Oriental Medicine |
| | Master of Arts in Organizational Management |

| | |
|---|---|
| MAOT | Master of Arts in Old Testament |
| MAP | Master of Applied Politics |
| | Master of Applied Psychology |
| | Master of Arts in Planning |
| | Master of Psychology |
| | Master of Public Administration |
| MAP Min | Master of Arts in Pastoral Ministry |
| MAPA | Master of Arts in Public Administration |
| MAPC | Master of Arts in Pastoral Counseling |
| MAPE | Master of Arts in Physics Education |
| MAPM | Master of Arts in Pastoral Ministry |
| | Master of Arts in Pastoral Music |
| | Master of Arts in Practical Ministry |
| MAPP | Master of Arts in Public Policy |
| MAPS | Master of Applied Psychological Sciences |
| | Master of Arts in Pastoral Studies |
| | Master of Arts in Public Service |
| MAPW | Master of Arts in Professional Writing |
| MAQRM | Master's of Actuarial and Quantitative Risk Management |
| MAR | Master of Arts in Reading |
| | Master of Arts in Religion |
| Mar Eng | Marine Engineer |
| MARC | Master of Arts in Rehabilitation Counseling |
| MARE | Master of Arts in Religious Education |
| MARL | Master of Arts in Religious Leadership |
| MARS | Master of Arts in Religious Studies |
| MAS | Master of Accounting Science |
| | Master of Actuarial Science |
| | Master of Administrative Science |
| | Master of Advanced Study |
| | Master of American Studies |
| | Master of Animal Science |
| | Master of Applied Science |
| | Master of Applied Statistics |
| | Master of Archival Studies |
| MASA | Master of Advanced Studies in Architecture |
| MASC | Master of Arts in School Counseling |
| MASD | Master of Arts in Spiritual Direction |
| MASE | Master of Arts in Special Education |
| MASF | Master of Arts in Spiritual Formation |
| MASJ | Master of Arts in Systems of Justice |
| MASLA | Master of Advanced Studies in Landscape Architecture |
| MASM | Master of Aging Services Management |
| | Master of Arts in Specialized Ministries |
| MASS | Master of Applied Social Science |
| MASW | Master of Aboriginal Social Work |
| MAT | Master of Arts in Teaching |
| | Master of Arts in Theology |
| | Master of Athletic Training |
| | Master's in Administration of Telecommunications |
| Mat E | Materials Engineer |
| MATCM | Master of Acupuncture and Traditional Chinese Medicine |
| MATDE | Master of Arts in Theology, Development, and Evangelism |
| MATDR | Master of Territorial Management and Regional Development |
| MATE | Master of Arts for the Teaching of English |
| MATESL | Master of Arts in Teaching English as a Second Language |
| MATESOL | Master of Arts in Teaching English to Speakers of Other Languages |
| MATF | Master of Arts in Teaching English as a Foreign Language/Intercultural Studies |
| MATFL | Master of Arts in Teaching Foreign Language |
| MATH | Master of Arts in Therapy |

| | |
|---|---|
| MATI | Master of Administration of Information Technology |
| MATL | Master of Arts in Teaching of Languages |
| | Master of Arts in Transformational Leadership |
| MATM | Master of Arts in Teaching of Mathematics |
| MATRN | Master of Athletic Training |
| MATS | Master of Arts in Theological Studies |
| | Master of Arts in Transforming Spirituality |
| MAUA | Master of Arts in Urban Affairs |
| MAUD | Master of Arts in Urban Design |
| MAURP | Master of Arts in Urban and Regional Planning |
| MAW | Master of Arts in Worship |
| MAWSHP | Master of Arts in Worship |
| MAYM | Master of Arts in Youth Ministry |
| MB | Master of Bioinformatics |
| MBA | Master of Business Administration |
| MBA-AM | Master of Business Administration in Aviation Management |
| MBA-EP | Master of Business Administration– Experienced Professionals |
| MBAA | Master of Business Administration in Aviation |
| MBAE | Master of Biological and Agricultural Engineering |
| | Master of Biosystems and Agricultural Engineering |
| MBAH | Master of Business Administration in Health |
| MBAi | Master of Business Administration– International |
| MBAICT | Master of Business Administration in Information and Communication Technology |
| MBC | Master of Building Construction |
| MBE | Master of Bilingual Education |
| | Master of Bioengineering |
| | Master of Bioethics |
| | Master of Biomedical Engineering |
| | Master of Business Economics |
| | Master of Business Education |
| MBEE | Master in Biotechnology Enterprise and Entrepreneurship |
| MBET | Master of Business, Entrepreneurship and Technology |
| MBI | Master in Business Informatics |
| MBIOT | Master of Biotechnology |
| MBiotech | Master of Biotechnology |
| MBL | Master of Business Leadership |
| MBLE | Master in Business Logistics Engineering |
| MBME | Master's in Biomedical Engineering |
| MBMSE | Master of Business Management and Software Engineering |
| MBOE | Master of Business Operational Excellence |
| MBS | Master of Biblical Studies |
| | Master of Biological Science |
| | Master of Biomedical Sciences |
| | Master of Bioscience |
| | Master of Building Science |
| | Master of Business and Science |
| | Master of Business Statistics |
| MBST | Master of Biostatistics |
| MBT | Master of Biomedical Technology |
| | Master of Biotechnology |
| | Master of Business Taxation |
| MBV | Master of Business for Veterans |
| MC | Master of Classics |
| | Master of Communication |
| | Master of Counseling |
| MC Ed | Master of Continuing Education |
| MC Sc | Master of Computer Science |
| MCA | Master of Commercial Aviation |
| | Master of Communication Arts |
| | Master of Criminology (Applied) |

| | |
|---|---|
| MCAM | Master of Computational and Applied Mathematics |
| MCC | Master of Computer Science |
| MCD | Master of Communications Disorders |
| | Master of Community Development |
| MCE | Master in Electronic Commerce |
| | Master of Chemistry Education |
| | Master of Christian Education |
| | Master of Civil Engineering |
| | Master of Control Engineering |
| MCEM | Master of Construction Engineering Management |
| MCEPA | Master of Chinese Economic and Political Affairs |
| MCHE | Master of Chemical Engineering |
| MCIS | Master of Communication and Information Studies |
| | Master of Computer and Information Science |
| | Master of Computer Information Systems |
| MCIT | Master of Computer and Information Technology |
| MCJ | Master of Criminal Justice |
| MCL | Master in Communication Leadership |
| | Master of Canon Law |
| | Master of Christian Leadership |
| | Master of Comparative Law |
| MCM | Master of Christian Ministry |
| | Master of Church Music |
| | Master of Communication Management |
| | Master of Community Medicine |
| | Master of Construction Management |
| | Master of Contract Management |
| MCMin | Master of Christian Ministry |
| MCMM | Master in Communications and Media Management |
| MCMP | Master of City and Metropolitan Planning |
| MCMS | Master of Clinical Medical Science |
| MCN | Master of Clinical Nutrition |
| MCOL | Master of Arts in Community and Organizational Leadership |
| MCP | Master of City Planning |
| | Master of Community Planning |
| | Master of Counseling Psychology |
| | Master of Cytopathology Practice |
| | Master of Science in Quality Systems and Productivity |
| MCPD | Master of Community Planning and Development |
| MCR | Master in Clinical Research |
| MCRP | Master of City and Regional Planning |
| | Master of Community and Regional Planning |
| MCRS | Master of City and Regional Studies |
| MCS | Master of Chemical Sciences |
| | Master of Christian Studies |
| | Master of Clinical Science |
| | Master of Combined Sciences |
| | Master of Communication Studies |
| | Master of Computer Science |
| | Master of Consumer Science |
| MCSE | Master of Computer Science and Engineering |
| MCSL | Master of Catholic School Leadership |
| MCSM | Master of Construction Science and Management |
| MCT | Master of Commerce and Technology |
| MCTM | Master of Clinical Translation Management |
| MCTP | Master of Communication Technology and Policy |
| MCTS | Master of Clinical and Translational Science |
| MCVS | Master of Cardiovascular Science |
| MD | Doctor of Medicine |

| | |
|---|---|
| MDA | Master of Dietetic Administration |
| MDB | Master of Design-Build |
| MDE | Master in Design Engineering |
| | Master of Developmental Economics |
| | Master of Distance Education |
| | Master of the Education of the Deaf |
| MDH | Master of Dental Hygiene |
| MDI | Master of Disruptive Innovation |
| MDM | Master of Design Methods |
| | Master of Digital Media |
| MDP | Master in Sustainable Development Practice |
| | Master of Development Practice |
| MDR | Master of Dispute Resolution |
| MDS | Master in Data Science |
| | Master of Dental Surgery |
| | Master of Design Studies |
| | Master of Digital Sciences |
| MDSPP | Master in Data Science for Public Policy |
| ME | Master of Education |
| | Master of Engineering |
| | Master of Entrepreneurship |
| ME Sc | Master of Engineering Science |
| ME-PD | Master of Education–Professional Development |
| MEA | Master of Educational Administration |
| | Master of Engineering Administration |
| MEAE | Master of Entertainment Arts and Engineering |
| MEAP | Master of Environmental Administration and Planning |
| MEB | Master of Energy Business |
| MEBD | Master in Environmental Building Design |
| MEBT | Master in Electronic Business Technologies |
| MEC | Master of Electronic Commerce |
| Mech E | Mechanical Engineer |
| MEDS | Master of Environmental Design Studies |
| MEE | Master in Education |
| | Master of Electrical Engineering |
| | Master of Energy Engineering |
| | Master of Environmental Engineering |
| MEECON | Master of Energy Economics |
| MEEM | Master of Environmental Engineering and Management |
| MEENE | Master of Engineering in Environmental Engineering |
| MEEP | Master of Environmental and Energy Policy |
| MEERM | Master of Earth and Environmental Resource Management |
| MEH | Master in Humanistic Studies |
| | Master of Environmental Health |
| | Master of Environmental Horticulture |
| MEHS | Master of Environmental Health and Safety |
| MEIM | Master of Entertainment Industry Management |
| | Master of Equine Industry Management |
| MEL | Master of Educational Leadership |
| | Master of Engineering Leadership |
| | Master of English Literature |
| MELP | Master of Environmental Law and Policy |
| MEM | Master of Engineering Management |
| | Master of Environmental Management |
| | Master of Marketing |
| MEME | Master of Engineering in Manufacturing Engineering |
| | Master of Engineering in Mechanical Engineering |
| MENR | Master of Environment and Natural Resources |
| MENVEGR | Master of Environmental Engineering |
| MEP | Master of Engineering Physics |
| MEPC | Master of Environmental Pollution Control |
| MEPD | Master of Environmental Planning and Design |
| MER | Master of Employment Relations |

| | | | |
|---|---|---|---|
| MERE | Master of Entrepreneurial Real Estate | | Master of Global Studies |
| MERL | Master of Energy Regulation and Law | MH | Master of Humanities |
| MES | Master of Education and Science | MH Sc | Master of Health Sciences |
| | Master of Engineering Science | MHA | Master of Health Administration |
| | Master of Environment and Sustainability | | Master of Healthcare Administration |
| | Master of Environmental Science | | Master of Hospital Administration |
| | Master of Environmental Studies | | Master of Hospitality Administration |
| | Master of Environmental Systems | MHB | Master of Human Behavior |
| MESM | Master of Environmental Science and Management | MHC | Master of Mental Health Counseling |
| | | MHCA | Master of Health Care Administration |
| MET | Master of Educational Technology | MHCD | Master of Health Care Design |
| | Master of Engineering Technology | MHCI | Master of Human-Computer Interaction |
| | Master of Entertainment Technology | MHCL | Master of Health Care Leadership |
| | Master of Environmental Toxicology | MHCM | Master of Health Care Management |
| METM | Master of Engineering and Technology Management | MHE | Master of Health Education |
| | | | Master of Higher Education |
| MEVE | Master of Environmental Engineering | | Master of Human Ecology |
| MF | Master of Finance | MHE Ed | Master of Home Economics Education |
| | Master of Forestry | MHEA | Master of Higher Education Administration |
| MFA | Master of Financial Administration | MHHS | Master of Health and Human Services |
| | Master of Fine Arts | MHI | Master of Health Informatics |
| MFALP | Master of Food and Agriculture Law and Policy | | Master of Healthcare Innovation |
| MFAS | Master of Fisheries and Aquatic Science | MHID | Master of Healthcare Interior Design |
| MFC | Master of Forest Conservation | MHIHIM | Master of Health Informatics and Health Information Management |
| MFCS | Master of Family and Consumer Sciences | | |
| MFE | Master of Financial Economics | MHIIM | Master of Health Informatics and Information Management |
| | Master of Financial Engineering | | |
| | Master of Forest Engineering | MHK | Master of Human Kinetics |
| MFES | Master of Fire and Emergency Services | MHM | Master of Healthcare Management |
| MFG | Master of Functional Genomics | MHMS | Master of Health Management Systems |
| MFHD | Master of Family and Human Development | MHP | Master of Health Physics |
| MFM | Master of Financial Management | | Master of Heritage Preservation |
| | Master of Financial Mathematics | | Master of Historic Preservation |
| MFPE | Master of Food Process Engineering | MHPA | Master of Heath Policy and Administration |
| MFR | Master of Forest Resources | MHPCTL | Master of High Performance Coaching and Technical Leadership |
| MFRC | Master of Forest Resources and Conservation | | |
| MFRE | Master of Food and Resource Economics | MHPE | Master of Health Professions Education |
| MFS | Master of Food Science | MHR | Master of Human Resources |
| | Master of Forensic Sciences | MHRD | Master in Human Resource Development |
| | Master of Forest Science | MHRIR | Master of Human Resources and Industrial Relations |
| | Master of Forest Studies | | |
| | Master of French Studies | MHRLR | Master of Human Resources and Labor Relations |
| MFST | Master of Food Safety and Technology | | |
| MFT | Master of Family Therapy | MHRM | Master of Human Resources Management |
| MFWCB | Master of Fish, Wildlife and Conservation Biology | MHS | Master of Health Science |
| | | | Master of Health Sciences |
| MFYCS | Master of Family, Youth and Community Sciences | | Master of Health Studies |
| | | | Master of Hispanic Studies |
| MGA | Master of Global Affairs | | Master of Human Services |
| | Master of Government Administration | | Master of Humanistic Studies |
| | Master of Governmental Administration | MHSA | Master of Health Services Administration |
| MGBA | Master of Global Business Administration | MHSM | Master of Health Systems Management |
| MGC | Master of Genetic Counseling | MI | Master of Information |
| MGCS | Master of Genetic Counselor Studies | | Master of Instruction |
| MGD | Master of Graphic Design | MI Arch | Master of Interior Architecture |
| MGE | Master of Geotechnical Engineering | MIA | Master of Interior Architecture |
| MGEM | Master of Geomatics for Environmental Management | | Master of International Affairs |
| | | MIAA | Master of International Affairs and Administration |
| | Master of Global Entrepreneurship and Management | | |
| | | MIAM | Master of International Agribusiness Management |
| MGIS | Master of Geographic Information Science | | |
| | Master of Geographic Information Systems | MIAPD | Master of Interior Architecture and Product Design |
| MGM | Master of Global Management | | |
| MGMA | Master of Greenhouse Gas Management and Accounting | MIB | Master of International Business |
| | | MIBS | Master of International Business Studies |
| MGP | Master of Gestion de Projet | MICLJ | Master of International Criminal Law and Justice |
| MGPS | Master of Global Policy Studies | | |
| MGREM | Master of Global Real Estate Management | MICM | Master of International Construction Management |
| MGS | Master of Gender Studies | | |
| | Master of Gerontological Studies | MID | Master of Industrial Design |

| | | | |
|---|---|---|---|
| | Master of Industrial Distribution | | Master of Judicial Studies |
| | Master of Innovation Design | | Master of Juridical Studies |
| | Master of Interior Design | MK | Master of Kinesiology |
| | Master of International Development | MKM | Master of Knowledge Management |
| MIDA | Master of International Development Administration | ML | Master of Latin |
| | | | Master of Law |
| MIDP | Master of International Development Policy | ML Arch | Master of Landscape Architecture |
| MIDS | Master of Information and Data Science | MLA | Master of Landscape Architecture |
| MIE | Master of Industrial Engineering | | Master of Liberal Arts |
| MIF | Master of International Forestry | MLAS | Master of Laboratory Animal Science |
| MIHTM | Master of International Hospitality and Tourism Management | | Master of Liberal Arts and Sciences |
| | | MLAUD | Master of Landscape Architecture in Urban Development |
| MIJ | Master of International Journalism | | |
| MILR | Master of Industrial and Labor Relations | MLD | Master of Leadership Development |
| MIM | Master in Ministry | | Master of Leadership Studies |
| | Master of Information Management | MLE | Master of Applied Linguistics and Exegesis |
| | Master of International Management | MLER | Master of Labor and Employment Relations |
| | Master of International Marketing | MLI Sc | Master of Library and Information Science |
| MIMFA | Master of Investment Management and Financial Analysis | MLIS | Master of Library and Information Science |
| | | | Master of Library and Information Studies |
| MIMLAE | Master of International Management for Latin American Executives | MLM | Master of Leadership in Ministry |
| | | MLPD | Master of Land and Property Development |
| MIMS | Master of Information Management and Systems | MLRHR | Master of Labor Relations and Human Resources |
| | Master of Integrated Manufacturing Systems | MLS | Master of Leadership Studies |
| MIP | Master of Infrastructure Planning | | Master of Legal Studies |
| | Master of Intellectual Property | | Master of Liberal Studies |
| | Master of International Policy | | Master of Library Science |
| MIPA | Master of International Public Affairs | | Master of Life Sciences |
| MIPD | Master of Integrated Product Design | | Master of Medical Laboratory Sciences |
| MIPER | Master of International Political Economy of Resources | MLSCM | Master of Logistics and Supply Chain Management |
| MIPM | Master of International Policy Management | MLT | Master of Language Technologies |
| MIPP | Master of International Policy and Practice | MLTCA | Master of Long Term Care Administration |
| | Master of International Public Policy | MLW | Master of Studies in Law |
| MIPS | Master of International Planning Studies | MLWS | Master of Land and Water Systems |
| MIR | Master of Industrial Relations | MM | Master of Management |
| | Master of International Relations | | Master of Mediation |
| MIRD | Master of International Relations and Diplomacy | | Master of Ministry |
| | | | Master of Music |
| MIRHR | Master of Industrial Relations and Human Resources | MM Ed | Master of Music Education |
| | | MM Sc | Master of Medical Science |
| MIS | Master of Imaging Science | MM St | Master of Museum Studies |
| | Master of Industrial Statistics | MMA | Master of Marine Affairs |
| | Master of Information Science | | Master of Media Arts |
| | Master of Information Systems | | Master of Musical Arts |
| | Master of Integrated Science | MMAL | Master of Maritime Administration and Logistics |
| | Master of Interdisciplinary Studies | | |
| | Master of International Service | MMAS | Master of Military Art and Science |
| | Master of International Studies | MMB | Master of Microbial Biotechnology |
| MISE | Master of Industrial and Systems Engineering | MMC | Master of Manufacturing Competitiveness |
| MISKM | Master of Information Sciences and Knowledge Management | | Master of Mass Communications |
| | | MMCM | Master of Music in Church Music |
| MISM | Master of Information Systems Management | MMCSS | Master of Mathematical Computational and Statistical Sciences |
| MISW | Master of Indigenous Social Work | | |
| MIT | Master in Teaching | MME | Master of Management in Energy |
| | Master of Industrial Technology | | Master of Manufacturing Engineering |
| | Master of Information Technology | | Master of Mathematics Education |
| | Master of Initial Teaching | | Master of Mathematics for Educators |
| | Master of International Trade | | Master of Mechanical Engineering |
| MITA | Master of Information Technology Administration | | Master of Mining Engineering |
| | | | Master of Music Education |
| MITM | Master of Information Technology and Management | MMEL | Master's in Medical Education Leadership |
| | | MMF | Master of Mathematical Finance |
| MJ | Master of Journalism | MMFC/T | Master of Marriage and Family Counseling/ Therapy |
| | Master of Jurisprudence | | |
| MJ Ed | Master of Jewish Education | MMFT | Master of Marriage and Family Therapy |
| MJA | Master of Justice Administration | MMG | Master of Management |
| MJM | Master of Justice Management | MMH | Master of Management in Hospitality |
| MJS | Master of Judaic Studies | | |

| | | | |
|---|---|---|---|
| | Master of Medical Humanities | | Master of Planning |
| MMI | Master of Management of Innovation | MP Ac | Master of Professional Accountancy |
| MMIS | Master of Management Information Systems | MP Acc | Master of Professional Accountancy |
| MML | Master of Managerial Logistics | | Master of Professional Accounting |
| MMM | Master of Manufacturing Management | | Master of Public Accounting |
| | Master of Marine Management | MP Aff | Master of Public Affairs |
| | Master of Medical Management | MP Th | Master of Pastoral Theology |
| MMP | Master of Marine Policy | MPA | Master of Performing Arts |
| | Master of Medical Physics | | Master of Physician Assistant |
| | Master of Music Performance | | Master of Professional Accountancy |
| MMPA | Master of Management and Professional Accounting | | Master of Professional Accounting |
| | | | Master of Public Administration |
| MMQM | Master of Manufacturing Quality Management | | Master of Public Affairs |
| MMR | Master of Marketing Research | MPAC | Master of Professional Accounting |
| MMRM | Master of Marine Resources Management | MPAID | Master of Public Administration and International Development |
| MMS | Master in Migration Studies | | |
| | Master of Management Science | MPAP | Master of Physician Assistant Practice |
| | Master of Management Studies | | Master of Public Administration and Policy |
| | Master of Manufacturing Systems | | Master of Public Affairs and Politics |
| | Master of Marine Studies | MPAS | Master of Physician Assistant Science |
| | Master of Materials Science | | Master of Physician Assistant Studies |
| | Master of Mathematical Sciences | MPC | Master of Professional Communication |
| | Master of Medical Science | MPD | Master of Product Development |
| | Master of Medieval Studies | | Master of Public Diplomacy |
| MMSE | Master of Manufacturing Systems Engineering | MPDS | Master of Planning and Development Studies |
| MMSM | Master of Music in Sacred Music | MPE | Master of Physical Education |
| MMT | Master in Marketing | MPEM | Master of Project Engineering and Management |
| | Master of Math for Teaching | | |
| | Master of Music Therapy | MPFM | Master of Public Financial Management |
| | Master's in Marketing Technology | MPH | Master of Public Health |
| MMus | Master of Music | MPHE | Master of Public Health Education |
| MN | Master of Nursing | MPHM | Master in Plant Health Management |
| | Master of Nutrition | MPHS | Master of Population Health Sciences |
| MN NP | Master of Nursing in Nurse Practitioner | MPHTM | Master of Public Health and Tropical Medicine |
| MNA | Master of Nonprofit Administration | MPI | Master of Public Informatics |
| | Master of Nurse Anesthesia | MPIA | Master of Public and International Affairs |
| MNAE | Master of Nanoengineering | MPL | Master of Pastoral Leadership |
| MNAL | Master of Nonprofit Administration and Leadership | MPM | Master of Pastoral Ministry |
| | | | Master of Pest Management |
| MNAS | Master of Natural and Applied Science | | Master of Policy Management |
| MNCL | Master of Nonprofit and Civic Leadership | | Master of Practical Ministries |
| MNCM | Master of Network and Communications Management | | Master of Professional Management |
| | | | Master of Project Management |
| MNE | Master of Nuclear Engineering | | Master of Public Management |
| MNL | Master in International Business for Latin America | MPNA | Master of Public and Nonprofit Administration |
| | | MPNL | Master of Philanthropy and Nonprofit Leadership |
| MNM | Master of Nonprofit Management | | |
| MNO | Master of Nonprofit Organization | MPO | Master of Prosthetics and Orthotics |
| MNPL | Master of Not-for-Profit Leadership | MPOD | Master of Positive Organizational Development |
| MNpS | Master of Nonprofit Studies | MPP | Master of Public Policy |
| MNR | Master of Natural Resources | MPPA | Master of Public Policy Administration |
| MNRD | Master of Natural Resources Development | | Master of Public Policy and Administration |
| MNRES | Master of Natural Resources and Environmental Studies | MPPAL | Master of Public Policy, Administration and Law |
| | | MPPGA | Master of Public Policy and Global Affairs |
| MNRM | Master of Natural Resource Management | MPPM | Master of Public Policy and Management |
| MNRMG | Master of Natural Resource Management and Geography | MPR | Master of Public Relations |
| | | MPRTM | Master of Parks, Recreation, and Tourism Management |
| MNRS | Master of Natural Resource Stewardship | | |
| MNS | Master of Natural Science | MPS | Master of Pastoral Studies |
| MNSE | Master of Natural Sciences Education | | Master of Perfusion Science |
| MO | Master of Oceanography | | Master of Planning Studies |
| MOD | Master of Organizational Development | | Master of Political Science |
| MOGS | Master of Oil and Gas Studies | | Master of Preservation Studies |
| MOL | Master of Organizational Leadership | | Master of Prevention Science |
| MOM | Master of Organizational Management | | Master of Professional Studies |
| | Master of Oriental Medicine | | Master of Public Service |
| MOR | Master of Operations Research | MPSA | Master of Public Service Administration |
| MOT | Master of Occupational Therapy | MPSG | Master of Population and Social Gerontology |
| MP | Master of Physiology | | |

| | |
|---|---|
| MPSIA | Master of Political Science and International Affairs |
| MPSL | Master of Public Safety Leadership |
| MPT | Master of Pastoral Theology |
| | Master of Physical Therapy |
| | Master of Practical Theology |
| MPVM | Master of Preventive Veterinary Medicine |
| MPW | Master of Professional Writing |
| | Master of Public Works |
| MQF | Master of Quantitative Finance |
| MQM | Master of Quality Management |
| | Master of Quantitative Management |
| MQS | Master of Quality Systems |
| MR | Master of Recreation |
| | Master of Retailing |
| MRA | Master in Research Administration |
| | Master of Regulatory Affairs |
| MRC | Master of Rehabilitation Counseling |
| MRCP | Master of Regional and City Planning |
| | Master of Regional and Community Planning |
| MRD | Master of Rural Development |
| MRE | Master of Real Estate |
| | Master of Religious Education |
| MRED | Master of Real Estate Development |
| MREM | Master of Resource and Environmental Management |
| MRLS | Master of Resources Law Studies |
| MRM | Master of Resources Management |
| MRP | Master of Regional Planning |
| MRRD | Master in Recreation Resource Development |
| MRS | Master of Religious Studies |
| MRSc | Master of Rehabilitation Science |
| MRUD | Master of Resilient Design |
| MS | Master of Science |
| MS Cmp E | Master of Science in Computer Engineering |
| MS Kin | Master of Science in Kinesiology |
| MS Acct | Master of Science in Accounting |
| MS Accy | Master of Science in Accountancy |
| MS Aero E | Master of Science in Aerospace Engineering |
| MS Ag | Master of Science in Agriculture |
| MS Arch | Master of Science in Architecture |
| MS Arch St | Master of Science in Architectural Studies |
| MS Bio E | Master of Science in Bioengineering |
| MS Bm E | Master of Science in Biomedical Engineering |
| MS Ch E | Master of Science in Chemical Engineering |
| MS Cp E | Master of Science in Computer Engineering |
| MS Eco | Master of Science in Economics |
| MS Econ | Master of Science in Economics |
| MS Ed | Master of Science in Education |
| MS Ed Admin | Master of Science in Educational Administration |
| MS El | Master of Science in Educational Leadership and Administration |
| MS En E | Master of Science in Environmental Engineering |
| MS Eng | Master of Science in Engineering |
| MS Engr | Master of Science in Engineering |
| MS Env E | Master of Science in Environmental Engineering |
| MS Exp Surg | Master of Science in Experimental Surgery |
| MS Mat SE | Master of Science in Material Science and Engineering |
| MS Met E | Master of Science in Metallurgical Engineering |
| MS Mgt | Master of Science in Management |
| MS Min | Master of Science in Mining |
| MS Min E | Master of Science in Mining Engineering |
| MS Mt E | Master of Science in Materials Engineering |
| MS Otol | Master of Science in Otolaryngology |
| MS Pet E | Master of Science in Petroleum Engineering |
| MS Sc | Master of Social Science |
| MS Sp Ed | Master of Science in Special Education |
| MS Stat | Master of Science in Statistics |
| MS Surg | Master of Science in Surgery |
| MS Tax | Master of Science in Taxation |
| MS Tc E | Master of Science in Telecommunications Engineering |
| MS-R | Master of Science (Research) |
| MSA | Master of School Administration |
| | Master of Science in Accountancy |
| | Master of Science in Accounting |
| | Master of Science in Administration |
| | Master of Science in Aeronautics |
| | Master of Science in Agriculture |
| | Master of Science in Analytics |
| | Master of Science in Anesthesia |
| | Master of Science in Architecture |
| | Master of Science in Aviation |
| | Master of Sports Administration |
| | Master of Surgical Assisting |
| MSAA | Master of Science in Astronautics and Aeronautics |
| MSABE | Master of Science in Agricultural and Biological Engineering |
| MSAC | Master of Science in Acupuncture |
| MSACC | Master of Science in Accounting |
| MSACS | Master of Science in Applied Computer Science |
| MSAE | Master of Science in Aeronautical Engineering |
| | Master of Science in Aerospace Engineering |
| | Master of Science in Applied Economics |
| | Master of Science in Applied Engineering |
| | Master of Science in Architectural Engineering |
| MSAEM | Master of Science in Aerospace Engineering and Mechanics |
| MSAF | Master of Science in Aviation Finance |
| MSAG | Master of Science in Applied Geosciences |
| MSAH | Master of Science in Allied Health |
| MSAL | Master of Sport Administration and Leadership |
| MSAM | Master of Science in Applied Mathematics |
| MSANR | Master of Science in Agriculture and Natural Resources |
| MSAS | Master of Science in Administrative Studies |
| | Master of Science in Applied Statistics |
| | Master of Science in Architectural Studies |
| MSAT | Master of Science in Accounting and Taxation |
| | Master of Science in Advanced Technology |
| | Master of Science in Athletic Training |
| MSB | Master of Science in Biotechnology |
| MSBA | Master of Science in Business Administration |
| | Master of Science in Business Analysis |
| MSBAE | Master of Science in Biological and Agricultural Engineering |
| | Master of Science in Biosystems and Agricultural Engineering |
| MSBCB | Master's in Bioinformatics and Computational Biology |
| MSBE | Master of Science in Biological Engineering |
| | Master of Science in Biomedical Engineering |
| MSBENG | Master of Science in Bioengineering |
| MSBH | Master of Science in Behavioral Health |
| MSBM | Master of Sport Business Management |
| MSBME | Master of Science in Biomedical Engineering |
| MSBMS | Master of Science in Basic Medical Science |
| MSBS | Master of Science in Biomedical Sciences |
| MSBTM | Master of Science in Biotechnology and Management |
| MSC | Master of Science in Commerce |
| | Master of Science in Communication |
| | Master of Science in Counseling |
| | Master of Science in Criminology |
| | Master of Strategic Communication |

*Peterson's Graduate Programs in the Biological/Biomedical Sciences & Health-Related Medical Professions 2021*

| | | | | |
|---|---|---|---|---|
| MSCC | Master of Science in Community Counseling | | MSECE | Master of Science in Electrical and Computer Engineering |
| MSCD | Master of Science in Communication Disorders | | MSED | Master of Sustainable Economic Development |
| | Master of Science in Community Development | | MSEE | Master of Science in Electrical Engineering |
| MSCE | Master of Science in Chemistry Education | | | Master of Science in Environmental Engineering |
| | Master of Science in Civil Engineering | | | |
| | Master of Science in Clinical Epidemiology | | MSEH | Master of Science in Environmental Health |
| | Master of Science in Computer Engineering | | MSEL | Master of Science in Educational Leadership |
| | Master of Science in Continuing Education | | MSEM | Master of Science in Engineering and Management |
| MSCEE | Master of Science in Civil and Environmental Engineering | | | Master of Science in Engineering Management |
| MSCF | Master of Science in Computational Finance | | | Master of Science in Engineering Mechanics |
| MSCH | Master of Science in Chemical Engineering | | | Master of Science in Environmental Management |
| MSChE | Master of Science in Chemical Engineering | | | |
| MSCI | Master of Science in Clinical Investigation | | MSENE | Master of Science in Environmental Engineering |
| MSCID | Master of Science in Community and International Development | | MSEO | Master of Science in Electro-Optics |
| MSCIS | Master of Science in Computer and Information Science | | MSES | Master of Science in Embedded Software Engineering |
| | Master of Science in Computer and Information Systems | | | Master of Science in Engineering Science |
| | Master of Science in Computer Information Science | | | Master of Science in Environmental Science |
| | | | | Master of Science in Environmental Studies |
| | Master of Science in Computer Information Systems | | | Master of Science in Exercise Science |
| MSCIT | Master of Science in Computer Information Technology | | MSESE | Master of Science in Energy Systems Engineering |
| MSCJ | Master of Science in Criminal Justice | | MSET | Master of Science in Educational Technology |
| MSCJA | Master of Science in Criminal Justice Administration | | | Master of Science in Engineering Technology |
| | | | MSEV | Master of Science in Environmental Engineering |
| MSCJS | Master of Science in Crime and Justice Studies | | MSF | Master of Science in Finance |
| MSCLS | Master of Science in Clinical Laboratory Studies | | | Master of Science in Forestry |
| MSCM | Master of Science in Church Management | | MSFA | Master of Science in Financial Analysis |
| | Master of Science in Conflict Management | | MSFCS | Master of Science in Family and Consumer Science |
| | Master of Science in Construction Management | | | |
| | Master of Supply Chain Management | | MSFE | Master of Science in Financial Engineering |
| MSCMP | Master of Science in Cybersecurity Management and Policy | | MSFM | Master of Sustainable Forest Management |
| | | | MSFOR | Master of Science in Forestry |
| MSCNU | Master of Science in Clinical Nutrition | | MSFP | Master of Science in Financial Planning |
| MSCP | Master of Science in Clinical Psychology | | MSFS | Master of Science in Financial Sciences |
| | Master of Science in Community Psychology | | | Master of Science in Forensic Science |
| | Master of Science in Computer Engineering | | MSFSB | Master of Science in Financial Services and Banking |
| | Master of Science in Counseling Psychology | | | |
| MSCPE | Master of Science in Computer Engineering | | MSFT | Master of Science in Family Therapy |
| MSCPharm | Master of Science in Pharmacy | | MSGC | Master of Science in Genetic Counseling |
| MSCR | Master of Science in Clinical Research | | MSH | Master of Science in Health |
| MSCRP | Master of Science in City and Regional Planning | | | Master of Science in Hospice |
| | | | MSHA | Master of Science in Health Administration |
| | Master of Science in Community and Regional Planning | | MSHCA | Master of Science in Health Care Administration |
| MSCS | Master of Science in Clinical Science | | | |
| | Master of Science in Computer Science | | MSHCPM | Master of Science in Health Care Policy and Management |
| | Master of Science in Cyber Security | | MSHE | Master of Science in Health Education |
| MSCSD | Master of Science in Communication Sciences and Disorders | | MSHES | Master of Science in Human Environmental Sciences |
| MSCSE | Master of Science in Computer Science and Engineering | | MSHFID | Master of Science in Human Factors in Information Design |
| MSCTE | Master of Science in Career and Technical Education | | MSHFS | Master of Science in Human Factors and Systems |
| MSD | Master of Science in Dentistry | | MSHI | Master of Science in Health Informatics |
| | Master of Science in Design | | MSHP | Master of Science in Health Professions |
| | Master of Science in Dietetics | | MSHR | Master of Science in Human Resources |
| MSDM | Master of Security and Disaster Management | | MSHRL | Master of Science in Human Resource Leadership |
| MSE | Master of Science Education | | MSHRM | Master of Science in Human Resource Management |
| | Master of Science in Economics | | | |
| | Master of Science in Education | | MSHROD | Master of Science in Human Resources and Organizational Development |
| | Master of Science in Engineering | | | |
| | Master of Science in Engineering Management | | MSHS | Master of Science in Health Science |
| | Master of Software Engineering | | | Master of Science in Health Services |
| | Master of Special Education | | | Master of Science in Homeland Security |
| | Master of Structural Engineering | | MSHSR | Master of Science in Human Security and Resilience |

| | |
|---|---|
| MSI | Master of Science in Information |
| | Master of Science in Instruction |
| | Master of System Integration |
| MSIA | Master of Science in Industrial Administration |
| | Master of Science in Information Assurance |
| MSIDM | Master of Science in Interior Design and Merchandising |
| MSIE | Master of Science in Industrial Engineering |
| MSIEM | Master of Science in Information Engineering and Management |
| MSIM | Master of Science in Industrial Management |
| | Master of Science in Information Management |
| | Master of Science in International Management |
| MSIMC | Master of Science in Integrated Marketing Communications |
| MSIMS | Master of Science in Identity Management and Security |
| MSIS | Master of Science in Information Science |
| | Master of Science in Information Studies |
| | Master of Science in Information Systems |
| | Master of Science in Interdisciplinary Studies |
| MSISE | Master of Science in Infrastructure Systems Engineering |
| MSISM | Master of Science in Information Systems Management |
| MSISPM | Master of Science in Information Security Policy and Management |
| MSIST | Master of Science in Information Systems Technology |
| MSIT | Master of Science in Industrial Technology |
| | Master of Science in Information Technology |
| | Master of Science in Instructional Technology |
| MSITM | Master of Science in Information Technology Management |
| MSJ | Master of Science in Journalism |
| | Master of Science in Jurisprudence |
| MSJC | Master of Social Justice and Criminology |
| MSJFP | Master of Science in Juvenile Forensic Psychology |
| MSJJ | Master of Science in Juvenile Justice |
| MSJPS | Master of Science in Justice and Public Safety |
| MSK | Master of Science in Kinesiology |
| MSL | Master in the Study of Law |
| | Master of School Leadership |
| | Master of Science in Leadership |
| | Master of Science in Limnology |
| | Master of Sports Leadership |
| | Master of Strategic Leadership |
| | Master of Studies in Law |
| MSLA | Master of Science in Legal Administration |
| MSLB | Master of Sports Law and Business |
| MSLFS | Master of Science in Life Sciences |
| MSLP | Master of Speech-Language Pathology |
| MSLS | Master of Science in Library Science |
| MSLSCM | Master of Science in Logistics and Supply Chain Management |
| MSLT | Master of Second Language Teaching |
| MSM | Master of Sacred Ministry |
| | Master of Sacred Music |
| | Master of School Mathematics |
| | Master of Science in Management |
| | Master of Science in Medicine |
| | Master of Science in Organization Management |
| | Master of Security Management |
| | Master of Strategic Ministry |
| | Master of Supply Management |
| MSMA | Master of Science in Marketing Analysis |
| MSMAE | Master of Science in Materials Engineering |
| MSMC | Master of Science in Management and Communications |
| | Master of Science in Mass Communications |

| | |
|---|---|
| MSME | Master of Science in Mathematics Education |
| | Master of Science in Mechanical Engineering |
| | Master of Science in Medical Ethics |
| MSMHC | Master of Science in Mental Health Counseling |
| MSMIT | Master of Science in Management and Information Technology |
| MSMLS | Master of Science in Medical Laboratory Science |
| MSMOT | Master of Science in Management of Technology |
| MSMP | Master of Science in Medical Physics |
| | Master of Science in Molecular Pathology |
| MSMS | Master of Science in Management Science |
| | Master of Science in Marine Science |
| | Master of Science in Medical Sciences |
| MSMSE | Master of Science in Manufacturing Systems Engineering |
| | Master of Science in Material Science and Engineering |
| | Master of Science in Material Science Engineering |
| | Master of Science in Mathematics and Science Education |
| MSMus | Master of Sacred Music |
| MSN | Master of Science in Nursing |
| MSNA | Master of Science in Nurse Anesthesia |
| MSNE | Master of Science in Nuclear Engineering |
| MSNS | Master of Science in Natural Science |
| | Master of Science in Nutritional Science |
| MSOD | Master of Science in Organization Development |
| | Master of Science in Organizational Development |
| MSOEE | Master of Science in Outdoor and Environmental Education |
| MSOES | Master of Science in Occupational Ergonomics and Safety |
| MSOH | Master of Science in Occupational Health |
| MSOL | Master of Science in Organizational Leadership |
| MSOM | Master of Science in Oriental Medicine |
| MSOR | Master of Science in Operations Research |
| MSOT | Master of Science in Occupational Technology |
| | Master of Science in Occupational Therapy |
| MSP | Master of Science in Pharmacy |
| | Master of Science in Planning |
| | Master of Speech Pathology |
| | Master of Sustainable Peacebuilding |
| MSPA | Master of Science in Physician Assistant |
| MSPAS | Master of Science in Physician Assistant Studies |
| MSPC | Master of Science in Professional Communications |
| MSPE | Master of Science in Petroleum Engineering |
| MSPH | Master of Science in Public Health |
| MSPHR | Master of Science in Pharmacy |
| MSPM | Master of Science in Professional Management |
| | Master of Science in Project Management |
| MSPNGE | Master of Science in Petroleum and Natural Gas Engineering |
| MSPPM | Master of Science in Public Policy and Management |
| MSPS | Master of Science in Pharmaceutical Science |
| | Master of Science in Political Science |
| | Master of Science in Psychological Services |
| MSPT | Master of Science in Physical Therapy |
| MSRA | Master of Science in Recreation Administration |
| MSRE | Master of Science in Real Estate |
| | Master of Science in Religious Education |
| MSRED | Master of Science in Real Estate Development |
| | Master of Sustainable Real Estate Development |
| MSRLS | Master of Science in Recreation and Leisure Studies |

| | | | |
|---|---|---|---|
| MSRM | Master of Science in Risk Management | MTCM | Master of Traditional Chinese Medicine |
| MSRMP | Master of Science in Radiological Medical Physics | MTD | Master of Training and Development |
| | | MTE | Master in Educational Technology |
| MSRS | Master of Science in Radiological Sciences | | Master of Technological Entrepreneurship |
| | Master of Science in Rehabilitation Science | MTESOL | Master in Teaching English to Speakers of Other Languages |
| MSS | Master of Security Studies | MTHM | Master of Tourism and Hospitality Management |
| | Master of Social Science | MTI | Master of Information Technology |
| | Master of Social Services | MTID | Master of Tangible Interaction Design |
| | Master of Sports Science | MTL | Master of Talmudic Law |
| | Master of Strategic Studies | MTM | Master of Technology Management |
| | Master's in Statistical Science | | Master of Telecommunications Management |
| MSSA | Master of Science in Social Administration | | Master of the Teaching of Mathematics |
| MSSCM | Master of Science in Supply Chain Management | | Master of Transformative Ministry |
| MSSD | Master of Arts in Software Driven Systems Design | | Master of Translational Medicine |
| | Master of Science in Sustainable Design | MTMH | Master of Tropical Medicine and Hygiene |
| MSSE | Master of Science in Software Engineering | MTMS | Master in Teaching Mathematics and Science |
| | Master of Science in Special Education | MTOM | Master of Traditional Oriental Medicine |
| MSSEM | Master of Science in Systems and Engineering Management | MTPC | Master of Technical and Professional Communication |
| MSSI | Master of Science in Security Informatics | MTR | Master of Translational Research |
| | Master of Science in Strategic Intelligence | MTS | Master of Theatre Studies |
| MSSIS | Master of Science in Security and Intelligence Studies | | Master of Theological Studies |
| MSSL | Master of Science in School Leadership | MTW | Master of Teaching Writing |
| MSSLP | Master of Science in Speech-Language Pathology | MTWM | Master of Trust and Wealth Management |
| MSSM | Master of Science in Sports Medicine | MUA | Master of Urban Affairs |
| | Master of Science in Systems Management | MUAP | Master's of Urban Affairs and Policy |
| MSSP | Master of Science in Social Policy | MUCD | Master of Urban and Community Design |
| MSSS | Master of Science in Safety Science | MUD | Master of Urban Design |
| | Master of Science in Systems Science | MUDS | Master of Urban Design Studies |
| MSST | Master of Science in Security Technologies | MUEP | Master of Urban and Environmental Planning |
| MSSW | Master of Science in Social Work | MUP | Master of Urban Planning |
| MSSWE | Master of Science in Software Engineering | MUPD | Master of Urban Planning and Development |
| MST | Master of Science and Technology | MUPP | Master of Urban Planning and Policy |
| | Master of Science in Taxation | MUPRED | Master of Urban Planning and Real Estate Development |
| | Master of Science in Teaching | MURP | Master of Urban and Regional Planning |
| | Master of Science in Technology | | Master of Urban and Rural Planning |
| | Master of Science in Telecommunications | MURPL | Master of Urban and Regional Planning |
| | Master of Science Teaching | MUS | Master of Urban Studies |
| MSTC | Master of Science in Technical Communication | Mus M | Master of Music |
| | Master of Science in Telecommunications | MUSA | Master of Urban Spatial Analytics |
| MSTCM | Master of Science in Traditional Chinese Medicine | MVP | Master of Voice Pedagogy |
| MSTE | Master of Science in Telecommunications Engineering | MVS | Master of Visual Studies |
| | | MWBS | Master of Won Buddhist Studies |
| | Master of Science in Transportation Engineering | MWC | Master of Wildlife Conservation |
| | | MWR | Master of Water Resources |
| MSTL | Master of Science in Teacher Leadership | MWS | Master of Women's Studies |
| MSTM | Master of Science in Technology Management | | Master of Worship Studies |
| | Master of Science in Transfusion Medicine | MWSc | Master of Wildlife Science |
| MSTOM | Master of Science in Traditional Oriental Medicine | Nav Arch | Naval Architecture |
| MSUASE | Master of Science in Unmanned and Autonomous Systems Engineering | Naval E | Naval Engineer |
| | | ND | Doctor of Naturopathic Medicine |
| MSUD | Master of Science in Urban Design | | Doctor of Nursing |
| MSUS | Master of Science in Urban Studies | NE | Nuclear Engineer |
| MSW | Master of Social Work | Nuc E | Nuclear Engineer |
| MSWE | Master of Software Engineering | OD | Doctor of Optometry |
| MSWREE | Master of Science in Water Resources and Environmental Engineering | OTD | Doctor of Occupational Therapy |
| | | PBME | Professional Master of Biomedical Engineering |
| MT | Master of Taxation | PC | Performer's Certificate |
| | Master of Teaching | PD | Professional Diploma |
| | Master of Technology | PGC | Post-Graduate Certificate |
| | Master of Textiles | PGD | Postgraduate Diploma |
| MTA | Master of Tax Accounting | Ph L | Licentiate of Philosophy |
| | Master of Teaching Arts | Pharm D | Doctor of Pharmacy |
| | Master of Tourism Administration | PhD | Doctor of Philosophy |
| | | PhD Otol | Doctor of Philosophy in Otolaryngology |
| | | PhD Surg | Doctor of Philosophy in Surgery |
| MTC | Master of Technical Communications | PhDEE | Doctor of Philosophy in Electrical Engineering |

| | | | |
|---|---|---|---|
| PMBA | Professional Master of Business Administration | SM | Master of Science |
| PMC | Post Master Certificate | SM Arch S | Master of Science in Architectural Studies |
| PMD | Post-Master's Diploma | SMACT | Master of Science in Art, Culture and Technology |
| PMS | Professional Master of Science | SMBT | Master of Science in Building Technology |
| | Professional Master's | SP | Specialist Degree |
| Post-Doctoral MS | Post-Doctoral Master of Science | Sp Ed | Specialist in Education |
| Post-MSN Certificate | Post-Master of Science in Nursing Certificate | Sp LIS | Specialist in Library and Information Science |
| PPDPT | Postprofessional Doctor of Physical Therapy | SPA | Specialist in Arts |
| Pro-MS | Professional Science Master's | Spec | Specialist's Certificate |
| Professional MA | Professional Master of Arts | Spec M | Specialist in Music |
| Professional MBA | Professional Master of Business Administration | Spt | Specialist Degree |
| Professional MS | Professional Master of Science | SSP | Specialist in School Psychology |
| PSM | Professional Master of Science | STB | Bachelor of Sacred Theology |
| | Professional Science Master's | STD | Doctor of Sacred Theology |
| Psy D | Doctor of Psychology | STL | Licentiate of Sacred Theology |
| Psy M | Master of Psychology | STM | Master of Sacred Theology |
| Psy S | Specialist in Psychology | tDACM | Transitional Doctor of Acupuncture and Chinese Medicine |
| Psya D | Doctor of Psychoanalysis | TDPT | Transitional Doctor of Physical Therapy |
| S Psy S | Specialist in Psychological Services | Th D | Doctor of Theology |
| Sc D | Doctor of Science | Th M | Master of Theology |
| Sc M | Master of Science | TOTD | Transitional Doctor of Occupational Therapy |
| SCCT | Specialist in Community College Teaching | VMD | Doctor of Veterinary Medicine |
| ScDPT | Doctor of Physical Therapy Science | WEMBA | Weekend Executive Master of Business Administration |
| SD | Specialist Degree | XMA | Executive Master of Arts |
| SJD | Doctor of Juridical Sciences | | |
| SLPD | Doctor of Speech-Language Pathology | | |

# INDEXES

# Displays and Close-Ups

# Directories and Subject Areas

Following is an alphabetical listing of directories and subject areas. Also listed are cross-references for subject area names not used in the directory structure of the guides, for example, "City and Regional Planning (*see* Urban and Regional Planning)"

## Graduate Programs in the Humanities, Arts & Social Sciences

Addictions/Substance Abuse Counseling
Administration (*see* Arts Administration; Public Administration)
African-American Studies
African Languages and Literatures (*see* African Studies)
African Studies
Agribusiness (*see* Agricultural Economics and Agribusiness)
Agricultural Economics and Agribusiness
Alcohol Abuse Counseling (*see* Addictions/Substance Abuse Counseling)
American Indian/Native American Studies
American Studies
Anthropology
Applied Arts and Design—General
Applied Behavior Analysis
Applied Economics
Applied History (*see* Public History)
Applied Psychology
Applied Social Research
Arabic (*see* Near and Middle Eastern Languages)
Arab Studies (*see* Near and Middle Eastern Studies)
Archaeology
Architectural History
Architecture
Archives Administration (*see* Public History)
Area and Cultural Studies (*see* African-American Studies; African Studies; American Indian/Native American Studies; American Studies; Asian-American Studies; Asian Studies; Canadian Studies; Cultural Studies; East European and Russian Studies; Ethnic Studies; Folklore; Gender Studies; Hispanic Studies; Holocaust Studies; Jewish Studies; Latin American Studies; Near and Middle Eastern Studies; Northern Studies; Pacific Area/ Pacific Rim Studies; Western European Studies; Women's Studies)
Art/Fine Arts
Art History
Arts Administration
Arts Journalism
Art Therapy
Asian-American Studies
Asian Languages
Asian Studies
Behavioral Sciences (*see* Psychology)
Bible Studies (*see* Religion; Theology)
Biological Anthropology
Black Studies (*see* African-American Studies)
Broadcasting (*see* Communication; Film, Television, and Video Production)
Broadcast Journalism
Building Science
Canadian Studies
Celtic Languages
Ceramics (*see* Art/Fine Arts)
Child and Family Studies
Child Development
Chinese
Chinese Studies (*see* Asian Languages; Asian Studies)
Christian Studies (*see* Missions and Missiology; Religion; Theology)
Cinema (*see* Film, Television, and Video Production)
City and Regional Planning (*see* Urban and Regional Planning)
Classical Languages and Literatures (*see* Classics)

Classics
Clinical Psychology
Clothing and Textiles
Cognitive Psychology (*see* Psychology—General; Cognitive Sciences)
Cognitive Sciences
Communication—General
Community Affairs (*see* Urban and Regional Planning; Urban Studies)
Community Planning (*see* Architecture; Environmental Design; Urban and Regional Planning; Urban Design; Urban Studies)
Community Psychology (*see* Social Psychology)
Comparative and Interdisciplinary Arts
Comparative Literature
Composition (*see* Music)
Computer Art and Design
Conflict Resolution and Mediation/Peace Studies
Consumer Economics
Corporate and Organizational Communication
Corrections (*see* Criminal Justice and Criminology)
Counseling (*see* Counseling Psychology; Pastoral Ministry and Counseling)
Counseling Psychology
Crafts (*see* Art/Fine Arts)
Creative Arts Therapies (*see* Art Therapy; Therapies—Dance, Drama, and Music)
Criminal Justice and Criminology
Cultural Anthropology
Cultural Studies
Dance
Decorative Arts
Demography and Population Studies
Design (*see* Applied Arts and Design; Architecture; Art/Fine Arts; Environmental Design; Graphic Design; Industrial Design; Interior Design; Textile Design; Urban Design)
Developmental Psychology
Diplomacy (*see* International Affairs)
Disability Studies
Drama Therapy (*see* Therapies—Dance, Drama, and Music)
Dramatic Arts (*see* Theater)
Drawing (*see* Art/Fine Arts)
Drug Abuse Counseling (*see* Addictions/Substance Abuse Counseling)
Drug and Alcohol Abuse Counseling (*see* Addictions/Substance Abuse Counseling)
East Asian Studies (*see* Asian Studies)
East European and Russian Studies
Economic Development
Economics
Educational Theater (*see* Theater; Therapies—Dance, Drama, and Music)
Emergency Management
English
Environmental Design
Ethics
Ethnic Studies
Ethnomusicology (*see* Music)
Experimental Psychology
Family and Consumer Sciences—General
Family Studies (*see* Child and Family Studies)
Family Therapy (*see* Child and Family Studies; Clinical Psychology; Counseling Psychology; Marriage and Family Therapy)
Filmmaking (*see* Film, Television, and Video Production)
Film Studies (*see* Film, Television, and Video Production)
Film, Television, and Video Production
Film, Television, and Video Theory and Criticism
Fine Arts (*see* Art/Fine Arts)
Folklore
Foreign Languages (*see* specific language)
Foreign Service (*see* International Affairs; International Development)
Forensic Psychology
Forensic Sciences
Forensics (*see* Speech and Interpersonal Communication)

French
Gender Studies
General Studies (*see* Liberal Studies)
Genetic Counseling
Geographic Information Systems
Geography
German
Gerontology
Graphic Design
Greek (*see* Classics)
Health Communication
Health Psychology
Hebrew (*see* Near and Middle Eastern Languages)
Hebrew Studies (*see* Jewish Studies)
Hispanic and Latin American Languages
Hispanic Studies
Historic Preservation
History
History of Art (*see* Art History)
History of Medicine
History of Science and Technology
Holocaust and Genocide Studies
Home Economics (*see* Family and Consumer Sciences—General)
Homeland Security
Household Economics, Sciences, and Management
    (*see* Family and Consumer Sciences—General)
Human Development
Humanities
Illustration
Industrial and Labor Relations
Industrial and Organizational Psychology
Industrial Design
Interdisciplinary Studies
Interior Design
International Affairs
International Development
International Economics
International Service (*see* International Affairs;
    International Development)
International Trade Policy
Internet and Interactive Multimedia
Interpersonal Communication (*see* Speech and
    Interpersonal Communication)
Interpretation (*see* Translation and Interpretation)
Islamic Studies (*see* Near and Middle Eastern Studies; Religion)
Italian
Japanese
Japanese Studies (*see* Asian Languages; Asian Studies; Japanese)
Jewelry (*see* Art/Fine Arts)
Jewish Studies
Journalism
Judaic Studies (*see* Jewish Studies; Religion)
Labor Relations (*see* Industrial and Labor Relations)
Landscape Architecture
Latin American Studies
Latin (*see* Classics)
Law Enforcement (*see* Criminal Justice and Criminology)
Liberal Studies
Lighting Design
Linguistics
Literature (*see* Classics; Comparative Literature; specific language)
Marriage and Family Therapy
Mass Communication
Media Studies
Medical Illustration
Medieval and Renaissance Studies
Metalsmithing (*see* Art/Fine Arts)
Middle Eastern Studies (*see* Near and Middle Eastern Studies)
Military and Defense Studies
Mineral Economics
Ministry (*see* Pastoral Ministry and Counseling; Theology)
Missions and Missiology
Motion Pictures (*see* Film, Television, and Video Production)
Museum Studies
Music
Musicology (*see* Music)

Music Therapy (*see* Therapies—Dance, Drama, and Music)
National Security
Native American Studies (*see* American Indian/Native
    American Studies)
Near and Middle Eastern Languages
Near and Middle Eastern Studies
Northern Studies
Organizational Psychology (*see* Industrial and Organizational
    Psychology)
Oriental Languages (*see* Asian Languages)
Oriental Studies (*see* Asian Studies)
Pacific Area/Pacific Rim Studies
Painting (*see* Art/Fine Arts)
Pastoral Ministry and Counseling
Philanthropic Studies
Philosophy
Photography
Playwriting (*see* Theater; Writing)
Policy Studies (*see* Public Policy)
Political Science
Population Studies (*see* Demography and Population Studies)
Portuguese
Printmaking (*see* Art/Fine Arts)
Product Design (*see* Industrial Design)
Psychoanalysis and Psychotherapy
Psychology—General
Public Administration
Public Affairs
Public History
Public Policy
Public Speaking (*see* Mass Communication; Rhetoric;
    Speech and Interpersonal Communication)
Publishing
Regional Planning (*see* Architecture; Urban and Regional Planning;
    Urban Design; Urban Studies)
Rehabilitation Counseling
Religion
Renaissance Studies (*see* Medieval and Renaissance Studies)
Rhetoric
Romance Languages
Romance Literatures (*see* Romance Languages)
Rural Planning and Studies
Rural Sociology
Russian
Scandinavian Languages
School Psychology
Sculpture (*see* Art/Fine Arts)
Security Administration (*see* Criminal Justice and Criminology)
Slavic Languages
Slavic Studies (*see* East European and Russian Studies; Slavic
    Languages)
Social Psychology
Social Sciences
Sociology
Southeast Asian Studies (*see* Asian Studies)
Soviet Studies (*see* East European and Russian Studies; Russian)
Spanish
Speech and Interpersonal Communication
Sport Psychology
Studio Art (*see* Art/Fine Arts)
Substance Abuse Counseling (*see* Addictions/Substance
    Abuse Counseling)
Survey Methodology
Sustainable Development
Technical Communication
Technical Writing
Telecommunications (*see* Film, Television, and Video Production)
Television (*see* Film, Television, and Video Production)
Textile Design
Textiles (*see* Clothing and Textiles; Textile Design)
Thanatology
Theater
Theater Arts (*see* Theater)
Theology
Therapies—Dance, Drama, and Music
Translation and Interpretation

Transpersonal and Humanistic Psychology
Urban and Regional Planning
Urban Design
Urban Planning (*see* Architecture; Urban and Regional Planning; Urban Design; Urban Studies)
Urban Studies
Video (*see* Film, Television, and Video Production)
Visual Arts (*see* Applied Arts and Design; Art/Fine Arts; Film, Television, and Video Production; Graphic Design; Illustration; Photography)
Western European Studies
Women's Studies
World Wide Web (*see* Internet and Interactive Multimedia)
Writing

# Graduate Programs in the Biological/ Biomedical Sciences & Health-Related Medical Professions

Acupuncture and Oriental Medicine
Acute Care/Critical Care Nursing Administration (*see* Health Services Management and Hospital Administration; Nursing and Healthcare Administration; Pharmaceutical Administration)
Adult Nursing
Advanced Practice Nursing (*see* Family Nurse Practitioner Studies)
Allied Health—General
Allied Health Professions (*see* Clinical Laboratory Sciences/Medical Technology; Clinical Research; Communication Disorders; Dental Hygiene; Emergency Medical Services; Occupational Therapy; Physical Therapy; Physician Assistant Studies; Rehabilitation Sciences)
Allopathic Medicine
Anatomy
Anesthesiologist Assistant Studies
Animal Behavior
Bacteriology
Behavioral Sciences (*see* Biopsychology; Neuroscience; Zoology)
Biochemistry
Bioethics
Biological and Biomedical Sciences—General Biological Chemistry (*see* Biochemistry)
Biological Oceanography (*see* Marine Biology)
Biophysics
Biopsychology
Botany
Breeding (*see* Botany; Plant Biology; Genetics)
Cancer Biology/Oncology
Cardiovascular Sciences
Cell Biology
Cellular Physiology (*see* Cell Biology; Physiology)
Child-Care Nursing (*see* Maternal and Child/Neonatal Nursing)
Chiropractic
Clinical Laboratory Sciences/Medical Technology
Clinical Research
Community Health
Community Health Nursing
Computational Biology
Conservation (*see* Conservation Biology; Environmental Biology)
Conservation Biology
Crop Sciences (*see* Botany; Plant Biology)
Cytology (*see* Cell Biology)
Dental and Oral Surgery (*see* Oral and Dental Sciences)
Dental Assistant Studies (*see* Dental Hygiene)
Dental Hygiene
Dental Services (*see* Dental Hygiene)
Dentistry
Developmental Biology Dietetics (*see* Nutrition)
Ecology
Embryology (*see* Developmental Biology)
Emergency Medical Services
Endocrinology (*see* Physiology)
Entomology

Environmental Biology
Environmental and Occupational Health
Epidemiology
Evolutionary Biology
Family Nurse Practitioner Studies
Foods (*see* Nutrition)
Forensic Nursing
Genetics
Genomic Sciences
Gerontological Nursing
Health Physics/Radiological Health
Health Promotion
Health-Related Professions (*see* individual allied health professions)
Health Services Management and Hospital Administration
Health Services Research
Histology (*see* Anatomy; Cell Biology)
HIV/AIDS Nursing
Hospice Nursing
Hospital Administration (*see* Health Services Management and Hospital Administration)
Human Genetics
Immunology
Industrial Hygiene
Infectious Diseases
International Health
Laboratory Medicine (*see* Clinical Laboratory Sciences/Medical Technology; Immunology; Microbiology; Pathology)
Life Sciences (*see* Biological and Biomedical Sciences)
Marine Biology
Maternal and Child Health
Maternal and Child/Neonatal Nursing
Medical Imaging
Medical Microbiology
Medical Nursing (*see* Medical/Surgical Nursing)
Medical Physics
Medical/Surgical Nursing
Medical Technology (*see* Clinical Laboratory Sciences/Medical Technology)
Medical Sciences (*see* Biological and Biomedical Sciences)
Medical Science Training Programs (*see* Biological and Biomedical Sciences)
Medicinal and Pharmaceutical Chemistry
Medicinal Chemistry (*see* Medicinal and Pharmaceutical Chemistry)
Medicine (*see* Allopathic Medicine; Naturopathic Medicine; Osteopathic Medicine; Podiatric Medicine)
Microbiology
Midwifery (*see* Nurse Midwifery)
Molecular Biology
Molecular Biophysics
Molecular Genetics
Molecular Medicine
Molecular Pathogenesis
Molecular Pathology
Molecular Pharmacology
Molecular Physiology
Molecular Toxicology
Naturopathic Medicine
Neural Sciences (*see* Biopsychology; Neurobiology; Neuroscience)
Neurobiology
Neuroendocrinology (*see* Biopsychology; Neurobiology; Neuroscience; Physiology)
Neuropharmacology (*see* Biopsychology; Neurobiology; Neuroscience; Pharmacology)
Neurophysiology (*see* Biopsychology; Neurobiology; Neuroscience; Physiology)
Neuroscience
Nuclear Medical Technology (*see* Clinical Laboratory Sciences/Medical Technology)
Nurse Anesthesia
Nurse Midwifery
Nurse Practitioner Studies (*see* Family Nurse Practitioner Studies)
Nursing Administration (*see* Nursing and Healthcare Administration)
Nursing and Healthcare Administration
Nursing Education
Nursing—General
Nursing Informatics

Nutrition
Occupational Health (*see* Environmental and Occupational Health; Occupational Health Nursing)
Occupational Health Nursing
Occupational Therapy
Oncology (*see* Cancer Biology/Oncology)
Oncology Nursing
Optometry
Oral and Dental Sciences
Oral Biology (*see* Oral and Dental Sciences)
Oral Pathology (*see* Oral and Dental Sciences)
Organismal Biology (*see* Biological and Biomedical Sciences; Zoology)
Oriental Medicine and Acupuncture (*see* Acupuncture and Oriental Medicine)
Orthodontics (*see* Oral and Dental Sciences)
Osteopathic Medicine
Parasitology
Pathobiology
Pathology
Pediatric Nursing
Pedontics (*see* Oral and Dental Sciences)
Perfusion
Pharmaceutical Administration
Pharmaceutical Chemistry (*see* Medicinal and Pharmaceutical Chemistry)
Pharmaceutical Sciences
Pharmacology
Pharmacy
Photobiology of Cells and Organelles (*see* Botany; Cell Biology; Plant Biology)
Physical Therapy
Physician Assistant Studies
Physiological Optics (*see* Vision Sciences)
Podiatric Medicine
Preventive Medicine (*see* Community Health and Public Health)
Physiological Optics (*see* Physiology)
Physiology
Plant Biology
Plant Molecular Biology
Plant Pathology
Plant Physiology
Pomology (*see* Botany; Plant Biology)
Psychiatric Nursing
Public Health—General
Public Health Nursing (*see* Community Health Nursing)
Psychiatric Nursing
Psychobiology (*see* Biopsychology)
Psychopharmacology (*see* Biopsychology; Neuroscience; Pharmacology)
Radiation Biology
Radiological Health (*see* Health Physics/Radiological Health)
Rehabilitation Nursing
Rehabilitation Sciences
Rehabilitation Therapy (*see* Physical Therapy)
Reproductive Biology
School Nursing
Sociobiology (*see* Evolutionary Biology)
Structural Biology
Surgical Nursing (*see* Medical/Surgical Nursing)
Systems Biology
Teratology
Therapeutics
Theoretical Biology (*see* Biological and Biomedical Sciences)
Therapeutics (*see* Pharmaceutical Sciences; Pharmacology; Pharmacy)
Toxicology
Transcultural Nursing
Translational Biology
Tropical Medicine (*see* Parasitology)
Veterinary Medicine
Veterinary Sciences
Virology
Vision Sciences
Wildlife Biology (*see* Zoology)
Women's Health Nursing
Zoology

# Graduate Programs in the Physical Sciences, Mathematics, Agricultural Sciences, the Environment & Natural Resources

Acoustics
Agricultural Sciences
Agronomy and Soil Sciences
Analytical Chemistry
Animal Sciences
Applied Mathematics
Applied Physics
Applied Statistics
Aquaculture
Astronomy
Astrophysical Sciences (*see* Astrophysics; Atmospheric Sciences; Meteorology; Planetary and Space Sciences)
Astrophysics
Atmospheric Sciences
Biological Oceanography (*see* Marine Affairs; Marine Sciences; Oceanography)
Biomathematics
Biometry
Biostatistics
Chemical Physics
Chemistry
Computational Sciences
Condensed Matter Physics
Dairy Science (*see* Animal Sciences)
Earth Sciences (*see* Geosciences)
Environmental Management and Policy
Environmental Sciences
Environmental Studies (*see* Environmental Management and Policy)
Experimental Statistics (*see* Statistics)
Fish, Game, and Wildlife Management
Food Science and Technology
Forestry
General Science (*see* specific topics)
Geochemistry
Geodetic Sciences
Geological Engineering (*see* Geology)
Geological Sciences (*see* Geology)
Geology
Geophysical Fluid Dynamics (*see* Geophysics)
Geophysics
Geosciences
Horticulture
Hydrogeology
Hydrology
Inorganic Chemistry
Limnology
Marine Affairs
Marine Geology
Marine Sciences
Marine Studies (*see* Marine Affairs; Marine Geology; Marine Sciences; Oceanography)
Mathematical and Computational Finance
Mathematical Physics
Mathematical Statistics (*see* Applied Statistics; Statistics)
Mathematics
Meteorology
Mineralogy
Natural Resource Management (*see* Environmental Management and Policy; Natural Resources)
Natural Resources
Nuclear Physics (*see* Physics)
Ocean Engineering (*see* Marine Affairs; Marine Geology; Marine Sciences; Oceanography)
Oceanography
Optical Sciences
Optical Technologies (*see* Optical Sciences)
Optics (*see* Applied Physics; Optical Sciences; Physics)
Organic Chemistry

Paleontology
Paper Chemistry (*see* Chemistry)
Photonics
Physical Chemistry
Physics
Planetary and Space Sciences
Plant Sciences
Plasma Physics
Poultry Science (*see* Animal Sciences)
Radiological Physics (*see* Physics)
Range Management (*see* Range Science)
Range Science
Resource Management (*see* Environmental Management and Policy; Natural Resources)
Solid-Earth Sciences (*see* Geosciences)
Space Sciences (*see* Planetary and Space Sciences)
Statistics
Theoretical Chemistry
Theoretical Physics
Viticulture and Enology
Water Resources

# Graduate Programs in Engineering & Applied Sciences

Aeronautical Engineering (*see* Aerospace/Aeronautical Engineering)
Aerospace/Aeronautical Engineering
Aerospace Studies (*see* Aerospace/Aeronautical Engineering)
Agricultural Engineering
Applied Mechanics (*see* Mechanics)
Applied Science and Technology
Architectural Engineering
Artificial Intelligence/Robotics
Astronautical Engineering (*see* Aerospace/Aeronautical Engineering)
Automotive Engineering
Aviation
Biochemical Engineering
Bioengineering
Bioinformatics
Biological Engineering (*see* Bioengineering)
Biomedical Engineering
Biosystems Engineering
Biotechnology
Ceramic Engineering (*see* Ceramic Sciences and Engineering)
Ceramic Sciences and Engineering
Ceramics (*see* Ceramic Sciences and Engineering)
Chemical Engineering
Civil Engineering
Computer and Information Systems Security
Computer Engineering
Computer Science
Computing Technology (*see* Computer Science)
Construction Engineering
Construction Management
Database Systems
Electrical Engineering
Electronic Materials
Electronics Engineering (*see* Electrical Engineering)
Energy and Power Engineering
Energy Management and Policy
Engineering and Applied Sciences
Engineering and Public Affairs (*see* Technology and Public Policy)
Engineering and Public Policy (*see* Energy Management and Policy; Technology and Public Policy)
Engineering Design
Engineering Management
Engineering Mechanics (*see* Mechanics)
Engineering Metallurgy (*see* Metallurgical Engineering and Metallurgy)
Engineering Physics
Environmental Design (*see* Environmental Engineering)
Environmental Engineering
Ergonomics and Human Factors
Financial Engineering

Fire Protection Engineering
Food Engineering (*see* Agricultural Engineering)
Game Design and Development
Gas Engineering (*see* Petroleum Engineering)
Geological Engineering
Geophysics Engineering (*see* Geological Engineering)
Geotechnical Engineering
Hazardous Materials Management
Health Informatics
Health Systems (*see* Safety Engineering; Systems Engineering)
Highway Engineering (*see* Transportation and Highway Engineering)
Human-Computer Interaction
Human Factors (*see* Ergonomics and Human Factors)
Hydraulics
Hydrology (*see* Water Resources Engineering)
Industrial Engineering (*see* Industrial/Management Engineering)
Industrial/Management Engineering
Information Science
Internet Engineering
Macromolecular Science (*see* Polymer Science and Engineering)
Management Engineering (*see* Engineering Management; Industrial/Management Engineering)
Management of Technology
Manufacturing Engineering
Marine Engineering (*see* Civil Engineering)
Materials Engineering
Materials Sciences
Mechanical Engineering
Mechanics
Medical Informatics
Metallurgical Engineering and Metallurgy
Metallurgy (*see* Metallurgical Engineering and Metallurgy)
Mineral/Mining Engineering
Modeling and Simulation
Nanotechnology
Nuclear Engineering
Ocean Engineering
Operations Research
Paper and Pulp Engineering
Petroleum Engineering
Pharmaceutical Engineering
Plastics Engineering (*see* Polymer Science and Engineering)
Polymer Science and Engineering
Public Policy (*see* Energy Management and Policy; Technology and Public Policy)
Reliability Engineering
Robotics (*see* Artificial Intelligence/Robotics)
Safety Engineering
Software Engineering
Solid-State Sciences (*see* Materials Sciences)
Structural Engineering
Surveying Science and Engineering
Systems Analysis (*see* Systems Engineering)
Systems Engineering
Systems Science
Technology and Public Policy
Telecommunications
Telecommunications Management
Textile Sciences and Engineering
Textiles (*see* Textile Sciences and Engineering)
Transportation and Highway Engineering
Urban Systems Engineering (*see* Systems Engineering)
Waste Management (*see* Hazardous Materials Management)
Water Resources Engineering

# Graduate Programs in Business, Education, Information Studies, Law & Social Work

Accounting
Actuarial Science
Adult Education

Advertising and Public Relations
Agricultural Education
Alcohol Abuse Counseling (*see* Counselor Education)
Archival Management and Studies
Art Education
Athletics Administration (*see* Kinesiology and Movement Studies)
Athletic Training and Sports Medicine
Audiology (*see* Communication Disorders)
Aviation Management
Banking (*see* Finance and Banking)
Business Administration and Management—General
Business Education
Communication Disorders
Community College Education
Computer Education
Continuing Education (*see* Adult Education)
Counseling (*see* Counselor Education)
Counselor Education
Curriculum and Instruction
Developmental Education
Distance Education Development
Drug Abuse Counseling (*see* Counselor Education)
Early Childhood Education
Educational Leadership and Administration
Educational Measurement and Evaluation
Educational Media/Instructional Technology
Educational Policy
Educational Psychology
Education—General
Education of the Blind (*see* Special Education)
Education of the Deaf (*see* Special Education)
Education of the Gifted
Education of the Hearing Impaired (*see* Special Education)
Education of the Learning Disabled (*see* Special Education)
Education of the Mentally Retarded (*see* Special Education)
Education of the Physically Handicapped (*see* Special Education)
Education of Students with Severe/Multiple Disabilities
Education of the Visually Handicapped (*see* Special Education)
Electronic Commerce
Elementary Education
English as a Second Language
English Education
Entertainment Management
Entrepreneurship
Environmental Education
Environmental Law
Exercise and Sports Science
Exercise Physiology (*see* Kinesiology and Movement Studies)
Facilities and Entertainment Management
Finance and Banking
Food Services Management (*see* Hospitality Management)
Foreign Languages Education
Foundations and Philosophy of Education
Guidance and Counseling (*see* Counselor Education)
Health Education
Health Law
Hearing Sciences (*see* Communication Disorders)
Higher Education
Home Economics Education
Hospitality Management
Hotel Management (*see* Travel and Tourism)
Human Resources Development
Human Resources Management
Human Services
Industrial Administration (*see* Industrial and Manufacturing Management)
Industrial and Manufacturing Management
Industrial Education (*see* Vocational and Technical Education)
Information Studies
Instructional Technology (*see* Educational Media/Instructional Technology)
Insurance
Intellectual Property Law
International and Comparative Education
International Business
International Commerce (*see* International Business)

International Economics (*see* International Business)
International Trade (*see* International Business)
Investment and Securities (*see* Business Administration and Management; Finance and Banking; Investment Management)
Investment Management
Junior College Education (*see* Community College Education)
Kinesiology and Movement Studies
Law
Legal and Justice Studies
Leisure Services (*see* Recreation and Park Management)
Leisure Studies
Library Science
Logistics
Management (*see* Business Administration and Management)
Management Information Systems
Management Strategy and Policy
Marketing
Marketing Research
Mathematics Education
Middle School Education
Movement Studies (*see* Kinesiology and Movement Studies)
Multilingual and Multicultural Education
Museum Education
Music Education
Nonprofit Management
Nursery School Education (*see* Early Childhood Education)
Occupational Education (*see* Vocational and Technical Education)
Organizational Behavior
Organizational Management
Parks Administration (*see* Recreation and Park Management)
Personnel (*see* Human Resources Development; Human Resources Management; Organizational Behavior; Organizational Management; Student Affairs)
Philosophy of Education (*see* Foundations and Philosophy of Education)
Physical Education
Project Management
Public Relations (*see* Advertising and Public Relations)
Quality Management
Quantitative Analysis
Reading Education
Real Estate
Recreation and Park Management
Recreation Therapy (*see* Recreation and Park Management)
Religious Education
Remedial Education (*see* Special Education)
Restaurant Administration (*see* Hospitality Management)
Science Education
Secondary Education
Social Sciences Education
Social Studies Education (*see* Social Sciences Education)
Social Work
Special Education
Speech-Language Pathology and Audiology (*see* Communication Disorders)
Sports Management
Sports Medicine (*see* Athletic Training and Sports Medicine)
Sports Psychology and Sociology (*see* Kinesiology and Movement Studies)
Student Affairs
Substance Abuse Counseling (*see* Counselor Education)
Supply Chain Management
Sustainability Management
Systems Management (*see* Management Information Systems)
Taxation
Teacher Education (*see* specific subject areas)
Teaching English as a Second Language (*see* English as a Second Language)
Technical Education (*see* Vocational and Technical Education)
Transportation Management
Travel and Tourism
Urban Education
Vocational and Technical Education
Vocational Counseling (*see* Counselor Education)

# Directories and Subject Areas in This Book